DICCIONARIO
ESPAÑOL ▶ INGLÉS
INGLÉS ▶ ESPAÑOL
SPANISH ▶ ENGLISH
ENGLISH ▶ SPANISH
DICTIONARY

COLLINS
DICCIONARIO
ESPAÑOL ▶ INGLÉS
INGLÉS ▶ ESPAÑOL

por
Colin Smith

QUINTA EDICIÓN

grijalbo

COLLINS
SPANISH ▶ ENGLISH
ENGLISH ▶ SPANISH
DICTIONARY
Unabridged

by
Colin Smith

FIFTH EDITION

HarperCollins*Publishers*

© *Copyright 1971, 1988 William Collins Sons & Co. Ltd.*

© *Copyright 1992, 1993, 1996, 1997 HarperCollins Publishers*

fifth edition/quinta edición 1997

Grijalbo Mondadori S.A.
Aragón 385, Barcelona 08013
ISBN 84-253-3066-1
84-253-3082-3 (con uñero)

HarperCollins Publishers

PO Box, Glasgow G4 0NB, Great Britain
ISBN 0-00-471024-X
with thumb index 0-00-471023-1

10 East 53rd Street, New York
New York 10022
ISBN 0-06-270207-6

First HarperCollins edition published 1993.

Library of Congress Cataloging-in-Publication Data

Smith, Colin, 1927-
    Collins Spanish-English, English-Spanish dictionary: unabridged / by
Colin Smith in collaboration with Diarmuid Bradley ... [et al.]. – 5th ed.
        p.   cm.
        Added title page title: Collins diccionario español-inglés, inglés-español.
    ISBN 0-06-270207-6
        1. Spanish language — Dictionaries – English.   2. English language –
Dictionaries – Spanish.   I. Bradley, Diarmuid. II. Title. III. Title: Collins dic-
cionario español-inglés, inglés-español.
PC4640.S595   1997
463'.21 – dc21   96-49838
                                                                                CIP

97 98 99 00 01 CIBM 10 9 8 7 6 5 4 3 2 1

Typeset by Morton Word Processing Ltd, Scarborough

Printed and bound in Great Britain by
Caledonian International Book Manufacturing Ltd, Glasgow, G64

FIFTH EDITION   QUINTA EDICIÓN

editorial staff/redacción

Teresa Álvarez García   Gerard Breslin   Jeremy Butterfield

Sharon Hunter   Cordelia Lilly   José María Ruíz Vaca

contributors/colaboradores

Professor I. F. Ariza   Diarmuid Bradley   José Ramón Parrondo

computing/informática

Robert McMillan

THIRD AND FOURTH EDITIONS/ EDICIONES TERCERA Y CUARTA

by

Colin Smith

in collaboration with/en colaboración con

Diarmuid Bradley   Teresa de Carlos   Louis Rodrigues

José Ramón Parrondo

Editorial management/Dirección editorial

Jeremy Butterfield

Coordinating editor/Coordinador de la obra

Gerard Breslin

Assistant editors/Ayudantes de redacción

Sharon Hunter
Lesley Johnston

SECOND EDITION   SEGUNDA EDICIÓN

by

Colin Smith

in collaboration with/en colaboración con

María Boniface   Hugo Pooley   Arthur Montague

Mike Gonzalez

FIRST EDITION   PRIMERA EDICIÓN

by

Colin Smith

in collaboration with/en colaboración con

Manuel Bermejo Marcos   Eugenio Chang-Rodríguez

ACKNOWLEDGEMENTS

FOURTH AND FIFTH EDITIONS

Our thanks are due to the following for their invaluable contributions to the special entries on language and culture and to the coverage of new words and senses: Joaquín Blasco, Harry Campbell, Max Cawdron, Sabine Citron, Maureen Dolan, María Jesús Fernández Prieto, José Miguel Galván Déniz, Nerea Gandarias Mendieta, Elena García Álvarez, Isobel Gordon, Bob Grossmith, Rosa María Manchón, Duncan Marshall, Hazel Mills, Bernard Murphy, Chantal Pérez Hernández, Leonor del Pino Jiménez, M. Dolores Ramis, Mar Rodríguez Vázquez and Alison Sadler.

THIRD EDITION

In the relatively short time which has passed since the second edition of 1988, there has naturally been less opportunity for users to contribute comments and suggestions than was the case when the second edition was being prepared. However, eager and learned colleagues and users have not been altogether lacking, and thanks for contributions (in some cases extensive) are due to: the reviewers of the second edition, Jennie Bachelor, Tom Bookless, Everett L. Boyd, John Butt, Nick Gardner, María Martín, Brian Mott, Patrick Nield, Hugo Pooley, Chris Pratt, Dan Quilter, Brian Steel, Roger Wright.

SECOND EDITION

Apart from those mentioned as members of the team on the title page, who have laboured devotedly, the author's special thanks are due to Guillermo Arce, Tom Bookless, John Butt, Teresa de Carlos, Concepción and Pilar Jiménez Bautista, Daniel Quilter, and Brian Steel, who over the years have provided substantial contributions; and to the following, who in differing degrees gave additional help: Pamela Bacarisse, David Balagué, Clive Bashleigh, Peter Beardsell, William Bidgood, T.R.M. Bristow, A. Bryson Gerrard, Robert Burakoff, Trevor Chubb, G.T. Colegate, Joe Cremona, Eve Degnen, Maureen Dolan, Carmen and Pablo Domínguez, Fr Carlos Elizalde C.P., John England, G.C. Gilham, Paul Gomez, Stephen Harrison, Patrick Harvey, Tony Heathcote, David Henn, Leo Hickey, Ian Jacob, F. Killoran, Norman Lamb, Emilio Lorenzo, Rodney Mantle, Alan Morley, Brian Morris, Ana Newton, Richard Nott, Hugh O'Donnell, Brian Powell, Chris Pratt, Robert Pring-Mill, C.H. Stevenson, Diana Streeten, Ian Weetman, Richard Wharton, Roger Wright, Alan Yates.

FIRST EDITION

It is proper to retain the following from the Preface to the First Edition of 1971: 'I am greatly indebted to the following: Dr M. Bermejo Marcos, who read all the drafts; Prof. E. Chang Rodríguez, who read the first part to check information about American Spanish; Mr H.B. Hall, who advised on principles at the start and read sections of the second part; and for a variety of contributions, to Mr T.C. Bookless, Prof. R.F. Brown, Dr G.A. Davies, Miss A. Johnson, Mr A. Madigan, Mr A. McCallum, Miss G. Weston, Sr J. and Sra M. del Río, Sra A. Espinosa de Walker and Sra M.J. Fernández de Wangermann. My wife helped in all the ways that wives do. To them all, my warmest thanks.'

Colin Smith

AGRADECIMIENTOS

EDICIONES CUARTA Y QUINTA

Queremos agradecer a las siguientes personas su inestimable colaboración en las entradas especiales de lengua y cultura, así como en la redacción y traducción de los neologismos y nuevas acepciones: Joaquín Blasco, Harry Campbell, Max Cawdron, Sabine Citron, Maureen Dolan, María Jesús Fernández Prieto, José Miguel Galván Déniz, Nerea Gandarias Mendieta, Elena García Álvarez, Isobel Gordon, Bob Grossmith, Rosa María Manchón, Duncan Marshall, Hazel Mills, Bernard Murphy, Chantal Pérez Hernández, Leonor del Pino Jiménez, M. Dolores Ramis, Mar Rodríguez Vázquez and Alison Sadler.

TERCERA EDICIÓN

En el poco tiempo transcurrido desde la publicación de la segunda edición, es natural que los usuarios no hayan tenido tantas oportunidades para enviar comentarios y sugerencias como las que tuvieron antes de la preparación de esa segunda edición. Sin embargo, no han faltado por completo colegas y usuarios entusiastas y eruditos, y ofrezco mis gracias por las aportaciones (a veces cuantiosas) de: los autores de reseñas de la segunda edición, Jennie Bachelor, Tom Bookless, Everett L. Boyd, John Butt, Nick Gardner, María Martín, Brian Mott, Patrick Nield, Hugo Pooley, Chris Pratt, Dan Quilter, Brian Steel, Roger Wright.

SEGUNDA EDICIÓN

Aparte de las personas que se mencionan en la portada, que han trabajado con devoción, quedo agradecido de manera especial por sus cuantiosas contribuciones a Guillermo Arce, Tom Bookless, John Butt, Teresa de Carlos, Concepción y Pilar Jiménez Bautista, Daniel Quilter, y Brian Steel, y a otros que de diversas maneras han aportado sus auxilios: Pamela Bacarisse, David Balagué, Clive Bashleigh, Peter Beardsell, William Bidgood, T.R.M. Bristow, A. Bryson Gerrard, Robert Burakoff, Trevor Chubb, G.T. Colegate, Joe Cremona, Eve Degnen, Maureen Dolan, Carmen and Pablo Domínguez, Fr Carlos Elizalde C.P., John England, G.C. Gilham, Paul Gomez, Stephen Harrison, Patrick Harvey, Tony Heathcote, David Henn, Leo Hickey, Ian Jacob, F. Killoran, Norman Lamb, Emilio Lorenzo, Rodney Mantle, Alan Morley, Brian Morris, Ana Newton, Richard Nott, Hugh O'Donnell, Brian Powell, Chris Pratt, Robert Pring-Mill, C.H. Stevenson, Diana Streeten, Ian Weetman, Richard Wharton, Roger Wright, Alan Yates.

PRIMERA EDICIÓN

Conservo lo siguiente del Prefacio de la Primera Edición de 1971: 'Agradezco la ayuda de: Dr M. Bermejo Marcos, que leyó todos los borradores; Prof. E. Chang-Rodríguez, que leyó la 1ª parte para mejorar lo referente al español de América; Sr H.B. Hall, que me dio consejos al principio y leyó varias letras de la 2ª parte. Han contribuido también: Sr T.C. Bookless, Prof. R.F. Brown, Dr G.A. Davies, Srta A. Johnson, Sr A. Madigan, Sr A. McCallum, Srta G. Weston, Sr J. y Sra M. del Río, Sra A. Espinosa de Walker y Sra M.J. Fernández de Wangermann. Mi esposa ha prestado su ayuda en las maneras en que suelen prestarla las esposas. Para todos, mis gracias.'

CONTENTS

ÍNDICE DE MATERIAS

PREFACE

PREFACE TO THE FIFTH EDITION

This fifth edition of Collins Spanish Dictionary reflects Collins' ongoing commitment to providing the most up-to-date and helpful Spanish-English English-Spanish dictionary on the market for students and professionals alike. In this latest edition we have brought in four major improvements: language notes to aid translation into the foreign language; encyclopedic entries to clarify aspects of life and culture; the addition of the latest terms and expressions; and a new and even more clear and attractive typography.

The language notes, which are aimed at tackling those areas of difficulty where even advanced students may benefit from further explanation, are designed to complement the dictionary entry in a clear and succinct fashion and to provide further helpful examples. The points covered in the notes were selected on the advice of practising teachers and academics, and contrastive information about the two languages was researched in our invaluable multi-million-word corpora of Spanish and English. All explanations are written in the language of the user to whom they are addressed. Our encyclopedic entries on key aspects of Spanish, Latin American, British and US culture, such as everyday life, literature, politics, history, education and organizations, are an attempt to bridge the gap between the differing cultures. Like the language notes, these entries are written in the native language of the user they are designed to benefit; this means that entires on Spanish and Latin American items are in English and entries on British and US items in Spanish.

The more than 5,000 neologisms, idioms and new senses we have added to the main dictionary text are the product of our successful and continuous monitoring of current English and Spanish, both spoken and written. In this regard we gratefully acknowledge the contributions made by Collins English Dictionaries and also that of Diarmuid Bradley of the National College of Galway, Ireland, along with the experienced team of lexicographers who moulded the raw materials into helpful entries, giving us unrivalled coverage of today's language.

Presentation is always a priority for a bilingual dictionary and Collins has long had a reputation for offering clear and uncluttered entires. To maintain and enhance this reputation, the typography of this new edition has been modernized and the layout improved to make the text even more readable. The result, we feel, sets new standards in bilingual dictionary typography and the Collins Spanish-English dictionary is easily the most readable and manageable of large Spanish-English dictionaries available today.

The Editorial Team

PREFACE TO THE FOURTH EDITION

The new-look fourth edition of the Collins Spanish Dictionary helps you make even more effective use of the text. One of its most innovative features is the way the main text of the dictionary has been linked to the Language in Use supplement in the middle of the book. This section has been completely revised and draws on the wealth of lexicographical information to be found in our corpora of authentic Spanish and English, both spoken and written, from such diverse sources as contemporary literature, press articles and recordings of real-life conversations currently totalling over 230 million words.

PREFACE TO THE THIRD EDITION

The fact that this new edition appears so shortly after the second (1988) has a particular motive. While on the one hand there is a permanent need to modernize such works of reference (and the pace of neologistic creation always seems to quicken), the author and publishers have seized the opportunity offered by 1992 to salute both the Single European Act and the Spanish-speaking world, **La Hispanidad**, as it reflects on its special quincentenary of cultural achievements in which language has been both a mover and a product. The chance has been taken to improve many thousands of entries on both sides and to add (from the very extensive corpus assembled by Diarmuid Bradley, Heriot Watt University) many hundreds of neologisms of Spanish. The revision of the English side was greatly enhanced by access to the COBUILD corpora and a wealth of neologisms from Collins English Dictionaries. Many improvements have been drawn in the coverage of business and administrative language from the expert knowledge of Louis Rodrigues (Cambridge), while Teresa de Carlos' (Cambridge) acute sense of both languages has led to the refinement of many entries. We have also paid renewed attention to the lexis of computers and new technology. A new appendix on Word Formation in Spanish has been provided in order to gather together problematic aspects and to indicate solutions. The main text of the dictionary is larger by 30,000 references and 50,000 translations. The work is offered with the confidence that it will maintain and even enhance the appreciation it has enjoyed among users since its first appearance in 1971.

PREFACE TO THE SECOND EDITION

That the First Edition was so well received did not
mean that the author could leave the work there
and rest on any laurels. From the moment of its
publication a mass of new materials began to be
assembled, some of it for correction and
improvement of existing entries, much relating to
new items of the kind that rapid evolution of
major modern languages produces. There have
also been notable improvements in method
devised for other books in the Collins bilingual
range, now adopted here. In particular, a
considerable effort has been made to improve
coverage of usage in Latin America and in the
United States. No doubt this second edition was
already long overdue, but it is offered with some
confidence that it represents a great all-round
improvement.

EXTRACT FROM THE PREFACE TO THE FIRST
EDITION

Given the rapidity of change in language and in
its social and theoretical aspects, a new dictionary
hardly needs an apology. This dictionary would be
justified even if it were of the traditional type;
in fact it incorporates new principles which may
be of interest to linguists, and whose practical
application should ease the task of users at every
level.

The lexicographer who attempts to equate and
harmonize two great world languages must
honestly recognize that both in theory and in
practice his task cannot be perfectly fulfilled. The
simplest word often has such a range, such
semantic potentiality and such nuances that it
cannot be fully defined within a single-language
dictionary; it is more difficult still to translate it
in a two-language dictionary of modest size.

This is, however, an optimistic undertaking. It
presupposes that the two linguistic areas are in
contact for reasons of trade, diplomacy, and
tourism; for cultural, literary, scientific and
sporting exchanges; that each has something to
learn from the other and the will to do so. It
presupposes free intercommunication across the
frontiers and the oceans. The dictionary is a tool
of understanding and it speaks for peace, tolerance
and mutual respect.

Colin Smith

PREFACIO

PREFACIO DE LA QUINTA EDICIÓN

La quinta edición del diccionario Collins de inglés-español refleja el esfuerzo continuo de Collins por crear el diccionario de inglés-español más actualizado y útil tanto para estudiantes como para profesionales. Hemos mejorado esta edición en cuatro distintos aspectos: la inclusión tanto de notas lingüísticas para ayudar a traducir a la lengua extranjera como de entradas enciclopédicas para aclarar distintos aspectos culturales, la adición de los términos, expresiones y acepciones más recientes y una tipografía aún más clara y atractiva.

Las notas lingüísticas, cuyo objetivo es aclarar y explicar aquellas dificultades que pueda tener incluso un estudiante avanzado, están diseñadas para complementar la entrada del diccionario de una forma clara y esquemática, proporcionando para ello más ejemplos ilustrativos. Los puntos que se han tratado en dichas notas se han seleccionado con la ayuda de profesores y la información contrastiva sobre ambos idiomas fue analizada con la inapreciable ayuda de nuestro corpus de español e inglés, de millones de palabras. Todas las explicaciones están escritas en la lengua del usuario a quien van dirigidas. Nuestras entradas enciclopédicas, que ofrecen información sobre aspectos clave de la cultura británica, norteamericana, española y latinoamericana -tales como la vida cotidiana, la literatura, la política, la historia, la educación y las distintas organizaciones de los países-, son un intento de salvar las diferencias entre las distintas culturas. Estas entradas, igual que las notas lingüísticas, están escritas en la lengua del usuario que más se beneficiará con ellas. Es decir, las entradas sobre la cultura británica y norteamericana están en español y las entradas sobre España y Latinoamérica en inglés.

Se han añadido más de 5,000 neologismos, giros idiomáticos y nuevas acepciones, producto de nuestro seguimiento continuo del inglés y español actual, tanto hablado como escrito. En este sentido agradecemos sinceramente las contribuciones de los Diccionarios monolingües Collins y la de Diarmuid Bradley, del National College de Galway, Irlanda, junto con el equipo de lexicógrafos que dieron forma al material bruto y crearon las entradas, dando lugar así al tratamiento sin igual del idioma actual que caracteriza a nuestro diccionario.

La presentación es siempre un elemento prioritario en un diccionario bilingüe y Collins tiene desde hace tiempo fama de ofrecer entradas claras y sin complejidades innecesarias. Para mantener y mejorar nuestra reputación se ha modernizado la tipografía de esta nueva edición y se ha perfeccionado la presentación con el fin de facilitar su consulta. El resultado, a nuestro parecer, logra superar el nivel existente en la tipografía de los diccionarios bilingües y convierte a esta obra de Collins en el diccionario grande de inglés-español más manejable y fácil de leer de cuantos existen hoy día.

El equipo editorial

PREFACIO DE LA CUARTA EDICIÓN

Con su nueva presentación, esta cuarta edición del Diccionario Collins de inglés tiene como objetivo lograr el máximo aprovechamiento del texto. Una de las principales innovaciones es la forma en que se ha conectado el texto principal del diccionario con el suplemento de Lengua y Uso, en el centro del libro. Esta sección, completamente revisada, tiene como base la extensa información lexicográfica de nuestros corpus de la lengua inglesa y española, tanto oral como escrita, tomados de fuentes tan diversas como la literatura contemporánea, artículos de prensa y grabaciones de conversaciones reales, llegando a alcanzar en la actualidad un total de más de 230 millones de palabras.

PREFACIO DE LA TERCERA EDICIÓN

El hecho de que esta nueva edición aparece tan pronto después de la segunda (1988) tiene un motivo bien concreto. Mientras por una parte existe la permanente necesidad de actualizar tales obras de consulta (y la rapidez de la creación neologística parece ir siempre en aumento), el autor y la editorial han aprovechado la oportunidad que ofrece 1992 para saludar tanto al Acta Única como al mundo hispanohablante, **La Hispanidad**, en el momento en que considera el quinto centenario de logros culturales en los que la lengua ha sido a la vez promotora y producto. Hemos rehecho y mejorado muchos miles de artículos en cada parte, añadiendo centenares de neologismos del español procedentes de la extensa colección de Diarmuid Bradley (Universidad de Heriot Watt). La remodelación del inglés se facilitó por el acceso a los corpora de COBUILD y los neologismos recogidos por Collins English Dictionaries. Hemos prestado atención especial a la cobertura de términos y giros del comercio y de la administración, aprovechando la pericia técnica de Louis Rodrigues (Cambridge), mientras la penetrante comprensión de Teresa de Carlos (Cambridge) en las dos lenguas ha servido para limar muchos artículos. Hemos renovado la atención concedida a la informática y las nuevas tecnologías. Presentamos un nuevo Apéndice sobre la formación de palabras en español con el propósito de reunir aspectos problemáticos para el usuario anglohablante. El texto del diccionario se aumenta en unas 30.000 referencias y 50.000 traducciones. Se ofrece la obra con la confianza de que mantendrá y aun mejorará el aprecio que viene disfrutando desde su primera aparición en 1971.

PREFACIO DE LA SEGUNDA EDICIÓN

La excelente acogida que se dio a la primera edición no quería decir que el autor pudiera dejar su trabajo en ese punto. Desde el momento de la publicación se empezó a reunir gran cantidad de materiales nuevos, en muchos casos destinados a corregir y mejorar el texto existente, en otros casos nuevos datos de los que produce la rápida evolución de las grandes lenguas modernas. En otros libros de la serie bilingüe de Collins se han realizado unos adelantos notables en cuanto al método, que he adoptado ahora. Los colaboradores se han esforzado por mejorar todo lo referente a usos lingüísticos americanos tanto para el español como para el inglés. Nadie duda que ya había llegado el momento de ofrecer esta segunda edición, y se presenta con la confianza de que supone una gran mejora.

EXTRACTO DEL PREFACIO DE LA PRIMERA EDICIÓN

El rápido desarrollo de las lenguas y de sus aspectos sociales y teóricos eximen al autor de la necesidad de disculparse al publicar un nuevo diccionario. Este libro se justificaría aun cuando fuera del tipo tradicional; se justifica más incorporando varios principios nuevos que pueden tener interés para los lingüistas, y cuya aplicación práctica podrá ayudar a los usuarios de todo tipo.

El lexicógrafo que se esfuerza por juntar y armonizar dos grandes idiomas mundiales tiene que reconocer honradamente que tanto en la teoría como en la práctica es imposible llevar perfectamente a cabo su cometido. La palabra más sencilla puede tener tal extensión, tanta potencialidad semántica y tantos matices que resulta imposible definirla en un libro monolingüe; es más difícil todavía traducirla en un diccionario bilingüe de tamaño modesto.

Con todo, esta empresa se funda en el optimismo. Ello supone que las dos áreas lingüísticas están en contacto por razones comerciales, diplomáticas y turísticas; para el intercambio cultural, literario, científico y deportivo; porque cada una tiene interés en aprender de la otra, y la voluntad de hacerlo. Ello supone que existe la libre comunicación a través de las fronteras y de los océanos. El diccionario sirve para la comprensión mutua y habla en pro de la paz.

Colin Smith

USING THE DICTIONARY
CÓMO UTILIZAR EL DICCIONARIO

Using the Dictionary

1 Alphabetical order is followed throughout. **NB:** *CH* and *LL* are no longer treated as separate letters in Spanish. *Ñ* continues to be a separate letter.

2 Cross-references include alternative spellings, parts of irregular verbs, contracted forms, many prefixes and some suffixes, and parts of compound words.

> **armor** ... *n* (*US*) = **armour.**
> **voy** *etc V* **ir.**
> **gave** ... *pret of* **give.**

3 Superior numbers are used to separate words of like spelling and pronunciation, eg **port¹**, **port²**, **choclo¹**, **choclo²**.

4 Noun plurals in Spanish are indicated after the headword only when irregular (eg **club**, *pl* **clubs** *o* **clubes**). In all other cases the basic rules apply: if a noun ends in a vowel it takes **-s** in the plural (eg **casa-s**, **tribu-s**); if it ends in a consonant (including for this purpose **y**) it takes **-es** in the plural (eg **pared-es**, **árbol-es**). Note the following, however:

  (i) Nouns that end in stressed **í** take **-es** in the plural (eg **rubí**, **rubíes**). Exception: **esquí**, **esquís**.
  (ii) Nouns that end in **-z** change this to **c** and add **-es** in the plural (eg **luz**, **luces**; **paz**, **paces**). The pronunciation is not affected.
  (iii) The accent which is written on a number of endings of singular nouns is not needed in the plural (eg **nación-naciones**, **patán-patanes**, **inglés-ingleses**). Some words having no written accent in the singular need one in the plural (eg **crimen-crímenes**, **joven-jóvenes**).
  (iv) There is little agreement about the plural of recent anglicisms and gallicisms, and some latinisms. Each case is treated separately in the dictionary; see eg **barman**.

5 Noun plurals in English are indicated after the headword only when they are truly irregular (eg **ox**, **oxen**), and in the few cases where a word in **-o** takes a plural in **-oes** (eg **potato-es**). In all other cases the basic rules apply:

  (i) Most English nouns take **-s** in the plural: **bed-s**, **site-s**, **photo-s**.

Cómo utilizar el diccionario

1 Se sigue un riguroso orden alfabético, pero conviene recordar que *CH* y *LL* ya no aparecen como letras independientes.

2 Con referencias a otros artículos figuran las variantes ortográficas, las formas de los verbos irregulares, las formas contractas, muchos prefijos y algunos sufijos, y elementos de palabras compuestas.

3 Los números altos sirven para distinguir las palabras que se escriben y se pronuncian iguales, p.ej. **port¹**, **port²**, **choclo¹**, **choclo²**.

4 Forma plural del sustantivo en español. Estas formas se hacen constar después de la voz cabeza de artículo sólo cuando son irregulares (p.ej. **club**, *pl* **clubs** *o* **clubes**). En los demás casos se aplican las siguientes reglas: si el sustantivo termina en vocal se añade **-s** para formar el plural (p.ej. **casa-s**, **tribu-s**); si termina en consonante (la **y** se considera como consonante en esta posición) se añade **-es** para formar el plural (p.ej. **pared-es**, **árbol-es**). Hay algunas excepciones:

  (i) Los sustantivos que terminan en **-í** acentuada forman el plural añadiendo **-es** (p.ej. **rubí**, **rubíes**). Excepción: **esquí**, **esquís**.
  (ii) Los sustantivos que terminan en **-z** la cambian en **c** al formarse el plural (p.ej. **luz**, **luces**; **paz**, **paces**). Esto no cambia la pronunciación.
  (iii) El acento que se escribe en varias desinencias de los sustantivos en singular se suprime en el plural (p.ej. **nación-naciones**, **patán-patanes**). Algunas palabras que no llevan acento escrito en singular lo tienen en plural (p.ej. **crimen-crímenes**).
  (iv) Reina bastante confusión acerca de la forma plural de los anglicismos y galicismos de reciente acuñación, y de algún latinismo. Se trata separadamente cada caso; véase p.ej. **barman**.

5 Forma plural del sustantivo en inglés. Estas formas se hacen constar después de la voz cabeza de artículo sólo cuando son irregulares (p.ej. **ox**, **oxen**), y en los pocos casos donde una palabra terminada en **-o** forma el plural en **-oes** (p.ej. **potato-es**). En los demás casos se aplican las siguientes reglas:

  (i) La mayor parte de los sustantivos en inglés forman el plural añadiendo **-s**: **bed-s**, **site-s**, **photo-s**.

(ii) Nouns that end in **-s, -x, -z, -sh** and some in **-ch** [tʃ] take **-es** in the plural: **boss-es, box-es, dish-es, patch-es**.

(iii) Nouns that end in **-y** not preceded by a vowel change the **-y** to **-ies** in the plural: **lady-ladies, berry-berries** (but **tray-s, key-s**).

6 Spanish and English verbs. All Spanish verb headwords are referred by number and letter (eg [1a], [2e]) to the table of verb paradigms on pp.1646–1654. In a few cases in which verbs have slight irregularities or are defective, the fact is noted after the headword. English irregular or strong verbs have their principal parts noted in bold face after the headword; these are also listed on pp.1658–1659. Minor variations of spelling are listed on p.1660.

7 Abbreviations and proper names. For easier reference, abbreviations, acronyms and proper names have been listed alphabetically in the wordlist, as opposed to being relegated to the appendices. **MOT** is used in every way like 'certificate' or 'permit', **IVA** like 'impuesto', and consequently these words are treated like any other noun.

8 Grammatical functions are distinguished by bold face numerals and abbreviations, eg **arder 1** *vt* ... **2** *vi* ... **3 arderse** *vr* ... . A separate division has been provided for *vr* in the English–Spanish, on the grounds that even though English has no strictly reflexive verbs this represents a convenience in translation and for the user.

9 The diverse meanings of the headword within each entry or grammatical function are separated by letters in bold face, **(a)** ... **(b)** ... . Sometimes the distinctions made are rather fine but necessary both for the compiler and the user; they are practical rather than scientific in terms of semantics. A certain order is normally followed: basic and concrete senses first, figurative and familiar ones later; (*LAm*) and (*US*) senses and highly specialized applications come last.

10 Field labels in italics: some are abbreviations (eg *Bio, Mus*), others complete words (eg *Art, Fencing*). Latin American usage has been divided into the following five groups and labelled accordingly: Andean (Bolivia, Colombia, Ecuador, Peru); Caribbean (Cuba, Puerto Rico, Santo Domingo, Venezuela); Central American (Costa Rica, El Salvador, Guatemala, Honduras, Nicaragua,

(ii) Los sustantivos terminados en **-s, -x, -z, -sh** y algunos en **-ch** [tʃ] forman el plural añadiendo **-es**: **boss-es, box-es, dish-es, patch-es**.

(iii) Los sustantivos terminados en **-y** no precedida por vocal forman el plural cambiando la **-y** en **-ies**: **lady-ladies, berry-berries** (pero **tray-s, key-s**).

6 Verbo español y verbo inglés. Los verbos españoles que encabezan artículo llevan una referencia por número y letra (p.ej. [1a], [2e]) al cuadro de conjugaciones en las págs. 1646–1654. En los casos donde el verbo es ligeramente irregular o defectivo, se nota tal hecho en el artículo. Se imprimen en negrilla inmediatamente después de la palabra cabeza de artículo el pretérito y participio de pasado de los verbos irregulares ingleses, y hay además lista de ellos en las págs. 1658–1659. Las ligeras variantes ortográficas de los verbos ingleses constan en la pág. 1660.

7 Abreviaturas y nombres propios. Para hacer más fácil la consulta del diccionario se ha decidido insertar en el texto, por orden alfabético, las abreviaturas, siglas y nombres propios, antes que relegarlos a los apéndices del final. Efectivamente, decir **MOT** en inglés o **IVA** en español equivale exactamente a decir 'certificate' o 'impuesto' respectivamente, y por tanto esas palabras reciben el mismo tratamiento que cualquier otro sustantivo.

8 Las funciones gramaticales se señalan mediante números en negrilla y abreviaturas, p.ej. **arder 1** *vt* ... **2** *vi* ... **3 arderse** *vr* .... En la Parte 2ª hay división especial para el *vr*, por el motivo de que (aunque el verbo inglés no tiene en rigor formas reflexivas) tal sistema es muy útil en la traducción y para el usuario.

9 Los diversos significados de la palabra cabeza de artículo quedan separados por letras en negrilla, **(a)** ... **(b)** ... . Alguna vez la distinción puede parecer nimia, pero es necesaria para el autor y más para el lector; esto tiene una finalidad práctica y no pretende tener validez científica. Se ha establecido cierto orden para estas subdivisiones: primero los significados básicos y concretos, después los figurados y familiares; las acepciones (*LAm*) y (*US*) y las aplicaciones técnicas vienen en último lugar.

10 Las indicaciones de campo semántico se imprimen en cursiva. Algunas son abreviaturas (p.ej. *Bio, Mús*) y otras palabras completas (p.ej. *Arte, Esgrima*). El vocabulario latinoamericano se ha dividido e indicado de acuerdo con los siguientes grupos de países: Región Andina (Bolivia, Colombia, Ecuador, Perú); Región del Caribe (Cuba, Puerto Rico, Santo Domingo,

Panama); Southern Cone (Argentina, Chile, Uruguay, Paraguay); and Mexico on its own.

11 Style labels. All words and phrases which are not standard language have been labelled according to two separate registers:

(a) formal and informal usage
(b) old-fashioned and literary usage
This labelling is given for both source and target languages and serves primarily to provide a warning to the non-native speaker. The symbols used are as follows:

(i) The abbreviation *frm* denotes formal language such as that used on an official form, in pronouncements and other formal communications.

> **whereto** ... (*frm*, ††) adonde.

(ii) * indicates that the expression, while not forming part of standard language, is used by all educated speakers in a relaxed situation, but would not be used in a formal essay or letter, or on an occasion when the speaker wishes to impress.

> **chollo*** ... (*Com*) ... snip*, ...
> **hacer dedo*** ... to thumb a lift* ...
> **then the band played*** (*US*) y se armó la gorda*.
> **it costs a bomb*** (*Brit*) cuesta un ojo de la cara*; ...

(iii) ‡ indicates that the expression is used by some but not all educated speakers in a very relaxed situation. Such words should be handled with extreme care by the non-native speaker unless he is very fluent in the language and is very sure of his company.

> **atizarse**‡ ... **(c)** to smoke pot
> **clink**^{2}‡ ... trena‡ *f*

(iv) ⁙ means 'Danger!'. Such words are liable to offend in any situation, and therefore are to be avoided by the non-native speaker.

> **cojón**⁙ ... ¡**cojones!**⁙ (*rechazo*) balls!⁙; (*sorpresa*) bugger me!⁙; ...
> **dick** ... **(b)** (⁙) polla⁙ *f*.

(v) † denotes old-fashioned terms which are no longer in wide current use but which the foreign user will certainly find in reading, or may encounter in humorous use.

> **merced** ... **(a)** (†) (*favor*) favour.

Venezuela); Región centroamericana (Costa Rica, El Salvador, Guatemala, Honduras, Nicaragua, Panamá); Cono Sur (Argentina, Chile, Uruguay, Paraguay); y México.

11 Niveles lingüísticos. Las palabras y frases que se distinguen de la lengua estándar llevan un signo que indica uno de dos registros:

(a) uso 'oficial' o coloquial
(b) uso literario o arcaico
Estos signos se imprimen para las dos lenguas, y sirven sobre todo como aviso al usuario no nativo. Los símbolos utilizados son los siguientes:

(i) La abreviatura *frm* indica el lenguaje 'oficial', p.ej. el empleado en los formularios burocráticos, en los discursos políticos, en las cartas enviadas por las autoridades, etcétera.

(ii) * indica que la palabra o locución no forma parte de la lengua estándar, pero es empleada por todos en situación familiar o de cierta intimidad; no se emplearía en ensayo o en carta oficial, o en situación donde se quiere hacer buena impresión.

(iii) ‡ indica que la palabra o locución es de carácter marcadamente coloquial; el usuario no nativo empleará estas palabras sólo con la mayor prudencia, dominando ya la otra lengua y considerando con cuidado el contexto social en que se encuentra.

(iv) ⁙ significa ¡Ojo! El usuario no nativo deberá poder reconocer estas palabras o giros, pero dado su carácter obsceno u ofensivo se guardará de emplearlos en la mayor parte de los contextos sociales.

(v) † indica palabras que ya no se emplean corrientemente pero que el usuario no nativo encontrará con frecuencia en sus lecturas, o en la actualidad con intención humorística.

(vi) †† denotes obsolete words which the user will normally find in literature, or may encounter in humorous use.

(vi) †† indica palabras más bien arcaicas que el usuario puede encontrar en sus lecturas de obras clásicas, o en la actualidad con intención humorística.

thy†† ... tu(s).
cumquibus... (††, *hum*): **el** ~ the wherewithal.

The use of † and †† should not be confused with the label *Hist*. *Hist* does not apply to the expression itself but denotes the historical context of the object so named.

El empleo de † y †† no debe confundirse con la abreviatura *Hist*. Ésta no se aplica a la palabra o expresión sino que se refiere al hecho o a la institución etc. así llamado.

ordeal ... *n* (*Hist*) ordalías *fpl*; ...

(vii) *liter* denotes an expression which belongs to literary language.

(vii) *liter* indica que la palabra o locución pertenece a la lengua literaria o poética.

heretofore ... (*liter*) hasta ahora

(viii) The labels and symbols above are used to mark either an individual word or phrase, or a whole category, or even a complete entry

(viii) Las indicaciones y símbolos se refieren según el caso a una palabra, una locución, parte del artículo, o al artículo en su totalidad.

The user should not confuse the style label *liter* with the field label *Liter* which indicates that the term or expression so labelled belongs to the field of literature. Similarly, the user should note that the abbreviation *lit* indicates the literal as opposed to the figurative meaning of a word.

El usuario no debe confundir la indicación estilística *liter* con *lit* que significa sentido propio o empleo literal, ni por otra parte con *Liter* que se refiere al campo de la literatura.

12 Indicators are complete words in italics placed before the translation; they aid in distinguishing meanings and help the user find that part of the headword's range which he is seeking. They have been made as brief and typical as possible, but they cannot be comprehensive and must not be taken to constitute full definitions or exact limitations. The main types of indicator are:

12 Contribuyen a hacer las distinciones semánticas las indicaciones de palabras enteras en cursiva, colocadas delante de la traducción; se proponen llamar la atención del lector hacia la parte de la extensión de la palabra con que tiene que ver. Hemos ideado estas aclaraciones para que sean breves y típicas; pero ellas no pueden ser universales, e importa mucho que no se las considere como definiciones completas ni como limitaciones exactas. Las indicaciones son de varias clases:

(i) For a **noun** headword: a variety of near-synonyms, part-definitions and hints (in parentheses), eg **poke** (*push*) ...; (*with elbow*) ...; (*jab*) ...; (*with poker*) ...

(i) Para **sustantivo** que encabeza artículo: sinónimos aproximativos, definiciones parciales, consejos (en paréntesis), p.ej. **abogado** (*notario*) ...; (*en tribunal*) ...; (*defensor*) ...

(ii) For an **adjective** headword: nouns (without parentheses) with which the adjective in its various applications might typically be used, eg **soft (b)** (*fig*) *air, sound* ...; *voice* ...; *step* ...; *water* ...

(ii) Para **adjetivo** que encabeza artículo: sustantivos (sin paréntesis) con los que el adjetivo en sus diversas aplicaciones pudiera emplearse, p.ej. **blando** *materia, agua etc* ...; *pasta etc* ...; *carne* ...; *tono* ...; *clima* ...

(iii) For a **transitive verb** headword: nouns (without parentheses) which might typically be the objects of the verb in its various applications, eg **pluck** *fruit, flower* ...; *bird* ...; *guitar* ...

(iii) Para **verbo transitivo** que encabeza artículo: sustantivos (sin paréntesis) que típicamente pudieran ser los objetos del verbo, p.ej. **abandonar** *lugar* ...; *persona* ...; *objeto* ...; *tentativa, hábito* ...

(iv) For an **intransitive** or **reflexive verb** headword: nouns (in parentheses) which might be typical subjects of the verb, eg **rise 2 (c)** (*of sun, moon*) ...; (*smoke etc*) ...; (*building, mountain*) ...

Indicators are not repeated in derivatives but can be transferred by the user, eg adjective to adverb, adjective to abstract noun (*fair-fairness*).

13 The order of material within the entry or subdivision has been planned for convenience and does not follow a rigid pattern. However, a typical order for a lengthy noun entry is: (i) basic translations of the headword; (ii) phrases consisting of noun + adjective; (iii) the noun preceded by a preposition (often with verb as well); (iv) the noun with a verb. Alphabetical order is followed within each of these categories. No attempt is made to separate idioms from usage examples.

14 The placing of phrases in entries raises many problems. The principles generally followed are:

(i) Phrases consisting of noun + noun, verb + verb, adjective + adjective are entered under the first component, eg **'casa y comida'** under **casa**, **'black and blue'** under **black**.

(ii) Spanish collocations consisting of noun + adjective are generally entered under the noun component, eg **cabina electoral** under **cabina**. English collocations consisting of adjective + noun are generally entered under the adjective component. However, some such combinations in English now have a sufficiently independent existence to figure as main entries.

(iii) Phrases consisting of verb + noun are entered under the noun component, eg **abrir carrera** under **carrera**, **to show cause** under **cause**; but many phrases will be found in the verb entries as usage examples also.

(iv) Phrasal verbs are listed in the dictionary at the end of the entry for the main verb, in their own alphabetical sequence and highlighted by a lozenge.

♦**go about** ... *vt* ...
♦**go across 1** *vt* ...

(v) Where the phrasal verb form in all its usages is identical in one meaning to one category of the main verb it is normally included in the main verb entry.

(iv) Para **verbo intransitivo** o **reflexivo** que encabeza artículo: sustantivos (entre paréntesis) que típicamente pudieran ser los sujetos del verbo, p.ej. **atascarse** (*tubo*) ...; (*motor*) ...

Estas aclaraciones no se repiten para las palabras derivadas, pero las podrá trasladar el lector, p.ej. del adjetivo al adverbio, o del adjetivo al sustantivo abstracto (*fair-fairness*).

13 El orden de material dentro del artículo o subdivisión ha sido pensado para ayudar al lector y no sigue un sistema rígido. Sin embargo, el orden normal para un artículo sobre sustantivo es: (i) las traducciones básicas de la palabra cabeza de artículo; (ii) las frases que consisten en sustantivo con adjetivo; (iii) el sustantivo precedido por preposición (muchas veces con verbo también); (iv) el sustantivo con verbo. Dentro de cada categoría se mantiene el orden alfabético. No se separan los modismos de los ejemplos que ilustran el uso.

14 La colocación de los giros en los artículos suscita muchos problemas. En general los principios son:

(i) Los giros que consisten en sustantivo + sustantivo, verbo + verbo etc figuran en el artículo del primer elemento, p.ej. **'casa y comida'** en **casa**, **'black and blue'** en **black**.

(ii) Los giros en español que consisten en sustantivo + adjetivo figuran en el artículo del elemento sustantivo, p.ej. **cabina electoral** en **cabina**. Los giros en inglés que consisten en adjetivo + sustantivo figuran en el artículo del elemento adjetivo. Pero son muchas las combinaciones inglesas de adjetivo + sustantivo que han adquirido ya una existencia bastante independiente para que figuren como palabras cabezas de artículo.

(iii) Los giros que consisten en verbo + sustantivo figuran en el artículo del sustantivo, p.ej. **to show cause** en **cause**, **abrir carrera** en **carrera**; pero se citan muchos giros de este tipo en los verbos, como ejemplos del uso.

(iv) Los verbos con partícula, o verbos frasales, aparecen en el diccionario al final del artículo del verbo principal, siguiendo el orden alfabético correspondiente y marcados por un rombo negro.

(v) Cuando el verbo frasal tiene el mismo significado que una de las categorías del verbo principal, normalmente va incluido en la entrada de este último.

bandage ... **2** *vt* (*also* **to ~ up**) vendar.

(vi) In the case of less common adverbs and prepositions the phrase may well appear under the adverb or preposition.

(vi) En el caso de los adverbios y preposiciones menos frecuentes la locución bien puede estar en el artículo del adverbio o preposición.

astern ...: **to go** ~ ciar, ir hacia atrás; ...

There is, however, intentional duplication of phrases. Thus **año bisiesto** belongs, by rule (ii) above, under **año**; but it is also the sole phrase under the headword **bisiesto**. In many other cases phrases are duplicated because they illustrate something about both headwords.

15 Translation by single word is obviously sufficient in many cases. Often a liberal policy has been followed in offering a number of near-synonyms separated by commas; this is especially true of the more emotive and less precise adjectives. The abbreviation (*approx*) is used where no full translation exists. Explanations in italics are given where a word has no correspondence in the other language, eg **cachetero (b)**, **cante (a)**. Where the source language headword or phrase has a cultural equivalent in the target language, the translation is preceded by the cultural equivalent sign ≃. See for instance the entry for **GCSE**. For greater precision explanations in italics and in parentheses are occasionally added after the translation, eg **camayo (c)**.

16 The gender of every Spanish noun is given immediately after it in both parts of the dictionary.

17 Spanish feminine forms. In the English-Spanish the typical entry '**teacher** = profesor *m*, -ora *f*' is to be read as '= profesor *m*, profesora *f*'. Often a written accent on the masculine form is not needed in the feminine, eg '**Dane** = danés *m*, -esa *f*' (to be read as '= danés *m*, danesa *f*'). The endings affected are: **-án**, **-ana**; **-és**, **-esa**; **-ón**, **-ona**. Where one vowel is given as the feminine ending, it replaces the **-e** or **-o** of the masculine; thus '**cook** = cocinero *m*, -a *f*' is read as '= cocinero *m*, cocinera *f*'.

Hay, sin embargo, muchos casos donde se duplica de propósito la locución. Así **año bisiesto** pertenece, según la regla (ii) arriba, a **año**; pero también es la única locución en **bisiesto**. En otros casos se duplican las locuciones por el motivo de que en ambos lugares ilustran algo.

15 La traducción por una sola palabra basta en muchos casos. Pero a menudo hemos seguido una norma liberal ofreciendo varios sinónimos o casi sinónimos, separados por comas, sobre todo para los adjetivos emotivos y por lo tanto menos precisos. Donde no existe traducción adecuada se emplea la abreviatura (*aprox*). Cuando la palabra no tiene correspondencia en el otro idioma damos una explicación en cursiva, p.ej. para **cachetero (b)**, **cante (a)**. Si existe en la lengua de llegada una institución que sea equiparable, en términos aproximativos, a la de la lengua de salida, la traducción va precedida del signo ≃. Véase **RACE**. Alguna vez se añade a la traducción, en cursiva y en paréntesis, una aclaración o precisión, p.ej. para **camayo (c)**.

16 El género de todo sustantivo español consta inmediatamente después de la palabra en las dos partes del diccionario.

17 Desinencias femeninas en español. En la Parte 2ª el artículo típico '**teacher** = profesor *m*, -ora *f*' ha de leerse '= profesor *m*, profesora *f*'. A menudo el acento que lleva el masculino se suprime en el femenino, p.ej. '**Dane** = danés *m*, -esa *f*' (ha de leerse '= danés *m*, danesa *f*'). Tales desinencias son: **-án**, **-ana**; **-és**, **esa**; **-ón**, **-ona**. Donde se cita una sola vocal de la forma femenina, esta vocal sustituye la **-e** o la **-o** del masculino; así '**cook** = cocinero *m*, -a *f*' ha de leerse '= cocinero *m*, cocinera *f*'.

SPANISH PRONUNCIATION AND SPELLING

PRONUNCIATION AND SPELLING
THE PRONUNCIATION OF EUROPEAN SPANISH

1 Except for a very few anomalies such as the writing of silent *h* and the existence of the two symbols *b* and *v* for the same sound, the pronunciation of Spanish is so well represented by normal orthography that it would be a waste of space to give a phonetic transcription for every Spanish word in Part I as is done for English in Part II. The general introduction given below should suffice. However, a transcription in IPA (International Phonetic Association) symbols is given for those few Spanish words in which spelling and pronunciation are not in accord, such as *reloj* [re'lo], and for those numerous anglicisms and gallicisms which retain an un-Spanish spelling or which have unexpected and unpredictable pronunciations even for those acquainted with the original languages. In some cases alternative pronunciations are given, an indication that cultured Spanish usage has not yet fixed firmly on one.

In this section the pronunciation described is that of educated Castilian, and little account is taken of that of the Spanish regions, even though some (notably Andalusia) have considerable cultural strength and a pronunciation which is socially acceptable throughout Spain. The pronunciation of Spanish in America is treated in a separate section.

It must be noted that in this attempt to describe the sounds of Spanish in terms of English, and in a limited space, one is conscious of making no more than approximations. Such comparisons have a practical end and inevitably lack the scientific exactness which trained phoneticians require.

2 Accentuation of Spanish words

For Spanish, unlike English, simple rules can be devised and stated which will enable the stress to be placed correctly on each word at sight:

(a) If the word ends in a vowel, or in *n* or *s* (often the signs of the plural of verbs and nouns respectively), the penultimate syllable is stressed: *zapato, zapatos, divide, dividen, dividieron, antiviviseccionista, telefonea, historia, diluviaba* (such words are called *palabras llanas* or *graves*).

(b) If the word ends in a consonant other than *n* or *s*, the last syllable is stressed: *verdad, practicar, decibel, virrey, coñac, pesadez* (such words are called *palabras agudas*).

(c) If the word is to be stressed in some way contrary to rules **(a)** and **(b)**, an acute accent is written over the vowel to be stressed: *hablará, guaraní, rubí, esté, rococó*; *máquina, métodos, viéndolo, paralítico, húngaro* (words of this latter type are called *palabras esdrújulas*). With only two exceptions, the same syllable is stressed in the singular and plural forms of each word, but an

accent may have to be added or suppressed in the plural: *crimen, crímenes; nación, naciones*. The two exceptions are *carácter, caracteres*, and *régimen, regímenes*. Only in a few verbal forms can the stress fall further back than on the antepenultimate syllable: *cántamelo, prohíbaselo*.

3 Diphthongs, hiatus and syllable division

It will have been noted in **2 (a)** above, in cases like *telefonea* and *historia*, that not all vowels count equally for the purposes of syllable division and stress. The convention is that *a, e* and *o* are 'strong' vowels, and *i, u* 'weak'. Four rules then apply:

(a) A combination of weak + strong forms a diphthong (one syllable), the stress falling on the stronger element: *baila, cierra, puesto, peine, causa*.

(b) A combination of weak + weak forms a diphthong (one syllable), the stress falling on the second element: *ruido, fuimos, viuda*.

(c) Two strong vowels remain in hiatus as two distinct syllables, the stress falling according to rules **(a)** and **(b)** in section 2; *ma/es/tro* (three syllables in all), *con/tra/er* (three syllables in all), *cre/er* (two syllables).

(d) Any word having a vowel combination whose parts are not stressed according to rules **(a)** to **(c)** above bears an acute accent on the stressed part: *creído, período, baúl, ríe, tío*.

Note – in those cases where IPA transcriptions are given for Spanish words, the stress mark ['] is inserted in the same way as explained for English, above in **LA PRONUNCIACIÓN DEL INGLÉS BRITÁNICO**, section 2.

4 The Spanish letters and their sounds

Note – the order in which the explanations are set out is that of the alphabet and not that of the phonetic system. The system of transcription adopted is a fairly 'broad' one; a more exact or 'narrow' system would involve, for example, division of the vowel [e] according to quality and length, and the use of two symbols instead of one [e, ɛ].

5 Vowels

Spanish vowels are clearly and rather sharply pronounced, and single vowels are free from the tendency to diphthongize which is noticeable in English (eg **side** [saɪd], **know** [nəʊ]). Moreover when they are in unstressed positions they are relaxed only slightly, again in striking contrast to English (compare English **natural** ['nætʃrəl] with Spanish **natural** [natu'ral]). Stressed vowels are somewhat more open and short before **rr** (compare **carro** with **caro**, **perro** with **pero**).

(NOTE: Examples are pronounced as in British English.)

a	[a]	Not so short as **a** in English *pat, patter,* nor so long as in English *rather, bar*	**pata** **amara**
e	[e]	In an open syllable (one which ends in a vowel) like **e** in English *they,* but without the sound of the **y**. In a closed syllable (one which ends in a consonant) is a shorter sound, like the **e** in English *set, wet*	**me** **pelo** **sangre** **peldaño**
i	[i]	Not so short as **i** in English *bit, tip,* nor so long as in English *machine*	**iris** **filo**
o	[o]	In an open syllable (one which ends in a vowel) like **o** in English *note,* but without the sound of [u] which ends the vowel in this word. In a closed syllable (one which ends in a consonant) is a shorter sound, though not quite so short as in English *pot, cot*	**poco** **cosa** **bomba** **conté**
u	[u]	Like **u** in English *rule* or **oo** in *food.* Silent after **q** and in the groups **gue, gui,** unless marked by a diaeresis (*argüir, fragüe, antigüedad*)	**luna** **pula** **aquel** **pague**
y	[i]	As a vowel – that is in the conjunction **y** 'and', and at the end of a word such as *ley, voy* – is pronounced like **i**.	

Diphthongs

(See also section 3 above)

ai, ay	[ai]	like **i** in English *side*	**baile** **estay**
au	[au]	like **ou** in English *sound*	**áureo** **causa**
ei, ey	[ei]	like **ey** in English *they*	**reina** **rey**
eu	[eu]	like the vowel sounds in English **may-you**, without the sound of the **y**	**deuda** **feudo**
oi, oy	[oi]	like **oy** in English *boy*	**oiga** **soy**

Semiconsonants

There are two, and they appear in a variety of combinations as the first element; not all the combinations are listed here.

i, y	[j]	like **y** in English *yes, yacht* (See also the note under **y** in the list of consonants)	**bien** **hielo** **yunta** **apoyo**
u	[w]	like **w** in English *well*	**huevo** **fuente** **agua** **guardar**

Consonants

b, v   These two letters have the same value in Spanish. There are two distinct pronunciations depending on position and context:

[b]   At the start of the breath-group and after written *m* and *n* (pronounced [m]) the sound is plosive like English *b*

bomba
boda
enviar

[ʙ]   In all other positions the sound is a bilabial fricative (unknown in English) in which the lips do not quite meet

haba
severo
yo voy
de Vigo

c   There are two different values:

[k]   *c* before *a, o, u* or a consonant is like English *k* in *keep,* but without the slight aspiration which accompanies it

calco
acto
cuco

[θ]   *c* before *e, i* is like English *th* in *thin*. In parts of Andalusia and in *LAm* this is pronounced like English voiceless *s* in *same,* a phenomenon known as **seseo**

celda
hacer
cinco
cecear

Note – in words like *acción, sección* both types of *c*-sound are heard [kθ]

ch   [tʃ]   like English *ch* in *church*

mucho
chocho

d   There are three different values depending on position and context:

[d]   At the start of the breath-group and after *l, n* the sound is plosive like English *d*

dama
aldea
andar

[ð]   Between vowels and after consonants other than *l, n* the sound is relaxed and approaches English voiced *th* [ð] in *this*; in parts of Spain and in uneducated speech it is further relaxed and even disappears, particularly in the *-ado* ending.
In the final position, the second type of [ð] is further relaxed or altogether omitted (though purists condemn this as a vulgar error). In eastern parts of Spain, however, this final *-d* may be heard as a [t]

pide
cada
pardo
sidra
verdad
usted
Madrid
callad

f   [f]   like English *f* in *for*

fama
fofo

g   There are three different values depending on position and context:

[x]   Before *e, i* it is the same as the Spanish *j* (below)

Gijón
general

[g]   At the start of the breath-group and after *n,* the sound is that of the English *g* in *get*

gloria
rango
pingüe

[ɣ]   In other positions the sound is as in the second type above, but is fricative not plosive, there being no more than a close approximation of the vocal organs
Note – in the group *gue, gui* the *u* is silent (*guerra, guindar*) except when marked by a diaeresis (*antigüedad, argüir*). In the group *gua* all the letters are sounded (*guardia, guapo*)

haga
agosto
la guerra

h   always silent, a written convention only

honor
hombre
rehacer

j   [x]   a strong guttural sound not found in the English of England, but like the *ch* of Scots *loch*, Welsh *bach*, or German *Aachen, Achtung*; it is silent at the end of a word (*reloj*)

jota
jején
baraja

k   [k]   like English *k* in *kick,* but without the slight aspiration which accompanies it

kilogramo

l	[l]	like English *l* in *love*	**lelo** **panal**
ll	[ʎ]	approximating to English *lli* in *million*; in parts of Spain and most of *LAm* is pronounced as [j] and in other parts as [ʒ]; the pronunciation as [j] is condemned in Spain as a vulgar error but is extending rapidly even in Castile	**calle** **ella** **lluvia** **millón**
m	[m]	like English *m* in *made*	**mano** **mamar**
n	[n]	like English *n* in *none*; but before written *v* is pronounced as *m,* the group making [mb] (*eg enviar, sin valor*)	**nadie** **pan** **pino**
ñ	[ɲ]	approximating to English *ni* [nj] in *onion*	**uña** **ñoño**
p	[p]	like English *p* in *put*, but without the slight aspiration which accompanies it; it is often silent in *septiembre, séptimo*	**padre** **papa**
q	[k]	like English *k* in *kick,* but without the slight aspiration which accompanies it; it is always written in combination with *u,* which is silent	**que** **quinqué** **busqué** **quiosco**
r	[r]	a single trill or vibration stronger than any *r* in the English of England, but like the *r* in Scots; it is more relaxed in the final position and is indeed silent in parts of Spain and *LAm*; pronounced like *rr* at the start of a word and also after *l, n, s*	**coro** **quiere** **rápido** **real**
rr	[rr]	strongly trilled in a way that does not exist in English (except in parodies of Scots)	**torre** **arre burra** **irreal**
s	[s]	Two pronunciations: Except in the instances mentioned next, is a voiceless *s* like *s* in English *same*	**casa** **Isabel** **soso**
	[z]	Before a voiced consonant (*b, d, g, l, m, n*) is in most speakers a voiced *s* like *s* in English *rose, phase*	**desde** **asgo** **mismo** **asno**
t	[t]	like English *t* in *tame,* but without the slight aspiration which accompanies it	**título** **patata**
v		(*see* **b**)	
w		found in a few recent loanwords only; usually pronounced like Spanish *b, v* or like an English *v,* or kept as English *w*	**wáter** **week-end** **wolframio**
x		There are several possible pronunciations:	
	[ks]	Between vowels, *x* is pronounced like English *x* in *box* [ks], or	**máximo**
	[gs]	like *gs* in *big stick* [gs]	**examen**
	[s]	In a few words the *x* is pronounced between vowels like English *s* in *same* by many (but not all) speakers	**exacto** **auxilio**
	[s]	Before a consonant *x* is pronounced like English *s* in *same* by many (but not all) speakers	**extra** **sexto**
y	[j]	as a consonant or semiconsonant, is pronounced like *y* in English *yes, youth*; in emphatic speech in Spain and *LAm* this is heard as a voiced palatal plosive rather like the *j* in English *jam* [dʒ]; in Argentina, Chile etc this *y* is pronounced like the *s* in English *leisure* [ʒ]	**mayo** **yo** **mayor** **ya**
z	[θ]	like English *th* in *thin*; in parts of Andalusia and in *LAm* this is pronounced like English voiceless *s* in *same*, a phenomenon known as **seseo**	**zapato** **zopenco** **zumbar** **luz**

6 Additional notes on pronunciation

(a) The letter **b** is usually not pronounced in groups with **s** such as **obscuro, substituir,** and such words are now often written (with the Academy's sanction) **oscuro, sustituir** *etc*; they are so printed in this dictionary. A tendency to drop the **b** in pronouncing other similar groups is also noticeable, for example in **subjuntivo,** but in these cases the **b** is still always written.

(b) With one exception there are no real double consonants in Spanish speech; **cc** in words like **acción** is two separate sounds [kθ], while **ll** and **rr** have their own values (see the table above). The exception is the **-nn-** group found in learned words having the Latin prefix **in-,** eg **innato,** or occasionally **con-, sin-,** as in **connatural, sinnúmero.** In these cases the *n* is pronounced double [nn].

(c) Final **-s** of the definite and indefinite articles, plural, and of plural adjectives, is usually silent when the following noun starts with **r-**: eg **unos rábanos** [uno'rraβanos], **los romanos, varias razones, dos ratas** [do'rratas].

(d) Foreign sounds in Spanish hardly warrant separate treatment for our purposes; whereas the cultured Briton makes some attempt to maintain at least a vaguely French sound when he pronounces English loanwords from French, with nasal vowels and so on, the cultured Spaniard for the most part and certainly his less cultured compatriot adapts the sounds (but often not the spelling) of loanwords taken from French or English to suit his native speech habits. This is best studied in the transcriptions of individual items in the main text of the dictionary; see for example **chalet, gag, jazz, shock**.

(e) No old-established Spanish word begins with what is called 'impure *s*', that is, *s* plus a consonant as an initial group. When Spaniards have to pronounce a foreign name having such a group they inevitably precede it with an **e-** sound, so that **Smith** is [ez'miθ] or [ez'mis]. Very recent anglicisms tend to be written in Spanish as **slip, slogan** and so on, but must be pronounced [ez'lip], [ez'loɣan]; those that are slightly better established are written **esnob, esplín** etc, and then present no problem in pronunciation.

7 The letters of the Spanish alphabet

When the letters are cited one by one, or when a word is spelled out for greater clarity, or when an aircraft is identified by a letter and a name, and so on, the names of the letters used are:

a	[a]	j	['xota]	r	['ere]
b	[be] (in *LAm*	k	[ka]	rr*	['erre]
	[be'larɣa])				
c	[θe] [se]	l	['ele]	s	['ese]
ch*	[tʃe]	ll*	['eʎe]	t	[te]
d	[de]	m	['eme]	u	[u]
e	[e]	n	['ene]	v	['uβe] (in
f	['efe]	ñ	['eɲe]		*LAm* [be'korta])
g	[xe]	o	[o]	w	['uβe 'doβle] (in
h	['atʃe]	p	[pe]		*LAm* ['doβle be])
i	[i]	q	[ku]	x	['ekis]
				y	[i'ɣrjeɣa]
				z	['θeta] *or*
					['θeða] *or* ['seta]

The letters are of the feminine gender: 'mayo se escribe con una **m** minúscula', '¿esto es una **c** o una **t**?'. One says 'una **a**' and 'la **a**,' 'una **h**' and 'la **h**' (not applying the rule as in **un ave, el agua**).
* Though not strictly letters of the alphabet, these are considered separate sounds in Spanish.

THE PRONUNCIATION OF SPANISH IN AMERICA

To generalize briefly about the vast area over which Spanish ranges in the New World is difficult; the following notes are very tentative. The upland regions (settled by Castilians from the *meseta*) tend to be linguistically conservative and to have more Castilian features; the lowland and coastal regions share many of the features of Andalusian speech. Among the vowels there is little to note. Among the consonants:

1 The Castilian [θ] sound – in writing **c** or **z** – is pronounced as various kinds of s [s] throughout America, a phenomenon known as *seseo*.

2 At the end of a syllable and a word, *s* is a slight aspiration, eg **las dos** [lah'doh], **mosca** ['mohka]; but in parts of the Andean region, in upland Mexico and in Peru the [s] is maintained as in Castilian.

3 Castilian written **ll** [ʎ] is pronounced in three different ways in regions of America. It survives as [ʎ] in part of Colombia, all Peru, Bolivia, N. Chile and Paraguay; in Argentina, Uruguay, upland Ecuador and part of Mexico it is pronounced [ʒ]; and in the remaining areas it is pronounced [j]. When this last kind [j] is in contact with the vowels **e** and **i** it disappears altogether and one finds in uneducated writing such forms as **gaína** (for **gallina**) and **biete** (for **billete**).

4 In uneducated speech in all parts there is much confusion of **l** and **r**: **clin** (for **crin**), **carma** (for **calma**) etc.

5 Written **h** is silent in Castilian, but in parts of Mexico and Peru this **h** is aspirated at the start of a word (when it derives from Latin initial *f-*), so that in uneducated writing one finds such forms as **jarto** (for **harto**) and **jablar** (for **hablar**). Compare **halar/jalar** and other cases in the text of the dictionary.

SPANISH SPELLING

The system of spelling in Spanish is extremely logical and apart from a few small anomalies it presents no problems. An excellent book for those in doubt is Manuel Seco's *Diccionario de dudas y dificultades de la lengua española*, Madrid, Espasa-Calpe, 9th ed., 1990.

1 Spelling reform in Spanish to correct the few remaining anomalies is rarely attempted. Some favour always writing **j** (not a mixture of **g** and **j**) for the [x] sound: **jeneral**, **Jibraltar** – quite logically, since **jirafa**, **jícara** and **jirón**, and many others, are so spelled by everybody. Poetic texts of Juan Ramón Jiménez are always printed with such spellings.

2 The Academy's *Nuevas Normas* of 1959 recommended spelling rare words beginning in **mn-** and rather frequent words in **ps-** with **m, s** respectively, but this is taking a long time to establish itself; we have preferred in the dictionary to give such words as **ps-** in both parts, but with a cross-reference from **s-** in the Spanish-English, in accordance with our principle of following usage rather than rules. (Note that the element **seudo-** is well established, however, and has virtually ousted **pseudo-**.)

3 Novels representing the life of the lower urban classes, peasants and the regions are numerous. In them the author may portray their speech (phonetically substandard on the purists' criteria) by such forms as:

señá *for* señora	pá *for* para
usté *for* usted	ná *for* nada
verdá *for* verdad	tó *for* todo
pué *for* puede	güevo *for* huevo
	agüela *for* abuela

4 Those who read familiar letters from less well-educated Spaniards may welcome a note on the kind of error which often appears in such documents (and is not wholly unknown in public notices and in print). The errors depend on the few anomalies of the official spelling system. Great confusion reigns over **b, v**; one finds **boy** for **voy**, **escrivir** for **escribir**, **tranbía** for **tranvía**, and even **vrabo** for **bravo**. H being silent is often omitted: **acer, reacer, ombre**; but equally it is often added where it does not belong, **hera** for **era**, **honce** for **once** and so on. Since written **ll** [ʎ] is often regionally and vulgarly pronounced [j], one sometimes finds **ll** written by hypercorrection in place of **y**: **cullo** for **cuyo**, **rallo** for **rayo**.

5 Much of the above applies also to Spanish in America, partly because of error and partly because it reflects pronunciation there (see the previous section). The confusion between written **ll** and **y** goes further than in Spain, eg with **llapa-yapa**; the same is true of initial **h-** and **j-**, eg **halar-jalar**, and of **gua-** and **hua-**, eg **guaca-huaca**; we have tried to provide cross-references to these variants in the dictionary. Forms such as **güevo** (for **huevo**) and **güeno** (for **bueno**) are common too. Newspapers and even books are more carelessly printed in parts of America than they are in Spain; examples noted from Central America include **excabar** (for **excavar**), **haya** (for **aya**), **desabitada** (for **deshabitada**); while because the regular **seseo** equates Castilian [θ] with [s] in America, one finds in print **capas** (for **capaz**), **saga** (for **zaga**), and by hypercorrection **sociego** (for **sosiego**) and **discución** (for **discusión**).

6 Use of capitals in Spanish. Capital letters are used to begin words as in English in the following cases: for the first word in the sentence; for proper names of every kind; for the names, bynames and possessive pronouns of God, Christ, the Virgin Mary etc; for ranks and authorities in the state, army, church, the professions etc.

Usage differs from English in the following cases:

(a) The names of the days and months do not have capitals in Spanish: **lunes, martes, abril, mayo**.

(b) The first person subject pronoun does not have a capital unless it begins the sentence: **yo**. In Spanish it is usual to write the abbreviations **Vd, Vds, Ud, Uds** with capitals, but **usted, ustedes** in their extended form.

(c) Capitals are used for the names of countries and provinces etc, but not for the names of their inhabitants, for the adjectives relating to them or for their languages: **Francia**, but **un francés, una francesa, el vino francés, hablar francés**. The same is true of adjectives and nouns formed from other types of proper names: **la teoría darviniana, los estudios cervantinos, el conocido gongorista, la escuela alfonsí**.

(d) In the titles of books, articles, films etc the capital is used only at the start of the first word, unless later words are proper names: **El tercer hombre, Lo que el viento se llevó** (but **Boletín de la Real Academia Española**).

e) A very few words which do not have capitals in English often have them in Spanish: **el Estado, la Iglesia** and such. This is not obligatory and may depend on the amount of respect being shown.

7 Spanish punctuation. This is as in English except for the following features:

(a) Exclamation and question marks are placed inverted (¡¿) at the start of the exclamation or question as well as at the end. Note that this does not always coincide with the start of the sentence: eg **Pues ¿vamos o no vamos?; Son trece en total, ¿verdad?**

(b) The long dash (—, called a *raya*) is often used in Spanish where English would put parentheses.

(c) The same dash is much used to introduce dialogue or direct speech; sometimes at the start and at the end of the quotation, but sometimes only at the start.

(d) The inverted commas ("") with which English encloses passages of direct speech and uses for a variety of other purposes are often represented in Spanish by « ».

8 Word division in Spanish. There are rules, rather different from those of English, about how a word may be divided in writing at the end of a line. The main points are:

(a) A single consonant between vowels is grouped with the second of them: **pa-lo, Barcelo-na**.

(b) In a group of two consonants between vowels, the first is grouped with the preceding vowel and the second with the following vowel: **in-nato, des-mochar, paten-te**. But groups having **l** or **r** as the second element are considered as units and join the following vowel only: **re-probar, de-clarar**.

(c) A group consisting of consonant + **h** may be split: **ex-hibición, Al-hambra**.

(d) It must be remembered that **ch**, **ll** and **rr** are considered as individual letters and must therefore never be split: **aprove-char, aga-lla, contra-rrevolucionario**.

(e) In a group of three consonants, the first two join the preceding vowel and the third joins the following vowel: **trans-porte, cons-tante**. Exception: if the third consonant in the group is **l** or **r**, only the first consonant joins the preceding vowel while the second and third join the following vowel: **som-bra, des-preciar, con-clave**.

(f) Two vowels should never be separated, whether they form one syllable or not: **rui-do, maes-tro, pro-veer**.

(g) Where it can be clearly recognized that a word consists of two or more words having an independent existence of their own, the long word may be divided in ways that contravene the foregoing rules: **latino-americano, re-examinar, vos-otros**. The same applies to some prefixes: **des-animar, ex-ánime**.

9 Use of the hyphen (-, called a *guión*) in Spanish. Strictly speaking this should only be used in Spanish in the cases mentioned in the *Nuevas Normas*, *e.g.* **relaciones franco-prusianas, cuerpos técnico-administrativos**. Compound words with or without a hyphen in English should be written as single words without hyphen in Spanish; a **hotplate** is **un calientaplatos** and a **windscreen-wiper** is **un limpiaparabrisas**, while a **Latin-American** is **un hispanoamericano** or **un latinoamericano**. Nonetheless in the dictionary we have used the hyphen in a few Spanish words which have been regularly noted in that form in print.

LA PRONUNCIACIÓN Y ORTOGRAFÍA DEL INGLÉS

PRONUNCIACIÓN Y ORTOGRAFÍA
LA PRONUNCIACIÓN DEL INGLÉS BRITÁNICO

Como es sabido, la ortografía del inglés se ajusta a criterios históricos y etimológicos y en muchos puntos apenas ofrece indicaciones ciertas de cómo ha de pronunciarse cada palabra. Por ello nos ha parecido aconsejable y de utilidad para los hispanohablantes dar para cada palabra inglesa una pronunciación figurada o transcripción. Al tratar de explicar en estas notas los sonidos del inglés mediante comparaciones con los sonidos del español en un espacio reducido nos damos cuenta de que realizamos una labor que no pasa de ser aproximativa. Tales comparaciones tienen una finalidad práctica y carecen del rigor científico que exigen los fonetistas especializados.

1 Sistema de signos

Se emplean los signos de la IPA (International Phonetic Association). Hemos seguido en general las transcripciones de Daniel Jones, *English Pronouncing Dictionary,* London, Dent, 14th ed., 1989. En el prólogo de esta obra el autor explica los principios que le han guiado en su trabajo.

2 Acentuación

En las transcripciones el signo ['] se coloca delante de la sílaba acentuada. El signo [ˌ] se pone delante de la sílaba que lleva el acento secundario o más ligero en las palabras largas, p.ej. **acceleration** [ækˌseləˈreɪʃən]. Dos signos de acento principal [' '] indican que las dos sílabas, o bien dos de las sílabas, se acentúan igualmente, p.ej. **A 1** [ˈeɪˈwʌn], **able-bodied** [ˈeɪblˈbɒdɪd].

3 Signos impresos en cursiva

En la palabra *annexation* [ˌænekˈseɪʃən], la [ə] en cursiva indica que este sonido puede o no pronunciarse; o porque muchos hablantes la pronuncian pero porque otros muchos no la pronuncian, o bien porque es un sonido que se oye en el habla lenta y cuidada pero que no se oye en el habla corriente y en el ritmo de la frase entera.

4 Transcripciones alternativas

En los casos donde se dan dos transcripciones, ello indica que ambas pronunciaciones son igualmente aceptables en el uso de las personas cultas, p.ej. **medicine** [ˈmedsɪn, ˈmedɪsɪn], o bien que la pronunciación varía bastante según la posición de la palabra en la frase y el contexto fonético, p.ej. **an** [æn, ən, n].

5 Véase también la nota sobre la pronunciación del inglés norteamericano (pag. xliii).

6 El orden en que se explican los signos abajo es más o menos ortográfico y no el estrictamente fonético.

Vocales

[æ]	sonido breve, bastante abierto, parecido al de *a* en *carro*	**bat** **apple**	[bæt] [ˈæpl]
[ɑː]	sonido largo parecido al de *a* en *caro*	**farm** **calm**	[fɑːm] [kɑːm]
[e]	sonido breve, bastante abierto, parecido al de *e* en *perro*	**set** **less**	[set] [les]
[ə]	'vocal neutra', siempre átona; parecida a la *e* del artículo francés *le* y a la *a* final del catalán (p.ej. *casa, porta*)	**above** **porter** **convey**	[əˈbʌv] [ˈpɔːtəʳ] [kənˈveɪ]
[ɜː]	forma larga del anterior, en sílaba acentuada; algo parecido al sonido de *eu* en la palabra francesa *leur*	**fern** **work** **murmur**	[fɜːn] [wɜːk] [ˈmɜːməʳ]
[ɪ]	sonido breve, abierto, parecido al de *i* en *esbirro, irreal*	**tip** **pity**	[tɪp] [ˈpɪtɪ]
[iː]	sonido largo parecido al de *i* en *vino*	**see** **bean** **ceiling**	[siː] [biːn] [ˈsiːlɪŋ]

[ɒ]	sonido breve, bastante abierto, parecido al de *o* en *corra, torre*	**rot**	[rɒt]
		wash	[wɒʃ]
[ɔ:]	sonido largo, bastante cerrado, algo parecido al de *o* en *por*	**ball**	[bɔ:l]
		board	[bɔ:d]
[ʊ]	sonido muy breve, más cerrado que la *u* en *burro*	**soot**	[sʊt]
		full	[fʊl]
[u:]	sonido largo, parecido al de *u* en *uno, supe*	**root**	[ru:t]
		fool	[fu:l]
[ʌ]	sonido abierto, breve y algo oscuro, sin correspondencia en español; se pronuncia en la parte anterior de la boca sin redondear los labios	**come**	[kʌm]
		rum	[rʌm]
		blood	[blʌd]
		nourish	['nʌrɪʃ]

Diptongos

[aɪ]	sonido parecido al de *ai* en *fraile, vais*	**lie**	[laɪ]
		fry	[fraɪ]
[aʊ]	sonido parecido al de *au* en *pausa, sauce*	**sow**	[saʊ]
		plough	[plaʊ]
[eɪ]	sonido medio abierto, pero más cerrado que la *e* de *casé*; suena como si le siguiese una [i] débil, especialmente en sílaba acentuada	**fate**	[feɪt]
		say	[seɪ]
		waiter	['weɪtəʳ]
		straight	[streɪt]
[əʊ]	sonido que es una especie de *o* larga, sin redondear los labios ni levantar la lengua; suena como si le siguiese una [u] débil	**ago**	[ə'gəʊ]
		also	['ɔ:lsəʊ]
		atrocious	[ə'trəʊʃəs]
		note	[nəʊt]
[ɛə]	sonido que se encuentra únicamente delante de la *r*; el primer elemento se parece a la *e* de *perro*, pero es más abierto y breve; el segundo elemento es una forma débil de la 'vocal neutra' [ə]	**there**	[ðɛəʳ]
		rare	[rɛəʳ]
		fair	[fɛəʳ]
		ne'er	[nɛəʳ]
[ɪə]	sonido cuyo primer elemento es una *i* medio abierta; el segundo elemento es una forma débil de la 'vocal neutra' [ə]	**here**	[hɪəʳ]
		interior	[ɪn'tɪərɪəʳ]
		fear	[fɪəʳ]
		beer	[bɪəʳ]
[ɔɪ]	sonido cuyo primer elemento es una *o* abierta, seguido de una *i* abierta pero débil; parecido al sonido de *oy* en *voy* o de *oi* en *coime*	**toy**	[tɔɪ]
		destroy	[dɪs'trɔɪ]
		voice	[vɔɪs]
[ʊə]	sonido cuyo primer elemento es una *u* medio larga; el segundo elemento es una forma débil de la 'vocal neutra' [ə]	**allure**	[ə'ljʊəʳ]
		sewer	[sjʊəʳ]
		pure	[pjʊəʳ]

Consonantes

[b]	como la *b* de *tumbar, umbrío*	**bet**	[bet]
		able	['eɪbl]
[d]	como la *d* de *conde, andar*	**dime**	[daɪm]
		mended	['mendɪd]
[f]	como la *f* de *fofo, inflar*	**face**	[feɪs]
		snaffle	['snæfl]
[g]	como la *g* de *grande, rango*	**go**	[gəʊ]
		agog	[ə'gɒg]
[h]	es una aspiración fuerte, algo así como la jota castellana [x] pero sin la aspereza gutural de aquélla	**hit**	[hɪt]
		reheat	['ri:'hi:t]
[j]	como la *y* de *cuyo, reyes*	**you**	[ju:]
		pure	[pjʊəʳ]
		million	['mɪljən]

[k]	como la *c* de *cama* o la *k* de *kilómetro*, pero acompañada por una ligera aspiración inexistente en español	**catch**	[kætʃ]
		kiss	[kɪs]
		chord	[kɔːd]
		box	[bɔks]
[l]	como la *l* de *leer, pala*	**lick**	[lɪk]
		place	[pleɪs]
[m]	como la *m* de *mes, comer*	**mummy**	['mʌmɪ]
		roam	[rəum]
[n]	como la *n* de *nada, hablan*	**nut**	[nʌt]
		sunny	['sʌnɪ]
[ŋ]	como el sonido que tiene la *n* en *banco, rango*	**bank**	[bæŋk]
		sinker	['sɪŋkəʳ]
		singer	['sɪŋəʳ]
[p]	como la *p* de *palo, ropa*, pero acompañada por una ligera aspiración inexistente en español	**pope**	[pəup]
		pepper	['pepəʳ]
[r]	Es un sonido muy débil, casi semivocal, que no tiene la vibración fuerte que caracteriza la *r* española. Se articula elevando la punta de la lengua hacia el paladar duro. (NB: En el inglés de Inglaterra la *r* escrita se pronuncia únicamente delante de vocal; en las demás posiciones es muda. Véase la nota sobre la pronunciación del inglés norteamericano y el signo [ʳ] abajo.)	**rate**	[reɪt]
		pear	[pɛəʳ]
		fair	[fɛəʳ]
		blurred	[blɜːd]
		sorrow	['sɒrəu]
[ʳ]	Este signo en las transcripciones indica que la *r* escrita en posición final de palabra se pronuncia en el inglés británico en muchos casos cuando la palabra siguiente empieza con vocal. En algún dialecto inglés y sobre todo en los Estados Unidos esta *r* se pronuncia siempre, así cuando la palabra se pronuncia aislada como cuando la siguen otras (empezando con vocal o sin ella).	**bear**	[bɛəʳ]
		humour	['hjuːməʳ]
		after	['ɑːftəʳ]
[s]	como la *s* (sorda) de *casa, sesión*	**sit**	[sɪt]
		scent	[sent]
		cents	[sents]
		pox	[pɒks]
[t]	como la *t* de *tela, rata*, pero acompañada por una ligera aspiración inexistente en español	**tell**	[tel]
		strut	[strʌt]
		matter	['mætəʳ]
[v]	Inexistente en español (aunque se encuentra en catalán y valenciano). En inglés es sonido labiodental, y se produce juntando el labio inferior con los dientes superiores	**vine**	[vaɪn]
		river	['rɪvəʳ]
		cove	[kəuv]
[w]	como la *u* de *huevo, puede*	**wine**	[waɪn]
		bewail	[bɪ'weɪl]
[z]	como la *s* (sonora) de *desde, mismo*	**zero**	['zɪərəu]
		roses	['rəuzɪz]
		buzzer	['bʌzəʳ]
[ʒ]	Inexistente en español, pero como la *j* de las palabras francesas *jour, jalousie*, o como la *g* de las palabras portuguesas *gente, geral*	**rouge**	[ruːʒ]
		leisure	['leʒəʳ]
		azure	['eɪʒəʳ]
	Este sonido aparece a menudo en el grupo [dʒ], parecido al grupo *dj* de la palabra francesa *adjacent*	**page**	[peɪdʒ]
		edge	[edʒ]
		jail	[dʒeɪl]
[ʃ]	Inexistente en español, pero como la *ch* de las palabras francesas *chambre, fiche*, o como la *x* de la palabra portuguesa *roxo*	**shame**	[ʃeɪm]
		ocean	['əuʃən]
		ration	['ræʃən]
		sugar	['ʃugəʳ]
	Este sonido aparece a menudo en el grupo [tʃ], parecido al grupo *ch* del español *mucho, chocho*	**much**	[mʌtʃ]
		chuck	[tʃʌk]
		natural	['nætʃrəl]
[θ]	como la *z* de *zumbar* o la *c* de *ciento*	**thin**	[θɪn]
		maths	[mæθs]

[ð]	forma sonorizada del anterior, algo parecido a la **d** de *todo, hablado*	**this** [ðɪs] **other** ['ʌðəʳ] **breathe** [briːð]
[x]	sonido que en rigor no pertenece al inglés de Inglaterra, pero que se encuentra en el inglés de Escocia y en palabras escocesas usadas en Inglaterra etc; es como la *j* de *joven, rojo*	**loch** [lɔx]

7 Sonidos extranjeros

El grado de corrección con que el inglés pronuncia las palabras extranjeras que acaban de incorporarse al idioma depende – como en español – del nivel cultural del hablante y de los conocimientos que pueda tener del idioma de donde se ha tomado la palabra. Las transcripciones que damos de tales palabras representan una pronunciación más bien culta. En las transcripciones la tilde [˜] indica que la vocal tiene timbre nasal (en muchas palabras de origen francés). En las pocas palabras tomadas del alemán aparece a veces la [x], para cuya explicación véase el cuadro de las consonantes.

8 Las letras del alfabeto inglés

Cuando se citan una a una, o cuando se deletrea una palabra para mayor claridad, o cuando se identifica un avión etc por una letra y su nombre, las letras suenan así:

a	[eɪ]	**j**	[dʒeɪ]	**s**	[es]
b	[biː]	**k**	[keɪ]	**t**	[tiː]
c	[siː]	**l**	[el]	**u**	[juː]
d	[diː]	**m**	[em]	**v**	[viː]
e	[iː]	**n**	[en]	**w**	['dʌbljuː]
f	[ef]	**o**	[əʊ]	**x**	[eks]
g	[dʒiː]	**p**	[piː]	**y**	[waɪ]
h	[eɪtʃ]	**q**	[kjuː]	**z**	[zed] (*en*
i	[aɪ]	**r**	[ɑːʳ]		*EEUU* [ziː])

LA PRONUNCIACIÓN DEL INGLÉS NORTEAMERICANO

Sería sin duda deseable dar aquí un resumen de las diferencias más notables que existen entre el inglés de Inglaterra y el de las regiones del Reino Unido – Escocia, Gales, Irlanda del Norte – y el de los principales países extranjeros y continentes donde se ha arraigado este idioma: Irlanda, Estados Unidos y el Canadá, las Antillas, Australia y Nueva Zelanda, Sudáfrica y los países sucesores de las antiguas colonias en el Este y Oeste de África, la India, etc. Para tal labor no disponemos ni del espacio ni mucho menos de los conocimientos necesarios. Siendo este diccionario un trabajo angloamericano, sin embargo, y considerando el predominio actual de los Estados Unidos en tantas esferas (entre ellas la lingüística), es de todos modos imprescindible apuntar algunas de las múltiples diferencias que existen entre el inglés de Inglaterra y el hablado en Estados Unidos.

Empleamos las abreviaturas (*Brit*) (British) y (*US*) (United States).

1 Acentuación

Las palabras que tienen dos sílabas o más después del acento principal llevan en (*US*) un acento secundario que no tienen en (*Brit*), p.ej. **dictionary** [(*US*) 'dɪkʃə,nerɪ = (*Brit*) 'dɪkʃənrɪ], **secretary** [(*US*) 'sekrə,terɪ = (*Brit*) 'sekrətrɪ]. En algunos casos se acentúa en (*US*) una sílaba distinta de la que lleva el acento en (*Brit*): p.ej. **primarily** [(*US*) praɪ'mærɪlɪ = (*Brit*) 'praɪmərɪlɪ]. Este cambio de acento se percibe ahora también, por influencia norteamericana, en el inglés de Inglaterra.

2 Entonación

El inglés de (*US*) se habla con un ritmo más lento y en un tono más monótono que en Inglaterra, debido en parte al alargamiento de las vocales que se apunta abajo.

3 Sonidos

Muchas de las vocales breves acentuadas en (*Brit*) se alargan mucho en (*US*), y alguna vocal inacentuada en (*Brit*) se oye con más claridad en (*US*), p.ej. **rapid** [(*US*) 'ræ:pɪd = (*Brit*) 'ræpɪd], **capital** [(*US*) 'kæ:bɪdəl = (*Brit*) 'kæpɪtl].

Peculiaridad muy notable del inglés en (*US*) es la nasalización de las vocales antes y después de las consonantes nasales [m, n, ŋ].

En las vocales individuales también hay diferencias. El sonido [ɑ:] en (*Brit*) en muchas palabras se pronuncia en (*US*) como [æ] o bien [æ:], p.ej. **grass** [(*US*) græs o græ:s = (*Brit*) grɑ:s], **answer** [(*US*) 'ænsər o 'æ:nsər = (*Brit*) 'ɑ:nsər]. El sonido [ɒ] en (*Brit*) se pronuncia en (*US*) casi como una [ɑ] oscura, p.ej. **dollar** [(*US*) 'dɑlər = (*Brit*) 'dɒlər], **hot** [(*US*) hɑt = (*Brit*) hɒt], **topic** [(*US*) 'tɑpɪk = (*Brit*) 'tɒpɪk]. El diptongo que se pronuncia en (*Brit*) [juː] en sílaba acentuada se pronuncia en la mayor parte de (*US*) sin [j], p.ej. **Tuesday** [(*US*) 'tuːzdɪ = (*Brit*) 'tjuːzdɪ], **student** [(*US*) 'stuːdənt = (*Brit*) 'stjuːdənt]; pero muchas palabras de este tipo se pronuncian en (*US*) igual que en (*Brit*), p.ej. **music, pure, fuel.** En último lugar entre las vocales, se nota que la sílaba final **-ile** que se pronuncia en (*Brit*) [aɪl] es a menudo en (*US*) [əl] o bien [ɪl], p.ej. **missile** [(*US*) 'mɪsəl, 'mɪsɪl = (*Brit*) 'mɪsaɪl]. Existen otras diferencias en la pronunciación de las vocales de palabras individuales, p.ej. **tomato,** pero éstas se tratan individualmente en el texto del diccionario.

En cuanto a las consonantes, destacamos dos diferencias. La consonante sorda [t] entre vocales suele sonorizarse bastante en (*US*), p.ej. **united** [(*US*) juˈnaɪdɪd = (*Brit*) juːˈnaɪtɪd], o sufre lenición [t]. La *r* escrita en posición final después de vocal o entre vocal y consonante es por la mayor parte muda en (*Brit*), pero se pronuncia a menudo en (*US*), p.ej. **where** [(*US*) wɛər = (*Brit*) wɛəʳ], **sister** [(*US*) 'sɪstər = (*Brit*) 'sɪstəʳ]. Hemos tomado esto en cuenta en las transcripciones en el texto del diccionario. También en posición final de sílaba (no sólo de palabra) se nota esta pronunciación de la *r* escrita: **burden** [(*US*) 'bəːrdn = (*Brit*) 'bəːdn], **jersey** [(*US*) 'dʒəːrzɪ = (*Brit*) 'dʒəːzɪ].

Conviene advertir que aun dentro del inglés de Estados Unidos hay notables diferencias regionales; la lengua de Nueva Inglaterra difiere bastante de la del Sur, la del Mediooeste no es la de California, etc. Los datos que constan arriba no son más que indicaciones muy someras.

LA ORTOGRAFÍA DEL INGLÉS

El extranjero, mientras lucha con las muchas confusiones y rarezas de la ortografía inglesa, se consuela recordando que los propios niños ingleses, y muchas personas mayores, sostienen la misma lucha. El inglés ha de ser el único idioma para el que ha valido la pena – la cosa estuvo de moda hace unos años – organizar certámenes ortográficos, en los que se pedía que los concursantes deletreasen palabras como **parallel**, **precede** y **proceed** y **supersede**, **sylph** y **Ralph**. Ha habido muchas tentativas de reforma – siendo quizá la más conocida la de G. B. Shaw – pero ninguna se ha llevado a la práctica; las reformas norteamericanas (véase abajo) son útiles pero afectan sólo a una pequeña parte del problema.

1   En general se aplica el sistema en todo su rigor y las dudas y desviaciones permitidas son escasísimas. Es lícito escribir algunas palabras con o sin **e** muda, como **blond(e)**, **judg(e)ment**; varía la vocal en **enquiry-inquiry**, **encrust-incrust**, y la consonante en muchas palabras terminadas en **-ise**, **-ize** (pero siempre **advertise**, **chastise**). En casos como **spirt-spurt** se hace generalmente una distinción de sentido. Son toleradas **grandad** y **granddad**, **mummie** y **mummy**. Las variantes más importantes constan en el texto del diccionario.

2   En las novelas en que se presenta la vida de la clase baja urbana (p.ej. de los *Cockneys* de Londres) o de gente del campo, el autor puede representar su habla – con sus incorrecciones y barbarismos, según el criterio casticista – con formas como las siguientes:

'e	=	he	Oim	=	I'm
'ere	=	here	roit	=	right
'ope	=	hope	Lunnun	=	London
'ed	=	head	bruvver	=	brother
et	=	ate	Fursday	=	Thursday
'arf	=	half	dook	=	duke
yer	=	your	dunno	=	don't know

La **-d** final tras **n** se suprime a menudo en este lenguaje, p.ej. **an'** = **and**, y la **-g** final se suprime en la desinencia **-ing**, p.ej. **boozin'** = **boozing**. Como curiosidad apuntamos que este último fenómeno se da también en representaciones del habla de las familias aristocráticas, de los militares viejos etc: **huntin'**, **shootin'** and **fishin'**. Nótese el modo de emplear la comilla (') para indicar la supresión de una letra. Tales cambios en la escritura pueden representar una diferencia no de clase sino de región, p.ej. en escocés **awa'** = **away**, y en el inglés de las Antillas **dis** = **this**.

3   Se observan a veces deformaciones hechas con intención humorística (**luv** = **love**, **Injun** = **Indian**) o con afán de ultramodernidad (**nite** = **night**) o como truco publicitario en el comercio (**sox** = **socks**) o como parte de la jerga de un grupo social (**showbiz** = **show business**).

4   Son mucho más importantes las diferencias ortográficas entre el inglés británico (*Brit*) y el norteamericano (*US*):

(a) La **u** que se escribe en (*Brit*) en las palabras terminadas en **-our** y derivadas del latín, se suprime en (*US*): (*US*) **color** = (*Brit*) **colour**, (*US*) **labor** = (*Brit*) **labour**. (Esto no afecta a los monosílabos como **dour, flour, sour**, donde no hay diferencia.) También en (*US*) se suprime la **u** del grupo **ou** [əʊ] en el interior de la palabra: (*US*) **mold** = (*Brit*) **mould**, (*US*) **smolder** = (*Brit*) **smoulder**.

(b) Muchas palabras que en (*Brit*) terminan en **-re** se escriben en (*US*) **-er**: *US* **center** = (*Brit*) **centre**, (*US*) **meter** = (*Brit*) **metre**, (*US*) **theater** = (*Brit*) **theatre**. (Pero no existe diferencia en **acre, lucre, massacre**.)

(c) Ciertas vocales finales, que no tienen valor en la pronunciación, se escriben en (*Brit*) pero se suprimen en (*US*): (*US*) **catalog** = (*Brit*) **catalogue**, (*US*) **prolog** = (*Brit*) **prologue**, (*US*) **program** = (*Brit*) **programme**, (*US*) **kilogram** = (*Brit*) **kilogramme**.

(d) En (*US*) se suele simplificar los diptongos de origen griego y latino **ae, oe**, escribiendo sencillamente **e**: (*US*) **anemia** = (*Brit*) **anaemia**, (*US*) **anesthesia** = (*Brit*) **anaesthesia**. En (*US*) se duda entre **subpoena** y **subpena**; en (*Brit*) se mantiene siempre el primero.

(e) En algunos casos las palabras que en (*Brit*) terminan en **-ence** se escriben **-ense** en (*US*): (*US*) **defense** = (*Brit*) **defence**, (*US*) **offense** = (*Brit*) **offence**.

(f) Algunas consonantes que en (*Brit*) se escriben dobles se escriben en (*US*) sencillas: (*US*) **wagon** = (*Brit*) **waggon** (pero **wagon** se admite también en Inglaterra), y sobre todo en formas verbales: (*US*) **kidnaped** = (*Brit*) **kidnapped**, (*US*) **worshiped** = (*Brit*) **worshipped**. El caso de **l, ll** intervocálicas ofrece más complejidades. Alguna vez lo que se escribe con **ll** en (*Brit*) se encuentra con una **l** en (*US*): así (*US*) **councilor** = (*Brit*) **councillor**, (*US*) **traveler** = (*Brit*) **traveller**. Por el contrario, en posición final de sílaba o de palabra la **l** en (*Brit*) es a menudo **ll** en (*US*): así (*US*) **enroll, enrolls** = (*Brit*) **enrol, enrols**, (*US*) **skillful** = (*Brit*) **skilful**.

(g) En (*US*) se modifica algún otro grupo ortográfico del inglés, pero sólo en la escritura de tono familiar: (*US*) **tho** = (*Brit*) **though**, (*US*) **thru** = (*Brit*) **through**. También son más corrientes en (*US*) las formas como **Peterboro** (o bien **Peterboro'**), aunque éstas no son desconocidas en (*Brit*).

(**h**) Viene luego una serie de palabras aisladas que se escriben de modo diferente:

(*US*)	(*Brit*)	(*US*)	(*Brit*)
ax	axe	mustache	moustache
check	cheque	pajamas	pyjamas
cozy	cosy	plow	plough
gray	grey	skeptic	sceptic
gypsy	gipsy	tire	tyre

En otros casos se duda bastante; en (*US*) hay lucha entre **rime, rhyme,** mientras en (*Brit*) se escribe únicamente el segundo; en (*US*) hay lucha entre **tire, tyre,** mientras en (*Brit*) se escribe siempre el segundo.

Conviene notar que mientras la influencia del inglés norteamericano se percibe a cada paso en el inglés británico en cuanto al léxico, a la fraseología y a la sintaxis, ésta parece no haber afectado para nada la ortografía del inglés en el Reino Unido.

5 Las mayúsculas se emplean más en inglés que en español. Se emplean como en español al principio de la palabra en los siguientes casos: en la primera palabra de la frase; en los nombres propios de toda clase; en los nombres, sobrenombres y pronombres posesivos de Dios, Cristo, Nuestra Señora etc; en las graduaciones y títulos de las autoridades del estado, del ejército, de la iglesia, de las profesiones etc.

Las mayúsculas se emplean en inglés en los siguientes casos donde se escribe minúscula en español:

(**a**) Los nombres de los días y meses: **Monday, Tuesday, April, May.**

(**b**) El pronombre personal de sujeto, primera persona: **I** (**yo**). Pero el pronombre de segunda persona se escribe en inglés con minúscula: **you** (*Vd, Vds*).

(**c**) Los nombres de los habitantes de los países y provincias, los adjetivos derivados de éstos y los nombres de los idiomas: **I like the French, two Frenchwomen, French cheese, to talk French, a text in old Aragonese.** Se emplea la mayúscula también en los nombres y adjetivos derivados de otras clases de nombres propios: **a Darwinian explanation, the Bennites, two well-known Gongorists, the Alphon-**

sine school. Sin embargo el adjetivo de nacionalidad puede escribirse con minúscula en algún caso cuando se refiere a una cosa corriente u objeto conocido de todos, p.ej. **a french window, french beans, german measles** (en este diccionario hemos preferido escribir algunas de estas palabras con mayúscula).

(**d**) En los sustantivos y adjetivos principales en los títulos de libros, artículos, películas etc: **The Third Man, Gone with the Wind.**

6 La puntuación en inglés. Los signos y el modo de emplearlos son como en español con las siguientes excepciones:

(**a**) Los signos de admiración y de interrogación (¡¿) no se emplean en inglés en principio de frase.

(**b**) En inglés se emplea menos la doble raya (— ... —) con función parentética; se prefiere en muchos casos el paréntesis (...).

(**c**) La raya (—) que sirve a menudo en español para introducir el diálogo y la oración directa, y a veces también para cerrarlos, se sustituye en inglés por las comillas (“...”). Conviene apuntar que éstas se emplean obligatoriamente al terminar la cita u oración directa y no sólo para introducirla. Los signos « » del español se escriben siempre como comillas (“...”) en inglés.

7 La división de la palabra en inglés. Las reglas para dividir una palabra en final de renglón son menos estrictas en inglés que en español. En general se prefiere cortar la palabra tras vocal, **hori-zontal, vindi-cation,** pero se prefiere mantener como unidades ciertos sufijos comunes, **vindica-tion, glamor-ous.** De acuerdo con esto se divide la palabra dejando separada la desinencia **-ing,** p.ej. **sicken-ing,** pero si ésta está precedida por un grupo de consonantes, una de ellas va unida al **-ing,** p.ej. **tick-ling.** Se divide el grupo de dos consonantes iguales: **pat-ter, yel-low, disap-pear,** y los demás grupos consonánticos de acuerdo con los elementos separables que forman la palabra: **dis-count, per-turb.**

DICCIONARIO
ESPAÑOL~INGLÉS

SPANISH~ENGLISH
DICTIONARY

A, a¹ [a] NF (*letra*) A, a; **a por a y be por be** point by point, in full detail.

a² PREP **(a)** (*lugar: dirección*) to; **ir a Madrid** to go to Madrid; **llegar a Madrid** to arrive in Madrid; to reach Madrid; **llegar al teatro** to arrive at the theatre; **ir al parque** to go to the park; **ir a casa** to go home; **subir a un avión** to get into a plane; **subir a un tren** to get into a train, to get on a train; **mirar al norte** to look northwards; **(de) cara al norte** facing north; **torcer a la derecha** to turn (to the) right; **caer al mar** to fall into the sea.
(b) (*lugar: distancia*) **está a 7 km de aquí** it is 7 km (away) from here.
(c) (*lugar: posición*) at; **al lado de** at the side of; **a la puerta** at the door; **estar a la mesa** to be at table; **estaba sentado a su mesa de trabajo** he was sitting at his desk; **a retaguardia** in the rear; **a orillas de** on the banks of; **al margen** in the margin.
(d) (*tiempo*) at; **a las 8** at 8 o'clock; **¿a qué hora?** at what time?; **a mediodía** at noon; **a la noche** at nightfall; (*LAm**) **a la tarde** in the afternoon; **a la mañana siguiente** the following morning; **a 3 de junio** on the third of June; **a los 55 años** at 55, at the age of 55; **al año de esto** after a year of this, a year later; **a los pocos días** within a few days, after a few days, a few days later; **a los 18 minutos** (*de un juego*) in the 18th minute; **'Cervantes a los 400 años'** (*título de estudio*) 'Cervantes after 400 years', 'Cervantes 400 years on'; **a tiempo** in time.
(e) (*manera*) **a la americana** in the American fashion, (in) the American way, American style; **a caballo** on horseback; **a escape** at full speed; **a oscuras** in the dark, in darkness; **diseño a cuadros** chequered pattern; **diseño a rayas** striped pattern; **a petición de** at the request of; **a pie** on foot; **a solicitud** on request; **tres a tres** three at a time, in threes, by threes; **beber algo a sorbos** to drink sth in sips; **mirarse a los ojos** to look into each other's eyes.
(f) (*medio, instrumento*) **funciona a pilas y a la red** it works on batteries and on the mains: **a lápiz** in pencil; **cocina a gas** gas stove; **a puñetazos** with (blows of) one's fists; **a mano** by hand; **bordado a mano** hand-embroidered; **girar algo a mano** to turn sth by hand; **despertarse al menor ruido** to wake at the least sound.
(g) (*razón*) **poco a poco** little by little; **palmo a palmo** inch by inch; **a un precio elevado** at a high price; **a 30 ptas el kilo** at 30 pesetas a kilo, for 30 pesetas a (o per) kilo; **al 5 por ciento** at 5%; **a 50 km por hora** at 50 km an hour.
(h) (*dativo*) to; **se lo di a él** I gave it to him; **le di dos a Pepe** I gave two to Joe, I gave Joe two; **El Toboso marcó 5 goles al Madrid** El Toboso scored 5 against Madrid.
(i) (*dativo: separación*) **se lo compré a él** I bought it from him.
(j) (*con objeto pers: no se traduce*) **vi al jefe** I saw the boss.
(k) (*construcción tras ciertos verbos*) to; **empezó a cantar** he began to sing; **voy a verle** I'm going to see him; **sabe a queso** it tastes of cheese; **huele a vino** it smells of wine.
(l) (*al + infin*) **al verle** on seeing him; when I saw him; *V t* **al.**
(m) (*a + infin*) **asuntos a tratar** agenda, items to be discussed; **el criterio a adoptar** the criterion to be adopted; **éste será el camino a recorrer** this will be the path to take.
(n) (*imperativo*) **¡a callar!** be quiet!; **¡a trabajar!** to work!, get down to it!
(o) (*si*) **a no ser esto así** if this were not so; **a decir verdad ...** to tell the truth ...; **a la que te descuides** before you know where you are ...
(p) **¡~ que ...!** I bet ...!

AA (*Aer*) ABR *de* **Aerolíneas Argentinas.**
AA.AA. ABR *de* **Antiguos Alumnos** Former Pupils, FPs.
AAE NF ABR *de* **Asociación de Aerolíneas Europeas** Association of European Airlines, AEA.
AA.EE. ABR *de* **Asuntos Exteriores**; *V* **asunto (a).**

ab. ABR *de* **abril** April, Apr.
abacá NM abaca, Manilla hemp.
abacado NM (*Carib*) avocado pear.
abacería NF grocer's (shop), grocery store.
abacero, -a NM/F grocer, provision merchant.
ábaco NM abacus.
abacora NF (*LAm*) type of tuna.
abacorar [1a] VT **(a)** (*And, Carib*) (*acosar*) to harass, plague, bother; (*sorprender*) to catch, surprise.
(b) (*Carib: acometer*) to undertake boldly; (*: *seducir*) to entice away.
(c) (*LAm Com*) to monopolize; to corner (the market in).
abad NM abbot.
abadejo NM **(a)** (*pez: de mar*) cod, codfish; pollack; (*de agua dulce*) ling; (*Carib: pez espada*) swordfish. **(b)** (*Ent*) Spanish fly, cantharides. **(c)** (*Culin*) dried salted cod.
abadengo [1] ADJ abbatial, of an abbot.
[2] NM abbacy.
abadesa NF **(a)** (*Rel*) abbess. **(b)** (*LAm**) madame, brothel-keeper.
abadía NF **(a)** (*edificio*) abbey. **(b)** (*rango, oficio*) abbacy.
abajadero NM slope, incline.
abajar [1a] VT (*LAm*) = **bajar.**
abajeño (*LAm*) [1] ADJ lowland (*atr*), of the lowland(s), from the lowland(s).
[2] NM, **abajeña** NF lowlander; (*Méx: costeño*) lowlander, coastal dweller.
abajera NF (*Cono Sur*) saddlecloth.
abajero ADJ (*LAm*) lower, under.
abajino (*Cono Sur*) [1] ADJ northern.
[2] NM, **abajina** NF northerner.
abajo [1] ADV (*posición*) down, below, down below, underneath, (*en casa*) downstairs; (*dirección*) down, downwards, (*en casa*) downstairs; **¡~ el gobierno!** down with the government!; **aquí ~** down here; **here below**; **desde ~** from below; **hacia ~** down, downwards; **más ~** lower down, further down; **por ~** underneath; **cuesta ~** downhill; **río ~** downstream; **del rey (para) ~** from the king down.
[2] **~ de** PREP below, under.
[3] **de ~** ADJ: **la parte de ~** the lower part, the underside; **el piso de ~** the downstairs flat; the floor below, the next floor down; **los de ~** the underdogs, the downtrodden, the underprivileged.
abajofirmante NMF: **el ~, la ~** the undersigned.
abalanzadero NM (*Méx*) ford, cattle crossing.
abalanzar [1f] [1] VT **(a)** (*pesar*) to weigh; (*equilibrar*) to balance.
(b) (*lanzar*) to hurl, throw; (*impeler*) to impel.
[2] **abalanzarse** VR **(a)** to spring forward, rush forward, dash forward; (*multitud*) to surge forward; **~ a peligro** to rush thoughtlessly into; **~ sobre** to spring at, rush at, hurl o.s. on; to pounce on; **se abalanzaron los amantes** the lovers threw themselves at one another.
(b) (*Cono Sur: caballo*) to rear up.
abaldonar [1a] VT (*degradar*) to degrade, debase; (*insultar*) to affront.
abalear [1a] [1] VT (*LAm: disparar*) to shoot (at), fire at; (*And: fusilar*) to shoot, execute.
[2] VI (*LAm: tirotear*) to shoot off guns, fire in the air.
abaleo NM (*LAm*) shooting.
abalorio NM glass bead; beads, beadwork; **no vale un ~** it's worthless.
abalum(b)ar* [1a] VT (*Méx*) to pile up, stack.
abanarse* [1a] VR (*Cono Sur*) to give o.s. airs, show off.
abanderado, -a NM/F (*Pol etc*) standard-bearer, champion, leader; (*LAm Dep*) representative; (*linier*) linesman.
abanderar [1a] VT **(a)** (*Náut*) to register. **(b)** *causa etc* to champion; *campaña* to take a leading role in.
abanderizar [1f] [1] VT to organize into bands.

2 abanderizarse VR to band together; to join a band; (*Cono Pol*) to take sides, adopt a position.

abandonado ADJ abandoned; *lugar etc* abandoned, deserted, godforsaken; *edificio* deserted, derelict; *piso* vacant; *aspecto* neglected; forlorn; slovenly, uncared-for; (*moralmente*) profligate; (*LAm: dejado*) slovenly, untidy; (*LAm*: pervertido*) perverted.

abandonamiento NM = **abandono**.

abandonar [1a] **1** VT *lugar etc* to leave; *persona* to leave, abandon; to desert, forsake; (*huir de*) to flee from; *objeto* to leave behind; *tentativa, hábito* to drop, give up; (*renunciar*) to renounce, relinquish; **~ una empresa** to give up an attempt; **abandonaron a sus hijos** they deserted their children; **cuando abandonó la casa** when he left the house; **tuvo que ~ el cargo** he had to give up the post; **¡abandonado me tenías!** you'd forgotten all about me!

2 VI to give up; (*Inform*) to quit; (*Dep*) to withdraw, scratch, retire; (*Ajedrez*) to resign.

3 abandonarse VR **(a)** (*rendirse*) to give in, give up; (*desanimarse*) to lose heart, get discouraged; (*descuidarse*) to let o.s. go, get slovenly, get slack; **no te abandones** don't let yourself go.

(b) **~ a** to give o.s. over to, yield to, indulge in an excess of.

abandonismo NM defeatism.

abandonista ADJ, NMF defeatist.

abandono NM (*V v*) **(a)** (*acto*) abandonment; dereliction; desertion; giving up, renunciation, relinquishment; (*Dep*) withdrawal, retirement; (*Ajedrez*) resignation; **~ de la escuela** truancy, absence from school; **ganar por ~** to win by default, win thanks to an opponent's withdrawal.

(b) (*estado*) moral abandon; profligacy; forlornness; neglect, slovenliness; abandoned state; indulgence (*a* in); (*LAm: descuido*) untidiness, disorder; **darse al ~** to go morally downhill, indulge one's vices; **viven en el mayor ~** they live in utter degradation.

(c) (*Méx: ligereza*) abandon, ease.

abanicada NF fanning, fanning action.

abanicar [1g] **1** VT to fan; (*reprender*) to tell off.

2 abanicarse VR to fan o.s.; **~ con algo** (*Cono Sur*) not to give a damn about sth; to shrug one's shoulders at sth.

abanico NM **(a)** (*gen*) fan; fan-shaped object; (***) sword; (*ventana*) fanlight; (*Náut*) derrick; (*Carib Ferro*) points signal; **~ de chimenea** fire screen; **~ eléctrico** (*Méx: ventilador*) electric fan; **extender las cartas en ~** to fan out one's cards; **con hojas en ~** with leaves arranged like a fan. **(b)** (*fig*) range; spread; **~ de posibilidades** range of possibilities; **~ salarial, ~ de salarios** wage scale.

abaniquear [1a] (*LAm*) **1** VT to fan.

2 abaniquearse VR to fan o.s.

abaniqueo NM fanning, fanning movement; (*manoteo*) gesticulation.

abaniquero, -a NM/F (*fabricante*) fan maker; (*comerciante*) dealer in fans.

abarajar* [1a] VT (*Cono Sur*) *golpe* to counter, parry.

abaratamiento NM cheapening, reduction in price; greater cheapness.

abaratar [1a] **1** VT *artículo* to make cheaper, reduce the price of; *precio* to lower.

2 VI y **abaratarse** VR to get cheaper, come down.

abarca NF sandal.

abarcar [1g] VT (*incluir*) to include, embrace, take in; to span; (*contener*) to contain, comprise; (*extenderse a*) to extend to; *trabajo* to undertake, take on; (*LAm: monopolizar*) to monopolize, corner (the market in); **el capítulo abarca 3 siglos** the chapter covers 3 centuries, the chapter deals with 3 centuries; **sus conocimientos abarcan todo el campo de ...** his knowledge ranges over the whole field of ...; **abarca una hectárea** it takes up a hectare, it's a hectare in size; **quien mucho abarca poco aprieta** you can bite off more than you can chew; Jack of all trades and master of none.

abarque NM (*And: huevos*) clutch.

abarquillar [1a] **1** VT (*arrollar*) to curl up, roll up; (*arrugar*) to wrinkle.

2 abarquillarse VR (*arrollarse*) to curl up, roll up; (*arrugarse*) to crinkle.

abarraganarse [1a] VR to live together (as man and wife *o* though unmarried), set up house together.

abarrajado* ADJ (*Cono Sur*) (*libertino*) dissolute, free-living; (*peleonero*) quarrelsome, argumentative.

abarrajar* [1a] **1** VI (*Cono Sur*) to run away, flee.

2 VR (*And: caer de bruces*) to fall flat on one's face. **(b)** (*And, Cono Sur: prostituirse*) to prostitute o.s., sell o.s.; (*fig*) to become corrupt, be perverted.

abarrajo NM (*And*) fall, stumble.

abarrancadero NM tight spot, jam.

abarrancar [1g] **1** VT to make cracks in, open up fissures in.

2 abarrancarse VR **(a)** (*caer*) to fall into a ditch (*o* pit *etc*).

(b) (*atascarse*) to get stopped up.

(c) (*Náut*) to run aground; (*fig*) to get into a jam.

abarrotar [1a] **1** VT **(a)** (*atrancar*) to bar, fasten with bars.

(b) (*Náut*) to stow, pack tightly; (*Com*) to overstock; (*fig*) to overstock, overfill; to overcrowd; **abarrotado de** filled to bursting with, stuffed full of; **el cine estaba abarrotado (de gente)** the cinema was packed; **el orador abarrató el aula** the speaker filled the room to overflowing.

2 abarrotarse VR (*LAm Com*) to become a glut on the market; **~ de** (*Méx*) to be stuffed (*o* bursting) with, be crammed full of.

abarrote NM **(a)** (*Náut*) packing. **(b)** (*LAm*) food item, item of food; foodstuff; **~s** food; food supplies; (*Com*) groceries; **tienda de ~s, la ~s*** grocer's (shop), grocery store, general store.

abarrotería NF (*Méx: tienda general*) grocer's (shop), grocery store; (*CAm: ferretería*) ironmonger's (shop), hardware store (*US*).

abarrotero, -a NM/F (*Méx*) grocer, owner of a general store.

abastar [1a] VT to supply.

abastardar [1a] **1** VT to degrade, debase.

2 VI to degenerate.

abastecedor(a) NM/F supplier, purveyor (*frm*); (*Méx*) wholesale butcher, meat supplier.

abastecer [2d] VT to supply, provide (*de* with).

abastecimiento NM (*acto*) supplying, provision; provisioning, catering; (*cantidad*) supply, provision; (*víveres*) provisions; **~ de agua** water supply.

abastero NM (*LAm: de ganado*) cattle-dealer; (*de comestibles*) provision merchant; (*Cono Sur, Méx: carnicero*) wholesale butcher, meat supplier.

abasto NM **(a)** supply; provisioning; **dar ~ a** to supply; **dar ~ a un pedido** to fill an order, meet an order; **no dar ~** (*fig*) to be unable to cope, be lacking in resources. **(b)** (*Cono Sur*) public meat market. **(c)** (*Carib*) grocery store, general store.

abatanado ADJ skilled, skilful.

abatanar [1a] VT *paño* to beat, full; (*fig*) to beat.

abatatado ADJ (*Cono Sur*) shy, coy.

abatatarse [1a] VR (*Cono Sur*) to be shy, be bashful.

abate NM (*Ecl: frec hum*) father, abbé.

abatí NM (*And, Cono Sur*) maize, Indian corn (*US*).

abatible ADJ folding; **asiento ~** tip-up seat; folding seat; (*Aut*) reclining seat; **mesa de alas ~s** gate-leg(ged) table, table with flaps.

abatido ADJ depressed, dejected, downcast, crestfallen; (*moralmente*) low, contemptible, despicable; (*Com, Fin*) depreciated; **estar ~ por el dolor** to be prostrate with pain; **estar muy ~** to be very depressed.

abatimiento NM **(a)** (*acto*) demolition, knocking down. **(b)** (*estado*) depression, dejection; (*carácter moral*) contemptible nature, despicable character.

abatir [3a] **1** VT **(a)** *casa etc* to demolish, knock down; to dismantle; *tienda* to take down; *árbol* to cut down, fell; *avión* to shoot down; *pájaro* to shoot, bring down; *bandera* to lower, strike; *persona* to knock down; (*enfermedad, dolor etc*) to prostrate, lay low.

(b) (*fig*) (*desanimar*) to depress, sadden, discourage; (*humillar*) to humble, humiliate.

2 abatirse VR **(a)** (*caerse*) to drop, fall; (*pájaro, avión*) to swoop, dive; **~ sobre** to swoop on, pounce on.

(b) (*fig*) to be depressed, get discouraged.

abayuncar [1g] (*Méx*) **1** VT *vaca etc* to throw, ground; **~ a uno*** to put sb on the spot.

2 abayuncarse* VR to become countrified.

abbasí ADJ, NMF Abbasid.

ABC, abc = **abecé**.

Abderramán NM Abd-al-Rahman.

abdicación NF abdication.

abdicar [1g] **1** VT to renounce, relinquish; **~ la corona** to give up the crown.

2 VI to abdicate; **~ de algo** to renounce sth, relinquish sth; **~ en uno** to abdicate in favour of sb.

abdomen NM abdomen.

abdominal **1** ADJ abdominal.

2 NM press-up.

abducción NF (*Med*) abduction.

abductor NM (*Anat*) abductor.

abecé NM ABC, alphabet; (*fig*) rudiments, basic elements.

abecedario NM alphabet; (*libro*) primer, spelling book.

abedul NM birch, birch-tree; **~ plateado** silver birch.

abeja NF bee; **~ asesina** killer bee; **~ machiega, ~ maestra, ~ reina** queen bee; **~ obrera** (*o* **neutra**) worker; (*fig: hormiguita*) hard worker.

abejar NM apiary.

abejarrón NM bumblebee.

abejaruco NM bee-eater.

abejón NM (*Méx*) buzzing insect; **hacer ~*** (*CAm: cuchichear*) to whisper; (*Carib: silbar*) to boo, hiss.

abejonear [1a] (*And, Carib*) **1** VT (*fig*) to whisper (*a* to).

2 VI (*Carib**) to mumble, whisper.

abejorro NM (*abeja*) bumblebee; (*coleóptero*) cockchafer.

abejucarse [1g] VR (*Méx*) to twist up, climb.

abellacado ADJ villainous.
abellacar [1g] VT to lower, degrade.
aberenjenado ADJ violet-coloured.
aberración NF aberration; **es una ~ bañarse cinco veces al día** it's crazy to have a bath five times a day.
aberrante ADJ aberrant; (*disparatado*) crazy, ridiculous.
aberrar [1a] VI to be mistaken, err.
aberrear [1a] VT (*And*) to anger, annoy.
Aberri Eguna NM Basque national holiday (*Easter Sunday*).
abertura NF (a) (*gen*) opening; (*brecha*) gap, hole, aperture; (*grieta*) crack, cleft, slit; fissure; (*Geog*) (*cala*) cove; (*valle*) wide valley, gap; (*puerto*) pass. (b) (*fig*) openness, frankness.
abertzale [aβer'tʃale] [1] ADJ: **movimiento ~** (Basque) nationalist movement.
    [2] NMF Basque nationalist.
abetal NM fir plantation, fir wood.
abeto NM fir, fir-tree; **~ blanco** silver fir; **~ falso, ~ del norte, ~ rojo** spruce.
abetunado ADJ (*fig*) dark-skinned.
abetunar [1a] VT (*LAm*) to polish, clean.
abey NM (*Carib Bot*) jacaranda tree.
abiertamente ADV openly.
abiertazo ADJ (*CAm*) generous, open-handed.
abierto [1] PTP *de* **abrir**.
    [2] ADJ open; opened; (*ciudad, cara, campo, competición etc*) open; *carácter* open, frank; (*LAm*: *tolerante*) generous, open; (*Carib*) conceited; **la puerta estaba abierta** the door was open, the door stood open; **muy ~, ~ de par en par** wide open; **una brecha muy abierta** a gaping hole, a wide gap; **es una carrera muy abierta** it's a very open race, the race is wide open; **dejar un grifo ~** to leave a tap running.
    [3] NM (*Dep*) open (competition).
abigarrado ADJ (*de diversos colores*) variegated, many-coloured, of many colours; *animal* piebald, brindled; mottled; *escena* motley, vivid, colourful; *habla etc* disjointed, uneven.
abigarramiento NM variegation; many colours; motley colouring; vividness, colourfulness.
abigarrar [1a] VT to paint (*etc*) in a variety of colours.
abigeato NM (*Méx*) (cattle) rustling.
abigeo NM (*Méx*: *ladrón*) (cattle) rustler.
-abilidad V Aspects of Word Formation in Spanish 2.
abintestato ADJ intestate.
abiótico ADJ abiotic.
abiselar [1a] VT to bevel.
Abisinia NF Abyssinia.
abisinio, -a ADJ, NM/F Abyssinian.
abismal ADJ abysmal; (*enorme*) vast, enormous; *diferencia* unbridgeable.
abismalmente ADV abysmally; vastly, enormously, greatly.
abismante* ADJ (*LAm*) amazing, astonishing.
abismar [1a] [1] VT (*humillar*) to cast down, humble; (*arruinar*) to spoil, ruin; **~ a uno en la tristeza** to plunge sb into sadness.
    [2] **abismarse** VR (a) (*LAm*: asombrarse*) to be amazed, be astonished.
    (b) (*Carib: arruinarse*) to be ruined.
    (c) **~ en** to plunge into; to sink into; **~ en el dolor** to abandon o.s. to one's grief; **estar abismado en** to be lost in, be sunk in.
abismo NM (*gen*) abyss (*t fig*), chasm; (*de ola*) trough; (*Rel*) hell; **desde los ~s de la Edad Media** from the dark depths of the Middle Ages; **estar al borde del ~** to be on the brink of ruin (*o failure o disaster etc*); **de sus ideas a las mías hay un ~** our views are worlds apart.
abizcochado ADJ (*LAm*) spongy.
Abjacia NF, **Abjasia** NF Abkhazia.
abjacio, -a, abjasi(o), -a ADJ, NM/F Abkhaz, Abkhazi, Abkhazian.
abjuración NF (*Jur*) retraction.
abjurar [1a] [1] VT to abjure, forswear.
    [2] VI: **~ de** to abjure, forswear.
ablación NF (*de un órgano*) removal; **~ del clítoris, ~ femenina** female circumcision.
ablactación NF (*Med*) weaning.
ablactar [1a] VT (*Med*) to wean.
ablandabrevas* NMF INVAR useless person, good-for-nothing.
ablandador NM: **~ de agua** water-softener; **~ de carnes** (*Méx*) meat tenderizer.
ablandahigos* NMF INVAR = **ablandabrevas**.
ablandamiento NM (*V v 1, 2*) softening; softening up; mitigation; soothing; moderation.
ablandar [1a] [1] VT (*gen*) to soften; (*Mil etc*) to soften up; (*LAm Aut*) to run in; *vientre* to loosen; *dureza* to mitigate, temper; *persona dura* to soothe, mollify, appease.
    [2] VI (*frío*) to become less severe; (*viento*) to moderate.
    [3] **ablandarse** VR to soften, soften up, get soft(er); (*frío*) to become less severe; (*viento*) to moderate, (*elementos*) decrease in force; (*perso-*

na) to relent, become less harsh; (*con la edad*) to mellow.
ablande NM (*LAm Aut*) running-in.
ablativo ADJ ablative; **~ absoluto** ablative absolute.
-able V Aspects of Word Formation in Spanish 2.
ablución NF ablution.
ablusado [1] ADJ (*no tallado*) loose.
    [2] NM (*Cono Sur*) loose garment.
abnegación NF self-denial, abnegation; unselfishness.
abnegado ADJ self-denying, self-sacrificing; unselfish.
abnegarse [1h y 1j] VR to deny o.s., go without, act unselfishly.
abobado ADJ silly; dim-witted; stupid-looking, bewildered; **mirar ~** to look bewildered.
abobamiento NM silliness, stupidity; bewilderment.
abobar [1a] [1] VT to make stupid; to daze, bewilder.
    [2] **abobarse** VR to get stupid.
abocado ADJ *vino* smooth, pleasant.
abocar [1g] [1] VT (*tomar en la boca*) to seize (*o catch*) in one's mouth; (*acercar*) to bring nearer, bring up; *vino* to pour out, decant.
    [2] VI (a) (*Náut*) to enter a river, enter a channel.
    (b) (*fig*) **~ a** to lead to, result in, end up in; **estar abocado al desastre** to be heading for disaster; **verse abocado a un peligro** to see danger looming ahead.
    (c) **estar abocado a** + *infin* to be designed to + *infin*; **esta medida está abocada a mejorar la situación** this measure is designed to (*o* is intended to) improve the situation.
    [3] **abocarse** VR (a) (*aproximarse*) to approach; **~ con uno** to meet sb, have an interview with sb.
    (b) **~ a** (*Cono Sur*) to confront, face up to.
abocardo NM (*Téc*) drill.
abocastro NM (*And, Cono Sur*) ugly devil.
abocetar [1a] VT to sketch.
abochornado ADJ embarrassed.
abochornante ADJ = **bochornoso** (b).
abochornar [1a] [1] VT (*sobrecalentar*) to make flushed, overheat; (*avergonzar*) to shame, embarrass.
    [2] **abochornarse** VR to get flushed, get overheated; (*Bot*) to wilt; **~ de** to feel ashamed at, get embarrassed about.
abocinado ADJ trumpet-shaped.
abocinar [1a] [1] VT to shape like a trumpet; (*Cos*) to flare.
    [2] **abocinarse*** VR to fall flat on one's face.
abodocarse [1g] VR (*CAm*) (*líquido etc*) to go lumpy; (*Méx* ††) to come out in boils.
abofado ADJ (*Carib, Méx*) swollen.
abofarse [1g] VR (*Méx*) to stuff o.s.
abofetear [1a] VT to slap, hit (in the face).
abogacía NF (*abogados*) legal profession; (*oficio*) the law.
abogaderas NFPL, **abogaderías** NFPL (*LAm pey*) specious (*o* false) arguments.
abogado NMF (a) (*t* **abogada** NF) (*gen*) lawyer; (*notario*) solicitor; (*en tribunal*) barrister, attorney-at-law (*US*); (*defensor*) counsel; **~ auxiliar** (*Méx*) junior lawyer; **~ criminalista** criminal lawyer; **~ charlatán** shady lawyer; **~ del diablo** devil's advocate; **~ defensor** defending counsel; **~ del Estado** public prosecutor, attorney general (*US*); **~ laboralista** labour lawyer; **~ matrimonialista** divorce lawyer; **~ de oficio** (*Méx*) court-appointed counsel; **~ penalista** (*Méx*) criminal lawyer; **~ picapleito** pettifogging lawyer; **~ de secano** shady solicitor; barrack-room lawyer; **~ trampista** shady solicitor; **constituir ~** to brief a barrister; **ejercer de ~** to practise law, be a lawyer; **recibirse de ~** to qualify as a solicitor; to be called to the bar.
    (b) (*fig*) champion, advocate.
abogar [1h] VI to plead; **~ por** (*o* **en**) to plead for, defend; (*fig*) to advocate, champion, back.
abolengo NM ancestry, lineage; inheritance.
abolición NF abolition, abolishment.
abolicionismo NM abolitionism.
abolicionista NMF abolitionist.
abolir [3a; *defectivo*] VT to abolish; to cancel, annul, revoke.
abolladura NF (*en metal*) dent; (*hinchazón*) bump; (*cardenal*) bruise; (*Arte*) embossing.
abollar [1a] [1] VT (a) to dent; to raise a bump on; to bruise; (*Arte*) to emboss, do repoussé work on.
    (b) (*Méx*) (*) *filo* to blunt; (*: *amolar*) to grind down, oppress.
    [2] **abollarse** VR to get dented; to get bruised.
abollón NM dent.
abollonar [1a] VT *metal* to emboss.
abolsado ADJ full of pockets, baggy.
abolsarse [1a] VR to form pockets, be baggy.
abombachado ADJ *pantalón* baggy.
abombado ADJ (a) (*gen*) convex; domed. (b) **estar ~** (*LAm fig*) (*aturdido*) to be bewildered; (*tonto*) to be silly; (*: *borracho*) to be tight*. (c) (*LAm*) *comida* rotten; **estar ~** to stink, smell foul.
abombar [1a] [1] VT (a) (*hacer convexo*) to make convex.

(b) (*) (*ensordecer*) to deafen; (*desconcertar*) to confuse; (*aturdir*) to bewilder; to stun.

2 **abombarse** VR (*LAm*) **(a)** (*pudrirse*) to rot, decompose; to smell bad.

(b) (*) (*emborracharse*) to get tight*; (*enloquecer*) to go mad, lose one's head; (*atontarse*) to go soft (in the head).

abominable ADJ abominable.

abominablemente ADV abominably.

abominación NF **(a)** (*sentimiento*) abomination; loathing, detestation. **(b)** (*cosa*) abomination; **es una ~** it's an abomination, it's detestable.

abominar 1 VT = 2.
2 (VI) **~ de** to loathe, detest, abominate.

abonable ADJ **(a)** (*pagadero*) payable; due. **(b)** (*Agr*) improvable.

abonado 1 ADJ reliable, trustworthy; **estar ~ a** + *infin* to be ready to + *infin*; to be inclined to + *infin*; **es ~ para ello** he is perfectly capable of (doing) it.
2 NM, **abonada** NF subscriber; (*Teat etc*) season-ticket holder; (*Ferro*) season-ticket holder, commuter.

abonamiento NM = **abono**.

abonanzar [1f] VI *y* **abonanzarse** VR (*Met*) to grow calm, become settled.

▼ **abonar** [1a] 1 VT **(a)** (*avalar*) *persona* to vouch for, support; *hecho* to guarantee, confirm, vouch for.
▼**(b)** (*Fin*) to pay; *compra etc* to pay for; **~ dinero en una cuenta** to pay money into an account, credit money to an account.
(c) (*Agr*) to fertilize, manure.
(d) (*suscribir*) to subscribe (for sb); **te abonaré al teatro** I'll take out a season-ticket for you to the theatre; **te abonaré a la revista** I'll take out a subscription to the journal for you.
2 VI (*Met*) to grow calm, become settled.
3 **abonarse** VR to subscribe (*a* to).

abonaré NM promissory note, IOU.

abonero NM (*Méx*: *vendedor*) street vendor, door-to-door salesman; (*LAm*: *que recoge abonos*) tallyman, collector.

abono NM **(a)** (*fianza*) guarantee; **en ~ de** in support of, in justification of; as confirmation of.
(b) (*Fin*) (*pago*) payment; (*plazo*) instalment; (*crédito*) credit; (*LAm*: *depósito*) down payment, deposit; **pagar por** (*o* **en**) **~s** to pay by instalments.
(c) (*Agr*: *material*) fertilizer, manure; (*acto*) fertilizing, manuring; **~ químico** chemical fertilizer, artificial manure.
(d) (*a revista*) subscription; (*Ferro, Teat etc*) season-ticket; (*abonados*) subscribers, subscription list.
(e) (*Méx*) (*recibo*) receipt.

aboquillado ADJ *cigarrillo* tipped, filter-tipped.

abordable ADJ *persona* approachable, accessible; *tarea* manageable, that can be tackled; *precio* reasonable; **no es nada ~** he's a difficult man.

abordaje NM (*Náut*) collision, fouling; (*ataque, subida a bordo*) boarding; (*en la calle etc*) accosting, approach; (*de problema*) approach (*de* to).

abordar [1a] 1 VT **(a)** (*Náut*: *chocar con*) to collide with, foul; (*llegar*) to come alongside (*en el embarcadero* at the quay); (*atacar, subir a*) to board.
(b) *persona* to accost, approach; to stop and speak to; *tarea, tema* to tackle; *problema* to approach, tackle; (*emprender*) to undertake, get down to, start on.
(c) (*Méx*) *bus* to board, get on; (*Carib Aer*) to board.
2 VI (*Méx Náut*) to dock.

aborigen 1 ADJ aboriginal; indigenous.
2 NMF aboriginal, aborigine.

aborrascarse [1g] VR to get stormy.

aborrecer [2d] VT (*detestar*) to hate, loathe, detest; (*aburrirse con*) to become bored by; *nido, hijuelos* to desert, abandon.

aborrecible ADJ hateful, loathsome, detestable; invidious; abhorrent.

aborrecido ADJ hated, loathed; boring.

aborrecimiento NM loathing, detestation; abhorrence; boredom.

aborregado ADJ: **cielo ~** mackerel sky.

aborregarse [1h] VR **(a)** (*) to follow slavishly, tag along. **(b)** (*LAm*) to be silly, get silly.

abortadora NF woman who suffers repeated miscarriages.

abortar [1a] 1 VT **(a)** (*gen*) to abort, cause to abort; **hacerse ~** to have an abortion, to have o.s. aborted. **(b)** (*Aer etc*) to abort.
2 VI **(a)** (*Med*: *por accidente*) to have a miscarriage; (*con intención*) to abort; **hacer ~ a una mujer** to procure an abortion for a woman.
(b) (*fig*) to miscarry, fail, go awry.

abortero, -a NM/F abortionist.

abortista 1 NMF **(a)** (*criminal*) abortionist; **~ ilegal** backstreet abortionist.
(b) (*partidario*) abortion campaigner, person seeking to legalize abortion.
2 NF woman who has had an abortion.

abortivo 1 ADJ abortive.
2 NM abortifacient.

aborto NM **(a)** (*Med*: *accidental, t* **~ espontáneo**) miscarriage; (*provocado*) abortion; (*Jur*) (criminal) abortion; **~ clandestino** backstreet abortion; **~ eugenésico** eugenic abortion; **~ habitual** repeated miscarriage; **~ ilegal** illegal abortion; **~ libre** (**y gratuito**) free right to abortion, abortion on demand; **~ provocado** abortion; **~ terapéutico** therapeutic abortion.
(b) (*Bio*) monster, unnatural creature, freak.
(c) (*fig*) miscarriage, failure.
(d) (:) ugly man, ugly woman; (*aplicado a mujer*) old bat:, old cow:.

abortón NM (*Vet*) premature calf.

abotagado ADJ swollen.

abotagamiento NM swelling.

abotagarse [1h] VR to swell up, become bloated.

abotonador NM buttonhook.

abotonar [1a] 1 VT **(a)** (*abrochar*) to button up, do up. **(b)** (*Méx*: *tapar*) to block, obstruct.
2 VI (*Bot*) to bud.

abovedado 1 ADJ vaulted; domed, arched.
2 NM vaulting.

abovedar [1a] VT to vault, arch.

aboyar [1a] VT **(a)** (*Náut*) to buoy, mark with buoys. **(b)** (*Méx*) to float.

abozalar [1a] VT to muzzle.

abr. ABR *de* **abril** April, Apr.

abra[1] NF (*Geog*: *cala*) cave, small bay, inlet; (*valle*) dale, gorge; (*Geol*) fissure; (*Cono Sur, Méx*: *claro*) clearing; (*CAm, Cono Sur*: *paso de sierra*) mountain pass.

abra[2] NF (*LAm*) panel, leaf (of a door).

abracadabra NM abracadabra; hocus-pocus.

abracadabrante ADJ (*aparatoso*) spectacular; (*atractivo*) enchanting, captivating; (*mágico*) magic-seeming; (*insólito*) unusual; (*raro*) extravagant.

abracar [1g] VT (*Méx*) = **abrazar**.

Abraham, Abrahán NM Abraham.

abrasado ADJ burnt, burnt up; **estar ~** to burn with shame; **estar ~ en cólera** to be in a raging temper.

abrasador ADJ, **abrasante** ADJ burning, scorching; (*fig*) withering.

abrasar [1a] 1 VT **(a)** (*gen*) to burn, burn up; *plantas* (*sol*) to dry up, parch; (*viento*) to sear; (*helada*) to cut, nip.
(b) (*fig*: *derrochar*) to squander, waste.
(c) (*fig*: *avergonzar*) to fill with shame.
2 **abrasarse** VR to burn (up); to catch fire; (*tierra*) to be parched; **~ de amores** to burn with love, be violently in love; **~ de calor** to be dying of the heat; **~ de sed** to have a raging thirst.

abrasión NF graze, abrasion.

abrasivo ADJ, NM abrasive.

abrazadera NF bracket; clasp, brace; (*Tip*) bracket; **~ para papeles** paper clip.

abrazar [1f] 1 VT (*persona*) to embrace; to hug, take in one's arms; (*fig*) to include; comprise, take in; *oportunidad* to seize; *empresa* to take charge of; *fe* to adopt, embrace; *doctrina* to espouse; *profesión* to adopt, enter, take up.
2 **abrazarse** VR to embrace (each other); **~ a** *persona* to embrace; to cling to, clutch.

▼ **abrazo** NM **(a)** embrace, (*fuerte*) hug; **~ fatal** (*Inform*) deadly embrace.
(b) (*en carta*) **un ~ fuerte** (*o* **afectuoso**) with best wishes, with kind regards, yours; **un ~** love from.

abreboca (*LAm*) 1 ADJ absent-minded.
2 NM appetizer.

abrebotellas NM INVAR bottle-opener.

abrecartas NM INVAR letter-opener, paper-knife.

ábrego NM south-west wind.

abrelatas NM INVAR tin-opener, can-opener.

abrenuncio INTERJ: **¡~!** not for me!; far be it from me!

abrevadero NM watering place, drinking-trough.

abrevar [1a] 1 VT *animal* to water, give a drink to; *tierra* to water, irrigate; *pieles* to soak; *superficie* (*antes de pintar*) to size.
2 **abrevarse** VR (*animal*) to drink, quench its thirst; **~ en sangre** (*fig*) to wallow in blood.

abreviación NF abbreviation; abridgement, shortening; reduction.

abreviadamente ADV (*sucintamente*) briefly, succinctly; (*en forma resumida*) in an abridged form.

abreviado ADJ (*breve*) brief; short, shortened; (*resumido*) abridged; **la palabra es forma abreviada de ...** the word is a shortened form of ..., the word is short for ...

abreviar [1b] 1 VT *palabra etc* to abbreviate; *texto* to abridge, reduce; *discurso, estancia, período* to shorten, cut short; *acontecimiento* to hasten; *fecha* to advance, bring forward.
2 VI to be quick; to get on quickly; **bueno, para ~** well, to cut a long story short.

abreviatura NF abbreviation.

abriboca* ADJ (*LAm*) open-mouthed.

abridor NM: ~ (**de botellas**) bottle-opener; ~ (**de latas**) tin-opener, can-opener.

abrigada NF, **abrigadero** NM shelter, windbreak; **abrigadero de ladrones** (*Méx*) den of thieves.

abrigado ADJ *lugar* sheltered, protected; *persona* well wrapped up.

abrigador 1 ADJ (*And, Méx*) warm.
   2 NM, **abrigadora** NF person who covers up for another.

abrigar [1h] 1 VT (**a**) (*resguardar*) to shelter, protect (*de* against, from); (*ropa etc*) to keep warm, protect, cover; to wrap up; (*ayudar*) to help, support.
   (**b**) (*fig*) *duda* to retain, entertain; *esperanza* to cherish, nurse; *opinión* to hold; *sospecha* to harbour.
   2 **abrigarse** VR to take shelter (*de* from), protect o.s.; (*con ropa*) to cover up (warmly), wrap o.s. up; (*And*) to warm o.s.; **¡abrígate bien!** wrap up well!

abrigo NM (**a**) (*gen*) shelter; (*protección*) protection; (*ayuda*) help, support; (*cobertura*) covering, protection; **de ~** tremendous*; **al ~ de** sheltered from, protected from; **ropa de mucho ~** heavy clothing, warm clothes; **escapar al ~ de la noche** to flee under cover of darkness.
   (**b**) (*Náut*) harbour, haven.
   (**c**) (*prenda*) coat, overcoat, outer coat; ~ **de pieles** fur coat; ~ **de visón** mink coat.
   (**d**) (*Cono Sur: manta*) blanket, quilt.

abril NM April; **en el ~ de la vida** in the springtime of one's life; **en ~ aguas mil** April showers bring May flowers; **una joven de 20 ~es** a girl of 20 (summers); **estar hecho un ~** to look very handsome.

abrileño ADJ April (*atr*).

abrillantado 1 ADJ polished; (*Culin*) glazed.
   2 NM polish(ing); (*Culin*) glaze, glazing.

abrillantadora NF floor-polisher.

abrillantamuebles NM INVAR furniture polish.

abrillantar [1a] VT *piedra* to cut into facets; (*pulir*) to polish, burnish, brighten; (*Culin*) to glaze; (*fig*) to enhance, add lustre to.

abrir [3a; PTP **abierto**] 1 VT (*gen*) to open; to open up; (*Med*) to cut open, open up; *mapa etc* to open out, spread out, extend; *libro* to open; *camino* to clear, make, open up; (*LAm*) *bosque* to clear; *foso, cimientos* to dig; *agujero* to make, bore; *pozo* to sink; *lámina* to engrave; *grifo* to turn on; *cuenta* to open; *negociaciones* to open, start; *mercado* to open up; *apetito* to whet, stimulate; *lista* to head; *desfile* to head, lead; ~ **una puerta con llave** to unlock a door; ~ **algo cortándolo** to cut sth open; ~ **una información** (*Jur*) to begin proceedings; **volver a ~ un pleito** (*Jur*) to reopen a case; **en un ~ y cerrar de ojos** in the twinkling of an eye; **~(se) el tobillo** to twist one's ankle, sprain one's ankle.
   2 VI (**a**) (*gen*) to open; (*flor*) to open, unfold.
   (**b**) (*Bridge*) to open; ~ **de 3 a un palo** to open 3 in a suit; ~ **de corazones** to open (with a bid in) hearts.
   (**c**) (*Carib**: *huir*) to escape, run off.
   3 **abrirse** VR (**a**) (*gen*) to open; to open out, unfold, spread (out); to expand; ~ **a uno**, ~ **con uno** to confide in sb.
   (**b**) (*: *largarse*) to go away, beat it*; **¡me abro!** I'm off!; **¡ábrete!** shove off!*
   (**c**) (*Méx: echar marcha atrás*) to backtrack, back-pedal, back out.

abrita NF (*CAm*) short dry spell.

abrochador NM buttonhook; (*LAm*) stapler, stapling machine.

abrochar [1a] 1 VT (**a**) (*con botones*) to button (up); (*con broche*) to do up, fasten (up); (*con hebilla*) to clasp, buckle; (*asir*) to grasp; (*LAm*) *papeles* to staple (together).
   (**b**) (*And: reprender*) to reprimand.
   (**c**) (*Méx*) (*atar*) to tie up; (*agarrar*) to grab hold of.
   2 **abrocharse** VR (**a**) (*LAm*) to struggle, wrestle. (**b**) V **1**.

abrogación NF abrogation, repeal.

abrogar [1h] VT to abrogate, repeal.

abrojo NM (*Bot*) thistle, thorn, caltrop; (*Mil*) caltrop; ~**s** (*Méx: matorral*) thorn bushes; (*Náut*) submerged rocks.

abroncar* [1g] 1 VT (*avergonzar*) to shame, make ashamed; (*ridiculizar*) to ridicule; (*aburrir*) to bore; (*molestar*) to annoy; *orador* to boo, heckle, barrack; (*reprender*) to give a lecture to, tick off.
   2 **abroncarse*** VR to get angry.

abroquelarse [1a] VR: ~ **con**, ~ **de** to shield o.s. with, defend o.s. with.

abrumador ADJ crushing, burdensome; exhausting; tiresome; *mayoría* vast, overwhelming; *superioridad* crushing, overwhelming; *atenciones* embarrassingly pressing; **el trabajo es ~** the work is killing; **es una responsabilidad ~a** it is a heavy responsibility.

abrumadoramente ADV crushingly; vastly, overwhelmingly.

abrumar [1a] 1 VT (*agobiar*) to crush, overwhelm; (*oprimir*) to oppress, weigh down; (*cansar*) to wear out, exhaust; ~ **a uno de trabajo** to swamp sb with work.
   2 **abrumarse** VR to get foggy, get misty.

abrupto ADJ *pendiente* steep, abrupt; *terreno* rough, rugged; *tono* abrupt; *cambio* sudden.

abrutado ADJ brutish, brutalized.

absceso NM abscess.

abscisión NF incision.

absenta NF absinth(e).

absentismo NM absenteeism; absentee landlordism; ~ **laboral** absenteeism from work.

absentista NMF absentee; absentee landlord.

ábside NM apse.

absintio NM absinth(e).

absolución NF (*Ecl*) absolution; (*Jur*) acquittal; pardon.

absoluta NF (**a**) (*declaración*) dogmatic statement, authoritative assertion. (**b**) (*Mil*) discharge; **tomar la ~** to take one's discharge, leave the service.

absolutamente ADV (**a**) (*completamente*) absolutely, completely; definitely; positively; ~ **nada** nothing at all; **es ~ imposible** it's absolutely impossible; **está ~ prohibido** it is absolutely forbidden; **el puente estaba ~ destruido** the bridge was completely destroyed.
   (**b**) (*en sentido neg*) not at all, by no means; **'¿así que no viene nadie?'** ... **'~'** 'so nobody is coming?' ... 'nobody at all'.

absolutismo NM absolutism; ~ **ilustrado** enlightened dictatorship.

absolutista 1 ADJ absolutist, absolute.
   2 NMF absolutist.

absolutizar [1f] VT to pin down, be precise about.

absoluto ADJ (**a**) (*gen*) absolute (*t Filos, Pol*); utter, complete; *fe* complete, implicit; *temperamento* domineering, tyrannical; **lo ~** the absolute.
   (**b**) (*en sentido neg*) **en ~** nothing at all, by no means; not in the slightest; (*Méx*) absolutely, undoubtedly; **¡en ~!** certainly not!, not at all!; no way!*; **no sabía nada en ~ de eso** I knew nothing at all about it; **no tenía miedo en ~** he wasn't a bit afraid.

absolutorio ADJ: **fallo ~** (*Jur*) verdict of acquittal, verdict of not guilty.

absolver [2h; PTP **absuelto**] VT to absolve; (*Jur*) to acquit, clear (*de una acusación* of a charge); to release (*de un empeño* from an obligation).

absorbencia NF absorbency.

absorbente 1 ADJ (**a**) (*Quím etc*) absorbent.
   (**b**) (*fig: interesante*) interesting, absorbing; *tarea* demanding; *amor etc* possessive, tyrannical.
   2 NM: ~ **higiénico** sanitary towel, sanitary napkin (*US*).

absorber [2a] 1 VT to absorb; to soak up; to suck in; *conocimientos* to absorb, take in, acquire; *capitales, recursos* to use up; *energías* to take up; *atención* to command; *lector etc* to absorb, engross.
   2 **absorberse** VR: ~ **en** to become absorbed in, become engrossed in.

absorbible ADJ absorbable.

absorbidad NF absorbency.

absorción NF absorption (*t fig*); (*Com*) takeover.

absorto ADJ absorbed; engrossed; **estar ~** (*extasiado*) to be entranced; (*pasmado*) to be amazed; **estar ~ (en meditación)** to be lost in thought; **estar ~ en un proyecto** to be engrossed in a scheme, be intent on a scheme.

abstemio 1 ADJ abstemious; (*completamente*) teetotal.
   2 NM, **abstemia** NF abstainer; teetotaller.

abstención NF abstention; non-participation.

abstencionismo NM non-participation, refusal to take part, opting out.

abstencionista NMF non-participant, person who opts out.

abstenerse [2k] VR to abstain; to refrain; ~ **de** + *infin* to abstain from + *ger*, refrain from + *ger*, forbear to + *infin*; **'~ medianías'** 'no dealers'; **'~ si no cumplen los requisitos'** 'do not apply unless you have the qualifications'; **en la duda, abstente** when in doubt, don't.

abstinencia NF abstinence; abstemiousness; (*de drogas*) withdrawal; (*Ecl*) abstinence; restraint, forbearance.

abstinente ADJ (*Ecl*) abstinent, observing abstinence.

abstracción NF (**a**) (*gen*) abstraction; (*despiste*) absent-mindedness, engrossment in something else; (*ensueño*) reverie.
   (**b**) ~ **hecha de ese libro** leaving that book aside, with the exception of that book.

abstractar [1a] VT *publicaciones* to abstract, make abstracts of.

abstracto ADJ abstract; **en ~** in the abstract.

abstraer [2o] 1 VT to abstract; to remove, consider separately.
   2 VI: ~ **de** to leave aside, exclude.
   3 **abstraerse** VR to be absorbed, be lost in thought; to be preoccupied.

abstraído ADJ withdrawn, absent-minded; preoccupied.

abstruso ADJ abstruse.

absuelto PTP *de* **absolver**.

absurdamente ADV absurdly.

absurdidad NF, **absurdidez** NF absurdity.

absurdo 1 ADJ absurd, ridiculous, preposterous; farcical; **teatro de**

lo ~ theatre of the absurd; **es ~ que** ... it is absurd that ...
[2] NM absurdity; farce; **decir ~s** to say absurd things.

abubilla NF hoopoe.

abucharar* [1a] VT (*abuchear*) to boo, jeer; (*excluir*) to ostracize, marginalize; (*criticar*) to slate*, criticize; (*avergonzar*) to put to shame; **quedarse abuchara(d)o** to be left out, be ostracized.

abuchear [1a] VT to boo, hoot at; to howl down, jeer at; **ser abucheado** (*Teat etc*) to be hissed at, get the bird*.

abucheo NM booing, hooting; jeering; **ganarse un ~** (*Teat etc*) to be hissed at, get the bird*.

abuela NF grandmother; (*fig*) old woman, old lady; **¡tu ~!*** rubbish!; **¡cuéntaselo a tu ~!** go tell that to the marines!; pull the other one!*; **¡no tienes ~!** come off it!, tell us another!; **no tiene ~*** he's full of himself; **no necesita ~*** he blows his own trumpet; (**éramos pocos) y parió la ~*** and that was the last straw, and that was all we needed.

abuelado* ADJ (*Cono Sur*) spoiled by one's grandparents.

abuelita* NF (a) (*: *persona*) grandma*, granny*; (*Méx etc*) grandmother. (b) (*Cono Sur: gorra*) baby's bonnet. (c) (*And: cuna*) cradle.

abuelito* NM granddad*, grandpa*; (*Méx etc*) grandfather.

abuelo NM grandfather; (*fig*) old man; ancestor, forbear; **~s** grandparents; **¡tu ~!*** get away!*; **está hecho un ~** he looks like an old man.

abulense [1] ADJ of Ávila.
[2] NMF native (o inhabitant) of Ávila; **los ~s** the people of Ávila.

abulia NF lack of willpower, spinelessness; apathy.

abúlico ADJ lacking in willpower, weakwilled, spineless; apathetic.

abulón NM (*Zool*) abalone.

abultado ADJ bulky, large, massive; unwieldy; *libro etc* thick; (*fig*) exaggerated.

abultamiento NM bulkiness, (large) size; swelling, increase; exaggeration; increased importance.

abultar [1a] [1] VT (*agrandar*) to enlarge; (*hacer más abultado*) to make bulky; (*aumentar*) to swell, increase; (*fig*) to exaggerate.
[2] VI to be bulky, be big; to take up a lot of room; (*fig*) to increase in importance, loom large.

abundamiento NM abundance, plenty; **a (o por) mayor ~** furthermore; with still more justification, as if that were not enough.

abundancia NF abundance, plenty; **en ~** in abundance, in plenty; **nadar en la ~** to be rolling in money.

abundante ADJ abundant, plentiful; *cosecha etc* heavy, copious; *provisión etc* generous; **~ en** abounding in; productive of.

abundantemente ADV abundantly; in abundance, in plenty.

abundar [1a] VI to abound, be plentiful; **~ de, ~ en** to abound in, abound with, be rich in; **~ en dinero** to be well supplied with money; **~ en la opinión de uno** to share sb's opinion (o view) wholeheartedly.

Abundio V **tonto**.

abundoso ADJ (*LAm*) abundant.

abur* INTERJ so long!

aburguesado ADJ: **un barrio ~** a gentrified area; **un hombre ~** a man who has become bourgeois, a man who has adopted middle-class ways.

aburguesamiento NM gentrification; process of becoming bourgeois, conversion to middle-class ways.

aburguesar [1a] [1] VT *casa etc* to gentrify.
[2] **aburguesarse** VR (*persona*) to become bourgeois, adopt middle-class ways.

aburrición NF (*LAm*) revulsion, repugnance.

aburridamente ADV tediously, annoyingly; in a boring manner.

aburrido ADJ (*que aburre*) boring, tedious, dull; monotonous; (*que siente aburrimiento*) bored.

┌─ **ABURRIDO** ─────────── *ver también la entrada* ─┐

Hay que tener en cuenta la diferencia entre "*bored*" y "*boring*" a la hora de traducir *aburrido*

  No me extraña que estés aburrido, con esa novia tan aburridísima que tienes
  I'm not surprised if you're bored, with such a boring girlfriend

• Usamos *bored* para referirnos al hecho de *estar* aburrido, es decir, de sentir aburrimiento:
  Si estás aburrida podrías ayudarme con este trabajo
  If you're bored you could help me with this work

• Usamos *boring* con personas, actividades y cosas para indicar que alguien o algo *es* aburrido, es decir, que produce aburrimiento:
  ¡Qué novela más aburrida!
  What a boring novel!
  No me gusta salir con él; es muy aburrido
  I don't like going out with him; he's very boring

└──┘

aburridón ADJ (*And*) rather boring.

---

aburrimiento NM boredom, tedium, monotony.

aburrir [3a] [1] VT (a) (*gen*) to bore; to tire, weary. (b) (‡) *dinero* to blow*; *tiempo* to spend, waste.
[2] **aburrirse** VR to be bored, get bored (**con, de, por** with); **~ como una almeja** (*u* **ostra**) to be bored stiff.

abusado* (*Méx*) [1] INTERJ look out!, careful!
[2] ADJ (*cauteloso*) watchful, wary; (*astuto*) sharp, on the ball; cunning.
[3] NM, **abusada** NF swot*.

abusador ADJ (*Cono Sur*) abusive.

abusar [1a] VI to go too far, exceed one's rights, take advantage; to ask too much; **~ de amistad** to presume upon, take unfair advantage of; to impose upon, make unfair demands on; *autoridad, hospitalidad, niño* to abuse; *confianza* to betray; *dinero* to misuse, misapply; **~ del tabaco** to smoke too much.

abusión NF abuse; superstition.

abusivamente ADV improperly; corruptly.

abusivo ADJ improper; corrupt.

abuso NM abuse; imposition, unfair demand; betrayal; misuse; misapplication; **~ de autoridad** abuse of authority; **~ de confianza** betrayal of trust, breach of faith; **~ deshonesto** indecent assault; **~ sexual** sexual abuse; **~ del tabaco** excessive smoking, smoking too much.

abusón* [1] ADJ (*egoísta*) selfish; (*engreído*) big-headed*, uppish*; (*insolente*) abusive.
[2] NM, **abusona** NF selfish person; bighead*; **eres un ~** you're too big for your boots.

abute‡ ADV: **vivir de ~** to live well, live like a prince; *V t* **dabuti**.

abyección NF wretchedness, abjectness; degradation; servility.

abyecto ADJ wretched, abject; degraded; servile.

A.C. NM ABR *de* **año de Cristo** Anno Domini, AD.

a/c. (a) ABR *de* **a cuenta** on account. (b) ABR *de* **al cuidado de** care of, c/o.

acá ADV (a) (*lugar*) here; over here, round here; **~ y allá, ~ y acullá** here and there; hither and thither; **pasearse de ~ para allá** to walk up and down, walk to and fro; **¡más ~!** more over this way!; **más ~ de** on this side of; **tráelo más ~** move it this way, bring it closer; **está muy ~** it's right here; **no tan ~** not so close, not so far this way; **¡ven ~!, ¡vente para ~!** come over here!
(b) (*tiempo*) at this time, now; **de ayer ~** since yesterday; (*LAm*) lately, recently; **¿de cuándo ~ sabes tú el francés?** since when do you know French?; **de ~ a poco** of late.
(c) (*LAm: como demostrativo*) this person (*etc*) here; **~ le contará** he'll tell you about it; **~ es mi señora** and this is my wife.

acabadero* NM (*Méx*): **el ~** the limit, the last straw.

acabado [1] ADJ (a) (*completo*) finished, complete; (*perfecto*) perfect; *producto* finished; (*fig*) consummate, masterly, polished.
(b) (*viejo*) old, worn out; (*Med*) ruined in health, wrecked; (*LAm: flaco*) thin; (*Méx: rendido*) exhausted; **está muy ~** (*Méx*) he's looking very old.
(c) **él, ~ de llegar ...**, immediately after his arrival he ...
[2] N (*Téc*) finish; **buen ~** high finish; **~ brillo** gloss finish; **~ satinado** matt finish.

acabador(a) NM/F (*Téc*) finisher.

acabalar [1a] VT to complete.

acaballadero NM stud farm.

acaballado* ADJ (*Cono Sur*) clumsy, gauche.

acaballar [1a] VT *yegua* to cover.

acabamiento NM finishing, completion; end; death; (*Méx: agotamiento*) exhaustion.

acabar [1a] [1] VT (*gen*) to finish, complete, conclude; (*dar el toque final a*) to round off, put the finishing touches to; (*matar*) to kill, kill off, destroy; (*LAm: hablar mal de*) to speak ill of.
[2] VI (a) (*terminar*) to finish, end, come to an end; (*morir*) to die; **y no acaba** and there's no sign of it coming to an end; **es cosa de nunca ~** there's no end to it; **¡acabáramos!** at last!; get to the point!; now I understand! *o* I get it!; **~ mal** to come to a sticky end; **la palabra acaba con Z** the word ends in a Z; **el palo acaba en punta** the stick ends in a point.
(b) **~ con** to put an end to, make an end of; to destroy, finish off, put paid to; *abuso* to stop, put an end to; *recursos* to exhaust, use up; **esto acabará conmigo** this will be the end of me.
(c) **~ de** + *infin* to have just + PTP; **acabo de verle** I have just seen him; **acababa de hacerlo** I had just done it; **cuando acabó de escribirlo** when he finished writing it; **cuando acabemos de pagarlo** when we finish paying for it; **¡acaba de parir!*** spit it out!*; **no lo acabo de entender** I don't fully understand it, I can't quite understand it; **no me acaba de convencer** I'm not altogether satisfied with it; **para ~ de arreglarlo** to make matters worse.
(d) **~** + *ger*, **~ por** + *infin* to end up by + *ger*, finish up by + *ger*; **acabó aceptándolo** he finally accepted it, eventually he accepted it, he ended up (by) accepting it.

(e) (*LAm*⁜: *eyacular*) to come⁜.

3 acabarse VR **(a)** (*terminar*) to finish, stop, come to an end; (*morir*) to die; (*fig*: *esp LAm*) to wear o.s. out; to be all over (and done with); (*existencias*) to run out, be exhausted; (*provisión*) to fail; **¡se acabó!** it's all over!; (*) that was the end of that!; it's all up; **... y se acabó ...** and that's the end of the matter; **todo se acabó para él** he's had it*; **¡un minuto más y se acabó!** one more minute and that will be it!

(b) (*con pron pers indirecto*) **se me acabó el tabaco** I ran out of cigarettes; **se nos acabará la gasolina** we shall soon be out of petrol; **se me acaba la paciencia** my patience is wearing thin.

acabildar [1a] VT to get together, organize into a group.

acabóse NM the end, the limit; **¡es el ~!** it's the absolute limit!; **la fiesta fue el ~** it was the best party ever.

acachetear [1a] VT to slap, punch.

acachihuite NM (*Méx*) (*paja*) straw, hay; (*cesto*) straw basket.

acacia NF acacia; **~ falsa** locust-tree.

acacito ADV (*LAm*) = **acá**.

academia NF (*gen*) academy; learned society; (*escuela*) (private) school; **~ de baile** school of dance; **~ de comercio** business school; **~ de conductores** driving-school; **~ gastronómica** domestic science college; **~ de idiomas** language school; **~ de interpretación** drama school; **~ militar** military academy; **~ de música** school of music, conservatoire; **la Real A~** the Spanish Academy; **la Real A~ de la Historia** the Spanish Academy of History.

┌─ ACADEMIA ─────────────────────

ⓘ *In Spain **academias** are private schools catering for students of all ages and levels outside normal school and working hours. Some specialize in particular skills such as computing, languages and dressmaking while others offer extra tuition in core school subjects and syllabuses. For people hoping to do well enough in the **oposiciones** to get a post in the public sector, there are **academias** offering special preparatory courses for these notoriously difficult competitive examinations.*
⇨ *See also* OPOSICIONES
└────────────────────────────────

académico 1 ADJ academic (*t fig*).

2 NM, **académica** NF academician, member (of an academy); fellow (of a learned society); **~ de número** full member of an academy.

acaecer [2d] VI to happen, occur; to take place; to befall; **acaeció que ...** it came about that ...

acaecimiento NM happening, occurrence.

acahual NM (*Méx*) (*girasol*) sunflower; (*yerba*) tall grass.

acáis⁜ NMPL peepers⁜, eyes.

acalambrarse [1a] VR to get cramp.

acalaminado ADJ (*Cono Sur*) *camino etc* rough, uneven, bumpy.

acalenturarse [1a] VR to get feverish.

acallamiento NM silencing, quietening; pacification.

acallar [1a] VT to silence, quieten, hush; (*fig*) *persona* to assuage, pacify; *crítica, duda* to silence.

acaloradamente ADV (*fig*) heatedly, excitedly.

acalorado ADJ heated, hot; tired; (*fig*) *discusión, palabras* heated, excited; *defensor* passionate; (*agitado*) agitated.

acaloramiento NM ardour, heat; vehemence, passion; anger.

acalorar [1a] 1 VT to make hot, warm up; (*sobrecalentar*) to overheat; (*cansar*) to tire; (*fig*) *mente* to inflame, excite; *pasiones* to inflame; *audiencia* to excite, work up; *ambición etc* to stir up, encourage.

2 **acalorarse** VR to get hot, become overheated; (*fig*: *persona*) to get excited, get worked up; to get angry, get het up* (*por* about); (*discusión*) to become heated; (*al hablar*) to speak passionately.

acalórico ADJ low-calorie (*atr*), low in calories.

acaloro NM anger.

acalote NM (*Méx*) channel.

acamar [1a] VT *cosecha etc* to beat down, lay.

acamastronarse [1a] VR (*LAm*) to get crafty, become artful.

acampada NF camping; **ir de ~** to go camping.

acampado, -a NM/F camper.

acampanado ADJ bell-shaped; **pantalones ~s** bell-bottomed trousers.

acampar [1a] 1 VI to camp; to encamp.

2 **acamparse** VR to camp.

acampo NM (common) pasture.

acanalado ADJ grooved, furrowed; striated; fluted; *hierro* corrugated.

acanaladura NF groove, furrow; striation; fluting (*t Arquit*); corrugation.

acanalar [1a] VT to groove, furrow; to flute; to corrugate.

acanallado ADJ disreputable, low; worthless; degenerate.

acanelado ADJ cinnamon flavoured (*o coloured*).

acantilado 1 ADJ *risco* steep, sheer; *costa* (*sobre el agua*) rocky; (*debajo del agua*) shelving.

2 NM cliff.

acanto NM acanthus.

acantonamiento NM **(a)** (*lugar*) cantonment. **(b)** (*acto*) billeting, quartering.

acantonar [1a] VT to billet, quarter (*en* on).

acaparación NF = **acaparamiento**.

acaparador 1 ADJ acquisitive; **instintos ~es** acquisitive instincts; **tendencia ~a** monopolizing tendency.

2 NM, **acaparadora** NF monopolizer, monopolist; profiteer; hoarder.

acaparamiento NM monopolizing; cornering the market (*de* in); hoarding.

acaparar [1a] VT (*Com*) *comercio* to monopolize; *productos* to corner, corner the market in; *víveres etc* to hoard; (*fig*) to hog, keep for o.s.; *interés* to hold, absorb; **los turistas acaparan los cafés** the tourists monopolize the cafés, the tourists take over the cafés; **ella acapara la atención** she occupies everyone's attention.

acapetate NM (*Méx*) straw mat.

acapillar⁜ [1a] VT (*Méx*) to grab, take hold of.

acápite NM (*LAm*) (*párrafo*) paragraph; (*título*) subheading; caption; **punto ~** full stop, new paragraph.

a cappella [aka'pela] ADV a cappella.

acapullado ADJ *flor* in bud.

acapulqueño (*Méx*) 1 ADJ of Acapulco.

2 NM, **acapulqueña** NF native (*o* inhabitant) of Acapulco; **los ~s** the people of Acapulco.

acaracolado ADJ spiral, winding, twisting.

acaramelado ADJ (*sabor*) toffee-flavoured; (*color*) toffee-coloured; (*fig*) sugary, over-sweet; cloying; over-polite; **estaban ~s** (*amantes*) they were besotted with each other, they had eyes only for each other.

acardenalar [1a] 1 VT to bruise.

2 **acardenalarse** VR to get bruised, go black and blue.

acar(e)ar [1a] VT *personas* to bring face to face; *peligro etc* to face, face up to; to confront.

acariciador ADJ caressing.

acariciar [1b] VT **(a)** (*gen*) to caress, fondle, stroke; *animal* to pat, stroke; (*rozar*) to brush, touch lightly.

(b) (*fig*) *esperanza* to cherish, cling to; *proyecto* to have in mind; to toy with.

acaricida NM (*Cono Sur*) insecticide.

ácaro NM (*Zool*) mite.

acarraladura* NF (*And, Cono Sur*) run, ladder (*in stocking*).

acarreadizo ADJ transportable, that can be transported.

acarreado, -a NM/F (*Méx*) peasant bussed in by the government in order to vote.

acarrear [1a] VT **(a)** (*transportar*) to transport, haul, cart, carry; (*persona*) to lug about, lug along; (*río*) to carry along, bring down.

(b) (*fig*) to cause, occasion, bring with it, bring in its train (*o* wake); to result in; to give rise to; **ello le acarreó muchos disgustos** it brought him lots of troubles; **acarreó la caída del gobierno** it led to the fall of the government.

acarreo NM transport, haulage, cartage, carriage; **gastos de ~, precio de ~** transport charges, haulage.

acarreto NM (*Carib, Méx*) = **acarreo**.

acartonado ADJ (*enjuto*) wizened; (*seco*) shrivelled; (*como cartón*) like cardboard.

acartonarse [1a] VR to get like cardboard; (*fig*) to become wizened; to shrivel up.

acartuchado* ADJ (*Cono Sur*) stuffy, stuck-up*.

acarvamiento NM erosion.

acaserarse* [1a] VR (*And*) (††) to become attached; (*Com*) to become a regular customer (*of a shop*); (*sentar la cabeza*) to settle down; (*And, Carib*: *quedar en casa*) to stay at home.

acaso 1 ADV **(a)** (*gen*) perhaps, maybe; by chance; **~ venga** maybe he'll come; **por si ~** just in case; **por si ~ viene** if by any chance he comes; **por si ~ viniera** just in case he should come; **por si ~ se necesita, llévalo** in case it should be needed, take it; **si ~** (*Méx*) at best, at most; **si ~ llegaré a cenar** (*Méx*) at best I'll arrive in time for supper.

(b) (*preguntas retóricas*) **¿~ yo lo sé?** how would I know?; **¿~ no quiere?** doesn't he want to, then?; **¿~ no te lo he dicho cien veces?** haven't I told you a hundred times?

2 NM chance, accident, coincidence; **al ~** at random; **por ~, por un ~** by chance.

acastañado ADJ (*color*) hazel.

acatamiento NM respect (*a* for); awe, reverence; deference.

acatar [1a] VT **(a)** (*respetar*) to respect; (*reverenciar*) to hold in awe, revere; (*subordinarse a*) to defer to, treat with deference; *ley* to obey, respect, observe. **(b)** (*LAm*) to notice, observe. **(c)** (*Cono Sur, Méx*: *molestar*) to annoy.

acatarrado ADJ: **estar ~** to have a cold.

acatarrar [1a] 1 VT (*Méx*⁜) to harass, pester.

2 **acatarrarse** VR to catch (a) cold; (*And*⁜: *emborracharse*) to get

tight*.

acato NM = **acatamiento**.

acatólico, -a ADJ, NM/F non-Catholic.

acaudalado ADJ well-off, affluent.

acaudalar [1a] VT to acquire, accumulate; (*pey*) to hoard.

acaudillar [1a] VT to lead, command, head.

▼ **acceder** [2a] VI to accede, agree (*a* to); ~ **a** to enter, gain admittance to (socially); (*Cono Sur: tener acceso*) to gain (*o* have) access to; ~ **a una base de datos** to have access to a database; ~ **a una graduación superior** to attain a higher rank, be promoted to a higher rank; ~ **al trono** to succeed to the throne; ~ **a** + *infin* to agree to + *infin*.

accesibilidad NF accessibility (*to* a).

accesible ADJ accessible; approachable; ~ **a** open to, accessible to.

accesión NF (**a**) (*consentimiento*) assent (*a* to); acquiescence (*a* in).
(**b**) (*accesorio*) accessory.
(**c**) (*Med*) attack; onset.

accésit NM INVAR consolation prize, second prize.

acceso NM (**a**) (*entrada*) entry, admittance, access; '~ **prohibido**', '**prohibido el ~**' 'no admittance'; **de fácil ~** of easy access, easy to approach; **éstos están al ~ de todos** these are within reach of everybody, these are available to all; **dar ~ a** to lead to.
(**b**) (*camino*) way, approach, access; (*Aer*) approach; ~**s** approaches.
(**c**) (*Inform*) access; ~ **aleatorio** random access; ~ **directo** direct access; ~ **secuencial** sequential access; ~ **en serie** serial access; **de ~ múltiple** multi-access.
(**d**) (*Med*) attack, fit; (*de ira etc*) fit, outburst, explosion; (*de generosidad*) fit, surge.

accesoria NF annex, outbuilding.

accesorio [1] ADJ accessory; dependent, subordinate; incidental.
[2] NM accessory, attachment, extra; (*prenda de vestir*) accessory; ~**s** (*Téc*) accessories, spare parts; (*Aut*) optional extras; (*Teat*) properties.

accidentado [1] ADJ *superficie* uneven; *horizonte etc* broken, uneven; *terreno* hilly; rough, rugged; *vida* stormy, troubled, eventful; *historial* variable, up-and-down; *viaje* eventful; (*mentalmente*) agitated, upset; (*Med*) injured; (*Carib Aut*) broken down; (*LAm euf*) hunchbacked.
[2] NM, **accidentada** NF injured person; casualty; person involved in an accident.

accidental ADJ (*gen*) accidental; (*sin querer*) unintentional; (*incidente*) incidental; (*fortuito*) casual; (*fugaz*) brief, transient; **un empleo ~** a temporary job.

accidentalidad NF accident rate, number of accidents.

accidentalmente ADV accidentally, by chance; unintentionally.

accidentarse [1a] VR to have an accident; (*Méx Aer etc*) to crash.

accidente NM (**a**) (*gen*) accident; mishap, misadventure; **por ~** by accident, accidentally, by chance; ~ **aéreo** plane crash; ~ **de carretera** road accident; ~ **de circulación** traffic accident; ~ **laboral**, ~ **de trabajo** industrial accident; industrial injury; ~ **múltiple** multiple accident, pile-up; **una vida sin ~s** an uneventful life; **hay ~s que no se pueden prever** accidents will happen; **sufrir un ~** to have an accident, meet with an accident.
(**b**) (*Med*) faint, swoon.
(**c**) (*Ling*) accidence.
(**d**) ~**s** (*de superficie*) unevenness; (*de terreno*) hilliness; roughness, ruggedness.
(**e**) ~ **de la cara** (*Méx*) feature.

acción NF (**a**) (*gen*) action; act, deed; (*de droga etc*) effect; **buena ~** good deed, kind act; **mala ~** evil deed, unkind thing (to do); **hombre de ~** man of action; ~ **de gracias** thanksgiving; **mecanismo de ~ retardada** delayed-action mechanism; **por ~ química** by chemical action; **¡~ y kilometraje!** (*Carib*) let's get some action!; **dejar sin ~** to put out of action; **estar en ~*** (*Carib*) to be busy; **ganar la ~ a uno** to forestall sb; **unir la ~ a la palabra** to suit the deed to the word.
(**b**) (*de mano*) movement, gesture.
(**c**) (*Mil*) action, engagement; **entrar en ~** to go into action.
(**d**) (*Teat: argumento*) action, plot, story line; ~ **aparte** by-play.
(**e**) (*Teat: interpretación*) oratory, delivery; acting.
(**f**) (*Jur*) action, lawsuit; ~ **penal** trial; **ejercitar una ~**, **emprender acciones judiciales** to bring an action, take legal action.
(**g**) (*Com, Fin*) share; **acciones** stock(s), shares; ~ **liberada** bonus share, paid-up share; ~ **ordinaria** ordinary share, common stock (*US*); ~ **preferente** preference share, preferred stock (*US*); ~ **primitiva** ordinary share, common stock (*US*); ~ **prioritaria** priority share.

accionado NM shares, shareholding; ~ **mayoritario** majority shareholding.

accionamiento NM (*Mec*) operation; **de ~ manual** manually-operated.

accionar [1a] [1] VT (*Mec*) to work, drive, propel; *bomba* to set off, detonate; (*Inform*) to drive.
[2] VI to gesticulate; to wave one's hands about.

accionariado NM (**a**) (*acciones*) (total of) shares, shareholding. (**b**) (*personas*) shareholders (collectively).

accionarial ADJ share (*atr*); **paquete ~**, **participación ~** shareholding.

accionario ADJ share (*atr*), of (*o* relating to) stocks and shares.

accionista NMF shareholder, stockholder; ~ **mayoritario** majority shareholder.

accisa NF excise duty.

ACE ['aθe] NF ABR *de* **Acción Católica Española**.

acebo NM holly, holly tree.

acebuche NM (**a**) (*Bot*) wild olive-tree; (*madera*) olive wood. (**b**) (*) yokel.

acechadera NF ambush; hiding place; (*Caza*) hide.

acechador(a) NM/F spy, watcher, observer.

acechanza NF (*LAm*) = **acecho**.

acechar [1a] VT (*espiar*) to spy on, watch, observe; (*esperar*) to lie in wait for; (*amenazar*) to threaten, beset; (*Caza*) to stalk; ~ **la ocasión** to wait one's chance.

acecho NM spying, watching; (*Mil*) ambush; **estar al ~**, **estar en ~** to lie in wait, be on the watch; **cazar al ~** to stalk.

acechón* ADJ spying, prying; **hacer la acechona** to spy, pry.

acecinar [1a] [1] VT *carne* to salt, cure.
[2] **acecinarse** VR to get very thin.

acedar [1a] [1] VT to turn sour, make bitter; (*fig*) to sour, embitter; to vex.
[2] **acedarse** VR to turn sour; (*Bot*) to wither, yellow.

acedera NF sorrel.

acedía[1] NF acidity, sourness; (*Med*) heartburn; (*fig*) sourness, unpleasantness, asperity.

acedía[2] NF (*pez*) plaice.

acedo ADJ acid, sour; (*fig*) sour, unpleasant, disagreeable.

acéfalo ADJ headless; (*Pol etc*) leaderless.

aceitada* NF (*Cono Sur*) bribe, backhander*.

aceitar [1a] VT to oil, lubricate; (*Carib, Cono Sur**: sobornar*) to bribe, grease the palm of.

aceite NM (**a**) (*gen*) oil; (*de oliva*) olive-oil; (*perfume*) essence; ~ **alcanforado** camphorated oil; ~ **de algodón** cottonseed oil; ~ **de almendra** almond oil; ~ **de ballena** whale-oil; ~ **de cacahuete** peanut oil; ~ **de coco** coconut oil; ~ **de colza** rape-seed oil; ~ **combustible** fuel-oil; ~ **de girasol** sunflower oil; ~ **de hígado de bacalao** cod-liver oil; ~ **de linaza** linseed oil; ~ **lubricante** lubricating oil; ~ **de maíz** corn oil; ~ **de oliva puro** pure olive-oil; ~ **de oliva refinado** refined olive-oil; ~ **de ricino** castor oil; ~ **de soja** soya oil; ~ **vegetal** vegetable oil; ~ **virgen de oliva** pure olive-oil; **echar ~ al fuego** to add fuel to the flames.
(**b**) (‡: *droga*) hash*; (*Méx etc*) LSD.

aceitera NF (**a**) (*de mesa*) olive-oil dish, olive-oil bottle; ~**s** oil and vinegar set.
(**b**) (*Mec*) oilcan.

aceitero [1] ADJ oil (*atr*).
[2] NM oil merchant.

aceitón NM thick oil, dirty oil.

aceitoso ADJ oily.

aceituna NF olive; ~ **rellena** stuffed olive.

aceitunado ADJ olive, olive-coloured, olive-skinned.

aceitunero, -a NM/F (*Com*) dealer in olives; (*Agr*) olive-picker.

aceituno [1] ADJ (*LAm*) color olive, olive-coloured.
[2] NM (**a**) (*Bot*) olive-tree. (**b**) (‡) Civil Guard.

aceleración NF acceleration (*t Mec*); speeding up, hastening.

acelerada NF acceleration, speed-up.

aceleradamente ADV quickly, speedily.

acelerado* ADJ (*LAm*) (*nervioso*) jumpy, nervous; (*impaciente*) impatient.

acelerador NM accelerator, gas pedal (*US*); ~ **de partículas** particle accelerator; **apretar el ~**, **pisar el ~** (*fig*) to speed things up, step up the pace.

acelerar [1a] [1] VT to accelerate (*t Mec*); to speed up, hasten, expedite; *paso* to quicken; ~ **la marcha** to go faster, accelerate.
[2] **acelerarse** VR (**a**) (*apresurarse*) to hurry, hasten.
(**b**) (*LAm*) (*excitarse*) to get agitated, get jumpy; (*enloquecer*) to lose one's head.

acelerón NM (*fig*) leap forward; rapid increase, rapid improvement.

acelga NF chard; silver-beet.

acémila NF beast of burden, mule; (*fig*) mule-headed person.

acemilero NM muleteer.

acendrado ADJ pure, unblemished, refined; **de ~ carácter español** of a typically (*o* thoroughly) Spanish nature.

acendrar [1a] VT to purify; (*Téc, Liter etc*) to refine.

acensuar [1d] VT to tax.

acento NM (*gen*) accent; (*énfasis*) stress, emphasis; (*modulación*) tone, inflection; (*poét*) voice, words; ~ **agudo** acute accent; ~ **ortográfico** written accent; ~ **tónico** tonic accent, stress; **con fuerte ~ andaluz** with a strong Andalusian accent; **en ~ de cierto asombro** in a somewhat surprised tone; **el ~ cae en la segunda sílaba** the stress falls on the second syllable; **poner ~ en algo** (*énfasis*) to emphasize (*o stress*) sth.

acentor NM: **~ común** hedgesparrow, dunnock.

acentuación NF accentuation.

acentuado ADJ accented, stressed.

acentuamiento NM (*Cono Sur*) accent, emphasis.

acentuar [1e] ① VT to accent, stress; to emphasize; (*fig*) to accentuate; (*Inform*) to highlight.
② **acentuarse** VR (**a**) (*palabra*) to be stressed, be accented; **esta palabra se acentúa en la u** this word is stressed on the *u*. (**b**) (*fig*) to become more noticeable, be accentuated; **se acentúa la tendencia a la baja en la Bolsa** the slide on the Stock Exchange is accelerating.

aceña NF water mill.

aceñero NM miller.

acepción NF (**a**) (*Ling*) sense, meaning. (**b**) (*preferencia*) preference; **sin ~ de persona** without respect of persons, without partiality of any kind.

acepilladora NF planer, planing machine.

acepilladura NF wood-shaving.

acepillar [1a] VT (**a**) to brush; (*Téc*) to plane, shave. (**b**) (*adular*) to flatter.

aceptabilidad NF acceptability.

▼ **aceptable** ADJ acceptable, passable.

aceptación NF (*gen*) acceptance; (*aprobación*) approval, approbation; (*status*) popularity, standing; (*Com*) acceptance; **mandar algo a la ~** to send sth on approval; **este producto tendrá una ~ enorme** this product will get a big welcome, this product is sure to be very popular; **no tener ~** to be unsuccessful.

▼ **aceptar** [1a] ① VT to accept; to approve; *trabajo* to accept, take on, undertake, agree to do; *hechos* to accept, face.
② VI: **~ a** + *infin* to agree to + *infin*.

acepto ADJ acceptable, agreeable (*a, de* to), welcomed (*a, de* by).

acequia NF (**a**) (*Agr*) irrigation ditch, irrigation channel; (*de calle*) gutter. (**b**) (*LAm*) (*arroyo*) stream; (*alcantarilla*) sewer.

acera NF pavement, sidewalk (*US*); row (of houses); **los de la ~ de enfrente*** the gays*.

acerado ADJ (*Téc*) steel (*atr*), steely; (*con punta*) steel-tipped; (*fig*) sharp, cutting, biting.

acerar [1a] ① VT (*Téc*) to make into steel; *punta etc* to put a steel tip (*etc*) on; (*fig*) to harden; to make sharp, make biting.
② **acerarse** VR to toughen o.s., steel o.s.

acerbamente ADV (*fig*) harshly, scathingly.

acerbidad NF acerbity; sourness; harshness.

acerbo ADJ *sabor* sharp, bitter, sour; (*fig*) harsh, scathing; **tener un odio ~ a algo** to hate sth bitterly.

acerca de PREP about, on, concerning.

acercamiento NM (**a**) (*lit*) approach, bringing near, drawing near. (**b**) (*fig*) reconciliation; (*Pol*) rapprochement.

acercar [1g] ① VT to bring near(er); to bring over; **~ algo al oído** to put sth to one's ear.
② **acercarse** VR (**a**) (*gen*) to approach, come near, draw near; **~ a** (*lit*) to approach; to come close to; (*) to pop in, pop round (*a* to), drop in (*a* at, on); (*fig*) to approach, verge on; **~ a uno** to go up to sb, come up to sb; (*LAm*) to approach sb, open negotiations with sb. (**b**) (*fig: amantes*) to be reconciled, achieve a reconciliation; (*Pol*) to make a rapprochement.

ácere NM maple.

acería NF steelworks, steel mill.

acerico NM small cushion; (*Cos*) pincushion.

acero NM steel (*t fig*); **~ bruto** crude steel; **~ colado, ~ fundido** cast steel; **~s especiales** special steels; **~ inoxidable** stainless steel; **~ al manganeso** manganese steel; **tener buenos ~s** (*aguante*) to have guts; (*hambre*) to be ravenously hungry.

acerote NM (*holgazán*) idler, loafer.

acérrimo ADJ (*fig*) *defensor etc* very strong, staunch, out-and-out; *enemigo* bitter.

acerrojar [1a] VT to lock, bolt.

acertado ADJ *conjetura, solución* correct, right; successful; *respuesta* sensible, wise, sound; *idea* bright, good; *proyecto* well-conceived; *observación* apt, fitting, well-aimed; **eso no me parece muy ~** that doesn't seem right to me; **en eso no anduvo muy ~** that was not very sensible of him; **lo ~ es hacerlo ahora** it's best to do it now.

acertante ① ADJ: **tarjeta ~** winning card.
② NMF (*de problema etc*) solver; winner; (*en quinielas*) forecaster; **hubo 9 ~s** there were 9 successful solvers (*o* forecasters).

acertar [1j] ① VT *blanco* to hit; *solución* to get, get right, guess correctly; *objeto perdido* to find, succeed in tracing; *resultado* to achieve, succeed in reaching; **a ver si lo acertamos esta vez** let's see if we can get it right this time; **lo has acertado** you've guessed it, that's right; **no aciertas el modo de hacerlo** you don't manage to find the proper way to do it.

② VI (**a**) (*dar en el blanco*) to hit the mark; (*fig*) to hit the nail on the head; (*tener razón*) to be right, get it right; (*conjeturar*) to guess right; (*lograrlo*) to manage it, be successful.
(**b**) **~ a** + *infin* to happen to + *infin*; to manage to + *infin*, succeed in + *ger*.
(**c**) **~ con algo** to happen on sth, hit on sth; to find sth (without trouble).
(**d**) (*Bot*) to flourish, do well.

acertijo NM riddle, puzzle.

acervo NM (*montón*) heap, pile; (*provisión*) stock, store; (*Jur*) undivided estate; common property; **~ arqueológico** arch(a)eological wealth, arch(a)eological riches; **~ comunitario** (*CEE*) community patrimony; **~ cultural** cultural tradition; cultural wealth; **aportar algo al ~ común** to bring sth to the common stock.

acetato NM acetate; **~ de vinilo** vinyl acetate.

acético ADJ acetic.

acetilénico ADJ acetylene (*atr*).

acetileno NM acetylene.

acetona NF acetone.

acetre NM small pail; (*Ecl*) holy water vessel, portable stoup.

acezar [1f] VI to puff, pant.

achacable ADJ: **~ a** attributable to.

achacar [1g] VT (**a**) **~ algo a una causa** to attribute sth to a cause, put sth down to a cause; **~ la culpa a uno** to lay the blame on someone.
(**b**) (*LAm**) (*robar*) to pinch*, nick⁑; (*saquear*) to pillage, loot.

achacoso ADJ sickly, ailing.

achaflanar [1a] VT to chamfer, bevel.

achafranar⁑ [1a] VI (*Méx*) to fuck⁑, screw⁑.

achahuistlarse VR (*Mex*) to get·depressed.

achalay, achachay INTERJ (*And*) ¡~! brr!

achampañado ADJ champagne-flavoured.

achamparse [1a] VR (*Cono Sur*) **~ algo** to keep sth which does not belong to one.

achancharse* [1a] VR (**a**) (*And: ponerse perezoso*) to get lazy. (**b**) (*Cono Sur: engordar*) to get fat. (**c**) (*And: ponerse violento*) to become embarrassed.

achantado* ADJ (*CAm*) bashful, shy.

achantar* [1a] ① VT (**a**) (*cerrar*) to close.
(**b**) (*intimidar*) to intimidate; (*humillar*) to take down a peg.
② VI to be quiet, shut up*.
③ **achantarse** VR (**a**) (*esconderse*) to hide away.
(**b**) (*fig*) to give in, comply; **~ por las buenas** to be easily intimidated.

achaparrado ADJ dwarf, stunted; *persona* stocky, thickset, stumpy.

achapinarse [1a] VR (*CAm*) to adopt the local customs.

achaque NM (**a**) (*Med*) sickliness, infirmity, weakness; ailment, malady; (*) period, monthlies; **~s mañaneros** morning sickness; **~s de la vejez** ailments of old age.
(**b**) (*defecto*) defect, fault, weakness.
(**c**) (*asunto*) matter, subject; **en ~ de** in the matter of, on the subject of.
(**d**) (*pretexto*) pretext; **con ~ de** under the pretext of.

achara INTERJ: ¡~! (*CAm: lástima*) what a pity!

achares* NMPL jealousy; **dar ~ a uno** to make sb jealous.

acharolado ADJ patent leather (*atr*).

achatamiento NM (**a**) (*allanamiento*) flattening. (**b**) (*LAm: desmoralización*) loss of moral (*o* intellectual) fibre; **sufrieron un ~** they lost heart, they felt down.

achatar [1a] ① VT to flatten.
② **achatarse** VR (**a**) (*gen*) to get flat.
(**b**) (*Cono Sur, Méx: declinar*) to grow weak, decline; (*LAm: perder ánimo*) to lose heart, feel down.
(**c**) (*Cono Sur, Méx: avergonzarse*) to be overcome with shame, be embarrassed; **quedarse achatado** to feel ashamed, be embarrassed.

achicado ADJ childish, childlike.

achicador NM scoop, baler.

achicalado ADJ (*Méx*) sugared, honeyed.

achicalar [1a] VT (*Méx*) to cover (*o* soak) in honey.

achicanado ADJ Chicano, characteristic of Mexican-Americans.

achicar [1g] ① VT (**a**) (*empequeñecer*) to make smaller; to dwarf; *espacios* to reduce; (*Cos*) to shorten, take in; (*quitar importancia a*) to minimize, diminish the importance of.
(**b**) (*Náut etc*) to scoop, bale (out); (*con bomba*) to pump out.
(**c**) (*fig*) (*humillar*) to humiliate; (*intimidar*) to intimidate, browbeat.
(**d**) (*And: matar*) to kill.
(**e**) (*And, Carib: sujetar*) to fasten, hold down.
② **achicarse** VR (**a**) to get smaller; to shrink.
(**b**) (*fig*) to humble o.s., eat humble pie.
(**c**) (*LAm: rebajarse*) to do o.s. down, belittle o.s.

achicharradero NM place of oppressive heat, inferno.

achicharrante ADJ: **calor ~** sweltering heat.

achicharrar [1a] ① VT (**a**) (*sobrecalentar*) to scorch, overheat; (*Culin*) to

fry crisp; (*por error*) to overcook, burn, scorch; **el sol achicharraba la ciudad** the sun was roasting the city.
  (b) (*: *fastidiar*) to bother, plague.
  (c) (‡: *matar*) to shoot, riddle with bullets.
  (d) (*LAm*: *allanar*) to flatten, crush.
  2 achicharrarse VR to scorch, get burnt.
achicharronar [1a] VT (*LAm*) to flatten, crush.
achichiguar [1i] VT (*Méx*) **(a)** (*) to cosset, spoil. **(b)** (*Agr*) to shade.
achichincle* NMF (*Méx*) camp-follower, groupie*.
achichuncle‡ NMF (*Méx*) creep‡, crawler‡.
achicopalado* ADJ (*Méx*) depressed, gloomy.
achicoria NF chicory.
achiguado* ADJ (*Méx*) spoiled.
achiguarse [1i] VR (*Cono Sur*) to grow a paunch; (*muro etc*) to bulge, sag.
achilarse [1a] VR (*And*) to turn cowardly.
achimero NM (*CAm*) pedlar, peddler (*US*), hawker.
achimes NMPL (*CAm*) cheap goods, trinkets.
achín NM (*CAm*) pedlar, peddler (*US*), hawker.
achinado ADJ **(a)** (*Cono Sur*) with Indian looks; (*) coarse, common.
  (b) (*And, Carib*) Chinese-like, oriental; **ojos ~s** almond eyes.
achinar* [1a] **1** VT to scare.
  2 achinarse VR (*Cono Sur*) to become coarse..
achipolarse* [1a] VR (*Méx*) to grow sad, get gloomy.
achique NM **(a)** making smaller; reduction. **(b)** baling; pumping.
achiquillado ADJ (*Méx*) childish.
achiquitar [1a] VT (*LAm**) to make smaller, reduce in size.
achirarse [1a] VR (*And*) (*nublarse*) to cloud over; (*oscurecerse*) to get dark.
achís INTERJ atishoo!
achispado* ADJ tight*, tipsy.
achispar* [1a] VT (*LAm*) to cheer up, liven up.
  2 achisparse VR to get tight*, get tipsy.
-acho, -acha *V Aspects of Word Formation in Spanish 2.*
achocar [1g] VT **(a)** (*tirar*) to throw against a wall, dash against a wall.
  (b) (*pegar*) to hit, bash*.
  (c) (*: *guardar*) to hoard, stash away*.
achocharse [1a] VR to get doddery, begin to dodder.
achoclonarse [1a] VR (*LAm*) to crowd together.
achocolatado ADJ **(a)** (*LAm*: *cualidad*) chocolate (*atr*); like chocolate.
  (b) (*LAm*: *color*) dark brown, chocolate-coloured, tan. **(c) estar ~‡** (*borracho*) to be canned‡.
acholado ADJ (*LAm*) **(a)** (*mestizo*) racially mixed, part-Indian.
  (b) (*acobardado*) cowed; (*avergonzado*) abashed.
acholar [1a] (*LAm*) **1** VT (*avergonzar*) to embarrass; (*intimidar*) to intimidate, scare.
  2 acholarse VR **(a)** (*acriollarse*) to have (*o* adopt) half-breed ways.
  (b) (*acobardarse*) to be cowed; (*avergonzarse*) to be abashed, become shy; (*sonrojarse*) to blush.
acholo NM (*LAm*) embarrassment.
-achón, -achona *V Aspects of Word Formation in Spanish 2.*
achoramiento‡ NM (*Cono Sur*) threat.
achubascarse [1g] VR (*cielo*) to become threatening, cloud over.
achuchado ADJ: **estar ~** (*Cono Sur*) (*paludismo*) to have malaria; (*tener escalofríos*) to catch a chill; (*tener fiebre*) to be feverish; (*fig*) to be scared (*o* frightened); **esta tarea está achuchada** this is a tough job.
achuchar [1a] **1** VT **(a)** (*estrujar*) to crush, squeeze flat.
  (b) *persona* (*empujar*) to shove, jostle; (*acosar*) to harass, pester.
  (c) *perro* to urge on; **~ un perro contra uno** to set a dog on sb.
  2 achucharse¹ VR (*amantes*) to cuddle, fondle (one another), pet* (one another).
achucharse² [1a] VR (*Cono Sur*) (*paludismo*) to catch malaria; (*acatarrarse*) to catch a chill; (*tener fiebre*) to get feverish; (*asustarse*) to get scared.
achuchón NM **(a)** (*empujón*) squeeze; shove, push. **(b) tener un ~** (*Med*) to fall ill; to have a relapse.
achucutado ADJ (*LAm*) (*deprimido*) gloomy, depressed; (*agobiado*) overwhelmed.
achucutarse [1a] VR (*LAm*) (*estar afligido*) to be (*o* look) dismayed; (*deprimirse*) to be gloomy; (*marchitarse*) to wilt; (*ser tímido*) to be timid, be shy.
achucuyarse [1a] VR (*CAm*) = **achucutarse**.
achuicarse [1g] VR (*Cono Sur*) (*avergonzarse*) to be embarrassed; (*apocarse*) to feel small.
achulado ADJ, **achulapado** ADJ **(a)** (*desenvuelto*) jaunty, cocky. **(b)** (*grosero*) common, uncouth.
achumado ADJ (*LAm*) drunk.
achumarse [1a] VR (*LAm*) to get drunk.
achunchar [1a] (*LAm*) **1** VT **(a)** (*avergonzar*) to shame, cause to blush.
  (b) (*intimidar*) to scare.
  2 achuncharse VR **(a)** (*avergonzarse*) to feel ashamed, blush.
  (b) (*intimidarse*) to get scared.

achuntar [1a] (*Cono Sur*) **1** VT to do properly, get right, do at the right time.
  2 VI to guess right; to hit the nail on the head.
achuñuscar* [1g] VT (*Cono Sur*) to squeeze.
achupalla NF (*LAm*) pineapple.
achura NF (*LAm*) offal.
achurar [1a] **1** VT (*LAm*) *animal* to gut; *persona* to stab to death, cut to pieces.
  2 VI (*LAm*) to benefit from a share-out, get sth free.
achurrucarse [1g] VR (*CAm*: *marchitarse*) to wilt.
achurruscado* ADJ rumpled, crumpled up.
achurruscar [1g] VT (*And, Cono Sur*) to rumple, crumple up.
aciago ADJ ill-fated, ill-omened, fateful.
aciano NM cornflower.
acíbar NM aloes; (*fig*) sorrow, bitterness.
acibarar [1a] VT to add bitter aloes to, make bitter; (*fig*) to embitter; **~ la vida a uno** to make sb's life a misery.
acicalado ADJ *metal* polished, bright and clean; *persona* smart, neat, spruce; (*pey*) dapper, overdressed.
acicalar [1a] **1** VT *metal* to polish, burnish, clean; *persona etc* to dress up, bedeck, adorn.
  2 acicalarse VR to smarten o.s. up, spruce o.s. up; to get dressed up.
acicate NM spur; (*fig*) spur, incentive, stimulus.
acicatear [1a] VT *persona, imaginación* to spur on, excite.
acícula NF (*Bot*) needle.
acidez NF acidity.
acidia NF indolence, apathy, sloth.
acidificar [1g] **1** VT to acidify.
  2 acidificarse VR to acidify.
acidillo ADJ slightly sour.
ácido **1** ADJ **(a)** *sabor, olor* sharp, sour, acid. **(b) estar ~** (*LAm**) to be great*, be fabulous*.
  2 NM **(a)** acid; **~ ascórbico** ascorbic acid; **~ carbólico** carbolic acid; **~ carbónico** carbonic acid; **~ cianhídrico** hydrocyanic acid; **~ clorhídrico** hydrochloric acid; **~ graso saturado** saturated fatty acid; **~ lisérgico** lysergic acid; **~ nicotínico** nicotinic acid; **~ nítrico** nitric acid; **~ nitroso** nitrous acid; **~ nucleico** nucleic acid; **~ oxálico** oxalic acid; **~ ribonucleico** ribonucleic acid; **~ sulfúrico** sulphuric acid; **~ úrico** uric acid. **(b)** (*: *droga*) acid*; (*pastilla*) LSD tablet.
acidófilo ADJ acidophilous.
acidulante NM acidulant, acidifier.
acídulo ADJ acidulous; disagreeable, sharp.
acierto NM **(a)** (*éxito*) success; (*tiro*) good shot, hit; (*conjetura*) good guess; (*idea*) good idea; sensible choice, wise move; **fue un ~ suyo** it was a sensible choice on his part.
  (b) (*talento*) skill, ability; (*lo apropiado*) aptness; (*juicio*) wisdom; (*discreción*) discretion; **obrar con ~** to act sensibly; to do well; **el periódico que con todo ~ dirige X** the paper which X edits so well.
aciguatado* ADJ (*Méx*) silly, stupid.
aciguatarse [1a] VR (*Carib, Méx*) to grow stupid; (*: *enloquecer*) to go crazy, lose one's head.
acitrón NM **(a)** (*Culin*) candied citron. **(b)** (*LAm Bot*) bishop's weed, goutweed.
acizañar* [1a] VT to stir things*, cause trouble.
aclamación NF acclamation; applause, acclaim; **entre las aclamaciones del público** amid the applause of the audience; **elegir a uno por ~** to elect sb by acclamation.
aclamar [1a] VT to acclaim; to applaud; **~ a uno por jefe** to acclaim sb (as) leader, hail sb as leader.
aclaración NF **(a)** (*de ropa*) rinse, rinsing. **(b)** (*explicación*) clarification, explanation, elucidation. **(c)** (*Met*) brightening, clearing up.
aclarado NM rinse.
aclarar [1a] **1** VT **(a)** *ropa* to rinse; *líquido etc* to thin, thin down; (*LAm*) to clear; *bosque* to clear, thin (out).
  (b) (*fig*) *problema* to clarify, cast light on, explain; *duda* to resolve, remove.
  2 VI (*Met*) to brighten, clear, clear up.
  3 aclararse* VR to catch on, get it*; **no me aclaro** I can't work it out.
aclaratorio ADJ explanatory; illuminating.
aclayos‡ NMPL (*Méx*) eyes.
aclimatación NF, **aclimatización** NF acclimatization, acclimation (*US*).
aclimatar [1a], **aclimatizar** [1f] **1** VT to acclimatize, acclimate (*US*).
  2 aclimatizarse VR to acclimatize o.s., get acclimatized, acclimate (*US*), get acclimated (*US*); **~ a algo** (*fig*) to get used to sth.
acne NF, **acné** NF acne.
ACNUR [ak'nur] NM ABR *de* **Alto Comisariado de las Naciones Unidas para los Refugiados** United Nations High Commission for Refugees, UNHCR.

-aco, -aca *V* Aspects of Word Formation in Spanish 2.

acobardamiento NM intimidation.

acobardar [1a] 1 VT to daunt, intimidate, cow, unnerve.

2 **acobardarse** VR to be frightened, get frightened; to flinch, shrink back (*ante* from, at).

acobe* NM (*Carib*) iron.

acobrado ADJ copper-coloured, coppery.

acocear [1a] VT to kick; (*fig: maltratar*) to ill-treat, trample on; (*insultar*) to insult.

acochambrar* [1a] VT (*Méx*) to make filthy.

acocharse [1a] VR to squat, crouch.

acochinar: [1a] VT to bump off:.

acocil NM (*Méx*) freshwater shrimp; **estar como un ~** to be red in the face.

acodado ADJ bent; elbowed.

acodalar [1a] VT to shore up, prop up.

acodar [1a] 1 VT *brazo* to lean, rest; *vid etc* to layer.

2 **acodarse** VR: **~ en** to lean on; **acodado en** leaning on, resting on; **~ hacia** to bend towards, curve towards.

acodiciarse [1b] VR: **~ a** to covet.

acodo NM (*Agr*) layer.

acogedizo ADJ gathered at random.

acogedor ADJ welcoming, friendly, hospitable, warm; *cuarto* snug, cosy; **un ambiente ~** a friendly atmosphere.

acoger [2c] 1 VT *visitante etc* to welcome, receive; *refugiado* to take in, give refuge to; *fugitivo* to harbour; *idea* to receive; *palabra nueva, hecho etc* to accept, admit.

2 **acogerse** VR to take refuge; (*fig*) **~ a** *pretexto* to take refuge in; *recurso* to resort to; *promesa* to avail o.s. of; **~ a la ley** to have recourse to the law; **~ a uno** to ask sb's help.

acogible ADJ (*Cono Sur*) acceptable.

acogida NF (*recepción*) welcome, reception; (*aprobación*) acceptance, admittance; (*refugio*) shelter, refuge, asylum; (*de ríos*) meeting place; **~ familiar** (*Jur*)(fostering; **dar ~ a** to accept; **tener buena ~** to be welcomed, be well received; **¿qué ~ tuvo la idea?** how was the idea received?

acogollar [1a] (*Agr*) 1 VT to cover up, protect.

2 VI to sprout.

acogotar [1a] VT (*matar*) to fell, kill (with a blow on the neck); (*dejar sin sentido*) to knock down, lay out; (*LAm*) to have at one's mercy; (*agarrar*) to grab round the neck; (*) to press, put pressure on, lean on*; **~ a uno** (*Cono Sur*) to harass sb for payment.

acohombrar [1a] VT (*Agr*) to earth up.

acojinar [1a] VT (*Téc*) to cushion.

acojonador: ADJ (*Esp*) = **acojonante**.

acojonamiento: NM (*Esp*) funk*, fear.

acojonante: ADJ (*Esp*) amazing; tremendous*, stupendous*, super*, great*.

acojonar: [1a] (*Esp*) 1 VT (a) (*atemorizar*) to put the wind up*, intimidate. (b) (*impresionar*) to impress; (*asombrar*) to amaze, overwhelm.

2 **acojonarse** VR (a) (*acobardarse*) to back down; (*inquietarse*) to get the wind up*; **¡no te acojones!** take it easy!*

(b) (*asombrarse*) to be amazed, be overwhelmed.

acojono: NM (*Esp*) funk*, fear.

acolada NF accolade.

acolchado ADJ quilted, padded; *sobre* padded.

acolchar [1a] VT (a) (*Téc*) to quilt, pad. (b) (*fig*) *golpe etc* to soften.

acólito NM (*Ecl*) acolyte, server, altar-boy; (*fig*) acolyte, minion.

acollador NM (*Náut*) lanyard.

acollar [1l] VT to earth up; (*Náut*) to caulk.

acollarar [1a] VT *bueyes* to yoke, harness; (*atar*) to tie by the neck; *perro etc* to put a collar on; (*Cono Sur: mujer*) to trap into marriage.

acollerar [1a] 1 VTI to gather, herd together.

2 **acollerarse** VR = 1.

acomedido ADJ (*LAm*) (*generoso*) helpful, obliging; (*solícito*) concerned, solicitous.

acomedirse [3k] VR (*LAm*) to offer to help; **~ a hacer algo** to do sth willingly.

acometedor ADJ energetic, enterprising; *toro* fierce.

acometer [2a] VT (a) (*violentamente*) to attack; to set upon, rush on, assail; (*toro*) to charge.

(b) *tarea* to undertake, attempt; *asunto* to tackle, deal with; *construcción* to begin, start on.

(c) (*sueño etc*) to overcome; (*temor*) to seize, take hold of; (*duda*) to assail; (*enfermedad*) to attack; **le acometieron dudas** he was assailed by doubts, he began to have doubts; **me acometió la tristeza** I was overcome with sadness.

acometida NF (a) (*violento*) attack, assault. (b) (*Elec etc*) connection.

acometimiento NM attack; **~ y agresión** (*Méx Jur*) assault and battery.

acometividad NF (a) (*energía*) energy, enterprise. (b) (*agresividad*) aggressiveness; (*de toro*) fierceness; (*Cono Sur*) touchiness; **mostrar ~** to show fight.

acomodable ADJ adaptable; suitable.

acomodación NF accommodation; adaptation; arrangement.

acomodadizo ADJ accommodating, obliging; acquiescent; (*pey*) pliable, easy-going.

acomodado ADJ (a) (*apropiado*) suitable, fit; *precio* moderate; *artículo* moderately priced. (b) *persona, familia etc* well-to-do, wealthy, well-off.

acomodador NM (*Teat etc*) usher.

acomodadora NF (*Teat etc*) usherette.

acomodamiento NM (a) (*cualidad*) suitability, convenience. (b) (*acto*) arrangement, agreement.

acomodar [1a] 1 VT (a) (*ajustar*) to adjust, accommodate, adapt (*a* to); **~ a uno con algo** to supply sb with sth.

(b) (*encontrar sitio para*) to fit in, find room for, accommodate; *persona* to take in, lodge.

(c) (*adaptar*) to suit, adapt (*a* to); *colores* to match; **¿puede ~me esta lana?** can you match this wool for me?; **~ un ejemplo a un caso** to apply an example to a case in point.

(d) (*Mec etc*) to repair, adjust, put right.

(e) *enemigos, puntos de vista* to reconcile.

(f) *criado etc* to place; *obrero* to give a job to, take on; (*Teat*) to show to a seat; *visitante* to make comfortable, make feel at home; *enfermo* to make comfortable; *niño* to settle; (*Cono Sur, Méx*) *amigo* to fix up (with a job); **acomodé a mi primo** I fixed my cousin up (with a job).

(g) (*Carib*: *estafar*) to con*, trick.

2 VI to suit, fit; to be suitable.

3 **acomodarse** VR (a) (*conformarse*) to comply, conform; (*adaptarse*) to adapt o.s.

(b) (*en un lugar*) to install o.s., settle down; **¡acomódese a su gusto!** make yourself comfortable!, make yourself at home!

(c) (*Cono Sur*) (*colocarse*) to fix o.s. up (with a job), pull strings (to get a job); (*) to marry into money.

(d) **~ a** to adapt o.s. to; to settle down to; to comply with, conform with; **~ a** + *infin* to settle down to + *infin*.

(e) **~ con** to reconcile o.s. to; to come to an agreement with; to comply with, conform with.

(f) **~ de** to provide o.s. with.

acomodaticio ADJ = **acomodadizo**.

acomodo NM (a) (*arreglo*) arrangement; compromise; (*acuerdo*) agreement, understanding; (*pey*) secret arrangement, secret deal.

(b) (*puesto*) post, job; (*LAm pey*) soft job, plum job.

(c) (*LAm**: *soborno*) bribe.

acompañado 1 ADJ (a) **estar ~, ir ~** to go accompanied, go with sb.

(b) *lugar* busy, frequented.

(c) **con falda acompañada** with skirt to match, with a skirt of the same colour (*o* pattern *etc*).

(d) **estar ~** (*Carib**) to be drunk.

2 NM, **acompañada** NF (*LAm*) lover; common-law husband, common-law wife.

acompañamiento NM (a) (*gen*) accompaniment; **sin ~** unaccompanied, alone.

(b) (*persona*) escort; (*personas*) retinue; (*LAm*) (*entierro*) funeral procession; (*boda*) wedding reception *etc*; (*Teat*) extras.

(c) (*Mús*) accompaniment; **con ~ de piano** with piano accompaniment; **cantar sin ~** to sing unaccompanied.

(d) (*consecuencias*) sequel, consequences, aftermath; **el terremoto y su ~** the earthquake and its aftermath.

(e) (*Teat*) walk-on parts.

acompañanta NF female companion, chaperon; (*Mús*) accompanist.

acompañante NM companion; escort; (*Mús*) accompanist.

acompañar [1a] 1 VT (a) (*gen*) to accompany, go with; (*oficialmente*) to attend; *mujer* to escort, *mujer joven* to chaperon; **prefiero que no me acompañen** I prefer to go alone; **¿quieres que te acompañe?** do you want me to come with you?; **~ a uno a la puerta** to see sb to the door, see sb out; **seguir acompañando a uno** to keep with sb, stay with sb, not leave sb; **este vino acompaña bien al queso** this wine goes well with the cheese.

(b) (*Mús*) to accompany (*a, con* on).

(c) (*en carta*) to enclose, attach; (*como apéndice*) to attach; **en el folleto que le acompañamos** in the enclosed brochure.*

(d) **~ lo que se ha dicho con** (*o de*) **pruebas** to support what one has said with evidence.

(e) **~ a uno en un sentimiento** to join sb in; **le acompaño en el sentimiento** please accept my condolences, I sympathize with you (in your loss).

2 **acompañarse** VR (*Mús*) to accompany o.s. (*con, de* on).

acompaño NM (*CAm, Méx*) meeting, group, crowd.

acompasado ADJ rhythmic, regular, measured; (*en habla*) slow; (*de paso*) slow, deliberate, leisurely.

acompasar [1a] VT **(a)** (*Mat*) to measure with a compass.
(b) (*Mús etc*) to mark the rhythm of; ~ **la dicción** to speak with a marked rhythm.

acomplejado ADJ full of complexes; gravely embarrassed, much put out.

acomplejante ADJ (*Cono Sur*) inhibiting, embarrassing.

acomplejar [1a] **1** VT to cause complexes in, give a complex to; to embarrass gravely, cause to be much put out.
2 **acomplejarse** VR to get a complex (*por* about); ¡**no te acomplejes!** don't get so worked up!

acompletadores* NMPL (*Méx*) beans.

acomunarse [1a] VR to join forces.

aconchabarse* [1a] VR to gang up*.

aconchado* NM (*Méx*) sponger*, scrounger*.

aconchar [1a] **1** VT **(a)** (*poner a salvo*) to push to safety.
(b) (*Náut*) to beach, run aground; (*viento*) to drive ashore.
(c) (*Méx**: *reprender*) to tell off*.
2 **aconcharse** VR **(a)** (*Náut*) to keel over; to run aground.
(b) (*Cono Sur: líquido*) to settle, clarify.
(c) (*: *vivir de otro*) to sponge*, live off somebody else.

acondicionado ADJ: **bien** ~ *persona* genial, affable, nice; *objeto* in good condition; **mal** ~ *persona* bad-tempered, difficult; *objeto* in bad condition; **un laboratorio bien** ~ a well-equipped laboratory.

acondicionador NM (*de pelo etc*) conditioner; ~ **de aire** air-conditioner.

acondicionamiento NM conditioning; ~ **de aire** air-conditioning.

acondicionar [1a] VT **(a)** (*arreglar*) to arrange, prepare, make suitable; (*Téc*) to condition. **(b)** *sala etc* to air-condition.

acongojado ADJ distressed, anguished.

acongojar [1a] **1** VT to distress, grieve.
2 **acongojarse** VR to become distressed, get upset; ¡**no te acongojes!** don't get upset!, don't worry!

acónito NM (*Bot*) aconite, monkshood.

▼ **aconsejable** ADJ advisable; sensible, politic; **nada** ~, **poco** ~ inadvisable; **eso no es** ~ that is not advisable; **no sería** ~ **que Vd** + *subj* you would be ill-advised to + *infin*.

aconsejado ADJ: **bien** ~ sensible; well-advised; **mal** ~ ill-advised, rash, ill-considered.

▼ **aconsejar** [1a] **1** VT **(a)** *persona* to advise; ~ **a uno hacer algo** to advise sb to do sth.
(b) *cuidado etc* to advise, recommend; *virtud* to preach.
2 **aconsejarse** VR to seek advice, take advice; ~ **con**, ~ **de** to consult; ~ **mejor** to think better of it.

ACONSEJAR	ver también la entrada

Aconsejar a algn que haga algo se traduce al inglés con *advise* + OBJETO + INFINITIVO *con* to, es decir: *advise sb to do sth*:

> Le aconsejé que (no) cambiase de trabajo
> *I advised her (not) to change jobs*
> Le aconsejaré a mi hermana que se lo piense dos veces
> *I'll advise my sister to think it over carefully*

NOTA: Cuando se quiere aconsejar a una persona, en inglés se suele utilizar el condicional para que no parezca un mandato, como se ve en los siguientes ejemplos:

> Le aconsejo que consulte a un abogado
> *I would advise you to see a lawyer*
> Te aconsejo que lo hagas
> *I'd advise you to do it*

Para otros usos y ejemplos ver la entrada.

---

aconsonantar [1a] VTI to rhyme (*con* with).

acontecedero ADJ which could happen, possible.

acontecer [2d] VI to happen, occur, come about.

acontecimiento NM event, happening, occurrence; incident; (*dramático*) happening; **fue realmente un** ~ it was an event of some importance.

acopiar [1b] VT to gather (together), collect; (*Com*) to buy up, get a monopoly of; *miel* to collect, hive.

acopio NM **(a)** (*acto*) gathering, collecting. **(b)** (*cantidad*) collection; store, stock; (*de madera etc*) stack; (*Cono Sur*) abundance, wealth; **hacer** ~ to stock up (*de* with), lay in stocks (*de* of).

acoplable ADJ attachable.

acoplado **1** ADJ: **un equipo bien** ~ a well coordinated team.
2 NM **(a)** (*LAm Aut*) trailer. **(b)** (*Cono Sur**: *parásito*) hanger-on, sponger*; (*intruso*) gatecrasher.

acoplador NM: ~ **acústico** acoustic coupler.

acoplamiento NM (*Mec*) coupling; joint; (*Elec*) connection; hookup; (*de astronaves*) docking, link-up; (*Zool*) mating; ~ **de manguito** sleeve coupling; ~ **en serie** series connection; ~ **universal** universal joint.

acoplar [1a] **1** VT (*Téc*) to couple; to join, fit together; (*Elec*) to connect, join up; *astronaves* to dock, link up; *bueyes* to yoke, hitch; *animales* to mate, pair; *personas* to associate, bring together; (*LAm*

Ferro) to couple (up); *opiniones* to reconcile; *proyectos, esfuerzos* to co-ordinate.
2 **acoplarse** VR **(a)** (*Zool*) to mate, pair.
(b) (*astronaves*) to dock, link up (*a* with).
(c) (*hacer las paces*) to make it up, be reconciled.
(d) (*Elec*) to cause feedback.

acoplo NM (*Elec*) feedback.

acoquinamiento NM intimidation.

acoquinar [1a] **1** VT to scare, intimidate, cow.
2 **acoquinarse** VR to get scared, allow o.s. to be intimidated.

acorar [1a] VT to distress, afflict, upset.

acorazado **1** ADJ armour-plated; ironclad; armoured.
2 NM battleship; ~ **de bolsillo** pocket battleship.

acorazar [1f] **1** VT to armour-plate, armour.
2 **acorazarse** VR (*fig*) to steel o.s., arm o.s. (*contra* against); to harden o.s.; ~ **contra** (*fig*) to become inured to.

acorazonado ADJ heart-shaped.

acorchado ADJ spongy, cork-like; *boca* furry.

acorchar [1a] **1** VT to cover with cork.
2 **acorcharse** VR to become spongy, become like cork; to wither, shrivel; (*miembro*) to go to sleep.

acordada NF (*Jur*) decree.

acordadamente ADV unanimously, by common consent.

acordado ADJ agreed; **lo** ~ that which has been agreed (upon).

acordar [1l] **1** VT **(a)** (*decidir*) to decide, resolve, agree on; ~ **que** + *subj* to resolve that ...; to resolve to + *infin*.
(b) (*And, Cono Sur: conceder*) to grant, accord.
(c) *opiniones* to reconcile; (*Mús*) to tune; (*Arte*) to blend, harmonize.
(d) ~ **algo a uno** to remind sb of sth.
2 VI to agree; to correspond.
3 **acordarse** VR **(a)** (*ponerse de acuerdo*) to agree, come to an agreement (*con* with); **se acordó hacerlo** it was agreed to do it; **se ha acordado que ...** it has been agreed that ...
(b) (*recordar*) to remember, recall, recollect; **no me acuerdo** I don't remember; **si mal no me acuerdo** if my memory serves me right; ~ **de algo** to remember sth; ¿**te acuerdas de mí**? do you remember me?; ¡**te acordarás de mí!** you'll be hearing from me!; ¡**te acordarás de ésta!** I'll teach you!; **no se acuerda ni del santo de su nombre** he hardly remembers his own name.

acorde **1** ADJ **(a)** **con sentimientos** ~**s** with identical feelings; **estar** ~**s** to be agreed, be in agreement.
(b) (*Mús*) harmonious; (*con estar*) in tune, in harmony.
2 NM (*Mús*) chord; **a los** ~**s de la marcha nupcial** to the strains of the wedding march.

acordeón NM accordion.

acordeonista NMF accordionist.

acordeón-piano NM piano-accordion.

acordonado ADJ **(a)** *superficie etc* ribbed; *lugar* cordoned-off; *moneda, borde* milled. **(b)** (*LAm*) *animal* thin.

acordonamiento NM (*V* ADJ) ribbing; cordoning off; milling.

acordonar [1a] VT **(a)** (*atar*) to tie up, tie with string; *corsé etc* to lace up.
(b) *lugar* to cordon off, rope off; surround with a cordon; (*policía etc*) to surround.
(c) *moneda, borde* to mill.
(d) (*LAm*) *terreno* to prepare.

acornar [1l] VT, **acornear** [1a] VT to butt; to gore.

acorralamiento NM enclosing; cornering, trapping.

acorralar [1a] VT *ganado* to round up, pen, corral; *animal peligroso* to corner, bring to bay; *persona* to corner; (*fig*) to intimidate.

acorrer [2a] **1** VT to help, go to the aid of.
2 VI to run up; ~ **a uno** to hasten to sb.

acortamiento NM shortening; reduction.

acortar [1a] **1** VT **(a)** (*gen*) to shorten, cut down, reduce; *velas, paso* to shorten; *narración* to cut short, abbreviate. **(b)** (*LAm: atenuar*) to tone down.
2 **acortarse** VR (*fig*) to be slow; to be shy, falter.

acosar [1a] VT (*perseguir*) to pursue relentlessly; (*fig*) to hound; to harass, badger; (*obsesionar*) to obsess; *animal* to urge on; ~ **a uno a preguntas** to pester sb with questions.

acosijar [1a] VT (*Méx*) = **acosar**.

acoso NM relentless pursuit; (*fig*) hounding, harassing; relentless questioning; ~ **sexual** sexual harassment; **operación de** ~ **y derribo** (*Mil*) search and destroy operation; (*fig*) hate campaign.

acostar [1l] **1** VT **(a)** (*tender*) to lay down.
(b) (*en cama*) to put to bed.
(c) (*Náut*) to bring alongside.
2 **acostarse** VR to lie down; to go to bed; (*LAm: dar a luz*) to give birth; **estar acostado** to be lying down; to be in bed; **nos acostamos tarde** we go to bed late; **A se acostó con B** A went to bed with B, A slept with B; **ella se acuesta con cualquiera** she sleeps around; **es hora de** ~ it's bedtime.

➤ LENGUA Y USO: **aconsejable** → 29.2   **aconsejar: 1a** → 28.2, 29.1, 29.2

acostillado ADJ ribbed, with ribs.

acostumbrado ADJ usual, customary, habitual.

acostumbrar [1a] ① VT: ~ **a uno a algo** to get sb used to sth; ~ **a uno a las dificultades** to inure sb to hardships; ~ **a uno a hacer algo** to accustom sb to doing sth; to get sb used to doing sth.

② VI: ~ + *infin*, ~ **a** + *infin* to be accustomed to + *infin*, be in the habit of + *ger*; **los sábados acostumbra (a) ir al cine** on Saturdays he usually goes to the cinema.

③ **acostumbrarse** VR (a) ~ **a algo** to get used to sth; **estar acostumbrado a algo** to be used to sth, be accustomed to sth; **está acostumbrado a verlas venir** he's not easily fooled.

(b) (*LAm*) **no se acostumbra aquí** it isn't usual here; **ya no se acostumbra la chistera** nobody wears top hats any more, top hats aren't worn nowadays.

┌─ ACOSTUMBRAR ─────────────── ver también la entrada ─┐

• La forma pronominal *acostumbrarse a hacer algo* se traduce al inglés por *get used to* + -ING:
  Te acostumbrarás a trabajar aquí
  You'll get used to working here
  Con el tiempo me acostumbré a estar sin él
  In time I got used to being without him
• La expresión *estar acostumbrado a hacer algo* se traduce por *to be used to* + -ING:
  Está acostumbrado a levantarse temprano
  He's used to getting up early
  NOTA: Otra forma de traducir esta estructura al inglés es con la construcción *to be accustomed to* + -ING, aunque tiene un registro formal:
  He's accustomed to getting up early
• Cuando el verbo *acostumbrar* equivale a *soler*, se puede traducir de dos formas distintas en inglés, dependiendo de si la acción a la que se refiere ocurre en el pasado o en el presente.
• En el *pasado*, lo traducimos por *used to* + INFINITIVO:
  Cuando era niña acostumbraba a rezar todas las noches
  When I was a child I used to pray every night
  El año pasado acostumbrábamos a vernos todos los viernes
  Last year we used to meet every Friday
• En el *presente* se traduce por el adverbio *usually* + PRESENTE SIMPLE:
  Los domingos acostumbro a levantarme tarde
  I usually get up late on Sundays
  Para otros usos y ejemplos ver la entrada.

└──┘

---

acotación NF (a) (*mojón*) boundary mark; (*Geog*) elevation mark. (b) (*apunte*) marginal note; (*Teat*) stage direction.

acotado ① ADJ enclosed, fenced.
② NM (*t ~ de caza*) game preserve.

acotamiento NM (*Méx Aut*) hard shoulder, berm (*US*); emergency lane.

acotar [1a] VT (a) *tierra* to survey, mark out; to limit, set bounds to; *coto etc* to fence in, protect, preserve.
(b) *árboles* to lop.
(c) *página* to annotate; *mapa* to mark elevations on.
(d) (*fig*) (*aceptar*) to accept, adopt; (*elegir*) to choose; (*avalar*) to vouch for; (*comprobar*) to check, verify.

acotejar [1a] VT (*LAm*) to arrange, put in order.

acotillo NM sledgehammer.

acoyundar [1a] VT to yoke.

acr. ABR *de* **acreedor** creditor, Cr.

acracia NF anarchy.

ácrata ① ADJ non-conformist; hippy; free-and-easy, unconventional; loose-living; (*Pol*) anarchistic; anarchic.
② NMF non-conformist; hippy, drop-out; unconventional person; (*Pol*) anarchist.

acrático ADJ = **ácrata 1**.

acre¹ ADJ *sabor* sharp, bitter, tart; *olor* acrid, pungent; *temperamento* sour; *crítica etc* biting, mordant.

acre² NM (*medida*) acre.

acrecencia NF (a) (*Jur*) accretion. (b) = **acrecentamiento**.

acrecentamiento NM increase, growth.

acrecentar [1j] ① VT to increase, augment; *persona etc* to advance, promote; to further the interests of.
② **acrecentarse** VR to increase, grow.

acrecer [2d] VT to increase.

acrecimiento NM increase, growth.

acreditación NF accreditation; sanctioning, authorization; vetting, (security) clearance.

acreditado ADJ (*Com, Pol*) accredited; (*estimado*) reputable, highly-esteemed; (*influyente*) influential; **nuestro representante** ~ our accredited representative, our official agent; **una casa acreditada** a reputable firm; **marca acreditada** reputable make.

acreditar [1a] ① VT (*dar reputación a*) to do credit to, add to the repu-

tation of; (*avalar*) to vouch for, guarantee; (*por seguridad*) to vet, clear, give security clearance to; (*probar*) to prove; (*sancionar*) to sanction, authorize; (*Com*) to credit; (*And*) to sell on credit; ~ **a un embajador cerca de uno** to accredit an ambassador to sb; **y virtudes que le acreditan** and qualities which do him credit; ~ **su personalidad** to establish one's identity.

② **acreditarse** VR to justify o.s., prove one's worth; ~ **de** to get a reputation for; ~ **en** to get a reputation in.

acreditativo ADJ: **documentos ~s** supporting documents.

acreedor ① ADJ: ~ **a** worthy of, deserving of; eligible for.
② NM, **acreedora** NF creditor; ~ **hipotecario** mortgagee.

acreencia NF (*And, Méx*) (*balance*) credit balance; (*deuda*) debt, amount owing (o owed).

acremente ADV sharply, bitterly; pungently; bitingly.

acribadura NF sifting, sieving.

acribar [1a] VT to sift, riddle.

acribillado ADJ *superficie* pitted, pockmarked; ~ **a** riddled with, peppered with; ~ **de** filled with; honeycombed with; ~ **de picaduras** covered with stings.

acribillar [1a] VT (a) ~ **a balazos** to riddle with bullets, pepper with shots; ~ **a puñaladas** to cover with stab wounds.
(b) (*fig*) to pester, badger; to harass; ~ **a uno a preguntas** to pester sb with questions.

acridio NM (*LAm*) locust.

acrílico ADJ, NM acrylic.

acrilonitrilo NM acrylonitrile.

acriminación NF incrimination; accusation.

acriminador ① ADJ incriminating.
② NM, **acriminadora** NF accuser.

acriminar [1a] VT to incriminate; to accuse.

acrimonia NF sharpness; acridness, pungency; sourness; (*fig*) acrimony, bitterness.

acrimonioso ADJ acrimonious.

acriollarse [1a] VR (*LAm*) to take on local habits (o the habits of the country); (*pey**) to go native.

acrisolado ADJ pure; tried, tested; unquestionable; **una fe acrisolada** a pure faith; **el patriotismo más** ~ the noblest kind of patriotism; **de acrisolada honradez** of unquestionable honesty.

acrisolar [1a] VT (*Téc*) to purify, refine; (*fig*) to purify, purge; to bring out, clarify; *verdad etc* to prove, reveal.

acristalado ADJ glazed.

acristalamiento NM glazing; **los ~s** windows, glazing; **doble ~** double glazing.

acristalar [1a] VT to glaze.

acristianar [1a] VT to christianize; *niño* to baptize.

acritud NF = **acrimonia**.

acrobacia NF acrobatics; ~ **aérea** aerobatics.

acróbata NMF acrobat.

acrobático ADJ acrobatic.

acrobatismo NM acrobatics.

acrónimo NM acronym.

Acrópolis NF Acropolis.

acróstico ADJ, NM acrostic.

acta NF (a) (*de reunión*) minutes, record; (*publicada, de sociedad*) transactions; (*Pol*) certificate of election; (*LAm Parl*) act, law; ~ **de acusación** bill of indictment; ~ **constitutiva** charter; ~ **de defunción** death certificate; ~ **matrimonial**, ~ **de matrimonio** (*Méx*) marriage certificate; ~ **de nacimiento** (*Méx*) birth certificate; ~ **notarial** affidavit; ~ **orgánica** (*LAm Jur*) constitution; **A~ Unica Europea** Single European Act; **levantar** ~ to take the minutes; to draw up a formal statement; **levantar** ~ **de** to take the minutes of, minute; **tomar** ~ (*Cono Sur*) to take note; **tomar** ~ **de algo** (*Cono Sur*) to bear sth in mind.
(b) **~s** (*de reunión*) minutes, record; (*publicadas, de sociedad*) transactions; **~s de un santo** life of a saint; **~s de los mártires** lives of the martyrs.

actinia NF actinia, sea-anemone.

actínico ADJ actinic.

actinio NM actinium.

▼ **actitud** NF (a) (*de cuerpo*) posture, position, attitude, pose.
▼(b) (*fig*) attitude; position; outlook; policy; **la ~ del gobierno** the government's attitude, the government's position; **adoptar una ~ firme** to take a firm stand, put one's foot down; **en ~ de** + *infin* (as if) ready to + *infin*, threatening to + *infin*.

activación NF activation; expediting, speeding-up; stimulation.

activador NM (*Téc*) activator; (*fig*) stimulus.

activamente ADV actively.

activar [1a] VT to activate; *trabajo* to expedite, speed up, hurry along; *fuego* to brighten up, poke; *mercado* to stimulate.

actividad NF (a) (*gen*) activity; liveliness; promptness; movement, bustle; **estar en** ~ to be active, be in operation, (*volcán*) be active, be in eruption; **estar en plena** ~ to be in full swing.
(b) (*profesional etc*) occupation; activity; ~ **complementaria** sideline;

~ lucrativa gainful employment; **~es** activities; **sus ~es políticas** his political activities.

activisimo NM (*LAm Pol*) political activity.

activista NMF activist; (*esp LAm*) political activist.

activo ① ADJ (*gen*) active; (*vivo*) lively; (*pronto*) prompt; (*enérgico*) energetic; (*ocupado*) busy; (*Ling*) active.

② NM (a) (*Com*) assets; **~ bloqueado**, **~ congelado** frozen assets; **~ circulante** circulating assets; **~ corriente** current assets; **~ fijo**, **~ inmovilizado** fixed assets; **~ flotante** floating assets; **~ inmaterial** intangible assets; **~s inmobiliarios** property assets, real-estate assets; **~ intangible** intangible assets; **~ invisible** invisible assets; **~ líquido**, **~ realizable** liquid assets; **~ neto** net worth; **~ oculto** hidden assets; **~ operante** operating assets; **~ y pasivo** assets and liabilities; **~ de la quiebra** bankrupt's estate; **~ tangible** tangible assets.

(b) **oficial en ~** (*Mil*) serving officer; **estar en ~** to be on active service; to be on the active list (*t fig*).

acto NM (*gen*) act; action, deed; (*ceremonia*) ceremony, function; (*Teat*) act; **A~s de los Apóstoles** Acts (of the Apostles); **~ de desagravio** act of atonement; **~ de fe** act of faith; **~ de habla** speech act; **~ inaugural** opening ceremony; **~ reflejo** reflex action; **~ religioso** church service; **~ continuo**, **~ seguido** next, forthwith, immediately after; **~ seguido de** immediately after; **~ sexual** sexual act, sex act; **morir en ~ de servicio** to die on active service; **ocurrió en ~ de servicio** it happened during working hours, it happened when he (*etc*) was at work; **en el ~** immediately; instantaneously; on the spot, there and then; **en el ~ de** in the act of; **'reparaciones en el ~'** 'repairs while you wait'; **celebrar un ~** to hold a function; **hacer ~ de presencia** to attend (formally), be present; to put in an appearance, make a token appearance.

actor NM (*Teat*) actor; (*fig*) protagonist; (*Jur*) plaintiff; **~ cinematográfico** film actor; **~ de doblaje** dubber; **~ de reparto** supporting actor.

actora ADJ: **parte ~** (*Jur*) prosecution; (*demandante*) plaintiff.

actriz NF actress; **primera ~** leading lady, *V t* **actor**.

actuación NF (a) (*acción*) action; (*conducta*) performance, conduct, behaviour; (*Teat*) performance; (*Dep*) performance; (*LAm*) role; **~ en vivo** live performance; **su ~ fue importante** his role (*o* part) was an important one.

(b) **actuaciones** (*Jur*) legal proceedings.

(c) **~ pericial** expert valuation.

actual ADJ (*presente*) present; present-day; (*corriente*) current; *cuestión* current, topical; (*al día*) modern, up-to-date; (*a la moda*) fashionable; **el 6 del ~** the 6th day of this month; **el rey ~** the present king.

actualidad NF (a) (*presente*) present, present time; **en la ~** at present, at the present time; nowadays, now.

(b) (*contemporaneidad*) present importance, current importance; **cuestión de palpitante ~** highly important current issue; highly topical question; **ser de gran ~** to be current, be alive; to have great importance now (*o* at the time); **perder (su) ~** to lose interest, get stale.

(c) **~es** current events; contemporary issues; (*Cine*) newsreel.

actualización NF modernization, bringing up to date; (*curso*) refresher course, course of retraining; (*Inform*) update, updating; (*Contabilidad*) discounting.

actualizador ADJ *influencia etc* modernizing.

actualizar [1f] VT to bring up to date, update, modernize; to add topicality to; (*Inform*) to update; (*Contabilidad*) to discount.

actualmente ADV at present; now, nowadays; at the moment; **~ está fuera** he's away at the moment; **los 50 ~ en servicio** the 50 at present in service.

actuar [1e] ① VT to work, actuate, operate; to set in motion.

② VI (*Mec*) to work, operate, function; (*persona*) to act, perform; **~ de** to act as; **~ sobre** to act on; **actuó bien el árbitro Sr X** Mr X refereed well; **actúa de manera rara** he's acting strangely; **~ en justicia** to institute legal proceedings.

actuarial ADJ actuarial.

actuario NM (*Jur*) clerk (of the court); (*Com, Fin*: *t* **~ de seguros**) actuary.

acuache* NM, **acuachi*** NM (*Méx*) mate, pal*.

acuadrillar [1a] ① VT to form into a band; (*Cono Sur*) to set upon (*o* about), gang up on.

② **acuadrillarse** VR to band together, gang up.

acuanauta NMF deep-sea diver.

acuaplano NM surfboarding.

acuarela NF watercolour.

acuarelista NMF watercolourist.

Acuario NM (*Zodíaco*) Aquarius.

acuario NM, **acuárium** NM aquarium.

acuartelado ADJ (*Her*) quartered.

acuartelamiento NM (a) (*Mil*) quartering, billeting. (b) (*Her*) quartering.

acuartelar [1a] ① VT (*Mil*) to quarter, billet; to confine to barracks.

② **acuartelarse** VR to withdraw to barracks.

acuático ADJ aquatic, water (*atr*).

acuátil ADJ aquatic, water (*atr*)

acuatinta NF aquatint.

acuatizaje NM (*Aer*) touchdown (*o* landing) (on the sea).

acuatizar [1f] VI (*Aer*) to come down on the water, land on the sea.

acuchamado ADJ (*Carib*: *triste*) sad, depressed.

acuchamarse [1a] VR (*Carib*) to get depressed.

acuchillado ADJ (a) *vestido* slashed. (b) (*escarmentado*) wary, schooled by bitter experience.

acuchillar [1a] ① VT (a) (*cortar*) to cut, slash, hack; (*Cos*) to slash; *persona* to stab (to death), knife.

(b) (*Téc*) to plane down, smooth.

② **acuchillarse** VR: **se acuchillaron** they fought with knives, they slashed at each other.

acuchucar [1g] VT (*Cono Sur*) to crush, flatten; to crumple.

acucia NF (*diligencia*) diligence, keenness; (*prisa*) haste; (*anhelo*) keen desire, longing.

acuciadamente ADV (*V N*) diligently, keenly; hastily; longingly.

acuciador ADJ, **acuciante** ADJ pressing, urgent.

acuciar [1b] VT (a) (*instar*) to urge on, goad, prod; (*dar prisa a*) to hasten; (*acosar*) to harass; to mob; (*problema etc*) to press, worry. (b) (*anhelar*) to desire keenly, long for.

acucioso ADJ diligent, zealous, keen; eager.

acuclillarse [1a] VR to squat down.

ACUDE [a'kuðe] NF ABR *de* **Asociación de Consumidores y Usuarios de España.**

acudir [3a] VI (a) (*venir*) to come, come along, come up; (*asistir*) to turn up, present o.s.; **~ a la puerta** to come (*o* go) to the door, answer the door; **~ a una cita** to keep an appointment, turn up for an appointment; **~ a una llamada** to answer a call; **~ a la mente** to come to (one's) mind; **pero no acudió** but he didn't come, but he didn't turn up.

(b) (*en auxilio*) to come (*o* go) to the rescue, go to help.

(c) (*fig*) **~ a** to call on, turn to, have recourse to; **~ al médico** to consult one's doctor; **~ a uno a pedir socorro** to turn to sb for help; **tendremos que ~ a otra solución** we shall have to seek another solution; **no tener a quien ~** to have no-one to turn to.

(d) (*Agr*) to produce, yield.

(e) (*caballo*) to answer, obey.

acueducto NM aqueduct.

ácueo ADJ aqueous.

▼ **acuerdo** NM (a) (*gen*) agreement, accord; decision; (*tratado etc*) agreement, pact; understanding; **~ económico social** (*Pol*) wages agreement; **~ extrajudicial** (*esp Méx*) out-of-court settlement; **~ marco** general framework of agreement; set of agreed guidelines; **~ de pago respectivo** knock-for-knock agreement, no-fault agreement (*US*); **~ salarial** wage agreement, pay settlement; **~ verbal** verbal agreement; gentleman's agreement; **¡de ~!** I agree!, agreed!; yes of course!; **de ~ con** in accordance with; **de ~ con el artículo 2 del código** under article 2 of the code, as laid down in article 2 of the code; **de común ~** with one accord, unanimously; **estar de ~** (*persona*) to agree, be in agreement (*con* with); (*cosas*) to agree, correspond; **esto está de ~ con lo que me dijo** this is in line with what he told me; **estar en perfecto ~** to be in perfect harmony; **llegar a un ~** to reach agreement, come to an understanding (*con* with); **ponerse** (*o* **quedar**) **de ~** to reach agreement, agree.

(b) (*Parl etc*) resolution; **tomar un ~** to pass a resolution.

(c) (*Arte*) harmony, blend.

(d) (*Cono Sur*: *consejo*) consultative meeting.

(e) (*recuerdo*) memory, recollection.

(f) (*juicio*) sense, right mind; **estar en su ~** to be in one's right mind; **volver en su ~** to come to one's senses.

acuícola ADJ water (*atr*); underwater; marine.

acuicultor(a) NM/F fish-farmer.

acuicultura NF development of water resources, aquaculture; fish-farming.

acuidad NF acuity.

acuífero ① ADJ aquiferous, water-bearing.

② NM aquifer.

acuilmarse [1a] VR (*CAm*) to get depressed; to cower, shrink away.

acuitadamente ADV sorrowfully, with regret.

acuitar [1a] ① VT to afflict, distress, grieve.

② **acuitarse** VR to grieve, be grieved (*por* at, by).

acular* [1a] ① VT (a) *caballo etc* to back (*a* against, into). (b) (*acorralar*) to corner, force into a corner.

② VI (*And*) to back away.

acullá ADV over there, yonder.

acullicar [1g] VI (*And, Cono Sur*) to chew coca (leaves).

aculturación NF acculturation.

aculturar [1a] VT to acculturate.

acumuchar [1a] VT (*Cono Sur*) to pile up, accumulate.

acumulación NF (*acto*) accumulation; (*cantidad*) accumulation; pile, stock, hoard.

acumulador [1] ADJ accumulative.
  [2] NM (*batería*) accumulator, storage battery; (*de calor*) storage heater.

acumular [1a] [1] VT to accumulate; to amass, gather, collect; to pile (up), hoard; **~ vapor** to get steam up.
  [2] **acumularse** VR (**a**) (*en general*) to accumulate, gather, pile up. (**b**) (*Cono Sur: personas*) to gather (o collect) together.

acumulativo ADJ accumulative.

acúmulo NM accumulation, build-up.

acunar [1a] VT to rock (to sleep).

acuñación NF coining, minting; wedging.

acuñar [1a] [1] VT (**a**) *moneda* to coin, mint; *medalla* to strike; *frase* to coin; *rueda etc* to wedge. (**b**) (*Carib: llevar a cabo*) to finish successfully.
  [2] **acuñarse** VR (*CAm*) to hit o.s., sustain a blow.

acuosidad NF wateriness; juiciness.

acuoso ADJ watery; *fruto* juicy, runny.

acupuntor(a) NM/F acupuncturist.

acupuntura NF acupuncture.

acupunturista NMF acupuncturist.

acurrado ADJ (**a**) (*Carib, Méx: guapo*) handsome. (**b**) (*CAm: rechoncho*) squat, chubby.

acurrucarse [1g] VR to squat, crouch; to huddle up, curl up.

acusación NF accusation; (*Jur*) accusation, charge, indictment; **negar la ~** to deny the charge, plead not guilty.

acusado [1] ADJ (**a**) (*Jur etc*) accused.
  (**b**) (*fuerte*) marked, pronounced; *característica, rasgo, personalidad* strong; *contraste* marked, striking; *color* deep.
  [2] NM, **acusada** NF accused, defendant.

acusador [1] ADJ accusing, reproachful; **los letrados ~es** prosecuting counsel; **la parte ~a** plaintiff; prosecution.
  [2] NM, **acusadora** NF accuser.

acusar [1a] [1] VT (**a**) (*gen*) to accuse (*de of*); (*Jur*) charge (*de with*), indict (*de on a charge of*); **¿me acusas a mí?** are you accusing me?; **~ a uno de haber hecho algo** to accuse sb of having done sth.
  (**b**) (*denunciar*) to denounce; *sospechoso* to point to, proclaim the guilt of.
  (**c**) (*revelar*) to show, reveal; *emoción etc* to register, show, betray; **su rostro acusó extrañeza** his face showed (o registered) surprise; **su silencio acusa cierta cobardía** his silence betrays a certain cowardice; **acusamos cierto retraso** we're a bit late.
  (**d**) *cartas* to declare, lay down.
  (**e**) **~ recibo** to acknowledge receipt (*de* of).
  [2] **acusarse** VR (**a**) (*confesar*) to confess; **~ de negligente** to confess one's negligence, confess to being negligent; **~ de un crimen** to confess to a crime; **~ de haberlo hecho** to confess to having done it.
  (**b**) (*hacerse más fuerte*) to become more marked, get stronger; **esta tendencia se acusa cada vez más** this tendency is becoming ever more marked, this tendency gets stronger all the time.

┌─ **ACUSAR** ─────────── **ver también la entrada** ─┐

• Traducimos *acusar* (*de*) por *accuse* (*of*) en la mayoría de los casos:
  Me acusó de haber mentido
  He accused me of lying
  ¿De qué me estás acusando?
  What are you accusing me of?

• Traducimos *acusar* (*de*) por *charge* (*with*) cuando se trata de una acusación formal que llevará a la celebración de un juicio:
  No lo han acusado de ningún delito
  He hasn't been charged with any offence
  Hasta ahora, la policía lo ha acusado solamente de uno de los asesinatos
  So far, the police have only charged him with one of the murders
  NOTA: El verbo *indict* tiene un significado parecido a *charge*, pero sólo se usa en contextos legales muy especializados.
  Para otros usos y ejemplos ver la entrada.
└───┘

acusativo NM accusative.

acusatorio ADJ accusatory, accusing.

acuse NM: **~ de recibo** acknowledgement of receipt.

acusetas* NMF INVAR, **acusete*** NMF (*And, Cono Sur*) telltale, sneak.

acusica* NMF, **acusique*** NM tell-tale, sneak.

acusón* [1] ADJ telltale, sneaking.
  [2] NM, **acusona** NF telltale, sneak; gossip.

acústica NF acoustics.

acústico [1] ADJ acoustic.
  [2] NM hearing-aid.

acutí NM (*Zool*) = **agutí**.

AD NF (*Venezuela*) ABR de **Acción Democrática**.

ADA ['aða] NF ABR *de* **Ayuda del Automovilista** ≃ AA, RAC.

-ada V Aspects of Word Formation in Spanish 2.

ADAC NM ABR *de* **avión de despegue y aterrizaje cortos** vertical take-off and landing (aircraft), VTOL.

adagio NM adage, proverb; (*Mús*) adagio.

adalid NM leader, champion.

adamado ADJ *hombre* effeminate, soft; *mujer* elegant, chic; (*pey*) flashy.

adamascado ADJ damask.

adamascar [1g] VT to damask.

Adán NM Adam.

adán NM (*sucio*) slovenly fellow; (*vago*) lazy chap*; **estar hecho un ~** to go about in rags, be terribly shabby, look a mess.

adaptabilidad NF adaptability; versatility.

adaptable ADJ adaptable; versatile.

adaptación NF adaptation.

adaptador NM (*Elec, Rad*) adapter.

adaptar [1a] [1] VT (*gen*) to adapt; (*adecuar*) to fit, make suitable (*para* for); (*ajustar*) to adjust.
  [2] **adaptarse** VR to adapt o.s. (*a* to); **saber ~ a las circunstancias** to be able to adapt o.s. to the circumstances, know how to adjust to circumstances.

adaptativo ADJ adaptive.

adaraja NF (*Arquit*) toothing.

adarga NF (oval) shield.

adarme NM whit, jot; **ni un ~** not a whit; **no me importa un ~** I couldn't care less; **sin un ~ de educación** without the least bit of good manners; **por ~s** in driblets.

A. de C. ABR *de* **año de Cristo** Anno Domini, AD.

adecentar [1a] [1] VT to tidy up, clean up, make decent.
  [2] **adecentarse** VR to tidy o.s. up.

adecuación NF adaptation; adequacy, fitness, suitability.

adecuadamente ADV adequately, fitly, suitably.

adecuado ADJ adequate; fit, suitable (*para* for); sufficient; appropriate; satisfactory; **los documentos ~s** the appropriate documents, the relevant papers; **el hombre ~ para el puesto** the right man for the job; **lo más ~ sería ...** the most appropriate thing would be to ..., it would be best to ...

adecuamiento NM adjustment.

adecuar [1d] VT to adapt, fit, make suitable; to prepare, make ready.

adefesiero* ADJ (*And, Cono Sur: ridículo*) comic, ridiculous; (*torpe*) clumsy; (*en el vestido*) overdressed, camp*.

adefesio NM (**a**) (*disparate*) piece of nonsense, absurdity; rubbish; **hablar ~s** to talk nonsense.
  (**b**) (*persona*) queer bird, ridiculous person; (*de aspecto*) scarecrow, fright; **ella estaba hecha un ~** she did look a fright.
  (**c**) (*vestido*) outlandish dress, ridiculous attire.
  (**d**) (*maula*) unwanted object, white elephant.

adefesioso ADJ (*And*) nonsensical, ridiculous.

adehala NF (*propina*) gratuity, tip; (*de pago*) bonus.

a. de J.C. ABR *de* **antes de Jesucristo** before Christ, BC.

adela NF (*CAm*) bittersweet.

adelaida NF (*Méx*) fuchsia.

adelantado [1] ADJ (**a**) (*avanzado*) advanced.
  (**b**) (*precoz*) well advanced, ahead of one's age, precocious; **estar ~** *reloj* to be fast.
  (**c**) *pago* in advance; **pagar por ~** to pay in advance.
  (**d**) (*pey*) bold, forward.
  [2] NM (*Hist*) governor (of a frontier province), captain-general.

adelantamiento NM advance; advancement, furtherance, promotion; progress; (*Aut*) overtaking, passing.

adelantar [1a] [1] VT (**a**) (*avanzar*) to move forward, move on, advance; (*Dep*) *balón* to pass on, pass forward.
  (**b**) *paso* to speed up, quicken; *proyecto, trabajo* to speed up, hurry along; **~ los acontecimientos** to anticipate events; **no adelantemos los acontecimientos** let's not cross our bridges before we come to them.
  (**c**) *suma, dinero* to advance, pay in advance; to lend.
  (**d**) *reloj* to put on, put forward.
  (**e**) *competidor* to get ahead of, outstrip; (*Aut*) to overtake, pass; **no le gusta dejarse ~** he doesn't like being overtaken; **estamos a punto de que se nos adelante** we are about to be overtaken.
  (**f**) (*fig*) to advance, further, promote; **~ una idea** to put forward an idea.
  (**g**) **~ que ...** to suggest that ..., propose that ...; to advise that ...
  [2] VI (**a**) (*avanzar*) to go ahead, get on, make headway; to improve, progress; **el enfermo adelanta** the patient is improving.
  (**b**) (*Aut*) to overtake, pass; **'prohibido ~'** 'no overtaking'.
  (**c**) (*reloj*) to be fast, gain; **mi reloj adelanta 5 minutos** my watch is 5 minutes fast.
  [3] **adelantarse** VR (**a**) (*tomar la delantera*) to go forward, go ahead; to improve, progress.

(b) ~ **a uno** to get ahead of sb, outstrip sb; *(fig)* to steal a march on sb, beat sb to it; *(Aut)* to overtake sb, pass sb, *(pey)* cut in on sb.
(c) ~ **a algo** to anticipate sth; ~ **a los deseos de uno** to anticipate sb's wishes.

adelante ① ADV **(a)** *(lugar)* forward, onward; ahead; **más ~** further on; **por el camino ~** further along the road; **ir ~** to go on, go forward; *V* **sacar (r)** etc.
(b) *(cantidad)* **de 100 ptas en ~** from 100 pesetas up.
(c) *(tiempo)* **en ~, de aquí en ~, de hoy en ~** in future, from now on, henceforth; **más ~** later, afterwards.
(d) **¡~!** *(INTERJ)* *al que habla* go on!, go ahead!, carry on!; *(contestando a llamada)* come in!; *(Mil etc)* forward!; *(Cono Sur)* bravo!, that's the way!
② PREP *(Cono Sur)*: ~ **nuestro** *(etc)* in front of us *(etc)*, before us *(etc)*.

adelanto NM **(a)** *(gen)* advancement, progress.
(b) *(progreso)* advance, improvement; **con todos los ~s modernos** with all the modern improvements; **los ~s de la ciencia** the advances of science; **llegar con un ~ de 15 minutos** *(LAm)* to arrive 15 minutes early.
(c) *(Com etc)* advance; loan.

adelfa NF rosebay, oleander.
adelgazador ADJ slimming.
adelgazamiento NM slimming.
adelgazante ADJ slimming.
adelgazar [1f] ① VT to make thin, make slender; *palo* to pare, whittle; *persona, figura* to slim, reduce, slenderize *(US)*; *(fig)* to purify, refine; *voz* to raise the pitch of; *entendimiento* to sharpen.
② VI to grow thin, lose weight; *(con intención)* to slim, reduce, lose weight; *(fig)* to split hairs.
③ **adelgazarse** VR to grow thin.

Adelpha NF ABR *de* **Asociación de Defensa Ecológica y del Patrimonio Histórico-artístico.**

ademán NM **(a)** *(con mano)* gesture, movement, motion; *(de cuerpo; t Arte)* posture, attitude, position; **en ~ de + infin** as if to + infin, getting ready to + infin; **hacer ~ de + infin** to make as if to + infin, make a move to + infin; **hacer ademanes** to gesture, make signs.
(b) **ademanes** *(modales)* manners.

▼ **además** ① ADV besides; moreover, furthermore; also; **y ~ la pegó** and he also beat her; **creo ~ que ...** moreover I think that ...
② ~ **de** PREP besides, in addition to; not to mention; ~ **de eso** moreover; on top of that.

Adén NM Aden.

ADENA [a'ðena] NF *(Esp)* ABR *de* **Asociación para la Defensa de la Naturaleza.**

adenoideo ADJ adenoidal.

adentellar [1a] VT to sink one's teeth into.

adentrarse [1a] VR: ~ **en** to go into, get into, get inside; to penetrate into; ~ **en la selva** to go deep(er) into the forest; ~ **en sí mismo** to become lost in thought.

adentro ① ADV = **dentro; mar ~** out at sea, out to sea; **tierra ~** inland; **¡~!** come in!
② PREP *(Cono Sur)*: ~ **mío** inside myself; ~ **de** = **dentro de.**
③ NM **(a)** *(Cono Sur)* indoors, inside of the house.
(b) ~**s** innermost being, innermost thoughts; **dijo para sus ~s** he said to himself; **reírse para sus ~s** to laugh inwardly.

adepto, -a NM/F follower, supporter; *(de mágica etc)* adept, initiate; *(LAm*)* drug-addict.

aderezado ADJ favourable, suitable.

aderezar [1f] ① VT to prepare, get ready, dress; *persona* to make beautiful, dress up, deck; *objeto* to embellish, adorn; *comida* to prepare; *(con especias)* to season, garnish; *ensalada* to dress; *bebidas* to prepare, mix; *vinos* to blend; *máquina etc* to repair; *tela* to gum, size.
② **aderezarse** VR to dress up, get ready.

aderezo NM **(a)** *(acto)* preparation; dressing; embellishment; seasoning; mixing; blending; repair.
(b) *(Culin)* seasoning, dressing; *(en vestido)* adornment; *(joyas)* set of jewels; ~ **de casa** household equipment; ~ **de diamantes** set of diamonds; ~ **de mesa** dinner service; **dar el ~ definitivo a algo** to put the finishing touch to sth.

adeudado ADJ in debt.

adeudar [1a] ① VT *dinero* to owe; *impuestos etc* to be liable for; ~ **una suma en una cuenta** to charge a sum to an account, debit an account for a sum.
② VI to become related by marriage.
③ **adeudarse** VR to run into debt.

adeudo NM *(deuda)* debit, indebtedness; *(de aduana)* customs duty; *(en cuenta)* debit, charge.

adeveras *(LAm)*: **de ~** ADV = **de veras.**

ADEVIDA [aðe'βiða] NF *(Esp)* ABR *de* **Asociación en Defensa de la Vida Humana.**

a.D.g. ABR *de* **a Dios gracias** thanks be to God, Deo gratias, D.G.

adherencia NF adherence, adhesion; *(fig)* bond, connection; *(Aut)*

road holding, road-holding qualities; **tener ~s** to have connections.

adherente ① ADJ: ~ **a** adhering to; joining.
② NM/F adherent, follower.

adherido, -a NM/F adherent, follower.

adherir [3i] ① VI to adhere, stick *(a* to); ~ **a** *(fig)* to adhere to, espouse, follow; *partido etc* to join, become a member of.
② **adherirse** VR = **1.**

adhesión NF adhesion; *(fig)* adherence, support; membership; *(mensaje)* message of support.

adhesividad NF adhesiveness.

adhesivo ① ADJ adhesive, sticky; *melodía* catchy.
② NM adhesive.

adicción NF addiction.

adición NF **(a)** *(gen)* addition; *(Mat)* addition; adding up. **(b)** *(Cono Sur: cuenta)* bill, check *(US)*.

adicional ADJ additional, extra, supplementary; *(Inform)* add-on.

adicionalidad NF additionality.

adicionar [1a] VT to add *(a* to); *(Mat)* to add, add up.

adictivo ADJ addictive.

adicto ① ADJ **(a)** *(leal)* ~ **a** devoted to, attached to; **las personas adictas a él** those who follow him, his supporters.
(b) ~ **a** *(pey)* given to, addicted to.
② NM, **adicta** NF supporter, follower; *(LAm Dep)* supporter, fan; *(de drogas)* addict.

adiestrado ADJ trained.

adiestramiento NM training; drilling; practice; ~ **con armas** weapons training.

adiestrar [1a] ① VT *animal etc* to train, teach, coach; *(Mil)* to drill; *(guiar)* to guide, lead.
② **adiestrarse** VR to practise, train o.s.; ~ **a + infin** to train o.s. to + infin; to teach o.s. to + infin.

adifés ADV **(a)** *(CAm: con dificultad)* with difficulty. **(b)** *(Carib: a propósito)* on purpose, deliberately.

adinerado ADJ wealthy, moneyed, well-off.

ad infinitum ADV ad infinitum.

adiós ① INTERJ good-bye!; *(al pasar en la calle etc)* hullo!; **¡~ Madrid, que te quedas sin gente!** good riddance!
② NM good-bye, farewell; **ir a decir ~ a uno** to go to say good-bye to sb; **decir ~ a algo** *(fig)* to renounce sth, give sth up.

adiosito* INTERJ *(esp LAm)* bye-bye!, cheerio!

adiposidad NF, **adiposis** NF adiposity.

adiposo ADJ adipose, fat.

aditamento NM *(complemento)* complement, addition; *(accesorio)* accessory.

aditivo NM additive; ~ **alimenticio** food additive.

adivinación NF prophecy, divination; guessing; solving; **por ~** by guesswork; ~ **de pensamientos** thought-reading, mind-reading.

adivinador(a) NM/F diviner.

adivinanza NF riddle, conundrum.

adivinar [1a] VT to prophesy, foretell, guess; *acertijo, puzzle* to solve; *solución* to guess correctly; *pensamientos* to read; **adivina quién lo hizo** it's anyone's guess who did it; *(nadie sabrá)* no-one will be any the wiser; *(es así de fácil)* it's as easy as that; *(juego de niños)* equivale a Guess Who; ~ **a uno** to guess what sb means, see through sb.

adivino ① NM, **adivina** NF fortune-teller.
② NM *(Zool)* praying mantis.

adj ABR *de* **adjunto** enclosure(s), enclosed, enc.

adjetivar [1a] VT **(a)** *(Gram)* to modify; to use adjectivally, use attributively. **(b)** *(fig)* to apply epithets to.

adjetivo ① ADJ adjectival.
② NM adjective.

adjudicación NF award; *(en subasta)* knocking down, sale; *(Méx Jur)* adjudication, award.

adjudicado ADJ: **¡~!** *(en subasta)* sold!

adjudicar [1g] ① VT to award *(a* to); ~ **algo a uno en 500 pesetas** to knock sth down to sb for 500 pesetas; ~ **algo al mejor postor** to knock sth down to the highest bidder.
② **adjudicarse** VR: ~ **algo** to appropriate sth; ~ **el premio** to win (the prize).

adjudicatorio, -a NM/F person who wins an award; *(en subasta)* successful bidder.

▼ **adjuntar** [1a] VT to append, attach; *(en carta)* to enclose; **adjuntamos factura** we enclose our account.

▼ **adjunto** ① ADJ **(a)** *(unido)* joined on; attached *(a* to); *(en carta)* attached, enclosed; **remitir algo ~** to enclose sth.
(b) *persona* assistant; *V* **profesor.**
② NM **(a)** *(añadidura)* addition, adjunct; *(en carta)* enclosure.
(b) *(persona)* assistant.

adlátere NM companion; associate; *(pey)* minion, minder.

adminículo NM accessory, gadget; ~**s** emergency kit.

administración NF **(a)** *(gen)* administration; *(gerencia)* management; running; **en ~** in trust; **obras en ~** books handled by us, books for

which we are agents; **A~ de Correos** General Post Office; **~ de empresas** (*Univ: curso*) business administration; **~ financiera** financial management; **~ de lotería** *place where lottery tickets are sold*; **~ militar** commissariat; **la A~ Pública** (*Cono Sur*) the Civil Service.
(b) (*Pol*) government, administration; **~ central** central government; **~ territorial** local government.
(c) (*oficina*) headquarters, central office; (*And: de hotel*) reception.
(d) (*Carib Ecl*) extreme unction.

administrador(a) NM/F administrator; manager; (*de propiedad*) steward, (land) agent; bailiff; **~ de aduanas** chief customs officer, collector of customs; **~ de correos** postmaster; **~ de fincas** land agent; **~ judicial** (*Méx Jur*) receiver; **es buena administradora** (*en casa*) she runs the house well, she's a good housekeeper.

administrar [1a] ⒈ VT to administer; to manage; to run; *justicia, sacramento* to administer.
⒉ **administrarse** VR to manage one's own affairs, organize one's life; to get one's priorities right.

administrativo ⒈ ADJ administrative; managerial; of the administration, of the government.
⒉ NM, **administrativa** NF clerk; administrator, administrative officer.

admirable ADJ admirable.

▼ **admiración** NF **(a)** (*gen*) admiration; **mi ~ por ti** my admiration for you. **(b)** (*asombro*) wonder, wonderment; amazement; **esto llenó a todos de ~** this filled everyone with wonderment. **(c)** (*Tip*) exclamation mark (¡!).

admirador(a) NM/F admirer.

admirar [1a] ⒈ VT **(a)** (*gen*) to admire; (*respetar*) to respect, look up to. **(b)** (*asombrar*) to astonish, surprise, cause to marvel; **ser de ~** to cause admiration, surprise; **no es de ~ que ...** it's not surprising that ...; **esto admiró a todos** this astonished everyone, this filled everyone with amazement; **me admira su declaración** your statement amazes me, I am amazed at what you say.
⒉ **admirarse** VR to be astonished, be surprised, marvel (*de* at); **se admiró de saberlo** he was amazed to hear it.

admirativo ADJ admiring, full of admiration.

admisibilidad NF admissibility.

admisible ADJ admissible; acceptable; *excusa etc* plausible, credible, legitimate; **eso no es ~** that cannot be allowed.

admisión NF admission (*a* to); acceptance; (*Mec*) intake, inlet; **~ de aire** (*Mec*) air intake; **acto de ~** (*Jur*) validation (of a suit).

admitido ADJ accepted, allowed, agreed.

▼ **admitir** [3a] VT (*gen*) to admit (*a* to, *en* into); (*aceptar*) to accept, allow; (*reconocer*) to recognize; *dudas* to leave room for; *mejora etc* to allow, be susceptible of; **esto no admite demora** this allows no delay; **no admite otra explicación** it allows no other explanation; **¿admite la Academia la palabra?** does the Academy accept the word?; **hay que ~ que ...** it must be admitted that ..., it must be confessed that ...; **'no se admiten propinas'** 'no tipping', 'tipping not allowed'; **la sala admite 500 personas** the hall holds 500 people.

admón. ABR *de* **administración** administration, admin.

admonición NF warning.

admonitivo ADJ, **admonitorio** ADJ *señal, voz etc* warning.

ADN ⒈ NM ABR *de* **ácido desoxirribonucleico** deoxyribonucleic acid, DNA.
⒉ NF (*Bolivia*) ABR *de* **Acción Democrática Nacionalista**.

adnominal ADJ, NM adnominal.

-ado *V* Aspects of Word Formation in Spanish 2.

adobado NM pickled meat, pickled pork.

adobar [1a] VT (*gen*) to prepare, dress; (*cocinar*) to cook; (*sazonar*) to season; *carne* to pickle; *pieles* to tan, dress; *lámpara* to trim; *narración* to twist.

adobe NM **(a)** (*ladrillo*) adobe, sun-dried brick. **(b)** (*Cono Sur hum: pie*) big foot. **(c) descansar haciendo ~s** (*Méx*) to moonlight, do work on the side.

adobera NF **(a)** (*para ladrillos*) mould for making adobes; (*Cono Sur, Méx**) (*queso*) brick-shaped cheese, (*molde*) cheese mould. **(b)** (*Cono Sur hum: pie*) big foot.

adobo NM **(a)** (*acto*) preparation, dressing; cooking; pickling; tanning. **(b)** (*salsa*) pickle, sauce; (*Méx*) red chili sauce; (*para curtir*) tanning mixture.

adocenado ADJ common, ordinary, commonplace.

adocenarse [1a] VR **(a)** (*hacerse común*) to become commonplace. **(b)** (*decaer*) to become mediocre; (*estancarse*) to remain stagnant, become fossilized.

adoctrinación NF indoctrination.

adoctrinador ADJ indoctrinating, indoctrinatory.

adoctrinamiento NM indoctrination.

adoctrinar [1a] VT to teach, instruct (*en* in); to indoctrinate (*en* with).

adolecer [2d] VI to be ill, fall ill; **~ de** (*Med*) to be ill with, fall ill with; (*fig*) to suffer from, display.

adolescencia NF adolescence.

adolescente ⒈ ADJ adolescent.
⒉ NMF adolescent; youngster, teenager.

Adolfo NM Adolphus, Adolph, Adolf.

adolorido ADJ (*LAm*) = **dolorido**.

adonde CONJ where.

adónde ⒈ ADV *interrog* where?
⒉ CONJ where.

adondequiera ADV: **~ que** wherever.

Adonis NM Adonis.

adopción NF adoption; **madrileño de** (*o* **por**) **~** a citizen of Madrid by adoption.

adoptado, -a NM/F (*Méx*) adopted child.

adoptar [1a] VT to adopt.

adoptivo ADJ adoptive; *niño* adopted; **patria adoptiva** country of adoption.

adoquín NM **(a)** (*lit*) paving stone, flagstone, wooden paving block; **me comería hasta adoquines** I could eat a horse. **(b)** (*: *tonto*) fool, dope*.

adoquinado NM paving.

adoquinar [1a] VT to pave.

adorable ADJ adorable.

adoración NF adoration; worship; **A~ de los Reyes** Epiphany; **una mirada llena de ~** an adoring look.

adorador ADJ adoring.

adorar [1a] VT to adore; to worship.

adormecedor ADJ that sends one to sleep, soporific; *droga* sedative; *música, tono* lulling, dreamy.

adormecer [2d] ⒈ VT to make sleepy, send to sleep; (*fig*) to calm, lull.
⒉ **adormecerse** VR **(a)** (*amodorrarse*) to become sleepy, get drowsy; to fall asleep, go to sleep; (*miembro*) to go numb, go to sleep. **(b)** **~ en** (*fig*) to persist in, go on with.

adormecido ADJ (*persona*) sleepy, drowsy; *miembro* numb; (*fig*) inactive.

adormecimiento NM sleepiness, drowsiness; numbness.

adormidera NF (*Bot*) opium plant, poppy; (*Med*) sleeping pill, sleeping draught.

adormilarse [1a] VR, **adormitarse** [1a] VR to doze, drowse.

adornar [1a] VT to adorn (*de* with); to decorate, embellish, bedeck; (*Cos*) to trim (*de* with); *comida* to garnish, decorate (*de* with); *persona* to endow, bless (*de* with); **le adornan mil virtudes** he is blessed with every virtue.

adornista NMF decorator.

adorno NM adornment; decoration, embellishment; (*Cos*) trimming; (*Culin*) garnishment, decoration; **~s** (*pey*) frills, adornments; **lo mismo sin los ~s** the same without the frills; **es el principal ~ de su ciudad** he is the chief adornment of his city, he is the city's chief claim to fame.

adosado ⒈ ADJ: **casa adosada** *o* **chalet ~** semi-detached house.
⒉ NM semi-detached house.

adosar [1a] VT **(a)** **~ algo a una pared** to lean sth against a wall; to place sth with its back against a wall.
(b) (*LAm*) (*juntar*) to join firmly; (*en carta*) to attach, include, enclose (with a letter).

adquirido ADJ: **mal ~** ill-gotten.

adquiriente NMF purchaser.

adquirir [3i] VT (*gen*) to acquire; to obtain; to procure; to buy, purchase; *hábito* to get into, form.

adquisición NF acquisition; procurement; (*compra*) purchase.

adquisidor(a) NM/F buyer.

adquisitivo ADJ acquisitive; **poder ~** purchasing power.

adquisividad NF acquisitiveness.

adral NM rail, sideboard (of a cart *etc*).

adrede, adredemente ADV on purpose, purposely, deliberately.

adrenalina NF adrenalin(e).

Adriano NM Hadrian.

Adriático NM: **el (Mar) ~** the Adriatic (Sea).

adscribir [3a; PTP **adscrito**] VT: **~ a** to appoint to, assign to; **estuvo adscrito al servicio de ...** he was attached to ..., he was in the service of ...

aduana NF **(a)** (*institución*) customs; (*oficina*) customs house; (*impuesto*) customs duty; **libre de ~** duty-free; **pasar por la ~** to go through the customs. **(b)** (‡) (*escondite*) pad‡, hide-out; (*refugio*) safe house; (*Méx: burdel*) brothel.

aduanal ADJ customs (*atr*).

aduanero ⒈ ADJ customs (*atr*).
⒉ NM, **aduanera** NF customs officer.

aducir [3n] VT to adduce, bring forward; to offer as proof; to quote, cite; *prueba* to provide, furnish.

adueñarse [1a] VR: **~ de** to take possession of; to appropriate; (*fig*) to master.

adujar [1a] VT (*Náut*) to coil.
adulación NF flattery, adulation.
adulada* NF (*Méx*) flattery.
adulador [1] ADJ flattering, fawning.
[2] NM, **aduladora** NF flatterer.
adular [1a] VT to flatter.
adulate ADJ, NM (*LAm*) = **adulón**.
adulón* [1] ADJ fawning, cringing, soapy*.
[2] NM, **adulona** NF toady, creep*.
adulonería NF (*LAm*) (a) (*adulación*) flattering, fawning. (b) (*carácter*) fawning nature, soapiness.
adúltera NF adulteress.
adulteración NF adulteration.
adulterado ADJ adulterated.
adulterar [1a] [1] VT to adulterate.
[2] VI to commit adultery.
adulterino ADJ adulterous; *moneda etc* spurious, counterfeit.
adulterio NM adultery.
adúltero [1] ADJ adulterous.
[2] NM adulterer.
adultez NF adulthood.
adulto ADJ, NM, **adulta** NF adult, grown-up.
adunar [1a] VT (*lit*) to join, unite.
adunco ADJ bent, curved.
adustez NF austerity, severity; grimness, sternness; sullenness.
adusto ADJ (a) (*caliente*) scorching hot. (b) (*severo*) austere, severe; (*inexorable*) grim, stern; (*hosco*) sullen.
advenedizo [1] ADJ foreign, from outside; newly arrived; (*pey*) upstart.
[2] NM, **advenediza** NF foreigner, outsider; newcomer; (*pey*) upstart.
advenimiento NM advent, arrival; ~ **al trono** accession to the throne.
adventicio ADJ adventitious.
adverbial ADJ adverbial.
adverbialización NF adverbialization.
adverbialmente ADV adverbially.
adverbio NM adverb.
adversario, -a NM/F adversary, opponent, antagonist.
adversativo ADJ (*Ling*) adversative.
adversidad NF (*gen*) adversity; (*revés*) setback, mishap.
adverso ADJ *lado* opposite, facing; *resultado etc* adverse, untoward; *suerte* bad.
▼ **advertencia** NF (*aviso*) warning; (*consejo*) piece of advice; (*recordatorio*) reminder; (*en libro*) preface, foreword; **sobre ~ no hay engaño** forewarned is forearmed.
advertido ADJ sharp, wide-awake.
advertimiento NM = **advertencia**.
▼ **advertir** [3i] [1] VT (a) (*observar*) to notice, observe; (*darse cuenta de*) to become aware of; ~ **que** ... to observe that ...
(b) (*indicar*) to point out, draw attention to.
▼ (c) (*aconsejar*) to advise; (*prevenir*) to warn; (*amonestar*) to caution; ~ **que** ... to advise that ..., recommend that ...; **les advertimos que** ... (*Com*) we would advise you that ...; **te advierto que** ...* mind you, ...
[2] VI: ~ **en** to notice, observe, become aware of; to take notice of, bear in mind.
Adviento NM Advent.
advocación NF (*Ecl*) name, dedication; **una iglesia bajo la ~ de San Felipe** a church dedicated to St Philip.
advocar [1g] VT (*LAm*) to advocate.
ADVP [1] ADJ ABR *de* **adicto** (*m*) **a drogas por vía parenteral** who uses drugs intravenously.
[2] NM intravenous drug user.
adyacencia NF (*Cono Sur*) nearness, proximity; **en las ~s** in the vicinity.
adyacente ADJ adjacent.
AECE [a'eθe] NF ABR *de* **Asociación Española de Cooperación Europea**.
aechaduras NFPL chaff.
AEDAVE NF (*Esp*) ABR *de* **Asociación Empresarial de Agencias de Viajes Españolas** *Spanish association of travel agents*, ≃ ABTA (*Brit*).
AEE NF ABR *de* **Agencia Europea del Espacio** European Space Agency, ESA.
AELC NF ABR *de* **Asociación Europea de Libre Comercio** European Free Trade Association, EFTA.
aeración NF aeration.
aéreo ADJ aerial; air (*atr*); *ferrocarril etc* overhead, elevated.
aero... PREF aero...
aerobic NM, **aeróbica** NF aerobics.
aeróbico ADJ aerobic.
aerobismo NM (*Cono Sur*) aerobics.
aerobús NM (*Aer*) airbus; (*Carib*) long-distance bus, coach.

aerocar NM airbus.
aerochati* NF air-hostess.
aeroclub NM flying club.
aerodeslizador NM, **aerodeslizante** NM hovercraft.
aerodinámica NF aerodynamics.
aerodinámico ADJ aerodynamic; (*perfil etc*) streamlined.
aerodinamismo NM streamlining.
aerodinamizar [1f] VT to streamline.
aeródromo NM, **aerodromo** NM aerodrome, airdrome (*US*), airfield.
aeroenviar [1c] VT to send by air.
aeroescuela NF flying school.
aeroespacial ADJ aerospace (*atr*).
aeroestación NF air terminal.
aerofaro NM (*Aer*) beacon.
aerofobia NF fear of flying.
aerofoto NF aerial photograph.
aerofotográfico ADJ aerial photographic.
aerofumigación NF crop-dusting.
aerogenerador NM wind turbine.
aerografía NF spray-painting, airbrushing.
aerografiado [1] ADJ spray-painted, airbrushed.
[2] NM spray-painting, airbrushing.
aerografista NMF spray-paint artist.
aerógrafo NM airbrush.
aerograma NM air-letter, aerogram.
aeroligero NM microlight.
aerolínea NF airline.
aerolito NM meteorite.
aeromodelismo NM aeromodelling, making model aeroplanes.
aeromodelista NMF model aeroplane enthusiast.
aeromodelo NM model aeroplane.
aeromotor NM aero-engine, aircraft engine.
aeromoza NF (*LAm*) air hostess, stewardess, flight attendant (*US*).
aeronauta NMF aeronaut.
aeronáutica NF aeronautics.
aeronáutico ADJ aeronautical.
aeronaval ADJ air-sea (*atr*); **base ~** air-sea base.
aeronave NF airship; (*Carib etc*) airliner.
aeronavegabilidad NF airworthiness.
aeronavegable ADJ airworthy.
aeroplano NM aeroplane, airplane (*US*).
aeroportuario ADJ airport (*atr*).
aeroposta NF (*LAm*) airmail.
aeropuerto NM airport.
aerosol NM aerosol.
aerostática NF ballooning.
aeróstato NM balloon, aerostat.
aerotaxi NM air taxi.
aeroterrestre ADJ air-ground *atr*.
aerotransportado ADJ airborne.
aerotransporte NM air transport.
aerotransportista NM (air) carrier.
aeroturbina NF wind turbine.
aerovía NF (*ruta*) airway; (*compañía*) airline.
AES NM ABR *de* **acuerdo económico social** wages pact.
a/f ABR *de* **a favor** in favour.
afabilidad NF affability, good nature, geniality; pleasantness, niceness.
afable ADJ affable, good-natured, genial; easy, pleasant, nice.
afablemente ADV affably; pleasantly.
afamado ADJ famous, noted (*por* for).
afamar [1a] [1] VT to make famous.
[2] **afamarse** VR to become famous, make a reputation.
afán NM (a) (*industria*) hard work, industry; (*labor*) exertion, toil.
(b) (*ansia*) anxiety; (*solicitud*) solicitude.
(c) (*deseo*) desire, urge; (*celo*) zeal, eagerness; **el ~ de** the desire for, the urge for; ~ **de estudios** studiousness, keenness to study; ~ **de lucro** profit motive; ~ **de superación** urge to improve, will to do better; ~ **de victoria** urge to win; **con ~** zealously, keenly.
afanador NM (*Cono Sur: ladrón*) thief, burglar; (*Méx: obrero*) menial worker; (*de limpieza*; *t* **afanadora** NF) cleaner.
afanaduría NF (*Méx Med*) casualty ward.
afanar [1a] [1] VT (a) (*gen*) to press, harass, bother; (*LAm: empujar*) to hustle; to jostle.
(b) (*CAm: ganar*) to earn.
(c) (*) to swipe*, pinch*, nick*.
[2] **afanarse** VR (a) (*trabajar duro*) to toil, labour (*en* at); to strive hard, exert o.s., go all out; ~ **por** + *infin* to strive to + *infin*; to toil to + *infin*.
(b) (*And: enfadarse*) to get angry.
afanoso ADJ *trabajo* hard, heavy, laborious; *tarea* tough, uphill;

temperamento industrious; solicitous; *actividad, búsqueda* feverish, hectic.

afantasmado ADJ conceited.

afarolado ADJ (*LAm*) excited, worked up.

afarolarse [1a] VR (*LAm*) to get excited, make a fuss, get worked up*.

afasia NF aphasia.

afásico ADJ (*Med*) aphasic, suffering from aphasia.

AFE ['afe] NF ABR *de* **Asociación de Futbolistas Españoles** ≈ Football Association, FA.

afeamiento NM (**a**) (*físicamente*) defacing, disfigurement. (**b**) (*fig*) condemnation, censure.

afear [1a] VT (**a**) (*hacer feo*) to make ugly, deface, spoil, disfigure; **los errores que afean el texto** the mistakes which disfigure the text. (**b**) (*fig*) to condemn, censure, decry.

afección NF (**a**) (*afecto*) affection, fondness; (*inclinación*) inclination; **afecciones del alma** emotions; emotional disorders.
(**b**) (*Med*) condition, trouble, disease; ~ **cardíaca** heart trouble, heart disease; ~ **hepática** liver complaint; ~ **lumbar** back trouble.

afeccionarse [1a] VR: ~ **a** (*Cono Sur*) to take a liking to, become fond of.

afectación NF affectation.

afectadamente ADV affectedly.

afectado ADJ (**a**) (*gen*) affected; (*estilo*) stilted, precious.
(**b**) (*Med*) **estar** ~ **del corazón** to have heart trouble; **estar** ~ (**del pecho**) (*Méx*) to be consumptive; **estar** ~ (*Cono Sur*) to be hurt; to be ill.

afectante ADJ (*Cono Sur*) disturbing, distressing.

afectar [1a] ① VT (**a**) (*gen*) to affect, have an effect on; **nos afecta gravemente** it seriously affects us; **su muerte nos afectó mucho** we were terribly saddened by his death; **por lo que afecta a esto** with regard to this; **las lluvias afectan al sur** it's raining in the south.
(**b**) (*por emoción*) to affect, move.
(**c**) (*fingir*) to affect, pretend, feign; to put on a show of; ~ **ignorancia** to feign ignorance.
(**d**) (*Jur*) to tie up, encumber.
(**e**) (*LAm: dañar*) to hurt, harm, damage.
(**f**) (*LAm*) *forma* etc to take on, assume.
(**g**) (*LAm*) *fondos* to set aside (*a* for); (*destinar*) to devote (*a* to).
② **afectarse** VR (*LAm*) to fall ill.

afectísimo ADJ affectionate; **suyo** ~ yours truly.

afectividad NF emotional nature, emotion(alism); sensitivity.

afectivo ADJ affective; emotional.

afecto ① ADJ (**a**) (*gen*) affectionate; ~ **a** attached to, fond of; inclined towards.
(**b**) ~ **a** (*Jur*) subject to, liable for.
(**c**) ~ **de** (*Med*) afflicted with.
② NM (**a**) (*cariño*) affection, fondness (*a* for), attachment (*a* to); **tomar** ~ **a** to become attached to, grow fond of.
(**b**) (*emoción*) feeling, emotion; (*instinto moral*) moral instinct.

afectuosamente ADV affectionately; ~ (*LAm: en carta*) yours affectionately.

afectuosidad NF affection.

afectuoso ADJ affectionate.

afeitada NF = **afeitado** (**a**).

afeitado NM (**a**) shave; shaving. (**b**) (*Taur*) blunting (*o* trimming) of the horns.

afeitadora NF electric razor, electric shaver.

afeitar [1a] ① VT (**a**) *barba* to shave; *planta, rabo* to trim; (*Taur*) *cuernos* to blunt, trim; *toro* to blunt (*o* trim) the horns of; **¡que te afeiten!** get your head seen to!*
(**b**) (*mujer*) to make up, paint, apply cosmetics to.
(**c**) (*: pasar*) to brush (past), shave.
② **afeitarse** VR (**a**) (*hombre*) to shave, have a shave.
(**b**) (*mujer*) to make o.s. up, put one's make-up on.

afeite NM make-up, cosmetic(s), rouge.

afelpado ADJ plush, velvety.

afeminación NF effeminacy.

afeminado ① ADJ effeminate.
② NM effeminate person.

afeminamiento NM effeminacy.

afeminarse [1a] VR to become effeminate.

aferrado ADJ stubborn, obstinate; **seguir** ~ **a** to remain firm in, stick to, stand by.

aferrar [1j *or* 1a] ① VT to grasp, seize, grapple; (*Náut*) *barco* to moor, *vela* etc furl.
② **aferrarse** VR (**a**) (*Náut*) to grapple; to anchor, moor; (*dos personas*) to grapple (together).
(**b**) ~ **a**, ~ **en** (*fig*) to stick to, stand by; ~ **a un principio** to stick to a principle; ~ **a una esperanza** to clutch at a hope, cling to a hope; ~ **a su opinión** to remain firm in one's opinion, stick to one's view.

afestonado ADJ festooned.

affaire NM (*Cono Sur*: NF) affair(e).

affma., affmo. ABR *de* **afectísima, afectísimo** Yours.

Afganistán NM Afghanistan.

afgano ADJ, NM, **afgana** NF Afghan.

afianzado, -a NM/F (*LAm*) fiancé(e).

afianzamiento NM (**a**) (*refuerzo*) strengthening, fastening, securing.
(**b**) (*Fin etc*) guarantee, security; (*Jur*) surety, bond.

afianzar [1f] ① VT (**a**) (*reforzar*) to strengthen, fasten, secure; (*apoyar*) to support, prop up; (*fig*) to support, back.
(**b**) (*avalar*) to guarantee, vouch for; (*salir garante por*) to stand surety for.
② **afianzarse** VR to steady o.s.; (*fig*) to become strong, become established; to make o.s. secure; ~ **a** to catch hold of, hold fast to; **la reacción se afianzó después de la guerra** the reaction set in after the war.

afiche NM (*cartel*) poster; (*Cono Sur: dibujo*) illustration, picture.

afición NF (**a**) (*amor*) fondness, liking (*a* for); (*inclinación*) taste (*a* for), inclination (*a* towards); **cobrar** ~ **a, tomar** ~ **a** to acquire a liking for, take a liking to; **tener** ~ **a** to like, be fond of.
(**b**) (*pasatiempo*) hobby, pastime; (*interés*) interest; **¿qué aficiones tiene?** what are his interests?; **pinta por** ~ he paints as a hobby.
(**c**) (*Dep etc*) **la** ~ the experts; the fans, the supporters; the sporting fraternity; **aquí hay mucha** ~ there is a large public for it here, support is strong here, the fans are terribly keen here.

aficionado ① ADJ (**a**) (*entusiasta*) keen, enthusiastic; **es muy** ~ he's very keen.
(**b**) ~ **a** keen on, fond of; with a taste for; **ser** (*o* **estar**) **muy** ~ **a** to be very keen on, be very fond of.
(**c**) *jugador* etc amateur.
② NM, **aficionada** NF (*gen*) enthusiast; (*no profesional*) amateur; (*como espectador* etc: *Dep*) fan, follower, supporter, (*Cine, Teat*) fan; **gritaban los** ~**s** the fans were shouting; **todos los** ~**s a la música** all music lovers; **la cantante y sus** ~**s** the singer and her fans; **función de** ~**s** amateur performance; **partido de** ~**s** amateur game; **somos simples** ~**s** we're just amateurs; **tenis para** ~**s** amateur tennis.

aficionar [1a] ① VT: ~ **a uno a algo** to make sb keen on sth, make sb like sth.
② **aficionarse** VR: ~ **a algo** to get fond of sth, take a liking to sth, take to sth; to become a follower (*o* fan) of sth; ~ **a** + *infin* to get fond of + *ger*, take to + *ger*.

afidávit NM affidavit, sworn statement.

áfido NM aphid.

afiebrado ADJ feverish.

afijo NM affix.

afiladera NF grindstone, whetstone.

afilado ADJ *borde* sharp; *punta* tapering, sharp.

afilador NM (**a**) (*persona*) knife-grinder; (*Téc*) steel, sharpener; strop, razor strop; ~ **de lápices** pencil sharpener. (**b**) (*Cono Sur* ††) womanizer, seducer.

afiladora NF (*Cono Sur* ††) flirt, coquette.

afiladura NF sharpening.

afilalápices NM INVAR pencil sharpener.

afilar [1a] ① VT (**a**) *herramienta* to sharpen, put an edge on; (*sacar punta a*) to put a point on; *cuchillo* to whet, grind; *navaja* to strop.
(**b**) (*Cono Sur* ††: *flirtear*) to court; to flirt with, seduce.
(**c**) (*Cono Sur*❁) to screw❁, fuck❁.
② **afilarse** VR (**a**) to get sharp; (*cara*) to sharpen, grow thin, get peaked; (*dedos*) to taper.
(**b**) (*And: prepararse*) to get ready; to get ready to tell sb off.

afiliación NF affiliation.

afiliado ① ADJ affiliated (*a* to), member ...; (*Com*) subsidiary; **los países** ~**s** the member countries.
② NM, **afiliada** NF (*And, Cono Sur*) member.

afiliarse [1b] VR: ~ **a** to affiliate to, join.

afiligranado ADJ filigreed; (*fig*) delicate, fine; *persona* dainty.

afilón NM (*correa*) strop; (*chaira*) steel.

afilorar [1a] VT (*Carib*) to adorn.

afín ① ADJ (**a**) (*contiguo*) bordering, adjacent. (**b**) (*conexo*) related, similar, allied; *persona* related.
② NMF relation by marriage.

afinación NF refining, polishing; completion; (*Aut, Mús*) tuning.

afinado ADJ finished, polished; (*Mús*) in tune.

afinador NM (*Mús*) tuning key; (*persona*) tuner; ~ **de pianos** piano tuner.

afinar [1a] ① VT (*completar*) to perfect, put the finishing touch to, complete; (*refinar*) to refine, polish; *puntería* etc to sharpen, make more precise; (*Téc*) to purify, refine; (*Aut, Mús*) to tune.
② VI to sing in tune, play in tune; (*fig*) to be precise, be exact.
③ **afinarse** VR (*modales*) to become more refined.

afincado NM (*Cono Sur*) farmer.

afincarse [1g] VR to establish o.s., settle (in a town *etc*).

afinidad NF affinity (*t Quím*); relationship, similarity, kinship (*con* with); **parentesco por** ~ relationship by marriage.

▼ **afirmación** NF affirmation.
afirmado NM (*Cono Sur*) (*acera*) paving, paved surface; (*Aut*) road surface.
▼ **afirmar** [1a] **1** VT (a) (*reforzar*) to make firm, steady, secure, strengthen.
▼ (b) (*declarar*) to affirm, assert, state; *lealtad etc* to declare, protest; ~ **que ...** to affirm that ..., state that ...; ~ **bajo juramento** to swear under oath.
2 VI (*Cono Sur, Méx: pegar*) to deal out blows, lash out.
3 **afirmarse** VR (a) (*recobrar el equilibrio*) to steady o.s.; ~ **en los estribos** (*lit*) to settle one's feet firmly in the stirrups; (*Cono Sur: fig*) to grit one's teeth.
(b) ~ **en lo dicho** to repeat what one has said, maintain one's opinion.
afirmativamente ADV affirmatively; **contestar** ~ to answer in the affirmative.
afirmativo ADJ affirmative, positive; **voto** ~ vote in favour, vote for.
aflatarse [1a] VR (*LAm*) to be sad.
aflautado ADJ *voz* high, fluty.
aflicción NF affliction; grief, sorrow.
aflictivo ADJ (*LAm*) distressing, grievous.
afligente ADJ (*CAm, Méx*) distressing, upsetting.
afligido **1** ADJ grieving, sorrowing, heartbroken; ~ **por** stricken with; **los ~s padres** the bereaved parents.
2 NM: **los ~s** the afflicted; (*en una muerte*) the bereaved.
afligir [3e] **1** VT (a) (*gen*) to afflict; (*angustiar*) to grieve, pain, distress.
(b) (*LAm: golpear*) to beat, hit.
2 **afligirse** VR to grieve (*con, de, por* about, at); **no te aflijas** don't grieve over it; **no te aflijas tanto** you must not let it affect you like this.
aflojamiento NM slackening; loosening; relaxation; abatement, weakening.
aflojar [1a] **1** VT (a) *tuerca, cuerda, paso etc* to slacken; *nudo etc* to loosen, undo; *presión* to relax; *agarro* to loosen, ease, let go; *freno* to release, take off; *vientre* to ease.
(b) (*) *dinero* to fork out*, pay up.
2 VI to slacken; to relent, let up; (*fiebre etc*) to abate, weaken; (*devoción*) to grow cool; (*dedicación etc*) to get slack.
3 **aflojarse** VR (*moderarse*) to slacken (off, up); (*pieza*) to come loose, work loose; (*fiebre, calor*) to abate; (*devoción*) to cool (off), diminish; (*interés*) to flag; (*precio*) to go down, weaken; (*Carib:*) to shit o.s.**.
afloración NF outcrop.
aflorado ADJ fine, elegant.
afloramiento NM = **afloración**.
aflorar [1a] VI (*Geol*) to crop out, outcrop, appear on the surface; (*sentimiento etc*) to show, appear; to emerge.
afluencia NF (a) (*gen*) inflow, influx, flow; (*de gente etc*) press; crowd, jam; (*en reunión*) attendance, number present; **la ~ de turistas** the influx of tourists; **la ~ de coches al estadio** the flow of cars towards the stadium; **tan grande fue la ~** so great was the rush.
(b) (*abundancia*) abundance, plenty.
(c) (*elocuencia*) eloquence, fluency.
afluente **1** ADJ (a) *agua etc* flowing, inflowing. (b) *discurso* eloquent, fluent.
2 NM (*Geog*) tributary.
afluir [3g] VI to flow (*a* into); (*personas*) to flow, flock (*a* into, to).
aflujo NM (*Med*) afflux, congestion; (*Mec*) inflow, influx, inlet.
aflús ADJ (*LAm*) broke*, flat* (*US*).
afluxionarse [1a] VR (*LAm*) to catch a cold.
afma., afmo. ABR *de* **afectísima, afectísimo** Yours.
afoetear [1a] VT (*And, Carib* ††) to whip, beat.
afonía NF hoarseness, state of having lost one's voice.
afónico ADJ (a) (*ronco*) hoarse, voiceless; **estar** ~ to be hoarse, have lost one's voice. (b) *letra* silent, mute.
aforado **1** ADJ (*provincia, territorio*) with a regional charter; **persona aforada** V 2.
2 NM, **aforada** NF person with parliamentary immunity who can only be tried by the Supreme Court.
aforador NM gauger.
aforar [1a] VT (*Téc*) to gauge; (*fig*) to appraise, evaluate.
aforismo NM aphorism.
aforístico ADJ aphoristic.
aforjudo ADJ (*Cono Sur*) silly, stupid.
aforo NM (a) (*Téc*) gauging; (*fig*) appraisal, valuation.
(b) (*Teat etc*) capacity; **el teatro tiene un ~ de 2.000** the theatre has a capacity of 2,000, the theatre can seat 2,000.
(c) (*Com*) import duty.
aforrar [1a] **1** VT (a) (*lit*) to line. (b) (*Cono Sur*: *golpear*) to smack, punch.
2 **aforrarse** VR (a) to wrap up warm, put on warm underclothes.
(b) (*) to stuff o.s.*, tuck it away*.

afortunadamente ADV fortunately, luckily.
afortunado ADJ fortunate, lucky.
afrailado ADJ (*LAm*) churchy*.
afrancesado **1** ADJ francophile; (*pey*) frenchified; (*Pol*) pro-French, supporting the French.
2 NM, **afrancesada** NF francophile; (*pey*) frenchified person; (*Pol*) pro-French person, French sympathizer.
afrancesamiento NM (*sentimiento*) francophilism, pro-French feeling; (*proceso*) gallicization, frenchification (*pej*).
afrancesarse [1a] VR to go French, become gallicized, acquire French habits; to become a francophile.
afrechillo NM (*Cono Sur Agr*) bran.
afrecho NM bran; (*LAm*) sawdust; ~ **remojado** mash.
afrenta NF affront, insult, outrage.
afrentar [1a] **1** VT (*insultar*) to affront, insult, outrage; (*deshonrar*) to dishonour.
2 **afrentarse** VR to be ashamed (*de* of).
afrentoso ADJ insulting, outrageous.
Africa NF Africa; ~ **Austral** Southern Africa; ~ **negra** Black Africa; ~ **del Norte** North Africa; ~ **del Sur** South Africa.
africaans NM Afrikaans.
africado ADJ (*Ling*) affricate.
africánder NM Afrikander.
africanidad NF Africanness.
africanista NMF specialist in African affairs; person interested in Africa.
africano, a ADJ, NM/F African.
afrijolar [1a] VT (*And*) to bother, annoy; ~ **una tarea a uno** to give sb an unpleasant job to do.
afrikaner ADJ, NMF Afrikaner.
afro ADJ Afro; **peinado** ~ Afro hairstyle.
afroamericano ADJ Afro-American.
afroasiático ADJ Afro-Asian.
afrobrasileño ADJ Afro-Brazilian.
afrocaribeño ADJ Afro-Caribbean.
afrocubano ADJ Afro-Cuban.
afrodisiaco, afrodisíaco ADJ, NM aphrodisiac.
Afrodita NF Aphrodite.
afronegrismo NM (*LAm*) word borrowed from an African language.
afrontar [1a] VT (a) *dos personas etc* to bring face to face. (b) *peligro, problema etc* to confront, face; to face up to; to deal with, tackle.
afrutado **1** ADJ *vino* fruity.
2 NM fruity flavour, fruitiness.
afta NF (*Med*) sore.
aftershave, after-shave [after'ʃeif] NM INVAR aftershave.
aftersun, after sun NM INVAR [after'san] aftersun.
aftosa NF foot-and-mouth (disease).
afuera **1** ADV out, outside; **¡~!** out of the way!, get out!, clear the way!; **de** ~ from outside; (*LAm*) outside; **por** ~ on the outside; **las hojas de** ~ the outer leaves, the outside leaves.
2 ~ **de** PREP (*LAm*) outside.
3 ~**s** NFPL outskirts, outer suburbs, outlying areas.
afuerano, afuereño, afuerino (*LAm*) **1** ADJ foreign; strange; from elsewhere, from outside.
2 NM, **afuerana, afuereña, afuerina** NF (*extranjero*) foreigner; stranger, outsider; (*trabajador*) itinerant worker, casual worker.
afuetear [1a] VT (*LAm*) to whip, beat.
afufa: NF flight, escape; **tomar las ~s** to beat it*.
afufar: [1a] VI, **afufarse** VR to beat it*, get out quick.
afufón: NM flight, escape.
afusilar [1a] VT (*LAm*) to shoot.
afutrarse [1a] VR (*Cono Sur*) to dress up.
ag. ABR *de* **agosto** August, Aug.
agachada* NF trick, dodge*.
agachadiza NF (*Orn*) snipe; **hacer la** ~ to duck, try not to be seen.
agachado*, -a NM/F (*LAm*) down-and-out, bum (*US*).
agachar [1a] **1** VT *cabeza* to bend, bow.
2 **agacharse** VR (a) (*agazaparse*) to stoop, crouch, get down; (*acuclillarse*) to squat; (*bajar la cabeza*) to duck; (*encogerse*) to cower.
(b) (*fig*) to go into hiding, lie low.
(c) (*LAm: rendirse*) to give in, submit.
(d) (*LAm: prepararse*) to get ready.
(e) ~ **algo** (*Méx**) to keep quiet about sth (out of spite), keep sth to o.s.
(f) ~ **con algo** (*And, Méx*) to make off with sth, pocket sth.
agache NM (*And*) fib, tale; **andar de** ~ to be on the run.
agachón: ADJ (*LAm*) weakwilled, submissive.
agafar: [1a] VT to pinch*, nick:.
agalbanado ADJ lazy, shiftless.
agalla NF (a) (*Bot*) gall; ~ **de roble** oak apple.
(b) (*Pez*) gill.
(c) (*And: codicia*) greed.

► LENGUA Y USO: **afirmación** → 53.6   **afirmar: 1b** → 53.1, 53.3, 53.5

(d) ~s (*Anat*) tonsils; (*Med*) tonsillitis.
(e) ~s* pluck, guts; **es hombre de ~s** he's got guts; **tener (muchas) ~s** to be brave, have guts.
(f) tener ~s (*LAm*) (*ser glotón*) to be greedy; (*ser tacaño*) to be mean; (*ser descarado*) to have lots of cheek*; (*Cono Sur: ser astuto*) to be sharp, be smart.

agalludo* ADJ (*LAm*) (*atrevido*) daring, bold; (*tacaño*) mean, stingy; (*And*) greedy.

ágape NM (*Hist*) love feast; banquet, feast.

agareno ① ADJ Moslem.
② NM, **agarena** NF Moslem.

agarrada NF (*riña*) row, argument; (*pelea*) scrap, brawl; (*Dep*) tackle.

agarradera NF (*LAm*), **agarradero** NM **(a)** (*manija*) handle; grip; (*de cortina*) cord.
(b) (*amparo*) protection; ~s* pull, influence; **tener (buenas) ~s** to have pull, have friends in the right places.

agarrado ADJ **(a)** mean, tight-fisted, stingy. **(b) baile ~** slow dance.

agarrador ADJ (*And, Cono Sur*) *licor* strong.

agarrafar [1a] VT to grab hold of.

agarrao* NM slow dance.

agarrar [1a] ① VT **(a)** (*gen*) to grasp, grip, seize, catch hold of; to grab, clutch; to pick up; **está bien agarrado*** he's got lots of pull; (*fig*) **no sé por donde ~lo** I don't know how to take him.
(b) (*) to get, wangle*.
(c) (*Com*) to corner the market in, pile up stocks of.
(d) (*LAm: sustituye a 'coger' en muchas aplicaciones*) to take; to pick up; **~ un autobús** to catch a bus; **~ una flor** to pick a flower; **~ un resfriado** to catch a cold; **agarra el libro del estante** get the book off the shelf.
(e) ~**la**: to get plastered:, get drunk.
(f) (*CAm, Carib, Méx*: captar*) to get*, understand.
(g) (*Cono Sur*) ~ **el vuelo** (*despegar*) to take off; ~ **a palos a uno** (*) to beat sb up*.
(h) (*Carib*:*) to fuck:*.
② VI **(a)** (*gen*) to take hold (*de* of); (*Bot*) to take root; (*pintura etc*) to stick.
(b) (*LAm*) ~ **para** to set out for; **agarre por esta calle** take this street; **agarró y se fue*** he upped and offed*.
③ **agarrarse** VR **(a)** (*dos personas*) to fight, have a fight; (*And*) to fight it out; **se agarraron a puñetazos** they fought it out with fists.
(b) (*asirse*) to hold on; (*Aut*) to hold the road; **¡agárrate bien!** hold on!, hold tight!; ~ **a**, ~ **de** to hold on to, grip, seize; ~ **al camino** (*Aut*) to hold the road; **agárrate!** (*) wait for it!; listen to this!; ~**la*** to burst into tears.
(c) se le agarró la fiebre the fever took hold of him; **se le agarró un fuerte catarro** he got a severe cold.
(d) (*LAm**) ~**la con uno** (*pelear*) to come to blows with sb; (*resentir*) to have sth against sb.

agarre NM **(a)** (*LAm: agarro*) hold; (*Aut*) road-holding (quality). **(b)** (*And: mango*) handle. **(c)** (*fig: valor*) guts, toughness. **(d) tener ~*** to have pull, be able to pull strings.

agarrete ADJ (*And*) mean, stingy.

agarro NM grasp, hold, clutch.

agarroch(e)ar [1a] VT to jab with a goad; (*Taur*) to prick with a pike.

agarrón NM **(a)** (*tirón*) jerk, pull, tug. **(b)** = **agarrada**.

agarroso ADJ (*CAm*) sharp, acrid, bitter.

agarrotamiento NM tightening; strangling; (*Aut*) seizing up.

agarrotar [1a] ① VT *lío etc* to tie tight; *persona* to squeeze tight, press tightly; *criminal* to garrotte; **esta corbata me agarrota** this tie is strangling me; **tengo los músculos agarrotados** I'm stiff.
② **agarrotarse** VR (*Med*) to stiffen, get numb; (*Aut etc*) to seize up.

agasajado, -a NM/F chief guest, guest of honour.

agasajador ADJ warm, welcoming.

agasajamiento NM = **agasajo**.

agasajar [1a] VT to treat well, fête, give a royal welcome to; to entertain royally, wine and dine.

agasajo NM good treatment, kindness; royal welcome, lavish hospitality, entertainment.

ágata NF agate.

agatas ADV (*Cono Sur*) **(a)** (*con dificultad*) (only) with great difficulty. **(b)** (*apenas*) hardly, scarcely; ~ **llegó, empezó a cantar** no sooner had he arrived than he started to sing.

agauchado ADJ (*Cono Sur*) like a gaucho.

agaucharse [1a] VR (*Cono Sur*) to imitate (*o* dress like) a gaucho.

agave NF agave, American aloe.

agavilladora NF binder, reaper.

agavillar [1a] ① VT *trigo* to bind (in sheaves); *libro* to bind.
② **agavillarse** VR to gang up, band together.

agazapar [1a] ① VT (*) to grab, grab hold of, nab*.
② **agazaparse** VR to hide; to crouch down, duck (down); **hay otra posibilidad agazapada allí** there's another possibility concealed in it; **tras esto se agazapa otra cosa** sth else is concealed behind this.

agencia NF agency; office, bureau; (*Cono Sur: montepío*) pawnshop; ~ **de cobro** debt-collecting agency; ~ **de colocaciones** employment agency; ~ **de contactos** dating agency; ~ **de créditos** credit agency; ~ **de damas de compañía** escort agency; ~ **exclusiva** exclusive agency; ~ **de información**, ~ **de noticias**, ~ **de prensa** news agency; ~ **inmobiliaria** estate agent's; ~ **de patentes** patents office; ~ **de promoción** development agency; ~ **de publicidad** advertising agency; ~ **de seguridad** security company; ~ **de transportes** carriers, removal business; **A~ Tributaria** Inland Revenue; ~ **de turismo**, ~ **de viajes** travel agency; ~ **única** sole agency.

agenciar [1b] ① VT (*lograr*) to bring about, effect, engineer; (*obtener*) to obtain, procure (*a uno* for sb); (*pey*) to wangle*, fiddle*; *trato* to negotiate.
② **agenciarse** VR to manage, get along; **yo me las agenciaré para llegar allí** I'll manage to get there somehow, I'll work out how to get there; ~ **algo*** to get hold of sth, manage to obtain sth.

agenciero NM (*Cono Sur*) (*de lotería*) lottery agent; (*agente*) representative; (*Cono Sur: de montepío*) pawnbroker.

agencioso ADJ active, diligent; industrious.

agenda NF **(a)** (*diario*) diary, notebook; (*de direcciones*) address-book; ~ **de bolsillo** pocket diary; ~ **de despacho**, ~ **de mesa** desk-diary; ~ **de trabajo** engagement book. **(b)** (*de reunión*) agenda. **(c)** (*Telec*) telephone directory.

agente ① NMF **(a)** (*gen*) agent; (*policía*) policeman, policewoman; (*LAm*) public service employee, worker in a nationalized industry; ~ **de bolsa** stockbroker; ~ **comercial** business agent, broker; ~ **especial** special agent; ~ **de exportación** export agent; ~ **extranjero** foreign agent; ~ **inmobiliario** estate agent; ~ **literario** literary agent; ~ **marítimo** shipping agent; ~ **de negocios** business agent, broker; ~ **oficial** official agent, authorized agent; ~ **del orden (público)**, ~ **de policía** policeman; ~ **de prensa** press agent; ~ **provocador** agent provocateur; ~ **de publicidad** (*Com*) advertising agent; (*Teat etc*) publicity agent; ~ **secreto** secret agent; ~ **de seguros** (*LAm*) insurance agent; ~**s sociales** social partners (*employers and unions*); ~ **de transportes** carrier; ~ **tributario** tax inspector; ~ **de turismo** travel agent, courier; ~ **único** sole agent; ~ **de ventas** sales agent, sales rep(resentative); ~ **viajero** (*LAm*) commercial traveller, salesman; ~ **de viajes** travel agent.
② NM (*Quím*) agent; ~ **químico** chemical agent.

agible ADJ feasible, workable.

agigantado ADJ gigantic, huge.

agigantar [1a] ① VT to enlarge, increase greatly; ~ **algo** to make sth seem huge.
② **agigantarse** VR to become huge; to seem huge; (*crisis etc*) to get much bigger.

ágil ADJ agile, nimble, quick; (*fig*) flexible, adaptable.

agilidad NF agility, nimbleness, quickness; (*fig*) flexibility, adaptability.

agilipollado: ADJ stuck-up*.

agilipollarse: VR **(a)** (*atontarse*) to get all confused, act like an idiot. **(b)** (*engreírse*) to get very stuck-up*.

agilitar [1a] ① VT to make agile; (*fig*) to help, make it easy for; (*LAm: activar*) to activate, set in motion.
② **agilitarse** VR to limber up.

agilización NF speeding-up; improvement.

agilizar [1f] ① VT (*acelerar*) to speed up; (*mejorar*) to improve, make more flexible.
② **agilizarse** VR to speed up.

ágilmente ADV nimbly, quickly.

agio NM agio; speculation; (*Méx Jur*) usury.

agiotaje NM (stock)jobbery, jobbing; speculation.

agiotista NM (stock)jobber; speculator; (*Méx: usurero*) usurer.

agitación NF **(a)** (*V v*) waving, flapping, shaking, stirring. **(b)** (*Náut*) roughness. **(c)** (*fig*) agitation (*t Pol*); bustle, stir, movement; excitement; nervousness.

agitado ① ADJ **(a)** *agua* rough, choppy; *vuelo* bumpy. **(b)** (*fig*) agitated; upset, anxious; excited; nervous; hectic.
② NM stirring, mixing.

agitador NM **(a)** (*Mec*) agitator, shaker; (*Culin*) stirrer. **(b)** (*persona*) agitator.

agitanado ADJ gipsy-like.

agitar [1a] ① VT **(a)** *brazo, bandera etc* to wave; *ala* to flap; *arma* to shake, brandish; *botella etc* to shake; *líquido (con mano)* to shake; (*con cuchara etc*) to stir, stir round, stir up; **agitaba un pañuelo** she was waving her handkerchief.
(b) (*fig*) (*excitar*) to stir up; to excite, rouse; (*perturbar*) to disturb; (*inquietar*) to worry, upset, make anxious.
② **agitarse** VR **(a)** to wave, wave to and fro; to flutter, flap; to shake; (*mar*) to get rough; **agítese antes de usar** shake (*o* stir) well before using.
(b) to get excited, get worked up; to get worried, get upset, upset o.s.

aglomeración NF agglomeration; crowd, mass; crowding; ~ **de tráfico** traffic jam; ~ **urbana** urban sprawl.

aglomerado [1] ADJ massed together, in a mass; **viven ~s** they live crowded together, they live on top of one another.
[2] NM (*madera*) plywood; (*Téc*) agglomeration; ~ **asfáltico** asphalt.

aglomerar [1a] [1] VT to agglomerate, crowd together.
[2] **aglomerarse** VR to agglomerate, form a mass; to crowd together.

aglutinación NF agglutination.

aglutinador ADJ agglutinative; cohesive; **fuerza ~a** unifying force, force that draws things together.

aglutinadora NF unifying force.

aglutinante ADJ agglutinative.

aglutinar [1a] [1] VT to agglutinate; (*fig*) to draw together, bring together; to make coherent.
[2] **aglutinarse** VR to agglutinate; (*fig*) to come together; to gel; to become coherent.

agnosticismo NM agnosticism.

agnóstico ADJ, NM, **agnóstica** NF agnostic.

agobiador ADJ, **agobiante** ADJ *cargo, calor etc* oppressive; *dolor etc* unbearable; *responsabilidad, trabajo* overwhelming; *pobreza* grinding.

agobiar [1b] [1] VT to weigh down, bow down; to oppress, burden, overwhelm; **sentirse agobiado por** to feel o.s. weighed down by; to be overwhelmed by; **está agobiado de trabajo** he is overloaded (*o* overburdened) with work.
[2] **agobiarse** VR: ~ **con**, ~ **de** to be weighed down with, bow beneath.

agobio NM (*carga*) burden, weight; (*opresión*) oppression; (*agotamiento*) exhaustion; (*aburrimiento*) boredom; (*Med*) nervous strain, anxiety.

agolpamiento NM throng, crush, rush, crowd.

agolparse [1a] VR to throng, rush, crowd together; to bunch together; (*problemas etc*) to come all together, come one on top of another; (*lágrimas*) to well up; to come in a flood; ~ **en torno a uno** to crowd round sb.

agonía NF (a) (*de muerte*) agony; death agony, death throes; **en su ~** on his (*etc*) death-bed; **acortar la ~ a un animal** to put an animal out of its misery; **la época está en su ~** the period is in its death throes.
(b) (*fig: dolor*) anguish, agony, torment.
(c) (*fig: anhelo*) desire, yearning.

agónico ADJ dying; (*fig*) agonizing.

agonioso ADJ (*LAm*) (*egoísta*) selfish; (*fastidioso*) bothersome; **es tan ~** he's such a pest.

agonizante [1] ADJ dying; *luz* failing.
[2] NMF dying person.

agonizar [1f] [1] VT (*) to bother, pester.
[2] VI (*t estar agonizando*) to be dying, be in one's death agony; ~ **por** (*fig*) + *infin* to be dying to + *infin*.

agonizos NMPL (*Méx*) worries, troubles.

agora ADV (*LAm*, ††) = **ahora**.

ágora NF main square.

agorafobia NF agoraphobia.

agorafóbico, -a NM/F agoraphobe.

agorar [1m] VT to predict, prophesy.

agorero [1] ADJ prophetic; ominous; **ave agorera** bird of ill omen.
[2] NM, **agorera** NF soothsayer, fortuneteller; forecaster.

agostar [1a] [1] VT to parch, burn up; (*fig*) to wither, kill before time; (*Méx: pastar*) to graze on rough ground.
[2] **agostarse** VR to dry up, shrivel; (*fig*) to die, fade away.

agosteño ADJ August (*atr*).

agosto NM August; (*cosecha*) harvest; (*época*) harvest-time; boom period; **hacer su ~** to feather one's nest, make one's pile; to make a killing.

agotado ADJ: **estar ~** (*persona*) to be exhausted, be worn out; (*existencias, provisión*) to be finished, be exhausted, (*Com*) be sold out; (*libro*) to be out of stock; (*pila*) to be flat, be run down.

agotador ADJ exhausting.

agotamiento NM exhaustion; depletion; draining; (*Med*) exhaustion; ~ **por calor** heat exhaustion; ~ **nervioso** nervous strain.

agotar [1a] [1] VT (*gen*) to exhaust, use up, finish; *reservas etc* to deplete, drain, empty; *paciencia* to exhaust; *persona* to exhaust, tire out; (*Med*) to exhaust.
[2] **agotarse** VR to become exhausted; to be finished, be used up; to give out, run out; to sell out; (*libro*) to go out of print; (*persona*) to exhaust o.s., wear o.s. out.

agraceño ADJ tart, sour.

agraciado ADJ (a) (*atractivo*) graceful; nice, attractive; (*encantador*) charming. (b) (*con suerte*) lucky; **salir ~** to be lucky, be the winner; **estar ~ de** to be blessed with.

agraciar [1b] VT (a) (*adornar*) to grace, adorn; (*hacer más atractivo*) to make more attractive.
(b) *prisionero* to pardon.

(c) ~ **a uno con algo** to bestow sth on sb, reward sb with sth.

agradable ADJ pleasant, agreeable, nice; enjoyable; **es un sitio ~** it's a nice place; **el cadáver no era muy ~ para la vista** the body was not a pretty sight; **ser ~ al gusto** to be nice, be tasty.

agradablemente ADV pleasantly, agreeably; enjoyably.

agradar [1a] [1] VT to please, be pleasing to, be to the liking of; **esto no me agrada** I don't like this.
[2] VI to please; **su presencia siempre agrada** it's always pleasant to have you with us, your presence is always welcome; **si le agrada le traeré más café** if you wish I'll bring you more coffee.
[3] **agradarse** VR to be pleased (*de* at, with).

▼ **agradecer** [2d] [1] VT *persona* to thank; *favor, regalo etc* to be grateful for; **agradezco tu ayuda** I am grateful for your help, thanks for your help; **se lo agradezco** I am grateful to you, I am much obliged to you; **un favor que él no agradecería nunca lo suficiente** a favour he can never thank you enough for; **agradecería que no lo hicieras** I should be glad if you would not do it, I should be obliged if you could avoid doing it; **eso no lo tiene que ~ a nadie** he has nobody to thank for that, he owes nobody thanks for that.
[2] **agradecerse** VR: **¡se agradece!** much obliged!, thanks very much!; **una copita de jerez siempre se agradece** a glass of sherry is always welcome.

agradecido ADJ grateful; appreciative; **¡muy ~!** thanks a lot!; thanks for everything!; **me miró agradecida** she looked at me gratefully; **estamos muy ~s** we are very grateful; **le quedaría muy ~ si ...** (*en carta*) I should be very grateful if ...

▼ **agradecimiento** NM gratitude, thanks; appreciation, gratefulness.

agrado NM (a) (*cualidad*) affability; **con ~** willingly. (b) (*gusto*) taste, liking; **ser del ~ de uno** to be to sb's liking; **tengo el ~ de informarle que ...** (*LAm*) I have pleasure in informing you that ..., I am glad to tell you that ...

ágrafo, -a ADJ, NM/F illiterate.

agramatical ADJ ungrammatical.

agrandamiento NM enlargement.

agrandar [1a] [1] VT to make bigger, enlarge, expand; *dificultad etc* to exaggerate, magnify.
[2] **agrandarse** VR to get bigger.

agranijado ADJ pimply.

agrario ADJ agrarian; land (*atr*); **política agraria** farming policy, agricultural policy; **reforma agraria** land reform.

agrarismo NM (*Méx*) agrarian reform movement.

agrarista NMF (*Méx*) supporter (*o* advocate) of land reform.

agravación NF, **agravamiento** NM aggravation, worsening; increase; (*Med*) decline, change for the worse.

agravado NM: **robo con ~** robbery with aggravation.

agravante [1] ADJ aggravating.
[2] NF additional burden; unfortunate circumstances; **con la ~ de que ...** with the further difficulty that ...; **con la ~ de la nocturnidad** (*Jur*) made more serious by the fact that it was done at night.

agravar [1a] [1] VT (*pesar sobre*) to weigh down, make heavier; *pena, impuesto etc* to increase; *dolor* to make worse; *problema, situación* to aggravate, make worse; *personas* to oppress, burden (*con* with).
[2] **agravarse** VR to worsen, get worse; to get more difficult.

agraviar [1b] [1] VT (*perjudicar*) to wrong; (*insultar*) to offend, insult.
[2] **agraviarse** VR to be offended, take offence (*de, por* at).

agravio NM wrong, injury; offence, insult; (*Jur*) grievance, injustice; ~ **comparativo** (resentment arising from) inequality; ~**s de hecho** assault and battery.

agravión ADJ (*Cono Sur*) touchy, quick to take offence.

agravioso ADJ offensive, insulting.

agraz NM (a) (*uva*) sour grape; (*jugo*) sour grape juice; **en ~** prematurely, before time. (b) (*fig*) bitterness, ill-feeling.

agrazar [1f] [1] VT (a) (*amargar*) to embitter. (b) (*fastidiar*) to vex, annoy.
[2] VI to taste sour, have a sharp taste.

agrazón NF (a) (*uva*) wild grape; (*grosellero*) gooseberry bush. (b) (*fig*) vexation, annoyance.

agredir [3a; *defectivo*] VT to attack, assault, set upon.

agregado [1] NM (a) (*Téc etc*) aggregate.
(b) (*Téc: bloque*) concrete block.
[2] NM, **agregada** NF (a) (*Pol*) attaché; (*Univ*) assistant professor; ~ **comercial** commercial attaché; ~ **cultural** cultural attaché; ~ **militar** military attaché; ~ **de prensa** press attaché.
(b) (*LAm*) person newly added to a group; thing newly added to a collection; (*Cono Sur: inquilino*) paying guest; (*And, Carib: aparcero*) sharecropper, tenant farmer paying rent in kind; (*Carib: jornalero*) (agricultural) day labourer.

agregaduría NF (*Pol, Mil: puesto*) post of attaché; (: *oficina*) attaché's office.

agregar [1h] VT (a) (*añadir*) to add (*a* to); (*unir*) to join (*a* to). (b) (*recoger*) to gather, collect. (c) *persona* to appoint, attach (*a* to, to the staff of).

agremiar [1b] **1** VT to form into a union, unionize. **2 agremiarse** VR to form a union.

agresión NF aggression; (*contra persona etc*) attack, assault; **~ sexual** sexual assault.

agresivamente ADV aggressively.

agresividad NF aggressiveness; drive, punch, vigour.

agresivo ADJ (*violento*) aggressive; (*vigoroso*) forceful, vigorous.

agresor **1** ADJ: **país ~** agressor country. **2** NM, **agresora** NF aggressor; attacker, assailant.

agreste ADJ (a) (*gen*) rural, country (*atr*). (b) *flor, paisaje etc* wild. (c) (*fig*) rough, uncouth.

agrete ADJ sourish.

agriado ADJ (*Cono Sur*) (a) sour, sharp. (b) (*fig*) (*resentido*) sour, resentful; (*exasperado*) angry, irritated.

agriar [1b *o* 1c] **1** VT (a) *sabor* to sour, turn sour. (b) (*fig*) (*amargar*) to sour; (*fastidiar*) to vex, annoy. **2 agriarse** VR (a) *sabor* to turn sour. (b) (*fig: fastidiarse*) to get cross, get exasperated; to become embittered.

agrícola ADJ agricultural, farming (*atr*).

agricultor **1** ADJ agricultural, farming (*atr*). **2** NM, **agricultora** NF farmer; **~ de montaña** hill-farmer.

agricultura NF agriculture, farming; **~ biológica**, **~ ecológica**, **~ orgánica** organic farming; **~ intensiva** intensive farming; **~ de montaña** hill-farming; **~ de rozas y quema** slash-and-burn agriculture; **~ de subsistencia** subsistence farming.

agricultural ADJ (*LAm*) agricultural, farming (*atr*).

agridulce ADJ bittersweet; sweet and sour.

agriera NF (*LAm Med*) heartburn.

agrietado ADJ cracked; *labios, manos* chapped.

agrietar [1a] **1** VT to crack, crack open; to make cracks in; *labios, manos* to chap. **2 agrietarse** VR to crack; to fissure; to get cracked, get covered in cracks; (*manos*) to get chapped.

agrifolio NM holly.

agrimensor(a) NM/F surveyor.

agrimensura NF surveying.

agringado ADJ (*LAm*) like (*o imitating*) a foreigner.

agringarse [1h] VR to act (*o behave*) like a foreigner.

agrio **1** ADJ (a) *sabor* sour, tart, bitter; (*fig*) sharp, sour, disagreeable. (b) *camino etc* rough, uneven; *materia* brittle; *color* garish. **2** NM sour juice; **~s** citrus fruit.

agripado ADJ (*LAm*): **estar ~** to have flu.

agriparse VR (*Cono Sur*) to catch a cold; to get flu.

agriura NF (*LAm*) sourness, tartness.

agro NM farming, agriculture.

agroalimentario ADJ food and agriculture (*atr*).

agrobiología NF agrobiology.

agrobiológico ADJ agrobiological.

agrobiólogo, -a NM/F agrobiologist.

agroenergética NF use of agricultural products as sources of energy.

agroforestal ADJ agroforestry (*atr*).

agroindustria NF agribusiness.

agronomía NF agronomy, agriculture.

agrónomo **1** ADJ agricultural, farming (*atr*). **2** NM, **agrónoma** NF agronomist, agricultural expert.

agropecuario ADJ farming (*atr*), stockbreeding (*atr*); **riqueza agropecuaria** agricultural wealth; **política agropecuaria** farming policy.

agropesquero ADJ relating to farming and fishing.

agroproducto NM agroproduct.

agroquímico ADJ, NM agrochemical.

agrosistema NM agricultural ecosystem, farming ecosystem.

agroturismo NM rural tourism.

agroturístico ADJ rural tourism (*atr*).

agrupación NF (a) (*grupo*) group, grouping; association; (*reunión*) gathering; (*unión*) union; (*Mús*) group, ensemble. (b) (*acto*) grouping; gathering; coming together.

agrupar [1a] **1** VT (*gen*) to group (together); *datos, gente etc* to gather, assemble; (*amontonar*) to crowd together. **2 agruparse** VR to form a group; to gather, come together; to crowd together, cluster, bunch together (*en torno a* round).

agrura NF sourness, tartness; **~s** (*Méx Med*) heartburn.

agua NF (a) (*gen*) water; fluid, liquid; (*lluvia*) rain; (*Náut: estela*) wake; (*Náut: vía de ~*) leak; (*Arquit*) slope of a roof, pitch; **¡~!** look out!; **¡hombre al ~!** man overboard!; **el invierno ha sido de mucha ~** it's been a very wet winter.

(b) (*con ADJ etc*) **~ para beber** drinking water; **~ bendita** holy water; **~ blanda** soft water; **~ de colonia** eau de cologne; **~ corriente** running water; **~ cuba** (*Cono Sur*) bleach; **~ destilada** distilled water; **~ dulce** fresh water; **pez de ~ dulce** freshwater fish; **~ dura** hard water; **~ de espliego** lavender water; **~ de fregar** (*: bebida*) ditch-

water; **~ de fuego** firewater; **~ de fusión de la nieve** meltwater; **~ con gas** sparkling water; **~ sin gas** still water; **~ gorda**, **~ gruesa** (*Méx*) salt water; **~ de grifo** tap-water; **~ gruesa** (*LAm*) hard water; **~ hirviendo** boiling water; **~ llovediza**, **~ (de) lluvia** rainwater; **~ del mar** seawater; **~ mineral** mineral water; **~ natural** tap-water; unchilled water; **~ oxigenada** hydrogen peroxide; **~ de pera** *etc* (*LAm: jugo*) pear juice *etc*; **~ perra** (*Cono Sur*) boiled water; **~ pesada** heavy water; **~ potable** drinking-water; **~ de rosas**, **~ rosada** rose-water; **~ salada**, **~ salina** salt water; **~ de seltz** seltzer (water); **~ subterránea** groundwater; **~ tónica** tonic water; **~ de Vichy** Vichy water.

(c) (*con verbo*) **¡~, que se quema la casa!** I'm dying for a drink!; **¡~ va!** look out!, timber!; **sin decir ~ va** without any warning; **eso es ~ pasada** that's all in the past; **~ pasada no mueve molino** it's no good crying over spilt milk; **bailarle el ~ a uno** to dance attendance on sb; **bañarse en ~ de rosas** to see the world through rose-coloured spectacles; **de esta ~ no beberé** I won't have anything to do with it; **nunca digas de esta ~ no beberé** don't be too sure; **cambiar el ~ al canario** (*Esp*;) to take a leak;; **coger ~ en cesto** to labour in vain, be wasting one's time; **¿me da para mis ~s?** (*Méx: pidiendo propina*) how about a little something for me?; **echar ~ arriba a uno** (*Méx*) to give sb a dressing down; **echar un barco al ~** to launch a boat; **echar** (*o* **llevar**) **el ~ a su molino** to bring the conversation round to one's own interests; to be on the make; **echarse al ~** to dive in; (*fig*) to take the plunge; **estar con el ~ al cuello*** to be over a barrel; **hacer ~** (*Náut*) to leak, take in water; **se me hace la boca ~** my mouth is watering; **se le hace ~ en la boca** it melts in one's mouth; **irse al ~** to be ruined; **mear ~ bendita**; to be terribly pious; **pescar en ~ turbia** to fish in troubled waters; **quedar en ~ de borrajas** to fail, come to nothing; **retener el ~** to hold water; **seguir las ~s a uno** (*Méx**) to keep on sb's good side.

(d) (*comparaciones*) **como ~** like water; freely, in abundance; **estar como el ~ de un lago** to be calm; **ser como el ~ por San Juan** to be harmful, be unwelcome; **es fácil como el ~** (*Cono Sur*) it's as easy as pie*; **venir como ~ de mayo** to be a godsend, be very welcome.

(e) **~s** waters; (*Náut*) tide; (*Med*) water, urine; (*de joya*) water, sparkle; **las ~s del Tajo** the waters of the Tagus; **~s abajo** downstream, down-river (*de from*); **~s arriba** upstream, up-river (*de from*); **~s de consumo** water supply, drinking water; **~s de escorrentía** run-off water; **~s fecales** sewage; **~s jurisdiccionales**, **~s territoriales** territorial waters; **~s litorales** coastal waters; **~s mayores** excrement, faeces; **~s menores** water, urine; **~s minerales** mineral waters; **~s negras** contaminated water; (*de cloaca*) sewage; **~s de pantoque** bilgewater; **~s residuales** sewage; **~s superficiales** surface water; **cubrir ~s** (*Arquit*) to put the roof on, top out; **hacer ~s** to make water, relieve o.s.; **estar** (*o* **nadar**) **entre dos ~s** to be undecided, sit on the fence; **tomar las ~s** to take the waters; **las ~s vuelven a su cauce** (*fig*) things return to normal.

aguacate NM (a) (*fruto*) avocado pear; (*árbol*) avocado pear tree. (b) (*CAm**) idiot, fool. (c) **~s** (*Méx*;) balls;;, bollocks;;.

aguacatero NM (*Méx*) avocado pear tree.

aguacero NM (heavy) shower, downpour.

aguacha NF foul water, stagnant water.

aguachacha NF (*CAm*) weak drink, nasty drink.

aguachado ADJ (*Cono Sur*) tame.

aguachento ADJ (*And, Cono Sur Bot*) watery, very juicy.

aguachinado ADJ (*Carib*) (*acuoso*) watery; (*blando*) soft.

aguachinarse VR (*Méx Agr*) to be flooded.

aguachirle NF (a) (*bebida*) weak drink, nasty drink; slops, dishwater. (b) (*bagatela*) trifle, mere nothing.

aguacil NM (*Cono Sur*) dragonfly.

aguacola NF (*Méx*) fish glue.

aguada NF (a) (*Agr*) watering place. (b) (*Náut*) water supply. (c) (*Min*) flood, flooding. (d) (*Arte*) watercolour, wash.

aguadilla NF ducking; **hacer una ~ a uno** to duck sb, hold sb's head under water.

aguado ADJ watery, watered-down, thin; (*: abstemio*) teetotal; (*Méx*) (*perezoso*) lazy, idle; (*flojo*) weak, simpering.

aguador NM water carrier, water seller.

aguaducho NM (a) (*arroyo*) freshet. (b) (*café*) refreshment stall, small open-air café.

aguafiestas NMF INVAR spoilsport, killjoy, wet blanket.

aguafuerte NF etching; **grabar algo al ~** to etch sth.

aguafuertista NMF etcher.

aguaitada NF (*LAm*) look, glance; **echar una ~ a** to take a look at.

aguaitar [1a] **1** VT (a) (*LAm*) (*espiar*) to spy on; (*vigilar*) to watch, keep an eye on; (*acechar*) to lie in wait for. (b) (*And, Carib: esperar*) to wait for. (c) (*Cono Sur etc: ver*) to look, see. **2** VI (*LAm*) to look; to watch; **~ por la ventana** to look out of the window.

aguaje NM (a) (*marea*) tide, spring tide; (*corriente*) current; (*estela*) wake. (b) (*provisión*) water supply; (*Agr*) watering trough. (c) (*And*,

CAm) rainstorm. (**d**) (CAm*: regañada) dressing-down*.
aguajirado ADJ (Carib) withdrawn, timid.
aguajirarse [1a] VR (Carib) to become countrified, acquire peasant's habits (etc); (ser reservado) to be withdrawn, be reserved.
agualotal NM (CAm) swamp, marsh.
aguamala NF (And etc) jellyfish.
aguamanil NM (jarro) ewer, water jug; (jofaina) washstand.
aguamar NM jellyfish.
aguamarina NF aquamarine.
aguamarse [1a] VR (And) to get scared, be intimidated.
aguamiel NF mead; sugared water; (CAm, Méx) fermented maguey (o agave juice).
aguamuerta NF (Cono Sur) jellyfish.
aguanieve NF sleet.
aguano NM (And) mahogany.
aguanoso ADJ (**a**) (gen) wet, watery; tierra waterlogged. (**b**) (Méx*) persona wet*.
aguantable ADJ bearable, tolerable.
aguantaderas NFPL (LAm): **tener ~** to be tolerant, be patient.
aguantadero* NM (Cono Sur) hide-out.
aguantador ① ADJ (LAm) = aguantón.
② NM, **aguantadora** NF (⁑) fence*, receiver (of stolen goods).
aguantar [1a] ① VT (**a**) (gen) to bear, endure, stand, put up with; insulto etc to swallow; tormenta to weather; examen to bear, stand up to; dolor to endure, bear; **no aguanto más** I'm not putting up with this, I can't bear it any more.
(**b**) techo etc to hold up, sustain; respiración to hold.
② VI (**a**) (resistir) to last, hold out; to resist; **aguanta mucho** he's very patient, he has lots of endurance.
(**b**) (cuerda etc) to hold (fast).
③ **aguantarse** VR (**a**) to restrain o.s., hold o.s. back, sit tight; to put up with it.
(**b**) (LAm) (callarse) to keep one's mouth shut; **~ de hacer algo** to hold back from doing sth; **¡aguántate!** calm down!; **tendrá que ~** he'll just have to put up with it.
aguante NM (paciencia) patience; (resistencia) endurance, fortitude; (Dep) stamina; (de objeto) strength; **al ~ de uno** (Carib*) behind sb's back.
aguantón ① ADJ (Carib, Méx) long-suffering, extremely patient.
② NM (Carib*): **te darás un ~** you'll have a long wait.
aguapié NM weak wine, plonk*.
aguar [1i] VT (**a**) vino etc to water (down). (**b**) (fig) to spoil, mar; V fiesta. (**c**) (CAm, Cono Sur) ganado to water.
aguarana NMF (And) primitive jungle Indian.
aguardada NF wait, waiting.
aguardadero NM, **aguardado** NM (Caza) hide.
aguardar [1a] ① VT to wait for, await; to expect.
② VI to hold on; to wait; **aguarde Vd** (en narración) that's what I'm trying to tell you, I'm coming to that.
aguardentería NF liquor store.
aguardentero, -a NM/F liquor seller.
aguardentoso ADJ alcoholic; voz fruity, beery.
aguardiente NM brandy, liquor; **~ de caña** rum; **~ de cerezas** cherry brandy; **~ de manzana** applejack.
aguardientoso ADJ (LAm) = aguardentoso.
aguardo NM (Caza) hide.
aguarrás NM turpentine.
aguate NM (Méx) prickle, thorn.
aguatero NM (LAm) water-carrier, water-seller.
aguatocha NF pump.
aguatoso ADJ (Méx) prickly.
aguaturma NF Jerusalem artichoke.
aguaviva NF (Cono Sur) jellyfish.
aguayo NM (And) multicoloured woollen cloth (for adornment, or carried as shoulder bag).
aguaza NF (Med) liquid (from a tumour); (Bot) sap.
aguazal NM (charco) puddle; (pantano) fen, swamp.
aguazar [1f] ① VT to flood, waterlog.
② **aguazarse** VR to become waterlogged.
agudeza NF (**a**) (gen) acuteness, sharpness; keenness. (**b**) (ingenio) wit, wittiness. (**c**) (una ~) witticism, witty saying.
agudización NF, **agudizamiento** NM sharpening; worsening.
agudizar [1f] ① VT to sharpen, make more acute.
② **agudizarse** VR to sharpen, become more acute, worsen; **el problema se agudiza** the problem is becoming more acute; **la competencia se agudiza** competition is intensifying.
agudo ADJ (**a**) (instrumento etc) sharp, pointed; ángulo acute.
(**b**) enfermedad, dolor acute.
(**c**) (Mús) nota high, high-pitched; shrill; sonido piercing; (Ling) acento acute.
(**d**) mente, sentido sharp, keen, acute, penetrating; observación smart, clever; crítica penetrating, trenchant; ingenio ready, lively; pregunta

acute, searching; sabor etc sharp, pungent.
(**e**) (ingenioso) witty.
agüé INTERJ (CAm) ¡~! hello!
agüeitar [1a] (LAm) = aguaitar.
agüera NF irrigation ditch.
agüero NM omen, sign; prediction, forecast; **de buen ~** lucky, propitious; **ser de buen ~** to augur well; **de mal ~** ill-omened; **pájaro de mal ~** bird of ill omen.
aguerrido ADJ hardened, veteran.
aguerrir [3a; defectivo] VT to inure, harden.
agüevar; [1a] ① VT (CAm, Méx) to put down, shame.
② **agüevarse** VR to cower, shrink.
aguijada NF, **aguijadera** NF goad.
aguijar [1a] ① VT to goad; (fig) to urge on, spur on, goad.
② VI to hurry along, make haste.
aguijón NM (**a**) (puya) point of a goad, goad; (Zool) sting; (Bot) prickle, spine, sting; **dar coces contra el ~** to kick against the pricks, struggle in vain. (**b**) (fig) spur, stimulus; incitement; **el ~ de la carne** sexual desire.
aguijonazo NM prick (with a goad), jab; (Zool, Bot) sting.
aguijonear [1a] VT = aguijar.
aguijoneo NM goading, provocation.
águila NF (**a**) (Orn) eagle; **~ calzada** booted eagle; **~ culebrera** short-toed eagle; **~ perdicera** Bonelli's eagle; **~ pescadora** osprey; **~ ratonera** buzzard; **~ real** golden eagle. (**b**) (fig) **ser un ~** to be a genius, be terribly clever. (**c**) (Cono Sur: estafador) cheat, swindler; **andar a palos con el ~*** to be broke; **¿~ o sol?** (Méx) heads or tails?
aguileña NF columbine.
aguileño ADJ nariz aquiline; cara sharp-featured; persona hawk-nosed.
aguilera NF eagle's nest, eyrie.
aguililllo, -a NM/F (LAm) fast horse.
aguilón NM (Orn) large eagle; (de grúa) jib; (Arquit) gable, gable-end; (And) large heavy horse.
aguilucho NM (Orn) eaglet, young eagle; harrier; (LAm) hawk, falcon.
aguinaldo NM (**a**) (de Navidades) Christmas box, New Year gift; (propina) tip; (plus) (salary) bonus. (**b**) (LAm: villancico) Christmas carol.
aguita; NF (And) cash, dough⁑, bread⁑.
agüita NF (Cono Sur) infusion, herb tea.
agüitado ADJ (Méx) depressed, gloomy.
aguja NF (**a**) (Cos etc) needle; (de sombrero) hatpin; **~ de arria** (LAm) pack needle; **~ capotera** darning needle; **~ de gancho** crochet hook; **~ de hacer calceta** (Esp), **~ de hacer punto** knitting-needle; **~ hipodérmica** hypodermic needle; **~ magnética**, **~ de marear** compass (needle); **conocer la ~ de marear** to know one's way around; **~ de media**, **~ de tejer** (LAm) knitting-needle; **~ de zurcir** darning needle; **buscar una ~ en un pajar** to look for a needle in a haystack; **darle a la ~*** to shoot up⁑.
(**b**) (de reloj) hand; pointer; **tumbar la ~*** (Aut) to step on the gas*, go full out.
(**c**) (Mil) firing pin.
(**d**) **~ de pino** (Bot) pine needle.
(**e**) **~ (de tranquera)** (LAm) fencepost.
(**f**) (Arquit) spire, steeple.
(**g**) **~s** (Anat) ribs.
(**h**) **~s** (Ferro) points.
(**i**) (Esp: t **~ de mar**) garfish.
(**j**) (CAm, Méx: carne) beef.
agujazo NM prick, jab.
agujereado ADJ full of holes, pierced with holes; perforated; leaky.
agujerear [1a] VT to make holes in, pierce; to perforate; (Cono Sur) to disrupt.
agujero NM (**a**) (gen) hole; (Anat⁑) hole ⁑; **~ de hombre** manhole; **~ negro** black hole; **~ de ozono** ozone hole, hole in the ozone layer; **hacer un ~ en, practicar un ~ en** to make a hole in. (**b**) (Cos) needle case; pincushion. (**c**) (⁑) pad⁑; hide-out, safe house. (**d**) (fig) gap; discrepancy; (Fin) hole, drain; deficit.
agujetas NFPL (Med) stitch; stiffness. (**b**) (Méx) shoelaces.
agujetero NM (LAm: alfiletero) pincushion.
agujón NM hatpin.
agur* INTERJ so long!, cheerio!
agusanado ADJ maggoty, wormy.
agusanarse [1a] VR to get maggoty.
Agustín NM Augustine.
agustiniano, agustino ADJ, NM Augustinian.
agutí NM (LAm Zool) guinea-pig.
aguzado ADJ (LAm) sharp, on the ball*.
aguzamiento NM sharpening.
aguzanieves NF INVAR wagtail.
aguzar [1f] VT (**a**) (afilar) to sharpen.
(**b**) (fig) to incite, stir up; apetito to whet; **~ las orejas** to prick up one's ears; **~ la vista** to look sharp, look more carefully.

ah INTERJ (**a**) oh!; **¡~ del barco!** ship ahoy! (**b**) (*LAm*) **¿~?** what?

a.h. ABR *de* **año de la Hégira** from the year of the Hegira, anno Hegirae, AH.

ahechaduras NFPL chaff.

ahechar [1a] VT to sift; to winnow.

aherrojamiento NM (*fig*) oppression.

aherrojar [1a] VT to put in irons, fetter, shackle; (*fig*) to oppress.

aherrumbrarse [1a] VR to rust, get rusty; to take on the taste (*o* colour) of iron.

ahí ① ADV there; **¿de ~?** well?; what next?, (*iró*) so what?; **¡ ~ es nada!** imagine!, wow!*; **¡ ~ está (la madre del cordero)!** that's the trouble!; **¡ ~ está el detalle!** that's the whole point!; **~ no más** (*LAm*) right here; **¡~ no más!** that's the limit!; **de ~ se deduce que ...** from that it follows that ...; **por ~** that way; over there; **200 pesos o por ~** 200 pesos or thereabouts; **está por ~** it's round here somewhere; (*persona*) he's round about somewhere; he's knocking around somewhere; **¡hasta ~ podíamos llegar!** that's the limit!, what a nerve!; **ir por ~** (*euf*) to get around, keep dubious company; **¡~ va!** there it goes!, there he goes!; (*con sorpresa*) goodness me!; (*burlándose*) get along with you!, tell us another!

② CONJ **de ~ que** + *subj* and so ..., so that ...; with the result that ...

ahijada NF goddaughter; (*fig*) protégée.

ahijado NM godson; (*fig*) protégé.

ahijar [1a] VT *persona* to adopt; *animal* to adopt, mother; **~ algo a uno** (*fig*) to impute sth to sb; to attribute sth to sb.

ahijuna: INTERJ (*Cono Sur*) son of a bitch!:

ahilar [1a] ① VT to line up.

② VI to go in single file.

③ **ahilarse** VR (*Med*) to faint with hunger; (*Bot*) to grow poorly; (*vino etc*) to turn sour, go off.

ahincadamente ADV hard, earnestly; emphatically.

ahincado ADJ earnest; emphatic.

ahincar [1g] ① VT to press, urge.

② **ahincarse** VR to hurry up, make haste.

ahínco NM (*seriedad*) earnestness, intentness; (*énfasis*) emphasis; (*empeño*) effort; (*resolución*) determination, perseverance; **con ~** hard, earnestly; eagerly.

ahitar [1a] ① VT to cloy, surfeit.

② **ahitarse** VR to stuff o.s. (*de* with), give o.s. a surfeit (*de* of); (*Med*) give o.s. indigestion.

ahíto ① ADJ (**a**) (*repleto*) gorged, surfeited, satiated. (**b**) (*fig: harto*) **estar ~ de** to be fed up with. (**c**) (*lleno*) full, packed tight.

② NM surfeit, satiety; (*Med*) indigestion.

AHN NM ABR *de* **Archivo Histórico Nacional.**

ahogadero NM (**a**) (*de animal*) throatband; headstall, halter; (*de verdugo*) hangman's rope. (**b**) (*fig*) **esto es un ~** it's stifling in here.

ahogado ① ADJ (**a**) *persona* drowned; (*asfixiado*) suffocated; **perecer ~** to drown; to suffocate.

(**b**) *cuarto* close, stifling.

(**c**) *emoción* pent-up; *grito* muffled, half-smothered.

(**d**) **estar ~**, **verse ~** to be in a tight spot.

② NM, **ahogada** NF drowned person.

③ NM (*LAm*) (*salsa*) sauce; (*guisado*) stew.

ahogador NM (*Méx Aut*) choke.

ahogar [1h] ① VT (**a**) (*en agua*) to drown; (*asfixiar*) to suffocate; to smother; *fuego* to put out; *proyecto, proyecto de ley etc* to kill; **~ las penas** to drown one's sorrows.

(**b**) *planta* to drown, overwater.

(**c**) *grito, sollozo etc* to choke back, stifle, hold in.

(**d**) (*fig*) to afflict, oppress, crush.

(**e**) (*Ajedrez*) to stalemate.

② **ahogarse** VR (*por accidente*) to drown; to suffocate; (*suicidio*) to drown o.s.

ahogo NM (**a**) drowning; **perecer por ~** to drown.

(**b**) (*Med*) shortness of breath, tightness of the chest.

(**c**) (*fig*) distress, affliction.

(**d**) (*Fin*) embarrassment, financial difficulty; economic stringency.

ahoguío NM (*Med*) = **ahogo** (**b**).

ahondar [1a] ① VT to deepen, make deeper, dig out.

② VI: **~ en** to go deeply into, penetrate deeply into; (*fig*) to study thoroughly, examine in depth.

③ **ahondarse** VR to go (*o* sink) in more deeply.

ahora ① ADV (*gen*) now; (*hace poco*) just now; a moment ago; (*dentro de poco*) in a little while, very soon; **desde ~** from now on; **hasta ~** up till now; as yet; hitherto; **¡hasta ~!** see you soon!; **por ~** for the present, for the moment; **~ mismito**, **~ poco*** just a moment ago; **~ mismo** right now, this very minute; at this very moment; **~ es cuando** now's your chance.

② CONJ now; now then, well now; on the other hand; **~ bien** now then, well now; but; however; **~ pues** well then; **~ ... ~** whether ... or.

ahorcado ① ADJ (*Cono Sur**) flat broke*.

② NM, **ahorcada** NF hanged person; *V* **soga.**

ahorcadura NF hanging.

ahorcajarse [1a] VR to sit astride; **~ en** to sit astride, straddle.

ahorcamiento NM hanging.

ahorcar [1g] ① VT to hang; **~ a uno** (*Méx**) to milk sb, squeeze sb dry; *V* **hábito** *etc.*

② **ahorcarse** VR to hang o.s.; *ver también* COLGAR

ahorita ADV (*esp LAm*) = **ahora**; (*ahora mismo*) right now, this very minute; (*hace poco*) a moment ago, just now; (*dentro de poco*) in a moment; **¡~ voy!** I'm just coming!, I'll be with you in a moment!

ahoritita* ADV (*Méx*) = **ahorita.**

ahormar [1a] VT (**a**) (*ajustar*) to fit, adjust (*a* to); (*formar*) to shape, mould; *zapatos* to break in, stretch; *carácter* to mould.

(**b**) (*fig*) **~ a uno** to make sb see sense.

ahorquillado ADJ forked.

ahorquillar [1a] ① VT (**a**) (*apoyar*) to prop up. (**b**) (*formar*) to shape like a fork.

② **ahorquillarse** VR to fork, become forked.

ahorrador ADJ thrifty.

ahorrar [1a] ① VT *dinero* to save; to put by; *molestia* to save, avoid; *peligro* to avoid; *esclavo* to free.

② **ahorrarse** VR (**a**) **~ molestias** to save o.s. trouble, spare o.s. effort; **no ~las con nadie** to be afraid of nobody.

(**b**) (*Carib, Agr*) to abort; (*CAm: cosecha*) to fail.

(**c**) (*And: gandulear*) to shirk, refuse to work.

ahorrativo ADJ thrifty; (*pey*) tight, stingy.

ahorrillos NMPL small savings.

ahorrista NMF saver.

ahorro NM (*acto*) economy, saving; (*cualidad*) thrift; **~s** savings; **~ energético** energy saving, saving in energy; (*política*) energy conservation.

ahoyar [1a] VT to dig holes in.

ahuchar[1] [1a] VT to hoard, put by.

ahuchar[2] [1a] VT (*And, Méx*) = **azuzar** (**b**).

ahuecado ADJ *voz* deep.

ahuecar [1g] ① VT (**a**) (*hacer hueco*) to hollow (out), make a hollow in; **~ la mano** to cup one's hand.

(**b**) (*Agr*) to loosen, soften; (*Cos*) to fluff out.

(**c**) *voz* to deepen, make pompous, give a solemn tone to.

(**d**) *V* **ala** (**g**).

② VI **¡ahueca!*** beat it!*

③ **ahuecarse*** VR to give o.s. airs.

ahuesarse [1a] VR (*And, Cono Sur*) (**a**) (*) (*pasar de moda*) to go out of fashion; (*comestibles*) to go off (*o* rotten); (*pasarse*) to become unsaleable.

(**b**) (*persona*) to get thin.

ahuevado ADJ (*LAm*) silly, stupid.

ahuizote NM (*CAm, Méx*) (**a**) (*persona*) bore. (**b**) (*maleficio*) evil spell, curse.

ahulado NM (*CAm, Méx*) oilskin; **~s** rubber shoes.

ahumado ① ADJ (**a**) *tocino etc* smoked; *sabor, superficie, ventana etc* smoky; *vidrio* tinted. (**b**) (*: borracho*) tight*, tipsy.

② NM (**a**) smoking, curing. (**b**) (*: borracho*) drunk*.

ahumar ① VT (**a**) *tocino etc* to smoke, cure.

(**b**) *superficie etc* to make smoky; *cuarto* to make smoky, fill with smoke.

(**c**) *colmena* to smoke out.

② VI to smoke, give out smoke.

③ **ahumarse** VR (**a**) (*comida*) to acquire a burnt taste.

(**b**) (*cuarto*) to be smoky, get smoked up.

(**c**) (*: emborracharse*) to get tight*.

ahusado ADJ tapering, spindle-shaped.

ahusarse [1a] VR to taper.

ahuyentar [1a] ① VT (**a**) (*espantar*) to drive away, frighten away; to put to flight; (*mantener a distancia*) to keep off.

(**b**) *temores, dudas etc* to banish, dispel; **~ las penas con vino** to drown one's sorrows in wine.

② **ahuyentarse** VR to run away; (*Méx*) to stay away.

AI NF ABR *de* **Amnistía Internacional** Amnesty International, AI.

AID NF ABR *de* **Agencia Internacional para el Desarrollo** Agency for International Development, AID.

AIF NF ABR *de* **Asociación Internacional de Fomento** International Development Association, IDA.

AIH [ai'atʃe] NF ABR *de* **Asociación Internacional de Hispanistas.**

aimara ① ADJ, NMF Aymara (Indian).

② NM (*Ling*) Aymara.

aína ADV (*liter*) speedily.

aindiado ADJ (*LAm*) like (*o* resembling) an Indian, Indian-looking; dark-skinned.

AINS NF (*Esp*) ABR *de* **Administración Institucional Nacional de Sanidad.**

airadamente ADV angrily.

airado ADJ (a) (*enojado*) angry; (*violento*) wild, violent; **joven ~** angry young man (*1950s*). (b) *vida* immoral, depraved.

airar [1a] 1 VT to anger.
2 **airarse** VR to get angry (*de, por* at).

airbag ['erβag] NM, PL **airbags** airbag.

aire NM (a) (*gen*) air; (*corriente*) wind, draught; **misil de ~ a ~** air-to-air missile; **~ colado** cold draught; **~ comprimido** compressed air; **~ detonante** firedamp; **~ líquido** liquid air; **~ puro** clean air; **~ viciado** stale air, foul air, fug; **~s de cambio** (*Pol*) winds of change; **con ~ acondicionado** air-conditioned, with air conditioning; **al ~ libre** in the open air, outdoors, (*como adj*) open-air, outdoor; **azotar el ~** to waste one's efforts; **beber los ~s por** to sigh for, yearn for; to be madly in love with; **cambiar de ~(s)** to have a change of air; **cortarlas en el ~** to be very sharp; **darse ~** to fan o.s.; **dejar una pregunta en el ~** to leave a question unanswered o unsettled; **echar al ~** to bare, uncover; **estar en el ~** (*Rad*) to be on the air; (*fig*) to be up in the air; to be doubtful, be undecided; **hacer ~ a uno** to fan sb; **hacerse ~** to fan o.s.; **hace mucho ~** it's very windy; **lanzar algo al ~** to throw sth up; **mantenerse** o **vivir del ~** to eat very little, live on thin air; **mudarse a cualquier ~** to be fickle; **ofenderse del ~** to be terribly touchy; **salir al ~** (*Rad*) to go out on the air; **saltar por los ~s*** to go up in smoke*, go up the wall*; **tomar el ~** to go for a stroll; **¡vete a tomar el ~!*** clear off!*; **¿qué ~s te traen por aquí?** what brings you here?; **volar por los ~s** to fly through the air.
(b) (*fig: aspecto, porte*) air, appearance; **darse ~s** to give o.s. airs; **darse ~s de** to boast of being; **no te des esos ~s de suficiencia conmigo** don't get on your high horse with me; **tener ~ de salud** to look healthy.
(c) (*fig: semejanza*)) resemblance; **~ de familia** family likeness; **darse un ~ a** to resemble; **tener ~ de** to look like, resemble.
(d) (*fig: humor*) humour, mood; **dar ~ al dinero** to spend money freely; **estar de buen ~** to be in a good mood; **estar de mal ~** to be in a bad mood; **ir a su ~** to go one's own way, follow one's whim, do one's own thing*; **seguir el ~ a uno** to humour sb, follow sb's whim.
(e) (*fig: elegancia etc*) air; elegance, gracefulness.
(f) (*Mús*) tune, air.
(g) (*Cono Sur* Med*) (*cuello*) stiff neck; (*parálisis*) paralysis.

aireación NF ventilation.

aireado NM ventilation; (*de vino*) aeration.

aire-aire ATR: **misil ~** air-to-air missile.

airear [1a] 1 VT (a) (*gen*) to air, ventilate; *ropa* to air.
(b) (*fig*) *idea, cuestión* etc) to discuss at length, give a lot of coverage to; **~ la atmósfera** to clear the air, let in fresh air.
(c) (*publicar*) to gossip about.
2 **airearse** VR to take the air; (*Med*) to catch a chill.

aireo NM ventilation.

aire-tierra ATR: **misil ~** air-to-ground missile.

airón NM (a) (*Orn*) heron. (b) (*de plumas etc*) tuft, crest.

airosamente ADV gracefully, elegantly; jauntily; successfully.

airosidad NF grace, elegance; jauntiness.

airoso ADJ (a) (*ventilado*) airy; *cuarto* draughty; *lugar expuesto* windy; *tiempo* windy, blowy.
(b) (*fig*) graceful, elegant; jaunty; successful; **quedar ~, salir ~** to be successful, acquit o.s. well, come out with flying colours.

aislación NF insulation; **~ de sonido** soundproofing.

aislacionismo NM isolationism.

aislacionista ADJ, NMF isolationist.

aislado ADJ (a) (*remoto*) isolated; cut off, shut off (*de* from); lonely; **'con inodoro ~'** (*anuncio*) 'with separate WC'. (b) (*Elec etc*) insulated.

aislador 1 ADJ (*Elec*) insulating.
2 NM (*Elec*) insulator, non-conductor.

aislamiento NM (a) (*gen*) isolation; loneliness; **~ sensorial** sensory deprivation. (b) (*Elec etc*) insulation; insulating material; **~ acústico** soundproofing.

aislante 1 ADJ insulating.
2 NM insulator, insulating material.

aislar [1a] 1 VT (a) (*gen*) to isolate; (*separar*) to separate, detach; (*cortar*) to cut off, shut off.
(b) (*Elec etc*) to insulate.
2 **aislarse** VR to isolate o.s., cut o.s. off (*de* from); to live in isolation, live in seclusion.

AITA NF ABR *de* **Asociación Internacional del Transporte Aéreo** International Air Transport Association, IATA.

ajá, ajajá INTERJ fine!, splendid!; (*sorpresa*) aha!

ajajay INTERJ V ajay.

ajamonarse* [1a] VR to get plump, run to fat.

ajar[1] NM garlic field, garlic patch.

ajar[2] [1a] 1 VT (a) (*gen*) to crumple, crush, mess up; to ruffle, rumple; to tamper with, spoil.
(b) (*fig*) to abuse, disparage.
2 **ajarse** VR to get crumpled, get messed up; (*Bot*) to wither, fade.

ajarabezado ADJ: **vino ~** wine with syrup added.

ajarafe NM (*Geog*) tableland; (*Arquit*) terrace, flat roof.

ajardinar [1a] VT to landscape; **zona ajardinada** landscaped area.

ajay INTERJ (*LAm: risa*) **¡~!** ha!

-aje V Aspects of Word Formation in Spanish 2.

ajedrea NF (*Bot*) savory.

ajedrecista NMF chessplayer.

ajedrez NM chess; **un ~** a chess set, a set of chessmen.

ajedrezado ADJ chequered.

ajenjo NM (*Bot*) wormwood; (*bebida*) absinth(e).

ajeno ADJ (a) (*de otro*) somebody else's, other people's; **un coche ~** sb else's car, a car belonging to sb else; **no meterse en lo ~** not to interfere in the affairs of others; **vivir a costa ajena** to live at sb else's expense; to live off other people.
(b) (*extraño*) outside; alien, foreign (*a* to); (*inconsecuente*) inconsistent (*a* with); (*impropio*) inappropriate (*a, de* for, to); **ser ~ a la muerte de uno** to have no part in someone's death; **por razones ajenas a mi voluntad** for reasons beyond my control; **eso está ~ a nuestro control** that is outside our control.
(c) **~ de cuidados** free from care, without a care.
(d) (*no enterado*) unaware (*a, de* of), unsuspecting.
(e) **estar ~ de sí** to remain detached.

ajerezado ADJ sherry-flavoured.

ajete NM spring onion.

ajetreado ADJ *vida* busy, tiring.

ajetrearse [1a] VR to bustle about, be busy; to fuss; to tire o.s. out; to work hard, slave away.

ajetreo NM bustle; fuss; drudgery, hard work; **es un continuo ~** it's all bustle, there's constant coming and going.

ají NM, PL **ajíes** o **ajises** (*LAm*) chili, red pepper; (*salsa*) chili sauce; **ponerse como un ~** to go bright red (in the face); **estar hecho un ~** to be hopping mad, go up the wall*; **refregarle a uno el ~** to criticize sb.

ajiaceite NM sauce of garlic and olive oil.

ajiaco NM (*Carib*) (*Culin*) potato and chili stew; (*lío*) mess, mix-up; **meterse el ~*** to eat.

ajibararse [1a] VR (*Carib*) = **aguajirarse**.

ajigolones NMPL (*CAm, Méx*) troubles, difficulties.

ajilar [1a] VI (*CAm, Méx*) to set out for a place; (*Carib*) to walk quickly.

ajilimoje NM, **ajilimójili** NM sauce of garlic and pepper; **~s*** bits and pieces, things, odds and ends; **ahí está el ~*** that's the point, that's the trouble.

ajillo NM chopped garlic; **al ~** with garlic, cooked in garlic.

ajimez NM mullioned window.

ajiseco NM (*And*) mild red pepper.

ajises* NMPL (*LAm*) de **ají**.

ajizarse* [1f] VR (*Cono Sur*) to lose one's temper, get mad.

ajo NM (a) (*Bot*) garlic; (*diente de ~*) clove of garlic; (*salsa*) garlic sauce; **~ tierno** spring onion.
(b) (*fig*) shady deal, secret affair; **¡~ y agua!*** you've just got to put up with it!; **harto de ~s** ill-bred, common; (**tieso**) **como un ~** high and mighty, stuck-up*; **andar** (o **estar**) **en el ~** to be mixed up in it, be concerned in a shady affair; to be in on the secret; **estar como el ~** (*Cono Sur*) to feel miserable; **revolver el ~** to stir up trouble.
(c) (**: palabrota*) swearword, oath, curse; **echar** (o **soltar**) **~s y cebollas** to swear horribly, let fly*.

-ajo, -aja V Aspects of Word Formation in Spanish 2.

ajoaceite NM sauce of garlic and oil.

ajoarriero NM dish of cod with oil, garlic and peppers.

ajobar [1a] VT to carry on one's back, hump*.

ajoblanco NM cold garlic and almond soup.

ajobo NM load; (*fig*) burden.

ajochar [1a] VT (*And*) = **azuzar**.

ajonje NM, **ajonjo** NM birdlime.

ajonjeo NM (*And*) nice remark, compliment.

ajonjolí NM sesame.

ajorca NF bracelet, bangle.

ajornalar [1a] VT to employ by the day.

ajotar [1a] VT (*CAm*) = **azuzar**; (*Carib*) (*desdeñar*) to scorn; (*rechazar*) to rebuff.

ajoto NM (*Carib*) rebuff.

ajuar NM (*muebles*) household furnishings; (*de novia*) trousseau; (*Hist*) dowry, bridal portion; **~ (de niño)** layette.

ajuarar [1a] VT *cuarto etc* to furnish, fit up.

ajuiciado ADJ sensible.

ajuiciar [1b] VT to bring to one's senses.

ajumado* 1 ADJ tight*, tipsy.
2 NM drunk*.

ajumarse* [1a] VR to get tight*.

ajuntarse* [1a] VR to live together, live in sin; (*entre niños*) **¡no me ajunto contigo!*** I'm not your friend any more!

Ajuria Enea NF residence of chief minister of Basque autonomous

government; (*fig*) Basque autonomous government.
ajurídico ADJ (*Cono Sur*) illegal.
ajustado ADJ **(a)** (*apropiado*) right, fitting; **~ a la ley** in accordance with the law. **(b)** *vestido* tight, closefitting; clinging; **muy ~** stretched tight, skintight; too tight.
ajustador NM **(a)** (*chaleco*) bodice, jerkin. **(b)** (*Téc*) fitter. **(c)** **~es** (*Carib*) bra*, brassière.
ajustamiento NM (*Fin*) settlement.
ajustar [1a] 1 VT **(a)** (*Téc etc*) to fit (*a* to, into); to fasten, engage. **(b)** *máquina etc* to adjust, regulate; (*fig*) to adjust, adapt (*a* to); *abuso, error* to put right.
(c) *trato* to strike; *acuerdo* to make; *matrimonio* to arrange; *diferencias* to settle, reconcile, adjust.
(d) *cuenta* to settle (*t fig*).
(e) *precio* to fix.
(f) *criado* to hire, engage.
(g) (*Tip*) to make up.
(h) **~ un golpe a uno** (*And*) to strike sb, lash out at sb.
2 VI to fit; **~ bien** to fit well, be a good fit.
3 **ajustarse** VR **(a)** (*encajarse*) to fit (*a* into).
(b) (*fig*) (*adaptarse*) to adjust o.s., get adjusted (*a* to); (*conformarse*) to conform (*a* to), comply (*a* with); **~ a las reglas** to abide by the rules.
(c) (*fig: llegar a un acuerdo*) to come to an agreement (*con* with).
ajuste NM **(a)** (*Téc etc*) fitting; adjustment; (*Cos*) fit, fitting; (*Méx Aut*) overhaul; **mal ~** maladjustment; **~ de plantilla** (*euf*) redeployment of labour.
(b) (*Fin*) settlement; (*reconciliación*) reconciliation; (*acuerdo*) compromise; (*fig*) **~ de cuentas** getting even, settling of scores.
(c) (*empleo*) hiring, engagement; contract of employment.
(d) (*Tip*) make-up.
(e) (*Jur*) retaining fee; (*sobrepaga*) bonus; **~ por aumento del costo de la vida** cost-of-living bonus.
ajusticiable NMF person who may face capital punishment.
ajusticiamiento NM execution.
ajusticiar [1b] VT to execute.
ajustón NM (*And*) (*castigo*) punishment; (*mal trato*) ill-treatment.
al = **a** + **el**; **al entrar** on entering; **al entrar yo** when I came in; on coming in, I ...; **al verlo yo** when I saw it; on seeing it, I ...; **estar al llegar** to be about to arrive.
ala 1 NF **(a)** (*Orn, Ent, Zool, t fig*) wing; **de cuatro ~s** four-winged; **de ~s azules** blue-winged.
(b) (*Aer*) wing; **~ delta** hang-glider; **con ~s en delta** delta-winged; **con ~s en flecha** swept-wing, with swept-back wings.
(c) (*de sombrero*) brim; (*Arquit: alero*) eaves; (*parte de edificio*) wing; (*Anat: de corazón*) auricle; (*Cono Sur, Méx*) arm; (*de hélice*) blade; (*de mesa*) leaf, flap; **tener bajo el ~** to have under one's arm.
(d) (*Pol*) wing; **el ~ izquierda del partido** the left wing of the party.
(e) (*Mil*) wing, flank.
(f) (*Dep*) wing (*part of field*).
(g) (*frases*) **ser como ~ de mosca** to be paper thin, be transparent; **ahuecar el ~*** to beat it*; to keep out of the way; **arrastrar el ~** to be courting; (*fig*) to be depressed; **se le cayeron las ~s del corazón** his heart fell; **andar con el ~ caída** to be downcast; **cortar las ~s a uno** to clip sb's wings, put sb on a tight rein; **dar ~s a uno** to encourage sb, embolden sb; **quedar tocado uno de ~** to be a lame duck; **tomar ~s*** to get cheeky*; **volar con las propias ~s** to stand on one's own two feet; **en ~s de la fantasía** on (the) wings of fantasy; **las 1000** (*etc*) **del ~** (*Esp**) a cool 1000 pesetas.
2 NMF (*Dep*) winger, wing; **medio ~** half-back, wing-half.
Alá NM Allah.
alabado NM **(a)** **al ~** (*Cono Sur*) at dawn. **(b)** **al ~** (*Méx*) at nightfall.
alabador ADJ approving, eulogistic.
alabamiento NM praise.
alabancioso ADJ boastful.
alabanza NF praise (*a* of); eulogy; **~s** praise, praises; **en ~ de** in praise of; **digno de toda ~** thoroughly praiseworthy, highly commendable; **cantar las ~s de uno** to sing sb's praises.
alabar [1a] 1 VT to praise; *decisión etc* to think right, approve of.
2 **alabarse** VR **(a)** (*jactarse*) to boast; **~ de** to boast of being. **(b)** (*pagarse*) to be pleased, be satisfied.
alabarda NF (*Hist*) halberd.
alabardero NM (*Hist*) halberdier; (*Teat*) paid applauder, member of the claque.
alabastrado ADJ, **alabastrino** ADJ alabastrine, alabaster (*atr*).
alabastro NM alabaster.
álabe NM (*Mec*) wooden cog, tooth; (*de noria*) paddle, bucket; (*Bot*) drooping branch.
alabear [1a] 1 VT to warp.
2 **alabearse** VR to warp.
alabeo NM warp, warping; **tomar ~** to warp.
alacalufe NMF (*Cono Sur*) Indian inhabitant of Tierra del Fuego.

alacena NF food cupboard, larder, closet (*US*).
alacrán NM **(a)** (*Zool*) scorpion. **(b)** (*Cono Sur: chismoso*) gossip, scandalmonger.
alacranear [1a] VI (*Cono Sur*) to gossip, scandalmonger.
alacraneo NM (*Cono Sur*) gossip, scandal; scandalmongering.
alacre ADJ (*Méx*) ready and willing.
alacridad NF alacrity, readiness; **con ~** with alacrity, readily.
alada NF flutter, fluttering; wing-beat.
ALADI [a'laði] NF ABR *de* **Asociación Latinoamericana de Integración.**
Aladino NM Aladdin.
alado ADJ winged, with wings; (*fig*) winged, swift.
alafia NF (*CAm*) verbosity, wordiness.
alafre (*Carib*) 1 ADJ wretched, miserable.
2 NM wretch.
alagartado ADJ motley, variegated.
alalá NM *traditional song in parts of northern Spain.*
ALALC NF ABR *de* **Asociación Latinoamericana de Libre Comercio** Latin-American Free Trade Association, LAFTA.
alambicado ADJ **(a)** (*destilado*) distilled. **(b)** (*fig*) given sparingly, given grudgingly. **(c)** (*fig*) *estilo* subtle, precious, refined; (*pey*) affected. **(d) precios ~s** rock-bottom prices, lowest possible prices.
alambicamiento NM (V ADJ) **(a)** (*destilación*) distilling. **(b)** (*fig*) subtlety, preciosity; (*pey*) affectation.
alambicar [1g] VT **(a)** (*destilar*) to distil. **(b)** (*fig*) *estilo* to subtilize, polish; (*pey*) to overrefine, exaggerate. **(c)** (*fig: escudriñar*) to scrutinize, investigate. **(d)** (*reducir*) to minimize, reduce to a minimum; (*Com*) to reduce (prices) to the minimum.
alambique NM still; **dar algo por ~** to give sth sparingly; **pasar algo por ~** to go through sth with a toothcomb.
alambiquería NF (*Carib*) distillery.
alambiquero NM (*Carib*) distiller.
alambrada NF (*red*) wire netting; (*cerca: t ~ de púas*) wire fence, barbed-wire fence; (*Mil*) barbed-wire entanglement.
alambrado NM (*red*) wire netting; (*cerca*) wire fence; (*Elec*) wiring, wiring system.
alambrar [1a] VT to wire; (*LAm*) to fence (with wire).
alambre NM wire; **~ cargado** live wire; **~ de espino, ~ espinoso, ~ de púas** barbed wire; **~ forrado** insulated wire; **~ de tierra** earth wire, ground wire (*US*); **estar hecho un ~** to be as thin as a rake.
alambrera NF wire screen; wire cover; fireguard.
alambrista NMF tightrope walker.
alambrito NM (*LAm*) tall thin person.
alambrón NM wire rod.
alameda NF (*Bot*) poplar grove; (*calle*) avenue, boulevard, tree-lined walk.
álamo NM poplar; poplar-tree; **~ blanco** white poplar; **~ de Italia** Lombardy poplar; **~ negro** black poplar; **~ temblón** aspen.
alamparse [1a] VR: **~ por** to crave, have a craving for.
alancear [1a] VT to spear.
alano¹ NM mastiff, wolfhound.
alano² (*Hist*) 1 ADJ of the Alani.
2 **~s** NMPL Alani.
alar NM (*tejado*) overhanging roof, eaves; (*LAm: acera*) pavement, sidewalk (*US*); **~es**$ trousers, pants.
alarde NM (*Mil*) review; (*fig*) show, display, parade; (*Dep*) supreme effort, sprint, dash; **~s** (*And, Cono Sur*) boasts, boasting; **en un ~ final** in a final effort; **hacer ~ de** to make a show of, make a parade of; to boast of.
alardeado ADJ vaunted, much boasted-of.
alardear [1a] VI to boast, brag.
alardeo NM boasting, bragging.
alargadera NF (*Quím*) adapter; (*Téc*) extension.
alargado ADJ long, extended.
alargador NM (*Cono Sur Elec*) extension lead.
alargamiento NM lengthening, prolongation, extension; increase.
alargar [1h] 1 VT **(a)** (*gen*) to lengthen, prolong, extend; *vestido* to lengthen, let down; *cuello* to stretch, crane; *mano* to put out, stretch out; *discurso, narración* to spin out.
(b) *cuerda* to pay out.
(c) (*alcanzar*) to reach for; to hand, pass (*a* to).
(d) *sueldo etc* to increase, raise.
(e) *paso* to hasten.
2 **alargarse** VR **(a)** (*gen*) to lengthen, get longer, extend; (*días*) to get longer, draw out; (*discurso etc*) to drag out; (*orador*) to be longwinded.
(b) **~ en** to expatiate on, enlarge upon; **se alargó en la charla** he spun his talk out, he took his time in the talk.
(c) (*irse*) to go away, withdraw.
alargo NM (*Elec*) extension, lead.
alarido NM shriek, yell; **dar ~s** to shriek, yell.
alarife NMF **(a)** (*Arquit*) master-builder; bricklayer. **(b)** (*Cono Sur*) (*tipo listo*) sharp customer*; (*mujer de vida*) loose woman.

alarma NF alarm; **~ aérea** air-raid warning, air alert; **~ antiincendios** fire-alarm; **falsa ~** false alarm; **~ de incendios** fire-alarm; **~ de ladrones** burglar alarm; **con creciente ~** with growing alarm, with growing concern; **señal de ~** alarm signal; **voz de ~** warning note; **timbre de ~** alarm bell; **dar la ~** to raise the alarm.

alarmante ADJ alarming.

alarmantemente ADV alarmingly.

alarmar [1a] ① VT to alarm; to frighten; (*Mil etc*) to alert, rouse; to call to arms.
② **alarmarse** VR to get alarmed, be alarmed; to take fright; **¡no te alarmes!** don't be alarmed!, there's nothing to worry about!

alarmismo NM alarmism; (excessive) alarm.

alarmista ① ADJ alarmist, (excessively) alarming.
② NMF alarmist.

alauí ADJ, **alauita** ADJ Moroccan.

alavense = **alavés**.

alavés ① ADJ of Álava.
② NM, **alavesa** NF native (*o* inhabitant) of Álava; **los alaveses** the people of Álava.

alazán ① ADJ *caballo* sorrel.
② NM sorrel (horse).

alba NF (a) (*amanecer*) dawn, daybreak; **al ~** at dawn; **al rayar** (*o* **romper**) **el ~** at daybreak. (b) (*Ecl*) alb.

albacea NMF executor, (*f*) executrix.

albacetense = **albaceteño**.

albaceteño ① ADJ of Albacete.
② NM, **albaceteña** NF native (*o* inhabitant) of Albacete; **los ~s** the people of Albacete.

albacora NF albacore, longfin tunny.

albahaca NF basil.

albanega NF hairnet.

albanés, -esa ① ADJ, NM/F Albanian.
② NM (*Ling*) Albanian.

Albania NF Albania.

albano = **albanés**.

albañal NM drain, sewer; (*Agr*) dung heap; (*fig*) mess, muck.

albañil NM (a) (*artesano*) bricklayer, mason. (b) (*obrero*) building worker.

albañilería NF (*materias*) brickwork, masonry; (*acto, oficio*) bricklaying, building.

albaquía NF balance due, remainder.

albar ADJ white.

albarán NM (*Com*) delivery note, advice note; invoice; (*señal*) 'to let' sign.

albarda NF packsaddle; (*LAm: silla de montar*) saddle; **~ sobre ~** piling it on, with a lot of unnecessary repetition; **¡como ahora llueven ~s!** not on your life!

albardar [1a] VT to saddle, put a packsaddle on.

albardear* [1a] VT (*CAm*) to bother, vex.

albardilla NF (a) (*silla*) small saddle; (*cojín*) cushion, pad. (b) (*Arquit*) coping. (c) (*Culin*) lard; batter.

albareque NM sardine net.

albaricoque NM apricot.

albaricoquero NM apricot tree.

albariño NM type of Galician wine.

albarrada NF (a) (*muro*) wall. (b) (*And*) cistern.

albatros NM INVAR albatross (*t Golf*).

albayalde NM white lead.

albazo NM (*And, Méx*) dawn raid; (*Cono Sur*) dawn visit.

albeador NM (*Cono Sur* ††) early riser.

albear [1a] VI (*Cono Sur* ††) to get up at dawn, get up early.

albedrío NM (*gen: t* **libre ~**) free will; (*capricho*) whim, fancy; (*gusto*) pleasure; **al ~ de uno** at one's pleasure, just as one likes, to suit o.s.

albéitar NM veterinary surgeon, veterinarian (*US*).

albeitería NF veterinary medicine.

alberca NF cistern, tank, reservoir; (*LAm*) swimming pool.

albérchigo NM (*fruto*) (clingstone) peach; (*árbol*) (clingstone) peach tree.

albergar [1h] ① VT (a) (*gen*) to shelter, give shelter to; to lodge, put up. (b) (*fig*) *esperanza* to cherish; *preocupación* to have, experience.
② **albergarse** VR to shelter; to lodge, stay.

albergue NM (*refugio*) shelter, refuge; (*alojamiento*) lodging; (*Zool*) lair, den; (*Alpinismo*) refuge, mountain hut; **~ de carretera** roadhouse; **~ para jóvenes**, **~ juvenil** youth hostel; **~ nacional** state-owned tourist hotel; **dar ~ a uno** to give sb lodging, take sb in.

alberguista NMF youth-hosteller.

albero ① ADJ white.
② NM (a) (*Geol*) pipeclay. (b) (*paño*) dishcloth, tea-towel.

Alberto NM Albert.

albillo ADJ *uva, vino* white.

albina NF salt lake, salt marsh.

albinismo NM albinism.

albino, -a ADJ, NM/F albino.

Albión NF Albion; **la pérfida ~** perfidious Albion.

albis: quedarse en ~ not to know a thing, not have a clue; **me quedé en ~** my mind went blank.

albo ADJ (*liter*) white.

albogue NM (*flauta*) rustic flute, shepherd's flute; (*gaita*) bagpipes; **~s** cymbals.

albóndiga NF rissole, meatball.

albondigón NM hamburger.

albor NM (a) (*blancura*) whiteness. (b) (*alba*) dawn, dawn light; **~ de la vida** childhood, youth; **~es** dawn; **a los ~es** at dawn.

alborada NF dawn; (*Mil*) reveille; (*Poét, Mús*) aubade, dawn song; (*Méx Rel*) night procession.

alborear [1a] VI to dawn.

albornoz NM (a) (*de árabe*) burnous(e). (b) (*de baño*) bathing wrap, bathrobe.

alborotadamente ADV excitedly; noisily, roughly; riotously.

alborotadizo ADJ turbulent; excitable, nervy, jumpy.

alborotado ADJ (a) (*excitado*) agitated, excited; (*ruidoso*) noisy, rough; (*amotinado*) mutinous, riotous; *período* disturbed, eventful. (b) (*precipitado*) hasty, rash; (*impetuoso*) reckless.

alborotador ① ADJ turbulent, rebellious; boisterous, noisy; mischief-making.
② NM, **alborotadora** NF agitator, troublemaker, mischief-maker; rioter.

alborotar [1a] ① VT (a) (*agitar*) to disturb, agitate, stir up; (*amotinar*) to incite to rebel.
(b) (*excitar*) to excite, arouse the curiosity of.
② VI to make a racket, make a row.
③ **alborotarse** VR (a) (*persona*) to get excited, get worked up; (*turba etc*) to riot, become violent; (*mar*) to get rough.
(b) (*CAm: ponerse amoroso*) to become amorous.
(c) (*Cono Sur: caballo*) to rear up.

alboroto NM (a) (*disturbio*) disturbance, (*vocerío*) racket, row, uproar; (*pelea*) brawl; (*motín*) riot; **armar un ~** to cause a commotion. (b) (*susto*) scare, shock, alarm. (c) **~s** (*And, CAm*) popcorn.

alborotoso (*And, Carib*) ① ADJ troublesome, riotous.
② NM, **alborotosa** NF troublemaker.

alborozado ADJ jubilant, overjoyed.

alborozar [1f] ① VT to gladden, fill with joy.
② **alborozarse** VR to be overjoyed, rejoice.

alborozo NM joy, merriment.

albricias NFPL (a) (*regalo*) gift, reward (to sb bringing good news). (b) (*como interj*) good news!, listen to this!; congratulations!

albufera NF (*Valencia y Mallorca*) lagoon.

álbum NM album; (*Mús*) album, (*elepé*) long-playing record; **~ doble** double album; **~ de recortes** scrapbook; **~ de sellos**, **~ de estampillas** (*LAm*) stamp album.

albumen NM white of egg; (*Bot*) albumen.

albúmina NF (*Quím*) albumin.

albuminoso ADJ albuminous.

albur NM (a) (*Esp Pez*) bleak. (b) (*riesgo*) chance, risk; (*Méx: juego de palabras*) pun, play on words; (*Carib: mentira*) lie.

albura NF (*blancura*) whiteness; (*de huevo*) white of egg.

alburear [1a] ① VT (*CAm*) to disturb, upset.
② VI (a) (*enriquecerse*) (*And*) to make money, get rich; (*Carib*) to line one's pockets. (b) (*Méx*) to pun, play with words.

alca NF razorbill.

alcabala NF (a) (*Hist*) sales tax. (b) (*Cono Sur*) police roadblock, checkpoint.

alcachofa NF (a) artichoke; **~ de (la) ducha** shower head. (b) (*Radio**) microphone.

alcahué* NM = **cacahuete**; *V t* **maní**.

alcahueta NF (*de mujeres*) procuress; (*intermediaria*) go-between; (*chismosa*) gossip.

alcahuete NM (a) (*chulo*) procurer, pimp; (*intermediario*) go-between; (*perista*) front man, receiver (of stolen goods). (b) (*Teat*) drop-curtain.

alcahuetear [1a] VI to procure, pimp; to act as a go-between; to act as front man, be a receiver (of stolen goods).

alcahuetería NF procuring, pimping; **~s** pimping.

alcaide NM (*Hist: de castillo, cárcel*) governor; (*carcelero*) warder, jailer.

alcaidía NF (*Hist*) governorship.

alcaldable NMF candidate for mayor; possible mayor, potential mayor.

alcaldada NF abuse of authority; arbitrary act, arbitrary decision.

alcalde NM (a) mayor; **tener el padre ~** to have influence. (b) (*LAm**) procurer, pimp.

alcaldear* [1a] VI to lord it, be bossy.

alcaldesa NF (woman) mayor; mayoress.

alcaldía NF (*oficio*) mayoralty, office of mayor; (*oficina*) mayor's office.

alcalducho* NM jumped-up mayor, power-mad mayor.

álcali NM alkali.
alcalino ADJ alkaline.
alcaloide NM alkaloid.
alcaloideo ADJ alkaloid.
alcamonero ADJ (*Carib*: *entrometido*) meddlesome.
alcamonías NFPL (a) (*Culin*) aromatic seeds (for seasoning). (b) (*: *alcahuetería*) pimping.
alcance NM (a) (*del brazo etc*) reach; **estar al ~ de uno** to be within one's reach, (*fig*) be within one's powers; **el que está más al ~** the one which is nearest, the one which is most readily accessible; **estar fuera del ~ de uno** to be out of one's reach, be beyond one's reach, (*fig*) to be over one's head, be inaccessible; **poner el coche al ~ de todos** to put the car within the reach of everybody, make the car accessible to all; **al ~ del oído** within earshot; **al ~ de la voz** within call.
(b) (*Mil etc*) range; (*fig*) scope; grasp; importance, significance; **el ~ del problema** the extent of the problem; **al ~** within range; **al ~ de la vista** within sight; **de gran ~** (*Mil*) long-range, (*fig*) far-reaching.
(c) (*persecución*) chase, pursuit; **dar ~ a** to catch up (with), overtake; **seguir el ~ a** (*Mil*) to pursue; **andar** (*o* **ir**) **a los ~s de uno** to press close on sb, be on sb's tracks; **andar** (*o* **ir**) **en los ~s a uno** to spy on sb.
(d) (*Fin*) adverse balance, deficit.
(e) (*Tip*) stop-press (news).
(f) (*inteligencia*) intelligence, capacity; **de cortos ~s** of limited intelligence, not very bright.
(g) **buzón de ~** late-collection postbox.
(h) **~s** (*CAm*: *calumnias*) calumnies, malicious accusations.
alcancía NF (a) (*hucha*) moneybox; (*LAm Ecl*) collection box, poorbox. (b) (*) cunt*; (c) (*Méx*: *cárcel*) nick*, can*.
alcancil NM (*Cono Sur*) procurer, pimp.
alcándara NF clothes rack; (*Orn*) perch.
alcandora NF beacon.
alcanfor NM (a) (*Bot*) camphor. (b) (*LAm*: *alcahuete*) procurer, pimp.
alcanforado 1 ADJ camphorated.
2 NM (*LAm*) procurer, pimp.
alcanforar [1a] 1 VT to camphorate.
2 **alcanforarse** VR (*And, CAm, Carib*) to disappear, make o.s. scarce*.
alcantarilla NF (*boca*) drain; (*cloaca*) sewer, drain; (*conducto*) culvert, conduit; (*Carib, Méx*) public fountain; (*And*: *para goma*) vessel for collecting latex.
alcantarillado NM sewer system, drains.
alcantarillar [1a] VT to lay sewers in, provide drains for.
alcanzadizo ADJ easy to reach, easily reachable, accessible.
alcanzado ADJ (a) (*) hard up*, broke*; **salir ~** to make a loss. (b) (*And*) (*fatigado*) tired; (*atrasado*) slow, late.
alcanzar [1f] 1 VT (a) (*en carrera etc*) to catch, catch up (with); to overtake; **tren, correo** to catch; **cuando le alcancé** when I caught up with him; **no nos alcanzarán nunca** they'll never catch us.
(b) (*bala etc*) to hit, strike; **un obús alcanzó la lancha** the launch was hit by a shell; **el presidente fue alcanzado por 2 balas** the president was struck by 2 bullets.
(c) (*llegar a*) to reach; to amount to; **la producción ha alcanzado las 20 toneladas** production has reached 20 tons; **el libro ha alcanzado 20 ediciones** the book has run into 20 editions; **las montañas alcanzan los 5.000 m** the mountains rise to 5,000 m.
(d) (*sentidos*) to reach to, perceive, take in.
(e) (*vivir hasta*) to live into the period of, live on into the time of.
(f) (*agarrar*) to grasp, catch hold of; *puesto* to get, obtain.
(g) *problema* to grasp, understand.
(h) (*And, Cono Sur*: *entregar*) to pass, hand over; (*traer*) to get, bring, fetch; (*dar*) to give; **alcánzame la sal, por favor** pass me the salt, please.
2 VI (a) (*llegar*) to reach, extend (*a, hasta* to, as far as); **~ para todos** to be enough (for everybody), go round; **no me alcanza el dinero** my money won't stretch to it; **el sueldo no alcanza para nada** I can't make ends meet on my salary; **¿a cuánto alcanza?** (*LAm*) how much does it all come to?
(b) **~ a + infin** to manage to + *infin*; **no alcanzo a ver cómo ...** I can't see how ...; **no alcanza a hacerlo** he can't manage to do it.
alcanzativo ADJ (*CAm*) suspicious.
alcaparra NF (*Bot*) caper.
alcaraván NM stone-curlew.
alcaravea NF caraway.
alcarreño 1 ADJ of La Alcarria.
2 NM, **alcarreña** NF native (*o* inhabitant) of La Alcarria; **los ~s** the people of La Alcarria.
alcatraz NM gannet, solan goose.
alcaucil NM (a) (*Bot*) artichoke. (b) (*Cono Sur*) (*informador*) informer, nark*; (*alcahuete*) pimp.
alcaudón NM shrike.

alcayata NF meat hook, spike; (*Méx*) hook.
alcayota NF squash, vegetable marrow.
alcazaba NF citadel, castle.
alcázar NM (*Mil*) fortress, citadel; (*palacio*) royal palace; (*Náut*) quarter-deck.
alcazuz NM liquorice.
alce[1] NM (*Zool*) elk, moose; **~ de América** moose.
alce[2] NM (*Naipes*) cut; **no dar ~ a uno** (*Cono Sur*) to give sb no respite (*o* rest).
alción NM kingfisher; (*clásico*) halcyon.
alcista (*Com, Fin*) 1 ADJ: **mercado ~** bull (*o* bullish) market, rising market; **la tendencia ~** the upward tendency, the upward trend.
2 NM bull, speculator.
alcoba NF (a) (*dormitorio*) bedroom; (*Méx Ferro*) sleeping compartment. (b) (*muebles*) suite of bedroom furniture.
alcohol NM alcohol; **~ absoluto** absolute alcohol, pure alcohol; **~ desnaturalizado, ~ metilado, ~ metílico, ~ de quemar** methylated spirit; **~ vínico** vinic alcohol; **lámpara de ~** spirit lamp.
alcoholemia NF blood-level of alcohol; **control de ~, prueba de ~, test de ~** breath test.
alcoholero ADJ alcohol (*atr*).
alcohólico 1 ADJ alcoholic; **no ~** *bebida* non-alcoholic, soft.
2 NM, **alcohólica** NF alcoholic.
alcoholímetro NM Breathalyser ®.
alcoholismo NM alcoholism.
alcoholista NMF (*Cono Sur*) drunk*.
alcoholizado, -a NM/F alcoholic; **morir ~** to die of alcoholism.
alcoholizar [1f] 1 VT to alcoholize.
2 **alcoholizarse** VR to drink heavily.
alcor NM hill.
Alcorán NM Koran.
alcornoque NM (a) (*Bot*) cork tree, cork oak. (b) (*) idiot.
alcorza NF (a) (*Culin*) icing, sugar paste. (b) (*Cono Sur*: *tipo sensible*) crybaby, sensitive soul.
alcorzar [1f] VT (*Culin*) to ice.
alcotán NM (*Orn*) hobby.
alcotana NF pickaxe, mattock.
alcubilla NF cistern, reservoir.
alcucero ADJ sweet-toothed; greedy.
alcurnia NF ancestry, lineage; **de ~** of noble family, of noble birth.
alcurniado ADJ aristocratic, noble.
alcuza NF (*para aceite*) olive-oil bottle; (*LAm*: *vinagreras*) cruet, cruet stand.
alcuzcuz NM couscous.
aldaba NF (a) (*de puerta*) (door-)knocker; (*cerrojo*) bolt, latch, crossbar; (*para caballo*) hitching ring; **tener buenas ~s** to have influence, have friends in the right places. (b) **~s** tits*.
aldabada NF knock (on the door); **dar ~s en** to knock at.
aldabilla NF latch.
aldabón NM (*de puerta*) large (door-)knocker; (*de baúl etc*) large handle.
aldabonazo NM bang, loud knock (on the door); (*fig*) knock, blow; **dar ~s en** to bang at.
aldea NF (small) village, hamlet.
aldeanismo NM provincialism, parish-pump attitudes.
aldeano 1 ADJ (a) (*de pueblo*) village (*atr*); (*fig*) rustic, rude; **gente aldeana** country people, village people.
(b) (*pey*) provincial, parish-pump (*atr*); **actitud aldeana** parish-pump attitude.
2 NM, **aldeana** NF villager; peasant; **los ~s** the villagers, the village people.
aldehuela NF hamlet.
aldeorrio NM backward little place, rural backwater.
alderredor ADV = **alrededor**.
aldosterona NF aldosterone.
aldrina NF aldrin.
aleación NF alloy; **~ ligera** light alloy.
aleado ADJ alloyed, alloy (*atr*).
alear[1] [1a] VT (*Téc*) to alloy.
alear[2] [1a] VI (*ave*) to flutter, flap (its wings); (*persona*) to move one's arms up and down; (*Med*) to improve; **ir aleando** to be improving.
aleatoriamente ADV randomly.
aleatoriedad NF randomness.
aleatorio ADJ accidental, fortuitous; uncertain; (*Estadística*) random, aleatory.
aleatorizar [1f] VT to randomize.
alebrarse [1j] VR to lie flat, squat; (*fig*) to cower; to lose heart.
alebrestar [1a] 1 VT (a) (*LAm*) (*alterar*) to distress, disturb; (*emocionar*) to excite, stimulate.
2 **alebrestarse** VR (a) (*LAm*) (*alterarse*) to get distressed, become agitated; (*emocionarse*) to get excited; to become enthusiastic. (b) (*Carib*: *rebelarse*) to rebel. (c) (*And*: *caballo*) to rear up.

aleccionador ADJ instructive, enlightening.

aleccionamiento NM instruction, enlightenment; training.

aleccionar [1a] VT (*instruir*) to instruct, enlighten, teach a lesson to; (*adiestrar*) to train; (*regañar*) to lecture.

alechado ADJ (*LAm*) milky, like milk; mixed with milk.

alechugado ADJ pleated; frilled, frilly; crimped.

alechugar [1h] VT to fold, pleat; to frill; to crimp.

aledaño [1] ADJ adjoining, bordering.
[2] NM boundary, limit; **~s** outskirts; surrounding area.

alefra INTERJ: **¡~!** (*Carib*) touch wood!

alegación NF declaration (in court); citation; claim, counterclaim; (*Carib, Cono Sur, Méx*) argument; **~ de culpabilidad** (*Méx Jur*) plea of guilty; **~ de inocencia** (*Méx Jur*) plea of not guilty.

alegador [1] ADJ (*Cono Sur*) argumentative.
[2] NM, **alegadora** NF argumentative person.

alegal ADJ (*Cono Sur Jur*) illegal.

alegar [1h] [1] VT (**a**) (*Jur etc*) *autoridad* to cite, invoke; to state; to bring forward as an argument; *méritos etc* to cite, adduce, produce in support; **~ que ...** to claim that ..., argue that ...; **alegando que ...** claiming that ..., on the grounds that ...
(**b**) (*LAm: disputar*) to argue against, dispute.
[2] VI (*LAm: discutir*) to argue, quarrel; (*protestar*) to complain loudly, kick up a fuss.

alegata NF (*LAm*) fight.

alegato NM (**a**) (*alegación*) claim. (**b**) (*Jur*) bill (of indictment); plea, argument.

alegoría NF allegory.

alegóricamente ADV allegorically.

alegórico ADJ allegoric(al).

alegorizar [1f] VT to allegorize.

alegrador ADJ cheering.

▼ **alegrar** [1a] [1] VT (**a**) *persona* to cheer (up), gladden; to make merry, make happy; **esta noticia alegró a todos** this news cheered everyone up, this news made everyone happy.
(**b**) *reunión etc* to enliven, cheer up, brighten up; *fuego* to stir up, make brighter.
(**c**) *toro* to excite, stir up.
(**d**) (*Náut*) *cuerda* to slacken.

▼ [2] **alegrarse** VR (**a**) (*estado*) to be glad, be happy, rejoice; **me alegro muchísimo** I'm delighted; **~ con, ~ de, ~ por** to be glad about, rejoice at; **~ de** + *infin* to be glad to + *infin*, be happy to + *infin*; **me alegro de saberlo** I am glad to hear it; **me alegro de que lo hayas hecho** I am glad you've done it.
(**b**) (*acto*) to cheer up (*de* at); **con esto empezó a ~** at this he began to cheer up.
(**c**) (*: emborracharse*) to get merry*, get tight*.

alegre ADJ (**a**) *persona* happy, merry, glad; carefree; (*temperamento*) cheerful, gay, sunny; *cara etc* happy; *música etc* merry, gay, cheerful; *noticia* good, cheering; *color* bright; *día, período* happy; *tiempo* cheerful, bright, pleasant; **~ de corazón** light-hearted.
(**b**) (*atrevido*) bold, reckless.
(**c**) *chiste* risqué, blue.
(**d**) *vida* fast, immoral; (*) *chica* fast, free-and-easy, swinging*.
(**e**) **estar ~*** to be merry*, be tight*.

alegremente ADV happily, merrily; cheerfully, gaily; brightly; recklessly.

alegría NF (**a**) (*gen*) happiness, joy; gladness; cheerfulness; gaiety, merriment; brightness; **¡qué ~!** that's great!, that's splendid!; **~ vital** joie de vivre; **saltar de ~** to jump with joy, jump for joy.
(**b**) (*pey*) recklessness, irresponsibility
(**c**) **~s** public rejoicings, festivities.
(**d**) **ser el ~s** (*iró*) to be very glum, be downcast.
(**e**) **~s** (*Esp*) naughty bits.
(**f**) (*Bot*) **~ de la casa** balsam.

alegro NM allegro.

alegrón NM (**a**) (*fig*) sudden joy. (**b**) (*de fuego*) sudden blaze, flare-up.

alegrona NF (*LAm*) prostitute.

alehop INTERJ hup!

alejado ADJ distant, remote (*from* de).

alejamiento NM (**a**) (*acto*) removal; withdrawal; estrangement. (**b**) (*estado*) distance, remoteness; aloofness.

Alejandría NF Alexandria.

alejandrino NM alexandrine.

Alejandro NM Alexander; **~ Magno** Alexander the Great.

alejar [1a] [1] VT (**a**) (*gen*) to remove, move away (*de* from), move to a distance; *peligro* to remove; *persona* to remove, dismiss; *sospecha* to divert; (*deshacerse de*) to get rid of; **conviene ~ tales libros de los niños** such books should be kept away from children, such books should be kept out of children's hands.
(**b**) (*fig*) to cause a rift between, separate, estrange.
[2] **alejarse** VR to move away, go away (*de* from); to move to a distance; (*ruido*) to grow fainter; (*peligro*) to recede; **alejémonos un**

poco más let's go a bit further away; **~ del buen camino** to get off the right road, lose one's way.

alelado ADJ (*aturdido*) stupefied, bewildered; (*bobo*) foolish, stupid.

alelamiento NM bewilderment; foolishness, stupidity.

alelar [1a] [1] VT to stupefy; to bewilder.
[2] **alelarse** VR to be stupefied, be bewildered; to look foolish, gape stupidly.

aleluya [1] NM o F hallelujah.
[2] NM Easter time.
[3] NF Easter print; strip cartoon with rhyming couplets (*originally on religious themes*); (*Arte*) daub, bad painting; (*LAm*) frivolous excuse; (*And*) spoiled child; thing that one loves excessively; (*Poét*) **~s** doggerel; **estar de ~** to rejoice; **ir al ~** (*Carib*) to go Dutch*, share costs.
[4] NMF (*: persona*) hot-gospeller, evangelical.

alelúyico ADJ evangelical.

alemán, -ana [1] ADJ, NM/F German.
[2] NM (*Ling*) German.

Alemania NF Germany.

alentada NF big breath, deep breath; **de una ~** in one breath.

alentado ADJ (*valiente*) brave; (*orgulloso*) proud, haughty; (*Cono Sur: fuerte*) strong, vigorous; (*CAm, Méx: mejorado*) improved, better.

alentador ADJ encouraging.

alentar [1j] [1] VT (**a**) (*gen*) to encourage, cheer, inspire; *resistencia* to stiffen, bolster up; *ánimos* to raise, buoy up; **~ a uno a hacer algo** to encourage sb to do sth; to inspire sb to do sth.
(**b**) (*And: aplaudir*) to clap, applaud.
[2] VI (**a**) (*gen*) to breathe, take a breath.
(**b**) (*fig*) to burn, glow; **en su pecho alienta mucho patriotismo** patriotism burns strongly in his heart.
[3] **alentarse** VR (**a**) (*gen*) to take heart, cheer up.
(**b**) (*Med*) to get well.
(**c**) (*And, CAm: dar a luz*) to give birth (*de* to).

aleonarse [1a] VR (*Cono Sur*) to get excited, get worked up; to cause uproar (*o* a commotion).

aleoyota NF (*Cono Sur Bot*) pumpkin.

alepantado ADJ (*And*) absent-minded.

alerce NM larch, larch tree.

alergeno NM, **alérgeno** NM allergen.

alergia NF allergy; **~ polínica** pollen allergy, allergy to pollen; **~ a la primavera** hay-fever; **tener ~ a** to be allergic to (*t fig*).

alérgico ADJ allergic (*a* to).

alergista NMF, **alergólogo, -a** NM/F allergist, specialist in allergies.

alergológico ADJ allergy (*atr*).

alero NM (**a**) (*Arquit*) eaves; gable-end; (*Aut*) wing; **estar (o seguir) en el ~** (*fig*) to be unsure, remain undecided. (**b**) (*Dep*) winger.

alerón NM (**a**) (*Aer*) aileron. (**b**) (*Anat*) armpit.

alerta INVAR [1] INTERJ watch out!
[2] ADV Y ADJ alert, watchful; **estar ~, estar ojo ~** to be on the alert, stand by, watch out; **todos los servicios de auxilio están ~** all the rescue services are on the alert.
[3] NF alert; (*Mil*) early warning; **~ rojo** red alert.

alertar [1a] [1] VT to alert, warn, put on one's guard.
[2] VI to be alert, keep one's eyes open.

alesnado ADJ (*Carib*) brave, intrepid.

aleta NF (*Orn etc*) wing, small wing; (*Aut*) wing, mudguard, fin; (*de hélice*) blade; (*de pez*) fin; (*de foca, t Dep*) flipper; (*: mano*) mitt, flipper*.

aletargado ADJ drowsy, lethargic; benumbed.

aletargamiento NM drowsiness, lethargy; numbness.

aletargar [1h] [1] VT to make drowsy, make lethargic; to numb.
[2] **aletargarse** VR to grow drowsy, become lethargic; to get numb.

aletazo NM (**a**) (*ave*) wingbeat, flap (of the wing); (*pez etc*) movement of the fin. (**b**) (*Cono Sur: fig: bofetada*) punch, slap. (**c**) (*CAm*) (*hurto*) robbery; (*estafa*) swindle.

aletear [1a] VI (*ave*) to flutter, flap its wings; (*pez*) to move its fins.

aleteo NM fluttering, flapping (of the wings); movements of the fins; (*Med*) palpitation.

aleudar [1a] [1] VT to leaven, ferment with yeast.
[2] **aleudarse** VR to rise.

aleve ADJ treacherous, perfidious.

alevín NM young fish, fry; (*fig*) beginner, neophyte, novice.

alevino NM (*LAm*) young fish, alevin, fry (*for restocking rivers etc*).

alevosía NF treachery.

alevoso [1] ADJ treacherous.
[2] NM traitor.

alfa¹ NF (*letra*) alpha.

alfa² NM (*LAm*) lucerne, alfalfa.

alfabéticamente ADV alphabetically.

alfabético ADJ alphabetic(al).

alfabetismo NM literacy.

alfabetización NF teaching literacy (*o* reading and writing); **campaña de ~** literacy campaign, drive to teach people to read and

➤ LENGUA Y USO: **alegrar: 1a** → 48.1, 51.1, 51.2 **2** → 51.3, 52.4

write.
alfabetizado ADJ literate, that can read and write.
alfabetizador(a) NM/F literacy tutor.
alfabetizar [1f] VT **(a)** (*ordenar*) to alphabetize, arrange alphabetically. **(b)** ~ **a uno** to teach sb to read and write.
alfabeto NM alphabet; ~ **Morse** Morse code; ~ **romano** Roman alphabet.
alfajor NM **(a)** (*LAm: dulce*) type of fudge; (*And: pasta*) puff pastry; (*Esp: polvorón*) cake eaten at Christmas. **(b)** (*Cono Sur* ††) = **facón**.
alfalfa NF lucerne, alfalfa.
alfalfar NM lucerne field.
alfandoque NM **(a)** (*CAm, Carib, Méx: pasta*) a kind of sweet pastry. **(b)** (*And, CAm Mús*) maraca-like instrument, cylindrical rattle. **(c)** (*And: dulce*) toffee-like almond paste. **(d)** (*Carib: pastelito*) small honey cake.
alfanje NM cutlass; (*Pez*) swordfish.
alfanumérico ADJ alphanumeric.
alfaque NM y ~**s** PL (*Náut*) bar, bank, shoal.
alfaquí NM Moslem doctor, ulema, expounder of the Law.
alfar NM **(a)** (*taller*) pottery, potter's workshop. **(b)** (*arcilla*) clay.
alfarería NF (*cerámica*) pottery; (*tienda*) pottery shop.
alfarero, -a NM/F potter.
alfarjía NF (*esp for door o window frames*) batten.
alféizar NM (*Arquit*) splay, embrasure; sill, windowsill, ledge.
alfeñicado* ADJ **(a)** (*débil*) weakly, delicate. **(b)** (*afectado*) affected.
alfeñicarse* [1g] VR **(a)** (*enflaquecerse*) to get terribly thin, look frail. **(b)** (*remilgarse*) to act affectedly, be overnice; to be very prim and proper.
alfeñique NM **(a)** (*Culin*) toffee-like paste, almond-flavoured sugar paste. **(b)** (*: *persona*) delicate person; mollycoddle, sissy*; very thin person. **(c)** (*cualidad*) affectation; primness; excessive delicacy.
alferecía NF epilepsy.
alférez NM (*Mil*) second lieutenant, subaltern; (*LAm Ecl*) official standard-bearer (in processions); ~ **de fragata** midshipman; ~ **de navío** sub-lieutenant.
alfil NM (*Ajedrez*) bishop.
alfiler NM (*gen*) pin; (*broche*) brooch, clip; ~**es** pin-money, dress allowance; ~ **de corbata** tiepin; ~ **de gancho** (*Cono Sur*) safety-pin; ~ **de seguridad** (*LAm*) safety-pin; ~ **de sombrero** hatpin; **aquí ya no cabe ni un** ~ you can't squeeze anything else in; **pedir para ~es** to ask for a tip; **prendido con ~es** shaky, hardly hanging together; **puesto con 25 ~es** dressed up to the nines.
alfilerar [1a] VT to pin together, pin up.
alfilerazo NM pinprick (*t fig*); **tirar ~s a uno** to have a dig at sb.
alfilerillo NM (*And, Cono Sur*) type of spikenard used for animal feeding.
alfiletero NM needle case; pincushion.
alfolí NM (*de granos*) granary; (*de sal*) salt warehouse.
alfombra NF carpet; rug, mat; ~ **de baño** bathmat; ~ **encantada**, ~ **mágica** magic carpet; ~ **de oración** prayer-mat; ~ **voladora** flying carpet.
alfombrado NM carpeting.
alfombrar [1a] VT to carpet (*t fig*).
alfombrero, -a NM/F carpet maker.
alfombrilla NF **(a)** (*alfombra*) rug, mat; ~ **roja** red carpet. **(b)** (*Med: sarampión*) German measles; (*Carib: sarpullido*) rash; (*Méx: viruela*) smallpox.
alfonsí ADJ Alphonsine (*esp re Alfonso X, 1252-84*).
alfonsino ADJ Alphonsine (*esp re recent kings of Spain named Alfonso*).
Alfonso NM Alphonso; ~ **el Sabio** Alphonso the Wise (*1252-84*).
alforfón NM buckwheat.
alforja NF (*de jinete*) saddlebag; (*mochila*) knapsack; (*de bicicleta*) pannier; ~**s** (*t fig*) provisions (for a journey); **pasarse a la otra** ~ (*Cono Sur*) to overstep the mark, go too far; **sacar los pies de las ~s** to go off on a different tack; **para ese viaje no hacían falta ~s** (*fig*) there was no point in making such elaborate preparations, you didn't have to go to such trouble.
alforjudo ADJ (*Cono Sur*) silly, stupid.
alforza NF pleat, tuck; (*fig*) slash, scar.
alforzar [1f] VT (*Cos*) to pleat, tuck.
Alfredo NM Alfred.
alga NF seaweed, alga; ~ **tóxica** toxic alga.
algaida NF (*Bot*) bush, undergrowth; (*Geog*) dune.
algalia[1] NF (*Zool*) civet.
algalia[2] NF (*Med*) catheter.
algara NF (*Hist*) raid; raiding party.
algarabía NF **(a)** (*Ling*) Arabic. **(b)** (*) (*habla*) double Dutch*, gibberish; gabble; (*jaleo*) din, hullabaloo*. **(c)** (*Bot*) cornflower.
algarada NF **(a)** (*griterío*) outcry; **hacer una** ~, **levantar una** ~ to kick up a tremendous fuss. **(b)** (*Hist*) cavalry raid; cavalry troop.
algarero ADJ noisy, rowdy.
algarroba NF carob, carob bean.
algarrobo NM carob tree, locust tree.
Algarve NM: **el** ~ the Algarve.
algazara NF din, clamour, uproar.
álgebra NF algebra; ~ **de Boole**, ~ **booleana** Boolean algebra.
algebraico ADJ algebraic.
algecireño [1] ADJ of Algeciras. [2] NM, **algecireña** NF native (*o* inhabitant) of Algeciras; **los ~s** the people of Algeciras.
álgido ADJ icy, cold, chilly; (*fig*) **punto** etc culminating, decisive; most intense.
algo [1] PRON **(a)** (*en frases afirmativas*) something; **habrá ~ para ti** there will be something in it for you; **esto es ~ nuevo** this is something new; ~ **es** ~ something is better than nothing; **eso ya es ~** that's something; **más vale** ~ **que nada** something is better than nothing; **¡por ~ será!** there must be a reason behind it, he (*etc*) can't have done it for no reason at all; **ya es ~** it's a start; **creerse ~** to think one is somebody; **tener un** ~ to have a certain charm; **estar en ~** (*LAm*) to be high (on drugs)♣; to be involved in something; **tomar ~** to have a drink. **(b)** (*en frases interrog y neg*) anything; **¿pasa ~?** is anything the matter?; **¿hay ~ para mí?** is there anything for me? [2] ADV rather, somewhat, a bit; **es ~ difícil** it's rather hard, it's a bit awkward. [3] NM (*And*) snack, something to eat; *ver también* ALGUNO, ALEGO .
algodón NM cotton; wadding; (*Med*) swab; (*Bot*) cotton plant; ~ **de azúcar**, ~ **de caramelo**, ~ **dulce** candy-floss, cotton candy (*US*); ~ **hidrófilo** cotton wool, absorbent cotton (*US*); ~ **labrado** patterned cotton; ~ **pólvora** guncotton; ~ **en rama** raw cotton, cotton wool; **se crió entre algodones** he was always pampered; he was brought up in luxury.
algodonal NM cotton plantation.
algodonar [1a] VT to stuff with cotton wool, wad.
algodoncillo NM milkweed.
algodoncito NM cotton-wool swab, cotton bud.
algodonero [1] ADJ cotton (*atr*). [2] NM **(a)** (*cultivador*) cotton grower; (*comerciante*) cotton dealer. **(b)** (*Bot*) cotton plant.
algodonosa NF cotton grass.
algodonoso ADJ cottony.
algorítmica NF algorithms.
algoritmo NM algorithm.
alguacil NM (*Hist*) governor; bailiff, constable; (*Taur: t* **alguacilillo**) mounted official.
alguicida NM algicide.
alguien PRON someone, somebody; anybody; **si ~ viene** if somebody comes, if anybody comes; **¿viste a ~?** did you see anybody?; **para ~ que conozca la materia** for anyone who is familiar with the subject; **ser ~** to be somebody; ~ **se lo habrá dicho** someone or other must have told him.
alguita♣ NF (*And*) money, dough♣.
alguito (*LAm*) = **algo**.
alguno [1] ADJ (**algún** *delante de* NM SING) **(a)** (*delante de* N) some, any; **some ... or other; algún obispo lo dijo** some bishop said so; **algún coche lo tiene ya** some cars already have it; **hubo algunas dificultades** there were some difficulties; there were a few difficulties; **algún que otro libro** an odd book or two; a few odd books; **leo algún libro que otro** I read an occasional book, I read a book from time to time; **por alguna que otra razón** for some reason or other. **(b)** (*precedido por neg, tras* N) no, not ... any; **no tiene talento** ~ he has no talent, he hasn't any talent, he has no talent at all; **sin interés** ~ without the slightest interest. [2] PRON **(a)** (*sing*) some; one; someone, somebody; ~ **es bueno** some are good, an occasional one is good; ~ **de ellos** one of them; ~ **que otro** one or two, an occasional one; ~ **dijo que ...** someone said that ...; **busco ~ que me ayude** I'm looking for somebody to help me. **(b)** ~**s** some; a few; ~**s son buenos** some are good; **vimos ~s** we saw some; we saw a few; **hay ~s que ...** there are some who ...; ~**s nunca están contentos** some are never happy.
alhaja NF **(a)** (*joya*) jewel, gem; (*objeto precioso*) precious object, treasure; (*mueble*) fine piece (of furniture). **(b)** (*fig: persona*) treasure, gem; **¡buena ~!** (*iró*) she's a fine one!
alhajado ADJ (*And*) wealthy.
alhajar [1a] VT **cuarto** to furnish, appoint (in delicate taste).
alhajera NF (*Cono Sur*) jewel box.
alharaca NF fuss; **hacer ~s** to make a fuss, make a great song and dance about sth.
alharaquiento ADJ demonstrative, highly emotional.
alhelí NM wallflower, stock.

alheña NF (a) (*Bot*) (*planta*) privet; (*flor*) privet flower; (*para teñir*) henna. (b) (*roya*) blight, mildew.

ALGUNO, ALGO — *ver también las entradas*

"Some" y "any" en oraciones afirmativas e interrogativas

Frases Afirmativas

- En frases afirmativas debe usarse *some* o las formas compuestas de *some*:

  He leído algunos artículos interesantes sobre el tema
  I have read some interesting articles on the subject
  Algunos no están de acuerdo
  Some people disagree
  He comprado algo para ti
  I've bought something for you

Frases Interrogativas

- En frases interrogativas que expresan algún tipo de ofrecimiento o petición y cuya respuesta se espera que sea positiva, también debe emplearse la forma *some, etc*:

  Tienes muchos libros. ¿Me dejas alguno?
  You've got lots of books. Can I borrow some?

- En el resto de las frases interrogativas, empléese *any* o las formas compuestas de *any*:

  ¿Se te ocurre alguna otra idea?
  Do you have any other ideas?
  ¿Hay algún sitio donde podamos escondernos?
  Is there anywhere we can hide?

Frases Condicionales

- La construcción *si* + VERBO + *algo* o *algún/alguna, etc* se traduce al inglés por *if* + SUJETO + VERBO + *any* o *some, etc*:

  Si necesitas algo, dímelo
  If you need anything, let me know
  Si quiere algunas cintas, no deje de pedirlas
  If you would like some tapes, don't hesitate to ask

  NOTA: Hay que tener en cuenta que *some* se utiliza cuando tenemos más certeza de que la condición se vaya a cumplir.

Alguna Vez

- Cuando utilizamos *alguna vez* en preguntas para informarnos sobre las experiencias de los demás, esto se traduce al inglés por *ever*:

  ¿Has visto alguna vez al Presidente en persona?
  Have you ever seen the President in person?
  ¿Has estado alguna vez en Groenlandia?
  Have you ever been to Greenland?

⇨ *Ver también* NINGUNO

Para otros usos y ejemplos ver las entradas *algo* y *alguno*.

---

alheñar [1a] [1] VT (a) (*teñir*) to dye with henna. (b) (*con roya*) to blight, cover with mildew. [2] **alheñarse** VR to become mildewed, get covered in mildew.

alhóndiga NF corn exchange.

alhucema NF lavender.

aliacán NM jaundice.

aliado [1] ADJ allied. [2] NM, **aliada** NF ally; **los A~s** the Allies. [3] NM (*Cono Sur*) (*emparedado*) toasted sandwich; (*bebida*) mixed drink.

aliaga NF = **aulaga**.

aliancista (*Esp Pol Hist*) [1] ADJ: **política ~** policy of Alianza Popular. [2] NMF member of Alianza Popular.

alianza NF (a) (*gen*) alliance; connection; (*Bib*) **A~** Covenant; **la A~ Atlántica** the Atlantic Alliance, NATO; **A~ para el Progreso** Alliance for Progress; **Santa A~** Holy Alliance. (b) (*anillo*) wedding ring.

aliar [1c] [1] VT to ally, bring into an alliance. [2] **aliarse** VR to ally o.s.; to become allied, form an alliance.

alias ADV, NM alias.

alicaído ADJ (*Med*) drooping, weak; (*fig*) downcast, crestfallen; depressed.

alicantina NF trick, ruse.

alicantino [1] ADJ of Alicante. [2] NM, **alicantina** NF native (*o* inhabitant) of Alicante; **los ~s** the people of Alicante.

alicatado NM tiling.

alicatar [1a] VT *pared* to tile; *azulejo* to shape, cut.

alicates NMPL pliers, pincers; **~ de corte** wire-cutters.

Alicia NF Alice; '**~ en el país de las maravillas**' 'Alice in Wonderland'; '**~ en el país del espejo**' 'Alice through the Looking-glass'.

aliciente NM incentive, inducement; lure; attraction; **ofrecer un ~** to hold out an inducement; **ofrece el ~ de ...** it holds out the attraction of ...

alicorarse* [1a] VR (*And*) to get boozed*.

alicorear [1a] VT (*CAm: adornar*) to decorate, adorn.

alicrejo NM (*CAm*) spider-like (*o* ugly) creature; (*hum*) old horse, nag.

alicurco ADJ (*Cono Sur*) sly, cunning.

alienación NF alienation, mental derangement.

alienado [1] ADJ alienated; (*Med*) insane, mentally ill. [2] NM, **alienada** NF alienated person; (*Med*) lunatic, mad person.

alienante ADJ inhuman, dehumanizing; alienating.

alienar [1a] VT = **enajenar**.

alienígena [1] ADJ foreign; alien; extraterrestrial. [2] NMF foreigner; alien; extraterrestrial being.

alienista NMF specialist in mental illness, psychiatrist, alienist (*US*).

aliento NM (a) (*un ~*) breath; (*gen*) breathing, respiration; **~ fétido** bad breath; **de un ~** (*lit*) in one breath, (*fig*) in one go; **aguantar el ~, contener el ~** to hold one's breath; **dar los últimos ~s** to breathe one's last; **estar sin ~** to be out of breath; **tiene mal ~** his breath smells; **tomar ~** to take breath; to get one's breath back. (b) (*fig: t ~s*) courage, spirit; strength; **cobrar ~** to take heart; **dar ~ a uno** to encourage sb, give sb courage; to support sb.

alifafe* NM ailment.

aligación NF alloy; (*fig*) bond, tie.

aligeramiento NM lightening; easing, alleviation.

aligerar [1a] [1] VT (*hacer más ligero*) to lighten; *dolor* to ease, relieve, alleviate; (*abreviar*) to shorten; *paso* to quicken. [2] **aligerarse** VR (a) (*carga*) to get lighter; **~ de ropa** to put on lighter clothing. (b) (*: *irse*) to beat it*, get out.

aligustre NM privet.

alijar¹ [1a] VT (*Téc*) to sandpaper.

alijar² [1a] VT to lighten; *barco* to unload; *contrabanda* to land, smuggle ashore.

alijar³ NM tile.

alijo NM (a) (*acto*) lightening; unloading. (b) (*géneros*) contraband, collection of smuggled goods; **~ de armas** consignment of smuggled arms, cache of arms; **~ de drogas** consignment of drugs (seized).

alilaya [1] NF (*And, Carib: excusa*) lame (*o* flimsy) excuse. [2] NMF (*Méx*) cunning person, sharp character*.

alimaña NF (a) (destructive, objectionable) animal; pest; **~s** (*frec*) vermin. (b) (*fig: persona*) brute, animal.

alimañero NM gamekeeper, vermin destroyer.

alimentación NF (a) (*acto*) feeding, nourishment; (*comida*) food; (*fig*) nurture, fostering; **el coste de la ~** the cost of food; **la ~ de los niños** the feeding of children, the nourishment of children; **~ insuficiente** malnutrition, undernourishment; **~ natural** natural food, health foods. (b) (*Téc*) feed; supply; **bomba de ~** feed pump; **~ por fricción** friction feed; **~ a la red** mains supply.

alimentador NM (*Téc*) feed, feeder; **~ automático de hojas, ~ de documentos, ~ de papel** (automatic) paper-feeder.

alimentar [1a] [1] VT (a) (*dar de comer a*) to feed, (*en sentido más general*) nourish. (b) (*fig*) *familia* to maintain, support; to bring up, nurture; *esperanza* to nourish, encourage; to cherish; *sentimiento* to foster; *pasión* to feed, add fuel to. (c) (*Téc*) to feed; *horno* to feed, stoke (*de* with); **~ una máquina de algo** to feed sth into a machine. [2] **alimentarse** VR to feed (*con, de* on); **~ de** to live on.

alimentario ADJ food (*atr*); **la industria alimentaria** the food industry.

alimenticio ADJ (a) (*nutritivo*) nourishing, nutritive. (b) (*relativo a comida*) food (*atr*); **artículos ~s** foodstuffs; **valor ~** food value, nutritional value.

alimento NM (a) (*gen*) food; nourishment; (*Méx*) meal; **~s integrales** whole foods; **~s naturales** health foods; **~ de primera necesidad** staple food. (b) (*fig*) encouragement, support; incentive; (*de pasión*) fuel. (c) **~s** (*Jur*) alimony.

alimentoso ADJ nourishing.

alimoche NM Egyptian vulture.

alimón: al ~ ADV together, jointly, in collaboration.

alindado ADJ foppish, dandified.

alindar¹ [1a] VT (*adornar*) to embellish, make pretty, make look nice; *persona* to doll up, prettify.

alindar² [1a] [1] VT *tierra* to mark off, mark out. [2] VI to adjoin, be adjacent.

alinderar [1a] VT (*CAm, Cono Sur*) to mark out the boundaries of.

alineación NF (a) (*Téc*) alignment; **estar fuera de ~** to be out of alignment, be out of true. (b) (*Dep etc*) line-up.

alineado ADJ: **está ~ con el partido** he is in line with the party; **los países no ~s** the non-aligned countries.

alineamiento NM: **no ~** non-alignment; *V t* **alineación**.

alinear [1a] [1] VT to align; to line up, put into line; (*Mil*) to form up; (*Dep*) *equipo* to play, field; (*fig*) to bring into line (*con* with). [2] **alinearse** VR to line up; (*Mil*) to fall in, form up; (*Inform*) to justify; **se alinearon a lo largo de la calle** they lined up along the street.

aliñador NM (*Cono Sur*) bonesetter.
aliñar [1a] VT (**a**) (*adornar*) to adorn, embellish. (**b**) (*preparar*) to prepare; (*Culin*) to dress, season. (**c**) (*Cono Sur*) *hueso* to set.
aliño NM (**a**) (*adorno*) adornment, embellishment; preparation. (**b**) (*Culin*) dressing, seasoning.
alioli NM (*Culin*) sauce of garlic and oil.
alionar [1a] VT (*Cono Sur*) to stir up.
alionín NM blue tit.
alipego NM (*CAm*) extra, bonus (*added as part of a sale*); (*) gatecrasher, intruder, person who comes uninvited.
aliquebrado ADJ crestfallen.
alirón [1] EXCL hurray!
   [2] NM *victory song of supporters of Real Madrid*; (*fig*) victory, triumph; victory celebration.
alisado [1] ADJ smooth; polished.
   [2] NM smoothing; polishing; finishing.
alisador NM (*persona*) polisher; (*herramienta*) smoothing blade, smoothing tool.
alisadura NF smoothing; polishing; **~s** cuttings, shavings.
alisar¹ [1a] VT to smooth (down); to polish, burnish; *pelo* to smooth, sleek; (*Téc*) to polish, finish, surface.
alisar² NM, **aliseda** NF alder grove.
alisios NMPL (*t* **vientos ~**) trade winds.
aliso NM alder, alder tree.
alistamiento NM enrolment; (*Mil*) enlistment, recruitment.
alistar¹ [1a] [1] VT (*poner en lista*) to list, put on a list; *miembro* to enrol; (*Mil*) to enlist; (*CAm: zapato*) to sew (up).
   [2] **alistarse** VR to enrol; (*Mil*) to enlist, join up.
alistar² [1a] [1] VT (*disponer*) to prepare, make ready.
   [2] **alistarse** VR (*LAm*) to get dressed, get ready.
aliteración NF alliteration.
aliterado ADJ alliterative.
alitranca NF (*And, Cono Sur*) brake, braking device.
aliviadero NM overflow channel (*on dam*).
aliviador ADJ comforting, consoling.
alivianarse* [1a] VR (*Méx*) to play it cool, be cool, be laid-back*.
aliviar [1b] [1] VT (**a**) (*aligerar*) to lighten; (*dolor*) to ease, relieve; to make more bearable; to soothe; **~ a uno de algo** (*robar*) to relieve sb of sth.
   (**b**) (*acelerar*) to speed up; *paso* to quicken.
   (**c**) (‡) to nick‡, pinch*.
   [2] **aliviarse** VR (**a**) (*dolor*) to diminish, become more bearable; (*paciente*) to gain relief; to get better, recover; **¡que se alivie!** get better soon!
   (**b**) (*fig*) to unburden o.s. (*de* of).
alivio NM (**a**) (*gen*) alleviation, relief, easing; mitigation; improvement; (*Med*) relief; **~ de luto** half-mourning; **¡que siga el ~!** I hope you continue to improve!
   (**b**) **de ~*** awful, horrible; **un susto de ~** an awful fright, a hell of a fright.
aljaba NF (**a**) (*para flechas*) quiver. (**b**) (*Cono Sur Bot*) fuchsia.
aljama NF (*Hist*) (**a**) (*barrio*) (*de moros*) Moorish quarter; (*de judíos*) Jewish quarter, ghetto. (**b**) (*mezquita*) mosque; (*sinagoga*) synagogue. (**c**) (*reunión*) gathering of Moors o Jews.
aljamía NF *Spanish written in Arabic characters (14th-16th centuries)*.
aljamiado ADJ: **texto ~** *text of Spanish written in Arabic characters*.
aljibe NM (**a**) (*cisterna*) cistern, tank; (*Náut*) water tender; (*Aut*) oil tanker; (*And: pozo*) well. (**b**) (*And: calabozo*) dungeon, underground prison.
aljofaina NF washbasin, washbowl.
aljófar NM (small o irregular) pearl; (*fig*) pearl of moisture; dewdrop.
aljofarar [1a] VT to bedew, cover with pearls of moisture.
aljofifa NF floor-cloth.
aljofifar [1a] VT to wash, mop, mop up.
allá [1] ADV (**a**) (*lugar*) there, over there; (*dirección*) to that place; **~ arriba** up there; **~ en Sevilla** down (there) in Seville; **~ mismo** right there; **más ~** further away, further over; further on; **más ~ de** beyond; **más ~ de los límites** outside the limits; **cualquier número más ~ de 7** any number higher than 7; **no sabe contar más ~ de 10** she can't count above (o beyond) 10; **muy ~** much further on, miles away; **no tan ~** not so far; **por ~** thereabouts; **vamos ~** let's go there; **¡~ voy!** I'm coming!; **¿quién va ~?** (*Mil*) who goes there?; **~ lo veremos** (*fig*) we'll see when we get there, we'll sort that one out later.
   (**b**) **~ tú** that's up to you, that's your concern, that's for you to decide (*etc*); **¡~ él!** (*más tajante*) that's his funeral!*; **~ cada uno** that's the concern of each one of us, that's for the individual to decide.
   (**c**) (*tiempo*) **~ en 1600** (way) back in 1600, as long ago as 1600; **~ en mi niñez** in my childhood days; **~ por el año 60** round about 1960 (*etc*).
   [2] NM: **el más ~** the great beyond.
allacito ADV (*LAm*) = **allá**.

allanamiento NM (**a**) (*nivelación*) levelling, flattening; smoothing; razing.
   (**b**) (*de obstáculos*) removal.
   (**c**) (*pacificación*) pacification.
   (**d**) (*Jur etc*) submission (*a* to).
   (**e**) **~ de morada** (*crimen*) housebreaking, breaking and entering, burglary; (*Jur*) search; **el juez dispuso el ~ del domicilio** the judge granted the police a search-warrant for the house.
   (**f**) (*esp LAm: de policía*) raid, search.
allanar [1a] [1] VT (**a**) (*nivelar*) to level (out), flatten, make even; (*alisar*) to smooth (down); (*arrasar*) to raze, level to the ground.
   (**b**) *dificultad etc* to remove, smooth away, iron out.
   (**c**) *país* to pacify, subdue.
   (**d**) *casa* to force an entry into, break into, burgle; (*esp LAm: policía*) to raid, search.
   [2] **allanarse** VR (**a**) (*nivelarse*) to level out, level off.
   (**b**) (*edificio*) to fall down, tumble down.
   (**c**) (*fig*) to submit, give way; **~ a** to accept, conform to; **se allana a todo** he agrees to everything.
allegadizo ADJ gathered at random, put together unselectively.
allegado [1] ADJ (**a**) (*afín*) near, close; allied; **según fuentes allegadas al ministro** according to sources close to the minister.
   (**b**) *persona* closely related, near; **los más ~s y queridos** one's nearest and dearest; **las personas allegadas a ...** those attached to ..., those closest to ...
   [2] NM, **allegada** NF (**a**) (*pariente*) relation, relative.
   (**b**) (*secuaz*) follower.
allegar [1h] [1] VT (**a**) (*reunir*) to gather (together), collect.
   (**b**) (*acercar*): **~ una cosa a otra** to put something near something else.
   (**c**) (*añadir*) to add.
   [2] **allegarse** VR (**a**) to arrive, approach; **~ a uno** to go up to sb.
   (**b**) (*fig*) **~ a una opinión** to adopt a view, agree with an opinion; **~ a una secta** to become attached to a sect.
allende (*liter*) [1] ADV on the other side.
   [2] (*t* **~ de**) PREP beyond; **~ los mares** overseas, beyond the seas; **~ los Pirineos** beyond the Pyrenees, on the other side of the Pyrenees, over the Pyrenees; **~ de eso** besides that.
allí ADV there; **~ arriba** up there; **~ dentro** in there; **de ~** from there; **de ~ a poco** shortly afterwards; **de ~ que ...** that is why ..., hence ...; **de ~ a decir que es un timo** but that's a long way from calling it a swindle; **de ~ para acá** back and forth; **hasta ~** as far as that, up to that point; **por ~** over there, round there; (*down*) that way; **una chica de por ~*** a wench, a scrubber‡; **está tirado por ~*** he's hanging around somewhere; **¡vete por ~!*** shove off!*
allicito ADV (*LAm*) = **allí**.
alma NF (**a**) (*gen*) soul; spirit; **¡hijo de mi ~!** my precious child!
   (**b**) (*locuciones con verbo*) **le arrancó el ~** he was deeply shocked by it; **se le fue el ~ a los pies** he became very disheartened, his heart sank; **se echó el ~ a las espaldas** he abandoned all scruples; he wasn't in the least worried; **entregar el ~** to give up the ghost; **estar con el ~ en la boca** to be scared to death; **hablar al ~** to speak most earnestly; **se le fue el ~ tras la muñeca** she fell for the doll, she would have sold her soul for the doll; **me llegó al ~** it affected me deeply, it really struck home; **partirse el ~ (para)** (*Méx*) to go to great lengths (to); **se le partió el ~** she was heartbroken; **no puedo con mi ~** (*Esp*) I can't stand it any more; **rendir el ~** to give up the ghost; **romper el ~ a uno‡** to do sb in‡; **rompe el ~ verlo** it breaks one's heart to see it; **lo siento en el ~** I am truly sorry; **tener el ~ en un hilo** to have one's heart in one's mouth; to be scared to death; **tener el ~ en su almario** to be up to anything, be fully up to the job; to have lots of guts*; **tener mucha ~, tener el ~ bien puesta** to be undaunted; **no tener ~** to be pitiless; **le volvió el ~ al cuerpo** he calmed down; he recovered his composure; it relieved him of a great worry (o fear etc).
   (**c**) (*comparaciones*) **andar** (o **estar**) **como ~ en pena** to go about like a lost soul; **estar como un ~ perdida** to be completely undecided; **ir como ~ que lleva el diablo** to go like a bat out of hell, run like hell.
   (**d**) (*persona*) soul, person, inhabitant; **un pueblo de 2 mil ~s** a village of 2,000 souls, a village of 2,000 inhabitants; **¡~ mía!** my precious!, darling!; **~ bendita** simple soul; **~ de caballo** twister; **~ de Caín, ~ de Judas** fiend, devil; **~ de cántaro** you idiot!; **~ de Dios** good soul; **ni ~ nacida, ni ~ viviente** not a single living soul.
   (**e**) (*fig*) soul, moving spirit, leading spirit; (*de asunto*) crux, heart, vital part; **él es el ~ del movimiento** he is the leading spirit of the movement; **es el ~ de la fiesta** he's the life and soul of the party.
   (**f**) **con el ~, con toda el ~** with all one's heart, heart and soul; **lo haré con toda mi ~** I'll do it with all my heart; **en lo más hondo de mi ~** in my heart of hearts.
   (**g**) (*And: cadáver*) corpse.
   (**h**) (*Bot*) pith; (*Téc*) core, heart; (*de cable*) core; (*de cuerda*) central

strand; (*de cañón*) bore.

almacén NM (a) (*depósito*) warehouse, store; depository; ~ **de depósito** bonded warehouse; **tener algo en** ~ to have sth in store, (*Com*) to stock sth.
(b) (*Mec, Mil etc*) magazine.
(c) (*tienda*) shop, store; (*LAm*) *esp* grocer's (shop), grocery shop, grocery store; ~ **frigorífico** cold store; (**grandes**) **almacenes** department store; **Almacenes Pérez** Pérez Department Store.

almacenable ADJ that can be stored, storable.

almacenado NM storage, warehousing.

almacenaje NM (a) (*acto*) storage, storing; ~ **frigorífico** cold storage; ~ **de larga duración** long-term storage. (b) (*precio*) storage charge, storage fee.

almacenamiento NM (*Inform*) storage; ~ **de datos** data storage; ~ **primario** primary storage; ~ **secundario** secondary storage; ~ **temporal en disco** (disk) spooling.

almacenar [1a] VT (a) (*poner en depósito*) to store, put into storage, keep in store; *víveres etc* to stock up (with); (*Inform*) to store, save.
(b) (*fig*) to keep, collect, (*pey*) hoard; ~ **odio** to store up hatred.

almacenero, -a NM/F storekeeper, warehouseman; (*LAm*) shopkeeper.

almacenista NMF warehouse owner; (*LAm*) shopkeeper, grocer.

almáciga NF, **almácigo** NM (*LAm*) seedbed, nursery.

almádena NF sledgehammer, large hammer.

almadía NF raft.

almadiarse [1c] VR to be sick, vomit.

almadraba NF (*acto, arte*) tunny fishing; (*lugar*) tunny fishery; (*redes*) tunny net(s).

almadreña NF wooden shoe, clog.

almagre NM red ochre.

almajara NF (*Agr*) hotbed, forcing frame.

alma máter NF alma mater.

almanaque NM almanac; **hacer ~s** to muse; (*And, Cono Sur*) **echar a uno vendiendo ~s** to send sb away with a flea in his ear.

almariarse [1c] VR (*CAm, Cono Sur*) to be sick, vomit.

almazara NF oil mill, oil press.

almeja NF (a) (*Zool*) shellfish, cockle, clam (*US*). (b) (♥‚) cunt♥‚; **mojar la** ~ to have a screw♥‚.

almenado ADJ battlemented, crenellated.

almenara NF (*fuego*) beacon; (*araña*) chandelier.

almenas NFPL battlements, crenellations.

almendra NF (a) (*Bot*) almond; ~ **amarga** bitter almond; ~ **garapiñada** praline, sugar almond; ~ **tostada** burnt almond; **ser ~** (*Carib fig*) to be a love (o of a peach).
(b) (*Bot: semilla*) kernel, stone.
(c) (*de vidrio*) cut-glass drop (of chandelier *etc*).

almendrada NF almond milk shake, drink made with milk and almonds.

almendrado [1] ADJ (a) *forma* almond-shaped, pear-shaped; **de ojos ~s** almond-eyed. (b) *sabor* nutty.
[2] NM macaroon.

almendral NM almond orchard.

almendrera NF almond tree.

almendrillo NM (*LAm*) almond tree.

almendro NM almond tree.

almendruco NM green almond.

almeriense [1] ADJ of Almería.
[2] NMF native (o inhabitant) of Almería; **los ~s** the people of Almería.

almete NM (*Hist*) helmet.

almez NM hackberry.

almiar NM haycock, hayrick.

almíbar NM syrup; ~ **de pelo** (*LAm*) heavy syrup; **estar hecho un** ~ to be all sweet and kind, be especially nice, (*pey*) overdo the sweetness.

almibarado ADJ syrupy; (*fig*) honeyed, over-sweet; *estilo, tono* sugary.

almibarar [1a] VT to preserve (o serve) in syrup; ~ **las palabras** to use honeyed words, overdo the sweetness.

almidón NM (*gen*) starch; (*Méx: engrudo*) paste.

almidonado ADJ starched; (*fig*) (*estirado*) stiff, starchy; (*pulcro*) dapper, spruce.

almidonar [1a] VT to starch; **los prefiero sin** ~ I prefer them unstarched.

almilla NF (a) (*jubón*) bodice; undervest. (b) (*Téc*) tenon. (c) (*Culin*) breast of pork.

alminar NM minaret.

almirantazgo NM admiralty.

almirante NM admiral.

almirez NM mortar.

almizcle NM musk.

almizcleño ADJ musky.

almizclera NF muskrat, musquash.

almizclero NM musk deer.

almo ADJ (*poét*) nourishing; sacred, venerable.

almocafre NM weeding hoe.

almodrote NM cheese and garlic sauce; (*fig*) hotchpotch.

almofré NM, **almofrez** NM (*LAm*) sleeping bag, bedroll.

almohada NF (*de cama*) pillow; bolster; (*cojín*) cushion; (*funda*) pillowcase; ~ **neumática** air cushion; **consultar algo con la** ~ to sleep on sth, think sth over carefully.

almohade [1] ADJ Almohad.
[2] **~s** NMPL Almohads.

almohadilla NF small cushion, small pillow; (*LAm*) holder (for iron *etc*); (*CAm, Carib, Méx Dep*) base, cushion; (*Cos*) pincushion; (*Arquit*) boss; (*Téc*) pad, cushion; ~ **de entintar** inkpad.

almohadillado [1] ADJ padded; stuffed; *piedra* dressed (in a special way, *eg* vermiculate).
[2] NM ashlar; dressed ashlar.

almohadón NM large pillow, bolster; (*Ecl*) hassock.

almohaza NF currycomb.

almohazar [1f] VT *caballo* to brush down, groom; *piel* to dress.

almoneda NF auction; clearance sale.

almoned(e)ar [1a] VT to auction.

almorávide [1] ADJ Almoravid.
[2] **~s** NMPL Almoravids.

almorranas NFPL (*Med*) piles.

almorta NF (*Bot*) vetch.

almorzar [1f y 1l] [1] VT to have for lunch, lunch on; (†† *y en regiones de LAm*) to have for second breakfast, breakfast late on.
[2] VI to lunch, have lunch; (†† *y en regiones de LAm*) to breakfast late, have second breakfast; **vengo almorzado** I've had lunch.

almuecín NM, **almuédano** NM muezzin.

almuerzo NM (a) (*a mediodía*) lunch, (*más formal*) luncheon; (*de boda*) wedding breakfast; (†† *y en regiones de LAm*) late breakfast, second breakfast; ~ **de gala** official luncheon; ~ **de negocios** business lunch; ~ **de trabajo** working lunch.
(b) (*vajilla*) dinner service.

alnado, -a NM/F stepchild.

aló INTERJ (*LAm Telec*) hullo?

alobado♥ ADJ dim♥, thick♥.

alocado [1] ADJ crazy, mad.
[2] NM, **alocada** NF madcap.

alocar♥ [1g] (*LAm*) [1] VT to drive crazy (with pleasure); **me alocan las pizzas** I love pizzas, I'm mad on pizzas♥.
[2] **alocarse** VR to go crazy.

alocución NF allocution; speech, address.

áloe NM (*Bot*) aloe; (*Farm*) aloes.

alojado, -a NM/F (*LAm*) guest, lodger.

alojamiento NM lodging(s); housing; accommodation; (*Mil: acto*) billeting, (*casa*) billet, quarters; (*And*) small hotel, boarding house; **buscarse** ~ to look for lodgings.

alojar [1a] [1] VT to lodge, accommodate, put up, house; (*Mil*) to billet, quarter.
[2] **alojarse** VR to lodge, be lodged; to stay; (*Mil*) to be billeted, quartered; ~ **en** to lodge at, put up at; **la bala se alojó en el pulmón** the bullet lodged in the lung.

alón [1] ADJ (*LAm*) large-winged; *sombrero* broad-brimmed.
[2] NM wing (of chicken *etc*).

alondra [1] NF (*Orn*) lark, skylark.
[2] NM (♥) = **albañil**.

alongar [1l] [1] VT = **alargar**.
[2] **alongarse** VR to move away.

alopecia NF alopecia.

alpaca NF alpaca.

alpargata NF rope-soled sandal, canvas sandal, espadrille; **turismo de** ~ travelling on the cheap♥, tourism on a shoestring.

alpargatería NF sandal shop.

alpargatero♥ ADJ low-class; down-market; done (*etc*) on the cheap♥.

alpargatilla NMF crafty person.

alpende NM tool shed, lean-to.

Alpes NMPL Alps.

alpestre ADJ Alpine; (*fig*) mountainous, rough, wild.

alpinismo NM mountaineering, climbing.

alpinista NMF mountaineer, climber.

alpinístico ADJ mountaineering (*atr*), climbing (*atr*).

alpino ADJ Alpine.

alpiste NM (a) (*semillas*) birdseed, canary seed. (b) (*LAm♥: dinero*) brass♥; (♥: *alcohol*) drink, booze♥.

alquería NF farmhouse, farmstead.

alquiladizo [1] ADJ for rent, for hire, that can be rented (o hired); (*pey*) hireling.
[2] NM, **alquiladiza** NF hireling.

alquilado, -a NM/F (*Carib*) tenant.

alquilador(a) NM/F renter, hirer; tenant, lessee.

alquilar [1a] [1] VT (a) (*sujeto: propietario*) *casa* to rent (out), let; *coche*, *autocar etc* to hire (out); *garaje, TV* to rent (out).

(b) (*sujeto: alquilador*) *casa* to rent; *coche, autocar etc* to hire; *garaje, TV* to rent; **'por ~'** 'to let', 'for rent' (*US*); **turba alquilada** rent-a-mob.

2 alquilarse VR **(a)** (*casa*) to be let (*en* at, for); **'se alquila'** (*anuncio*) 'to let', 'for rent' (*US*); **aquí no se alquila casa alguna** there is no house to let here.

(b) (*taxi etc*) to be on hire, be out for hire.

(c) (*persona*) to hire o.s. out; (*Carib*) to go into service.

alquiler NM **(a)** (*acto*) letting, renting; hire, hiring; **de ~** for hire, on hire; **'~ sin chófer'** (*Esp*) 'drive yourself' 'self-drive'; **~ de úteros** surrogate motherhood.

(b) (*precio*) rent, rental; hire charge; **control de ~es** rent control; **exento de ~es** rent-free; **pagar el ~** to pay the rent; **subir el ~ a uno** to raise sb's rent.

alquimia NF alchemy.

alquimista NM alchemist.

alquitara NF still.

alquitarar [1a] VT to distil.

alquitrán NM tar; **~ de hulla, ~ mineral** coal tar.

alquitranado **1** ADJ tarred, tarry.

2 NM (*materia*) tarmac; (*tela*) tarpaulin.

alquitranar [1a] VT to tar.

alrededor **1** ADV **(a)** around, about; **todo ~** all around. **(b)** **~ mío** (*etc*) (*Cono Sur*) around me (*etc*).

2 ~ de PREP **(a)** (*gen*) around, about; **todo ~ de la iglesia** all around the church; **mirar ~ de sí, mirar ~ suyo** to look about one.

(b) (*fig*) about, in the region of; **~ de 200** about 200.

3 NM: **mirar a su ~** to look about one; **~es** surroundings, neighbourhood; (*de ciudad*) outskirts, environs; (*de escena, lugar*) setting; **en los ~es de Londres** on the outskirts of London; in the area round London.

Alsacia NF Alsace.

Alsacia-Lorena NF Alsace-Lorraine.

alsaciano **1** ADJ Alsatian.

2 NM, **alsaciana** NF Alsatian.

alt. ABR *de* **altura** height, ht.

alta NF (*Med*) (certificate of) discharge from hospital; (*Téc etc*) installation, fitting up, making ready; **el ~ de la línea telefónica** putting in the phone, the connecting up of the phone; **dar a uno de ~** to discharge sb from hospital, (*Mil*) to pass sb (as) fit; **darse de ~** to join, become a member; (*Med*) to return to duty; **dar una propiedad de ~** (*Jur*) to register a property (for taxation purposes); **estar de ~** to be back on duty; to be up and about again; to be back to normal; to have got over it.

altamente ADV highly, extremely.

altanería NF **(a)** (*altivez*) haughtiness, disdain, arrogance. **(b)** (*Caza*) hawking, falconry. **(c)** (*Met*) upper air.

altanero ADJ **(a)** (*altivo*) haughty, disdainful, arrogant. **(b)** *ave* high-flying.

altar NM altar; **~ mayor** high altar; **llevar a una al ~** to lead sb to the altar; **poner a una en un ~** to put sb on a pedestal; **quedarse para adornar ~es** to be left on the shelf; **subir a los ~es** to be beatified (*o* canonized).

altaricón* ADJ big-built, large.

altavoz NM (*Rad*) loudspeaker; (*Elec*) amplifier.

altea NF mallow.

altear [1a] VT (*Cono Sur Hist*) to order to stop (*o* halt).

al-tec* ABR *de* **alta tecnología** high technology, high-tech*.

alterabilidad NF changeability.

alterable ADJ changeable.

alteración NF **(a)** (*cambio*) alteration, change.

(b) (*aturdimiento*) upset, disturbance; (*Med*) irregularity of the pulse; **~ digestiva** digestive upset; **~ del orden público** breach of the peace.

(c) (*agitación*) strong feeling, agitation.

(d) (*disputa*) quarrel, dispute.

alterado ADJ agitated, upset, disturbed; angry; (*Med*) upset, disordered.

alterar [1a] **1** VT **(a)** (*cambiar*) to alter, change; to change for the worse; *verdad* to distort, twist.

(b) (*perturbar*) to upset, disturb; to cause a commotion in; *paz, silencio etc* to disturb.

(c) (*agitar*) to stir up, excite, agitate; to irritate, anger.

2 alterarse VR **(a)** (*cambiar*) to alter, change.

(b) (*comida*) to go bad, go off; (*leche etc*) to go sour.

(c) (*voz*) to falter.

(d) (*persona: agitarse*) to get upset, become agitated, become disturbed; (*enfadarse*) to get angry; (*ofenderse*) to be put out; (*distraerse*) to be put off one's stroke; **siguió sin ~** he went on unabashed, he went on unmoved; **no ~** to keep a stiff upper lip, show no emotion, not turn a hair; **¡no te alteres!** don't upset yourself!, keep calm!; **~ por algo** to get angry (*o* excited *etc*) about sth.

altercación NF, **altercado** NM argument, altercation.

altercar [1g] VI to argue, quarrel, wrangle.

álter ego NM alter ego.

alteridad NF otherness.

alternación NF alternation.

alternadamente ADV alternately.

alternado ADJ alternate.

alternador NM (*Elec*) alternator.

alternancia NF alternation; **~ de cultivos** crop rotation; **~ en el poder** taking turns in office.

alternante ADJ alternating.

alternar [1a] **1** VT to alternate; to vary.

2 VI **(a)** (*gen*) to alternate (*con* with); (*Téc*) to alternate, reciprocate; (*hacer turno*) to take turns, change about; (*cambiar*) to vary; **alternar a los mandos** to take turns at the controls; **~ en el poder** to take turns in office.

(b) (*participar*) to mix, take part in the social round, socialize; (*) to go on a pub crawl*, go boozing*; to sleep around*; **~ con un grupo** to mix with a group, go around with a group; **~ con la gente bien** to hobnob with top people; to move in elevated circles; **tiene pocas ganas de ~** he doesn't want to mix, he is disinclined to be sociable; **~ de igual a igual** to be on an equal footing.

▼ alternativa NF **(a)** (*opción*) alternative, option, choice; **no tener ~** to have no alternative; **tomar una ~** to make a choice.

(b) (*sucesión*) alternation; (*trabajo*) shift work, work done in relays; **~ de cosechas** crop rotation.

(c) (*Taur*) ceremony by which a novice becomes a fully-qualified bullfighter; **tomar la ~** to become a fully-qualified bullfighter.

(d) **~s** ups and downs, vicissitudes, fluctuations; **las ~s de la política** the ups and downs of politics.

alternativamente ADV alternately.

alternativo ADJ alternating (*t Elec*); alternative, alternate; *cultura, prensa etc* alternative; **fuentes alternativas de energía** alternative energy sources.

alterne **1** NM mixing, socializing; (*euf*) sexual contact(s); sleeping around*; **club de ~** singles club; **estas chicas no son de ~** these girls don't sleep around*, these girls are not easy lays; (*V t* **chica**).

2 NF hostess.

alterno ADJ (*Bot, Mat etc*) alternate; **tiempo con nubes alternas** partly cloudy weather.

altero NM (*Méx*), **alterón** NM (*And*) heap, pile.

alteza NF **(a)** (*altura*) height.

(b) (*fig*) sublimity; **~ de miras** high-mindedness.

(c) (*título*) **A~** Highness; **Su A~ Real** His (*o* Her) Royal Highness; **sí, A~** yes, your Highness.

altibajos NMPL ups and downs (*t fig*).

altillo NM **(a)** (*Geog*) small hill, hillock. **(b)** (*LAm: desván*) attic. **(c)** (*piso*) mezzanine.

altilocuencia NF grandiloquence.

altilocuente ADJ, **altílocuo** ADJ grandiloquent.

altímetro NM altimeter.

altimontano ADJ high mountain (*atr*), upland (*atr*).

altinal NM (*Méx*) pillar, column.

altiplanicie NF high plateau.

altiplano NM high plateau; **A~** (*Geog Bol*) Altiplano.

altísimo ADJ very high; **el A~** the Almighty, the Most High.

altisonancia NF high-flown style (*etc*); high-sounding nature.

altisonante ADJ, **altísono** ADJ high-flown, high-sounding.

altitud NF height; (*Aer, Geog*) altitude, elevation; **a una ~ de** at a height of.

altivamente ADV haughtily, arrogantly.

altivarse [1a] VR to give o.s. airs.

altivez NF, **altiveza** NF haughtiness, arrogance.

altivo ADJ haughty, arrogant.

alto¹ **1** ADJ **(a)** (*gen*) high; *persona* tall; *edificio, árbol, roca* high, tall; *mando, oficial, precio, relieve, traición etc* high; *ejecutivo* senior; *cámara* (*Pol*), *clase, piso* upper; **el muro tiene 5 metros de ~** the wall is 5 metres high; **él tiene 1,80 m de ~** he is 1.80 m tall; **lanzar algo de lo ~** to throw sth down (from above); **desde lo ~ del árbol** from the top of the tree; **estar en (lo) ~** to be up high, be high up, be up on top; **estar en lo ~ de la escalera** to be at the top of the stairs; **pasó por lo ~** it passed overhead; **por todo lo ~** (*fig*) in style, in the proper way.

(b) (*Geog*) upper; **el A~ Rin** the Upper Rhine.

(c) **estar ~** (*río*) to be in spate, to be swollen; (*mar*) to be rough.

(d) (*fig*) sublime, lofty, elevated; high; **un ~ sentido del deber** a high sense of duty; **~s pensamientos** lofty thoughts, noble thoughts.

(e) *hora* late, advanced; **en las altas horas** in the small hours, late at night.

(f) *sonido* high, loud; **en alta voz** loud(ly), in a loud voice.

(g) (*Mús*) *nota* sharp; *instrumento, voz* alto.

➤ LENGUA Y USO: **alternativa: a → 45.4**

(h) (*Hist, Ling*) high; ~ **alemán antiguo** Old High German; **la alta Edad Media** the high Middle Ages.

2 ADV **(a)** (*gen*) high, high up; on high; **lanzar algo** ~ to throw sth high.

(b) *sonar* loud, loudly; **hablar** ~ to speak loudly, (*fig*) to speak out (frankly); **gritar** ~ to shout out loud; **poner la radio más** ~ to turn the radio up; **¡más ~, por favor!** louder, please!

3 NM **(a)** (*Geog*) hill, height; **A~s del Golán** Golan Heights.

(b) (*Arquit*) upper floor, upstairs flat.

(c) (*LAm: montón*) pile, stack.

(d) (*Mús*) alto.

(e) **~s y bajos** ups and downs.

(f) **pasar por** ~ to overlook, forget, omit; to pass over, ignore.

alto² **1** NM halt (*t Mil*); stop; pause; **dar el** ~ **a uno** to order sb to halt, challenge sb; **hacer** ~ to halt (*t Mil*), stop, pause; (*Méx: parada*) stop.

2 INTERJ halt! (*t Mil*), stop!; **¡~ ahí!** halt!; ~ **el fuego, ~ al fuego** ceasefire; **¡~ el fuego!** cease fire!; **echar el** ~ **a uno** to order sb to stop.

altocúmulo NM altocumulus.

altomedieval ADJ early medieval, of the High Middle Ages.

altoparlante NM (*esp LAm*) loudspeaker.

altorrelieve NM high relief.

altostrato NM altostratus.

altozanero NM (*And*) porter.

altozano NM **(a)** (*otero*) small hill, hillock; (*de ciudad*) upper part. **(b)** (*And, Carib*) cathedral forecourt, church forecourt.

altramuz NM lupin.

altruismo NM altruism, unselfishness.

altruista **1** ADJ altruistic, unselfish.

2 NMF altruist, unselfish person.

altura NF **(a)** (*gen*) height; altitude; (*de agua*) depth; ~ **de caída** (*de cascada etc*) fall; ~ **de crucero** cruising height; ~ **del suelo** ground clearance, height off the ground; ~ **de la vegetación** timber line; **a una** ~ **de 600 m** at a height of 600 m; **sentí un dolor a la** ~ **de los riñones** I felt a pain in the kidney region, I felt a pain in the area of my kidneys; **tiene 5 m de** ~ it is 5 m high; **él tiene 1,80 m de** ~ he is 1.80 m tall; (*Aer*) **ganar** ~, **tomar** ~ to climb, gain height.

(b) (*fig: mérito*) **poemas de** ~ good poems, worthy poems; **estar a la** ~ **de una tarea** to be up to a task, be equal to a task; **estar a la** ~ **de las circunstancias** to rise to the occasion; **estar a la** ~ **del tiempo** to be abreast of the times; **poner a uno a la** ~ **del betún** (*Esp**) to make sb feel like dirt.

(c) (*Geog: latitud*) latitude; **a la** ~ **de** on the same latitude as; **a la** ~ **de Cádiz** off Cadiz; opposite Cadiz; (*Aut etc*) **a la** ~ **del km 8** at the 8th km (point); **a la** ~ **del museo** up (the street) near the museum; **la calle sale a la** ~ **de Correos** the street is just after the post office; **¿a qué** ~ **quiere?** how far along (the street)?

(d) (*Náut*) **barco de** ~ seagoing vessel; **pesca de** ~ deep-sea fishing; **remolcador de** ~ deep-sea tug, ocean-going tug.

(e) (*Mús*) pitch.

(f) (*Dep: salto*) high jump.

(g) (*fig*) sublimity, loftiness; **ha sido un partido de gran** ~ it has been a match of real class, it has been a really excellent game.

(h) **~s** (*Geog*) heights; (*Rel*) heaven; **a estas ~s** (*fig*) at this point, at this stage; at this (late) hour; (*fig*) **por estas ~s** around here; at this juncture; **estar en las ~s** to be on high.

(i) **una casa de 5 ~s** a 5-storey house.

alubia NF French bean, kidney bean.

alucinación NF hallucination, delusion.

alucinado ADJ **(a)** (*lit*) deluded, suffering hallucinations. **(b)** (**: asombrado*) amazed, dumbfounded.

alucinador ADJ hallucinatory, deceptive.

alucinante **1** ADJ **(a)** (*Med*) hallucinatory. **(b)** (*Esp: fig*) attractive, beguiling; mysterious; (***) great*, super*. **(c)** (*Esp: absurdo*) absurd; fantastic; **¡es ~!** it's mind-boggling!*

2 NM (*Méx*) hallucinogenic drug.

alucinar [1a] **1** VT **(a)** (*engañar*) to hallucinate, delude, deceive. **(b)** (*fascinar*) to fascinate, beguile; (*Esp**) to grab*, be a hit with.

2 **alucinarse** VR to hallucinate, be deluded; to delude o.s.

alucine* NM delusion; **de** ~ super*, great*.

alucinógeno **1** ADJ hallucinogenic.

2 NM hallucinogen, hallucinogenic drug.

alucinosis NF hallucinosis.

alud NM avalanche.

aludido ADJ aforesaid, above-mentioned, this ... that has been mentioned; **darse por** ~ to take it personally, take the hint; **no darse por** ~ to pretend not to hear; **no te des por** ~ don't take it personally.

aludir [3a] VI: ~ **a** to allude to, mention.

aluego ADV *etc* (*LAm*) = **luego.**

alujado ADJ (*CAm, Méx*) bright, shining.

alujar [1a] VT (*CAm, Méx*) to polish, shine.

alumbrado **1** ADJ (***) boozed*.

2 NM lighting, lighting system, illumination; ~ **eléctrico** electric lighting; ~ **de emergencia** emergency lighting; ~ **fluorescente** fluorescent lighting; ~ **de gas** gas lighting; ~ **público** street lighting.

3 NM, **alumbrada** NF illuminist; **los A~s** the Illuminati.

alumbramiento NM **(a)** (*Elec etc*) lighting, illumination. **(b)** (*Med*) childbirth; **tener un feliz** ~ to have a safe delivery, come safely through childbirth.

alumbrar [1a] **1** VT **(a)** (*Elec etc*) to light (up), illuminate, shed light on.

(b) *persona* to light the way for, show a light to.

(c) *ciego* to give sight to, restore the sight of.

(d) (*fig*) *persona* to enlighten.

(e) (*fig*) *agua* to find, strike, cause to flow.

2 VI **(a)** (*lit*) to give light, shed light; **esto alumbra bien** this gives a good light.

(b) (*Med*) to give birth, have a baby.

3 **alumbrarse*** VR to get tight*.

alumbre NM alum.

aluminio NM aluminium, aluminum (*US*); ~ **doméstico, papel de** ~ cooking foil, kitchen foil.

aluminosis NF INVAR *degeneration of cement used in construction.*

alumnado NM **(a)** (*personas*) (*Escol*) pupils, roll; (*Univ*) student body. **(b)** (*LAm: colegio*) college, school.

alumno, -a NM/F **(a)** (*de escuela*) pupil, (*Univ*) student; ~ **externo** day pupil; ~ **interno** boarder; **antiguo** ~ (*de escuela*) old boy, former pupil, (*Univ*) old student, former student, alumnus (*US*). **(b)** (*Jur*) ward, foster child.

alunarse [1a] VR (*CAm*) to get saddlesore (*horse*).

alunizaje NM **(a)** landing on the moon, moon-landing. **(b)** (***) smash-and-grab raid.

alunizar [1f] VI to land on the moon.

alusión NF allusion, mention, reference; **hacer** ~ **a** to allude to, mention, refer to; to hint at.

alusivo ADJ allusive.

aluvial ADJ alluvial.

aluvión NM **(a)** (*Geol*) alluvium; **tierras de** ~ alluvial soil(s). **(b)** (*fig*) flood; ~ **de improperios** shower of insults; torrent of abuse; **llegan en incontenible** ~ they come in an unstoppable flood.

aluvionado NM alluviation.

álveo NM riverbed, streambed.

alveolar ADJ alveolar.

alveolo NM, **alvéolo** NM (*Anat*) alveolus; socket; (*de panal*) cell; (*fig*) network, honeycomb.

alverja NF **(a)** (*arveja*) vetch. **(b)** (*LAm: guisante*) pea.

alverjilla NF sweet pea.

alza NF **(a)** (*de precio, temperatura*) rise; **al** ~, **en** ~ *tendencia* upward; *precio* rising; **jugar al** ~ (*Fin*) to speculate on a rising market; **revisar los precios al** ~ to put prices up; **cotizarse en** ~, **estar en** ~ (*Fin*) to rise, advance; **estar en** ~ (*LAm*) to have a good name (*o* reputation); **hacer algo por la pura** ~ to do sth just for the sake of it.

(b) (*Mil*) sight; **~s** sights; **~s fijas** fixed sights; **~s graduables** adjustable sights.

alzacristales NM INVAR: ~ **eléctrico** electric windows.

alzacuello(s) NM clerical collar, dog-collar.

alzada NF **(a)** (*de caballo*) height; (*Arquit*) elevation, side view. **(b)** (*Jur*) appeal.

alzado **1** ADJ **(a)** (*elevado*) raised, elevated.

(b) *precio* fixed; *persona* fraudulently bankrupt; **por un tanto** ~ for a lump sum.

(c) (*LAm: soberbio*) vain, stuck-up*; (*LAm*) *animal* untamed, wild; (*Pol*) mutinous; (*And*) drunk.

(d) **estar** ~ (*Cono Sur*) to be on heat.

2 NM **(a)** (*Tip*) gathering. **(b)** (*Arquit*) elevation.

3 NM, **alzada** NF: ~ **en armas** armed insurgent.

alzamiento NM **(a)** (*acto*) lifting, raising; (*de precio*) rise, increase; (*en subasta*) higher bid, raise.

(b) ~ **de bienes** fraudulent bankruptcy.

(c) (*Pol*) rising, revolt.

alzaprima NF **(a)** (*palanca*) lever, crowbar; (*cuña*) wedge. **(b)** (*Mús*) bridge. **(c)** (*Cono Sur: carro pesado*) heavy trolley, flat truck.

alzaprimar [1a] VT to lever up, raise with a lever; (*fig*) to arouse, stir up.

alzar [1f] **1** VT **(a)** (*gen*) to lift (up), raise (up); to hoist (up); (*Ecl*) *hostia* to elevate; *edificio* to raise; *cosecha* to get in, gather in; (*Tip*) to gather; *mantel* to remove, put away; *prohibición, restricción* to lift; (*LAm: recoger*) to pick up.

(b) (*quitar*) to remove; (*robar*) to steal; (*ocultar*) to hide.

2 **alzarse** VR **(a)** (*persona*) to rise, get up, stand up; (*precio, temperatura etc*) to rise.

(b) (*Pol*) to rise, revolt.

(c) (*Fin*) to go fraudulently bankrupt.
(d) ~ **algo**, (*LAm*) ~ **con algo** to steal (*o* make off with*) sth; ~ **con el premio** to carry off the prize.
(e) (*And: emborracharse*) to get drunk.
(f) (*LAm: animal*) to run away.
alzaválvulas NM INVAR (*Mec*) tappet.
alzo NM (*CAm*) theft.
A.M. NF ABR *de* **amplitud modulada** amplitude modulation, AM.
a.m. (*LAm*) ABR *de* **ante meridiem** ante meridiem, a.m.
ama NF **(a)** (*en casa*) lady of the house, mistress; ~ **de casa** housewife.
(b) (*dueña*) owner, proprietress; (*de pensión*) landlady; (*de soltero*) housekeeper; (*: de burdel*) madame; ~ **de cura** priest's housekeeper; ~ **de gobierno**, ~ **de llaves** housekeeper, (*de colegio etc*) matron, bursar.
(c) (*de niño*) foster mother; ~ **de brazos** (*LAm*), ~ **de cría**, ~ **de leche** wet-nurse; ~ **seca** nurse, nursemaid.
▼ **amabilidad** NF kindness; niceness; **tuvo la ~ de** + *infin* he was kind enough to + *infin*, he was good enough to + *infin*; **tenga la ~ de** + *infin* please be so kind as to + *infin*.
amabilísimo ADJ (SUPERL) *de* **amable**.
▼ **amable** ADJ kind; nice; lovable; ¡**muy ~**! thanks very much, that's very kind (of you); **es Vd muy ~** you are very kind; **ser ~ con uno** to be kind to sb, be good to sb; **si es tan ~** if you would be so kind; ¡**qué ~ ha sido Vd en traerlo!** how kind of you to bring it!
amablemente ADV kindly; **muy ~ me ayudó** he very kindly helped me.
amachambrarse [1a] VR (*Cono Sur*) *etc* = **amachinarse**.
amacharse [1a] VR (*LAm*) (*persona*) to dig one's heels in, refuse to be moved; (*caballo*) to refuse.
amachinarse [1a] VR (*LAm*) to live together, cohabit; ~ **con uno** to become sb's lover; **estar** (*o* **vivir**) **amachinado con** to live with, be the lover of.
amacho ADJ (*CAm, Cono Sur*) (*destacado*) outstanding; (*fuerte*) strong, vigorous.
amaderado ADJ *vino* woody.
amado [1] ADJ dear, beloved.
[2] NM, **amada** NF lover, sweetheart.
amador [1] ADJ loving, fond.
[2] NM, **amadora** NF lover.
amadrigar [1h] [1] VT to take in, give shelter to.
[2] **amadrigarse** VR (*animal*) to go into its hole, burrow; (*persona, fig*) to go into retirement, hide o.s. away; to withdraw into one's shell.
amadrinar [1a] VT *niño* to be godmother to; *soldado, regimiento* to be patron to.
amaestrado ADJ **(a)** *animal* trained; (*en circo etc*) performing. **(b)** *plan* well-contrived, artful.
amaestrador(a) NM/F trainer.
amaestramiento NM training; drill.
amaestrar [1a] VT *persona* to train, coach; *animal* to train; *caballo* to break in.
amagar [1h] [1] VT (*amenazar*) to threaten, portend; (*dar indicios de*) to show signs of.
[2] VI to threaten, be impending; to be in the offing; (*Med*) to show the first signs; (*Esgrima, Mil*) to feint; ~ **y no dar** to make empty threats; ~ **a** + *infin* to threaten to + *infin*, show signs of + *ger*.
[3] **amagarse** VR **(a)** (*Cono Sur: tomar una postura amenazante*) to adopt a threatening posture, shape up.
(b) (*: esconderse*) to hide.
amago NM **(a)** (*amenaza*) threat; threatening posture, threatening gesture.
(b) (*señal*) sign, symptom; (*indicio*) hint; ~ **tormentoso** outbreak of bad weather; **un ~ de mapa** a rough map; **con un ~ de sonrisa** with the suggestion of a smile, with a faint smile.
(c) (*Esgrima, Mil*) feint.
amainar [1a] [1] VT *vela* to take in, shorten; *furia etc* to calm.
[2] VI *y* **amainarse** VR (*ira, viento etc*) to abate, moderate; (*esfuerzo etc*) to lessen, slacken; to relax.
amaine NM (*V v*) **(a)** shortening. **(b)** abatement, moderation; lessening, slackening; relaxation.
amaitinar [1a] VT to spy on.
amaizado ADJ (*And*) rich.
amalaya INTERJ (*LAm*) = **ojalá**.
amalayar [1a] VT (*And, CAm, Méx*) to covet, long for; ~ + *infin* to long to + *infin*.
amalgama NF amalgam.
amalgamación NF amalgamation.
amalgamar [1a] [1] VT to amalgamate; to combine, mix, blend.
[2] **amalgamarse** VR to amalgamate.
Amalia NF Amelia.
amamantar [1a] VT **(a)** (*dar el pecho a*) to suckle, nurse. **(b)** (*Carib: mimar*) to spoil.

amancebamiento NM illicit union, cohabitation.
amancebarse [1a] VR (*t* **estar amancebados, vivir amancebados**) to live together, cohabit.
amancillar [1a] VT to stain; (*fig*) to stain; tarnish, dishonour.
amanecer [1] NM dawn, daybreak; **al ~** at dawn.
[2] [2d] VI **(a)** (*gen*) to dawn, begin to get light.
(b) (*aparecer*) to appear; begin to show.
(c) (*persona*) **amaneció en el bosque** he found himself at dawn in the wood, he woke up in the wood; **amaneció acatarrado** he woke up with a cold; **amaneció rey** he woke up to find himself king; **amaneceremos en Vigo** we'll be in Vigo by morning; **el día amaneció lloviendo** at daybreak it was raining.
(d) **amaneció bailando** (*LAm*) he danced all night.
(e) ¿**cómo amaneció?** (*LAm*) how are you?, good morning!
amanecida NF dawn, daybreak.
amanerado ADJ mannered, affected; (*LAm*) extra polite, excessively polite.
amaneramiento NM affectation; (*Liter etc*) mannerism (of style).
amanerarse [1a] VR to become affected, fall into affectation.
amanezca NF (*Carib, Méx*) (*alba*) dawn; (*desayuno*) breakfast.
amanezquera NF (*Carib, Méx*) early morning, daybreak.
amanita NF amanita.
amanojar [1a] VT to gather by the handful, gather in bunches.
amansa NF (*Cono Sur*) taming; breaking-in.
amansado ADJ tame.
amansador NM tamer; (*Méx*) horse breaker (*o* trainer).
amansadora NF (*Cono Sur*) **(a)** (*sala*) waiting-room (*in public building*).
(b) (*: espera*) long wait (*at government office*).
amansamiento NM **(a)** (*acto*) taming; breaking-in; soothing. **(b)** (*cualidad*) tameness.
amansar [1a] [1] VT *animal* to tame; *caballo* to break in; *persona* to tame, subdue; *pasión etc* to soothe, appease.
[2] **amansarse** VR (*persona*) to calm down; (*pasión etc*) to moderate, abate.
amanse NM (*And, Méx*) taming; breaking-in.
amante [1] ADJ loving, fond; **nación ~ de la paz** peace-loving nation.
[2] NM lover; **~s** lovers.
[3] NF lover, mistress.
amanuense NM/F amanuensis; scribe, copyist; secretary.
amañado ADJ **(a)** (*diestro*) skilful, clever. **(b)** (*falso*) fake, faked; (*falsificado*) fixed, rigged.
amañador [1] ADJ (*And, Carib*) having a pleasant climate.
[2] NM, **amañadora** NF (*) fixer*.
amañamiento NM fiddling, trickery; (*Pol*) rigging, gerrymandering.
amañanar [1a] VI (*persona*) to wake up; (*día*) to dawn.
amañar [1a] [1] VT **(a)** (*gen*) to do skilfully, perform cleverly.
(b) (*pey*) to alter; to play about with, tamper with; to fiddle*; *foto etc* to fake; *partido, jurado* to fix; *cuentas* to cook*; *excusa* to cook up; *elección* to rig, rig the results of.
[2] **amañarse** VR **(a)** (*ser diestro*) to be skilful, be expert; (*adquirir destreza*) to become expert, get the hang of it; (*Cono Sur*) to meet trouble head on; ~ **a** + *infin* to settle down to + *infin*; ~ **con** to get along with.
(b) (*Carib: mentir*) to tell lies, lie.
(c) (*And, Carib: acostumbrarse a un lugar*) to become (*o* grow) accustomed to a place (*o* person etc); **ya se amaña en Quito** he's settling down (*o* finding his feet) in Quito.
amaño NM **(a)** (*gen*) skill, expertness, cleverness; **tener ~ para** to have an aptitude for.
(b) **~s** (*Téc*) tools; (*fig*) tricks, cunning ways; guile; (*Cono Sur: mañas*) underhand means.
amapola NF poppy; **ponerse como una ~** to blush like a beetroot.
amar [1a] VT to love.
amaraje NM (*Aer*) landing (on the sea); splashdown, touchdown; ~ **forzoso** ditching.
amarar [1a] VI (*Aer*) to land (on the sea); (*cápsula*) to touch down, come down, splash down; (*para evitar accidente*) to ditch.
amarchantarse [1a] VR: ~ **en** (*LAm*) to become a (regular) customer of.
amargado ADJ bitter, embittered.
amargamente ADV bitterly.
amargar [1h] [1] VT to make bitter, sour; (*fig*) *persona, relaciones* to embitter; *ocasión* to spoil, upset.
[2] VI to be bitter, taste bitter.
[3] **amargarse** VR **(a)** to get bitter.
(b) (*persona*) to get bitter, become embittered.
amargo [1] ADJ **(a)** *sabor* bitter; sharp, tart.
(b) (*fig*) bitter, embittered.
(c) (*Cono Sur: cobarde*) cowardly; (*Carib: poco servicial*) unhelpful, offhand.
[2] NM **(a)** (*gen*) bitterness; sharpness, tartness.
(b) **~s** NMPL bitters.

(c) (*LAm Culin*) maté tea.

3 NM, **amarga** NF (*Cono Sur*) (*de mal genio*) grouch*; (*vago*) shirker, skiver*.

amargón NM dandelion.

amargor NM, **amargura** NF **(a)** (*sabor*) bitterness; sharpness, tartness. **(b)** (*fig*) bitterness; grief, distress.

amargoso ADJ (*LAm*) = **amargo**.

amaricado*, amariconado* ADJ **1** effeminate, queer*.

2 NM nancy-boy*, queer*.

Amarilis NF Amaryllis.

amarillear [1a] VI **(a)** (*volverse amarillo*) to go yellow, turn yellow.

(b) (*tirar a amarillo*) to be yellowish; (*mostrarse amarillo*) to show yellow, look yellow.

(c) (*palidecer*) to pale.

amarillecer [2d] VI to yellow, turn yellow.

amarillejo ADJ yellowish.

amarillento ADJ yellowish; *tez* pale, sallow.

amarillez NF yellow, yellowness; paleness, sallowness.

amarillismo NM **(a)** (*Prensa*) sensationalist journalism, sensationalism. **(b)** (*Pol*) trade unionism which is in league with the bosses.

amarillista ADJ **(a)** *prensa* sensationalist. **(b)** *sindicato* pro-management.

amarillo **1** ADJ **(a)** yellow; *semáforo* amber. **(b)** *prensa* sensational, gutter (*atr*). **(c)** (*Pol*) **sindicato ~** trade union which is in league with the bosses.

2 NM **(a)** yellow; **~ canario** canary yellow; **~ mostaza** mustard yellow; **~ paja** straw colour. **(b)** (*Carib*) ripe banana.

amarilloso ADJ (*Cono Sur*) yellowish.

amariposado* ADJ effeminate.

amarra NF **(a)** (*Náut*) cable, hawser; mooring line, painter; (*LAm: cuerda*) rope, line, cord; (*Méx: rienda*) rein, lead.

(b) (*Náut*) **~s** moorings; **cortar las ~s, romper las ~s** to break loose, cut adrift; **echar las ~s** to moor.

(c) (*fig*) **soltar las ~s** to go away, vanish.

(d) (*fig: protección*) **~s** protection; **tener buenas ~s** to have good connections, have influence.

amarradera NF (*And: para barcos*) mooring; (*Méx: cuerda*) rope, line, tether.

amarradero NM (*poste*) post, bollard; (*amarras*) moorings; (*sitio*) berth, mooring.

amarrado ADJ (*LAm*) mean, stingy.

amarradura NF mooring.

amarraje NM mooring charges.

amarrar [1a] **1** VT **(a)** (*gen*) to fasten, hitch, tie up; (*Náut*) *barco* to moor, tie up; *cuerda* to lash, belay; (*LAm*) to tie; *cartas* to stack; **está de ~** he's raving mad. **(b)** (*) to swot*, mug up*.

2 VI (*) to swot*, cram.

3 **amarrarse** VR (*): **amarrársela** (*And, CAm*) to get tight*.

amarre NM (*V v* **1**) fastening, tying; mooring, berth; lashing.

amarrete (*LAm*) **1** ADJ mean, stingy.

2 NM, **amarreta** NF miser, skinflint, tightwad* (*US*).

amarro NM (*And*) (*cuerda*) knotted string, knotted rope; (*nudos*) mass of knots; (*paquete*) bundle, packet; **~ de cigarrillos** packet of cigarettes.

amarrocar [1g] VI (*Cono Sur*) to scrimp and save.

amarronado ADJ chestnut, brownish.

amarroso ADJ (*CAm*) *fruta* acrid, sharp.

amartelado ADJ lovesick; **andar ~ con, estar ~ con** to be in love with, be infatuated with; **andan muy ~s** they're deeply in love.

amartelamiento NM lovesickness, infatuation.

amartelar [1a] **1** VT **(a)** *persona* to make jealous, torment with jealousy. **(b)** *corazón* to win, conquer.

2 **amartelarse** VR to fall in love (*de* with).

amartillar [1a] VT to hammer; *escopeta* to cock.

amasadera NF kneading trough.

amasado ADJ (*Carib*) **(a)** *sustancia* doughy. **(b)** *persona* plump.

amasador(a) **1** NM/F kneader, baker.

2 **amasadora** NF kneading machine.

amasadura NF **(a)** (*acto*) kneading. **(b)** (*hornada*) batch.

amasamiento NM kneading; (*Med*) massage.

amasandería NF (*And, Cono Sur*) bakery, baker's shop.

amasandero, -a NM/F (*And, Cono Sur*) bakery worker.

amasar [1a] VT **(a)** *masa* to knead; *harina, argamasa* to mix, prepare; *patatas* to mash; (*Med*) to massage.

(b) (*fig*) to cook up, concoct, fix.

(c) (*) *dinero etc* to pile up, accumulate.

amasiato NM (*LAm*) common-law marriage, cohabitation; **su ~ duró mucho tiempo** they lived together for a long time. **(b)** (*Méx*) casual sexual encounter, pick-up.

amasigado ADJ (*And*) dark, swarthy.

amasijar* [1a] VT (*Cono Sur*) to do in*.

amasijo NM **(a)** (*acto*) kneading; mixing; mashing; (*fig*) cooking-up,

concoction.

(b) (*material*) mixture, mash, batch (of dough *etc*); (*fig*) hotchpotch, medley, jumble.

(c) (*tarea*) task.

(d) (*plan*) plot, scheme.

(e) (*Carib: pan*) wheat bread; **~ de palos** beating, thrashing.

amasio NM, **amasia** NF (*CAm, Méx*) lover, (*mujer*) mistress.

amate NM (*LAm Bot*) fig-tree.

amateur ADJ, NMF amateur.

amateurismo NM amateurism.

amatista NF amethyst.

amatorio ADJ amatory; **poesía amatoria** love poetry.

amauta NM (*And Hist*) Inca elder.

amayorado ADJ (*And*) *niño* precocious, forward.

amazacotado ADJ (*pesado*) heavy, clumsy, awkward; (*informe*) shapeless, formless; (*Liter etc*) ponderous, stodgy; **~ de detalles** crammed with details.

amazona NF **(a)** (*Hist*) Amazon; (*jineta*) horsewoman, rider, equestrienne; (*pey*) mannish woman.

(b) (*vestido*) riding-habit.

Amazonas NM: **el río ~** the Amazon.

Amazonia NF Amazonia.

amazónico ADJ Amazon (*atr*).

ambages NMPL circumlocutions, roundabout style; **sin ~** in plain language, without beating about the bush.

ambagioso ADJ involved, circuitous, roundabout.

ámbar NM amber; **~ gris** ambergris.

ambareado ADJ (*And* ††) *pelo* chestnut, auburn.

ambarino ADJ amber.

Amberes NM Antwerp.

▼ **ambición** NF ambition; (*pey*) ambitiousness, self-seeking, egotism.

▼ **ambicionar** [1a] VT to aspire to, seek, strive after; (*pey*) to be out for, covet; **~ ser algo** to have an ambition to be somebody, be out to become somebody; **no ambiciona nada** he seeks nothing for himself.

ambiciosamente ADV ambitiously.

ambicioso **1** ADJ **(a)** (*gen*) ambitious.

(b) (*pey*) pretentious, grandiose; *persona* overambitious; overweening, proud, self-seeking.

2 NM, **ambiciosa** NF ambitious person; (*en el trabajo*) careerist; **~ de figurar** social climber.

ambidextro ADJ ambidextrous.

ambientación NF **(a)** (*lit*) orientation. **(b)** (*Cine, Liter etc*) setting; (*Cine: efectos*) sound-effects.

ambientado ADJ (*LAm*) (*climatizado*) air-conditioned; **estar ~** (*persona*) to be settled in, be at home.

ambientador NM air-freshener.

ambientador(a) NM/F (*Cine, TV*) dresser.

ambiental ADJ **(a)** (*lit*) environmental, relating to one's environment; **música ~** piped music. **(b)** (*fig*) general, pervasive.

ambientalismo NM environmentalism.

ambientalista ADJ, NMF environmentalist.

ambientalmente ADV environmentally; in terms of the surroundings (*o* setting).

ambientar [1a] **1** VT **(a)** (*dar ambiente a*) to give an atmosphere to, add colour to; **ambienta el escenario con bailes folklóricos** he enlivens the scene with folk dances.

(b) (*Liter etc*) to set; **la novela está ambientada en una sociedad de ...** the novel is set in a society of ...

(c) (*dirigir*) to orientate, direct.

2 **ambientarse** VR to orientate o.s., get one's bearings, get a sense of direction; (*LAm*) to find one's way around; to acclimatize o.s.; **procuraré ambientarme** I'll try to get myself sorted out, I'll try to get the feel of the thing.

ambiente **1** ADJ ambient, surrounding.

2 NM **(a)** (*gen*) atmosphere; **~ artificial** air-conditioning.

(b) (*fig*) atmosphere; (*entorno*) milieu, environment, surroundings; (*clima*) climate; (*Bio*) environment; **~ laboral** working environment; **en ~s universitarios** in university circles, in the university world; **no me gusta el ~** I don't like the atmosphere; **se crió en un ~ de violencia** he grew up in an atmosphere of violence; **voy a cambiar de ~** I'm going to move to new surroundings; **había escaso ~ callejero** there was not much going on in the streets.

(c) (*And: cuarto*) room.

ambigú NM (*Esp*) buffet supper, cold supper.

ambiguamente ADV ambiguously.

ambigüedad NF ambiguity.

ambiguo ADJ (*gen*) ambiguous; (*incierto*) doubtful, uncertain; (*equívoco*) noncommittal, equivocal; *género* common; (*bisexual*) bisexual.

ambilado ADJ (*Carib*): **estar** (*o* **quedar**) **~** (*boquiabierto*) to be left open-mouthed; (*embobado*) to be distracted.

➤ LENGUA Y USO: **ambición → 35.2** **ambicionar → 35.4**

ámbito NM (**a**) (*campo*) compass, ambit, field; (*límite*) boundary, limit; **dentro del ~ de** within the limits of; **en el ~ nacional** on a nation-wide basis, on a nation-wide scale; **en todo el ~ nacional** over the whole nation, throughout the country; **en el ~ nacional y extranjero** at home and abroad.
(**b**) (*fig*) scope, sphere, range; area; **~ de acción** field of activity; **buscar mayor ~** to look for greater scope.

ambivalencia NF ambivalence.

ambivalente ADJ ambivalent.

ambladura NF: **a paso de ~** at an amble.

amblar [1a] VI to amble, walk in a leisurely manner.

ambo NM (*Cono Sur*) two-piece suit.

ambos ADJ Y PRON both; **~ a dos** both (of them), both together.

ambrosía NF ambrosia.

Ambrosio NM Ambrose.

ambucia NF (*Cono Sur*) (*codicia*) greed, greediness; (*hambre*) voracious hunger.

ambuciento ADJ (*Cono Sur*) (*codicioso*) greedy; (*hambriento*) voracious.

ambulancia NF ambulance; (*Mil*) field hospital; **~ de correos** (*Esp Ferro*) post-office coach.

ambulanciero NM ambulance man.

ambulante ADJ walking; roving; *músico etc* itinerant; *actor* strolling; *vendedor, exposición etc* travelling.

ambulatoriamente ADV: **tratar un paciente ~** to treat sb as an out-patient.

ambulatorio [1] NM (*sección*) out-patients department; (*hospital*) state health-service hospital.
[2] ADJ: **en régimen ~** as an outpatient.

ameba NF amoeba.

amedrentador ADJ frightening, menacing.

amedrentar [1a] [1] VT to scare, frighten; to intimidate.
[2] **amedrentarse** VR to get scared.

amejoramiento NM (*LAm*) = **mejoramiento**.

amejorar [1a] VT (*LAm*) = **mejorar**.

amelcocharse [1a] VR (*Carib*) to fall in love; (*Méx*) *azúcar* to harden, set; (*ser coqueta*) to be coy, be prim.

amelonado ADJ (**a**) (*lit*) melon-shaped. (**b**) **estar ~*** to be lovesick.

amén [1] NM amen; **decir ~ a todo** to agree to everything; **en un decir ~** in a trice.
[2] INTERJ amen!
[3] **~ de** PREP (**a**) (*excepto por*) except for, aside from. (**b**) (*además de*) in addition to, besides; not to mention ...
[4] **~ de que** CONJ in spite of the fact that ...

-amen V Aspects of Word Formation in Spanish 2.

amenaza NF threat, menace; **~ amarilla** yellow peril; **~ de bomba** bomb scare; **~ de muerte** death threat.

amenazador ADJ, **amenazante** ADJ threatening, menacing.

amenazar [1f] [1] VT to threaten, menace; **~ violencia** to threaten violence; **~ a uno de muerte** to threaten sb with death; **una especie amenazada de extinción** a species threatened with extinction; **me amenazó con despedirme** he threatened to fire me.
[2] VI to threaten; to loom, impend; **~ + infin, ~ con + infin** to threaten to + infin.

amenguar [1i] VT (**a**) (*lit*) to lessen, diminish. (**b**) (*fig*) (*despreciar*) to belittle; (*deshonrar*) to dishonour.

amenidad NF pleasantness, agreeableness; grace, elegance.

amenización NF improvement; enlivening; brightening up; entertainment.

amenizar [1f] VT to make pleasant, make more agreeable; to add charm to; *conversación* to enliven, make more entertaining; *estilo* to brighten up; *reunión* to provide entertainment for, entertain.

ameno ADJ (*agradable*) pleasant, agreeable, nice; *estilo* graceful, elegant; *libro* pleasant, readable; **es un sitio ~** it's a nice spot; **prefiero una lectura más amena** I prefer lighter reading; **la vida aquí es más amena** life is pleasanter here.

amento NM catkin.

América NF America (*depending on context, may mean the whole continent, the United States, or Latin America*); **~ Central** Central America; **~ Latina** Latin America; **~ del Norte** North America; **~ del Sur** South America; **hacerse la ~** (*Cono Sur*) to make a fortune.

americana NF coat, jacket; **~ de sport** sports jacket.

americanada NF typically American thing (to do).

americanismo NM (*Ling*) americanism; (*LAm Pol*) Yankee imperialism; (*Carib, Méx*) liking for North American ways (*etc*).

americanista NMF americanist, specialist in indigenous American culture; (*liter*) specialist in American literature; (*CAm, Méx*) person with a liking for North American ways (*etc*).

americanización NF americanization.

americanizar [1f] [1] VT to americanize; to Latin-americanize.
[2] **americanizarse** VR to become americanized; to become Latin-americanized; (*CAm, Méx*) to adopt North American ways.

americano [1] ADJ American (*depending on context, may refer to the whole continent, the United States, or Latin America*).
[2] NM, **americana** NF American.

americio NM (*Quím*) americium.

amerindio, -a ADJ, NM/F Amerindian, American Indian.

ameritado ADJ (*LAm*) worthy.

ameritar [1a] [1] VT (*LAm*) to deserve.
[2] VI to win credit, do well.

amerizaje NM landing (on the sea); splashdown, touchdown.

amerizar [1f] VI (*Aer*) to land (on the sea); (*cápsula*) to touch down, come down, splash down.

amestizado ADJ like a half-breed.

ametrallador NM machine gunner.

ametralladora NF machine gun.

ametrallamiento NM machine-gunning, machine-gun attack.

ametrallar [1a] VT to machine-gun.

amianto NM asbestos.

amiba NF, **amibo** NM amoeba.

amiga NF (*gen*) friend; (*de chico*) girlfriend; (*amante*) lover; (*querida*) lover, mistress.

amigable ADJ friendly, amicable; (*fig*) harmonious.

amigablemente ADV amicably.

amigacho* NM (*pey*) mate, buddy (*esp US*), bachelor friend; **ha salido con los ~s** he's out with the boys; **esos ~s tuyos** those cronies of yours.

amigarse [1h] VR to get friendly; (*amantes*) to set up house together.

amigazo* NM (*Cono Sur*) pal*, buddy (*esp US*), close friend.

amígdala NF tonsil.

amigdalitis NF tonsillitis.

amigdalotomía NF tonsillectomy.

amigo [1] ADJ friendly; (*fig*) **ser ~ de** to be fond of, be given to; **A es muy ~ de B** A is a close friend of B; **son muy ~s** they are close friends.
[2] NM (*gen*) friend; (*de chica*) boyfriend; (*amante*) lover; **pero ¡~!** but my dear sir!, (*afectuoso*) look here, old chap!; **~ de lo ajeno** thief; **~ del alma, ~ de confianza, ~ íntimo** intimate friend, close friend; **~ de clase** schoolfriend; **~ por correspondencia** penfriend; **~ en la prosperidad** fair-weather friend; **hacerse ~s** to become friends; **hacerse ~ de** to make friends with, become a friend of; **soy ~ de hablar en franqueza** I am all for talking openly; **y todos tan ~s** and that's that, so that was that.

amigote* NM old pal*, old buddy (*esp US*); (*pey*) sidekick*, crony.

amiguero ADJ (*LAm*) friendly.

amiguete* NM buddy, mate; influential friend, friend in the right place.

amiguismo NM old-boy network, nepotism, jobs for the boys.

amiguita NF girlfriend; lover.

amiguito NM boyfriend; lover.

amiláceo ADJ starchy.

amilanar [1a] [1] VT to scare, intimidate.
[2] **amilanarse** VR to get scared, be intimidated.

aminoácido NM amino acid.

aminorar [1a] VT to lessen, diminish; *gastos etc* to cut down, reduce; *velocidad* to reduce, slacken.

amistad NF (**a**) (*cariño*) friendship; friendly relationship, friendly connection; **hacer** (*o* **trabar**) **~ con** to strike up a friendship with, become friends with; **llevar ~ con** to be on friendly terms with; **hacer las ~es** to make it up; **romper las ~es** to fall out, break off a friendship.
(**b**) **~es** friends, acquaintances; **invitar a las ~es** to invite one's friends.

amistar [1a] [1] VT (*hacer amigos*) to bring together, make friends of; (*reconciliar*) to bring about a reconciliation between, heal a breach between; (*Méx: hacerse amigo de*) to befriend.
[2] **amistarse** VR to become friends, establish a friendship; to make it up; **~ con** to make friends with.

amistosamente ADV amicably; in a friendly way (*o* tone *etc*).

amistoso [1] ADJ friendly, amicable; (*Dep*) friendly; (*Inform*) user-friendly.
[2] NM (*Dep*) friendly (game).

amnesia NF amnesia; loss of memory; **~ temporal** blackout.

amnésico, -a ADJ, NM/F amnesiac, amnesic.

amniocentesis NF INVAR amniocentesis.

amniótico ADJ amniotic; **líquido ~** amniotic fluid.

amnistía NF amnesty; **A~ Internacional** Amnesty International.

amnistiado, -a [1] ADJ amnestied.
[2] NM, **amnistiada** NF *person granted an amnesty*.

amnistiar [1c] VT to amnesty, grant an amnesty to.

amo NM (**a**) (*de familia etc*) master; head of the family; **~ de casa** householder; **¿está el ~?** is the master in? (**b**) (*de propiedad*) owner; proprietor. (**c**) (*en el trabajo*) boss, employer; overseer; **ser el ~** to be the boss; **ser el ~ en un juego** to be the best at a game.

amoblado [1] ADJ furnished.

2 NM (*CAm*) furniture, furnishings.
amoblar [1l] VT to furnish.
amodorramiento NM sleepiness, drowsiness.
amodorrarse [1a] VR to get sleepy, get drowsy; to fall into a stupor; to go to sleep.
amohinar [1a] 1 VT to vex, annoy.
2 **amohinarse** VR to get annoyed; to sulk.
amohosado ADJ (*Cono Sur*) rusty.
amojonar [1a] VT to mark out, mark the boundary of.
amojosado ADJ (*Cono Sur*) rusty.
amoladera NF whetstone, grindstone; (*LAm**: *tipo pesado*) nuisance, pain*.
amolado ADJ (a) (*Cono Sur*: *fastidiado*) bothered, irritated. (b) (*And*, *Méx*) (*ofendido*) offended; (*molesto*) irritating, annoying. (c) (*And*: *dañado*) damaged, ruined.
amolador 1 ADJ boring, tedious.
2 NM knife-grinder.
amoladura NF grinding, sharpening.
amolar [1l *o* 1a] 1 VT (a) (*Téc*) to grind, sharpen. (b) (*) (*fastidiar*) to upset; to annoy, irritate; (*perseguir*) to harass, pester. (c) (*estropear*) to damage, ruin. (d) (*Méx*⁑: *arruinar*) to screw up⁑, fuck up⁑; ¡lo **amolaste!** you screwed it up!⁑, you fucked it up!⁑
2 **amolarse** VR (a) (⁑) = **joderse**. (b) (*Cono Sur, Méx*: *enfadarse*) to get cross, take offence. (c) (*enflaquecer*) to get thinner.
amoldable ADJ *carácter, persona* adaptable.
amoldar [1a] 1 VT (*formar*) to mould (*t fig*; *a, según* on); to fashion; (*ajustar*) to adapt, adjust (*a* to).
2 **amoldarse** VR to adapt o.s., adjust o.s. (*a* to).
amonal NM ammonal.
amonarse* [1a] VR to get tight*.
amondongado ADJ fat, flabby.
amonedación NF coining, minting.
amonedar [1a] VT to coin, mint.
amonestación NF (a) (*advertencia*) warning; (*consejo*) piece of advice; (*Dep*) warning (with yellow card *etc*); (*Jur*) warning, caution. (b) (*Ecl*) marriage banns; **correr las amonestaciones** to publish the banns.
amonestador ADJ warning, cautionary.
amonestar [1a] VT (a) (*advertir*) to warn; (*avisar*) to advise, remind; (*reprender*) to reprove, admonish; (*Dep*) to warn (with yellow card *etc*); (*Jur*) to warn, caution. (b) (*Ecl*) to publish the banns of.
amoniacal ADJ ammoniacal, ammoniac, ammonia (*atr*).
amoniaco, amoníaco 1 ADJ ammoniac(al).
2 NM ammonia; ~ **líquido** liquid ammonia.
amononar [1a] VT (*Cono Sur*) to improve the appearance of, smarten up; (*pey*) to prettify.
amontillado NM amontillado (*pale dry sherry*).
amontonadamente ADV in heaps; in confusion.
amontonado ADJ heaped (up), piled up; **viven ~s** they live on top of each other, they live in very crowded conditions.
amontonamiento NM heaping, piling up; banking, drifting; hoarding; accumulation; overcrowding; crowding; (*Aut*) traffic jam.
amontonar [1a] 1 VT (a) (*apilar*) to heap (up), pile (up); *nieve, nubes etc* to bank (up); *datos etc* to gather, collect, accumulate; *víveres etc* to hoard, store away; **viene amontonando fichas** he's been collecting data in large quantities; ~ **alabanzas sobre uno** to heap praises on sb.
(b) (*And*: *insultar*) to insult.
2 **amontonarse** VR (a) (*apilarse*) to pile up, get piled up; (*hojas, nieve*) to drift, bank up; (*nubes*) to gather, pile up; to accumulate, collect; (*gente*) to crowd together, huddle together; (*acudir*) to come thronging; (*: *2 personas*) to shack up*; **viven amontonados*** they're shacked up together*; **la gente se amontonó en la salida** people crowded into the exit, people jammed the exit; **se amontonaron los coches** the cars got jammed.
(b) (*: *enfadarse*) to fly off the handle*, go up in smoke*.
(c) (*And*: *terreno*) to revert to scrub.
amor NM (a) (*gen*) love (*a* for, *de* of); ~ **cortés** courtly love; ~ **fracasado** disappointment in love, unhappy love affair; ~ **interesado** cupboard love; ~ **libre** free love; ~ **maternal** motherly love; ~ **platónico** platonic love; ~ **propio** amour propre, self-respect, pride; **una relación de ~-odio** a love-hate relationship; **es cuestión de ~ propio** it's a matter of pride; **picar a uno en el ~ propio** to wound sb's pride; ~ **a primera vista** love at first sight; **de** (*o con*) **mil ~es** with great pleasure; **¡con mil ~es!, ¡de mil ~es!** I'd love to!, I should be only too glad!; **por el ~ de** for the love of; for the sake of; **por** (**el**) ~ **de Dios** for God's sake; **por el ~ del arte** (*hum*) just for the fun of it; **por ~ al arte** (*Cono Sur*) for nothing, for love; **casarse por ~** to marry for love; **lo hizo por ~** he did it for love; **matrimonio sin ~** loveless marriage; **hacer el ~** to make love; **hacer el ~ a** to court; to make love to; **hacerse el ~** to make love; **con ~ se paga** one good turn deserves another, (*iró*) an eye for an eye; **tener mal de ~es** to be lovesick.

(b) (*persona*) love, lover; **mi ~, ~ mío** my love; **primer ~** first love; **buscar un nuevo ~** to look for a new love; **tiene un ~ en la ciudad** he's carrying on an affair in town.
(c) **ir al ~ del agua** to go with the current; **estar al ~ de la lumbre** to be close to the fire, be by the fireside.
(d) **~es** love affair, romance; **los mil ~es de don Juan** Don Juan's numberless affairs; **requebrar a una de ~es** to court sb.
amoral ADJ amoral.
amoralidad NF amorality.
amoratado ADJ purple, purplish; livid; (*de frío*) blue (with cold); (*LAm*: *con cardenales*) bruised, black and blue; **ojo ~** black eye.
amoratarse [1a] VR (*LAm*) to turn (*o* go) purple; (*por golpes*) to get bruised, go black and blue.
amorcillo NM (a) (*amorío*) flirtation, light-hearted affair.
(b) (*Cupido*) Cupid.
amordazar [1f] VT *persona* to gag; *perro etc* to muzzle; (*fig*) to gag, silence.
amorfo ADJ amorphous, formless, shapeless.
amorío NM (*t* ~s) love affair, romance.
amorochado ADJ (*LAm*) = **morocho** 1 (a).
amorosamente ADV lovingly, affectionately; amorously; caressingly.
amoroso ADJ (a) (*gen*) loving, affectionate, tender; *mirada etc* amorous; *carta etc* love (*atr*), of love; **poesía amorosa** love-poetry; **en tono ~** in an affectionate tone; in a caressing tone; **empezar a sentirse ~** to begin to feel amorous.
(b) (*fig*) *tierra* workable; *metal* malleable; *tiempo* mild.
(c) (*Cono Sur*) sweet, pretty, cute.
amorrar [1a] VI to hang one's head; (*fig*) to be sullen, sulk; (*Náut*) to pitch, dip the bows under.
amortajar [1a] VT *muerto* to lay out; (*fig*) to shroud.
amortecer [2d] 1 VT *ruido* to deaden, muffle; *fuego* to damp down; *luz* to dim; (*Mús*) to tone down; *pasión* to curb, control.
2 VI (*ruido*) to become muffled, die away; (*Med*) to faint, swoon.
amortecido ADJ: **caer ~** to fall in a swoon, faint away.
amortecimiento NM (*V v* 1) deadening, muffling; dimming; toning down; controlling; (*Med*) fainting.
amortiguación NF = **amortiguamiento**.
amortiguador 1 ADJ deadening, muffling; softening.
2 NM (*Téc*) damper, muffler; (*Mec*) shock absorber, cushion; (*Ferro*) buffer; (*Aut*) shock absorber; (*Elec*) damper; ~ **de luz** dimmer; ~ **de ruido** muffler, silencer.
amortiguamiento NM (*V v* 1) deadening, muffling; cushioning; absorption; softening; toning down; damping; dimming.
amortiguar [1i] 1 VT *ruido* to deaden, muffle; *golpe* to cushion; *choque* to absorb; *efecto* to cushion, mitigate, diminish, reduce the force of; *fuego* to damp down; *color* to soften, tone down; (*Elec*) to damp; *luz* to dim.
2 **amortiguarse** VR (*Cono Sur*) (a) (*Bot*) to wither.
(b) (*fig*) to get depressed; to become subdued.
amortizable ADJ (*Fin*) redeemable, amortizable.
amortización NF (*Jur*) amortization; (*Fin*) redemption; paying-off, repayment; (*de inversión*) depreciation; (*de puesto*) suppression, abolition.
amortizar [1f] VT (*Jur*) to amortize; (*Fin*) *bonos etc* to redeem; *préstamo, hipoteca* to pay off, repay; to refund; *puesto* to suppress, abolish; ~ **algo por desvalorización** to write sth off through depreciation.
amos⁑ INTERJ = **¡vamos!**; *V* **ir**.
amoscarse* [1g] VR (a) (*Esp*: *enojarse*) to get cross, get peeved*. (b) (*Carib, Méx*) (*aturdirse*) to get confused; (*avergonzarse*) to get embarrassed.
amostazar* [1f] 1 VT to make cross, peeve*.
2 **amostazarse** VR (a) to get cross, get peeved*. (b) (*LAm*) to be embarrassed, get embarrassed.
amotinado 1 ADJ riotous, violent; (*Mil, Náut*) mutinous.
2 NM, **amotinada** NF rioter; (*Pol*) rebel, (*Mil, Náut*) mutineer.
amotinador ADJ, NM = **amotinado**.
amotinamiento NM (*civil*) riot; (*Pol*) rising, insurrection; (*Mil, Náut*) mutiny.
amotinar [1a] 1 VT to stir up, incite to riot (*o* mutiny *etc*).
2 **amotinarse** VR to riot; to rise up, revolt, rebel; to mutiny.
amover [2h] VT to dismiss, remove (from office).
amovible ADJ *pieza* removable, detachable; *empleado* temporary.
amparador 1 ADJ helping, protecting, protective.
2 NM, **amparadora** NF protector.
amparar [1a] 1 VT (a) (*proteger*) to protect (*de* from), shelter, help; ~ **a los pobres** to help the poor; **le ampara el ministro** the minister protects him. (b) (*Jur*) *criminal* to harbour; (*abarcar*) to cover, embrace; to apply to. (c) (*Carib*: *pedir prestado*) to borrow.
2 **ampararse** VR (a) (*buscar protección*) to seek protection, seek help; ~ **a** to have recourse to; ~ **con**, ~ **de** to seek the protection of. (b) (*protegerse*) to protect o.s., defend o.s.; (*refugiarse*) to shelter.
amparo NM (*ayuda*) help; (*favor*) favour, protection; (*abrigo*) refuge,

shelter; (*defensa*) defence; (*Jur, esp*) right of habeas corpus; **al ~ de la ley** under the protection of the law; **recurso de ~** (*Cono Sur Jur*) habeas corpus.

ampáyar NM, **ampáyer** NM (*LAm*) referee, umpire.

ampe INTERJ (*And*) please!

amperímetro NM ammeter.

amperio NM ampère, amp.

ampliable ADJ extendable, which can be extended (*o* increased; *a* to); (*Inform*) expandable (*a* to).

ampliación NF enlargement, extension; expansion; amplification; (*Fot*) enlargement; **~ de capital(es)** increase of capital.

ampliado NM (*LAm Pol*) general meeting; mass meeting.

ampliadora NF (*Fot*) enlarger.

ampliamente ADV amply; extensively; **satisfará ~ la demanda** it will more than meet the demand.

ampliar [1c] VT (*gen*) to enlarge, extend; (*Fot*) to enlarge; *comercio etc* to expand; *capital* to increase; *sonido* to amplify; *poderes* to extend, widen; *declaración* to amplify, elaborate.

amplificación NF amplification; (*LAm Fot*) enlargement.

amplificador NM (*Rad*) amplifier.

amplificar [1g] VT to amplify; (*LAm Fot*) to enlarge.

amplio ADJ (a) (*espacioso*) spacious, wide; (*extenso*) extensive; roomy; *ropa* big; *falda etc* full.
(b) (*fig*) broad, extensive, ample; *informe etc* detailed, full; *poderes* ample, wide; *sentido* broad.

amplitud NF spaciousness, extent; roominess; fullness; amplitude; **~ de banda** band width; **~ de criterio** broad-mindedness.

ampo NM (*blancura*) dazzling whiteness; (*copo de nieve*) snowflake; **como el ~ de la nieve** as white as the driven snow.

ampolla NF (*burbuja*) bubble; (*Med*) blister; (*frasco*) flask, decanter, (*Med*) ampoule; **la medida levantó ~s en la compañía** (*fig*) the measure raised a lot of bad feeling within the company.

ampollarse [1a] VR to blister, form blisters.

ampolleta NF (*botellita*) phial, small bottle; (*de arena*) hourglass, sandglass; (*de termómetro etc, t Elec*) bulb; **encendérsele a uno la ~** (*Cono Sur**) to have a brainwave.

ampón ADJ bulky; *persona* stout, tubby.

ampulosamente ADV bombastically, pompously.

ampulosidad NF bombast, pomposity.

ampuloso ADJ bombastic, pompous.

amputación NF amputation.

amputado, -a NM/F amputee.

amputar [1a] VT to amputate, cut off.

amuchachado ADJ boyish.

amuchar* [1a] VT (*And, Cono Sur*) to increase, multiply.

amueblado ①️ ADJ furnished (*con, de* with).
②️ NM (*Cono Sur euf*) hotel, hotel room (*used for sexual encounters and paid for by the hour*).

amueblamiento NM furnishing.

amueblar [1a] VT to furnish (*de* with).

amuermado* ADJ boring.

amuermante* ADJ boring; dull, unexciting; mundane, banal.

amuermar* [1a] ①️ VT to bore.
②️ **amuermarse** VR (a) (*tener sueño*) to feel sleepy (after a meal); (*fig*) (*aburrirse*) to get bored; (*deprimirse*) to get depressed.
(b) (*pudrirse*) to vegetate, rot; (*ponerse pesado*) to get very dull.

amuinar [1a] (*Méx*) ①️ VT to annoy, irritate.
②️ **amuinarse** VR to get cross.

amujerado ADJ effeminate.

amularse [1a] VR (*Méx*) (*persona*) to get stubborn, dig one's heels in; (*Com*) to become unsaleable, become a glut on the market.

amulatado ADJ mulatto-like.

amuleto NM amulet, charm.

amunicionar [1a] VT to supply with ammunition.

amuñecado ADJ doll-like.

amura NF (*Náut*) (a) (*proa*) bow. (b) (*cabo*) tack.

amurallado ADJ *ciudad* walled.

amurallar [1a] VT to wall, wall in, fortify.

amurar [1a] VI (*Náut*) to tack.

amurrarse [1a] VR (*LAm*) to get depressed, become sad.

amurriarse [1b] VR (*Esp*) to get sad (*o* depressed).

amurruñarse [1a] VR (*Carib*) (*abrazarse*) to nestle together, cuddle up; (*hacerse un ovillo*) to curl up.

amusgar [1h] ①️ VT *orejas* to lay back, throw back; *ojos* to screw up, narrow.
②️ **amusgarse** VR (*CAm*) to feel ashamed.

Ana NF Ann(e).

anabólico ADJ anabolic.

anabolizante NM anabolic steroid.

anacarado ADJ pearly, mother-of-pearl (*atr*).

anacardo NM (*nuez*) cashew (nut); (*árbol*) cashew tree.

anaco NM (*And*) poncho, Indian blanket.

anacoluto NM anacoluthon.

anaconda NF anaconda.

anacoreta NMF anchorite.

Anacreonte NM Anacreon.

anacronía NF timelessness.

anacrónico ADJ anachronistic.

anacronismo NM (a) (*gen*) anachronism. (b) (*objeto*) out-of-date thing, piece of bric-a-brac.

ánade NM duck; **~ friso** gadwall; **~ rabudo** pintail; **~ real** mallard; **~ silbón** wigeon.

anadear [1a] VI to waddle.

anadeo NM waddle, waddling.

anadón NM duckling.

anaeróbico ADJ, **anaerobio** ADJ anaerobic.

anáfora NF anaphora.

anafórico ADJ anaphoric, anaphorical.

anagrama NM anagram.

anal ADJ anal.

analcohólico ADJ *bebida* non-alcoholic, soft.

anales NMPL annals.

analfa* ADJ, NMF = **analfabeto**.

analfabetismo NM illiteracy.

analfabeto ①️ ADJ illiterate.
②️ NM, **analfabeta** NF illiterate (person).

analgesia NF analgesia.

analgésico ①️ ADJ analgesic, pain-killing.
②️ NM analgesic, pain-killer.

análisis NM INVAR analysis; (*explicativo*) breakdown; (*Ling*) analysis, parsing; (*Med*) test (*de* for); **~ de costos** cost analysis; **~ espectral** spectrum analysis; **~ financiero** financial analysis; **~ funcional** functional analysis; **~ de mercados** market research; **~ orgánico** organic analysis; **~ de sangre** blood test; **~ de sistemas** systems analysis; **~ de viabilidad** feasibility study; **~ de la voz** speech analysis.

analista NMF analyst; (*de historia regional*) chronicler, annalist; **~ financiero** financial analyst, market analyst; **~ de inversiones** investment consultant; **~ de sistemas** systems analyst.

analista-programador(a) NM/F computer analyst and programmer.

analítico ADJ analytic(al); **cuadro ~** analytic table, table showing the breakdown by groups (*etc*).

analizable ADJ analysable; **fácilmente ~** easy to analyse.

analizador NM analyst.

analizar [1f] VT to analyse; (*Ling*) to parse.

analogía NF analogy; similarity; **por ~ con** on the analogy of.

analógico ADJ analogical.

análogo ①️ ADJ analogous, similar (*a* to).
②️ NM analogue; **añadir frutas o ~** add fruit or something of the kind, add fruit or something similar.

ananá(s) NM, **ananasa** NF (*And*) pineapple.

anapesto NM anapaest.

anaquel NM shelf.

anaquelería NF shelves, shelving.

anaranjado ①️ ADJ orange(-coloured).
②️ NM orange (colour).

anarca*, anarco* = **anarquista**.

anarcosindicalismo NM anarcho-syndicalism.

anarcosindicalista ①️ ADJ anarcho-syndical.
②️ NMF anarcho-syndicalist.

anarquía NF anarchy.

anárquico ADJ anarchic(al).

anarquismo NM anarchism.

anarquista ①️ ADJ anarchist(ic).
②️ NMF anarchist.

anarquizante ADJ anarchic.

anarquizar [1f] VT to produce anarchy in, cause utter disorder in; to sow the seeds of rebellion among.

anatema NM anathema.

anatematizante ADJ: **palabras ~s** words of condemnation.

anatematizar [1f] VT, **anatemizar** [1f] VT (*Ecl*) to anathematize; (*fig*) to curse, condemn.

anatomía NF anatomy.

anatómico ADJ anatomical; **asiento ~** seat moulded to the body.

anatomizar [1f] VT to anatomize; (*Arte*) *huesos, músculos etc* to bring out, emphasize; (*fig*) to anatomize, dissect.

anca¹ NF haunch; rump, croup; **~s*** bottom, bum‡; **~s de rana** (*Culin*) frog's legs; **llevar a uno a las ~s, llevar a uno en ~(s)** (*LAm*) to let sb ride pillion (*o* behind one); **esto lleva el desastre en ~(s)** (*LAm*) this spells disaster; **no sufre ~s*** he can't take a joke.

anca² NF (*And*) toasted maize.

ancestral ADJ ancestral; (*fig*) ancient.

ancestro NM (*LAm*) (a) (*persona*) ancestor. (b) (*linaje*) ancestry.

anchamente ADV widely.

ancheta NF **(a)** (*Com: lote*) small lot of goods; (*negocio*) small business; small-time affair.

(b) (*ganancia*) gain, profit; (*And, Méx*) (*ganga*) bargain; (*negocio*) profitable deal; (*oportunidad*) chance to make easy money; **¡vaya (o buena) ~!** some deal this turned out to be!

(c) (*And, Cono Sur: palabrería*) prattle, babble.

(d) (*Carib*) (*broma*) joke; (*estafa*) hoax.

ancho **1** ADJ **(a)** (*gen*) wide, broad; (*demasiado ~*) too wide; **~ de 4 cm, 4 cm de ~** 4 cm wide, 4 cm in width; **~ de espaldas** broad-shouldered; **recorrer un país a lo ~ y a lo largo** to cross and recross a country; **por todo el ~ mundo** throughout the whole wide world.

(b) (*Cos*) big; loose, loose-fitting; *falda* full; **me viene algo ~** it's on the big side for me; **le viene muy ~ el cargo** the job is too much for him, he's not up to the job.

(c) (*fig*) liberal, broad-minded; *vida* fast; **~ de conciencia** not overscrupulous; **~ de miras** broad-minded; **ponerse ~** to be smug, get conceited; **quedarse tan ~** to go on as if nothing had happened, remain completely unabashed.

(d) estar a sus anchas to be at one's ease, be comfortable; **aquí estoy a mis anchas** I feel at home here; **ponerse a sus anchas** to make o.s. comfortable, spread o.s.

2 NM width, breadth; (*Ferro*) gauge; **~ de banda** band width; **~ normal** standard gauge; **~ de vía** (*Ferro*) gauge, (*Aut*) wheel track.

anchoa NF anchovy (*pickled, tinned*).

anchor NM = **anchura**.

anchote ADJ *persona* burly.

anchoveta NF (*And*) anchovy (*for fishmeal*).

anchura NF width, breadth; wideness; (*Cos*) bigness, looseness, fullness; (*fig*) freedom; ease, comfort; **~ alar** wingspan; **~ de conciencia** lack of scruple.

anchuroso ADJ wide, broad; spacious.

anciana NF old woman, old lady, elderly lady.

ancianidad NF old age.

anciano **1** ADJ old, aged.

2 NM old man, elderly man; (*Ecl*) elder.

ancilar ADJ ancillary.

ancla NF anchor; **~ de la esperanza** (*fig*) sheet anchor, last hope; **echar ~s** to cast anchor, drop anchor; **estar al ~** to be (o lie o ride) at anchor; **levar ~s** to weigh anchor.

ancladero NM anchorage.

anclaje NM (*Naut*) anchorage; (*Aut*) catch, clamp (of a seatbelt).

anclar [1a] VI to anchor, drop anchor.

ancón NM **(a)** (*Náut*) cove. **(b)** (*And, Méx: rincón*) corner. **(c)** (*And: camino*) mountain pass.

áncora NF anchor; **~ de salvación** (*fig*) sheet anchor, last hope.

andadas NFPL (*Caza*) tracks; **volver a las ~** to backslide, revert to one's old ways.

andaderas NFPL baby-walker.

andadero ADJ passable, easy to traverse.

andado ADJ (*trillado*) worn, well-trodden; (*corriente*) common, ordinary; *ropa* old, worn.

andador **1** ADJ **(a)** (*rápido*) fast-walking; **es ~** he's a good walker.

(b) (*Cono Sur*) *caballo* well-paced, long-striding.

(c) (*viajero*) fond of travelling, fond of gadding about.

2 NM, **andadora** NF (*persona*) walker; gadabout.

3 NM (*aparato*) baby-walker; **~es** baby harness.

4 andadora NF (*Méx*) prostitute, streetwalker.

andadura NF **(a)** (*acto*) walking; (*paso*) pace, gait, walk; (*de caballo*) pace. **(b)** (*fig: camino*) path, course; (*progreso*) progress; (*avance*) advance; **comenzar nuevas ~s** to start again.

ándale INTERJ (*esp Méx*) V **andar 1(h)**.

andalón ADJ (*Méx*) *caballo* well-paced, long-striding.

Andalucía NF Andalusia.

andalucismo NM **(a)** (*Ling*) andalusianism, word (o phrase *etc*) peculiar to Andalusia. **(b)** sense of the differentness of Andalusia; (*Pol*) doctrine of (o belief in) Andalusian autonomy.

andaluz, -uza **1** ADJ, NM/F Andalusian.

2 NM (*Ling*) Andalusian.

andaluzada* NF (*cuento*) tall story, piece of typical Andalusian exaggeration; (*acto*) the sort of thing one expects from an Andalusian.

andamiada NF, **andamiaje** NM scaffolding, staging.

andamio NM (*de edificio*) scaffold; (*tablado*) stage, stand; **~ óseo** skeleton, bone framework.

andana NF row, line; **llamarse ~** to go back on one's word; to wash one's hands of a matter.

andanada NF **(a)** (*Náut*) broadside; (*fuego artificial*) big rocket; (*fig*) reprimand, telling-off*; **~ verbal** verbal broadside; **por ~s** (*Cono Sur*) in (o to) excess; **soltar una ~** to say something unexpected, drop a bomb*; **soltar la ~ a uno** to give sb a telling-off*.

(b) (*tribuna*) covered grandstand.

(c) (*de ladrillos etc*) layer, row.

andante **1** ADJ walking; *caballero etc* errant.

2 NM (*Mús*) andante.

andanza NF fortune, fate; **~s** deeds, adventures.

andar [1p] **1** VT **(a)** *distancia* to go, cover, travel; *camino etc* to travel, go along, walk.

(b) (*CAm: llevar*) to wear; to carry, use, have; **yo no ando reloj** I don't wear a watch, I don't carry a watch.

2 VI **(a)** (*ir a pie*) to go, walk; (*moverse*) to move; (*viajar*) to go about, travel; (*caballo*) to walk, amble; **~ a caballo** to ride, go on horseback; **~ tras uno** to go after sb; to pursue sb; **~ tras una chica** to court a girl; **~ tras algo** to yearn for sth, have a keen desire for sth; **venimos andando** we walked, we came on foot.

(b) (*reloj*) to go; (*Mec*) to go, run, work; **el reloj anda bien** the clock keeps good time; **el reloj no anda** the clock won't go.

(c) (*estar*) to be; **anda por aquí** it's around here somewhere; **~ alegre** to be cheerful, feel cheerful; **hay que ~ con cuidado** one must go carefully; **anda enfermo** he's ill; **~ bien de salud** to be well, be in good health; **andamos mal de dinero** we're badly off for money; **¿cómo te anda?** how are you getting on?, how's it going?; **¿cómo anda esto?** how are things going?; **¿cómo andas de tabaco?** how are you off for cigarettes? **ropa de ~ por casa** clothes one normally wears at home; **un montaje muy de ~ por casa** an amateurish production.

(d) anda en los 50 he's about 50.

(e) ~ en to tamper with, mess about with; **han andado en el armario** they've been rummaging in the cupboard; **no me andes en mis cosas** keep out of my things.

(f) ~ en to be engaged in; **~ en pleitos** to be engaged in lawsuits, be tied up in lawsuits.

(g) (*tiempo*) to pass, elapse.

(h) ¡anda! (*sorpresa*) get along with you!, well!, go on!; (*¡vamos!*) come on!; (*desaprobación*) get on with it!; **¡anda, anda!** don't be silly!; **¡anda ya!** (*incredulidad*) really!, leave off!; **¡andando!** and that's it!, now we can get on with it!; (*Méx etc*) **¡ándale (pues)!*** (*adiós*) cheerio!; (*¡apúrese!*) come on!, hurry up!; (*encontrando algo*) that's it!, that's the one!; (*gracias*) thanks!

(i) anda que te anda never letting up for a moment, without stopping at all.

(j) ~ haciendo algo to be doing sth, be in the course of doing sth; **no andes criticándole todo el tiempo** don't keep criticizing him all the time.

3 andarse VR *frec* = VI; **(a)** (*irse*) to go off, go away.

(b) ~ con to use, make use of, employ; **~ en** to indulge in; **Juanito se anda por el abecedario** Johnny is beginning to read.

(c) todo se andará all in good time, it will all come right in the end.

4 NM walk; gait, pace; **a largo ~** in the end; in the long run; **a más ~, a todo ~** at full speed, as quickly as possible; **a mejor ~** at best; **a peor ~** at worst; **estar a un ~** to be on the same level.

andaras NM (*And*) Indian flute.

andarica NF (*prov*) crab.

andariego ADJ wandering, roving; fond of travelling; restless.

andarilla NF (*And Mús*) type of flute.

andarín NM walker; **es muy ~** he is a great walker.

andarivel NM **(a)** (*Téc*) cableway, cable ferry; (*Náut etc*) handrope; (*Cono Sur*) (*cerco*) rope barrier; (*de piscina*) lane. **(b)** (*And: adornos*) adornments, trinkets.

andas NFPL (*camilla*) stretcher; (*silla*) litter, sedan chair; (*Rel*) portable platform; (*féretro*) bier; **llevar a uno en ~** (*fig*) to praise sb to the skies; to treat sb with great consideration.

ándele INTERJ (*Méx*) (*¡siga!*) come on!; (*¡ya ves!*) see what I mean!; (*¡ya lo creo!*) get away!; (*correcto*) exactly!

andén NM (*Ferro*) platform; (*CAm: acera*) pavement, sidewalk (*US*); (*Náut*) quayside; (*And, Cono Sur Agr*) terrace; **~ de salida** departure platform; **~ de vacío** arrival platform.

Andes NMPL Andes.

andinismo NM (*LAm*) mountaineering, mountain climbing; **hacer ~** to go mountaineering, go mountain climbing.

andinista NMF (*LAm*) mountaineer, climber.

andino ADJ Andean, of the Andes.

ándito NM (*pasillo*) outer walk, corridor; (*acera*) pavement, sidewalk (*US*).

andoba* NM guy*, chap*.

andolina NF swallow.

andón ADJ (*LAm*) = **andador (b)**.

andonear [1a] VI (*Carib*) (*persona*) to amble (o stroll) along; (*caballo*) to trot.

andorga* NF belly.

andorina NF swallow.

Andorra NF Andorra.

andorrano, -a ADJ, NM/F Andorran.

andorrear* [1a] VI (*ajetrearse*) to bustle about, fuss around; (*ir de acá para allá*) to gad about, move about a lot.

andorrero [1] ADJ bustling, busy.
[2] NM, **andorrera** NF busy sort, gadabout.
[3] **andorrera** NF (*pey*) streetwalker.
andrajo NM (a) (*trapo*) rag, tatter; ~s rags, tatters; **estar en ~s, estar hecho un ~** to be in rags; **ser un ~ humano** to be a wreck. (b) (*pillo*) rascal, good-for-nothing. (c) (*bagatela*) trifle, mere nothing.
andrajoso ADJ ragged, in tatters.
Andrés NM Andrew.
androcéntrico ADJ male-centred, androcentric.
androcentrismo NM male-centredness, androcentricity.
androfobia NF hatred of men.
androgénico ADJ androgenic.
andrógeno NM androgen.
androginia NF androgyny.
andrógino ADJ androgynous.
androide NM android.
Andrómaca NF Andromache.
andrómina• NF fib, tale; piece of humbug; trick.
andropausia NF male menopause.
androsterona NF androsterone.
andullo NM (*Carib, Cono Sur, Méx*) plug of chewing tobacco.
andurrial NM (*lodazal*) bog, quagmire; (*zanja*) ditch; (*descampado*) piece of waste ground; ~es out-of-the way place, the wilds; **en esos ~es** in that godforsaken place.
anduve, anduviera etc V **andar**.
anea NF bulrush, reedmace.
aneblar [1j] [1] VT to cover with mist (o cloud); (*fig*) to obscure, darken, cast a cloud over.
[2] **aneblarse** VR to get misty, get cloudy; to get dark.
anécdota NF anecdote, story; (*odd*) incident, (strange) business; **este cuadro tiene una ~** there's a tale attached to this picture.
anecdotario NM collection of stories.
anecdótico ADJ anecdotal; trivial; **contenido ~** story content; **valor ~** story value, value as a story; **el estudio se queda en lo ~** the study does not rise above the merely superficial, the study stays on the surface.
anecdotismo NM anecdotal nature, (merely) anecdotal quality; triviality.
anega NF (*Cono Sur*) = **fanega**.
anegación NF drowning; flooding.
anegadizo ADJ *tierra* subject to flooding, frequently flooded; *madera* heavier than water.
anegar [1h] [1] VT (a) (*ahogar*) to drown. (b) (*inundar*) to flood; (*fig*) to overwhelm, destroy.
[2] **anegarse** VR (a) (*ahogarse*) to drown. (b) (*lugar*) to flood, be flooded; ~ **en llanto** to dissolve into tears. (c) (*Náut*) to sink, founder.
anejo [1] ADJ attached; dependent; ~ **a** attached to; joined on to.
[2] NM (*Arquit*) annexe, outbuilding; (*Liter, Tip*) supplement.
anemia NF anaemia.
anémico ADJ anaemic.
anemómetro NM anemometer; (*Aer*) wind gauge; ~ **registrador** wind-speed indicator.
anémona NF, **anémone** NF anemone; ~ **de mar** sea anemone.
aneroide ADJ aneroid.
anestesia NF anaesthesia; ~ **general** general anaesthetic; ~ **local** local anaesthetic.
anestesiante ADJ, NM anaesthetic (t *fig*).
anestesiar [1b] VT to anaesthetize, give an anaesthetic to; (*fig*) to blunt (the emotions of), desensitize.
anestésico ADJ, NM anaesthetic.
anestesista NMF anaesthetist.
anexar [1a] VT (*Pol*) to annex; (*Inform*) to append.
anexión NF, **anexionamiento** NM annexation.
anexionar [1a] VT (*Pol*) to annex.
anexo [1] ADJ attached; dependent (t *Ecl*); **llevar algo ~, tener algo ~** to have sth attached; **anexo a la presente ...** (*Méx*) please find enclosed ...
[2] NM (*Arquit*) annexe, outbuilding; (*Ecl*) dependency; (*papel*) appendix, attached document; (*And Telec*) extension.
anfeta• NF = **anfetamina**.
anfetamina NF amphetamine.
anfetamínico, -a NM/F (a) amphetamine addict, speed freak•. (b) (•) bore; idiot; pain•.
anfibio [1] ADJ amphibious; amphibian (t *Aer etc*).
[2] NM amphibian; **los ~s** (*como clase*) the amphibia.
anfibología NF ambiguity.
anfibológico ADJ ambiguous.
anfiteatro NM amphitheatre; arena; (*Teat*) dress circle; ~ **anatómico** dissecting room.
Anfitrión NM Amphitryon.
anfitrión NM host.

anfitriona NF hostess.
ánfora NF amphora; (*LAm*) ballot box; (*Cono Sur*•: *de marijuana*) marijuana pouch.
anfractuosidad NF (*aspereza*) roughness, unevenness; (*curva*) bend; (*vuelta*) turning; (*Anat*) fold, convolution; ~es rough places, up-and-down parts.
anfractuoso ADJ rough, uneven, up-and-down.
angarilla NF (*LAm*), **angarillas** NFPL (*carretilla*) handbarrow; (*alforjas*) panniers, packs; (*Culin*) cruet, cruet stand.
angarrio ADJ (*And, Carib*) terribly thin, thin as a rake•.
angas: por ~ o por mangas (*And*) like it or not; willy-nilly.
ángel NM (a) (*Rel*) angel; ~ **caído** fallen angel; ~ **custodio**, ~ **de la guarda** guardian angel; ~ **exterminador** angel of death; ~ **del infierno** hell's angel.
(b) (*fig*) charm, mystery; charisma; **tener ~** to have charm, be very charming; **tener mal ~** to be a nasty piece of work; to have an unfortunate effect (on people *etc*); **pasó un ~** there was a sudden silence; (*en charla*) there was a lull in the conversation.
angélica NF angelica.
angelical ADJ, **angélico** ADJ angelic(al).
angelino [1] ADJ of Los Angeles.
[2] NM, **angelina** NF native (o inhabitant) of Los Angeles; **los ~s** the people of Los Angeles.
angelito NM little angel; (*LAm*) dead child; **¡~!** (*Cono Sur*) don't play the innocent!, pull the other one!•; **¡no seas ~!** (*Cono Sur*) don't be silly!
angelón• NM: ~ **de retablo** fat old thing.
angelopolitano (*Méx*) [1] ADJ of Puebla.
[2] NM, **angelopolitana** NF native (o inhabitant) of Puebla; **los ~s** the people of Puebla.
angelote NM (a) (*niño*) chubby child. (b) (*LAm: person*) decent person. (c) (*pez*) angel-fish.
ángelus NM angelus.
angina NF (a) (*Med*) angina, quinsy; (*Méx*) tonsil; ~s tonsillitis, sore throat, pharyngitis; ~ **de pecho** angina pectoris; **tener ~s** to have a sore throat. (b) ~s (*Esp*‡) tits‡.
angiosperma NF angiosperm.
anglicanismo NM Anglicanism.
anglicano, -a ADJ, NM/F Anglican.
anglicismo NM anglicism.
anglicista [1] ADJ: **tendencia ~** anglicizing tendency.
[2] NMF anglicist.
angliparla NF (*hum*) Spanglish.
anglo... PREF anglo...
anglófilo, -a NM/F anglophile.
anglofobia NF anglophobia.
anglófobo [1] ADJ anglophobe, anglophobic.
[2] NM, **anglófoba** NF anglophobe.
anglófono [1] ADJ English-speaking.
[2] NM, **anglófona** NF English speaker.
anglohablante, angloparlante [1] ADJ English-speaking.
[2] NMF English speaker.
anglonormando [1] ADJ Anglo-Norman; **Islas** FPL **Anglonormandas** Channel Isles.
[2] NM, **anglonormanda** NF Anglo-Norman.
[3] NM (*Ling*) Anglo-Norman.
anglosajón, -ona [1] ADJ, NM/F Anglo-Saxon.
[2] NM (*Ling*) Anglo-Saxon.
Angola NF Angola.
angoleño, -a ADJ, NM/F Angolan.
angolés = **angoleño**.
angora NMF angora.
angorina NF artificial angora.
angostar [1a] [1] VT to narrow; (*Cono Sur*) to make smaller; *ropa* to take in.
[2] **angostarse** VR to narrow, get narrow(er).
angosto ADJ narrow.
angostura NF (a) (*cualidad*) narrowness. (b) (*Náut*) narrows, strait; (*Geog*) narrow passage, narrow defile, narrow place. (c) (*bebida*) angostura.
angra NF cove, creek.
angstrom NM angstrom.
anguila NF eel; (*Náut*) ~s slipway.
angula NF elver, baby eel.
angulación NF (*Cine*) camera angle.
angular [1] ADJ angular; V **piedra**.
[2] NM: **gran ~** wide-angle lens.
Angulema NF Angoulême.
ángulo NM baby eel, elver.
ángulo NM (*gen, t Mat*) angle; (*esquina*) corner; (*curva*) bend, turning; (*Mec*) knee, bend; ~ **agudo** acute angle; ~ **alterno** alternate angle; ~ **de mira** angle of sight; ~ **oblicuo** oblique angle; ~ **obtuso** obtuse

angle; **~ del ojo** corner of one's eye; **~ recto** right angle; **de ~ recto, en ~ recto** right-angled; **~ de subida, ~ de trepada** (*Aer*) angle of climb; **de gran ~, de ~ ancho** *lente etc* wide-angle; **en ~** at an angle; **está inclinado a un ~ de 45 grados** it is leaning at an angle of 45°; **formar ~ con** to be at an angle to.

anguloso ADJ *cara etc* angular, sharp; *camino* tortuous, full of bends.

angurria NF (*And, Cono Sur*) **(a)** (*hambre*) voracious hunger, greed; (*angustia*) intense anxiety, grave worry; **comer con ~*** to scoff one's food*. **(b)** (*tacañería*) meanness, stinginess.

angurriento ADJ (*And, Cono Sur*) **(a)** (*voraz*) greedy. **(b)** (*tacaño*) mean, stingy.

angustia NF anguish, distress; **~ de muerte** death-throes; **de puta ~*** by sheer chance.

angustiado ADJ **(a)** (*apenado*) anguished, distressed; anxious; wretched. **(b)** (*avaro*) grasping, mean.

angustiante ADJ *situación, experiencia* distressing.

angustiar [1b] **1** VT to distress, grieve, cause anguish to.
2 angustiarse VR to be distressed, grieve, feel anguish (*por* at, on account of); to worry, get worried.

angustiosamente ADV in an anguished tone (*etc*); anxiously; distressingly.

angustioso ADJ **(a)** (*angustiado*) distressed, anguished; anxious. **(b)** (*doloroso*) distressing, agonizing; heartbreaking.

anhá INTERJ (*Cono Sur*) = **anjá**.

anhelación NF **(a)** (*Med*) panting. **(b)** (*fig*) longing, yearning.

anhelante ADJ **(a)** *respiración* panting. **(b)** (*fig*) eager; longing, yearning.

anhelar [1a] **1** VT to be eager for; to long for, yearn for, crave.
2 VI **(a)** (*Med*) to gasp, pant.
(b) (*fig*) **~ + infin** to be eager to + *infin*, long to + *infin*, yearn to + *infin*; **~ por algo** to long for sth, hanker after sth; **~ por + infin** to aspire to + *infin*.

▼ **anhelo** NM eagerness; longing, yearning, desire (*de, por* for); **~ de superación** urge to do better; **con ~** longingly, yearningly; **tener ~s de** to be eager for, long for.

anheloso ADJ **(a)** (*Med*) gasping, panting; *respiración* heavy, difficult. **(b)** (*fig*) eager, anxious.

anhídrido NM: **~ carbónico** carbon dioxide.

Aníbal NM Hannibal.

anidación NF, **anidada** NF (*Orn*) nesting.

anidamiento NM (*Inform*) nesting.

anidar [1a] **1** VT to take in, shelter.
2 VI **(a)** (*Orn*) to nest, make its nest; (*fig*) to live, make one's home; (*Inform*) to nest; **la maldad anida en su alma** his heart is full of evil.

anieblar [1a] = **aneblar**.

aniego NM (*And, Cono Sur*), **aniegue** NM (*Méx*) flood.

anilina NF aniline.

anilla NF (*de cortina*) curtain ring; (*anillito*) small ring; (*de puro*) cigar band; (*Orn*) ring; (*Gimnasia*) **~s** rings.

anillado **1** ADJ ringed; ring-shaped.
2 NM ringing (of birds).

anillamiento NM ringing (of birds).

anillar [1a] VT (*dar forma a*) to make into a ring, make rings in; (*sujetar*) to fasten with a ring; (*Orn*) to ring.

anillejo NM, **anillete** NM small ring, ringlet.

anillo NM ring (*t Astron, Mec*); (*de puro*) cigar band; **~ de boda** wedding-ring; **~ de compromiso, ~ de prometida, ~ de pedida** engagement ring; **~ de crecimiento** growth ring; **~ pastoral** bishop's ring; **no creo que se me caigan los ~s por eso** I don't feel it's in any way beneath my dignity; **venir como ~ al dedo** to be just right, meet the case perfectly, be just what the doctor ordered.

ánima NF **(a)** (*Rel*) soul; **~ bendita, ~ en pena, ~ del purgatorio** soul in purgatory; (*Ecl*) **las ~s** evening bell, sunset bell. **(b)** (*Mil*) bore. **(c)** (*Cono Sur: santuario*) wayside shrine.

animación NF **(a)** liveliness, life; bustle, activity, movement, animation; sprightliness; **~ cultural** cultural awakening; **~ suspendida** suspended animation; **campaña de ~ social** campaign of social awakening; **experta en ~ social** social activities coordinator; **había poca ~** there wasn't much life about it; **una escena llena de ~** a scene full of life. **(b)** (*gráfica*) animation; **~ por ordenador** computer animation, computer graphics.

animadamente ADV in lively fashion, gaily; animatedly; in sprightly fashion; merrily.

animado ADJ **(a)** *carácter, persona etc* lively, gay; (*concurrido*) bustling, busy, animated; (*enérgico*) sprightly; (*alegre*) merry, in high spirits. **(b)** *reunión* well-attended, popular. **(c)** (*Zool*) animate. **(d)** (*LAm Med*) recovering, improving.

animador NM compère, (*hombre*) master of ceremonies; (*TV etc*) presenter; (*LAm*) cheerleader; **~ cultural** (*en ayuntamiento*) events organiser; (*en hotel*) entertainments manager.

animadora NF (*cantante*) night-club singer, crooner; (*TV etc*) presenter; (*LAm*) cheerleader; **~ cultural** (*en ayuntamiento*) events organiser;

(*en hotel*) entertainments manager.

animadversión NF ill will, animosity; animadversion.

animal **1** ADJ **(a)** (*lit*) animal.
(b) (*fig*) stupid.
2 NM **(a)** (*lit*) animal; **~ de compañía** pet; **~ de laboratorio** laboratory animal; **~ de tiro** carthorse, workhorse (*t fig*); **soy un ~ político** I am a political animal.
(b) (*fig: tonto*) fool, idiot; (*fig: bestia*) beast, brute; **¡~!** you brute!; **el ~ de Juan** that beast of a John; **¡qué ~ de policía!** what a brute of a policeman!; **¡no seas ~!** don't be beastly!, don't be horrid!

animalada NF **(a)** (*LAm: rebaño*) group (*o* herd) of animals.
(b) (*cualidad*) foolishness, stupidity; (*disparate*) silly thing (to do *o* say *etc*); (*grosería*) coarse thing, piece of disgraceful conduct; **hacer una ~** to do sth silly; to do sth disgraceful.

animalaje NM (*Cono Sur*) animals; herd (*o* group) of animals.

animalejo NM odd-looking creature, nasty animal; creepy-crawly*.

animalidad NF animality; sensuality.

animalizarse [1f] VR to become brutalized.

animalote NM big animal.

animalucho NM ugly brute; creepy-crawly*.

animar [1a] **1** VT **(a)** (*Bio*) to animate, give life to.
(b) *discusión, reunión etc* to enliven, liven up, add interest to; *cuarto, fuego, escena, vista etc* to brighten up; *cosa aburrida* to stimulate, give new life to, ginger up.
(c) *persona* (*alegrar*) to cheer up; (*alentar*) to encourage, put new heart into; **~ a uno a hacer algo** to encourage sb to do sth.
2 animarse VR **(a)** (*fiesta etc*) to become more lively, liven up, acquire new life; to brighten up.
(b) (*persona*) (*alegrarse*) to brighten up, cheer up, feel encouraged, take heart; (*decidirse*) to make up one's mind, decide; **¡anímate!** cheer up!, buck up!; (*atreverse*) go on then!; (*decidirse*) make up your mind!; **¿te animas?** do you want to have a go?, are you game?; **~ a hacer algo** to make up one's mind to do sth, resolve to do sth; **a ver si se animan** we'll wait and see if they do anything about it; **no me animo a hacerlo** I can't bring myself to do it.

anime NM (*Carib*) polyethylene.

anímicamente ADV mentally.

anímico ADJ mental; **estado ~** state of mind.

animismo NM animism.

animista ADJ, NMF animist.

animita NF (*Cono Sur*) roadside shrine.

ánimo NM **(a)** (*mente etc*) mind; soul, spirit; **eso está en el ~ de todos** everybody is aware of that; **apaciguar los ~s** to calm people down.
(b) (*valor*) courage, pluck; nerve; (*energía*) energy; **caer(se) de ~** to lose heart, get disheartened; **cobrar ~** to take heart, pluck up courage; **dar ~(s) a, infundir ~ a** to encourage; **dilatar el ~ a uno** to put heart into sb.
(c) (*intención*) intention, purpose; **con ~ de + infin** with the intention of + *ger*, with the idea of + *ger*; **sin ~ de ofenderle** without wishing to offend you; **sin ~ de polémica** without wishing to be controversial; **sociedad sin ~ de lucro** non-profit-making organization; **se hizo con ~ de lucro** it was done with profit in mind; **estar con ~ de + infin** to feel like + *ger*; **hacer ~ de + infin** to intend to + *infin*, mean to + *infin*; **tener ~s para algo** to be in the mood for sth, feel like sth.
(d) **¡~(s)!** INTERJ cheer up!; (*Dep*) come on!, go it!

animosamente ADV bravely; with spirit, in lively fashion.

animosidad NF animosity, ill will.

animoso ADJ brave; spirited, lively.

aniñado ADJ **(a)** childlike; (*pey*) childish, puerile. **(b)** (*Cono Sur: animoso*) spirited, lively. **(c)** (*Cono Sur: guapo*) handsome.

aniñarse [1a] VR to act childishly.

aniquilación NF, **aniquilamiento** NM annihilation, destruction.

aniquilador ADJ destructive.

aniquilar [1a] **1** VT to annihilate, destroy, obliterate, wipe out; to overwhelm.
2 aniquilarse VR **(a)** (*lit*) to be annihilated, be wiped out.
(b) (*fig*) to deteriorate, decline; (*Med*) to waste away; (*fortuna etc*) to disappear, be frittered away.

anís NM **(a)** (*Bot*) anise, aniseed. **(b)** (*bebida*) anis, anisette; **estar hecho un ~** (*And*) to be elegantly dressed; to be as clean as a new pin; **llegar a los anises** to turn up late. **(c)** (*And: energía*) strength, energy.

anisado ADJ flavoured with aniseed.

aniseros* NMPL (*And*): **entregar los ~** to kick the bucket*; **vaciar los ~ a uno** to bump sb off*.

anisete NM anisette.

anivelar [1a] VT = **nivelar**.

aniversario NM anniversary.

anjá INTERJ (*Carib, Méx**: ¡*claro!*) of course!; that's it!; (*Carib*) (¡*bravo!*) bravo!; (*reprobación*) come off it!*

Anjeo NM Anjou.

➤ LENGUA Y USO: **anhelo → 35.4**

Ankara NF Ankara.
ano NM anus.
anoche ADV last night; **antes de ~** the night before last.
anochecedor(a) NM/F late bird, person who keeps late hours.
anochecer [1] [2d] VI **(a)** (gen) to get dark.
  (b) (persona) to arrive at nightfall; **anochecimos en Toledo** we got to Toledo as night was falling.
  [2] NM nightfall, dusk; **al ~** at nightfall; **antes del ~** by nightfall, before nightfall.
anochecida NF nightfall, dusk.
anodino [1] ADJ anodyne; (fig) anodyne, harmless, inoffensive; dull.
  [2] NM anodyne.
ánodo NM anode.
anomalía NF anomaly.
anómalo ADJ anomalous.
anona NF (CAm Bot) custard apple.
anonadación NM, **anonadamiento** NM **(a)** (destrucción) annihilation, destruction. **(b)** (desánimo) discouragement, despair; humiliation.
anonadador ADJ crushing, overwhelming.
anonadar [1a] [1] VT **(a)** (destruir) to annihilate, destroy; to overwhelm. **(b)** (desanimar) to discourage, depress; (humillar) to humiliate.
  [2] **anonadarse** VR **(a)** (ser derrotado) to be crushed, be overwhelmed.
  (b) (desanimarse) to get discouraged; to be humiliated.
anónimamente ADV anonymously.
anonimato NM, **anonimia** NF anonymity; **mantenerse en el anonimato** to remain anonymous.
anónimo [1] ADJ anonymous; nameless; (Com, Fin) compañía limited.
  [2] NM **(a)** (estado) anonymity; **conservar** (o **guardar**) **el ~** to preserve one's anonymity.
  (b) (persona) anonymous person, unknown person.
  (c) (carta) anonymous letter; (documento) anonymous document; (Liter) unsigned literary work.
anorac NM, **anorak** NM anorak.
anorexia NF anorexia; **~ nerviosa** anorexia nervosa.
anoréxico [1] ADJ anorexic.
  [2] NM, **anoréxica** NF anorexic.
anormal ADJ **(a)** abnormal; irregular, unusual; niño subnormal, mentally handicapped. **(b)** (*) silly, cretinous.
anormalidad NF abnormality; irregularity; unusual nature; subnormality, mental handicap.
anormalmente ADV abnormally, unusually.
anotación NF annotation; note, record, observation; (LAm Dep) score; (en cuenta) debit.
anotador(a) [1] NM/F **(a)** (Liter) annotator. **(b)** (LAm Dep) scorer.
  [2] NM (LAm) scorecard.
  [3] **anotadora** NF (Cine) script girl, continuity girl.
anotar [1a] VT **(a)** (tomar apuntes) to annotate; to note (down), jot down, take down; to register, record; (Com) pedido to note, book. **(b)** (Dep) to score.
anovulatorio NM anovulant; contraceptive pill.
ANPE NF ABR de **Asociación Nacional del Profesorado Estatal.**
anquilosado ADJ (fig) stagnant; paralyzed.
anquilosamiento NM, **anquilosis** NF (fig) stagnation; paralysis.
anquilosar [1a] [1] VT to paralyze.
  [2] VI (Aut, Mec) to seize up.
  [3] **anquilosarse** VR to decline; to become eroded.
anquilostoma NM hookworm.
ánsar NM goose.
ansarino NM gosling.
Anselmo NM Anselm.
ansia NF **(a)** (preocupación) anxiety, worry; (angustia) fear, anguish. **(b)** (anhelo) yearning, longing (de for). **(c)** (Med) anxiety, nervous tension. **(d)** (Med) ~s nausea, sick feeling.
ansiado ADJ longed-for; **el momento tan ~** the moment which we (etc) had so much longed for.
ansiar [1c] [1] VT to long for, yearn for; to covet, crave; **~ + infin** to long to + infin, yearn to + infin.
  [2] VI: **~ por uno** to be madly in love with sb.
ansiedad NF **(a)** (preocupación) anxiety, worry; solicitude; suspense. **(b)** (Med) anxiety, nervous tension.
ansina ADV (LAm) = **así.**
ansiolítico [1] ADJ sedative.
  [2] NM sedative, tranquillizer.
ansioso ADJ **(a)** (preocupado) anxious, uneasy, worried; solicitous; **esperamos ~s** we waited anxiously; **~ de algo, ~ por algo** eager for sth, avid for sth; greedy for sth. **(b)** (Med) (tenso) anxious, nervously tense; (bascoso) sick, queasy.
anta NF elk, moose; (LAm) tapir.
antagónico ADJ antagonistic; opposed, contrasting.
antagonismo NM antagonism.

antagonista NMF antagonist, opponent.
antagonístico ADJ = **antagónico.**
antagonizar [1f] VT to antagonize.
antañazo ADV a long time ago.
antaño ADV (el año pasado) last year; (hace mucho) long ago, formerly; **el ~ poderoso país** the once-powerful country.
antañón ADJ ancient, very old, of long ago.
antañoso ADJ (And) ancient, very old.
antara NF (And) pan pipes, Indian flute.
antarca ADV (And, Cono Sur) on one's back; **caerse ~** to fall flat on one's back.
antártico [1] ADJ Antarctic.
  [2] NM: **el A~** the Antarctic.
Antártida NF Antarctica.
ante¹ NM **(a)** (Zool) (anta) elk, moose; (búfalo) buffalo; (Méx: tapir) tapir. **(b)** (piel) buckskin, suede. **(c)** (Méx: dulce) macaroon.
▼**ante²** PREP persona before, in the presence of; enemigo, peligro etc in the face of; dificultad, duda faced with; asunto with regard to; **~ esta posibilidad** in view of this possibility; **~ tantas posibilidades** faced with so many possibilities; **~ todo hay que recordar que ...** first of all let's remember that ...; **estamos ~ un gran porvenir** we have a great future before us.
ante... PREF ante...
-ante V Aspects of Word Formation in Spanish 2.
anteado ADJ buff-coloured, fawn.
anteanoche ADV the night before last.
anteayer ADV the day before yesterday.
antebrazo NM forearm.
anteburro NM (LAm Zool) tapir.
antecámara NF anteroom, antechamber; lobby.
antecedente [1] ADJ previous, preceding, foregoing; **visto lo ~** in view of the foregoing.
  [2] NM **(a)** (Mat, Filos, Gram) antecedent.
  (b) ~s record, history, background; **¿cuáles son sus ~s?** what's his history?, what's his background like?; **~s delictivos, ~s penales, ~s policiales** criminal record; **un hombre sin ~s** a man with a clean record; **estar en ~s** to know all about it, be well informed; **poner a uno en ~s** to put sb in the picture, give sb the latest information; **tener buenos ~s** to have a good record.
anteceder [2a] VT to precede, go before.
antecesor [1] ADJ preceding, former.
  [2] NM, **antecesora** NF predecessor; (antepasado) ancestor, forbear.
antecocina NF scullery.
antecomedor NM (LAm) room adjoining the dining room.
antedatar [1a] VT to antedate.
antedicho ADJ aforesaid, aforementioned.
antediluviano ADJ antediluvian.
anteiglesia NF (Ecl) porch.
antejuela NF (CAm) = **lentejuela.**
antelación NF (esp Esp) precedence, priority; **con ~** in advance, in good time, beforehand; **con mucha ~** long in advance, long beforehand.
antelina NF suède, artificial buckskin.
antellevar [1a] VT (Méx Aut) to run down, knock down.
antellevón NM (Méx Aut) accident.
antemano: de ~ ADV in advance, beforehand.
antena NF **(a)** (Zool) feeler, antenna; **tener ~ para** (fig) to have a feeling for, have a nose for.
  (b) (Náut) lateen yard.
  (c) (Rad etc) aerial, antenna; **~ colectiva** communal aerial, **~ direccional, ~ dirigida** directional aerial; **~ encerrada** built-in aerial; **~ interior** indoor aerial; **~ parabólica** parabolic aerial, satellite dish; **~ de plato** dish aerial, satellite dish; **~ de televisión** television aerial; **estar en ~** to be on the air; **permanecer en ~** to stay on the air; **salir en ~** to go out on the air, be broadcast; **el programa es el sexto en duración en ~** the programme is the sixth longest-running on TV.
  (d) (*) ~s ears.
antenatal ADJ antenatal, prenatal.
antenombre NM style, title (preceding first name).
anteojera¹ NF **(a)** (funda) spectacle case. **(b)** ~s blinkers.
anteojero, -a² NM/F spectacle maker, optician.
anteojo NM **(a)** (lente) eyeglass, spyglass, (small) telescope; **~ de larga vista** telescope.
  (b) ~s (gafas) spectacles, glasses; (Aut, Téc etc) goggles; (de caballo) blinkers; **~s ahumados** smoked glasses; **~s de concha** horn-rimmed spectacles; **~s de sol, ~s para el sol** sunglasses.
antepagar [1h] VT to prepay, pay beforehand.
antepasado [1] ADJ previous, immediately past, before last.
  [2] NM, **antepasada** NF ancestor, forbear; **mis ~s** my forbears, my forefathers.
antepecho NM (de puente etc) rail, guardrail, parapet; (de ventana)

ledge, sill; (*Mil*) parapet, breastwork.

antepenúltimo ADJ last but two, antepenultimate.

anteponer [2q] **1** VT **(a)** (*lit*) to place in front (*a* of). **(b)** (*fig*) to prefer (*a* to).

2 anteponerse VR to be in front (*a* of), come in between.

anteportal NM porch.

anteproyecto NM preliminary sketch, preliminary plan; (*esp fig*) blueprint; **~ de ley** draft bill.

antepuerto NM outer harbour.

antepuesto ADJ preceding, coming before.

antequerano 1 ADJ of Antequera.

2 NM, **antequerana** NF native (*o* inhabitant) of Antequera; **los ~s** the people of Antequera.

antera NF anther.

anterior ADJ **(a)** *pierna, parte etc* front, fore, anterior; **en la parte ~ del coche** on the front part of the car.

(b) (*en orden*) preceding, previous, former; (*Ling*) anterior; (*antedicho*) aforementioned; **cada uno mejor que el ~** each one better than the last; **se había olvidado de todo lo ~** he had forgotten all that had happened previously.

(c) (*en el tiempo*) former; previous (*a* to), earlier (*a* than); **un texto ~ a 1140** a text earlier than 1140; **el día ~** the previous day, the day before.

anterioridad NF precedence, priority; **con ~** previously, beforehand; earlier; **con ~ a esto** prior to this, before this.

anteriormente ADV previously, before.

antes 1 ADV **(a)** (*gen*) before; (*primero*) first; (*antaño*) once, previously, formerly; in times gone by; (*antes de ahora*) sooner, before now; **3 días ~** 3 days before, 3 days earlier; **la casa de ~** the previous house; **lo de ~** that earlier business; **en ~** (*And, Cono Sur*) in the past; **no quiso venir ~** he didn't want to come any earlier; **conviene cazar ~ la liebre** first catch your hare; **la planta existió aquí ~** the plant used to grow here; **lo vio ~ que yo** he saw it before I did; **~ hoy que mañana** the sooner the better; **lo ~ posible, cuanto ~** as soon as possible; **cuanto ~ mejor** the sooner the better; as quickly as possible; **mucho ~** long before; **poco ~** shortly before, a short time previously.

(b) (*preferencia*) sooner, rather; **~ (bien)** rather, on the contrary; **~ muerto que esclavo** better dead than enslaved; **~ mejor que vino** (*LAm*) it's just as well he came; **preferimos ir en tren ~ que en avión** we prefer to go by train rather than by plane; **no cederemos: ~ lo destruimos todo** we shall never give up: we would rather destroy everything.

2 ~ de PREP before; previous to; **~ de 1900** before 1900; up to 1900; **~ de hacerlo** before doing it; **~ de terminado el discurso** before the speech was over.

3 ~ (de) que CONJ before; **~ de que te vayas** before you go.

antesala NF anteroom, antechamber; lobby; (*fig*) **estamos en la ~ de** we are on the verge of, we are on the threshold of; **hacer ~** to wait, wait to be received, wait to go in to see sb, (*fig*) cool one's heels.

antesalazo NM (*Méx*) long wait (*before admission*).

antetítulo NM introductory heading, prefatory heading.

anteúltimo ADJ (*Cono Sur*) penultimate.

anti... PREF anti...; un...; non-...

antiabortista 1 ADJ: **campaña ~** anti-abortion campaign.

2 NMF antiabortionist.

antiaborto ADJ INVAR anti-abortion.

antiácido ADJ, NM antacid.

antiadherencia NF non-stick properties; **prueba ~** non-stick test.

antiadherente ADJ non-stick.

antiaéreo 1 ADJ anti-aircraft.

2 NM (*LAm*) anti-aircraft gun.

antialcohólico (*LAm*) **1** ADJ teetotal.

2 NM, **antialcohólica** NF teetotaller.

antialérgico ADJ antiallergic, antiallergenic.

antiamericano ADJ anti-American; un-American.

antiapartheid ADJ anti-apartheid.

antiarrugas ADJ INVAR anti-wrinkle, wrinkle (*atr*).

antiatómico ADJ: **refugio ~** fall-out shelter.

antiatraco(s) ADJ: **dispositivo ~** anti-theft device, security device.

antibacteriano ADJ, NM antibacterial.

antibala(s) ADJ INVAR bullet-proof.

antibalístico ADJ antiballistic.

antibelicista 1 ADJ anti-war; pacifist.

2 NMF pacifist.

antibiótico ADJ, NM antibiotic.

antibloqueo ADJ INVAR: **sistema ~ de frenos, sistema de frenado ~** ABS braking system.

antibombas ADJ INVAR: **refugio ~** bomb shelter.

anticalcáreo ADJ: **dispositivo ~** anti-scaling device.

anticanceroso ADJ anti-cancer, cancer (*atr*); **tratamiento ~** cancer treatment.

anticarro ADJ INVAR antitank.

anticaspa ADJ INVAR dandruff (*atr*), anti-dandruff.

anticelulítico ADJ anti-cellulite, cellulite (*atr*).

antichoque(s) ADJ INVAR: **panel ~** shock-resistant panel.

anticiclón NM anticyclone.

anticiclonal ADJ, **anticiclónico** ADJ anticyclonic.

anticipación NF anticipation; foretaste; (*Com, Fin*) advance; **hacer algo con ~** to do sth well beforehand, do sth in good time; **reservar con ~** to book in advance, book early; **llegar con bastante ~** to arrive early, arrive in good time; **llegar con 10 minutos de ~** to come 10 minutes early.

anticipadamente ADV in advance, beforehand; **le doy las gracias ~** I thank you in advance.

anticipado ADJ (*futuro*) future, prospective; (*con antelación*) early; *pago etc* advance; **por ~** in advance, beforehand.

anticipar [1a] **1** VT **(a)** *fecha, acontecimiento* to bring forward, advance; to hasten (the date of); **anticiparon las vacaciones** they took their holiday early; **no anticipemos los acontecimientos** let's not cross our bridges before we come to them.

(b) *dinero* to advance, lend, loan.

(c) **~ las gracias a uno** to thank sb in advance.

(d) (*LAm: prever*) to anticipate, foresee; **~ que ...** to anticipate that ...

2 anticiparse VR **(a)** (*acontecimiento*) to take place early, happen before the expected time.

(b) **~ a un acontecimiento** to anticipate an event, forestall an event; **~ a uno** to beat sb to it, steal a march on sb; **Vd se ha anticipado a mis deseos** you have anticipated my wishes; **~ a hacer algo** to do sth ahead of time, do sth before the proper time.

anticipo NM **(a)** (*gen*) anticipation, foretaste; **fue el ~ del fin para toda una época** it was the beginning of the end for a whole epoch; **esto es sólo un ~** this is just a foretaste.

(b) (*Com, Fin*) advance, loan; (*t* **~ a cuenta**) advance payment.

(c) (*Jur*) retaining fee.

anticlerical ADJ, NMF anticlerical.

anticlericalismo NM anticlericalism.

anticlímax NM INVAR anticlimax.

anticlinal NM (*LAm*) watershed; (*Geol*) anticline.

anticoagulante ADJ, NM anticoagulant.

anticoba NF brutal frankness, outspokenness.

anticolesterol ADJ cholesterol-free, low in cholesterol.

anticomunista ADJ anticommunist.

anticoncepción NF contraception, birth-control.

anticoncepcional ADJ birth-control (*atr*), family-planning (*atr*), contraceptive.

anticoncepcionismo NM contraception, birth-control.

anticonceptivo 1 ADJ birth-control (*atr*), family-planning (*atr*), contraceptive; **métodos ~s** birth-control methods, contraceptive devices; **píldora anticonceptiva** contraceptive pill.

2 NM contraceptive.

anticongelante 1 ADJ antifreeze.

2 NM antifreeze (solution).

anticonstitucional ADJ unconstitutional.

anticonstitucionalidad NF unconstitutionality.

anticontaminante ADJ anti-pollution.

anticorrosivo ADJ anticorrosive, antirust.

anticristo NM Antichrist.

anticuado ADJ antiquated, old-fashioned, out-of-date; obsolete.

anticuario 1 ADJ antiquarian.

2 NM, **anticuaria** NF (*erudito etc*) antiquarian, antiquary; (*Com*) antique dealer.

anticuarse [1d] VR to become antiquated, get out of date; to become obsolete.

anticucho NM (*And Culin*) (beef) kebab.

anticuerpo NM antibody.

antidemocráticamente ADV undemocratically.

antidemocrático ADJ undemocratic.

antideportividad NF unsporting attitude, unsportsmanlike behaviour.

antideportivo ADJ unsporting, unsportsmanlike.

antidepresivo 1 ADJ antidepressant.

2 NM antidepressant (drug), stimulant.

antiderrapante ADJ non-skid.

antideslizante 1 ADJ non-slipping; (*Aut*) non-skid; *piso* non-slip.

2 NM (*LAm*) non-skid tyre.

antideslumbrante ADJ anti-dazzle, anti-glare.

antidetonante ADJ (*Aut*) antiknock.

antidisturbios ADJ INVAR: **policía ~** riot (control) police.

antidopaje ADJ, **antidoping** ADJ: **control ~** (anti-)drugs test, check for drugs.

antídoto NM antidote (*contra, de* against, for, to).

antidroga ADJ INVAR: **brigada ~** drug squad; **campaña ~** anti-drug campaign; **tratamiento ~** treatment for drug addiction.

antidúmping ADJ INVAR (*Com*): **medidas ~** antidumping measures, measures against dumping.

antiecológico ADJ: **producto ~** product damaging to the environment, environmentally unsafe product.

antieconómico ADJ uneconomic(al); wasteful.

antienvejecimiento ADJ INVAR anti-ageing.

antier ADV (*LAm*) = **anteayer.**

antiestático ADJ antistatic.

antiestético ADJ unsightly, ugly, offensive.

antiestrés ADJ INVAR anti-stress, stress (*atr*).

antifascismo NM antifascism.

antifascista ADJ, NMF antifascist.

antifatiga ADJ INVAR: **píldora ~** anti-fatigue pill, pep pill*.

antifaz NM (a) mask; veil. (b) (‡) condom.

antifeminismo NM antifeminism.

antifeminista ADJ, NMF antifeminist.

antífona NF antiphony.

antifranquismo NM opposition to Franco.

antifranquista ①ADJ anti-Franco. ②NMF opponent of Franco, person opposed to Franco.

antifraude ADJ INVAR: **acción ~** action to combat fraud.

antifriccional ADJ antifriction.

antifrís NM (*LAm*) antifreeze (solution).

antifuego ADJ INVAR *puerta, barrera* fire (*atr*), fireproof; **lucha ~** firefighting.

antigás ADJ INVAR: **careta ~** gasmask.

antígeno NM antigen.

antigolpes ADJ INVAR shockproof.

Antígona NF Antigone.

antigripal ADJ: **vacuna ~** flu vaccine.

antigualla NF antique; (*pey*) old thing, relic, out-of-date object (*o custom etc*); (*cuento viejo*) old story; (*persona*) has-been, back number; (*trastos*) **~s** old things, junk.

antiguamente ADV formerly, once; in ancient times, long ago.

antigüedad NF (a) (*Hist*) antiquity; **los artistas de la ~** the artists of antiquity, the artists of the ancient world; **alta ~, remota ~** high antiquity; **de toda ~** from time immemorial.
(b) (*edad*) antiquity, age; **la fábrica tiene una ~ de 200 años** the factory is 200 years old.
(c) (*objeto*) antique; **~es** antiques; antiquities; **tienda de ~es** antique shop.
(d) (*en escalafón*) (length of) service, seniority.

antiguerra ADJ INVAR anti-war.

antiguo ①ADJ (a) (*viejo*) old; ancient; *coche etc* vintage, classic; **a la antigua** in the ancient manner, in the old-fashioned way; **de ~** from time immemorial, since ancient times; **en lo ~** in olden times, in ancient times.
(b) (*de antes*) former, old, one-time; **un ~ alumno mío** an old pupil of mine; **~ primer ministro** former prime minister.
(c) (*de rango*) **más ~** senior; **socio más ~** senior partner; **es más ~ que yo** he is senior to me, he is my senior. ②NMPL: **los ~s** the ancients.

antihéroe NM antihero.

antihigiénico ADJ unhygienic, insanitary.

antihistamínico ADJ, NM antihistamine.

antihumano ADJ inhuman.

antiimperialismo NM anti-imperialism.

antiimperialista ADJ, NMF anti-imperialist.

antiincendios ADJ INVAR: **equipo ~** fire-fighting team; **servicio ~** fire-fighting service.

antiinflacionista ADJ anti-inflationary.

antiinflamatorio ADJ anti-inflammatory.

antillanismo NM word (*o phrase etc*) peculiar to the Antilles.

antillano ①ADJ West Indian, of the Antilles. ②NM, **antillana** NF West Indian, native (*o inhabitant*) of the Antilles; **los ~s** the West Indians.

Antillas NFPL Antilles, West Indies; **el mar de las ~** the Caribbean (Sea).

antilogaritmo NM antilogarithm.

antilógico ADJ illogical.

antílope NM antelope.

antimacasar NM antimacassar.

antimanchas ADJ INVAR: **superficie ~** stain-resistant surface.

antimateria NF antimatter.

antimilitarismo NM antimilitarism.

antimilitarista ADJ, NMF antimilitarist.

antimisil ①ADJ INVAR antimissile; **misil ~** antimissile missile. ②NM antimissile.

antimonio NM antimony.

antimonopolio ADJ INVAR: **ley ~** anti-trust law.

antimosquitos ADJ INVAR mosquito (*atr*); **red ~** mosquito net.

antinacional ADJ unpatriotic.

antinatural ADJ unnatural.

antiniebla ADJ INVAR: **luz ~** fog-lamp.

antinomia NF antinomy, conflict of authority.

antinuclear ADJ antinuclear.

Antioquía NF Antioch.

antioxidante ADJ antirust.

antipalúdico ADJ antimalarial.

antipara NF screen.

antiparabólico* ADJ (*Carib*) wild, over the top.

antiparasitario ①ADJ antiparasitic. ②NM antiparasitic drug.

antiparras* NFPL glasses, specs*.

antipatía NF antipathy (*hacia* towards, *entre* between), dislike (*hacia* for); unfriendliness (*hacia* towards).

antipático ADJ disagreeable, unpleasant, antipathetic; uncongenial; **es un tipo ~** he's a disagreeable sort; **me es muy ~** I don't like him at all; **es de lo más ~** he's horrible; **en un ambiente ~** in an uncongenial atmosphere, in an unfriendly environment.

antipatizar [1f] VI (*LAm*) to feel unfriendly; **~ con uno** to dislike sb.

antipatriótico ADJ unpatriotic.

antiperras NFPL (*And*) half-moon glasses (*o spectacles*).

antípodas NMPL antipodes.

antipolilla ADJ INVAR mothproof.

antiproteccionista ADJ antiprotectionist, free-trade (*atr*).

antiproyectil ADJ INVAR antimissile.

antiquísimo ADJ ancient.

antiquista (*Méx*) ①ADJ antiquarian. ②NMF antiquarian, antique dealer.

antirrábico ADJ: **vacuna antirrábica** anti-rabies vaccine.

antirracista ADJ, NMF anti-racist.

antirreflectante ADJ *pantalla, cristal* anti-glare.

antirreglamentario ADJ illegal, unlawful; (*Dep*) foul.

antirresbaladizo ADJ (*Aut*) non-skid.

antirretroviral ①ADJ antiretroviral. ②NM antiretroviral drug.

antirrino NM antirrhinum.

antirrobo ①ADJ INVAR: **sistema ~** anti-theft system. ②NM anti-theft device.

antirruido ADJ *sistema* noise-reduction (*atr*); *comisión* noise-abatement (*atr*); *ley* noise-pollution (*atr*).

antisemita NMF anti-Semite.

antisemítico ADJ anti-Semitic.

antisemitismo NM anti-Semitism.

antiséptico ADJ, NM antiseptic.

antisocial ADJ antisocial.

antisudoral ADJ, NM (*LAm*) deodorant.

antitabaco ADJ INVAR: **campaña ~** anti-smoking campaign.

antitabaquismo NM anti-smoking attitudes *pl*.

antitabaquista ADJ anti-smoking.

antitanque ADJ INVAR antitank.

antitaurino ADJ anti-bullfighting.

antiterrorista ADJ: **medidas ~s** measures against terrorism; **Ley A~** ≃ Prevention of Terrorism Act.

▼ **antítesis** NF INVAR antithesis.

antitetánica NF anti-tetanus.

antitético ADJ antithetic(al).

antitranspirante ADJ, NM anti-perspirant.

antivaho ADJ INVAR: **dispositivo ~** demister, demisting device.

antivirus NM INVAR antivirus.

antiviviseccionista NMF antivivisectionist.

antivuelco ADJ INVAR: **barra ~** anti-roll bar.

antofagastino (*Cono Sur*) ①ADJ of Antofagasta. ②NM, **antofagastina** NF native (*o inhabitant*) of Antofagasta; **los ~s** the people of Antofagasta.

antojadizo ADJ capricious; given to sudden fancies, given to whims, unpredictable.

antojado ADJ: **~ con, ~ por** taken by, hankering after; craving for.

antojarse [1a] VR (a) **~ algo** to take a fancy to sth, want sth.
(b) **~ que ...** to imagine that ..., fancy that ..., have a hunch that ...; **se me antoja que no estará** I have the feeling that he won't be in.
(c) **~ + infin** to have a mind to + *infin*; **se me antoja comprarlo** I have a mind to buy it, I fancy buying it; **se le antojó ir al cine** he took it into his head to go to the cinema; **no se le antojó decir otra cosa** it didn't occur to him to say anything else; **no se le antoja ir** he doesn't feel like going; **¿cómo se le antoja esto?** how does this seem to you?

antojitos NMPL (*Cono Sur* ††) sweets, candy (*US*); (*Méx*) snacks, nibbles.

antojo NM (a) (*capricho*) caprice, whim, passing fancy, notion; **cada uno a su ~** each to his own; **hacer a su ~** to do as one pleases; **¿cuál es su ~?** what's your idea?; **no morirse de ~** (*Cono Sur*) to

satisify a whim.
(b) (*de embarazada*) craving; **tener ~s** to have (pregnancy) cravings.
(c) (*Anat*) birthmark, strawberry mark; mole.
antología NF anthology.
antológica NF (*Arte*) selective exhibition.
antológico ADJ: **exposición antológica** (*Arte*) retrospective; **un gol ~** a goal for the history books, a goal that will go down in history.
antónimo NM antonym.
Antonio NM Anthony.
antonomasia NF antonomasia; **por ~** par excellence.
antorcha NF torch; (*fig*) torch, lamp.
antracita NF anthracite.
ántrax NM anthrax.
antro NM cavern; **~ de corrupción** (*fig*) den of iniquity.
antropofagia NF cannibalism.
antropófago ⓵ ADJ man-eating, anthropophagous; cannibalistic.
　　⓶ NM **antropófaga** NF cannibal; **~s** anthropophagi.
antropoide ADJ anthropoid.
antropoideo NM anthropoid.
antropología NF anthropology; **~ social** social anthropology.
antropológico ADJ anthropological.
antropólogo, -a NM/F anthropologist.
antropomorfismo NM anthropomorphism.
antruejo NM carnival (*3 days before Lent*). ·
antucá NM (*Cono Sur*) sunshade, parasol.
antuviada NF sudden blow, bump.
antuvión NM sudden blow, bump; **de ~** suddenly, unexpectedly.
anual ADJ, NM (*Bot*) annual.
anualidad NF **(a)** (*Fin*) annuity; annual payment. **(b)** (*suceso*) annual occurrence.
anualizado ADJ (*Fin*) annual; calculated on a yearly basis.
anualmente ADV annually, yearly.
anuario NM (*gen*) yearbook; annual; (*Com*) trade directory; (*manual*) reference book, handbook; **~ militar** military list; **~ telefónico** telephone directory.
anubarrado ADJ cloudy, overcast.
anublar [1a] ⓵ VT **(a)** *cielo* to cloud (over); (*oscurecer*) to dim, darken, obscure. **(b)** (*Bot*) to blight; to wither, dry up.
　　⓶ **anublarse** VR **(a)** (*oscurecer*) to cloud over, become cloudy, become overcast; (*cielo*) to darken, get dark. **(b)** (*Bot*) to wither, dry up; (*fig*) to fade away.
anudar [1a] ⓵ VT (*atar*) to knot, tie; (*unir*) to join, link, unite; *cuento* to resume, take up again; *voz* to choke, strangle.
　　⓶ **anudarse** VR **(a)** (*enmarañarse*) to get into knots, get tied up.
(b) (*Bot*) to remain stunted.
(c) se me anudó la voz (en la garganta) I got a lump in my throat.
anuencia NF approval, agreement, consent.
anuente ADJ consenting, consentient.
anulación NF annulment, cancellation; revocation, repeal.
▼**anular¹** [1a] ⓵ VT (*gen*) to annul, cancel; *decisión etc* to overrule, override; *ley* to revoke, repeal; *efecto* to nullify, cancel out; *gol* to disallow; (*Mat*) to cancel out; *persona* to deprive of authority, remove from office; **~ el tiempo** to put the clock back.
　　⓶ **anularse** VR (*persona*) to lose one's identity; to renounce everything.
anular² ⓵ ADJ ring-shaped, annular; **dedo ~ = 2**.
　　⓶ NM ring finger.
anunciación NF announcement; **A~** (*Rel*) Annunciation; **(día de) la A~** the Annunciation, Lady Day (*25 March*).
anunciador NM announcer; (*Teat*) compère; (*Méx Rad*) announcer.
anunciante NMF (*Com*) advertiser.
▼**anunciar** [1b] ⓵ VT (*gen*) to announce; (*proclamar*) to proclaim; (*augurar*) to forebode, foreshadow; (*Com*) to advertise; **no nos anuncia nada bueno** it augurs ill for us, it bodes ill for us.
　　⓶ **anunciarse** VR: **el festival se anuncia animado** the festival looks like being lively, everything points to the festival being a lively one; **la cosecha se anuncia buena** the crop promises to be a good one.
▼**anuncio** NM **(a)** (*gen*) announcement; (*presagio*) sign, omen; (*aviso*) notice.
▼**(b)** (*Com etc*) advertisement; (*cartel*) placard, poster; (*Teat etc*) bill; **~s breves, ~s económicos, ~s por palabras** classified advertisements, small advertisements; **~ luminoso** illuminated sign; **~ a página completa** full-page advertisement; **~ de trabajo** job advertisement.
anuo ADJ annual.
anverso NM obverse.
anzuelo NM hook, fish hook; (*fig*) bait, lure; **echar el ~** to offer a bait, offer an inducement; **picar en el ~, tragar el ~** (*fig*) to swallow the bait, be taken in, fall for it.
añada NF (*Agr*) **(a)** (*año*) year, season. **(b)** (*trozo de campo*) piece of field, strip.

añadido ⓵ ADJ added; additional, extra; **lo ~** what is added.
　　⓶ NM false hair, switch, hairpiece.
añadidura NF addition, extra, thing added; (*Com*) extra measure, extra weight; **dar algo de ~** to give sth extra; **con algo de ~** with sth else, with sth into the bargain; **por ~** besides, in addition; on top of all that.
▼**añadir** [3a] VT to add (*a* to); to increase; *encanto, interés etc* to add, lend (*a* to).
añagaza NF (*Caza*) lure, decoy; (*fig*) lure, bait, inducement.
añal ⓵ ADJ **(a)** *suceso* yearly, annual. **(b)** (*Agr*) year-old.
　　⓶ NM year-old animal, yearling.
añangá NM (*Cono Sur*) the devil.
añango (*And*) ⓵ ADJ *niño* sickly.
　　⓶ NM small portion.
añañay* INTERJ (*Cono Sur*) great!* super!*
añapar [1a] VT (*LAm*) to smash to bits.
añar NM (*LAm*): **hace ~es que ...** it's ages since ...
añascar [1g] VT to scrape together, get together bit by bit.
añaz NM (*And*) skunk.
añeja* NF (*Carib*) old lady*, mum*.
añejar [1a] ⓵ VT to age.
　　⓶ **añejarse** VR to age, get old; (*vino*) to age, improve with age, mellow; (*pey*) to get stale, go musty.
añejo ADJ old; *vino* mellow, mature; (*pey*) stale, musty.
añicos NMPL bits, pieces, fragments; splinters; **hacer un papel ~** to tear a piece of paper into little bits; **hacer un vaso ~** to smash a glass, shatter a glass; **hacerse ~** to shatter, smash to pieces; **hacerse ~** (*fig*) to wear o.s. out.
añil NM ⓵ (*Bot*) indigo; (*color*) indigo, indigo blue; (*para lavar*) blue, bluing.
　　⓶ ADJ INVAR blue.
añilar [1a] VT to dye indigo; *ropa* to blue.
añinos NMPL lamb's wool.
año NM **(a)** (*gen*) year; **~ bisiesto** leap year; **~ civil, ~ común** calendar year; **el ~ 66 de Cristo** 66 AD; **~ económico** financial year, fiscal year; **~ escolar** school year; **~ fiscal** tax year; **~ de gracia** year of grace; **~ lectivo** school year; **~ luz** light-year; **100 ~s luz** 100 light-years; **~ natural** calendar year; **A~ Nuevo** New Year; **¡feliz ~ nuevo! happy new year!; día de A~ Nuevo** New Year's Day; **~ presupuestario** budget year, financial year; **~ de nuestra salud** year of Our Lord; **~ sabático** sabbatical year; **el ~ verde** (*LAm*) never; **los 40 ~s, los ~s difíciles, los ~s negros** (*Esp*) the Franco years (*1936-75*); **el ~ pasado** last year; **el ~ antepasado** the year before last; **el ~ entrante, el ~ próximo** next year; **¡mal ~ para él!** good riddance to him!, and the best of luck! (*iró*); **hace ~s años** ago; **esperamos ~s y ~s** we waited years and years; **5 toneladas al ~** 5 tons a year; **al ~ de casado** a year after his marriage, after he had been married a year; **una cosa del ~ uno** (o **catapún** o **de la pera** o **de la quica** *etc*) something from the year dot; **estar de buen ~** to look well-fed, be in good shape; (*: *mujer*) to be a bit of all right‡; **en el ~ 1980** in 1980; **en los ~s 60 y 70** in the sixties and seventies; **en estos últimos ~s** in recent years, of late years; **en el ~ de la nana** (o **nanita** o **polca**) in the year dot, way back; **por los ~s de 1950** about 1950; **¡por muchos ~s!** (*brindis*) here's health!, (*cumpleaños*) many happy returns!; (*presentación*) how do you do?; **dentro de cien ~s, todos calvos** it will all be the same in a hundred years, it won't matter in the long run.
(b) **~s** (*de persona*) age, years; **cumplir los 21 ~s** to reach 21, have one's 21st birthday; **cumplir ~s** to have a birthday; **¿cuántos ~s tienes?** how old are you?; **tengo 9 ~s** I'm 9; **con los ~s que yo tengo** at my age; **(nunca) en los ~s que tengo** never before, never in my life; **de pocos ~s** young, small; **entrado en ~s** elderly, advanced in years; **quitarse ~s** to lie about one's age; **A le saca muchos ~s a B** A is much older than B; *ver también* ⃞ KILOS, METROS, AÑOS ⃞.
año-hombre NM, PL **años-hombre** man-year.
añojal NM land alternatively cultivated and left fallow.
añojo, -a NM/F yearling.
añorante ADJ yearning, longing, nostalgic; affectionate.
añoranza NF longing, yearning (*de* for); hankering (*de* after); nostalgia (*de* for); sense of loss, regret (*de* for).
añorar [1a] ⓵ VT to long for, yearn for, pine for, hanker after; *muerto* to grieve for; *pérdida* to mourn.
　　⓶ VI to yearn, pine, grieve; to feel nostalgia, be homesick.
añoso ADJ aged, full of years.
añublar(se) [1a] = anublar(se).
añublo NM blight, mildew.
añudar NM = anudar.
añusgar [1h] ⓵ VI to choke; (*fig*) to get angry.
　　⓶ **añusgarse** VR to get cross.
aojada NF (*And*) skylight.
aojar [1a] VT to put the evil eye on; to bewitch.
aojo NM evil eye, hoodoo; sorcery, witchcraft.

aoristo NM (*Ling*) aorist.

aorta NF aorta.

aovado ADJ oval, egg-shaped.

aovar [1a] VI to lay eggs.

aovillarse [1a] VR to roll o.s. into a ball, curl up.

AP NF (*Esp Pol Hist*) ABR de **Alianza Popular**; *see also* PP .

Ap. NM ABR de **apartado de correos** Post Office Box, POB.

APA NF ABR de **Asociación de Padres de Alumnos** ≃ Parent-Teacher Association, PTA.

apa¹ INTERJ (*Méx*) good God!; goodness me!

apa² INTERJ (*ánimo*) cheer up!; (*levántate*) get up!; (*recógelo*) pick it up!; (*basta*) that's enough!

apa³: al ~ ADV (*Cono Sur*) llevar etc on one's back.

apabullante ADJ shattering, crushing, overwhelming.

apabullar [1a] VT to crush, flatten, squash (*t fig*).

apacentadero NM pasture, pasture land.

apacentar [1j] 1 VT (a) (*Agr*) to pasture, graze, feed.
(b) (*fig*) discípulo etc to teach, minister to; intelecto to feed, give food for thought to, nourish; pasión to gratify, pander to; deseo to satisfy, minister to.
2 **apacentarse** VR (a) (*Agr*) to graze, feed.
(b) (*fig*) to feed (*con, de* on).

apachar [1a] VT (*Perú*) to steal.

apache NM Apache (Indian); (*Esp fig*) apache, street ruffian, thug.

apacheta NF (a) (*And, Cono Sur*) (*Rel*) grotto, wayside shrine. (b) (*montón*) pile, heap. (c) (*Pol*) (political) clique; (*confabulación*) ring, gang. (d) (*Com*) ill-gotten gains; **hacer la ~*** to make one's pile*.

apachico NM (*LAm*) bundle.

apachurrar [1a] VT to crush, squash.

apacibilidad NF gentleness, mildness; even temper, peaceable nature; calmness, quietness.

apacible ADJ gentle, mild; temperamento gentle, even, peaceable; tiempo mild, calm, quiet; viento gentle.

apaciblemente ADV gently, mildly; peaceably.

apaciguador ADJ pacifying, calming, soothing.

apaciguamiento NM appeasement (*t Pol*), pacifying, calming.

apaciguar [1i] 1 VT to pacify, appease, mollify; to calm down; (*Pol*) to appease.
2 **apaciguarse** VR to calm down, quieten down.

apadrinamiento NM sponsorship; patronage; (*fig*) backing, support.

apadrinar [1a] VT empresa to sponsor, back; (*Dep*) to sponsor; artista etc to be a patron to; (*Ecl*) niño to act as godfather to; novio to be best man for; duelista to act as second to; (*fig*) to back, support, favour.

apadronarse [1a] VR to register (as a resident).

apagadizo ADJ slow to burn, difficult to ignite.

apagado 1 ADJ (a) volcán extinct; cal slaked; **estar ~** (*fuego etc*) to be out; (*luz, radio*) to be off.
(b) sonido muted, muffled, dull; voz quiet, timid.
(c) color dull, quiet, lustreless, lifeless; persona, temperamento listless, spiritless, colourless; mirada lifeless.
2 NM switching-off; **botón de ~** off button, off switch.

apagador NM (a) (*extintor*) extinguisher. (b) (*Mec*) silencer, muffler; (*Mús*) damper; (*Cono Sur, Méx Elec*) switch.

apagafuegos 1 ADJ INVAR: **avión ~** fire-fighting plane.
2 NM (a) fire-fighting plane. (b) (*persona*) trouble-shooter.

apagar [1h] 1 VT (a) fuego to put out, extinguish, quench; luz to put out, turn off, switch off; radio etc to switch off; vela to snuff; (*And, Carib*) arma de fuego to empty, discharge; cal to slake; sed to quench, slake.
(b) sonido to silence, muffle, deaden; (*Mús*) to mute, damp.
(c) color to dull, tone down, soften.
(d) afecto, dolor etc to kill; ira etc to calm, soothe.
2 **apagarse** VR (a) (*fuego*) to go out; (*luz*) to go out, be put out; (*volcán*) to become extinct; (*vida*) to end, come to an end; **antes de que el año se apague** before the year ends.
(b) (*sonido*) to die away, cease.
(c) (*ira etc*) to calm down, subside.
(d) (*persona*) to pass away.

apagavelas NM INVAR candle-snuffer.

apagón NM blackout; (*Elec*) power cut, electricity failure, outage; **~ informativo, ~ de noticias** news blackout.

apagoso ADJ (*LAm*) = **apagadizo**.

apaisado ADJ oblong; squat, flattened.

apajarado ADJ (*Cono Sur*) daft, scatterbrained.

apalabrar [1a] 1 VT (a) (*convenir en*) to agree to; **estar apalabrado** to be committed, have given one's word. (b) (*encargar*) to bespeak; (*contratar*) to engage.
2 **apalabrarse** VR to come to a verbal agreement (*con* with).

apalabrear [1a] (*LAm*) = **apalabrar**.

Apalaches NMPL: **Montes ~** Appalachians.

apalancado* ADJ settled, established.

apalancamiento NM leverage.

apalancar [1g] 1 VT (a) (*levantar*) to lever up, move (o lift etc) with a crowbar. (b) (*fig*) to support; (*Cono Sur**) **~ a uno** to wangle a job for sb*. (c) (*guardar*) to keep; (*esconder*) to hide, stash away.
2 VI (‡) (*esconderse*) to hide; (*dormirse*) to settle down, kip down‡; (*encontrar lugar*) to find a place.
3 **apalancarse*** VR to sit down, squat*; to settle in, establish o.s.

apalé INTERJ (*Méx*) (a) (*sorpresa*) goodness me! (b) (*aviso*) look out!, watch it!

apaleada NF (*Cono Sur, Méx Agr*) winnowing.

apaleamiento NM beating, thrashing.

apalear [1a] VT animal, persona to beat, thrash; tapiz to beat; (*Agr*) to winnow; **~ oro, ~ plata** to be rolling in money.

apaleo NM (*Agr*) winnowing.

apalizar [1f] VT to beat up*.

apallar [1a] VT (*And*) to harvest.

apamparse [1a] VR (*Cono Sur*) to become bewildered; to lose one's grip.

apanado 1 ADJ (*LAm*) breaded, cooked in breadcrumbs.
2 NM (*And*) beating.

apanalado ADJ honeycombed.

apanar [1a] VT (*LAm Culin*) to cover in breadcrumbs.

apancle NM (*Méx*) irrigation ditch.

apandar‡ [1a] VT to rip off‡, knock off‡.

apandillar [1a] 1 VT to form into a gang.
2 **apandillarse** VR to gang up, form a gang, band together.

apando NM (*Méx*) punishment cell.

apandorgarse [1h] VR (*And*) to lose heart, get scared.

apani(a)guarse [1i] VR (*And, Carib*) to gang up.

apanicar* [1g] VT (*Cono Sur*) to cause panic in, frighten.

apantallado ADJ (*Méx*) (*impresionado*) impressed, overwhelmed; (*achatado*) overwhelmed, crushed; **quedar ~** to be left open-mouthed.

apantallar¹ [1a] VT to screen, shield.

apantallar² [1a] VT (*Méx*) (*impresionar*) to impress; to fill with wonder; (*achatar*) to crush, overwhelm.

apantanar [1a] VT to flood, make boggy, make swampy.

apañadito* ADJ neat, tidy; controlled, well-organized.

apañado ADJ (a) (*mañoso*) skilful, clever, handy. (b) (*conveniente*) suitable (*para* for). (c) (*) **estar ~** (*borracho*) to be tight*; **¡estás ~!*** you've had it!*; you don't have a chance!; **estar ~ para hacer algo** to have difficulty in doing sth; **estoy ~ si lo hago** I'll be in trouble if I do it; **están ~s** they're mistaken, they've got it all wrong; **~s estaríamos si confiáramos en eso** we'd be fools if we relied on that. (d) **los hijos quedarán bien ~s** the children will be well provided for.

apañador(a) NM/F (a) (*Dep*) catcher. (b) (*) fixer*.

apañar [1a] 1 VT (a) (*asir*) to take hold of, grasp, seize; (*recoger*) to pick up; (*) to pinch*.
(b) (*vestir*) to dress, dress up; (*envolver*) to wrap up; (*remendar*) to mend, patch up; (*arreglar*) to fix up.
(c) (*Cono Sur*) crimen to conceal, cover up; criminal to harbour, hide.
2 **apañarse** VR (a) (*ser diestro*) to be skilful, be clever; **~ para + infin** to contrive to + infin, manage to + infin; **apañárselas (por su cuenta)** to fend for o.s., get along without help; to manage, find a way; **apañaos como podáis** manage as best you can.
(b) (*Cono Sur*) **~ algo** to get one's hands on sth, get hold of sth.

apando NM (*Méx*) punishment cell.

apaño NM (a) (*remiendo*) patch, mend; (*fig*) fix*; shady deal, put-up job*; fiddle*, piece of juggling (with figures etc); **esto no tiene ~** there's no answer to this one. (b) (*destreza*) skill, knack, dexterity; (*pey*) craft, guile. (c) (‡: *amorío*) affair. (d) (‡: *amante*: t **apaña** f) lover.

apañuscar* [1g] VT (a) (*ajar*) to rumple; (*aplastar*) to crush. (b) (*: *robar*) to pinch*, steal.

apapachar [1a] VT (*Carib*: *abrazar*) to cuddle, hug; (*mimar*) to spoil.

apapachos NMPL (*Méx*) (*abrazos*) hugs, cuddles; (*caricias*) caresses.

aparador NM (*mueble*) sideboard; (*vitrina*) showcase; (*escaparate*) shop window; (*Téc*) workshop; **estar de ~** to be dressed up to receive visitors.

aparadorista NMF (*Méx*) window dresser.

aparar [1a] VT (a) (*disponer*) to arrange, prepare. (b) manos etc to stretch out (*to catch sth*). (c) (*Agr*) to weed, clean.

aparatarse [1a] VR (*And, Cono Sur*): **se aparata** it's brewing up for a storm, there's a storm coming.

aparatejo NM gadget.

aparato NM (a) (*Quím, Fís etc*) apparatus, piece of apparatus; (*Mec*) machine; device; piece of equipment; (*Rad, TV*) set, receiver; (*Telec*) instrument, handset; (*Aer*) machine; (*doméstico*) appliance; (*Fot*) apparatus, piece of equipment; (*Med*) dressing, bandage; surgical appliance; (*Teat*) properties; (*Anat*) system; **~ de afeitar** safety razor; **~ antirrobo** anti-theft device; **~ auditivo** hearing aid; **~ circulatorio** circulation, circulatory system; **~ crítico** (*Liter*) critical apparatus; **~ eléctrico** (*Met*) display of lightning, electrical storm; **~ de escucha**

listening device; ~ **fotográfico** camera; ~ **lector de microfilms** microfilm reader; **~s de mando** (*Aer etc*) controls; ~ **de oído** hearing aid; ~ **de ortodoncia** brace; ~ **periférico** peripheral device; **~s de pescar** fishing tackle; ~ **de relojería** clockwork mechanism; ~ **respiratorio** respiratory system; **~s sanitarios** bathroom fittings; ~ **para sordos** hearing aid; ~ **de televisión** television set; ~ **para filmar**, ~ **tomavistas** cine-camera; ~ **de uso doméstico** domestic appliance; **tengo a X en el** ~ I have X on the line.

(**b**) (*boato*) display, show, ostentation; **de mucho** ~ spectacular; **sin** ~ unostentatiously, without ceremony, without fuss.

(**c**) (*indicios*) signs, symptoms; (*Med*) symptoms; (*Psic*) syndrome.

(**d**) (*Pol*) machine; ~ **electoral** electoral machine; ~ **del partido** party machine.

(**e**) (⁕) (*pene*) prick⁕; (*vagina*) cunt⁕.

aparatosamente ADV showily, ostentatiously; pretentiously; in a spectacular way.

aparatosidad NF showiness, ostentation; pretentiousness; spectacular character.

aparatoso ADJ (*vistoso*) showy, ostentatious; (*exagerado*) exaggerated, pretentious; *caída, función* spectacular.

aparcacoches NM INVAR car-park attendant, parking valet.

aparcadero NM parking lot.

aparcamento NM (*CAm, Carib*), **aparcamiento** NM (**a**) (*acto*) parking; ~ **en doble fila** double parking. (**b**) (*lugar*) car-park, parking lot (*US*), parking place; (*apartadero*) lay-by; ~ **subterráneo** underground car-park; ~ **vigilado** car-park (*with attendant*).

aparcar [1g] **1** VT (*Aut*) to park; (*Parl⋆*) *proyecto de ley* to shelve; *idea* to put on the back burner.
2 VI to park.

aparcería NF (*Com*) partnership; (*Agr*) share-cropping; (*Cono Sur*) comradeship, friendship; kinship.

aparcero, -a NM/F (*Com*) co-owner, partner; (*Agr*) sharecropper; (*Cono Sur*) comrade, friend; (*hombre*) kinsman, (*mujer*) kinswoman.

apareamiento NM (**a**) (*emparejamiento*) matching; levelling. (**b**) (*emparejarse*) mating, pairing.

aparear [1a] **1** VT (**a**) (*emparejar*) to pair, match; (*nivelar*) to level up. (**b**) *animales* to mate, pair.
2 aparearse VR (**a**) (*emparejarse*) to form a pair, go together. (**b**) (*animales*) to mate, pair.

aparecer [2d] VI, **aparecerse** VR (*gen*) to appear; (*presentarse*) to show up, turn up; (*revelarse*) to come into sight; to loom up; (*libro*) to come out; (*fantasma*) to appear, walk; **apareció borracho** he turned up drunk; **allí aparecen fantasmas** the place is haunted; **no ha aparecido el libro ese** that book still hasn't shown up; **Nuestra Señora se apareció a Bernadette** Our Lady appeared to Bernadette.

aparecido, -a NM/F ghost.

aparejado ADJ (**a**) (*apto*) fit, suitable, ready (*para* for). (**b**) **llevar** (*o* **traer**) **algo** ~ to entail sth.

aparejador NM foreman, overseer; (*Arquit*) master builder; quantity surveyor; (*Náut*) rigger.

aparejar [1a] **1** VT to prepare, get ready; *caballo* to saddle, harness; (*Náut*) to fit out, rig out; (*antes de pintar*) to size, prime.
2 aparejarse VR (**a**) (*prepararse*) to get ready; (*equiparse*) to equip o.s..
(**b**) (*CAm, Carib*) to mate, pair.

aparejo NM (**a**) (*acto*) preparation.
(**b**) (*avíos*) gear, equipment, tackle.
(**c**) (*Náut*) rigging; rig, type of rig.
(**d**) (*para levantar*) lifting gear, tackle, block and tackle; (*Náut*) tackle, derrick.
(**e**) (*Pesca*) tackle; ~ **de anzuelos** set of hooks.
(**f**) (*Arquit*) bond, bonding.
(**g**) (*de caballo*) (*arreos*) harness; (*CAm, Méx: silla*) saddle; (*And*) woman's saddle.
(**h**) (*antes de pintar*) sizing, priming.
(**i**) **~s** gear, equipment, tools, kit.

aparellaje NM control gear.

aparencial ADJ apparent.

aparentar [1a] **1** VT (**a**) (*fingir*) to feign, affect.
(**b**) *edad* to look, seem to be; **ella no aparenta sus años** she doesn't look her age.
(**c**) ~ + *infin* to feign to + *infin*, pretend to + *infin*, make as if to + *infin*.
2 VI to show off, make a show.

aparente ADJ (**a**) (*que parece*) apparent, seeming; (*pey*) unreal; deceptive. (**b**) (*evidente*) visible, evident; outward. (**c**) (*conveniente*) fit, suitable, proper. (**d**) (⋆: *atractivo*) attractive, smart; eye-catching; (*pey*) flashy.

aparentemente ADV (**a**) (*según parece*) seemingly. (**b**) (*evidentemente*) visibly, outwardly.

aparición NF (**a**) (*acto*) appearance; publication; ~ **en público** public appearance; **un libro de próxima** ~ a book soon to be published, a

forthcoming book. (**b**) (*aparecido*) apparition, spectre.

apariencia NF (**a**) (*aspecto*) appearance, aspect, look(s).
(**b**) (*exterior*) outward appearance, semblance; **en** ~ outwardly, seemingly; **por todas las ~s** to all appearances; **juzgar por las ~s** to judge by appearances; **cubrir ~s, salvar las ~s** to keep up appearances, save one's face; **las ~s engañan** appearances are deceptive.
(**c**) (*probabilidad*) probability.

aparragado (*Cono Sur*) **1** ADJ stunted, dwarfish.
2 NM dwarf.

aparragarse [1h] VR (**a**) (*CAm: hacerse un ovillo*) to roll up, curl up.
(**b**) (*Cono Sur: agacharse*) to squat, crouch down.
(**c**) (*CAm, Cono Sur, Méx: no crecer*) to remain stunted, stay small; (*encogerse*) to shrink, grow small.

apartadero NM (*Aut*) lay-by; (*Ferro*) siding.

apartadijo NM (**a**) (*porción*) small portion, bit. (**b**) = **apartadizo** 2.

apartadizo **1** ADJ unsociable.
2 NM recess, alcove, nook.

apartado **1** ADJ (*separado*) separated; (*remoto*) remote, isolated, out-of-the-way.
2 NM (**a**) (*cuarto*) spare room; side room.
(**b**) (*t* ~ **de correos**, ~ **postal**) post-office box; box number; ~ **de localidades** (*Teat*) ticket agency.
(**c**) (*Tip*) paragraph, section; heading.
(**d**) (*Metal*) extraction.

apartahotel NM aparthotel.

apartamento NM apartment, flat.

apartamiento NM (**a**) (*acto*) separation; withdrawal. (**b**) (*cualidad*) seclusion, remoteness, isolation; (*lugar*) secluded spot, remote area.

apartar [1a] **1** VT (*separar*) to separate, divide, take away (*de* from); (*quitar*) to remove, move away, put aside; (*Min*) to extract; (*Agr*) *ganado* to separate, cut out; (*Correos*) to sort; (*Ferro*) to shunt; (*Jur*) to set aside, waive; ~ **a uno para decirle algo** to take sb aside to tell him sth; ~ **a uno de un propósito** to dissuade sb from an intention; **lograron ~ la discusión de ese punto** they managed to turn the discussion away from that point; **el ministro le apartó del mando** the minister removed him from the command; ~ **un pensamiento de sí** to put a thought out of one's mind; **apartó el plato con la mano** he pushed his plate aside; **¿no podemos ~lo un poco más?** can't we move it a bit further away?
2 apartarse VR (**a**) (*dos personas*) to part, separate; (*dos cosas*) to become separated.
(**b**) (*retirarse*) to move away, withdraw, retire (*de* from); (*mantenerse aparte*) to keep away (*de* from), stand aside; **¡apártate!** out of the way!; ~ **de un camino** to turn off a road; to stray from a path; **nos hemos apartado bastante de la ruta** we've got rather a long way off the route; **el cohete se está apartando de la trayectoria** the rocket is deviating from the trajectory.
(**c**) (*Jur*) to withdraw from a suit.

aparte **1** ADV (*gen*) apart, aside; (*por separado*) separately; (*además*) besides; (*Teat*) aside; **tendremos que considerar eso** ~ we shall have to consider that separately; **hacerle a uno** ~ to exclude sb; to ignore sb; **poner algo** ~ to put sth aside, put sth on one side; **ser algo** ~ to be something superior; **eso** ~ apart from that.
2 ~ **de** PREP apart from; ~ **de eso** apart from that; ~ **de que** ... apart from the fact that ... .
3 NM (**a**) (*Teat*) aside.
(**b**) (*Tip*) (*new*) paragraph; '(**punto y**) ~' (*al dictar*) 'new paragraph'.
(**c**) (*LAm Agr*) separation, sorting out.

apartheid NM apartheid.

aparthotel NM aparthotel.

apartidismo NM non-political nature, non-party character.

apartidista ADJ apolitical, non-party.

apasionadamente ADV (**a**) (*con pasión*) passionately; intensely; fervently. (**b**) (*pey*) in a biassed way, partially.

apasionado **1** ADJ (**a**) (*gen*) passionate; *denuncia etc* impassioned; (*intenso*) intense, emotional; (*ardiente*) fervent, enthusiastic; ~ **a**, ~ **por** passionately fond of, passionately attached to.
(**b**) (*pey*) biassed, partial, prejudiced.
2 NM, **apasionada** NF admirer, devotee; **los ~s de Góngora** devotees of Góngora, Góngora enthusiasts.

apasionamiento NM (**a**) passion, enthusiasm; vehemence, intensity; great fondness (*de, por* for). (**b**) (*pey*) bias, partiality, prejudice.

apasionante ADJ exciting, thrilling.

apasionar [1a] **1** VT (**a**) (*entusiasmar*) to fill with passion; to stir deeply, make a strong appeal to; *amante* to stir, arouse; **me apasionan las gambas** I adore prawns, I can't resist prawns; **es una lectura que apasiona** it's stirring stuff to read; **es un estudio que apasiona** it's a fascinating study; **le apasiona el fútbol** he's crazy about football, he's football-mad.
(**b**) (*afligir*) to afflict, torment.
2 apasionarse VR (**a**) (*excitarse*) to get excited, be roused, work o.s. up; ~ **de**, ~ **por** *persona* to fall madly in love with; *cosa* to get mad

about, enthuse over, become enthusiastic about.

(**b**) (*pey*) to become biassed, give way to prejudice.

apaste NM, **apaxte** NM (*CAm*) clay pot, clay jug.

apatía NF apathy; (*Med*) listlessness.

apático ADJ apathetic; (*Med*) listless.

apátrida ☐1 ADJ stateless; (*Cono Sur: sin patriotismo*) unpatriotic.
☐2 NMF (*Cono Sur*) unpatriotic person.

apatronarse [1a] VR (*And, Cono Sur*): ~ **de uno** (*amancebarse*) to find a protector in sb; (*buscar empleo*) to seek a domestic post with sb; (*And: cargarse*) to take charge of sb.

apatusco NM (**a**) (*adornos*) frills, adornments. (**b**) (*Carib*) (*enredo*) trick; (*fingimiento*) pretence; (*intrigas*) intrigue.

APD NF (*Esp*) ABR de **Asistencia Pública Domiciliaria** (*social welfare organization*).

apdo. NM ABR de **apartado de correos** Post Office Box, PO Box.

apeadero NM (**a**) (*para montar*) mounting block, step. (**b**) (*parada*) halt, stopping place; (*Ferro*) halt, wayside station. (**c**) (*alojamiento*) temporary quarters, temporary lodging, pied-à-terre.

apear [1a] ☐1 VT (**a**) *persona* to help down, help to alight (*de* from); *objeto* to take down, get down (*de* from); *árbol* to fell; **quedar apeado** (*fig*:) to be left behind.

(**b**) *caballo* to hobble; *rueda* to chock, scotch.

(**c**) (*Arquit*) to prop up.

(**d**) (*Agrimen*) to survey, measure; to mark the boundaries of.

(**e**) *problema* to solve, work out; *dificultad* to overcome.

(**f**) ~ **a uno de su opinión** to make sb give up his view, persuade sb that his opinion is wrong; ~ **a uno de un propósito** to wean sb away from an intention, make sb give up his plan.

(**g**) ~ **el tratamiento a uno** to drop sb's title, address sb without formality.

(**h**) (*: despedir*) to dismiss, sack*; ~ **a uno de su cargo** to remove sb from his post.

(**i**) (*And: matar*) to kill.

(**j**) (*CAm: reprender*) to dress down*, tell off*.

☐2 **apearse** VR (**a**) to dismount; to get down, get out (*de* of), alight (*de* from); (*Ferro*) to get off, get out.

(**b**) ~ **en** to stay at, put up at.

(**c**) *V* **burro**.

(**d**) ~ **de algo** (*And*) to get rid of sth.

(**e**) **no apeársela** (*CAm*) to be drunk all the time.

apechugar [1h] ☐1 VT (**a**) (*Cono Sur: hacer frente a*) to face (up to) resolutely.

(**b**) (*Cono Sur, Carib: agarrar*) to grab (hold of), seize.

(**c**) (*And: sacudir*) to shake violently.

☐2 VI (**a**) (*) to push, shove; **¡apechuga!** buck up!, come on!

(**b**) ~ **con** to put up with, swallow; *cometido* to take on.

☐3 **apechugarse** VR: ~ **algo** (*CAm*) to snatch sth.

apechugón NM violent shake, violent shove.

apedazar [1f] VT (**a**) (*remendar*) to mend, patch. (**b**) (*despedazar*) to tear to pieces, cut into pieces.

apedrear [1a] ☐1 VT to stone, pelt with stones; to stone to death.

☐2 VI (**a**) (*Met*) to hail. (**b**) (*Méx*:) to stink, reek.

☐3 **apedrearse** VR to be damaged by hail.

apedreo NM (**a**) stoning, stone throwing; stoning to death. (**b**) (*Met*) hail; damage by hail.

apegadamente ADV devotedly.

apegado ADJ: ~ **a** attached to, devoted to, fond of.

apegarse [1h] VR: ~ **a** to become attached to, grow fond of.

apego NM: ~ **a** attachment to, devotion to, fondness for.

apelable ADJ (*Jur*) appealable, that can be appealed against, subject to appeal.

apelación NF (**a**) (*Jur*) appeal; **sin** ~ without appeal, final; **interponer** ~ to appeal, lodge an appeal; **presentar su** ~ to present one's appeal; **ver una** ~ to consider an appeal.

(**b**) (*fig*) help, remedy; **no hay** ~, **esto no tiene** ~ it's a hopeless case.

apelante NMF appellant.

apelar [1a] VI (*Jur*) to appeal (*de* against); ~ **a** (*fig*) to resort to, have recourse to, call on.

apelativo NM (*Ling*) common noun; (*LAm*) group (*o* collective) name.

apeldar: [1a] VT: **~las** to beat it*.

apellidar [1a] ☐1 VT (**a**) (*llamar*) to name, surname, call. (**b**) ~ **a uno por rey** to proclaim sb king.

☐2 **apellidarse** VR to be called, call o.s., have as a surname; **¿cómo se apellida Vd?** what is your (sur)name?

apellido NM name; surname, family name; (*apodo*) nickname; ~ **de soltera** maiden name.

┌─ **APELLIDO** ─────────────────────────

ⓘ *In the Spanish-speaking world most people use two **apellidos**, the first being their father's first surname, and the second their mother's first surname: e.g. the surname of the children of Juan **García López**, married to*

Carmen **Pérez Rodríguez** would be **García Pérez**. Married women normally retain their own surnames but in exceptional cases they add their husband's first surname to their first surname with **de** in between: e.g. Carmen Pérez de García. In such cases she could also be referred to as **(la) señora de García**. In Latin America it is usual for the second surname to be shortened to an initial in correspondence: e.g. Juan García L.

apelmazado ADJ *masa* compact, compressed, solid; *pelo* matted; *líquido* thick, lumpy; *escritura* clumsy.

apelmazar [1f] ☐1 VT to compress, squeeze together; (*CAm*) to roll; to firm.

☐2 **apelmazarse** VR to cake, solidify; to get lumpy.

apelotonar [1a] ☐1 VT to roll into a ball.

☐2 **apelotonarse** VR (*animal etc*) to roll up, curl up; (*gente*) to mass, crowd together; (*sustancia*) to get lumpy.

apenado ADJ (*LAm*) (*avergonzado*) ashamed, embarrassed; (*triste*) sad, sorry; (*tímido*) shy, timid.

apenar [1a] ☐1 VT to grieve, upset, trouble; to cause pain to.

☐2 **apenarse** VR (**a**) (*afligirse*) to grieve, sorrow, distress o.s.; ~ **de algo**, ~ **por algo** to grieve about sth, distress o.s. on account of sth.

(**b**) (*LAm*) (*avergonzarse*) to feel embarrassed, feel ashamed; (*ser triste*) to be sorry, be sad; (*ser tímido*) to be shy; (*sonrojarse*) to blush; **no se apene, no tiene importancia** (*Méx*) don't worry, it doesn't matter.

▼ **apenas** ☐1 ADV hardly, scarcely; ~ **nada** hardly anything; ~ **nadie** hardly anybody; ~ **si pude levantarme** I could hardly get up.

☐2 CONJ (**a**) ~ **hube llegado cuando** ... no sooner had I arrived than ..., I had only just arrived when ...

(**b**) (*esp LAm: en cuanto*) as soon as; ~ **terminó se fue** as soon as it was over she left.

┌─ **APENAS** ──────── **ver también la entrada** ─┐

El adverbio **apenas** tiene dos traducciones principales en inglés: *hardly* y *scarcely*, este último usado en lenguaje más formal.

● Estos adverbios se colocan normalmente detrás de los verbos auxiliares y modales y delante de los demás verbos:

   Apenas podía hablar después del accidente

   He could hardly o scarcely speak after the accident

   Apenas nos conocemos

   We hardly o scarcely know each other

● Sin embargo, en oraciones temporales, podemos colocar *hardly* y *scarcely* al principio de la oración si queremos reforzar la inmediatez de algo, o como recurso estilístico en cuentos y relatos. En este caso los adverbios van siempre seguidos de un verbo auxiliar, con lo que se invierte el orden normal del sujeto y el verbo en inglés, quedando la estructura *hardly/scarcely* + *had* + SUJETO + PARTICIPIO + *when* ...:

   Apenas me había acostado cuando oí un ruido extraño

   Hardly o Scarcely had I gone to bed when I heard a strange noise

NOTA: En este sentido se suele utilizar también *no sooner* + *had* + SUJETO + PARTICIPIO + *than* + ...:

   No sooner had I gone to bed than I heard a strange noise

Para otros usos y ejemplos ver la entrada.

└─────────────────────────────────────┘

apencar: [1g] VI to slog, slave.

apendectomía NF appendectomy.

apendejarse [1a] VR (*Carib*) (*hacer el tonto*) to get silly, act the fool; (*acobardarse*) to lose one's nerve.

apéndice NM (*Anat*) appendix; (*fig*) appendage; (*Liter etc*) appendix, supplement; (*Jur*) schedule.

apendicitis NF appendicitis.

Apeninos NMPL Apennines.

apenitas ADV (*And, Cono Sur*) = **apenas**.

apensionado ADJ (*And, Cono Sur, Méx*) depressed, sad; grieved.

apensionar [1a] ☐1 VT (*And, Cono Sur, Méx*) to sadden, grieve.

☐2 **apensionarse** VR to become sad, get depressed.

apeñuscarse [1g] VR (*Cono Sur*) to crowd together.

apeo NM (**a**) (*Agrimen*) survey. (**b**) (*soporte*) prop, support; (*andamio*) scaffolding. (**c**) (*de árboles*) felling.

apeorar [1a] VI to get worse.

aperado ADJ (*Cono Sur*) well-equipped.

aperar [1a] ☐1 VT (**a**) (*Agr*) to make, repair, fit up.

(**b**) (*Cono Sur*) *caballo* to harness; ~ **a uno de herramientas** to provide sb with tools, fix sb up with tools.

☐2 **aperarse** VR: ~ **de algo** (*Cono Sur*) to equip o.s., provide o.s. with sth; **estar bien aperado para** to be well equipped for.

apercancarse [1g] VR (*Cono Sur*) to go mouldy.

aperchar [1a] VT (*CAm, Cono Sur*) to pile up, stack up.

apercibimiento NM (**a**) (*acto*) preparation; provision. (**b**) (*aviso*) warning, notice. (**c**) (*Jur*) warning.

apercibir [3a] ☐1 VT (**a**) (*preparar*) to prepare, make ready; (*proveer*) to furnish, provide; **con los fusiles apercibidos** with rifles at the ready.

(**b**) (*avisar*) to warn, advise.

┌─► LENGUA Y USO: **apenas**: 1 → 43.2 ─┐

(c) (*Jur*) to warn.
(d) (*LAm: darse cuenta*) to notice, observe, see.
(e) *error etc* = **percibir**.
2 apercibirse VR to prepare o.s., get ready (*para* for); **~ de** to provide o.s. with; **~ de** (*Cono Sur*) to notice, perceive.
apercollar [1l] VT **(a)** (*agarrar*) to seize by the neck. **(b)** (*matar*) to fell, kill (with a blow on the neck). **(c)** (‡: *detener*) to knock off‡, nick‡.
apergaminado ADJ parchment-like; *piel etc* dried up, wrinkled; *cara* wizened.
apergaminarse [1a] VR to get like parchment; (*piel etc*) to dry up, get yellow and wrinkled.
apergollar [1a] VT (*LAm*) (*agarrar*) to grab by the throat; (*engañar*) to trap, ensnare.
aperital NM (*Cono Sur*) = **aperitivo**.
aperitivo NM appetizer, snack; (*bebida*) aperitif.
apero NM (*colectivo: t* ~**s**) tools, gear; equipment; (*Agr*) implement; (*LAm: arneses*) harness, trappings; (*LAm: silla*) saddle; (*Méx Agr*) (*animales*) ploughing team, draught animals; ~**s** (*equipo*) plough and tackle, ploughing equipment.
aperrarse* [1a] VR (*Cono Sur*) to dig one's heels in.
aperreado†† ADJ wretched, miserable; **llevar una vida aperreada** to have a wretched life.
aperreador ADJ bothersome, tiresome.
aperrear [1a] **1** VT **(a)** (*lit*) to set the dogs on. **(b)** (*fig*) (*acosar*) to harass, plague; (*cansar*) to wear out, tire out.
2 aperrearse VR **(a)** (*ser acosado*) to get harassed; (*trabajar demasiado*) to slave away, overwork. **(b)** (*LAm: insistir*) to insist.
aperreo NM **(a)** (*problema*) harassment, worry; toil, overwork. **(b)** (*LAm: molestia*) nuisance; (*ira*) rage; **¡qué ~ de vida!** it's a dog's life!
apersogar [1h] VT to tether, tie up; (*Carib*) to string together.
apersonado ADJ: **bien ~** presentable, nice-looking; **mal ~** unattractive, unprepossessing, scruffy.
apersonarse [1a] VR to appear in person; to appear, come, show up; (*Com*) to have a business interview; (*Jur*) to appear.
apertura **1** NF **(a)** (*gen*) opening; (*de un testamento*) reading; (*Pol*) openness, liberalization. **(b)** (*de texto*) opening, start.
2 NM (*Dep*) fly-half.
aperturar [1a] VT to open.
aperturismo NM liberalization; relaxation, loosening-up; (*Pol*) (policy of) liberalization.

┌─── **APERTURISMO** ───────────────────────────────┐
*In the final years of the Franco régime and after Franco's death in 1975, politicians who wanted to liberalize and democratize the political system were known as **aperturistas** while diehard right-wingers who wanted the régime or something very similar to continue were known as **inmovilistas.***
⇨ *See also* TRANSICIÓN A LA DEMOCRACIA
└──┘

aperturista **1** ADJ *tendencia etc* liberalizing, liberal.
2 NMF liberalizer, liberal.
apesadumbrado ADJ grieved, sad, distressed.
apesadumbrar [1a] **1** VT to grieve, sadden, distress.
2 apesadumbrarse VR to grieve, be grieved, distress o.s. (*con, de* about, at).
apesarar(se) [1a] = **apesadumbrar(se)**.
apescollar [1l] VT (*Cono Sur*) to seize by the neck.
apesgar [1h] VT to weigh down, overburden.
apestado ADJ **(a)** (*LAm: maloliente*) stinking; (*Med*) infected with the plague. **(b) estar ~ de** to be infested with, be full of.
apestar [1a] **1** VT **(a)** (*Med*) to infect (with the plague).
(b) (*fig: corromper*) to corrupt, spoil, vitiate; (*molestar*) to plague, harass; (*repugnar*) to sicken, nauseate.
(c) (*olor*) to stink out.
2 VI to stink (*a* of).
3 apestarse VR **(a)** (*Med*) to catch the plague.
(b) (*LAm Bot*) to be blighted, get blight.
(c) (*And: resfriarse*) to catch a cold.
apestillar [1a] VT (*Cono Sur*) **(a)** (*agarrar*) to catch, grab hold of. **(b)** (*regañar*) to tell off, reprimand.
apestoso ADJ **(a)** (*lit*) stinking; *olor* awful, pestilential. **(b)** (*) (*molesto*) annoying; (*repugnante*) sickening, nauseating.
apetachar [1a] VT to patch, mend.
▼ **apetecer** [2d] **1** VT **(a)** (*desear*) to crave, long for, yearn for.
▼**(b)** (*esp Esp: atraer*) to appeal to, attract, take one's fancy; **me apetece un helado** I feel like an ice cream, I could manage an ice cream, the idea of an ice cream appeals to me; **me apetece ir** I should like to go; **¿te apetece?** how about it?
2 VI to attract, have an appeal, be welcome; **la idea no apetece** the idea has no appeal; **un vaso de jerez siempre apetece** a glass of sherry is always welcome.
apetecible ADJ attractive, tempting, desirable.

apetencia NF hunger, appetite; (*fig*) hunger, craving, desire (*de* for); inclination.
apetente ADJ hungry, yearning, craving.
APETI NF ABR *de* **Asociación Profesional Española de Traductores e Intérpretes.**
apetite NM appetizer; (*fig*) incentive.
apetito NM **(a)** (*gen*) appetite (*de* for); **abrir el ~** to whet one's appetite; **quitar el ~ de** to destroy one's appetite for. **(b)** (*fig*) desire, relish (*de* for).
apetitoso ADJ **(a)** (*gen*) appetizing; tasty, tempting; (*fig*) tempting, attractive. **(b)** *persona* fond of good food.
API NMF ABR *de* **agente de la propiedad inmobiliaria** estate agent.
apí NM **(a)** (*And*) a non-alcoholic maize drink. **(b)** (*And, Cono Sur: añicos*) **el vaso se hizo ~** the glass was smashed to pieces.
apiadar [1a] **1** VT to move to pity.
2 apiadarse VR: **~ de** to take pity on, express pity for, feel sorry for.
apiado NM (*Cono Sur*) celery liqueur.
apicarado ADJ roguish, mischievous.
apicararse [1a] VR to go to the bad, pick up dishonest ways.
ápice NM **(a)** (*cumbre*) apex, top. **(b)** (*fig: de problema*) crux, knotty point; **estar en los ~s de** to be well up in, know all about. **(c)** (*fig: jota*) whit, iota; **ni ~** not a whit; **no ceder un ~** not to yield an inch; **no importa un ~** it doesn't matter a bit.
apichicarse [1g] VR (*Cono Sur*) to squat, crouch.
apicultor(a) NM/F beekeeper, apiarist.
apicultura NF beekeeping, apiculture.
apilado NM piling, heaping, stacking.
apiladora NF (*en impresora*) stacker.
apilar [1a] VT to pile up, heap up, stack.
apilonar [1a] VT (*LAm*) = **apilar**.
apimplado* ADJ (*LAm*) tight*, tipsy.
apiñado ADJ **(a)** (*lleno*) crowded, packed, congested (*de* with). **(b)** *forma* cone-shaped, pyramidal.
apiñadura NF, **apiñamiento** NM crowding, congestion; crowd, squash, jam.
apiñar [1a] **1** VT (*agrupar, reunir*) to crowd together, bunch together; (*apretar*) to pack in, press together, squeeze together; *espacio etc* to overcrowd, congest.
2 apiñarse VR to crowd together, press together; to be packed tight, be squashed together; **la multitud se apiñaba alrededor de él** the crowd pressed round him.
apio NM **(a)** (*Bot*) celery. **(b)** (*Esp*‡) queer‡.
apiolar‡ [1a] VT **(a)** (*detener*) to nab*, nick‡. **(b)** (*matar*) to do in‡ bump off‡.
apio nabo NM celeriac.
apiparse* [1a] VR to stuff o.s., guzzle.
apir(i) NM (*LAm*) mineworker.
apirularse [1a] VR (*Cono Sur*) to get dressed up to the nines.
apisonadora NF steamroller, road roller.
apisonar [1a] VT to roll, roll flat; to tamp down, ram down.
apitiquarse [1a] VR (*And*) to get depressed; to be dismayed.
apitonar [1a] **1** VT *cáscara* to crack, pierce, break through.
2 VI (*cuernos*) to sprout, begin to show; (*animal*) to begin to grow horns.
3 apitonarse* VR (*enfadarse*) to get into a huff; (*dos personas*) to have a slanging match*.
apizarrado ADJ slaty, slate-coloured.
aplacar [1g] VT to appease, placate; to soothe, calm down; *hambre etc* to satisfy.
aplanacalles NM INVAR (*LAm*) idler, layabout.
aplanador NM: **~ de calles** idler, layabout.
aplanamiento NM smoothing, levelling, flattening.
aplanar [1a] **1** VT **(a)** (*nivelar*) to smooth, level, make even; to roll flat, flatten; (*And*) *ropa* to iron; **~ las calles** (*LAm*) to hang about (o around) in the street.
(b) (*) to knock out, bowl over with surprise.
2 aplanarse VR **(a)** (*Arquit*) to collapse, cave in, fall down.
(b) (*) (*desanimarse*) to get discouraged; (*aletargarse*) to become lethargic, sink into lethargy.
aplanchar [1a] VT (*LAm*) = **planchar**.
aplastamiento NM crushing.
aplastante ADJ overwhelming, crushing.
aplastar [1a] **1** VT **(a)** to flatten (out), squash, crush (flat).
(b) (*fig*) *enemigo etc* to crush, overwhelm; (*) *persona* to floor, flatten, leave speechless.
2 aplastarse VR **(a)** to flatten o.s.; **se aplastó contra la pared** he flattened himself against the wall.
(b) (*Arquit etc*) to collapse.
(c) (*Cono Sur*) (*desanimarse*) to get discouraged, lose heart; (*atemorizarse*) to get scared, take fright.
(d) (*Cono Sur: agotarse*) to be drained, be exhausted.

(e) (*Cono Sur: atleta, caballo*) to blow up.

aplatanado ADJ **(a)** está ~ (*Carib etc*) he has gone native. **(b)** (*fig*) (*soso*) lumpish, lacking all ambition; (*aletargado*) weary, lethargic.

aplatanarse [1a] VR **(a)** (*abandonarse*) to become lethargic, sink into lethargy. **(b)** (*Carib etc: acriollarse*) to go native.

aplatarse [1a] VR (*Carib*) to get rich.

aplaudir [3a] VT to applaud, cheer, clap; (*fig*) to applaud, approve.

▼ **aplauso** NM applause; (*fig*) approval, acclaim; **~s** applause, cheering, clapping.

aplazamiento NM **(a)** postponement, deferment; adjournment. **(b)** summons, summoning.

aplazar [1f] ⒈ VT **(a)** (*diferir*) to postpone, put off, defer; *asunto etc* to adjourn, hold over; **se ha aplazado la decisión por tiempo indefinido** the decision has been postponed indefinitely. **(b)** (*fijar hora etc para*) to set a time for, set a date for; (*convocar*) to summon, convene.
⒉ VI (*CAm: suspender*) to fail (an exam).

aplebeyado ADJ coarse, coarsened.

aplebeyar [1a] ⒈ VT to coarsen, degrade; to demean.
⒉ **aplebeyarse** VR to become coarse; to lower o.s., demean o.s.

aplicabilidad NF applicability.

aplicable ADJ applicable (*a* to).

aplicación NF **(a)** (*acto*) application (*t Med*); **enviar su ~** (*LAm*) to send in one's application. **(b)** (*cualidad*) industry, studiousness, application; **le falta ~** he doesn't work hard enough, he lacks steadiness. **(c)** **aplicaciones** (*Inform*) applications; **aplicaciones de gestión** management applications; **aplicaciones comerciales** business applications.

aplicado ADJ **(a)** *ciencia* applied. **(b)** *carácter* studious; diligent, industrious.

aplicador NM applicator.

aplicar [1g] ⒈ VT (*gen*) to apply (*a* to); *esfuerzo, dinero etc* to devote, assign (*a* to), earmark (*a* for); *hombres, recursos* to assign (*a, para* to); *crimen etc* to attribute, impute (*a* to); **~ sanciones** to impose sanctions; **~ a uno a una carrera** to enter sb for a profession, put sb in for a profession; **~ el oído a una puerta** to put one's ear to a door.
⒉ **aplicarse** VR **(a)** **~ algo** to attribute sth to o.s., claim sth for o.s. **(b)** (*ley, regla etc*) **~ a** to apply to, be applicable to, be relevant to. **(c)** (*persona*) **~ a** to apply o.s. to, devote o.s. to, give one's mind to; **~ a + infin** to devote o.s. to + *ger*.

aplique NM (*lámpara*) wall lamp; (*Teat*) piece of stage décor, (*Cos*) appliqué.

aplomado ADJ self-confident.

aplomar [1a] ⒈ VT (*Arquit etc*) to plumb, test with a plumbline; to make perpendicular, make straight.
⒉ **aplomarse** VR **(a)** (*desplomarse*) to collapse, cave in, fall down. **(b)** (*fig*) to gain confidence. **(c)** (*Cono Sur*) to get embarrassed.

aplomo NM (*serenidad*) self-possession, assurance, aplomb; (*gravedad*) gravity, seriousness; (*pey*) nerve, cheek; **¡qué ~!** what a nerve!; **dijo con el mayor ~** he said with the utmost assurance; **perder su ~** to get worried, get rattled.

apocado ADJ **(a)** (*tímido*) diffident, timid; (*pusilánime*) pusillanimous; (*falto de voluntad*) spiritless, spineless. **(b)** (*humilde*) common, lowly.

apocalipsis NM apocalypse; **A~** (*Bib*) Revelations.

apocalíptico ADJ apocalyptic; *estilo* obscure, enigmatic.

apocamiento NM **(a)** (*timidez*) diffidence, pusillanimity, timidity; spinelessness. **(b)** (*depresión*) depression, depressed state.

apocar [1g] ⒈ VT **(a)** (*hacer pequeño*) to make smaller, diminish, reduce; (*fig*) to limit, restrict. **(b)** (*denigrar*) to belittle, run down; (*humillar*) to humiliate; (*intimidar*) to intimidate; **nada me apoca** nothing scares me.
⒉ **apocarse** VR to feel small, feel humiliated; to humble o.s.

apochongarse [1h] VR (*Cono Sur*) to get scared, be frightened.

apocopar [1a] VT to apocopate.

apócope NF (*Ling*) apocope; **Doro es ~ de Dorotea** Doro is a shortened form of Dorotea, Doro is short for Dorotea.

apócrifo ADJ apocryphal; false, spurious.

apodar [1a] VT to nickname, dub, call; to label.

apoderado, -a NM/F agent, representative; (*Jur*) proxy, attorney; (*Mús, Dep*) manager.

apoderar [1a] ⒈ VT **(a)** (*autorizar*) to authorize, empower. **(b)** (*Jur*) to grant power of attorney to.
⒉ **apoderarse** VR: **~ de** to get hold of, seize, take possession of.

apodíctico ADJ apodictic, necessarily true.

apodo NM nickname; label; (*Jur*) false name, alias.

apódosis NF apodosis.

apogeo NM (*Astron*) apogee; (*fig*) peak, summit, top; **estar en el ~ de su fama** to be at the height of one's fame; **estar en todo su ~** to be on top form.

apolillado ADJ moth-eaten.

apolilladura NF moth-hole.

apolillar [1a] ⒈ VT (*Cono Sur*): **estarla apolillando** to be snoozing*.
⒉ **apolillarse** VR to get moth-eaten; (*fig*) to get old.

apolíneo ADJ (*Mit*) Apollonian; (*fig*) classically handsome.

apolismado ADJ (*And, Carib, Méx: enclenque*) sickly, weak; (*CAm: vago*) lazy; (*Méx, Carib: deprimido*) gloomy, depressed; (*Carib: estúpido*) stupid.

apolismar [1a] ⒈ VT (*LAm*) to ruin, destroy.
⒉ VI (*CAm*) to laze about, idle.
⒊ **apolismarse** VR (*LAm*) (*enfermar*) to grow weak, weaken; (*deprimirse*) to get worried, get depressed; (*desanimarse*) to lose heart.

apoliticismo NM apolitical nature, non-political nature; non-political approach.

apolítico ADJ apolitical, non-political.

apoliyar [1a] VT = **apolillar.**

Apolo NM Apollo.

apologética NF apologetics.

apologético ADJ apologetic.

apología NF defence; eulogy; (*LAm*) apology; **una ~ del terrorismo** a statement in support of terrorism.

apologista NMF apologist.

apoltronado ADJ lazy, idle.

apoltronarse [1a] VR to get lazy; to laze, loaf around, idle.

apolvillarse [1a] VR (*Cono Sur Agr*) to be blighted.

apoplejía NF apoplexy, stroke.

apoplético ADJ apoplectic.

apoquinar* [1a] VT *dinero* to fork out*, pay up.

aporcar [1g] VT (*Agr*) to earth up.

aporrar* [1a] ⒈ VI to dry up*, get stuck (in a speech *etc*).
⒉ **aporrarse** VR to become a bore, become a nuisance.

aporreado ⒈ ADJ *vida etc* wretched, miserable; *persona* rascally.
⒉ NM (*Carib*) meat stew, chili stew.

aporreamiento NM beating.

aporrear [1a] ⒈ VT **(a)** *persona* to beat, bash*, club; to beat up*. **(b)** *puerta, mesa etc* to thump (on), pound (on), bang away at. **(c)** (*LAm: aplastar*) to crush completely (in an argument). **(d)** (*fig: acosar*) to bother, pester.
⒉ **aporrearse** VR to slave away, slog, toil.

aporreo NM **(a)** (*paliza*) beating; beating-up. **(b)** (*ruido*) thumping, pounding, banging. **(c)** (*molestia*) bother, nuisance.

aportación NF contribution; **aportaciones de la mujer** dowry.

aportar¹ [1a] VT to bring; to furnish, contribute; *evidencia etc* to bring forward, adduce; (*Jur*) to contribute (to the marriage settlement).

aportar² [1a] VI **(a)** (*Náut*) to reach port, come into harbour. **(b)** (*aparecer*) to come out at an unexpected place. **(c)** (*llegar*) to arrive, show up, come.

aporte NM contribution.

aportillar [1a] ⒈ VT to break down, break open; *muro* to breach.
⒉ **aportillarse** VR (*desplomarse*) to collapse, tumble down.

aposentar [1a] ⒈ VT to lodge, put up.
⒉ **aposentarse** VR to lodge, put up (*en* at).

aposento NM room; lodging; (*Carib*) main bedroom.

aposesionarse [1a] VR: **~ de** to take possession of.

aposición NF apposition; **en ~** in apposition.

apósito NM (*Med*) application, poultice; dressing.

aposta ADV, **apostadamente** ADV on purpose.

apostadero NM (*Mil*) station, post; (*Náut*) naval station.

apostador(a) NM/F better, backer, punter; **~ profesional** bookmaker.

apostar¹ [1a] ⒈ VT to station, post.
⒉ **apostarse** VR: **~ en** to station o.s. in (*o* at).

apostar² [1l] ⒈ VT **(a)** *dinero* to lay, stake, bet (*a* on). **(b)** **~las a uno, ~las con uno** to compete with sb.
⒉ VI to bet (*a, por* on; *a que* that); **apuesto a que sí** I bet it is; **~ por** (*fig*) *partido etc* to bet on, back; *programa etc* to put one's faith in, believe in; to advocate; **~ fuerte por** to give strong support to.
⒊ **apostarse** VR to compete (*con* with), be rivals, vie; **~las a uno, ~las con uno** to compete with sb.

apostasía NF apostasy.

apóstata NMF apostate.

apostatar [1a] VI (*Ecl*) to apostatize (*de* from); (*fig*) to change sides.

apostema NF abscess.

a posteriori ADV **(a)** at a later stage; *comprender etc* with (the benefit of) hindsight. **(b)** (*Lógica, Jur*) a posteriori.

apostilla NF note, comment.

apostillar [1a] VT to add notes to, annotate; (*fig*) to add, chime in with; *observación* to echo; **'Sí', apostilló una voz** 'Yes', a voice added.

apóstol NM apostle.

apostolado NM apostolate.

apostólico ADJ apostolic.

apostrofar [1a] VT **(a)** (*dirigirse a*) to apostrophize, address. **(b)** (*insultar*) to insult, shout insults at.

apóstrofe *gen* NM **(a)** (*Ling*) apostrophe. **(b)** (*insulto*) taunt, insult; (*reprensión*) rebuke, reprimand.

apóstrofo NM (*Tip*) inverted comma, apostrophe.
apostura NF (**a**) (*pulcritud*) neatness, elegance; (*hum*) nattiness. (**b**) (*belleza*) good looks.
apotegma NM apothegm, maxim.
apoteósico ADJ (*fig*) *éxito etc* huge, tremendous.
apoteosis NF apotheosis; (*fig*) climax, high point, culmination.
apoyabrazos NM INVAR armrest.
apoyacabeza(s) NM INVAR headrest.
apoyador NM (**a**) support, bracket. (**b**) (*Pol*) seconder.
apoyalibros NM INVAR book-ends.
apoyapié(s) NM INVAR footrest.
▼ **apoyar** [1a] **1** VT (**a**) *codo, cabeza etc* to lean, rest (*en, sobre* on); (*Arquit, Téc*) to hold up, support; to prop up; ~ **una escalera contra una pared** to lean a ladder against a wall.
  ▼ (**b**) (*fig*) *persona* to support, back; to stand by; (*pey*) to abet; *moción* to second, support; *principio* to uphold; *teoría etc* to bear out, confirm, support; **apoya su argumento en los siguientes hechos** he bases his argument on the following facts; **no apoyamos más al gobierno** we no longer support the government.
  2 VI: ~ **en** to rest on, be supported by.
  3 **apoyarse** VR: ~ **en** (**a**) *base* to rest on, be supported by; *hombro, bastón etc* to lean on; ~ **contra una pared** to lean against a wall.
  (**b**) (*fig*) *persona* to rely on; to lean on; *argumento, evidencia etc* to base o.s. on.
apoyatura NF (**a**) support. (**b**) (*Mús*) appoggiatura.
▼ **apoyo** NM (**a**) (*soporte*) support; prop. (**b**) (*fig*) (*respaldo*) support, backing; (*ayuda*) help; (*aprobación*) approval, favour; ~ **económico** financial support, financial backing; **contamos con su** ~ we rely on your support.
apozarse [1f] VR (*And, Cono Sur*) to form a pool.
APRA ['apra] NF (*Perú Pol*) ABR *de* **Alianza Popular Revolucionaria Americana**.

┌─── ▭APRA▭ ───
│ ⓘ *Peru's oldest political party, the **Alianza Popular Revolucionaria**
│ ***Americana** was created in 1924 as an international party to support
│ *the rights and needs of South America's indigenous populations. It failed to
│ *establish a base in other countries, however, and in spite of policies which
│ *appealed to a wide range of sectors at home, it did not come to power in
│ *Peru until 1985. The high hopes that accompanied **APRA**'s election were
│ *soon dashed, as human rights abuses continued, Shining Path terrorist
│ *activities went on unabated and failure to make foreign debt repayments
│ *plunged Peru into bankruptcy. In 1990 **APRA** lost to Alberto Fujimori's
│ ***Cambio 90**.*
│ ⇨ *See also* ▭CAMBIO 90▭ , ▭SENDERO LUMINOSO▭

apreciable ADJ (**a**) (*gen*) appreciable, considerable; (*perceptible*) noticeable; (*mensurable*) measurable; **una cantidad** ~ an appreciable quantity; ~ **al oído** audible.
  (**b**) (*fig*) worthy, estimable, esteemed; valuable; **los ~s esposos** the esteemed couple; **'A~ Señor ...'** (*Esp*) 'Dear Sir ...'.
apreciación NF (**a**) (*evaluación*) appreciation, appraisal; (*Com, Fin*) valuation; estimate; **según nuestra** ~ according to our estimation; ~ **del trabajo** job evaluation. (**b**) (*subida*) appreciation.
apreciado ADJ worthy, estimable, esteemed.
apreciar [1b] **1** VT (**a**) (*Com, Fin etc*) to value, assess, estimate (*en* at); to evaluate.
  (**b**) (*fig*) (*estimar*) to esteem, value (*por* for); (*tener cariño a*) to like, be fond of; **aprecia mucho a los niños** she's very fond of children; ~ **algo en mucho** to value sth highly; ~ **en poco** to set little value on, attach little value to.
  (**c**) (*Arte, Mús etc*) to appreciate.
  (**d**) (*percibir*) to see, notice, observe; (*LAm: darse cuenta de*) to become aware of.
  (**e**) (*LAm: realzar*) to add value to, enhance, improve.
  (**f**) (*LAm: agradecer*) to be grateful for, appreciate; **lo aprecio mucho** I much appreciate it.
  2 **apreciarse** VR (**a**) **se aprecia la diferencia** one can tell the difference, the difference can be appreciated. (**b**) (*valor etc*) to appreciate, rise (in value).
apreciativo ADJ: **una mirada apreciativa** an appraising look, a look of appraisal.
apreciatorio ADJ: **presión apreciatoria** upward pressure; **tendencia apreciatoria** upward tendency, tendency to rise.
aprecio NM (**a**) (*Com, Fin etc*) valuation, appraisal; estimate.
  (**b**) (*fig*) appreciation; esteem, regard; **tener a uno en gran** ~ to hold sb in high regard; **en señal de mi** ~ as a token of my esteem; **no hacer** ~ **de algo** (*Méx*) to pay no attention to sth.
aprehender [2a] VT (**a**) *persona* to apprehend, detain; *mercancías* to seize. (**b**) (*Filos*) (*comprender*) to understand; (*concebir*) to conceive, think; (*concretar*) to pin down.
aprehensible ADJ understandable; conceivable; **una idea**

difícilmente ~ an idea which is difficult to pin down, an idea not readily understood.
aprehensión NF (**a**) (*captura*) apprehension, detention, capture; seizure. (**b**) (*Filos*) understanding; conception, perception.
apremiador ADJ, **apremiante** ADJ urgent, pressing, compelling.
apremiar [1b] **1** VT (**a**) (*instar*) to urge (on), press; to force, compel; ~ **a uno a hacer algo**, ~ **a uno para que haga algo** to press sb to do sth.
  (**b**) (*dar prisa a*) to hurry (along).
  (**c**) (*oprimir*) to oppress; (*acosar*) to harass.
  2 VI to press, be urgent; **el tiempo apremia** time presses; **apremiaba repararlo** it was an urgent task to repair it, it was urgent to get it repaired.
apremio NM (**a**) (*urgencia*) urgency, pressure; (*obligación*) compulsion; **por** ~ **de tiempo** because time is pressing; **por** ~ **de trabajo** because of pressure of work; ~ **de pago** demand for payment, demand note; **procedimiento de** ~ compulsory procedure.
  (**b**) (*Jur*) writ, judgement; summons; judicial constraint.
  (**c**) (*opresión*) oppression; (*acoso*) harassment.
aprender [2a] **1** VTI to learn; ~ **a hacer algo** to learn to do sth.
  2 **aprenderse** VR to learn by heart.
aprendiz(a) NM/F (**a**) learner; beginner, novice; (*Dep*) novice, junior; ~ **de conductor** learner, learner-driver.
  (**b**) (*en un oficio*) apprentice; (*Com etc*) trainee; ~ **de brujo** sorcerer's apprentice; ~ **de comercio** business trainee; **estar de** ~ **con uno** to be apprenticed to sb; **poner a A de** ~ **con B** to apprentice A to B; ~ **de todo y oficial de nada** jack of all trades and master of none.
aprendizaje NM (**a**) (*industrial etc*) apprenticeship; (*Com etc*) training period, period as a trainee; **hacer su** ~ to serve one's apprenticeship.
  (**b**) (*el aprender*) learning; **dificultades de** ~ learning difficulties.
aprensar [1a] VT (**a**) (*Téc*) to press, crush. (**b**) (*fig*) (*oprimir*) to oppress, crush; (*afligir*) to distress.
aprensión NF (*miedo*) apprehension, fear, worry; (*nerviosismo*) nervousness; (*Med*) hypochondria, fear of being ill; (*capricho*) odd idea, (*remilgos*) strange notion, idle fancy; squeamishness.
aprensivo ADJ apprehensive, worried; nervous, timid; (*Med*) hypochondriac, fearful of being ill; squeamish.
apresador(a) NM/F captor.
apresamiento NM seizure; capture.
apresar [1a] VT (**a**) (*agarrar*) to seize, clutch, grab, grasp. (**b**) *persona, barco* to capture. (**c**) (*Jur*) to seize.
aprestado ADJ ready; **estar** ~ **para** + *infin* to be ready to + *infin*.
aprestar [1a] **1** VT to prepare, get ready, make ready; *paño* to size; (*para pintar*) to prime, size.
  2 **aprestarse** VR to prepare, get ready; ~ **a** + *infin*, ~ **para** + *infin* to get ready to + *infin*.
apresto NM (**a**) (*acto*) preparation. (**b**) (*equipo*) outfit, equipment, kit. (**c**) (*acto: antes de pintar*) priming, sizing. (**d**) (*materia*) size, primer.
apresuradamente ADV hurriedly, hastily.
apresurado ADJ hurried, hasty; quick; precipitate.
apresuramiento NM hurry, haste, precipitation.
apresurar [1a] **1** VT to hurry (along); to hustle; to speed up, accelerate, expedite.
  2 **apresurarse** VR to hurry, hasten, make haste; ~ **a** + *infin*, ~ **por** + *infin* to hasten to + *infin*; **me apresuré a sugerir que ...** I hastened to suggest that ..., I hastily suggested that ...
apretadamente ADV tightly; densely, solidly.
apretadera NF (**a**) (*correa, cuerda*) strap, rope. (**b**) ~**s*** pressure, insistence.
apretado ADJ (**a**) *nudo, tornillo, vestido etc* tight; V **baile**.
  (**b**) (*denso etc*) dense, thick, compact, solid; *escritura* cramped; *cuarto, espacio* full, chock-a-block; *programa etc* tight; **estaba** ~ **a presión** it was full to bursting.
  (**c**) (*difícil*) difficult, dangerous; **es un caso** ~ it's a tricky business; **estar** ~ to be in a difficult situation, (*Med*) be in a bad way; **estar** ~ **de dinero** to be short of money.
  (**d**) (*: *tacaño*) tight-fisted, stingy.
  (**e**) (*Méx: presumido*) conceited.
  (**f**) (*Carib: sin dinero*) broke*, flat* (*US*).
apretar [1j] **1** VT (**a**) *cinturón, tuerca, tornillo* to tighten (up); *mano* to clasp, grip, (*al saludar*) shake; *puño* to clench; *dientes* to grit, set; *botón, pedal, gatillo etc* to press, press down; (*vestido*) to be too tight for; (*zapato*) to pinch; *persona* to hug, squeeze; (*fig*) to pressurize; ~ **a uno entre los brazos** to hug sb in one's arms; ~ **a uno contra la pared** to pin sb against the wall.
  (**b**) *contenido* to pack in, pack tight; to press together, squeeze together.
  (**c**) *disciplina* to tighten up; (*Mil*) *ataque* to press, intensify; *paso* to quicken.
  (**d**) (*afligir*) to afflict, distress, trouble; to beset; (*Med*) to distress.
  (**e**) (*importunar*) to harass, pester (*por* for).
  2 VI (**a**) (*vestido*) to be too tight; (*zapato*) to pinch, hurt.

► LENGUA Y USO: **apoyar: 1b** → 38.2, 39.1, 39.3, 40.2   **apoyo: b** → 38.1, 38.2, 40.2

(b) (*empeorar*) to get worse, get more severe; **cuando el calor aprieta** when the heat becomes oppressive; **allí donde más aprieta el calor** out there where the heat is at its worst; **el frío aprieta** (*esp Méx*) it's getting colder.

(c) (*insistir*) to insist, exert pressure.

(d) ~ **con el enemigo** to close with the enemy, to close in on the enemy.

(e) (*LAm: esforzarse*) to make an extra (o special) effort.

(f) ~ **a correr** to break into a run, start to run.

(g) **¡aprieta!** nonsense!; good grief!

3 apretarse VR **(a)** (*estrecharse*) to narrow, get narrower.

(b) (*agolparse*) to crowd together, squeeze up; to huddle together.

(c) (*afligirse*) to grieve, be distressed.

apretón NM **(a)** (*presión*) squeeze, pressure; (*abrazo*) hug; ~ **financiero** financial squeeze; ~ **de manos** handshake; **se dieron un ~ de manos** they shook hands.

(b) (*agolpamiento*) press, crush, jam; **el ~ en el metro** the crush in the underground.

(c) (*apuro*) difficulty, jam, fix; **estar en un ~** to be in a fix, be in a quandary.

(d) (*carrera*) dash, sprint, short run.

apretujar [1a] VT (*apretar*) to press hard, squeeze hard; (*abrazar*) to hug; (*estrujar*) to crush, crumple; **estar apretujado entre dos personas** to be crushed between two people, be sandwiched between two people.

apretujón NM **(a)** (*apretón*) hard squeeze; (*abrazo*) big hug. **(b)** (*agolpamiento*) press, crush, jam.

apretura NF **(a)** = **apretón, apretujón** (a), (b). **(b)** = **apretón** (c).

aprieto NM **(a)** = **apretón** (a), (b). **(b)** (*fig*) difficulty, jam, fix; distress; **estar en un ~, verse en un ~** to be in a jam; **poner a uno en un ~** to put sb in a fix; **ayudar a uno a salir de un ~** to help sb out of trouble.

a priori ADV **(a)** beforehand; **juzgar** in advance. **(b)** (*Lógica, Jur*) a priori.

apriorismo NM tendency to resolve matters hastily.

apriorístico ADJ **(a)** (*deductivo*) a priori, deductive.

(b) (*precipitado*) hasty, premature.

aprisa ADV quickly, hurriedly.

aprisco NM sheepfold.

aprisionar [1a] VT (*encarcelar*) to imprison; (*atar*) to bind, tie; (*atrapar*) to trap; (*aherrojar: t fig*) to shackle.

aprismo NM (*And Pol*) doctrine of APRA.

aprista NMF (*And Pol*) follower (o member) of APRA.

▼ **aprobación** NF **(a)** approval; consent; **dar su ~** to give one's consent, approve. **(b)** (*Educ*) pass mark.

aprobado **1** ADJ approved; worthy, excellent.

2 NM (*Educ*) pass, pass mark; pass certificate.

▼ **aprobar** [1l] **1** VT to approve, approve of, consent to, endorse; (*Parl*) *proyecto de ley* to pass; *informe* to approve, adopt; (*Educ*) *candidato, examen, asignatura* to pass.

2 VI (*Educ*) to pass; **aprobé en francés** I passed in French.

aprobatorio ADJ: **una mirada aprobatoria** an approving look.

aproches NMPL (*Mil*) approaches; (*LAm barrio*) neighbourhood, district.

aprontamiento NM quick delivery, rapid service.

aprontar [1a] VT (*preparar*) to get ready quickly, prepare without delay; *mercancías, dinero* to deliver at once, hand over immediately; (*Méx*) (*preparar*) to prepare in advance; (*entregar*) to hand over.

apronte NM (*Cono Sur*) **(a)** (*Dep*) heat, preliminary race. **(b)** ~**s** preparations; **irse en los ~s** to waste one's energy on unnecessary preliminaries.

apropiación NF appropriation; adaptation, application; giving, gift; ~ **ilícita** illegal seizure, misappropriation; (*de dinero*) fraudulent conversion; ~ **indebida de fondos** misappropriation of funds, embezzlement.

apropiadamente ADV appropriately, fittingly.

apropiado ADJ appropriate (*a, para* to), suitable, fitting (*a, para* for).

apropiamiento NM = **apropiación**.

apropiar [1b] **1** VT **(a)** (*adecuar*) to adapt, fit (*a* to), make suitable (*a* for); (*aplicar*) to apply (*a* to).

(b) ~ **algo a uno** to give sth to sb; (*LAm*) (*asignar*) to assign sth to sb; (*otorgar*) to award sth to sb.

2 apropiarse VR: ~ (**de**) **algo** to appropriate sth.

apropincuarse [1d] VR (*hum*) to approach.

aprovechable ADJ usable, that can be used; useful, serviceable; wearable.

aprovechadamente ADV profitably.

aprovechado **1** ADJ **(a)** (*trabajador*) industrious, diligent, hardworking; (*ingenioso*) resourceful.

(b) (*frugal*) thrifty, economical.

(c) (*pey*) unscrupulous, selfish; grasping.

(d) *tiempo etc* well-spent.

2 NM, **aprovechada** NF selfish person, person who has an eye to

the main chance.

aprovechamiento NM **(a)** (*uso*) use, development; exploitation; ~ **de recursos naturales** use of natural resources. **(b)** (*progreso*) progress, improvement.

aprovechar [1a] **1** VT (*utilizar*) to make (good) use of, use, utilize; (*explotar*) to develop, exploit; *oferta etc* to take up, take advantage of; *experiencia, lección* to profit by, profit from; *ocasión* to seize, avail o.s. of, take; *posibilidades* to make the most of; (*pey*) to exploit, abuse, make unfair use of, get the benefit of.

2 VI **(a)** (*ser útil*) to be of use, be useful, be profitable; **eso aprovecha poco** that is of little use, that is of no avail; **no ~ para nada** to be completely useless; ~ **a uno** to be of use to sb, profit sb, be beneficial to sb; **¡que aproveche!** (*phrase used to those at table, hoping they will enjoy their meal*) bon appétit.

(b) (*progresar*) to progress, improve; ~ **en los estudios** to make progress in one's work.

3 aprovecharse VR: ~ **de** = **1**.

aprovechón ADJ opportunistic, having an eye to the main chance.

aprovisionador(a) NM/F supplier.

aprovisionamiento NM supply, supplying.

aprovisionar [1a] VT to supply.

aproximación NF **(a)** (*gen; t Mat*) approximation (*a* to). **(b)** (*proximidad*) nearness, closeness; **no parece ni por ~ que vaya a ceder** he seems to be nowhere near giving up. **(c)** (*acercamiento*) approach (*a* to); (*Pol*) rapprochement; (*a problema, texto*) approach. **(d)** (*de lotería*) consolation prize.

aproximadamente ADV approximately; roughly.

aproximado ADJ approximate; *estimación, conjetura* rough.

aproximamiento NM = **aproximación**.

aproximar [1a] **1** VT to bring near(er), bring up, draw up (*a* to); ~ **una silla** to bring a chair nearer, bring a chair over.

2 aproximarse VR **(a)** (*acercarse*) to come near, come closer, approach; ~ **a** to near, approach; **el tren se aproximaba a su destino** the train was nearing its destination.

(b) ~ **a** (*fig*) to approach, approximate to.

aproximativo ADJ approximate; *estimación, conjetura* rough.

Aptdo. ABR *de* **apartado de correos** Post Office Box, POB.

aptitud NF **(a)** (*conveniencia*) suitability, fitness (*para* for). **(b)** (*talento*) aptitude, ability; capacity; ~ **para los negocios** business sense, business talent; **carece de ~** he hasn't got the talent; **demostrar tener ~es** to show ability, show promise.

apto ADJ suitable, fit; (*Escol*) pass (*atr*); **ser ~ a aprender, ser ~ para aprender** to be quick to learn; ~ **para desarrollar** suitable for developing; **no es ~ para conducir** he's not fit to drive; **película no apta para menores** film for adults only; ~ **para el servicio** (*Mil*) fit for military service.

Apto. ABR *de* **apartamento**.

apuesta NF bet, wager; (*Bridge*) bid.

apuesto ADJ **(a)** (*pulcro*) neat, elegant, spruce; (*hum*) dapper, natty. **(b)** (*guapo*) handsome, nice-looking.

Apuleyo NM Apuleius.

apunarse [1a] VR (*And, Cono Sur*) to get mountain sickness.

apuntación NF note; (*Mús*) notation.

apuntado ADJ **(a)** (*agudo*) pointed, sharp. **(b)** (*Cono Sur*: borracho*) merry*, tight*.

apuntador(a) NM/F (*Teat*) prompter; (*Méx Dep*) scorer; **murió** (o **no se salvó**) **hasta el ~*** no-one was spared.

apuntalamiento NM propping-up, underpinning.

apuntalar [1a] **1** VT (*Arquit, fig*) to prop up, shore up, underpin; (*Mec*) to strut.

2 apuntalarse VR to have a snack.

apuntamiento NM **(a)** (*de arma*) aiming, pointing. **(b)** (*nota*) note. **(c)** (*Jur*) judicial report.

apuntar [1a] **1** VT **(a)** *fusil etc* to aim, level, point (*a* at); *cañón* to train (*a* on); ~ **a un blanco** to aim at a target; ~ **a uno con el revólver** to point a pistol at sb, cover sb with a pistol; (*en atraco etc*) hold sb up with a pistol.

(b) (*señalar*) to point at, point to; (*indicar*) to point out; (*sugerir*) to hint at; ~ **que ...** to point out that ...; to hint that ...

(c) (*escribir*) to note, note down, make (o take) a note of; (*Dep*) *puntos* to score; (*en cuenta etc*) to enter, set down; (*registrar*) to record; (*bosquejar*) to sketch, outline; ~ **una cantidad en la cuenta de uno** to charge a sum to sb's account; ~ **a uno** (*exámenes*) to give sb the answers.

(d) *herramienta* to sharpen, put a point on.

(e) (*Cos*) to patch, mend, darn; to tack down; to fasten temporarily.

(f) (*Naipes*) *dinero* to stake, put up.

(g) (*Teat*) to prompt.

2 VI **(a)** (*barba etc*) to begin to show, appear; (*día*) to dawn, break; (*LAm Bot*) to sprout, show; **el maíz apunta bien este año** (*LAm*) the corn is coming on nicely this year.

(b) (*Teat; t en examen etc*) to prompt.

▶ LENGUA Y USO: **aprobación: a** → 40.2   **aprobar: 1** → 38.2, 40.3

(c) ~ **y no dar** to fail to keep one's word.

(d) (*LAm: apostar*) to bet, place bets.

3 apuntarse VR **(a)** ~ **un tanto** (*Dep*) to score a point; (*fig*) to stay one up; ~ **una victoria** to score a win, chalk up a win.

(b) (*agriarse*) to turn sour.

(c) (**: emborracharse*) to get tight*.

(d) (*firmar etc*) to sign on, sign up; to put one's name down (*a* for); (*Mil*) to join up; ~ **a un club** to join a club.

(e) (**: estar de acuerdo*) to agree; **¿os apuntáis?** OK?*, (is that) agreed?; **¡me apunto!** OK!*, I'm game!

(f) **¿te apuntas un café?** (*Esp*: apetecer*) how about a coffee?, do you fancy a coffee?

apunte NM **(a)** (*nota*) note; jotting; memorandum; (*Com*) entry; (*en cuenta bancaria, esp*) debit, debiting; (*Arte*) sketch; (*Cono Sur Com*) list of debts, note of money owing; **'A~s sobre el unicornio'** 'Notes on the Unicorn'; **llevar el** ~ (*Cono Sur*) to pay attention, take notice; (*mujer*) to begin to take an interest, accept sb's advances; **sacar ~s** to take notes.

(b) (*Teat*) (*pie*) cue; (*apuntador*) prompter; (*texto*) prompt copy, prompt book.

(c) (*Naipes*) stake.

(d) (*LAm: apuesta*) bet.

apuntillar [1a] VT **(a)** *toro* to finish off. **(b)** (*fig*) to round off.

apuñadura NF knob, handle.

apuñalar [1a] VT, **apuñalear** [1a] VT (*LAm*) to stab; to knife; ~ **a uno por la espalda** (*fig*) to stab sb in the back; ~ **a uno con la mirada** to look daggers at sb.

apuñar [1a] VT to seize (in one's fist); (*Cono Sur*) to knead (with the fists).

apuñear [1a] VT, **apuñetear** [1a] VT to punch, strike.

apuradamente ADV **(a)** (*exactamente*) precisely, exactly. **(b)** (*con dificultad*) with difficulty. **(c)** (*LAm: de prisa*) hurriedly.

apurado ADJ **(a)** (*sin dinero*) needy, hard up.

(b) (*difícil etc*) difficult; dangerous; **estar** ~, **estar en una situación apurada** to be in a jam, be in a tight spot; (*sentir vergüenza*) to feel embarrassed.

(c) (*agotado*) exhausted.

(d) (*exacto*) precise, exact.

(e) (*LAm: apresurado*) hurried, rushed; **estar** (*o* **ir**) ~ to be in a hurry; **hacer algo a la apurada** (*Cono Sur*) to do sth hurriedly, make a botch of sth.

apuramiento NM **(a)** (*Téc*) purification, refinement.

(b) (*agotamiento*) exhaustion.

(c) (*aclaración*) verification; clarification.

apurar [1a] **1** VT **(a)** (*Téc*) to purify, refine.

(b) *líquido* to drain, drink up; *vaso* to drain; *provisión etc* to use up, exhaust, finish off; *proceso* to conclude, conclude.

(c) *hechos* to check on, verify; *asunto* to study minutely, make a thorough investigation of; *misterio* to clear up, fathom, get to the bottom of.

(d) (*fastidiar etc*) to annoy, bother; (*impacientar*) to make impatient; (*azorar*) to embarrass; (*presionar*) to put pressure on, force; (*importunar*) to pester; (*dar prisa a*) to hurry, hustle; to press, urge on; **¡no me apures!** don't hustle me!; **si mucho me apuras** if you really press me, if you really insist; **deja que el niño haga lo que pueda sin ~le** let the child do what he can without forcing him.

2 apurarse VR **(a)** (*afligirse*) to worry, fret, upset o.s. (*por* about, over); **ella se apura por poca cosa** she upsets herself for no reason; **¡no te apures!** don't worry!

(b) (*esforzarse*) to make an effort, go hard at it, exert o.s.; ~ **por hacer algo** to strive to do sth.

(c) to rush, hurry up; **¡apúrate!** come along!, get a move on!; **no te apures** there's no hurry.

apuro NM **(a)** (*económico*) want, financial need; (*penas*) hardship, distress; **pasar ~s** to suffer hardship(s); **verse en ~s** to be in trouble, be in distress.

(b) (*aprieto*) fix, jam, difficulty, tight spot; **colocar a uno en ~s** to put sb on the spot; **andar** (*o* **estar**) **en ~s, estar en el mayor** ~ to be in a jam; **me da un** ~ I'd hate to, it would be terribly awkward; **sacar a uno de** ~ to get sb out of a jam.

(c) (*esp LAm*) haste, hurry; **tener** ~ to be in a hurry.

apurón NM (*LAm*) great haste, great hurry; (*Cono Sur*) impatience; **andar a los apurones** (*Cono Sur*) to do things in a rush (*o* hurry).

apurruñar [1a] VT (*Carib*) (*maltratar*) to maltreat, handle roughly; (*manosear*) to mess up, rumple.

aquejado ADJ: ~ **de** (*Med*) suffering from.

aquejar [1a] VT **(a)** (*afligir*) to distress, grieve, afflict; (*importunar*) to worry, harass; (*cansar*) to weary; **¿qué le aqueja?** what's up with him?

(b) (*Med*) to ail, afflict; **le aqueja una grave enfermedad** he suffers from a serious disease, he is afflicted with a serious disease.

aquel ADJ DEM M, **aquella** F that (*remote from speaker and listener, in time*

etc); **aquellos** MPL, **aquellas** FPL those.

aquél **1** PRON DEM M, **aquélla** F that (*remote from speaker and listener, in time etc*); **aquéllos** MPL, **aquéllas** FPL those; that one, those (ones); **éstos son negros mientras aquéllos son blancos** the latter are black whereas the former (*o* the others *o* the earlier ones) are white; **aquél que yo quiero** the one I love; **aquél que está en el escaparate** the one that's in the window; **todo aquél que ...** each one who ...; **como aquél que dice** so to speak.

2 (*) NM **(a)** (*Esp*) charm; sex appeal; **tiene mucho** ~ she's got it*, she certainly has sex appeal.

(b) **esto tiene su** ~ this has its awkward points.

aquelarre NM witches' sabbath; (*fig*) uproar, din.

aquello PRON DEM ('*neuter*') that; that affair, that business, that matter; ~ **no tiene importancia** that's not important; **no me gusta** ~ I don't care for that; **¡no se te olvide** ~! see you don't forget what I told you about (*o* what I told you to do *etc*)!; ~ **de mi hermano** that business about my brother; ~ **fue de miedo*** that was awful, wasn't that awful?

aquerenciado ADJ (*Cono Sur, Méx*) in love, loving.

aquerenciarse [1b] VR **(a)** ~ **a un lugar** to become fond of a place, become attached to a place. **(b)** (*Cono Sur, Méx: enamorarse*) to fall in love.

aqueridarse [1a] VR (*Carib*) to set up house together, move in together.

aquí ADV **(a)** (*lugar*) here; ~ **dentro** in here; ~ **mismo** right here, on this very spot; **a 2 km de** ~ 2 km from here; (*presentando 2 personas*) ~ **Pepe,** ~ **Manolo** this is Pepe and this is Manolo; **hubo un lío de** ~ **te espero*** there was a tremendous fuss*; **andar de** ~ **para allá** to walk up and down, walk to and fro; **hasta** ~ so far, as far as here; **pase** *o* **venga por** ~ come this way; **no pasó por** ~ he didn't come this way; **vive por** ~ (*cerca*) he lives round here, he lives hereabouts; **... y** ~ **no ha pasado nada** and we'll say no more about it.

(b) (*tiempo*) **de** ~ **en adelante** from now on, henceforth; **de** ~ **a un mes** in a month's time; a month from now; **de** ~ **a 1999** from now till 1999; **de** ~ **a nada** in next to no time; **hasta** ~ up till now.

(c) **de** ~ **que ...** CONJ and so ..., hence ..., that's why ...; *V* **ahí 2.**

aquiescencia NF acquiescence.

aquiescente ADJ acquiescent.

aquietar [1a] VT to quieten (down), calm (down); to pacify; *temores* to calm, allay.

aquijotado ADJ quixotic.

aquilatar [1a] **1** VT **(a)** *metal* to assay; *joya* to value, grade. **(b)** (*fig*) to weigh up, test, examine; to appreciate.

2 aquilatarse VR (*Cono Sur*) to improve.

Aquiles NM Achilles.

aquilón NM (*poét*) (*viento*) north wind; (*norte*) north.

Aquisgrán NM Aachen, Aix-la-Chapelle.

aquisito* ADV (*LAm*) = **aquí.**

aquistar [1a] VT to win, gain, acquire.

Aquitania NF Aquitaine.

A.R. ABR *de* **Alteza Real** Royal Highness, R.H.

ara¹ NF altar; altar stone; **en ~s de** on the altars of, in honour of; for the sake of; **en ~s de la exactitud** in the interests of precision.

ara² NM (*LAm*) parrot.

árabe **1** ADJ Arab, Arabian, Arabic; **estilo** ~ (*Arquit*) Moresque; **lengua** ~ Arabic; **palabra** ~ Arabic word.

2 NMF Arab; (*Méx*) hawker, street vendor.

3 NM (*Ling*) Arabic.

arabesco **1** ADJ Arabic; *estilo* arabesque.

2 NM arabesque.

Arabia NF Arabia; ~ **Saudí,** ~ **Saudita** Saudi Arabia.

arábigo **1** ADJ Arab, Arabian, Arabic; *número* Arabic.

2 NM Arabic; **está en ~*** it's Greek to me; **hablar en ~*** to talk double Dutch*.

arábigoandaluz ADJ of Al-Andalus, of Muslim (southern) Spain.

arabismo NM (*Ling*) arabism.

arabista NMF Arabist.

arabizar [1f] VT to arabize.

arable ADJ (*esp LAm*) arable.

arácnido NM arachnid.

arada NF **(a)** (*acto*) ploughing. **(b)** (*tierra*) ploughed land. **(c)** (*extensión*) day's ploughing, yoke, area of land that can be ploughed in one day.

arado NM **(a)** (*apero*) plough. **(b)** (*reja*) ploughshare. **(c)** (*And: tierra*) ploughland, tilled land; (*huerto*) orchard.

arador NM ploughman.

Aragón NM Aragon.

aragonés, -esa **1** ADJ, NM/F Aragonese.

2 NM (*Ling*) Aragonese.

aragonesismo NM aragonesism, word (*o* phrase *etc*) peculiar to Aragon.

araguato **1** ADJ (*Carib*) dark, tawny-coloured.

2 NM (And, Carib, Méx) howler monkey.

arahuaco ADJ, NM (Ling) Arawak.

arambel NM (a) (Cos) patchwork hangings, patchwork quilt. (b) (triza) rag, shred, tatter.

arameo 1 ADJ (Ling) Aramaic; pueblo Aramean.
2 NM, **aramea** NF Aramean.
3 NM (Ling) Aramaic.

arana NF (trampa) trick, swindle; (mentira) lie.

araná NM (Carib) straw hat.

arancel NM tariff, duty; ~ **protector** protective tariff.

arancelario ADJ tariff (atr), customs (atr); **barrera arancelaria** tariff barrier; **protección arancelaria** tariff protection.

arándano NM bilberry, whortleberry; ~ **agrio**, ~ **colorado**, ~ **encarnado** cranberry.

arandela NF (a) (Téc) washer. (b) (de vela) drip-collar. (c) (And, Méx: volante) frill, flounce. (d) ~s (Culin) teacakes, buns.

araña NF (a) (Zool) spider; **matar la ~*** (comer) to take the edge off one's appetite; (perder el tiempo) to waste time.
(b) (t ~ **de luces**) chandelier; ~ **de mesa** candelabrum.
(c) (*: persona aprovechada) resourceful person, calculating person; (puta) prostitute.
(d) (Méx‡) bird‡, girl.

arañar [1a] VT (a) (herir) to scratch. (b) (reunir) to scrape together; (cobrar) to claw back (a from), make up (a on); **pasó los exámenes arañando** (Cono Sur) he just scraped through his exams. (c) (*) beneficios to rake off, take, cream off.

arañazo NM, **arañón** NM scratch.

arañonero NM spider-plant.

arao NM guillemot.

arar [1a] VT to plough; to till, cultivate.

arara NM (LAm) parrot.

arate‡ NM blood.

araucano 1 ADJ Araucanian.
2 NM, **araucana** NF Araucanian, Araucan.

ARAUCANO

(i) The **Araucanos** from the south-east of Latin America fiercely resisted both Inca and Spanish attempts to colonize them and are known for their independence and indomitable spirit. Their exploits are celebrated in **La Araucana**, an epic poem by Alonso de Ercilla (1533-94). The **Araucano** language, also known as **Mapuche**, is today spoken by over 300,000 people in Chile and Argentina, and many words of Araucanian origin are used in Chilean and Argentinian Spanish. The name **Chile** is Araucanian for "Land's End".

---

araucaria NF araucaria, monkey-puzzle tree.

arbitrador(a) NM/F arbiter, arbitrator.

arbitraje NM (a) (juicio) arbitration; ~ **industrial**, ~ **laboral** industrial arbitration. (b) (Com) arbitrage. (c) (Dep) refereeing, umpiring.

arbitrajista NM arbitrageur.

arbitral ADJ arbitral; of a referee (o an umpire); **una decisión ~** a referee's ruling; **el equipo ~** the referee and his linesmen.

arbitrar [1a] 1 VT (a) disputa to arbitrate in; (Dep) tenis etc to umpire, boxeo, fútbol etc to referee.
(b) (obtener) to contrive, find; (reunir) to bring together; to summon up one's resources for; fondos to raise, collect.
2 VI (a) (actuar como árbitro) to arbitrate; (Dep) to umpire, referee; ~ **en una disputa** to arbitrate in a dispute; ~ **entre A y B** to arbitrate between A and B.
(b) (Filos) to act freely, judge freely.
3 **arbitrarse** VR to get along, manage.

arbitrariamente ADV arbitrarily.

arbitrariedad NF (a) (cualidad) arbitrariness, arbitrary nature. (b) (acto) arbitrary act, outrage; (Jur) illegal act.

arbitrario ADJ arbitrary.

arbitrio NM (a) (libre albedrío) free will.
(b) (medio) means, expedient.
(c) (Jur) adjudication, decision; choice; **al ~ de** at the discretion of; **dejar algo al ~ de uno** to leave sth to sb's discretion.
(d) (Fin) ~s municipal taxes; ~ **municipal de plusvalía** municipal capital gains tax.

arbitrismo NM arbitrariness, arbitrary nature.

arbitrista NMF promoter of crackpot (o utopian) schemes; armchair politician.

árbitro NMF (t **árbitra** NF) arbiter, arbitrator; (Dep: tenis etc) umpire, (boxeo, fútbol etc) referee.

árbol NM (a) (Bot) tree; **el ~ de la ciencia** the tree of knowledge; ~ **frutal** fruit tree; ~ **genealógico** family tree; ~ **de Navidad**, ~ **navideño**, ~ **de Pascua** (Cono Sur) Christmas tree; **estar en el ~** (And) to be in a powerful position; **los ~es no están dejando ver el bosque** you can't see the wood for the trees.
(b) (Mec) axle, shaft; spindle; ~ **del cigüeñal** crankshaft; ~ **de levas**

camshaft; ~ **motor** drive, drive-shaft; ~ **de transmisión** transmission shaft.
(c) (Náut) mast; ~ **mayor** mainmast.
(d) (Inform) tree.

arbolado 1 ADJ (a) tierra wooded, tree-covered; calle tree-lined, lined with trees. (b) (Náut: barco) with a mast, masted. (c) (Náut) **mar arbolada** heavy sea.
2 NM woodland.

arboladura NF masts and spars.

arbolar [1a] 1 VT (colocar) to put up, place upright (a against); bandera to hoist, raise; barco to fit with masts.
2 **arbolarse** VR (caballo) to rear up, get up on its hind legs.

arboleda NF grove, plantation, coppice.

arboledo NM woodland.

arbolejo NM small tree.

arbóreo ADJ (a) (Zool) arboreal, tree (atr). (b) forma treelike, tree-shaped.

arborícola ADJ arboreal, tree-dwelling.

arboricultor(a) NM/F forester.

arboricultura NF forestry.

arborización NF replanting (of trees), reafforestation.

arborizar [1f] VI to plant trees, replant trees.

arbotante NM flying buttress.

arbustivo ADJ bushy.

arbusto NM shrub, bush.

arca NF (a) (caja) chest, box, coffer; safe; (t ~s) strongroom; ~ **de hierro** strongbox; ~s **públicas** public funds; **ser como un ~ abierta** to be a dreadful gossip; **ser como un ~ cerrada** to know how to keep a secret.
(b) **A~ de la Alianza** Ark of the Covenant; **A~ de Noé** Noah's Ark.
(c) (depósito) tank, reservoir; ~ **de agua** water-tower.
(d) (Anat: t ~s) flank, side.

arcabucero NM (Hist) (h)arquebusier.

arcabuco NM thick forest, impenetrable vegetation.

arcabuz NM (Hist) (h)arquebus.

arcada NF (a) (Arquit) arcade, series of arches. (b) (de puente) arch, span; ~ **dentaria** denture; **de una sola ~** single-span. (c) ~s (Med) retching; **sentir ~s** to retch, **sentía ~s pensando aquello** the very thought of it made him sick.

árcade ADJ, NMF Arcadian.

Arcadia NF Arcady.

arcádico ADJ, **arcadio** ADJ Arcadian.

arcaduz NM (a) (conducto) pipe, conduit; (de noria) bucket. (b) (fig) channel, way, means.

arcaico ADJ archaic.

arcaísmo NM archaism.

arcaizante ADJ archaic; región, habla conservative, conserving many archaisms; persona fond of archaisms; estilo old-fashioned.

arcángel NM archangel.

arcano 1 ADJ arcane, recondite, enigmatic.
2 NM secret, mystery.

arcar [1g] = **arquear**.

arce NM maple, maple tree.

arcediano NM archdeacon.

arcén NM (a) (borde) border, edge, brim; (de muro) curb, curbstone. (b) (Aut) (de autopista) hard shoulder, berm (US); (de carretera) verge; ~ **de servicio** service area.

archi... PREF arch...; en palabras compuestas, p.ej. **archiconservador** ultra-conservative; **archifresco** as fresh as one can get; **archipopular** extremely popular; **un niño archimalo** a terribly naughty child; **un hombre archiestúpido** an utterly stupid man.

archicomprobado ADJ all too well-known.

archiconocido ADJ extremely well-known.

archidiácono NM archdeacon.

archidiócesis NF INVAR archdiocese.

archiduque NM archduke.

archiduquesa NF archduchess.

archienemigo NM arch-enemy.

archimillonario, -a NM/F multimillionaire.

archipámpano NM (hum) bigwig, tycoon; panjandrum; **el ~ de Sevilla** the Great Panjandrum.

archipiélago NM archipelago; (fig) mass (of troubles), sea (of difficulties).

archirrepetido ADJ hackneyed, trite, over-used.

archisabido ADJ extremely well-known; **un hecho ~** a perfectly well-known fact; **eso lo tenemos ~** we know that perfectly well, that is common knowledge.

architonto 1 ADJ utterly silly.
2 NM, **architonta** NF utter fool, complete idiot.

archivado 1 ADJ (LAm) out-of-date, old-fashioned.
2 NM filing.

archivador 1 NM (mueble) filing cabinet; (carpeta) file.

archivadora NF filing clerk.
archivar [1a] VT (a) (*guardar en un archivo*) to file, file away; to store away; to place in the archives.
  (b) (*: esconder*) to hide away, pigeonhole, shelve.
  (c) (*LAm: retirar*) to take out of circulation.
  (d) (*Cono Sur, Méx: encarcelar*) to jail.
archivero, -a NM/F (*de oficina*) filing clerk; (*de archivo histórico*) archivist, keeper of archives; (*~s*), record officer; (*~ público*) registrar.
archivista NMF (*LAm*) archivist.
archivo NM (a) (*edificio*) archive(s); registry; **A~ Nacional** Public Record Office.
  (b) (*documentos*) file; **~s** files; archives, records, muniments; **~s policíacos** police files; **~ sonoro** sound archive; **buscaremos en los ~s** we'll look in the files.
  (c) (*Inform*) file; **~ fuente** source file.
  (d) (*And: oficina*) office.
  (e) (*Cono Sur, Méx: cárcel*) jail.
arcilla NF clay; **~ de alfarería, ~ figulina** potter's clay; **~ cocida** baked clay; **~ refractaria** fire clay.
arcilloso ADJ clayey.
arcipreste NM archpriest.
arco NM (a) (*Arquit*) arch; archway; **~ detector de metales** metal-detecting arch; **~ de herradura** horseshoe arch, Moorish arch; **~ ojival** pointed arch; **~ redondo** round arch; **~ triunfal** triumphal arch.
  (b) (*Anat*) arch.
  (c) (*Geom*) arc.
  (d) (*Elec*) arc; spotlight; **~ voltaico** arc lamp.
  (e) (*Mús*) bow; **~ de violín** violin bow, fiddlestick (*hum*).
  (f) (*Mil*) bow; **~ y flechas** bow and arrows.
  (g) (*de tonel*) hoop.
  (h) **~ iris** rainbow.
  (i) (*Dep*) goal.
  (j) (*fig*) **~ constitucional, ~ parlamentario** range of democratic parties represented in parliament; **~ político** political spectrum.
arcón NM large chest; bin, bunker.
ARDE NF (*Nicaragua*) ABR de **Alianza Revolucionaria Democrática**.
ardedor ADJ (*Carib, Méx*) quick-burning, easy to light.
Ardenas NFPL Ardennes.
ardentía NF (*Med*) heartburn; (*Náut*) phosphorescence.
arder [2a] [1] VT (a) (*quemar*) to burn.
  (b) (*LAm Med*) to sting, cause to smart.
  [2] VI (a) (*gen*) to burn; to blaze; **~ sin llama** to smoulder; **la casa está que arde** things are on the boil, things are coming to a head.
  (b) (*abono etc*) to ferment; (*trigo etc*) to heat up.
  (c) (*brillar etc*) to glow, shine, blaze; (*relampaguear*) to flash.
  (d) (*fig*) to burn, seethe; **~ de amor, ~ en amor** to burn with love; **~ en guerra** to be ablaze with war; **está que arde** (*LAm*) it's at bursting (*o* breaking) point; **¿a ti qué te arde?** what's it got to do with you?
  [3] **arderse** VR to burn away, burn up; (*cosecha etc*) to parch, burn up.
ardid NM ruse, device, stratagem; **~es** tricks, wiles.
ardido ADJ (a) (*valiente*) brave, bold, daring. (b) (*LAm: enojado*) cross, angry.
ardiente ADJ (a) (*que quema*) burning. (b) (*que brilla*) glowing, shining, blazing; *color* bright, glowing; *flor* bright red. (c) *fiebre, interés, deseo etc* burning; *amor* ardent, passionate; *partidario* fervent, passionate.
ardientemente ADV ardently, fervently, passionately.
ardilla [1] NF (a) (*Zool*) squirrel; **~ listada** chipmunk; **~ de tierra** gopher; **estar como ~** to be always on the go, not be still for a moment.
  (b) (*LAm*) (*hombre*) clever businessman; (*mujer*) clever businesswoman; (*pey*) untrustworthy person.
  [2] ADJ INVAR sharp, clever.
ardiloso ADJ (*And, Cono Sur: mañoso*) crafty, wily; (*Cono Sur: soplón*) loose-tongued.
ardimiento¹ NM (*acto*) burning.
ardimiento² NM (*bizarría*) courage, dash.
ardita NF (*And, Carib, Cono Sur*) = **ardilla**.
ardite NM: **no me importa un ~** I don't give a tinker's curse; **no vale un ~** it's not worth a brass farthing.
ardor NM (a) (*calor*) heat, warmth.
  (b) (*Med*) **~ de estómago** heartburn.
  (c) (*fig: celo*) ardour, eagerness, zeal; (*bizarría*) courage, dash; (*de argumento*) heat, warmth; **en el ~ de la batalla** in the heat of battle.
ardoroso ADJ (a) (*lit*) hot, burning; **en lo más ~ del estío** in the hottest part of the summer. (b) (*fig*) fiery, fervent, ardent.
arduamente ADV arduously.
arduidad NF arduousness.
arduo ADJ arduous, hard, tough.
área NF (a) (*gen*) area; **~ de descanso** (*Aut*) rest area; **~ de servicio(s)** (*Aut*) service area; **en el ~ de los impuestos** in the field of taxation.
  (b) (*Mat*) are, square decameter. (c) (*Dep*) **~ de castigo, ~ de penálty** penalty area; **~ de gol, ~ de meta** goal area. (d) **~ metropolitana** (*LAm*) metropolitan area, urban district; **~ verde** (*Carib*) green area, park area.
ARENA NF (*El Salvador*) ABR de **Alianza Republicana Nacionalista**.
arena NF (a) (*Geol*) sand; grit, gravel; **~s movedizas** quicksands, shifting sands; **~s de oro** (*fig*) fine gold, gold dust; **sembrar en ~** (*fig*) to labour in vain.
  (b) (*Med*) **~s** stones, gravel.
  (c) (*Dep etc*) arena.
arenal NM (a) (*terreno*) sandy spot, sandy ground. (b) (*hoyo*) sandpit; (*Golf*) bunker. (c) (*Náut*) sands, quicksand.
arenar [1a] VT (a) (*restregar con arena*) to sand, sprinkle with sand. (b) (*Téc*) to sand, polish with sand, rub with sand.
arenga NF (a) (*discurso*) harangue, speech; (*•*) lecture, sermon. (b) (*Cono Sur: discusión*) argument, quarrel.
arengar [1h] VT to harangue.
arenguear [1a] VI (*Cono Sur*) to argue, quarrel.
arenillas NFPL (*Med*) stones, gravel.
arenisca NF sandstone.
arenisco ADJ sandy; gravelly, gritty.
arenoso ADJ sandy.
arenque NM herring; **~ ahumado** kipper.
areómetro NM hydrometer.
arepa NF (*LAm*) large tortilla (*o* maize cake); **hacer ~s** to make love (*lesbians*).
arepera NF (*LAm*) (a) *arepa* seller. (b) (*:*) lesbian.
arepero NM (*Carib*) poor wretch.
arequipa NF (*And*) rice pudding.
arequipeño [1] ADJ of (*o* from) Arequipa.
  [2] NM, **arequipeña** NF native (*o* inhabitant) of Arequipa; **los ~s** the people of Arequipa.
arete NM earring; **ir** (*o* **estar**) **de ~** (*Carib*) to be a hanger-on.
argamandijo• NM set of tools, tackle.
argamasa NF mortar, plaster.
argamasar [1a] VT (a) *mortero* to mix. (b) *pared* to mortar, plaster.
árgana NF derrick.
árganas NFPL (*esp Cono Sur*) wicker baskets, panniers (*carried by horse*).
Argel NM Algiers.
Argelia NF Algeria.
argelino, -a ADJ, NM/F Algerian.
argén NM (*Her*) argent.
argentado ADJ silvered; (*fig*) silvery.
argentar [1a] VT to silver.
argénteo ADJ (a) (*Téc*) silver-plated. (b) (*poét*) silver, silvery.
argentería NF silver (*o* gold) embroidery, silver (*o* gold) filigree.
Argentina NF Argentina, the Argentine.
argentinismo NM argentinism, word (*o* phrase *etc*) peculiar to Argentina.
argentino¹ ADJ silvery.
argentino², -a ADJ, NM/F Argentinian, Argentine.
argento NM (*poét*) silver; **~ vivo** quicksilver.
argo NM argon.
argolla NF (a) (*aro*) (large) ring; (*para caballo*) hitching ring; (*aldaba*) door-knocker; (*de servilleta*) serviette ring; (*LAm: de novios*) engagement ring, (*de boda*) wedding ring; **cambio de ~s** (*Cono Sur*) engagement. (b) (*Dep*) argolla (*a game like croquet*).
argollar [1a] [1] VT (*And*) *cerdo* to ring; (*Méx*) to hitch to a ring; **~ a uno** (*Méx*) to have a hold over sb (because of a service rendered).
  [2] **argollarse** VR (*And*) to get engaged.
argón NM argon.
argonauta NM Argonaut.
Argos NM Argus.
argot [ar'go] NM, PL **argots** [ar'go] slang.
argótico ADJ slang (*atr*); slangy.
argucia NF subtlety, sophistry, hair-splitting; trick, subtle manoeuvre.
argüende NM (*LAm*) argument.
argüir [3g] [1] VT (a) (*razonar*) to argue, contend; (*indicar*) to indicate, point to, imply; (*deducir*) to infer, deduce; **de ahí arguyo su buena calidad** I deduce its good quality from that; **esto arguye su poco cuidado** this indicates his lack of care.
  (b) (*reprochar*) to reproach; to accuse; **me argüían con vehemencia** they vehemently reproached me; **~ a uno (de) su crueldad** to reproach sb for his cruelty.
  [2] VI to argue (*contra* against, with).
argumentable ADJ arguable.
argumentación NF argumentation; line of argument.
argumentador ADJ argumentative.
argumental ADJ (*Liter*) plot (*atr*); **línea ~** line of the plot, story-line.
argumentar [1a] VTI to argue; **~ que ...** to argue that ..., contend that ...

argumentista NMF (*TV etc*) scriptwriter.

▼ **argumento** NM (**a**) (*gen*) argument (*t Jur*); line of argument; (*razonamiento*) reasoning, thinking.
    (**b**) (*Liter, Teat*) plot, story-line; ~ **de la obra** (*como prólogo*) summary of the plot, summary of the story, outline.
    (**c**) (*LAm: discusión*) argument, discussion, quarrel.

aria NF aria.

aridecer [2d] **1** VT to dry up, make arid.
    2 VI *y* **aridecerse** VR to dry up, become arid.

aridez NF aridity, dryness (*t fig*).

árido **1** ADJ arid, dry (*t fig*).
    2 ~s NMPL (*Com*) dry goods; (*Agr*) dry grains, hard grains; (*hormigón*) sand and cement; **medida para** ~s dry measure.

Aries NM (*Zodíaco*) Aries.

ariete NM (**a**) (*Mil*) battering ram. (**b**) (*Dep*) striker.

arigua NF (*Carib*) wild bee.

arillo NM earring.

ario, -a ADJ, NM/F Aryan.

ariqueño **1** ADJ of Arica.
    2 NM, **ariqueña** NF native (*o* inhabitant) of Arica; **los** ~s the people of Arica.

ariscar [1g] **1** VT (*CAm, Carib, Méx*) (*domar*) *animal* to pacify, control; *persona* to make suspicious.
    2 **ariscarse** VR (*CAm, Carib*) to run away.

arisco ADJ *animal* shy; wild, temperamental, vicious; timid; *persona* surly; unsociable, unapproachable; (*LAm*) reserved.

arista NF (*Bot*) beard, awn; (*Geom*) edge; (*Arquit*) arris; (*Alpinismo*) arête.

aristocracia NF aristocracy.

aristócrata NMF aristocrat.

aristocrático ADJ aristocratic.

Aristófanes NM Aristophanes.

aristón NM (*Mús*) mechanical organ.

Aristóteles NM Aristotle.

aristotélico ADJ Aristotelian.

aritmética NF arithmetic.

aritmético **1** ADJ arithmetical.
    2 NMF arithmetician.

Arlequín NM Harlequin.

arlequín NM (**a**) (*fig*) buffoon. (**b**) (*helado*) Neapolitan ice cream.

arlequinada NF (*Hist*) harlequinade; (*bufonada*) (piece of) buffoonery, fooling.

arlequinesco ADJ (*fig*) grotesque, ridiculous.

Arlés NF Arles.

arma NF (**a**) (*Mil etc*) arm, weapon; (✲✲) prick✲✲; ~ **arrojadiza** missile; ~ **atómica** atomic weapon; ~ **biológica** biological weapon; ~ **blanca** steel blade, knife, sword; ~ **de combate** assault weapon; ~ **convencional** conventional weapon; ~s **cortas** small arms; ~ **de fuego** firearm, gun; ~ **de infantería** infantry weapon; ~ **larga** shotgun; ~ **negra** fencing foil; ~ **química** chemical weapon; ~ **reglamentaria** service weapon, regulation weapon; ~ **de doble filo** (*fig*) double-edged sword; **¡a las** ~s! to arms!; **¡**~s **al hombro!** shoulder arms!; **alzarse en** ~s to rise up in arms, rebel; **¡descansen** ~s! order arms!; (*fig*) **estar en** ~s to be anxious; **estar sobre las** ~s to be under arms; to stand by; **limpiar el** ~✲✲ to have a screw✲✲; **pasar a uno por las** ~s to shoot sb, execute sb; **pasar a una por las** ~s✲✲ to screw sb✲✲; **¡presenten** ~s! present arms!; **rendir las** ~s to lay down one's arms; **tocar (al)** ~ to sound the call to arms; **tomar las** ~s to take up arms; **ser de** ~s **tomar**, **ser de llevar** ~s (*LAm*) to be bold, be determined, be sb to be reckoned with; **volver el** ~ **contra uno** to turn the tables on sb.
    (**b**) (*servicio*) arm, branch, service.
    (**c**) ~s (*Her*) arms.

armada NF (**a**) (*escuadra*) fleet; (*nacional*) navy; (*Hist*) armada; **la A~ Británica** the British Navy; **un oficial de la** ~ a naval officer.
    (**b**) (*Cono Sur: lazo*) noose, lasso.

armadía NF = **almadía**.

armadijo NM trap, snare.

armadillo NM armadillo.

armado ADJ (**a**) (*Mil*) armed; ~ **hasta los dientes** armed to the teeth; **ir** ~ to go armed. (**b**) (*Mec*) mounted, assembled. (**c**) (*Téc*) *hormigón* reinforced; *tela* toughened. (**d**) (*LAm*) stubborn.

armador NM (**a**) (*Náut: dueño*) shipowner; (*constructor*) shipbuilder; (*Hist*) privateer. (**b**) (*Mec*) fitter, assembler. (**c**) (*LAm*) (*chaleco*) waistcoat; (*percha*) coathanger.

armadura NF (**a**) (*Mil, Hist*) armour; **una** ~ a suit of armour.
    (**b**) (*Téc*) frame, framework; (*de gafas*) frame; (*Anat*) skeleton; (*Bot, Elec, Zool*) armature; ~ **de la cama** bedstead.
    (**c**) (*Mús*) key signature.

armaduría NF (*LAm*) car assembly plant.

Armagedón NM Armageddon.

armamentismo NM tendency to indulge in the arms race; reliance on abundant armaments; arms build-up.

armamentista ADJ arms (*atr*); **carrera** ~ arms race.

armamento NM (**a**) (*Mil*) arms, armaments; (*de buque, unidad*) armament. (**b**) (*Mil: acto*) arming; (*Náut*) fitting-out. (**c**) (*Téc*) framework.

armar [1a] **1** VT (**a**) (*con arma*) to arm (*con, de* with).
    (**b**) *bayoneta* to fix; *arco* to bend; *cañón etc* to load; *trampa* to set.
    (**c**) (*disponer*) to prepare, arrange, get ready; (*Mec*) to assemble, put together; to set up; to mount; *tienda* to pitch, set up; (*Arquit*) to set (*en, sobre* on).
    (**d**) (*Náut*) to fit out, equip; to put into commission.
    (**e**) *hormigón* to reinforce; (*Cos*) to stiffen.
    (**f**) ~ **a uno caballero** to knight sb, dub sb knight.
    (**g**) *pleito* to bring; *lío* to cause, make, start, stir up; ~**la** to start a row, make trouble.
    2 **armarse** VR (**a**) (*con arma*) to arm o.s. (*con, de* with); ~ **de valor** to gather up one's courage; ~ **de paciencia** to arm o.s. with patience, resolve to be patient.
    (**b**) (*disponerse*) to prepare, get ready; *V* **Dios** *etc*.
    (**c**) (*CAm, Carib, Méx*) (*obstinarse*) to become obstinate; (*negarse*) to refuse point blank.
    (**d**) (*Carib: animal*) to balk, shy.
    (**e**) (*LAm: tener suerte*) to be lucky, have a stroke of luck; (*enriquecerse*) to strike it rich.
    (**f**) **¡te vas a armar!** (*Cono Sur*) forget it!, no way!✲

armario NM cupboard; ~ (**para libros**) bookcase; ~ (**ropero**) wardrobe; ~ **botiquín** medicine chest; ~ **empotrado** built-in cupboard.

armatoste NM (**a**) (*mueble*) unwieldy piece of furniture (*etc*); (*trasto*) large useless object; (*Mec*) contraption; (*Aut*) crock, jalopy.
    (**b**) (*persona*) useless great object, clumsy sort.

armazón NM *o* F (*armadura*) frame, framework; (*Aer, Aut*) body, chassis; (*Arquit*) shell, skeleton; (*de mueble*) frame; (*And, Cono Sur: estante*) shelves, shelving.

armella NF eyebolt.

Armenia NF Armenia.

armenio, -a ADJ, NM/F Armenian.

armería NF (**a**) (*museo*) military museum, museum of arms; armoury. (**b**) (*tienda*) gunsmith's (shop), gun shop. (**c**) (*arte*) art of the gunsmith. (**d**) (*Her*) heraldry.

armero NM (**a**) (*persona*) gunsmith, gunmaker, armourer. (**b**) (*estante*) gun rack; stand for weapons.

armiño NM (*Zool*) stoat; (*piel, Her*) ermine.

armisticio NM armistice.

armón NM (*t* ~ **de artillería**) gun carriage, limber.

armonía NF harmony; **en** ~ in harmony (*con* with), in keeping (*con* with).

armónica NF harmonica, mouth organ.

armónicamente ADV harmoniously; harmonically.

armonicista NMF harmonica player, mouth-organist.

armónico **1** ADJ harmonious; harmonic.
    2 NM (*Mús, Fís*) harmonic.

armonio NM harmonium.

armoniosamente ADV harmoniously; tunefully.

armonioso ADJ harmonious; tuneful.

armonizable ADJ (*fig*) that can be reconciled.

armonización NF harmonization; (*fig*) reconciliation; coordination; **ley de** ~ coordinating law, law designed to reconcile differences.

armonizador ADJ: **ley** ~a; *V n*.

armonizar [1f] **1** VT to harmonize; (*fig*) to harmonize, bring into harmony; *diferencias* to reconcile.
    2 VI to harmonize (*con* with); (*fig*) ~ **con** to harmonize with, blend with, be in keeping with; ~ **con** (*colores*) to blend with, tone in with.

ARN NM ABR *de* **ácido ribonucleico** ribonucleic acid, RNA.

arnaco NM (*And*) useless object, piece of lumber.

arnero NM (*LAm*) sieve.

arnés NM (**a**) (*Mil, Hist*) armour. (**b**) harness; ~ **de seguridad** safety harness; **arneses** harness, trappings; (*fig*) gear, tackle, outfit.

árnica NF arnica; (*Dep*) **pedir** ~ to throw in the towel.

aro[1] NM ring, hoop; rim; (*Dep*) quoit; (*LAm: arete*) earring; (*LAm: anillo de boda*) wedding ring; (*de servilleta*) serviette ring; ~ **de émbolo** piston ring; ~ **de rueda** rim of a wheel; (**juego de**) ~s quoits; **entrar por el** ~ to fall into line; to knuckle under; to have no option; **hacer un** ~ (*Cono Sur*) to have a break; **pasar a uno por el** ~ (*LAm*✲) to play tricks on sb.

aro[2] NM (*Bot*) lords-and-ladies.

aroma NM aroma, scent, fragrance; (*de vino*) bouquet.

aromaterapia NF aromatherapy.

aromático ADJ aromatic, sweet-scented.

aromatizador NM (*LAm*) spray.

aromatizante NM flavouring, aromatic spice.

aromatizar [1f] VT to scent, give fragrance to; (*Culin*) to spice, flavour with herbs.

arpa NF harp; **tocar el** ~✲ to be a thief, live by thieving.

arpado ADJ jagged, toothed, serrated.

arpar[1] [1a] VT (*arañar*) to scratch, claw (at); (*hacer pedazos*) to tear, tear to pieces.

arpar[2]; [1a] VT (*LAm*) to pinch*, nick;.

arpegio NM (*Mús*) arpeggio.

arpeo NM grappling iron.

arpero, -a NM/F (*Méx*) (*ladrón*) thief, burglar; (*arpista*) harpist.

arpía NF harpy; (*fig*) shrew, hag.

arpicordio NM harpsichord.

arpillar [1a] VT (*CAm*) to pile up.

arpillera NF sacking, sackcloth; hessian.

│ **ARPILLERA** │

ⓘ *Arpilleras is the term used for the colourful pictures made in many parts of Latin America by appliquéing scraps of fabric onto a hessian backing. During the Pinochet dictatorship in Chile they became politically significant since working-class women used them to depict the reality of life under military rule. As these **arpilleras** escaped the scrutiny of the male-dominated regime, they provided women with a means of recording events as well as obtaining income from abroad.*

---

arpir NM (*And, Cono Sur*) mineworker.

arpista NMF (*Mús*) harpist; (*Cono Sur: ladrón*) thief, burglar.

arpón NM harpoon; gaff.

arponar [1a] VT, **arponear** [1a] VT to harpoon; to gaff.

arponero ADJ: **navío ~** whaler, whaling-vessel.

arquear [1a] ① VT (a) (*doblar*) to arch; to bend.
(b) *lana* to beat.
(c) (*Náut*) to gauge.
(d) (*LAm Com*) to check, check the contents of.
② VI (*Med*) to retch.
③ **arquearse** VR to arch; to bend; (*superficie*) to camber.

arqueo NM (a) (*Arquit etc*) arching. (b) (*Náut*) tonnage, burden; capacity; **~ bruto** gross tonnage. (c) (*Com*) checking.

arqueolítico ADJ Stone-Age (*atr*).

arqueología NF archaeology; **~ industrial** industrial archaeology; **~ submarina** underwater archaeology.

arqueológico ADJ archaeological.

arqueólogo, -a NM/F archaeologist.

arquería NF arcade, series of arches.

arquero NM (a) (*Mil*) bowman, archer. (b) (*Com*) cashier. (c) (*Dep*) goalkeeper.

arqueta NF chest.

arquetípico ADJ archetypal, archetypical.

arquetipo NM archetype.

Arquímedes NM Archimedes.

arquimesa NF desk, escritoire.

arquitecto, -a NM/F architect; **~ de jardines** landscape gardener; **~ paisajista** landscaping expert.

arquitectónico ADJ architectural.

arquitectura NF architecture; **~ de jardines** landscape gardening; **~ paisajista** landscaping.

arquitrabe NM architrave.

arrabal NM suburb; (*LAm: barrio bajo*) slums, slum quarter; **~es** outskirts, outlying area.

arrabalero ① ADJ (a) (*de un arrabal*) suburban; (*pey*) of (o from) the poorer quarters.
(b) (*fig*) common, coarse.
② NM, **arrabalera** NF (a) (*gen*) suburbanite, (*pey*) person from the poorer quarters.
(b) (*fig*) common sort, coarse person.

arrabio NM cast iron.

arracacha NF (*And*) idiocy, silliness.

arracacho NM (*And*) idiot.

arracada NF pendant earring.

arracimado ADJ clustered, clustering; crowded, packed together.

arracimarse [1a] VR to cluster together, hang in bunches.

arraigadamente ADV firmly, securely.

arraigado ADJ firmly rooted, well-rooted, deep-rooted; (*fig*) established, ingrained; *persona* landed, property-owning.

arraigar [1h] ① VT (a) (*fig*) to establish; to strengthen (*en* in).
(b) (*LAm Jur*): **~ a uno** to put (o keep) sb under a restriction order.
② VI (*Bot*) to take root, strike root.
③ **arraigarse** VR (*Bot*) to take root; (*costumbre etc*) to take root, establish itself, take a hold; (*persona*) to settle, establish o.s.; to acquire property; **la costumbre se arraigó en él** the habit grew on him.

arraigo NM (a) (*Bot*) rooting; **de fácil ~** easily-rooted; **de mucho ~, de viejo ~** deep-rooted.
(b) (*bienes*) property, land, real estate; **hombre de ~** man of property.
(c) (*fig: acto*) settling, establishment.
(d) (*fig: influencia*) hold, influence; **tener ~** to have influence.

(e) **orden de ~** (*Cono Sur, Méx*) restriction order.

arralar [1a] VT (*Méx*) *árboles* to thin out.

arramblar* [1a] VI: **~ con** (a) (*robar*) to make off with, pinch*. (b) (*apartar*) to remove, relegate, push aside.

arrancaclavos NM INVAR claw hammer, nail extractor.

arrancada NF (*arranque*) sudden start; (*aceleración*) burst of speed; (*sacudida*) jerk, jolt; (*Dep: pesos*) snatch; (*LAm*) sudden dash, escape attempt.

arrancadero NM starting point.

arrancado ① ADJ (*) broke*, penniless.
② NM (*Aut*) starting, ignition.

arrancador NM (*Aut*) starter.

arrancamiento NM pulling out, extraction; snatching.

arrancar [1g] ① VT (a) *planta etc* to pull up, root out; *diente* to extract, pull; *metal* to win, extract; *pelo etc* to pluck out; *botón etc* to tear off, tear away; *papel etc* to tear out, rip out; (*Inform*) to boot; *flema* to bring up; *suspiro* to fetch; **una historia que arranca lágrimas** a story to make one cry.
(b) (*arrebatar etc*) to snatch, snatch away (*a, de* from); to wrench, wrest (*a, de* from); **le arrancó el bolso** he snatched her handbag; **el viento lo arrancó de mis manos** the wind snatched it from my hands; **lograron ~le el cuchillo** they managed to wrest the knife from him.
(c) **~ a uno de una fiesta** to drag sb away from a party; **~ a uno de un vicio** to break sb of a bad habit.
(d) *adhesión* to win, get; *victoria* to snatch, wrest (*a* from); **~ una promesa a uno** to force a promise out of sb, extort a promise from sb; **~ información a uno** to worm information out of sb, extract information from sb.
(e) (*Aut etc*) to start.
② VI (a) (*partir*) to start, set off; (*Aut*) to start; (*Náut*) to set sail; (*acelerarse*) to pick up speed, accelerate; (*) to leave (at last), get going; (;: *largarse*) to clear out*; (*LAm*) to escape, run off; **~ a cantar** to break into song, burst out singing; **~ a correr** to start running, break into a run.
(b) (*Cono Sur: lanzarse*) to launch o.s., start off with a will.
(c) (*Arquit: arco etc*) **~ de** to spring from.
(d) **~ de** (*fig*) to come from, spring from, originate in; to go back to; **esto arranca del siglo XV** this goes back to the 15th century, this began in the 15th century; **todo arranca de aquello** it all starts with that.
③ **arrancarse**; VR (*And, Carib, Méx*) to peg out;, kick the bucket;.

arranchar [1a] ① VT (a) *velas* to brace.
(b) *costa* to skirt, sail close to.
(c) (*And: arrebatar*) to snatch away (*a* from).
② **arrancharse** VR (a) (*reunirse*) to gather together; (*comer*) to eat together.
(b) (*Carib, Méx: acomodarse*) to settle in, make o.s. comfortable; (*Carib: adaptarse*) to make the best of it.

arrancón NM (*Méx*) = **arrancada**.

arranque NM (a) (*sacudida*) sudden start, jerk, jolt; wrench.
(b) (*Aut, Mec*) start; starting, ignition; **~ (automático)** (*Aut*) (self-)starter; **~ en frío** cold start; **~ manual** crank starting.
(c) (*Anat, Arquit*) starting point; base.
(d) (*fig: impulso*) impulse; (*arrebato*) (emotional) outburst; **~ de cólera** fit of anger, outburst of bad temper; **~ de energía** burst of energy; **en un ~** impulsively.
(e) (*fig: gracia*) sally, witty remark.
(f) (*) **estar en el ~** (*LAm*) to be completely broke*.
(g) **no servir ni para el ~** (*Méx*) to be completely useless.

arranquera* NF, **arranquitis*** NF (*And, CAm, Carib*) = **arranque** (f).

arrapiezo NM (a) (*trapo*) rag, tatter. (b) (*persona*) whippersnapper.

arras NFPL (a) (*prenda*) pledge, security, deposit. (b) (*Hist*) 13 coins given by bridegroom to bride.

arrasador ADJ = **arrollador**.

arrasamiento NM levelling; demolishing; devastation; **bombardeo de ~** carpet bombing.

arrasar [1a] ① VT (a) (*nivelar*) to level, flatten; *edificio etc* to raze to the ground, demolish; *ciudad, región* to devastate.
(b) (*colmar*) to fill up, fill to the brim.
② VI (a) (*Met*) to clear.
(b) (*triunfar*) to triumph, achieve a great success; (*Pol etc*) to sweep the board.
③ **arrasarse** VR (*Met*) to clear; **se le arrasaron los ojos de** (o **en**) **lágrimas** her eyes filled with tears.

arrastracueros NM INVAR (*Carib*) crook; rascal, rogue.

arrastradizo ADJ dangling, trailing.

arrastrado ① ADJ (a) **llevar algo ~** to drag sth along.
(b) (*miserable*) poor, wretched, miserable; vile; **andar ~** to have a wretched life.
(c) (*astuto*) wily, rascally.
(d) (*LAm: servil*) cringing, servile.

2 NM rogue, rascal; (*Méx: pobre diablo*) down-and-out.
arrastrador NM (*en impresora*) tractor.
arrastrar [1a] **1** VT (a) (*gen*) to drag, drag along; *carro etc* to haul, pull; (*hacia abajo*) to drag down.
(b) *vestido etc* to trail along the ground.
(c) **~ los pies** to drag one's feet, shuffle along.
(d) (*agua, viento etc*) to carry away, carry down, sweep along.
(e) *palabras* to drawl.
(f) (*Bridge*) *triunfos* to draw.
(g) (*pasiones etc*) to carry away; *adherentes etc* to win over, carry with one; *afecto, lealtad* to command, draw, win; (*Rad etc*) *audiencia* to draw, attract; **no te dejes ~ por esa idea** don't get carried away by that idea, don't run away with that idea.
(h) (*degradar*) to drag down, degrade, debase.
(i) (*acarrear*) to bring with it, bring in its train, have as consequences.
(j) **~ a uno a hacer algo** to lead sb to do sth.
2 VI to drag, trail along the ground, hang down; (*Bot*) to trail.
3 **arrastrarse** VR (a) (*animal, persona*) to crawl, creep; to drag o.s. along; **se arrastró hasta la puerta** he dragged himself to the door.
(b) (*vestido etc*) to drag, trail along the ground, hang down.
(c) (*tiempo, función etc*) to drag.
(d) (*humillarse*) to grovel, fawn, creep*.
arrastre NM (a) (*acto*) drag, dragging, pulling; haulage; (*Aer*) drag; (*Pesca*) trawling; **flota de ~** trawling fleet, fleet of trawlers; **~ por correa** belt-drive.
(b) (*Carib: influencia*) influence, pull; **tener mucho ~** to have a lot of influence, have connections.
(c) (*Taur*) dragging away of the dead bull; **estar para el** (o **pal**) **~** to be finished, be done for; to be all in.
(d) (*Inform*): **~ de dientes** tractor; **~ de papel por tracción** tractor feed; **~ de papel por fricción** friction feed.
arrastrero **1** ADJ trawler (*atr*); **flota arrastrera** trawling fleet, fleet of trawlers.
2 NM trawler.
arrayán NM myrtle.
arre INTERJ get up!, gee up!; (*LAm*) hurry up!
arreada NF (*Cono Sur, Méx*) rustling, cattle-thieving; round-up.
arreado ADJ (*And, Cono Sur, Méx*) sluggish, ponderous.
arreador NM (a) (*capataz*) foreman; (*arriero*) muleteer. (b) (*Cono Sur: látigo*) long whip.
arrear [1a] **1** VT (a) *ganado etc* to drive, urge on. (b) (*caballo*) to harness. (c) (*CAm, Cono Sur, Méx: ganado*) to steal, rustle. (d) (*) *golpe* to give.
2 VI to hurry along; **¡arrea!** get moving!; (*fig: repulsa*) get away!; (*Esp: asombro*) Christ!, well I'm damned!; (*admiración*) look at that!
arrebañaduras NFPL scrapings, remains.
arrebañar [1a] VT to scrape together; *comida* to eat up, clear up.
arrebatadamente ADV suddenly, violently; headlong; rashly; **hablar ~** to speak in a rush.
arrebatadizo ADJ excitable, hot-tempered.
arrebatado ADJ (a) (*apresurado*) hasty, sudden, violent. (b) (*impetuoso*) rash, impetuous. (c) (*absorto etc*) rapt, bemused; ecstatic. (d) *cara* flushed.
arrebatador ADJ *belleza* dazzling, breathtaking; *sonrisa* winning, captivating.
arrebatamiento NM (a) (*acto*) snatching (away); seizure; abduction.
(b) (*fig*) captivation; (*éxtasis*) ecstasy, rapture; (*emoción*) excitement; (*ira*) anger.
arrebatar [1a] **1** VT (a) (*gen*) to snatch, snatch away (*a* from); to seize; to wrench, wrest (*a* from); (*viento*) to blow away; *página, parte etc* to tear off, rip off; *persona* to carry away, carry off, abduct; **le arrebató el revólver** he snatched the pistol from him; **nos arrebataron la victoria** they wrested victory from us; **~ la vida a uno** to take sb's life.
(b) (*fig: conmover*) to move deeply, stir; (*extasiar*) to captivate, enrapture; (*alegrar*) to exhilarate; **se dejó ~ por su entusiasmo** he got carried away by his enthusiasm.
(c) (*Agr*) to parch.
2 **arrebatarse** VR (a) (*excitarse*) to get carried away; to get excited; **~ de cólera** to be overcome with anger.
(b) (*Culin*) to burn, overcook.
arrebatiña NF scramble (to pick sth up); rush, scrimmage; snatching; **coger algo a la ~** to snatch sth up.
arrebato NM (a) (*ira*) fit of rage, fury. (b) (*éxtasis*) ecstasy, rapture; **en un ~ de entusiasmo** in a sudden fit of enthusiasm.
arrebiatarse [1a] VR (*CAm: unirse*) to join up, join together; (*Méx*) to follow the crowd, agree automatically (with everything).
arrebol NM rouge; (*de cielo*) red flush, red glow; **~es** red clouds.
arrebolar [1a] **1** VT to redden.
2 **arrebolarse** VR (a) (*maquillarse*) to apply rouge, rouge o.s. (b) (*enrojecer*) to redden, flush. (c) (*Carib: vestirse*) to dress up.

arrebozar [1f] **1** VT (a) (*embozar*) to cover (with a cloak); to conceal.
(b) (*Culin*) to cover, coat; *taza* to fill right up.
2 **arrebozarse** VR (a) (*embozarse*) to cover one's face; to muffle up, muffle one's face.
(b) (*Ent*) to swarm.
arrebujado ADJ wrapped-up.
arrebujar [1a] **1** VT (a) (*objetos*) to jumble together, jumble up; to bundle together. (b) *niño etc* to wrap up, cover.
2 **arrebujarse** VR to wrap o.s. up (*con* in, with).
arrechada NF (*CAm, Méx*) = **arrechera**.
arrechar [1a] **1** VT (*LAm*) to arouse, excite.
2 VI (a) (*CAm: animarse*) to show energy, begin to make an effort. (b) (*CAm, Méx*: estar cachondo*) to feel randy*.
3 **arrecharse** VR (*CAm, Méx*) to get angry.
arrechera NF (a) (*Cono Sur Zool*) heat, mating urge; (*Méx**) randiness*, lust. (b) (*Méx: capricho*) whim, fancy. (c) (*Carib: mal humor*) bad mood.
arrecho **1** ADJ (a) (*CAm, Méx*) (*vigoroso*) vigorous; (*enérgico*) energetic; (*valiente*) brave. (b) (*CAm: lascivo*) randy, lecherous, sexy; **estar ~** (*Zool*) to be on heat; (*persona*) to be in the mood, feel randy*. (c) (*Carib*) **¡qué ~!** what fun! (d) (*CAm, Carib, Méx: furioso*) angry, furious.
2 NM (a) **en ~** (*CAm, Méx Zool*) on heat. (b) **es un ~** (*CAm*: fastidio*) he's a bloody nuisance*, he's a pain in the ass**.
arrechucho NM (a) (*impulso*) sudden impulse; (*arranque*) fit, outburst; (*dificultad*) unforeseen difficulty, new trouble.
(b) (*Med*) queer turn, sudden indisposition.
arreciar [1b] **1** VI to grow worse, get more severe; (*demanda*) to intensify; (*viento*) to get stronger.
2 **arreciarse** VR (a) = VI.
(b) (*Med*) to get stronger, pick up.
arrecife NM reef; **~ de coral, ~ coralina** coral reef.
arrecirse [3b] VR (*LAm*) to be frozen stiff.
arredo ADV (*CAm, Méx*): **¡~ vaya!*** get lost!*
arredomado ADJ (*LAm*) sly, artful.
arredrar [1a] **1** VT (a) (*hacer retirarse*) to drive back; (*apartar*) to remove, separate.
(b) (*asustar*) to scare, daunt.
2 **arredrarse** VR (a) (*retirarse*) to draw back, move away (*de* from).
(b) (*asustarse*) to get scared, lose heart; **~ ante algo** to shrink away from sth; **sin ~** unmoved, nothing daunted.
arregazado ADJ *vestido etc* tucked up; *nariz* turned up, snub.
arregazar [1f] VT to tuck up.
arregionado **1** ADJ (a) (*And, Méx: de mal genio*) ill-tempered, sharp; (*And: irreflexivo*) impulsive; (*And: mohino*) sulky; (*And*) cross, angry. (b) (*Carib: estimado*) highly regarded.
2 NM, **arregionada** NF (*Carib*) highly respected person.
arreglada NF: **~ de bigotes** (*Cono Sur**) dirty deal, shady business.
arregladamente ADV regularly, in an orderly way; sensibly, reasonably.
arreglado ADJ (a) (*ordenado*) neat, orderly, proper; (*moderado*) moderate, sensible, reasonable; **una vida arreglada** a well-regulated life, a sensible life, a well-adjusted life; **conducta arreglada** good behaviour, orderly behaviour; **un precio ~** a reasonable price.
(b) **~ a** in accordance with, adjusted to.
arreglador(a) NM/F (*Mus*) arranger.
Arreglalotodo* NM: **el Señor ~** Mr Fixit*.
arreglar [1a] **1** VT (a) (*gen*) to arrange; (*resolver*) to settle; (*ajustar*) to adjust (*a* to), regulate; *cita, fecha, reunión etc* to arrange, fix up; *problema* to put right; *abuso* to correct; *disputa* to settle, put right; (*Cono Sur, Méx*) *deuda* to settle; (*LAm*) *animal* to castrate; **yo lo arreglaré** I'll see to it, I'll arrange it; **todavía no se ha arreglado nada** nothing has been fixed up yet.
(b) (*Mec etc*) to fix, mend, repair.
(c) *aspecto, pelo, cuarto etc* to tidy up, smarten up, do; **voy a que me arreglen el pelo** I'm going to have my hair done.
(d) (*Mús*) to arrange.
2 **arreglarse** VR (a) (*ponerse de acuerdo*) to come to terms (*a, con* with), reach an understanding; **~ a** to conform to, adjust o.s. to; **por fin se arreglaron** eventually they reached an agreement.
(b) **~ el pelo** to have one's hair done; to do one's hair, tidy one's hair.
(c) (*problema etc*) to work out, be solved, be all right; **por fin el asunto se arregló** everything was finally fixed up; **todo se arreglará** things will work out, everything will be all right; (*LAm*) **ya es hora de ~** it's time to get ready.
(d) (*LAm: tener suerte*) to have a stroke of luck; (*entenderse*) to get on, hit it off.
(e) **arreglárselas** to get by, manage; **arreglárselas para + infin** to manage to + infin; **¿cómo se las arreglan Vds?** how do you manage?; **hay que arreglárselas** you've got to get organized; it's up to you to see to it; **sabe arreglárselas** he's well able to take care of himself.

arreglista NMF (*Mús*) arranger.

arreglo NM (**a**) (*acto*) arrangement, settlement; adjustment; regulation; **~ de cuentas** (*fig*) settling of old scores; **esto no tiene ~** there's no way of sorting this out, there's no solution to this; **ya no tiene ~** it's too late now, there's nothing to be done now; it's beyond repair.
(**b**) (*orden*) rule, order; orderliness; **vivir con ~** to live an orderly life.
(**c**) (*acuerdo*) agreement, understanding; compromise; **con ~ a** according to, in accordance with; **llegar a un ~** to reach a settlement, reach a compromise.
(**d**) (*Mús*) setting, arrangement.
(**e**) (*euf: de amantes*) liaison, understanding.
(**f**) (*de pelo*) trim.

arregostarse [1a] VR: **~ a** to take a fancy to.

arregosto NM fancy, taste (*de* for).

arrejarse [1a] VR (*Cono Sur: arriesgarse*) to take a risk.

arrejuntado, -a NM/F live-in lover; **los ~s** the couple living together.

arrejuntarse [1a] VR to move in together; **vivir arrejuntados** to live together.

arrejunte NM cohabitation, living together.

arrellanarse [1a] VR, **arrellenarse** [1a] VR (**a**) to lounge, sprawl, loll; **~ en el asiento** to settle o.s. comfortably in one's chair, (*pey*) to sit sprawled in one's chair.
(**b**) (*fig*) to be happy in one's work.

arremangado ADJ turned up, tucked up; *nariz* turned up, snub.

arremangar [1h] ① VT *manga etc* to turn up, tuck up, roll up; *falda etc* to tuck up.
② **arremangarse** VR (**a**) (*mangas etc*) to roll up one's sleeves (*etc*).
(**b**) (*fig: adoptar una actitud firme*) to take a firm line.

arrematar· [1a] VT to finish, complete.

arremeter [2a] ① VT (**a**) (*atacar*) to attack, assail.
(**b**) *caballo* to spur on, spur forward.
② VI (**a**) (*atacar*) to rush forth, attack; **~ contra uno** to rush at sb, attack sb, launch o.s. at sb, lash out at sb.
(**b**) (*fig*) to offend good taste, shock the eye.

arremetida NF (**a**) (*ataque*) attack, assault; (*ímpetu*) onrush; (*empujón*) push; lunge. (**b**) (*de caballo*) sudden start.

arremolinarse [1a] VR (*gente*) to crowd around, mill around, swirl; (*agua*) to swirl, eddy; (*bailadores, polvo etc*) to swirl, whirl.

arrempujar [1a] VT = **empujar; rempujar.**

arrendable ADJ: **casa ~** house available for letting, house to let.

arrendador(a) NM/F (**a**) (*propietario*) landlord, landlady; (*Jur*) lessor.
(**b**) (*arrendatario*) tenant.

arrendajo NM (**a**) (*Orn*) jay. (**b**) (*fig*) mimic.

arrendamiento NM (**a**) (*acto*) letting, leasing; hiring; farming out; **~ financiero** leasing; **tomar una casa en ~** to rent a house.
(**b**) (*alquiler*) rent, rental; lease; hiring fee.
(**c**) (*contrato*) contract, agreement.

arrendar¹ [1j] VT (**a**) (*sujeto: dueño*) *casa* to let, lease; *máquina etc* to hire out.
(**b**) (*sujeto: inquilino etc*) *casa* to rent, lease; *máquina etc* to hire.

arrendar² [1j] VT *caballo* to tie, tether (by the reins).

arrendatario, -a NM/F tenant; lessee, leaseholder; hirer.

arrendero NM (*Cono Sur, Méx*) = **arrendatario.**

arreo NM (**a**) (*adorno*) adornment, dress; (*de caballo*) piece of harness.
(**b**) **~s** harness, trappings; (*fig*) gear, equipment. (**c**) (*LAm Agr*) drove (o herd) of cattle.

arrepentidamente ADV regretfully, repentantly.

arrepentido ① ADJ regretful, repentant, sorry; **terrorista ~** reformed terrorist; **estar ~ de algo** to regret sth, be sorry about sth; **se mostró muy ~** he was very sorry.
② NM, **arrepentida** NF (*Ecl*) penitent; (*Pol*) reformed terrorist (*etc*); person who has turned informer.

arrepentimiento NM (**a**) regret, repentance, sorrow; (*Ecl*) repentance. (**b**) (*Arte*) change (made by the artist to a picture).

arrepentirse [3i] VR to repent, be repentant; **~ de algo** to regret sth, repent of sth; **se arrepintió de haberlo dicho** he regretted having said it; **no me arrepiento de nada** I regret nothing.

arrequín NM (**a**) (*LAm: ayudante*) helper, assistant. (**b**) (*LAm Agr*) leading animal (of a mule team).

arrequives NMPL (**a**) (*ropa*) finery, best clothes; (*adornos*) frills, trimmings. (**b**) (*fig*) circumstances.

arrestado ADJ bold, daring.

arrestar [1a] ① VT (*detener*) to arrest; (*encarcelar*) to imprison; **~ en el cuartel** (*Mil*) to confine to barracks.
② **arrestarse** VR: **~ a algo** to rush boldly into sth; **~ a todo** to be afraid of nothing.

arresto NM (**a**) arrest; imprisonment; (*Mil*) detention, confinement; **~ domiciliario** house arrest; **~ mayor** (*Esp*) imprisonment for from one month and a day to six months; **~ menor** (*Esp*) imprisonment for from one day to thirty days; **~ preventivo** preventive detention; **estar bajo ~** to be under arrest.

(**b**) (*fig*) **~s** boldness, daring; enterprise; **tener ~s** to be bold, be daring.

arrevesado ADJ (*LAm*) = **enrevesado.**

arria NF (*LAm*) mule train, train of pack animals.

arriada NF flood.

arriado ADJ (*LAm*) = **arreado.**

arrianismo NM Arianism.

arriano, -a ADJ, NM/F Arian.

arriar [1c] ① VT (**a**) (*inundar*) to flood. (**b**) (*Náut*) *pabellón* to lower, strike; *vela* to haul down; *cuerda* to loosen; to pay out; (***) to let go.
② **arriarse** VR to flood, become flooded.

arriate NM (**a**) (*Hort*) bed, border; trellis. (**b**) (*camino*) road, path.

arriba ① ADV (**a**) (*posición*) above; overhead; on top; high, on high; (*Náut*) aloft; (*en casa*) upstairs; (*dirección*) up, upwards; **'este lado ~'** 'this side up'; **lo ~ escrito** what has been said above; **la persona ~ mencionada** the aforementioned person; **de ~ abajo** from top to bottom; (*persona*) from head to foot; from beginning to end; **correr de ~ abajo** to run up and down; **desde ~** from (up) above; **hacia ~** up, upwards; **está hasta ~ del trabajo*** he's fed up with the job*; **está más ~** it's higher up; it's further up; **por la calle ~** up the street; **de 10 dólares para ~** from 10 dollars upwards; **de la cintura (para) ~** from the waist up; **llegar ~** to get to the top; *V* **agua, cuesta, río** *etc*.
(**b**) **de ~** ADJ: **la parte de ~** the upper part, the top side; **los de ~** those above; those at the top; those on top.
(**c**) (*Cono Sur*) **~ mío** (*etc*) over me (*etc*), above me (*etc*); on top of me (*etc*).
② INTERJ: **¡~!** up you get!; **¡~ España!** Spain for ever!, long live Spain!; **¡~ Toboso!** (*Dep etc*) up (with) Toboso!
③ **~ de** PREP above; higher than, further up than; (*Méx*) (*encima de*) on top of; above; (*más de*) more than; **el río ~ de la ciudad** the river above the town.

arribada NF (*Náut y fig*) arrival, entry into harbour; **~ forzosa** emergency call, unscheduled stop; **entrar de ~** to put into port.

arribaje NM (*Náut*) arrival, entry into harbour.

arribano ADJ (*Cono Sur*) upper, higher.

arribar [1a] VI (**a**) (*esp LAm: llegar*) to arrive; (*Náut*) to put into port, reach port; to make an emergency call; (*ir a la deriva*) to drift; **~ a** to reach. (**b**) (*Med, Fin*) to recover, improve. (**c**) **~ a** + *infin* to manage to + *infin*.

arribazón NF coastal abundance of fish, off-shore shoal; (*fig*) bonanza.

arribeño, -a NM/F (**a**) (*LAm: serrano*) highlander, inlander. (**b**) (*Cono Sur: forastero*) stranger.

arribismo NM social climbing.

arribista NMF go-getter, arriviste, social climber.

arribo NM (*esp LAm*) arrival; **hacer su ~** to arrive.

arriendo NM = **arrendamiento.**

arriero NM muleteer; (*CAm*) carrier.

arriesgadamente ADV riskily, dangerously; daringly; boldly; rashly.

arriesgado ADJ (**a**) *acto* risky, dangerous, hazardous; daring; **unas ideas arriesgadas** some dangerous ideas; **me parece ~ prometerlo** it would be rash to promise it.
(**b**) *persona* bold, daring; (*pey*) rash, foolhardy.

arriesgar [1h] ① VT *vida etc* to risk, hazard; to endanger; *conjetura* to hazard, venture; *posibilidades* to endanger, jeopardize; *dinero* to stake.
② **arriesgarse** VR to take a risk, expose o.s. to danger; to put one's life (o chances *etc*) in danger; **~ a una multa** to risk a fine, face a fine; **~ a hacer algo** to dare to do sth, risk doing sth; **~ en una empresa** to venture upon an enterprise.

arrimadero NM support; (*al montar*) mounting-block, step.

arrimadillo NM matting (*used as wainscot*).

arrimadizo ① ADJ (*fig*) parasitic, sycophantic.
② NM, **arrimadiza** NF parasite, hanger-on, sycophant.

arrimado ① ADJ *imitación etc* close.
② NM, **arrimada** NF parasite; (*recién venido*) newcomer (to a group); (*And: amante*) lover; (*Carib: intruso*) unwelcome guest; (*Cono Sur*: amancebado*) ponce, kept man.

arrimar [1a] ① VT (**a**) (*acercar*) to bring close, move up, draw up (*a* to); **hay que ~lo todavía más** you'll have to bring it closer still; **lo arrimamos a la ventana** we put it against the window; **arrimó el oído a la puerta** he put his ear to the door; **~ la escalera a una pared** to put (o lean, place) the ladder up against a wall; **vivir arrimado a uno** (*LAm*) to live off sb; **~ la culpa a uno** (*Cono Sur*) to lay the blame on sb; **~ un golpe a uno*** to give sb a blow.
(**b**) (*arrinconar*) to put away, lay aside, shelve; (*apartar*) to move out of the way; (*tirar*) to get rid of; *persona* to ignore, push aside; **el plan quedó arrimado** the plan was shelved; **~ los libros** (*fig*) to lay one's books, give up studying.
(**c**) (*Náut*) *carga* to stow.
(**d**) (*Méx*) *niño* to thrash, give a hiding to.
② **arrimarse** VR (**a**) (*acercarse*) to come close, come closer; (*reunirse*)

to gather, come together; (*Taur*) to fight close to the bull; (*en baile*) to dance very close, dance cheek-to-cheek.
(**b**) ~ **a** (*acercarse a*) to come close(r), to get near(er) to; (*apoyarse en*) to lean against, lean on; (*amante, niño*) to cuddle up to, snuggle up to; **se arrimó a la lumbre** she huddled over the fire; **arrímate a mí** lean on me; cuddle up to me.
(**c**) (*fig*) ~ **a** to join, keep company with; to seek the protection of; **arrímate a los buenos** choose your friends among good people; cultivate the virtuous.
(**d**) (*amantes*) to set up house (*o* live) together.
(**e**) (*LAm**) to sponge*.

arrimo NM (**a**) (*gen*) support. (**b**) (*fig: apoyo*) support, help, protection. (**c**) (*fig: afecto*) attachment. (**d**) (**: persona*) lover. (**e**) (**: amorío*) affair.

arrimón NM loafer, idler; sponger*; **estar de** ~ to hang about, loaf around.

arrinconado ADJ (*fig*) (*olvidado*) forgotten, neglected; (*remoto*) remote; (*abandonado*) abandoned; (*marginado*) out in the cold.

arrinconar [1a] ① VT (**a**) *cosa* to put in a corner; *enemigo etc* to corner.
(**b**) (*fig: apartar*) to lay aside, put away; (*tirar*) to get rid of; (*dar carpetazo a*) to shelve; (*desterrar*) to banish; *persona* to push aside, push into the background, ignore; (*marginar*) to leave out in the cold.
② **arrinconarse** VR to retire, withdraw from the world.

arriñonado ADJ kidney-shaped.

arriñonar* [1a] VT to wear out, exhaust; **estar arriñonado** to be knackered*.

arriscadamente ADV boldly, resolutely.

arriscado ADJ (**a**) (*Geog*) craggy. (**b**) (*fig: resuelto*) bold, resolute; (*animoso*) spirited. (**c**) (*fig: ágil*) brisk, agile.

arriscamiento NM boldness, resolution.

arriscar¹ [1g] ① VT to risk.
② **arriscarse** VR to take a risk.

arriscar² [1g] ① VT (*And, Cono Sur, Méx: doblar*) to turn (*o* fold) up; to tuck up; (*encrespar*) to stiffen; *nariz* to wrinkle.
② VI (**a**) (*And: enderezarse*) to draw o.s. up, straighten up. (**b**) ~ **a** (*LAm*) to amount to.
③ **arriscarse** VR (**a**) (*engreírse*) to get conceited. (**b**) (*And, CAm: estar de punto en blanco*) to dress up to the nines.

arriscocho ADJ (*And*) restless; turbulent.

arritmia NF (*Med*) arrhythmia.

arrítmico ADJ (**a**) (*Med*) arrhythmic. (**b**) (*Mús*) unrhythmical.

arrivista = **arribista**.

arrizar [1f] VT (*Náut*) to reef; to fasten, lash down.

arroba NF (**a**) *measure of weight = 11,502 kg (25 lbs).*
(**b**) *a variable liquid measure.*

arrobador ADJ entrancing, enchanting.

arrobamiento NM ecstasy, rapture, bliss; trance; **salir de su** ~ to emerge from one's state of bliss.

arrobar [1a] ① VT to entrance, enchant.
② **arrobarse** VR to become entranced, go into ecstasies, be enraptured.

arrobo NM = **arrobamiento**.

arrocero ① ADJ rice (*atr*); rice-producing; **industria arrocera** rice industry.
② NM, **arrocera** NF (*Carib*) gatecrasher.

arrochelarse [1a] VR (*And: ganado*) to take a liking to a place; (*perro etc*) to refuse to go out; (*caballo*) to balk, shy.

arrodajarse [1a] VR (*CAm*) to sit down cross-legged.

arrodillarse [1a] VR to kneel, kneel down, go down on one's knees; **estar arrodillado** to kneel, be kneeling (down), be on one's knees.

arrogancia NF arrogance; pride.

arrogante ADJ (*gen*) arrogant, haughty; (*orgulloso*) proud; (*audaz*) bold.

arrogantemente ADV arrogantly, haughtily; proudly; boldly.

arrogarse [1h] VR: ~ **algo** to assume sth, take sth on o.s.

arrojadamente ADV daringly, dashingly; boldly.

arrojadizo ADJ for throwing, that can be thrown.

arrojado ADJ (*fig: bizarro*) daring, dashing; (*audaz*) bold.

arrojallamas NM INVAR flamethrower.

arrojar [1a] ① VT (**a**) (*gen*) to throw, fling, hurl, cast; (*Dep*) *pelota* to bowl, pitch; (*peso*) to put; (*Pesca*) to cast; ~ **algo de sí** to cast sth from one, fling sth aside
(**b**) *humo etc* to give out, send out, emit; *luz* to give, shed; *flor, renuevo* to put out; (*) to throw up, vomit; *persona* to throw out, turn out; (*esp LAm*) to bring up, throw up; **este estudio arroja alguna luz sobre el tema** this study throws some light on the subject.
(**c**) (*Com, Fin, Mat*) to give, produce, yield; *resultado, estadística* to show, throw up; **este negocio arroja déficit** this business shows an unfavourable balance; **el accidente arrojó 80 muertos** (*LAm*) the accident left 80 dead.
② **arrojarse** VR (**a**) to throw o.s., hurl o.s. (*a* into, on; *por* out of,

through); ~ **al agua** to jump into the water; ~ **por una ventana** to throw o.s. out of a window.
(**b**) (*fig*) ~ **a**, ~ **en** to rush into, fling o.s. into, plunge into.

arrojo NM daring, dash, fearlessness; **con** ~ boldly, fearlessly.

arrollado NM (*Cono Sur Culin*) rolled pork.

arrollador ADJ (*fig*) sweeping, overwhelming, crushing, devastating; **por una mayoría** ~**a** by an overwhelming majority; **es una pasión** ~**a** it is a consuming passion; **un ataque** ~ a crushing attack.

arrollar¹ [1a] VT (**a**) (*enrollar*) to roll up; (*Elec, Téc etc*) to coil, wind.
(**b**) (*agua etc*) to sweep away, wash away; *enemigo* to throw back, rout; (*Dep*) *adversario* to overwhelm, crush; (*Aut, Ferro etc*) to run over, knock down; **arrollaron a sus rivales** they crushed their rivals.
(**c**) (*fig: asombrar*) *persona* to dumbfound, leave speechless; to squash.

arrollar² [1a] VT = **arrullar**.

arromar [1a] VT to blunt, dull.

arropar [1a] ① VT (*vestir*) to cover; to wrap up (with clothes); (*en cama*) to tuck up (in bed). (**b**) (*fig*) to protect.
② **arroparse** VR to wrap o.s. up; to tuck o.s. up (*o* in); ¡**arrópate bien**! wrap up warm!

arrope NM syrup; grape syrup, honey syrup.

arrorró NM (*LAm*) lullaby.

arrostrado ADJ: **bien** ~ nice-looking; **mal** ~ ugly.

arrostrar [1a] ① VT (*hacer frente a*) to face; to face up to, brave, defy; (*aguantar*) to stand up to; ~ **las consecuencias** to face the consequences; ~ **un peligro** to face a danger resolutely, face up to a danger.
② VI: ~ **a algo** to show a liking for sth; ~ **con** = VT.
③ **arrostrarse** VR to rush into the fight, throw o.s. into the fray.

arroyada NF (**a**) (*barranco*) gully, stream bed. (**b**) (*inundación*) flood, flooding.

arroyo NM (**a**) (*gen*) stream, brook; (*cauce*) watercourse; (*LAm: río*) river; (*Méx*) gully, ravine.
(**b**) (*cuneta*) gutter; (*fig*) the street; **estar en el** ~ (*Méx*) to be on one's uppers; (*mujer*) to be on the streets; **poner a uno en el** ~ to turn sb out of the house; **sacar a uno del** ~ to drag sb up from the gutter; **ser del** ~ to be an orphan, be a foundling.

arroyuelo NM small stream, brook.

arroz NM rice; ~ **blanco** boiled rice; ~ **a la cubana** rice with banana and fried egg; ~ **hinchado** puffed rice; ~ **integral** brown rice; ~ **con leche** rice-pudding; **hubo** ~ **y gallo muerto** (*Esp, Carib**) it was a slap-up do*.

arrozal NM ricefield.

arrufarse [1a] VR (*Carib: enojarse*) to get annoyed, get angry.

arruga NF (**a**) (*en piel*) wrinkle, line; (*en tela*) crease, fold; ruck. (**b**) (*And**) (*estafa*) trick, swindle; (*deuda*) debt; **hacer una** ~ (*And*) to cheat.

arrugado ADJ *cara etc* wrinkled, lined; *papel etc* creased; *vestido etc* rucked up, crumpled.

arrugar [1h] ① VT *cara etc* to wrinkle, line; *ceño* to knit, pucker up; *papel etc* to crease; to crumple, screw up; *vestido etc* to ruck up, crumple; ~ **la cara** to screw up one's face; ~ **la frente** to knit one's brow, frown.
② **arrugarse** VR (**a**) (*piel*) to wrinkle (up), get wrinkled; (*tela*) to crease, get creased; to ruck up, get crumpled; (*Bot*) to shrivel up. (**b**) (*: *asustarse*) to get scared, get the wind up*.

arrugue NM (*Carib*) = **arruga**.

arruinado ADJ (**a**) ruined. (**b**) (*Cono Sur, Méx*) (*enclenque*) sickly, stunted; (*Cono Sur: miserable*) wretched, down and out.

arruinamiento NM ruin, ruination.

arruinar [1a] ① VT to ruin; to wreck, destroy; (*LAm: desvirgar*) to deflower.
② **arruinarse** VR to be ruined (*t Fin*); to go to rack and ruin; (*Arquit etc*) to fall into ruins, fall down.

arrullar [1a] ① VT *niño* to lull to sleep, rock to sleep; (*: *amante*) to whisper endearments to, say sweet nothings to.
② VI (*Orn*) to coo.
③ **arrullarse** VR to bill and coo, whisper endearments; to flirt.

arrullo NM (*Orn*) cooing; (*fig*) billing and cooing; (*Mús*) lullaby.

arrumaco NM (**a**) (*caricia*) caress. (**b**) (*vestido etc*) eccentric item of dress (*o* adornment). (**c**) (*halago*) piece of flattery; **andar con** ~ to flatter. (**d**) ~**s** show of affection, endearments.

arrumaje NM (*Náut*) stowage; ballast.

arrumar [1a] ① VT (*Náut*) to stow; (*amontonar*) to pile up.
② **arrumarse** VR (*Náut*) to become overcast.

arrumbar¹ [1a] VT (**a**) *objeto* to put aside, put on one side, ignore, discard; (*olvidar*) to neglect, forget. (**b**) (*en discusión*) *persona* to silence, floor; (*apartar*) to remove.

arrumbar² [1a] (*Náut*) ① VI to take one's bearings.
② **arrumbarse** VR (**a**) (*marearse*) to be seasick. (**b**) (*And, Cono Sur: oxidarse*) to rust; (*agriarse*) to turn sour.

arrume NM (*And, Carib*) pile, heap.

arruncharse [1a] VR (*And*) to curl up, roll up.

arrurruz NM arrowroot.

arrutanado ADJ (*And*) plump.

arrutinarse [1a] VR to get into a routine, get set in one's ways.

arsenal NM (*Náut*) dockyard, naval dockyard; (*Mil*) arsenal; (*fig*) storehouse, mine.

arsenalera NF (*Cono Sur Med*) surgeon's assistant, theatre auxiliary.

arsénico NM arsenic.

arte NM y NF (*gen* M *en sing*, F *en pl*) (a) (*gen*) art; ~s (*Univ*) arts; ~ **abstracto** abstract art; **bellas ~s** fine arts; **~s decorativas** decorative arts; **~s gráficas** graphic arts; **~s liberales** liberal arts; **por ~ de magia** (as if) by magic; **~s marciales** martial arts; ~ **mecánico** mechanical skill, manual skill; **~s y oficios** arts and crafts; **~s plásticas** plastic arts; ~ **poética** poetics; ~ **pop** pop art; **el séptimo ~** the cinema, film; ~ **de vivir** art of living.
(b) (*Liter*): ~ **mayor** *Spanish verse of 8 lines each of 12 syllables (15th century)*; ~ **menor** *Spanish verse usually of 4 lines each of 6 or 8 syllables.*
(c) (*habilidad*) craft, skill; knack.
(d) (*astucia*) craftiness, cunning; (*trampa*) trick; **malas ~s** trickery, guile; **por malas ~s** by trickery.
(e) (*hechura*) workmanship; artistry.
(f) **no tener ~ ni parte en algo** to have nothing whatsoever to do with a matter.
(g) (*Pesca*) ~ (**de pescar**) (*red*) fishing-net; (*caña etc*) fishing tackle.

artefacto NM (a) (*Téc*) appliance, device, contrivance; (*explosivo*) device; **~s de alumbrado** light fittings, light fixtures (*US*); ~ **explosivo**, ~ **infernal** bomb, explosive device; ~ **nuclear** nuclear device.
(b) (*esp arqueológico*) artefact.
(c) (*Aut**) old crock, jalopy.

artejo NM knuckle, joint.

arteramente ADV cunningly, artfully.

arteria NF artery (*t fig*); (*Elec*) feeder; **la ~ principal de una ciudad** the main artery of a city, the main thoroughfare of a town.

artería NF cunning, artfulness.

arterial ADJ arterial.

arterio(e)sclerosis NF arteriosclerosis.

artero ADJ cunning, artful.

artesa NF trough, kneading trough.

artesanado NM artisans *pl*.

artesanal ADJ craft (*atr*); **industria ~** craft industry.

artesanía NF craftsmanship; handicraft, skill; **objeto de ~** handmade article; **obra de ~** piece of craftsmanship; **zapatos de ~** craft shoes, hand-made shoes.

artesano 1 ADJ home-made, home-produced.
2 NM craftsman.

artesiano ADJ: **pozo ~** artesian well.

artesón NM (a) (*de cocina*) kitchen tub. (b) (*Arquit*) coffer, caisson; (*adorno*) moulding. (c) (*And, Méx*: *bóveda*) vault; (*arcos*) arcade, series of arches; (*terraza*) flat roof, terrace.

artesonado NM coffered ceiling; stuccoed ceiling, moulded ceiling.

artesonar [1a] VT (a) (*poner paneles a*) to coffer. (b) (*estucar*) to stucco, mould.

ártico 1 ADJ Arctic.
2 NM: **el Á~** the Arctic.

articulación NF (a) (*Anat*) articulation; joint. (b) (*Mec*) joint; ~ **esférica** ball-and-socket joint; ~ **universal** universal joint. (c) (*Ling*) articulation.

articuladamente ADV distinctly, articulately.

articulado ADJ (a) *persona* articulate. (b) (*Anat, Mec*) articulated, jointed; (*Aut*) *volante* collapsible.

articular [1a] 1 VT (a) (*Ling*) to articulate; (*Mec*) to articulate, join together, join up.
(b) (*constituir*) to make up, constitute.
(c) (*Jur*) to article, specify charges against.
(d) (*And, Cono Sur**) to tell off*, dress down*.
2 VI (*Cono Sur*: *reñir*) to quarrel, squabble; (*quejarse*) to grumble.

articulista NMF columnist, feature writer, contributor (to a paper).

artículo NM (a) (*objeto*) article, thing; (*Com etc*) commodity; **~s** (*Com etc*) commodities, goods; **~s alimenticios** foodstuffs; ~ **de comercio** commodity; **~s de consumo** consumer goods; consumables, consumable supplies; **~s de escritorio** stationery; **~s de marca** branded goods; **~s de primera necesidad** basic commodities, essentials; **~s de plata** silverware; **~s de tocador** toilet articles, toiletries.
(b) (*en periódico etc*) article; feature, report, study; (*en revista erudita*) article, paper; (*en libro de referencia*) entry, article; (*de ley, documento*) article, section, item; ~ **de fondo** leading article, leader, editorial; ~ **de portada** front-page article.
(c) (*Ling*) article; ~ **definido** definite article; ~ **indefinido** indefinite article.
(d) (*Anat*) articulation, joint.

artífice NMF (*Arte etc*) artist, craftsman; (*hacedor*) maker; (*inventor*) inventor; (*fig*) architect; **el ~ de la victoria** the architect of (the) victory.

artificial ADJ artificial.

artificialidad NF artificiality.

artificializar [1f] VT to make artificial, give an air of artificiality to.

artificialmente ADV artificially.

artificiero NM explosives expert, bomb-disposal officer.

artificio NM (a) (*arte*) art, craft, skill; (*pey*) artifice. (b) (*hechura*) workmanship, craftsmanship. (c) (*aparato*) contrivance, device, appliance. (d) (*astucia*) cunning, sly trick.

artificiosamente ADV (a) skilfully, ingeniously; artistically. (b) cunningly, artfully.

artificioso ADJ (a) (*ingenioso*) skilful, ingenious; artistic. (b) (*astuto*) cunning, artful.

artillería NF (a) (*Mil*) artillery; ~ **antiaérea** anti-aircraft guns; ~ **de campaña** field guns; ~ **pesada** heavy artillery. (b) (*Dep**) forward line.

artillero NM (a) (*Mil*) artilleryman, gunner; (*Aer, Náut*) gunner; (*Min*) explosives expert. (b) (*Dep**) forward.

artilugio NM (a) (*aparato*) gadget, contraption. (b) (*truco*) gimmick, stunt. (c) (*chisme*) thingummy*, whatsit*.

artimaña NF (a) (*trampa*) trap, snare. (b) (*fig: ingenio*) cunning.

artista NMF (*Arte*) artist; (*Teat etc*) artist, artiste; ~ **de cine** film actor, film actress; ~ **comercial** commercial artist; ~ **invitado** guest artist; ~ **marcial** martial arts expert; ~ **de teatro** artist, artiste; ~ **de variedades** variety artist(e).

artísticamente ADV artistically.

artístico ADJ artistic.

artrítico ADJ arthritic.

artritis NF arthritis; ~ **reumatoidea** rheumatoid arthritis.

artrópodo NM arthropod; **~s** PL (*como clase*) arthropoda.

artroscopia NF arthroscopy.

artrósico ADJ (a) **estar ~** (*Med*) to have arthrosis. (b) *política, partido* stagnant.

artrosis NF INVAR arthrosis.

Arturo NM Arthur.

Artús NM: **el Rey ~** King Arthur.

aruñón NM (a) (*And*: *ladrón*) thief, pickpocket. (b) = **arañazo**.

arveja NF (a) (*Bot*) vetch. (b) (*LAm*: *guisante*) pea.

arz. ABR de **arzobispo** Archbishop, Abp.

arzobispado NM archbishopric.

arzobispal ADJ archiepiscopal; **palacio ~** archbishop's palace.

arzobispo NM archbishop.

arzón NM saddle tree; ~ **delantero** saddlebow.

as NM (a) (*Cartas*) ace; (*fig*) ace, trump card; (*dados*) one; ~ **de espadas** ace of spades; **guardarse un ~ en la manga** to have an ace up one's sleeve.
(b) (*: *campeón*) ace, wizard*; ~ **del fútbol** wizard footballer*, star player; ~ **del tenis** star tennis player; ~ **del volante** champion driver, speed king; **es un ~** he's a wizard*, he's the tops*.
(c) (*fig: Tenis*) ace, ace service.

asa[1] NF handle; grip; (*fig*) lever, pretext; **ser muy del ~*** to be well in.

asa[2] NF (*Bot*) juice.

asadera NF (*Cono Sur Culin*) baking tin.

asadero 1 ADJ roasting, for roasting.
2 NM spit; (*Méx*: *queso*) soft cheese.

asado 1 ADJ (a) (*Culin*) roast, roasted; **carne asada** roast meat; ~ **al horno** baked; ~ **a la parrilla** broiled; grilled; **bien ~** well done; **poco ~** underdone; rare, red.
(b) (*LAm*: *enfadado*) cross, angry.
(c) (*) **estar ~** (*Carib*) to be broke*.
2 NM (a) (*Culin*) roast, roast meat, joint. (b) (*Cono Sur*: *carne*) steak; ~ **al palo** barbecue.

asador NM (a) (*Culin*) spit; (*mecánico*) roasting-jack; ~ **a rotación**, ~ **rotatorio** rotary spit. (b) (*restaurante*) carvery.

asadura 1 NF (a) (*Anat*) **~s** entrails, offal; (*Culin*) chitterlings; **echar las ~s** to make a tremendous effort, bust a gut*. (b) (*pachorra*) sluggishness, laziness; **tiene ~s** he's terribly lazy.
2 NMF (*) stolid person, dull sort*.

asaetear [1a] VT (a) (*tirar*) to shoot, hit (with an arrow). (b) (*fig: acosar*) to bother, pester.

asalariado 1 ADJ paid; wage-earning.
2 NM, **asalariada** NF (a) (*empleado*) wage earner; employee. (b) (*pey*: *mercenario*) hireling; **es ~ de Eslobodia** he's in the pay of Slobodia.

asalariar [1b] VT to hire, put on the pay-roll.

asalmonado ADJ salmon coloured.

asaltabancos NMF INVAR bank robber.

asaltador(a) NM/F, **asaltante** NMF attacker, assailant; raider.

asaltar [1a] VT (a) *persona* to attack, assail; to rush; (*Mil*) to storm; *banco, tienda etc* to break into, raid; (*en disturbios etc*) to loot, sack; **le asaltaron 4 bandidos** he was held up by 4 bandits; **anoche fue asaltada la joyería** the jeweller's was raided last night, last night

there was a break-in at the jeweller's.
(b) (*desastre, muerte*) to fall upon, surprise, overtake.
(c) (*fig: duda*) to assail, afflict; (*pensamiento*) to cross one's mind; **le asaltó una idea** he was struck by an idea, he suddenly had an idea.
asalto NM **(a)** (*ataque*) attack, assault; **tomar por ~** to take by storm. **(b)** (*Boxeo*) round; (*Esgrima*) bout, assault. **(c)** (*Carib, Méx: visita*) unexpected visit.
asamblea NF (*gen*) assembly; (*reunión*) meeting; (*congreso*) congress, conference; **~ general** general assembly; **llamar a ~** (*Mil Hist*) to assemble, muster.
asambleario, -a NM/F, **asambleísta** NMF member of an assembly; (*congresista*) conference member.
asapán NM (*Méx*) flying squirrel.
asar [1a] **1** VT **(a)** (*Culin*) to roast; **~ al horno** to bake; **~ a la parrilla** to broil, grill.
(b) (*fig: acosar*) to pester, plague (*con* with).
(c) (:) to shoot, gun down.
2 asarse VR (*fig*) to be terribly hot, roast; **me aso de calor** I'm roasting; **aquí se asa uno vivo** it's boiling hot here, the heat is killing here.
asascuarse• [1d] VR (*Méx*) to roll up into a ball.
asaz ADV (†, *lit*) very, exceedingly; **una tarea ~ difícil** an exceedingly difficult task.
asbesto NM asbestos.
ascendencia NF **(a)** (*linaje*) ancestry, descent, origin; **de remota ~ normanda** of remote Norman ancestry. **(b)** (*LAm: dominio*) ascendancy; (*influencia*) hold, influence.
ascendente ADJ *movimiento* ascending, upward; *tendencia* rising, increasing; **en una curva ~** in an upward curve; **la carrera ~ del pistón** the up-stroke of the piston; **el tren ~** the up train.
ascender [2g] **1** VT to promote; **fue ascendido a teniente** he was promoted (to) lieutenant, he was raised to the rank of lieutenant.
2 VI **(a)** (*subir*) to ascend, rise, go up.
(b) (*ser ascendido*) to be promoted (*a* to), go up; **Málaga asciende a primera división** Málaga goes up to the first division.
(c) **~ a** (*Com etc*) to amount to, add up to, total.
ascendiente **1** ADJ = **ascendente**.
2 NMF (*persona*) ancestor.
3 NM (*influencia*) ascendancy, influence, power (*sobre* over).
ascensión NF **(a)** (*subida*) ascent; **~ en globo** balloon ride, trip in a balloon. **(b)** (*ascenso*) promotion (*a* to, to the rank of). **(c)** (*Ecl*) **la A~** the Ascension; **Día de la A~** Ascension Day.
ascensional ADJ *curva, movimiento etc* upward; (*Astron*) ascendant, rising.
ascensionista NMF balloonist.
ascenso NM promotion (*a* to, to the rank of).
ascensor NM lift, elevator (*US*); (*Téc*) elevator.
ascensorista NMF lift attendant, elevator operator (*US*).
ascesis NF asceticism; ascetic life.
asceta NMF ascetic.
ascético ADJ ascetic.
ascetismo NM asceticism.
asco NM **(a)** (*sentimiento*) loathing, disgust, revulsion; **¡qué ~!** how awful!, how revolting!; **¡qué ~ de gente!** what awful people!; **coger ~ a algo** to get sick of sth; **dar ~ a uno** to sicken sb, disgust sb; **me das ~** you disgust me; **me dan ~ las aceitunas** I loathe olives, olives revolt me; **hacer ~s de algo** to turn up one's nose at sth; **morirse de ~•** (*Esp*) to be bored to tears.
(b) (*objeto etc*) loathsome thing, disgusting thing, abomination; **es un ~** it's disgusting; **estar hecho un ~** to be filthy; **poner a uno un ~** (*Méx*) to insult (*o* abuse) sb.
ascua NF live coal, ember; **¡~s!** ouch!; **arrimar el ~ a su sardina** to look after number one, put one's own interests first; **estar como ~ de oro** to be shining bright; **estar en ~s** to be on tenterhooks; **tener a uno sobre ~s** to keep sb on tenterhooks; **sacar el ~ con la mano del gato** (*o* **con mano ajena**) to get sb else to do the dirty work.
aseadamente ADV cleanly, neatly, tidily; smartly.
aseado ADJ clean, neat, tidy; smart.
asear [1a] **1** VT **(a)** (*adornar*) to adorn, embellish. **(b)** (*limpiar*) to clean up, tidy up; (*pulir*) to smarten up.
2 asearse VR to tidy o.s. up; to smarten o.s. up.
asechanza NF trap, snare (*t fig*).
asechar [1a] VT to waylay, ambush; (*fig*) to set a trap for.
asediador NM besieger.
asediar [1b] VT **(a)** (*Mil*) to besiege, lay siege to; to blockade. **(b)** (*fig*) to bother, pester; (*amante*) to chase, lay siege to.
asedio NM **(a)** (*Mil*) siege; blockade. **(b)** (*Fin etc*) run; **~ de un banco** run on a bank.
asegún ADV, PREP (*LAm•*) = **según**.
asegurable ADV insurable.
aseguración NF insurance.

asegurado **1** ADJ insured.
2 NM, **asegurada** NF: **el ~, la asegurada** the insured, the insured person.
asegurador(a)¹ NM/F insurer; underwriter.
aseguradora² NF insurance company.
▼ **asegurar** [1a] **1** VT **(a)** (*fijar*) to secure, fasten, fix; to make firm, settle securely; **~ algo con pernos** to secure sth with bolts.
(b) *lugar etc* to make secure, strengthen the defences of (*contra* against).
(c) *derechos* to safeguard, guarantee, assure.
▼ **(d)** (*afirmar*) to assure, affirm; **le aseguro que ...** I assure you that ...; **aseguró que ...** he assured that ..., he confirmed that ...; **se lo aseguro** I assure you, I promise you; take my word for it; **ella le aseguró de su inocencia** she assured him of her innocence.
(e) (*Com, Fin*) to insure; **~ algo contra incendios** to insure sth against fire.
2 asegurarse VR **(a)** (*protegerse*) to make o.s. secure (*de* from).
▼ **(b)** (*comprobar*) to make sure (*de* of); **para asegurarnos del todo** in order to make quite sure.
(c) (*Com, Fin*) to insure o.s.
ASELE NF ABR *de* **Asociación para la Enseñanza del Español como Lengua Extranjera**.
asemejar [1a] **1** VT **(a)** (*hacer parecido*) to make alike, make similar; (*copiar*) to copy. **(b)** (*comparar*) to liken, compare (*a* to).
2 asemejarse VR to be alike, be similar; **~ a** to be like, resemble.
asendereado ADJ **(a)** *sendero* beaten, well-trodden. **(b)** *vida* wretched, full of hardships.
asenderear [1a] VT: **~ a uno** to chase sb relentlessly; to bother sb, pester sb.
asenso NM **(a)** (*consentimiento*) assent; **dar su ~** to assent. **(b)** (*acto de creer*) credence; **dar ~ a** to give credence to.
asentada NF sitting; **de una ~** at one sitting.
asentaderas NFPL (•) behind•, bottom.
asentado ADJ established, settled, permanent.
asentador NM **(a)** razor strop. **(b)** (*Com*) dealer, middleman.
asentamiento NM **(a)** (*pueblo*) shanty town, township. **(b)** (*industrial etc*) site; establishment.
asentar [1j] **1** VT **(a)** *persona* to seat, sit down; *objeto* to place, fix, set; *tienda* to pitch; *ciudad etc* to found; *cimiento* to make firm; *válvula* to seat.
(b) *tierra* to level, tamp down, firm.
(c) *golpe* to give, fetch.
(d) *cuchillo etc* to sharpen, hone.
(e) (*fig: establecer*) to settle, establish, consolidate; *principio* to lay down, establish; *impresión* to fix in the mind; *opinión* to affirm, assert.
(f) (*apuntar*) to note down, set down, put in writing; (*Com*) *pedido* to enter, book; *libro mayor* to enter up; **~ algo al debe de uno** to debit sth to sb; **~ algo al haber de uno** to credit sth to sb.
2 VI to be suitable, suit.
3 asentarse VR **(a)** (*pájaro*) to alight, settle; (*líquido*) to settle; (*Arquit*) to settle, sink, subside.
(b) (*fig: establecerse*) to settle, establish o.s.
asentimiento NM assent, consent.
asentir [3i] VI **(a)** (*consentir*) to assent, agree; **~ con la cabeza** to nod (one's head).
(b) **~ a** to agree to, consent to; *petición* to approve, grant; *convenio* to accept; **~ a la verdad de algo** to recognize the truth of sth.
asentista NM contractor, supplier.
aseñorado ADJ lordly; dressed like a gentleman, behaving like a gentleman.
aseo NM **(a)** (*limpieza*) cleanliness, neatness, tidiness. **(b)** **~s** (*euf*) cloakroom, toilet, powder room.
aséptico ADJ aseptic; germ-free, free from infection.
asequible ADJ (*gen*) obtainable, available; *finalidad* attainable; *plan* feasible; *precio* moderate, reasonable, within reach.
aserción NF assertion.
aserradero NM sawmill.
aserrador NM sawyer.
aserradora NF power saw.
aserradura NF saw cut; **~s** sawdust.
aserrar [1j] VT to saw, saw through; to saw up.
aserrín NM sawdust.
aserruchar [1a] VT (*LAm*) = **aserrar**.
asertar [1a] VT to assert, affirm.
asertividad NF assertiveness.
asertivo ADJ assertive.
aserto NM assertion.
asesina NF murderess.
asesinado, -a NM/F murder victim, murdered person.
asesinar [1a] VT **(a)** to murder; (*Pol*) to assassinate. **(b)** (*fig: molestar*) to pester, plague to death.

asesinato NM murder; (*Pol*) assassination; ~ **frustrado** attempted murder; ~ **legal** judicial murder; ~ **moral** character assassination.

asesino ① ADJ murderous; killer.
② NM (a) (*asesino*) murderer, killer; (*Pol*) assassin; ~ **múltiple**, ~ **en serie** serial killer. (b) (*fig: matón*) thug, cut-throat; ¡~! you brute!

asesor(a) ① NM/F adviser, consultant; ~ **de cuentas**, ~ **fiscal** tax accountant; ~ **financiero** financial adviser; **asesora** (**del hogar**) (*Cono Sur*) maid; ~ **de imagen** public-relations adviser.
② ADJ advisory.

asesoramiento NM advice.

asesorar [1a] ① VT (a) *persona* to advise, give legal (*o* professional) advice to.
(b) *compañía etc* to act as consultant to.
② **asesorarse** VR (a) ~ **con**, ~ **de** to take advice from, consult.
(b) ~ **de una situación** to take stock of a situation.

asesorato NM (*LAm*) (a) (*acto*) advising. (b) (*oficina*) consultant's office.

asesoría NF (a) (*acto*) advising; task of advising; ~ **jurídica** legal advice. (b) (*derechos*) adviser's fee. (c) (*oficina*) consultant's office.

asestar [1a] VT (a) *arma* to aim (*a* at, in the direction of); to fire, shoot. (b) *golpe* to deal, give, strike; ~ **una puñalada a uno** to stab sb.

aseveración NF assertion, contention.

aseveradamente ADV positively.

aseverar [1a] VT to affirm, assert.

asexuado ADJ sexless.

asexual ADJ asexual.

asfaltado ① ADJ asphalt, asphalted; **carrera asfaltada** made-up road.
② NM (a) (*acto*) asphalting. (b) (*firme*) asphalt, asphalt pavement, asphalt surface (*etc*); (*Aer etc*) tarmac.

asfaltar [1a] VT to asphalt.

asfáltico ADJ asphalt (*atr*).

asfalto NM asphalt; (*Aer etc*) tarmac; **regar el ~** to kick the bucket.

asfixia NF suffocation, asphyxiation, (*Med*) asphyxia.

asfixiador ADJ, **asfixiante** ADJ suffocating, asphyxiating; **calor** ~ suffocating heat; **gas** ~ poison gas.

asfixiar [1b] ① VT (a) (*ahogar*) to asphyxiate; to suffocate; (*Mil: con gas*) to gas. (b) **estar asfixiado** (*sin dinero*) to be broke*; (*en aprieto*) to be up the creek.
② **asfixiarse** VR to be asphyxiated, suffocate.

asgo V **asir**.

▼ **así** ① ADV (a) (*de este modo*) so, in this way, thus; by this means, thereby; **lo hizo** ~ he did it like this, he did it this way; ~ **lo hace cualquiera** anybody could do it, it's easy; (*título*) '**A~ se roba**' 'How to Steal'; **¡y** ~ **te va!** look where it's got you!; **aun** ~ **no me** *etc* **resultó** even then it didn't work; **¡~!** that's right!, that's the way!; ~ ~, ~ **asá**, ~ **asado** so-so, fair, middling; ~ **o asá** one way or another; ~ **que asá** it makes no odds; ~ **como** ~, ~ **que** ~ anyway; **20 dólares o** ~ 20 dollars or so, 20 dollars or thereabouts; **y** ~ **en adelante**, **y** ~ **sucesivamente** and so on; ~ **que** ... so ..., therefore ...; ~ **nada más** just like that, if you please; **pues** ... and so ..., so then ...; ~ **y todo** even so; ~ **es** that is so; ~ **era** that's the way it was, that's what it was like; ~ **es que no fuimos** so we didn't go, that's why we didn't go; **¿no es** ~? is it not so?, isn't it it?; **¡~ sea!** so be it!
(b) (*comparaciones*) ~ **A como B** both A and B, A as well as B; ~ **como Vd sabe ruso yo sé chino** in the same way as you know Russian I know Chinese; **el original** ~ **como una copia** the original together with a copy; **no se hace** ~ **como** ~ it's not as easy as all that.
(c) ~ **de pobre que** ... so poor that ...; **un baúl** ~ **de grande** a trunk this big, a trunk as big as this; **estaba** ~ **de gordo** he was that fat.
② *como* ADJ INVAR: **un hombre** ~ such a man, a man like that; **todos tenemos épocas** ~ we all have spells like that, we all have spells of that sort; ~ **es la vida** such is life, that's life; **los franceses son** ~ the French are like that, that's the way the French are.
③ CONJ (a) ~ **que** ... as soon as ...; no sooner than ...
(b) ~ **se esté muriendo de dolor** (*LAm*) even though he's dying of pain; **¡~ te mueras!** and I hope you die!; ~ **te mueras tienes que hacerlo** you have to do it even if it costs your life; **¡~ nomás!** (*Méx*) just like that!

Asia NF Asia; ~ **Menor** Asia Minor.

asiático, -a ADJ, NM/F Asian, Asiatic.

asidero NM (a) (*agarro*) hold, grasp.
(b) (*asa*) handle, holder.
(c) (*fig*) pretext, excuse; lever.
(d) (*Cono Sur*) basis, support; **eso no tiene** ~ there is no basis for it.

asiduamente ADV assiduously; frequently, regularly.

asiduidad NF (a) (*cualidad*) assiduousness; regularity. (b) ~**es** attentions, kindnesses.

asiduo ① ADJ assiduous; frequent, regular, persistent; *admirador* devoted; **parroquiano** ~ regular customer; **como** ~ **lector de su periódico** as a regular (*o* constant) reader of your newspaper.
② NM, **asidua** NF regular customer (*etc*), habitué(e); **era un** ~ **del café** he was an habitué of the café; **es un** ~ **del museo** he is a frequent visitor to the museum.

asiento NM (a) (*silla etc*) seat, chair; place; (*de bicicleta*) saddle; ~ **de atrás**, ~ **trasero** rear seat; pillion seat; ~ **delantero** front seat; ~ **expulsor**, ~ **lanzable**, ~ **proyectable** (*Aer*) ejector seat; ~ **reservado** reserved seat; **no ha calentado el** ~ he hasn't stayed long; **tomar** ~ to take a seat.
(b) (*sitio*) site, location.
(c) (*de botella etc*) bottom, base; (*Anat**) bottom.
(d) (*Mec*) seating; ~ **de válvula** valve seating.
(e) (*gen* ~**s** PL) sediment, dregs.
(f) (*Náut*) trim.
(g) (*Arquit*) settling; **hacer** ~ to settle, sink.
(h) (*acto*) settling, settlement, establishment; **estar de** ~ to be settled (in a place); **vivir de** ~ **con uno** to live in sin with sb.
(i) ~ (**minero**) (*And*) mining town, mining settlement.
(j) (*Com*) contract, trading agreement; (*Pol*) (peace) treaty.
(k) (*Fin: en cuenta etc*) entry; ~ **de cierre** closing entry; ~ **contable** book-keeping entry.
(l) (*cualidad*) stability; good sense, judgement; **hombre de** ~ sensible man.

asignable ADJ: ~ **a** assignable to, which can be assigned to.

asignación NF (a) (*acto*) assignment; allocation (*t Inform*); appointment; determination; ~ **de presupuesto** (*Com*) budget appropriation. (b) (*porción*) share, portion; (*Fin*) allowance, salary; pocket money; ~ **semanal** weekly allowance. (c) ~ **presupuestaria** (*Carib*) budget.

asignado NM (*And Agr*) wages paid in kind.

asignar [1a] VT (*gen*) to assign; to allot, apportion; (*Inform*) to allocate; *persona* to appoint; *tarea* to assign, set; *causas* to determine.

asignatario NM, **asignataria** NF (*LAm*) heir, legatee.

asignatura NF (*Univ etc*) subject, course; ~ **pendiente** (*Univ etc*) failed subject, subject to be retaken; (*fig*) matter pending, matter still to be resolved; **aprobar una** ~ to pass (in) a subject.

asigunas* NFPL: **según** ~ (*Carib*) it all depends.

asilado, -a NM/F inmate; (*Pol*) (political) refugee.

asilar [1a] ① VT (a) (*acoger*) to take in, give shelter to; (*LAm*) to give political asylum to.
(b) *viejo etc* to put into a home (*o* institution).
② **asilarse** VR (a) (*refugiarse*) to take refuge (*en* in); (*Pol*) to seek political asylum.
(b) (*viejo etc*) to enter a home (*o* institution).

asilo NM (a) (*Pol etc*) asylum; sanctuary; (*fig*) shelter, refuge; **derecho de** ~ right of sanctuary; **pedir** (**el**) ~ **político** to ask for political asylum.
(b) (*de viejos etc*) home, institution; ~ **de ancianos** old people's home; ~ **para desamparados** workhouse; ~ **de huérfanos** orphanage; ~ **de locos** lunatic asylum; ~ **de niños expósitos** foundling hospital; ~ **de pobres** poorhouse.

asilvestrarse [1a] VR (*tierra*) to become wooded, revert to woodland; (*planta*) to establish itself in the wild.

asimetría NF asymmetry; irregularity, unevenness.

asimétrico ADJ asymmetric(al); irregular, uneven.

asimiento NM (a) (*acto*) seizing, grasping; hold. (b) (*fig*) attachment, affection.

asimilable ADJ: **fácilmente** ~ readily assimilated, easy to assimilate.

asimilación NF assimilation.

asimilado ① ADJ similar, related; **establecimientos hoteleros y** ~**s** hotels and the like.
② NM (*LAm*) professional person attached to the army.

asimilar [1a] ① VT to assimilate.
② **asimilarse** VR (a) (*establecerse*) to assimilate, become assimilated.
(b) ~ **a** to resemble.

asimismo ADV likewise, in like manner, in the same way.

asín* ADV = **así**.

asíncrono ADJ asynchronous.

asintomático ADJ asymptomatic.

asir [3a; *pero en presente como* **salir**] ① VT to seize, grasp, catch, take hold of (*con* with, *de* by); **ir asidos del brazo** to walk along arm-in-arm.
② VI (*Bot*) to take root.
③ **asirse** VR to take hold; (*2 personas*) to fight, grapple, lay hold of one another; ~ **a**, ~ **de** to seize, take hold of; to clutch on to; ~ **de** (*fig*) to avail o.s. of, take advantage of; ~ **con uno** to grapple with sb.

Asiria NF Assyria.

asirio, -a ADJ, NM/F Assyrian.

asisito ADV (*And etc*) = **así**.

asísmico ADJ (*LAm*): **construcción asísmica** earthquake-resistant building; **medidas asísmicas** anti-earthquake measures.

asistencia NF (a) (*presencia*) attendance, presence (*a* at).

(b) (*personas*) people present, those attending; audience; **¿había mucha ~?** were there many people there?

(c) (*ayuda*) help, assistance; (*en casa*) domestic help, service; (*Med*) care, attendance; nursing; **~ intensiva** intensive care; **~ letrada** legal aid; **~ médica** medical care, medical attendance; **~ pública** (*Cono Sur*) state medical service; public health system; **~ sanitaria** health care; **~ social** social welfare, welfare work, social work.

(d) (*Méx: cuarto*) spare room, guest room.

(e) (*And, Méx: pensión*) cheap boarding-house.

(f) **~s** (*Fin*) allowance, maintenance.

asistencial ADJ welfare (*atr*), social security (*atr*).

asistenta NF assistant; (*de limpieza*) charwoman, daily help, cleaning lady; (*And, Méx*) boarding-house keeper, landlady.

asistente NM (*a veces* **asistenta** NF) **(a)** (*ayudante*) assistant; (*Mil*) orderly, batman; (*And*) servant; (*And, Méx*) boarding-house keeper, landlord; **~ social** social worker, welfare worker.

(b) **los ~s** (*presentes*) those present, the people present.

asistido [1] ADJ: **~ por ordenador** computer-assisted.

[2] NM, **asistida** NF (*And, Méx*) boarder, lodger, resident.

asistir [3a] [1] VT **(a)** (*estar presente*) to attend; (*servir*) to serve, wait on.

(b) (*ayudar*) to help, assist; (*Med*) to attend, care for; **el médico que le asiste** the doctor who attends him, the doctor in whose care he is; **~ un parto** to deliver a baby.

(c) (*Jur*) to represent, appear for; **asistido por su abogado** with his lawyer present.

(d) **le asiste la razón** he has right on his side.

[2] VI **(a)** (*estar presente*) to be present (*a* at), attend; *suceso, proceso, escena* to witness, be a witness of; **no asistió a la clase** he did not attend the class, he did not come to the class; **¿vas a ~?** are you going?; **asistieron unas 200 personas** some 200 people were present.

(b) (*Naipes*) to follow suit.

askenazí ADJ, NMF Ashkenazi.

asma NF asthma; **~ bronquial** bronchial asthma.

asmático ADJ, NM, **asmática** NF asthmatic.

asna NF female donkey.

asnada* NF silly thing.

asnal* ADJ asinine, silly; beastly.

asnar ADJ: *ganado* ~ donkeys.

asnear [1a] VI (*LAm*) to act the fool, do sth silly; to be clumsy.

asnería* NF silly thing.

asno NM **(a)** (*Zool*) donkey. **(b)** (*fig*) ass*, fathead*; **¡soy un ~!** I'm an ass!*

asociación NF association; society; (*Com, Fin*) partnership; **~ aduanera** customs union; **~ para el delito** criminal conspiracy; **~ libre** free association; **~ obrera** trade union; **~ de padres de alumnos** parent-teacher association; **~ de vecinos** neighbourhood association, residents' association; **por ~ de ideas** by association of ideas.

asociado [1] ADJ associated; *miembro etc* associate.

[2] NM, **asociada** NF associate; member; (*Com, Fin*) partner.

asocial ADJ asocial.

asociar [1b] [1] VT (*gen*) to associate (*a, con* with); *esfuerzos, recursos etc* to pool, put together; (*Com, Fin*) to take into partnership.

[2] **asociarse** VR to associate; (*Com, Fin*) to become partners, form a partnership; **~ con uno** to team up with sb, join forces with sb.

asocio NM (*LAm*): **en ~** in association (*de* with).

asolación NF destruction, devastation.

asolador ADJ destructive, devastating.

asolanar [1a] VT, **asolar¹** [1a] [1] VT to dry up, parch.

[2] **asolanarse** VR, **asolarse** VR to dry up, be ruined.

asolar² [1a] [1] VT to raze (to the ground), lay flat, destroy; to lay waste.

[2] **asolarse** VR (*líquido*) to settle.

asoleada NF (*LAm*) sunstroke.

asoleado ADJ (*CAm*) **(a)** *persona* stupid. **(b)** *animal* tired out.

asoleadura NF (*Cono Sur*) sunstroke.

asolear [1a] [1] VT to put in the sun, keep in the sun; to dry in the sun.

[2] **asolearse** VR **(a)** to sun o.s., bask in the sun; to get sunburnt.

(b) (*Cono Sur, Méx Med*) to get sunstroke.

(c) (*CAm: atontarse*) to get stupid.

asoleo NM (*Méx*) sunstroke.

asomada NF **(a)** (*aparición*) brief appearance. **(b)** (*vislumbre*) glimpse, sudden view.

asomadero NM (*And*) viewing point, vantage point.

asomar [1a] [1] VT to show, put out, stick out; **~ la cabeza** to put one's head out (*a la ventana* of the window); **~ la cara** to show one's face (*t fig*); **asomó un pie** she stuck a foot out.

[2] VI to begin to show, appear, become visible; **asoman ya las nuevas plantas** the new plants are beginning to show; **asomó el buque en la niebla** the ship loomed up out of the fog.

[3] **asomarse** VR **(a)** (*objeto*) to show, appear, stick out; (*costa, en niebla etc*) to loom up; **se asomaba el árbol por encima de la tapia** the

tree showed above the wall.

(b) (*persona*) to show up, show o.s.; **~ a, ~ por** to show o.s. at, lean out of, look out of; **ella estaba asomada a la ventana** she was leaning out of the window; **¡asómate!** put your head out!; **~ a ver algo** to take a look at sth; to peep in at sth.

(c) (*: *emborracharse*) to get tight*, get tipsy.

(d) (*And: acercarse*) to approach, come close (to).

asombradizo ADJ easily alarmed.

asombrador ADJ amazing, astonishing.

asombrar [1a] [1] VT **(a)** (*pasmar*) to amaze, astonish; to frighten; **no deja de ~me** it never ceases to amaze me.

(b) (*ensombrecer*) to shade, cast a shadow on; *color* to darken.

[2] **asombrarse** VR **(a)** (*sorprenderse*) to be amazed, be astonished (*de* at); (*escandalizarse*) to be shocked (*de* at); (*asustarse*) to take fright; **~ de saber algo** to be surprised to learn sth.

(b) (*CAm: desmayarse*) to faint.

asombro NM **(a)** (*pasmo*) amazement, astonishment, surprise; (*miedo*) fear, fright.

(b) (*objeto*) wonder; **es el ~ del siglo** it is the wonder of the century.

asombrosamente ADV amazingly, astonishingly.

asombroso ADJ amazing, astonishing.

asomo NM **(a)** (*aparición*) appearance.

(b) (*indicio*) hint, sign, indication, trace; **ante cualquier ~ de discrepancia** at the slightest hint of disagreement; **sin ~ de violencia** without a trace of violence; **ni por ~** by no means, not by a long shot; **¡ni por ~!** no chance!

asonada NF **(a)** (*personas*) mob, rabble. **(b)** (*motín*) riot, disturbance.

asonancia NF **(a)** (*Liter*) assonance. **(b)** (*fig*) harmony; correspondence, connection; **no tener ~ con** to bear no relation to.

asonantar [1a] VTI to assonate (*con* with).

asonante [1] ADJ assonant.

[2] NF (*gen*) assonance; (*palabra*) assonant (rhyme).

asonar [1l] VI to assonate, be in assonance.

asordar [1a] VT to deafen.

asorocharse [1a] VR (*And, Cono Sur*) to get mountain sickness.

asosegar [1h y 1j] = **sosegar**.

aspa NF cross, X-shaped figure (*o design etc*); (*Mat*) multiplication sign; (*Arquit*) crosspiece; (*de molino*) sail, arm; (*Téc*) reel, winding frame; (*Cono Sur*) horn; **ventilador de ~** rotary fan.

aspadera NF reel, winder.

aspado ADJ cross-shaped, X-shaped; *persona* with arms outstretched; **estar ~ en algo** to be all trussed up in sth.

aspador NM reel, winder.

aspamentero ADJ (*etc*) (*Cono Sur, Méx*) = **aspaventero** (*etc*).

aspar [1a] [1] VT **(a)** (*Téc*) to reel, wind.

(b) (*fig: fastidiar*) to vex, annoy; **¡que te aspen!*** get lost!*; **lo hago aunque me aspen** wild horses wouldn't stop me doing it.

[2] **asparse** VR **(a)** (*retorcerse*) to writhe.

(b) (*fig: esforzarse*) to do one's utmost, go all out (*por algo* to get sth).

aspaventero [1] ADJ excitable, emotional, given to exaggerated displays of feeling; fussy.

[2] NM, **aspaventera** NF excitable person; fussy person.

aspaviento NM exaggerated display of feeling; fulsome expression of feeling; fuss, to-do*; **~s** exaggerated gestures; **hacer ~s** to make a great fuss.

▼ **aspecto** NM **(a)** (*apariencia*) look, appearance; looks; aspect; (*Arquit, Geog etc*) aspect; **~ exterior** outward appearance; **un hombre de ~ feroz** a man with a fierce look, a fierce-looking man; **tener buen ~** to look well; **¿qué ~ tenía?** what was he like?, what did he look like?

▼ **(b)** (*fig*) aspect; side; **a(l) primer ~** at first sight; **bajo ese ~** from that point of view; **estudiar una cuestión bajo todos sus ~s** to study all aspects of a question; **ver sólo un ~ de la cuestión** to see only one side to the question.

aspectual ADJ aspectual.

ásperamente ADV roughly; harshly, gruffly; **dijo ~** he said in a harsh tone.

aspereza NF (*V ADJ*) roughness; ruggedness; sourness, bitterness; toughness; harshness; surliness; **contestar con ~** to answer with asperity, answer harshly; **limar ~s** (*fig*) to smooth things over.

asperges NM **(a)** (*aspersión*) sprinkling; **quedarse ~** to come away empty-handed. **(b)** (*Ecl*) aspergillum; hyssop.

asperillo NM slight sour (*o bitter*) taste.

asperjar [1a] VT to sprinkle; (*Ecl*) to sprinkle with holy water.

áspero ADJ **(a)** (*al tacto*) rough; *filo* uneven, jagged, rough; *terreno* rough, rugged.

(b) (*al gusto*) sour, tart, bitter.

(c) *clima* hard, tough; *trato* rough.

(d) *voz* harsh, rough; rasping; *tono* harsh; surly, gruff; (*inculto*) unpolished; *temperamento* sour; *disputa etc* bad-tempered.

asperón NM sandstone, grit; (*Téc*) grindstone.
aspersión NF (*de agua etc*) sprinkling; (*Agr, Hort*) spray, spraying; **riego por ~** watering by spray, watering by sprinklers.
aspersor NM sprinkler.
áspid(e) NM asp.
aspidistra NF aspidistra.
aspillera NF (*Mil*) loophole.
aspiración NF (**a**) (*respiración*) breath; breathing in, inhalation; (*Ling*) aspiration; (*Mús*) (*short pause for*) breath. (**b**) (*Mec*) air intake. (**c**) **aspiraciones** (*LAm*) aspirations.
aspirada NF aspirate.
aspirado ADJ aspirate.
aspirador ① ADJ suction (*atr*); **bomba ~a** suction pump.
　② NM (*t ~ de polvo*) vacuum-cleaner; **pasar el ~ a la alfombra** to hoover the carpet.
aspiradora NF vacuum-cleaner.
aspirante ① ADJ: **bomba ~** suction pump.
　② NMF aspirant; candidate, applicant (*a* for); **~ de marina** naval cadet.
aspirar [1a] ① VT (**a**) *aire etc* to breathe in, inhale; *líquido* to suck in, suck up; (*Téc*) to suck in, take in; *droga* to sniff.
　(**b**) (*Ling*) to aspirate.
　② VI: **~ a algo** to aspire to sth; **no aspiro a tanto** I do not aim so high; **A aspiró a la mano de B** A sought B's hand in marriage; **~ a hacer algo** to aspire to do sth, aim to do sth, seek to do sth; **el que no sepa eso que no aspire a aprobar** whoever doesn't know that can have no hope of passing.
aspirina NF aspirin.
aspudo ADJ (*Cono Sur*) big-horned.
asqueante ADJ sickening.
asquear [1a] ① VT to nauseate; **me asquean las ratas** I loathe rats, rats nauseate (*o* disgust) me.
　② VI **y asquearse** VR to be nauseated, feel disgusted.
asquerosamente ADV disgustingly, sickeningly; (*) awfully.
asquerosidad NF (**a**) (*cualidad*) loathsomeness; squalor; awfulness; vileness. (**b**) (*una ~*) mess, filth; **hacer ~es** to make a mess. (**c**) (*trampa*) dirty trick.
asqueroso ADJ (**a**) (*repugnante*) disgusting, loathsome, sickening; squalid; *comida* revolting; (*) awful, lousy*, vile. (**b**) (*de gusto delicado*) squeamish.
asquiento ADJ (*And*) (**a**) (*quisquilloso*) fussy. (**b**) = **asqueroso**.
asta NF (*arma*) lance, spear; (*palo*) pole; shaft; (*asidero*) handle; (*de bandera*) flagstaff, flagpole; (*Zool*) horn, antler; **a media ~** at half mast; **dejar a uno en las ~s del toro** to leave sb in a jam.
astabandera NF (*LAm*) flagstaff, flagpole.
ástaco NM crayfish.
astado ① ADJ horned.
　② NM bull.
astear [1a] VT (*Cono Sur*) to gore.
aster NF aster.
asterisco NM asterisk; **señalar con un ~, poner ~ a** to asterisk.
asteroide NM asteroid.
astigmático ADJ astigmatic.
astigmatismo NM astigmatism.
astil NM (*de herramienta*) handle, haft; (*de flecha*) shaft; (*de balanza*) beam.
astilla NF (**a**) (*fragmento*) splinter, chip; **~s** (*para fuego*) firewood, kindling; **hacer algo ~s** to smash sth into little pieces, smash sth to matchwood; **hacerse ~s** to shatter into little pieces. (**b**) (*Esp**) small bribe, sweetener*; **dar ~ a uno** to give sb a cut*; **ese tío no da ~** he's a very tight-fisted so-and-so*.
astillar [1a] ① VT to splinter, chip; to shatter.
　② **astillarse** VR to splinter; to shatter.
astillero NM shipyard, dockyard.
astracán NM astrakhan.
astracanada* NF silly thing (to do); piece of buffoonery.
astrágalo NM (*Arquit, Mil*) astragal; (*Anat*) ankle bone, astragalus.
astral ADJ astral, of the stars.
astreñir [3h y 3i] = **astringir**.
astrilla NF (*Cono Sur*) = **astilla**.
astringente ① ADJ astringent, binding.
　② NM astringent.
astringir [3e] VT (**a**) (*Anat*) to constrict, contract; (*Med*) to bind. (**b**) (*fig*) to bind, compel.
astro NM (**a**) (*Astron*) star, heavenly body; **el ~ Rey** the sun. (**b**) (*fig*) star, leading light; (*Cine*) star.
astrofísica[1] NF astrophysics.
astrofísico, -a[2] NM/F astrophysicist.
astrolabio NM astrolabe.
astrología NF astrology.
astrológico ADJ astrological.
astrólogo, -a NM/F astrologer.

astronauta NMF astronaut.
astronáutica NF astronautics.
astronave NF spaceship.
astronometría NF astrometry.
astronomía NF astronomy.
astronómico ADJ astronomical.
astrónomo, -a NM/F astronomer.
astroso ADJ (**a**) (*malhadado*) ill-fated, unfortunate. (**b**) (*vil*) contemptible. (**c**) (*sucio*) dirty; (*desaseado*) untidy, shabby.
astucia NF (**a**) (*cualidad*) cleverness; guile, cunning; **actuar con ~** to act cunningly, be crafty. (**b**) **una ~** a clever trick, a piece of cunning.
astur ADJ, NM Asturian.
asturiano, -a ① ADJ, NM/F Asturian.
　② NM (*Ling*) Asturian.
Asturias NF: (**el Principado de**) **~** Asturias.
asturleonés ADJ of (*o* from) Asturias and León.
astutamente ADV cleverly, smartly; craftily, cunningly.
astuto ADJ clever, smart; crafty, cunning.
asueto NM time off, break, short holiday; **día de ~** day off; **tarde de ~** afternoon off, (*Escol*) half-holiday; **tomarse un ~ de fin de semana** to take a weekend break, take the weekend off.
asumible ADJ *riesgo* acceptable, permissible.
asumidamente ADV supposedly.
asumir [3a] ① VT (**a**) *responsabilidad etc* to assume, take on; *mando etc* to take over; *cargo* to take up; *actitud* to strike, adopt. (**b**) (*suponer*) to assume, suppose; to take for granted; **~ que ...** to assume that ...
　② VI (*Pol etc*) to take up office.
asunceño (*Cono Sur*) ① ADJ of Asunción.
　② NM, **asunceña** NF native (*o* inhabitant) of Asunción; **los ~s** the people of Asunción.
Asunción NF (**a**) (*Ecl*) Assumption. (**b**) (*Geog*) Asunción.
asunción NF assumption.
asunto NM (**a**) (*gen*) matter, subject; (*tema*) topic; (*negocio*) affair, business; (*Liter*) theme, subject; plot; (*: ligue*) affair; **¡~ concluido!** that's an end of the matter!; **el ~ está concluido** the matter is closed; **~ de alcoba** matter involving sexual relations; **~ de honor** affair of honour; **el ~ Rumasa** the Rumasa affair; **~s exteriores** foreign affairs; **Ministerio de A~s Exteriores** Foreign Ministry, Foreign Office, State Department (*US*); **~s a tratar** agenda, items to be discussed; **es un ~ de faldas** there's a woman in it somewhere; **ausente por ~ grave** absent with good reason, absent for good cause; **es un ~ triste** it's a bad business; **ir al ~** to get down to business; **entrometerse en un ~** to meddle in an affair.
　(**b**) (*Carib: atención*) study, attention; **poner ~** to pay attention.
　(**c**) **¿a ~ de qué lo hiciste?** (*Cono Sur*) why did you do it?
asurar [1a] VT (**a**) (*Culin etc*) to burn; (*Agr*) to burn up, parch. (**b**) (*fig*) to worry.
asurcar [1g] VT = **surcar**.
asustadizo ADJ easily frightened; nervy, jumpy; *animal* shy, skittish.
asustar [1a] ① VT to frighten, scare; to alarm, startle.
　② **asustarse** VR to be frightened, get scared; to get alarmed, be startled; **~ de** (*o* **por**) **algo** to be frightened at sth, get alarmed about sth; **~ de** + *infin* to be afraid to + *infin*; **¡no te asustes!** don't be alarmed!
asusto NM (*And*) = **susto**.
A.T. ABR *de* **Antiguo Testamento** Old Testament, O.T.
-ata V **Aspects of Word Formation in Spanish 2**.
atabacado ADJ (**a**) (*color*) tobacco-coloured. (**b**) **con aliento ~** (*Cono Sur*) with breath smelling of tobacco.
atabal NM kettledrum.
atabalear [1a] VI (*caballo*) to stamp, drum; (*con dedos*) to drum.
atacable ADJ attackable, assailable.
atacado ADJ (**a**) (*pusilánime*) fainthearted; (*vacilante*) dithery, irresolute. (**b**) (*tacaño*) mean, stingy.
atacador ① NM (*Mil*) ramrod.
　② NM, **atacadora** NF attacker, assailant.
atacadura NF fastener, fastening.
atacante NMF attacker, assailant.
atacar [1g] ① VT (**a**) (*Mil etc*) to attack; to assail, assault; *teoría etc* to attack, impugn; (*en disputa*) to attack, set about, go for; to press hard.
　(**b**) (*Quím, Med etc*) to attack.
　(**c**) (*pegar etc*) to attach, fasten; *vestido* to button up, do up.
　(**d**) *bolsa etc* to stuff, pack; (*Mil, Min*) to ram home, tamp; to wad, plug.
　② **atacarse*** VR (*LAm*) to scoff*, stuff o.s.
atachable ADJ (*Méx: Inform*) compatible (*a* with).
atachar [1a] VT (*Méx Elec*) to plug in.
ataché NM (*CAm, Carib*) paper clip.
ataderas* NFPL garters.
atadero NM (*cuerda*) rope, cord; (*cierre*) fastening; (*sitio*) place for ty-

ing; (Méx: liga) garter; **eso no tiene ~** you can't make head or tail of it, there's nothing to latch on to.

atadijo NM loose bundle.

atado ① ADJ (a) (lit) tied. (b) (fig: tímido) shy, inhibited; (indeciso) irresolute.
② NM bundle; bunch; **~ de cigarrillos** (Cono Sur) packet of cigarettes.

atadora NF (Agr) binder.

atadura NF (a) (acto) tying, fastening. (b) (cuerda etc) string, cord, rope; (Agr) rope, tether; (fig) bond, tie. (c) (fig: limitación) limitation, restriction.

atafagar [1h] VT (a) (olor) to stifle, suffocate. (b) (fig) to pester the life out of.

ataguía NF cofferdam, caisson.

atajar [1a] ① VT (a) (gen) to stop, intercept; fugitivo etc to head off, cut off; (LAm: recoger) to catch, catch in flight; (Dep) to tackle; (Arquit) to partition off; **~ a uno** (LAm) to hold sb back (to stop a fight); **~ un golpe** (LAm) to parry a blow; **me quiso ~ al almuerzo** (LAm) she wanted me to stay for lunch.
(b) discusión to cut short; discurso etc to interrupt, break into; proceso to end, stop, call a halt to; abuso to put a stop to; **este mal hay que ~lo** we must put an end to this evil.
② VI to take a short cut (por by way of, across); (Aut) to cut corners.
③ **atajarse** VR (avergonzarse) to feel ashamed of o.s.; (aturdirse) to be overcome by confusion, be all of a dither; (Cono Sur) to keep one's temper, control o.s.

atajo NM (a) (en camino) short cut; **echar por el ~** to take the easiest way out, seek a quick solution; **no hay ~ sin trabajo** short cuts don't help in the long run. (b) (Dep) tackle.

atalaje NM = atelaje.

atalaya ① NF (a) (torre) watchtower; observation point, observation post. (b) (fig) vantage point.
② NM lookout, observer, sentinel.

atalayador(a) NM/F look-out; (fig) snooper, spy.

atalayar [1a] VT (observar) to watch, observe; (vigilar) to watch over, guard; (espiar) to spy on.

atañer [2f] [defective: se usa en 3ª persona de presente] VI: **~ a** to concern, have to do with; **en lo que atañe a eso** with regard to that, as to that; **eso no me atañe** it's no concern of mine.

atapuzar [1f] (Carib) ① VT to fill, stop up.
② **atapuzarse** VR to stuff o.s.

ataque NM (a) (Mil etc) attack (a, contra on); strike (a, contra against); (Aer) attack, raid; **~ aéreo** air raid, air attack; **~ fingido** sham attack; **~ de flanco** flank attack; **~ de frente** frontal attack; **~ preventivo** pre-emptive strike; **~ por sorpresa** surprise attack; **~ a superficie** ground attack; **dejarse expuesto a** to leave o.s. open to attack; **lanzar un ~** to launch an attack; **pasar al ~** to go on the offensive; **volver al ~** to return to the attack.
(b) (Med etc) attack (de of), fit; **~ cardíaco**, **~ al corazón** heart-attack; **~ cerebral** brain haemorrhage; **~ epiléptico** epileptic fit; **~ fulminante** stroke, seizure; **~ de risa** fit of laughing.

atar [1a] ① VT (a) (gen) to tie, tie up; cautivo to bind; (abrochar) to fasten; (Agr) animal to tether; gavilla to bind; **zapatos de ~** lace-up shoes; **está de ~** he's raving mad; **~ corto a uno** (fig) to keep sb on a close rein; **~ la lengua a uno** (fig) to silence sb; **~ las manos a uno** (fig) to limit sb's freedom of action; **verse atado de pies y manos** (fig) to be tied hand and foot; **dejar algo atado y bien atado** (fig) to leave no loose ends, leave everything properly tied up.
(b) (fig) to bind, tie; to hamper.
② VI: **ni ata ni desata** this is nonsense, this is getting us nowhere.
③ **atarse** VR (a) (quedar atascado) to stick, get stuck; **~ en una dificultad** to get tied up in a difficulty.
(b) (sentirse violento) to be embarrassed, get embarrassed.
(c) **~ a la letra** to stick to the literal meaning; **~ a una opinión** to stick to one's opinion.

ataracea NF = taracea.

atarantar [1a] ① VT (a) (aturdir) to stun, daze; **quedó atarantado** he was stunned, he was unconscious.
(b) (fig) to stun, dumbfound.
② **atarantarse** VR (a) to be stunned, be dumbfounded.
(b) (And: darse prisa) to hurry, dash, rush.
(c) (Méx: comiendo) to stuff o.s.
(d) (CAm, Méx: bebiendo) to get drunk.

atarazana NF dockyard.

atardecer ① [2d] VI to get dark; **atardecía** it was getting dark, night was falling.
② NM late afternoon; dusk, evening; **al ~** at dusk.

atardecida NF dusk, nightfall.

atareado ADJ busy, rushed; **andar muy ~** to be very busy.

atarear [1a] ① VT to give a job to, assign a task to.
② **atarearse** VR to work hard, keep busy; to be busy (con, en with); **~ a hacer algo** to be busy doing sth.

atarjea NF sewage pipe, drain; (And: presa de agua) reservoir.

atarragarse [1h] VR (Carib, Méx) to stuff o.s., overeat.

atarugar [1h] ① VT (a) (asegurar) to fasten (with a peg o wedge); to peg, wedge.
(b) agujero to plug, stop, bung up.
(c) (llenar) to stuff, fill (de with).
(d) (*) **~ a uno** to shut sb up.
② **atarugarse** VR (a) (atragantarse) to swallow the wrong way, choke.
(b) (fig) to get confused, be in a daze.
(c) (*: tragar) to stuff o.s., overeat.

atasajar [1a] VT carne to jerk.

atascadero NM (a) (lit) mire, bog, muddy place. (b) (fig) stumbling block, obstacle; dead end.

atascar [1g] ① VT fuga to stop; agujero to block, plug, stop up; tubo etc to clog, clog up, obstruct; proceso to hinder.
② **atascarse** VR (a) (carro etc) to get stuck (in the mud), get bogged down; (Aut) to get into a jam; (motor) to stall; **quedó atascado a mitad de la cuesta** he got stuck halfway up the climb.
(b) (fig) to get bogged down (en un problema in a problem); (en discurso) to get stuck, dry up*.
(c) (tubo etc) to clog, get clogged up, get stopped up; (LAm Med) to have an internal blockage.

atasco NM obstruction, blockage; (Aut) traffic-jam.

ataúd NM coffin; bier.

ataujía NF (a) (Téc) damascene, damascene work. (b) (CAm: desagüe) conduit, drain.

ataviar [1c] ① VT (a) to deck, array (con, de in); to dress up, get up (con, de in). (b) (LAm) to adapt, adjust, accommodate.
② **ataviarse** VR to dress up, get o.s. up (con, de in).

atávico ADJ atavistic.

atavío NM attire, dress; (hum) rig, get-up; **~s** finery.

atavismo NM atavism.

ate NM (CAm, Méx Culin) jelly.

atecomate NM (Méx: vaso) tumbler.

atediante ADJ boring, wearisome.

atediar [1b] ① VT to bore, weary.
② **atediarse** VR to get bored.

ateísmo NM atheism.

ateísta ADJ atheistic.

atejonarse [1a] VR (Méx) (a) (arrollarse) to curl up into a ball. (b) (hacerse más astuto) to become sharp (o cunning).

atelaje NM (a) (caballos) team (of horses). (b) (arreos) harness; (equipo) equipment; (*) trousseau.

atembado ADJ (And) silly, stupid; lacking in willpower.

atemorizar [1f] ① VT to frighten, scare.
② **atemorizarse** VR to get scared (de, por at).

atempar* [1a] VI (CAm) to wait, hang around.

atemperar [1a] VT (a) (moderar) to temper, moderate. (b) (ajustar) to adjust, accommodate (a to); **~ los gastos a los ingresos** (Com) to balance outgoings with income.

atemporal ADJ timeless.

atemporalado ADJ stormy.

atemporalidad NF timelessness.

Atenas NF Athens.

atenazar [1f] VT (fig) to grip; (duda etc) to torment, beset; **el miedo me atenazaba** I was gripped by fear.

atención NF (a) (gen) attention; care, heed; **¡~!** attention!; (aviso) look out!, careful!; (escrito en envase etc) 'with care'; **~ domiciliaria** home help; **~ primaria** primary (health) care; **¡~ a los pies!** mind your feet!; **'¡~! frenos potentes'** 'Beware!: powerful brakes'; **'¡~ a la velocidad!'** (Aut) 'watch your speed!'; **'¡~ a los precios!'** (Com) 'look at our prices!'; **'para (o a) la ~ de X'** (en sobre) 'for the attention of X'; **llamar la ~** to attract attention, catch the eye; **llamar la ~ de uno por algo** to rebuke sb for sth, find fault with sb over sth; **no me llama la ~** it doesn't surprise me; **me llamó la ~ un detalle** I was struck by a detail; **llamar la ~ de uno sobre un detalle** to draw sb's attention to a detail; **prestar ~** to pay attention, listen (a to).
(b) (amabilidad) kindness, civility; **atenciones** attentions, courtesies.
(c) (asuntos) **atenciones** affairs; duties, responsibilities.
(d) **en ~ a esto** in view of this, having regard to this.

atencioso ADJ (LAm) = atento.

atender [2g] ① VT (a) (gen) to attend to, pay attention to; consejo, aviso etc to heed; (Mec) to service, maintain; niño, enfermo etc to look after, care for; petición to comply with; **~ a un cliente** to serve a customer; **~ a uno que pregunta** to give full satisfaction to an inquirer; **~ sus compromisos** to meet one's obligations; **~ el teléfono** to mind the telephone, stay at the telephone; (Cono Sur, Méx) to answer the telephone; **~ una demanda** (Com) to meet a demand; **~ una tienda** (Com) to serve in a shop; to be in charge of a shop; **~ una orden** (Com) to attend to an order; **~ un giro** (Com) to honour a draft.

(b) (*LAm: asistir a*) to attend, be present at.

2 VI **(a)** ~ **a** to attend to, pay attention to; *detalles* to take note of; ~ **a un caso urgente** to see about an urgent matter; **¡atiende a lo tuyo!** (*Cono Sur*) mind your own business!

(b) ~ **por** to answer to the name of.

atendible ADJ acceptable, worthy of consideration; **esa objeción no es** ~ that objection is not valid, that objection is not to be entertained.

ateneo NM cultural association (*o* centre).

atenerse [2k] VR: ~ **a (a)** *regla* to abide by, obey; *verdad, opinión* to hold to; *promesa* to stand by, adhere to, keep to.

(b) (*contar con*) to rely on; **no saber a qué** ~ not to know what to expect; not to know what line to take; not to know where one stands; **lo hizo ateniéndose a que ...** he did it knowing that ..., he did it taking into account the fact that ...; ~ **a las consecuencias** to bear the consequences in mind.

ateniense ADJ, NMF Athenian.

atentado **1** ADJ (*prudente*) prudent, cautious; (*moderado*) moderate.

2 NM (*ofensa*) illegal act, offence; (*crimen*) outrage, crime; (*ataque*) assault, attack; attempt (*a, contra la vida de uno* on sb's life); ~ **terrorista** terrorist outrage; ~ **contra la honra,** ~ **contra el pudor** indecent assault.

atentamente ADV (*V ADJ*) **(a)** attentively. **(b)** politely; thoughtfully, kindly; (**le saluda**) ~ yours sincerely, sincerely yours (*US*); yours faithfully.

| ┌─ ¡ATENTAMENTE│ | *ver también la entrada* ─┐ |

Para traducir *atentamente* o *le saluda atentamente* al inglés británico hay que tener en cuenta la diferencia de uso entre *Yours sincerely* y *Yours faithfully*:

• Se traduce por *Yours sincerely* cuando hemos empezado la carta con *Dear Mr/Mrs Brown*, es decir, conocemos al destinatario y le queremos dar un tratamiento más cordial.

• Se traduce por *Yours faithfully* cuando no conocemos al destinatario de la carta y hemos empezado escribiendo *Dear Sir*, *Dear Sirs* o *Dear Sir or Madam*.

• En inglés americano se usa *Sincerely yours* en ambos casos.

---

atentar [1a] **1** VT *acto* to do illegally; *crimen* to attempt, try to commit.

2 VI: ~ **a,** ~ **contra** to commit an outrage against; ~ **contra la honra de una** to make an indecent assault on sb; ~ **contra la ley** to break the law; ~ **contra la vida de uno** to make an attempt on sb's life.

atentatorio ADJ illegal, criminal; **un acto** ~ **a ...** an act which poses a threat to ..., an act which undermines ...

atento ADJ **(a)** (*observador*) attentive (*a* to), observant, watchful (*a* of); **estar** ~ **a los peligros** to be mindful of the dangers.

(b) (*cortés*) polite; (*amable*) thoughtful, kind; (*servicial*) obliging; **ser** ~ **con uno** to be kind to sb, be considerate towards sb.

(c) **su atenta** (**carta**) (*Com*) your esteemed letter.

(d) ~ **a** *como prep* in view of, in consideration of; ~ **a que ...** *como conj* considering that ..., in view of the fact that ...

atenuación NF (*V vt*) attenuation; lessening, diminution; understatement; (*Jur*) extenuation.

atenuante **1** ADJ extenuating; **circunstancias** ~**s** extenuating circumstances, mitigating circumstances.

2 NF **(a)** ~**s** (*Jur*) extenuating circumstances. **(b)** (*LAm Jur; t* NM) excuse, plea.

atenuar [1e] **1** VT to attenuate; *crimen etc* to extenuate; *impacto* to cushion, lessen; *importancia* to lessen, minimize; *impresión etc* to tone down; to understate.

2 atenuarse VR to weaken.

ateo **1** ADJ atheistic.

2 NM, **atea** NF atheist.

ateperetarse [1a] VR (*CAm, Méx*) to get confused, get bewildered.

atepocate NM (*Méx Zool*) tadpole.

aterciopelado ADJ velvet (*atr*), velvety.

aterido ADJ numb, stiff with cold.

aterirse [3a; *defectivo; se usan el infin y pp*] VR to get numb, get stiff with cold.

aterrada NF (*Náut*) landfall.

aterrador ADJ frightening, terrifying; appalling.

aterraje NM (*Aer*) landing; (*Náut*) landfall.

aterrar¹ [1j] **1** VT **(a)** (*derribar*) to pull down, demolish, destroy.

(b) (*cubrir*) to cover with earth; (*Agr*) to earth up.

(c) (*CAm, Méx: obstruir*) to choke, obstruct.

2 VI (*Aer*) to land; (*Náut*) to reach land.

3 aterrarse VR (*Náut*) to stand inshore; **navegar aterrado** to sail inshore.

aterrar² [1a] **1** VT (*asustar*) to terrify, frighten; to appal.

2 aterrarse VR to be terrified, be frightened (*de* at); to be appalled

(*de* about, by); to panic.

aterrazamiento NM terracing.

aterrazar [1f] VT to terrace.

aterrizaje NM (*Aer*) landing; ~ **duro** hard landing; ~ **de emergencia,** ~ **forzoso** emergency landing, forced landing; ~ **de panza,** ~ **a vientre** pancake landing; ~ **suave** soft landing; ~ **violento** crash landing.

aterrizar [1f] VI (*Aer*) to land; (*persona*) to get out (of an aeroplane).

aterronar [1a] **1** VT to cake, harden.

2 aterronarse VR to get lumpy; to cake, harden.

aterrorizador ADJ terrifying, frightening.

aterrorizar [1f] VT to terrify; (*Mil, Pol etc*) to terrorize.

atersar [1a] VT to smooth.

atesar [1j] VT (*LAm*) = **atiesar**.

atesoramiento NM hoarding, accumulation.

atesorar [1a] VT to hoard, store up, accumulate; *virtudes etc* to possess.

atestación NF attestation.

atestado¹ NM (*Jur*) affidavit, sworn statement.

atestado² ADJ obstinate, stubborn.

atestado³ ADJ packed, cram-full; ~ **de** packed with, crammed with, full of; well-stocked with.

atestar¹ [1a] VT (*Jur*) to attest, testify to; (*fig*) to attest, vouch for; **una palabra no atestada** an unattested word, an unrecorded word.

atestar² [1j] **1** VT to pack, cram, stuff (*de* with); to fill up (*de* with); to crowd; ~ **a uno de frutas*** to stuff sb with fruit.

2 atestarse VR to stuff o.s.

atestiguación NF **(a)** attestation. **(b)** (*Jur*) deposition, testimony.

atestiguar [1i] VT (*Jur*) to testify to, bear witness to, give evidence of; (*fig*) to attest, vouch for.

atezado **1** ADJ **(a)** (*bronceado*) tanned; (*moreno*) swarthy. **(b)** (*negro*) black, blackened.

2 NM tanning; blackening.

atezar [1f] **1** VT **(a)** (*al sol*) to tan, burn. **(b)** (*ennegrecer*) to blacken, turn black.

2 atezarse VR to get tanned.

atiborrado ADJ: ~ **de** full of, stuffed with, crammed with.

atiborrar [1a] **1** VT to fill, stuff (*de* with); ~ **a un niño de dulces*** to stuff a child with sweets.

2 atiborrarse* VR to stuff o.s. (*de* with).

ático NM attic; (*apartamento*) penthouse.

atiesar [1a] **1** VT to stiffen; to tighten, tighten up; to tauten, stretch taut.

2 atiesarse VR to get stiff, stiffen (up); to tighten; to tauten; (*en la construcción*) to bind.

atigrado **1** ADJ striped, marked like a tiger; *gato* tabby.

2 NM tabby.

atigronarse [1a] VR (*Carib*) to get strong.

Atila NM Attila.

atildado ADJ neat, elegant, stylish.

atildar [1a] **1** VT **(a)** (*Tip*) to put a tilde (~) over, mark with a tilde.

(b) (*asear*) to tidy, clean (up); to improve the looks of; to put right.

(c) (*criticar*) to criticize, find fault with.

2 atildarse VR to spruce o.s. up, titivate o.s.

atilincar [1g] VT (*CAm*) to tighten, stretch.

atinadamente ADV correctly; sensibly; pertinently; **según dijo** ~ as he rightly said.

atinado ADJ (*correcto*) accurate, correct; (*juicioso*) wise, sensible, judicious; (*pertinente*) pertinent; (*agudo*) penetrating; **unas observaciones atinadas** some pertinent remarks; **una decisión poco atinada** a rather unwise decision.

atinar [1a] **1** VT *solución etc* to hit upon, find; (*acertar*) to guess right; (*encontrar*) to succeed in finding.

2 VI **(a)** (*gen*) to guess right; to be right, do the right thing; **siempre atina** he always gets it right, he always hits the nail on the head; **el médico no le atina** the doctor doesn't know what's wrong with him.

(b) ~ **al blanco** to hit the target; (*fig*) hit the mark; ~ **a,** ~ **con,** ~ **en** *solución etc* to hit upon, find, succeed in finding.

(c) ~ **a hacer algo** to succeed in doing sth, manage to do sth.

atingencia NF (*LAm*) **(a)** (*relación*) connection, bearing. **(b)** (*obligación*) obligation. **(c)** (*reserva*) qualification; (*aclaración*) clarification; (*observación*) remark, comment.

atingido ADJ **(a)** (*And, Cono Sur: deprimido*) depressed, down-in-the-mouth; (*débil*) feeble, weak; (*tímido*) timid. **(b)** (*And: sin dinero*) penniless. **(c)** (*Méx: taimado*) sly, cunning.

atingir [3c] VT **(a)** (*LAm*) to concern, bear on, relate to. **(b)** (*And*) to oppress.

atiparse* [1a] VR to stuff o.s.*

atípicamente ADV atypically, untypically.

atipicidad NF atypical nature.

atípico ADJ atypical, untypical, exceptional.

atiplado ADJ *voz* treble, high-pitched.

atiplar [1a] ☐1 vt *voz* to raise the pitch of.
  ☐2 **atiplarse** vr (*voz*) to go higher, become shrill; to go squeaky.
atipujarse [1a] vr (*CAm, Méx*) to stuff o.s.
atirantar [1a] ☐1 vt **(a)** to tighten, tauten; to stretch; **estar atirantado entre dos decisiones** to be torn between two decisions.
  (b) (*And, Cono Sur, Méx*) to spreadeagle, stretch out on the ground.
  ☐2 **atirantarse** vr (*Méx*) to peg out‡.
atisba nm (*And: vigilante*) watchman, look-out; (*espía*) spy.
atisbadero nm peephole.
atisbador(a) nm/f (*observador*) observer; watcher; (*espía*) spy.
atisbar [1a] vt (*espiar*) to spy on, watch; (*mirar*) to peep at; (*lograr ver*) to see, discern, make out; **~ a uno a través de una grieta** to peep at sb through a crack; **atisbamos un rayo de esperanza** we can just see a glimmer of hope.
atisbo nm **(a)** spying; watching; look, peep. **(b)** (*fig*) inkling, slight sign, first indication.
atizadero nm **(a)** poker. **(b)** (*fig*) spark, stimulus.
atizador nm poker.
atizar [1f] ☐1 vt **(a)** *fuego* to poke, stir; *horno* to stoke; *vela* to snuff, trim.
  (b) (*fig*) *motín etc* to stir up; *pasión* to fan, rouse.
  (c) (*) *golpe etc* to give; **se atizó el vaso** he knocked back the glassful*.
  ☐2 (*) vi: **¡atiza!** gosh!
  ☐3 **atizarse‡** vr to smoke pot‡.
atizonar [1a] vt (*Bot*) to blight, smut.
Atlante nm (*Mit*) Atlas.
Atlántico nm: **el (Océano) ~** the Atlantic (Ocean).
Atlántida nf Atlantis.
atlantista ☐1 adj relating to the Atlantic Alliance (*NATO*).
  ☐2 nmf supporter of the Atlantic Alliance (*NATO*).
atlas nm atlas.
atleta nmf athlete.
atlético adj athletic.
atletismo nm athletics; **~ en pista cubierta, ~ en sala** indoor athletics.
atmósfera nf **(a)** (*Fís y fig*) atmosphere.
  (b) (*fig*) atmosphere; (*campo*) sphere (of influence); (*sentimiento*) feeling (about o towards a person); **Juan tiene buena ~** (*LAm*) Juan enjoys considerable social standing, Juan stands well with everybody.
atmosférico adj atmospheric.
atoar [1a] vt (*Náut*) to tow.
atoc nm (*And*) fox.
atocar [1g] vt (*LAm*) = **tocar.**
atocha nf esparto.
atochal nm esparto field.
atochamiento nm (*Cono Sur*) traffic jam.
atochar nm = **atochal.**
atocinado adj fat, well-upholstered*.
atocinar [1a] ☐1 vt **(a)** *cerdo* to cut up; to make into bacon; *carne* to cure. **(b)**(‡) to do in‡, carve up*.
  ☐2 **atocinarse** vr (*sulfurarse*) to get het up; (*enamorarse*) to fall madly in love.
atocle nm (*Méx*) sandy soil rich in humus.
atol nm (*LAm*) *drink o gruel) made of maize flour.*
atolada nf (*CAm*) party.
atole nm (*Méx*) = **atol.**
atoleada nf (*CAm*) party.
atolería nf (*LAm*) stall (*etc*) where *atol* is sold.
atolladero nm **(a)** (*lodazal*) muddy place; mire, morass.
  (b) (*fig*) (*aprieto*) awkward spot, jam*; (*situación violenta*) embarrassing situation; **estar en un ~** to be in a jam*; **sacar a uno del ~** to get sb out of a fix*; **salir del ~** to get out of a jam*.
atollar(se) [1a] vi *y* vr **(a)** (*atascarse*) to get stuck in the mud, get bogged down. **(b)** (*fig*) to get into a jam*, get stuck.
atolón nm atoll.
atolondrado adj (*casquivano*) scatterbrained; (*tonto*) silly; (*aturdido*) bewildered; (*pasmado*) stunned, amazed; (*irreflexivo*) thoughtless, reckless.
atolondramiento nm silliness; bewilderment; stunned state, amazement; thoughtlessness, recklessness.
atolondrar [1a] ☐1 vt *confundir* to bewilder; *pasmar* to stun, amaze.
  ☐2 **atolondrarse** vr to be bewildered; to be stunned, be amazed.
atomía nf (*LAm*) **(a)** (*acto*) evil deed, savage act. **(b) decir ~s** to shoot one's mouth off* (*a uno* to sb).
atómico adj atomic.
atomista ☐1 adj atomistic.
  ☐2 nmf atomist.
atomización nf (*Pol, Com etc*) fragmentation.
atomizador nm atomizer; (*de perfume etc*) spray, scent spray.
atomizar [1f] ☐1 vt to atomize; to spray.
  ☐2 **atomizarse** vr to break up (*en* into), fragment.

átomo nm atom; (*fig*) atom, particle, speck; **~ de vida** spark of life; **ni un ~ de** not a trace of.
atonal adj atonal.
atonía nf lethargy, apathy.
atónito adj amazed, astounded (*con, de, por* at, by); **me miró ~** he looked at me in amazement.
átono adj atonic, unstressed.
atontadamente adv in a bewildered way; foolishly, sillily.
atontado adj **(a)** (*aturdido*) stunned, bewildered. **(b)** (*tonto*) silly, dim-witted*.
atontar [1a] ☐1 vt **(a)** to stun, stupefy. **(b)** (*fig*) to stun, bewilder.
  ☐2 **atontarse** vr to get bewildered, get confused.
atontolinamiento nm bewilderment.
atontolinar [1a] vt to daze; to stun; **quedar atontolinado** to be in a daze.
atorafo adj (*Carib*) anxious.
atorar [1a] ☐1 vt **(a)** (*obstruir*) to stop up, choke, obstruct; (*inmovilizar*) to stop, immobilize.
  (b) (*Carib, Méx: fig*) to block, impede.
  (c) (*) to annoy, bother, upset; **¡no me atores!** stop bothering me!; **estoy atorado de ti** I'm fed up with you*.
  ☐2 **atorarse**[1] vr (*atragantarse*) to choke, swallow the wrong way; (*trabarse la lengua*) to get tongue-tied; to have nothing to say, be unable to respond.
atorarse[2] [1a] vr (*Cono Sur*) to get wild, get fierce.
atormentador(a) ☐1 adj tormenting.
  ☐2 nm/f tormentor.
atormentar [1a] ☐1 vt to torture; (*fig*) to torture, torment; (*acosar*) to plague, harass; (*tentar*) to tantalize.
  ☐2 **atormentarse** vr to torment o.s., suffer agonies of mind.
atornillador nm screwdriver.
atornillar [1a] vt **(a)** (*lit*) to screw on; to screw up; to screw down; to screw together. **(b)** (*LAm*: *fastidiar*) to pester, harass.
atoro nm (*LAm*) destruction; (*fig*) tight spot, difficulty.
atorón nm (*Méx*) traffic-jam.
atorozarse [1f] vr (*CAm*) to choke, swallow the wrong way.
atorrante ☐1 adj **(a)** *calor* baking. **(b)** (*LAm*: *vago*) lazy.
  ☐2 nm tramp, bum (*US*).
atorrantear [1a] vi (*Cono Sur*) to live like a tramp, be on the bum (*US*).
atortolado adj: **están ~s** they're like two turtle-doves.
atortolar [1a] vt (*asustar*) to rattle*, scare; (*pasmar*) to shatter, flabbergast.
atortujar [1a] ☐1 vt to squeeze flat.
  ☐2 **atortujarse** vr (*CAm*) to be shattered, be flabbergasted.
atorunado adj (*Cono Sur*) stocky, bull-necked.
atosigador adj **(a)** poisonous. **(b)** (*fig*) pestering, worrisome; pressing.
atosigante adj = **atosigador (b).**
atosigar [1h] ☐1 vt **(a)** (*envenenar*) to poison. **(b)** (*fig*) (*importunar*) to plague, badger, harass; (*presionar*) to rush, put the pressure on.
  ☐2 **atosigarse** vr to be in a rush, get rushed.
atóxico adj non-poisonous.
atrabancar [1g] ☐1 vt to rush, hurry over.
  ☐2 **atrabancarse** vr to be in a fix, get into a jam.
atrabiliario adj bad-tempered, difficult, moody.
atrabilis nf (*fig*) bad temper, difficult temperament, moodiness.
atracadero nm berth, wharf, landing place.
atracado adj (*LAm*) mean, stingy.
atracador nm hold-up man, bandit, gangster.
atracar [1g] ☐1 vt **(a)** *banco etc* to hold up; *viajero* to attack, waylay; (*Aer*) to hijack.
  (b) (*Náut*) to tie up, moor, bring alongside; *astronave* to dock (*a* with).
  (c) (*atiborrar*) to stuff, cram (with food).
  (d) (*Carib Aut*) to park.
  ☐2 vi (*Náut*) to tie up, moor, come alongside; (*astronave*) to dock (*a* with); **~ al muelle, ~ en el muelle** to tie up at the quay, berth at the quay.
  ☐3 **atracarse** vr **(a)** to cram, stuff o.s. (*de* with).
  (b) (*Carib, Cono Sur*: *acercarse*) to approach, come up; **~ a** to approach, come up to.
  (c) (*Carib*: *pelear*) to brawl, fight.
atracción nf **(a)** (*gen*) attraction; (*de persona*) attractiveness, appeal, charm; **~ gravitatoria** gravity, gravitational attraction; **~ sexual** sexual attraction, (*de persona*) sex-appeal. **(b)** (*diversión*) amusement; **atracciones** (*Teat*) attractions, entertainment, floor show; (*de feria*) stalls, sideshows.
atraco nm hold-up, robbery; (*Aer*) hijack(ing); **~ a mano armada** armed robbery; **¡es un ~!** (*fig*) it's sheer robbery!
atracón nm blow-out‡; **darse un ~** to stuff o.s.; **darse un ~ de** to stuff o.s. with, make a pig of o.s. over.

atractivamente ADV attractively.

atractividad NF attractiveness.

atractivo [1] ADJ attractive.
[2] NM attraction; attractiveness, appeal, charm.

atraer [2p] [1] VT (gen) to attract; to draw; to lure; atención to attract, engage; imaginación to appeal to; adhesión to attract, win, draw; **dejarse ~ por** to allow o.s. to be drawn towards; **sabe ~(se) a la juventud** he knows how to win young people over.
[2] **atraerse** VR: **se atrajo las simpatías de todos** he won everyone's affection, everyone liked him; **se atrajo el rencor del jefe** the boss began to resent him.

atragantarse [1a] VR (a) (al comer) to choke (con on), swallow the wrong way; **se me atragantó una miga** a crumb went the wrong way.
(b) (fig: al hablar) to get mixed up, lose the thread of what one is saying.
(c) **Pepe se me ha atragantado** (fig) Pepe sticks in my gullet, I can't bear Pepe.

atrague NM: **¡que ~!** (Carib) what an idiot!

atraillar [1a] VT to put on a leash.

atramparse [1a] VR (a) (persona) to fall into a trap; (fig) to get stuck, get o.s. into a jam. (b) (tubo) to clog, get blocked up; (atascarse) to stick, catch, jam.

atrancar [1g] [1] VT puerta to bar, bolt; tubo to clog, block up; (fig) escotillas to batten down; (Cono Sur) to constipate.
[2] VI to stride along, take big steps; (fig: al leer) to skip a lot.
[3] **atrancarse** VR (a) to get stuck, get bogged down (en in); (fig) to get stuck.
(b) (Cono Sur* Med) to get constipated.
(c) (Méx: porfiarse) to dig one's heels in.

atranco NM = atascadero.

atrapada NF (Dep) save.

atrapamaridos* [1] ADJ INVAR: **mujer ~ = 2.**
[2] NF woman on the look-out for a husband.

atrapamoscas NM INVAR flypaper.

atrapar [1a] VT (a) (en trampa) to trap; (coger) to catch, nab*, overtake; puesto to get, land; catarro to catch; **quedaron atrapados en la montaña** they were trapped on the mountainside.
(b) (fig) to take in, deceive.

atraque NM (a) (Náut) mooring place, berth. (b) (de astronave) link-up, docking.

atrás [1] ADV (a) (lugar) **¡~!** back!, get back!; **estar ~** to be behind; to be in the rear; **está más ~** it's further back; **ir (hacia) ~** to go back, go backwards; to go to the rear; **rueda de ~** rear wheel, back wheel.
(b) (tiempo) previously; **días ~** days ago, days before; **4 meses ~** 4 ▼ months back; **más ~** earlier, longer ago; **desde muy ~** for a very long time.
(c) (Cono Sur) **~ mío** behind me.
[2] **~ de** PREP (LAm) = detrás de.

atrasado [1] ADJ (a) (con retraso) slow, late, late (time); pago overdue; (Tip) número back (atr); andar **~, estar ~** (reloj) to be slow; **estar un poco ~** (persona) to be a bit behind; **estar ~ en los pagos** to be behind, be in arrears; **estar ~ de noticias** to be behind the times, lack up-to-date information; **estar ~ de medios** to be short of resources; **estar ~** (CAm*) to be broke*.
(b) país backward; underdeveloped; alumno etc slow, backward.
(c) (Cono Sur Med etc) ill.
[2] NM: **es un ~** he's behind the times.

atrasar [1a] [1] VT progreso to slow down, slow up, retard; salida to delay; reloj to put back.
[2] VI (reloj) to lose, be slow; **mi reloj atrasa 8 minutos** my watch is 8 minutes slow.
[3] **atrasarse** VR (a) (quedarse atrás) to be behind; to lag, stay back, remain behind; (tren etc) to be late; (reloj) to lose, be slow; **~ en los pagos** to be in arrears.
(b) (LAm) proyecto etc to suffer a setback; (Cono Sur: lastimarse) to hurt o.s. (de in); (mujer) to be pregnant.

atraso NM (a) (gen) delay, time lag; (de reloj) slowness; (de país etc) backwardness; **el tren lleva ~** the train is late; **salir del ~** to catch up, make up lost time; **llegar con 20 minutos de ~** to arrive 20 minutes late.
(b) **~s** (Com, Fin) arrears; (de pedidos etc) backlog, quantity pending; (And, Carib) setback; **cobrar ~s** to collect arrears.
(c) **tener un ~** (LAm Med) to have a period.

atravesada NF (LAm) crossing, passage.

atravesado ADJ (a) (oblicuo) crossed, laid across, oblique. (b) (de vista) squinting, cross-eyed. (c) perro etc mongrel, crossbred. (d) (malo) wicked, evil; treacherous.

atravesar [1j] [1] VT (a) (persona) to cross, cross over, go across, go over; to pass through; rápidos etc to negotiate; período to go through, pass through; **atravesamos un momento difícil** we are going through a difficult time.

(b) (bala, espada) to pierce, go through, transfix; **~ a uno con una espada** to run sb through with a sword; **la bala atravesó el metal** the bullet passed through the metal.
(c) (puente etc) to cross, span, bridge.
(d) objeto to lay across, put across; to put crosswise, put obliquely; **~ un tronco en el camino** to lay a tree trunk across the road.
(e) dinero to bet, lay, stake.
(f) (LAm Com) to monopolize, corner (the market in).
(g) **le tengo atravesado** he sticks in my gullet, I can't stand him.
[2] **atravesarse** VR (a) (obstáculo) to come in between; to interfere; (problema etc) to arise, spring up; (hueso etc) to stick in one's throat.
(b) **~ en una conversación** to butt into a conversation; **~ en un negocio** to meddle in an affair.
(c) **se me atraviesa el tipo ese** I can't stand that fellow.
(d) (dos personas) to wrangle, bicker, get across each other; **se atravesaron en la calle** (LAm) they bumped into each other in the street.

atrayente ADJ attractive.

atrechar [1a] VI (Carib) to take a short cut.

atrecho NM (Carib) short cut.

atreguar [1i] [1] VT to grant a truce to.
[2] **atreguarse** VR to agree to a truce.

atrenzo NM (LAm) trouble, difficulty; **estar en un ~** to be in trouble, have a problem.

atreverse [2a] VR (a) to dare; **no me atrevo, no me atrevería** I wouldn't dare; **¿te atreves?** are you game?, will you?; **¡atrévete!** just you dare!; **~ a hacer algo** to dare to do sth, venture to do sth; **~ a una empresa** to undertake a task, dare to undertake a task; **~ con un rival** to take on a rival, (venture to) compete with a rival; **se atreve con todo** he'll tackle anything; **me atrevo con una tarta** I could manage a cake.
(b) **~ con uno, ~ contra uno** to be insolent to sb.

atrevidamente ADV (a) boldly, daringly. (b) insolently, disrespectfully, impudently.

atrevido ADJ (a) (audaz) bold, daring. (b) (insolente) insolent, disrespectful; (descarado) impudent, forward; chiste etc daring, risqué.

atrevimiento NM (a) (audacia) boldness, daring, audacity.
(b) (pey) insolence; impudence, forwardness.

atrevismo NM ostentatious; daring.

atrezzo NM (Teat) properties; (fig) kit, gear.

atribución NF (a) (acto) attribution. (b) (de puesto) powers, authority, functions.

atribuible ADJ attributable (a to); **obras ~s a Góngora** works which are attributed to Góngora, works probably by Góngora.

atribuir [3g] [1] VT (a) **~ a** to attribute to; to put down to; to ascribe to, impute to.
(b) **las funciones atribuidas a mi cargo** the powers conferred on me by my post, the authority which goes with the post I hold.
[2] **atribuirse** VR: **~ algo** to assume sth, claim sth for o.s.; to arrogate sth to o.s.; **~ la responsabilidad de un atentado** to claim responsibility for an attack.

atribulación NF affliction, suffering, tribulation.

atribulado [1] ADJ afflicted, suffering.
[2] NM: **los ~s** the afflicted, the suffering, the sufferers.

atribular [1a] [1] VT to grieve, afflict.
[2] **atribularse** VR to grieve, be distressed.

atributivo ADJ attributive.

atributo NM (gen) attribute; (emblema) emblem, sign of authority.

atril NM (Ecl etc) lectern; (para libro) bookrest, reading desk; (Mús) music stand.

atrincar [1g] [1] VT (LAm) to tie up tightly.
[2] **atrincarse** VR (Méx) to be stubborn, dig one's heels in.

atrincheramiento NM entrenchment.

atrincherar [1a] [1] VT to surround with a trench, fortify with trenches.
[2] **atrincherarse** VR (a) to entrench (o.s.), dig in; **están muy fuertemente atrincherados** (fig) they are very strongly entrenched.
(b) **~ en** (fig) to take one's stand on; to take refuge in.

atrio NM (Hist) atrium, inner courtyard; (Ecl) vestibule, porch; (de garaje) forecourt.

atrochar [1a] VI to go by the byways; to take a short cut.

atrocidad NF (a) (desmán) atrocity, outrage.
(b) (tontería) silly remark, foolish thing (to do); **decir ~es** to say silly things.
(c) (*) enormity, crime; **¡qué ~!** how dreadful!; **la comedia es una ~** the play is awful; **como me fastidian hago ~es** if they upset me I'll do sth dreadful; **me gustan los helados una ~** I'm awfully fond of ice cream.

atrofia NF atrophy.

atrofiar [1b] [1] VT to atrophy.
[2] **atrofiarse** VR to atrophy.

atrojarse [1a] VR (Carib) to find no way out, be cornered; (Méx) to be-

➤ LENGUA Y USO: **atribuir: 1a → 44.2**

come confused, be bewildered.

atrompetado ADJ: **nariz atrompetada** flared nostrils *pl*.

atronadamente ADV recklessly, thoughtlessly.

atronado ADJ reckless, thoughtless.

atronador ADJ deafening; *aplausos* thunderous.

atronamiento NM *(fig)* bewilderment, confusion, stunned state.

atronar [1l] VT (a) *(ensordecer)* to deafen. (b) *(aturdir)* to stun, daze; *(acogotar)* to fell with a blow on the neck. (c) *(fig)* to stun; to bewilder, confuse.

atropellada NF *(Cono Sur)* attack, onrush.

atropelladamente ADV *correr etc* pell-mell, helter-skelter; *decidir* hastily; *hablar* incoherently, in a rushed way.

atropellado ADJ *acto* hasty, precipitate, impetuous; *manera* brusque, abrupt; violent.

atropellador NM lout, hooligan.

atropellaplatos* NM INVAR clumsy servant; clumsy sort.

atropellar [1a] **1** VT (a) *(pisotear)* to trample underfoot; *(derribar)* to knock down; *(empujar)* to push violently past; *(Aut etc)* to knock down, run over, run down; *figura famosa* to mob, overwhelm.
(b) *(fig)* *trabajo* to do hurriedly, hurry over; *derechos* to disregard, trample; *oposición, opiniones* to ride roughshod over; *inferior* to bully, oppress; *sentimientos* to insult, outrage; *constitución* to violate.
(c) *(LAm)* to make love to; to seduce, dishonour.
2 VI: **~ por** to push one's way violently through.
(b) *(fig)* to disregard, ride roughshod over; **atropella por todo** he doesn't respect anything, he doesn't give a damn for anybody.
3 **atropellarse** VR to act hastily, do things thoughtlessly.

atropello NM (a) *(Aut etc)* accident; knocking down, running over.
(b) *(fig)* outrage *(de* upon); abuse *(de* of); disregard *(de* for); **los ~s del dictador** the dictator's crimes, the outrages committed by the dictator.

atroz ADJ (a) *(gen)* atrocious; *(cruel)* cruel, inhuman; *(escandaloso)* outrageous. (b) (*) *(grande)* huge, terrific; *(malo)* dreadful, awful.

atrozmente ADV (a) atrociously; cruelly; outrageously. (b) (*) dreadfully.

ATS NMF ABR *de* **ayudante técnico sanitario** nursing assistant.

atta., atto. ABR *de* **atenta, atento** *(in courtesy formula in letters).*

attaché NM attaché case.

attrezzo NM *(Teat)* properties; *(fig)* kit, gear.

ATUDEM NF ABR *de* **Asociación Turística de Estaciones de Esquí y Montaña.**

atuendo NM (a) *(vestido)* attire; *(hum)* rig, getup*. (b) *(boato)* pomp, show.

atufado ADJ (a) *(Cono Sur*: enojado)* angry, mad*. (b) *(CAm, Carib*: vanidoso)* proud, vain, stuck-up*.

atufamiento NM *(fig)* irritation, vexation.

atufar [1a] **1** VT (a) to overcome (with smell *o* fumes).
(b) *(fig)* to irritate, vex.
2 **atufarse** VR (a) *(vino)* to turn sour.
(b) *(persona)* to be overcome (with smell *o* fumes).
(c) *(fig)* to get angry, get mad* *(con, de, por* at, with; *t Cono Sur)*; *(And)* to get bewildered, become confused; *(CAm, Carib)* to be proud, get vain.

atufo NM irritation.

atulipanado ADJ tulip-shaped.

atún NM (a) (blue-fin) tuna, tunny; **querer ir por ~ y ver al duque** to want to have it both ways, want to have one's cake and eat it too. (b) (*) nitwit*.

atunero **1** ADJ tuna *(atr).*
2 NM (a) *(persona)* tuna fisherman. (b) *(barco)* tuna fishing boat.

aturar [1a] VT to close up tight.

aturdidamente ADV (a) in a bewildered way. (b) thoughtlessly, recklessly.

aturdido ADJ (a) *(atolondrado)* bewildered, dazed, stunned. (b) *(irreflexivo)* thoughtless, reckless.

aturdidura NF *(Cono Sur)*, **aturdimiento** NM (a) stunned state, dazed condition; bewilderment, confusion; amazement. (b) thoughtlessness, recklessness.

aturdir [3a] **1** VT (a) *(físicamente: con golpe)* to stun, daze; *(ruido)* to deafen; *(droga, vino etc)* to stupefy, fuddle; *(movimiento)* to make giddy.
(b) *(fig)* *(atolondrar)* to stun, dumbfound; *(dejar perplejo)* to bewilder, confuse, perplex; **la noticia nos aturdió** the news stunned us.
2 **aturdirse** VR to be stunned; to get bewildered, get confused.

aturrullado ADJ bewildered, perplexed; flustered.

aturrullar [1a] **1** VT to bewilder, perplex; to fluster.
2 **aturrullarse** VR to get bewildered; to get flustered, get het up; ₁**no te aturrulles cuando surja una dificultad** don't get flustered when sth awkward comes up.

atusamiento NM smartness, elegance.

atusar [1a] **1** VT *(cortar)* to trim; *(alisar)* to comb, smooth.
2 **atusarse** VR *(fig)* to overdress, dress in great style.

audacia NF boldness, audacity.

audaz ADJ bold, audacious.

audazmente ADV boldly, audaciously.

audibilidad NF audibility.

audible ADJ audible.

audición NF (a) *(gen)* hearing. (b) *(Teat etc)* audition; **dar ~ a uno** to audition sb, give sb an audition; **le hicieron una ~ para el papel** they gave him an audition for the part.
(c) *(Mús)* concert; **~ radiofónica** radio concert.
(d) *(LAm Com, Fin)* audit.

audiencia NF (a) *(acto)* audience, hearing; *(entrevista)* formal interview; **recibir a uno en ~** to grant sb an audience, receive sb in audience.
(b) *(sala)* audience chamber; *(Jur)* high court.
(c) *(personas)* audience; *(de periódico)* readership.

audífono NM *(de sordo)* hearing-aid, deaf-aid; *(LAm Telec)* earpiece, receiver; **~s** headphones.

audímetro NM audience meter.

audio NM audio.

audiofrecuencia NF audio-frequency.

audiómetro NM audiometer.

audiovisual ADJ audio-visual.

auditar [1a] VT to audit.

auditivo **1** ADJ auditory, hearing *(atr).*
2 NM *(Telec)* earpiece, receiver.

audito NM audit, auditing.

auditor(a)[1] NM/F (a) *(t* **~ de guerra**) judge-advocate. (b) *(Com, Fin)* auditor; **~ de cuentas** auditor. (c) *(Méx Ferro)* ticket inspector.

auditora[2] NF firm of auditors, accountancy firm.

auditoría NF *(Com, Fin)* audit(ing); **~ administrativa, ~ de gestión, ~ operativa** management audit; **~ externa** external audit; **~ general** general audit; **~ interna** internal audit.

auditorio NM (a) *(personas)* audience. (b) *(sala: t* **auditorium** NM) auditorium, hall.

auge NM *(cima)* peak, summit, zenith; *(Astron)* apogee; *(aumento)* increase *(de* of); *(período)* period of increase, period of prosperity; *(Com)* boom *(de* in); **estar en ~** to thrive, run at a high level, do well; *(Com)* to boom.

Augías NM: **establos de ~** Augean Stables.

augurar [1a] VT *(suceso)* to augur, portend; *(persona)* to predict; **~ que ...** to predict that ...

augurio NM (a) *(gen)* augury; *(presagio)* omen, portent; *(profecía)* prediction; **consultar los ~s** to take the auguries.
(b) **~s** best wishes; **con nuestros ~s para ...** with our best wishes for ...; **mensaje de buenos ~s** goodwill message.

augustal ADJ Augustan.

Augusto NM Augustus.

augusto ADJ august.

aula NF *(Escol)* classroom; *(Univ)* lecture room; **~ magna** assembly hall, main hall.

aulaga NF furze, gorse.

aulario NM *(Univ)* lecture room building, block of lecture rooms.

áulico **1** ADJ court *(atr)*, palace *(atr).*
2 NM courtier.

aullar [1a] VI to howl; to yell.

aullido NM, **aúllo** NM howl, yell; **dar aullidos** to howl, yell.

aumentador NM *(Elec)* booster.

aumentar [1a] **1** VT *(gen)* to increase, add to, augment; *precio* to increase, raise, put up; *producción* to increase, step up; *(Elec)* to boost, step up; *(Ópt)* to magnify; *(Fot)* to enlarge; *(Rad)* to amplify; *detalles, impresión etc* to magnify, exaggerate; **esto viene a ~ el número de ...** this helps to swell the numbers of ...
2 VI *y* **aumentarse** VR to increase, be on the increase; to multiply; to rise, go up; *(valor)* to appreciate.

aumentativo ADJ, NM augmentative.

aumento NM (a) increase; *(de precio)* increase, rise; *(de sueldo)* rise, raise (US); *(de valor)* appreciation; *(Ópt)* magnification; *(Fot)* enlargement; *(Rad)* amplification; **~ lineal** across-the-board pay rise; **~ de población** population increase; **~ de precio** rise in price; **~ salarial** wage increase; **eso le valió un ~** that got him a rise (in salary); **ir en ~** to increase, be on the increase; to prosper, do well; **una población que va en continuo ~** an ever-growing population.
(b) *(CAm, Méx: en una carta)* postscript.

aun ADV even; **~ los que tienen dinero** even those who have money; **ni ~ si me lo regalas** not even if you give it to me; **~ así, ~ siendo esto así** even so; **~ cuando** although, even though; **más ~** even more.

aún ADV still, yet; **~ está aquí** he's still here; **~ no lo sabemos** we still don't know, we don't know yet; **¿no ha venido ~?** hasn't he come yet?

aunar [1a] **1** VT to join, unite, combine.
2 **aunarse** VR to unite, combine.

aunque CONJ though, although, even though; **~ llueva vendremos** we'll come even if it rains; **es guapa ~ algo bajita** she's pretty but rather short, she's pretty even if she is on the short side; **~ no me creas** even though you may not believe me; **~ más ...** however much ..., no matter how much ...

┌─ AUNQUE ─┐ **ver también la entrada**

Aunque se puede traducir al inglés por *although*, *though*, *even though* o *even if*.

● Por regla general, cuando la cláusula introducida por *aunque* indica un hecho (*aunque* + INDICATIVO), en inglés coloquial se traduce por *though* y en lenguaje más formal por *although*:
    Aunque había un montón de gente, al final pude encontrar a Carlos
    Though there were a lot of people there, I managed to find Carlos
    No esperaba eso de él, aunque entiendo por qué lo hizo
    I did not expect that from him, although I can understand why he did it

● *Even though* introduce la oración subordinada, enfatizando con más fuerza el contraste con la principal, cuando *aunque* va seguido de un hecho concreto, no una hipótesis, y equivale a *a pesar de que*:
    Llevaba un abrigo de piel, aunque era un día muy caluroso
    She wore a fur coat, even though it was a very hot day

● Si *aunque* tiene el sentido de *incluso si* (*aunque* + SUBJUNTIVO), se traduce por *even if*:
    Debes ir, aunque no quieras
    You must go, even if you don't want to
    Me dijo que no me lo diría, aunque lo supiera
    He said he wouldn't tell me even if he knew
    Para otros usos y ejemplos ver la entrada.

---

aúpa* ① INTERJ up!, up you get!; up with it! (*etc*); **¡~ Toboso!** up Toboso!
    ② *como* ADJ(*): **una función de ~** a slap-up do*, a posh affair*; **una paliza de ~** a thrashing and a half; **una tormenta de ~** a real storm, the father and mother of a storm*; (*iró*) **es de ~** it's terribly bad, it's absolutely awful.

au pair ① ADJ, ADV au pair; **chica ~ = 2.**
    ② NF au pair (girl).

aupar* [1a] VT *persona* to help up, get up; *pantalón etc* to hitch up, hoist up; (*fig*) to boost, praise up; **~ a uno al poder** to raise sb to power.

aura NF (a) gentle breeze, sweet breeze. (b) (*fig*) popularity, popular favour; aura.

áureo ADJ (a) (*liter*) golden. (b) (*Esp Hist*) **nuestra literatura áurea** Golden Age literature.

aureola NF, **auréola** NF halo, aureole.

aureolar†† [1a] VT (*esp LAm*) *persona* to praise, extol the virtues of; *reputación etc* to enhance, add lustre to.

aurícula NF (*Anat*) auricle.

auricular ① ADJ auricular, aural, of the ear.
    ② NM (a) (*dedo*) little finger. (b) (*Telec*) earpiece, receiver; **~es** headphones, earphones.

auriculoterapia NF auriculotherapy.

aurífero ADJ gold-bearing.

aurora NF (*lit, fig*) dawn; **~ boreal(is)** aurora borealis, northern lights.

auscultación NF sounding, auscultation.

auscultar [1a] VT (*Med*) *pecho etc* to sound, auscultate.

ausencia NF absence; **en ~ del gato se divierten los ratones** when the cat's away the mice will play; **condenar a uno en su ~** to sentence sb in his absence; **hacer buenas ~s de uno** to speak kindly of sb in his absence, remember sb with affection; **tener buenas ~s** to have a good reputation; *V* **brillar.**

ausentarse [1a] VR to go away, absent o.s. (*de* from); to stay away (*de* from).

ausente ① ADJ absent (*de* from); **estar ~ de** to be absent from, be missing from; **estar ~ de su casa** to be away from home.
    ② NMF absentee; (*Jur*) missing person.

auspiciado ADJ sponsored, backed.

auspiciador ① ADJ: **firma ~a** sponsoring firm.
    ② NM, **auspiciadora** NF sponsor.

auspiciar [1b] VT (a) (*apoyar*) to back, sponsor. (b) (*LAm*) (*desear éxito*) to wish good luck to.

auspicios NMPL (*esp LAm*) auspices; (*protección*) protection, patronage; (*patrocinio*) sponsorship; **bajo los ~ de** under the auspices of, sponsored by.

auspicioso ADJ (*LAm*) auspicious.

austeramente ADV austerely; sternly, severely.

austeridad NF austerity; sternness, severity; **~ económica** economic austerity.

austero ADJ austere; stern, severe.

austral ① ADJ (a) southern; **el Hemisferio A~** the Southern Hemisphere. (b) (*Cono Sur*) of (*o* from) southern Chile.
    ② NM (*Cono Sur Fin*) standard monetary unit of Argentina (*since 1985*).

Australia NF Australia.

australiano, -a ADJ, NM/F Australian.

australopiteco, -a NM/F, **australopitecus** NMF Australopithecus.

Austria NF Austria.

austriaco, -a, austríaco, -a ADJ, NM/F Austrian.

austro NM (*liter*) south; (*viento*) south wind.

austro-húngaro ADJ Austro-Hungarian.

autarquía NF (*Pol*) autarchy, self-government; (*Econ*) autarky, national self-sufficiency.

autazo NM (*LAm*) theft of a car.

auténtica NF certificate, certification; authorized copy.

auténticamente ADV authentically; genuinely, really.

autenticar [1g] VT to authenticate.

autenticidad NF authenticity; genuineness.

auténtico ADJ (a) authentic; genuine, real; **un ~ espíritu de servicio** a true spirit of service; **es un ~ campeón** he's a real champion; **éste es copia y no el ~** this one is a copy and not the real one; **días de ~ calor** days of real heat, really hot days; **ir de ~*, ser de ~*** to be absolutely with it*. (b) (*) great*, brilliant*.

autentificar [1g] VT to authenticate.

autería NF (*Cono Sur: presagio*) evil omen, bad sign; (*brujería*) witchcraft.

autero¹, -a NM/F (*LAm*) car thief.

autero², -a NM/F (*Cono Sur*) (*pesimista*) pessimist, defeatist; (*mal augurio*) jinx*, person who brings bad luck.

autillo NM tawny owl.

autismo NM autism.

autista ADJ, **autístico** ADJ autistic.

auto¹ NM (*Aut*) car, automobile (*US*); **~ de choque** bumper car, dodgem.

auto² NM (a) (*Jur*) edict, judicial decree; writ, order; document; **~ de ejecución** writ of execution; **~ de prisión** warrant for arrest; **~ de procesamiento** charge, indictment.
    (b) **~s** documents, proceedings, court record; **estar en ~s** to be in the know; **poner a uno en ~s** to put sb in the picture.
    (c) (*Ecl y Teat*) mystery play, religious play, allegory; **~ del nacimiento** nativity play; **~ sacramental** eucharistic play.
    (d) (*Ecl*) **~ de fe** auto-da-fé; **hacer un ~ de fe de** (*fig*) to burn.

auto... PREF auto..., self...

autoabastecerse [2d] VR to supply o.s. (*de* with); to be self-sufficient.

autoabastecimiento NM self-sufficiency.

autoacusación NF self-accusation.

autoacusarse [1a] VR to accuse o.s.

autoadherente ADJ self-adhesive.

autoadhesivo ADJ self-adhesive; *sobre* self-sealing.

autoadministrarse [1a] VR (a) **~ una droga** to take a drug. (b) (*Pol*) to govern o.s., be self-governing.

autoadulación NF self-praise.

autoafirmación NF assertiveness.

autoaislarse [1a] VR to isolate o.s.

autoalarma NF car alarm.

autoalimentación NF: **~ de hojas** (*Inform*) automatic paper feed.

autoanálisis NM self-analysis.

autoanalizarse [1f] VR to analyze o.s., do self-analysis.

autoaprovisionamiento NM self-sufficiency.

autoayuda NF self-help.

autobiografía NF autobiography.

autobiográfico ADJ autobiographic(al).

autobomba NF fire-engine.

autobombearse* [1a] VR to blow one's own trumpet, shoot a line*.

autobombo* NM self-advertisement, self-glorification; **hacer ~** to blow one's own trumpet.

autobronceador NM bronzing lotion.

autobús NM bus, omnibus (††); coach (*Brit*); (*LAm: de distancia*) coach (*Brit*), long-distance bus (*US*); **~ de dos pisos** double-decker bus; **~ escolar** school bus; **~ de línea** coach (*Brit*), long-distance bus (*US*).

autobusero ① ADJ bus (*atr*).
    ② NM, **autobusera** NF bus driver.

autocalificarse [1g] VR: **~ de** to describe o.s. as.

autocar NM coach, bus.

autocaravana NF camper, camping vehicle.

autocargador ADJ: **camión ~** self-loading truck.

autocarril NM (*LAm*) railway car.

autocartera NF holding of its own shares (*by a company*).

autocensura NF self-censorship.

auto-choque NM bumper car, dodgem.

autocine NM drive-in cinema.

autoclave NM pressure cooker; (*Med*) sterilizing apparatus.

autocompasión NF self-pity.
autocomplaciente ADJ self-satisfied.
autocomprobación NF (*Inform*) self-test.
autoconcederse [2a] VR: **~ un título** to grant o.s. a title.
autoconfesado ADJ self-confessed.
autoconfesarse [1a] VR to confess o.s.
autoconfesión NF self-confession.
autoconfianza NF self-confidence.
autoconservación NF self-preservation.
autoconsumo NM (*de alimentos*) personal consumption; (*de bienes*) personal use.
autocontrol NM (a) (*autodominio*) self-control, self-restraint. (b) (*Téc*) self-monitoring.
autoconvencerse [2d] VR to convince o.s.
autocracia NF autocracy.
autócrata NMF autocrat.
autocrático ADJ autocratic.
autocremarse [1a] VR to set fire to o.s., burn o.s. (to death).
autocrítica NF self-criticism, self-examination.
autocrítico ADJ self-critical.
auto-cross NM autocross.
autóctono ADJ autochthonous, original, native, indigenous.
autocue NM autocue.
autodefensa NF self-defence.
autodefinirse [3a] VR to define o.s., state one's position.
autodegradación NF self-abasement.
autodenominarse [1a] VR to call o.s.
autodestrucción NF self-destruction.
autodestructible ADJ, **autodestructivo** ADJ self-destructive, self-destructing.
autodestruirse [3g] VR to self-destruct.
autodeterminación NF self-determination.
autodidacta ADJ, NMF = **autodidacto**.
autodidacto [1] ADJ self-educated, self-taught.
    [2] NM, **autodidacta** NF autodidact, self-taught person.
autodisciplina NF self-discipline.
autodisciplinado ADJ self-disciplined.
autodisparador NM (*Fot*) self-timer.
autodominio NM self-control.
autódromo NM motor-racing circuit, racetrack.
autoedición NF desktop publishing.
autoempleo NM self-employment.
autoengaño NM self-deception, self-delusion.
autoerótico ADJ autoerotic.
autoescuela NF driving school.
autoestima NF self-esteem.
autoestop NM = **autostop**.
autoestopista NMF hitch-hiker.
autoevaluación NF self-assessment.
autoexcluirse [3g] VR to exclude o.s.
autoexploración NF self-examination.
autoexpresión NF self-expression.
autofecundación NF self-fertilization.
autofelicitación NF self-congratulation.
autofinanciable ADJ self-financing.
autofinanciado ADJ self-financed.
autofinanciarse [1b] VR to finance o.s.
autógena NF welding.
autogestión NF self-management; (*esp*) worker management.
autogiro NM autogiro.
autogobernarse [1j] VR to govern itself, be self-governing.
autogobierno NM self-government.
autogol NM own goal.
autogolpe NM coup *organized by the government itself to allow it to take extra powers; see also* CAMBIO 90.
autógrafo ADJ, NM autograph.
autohipnosis NF autohypnosis, self-hypnosis.
autoimpuesto ADJ self-imposed.
autoincluirse VR to include o.s.
autoinculpación NF self-accusation; (*Jur*) plea of guilty.
autoinculparse [1a] VR to incriminate o.s.
autoinducido ADJ self-induced.
autoinfligido ADJ herida self-inflicted.
autoinmune ADJ autoimmune.
autoinmunidad NF autoimmunity.
autoinmunitario ADJ, **autoinmunológico*** ADJ autoimmune.
autolavado NM car-wash.
autolesionarse [1a] VR to inflict injury on o.s.
autolimpiable ADJ horno etc self-cleaning.
autollamarse [1a] VR to call o.s.
automación NF automation.
automarginación NF dropping-out.

automarginado [1] ADJ: **persona automarginada** drop-out.
    [2] NM, **automarginada** NF drop-out.
automarginarse [1a] VR to drop out; **~ de** to drop out of; to stay away from, keep clear of, have nothing to do with.
autómata NM automaton, robot; (*fig*) automaton; puppet.
automática NF (a) (*ciencia*) automation. (b) (*lavadora*) washing-machine. (c) (*Mil*) automatic.
automáticamente ADV automatically.
automaticidad NF automatic nature.
automático [1] ADJ automatic; self-acting.
    [2] NM (*Cono Sur*) (a) self-service restaurant, automat (*US*). (b) (*cierre*) snap fastener.
automatismo NM automatism.
automatización NF automation; **~ de oficinas** office automation; **~ de fábricas** factory automation.
automatizado ADJ automated.
automatizar [1f] VT to automate.
automedicarse [1g] VR to treat o.s.
automedonte NM (*hum y LAm*) coachman; driver.
automercado NM (*Carib*) supermarket.
automoción NF: **la industria de la ~** the car industry, the automobile industry (*US*).
automodelismo NM model-car racing.
automodelista NMF radio-controlled model car enthusiast.
automotor [1] ADJ (F : **automotriz**) self-propelled.
    [2] NM (*Ferro*) diesel train; (*LAm*) self-propelled vehicle.
automóvil [1] ADJ self-propelled.
    [2] NM car, motor car, automobile (*US*); **~ de alquiler** hire car; **~ de carreras** racing car; **~ de choque** bumper car, dodgem; **~ de importación** foreign car; **ir en ~** to go by car, travel by car.
automovilismo NM (a) (*actividad*) motoring; **~ deportivo** motor racing. (b) (*industria*) car industry, automobile industry (*US*).
automovilista NMF motorist, driver.
automovilístico ADJ car (*atr*); **accidente ~** car accident.
automutilación NF self-mutilation.
automutilarse [1a] VR to mutilate o.s.
autonomía NF (a) (*Pol*: *sistema*) autonomy; home rule; self-government.
    (b) (*Pol*: *territorio*) autonomous region, autonomy.
    (c) (*Aer*, *Náut*) range; **un avión de gran ~** a long-range aircraft; **el avión tiene una ~ de 5.000 km** the aircraft has a range of 5,000 km.
autonómico ADJ relating to autonomy; **elecciones autonómicas** elections for the autonomous regions; **política autonómica** policy concerning autonomies; **el proceso ~** the process leading to autonomy.
autonomismo NM movement towards autonomy.
autónomo [1] ADJ (*Pol etc*) autonomous; self-governing; independent; *persona* self-employed; (*Inform*) stand-alone; **trabajo ~** self-employment.
    [2] NM, **autónoma** NF self-employed person.
autopatrulla NM (*Méx*) patrol car.
autopegado ADJ sobre self-sealing.
autopiano NM (*Carib*) pianola.
autopista NF motorway; expressway (*US*); **~ de la información** information superhighway; **~ de peaje** toll road, toll motorway, turnpike road (*US*); **~ perimetral** ring road, bypass.
autopolinización NF self-pollination.
autopreservación NF self-preservation.
autoproclamado ADJ self-proclaimed.
autoproclamarse [1a] VR to proclaim o.s.
autoprofesor NM teaching machine.
autoprogramable ADJ intelligent.
autopropulsado ADJ self-propelled.
autopropulsión NF self-propulsion.
autopropulsor ADJ self-propelling.
autoprotegerse [2c] VR to protect o.s.
autopsia NF post mortem, autopsy.
autopublicidad NF self-advertisement; **hacer ~** to indulge in self-advertisement.
autor(a) NM/F (*Liter*) author, writer; (*de idea*) creator, originator, inventor; (*de crimen*) perpetrator (*de* of), person responsible (*de* for), person concerned (*de* in).
autoría NF (*Liter etc*) authorship; **la ~ del atentado** the responsibility for the attack.
autoridad NF (a) (*gen*) authority; jurisdiction.
    (b) (*boato*) pomp, show, ostentation.
    (c) (*persona*) authority; **las ~es** the authorities; **~es aduaneras** customs authorities; **~ de sanidad** health authorities; **¡abran a la ~!** open up in the name of the law!; **entregarse a la ~** to give o.s. up (to the police).
autoritario [1] ADJ authoritarian; peremptory; dogmatic.

2 NM, **autoritaria** NF authoritarian.

autoritarismo NM authoritarianism.

autoritativo ADJ authoritative.

autorización NF authorization; permission, licence; **tener la ~ de uno para** + infin to have sb's authorization to + infin.

autorizadamente ADV officially, authoritatively.

▼ **autorizado** ADJ authorized, official; authoritative; approved; **la persona autorizada** the officially designated person, the approved person.

▼ **autorizar** [1f] VT (dar facultad a) to authorize, empower; (permitir) to approve, license; (justificar) to justify, give (o lend) authority to; **~ a uno para** + infin to authorize sb to + infin, empower sb to + infin; **el futuro no autoriza optimismo alguno** the future does not justify (o warrant) the slightest optimism.

autorradio NF car radio.

autorrealización NF self-fulfilment.

autorrealizado ADJ self-fulfilled.

autorrealizarse [1f] VR to feel fulfilled; to gain self-fulfilment.

autorregulable ADJ self-adjusting.

autorregulación NF self-regulation.

autorretrato NM self-portrait.

autorzuelo NM scribbler, hack, penpusher.

autoservicio NM self-service (restaurant etc).

autosostenerse [2k] VR to pay one's own way, be self-supporting.

autostop NM hitch-hiking; **hacer ~, viajar en ~** to hitch-hike; **fuimos haciendo ~ de Irún a Burgos** we hitch-hiked from Irún to Burgos, we got a lift from Irún to Burgos.

autostopismo NM hitch-hiking.

autostopista NMF hitch-hiker.

autosuficiencia NF (a) (Econ) self-sufficiency. (b) (pey) smugness.

autosuficiente ADJ (a) (Econ) self-sufficient. (b) (pey) smug.

autosugestión NF autosuggestion.

autotanque NM tanker, tank truck (US).

autotitularse [1a] VR to title o.s., call o.s.

autoventa ATR: **vendedor ~** travelling salesman, representative who travels by car.

autovía NF main road, trunk road; dual carriageway, divided highway (US); **~ de circunvalación** bypass, ring road.

autovivienda NF caravan, trailer.

Auvernia NF Auvergne.

auxiliar 1 ADJ auxiliary; assistant.
2 NMF assistant; auxiliary; assistant teacher; (Dep) linesman; **~ administrativo** administrative assistant; **~ de cabina, ~ de vuelo** steward, stewardess; flight attendant (US); **~ de conversación** conversation assistant; **~ de enfermería** (CAm) nursing auxiliary; **~ de lengua inglesa** English language assistant; **~ sanitario** health worker; **~ técnico** (LAm Dep) coach, trainer.
3 VT [1b] to help, assist; to bring aid to; moribundo to comfort, help to make a good end.

auxilio NM help, aid, assistance; relief; **~ espiritual** consolations of religion; (sacramentos) last rites; **~ social** social work, welfare (work); welfare service; **primeros ~s** (Med) first aid; **acudir en ~ de uno** to come to sb's aid.

Av. ABR de **Avenida** Avenue, Av., Ave.

a/v (Com) ABR de **a vista** at sight.

avada: NM (Carib) queer:.

avahar [1a] 1 VT to blow on, warm with one's breath.
2 VI y **avaharse** VR to steam, give off steam, give off vapour.

aval NM (Com) guarantee, reference, backing (for a loan etc); (Cono Sur) guarantor; (Pol) backing, support; **~ bancario** banker's reference.

avalancha NF avalanche.

avalar [1a] VT (Com) to guarantee; (fig) decisión etc to support, endorse; persona to answer for.

avalentado ADJ, **avalentonado** ADJ boastful, bullying, arrogant; disrespectful.

avalista NMF guarantor.

avalorar [1a] VT (a) (realzar) to enhance; to set off. (b) (fig) to encourage.

avaluación, avaluada (LAm) NF valuation, appraisal.

avaluar [1e] VT to value, appraise (at en).

avalúo NM valuation, appraisal.

avancarga: cañón de ~ muzzle loader.

avance NM (a) (Mil y fig) advance; (de precio) rise, advance; **en ~** in advance.
(b) (Cono Sur Mil) attack, raid.
(c) (Com, Fin: pago) advance, advance payment; (Com: cálculo) estimate.
(d) (Com: balance) balance; balance sheet.
(e) (Elec) lead; (Mec) feed.
(f) (Cine) trailer; preview; **~s** (Méx) trailer; (TV) early news programme; **~ informativo** advance notice, publicity hand-out; press-release.

(g) (CAm: robo) theft; (Mil) looting, sacking.
(h) (Cono Sur: regalo) tempting offer, inducement (made to secure sb's goodwill).

avante ADV (esp LAm) forward; (Náut) forward, ahead; **¡~!** forward!; **todo ~** (Náut) full steam ahead; **salir ~** to get ahead, get on in the world.

avanzada NF (Mil) (a) (puesto) outpost. (b) (soldados) advance party, advance guard.

avanzadilla NF (Mil: patrulla) scout, patrol; (avanzada) advance party.

avanzado ADJ advanced; ideas, tendencia advanced, avant-garde, progressive; diseño etc advanced; hora late; hueso etc prominent; **de edad avanzada, ~ de edad** advanced in years; **a una hora avanzada** at a late hour.

avanzar [1f] 1 VT (a) (adelantar) to advance, move forward.
(b) dinero to advance.
(c) (promover) to promote.
(d) propuesta to advance, put forward.
(e) (Carib) to vomit, throw up.
2 VI y **avanzarse** VR (a) to advance (t Mil), move on, push on; to go forward; **no avanzo nada** I'm not making any headway.
(b) (proyecto etc) to go forward, progress, advance.
(c) (noche, invierno etc) to advance, draw on; (terminar) draw to a close.
(d) **~se algo** (CAm, Méx) to steal sth.

avanzo NM (Com) (a) (balance) balance; balance sheet. (b) (cálculo) estimate.

avaricia NF miserliness, avarice; greed, greediness.

avariciosamente ADV avariciously; greedily.

avaricioso ADJ, **avariento** ADJ miserly, avaricious; greedy.

avariosis NF (LAm) syphilis.

avaro 1 ADJ miserly, mean; **ser ~ de alabanzas** to be sparing in one's praise, be mean with one's praises; **ser ~ de palabras** to be a person of few words.
2 NM, **avara** NF miser, mean person.

avasallador ADJ overwhelming; domineering.

avasallamiento NM subjugation.

avasallar [1a] 1 VT (subyugar) (a) to subdue, subjugate; to dominate; to enslave. (b) **~ a uno** (fig) to steamroller sb (into agreement o compliance).
2 **avasallarse** VR to submit, yield.

avatar NM (transformación) avatar, change, transformation; (encarnación) incarnation; (etapa) phase; (ola) wave; **~ destructivo** wave of destruction; **~es** vicissitudes, ups and downs.

Avda. ABR de **Avenida** Avenue, Av., Ave.

AVE NM (Esp) ABR de **Alta Velocidad Española** high speed train.

ave NF bird; (esp LAm) chicken; **~ acuática, ~ acuátil** water bird; **~ canora, ~ cantora** songbird; **~ de corral** chicken, fowl; **~s de corral** fowls, poultry; **~ marina** sea bird; **~ negra** (Cono Sur) crooked lawyer; **~ nocturna** night bird (t fig); **~ del paraíso** bird of paradise; **~ de paso** bird of passage (t fig), migrant; **~ de presa, ~ de rapiña** bird of prey; **~ zancuda** wader, wading bird.

avechuco* NM ragamuffin, ne'er-do-well.

avecinarse [1a] VR to approach, come near.

avecindarse [1a] VR to take up one's residence, settle.

avefría NF lapwing.

avejentado ADJ piel, rostro old; **le encontré ~ para su edad** he looked old for his age.

avejentar [1a] VI y **avejentarse** VR to age (before one's time).

avejigar [1h] 1 VT to blister.
2 **avejigarse** VR to blister.

avellana NF (a) (Bot) hazelnut. (b) (And) firecracker.

avellanado ADJ (a) color nutbrown. (b) piel etc shrivelled, wizened. (c) sabor nutty.

avellanal NM hazel wood, hazel plantation.

avellanar 1 NM hazel wood, hazel plantation.
2 [1a] VT (Téc) to countersink.
3 **avellanarse** VR to shrivel up.

avellanedo NM hazel wood, hazel plantation.

avellanero NM, **avellano** NM hazel, hazel tree.

avemaría NF (a) (Ecl) Ave Maria, Hail Mary. (b) **al ~** at dusk; **en un ~*** in a twinkling; **saber algo como el ~*** to know sth inside out.

avena NF oats; **~ loca, ~ morisca, ~ silvestre** wild oats.

avenado ADJ half-crazy, rather mad.

avenal NM oatfield.

avenamiento NM draining, drainage.

avenar [1a] VT tierra to drain.

avenencia NF agreement; compromise; (Com) bargain, deal.

avenida NF (a) (calle) avenue. (b) (de río) flood, spate.

avenido ADJ: **están bien ~s** personas they get on well; pareja they're well matched.

avenimiento NM agreement, compromise.

avenir [3a] 1 VT to reconcile, bring together.

► LENGUA Y USO: **autorizado** → 36.2   **autorizar** → 36.3

2 avenirse VR **(a)** (*2 personas: acto*) to come to an agreement, be reconciled; to reach a compromise; (*estado*) to be on good terms, get on well together; **no se avienen** they don't get on, they don't agree.
(b) ~ **con algo** to be in agreement with sth, conform to sth; to resign o.s. to sth, come to terms with sth; ~ **con uno** to reach an agreement with sb; **¡allá te las avengas!*** that's your look-out!, that's up to you!
(c) ~ **a hacer algo** to agree to do sth.
aventado ADJ (*CAm, Méx*) brave, daring.
aventador NM (*para fuego*) fan, blower; (*Agr*) winnowing fork.
aventadora NF winnowing machine.
aventajadamente ADV outstandingly, extremely well.
aventajado ADJ outstanding, excellent, superior; (*en grado*) advanced; ~ **de estatura** exceptionally tall, having the advantage of great height.
▼ **aventajar** [1a] **1** VT **(a)** (*sobrepasar*) to surpass, beat, excel; to outstrip; (*CAm Aut*) to overtake; **A aventaja a B por 4 puntos** A leads B by 4 points; ~ **con mucho a uno** to beat sb easily, be far better than sb.
(b) (*mejorar*) to improve, better.
(c) (*preferir*) to prefer.
2 aventajarse VR to get ahead; ~ **a** to surpass, beat, excel; to get the advantage of.
aventar [1j] **1** VT **(a)** *fuego* to fan, blow (on); *trigo* to winnow.
(b) (*lanzar al aire*) to cast to the winds; (*viento*) to blow away; (*Carib Agr*) to dry in the wind.
(c) (*LAm: tirar*) to throw; to chuck out, throw out.
2 aventarse VR **(a)** (*hincharse*) to fill with air, swell up.
(b) (‡: *largarse*) to beat it*.
(c) (*Méx*) to decide.
(d) (*LAm: tirarse*) to throw o.s.; (*arriesgarse*) to take risks.
aventón* NM (*Méx*) throw; (*Aut*) lift; **pedir** ~ to hitch a lift.
aventura NF **(a)** (*andanza*) adventure; bold venture, daring enterprise; (*pey*) escapade; ~ **sentimental** love affair, affair of the heart; (*Fin, Pol etc*) ~s reckless gambles, adventurism.
(b) (*azar*) chance, contingency.
(c) (*peligro*) risk, danger, hazard.
aventurado ADJ risky, hazardous.
aventurar [1a] **1** VT to venture, risk; *capital* to risk, stake.
2 aventurarse VR to dare, take a chance, risk it; ~ **a** + *infin* to venture to + *infin*, dare to + *infin*, risk + *ger*.
aventurera NF adventuress.
aventurero 1 ADJ adventurous; enterprising.
2 NM adventurer; (*Mil*) mercenary, soldier of fortune; (*pey*) social climber.
avergonzado ADJ *cara* shamefaced; embarrassed; **estar** ~ to be ashamed (*de, por* about, at).
avergonzar [1f y 1l] **1** VT to shame, put to shame; to abash, embarrass.
2 avergonzarse VR (*sentir vergüenza*) to be ashamed; (*sentirse violento*) to be embarrassed, look embarrassed; ~ **de**, ~ **por** to be ashamed about (*o* at, of); to be embarrassed about; ~ **de** + *infin* to be ashamed to + *infin*; **se avergonzó de haberlo dicho** he was ashamed at having said it.
avería¹ NF (*Orn*) (*pajarera*) aviary; (*aves*) flock of birds.
avería² NF **(a)** (*Com etc*) damage; (*Mec*) breakdown, fault, failure; **el coche tiene una** ~ the car has had a breakdown, there's sth wrong with the car.
(b) **hombre de** ~**s** (*Cono Sur: matón*) tough guy*, thug; (*criminal*) dangerous criminal; **ser de** ~ to be dangerous.
avería³ NF (*Com, Náut*) average; ~ **gruesa** general average.
averiado ADJ *fruto etc* damaged, spoiled; (*Mec*) broken down, faulty; **los faros están** ~**s** the lights have failed, there's sth wrong with the lights.
averiar [1c] **1** VT to damage, spoil; (*Mec*) to cause a breakdown in, cause a failure in; to damage.
2 averiarse VR **(a)** (*dañarse*) to get damaged; (*Mec*) to have a breakdown, have a failure, fail; **se averió el arranque** the starter failed, the starter went wrong.
(b) (*Méx: perder la virginidad*) to lose one's virginity.
averiguable ADJ ascertainable.
averiguación NF **(a)** (*comprobación*) ascertainment, discovery; establishment; (*investigación*) investigation; inquiry; check. **(b)** (*CAm, Méx: discusión*) quarrel, argument.
averiguadamente ADV certainly.
averiguado ADJ certain, established; **es un hecho** ~ it is an established fact.
averiguador(a) NM/F investigator; inquirer.
averiguar [1i] **1** VT (*descubrir*) to find out, ascertain, discover; *dato etc* to look up; (*indagar*) to investigate, inquire into, find out about; (*comprobar*) to check; ~ **las señas de uno** to find out sb's address; **hay que** ~ **esto en la biblioteca** this must be looked up in the li-

brary, you'll have to check this in the library; **eso es todo lo que se pudo** ~ that is all that could be discovered.
2 VI (*CAm, Méx*) to quarrel, fight.
3 averiguarse VR **(a)** ~ **con uno*** (*obligar*) to tie sb down; (*llevarse bien*) to get along with sb.
(b) ~ **con uno** (*CAm, Méx*) to argue (*o* fight) with sb, take sb on.
averiguata NF (*Méx*) argument, fight.
averigüetas NMF INVAR (*And*) snooper, busybody.
averrugado ADJ warty.
▼ **aversión** NF aversion (*a, hacer, por* to); distaste, disgust, loathing; **cobrar** ~ **a** to take a strong dislike to.
avestruz NM **(a)** (*Orn*) ostrich; ~ **de la pampa** rhea.
(b) (*LAm**) dimwit*, idiot.
avetado ADJ veined, grained, streaked.
avetoro NM bittern.
avezado ADJ accustomed; inured, experienced; **los ya** ~**s en estos menesteres** those already experienced in such activities.
avezar [1f] **1** VT to accustom, inure (*a* to).
2 avezarse VR to get used (to it); to become accustomed; ~ **a algo** to get used to sth, get hardened to sth.
aviación NF **(a)** (*gen*) aviation. **(b)** (*fuerza*) air force.
AVIACO NF (*Esp*) ABR *de* **Aviación y Comercio S.A.** *Spanish airline.*
aviado ADJ: **estar** ~ **(a)** (*Cono Sur: bien surtido*) to be well off, have everything one needs; to be properly equipped (*with tools etc*).
(b) (*Cono Sur: soñar*) to have one's head in the clouds.
(c) (*) to be in a mess; **¡**~**s estamos!** what a mess we're in!; **dejar a uno** ~ to leave sb in the lurch.
aviador¹ NM (*Aer*) airman, aviator, flyer; (*Mil*) airman, member of the air force.
aviador² NM (*And, Carib, Cono Sur*) (*Com*) mining speculator (*o* financier); (*prestamista*) moneylender, loan shark*.
aviadora NF aviator, (woman) pilot.
aviar [1c] **1** VT **(a)** (*preparar*) to get ready, prepare, fit out; (*ordenar*) to tidy up; (*proveer*) to equip, supply, provide (*de* with).
(b) (*LAm*) to advance money to; to lend equipment to, provide with equipment; to provide with food for a journey.
(c) ~ **a uno*** (*dar prisa*) to hurry sb up, get sb moving; (*despedir*) to see sb off.
(d) (*prov, LAm Agr*) to castrate.
2 VI (*) to hurry up, get a move on; **¡vamos aviando!** let's get a move on!
3 aviarse VR to get ready; ~ **para hacer algo** to get ready to do sth.
aviario NM aviary.
aviatorio ADJ (*LAm*): **accidente** ~ air crash, plane crash.
avícola ADJ chicken (*atr*), poultry (*atr*); **granja** ~ chicken farm, poultry farm.
avicultor(a) NM/F chicken farmer, poultry farmer; bird fancier.
avicultura NF chicken farming, poultry farming; bird fancying.
ávidamente ADV avidly, eagerly; (*pey*) greedily.
avidez NF avidity, eagerness (*de* for); (*pey*) greed, greediness (*de* for); **con** ~ eagerly; greedily.
ávido ADJ avid, eager (*de* for); (*pey*) greedy (*de* for); ~ **de sangre** bloodthirsty.
aviejarse [1a] VR to age before one's time.
avieso 1 ADJ (*torcido*) distorted, crooked; (*siniestro*) sinister; (*perverso*) perverse, wicked; (*rencoroso*) spiteful.
2 NM (*And*) abortion.
avifauna NF birds, bird life.
avilantarse [1a] VR to be insolent.
avilantez NF insolence, effrontery.
avilés 1 ADJ of Ávila.
2 NM, **avilesa** NF native (*o* inhabitant) of Ávila; **los avileses** the people of Ávila.
avilesino 1 ADJ of Avilés.
2 NM, **avilesina** NF native (*o* inhabitant) of Avilés; **los** ~**s** the people of Avilés.
avillanado ADJ boorish, uncouth.
avinagrado ADJ sour, acid; (*fig*) sour, jaundiced, crabbed.
avinagrar [1a] **1** VT to sour.
2 avinagrarse VR to turn sour.
Aviñón NM Avignon.
avío NM **(a)** preparation, provision; (*de pastor*) provisions for a journey.
(b) (*And, Carib, Cono Sur: préstamo*) loan (of money *o* of equipment).
(c) **hacer su** ~***** to make one's pile*; (*iró*) to make a mess of things.
(d) **¡al** ~**!*** get cracking!*, get on with it!
(e) ~**s** gear, tackle, kit.
avión NM **(a)** (*Aer*) aeroplane, plane, aircraft, airplane (*US*); ~ **ambulancia** ambulance plane; ~ **de carga** freight plane, cargo plane; ~ **de caza**, ~ **de combate** fighter, pursuit plane; ~ **cisterna** tanker aircraft; ~ **a** (*o* de) **chorro**, ~ **de propulsión a chorro**, ~ **a** (*o*

de) reacción jet (plane); **~ de despegue vertical** vertical take-off plane; **~ espía** spy plane; **~ de papel** paper dart; **~ de pasajeros** passenger aircraft; **por ~** (*Correos*) by airmail; **enviar artículos por ~** to send goods by plane; **ir en ~** to go by plane, go by air, fly.
(b) (*Orn*) martin.
(c) hacer el ~ a uno: to do sb down, cause harm to sb; (*esp And*: *estafar*) to cheat sb.
(d) (*CAm*: *juego*) hopscotch.

avionazo NM plane crash, accident to an aircraft.

avioncito NM: **~ de papel** paper dart.

avionero NM (*And, Cono Sur*) airman.

avioneta NF light aircraft.

aviónica NF aviation, avionics.

avionístico ADJ relating to aeroplanes, relating to flying; **miedo ~** fear of flying.

avisadamente ADV sensibly, wisely.

avisado ADJ sensible, wise; **mal ~** rash, ill-advised.

avisador [1] NM, **avisadora** NF **(a)** informant; messenger; (*pey* †) informer. **(b)** (*Cine, Teat*) programme seller.
[2] NM electric bell; (*Culin*) timer; **~ de incendios** fire-alarm.

▼ **avisar** [1a] VT to warn; to inform, notify, tell; **~ a uno con una semana de anticipación** to let sb know a week in advance, give sb a week's notice; **¿por qué no me avisó?** why didn't you let me know?; **en cuanto ella llegue me avisas** tell me the moment she comes; **lo hizo sin ~** he did it without warning; **~ al médico** (*etc*) to send for the doctor (*etc*), call the doctor (*etc*); **~ un taxi** to call a cab; **'avisamos grúa'** (*Esp*) 'we will call the towing vehicle' (to remove any parked car).

aviso NM **(a)** (*gen*) piece of information, tip; (*advertencia*) notice; warning; (*Inform*) prompt; **~ de bomba** bomb alert, bomb warning; **~ de envío** dispatch note; **~ escrito** written notice, notice in writing; **~ de mercancías** advice note; **con 15 días de ~** at a fortnight's notice; **con poco tiempo de ~** at short notice, with little warning; **~ previo de despido** prior notice of discharge; **sin previo ~** without warning, without notice; **hasta nuevo ~** until further notice; **salvo ~ en contrario** unless otherwise informed; **según (su) ~** (*Com*) as per order, as you ordered; **dar ~ a** to notify, inform; **mandar ~** to send word.
(b) (*LAm*) advertisement; **'~s económicos'** 'classified advertisements'; **~ mural** poster, wall poster.
(c) (*cualidad*) caution; discretion, prudence; **estar sobre ~** to be on the alert, be on the look-out; **poner a uno sobre ~** to forewarn sb, put sb on his guard.

avispa NF wasp.

avispado ADJ (*astuto*) sharp, clever, wide-awake; (*pey*) sly, wily; (*LAm*: *nervioso*) jumpy*, nervous.

avispar [1a] [1] VT *caballo* to spur on, urge on; (*fig*) to stir up, prod, ginger up.
[2] **avisparse** VR to fret, worry; (*Méx*) to become concerned, get alarmed.

avispero NM **(a)** (*Ent*) wasps' nest; **meterse en un ~** to get o.s. into a jam*. **(b)** (*Med*) carbuncle. **(c)** (*) mess; (*Cono Sur*) noisy gathering.

avispón NM hornet.

avistar [1a] [1] VT to sight, make out, glimpse.
[2] **avistarse** VR to have an interview (*con* with).

avitaminosis NF INVAR vitamin deficiency.

avituallamiento NM victualling, provisioning, supply(ing).

avituallar [1a] VT to victual, provision, supply with food.

avivado ADJ (*Cono Sur*) forewarned, alerted.

avivar [1a] [1] VT *fuego* to stoke (up); *color, luz* to brighten, make brighter; *dolor* to intensify; *pasión* to inflame; *disputa* to add fuel to; *interés* to stimulate, arouse; to revive; *efecto* to enhance, heighten; *combatientes* to urge on; (*LAm*: *avisar*) to warn, alert.
[2] **avivarse** VR to revive, acquire new life; to cheer up, become brighter; **¡avívate!** look alive!, snap out of it!

avizor [1] ADJ: **estar ojo ~** to be on the alert, be vigilant.
[2] NM watcher.

avizorar [1a] VT to watch, spy on.

avocastro NM (*Cono Sur*) = **abocastro**.

avorazado ADJ (*Méx*) greedy, grasping.

avutarda NF great bustard.

axial ADJ axial.

axila NF axilla, armpit.

axiológico ADJ axiological.

axioma NM axiom.

axiomático ADJ axiomatic.

axis NM INVAR (*Anat*) axis.

ay [1] INTERJ **(a)** (*dolor físico*) ow!, ouch!
(b) (*pena etc*) oh!, oh dear!, (*más dramático*) alas!; **¡~ de mí!** poor me!; it's very hard (on me)!; whatever shall I do?; (*muy dramático*) woe is me!; **¡~ del que lo haga!** woe betide the man who does it!
(c) (*sorpresa*) oh!, goodness!

[2] NM (*suspiro*) sigh; (*gemido*) moan, groan; (*grito*) cry; **un ~ desgarrador** a heartrending cry.

aya NF (*institutriz*) governess; (*niñera*) child's nurse.

ayatolá NM, **ayatollah** NM ayatollah.

Ayax NM Ajax.

ayer [1] ADV yesterday; (*fig*) formerly, in the past; **~ no más, no más que ~** only yesterday; **~ por la mañana** yesterday morning; **de ~ acá** (*fig*) very suddenly; **no es cosa de ~** it's nothing new.
[2] NM yesterday, past; **el ~ madrileño** Madrid in the past, old Madrid.

ayllu NM (*And*) (*Hist*: *familia*) family, tribe; (*comunidad*) community; (*tierras*) communal lands.

aymara = **aimara**.

aymará ADJ, NMF Aymara.

ayo NM tutor.

ayote NM (*Méx*: *calabaza*) small pumpkin; (*CAm*: *jícaro*) pumpkin, squash; (*hum*) nut:, bonce:; **dar ~s a** to jilt; **la fiesta fue un ~** (*Méx*) the party was a disaster.

ayotoste NM armadillo.

ayte. ABR *de* **ayudante** assistant, asst.

Ayto ABR *de* **Ayuntamiento**.

ayuda [1] NF **(a)** help, aid, assistance; **~s audiovisuales** audiovisual aids; **~ compensatoria** ≃ income support; **~ a domicilio** home help; **~ económica** financial (*o* economic) aid; **~s familiares** family allowances; **~ humanitaria** humanitarian aid; **~s a la navegación** aids to navigation, navigational aids; **~ visual** visual aid.
(b) (*Med*) enema; (*LAm*) laxative.
[2] NM page; **~ de cámara** valet.

ayudado NM (*Taur*) two-handed pass with the cape.

ayudador(a) NM/F helper.

ayudante NM, **ayudanta** NF helper, assistant; (*Mil*: *t* **~ de campo**) adjutant; (*Téc*) mate; technician; (*colegio, Univ*) assistant; (*Golf*) caddie; **~ de dirección** production assistant; **~ ejecutivo** executive assistant; **~ de electricista** electrician's mate; **~ de laboratorio** laboratory assistant; **~ de realización** (*TV*) production assistant; **~ técnico sanitario** nursing assistant.

ayudantía NF assistantship; (*Mil*) adjutancy; (*Téc*) post of technician.

ayudar [1a] VT to help, aid, assist; **~ a uno a hacer algo** to help sb to do sth; to help sb in doing sth; **~ a uno a bajar** to help sb down, help sb out; **me ayuda muchísimo** he's a great help (to me), he helps me a lot; **¿me puedes ~ con la limpieza esta tarde?** can you help me out with the cleaning this afternoon?

┌─ *AYUDAR* ──────────── *ver también la entrada* ─┐

Ayudar se puede traducir por *help*, *assist* y *aid*.

• La manera más frecuente de traducir *ayudar* es por *help*. Si *help* va seguido de un verbo, éste puede ir en infinitivo *con o sin to*:
  ¿Puedes ayudarnos?
  Can you help (us)?
  Siempre le ayuda con la tarea
  He always helps her with her homework
  ¿Me puedes ayudar a preparar la cena?
  Can you help me (to) get dinner ready?

• *Ayudar* se traduce por *assist* en un registro bastante más formal y se construye frecuentemente en la estructura *to assist somebody with something*:
  La comadrona ayudó al médico con el parto
  The midwife assisted the doctor with the delivery

• *Ayudar* se traduce por *aid* en inglés formal en el contexto de asesorar o prestar ayuda a un grupo de personas necesitadas:
  ...los intentos de Estados Unidos de ayudar a los refugiados kurdos...
  ...attempts by the United States to aid Kurdish refugees...
  Para otros usos y ejemplos ver la entrada.

└──┘

ayudista NMF (*Cono Sur Pol*) supporter.

ayudita* NF small contribution.

ayunar [1a] VI to fast (*a* on); **~ (de)** (*fig*) to go without.

ayunas NFPL: **salir en ~** to go out without any breakfast; **estar** (*o* **quedarse**) **en ~** to know nothing about it, be completely in the dark.

ayuno [1] ADJ **(a)** (*en ayunas*) fasting. **(b) estar ~** = **estar** *etc* **en ayunas**.
[2] NM fast; fasting; abstinence; **estar** *etc* **en ~** = **estar en ayunas**.

ayuntamiento NM **(a)** (*corporación*) town council, city council, corporation, municipal government.
(b) (*edificio*) **A~** town hall, city hall.
(c) (*t* **~ sexual**) sexual intercourse; **tener ~ con** to have intercourse with.

ayuntar [1a] VT **(a)** (*Náut*) to splice. **(b)** (*And Agr*) to yoke, yoke together.

ayuya NF (*Cono Sur*) flat roll, scone.

azabachado ADJ jet, jet-black.
azabache NM (*Min*) jet; **~s** jet trinkets.
azacán NM, **azacana** NF drudge, slave; **estar hecho un ~** to be worked to death.
azacanarse [1a] VR to drudge, slave away.
azada NF hoe.
azadón NM large hoe, mattock.
azadonar [1a] VT to hoe.
azafata NF (**a**) (*Aer*) air hostess, stewardess, flight attendant (*US*); (*Náut*) stewardess; (*TV*) hostess; (*compañera*) escort (*supplied by escort agency*); **~ de exposiciones y congresos** congress organizer, hostess. (**b**) (*Cono Sur*) = **azafate**. (**c**) (*Hist*) lady-in-waiting; handmaiden.
azafate NM flat basket, tray.
azafrán NM (*Bot*) saffron, crocus; (*Culin*) saffron.
azafranado ADJ saffron, saffron-coloured.
azafranar [1a] VT (*Culin*) to saffron.
azagaya NF assegai, javelin.
azahar NM orange blossom.
azalea NF azalea.
azar NM (**a**) (*suerte*) chance, fate; **al ~** at random; **por ~** accidentally, by chance; **juego de ~** game of chance; **los ~es de la vida** life's ups and downs; **no es un ~ que ...** it is no mere accident that ..., it is not a matter of chance that ...; **decir al ~** to say to nobody in particular. (**b**) (*percance*) misfortune, accident, piece of bad luck.
azararse[1] [1a] VR (*ruborizarse*) to blush, redden.
azararse[2] [1a] VR (**a**) (*malograrse*) to go wrong, go awry. (**b**) = **azorarse**.
azarear [1a] VT, **azarearse** VR = **azorar(se)**.
azarosamente ADV hazardously; eventfully.
azaroso ADJ (**a**) (*arriesgado*) risky, hazardous, chancy; *vida* eventful; full of ups and downs. (**b**) (*malhadado*) unlucky, accident-prone.
Azerbaiyán NM Azerbaijan.
azerbaiyano, -a ADJ, NMF Azerbaijani.
azerí ADJ, NMF Azeri.
ázimo ADJ *pan* unleavened.
aznarismo NM *policies and following of José María Aznar (Spanish Prime Minister from 1996).*
aznarista [1] ADJ *related to José María Aznar or his policies, Aznar (atr); intelectual, círculos* pro-Aznar.
[2] NMF Aznar supporter.
-azo, -aza V Aspects of Word Formation in Spanish 2.
azocar [1g] VT (*Carib*) to pack tightly.
azófar NM brass.
azogado [1] ADJ restless, fidgety; **temblar como un ~** to shake like a leaf, tremble all over.
[2] NM silvering (of a mirror).
azogar [1h] [1] VT to coat with quicksilver; *espejo* to silver.
[2] **azogarse** VR to be restless, be fidgety; to get agitated.
azogue NM mercury, quicksilver; **ser un ~** to be always on the go; to be restless, be fidgety.
azolve NM (*Méx*) sediment, deposit.
azonzado ADJ (*Cono Sur*) silly, stupid.
azor NM goshawk.
azora NF (*LAm*) = **azoramiento**.
azorado ADJ (**a**) (*alarmado*) alarmed, upset. (**b**) (*turbado*) embarrassed, flustered. (**c**) (*emocionado*) excited.
azoramiento NM (V ADJ) (**a**) alarm. (**b**) embarrassment, confusion; fluster. (**c**) excitement.
azorar [1a] [1] VT (**a**) (*alarmar etc*) to alarm, disturb, upset; to rattle. (**b**) (*turbar*) to embarrass, fluster. (**c**) (*emocionar*) to excite; (*instar*) to urge on, egg on.
[2] **azorarse** VR (**a**) to get alarmed, get upset; to get rattled. (**b**) to be embarrassed, get flustered.
Azores NFPL Azores.
azoro NM (**a**) (*esp LAm*) = **azoramiento**. (**b**) (*CAm*) ghost.
azorrillarse [1a] VR (*Méx*) to hide away, keep out of sight.
azotacalles NM INVAR idler, loafer.
azotaina NF beating, spanking.
azotamiento NM whipping, flogging.

azotar [1a] [1] VT to whip, flog, beat; to scourge; *niño* to thrash, spank; (*Agr etc*) to beat; *ramas etc* to jar, shake; (*lluvia, olas*) to lash, beat, beat down upon; **un viento huracanado azota la costa** a hurricane is lashing the coast.
[2] **azotarse** VR (*Méx*) to put on airs, fancy o.s.
azotazo NM stroke, lash; spank.
azote NM (**a**) (*látigo*) whip, lash, scourge.
(**b**) (*golpe*) stroke, lash; spank; **ser condenado a 100 ~s** to be sentenced to 100 lashes; **~s y galeras** (*fig*) monotonous fare, the same old stuff.
(**c**) (*fig*) scourge; calamity; **Atila, el ~ de Dios** Attila, the Scourge of God.
azotea NF (**a**) (*techo*) flat roof, terrace roof; (*And, Cono Sur*) flat-roofed adobe house. (**b**) (: *cabeza*) bonce:, head; **estar mal de la ~** to be round the bend:.
azotera NF (*LAm*) (*acto*) beating, thrashing; (*azote*) cat-o'-nine-tails.
AZT NM ABR de **azidotimidina** azidothymidine, AZT.
azteca ADJ, NMF Aztec; (*fig*) Mexican.
azúcar NM (*en LAm gen* NF) sugar; **~ blanco, ~ extrafino, ~ fina** castor sugar; **~ cande, ~ candi** sugar candy, rock candy; **~ de caña, ~ mascabada** cane sugar; **~ de cortadillo, ~ en terrón** lump sugar; **~ flor,** (*LAm*) **~ glas,** (*Cono Sur*) **~ impalpable, ~ en polvo** icing sugar; **~ lustre** castor sugar; **~ morena, ~ negra, ~ terciada** brown sugar.
azucarado ADJ sugary, sweet (*t fig*).
azucarar [1a] VT (**a**) (*agregar azúcar*) to sugar, add sugar to; to ice with sugar, coat with sugar. (**b**) (*fig*) to soften, mitigate; *persona* to sweeten.
azucarería NF sugar refinery; (*Carib, Méx*) sugar shop.
azucarero [1] ADJ sugar (*atr*).
[2] NM (*t* **azucarera** NF) sugar basin, sugar bowl.
azucena NF (white) lily, Madonna lily; **~ rosa** belladonna lily; **~ tigrina** tiger lily.
azud NM, **azuda** NF (*noria*) waterwheel; (*presa*) dam (for irrigation), mill dam.
azuela NF adze.
azufre NM sulphur; brimstone.
azufroso ADJ sulphurous.
azul [1] ADJ blue; (*Pol*) conservative.
[2] NM blue; blueness; **~ celeste** sky blue; **~ de cobalto** cobalt blue; **~ eléctrico** electric blue; **~ de mar, ~ marino** navy blue; **~ pavo** peacock blue; **~ de Prusia** Prussian blue; **~ turquesa** turquoise; **~ de ultramar** ultramarine.
azulado ADJ blue, bluish.
azular [1a] [1] VT to colour blue, dye blue.
[2] **azularse** VR to turn blue.
azulear [1a] VI (**a**) (*volverse azul*) to go blue, turn blue. (**b**) (*tirar a azul*) to be bluish; (*mostrarse azul*) to show blue, look blue.
azulejar [1a] VT to tile.
azulejería NF (**a**) (*azulejos*) tiling. (**b**) (*industria*) tile industry.
azulejista NMF tiler.
azulejo NM (**a**) tile, glazed tile, ornamental tile. (**b**) (*Carib, Méx*:) copper*. (**c**) (*Méx: color*) bluish. (**d**) (*Méx Pez*) sardine-like fish.
azulenco ADJ bluish.
azulete NM blue (*for washing*).
azulgrana [1] ADJ INVAR (**a**) (*color*) blue and scarlet. (**b**) (*Dep*) of Barcelona Football Club.
[2] NMPL: **los A~** the Barcelona club (*o team*).
azulina NF cornflower.
azulino ADJ bluish.
azulón ADJ, NM deep blue.
azuloso ADJ (*LAm*) bluish.
azumagarse [1h] VR (*Cono Sur*) to rust, get rusty.
azumbrado ADJ tight*.
azumbre NM *liquid measure = 2.016 litres.*
azur NM (*Her*) azure.
azurumbado ADJ (*CAm*) (*tonto*) silly, stupid; (*borracho*) drunk.
azuzar [1f] VT (**a**) **~ a los perros a uno** to set the dogs on sb, urge the dogs to attack sb.
(**b**) (*fig*) *persona* to egg on, urge on, incite; *emoción* to stir up, fan.

B

B, b [be] NF (*letra*) B, b; **se escribe con ~ de Barcelona** (*o* **~ de burro**, (*LAm*) **~ alta**, **~ grande**, **~ larga**) it's written with a *b*; **se escribe con ~ de Valencia** (*o* **~ de vaca**, (*LAm*) **~ chica**, **~ corta**, **~ baja**) it's written with a *v*.

B. (a) ABR *de* **Barcelona**. (b) (*Rel*) ABR *de* **Beato, Beata** Blessed.

baba NF (a) spittle, saliva, slobber; (*Bio*) mucus; (*de babosa etc*) slime, slimy secretion; **echar ~** to drool, slobber; **se le cae la ~** (*fig*) he's thrilled to bits, he's delighted (*por* with); (*en amor*) he's soft (*por* on), he's drooling (*por* over); (*pey*) he's a bit soft (in the head); (*LAm*) she could hardly wait; **cambiar ~s** to kiss.
(b) **mala ~*** (*malhumor*) bad temper; (*mal genio*) nasty character.

babador NM bib.

babasfrías NM INVAR (*And, Méx*) fool.

babaza NF (a) slime, mucus. (b) (*Zool*) slug.

babear [1a] ① VI (a) to drool, slobber.
(b) (*fig*) to be sloppy, drool (over women).
② **babearse** VR (a) (*Cono Sur*) to feel flattered, glow with satisfaction.
(b) **~ por algo** (*Méx*) to yearn for sth, drool over sth.

Babel NM Babel; **Torre de ~** Tower of Babel.

babel NM *o* F bedlam; confusion, mess.

babeo NM drooling, slobbering.

babero NM bib.

babi* NM = **baby** (b).

Babia NF: **estar en ~** to be daydreaming, have one's mind somewhere else.

babieca* ① ADJ simple-minded, stupid.
② NMF idiot, dolt.

babilla NF (*Vet*) stifle.

Babilonia NF Babylon, Babylonia.

babilonia[1] NF bedlam.

babilónico ADJ Babylonian.

babilonio, -a[2] ADJ, NM/F Babylonian.

bable NM dialect of Asturias.

babor NM port, port side, larboard; **a ~** on the port side; **la mar a ~** the sea to port; **¡tierra a ~!** land to port!; **poner el timón a ~, virar a ~** to turn to port, port the helm; **de ~** port (*atr*).

babosa NF slug.

babosada NF (*LAm*: *disparates*) stupid thing; (*inútil*) dead loss, useless thing; (*CAm, Méx: comentario*) stupid comment, silly remark; (*CAm, Méx: acto*) stupid thing to do; **¡~s!** rubbish!

babosear [1a] ① VT (a) to drool over, slobber over.
(b) (*fig*) to drool over; (*CAm*) to insult; (*Méx**: *manosear*) to manhandle; (*CAm, Méx*‡: *tratar de bobo*) to take for (*o* treat like) a fool; **muchos han baboseado este problema** (*Méx*) many have taken a superficial look at this problem.
② VI (a) to drool. (b) (*Méx: holgazanear*) to mess about.

baboseo NM (a) drooling, slobbering. (b) (*fig*) infatuation, drooling.

baboso ① ADJ (a) drooling, slobbering; slimy.
(b) (***) (*fig: en amor*) sloppy (about women); (*sensiblero*) mushy, foolishly sentimental; (*adulón*) fawning, snivelling; (*sucio*) dirty; (*LAm: tonto*) silly, foolish; (*CAm*) rotten*, caddish*.
② NM, **babosa** NF (*LAm*) fool, idiot.

babucha NF slipper; (*Carib*) child's bodice; (*LAm: blusa*) loose blouse, smock; **~s** (*Carib*) rompers; (*Méx*) high-heeled boots; **llevar algo a ~** (*Cono Sur*) to carry sth on one's back.

babuino NM baboon.

babujal NM (*Carib*) witch, sorcerer.

baby ['beiβi] NMF (a) (*LAm*) baby; (*Aut*) small car, mini; **~ crece** babygrow; **~ fútbol** table football. (b) (*: *babero*) bib; (*mandil*) apron, smock.

baca NF (a) (*de autocar*) top; rainproof cover. (b) (*portaequipajes*) luggage rack, carrier, roof rack.

bacal NM (*Méx*) corncob.

bacalada‡ NF sweetener*, bribe.

bacaladero ADJ cod (*atr*); **flota bacaladera** cod-fishing fleet.

bacaladilla NF blue whiting.

bacalao NM (a) cod, codfish; **mi ~*** my other half, the wife*; **cortar el ~*** to be the boss, have the final say, run the show; **¡te conozco, ~!*** I've rumbled you!*.
(b) (*Cono Sur*) miser, tight-fisted person.
(c) (*Esp*‡) cunt‡.

bacán* ① ADJ posh*, classy*.
② NM (*Cono Sur: rico*) wealthy man; (*protector*) sugar daddy*; (*señorito*) playboy; (*elegante*) toff*, dude (*US*).

bacanal ① ADJ bacchanalian.
② NF (*t* **~es**) bacchanalia; (*fig*) bacchanalia, orgy.

bacanalear [1a] VI (*CAm*) to have a wild time.

bacane NM (*Carib*) driving licence, driver's license (*US*).

bacanería NF (*Cono Sur**) (*elegancia*) sharp dressing, nattiness; (*ostentación*) vulgar display, ostentation.

bacante NF bacchante; (*fig*) drunken and noisy woman.

bacar(r)á NM baccarat.

bacelador* NM (*Carib*) con man.

bacelar [1a] VT (*Carib*) to con, trick.

bacenica NF (*LAm*) = **bacinica**.

bacha NF (*Carib*) spree, merry outing.

bachata NF (*Carib*) party, good time.

bachatear [1a] VI (*Carib*) to go on a spree, go out for a good time.

bachatero NM (*Carib*) reveller, carouser.

bache NM (a) hole, pothole; (*fig*) bad patch, bad spot, rut; **~ de aire** (*Aer*) air pocket. (b) (*fig*) (*Econ etc*) slump; **~ económico** slump, economic depression; **salir del ~** to get out of the rut, get moving again; **salvar el ~** to get the worst over, be over the worst.

bacheado ADJ *carretera* bumpy, uneven, full of pot-holes.

bachicha NM (a) (*Cono Sur*‡: *italiano*) dago, Wop‡. (b) (*Méx*) (*restos*) leftovers; (*colilla*) cigarette end, cigar stub; (*de bebida*) dregs. (c) (*Méx Fin*) nest-egg, secret hoard.

bachiche NM (*And*) = **bachicha** (a).

bachiller ① ADJ garrulous, talkative.
② NMF *pupil who has passed the school-leaving examination or holds a certificate of higher education* (V **bachillerato**); (*Univ: Hist*) bachelor.
③ NM (*fig*) windbag.
④ **bachillera** NF (a) (*erudita*) bluestocking; (*gárrula*) talkative woman.
(b) (*astuta*) cunning woman, scheming woman.

bachillerato NM *higher secondary-education course*; (*Univ: Hist*) bachelor's degree; **~ comercial** certificate in business studies; **~ elemental** lower examination (≈ 'O' *level*); **~ laboral** certificate in agricultural (*o* technical) studies; **~ del magisterio** certificate for students proceeding to teacher-training; **~ superior** higher certificate (≈ 'A' *level*); *see also* [ESO].

bachillerear* [1a] VI to talk a lot, prattle away.

bachillería* NF (a) (*cotorreo*) talk, prattle; idle talk. (b) (*disparate*) piece of nonsense.

bacía NF (*vasija*) basin, vessel; (*de afeitar*) barber's bowl, shaving bowl.

bacilar ADJ bacillary.

bacilarse [1a] VR (*And*) to have a good time.

bacilo NM bacillus, germ.

bacilón* ① ADJ brilliant*, great*; *V t* **vacilón**.
② NM (*And*) fun, good time.

bacín NM (a) (*orinal*) chamberpot; (*cepo*) poorbox; (*de mendigo*) beggar's bowl.
(b) (*persona*) wretch, cur.

bacinete NM (*LAm*) lavatory pan.

bacinica NF small chamberpot.

Baco NM Bacchus.

bacón ['beɪkon] NM bacon.

bacteria NF bacterium, germ; **~s** bacteria, germs.

bacterial ADJ, **bacteriano** ADJ bacterial.

bactericida [1] ADJ germ-killing.
   [2] NM germicide, germ killer.

bactérico ADJ bacterial.

bacteriología NF bacteriology.

bacteriológico ADJ bacteriological.

bacteriólogo, -a NM/F bacteriologist.

bacteriosis NF bacteriosis.

báculo NM (a) stick, staff; **~ pastoral** crozier, bishop's staff. (b) (*fig*) prop, support, staff; **ser el ~ de la vejez de uno** to be sb's comfort in old age.

badajada NF (a) (*de campana*) stroke (of a bell), chime. (b) (*fig*) piece of idle talk, piece of gossip; rubbish, stupid remark.

badajazo NM stroke (of a bell), chime.

badajear [1a] VI to swing to and fro.

badajo NM (a) (*de campana*) clapper (of a bell). (b) (*) chatterbox.

badajocense [1] ADJ of Badajoz.
   [2] NMF native (*o* inhabitant) of Badajoz; **los ~s** the people of Badajoz.

badajoceño = **badajocense**.

badana NF dressed sheepskin; **zurrar** (*o* **calentar, sobar**) **la ~ a uno*** to tan sb's hide*, (*fig*) haul sb over the coals.

badaza NF (*Carib*) strap (for standing passenger).

badén NM (*Aut*) (*bache*) bump; dip, pothole; (*agua*) splash of water; (*señal*) '~' 'splash'.

badil NM, **badila** NF fire shovel.

badilejo NM (*And*) (builder's) trowel.

bádminton NM badminton.

badulaque NM (a) (*idiota*) idiot, nincompoop. (b) (*Cono Sur* ††) rogue.

badulaquear [1a] VI (a) (*ser idiota*) to be an idiot, act like an idiot. (b) (*Cono Sur* ††) to be a rogue, be dishonest, act like a rogue.

baf(f)le NM (*Elec*) speaker, loudspeaker.

bagaje NM (a) (*Mil*) baggage; equipment; (*LAm: equipaje*) luggage, baggage (*US*). (b) (*animal*) beast of burden. (c) (*fig*) knowledge, experience.

bagatela NF trinket, knick-knack; trifle, mere nothing, bagatelle; **¡una ~!** a mere trifle!; **son ~s** those are trivialities, those are things of no importance.

bagayo* NM (*Cono Sur*) (a) (*lío*) bundle, tramp's bundle; (*carga*) heavy (*o* awkward) burden; (*cosas robadas*) loot (from a crime); (*contrabando*) contraband goods. (b) (*fig: inútil*) useless lump, berk*; (*mujer fea*) old bag*.

bagazo NM (a) (*residuo*) chaff, husks; pulp; (*LAm: de azúcar*) husks of sugar cane. (b) (*fig*) dead loss. (c) (*Carib: miserable*) down-and-out.

bagre [1] ADJ (a) (*And*) vulgar, coarse, loud. (b) (*CAm*) clever, sharp.
   [2] NM (*LAm: pez*) catfish.
   [3] NMF (*) (*LAm*) (*taimado*) unpleasant person, sly sort; (*tipo feo*) ugly mug‡; (*mujer*) old bag*; **pica el ~** (*Cono Sur**) I'm starving.

bagrero ADJ (*And*) fond of ugly women.

bagual [1] ADJ (*And, Cono Sur*) (a) *animal* wild, untamed. (b) *persona* rough, loutish, rude.
   [2] NM (a) (*And, Cono Sur*) wild (*o* unbroken) horse; **ganar los ~es** (*Cono Sur Hist*) to escape, get to safety. (b) (*Cono Sur: persona*) thug, lout.

bagualada NF (*Cono Sur*) (a) herd of wild horses. (b) (*fig*) stupid thing (to do).

bagualón ADJ (*Cono Sur*) half-tamed.

baguío NM hurricane, typhoon.

bah INTERJ (*desprecio*) bah!, that's nothing!, pooh!; (*incredulidad*) hum!, never!

Bahama: Islas NFPL **~,** *t* **Las Bahamas** the Bahamas.

bahareque NM = **bajareque**.

baharí NM sparrowhawk.

bahía NF (*Geog*) bay.

baho NM (*CAm Culin*) dish of meat and yucca.

bahorrina NF (a) dirt, filth; slops. (b) (*fig*) riffraff, scum.

bahreiní ADJ, NMF Bahreini.

bailable [1] ADJ: **música ~** dance music, music that you can dance to.
   [2] NM dance, dance number; ballet.

bailada NF (*LAm*) dance, dancing.

bailadero NM (*sala*) dance hall; (*pista*) dance floor.

bailador [1] ADJ dancing.
   [2] NM, **bailadora** NF dancer.

bailaor(a) NM/F flamenco dancer.

bailar [1a] [1] VT (a) to dance: *peonza etc* to spin. (b) (*LAm**) **le bailaron la herencia** they cheated her out of her inheritance.

   [2] VI to dance; (*peonza*) to spin, spin round; (*fig*) to dance, jump about; **~ al son que tocan** to toe the line; to adapt o.s. to circumstances; **éste es otro que bien baila** here's another one (of the same kind); **¿quieres ~?** shall we dance?; **sacar a una a ~** to invite a girl to dance; **le bailaban los ojos de alegría** her eyes sparkled with happiness; **¡que nos quiten lo bailado!** nobody can take away the good times we've had!

bailarín NM (professional) dancer; (*de ballet*) ballet dancer; **~ de claqué** tap-dancer.

bailarina NF (professional) dancer; dancing-girl; (*de ballet*) ballet dancer, ballerina; **~ del vientre** belly-dancer; **primera ~** prima ballerina.

bailata‡ NF = **baile**.

baile NM (a) (*gen*) dance; dancing, the dance; (*Teat*) dance, ballet; **~ agarrado, ~ apretado** slow dance; **~ clásico** ballet; **~ folklórico, ~ popular, ~ regional** traditional dance; **~ de salón** ballroom dance; **~ de San Vito** St Vitus's dance; **hacer el ~** (*Fútbol**) to pass the ball to and fro, waste time.
(b) (*función*) dance, (*más formal*) ball; **~ de candil, ~ de medio pelo** (*LAm*) village dance, hop*; **~ de contribución** (*CAm, Carib*) public dance; **~ de disfraces** fancy dress ball; **~ de etiqueta** ball, dress ball, formal dance; **~ de fantasía** (*LAm*), **~ de máscaras** masked ball; **~ de trajes** fancy-dress ball.

bailecito(s) NM(PL) (*LAm*) folk dance.

bailón ADJ fond of dancing, that dances a lot.

bailongo [1] ADJ dance (*atr*); **música bailonga** music for dancing, music you can dance to.
   [2] NM (*esp LAm*) local dance.

bailotear [1a] VI (*pey*) to dance about, hop around.

bailoteo* NM dancing; **estuvieron toda la noche de ~** they were out all night dancing.

baivel NM bevel.

baja NF (a) (*de precio, temperatura etc*) drop, fall; cut; **~ repentina** (*Econ*) slump, recession; **una ~ de 5 por ciento** a fall of 5%; **una ~ de los tipos de interés** a cut in interest rates; **una ~ de temperatura** a drop in temperature; **tendencia a la ~** downward tendency, tendency to fall; **jugar a la ~** (*Fin*) to speculate on a fall in prices; **dar ~, ir de ~** (*Fin*) to decline, lose value; **seguir en ~** (*Fin*) to continue downwards; **se cotiza hoy a la ~** (*fig*) it's in decline, it's going downhill.
(b) (*Mil*) casualty; (*en un puesto*) vacancy; (*abono*) cancelled subscription; **~ incentivada, ~ por incentivo** voluntary severance; **~ retribuida** paid leave; **~ voluntaria** voluntary redundancy; **las ~s son grandes** the casualties are heavy, there are heavy casualties; **Pepe es ~ (por enfermedad)** Pepe is off sick; **dar a uno de ~** to mark sb absent; to strike off sb, eliminate sb (from a list); (*Mil*) to post a man as absent (from parade *etc*); **dar de ~ a un soldado** to discharge a soldier; **dar de ~ a un empleado** to give notice to an employee; **dar de ~ a un miembro** to expel a member, remove sb from the list of members; **darse de ~** to drop out, withdraw, retire; to go sick; to step down; to give up one's job, leave one's post; to cease to subscribe, give up one's membership.

bajá NM pasha.

bajacaliforniano (*Méx*) [1] ADJ of Baja California.
   [2] NM, **bajacaliforniana** NF native (*o* inhabitant) of Baja California.

bajada NF (a) (*cuesta*) slope. (b) (*acto*) descent, going down; **~ de bandera*** minimum (taxi) fare; **~ de pantalones*** shameful capitulation; **durante la ~** as we (*etc*) went down, on the way down. (c) (*de precios*) reduction, lowering.

bajamar NF low tide, low water.

bajante NM drainpipe.

bajar [1a] [1] VT (a) *objeto* to lower, let down; to bring down, carry down; *equipaje etc* to take down, get down; *bandera* to lower; *persona* to help down, help out; to lead down; **~ el telón** to lower the curtain; **~ el equipaje al taxi** to take the luggage down to the taxi; **¿me ayuda a ~ esta maleta?** would you help me to get this case down?
(b) *brazo, ojos etc* to drop, lower; *cabeza* to bow, bend.
(c) *precio* to reduce, lower, cut; *gas, radio etc* to turn down; *voz* to lower; (*Aut*) *faros* to dip.
(d) *cuesta, escalera* to come down, go down, descend.
(e) (*fig: humillar*) to humble, humiliate.
(f) (*Carib‡: pagar*) to pay up, cough up*.
(g) (*And‡: matar*) to do in‡.
   [2] VI (a) (*descender*) to come down, go down, descend.
(b) (*de vehículo*) to get off, get out; **~ de** to get off, get out of.
(c) (*precio, temperatura, agua etc*) to fall; **la venta no ha bajado nunca de mil** sales have never been less than a thousand, sales have never fallen below a thousand.
   [3] **bajarse** VR (a) (*inclinarse*) to bend down, stoop; **~ a recoger algo** to bend down to pick sth up.
(b) (*de vehículo*) to get off, get out; **~ de** to get off, get out of; **~ del**

vicio* to kick the drug habit*.
(c) (*fig*) to lower o.s., humble o.s.; ~ **a hacer algo vil** to lower o.s. to do sth mean.
(d) (*Cono Sur: alojarse*) to stay, put up (*en* in, at).

| BAJAR | | ver también la entrada |

De vehículos
- *Bajar(se) de* un vehículo privado o de un taxi se traduce por **get out of**, mientras que *bajar(se) de* un vehículo público (tren, autobús, avión, *etc*) se traduce por **get off**:
  Bajó del coche y nos saludó
  She got out of the car and said hello
  No baje del tren en marcha
  Don't get off the train while it is still moving
- Debe emplearse *get off* cuando nos referimos a bicicletas, motos y animales de montura:
  Se bajó de la bicicleta
  He got off his bicycle

Otros verbos de movimiento
- *Bajar la escalera/la cuesta etc*, por regla general, se suele traducir por **come down** o por **go down**, según la dirección del movimiento (hacia o en sentido contrario del hablante), pero *come* y *go* se pueden substituir por otros verbos de movimiento si la oración española especifica la forma en que se baja mediante el uso de adverbios o construcciones adverbiales:
  Bajó las escaleras deprisa y corriendo
  She rushed down the stairs
  Bajó la cuesta tranquilamente
  He ambled down the path
  Para otros usos y ejemplos ver la entrada.

---

bajareque NM **(a)** (*LAm: tapia*) mud wall; (*Carib: cabaña*) hovel, shack. **(b)** (*CAm*) (*llovizna*) fine drizzle; (*caña*) bamboo.
bajativo ADJ (*Cono Sur*) digestive.
bajel NM (*liter*) vessel, ship.
bajera NF **(a)** (*Arquit*) lower ground floor, basement. **(b)** (*And, CAm, Carib*) lower leaves of the tobacco plant; rough (*o inferior*) tobacco. **(c)** (*And, CAm, Carib: fig*) insignificant person, nobody. **(d)** (*Cono Sur*) horse blanket.
bajero ADJ **(a)** lower, under-...; **falda bajera** underskirt. **(b)** (*CAm: de colina etc*) downhill, descending.
bajetón ADJ (*And*) short, small.
bajeza NF **(a)** (*cualidad*) lowliness; vileness, baseness, meanness. **(b)** (*una ~*) mean thing, vile deed.
bajial NM (*LAm*) lowland; flats, floodplain.
bajini(s)*: por lo ~ ADV *decir* very quietly, in an undertone.
bajío NM **(a)** (*Náut*) shoal, sandbank; shallows. **(b)** (*LAm*) lowland; (*Méx: t ~s*) flat arable land on a high plateau; **el B~** (*Méx*) the fertile plateau of northern Mexico.
bajista ① ADJ (*Fin*): **tendencia ~** tendency to lower prices, bearish tendency.
② NM (*Fin*) bear.
③ NMF (*Mús*) bass guitar player, bassist.
bajo ① ADJ **(a)** (*no alto*) low; *persona* short, small (*t ~* **de cuerpo**, **~ de estatura**); *parte, lado* lower, under; *piso* lower, ground (*atr*); *tierra* low, low-lying; *agua* shallow; **con la cabeza baja** with bowed head, with head lowered; **con los ojos ~s** with downcast eyes, with lowered eyes; **en la parte baja de la ciudad** in the lower part of the town.
(b) *sonido* faint, soft; *voz* low, (*de tono*) deep; **en voz baja** in an undertone, in a low voice; **por lo ~** (*Méx: a lo menos*) at (the) least; **decir algo por lo ~** to say sth in an undertone; **hacer algo por lo ~** to do sth secretly.
(c) *color* dull; pale.
(d) (*t ~* **de ley**) *metal* base.
(e) **~ latín** Low Latin; **baja Edad Media** late Middle Ages.
(f) *nacimiento* low, humble; *cámara* (*Pol*), *clase* lower; *condición* lowly; *tarea* menial; *barrio* poor, working-class (*y V* **barrio**).
(g) (*pey*) common, ordinary; *cualidad* low, poor; (*moralmente*) vile, base, mean.
② NM **(a)** deep place, depth; hollow.
(b) (*Náut*) = **bajío**.
(c) (*Cos*) hemline; **~s de la falda** lower part of the skirt; **~s del pantalón** trouser bottoms.
(d) (*Arquit*) **~s** ground floor, first floor (*US*), ground-floor flat (*o* rooms).
(e) (*Mús: voz*) bass; **~ profundo** basso profundo.
(f) (*Mús: guitarrista*) bass guitar player, bassist.
(g) **~s** (*Anat*) lower parts (of the body); (*euf*) genitals.
③ ADV **(a)** down; below.
(b) *tocar, cantar* quietly; *hablar* low, in a low voice; **¡más ~, por favor!** quieter, please!

④ PREP **(a)** under, underneath, below.
(b) (*fig*) under; **~ Napoleón** under Napoleon; **~ el reinado de** in the reign of.
(c) **V juramento** etc.
bajo-barítono NM bass-baritone.
bajomedieval ADJ late medieval.
bajón NM **(a)** (*caída*) decline, fall, drop; (*Med*) decline, worsening; withdrawal symptoms (after drug use); (*Com, Fin*) sharp fall in price; slump; **~ en la moral** slump in morale; **dar un ~** to fall away sharply, slump, go rapidly downhill; **en 3 meses ha pegado un ~ de 5 años** in 3 months he seems to have aged 5 years.
(b) (*Mús*) bassoon.
bajorrelieve NM bas-relief.
bajuno ADJ *truco etc* base, underhand, sly.
bajura NF **(a)** (*V ADJ* **(a)**) lowness; shortness, smallness, small size. **(b)** (*Carib Geog*) lowland. **(c)** **pesca de ~** inshore fishing, coastal fishing.
bakaladero* ① ADJ rave (*atr*).
② NM, **bakaladera** NF raver.
bakalao* ① ADJ INVAR rave (*atr*).
② NM rave (music); **la ruta del ~** weekend-long tour of a series of rave parties.
bala NF **(a)** (*Mil*) bullet, shot; **~ de cañón** cannonball; **~ de fogueo** blank cartridge; **~ fría** spent bullet; **~ de goma** plastic bullet, rubber bullet; **~ perdida** stray shot; **~ trazadora** tracer bullet; **como una ~** like a bullet, like lightning; **ni a ~** (*LAm*) by no means, not on any account; **ser una ~** (*Carib**) to be a pain in the neck*; **ser un(a) ~** (**perdida***) (*raro*) to be an oddball*; (*calavera*) to be a madcap; (*malo*) to be a rotter*; **quedar con la ~ pasada** (*Cono Sur*) to have a nagging doubt; **no le entra ~** (*Cono Sur*) (*de salud*) he's never ill, he's terribly tough; (*insensible*) he's very thick-skinned.
(b) (*Com*) bale; **~ de algodón** bale of cotton, cotton bale.
(c) **~ de entintar** (*Tip*) inkball, inking ball.
balaca NF (*LAm: baladronada*) boast, piece of boasting, brag; (*And: boato*) show, pomp.
balacada NF (*Cono Sur*) = **balaca**.
balacear [1a] VT (*CAm, Méx*) to shoot, shoot at.
balacera NF (*tiroteo*) exchange of shots, shooting; (*balas*) hail of bullets; (*enfrentamiento*) shoot-out.
balada NF (*Liter*) ballad; (*Mús*) ballad, ballade.
baladí ADJ trivial, paltry, worthless; trashy.
baladista NMF ballad-maker, songwriter; ballad-singer.
baladrar [1a] VI to scream, howl; to shout.
baladre NM oleander, rosebay.
baladrero ADJ loud, noisy.
baladro NM scream, howl; shout.
baladrón ① ADJ boastful.
② NM braggart, bully.
baladronada NF boast, brag; bravado, piece of bravado.
baladronear [1a] VI to boast, brag; to indulge in bravado.
bálago NM **(a)** (*paja*) (long) straw. **(b)** (*jabón*) soapsuds, lather.
balance NM **(a)** (*vaivén*) to-and-fro motion, oscillation; rocking, swinging; (*Náut*) roll, rolling.
(b) (*fig: indecisión*) hesitation, vacillation.
(c) (*Carib: mecedora*) rocking chair.
(d) (*Com, Fin*) balance; balance-sheet; (*inventario*) stocktaking; **~ de comprobación** trial balance; **~ consolidado** consolidated balance-sheet; **~ de la situación** balance-sheet; **el ~ de víctimas en el accidente** the toll of victims in the accident, the number of dead in the accident; **hacer ~** to draw up a balance; to take an inventory; (*fig*) to take stock (of one's situation).
(e) **~ de pagos** etc **V balanza (c)**.
(f) (*And: asunto*) affair, matter; (*negocio*) deal.
balanceado NM (*Boxeo*) swing.
balancear [1a] ① VT to balance.
② VI y **balancearse** VR **(a)** (*movimiento*) to move to and fro, oscillate; to rock, swing; (*Náut*) to roll. **(b)** (*fig: vacilar*) to hesitate, vacillate, waver.
balanceo NM = **balance (a)**, **(b)**.
balancín NM (*de balanza*) balance beam; (*Mec*) rocker, rocker arm; (*de carro*) swingletree; (*Náut*) outrigger; (*de volatinero*) balancing pole; (*para llevar cargas*) yoke; (*columpio*) seesaw, (*juguete*) child's rocking toy; (*silla*) rocking chair.
balandra NF sloop; (large, sea-going) yacht.
balandrán NM cassock.
balandrismo NM yachting; sailing.
balandrista NMF yachtsman, yachtswoman; sailing enthusiast.
balandro NM yacht; (*Carib*) fishing vessel.
balanza NF **(a)** (*instrumento*) balance (*esp Quím*), scales, weighing machine; (*Zodíaco*) **B~** Libra, the Scales; **~ de cocina** kitchen scales; **~ de cruz** grocer's scales; **~ de laboratorio**, **~ de precisión** precision balance; **~ de muelle** spring-balance; **~ romana** steelyard; **estar en la ~** to be in the balance.

(b) (*fig: juicio*) judgement; (*comparación*) comparison.
(c) (*Com, Fin, Pol etc*) balance; **~ comercial, ~ de comercio** balance of trade; **~ por cuenta corriente, ~ de pagos** balance of payments; **~ de poder(es), ~ política** balance of power.
balaquear [1a] VI to boast.
balar [1a] VI to bleat, baa.
balasto[1] NM (*Ferro*) sleeper.
balasto[2] NM (*Cono Sur, Méx*) ballast.
balastro NM = **balasto**[2].
balata NF (*LAm: Aut*) brake lining.
balaustrada NF balustrade; bannisters.
balaustre NM baluster; banister.
balay NM (*LAm*) wicker basket.
balazo NM shot; bullet wound; **matar a uno de un ~** to shoot sb dead.
balboa NF balboa (*Panamanian unit of currency*).
balbucear [1a] VTI, **balbucir** [3f; *defectivo: se usan únicamente las formas que tienen -i- en la desinencia*] VTI to stammer, stutter; (*niño*) to lisp, make its first sounds; to babble.
balbuceo NM stammering, stuttering; babbling.
balbuciente ADJ stammering, stuttering; babbling.
Balcanes NMPL: **los ~** the Balkans; **la Península de los ~** the Balkan Peninsula; **los (Montes) ~** the Balkan Mountains.
balcánico ADJ Balkan.
balcanización NF balkanization.
balcarrias NFPL, **balcarrotas** NFPL (*And*) sideburns.
balcón NM balcony; balcony window; railing (of a balcony); (*fig*) vantage point.
balconada NF row of balconies.
balconeador(a) NM/F onlooker, observer.
balconear [1a] [1] VT (*Cono Sur*) to watch closely (from a balcony); *juego etc* to sneak a look at.
[2] VI (*CAm: amantes*) to talk at the window.
balconero NM cat burglar.
balda NF shelf.
baldada NF (*Cono Sur*) bucketful.
baldado [1] ADJ crippled, disabled; **estar ~*** to be knackered*.
[2] NM, **baldada** NF cripple, disabled person.
baldaquín NM, **baldaquino** NM canopy, baldachin.
baldar [1a] VT **(a)** (*lisiar*) to cripple, maim, disable. **(b)** (*fig: dañar*) to harm, cripple; (*Naipes*) to trump.
balde[1] NM bucket, pail; **~ de la basura** trash-can.
balde[2] NM **(a)** **obtener algo de ~** to get sth free, get sth for nothing; **vender algo medio de ~** to sell sth for a song; **había muchos de ~** there were a lot left over; **estar de ~** (*persona*) (*estar de más*) to be de trop, be unwanted, be in the way; (*sin empleo*) to be idle, be out of work.
(b) **¡no de ~!** (*CAm*) goodness!, I never noticed!
(c) **en ~** in vain, to no purpose; **¡ni en ~!** (*LAm*) no way!*, not on your life!
baldear [1a] VT **(a)** (*limpiar*) to hose down; to wash, wash down, swill with water. **(b)** (*Naút*) to bail out.
baldeo NM **(a)** wash, hosing down. **(b)** (‡) chiv‡, knife.
baldío [1] ADJ **(a)** *tierra* uncultivated; waste. **(b)** (*ocioso*) lazy, idle. **(c)** (*vano*) vain, useless.
[2] NM uncultivated land; waste land; uncultivated common land.
baldón NM (*afrenta*) affront, insult; (*tacha*) blot, stain, disgrace.
baldonar [1a] VT to insult; to blot, disgrace.
baldosa NF floor tile; paving stone; (*LAm: lápida*) tombstone.
baldosado NM tiled floor, tiling; paving (of flagstones).
baldosar [1a] VT *suelo* to tile; *vereda etc* to pave (with flagstones).
baldoseta NF small tile.
baldosín NM tile.
balduque NM (*official*) red tape (*t fig*).
baleado, -a NM/F shooting victim, person who has been shot.
balear[1] [1a] [1] VT (*esp LAm*) **(a)** (*disparar contra*) to shoot (at); (*matar*) to shoot down (o dead); **morir baleado** to be shot dead. **(b)** (*estafar*) to cheat, swindle.
[2] **balearse** VR (*esp LAm*) to exchange shots, shoot at each other.
balear[2] [1] ADJ Balearic, of the Balearic Isles.
[2] NMF native (o inhabitant) of the Balearic Isles; **los ~es** the people of the Balearic Isles.
Baleares NFPL (*t* **Islas ~**) NFPL Balearics, Balearic Islands.
baleárico ADJ Balearic, of the Balearic Isles.
baleo NM **(a)** (*esp LAm: tiroteo*) shooting. **(b)** (*Méx: abanico*) fan.
balero NM (*LAm: juguete*) cup-and-ball toy; (*Méx Téc*) ball bearing(s); (*Cono Sur*‡) head, nut‡.
balido NM bleat, bleating, baa.
balín NM small bullet, pellet; **~es** shot.
balinera NF (*And*) ball-bearing(s).
balística NF ballistics.
balístico ADJ ballistic.

balita NF **(a)** (*balín*) small bullet, pellet. **(b)** (*Cono Sur: canica*) marble.
baliza NF (*Naút*) (lighted) buoy, marker; (*Aer*) beacon, marker.
balizaje NM, **balizamiento** NM: **~ de pista** (*Aer*) runway lighting, runway beacons.
balizar [1f] VT *canal* to buoy, mark with buoys; (*Aer*) to light, mark with beacons.
ballena NF **(a)** (*Zool*) whale; **~ azul** blue whale; **parece una ~*** she's as fat as a cow*. **(b)** (*hueso*) whalebone; (*de corsé*) bone, stay.
ballenato NM whale calf.
ballenear [1a] VI to whale, hunt whales.
ballenera NF whaler, whaling ship.
ballenero [1] ADJ whaling (*atr*); **industria ballenera** whaling industry.
[2] NM **(a)** (*persona*) whaler. **(b)** (*barco*) whaler, whaling ship.
ballesta NF **(a)** (*Hist*) crossbow. **(b)** (*Aut, Ferro etc*) spring; **~s** springs, suspension.
ballestero NM (*Hist*) crossbowman.
ballestrinque NM clove hitch.
ballet [ba'le] NM, PL **ballets** [ba'le] ballet; (*de coristas etc*) troupe of dancers, dance troupe; **~ acuático** synchronized swimming.
balletístico ADJ ballet (*atr*).
balneario [1] ADJ *estación* thermal, medicinal; spa (*atr*), health (*atr*).
[2] NM spa, health resort.
balneoterapia NF balneotherapy.
balompédico ADJ football (*atr*).
balompié NM football.
balón NM **(a)** (*Dep*) (large) ball, football; (*Quím etc*) bag (for gas); (*Met*) balloon; (*Naút*) spinnaker; (*And, Cono Sur: bombona*) drum, canister; **~ de playa** beach-ball; **achicar balones*, echar balones fuera*** to dodge the issue. **(b)** (*Com*) (large) bale. **(c)** (*copa*) brandy glass.
balonazo NM: **me dio un ~ en la cara** he kicked the ball right in my face.
baloncestista NMF basketball player.
baloncestístico ADJ basketball (*atr*).
baloncesto NM basketball.
balonmanear [1a] VI (*Dep*) to handle, handle the ball.
balonmano NM handball.
balonvolea NM volleyball.
balota NF ballot (*ball used in voting*).
balotaje NM (*Méx*) (*votación*) balloting, voting; (*recuento*) counting of votes.
balotar [1a] VI to ballot, vote.
balsa[1] NF **(a)** (*Bot*) balsa; balsa wood. **(b)** (*Naút*) raft; ferry; **~ de salvamento, ~ salvavidas** life-raft; **~ neumática** (*Aer etc*) rubber dinghy, rubber raft.
balsa[2] NF pool, pond; (*Méx: pantano*) swamp, marshy place; **el pueblo es una ~ de aceite** the village is as quiet as the grave.
balsadera NF, **balsadero** NM ferry(-station).
balsámico ADJ balsamic, balmy; (*fig*) balmy, soothing, healing.
bálsamo NM **(a)** (*Med*) balsam, balm; (*Cono Sur: de pelo*) hair conditioner. **(b)** (*fig*) balm, comfort.
balsar NM (*And, Carib*) overgrown marshy place.
balsear [1a] VT **(a)** *río* to cross by ferry, cross on a raft. **(b)** *personas, mercancías* to ferry across.
balsero NM **(a)** (*conductor*) ferryman. **(b)** (*Cuba*) refugee (*on a raft*).
balsón[1] NM (*Méx*) (*pantano*) swamp, bog; (*agua estancada*) stagnant pool.
balsón[2] ADJ (*And*) fat, flabby.
balsoso ADJ (*And*) soft, spongy.
Baltasar NM Balthasar; (*Bib*) Belshazzar; V **cena**.
báltico ADJ Baltic; **el Mar B~** the Baltic (Sea); **los estados ~s** the Baltic states.
baluarte NM bastion; (*fig*) bastion, bulwark.
balumba NF **(a)** (*masa*) (great) bulk, mass. **(b)** (*montón*) pile, heap. **(c)** (*LAm: alboroto*) noise, uproar.
balumbo NM bulky thing, cumbersome object.
balumoso ADJ (*And, CAm, Méx*) bulky, cumbersome.
baluquero NM (*Fin*) forger.
balurdo [1] ADJ (*LAm*) flashy.
[2] NM (*Cono Sur**) crooked deal*.
bamba[1] NMF (*Carib*) negro, negress.
bamba[2] NF **(a)** (*And Bot*) bole, swelling (on tree trunk). **(b)** (*And: gordura*) fat, flabbiness.
bamba[3]‡ NF (*Esp*) fuzz‡, police.
bambalear [1a] = **bambolear**.
bambalina NF (*Teat*) drop(-scene), cloth border; **entre ~s** behind the scenes.
bambalúa NM (*LAm*) clumsy fellow, lout.
bambarria* NMF idiot, fool.
bamboleante ADJ wobbly; unsteady; *pantalones* baggy.
bambolear [1a] VI **y bambolearse** VR to swing, sway; (*al andar*) to sway, roll, reel; (*mueble*) to wobble, be unsteady; (*tren etc*) to sway.
bamboleo NM swinging, swaying; rolling, reeling; wobbling, un-

steadiness.

bambolla* NF (*ostentación*) show, ostentation; (*farsa*) sham.

bambollero* ADJ showy, flashy; sham, bogus.

bambú NM bamboo.

bambudal NM (*And*) bamboo grove.

banal ADJ banal; trivial, ordinary; *persona* ordinary, commonplace; superficial.

banalidad NF (a) (*cualidad*) banality; triviality, ordinariness; superficiality.

(b) (*en conversación*) banality, trivial thing; **intercambiar ~es con uno** to exchange trivialities with sb, swap small talk with sb.

banalizar [1f] VT to trivialize.

banana NF (*esp LAm*) (*fruta*) banana; (*árbol*) banana tree.

bananal NM (*LAm*) banana plantation.

bananera NF banana plantation.

bananero ① ADJ (a) (*LAm: de bananas*) banana (*atr*); **compañía bananera** banana company; **plantación bananera** banana plantation. (b) (*) vulgar, coarse. (c) (*Pol etc*) third-world (*atr*), backward; **república bananera** banana republic.

② NM banana tree.

banano NM (*LAm: árbol*) banana tree.

banas NFPL (*Méx Rel*) banns.

banasta NF large basket, hamper.

banasto NM large round basket.

banca NF (a) (*puesto*) stand, stall; (*LAm*) bench.

(b) (*Com, Fin*) **la ~** the banks, banking; **~ comercial** commercial banking; **~ industrial** merchant banking, investment banking; **horas de ~** banking hours.

(c) (*en juegos*) bank; **hacer saltar la ~** to break the bank; **tener la ~** to be banker, hold the bank.

(d) (*Cono Sur**) pull, influence; **tener (gran) ~** to have (lots of) pull.

bancada NF stone bench; (*Mec*) bench, bed, bedplate; (*Náut*) thwart, (oarsman's) seat; (*de remo*) **~ corrediza** sliding seat.

bancal NM (a) (*Agr*) patch, plot, bed; terrace. (b) (*Mec*) runner, bench-cover.

bancar [1g] ① VT (*Cono Sur*) to pay for; (*fig*) to put up with.

② **bancarse** VR: **~ algo/a uno** to put up with sth/sb.

bancario ADJ bank (*atr*), banking (*atr*); financial.

bancarrota NF (*esp* fraudulent) bankruptcy; failure; **declararse en ~, hacer ~** to go bankrupt.

bancazo NM (*Méx*) bank robbery.

banco NM (a) (*asiento*) bench, seat; (*Náut*) thwart, (oarsman's) seat; (*Téc*) bench, work table; **~ azul** (*Parl*) ministerial benches; **~ de pruebas** testbed, (*fig*) testing-ground.

(b) (*Geog, Náut*) bank, shoal; (*And: suelo aluvial*) deposit of alluvial soil; (*Carib: tierra elevada*) raised ground; **~ de arena** sandbank; **~ de hielo** icefield, ice floe; **~ de nieve** snowdrift.

(c) (*Geol: estrato*) stratum, layer.

(d) (*de peces*) shoal, school.

(e) (*Com, Fin*) bank; **~ por acciones** joint-stock bank; **~ de ahorros** savings bank; **~ en casa** home banking; **~ central** central bank; **~ comercial** commercial bank; **~ de crédito** credit bank; **~ de datos** databank; **~ emisor** issuing bank; **~ de esperma(s)** sperm bank; **~ fiduciario** trust company; **~ de inversiones** investment bank; **~ de liquidación** clearing house; **~ de memoria** memory bank; **~ mercantil** merchant bank; **B~ Mundial** World Bank; **~ de sangre** bloodbank.

banda NF (a) (*franja*) band, strip; ribbon; (*de vestido*) sash, band; (*Méx Aut*) fanbelt; (*Billar*) cushion; (*de tierra*) strip, ribbon; zone; (*de pista de atletismo, de autopista*) lane; (*Rad*) band; **~ ancha** broad band; **~ de dibujos** comic strip; **~ horaria caliente** (*TV*) prime time, peak viewing time; **~ magnética** (*cinta*) magnetic tape; (*de tarjeta*) magnetic strip; **~ de rodaje, ~ de rodamiento** (*Aut*) tread; **~ salarial** wage scale; wage-rise limits; **~ de sonido, ~ sonora** (*Cine*) soundtrack; **~ transportadora** conveyor belt.

(b) (*Dep*) boundary; touchline; **estar fuera de ~** (*balón*) to be out; (*jugador*) to be offside; **sacar de ~** to take a throw-in, throw the ball in.

(c) (*Geog: de río*) side, bank; (*de monte*) side, edge; (*de barco*) side; **~ de Gaza** Gaza Strip; **la B~ Oriental** (*Hist*) Uruguay; **de la ~ de acá** on this side; **cerrarse a la** (o **en**) **~** to stand firm, be adamant; **dar un barco a la ~** to careen a ship; **encerrarse en ~** to refuse to comment, refuse to say anything more; to rule oneself out; **irse a la ~** (*Náut*) to list.

(d) (*personas*) band; gang; troop, party; (*Orn*) flock; **~ de los cuatro** (*Pol*) gang of four; **negociaciones a tres ~s** three-party talks, trilateral negotiations.

(e) (*Mús*) band, (*esp*) brass band.

(f) **coger a uno por ~*** to make sb do the dirty work; **¡como te coja por ~!** I'll get even with you!

bandada NF (a) (*de aves*) flock; flight; (*de peces*) shoal. (b) (*LAm*) = **banda** (d).

bandazo NM (*caída*) heavy fall; (*Náut*) heavy roll (of a ship); (*LAm Aer*) air pocket, sudden drop; (*fig*) marked shift (of policy *etc*); **caminar dando ~s** to stumble along; to reel from side to side, stagger.

bandear [1a] ① VT (a) (*CAm*) (*perseguir*) to pursue, chase; (*pretender*) to court.

(b) (*CAm: herir*) to wound severely; (*Cono Sur: con comentario*) to hurt (with a remark).

(c) (*Cono Sur: cruzar*) to cross, go right across.

② **bandearse** VR (a) (*ir de un lado a otro*) to move to and fro; (*Méx Náut*) to move to the other side of a boat.

(b) (*Cono Sur Pol*) to change parties.

(c) (*Méx*) (*vacilar*) to vacillate; (*cambiar de dirección*) to go one way and then another.

(d) (*Esp**) (*arreglárselas*) to shift for o.s., manage; to get wise*, get organized.

bandeja NF (a) tray, salver; (*LAm: platón*) large serving dish, bowl; **~ de entrada** in-tray; **~ de salida** out-tray; **~ para horno** oven tray; **servir algo a uno en ~ (de plata)** (*fig*) to hand sth to sb on a plate; **te lo han servido** (o **puesto**) **en ~** they've made it very easy for you.

(b) (*Cono Sur*) central reservation (*of a road*).

bandera NF (a) (*gen*) flag; banner, standard; (*Mil*) colours; (*Inform*) marker, flag; **~ ajedrezada, ~ a cuadros** chequered flag; **~ blanca** white flag; **~ de conveniencia** flag of convenience; **~ de esquina** corner flag; **~ de parlamento** flag of truce, white flag; **~ de popa** ensign; **~ de proa** jack; **~ roja** red flag; **la ~ roja y gualda** the Spanish flag; **arriar la ~** (*Náut*) to strike one's colo(u)rs; **bajar la ~** (*taxi*) to pick up a fare; (*Carib fig*) to give in; **dar la ~ a uno** to give sb pride of place; **estar hasta la ~*** to be packed out; **hacer algo a ~s desplegadas** to do sth openly; **venir a ~s desplegadas** to come out with flying colo(u)rs.

(b) **de ~*** terrific*, marvel(l)ous; **una mujer de ~** (*Esp**) a woman with a smashing figure*.

banderazo NM: **~ de salida** starting-signal.

bandería NF faction; (*fig*) bias, partiality.

banderilla NF (a) (*Taur*) banderilla (*barbed dart with banderole*); **~ de fuego** banderilla with attached firecracker; **poner una ~ a uno, poner ~s a uno** to taunt sb, provoke sb, make sb cross.

(b) (*LAm**) swindle.

(c) (*Culin*) savoury appetizer (served on a cocktail stick).

banderillear [1a] VT (*Taur*) to thrust the banderillas into (the neck of).

banderillero NM (*Taur*) banderillero, bullfighter who uses the banderillas.

banderín NM little flag, pennant; (*Ferro*) signal flag; (*Mil: t ~ de enganche*) recruiting centre, recruiting post.

banderita NF little flag; flag sold for charity; **día de la ~** flag day.

banderizo ADJ (a) factional, factionist. (b) (*fig*) fiery, excitable.

banderola NF (a) (*gen*) banderole; signalling flag; (*Mil*) pennant, pennon; **~ de esquina** corner flag. (b) (*Cono Sur: travesaño*) transom.

bandidaje NM, **bandidismo** NM banditry.

bandido NM (a) (*delincuente*) bandit; outlaw; desperado. (b) (*) rogue, rascal; **¡~!** you rogue!, you beast!

bando NM (a) (*edicto*) edict, proclamation; **~s** (*Ecl*) banns. (b) (*partido*) faction, party; side; (*en juegos*) side; **uno del otro ~*** one of them*; **pasar al otro ~** to change sides.

bandola NF (a) (*Mús*) mandolin. (b) (*And: capa*) bullfighter's cape. (c) (*Carib: fuete*) knotted whip.

bandolera NF (a) bandoleer; **llevar algo en ~** to wear sth across one's chest. (b) (*persona*) woman bandit, moll*.

bandolerismo NM brigandage, banditry.

bandolero NM brigand, bandit; (*Hist*) highwayman.

bandolina NF mandolin.

bandoneón NM (*LAm*) large accordion.

bandullo‡ NM belly, guts; **llenarse el ~** to stuff o.s.*

bandurria NF bandurria (*Spanish instrument of the lute type*).

BANESTO NM ABR de **Banco Español de Crédito**.

bangaña NF, **bangaño** NM (*LAm: Bot*) calabash, gourd; (*vasija*) vessel made from a gourd.

Bangladesh NM Bangladesh.

bangladesí ADJ, NMF Bangladeshi.

banjo NM banjo.

banquear [1a] VT (a) (*Aer*) to bank. (b) (*And*) to level, flatten out.

banqueo NM (a) terraces, terracing. (b) (*Aer*) bank(ing).

banquero, -a NM/F banker.

banqueta NF (a) (*taburete*) stool; (*banco*) low bench; **~ de piano** piano stool. (b) (*CAm, Méx: acera*) pavement, sidewalk (*US*).

banquetazo* NM spread*, blow-out‡.

banquete NM banquet, feast; formal dinner; dinner party; **~ anual** annual dinner; **~ de boda** wedding breakfast; **~ de gala** state banquet.

banquetear [1a] VTI to banquet, feast.

banquillo NM bench; footstool; (*Dep*) (team) bench; (*Jur: t ~ de los* acusados) prisoner's seat, dock.

banquina NF (*Cono Sur: en carretera*) verge; (: *en autopista*) hard shoulder, berm (*US*).

banquisa NF ice field, ice floe.

bantam NF (**a**) (*t* **gallina de ~**) bantam. (**b**) (*LAm, fig: persona*) small restless person.

bantú ADJ, NMF Bantu.

banyo NM (*LAm*) banjo.

bañada NF (*LAm*) (*baño*) bath, dip, swim; (*de pintura*) coat (of paint).

bañadera NF (*Cono Sur*) bathtub.

bañado NM (*And, Cono Sur*) (*pantano*) swamp, marshland; (*charco*) flash, rain pool.

bañador ①️ NM (**a**) (*Téc*) tub, trough. (**b**) (*traje de baño*) bathing costume, swimsuit; (*de hombre*) trunks.
  ②️ NM, **bañadora** NF bather, swimmer.

bañar [1a] ①️ VT (**a**) (*sumergir*) to bathe, immerse, dip; (*en baño*) to bath, bathe (*US*); (*Med*) to bathe (*con, de* in, with); (*Téc*) to dip; to coat; cover (*de* with); (*Culin*) to dip (*de* in), coat (*de* with).
  (**b**) (*mar*) to bathe, wash.
  (**c**) (*luz etc*) to bathe, suffuse, flood (*de* with).
  (**d**) (*fig*) to bathe (*con, de, en* in); V **agua**.
  ②️ **bañarse** VR (**a**) (*en baño*) to bath, bath o.s., take a bath, bathe (*US*); (*en mar*) to bathe, have a swim; **ir a ~** to go for a swim, go for a bathe, have a bathe, go swimming; **'prohibido ~'** 'no bathing', 'no swimming'.
  (**b**) **¡anda a bañarte!** (*Cono Sur*) get lost!**‡**, go to hell!

bañata* NM (*Esp*) swimsuit, bathing costume.

bañera NF bath, bathtub.

bañero NM (*Cono Sur*) lifeguard.

bañista NMF (**a**) (*en mar etc*) bather. (**b**) (*Med*) person taking the waters at a spa, patient at a spa.

baño NM (**a**) (*acto*) (*gen*) bathing; (*en bañera*) bath; (*en mar etc*) swim, dip, bathe; **dar un ~ a** (*Dep**) to whitewash*; **tomar un ~** (*en bañera*) to bath, bathe (*US*), take a bath; (*en mar etc*) to swim, bathe, have a swim.
  (**b**) (*bañera etc*) bath, bathtub; (*Téc*) bath; (*Carib: lugar*) cool place; (*WC*) toilet; **~ de asiento** hip-bath; **~ de burbujas** bubble-bath, foam-bath; **~ de ducha** showerbath; **~ de espuma** bubble-bath, foam-bath; **~ de fuego** baptism of fire; **~ de María** bain marie, double saucepan; **~ de masas**, **~ de multitud(es)** walkabout, mingling with the crowd; **~ de revelado** developing bath; **~ ruso** (*Cono Sur*) steam bath; **~ de sangre** (*fig*) bloodbath; **~ de sol** sun bath; **~ turco** Turkish bath; **~ de vapor** steam bath.
  (**c**) **~s** (*Med*) baths; spa; **ir a ~s** to take the waters.
  (**d**) (*Arte*) wash; (*Culin*) coating, covering.

bao NM (*Náut*) beam.

baobab NM baobab.

baptismo NM: **el ~** the Baptist faith.

baptista NMF Baptist; **la Iglesia B~** the Baptist church.

baptisterio NM baptistery, font.

baque NM bump, bang, thud.

baqueano NM *etc* = **baquiano**.

baquelita NF bakelite.

baqueta NF (**a**) (*Mil*) ramrod.
  (**b**) (*Mús*) (*de tambor*) drumstick; (*CAm, Méx: de marimba*) hammer.
  (**c**) **correr ~s, pasar por ~s** to run the gauntlet; **mandar a ~** to rule tyrannically; **tratar a uno a (la) ~** to treat sb harshly.

baquetazo NM: **tratar a uno a ~ limpio*** to treat sb harshly.

baqueteado ADJ experienced; **estar ~** to be inured to it, be used to it; **ser un ~** to know one's way around.

baquetear [1a] VT to annoy, bother.

baqueteo NM annoyance, bother; **es un ~** it's an imposition, it's an awful bind*.

baquetudo ADJ (*Carib*) sluggish, slow.

baquía NF (**a**) (*LAm: conocimiento de una región*) intimate knowledge of a region, local expertise. (**b**) (*And, Cono Sur* †: *habilidad*) expertise, dexterity, skill.

baquiano ①️ ADJ (**a**) (*LAm: que conoce una región*) familiar with a region.
  (**b**) (*And, Cono Sur* †: *experto*) expert, skillful; **para hacerse ~ hay que perderse alguna vez** (*Cono Sur*) one learns the hard way.
  ②️ NM (**a**) (*LAm* †: *guía*) pathfinder, guide; local expert, person with an intimate knowledge of a region; (*Náut*) pilot.
  (**b**) (*And, Cono Sur: experto*) expert; person who knows what he is talking about.

báquico ADJ Bacchic; bacchanalian, drunken.

báquiro NM (*And, Carib*) peccary.

bar NM bar; snack bar; **~ de alterne**, **~ de citas** singles bar; **~ suizo** open plan kitchen.

baraca NF (charismatic) gift of bringing good luck; blessing.

barahúnda NF uproar, hubbub; racket, din.

baraja NF (**a**) (*gen*) pack of cards; (*Méx*) cards; **jugar ~** (*LAm*) to play

cards; **jugar a** (*o* **con**) **dos ~s** to play a double game; **romper la ~** (*fig*) to break off the engagement, end the conflict. (**b**) **~s** (*fig*) fight, set-to.

⌐ *BARAJA ESPAÑOLA* ─────────────────

ⓘ *The Spanish deck of cards differs from its British and American counterpart, known in Spain as the **baraja francesa**. The four Spanish suits, **oros**, **copas**, **espadas** and **bastos** ("golden coins", "goblets", "swords" and "clubs") each contain 9 numbered cards, although for certain games only 7 are used, and 3 picture cards: **sota**, **caballo** and **rey** (Jack, Queen, King).*

---

barajadura NF shuffle, shuffling.

barajar [1a] ①️ VT (**a**) *cartas* to shuffle.
  (**b**) (*fig: mezclar*) to jumble up, mix up, shuffle round; (*Cono Sur: ofrecer*) to pass round, hand round; (*Cono Sur, Méx*) *asunto* to entangle, confuse; (*demorar*) to delay.
  (**c**) (*Cono Sur: agarrar*) to catch (in the air); **~ algo en el aire** (*fig*) to see the point of sth.
  ②️ VI to quarrel, squabble.
  ③️ **barajarse** VR (**a**) (*Cono Sur: pelear*) to fight, brawl.
  (**b**) (*mezclarse*) to get jumbled up, get mixed up.
  (**c**) **se baraja la posibilidad de que ...** there is discussion of the possibility that ..., the possibility that ... is being discussed; **las cifras que se barajan ahora** the figures now being put about, the figures now being bandied about.

barajo ①️ INTERJ (*LAm: euf*) = **carajo**.
  ②️ NM (*And*) (*pretexto*) pretext, excuse; (*salida*) loophole.

barajuste NM (*Carib*) stampede, rush.

baranda1 NF rail, railing; handrail; (*Billar*) cushion.

baranda2**‡** NM chief, boss.

barandal NM base, support (of banisters); handrail; balustrade.

barandilla NF balustrade; handrail; (*And*) altar rail.

barata1 NF (**a**) (*And, Méx: saldo*) sale, bargain sale.
  (**b**) (*And, Méx: sección de gangas*) bargain counter; (*tienda*) cut-price store.
  (**c**) (*And*) **a la ~*** (*sin orden*) any old how*; **tratar a uno a la ~** to treat sb with scorn.

barata2 NF (*Cono Sur*) cockroach.

baratear [1a] VT to sell cheaply; to sell at a loss.

baratejo* ADJ cheap and nasty, trashy.

baratero ①️ ADJ (**a**) (*esp LAm*) (*gen*) cheap; *tendero etc* who sells cheap; **tienda baratera** shop offering bargains, cut-price store.
  (**b**) (*Cono Sur: regateo*) haggling.
  ②️ NM (**a**) (*en el juego*) person who extracts money from winning gamblers.
  (**b**) (*LAm: tendero*) shopkeeper offering bargains, cut-price merchant.
  (**c**) (*Cono Sur: persona que regatea*) haggler.

baratez NF (*Carib*), **baratía** NF (*And*) cheapness.

baratija NF trinket; (*Com*) cheap novelty; (*fig*) trifle; **~s** (*Com*) cheap goods, inexpensive articles; **~s** (*pey*) trash, junk.

baratillero NM seller of cheap goods.

baratillo NM (**a**) (*géneros*) secondhand goods; cheap goods.
  (**b**) (*tienda*) secondhand shop, junkshop; (*sección de gangas*) bargain counter.
  (**c**) (*saldo*) bargain sale; **cosa de ~** tawdry thing, gimcrack article.
  (**d**) (*Méx*) flea market.

barato ①️ ADJ cheap; inexpensive, economical; **obtener algo de ~** to get sth free; **dar algo de ~** (*fig*) to concede sth, grant sth (for the sake of argument); **echar a ~**, **meter a ~** to heckle, barrack, interrupt noisily.
  ②️ ADV cheap, cheaply; inexpensively.
  ③️ NM (**a**) (*saldo*) bargain sale.
  (**b**) (*en el juego*) money extracted from winning gamblers; **cobrar el ~** (*fig*) to be a bully, wield power by intimidation.

baratón ①️ ADJ (*And, CAm, Méx*) *argumento* weak, feeble; *comentario* well-worn, trite.
  ②️ NM (*CAm*) (*ganga*) bargain; (*saldo*) sale.

baratura NF cheapness; inexpensiveness.

baraúnda NF = **barahúnda**.

barba ①️ NF (**a**) (*mentón*) chin.
  (**b**) (*pelos*) beard, whiskers (*t* **~s**); **~ cerrada**, **~ bien poblada** thick beard, big beard; **~s de chivo** goatee; **~ honrada** distinguished personage; **a ~ regada** abundantly, fully; **decir algo en las ~s de uno** to say sth to sb's face; **robar algo en las ~s de uno** to steal sth from under sb's nose; **2 naranjas por ~** 2 oranges apiece, 2 oranges per head; **un hombre con toda la ~** a real man; **colgar ~s al santo** to give sb his due; **hacer la ~** to shave, have a shave; **hacer la ~ a uno** to shave sb; (*fig*) to pester sb, annoy sb; (*fig*) to fawn on sb, flatter sb; **llevar ~** to have a beard; **llevar a uno de la ~** to lead sb by the nose; **mentir por la ~** to tell a barefaced lie; **subirse a las ~s de uno** to be disrespectful to sb; **tener pocas ~s** to be green, be inexperi-

enced; **tirarse de las ~s** to rage, tear one's hair.
(**c**) (*Orn*) wattle; **~ de ballena** whalebone.
(**d**) (*Bot*) beard.
[2] NM (**a**) (*Teat: papel*) old man's part; (*actor*) performer of old men's parts; (*de melodrama*) villain.
(**b**) **~s** guy*, bloke*.
Barba Azul NM Bluebeard.
barbacana NF (*defensa*) barbican; (*tronera*) loophole, embrasure.
barbacoa NF (**a**) (*Culin*) barbecue; (*CAm, Carib, Méx: carne*) barbecued meat, meat.
(**b**) (*LAm: cama*) bed made with a hurdle supported on sticks.
(**c**) (*And: estante*) rack for kitchen utensils.
(**d**) (*And: desván*) loft.
(**e**) (*And Mús*) tap-dance.
Barbada NF: **la ~** Barbados.
barbado [1] ADJ bearded, with a beard.
[2] NM (**a**) (*persona*) man with a beard; (*fig: adulto*) full-grown man.
(**b**) (*Bot*) cutting (with roots); **plantar de ~** to transplant, plant out.
Barbados NM Barbados.
barbar [1a] VI (**a**) (*gen*) to grow a beard. (**b**) (*Bot*) to strike root.
Bárbara NF Barbara.
bárbaramente ADV (**a**) (*cruelmente*) barbarously; cruelly, savagely. (**b**) (*) tremendously*; **pasarlo ~** to have a great time.
barbáricamente ADV barbarically.
barbárico ADJ barbaric.
barbaridad NF (**a**) (*gen*) barbarity; barbarism; (*acto*) atrocity, outrage, barbarous act; **es capaz de hacer cualquier ~** he's capable of doing sth terrible.
(**b**) (*) **¡qué ~!** how awful!, shocking!
(**c**) **~es** awful things, terrible things, naughty things; nonsense; **decir ~ es** to say awful things; to talk nonsense.
(**d**) **una ~*** (*cantidad*) a huge amount, loads*, tons* (*de* of); **había una ~ de gente** there was an awful lot of people; **comimos una ~** we ate an awful lot; **cuesta una ~** it costs a fortune; **sabe una ~ de cosas** he knows a tremendous amount.
(**e**) **una ~** (*: como adv*) a lot, lots; **nos gustó una ~** we liked it a lot; **me quiere una ~** he's terribly fond of me, he likes me awfully; **nos divertimos una ~** we had a tremendous time, we had a lot of fun; **habló una ~** he talked his head off; **se nota una ~** it sticks out a mile.
barbarie NF (**a**) (*gen*) barbarism, barbarousness. (**b**) (*crueldad*) barbarity, cruelty, savagery.
barbarismo NM (**a**) (*Ling*) barbarism. (**b**) = **barbarie**.
bárbaro [1] ADJ (**a**) (*Hist*) barbarian, barbarous.
(**b**) (*fig: cruel*) barbarous, cruel, savage; (*espantoso*) awful, frightful; (*inculto*) rough, uncouth; (*audaz*) bold, daring.
(**c**) (*: estupendo*) tremendous*, terrific*, smashing*; **¡qué ~!** how marvellous!, terrific!*; how awful!; **un éxito ~** a tremendous success*; **es un tío ~** he's a great guy*, he's a splendid chap*; **hace un frío ~** it's terribly cold.
[2] ADV (*) marvellously; terrifically*; **lo pasamos ~** we had a tremendous time; **ella canta ~** she sings marvellously.
[3] INTERJ (*Cono Sur**) fine!, OK!*
[4] NM, **bárbara** NF (**a**) (*lit*) barbarian.
(**b**) (*) rough sort, uncouth person; **conduce como un ~** he drives like a madman; **gritó como un ~** he gave a tremendous shout, he shouted like mad.
barbarote* NM brute, savage.
barbear [1a] [1] VT (**a**) (*LAm: afeitar*) to shave.
(**b**) (*CAm, Méx**) (*adular*) to fawn on, suck up to*; (*mimar*) to spoil.
(**c**) (*CAm: fastidiar*) to annoy, bore.
(**d**) (*LAm*) ganado to throw, fell.
(**e**) (*alcanzar*) to reach with one's chin, come up to, be as tall as.
(**f**) (*: ver*) to see, spot.
(**g**) (*CAm*: *regañar*) to tell off.
[2] VI (**a**) **~ con** = VT (**e**). (**b**) (*CAm*: *meterse*) to stick (o poke) one's nose in.
barbechar [1a] VT (**a**) (*dejar en barbecho*) to leave fallow. (**b**) (*arar*) to plough for sowing.
barbechera NF fallow, fallow land.
barbecho NM (**a**) (*tierra*) fallow, fallow land; **estar en ~** (*Cono Sur: fig*) to be in preparation, be on its way; **firmar como en un ~** to sign without reading.
(**b**) (*tierra arada*) ploughed land ready for sowing.
(**c**) (*acto*) first ploughing.
barbería NF (**a**) (*tienda*) barber's (shop). (**b**) (*arte*) hairdressing.
barbero [1] NM (**a**) (*peluquero*) barber, hairdresser; '**El ~ de Sevilla**' 'The Barber of Seville'. (**b**) (*CAm, Méx**) flatterer.
[2] ADJ (*CAm, Méx*: *adulador*) grovelling; niño affectionate, cuddly.
barbeta* NMF (*Cono Sur*) fool.
barbetear [1a] VT (*Méx*) ganado to throw, fell (by twisting the head of), throw to the ground.

barbicano ADJ grey-bearded, white-bearded.
barbihecho ADJ freshly shaven.
barbijo NM (**a**) (*And, Cono Sur: correa*) chinstrap; (*And, Carib, Cono Sur: pañuelo*) headscarf (knotted under the chin). (**b**) (*And, Cono Sur: cicatriz*) scar.
barbilampiño [1] ADJ (**a**) (*lit*) smooth-faced, beardless. (**b**) (*fig: novato*) inexperienced.
[2] NM (*fig*) novice, greenhorn.
barbilindo ADJ dapper, spruce; (*pey*) dandified, foppish.
barbilla NF (tip of the) chin.
barbiponiente ADJ (**a**) (*lit*) beginning to grow a beard, with a youthful beard. (**b**) (*fig: novato*) raw, inexperienced, green.
barbiquejo NM (**a**) = **barbijo** (**a**). (**b**) (*Carib: bocal*) bit.
barbiturato NM, **barbitúrico** NM barbiturate.
barbo NM barbel; **~ de mar** red mullet.
barbón NM (**a**) (*persona*) bearded man, man with a (big) beard; (*fig*) greybeard, old hand. (**b**) (*Zool*) billy-goat.
barbot(e)ar [1a] VTI to mutter, mumble.
barboteo NM mutter, muttering, mumbling.
barbudo ADJ bearded; having a big beard, long-bearded.
barbulla NF clamour, hullabaloo.
barbullar [1a] VI to jabber away, talk noisily.
barca NF boat, small boat; **~ de pasaje** ferry; **~ de pesca**, **~ pesquera** fishing boat.
Barça NM: (**el**) **~** Barcelona Football Club.
barcada NF (**a**) (*carga*) boatload. (**b**) (*viaje*) boat trip; (*travesía*) crossing (by ferry).
barcaje NM toll.
barcarola NF barcarole.
barcaza NF barge, lighter; ferry; **~ de desembarco** (*Mil*) landing-craft.
Barcelona NF Barcelona.
barcelonés [1] ADJ of Barcelona.
[2] NM, **barcelonesa** NF native (o inhabitant) of Barcelona; **los barceloneses** the people of Barcelona.
barchilón NM, **barchilona** NF (*And: enfermero*) nurse, hospital aide; (*And, Cono Sur: curandero*) quack doctor, quack surgeon.
barcia NF chaff.
barcino ADJ reddish-grey.
barco NM (*gen*) boat; (*navío*) ship, vessel; **~ de apoyo** support ship; **~ cablero** cable-ship; **~ carbonero**, **~ minero** collier; **~ de carga** cargo boat; **~ contenedor** container ship; **~ de guerra** warship; **~ meteorológico** weather-ship; **~ náufrago** wreck; **~ patrullero** patrol-boat; **~ de vela** sailing-ship; **~ vivienda** houseboat; **abandonar el ~** to abandon ship; **ir en ~** to go by boat, go by ship; **como ~ sin timón** irresolute(ly), lacking a firm purpose.
barco-madre NM, PL **barcos-madre** mother ship.
barda NF (**a**) protective covering on a wall; (*Méx*) high hedge, fence, wall; **~s** top of a wall, walls. (**b**) (*) jacket.
bardal NM wall topped with brushwood *etc*.
bardana NF burdock.
bardar [1a] VT to thatch.
bardo NM bard.
baré NM (*Esp*) 5-peseta coin.
baremar [1a] VT to calculate, reckon; to measure.
baremo NM (*Mat*) table(s); ready-reckoner; (*fig*) scale, schedule; yardstick, gauge, criterion; set of norms, basis for comparison.
bareo* NM: **ir de ~** to go drinking, go pub-crawling*.
barillero NM (*Méx*) hawker, street vendor.
bario NM barium.
barítono NM baritone.
barjuleta NF knapsack.
barloventear [1a] VI (**a**) (*Náut*) to tack; to beat to windward. (**b**) (*fig: vagar*) to wander about.
Barlovento: **Islas** NFPL **de ~** Windward Isles.
barlovento NM windward; **a ~** to windward; **de ~** windward (*atr*); **ganar el ~ a** to get to windward of.
barman NM, PL **barmans**, **bármanes**, **barmen** barman, bartender.
Barna. ABR *de* Barcelona.
barniz NM (**a**) (*gen*) varnish; (*Aer*) dope; (*en cerámica*) glaze; (*en metal etc*) gloss, polish; **~ para las uñas** nail varnish, nail polish; **dar de ~ a** to varnish.
(**b**) (*fig: cualidad superficial*) gloss, veneer; smattering, superficial knowledge.
barnizado NM varnish, varnishing.
barnizar [1f] VT to varnish; to glaze; to polish, put a gloss on.
baró NM (*Esp*) 5-peseta coin.
barométrico ADJ barometric.
barómetro NM barometer; **~ aneroide** aneroid barometer.
barón NM (**a**) (*título*) baron; (*: Pol etc*) chief, influential member (*etc*), high-up*.
(**b**) (*Carib**) pal*, buddy (*US*).

baronesa NF baroness.
baronía NF barony.
baronial ADJ baronial.
barquero NM boatman; ferryman, waterman.
barquía NF skiff, rowing boat.
barquilla NF (**a**) (*Aer: de globo*) basket; (*de aeronave*) gondola, nacelle, car. (**b**) (*Náut*) log. (**c**) (*Carib: helado*) ice-cream cornet, cone.
barquillo NM (*Culin*) horn, rolled wafer; (*helado*) ice-cream cornet, cone.
barquinazo NM (*caída*) tumble, hard fall; spill; (*Aut etc*) bump, jolt; (*And*) sudden start.
barra NF (**a**) (*gen*) bar; rail, railing; (*en un bar*) bar, counter; (*Mec*) rod; lever; (*pan*) French bread; (*de jabón*) bar, stick; (*de metal*) bar, ingot; ~ **americana** singles bar; (**la bandera de**) **las ~s y estrellas** the Stars and Stripes; ~ **antivuelco**, ~ **estabilizadora** anti-roll bar; ~ **de carmín**, ~ **de labios** lipstick; ~ **de chocolate** (*Cono Sur*) bar of chocolate; ~ **de cortina** curtain rod; ~ **de equilibrio(s)** beam; ~ **de espaciado**, ~ **espaciadora** space-bar, spacing-bar; ~ **fija** fixed bar; ~ **libre** free bar, drinks on the house; ~**s paralelas** parallel bars; **a ~s derechas** honestly; **no pararse en ~s** to stop at nothing.
(**b**) (*Her*) stripe, bar; (*Tip: t ~ oblicua*) oblique stroke, slash (*US*); ~ **inversa** backslash.
(**c**) (*Náut*) bar, sandbank.
(**d**) (*Jur*) bar, rail; (*aprox*) dock; **la B~** (*Méx*) the Bar, the legal profession; **llevar a uno a la ~** to bring sb to justice.
(**e**) (*LAm: público, Jur etc*) public, members of the public; (*Cono Sur: público*) spectators, audience; (*Dep*) fans, supporters; **había mucha ~** there was a big audience.
(**f**) (*Cono Sur: pandilla*) band, gang; (*camarilla*) clique, coterie.
(**g**) (*Carib, Cono Sur, Méx: ría*) river mouth, estuary.
Barrabás NM Barrabas; **ser un ~** to be wicked, (*niño*) be mischievous, be naughty.
barrabasada NF mischief; outrage, excess; dirty trick.
barraca¹ NF (**a**) (*cabaña*) hut, cabin; (*de obreros*) workmen's hut; (*moderna, de ciudad*) shanty, hovel; (*Valencia*) thatched farmhouse; ~**s** (*Méx*) shanty town.
(**b**) (*de feria*) booth, stall; ~ **persa** (*Cono Sur*) cut-price store; ~ **de tiro al blanco** shooting-gallery.
(**c**) (*LAm: depósito*) large storage shed; (*And: de mercado*) market stall.
(**d**) **creerse algo a la ~** to believe sth implicitly.
barraca² NF (*LAm Mil*) barracks.
barracón NM (**a**) (*caseta*) big hut; (*Carib Agr*) farmworkers' living quarters.
(**b**) (*de feria*) large booth, stall; side show; ~ **de espejos**, ~ **de la risa** hall of mirrors.
barracuda NF barracuda.
barragana NF official mistress, concubine; (††) morganatic wife.
barrajes NMPL (*And*) shanty-town.
barranca NF gully, ravine.
barrancal NM place full of ravines.
barranco NM (**a**) (*Geog*) gully, ravine. (**b**) (*LAm*) (*despeñadero*) cliff; (*de río*) steep riverbank. (**c**) (*fig: obstáculo*) difficulty, obstacle.
barraquismo NM phenomenon of shanty towns, shanty town problem.
barrar [1a] VT to daub, smear (*de* with).
barreal NM (*Cono Sur: tierra*) heavy clay land; (*CAm: pantano*) bog.
barrear [1a] VT to barricade, fortify; to bar, fasten with a bar.
barredera NF (*persona*) street sweeper; (*Aut*) street-cleaning vehicle; ~ **de alfombras**, ~ **mecánica** carpet sweeper.
barredor NM: ~ **de frecuencia** frequency sweeper.
barredura NF (**a**) (*gen*) sweep, sweeping. (**b**) ~**s** sweepings; rubbish, refuse.
barreminas NM INVAR minesweeper.
barrena NF (**a**) (*taladro*) drill, auger; bit; (*Min*) rock drill, mining drill; ~ **de mano**, ~ **pequeña** gimlet. (**b**) (*Aer*) spin; **entrar en ~** to go into a spin.
barrenado* ADJ: **estar ~** to be dotty*.
barrenar [1a] VT (**a**) (*gen*) to drill, drill through, bore; *roca* to blast; *barco* to scuttle.
(**b**) (*fig: frustrar*) to foil, frustrate; (*) to make a mess of; (*Jur*) to violate, infringe.
barrendero, -a NM/F sweeper.
barrenillo NM (**a**) (*Zool*) borer. (**b**) (*Carib: empeño*) foolish persistence; (*Cono Sur, Méx*) (*preocupación*) constant worry; (*manía*) mania, pet idea.
barreno NM (**a**) (*Téc: instrumento*) large drill, borer.
(**b**) (*perforación*) bore, borehole; **dar ~ a un barco** to scuttle a ship.
(**c**) (*fig: vanidad*) vanity, pride.
(**d**) (*Cono Sur, Méx*) (*preocupación*) constant worry; (*manía*) mania, pet idea.
barreño NM washing-up basin.
barrer [1a] ① VT (**a**) (*gen*) to sweep; to sweep clean, sweep out, sweep away.

(**b**) (*Mil, Náut*) to sweep (with gunfire); ~ **la mente:** to blow one's mind:.
(**c**) (*fig*) *obstáculos etc* to sweep aside, sweep away; *dudas* to dispel; (*And: derrotar*) to beat, overwhelm; **los candidatos del partido barrieron a sus adversarios** the party's candidates swept aside their rivals.
② VI (**a**) **comprar algo al ~** (*Cono Sur*) to buy sth in a job lot.
(**b**) ~ **hacia dentro*** to look after Number One.
③ **barrerse** VR (**a**) (*Méx: caballo*) to shy, start.
(**b**) (*Méx*: *humillarse*) to grovel.
barrera¹ NF (**a**) (*barra*) barrier; rail, bar; (*Mil etc*) barricade; (††, *Mil*) parapet; (*Ferro*) barrier, crossing gate; (*Taur*) barrier, fence round the inside of the bullring; first row of seats; (*Dep: de jugadores*) wall; ~ **aduanera** customs barrier; ~ **arancelaria** tariff barrier; ~ **de color** colour bar; ~ **comercial** trade barrier; ~ **de contención** containing wall; ~ **coralina** coral reef; ~ **generacional** generation gap; ~ **de peaje**, ~ **de portazgo** tollgate, turnpike; ~ **protectora**, ~ **de seguridad** safety barrier; ~ **racial** racial bar, colour bar; ~ **del sonido** sound barrier; **poner ~s a** to hinder.
(**b**) (*Mil: t ~ de fuego*) barrage; ~ **de fuego móvil** creeping barrage.
(**c**) (*fig: impedimento*) barrier, bar; obstacle; hindrance.
barrera² NF claypit.
barrero ① ADJ (*Cono Sur*) *caballo* that likes heavy going.
② NM (*tierra fangosa*) muddy ground; (*And, Cono Sur: saladar*) salt marsh.
bar-restaurante NM bar-cum-restaurant.
barretina NF Catalan cap.
barriada NF quarter, district; (*LAm: barrio pobre*) shanty-town; slum quarter.
barrial NM (**a**) (*Méx: tierra*) heavy clay land. (**b**) (*LAm: pantano*) bog.
barrica NF large barrel, cask.
barricada NF barricade.
barrida NF (*LAm*) (*acto*) sweep, sweeping; (*de policía*) sweep, raid; (*en elección*) landslide.
barrido NM sweep, sweeping; (*Elec*) scan, sweep; **vale** (*o* **sirve**) **tanto para un ~ como para un fregado** he can turn his hand to anything.
barriga NF (**a**) (*Anat*) belly; paunch, guts; **echar ~** to get middle-age spread; **la cerveza echa ~** beer makes you fat; **hacer una ~ a una*** to get a girl in the family way; **llenarse la ~** to stuff o.s*; **rascarse** (*o* **tocarse**) **la ~:** to do damn-all:, be idle; **tener ~*** to be in the family way.
(**b**) (*de jarra*) belly, rounded part; (*de muro*) bulge.
barrigón ① ADJ fat, potbellied.
② NM, **barrigona** NF (*And, Carib**) child, kid*.
barrigudo ADJ fat, potbellied.
barriguera NF (horse's) girth.
barril NM (**a**) (*tonel*) barrel; cask, keg; **cerveza de ~** draught beer, beer on draught; ~ **de petróleo** barrel of oil; ~ **de pólvora** (*fig*) powderkeg; **comer del ~** (*And*) to eat poor-quality food.
(**b**) (*LAm: cometa hexagonal*) hexagonal kite.
barrila* NF row, to-do; **dar la ~** to kick up a fuss.
barrilería NF (**a**) (*almacén*) barrel store. (**b**) (*tienda, taller*) cooper's shop. (**c**) (*arte*) cooperage.
barrilero NM cooper.
barrilete ① NM (**a**) (*barril*) keg.
(**b**) (*Téc*) dog, clamp.
(**c**) (*de revólver*) chamber.
(**d**) (*Méx Jur*) junior barrister.
(**e**) (*Cono Sur: cometa*) kite.
② NF (*Cono Sur*) restless woman.
barrilla NF (*Bot, Quím*) barilla, saltwort.
barrillo NM blackhead, pimple.
barrio NM quarter, district, area (of a town); suburb; (*LAm*) slum quarter, shanty-town; **el otro ~*** the next world; **irse al otro ~:** to snuff it:; **mandar a uno al otro ~:** to do sb in:; ~**s bajos** poorer quarter, working-class quarter, (*pey*) slums, slum area; ~ **bruja** (*And*) shanty-town; ~ **de los calvos*** graveyard; ~ **comercial** business quarter; shopping district; ~ **chino** (*Esp*) red-light district; ~ **dormitorio** commuter suburb; ~ **exterior** outer suburb; ~ **latino** Latin quarter; ~ **miseria** slum quarter, shanty-town; ~ **residencial** residential area; ~ **de tolerancia** (*And*) red-light district.
barriobajero ADJ slum (*atr*); (*fig*) vulgar, coarse, common.
barrisco: a ~ ADV jumbled together, in confusion; indiscriminately.
barritar [1a] VI (*elefante*) to trumpet.
barrito NM trumpeting.
barrizal NM muddy place, mire.
barro NM (**a**) (*lodo*) mud.
(**b**) (*arcilla*) clay, potter's clay; ~ **cocido** baked clay; **vasija de ~** earthen vessel, earthenware vessel.
(**c**) (*vasija*) earthenware pot; mug (for beer *etc*); ~**s** earthenware,

crockery.

(**d**) (‡: *dinero*) dough‡, brass*; **tener ~ a mano** to be in the money.

(**e**) (*Cono Sur*‡: *plancha*) clanger‡; **hacer un ~** to drop a clanger‡.

(**f**) (*Anat*) pimple.

barroco [1] ADJ baroque (*t fig*).

[2] NM baroque (style); baroque period.

barroquismo NM baroque (style); baroque taste.

barroso ADJ (**a**) (*lodoso*) muddy. (**b**) (*de color*) mud-coloured; *vaca* reddish, brownish, (*CAm*: *blancuzco*) off-white. (**c**) (*Anat*) pimply.

barrote NM heavy bar, thick bar; crosspiece; (*de silla etc*) rung.

barruntar [1a] VT *y* **barruntarse** VR to sense, feel; to guess, conjecture; to suspect; **~ que ...** to sense that ..., have a feeling that ...

barrunte NM sign, indication.

barrunto NM (**a**) (*conjetura*) guess, conjecture; (*indicio*) sign, indication; (*sospecha*) suspicion; (*presentimiento*) foreboding. (**b**) (*Carib, Méx: Met*) north wind which brings rain.

Barsa NM = **Barça**.

bartola NF: **echarse** (*o* **tenderse, tumbarse**) **a la ~** to be lazy, take it easy; to do nothing.

bartolear [1a] VI (*Cono Sur*) to be lazy, take it easy.

bartolina NF (*CAm, Carib, Méx*) jail.

Bartolo NM *forma familiar de* **Bartolomé**.

bartolo* ADJ (*Méx*) thick*, stupid.

Bartolomé NM Bartholomew.

bartulear [1a] VI (*Cono Sur*) to think hard, rack one's brains.

bártulos NMPL things, belongings, gear; goods; (*Téc*) tools; **liar los ~** to pack up one's belongings; (‡) to peg out‡; **preparar los ~** to get ready (to go).

barucho* NM seedy bar.

barullento ADJ (*Cono Sur*) noisy, rowdy.

barullo NM (**a**) (*alboroto*) row, uproar, din; confusion. (**b**) **a ~*** in abundance, by the ton*.

barzón NM saunter, stroll; **dar ~es** to stroll around.

barzonear [1a] VI to stroll around, wander about.

basa NF (**a**) (*Arquit*) base (of a column). (**b**) (*fig: base*) basis, foundation.

basalto NM basalt.

basamentar [1a] VT = **basar**.

basamento NM (*Arquit*) base.

▼ **basar** [1a] [1] VT to base; (*fig*) to base, found, ground (*sobre* on).

▼[2] **basarse** VR: **~ en** (**a**) to be based on, rest on. (**b**) (*fig*) to base o.s. on, rely on.

basca NF (*frec* ~s) (**a**) (*Med*) nausea, queasy feeling, sick feeling; **dar ~s a uno** to make sb feel sick, turn sb's stomach; **le entraron ~s, tuvo una ~** he felt nauseated, he felt sick.

(**b**) (*fig: rabieta*) fit of rage, tantrum.

(**c**) (*) (*grupo*) group, set of people; (*gentío*) mob; (*pandilla*) gang; (*séquito*) followers; **toda la ~** every last one of them.

(**d**) **le dio la ~** (*impulso*) he had a sudden urge.

bascosidad NF (**a**) (*porquería*) filth, dirt. (**b**) (*And: obscenidad*) obscenity.

bascoso ADJ (**a**) (*delicado*) squeamish, easily upset; (*Med*) queasy. (**b**) (*And: vomitivo*) nauseating, sickening; (*obsceno*) obscene; *persona* vile, disgusting.

báscula NF (*platform*) scales, weighing machine; (*romana*) steelyard; **~ de baño** bathroom scales; **~ biestable** flip-flop, toggle; **~ de puente** weighbridge.

basculable ADJ (*Aut etc*) *luz* directional, with swinging beam.

basculante NM tip-up lorry, dump truck (*US*).

báscula-puente NF weighbridge.

bascular [1a] VI (*inclinarse*) to tilt, tip up; (*columpiarse*) to seesaw; (*mecerse*) to rock to and fro; (*Pol etc*) to swing; (*Inform*) to toggle.

base [1] NF (**a**) (*Arquit*) base; (*Téc*) base, mounting, bed; (*Agrimen*) base, base line; **~ de maquillaje** make-up foundation.

(**b**) (*Mil*) base; **~ aérea** air base; **~ aeronaval** naval air base; **~ avanzada** forward base; **~ espacial** space-station; **~ naval** naval base.

(**c**) (*Béisbol*) base.

(**d**) (*fig: fundamento*) basis, foundation; **~ derivativa** (*Ling*) base form; **~ imponible** taxable income; **~ de poder** power base; **a ~ de** on the basis of; by means of; **a ~ de no hacer nada** by doing nothing; with the idea of not doing anything; **a ~ de 50 toneladas al año** on a basis of 50 tons a year, at 50 tons a year; **a ~ de bien*** (ADJ) really good, (ADV) really well, loads*; **en ~ a** (*como prep*) with regard to; with a view to; **en ~ a + infin** with a view to + *ger*; **en ~ a que ...** (*como conj*) in view of the fact that ..., bearing in mind that ...; **coger a uno fuera de ~** (*CAm, Carib*: *fig*) to catch sb out; **partir de una ~ falsa** to start from a false assumption; **sentar las ~s de** to do the groundwork for, lay the foundations of.

(**e**) (*Inform, Mat*) base; **~ de datos** database; **~ de datos relacional** relational database; **~ de conocimientos** knowledge base.

(**f**) (*de concurso*) **~s** conditions, rules.

(**g**) (*Pol*) rank and file, ordinary members; **militante de ~** rank-and-file member; **opinión de ~** grass-roots opinion, rank-and-file opinion.

(**h**) (‡: *droga*) crack, cocaine.

[2] NM (*Dep*) base.

[3] ADJ basic, base (*atr*); **color ~** basic colour; **salario ~** basic wage, wage taken as a base.

baseballista NMF (*LAm*) baseball player.

basebolero [1] ADJ (*Carib*) baseball (*atr*).

[2] NM, **basebolera** NF (*Carib*) baseball player.

básica NF = **EGB**.

▼ **básico** ADJ basic (*t Quím*).

Basilea NF Basle, Basel, Bâle.

basílica NF basilica.

basilisco NM (*Mit*) basilisk; (*Méx*) iguana; **estar hecho un ~** to be terribly angry; **ponerse como un ~** to get terribly angry.

básket NM basketball.

basoto ADJ of (*o* from) Lesotho.

basquear [1a] VI to be nauseated, feel sick; **hacer ~ a uno** to make sb feel sick, turn sb's stomach.

básquet NM, **básquetbol** NM basketball.

basquetbolero [1] ADJ (*LAm*) basketball (*atr*).

[2] NM, **basquetbolera** NF (*LAm*) basketball player.

basquetbolista NMF (*LAm*) basketball player.

basquetbolístico ADJ (*LAm*) basketball (*atr*).

basquiña NF skirt.

basta NF tacking stitch, basting stitch.

bastante [1] ADJ (**a**) enough, sufficient (*para* for; *para + infin* to + *infin*).

(**b**) (*LAm*) (*demasiado*) too much, more than enough; **toma ~** take plenty.

[2] ADV (**a**) (*gen*) enough, sufficiently; **~ grande** big enough, sufficiently large; **es ~ alto** (**como**) **para alcanzarlo** he's tall enough to reach it.

(**b**) (*en parte pey*) **~ bueno** fairly good, quite good, rather good, goodish.

(**c**) (*muy*) very, really; **estoy ~ cansado** I'm really tired.

bastantemente ADV sufficiently.

bastar [1a] [1] VTI to be enough, be sufficient, suffice; **¡basta!** that's enough!, that will do!, stop now!; **¡basta ya!** that's quite enough of that!; **basta y sobra** that's more than enough; **con eso basta** that's enough; **eso me basta** that's enough for me; **basta decir que ...** suffice it to say that ...; **nos basta saber que ...** it is enough for us to know that ...; **~ a + infin, ~ para + infin** to be enough to + *infin*, be sufficient to + *infin*.

[2] **bastarse** VR: **~ a sí mismo** to be self-sufficient.

bastardear [1a] [1] VT to debase; to adulterate.

[2] VI (*Bot*) to degenerate; (*fig*) to degenerate, fall away (*de* from).

bastardía NF (**a**) (*calidad*) bastardy. (**b**) (*fig: bajeza*) meanness, baseness; wicked thing.

bastardilla NF (*t letra* **~**) italic type, italics; **en ~** in italics; **poner en ~** to italicize.

bastardo [1] ADJ (**a**) (*gen*) bastard. (**b**) (*fig: vil*) mean, base. (**c**) (*fig: híbrido*) hybrid, mixed.

[2] NM, **bastarda** NF bastard.

bastear [1a] VT to tack, stitch loosely.

bastedad NF coarseness.

bastero, -a NM/F (*Méx*) pickpocket.

bastes‡ NMPL (*Esp*) dabs‡, fingers.

bastez NF coarseness, vulgarity.

bastidor NM (**a**) (*Téc, Cos etc*) frame, framework; (*de ventana*) frame, case; (*de lienzo*) stretcher; (*de vehículo*) chassis; (*And, Cono Sur*: *ventana*) lattice window; (*Carib*: *catre*) metal bedstead; (*Carib, Méx*: *colchón*) interior sprung mattress.

(**b**) (*Teat*) wing; **entre ~es** behind the scenes (*t fig*); **estar entre ~es** to be offstage; **dirigirlo entre ~es** to pull strings, work the oracle.

bastilla NF hem.

bastillar [1a] VT to hem.

bastimentar [1a] VT to supply, provision.

bastimento NM (**a**) (*provisiones*) supply (of provisions). (**b**) (*Náut*) vessel.

bastión NM bastion, bulwark.

basto[1] [1] ADJ (*tosco*) coarse, rough; (*grosero*) rude, uncouth.

[2] NM packsaddle; (*LAm*: *t* **~s**) soft leather pad (*used under the saddle*).

basto[2] NM (*Cartas*) ace of clubs; **~s** clubs; **pintan ~s** (*fig*) things are getting tough, the going is getting rough.

bastón NM stick; staff; walking stick; (*porra*) truncheon; (*Mil etc*) baton; (*Her*) vertical bar, pallet; (*fig*) control, command; **~ alpino, ~ de alpinista, ~ de montaña** alpenstock; **~ de estoque** swordstick; **~ de mando** baton, sign of authority; **empuñar el ~** to take command; **meter el ~** to intervene.

bastonazo NM (*golpe*) blow with a stick; (*paliza*) beating, caning.

▶ LENGUA Y USO: **basar: 2b** → 44.1   **básico** → 53.2

bastoncillo NM (**a**) ~ (*de algodón*) cotton bud, cotton swab (*US*). (**b**) (*Anat*) (retinal) rod.

bastoncito NM (**a**) (*de pan*) bread stick. (**b**) ~ (*de algodón*) = **bastoncillo (a)**.

bastonear [1a] VT to beat (with a stick), hit (with a stick).

bastonera NF umbrella stand.

bastonero NM (**a**) (*de bailes*) master of ceremonies (*at a dance*). (**b**) (*Carib*) scoundrel, tough*.

bastón-taburete NM shooting stick.

basuco* NM unpurified cocaine.

basura NF (**a**) (*gen*) rubbish, refuse, garbage (*US*); litter; dust; (*Agr*) dung, manure; ~ **radioactiva** radioactive waste.
(**b**) (*fig*) trash, rubbish; **la novela es una** ~ the novel is rubbish; **él es una** ~* he's a shocker*, he's a rotter*.

basural NM (*LAm*) rubbish dump.

basurear [1a] VT: ~ **a uno** (*Cono Sur*) to push sb along; (*fig*) (*humillar*) to humiliate sb; (*insultar*) to be rude to sb, rubbish sb*.

basurero NM (**a**) (*persona*) dustman, garbage man (*US*); scavenger. (**b**) (*vertedero*) rubbish dump; (*Agr*) dung heap. (**c**) (*recipiente*) dustbin, trashcan (*US*).

basuriento ADJ (*And, Cono Sur*) dirty, full of rubbish.

Basutolandia NF (*Hist*) Basutoland.

bata¹ NF dressing gown; (*de trabajo, de estar por casa*) housecoat, smock; (*salto de cama*) negligée; (*de playa*) beachwrap; (*de laboratorio etc*) white coat, laboratory coat; ~ **blanca** white coat.

bata²‡ NF mother.

batacazo NM (**a**) (*gen*) bump, thump; (*caída*) heavy fall. (**b**) (*fig: chiripa*) stroke of luck, fluke; unexpected win.

bataclán NM (*LAm*) burlesque show (*US*), striptease show.

bataclana NF (*LAm*) striptease girl, stripper.

batahola* NF (*ruido*) din, hullabaloo*; (*jaleo*) rumpus*.

bataholear [1a] VI, **batajolear** [1a] VI (*And*) (*pelear*) to brawl; (*ser travieso*) to be mischievous, play pranks.

batalla NF (**a**) (*Mil*) battle; (*fig*) battle, fight, struggle; (*fig*) inner struggle, agitation (of mind); ~ **campal** pitched battle; **ropa de** ~ everyday clothes, clothes not kept for best; **librar** ~ to do battle; **trabar** ~ to join battle.
(**b**) (*Arte*) battle piece, battle scene.
(**c**) (*Aut etc*) wheelbase.

batallador [1] ADJ battling, fighting; warlike.
[2] NM, **batalladora** NF battler, fighter; (*Dep*) fencer.

batallar [1a] VI (**a**) (*luchar*) to battle, fight, struggle (*con* with, against; *por* about, over); (*Dep*) to fence. (**b**) (*fig: vacilar*) to waver, vacillate.

batallita* NF: **contar** ~s to shoot a line*.

batallón [1] ADJ: **cuestión batallona** vexed question.
[2] NM battalion; ~ **de castigo**, ~ **disciplinario** punishment squad.

batán NM (**a**) (*lugar*) fulling mill; (*herramienta*) fulling hammer. (**b**) (*Cono Sur: tintorería*) dry cleaner's. (**c**) (*And: espesura de tela*) thickness (of cloth).

batanar [1a] VT (**a**) (*Téc*) to full. (**b**) (*) to beat, thrash.

batanear* [1a] VT (*pegar*) to beat, thrash; (*sacudir*) to shake.

batanero NM fuller.

bataola NF = **batahola**.

batasuno, -a [1] ADJ of Herri Batasuna.
[2] NM, **batasuna** NF member (*o* supporter) of Herri Batasuna.

batata [1] NF (**a**) (*Bot*) sweet potato, yam.
(**b**) (*And, Carib: pantorrilla*) calf (of the leg).
(**c**) (*Cono Sur: timidez*) bashfulness, embarrassment.
(**d**) (*Cono Sur*: *coche*) car.
[2] ADJ (**a**) (*Cono Sur: tímido*) bashful, shy, embarrassed.
(**b**) (*Carib, Cono Sur: simple*) simple, gullible.
(**c**) (*Carib*) (*llenito*) chubby, plump; (*rechoncho*) squat.

batatar NM (*LAm*) sweet potato field.

batatazo NM (*LAm*) = **batacazo**.

batayola NF (*Náut*) rail.

bate NM (*esp LAm*) (baseball) bat; **estar al** ~ **de algo** (*CAm, Carib*) to be in charge of sth.

batea NF (**a**) (*bandeja*) tray; small trough; round trough; (*de lavar*) washtub; (*Min*) washing pan. (**b**) (*Ferro*) flat car, low wagon. (**c**) (*Náut*) flat-bottomed boat, punt.

bateador NM (*esp LAm*) batter.

batear [1a] [1] VT (*esp LAm*) to hit.
[2] VI (**a**) (*esp LAm Dep*) to bat. (**b**) (*Carib*: *tragar*) to overeat.

batel NM small boat, skiff.

batelero NM boatman.

batelón NM (*And*) canoe.

batería [1] NF (**a**) (*Mil, Elec, para gallinas*) battery; (*de luces*) bank, battery, set; (*Teat*) footlights; (*Mús*) percussion, drums; ~ **de cocina** kitchen utensils, pots and pans; ~ **seca** dry battery; **aparcar en** ~ (*Aut*) to park square on (*o* obliquely) to the kerb; (**re**)**cargar las** ~s (*fig*) to recharge one's batteries.
(**b**) (*And: ronda de bebidas*) round of drinks.

(**c**) (*LAm Béisbol*) hit, stroke.
(**d**) (*Méx*) **dar** ~* to keep at it; **dar** ~ **a*** to make trouble for, make a lot of work for.
[2] NMF (*persona*) drummer.

baterista NMF (*LAm*) drummer.

batey NM (*Carib*) clearing in front of a country house, forecourt.

batiburrillo NM hotchpotch.

baticola NF (*de montura*) crupper; (*And: taparrabo*) loincloth; (*Cono Sur: pañal*) nappy, diaper (*US*).

batida NF (**a**) (*Caza*) battue; (*Mil*) reconnaissance; (*And, Cono Sur: redada*) raid (by the police); (*fig: registro*) search; combing; (*And: persecución*) chase. (**b**) (*And, Carib: paliza*) beating, thrashing.

batido [1] ADJ (**a**) *camino* well-trodden, beaten. (**b**) *seda* shot, chatoyant.
[2] NM (*Culin*) batter; ~ (**de leche**) milk-shake.

batidor NM (**a**) (*Caza, Téc*) beater; (*Mil*) scout. (**b**) (*herramienta*) beater; (*peine*) wide-toothed comb; (*Culin*) beater, whisk, mixer; (*CAm, Méx: vasija*) wooden bowl, mixing bowl. (**c**) (*Cono Sur: delator*) informer.

batidora NF (*Culin*) beater, whisk, mixer; (*Téc*) beater; ~ **eléctrica** electric mixer.

batiente NM (**a**) (*marco de puerta*) jamb; (*marco de ventana*) frame, case; (*hoja de puerta*) leaf, panel. (**b**) (*Mús*) damper. (**c**) (*Náut*) open coastline.

batifondo NM (*Cono Sur*) uproar, din.

batín NM (*bata*) (man's) dressing gown; (*chaqueta*) smoking jacket; (*de playa*) beach-wrap.

batintín NM gong.

batir [3a] [1] VT (**a**) (*gen*) to beat; (*martillear*) to hammer, pound (on); *tambor, metal* to beat; *moneda* to mint; *alas* to beat, flap; *manos* to clap; *pelo* to back-comb.
(**b**) *casa* to knock down; *muro etc* (*Mil*) to batter down; *tienda* to take down; *privilegio* to do away with.
(**c**) (*mar*) to beat on, dash against; (*sol*) to beat down on; (*viento*) to sweep.
(**d**) (*Culin*) to beat, mix, whisk; to stir, churn; *mantequilla* to cream; *nata* to whip.
(**e**) (*Caza*) to beat; to comb, search; (*Mil*) to reconnoitre.
(**f**) *adversario, enemigo* to beat, defeat; *récord* to beat.
(**g**) (*And*) *ropa* to rinse (out).
(**h**) (*Cono Sur: denunciar*) to inform on.
[2] VI (*Med*) to beat violently.
[3] **batirse** VR to fight, have a fight; ~ **con uno** to fight sb; ~ **en duelo** to fight a duel.

batiscafo NM bathyscape.

batista NF cambric, batiste.

bato¹ NM simpleton.

bato²‡ NM father.

batonista NF drum majorette.

batracio NM batrachian.

Batuecas NFPL: **las** ~ backward region of Extremadura, equivalent to the backwoods, the hillbilly country; **estar en las** ~ (*fig*) to be daydreaming.

batueco* ADJ stupid, silly.

batuque NM (*Cono Sur*) rumpus, racket.

batuquear [1a] VT (*CAm*) to pester, annoy.

baturrillo NM hotchpotch.

baturro [1] ADJ uncouth, rough.
[2] NM, **baturra** NF Aragonese peasant.

batusino, -a NM/F idiot, fool.

batuta NF (*Mús*) baton; **llevar la** ~ (*fig*) to be the boss, be firmly in command.

batzoki NM social club for PNV supporters.

baudio NM baud.

baúl NM (**a**) (*gen*) trunk; ~ **armario**, ~ **ropero** wardrobe trunk; ~ **camarote** cabin trunk; ~ **mundo** large trunk, Saratoga trunk; ~ **de viaje** portmanteau.
(**b**) (*Aut*) boot, trunk (*US*).
(**c**) (*: vientre*) belly.

bauprés NM bowsprit.

bausa NF (*And, Méx*) laziness, idleness.

bausán NM, **bausana** NF (*lit*) dummy; (*fig*) simpleton; (*And: holgazán*) good-for-nothing.

bausano NM (*CAm*) idler, lazy person.

bauseador NM (*And*) idler, lazy person.

bautismal ADJ baptismal.

bautismo NM (**a**) (*Rel*) baptism, christening; ~ **de fuego** baptism of fire. (**b**) **romper el** ~ **a uno‡** to knock sb's block off‡.

Bautista NM: ~, **San Juan** ~ St John the Baptist.

bautista ADJ: **Iglesia B**~ Baptist Church.

bautizar [1f] VT (**a**) (*Rel*) to baptize, christen; **le bautizaron con el nombre de Wamba** he was baptized Wamba.
(**b**) (*fig: nombrar*) to christen, name, give a name to.
(**c**) (*) *vino* to water (down), dilute; *persona* to drench, soak.

bautizo NM **(a)** (*acto*) baptism, christening. **(b)** (*fiesta*) christening party.

bauxita NF bauxite.

bávaro, -a ADJ, NM/F Bavarian.

Baviera NF Bavaria.

baya NF berry.

bayajá NM (*Carib*) headscarf.

báyer NF (*Cono Sur*) dope‡, pot‡.

bayeta NF **(a)** (*tela verde*) baize. **(b)** (*para limpiar*) floorcloth, cleaning rag; washing-up cloth. **(c)** (*And: pañal*) nappy, diaper (*US*).

bayetón NM **(a)** bearskin, thick woollen cloth. **(b)** (*And: poncho largo*) long poncho.

bayo ① ADJ bay.
② NM bay (horse).

Bayona NF Bayonne.

bayoneta NF **(a)** (*arma*) bayonet; **con ~s caladas** with fixed bayonets. **(b)** (*LAm Bot*) yucca.

bayonetazo NM (*arremetida*) bayonet thrust; (*herida*) bayonet wound.

bayonetear [1a] VT (*LAm*) to bayonet.

bayoya NM (*Carib*) row, uproar; **es un ~ aquí** it's pandemonium here.

bayunca[1] NF (*CAm*) bar, saloon.

bayunco ① ADJ (*CAm*) (*tonto*) silly, stupid; (*tímido*) shy; (*grosero*) crude, vulgar.
② NM, **bayunca**[2] NF (*CAm*) uncouth peasant; *name applied by Guatemalans to other Central Americans.*

baza NF **(a)** (*Naipes*) trick; **~ de honor** honours trick; **hacer 3 ~s** to make 3 tricks.
(b) (*fig*) **hacer ~** to get on; **meter ~** to butt in; **meter ~ en** interfere in; **no dejar meter ~ a nadie** not to let sb get a word in edgeways; **sentar ~** to intervene decisively; to speak up dogmatically; **sentada esta ~, ...** this point being established, ...; **tiene sentada la ~ de discreto** he has a reputation for good sense.

bazar NM (*mercado*) bazaar; (*almacenes*) large retail store; (*juguetería*) toy shop; (*LAm*) bazaar, charity fair; (*Méx*) second-hand shop; (*Cono Sur: ferretería*) ironmonger's (shop).

bazo ① ADJ yellowish-brown.
② NM (*Anat*) spleen.

bazofia NF **(a)** (*sobras*) left-overs, scraps of food; (*para cerdos*) pigswill. **(b)** (*fig: basura*) pigswill, hogwash (*US*); vile thing, filthy thing.

bazuca NF bazooka.

bazucar [1g] VT, **bazuquear** [1a] VT (*agitar*) to stir; (*sacudir*) to shake, jolt.

bazuqueo NM stirring; shaking, jolting; **~ gástrico** rumblings in the stomach.

BC NF ABR *de* **Banda Ciudadana** Citizens' Band, CB (*Radio*).

BCG NF ABR *de* **Bacilo Calmette-Guérin** (*vacuna*) BCG.

Bco ABR *de* **Banco** bank, bk.

be[1] NF the (name of the) letter *b*; **por ~** in detail, down to the last detail; **esto tiene las tres ~s** ('*bonita, barata, y buena*') this is really very nice, this is just perfect.

be[2] NM baa.

beata NF **(a)** (*Ecl*) lay sister.
(b) (*gen*) devout woman; woman who lives in pious retirement; (*pey*) excessively pious woman, sanctimonious woman, goody-goody*.
(c) (‡ *Fin*) one peseta.

beatería NF affected piety; cant, sanctimoniousness.

beaterío NM goody-goodies*, sanctimonious people.

beatificación NF beatification.

beatificar [1g] VT to beatify.

beatífico ADJ beatific.

beatitud NF beatitude; blessedness; **su B~** His Holiness.

beatnik ['bitnik] NM, PL **beatniks** ['bitnik] beatnik.

beato ① ADJ **(a)** (*feliz*) happy, blessed.
(b) (*Ecl*) beatified; blessed.
(c) (*piadoso*) devout, pious; (*pey*) excessively devout; canting, hypocritical.
② NM **(a)** (*Ecl*) lay brother.
(b) (*pey*) over-devout man, excessively pious person.

Beatriz NF Beatrice.

bebe, -a NM/F (*LAm*) baby.

bebé NMF baby; (*p.ej.*) **~ foca** baby seal; **dos ~s panda** two baby pandas.

bebecina NF (*And*) drunkenness; drinking spree.

bebedera NF (*And: embriaguez*) habitual drunkenness; (*CAm, Méx: juerga*) drinking bout, drunken spree.

bebedero ① ADJ drinkable, good to drink.
② NM **(a)** (*recipiente*) drinking trough; (*Zool*) drinking place, watering hole.
(b) (*de jarro*) spout.
(c) (*And*) (*Com*) establishment selling alcoholic drinks; (*fig*) watering place (*o* hole).

bebedizo ① ADJ drinkable.
② NM (*Med*) potion; (*Hist*) love potion, philtre.

bebedor ① ADJ hard-drinking, bibulous, given to drinking.
② NM, **bebedora** NF drinker; (*pey*) hard drinker, toper; **~ fuerte** heavy drinker; **~ social** social drinker.

bebendurria NF **(a)** (*Cono Sur: fiesta*) drinking party. **(b)** (*And, Méx*) (*embriaguez*) drunkenness; (*juerga*) drinking spree.

bebé-probeta NMF, PL **bebés-probeta** test-tube baby.

beber ① NM drink, drinking.
② [2a] VTI (*gen*) to drink; to drink up; (*fig*) to drink in, absorb, imbibe; **~ de** to drink from, drink out of; **~ a sorbos** to sip; **~ mucho, ~ a pote** to drink a lot, be a heavy drinker; **se lo bebió todo** he drank it all up.

beberaje NM (*Cono Sur*) drink (*esp alcoholic*).

bebercio* NM drink, booze*.

bebereca* NF (*And*) booze*.

beberecua* NF (*And*) **(a)** (*juerga*) boozing‡. **(b)** = **bebereca**.

beberrón ADJ, NM, **beberrona** NF = **bebedor**.

bebestible ① ADJ (*LAm*) drinkable.
② **~s** NMPL drinks.

bebezón NF (*Carib*) **(a)** (*bebida*) drink, booze*. **(b)** (*embriaguez*) drunkenness; (*juerga*) drinking spree.

bebezona* NF booze-up*.

bebible ADJ (just) drinkable; **no ~** undrinkable.

bebida NF **(a)** (*gen*) beverage.
(b) (*alcohólico*) (alcoholic) drink; **~ alcohólica** alcoholic drink, liquor; **~ no alcohólica** non-alcoholic drink, soft drink; **~ larga** long drink; **~ refrescante** soft drink; **dado a la ~** given to drink, hard-drinking; **darse a la ~** to take to drink; **tener mala ~** (*LAm*) to get violent with drink.
(c) (*Cono Sur*) bib.

bebido ADJ tipsy, merry*.

bebistrajo* NM nasty drink, filthy drink, brew.

bebito, -a NMF (*Cono Sur*) little baby.

BEBS [beß] ABR *de* **basura entra, basura sale** garbage in, garbage out, GIGO.

beca NF **(a)** (*dinero*) scholarship, grant; fellowship; award. **(b)** (*vestido*) sash, hood.

becacina NF snipe.

becada[1] NF (*Orn*) woodcock.

becado ① ADJ *estudiante* who holds a scholarship; *investigador* who holds an award; **está aquí ~** (*LAm*) he's here on a grant.
② NM, **becada**[2] NF scholarship holder; award holder.

becar [1g] VT to award a scholarship (*o* grant *etc*) to.

becario, -a NM/F scholarship holder; award holder; scholar, fellow.

becerrada NF (*Taur*) fight with young bulls.

becerrillo NM calfskin.

becerro NM **(a)** (*animal*) yearling calf, bullock; **~ de oro** golden calf. **(b)** (*piel*) calfskin. **(c)** (*Ecl Hist*) cartulary, register, record book.

bechamel NF white sauce, béchamel sauce.

becuadro NM (*Mús*) natural (sign).

Beda NM Bede.

bedel, -ela NM/F (*Univ: aprox*) head porter; (*de edificio oficial, museo*) uniformed employee; (*de colegio*) janitor.

bedoya NM (*And*) idiot.

beduino ① ADJ Bedouin.
② NM, **beduina** NF Bedouin; (*pey*) savage.

befa NF jeer, taunt.

befar [1a] VT (*t* **befarse** VR) **~ de** to scoff at, jeer at, taunt.

befo ① ADJ **(a)** (*bezudo*) thick-lipped. **(b)** (*patizambo*) knock-kneed, (*zancajoso*) splayfooted.
② NM lip.

begonia NF begonia.

behaviorismo NM behaviourism.

behaviorista ADJ, NMF behaviourist.

BEI NM ABR *de* **Banco Europeo de Inversiones** European Investment Bank, EIB.

beibi NF girlfriend, bird‡.

beicon NM bacon.

beige [beis], **beis** ADJ, NM beige.

béisbol NM baseball.

beisbolero ① ADJ (*LAm*) baseball (*atr*).
② NM (*LAm*) (*jugador*) baseball player; (*aficionado*) baseball fan.

beisbolista NM (*LAm*) baseball player.

beisbolístico ADJ baseball (*atr*).

bejuco NM (*LAm Bot*) liana; **no sacar ~*** (*Carib*) to miss the boat; to come a cropper*.

bejuquear [1a] VT (*LAm*) to beat, thrash.

bejuquero NM (*And*) confused situation, mess.

bejuquillo NM **(a)** (*Carib, Méx Bot*) (variety of) liana. **(b)** (*And: vainilla*) vanilla.

bejuquiza NF (*And*) beating, thrashing.

Belcebú NM Beelzebub.

beldad NF (**a**) (*cualidad*) beauty. (**b**) (*persona*) beauty, belle.

beldar [1j] VT to winnow (with a fork).

belduque NM (*CAm, Méx*) pointed sword.

Belén NM Bethlehem.

belén NM (**a**) (*de Navidad*) nativity scene, crib.
(**b**) (*fig*) (*confusión*) confusion, bedlam; (*guirigay*) madhouse; (*riesgo*) risky venture; **meterse en belenes** (*Cono Sur*) to get involved in other people's troubles.

belenista NMF maker of nativity scenes.

beleño NM henbane.

belfo = **befo**.

belga ADJ, NMF Belgian.

Bélgica NF Belgium.

bélgico ADJ Belgian.

Belgrado NM Belgrade.

Belice NM Belize.

beliceño, -a ADJ, NM/F Belizean.

belicismo NM warmongering, militarism.

belicista [1] ADJ warmongering, militaristic, warminded.
[2] NMF warmonger.

bélico ADJ (**a**) (*gen*) warlike, martial. (**b**) *material, juguete etc* war (*atr*).

belicosidad NF warlike spirit; bellicosity, aggressiveness; militancy.

belicoso ADJ warlike; bellicose, aggressive; militant.

beligerancia NF belligerency; militancy, warlike spirit.

beligerante [1] ADJ belligerent; militant, warlike; **no ~** non-belligerent.
[2] NMF belligerent; **no ~** non-belligerent.

belinún NM (*Cono Sur*) simpleton, blockhead*.

belitre NM (**a**) (*granuja*) rogue, scoundrel. (**b**) (*And, CAm: niño*) shrewd child; restless child.

bellaco [1] ADJ (*malvado*) wicked; (*taimado*) cunning, sly; (*pícaro*) rascally; (*Cono Sur, Méx*) *caballo* vicious, hard to control; (*And, CAm*) brave.
[2] NM (*esp hum*) rascal, rogue, villain.

belladona NF deadly nightshade, belladonna.

bellamente ADV beautifully; finely.

bellaqueada NF (*Cono Sur*) bucking, rearing; shy.

bellaquear [1a] VI (**a**) (*engañar*) to cheat, be crooked*. (**b**) (*And, Cono Sur: caballo*) to rear up, balk; to shy; (*fig*) to dig one's heels in, be stubborn.

bellaquería NF (**a**) (*acto*) dirty trick, wicked thing. (**b**) (*cualidad*) wickedness; cunning, slyness.

belleza NF (**a**) (*gen*) beauty, loveliness; **las ~s de Mallorca** the beauties of Majorca. (**b**) (*persona*) beauty, beautiful woman (*etc*); (*objeto*) lovely thing.

bello ADJ beautiful, lovely; fine; noble; *V* **arte** *etc*.

bellota NF (**a**) (*Bot*) acorn; (*de clavel*) bud. (**b**) *Anat* (*) Adam's apple. (**c**) (*para perfumes*) perfume-box, pomander. (**d**) **~ de mar, ~ marina** sea urchin.

bemba: NF (*LAm*) lip.

bembo ADJ, **bembón** ADJ, **bembudo** ADJ (*LAm*) thick-lipped.

bemol NM (**a**) (*Mús*) flat; **esto tiene muchos** (*o* **tres**) **~es*** this is a tough one, this bristles with difficulties. (**b**) **~es** (:: *euf*) = **cojones**.

bencedrina NF Benzedrine ®.

benceno NM benzene.

bencina NF benzine; (*Cono Sur: gasolina*) petrol, gasoline (*US*).

bencinera¹ NF (*Cono Sur*) garage, petrol-station.

bencinero, -a² NM/F (*Cono Sur*) petrol-station attendant.

bendecir [*aprox* 3o] VT (*gen*) to bless; (*consagrar*) to consecrate; (*loar*) to praise, call down a blessing on; **~ la comida, ~ la mesa** to say grace.

bendición NF (**a**) (*Rel*) blessing, benediction; **~ de la mesa** grace; **bendiciones nupciales** wedding ceremony; **echar la ~** to give one's blessing (*a* to; *t fig*); **tuvo que echar la ~ a eso** he had to say goodbye to that, he had to give up all hope of (finding) that; **será mejor echar la ~ a eso** it will be best to have nothing more to do with it. (**b**) **... que es una ~ (de Dios)** ... and it's just marvellous; **llovió que era una ~ (de Dios)** there was such a lovely lot of rain; **lo hace que es una ~** she does it splendidly, she does it with the greatest ease.

bendiga *etc*, **bendije** *etc V* **bendecir**.

bendito [1] ADJ (**a**) (*Rel*) blessed, holy; saintly.
(**b**) (*fig*) blessed.
(**c**) (*feliz*) happy; lucky.
(**d**) (*cándido*) simple, simple-minded.
(**e**) (*piropos*) **¡~s los ojos que te ven!** lucky eyes to be looking at you!; **¡bendita la madre que te parió!** what a daughter for a mother to have!
[2] NM (**a**) (*Rel*) saint.
(**b**) (*fig*) simple soul, good soul; **es un ~** he's a good kind person, he's sweet; **dormir como un ~** to sleep peacefully, be fast asleep.
(**c**) (*Cono Sur: oración*) prayer.

(d) (*Cono Sur*) (*Rel*) wayside shrine; (*cabaña*) native hut.

benedícite NM grace.

benedictino [1] ADJ Benedictine.
[2] NM (*Ecl, licor*) Benedictine; **es obra de ~s** it's a huge task, it's a long job.

Benedicto NM Benedict.

benefactor [1] ADJ salutary; beneficent; *V* **estado**.
[2] NM, **benefactora** NF benefactor.

beneficencia NF (**a**) (*gen*) beneficence, doing good.
(**b**) (*obra etc*) charity; charitable organization; (*t ~ social*) social welfare; **vivir a cargo de la ~** to live on charity, live on public welfare.

beneficiado NM (*Ecl*) incumbent, beneficiary.

beneficial ADJ relating to ecclesiastical benefices; **terreno ~** glebe, glebe land.

beneficiar [1b] [1] VT (**a**) (*gen*) to benefit, be of benefit to.
(**b**) (*Cono Sur*) *tierra* to cultivate; *mina* to exploit, work; *mineral* to process, refine; (*CAm: Agr*) to process.
(**c**) (*LAm*) *animal* (*matar*) to slaughter; (*CAm*) *persona* to shoot, kill.
(**d**) (*Com*) to sell at a discount.
(**e**) (*) *puesto* to buy one's way into.
[2] VI to be of benefit.
[3] **beneficiarse** VR (**a**) (*gen*) to benefit, profit; **~ de** to benefit from, take advantage of; (*pey*) to make a good thing out of.
(**b**) **~ a uno** (*CAm*) to shoot sb.

beneficiario, -a NMF beneficiary.

beneficiencia NF (*Méx*) welfare.

▼ **beneficio** NM (**a**) (*provecho*) benefit, profit, gain, advantage; **~ de justicia gratuita** legal aid; **~s marginales** fringe benefits; **a ~ de** for the benefit of; **en ~ propio** to one's own advantage; **en su propio ~, no ...** in your own interests, do not ...
(**b**) (*donativo*) benefaction.
(**c**) (*Teat*) benefit, benefit performance.
(**d**) (*Ecl*) living, benefice.
(**e**) (*Com, Fin*) profit; earnings; **~ bruto** gross profit; **~s excesivos** excess profits; **~s imprevistos** windfall profits; **~ líquido, ~ neto** net profit; **~s posimpositivos** after-tax profits, profits after tax; **~ preimpositivos** pre-tax profits, profits before tax; **~s previstos** anticipated profits; **~s retenidos** retained profits; **~ por acción** earnings per share.
(**f**) (*Agr, Min: producto*) yield.
(**g**) (*acto: Agr*) cultivation; (*Min: de mina*) exploitation; (*Min: de mineral*) processing, treatment, smelting.
(**h**) (*LAm: matanza*) slaughter, slaughtering.
(**i**) (*Cono Sur Agr*) manure.
(**j**) (*LAm*) (*matadero*) slaughterhouse; (*cafetal*) coffee plantation; (*ingenio*) sugar refinery.

beneficioso ADJ beneficial, profitable, useful.

benéfico ADJ (**a**) (*amable etc*) beneficent, charitable, kind (*a* to; *para, con* towards). (**b**) *trabajo, organismo etc* charitable; **función benéfica** charity performance; **obra benéfica** charity.

benemérito ADJ (**a**) (*gen*) worthy, meritorious; notable; distinguished; **el ~ hispanista** the distinguished hispanist.
(**b**) **un ~ de la patria** a national hero; **la Benemérita** the Civil Guard; *see also* GUARDIA CIVIL .

beneplácito NM approval, consent; **dar su ~** to give one's consent.

benevolencia NF benevolence, kindness, kindliness; geniality.

benevolente ADJ, **benévolo** ADJ benevolent, kind, kindly; genial; **~ con** well-disposed towards, kind to.

Bengala NF Bengal; **el Golfo de ~** the Gulf of Bengal.

bengala NF flare; star shell.

bengalí ADJ, NMF Bengali.

Bengasi NM Bengazi.

benignamente ADV kindly, benignly; graciously, gently; mildly.

benignidad NF kindness, kindliness; graciousness, gentleness; mildness.

benigno ADJ kind, kindly, benign; gracious; gentle; *clima* mild; (*Med*) *ataque, caso* mild; *tumor* benign, non-malignant.

Benito NM Benedict.

benito = **benedictino**.

Benjamín NM Benjamin.

benjamín [1] NM, **benjamina** NF (*t* **benjasmín** NM, **benjasmina** NF *Cono Sur*) baby of the family, youngest child; favourite child; (*Dep*) junior, young player.
[2] NM (*botella*) half-bottle.

benzina NF (*Cono Sur*) = **bencina**.

beo:: NM cunt::.

beocio:: ADJ stupid.

beocio: ADJ stupid.

beodez NF drunkenness.

beodo [1] ADJ drunk.
[2] NM drunk, drunkard.

beorí NM American tapir.

beque [1] ADJ (*CAm*) stammering.

2 NMF (*CAm*) stammerer.

bequista NMF (*CAm, Carib*) = **becario**.

berbecí NMF (*Méx*) quick-tempered person.

berbén NM (*Méx*) scurvy.

berberecho NM cockle.

berberí ADJ y NMF = **bereber**.

Berbería NF Barbary.

berberisco ADJ Berber.

berbiquí NM carpenter's brace; ~ **y barrena** brace and bit.

berdel NM mackerel.

bereber, beréber, berebere ADJ, NMF Berber.

berengo (*Méx*) 1 ADJ foolish, stupid.
2 NM, **berenga** NF idiot.

berenjena NF (a) aubergine, eggplant. (b) (*Carib**) nuisance, bother.

berenjenal NM (a) (*lit*) aubergine bed. (b) (*fig: lío*) mess, trouble; **en buen** ~ **nos hemos metido** we've got ourselves into a fine mess.

bereque ADJ (*CAm*) cross-eyed.

bergante NM scoundrel, rascal.

bergantín NM brig.

Beri N: **andar** (*o* **ir**) **con las de** ~ (*tener genio*) to have a violent temper; (*tener malas intenciones*) to have evil intentions.

beriberi NM (*Med*) beriberi (fever).

beril(i)o NM beryl.

berkelio NM berkelium.

Berlín NM Berlin; ~ **Oeste** West Berlin.

berlina NF (a) (*Aut*) saloon car, sedan. (b) (*Cono Sur*) doughnut, donut (*US*).

berlinés 1 ADJ Berlin (*atr*).
2 NM, **berlinesa** NF Berliner.

berma NF berm; (*Cono Sur*) hard shoulder; emergency lane.

bermejo ADJ (a) (*de color*) red, bright red; reddish; *gato* ginger; (*Carib, Méx*) *vaca* light brown. (b) (*Carib: único*) matchless, unsurpassed.

bermellón NM vermilion.

bermuda NF (*LAm*) meadow grass.

Bermudas NFPL (*t* **Islas Bermuda** NFPL) Bermuda, the Bermudas.

bermudas NMPL Bermuda shorts.

Berna NF Berne.

bernardina* NF yarn, tall story.

Bernardo NM Bernard.

berraco* NM noisy brat.

berrear [1a] 1 VI (a) (*Zool*) to bellow, low; (*niño*) to howl; (*Mús: hum*) to bawl; to screech. (b) (*fig*) to fly off the handle*.
2 **berrearse** VT to squeal**‡**; grass**‡**.

berrenchín NM rage, tantrum.

berreo* NM bawling.

berreta* ADJ (*Cono Sur*) cheap, flashy.

berretín* NM (*Cono Sur*) (*obsesión*) obsession, mania; (*terquedad*) pigheadedness.

berrido NM (*Zool*) bellow, bellowing; lowing; (*niño*) howl; (*Mús: hum*) bawl, bawling; screech.

berrinche 1 NM (a) (***) (*rabieta*) rage, tantrum*; **coger** (*o* **llevarse**) **un** ~ to fly into a rage. (b) (*LAm*‡: *hedor*) pong**‡**, stink.
2 ~**s*** NM INVAR bad-tempered person, stroppy individual*.

berrinchudo* ADJ (a) *persona* cross, bad-tempered. (b) (*Méx*) *animal* on heat.

berro NM (*Bot*) watercress; (*Carib: enojo*) rage, anger.

berza 1 NF (*Esp*) cabbage; ~ **lombarda** red cabbage; **mezclar** ~**s con capachos*** to get things in a shocking mess.
2 ~**s*** NMF INVAR idiot, imbecile; ¡~**s!** you idiot!

berzal NM (*Esp*) cabbage patch.

berzotas* NMF INVAR twit*, chump*.

besamanos NM INVAR royal audience, levée.

besamel NF white sauce, béchamel sauce.

besana NF land to be ploughed.

besar [1a] VT (a) (*gen*) to kiss; ~ **la mano**, ~ **los pies** (*fig*) to pay one's humble respects (*a* to).
(b) (*fig: tocar*) to graze, touch.
2 **besarse** VR (a) (*gen*) to kiss, kiss one another.
(b) (*fig: tocar*) to touch, knock against each other; to bump heads.

besazo NM big kiss, smacker*.

▼ **beso** NM (a) (*gen*) kiss; ~ **lingual**, ~ **de tornillo** French kiss; ~ **de la muerte** kiss of death; ~ **de la vida** kiss of life; **dar un** ~ **volado a**, **echar** (*o* **tirar**) **un** ~ **a** to blow a kiss to. (b) (*choque*) bump, collision.

besograma NM kissogram.

besotear [1a] VT (*Méx*) = **besuquear**.

bestia 1 NF (*Zool*) beast, animal, (*esp*) horse, mule; ~ **de arrastre**, ~ **de carga** beast of burden; ~ **negra** (*fig*) bête noire, pet aversion; ~ **de tiro** draught animal.
2 NMF (a) (***) (*idiota*) idiot, ignoramus; (*patán*) boor; (*bruto*) beast, brute; ¡~! you idiot!, you brute!; ¡**no seas** ~! don't be an idiot!
(b) (***: *admirativo*) ¡**estás hecho un** ~! you're great!*
3 ADJ (***) stupid; **Juan es muy** ~ John is a bit stupid; **el muy** ~ the

great idiot; **ese tío** ~ that beastly fellow; **a lo** ~ (ADJ) vulgar, crude; boorish; (ADV) vulgarly, crudely; boorishly; **me pone** ~**‡** it turns me on*.

bestiada* NF: **una** ~ **de** masses of, tons of*; **disfrutar** ~**s** to enjoy o.s. hugely.

bestial ADJ (a) (*animal*) beast-like, bestial. (b) (***) terrific*; tremendous*, marvellous; smashing*, super*.

bestialidad NF (a) (*cualidad*) beast-like nature, bestiality. (b) (*sexual*) bestiality. (c) (*fig*) (*estupidez*) stupidity; (*disparate*) silly thing, piece of stupidity. (d) **una** ~ **de gente*** lots and lots of people.

bestialismo NM bestiality.

bestialmente* ADV marvellously; **lo pasamos** ~ we had a super time*.

best-seller NM, PL **best-sellers** best-seller.

besucar* [1g] VT = **besuquear**.

besucón* ADJ free with kisses, fond of kissing.

besugo NM (a) (*pez*) red bream; **con ojos de** ~ with bulging eyes; with eyes like a spaniel's. (b) (***: *idiota*) idiot.

besuguera NF (a) fishing-boat. (b) (*Pez: Galicia*) bream. (c) (*Culin*) fish pan.

besuquear* [1a] 1 VT to cover with kisses, keep on kissing.
2 **besuquearse** VR to kiss (each other) a lot; (*magrearse*) to pet*, neck*.

besuqueo* NM kissing; petting*, necking*.

beta NF beta.

betabel 1 NM (*LAm*) sugar-beet.
2 ADJ (*Méx**) old, ancient.

betabloqueador NM beta-blocker.

betarraga NF (*LAm*), **betarrata** NF beetroot, beet (*US*).

betel NM betel.

Bética NF (*liter*) Andalusia; (*Hist*) Baetica.

bético ADJ (*liter*) Andalusian.

betonera NF (*Cono Sur*) concrete mixer.

betún NM (a) (*Quím*) bitumen; ~ **de Judea**, ~ **judaico** asphalt. (b) shoe polish, blacking; **dar de** ~ **a** to polish, black; **darse** ~***** to swank*, show off.

betunero NM shoeblack, bootblack.

bezo NM thick lip; (*Med*) proud flesh.

bezudo ADJ thick-lipped.

bi... PREF bi...

biaba NF (*Cono Sur*) punch, slap; **dar la** ~ **a** (*pegar*) to beat up; (*derrotar*) to defeat, crush.

bianual ADJ, NM (*Bot*) biennial.

bianualmente ADV biennially, every two years.

biatlón NM biathlon.

Bib. NF ABR *de* **Biblioteca** Library, Lib.

biberón NM feeding bottle.

Biblia NF (a) (*Rel*) Bible; **la Santa** ~ the Holy Bible. (b) **es la** ~ (**en verso**)* it's the tops*; **saber la** ~***** to know everything.

bíblico ADJ Biblical.

biblio... PREF biblio...

bibliobús NM travelling library, mobile library, library van.

bibliofilia NF bibliophily, love of books.

bibliófilo, -a NMF bibliophile.

bibliografía NF bibliography.

bibliográfico ADJ bibliographic(al).

bibliógrafo, -a NMF bibliographer.

bibliomanía NF bibliomania.

bibliometría NF bibliometry.

bibliométrico ADJ bibliometric.

bibliorato NM (*Cono Sur*) box-file.

biblioteca NF (a) (*gen*) library; ~ **circulante** lending library; circulating library; ~ **de consulta** reference library; ~ **pública** public library; ~ **universitaria** university library.
(b) (*estante*) bookcase, bookshelves.

bibliotecario 1 ADJ library (*atr*); **servicios** ~**s** library services.
2 NM, **bibliotecaria** NF librarian.

bibliotecnia NF, **bibliotecología** NF, **biblioteconomía** NF library science, librarianship.

biblioteconomista NMF librarian.

BIC [bik] NF (*Esp*) ABR *de* **Brigada de Investigación Criminal** ≃ CID, FBI (*US*).

bicameral ADJ (*Pol*) two-chamber, bicameral.

bicameralismo NM system of two-chamber government.

bicampeón, -ona NM/F two-times champion, twice champion.

bicarbonatado ADJ bicarbonated, fizzy.

bicarbonato NM: ~ (**sódico**), ~ **de sosa** bicarbonate of soda; (*Culin*) baking soda.

bicentenario ADJ, NM bicentenary.

bíceps NM INVAR biceps.

bicha NF (a) (*euf: serpiente*) snake; (*fig*) bogy; ~ **negra** bête noire, pet aversion; **mentar la** ~ to bring up an unpleasant subject. (b) (*CAm:*

niña) child, little girl. (**c**) (*And: olla*) large cooking-pot.

bichadero NM (*Cono Sur*) watchtower, observation tower.

bichará NM (*Cono Sur*) poncho (with black and white stripes).

bicharraco*, -a NM/F (*animal*) creature; (*insecto*) creepy-crawly*; (*niño*) little monster.

biche ① ADJ (*Cono Sur: débil*) weak; (*de mal color*) of unhealthy colour; (*And: no desarrollado*) stunted, immature; (*Méx*: fofo*) soppy*, empty-headed.
② NM (*And*) large cooking-pot.

bicheadero NM (*Cono Sur*) = **bichadero**.

bichear [1a] VT (*Cono Sur*) to spy (o keep watch) on.

bicherío NM (*LAm*) insects, bugs, creepy-crawlies*.

bichero NM boat hook; (*Pesca*) gaff.

bichi‡ ADJ (*Méx*) naked, starkers‡.

bichicori* ADJ (*Méx*) skinny.

bichito NM (**a**) small creature, little insect. (**b**) (‡) LSD tablet.

bicho NM (**a**) (*Zool etc: gen: animal*) small animal; (*insecto*) (unpleasant) insect, bug, creepy-crawly*; (*Carib, Cono Sur: gusano*) maggot, grub; (*And: serpiente*) snake; (*LAm: animal extraño*) odd-looking creature; **~s** (*frec*) vermin, pests, bugs.
(**b**) (*And: peste aviar*) fowl pest.
(**c**) (*Taur*) bull.
(**d**) (*persona*: *t* **~ raro**) odd-looking person, queer fish; **~ raro** weirdo*, weirdy*; **mal ~** rogue, villain; **es un mal ~** he's a nasty piece of work, he's a rotter*; **todo ~ viviente** every living soul, every manjack of them; **sí, bichito*** yes, my love.
(**e**) (*) (*pey: niño*) brat; (*Mil*) squaddie*, recruit; (*CAm: niño*) child, little boy.
(**f**) **de puro ~** (*LAm*) out of sheer pig-headedness; **tener ~** to be terribly thirsty; **matar el ~** to have a drink.
(**g**) (*Carib: chisme*) what's-it*, thingummy*.

bichoco ADJ (*And, Cono Sur*) past it, useless; unfit to work.

bici* NF bike*.

bicicleta NF bicycle, cycle; **~ de carreras** racing bicycle; **~ de ejercicio**, **~ estática**, **~ fija**, **~ gimnástica** exercise bicycle; **~ de montaña** mountain bicycle; **andar en ~**, **ir en ~** to cycle; to ride a bicycle.

bicicletero* ① ADJ bicycle (*atr*).
② NM, **bicicletera** NF cyclist.

biciclo NM (††) velocipede††.

bicicross NM cyclo-cross.

bicilíndrico ADJ two-cylinder (*atr*), twin-cylinder (*atr*).

bicimoto NM (*CAm*) moped.

bicoca NF (**a**) (*bagatela*) trifle, mere nothing. (**b**) (*ganga*) bargain; (*prebenda*) soft job, plum job. (**c**) (*And, Cono Sur Ecl*) priest's skull cap. (**d**) (*And, Cono Sur*) (*capirotazo*) snap of the fingers; (*golpe*) slap, smack.

bicolor ADJ two-colour, in two colours, (*Aut*) two-tone.

bicultural ADJ bicultural.

bicúspide ADJ bicuspid.

BID NM ABR *de* **Banco Interamericano de Desarrollo** Inter-American Development Bank, BID.

bidé NM, **bidet** [biˈðe] NM, PL **bidets** bidet.

bidel NM (*LAm*) bidet.

bidimensional ADJ two-dimensional.

bidireccional ADJ duplex, bidirectional; **~ simultáneo** full duplex.

bidón NM drum; can, tin; **~ de aceite** oildrum.

biela NF (**a**) (*Téc*) connecting rod. (**b**) (‡) leg.

bielástico ADJ with two-way stretch.

bielda NF winnowing fork, (kind of) pitchfork.

bieldar [1a] VT to winnow (with a fork).

bieldo NM winnowing rake.

Bielorrusia NF Belorussia.

bielorruso, -a ADJ, NM/F Belorussian.

bien ① ADV (**a**) (*gen*) well; (*correctamente*) properly, right; (*con éxito*) successfully; **hacer algo ~** to do sth well, do sth properly; **contestar ~** to answer right, answer correctly; **lo sé muy ~** I know that perfectly well; **no veo muy ~** I can't see all that well; **¡qué ~!** (*bravo*) jolly good!, marvellous!; (*ojalá*) now that really would be something!; (*iró*) a lot of good that would do!; **~ que mal** one way or another, by hook or by crook; **de ~ en ~**, **de ~ en mejor** better and better; **aquí se está ~** it's nice here; **¿estás ~?** are you all right?; are you comfortable?; **ya está ~ de quejas** we've had enough complaints, that's quite enough complaining; **¿está ~ que ...?** is it all right that ...?; **hacer ~ en** + *infin* to be right to + *infin*, do well to + *infin*; **tener a ~** + *infin* to see fit to + *infin*, deign to + *infin*; to think it proper to + *infin*.
(**b**) (*de buena gana*) willingly, gladly, readily; **yo ~ iría, pero ...** I'd gladly go, but ...; (*asentimiento poco entusiasta*) **¿quieres que vayamos al cine? - ~** shall we go to the cinema? - all right.
(**c**) (*muy*) very, much, quite, a good deal, fully; **un cuarto ~ caliente** a nice warm room; **eso es ~ tonto** that's pretty silly; **un**

coche ~ caro a very expensive car; **~ temprano** very early, pretty early, quite early; **había ~ 8 toneladas** there were fully (o easily, at least) 8 tons.
(**d**) (*fácilmente*) easily; **~ se ve que ...** one can easily see that ..., it is easy to see that ...; **~ es verdad que ...** it is of course true that ...
(**e**) (*o ... o*) **~ por avión, ~ en tren** either by air or by train; **~ se levantó, ~ se sentó** whether he stood up or sat down.
(**f**) **~ (así) como** just as, just like; **más ~** rather; **más ~ creo que ...** on the contrary I think that ...; **más ~ bajo (que alto)** rather short, on the short side; **o ~** or else; **pues ~** well, well then.
(**g**) INTERJ etc **¡~!** yes!, all right!; O.K.!*; jolly good!*; well done!; **¡muy ~!** (*aprobando discurso etc*) hear hear!; **¡hizo muy ~!** and he was quite right too!; **¡muy ~ (por) usted!** good for you!
② *ADJ *persona* well-off; *restaurante etc* posh*, classy*; **barrio ~** posh neighbourhood*; *V* **gente, niño**.
③ CONJ (**a**) **~ que, si ~** although, even though.
(**b**) **no ~ llegó, empezó a llover** no sooner had he arrived than it started to rain, as soon as he arrived it started to rain.
④ NM (**a**) (*gen*) good; (*provecho*) advantage, benefit, profit; **hombre de ~** honest man, good man; **el ~ público** the common good; **sumo ~** highest good; **en ~ de** for the good of, for the benefit of; **para ~** for the best; positively; **hacer ~** to do good; to be honest, lead an honest life; **hacer algo para el ~ de** to do sth for the well-being of.
(**b**) **mi ~** my dear, my darling.
(**c**) **~es** (*Com etc*) goods; (*propiedad*) property, possessions; (*riqueza*) riches, wealth; **~es activos** active assets; **~es de capital** capital goods; **~es de consumo** consumer goods; **~es de consumo duraderos** consumer durables; **~es duraderos** durables; **~es de equipo** capital goods; **~es dotales** dowry; **~es fungibles** perishable goods; **~es gananciales** (*Jur*) shared possessions; **~es heredables** hereditament; **~es inmuebles**, **~es raíces** real estate, landed property; **~es de inversión** capital goods; **~es mostrencos** unclaimed property, ownerless property; **~es muebles** personal property, goods and chattels; **~ de producción** industrial goods; **~es públicos** government property, state property; **~es relictos** estate, inheritance; **~es semovientes** livestock; **~es de servicio** services; **~ terrestres** worldly goods; **~es de la tierra** produce; **~es vinculados** entail.
(**d**) **decir mil ~es de uno** to speak highly of sb, talk in glowing terms of sb.

bienal ① ADJ biennial.
② NF biennial exhibition, biennial show.

bienamado ADJ beloved.

bienandante ADJ happy; prosperous.

bienandanza NF happiness; prosperity.

bienaventuradamente ADV happily.

bienaventurado ADJ (**a**) (*feliz*) happy, fortunate; (*Ecl*) blessed. (**b**) (*cándido*) simple, naïve.

bienaventuranza NF (**a**) (*Ecl*) blessedness, (eternal) bliss; **las ~s** the Beatitudes. (**b**) (*felicidad*) happiness; (*bienestar*) well-being, prosperity.

bienestar NM wellbeing, welfare; comfort; **~ social** social welfare.

bienhablado ADJ nicely-spoken, well-spoken.

bienhadado ADJ lucky.

bienhechor ① ADJ beneficent, beneficial.
② NM benefactor.

bienhechora NF benefactress.

bienhechuría NF (*Carib*) improvement (to property).

bienintencionado ADJ well-meaning.

bienio NM two years, two-year period.

bienoliente ADJ sweet-smelling, fragrant.

bienpensante ① ADJ orthodox; conservative.
② NMF orthodox person; conservative.

bienquerencia NF (*afecto*) affection; (*buena voluntad*) goodwill.

bienquerer ① [2t] VT to like, be fond of.
② NM (*afecto*) affection; (*buena voluntad*) goodwill.

bienquistar [1a] ① VT to bring together, reconcile.
② **bienquistarse** VR to become reconciled; **~ con uno** to gain sb's esteem.

bienquisto ADJ well-liked, well-thought-of (*con, de, por* by).

bienudo* ADJ (*Cono Sur*) well-off.

bienvenida NF (*gen*) welcome; (*saludo*) greeting; **dar la ~ a uno** to welcome sb, make sb welcome.

bienvenido ADJ welcome; **¡~!** welcome!; **¡~s a bordo!** welcome on board!

bienvivir [3a] VI to live in comfort; to live decently, lead a decent life.

bies NM: **al ~** (*Cos*) cut on the cross.

bifásico ADJ (*Elec*) two-phase.

bife¹ NM (*LAm*: *t* **baby ~**) steak, beefsteak; cutlet, fillet.

bife² NM (*Cono Sur*) slap, smack.

bífido ADJ *lengua etc* forked.

bífidus NM INVAR bifidus.

bifocal [1] ADJ bifocal.
  [2] **~es** NMPL bifocals.
bifronte ADJ two-faced.
biftec NM steak, beefsteak.
bifurcación NF fork; junction; branch.
bifurcado ADJ forked.
bifurcarse [1g] VR to fork, branch, bifurcate; to branch off; to diverge.
bigamia NF bigamy.
bígamo [1] ADJ bigamous.
  [2] NM, **bígama** NF bigamist.
bigardear* [1a] VI to loaf around.
bigardo [1] ADJ lazy, idle; licentious.
  [2] NM (*vago*) idler; (*libertino*) libertine.
bígaro NM, **bigarro** NM winkle.
bignonia NF: **~ del Cabo** Cape honeysuckle.
bigornia NF (double-headed) anvil.
bigotazo NM huge moustache.
bigote NM (*t* **~s**) moustache; (*de gato etc*) whiskers; **~ de cepillo** toothbrush moustache; **~ de morsa** walrus moustache; **de ~*** terrific*, marvellous; (*pey*) awful; **chuparse los ~s** (*Cono Sur*) to lick one's lips; **menear el ~** to eat, scoff*.
bigotudo ADJ with a big moustache.
bigudí NM hair-curler.
bijirita NF (*Carib*) (a) (*cometa*) kite. (b) **empinar la ~*** (*beber*) to booze*, drink a lot; (*enriquecerse*) to make money by dubious methods.
bikini NM bikini.
bilateral ADJ bilateral.
bilbaíno [1] ADJ of Bilbao.
  [2] NM, **bilbaína** NF native (o inhabitant) of Bilbao; **los ~s** the people of Bilbao.
bilbilitano [1] ADJ of Calatayud.
  [2] NM, **bilbilitana** NF native (o inhabitant) of Calatayud; **los ~s** the people of Calatayud.
Bilbo* ['bɪlβo] NM = **Bilbao**.
biliar ADJ bile (*atr*), gall (*atr*).
bilingüe ADJ bilingual.
bilingüismo NM bilingualism.
bilioso ADJ (a) (*gen*) bilious. (b) (*fig: irritable*) bilious, peevish.
bilis NF (a) (*Anat*) bile.
  (b) (*fig: cólera*) bile, spleen; **descargar la ~** to vent one's spleen (*contra* on); **se le exalta la ~** he gets very cross; **eso me revuelve la ~** it makes my blood boil; **tragar ~** to put up with it.
billar NM (a) (*juego*) billiards; **~ americano** pool; **~ automático, ~ romano** pin table. (b) (*sala*) billiard room; (*mesa*) billiard table.
billete NM (a) (*Esp Ferro etc*) ticket; **~ de abono** season-ticket, commutation ticket (*US*); **~ de andén** platform ticket; **~ de avión** plane ticket; **~ azul** ticket for off-peak travel; **~ de favor** complimentary ticket; **~ de ida y vuelta** return ticket, round-trip ticket (*US*); **~ kilométrico** runabout ticket, mileage book; **~ de libre circulación** travel-card which allows unlimited travel within an area; **medio ~** half fare; **~ sencillo** single ticket, one-way ticket (*US*); **pagar el ~** to pay one's fare, buy one's ticket; **sacar un ~** to get a ticket.
  (b) (*Fin*) banknote, note, bill (*US*); (*) 1000-peseta note (*t* **~ verde**); **~ de banco** banknote; **~ de 5 libras** a five-pound note; **un ~ de 100 dólares** a 100-dollar bill; **tener ~ largo** (*Cono Sur**) to be rolling in it*.
  (c) (*carta*) note, short letter; **~ amoroso** love letter, billet-doux.
billetera NF, **billetero** NM wallet, pocketbook (*US*), billfold (*US*).
billón NM: **un ~ (de)** a billion (*Brit*), a million million, a trillion (*US*).
billonario, -a NM/F billionaire.
bilobulado ADJ bilobate.
bilongo NM (*Carib*) evil influence, evil eye; **echar ~ en** to put the evil eye on; **tener ~** to bristle with difficulties.
bilonguear [1a] VT (*Carib*) to cast a spell on, put the evil eye on.
bimba¹* NF top hat, topper*.
bimba²: NF (*Méx*) (*embriaguez*) drunkenness; (*juerga*) drinking spree.
bimba³: NF wallet.
bimbalete NM (*Méx*) (*columpio*) swing; (*de tabla*) seesaw.
bimbollo NM (*Méx*) bun.
bimensual ADJ twice-monthly.
bimensuario [1] ADJ twice-monthly.
  [2] NM publication appearing twice monthly.
bimestral ADJ two-monthly.
bimestralmente ADV every two months.
bimestre [1] ADJ bimonthly, two-monthly.
  [2] NM (a) (*período*) period of two months. (b) (*pago*) bimonthly payment.
bimilenario ADJ, NM bimillenary.
bimotor [1] ADJ twin-engined.
  [2] NM twin-engined plane.

binadera NF, **binador** NM weeding hoe.
binar [1a] VT to hoe, dig over.
binario ADJ binary; (*Mús*) *compás* two-four.
bincha NF (*And, Cono Sur*) hairband.
bingo NM (*juego*) bingo; (*sala*) bingo hall.
binguero, -a NM/F bingo-hall attendant.
binoculares NMPL, **binóculo** NM (*gen*) binoculars, field glasses; (*Teat*) opera glasses; (*quevedos*) pince-nez.
binomio NM (a) (*gen*) binomial. (b) **el ~ ejército-pueblo** (*fig*) the people-army relationship.
bio... PREF bio...
bioactivo ADJ bioactive.
bioagricultura NF organic farming.
biocarburante NM biofuel.
biociencia NF bioscience.
biodegradable ADJ biodegradable.
biodegradación NF biodegradation.
biodegradar [1a] VT y **biodegradarse** VR to biodegrade.
biodetergente NM biodegradable detergent.
biodiversidad NF biodiversity.
bioestadística NF biostatistics, vital statistics.
bioética NF bioethics.
biofísica NF biophysics.
biogás NM biogas.
biogénesis NF biogenesis.
biogenética NF genetic engineering.
biografía NF biography, life.
biografiado, -a NM/F subject of a biography, biographee.
biografiar [1c] VT to write the biography of.
biográfico ADJ biographic(al).
biógrafo¹, -a NM/F biographer.
biógrafo² NM (*Cono Sur*) cinema.
bioingeniería NF bioengineering.
biología NF biology; **~ aplicada** applied biology; **~ celular** cell biology; **~ molecular** molecular biology.
biológico ADJ biological; *alimento* organic; **cultivo ~** organically-grown crop.
biólogo, -a NM/F biologist.
biomagnetismo NM biomagnetism.
biomasa NF biomass.
biombo NM folding screen.
biomédico ADJ biomedical.
biometría NF biometry, biometrics.
biónico ADJ bionic.
bioorgánico ADJ bioorganic.
biopsia NF biopsy.
bioquímica¹ NF biochemistry.
bioquímico [1] ADJ biochemical.
  [2] NM, **bioquímica²** NF biochemist.
biorritmo NM biorhythm.
bioscopia NF bioscopy.
bioseguridad NF bioethics.
biosensor NM biosensor.
biosfera NF biosphere.
biosíntesis NF biosynthesis.
biosintético ADJ biosynthetic.
biotecnología NF biotechnology.
biotecnológico ADJ biotechnological.
biotecnólogo, -a NM/F biotechnologist.
biótico ADJ biotic.
biotipo NM biotype.
biotopo NM biotope.
biotransformación NF biotransformation.
bióxido NM dioxide; **~ de carbono** carbon dioxide.
BIP NM ABR *de* **Banco Internacional de Pagos** Bank of International Settlements, BIS.
bip NM pip, beep.
bipartidismo NM two-party system.
bipartidista ADJ two-party (*atr*).
bipartido ADJ divided in two.
bipartito ADJ bipartite.
bípedo NM biped.
biplano NM biplane.
biplaza NM (*Aer*) two-seater.
bipolaridad NF bipolarity.
biquini NM bikini.
BIRD NM ABR *de* **Banco Internacional para la Reconstrucción y el Desarrollo** International Bank of Reconstruction and Development, IBRD.
birdie NM (*Golf*) birdie.
BIRF NM ABR *de* **Banco Internacional de Reconstrucción y Fomento**.
birimbao NM Jew's-harp.

birlar [1a] VT (**a**) (*derribar*) to knock down with a blow, bring down with a shot.
(**b**) (*: *hurtar*) *persona* to swindle out of, do out of*; *cosa* to pinch*; **Juan le birló la novia** John pinched his girl; **le birlaron el empleo** he was done out of the job*.
birlibirloque: por arte de ~ by magic, as if by magic.
birlocha NF (**a**) (*cometa*) kite. (**b**) (*Méx*, *Aut*) old banger*, old crock.
birlonga: hacer algo a la ~ to do sth carelessly, do sth sloppily.
Birmania NF Burma.
birmano, -a ADJ, NM/F Burmese.
birome NF (*Cono Sur*) (*lápiz*) propelling pencil; (*bolígrafo*) ball-point pen.
birra* NF beer.
birreactor 1 ADJ twin-jet.
  2 NM twin-jet (plane).
birreta NF (*Ecl*) biretta; **~ (cardenalicia)** cardinal's skull cap.
birrete NM (*Ecl*) biretta; (*Univ*) doctor's hat, academic cap; (*Jur*) judge's cap.
birrí NM (*And*) snake.
birria* NF (**a**) (*esp Esp*: *cosa fea*) monstrosity, ugly old thing; (*obra*) wretched piece of work; (*basura*) rubbish, trash; (*cosa inútil*) useless object; **la novela es una ~** the novel is rubbish; **entre tanta ~** among so much trash; **la casa era una ~** the house was like a pig-sty.
(**b**) (*Cono Sur, Méx: bebida*) tasteless drink; (*Méx: guiso*) stew.
(**c**) (*And: obsesión*) set idea, mania; obstinacy.
(**d**) **jugar de ~** (*LAm*) to play half-heartedly.
(**e**) (*CAm*: cerveza*) beer.
birriondo ADJ (*LAm*) (**a**) (*: *asustadizo*) jumpy, highly strung. (**b**) (*: *cachondo*) randy*.
birrioso* ADJ awful.
biruji NM (*Cono Sur*) chilly wind.
birutilla NF (*Cono Sur*) pot scourer.
birutillar [1a] VT (*Cono Sur*) to polish.
bis 1 ADV twice; **¡~!** (*Theat*) encore!
  2 NM (*Teat*) encore.
  3 ADJ: **ministro ~** deputy minister, stand-in minister.
bisabuela NF great-grandmother.
bisabuelo NM great-grandfather; **~s** great-grandparents.
bisagra 1 NF hinge; (*: *de caderas*) waggle, wiggle.
  2 ATR (**a**) **acontecimiento ~** decisive event, event that marks a watershed. (**b**) (*Pol*) **partido ~** party that holds the balance of power.
bisar [1a] 1 VT (**a**) to give as an encore, repeat. (**b**) (*Cono Sur*) to encore, demand as an encore.
  2 VI to give an encore.
bisbis(e)ar [1a] VT (*murmurar*) to mutter, mumble; (*Cono Sur*) to whisper.
bisbiseo NM mutter, muttering, mumbling.
bisbita NF pipit.
biscote NM rusk.
biscúter NM (*Aut*) three-wheeler.
bisecar [1g] VT to bisect.
bisel NM bevel, bevel edge.
biselado ADJ bevel (*atr*), bevelled.
biselar [1a] VT to bevel.
bisemanal ADJ twice-weekly.
bisemanalmente ADV twice-weekly.
bisexuado ADJ hermaphrodite, twin-sex.
bisexual ADJ, NMF bisexual.
bisexualidad NF bisexuality.
bisgra; NF (*Carib*) armpit.
bisiesto ADJ: **año ~** leap year.
bisilábico ADJ, **bisílabo** ADJ two-syllabled.
bismuto NM bismuth.
bisnieta NF great-granddaughter.
bisnieto NM great-grandson; **~s** great-grandchildren.
bisnis; NM (prostitute's) clients, clientèle.
bisojo ADJ cross-eyed, squinting.
bisonte NM bison, buffalo (*US*).
bisoñada NF naïve remark, naïve thing to do.
bisoñé NM wig, toupée.
bisoñez NF inexperience; rawness.
bisoño 1 ADJ green, inexperienced; *recluta* raw.
  2 NM greenhorn; (*Mil*) raw recruit, rookie*.
bisté NM, **bistec** NM, **bisteck** NM, **bisteque** NM (**a**) (*Culin*) steak, beefsteak. (**b**) (*: *tongue*; **achantar el ~** to shut one's trap*.
bistongo ADJ (*CAm, Carib, Méx*) spoiled, indulged.
bisturí NM scalpel.
bisunto ADJ greasy, grubby.
bisutería NF imitation jewellery, costume jewellery, paste.
bit NM, PL **bits** (*Inform*) bit; **~ de parada** stop bit; **~ de paridad** parity

bit.
bitácora NF (*Náut*) binnacle.
bitensional ADJ (*Elec*) equipped to work on two different voltages.
bíter NM bitters.
bitio NM bit.
bitoque NM (*tapón*) bung, spigot; (*CAm: desagüe*) drain; (*LAm: de jeringa*) injection tube (of a syringe); (*Cono Sur: canilla*) tap; (*Cono Sur: bulto*) bump, swelling.
bituminoso ADJ bituminous.
bivalvo ADJ, NM bivalve.
bivio NM (*LAm*) road junction.
Bizancio N Byzantium.
bizantino 1 ADJ (**a**) (*gen*) Byzantine. (**b**) (*fig: decadente*) decadent. (**c**) (*fig: baldío*) *discusión* idle, pointless; (*irreal*) over-subtle, unreal.
  2 NM, **bizantina** NF Byzantine.
bizarramente ADV (**a**) (*valientemente*) gallantly, bravely; dashingly. (**b**) (*generosamente*) generously, splendidly.
bizarría NF (**a**) (*valor*) gallantry, bravery; dash, verve. (**b**) (*generosidad*) generosity.
bizarro ADJ (**a**) (*valiente*) gallant, brave; dashing. (**b**) (*generoso*) generous, splendid.
bizbirindo ADJ (*Méx*) lively, bright.
bizcar [1g] 1 VT *ojo* to wink.
  2 VI to squint, be cross-eyed.
bizco 1 ADJ cross-eyed, squinting; **mirada bizca** squint, cross-eyed look; **dejar a uno ~** to impress sb strongly, leave sb open-mouthed (with wonder); **ponerse ~** to squint, look cross-eyed; **quedarse ~** to be very impressed, be dumbfounded.
  2 ADV: **mirar ~** to squint, look cross-eyed.
bizcochera NF biscuit barrel, biscuit tin.
bizcochería NF (*Méx*) cake shop.
bizcocho NM (**a**) (*Culin*) sponge, sponge cake; sponge finger; (*Náut*) hardtack, ship's biscuit; **~ borracho** sponge soaked in wine and syrup; **embarcarse con poco ~** to set out unprepared.
(**b**) (*Méx*) (*galleta*) biscuit; (*:) cunt*;.
(**c**) (*Cerámica*) bisque, biscuit ware.
bizcorneado ADJ (*Carib*) = **bizco**.
bizcornear [1a] VI (*Carib*) to squint, be cross-eyed.
bizcorneto ADJ (*And, Méx*) = **bizco**.
Bizkaia [biθ'kaja] NF Biscay (*Basque province*).
bizma NF poultice.
bizmar [1a] VT to poultice.
biznieto NM (*etc*) = **bisnieto** (*etc*).
bizquear [1a] VI to squint, look cross-eyed.
bizquera NF (*And*) squint.
bla-bla-bla NM claptrap, rubbish; aimless gossip; hot air, bla-bla-bla.
blanca NF (**a**) (*mujer*) white woman.
(**b**) (*Hist*) old Spanish copper coin; **estar sin ~, quedarse sin ~** to be broke*.
(**c**) (*Mús*) minim.
(**d**) (*:) (*cocaína*) cocaine; (*heroína*) heroin.
(**e**) **las ~s** (*Ajedrez*) white, the white pieces.
Blancanieves NF Snow White.
blanco 1 ADJ (**a**) (*gen*) white; *pan, pelo, vino* white; *piel* white, light; *tez* fair; **la raza blanca** the white race; **más ~ que el jazmín** (o **la nieve** *etc*) whiter than white, as white as snow; **más ~ que el papel** (o **la cera** *etc*) as white as a sheet.
(**b**) *página, espacio* blank.
(**c**) *verso* blank.
(**d**) (*: *cobarde*) yellow, cowardly.
(**e**) **estar ~*** to have a clean record.
  2 NM (**a**) (*gen*) white; whiteness; **~ de España** whiting (*chalk*); **~ del huevo** white of egg; **~ del ojo** white of the eye; **~ de plomo** white lead; **calentar al ~** to make white-hot; **poner los ojos en ~** to roll one's eyes; to look ecstatic; **poner lo ~ negro** to make out that white is black.
(**b**) (*persona*) white man, white person; **los ~s** the whites.
(**c**) (*de animal*) white spot, white patch.
(**d**) (*intervalo*) interval, gap.
(**e**) (*espacio*) blank, blank space; **con 2 páginas en ~** with two blank pages; **cheque en ~** blank cheque; **dejar un ~** to leave a space; **dejar algo en ~** to leave sth blank; **firmar en ~** to sign a blank cheque; **votar en ~** to return a blank voting paper, spoil one's vote.
(**f**) (*formulario*) blank, blank form.
(**g**) (*Mil y fig*) target; **~ móvil** moving target; **ser el ~ de las burlas** to be the target for jokes, be the object of ridicule; **dar en el ~** to hit the mark; **hacer ~** to hit the target, strike home; **hacer ~ en** to hit, strike.
(**h**) **dejar a uno en ~** to disappoint sb; **dejar al contrario en ~** to whitewash one's opponent*; **estoy en ~** I haven't a clue; **pasar la noche en ~** to have a sleepless night; **quedarse en ~** to fail to see the point, not understand a word; to be disappointed.

(i) **los B~s** (*Cono Sur Pol*) Uruguayan political party.
3 ATTR : **el vehículo ~** the target vehicle.
blancón ADJ (*And*) white-skinned.
blancor NM whiteness.
blancote **1** ADJ **(a)** sickly white, unhealthily white. **(b)** (*: *cobarde*) yellow, cowardly.
2 NM (*) coward.
blancura NF whiteness.
blancuzco ADJ whitish.
blandamente ADV softly; mildly, gently; tenderly; indulgently.
blandear¹ [1a] VT = **blandir**.
blandear² [1a] **1** VT (*fig*) to convince, persuade.
2 VI *y* **blandearse** VR to soften, yield, give way; **~ con uno** to humour sb.
blandengue* **1** ADJ soft, weak.
2 NM soft sort, softie.
blandiporno* ADJ INVAR: **película ~** soft-porn film.
blandir [3a; *defectivo*] **1** VT to brandish, flourish, wave about.
2 VI *y* **blandirse** VR to wave to and fro, swing.
blando **1** ADJ **(a)** *materia, droga, agua etc* soft; *pasta etc* smooth; *carne* (*pey*) flabby, slack; **~ al tacto** soft to the touch; **~ de boca** *caballo* tender-mouthed.
(b) *tono etc* mild, gentle, bland; *clima* mild; *mirada* tender; *palabras* bland; **~ de corazón** sentimental, tender-hearted.
(c) *carácter* soft, delicate; sensual; (*indulgente*) soft, indulgent; (*Pol*) soft, wet; **ser ~ con el crimen** to be soft on crime.
(d) (*cobarde*) cowardly.
2 NM, **blanda** NF (*Pol etc*) softliner, wet.
blandón NM (*Ecl*) wax taper; large candlestick.
blandorro* **1** ADJ *sabor* weak, tasteless, insipid; *sonrisa etc* weak, sheepish.
2 NM, **blandorra** NF weakling, wimp*; coward.
blanducho ADJ soft, softish; *carne* (*pey*) flabby, slack.
blandujo ADJ softish.
blandura NF **(a)** (*cualidad*) softness; smoothness; mildness; gentleness; blandness; tenderness.
(b) (*cualidad moral*) moral softness, effeminacy.
(c) (*palabra*) blandishment, flattering words; **~s** endearments, sweet nothings.
blanduzco ADJ softish.
blanqueada NF (*LAm: jalbegue*) whitewashing; (*Méx: *: *Dep*) whitewash.
blanqueador(a) NM/F bleacher.
blanquear [1a] **1** VT **(a)** (*gen*) to whiten; *pared* to whitewash; *tela* to bleach; *metal* to blanch; *falta, persona culpable etc** to whitewash; *dinero** to launder*. **(b)** (*Carib**) (*matar*) to kill; (*ganar*) to beat, overcome.
2 VI **(a)** (*volverse blanco*) to go white, turn white, whiten. **(b)** (*tirar a blanco*) to be whitish; (*mostrarse blanco*) to show white, look white.
blanquecer [2d] VT = **blanquear 1**.
blanquecino ADJ whitish.
blanqueo NM whitening; whitewashing; bleaching; (*) laundering.
blanquiazul **1** ADJ **(a)** blue and white. **(b)** (*Dep*) of Español football club.
2 NMF Español player (*o* supporter *etc*); **los ~es** Español (club *o* team *etc*).
blanquillo **1** ADJ whitish; *pan etc* white.
2 NM **(a)** (*de huevo*) white of egg; (*CAm, Méx euf*: *huevo*) egg. **(b)** (*And, Cono Sur: melocotón*) white peach. **(c)** (*Carib, Cono Sur: pez*) whitefish.
blanquimiento NM bleach, bleaching solution.
blanquín NM: **~ de gallina** (*Carib: euf*) hen's egg.
blanquinegro ADJ white-and-black.
blanquita; NF (*Carib*) cocaine.
blasfemador **1** ADJ blasphemous, blaspheming.
2 NM, **blasfemadora** NF blasphemer.
blasfemamente ADV blasphemously.
blasfemar [1a] VI (*Ecl*) to blaspheme (*contra* against); (*fig*) to curse, swear; **~ de** to curse, swear about (*o* at).
blasfemia NF **(a)** (*taco*) swearword, curse, oath. **(b)** (*injuria*) insult.
blasfemo = **blasfemador**.
blasón NM **(a)** (*escudo*) coat of arms, escutcheon; bearings. **(b)** (*heráldica*) heraldry. **(c)** (*fig*: *honor*) honour, glory.
blasonar [1a] **1** VT to emblazon; (*fig*) to praise, extol.
2 VI to boast, brag; **~ de** to boast about; to boast of being.
blázer NM blazer.
bleck NM (*Cono Sur*) pitch, tar; **dar una mano de ~ a uno** to discredit sb, blacken sb's name.
bledo NM: **(no) me importa un ~, no se me da un ~** I don't care two hoots (*de* about).
bleque NM (*Cono Sur*) = **bleck**.
blindado **1** ADJ (*Mil*) armoured, armour-plated; (*Mec*) shielded, pro-

tected, encased; **puertas blindadas** reinforced doors.
2 NM (*Mil*) armoured vehicle.
blindaje NM (*Mil*) armour, armour plating; (*Téc*) shield, protective plating, casing.
blindar [1a] VT (*Mil*) to armour, armour-plate; (*Téc*) to shield.
b.l.m. ABR *de* **besa las manos** (*courtesy formula*).
bloc NM, PL **blocs** pad, writing pad; calendar pad; notebook; (*Escol*) exercise book; **~ de dibujos** sketching-pad; **~ de notas** pad for notes; (reporter's) notebook; **~ de taquigrafía** shorthand book.
blocaje NM (*Dep*) tackle; stop; (*Mil*) blockade; (*Mec*) gripping, locking.
blocao NM blockhouse; pillbox.
blocar [1g] VT (*Dep*) *jugador* to tackle; *balón* to stop, trap, catch.
blof NM (*LAm*) bluff; **hacer un ~ a uno** to bluff sb.
blofear [1a] VI (*LAm*) to boast, brag.
blofero ADJ (*LAm*) boastful, bragging.
blofista NMF (*LAm*) boaster, braggart; bluffer.
blonda NF **(a)** (*encaje*) blond lace. **(b)** (*Cono Sur: rizo*) curl.
blondo ADJ **(a)** (*rubio*) blond(e); fair, light; (*liter*) flaxen. **(b)** (*LAm: liso*) soft, smooth, silken; (*CAm: lacio*) lank; (*Cono Sur, Méx: rizado*) curly.
bloque NM **(a)** (*gen*) block; **~ (de casas)** block (of houses); **~ de hormigón** block of concrete; **~ de sellos** block of stamps; **~ de cilindro** cylinder block; **~ de papel** = **bloc**; **~ publicitario** commercial break; **~ de viviendas** block of flats.
(b) (*Pol*) bloc, group; **el ~ comunista** (*Hist*) the communist bloc.
(c) (*en tubo etc*) block, blockage, obstruction.
(d) **en ~** en bloc.
bloqueante **1** ADJ paralysing; inhibiting.
2 NM (*droga*) inhibitor, anticatalyst.
bloquear [1a] **1** VT **(a)** (*estorbar etc*) to block, obstruct; (*Dep*) *jugador* to tackle; *pelota* to stop, trap; (*Rad*) to jam; **~ una ley en la cámara** to block a bill in parliament; **los manifestantes bloquearon las calles** the demonstrators blocked the streets.
(b) (*Mec*) to block, jam; **el mecanismo está bloqueado** the mechanism is jammed, the mechanism is stuck.
(c) (*aislar*) to cut off; **la inundación bloqueó el pueblo** the flood cut off the village; **quedaron bloqueados por la nieve** they were cut off by the snow.
(d) (*Aut*) to brake, pull up; *volante* to lock.
(e) (*Mil*) to blockade.
(f) (*Com, Fin*) to freeze, block; **fondos bloqueados** frozen assets.
(g) **quedar bloqueado** (*fig*) to be paralysed with fear (*etc*).
2 **bloquearse** VR: **~ de** (*fig*) to shut o.s. off from, shield o.s. from.
bloqueo NM **(a)** (*Mil*) blockade; **burlar el ~, forzar el ~** to run the blockade.
(b) (*Com, Fin*) freezing, blocking; squeeze; **~ de fondos** freezing of assets; **~ informativo** news blackout.
(c) **~ mental** mental block.
(d) **~ central de cerraduras** central locking.
b.l.p. ABR *de* **besa los pies** (*courtesy formula*).
bluejean NM (*Cono Sur*) jeans.
blufar [1a] (*etc*) = **blofear** (*etc*).
bluff [bluf] NM bluff.
blumes NMPL: **tener ~** (*Carib**) to be fussy, be finicky.
blusa NF (*de mujer*) blouse; (*mono*) overall; (*bata*) smock.
blusero **1** ADJ (rhythm and) blues (*atr*).
2 NM, **blusera** NF (rhythm and) blues fan.
blusón NM smock; (*Mil*) jacket.
BM NM ABR *de* **Banco Mundial** World Bank, WB.
BN **1** NF (*Esp*) ABR *de* **Biblioteca Nacional**.
2 NM (*Perú*) ABR *de* **Banco de la Nación**.
b/n ABR *de* **blanco y negro** black-and-white, b/w.
B.º (a) (*Fin*) ABR *de* **banco** bank, bk. **(b)** (*Com*) ABR *de* **beneficiario** beneficiary.
boa NF boa.
boardilla NF = **buhardilla**.
boatiné NF: **bata de ~** padded dressing-gown.
boato NM show, showiness, ostentation; pomp, pageantry.
bob NM bobsleigh.
bobada NF silly thing, stupid thing; **esto es una ~** this is nonsense; **decir ~s** to say silly things, talk nonsense; **¡no digas ~s!** come off it!
bobales* NMF INVAR, **bobalías** NMF INVAR nitwit*, dolt.
bobalicón* **1** ADJ silly.
2 NM, **bobalicona** NF nitwit*, dolt.
bobamente ADV stupidly; naïvely.
bobático* ADJ silly, half-witted.
bobear [1a] VI to fool about, do silly things; to talk nonsense, say silly things.
bobelas* NMF INVAR idiot, chump*.
bobera NF = **bobada, bobería**.
boberá NMF (*Carib*) fool.
bobería NF **(a)** (*cualidad*) silliness, idiocy. **(b)** = **bobada**.
bobeta **1** ADJ (*Cono Sur*) silly, stupid.

2 NMF (*Cono Sur*; *t* ~s *And*) fool, idiot.
bobicomio NM (*And*) lunatic asylum.
bóbilis ADV (*t de* ~) (*gratis*) free, for nothing; (*sin esfuerzo*) without effort, without lifting a finger.
bobina NF (*Téc*) bobbin, spool; reel; drum, cylinder; (*Fot*) spool, reel; (*de cinta*) reel; (*Aut, Elec*) coil; ~ **de encendido** ignition coil.
bobinado NM (*Elec*) winding.
bobinadora NF winder, winding machine.
bobinar [1a] VT to wind.
bobo **1** ADJ (*tonto*) silly, stupid; (*simple*) simple; (*ingenuo*) naïve.
2 NM, **boba** NF (a) (*tonto*) idiot, fool; greenhorn; (*Teat*) clown, funny man; **a los ~s se les aparece la madre de Dios** fortune favours fools; **entre ~s anda el juego** (*iró*) they're well matched; one's as bad as the other.
(b) (*) (*Carib*: *reloj*) watch; (*Cono Sur*: *corazón*) heart, ticker*.
boboliche NM (*And*) fool.
bobsleigh ['bobslei] NM bobsleigh.
boca **1** NF (a) (*Anat*) mouth; ~ **de dragón** (*Bot*) snapdragon; ~ **de escorpión** (*fig*) wicked tongue; ~ **de mar** (*Culin*) crab-stick; **a** ~ verbally, by word of mouth; ~ **a** ~ (NM) rumour, piece of hearsay; **respiración** ~ **a** ~ kiss of life, mouth-to-mouth resuscitation; **a pedir de** ~ as much as one wishes, to one's heart's content; for the asking; **todo salió a pedir de** ~ it all turned out perfectly; **en** ~ **de** (*LAm*) according to; ~ **abajo** face downward; **apoyó la idea de** ~ **afuera** he paid lip-service to the idea; ~ **arriba** face upward; **aceituna de** ~ eating olive; **abrir tanta** ~ (*And, Carib, Méx*) to stand amazed; **andar en** ~ **de la gente** to be talked about; **la cosa anda** (*o* **va**) **de** ~ **en** ~ the story is going the rounds; **ella anda de** ~ **en** ~ she is the subject of gossip, people are talking about her; **buscar la** ~ **a uno** to (try to) draw sb out; to provoke sb; **calentársele a uno la** ~ to talk a lot; to get worked up; **¡cállate la** ~!* shut up!*; **coserse la** ~* to shut up*, keep mum; **dar** ~* to gab*, chat; **decir algo con la** ~ **chica** (*o* **pequeña**) to say sth without really meaning it; **no decir esta** ~ **es mía** not to open one's mouth; **lo hizo sin decir esta** ~ **es mía** he did it without a word to anybody; **en** ~ **cerrada no entran moscas** silence is golden; mum's the word; **hablar por** ~ **de ganso** to repeat sth parrot fashion; **hacer** ~ to work up an appetite; **se me hace la** ~ **agua** my mouth is watering; **se le llena la** ~ he's just paying lip service; **se le llena la** ~ **del coche** all he can talk about is the car; **meter a uno en la** ~ **del lobo** to put sb on the spot; **meterse en la** ~ **del lobo** to put one's head in the lion's mouth; **por la** ~ **muere el pez** silence is golden; **partir la** ~ **a uno*** to smash sb's face in*; **quedarse con la** ~ **abierta** to be dumbfounded; **¡qué tu** ~ **sea santa!** (*Carib*) I hope you're right!; **tapar la** ~ **a uno** to shut sb's mouth; **torcer la** ~ to make a wry face; to sneer.
(b) (*fig*: *abertura*) mouth, entrance, opening; approach; ~ **de agua**, ~ **de incendios**, ~ **de riego** hydrant; ~ **del estómago** pit of the stomach; **a** ~ **de invierno** at the start of winter; **a** ~ **de jarro** *beber* excessively, immoderately; (*Mil*) point-blank, at close range; *anunciar etc* point-blank; ~ **de metro** tube station entrance, subway entrance (*US*); ~ **de mina** pithead, mine entrance; ~(**s**) **de río** river mouth, mouth of a river.
(c) (*de cañón*) muzzle, mouth; **a** ~ **de cañón** (*LAm*) at point-blank range.
(d) (*de bogavante etc*) pincer; (*de herramienta*) cutting edge.
(e) (*de barril*) bunghole.
(f) (*CAm*: *t* ~s) (*tapa*) bar snack.
(g) (*de vino*) flavour, taste; **tener buena** ~ to have a good flavour.
(h) (*Inform*) slot.
2 NM(‡) screw‡, warder.
bocabajear [1a] VT (*LAm*) to put down, crush.
bocabajo NM (*Carib*) beating.
bocacalle NF entrance to a street; intersection; **la primera** ~ the first turning.
bocacha NF (a) (‡) bigmouth‡. (b) (*Mil, Hist*) blunderbuss.
bocacho ADJ (*Cono Sur*) (*t**) big-mouthed.
Bocacio NM Boccaccio.
bocadear [1a] VT to cut up (for eating).
bocadillería NF (*Esp*) snack bar, sandwich bar.
bocadillo NM (a) (*Esp*: *tapa*) snack. (b) (*emparedado*) sandwich, meat (*o* cheese *etc*) roll; **tomar un** ~ to have a snack, have a bite to eat. (c) (*en dibujo*) balloon, bubble.
bocadito NM (a) (*mordisco*) small bite, morsel, bit; ~s (*And*) snack, appetizer; **a** ~s (*fig*) piecemeal. (b) (*Carib*: *cigarrillo*) cigarette wrapped in tobacco leaf; ~s bar snacks.
bocado NM (a) (*mordisco*) mouthful; morsel, bite; **no hay para un** ~ that's not nearly enough; **no he pasado** (*o* **probado**) ~ **en todo el día** I've not had a bite to eat all day; **no tener para un** ~ to be completely penniless; **tomar un** ~ to have a bite to eat; ~ **exquisito**, ~ **regalado** titbit; **el** ~ **del león** the lion's share; ~ **sin hueso** sinecure, soft job.
(b) (*freno*) bit; bridle.

(c) ~ **de Adán** (*Anat*) Adam's apple.
(d) (*And*: *veneno*) (animal) poison.
(e) (*: *astilla*) sweetener*, backhander*.
bocajarro: **a** ~ ADV (*Mil*) at close range, point-blank; **decir algo a** ~ to say sth straight out.
bocal NM (a) (*jarra*) pitcher, jar. (b) (*Mús*, †) mouthpiece.
bocallave NF keyhole.
bocamanga NF (a) (*puño*) cuff, wristband. (b) (*Méx*: *agujero*) hole for the head (in a cape).
bocamina NF pithead, mine entrance.
bocana NF (river) mouth.
bocanada NF (a) (*de vino etc*) mouthful, swallow.
(b) (*de humo, viento*) puff; (*de aliento*) gust, blast.
(c) **echar** ~s to boast, brag.
(d) ~ **de gente** crush of people.
bocaracá NM (*CAm*) snake.
bocarada NF (*LAm*) = **bocanada**.
bocarte NM small sardine.
bocata* NM = **bocadillo** (a).
bocatería* NF ≃ sandwich bar.
bocatero, -a NM/F (*Carib*) loudmouth*, braggart.
bocatoma NF (*LAm*) water intake, inlet pipe.
bocaza* NMF, **bocazas*** NMF INVAR bigmouth‡; **¡~!** (*insulto*) bigmouth!‡
bocera NF (*gen* PL) smear on the lips.
boceras* NMF INVAR idiot, fool; bigmouth‡.
bocetista NMF sketcher.
boceto NM (*bosquejo*) sketch, outline; (*diseño*) design; (*maqueta*) model, mock-up.
bocha NF (a) (*bola*) bowl; **juego de las** ~s bowls. (b) (*Cono Sur*‡) nut‡.
bochar [1a] VT (a) (*Carib, Méx*: *rechazar*) to rebuff, reject. (b) (*Cono Sur*: *no aprobar*) to fail, flunk‡.
boche NM (a) (*Cono Sur Agr*) husks, chaff.
(b) (*Carib*: *regañada*) telling-off*, dressing-down*.
(c) (*Carib*: *rechazo*) snub, slight; **dar** ~ **a uno** to snub sb, cold-shoulder sb.
(d) (*And, Cono Sur*) (*jaleo*) uproar, din; (*pelea*) brawl.
bochinche NM (a) (*jaleo*) uproar, din; (*motín*) riot; (*disturbio*) commotion.
(b) (*And, Carib*: *chisme*) piece of gossip.
(c) (*Méx*: *baile*) rave-up*; (*fiesta*) wild party.
(d) (*Méx*: *bar*) seedy bar, dive; (*tienda*) local stores.
(e) (*Carib*) muddle, mess.
bochinchear [1a] VI (*LAm*) to kick up a din, make a racket.
bochinchero **1** ADJ (*LAm*) rowdy, brawling.
2 NM (*LAm*) rowdy, brawler.
bochinchoso ADJ (a) (*LAm*: *chismoso*) gossiping, telltale, gossipy. (b) (*And*: *agresivo*) rowdy, noisy. (c) (*quisquilloso*) fussy, finicky.
bocho NM: **ser un** ~ (*Cono Sur*) to be brainy, be clever.
bochorno NM (a) (*Met*: *calor*) sultry weather, oppressive weather; (*atmósfera*) stifling atmosphere; sultriness; (*viento*) hot summer breeze.
(b) (*Med*) queer turn; hot flush; blush.
(c) (*fig*: *vergüenza*) embarrassment, flush, (feeling of) shame; (*tacha*) stigma, dishonour; **¡qué** ~! how embarrassing!
bochornoso ADJ (a) (*Met*) sultry, oppressive; thundery; stuffy, stifling.
(b) (*fig*: *violento*) embarrassing; (*vergonzoso*) humiliating, shameful, disgraceful, degrading; **es un espectáculo** ~ it is a degrading spectacle, it is a shameful sight.
bocina NF (*Mús*) trumpet; (*Aut, de gramófono*) horn; (*megáfono*) megaphone; speaking trumpet; (*LAm*: *trompetilla*) ear-trumpet; (*Méx Telec*) mouthpiece; (*Cono Sur*‡: *soplón*) grass‡, informer; ~ **de niebla** foghorn; **tocar la** ~ (*Aut*) to sound one's horn.
bocinar [1a] VI (*Aut*) to sound one's horn, blow the horn, hoot.
bocinazo NM (*Aut*) hoot, toot, blast (of the horn); **dar el** ~‡ to grass‡.
bocinero, -a NM/F horn player.
bocio NM goitre.
bock [bok] NM, PL **bocks** [bok] beer-glass, tankard.
bocón **1** ADJ (a) (*lit*) big-mouthed.
(b) (*fig*: *jactancioso*) boastful, big-mouthed‡; (*Carib, Cono Sur*: *gritón*) loud-mouthed; (*chismoso*) backbiting, gossipy; (*Méx*: *poco discreto*) indiscreet.
2 NM braggart; **¡~!** (*) bigmouth!‡
bocoy NM hogshead, large cask.
▼ **boda** NF (*t* ~s: *acto*) wedding, marriage; (*fiesta*) wedding reception; ~s **de diamante** diamond wedding, (*de club etc*) diamond jubilee; ~s **de oro** golden wedding, (*de club etc*) golden jubilee; ~s **de plata** silver wedding, (*de club etc*) silver jubilee; ~ **de negros** rowdy party.
bodega NF (*depósito de vinos*) wine cellar; (*despensa*) pantry; (*almacén*) storeroom, warehouse; (*tienda*) wine shop; (*Náut*) hold; (*esp LAm*: *bar*) bar, tavern; (*restaurante*) restaurant; (*LAm*: *tienda de comestibles*) grocery store, general store; ~ **de carga** (*Aer*) hold.

bodegaje NM (*Chile*) storage.
bodegón NM (**a**) cheap restaurant. (**b**) (*Arte*) still life.
bodegonista NMF still-life painter.
bodeguero ① ADJ (*Carib*) coarse, common.
　② NM (**a**) (*productor*) wine-producer; (*Com*) vintner; (*obrero*) cellarman; (*dueño*) owner of a *bodega*. (**b**) (*And, Carib: tendero*) grocer.
bodijo* NM quiet wedding; (*pey*) misalliance, unequal match.
bodolle NM (*Cono Sur*) large pruning knife, billhook.
bodoque NM (**a**) (*balita*) small ball, pellet (of clay).
　(**b**) (*hinchazón*) lump; (*CAm, Méx*) (*Med*) lump, swelling; (*bolita*) lump, ball; (*CAm: manojo*) bunch.
　(**c**) (*Méx: cosa mal hecha*) badly-made thing.
　(**d**) (*: *tonto*) dimwit*.
bodorrio NM (**a**) = **bodijo**. (**b**) (*Méx: fiesta*) rowdy party.
bodrio NM (**a**) (*confusión*) mix-up, mess. (**b**) (*cosa mal hecha*) badly-made thing; monstrosity, piece of rubbish; **un ~ de sitio** an awful place.
body ['boði] NM, PL **bodies** ['boðis] body-stocking.
BOE NM (*Esp*) ABR *de* **Boletín Oficial del Estado**.

　　BOE

ⓘ *The **Boletín Oficial del Estado** is a daily Spanish-government publication in which new laws, directives and executive decisions are published together with advertisements for public-sector posts and contracts. It is provided free of charge to all government agencies and state organizations including schools, embassies and public libraries.*

---

bóer ① ADJ Boer.
　② NMF, PL **bóers** Boer.
bofe NM (*Zool*) lung; **~s** lungs, lights; **echar el ~**, **echar los ~s** to slog, slave; **echar los ~s por algo** to go all out for sth.
bofetada NF (*palmada*) slap in the face (*t fig*); (*puñetazo*) cuff, punch; **dar de ~s a uno** to hit sb, punch sb; **darse de ~s** to come to blows; (*colores*) to clash.
bofetón* NM punch (in the face), hard slap.
bofia* ① NF: **la ~** the cops*.
　② NM cop*, copper*.
boga¹ NF vogue, fashion; popularity; **la ~ de la minifalda** the fashion for the miniskirt, the popularity of the miniskirt; **estar en ~** to be in fashion, be in vogue; **poner algo en ~** to establish a fashion for sth.
boga² NF (*Ferro etc*) bogey.
boga³ ① NMF rower; oarsman, oarswoman.
　② NF rowing.
bogada NF stroke (of an oar).
bogador NM, **bogadora** NF, **bogante** NMF rower; oarsman, oarswoman.
bogar [1h] VI to row; to sail, move.
bogavante NM (**a**) (*Náut*) stroke, first rower. (**b**) (*Zool*) lobster.
bogotano ① ADJ of Bogotá.
　② NM, **bogotana** NF native (*o* inhabitant) of Bogotá; **los ~s** the people of Bogotá.
bogotazo NM (*And*) ruin, destruction, pillage.
bohardilla NF = **buhardilla**.
Bohemia NF Bohemia.
bohémico ADJ (*Geog*) Bohemian.
bohemio, -a (*fig*), **bohemo, -a** (*Geog*) ADJ, NM/F Bohemian.
bohío NM (*LAm*) hut, shack.
boicot NM, PL **boicots** boycott.
boicotear [1a] VT (*gen*) to boycott; (*sabotear*) to sabotage.
boicoteo NM boycott, boycotting; sabotaging.
boicotero NM (*LAm*) boycott.
boina ① NF beret.
　② NM: **~ verde** commando.
boite NF, **boîte** NF [bwat] night-club.
boje ADJ (*Méx*) silly, stupid.
boj(e) NM (*planta*) box; (*madera*) boxwood.
bojote NM (**a**) (*LAm: lío*) bundle, package. (**b**) (*CAm: trozo*) lump, chunk. (**c**) (*LAm: fig*) **un ~ de** a lot of, a great many of. (**d**) (*Carib*) fuss, row.
bol NM (**a**) (*gen*) bowl; punch bowl; (*LAm*) finger bowl. (**b**) (*Dep*) nine-pin.
bola NF (**a**) (*pelota etc*) ball; (*canica*) marble; (*Náut*) signal (with discs); (*Tip*) golfball; (*LAm Dep*) ball, football; (*: *cabeza*) nut**; **~s** (*Mec*) ball-bearings; (*LAm Caza*) bolas; (**) balls**; **~ de billar** billiard ball; **estar como ~ de billar** to be as bald as a coot; **~ de contar** abacus bead; **~ de cristal** crystal ball; **~ de fuego** fireball; (*Met*) ball lightning; **~ del mundo** globe; **~ de naftalina** mothball; **~ negra** black ball; **~ de nieve** snowball; **~ de partido** (*Tenis*) match ball; **~ de tempestad**, **~ de tormenta** storm signal; **juego de (las) ~s** American skittles; **tú a tu ~*** that's up to you; don't you worry about it; **cambiar la ~** (*Carib**) to change one's mind; **dar ~** (*Cono Sur**) to

take notice, pay attention; **dar la ~*** to be released (from jail); **¡dale ~!** what, again!; come off it!; **dejar que ruede la ~** to let things take their course; **escurrir la ~** to take French leave; **hacerse ~s*** (*LAm*) to get o.s. tied up in knots; **ir a su ~** to go one's own way; **ir en ~s*** to be starkers**; **poner ~s a** to pay attention to; **pasarse de la ~** (*Carib**) to go too far; **no rasca ~*** he doesn't do a stroke; **tragar la ~** to rise to the bait, swallow the bait; **¡qué ~s!*** (*Carib, Cono Sur*) what a nerve!*
　(**b**) (*Naipes*) slam, grand slam; **media ~** small slam.
　(**c**) (*betún*) shoe polish, blacking.
　(**d**) (*cuento*) fib, tale; (*rumor*) rumour.
　(**e**) (*Méx: ruido*) row, hubbub; (*pelea*) brawl; (*fiesta*) noisy party.
　(**f**) **una ~ de gente** (*Méx*) a (whole) crowd (of people).
bolacear [1a] VI (*Cono Sur*) to talk rubbish.
bolaco NM (*Cono Sur*) ruse, device.
bolada NF (**a**) (*echada*) throw (of a ball); (*Billar etc*) stroke.
　(**b**) **~ de aficionado** (*Cono Sur*) intervention (by a third party).
　(**c**) (*LAm: suerte*) piece of luck, lucky break; (*Com: ganga*) bargain, lucky piece of business.
　(**d**) (*LAm: mentira*) fib, lie; (*Méx: chiste*) joke, witty comment; (*Méx: engaño*) trick, con*.
　(**e**) (*Cono Sur: golosina*) titbit, treat.
bolado NM (**a**) (*CAm, Cono Sur, Méx: negocio*) (business) deal; (*Méx: amorío*) love affair, flirtation.
　(**b**) (*CAm Billar*) clever stroke.
　(**c**) (*CAm*) (*cuento*) fib, tale; (*chisme*) rumour, piece of gossip.
　(**d**) (*LAm: locuciones*) **¡hazme un ~!*** do me a favour!*; **esta noche tengo un ~*** I've got something on tonight.
bolamen** NM balls**.
bolardo NM bollard.
bolata* NM ex-con*, old lag**.
bolate NM (*And*) = **volate**.
bolazo NM (**a**) (*Cono Sur*) (*disparate*) silly remark, piece of nonsense; (*noticia falsa*) false news; (*mentira*) fib, lie; (*error*) mistake, error; **mandarse un ~** to put one's foot in it. (**b**) **al** (*o* **de**) **~** (*Méx*) at random; any old way.
bolchevique ADJ, NMF Bolshevik.
bolchevismo NM Bolshevism.
bolea NF (*Dep*) volley.
boleada¹ NF (*Cono Sur* ††) hunt, hunting expedition (with *bolas*).
boleada² NF (*Méx*) shoeshine.
boleado¹ ADJ (*Cono Sur*): **estar ~** to have lost one's touch; to be up the creek**.
boleado² NM (*Méx*) shoeshine.
boleador(a) NM/F (*Méx*) (*chico*) shoeshine boy; (*chica*) shoeshine girl.
boleadoras NFPL (*Cono Sur*) bolas, lasso with balls; *see also* ‖GAUCHO‖.
bolear¹ [1a] ① VT (**a**) *pelota* to throw.
　(**b**) (*LAm*††: *cazar*) to hunt; (*atrapar*) to catch with *bolas*; (*And, Cono Sur: fig*) to floor, flummox.
　(**c**) (*LAm*) *candidato* to reject, blackball; (*) *obrero* to sack*, fire*; (*Univ etc*) to fail.
　② VI (**a**) (*jugar*) to play for fun, knock the balls about.
　(**b**) (*: *mentir*) to tell fibs.
　(**c**) (*jactarse*) to boast.
　③ **bolearse** VR (**a**) (*Cono Sur: caballo*) to rear and fall on its back; (*Aut*) to overturn.
　(**b**) (*Cono Sur**) (*quedar perplejo*) to get confused, get bewildered; (*avergonzarse*) to be shamefaced.
bolear² [1a] VT (*Méx*) *zapatos* to shine, polish.
boleco ADJ (*CAm*) drunk.
bolera NF bowling-alley, skittle-alley.
bolería NF (*Méx*) shoeshine shop.
bolero¹ NM (**a**) (*baile, chaqueta*) bolero. (**b**) (*CAm, Méx: chistera*) top hat.
bolero² NM (*Méx*) bootblack.
boleta NF (**a**) (*gen*: †) pass, permit; (*permiso*) authorization; (*billete*) ticket; (*Cono Sur*) first draft of a deed; (*LAm: borrador*) draft (document); (*And: certificado*) certificate; (*And: permiso*) authorization, permit; (*LAm: papeleta*) ballot, voting paper; (*Cono Sur Escol*) (school) report; (*Carib: multa*) fine, penalty; **~ de venta** (*Cono Sur*) sales chit, receipt.
　(**b**) (*Mil*) billet.
　(**c**) (*tabaco*) small packet of tobacco.
　(**d**) (*Cono Sur**) **hacer la ~ a uno** to murder sb, knock sb off**; **ser ~** to be condemned to death.
boletería NF (**a**) (*LAm: gen*) ticket agency; (*Ferro etc*) ticket office; (*Teat*) box-office. (**b**) (*LAm: recaudación*) gate, takings.
boletero, -a NM/F (*LAm*) ticket clerk.
boletín NM bulletin; (*Liter*) bulletin, journal, review; (*Teat etc*) ticket; (*Carib: Ferro*) ticket; (*Mil*) pay warrant; (*Mil*) billet; (*Escol*) report; (*Com*) cut-out coupon; **~ facultativo** medical report; **~ informativo** news bulletin, news sheet; **~ de inscripción** registration form; **~**

meteorológico weather report, weather forecast; ~ **naviero** shipping register; ~ **de notas** school report; ~ **de noticias** news bulletin; ~ **oficial** official gazette; ~ **de pedido** application form; (*Com*) order form; ~ **de precios** price list; ~ **de prensa** press-release; ~ **de suscripción** subscription form; *see also* BOE .

boleto NM **(a)** (*LAm: gen*) ticket; ~ **de ida y vuelta, de regreso,** ~ **de viaje redondo** return ticket, round-trip ticket (*US*); *y compárese* **billete.**
  (b) (*de quiniela*) coupon; ~ **de apuestas** betting slip.
  (c) **de** ~ (*Mex: como adv*) at once.

boli* NM = **bolígrafo.**

bolichada NF lucky break, stroke of luck; **de una** ~ at one go.

boliche¹ NM **(a)** (*bola*) jack.
  (b) (*juego: bochas*) bowls; ten-pin bowling; (*bolos*) skittles.
  (c) (*bolera*) bowling alley.
  (d) (*juguete*) cup-and-ball toy.
  (e) (*red*) small dragnet.
  (f) (*horno*) small furnace, smelting furnace.

boliche² NM (*And, Cono Sur: tienda*) grocer's, small grocery shop (*o* store); (*Cono Sur: snack*) cheap snack bar; (*And: tahona*) low-class bakery; (*Cono Sur: garita*) gambling den.

boliche³* NM (*LAm*) Bolivian.

bolichera NF (*Perú*) fishing boat.

bolichero NM (*Cono Sur*) small shopkeeper.

bólido NM **(a)** (*Astron*) meteorite. **(b)** (*Aut*) racing car, hot-rod* (*US*); (*hum*) (any) car; (*Náut*) powerboat, speedboat; **iba como un** ~* he was really shifting*.

bolígrafo NM ball-point pen.

bolilla NF **(a)** (*Cono Sur: canica*) marble. **(b)** (*Cono Sur Univ*) (piece of paper bearing) examination question; **dar** ~ **a** to be aware of.

bolillo NM **(a)** (*Cos*) bobbin (for lacemaking). **(b)** (*LAm Mús*) drumstick.
  (c) (*Méx Culin*) bread roll.

bolina NF **(a)** (*Náut: cabo*) bowline; (*sonda*) lead, sounding line; **de** ~ close-hauled; **navegar de** ~ to sail close to the wind. **(b)** (*: *jaleo*) racket, row, uproar.

bolinga* 1 ADJ INVAR: **estar** ~ to be canned*.
  2 NM: **estar de** ~ to be boozing*; **ir de** ~ to go on the booze*.

bolita NF **(a)** (*gen*) small ball; pellet; (*Cono Sur: canica*) marble. **(b)** (*Cono Sur Pol*) ballot paper.

bolívar NM bolívar (*Venezuelan unit of currency*); **no verle la cara a B~*** to be broke*.

Bolivia NF Bolivia.

bolivianismo NM bolivianism, word (*o phrase etc*) peculiar to Bolivia.

boliviano, -a ADJ, NM/F Bolivian.

bollera* NF lesbian, dyke*.

bollería NF baker's (shop), bakery, pastry shop.

bollero, -a NM/F baker, pastrycook.

bollo NM **(a)** (*Culin*) bread roll; bun; **perdonar el** ~ **por el coscorrón** to realize that it's more trouble than it's worth; **no pela** ~ (*Carib*) he never gets it wrong.
  (b) (*abolladura*) dent; (*Med*) bump, lump; (*Cos*) puff.
  (c) (*fig: confusión*) confusion; mix-up; **armar(se)** ~ to make a fuss; **meter a uno en el** ~ to get sb into trouble.
  (d) (*CAm, Cono Sur: puñetazo*) punch.
  (e) ~**s** (*And*) troubles, problems.
  (f) (*CAm, Carib***) cunt**.

bollón NM (*tachón*) (ornamented) stud; (*de oreja*) button earring.

bolo¹ NM **(a)** (*Dep*) ninepin, skittle; (**juego de**) ~**s** ninepins, skittles, tenpin bowling; **andar en** ~ (*And*) to be naked; **ir en** ~ (*Carib*) to run off, run away; **tumbar** ~ (*And*) to do well, bring it off; **echar a rodar los** ~**s** (*fig*) to create a disturbance.
  (b) (*Med*) large pill.
  (c) (*moneda*) (*Fin Esp*) 5-peseta coin; (*Carib, Méx*) one-peso coin; (*Venezuela*) one-bolívar coin.
  (d) (*Cartas*) slam.
  (e) (*Méx: regalo*) christening present (from godparents).
  (f) (**) prick**.

bolo²* 1 ADJ (*CAm: borracho*) drunk, plastered*.
  2 NM drunk*.

bolo³* NM (*Mús*) gig, concert.

bolón NM **(a)** (*Cono Sur: piedra*) building stone; (*Carib*) marble. **(b)** (*Carib: muchedumbre*) mob, rabble.

Bolonia NF Bologna.

bolonio*, -a NM/F dunce, ignoramus.

boloñesa NF bolognese sauce, meat sauce.

bolsa NF **(a)** (*gen*) bag; (*morral*) pouch; (*de mujer*) handbag; (*monedero*) purse; (*LAm: bolsillo*) sack; (*And, CAm, Méx: bolsillo*) pocket; ~ **de agua caliente** hot-water bottle; ~ **de baño** beach bag; ~ **de basura** refuse sack, rubbish bag; ~ **de la compra** shopping bag; ~ **de cultivo** growbag; ~ **de deportes** sports bag; ~ **de herramientas** toolbag; ~ **de hielo** ice-pack, pack of ice; ~**s de mano** hand-luggage; ~ **de**

palos golfing bag; ~ **de papel** paper bag; ~ **de patatas fritas** packet of crisps; ~ **de plástico** plastic bag, carrier-bag; ~ **para tabaco** tobacco pouch; ~ **de té** tea bag; **¡la** ~ **o la vida!** your money or your life!; **no abre fácilmente la** ~ he's pretty mean; **hacer algo de** ~ (*Cono Sur*) to do sth at somebody else's expense; **hacer algo** ~ (*Cono Sur**) (*objeto*) to tear sth to pieces; (*persona*) to do sth at somebody else's expense; **volver a uno** ~ (*Méx*) to swindle sb.
  (b) (*Cos: de vestido etc*) bag; **hacer** ~ to bag, pucker up.
  (c) (*Mil*) pocket.
  (d) (*Geol*) pocket; ~ **de aire** (*Aer*) air pocket; **todavía hay** ~**s de pobreza** there are still pockets of poverty.
  (e) (*Anat, Zool*) cavity, sac; pouch; ~**s de los ojos** bags under the eyes.
  (f) (*Com, Fin*) stock exchange; stock market; ~ **de divisas** foreign-exchange market; ~ **de granos** corn exchange; ~ **negra** (*LAm*) black market; **'B~ de la propiedad'** (*sección de periódico*) 'Property Mart', 'Property for Sale'; ~ **de trabajo** labour exchange, employment bureau; **precio en la** ~ price on the stock exchange; **jugar a la** ~ to speculate, play the market; **sacar una emisión a** ~ to float an issue on the stock market; *V* **cotizar** *etc.*
  (g) ~ **de estudio** educational grant; ~ **de viaje** travel grant, grant for travelling.

bolsear [1a] 1 VT: **la bolsearon** she had her handbag stolen; ~ **a uno** (*CAm, Méx*) to pick sb's pocket.
  2 VI **(a)** (*CAm, Méx*) to pick pockets. **(b)** (*CAm, Cono Sur, Méx: estafar*) to cheat, swindle.

bolsicón NM (*And*) thick flannel skirt.

bolsicona NF (*And*) peasant woman.

bolsillo NM **(a)** (*gen*) pocket; (*monedero*) purse, moneybag, pocketbook; **guardar algo en el** ~ to put sth in one's pocket, pocket sth; **meterse a uno en el** ~ to win sb over, have sb eating out of one's hand; **rascarse el** ~* to pay up, fork out*; **tentarse el** ~ (*fig*) to feel in one's pocket, consider one's financial circumstances; **tener a uno en el** ~ to have sb captivated.
  (b) de ~ pocket (*atr*), pocket-size; **edición de** ~ pocket edition; **acorazado de** ~ pocket battleship.

bolsín NM kerb market (in stocks and shares).

bolsiquear [1a] VT (*Cono Sur*): ~ **a uno** (*registrar*) to search (*o* go through) sb's pockets; (*robar*) to pick sb's pockets.

bolsista NMF **(a)** (*Fin*) stockbroker. **(b)** (*CAm, Méx: ladrón*) pickpocket.

bolsita NF: ~ **de té** tea bag.

bolso NM bag, purse (*US*); handbag, purse (*US*); ~ **de aseo** toilet bag; ~ **de bandolera** shoulder-bag; ~ **de mano,** ~ **de mujer** handbag, purse (*US*); ~ **de viaje** travelling bag; **hacer** ~ (*vela*) to fill, belly out.

bolsón 1 NM **(a)** (*And: bolso*) handbag, purse (*US*).
  (b) (*And Min*) lump of ore.
  (c) (*Méx: lago*) lagoon.
  (d) (*And: tonto*) fool.
  2 ADJ **(a)** (*And: tonto*) silly, foolish.
  (b) (*Carib, Méx: perezoso*) lazy.

bolsonada NF (*And, Cono Sur*) silly thing to do, act of foolishness.

boludear* [1a] VI (*Cono Sur*) to mess about.

boludez* NF (*Cono Sur*) **(a)** (*cosa fácil*) piece of cake*.
  (b) (*acto*) stupid thing to do; **boludeces** (*palabras*) rubbish, nonsense.

boludo* (*And, Cono Sur*) 1 ADJ thick*, stupid.
  2 NM, **boluda** NF wally*, nerd*.

bomba 1 NF **(a)** (*Mil etc*) bomb; (*proyectil*) shell; (*carga*) charge; ~ **atómica** atomic bomb; ~ **cazabobos** booby-trap bomb; ~ **de cobalto** cobalt bomb; ~ **de dispersión,** ~ **de racimo** (*Cono Sur*) cluster-bomb; ~ **de acción retardada** time-bomb; ~ **fétida** stink-bomb; ~ **de fósforo** incendiary bomb; ~ **de fragmentación** fragmentation bomb; ~ **H** H-bomb; ~ **de hidrógeno** hydrogen bomb; ~ **de humo** smoke-bomb; ~ **incendiaria** incendiary bomb; ~ **lacrimógena** tear-gas bomb; ~ **de mano** grenade, hand-grenade; ~ **nuclear** nuclear bomb; ~ **de profundidad** depth charge; ~ **de racimo** cluster-bomb; ~ **de efecto retardado,** ~ **de relojería,** ~ **de retardo** time-bomb; ~ **revientamanzanas,** ~ **vuelamanzanas** blockbuster; ~ **volante** flying bomb; **a prueba de** ~**s** bombproof, shellproof; **atacar con** ~**s, lanzar** ~**s sobre** to bomb, drop bombs on; **caer como una** ~ to fall like a bombshell; **estar a tres** ~**s** to be very cross; **estar echando** ~**s** to be boiling hot.
  (b) (*fig: sorpresa*) surprise; (*notición*) bombshell, surprising item of news; (*éxito*) great success; **¡~!** attention please!; **es la** ~ **del año** it's the surprise of the year; **caer como una** ~ to come as a bombshell.
  (c) (*Téc*) pump; (*Mús*) slide; (*Cono Sur: Aut*) garage, petrol-station; ~ **de aire** air-pump; ~ **de alimentación** feed-pump; ~ **aspirante** suction pump; ~ **bencinera** (*Carib, Cono Sur*) petrol-station, gas station (*US*); ~ **de engrase** grease-gun; ~ **de gasolina** (*en motor*) fuel-pump; (*de garaje*) petrol-pump, gas pump (*US*); ~ **impelente,** ~ **impulsora** force pump; ~ **de incendios** fire-engine; ~ **de inyección** (*de combustible*) fuel-pump; ~ **de pie** footpump; ~ **de succión** suction

pump; **dar a la ~** to pump, work the pump.

(d) (*de lámpara*) shade; glass, globe.

(e) (*And: burbuja*) soap bubble.

(f) (*Carib: tambor*) big drum; (*baile*) dance accompanied by a drum.

(g) (*And, Carib: globo*) balloon; (*Carib, Cono Sur: cometa*) round kite.

(h) (*Carib, Méx: chistera*) top hat.

(i) (*And, CAm, Cono Sur*) (*juerga*) drinking spree; (*embriaguez*) drunkenness; **estar en ~** to be drunk.

(j) (*LAm*) (*rumor*) false rumour; (*mentira*) lie; (*Carib: noticia*) piece of news.

2 ADJ INVAR (*) **(a)** sensational; **noticia ~** shattering piece of news; **está ~** she's smashing*.

(b) estar ~ (*And**) to be clapped-out*.

3 ADV: **pasarlo ~*** to have a grand time, have a whale of a time*.

bombachas¹ NFPL (*Cono Sur: de mujer*) panties.

bombachas² NFPL (*And, Cono Sur*), **bombaches** NMPL (*Carib*) baggy trousers, peasant trousers.

bombacho **1** ADJ (*LAm*) baggy, loose-fitting.

2 bombachos NMPL baggy trousers; (*de golf etc*) plus-fours.

bomba-lapa NF, PL **bombas-lapa** limpet bomb.

bombardear [1a] VT (*Mil*) to bombard, shell; (*Aer*) to bomb, raid; (*Fís*) to bombard; (*fig*) to bombard (*de* with).

bombardeo NM bombardment (*t fig*), shelling; bombing; raid; **~ aéreo** air-raid, air attack (*contra, de* on); **~ de saturación** saturation bombing; **~ en picado** dive-bombing.

bombardero **1** ADJ bombing.

2 NM (*Aer*) bomber; (*Mil:* ††) bombardier.

bombardino NM (*Mús*) tuba, bass saxhorn.

bombasí NM fustian.

bombástico ADJ bombastic; (*Carib: elogioso*) complimentary, eulogistic.

bomba-trampa NF, PL **bombas-trampa** booby-trap bomb.

bombazo NM bomb explosion; (*fig*) bombshell.

bombeador NM **(a)** (*Cono Sur Aer*) bomber. **(b)** (*Cono Sur*) (*explorador*) scout; (*espía*) spy.

bombear [1a] **1** VT **(a)** (*Mil*) to shell.

(b) *líquido* to pump; to pump out, pump up.

(c) (*Cos*) to pad.

(d) (*fig: alabar*) to praise up, inflate the reputation of.

(e) (*Cono Sur**) *plan* to sabotage, wreck; (*Univ*) to fail, flunk‡; (*And**: *despedir*) to sack*, fire*.

(f) (*And*) (*Hist: espiar*) to spy on; (*reconocer*) to reconnoitre.

(g) (*CAm: robar*) to steal.

(h) (*Dep*) *balón* to lob; to kick high; **balón bombeado** high ball.

2 VI **(a)** (*Carib: emborracharse*) to get drunk.

(b) (*CAm, Méx**) to screw‡‡, fuck‡‡.

3 bombearse VR (*Arquit*) to camber; (*madera etc*) to warp, bulge.

bombeo NM **(a)** (*con bomba*) pumping. **(b)** (*Arquit*) camber; warping, bulging; crown (of the road).

bombero NM **(a)** (*gen*) fireman; **~s, cuerpo de ~s** fire brigade. **(b)** (*fig*) trouble-shooter. **(c)** (*Cono Sur: espía*) spy, scout; guard. **(d)** (*LAm: Aut*) petrol-pump attendant.

bombilla NF (*Elec*) (light) bulb; (*Náut*) ship's lantern; (*LAm: tubo*) metal tube for drinking maté; (*paja*) drinking straw; (*Méx: cuchara*) ladle; **~ de flash, ~ fusible** (*Fot*) flash bulb; **se le encendió la ~** it dawned on him, the penny dropped; he had a great idea.

bombillo NM (*And, CAm, Carib, Méx*) (light) bulb.

bombín NM **(a)** (*sombrero*) bowler hat. **(b)** (*Cono Sur: de aire*) pump, bicycle pump.

bombo **1** ADJ **(a)** (*aturdido*) dumbfounded, stunned.

(b) (*Carib*) (*tibio*) lukewarm; (*aguado*) watery, insipid; *persona* stupid, thick*.

(c) (*Méx*) *carne* bad, off.

2 NM **(a)** (*Mús*) big drum, bass drum; (*Téc*) cylinder, drum; (*Carib*) dance accompanied by a drum; **anunciar algo a ~ y platillo(s)** to announce sth with a lot of hype*, go in for a lot of publicity about sth; **hacer algo a ~ y platillo(s)** to make a great song and dance about sth; **tengo la cabeza hecha un ~** I've got a splitting headache; I'm all muddled.

(b) (*Carib: sombrero*) bowler hat.

(c) (*Náut*) barge, lighter.

(d) (*: elogio exagerado*) exaggerated praise; (*Teat etc*) hype*, ballyhoo*, big write-up; **dar ~ a uno** to give sb exaggerated praise, write sb up in a big way; to boost sb; **darse el ~ mutuo** to indulge in mutual backslapping.

(e) irse al ~ (*Cono Sur*) to come to grief, blow it‡; **mandar a uno al ~** (*Cono Sur‡*) to knock sb off‡; **poner a uno ~** (*Méx**) to hurl insults at sb; to hit sb.

(f) (*) **estar con ~** to be in the family way; **dejar a una con ~** to put a girl in the family way.

bombón NM **(a)** (*chocolatina*) chocolate. **(b)** (*) (*objeto*) beauty, gem; (*chica*) peach‡, smasher‡. **(c)** (*: chollo*) gift*, cinch‡.

bombona NF carboy; **~ (de gas)** canister, cylinder.

bombonera NF **(a)** (*caja para dulces*) sweet box; (*lata para dulces*) sweet tin. **(b)** (*: lugar*) cosy little place.

bombonería NF sweetshop, confectioner's (shop).

bómper NM (*LAm Aut*) bumper.

bonachón ADJ good-natured, kindly; easy-going; (*pey*) simple, naïve.

bonachonamente ADV good-naturedly, in an easy-going way; (*pey*) naïvely.

bonaerense **1** ADJ of Buenos Aires province.

2 NMF native (*o* inhabitant) of Buenos Aires province; **los ~s** the people of Buenos Aires province.

bonancible ADJ (*Met*) fair, calm, settled; *viento* light.

bonanza NF **(a)** (*Náut*) fair weather, calm conditions; **ir en ~** to have fair weather.

(b) (*Min*) rich pocket (*o* vein) of ore, bonanza.

(c) (*fig: prosperidad*) prosperity, boom, bonanza; **estar en ~** (*Com*) to be booming; **ir en ~** go well, prosper.

bonazo ADJ **= buenazo**.

bonchar [1a] VI (*Carib*) to have a party; (*fig*) to have a good time.

bonche¹ NM (*LAm: montón*) load, bunch.

bonche² NM (*Carib*) **(a)** (*fiesta*) party, good time. **(b)** (*cosa divertida*) amusing thing; (*persona divertida*) amusing person.

bonche³ NM petting*, necking*.

bonchón NM, **bonchona** NF fun-loving person.

bondad NF (*gen*) goodness; (*amabilidad*) kindness, helpfulness; **tener la ~ de + ***infin*** to be so kind as to + *infin*, be good enough to + *infin*; **tenga la ~ de no fumar** please do not smoke, please be so kind as not to smoke; **tuvo la ~ de prestárnoslo** he very kindly lent it to us.

bondadosamente ADV kindly; good-naturedly.

bondadoso ADJ kind, good; kindly, kind-hearted, good-natured.

bondi NM (*Cono Sur*) tram.

bonete NM (*Ecl*) hat, biretta; (*Univ*) cap; **¡~!** (*CAm, Méx**) not on your life!, no way!*; **a tente ~** doggedly, insistently.

bonetería NF (*Cono Sur, Méx*) draper's (shop), clothing store.

bóngalo NM, **bongaló** NM bungalow.

bongo NM (*LAm*) small boat; (*And*) small punt.

bongó NM (*Carib*) bongo (drum), African-type drum.

boni‡ NM **= boniato (b)**.

boniata **1** ADJ (*LAm*) edible, non-poisonous.

2 NF (*Carib*) edible yucca, cassava.

boniato NM **(a)** (*Carib, Cono Sur Bot*) sweet potato, yam. **(b)** (*‡: Esp*) 1000-peseta note.

bonificación NF **(a)** (*pago*) bonus; (*esp Agr*) betterment, improvement (in value); (*Dep*) allowance of points. **(b)** (*Com*) allowance, discount; rebate.

bonificar [1g] **1** VT **(a)** (*Agr, Com*) to improve. **(b)** (*Com*) to allow, discount.

2 bonificarse VR to improve.

bonísimo ADJ *superl de* **bueno**.

bonitamente ADV **(a)** (*con maña*) nicely, neatly; craftily. **(b)** (*poco a poco*) slowly, little by little.

bonitero **1** ADJ *bonito* (*atr*).

2 NM **(a)** (*persona*) bonito fisherman. **(b)** (*barco*) bonito fishing boat.

bonito¹ **1** ADJ **(a)** (*guapo*) pretty; nice, nice-looking; (*esp Cono Sur*) handsome; **~ como un sol** as pretty as a picture.

(b) (*bueno*) pretty good, passable; **una bonita cantidad** a nice little sum; **¡qué ~!** very nice too! (*t iró*).

2 ADV (*Cono Sur**) well, nicely; **ella canta ~** she sings nicely; **se te ve ~** it looks good on you.

bonito² NM (*Pez*) bonito.

bonitura NF (*LAm*) beauty, attractiveness.

bono NM **(a)** (*gen*) voucher, certificate; **~ alimenticio** food stamp. **(b)** (*Fin*) bond; **~ de ahorros** savings bond; **~ de caja, ~ de tesorería** debenture bond; **~ de caja de ahorros** savings certificate; **~ del estado** government bond.

bono-bus NM, PL **bonos-bus, bonobús** NM, PL **bonobuses** (*Esp*) bus pass, book of bus tickets.

bono-loto NF (*Esp: t* **bonoloto**) state-run weekly lottery; *see also* LOTERÍA PRIMITIVA, LOTERÍA NACIONAL.

bono-metro NM metro pass, book of metro tickets.

bonsai NM bonsai.

bonzo NM bonze; **quemarse a lo ~** to set o.s. alight.

boñiga NF, **boñigo** NM cow pat, horse dung.

boom [bum] NM boom; **~ inmobiliario** property boom; **dar ~ a un problema** to exaggerate a problem, make a meal of a problem.

boomerang [bume'ran] NM, PL **boomerangs** [bume'ran] boomerang.

boqueada NF gasp; **dar la última ~** to breathe one's last, be at one's last gasp; **dar las ~s** to be dying.

boquear [1a] **1** VT to say, utter, pronounce.

2 VI **(a)** (*quedar boquiabierto*) to gape, gawp.

(b) (*estar expirando*) to be at one's last gasp; (*fig*) to be in its final stages; (*provisión*) to be very nearly exhausted.

boquera [1] NF (**a**) (*Agr*) sluice. (**b**) (*Med*) lip sore, mouth ulcer.
[2] NM: ~s‡ screw‡, warder.

boqueriento ADJ (**a**) (*Med*) suffering from lip sores. (**b**) (*Cono Sur: miserable*) wretched, miserable.

boquerón NM (**a**) (*abertura*) wide opening, big hole. (**b**) (*Pez*) (fresh) anchovy. (**c**) (*: persona*) = **malagueño**.

boquete NM gap, opening; hole, breach.

boqui‡ NM screw‡, warder.

boquiabierto ADJ open-mouthed; **estar ~** to stand open-mouthed, stand gaping (in astonishment); to stand aghast.

boquiancho ADJ wide-mouthed.

boquiblando ADJ *caballo* tender-mouthed.

boquifresco· ADJ outspoken; cheeky·.

boquilla NF (**a**) (*Mús*) mouthpiece; (*de manga etc*) nozzle; (*de gas*) burner; (*de pipa*) mouthpiece; cigarette holder, cigar-holder; (*Cos*) trouser bottom; ~ **de filtro** filter tip; **hablar de ~** to talk out of the side of one's mouth.
(**b**) (*And: chisme*) rumour, piece of gossip.
(**c**) **promesa de ~** insincere promise, promise not meant to be kept; **lo dijo de ~** he was not sincere in what he said, he was only paying lip-service to it.

boquillazo NM (*And*) rumour, talk.

boquillero ADJ (*Carib*) smooth-talking, sweet-talking.

boquirroto ADJ talkative, garrulous.

boquirrubio [1] ADJ (**a**) (*gárrulo*) talkative; (*de mucha labia*) glib; (*indiscreto*) indiscreet, loose-tongued. (**b**) (*simple*) simple, naïve.
[2] NM fop, dandy.

boquita NF: ~ **de piñón** pursed lips *pl*.

boquitinguero ADJ (*Cono Sur*) gossipy.

boquituerto ADJ wry-mouthed.

boquiverde· ADJ foul-mouthed.

boraciar [1b] VI (*Cono Sur*) to boast, brag.

bórax NM borax.

borboll(e)ar [1a] VI (**a**) (*burbujear*) to bubble, boil up. (**b**) (*fig: chisporrotear*) to splutter.

borbollón NM bubbling, boiling; gushing, welling up; **hablar a ~es** to talk in a torrent; to splutter; **reírse a ~es** to bubble with laughter; **salir a ~es** (*agua*) to come out in a torrent, come out with a rush, gush forth.

borbollonear [1a] VI = **borboll(e)ar**.

Borbón N Bourbon.

borbónico ADJ Bourbon.

borbot(e)ar [1a] VI (*hacer burbujas*) to bubble; (*al hervir*) to boil (up), boil over; (*nacer*) to gush forth, well up.

borbotón NM = **borbollón**.

borceguí NM high shoe, laced boot; half boot; (*de bebé*) (baby's) bootee.

borda NF (**a**) (*Náut: regala*) gunwale, rail; **motor fuera (de) ~** outboard motor; **echar** (*o* **tirar**) **algo por la ~** to throw sth overboard (*t fig*).
(**b**) (*Náut: vela*) mainsail.
(**c**) (*choza*) hut.

bordada NF (*Náut*) tack; **dar ~s** to tack; (*fig*) to keep on going to and fro.

bordado NM embroidery, needlework.

bordadora NF needlewoman.

bordadura NF embroidery, needlework.

bordalesa NF (*Cono Sur* ††) *wine barrel holding 225 litres*.

bordante NMF (*Carib, Méx*) lodger.

bordar [1a] VT to embroider; (*fig*) to do supremely well; **ha bordado su papel** she was excellent in her part.

borde¹ NM (**a**) (*gen*) edge, border; (*de camino etc*) side; (*de plato*) brim, rim, lip; (*de ventana*) ledge; (*Cos*) edge, hem, selvage; (*Náut*) board; ~ **de la acera** kerb; ~ **de ataque** (*Aer*) leading edge; ~ **del camino**, ~ **de la carretera** roadside, verge; ~ **del mar** seaside, seashore; ~ **de salida** (*Aer*) trailing edge; **al ~ de** at the edge of, on the border of, at the side of.
(**b**) (*fig*) **estar al ~ de una crisis nerviosa** to be on the verge of a nervous breakdown; **estar en el mismo ~ del desastre** to be on the very brink of disaster.

borde² ADJ (**a**) (*·*) *persona* anti-social; rough, uncouth; difficult, bad-tempered, stroppy·; **ponerse ~** to get stroppy·.
(**b**) *niño* illegitimate.
(**c**) (*Bot*) wild.

bordear [1a] [1] VT (**a**) (*seguir el borde de*) to skirt, go along (*o* round) the edge of.
(**b**) (*lindar con*) to border on; to flank; (*fig*) to verge on.
(**c**) ~ **un asunto** (*Cono Sur*) to skirt round (*o* avoid) a (tricky) subject; (*Cono Sur, Méx*) to broach a subject.
(**d**) (*Cono Sur: calle etc*) to border, line; **los árboles bordean el camino** trees line the road.

[2] VI (*Náut*) to tack.

bordejada NF (*Carib, Cono Sur: Náut*) tack.

bordej(e)ar [1a] VI (*Carib, Cono Sur: Náut*) to tack.

bordelés [1] ADJ of (*o* from) Bordeaux.
[2] NM, **bordelesa** NF native (*o* inhabitant) of Bordeaux.

bordería· NF stroppiness·.

bordillo NM kerb.

bordin NM (*And, Carib, Méx*) boarding house.

bordinguero, -a NM/F (*And, Carib, Méx*) (*hombre*) landlord, (*mujer*) landlady.

bordo NM (**a**) (*Náut*) side, board; **a ~** on board; **con ordenador de a ~** with on-board computer; **estar a ~ del barco** to be on board (the) ship; **ir a ~** to go on board; **al ~** alongside; **buque de alto ~** big ship, seagoing vessel; **personaje de alto ~** distinguished person, influential person.
(**b**) (*Náut: bordada*) tack; **dar ~s** to tack.
(**c**) (*CAm, Cono Sur, Méx: presa*) roughly-built dam; (*Cono Sur: dique*) raised furrow; (*CAm: de montaña*) peak, summit.

bordó (*Cono Sur*) [1] ADJ maroon.
[2] NM maroon.

bordón NM (**a**) (*de peregrino*) pilgrim's staff; (*de ciego*) stick; (*fig*) guide, helping hand.
(**b**) (*Mús: cuerda*) bass string; (*registro*) bass stop, bourdon; (*Poét*) refrain; (*fig*) pet word, pet phrase.
(**c**) (*And, CAm: benjamín*) youngest son.

bordona NF (*Cono Sur*) sixth string of the guitar; ~**s** bass strings of the guitar.

bordoncillo NM pet word, pet phrase.

bordonear [1a] [1] VT (*Cono Sur Mús*) to strum.
[2] VI (*And, Carib*) to hum, buzz.

bordoneo NM (*Cono Sur: Mús*) strumming.

boreal ADJ northern; **el Hemisferio B~** the Northern Hemisphere.

borgesiano, borgiano ADJ Borgesian, characteristic of J.L. Borges.

Borgoña NF Burgundy.

borgoña NM (*t* **vino de ~**) burgundy.

bórico ADJ boric.

boricua ADJ, NMF Puerto Rican.

borinqueño, -a ADJ, NM/F Puerto Rican.

Borja N Borgia.

borla NF tassel, pompom; tuft; (*Univ*) tassel on a cap; ~ **(de empolvarse)** powder puff; **tomar la ~** (*Univ*) to take one's master's (*o* doctor's) degree.

borlete NM (*Méx*) row, din, uproar.

borne NM (*Elec*) terminal.

borneadizo ADJ easily warped, flexible.

bornear [1a] [1] VT (**a**) (*torcer*) to twist, bend.
(**b**) (*Arquit*) to hoist into place; to put in place, align.
(**c**) (*Méx*) *pelota* to spin, turn.
[2] VI (*Náut*) to swing at anchor.
[3] **bornearse** VR to warp, bulge.

borneco ADJ (*Cono Sur*) small, short.

borneo NM (**a**) (*torcer*) twisting, bending. (**b**) (*Arquit*) alignment. (**c**) (*Náut*) swinging at anchor.

boro NM (*Quím*) boron.

borona NF (**a**) (*maíz*) maize, corn (*US*); (*mijo*) millet. (**b**) (*pan*) maize bread, corn bread (*US*); (*LAm: migaja*) crumb.

borra NF (**a**) (*lana*) thick wool, coarse wool, flock; stuffing.
(**b**) (*pelusa*) fluff; (*Bot*) down; ~ **de algodón** cotton waste; ~ **de seda** floss silk.
(**c**) (*sedimento*) sediment, lees.
(**d**) (*: charla insustancial*) empty talk; (*basura*) trash, rubbish.

borrachear· [1a] VI to booze·, get drunk habitually.

borrachera NF (**a**) (*estado*) drunkenness, drunken state; **despejarse la ~**, **espabilarse la ~**, **quitarse la ~** to sober up, get rid of one's hangover; **pegarse una ~**, **ponerse una ~** (*Méx*) to get drunk.
(**b**) (*juerga*) spree, binge, drinking expedition.

borrachez NF drunkenness, drunken state.

borrachín NM drunkard, sot, toper.

borracho [1] ADJ (**a**) (*temporalmente*) drunk, intoxicated; (*por costumbre*) drunken, hard-drinking, fond of the bottle; **estar ~ como un tronco** (*o* **una uva**), **estar más ~ que una cuba** to be as drunk as a lord.
(**b**) (*fig: poseído de pasión*) drunk, blind, wild (*de ira etc* with rage *etc*).
(**c**) *bizcocho* tipsy, soaked in liqueur (*o* spirit); (*de color*) violet; (*LAm*) *fruta* overripe.
(**d**) **es un negocio ~·** (*Esp*) it's a real money-spinner, it's money for old rope·.
[2] NM, **borracha** NF drunkard, drunk.

borrado NM erasure.

borrador NM (**a**) (*primera versión*) first draft, preliminary sketch, rough copy.
(**b**) (*cuaderno etc*) book for rough work, scribbling pad, scratch pad

(US); (Com) daybook.

(c) (para borrar) rubber, eraser; duster.

borradura NF erasure, crossing-out.

borraja NF borage.

borrajear [1a] VTI to scribble, scrawl; to doodle.

borrar [1a] ① VT (a) (con borrador) to erase, rub out; (tachar) to cross out, score out, obliterate; to wipe out; cinta to wipe (clean); (fig) memoria etc to erase, efface, wipe away; (Pol: euf) to eliminate, dispose of; **~ a uno de una lista** to cross sb off a list, delete sb from a list.

(b) (manchar) to blot, smear; (Fot etc) to blur.

② **borrarse** VR to resign (from a club etc).

borrasca NF (a) (Met) storm; squall.

(b) (fig: peligro) peril, hazard; (revés) setback.

(c) (*: juerga) orgy, spree.

borrascoso ADJ (a) tiempo stormy; viento squally, gusty. (b) (fig) stormy, tempestuous.

borrasquero ADJ riotous, wild.

borregada* NF student rag*, prank.

borregaje NM (Cono Sur) flock of lambs.

borrego ① NM, **borrega** NF (a) (Zool) lamb, yearling lamb; **no hay tales ~s** there isn't any such thing.

(b) (fig: persona) simpleton.

② NM (Carib: trampa) con*, hoax; (Méx: mentira) lie, tall story.

③ **~s** NMPL (nubes) fleecy clouds; (prov: Náut) white horses, foamy crests of waves.

borreguil ADJ meek, like a lamb.

borreguillo NM fleece; **forro de ~** fleece lining.

borrica NF (a) (Zool) she-donkey. (b) (*) stupid woman.

borricada NF silly thing, piece of nonsense.

borrico NM (a) (Zool) donkey (t fig). (b) (Téc) sawhorse.

borricón* NM, **borricote*** NM long-suffering person.

borriquete NM (Arte) easel; (Téc) sawhorse.

borrón NM (a) (mancha) blot, smudge, stain; (fig) blemish; stain, stigma; slur; **hacer ~ y cuenta nueva** to wipe the slate clean (and start again); to let bygones be bygones.

(b) (Liter) rough draft, preliminary sketch; (Arte) sketch; **estos ~es** (iró) these humble jottings.

borronear [1a] VT (a) (borrajear) to scribble; to doodle*. (b) (hacer borrador de) to make a rough draft of.

borroso ADJ (a) (Fot) blurred, indistinct, fuzzy; smudgy; (Arte) woolly.

(b) líquido muddy, thick, cloudy.

boruca* NF row, din.

borujo NM lump, pressed mass, packed mass.

borujón NM (Med) bump, lump; (lío) bundle.

boruquear [1a] VT (Méx) (revolver) to mix up, mess up; (fig) to stir up (trouble in).

boscaje NM thicket, grove, small wood; (Arte) woodland scene.

Bosco NM: **el ~** Hieronymus Bosch.

boscoso ADJ wooded.

Bósforo NM Bosphorus; **el Estrecho del ~** the Bosphorus (Strait).

Bosnia NF Bosnia.

bosnio, -a ADJ, NM/F Bosnian.

bosorola NF (CAm, Méx) sediment, dregs.

bosque NM wood, woodland, forest; woods; **~ pluvial** rainforest.

bosquecillo NM copse, small wood.

bosquejar [1a] VT (Arte) to sketch, make a sketch of, draw in outline; to model in rough; (fig) to sketch, outline; plan etc to draft.

bosquejo NM sketch, outline; rough model; draft.

bosquete NM copse, small wood.

bosquimán NM, **bosquimano** NM African bushman.

bosta NF dung, droppings; manure.

bostezar [1f] VI to yawn.

bostezo NM yawn.

bota¹ NF boot; **~s de agua** wellingtons, gumboots; **~s de campaña, ~s camperas** top boots; **~s de esquí** ski boots; **~s de fútbol** football boots; **~s de goma** gumboots; **~s de media caña** ankle-boots; **~s de montar** riding boots; **colgar las ~s** to hang up one's boots (t fig); **morir con las ~s puestas** to die in harness; **ponerse las ~s*** (enriquecerse) to strike it rich*, make one's pile*; (pasarlo bien) to enjoy o.s. immensely; (soñar) to indulge in fantasies; (comer) to have a blow-out‡.

bota² NF (a) (de vino) leather wine bottle. (b) = 516 litres. (c) (tonel) large barrel.

botada¹ NF (LAm) (tirada) throw, throwing; throwing away; (despedida) sacking, dismissal.

botadero NM (And, Méx: vado) ford; (LAm: vertedero) rubbish dump.

botado ① ADJ (a) (descarado) cheeky.

(b) (CAm: gastador) spendthrift.

(c) (And: resignado) resigned; (dispuesto para todo) ready for anything, resolute.

(d) (CAm, Cono Sur: Com) dirt cheap.

(e) **niño ~** (LAm) = **2**.

(f) (CAm, Méx: borracho) blind drunk.

② NM, **botada**² NF (LAm) abandoned child, foundling; (And: vago) good-for-nothing, bum (US).

botador NM (a) (Náut) (punt) pole. (b) (sacaclavos) nail-puller, claw-hammer. (c) (LAm: gastador) spendthrift.

botadura NF (a) (Náut) launching. (b) (LAm) = **botada**¹.

botafuego NM (††) linstock; (*) quick-tempered person.

botalodo NM (And, Carib) mudguard.

botalón NM (a) (Náut) boom, outrigger; **~ de foque** jib-boom. (b) (And, Cono Sur: viga) beam, prop; (And: poste) post, stake; (And: de atar) hitching post.

botanas NFPL (LAm) snack, appetizer.

botanearse* [1a] VR: **~ a uno** (LAm) to speak ill of sb, drag sb's name through the dirt.

botaneo NM (LAm) (malicious) gossip, slander.

botánica¹ NF botany.

botánico ① ADJ botanical.

② NM, **botánica**² NF botanist.

botanista NMF botanist.

botar [1a] ① VT (a) (lanzar) to throw, fling, hurl; pelota to bowl, pitch; balón to kick.

(b) (Náut) barco to launch (t **~ al agua**).

(c) (Náut) timón to put over.

(d) (esp LAm: tirar) to throw away, chuck out; persona* to fire*, sack*; fortuna to fritter away, squander; **le botaron de su trabajo** they sacked him from his job.

(e) (LAm: perder) to lose.

② VI (a) (pelota) to bounce; (Aut etc) to bump, bounce, jolt; (caballo) to buck, rear; **está que bota** he's hopping mad.

(b) **~ a babor** (Náut) to put over to port.

③ **botarse** VR (Cono Sur) (a) (cambiar empleos) to change jobs.

(b) **se bota a experto** he fancies himself as expert, he claims to be an expert.

(c) (Carib: tomar medidas extremas) to go to extremes, go all the way.

botaratada NF wild thing; wild scheme, nonsensical idea.

botarate NM (a) (loco) madcap, wild fellow. (b) (idiota) idiot. (c) (LAm: gastador) spendthrift.

botarel NM buttress.

botarga NF motley, clown's outfit.

botavara NF (a) (Náut) boom. (b) (Carib, Cono Sur: de carro) pole, shaft.

bote¹ NM (a) (arremetida) thrust, lunge, blow.

(b) (de pelota) bounce; (Aut etc) bump, bounce, jolt; (de caballo) buck; **a ~ pronto** (ADJ) sudden; (ADV) decir, preguntar suddenly, point-blank; (desde el comienzo) right away, from the start; **de ~ y voleo** instantly; **dar un ~** to jump; **dar el ~ a uno*** to chuck sb out; to sack sb*; **darse el ~‡** to beat it*; **dar ~s** (Aut etc) to bump, bounce; **pegar un ~** to jump, start (with surprise).

(c) **estar de ~ en ~** to be packed, be jammed full, be crowded out.

bote² NM (a) (lata) can, tin, canister; (tarro) pot, jar; (en café: propina) tip, (caja) box (for waiters' tips); **~ de basura** (Méx) dustbin, ashcan (US); **~ de cerveza** beer-can; can of beer; **~ de cuestación** collecting tin; **~ de humo** smoke-bomb; **está en el ~*** it's in the bag*; **lo tiene en el ~*** he's got it all sewn up*.

(b) (Naipes) jackpot, kitty.

(c) (*: Aut) grid*, jalop(p)y; (CAm, Méx‡) jail, nick‡.

(d) (*) **chupar del ~** (congraciarse) to curry favour, creep*; (gorronear) to scrounge a meal (o drink etc); (mirar por sí) to look after Number One; (enriquecerse) to feather one's nest; **pegarse el ~ con uno** to get on like a house on fire with sb.

bote³ NM (Náut) boat; **~ de carrera, ~ de un remero** skiff, sculling boat; **~ neumático** rubber dinghy; **~ de a ocho** racing eight; **~ de paseo** rowing boat; **~ de paso** ferry-boat; **~ patrullero** patrol boat; **~ de remos** rowing boat; **~ de salvamento, ~ salvavidas** lifeboat.

botella NF (a) (gen) bottle; **~ de Leiden** Leyden jar; **cerveza de ~, cerveza en ~s** bottled beer.

(b) (Carib: prebenda) sinecure, soft job (in government).

botellazo NM a blow with a bottle.

botellería NF (Cono Sur) wine shop.

botellero NM wine-rack.

botellín NM small bottle, half-bottle.

botepronto NM (Dep) half-volley; V t **bote**¹ (b).

botería NF (Cono Sur) shoeshop.

bote-vivienda NM, PL **botes-vivienda** houseboat.

botica NF (a) (tienda) chemist's (shop), pharmacy, drugstore (US); **de todo como en ~** everything under the sun. (b) (‡) trouser fly, flies.

boticaria NF (woman) chemist, druggist; (Hist) chemist's wife, apothecary's wife.

boticario NM chemist, druggist, (Hist) apothecary.

botija ① NF (a) (vasija) earthenware jug; (*) fat person; **estar como una ~, estar hecho una ~** to be as fat as a sow; **poner a uno como**

~ verde (*LAm*) to call sb every name under the sun. **(b)** (*CAm, Carib*: *tesoro*) buried treasure. ☐2 NMF (*Cono Sur*) baby, child.

botijo NM **(a)** (*Culin*) earthenware drinking jug (*with spout and handle*); V **tren. (b)** (***: *de policía*) water-cannon.

botijón* ADJ (*Méx*) potbellied.

botijuela NF (*LAm*) **(a)** (*botijo*) earthenware jug. **(b)** (*tesoro*) buried treasure.

botillería NF refreshment stall; (*LAm*) liquor store.

botillero NM (*Méx*) shoemaker, cobbler.

botín1 NM (*Mil etc*) booty, plunder, loot.

botín2 NM **(a)** (*polaina*) half boot; legging, high boot. **(b)** (*Cono Sur*: *calcetín*) sock.

botina NF high shoe; (*de bebé*) bootee.

botiquín NM **(a)** (*Med*) medicine chest; (*enfermería*) first-aid post; (*t ~ de emergencia*) first-aid kit. **(b)** (*Carib*: *hum*) drinks cupboard.

boto1 ADJ dull, blunt; (*fig*) dull, dim.

boto2 NM leather wine bottle.

botón NM **(a)** (*Cos*) button; **~ (de camisa)** stud; **¡ni un ~!*** not a sausage!*
(b) (*Elec etc*) button; (*Téc*) button, knob; (*Rad*) knob; **~ (de puerta)** doorknob, doorhandle; **~ de alarma** alarm, alarm button; **~ de arranque** starter, starting switch; **~ de contacto**, **~ de presión** push-button; **~ de destrucción** destruct button; **~ de muestra** sample, illustration; **empujar (o presionar etc) el ~** to press the button.
(c) (*Esgrima*: *de flor etc*) tip.
(d) (*Bot*) bud; **~ de oro** buttercup, kingcup.

botonadura NF (set of) buttons.

botonar [1a] (*LAm*) ☐1 VT to button (up). ☐2 VI to bud, sprout.

botones NM INVAR buttons; bellboy, bellhop (*US*).

Botsuana NF Botswana.

botulismo NM botulism.

boutique [bu'tik] NF boutique.

bóveda NF (*Arquit*) vault; dome; (*cueva*) cave, cavern; **~ de cañón** barrel vault; **~ celeste** vault of heaven, sky, firmament; **~ craneal** vault of the skull.

bovedillas* NFPL: **subirse a las ~*** to go up the wall*.

bovino ADJ bovine; cow (*atr*), ox (*atr*).

box1 [boks] NM, PL **boxes** [boks] (*de caballo*) stall; loose box; (*en carreras de coches*) pit; (*CAm, Carib, Correos*) post-office box, P.O. Box; **entrar en ~es** to make a pit-stop, go into the pits.

box2 [boks] NM (*LAm*) boxing.

boxeador NM boxer.

boxear [1a] VI to box.

boxeo NM boxing.

bóxer NM boxer (dog).

boxeril ADJ (*Cono Sur*), **boxístico** ADJ boxing (*atr*).

boya NF (*Náut*) buoy; (*Pesca*) float; **~ de campana** bellbuoy.

boyada NF drove of oxen.

boyante ADJ (*Náut*) buoyant, light in the water; (*fig*) buoyant, prosperous.

boyar [1a] VI to float.

boyazo NM (*CAm, Cono Sur*) punch.

boyé NM (*Cono Sur*) snake.

boyera NF, **boyeriza** NF cattle shed.

boyero NM **(a)** (*persona*) oxherd, drover. **(b)** (*perro*) cattle dog. **(c)** (*And*: *aguijada*) goad, spike.

boyuyu* NM chaos, mess, confusion.

bozada NF (*And*) halter.

bozal ☐1 ADJ **(a)** (*nuevo*) new, raw, green; *animal* wild, untamed.
(b) (*tonto*) stupid.
(c) (*LAm*) negro pure.
(d) (*LAm Ling*) speaking broken Spanish.
☐2 NM (*de perro*) muzzle; (*LAm*: *de caballo*) halter, headstall.

bozo NM **(a)** (*pelos*) down (on the upper lip), youthful whiskers. **(b)** (*boca*) mouth, lips. **(c)** (*cabestro*) halter, headstall.

bracamonte NM (*And*) ghost.

bracear [1a] ☐1 VT **(a)** (*Náut*) to measure in fathoms.
(b) *horno* to tap.
☐2 VI (*mover los brazos*) to swing one's arms; (*nadar*) to swim, (*esp*) crawl; (*fig*) to wrestle, struggle.

bracero NM **(a)** (*peón*) labourer, navvy; (*Agr*) farmhand, farm labourer. **(b) ir de ~** to walk arm-in-arm.

bracete: ir de ~ to walk arm-in-arm.

bracmán NM, **bracmana** NF Brahman, Brahmin.

braco ☐1 ADJ pug-nosed.
☐2 NM (*t perro ~*) pointer.

braga NF **(a)** (*Náut, Téc*) sling, rope (for hoisting).
(b) (*de niño*) nappy, diaper (*US*); **~s** (*de hombre*) breeches; (*Esp*) (*de mujer*) panties; **calzar(se) las ~s** (*mujer*) to wear the pants, be the boss; **coger** (*o* **pillar** *etc*) **a uno en ~s*** to catch sb with his pants

down*; **dejar a uno en ~s*** to leave sb empty-handed; **estar hecho una ~***: to be knackered*; **estar en ~s*** to be flat broke*.

bragado* ADJ energetic, tough; wicked, vicious.

bragadura NF (*Anat, Cos*) crotch.

braga-faja NF panty girdle.

bragapañal NM disposable nappy.

bragazas NM INVAR henpecked husband.

braguero NM (*Med*) truss.

bragueta NF (*Cos*) fly, flies; (*de chico*) short trousers; shorts; **gran ~** womanizer; **estar como ~ de fraile** (*Cono Sur*) to be very solemn; **oír por la ~*** (*lerdo*) to be pretty thick*; (*sordo*) to be stone-deaf; (*entender mal*) to misunderstand; **ser hombre de ~** to be a real man.

braguetazo* NM marriage for money; **dar el ~** to marry for money.

braguetero ☐1 ADJ **(a)** (*lascivo*) lecherous, randy.
(b) (*LAm*: *al casarse*) who marries for money; (*And, Carib*: *vividor*) who lives on a woman's earnings; **todos saben que es ~** everyone knows he married for money.
☐2 NM lecher, womanizer.

braguillas NM INVAR brat.

braguita(s) NF(PL) panties.

brah(a)mán NM Brahman, Brahmin.

braille ['braile] NM Braille.

brama NF (*Zool*) rut, rutting season.

bramadero NM (*LAm*) tethering (*o* hitching) post.

bramante NM twine, string.

bramar VI **(a)** (*Zool*) to roar, bellow. **(b)** (*fig*: *persona*) to roar; to rage, bluster; (*viento, tormenta*) to howl, roar; (*mar*) to roar, thunder; **están que braman con el alcalde*** they're hopping mad with the mayor.

bramido NM roar, bellow; howl, howling.

brandy, PL **brandies, brandys** NM brandy.

branquia NF gill.

brasa NF live coal, hot coal; **a la ~** (*Culin*) grilled; **atizar la ~** to stir things up, add fuel to the flames; **estar en ~s** to be on tenterhooks; **estar hecho una ~** to be very flushed.

brasear [1a] VT to braise.

brasería NF grill.

brasero NM (*gen*) brazier (*esp as used for domestic heating*); (*Hist*) stake; (*LAm*: *chimenea*) hearth, fireplace; (*And*: *hoguera*) large bonfire; (*Méx*: *hornillo*) small stove.

Brasil NM: **el ~** Brazil.

brasileño, -a, (*LAm*) **brasilero, -a** ADJ, NM/F Brazilian.

brava NF **(a)** (*Méx*: *disputa*) row, fight. **(b) a la ~** like it or not, by hook or by crook; **a la ~ tendrás que ir** you'll have to go whether you like it or not. **(c) dar una ~ a** (*Carib*) to intimidate (*o* lean on*).

bravata NF (*amenaza*) threat; (*fanfarronada*) boast, brag, piece of bravado; **echar ~s** to boast, talk big; to bluster.

braveador ☐1 ADJ blustering, bullying.
☐2 NM bully.

bravear [1a] VI **(a)** (*jactarse*) to boast, talk big; to bluster. **(b)** (*aplaudir*) to applaud, shout bravo.

bravera NF vent, window (*in an oven*).

bravero (*Carib*) ☐1 ADJ bullying.
☐2 NM bully.

braveza NF **(a)** (*ferocidad*) ferocity, savageness; (*Met*) fury, violence.
(b) (*valor*) bravery.

bravío ☐1 ADJ **(a)** (*Zool*) fierce, ferocious, savage; wild; untamed; (*Bot*) wild.
(b) (*fig*: *grosero*) uncouth, coarse.
☐2 NM fierceness, savageness.

bravo ☐1 ADJ **(a)** (*valiente*) brave; tough, spirited, pugnacious.
(b) (*excelente*) fine, excellent; *banquete etc* splendid, sumptuous.
(c) *animal* fierce, ferocious; *mar* rough, stormy; *paisaje* rugged, rough, wild; *persona* angry, wild; bad-tempered; **ponerse ~ con uno** to get angry with sb.
(d) (*jactancioso*) boastful, swaggering.
(e) (*LAm*: *picante*) hot, strong.
☐2 INTERJ bravo!, splendid!, well done!
☐3 NM thug.

bravucón ☐1 ADJ boastful, swaggering.
☐2 NM boaster, braggart.

bravuconada NF **(a)** (*cualidad*) bluster, boastfulness. **(b)** (*acto*) boast; boasting, bragging.

bravura NF **(a)** (*ferocidad*) fierceness, ferocity. **(b)** (*valor*) bravery. **(c)** = **bravata**.

braza NF **(a)** (*Náut*: *medida*: *aprox*) fathom. **(b)** (*Náut*) brace. **(c)** (*Natación*) (*t ~ de pecho*) breast stroke; **~ de espalda** back stroke; **~ de mariposa** butterfly stroke.

brazada NF **(a)** (*gen*) movement of the arms.
(b) (*de remo*) stroke.
(c) (*Natación*) stroke.
(d) (*cantidad*) armful.
(e) (*LAm Náut*: *medida*: *aprox*) fathom.

brazado NM armful.

brazal NM (a) (*brazalete*) armband. (b) (*Agr*) irrigation channel.

brazalete NM (a) (*joya*) bracelet, wristlet. (b) (*brazal*) armlet, armband.

brazo NM (a) (*gen*) arm; (*Zool*) foreleg; (*Téc: de silla etc*) arm; bracket; (*Bot*) limb, branch; **~ armado** military wing (*of terrorist movement etc*); **~ derecho** (*fig*) right-hand man; indispensable aid; **~ de dirección** steering arm; **~ de gitano** (*Culin*) swiss roll; **~ de lámpara** lamp bracket; **~ de lámpara de gas** gas bracket; **~ lector, ~ de lectura** pick-up arm; **~ de mar** arm of the sea, sound; **estar** (o **ir**) **hecho un ~ de mar** to be dressed up to the nines; **~ político** political wing (*of terrorist movement etc*); **~ de reina** (*Cono Sur Culin*) swiss roll; **~ de río** branch of a river; **~ secular** secular arm; **~ de toma de sonido** pickup arm; **ir asidos** (o **cogidos**) **del ~, ir del ~** (*LAm*) to walk arm-in-arm; **coger a uno por el ~** to seize sb by the arm; **cruzarse de ~s** (*lit*) to fold one's arms; (*fig*) not to do anything; **estarse con los ~s cruzados** (*fig*) to sit back and do nothing; **dar el ~ a uno** (*fig*) to give sb a helping hand; **no dar su ~ a torcer** to stand fast, not give way easily; **ir del ~** (*LAm*) to walk arm-in-arm; **luchar a ~ partido** to fight hand-to-hand, (*fig*) fight bitterly; **mover algo a ~** to move sth by hand, manhandle sth; **recibir a uno con los ~s abiertos** to receive sb with open arms.
(b) (*fig*) (*energía*) energy, enterprise; (*valor*) courage.
(c) **~s** (*fig*) (*obreros*) hands, workers; (*protectores*) backers, protectors.

brazuelo NM (*Zool*) shoulder.

brea NF tar, pitch.

break [brek] NM break dancing.

brear [1a] VT (a) (*maltratar*) to abuse, ill-treat; **~ a uno a golpes** to beat sb up. (b) (*embromar*) to make fun of, tease.

brebaje NM (*Farm*) potion, mixture; (*hum*) nasty drink, brew, concoction.

brecha NF (*Mil*) breach; gap, opening; (*de tiempo*) gap; (*fig*) breach, gap; (*Med*) gash, wound; **abrir ~ en una muralla** to breach a wall; **batir en ~** (*Mil*) to breach, (*fig*) get the better of; **estar en la ~** to be in the thick of things; **hacer ~ en** (*fig*) to make an impression on; **seguir en la ~** to go on with one's work, keep at it, not give in.

brecina NF (*Bot*) heath.

breck NM (*Cono Sur*) = **breque** (b).

brécol NM, **brécoles** NMPL broccoli.

brega NF (a) (*lucha*) struggle; **andar a la ~** to slog away, toil hard.
(b) (*riña*) quarrel, scrap*, row.
(c) (*broma*) trick, practical joke; **dar ~ a** to play a trick on.

bregar [1h] VI (a) (*luchar*) to struggle, fight (*con* against, with; *t fig*).
(b) (*reñir*) to quarrel, scrap*.
(c) (*trabajar*) to slog away, toil hard; **tendremos que hacerlo bregando** we shall have to do it by sheer hard work.

breguetear [1a] VI (*And*) to argue.

breje: NM: **¿cuántos ~s tienes?** (*Esp*) how old are you?

brejetero ADJ (*Carib*) trouble-making, mischief-making.

breke NM (*CAm Aut*) brake.

bren NM bran.

breña NF, **breñal** NM scrub, rough ground; bramble patch.

breñoso ADJ rough, scrubby; brambly.

breque NM (a) (*LAm Hist*) break (*vehicle*). (b) (*And, Cono Sur Ferro*) luggage van, baggage car (*US*). (c) (*LAm Mec*) brake.

brequear [1a] VTI (*LAm*) to brake.

brequero NM (*And, CAm, Méx*) brakeman.

Bretaña NF Brittany.

brete NM (a) (*grilletes*) fetters, shackles.
(b) (*fig: apuro*) tight spot, jam*; predicament; **estar en un ~** to be in a jam*; **poner a uno en un ~** to put sb on the spot.
(c) (*Carib*) screw*, lay*.

breteles NMPL (*LAm*) straps.

bretón, -ona [1] ADJ, NM/F Breton.
[2] NM (*Ling*) Breton.

bretones NMPL Brussels sprouts.

breva NF (a) (*Bot*) early fig, (black) fig.
(b) (*puro*) flat cigar; (*Carib, Cono Sur: de calidad*) good-quality cigar; (*LAm: tabaco*) chewing tobacco.
(c) **¡no caerá esa ~!** (*Esp*) no such luck!; **pelar la ~** (*Cono Sur*) to steal; **poner a uno como una ~** to beat sb black and blue.
(d) (*: puesto*) plum, plum job; (*gaje*) perk*; **es una ~** it's a cinch*, it's a pushover*; **para él es una ~** it's chickenfeed to him*.

breve [1] ADJ short, brief; (*en estilo*) terse, concise; **en ~** shortly, before long, very soon; concisely.
[2] NM (a) (*Ecl*) papal brief. (b) (*Prensa*) short news item.
[3] NF (*Mús*) breve.

brevedad NF shortness, brevity; terseness, conciseness; **con** (o a) **la mayor ~** as soon as possible, at one's earliest convenience; with all possible speed; **bueno, para mayor ~ ...** well, to be brief ...; **llamado por ~** called for short.

brevemente ADV briefly, concisely.

brevería NF (*Tip*) note, short news item; snippet; **'Breverías'** (*sección de periódico*) 'News in Brief'.

brevete NM note, memorandum; (*LAm Aut*) driving licence, driver's license (*US*).

breviario NM (*Ecl*) breviary; compendium, brief treatise; (*fig*) regular reading, daily reading.

brezal NM moor, moorland, heath.

brezar [1f] VT to rock, lull (in a cradle).

brezo NM (*Bot*) heather; (*de pipa*) briar.

briaga NF (*Méx*) drunkenness.

briago ADJ (*Méx*) drunk.

briba NF vagabond's life, idle life; **andar** (o **vivir**) **a la ~** to loaf around, be on the bum (*US*).

bribón [1] ADJ (a) (*vago*) idle; lazy.
(b) (*criminal*) dishonest, rascally.
[2] NM, **bribona** NF (a) (*vagabundo*) vagabond, vagrant; loafer.
(b) (*granuja*) rascal, rogue.

bribonada NF dirty trick, piece of mischief.

bribonear [1a] VI (a) (*gandulear*) to idle, loaf around. (b) (*ser granuja*) to be a rogue, play dirty tricks.

bribonería NF (a) (*briba*) vagabond's life, idle life. (b) (*picardía*) roguery.

bribonesco ADJ rascally, knavish.

bricbarca NF large sailing ship.

bricolador(a) NM/F = **bricolagista**.

bricolage NM do-it-yourself (work).

bricolagista NMF do-it-yourself expert.

bricolaje NM = **bricolage**.

bricolero, -a NM/F, **bricolajista** NMF = **bricolagista**.

brida NF (a) (*freno*) bridle; rein; **ir a toda ~** to go at top speed; **tener a uno a ~ corta** to keep sb on a tight rein, keep sb under strict control.
(b) (*Téc*) clamp; flange; collar; (*Ferro*) fishplate; (*Med*) adhesion.

bridge [briʒ, britʃ] NM (*Cartas*) bridge.

bridgista [bri'ʒista] NMF bridge player.

bridgístico [bri'ʒistiko] ADJ bridge (*atr*); **el mundo ~** the bridge world.

bridón NM snaffle; (*Mil*) bridoon.

briega NF (*pelea*) fight, brawl; (*trabajo duro*) slog.

brigada [1] NF (a) (*Mil*) brigade.
(b) (*de obreros etc*) squad, gang.
(c) (*de policía etc*) squad; **~ antidisturbios** riot squad; **~ antidrogas, ~ de estupefacientes** drug squad; **~ de bombas** bomb-disposal unit; **~ de delitos monetarios** fraud squad; **~ fluvial** river police; **B~s Internacionales** International Brigade; **~ móvil** flying squad; **~ sanitaria** sanitation department.
[2] NM (*Mil: aprox*) staff-sergeant, sergeant-major; warrant officer.

brigadier NM brigadier(-general).

brigadilla NF squad, detachment.

brigadista NM: **~ internacional** member of the International Brigade.

brigán NM (*CAm, Carib Hist*) brigand, bandit.

brigandaje NM (*Carib Hist*) brigandage, banditry.

brigantino [1] ADJ of Corunna.
[2] NM, **brigantina** NF native (o inhabitant) of Corunna; **los ~s** the people of Corunna.

Brígida NF Bridget.

Briján: saber más que ~ to be very smart, know the lot.

brik NM carton.

brillante [1] ADJ (a) (*gen*) brilliant, bright, shining; *joya* bright, sparkling; *escena* brilliant, glittering, splendid; *superficie* shining; glossy; *conversación, ingenio* sparkling, scintillating; *compañía* brilliant.
(b) (*fig*) brilliant.
[2] NM brilliant, diamond.

brillantemente ADV (a) (*gen*) brilliantly; brightly. (b) (*fig*) brilliantly.

brillantez NF (a) (*color etc*) brilliance, brightness; splendour. (b) (*fig*) brilliance.

brillantina NF brilliantine, hair cream.

brillar [1a] VI (a) (*gen*) to shine; to sparkle, glitter, gleam, glisten.
(b) (*fig: al sonreír*) to beam; (*de alegría etc*) to glow, light up.
(c) (*fig: en estudios etc*) to shine; to be outstanding; **~ por su ausencia** to be conspicuous by one's absence.

brillazón NF (*Cono Sur*) mirage.

brillo NM (a) (*resplandor*) brilliance; brightness, shine; sparkle, glitter; glow; (*de superficie*) lustre, sheen, gloss; radiance; **sacar ~ a** to polish, shine.
(b) (*fig: esplendor*) splendour, lustre, brilliance.
(c) **~ de labios** lip gloss.

brilloso ADJ (*And, Carib, Cono Sur*) = **brillante** 1(a).

brin NM fine canvas, duck.

brincar [1g] [1] VT (a) *niño* to jump up and down, bounce, dandle.
(b) *pasaje* (*en lectura*) to skip, miss out.
[2] VI (a) (*saltar*) to skip, hop, jump, leap about; (*cordero etc*) to skip

about, gambol; (*rebotar*) to bounce.

(b) (*fig*: *t ~* **de cólera**) to fly into a rage, flare up; **está que brinca** he's hopping mad.

3 brincarse VR: **~ uno** (*And*:) to bump sb off:.

brinco NM hop, jump, leap, skip; bounce; **a ~s** by fits and starts; **de un ~** at one bound; **de un ~** (*LAm*), **en un ~** on the spot, right away; **dar ~s** to hop, jump *etc*; **pegar un ~** to jump, give a start; **quitar los ~s a uno** to take sb down a peg; **¿para qué son tantos ~s estando el suelo parejo?** (*: CAm, Méx*) what's all the fuss about?

brindar [1a] **1** VT **(a)** (*gen*) to offer, present, afford; **~ a uno con algo** to offer sth to sb; **voy a ~te un güisqui** let me stand you a whisky, have a whisky on me; **le brinda la ocasión** it offers (*o* affords) him the opportunity; **los árboles brindaban sombra** the trees afforded shade.

(b) (*Taur*) to dedicate (*a* to).

(c) **~ a uno a hacer algo** to invite sb to do sth.

2 VI: **~ a**, **~ por** to drink to, drink a toast to, toast; **¡brindemos por la unidad!** here's to unity!, let's drink to unity!

3 brindarse VR: **~ a** + *infin* to offer to + *infin*.

brindis NM INVAR **(a)** toast; (*Taur*) (ceremony of) dedication. **(b)** (*And, Carib*) official reception; cocktail party.

brío NM (*t ~s*: *ánimo*) spirit, dash, verve; (*resolución*) determination, resolution; (*elegancia*) elegance; (*alegría*) jauntiness; **es hombre de ~s** he's a man of spirit, he's a man of mettle; **cortar los ~s a uno** to clip sb's wings.

briosamente ADV with spirit, dashingly, with verve; resolutely; elegantly; jauntily.

brioso ADJ spirited, dashing, full of verve; determined, resolute; elegant; jaunty.

briqueta NF briquette.

brisa NF breeze.

brisca NF Spanish card game.

brisera NF (*LAm*), **brisero** NM (*LAm*) windshield (*for a lamp etc*).

brisita NF: **tener** (*o* **pasar**) **una ~** to be hungry, have an empty stomach.

británico 1 ADJ British.

2 NM, **británica** NF British person, Briton, Britisher (*US*); **los ~s** the British.

britano 1 ADJ (*esp Hist*) British.

2 NM, **britana** NF (*en estilo formal, Hist y Poét etc*) Briton.

brizna NF **(a)** (*hebra*) strand, thread, filament; (*de hierba*) blade, wisp; (*de judía*) string.

(b) (*trozo*) chip, piece, fragment; scrap; **no me queda ni una ~** I haven't a scrap left.

(c) (*Carib*) llovizna) drizzle.

briznar [1a] VI (*Carib*) to drizzle.

broca NF **(a)** (*Cos*) reel, bobbin. **(b)** (*Mec*) drill, bit. **(c)** (*de zapato*) tack.

brocado NM brocade.

brocal NM rim, mouth; (*de pozo*) curb, parapet; (*Méx*) kerb.

brocha 1 NF **(a)** (*pincel grande*) brush, large paintbrush; **~ de afeitar** shaving brush; **de ~ gorda** crudely painted, (*fig*) slapdash, crude, badly done.

(b) (*Cono Sur*) skewer, spit.

(c) (*: CAm: zalamero*) creep:.

2 ADJ (*: CAm*) meddling; creeping:, servile; **hacerse ~** (*CAm*) to play the fool.

brochada NF, **brochazo** NM brush-stroke.

broche NM clip, clasp, fastener; brooch; (*de libro*) clasp, hasp; (*LAm*) cufflink; (*And, Carib, Cono Sur*: **sujetapapeles**) paper clip; **~ (para la ropa)** (*Cono Sur*) clothes peg; **el ~ final, el ~ de oro** (*fig*) the finishing touch.

brocheta NF skewer.

brochón 1 NM whitewash brush.

2 ADJ (*Carib*) flattering.

bróculi NM, **broculí** NM broccoli.

bróder* NM (*CAm*) lad, fellow*.

broker NM (*Cono Sur Fin*) broker.

brollero ADJ (*Carib*) trouble-making, mischief-making.

broma NF **(a)** (*gen*) fun, gaiety, merriment; **tomar algo a ~** to take sth as a joke; **estar de ~** to be in a joking mood; to be joking, not be serious; **en ~** in fun, as a joke; **ni en ~** never, not on any account; **lo decía en ~** I was only joking, I said it as a joke.

(b) (*una ~*) joke; hoax, leg-pull*, prank; **~ estudiantil** student rag; **~ pesada** practical joke, hoax; (*pey*) poor sort of joke, unfunny joke; **pero ~s aparte ...** but joking apart ...; **entre ~s y veras** half-joking(ly); **no es ninguna ~** this is serious; **fue una ~ nada más** it was just a joke; **¡déjate de ~s!** quit fooling!, joke over!; **no está para ~s** he's in no mood for jokes; **¡para ~s estoy!** (*iró*) a fine time for joking!; **gastar una ~ a uno** to play a joke on sb; **la ~ me costó caro** the affair cost me dear; **no hay ~s con la autoridad** you can't play games with the authorities.

(c) (*Carib, Cono Sur*) (*decepción*) disappointment; (*molestia*) vexation,

annoyance.

(d) (*Zool*) shipworm.

bromato NM bromate.

bromazo NM unpleasant joke, stupid practical joke.

bromear [1a] VI, **bromearse** VR to joke, crack jokes*, rag; **se estaban bromeando** they were ragging each other, they were pulling each other's legs; **creía que bromeaba** I thought he was joking.

bromista 1 ADJ fond of joking, full of fun; **es muy ~** he's full of jokes, he's a great one for jokes.

2 NMF joker, wag; practical joker, leg-puller*; **lo ha hecho algún ~** some joker did this.

bromuro NM bromide.

bronca 1 NF **(a)** (*follón etc*) row, scrap*, set-to*; **armar una ~** to kick up a row; make a great fuss; **se armó una tremenda ~** there was an almighty row*; **dar una ~ a** (*Taur, Teat etc*) to hiss, boo, barrack.

(b) (*reprimenda*) ticking-off*; **nos echó una ~ fenomenal*** he gave us a terrific ticking-off*, he came down on us like a ton of bricks*.

(c) (*Cono Sur*) anger, fury; **me da ~** it makes me mad*.

2 ADJ INVAR (*) boring, tedious.

broncamente ADV roughly, harshly; rudely.

broncata: NF = **bronca 1 (b)**.

bronce NM **(a)** (*gen*) bronze; **el ~** (*Mús*) the brass; **~ de campana** bell metal; **~ de cañón** gunmetal; **~ dorado** ormolu; **ligar ~** (*Esp**) to get a suntan; **ser de ~** (*fig*) to be inflexible, be deaf to appeals.

(b) (*Arte*) bronze (statue).

(c) (*moneda*) copper coin.

(d) (*LAm*) bell.

bronceado 1 ADJ **(a)** (*gen*) bronze, bronze-coloured.

(b) *piel, persona* tanned, sunburnt.

2 NM **(a)** (*Téc*) bronzing, bronze finish.

(b) (*de piel*) tan, suntan.

bronceador NM suntan lotion.

broncear [1a] **1** VT **(a)** (*Téc*) to bronze. **(b)** *piel* to tan, bronze, brown.

2 broncearse VR to brown, get a suntan.

broncería NF (*Cono Sur*) ironmonger's (shop), ironmongery.

bronco ADJ **(a)** *superficie* rough, coarse, unpolished.

(b) *metal* brittle.

(c) *voz* gruff, rough, harsh; (*Mús*) rough, rasping, harsh; *actitud, porte* gruff, rude; surly.

(d) *caballo* wild, untamed.

broncodilatador NM bronchodilator.

bronconeumonía NF bronchopneumonia.

broncopulmonar ADJ broncho-pulmonary.

bronquedad NF **(a)** (*tosquedad*) roughness, coarseness. **(b)** (*delicadez*) brittleness. **(c)** (*de voz*) gruffness, harshness; roughness.

bronquial ADJ bronchial.

bronquina* NF = **bronca 1(a).**

bronquinoso* ADJ (*Carib*) quarrelsome, brawling.

bronquios NMPL bronchial tubes.

bronquítico 1 ADJ bronchitic.

2 NM, **bronquítica** NF bronchitis sufferer.

bronquitis NF bronchitis.

broquel NM shield (*t fig*), buckler.

broquelarse [1a] VR to shield o.s.

broquero NM (*Méx*) brace.

broqueta NF skewer.

brota NF bud, shoot.

brotar [1a] **1** VT (*tierra*) to bring forth; (*planta*) to sprout, put out; (*fig*) to sprout; to pour out.

2 VI **(a)** (*Bot*) to sprout, bud, shoot.

(b) (*agua*) to spring up, gush forth, flow; (*lágrimas*) to well up, start to flow; (*río*) to rise.

(c) (*Med*) to break out, appear, show.

(d) (*aparecer*) to appear, spring up; **han brotado las manifestaciones** demonstrations have occurred; there have been outbreaks of rioting; **como princesa brotada de un cuento de hadas** like a princess out of a fairy tale.

brote NM **(a)** (*Bot*) bud, shoot; **~s de soja** bean shoots.

(b) (*Med*: *aparición*) outbreak, appearance; (*erupción cutánea*) rash, pimples; **un ~ de sarampión** an outbreak of measles.

(c) (*fig*: *ola*) outbreak, rash; **un ~ huelguístico** an outbreak (*o* rash, wave) of strikes.

(d) (*fig*: *origen*) origin; (*comienzo*) earliest beginnings, first manifestation.

broza NF **(a)** (*hojas etc*) dead leaves, dead wood; chaff; brushwood. **(b)** (*fig*: *en discurso etc*) padding. **(c)** (*Tip*) printer's brush.

brucelosis NF brucellosis.

bruces: caer de ~ to fall headlong, fall flat; **estar de ~** to lie face downwards, lie flat on one's stomach.

bruja 1 NF **(a)** (*hechicera*) witch; sorceress.

(b) (*: arpía*) hag, old witch, shrew; (*Méx*) woman.

(c) (*Carib, Cono Sur*) (*fantasma*) spook*, ghost; (*puta*) whore.

2 ADJ: **estar ~:** (*Carib, Méx*) to be broke*, be flat* (*US*); **ando bien ~:** I'm skint:.

Brujas NF Bruges.

brujear [1a] **1** VT (*Carib: t fig*) to stalk, pursue.
2 VI (a) (*gen*) to practise witchcraft. (b) (*Carib, Méx: ir de juerga*) to go on a spree.

brujería NF (a) (*hechizo*) witchcraft, sorcery, (black) magic. (b) (*Carib: pobreza*) poverty.

brujeril ADJ witch-like.

brujo NM sorcerer; wizard, magician; (*LAm*) medicine man; (*Méx**) doctor.

brújula NF (a) (*compás*) compass; magnetic needle; **~ de bolsillo** pocket compass; **perder la ~** to lose one's bearings, (*fig*) lose one's touch.
(b) (*fig: mira*) guide, norm.

brujulear [1a] **1** VT (a) *cartas* to uncover (gradually); (*: adivinar*) to guess.
(b) (*tratar de conseguir*) to intrigue for, try to wangle.
2 VI (*) (a) to manage, get along, keep going.
(b) (*And, Carib*) to go on the booze*, go on a bender:.

brulote NM (*And, Cono Sur: comentario*) obscene remark (*o comment*); (*Cono Sur: escrito*) obscene letter.

bruma NF mist, fog; **~ del alba** morning mist.

brumoso ADJ misty, foggy.

bruno ADJ dark brown.

bruñido **1** ADJ polished, burnished.
2 NM (a) (*acto*) polish, polishing; **~ de zapato** shoeshine. (b) (*brillo*) polish, shine, gloss.

bruñidor NM, **bruñidora** NF polisher, burnisher.

bruñir [3h] **1** VT (a) (*sacar brillo a*) to polish, burnish, shine.
(b) (*maquillar*) to make up (with cosmetics).
(c) (*CAm: molestar*) to harass, pester.
2 **bruñirse** VR to make (o.s.) up.

bruscamente ADV (a) (*gen*) suddenly, brusquely, sharply. (b) (*rudamente*) sharply, abruptly.

brusco¹ ADJ (a) *ataque etc* sudden; *movimiento* sudden, brusque; *curva* sharp; *bajada (de temperatura etc)* sharp, sudden; *cambio* sudden, marked, violent.
(b) *actitud, porte* brusque, sharp, abrupt; rude.

brusco² NM (*Bot*) butcher's broom.

Bruselas NF Brussels.

bruselas NFPL tweezers; **unas ~** a pair of tweezers.

bruselense **1** ADJ of (*o* from) Brussels.
2 NMF native (*o* inhabitant) of Brussels.

brusquedad NF (a) (*gen*) suddenness; sharpness. (b) (*actitud*) brusqueness, sharpness, abruptness; rudeness; **hablar con ~** to speak sharply.

brutal **1** ADJ (a) (*bruto*) brutal; brutish, beastly. (b) (*: estupendo*) terrific*, tremendous*; **¡~!** (*LAm*) great!*, brilliant!* (c) (*CAm: asombroso*) incredible, extraordinary.
2 NM brute, animal.

brutalidad NF (a) (*cualidad*) brutality; brutishness, beastliness.
(b) (*una ~*) brutal act, piece of brutality, crime.
(c) (*estupidez*) stupidity.
(d) **me gusta una ~*** I like it tremendously*.

brutalizar [1f] **1** VT to brutalize, treat brutally; *mujer* to rape.
2 **brutalizarse** VR to become brutalized.

brutalmente ADV brutally.

bruteza NF (a) (*gen*) brutality. (b) (*tosquedad*) coarseness, roughness.

Bruto NM Brutus.

bruto **1** ADJ (a) (*brutal*) brute, brutish; bestial.
(b) (*estúpido*) stupid, ignorant; (*inculto*) coarse, rough, uncouth; **más ~ que un adoquín** as dumb as an ox; **Pepe es muy ~** Joe is pretty rough, Joe is terribly uncouth; **¡no seas ~!** don't be an idiot!
(c) *diamante etc* (*t en ~*) uncut, rough, unpolished; **en ~** rough, raw, unworked; in a rough state; **hierro (en) ~** crude iron, pig iron; **a la bruta** (*LAm*), **a lo ~** (*LAm*) roughly, crudely.
(d) **pegar a uno en ~** (*Carib*) to beat sb mercilessly.
(e) (*medidas*) gross; **peso ~** gross weight; **producto ~** gross product.
(f) (*Cono Sur: mala calidad*) poor-quality, inferior.
(g) **estar ~:** to be randy*, **ponerse ~** to get randy*.
2 NM (a) (*animal*) brute, beast; **¡~!** you beast! (*hum*).
(b) (*idiota*) idiot.

bruza NF coarse brush, scrubbing brush; horse brush; (*Tip*) printer's brush.

Bs.As. ABR *de* **Buenos Aires** Buenos Aires, B.A.

Bta, Bto ADJ (*Rel*) ABR *de* **Beata, Beato** Beatus, Blessed, B.

bu NM bogeyman; **hacer el ~ a uno** to scare sb.

búa NF pimple.

buba NF, **bubón** NM tumour, bubo.

bubónico ADJ: **peste bubónica** bubonic plague.

bubute NM (*Carib*) beetle.

bucal ADJ oral, of the mouth; **por vía ~** through the mouth, by mouth, orally.

bucanero NM buccaneer.

bucarán NM buckram.

búcaro NM (a) (*arcilla*) (fragrant) clay. (b) (*jarrón*) vase.

buccino NM whelk.

buceador(a) NM/F diver; underwater swimmer, skindiver.

bucear [1a] VI (a) (*gen*) to dive; to swim under water; to skin-dive; (*trabajar como buzo*) to work as a diver. (b) (*fig: explorar*) to delve, explore, look below the surface.

buceo NM diving; underwater swimming, skindiving; **~ de saturación** saturation diving.

buchaca NF (*CAm, Carib, Méx*) (*bolso*) bag; (*de caballo*) saddlebag; (*Billar*) (billiard) pocket.

buchada NF mouthful (of liquid).

buchante: NM shot.

buche NM (a) (*Orn*) crop; (*Zool*) maw; (*) guts, belly; **llenar el ~*** to fill one's belly.
(b) (*fig: pensamientos*) inner thoughts; bosom; **sacar el ~*** to show off; **sacar el ~ a uno*** to make sb talk.
(c) (*buchada*) mouthful (of liquid); (*And*) shot, slug* (*US*) (of drink).
(d) (*Cos*) bag; wrinkle, pucker; **hacer ~** to be baggy, wrinkle up.
(e) (*And: chistera*) top hat.
(f) (*LAm Med*) (*bocio*) goitre, thyroid; (*paperas*) mumps.
(g) (*Carib: tonto*) fool, idiot.

buché NM (*CAm*) rustic, peasant.

buchinche NM (*Carib*) (*casa*) hovel; (*tienda*) pokey little shop.

bucle NM (a) (*pelo*) curl, ringlet. (b) (*fig*) curve, bend, loop; (*Inform*) loop; **~s anidados** nested loops.

bucodental ADJ *salud, higiene* oral; *tratamiento, clínica* dental.

bucólica NF (a) (*Liter*) pastoral poem, bucolic. (b) (*) meal.

bucólico ADJ pastoral, bucolic.

Buda NM Buddha.

budín NM (*LAm*) (*pastel*) cake; (*postre*) trifle; **~ de pescado** fish pie; **esa chica es un ~** that girl's a smasher:.

budismo NM Buddhism.

budista ADJ, NMF Buddhist.

budleia NF buddleia.

buen ADJ V **bueno**.

buenamente ADV (a) (*fácilmente*) easily, freely, without difficulty. (b) (*voluntariamente*) willingly; voluntarily.

buenamoza NF (*And euf*) jaundice.

buenaventura NF (a) (*suerte*) good luck. (b) (*adivinación*) fortune; **decir** (*o* **echar**) **la ~ a uno** to tell sb's fortune.

buenazo **1** ADJ kindly, good-natured; long-suffering.
2 NM good-natured person; **ser un ~** to be (*too*) kind-hearted, be easily imposed upon; **el ~ de Marcos** good old Marcos.

buenmozo ADJ (*Cono Sur*) good-looking, handsome.

bueno **1** ADJ (**buen** *delante de nm sing*) (a) (*gen*) good; *tiempo* fine, good, fair; *constitución* strong, sound; *doctrina* right, sound; *sociedad* good, polite; **el ~** (*Cine etc*) the goody, the good guy; **sé ~** be good; **la buena gente, los ~s** good people, decent people; **la buena*** the right hand; **el ~ de Manolo** good old Manolo; **lo ~ es que ...** the best thing about it is that ..., the best part is that ...; **the funny thing is that ...; ~ fuera que ...** it would be fine if ...; **¡~ está!** that's enough!, that'll do!; **luego verás lo que es ~*** I'll get you!; **hacer ~ un refrán** to corroborate a proverb, give meaning to a proverb; **hacer algo a la buena de Dios** to do sth in a hit-or-miss way, do sth haphazardly; **tan ~ como el pan** as good as gold.
(b) (*amable*) kind, good, nice; **fue muy ~ conmigo** he was very nice to me; **es Vd muy ~** you are very kind.
(c) (*apropiado*) fit, proper, suitable; **en el momento ~** at the right moment, at the proper time; **por buen camino** along the right road (*y V* **camino**); **ser ~ para** to be suitable for, be good for; **~ de comer** good to eat, nice to eat; fit to eat.
(d) (*Med*) **estar ~** to be well; **no estar ~ de la cabeza** to be weak in the head.
(e) (*iró*) fine, pretty; **¡buen conductor!** a fine driver you are!; **¡ésa sí que es buena!** that's a good one!; **¡estaría ~!** a fine thing!; I should jolly well say not!*; **estaría ~ que ...** a fine thing it would be if ...; **le dio un tortazo de los ~s** he gave him a real bash*, he really did bash him*; **le di un buen susto** I gave him a good fright.
(f) (*: atractivo*) attractive; **está buena** she's hot stuff*, she's quite a girl; **¡estaba buenísima!** she looked a real treat!*, she looked great!*; *V* **mozo**.
(g) **¿adónde ~?** where are you off to?; **¿de dónde ~?** where did you spring from?; **¡cuánto ~ por aquí!** what a nice surprise to see you!
(h) (*locuciones con buenas*) **¡buenas!** hullo!; **de buenas a primeras** straight away, from the very start; suddenly, without warning; **decir una noticia a uno de buenas a primeras** to spring a piece of news on sb; **estar de buenas** to be in a good mood; to be in luck; **por las**

buenas (*de buena gana*) gladly, willingly; (*por capricho*) just because he (*etc*) felt like it, quite arbitrarily; **por las buenas o por las malas** willy-nilly; by hook or by crook, by fair means or foul; **resolver algo por las buenas** to come to an amicable agreement about sth. **(i)** (*And, Cono Sur*) **estar en la buena** (*de buen humor*) to be in a good mood; (*tener suerte*) to be in luck. ❷ ADV, *como* INTERJ *etc*: ¡~! right!, all right!, O.K.!*; (*iró*) come off it!*, so you say!; ¿~? (*Méx Telec*) hullo?; ~, **resulta que** ... well, it happens that ...; ~, **¿y qué?** well, so what?; **pero ¡~!** well, I like that!; ~, **pues** ... well ...

buenón* ADJ nice-looking, good-looking.

buey NM **(a)** (*Zool*) ox; bullock, steer; ~ **almizclado** musk ox; ~ **corneta** (*And, Cono Sur*) one-horned ox; ~ **de Francia** crab; ~ **marino** manatee, sea-cow. **(b)** (*LAm fig: cornudo*) cuckold. **(c)** (*Carib fig: dineral*) big sum of money. **(d)** (*fig: locuciones*) ~ **corneta** (*And, Cono Sur: entrometido*) busybody, noseyparker*; **nunca falta un** ~ **corneta** (*And, Cono Sur*) there's always someone who can't keep his mouth shut; ~ **muerto** (*Carib*) bargain; ~ **suelto** free agent; (*soltero*) bachelor; **chinches** (*etc*) **como** ~**es** enormous bedbugs (*etc*), bedbugs (*etc*) the size of buffaloes; **es un** ~ **para el trabajo** he's a tremendous worker; **hablar de** ~**es perdidos** (*Cono Sur*) to waste one's breath; **pegar** ~**es** (*CAm*) to go to sleep; **poner los** ~**es antes que el carro** to put the cart before the horse; **saber con los** ~**es que ara** (*Carib, Cono Sur*) to know who your friends are; **sacar el** ~ **de la barranca** (*Carib, Méx*) (*tener éxito*) to bring sth off; (*salvarse*) to get out of a hole; **cuando vuelen los** ~**es** when pigs learn to fly.

bueyada NF (*LAm*) drove of oxen.

bufa* ❶ ADJ (*Carib, Méx*) tight*, drunk. ❷ NF **(a)** (*broma*) joke, piece of clowning. **(b)** (*Carib, Méx: embriaguez*) drunkenness.

búfalo ❶ NM buffalo. ❷ ADJ (*Carib**) great*, fantastic*.

bufanda NF **(a)** (*prenda de vestir*) scarf, muffler. **(b)** (:) (*soborno*) sweetener*, back-hander*; (*gaje*) perk*.

bufar [1a] VI **(a)** to snort; (*gato*) to spit; ~ **de ira** to snort with rage. **(b)** (*Méx*) to reek, stink.

bufarrón* NM (*Cono Sur*) pederast, child molester.

bufé NM = **bufet**.

bufeo NM (*CAm, Carib, Méx*) (*atún*) tunny; (*delfín*) dolphin.

bufet [bu'fe] NM, PL **bufets** [bu'fe] **(a)** (*mueble*) sideboard. **(b)** (*cena*) buffet supper, cold supper. **(c)** (*comedor*) dining-room (of an hotel); (*restorán*) restaurant.

bufete NM **(a)** (*mesa*) desk. **(b)** (*Jur*) lawyer's office; lawyer's clients, lawyer's practice; **abrir** ~, **establecer su** ~ to set up in legal practice. **(c)** (*Culin*) = **bufet (b)**.

bufido NM snort (*t fig*).

bufo¹ ❶ ADJ comic, farcical; slapstick, knockabout; **ópera** comic. ❷ NM **(a)** (*payaso*) clown, funny man; (*Mús*) buffo. **(b)** (*Cono Sur*) queer:.

bufo² ADJ (*Carib*) spongy.

bufón ❶ ADJ funny, comical; clownish. ❷ NM funny man, buffoon, clown; (*Hist*) jester.

bufonada NF **(a)** (*gen*) buffoonery, clowning. **(b)** (*una* ~) (*dicho*) joke, jest; (*hecho*) piece of buffoonery; (*Teat*) comic piece, farce.

bufonear [1a] VI, **bufonearse** VR to joke, jest; to clown, play the fool.

bufonesco ADJ funny, comical; clownish.

bufoso* NM (*Cono Sur*) gun, rod*.

buga¹: NM (*Aut*) car.

buga²: NM (*persona*) straight person:, heterosexual.

buganvilla NF bougainvillea.

bugle NM bugle.

bugui-bugui NM boogie-woogie.

buharda NF, **buhardilla** NF **(a)** (*ventana*) dormer window; skylight. **(b)** (*ático*) garret, loft.

búho NM **(a)** (*Orn*: t ~ **real**) eagle owl. **(b)** (*fig: persona*) unsociable person, recluse.

buhonería NF **(a)** (*acto*) peddling, hawking. **(b)** (*mercancías*) pedlar's wares, hawker's wares.

buhonero NM pedlar, peddler (*US*), hawker.

buido ADJ **(a)** (*puntiagudo*) sharp, pointed. **(b)** (*estriado*) fluted, grooved.

buitre ❶ NM **(a)** (*Orn*) vulture, (*esp*) Griffon vulture; ~ **alimoche** Egyptian vulture; ~ **leonado** Griffon vulture. **(b)** (*) go-getter*; sponger*, cadger*. ❷ ADJ (*) sponging*, cadging*.

buitrear [1a] ❶ VT **(a)** (*LAm: matar*) to kill. **(b)** (*And, Cono Sur*: *vomitar*) to throw up, vomit. ❷ VI (*And, Cono Sur*) to be sick, vomit.

buitrón NM fish trap.

buja NF (*Méx*) = **buje**.

bujarra: NM, **bujarrón:** NM queer:.

buje NM axle box, bushing.

bujería NF trinket, knick-knack.

bujero: NM hole.

bujía NF **(a)** (*vela*) candle; (*candelero*) candlestick. **(b)** (*Elec*) candlepower. **(c)** (*Aut etc*: t ~ **de encendido**) sparking plug. **(d)** (*CAm: bombilla*) light bulb.

bul: NM arse:.

bula NF (*papal*) bull; **no poder con la** ~* to have no strength left for anything; **no me vale la** ~ **de Meco** I'm done for.

bulbo NM (*Anat, Bot, Med*) bulb; (*Méx Rad*) valve, tube (*US*); (*Cono Sur Elec*) bulb.

bulboso ADJ bulbous.

buldog [bul'dog] NM, PL **buldogs** bulldog.

bule NM (*Méx*) (*Bot*) gourd; (*jarro*) water pitcher; **llenarse hasta los** ~**s** to stuff o.s.; **el que nace para** ~ **hasta jícara no para** you can't escape your destiny.

bulerías NFPL *Andalusian song accompanied with clapping and dancing.*

bulevar NM boulevard, avenue.

Bulgaria NF Bulgaria.

búlgaro, -a ❶ ADJ, NM/F Bulgarian. ❷ NM (*Ling*) Bulgarian.

bulimia NF bulimia.

bulín NM (*Cono Sur*) **(a)** (*de soltero*) bachelor flat (o pad). **(b)** (*especie de burdel*) room (used for sexual encounters).

bulla NF **(a)** (*follón*) noise, uproar; racket; (*bullicio*) bustle; (*confusión*) fuss, confusion; (*LAm: pelea*) quarrel, brawl, fight; (*Carib: discusión*) argument; **armar** ~, **meter** ~ to make a row (o racket); **meter algo a** ~ to throw sth into confusion; to obstruct sth. **(b)** (*turba*) crowd, mob. **(c)** **ser el hombre de la** ~ (*Carib*) to be the man of the moment.

bullabesa NF fish soup, bouillabaisse.

bullaje NM noisy crowd, mob.

bullanga NF disturbance, riot.

bullanguero ❶ ADJ riotous, rowdy. ❷ NM, **bullanguera** F noisy person; rioter, troublemaker.

bullaranga NF (*LAm*) (*follón*) noise, row; (*disturbio*) riot.

bullarengue: NM (woman's) bottom.

bulldog [bul'dog] NM, PL **bulldogs** bulldog.

bulldozer [bul'doθer] NM, PL **bulldozers** [bul'doθer] bulldozer.

bullebulle NMF busybody; mischief-maker; fusspot.

bullero ADJ (*LAm*) = **bullicioso**.

bullicio NM (*ruido*) uproar, din, racket, hubbub; (*actividad*) bustle, bustling movement, bustling activity; (*confusión*) confusion; (*disturbio*) disturbance, riot.

bulliciosamente ADV noisily; boisterously; busily; restlessly; riotously.

bullicioso ADJ noisy, rowdy; boisterous; busy, bustling, full of movement; active; restless; turbulent, riotous.

bullir [3h] ❶ VT to move, stir; **no bulló pie ni mano** he did not lift a finger. ❷ VI **(a)** (*líquido*) (*hervir*) to boil; (*agitarse*) to bubble, bubble up; **el agua bullía ligeramente** the water rippled slightly. **(b)** (*moverse*) to move, stir, budge; to move about; to bustle about; **no bullía** he didn't move, he never stirred. **(c)** (*insectos*) to swarm; to teem; ~ **de** (*fig*), ~ **en** to teem with, swarm with, seethe with; **bullía de indignación** he was seething with indignation; **la ciudad bullía de actividad** the town was humming with activity; **Londres está que bulle de juventud** London is bursting with young people. ❸ **bullirse** VR to move, stir, budge.

bulo NM hoax, false report, canard.

bulón NM bolt; spring pin.

bulto NM **(a)** (*tamaño, volumen*) size, bulk, bulkiness, volume, massiveness; (*fig*) substance, importance; **de** ~ obvious, striking; **error gross**; (*Méx: de sobra*) superfluous, excess; **de gran** ~ bulky; **de mucho** ~ heavy, sizeable, massive, (*fig*) important; **de poco** ~ small, that does not take up much room, (*fig*) unimportant; **argumentos de** ~ arguments of substance; **estar de** ~, **hacer** ~, **ir de** ~ to swell the number(s), make up the number(s); **hacer** ~ to take up space. **(b)** (*forma*) shape, form; vague shape, indistinct shape; **a** ~ roughly, broadly; in the mass; **estimación a** ~ rough estimate; **buscar el** ~ **a uno** to provoke (o push) sb; to be out for sb's blood; **calcular a** ~ to calculate roughly; **decir algo a** ~ to come right out with sth, blurt sth out; **ir al** ~, **tirar al** ~ to come straight to the point; **escurrir el** ~ to dodge, duck out of it, shy away, (*fig*) dodge the issue, pass the buck*; **menear el** ~ **a uno** to thrash sb. **(c)** (*paquete etc*) package, bundle; bale; bulky object; piece of luggage; (*CAm*) (*bolso*) briefcase, bag; (*de escolar*) satchel; ~**s de mano** hand luggage. **(d)** (*Med*) lump, swelling.

(e) (*estatua*) bust, statue.

(f) (*Mil*) squaddie*, recruit.

bululú NM (*Carib*) excitement, agitation.

bumerán NM boomerang.

bumerang [bume'ran] NM, PL **bumerangs** [bume'ran] boomerang.

bunga NF (*Carib*) lie.

bungalow ['boŋgalo, buŋga'lo] NM, PL **bungalows** ['boŋgalo, buŋga'lo] bungalow.

bungee ['banji] NM bungee jumping.

bungo NM (*CAm*) = **bongo**.

buniato NM = **boniato**.

bunjo NM: **hacer ~** (*Carib*) to hit the jackpot.

búnker ['buŋker] NM, PL **búnkers** ['buŋker] **(a)** (*Golf*) bunker. **(b)** (*Pol*) reactionary clique, reactionary core; entrenched interests.

búnquer NM = **búnker**.

buñolería NF bakery where *buñuelos* are made; shop where *buñuelos* are sold.

buñuelo NM **(a)** (*Culin: aprox*) doughnut, fritter. **(b)** (*: chapuza*) botched job, mess.

BUP [bup] NM (*Esp Escol*) ABR de **Bachillerato Unificado y Polivalente.**

> **BUP**
>
> ℹ️ *In the Spanish educational system **BUP** was a three-year course taken by 14- to 17-year-olds which consisted of obligatory core subjects until year 3, when students could choose between a number of Arts and Science options. After **BUP** those wishing to go to university would go on to do the **Curso de Orientación Universitaria** (**COU**). Now schoolchildren start **ESO** (Educación Secundaria Obligatoria) at 12 and can move onto **Bachillerato** at 16.*
>
> ⇨ *See also* COU
---

buque NM **(a)** (*gen*) ship, vessel, boat; **~ de abastecimiento** supply ship; **~ almirante** flagship; **~ de carga**, **~ carguero** freighter; **~ cisterna** tanker; water-boat; **~ correo** mailboat; **~ costero** coaster; **~ de desembarco** landing-craft; **~ escolta** escort vessel; **~ escuela** training ship; **~ espía** spy ship; **~ factoría** factory ship; **~ fanal**, **~ faro** lightship; **~ granelero** bulk-carrier; **~ de guerra** warship, (*Hist*) man-of-war; **~ hospital** hospital ship; **~ insignia** flagship; **~ de línea** liner, (*Hist*) ship of the line; **~ mercante** merchantman, merchant ship; **~ minador** minelayer; **~ nodriza** depot ship, mother-ship; **~ de pasajeros** passenger ship; **~ portacontenedores** container ship; **~ portatrén** train ferry; **~ de ruedas** paddle-steamer; **~ de vapor** steamer, steamship; **~ de vela**, **~ velero** sailing ship; **ir en ~** to go by ship, go by sea. **(b)** (*tonelaje*) capacity, tonnage. **(c)** (*casco*) hull.

buqué NM bouquet (*of wine*).

buraco NM (*Cono Sur*) hole.

burata NF (*Carib*) cash, dough*.

burbuja NF bubble; **hacer ~s** to bubble.

burbujeante ADJ bubbly, fizzy; bubbling.

burbujear [1a] VI to bubble; to form bubbles.

burbujeo NM bubbling.

burda NF door.

burdégano NM hinny.

burdel NM brothel.

Burdeos NM Bordeaux.

burdeos ① NM claret, Bordeaux (wine) (*t* **vino de ~**). ② ADJ maroon, dark red.

burdo ADJ coarse, rough; (*fig*) *excusa, mentira etc* clumsy.

burear [1a] (*And*) ① VT to con*, trick. ② VI to go out on the town*.

bureo NM **(a)** (*diversión*) entertainment, amusement; spree; **ir de ~** to have a good time, go on a spree. **(b)** (*: paseo*) stroll; **darse un ~** to go for a stroll.

bureta NF burette.

burgalés ① ADJ of Burgos. ② NM, **burgalesa** NF native (*o* inhabitant) of Burgos; **los burgaleses** the people of Burgos.

burgo NM hamlet.

burgués ① ADJ middle class, bourgeois (*t pey*); town (*atr*). ② NM, **burguesa** NF member of the middle class, bourgeois(e); townsman, townswoman.

burguesía NF middle class, bourgeoisie; **alta ~** upper middle class; **pequeña ~** lower middle class.

buril NM burin, engraver's chisel.

burilar [1a] VT to engrave; to chisel.

burla NF **(a)** (*mofa*) gibe, taunt, jeer; **~s** mockery, ridicule; **hacer ~ de** to make fun of, mock; **hace ~ de todo** he mocks everything. **(b)** (*broma*) joke; **~s** joking, fun; **de ~s** in fun; **~s aparte** joking aside; **~ burlando** unawares, without noticing it; on the quiet; **~s y veras** light-hearted and serious things; **entre ~s y veras** half-

jokingly; **gastar ~s con uno** to make fun of sb.

(c) (*broma pesada*) trick; hoax, practical joke; **fue una ~ cruel** it was a cruel sort of joke.

burladero NM **(a)** (*Aut*) traffic island, refuge; (*Taur*) refuge, shelter; (*Ferro etc*) recess, refuge (*in a tunnel*).

burlador ① ADJ mocking.
② NM **(a)** (*mofador*) scoffer, mocker. **(b)** (*bromista*) practical joker, hoaxer, leg-puller*. **(c)** (*seductor*) seducer, libertine.

burlar [1a] ① VT **(a)** (*engañar*) to deceive, take in, hoax, trick; *enemigo etc* to outwit, outmanoeuvre; *orden* to show no respect for; to get round, disregard; *bloqueo* to run; *vigilancia* to defeat.
(b) *ambición, plan etc* to frustrate; *esperanzas* to cheat, disappoint.
(c) *mujer* to seduce, deceive.
(d) (*: saber usar*) to know how to use, be able to handle; **ya burla la moto** she can handle the bike now*.
② VI **y burlarse** VR **(a)** (*bromear*) to joke, banter; (*mofarse*) to scoff; **yo no me burlo** I'm not joking, I'm in earnest.
(b) **~se de** to mock, ridicule, scoff at; to make fun of.

burlería NF **(a)** (*mofa*) mockery; (*bromas*) fun. **(b)** (*engaño*) trick, deceit; (*ilusión*) illusion. **(c)** (*cuento*) tall story, fairy tale.

burlesco ADJ **(a)** (*divertido*) funny, comic. **(b)** (*Liter etc*) mock, burlesque.

burlete NM weather strip, draught excluder.

burlisto ADJ (*Cono Sur, CAm, Méx*) = **burlón**.

burlón ① ADJ mocking; joking, teasing, bantering; *risa etc* mocking, sardonic; **dijo ~** he said banteringly.
② NM, **burlona** NF **(a)** (*bromista*) joker, wag, leg-puller.
(b) (*mofador*) mocker, scoffer.

buró NM **(a)** (*mueble*) bureau, (roll-top) desk. **(b)** (*Pol etc*) bureau. **(c)** (*Méx*) bedside table.

burocracia NF bureaucracy; officialdom.

burócrata NMF civil servant, administrative official, official of the public service; (*pey*) bureaucrat.

burocrático ADJ official; civil service (*atr*); (*pey*) bureaucratic.

burocratizar [1f] VT to bureaucratize.

buromática NF, **burótica** NF office automation, office computerization.

burra NF **(a)** (*Zool*) (she-)donkey. **(b)** (*fig*: *mujer*) stupid woman; (*t* **~ de carga**) hard-working woman, drudge, slave. **(c)** (*Esp*: *bicicleta*) bike.

burrada NF **(a)** (*burros*) drove of donkeys.
(b) (*: disparate*) silly thing, stupid act (*o saying etc*); **decir ~s** to talk nonsense, say silly things.
(c) **una ~ (de cosas)** a whole heap of things, heaps of things; **sabe una ~** he knows a hell of a lot.
(d) (*: como adv*) **me gusta una ~** I like it a lot.

burrajo ADJ (*Méx*) vulgar, rude.

burrear VT (*robar*) to rip off; (*engañar*) to con*.

burrero ① ADJ (*Cono Sur: hum*) horse-loving, racegoing.
② NM **(a)** (*Méx: arriero*) mule (*o* donkey) driver. **(b)** (*CAm: burros*) large herd of donkeys. **(c)** (*Carib: malhablado*) coarse (*o* foul-mouthed) individual. **(d)** (*Cono Sur: hum*) horse-lover.

burricie NF stupidity.

burro ① NM **(a)** (*Zool*) donkey; (*fig*) ass, idiot; (*Cono Sur: hum*) race-horse; (*caballo*) old horse, nag; (*perdedor en carrera*) also ran; (*CAm Naipes*) old maid; **~ de agua** (*Carib, Méx*) big wave; **~ de carga** (*fig*) glutton for work, hard worker, (*pey*) slave, drudge; **~ cargado de letras** pompous ass; **salto de ~** (*Méx: juego*) leapfrog; **apearse de su ~**, **bajar del ~** to back down, think better of it; **no apearse de su ~** to stick to one's guns, persist in one's error; **caer ~s aparejados** (*Carib*) to rain cats and dogs; **caerse del ~** to realize one's mistake; **poner a uno a caer de un ~** to beat sb black and blue; **esto comió ~** (*Cono Sur*) it got lost, it vanished; **no ver tres** (*etc*) **en un ~** to be as blind as a bat; **ver ~s negros** (*Cono Sur*) to see stars.
(b) (*Téc*) sawhorse.
(c) (*LAm: escalera*) step ladder.
(d) (*And, Carib: columpio*) swing.
② ADJ **(a)** (*estúpido*) stupid; **el muy ~** the great oaf.
(b) (*: cachondo*) **estar ~** to feel randy*; **poner ~ a uno** to make sb feel randy*.

burrumazo NM (*Carib*) blow, thump.

bursátil ADJ stock-exchange (*atr*), stock-market (*atr*); **crisis ~** crisis on the stock exchange; **desplome ~** stock exchange crash.

bursitis NF bursitis.

burujaca NF (*LAm*) saddlebag.

burujo NM = **borujo**.

burundanga NF (*Carib*) **(a)** (*objeto*) worthless object; piece of junk; **de ~** worthless; **es ~** it's just a piece of junk. **(b)** (*lío*) mess, mix-up.

burusca NF (*CAm*) kindling.

bus NM **(a)** bus; (*LAm: autocar*) coach (*Brit*), long-distance bus. **(b)** (*Inform*) bus; **~ de expansión** expansion bus; **~ de memoria** memory bus.

busa: NF: **tener ~** (*Esp*) to feel hungry.
busaca NF (*And, Carib*) saddlebag; (*Carib*) satchel.
busca [1] NF search, hunt (*de* for); pursuit; **en ~ de** in search of.
  [2] NM (*Telec*) bleeper, pager, paging device.
buscabulla NM (*Carib, Méx*) brawler, troublemaker.
buscabullas• ADJ INVAR (*Méx*) troublemaking.
buscada NF = **busca 1**.
buscador(a) NM/F searcher, seeker; **~ de oro** gold prospector.
buscaniguas NM INVAR (*And, CAm*) squib, cracker.
buscapersonas NM INVAR = **busca 2**.
buscapié NM hint; feeler.
buscapiés NM INVAR squib, cracker.
buscapleitos NMF INVAR (*LAm*) troublemaker.
buscar [1g] [1] VT **(a)** (*gen*) to look for, search for, seek; (*objeto perdido*) to hunt for, have a look for; *enemigo* to seek out; *camorra* to be asking for, look for; *beneficio, ganancia etc* to seek, be out for; **ir a ~** to go and look for; to bring, fetch; **ven a ~me a la oficina** come and find me at the office, come and pick me up at the office; **nadie nos buscará aquí** nobody will look for us here; **tengo que ~ la referencia** I have to look the reference up; **el terrorista más buscado** the most wanted terrorist.
  (b) (*LAm: pedir*) to ask for, call for.
  (c) (*Méx*) *riña etc* to provoke.
  [2] VI **(a)** (*gen*) to look, search, hunt; **buscó en el bolsillo** he felt in his pocket, he hunted in his pocket.
  (b) **~ + infin** to seek to + *infin*, try to + *infin*.
  [3] **buscarse** VR (*Esp*) **(a)** (*anuncio*) **'se busca coche'**, **'búscase coche'** 'car wanted'.
  (b) **~la**• (*arreglárselas*) to manage, get along; (*buscar camorra*) to be looking for trouble, ask for it; **se la buscó** he brought it on himself, it serves him right.
  (c) **~las**• to fend for o.s.
buscarruidos NM INVAR rowdy, troublemaker.
buscas• NFPL (*Carib, Méx, And*) perks•, profits on the side.
buscatesoros NMF INVAR treasure hunter, treasure seeker.
buscavidas NMF INVAR **(a)** (*entrometido*) snooper, meddler, busybody.
  (b) (*ambicioso*) hustler; (*pey*) social climber, go-getter.
buscón [1] ADJ **(a)** (*gen*) thieving, crooked. **(b)** (*Méx: diligente*) active, diligent.
  [2] NM petty thief, small-time crook; rogue.
buscona NF whore.

buseca NF (*Cono Sur*) thick stew.
buseta NF (*LAm*) small bus, microbus.
busilis• NM **(a)** (*pega*) difficulty, snag; **ahí está el ~** there's the snag, that's the rub.
  (b) (*esencia*) core (of the problem); **dar en el ~** to put one's finger on the spot.
búsqueda NF search; inquiry, investigation; (*Inform*) search.
busto NM bust; **~ parlante** talking head.
butaca NF armchair, easy chair; (*Teat*) stall; **~ ojerera** wing-chair; **~ de platea** (*Teat*) orchestra stall.
butacón NM large armchair.
butanero NM gas-bottle delivery man.
butano NM (*t* **gas ~**) butane, butane gas; **color ~** orange.
butaque NM (*LAm*) small armchair.
buten: de ~• terrific•, tremendous•.
butí• NF boutique.
butifarra NF **(a)** (*salchichón*) Catalan sausage; **hacer (la) ~ a uno**• ≃ to give sb the two-fingers sign, make an obscene gesture to sb.
  (b) (•: *media*) badly-fitting stocking.
  (c) (*And: emparedado*) long sandwich.
  (d) (*Cono Sur*) **tomar a uno para la ~** to poke fun at sb.
butiondo ADJ lewd, lustful.
butrón• NM hole made to effect a break-in; burglary, break-in.
butronero• NM burglar.
butuco ADJ (*CAm*) short, squat.
buz NM respectful kiss, formal kiss; **hacer el ~** to bow and scrape.
buzamiento NM (*Geol*) dip.
buzar [1f] VI (*Geol*) to dip.
buzo[1] NM diver.
buzo[2] NM (*And, Cono Sur*) tracksuit, jogging suit; jumpsuit.
buzón NM **(a)** (*Correos*) letterbox, pillar-box, mailbox (*US*); (*Inform*) mailbox; **~ de alcance** late-collection postbox; **~ de sugerencias** suggestions box; **cerrar el ~:** to keep one's trap shut:; **echar una carta al ~** to post a letter; **vender un ~ a uno**• (*Cono Sur*) to sell sb a dummy, pull the wool over sb's eyes.
  (b) (*canal*) canal, conduit.
  (c) (*tapón*) stopper; (*tapa*) lid, cover.
buzonear [1a] VT to deliver door-to-door.
buzonero NM (*LAm*) postal employee (*who collects from letterboxes*).
byte [bait] NM byte.

C

C, c [θe, se (*esp LAm*)] NF (*letra*) C, c; **datación por C-14** C-14 dating.
C (a) ABR *de* **centígrado** centigrade, C. (b) ABR *de* **Compañía** Company, Co.
c ABR *de* **capítulo**; = **cap.**
C/ ABR *de* **Calle** Street, St.
c/ (a) ABR *de* **cuenta** account, a/c. (b) ABR *de* **capítulo** chapter, ch.
ca INTERJ (†) not a bit of it!, no, indeed!, oh no!
C.A. NF (a) (*Elec*) ABR *de* **corriente alterna** alternating current, A.C. (b) (*Pol*) ABR *de* **Comunidad Autónoma**.
cabal ⒈ ADJ (*exacto*) exact; (*apropiado*) right, proper; (*acabado*) finished, complete, consummate, full; (*perfecto*) perfect; **esfuerzo etc** thorough, all-out.
⒉ ADV exactly; **¡~!** perfectly correct!, right!
⒊ **~es** NMPL: **estar en sus ~es** to be in one's right mind; **hacer algo por sus ~es** to do sth properly; to do things in the right order.
cábala NF (a) (*Rel*) cab(b)ala. (b) **~s** (*suposición*) guess, supposition; (*intrigas*) intrigues.
cabalgada NF (*Hist*) troop of riders; cavalry raid.
cabalgador NM rider, horseman.
cabalgadura NF (*de montar*) mount, horse; (*de carga*) beast of burden.
cabalgar [1h] ⒈ VT (a) (*persona*) to ride.
(b) (*semental*) to cover, serve.
⒉ VI to ride; to go riding; **~ en mula** to ride (on) a mule; **~ sin montura, ~ a pelo** (*LAm*) to ride bareback.
cabalgata NF (*acto*) ride; (*desfile*) cavalcade, mounted procession; **~ de Reyes** Twelfth Night procession.

┌─── **CABALGATA DE REYES** ───┐

ⓘ The **cabalgata de Reyes** is a float parade held on 5 January, the eve of Epiphany, in most Spanish towns and cities. It celebrates the coming of the Three Kings with their gifts for the infant Jesus. In the course of the cabalgatas, the Three Kings throw sweets into the crowd.

⇨ See also REYES, DÍA DE

cabalidad NF: **a ~** perfectly, adequately.
cabalista NM schemer, intriguer.
cabalístico ADJ cabalistic; (*fig*) occult, mysterious.
caballa NF (Atlantic) mackerel.
cabalgada NF (a) (*Zool*) drove of horses. (b) (*LAm: animalada*) gaffe, blunder; **has hecho una ~** that was a stupid thing to do.
caballaje NM horsepower.
caballar ADJ horse (*atr*), equine; **cara ~** horse-face; **ganado ~** horses.
caballazo NM (*LAm*) collision between two horsemen, accident involving a horse.
caballejo NM (a) (*poney*) pony. (b) (*rocín*) old horse, poor horse, nag.
caballerango NM (*Méx*) groom.
caballerear [1a] VI to give o.s. the airs of a gentleman.
caballeresco ADJ (a) (*Hist*) knightly, chivalric; **literatura caballeresca** chivalresque literature, books of chivalry; **orden caballeresca** order of chivalry.
(b) *sentimiento* fine, noble, chivalrous; *trato etc* chivalrous; *carácter* gentlemanly, noble.
caballerete NM dandy, fop, dude (*US*).
caballería NF (a) (*animal*) (*gen*) mount; steed; (*caballo*) horse; (*mula*) mule (*etc*); **~ de carga** beast of burden.
(b) (*Mil*) cavalry; **~ ligera** light horse, light cavalry.
(c) (*Hist*) chivalry, knighthood; (*orden*) order of chivalry, military order; **~ andante** knight-errantry.
(d) **andarse en ~s** to overdo the compliments.
(e) (*CAm, Carib, Cono Sur, Méx: Agr*) *a land measurement of varying sizes* (*usually 42 hectares*).
caballericero NM (*CAm, Carib*) groom.
caballeriza NF (a) (*cuadra*) stable; (*de cría*) stud, horse-breeding establishment; **~ de alquiler** livery stable. (b) (*personas*) stable hands, grooms.
caballerizo NM groom, stableman; (*Hist*) **~ mayor del rey** master of the king's horse; **~ del rey** equerry.
caballero ⒈ NM (a) (*el que cabalga*) rider, horseman.
(b) (*señor*) gentleman; **cosas indignas de un ~** things unworthy of a gentleman; **~ de industria** swindler, adventurer, gentleman crook; **~ solitario** lone wolf; **de ~ a ~** as one gentleman to another; **ser cumplido ~, ser todo un ~** to be a real gentleman; **es un mal ~** he's no gentleman; **'C~s'** 'Gents', 'Men'.
(c) (*Hist*) knight; noble, nobleman; **~ andante** knight-errant; **los ~s de Malta** the Knights of Malta; **~ de Santiago** Knight of (the Order of) Santiago; (*título*) **el C~ de la Rosa** the Rosenkavalier; **el C~ de la Triste Figura** the Knight of the Doleful Countenance (*Don Quixote*); **armar ~ a uno** to knight sb, dub sb knight.
(d) (*en oración directa, frec iró*) sir; **¿quién es Vd, ~?** who are you, sir?
⒉ ADJ: **iba ~ en una mula** he was riding a mule, he was mounted on a mule; **estar ~ en su opinión** to stick firmly to one's opinion.
caballerosamente ADV like a gentleman; chivalrously.
caballerosidad NF gentlemanliness; chivalry.
caballeroso ADJ gentlemanly; chivalrous; **poco ~** ungentlemanly.
caballerote NM (*pey*) so-called gentleman, gentleman unworthy of the name.
caballete NM (*Agr*) ridge; (*Arquit*) (*de techo*) ridge, (*de chimenea*) cap; (*Arte*) easel; (*Téc*) trestle; (*Anat*) bridge (of the nose); **~ de aserrar** sawhorse; **~ para bicicleta** bicycle clamp, bicycle rest; **~ de pintor** painter's easel.
caballista NM expert horseman; expert in horses.
caballito NM (a) (*poney*) little horse, pony; **~ de niño** hobby-horse; **~ del diablo** dragonfly; **~ de mar, ~ marino** sea horse.
(b) **~s** (*de verbena etc*) merry-go-round.
(c) (*Méx: compresa*) sanitary towel, sanitary napkin (*US*).
caballo NM (a) (*Zool*) horse; **~ (de) aros** vaulting horse; **~ (de) balancín** rocking horse; **~ de batalla** (*fig*) forte, speciality; (*en controversia*) main point, central issue; **es su ~ de batalla** it's a hobby-horse of his; **~ blanco*** backer; **~ de buena boca** obliging chap; **~ castrado** gelding; **~ de carga** packhorse; **~ de carrera(s)** racehorse; **~ de caza** hunter; **~ entero** stallion; **el ~ de Espartero, el ~ de Santiago** symbols of virility; **~ de guerra** warhorse, charger; **~ marino** sea horse; **~ mecedor** rocking horse; **~ padre** stallion; **~ de tiro** carthorse, draught horse; **~ de Troya** Trojan horse; **~ de vaivén** rocking horse; **a ~** on horseback; **andar** (*o* **ir** *o* **montar**) **a ~** to ride, go on horseback; **las cosas andan a ~** (*Cono Sur*) the price of things is sky-high; **bajar a uno del ~** (*Carib*) to take sb down a peg (*or* two); **estar a ~ de algo** to be astride sth, be on sth; **estar a ~ entre dos cosas** (*fig*) to be between two things, alternate between two things; **pararle el ~ a uno** (*Méx*) to slow sb down; **pasársele el ~** to go over the top; **ser un ~*** to be stupid; **subir a ~** to mount, get on one's horse; **ir a mata ~** to go at breakneck speed; **a ~ regalado no le mires el diente** don't look a gift horse in the mouth; **como ~ desbocado** rashly, hastily; **como un ~ en una cacharrería** like a bull in a china-shop; **una dosis** (*etc*) **de ~*** a huge dose (*etc*), a massive dose (*etc*); **tropas de a ~** mounted troops; **es de a ~** he's a good rider.
(b) (*Ajedrez*) knight; (*Naipes*) queen.
(c) (*Téc*) sawhorse.
(d) (*Mec*) **~ de vapor decimal** (*C.V.*) metric horse-power; **~ de fuerza, ~ de potencia, ~ de vapor inglés** horse-power (HP); **un dos ~s** a small car; **~ de vapor** horse-power; **un motor de 18 ~s** an 18 horse-power engine; **¿cuántos ~s tiene este coche?** what horse-power is this car?
(e) (**‡**) heroin.
caballón NM (*Agr*) ridge.

caballuno ADJ horse-like, horsy.

cabalmente ADV exactly; properly; completely; fully; thoroughly.

cabanga NF (*CAm*) nostalgia, homesickness; **estar de ~** to be homesick.

cabaña NF (a) (*casita*) hut, cabin, hovel, shack; **~ de madera** log cabin.
(b) (*Billar*) balk.
(c) (*Agr*) livestock.
(d) (*Cono Sur: estancia*) cattle-breeding ranch.

cabañero NM herdsman.

cabañuelas NFPL (*LAm*) (fanciful) weather predictions; (*And*) first summer rains; (*Méx*) first twelve days of January (*used to predict the weather*).

cabaré NM = cabaret.

cabaret [kaβa're] NM, PL **cabarets** [kaβa're] (*show*) cabaret, floor show; (*boîte*) nightclub; **~ de desnudo** nude show, striptease show, strip club.

cabaretera NF cabaret dancer, cabaret entertainer; night-club hostess; showgirl.

cabaretero ADJ of a nightclub; **con ambiente ~** with a nightclub atmosphere.

cabás NM schoolbag, satchel.

cabe¹ NM: **~ de pala** windfall, lucky break; **dar un ~ a** to harm, do harm to; **dar un ~ al bolsillo** to make a hole in one's pocket.

cabe²* NM (*Dep*) header.

cabe³ PREP (*liter*) near, next to.

cabeceada NF (*LAm*) nod, shake of the head.

cabecear [1a] **1** VT (a) (*Cos*) to bind (the edge of).
(b) *vino* to strengthen; *vinos* to blend.
(c) *balón* to head.
2 VI (a) (*estando dormido*) to nod; (*negando*) to shake one's head; (*caballo*) to toss its head.
(b) (*Náut*) to pitch; (*Aut etc*) to lurch; (*carga*) to shift, slip.

cabeceo NM (a) (*al dormir*) nod, nodding; (*negativa*) shake of the head; (*de caballo*) toss of the head. (b) (*Náut*) pitching; (*Aut etc*) lurch, lurching; shifting; slipping.

cabecera NF (a) (*de cama, mesa, puente etc*) head; (*asiento*) seat of honour; (*de sala*) upper end, far end; (*de pista de aterrizaje*) end, head; **~ (de río)** headwaters (of a river); **~ del cartel** (*Teat*) top of the bill; **ser ~ de cartel** to top the bill.
(b) (*tabla: de cama*) headboard; (*almohada*) pillow, bolster; (*fig*) bedside; **libro de ~** bedside book; **médico de ~** family doctor; **estar a la ~ de uno** to be at sb's bedside; to nurse sb.
(c) (*Tip*) headline; headpiece, title; vignette; (*de documento*) heading.
(d) (*Pol*) administrative centre, chief town, capital.
(e) (*elemento principal*) leading member; chief unit, most important element.

cabecero NM bedhead.

cabeciduro ADJ (*And, Carib*) stubborn, pigheaded.

cabecilla **1** NMF hothead, wrong-headed person.
2 NM (*Mil, Pol*) ringleader; rebel leader.

cabellera NF (a) (*pelo*) hair, head of hair; (*tupé etc*) wig, false hair, switch, hairpiece; **soltarse la ~*** to act (*o speak etc*) in a forthright way. (b) (*Astron*) tail (of a comet).

cabello NM (a) (*pelo*) hair; (*t ~s*) hair, head of hair; locks; **~ de Venus** (*Bot*) maidenhair; **estar en ~** to have one's hair down; **estar en ~s** to be bareheaded; **estar pendiente de un ~** to hang by a thread; **asirse de un ~** to latch on to any excuse; **mesarse los ~s** to tear one's hair; **sentirse como colgado de los ~s** to feel on edge; **traído por los ~s** far-fetched, irrelevant.
(b) **~s de ángel** (*Culin*) thin vermicelli.

cabelludo ADJ hairy, shaggy; *V* cuero.

▼ **caber** [2l] VI (a) (*gen*) to go, fit (*en* in, into); to be contained (*en* in); to have enough room; **no cabe el libro** the book won't go in, there's no room for the book; **caben 3 más** there's room for 3 more, we (*etc*) can get 3 more in; **en esta maleta no cabe** it won't go into this case, there's no room for it in this case, this case won't take it; **en este depósito caben 20 litros** this tank holds 20 litres; **¿cabe uno más?** is there room for one more?, can you get one more in?; **¿cabemos todos?** is there room for us all?; **eso no cabe por esta puerta** that won't go through this door.
(b) (*Mat*) **¿cuántas veces cabe 5 en 20?** how many times does 5 go into 20?
(c) (*fig: ser posible*) to be possible; **los compro todos y más, si cabe** I'll buy them all and more, if (that is) possible; **no cabe en él hacerlo** it is not in him to do it; **todo cabe en ese chico** that lad is capable of any mischief, anything might be expected from that lad.
▼ (d) (*locuciones*) **no cabe más** that's the lot, that's the limit; one could wish for nothing more; it leaves nothing to be desired; **no ~ en sí** to be bursting, be beside o.s.; (*pey*) to be big-headed*; **no ~ en sí de contento** (*o* **gusto**) to be overjoyed, be overwhelmed with joy; **no cabe perdón** it's inexcusable; **cabe preguntar si ...** one may

ask whether ..., it is proper to ask if ...; **cabe intentar otro sistema** one might try another system.
(e) (*fig: tocar a uno en suerte*) **~ a uno** to happen to sb, befall sb; to fall to one's lot; **le cupieron 120 dólares** his share was 120 dollars, he got 120 dollars (as his share); *V* **duda, suerte.**

cabestrar [1a] VT to halter, put a halter on.

cabestrillo NM (*Med*) sling; **con el brazo en ~** with one's arm in a sling.

cabestro NM (a) (*ronzal*) halter; **llevar a uno del ~** to lead sb by the nose. (b) (*buey*) leading ox, bell-ox. (c) (*) (*cornudo*) cuckold; (*lerdo*) thickie*.

cabeza **1** NF (a) (*Anat y en muchos sentidos figurados*) head; (*de clavo, cohete, mesa, puente etc*) head; **~ atómica, ~ nuclear** atomic warhead; (*Mec*) **~ de biela** big end; **~ buscadora** homing head, homing device; **~ de chorlito*** scatterbrain, dimwit*; **~ de escritura** (*Tip*) golf ball; **~ explosiva, ~ de guerra** warhead; **~ grabadora, ~ de impresión** (*Inform*) head, printhead; **~ hueca, ~ sin seso** idiot; **~ pelada** (*Hist: Brit*) Roundhead; **~ de playa** beachhead; **~ de puente** bridgehead; **~ de serie** (*Dep*) seed, seeded player; **~ de serrín*** airhead*; **~ sonora** recording head; **~ de turco** scapegoat, whipping boy, fall guy (*US*); **andar de ~*** to be snowed under; **andar en ~** (*LAm**) to be hatless, be bareheaded; **echar ~ a un asunto** to give thought to a matter; **no estar bien de la ~, estar mal de ~*** to be soft in the head; **estar de ~** to be on end; **caer de ~** to fall head first, fall headlong; **ir de ~*** to be snowed under; **lanzarse de ~ a** to rush headlong at; to rush headfirst into; **marcar de ~** to score from a header; **meterse de ~ en algo** to plunge into sth; **5 dólares por ~** 5 dollars a head, 5 dollars per person; **por encima de la ~** over one's head, overhead; **ganar por una ~ (escasa)** to win by a (short) head; **un melocotón como mi ~** a peach as big as a football; **alzar (o levantar) la ~** (*Com etc*) to get on one's feet again, (*Med*) be up and about, be improving; **asentir con la ~** to nod (one's head); **calentarse la ~** to get tired out; **me duele la ~** my head aches, I've got a headache; **echar de ~ a uno** (*LAm**) to inform (*o* blow the whistle*) on sb; **escarmentar en ~ ajena** to learn by sb else's mistakes; **no estar bueno de la ~** to be weak in the head; **se me fue la ~** I felt giddy; **se me fue de la ~** it went right out of my mind; **es ~ de pescado** (*Cono Sur**) it's sheer nonsense; **hablar ~s de pescado** (*Cono Sur**) to talk drivel, talk through the back of one's head*; **jugarse la ~** to risk one's life; **lavarse la ~** to wash one's hair; **levantar ~** to recover one's health; **está que no levanta ~** she's totally engrossed in her work; **por fin se lo metimos en la ~** we finally got it into his head (*que* that); **esa melodía la tengo metida en la ~** I've got that tune on the brain; **meter la ~ en la arena** to bury one's head in the sand; **mover la ~ afirmativamente** to nod (one's head); **mover la ~ negativamente** to shake one's head; **jamás se me pasó por la ~** it never entered my head; **perder la ~** to lose one's head; **quitar algo de la ~ a uno** to get sth out of sb's head; **ella me ha quitado la ~** I'm crazy about her; **romper la ~ a uno** to give sb a beating; **romperse la ~** to rack one's brains; **le saca la ~ a su hermano** he is taller by a head than his brother; **sentar la ~** to settle down; to come to one's senses; **el vino se me subió a la ~** the wine went to my head; **tener ~ de pollo** (*Cono Sur**) to have a memory like a sieve; **no tener ~ para las alturas** to have no head for heights; **estar tocado de la ~** to be weak in the head; **traer de ~ a uno** to upset sb, bother sb; **vestirse por la ~*** to be female; (*sacerdote*) **volver la ~** to look round, turn one's head; **volver la ~ a uno** to look away from sb, ignore sb.
(b) (*de monte*) top, summit; (*de liga, lista, etc*) head, top; **con Pérez a la ~ del gobierno** with Pérez at the head of the government; **ir a la ~ de la lista** to be at the top of the list; **ir en ~** to be in the lead; **tomar la ~** to take the lead.
(c) (*de río*) head, headwaters.
(d) (*Pol*) main town, chief centre, capital; **~ de partido** county town, administrative centre.
(e) (*Bot*) **~ de ajo** bulb of garlic; **~ de plátanos** (*And*) bunch of bananas.
(f) (*fig: origen*) origin, beginning.
2 NMF (*persona*) head; chief, leader; **~ de familia** head of the household; **~ de lista** person at the head of the list; **~ visible** chief, leader, top person.

cabezada NF (a) (*golpe*) butt; blow on the head.
(b) (*movimiento*) nod; shake of the head; **dar una ~, dar ~s, echar una ~** to nod (sleepily), doze; **darse de ~s** to rack one's brains.
(c) (*Náut*) pitch, pitching; **dar ~s** to pitch.
(d) (*parte de arreos*) head stall; (*de bota*) instep; (*de zapato*) vamp.
(e) (*And, Cono Sur*) saddle-tree.
(f) (*Carib, Cono Sur: de río*) headwaters.

cabezadita* NF: **echar una ~** to have a snooze*, doze.

cabezal NM (*almohada*) pillow; bolster; (*de dentista etc*) headrest; (*Med*) pad, compress; (*Inform*) head; **~ de enganche** towbar.

cabezazo NM butt; (*Ftbl*) header.

cabezo NM (*Geog*) hillock, small hill; (*Náut*) reef.

cabezón [1] ADJ = **cabezudo**.

[2] NM (a) (*cabeza*) big head. (b) (*Cos*) hole for the head. (c) (*cuello*) collar band; **llevar a uno de los cabezones** to force sb to go. (d) **cabezones** rapids, whirlpool.

cabezonada NF: **fue una ~** it was a pig-headed thing to do.

cabezonería NF pig-headedness.

cabezota [1] NF big head.

[2] NMF (*) pig-headed person.

cabezudo [1] ADJ (a) (*lit*) big-headed, with a big head. (b) (*fig*) pig-headed. (c) *vino* heady.

[2] NM *carnival figure with an enormous head*.

cabezuela NF head (of a flower); rosebud.

cabida NF (a) (*espacio*) space, room; (*capacidad*) capacity (*t Náut*); (*extensión*) extent, area; **con ~ para 50 personas** with space for 50 people; **dar ~ a** to make room for, leave space for; **hay que dar ~ a los imponderables** one must leave room for (o allow for) the imponderables; **tener ~ para** to have room for, hold. (b) (*fig: influencia*) influence; **tener ~ con uno** to have influence with sb.

cabildear [1a] VI to lobby; (*pey*) to intrigue.

cabildeo NM lobbying; (*pey*) intriguing, intrigues.

cabildero -a NM/F lobbyist, member of a pressure group; (*pey*) intriguer.

cabildo NM (a) (*personas*) (*Ecl*) chapter; (*Pol*) town council. (b) (*junta*) chapter meeting; (*Carib: de negros*) gathering of Negroes; (*Carib: reunión desordenada*) riotous assembly. (c) (*Parl*) lobby.

cabilla NF: **dar ~ a**✱✱ to fuck✱✱, screw✱✱.

cabillo NM end; (*Bot*) stalk, stem.

cabina NF (*de camión, Náut etc*) cabin; (*Ferro*) personal compartment, sleeping compartment; (*Aer*) cabin, cockpit; (*de gimnasio*) locker; (*Cine*) projection room; **~ a presión** pressurized cabin; **~ del conductor** driver's cab; **~ electoral** voting booth; **~ de prensa** press box; **~ de teléfono, ~ telefónica** telephone box, telephone kiosk, telephone booth (*US*).

cabinada NF cabin cruiser.

cabinera NF (*And*) air hostess, stewardess, flight attendant (*US*).

cabinista NMF projectionist.

cabio NM (*viga*) beam, joist; rafter; (*de puerta, ventana*) lintel, transom.

cabizbajo ADJ crestfallen, dejected, downcast.

cabla NF (*LAm*) trick.

cable NM (*Náut etc*) cable, rope, hawser; (*medida*) cable length; (*Telec*) cable; (*Elec*) cable, wire, lead; **~ aéreo** overhead cable; **~ coaxial** coaxial cable; **~ de desgarre** ripcord; **~ de remolque** towline, tow-rope; **se le cruzaron los ~s** he got his wires crossed; **echar un ~ a uno** to give sb a helping hand, help sb out of a jam; **se le pelaron los ~s** (*CAm*✱) he got all mixed up.

cableado NM wiring, cables.

cablear [1a] VT to wire up.

cablegrafiar [1c] VI to cable.

cablegráfico ADJ cable (*atr*); **transferencia cablegráfica** cable transfer.

cablegrama NM cable, cablegram.

cablero NM cable ship.

cablista ADJ (*LAm*) sly, cunning.

cabo NM (a) (*extremo*) end, extremity; **de ~ a ~, de ~ a rabo** from beginning to end; **leer un libro de ~ a ~** to read a book from cover to cover.

(b) (*de período, proceso*) end; termination, conclusion; **al ~** finally, in the end; **al ~ de 3 meses** at the end of 3 months, after (the lapse of) 3 months; **dar ~ a** to complete, finish off; **dar ~ de** to put an end to; **estar al ~** to be nearing one's end; **estar al ~ de la calle** (*fig*) to know what's going on, know what's what; to know what the score is; to be up to date; **estar al ~ de la calle de que ...** to know perfectly well that ...; **¿estamos al ~ de la calle?** do you get it now?, understand?; **llevar a ~** to carry out, execute, carry through; to implement; to transact; **ponerse al ~ de un asunto** to get to know all about a matter.

(c) (*resto de objeto*) end, bit; stub, stump, butt; **~ de lápiz** stub of a pencil; **~ de vela** candle-end.

(d) (*hilo*) strand; (*Téc*) thread; (*Náut*) rope, cable; **~ de desgarre** ripcord; **~ suelto** loose end; **atar ~s** to tie up the loose ends; to put two and two together; **no dejar ningún ~ suelto** to leave no loose ends; to take every precaution.

(e) (*mango*) handle, haft.

(f) (*Geog*) cape, point; **C~ de Buena Esperanza** Cape of Good Hope; **C~ de Hornos** Cape Horn; **Islas de C~ Verde** Cape Verde Islands.

(g) (*persona*) chief, head; (*Mil*) corporal; (*de policía*) sergeant; (*remador*) stroke; **~ de escuadra** corporal; **~ de mar** petty officer.

(h) **~s** (*Cos*) accessories; (*fig*) odds and ends.

cabotaje NM coasting trade, coastal traffic.

caboverdiano, -a ADJ, NM/F Cape Verdean.

cabra NF (a) (*Zool*) goat, nanny goat; (*almizclero*) musk deer; **~ montés** wild goat; **estar como una ~** to be crazy. (b) (*And, Carib: trampa*) trick, swindle; (*dado*) loaded dice. (c) (*Cono Sur*) (*carro*) light carriage; (*de carpintero*) sawhorse. (d) (*Cono Sur*✱: *niña*) little girl. (e) (*✱: moto*) motorbike✱.

cabracho NM large-scaled scorpion fish.

cabrahigo NM wild fig.

cabrales NM INVAR *a kind of very strong Asturian cheese*.

cabré *etc V* **caber**.

cabreante✱ ADJ infuriating.

cabrear✱ [1a] [1] VT to infuriate, make livid.

[2] **cabrearse** VR (a) (*enojarse*) to get furious, get livid. (b) (*sospechar*) to get suspicious. (c) (*Cono Sur*✱: *aburrirse*) to get bored.

cabreo✱ NM fury, anger; fit of bad temper; **coger un ~** to get angry, fly into a rage.

cabreriza NF goat shed, goat house.

cabrerizo [1] ADJ goatish; goat (*atr*).

[2] NM goatherd.

cabrero✱ [1] ADJ (*Cono Sur*) bad-tempered; **ponerse ~** to fly off the handle✱.

[2] NM goatherd.

cabrestante NM capstan, winch.

cabria NF hoist, derrick; **~ de perforación** drilling-rig.

cabrio NM rafter.

cabrío [1] ADJ goatish; **macho ~** he-goat, billy goat.

[2] NM herd of goats.

cabriola NF (a) (*gen*) caper; gambol; hop, skip, prance; **hacer ~s** to caper about, prance around; **hacer ~s con** (*fig*) to weave elegant patterns around. (b) (*Carib: travesura*) prank, piece of mischief.

cabriolar [1a] VI to caper (about); to gambol; to skip, prance (around), frisk about.

cabriolé NM cab, cabriolet.

cabriolear [1a] VI = **cabriolar**.

cabritada✱ NF dirty trick.

cabritas NFPL (*Cono Sur*) popcorn.

cabritilla NF kid, kidskin.

cabrito NM (a) kid; **a ~** astride. (b) (✱) (*cornudo*) cuckold; (*de prostituta*) client; **¡~!** you bastard!✱.

cabro NM (a) (*LAm Zool*) he-goat, billy goat. (b) (*Cono Sur*: *niño*) small child; (*chico*) boy; (*amante*) lover, sweetheart; (*sujeto*) guy✱. (c) (✱) queer✱.

cabrón NM (a) (*cornudo*) cuckold, complaisant husband.

(b) (✱: *insulto*) **¡~!** you bastard!✱, (*hum*) you old bastard!✱; **el muy ~ le robó el coche** the bastard stole his car✱; **el tío ~ ese** that bastard✱; **es un ~** he's a bastard✱.

(c) (*LAm*✱: *de burdel*) brothel-keeper; (*And, Cono Sur*: *chulo*) pimp; (*CAm, Cono Sur*: *traidor*) traitor; (*And*✱: *maricón*) queer✱, fag✱; **¡~!** you stupid berk✱!

cabronada✱ NF (a) (*mala pasada*) dirty trick; **hacer una ~ a uno** to play a dirty trick on sb. (b) (*faena*) tough job, fag✱.

cabronazo✱ NM rotter✱, villain; **¡¡jo, ~!** (*hum*) hey, you old bastard!✱.

cabroncete✱ NM little twerp✱.

cabruno ADJ goatish; goat (*atr*).

cábula NF (a) (*And, Cono Sur*: *amuleto*) amulet. (b) (*Cono Sur*: *intriga*) cabal, intrigue. (c) (*And, CAm, Carib*: *ardid*) trick, stratagem.

cabulear [1a] VI (*And, CAm, Carib*) to scheme.

cabulero (*And, CAm, Carib*) [1] ADJ tricky, cunning, scheming.

[2] NM trickster, schemer.

cabuya NF (*LAm*) (*Bot*) agave, pita; (*fibra*) pita hemp; (*cuerda*) rope, cord (of pita *or in general*); **dar ~** (*Carib*) to put things off; **ponerse en la ~** to cotton on✱; **verse a uno las ~s** to see what sb is up to, see through sb's scheme.

caca NF (a) (✱✱) (*palabra de niños*) number two✱, poo-poo✱. (b) (✱) (*fig*) dirt, filth; **¡~!** (*desagrado*) ugh!; (*no toques*) don't touch!

caca-can✱ NM pooper-scooper✱.

cacaguatal NM (*CAm*) cocoa field.

cacahual NM (*LAm*) cacao plantation.

cacahuate NM (*CAm, Méx*), **cacahuete** NM (*Esp*) (*nuez*) peanut, monkey nut; (*planta*) groundnut.

cacao NM (a) (*árbol, semilla*) cacao; (*polvo, bebida*) cocoa; **pedir ~** (*LAm*) to give in, ask for mercy; **ser gran ~** to have influence; **tener un ~ en la cabeza**✱ to be all mixed up; **no valer un ~** (*LAm*) to be worthless, be insignificant. (b) (✱: *jaleo*) fuss, to-do✱. (c) **~ mental**✱ mental confusion; **ser un ~** to be a mess.

cacaotal NM (*LAm*) cacao plantation.

cacaraña NF (a) (*señal*) pockmark. (b) (*CAm: garabato*) scribble.

cacarañado ADJ pitted, pockmarked.

cacarañar [1a] VT (*Méx*) to scratch, pinch; to pit, scar, pockmark.

cacarear [1a] [1] VT to boast about, exaggerate, make much of; **ese triunfo tan cacareado** that much trumpeted triumph, that vaunted triumph.

2 VI to crow; to cackle.

cacareo NM crowing, cackling; (*fig*) crowing, boasting, trumpeting.

cacarico ADJ (*CAm*) numb.

cacarizo ADJ (*Méx*) pitted, pockmarked.

cacastle NM (*CAm, Méx*) (*esqueleto*) skeleton; (*canasta*) large wicker basket; (*armazón*) wicker carrying frame.

cacatúa NF (a) (*Orn*) cockatoo. (b) (*: bruja*) old bat*, old cow‡.

cacaxtle NM (*CAm, Méx*) = **cacastle**.

cacera NF ditch, irrigation channel.

cacereño **1** ADJ of Cáceres.

   2 NM, **cacereña** NF native (*o* inhabitant) of Cáceres; **los ~s** the people of Cáceres.

cacería NF (a) (*gen*) hunting, shooting.

   (b) (*personas*) hunt, shoot, shooting-party; **~ de brujas** witch-hunt; **~ de zorros** fox hunt; **organizar una ~** to organize a hunt.

   (c) (*animales cazados*) bag, total of animals (*etc*) bagged.

   (d) (*Arte*) hunting scene.

cacerola NF pan, saucepan; casserole.

cacerolazo NM (*Cono Sur*) banging on pots and pans (*as political protest*).

cacha NF, *frec* **~s** PL (a) handle; (*de revólver*) butt; **hasta las ~s** up to the hilt, completely.

   (b) (*And: cuerno*) horn.

   (c) (*And: de gallo*) metal spur attached to the leg of a fighting cock.

   (d) (*And: arca*) large chest.

   (e) (*) **~s** (*culo*) bottom; (*piernas*) legs.

   (f) (*locuciones*) **estar a medias ~s** (*Méx*) to be tipsy; **estar fuera de ~** to be out of danger; **hacer ~s** (*CAm*) to try hard; **sacar ~(s) a** (*o* **de**)* to make fun of.

   (g) (*LAm: cachete*) cheek.

   (h) (*CAm*: negocio*) crooked deal*; **¡qué ~!** what a nuisance!; **hacer la ~** to put one's back into it.

   (i) (*CAm: oportunidad*) opportunity.

cachaciento ADJ (*CAm, Cono Sur*) = **cachazudo**.

cachaco NM (a) (*And, Carib: petimetre*) fop, dandy. (b) (*And‡*) (*policía*) copper*, cop*; (*desaliñado*) scruff*. (c) (*Carib*: entrometido*) busybody, nosey-parker*.

cachada NF (a) (*LAm Taur*) butt, thrust; goring. (b) (*Cono Sur*: broma*) joke, leg-pull*.

cachador* (*Cono Sur*) **1** ADJ fond of practical jokes.

   2 NM practical joker.

cachafaz* ADJ (*LAm*) (*pillo*) rascally; (*taimado*) crafty; (*fresco*) cheeky*.

cachalote NM sperm whale.

cachancha NF (*Carib*) patience; **estar de ~ con uno*** to suck up to sb*.

cachaña NF (*Cono Sur*) (a) (*Orn*) small parrot. (b) (*broma*) hoax, leg-pull*; (*mofas*) mockery, derision. (c) (*arrogancia*) arrogance. (d) (*estupidez*) stupidity. (e) (*arrebatiña*) rush, scramble (for sth).

cachañar [1a] VT (*Cono Sur*) = **cachar**[1]; **~ a uno*** to pull sb's leg*.

cachar[1] [1a] VT (a) (*romper*) to smash, break, break in pieces; *madera* to split; (*Agr*) to plough up.

   (b) (*And, CAm: Taur*) to butt, gore.

   (c) (*And, CAm, Cono Sur*) (*ridiculizar*) to scoff at, deride, ridicule; (*fastidiar*) to annoy, irritate.

   (d) (*And, Cono Sur‡*) to screw‡.

   (e) (*Méx*: registrar*) to search.

cachar[2] [1a] VT (a) (*Cono Sur*) *bus etc* to catch.

   (b) (*CAm: obtener*) to get, obtain; (*CAm, Cono Sur: robar*) to steal.

   (c) (*Cono Sur, Méx: sorprender*) to surprise, catch in the act.

   (d) (*Cono Sur*) *sentido etc* to penetrate; *persona, razón* to understand; **sí, te cacho** sure, I get it*.

   (e) (*And, CAm, Carib: Dep*) *pelota* to catch.

cacharpari NM (*And, Cono Sur*) = **cacharpaya**.

cacharpas NFPL (*LAm*) useless objects, lumber, junk; odds and ends.

cacharpaya NF (*And, Cono Sur*) send-off, farewell party; (*Cono Sur*) farewell; minor festivity.

cacharpearse [1a] VR (*LAm*) to dress up.

cacharra‡ NF rod‡, pistol.

cacharrazo* NM bash*, bang.

cacharrear [1a] VT (*CAm, Carib*) to throw into jail, jail.

cacharrería NF (a) (*tienda*) crockery shop. (b) (*cacharros*) crockery, pots. (c) (*And*) ironmongery.

cacharro NM (a) (*vasija*) earthenware pot, crock; **~s** earthenware, crockery, pots, coarse pottery.

   (b) (*casco*) piece of pottery, potsherd.

   (c) (*pey*) useless object, piece of junk; (*Aut etc**) old crock, jalop(p)y; (*And*) trinket.

   (d) (*‡: pistola*) rod‡, pistol.

   (e) (*CAm, Carib: cárcel*) jail.

cachas* ADJ INVAR he-man*, hunk*, muscle-man*; **estar ~** to be tough, be well set-up; **está ~** (*hombre*) he's dishy*; (*mujer*) she's hot stuff*.

cachativa NF: **tener ~** (*Cono Sur*) to be quick on the uptake.

cachaza NF (a) (*tranquilidad*) slowness; calmness, phlegm. (b) (*LAm: licor*) rum.

cachazo NM (*LAm*) (*golpe*) butt, thrust; (*herida*) goring.

cachazudo **1** ADJ slow; calm, phlegmatic.

   2 NM slow sort; phlegmatic person.

cache NM (*Inform*) cache, cache memory.

caché NM = **cachet**.

cachear [1a] VT (a) (*LAm Taur*) to butt, gore. (b) (*LAm: pegar*) to punch, slap. (c) (*abrir*) to split, cut open. (d) (*registrar*) to frisk, search (for weapons).

cachejo* NM (*Esp*) **un ~ (de) pan** a little bit of bread; **aquel ~ de partido** that awful game.

cachemir NM, **cachemira** NF cashmere.

Cachemira NF Kashmir.

cacheo NM searching, frisking (for weapons).

cachería NF (a) (*And, CAm Com*) small business, sideline. (b) (*Cono Sur*) (*falta de gusto*) bad taste; (*desaseo*) slovenliness.

cachero **1** ADJ (a) (*CAm, Carib: embustero*) lying, deceitful. (b) (*CAm: trabajador*) hard-working, diligent.

   2 NM (*LAm*) sodomite.

cachet [ka'tʃe] NM, PL **~s** [ka'tʃe] (a) (*sello distintivo*) cachet; character, temperament. (b) (*de artista*) appearance money, fee.

cachetada NF (*LAm*) (*golpe*) slap, box on the ear; (*paliza*) beating.

cachetazo NM (a) (*LAm**: bofetada*) slap, punch; (*fig*) snub. (b) (*LAm: trago*) swig*, slug* (*US*). (c) **¡hazme un ~!** (*CAm, Carib**) do me a favour!

cachete NM (a) (*Anat*) (fat) cheek; (*Med*) swollen cheek. (b) (*golpe*) punch in the face, slap. (c) (*arma*) dagger. (d) (*CAm: favor*) favour. (e) **~s*** (*Cono Sur Anat*) bottom.

cacheteada NF (*Cono Sur*) slap, box on the ear.

cachetear [1a] **1** VT (*And, Cono Sur*) to slap (*o* smack) in the face.

   2 VI (*Cono Sur*) to eat well.

cachetero NM (a) (*puñal*) dagger. (b) (*Taur*) *bullfighter who finishes the bull off with a dagger*.

cachetina* NF fist fight, punch-up*.

cachetón ADJ (a) (*LAm: de cara rechoncha*) plump-cheeked, fat-faced. (b) (*Méx: descarado*) impudent, barefaced; (*Cono Sur: orgulloso*) proud, haughty. (c) (*CAm: atractivo*) attractive, congenial.

cachicamo NM (*And, Carib*) armadillo.

cachicán **1** ADJ sly, crafty.

   2 NM (a) (*Agr*) foreman, gaffer. (b) (*) sly sort, wide boy*.

cachicuerno ADJ *arma* with a horn handle.

cachifa NF (*LAm, Carib*) girl, kid*.

cachifo NM (*And, CAm, Carib*) lad, kid*; young boy.

cachilla NF (*Cono Sur*) jalop(p)y, old crock.

cachimba **1** NF (a) (*LAm: pipa*) pipe. (b) (*LAm: cartucho*) empty cartridge. (c) (*Cono Sur: pozo*) shallow well (*o* water hole). (d) (*Carib‡: puta*) tart‡, slut. (e) **fregar la ~ a uno*** to get on sb's nerves.

   2 ADJ (*) fantastic*, terrific*.

cachimbazo* NM (*CAm*) (a) (*golpe*) thump, blow. (b) (*trago*) shot, slug* (*US*).

cachimbo NM (a) (*LAm: pipa*) pipe; **chupar ~** (*Carib*) to smoke a pipe; (*hum: niño*) to suck its thumb.

   (b) (*Carib: ingenio*) small sugar mill.

   (c) (*Carib: pobre*) poor man.

   (d) (*) (*And Univ*) freshman.

   (e) (*CAm*: montón*) pile, heap.

   (f) (*And: Mil*) soldier, squaddie*.

cachimbón* ADJ (*CAm*) smart, sharp.

cachipolla NF mayfly.

cachiporra NF (a) (*bastón*) truncheon; club, big stick, cosh. (b) (*Cono Sur: jactancioso*) braggart.

cachiporrazo NM blow with a truncheon (*etc*).

cachiporrear* [1a] **1** VT (*Mús etc*) to bash*, pound.

   2 cachiporrearse VR (*Cono Sur*) to brag, boast.

cachito NM (a) (*And*) (*juego de dados*) dice game; (*cubito*) dice cup. (b) (*LAm**) **espera un ~** just a minute, hang on a sec*; **un ~ de café** a drop of coffee.

cachivache NM (a) pot, utensil. (b) **~s** pots and pans, kitchen utensils; (*fig*) trash, junk, lumber.

cacho[1] **1** ADJ (*corvado*) bent, crooked.

   2 NM (a) (*miga*) crumb; (*pedacito*) bit, small piece, slice; **¡~ de gloria!** my precious!; **¡~ de ladrón!** you thief!; **es un ~ de pan*** he's terribly kind.

   (b) (*LAm: cuerno*) horn; **~s** (number of) cattle; **hombre de muchos ~s** large cattle farmer; **¿cuántos ~s tiene?** how many head of cattle does he own?; **montar ~s a uno** to cuckold sb.

   (c) (*And, Cono Sur: dados*) dice, set of dice; (*cubo de dados*) dice box (*o* cup); **jugar al ~** to play dice.

   (d) (*Cono Sur: para beber*) cup (made of horn); **empinar el ~** to drink a lot.

   (e) (*Cono Sur: plátanos*) bunch of bananas.

(f) (*Cono Sur: Com*) unsaleable (*o* unsold) goods.

(g) (*LAm*) (*chiste*) funny story, joke; (*broma*) prank, practical joke; (*Carib: mofa*) mockery, derision.

(h) (*Carib‡: marijuana*) joint‡.

(i) (*Carib*‡: *pene*) prick‡.

(j) (*Cono Sur*) (*problema*) problem; (*apuro*) jam*, tricky situation; (*maula*) unwanted object, useless thing.

(k) (*locuciones*) **echar ~ a uno** (*And*) to do better than (*o* surpass) sb; **estar fuera de ~** to be safe, be out of danger; **pegar los ~s a uno** (*CAm**) to cheat on sb, be unfaithful to sb; **raspar el ~ a uno** (*Cono Sur*) to tell sb off*; **¡~s para arriba!** (*Cono Sur*) that's marvellous!, splendid!

cacho² NM (*Pez*) (*de río*) chub; (*de mar*) (red) surmullet.

cachón NM (*ola*) wave, breaker; (*cascada*) small waterfall.

cachondear* [1a] (*CAm, Méx*) ☐1 VI (*acariciar*) to pet*; (*besarse*) to snog‡ (*Brit*).

☐2 **cachondearse** VR **(a)** to take things as a joke; **~ de uno** to take the mickey out of sb‡, make fun of sb. **(b)** (*LAm**) to get turned on*.

cachondeo* NM **(a)** (*guasa*) joking; teasing, nagging; messing about; **estar de ~** to be in a joking mood; **tomar algo a ~** to take sth as a joke; **para ella la vida es un ~ continuo** life for her is just one big joke.

(b) (*juerga*) **estar de ~** to live it up, have a good time.

(c) (*jaleo*) trouble, disturbance; **armar un ~** to make a fuss.

(d) (*farsa*) farce, mess; poor show*; **¡esto es un ~!** what a mess!, what a farce this is!

cachondez NF **(a)** (*Zool*) heat, rut, readiness to mate. **(b)** (*de persona*) sexiness; randiness*.

cachondo ADJ **(a)** (*Zool*) on heat, in rut. **(b)** (*persona*) **ser ~** to be sexy; **estar ~** to feel randy*, be in the mood. **(c)** (*juerguista*) fun-loving; high-spirited, riotous. **(d)** (*gracioso*) funny, amusing; jokey; **~ mental** crazy but likable.

cachorro, -a NM/F **(a)** (*perrito*) pup, puppy; (*de otro animal*) cub. **(b)** (*Carib*‡) EXCL you rat!*, you swine!‡

cachuca‡ NF (*And*) nick‡, prison.

cachucha‡ NF (*Méx*) hat, tile‡.

cachucho NM **(a)** (*Pez*) sea-bream. **(b)** (*alfiletero*) pin box. **(c)** (*And*) daily bread; **ganarse el ~** to make a living.

cachudo ☐1 ADJ **(a)** (*And, Méx: con cuernos*) horned, with horns.

(b) (*And: rico*) wealthy.

(c) (*Cono Sur*) (*receloso*) suspicious, distrustful; (*taimado*) cunning.

(d) (*Méx: triste*) long-faced, miserable.

☐2 NM: **el ~** the devil, the horned one.

cachuela NF **(a)** (*Culin*) stew, fricassee. **(b)** (*And: remolinos*) rapids.

cachupín NM, **cachupina** NF (*And, Carib: pey*) Spanish settler (in America).

cachureo NM (*Cono Sur*) bric-a-brac, junk, bits and pieces.

cachuzo* ADJ (*Cono Sur*) worn-out, old.

cacica NF (*LAm*) woman chief; chief's wife; (*Pol*) wife of a local boss (*etc*).

cacicada NF despotic act, high-handed act; abuse of authority.

cacillo NM ladle.

cacimba NF **(a)** (*And, Carib, Cono Sur: pozo*) well; (*Carib: de árbol*) hollow of tree where rain water is collected; (*And*) outdoor privy. **(b)** (*Carib, Méx: casucha*) hovel, slum.

cacique NM **(a)** (*LAm: jefe*) chief, headman, local ruler; (*Pol*) local boss, party boss; (*fig*) petty tyrant, despot; (*Cono Sur: vago*) person who lives idly in luxury. **(b)** (*And, CAm, Méx: ave*) oriole.

caciquil ADJ despotic, tyrannical.

caciquismo NM (*Pol*) (system of) dominance by the local boss; petty tyranny, despotism.

cacle NM (*Méx*) rough leather sandal.

caco* NM **(a)** (*ratero*) pickpocket, thief; (*criminal de categoría*) crook*. **(b)** (*cobarde*) coward.

cacofonía NF cacophony.

cacofónico ADJ cacophonous.

cacto NM, **cactus** NM INVAR cactus.

cacumen* NM perspicacity; brains, insight.

cada ADJ INVAR each; (*con número*) every; **~ día** each day; every day; **~ uno** each one; every one; **~ 3 meses** every 3 months; **~ (y) cuando** every now and then; **~ y cuando que ...** whenever ...; as soon as ...; **~ y siempre que ...** as soon as ...; **~ cierta distancia por la carretera** every so often along the road, at intervals along the road; **~ cierto tiempo** every so often; **¿~ cuánto?** how often?; (*LAm*) **~ que** every time, whenever; **~ que viene** every time he comes; **¡tienes ~ idea!** what funny ideas you have!; **oye una ~ historia** one hears some very strange stories (these days); *V t* **vez.**

cadalso NM scaffold; (*Téc*) stand, platform.

cadarzo NM floss, floss silk.

cadáver NM body, dead body, corpse, cadaver (*US*); **~ en el armario** (*fig*) skeleton in the cupboard; **¡sobre mi ~!** over my dead body!; **ingresó ~** he was dead on arrival (at hospital).

cadavérico ADJ cadaverous; death-like; ghastly, deathly pale.

caddie ['kadi] NMF (*Golf*) caddie.

┌─ **CADA** ──────── **ver también la entrada** ─┐

• *Cada* se traduce por *each* cuando queremos individualizar, cuando se conocen o se le quiere dar importancia a los elementos dentro del grupo:

A cada miembro del personal se le asignó una tarea específica
Each member of staff was allocated a specific task
Quiero tener una charla con cada uno de vosotros
I want to have a chat with each of you

• Se traduce por *every* cuando el número de elementos del grupo no se conoce o no importa, cuando se está generalizando:

Cada empresa funciona de una manera distinta
Every company works differently
Cada día me dice una cosa
Every day he tells me something different
Cada vez que viene nos trae un regalo
Every time he comes he brings us a present

NOTA: En expresiones como *cada dos meses/cada tres años/etc*, *cada* se traduce por *every*:
Se hace una revisión cada tres meses
He has a check-up every three months

• Cuando hablamos sólo de dos cosas o personas, *cada* solamente se puede traducir por *each*:
Es importante que cada gemelo desarrolle su propia personalidad
It is important that each twin develops his own personality

NOTA: Cuando *each* o *every* forman parte del sujeto, el verbo va en singular.

Para otros usos y ejemplos ver la entrada.

└──┘

cadena ☐1 NF **(a)** (*gen*) chain (*t Com, Inform*); (*fig*) bond, link; series, sequence; (*Rad, TV*) network; **~ de agrimensor** surveyor's chain (*10m = 22 yards*); **~ alimentaria, ~ alimenticia** food chain; **~s (antideslizantes)** tyre chains; **~ de distribución** (*Aut*) timing chain; **~ de ensamblaje** assembly line; **~ de fabricación** production line; **~ de hoteles** chain of hotels; **~ de mando** chain of command; **~ de montaje** assembly line; **~ de montañas** range of mountains; **~ de oruga** caterpillar track; **~ de producción** production line; **~ de reloj** watch chain; **~ sin fin** endless chain; **~ de sonido** sound system; **reacción en ~** chain reaction.

(b) (*Jur: Hist*) chain-gang.

(c) **~ perpetua** (*Jur*) life imprisonment.

(d) (*Arquit*) wooden frame.

☐2 **~s*** NM: **ser un ~** (*Esp*) to be a boaster.

cadencia NF cadence, rhythm; measure; (*Mús*) cadence, cadenza.

cadencioso ADJ rhythmic(al), cadenced.

cadeneta NF (*Cos*) chain stitch; **~ de papel** paper chain.

cadenilla NF, **cadenita** NF small chain; (*collar*) necklace.

cadera NF hip.

caderamen* NM big hips, massive hips.

cadetada NF thoughtless action, irresponsible act.

cadete NM (*Mil etc*) cadet; (*Dep*) junior; (*LAm*) office-boy; apprentice.

cadí NM (*Hist*) cadi.

Cádiz NM Cadiz.

cadmio NM cadmium.

caducar [1g] VI **(a)** (*persona*) to become senile; to dodder, be in one's dotage.

(b) (*permiso etc*) to get out of date, run out; (*costumbre*) to fall into disuse; (*Com, Jur*) to expire, lapse; **el abono ha caducado** the season ticket has expired.

(c) (*deteriorarse*) to deteriorate.

(d) (*comida*) to be (*o* go) past its sell-by date.

caducidad NF lapse, lapsing, expiry; **fecha de ~** (*alimentos*) sell-by date.

caduco ADJ **(a)** *persona* senile, very old, decrepit; worn out.

(b) (*Bot*) deciduous.

(c) *placer etc* fleeting, perishable.

(d) (*Com, Jur*) lapsed, expired, invalid; **quedar ~** to lapse.

caduquez NF senility, decrepitude.

C.A.E. (a) (*Com*) ABR **de cóbrese al entregar** cash on delivery, COD.

(b) NM (*Jur*) ABR **de Código Alimentario Español.**

caedizo ☐1 ADJ unsteady, about to fall; weak; (*Bot*) deciduous.

☐2 NM (*And*) (*edificio*) shed; (*techo*) sloping roof.

caer [2n] VI *y en ciertos sentidos* **caerse** VR **(a)** (*gen*) to fall; to fall down; (*desplomarse*) to tumble (down), collapse; (*separarse*) to fall off, fall out; (*Aer*) to crash, come down; (*cortina etc*) to hang; (*pelo, rama*) to hang down; **~ al suelo** to fall to the ground; **el edificio se está cayendo** the building is falling down; **~ sobre** to fall on, pounce on; to descend upon; **cayó un rayo en la torre** the tower was struck by lightning; **estar al ~** to be about to fall, (*fig*) be about to happen, be due to happen; (*persona*) to be about to arrive; **estar a la que cae**

to be alert; **dejar ~** to drop, let fall; **dejarse ~** to let o.s. go, let o.s. fall; **hacer ~** to knock down, knock over, knock off, cause to fall; **se me cayó el guante** I dropped my glove, my glove fell off; **Eslobodia nunca cayó tan bajo** Slobodia never fell so low; **~ en cama, ~ enfermo** to fall ill; **~ en un error** to fall into error; **~ redondo** to fall in a heap; **~se de miedo** to be terrified; **~se de tonto** (*etc*) to be very silly (*etc*); **se cae de viejo** he's so old he can hardly walk; **eso (se) cae de suyo** that's obvious, that goes without saying.

(**b**) (*morir*) to fall (in battle); (*Mil: ciudad*) to fall, be captured; (*: ser detenido*) to be arrested; **ha caído el gobierno** the government has fallen; **~ como chinches, ~ como moscas** to fall like flies.

(**c**) (*nivel, precio, temperatura*) to fall, go down; to diminish; (*conversación*) to flag; (*costumbre etc*) to lapse.

(**d**) (*sol, viento*) to go down.

(**e**) (*día*) to decline, draw to its close; (*noche*) to fall, close in; **al ~ de la noche** at nightfall.

(**f**) (*color*) to fade.

(**g**) (*lugar*) to fall, lie, be located; **cae en el segundo tomo** it comes in the second volume; **eso cae más hacia el este** that lies further to the east.

(**h**) (*ventanas etc*) **~ a, ~ hacia** to look over, look out on, look towards.

(**i**) (*suceso*) to fall; **el aniversario cae en martes** the anniversary falls on a Tuesday.

(**j**) (*Com, Fin*) to fall due.

(**k**) (*herencia*) **~ a** to fall to, come to, fall to the lot of; *V* **suerte.**

(**l**) (*darse cuenta*) to realize; **no caigo** I don't get it; **ya caigo** I see, now I understand; **~ en que ...** to realize that ...; *V* **cuenta.**

(**m**) (*vestido*) **~ bien a uno** to suit sb, look well on sb; **el traje le caía mal** the suit did not fit him, the suit was not right for him.

(**n**) (*impresión*) **no me cae bien** (o **me cae mal**) I don't like him at all, I really don't like him, we don't get on at all well; **no me cayó bien** he did not make a good impression on me; (*más fuerte*) I didn't take to him at all; **no les caí** (*CAm*) I didn't hit it off with them, I didn't get on well with them, they didn't take to me.

(**o**) (*comida*) **~ mal a** to disagree with.

(**p**) (*Cono Sur: hacer una visita*) to come by, visit, drop in; **él suele ~ por aquí** he usually comes here.

(**q**) (*) **ese número es de ~se** that number is a real riot*.

café NM (**a**) (*bebida, grano, planta*) coffee; **~ ~** real coffee, coffee that really is coffee; **~ americano** large black coffee; **~ cerrero** (*And*) strong black coffee; **~ cortado** coffee with a dash of milk; **~ exprés** expresso coffee; **~ helado** iced coffee; **~ instantáneo, ~ soluble** instant coffee; **~ irlandés** Irish coffee; **~ con leche** white coffee, coffee with milk; (**:**) queer**:**; **~ molido** ground coffee; **~ negro, ~ solo, ~ tinto** (*LAm*) black coffee; **~ pintado** (*And*), **~ quemado** (*Carib*) coffee with a drop of milk; **~ tostado** roasted coffee.

(**b**) (*establecimiento*) café; coffee-house; restaurant, bar; **~ cantante** café which provides entertainment, seedy night-club.

(**c**) (*: reprimenda*) ticking-off*.

(**d**) **estar de mal ~** to be in a bad mood, (*CAm*) to be out of sorts; **tener mal ~** to have a nasty temper; to have evil intentions.

(**e**) (*t* **color ~**) brown; **~ avellana** (*como adj*) nut-brown.

cafecito NM (*LAm*) black coffee.

café-concierto NM café which provides entertainment.

cafeína NF caffein(e).

cafetal NM (**a**) (*plantío*) coffee plantation. (**b**) (*CAm: árbol*) coffee tree.

cafetalero (*LAm*) **1** ADJ coffee (*atr*), coffee-growing (*atr*); **industria cafetalera** coffee-growing industry.

2 NM, **cafetalera** NF coffee grower.

cafetalista NMF (*LAm*) coffee grower.

cafetear* [1a] VT (*Cono Sur*) to tick off*, tell off*.

café-teatro NM café which provides entertainment.

cafetera¹ NF (**a**) (*gen*) coffee pot; **~ automática** electric kettle; **~ filtradora** percolator. (**b**) (*) (*Aut*) old crock, jalop(p)y; (*de policía*) police car.

cafetería NF café, coffee house; (*Ferro*) buffet, refreshment room; (*And, Carib, Cono Sur*) retail coffee shop.

cafetero **1** ADJ (**a**) (*Com*) coffee (*atr*); **industria cafetera** coffee industry. (**b**) (*que bebe café*) coffee-drinking; fond of coffee; **soy muy ~** I drink a lot of coffee. (**c**) (*asiduo*) fond of going to cafés; **es muy ~** he spends a lot of time in cafés.

2 NM, **cafetera²** NF (*: dueño*) café proprietor, café owner; (*cultivador*) coffee grower; (*comerciante*) coffee merchant.

cafetín NM seedy bar, small café.

cafeto NM (*LAm*) coffee bush.

cafetucho NM seedy little café.

cafiche* NM pimp.

cafichear* [1a] VI (*Cono Sur*) to live off sb else, ponce.

caficho* NM (*Cono Sur*) pimp, ponce.

caficultor(a) NM/F (*CAm*) coffee grower.

caficultura NF (*CAm*) coffee growing.

cáfila NF caravan, group, flock, large number (*esp* on the march); **una ~ de disparates** a string of nonsense.

cafiolo* NM (*Cono Sur*) pimp, ponce.

cafre **1** ADJ (**a**) (*lit*) Kaffir. (**b**) (*fig: cruel*) cruel, savage; uncouth, boorish.

2 NMF Kaffir; **como ~s** (*fig*) like savages, like beasts.

caftán NM caftan, kaftan.

cagaaceite NM missel thrush.

cagada: NF (**a**) (*acto*) shit**:**, crap**:**.

(**b**) (*materia*) shit**:**; turd**:**.

(**c**) (*fig: lío*) cock-up**:**, fuck-up**:**; (*tonterías*) crap**:**; **decir una ~** to talk a lot of crap**:**.

cagadera: NF (*LAm*) the shits**:**, diarrhoea.

cagadero: NM bog**:**, john (*US*:).

cagado: ADJ yellow, funky*.

cagajón NM horse-dung, mule-dung.

cagalera: NF runs**:**, the shits**:**; (*iró*) **¡brava ~!** what a mess!

cagar [1h] **1** VT (**a**) (**:** *gen*) to shit**:**, crap**:**.

(**b**) (**:**) *ropa* to dirty, soil.

(**c**) (**:** *fig: t* **~la**) to cock (it) up**:**; **¡la cagamos!** we blew it!**:**

2 VI (**:**) to shit**:**, have a shit**:**.

3 **cagarse** VR (**a**) = VI.

(**b**) (**:**) **¡me cago!, ¡me cago en la mar!** (*etc*) well I'm damned!; damn it!; **¡me cago en el gobierno!** to hell with the government!; **... y se caga la perra ...** (*Esp*) and you never saw anything like it; **la tía estaba que te cagas** she was absolutely fantastic*.

cagarro: NM fag**:**, ciggy*.

cagarruta NF (**a**) (*de animal*) sheep-droppings, goat dirt. (**b**) **es una ~ de su padre:** (*Esp*) he's the spitting image of his father.

cagatintas NM INVAR penpusher, clerk; (*And*) miser.

cagón: **1** ADJ = **cagado.**

2 NM, **cagona** NF coward.

caguama NF (*Méx*) large turtle.

cague: NM: **le entró un ~ de mucho cuidado** he was scared shitless**:**.

cagueruelas: NFPL: **las ~** the runs**:**, the trots**:**.

cagueta NMF, **caguetas:** NMF INVAR, **caguica:** NMF INVAR coward.

caguitis: NF fear, funk*; **le entra ~** he gets the wind up*.

Cahispa [ka'ispa] NF ABR *de* **Caja Hispana de Previsión.**

cahuin NM (*Cono Sur*) (**a**) drunkenness, drunken spree. (**b**) rowdy gathering. (**c**) (*Cono Sur:* lío) mess, cock-up**:**.

caída NF (**a**) fall; tumble, spill; falling, falling-out; (*fig*) fall, collapse, downfall; (*Teat*) flop*, failure; **la C~** (*Rel*) the Fall; **la ~ del gobierno** the fall of the government; **la ~ del imperio** the collapse of the empire; **la ~ de los dientes** the falling-out of one's teeth, the loss of one's teeth; **~ de agua** waterfall; **~ de cabeza** fall headfirst, header; **~ libre** free fall; **a la ~ del sol** at sunset; **a la ~ de la tarde** in the evening; **sufrir una ~** to have a fall, have a tumble.

(**b**) (*nivel, precio etc*) fall, drop (*de 5 grados* of 5 degrees; *de la temperatura* in temperature: *de tensión* in blood pressure); decline, diminution; **~ de la actividad económica** downturn in the economy.

(**c**) (*terreno*) drop, fall, slope; (*Geol*) dip; (*de espaldas*) slope.

(**d**) (*de cortina etc*) fold(s); (*de vestido*) set, hang.

(**e**) **~ radiactiva** radioactive fallout.

(**f**) **~s** (*Téc*) low-grade wool.

(**g**) **~s*** witty remarks; **¡qué ~s tiene!** isn't he witty?

caído **1** ADJ (**a**) (*gen*) fallen; *cabeza etc* drooping; *cuello* turndown; *flor etc* languid, limp, drooping; **estar ~ de sueño** to be dead tired.

(**b**) (*fig*) crestfallen, dejected.

(**c**) **~ de color** pale.

2 NM (**a**) (*muertos*) **los ~s** the fallen; **los ~s por España** those who fell for Spain; **monumento a los ~s** war memorial.

(**b**) (*Méx: soborno*) backhander*, bribe.

caifán* NM (*Méx*) pimp, ponce.

caigo *etc V* **caer.**

caimacán NM (*And*) important person, big shot*; ace, star, expert.

caimán NM (**a**) (*LAm Zool: reptil parecido al cocodrilo*) cayman, caiman, alligator. (**b**) (*And Zool: iguana*) iguana. (**c**) (*LAm*: *estafador*) twister, swindler. (**d**) (*Méx Méc*) chain wrench. (**e**) (*And: gandul*) lazy fellow.

caimanear [1a] (*LAm*) **1** VT to swindle, cheat.

2 VI to hunt alligators.

caimiento NM (**a**) (*acto*) fall, falling; (*Med*) decline. (**b**) (*fig*) dejection; limpness.

Caín NM Cain; **pasar las de ~** to have a ghastly time*; **venir con las de ~** to have evil intentions.

cainismo NM fratricidal violence, fratricidal treachery.

cairel NM (*peluca*) wig; (*Cos*) fringe.

cairelear [1a] VT to trim, fringe.

Cairo NM: **el ~** Cairo.

caita **1** ADJ INVAR (*Cono Sur*) (*montaraz*) wild, untamed; (*huraño*) unsociable, withdrawn.

2 NM (*Cono Sur*) migratory agricultural worker.
caite NM (*CAm*) rough rubber-soled sandal.
caitearse [1a] VR: ~**las** (*CAm*) to run away, beat it*.
caja NF (**a**) (*gen*) box; (*arca*) chest; (*de embalaje*) case, crate; (*ataúd*) coffin, casket (*US*); ~ **acústica** loudspeaker; ~ **anidadera** nestbox, nesting-box; (*TV*) **la** ~ (**boba** *etc*)* the box*; ~ **de colores** paintbox; ~ **de cuchillería** cutlery cabinet; ~ **china** Chinese box; ~ **del cuerpo** chest, thorax; ~ **de herramientas** toolbox, tool-chest; ~ **de música** musical box; ~ **negra** (*Aer*) black box; ~ **nido** nestbox, nesting-box; ~ **de seguridad** safe-deposit box; ~ **de sorpresa(s)** jack-in-the-box; ~ **del tambor**, ~ **del tímpano** (*Anat*) eardrum; ~ **torácica** chest wall; **estar en** ~ (*persona*) to be in good shape, (*aparato*) to be working well.
(**b**) (*Mec*) case, casing, housing; (*de vehículo*) body; ~ **de cambios** gearbox; ~ **del cigüeñal** crankcase; ~ **de eje** axle-box; ~ **de engranajes** gearbox; ~ **de fuego** (*Ferro*) fire-box; ~ **de sebo** grease-cup; ~ **de velocidades** gearbox.
(**c**) (*Elec*) box; ~ **de empalmes** junction box; ~ **de fusibles** fuse-box.
(**d**) (*Arquit: de escalera*) well; (*de ascensor*) well, shaft; ~ **de registro** manhole.
(**e**) ~ (**de fusil**) stock.
(**f**) (*Bot*) seed case, capsule.
(**g**) (*Com, Fin*) (*de caudales*) cashbox, safe; (*mesa*) cashier's desk, cashdesk; (*oficina*) cashier's office; (*de supermercado*) check-out; ~ **de alquiler** safe-deposit box; ~ **de caudales** strongbox, safe; ~ **de fondo** (*Cono Sur*) safe deposit box, strongbox; ~ **fuerte** strongroom, bank vault; strongbox; ~ **de** (**gastos**) **menores** petty cash; ~ **de reclutamiento** recruiting office; ~ **registradora** cash register, till; **metálico en** ~ cash in hand; **hacer** ~ to make up the accounts for the day, cash up; **hicieron** ~ **de X pesetas** they took in X pesetas; **ingresar en** ~ (*persona*) to pay in, (*dinero*) be paid in.
(**h**) (*Fin*) fund; ~ **B** secret account, secret fund, slush fund; ~ **de ahorros** savings bank; ~ **postal de ahorros** post-office savings bank; ~ **de compensación** equalization fund; ~ **de construcciones** building society; ~ **de jubilaciones** pension fund; ~ **de resistencia** strike fund; ~ **rural** agricultural credit bank.
(**i**) **despedir** (o **echar**) **a uno con** ~**s destempladas** to send sb packing.
(**j**) (*Mús*) (*de piano etc*) case; (*de violín etc*) body, case; (*Rad*) cabinet; (*tambor*) drum; ~ **de resonancia** soundbox; (*fig*) sounding board; ~ **de ritmos** drum machine, beatbox.
(**k**) (*Tip*) case; ~ **alta** upper case; ~ **baja** lower case.
(**l**) (*Cono Sur: lecho de río*) (dried up) riverbed.
cajear* [1a] VT (*And, CAm*) to beat up*.
cajero, -a NM/F cashier; (*bank*) teller; ~ **automático** cash-dispenser, autoteller.
cajeta NF (**a**) small box; (*LAm: para dulces*) small round sweet box; (*LAm: dulce de leche*) fudge, soft toffee; (*Méx: dulce de jalea*) jelly; (*And: dulce*) sweet, candy (*US*).
(**b**) (*And, CAm: de animal*) lip.
(**c**) **de** ~ (*CAm, Méx: iró*) first-class, super.
(**d**) (*) (*Méx*) coward; wimp*.
(**e**) (*Cono Sur‡*) cunt‡*.
cajete NM (*Méx*) (**a**) (*cazuela*) earthenware pot (o bowl). (**b**) (*: wáter*) toilet, loo*. (**c**) (‡: *culo*) bum‡.
cajetilla **1** NF small box; ~ **de cigarrillos** packet of cigarettes, pack of cigarettes (*US*); (*Carib: dientes*) teeth.
2 NM (*Cono Sur*: *pey*) toff*, dude* (*US*); city slicker (*US*); (*afeminado*) poof‡, queen‡.
cajista NMF compositor, typesetter.
cajita NF small box; ~ **de cerillas**, ~ **de fósforos** (*LAm*) box of matches, matchbox; **de** ~ (*LAm*) great*, fine.
cajón NM (**a**) (*caja*) big box, case; crate; chest; ~ **de embalaje** packing case.
(**b**) (*And, Cono Sur: ataúd*) coffin, casket (*US*).
(**c**) (*gaveta*) drawer; locker; (*Com*) till; ~ **de sastre** collection of odds and ends; mixed bag, pot pourri; (*persona*) muddle-headed sort; **estar como** ~ **de sastre** to be in utter disorder, be in a terrible mess.
(**d**) (*Com*) stall, booth; ~ **de ropa** (*Méx*) draper's (shop), dry-goods store (*US*).
(**e**) (*Téc*) ~ **hidráulico**, ~ **de suspensión** caisson.
(**f**) (*Dep*) ~ **de salida** starting-gate.
(**g**) (*CAm, Cono Sur: barranco*) ravine.
(**h**) **eso es de** ~ that's a matter of course, that goes without saying; that's the usual thing.
(**i**) (*And Mús*) box drum.
caju NM cashew (nut).
cajuela NF (*Méx Aut*) boot, trunk (*US*).
cal NF lime; ~ **apagada**, ~ **muerta** slaked lime; ~ **viva** quicklime; **cerrar algo a** ~ **y canto** to shut sth firmly (o securely); **de** ~ **y canto** firm, strong, tough; **dar una de** ~ **y otra de arena** to apply a policy of the carrot and the stick; to blow hot and cold.

cala¹ NF (*Geog*) cove; creek, inlet; (*Pesca*) fishing ground; (*Náut*) hold; ~ **de construcción** slipway.
cala² NF (*de fruta*) sample slice; (*Med*) suppository; (*Aut*) dipstick; (*Med: sonda*) probe; **hacer** ~ **y cata** to test for quality.
cala³‡ NF (*Esp*) one peseta.
cala⁴‡ NM (*Mil*) glasshouse‡, prison.
calabacear* VT (*Univ*) *candidato* to fail, plough*; *amante* to jilt.
calabacera NF pumpkin (plant), gourd (plant).
calabacín NM (**a**) (*Bot*) marrow, courgette. (**b**) (*fig: idiota*) dolt.
calabacita NF (*Esp*) courgette.
calabaza NF (**a**) (*Bot*) pumpkin; gourd, calabash.
(**b**) (*fig: idiota*) dolt.
(**c**) (‡: *cabeza*) bonce‡, head.
(**d**) (*) **dar** ~**s a** *candidato* to fail, plough*; *amante* to jilt; (*ofender*) to snub, offend; **llevarse** ~**s**, **recibir** ~**s** (*Univ*) to fail, plough*; (*amante*) to be jilted; **salir** ~ to be a flop*, prove a miserable failure.
calabazada NF butt, knock (with the head); blow on the head.
calabazazo NM bump on the head.
calabazo NM (**a**) (*Bot*) pumpkin, gourd. (**b**) (*Carib Mús*) drum.
calabobos NM drizzle.
calabozo NM prison; prison cell; (*esp Hist*) dungeon; (*Mil*) military prison.
calabrote NM (*Náut*) cable-laid rope, cable rope.
calache* NM (*CAm*) thing, thingummyjig*; **reúne tus** ~**s** get your things, get your bits and pieces.
calada NF (**a**) (*mojada*) soaking. (**b**) (*de red*) lowering. (**c**) (*: de humo*) puff, drag*. (**d**) (*de ave*) stoop, swoop, pounce. (**e**) (*: regañada*) ticking-off*; **dar una** ~ **a uno** to tick sb off*, haul sb over the coals.
caladero NM fishing-grounds.
calado **1** ADJ: **estar** ~ (**hasta los huesos**) to be soaked (to the skin).
2 NM (**a**) (*Téc*) fretwork; (*Cos*) openwork.
(**b**) (*Náut*) depth of water; (*de barco*) draught; **en iguales** ~**s** on an even keel.
(**c**) (*fig*) depth; scope; importance; **una razón de mayor** ~ a more weighty reason; **un descubrimiento de gran** ~ a very important discovery.
(**d**) (*Mec*) stall, stalling.
calafate NM caulker; shipwright.
calafatear [1a] VT (*Náut*) to caulk; to plug (up).
calaguasca NF (*LAm*) rum.
calagurritano **1** ADJ of Calahorra.
2 NM, **calagurritana** NF native (o inhabitant) of Calahorra; **los** ~**s** the people of Calahorra.
calamaco NM (*Méx: Culin*) kidney bean.
calamar NM squid.
calambrazo NM attack of cramp, spasm.
calambre NM (*t* ~**s**) cramp; ~ **de escribiente** writer's cramp.
calambur NM (*LAm*) pun.
calamidad NF calamity, disaster; **es una** ~* (*suceso etc*) it's a great pity; it's a nuisance; (*persona*) he's utterly useless, he's a dead loss; **estar hecho una** ~ to be in a very bad way; **¡vaya** ~! what bad luck!
calamina NF (**a**) (*gen*) calamine. (**b**) (*LAm*) corrugated iron.
calaminado ADJ (*LAm*) firm, bumpy, uneven.
calamita NF lodestone; magnetic needle.
calamitosamente ADV calamitously, disastrously.
calamitoso ADJ calamitous, disastrous.
cálamo NM (*Bot*) stem, stalk; (*Mús*) reed; (*Mús: Hist*) flute; (*poét*) pen; **empuñar el** ~ to take up one's pen; **menear** ~ to wield a pen.
calamocano* ADJ (**a**) (*borracho*) merry*, tipsy. (**b**) (*cariñoso*) doting.
calamoco NM icicle.
calamorra NF nut, head.
calamorrada* NF butt; bump on the head.
calandraco ADJ (*And, Cono Sur*) (*fastidioso*) annoying, tedious; (*casquivano*) scatterbrained.
calandria¹ NF (*Orn*) calandra lark.
calandria² **1** NF (**a**) (*rodillo*) mangle; (*Téc*) calender. (**b**) (*Fin‡*) one peseta. (**c**) (*argot*) underworld slang, argot.
2 NMF (*) (*persona*) malingerer.
calaña NF model, pattern; (*fig: gen pey*) nature, kind, stamp.
calañés NM (*Andalucía*) hat with a turned-up brim.
calar¹ **1** ADJ calcareous, lime (*atr*).
2 NM limestone quarry.
calar² [1a] **1** VT (**a**) *persona* to soak, drench; *materia* to soak, drench; (*empapar*) to soak into, saturate, permeate.
(**b**) (*penetrar*) to penetrate, perforate, pierce, go through.
(**c**) (*Téc*) *metal* to do fretwork on; (*Cos*) to do openwork on.
(**d**) (*penetrar, fig*) *persona* to size up; *intención* to see through; *secreto* to penetrate; **¡nos ha calado!** he's rumbled us!*; **a ésos los tengo muy calados** I've got them thoroughly weighed up (o sized up).
(**e**) (*fijar*) *bayoneta* to fix; *mástil* to fix, step.
(**f**) *puente* to lower, let down; *red, vela* to lower.
(**g**) *fruta* to cut a sample slice of; (*LAm*) *maíz* to take a sample of.

(h) (*And*: *aplastar*) to crush, flatten, sit on; (*fig*: *humillar*) to humiliate.
(i) (*Náut*) to draw; **el buque cala 12 metros** the ship draws 12 metres, the ship has a draught of 12 metres.
2 VI **(a)** (*líquido*) to sink in, soak in; (*zapato*) to leak, let in the water.
(b) (*fig*) **~ en** to go deeply into; **hay que ~ más hondo** this must be investigated further, one must dig more deeply into this.
(c) (*Mec*) to stop, stall.
(d) (*Orn*) = **3 (c).**
3 calarse VR **(a)** (*mojarse*) to get soaked, get drenched (*hasta los huesos* to the skin).
(b) (*lograr entrar*) to get in, squeeze in; to sneak in.
(c) (*Orn*) to stoop, swoop (down), pounce (*sobre* on).
(d) (*Mec*) to stop, stall.
(e) **~ el sombrero** to pull one's hat down; to put one's hat on firmly; **~ las gafas** to stick one's glasses on; to push one's glasses back.
calarredes NM INVAR trawler.
calatear [1a] **1** VT (*And, Cono Sur*) to undress, strip.
2 calatearse VR to get undressed, strip off.
calato ADJ (*And*) naked, bare; (*fig*) penniless, broke*.
calavera 1 NF **(a)** (*Anat*) skull.
(b) (*Ent*) death's-head moth.
(c) (*Méx Aut*) rear light.
2 NM (*juerguista*) gay dog†; (*locuelo*) madcap; (*libertino*) rake, roué; (*canalla*) rotter†, cad†, heel.
calaverada NF madcap escapade, foolhardy act.
calaverear [1a] VI to live it up*; to have one's fling; (*pey*) to lead a wild life, live recklessly.
calca NF **(a)** (*And Agr*) barn, granary. **(b)** (*LAm*: *copia*) copy.
calcado NM tracing.
calcañal NM, **calcañar** NM, **calcaño** NM heel.
calcar [1g] VT **(a)** (*Téc*) to trace, make a tracing of. **(b)** **~ A en B** (*copiar*) to model A on B, base A on B; (*pey*) to copy A slavishly from B.
calcáreo ADJ calcareous, lime (*atr*).
calce NM **(a)** (*llanta*) (steel) tyre; (*cuña*) wedge, shim; (*punta*) iron tip; (*And*: *empaste*) filling (*of a tooth*).
(b) (*CAm, Carib, Méx*: *de documento*) foot, lower margin (of a document); (*firma*) signature; **firmar al ~** to sign at the foot (*o* bottom) of the page.
(c) (*Cono Sur*: *oportunidad*) chance, opportunity.
calcés NM masthead.
calceta NF **(a)** (*media*) (knee-length) stocking. **(b)** (*hierro*) fetter, shackle. **(c) hacer ~** to knit.
calcetería NF **(a)** (*oficio*) hosiery. **(b)** (*tienda*) hosier's (shop).
calcetero, -a NM/F hosier.
calcetín NM sock; **~ de viaje‡** French letter; **darle la vuelta al ~** (*fig*) to turn things upside-down.
calcha NF **(a)** (*Cono Sur*: *ropa*) clothing, (*de cama*) bedding; (*arreos*) harness. **(b)** (*Cono Sur*: *cerneja*) fetlock; (*fleco*) fringe (of hair); (*pingajos*) tatters, strands.
calchona NF (*Cono Sur*) ghost, bogey; (*fig*) hag.
calchudo ADJ (*Cono Sur*) shrewd, cunning.
calcícola 1 ADJ calcicolous.
2 NF calcicole.
calcificación NF calcification.
calcificante ADJ calcifying.
calcificar [1g] **1** VT to calcify.
2 calcificarse VR to calcify.
calcífugo ADJ calcifugous.
calcina NF concrete.
calcinación NF calcination.
calcinar [1a] **1** VT **(a)** (*gen*) to calcine; to burn, reduce to ashes, blacken; **las ruinas calcinadas del edificio** the blackened ruins of the building.
(b) (*: *fastidiar*) to bother, annoy.
2 calcinarse VR to calcine.
calcio NM calcium.
calco NM **(a)** (*Téc*) tracing.
(b) (*fig*: *acto*) imprint(ing); graft(ing); implantation; **~ a escala** scale model.
(c) (*Ling*) calque (*de* on), loan-translation (*de* of); semantic borrowing (*de* from).
(d) **~s‡** (*pies*) plates‡, feet; (*zapatos*) shoes.
calcomanía NF transfer.
calculable ADJ calculable.
calculador ADJ **(a)** (*gen*) calculating. **(b)** (*LAm*: *egoísta*) selfish, mercenary; **~ solar** solar calculator.
calculadora NF calculating machine, calculator; **~ de bolsillo** pocket calculator.
calcular [1a] VT **(a)** to calculate, compute; to add up, work out. **(b)** **~ que ...** to reckon that ...; to anticipate that ..., expect that ...
cálculo NM **(a)** (*gen*) calculation; (*cómputo*) reckoning; estimate;

(*conjetura*) conjecture; (*Mat*) calculus; **~ de costo** costing; **~ diferencial** differential calculus; **hoja de ~** spreadsheet; **libro de ~s hechos** ready reckoner; **~ mental** mental arithmetic; **~ de probabilidades** theory of probability; **según mis ~s** according to my calculations, by my reckoning; **obrar con mucho ~** to act cautiously.
(b) (*Med*) stone; (*biliar*) gallstone.
Calcuta NF Calcutta.
calda NF **(a)** heating; stoking. **(b)** **~s** hot springs, hot mineral baths.
caldeamiento NM warming, heating.
caldear [1a] **1** VT to warm (up), heat (up); (*Téc*) to weld; **estar caldeado** to be very hot, (*fig*: *situación etc*) be very tense.
2 caldearse VR to get very hot, get overheated.
caldeo NM warming, heating; (*Téc*) welding.
caldera NF (*Téc*) boiler; boiling-pan; (*Cono Sur*) pot; (*tetera*) kettle, teapot; (*And*) crater; **las ~s de Pe(d)ro Botero** hell.
calderero NM boilermaker; coppersmith; **~ remendón** tinker.
caldereta NF **(a)** (*caldera pequeña*) small boiler; stewpan. **(b)** (*Ecl*) holy water vessel. **(c)** (*Culin*) fish stew; lamb stew. **(d)** (*Carib*: *viento*) warm wind from the sea.
calderilla NF **(a)** (*Ecl*) holy water vessel. **(b)** (*Fin*) small change, coppers; **en ~** in coppers.
caldero NM small boiler, copper.
calderón NM **(a)** (*caldera grande*) large boiler, cauldron. **(b)** (*Tip*) paragraph sign, section mark. **(c)** (*Mús*) pause (sign).
calderoniano ADJ relating to Calderón; **héroe ~** Calderonian hero; **estudios ~s** Calderón studies.
caldo NM **(a)** (*sopa*) broth, bouillon; (*consomé*) consommé, clear soup; (*salsa*) (*para asado*) gravy, (*para ensalada*) dressing, sauce; **~ de carne** (*para enfermo*) beef tea; **~ de cultivo** (*Bio*) culture medium; (*fig*) breeding ground; **~ de pollo** chicken broth; **~ de teta‡** milk; **cambiar el ~ a las aceitunas‡** to have a leak‡; **dar un ~ a uno** (*Cono Sur*) to torture sb; **estar a ~*** to be broke*; **hacer el ~ gordo** to make things easier, smooth the way; **hacer el ~ gordo a uno** to play into sb's hands, make it easy for sb; **se le hacía ~ la cabeza** (*Cono Sur*) he worried a lot about it; **poner a uno a ~*** to give sb a bashing*, (*fig*: *reprender*) to give sb a dressing-down*, (*insultar*) to lay into sb*, insult sb.
(b) **~s** (*aceite*) oil, (*vino*) wine, (*sidra*) cider (and other vegetable juices); **los ~s jerezanos** the wines of Jerez, sherries.
(c) (‡: *cigarrillo*) fag‡, gasper‡.
(d) (*Méx*) sugar cane juice.
caldoso* ADJ watery, weak.
calducho NM (*Cono Sur*) day off.
cale NM slap, smack.
calé 1 ADJ gipsy (*atr*).
2 NMF gipsy.
calefacción NF heating; **~ central** central heating; **sistema de ~** heating (system).
calefaccionable ADJ: **espejo exterior ~** heated wing mirror.
calefactor 1 ADJ heating (*atr*); **sistema ~** heating system.
2 NM heater.
calefán NM (*Cono Sur*) water heater.
calefón NM (*Cono Sur*) hot-water boiler, water-heater; **~ a gas** gas heater.
cal(e)idoscopio NM kaleidoscope.
caleidoscópico ADJ kaleidoscopic.
calendar [1a] VT to schedule, programme.
calendario NM calendar; (*de reforma etc*) timetable; (*de trabajo etc*) schedule; **~ de pared** wall calendar; **~ de taco** tear-off calendar; **hacer ~s** to muse, dream.
caléndula NF marigold.
calentador NM heater; **~ de agua** water-heater; **~ de cama** (*Hist*) bed-warmer, warming-pan; **~ eléctrico** electric fire; **~ a gas** gas heater, geyser, water heater; **~ de inmersión** immersion heater; **~es de piernas** leg-warmers.
calentamiento NM heating, warming; (*Deporte*: *previo*) warm-up; **~ global, ~ del planeta** global warming.
calentar [1j] **1** VT **(a)** *horno, agua,* to heat (up); *cuerpo, silla, comida, cuarto etc* to warm (up); *motor* to warm up; **~ al blanco** to make white-hot; **~ al rojo** to make red-hot.
(b) *negocio etc* to hurry on, speed up, get moving.
(c) (*LAm*: *provocar*) to anger, enrage.
(d) (*: *zurrar*) to warm*, tan*.
(e) (*: *excitar*) to arouse (sexually), turn on*.
2 calentarse VR **(a)** to heat up, warm up, get hot, get warm; (*junto al fuego*) to warm o.s.; (*Deporte*) to warm up.
(b) (*fig*: *discusión*) to get heated; (*persona*) to get heated, get het up, get excited (*por* about).
(c) (*Zool*) to be on heat; (*persona*) to get randy*, feel in the mood.
(d) (*LAm*: *enfadarse*) to get cross (*o* mad).
calentito ADJ *lugar* nice and warm; *comida* nice and hot; **aquí**

estaremos ~s we'll be nice and warm here; **una sopa calentita** a nice plate of hot soup.

calentón* ⬛1 ADJ sexy, randy*.

⬛2 NM **(a)** (*And, Cono Sur**) randy person*. **(b) darse el ~, tener un ~** to feel randy*, feel sexy, be in the mood.

calentura NF **(a)** (*Med: fiebre*) fever, (high) temperature; **estar con ~, tener ~** to be feverish, have a temperature; **tener ~ de pollo** to pretend to be ill, have an imaginary illness.

(b) (*Cono Sur: tuberculosis*) tuberculosis.

(c) (*And, Cono Sur: cachondez*) randiness*, sexual excitement; **tener ~** to feel randy*.

(d) (*And: rabieta*) fit of rage, tantrum.

calenturiento ADJ **(a)** (*Med*) feverish. **(b)** (*Cono Sur: tísico*) consumptive, tubercular. **(c)** *mente* (*indecente*) dirty, prurient; (*exaltado*) rash, impulsive; (*Pol etc*) **las mentes calenturientas** the hotheads.

calenturón NM high fever.

calenturoso ADJ (*Med*) feverish.

calera NF (*cantera*) limestone quarry; (*horno*) lime-kiln.

calero ⬛1 ADJ lime (*atr*).

⬛2 NM lime-kiln.

calés⁑ NMPL bread⁑, money.

calesa NF chaise, calash, buggy.

calesera NF Andalusian jacket.

calesín NM gig, fly.

calesita NF (*And, Cono Sur*) merry-go-round, carousel (*US*).

caleta NF **(a)** (*Geog*) cove, small bay, inlet. **(b)** (*And: Náut*) coasting vessel, coaster. **(c)** (*And*: escondite*) hiding-place.

caletero NM **(a)** (*Carib: estibador*) docker, port worker. **(b)** (*LAm Ferro*) milk-train. **(c)** (*Carib: en tienda*) shop assistant.

caletre* NM gumption*, brains; **no le cabe en el ~** he can't get it into his thick head*.

calibración NF calibration.

calibrado ADJ calibrated.

calibrador NM gauge; calliper(s); **~ de alambre** wire gauge.

calibraje NM calibration.

calibrar [1a] VT to calibrate; to gauge, measure.

calibre NM **(a)** (*gen*) calibre; gauge; (*Mil*) calibre, bore; (*Ferro*) gauge; (*de alambre, tubo etc*) diameter; (*fig*) calibre; **de grueso ~** large-bore; **palabras de grueso ~** (*Cono Sur*) crude language, swearing. **(b)** = **calibrador**.

calicanto NM (*Carib, Cono Sur: muro*) stone wall; (*muelle*) jetty.

calicata⁑ NF (*pierna*) leg; (*culo*) backside.

caliche NM **(a)** (*And, Cono Sur: salitre*) saltpetre; (*terreno*) nitrate-bearing ground. **(b)** (*Cono Sur: jalbegue*) crust of whitewash which flakes from a wall. **(c) echar un ~** ⁑ to have a screw⁑.

calicó NM calico.

calidad NF **(a)** (*gen*) quality; grade; **de ~** of quality; **de mala ~** of bad quality, bad-quality, low-quality; **~ de la vida** quality of life.

(b) (*posición*) position, capacity; **en ~ de** in the capacity of, as.

(c) (*de contrato*) stipulation, term; **a ~ de que ...** provided that ...

(d) (*rango*) rank, importance, quality.

(e) ~es (moral) qualities; gifts; worth.

cálido ADJ *clima, país* hot; (*fig*) *manta, aplausos, color etc* warm.

calidoscópico ADJ kaleidoscopic.

calidoscopio NM kaleidoscope.

calienta *etc* V **calentar**.

calientabiberones NM INVAR bottle warmer.

calientabraguetas⁑ NF INVAR cock-teaser⁑.

calientacamas NM INVAR electric blanket.

calientafuentes NM INVAR hotplate.

calientapiernas NM INVAR leg-warmer(s).

calientapiés NM INVAR hot-water bottle; foot warmer.

calientaplatos NM INVAR hotplate.

calientapollas⁑ NF INVAR (*Esp*) prick-teaser⁑.

caliente ⬛1 ADJ **(a)** (*gen*) warm; hot.

(b) (*fig*) *carácter* fiery, spirited; *discusión* heated; *batalla* raging; (*LAm*) *persona* angry, mad*; **~ de cascos** hot-headed; **un verano ~** (*Pol etc*) a long hot summer.

(c) *persona* **estar ~** (*Zool*) to be on heat; (*: *persona*) to feel randy*, be in the mood; **ponerse ~** to get randy*, get in the mood.

(d) en ~ in the heat of the moment; (*Téc*) hot; **persecución en ~** hot pursuit; **montar algo en ~** to assemble sth while it is hot, shrink sth on.

⬛2 NMF (⁑) **~ mental** oversexed person.

califa NM caliph.

califal ADJ caliphal; **la Córdoba ~** Cordova under the Caliphs, the Cordova of the Caliphs.

califato NM caliphate.

calificación NF **(a)** (*gen*) qualification; (*evaluación*) assessment; (*descripción*) description, label. **(b)** (*posición*) rating, standing; (*Escuela*) grade, mark; **~ de sobresaliente** first-class mark.

calificado ADJ **(a)** (*capacitado*) qualified, competent; *obrero* skilled. **(b)**

(*conocido*) well-known, eminent; *prueba etc* undisputed; *robo* proven, manifest. **(c)** (*Méx Jur*) qualified, conditional.

┌─ CALIENTE ────────── ver también la entrada ─┐

A la hora de traducir el adjetivo **caliente**, hay que tener en cuenta la diferencia en inglés entre los adjetivos **warm** y **hot**.

• Se utiliza **warm** cuando nos referimos a algo que está templado, que no quema o que no está suficientemente frío:

  El biberón del niño ya está caliente
  The baby's bottle is warm now
  ¡Esta cerveza está caliente!
  This beer is warm!

• Se emplea **hot** cuando estamos hablando de una temperatura alta, que puede quemar:

  No toques la sartén, está muy caliente
  Don't touch the frying pan, it's very hot
  Me apetece un café calentito
  I fancy a nice hot cup of coffee
  Para otros usos y ejemplos ver la entrada.

└─────────────────────────────────────┘

---

calificar [1g] ⬛1 VT **(a)** (*gen*) (*t Gram*) to qualify.

(b) (*evaluar*) to assess; to rate; *examen* to grade, mark.

(c) ~ a uno (*distinguir*) to distinguish sb, give sb his standing (*o* fame); (*ennoblecer*) to ennoble sb.

(d) ~ a uno de tonto to call sb silly, describe sb as silly, label sb silly.

⬛2 **calificarse** VR (*LAm: Pol*) to register as a voter.

calificativo ⬛1 ADJ qualifying.

⬛2 NM qualifier, epithet; description; **sólo merece el ~ de ...** it can only be described as ...

california NF (*Cono Sur*) **(a)** (*carrera*) horse-race. **(b)** (*Téc*) wirestretcher.

californiano, -a ADJ, NM/F Californian.

calígine NF (*poét*) mist, darkness.

caliginoso ADJ (*poét*) misty, dark.

caligrafía NF calligraphy, penmanship.

caligrafiar [1c] VT to write in a stylish hand.

caligráfico ADJ calligraphic.

calilla NF (*CAm, Méx*) **(a)** (*persona*) bore, nuisance. **(b)** (*molestia*) nuisance. **(c)** (*engaño*) hoax; (*broma*) boring joke.

calima NF = **calina**.

calimocho NM drink of mixed Coca-Cola and wine.

calina NF haze, mist; (*industrial*) smog.

calinoso ADJ hazy, misty.

calipso NM calypso.

caliqueño NM **(a)** type of cheap cigar. **(b)** (⁑) prick⁑; **echar un ~** to have a screw⁑.

calistenia NF cal(l)isthenics.

cáliz NM **(a)** (*Bot*) calyx. **(b)** (*Ecl*) chalice, communion cup; (*poét*) cup, goblet; **~ de amargura, ~ de dolor** cup of sorrow, cup of bitterness.

caliza NF limestone.

calizo ADJ lime (*atr*); *tierra* limy.

callada: a la ~ ADV, **de ~** ADV on the quiet, secretly; **dar la ~ por respuesta** to say nothing.

calladamente ADV quietly, silently; secretly.

callado ADJ **(a)** (*temperamento*) quiet, reserved, reticent.

(b) (*silencioso*) quiet, silent; **todo estaba muy ~** everything was very quiet; **tener algo ~** to keep quiet about sth, keep sth secret; **¡qué se lo tenía Vd!** you kept pretty quiet about it!; **pagar para tener ~ a uno** to pay to keep sb quiet; **nunca te quedas ~** you always have an answer for everything.

callampa NF (*Cono Sur*) (*Bot*) mushroom; (*: *paraguas*) brolly*, umbrella; **~s** (* *Anat*) big ears; **~s** (*t* **población ~**) shanty-town, slum.

callana NF (*LAm Culin*) flat earthenware pan; (*Cono Sur hum*) pocket watch.

callandico ADV, **callandito** ADV softly, very quietly; stealthily.

callar [1a] ⬛1 VT *secreto* to keep; *hecho, pasaje etc* to pass over in silence, say nothing about, not mention; *dato, información* to keep back, keep to o.s., keep secret; *asunto vergonzoso* to keep quiet about, hush up.

⬛2 VI **y callarse** VR (*gen*) to keep quiet, be silent, remain silent; (*ruido*) to stop; (*dejar de hablar*) to become silent, stop talking (*o* playing *etc*); to become quiet; (*mar, viento*) to become still, be hushed; **¡calla!, ¡cállate!, ¡cállese!** (*orden*) shut up!*, be quiet!, hold your tongue!; **calla, calle** (*asintiendo*) say no more, enough said; **¡calla!** (*sorpresa*) you don't mean to say!, well!; **¡cállate la trompa!*** shut up!* **hacer ~ a uno** to make sb be quiet, make sb stop talking (*etc*); (*enérgicamente*) to shut sb up; **¿quieres ~?** you've said enough, that's enough now; **sería mejor ~se** it would be best to say nothing; **~ como una piedra, ~ como un muerto** to shut up like a clam; **quien calla otorga** silence gives consent; **al buen ~ llaman Sancho** silence is golden.

calle NF **(a)** (*gen*) street, road; **~ abajo** down the street; **~ arriba** up the street; **~ ciega** (*Carib*) cul-de-sac; **~ de dirección única, ~ de un (solo) sentido** (*Méx*) one-way street; **~ de doble sentido** two-way road; **~ mayor** high street, main street; **~ peatonal, ~ salón** pedestrian precinct; **~ de rodadura, ~ de rodaje** (*Aer*) taxiway; **precio en la ~** (*Aut*) price on the road; **dejar a uno en la ~** to put sb out of a job; **echar por la ~ de en medio** to push on, press on regardless; **echarse a la ~** to go out into the street; (*turba*) to take to the streets, riot, demonstrate; **hacer (la) ~*** (*prostituta*) to be on the streets, be on the game*; **llevarse a uno de ~** to bowl sb over; **llevar (o traer) a uno por la ~ de la amargura** to give sb a difficult time; **y ahora patea las ~s** now he's out on the streets; **poner a uno (de patitas) en la ~** to kick sb out, chuck sb out; to put sb out of a job; **quedarse en la ~** not to have a penny to one's name; **verse en la ~** to find oneself out of a job; *V* **aplanar, rondar.**

(b) (*camino para pasar*) passage, way; room; **¡~!** make way!; **abrir ~, hacer ~** to make way, clear the way.

(c) (*Dep: de piscina, pista*) lane; (*Golf*) fairway.

(d) (*fig: público*) **la ~** the public; **la presión de la ~** the pressure of public opinion.

calleja NF = **callejuela.**

callejear [1a] VI to wander about the streets, stroll around; (*pey*) to loaf, hang about idly.

callejera NF street-walker.

callejero ① ADJ **(a)** (*gen*) street (*atr*); **accidente ~** street accident; **disturbios ~s** trouble in the streets, rioting in the streets; **perro ~** stray dog.

(b) *persona* fond of walking about the streets, fond of gadding about.

② NM **(a)** (*guía*) street directory. **(b)** (*Aut*) runabout.

callejón NM alley, alleyway, passage; (*And*) main street; (*Taur*) space between inner and outer barriers; **~ sin salida** cul-de-sac; blind alley (*t fig*); **gente de ~** (*And*) low-class people; **las negociaciones están en un ~ sin salida** the negotiations are at an impasse, the negotiations are deadlocked.

callejuela NF **(a)** (*gen*) narrow street, side street; alley, passage. **(b)** (*fig: subterfugio*) subterfuge; way out (of the difficulty).

callicida NM corn cure.

callista NMF chiropodist.

callo NM **(a)** (*Med: de pie*) corn; callus; **criar ~s** to become inured, become hardened; **pisar los ~s a uno** to tread on sb's toes (*o* corns). **(b)** (*Esp Culin*) **~s** tripe; **~s al ajo** tripe with garlic. **(c)** (**: mujer*) old bat*, old cow*; ugly woman; (*hombre*) villain, nasty piece of work*. **(d) dar el ~** (*Esp**) to slog, work hard.

callosidad NF callosity, hard patch (*on hand etc*).

calloso ADJ horny, hard, rough; calloused.

calma NF **(a)** (*Met, Náut*) calm, calm weather; **~ chicha** dead calm; **estar en ~** to be calm. **(b)** (*Com, Fin*) calm, inactivity, lull (*de* in); cessation, suspension (*de* of); **estar en ~** (*mercado*) to be steady. **(c)** (*de temperamento*) calm, calmness; (*pey*) slowness, phlegm, laziness; **¡~!, ¡con ~!** calm down!, don't get so worked up!, take your time!; **hacer algo con ~** to do sth calmly; **lo hizo con sus ~s*** he did it calmly, he did it slowly; **tomarlo con ~** to take things gently; **perder la ~** to get ruffled, lose one's composure.

calmante ① ADJ soothing, sedative. ② NM sedative, tranquillizer.

calmar [1a] ① VT (*gen*) to calm; *persona* to calm (down), quieten (down), soothe; *nervios* to soothe, steady; *dolor* to relieve. ② VI (*viento etc*) to abate, fall calm. ③ **calmarse** VR (*persona*) to calm down, calm o.s.; (*tiempo*) to improve, settle down; **¡cálmate!** calm down!, don't get so worked up!

calmazo NM dead calm.

calmécac NM (*Méx Hist*) Aztec school for priests.

calmo¹ ADJ slow, steady, measured.

calmo² ADJ (*esp LAm*) *tierra* barren, uncultivated.

calmosamente ADV **(a)** calmly. **(b)** slowly, sluggishly; nonchalantly, deliberately; lazily.

calmosidad NF **(a)** calm, calmness. **(b)** slowness, sluggishness; nonchalance; deliberateness; laziness.

calmoso ADJ **(a)** (*gen*) calm, quiet. **(b)** (*pey: torpe*) slow, sluggish; nonchalant, deliberate; lazy.

caló NM gipsy language, gipsy talk; (*argot*) slang; (*jerga*) cant.

calofriarse [1c] VR = **escalofriarse.**

calofrío NM = **escalofrío.**

calor NM **(a)** (*gen*) heat (*t Fís, Téc etc*); warmth; **un ~ agradable** a pleasant warmth; **un ~ excesivo** an excessive heat; **~ blanco** white heat; **~ rojo** red heat; **¡qué ~!** isn't it hot!, how hot it is!; **entrar en ~** to get warm, begin to feel warm; (*antes de jugar, con ejercicios*) to warm up; **hace ~** it's hot; **hace mucho ~** it's very hot; **tener ~** to be hot, feel hot; **tomar algo con ~** to work hard at sth.

(b) (*fig: de discusión*) warmth, heat; (*de batalla*) heat; (*de acogida etc*) warmth; (*de pasión*) ardour, fervour; excitement, passion; **dar ~ a** to

encourage; **meter a uno en ~** to enourage sb, incite sb.

caloría NF calorie.

calórico ADJ caloric.

calorífero ① ADJ heat-producing, heat-giving. ② NM (*sistema*) heating system; (*estufa*) furnace, stove; (*radiador*) heater, radiator; **~ mural** wall radiator.

calorífico ADJ calorific.

calorifugar [1h] VT *caldera, tubo* to lag.

calorífugo ADJ (*resistente*) heat-resistant, non-conducting; (*incombustible*) fireproof.

calorro, -a ADJ, NM/F gipsy.

calostro NM colostrum.

calote* NM (*Cono Sur*) con*, swindle; **dar ~** to skip payments, leave without paying.

calotear [1a] VT (*Cono Sur*) to swindle, con*.

calta NF marsh marigold (*t* **~ palustre**).

caluga NF (*Cono Sur*) toffee, chewy sweet.

caluma NF (*And*) mountain pass (*in the Andes*).

calumnia NF calumny; (*Jur*) (*oral*) slander, (*escrito*) libel (*de* on).

calumniador(a) NM/F slanderer, libeller.

calumniar [1b] VT to slander, libel; **calumnia, que algo queda** some of the mud sticks.

calumnioso ADJ slanderous, libellous.

calurosamente ADV (*fig*) warmly, enthusiastically, heartily.

caluroso ADJ **(a)** (*gen*) warm, hot. **(b)** (*fig: animado*) warm, enthusiastic, hearty.

calva NF (*en cabeza*) bald patch; (*en vestido*) bare spot, worn place; (*de bosque etc*) clearing.

Calvados NM INVAR Calvados.

Calvario NM **(a)** (*Ecl*) Calvary; Stations of the Cross; **c~** wayside shrine. **(b)** (*fig*) **c~** cross, heavy burden; series of disasters; string of debts; **pasar un ~** to suffer agonies.

calvatrueno* NM **(a)** (*calvo*) bald pate. **(b)** (*tarambana*) wild fellow, madcap.

calvero NM **(a)** (*de bosque*) glade, clearing. **(b)** (*cantera*) chalkpit, marlpit.

calvicie NF baldness; **~ precoz** premature baldness.

calvinismo NM Calvinism.

calvinista ① ADJ Calvinist(ic). ② NMF Calvinist.

calvo ① ADJ **(a)** *cabeza, persona* bald; *piel* bald, hairless; **quedarse ~** to go bald. **(b)** *terreno* bare, barren; *vestido* threadbare. ② NM bald man.

calza NF **(a)** (*Mec*) wedge; scotch, chock; **poner ~ a** to wedge, scotch. **(b)** (**: media*) stocking; **~s†** hose; (*pantalón*) breeches; (*panti*) tights; **estar en ~s prietas** to be in a fix. **(c)** (*LAm: de diente*) filling.

calzada NF roadway; (*paved*) road; causeway; (*de casa*) drive; (*LAm: avenida*) avenue; (*Carib: acera*) pavement, sidewalk (*US*); **~ romana** Roman road.

calzado ① ADJ shod, wearing shoes; **~ de** shod with, wearing; **conviene ir ~** it's better to wear shoes, one has to wear sth on one's feet. ② NM footwear.

calzador NM shoehorn; (*And, Cono Sur*) pen-holder.

calzar [1f] ① VT **(a)** (*ponerse*) to put on; (*llevar*) to wear; **calzaba zapatos verdes** she was wearing green shoes, she had green shoes on; **¿qué número calza Vd?** what size do you take?; **el que primero llega se la calza** first come first served. **(b)** *persona* to put shoes on; to provide with footwear, supply with shoes; **me ayudó a ~me las botas** he helped me to put my boots on. **(c)** (*arma*) to carry, take, use. **(d)** (*Mec*) *rueda etc* to wedge, scotch, chock; to put a wedge in (*o* under *etc*), put chocks under; (*bloquear*) to block; (*asegurar*) to secure. **(e)** (*LAm*) *diente* to fill. **(f)** (*poner punta a*) to tip, put an iron tip on. ② VI **(a)** **calza bien** he wears good shoes. **(b)** (***) **calza poco, no calza mucho** he's pretty dim*. ③ **calzarse** VR **(a)** **~ los zapatos** to put on one's shoes; **¿qué zapatos calzaba?** what shoes was he wearing? **(b)** (***) **~ un empleo** to get a job; **~ a uno** to keep sb under one's thumb. **(c)** **~ a una**** to screw sb**.

calzo NM wedge, scotch, chock; shim; (*Mec*) brake-shoe; (*Náut*) skid, chock.

calzón NM (*t* **calzones**) **(a)** (*de hombre*) breeches; shorts (*t Dep*); (*ropa interior*) underpants; (*LAm*) trousers, pants (*US*); **~ de baño††** bathing trunks; **calzones rotos** (*Cono Sur Culin*) doughnuts, donuts (*US*); **amarrarse los calzones** (*LAm*) to get stuck in; **hablar a ~ quitado** (*sin parar*) to talk without stopping; (*con franqueza*) to open one's heart, speak openly (*o* frankly); **ponerse los calzones** (*mujer: fig*) to wear

the trousers; **tener (muchos) calzones** (*Méx*) to be tough.
(**b**) (*de mujer*) shorts; (*LAm*) pants, knickers; ~ **de baño** pants part of two-piece swimsuit.
(**c**) (*LAm: de bebé*) ~ **de vinilo** plastic pants; ~ **desechable** disposable nappy.

calzonaria NF, **calzonario** NM (*LAm*) pants, knickers.

calzonazos* NM INVAR (*tonto*) stupid fellow; (*débil*) weak-willed fellow; (*marido*) henpecked husband.

calzoncillos NMPL pants, underpants (*US*), shorts (*US*); ~ **del 9 largo***, ~ **marianos*** long johns*.

calzoneras NFPL (*Carib, Méx*) side-buttoning trousers.

calzoneta NF (*CAm, Méx*) swimming trunks.

calzonudo ADJ (*And, CAm, Cono Sur*) (*estúpido*) stupid; (*débil*) weak-willed, timid; (*Méx*) (*enérgico*) energetic; (*audaz*) bold, brave.

CAM NF ABR de **Comunidad Autónoma de Madrid**.

cama NF (**a**) (*gen*) bed; bedstead; couch; ~ **de agua** water bed; ~ **camera** large single bed; (*Cono Sur*) double bed; ~ **de campaña** campbed; ~ **de columnas**, ~ **imperial** fourposter bed; ~ **de cuero** (*Cono Sur*) cot; ~ **elástica** trampoline; ~**s gemelas** twin beds; ~ **de matrimonio**; ~ **matrimonial** (*LAm*) double bed; **media** ~, ~ **de monja**, ~ **de soltero** single bed; ~ **en petaca** apple-pie bed; ~ **plegable**, ~ **de tijera** folding bed, campbed; ~ **de rayos infrarrojos**, ~ **solar** sunbed; ~ **redonda** group sex; ~ **turca** divan bed, day bed; ~ **de viento** (*And, CAm*) cot; **caer en** (**la**) ~ to fall ill; **estar en** ~ (*Med*), **guardar** ~ to be ill in bed, be confined to bed; **hacer la** ~ to make the bed; **hacer** (o **poner**) **la** ~ **a uno** (*fig*) to play a dirty trick on sb; **quien mala** ~ **hace en ella se yace** having made your bed you must lie on it; **ir a la** ~ to go to bed; **levantarse por los pies de la** ~ to get out of bed on the wrong side; **se la llevó a la** ~ he took her to bed.
(**b**) (*de animal*) bed, bedding, litter.
(**c**) (*Zool*) den, lair.
(**d**) (*de carro*) floor.
(**e**) (*Geol*) layer, stratum; (*Culin*) layer.

camachuelo NM bullfinch.

camada NF (**a**) (*Zool*) litter; (*personas*) gang, band; *V* **lobo**. (**b**) (*Geol*) layer; (*Arquit*) course (of bricks); (*de huevos, frutas*) layer.

camafeo NM cameo.

camagua NF (*CAm*) ripening maize, ripening corn (*US*); (*Méx*) unripened maize.

camal NM (**a**) (*cabestro*) halter. (**b**) (*palo*) pole (from which dead pigs are hung); (*And: matadero*) slaughterhouse, abattoir.

camaleón NM chameleon.

camaleónico ADJ chameleon-like.

camalote NM camalote (*an aquatic plant*).

camama* NF (*mentira*) lie; (*engaño*) trick.

camamila NF camomile.

camanance NM (*CAm*) dimple.

camanchaca* NF (*Cono Sur*) thick fog, pea-souper*.

camándula NF rosary; **tener muchas ~s*** to be full of tricks, be a sly sort.

camandulear [1a] VI to be a hypocrite, be falsely devout; (*LAm*) (*intrigar*) to intrigue, scheme; (*vacilar*) to bumble, avoid taking decisions.

camandulería NF prudery, priggishness; hypocrisy, false devotion.

camandulero [1] ADJ (*remilgado*) prudish, priggish; (*hipócrita*) hypocritical; (*beato*) falsely devout; (*taimado*) sly, tricky; (*LAm*) (*enredador*) intriguing, scheming; (*zalamero*) fawning, bootlicking*.
[2] NM, **camandulera** NF (*gazmoño*) prude, prig; (*hipócrita*) hypocrite; (*vividor*) sly sort, tricky person; (*LAm: intrigante*) intriguer, schemer.

cama-nido NF, PL **camas-nido** bunk-bed.

cámara [1] NF (**a**) (*cuarto, sala*) room, hall; ~ **acorazada** strongroom, vault; ~ **de aislamiento** isolation room; ~ **ardiente**, ~ **mortuoria** funeral chamber; ~ **congeladora** freezing compartment; ~ **frigorífica** cold-storage room; ~ **nupcial** bridal suite; ~ **de tortura** torture chamber; **música de** ~ chamber music.
(**b**) (*de reyes*) royal chamber; **médico de** ~ royal doctor; **gentilhombre de** ~ gentleman-in-waiting.
(**c**) (*Náut*) (*camarote*) stateroom, cabin; (*de pasajeros*) saloon; (*de oficiales de marina*) wardroom; ~ **de cartas** chart house; ~ **de motores** engine room.
(**d**) (*Agr*) granary.
(**e**) (*Pol etc*) chamber, house; ~ **agraria** chamber of agriculture; ~ **alta** upper house; ~ **baja** lower house; ~ **de comercio** chamber of commerce; ~ **de compensación** (*Fin*) clearing house; **C~ de los Comunes** House of Commons; ~ **legislativa** legislative assembly; **C~ de los Lores** House of Lords; **C~ de Representantes** House of Representatives.
(**f**) (*Mec, Fís*) chamber; ~ **de aire** air chamber; ~ **de combustión**, ~ **de explosión** combustion chamber; ~ **de compresión** compression chamber; ~ **de descompresión** decompression chamber; ~ **de gas**

(*de aeronave*) gasbag; (*de nazis etc*) gas chamber; ~ **de oxígeno** oxygen tent; ~ **de vacío** vacuum chamber.
(**g**) (*Aut etc*: *t* ~ **de aire**) tyre, inner tube; **sin** ~ **neumático** tubeless.
(**h**) (*Mil*) breech, chamber.
(**i**) (*Anat*) cavity.
(**j**) (*Fot*: *t* ~ **fotográfica**) camera; ~ **de cine**, ~ **cinematográfica**, ~ **filmadora** cinecamera, film camera; **a** ~ **lenta** in slow motion; **a** ~ **rápida** speeded-up; ~ **oscura** camera obscura; ~ **de televisión**, ~ **televisora** television camera; ~ **de vídeo** video camera; **chupar ~*** to collar an unfair amount of TV time*, hog the limelight.
(**k**) ~**s** (*Med*) diarrhoea; stool; **tener ~s en la lengua*** to gossip a lot, tell tales (out of school).
[2] NM cameraman.

camarada NMF comrade, companion; chum*, pal*, mate; (*Pol*) comrade.

camaradería NF comradeship; companionship; camaraderie; matiness*; (*Dep*) team spirit.

camarata* NM waiter.

camarera NF (*de restaurante*) waitress; (*de hotel*) maid, chambermaid; (*en casa*) parlourmaid; lady's maid; (*Náut*) stewardess; (*Cono Sur Aer*) stewardess, flight attendant (*US*).

camarero NM (*de restaurante*) waiter; (*Náut*) steward; ~ **mayor** (*Hist*) royal chamberlain; ~ **principal** head waiter.

camareta NF (*Náut*) cabin; messroom; ~ **alta** deckhouse.

camarico NM (*Cono Sur*) (**a**) (*lugar*) favourite place. (**b**) (*amor*) love affair.

camarilla NF (**a**) (*cuarto*) small room. (**b**) (*personas*) clique, coterie; entourage; (*Pol*) lobby, pressure group; faction.

camarín NM (**a**) (*Teat*) dressing room; (*tocador*) boudoir; (*cuarto pequeño*) side room; (*de ascensor*) lift car, elevator car (*US*); (*Náut*) cabin; (*LAm Ferro*) sleeping compartment.
(**b**) (*Ecl*) side-chapel (for a special image); room where jewels *etc* of an image are kept.

camarógrafo NM (*Cine, TV*) cameraman.

camarón NM (**a**) (*Zool*) shrimp, prawn. (**b**) (*CAm: propina*) tip, gratuity. (**c**) (*And**: *traidor*) turncoat; **hacer** ~ to change sides. (**d**) (*CAm**: *trabjo*) casual (o occasional) work. (**e**) (*Cono Sur. litera*) bunk (bed).

camaronear [1a] VI (**a**) (*Méx: pescar camarones*) to go shrimping. (**b**) (*And Pol*) to change sides.

camaronero NM (*And*) kingfisher.

camarote NM (*Náut*) cabin, stateroom; ~ **de lujo** first-class cabin.

camarotero NM (*LAm*) steward, cabin servant.

camaruta* NF bar girl.

camastro NM rickety old bed.

camastrón [1] ADJ (*) sly, untrustworthy.
[2] NM (*CAm*) large (o double) bed.

camayo(c) NM (*And*) foreman, overseer (*of a country estate*).

cambado ADJ (*And, Carib, Cono Sur*) bow-legged.

cambalache NM (**a**) (*cambio*) swap, exchange. (**b**) (*LAm: tienda*) second-hand shop, junk shop.

cambalach(e)ar [1a] VT to swap, exchange.

cambar [1a] VT (*Carib, Cono Sur*) = **combar**.

cámbaro NM crab.

cambiable ADJ (**a**) (*variable*) changeable; variable. (**b**) (*Com, Fin etc*) exchangeable.

cambiadiscos NM INVAR record-changer.

cambiadizo ADJ changeable.

cambiador NM barterer; moneychanger; (*And, Cono Sur, Méx: Ferro*) switchman.

cambiante [1] ADJ (**a**) (*variable*) changing; variable; *tiempo* changeable.
(**b**) (*pey*) fickle, temperamental.
[2] NM (**a**) (*persona*) moneychanger.
(**b**) (*tela*) iridescent fabric.
(**c**) ~**s** changing colours, iridescence.

cambiar [1b] [1] VT (**a**) (*transformar*) to change, alter, convert, turn (en into).
(**b**) (*trocar*) to change, exchange (con, por for); ~ **libras en francos**, ~ **libras por francos** to change pounds into francs; ~ **saludos** to exchange greetings; ~ **sellos** to exchange stamps, swap stamps.
(**c**) (*trasladar*) to shift, move; **¿lo cambiamos a otro sitio?** shall we move it somewhere else?
[2] VI (**a**) (*gen*) to change, alter; (*Rad*) **¡cambio!** over!; **¡cambio y corto!** over and out!; ~ **a un nuevo sistema** to change (o switch) to a new system; **no ha cambiado nada** nothing has changed; **entonces, la cosa cambia** that alters matters; **está muy cambiado** he's changed a lot, he has greatly altered.
(**b**) ~ **de** to change; ~ **de casa** to move (house); ~ **de color** to change colour; ~ **de dueño** to change hands; ~ **de idea** to change one's mind; ~ **de ropa** to change one's clothes; ~ **de sitio** to shift, move; ~ **de sitio con uno** to change places with sb; **cambiamos de sombrero** we exchanged hats.
(**c**) (*viento*) to veer, change round.

(d) mandarse a ~ (*LAm*) to get out.

3 cambiarse VR **(a)** (*gen*) to change; (*viento*) to veer, change round.
(b) ~ en to change into, be changed into.

cambiario ADJ (*Fin*) exchange (*atr*); **estabilidad cambiaria** stability of (o in) the exchange rate; **liberalización cambiaria** freeing of exchange controls (o rates *etc*).

cambiavía NM (*Carib, Méx: Ferro*) **(a)** (*persona*) switchman. **(b)** (*agujas*) switch, points.

cambiazo NM (*Com*) (dishonest) switch; **dar el ~** to switch the goods.

▼ **cambio** NM **(a)** (*transformación*) change, alteration; changeover; substitution; (*de política etc*) change, switch, shift; (*de marea*) turn; (*de lugar*) shift, move (*a* to); **ha habido muchos ~s** there have been many changes; **el ~ se efectuó en 1970** the changeover took place in 1970; **~ climático** climatic change; **~ de decoración** (*Teat*) change of décor; **~ de domicilio** change of address; **~ de guardia** changing of the guard; **~ de marchas, ~ de velocidades** (*Aut*) gear-change; **con ~ de marchas automático** with automatic transmission; **~ de la marea** turn of the tide; **~ de pareja** wife-swapping; **~ radical** turning point; **~ de tiempo** change in the weather; **~ de vía** (*Ferro*) points.
(b) (*Fin: dinero*) change, small change; **¿tienes ~ encima?** have you any change on you?
(c) (*trueque*) exchange; barter; **~ de impresiones** exchange of views; **libre ~** free trade; '**admitimos su coche usado a ~**' 'we take your
▼ old car in part exchange'; **a ~ de** in exchange for, in return for; **la compañía pagó X pesetas a ~ de que la otra concediera ...** the company paid X pesetas in return for the other allowing ...; **en ~** in exchange; on the other hand; instead.
(d) (*Fin: tipo*) rate of exchange; **al ~ de** at the rate of.

CAMBIO 90

i   *The Peruvian political party **Cambio 90** was founded shortly before the 1990 elections by Alberto Fujimori, then a newcomer to politics. He pledged to introduce state control of resources, improve social services, renegotiate Peru's foreign debt with the IMF and provide incentives for small industry. He also undertook to deal with terrorism by tackling poverty rather than by using military force. With this platform **Cambio 90** won a comfortable victory. Once in office Fujimori was hampered by the need for coalitions with traditional parties and abandoned his election platform. The war against the terrorist **Sendero Luminoso** (Shining Path) escalated and restrictions on labour, civil and human rights came into force. Fujimori's increasingly autocratic style culminated in the April 1992 autogolpe in which he dissolved Congress and suspended the Peruvian constitution in order to implement his policies unhindered.*
⇨ *See also* APRA , SENDERO LUMINOSO

---

cambista NM moneychanger.
Camboya NF (*Hist*) Cambodia.
camboyano, -a ADJ, NM/F Cambodian.
cambray NM cambric.
cambrón NM buckthorn; hawthorn; bramble.
cambrona NF (*Cono Sur*††) tough cotton cloth.
cambucho NM (*Cono Sur*) (*cono*) paper cone; (*cesta*) straw basket for waste paper (o dirty clothes); (*envase*) straw cover (*for a bottle*); (*cuartucho*) miserable little room, hovel.
cambujo ADJ (*CAm, Méx*) animal black; persona dark, swarthy.
cambullón NM (*And, Cono Sur*) (*estafa*) swindle; (*compló*) plot, intrigue; (*cambio*) swap, exchange.
cambur NM **(a)** (*Carib: plátano*) banana; (*árbol*) banana tree. **(b)** (*: prebenda*) government post, soft job, cushy number*; (*dinero*) windfall. **(c)** public servant, state employee.
cambuto ADJ (*And*) small, squat; chubby.
camelar [1a] VT **(a)** (*mujer*) to flirt with; to attract, get off with*; to make up to*. **(b)** (*persuadir*) to cajole, blarney; to win over; **tener camelado a uno** to have sb wrapped round one's little finger. **(c)** (*Méx*) (*mirar*) to look into, look towards (*etc*); (*perseguir*) to pursue, hound.
camelia NF camellia.
camelista NMF flatterer, creep*.
camellar [1a] VI (*Carib*) to work (hard).
camellear VI to push drugs, be a pusher.
camelleo NM drug-pushing.
camellero NM camel-driver.
camello NM **(a)** (*Zool*) camel. **(b)** (*) drug-pusher.
camellón NM (*bebedero*) drinking trough; (*Agr*) ridge (*between furrows*); (*Méx Aut*) central reservation, divider (*US*).
camelo NM **(a)** (*flirteo*) flirtation.
(b) (*broma*) joke, hoax; (*cuento*) cock-and-bull story; (*bola*) humbug; (*coba*) blarney; **dar ~ a uno** to make fun of sb; to put one over on sb; **me huele a ~** it smells fishy*, there's something funny going on

here; **¡esto es un ~!** it's all a swindle!
camerino NM (*Teat*) dressing room; (*Méx Ferro*) roomette.
camero ADJ **(a)** (*gen*) bed (*atr*); for a large single bed. **(b)** (*Carib: grande*) big.
Camerún NM Cameroon.
camilla NF (*sofá*) sofa, couch; (*cuna*) cot; (*mesa*) table with a heater underneath; (*Med*) stretcher.
camillero, -a NM/F stretcher-bearer.
camilucho NM (*Cono Sur, Méx*) Indian day labourer.
caminante NMF traveller, wayfarer; walker.
caminar [1a] **1** VT *distancia* to cover, travel, do.
2 VI **(a)** (*gen*) to walk, journey; (*río etc*) to go, move, flow; (*fig*) to act, move, go; **venir caminando** (*LAm*) to come on foot; **~ derecho** to behave properly; **~ con pena** to trudge along, move with difficulty.
(b) (*LAm Mec*) to work.
caminata NF (*paseo largo*) long walk; (*por el campo*) hike, ramble; (*excursión*) excursion, outing, jaunt.
caminero **1** ADJ road (*atr*); V **peón**.
2 NM (*LAm*) road builder.
caminito NM: **~ de rosas** (*fig*) primrose path.
camino NM **(a)** (*carretera*) road; (*Méx*) (main) road; (*sendero*) track, path; trail; (*Inform*) path; **~ de acceso, ~ de entrada** approach road; **~ de Damasco** road to Damascus, road to conversion; **~ sin firme** unsurfaced road; **~ forestal** forest track; **C~ de Santiago** (*Rel*) pilgrims' road to Santiago de Compostela; (*Astron*) Milky Way; **~ de herradura** bridle path; **~ de ingresos, ~ de peaje** toll road; **~ real** highroad (*t fig*); **~ de sirga** towpath; **~ de tierra** dirt track; **~ trillado** well-trodden path; (*fig*) beaten track; **tener el ~ trillado** (*fig*) to have the ground prepared for one; **~ vecinal** country road, lane, by-road; **C~s, Canales y Puertos** (*Univ*) Civil Engineering.
(b) (*dirección, distancia etc; t fig*) way, road (*de* to), route; journey; (*fig*) way, path, course; **el ~ a seguir** the route to follow; **el ~ de La Paz** the way to La Paz, the La Paz road; **es el ~ del desastre** that is the road to disaster, that way lies disaster; **el ~ de en medio** (*fig*) the middle way, the way of compromise; **~ de Lima** on the way to Lima; **vamos ~ de la muerte** death awaits us all; **a medio ~** halfway (there); **de ~** on the way, (*fig*) in passing; **tienen otro niño de ~** they have another child on the way; **en el ~** on the way, en route; **está en ~ de desaparecer** it's on its way out; **después de 3 horas de ~** after travelling for 3 hours; **nos quedan 20 kms de ~** we still have 20 kms to go; **es mucho ~** it's a long way; **¿cuánto ~ hay de aquí a San José?** how far is it from here to San Jose?; **por (el) buen ~** along the right road; **ir por (el) buen ~** (*fig*) to be on the right track; **¿vamos por buen ~?** are we on the right road?; **traer a uno por buen ~** (*fig*) to put sb on the right road; to disabuse sb; **abrirse ~** to make one's way; **allanar el ~** to smooth the way (*a uno* for sb); **echar ~ adelante** to strike out; **errar el ~** to lose one's way; **ir por su ~** to go one's own sweet way; **todos los ~s van a Roma** all roads lead to Rome; **llevar a uno por mal ~** (*fig*) to lead sb astray; **partir el ~ con uno** to meet sb halfway; **ponerse en ~** to set out, set forth, start; **quedarse en el ~** (*fig*) to be left behind, be left in the lurch.
(c) (*And, Cono Sur: tira*) runner, strip of carpet (o matting *etc*); **~ de mesa** table runner.

CAMINO DE SANTIAGO

i   *The **Camino de Santiago** is a medieval pilgrim route stretching from the Pyrenees to Santiago de Compostela in north-west Spain, where tradition has it that the body of Saint James the Apostle (Spain's patron saint) is buried. At one time Santiago de Compostela came next only to Jerusalem and Rome as the most popular destination for Christian pilgrims from all over Europe. Those who had made the long, dangerous journey returned proudly wearing on their hat or cloak the venera or concha (scallop shell) traditionally associated with this pilgrimage - Saint James' body had reportedly been found covered in scallops. Today this symbolic shell can still be seen all along the **Camino de Santiago**, carved on ancient buildings and painted on modern-day road signs marking the historic route for the benefit of tourists and pilgrims.*
  *In Astronomy the **Camino de Santiago** is another name for the Vía Láctea (Milky Way), hence the title of Buñuel's famous satirical film about the route to Compostela.*

---

camión NM (*Aut*) lorry, truck (*esp US*); van; (*de caballos*) heavy wagon, dray; (*Méx: autobús*) bus; **~ de agua** water cart, water wagon; **~ de la basura** dustcart, garbage truck (*US*); **~ blindado** troop carrier; **~ de bomberos** fire engine; **~ cisterna** tanker, tank wagon; **~ frigorífico** refrigerator lorry; **~ ganadero** cattle truck; **~ de mudanzas** removal van; **~ de reparto** delivery truck; **~ de riego** water cart, water wagon; **~ volquete** dumper; **está como un ~** she looks smashing*.
camionaje NM haulage, cartage.
camionero, -a NM/F lorry driver, truckdriver (*US*), teamster (*US*).

camioneta NF van, light truck; (*LAm*) station-wagon; (*CAm*) bus; (*Carib*) minibus; ~ **detectora** detector van; ~ **de reparto** delivery van; ~ **de tina** (*CAm*) pick-up (truck).

camión-grúa NM, PL **camiones-grúa** tow-truck, towing vehicle.

camionista NM = **camionero.**

camion-tanque NM, PL **camiones-tanque** (*Aut*) tanker.

camisa NF (a) (*de hombre*) shirt; ~ (**de mujer, de señora**) chemise, slip; (*LAm*) garment, article of clothing; ~ **de deporte** sports shirt, vest; ~ **de dormir** nightdress; ~ **de fuerza** straitjacket; ~ **de rayas** striped shirt; **cambiar de** ~ to turn one's coat, change one's colours; **estar en (mangas de)** ~ to be in one's shirt-sleeves; **dejar a uno sin** ~ to leave sb destitute, clean sb out*; **jugarse hasta la** ~ to bet one's bottom dollar; **no le llegaba la** ~ **al cuerpo** he was simply terrified; **meterse en** ~ **de once varas** to interfere in other people's affairs; to bite off more than one can chew; **recibir a una mujer sin** ~* to take a wife without a dowry.
(b) (*Bot*) skin; (*Zool: de culebra*) slough.
(c) (*Mec*) jacket; case, casing; sleeve; ~ **de agua** water jacket; ~ **de gas** gas mantle.
(d) (*carpeta*) folder (*for papers*); (*Tip*) jacket, dust jacket, wrapper.

camisería NF outfitter's (shop).

camisero NM (a) (*persona*) shirt maker; outfitter. (b) (*prenda*) shirt dress.

camiseta NF vest, undershirt (*US*); (*Dep*) singlet, shirt, vest; (*LAm*) nightdress; ~ (**con dibujo**) T-shirt.

camisilla NF (*Carib, Cono Sur*) = **camiseta.**

camisola NF (*Méx*) sports shirt.

camisolín NM stiff shirt front, dickey.

camisón NM (*t* ~ **de noche**) nightdress, nightgown; (*de hombre*) nightgown.

camita[1], **camítico** ADJ Hamitic.

camita[2] NF small bed, cot.

camomila NF camomile.

camón NM big bed; (*Arquit*) oriel window; ~ **de vidrios** glass partition.

camorra NF row, set-to*; **armar** ~ to kick up a row; **buscar** ~ to go looking for trouble.

camorrear* [1a] VI (*CAm, Cono Sur*) to have a row.

camorrero NM = **camorrista.**

camorrista [1] ADJ quarrelsome, rowdy, brawling.
[2] NMF quarrelsome person, rowdy element, hooligan.

camotal NM (*LAm*) sweet potato field (*o* plot).

camote NM (a) (*LAm Bot*) sweet potato; (*Méx: bulbo*) tuber, bulb.
(b) (*CAm, Cono Sur: Med*) bump, swelling.
(c) (*Cono Sur: piedra*) large stone.
(d) (*Cono Sur: persona*) bore, tedious person.
(e) (*CAm: de pierna*) calf of the leg.
(f) (*CAm*: *molestia*) nuisance, bother.
(g) (*LAm: amor*) love; crush*; **tener un** ~ **con uno** to have a crush on sb*.
(h) (*And, Cono Sur*: *amante*) lover, sweetheart.
(i) (*Cono Sur*: *mentirilla*) fib.
(j) (*And, Cono Sur: tonto*) fool.
(k) (*LAm*) **poner a uno como** ~ to give sb a telling off*; **tragar** ~ (*tener miedo*) to have one's heart in one's mouth; (*balbucir*) to stammer.

camotear [1a] [1] VT (a) (*Cono Sur: estafar*) to rob, fleece; to take for a ride*.
(b) (*CAm: molestar*) to annoy.
[2] VI (*CAm: molestar*) to be trying, cause trouble.

campa [1] ADJ INVAR: **tierra** ~ treeless land.
[2] NF open field, open space.

campal ADJ: **batalla** ~ pitched battle.

campamentista NMF camper.

campamento NM camp; encampment; ~ **de base** base camp; ~ **para prisioneros** prison camp; ~ **de refugiados** refugee camp; ~ **de trabajo** labour camp; ~ **de veraneo** holiday camp.

campana NF (a) (*gen*) bell; **a** ~ **herida, a** ~ **tañida, a toque de** ~ to the sound of bells; **echar las** ~**s a vuelo** to peal the bells; (*fig*) to proclaim sth from the rooftops; to rejoice, celebrate (prematurely); **estar** ~ (*Carib*) to be fine; **hacer** ~* to play truant; **oír** ~**s y no saber dónde** to get hold of the wrong end of the stick; **tañer las** ~**s, tocar las** ~**s** to peal the bells; **tocar la** ~*** to wank*.
(b) (*objeto*) bell-shaped object; ~ **de bucear**, ~ **de buzo** diving bell; ~ **de cristal** bell glass, glass cover; ~ **extractora** extractor hood.
(c) (*LAm*: *ladrón*) thieves' look-out; **hacer de** ~ to keep watch, be look-out.

campanada NF (a) (*Mús*) stroke, peal (of a bell); (sound of) ringing; **dar la** ~ to sound the alarm (*t fig*).
(b) (*fig: escándalo*) scandal, sensation, commotion; **dar una** ~ to make a big stir, cause a great surprise.

campanario NM (a) (*de iglesia etc*) belfry, bell tower, church tower.
(b) (*pey*) **de** ~ mean, narrow-minded; **espíritu de** ~ parochial spirit, parish-pump attitude.

campanazo NM (a) = **campanada.** (b) (*And: advertencia*) warning.

campaneado ADJ (*fig*) much talked-of.

campanear [1a] VI (a) (*Mús*) to ring the bells. (b) (*LAm*: *ladrón*) to keep watch.

campaneo NM bell ringing, pealing, chimes.

campanero NM (a) (*Téc*) bell founder; (*Mús*) bell-ringer.

campaniforme ADJ bell-shaped.

campanilla NF (a) (*campana*) small bell, handbell, electric bell; **de muchas** ~**s*** big, grand; high-class.
(b) (*burbuja*) bubble.
(c) (*Anat*) uvula.
(d) (*Cos*) tassel.
(e) (*Bot*) bellflower; harebell; ~ **blanca**, ~ **de febrero** snowdrop.

campanillazo NM loud ring, sudden ring.

campanillear [1a] VI to ring, tinkle.

campanilleo NM ringing, tinkling.

campanología NF campanology, bell-ringing.

campanólogo, -a NM/F campanologist, bell-ringer.

campante ADJ (a) (*destacado*) outstanding.
(b) (*pey*) self-satisfied, smug; **siguió tan** ~ he went on cheerfully, he went on as if nothing had happened; **allí estaba tan** ~ there he was as large as life, there he sat (*etc*) as cool as a cucumber.

campanudo ADJ (a) *objeto* bell-shaped; *falda* wide, spreading. (b) *estilo* high-flown, bombastic, sonorous; *orador* pompous, windy; **dijo** ~ he said pompously.

campánula NF bellflower, campanula.

campaña NF (a) (*campo*) countryside; (*llanura*) level country, plain; (*LAm*) country, countryside; **batir la** ~, **correr la** ~ to reconnoitre.
(b) (*Mil, Pol, fig*) campaign; (*Com*) sales drive; ~ **denigratoria** smear campaign; ~ **de imagen** campaign to improve one's image; ~ **publicitaria** advertising campaign, publicity campaign; **de** ~ (*Mil*) field (*atr*), campaign (*atr*); **hacer** ~ to campaign; **hacer** ~ **en contra de** to campaign against; **hacer** ~ **a favor de** (*o* **en pro de**) to campaign for.
(c) (*Náut*) cruise, expedition, trip.
(d) (*Agr etc*) season.

campañol NM vole.

campar [1a] VI (a) (*Mil etc*) to camp. (b) (*destacar*) to stand out, excel; V **respeto.**

campear [1a] VI (a) (*Agr*) (*ganado*) to go to graze, go out to pasture; (*hombre*) to work in the fields.
(b) (*Bot*) to show green.
(c) (*Mil*) to reconnoitre; (*LAm*) to scour the countryside.
(d) **ir campeando*** to carry on, keep going.
(e) (*LAm: ir de camping*) to camp, go camping.
(f) (*And: atravesar*) to make one's way through.
(g) (*And: fardar*) to bluster.

campechana NF (a) (*Carib, Méx: bebida*) cocktail. (b) (*Méx: de mariscos*) seafood cocktail.

campechanería NF (*LAm*), **campechanía** NF frankness, openness; heartiness, cheerfulness, geniality; fellow feeling; generosity.

campechano ADJ (a) (*franco*) frank, open; (*cordial*) good-hearted, hearty, cheerful, genial; (*amigable*) comradely; (*generoso*) generous.
(b) (*Carib*) peasant (*atr*).

campeón NM, **campeona** NF champion; ~ **de venta** best seller, best-selling article.

campeonar [1a] VI to win the championship, emerge as champion.

campeonato NM championship; **de** ~ (*a ultranza*) absolute, out-and-out; (*enorme*) huge, really big; (*estupendo*) smashing*.

campeonísimo, -a NM/F undisputed champion.

campera NF (*Cono Sur*) windcheater.

campero [1] ADJ (a) (*descubierto*) unsheltered, (out) in the open; open-air (*atr*); **ganado** ~ stock that sleeps out in the open.
(b) (*LAm*) *persona* knowledgeable about the countryside; expert in farming matters; *animal* trained to travel in difficult country, sure-footed.
[2] NM (*And*) jeep, land rover.

camperuso* (*Carib*) [1] ADJ (a) rural, rustic. (b) (*huraño*) reserved, stand-offish.
[2] NM, **camperusa** NF peasant.

campesina NF peasant (woman).

campesinado NM peasantry, peasants.

campesino [1] ADJ (a) country (*atr*), rural; peasant (*atr*); (*pey*) rustic.
(b) (*Zool*) field (*atr*).
[2] NM (a) (*paisano*) peasant; countryman; farmer; (*pey*) peasant. (b) (*And: indio*) Indian.

campestre ADJ (a) country (*atr*), rural. (b) (*Bot*) wild.

camping ['kampin] NM, PL **campings** ['kampin] (a) (*acto*) camping; **estar de** ~ to be on a camping holiday; **hacer** ~ to go camping. (b) (*sitio*) campsite, camping site, camping ground.

campiña NF countryside, open country; flat stretch of farmland, large area of cultivated land.

campirano NM (*LAm*) (a) (*campesino*) peasant; (*pey*) rustic, country bumpkin.
(b) (*Agr*) (*perito*) expert in farming matters; (*guía*) guide, pathfinder; (*jinete*) skilled horseman; (*ganadero*) stockbreeding expert.

campiruso (*Carib*) = **camperuso**.

campista¹ NMF camper.

campista² ① ADJ (a) (*CAm, Carib*) rural, country (*atr*). (b) (*LAm*) = **campero 1 (b)**.
② NM (*CAm*) herdsman.

campisto ① ADJ (*CAm*) rural, country (*atr*).
② NM (a) (*CAm: campesino*) peasant. (b) (*CAm Agr*) amateur vet.

campo NM (a) (*gen*) country, countryside; ~ **abierto**, ~ **raso** open country; **a** ~ **raso** in the open; ~ **a través** cross-country (running); **ir a** ~ **traviesa**, **ir** ~ **travieso** to go across country, take a cross-country route; **ir al** ~ to go into the country; ¿**te gusta el** ~? do you like the country (side)?; **el** ~ **está espléndido** the countryside looks lovely.
(b) (*Agr, t Inform, Mil, Fís etc*) field; (*Dep*) field, ground, pitch; ~ **alfanumérico** alphanumeric field; ~ **de aterrizaje** landing field; ~ **aurífero** goldfield; ~ **de aviación** airfield; ~ **de batalla** battlefield; ~ **de deportes** sports ground, playing field; recreation ground; ~ **de ejercicios** (*Mil*) drilling ground; **C~s Elíseos**, **C~s Eliseos** Elysian Fields; ~ **de fuego** field of fire; ~ **de fútbol** football ground, football pitch; ~ **de golf** golf course, golf links; ~ **gravitatorio** field of gravity; ~ **de instrucción** (*Mil*) drilling ground; ~ **de juego** playground; ~ **magnético** magnetic field; ~ **de minas** minefield; ~ **numérico** numeric field; ~ **petrolífero** oilfield; ~ **de pruebas** testing ground (*t fig*); ~**s de riego** (*euf*) sewage farm; ~ **santo** cemetery, churchyard; ~ **de tiro** firing range; ~ **visual** field of vision; ~ **de vuelo** flying field; **trabajo de** ~, **trabajo en el propio** ~ fieldwork; **experiencia de** ~ experience in the field, experience of fieldwork; **abandonar el** ~, **levantar el** ~ (*Mil*) to retire from the field; (*fig*) to give up the struggle; **batir el** ~, **reconocer el** ~ to reconnoitre; **dejar el** ~ **libre** to leave the field open (*para* for); **se le hizo el** ~ **orégano** (*Cono Sur*) it all turned out nicely for him; **quedar en el** ~ to fall in battle; to be killed in a duel.
(c) (*And: estancia*) farm, ranch; farmhouse; (*Cono Sur: tierra pobre*) barren land; (*And, Cono Sur: Min*) mining concession.
(d) (*Arte*) ground, background; (*Her*) field.
(e) (*Mil etc*) camp; ~ **(de) base** base camp; ~ **de concentración** concentration camp; ~ **de internamiento** internment camp; ~ **de trabajo** labour camp.
(f) (*equipo, en juegos*) side.
(g) (*LAm: sitio*) space, room; ~ **de maniobras** room for manoeuvre; **no hay** ~ there's no room.
(h) (*fig: esfera*) scope; range, sphere; **el** ~ **de aplicación del invento** the scope of the invention, the range of application of the invention; **hay** ~ **para más** there is scope for more; **dar** ~ **a** to give free range to, allow ample scope for.

camposantero NM cemetery official.

camposanto NM cemetery, churchyard.

CAMPSA, Campsa ['kampsa] NF (*Esp*) ABR *de* **Compañía Arrendataria de Monopolio de Petróleos, S.A.**

campus NM INVAR (*Univ*) campus.

campusano NM, **campus(i)o** NM (*CAm etc*) peasant.

camuesa NF pippin, dessert apple.

camueso NM (a) (*Bot*) pippin tree. (b) (*: tonto*) dolt, blockhead.

camuflado ADJ camouflaged; *coche policial* unmarked.

camuflaje NM camouflage.

camuflar [1a] VT (*t fig*) to camouflage.

can NM (a) (*Zool*) † *o hum*) dog, hound (*hum*). (b) (*Mil*) trigger. (c) (*Arquit*) corbel.

cana¹ NF (*t* ~**s**) white hair, grey hair; **echar una** ~ **al aire** to let one's hair down, cut loose; **faltar a las** ~**s** to show a lack of respect for one's elders; **peina** ~**s** he's getting on.

cana² (*LAm*) ① NF (a) (*cárcel*) jail; (*celda*) prison cell; **caer en** ~ to land in jail. (b) (*policía*) police.
② NM policeman.

canabis NM cannabis.

canaca NMF (a) (*And, Cono Sur*: *chino*) Chink*, Chinese. (b) (*Cono Sur*) (*dueño*) brothel-keeper; (*burdel*) brothel.

Canadá NM: **el** ~ Canada.

canadiense ① ADJ, NMF Canadian.
② NM (*prenda*: *t* **chaqueta** ~) lumber jacket.

canal¹ NM (a) (*Náut*) canal; waterway; **C~ de Panamá** Panama Canal; **C~ de Suez** Suez Canal; ~ **de navegación** ship canal; ~ **de riego** irrigation channel.
(b) (*Náut*: *parte de río etc*) deep channel; navigation channel.
(c) (*Geog*) channel, strait; **C~ de la Mancha** English Channel.
(d) (*Anat*) canal, duct, tract; ~ **digestivo** digestive tract, alimentary canal.
(e) (*TV*) channel; ~ **de pago** pay channel, subscription channel.
(f) (*de cinta*) track.
(g) (*Carib Aut*) lane.

canal² NM o F (a) (*tubo*) conduit, pipe; underground watercourse; ~ **de desagüe** (*And*) sewer; ~ **de humo** (*Méx*) flue; ~ **inclinado** chute.
(b) (*Arquit: canalón etc*) gutter, guttering; spout; drainpipe.
(c) (*Arquit: estría*) groove, fluting.
(d) (*Geog*) narrow valley.
(e) (*carne*) dressed carcass; **abrir en** ~ to cut down the middle, slit open.
(f) (*escote*) cleavage.

canaladura NF fluting; V t **acanaladura**.

canalé NM: **jersey de** ~ ribbed sweater.

canaleta NF (*Cono Sur*) pipe, conduit; roof gutter.

canalete NM paddle.

canalización NF (a) (*acto*) canalization, channelling. (b) (*Téc*) piping; (*Elec*) wiring; (*de gas etc*) mains; (*LAm: de cloacas*) sewerage system, drainage.

canalizar [1f] VT *río etc* to canalize; to confine between banks, rebuild the banks (*o course*) of; *agua* to harness; to pipe; *aguas de riego* to channel; (*Elec*) *impulso, mensaje* to carry; (*fig*) *intereses etc* to channel, direct.

canalizo NM navigable channel.

canalla ① NF rabble, mob, riffraff.
② NM swine*, rotter*; ¡~! you swine!*

canallada NF, **canallería** NF (*LAm*) (*acto*) dirty trick, mean thing (to do), despicable act; (*dicho*) nasty remark, vile thing (to say).

canallesco ADJ mean, rotten*, despicable; **diversión canallesca** low form of amusement.

canalón NM (a) (*Arquit*) gutter, guttering; spout; drainpipe; (*de disco*) groove. (b) (*sombrero*) shovel hat. (c) **canalones** (*Culin*) cannelloni.

canana NF (a) (*Mil*) cartridge belt. (b) (*LAm Med*) goitre. (c) (*Carib: mala pasada*) mean trick, low prank. (d) ~**s** (*And*) handcuffs.

canapé NM (a) (*mueble*) sofa, settee, couch. (b) (*Culin*) canapé.

Canarias NFPL, *t* **Islas** NFPL **Canarias** Canaries, Canary Isles.

canario ① ADJ of the Canary Isles.
② NM, **canaria** NF native (*o inhabitant*) of the Canary Isles; **los** ~**s** the people of the Canary Isles.
③ NM (a) (*Orn*) canary. (b) (¡¡) prick¡¡. (c) (*LAm: amarillo*) yellow.
④ INTERJ (*) well I'm blowed!*

canarión, -ona NM/F native (*o inhabitant*) of Gran Canaria.

canasta NF (a) (*gen*) (round) basket; (*de comida*) hamper; (*Com*) crate; (*Baloncesto*) basket; ~ **para papeles** wastepaper basket. (b) (*juego*) canasta.

canastero, -a NM/F basket maker.

canastilla NF (a) (*gen*) small basket; (*Méx: de basura*) wastepaper basket; ~ **de la costura** sewing basket.
(b) (*de bebé*) (baby's) layette.
(c) (*And, Carib, Cono Sur: de novia*) trousseau, (*hum*) bottom drawer, (*US*) hope chest.

canastillo NM (a) (*bandeja*) wicker tray, small basket. (b) (*de bebé*) layette.

canasto NM (a) (*gen*) large basket; (*de comida*) hamper; (*Com*) crate.
(b) (*And: criado*) servant. (c) ¡~**s**! good heavens!

cáncamo NM (*Náut*) eyebolt; ~ **de argolla** ringbolt.

cancamurria* NF blues, gloom.

cancamusa* NF trick; **armar una** ~ **a uno** to throw sand in sb's eyes.

cancán NM (a) (*Mús*) cancan. (b) (*Cos*) flounced petticoat.

cáncana NF (*Cono Sur*) (*de asar*) spit, jack; (*de vela*) candlestick; (*And*) thin person.

cancanco* NM (*Carib Aut*) breakdown.

cancanear [1a] VI (a) (*gandulear*) to loiter, loaf about.
(b) (*Cono Sur: bailar*) to dance the cancan.
(c) (*And, CAm, Méx*) (*expresarse*) to express o.s. with difficulty; (*tartamudear*) to stammer; (*leer mal*) to read haltingly, falter in reading.

cancaneo NM (*And, CAm, Méx*) (*al leer*) faltering; (*tartamudeo*) stammering.

cáncano* NM louse; **andar como** ~ **loco** to go round in circles.

cancel NM windproof door, storm door; (*LAm*) (*mampara*) folding screen; (*tabique*) partition, thin wall.

cancela NF lattice gate, wrought-iron gate; outer door, outer gate.

cancelación NF, **cancelamiento** NM cancellation; (*Inform*) deletion.

cancelar [1a] VT (*gen*) to cancel; *deuda* to write off, wipe out; (*Inform*) to delete; (*LAm*) *cuenta* to pay, settle; *decisión* to cancel, annul; (*fig*) to dispel, banish (from one's mind); to do away with.

cancelaría NF papal chancery.

cáncer NM (a) (*Med*) cancer; ~ **de cuello uterino**, ~ **cervical** cervical cancer; ~ **de los huesos** bone cancer; ~ **de mama** breast cancer; ~ **de pulmón** lung cancer. (b) **C~** (*Zodíaco*) Cancer.

cancerado ADJ cancerous; (*fig*) corrupt.

cancerarse [1a] VR **(a)** (*Med*) (*órgano etc*) to become cancerous; (*persona*) to get cancer, have cancer. **(b)** (*fig*) to become corrupt.
cancerbero NM goalkeeper.
cancerígeno ADJ carcinogenic.
cancerología NF study of cancer, carcinology.
cancerólogo, -a NM/F cancer specialist.
canceroso 1 ADJ cancerous.
  2 NM, **cancerosa** NF cancer patient, cancer sufferer.
cancha[1] NF **(a)** (*en algunos sentidos, esp LAm*) field, ground; (*descampado*) open space, tract of level ground; (*Dep*) sports-field; (*de tenis*) court; (*de fútbol*) pitch; (*de gallos*) cockpit; (*hipódromo*) racetrack; (*And, Cono Sur*) wide part of a river; (*Cono Sur*) path, road; ¡~! (*Cono Sur*) gangway!; **~ de aterrizaje** landing ground; **~ de carreras** racecourse; racetrack; **~ de fútbol** football ground; **~ de golf** golfcourse; **~ de pelota** pelota court; **~ de tenis** tennis court; **abrir ~, dar ~, hacer ~** to make way, make room (*a* for); to provide facilities (*a* for); **estar en su ~** (*Cono Sur*) to be in one's element; **tener ~** (*Cono Sur*) (*experiencia*) to be experienced, be an expert; (*influencia*) to have clout*, have pull; **tener ~ a algo** (*Carib*) to be good at sth; **en la ~ se ven los pingos** (*LAm*) actions speak louder than words.
  (b) (*And*: *tajada*) cut.
cancha[2] NF (*And*) (*maíz*) toasted maize, popcorn; (*habas*) toasted beans.
canchar [1a] VT (*And, Cono Sur*) to toast.
canche ADJ **(a)** (*CAm*: *rubio*) blond(e). **(b)** (*And*: *soso*) poorly seasoned, tasteless.
canchero, -a NM/F **(a)** (*experimentado*) experienced person. **(b)** (*Dep*: *jugador*) experienced player; (*LAm*: *cuidador*) groundsman, groundswoman. **(c)** (*Cono Sur*: *vago*) layabout, loafer.
canchón NM (*And*) enclosed field.
cancilla NF gate.
canciller NM chancellor; (*LAm*) foreign minister.
cancilleresco ADJ **(a)** (*Admin*) chancellery (*atr*), chancery (*atr*); diplomatic. **(b)** (*fig*) formal, ceremonious; ruled by protocol.
cancillería NF (*en embajada*) chancery, chancellery; (*LAm*) ministry of foreign affairs, foreign ministry.
canción NF song; (*Liter*) lyric, song; **~ amatoria** lovesong; **~ de copas** drinking-song; **~ de cuna** lullaby, cradlesong; **~ infantil** nursery-rhyme; **¡siempre la misma ~!** the same old story!; **dejar como la ~ a uno** to stand sb up*; **volvemos a la misma ~** here we go again, you're harping on the same old theme.
cancionero NM (*Mús*) songbook, collection of songs; (*Liter*) anthology, collection of verse.
cancionista NMF **(a)** (*compositor*) songwriter. **(b)** (*cantante*) ballad-singer; singer, vocalist, crooner.
canción-protesta NF, PL **canciones-protesta** protest song.
canco NM **(a)** (*Cono Sur*) (*jarro*) earthenware jug; (*tiesto*) flowerpot; (*orinal*) chamberpot. **(b)** **~s** (*And, Cono Sur*: *Anat*) buttocks; hips. **(c)** (‡: *homosexual*) queer‡, fairy‡.
cancro NM (*Bot*) canker; (*Med*) cancer.
candado NM **(a)** (*gen*) padlock; (*de libro*) clasp; **~ digital** combination lock; **poner algo bajo siete ~s** to lock sth safely away. **(b)** (*And*: *barba*) goatee beard.
candanga NM: **el ~** (*Méx*) the devil.
candar [1a] VT to lock; to lock up, put away.
cande ADJ: **azúcar ~** sugar candy, rock candy.
candeal 1 ADJ: **pan ~** white bread; **trigo ~** bread wheat.
  2 NM (*And, Cono Sur*) egg flip.
candela NF **(a)** (*vela*) candle; (*candelero*) candlestick; (*Fís*) candle power, candela; **en ~** (*Náut*) vertical; **se le acabó la ~‡** he snuffed it‡; **arrimar ~ a uno*** to give sb a tanning*; **estar con la ~ en la mano** (*fig*) to be at death's door.
  (b) (*esp LAm*: *fuego*) fire; (*para cigarrillo*) light; **dar ~** to be a nuisance, be trying; **echar ~** (*ojos etc*) to sparkle; **pegar ~ a, prender ~ a** to set fire to, set alight.
candelabro NM candelabrum.
Candelaria NF Candlemas.
candelaria NF (*Bot*) mullein.
candelejón* ADJ (*And*) simple, slow.
candelero NM **(a)** (*velador*) candlestick; (*lámpara*) oil lamp; **tema en ~** hot subject, subject of great current interest; **estar en (el) ~** (*persona*) to be high up, be in a position of authority; (*suceso*) to be under way, be in progress; (*tema*) to be of keen current interest; **poner a uno en (el) ~** to give sb a high post; **poner algo en ~** to bring sth into the limelight.
  (b) (*Náut*) stanchion.
candelilla NF **(a)** (*vela*) small candle.
  (b) (*Bot*) catkin.
  (c) (*LAm*: *luciérnaga*) glow-worm; (*Cono Sur*: *libélula*) dragonfly; (*And*: *niño*) lively child.
  (d) (*Carib, Cono Sur*: *Cos*) hem, border.
candelizo NM icicle.

candelo ADJ (*And*) reddish-blond(e).
candencia NF white heat.
candente ADJ **(a)** (*encendido*) red-hot, white-hot; glowing, burning. **(b)** (*fig*) *cuestión* burning; important, pressing, urgent; *atmósfera etc* charged, electric.
candi ADJ: **azúcar ~** sugar candy, rock candy.
candidatizar [1f] VT to propose, nominate.
candidato, -a NM/F **(a)** (*pretendiente*) candidate (*a* for); applicant (*a* for). **(b)** (*Cono Sur*‡) sucker‡.
candidatura NF candidature.
candidez NF **(a)** (*cualidad*) simplicity, ingenuousness, innocence; naïveté; stupidity. **(b)** (*una ~*) silly remark.
cándido ADJ **(a)** (*ingenuo*) simple, ingenuous, innocent; naïve; (*pey*) stupid. **(b)** (*poét*) snow-white.
candil NM **(a)** (*lámpara*) oil lamp, kitchen lamp, (*Méx*) chandelier; (*poder*) **arder en un ~** (*fig*) (*vino*) to be very strong; (*tema etc*) to be pretty strong stuff.
  (b) (*Zool*) tine, point, small horn.
candileja NF oil reservoir of a lamp; small oil lamp; **~s** (*Teat*) footlights.
candinga[1] NF (*Cono Sur*) impertinence, insistence.
candinga[2] NM: **el ~** (*Méx*) the devil.
candiota NF wine cask.
candiotero NM cooper.
candombe NM (*LAm*) Latin American dance.
candomblé NM candomblé.
candonga NF **(a)** (‡: *puta*) whore. **(b)** (*Fin*‡) one peseta. **(c)** (‡: *Anat*) scrotum. **(d)** (*: lisonjas*) blarney, flattery; (*truco*) trick; (*broma*) playful trick, hoax, practical joke; (*guasa*) teasing; **dar ~ a uno** to tease sb, kid sb*. **(e)** **~s** (*And*) earrings.
candongo* ADJ 1 (*zalamero*) smooth, oily; (*taimado*) sly, crafty; (*vago*) lazy.
  2 NM (*cobista*) creep‡, toady, flatterer; (*taimado*) sly sort; (*vago*) shirker, idler, lazy blighter‡.
candonguear* [1a] 1 VT to tease, kid*.
  2 VI to shirk, dodge work.
candonguero* ADJ = **candongo 1**.
candor NM **(a)** (*inocencia*) innocence, guilelessness, simplicity; frankness, candidness. **(b)** (*poét*) pure whiteness.
candorosamente ADV innocently, guilelessly, simply; frankly, candidly.
candoroso ADJ innocent, guileless, simple; *confesión etc* frank, candid.
candungo NM (*And*) idiot.
canear* [1a] VT to bash*, hit.
caneca NF **(a)** (*Cono Sur*: *balde*) wooden bucket; (*Carib*: *bolsa de agua*) hot-water bottle; (*And*) can, tin; (*de petróleo etc*) drum; (*porrón*) wine bottle (with a spout); (*Méx*) glazed earthenware bottle.
  (b) (*And, Carib*) liquid measure = 19 litres.
caneco ADJ (*And*) tipsy.
canela NF **(a)** (*Bot, Culin*) cinnamon. **(b)** (*fig*) lovely thing, exquisite object; **es ~ fina** she's wonderful; **es ~ en rama** she's a very sweet person; **V flor. (c)** (*Carib*: *mulata*) mulatto girl. **(d)** INTERJ (*euf*) good gracious!
canelero NM cinnamon tree.
canelo 1 ADJ cinnamon, cinnamon-coloured.
  2 NM cinnamon tree.
canelón NM **(a)** = **canalón. (b)** (*carámbano*) icicle. **(c)** (*CAm*: *rizo*) corkscrew curl. **(d) canelones** (*Culin*) cannelloni.
canesú NM **(a)** (*Cos*) yoke. **(b)** (*prenda*) underbodice, camisole.
caney NM **(a)** (*And, Carib*: *cabaña*) log cabin, hut; (*Carib Hist*) chief's house; (*And, Carib*: *cobertizo*) large shed. **(b)** (*LAm*: *de río*) river bend.
canfín NM (*CAm, Carib*) petrol, gasoline (*US*).
cangalla* NMF (*LAm*) coward.
cangallar* [1a] VT (*And, Cono Sur*) to pinch*, swipe‡.
cangilón NM **(a)** (*jarro*) pitcher; metal tankard; (*de noria*) bucket, scoop; (*And*) drum. **(b)** (*LAm*: *carril*) cart track, rut.
cangrejo NM **(a)** **~ (de mar)** (common) crab; **~ (de río)** crayfish. **(b)** (*Náut*) gaff. **(c)** (*And*: *idiota*) idiot; (*And*: *granuja*) rogue, crafty person. **(d)** (*LAm*: *misterio*) mystery, enigma. **(e)** (‡: *moneda*) 25 pesetas.
cangri‡ NM **(a)** (*cárcel*) nick‡, prison. **(b)** (*Ecl*) church. **(c)** (*Fin*) 25 setas.
cangro NM (*And, CAm, Méx*) cancer.
canguelo* NM, **canguis*** NM funk*.
canguro NM **(a)** (*Zool*) kangaroo. **(b)** (*: persona t* **cangura** F) baby-sitter; **hacer de ~** to baby-sit. **(c)** (*ropa*) light jacket, light coat. **(d)** (*: Náut*) ferry.
caníbal 1 ADJ cannibal; cannibalistic, man-eating; (*fig*) fierce, savage.
  2 NMF cannibal.
canibalesco ADJ cannibalistic.
canibalismo NM cannibalism; (*fig*) fierceness, savageness.
canibalizar [1f] VT to cannibalize.
canica NF **(a)** (*bola*) marble; (*juego*) marbles. **(b)** **~s‡** marbles‡, balls‡.

caniche NM poodle.
canicie NF (*de pelo*) greyness, whiteness.
canícula NF dog days, midsummer heat; (*fig*) hottest part of the day; **C~** Dog Star, Sirius.
canicular [1] ADJ: **calores ~es** midsummer heat.
  [2] **~es** NMPL dog days.
canicultura NF dog-breeding.
canijo ADJ (**a**) (*endeble*) weak, frail, sickly. (**b**) (*Méx**: *malvado*) sly, crafty.
canilla NF (**a**) (*Anat*) long bone (*of arm or leg*); (*espinilla*) shin, shin-bone; (*esp LAm*: *pierna*) shank, thin leg; **~ de la pierna** shinbone, tibia; **~ del brazo** armbone, ulna.
  (**b**) (*Téc*) bobbin, reel, spool.
  (**c**) (*grifo*) tap; (*de barril*) spout, cock, tap; **irse como una ~***, **irse de ~*** to have the trots**:**.
  (**d**) (*de paño*) rib.
  (**e**) (*Carib*: *cobardía*) cowardice.
  (**f**) (*Méx*) **a ~** by hook or by crook; **tener ~** to have great physical strength.
canillento ADJ (*And*) long-legged.
canillera NF (*LAm*) (*miedo*) fear; (*cobardía*) cowardice.
canillita NM (*LAm*) newsvendor, newspaper boy.
canillón* ADJ (*LAm*), **canilludo*** ADJ (*LAm*) long-legged.
canina NF dog dirt.
caninez NF ravenous hunger.
canino [1] ADJ (**a**) (*Zool*) canine; dog (*atr*). (**b**) **hambre canina** ravenous hunger.
  [2] NM canine (tooth).
canje NM exchange.
canjeable ADJ (*Fin*) exchangeable for cash, that can be cashed.
canjear [1a] VT (*gen*) to exchange; to swap; (*trocar*) to change over, interchange; *cupón* to cash in.
cannabis NM cannabis.
cano ADJ (**a**) (*de pelo*) grey-haired, white-haired, white-headed; **quedar ~** to go grey. (**b**) (*poét*) snow-white. (**c**) (*fig*) venerable; (*pey*) hoary, ancient.
canoa NF (**a**) (*Náut*) canoe; boat, launch; **~ automóvil** motor boat, launch; **~ fuera borda** outboard motorboat. (**b**) (*LAm*) (*conducto*) conduit, pipe; (*comedero*) feeding trough; (*de gallinas*) chicken coop; (*de palomas*) dovecot.
canódromo NM dogtrack.
canoero NM (*LAm*), **canoísta** NMF canoeist.
canólogo, -a NM/F expert on dogs.
canon NM (**a**) rule, canon; (*Arte, Ecl, Mús*) canon; (*Fin*) tax, levy; (*Min*) royalty; (*Agr*) rent; **~ de tránsito** (*Aut etc*) toll; **como mandan los cánones** as the rules require, in accordance with sound principles. (**b**) (*Ecl*) **cánones** canon law.
canonical ADJ of a canon (*o prebendary*), canonical; (*fig*) easy.
canonicato NM (*Ecl*) canonry; (***) sinecure, cushy job**:**.
canónico ADJ canonical; **derecho ~** canon law.
canóniga* NF nap before lunch; **coger una ~*** to have one over the eight.
canónigo NM canon.
canonista NM canon lawyer, expert in canon law.
canonización NF canonization.
canonizar [1f] VT to canonize; (*fig*) to consecrate; to applaud, extol, show approval of.
canonjía NF (*Ecl*) canonry; (***) sinecure, cushy job**:**.
canoro ADJ melodious, sweet, tuneful; **ave canora** songbird.
canoso ADJ grey-haired, white-haired; *barba* grizzled, hoary.
canotaje NM boating.
canotier NM, **canotié** NM straw hat, boater.
cansadamente ADV (*V* ADJ) (**a**) wearily, in a tired way. (**b**) tediously, boringly; tiresomely.
cansado ADJ (**a**) (*fatigado*) tired, weary (*de* of); *ojos* tired, strained; (*Agr*) *tierra* exhausted; **con voz cansada** in a weary voice; **estar ~** to be tired; **estoy ~ de hacerlo** I'm tired of doing it, I'm sick of doing it.
  (**b**) (*que cansa*) tiring.
  (**c**) (*aburrido*) tedious, boring; (*molesto*) tiresome, trying.
  (**d**) **a las cansadas** (*Carib, Cono Sur*) after much delay, after a long wait.
cansador ADJ (*Cono Sur*) = **cansado** (**b**).
cansancio NM tiredness, weariness; (*Med*) fatigue, exhaustion; **estar muerto de ~** to be dead tired, be dog-tired.
cansar [1a] [1] VT (*gen*) to tire, tire out, weary; (*Med*) to fatigue, exhaust; *ojos* to tire, strain, try; *paciencia* to try, wear out; (*Agr*) *tierra* to exhaust; *apetito* to jade; (*fig*) (*aburrir*) to bore; (*molestar*) to badger, bother (*con* with).
  [2] VI (**a**) (*fatigar*) to tire.
  (**b**) (*dar la lata*) to be trying, be tiresome.
  [3] **cansarse** VR to tire, get tired, grow weary (*con, de* of); to get

bored (*con, de* with); to tire o.s. out; **~ de hacer algo** to get tired of doing sth, get bored with doing sth.

| CANSADO | ver también la entrada |

Hay que tener en cuenta la diferencia entre **tired** y **tiring** a la hora de traducir **cansado**.
- Usamos **tired** cuando queremos indicar que *estamos* o que nos sentimos cansados:
  Se sintió cansado y se marchó
  He felt tired and left
  Estoy cansado de trabajar
  I'm tired of working
  Estábamos cansados del viaje
  We were tired after the journey
- Usamos **tiring** cuando queremos indicar que algo *es* **cansado**, es decir, que nos produce cansancio:
  Conducir 140 kms. todos los días es muy cansado
  Driving 140 kms every day is very tiring
Para otros usos y ejemplos ver la entrada.

---

cansera* NF bother; (*LAm*) wasted effort.
cansinamente ADV wearily; lifelessly.
cansino ADJ weary; lifeless; (*lento*) slow.
cantable [1] ADJ suitable for singing, to be sung; (*Mús*) cantabile; melodious.
  [2] NM sung part of a *zarzuela*.
cantábrico ADJ Cantabrian; **Mar C~** Bay of Biscay; **los (Montes) ~s** the Cantabrian Mountains.
cántabro, -a ADJ, NM/F Cantabrian.
cantada* NF (*Méx*) squealing*, grassing*.
cantadera NF (*LAm*) loud singing, prolonged singing.
cantado ADJ: **estar ~** to be a foregone conclusion.
cantador(a) NM/F folksinger, singer of popular songs.
cantal NM (**a**) (*piedra*) boulder; (*bloque*) stone block. (**b**) (*pedregal*) stony ground.
cantaleta NF (*LAm*) constant nagging; boring chorus, tedious refrain.
cantaletear [1a] VT (*LAm*) (**a**) (*repetir*) to repeat ad nauseam, say over and over. (**b**) (*embromar*) to laugh at, make fun of.
cantalupa NF (*CAm*), **cantalupo** NM cantaloupe.
cantamañanas* NMF INVAR: **no le hagas caso, es un ~** don't take any notice of him, you can't believe a word he says.
cantante [1] ADJ singing.
  [2] NMF (professional) singer; (*de jazz etc*) vocalist; **~ de ópera** opera singer.
cantaor(a) NM/F = **cantador(a)** (*esp de cante flamenco*).
cantar [1a] [1] VT (*gen*) to sing; to chant; (*alabar*) to sing about, sing of, sing the praises of; **~ mal y porfiar** to persist in doing sth badly; **~las claras** to speak out, speak frankly; (*pey*) to be cheeky.
  [2] VI (**a**) (*Mús*) to sing; to chant; (*insecto etc*) to chirp; (*máquina, rueda, etc*) to creak, squeak, grind; **~ a dos voces** to sing a duet.
  (**b**) (***: *confesar*) to squeal**:**, blab, spill the beans*; **~ de plano*** to tell all one knows, make a full confession.
  (**c**) **~ alto** (*Cono Sur*) to ask too high a price, over-charge.
  (**d**) (**:** *oler*) to smell bad, pong**:**.
  (**e**) (**:** *llamar la atención*) to attract (too much) attention, stand out (in an undesirable way); **las estadísticas cantan** there's no arguing with statistics, statistics don't lie.
  [3] NM (**a**) (*acto*) singing; chanting.
  (**b**) (*canción*) song; (*poesía*) poem (set to music); (*épica*) epic poem; **C~ de los C~es** Song of Songs; **~ de gesta** epic poem; **C~ de mio Cid** Poem of the Cid; **eso es otro ~** that's another story.
cántara NF (**a**) (*recipiente*) large pitcher. (**b**) *liquid measure* = 16.13 litres.
cantarería NF (**a**) (*tienda*) pottery shop, earthenware shop. (**b**) (*cerámica*) pottery.
cantarero NM potter, dealer in earthenware.
cantárida NF (*t polvo de ~*) Spanish fly, (*Farm*) cantharides.
cantarín [1] ADJ *persona* fond of singing; *arroyo* tinkling, musical; *tono* singsong, lilting.
  [2] NM, **cantarina** NF (professional) singer.
cántaro NM (**a**) (*vasija*) pitcher, jug; (*cantidad*) jugful; **a ~s** in plenty; **llover a ~s** to rain cats and dogs, rain in torrents. (**b**) **~s:** tits**:**.
cantata[1] NF (*Mús*) cantata.
cantata[2]**:** NF tip-off.
cantautor(a) NM/F singer-songwriter.
cante NM (**a**) **~ flamenco**, **~ jondo** Andalusian gipsy singing. (**b**) (**:** *soplo*) tip-off (to the police).
cantegriles NMPL (*Cono Sur*) shanty-town.
cantera NF (**a**) quarry, pit; **~ de arena** sandpit; **~ de piedra** stone quarry. (**b**) (*fig*) talent, genius. (**c**) (*fig*) source of supply; (*Dep*) reserve of young players; nursery, seedbed.
canterano, -a NM/F junior player, novice.
cantería NF (**a**) (*acto*) quarrying, stone cutting. (**b**) (*Arquit*) masonry,

stonework. (**c**) (*piedra*) piece of masonry, stone, ashlar.
cantero NM (**a**) (*persona*) quarryman; stonemason.
(**b**) (*cabo*) end, extremity; ~ **de pan** crust of bread.
(**c**) (*Cono Sur*) (*sembradío*) bed, plot (*of vegetables*), (*de flores*) flower-bed; (*And, Méx: de caña*) plot of sugar cane.
cántico NM (*Ecl*) canticle; (*fig*) song.
cantidad 1 NF quantity; amount, number; (*cifra*) figure; (*de dinero*) amount, sum; ~ **alzada** fixed price, all-in price; ~ **de movimiento** (*Fís*) momentum; **en** ~ in quantity; ~ **de**, (**una**) **gran** ~ **de** a great quantity of, lots of; **¿había mucha gente?** ... **¡cualquier ~!** (*LAm**) were there many people? ... loads! (o masses!); **tengo una** ~ **de cosas que hacer** I've lots of things to do, I've masses of things to do.
2 *como* ADV (*) a lot, a good deal; **ese coche mola ~:** that car is really nice; **esto está degenerando** ~ this is really going downhill; **sabe** ~ **de eso** he knows a lot about that.

┌─ CANTIDAD ──────────── *ver también la entrada* ─┐

Cantidad, como sustantivo, se puede traducir al inglés por *amount*, *number*, *sum*, *quantity* y *figure*.

• Cuando *cantidad* expresa cuánto tenemos, necesitamos u obtenemos de algo se traduce por *amount*, palabra que se usa en el contexto de nombres incontables:
   Le preocupaba la cantidad de trabajo que tenía que hacer
   He was worried about the amount of work he had to do
! Se puede decir *a large amount* y *a small amount*, pero es incorrecto decir *a big amount* o *a little amount*:
• Cuando hablamos de una *cantidad* de personas, animales o cosas, (nombres en plural), *cantidad* se traduce por *number*. Con la expresión *the number of* el verbo va en singular y con *a number of* en plural:
   En los últimos 30 años la cantidad de consumidores de electricidad ha aumentado en un 50 por ciento
   In the last 30 years, the number of electricity consumers has risen by 50 per cent
   Me esperaban una gran cantidad de recibos sin pagar
   A large number of bills were waiting for me
! Hay que tener en cuenta que con *number* también podemos utilizar *large* y *small*, pero no *big* ni *little*.
• Hablando de dinero, *cantidad* se traduce por *sum*. Puede aparecer con *large*, *small* o *huge*:
   Los fabricantes gastan enormes cantidades de dinero en anunciar sus productos
   Manufacturers spend huge sums of money on advertising their products
• Una *cantidad* que se puede medir o contar se puede traducir por *quantity*. Puede ir acompañado de *large* o *small*:
   Quiero un kilo de patatas y la misma cantidad de manzanas
   I'd like a kilo of potatoes and the same quantity of apples
   Sólo necesitas una cantidad muy pequeña
   You only need a very small quantity
NOTA: *Amount* también es posible en el contexto de sustancias incontables:
   You only need a very small amount
• Una *cantidad* específica, expresada numéricamente, se traduce por *figure*, que puede aparecer con los adjetivos *high* y *low*:
   Al final se decidieron por una cantidad de veinte mil libras
   Finally, they decided on a figure of twenty thousand pounds
   Para otros usos y ejemplos ver la entrada.

└──┘

cantiga NF, **cántiga** NF song, poem.
cantil NM (*en roca*) shelf, ledge; (*de costa*) coastal shelf; (*risco*) cliff.
cantilena NF ballad, song, chant; **la misma** ~ (*fig*) the same old tale; **y toda esa ~*** and all that jazz*.
cantillos NMPL (*juego*) jacks.
cantimplora NF (*para agua*) water bottle, canteen; (*para licor*) hip flask; (*Téc*) syphon; (*And*) powder flask; **¡~!** (*And**) not on your life!
cantina NF (**a**) (*Ferro*) buffet, refreshment room; (*Mil etc*) canteen; (*snack*) snack bar; (*LAm: bar*) bar, saloon; (*Cono Sur: restorán*) cheap restaurant.
(**b**) (*bodega*) wine cellar.
(**c**) (*caja de comida*) lunch box; (*And: de leche*) milk churn; ~**s** (*Méx*) saddlebags.
cantinela NF = **cantilena**.
cantinero NM barman, publican.
cantinflismo NM (*Méx*) babble, empty chatter.
cantío NM (*Carib*) folksong, popular song.
cantiral NM stony ground, stony place.
canto[1] NM (*Mús*) (**a**) (*arte, gen*) singing; chanting.
(**b**) (*acto: gen*) singing; **el** ~ **de los pájaros** the singing of the birds.
(**c**) (*canción*) song; ~ **llano** plainsong; ~ **de sirena(s)** siren song; **al** ~ **del gallo** at cockcrow, at daybreak.

(**d**) (*Poét*) song, lyric; (*parte de épica*) canto.
canto[2] NM (**a**) (*borde*) edge; rim, border; (*de cuchillo*) back; (*de libro*) fore-edge; (*extremo*) end, point; (*ángulo*) corner; (*de pan*) crust; **ni un** ~ **de uña** absolutely nothing; **estar de** ~ to be on edge, be edgeways; to be on end; **le faltó el** ~ **de un duro** he had a narrow shave; **tener 3 cm de** ~ to be 3 cm thick.
(**b**) (*piedra*) stone, pebble; rock; (*t* ~ **rodado**) boulder.
cantón[1] NM corner; (*Her, Pol*) canton; (*Mil*) cantonment.
cantón[2] NM (*LAm Cos*) cotton material.
cantonada NF: **dar** ~ **a uno** to dodge sb, shake sb off.
cantonal ADJ cantonal.
cantonear [1a] VI to loaf around.
cantonera NF (**a**) (*anaquel*) corner shelf; (*escuadra*) corner bracket, angle iron; (*mesita*) corner table; (*armario*) corner cupboard; (*de libro, mueble etc*) corner piece.
(**b**) (*) streetwalker.
cantonero NM loafer, idler, good-for-nothing.
cantonés, -esa 1 ADJ, NM/F Cantonese.
2 NM (*Ling*) Cantonese.
cantor 1 ADJ singing, that sings; **ave ~a** a songbird.
2 NM, **cantora** NF singer; (*Orn*) songbird.
Cantórbery NM Canterbury.
cantorral NM stony ground, stony place.
cantuariense ADJ of (o from) Canterbury.
cantuja NF (*And*) slang.
cantúo: ADJ: **una mujer cantúa** a woman with a smashing figure*.
canturía NF (*canto*) singing, vocal music; (*ejercicio*) singing exercise; (*pey*) monotonous singing, droning.
canturrear [1a] VTI to hum, croon, sing softly; to chant; to drone.
canturreo NM humming, crooning, soft singing; chanting; droning.
canutazo: NM telephone call.
canutero NM (*LAm*) barrel (*of pen*).
canuto 1 (:) ADJ (**a**) super*, smashing*.
(**b**) **pasarlas canutas** to have a rough time of it.
2 NM (**a**) (*tubo*) small tube, small container.
(**b**) (*Bot*) internode.
(**c**) (*: *persona*) telltale.
(**d**) (:) *porro*) joint:.
(**e**) (:) *teléfono*) telephone, blower:.
canzonetista NF vocalist, crooner.
caña NF (**a**) (*Bot: especie*) reed.
(**b**) (*Bot: tallo*) stem, stalk, cane; (*bastón*) walking-stick, cane; ~ **de azúcar**, ~ **dulce**, ~ **melar** sugar cane; ~ **de pescar** fishing rod; ~ **del timón** tiller, helm; **las ~s se vuelven lanzas** a joke can easily turn into something unpleasant.
(**c**) (*Anat*) long bone (*of arm or leg*), (*esp*) shinbone; (*de bota, media*) leg; (*de ancla, caballo*) shank; (*de pilar*) shaft; (:) prick:: ~**s** (*Méx**) legs.
(**d**) (*vaso*) tall wineglass, long glass; ~ **de cerveza** glass of beer; beer glass; **¡dos ~s!** (*in bar*) 'two beers please'.
(**e**) (*LAm*) (*azúcar*) sugar cane; (*licor*) rum, brandy; **estar con la** ~ **mala** (*Cono Sur**) to have a hangover*.
(**f**) (*Min*) gallery.
(**g**) (*Carib**) swig*, drink.
(**h**) (*And, Carib*) (*bulo*) false rumour; (*bravata*) piece of bluff, piece of bluster.
(**i**) (*LAm: pajita*) (drinking) straw.
(**j**) (*) **dar** ~ **a**, **meter** ~ **a** to attack, go for; *tarea etc* to get stuck into.
cañabrava NF (*LAm*) reed; bamboo.
cañada NF (**a**) (*barranco*) gully, ravine; (*valle*) glen. (**b**) (*camino*) cattle track, drover's road. (**c**) (*LAm: arroyo*) stream; low-lying wet place.
cañadón NM (*Cono Sur*) low-lying part of a field.
cañamar NM hemp field.
cañamazo NM (coarse) canvas (for embroidery); burlap.
cañamelar NM sugar-cane plantation.
cañameno ADJ hempen.
cañamero ADJ hemp (*atr*).
cañamiel NF sugar cane.
cáñamo NM (*Bot*) hemp; (*tela*) hempen cloth; (*CAm, Carib, Cono Sur: cuerda*) hempen cord; ~ **agramado** dressed hemp; ~ **indio** Indian hemp, marijuana; ~ **índico** (*LAm*) marijuana plant.
cañamón NM hemp seed; birdseed.
cañata: NF (glass of) beer.
cañavera NF reed grass.
cañaveral NM reedbed; (*Agr*) sugar-cane plantation.
cañazo NM (*And*) cane liquor; **dar** ~ **a** to play a trick on.
cañear* [1a] VI to drink, carouse.
cañengo ADJ, **cañengue** ADJ (*And, Carib*) weak, sickly; skinny.
cañeo* NM drinking, carousal.
cañería NF (*tubo*) pipe, piece of piping, length of piping; (*conducto*) pipeline, conduit; (*desaguadero*) drain; (*Mús*) organ pipes; (:) *droga*)

main line**;** **~s** pipes, piping; **~ maestra (de gas)** (gas) main.

cañero [1] ADJ **(a)** (*LAm*) sugar-cane (*atr*); **machete ~** sugar-cane knife.
(b) (*And, Carib*) (*mentiroso*) lying; (*fanfarrón*) boastful.
[2] NM **(a)** (*Téc*) plumber, pipe fitter.
(b) (*LAm: Agr*) owner (*o* manager) of a sugar-cane plantation.
(c) (*And, Carib*) (*mentiroso*) liar; (*fanfarrón*) bluffer, boaster.

cañete NM small pipe.

cañí = **calé**.

cañita NF (*And*) (drinking) straw.

cañiza NF coarse linen.

cañizal NM, **cañizar** NM (*natural*) reedbed; (*Agr*) sugar-cane plantation.

cañizo NM (*Agr*) hurdle (for drying fruit *etc*).

caño NM **(a)** (*tubo*) tube, pipe; (*Mús*) pipe; (*de fuente*) jet, spout; (*Arquit*) gutter; (*alcantarilla*) drain, (open) sewer; (*And: grifo*) tap.
(b) (*galería*) gallery.
(c) (*bodega*) wine cellar.
(d) (*Náut*) navigation channel, deep channel; (*And, Carib: río*) narrow navigable river.

cañón [1] NM **(a)** (*tubo*) tube, pipe; (*Mús*) pipe, organ pipe; (*de chimenea*) flue; shaft, stack; (*de columna, ascensor*) shaft; (*de escalera*) well; (*de arma, pluma*) barrel; (*de pipa*) stem; (*Alpinismo*) chimney; **escopeta de dos cañones** double-barrelled gun; **~ rayado** rifled barrel; **ni a ~ rayado** (*And, Carib, Cono Sur*) by no means, not at all.
(b) (*Mil*) gun; (*esp Hist*) cannon; (*TV**) zoom-lens; (*luz*) spotlight; **~ de agua** water-cannon; **~ antiaéreo** anti-aircraft gun; **~ antitanque** anti-tank gun; **~ arponero** harpoon; **~ de avancarga** muzzle-loader; **~ de campaña** fieldgun; **~ de nieve artificial** snow machine; **~ obús** howitzer.
(c) (*de pluma*) quill; quill pen.
(d) (*Geog*) canyon, gorge; (*And: paso*) pass.
(e) (*And: Bot*) trunk.
(f) (*And, Méx: camino*) mountain path.
[2] *como* ADJ INVAR (*) fabulous*, marvellous*; **¡el hombre está ~!** he's fabulous!*; **¡la función estaba ~!** the show was great!*; **una noticia ~** a stunning piece of news.

cañonazo NM **(a)** (*Mil*) gunshot; (*Hist*) cannon shot; (*Dep**) fierce shot; **~s** gunfire, shellfire; **salva de 21 ~s** 21-gun salute; **~ de advertencia** (*Náut*) warning shot, shot across the bows.
(b) (*fig*) bombshell, bolt from the blue.

cañonear [1a] [1] VT to shell, bombard.
[2] **cañonearse** VR (*Cono Sur**) to get tight*.

cañoneo NM shelling, shellfire, gunfire; bombardment, cannonade.

cañonera NF **(a)** (*Mil: Hist*) embrasure. **(b)** (*Náut: t* **lancha ~**) gunboat.
(c) (*LAm: pistolera*) holster.

cañonero NM gunboat.

cañusero NM (*And*) owner of a sugar-cane plantation.

cañutero NM pincushion.

cañuto NM = **canuto**.

caoba NF mahogany.

caolín NM kaolin.

caos NM chaos.

caótico ADJ chaotic.

caotizar [1f] VT to throw into disarray, cause chaos in.

cap. ABR *de* **capítulo** chapter, ch.

C.A.P. NM ABR *de* **Certificado de Aptitud Pedagógica** (*teaching certificate*).

capa NF **(a)** cloak, cape; (*Ecl: t* **~ pluvial**) cape; **~ de agua**, **~ aguadera** raincape, waterproof cloak; **~ del cielo** canopy of heaven; **~ (de ladrones)** (*fig*) fence, receiver; **~ rota** (*fig*) secret emissary; **~ torera** bullfighter's cape; **andar de ~ caída** to be in a bad way, be on the decline; **echar una ~ a uno** to cover up for sb; **echar la ~ al toro** to make a final desperate effort; **hacer de su ~ un sayo** to do what one likes with one's own things, act freely; **comedia de ~ y espada** cloak-and-dagger play.
(b) (*fig*) cloak, pretence; mask, disguise; **so ~ de** under the pretext of, in the guise of.
(c) (*Geol*) layer, bed, stratum; (*Met, Anat etc*) layer; (*de humo*) pall; (*de polvo*) layer, film; (*de nieve*) layer, covering, mantle; (*Culin*) coating; (*de pintura*) coat; **primera ~** undercoat, first coat; **~ freática** water table; **~ de ozono** ozone layer; **~s sociales** social layers, social levels; **madera de tres ~s** three-ply wood.
(d) (*Náut*) **estar a la ~**, **ponerse a la ~** to lie to.

capaburro NM (*LAm*) piranha.

capacha NF **(a)** (*espuerta*) basket. **(b)** (*And, Cono Sur**) jail, clink**;** **caer en la ~** (*Cono Sur*) to fall into the trap.

capacheca NF (*And, Cono Sur*) street-vendor's barrow (*o* stall).

capacho NM **(a)** (*espuerta*) wicker basket, big basket; (*Téc*) wickerwork hod; (*And: alforja*) saddlebag. **(b)** (*And, Cono Sur: sombrero*) old hat.

capacidad NF **(a)** capacity (*t Com, Fís, Téc etc*); (*cabida*) capaciousness, size; **una sala con ~ para 900** a hall with room for 900, a hall that can hold 900; **un avión con ~ para 20 plazas** a 20-seater plane; **~**

adquisitiva, **~ de compra** purchasing power; **~ de almacenaje** storage capacity; **~ de arrastre**, **~ de convocatoria** (*de orador etc*) drawing power, power of attraction; popular appeal; **~ de carga** carrying capacity; **~ de endeudamiento** (limit of) borrowing powers; **~ financiera** financial standing; **~ de ganancia** earning power; **~ de pago** credit-worthiness; **~ de repercusión** resilience; **~ útil** effective capacity.
(b) (*fig*) (*talento*) (mental) capacity, ability, capability, talent; (*habilidad*) competence, efficiency; (*Jur*) capacity, legal competency; **tener ~ para** to have an aptitude for, have talent for; **no tiene ~ para los negocios** he has no business sense.
(c) (*LAm: persona hábil*) able person, talented person.

capacitación NF (*Jur*) capacitation; (*Téc etc*) training, education.

capacitado ADJ qualified; **estar ~ para** + *infin* to be qualified to + *infin*.

capacitar [1a] [1] VT **(a)** **~ a uno para algo** to fit sb for sth, qualify sb for sth; (*Téc*) to train (*o* educate) sb for sth; **~ a uno para** + *infin* to enable sb to + *infin*.
(b) **~ a uno para hacer algo** (*And, Cono Sur, Méx*) to empower (*o* authorize) sb to do sth.
[2] **capacitarse** VR: **~ para algo** to fit o.s. for sth, qualify for sth.

capacitor NM capacitor.

capadura NF castration.

capar [1a] VT **(a)** *animal* to castrate, geld.
(b) (*fig*) to reduce, cut down, curtail.
(c) (*Carib, Méx: Agr*) to cut back, prune.
(d) (*And, Carib*) *comida* to start on, begin to eat.

caparazón NM **(a)** (*Hist*) caparison; (*manta*) horse blanket; (*comedero*) nosebag. **(b)** (*Zool*) shell.

caparrón NM bud.

caparrosa NF copperas; vitriol; **~ azul** copper sulphate, blue vitriol.

capataz NM foreman, overseer.

▼ **capaz** [1] ADJ **(a)** (*en tamaño*) capacious, roomy, large; **~ de**, **~ para** with a capacity of, with room for, that holds; **un coche ~ para 4 personas** a car with room for 4 people.
▼ **(b)** (*en competencia*) able, capable; efficient, competent; fit; (*Jur*) competent; **ser ~ de algo** to be capable of sth; **ser ~ de hacer algo** to be capable of doing sth, be up to doing sth; to be competent to do sth; **es ~ de cualquier tontería** he is capable of any stupidity, one might expect any idiocy from him; **¿serías ~?** would you dare? **¡sería ~!** one could well believe it of him, I wouldn't put it past him, I'm not surprised; **~ de funcionar** (*Téc*) operational, in working order; **ser ~ para un trabajo** to be qualified for a job, be up to a job.
(c) (*LAm*) (*es*) **~ que venga** (*probable*) he'll probably come, he's likely to come; (*posible*) he might come, possibly he'll come; **~ que le pasaba algo** maybe he had some problem.
[2] ADV (*LAm*) **¿vendrá? - ~ que sí** will he come? - maybe (*o* he might).

capazo NM large basket; (*de niño*) carrycot.

capcioso ADJ wily, deceitful.

capea NF bullfight with young bulls.

capeador NM *bullfighter who uses the cape.*

capear [1a] [1] VT **(a)** (*Taur*) to play with the cape, wave the cape at; (*fig*) to take in, deceive.
(b) (*Náut y fig*) *temporal* to ride out, weather.
(c) (*esquivar*) to dodge.
(d) (*Culin*) to cap, cover (*con* with).
[2] VI (*Náut*) to ride out the storm; to lie to.

capellada NF (*puntera*) toecap; (*remiendo*) patch.

capellán NM chaplain; priest, clergyman; **~ castrense**, **~ de ejército** army chaplain.

capellanía NF chaplaincy.

capelo NM **(a)** (*Ecl*) cardinal's hat; (*fig*) cardinalate. **(b)** (*Cono Sur, Méx: tapa*) bell glass, glass cover. **(c)** (*LAm Univ*) **~ de doctor** doctor's gown.

capero NM hallstand, hatstand.

Caperucita Roja NF (Little) Red Riding Hood.

caperuza NF (*pointed*) hood; (*Mec*) hood, cowling; (*de pluma etc*) top, cap; **~ de chimenea** chimney cowl.

capi¹* NM = **capitán**.

capi² NF (*And, Cono Sur*) (*harina*) white maize flour; (*maíz*) maize, corn (*US*); (*vaina*) unripe pod.

capi³* NF capital.

capia NF (*And, Cono Sur*) (*harina*) white maize flour; (*maíz*) maize, corn (*US*).

capiango NM (*Cono Sur*) clever thief.

capicúa NM reversible number, symmetrical number (*p.ej.* 12321); palindrome.

capigorra NM, **capigorrista** NM, **capigorrón** NM idler, loafer.

capilar [1] ADJ capillary; hair (*atr*); **tubo ~** capillary.
[2] NM capillary.

➤ LENGUA Y USO: capaz: 1b → 43.4

capilaridad NF capillarity.

capilla NF (a) (*Ecl*) chapel; ~ **ardiente** funeral chapel; ~ **mayor** choir, chancel; ~ **de la Virgen** Lady Chapel; **estar en** (**la**) ~ (*fig*) to be awaiting execution; to be in great danger; to be in suspense, be on tenterhooks.
(b) (*Mús*) choir.
(c) (*Tip*) proof sheet; **estar en ~s** to be in proof.
(d) (*caperuza*) cowl; (*Téc*) hood, cowl.
(e) (*peña*) group of supporters, following; informal club.

capiller(o) NM churchwarden; sexton.

capillo NM (a) (*de bebé*) baby's bonnet; (*de halcón*) hood. (b) (*Bot, Zool*) = **capullo.**

capirotazo NM flip, flick.

capirote NM (a) (*Hist, Univ, de halcón*) hood. (b) (*capirotazo*) flip, flick. (c) **tonto de** ~ prize idiot, utter fool. (d) (*Culin*) cloth strainer (for coffee *etc*).

capirucho NM hood.

capiruchu NM (*CAm*) *child's toy consisting of wooden cup and ball.*

capisayo NM (*And*) vest, undershirt (*US*).

capitación NF poll tax, capitation.

capital [1] ADJ (*en muchos sentidos*) capital; *ciudad, crimen* capital; *enemigo, pecado* mortal; *rasgo* main, chief, principal; *punto* essential, fundamental; *importancia* capital, supreme, paramount; (*esp LAm*) *letra* capital; **lo** ~ the main thing, the essential point.
[2] NM (*Fin*) capital; capital sum; ~ **en acciones** share capital; ~ **activo** working capital, (*And, Cono Sur*) capital assets; ~ **arriesgado** venture capital; ~ **autorizado** authorized capital; ~ **circulante** circulating capital; ~ **de explotación** working capital; ~ **emitido** issued capital; ~ **fijo** fixed capital; ~ **físico** (*Cono Sur*) capital assets; ~ **improductivo** idle money; ~ **invertido**, ~ **utilizado** invested capital; ~ **pagado** paid-up capital; ~ (**de**) **riesgo** risk capital; ~ **social** share capital; **inversión de ~es** capital investment.
[3] NF (a) (*Pol: de país*) capital, capital city; (*de región*) chief town, centre; ~ **de provincia** provincial capital, administrative centre of the province; **en León** ~ in the city of León.
(b) (*Tip*) decorated initial capital.

capitalidad NF capital status, status as capital.

capitalino (*LAm*) [1] ADJ of the capital.
[2] NM, **capitalina** NF (a) native (o inhabitant) of the capital; **los ~s** the people of the capital. (b) (*) city slicker*.

capitalismo NM capitalism; ~ **de Estado** state capitalism; ~ **monopolista** monopoly capitalism.

capitalista [1] ADJ capitalist(ic).
[2] NMF capitalist; (*hum*) Madrilenian.

capitalización NF capitalization; compounding.

capitalizar [1f] VT (a) to capitalize; *interés* to compound. (b) (*fig*) to capitalize on, turn to account.

capitán NM (*Dep, Mil, Náut, etc*) captain; (*jefe*) leader, chief, commander; (*Méx*) maître d'hôtel; ~ **de corbeta** lieutenant-commander; ~ **de fragata** commander; ~ **general** (**de ejército**) (*aprox*) field marshal; ~ **general** (**de armada**) chief of naval operations; ~ **de navío** captain; ~ **del puerto** harbour master.

capitana NF (a) (*Dep, Mil*) (woman) captain; (*Hist*) captain's wife. (b) (*Náut*) flagship.

capitanear [1a] VT *equipo* to captain; *expedición, sublevación etc* to lead, head, command.

capitanía NF (a) (*cargo*) captaincy; (*rango*) rank of captain. (b) ~ **del puerto** harbour master's office. (c) (*derechos*) harbour dues.

capitel NM (*Arquit*) capital.

capitolio NM capitol; (*edificio grande*) large edifice, imposing building; (*Pol*) statehouse, parliament building; **C~** Capitol.

capitoné NM (a) removal van, furniture van. (b) (*Cono Sur*) quilt, quilted blanket.

capitonear [1a] VT (*Cono Sur*) to quilt.

capitoste NM (*pey*) chief, boss; petty tyrant.

capitulación NF (a) (*Mil*) capitulation, surrender; ~ **sin condiciones** unconditional surrender.
(b) (*acuerdo*) agreement, pact; **capitulaciones** (**de boda, matrimoniales**) marriage settlement.

capitular[1] ADJ (*Ecl*) chapter (*atr*); **sala** ~ chapter house, meeting room.

capitular[2] [1a] [1] VT (a) *condiciones* to agree to, agree on.
(b) (*Jur*) to charge (*de* with), impeach.
[2] VI (a) (*pactar*) to come to terms, make an agreement (*con* with).
(b) (*Mil*) to capitulate, surrender.

capitulear [1a] VI (*And, Cono Sur: Parl*) to lobby.

capituleo NM (*And, Cono Sur: Parl*) lobbying.

capítulo NM (a) (*Liter, Tip*) chapter; **eso es** ~ **aparte** that's another question altogether; **esto merece** ~ **aparte** this deserves separate treatment.
(b) (*reprimenda*) reproof, reprimand; ~ (**de culpas**) charge, impeachment.
(c) (*asunto*) subject, matter; point; **ganar** ~ to make one's point.

(d) **~s matrimoniales** marriage contract, marriage settlement.
(e) (*junta*) meeting (of a council); (*Ecl*) chapter; **llamar a uno a** ~ **to** take sb to task, call sb to account.
(f) (*Ecl*) chapter house.

cap.º ABR *de* **capítulo**; = **cap.**

capo* (*Cono Sur*) [1] ADJ INVAR great*, fabulous*.
[2] NM (*jefe*) boss; (*persona influyente*) bigwig; (*perito*) expert; **es un** ~ (*en arte, profesión*) he's the tops*, he's brilliant.

capó NM (*Aut*) bonnet, hood (*US*); (*Aer*) cowling.

capoc NM kapok.

capón[1] NM rap on the head.

capón[2] [1] ADJ castrated.
[2] NM (a) (*pollo*) capon; (*eunuco*) eunuch. (b) (*Cono Sur*) (*: novato*) novice, greenhorn; (*cor dero*) castrated sheep, wether; (*carne*) mutton.

caponera NF (*Agr*) chicken coop, fattening pen; (*fig*) place of easy living, open house; (‡) clink‡.

caporal NM chief, leader, (*Agr etc: esp LAm*) foreman, head man.

capot [ka'po] NM (*Aut*) = **capó.**

capota NF (a) (*de mujer*) bonnet. (b) (*de carruaje, cochecito*) hood; (*Aut*) hood, top (*US*); ~ **plegable** folding hood, folding top (*US*).

capotar [1a] VI (*Aut etc*) to turn over, turn turtle; to somersault; (*fig*) to fall down, collapse.

capote NM (a) (*capa*) long cloak, cloak with sleeves; (*t* ~ **de brega**) bullfighter's cape; (*Mil*) greatcoat; ~ **de monte** poncho; **a mi** ~, **para mi** ~ to my way of thinking; **de** ~ (*Méx*) on the sly, in an underhand way; **dar un** ~ **a** = **capotear** (b); **darse** ~ (*Méx*) to give up one's job; to acknowledge defeat; **decir para su** ~ to say to o.s.; **echar un** ~ **a uno** to give sb a helping hand.
(b) (*ceño*) frown, scowl; (*Met*) mass of dark clouds.
(c) (*Naipes*) slam.
(d) (*Cono Sur Naipes*) **quedar** ~ to be whitewashed*.

capotear [1a] VT (a) (*Taur*) *toro* to play with the cape. (b) *persona* to deceive, bamboozle*. (c) *dificultad etc* to shirk, duck, dodge. (d) (*Cono Sur Naipes*) to win all the tricks against, whitewash*.

capotera NF (a) (*CAm: gancho*) clothes peg. (b) (*Cono Sur: azotaina*) beating. (c) (*CAm: lona*) tarpaulin.

capotudo ADJ frowning, scowling.

capricho NM (a) (*noción etc*) whim, caprice, (passing) fancy; (*deseo*) keen desire, sudden urge (*de* for); (*pey*) craze, fad, silly notion; **por puro** ~ just to please o.s., out of sheer cussedness*; **es un** ~ **nada más** it's just a passing whim; **fue un** ~ **suyo** it was one of his silly notions; **tiene sus ~s** he has his little whims, he has his moods.
(b) (*cualidad*) whimsicality, fancifulness.
(c) (*Arte*) caprice; (*Mús*) capriccio.

caprichosamente ADV capriciously; whimsically; wilfully; waywardly.

caprichoso ADJ (*gen*) capricious; full of whims, having odd fancies; full of one's own pet notions; *idea, novela, etc* fanciful, whimsical; (*pey*) wilful; moody, temperamental; wayward.

caprichudo ADJ stubborn, obstinate, unyielding (about one's odd ideas).

Capricornio NM (*Zodíaco*) Capricorn.

cápsula NF (*Aer, Anat, Bot, Farm etc*) capsule; (*de botella*) cap; (*de tocadiscos*) pick-up; (*de cartucho*) case; (*Carib*) cartridge; ~ **espacial** space capsule; ~ **fulminante** percussion cap; ~ **de mando** command module.

capsular ADJ capsular; **en forma** ~ in capsule form.

captación NF: ~ **de datos** data capture.

captador NM (*Téc*) sensor.

captafaros NM INVAR (*t* **placa de ~**) reflector.

captar [1a] VT (a) (*atraer*) to captivate; *apoyo* to win, gain, attract; *confianza etc* to win, get; *voluntad* to gain control over; *atención etc* to get, secure; *sentido* to grasp; *persona* to win over.
(b) *aguas* to collect; to dam, harness.
(c) (*Rad*) *emisora* to tune in to; *señal* to get, pick up, receive; (*Inform*) *datos* to capture, store.
(d) (*Cine, Fot*) *imagen* to shoot, take, film.

captura NF capture; seizure; arrest.

capturar [1a] VT to capture; to seize; to arrest.

capturista NMF (*Méx*) typist; (: *Inform*) computer operator, keyboarder.

capucha NF (a) (*prenda*) hood; (*Ecl*) hood, cowl; ~ **antihumo** smoke hood. (b) (*Tip*) circumflex accent.

capuchina NF (a) (*Ecl*) Capuchin sister. (b) (*Bot*) nasturtium.

capuchino NM (a) (*Ecl*) Capuchin. (b) (*LAm Zool*) Capuchin monkey. (c) (**café**) ~ capuccino (coffee).

capucho NM cowl, hood.

capuchón NM (a) (*prenda*) capuchin, lady's hooded cloak. (b) (*Fot*) hood. (c) ~ **de válvula** (*Aut etc*) valve cap. (d) (*de pluma*) top, cap.

capujar [1a] VT (*Cono Sur*) (*atrapar*) to catch in (o snatch out of) the air; (*arrebatar*) to snatch; (*decir*) to say what sb else was about to say.

capullada* NF silly thing, piece of nonsense.

capullo NM (**a**) (*Zool*) cocoon. (**b**) (*Bot*) bud; (*de bellota*) cup; ~ (**de rosa**) rosebud. (**c**) (*Anat*) prepuce; **porque no me sale del ~*** because I don't want to. (**d**) (*) (*persona*: *principiante*) novice, beginner; (*imbécil*) twit*; (*Mil*) raw recruit. (**e**) (*tela*) coarse silk cloth.

caqui[1] NM khaki; **marcar el ~*** to finish military service.

caqui[2] NM (*Cono Sur*) date plum; (*fig*) red.

caquino NM: **reírse a ~s, reírse a ~ suelto** (*Méx*) to laugh uproariously, cackle.

cara[1] NF (**a**) (*Anat*) face; ~ **cortada** (*como apodo*) scarface; ~ **de cuchillo** hatchet face; ~ **a** ~ face to face; (*como nm*) face-to-face encounter; **a** ~ **descubierta** openly; **de** ~ opposite, facing; **mirar a uno a la** ~ to look sb in the face; **los banqueros sin** ~ the faceless bankers; **asomar la** ~ to show one's face (*t fig*); **se le caía la** ~ **de vergüenza** he blushed with shame; **cruzar la** ~ **a uno** to slash sb across the face; **dar la** ~ to face the consequences of what one has done; **no quería dar la** ~ he didn't want to show his face (in public); **dar la** ~ **por otro** to answer for sb else; **dar** ~ **a** to face up to; **decir algo en la** ~ **de uno** to say sth to sb's face; **echar algo en** ~ **a uno** to reproach sb for sth, cast sth in sb's teeth; to allude to sth; **es lo mejor que te puedes echar a la** ~* it's the very best you could wish for; **entrar** (*o* **pasar**) **por la** ~ to gatecrash; **hacer a dos ~s** to engage in double-dealing; **hacer** ~ **a** to face; *enemigo etc* to face up to, stand up to; **huir la** ~ **a uno** to avoid meeting sb; **lavar la** ~ **a uno** to lick sb's boots; **no mirar la** ~ **a uno** (*fig*) to be at daggers drawn with sb; **plantar** ~ **a uno** to confront sb; **romper la** ~ **a uno** to smash sb's face in; **sacar la** ~ **por uno** to stick up for sb; **nos veremos las ~s** (*amenaza*) we'll meet again, we'll see; **no volver la** ~ **atrás** not to flinch.

(**b**) (*usos como ADV y PREP*): ~ **adelante** forwards; facing forwards; ~ **atrás** backwards; facing backwards; ~ **al sol** facing the sun; (**de**) ~ **al norte** facing north; ~ **al futuro** with an eye to the future; **de** ~ **a** (*fig*) in view of, with a view to; as an aid to, as helping towards; directed towards; in connection with; **de** ~ **a** + *infin* in order to + *infin*, with a view to + *ger*.

(**c**) (*aspecto*) look, appearance; **tener** ~ **de** to look like; **tener** ~ **de querer** + *infin* to look as if one would like to + *infin*; **tener** ~ **de aburrirse** to look bored; **tener buena** ~ to look nice, (*Med*) look well; **tener mala** ~ to look bad, (*Med*) look ill; ~ **de aleluya** cheerful look; **tener** ~ **de pocos amigos** to look black, have a hangdog look; ~ **de corcho** cheeky look; ~ **dura** shamelessness; cheek*, nerve*; **¡qué** ~ **más dura!*** what a nerve!*; ~ **de hereje** ugly face; hangdog look; ~ **de** (**justo**) **juez** stern face, grim-looking face; **mala** ~ wry face, grimace; **poner mala** ~ to pout, grimace, make a (wry) face; **poner al mal tiempo buena** ~ to put a brave face on it; **poner** ~ **de circunstancias** to look appropriately grave (*etc*), look serious; **tener** ~ **de acelga** to have a face a mile long, (*Med*) to look pale, look washed out; **tener** ~ **de estatua** to have a wooden expression; **tener** ~ **de monja boba** to look all innocent; **tener** ~ **de palo** to have a wooden expression; to be poker-faced, not let on; ~ **de pascua(s)** smiling face; **tener** ~ **de pascua(s)** to look pretty pleased; **una discusión a** ~ **de perro** a fierce argument; **tener** ~ **de roñoso** to look mean; ~ **de viernes** sad look; ~ **de vinagre** sour expression.

(**d**) (*) (*valor*) boldness, nerve*; **tener** ~ **para** + *infin* to have the nerve* to + *infin*; **tener más** ~ **que ...*** to have more nerve* than ...; **¿con qué** ~ **le voy a pedir eso?*** how would I have the nerve to ask for that?*

(**e**) (*de objeto*) face; outside, surface; (*Arquit*) face, façade, front; (*Geom*) face; (*de papel*) side; (*de paño etc*) face, right side, finished side; (*de tajada, disco etc*) side; (*al sortear*) face, obverse, (*de moneda*) heads; ~ **A** A side; ~ **B** B side, (*fig*) flip side; ~ **o cruz** heads or tails; ~ **y cruz de una cuestión** both sides of a question; **echar** (*o* **jugar, sortear**) **algo a** ~ **o cruz** to toss up for sth; **escribir por ambas ~s** write on both sides.

cara*[2] NMF = **caradura**.

caraba: NF: **es la** ~ it's the absolute tops:, (*pey*) it's the last straw.

carabao NM Philippine buffalo.

cárabe NM amber.

carabela NF caravel.

carabina NF (**a**) (*Mil*) carbine, rifle; ~ **de aire compromido** airgun; **ser la** ~ **de Ambrosio*** to be a dead loss.
(**b**) (*) chaperon; **hacer de** ~, **ir de** ~ to go as chaperon; to play gooseberry.

carabinero NM (**a**) (*Mil*) carabineer, rifleman; (*de aduana*) revenue guard; (*Cono Sur*) policeman. (**b**) (*Zool*) prawn.

cárabo NM tawny owl.

caracha NF (*LAm* ††) mange, itch; scab.

carachento ADJ, **carachoso** ADJ (*LAm*) mangy, scabby.

caracho [1] ADJ violet-coloured.
[2] INTERJ **¡~!** (*And**) good heavens!, good Lord!

caracol NM (**a**) (*Zool*) snail; (*concha*) snail shell, sea shell; conch shell; ~ **comestible** edible snail; ~ **de mar** (*esp*) winkle.

(**b**) (*de pelo*) curl.
(**c**) (*de forma*) spiral; (*Cono Sur*) circular shopping-centre; **escalera de** ~ spiral staircase, winding staircase; **subir en** ~ (*humo etc*) to spiral up, corkscrew up; **hacer ~s** (*persona*) to weave about, zigzag; (*pey*) to reel, stagger; (*caballo*) to prance about.
(**d**) **¡~es!** (*euf**) (*sorpresa*) good heavens!; (*ira*) damn it!

caracola NF (*Zool*) large shell.

caracoleante ADJ winding, spiral.

caracolear [1a] VI (*caballo*) to prance about, caracole.

caracolillo NM (*pelo*) kiss-curl.

carácter NM, PL **caracteres** (**a**) (*naturaleza*) character; (*clase*) nature, kind, condition; **de medio** ~ of an ill-defined nature; **de** ~ **totalmente distinto** of quite a different kind.
(**b**) (*de persona*) character; **una persona de** ~ a person of character; **de** ~ **duro** hard-natured; **no tiene** ~ he lacks firmness, he's a weak character.
(**c**) (*LAm*: *Liter, Teat*) character, personage.
(**d**) (*Bio*) character; feature, characteristic; ~ **adquirido** acquired characteristic; ~ **hereditario** inherited characteristic.
(**e**) (*Tip*) character; **caracteres de imprenta** type, typeface; **escribir en caracteres de imprenta** to write in block letters, print.
(**f**) (*Inform*) character; ~ **alfanumérico** alphanumeric character; ~ **comodín** wild character; ~ **de petición** prompt.

caracteriológico ADJ character (*atr*); **cambio** ~ character change, change of character.

característica NF (**a**) characteristic; trait, quality, attribute. (**b**) (*Teat*) character actress.

característicamente ADV characteristically.

▼ **característico** [1] ADJ characteristic, typical (*de* of).
[2] NM (*Teat*) character actor.

caracterización NF characterization.

caracterizado ADJ (*distinguido*) distinguished, of note; (*especial*) special, peculiar, having special characteristics, (*típico*) typical.

caracterizar [1f] [1] VT (**a**) (*gen*) to characterize; (*tipificar*) to typify; (*distinguir*) to distinguish, set apart.
(**b**) (*honrar*) to confer (a) distinction on, confer an honour on.
(**c**) (*Teat*) *papel* to play with great effect.
[2] **caracterizarse** VR (*Teat*) to make up, dress for the part.

caracú NM (*LAm*) bone marrow.

caradura* [1] NMF rotter*, cad, shameless person; **¡~!** you swine!*
[2] NF V **cara** (**c**).

caraja: NF: **tener la** ~ (*agotado*) to look absolutely knackered*; (*perplejo*) to be all at sea, be just not with it*.

carajear [1a] VT (*Cono Sur*) to insult, swear at.

carajiento ADJ (*And*) foul-mouthed.

carajillo NM coffee with a dash of brandy (*o* anís *etc*).

carajito* NM (*LAm*) kid*, small child.

carajo:: NM (**a**) prick::. (**b**) (*locuciones*) **de** ~ tremendous*; awful; **ese conductor del** ~ that shit of a driver::; **en el quinto** ~ miles away; **no entiende ni** ~, **no sabe un** ~ **de eso** he doesn't know a damned thing about it; **¿qué** ~ **quieres?** what the hell do you want?::; **me importa un** ~ I don't give a damn; **irse al** ~ to fail, collapse, go down the drain*; to go to the dogs; **¡vete al ~!** fuck off!::; **mandar a uno al** ~ to tell sb to go to hell. (**c**) EXCL damn it!, hell!

caramanchel NM (*LAm*) hut, shack; (*And*) shed; (*And*) street-vendor's stall.

caramba INTERJ (*sorpresa*) well!, good gracious!; (*qué raro*) very odd!, how strange!; (*protesta*) hang it all!

carámbano NM icicle.

carambola NF (*Billar*) cannon; (*fig*) trick, ruse; **por** ~ by a lucky chance; indirectly, in a roundabout way.

caramel NM sardine.

caramelear* [1a] VT (*And*) (*engañar*) to con*, deceive; (*engatusar*) to suck up to*, flatter.

caramelizado ADJ caramelized.

caramelo NM (**a**) sweet, toffee; candy (*US*) caramel; **es de** ~ it's fine.
(**b**) **~s**: hash*, pot::.

caramillo NM (**a**) (*Mús*) flageolet; rustic pipe.
(**b**) (*montón*) untidy heap.
(**c**) (*chisme*) piece of gossip; (*intriga*) intrigue; **armar un** ~ to make mischief, start a gossip campaign.
(**d**) (*jaleo*) fuss, trouble.

caramilloso ADJ fussy.

caranchear [1a] VT (*Cono Sur*) to irritate, annoy.

carancho NM (*And*: *búho*) owl; (*Cono Sur*: *buitre*) vulture.

caranga NF (*And, CAm*), **carángano** NM (*LAm*) louse.

carantamaula NF (**a**) (*careta*) grotesque mask. (**b**) (::: (*cara*) ugly mug::; (*persona*) ugly person; scarecrow.

carantoña NF (**a**) (*careta*) grotesque mask.
(**b**) (::: (*cara*) ugly mug::.
(**c**) **ella es una** ~* she's mutton dressed up as lamb*, she's a painted hag.

(d) ~s* (*magreo*) caresses; petting*, fondling; **hacer ~s a uno** (*muecas*) to make faces at sb; (*amorosamente*) to make sheep's eyes at sb; (*dar coba a*) to (try to) butter sb up.

caraota NF (*Carib*) bean.

carapacho NM shell, carapace; **meterse en su ~** to go into one's shell.

carapintado* NM (*Argentina*) member of an army special unit.

caraqueño [1] ADJ of Caracas.

[2] NM, **caraqueña** NF native (*o* inhabitant) of Caracas; **los ~s** the people of Caracas.

caráspita EXCL (*Cono Sur*) damn!

carátula NF **(a)** (*careta*) mask; **la ~** (*fig: Teat*) the stage, the theatre. **(b)** (*CAm, Méx: de reloj*) face, dial. **(c)** (*LAm: Tip*) title page; (*LAm*) cover (of a magazine). **(d)** (*de disco*) sleeve.

caravana NF **(a)** (*Hist*) caravan; (*fig: grupo*) group, band; (*fig: excursionistas*) crowd of trippers, group of picnickers; **ir en ~** to go in single file.
(b) (*Aut: vehículo*) caravan, trailer.
(c) (*Aut*) (*coches*) stream of cars; (*cola*) jam, tailback, queue.
(d) (*Carib: trampa*) bird trap.
(e) (*LAm: cortesía*) flattering remark, compliment; **bailar** (*o* **correr, hacer**) **la ~ a uno** to overdo the courtesies; to dance attention on sb.
(f) ~s (*LAm*) long earrings.

caravaning [kara'βanin] NM caravanning.

caravanismo NM caravaning.

caravanista NMF caravaner.

caravan(s)era NF, **caravasar** NM caravanserai.

caray INTERJ (*sorpresa*) gosh!*, good heavens!; well I'm blowed!*; (*indignación*) damn it!; **¡~ con ...!** to hell with ...!

carbohidrato NM carbohydrate.

carbólico ADJ carbolic.

carbón NM **(a)** (*Min*) coal; **~ ardiente** (*fig*) hot potato; **~ bituminoso** soft coal; **~ de leña**, **~ vegetal** charcoal; **~ menudo** small coal, slack; **~ pardo** brown coal; **~ de piedra** coal; **~ térmico** steam coal; **¡se acabó el ~!*** that's it!, all done!
(b) (*Tip: t* **papel ~**) carbon paper, carbon; **copia al ~** carbon copy.
(c) (*Arte*) charcoal; **dibujo al ~** charcoal drawing.
(d) (*Elec*) carbon.
(e) (*Agr*) smut.

carbonada NF (*And, Cono Sur*) (*guiso*) meat stew; (*carne*) chop, steak; (*Cono Sur: sopa*) thick soup, broth; (*Cono Sur: picadillo*) mince.

carbonatado ADJ carbonated.

carbonato NM carbonate; **~ cálcico**, **~ de calcio** calcium carbonate; **~ sódico** sodium carbonate.

carboncillo NM (*Arte*) charcoal; (*Min*) small coal, slack; (*Aut*) carbon, carbon deposit.

carbonear [1a] VT **(a)** (*hacer carbón*) to make charcoal of. **(b)** (*Cono Sur*: incitar*) to push, egg on.

carbonera NF **(a)** (*mina*) coalmine. **(b)** (*depósito*) coal tip, coal heap. **(c)** (*receptáculo*) coal bin, coal bunker. **(d)** (*horno*) charcoal kiln.

carbonería NF coalyard.

carbonero [1] ADJ coal (*atr*); charcoal (*atr*); **barco ~** collier; **estación carbonera** coaling station.
[2] NM **(a)** (*persona*) coal merchant; charcoal burner.
(b) (*Náut*) collier, coal ship.
(c) (*Orn*) coal tit.

carbónico [1] ADJ carbonic.
[2] NM (*Cono Sur: t* **papel ~**) carbon (paper).

carbonífero ADJ carboniferous; **industria carbonífera** coal industry.

carbonilla NF **(a)** (*Min*) small coal, coaldust; cinder. **(b)** (*Aut*) carbon, carbon deposit. **(c)** (*LAm Arte*) charcoal.

carbonización NF (*Quím*) carbonization; charring.

carbonizar [1f] [1] VT (*Quím*) to carbonize; to char; *madera* to make charcoal of; **quedar carbonizado** to be charred, be burnt to a cinder; (*Elec*) to be electrocuted; (*edificio*) to be burnt down, be reduced to ashes.
[2] **carbonizarse** VR (*Quím*) to carbonize; = **quedar carbonizado**.

carbono NM carbon; **~ 14** carbon 14.

carbonoso ADJ carbonaceous.

carborundo NM carborundum.

carbunclo NM (*Min*), **carbunco** NM (*Med*), **carbúnculo** NM (*Min*) carbuncle.

carburador NM carburettor.

carburante NM fuel; **~ fósil** fossil fuel.

carburar* [1a] VI **(a)** (*funcionar*) to go, work. **(b)** (*pensar*) to think, ponder.

carburo NM carbide; **~ de silicio** silicon carbide.

carca* [1] ADJ INVAR square*; narrow-minded, having a closed mind; ancient; dead-beat*; (*Pol*) reactionary.
[2] NMF **(a)** (*persona*) square*; narrow-minded person; old fogey; (*Pol*) reactionary; (*Hist*) Carlist. **(b)** (*And: mugre*) muck, filth.

carcacha* NF (*Méx: Aut*) old crock.

carcaj NM (*para flechas*) quiver; (*LAm: de fusil*) rifle case, pistol holster.

carcajada NF (loud) laugh, peal of laughter, guffaw; **hubo ~s** there was loud laughter; **reírse a ~s** to laugh heartily, roar with laughter; **soltar la ~** to burst out laughing.

carcajeante ADJ *conducta* riotous; *abrazo* hearty; *decisión etc* ridiculous, laughable.

carcajear [1a] VI *y* **carcajearse** VR to roar with laughter, have a good laugh (*de* at).

carcamal* NM **(a)** (*vejestorio*) old crock, wreck; **es un ~** he's a wreck. **(b)** = **carca**.

carcamán [1] NM (*Náut*) tub, hulk; (*And, Carib**) old crock*, wreck.
[2] NM, **carcamana** NF **(a)** (***) (*Carib: persona*) low-class person; (*And, Carib: inmigrante*) poor immigrant. **(b)** (*Cono Sur Pol*) diehard, reactionary.

carcancha NF (*Méx*) bus.

carcasa NF (*Aut etc*) chassis, grid; (*de neumático*) carcass; (*Téc*) casing.

carcayú NM wolverine.

cárcel NF **(a)** prison, jail; **~ abierta**, **~ de régimen abierto** open prison; **~ modelo** model prison; **~ del pueblo** people's prison; **~ transitoria** remand centre; **poner en la ~** to jail, send to jail, put in prison. **(b)** (*Téc*) clamp.

┌─ **CÁRCEL** ─────────────────────────── **ver también la entrada** ─┐

Uso del artículo

A la hora de traducir expresiones como *a la cárcel*, *en la cárcel*, *desde la cárcel*, *etc*, hemos de tener en cuenta el motivo por el que alguien acude al recinto o está allí.

• Se traduce *a la cárcel* por *to jail/to prison*, *en la cárcel* por *in jail/in prison*, *desde la cárcel* por *from jail/from prison etc*, cuando alguien va o está allí en calidad de preso:
　¿Cuánto tiempo estuvo en la cárcel?
　How long was he in jail o in prison?
　No sabemos por qué los metieron en la cárcel
　We don't know why they were sent to jail/to prison

• Se traduce *a la cárcel* por *to the jail/to the prison*, *en la cárcel* por *in the jail/in the prison*, *desde la cárcel* por *from the jail/from the prison etc*, cuando alguien va o está allí por otros motivos:
　Fueron a la cárcel a inspeccionar el edificio
　They went to the prison to inspect the building
　Las visitas no pueden estar en la cárcel más de media hora
　Visitors may only stay at the prison for half an hour
　Para otros usos y ejemplos ver la entrada.

└──┘

carcelario ADJ prison (*atr*).

carcelería NF imprisonment, detention.

carcelero [1] ADJ prison (*atr*).
[2] NM warder, jailer.

carcinogén NM carcinogen.

carcinogénesis NF INVAR carcinogenesis.

carcinogénico ADJ carcinogenic.

carcinógeno NM carcinogen.

carcinoma NM carcinoma.

carcocha NF (*And*) = **carcacha**.

carcoma NF **(a)** (*Ent*) deathwatch beetle; woodworm. **(b)** (*fig: preocupación*) anxiety, perpetual worry; (*persona*) spendthrift.

carcomer [2a] [1] VT **(a)** (*gen*) to bore into, eat into, eat away.
(b) (*fig*) *salud etc* to undermine; *fortuna* to eat into, eat away.
[2] **carcomerse** VR **(a)** to get worm-eaten.
(b) (*fig*) to decay, waste away; to be eaten away.

carcomido ADJ worm-eaten, wormy, infested with woodworm; rotten; (*fig*) rotten, decayed.

carcoso ADJ (*And*) dirty, mucky.

carda NF **(a)** (*Bot*) teasel; (*Téc*) teasel, card (*for combing wool*). **(b)** (*acto*) carding. **(c)** (**: reprimenda*) reprimand; **dar una ~ a uno** to rap sb over the knuckles.

cardamomo NM cardamom.

cardán NM (*Cono Sur Aut*) propellor shaft; (*LAm Aut*) axle.

cardar [1a] VT **(a)** (*Téc*) to card, comb; **pelo cardado** swept-back hair. **(b)** (**: t* **~ la lana** a) to tell off*, rap over the knuckles.

cardenal NM **(a)** (*Ecl*) cardinal. **(b)** (*Med*) bruise, mark, weal. **(c)** (*Cono Sur Bot*) geranium. **(d)** (*Orn*) cardinal bird.

cardenalato NM cardinalate.

cardenalicio ADJ: **capelo ~** cardinal's hat.

cardencha NF (*Bot, Téc*) teasel.

cardenillo NM verdigris.

cárdeno ADJ purple, violet; livid; *agua* opalescent.

cardiaco, **cardíaco** [1] ADJ cardiac, heart (*atr*). **(b)** (***) **estar ~ con** to be enchanted with, enthuse over.
[2] NM, **cardíaca** NF heart case, sufferer from a heart complaint.

cardinal ADJ cardinal.

cardio... PREF cardio...

cardiocircujano, -a NM/F heart surgeon.
cardiograma NM cardiogram, cardiograph.
cardiología NF cardiology.
cardiológico ADJ cardiological.
cardiólogo, -a NM/F, **cardiópata** NMF cardiologist, heart specialist.
cardiorrespiratorio ADJ cardiorespiratory.
cardiosaludable ADJ good for the heart.
cardiovascular ADJ cardiovascular.
cardo NM thistle; **es un ~*** he's very prickly.
cardón NM (*Cono Sur*) (species of) giant cactus.
cardume(n) NM (a) (*Pez*) shoal. (b) (*And, Cono Sur*) great number, mass; **un ~ de gente** a lot of people, a crowd of people.
carea NM sheepdog.
carear [1a] ①️ VT *personas* to bring face to face; *textos* to compare, collate, check against each other.
  ②️ VI: **~ a** to face towards, look on to.
  ③️ **carearse** VR (a) (*2 personas*) to come face to face, come together, meet.
  (b) **~ con** to face, face up to; to confront.
carecer [2d] VI (a) **~ de** to lack, be in need of, be without, want for; **carece de talento** he lacks talent, he has no talent; **no carecemos de dinero** we don't lack money, we're not short of money; **eso carece de sentido** that doesn't make sense; **aquí se carece de todo** here there is a great need of everything.
  (b) (*Cono Sur*: *hacer falta*) **carece hacerlo** it is necessary to do it; **carece no dejarla** we must not allow her to.
carecimiento NM lack, need.
carel NM side, edge.
carena NF (a) (*Náut*) careening; **dar ~ a** to careen. (b) (*) ragging*; **dar ~ a uno** to rag sb*, tease sb.
carenar [1a] VT to careen.
carencia NF lack (*de* of), shortage (*de* of), need (*de* for); scarcity; (*Med etc*) deficiency; **(periodo de) ~** period free of interest payments and debt repayments.
carencial ADJ: **estado ~** state of want; **mal ~** deficiency disease.
carente ADJ: **~ de** lacking (in), devoid of.
carentón ADJ (*Cono Sur*) large-faced.
careo NM confrontation, meeting (face to face); comparison, collation; **~ (de policía)** identity parade; **someter sospechosos a ~** to bring suspects face to face.
carero ADJ *tienda* expensive, dear, pricey*.
carestía NF scarcity, shortage, dearth; famine; (*Com*) high price(s), high cost; **~ de la vida** high cost of living; **época de ~** period of shortage, lean period, bad time.
careta NF mask; (*Min etc*) breathing apparatus, respirator; **~ antigás** gasmask; **~ de esgrima** fencing mask; **quitar la ~ a uno** to unmask sb.
careto: ①️ ADJ ugly. ②️ NM clock:, face.
carey NM tortoiseshell; (*Zool*) turtle.
carga NF (a) (*cargamento*) load; (*Náut*) cargo; (*Ferro*) freight; (*peso*) burden, weight; (*Aut*) tare, permitted load; **~ cinegética** carrying capacity; **~ fiscal** tax burden; **~ del hombre blanco** white man's burden; **~ de pago** payload; **a ~s** in plenty, in abundance, galore; **en plena ~** under full load; **bestia de ~** beast of burden; **buque de ~** freighter; **tomar ~** to load up, (*Náut*) take on cargo.
  (b) (*Elec*) charge; load; **hilo con ~** live wire.
  (c) (*Mec*) load; **~ fija, ~ muerta** dead load; **~ de fractura, ~ de rotura** breaking load; **~ útil** payload.
  (d) (*Mil*; *t de obús, horno etc*) charge; **~ explosiva** explosive charge; **~ de pólvora** (*Min*) blasting powder; **~ de profundidad** depth charge.
  (e) (*Fin*) tax, charge, duty; **~ impositiva** tax burden; **~s sociales** social security contribution.
  (f) (*deber*) duty, obligation, charge; (*responsabilidad*) onus, responsibility; **~ de familia** dependent relative; **~ personal** personal commitments; **echar la ~ a uno** to put the blame on sb, put the onus on sb; **echarse con la ~*** to throw in the sponge; **llevar la ~** to be the one responsible (*de* for).
  (g) (*Mil*: *ataque*) charge, attack; (*Dep*) charge, tackle; **~ a la bayoneta** bayonet charge; **~ de caballería** cavalry charge; **~ policial** baton charge; **tocar a ~** to sound the charge; **volver a la ~** (*fig*) to return to the charge, return to the attack.
  (h) (*acto*) loading; (*Elec, Mil*) loading; charging; **de ~ frontal** front-loading; **andén de ~** loading platform; **'permitido ~ y descarga'** 'loading and unloading'; **estar a la ~** to be loading.
cargada NF (a) (*Cono Sur*) unpleasant practical joke.
  (b) (*Méx*) = **carga (h).**
  (c) **ir a la ~** (*Méx*) to jump on the bandwagon.
cargaderas NFPL (*And*) braces, suspenders (*US*).
cargadero NM (a) loading point; (*Ferro*) goods platform, loading bay.
  (b) (*Arquit*) lintel.
cargado ADJ Y PTP (a) (*gen*) loaded, with a load, under load; *dados* loaded; (*esp fig*) laden, burdened, weighed down (*de* with); **estar ~**

(*de vino*) to be drunk; **estar ~ de años** to be very old, be weighed down with age; to be out of date; **estar ~ de hijos** to have a lot of children; **estar ~ de hostias:** (o **puñetas:** *etc*) to have lots of hang-ups*; **ser ~ de espaldas** to be round-shouldered, have a stoop; **un árbol ~ de fruto** a tree laden with fruit; **tener los ojos ~s de sueño** to have eyes heavy with sleep.
  (b) (*Elec*) *hilo* live; *pila* charged.
  (c) **~ (con bala)** (*Mil*) live.
  (d) *café, té* strong; *licor* large; good and strong.
  (e) *cielo* overcast; *atmósfera* heavy, sultry, close.
cargador NM (a) (*persona*) loader; (*transportador*) carrier, haulier; (*Náut*) docker, stevedore, longshoreman (*US*); (*de horno*) stoker; (*LAm*) porter.
  (b) (*Téc: de cañón*) chamber; (*de pluma*) filler; (*Mil: Hist*) ramrod; **~ de acumuladores, ~ de baterías** battery charger.
  (c) **~es** (*And*) braces, suspenders (*US*).
cargadora NF (*And, Carib*) nursemaid.
cargamento NM (a) (*acto*) loading. (b) (*carga*) load; (*Náut*) cargo; shipment; **~ de retorno** return cargo.
cargante ①️ ADJ *persona* demanding, fussy; annoying, troublesome; *niño* trying; *tarea* irksome, tedious.
  ②️ NMF: **es un ~** he's a pain*.
cargar [1h] ①️ VT (a) (*gen*) to load (*de* with; *a, en* on); (**~ demasiado**) to overload, burden, weigh down (*de* with); *dados* to load; *imaginación, mente etc* to fill (*de* with); **~ a uno de deudas** to encumber sb with debts; **~ a uno de nuevas obligaciones** to burden sb with new duties.
  (b) (*Elec*) to charge; (*Inform*) to load.
  (c) *horno* to stoke, charge.
  (d) (*hacer más pesado*) to increase the weight of, cause to bear down more heavily; V **mano.**
  (e) *impuesto* to impose, lay (*sobre* on); to increase.
  (f) (*Com, Fin*) to charge, debit (*en cuenta a* to, to the account of); **~ de menos a uno** to undercharge sb; **~ una factura con un porcentaje por servicio** to add a service charge to a bill.
  (g) (*achacar*) to impute, ascribe (*a* to); *culpa* to lay (*a* on); *responsabilidad* to entrust (*a* to), place (*a* on).
  (h) (*Jur*) to charge, accuse; **~ a uno de poco escrupuloso** to accuse sb of being unscrupulous, charge sb with being unscrupulous.
  (i) (*Mil*) *enemigo* to charge, attack.
  (j) (*Mil*) *cañón* to load.
  (k) (*Náut*) *vela* to take in.
  (l) (*Univ**) *candidato* to plough*, fail.
  (m) (*LAm*) to carry, have, use; to wear; **~ anteojos** to wear glasses; **~ revólver** to pack a gun*; **¿cargas dinero?** have you any money on (o with) you?
  (n) (*And, Cono Sur*: *perro etc*) to attack, go for.
  (o) (*) (*aburrir*) to bore; (*molestar*) to annoy, vex; **esto me carga** this annoys me, I find this annoying.
  ②️ VI (a) (*Aut etc*) to load, load up; to take on a load; (*Náut*) to take on (a) cargo; **~ (demasiado, mucho)** (*fig*) to overeat, drink too much.
  (b) **~ con** *objeto, peso* to pick up, carry away, take away; *peso* (*fig*) to shoulder, take upon o.s.; *responsabilidad* to assume, take on; *culpa* to bear.
  (c) (*Ling*: *acento*) to fall (*en, sobre* on).
  (d) (*inclinarse*) to lean, tip, incline.
  (e) (*apoyarse*) **~ en, ~ sobre** to lean on, lean against; (*Arquit etc*) to rest on, be supported by.
  (f) **~ sobre uno** (*presionar*) to urge sb, press sb; to importune sb.
  (g) (*dar la lata*) to pester, be annoying.
  (h) (*Met*) to turn, veer (*a* to, *hacia* towards).
  (i) (*apiñarse*) to crowd together, concentrate; to come in large numbers.
  ③️ **cargarse** VR (a) **~ algo** to take sth on o.s.; **~ de algo** to be full of sth, be loaded with sth; to fill o.s. up with sth, (*fig*) get one's fill of sth; **~ de hijos** to overburden o.s. with children; **~ de años** to get very old; **el árbol se carga de manzanas** the tree produces apples in abundance.
  (b) = VI (d), (e).
  (c) (*Elec*) to become charged, become live.
  (d) (*Met*: *cielo*) to become overcast; (*atmósfera*) to become heavy, become oppressive.
  (e) (*) (*enfadarse*) to get cross; (*aburrirse*) to get bored.
  (f) **~la*** to get into hot water, get it in the neck*.
  (g) **~ a*** (*matar*) to do in:, bump off:; (*eliminar*) to get rid of, remove, suppress; **¡algún día me lo cargaré!** I'll get him one day!
  (h) **~ algo*** to break sth, smash sth.
  (i) **~ a:*** to screw:*.
cargazón NF (a) (*carga*) load; (*Náut*) cargo, shipment; (*fig*) dead weight, useless mass.
  (b) (*Med*) heaviness (*of stomach etc*).

(c) (*Met*) mass of heavy cloud.
(d) ~ **de espaldas** stoop.
(e) (*Cono Sur*) abundance of fruit (*on tree*).
cargo NM **(a)** (*carga, peso*) load, weight, burden.
(b) (*fig*) burden; ~ **de conciencia** burden on one's conscience; remorse, guilty feeling.
(c) (*Com*) charge, debit; **una cantidad en ~ a uno** a sum to be charged to sb; **ser en ~ a uno** to be indebted to sb; **girar a ~ de, librar a ~ de** to draw on.
(d) (*puesto*) post, office; (*Teat y fig*) role, part; **un ~ casi sin responsabilidades** a post almost without duties; **desempeñar un ~** to fill an office; **jurar el ~** to take the oath of office, be sworn into office; **vestir el ~** to look the part, dress the part.
(e) (*persona*) office-holder; highly-placed official; **altos ~s** people in authority, top people; senior officials; **altos ~s directivos** senior management, top management.
(f) (*deber*) duty, obligation, responsibility; (*custodia*) charge, care; **a ~ de** in the charge of; **tener algo a su ~** to have sth in one's charge, be in charge of sth; **hacerse ~ de** to take charge of; to see about; to realize, understand; **el ejército se hizo ~ del poder** the army took over power; **apenas si pude hacerme ~ de ello** I could scarcely grasp what was going on; **parecía no hacerse ~ de la dificultad** he seemed not to understand the difficulty.
(g) (*Jur*) charge; (*reproche*) reproach, accusation; **hacer a uno ~ de algo** to charge sb with sth.
cargosear [1a] VT (*And, Cono Sur*) to pester, keep on at.
cargoso ADJ (*Cono Sur*) maddening, annoying.
carguera NF (*And, Carib*) nursemaid.
carguero NM **(a)** (*Náut*) freighter, cargo boat; (*Aer*) freight plane, transport plane; ~ **militar** air-force transport plane.
(b) (*And, Cono Sur: bestia de carga*) beast of burden.
(c) (*Méx*) lorry, truck.
carguío NM load; cargo, freight.
cari ADJ (*Cono Sur*) grey.
cariacontecido ADJ crestfallen, down in the mouth, woebegone.
cariado ADJ *diente, hueso* bad, rotten, decayed, carious.
cariadura NF (*Med*) caries, decay.
cariancho ADJ broad-faced.
cariar [1h] **1** VT to cause to decay, cause decay in.
2 cariarse VR to decay, become decayed.
cariátide NF caryatid.
caribe **1** ADJ **(a)** (*Geog etc*) Caribbean; **Mar C~** Caribbean Sea.
(b) (*LAm*) (*caníbal*) cannibalistic; (*fig*) savage, cruel.
2 NMF Carib, inhabitant of the Caribbean area.
3 NM (*LAm*) cannibal; (*Carib: fig:* ††) savage, wild man.
caribeño = **caribe**.
caribú NM caribou.
caricato NM (*Cono Sur, Méx*) = **caricatura**.
caricatura NF caricature (*t fig*); cartoon.
caricaturesco ADJ absurd, ridiculous.
caricaturista NMF caricaturist; cartoonist.
caricaturización NF caricaturization, caricaturing.
caricaturizar [1f] VT to caricature.
caricia NF **(a)** caress; pat, stroke; **hacer ~s** to caress, fondle, stroke.
(b) (*fig*) endearment.
caricioso ADJ caressing, affectionate.
caridad NF charity; charitableness; **¡por ~!** for goodness sake!; **la ~ empieza por uno mismo** charity begins at home; **hacer ~ a uno** to give alms to sb; **hacer la ~ de** + *infin* to do the favour of + *ger*.
carie NF, **caries** NF INVAR **(a)** (*Med*) dental decay, caries. **(b)** (*Agr*) blight.
carigordo ADJ fat-faced.
carilampiño ADJ (*afeitado*) clean-shaven; *joven* smooth-faced, beardless.
carilargo ADJ long-faced; (*LAm*) annoyed.
carilla NF **(a)** (*careta*) bee veil. **(b)** (*Tip*) side (of a sheet of paper).
carillero ADJ round-faced, full-faced.
carillo* ADJ a bit expensive, on the dear side.
carillón NM carillon.
carimbo NM (*LAm*) branding iron.
▼ **cariño** NM **(a)** (*afecto*) affection, love (*a, por* for); fondness, liking (*a, por* for); tenderness; **sí, ~** yes, my dear; **sentir ~ por, tener ~ a** to like, be fond of; **por el ~ que te tengo** because I'm fond of you; **tomar ~ a** to take a liking to, get fond of.
(b) (*caricia*) caress, stroke; (*regalo*) gift, token (of affection); **hacerle ~ a uno** to caress (*o* stroke) sb.
(c) **~s** endearments; show of affection.
cariñosamente ADV affectionately, lovingly, fondly; tenderly.
cariñoso ADJ affectionate, loving, fond; tender.
carioca **1** ADJ of Rio de Janeiro, of the State of Guanabara.
2 NMF native (*o* inhabitant) of Rio de Janeiro, native (*o* inhabitant) of the State of Guanabara.
cariparejo ADJ poker-faced, inscrutable.

carirraído ADJ brazen, shameless.
carirredondo ADJ round-faced.
carisellazo NM (*And*) toss of a coin; **echar un ~** to toss (*o* spin) a coin.
carisma NM charisma.
carismático ADJ charismatic.
carita NF little face; **de ~** (*And*) first-class; jolly good*; **dar** (*o* **hacer**) **~** (*Méx: mujer*) to return a smile, flirt (back); **hacer ~s** (*And*) to make faces.
caritativamente ADV charitably.
caritativo ADJ charitable (*con, para* to).
cariz NM look, aspect; (*fig*) outlook; (*Met*) look of the sky; **mal ~** scowl; **poner mal ~** to scowl; **esto va tomando mal ~** this business is beginning to look bad, I don't like the look of this; **en vista del ~ que toman las cosas** in view of the way things are going.
carlanca NF **(a)** spiked dog-collar; (*And, CAm: grillo*) shackle, fetter.
(b) (*CAm, Cono Sur*) (*persona*) bore, pest, drag; (*aburrimiento*) boredom, tedium; (*enojo*) annoyance, irritation.
(c) **~s** tricks, cunning; **tener muchas ~s** to be full of tricks.
carlinga NF (*Aer*) cockpit, pilot's cabin; interior of an aeroplane.
carlismo NM Carlism.

| CARLISMO |

ⓘ *The controversial change which Ferdinand VII of Spain made to the law in order to allow his daughter Isabella to succeed him instead of his brother, Carlos María Isidro de Borbón, gave rise to Carlism, a movement supporting Carlos's claim to the throne. It also sparked off a series of armed conflicts. The First Carlist War (1833-1839) was declared by Carlos when Isabella came to the throne, the Second (1860) was started by his son of the same name, and the Third (1872-76) by a grandson, another Don Carlos. The last Carlist pretender, Alfonso, died in 1936 without descendants, although that did not prevent the* **Falange Española** *from later backing the Carlist cause in an attempt to prevent the current king, Juan Carlos, being designated Franco's successor. To this day there is still a Carlist party in Spain.*
⇨ *See also* FALANGE ESPAÑOLA

carlista ADJ, NMF Carlist.
carlistada NF Carlist attack, Carlist uprising.
Carlitos NM *forma familiar de* **Carlos** Charlie.
Carlomagno NM Charlemagne.
Carlos NM Charles.
Carlota NF Charlotte.
carlota NF (*Culin*) charlotte.
carmelita¹ (*Ecl*) **1** ADJ Carmelite.
2 NMF Carmelite; ~ **descalzo** discalced Carmelite.
carmelita² ADJ, **carmelito** ADJ (*esp LAm*) light brown, tan.
carmelitano ADJ Carmelite.
Carmelo NM Carmelite convent.
Carmen NM (*Ecl*) Carmelite Order.
carmen¹ NM (*Granada*) villa with a garden.
carmen² NM (*Liter*) song, poem.
carmenar [1a] VT **(a)** (*Téc*) *lana* to card, teasel; *seda etc* to unravel; *pelo* to disentangle; ~ **el pelo a uno*** to pull sb's hair. **(b)** (*) to fleece, swindle.
carmesí ADJ, NM crimson.
carmín NM **(a)** carmine; rouge, lipstick. **(b)** (*Bot*) dog rose.
carminativo ADJ, NM carminative.
carmíneo ADJ carmine, crimson.
carnada NF bait.
carnal **1** ADJ **(a)** (*Rel*) carnal, of the flesh. **(b)** *parentesco* full, blood (*atr*); **hermano ~** full brother; **primo ~** first cousin; **tío ~** real uncle.
2 NM (*Méx**) pal*, buddy (*US*).
carnalidad NF lust, carnality.
carnaval NM carnival (*t fig*); (*Ecl*) Shrovetide; **martes de ~** Shrove Tuesday.

| CARNAVAL |

ⓘ **Carnaval** *is the traditional period of fun, feasting and partying that precedes the start of Lent (Cuaresma). The most important day is probably Shrove Tuesday (Martes de Carnaval), but throughout Carnaval there are fancy-dress parties, parades and firework displays. In some places in Spain, the changeover from Carnaval to Lent on Ash Wednesday is marked by the Entierro de la Sardina. This is a grotesque funeral parade in which the symbolic cardboard figure of a sardine is marched through the streets and finally ceremonially burnt or buried. Although banned under Franco, partly because of the irreverent nature of the activities and partly because of the dangers posed by people wandering around freely in disguise, Carnaval has recently enjoyed a revival in Spain, with Cádiz and Tenerife being particularly well-known for their celebrations.*

carnavalero ADJ, **carnavalesco** ADJ carnival (*atr*).

carnaza NF **(a)** (*cebo: para peces*) groundbait; (: *para leones*) scraps *pl* of meat. **(b)** (*fig*): **dar ~ a la gente** to satisfy people's appetite for juicy stories.

carne NF **(a)** (*Anat*) flesh; **~ de gallina** (*fig*) gooseflesh; **~ viciosa** (*Med*) proud flesh; **me pone la ~ de gallina** it gives me gooseflesh, (*fig*) it makes my flesh creep, it gives me the creeps; **de abundantes ~s, de muchas ~s** fat; **entrado en ~s** plump, overweight; **algo metido en ~s** somewhat plump; **de pocas ~s** thin; **en ~ viva** in the raw; **en ~s** naked, with nothing on; **se me abrieron las ~s** I was terrified; **cobrar** (o **criar, echar**) **~s** to put on weight; **perder ~s** to lose weight; **ser de ~ y hueso** to be only human, have the same feelings as other people; **tener ~ de perro** to have an iron constitution.
(b) (*Culin*) meat; **~ adobada** salt meat; **~ asada** roast meat; **~ blanca** white meat; **~s blandas** (*Cono Sur*) white meat; **~ de bovino** beef; **~ de cañón** cannon-fodder; **~ de carnero** mutton; **~ de cerdo** pork; **~ concentrada** meat extract; **~ congelada** frozen meat; **~ de cordero** lamb, mutton; **~ deshilachada** (*CAm, Méx*) stewed meat; **~ fiambre** cold meat; **~ de horca** good-for-nothing, gallows bird; **~ magra, ~ mollar** lean meat; **~ marinada** (*LAm*) salt meat; **~ molida** (*LAm*) mince, minced meat; **~ de oveja, ~ ovina, ~ de ovino** mutton, lamb; sheepmeat; **~ picada** mince, minced meat; **~ porcina, ~ de porcino** pork; pigmeat; **~ de res** (*LAm*) beef; **~ roja** red meat; **~ salvajina** game; **~ tapada** stewed meat, stew; **~ de ternera** veal; **~ de vaca, ~ de vacuno** beef; **~ de venado** venison; **no ser ~ ni pescado** to be neither fish nor fowl, be neither one thing nor the other; **poner toda la ~ en el asador** to go the whole hog, stake one's all.
(c) (*Bot*) flesh, fleshy part, pulp; (*LAm: de árbol*) heart, hardest part; **~ de membrillo** quince jelly.
(d) (*Ecl etc*) flesh, carnality.

carné NM = **carnet**.
carneada NF (*Cono Sur*) (*de animales*) slaughter(ing); (*masacre*) slaughter, massacre.
carnear [1a] VT **(a)** (*Cono Sur*) *animal* to slaughter (and dress); (*fig: asesinar*) to murder, butcher.
(b) (*Cono Sur: engañar*) to cheat, swindle.
carnecería NF = **carnicería**.
carnerada NF flock of sheep.
carnerear [1a] VI (*Cono Sur*) to blackleg, be a strikebreaker.
carnerero NM shepherd.
carnero NM **(a)** (*Zool*) sheep, ram; **~ marino** seal; **~ de la sierra** (*LAm*), **~ de la tierra** (*LAm*) llama, alpaca, vicuña; **~ de simiente** breeding ram; **no hay tales ~s** there's no such thing; it's nothing of the sort; **cantar para el ~** to kick the bucket, peg out.
(b) (*Culin*) mutton.
(c) (*piel*) sheepskin.
(d) (*Cono Sur*) (*débil*) weak-willed person; (*esquirol*) blackleg, strikebreaker.
(e) botarse (o **echarse**) **al ~** (*Cono Sur*) to chuck it all up*, throw in the towel.
carnestolendas NFPL Shrovetide.
carnet [kar'ne] NM, PL **carnets** [kar'ne] (*librito*) notebook; (*de banco*) bankbook; (*de viaje*) (tourist's) travel voucher; **~ de conducir, ~ de conductor, ~ de chófer, ~ de manejo** (*LAm*) driving licence; **~ de identidad** identity card; **~ sindical** union card; **~ de socio** membership card; *see also* DOCUMENTO NACIONAL DE IDENTIDAD .
carnicería NF **(a)** (*tienda*) butcher's (shop); (*mercado*) meat market; (*And*) slaughterhouse.
(b) (*fig*) slaughter, carnage; **~ en las carreteras** carnage on the roads; **hacer una ~ de** to massacre, slaughter.
carnicero [1] ADJ **(a)** (*Zool*) carnivorous, flesh-eating; (*Orn*) of prey; (*) *persona* fond of meat.
(b) (*fig*) savage, cruel, bloodthirsty.
[2] NM **(a)** butcher (*t fig*).
(b) (*Zool*) carnivore.
cárnico ADJ meat (*atr*); **industria cárnica** meat industry.
carnitas NFPL (*Méx*) barbecued pork.
carnívoro [1] ADJ carnivorous, flesh-eating; meat-eating.
[2] NM carnivore.
carnosidad NF **(a)** fleshiness; corpulence, obesity. **(b)** (*Med*) proud flesh.
carnoso ADJ beefy, fat.
carnudo ADJ fleshy.
caro [1] ADJ **(a)** (*querido*) dear, beloved; **las cosas que nos son tan caras** the things which are so dear to us.
(b) (*Com*) dear, expensive; **un coche carísimo** a terribly expensive car.
[2] ADV dear, dearly; **le costó muy ~** it cost him dear; **eso sale bastante ~** that comes rather expensive; **vender ~** to sell at a high price.
carocas* NFPL (*lisonjas*) (exaggerated) flattery; (*caricias*) caresses; (*jabón*) soft soap*.

carocha* NF (*Méx*) old banger, old crock.
caroleno NM (*Méx*) backslang.
Carolina¹ NF Caroline.
Carolina² NF (*Geog*): **~ del Norte** North Carolina; **~ del Sur** South Carolina.
carolingio ADJ Carolingian.
carón [1] ADJ (*LAm*) broad-faced.
[2] NM (:) mug, face.
carona NF **(a)** (*paño*) saddlecloth; (*parte del caballo*) saddle; **andar con las ~s ladeadas** (*Cono Sur*) to have problems. **(b)** (*Cono Sur*) bed.
carota* [1] ADJ INVAR barefaced, brazen.
[2] NMF rotter*; shameless person.
carótida NF carotid (artery).
carozo NM **(a)** cob of maize, corncob (*US*). **(b)** (*LAm: de fruta*) stone, core (*of fruit*).
carpa¹ NF (*Pez*) carp; **~ dorada** goldfish.
carpa² NF (*tienda de campaña*) tent; (*toldo*) marquee; awning; (*de circo*) big top; (*LAm: Com*) market stall, open-air shop; (*Méx*) travelling show.

┌─── CARPA ───┐

*In Mexico a **carpa** is a travelling show held under a big top. Originating in the nationalistic aftermath of the Mexican revolution, carpas toured agricultural communities and mining towns offering a menu of satire, slapstick humour, dramatic sketches and humorous monologues, as well as acrobatics, tightrope walking and other circus entertainments. It was in the **carpa** that the Mexican comic character, Cantinflas, started life.*
⇨ *See also* PELADO

└──┘

carpanta* NF ravenous hunger.
Cárpatos ADJ: **Montes ~** Carpathians.
carpeta NF **(a)** (*para papeles*) folder, file; portfolio; (*cartera*) briefcase; (*de disco*) sleeve; **~ de información** information folder, briefing kit; **cerrar la ~** to close the file (*in an investigation*).
(b) (*paño: t ~ de mesa*) table cover.
(c) (*LAm: pupitre*) table, desk.
carpetazo NM: **dar ~ a** to shelve, put on one side, do nothing about.
carpetovetónico ADJ terribly Spanish, Spanish to the core; reactionary, ultraconservative.
carpidor NM, **carpidora** NF (*LAm*) weeding hoe.
carpintear [1a] VI to carpenter; to do woodwork (*as a hobby*).
carpintería NF **(a)** (*oficio etc*) carpentry, joinery, woodwork. **(b)** (*taller*) carpenter's shop.
carpintero NM **(a)** (*Téc*) carpenter; woodworker; **~ de blanco** joiner; **~ de carretas, ~ de prieto** cartwright, wheelwright; **~ de buque, ~ de ribera** ship's carpenter, shipwright.
(b) (*Orn*) woodpecker.
carpir [3a] VT (*LAm*) to weed, hoe.
carraca NF **(a)** (*Náut: Hist*) carrack; (*pey*) tub, old hulk.
(b) (*Mús, Dep*) rattle.
(c) (*Téc*) ratchet brace.
(d) (*: *coche*) old crock.
(e) echar ~ (*And*) to lie.
carraco [1] ADJ feeble, decrepit.
[2] NM (*: *coche*) old crock*.
carrada NF (*Cono Sur*) = **carretada**.
carral NM barrel, vat.
carralero NM cooper.
carrasca NF kermes oak; **ser de ~*** = **ser de aúpa**; *V* **aúpa**.
carrascoloso ADJ (*LAm*) grumpy*, touchy, irritable.
carraspear [1a] VI (*al hablar*) to be hoarse, have a frog in one's throat; (*aclararse*) to clear one's throat, hawk.
carraspeo NM sore throat.
carraspera NF hoarseness, frog in the throat.
carrasposo ADJ **(a)** hoarse, having a sore throat. **(b)** (*LAm*) rough, harsh.
carrera NF **(a)** (*acto*) run; running; chase, rush; **a ~ (abierta), a ~ tendida** at full speed, all out; **a la ~** at full speed; hastily; **de ~** hastily; rashly; without thinking; easily; **partir de ~** to proceed rashly; **dar ~ libre a** to give free rein to; **darse una ~** to rush; **hacer la ~*** (*prostituta*) to walk her beat, work, ply her trade, (*gen*) to be on the game*; **hacer el trabajo a la ~** to race through one's work; **~ de aterrizaje** landing run; **~ de despegue** take-off run; **~ del oro** gold-rush.
(b) (*Dep: béisbol etc*) run.
(c) (*Dep: concurso*) race; **~s** races, racing; **de ~(s)** racing (*atr*), race (*atr*); **caballo de ~(s)** racehorse; **coche de ~s** racing car; **~ armamentística, ~ de armamentos** arms race; **~ de caballos** horse race; **~ por carretera** road race; **~ de ensacados** (*Cono Sur*) sack race; **~ contra el reloj** race against the clock; **~ contra el tiempo** race against time; **~ corta** dash, short run, sprint; **~ espacial** space

race; **~ de fondo** long-distance race; **~ de medio fondo** middle-distance race; **~ lisa** flat race; **~ hacia la luna** race for the moon, race to get to the moon; **~ de maratón** marathon; **~ de obstáculos** obstacle race; (*de caballos*) steeplechase; **~ en parada** running on the spot; **~ pedestre** walking race, foot race; **~ de relevos** relay race; **~ de resistencia** endurance race, long-distance race; **~ de ruta** road race; **~ de sacos** sack race; **~ de trotones** harness race; **~ de vallas** hurdle race, hurdles; (*de caballos*) steeplechase; **abrir ~** to lead the race, be in front; **apuntarse a la ~** to stay in the running.

(d) (*hilera*) row, line; (*Arquit: de ladrillos etc*) course; (*pista*) track; (*en pelo*) parting; (*de media*) run, ladder.

(e) (*Arquit: viga*) beam, girder, joist.

(f) (*Mús*) run.

(g) (*Náut*) run, route; (*de desfile*) route; (*de taxi*) ride, journey; (*Astron*) course; **~ de Indias** (*Hist*) the Indies run; **la ~ del sol** the course of the sun.

(h) (*esp LAm: avenida*) avenue.

(i) (*Mec*) (*de émbolo*) stroke; (*de válvula*) lift; **~ ascendente** upstroke; **~ descendente** downstroke.

(j) (*fig*) career; profession; **diplomático de ~** career diplomat; **dar ~ a uno** to give sb his education, pay for sb's professional studies; to put sb to a career; **hacer ~** to get on in one's career; to get on in the world, make headway; **no hago ~ con este niño** I can't make any headway with this child; **no tiene ~** he has no profession, he doesn't do anything serious in life.

(k) (*Univ*) course, studies; period of study; **cuando termine la ~** when he finishes his course, when he qualifies.

(l) (*de la vida*) course of human life.

carrerilla NF: **a ~** non-stop, continuously; **de ~** on the trot, in succession; **lo dijo de ~** he reeled it off.

carrerista 1 ADJ fond of racing; (*pey*) horsy.
2 NMF **(a)** (*aficionado a carreras de caballos*) racing man, racing woman, racegoer; professional punter. **(b)** (*ciclista*) racing cyclist. **(c)** (*Pol*) careerist, career politician.
3 NF (*) streetwalker.

carrero NM carter, cart driver.

carreta NF (long narrow) wagon, low cart; (*And, Carib*) wheelbarrow; **~ de mano** = **carretilla**; **~ de bueyes** oxcart; **tener la ~ llena** (*Carib: fig*) to be weighed down by problems.

carretada NF cart load; (*fig*) cart load, great quantity; **a ~s** in loads, galore.

carretaje NM cartage, haulage.

carrete NM (*gen*) reel, spool; (*Cos*) reel, bobbin; (*Elec*) coil; (*Fot*) cartridge, film, spool; (*Pez*) reel; **~ de encendido** (*Aut*) ignition coil; **~ de inducción** (*Elec*) induction coil; **dar ~ a uno** to keep sb guessing, keep sb in suspense.

carretear [1a] VT **(a)** *carga* to cart, haul. **(b)** *carro* to drive; (*Aer*) to taxi.

carretel NM (fishing) reel; (*Náut*) log reel.

carretela NF (*Hist*) coach, carriage; calash; (*CAm: carro*) cart.

carretera NF (main) road, highway; **de ~** road (*atr*); **por ~** by road; **~ de circunvalación** bypass, ring road; **~ comarcal** country road; **~ de cuota** (*LAm*) toll road, turnpike (*US*); **~ nacional** corresponde a A-road (*Brit*), major road; **~ radial** ring road; **~ secundaria** ≈ B-road (*Brit*).

carretero 1 ADJ: **camino ~** vehicular road.
2 NM **(a)** (*transportista*) carter; cart driver; (*ruedero*) cartwright, wheelwright; **fuma como un ~** he smokes like a chimney. **(b)** (*LAm*) road.

carretilla NF **(a)** (*carro pequeño*) truck, trolley; (*t ~ de mano*) handcart, barrow; (*Agr, Hort*) wheelbarrow; (*de niño*) go-cart; (*de bebé*) baby-walker; (*de supermercado*) trolley; **~ elevadora**, **~ de horquilla** fork-lift truck.

(b) (*buscapiés*) squib, cracker.

(c) (*Cono Sur: quijada*) jaw, jawbone.

(d) (*And: lote*) lot, series.

(e) **aprender algo de ~** to learn sth mechanically; **saber algo de ~** to know sth by heart.

carretón NM small cart; wagon, dray; (*Ferro*) bogey; **~ de remolque** trailer.

carricero NM: **~ común** reed-warbler.

carricoche NM covered wagon, (gipsy) caravan; (*) crock.

carricuba NF water cart.

carriel NM (*And, CAm*) leather case.

carril NM **(a)** (*rodada*) rut, track; (*camino*) cart track, lane; (*de carretera*) lane; (*Agr*) furrow; **~ de adelantamiento** fast lane; **~ de autobús** bus lane; **~ de bicicleta** cycleway, cycle-path.

(b) (*Ferro*) rail, railway; (*Carib, Cono Sur: tren*) train; **~ de toma** third rail.

carrilano NM (*Cono Sur*) **(a)** (*atracador*) robber, hold-up man. **(b)** (*Ferro*) railwayman.

carril-bici NM, PL **carriles-bici** cycle lane.

carril-bus NM, PL **carriles-bus** bus lane.

carrilera NF **(a)** (*rodera*) rut, track. **(b)** (*Carib Ferro*) siding.

carrilero NM (*And Ferro*) railwayman; (*Cono Sur: embaucador*) con man*.

carrillera NF **(a)** (*Zool*) jaw. **(b)** (*de casco*) chinstrap.

carrillo NM **(a)** (*mejilla*) cheek; jowl; **comer a dos ~s** (*comer*) to eat greedily, stuff o.s.; (*más de un empleo*) to moonlight*, have more than one well-paid job; (*fig*) to run with the hare and hunt with the hounds.

(b) (*Téc*) pulley.

carrindanga* NF (*Cono Sur*) old crock.

carriola NF truckle bed.

carrito NM **(a)** (*de supermercado*: *t ~ de la compra*) trolley, shopping cart (*US*); (*de hotel etc*) tea trolley, serving-trolley; **~ de bebidas** drinks trolley; **~ de postres** dessert trolley. **(b)** (*Carib: taxi*) taxi.

carrizal NM reedbed.

carrizo NM **(a)** (*Bot*) reed. **(b)** **~s** (*And, Méx*) thin (*o* spindly) legs, pins‡; **hacer ~** (*And*) to cross one's legs. **(c)** **no nos ayudan en un ~** (*Carib*) they do nothing at all to help us. **(d)** (*And, CAm, Carib*) = **caramba**.

carro NM **(a)** (*gen*) cart, wagon; (*Hist: t ~ de guerra*) chariot; (*de supermercado*) trolley, shopping cart (*US*); (*LAm*) (*any*) vehicle, (*esp*) car, automobile; (*LAm: taxi*) cab, taxi; (*Mil*) tank; (*LAm Ferro*) car, truck, coach; **~ alegórico** float (*in a procession*); **~ aljibe** water cart; **~ blindado** armoured car; **~ de combate** tank; **~ comedor** (*Méx*) dining-car; **~ correo** (*LAm Ferro*) mail van; **~ cuba** tank truck; **~ dormitorio** (*Méx*) sleeping-car; **~ fuerte** heavy trolley; **~ fúnebre** hearse; **~ de golf** golf buggy; **~ de mudanzas** removal van; **~ de riego** water cart; **~ tranvía**, **~ urbano** (*LAm*) tramcar, streetcar (*US*); **aguantar** (*o* **pasar por**) **~s y carretas** to put up with anything, remain undismayed; **apearse del ~*** to back down; **arrimarse al ~ del que manda**, **subirse al ~** to climb on the bandwagon; **era como si cantara un ~** it was like talking to a brick wall; **poner el ~ delante de las mulas** to put the cart before the horse; **¡pare Vd el ~!** hold your horses!; **tirar del ~** (*fig*) to do all the donkey-work; **untar el ~ a uno** to grease sb's palm; *V t* **carrito**.

(b) (*cantidad*) cartload; **un ~ de problemas** (*fig*) a whole load of problems.

(c) (*de máquina de escribir*) carriage.

carrocería NF **(a)** (*taller*) coachbuilder's; carriage repair shop. **(b)** (*Aut etc*) bodywork, coachwork.

carrocero NM coachbuilder, carriage builder.

carrocha NF (*Ent*) eggs, ova.

carromato NM covered wagon, (gipsy) caravan.

carroña NF carrion.

carroñero ADJ **(a)** rotten, (*fig*) vile, foul. **(b)** **animal ~** animal which feeds on carrion.

carroño ADJ **(a)** (*putrefacto*) rotten, putrid, foul. **(b)** (*And: cobarde*) cowardly.

carroza 1 NF **(a)** (*carruaje*) (state) coach, carriage; (*en desfile*) float; **~ fúnebre** hearse.

(b) (*Náut*) awning.

2 NM (*) **(a)** (*viejo*) old geezer‡, old boy*; old fogey*; (*carca*) square*; (*Pol*) old reactionary.

(b) (*homosexual*) gay*, queer‡; old queen‡.

3 ADJ INVAR (*) archaic, passé; square*.

carruaje NM carriage; vehicle.

carrujo‡ NM (*LAm*) joint‡, reefer‡.

carrusel NM **(a)** (*de verbena*) merry-go-round, roundabout. **(b)** (*Fot*) carrousel, circular slide-tray. **(c)** (*de regalos etc*) revolving display.

carry-all NM (*Cono Sur*) estate car, station wagon (*US*).

▼ **carta** NF **(a)** (*gen*) letter; **~ abierta** open letter; **~ de acuse de recibo** letter of acknowledgement; **~ adjunta** covering letter; **~ aérea** air-mail letter; **~ de ajuste** test card; **~ de amor**, **~ amorosa** love-letter; **~ de asignación** letter of allotment; **~ de aviso** letter of advice; **~ certificada** registered letter; **~s credenciales** letters of credence; **~ de crédito** letter of credit; **~ de emplazamiento** (*Jur*) summons; **~ de intenciones** letter of intent; **~ particular**, **~ privada** private letter, personal letter; **~ pastoral** pastoral letter; **~ de pedido** (*Com*) order; **~ de pésame** letter of condolence; **~ de porte** waybill; **~ postal** (*LAm*) postcard; **~ de presentación**, **~ de recomendación** letter of introduction (*para* to); **~ de solicitud** (letter of) application; **~ urgente** special-delivery letter; **echar una ~ al correo** to post a letter.

(b) (*Jur*) document, deed; (*Hist: de ciudad etc*) charter; **~ blanca** carte blanche; **dar ~ blanca a uno** to give sb carte blanche; **tener ~ blanca** to have a free hand; **~ de ciudadanía**, **~ de naturaleza** naturalization papers; **adquirir ~ de naturaleza** (*fig*) to come to seem native, be thoroughly accepted; **~ ejecutoria**, **~ de hidalguía** letters patent of nobility; **C~ Magna** (*Brit*) Magna Carta; **~ de pago** receipt, discharge in full; **~ partida** (*por ABC*) indenture; **~ de privilegio** company charter; **~ de trabajo** work permit; **~ de venta** bill of sale; **~ verde** (*Aut*) green card; **a ~ cabal** thoroughly, in every respect; one hundred per cent; loyally; **caballero a ~ cabal** a thorough gentleman; **¡~ canta!** there it is in black and white!

(c) (*Geog*) map (*t* **~ geográfica**); (*Náut*) chart; **~ acotada** contour map; **~ astral** star chart; **~ de flujo** flowchart; **~ de marear, ~ marítima** chart; **~ meteorológica** weather map; **~ naval, ~ de navegación, ~ de viaje** chart; **~ de vuelo** flight plan.

(d) (*Naipes*) card, playing card; **~ de figura** court card, picture card; **a ~s vistas** openly, honestly; with inside information; **echar las ~s** to tell sb's fortune (with cards); **enseñar las ~s** (*fig*) to show one's hand; **ponér las ~s boca arriba, poner las ~s sobre la mesa** to put one's cards on the table; **no saber a qué ~ quedarse** not to know what to think, be undecided; to be in a dilemma; **tener** (*o* **tomar**) **~s en un asunto** to intervene (*o* take a hand) in a matter, come in on an affair; **más vale pecar por ~ de más que por ~ de menos** better safe than sorry.

(e) (*Culin*) menu; **~ de vinos** wine list; **a la ~** à la carte.

carta-bomba NF, PL **cartas-bomba** letter-bomb.

cartabón NM (*de carpintero*) square, set-square; (*de delineante*) triangle; (*Agrimen, Mil*) quadrant.

cartagenero ⊡ ADJ of Cartagena.
⊡ NM, **cartagenera** NF native (*o* inhabitant) of Cartagena; **los ~s** the people of Cartagena.

cartaginés ⊡ ADJ Carthaginian.
⊡ NM, **cartaginesa** NF Carthaginian.

Cartago NF Carthage.

cartapacio NM (*cuaderno*) notebook; (*carpeta*) folder, briefcase; (*de colegial*) satchel.

carta-tarjeta NF, PL **cartas-tarjeta** letter-card.

cartear [1a] ⊡ VI (*Naipes*) to play low.
⊡ **cartearse** VR to correspond (*con* with); **se cartearon durante 2 años** they wrote to each other for 2 years.

cartel[1] NM (*gen*) poster, placard; (*Teat etc*) bill; (*Cine*) credits, list of credits; (*Escol*) wall chart; **~ de completo** 'full up' sign; **~ de escaparate** window card; **torero de ~** star bullfighter; **poner ~*** (*Teat*) to be sold out; **tener ~*** to be a hit, be all the rage; **'se prohibe fijar ~es'** 'post no bills'.

cartel[2], **cártel** NM (*Com, Fin*) cartel, trust.

cartela NF **(a)** (*papel*) slip of paper, bit of card. **(b)** (*Arquit*) console; corbel; cartouche.

cartelera NF (*valla*) hoarding, billboard; (*tablón*) notice board; (*en periódico*) list of plays, theatre section; **mantenerse en la ~, seguir en la ~** to run, be on; **se mantuvo en la ~ durante 3 años** it ran for 3 years.

cartelero NM billsticker, billposter.

cartelista NMF poster artist, poster designer.

cartelón NM large notice; sign.

carteo NM correspondence, exchange of letters.

cárter NM (*Mec*) housing, case; **~ del cigüeñal** (*Aut*) sump; crank-case.

cartera NF **(a)** (*de bolsillo*) wallet, pocketbook; (*para papeles*) letterfile, portfolio; (*de mano*) briefcase; (*carpeta*) folder; (*Cos*) pocket flap; (*LAm: bolso*) handbag, purse; (*de motocicleta*) pannier bag; (*de colegial*) satchel; **~ de bolsillo** wallet; **~ de herramientas** saddle-bag, toolbag; **~ de mano** briefcase.

(b) (*Com*) **~ de clientes** client portfolio; **~ de pedidos** order-book; **~ de pedidos exteriores** export order-book; **proyecto en ~** plan in the pipeline.

(c) (*Pol*) portfolio, ministerial post; **ministro sin ~** minister without portfolio.

(d) (*Fin*: *t* **~ de valores**) portfolio, holdings; **efectos en ~** holdings, stocks.

carterero NM (*Cono Sur*) pickpocket; bagsnatcher.

carterista NM pickpocket.

carterita NF: **~ de fósforos** book of matches.

cartero NM postman, mailman (*US*).

cartesiano, -a ADJ, NM/F Cartesian.

cartilaginoso ADJ cartilaginous.

cartílago NM cartilage.

cartilla NF **(a)** (*Escol*) primer, first reader; spelling book; elementary treatise; **cantar la ~ a uno** to give sb a severe ticking-off; **no saber la ~*** not to know a single thing.

(b) **~ de ahorros** savings bank book, deposit book; **~ de identidad** identity card; **~ de racionamiento** ration book; **~ de seguro** (*o* **seguridad**) social security card; **~ de trabajo** work permit.

(c) (*Méx*) identity card.

(d) (*Ecl*) certificate of ordination; liturgical calendar.

cartografía NF cartography, mapmaking.

cartografiado NM mapping.

cartográfico ADJ cartographic(al).

cartógrafo, -a NM/F cartographer, mapmaker.

cartomancia NF fortune-telling (*with cards*).

cartomante NMF fortune-teller (*who uses cards*).

cartón NM **(a)** (*materia*) cardboard, pasteboard; (*de libro*) board; **~**

alquitranado tar paper; **~ de bingo** bingo card; **~ de embalaje** wrapping paper; **~ de encuadernar** millboard; **~ acanalado, ~ ondulado** corrugated cardboard; **~ piedra** papier mâché.

(b) (*Arte*) artist's cartoon.

(c) (*caja etc*) (cardboard) box, carton.

(d) (*LAm: dibujo*) cartoon, sketch.

cartoné NM (*Tip*): **en ~** (bound) in boards.

cartón-madera NM chipboard.

cartuchera NF cartridge belt.

cartuchería NF cartridges, ammunition.

cartucho NM **(a)** (*Mil*) cartridge; cartridge case; **~ sin bala, ~ de fogueo** blank cartridge; **luchar hasta quemar el último ~** to fight on to the last ditch.

(b) (*bolsita*) paper cone, paper cornet; (*de monedas*) roll; (*LAm*) cornucopia.

(c) (*Inform*) cartridge.

Cartuja NF (*Ecl*) Carthusian order.

cartuja NF Carthusian monastery.

cartujano ADJ, NM Carthusian.

cartujo NM Carthusian.

cartulaje: NM pack of cards.

cartulario NM cartulary.

cartulina NF (*materia*) thin cardboard, Bristol board; (*tarjeta*) card; pass; (*Golf*) card; **~ amarilla** yellow card.

carura NF **(a)** (*And, CAm, Cono Sur*) (*lo costoso*) high price, dearness. **(b)** (*And, CAm, Cono Sur*) (*objeto*) expensive thing; **en esta tienda sólo hay ~s** everything in this shop is dear. **(c)** (*Cono Sur: carestía*) lack, shortage.

CASA ['kasa] NF (*Esp*) ABR *de* **Construcciones Aeronáuticas, S.A.**

casa NF **(a)** (*gen*) house; (*piso*) flat, apartment; (*edificio*) building; **~ de alquiler** block of flats, apartment block; **~ de asistencia** boarding house; **~ de azotea** penthouse; **~ baja** slum, shack; **~ de baños** public baths, bathhouse (*US*); **~s baratas** low-cost housing; **~ de bebidas** bar, saloon; **~ de beneficencia** (*Hist*) poor-house; **~ de bombas** pumphouse; **~ de campaña** (*LAm*) tent; **~ de campo** country house; **~ chica** (*Méx*) mistress's house; **~ de citas, ~ pública, ~ de putas*, ~ de tolerancia, ~ de vicio** brothel; **~ consistorial** town hall; civic centre; **~ de corrección** reformatory, remand home; **~ de correos** post office; **~ cuna** (PL **casas cuna**) (*Hist*) foundling home; (*moderna*) day-nursery, crèche; **~ de departamentos** (*LAm*) tenement, block of flats, apartment house (*US*); **~ de ejercicios** (religious) retreat; **~ encantada** haunted house; **~ exenta** detached house; **~ de fieras** (*Madrid*) zoo, menagerie; **~ de guarda** lodge; **~ de huéspedes** boarding house; **~ de juego** gambling house; **~ de labor, ~ de labranza** farm, farmhouse; **~ de locos, ~ de orates** asylum; **~ de maternidad** maternity hospital; **~ de muñecas** doll's house; **~ pareada** semi-detached house; **~ de pisos** block of flats; **~ religiosa** monastery; convent; **~ rodante** caravan, trailer; **~ de seguridad** (*Cono Sur Pol*) safe house; **~ de socorro** first-aid post; **~ de Tócame Roque** place where one does as one likes, Liberty Hall; **~ de vecindad** block of tenements, apartment house (*US*); **un complejo como una ~*** a massive complex; **un penalti como una ~*** a clear-cut penalty.

(b) (*con aplicación personal, hogar*) home; residence, house; household; **~ y comida** board and lodging; **¿dónde tienes tu ~?** where is your home?; **~ mortuoria** house of mourning; **~ paterna** parents' home; **~ solariega** family seat, ancestral home; **es una ~ alegre** it's a happy home, it's a happy household; **ir a ~** to go home; **ir hacia ~** to head for home, go homewards; **ir a ~ de Juan** to go to John's house, go to John's place, go to John's; **salir de ~** to leave home; **ir de ~ en ~** to go from house to house; **estar en ~** to be at home, be in; **¿está la señora en ~?** is the lady in?, is the lady at home?; **están en ~ de los abuelos** they're at their grandparents'; **jugar en ~** (*Dep*) to play at home; **estar fuera de ~** to be out, be away from home; **jugar fuera de ~** (*Dep*) to play away; **voy para ~** I'm off home; **estar por la ~** to be about the house; **de ~** home (*atr*), household (*atr*); *deporte, ropa* indoor; *animal* pet, family (*atr*); (*fig*) ordinary, commonplace; **estar de ~** to be in one's ordinary clothes; **zapatos de andar por ~** shoes for (wearing) around the house; **una explicación para andar por ~** a rough-and-ready explanation; **ser de la ~** to be like one of the family.

(c) (*hogar: locuciones con verbo*) **abandonar la ~** to leave home, move out; **echar la ~ por la ventana** to go to enormous expense; to roll out the red carpet for sb; **empezar la ~ por el tejado** to put the cart before the horse; **franquear la ~ a uno** to open one's house to sb; **llevar la ~** to keep house, run the house; **cada uno manda en su ~** one's home is one's castle; **poner ~** to set up house; **poner ~ a una mujer** to set a woman up in a little place; **poner a uno en ~** (*fig*) to do sb a great favour; **poner su ~ en orden** (*fig*) to put one's own house in order; **sentirse como en su ~** to feel at home; **no tener ~ ni hogar** to be homeless; **vender cosas por las ~s** to sell things from door to door.

(d) (*fórmulas de cortesía*) **Vd está en su ~, aquí tiene Vd su ~** you're very welcome.

(e) (*Com, Fin*) firm, business house (*t* **~ de comercio**); **~ de banca, ~ bancaria** banking house; **~ central** head office; **~ de discos, ~ discográfica** record company; **~ editorial** publishing house; **~ de empeños, ~ de préstamos** pawnshop; **~ matriz** head office; parent company; **~ de modas** fashion house; **~ de (la) moneda** mint.

(f) **C~ Blanca** White House (*Washington*); **C~ Rosada** Government House (*Buenos Aires*).

(g) (*linaje*) house, line, family; **~ real** royal house, royal family; **la ~ de Borbón** the house of Bourbon.

(h) (*en juegos*) square.

┌─ CASA ─────────────── ver también la entrada ─┐

Uso de la preposición "to" con "home"

A la hora de traducir expresiones como *ir a casa, volver a casa, venir a casa*, hay que tener en cuenta que *home* sigue directamente al verbo (*sin to*):

Quiero irme a casa
I want to go home
No puede volver a casa
He can't go back home

NOTA: Sin embargo, *to* sí se pone cuando *home* viene calificado:

Quiere volver a su antigua casa
She wants to return to her former home

Para otros usos y ejemplos ver la entrada.

┌─ CASA DE CONTRATACIÓN ─┐

ⓘ *The **Casa de Contratación** was responsible for the regulation of Spain's trade with her Latin American colonies. Founded in 1503 by the Crown, the **Casa de Contratación** supervised all transatlantic ships operating between certain ports in Spain and Latin America, notably between Cádiz in Spain and Veracruz in Mexico. The **Casa** also collected the levy (known as the **quinto**) of a fifth of all colonial gold and silver, and regulated the African slave trade with Cartagena de Indias, Colombia. As the volume of trade increased, the **Casa** operated armed fleets to protect shipments from piracy.*

---

casabe NM (*LAm*) cassava.

casa-bote NF, PL **casas-bote** houseboat.

casaca NF **(a)** (*vestido*) frock coat; (*Cono Sur*) zip jacket; **~ de montar** riding coat; **cambiar de ~, volver la ~** to turn one's coat, be a turncoat.
(b) (**: boda*) wedding, marriage.

casación NF cassation, annulment.

casacón NM greatcoat.

casa-cuartel NF, PL **casas-cuarteles** residential barracks (for Civil Guard).

casada NF married woman.

casadero ADJ marriageable, of an age to be married.

casado ① ADJ married; **bien ~** happily married; **mal ~** unhappily married; **~ y arrepentido** marry in haste and repent at leisure; **estar ~** to be married (*con* to); **estar ~ a media carta** to live in sin.
② NM **(a)** (*persona*) married man; **los ~s** married men; married people; **los recién ~s** the newlyweds.
(b) (*Tip*) imposition.
(c) (*LAm Culin*) two separate varieties of food eaten together.

casal NM **(a)** (*casa de campo*) country house; (*granja*) farmhouse; (*solar*) ancestral home. **(b)** (*Cono Sur: matrimonio*) married couple; (*Zool*) pair.

casamata NF casemate.

casamentero NM, **casamentera** NF matchmaker.

casamiento NM marriage, wedding (ceremony); **~ por amor** love match; **~ de conveniencia** marriage of convenience; **~ a la fuerza** forced marriage, shotgun marriage; **prometer a una joven en ~** to betroth a girl (*con* to).

casampolga NF (*CAm Zool*) black widow spider.

Casandra NF Cassandra.

casapuerta NF entrance hall, vestibule.

casar¹ NM hamlet.

▼**casar²** [1a] ① VT **(a)** (*sujeto: cura*) to marry, join in marriage, join in wedlock.
(b) (*sujeto: padre o madre*) to marry (off), give in marriage (*con* to).
(c) (*fig: emparejar*) to pair, couple; to match; (*Tip*) to impose.
(d) (*Jur*) to quash, annul.
② VI **(a)** = VR.
(b) (*fig: armonizar*) to match, harmonize.

▼③ **casarse** VR **(a)** (*gen*) to marry, get married; **A se casó con B** A married B; **¿cuándo te vas a casar?** when are you getting married?; **volver a ~, ~ en segundas nupcias** to marry again (*y V* **nupcias**).
(b) (*fig: armonizar*) to match, harmonize.

casa-refugio NF, PL **casas-refugio** refuge for battered wives.

casatienda NF shop with dwelling accommodation, shop with flat over.

casba(h) NF kasbah.

casca NF **(a)** (*corteza*) bark (for tanning). **(b)** (*uvas*) marc (of grapes). **(c)** **~s almibaradas** candied peel.

cascabel NM **(a)** (*campanita*) (little) bell; **de ~ gordo** pretentious; cheap; **ser un ~*** to be a scatterbrain; **echar** (*o* **soltar**) **el ~** to drop a hint; **poner el ~ al gato** to bell the cat. **(b)** (*LAm: víbora*) rattlesnake.

cascabela NF (*LAm*) rattlesnake.

cascabelear [1a] ① VT to take in*, raise the hopes of, beguile.
② VI **(a)** (*LAm: tintinear*) to jingle, tinkle.
(b) (*fig: ser imprudente*) to act recklessly, behave frivolously, be inconsiderate.
(c) (*Cono Sur: refunfuñar*) to moan, grumble.

cascabeleo NM jingle, jingling, tinkling.

cascabelero* ① ADJ scatterbrained.
② NM, **cascabelera** NF scatterbrain.

cascabillo NM **(a)** (*campanilla*) little bell. **(b)** (*Bot*) (*de granos*) husk, chaff; (*de bellota*) cup.

cascada NF waterfall; cascade.

cascado ADJ **(a)** (*roto*) broken (down); *persona* infirm, decrepit, worn out. **(b)** *voz* weak, unmelodious, cracked; *piano etc* tinny.

cascajo NM **(a)** (*grava*) (piece of) gravel; (*Arquit etc t* **~s**) rubble; (*de cerámica etc*) fragments, shards.
(b) (*trastos*) junk, rubbish, lumber; **estar hecho un ~*** to be a wreck.

cascajoso ADJ gritty, gravelly.

cascanueces NM INVAR nutcracker; **un ~** a pair of nutcrackers.

cascar [1g] ① VT **(a)** (*romper*) to crack, split, break (open); to crunch; *nuez* to crack.
(b) (*fig*) *salud* to shatter, undermine.
(c) (*) (*pegar*) to belt*, smack; (*Dep*) to beat hollow*, wipe the floor with*.
(d) **~la:** to kick the bucket‡.
② VI **(a)** (*chacharear**) to chatter, talk too much.
(b) (‡) to kick the bucket‡.
③ **cascarse** VR **(a)** (*romperse*) to crack, split, break (open).
(b) (*salud*) to crack up; (*voz*) to break, crack.
(c) **cascársela**‡‡ to wank‡‡.

cáscara NF **(a)** (*de huevo, nuez, edificio*) shell; (*de grano*) husk; (*de fruto*) rind, peel, skin; (*de árbol*) bark; **~ de huevo** eggshell; (*porcelana*) eggshell china; **~ de limón** lemon peel; **~ sagrada** (*Farm*) cascara; **patatas cocidas con ~** potatoes in their jackets; **no hay más ~s*** there's no other way; **ser de la ~ amarga*** to be wild, be mischievous; (*Pol*) have radical ideas; (*sexualmente*) to be the other sort; **dar ~s de novillo a** (*LAm*) to thrash.
(b) (*) (*euf*) **¡~s!** well I'm blowed!*
(c) **~s‡** (*And*) clothes.
(d) **tener ~** (*CAm**) to have a cheek*, be shameless.

cascarazo NM **(a)** (*And, Carib: puñetazo*) punch; (*And: azote*) lash. **(b)** (*Carib*: trago*) swig*, slug* (*US*).

cascarear‡ [1a] ① VT (*And, CAm*) to belt*, smack.
② VI (*Méx**) to scrape a living.

cascarilla ① ADJ (*Carib, Cono Sur: enojadizo*) touchy, quick-tempered.
② NF **(a)** (*Carib, Cono Sur: persona*) quick-tempered person.
(b) (*And, Cono Sur: Med*) medicinal herb; dried cacao husks (*used as tea*).

cascarón NM (broken) eggshell.

cascarrabias* NMF INVAR quick-tempered person, irritable sort.

cascarria NF (*Cono Sur: mugre*) filth, muck; (*Agr*) sheep droppings.

cascarriento ADJ (*Cono Sur*) filthy, mucky.

cascarrón* ADJ gruff, abrupt, rough.

cascarudo ① ADJ thick-shelled, having a thick skin.
② NM (*Cono Sur*) beetles (*collectively*).

casco NM **(a)** (*Mil etc*) helmet; (*parte de sombrero*) crown; **~s*** (*Rad*) headset, set of headphones; **~ de acero** steel helmet; **~ azul** soldier of a UN peace-keeping force; **~ de corcho** sun helmet; **~ protector** (*de motorista*) safety helmet, crash helmet; (*de albañil etc*) hard hat; **~ sideral** space helmet.
(b) (*Anat*) skull; (‡) brains, head, nut‡; **alegre de ~s, ligero de ~s** scatterbrained, frivolous; flighty; **calentar los ~s a uno** to get sb worked up; **estar mal de los ~s** to be crazy; **romper los ~s a uno** to bash sb's head in*; **romperse los ~s** to rack one's brains; **sentar los ~s** to quieten down, settle down, learn to behave o.s.; **tener los ~s a la jineta** to be scatterbrained.
(c) (*de cerámica*) fragment, shard; (*envase*) returnable soft drink bottle, empty (bottle).
(d) (*de cebolla*) edible part, edible layer.
(e) (*barril*) cask, barrel.
(f) (*Náut*) hull; (*pey*) old hulk.
(g) (*Zool*) hoof.
(h) (*Mec*) casing.

▶ LENGUA Y USO: **casar: 3a** → 51.3

(i) (*de ciudad*) inner part, central area; (*Méx Agr*) ranchhouse, ranch and outbuildings; (*Cono Sur: de hacienda*) part, section; **~ comercial** business quarter; **~ urbano** inner city, area enclosed within city limits; **el ~ antiguo de la ciudad** the old part of the city.
(j) (*Carib: de fruta*) quarter, segment.
(k) (*LAm: edificio vacío*) empty building.

cascorros* NMPL (*Méx*) shoes.

cascorvo* ADJ (*CAm*) bow-legged.

cascote NM (piece of) rubble, (piece of) debris.

cascundear [1a] VT (*CAm*) to beat, thrash.

cáseo 1 ADJ cheesy.
2 NM curd.

caseoso ADJ cheesy, like cheese.

casera¹ NF landlady (*owner*); (*Ecl*) (priest's) housekeeper; *V t* **casero 2**.

casería NF **(a)** (*casa*) country house. **(b)** (*LAm* †: *clientela*) customers, clientèle.

caserío NM **(a)** (*casa*) country house. **(b)** (*aldea*) hamlet, settlement, group of dwellings.

caserna NF (*LAm*) barracks.

casero 1 ADJ **(a)** domestic, household (*atr*); *bomba, pan etc* homemade; *paño* homespun; *remedio* household; *ropa* house (*atr*), indoor, ordinary; *reunión* family (*atr*); **conejo ~** pet rabbit, tame rabbit; **el equipo ~** (*Dep*) the home team; **una victoria casera** a home win, a win for the home side.
(b) *persona* home-loving.
2 NM **(a)** (*dueño*) landlord; (*vigilante*) caretaker; (*conserje*) porter, concierge, janitor (*US*); (*inquilino*) tenant, occupier; (*Com*) house agent (*in charge of a property*).
(b) (*t* **casera²** NF) stay-at-home, home-lover.
(c) (*LAm: t* **casera³** NF: *cliente*) customer, client; (*Carib: repartidor*) (*hombre*) delivery man; (*mujer*) delivery woman.

caserón NM large (ramshackle) house, barracks (of a place).

┌─ CASI ─────────────────────── *ver también la entrada* ─┐

Las dos traducciones principales de *casi* en inglés son *almost* y *nearly*:

> Estoy casi lista
> *I'm almost o nearly ready*
> Eran casi las cuatro cuando sonó el teléfono
> *It was almost o nearly four o'clock when the telephone rang*
> Nos vemos casi todos los días
> *We meet almost o nearly every day*

● Cuando *almost* y *nearly* acompañan a un verbo, se colocan detrás de éste si se trata de un verbo auxiliar o modal y delante en el caso de los demás verbos:

> Casi me rompo la muñeca
> *I almost o nearly broke my wrist*
> Mi hijo ya casi habla
> *My son can almost o nearly talk*

Sin embargo, hay algunos casos en los que sólo podemos utilizar *almost*:

● delante de adverbios que terminan en *-ly*

> "¿Qué estáis haciendo aquí?", nos preguntó casi con enfado
> *"What are you doing here?" he asked almost angrily*

● delante de *like*:

> Se comporta casi como un niño
> *He behaves almost like a child*

● delante de palabras de sentido negativo, como *never, no, none, no-one, nothing* y *nowhere*; en estos casos, muchas veces se traduce también por *practically*:

> No dijo casi nada
> *She said almost o practically nothing*
> No había casi nadie en la fiesta
> *There was almost o practically no-one at the party*

NOTA: En estos casos también se puede usar la construcción *hardly + ever/any/anything/etc*:

> *She said hardly anything*
> *There was hardly anyone at the party*

● acompañando a adjetivos o sustantivos que, normalmente, no pueden ser modificados:

> El mono tenía una expresión casi humana
> *The monkey had an almost human expression*
> Me pareció casi un alivio
> *I found it almost a relief*

Para otros usos y ejemplos ver la entrada.

└──┘

caseta NF (*de mercado*) stall, stand, booth; (*en exposición*) stand; (*de feria*) sideshow, booth; (*Dep*) dressing-room, changing-room; pavilion; (*de piscina*) cubicle, changing-room; (*de playa*) bathing-hut, bathingtent; (*de campo*) cottage; **~ de perro** kennel, doghouse (*US*); **~ del timón** wheelhouse; **mandar a un jugador a la ~** to send a player for an early bath.

---

casetera NF (*LAm*) cassette deck.

caset(t)e [ka'set] 1 NF cassette.
2 NM cassette-player.

cash [katʃ] NM, PL **cash** [katʃ] (*t* **~ and carry**) cash-and-carry store.

casi ADV almost, nearly; **~ ~** very nearly; **está ~ terminado** it's almost finished; **~ nada** next to nothing; **100 dólares ..., ~ nada** 100 dollars, a mere trifle; **~ nunca** almost never, hardly ever; **300 o ~** some 300, 300 or thereabouts.

casilla NF **(a)** (*cabaña*) hut, cabin, shed; (*en parque etc*) keeper's lodge; (*de mercado etc*) booth, stall; (*Ferro*) platelayer's hut, guard's hut; **~ electoral** (*Méx*) polling-station.
(b) (*Aut, Ferro: de locomotora*) cab.
(c) (*Teat*) box office.
(d) (*para cartas*) pigeonhole; (*de caja etc*) compartment; (*de papel*) ruled column, section; (*de formulario*) box; (*Ajedrez etc*) square; (*LAm Correos*) post-office box (number).
(e) (*And: retrete*) lavatory.
(f) (*Carib: trampa*) bird trap.
(g) **sacar a uno de sus ~s** to shake sb up, shake sb out of his complacency; to make sb cross, get sb worked up; **salir de sus ~s** to fly off the handle*.

casillero NM (*para cartas*) (set of) pigeonholes; (*Ferro etc*) luggage-locker; (*Correos etc*) sorting-rack; (*Dep**) scoreboard.

casimba NF (*LAm*) = **cacimba.**

casimir NM cashmere.

casimiro ADJ (*LAm: hum*) cross-eyed.

casinista NM clubman, member of a casino.

casino NM (*gen*) club; social club, political club; (*de juego*) casino; (*Cono Sur*) canteen.

Casio NM Cassius.

casis 1 NM INVAR (*t* **~ de negro**) blackcurrant bush; **~ de rojo** redcurrant bush.
2 NF INVAR (*t* **~ de negro**) blackcurrant; **~ de rojo** redcurrant.

casita NF small house; (*de campo*) cottage; **los niños están jugando a las ~s** the children are playing houses.

▼ **caso** NM **(a)** (*Ling*) case.
(b) (*Med*) case; **es un ~ perdido** he's a dead loss, he's a disaster.
(c) (*en experimento etc*) case, subject; **soy un ~ difícil** I'm a difficult subject.
(d) (*ejemplo*) case, instance; (*suceso*) event, happening; (*circunstancias*) circumstances; **~ fortuito** (*Jur*) act of God; unforeseen circumstance; **~ límite** extreme case; **el ~ Hess** the Hess affair, the Hess case; **el ~ Romeo-Julieta** the Romeo and Juliet affair; the trouble between Romeo and Juliet; **en el ~ de Eslobodia** in the case of Slobodia; **en uno u otro ~** one way or the other; **en ~ de** in the event of; **~ que venga, en (el) ~ de que venga** in case he should come, should he come, in the event of his coming; **en ~ afirmativo** if so, if it should be so; **en ~ negativo, en el ~ contrario** if not, if it should not be so; **en el mejor de los ~s** at best; **en el peor de los ~s** at worst; **en tal ~** in such a case; **en todo ~** in any case, at all events; **en último ~** as a last resort, in the last resort; **y en su ~ también otros** and where appropriate, others also; **ponte en mi ~** put yourself in my position; **según el ~** as the case may be; **según lo requiera el ~** as the case may require; **dado el ~ que ...** supposing (that) ...; **el ~ es que ...** the fact is that ...; **creerse en el ~ de** + *infin* to think fit to + *infin*; **hablar al ~** to speak to the point; **hacer al ~, venir al ~** to be relevant; to be appropriate; **no hacer al ~, no venir al ~** to be beside the point; **pongamos por ~ que ...** let us suppose that ...; **pongamos por ~ a X** let us take X as an example; **servir para el ~** to serve one's purpose; **no tiene ~** (*Méx*) there's no point (in it); **¡vamos al ~!** let's get to the point!; let's get down to business!; **vaya por ~ ...** to give an example, ...; **verse en el ~ de** + *infin* to be compelled to + *infin*.
▼ **(e)** (*atención*) notice; **hacer ~ a** to heed, notice; **no me hacen ~** they don't pay me any attention; **¡no haga Vd ~!** take no notice!, don't worry!; **maldito el ~ que me hace** a fat lot of notice he takes of me; **hacer ~ de** to pay attention to; to take into account; **sin hacer ~ de eso** regardless of that; **hacer ~ omiso de** to ignore, fail to mention, deliberately pass over; **¡(pero) ni ~!*** but he took absolutely no notice; **¡ni ~!*** don't pay any attention to him! (*etc*).

casona NF large house.

casorio* NM hasty marriage, unwise marriage; (*Méx*) wedding, marriage.

caspa NF dandruff, scurf.

Caspio ADJ: **Mar M ~** Caspian Sea.

caspiroleta NF (*And, Carib, Cono Sur*) eggnog, egg flip.

cáspita INTERJ my goodness!; come off it!*

caspitoso ADJ **(a)** full of dandruff, scurfy. **(b)** (*fig*) shoddy, tawdry.

casposo ADJ covered in dandruff.

casquería NF tripe and offal shop.

casquero, -a NM/F seller of tripe and offal.

casquete NM **(a)** (*gorra*) skullcap; (*Mil*) helmet; (*Mec*) cap; **~ de hielo**

icecap; **~ de nieve** snow-cap; **~ polar** polar cap. **(b)** **echar un ~⁑** to have a screw⁑.

casquijo NM gravel.

casquillo NM **(a)** tip, cap; (*de botella*) bottle-top; (*de bastón*) ferrule, tip; (*Mec*) sleeve, bushing; (*Mil*) cartridge case. **(b)** (*LAm: de caballo*) horseshoe.

casquinona NF (*And*) (*botella*) beer bottle; (*cerveza*) beer.

casquivano 1 ADJ scatterbrained.
2 NM, **casquivana** NF scatterbrain.

cassette = **caset(t)e.**

casta NF **(a)** (*Rel etc*) caste; (*raza*) breed, race; (*grupo*) privileged group; (*fig*) class; quality; **de ~** of quality, of breeding; **carecer de ~** to lack breeding, have no class; **eso le viene de ~** that comes naturally to him.
(b) (*Méx Tip*) fount.

castamente ADV chastely, purely.

castaña NF **(a)** (*Bot*) chestnut; **~ de agua** water chestnut; **~ de Indias** horse chestnut; **dar** (o **meter**) **la ~ a uno** to swindle sb, make a fool out of sb; **sacar a uno las ~s del fuego** to pull sb's chestnuts out of the fire for him, to do sb's dirty work for him; **¡toma ~!*** well!; how do you like that!; just imagine!; **ser algo** (o **uno**) **una ~*** to be a drag.
(b) (*de pelo*) bun, chignon.
(c) (*vasija*) demijohn.
(d) (⁑: *golpe*) bash*, blow; (*Aut etc*) collision, accident, crash; **darse una ~** to give oneself a knock.
(e) (*Fin⁑*) one peseta.
(f) **cogerse una ~⁑** to get canned⁑, get drunk.
(g) (⁑) **tiene 71 ~s** he's 71 (years old).
(h) (⁑) **conducir a toda ~** to drive flat out.

castañar NM chestnut grove.

castañazo NM (*Cono Sur*) punch, thump.

castañero NM, **castañera** NF chestnut seller.

castañeta NF **(a)** (*con dedos*) snap (of the fingers). **(b)** (*Mús*) castanet.

castañetazo NM snap, crack, click.

castañetear [1a] 1 VT **(a)** *dedos* to snap.
(b) (*Mús*) to play on the castanets.
2 VI **(a)** (*dedos*) to snap; to click; (*platos etc*) to clatter; (*dientes*) to chatter, rattle; (*huesos*) to crack; (*rodillas*) to knock together; **~ con los dedos** to snap one's fingers.
(b) (*Mús*) to play the castanets.

castañeteo NM **(a)** (*dedos*) snap(ping); click(ing); (*platos*) clatter(ing); (*dientes*) chatter(ing); rattling; (*huesos*) crack(ing); (*gopeteo*) knocking.
(b) (*Mús*) sound of the castanets.

castaño 1 ADJ chestnut(-coloured), brown.
2 NM chestnut, chestnut tree; **~ de Indias** horse chestnut tree; **esto pasa de ~ oscuro** this is really too much, this is beyond a joke; **pelar el ~** (*Carib**) to hoof it*.

castañuela NF castanet; **no éramos unas ~s** we were not the life and soul of the party; **estar hecho unas ~s, estar como unas ~s** to be very merry, be in high spirits.

castañuelo ADJ chestnut(-coloured), brown.

castellanizar [1f] VT to hispanicize, give a Spanish form to.

castellano 1 ADJ Castilian; Spanish.
2 NM, **castellana** NF Castilian; Spaniard.
3 NM (*Ling*) Castilian, Spanish.

┌─ **CASTELLANO** ─┐

ⓘ *In the Spanish-speaking world* **castellano** *rather than* **español** *is a very common term for the Spanish language. Under the Spanish Constitution* **castellano** *is Spain's official language, but in some of the* **Comunidades Autónomas** *it shares official status with another language. Use of one or other term in Spain will depend on where the speaker is from, and where they place themselves in the linguistic debate, while in general the Latin Americans tend to favour the term* **castellano.**
⇨ *See also* │LENGUAS COOFICIALES│ , │COMUNIDAD AUTÓNOMA│

castellanohablante, castellanoparlante 1 ADJ Castilian-speaking, Spanish-speaking.
2 NMF Castilian speaker, Spanish speaker.

castellonense 1 ADJ of Castellón de la Plana.
2 NMF native (o inhabitant) of Castellón de la Plana; **los ~s** the people of Castellón de la Plana.

castellonés, -esa ADJ, NM/F = **castellonense.**

casticidad NF **(a)** (*Ling*) purity, correctness. **(b)** (*casticismo*) traditional character; thoroughbred character, true-born nature; authenticity, genuineness.

casticismo NM **(a)** (*Ling*) purity, correctness. **(b)** (*tradicionalismo*) love of tradition, traditionalism; = **casticidad (b).**

casticista ADJ, NMF purist.

castidad NF chastity, purity.

castigador NM **(a)** (*que castiga*) punisher. **(b)** (*en lo sexual*) ladykiller;

(*pey*) seducer, libertine.

castigar [1h] VT **(a)** (*gen*) to punish (*de, por* for); (*Dep*) to penalize (*por* for).
(b) (*fig*) to castigate; *carne* to mortify; (*enfermedad etc*) to afflict, affect; (*en las emociones*) to afflict, grieve; (*físicamente*) to strain, use hard; **~ mucho a un caballo** to ride a horse hard.
(c) (*fig: corregir*) *estilo etc* to refine; *texto* to correct, revise.
(d) (*Com*) *gastos* to reduce.
(e) (*Méx Mec*) to tighten (up).

castigo NM **(a)** (*gen*) punishment; (*Dep etc*) penalty; fine. **(b)** (*fig*) castigation; mortification, affliction. **(c)** (*fig*) (*refinación*) refinement; (*corrección*) correction, revision.

Castilla NF Castile; **~ la Nueva** New Castile; **~ la Vieja** Old Castile; **¡ancha es ~!** it takes all sorts!

castilla NF (*Cono Sur, Méx*) **(a)** (*Ling*) Castilian, Spanish; **hablar la ~** to speak Spanish. **(b)** **de ~** (*Hist*) Spanish, from the old country.

Castilla-León NM Castille and León.

castillejo NM **(a)** (*Arquit*) scaffolding. **(b)** (*de niño*) go-cart.

castillo NM castle; (*de elefante*) howdah; **~s en el aire** castles in the air; **~ de arena** sandcastle; **~ de fuego** firework set piece; **~ de naipes** house of cards; **~ de popa** aftercastle; aft awning; **~ de proa** forecastle; **hacer un ~ de un grano de arena** to make a mountain out of a molehill.

casting ['kastɪŋ] NM (*Cine etc*) casting.

castizo ADJ **(a)** (*Ling*) pure, correct.
(b) (*de pura sangre*) thoroughbred; true-born; (*fig*) (*tradicional*) traditional; (*genuino*) pure, authentic; genuine; **es un tipo ~*** he's one of the best; **un aragonés ~** a true-blue Aragonese, an Aragonese through and through.

casto ADJ chaste, pure.

castor NM beaver.

castoreño NM beaver (*hat*); (*Taur*) picador's hat.

castoreo NM (*Farm*) castor.

castra NF (*Bot*) (*acto*) pruning; (*época*) pruning season.

castración NF **(a)** (*Bio*) castration, gelding. **(b)** (*Bot*) pruning. **(c)** (*Agr*) extraction of honeycombs.

castrado 1 ADJ castrated.
2 NM eunuch.

castrar [1a] VT **(a)** (*Bio*) to castrate, geld; *gato etc* to doctor (*euf*).
(b) (*Bot*) to prune, cut back.
(c) *colmena* to extract honeycombs from.
(d) (*fig: debilitar*) to mutilate, impair, weaken.

castrense ADJ army (*atr*), military; **las glorias ~s** military glories.

castro NM hill-fort; Iron-Age settlement.

casual 1 ADJ **(a)** (*fortuito*) fortuitous, accidental, chance. **(b)** (*incidente*) incidental. **(c)** (*Ling*) case (*atr*); **desinencia ~** case ending.
2 NM: **por un ~*** by chance.

casualidad NF **(a)** (*gen*) chance, accident; coincidence; **fue una pura ~** it was sheer coincidence, it was entirely a matter of chance; **por ~** by chance; **¿tienes por ~ una pluma?** do you have a pen, by any chance?, do you happen to have a pen?; **me encontraba allí por ~** I happened to be there, I chanced to be there; **un día entró por ~** one day he dropped in; **da la ~ que ...** it (so) happens that ...; **dio la ~ que ...** it happened that ..., luck had it that ...; **¡qué ~!** what a coincidence!; **¡qué ~ verle aquí!** what a coincidence meeting you here!, fancy meeting you here!
(b) **~es** (*CAm*) casualties.

casualmente ADV by chance, by accident, fortuitously; **~ le vi ayer** I happened to see him yesterday, as it happens I saw him yesterday.

casuario NM cassowary.

casuca NF, **casucha** NF hovel, shack; slum.

casuista NMF casuist.

casuística NF casuistry.

casulla NF chasuble.

CAT [kat] NF (*Esp*) ABR *de* **Comisaría de Abastecimientos y Transportes.**

cata¹ NF **(a)** (*gen*) tasting, testing, sampling; blending; **~ de vinos** wine-tasting.
(b) (*muestra*) taste, sample.
(c) (*LAm Min*) trial excavation, test bore; prospecting.
(d) **ir en ~ de algo*** to go looking for sth.

cata² NF (*And, Cono Sur, Méx* †) parrot.

catabre NM (*And, Carib*) gourd; basket.

catacaldos NM INVAR **(a)** (*persona inconstante*) rolling stone; quitter, person who starts things but gives up easily; (*Arte etc*) dilettante.
(b) (*entrometido*) busybody, meddler.

cataclismismo NM doomwatching.

cataclismista NMF doomwatcher.

cataclismo NM cataclysm.

catacumbas NFPL catacombs.

catador(a) NM/F (*de té, vinos etc*) taster, blender, sampler; (*fig*) connoisseur.

catadura[1] NF tasting, sampling, blending.

catadura[2]* NF looks, face; **de mala ~** nasty-looking.

catafalco NM catafalque.

catafotos NMPL (*Aut*) cat's-eyes.

catajarria NF (*Carib*) string, series.

catalán, -ana [1] ADJ, NM/F Catalan, Catalonian.

   [2] NM (*Ling*) Catalan.

| CATALÁN |

ⓘ *Catalan is a romance language whose earliest literature dates back to the 12th century. In the Middle Ages Catalan military expansion spread the use of the language beyond modern Catalonia, but following the unification of Castile and Aragon the language lost ground to Castilian. During the Franco régime the use of Catalan and other minority national languages was prohibited in the media and in public institutions. This, together with the influx of Castilian-speaking immigrants, posed a threat to the survival of the language. Since 1979, when Catalonia's autonomous government, the **Generalitat**, was reestablished and Catalan gained **lengua cooficial** status, the language has returned to public life in Catalonia and is flourishing. Indeed, many Catalan authors publish first in Catalan and only later in Castilian. Outside Catalonia, Catalan is also spoken by large numbers of people in the Balearic Islands and Andorra. **Valenciano**, a language spoken in the Valencia region, is closely related.*

⇨ *See also* | LENGUAS COOFICIALES |

---

catalanismo NM **(a)** (*Ling*) catalanism, word (*o* phrase *etc*) peculiar to Catalonia. **(b)** sense of the differentness of Catalonia; (*Pol*) doctrine of (*o* belief in) Catalan autonomy.

catalanista [1] ADJ that supports (*etc*) Catalan autonomy; **el movimiento ~** the movement for Catalan autonomy; **la familia es muy ~** the family strongly supports Catalan autonomy.

   [2] NMF supporter (*etc*) of Catalan autonomy.

catalanizar [1f] VT to make Catalan, make a Catalan version of.

catalejo NM spyglass, telescope.

catalepsia NF catalepsy.

cataléptico, -a ADJ, NM/F cataleptic.

Catalina NF Catherine.

catálisis NF catalysis.

catalítico ADJ catalytic.

catalizador NM catalyst; (*Aut*) catalytic converter.

catalizar [1f] VT to catalyse.

catalogable ADJ classifiable.

catalogación NF cataloguing.

catalogar [1h] VT to catalogue.

catálogo NM catalogue; **~ colectivo** union catalogue; **~ de materias** subject index; **el libro está fuera de ~** the book is out of print.

Cataluña NF Catalonia.

catamarán NM catamaran.

cataplasma NF **(a)** (*Med*) poultice. **(b)** (*: persona*) bore.

cataplines: NMPL goolies:.

cataplum INTERJ bang!, crash!

catapulta NF catapult.

catapultar [1a] VT to catapult.

catapún ADJ: **una cosa del año ~** an antiquated thing, a totally obsolete thing; **películas del año ~** films of the year dot.

catar [1a] VT **(a)** (*probar*) to taste, sample, try; (*fig: examinar*) to examine, inspect, have a look at; (*fig: estimar*) to esteem.

   (b) (*mirar*) to look at; to look out for; **¡cata!, ¡cátale!** just look at him!; **¡cátate eso!** you just think!

   (c) *colmena* to extract honeycombs from.

catarata NF **(a)** (*Geog*) waterfall, falls; cataract; **C~ del Niágara** Niagara Falls; **C~s de Victoria** Victoria Falls.

   (b) (*Med*) cataract.

catarral ADJ catarrhal.

catarriento ADJ (*LAm*) = **catarroso**.

catarro NM cold; catarrh; **~ crónico del pecho** chest trouble; **coger** (*Esp*) (*o* **pescar***) **un ~** to catch a cold.

catarroso ADJ subject to colds; having catarrh, suffering from catarrh.

catarsis NF catharsis.

catártico ADJ cathartic.

catasalsas NM INVAR = **catacaldos**.

catastral ADJ relating to the property register; **valores ~es** property values, land values.

catastro NM property register, land registry, cadastre.

catástrofe NF catastrophe.

catastrófico ADJ catastrophic.

catastrofismo NM alarmism; doomwatching; scaremongering.

catastrofista [1] ADJ alarmist.

   [2] NMF alarmist; doomwatcher; scaremonger.

catatán NM (*Cono Sur*) punishment.

catatar [1a] VT (*And*) to ill-treat.

catauro NM (*Carib*) basket.

catavinos NMF INVAR wine taster; (*) boozer:.

cate[1]* NM (*golpe*) punch, bash*; **dar ~ a uno** (*Univ*) to plough sb*.

cate[2]* NMF (*profesor*) teacher.

catear [1a] VT **(a)** (*investigar*) to investigate; (*probar*) to try, sample.

   (b) (*Univ**) *candidato* to plough*; *examen* to fail.

   (c) (*Cono Sur, Méx: Min*) to make test borings in, explore.

   (d) (*Méx: policía*) to search, make a search of.

catecismo NM catechism.

catecúmeno, -a NM/F catechumen; (*fig*) convert.

cátedra [1] NF **(a)** (*Univ*) chair, professorship; (*de instituto*) senior teaching post (in a grammar school); **~ del Espíritu Santo** (*Ecl*) pulpit; **explicar una ~** to hold a chair (*de* of); **poner ~, sentar ~** to set up as an expert (*de* in), lay down the law (*de* about); to spout.

   (b) (*asignatura*) subject.

   (c) (*aula*) lecture room.

   (d) (*estudiantes*) group of students, class.

   (e) (*Carib* †) wonder, marvel; **es ~, está la ~** it's marvellous.

   [2] ADJ (*Carib*) wonderful, marvellous, excellent.

catedral NF cathedral; **un complejo como una ~*** a massive complex.

catedralicio ADJ cathedral (*atr*).

catedrático, -a NM/F (*Univ*) professor; **~ de instituto** ≃ grammar-school teacher.

cátedro* NM = **catedrático**.

categoría NF (*gen*) category; (*clase*) class, group; (*status*) rank, standing; (*calidad*) quality; (*prestigio*) prestige; **~ fiscal, ~ tributaria** tax bracket; **de ~** important; distinguished, high-ranking, prominent; **es hombre de cierta ~** he is a man of some standing; **servicio de primera ~** first-class service; **de baja ~** of low quality; of low rank; **de segunda ~** (*pey*) second-rate; **no tiene ~** he has no standing; **tiene ~ de ministro** he has the rank of minister.

categóricamente ADV categorically.

categórico ADJ categorical; *mentira* downright, outright; *orden* strict, express.

categorización NF categorization.

categorizar [1f] VT to categorize.

catenaria NF (*Elec, Ferro*) overhead power cable.

cateo NM (*Méx*) search, raid.

catequesis NF INVAR ≃ Sunday school.

catequista NMF (*CAm Rel*) catechizer.

catequizar [1f] VT **(a)** (*Ecl*) to catechize, instruct in Christian doctrine. **(b)** (*: convencer*) to win over, talk round.

catering ['katerin] NM INVAR catering; **empresa de ~** caterer's, catering firm.

caterva NF host, throng, crowd; **venir en ~** to come in a throng, come thronging.

catetada* NF piece of nonsense; stupid action, silly thing to do.

catéter NM catheter.

catetismo* NM slow-wittedness, boorishness, stupidity.

cateto NM (*pey*) peasant, country bumpkin.

catimbao NM (*And, Cono Sur*) clown, carnival clown.

catinga NF **(a)** (*And, Cono Sur*) (*olor personal*) body odour; (*de animales etc*) strong smell. **(b)** (*Cono Sur: palabra de marineros*) soldier.

catingoso ADJ (*And, Cono Sur*), **catingudo** ADJ (*And, Cono Sur*) stinking, foul-smelling.

catire ADJ (*Carib*), **catiro** ADJ (*LAm*) (*rubio*) blond, fair; (*pelirrojo*) reddish, red-haired.

catisumba(da) NF (*CAm*) lot, great number; **una ~ de** lots of, loads of.

catita NF (*LAm*) parrot.

catitear [1a] VI (*Cono Sur*) to dodder, shake (with old age).

catiusca (*Esp*) [1] ADJ: **botas ~s** rubber boots.

   [2] NF rubber boot.

catoche NM (*Méx*) bad mood, bad temper.

catódico ADJ cathodic, cathode (*atr*).

cátodo NM cathode.

catolicidad NF catholicity.

catolicismo NM (Roman) Catholicism.

católico [1] ADJ **(a)** (*Ecl*) (Roman) Catholic; **no ~** non-Catholic.

   (b) (*fig: verdadero*) *doctrina* true, infallible; certain; (*: correcto*) right, as it should be; **no estar muy ~** not to be quite right, be none too good, have sth up (with it); (*Med*) to be under the weather.

   [2] NM, **católica** NF Catholic; **no ~** non-Catholic.

Catón NM Cato.

catón NM **(a)** (*crítico*) severe critic. **(b)** (*libro*) primer, first reading book; **eso está en el ~** that is absolutely elementary.

catorce ADJ fourteen; (*fecha*) fourteenth.

catorceavo ADJ, NM fourteenth.

catorrazo NM (*Méx*), **catorro** NM (*Méx*) punch, blow.

catracho* (*CAm: pey*) [1] ADJ of El Salvador, Salvadorean.

   [2] NM, **catracha** NF native (*o* inhabitant) of El Salvador, Salvado-

rean.

catre NM (a) (*litera*) cot; (*Cono Sur: cama*) bed; (*And, Cono Sur: cuja*) bedstead; ~ **de tijera**, ~ **de viento** camp bed, bed; (*fig*) **cambiar el** ~ to change the subject. (b) ~ **de balsa** (*Cono Sur: barquito*) raft.

catrecillo NM camp stool, folding seat.

catrera NF (*Cono Sur*) bunk, bed.

catrín NM (*CAm, Méx†*) toff*, dude* (*US*).

catsup NM ketchup, catsup (*US*).

Catulo NM Catullus.

caucarse [1g] VR (*Cono Sur: persona*) to get old; (*comida*) to go stale.

caucasiano, -a (*Geog*), **caucásico, -a** (*de raza*) ADJ, NM/F Caucasian.

Cáucaso NM Caucasus.

cauce NM (a) (*de río*) river bed; (*Agr*) irrigation channel. (b) (*fig*) channel, course, way; **por el** ~ **reglamentario** through the usual channels.

cauch NM (*CAm, Carib*) couch.

cauchal NM rubber plantation.

cauchar 1 NM (*And*) rubber plantation.
2 VI (*And*) to tap (trees for rubber).

cauchera NF (a) (*Bot*) rubber plant, rubber tree. (b) (*And: cauchal*) rubber plantation.

cauchero 1 ADJ rubber (*atr*); **industria cauchera** rubber industry.
2 NM (*LAm*) rubber tapper, rubber worker.

caucho¹ NM (a) (*gen*) rubber; ~ **esponjoso** foam rubber; ~ **en bruto**, ~ **natural** natural rubber; ~ **regenerado** reclaimed rubber; ~ **sintético** synthetic rubber.
(b) (*LAm: impermeable*) raincoat, mac; (*And*) (*manta*) waterproof blanket; (*zapato*) rubber shoe; (*LAm Aut*) tyre, tire (*US*).

caucho² NM (*Carib*) couch.

cauchutado ADJ rubberized.

cauchutar [1a] VT to rubberize.

caución NF (a) (*cautela*) caution, wariness. (b) (*Jur*) pledge, security, bond; bail; **admitir a uno a** ~ to grant sb bail.

caucionar [1a] VT (a) (*prevenir*) to prevent, guard against. (b) (*Jur*) to bail, go bail for.

caudal¹ NM (a) (*de río*) volume, flow.
(b) (*abundancia*) plenty, abundance, wealth; (*de persona etc*) fortune, wealth; property; ~ **social** assets of a partnership.

caudal² ADJ caudal.

caudaloso ADJ (a) *río* large, carrying much water. (b) (*abundante*) copious, abundant; *persona etc* wealthy, rich.

caudillaje NM (a) (*jefatura*) leadership; **bajo el** ~ **de** under the leadership of. (b) (*LAm Pol: pey*) tyranny, rule by political bosses.

caudillismo NM (doctrine of) government by a strong man.

caudillo, -a NM/F (a) (*jefe*) leader, chief; strong man; (*jefe de estado*) head of state; **el C~** (*Esp*) the Caudillo, Franco. (b) (*LAm pey*) (*tirano*) tyrant; (*líder*) political boss, leader.

caula NF (*CAm, Cono Sur*) plot, intrigue.

cauri NM cowrie.

▼**causa¹** NF (a) (*gen*) cause; (*motivo*) reason, motive; (*de queja*) grounds; **veamos qué** ~ **tiene esto, veamos cuál es la** ~ **de esto** let us see what is the reason for this; ~ **final** final cause; ~ **primera** first cause; **a** ~ **de, por** ~ **de** on account of, because of, owing to; **por mi** ~ for my sake; **por poca** ~, **sin** ~ for no good reason; **¿por qué** ~? why?, for what reason?; **fuera de** ~ irrelevant.
(b) (*Pol etc*) cause; **hacer** ~ **común con** to make common cause with.
(c) (*Jur*) lawsuit; case, trial; prosecution; **instruir** ~ to take legal proceedings.

causa² NF (a) (*Cono Sur: tentempié*) snack, light meal; picnic lunch. (b) (*And: ensalada de patatas*) potato salad.

causal 1 ADJ causal.
2 NF reason, grounds.

causalidad NF causality; causation.

causante 1 ADJ causing, originating; **el coche** ~ **del accidente** the car which caused the accident, the car responsible for the accident.
2 NMF (a) (*el que causa*) causer, originator.
(b) (*Méx Fin*) taxpayer, person liable for tax.
3 NF (*LAm: causa*) cause.

causar [1a] VT (*gen*) to cause; *gasto, trabajo* to create, entail, make; *impresión* to create, make; *cólera, protesta* to provoke; ~ **risa a uno** to make sb laugh.

causativo ADJ causative.

causear [1a] VI (*Cono Sur*) to have a snack (o a light meal); to have a picnic lunch.

causeo NM (*Cono Sur*) = **causa²**.

cáustica NF caustic.

cáustico ADJ caustic (*t fig*).

cautamente ADV cautiously, warily, carefully.

cautela NF (a) (*gen*) caution, cautiousness, caginess*, wariness; **con mucha** ~ (*prevenir*) very cautiously; **tener la** ~ **de** + *infin* to take the precaution of + *ger*. (b) (*pey*) cunning.

cautelar [1a] 1 ADJ precautionary.
2 VT (a) (*prevenir*) to prevent, guard against. (b) (*LAm: defender*) to protect, defend.
3 **cautelarse** VR to be on one's guard (*de against*).

cautelosamente ADV (a) (*con cautela*) cautiously, cagily*, warily, carefully. (b) (*pey*) cunningly, craftily.

cauteloso ADJ (a) (*gen*) cautious, cagey*, wary, careful. (b) (*pey*) cunning, crafty.

cauterio NM (a) (*Med*) cautery, cauterization. (b) (*fig*) drastic remedy.

cauterizar [1f] VT (a) (*Med*) to cauterize. (b) (*fig*) to treat drastically, apply a drastic remedy to.

cautivador ADJ, **cautivante** ADJ captivating.

cautivar [1a] VT (a) (*Mil etc*) to capture, take prisoner. (b) (*fig: hechizar*) to charm, captivate, win over; to enthrall; *corazón* to steal, captivate.

cautiverio NM, **cautividad** NF captivity; (*fig*) bondage, serfdom.

cautivo, -a ADJ, NM/F captive.

cauto ADJ cautious, wary, careful.

cava¹ NF (*Agr*) digging and hoeing (*esp* of vines).

cava² NF (*bodega*) wine-cellar; (*de garaje*) pit; (*Carib: nevera*) icebox.

cava³ NM (*vino*) sparkling wine.

┌─── **CAVA** ───

i *A sparkling white or occasionally rosé Spanish wine,* **cava** *is produced mainly in the* **Penedés** *region using the traditional techniques developed in Champagne, France. To maintain the constant temperature important to the process, the wine is stored and fermented in cellars or* **cavas**, *hence the name. Varieties of* **cava** *include: medium* (**semiseco**), *dry* (**seco**), *very dry* (**brut**) *and the extra dry variety especially recommended by connoisseurs called* **brut nature**.
---

cava⁴ NF (*Carib*) closed truck, lorry.

cavador NM digger; excavator; ~ **de oro** gold digger.

cavadura NF digging, excavation.

cavar [1a] 1 VT *hoyo* to dig; *pozo* to sink; (*Agr*) to dig over, hoe, fork over; *cepas* to dig round.
2 VI (a) (*gen*) to dig.
(b) (*fig: investigar*) to delve (*en into*), go deeply (*en into*); (*meditar*) to meditate profoundly (*en on*).

cavazón NF digging, excavation.

caverna NF cave, cavern.

cavernícola 1 ADJ (a) (*lit*) cave-dwelling, cave (*atr*); **hombre** ~ caveman.
(b) (*Pol**) reactionary.
2 NMF (a) (*lit*) cave dweller, caveman, troglodyte.
(b) (*Pol**) reactionary, backwoodsman.

cavernoso ADJ (a) (*gen*) cavernous; cave (*atr*); *montaña* full of caves, honeycombed with caves. (b) *sonido, voz* resounding, deep; hollow.

caviar NM caviar(e).

cavidad NF cavity; hollow, space; ~ **nasal** nasal cavity.

cavilación NF (a) (*meditación*) deep thought, rumination. (b) (*sospecha*) (unfounded) suspicion, apprehension.

cavilar [1a] VT to ponder, consider closely; to brood over, be obsessed with.

cavilosear [1a] VI (*Carib: ilusionarse*) to harbour illusions; (*Carib: vacilar*) to vacillate, hesitate; (*CAm: chismear*) to gossip.

cavilosidad NF (unfounded) suspicion, apprehension.

caviloso ADJ (a) (*obsesionado*) brooding, obsessed; (*receloso*) suspicious, mistrustful.
(b) (*CAm: chismoso*) gossipy, backbiting.
(c) (*And*) (*agresivo*) quarrelsome, touchy; (*quisquilloso*) fussy, finicky.

cayado NM staff, stick; (*Agr*) crook; (*Ecl*) crozier.

cayena NF cayenne pepper.

cayendo *etc* V **caer**.

cayo NM (*Carib*) islet, key; **C~ Hueso** Key West.

cayubro ADJ (*And*) reddish-blond, red-haired.

cayuca: NF (*Carib*) head, bean*.

cayuco NM (*Carib*) dugout canoe.

caz NM (*de riego*) irrigation channel; (*de molino*) millrace.

caza 1 NF (a) (*gen*) hunting; (*con escopeta*) shooting, sport; (*con trampa*) trapper; (*una* ~) hunt; shoot; chase, pursuit; ~ **de brujas** witch-hunt; ~ **de control** culling; ~ **furtiva** poaching, illegal hunting; ~ **del hombre** manhunt; ~ **con hurón** ferreting; ~ **del jabalí** boar hunt(ing); ~ **de patos** duck shoot(ing); ~ **submarina** underwater fishing; ~ **del tesoro** treasure hunt; ~ **del zorro** foxhunt(ing); **andar a** (**la**) ~ **de** to go hunting for; **dar** ~ to give chase, go in pursuit; **dar** ~ **a** to hunt, chase, go after; to hunt down; **dar** ~ **a un empleo** to hunt for a job; **ir a la** ~, **ir de** ~ to go hunting, go (out) shooting.
(b) (*animales*) game; ~ **mayor** big game; ~ **menor** small game; **levantar la** ~ to put up the game; (*fig*) to give the game away.
2 NM (*Aer*) fighter, fighter-plane; ~ **de escolta** escort fighter; ~ **nocturno** night-fighter.

cazaautógrafos NMF INVAR autograph-hunter.
cazabe NM (*Carib*) cassava cake.
caza-bombardero NM fighter-bomber.
cazaclavos NM INVAR nail-puller.
cazadero NM hunting ground.
cazador NM (*gen*) hunter; (*a caballo*) huntsman; (*con trampa*) trapper; ~ **de alforja**, ~ **de pieles** trapper; ~ **de autógrafos** autograph-hunter; ~ **de cabezas** headhunter; ~ **furtivo** poacher.
cazadora NF (a) (*persona*) hunter, huntress. (b) (*prenda*) windcheater, windbreaker (*US*); (*de caza*) hunting jacket; ~ **de piel** leather jacket.
cazador-recolector NM, PL **cazadores-recolectores** hunter-gatherer.
cazadotes NM INVAR fortune-hunter.
cazaejecutivos NMF INVAR (*Com*) headhunter.
cazafortunas NF INVAR fortune-hunter, gold-digger.
cazagenios NMF INVAR talent scout, talent spotter; (*Com*) head-hunter.
cazamariposas NM INVAR butterfly-net.
cazaminas NM INVAR minesweeper.
cazamoscas NM INVAR (*Orn*) flycatcher.
cazanazis NMF INVAR Nazi-hunter.
cazar [1f] VT (a) (*buscar*) to hunt; to trap; to chase, pursue; to go after; (*esp fig*) to hunt down, track down, run to earth; **le cacé por fin en la tienda** I eventually ran him down in the shop.
(b) (*coger*) to catch; *piezas cazadas etc* to bag; *puesto etc* to land, get; (*pey*) to get hold of by trickery, wangle*; *persona* to win over (by flattery); (*pey*) to take in*; **~las al vuelo** to be pretty sharp.
(c) (*en un error*) to catch out.
cazarrecompensas NM INVAR bounty-hunter.
cazasubmarinos NM INVAR submarine-chaser.
cazatalentos NMF INVAR talent scout, talent spotter; headhunter.
cazatanques NM INVAR: **avión** ~ anti-tank aircraft.
cazatesoros NM INVAR treasure-hunter.
cazaturistas ATR: **lugar** ~ tourist trap, touristy place.
cazcalear* [1a] VI to fuss around, buzz about.
cazcarrias NFPL splashes of mud on one's clothes.
cazcarriento ADJ splashed with mud, mud-stained.
cazo NM (a) (*cacerola*) saucepan; ~ **de cola** gluepot; ~ **eléctrico** electric kettle. (b) (*cucharón*) ladle, dipper. (c) (‡: *chulo*) pimp.
cazolero NM milksop.
cazoleta NF (a) (*cazo*) (small) pan; (*de pipa*) bowl; (*de escudo*) boss; (*de sostén*) cup. (b) (*de espada*) guard. (c) (*Mec*) housing.
cazón NM dogfish, tope.
cazonete NM (*Náut*) toggle.
cazuela NF (a) (*Culin*: *vasija*) pan, cooking-pot, casserole; (*guiso*) casserole; (*LAm*: *guiso*) chicken stew. (b) (*Teat*) gallery, gods.
cazurro ADJ surly, sullen; stubborn.
cazuz NM ivy.
CC NM (a) (*Aut*) ABR de **Código de la Circulación** Highway Code. (b) (*Pol*) ABR de **Comité Central** Central Committee. (c) (*Esp*) ABR de **Coalición Canaria**.
c.c. NMPL ABR de **centímetros cúbicos** cubic centimetres, c.c.
c/c ABR de **cuenta corriente** current account, C/A.
CCAA NFPL (*Esp*) ABR de **Comunidades Autónomas**.
CCI NF ABR de **Cámara de Comercio Internacional** International Chamber of Commerce, ICC.
CCOO NFPL abr de **Comisiones Obreras**.

┌─ CCOO ─┐

i *Comisiones Obreras is the Spanish communist trade union federation. Banned under the dictatorship of General Franco, it was relegalized following Franco's death and is nowadays one of Spain's two largest trades unions, together with* **UGT**.

C.D. NM (a) ABR de **Cuerpo Diplomático** Diplomatic Corps, Corps Diplomatique, CD. (b) ABR de **Club Deportivo** sports club.
c/d (a) ABR de **en casa de** care of, c/o. (b) (*Com*) ABR de **con descuento** with discount.
C. de J. NF ABR de **Compañía de Jesús** Society of Jesus, S.J.
CD-I [ceðe'i] NM ABR de **Compact Disc Interactive** CD-I.
C.D.N. NM (*Esp*) ABR de **Centro Dramático Nacional** ≃ RADA.
CD-ROM [ceðe'rom] NM INVAR ABR de **Compact Disc Read-Only Memory** CD-ROM.
CDS NM ABR de **Centro Democrático y Social**.
CDU NF ABR de **Clasificación Decimal Universal** Dewey decimal system.
CE NM (a) ABR de **Consejo de Europa** Council of Europe. (b) ABR de **Comunidad Europea** European Community, EC.
ce¹ INTERJ hey!
ce² NF (*name of the*) letter **c**; ~ **por be** down to the tiniest detail, leaving nothing whatsoever out; **por ~ o por be** somehow or other.
ceba NF (a) (*Agr*) fattening. (b) (*LAm*: *de cañón*) charge, priming. (c) (*de horno*) stoking.

cebada NF barley; ~ **perlada** pearl barley.
cebadal NM barley field.
cebadera NF (a) (*Agr*) food bag; barley bin. (b) (*Téc*) hopper.
cebadero NM (a) (*comerciante*) barley dealer.
(b) (*mula*) leading mule (*of a team*).
(c) (*sitio*) feeding place.
(d) (*Téc*) mouth for charging a furnace.
cebado [1] ADJ (*LAm*) *animal* man-eating.
[2] NM (a) (*Agr*) fattening. (b) priming; stoking.
cebador NM (*Cono Sur Aut*) choke.
cebadura NF (a) (*Agr*) fattening.
(b) (*de cañón*) priming; (*de horno*) stoking.
cebar [1a] [1] VT (a) (*Agr*) to fatten (up), feed (up) (*con on*).
(b) *fuego, horno* to feed, stoke (up); *cañón, lámpara, bomba* to prime; *fuego artificial* to light, set off.
(c) *anzuelo, trampa* to bait.
(d) *pasión etc* to feed, nourish; *cólera* to inflame; *hope* to stimulate.
(e) (*LAm Culin*) *maté* to make, brew.
[2] VI (*tuerca etc*) to grip, catch, go on; (*clavo*) to go in.
[3] **cebarse** VR (a) (*CAm, Méx*: *tiro, fuego artificial*) to fail to go off; (*fig*) to go wrong; **se me cebó** it didn't work, I didn't manage it.
(b) ~ **con uno** to set upon sb, go for sb, attack sb; ~ **en** to vent one's fury on; to batten on, prey upon; (*peste etc*) to rage among; (*fuego*) to devour, rage in.
(c) ~ **en un estudio** to devote o.s. to a study, become absorbed in a study.
(d) ~ **en la sangre** to gloat over the blood(shed), revel in the blood(shed).
cebeísmo NM enthusiasm for CB radio.
cebeísta NMF CB radio enthusiast.
cebellina NF (*Zool*) sable.
cebiche NM (*And*) marinaded fish salad; marinaded shellfish.
cebo NM (a) (*Agr*) feed, food.
(b) (*de cañón*) charge, priming; (*Téc*) fuel, oven load.
(c) (*Pez*) bait; (*fig*) bait, lure, incentive; ~ **vivo** live bait.
cebolla NF (a) (*Bot*) onion; (*de tulipán etc*) bulb; ~ **escalonia** shallot.
(b) (*LAm hum*) watch. (c) (‡: *cabeza*) onion‡, head.
cebollado ADJ (*LAm*) cooked with onions.
cebollana NF chive.
cebolleta NF (a) (*Bot*) spring onion. (b) (‡) prick‡.
cebollino NM young onion, spring onion, onion for transplanting; (*semilla*) onion seed; (*cebollana*) chive.
cebollita NF (*LAm Bot*: t ~ **china**) spring onion.
cebollón NM (*Cono Sur*: *pey*) old bachelor.
cebollona NF (*Cono Sur*: *pey*) old maid*, spinster.
cebolludo ADJ (a) (*Bot*) bulbous. (b) (*) *persona* vulgar.
cebón [1] ADJ fat, fattened.
[2] NM fattened animal.
ceboruco NM (a) (*Carib*: *arrecife*) reef. (b) (*Méx*: *terreno quebrado*) rough rocky place. (c) (*Carib*: *maleza*) brush, scrub(land).
cebra NF (a) (*Zool*) zebra. (b) ~**s** (*Aut*) zebra crossing, crosswalk (*US*).
cebú NM zebu.
CECA ['θeka] NF (a) ABR de **Comunidad Europea del Carbón y del Acero** European Coal and Steel Community, ECSC. (b) ABR de **Confederación Española de Cajas de Ahorro**.
Ceca NF: **andar** (o **ir**) **de la ~ a la Meca** to go hither and thither, chase about all over the place.
ceca NF (*Fin*) mint.
CECE [θeθe] NF ABR de **Confederación Española de Centros de la Enseñanza**.
cecear [1a] VI to lisp; to pronounce [s] as [θ].
ceceo NM lisp; pronunciation of [s] as [θ].
ceceoso ADJ lisping, having a lisp.
Cecilia NF Cecily.
Cecilio NM Cecil.
cecina NF dried meat, smoked meat; corned beef; (*Cono Sur*) sausage.
CEDA [θeða] NF (*Esp Hist*) ABR de **Confederación Española de Derechas Autónomas**.
ceda NM: ~ **el paso** (*Aut*) priority, right of way.
cedazo NM sieve.
cedente NMF (*Jur*) assignor.
ceder [2a] [1] VT to hand over, give up; to yield (up); to part with; *territorio* to cede; *propiedad* to transfer, make over; (*Dep*) *balón* to pass; V **paso** etc.
[2] VI (a) (*rendirse*) to give in, yield (*a* to); **no ceden fácilmente a las innovaciones** they do not give in (o give way) easily to innovations; **no cede a nadie en experiencia** he is inferior to none in experience; ~ **de una pretensión** to give up a claim, renounce a claim.
(b) (*bajar*) to diminish, decline, go down; (*fiebre, viento etc*) to abate.
(c) (*suelo, cuerda etc*) to give, give way, sag.
(d) (*Dep*) to pass.
cedible ADJ transferable.

cedilla NF cedilla.

cedizo ADJ *carne* high, tainted.

cedro NM cedar.

cedrón NM (*Cono Sur*) lemon verbena.

cédula NF (*documento*) certificate, document; (*formulario*) form, blank, (slip of) paper; (*orden*) (official) order, decree; (*Com*) warrant; (*esp LAm*) identity card; **~ de aduana** customs permit; **~ en blanco** blank cheque; **~ de cambio** bill of exchange; **~ hipotecaria** mortgage bond; **~ de identidad** (*LAm*), **~ personal**, **~ de vecindad** identity card; **~ real** royal letters patent; **dar ~ a uno** to license sb.

cedulista NMF (*Fin*) holder (of a certificate *etc*).

CEE NF ABR *de* **Comunidad Económica Europea** European Economic Community, EEC.

cefalea NF severe headache, migraine.

cefálico ADJ cephalic.

céfiro NM zephyr.

cegador ADJ blinding; **brillo ~** blinding glare.

cegajoso ADJ weepy, bleary-eyed.

cegamiento NM (*de tubería*) blockage.

cegar [1h *y* 1j] **1** VT (a) *persona* to blind, make blind; **le ciega la pasión** he is blinded by passion.
(b) (*fig: tapar*) *tubo etc* to block up, stop up; *hoyo* to fill up; *puerta, ventana* to wall up.
2 VI to go blind, become blind(ed).
3 **cegarse** VR (*fig*) to become blinded (*de* by).

cegato ADJ, **cegatón** ADJ (*LAm*) short-sighted.

cegatoso ADJ = **cegajoso**.

cegué V **cegar**.

ceguedad NF, **ceguera** NF blindness (*t fig*); **~ nocturna** night blindness.

CEI NF ABR *de* **Comunidad de Estados Independientes** Commonwealth of Independent States, CIS.

ceiba NF ceiba, silk-cotton tree, bombax.

Ceilán NM (*Hist*) Ceylon.

ceilanés, -esa ADJ, NM/F (*Hist*) Ceylonese.

ceja NF (a) (*Anat*) eyebrow; **arquear las ~s** to raise one's eyebrows; **dejarse las ~s** to give of one's best; **fruncir las ~s** to knit one's brows, frown; **meterse algo entre ~ y ~** to get sth firmly into one's head; **quemarse las ~s** to work far into the night; **tener a uno entre ~ y ~** to look askance at sb; to have a grudge against sb; **tomar a uno entre ~ y ~** to take a dislike to sb.
(b) (*fig: Téc*) rim, flange; (*Cos*) edging; (*Arquit*) projection; (*de colina*) brow, crown; (*Met*) cloud-cap; (*Mús*) bridge; (*LAm: vereda*) forest path.

cejar [1a] VI (*retroceder*) to move back, back; (*fig*) to give way, back down; (*en discusión etc*) to climb down; **no ~** to keep it up, keep going, hold out; **sin ~** unflinchingly, undaunted; **no ~ en sus esfuerzos** to keep up one's efforts, not let up in one's efforts; **no ~ en su trabajo** to keep on with one's work.

cejijunto ADJ with bushy eyebrows; having brows that meet; (*fig*) scowling, frowning.

cejilla NF (a) (*abrazadera*) capo; (*con los dedos*) bridge; **hacer la ~** to make (o form) a bridge. (b) (*para instrumento de cuerda*) bridge.

cejudo ADJ beetle-browed, with bushy eyebrows.

celacanto NM coelacanth.

celada NF (a) (*emboscada*) ambush, trap; (*fig*) trick, ruse; **caer en la ~** to fall into the trap. (b) (*Hist: casco*) helmet, sallet.

celador(a) NM/F (*de edificio etc*) watchman, guard; (*de biblioteca, museo*) attendant; (*en examen*) invigilator; (*Téc*) maintenance man; (*Elec*) linesman; (*Med*) hospital porter; (*Aut*) parking attendant; (*de cárcel*) prison warder.

celaje NM (a) (*Met*) sky with clouds of varied hue; (*Náut*) clouds; **~s** sunset clouds, sky with scudding clouds.
(b) (*CAm*) (*Arte*) cloud painting; (*efecto*) cloud effect.
(c) (*Arquit*) skylight.
(b) (*fig: presagio*) (promising) sign, token.
(e) (*And, Carib: fantasma*) ghost; **como un ~** in a flash.

celar¹ [1a] **1** VT (*vigilar*) to watch over, keep a watchful eye on, keep a check on; **~ las leyes** to see that the laws are kept; **~ la justicia** to see that justice is done.
2 VI: **~ por**, **~ sobre** to watch over.

celar² [1a] VT (*ocultar*) to conceal, cover, hide.

celda NF cell; **~ de castigo** solitary confinement cell.

celdilla NF (*de colmena*) cell; (*hueco*) cavity, hollow; (*casilla*) pigeonhole; (*Arquit*) niche.

cele ADJ (*CAm*) (*color*) light green; (*inmaduro*) unripe.

celebérrimo ADJ *superl de* **célebre**.

celebración NF (a) (*acto*) celebration; holding; conclusion; solemnization. (b) (*elogio*) praise; (*aplausos*) applause, welcome; (*de ventajas etc*) preaching.

celebrante NM (*Ecl*) celebrant, officiating priest.

▼ **celebrar** [1a] **1** VT (a) *aniversario, suceso etc* to celebrate; *reunión* to hold; *entrevista, charla* to have, hold (*con* with); *tratado* to conclude

(*con* with); *fiesta* to keep, celebrate; *boda* to perform, solemnize; *misa* to say.
▼ (b) (*elogiar*) to praise; (*aplaudir*) to applaud, welcome; *ventajas* to preach, dwell on; *chiste* to laugh at, find amusing; **~ + infin** to be glad to + *infin*, be delighted to + *infin*; **lo celebro** I'm very glad; **lo celebro mucho por él** I'm very glad for his sake.
2 VI (a) (*Ecl*) to say mass.
(b) (*alegrarse*) to be glad, be delighted.
(c) (*Carib: enamorarse*) to fall in love.
3 **celebrarse** VR (*fiesta etc*) to fall, occur, be celebrated; (*reunión*) to be held, take place.

célebre ADJ (a) (*famoso*) famous, celebrated, noted (*por* for); remarkable.
(b) (*gracioso*) *persona* witty, facetious; *suceso* funny, amusing; **es ~ ¿no?**: he's a scream, isn't he?*; **¡fue ~!** it was killing!

celebridad NF (a) (*gen*) celebrity, fame. (b) (*persona*) celebrity. (c) (*fiestas etc*) celebration(s); festivity; pageant.

celeque ADJ (*CAm*) green, unripe.

célere ADJ rapid, swift.

celeridad NF speed, swiftness; **con ~** quickly, speedily, promptly.

celeste ADJ celestial, heavenly; (*Astron*) heavenly; (*color*) sky blue.

celestial ADJ (a) (*Rel*) celestial, heavenly. (b) (*fig: delicioso*) heavenly, delightful. (c) (*: tonto*) silly.

celestina NF bawd, procuress; (*de burdel*) madame.

celestinazgo NM pimping, procuring.

celibato NM (a) (*condición*) celibacy. (b) (*: soltero*) bachelor.

célibe **1** ADJ single, unmarried; celibate.
2 NMF unmarried person, bachelor, spinster; celibate.

célico ADJ (*liter*) heavenly, celestial.

celidonia NF celandine.

celinda NF (*Bot*) mock orange.

cellisca NF sleet; sleet storm.

cellisquear [1a] VI to sleet.

cello¹ NM (*Mus*) cello.

cello² NM = **celo²**.

celo¹ NM (a) (*fervor*) zeal, fervour, ardour; (*escrupulosidad*) conscientiousness; (*Rel*) religious fervour, piety; (*pey*) envy, mistrust.
(b) (*Zool*) (*de macho*) rut; (*de hembra*) heat; **caer en ~** to come into rut, come into season; **estar en ~** to be on heat, be in rut, be in season; V **época**.
(c) **~s** jealousy; **dar ~s** to give grounds for jealousy; **dar ~s a uno, infundir ~s a uno** to make sb jealous; **tener ~s de uno** to be jealous of sb.

celo² NM (*t papel ~*) adhesive tape.

celofán NM cellophane.

celosamente ADV (a) (*con fervor*) zealously; eagerly; fervently. (b) (*pey*) suspiciously, distrustfully. (c) (*con celos*) jealously.

celosía NF (a) (*reja*) lattice; (*contraventana*) slatted shutter; (*ventana*) lattice window. (b) (*celos*) jealousy.

celoso ADJ (a) (*entusiasta*) zealous (*de* for), keen (*de* about, on); eager; (*fervoroso*) fervent.
(b) (*pey*) suspicious, distrustful.
(c) (*con celos*) jealous (*de* of).
(d) (*LAm: Mec etc*) highly sensitive; (*And*) *barca* unsteady, easily upset; (*LAm*) *arma* delicate, liable to go off; **este es un fusil ~** (*LAm*) this gun is quite liable to go off.

celta **1** ADJ Celtic.
2 NMF Celt.
3 NM (*Ling*) Celtic.

Celtiberia NF Celtiberia.

celtibérico, -a, celtíbero, -a ADJ, NM/F Celtiberian.

céltico ADJ Celtic.

célula NF (a) (*Bio etc*) cell; **~ fotoeléctrica** photoelectric cell; **~ fotovoltaica** photovoltaic cell; **~s grises** grey matter; **~ germen** germ cell; **~ nerviosa** nerve cell; **~ sanguínea** blood cell; **~ de silicio** silicon chip; **~ solar** solar cell. (b) (*fig, Pol*) cell; **~ terrorista** terrorist cell. (c) (*Aer*) airframe.

celular ADJ cellular; cell (*atr*); V **coche** etc.

celulítico ADJ cellulite (*atr*); *persona* with cellulite.

celulitis NF cellulitis.

celuloide NM celluloid.

celulosa NF celulose.

CEM NM (*Esp*) ABR *de* **Centro de Estudios para la Mujer**.

cementación NF (*Téc*) case-hardening, cementation.

cementar [1a] VT (*Téc*) to case-harden, cement.

cementera NF cement works.

cementerio NM cemetery, graveyard; **~ de coches** used-car dump; **~ nuclear** nuclear waste dump.

cementero ADJ cement (*atr*).

cementista NM cement worker.

cemento NM (*Anat, Téc*) cement; (*hormigón*) concrete; (*LAm*) glue; **~ armado, ~ reforzado** (*And*) reinforced concrete.

cemita NF (*LAm*) white bread roll.
CEN NM (*Esp*) ABR *de* **Consejo de Economía Nacional.**
cena NF supper; evening meal; (*formal etc*) dinner; **~ de gala** dinner-party; formal dinner; (*Pol*) state banquet; **~ de negocios** business dinner; **~ de trabajo** working dinner; **la C~, la Última C~** the Last Supper; **C~ de Baltasar** Belshazzar's Feast.
cena-bufete NF, PL **cenas-bufete** buffet-supper.
cenáculo NM group, coterie; literary group, cenacle.
cenador NM arbour; pavilion; summerhouse.
cenaduría NF (*Méx*) eating house, restaurant.
cena-espectáculo NF, PL **cenas-espectáculo** dinner show, dinner with a floor show.
cenagal NM bog, quagmire, morass; (*fig*) tricky situation, sticky business.
cenagoso ADJ muddy, boggy.
cena-homenaje NF, PL **cenas-homenaje** formal dinner, celebratory dinner; **ofrecer una ~ a uno** to hold a dinner for sb.
cenar [1a] **1** VT to have for supper (*etc*), sup on, sup off.
2 VI to have one's supper, have dinner, dine; **invitar a uno a ~** to invite sb to dinner; **vengo cenado** I've had dinner (*etc*).
cenceño ADJ thin, skinny; *V* **pan.**
cencerrada NF charivari; rowdy music, noise, din.
cencerrear [1a] VI to jangle; (*máquina etc*) to rattle, clatter; (*puerta, carro etc*) to creak; (*Mús*) to play terribly, make a dreadful noise.
cencerreo NM jangle; rattle, clatter; creak; (*Mús*) dreadful noise.
cencerro NM cowbell; **a ~s tapados** stealthily, on the sly; **estar como un ~*** to be crazy.
cendal NM gauze; fine silk stuff, sendal.
Cenebad [θene'βað] NM (*Esp Escol*) ABR *de* **Centro Nacional de Educación Básica a Distancia.**
cenefa NF (*Cos*) edging, trimming, border; stripe, band; (*Arquit*) border, frieze.
cenetista **1** ADJ of the CNT; anarchosyndicalist; **política ~** policy of the CNT.
2 NMF member of the CNT; anarchosyndicalist.
cenicero NM (*de mesa*) ashtray; (*recogedor*) ash pan; (*vertedero*) ash pit, ash tip.
Cenicienta NF: **la ~** Cinderella; **soy la ~ de la casa** I'm always the one to be left out.
cenicienta NF (*fig*) Cinderella; (*de la casa*) dogsbody*.
ceniciento ADJ ashen, ash-coloured.
cénit NM, **cenit** NM zenith.
ceniza NF ash, ashes; cinder; **~s** (*de persona*) ashes, mortal remains; **huir de las ~s y dar en las brasas** to jump out of the frying pan into the fire; **reducir algo a ~s** to reduce sth to ashes.
cenizo **1** ADJ **(a)** (*de color*) ashen, ash-coloured.
(b) (*de mal augurio*) ill-omened; (*alarmante*) alarming.
2 NM **(a)** (*Bot*) goosefoot.
(b) (*: *gafe*) jinx*, hoodoo; **es un avión ~** it's a plane with a jinx on it*; **entrar el ~ en casa** to have a spell of bad luck; **tener el ~** to have a jinx on one*.
(c) (*persona*) bringer of bad luck; wet blanket.
cenobio NM monastery.
cenobita NMF coenobite, monk, nun.
cenojil NM garter.
cenorrio* NM posh dinner*, slap-up do*.
cenotafio NM cenotaph.
cenote NM (*CAm, Méx*) cenote, deep rock-pool, natural well.
censal ADJ = **censual.**
censado NM census-taking.
censar [1a] VT (*Cono Sur*) to take a census of.
censista NMF census official, census taker.
censo NM **(a)** (*de habitantes*) census; **~ de tráfico** traffic census, traffic count; **levantar el ~ de** to take a census of.
(b) (*Fin*) tax; (annual) ground rent; mortgage; leasehold.
(c) (*Pol*) **~ electoral** electoral roll, (*fig*) electorate.
(d) ser un ~* to be a constant drain, be a financial burden.
censor(a) NM/F **(a)** (*Pol*) censor.
(b) (*Univ*) proctor.
(c) (*Com, Fin*) **~ de cuentas** auditor; **~ jurado de cuentas** chartered accountant.
(d) (*fig: crítico*) critic.
censual ADJ **(a)** (*gen*) census (*atr*), relating to a census. **(b)** (*Fin*) tax (*atr*), mortage (*atr*) etc. **(c)** (*Pol: de elecciones*) electoral, relating to the electoral roll.
censura NF **(a)** (*Pol: acto*) censorship; censoring; **someter a la ~** to censor.
(b) (*oficina*) censor's office.
(c) (*crítica*) censure, stricture, criticism; (*reproche*) blame, reproach; (*Liter etc*) criticism, judgement; **digno de ~** censurable, blameworthy.
(d) (*Com, Fin*) **~ de cuentas** auditing.

censurable ADJ censurable, reprehensible, blameworthy.
censurar [1a] VT **(a)** (*Pol*) to censor. **(b)** (*criticar*) to censure, condemn, criticize, blame, reproach; to find fault with; (*Liter etc*) to criticize, judge.
censurista **1** ADJ censorious.
2 NMF critic, faultfinder.
centaura NF centaury.
centauro NM centaur.
centavo **1** ADJ hundredth.
2 NM **(a)** (*Mat*) hundredth (part). **(b)** (*Fin*) *in LAm currencies*, centavo, *one-hundredth part of a peso etc.*
centella NF spark (*t fig*); flash of lightning.
centelleante ADJ **(a)** (*gen*) sparkling; gleaming, glinting, twinkling; flashing. **(b)** (*fig*) sparkling.
centell(e)ar [1a] VI **(a)** (*gen*) to sparkle; to gleam, glint, glitter; (*estrella*) to twinkle; (*relámpago*) to flash. **(b)** (*fig*) to sparkle.
centelleo NM sparkle, sparkling; gleam(ing); glinting; flashing.
centena NF hundred.
centenada NF hundred.
centenal NM, **centenar¹** NM (*Agr*) rye field.
centenar² NM hundred; **a ~es** by the hundred, by hundreds.
centenario **1** ADJ centenary, centennial.
2 NM centenary, centennial.
3 NM, **centenaria** NF (*persona*) centenarian.
centeno NM rye.
centésima NF hundredth (part).
centesimal ADJ centesimal.
centésimo **1** ADJ hundredth.
2 NM hundredth (part); *in LAm currencies*, centésimo, *one-hundredth part of a balboa etc.*
centígrado ADJ centigrade.
centigramo NM centigram.
centilitro NM centilitre.
centímetro NM centimetre; *see also* KILOS, METROS, AÑOS .
céntimo **1** ADJ hundredth.
2 NM hundredth part (*esp* of a peseta), cent; **no tiene un ~** he hasn't a penny, he hasn't a bean*; **no vale un ~** it's worthless.
centinela NMF (*Mil*) sentry, guard, sentinel; (*en atraco etc*) look-out man; **estar de ~** to be on guard, do sentry duty; **hacer ~** (*fig*) to keep watch, be on the look-out.
centiplicado ADJ hundredfold.
centolla NF, **centollo** NM spider crab, (large) crab.
centón NM **(a)** (*Cos*) patchwork quilt, crazy quilt. **(b)** (*Liter*) cento.
central **1** ADJ central; middle; **en los días ~es de la semana** in midweek, midway through the week.
2 NF (*Com*) head office, headquarters; (*Téc*) plant, station; (*Telec*) exchange, (*privada*) switchboard; (*sindicato*) trade union; **~ (azucarera)** (*Carib*) sugar-mill; **~ de bombeo** pumping-station; **~ de correos** head post office, general post office; **~ depuradora** waterworks; **~ eléctrica, ~ de energía** power-station; **~ lechera** dairy; **~ nuclear** nuclear power-station; **~ sindical** trade union; **~ telefónica, ~ de teléfonos** telephone exchange; **~ de teléfonos automática** automatic telephone exchange; **~ de teléfonos manual** (*o* **con servicio a mano**) manual telephone exchange; **~ térmica de fuel** oil-fired power-station.
centralidad NF centrality, central importance.
centralismo NM centralism.
centralista **1** ADJ centralist, centralizing.
2 NMF centralist.
3 NM (*Carib*) sugar-mill owner.
centralita NF (*Telec*) switchboard.
centralización NF centralization.
centralizado **1** ADJ centralized; **cierre ~** central locking.
2 NM centralization.
centralizar [1f] VT to centralize.
▼ **centrar** [1a] **1** VT **(a)** (*gen*) to centre (*en* on); *atención, esfuerzos* to concentrate, focus (*en* on); *novela etc* to base, centre (*en* on). **(b)** (*Mil*) *fuego* to concentrate, aim; (*Fot*) to focus (*en* on).
▼ **2 centrarse** VR **(a)** **~ en** to centre on, be centred on; to focus on; to concentrate on. **(b)** (*en un empleo*) to settle in, get to know the ropes.
céntrico ADJ central, middle; **punto ~** (*fig*) focal point; **es muy ~** it's very central, it's very convenient; **un restaurante ~** a restaurant in the centre of town, a downtown restaurant.
centrífuga NF centrifuge.
centrifugadora NF (*para ropa*) spin-dryer; (*Téc*) centrifuge.
centrifugar [1h] VT to centrifuge; *colada* to spin.
centrífugo ADJ centrifugal.
centrípeto ADJ centripetal.
centrismo NM centrism, political doctrine of the centre.
centrista **1** ADJ centrist, of a centrist party (*o* policy *etc*).
2 NMF centrist, member of a centrist party.

➤ LENGUA Y USO: **centrar: 2a →** 53.2, 53.6

centro NM (**a**) (*gen*) centre, middle; (*Mat, Pol*) centre; (*de actividad*) centre, hub; (*de incendio*) seat; **~ de acogida para mujeres maltratadas** refuge for battered wives; **~ de atracción** centre of attraction, main attraction; **~ de cálculo** computer centre; **~ cívico** community centre; **~ comercial** shopping centre; shopping precinct, mall (*US*); **~ de convivencia social** social centre, community centre; **~ de coordinación** (*policía*) operations room; **~ de costos** cost centre; **~ demográfico, ~ de población** centre of population; **~ de detención** detention centre; **~ docente** teaching institution; **~ espacial** space centre; **~ de fricción** trouble spot; **~ de gravedad** centre of gravity; **~ de interés** centre of interest, main point of interest; **~ de intrigas** centre of intrigue; **~ de mesa** centrepiece; **~ neurálgico** nerve-centre (*t fig*); **~ de orientación familiar, ~ de planificación familiar** family-planning clinic; **~ recreacional** (*Carib*) sports (*o* leisure) centre; **~ de salud** health centre; **~ social** community centre; **estar en su ~** (*fig*) to be in one's element; **ser de ~** (*Pol*) to be a moderate; **ir al ~** (*de ciudad*) to go into the centre, go into town, go downtown.
(**b**) (*fig: objetivo*) goal, purpose, objective.
(**c**) (*Dep*) centre; **~ de(l) campo** midfield; **delantero ~** centre-forward; **medio ~** centre-half.
(**d**) (*Dep: golpe*) centre.
(**e**) (*CAm: juego de ropa*) trousers and waistcoat; (*Carib, Méx: juego de ropa*) matching waistcoat and jacket; (*And, Carib, Méx: enaguas*) underskirt; (*And: falda*) thick flannel skirt.

centroafricano ADJ Central African; **la República Centroafricana** the Central African Republic.

Centroamérica NF Central America.

centroamericano, -a ADJ, NM/F Central American.

centrocampismo NM midfield play.

centrocampista NMF midfield player.

centrocampo NM midfield.

centroderecha NM centre-right.

Centroeuropa NF Central Europe.

centroeuropeo, -a ADJ, NM/F Central European.

centroizquierda NM centre-left.

cént(s) ABR *de* **céntimo(s)** cent(s), c.

centuplicar [1g] VT to increase a hundredfold (*t fig*), increase enormously.

centuplo ① ADJ hundredfold, centuple.
② NM centuple.

centuria NF century.

centurión NM centurion.

cenutrio* NM twit*, twerp*.

cénzalo NM mosquito.

cenzontle NM (*Méx*) mockingbird.

ceñido ADJ (**a**) *vestido* tight, tight-fitting, close-fitting, clinging; narrow-waisted; *curva* sharp.
(**b**) (*fig: frugal*) sparing, frugal, thrifty; moderate; **~ al tema** keeping close to the point; **~ y corto** brief and to the point.

ceñidor NM sash, girdle.

ceñir [3h *y* 3k] ① VT (**a**) (*rodear*) to girdle, encircle, surround; (*Mil*) to besiege; **la muralla ciñe la ciudad** the wall surrounds the city; **~ una ciudad con una muralla** to encircle a city with a wall, throw a wall round a city.
(**b**) (*ponerse*) to fasten round one's waist; *espada* to gird on; *cinturón etc* to put on; **~ espada** to wear a sword.
(**c**) *frente* to bind, encircle, wreathe (*con, de* with).
(**d**) (*ajustar*) to fit tight; (*acortar*) to tighten (up), draw in; **el vestido ciñe bien el cuerpo** the dress fits well; **habrá que ceñirlo más** we shall have to draw it in.
(**e**) (*fig: abreviar*) to shorten, cut down, condense.
② **ceñirse** VR (**a**) **~ algo** to put sth on; **se ciñó la espada** he put his sword on; **~ la corona** to take the crown.
(**b**) (*Fin etc*) to reduce expenditure, tighten one's belt; (*al hablar*) to limit o.s., be brief; **~ a un tema** to limit o.s. to a subject, concentrate on a subject; **~ al asunto** to stick to the matter in hand; **te ciñes muy a la derecha en la carretera** you keep very close to the right when you're driving.

ceño NM (**a**) (*expresión*) frown, scowl; **arrugar el ~, fruncir el ~** to frown, knit one's brows; **mirar con ~** (VT) to frown at, scowl at, give black looks to; (VI) to frown, scowl, look black.
(**b**) (*Met*) threatening appearance.

ceñudo ADJ *persona* frowning, grim; *mirada* black, grim.

CEOE NF ABR *de* **Confederación Española de Organizaciones Empresariales** ≃ Confederation of British Industry, CBI.

CEP NM (*Esp*) ABR *de* **Centro de Educación de Profesores** teacher training centre.

cepa NF (**a**) (*Bot*) stump; (*de vid*) stock; vine; (*Zool: de cuerno, cola*) root; (*Arquit*) pier.
(**b**) (*fig: origen*) stock; **de buena ~** (*persona*) of good stock, (*cosa*) of high quality; **de buena ~ castellana** of good Castilian stock.

(**c**) (*Méx: hoyo*) pit, trench.

CEPAL [se'pal] NF ABR *de* **Comisión Económica para América Latina** Economic Commission for Latin America, ECLA.

cepero NM trapper.

cepillado NM brushing, brush (*act*); planing; **se elimina con un suave ~** it goes away with a gentle brush.

cepilladura NF = **cepillado**.

cepillar [1a] ① VT (**a**) (*gen*) to brush; (*Téc*) to plane (down).
(**b**) (*Univ**) to plough*.
(**c**) (*LAm: lisonjear*) to flatter, butter up*.
(**d**) (‡: *robar*) to rip off‡.
(**e**) (‡: *ganar*) to win, take (*a* from).
(**f**) (‡: *matar*) to bump off‡.
(**g**) (*pegar azotes*) to spank.
② **cepillarse** VR (**a**) **~ a uno‡** to bump sb off‡, knock sb off‡.
(**b**) **~ algo‡** to rip sth off‡.
(**c**) **~ a una‡‡** to screw sb‡‡.

cepillo NM (**a**) (*gen*) brush; **~ de baño** bath-brush; **~ de dientes** toothbrush; **~ para el pelo** hairbrush; **~ de púas metálicas** wire brush; **~ de (*o* para) la ropa** clothes-brush; **~ para el suelo** scrubbing brush; **~ para las uñas** nailbrush; **pelo cortado al ~** crew-cut.
(**b**) (*Téc*) plane.
(**c**) (*Ecl*) poorbox, alms box.
(**d**) (*LAm: adulador*) flatterer, creep‡.

cepillón‡ ① ADJ soapy*.
② NM, **cepillona** NF creep‡.

cepo NM (**a**) (*Bot*) branch, bough.
(**b**) (*Caza*) trap, snare; (*Mil*) mantrap; stocks; (*Aut*) wheel clamp; **~ conejero** snare; **~ lobero** wolf-trap.
(**c**) (*Mec*) reel; (*de yunque, ancla*) stock.
(**d**) (*Ecl*) poorbox, alms box.

ceporrez* NF idiocy, foolishness.

ceporro* NM (**a**) (*idiota*) twit*. (**b**) **estar como un ~** to be very fat.

CEPSA ['θepsa] NF (*Com*) ABR *de* **Compañía Española de Petróleos, Sociedad Anónima**.

CEPYME [θe'pime] NF ABR *de* **Confederación Española de la Pequeña y Mediana Empresa**.

cequión NM (*Cono Sur*) large irrigation channel.

cera NF (**a**) (*gen*) wax; **~ de abejas** beeswax; **~ depilatoria** depilatory; **~ de lustrar** wax polish; **~ de los oídos** earwax; **~ para suelos** floorpolish; **ser como una ~** to be as gentle as a lamb.
(**b**) **~s** honeycomb.
(**c**) (*And, Méx: vela*) candle.

cerafolio NM chervil.

cerámica NF (**a**) (*Arte*) ceramics, pottery. (**b**) (*objetos*) pottery (*t* **~s**).

cerámico ADJ ceramic.

ceramista NMF potter.

cerbatana NF (*Mil etc*) blowpipe; (*juguete*) peashooter; (*Med*) ear trumpet.

cerca¹ NF fence, wall; **~ eléctrica** electrified fence.

cerca² ① ADV (**a**) near, nearby, close; **de ~** closely; (*Mil*) at close range; **examinar algo de ~** to examine sth closely; **aquí ~** near here; **por aquí ~** nearby, hereabouts, somewhere round here.
(**b**) (*Cono Sur*) **~ nuestro** (*etc*) near us (*etc*).
② **~ de** PREP (**a**) (*lugar*) near, close to; in the neighbourhood of; **estar ~ de + infin** to be near + *ger*, be on the point of + *ger*.
(**b**) (*cantidad*) nearly, about; (*tiempo*) nearly; **hay ~ de 8 toneladas** there are about 8 tons; **son ~ de las 6** it's nearly 6 o'clock.
(**c**) (*Pol*) to; **embajador ~ de la corte de Ruritania** ambassador to the court of Ruritania.
③ NM (**a**) **tiene buen ~** it looks all right close up.
(**b**) (*Arte*) **~s** objects in the foreground.

cercado NM (**a**) (*recinto*) enclosure; (*huerto*) enclosed garden, fenced field, orchard.
(**b**) (*cerca*) fence, wall; **~ eléctrico** electrified fence.
(**c**) (*And: ejido*) communal lands.
(**d**) (*And Hist*) state capital and surrounding towns.

cercanía NF (**a**) (*proximidad*) nearness, closeness, proximity.
(**b**) **~s** (*vecindad*) neighbourhood, vicinity; surroundings.
(**c**) **~s** (*de ciudad*) outskirts, outer suburbs, outlying areas; **tren de ~s** suburban train.

cercano ADJ *pueblo etc* nearby, neighbouring; *pariente* close; *muerte, fin* approaching; **~ a** near, close to.

Cercano Oriente NM Near East.

cercar [1g] VT (**a**) (*poner valla a*) to fence in, wall in, hedge; to enclose; (*rodear*) to encircle, surround, ring (*de* with); (*enemigo, montañas etc*) to hem in.
(**b**) (*Mil*) *ciudad* to surround, besiege; *tropas* to surround, cut off, encircle.

cercén ADV: **cortar a ~** to extirpate, take out (*o* off) completely; **cortar un brazo a ~** to cut an arm off completely.

cercenar [1a] VT (**a**) (*gen*) to clip; to cut the edge off, trim the edges of; *cabo, punta* to cut off, slice off; *miembro* to cut off, amputate; *moneda* to clip.

(b) *(fig) gastos* to cut down, reduce; *texto etc* to shorten, cut down; *(suprimir)* to delete, cut out.

cerceta NF teal, garganey.

cerciorar [1a] ①1 VT to inform, assure.

②2 **cerciorarse** VR to find out; to make sure; ~ **de** to find out about, ascertain; to make sure of.

cerco NM **(a)** *(Agr etc)* enclosure; *(LAm: valla)* fence, hedge; *(And)* small walled property; **saltar el ~** *(Cono Sur Pol)* to jump on the bandwagon.

(b) *(Téc)* *(de rueda)* rim; *(de barril)* hoop; *(Arquit)* casing, frame; *(de suciedad etc)* ring, rim, mark.

(c) *(Astron, Met)* halo.

(d) *(grupo)* social group, circle.

(e) *(Mil)* siege; **alzar** (o **levantar**) **el ~** to raise the siege; **poner ~ a** to lay siege to.

cercón ADV *(LAm)* rather close.

cerda NF **(a)** *(Zool)* sow. **(b)** *(pelo)* bristle; horsehair; *(Caza)* snare, noose. **(c)** (‡: *puta)* slut; whore.

cerdada* NF dirty trick; nasty thing (to do).

cerdear [1a] VI **(a)** *(Mús)* to scratch, rasp, grate; *(Mec)* to work badly, play up. **(b)** *(*: dudar)* to hedge, jib, hold back. **(c)** *(*: hacer trampa)* to play a dirty trick.

Cerdeña NF Sardinia.

cerdito NM, **cerdita** NF piglet.

cerdo ①1 NM **(a)** *(Zool)* pig; ~ **ibérico** Iberian pig; ~ **salvaje** wild pig.

(b) ~ **marino** *(Zool)* porpoise.

(c) *(Culin)* pork.

(d) *(fig: persona)* dirty person, slovenly fellow; *(en lo moral)* swine; ~ **machista** male chauvinist pig.

②2 ADJ (*) **(a)** *(sucio)* dirty, filthy.

(b) *(vil)* rotten*.

cerdoso ADJ *animal* shaggy, hairy, bristly; *barba* bristly, stubbly.

cereal ①1 ADJ cereal; grain *(atr)*.

②2 NM cereal; ~es cereals, grain; ~es *(Culin)* cereals, cornflakes; ~es **forrajeros** grain used as animal feed, fodder grain.

cerealista NMF grain farmer.

cerealístico ADJ grain *(atr)*, cereal *(atr)*.

cereal-pienso NM, PL **cereales-pienso** grain used as animal feed, fodder grain.

cerebelo NM cerebellum.

cerebral ADJ cerebral, brain *(atr)*; *(pey)* scheming, calculating; shrewd.

cerebralismo NM intellectualism, cerebralism.

cerebro NM brain; cerebrum; *(fig)* brains; intelligence; ~ **electrónico** electronic brain; ~ **gris** éminence grise; **es el ~ del equipo** he is the brains of the team; **estrujar el ~** to rack one's brains; **ser un ~** to be brilliant.

ceremonia NF **(a)** *(acto)* ceremony; *(Ecl)* ceremony, service; **hacer ~s** to stand on ceremony.

(b) *(cualidad)* ceremony, ceremoniousness; formality; pomp; **falta de ~** informality; **reunión de ~** formal meeting, ceremonial meeting; **reunirse de ~** to meet with all due ceremony; **por ~** as a matter of form; **hablar sin ~** to speak informally; **hacer algo sin ~** to do sth without fuss.

ceremonial ADJ, NM ceremonial.

ceremoniosamente ADV ceremoniously; formally; stiffly; with an excess of politeness.

ceremonioso ADJ ceremonious; *persona, vestido, saludo, visita etc* formal; *(pey)* stiff, over-polite.

céreo ADJ wax *(atr)*, waxen.

cerería NF wax-chandler's shop, chandlery.

cerero NM wax chandler.

cereza NF cherry; **un suéter rojo ~** a cherry-red jumper; ~ **silvestre** wild cherry.

cerezal NM cherry orchard.

cerezo NM *(árbol)* cherry tree; *(madera)* cherry wood.

cerilla NF **(a)** *(fósforo)* match; *(vela)* wax taper. **(b)** *(Anat)* earwax.

cerillazo NM: **pegar un ~ a** to set a match to.

cerillera NF, **cerillero** NM **(a)** *(vendedor)* street vendor of tobacco. **(b)** *(LAm: cajita de cerillas)* matchbox.

cerillo NM *(CAm, Méx)* match.

cernedor NM sieve.

cernejas NFPL fetlock.

cerner [2g] ①1 VT **(a)** *(Téc)* to sift, sieve.

(b) *(fig: observar)* to scan, watch.

②2 VI **(a)** *(Bot)* to bud, blossom.

(b) *(Met)* to drizzle.

③3 **cernerse** VR **(a)** *(Orn: sin moverse)* to hover; *(subir)* to soar; *(Aer)* to circle; *(helicóptero)* to hover; ~ **sobre** to be poised over, hang over; *(fig)* to threaten, hang over.

(b) *(persona)* to swagger.

cernícalo NM **(a)** *(Orn)* kestrel. **(b)** (*: *tonto)* lout, dolt. **(c)** **coger un ~*** to get tight*. **(d)** *(And Orn)* hawk, falcon.

cernidillo NM **(a)** *(modo de andar)* swagger, rolling gait. **(b)** *(Met)* drizzle.

cernido NM **(a)** *(acto)* sifting; *(harina)* sifted flour. **(b)** *(And Met)* drizzle.

cernidor NM sieve.

cernidura NF sifting.

cero NM **(a)** *(gen)* nothing; nought; *(Fís etc)* zero; *(Dep)* **por 3 goles a ~** by 3 goals to nil, by 3 goals to nought; **empatar a ~(s)** to draw nil-nil, play a no-score draw; **estamos a 40 contra ~** *(Tenis)* the game stands at 40-love; **estoy a ~*** I'm broke*; **estamos a ~ de leche*** we're out of milk; **yo en eso estoy ~*** I'm no good at that; ~ **absoluto** absolute zero; **8 grados bajo ~** 8 degrees below zero, 8 degrees below freezing, 8 degrees of frost; **desde las ~ horas** from the start of the day; **es un ~ a la izquierda** he's useless, he's a nobody; **tendremos que partir (nuevamente) de ~** *(fig)* we shall have to start from scratch again.

(b) (*: *coche-patrulla)* police car.

ceroso ADJ waxen; waxy, waxlike.

cerote NM **(a)** *(Téc)* (shoemaker's) wax.

(b) (*: *miedo)* panic, funk*.

(c) *(CAm, Méx: excremento)* piece of human excrement, stool; **estar hecho un ~** *(And)*, **tener ~** *(Cono Sur, Méx)* to be covered in dirt (o muck).

cerotear [1a] VT *hilo* to wax.

cerquillo NM **(a)** *(de pelo)* fringe of hair round the tonsure; *(Méx)* *(fleco)* fringe; *(rizos)* kiss-curls. **(b)** *(Téc)* seam, welt.

cerquita ADV quite near, close by.

cerradero ①1 ADJ *dispositivo* locking, fastening; **caja cerradera** box that can be locked, box with a lock.

②2 NM locking device; clasp, fastener; *(de cerradura)* strike, keeper; *(de monedero)* purse strings.

cerrado ADJ **(a)** *(gen)* closed, shut; *(con llave)* locked; *puño* clenched; ~ **al vacío** vacuum-packed; ~ **por obras** closed for repairs (o alterations); **aquí huele a ~** it smells stuffy in here, it's thick in here.

(b) *asunto* obscure, incomprehensible.

(c) *(Met) sky* cloudy, overcast; *atmósfera* heavy; *noche* dark, black.

(d) *curva* sharp, tight.

(e) *barba* thick, full.

(f) *persona (callado)* quiet, reserved, uncommunicative; *(pey)* secretive; ~ **de mollera** *(poco inteligente)* dense*, dim*; *(obstinado)* pigheaded.

(g) *persona (típico)* typical, all-too-typical; **es un eslobodio ~** he's a typical Slobodian, he has all the worst features of the Slobodian.

(h) *(Ling) vocal* close.

(i) *(Ling) persona* with a broad accent; *acento* broad, marked, strong; *habla* thick, broad; **habló con ~ acento gallego** he spoke with a strong Galician accent.

(j) **a precio ~** at a fixed price, at a firm price.

(k) *(And, Cono Sur: terco)* pigheaded, stubborn.

cerradura NF **(a)** *(acto)* closing, shutting; locking.

(b) *(dispositivo)* lock; ~ **de combinación** combination lock; ~ **de golpe**, ~ **de muelle** spring lock; ~ **de seguridad** safety lock.

cerraja NF **(a)** *(cerradura)* lock. **(b)** *(Bot)* sow-thistle.

cerrajería NF **(a)** *(oficio)* locksmith's craft (o trade). **(b)** *(tienda)* locksmith's (shop).

cerrajero NM locksmith.

cerrar [1j] ①1 VT **(a)** *caja, ojos, boca, puerta etc* to close, shut; *puerta (con llave)* to lock (up); to bolt; *puño* to clench, close; *carta* to seal; *filas* to close; *(Elec, TV etc)* to switch off; ~ **algo con llave** to lock sth.

(b) *agujero, brecha, tubo etc* to block (up), stop (up), close, obstruct; *puerto* to close; **han cerrado la frontera** they have closed the frontier; **la carretera está cerrada por la nieve** the road is blocked by snow.

(c) *terreno, zona* to enclose, close off, fence (in), wall (in).

(d) *grifo, gas, agua etc* to turn off.

(e) *(Elec) circuito* to make, close, complete.

(f) *tienda, negocio* to shut, close; *(para siempre)* to shut up; *fábrica* to close (down).

(g) *desfile* to bring up the rear of; ~ **la marcha** to come last, bring up the rear.

(h) *cuenta, debate, narración* to close; *programa* to end, be the final item in.

(i) *trato* to seal, strike.

②2 VI **(a)** *(gen)* to close, shut; **la puerta cierra mal** the door doesn't close properly; **cerramos a las 9** we close at 9; **dejar una puerta sin ~** to leave a door open.

(b) *(noche)* to come down, set in; *(invierno)* to close in.

(c) ~ **con uno** to close with sb, grapple with sb; ~ **con el enemigo** to come to close quarters with the enemy.

③3 **cerrarse** VR **(a)** *(gen)* to close, shut; *(herida)* to close up, heal;

(*Mil*) to close ranks.

(b) (*Met*) to cloud over, become overcast.

(c) ~ **en** + *infin* to persist in + *ger*, go on stubbornly + *ger*.

cerrazón NF **(a)** (*Met*) threatening sky, storm clouds. **(b)** (*Cono Sur*: *niebla*) thick fog, thick mist. **(c)** (*And*: *de sierra*) spur. **(d)** (*fig*: *punto muerto*) impasse. **(e)** (*cualidad*) small-mindedness, narrow-mindedness; **su ~ hacia** his blind opposition to, his unreasoning hostility to.

cerrero ADJ **(a)** *animal* wild; untamed, unbroken; *persona* rough, uncouth. **(b)** (*And, Carib*: *sin azúcar*) unsweetened; (*agrio*) bitter; *pan etc* ordinary; (*Carib*) *persona* simple, ordinary.

cerril ADJ **(a)** *terreno* rough; mountainous. **(b)** *animal* wild; untamed, unbroken; *persona* (*inculto*) rough, uncouth; (*terco*) obstinate; (*de miras estrechas*) small-minded.

cerrilismo NM roughness, uncouthness; obstinacy; small-mindedness.

cerrillar [1a] VT *moneda* to mill.

cerro NM **(a)** (*colina*) hill; **andar** (*o* **echarse, ir**) **por los ~s de Úbeda** to wander from the point; to talk a lot of rubbish.

(b) (*Zool*) neck; backbone, back; **en ~** bareback.

(c) (*Téc*) bunch of cleaned hemp (*o* flax).

(d) (*And*: *montón*) lot, heap; **un ~ de** a heap (*o* pile) of.

cerrojazo NM slamming; **dar ~** to slam the bolt; (*fig*) to end unexpectedly; (*Parl*) to close (the session) unexpectedly; **dar ~ a uno** to slam the door in sb's face.

cerrojo NM bolt, latch; (*Dep*: t **táctica de ~**) defensive play, negative play; **echar el ~** to bolt the door.

certamen NM competition, contest; **~ de belleza** beauty contest.

certeramente ADV accurately, unerringly.

certero ADJ **(a)** *hecho etc* accurate, sure, certain.

(b) *tiro* accurate, well-aimed; telling; *puntería* excellent; *tirador* sure, good, crack.

(c) (*enterado*) well-informed.

▼ **certeza** NF certainty; **tener la ~ de que ...** to know for certain that ..., have the certain knowledge that ...

certidumbre NF certainty; conviction.

certificable ADJ certifiable; (*Correos*) registrable, that can be registered.

certificación NF certification; (*Correos*) registration; (*Jur*) attestation.

certificado [1] ADJ certified; (*Correos*) registered.

[2] NM **(a)** (*gen*) certificate; **~ de aeronavegabilidad** certificate of airworthiness; **~ de aptitud** testimonial; **~ de ciudadanía** naturalization papers; **~ de defunción** death certificate; **~ de depósito** certificate of deposit; **~ escolar, ~ de escolaridad** certificate of completion of *EGB* course (at age 14); **~ médico** medical certificate; **~ de origen** certificate of origin; **~ de penales** good-conduct certificate; **~ de vacuna** vaccination certificate.

(b) (*Correos*) registered packet, registered item.

certificar [1g] VT **(a)** to certify; to guarantee, vouch for; **~ que ...** to certify that ... **(b)** (*Correos*) to register.

certitud NF certainty, certitude.

cerúleo ADJ sky blue.

cerumen NM earwax.

cerval ADJ deer (*atr*), deer-like.

cervantino ADJ Cervantine; relating to Cervantes; **estilo ~** Cervantine style; **estudios ~s** Cervantes studies.

cervantista NMF Cervantes scholar, specialist in Cervantes.

cervatillo NM fawn.

cervato NM fawn.

cervecera NF brewery.

cervecería NF **(a)** (*fábrica*) brewery. **(b)** (*bar*) bar, public house.

cervecero [1] ADJ beer (*atr*); **la industria cervecera** the brewing industry. [2] NM brewer.

cerveza NF beer; **~ de barril, ~ (servida) al grifo** draught beer, beer on draught; **~ de botella, ~ en botellas, ~ embotellada** bottled beer; **~ clara** light beer; **~ negra** dark beer, stout; **~ de sifón** (*CAm*) draught beer.

cervical ADJ (*del cuello*) neck (*atr*), cervical; (*del útero*) cervical.

Cervino NM: **el Monte ~** Mont Cervin, the Matterhorn.

cerviz NF **(a)** (*cuello*) neck, nape of the neck; **de dura ~** stubborn, headstrong, wild; **bajar** (*o* **doblar**) **la ~** to submit, bow down; **levantar la ~** to lift one's head up (again).

(b) (*útero*) cervix.

cervuno ADJ deer-like; deer-coloured.

cesación NF cessation; suspension, stoppage; **~ del fuego** ceasefire.

cesante [1] ADJ out of a job, out of office; discharged; retired; redundant; (*LAm*) unemployed; **el gobierno ~** the outgoing government.

[2] NM *civil* (*o* *public*) *servant who has been made redundant*; (*LAm*) unemployed person.

cesantear [1a] VT (*Cono Sur*) to dismiss, sack*.

cesantía NF **(a)** (*condición*) state of being a *cesante*, redundancy; (*suspensión*) suspension; (*Cono Sur*) dismissal, sacking*; unemployment.

(b) (*pago*) retirement pension, redundancy compensation, severance pay.

cesar [1a] [1] VT **(a)** (*gen*) to cease, stop; *pagos, trabajo* to stop, suspend.

(b) (*despedir*) *obrero* to dismiss, sack*, fire*; *funcionario, ministro* to remove from office; **ha sido cesado de su cargo** he has been dismissed from his post; **le cesaron en el trabajo** they sacked him from his work.

[2] VI **(a)** (*gen*) to cease, stop; to desist; **~ de hacer algo** to stop doing sth, leave off doing sth; **no cesa de hablar** she never stops talking; **sin ~** ceaselessly, incessantly.

(b) (*empleado*) to leave, quit; (*jubilarse*) to retire; **~ en el trabajo** to give up one's work, retire from work.

César NM Caesar.

cesaraugustano = **zaragozano**.

cesárea NF (*Med*) Caesarean (section).

cesáreo ADJ **(a)** Caesarean; imperial. **(b)** (*Med*) **operación cesárea** Caesarean operation.

cese NM **(a)** (*gen*) cessation; suspension, stoppage: **~ de alarma** (*Mil*) all-clear signal; **~ de fuego, ~ de hostilidades** ceasefire; **~ de pagos** suspension of payments, stoppage of payments; **~ temporal de los bombardeos** temporary halt to the bombing.

(b) (*de funcionario*) dismissal, compulsory retirement; (*de obrero*) sacking*, firing*; **dar el ~ a uno** to retire sb; to sack sb*.

Ceseden [θese'ðen] NM (*Esp*) ABR *de* **Centro Superior de Estudios de la Defensa Nacional.**

CESID, Cesid [θe'siδ] NM (*Esp*) ABR *de* **Centro Superior de Información de la Defensa** (*military intelligence service*).

cesio NM caesium, cesium (*US*).

cesión NF **(a)** (*Pol etc*) cession. **(b)** (*Jur*) cession, granting, transfer; **~ de bienes** surrender of property.

cesionario, -a NM/F grantee, assign.

cesionista NMF grantor, assignor.

césped NM **(a)** (*hierba*) grass, lawn, (stretch of) turf; (*para juegos*) pitch; (*para bolos*) green. **(b)** (*tepe*) turf, sod.

cesta NF (*gen*) basket; (*pelota*) long wicker racquet; **~ de la compra, ~ para compras** shopping basket; **~ de la compra** (*fig*) (weekly *etc*) cost of foodstuffs; **~ de costura** sewing basket; **~ de Navidad** Christmas box; **~ para papeles, ~ de los papeles** wastepaper basket; **~ de picnic** picnic hamper; **llevar la ~*** to go along as chaperon; to play gooseberry.

cestada NF basketful.

cestería NF **(a)** (*arte*) basketmaking. **(b)** (*materia; objetos*) wickerwork, basketwork; **silla de ~** wicker(work) chair. **(c)** (*tienda*) basket shop.

cestero, -a NM/F (*obrero*) basketmaker; (*vendedor*) basket seller.

cestillo NM small basket; **~ del polen** (*Ent*) pollen sac.

cesto NM **(a)** (*cesta*) (large) basket; hamper; **~ de la colada** clothes basket; **~ para papeles, ~ de los papeles** wastepaper basket.

(b) **estar hecho un ~** to be very drowsy; to be fuddled with drink.

(c) (*: gamberro*) lout.

cesura NF caesura.

cetáceo ADJ, NM cetacean.

cetárea, cetaria NF shellfish farm.

CETME ['θetme] NM ABR *de* **Centro de Estudios Técnicos de Materiales Especiales.**

cetme NM rifle.

cetorrino NM basking shark.

cetrería NF falconry, hawking.

cetrero NM **(a)** (*Caza*) falconer. **(b)** (*Ecl*) verger.

cetrino ADJ greenish-yellow; *cara, tez* sallow; (*fig*) melancholy, jaundiced.

cetro NM **(a)** sceptre; (*fig*) sway, power, dominion; **empuñar el ~** to ascend the throne, begin to reign. **(b)** (*LAm: Dep*) crown, championship.

CEU NM (*Esp*) ABR *de* **Centro de Estudios Universitarios.**

ceutí [1] ADJ of Ceuta.

[2] NMF native (*o* inhabitant) of Ceuta; **los ~es** the people of Ceuta.

C.F. NM ABR *de* **Club de Fútbol** football club, FC.

CFC NM ABR *de* **clorofluorocarbono** chlorofluorocarbon, CFC.

cfr. ABR *de* **confróntese, compárese** confer, compare, cf.

CG NF (*Esp*) ABR *de* **Coalición Galega.**

cg ABR *de* **centigramo** centigramme, cg.

CGC-L NM (*Esp*) ABR *de* **Consejo General de Castilla y León.**

CGPJ NM (*Esp*) ABR *de* **Consejo General del Poder Judicial.**

CGS NF (*Guatemala, El Salvador*) ABR *de* **Confederación General de Sindicatos.**

CGT NF **(a)** (*Méx, Perú*) ABR *de* **Confederación General de Trabajadores.** **(b)** (*Argentina, Esp*) ABR *de* **Confederación General del Trabajo.**

CGV NM (*Esp*) ABR *de* **Consejo General Vasco.**

Ch, ch NF *former letter in the Spanish alphabet*.

cha NM Shah.

chabacanear [1a] VI (*LAm*) to say (*o* do) coarse things.

chabacanería NF (**a**) (*cualidad*) vulgarity, bad taste; commonness; shoddiness.

(**b**) (*una* ~) coarse thing (to say), vulgar remark (*etc*); platitude; shoddy piece of work.

chabacanizar [1f] VT to trivialize.

chabacano[1] ADJ *chiste, comedia etc* vulgar, coarse, in bad taste; *artículo* cheap, common; *hechura etc* shoddy, crude.

chabacano[2] NM (*Méx*) apricot.

chabola NF shack, shanty; ~s (*esp LAm*) shanty-town.

chabolismo NM (problem of *o* tendency to create *etc*) shanty towns; shanty-town conditions.

chabolista NMF shanty-town dweller.

chabón[*] [1] ADJ daft, stupid.

[2] NM, **chabona** NF twit*.

chaca[*] NF: **estar en la** ~ (*Carib*) to be flat broke*.

chacal NM jackal.

chacalín[*] NM, **chacalina**[*] NF (*CAm*) (**a**) (*chico*) kid*, child. (**b**) (*camarón*) shrimp.

chacanear [1a] VT (**a**) (*Cono Sur*) *caballo* to spur violently. (**b**) (*Cono Sur: fastidiar*) to pester, annoy. (**c**) (*And: usar*) to use daily.

chacaneo NM: **para el** ~ (*And*) for daily use, ordinary.

chácara[1] NF (**a**) (*And, CAm, Cono Sur: Med*) sore, ulcer. (**b**) (*And, CAm, Carib: bolso*) large leather bag; (*And: maleta*) case.

chácara[2] NF (*LAm*) = **chacra**.

chacarería NF (**a**) (*LAm Agr*) market gardens, truck farms (*US*). (**b**) (*And, Cono Sur: industria*) horticulture, market gardening, truck farming (*US*); farm work.

chacarero NM (**a**) (*LAm*) (*dueño*) farmer, grower; market gardener, truck farmer (*US*); (*aparcero*) sharecropper; (*mayoral*) farm overseer; (*peón*) farm labourer. (**b**) (*Cono Sur: sandwich*) sandwich.

chacha[*] NF (*niñera*) maid, nursemaid; (*de limpieza*) cleaning lady; (*del pueblo*) low-class girl.

chachacaste NM (*CAm*) liquor, brandy.

cha-cha-cha NM (**a**) (*baile*) cha-cha. (**b**) (*juego*) solitaire.

chachal NM (*CAm*) charm necklace.

chachalaca[*] (*CAm, Méx*) [1] ADJ chatty, talkative.

[2] NMF chatterbox.

chachar [1a] VT (*And*) *coca* to chew.

cháchara NF (**a**) (*charla*) chatter, idle talk, small talk; **estar de** ~[*] to have a chat. (**b**) (*And: chiste*) joke. (**c**) ~s (*Cono Sur, Méx: cosas*) things, bits and pieces; junk.

chacharachas NFPL (*Cono Sur*) useless ornaments; trinkets.

chacharear [1a] [1] VT (*Méx*) to deal in, sell.

[2] VI to chatter, jaw*.

chacharería NF (*Cono Sur, Méx*) trinkets.

chacharero [1] ADJ chattering, garrulous.

[2] NM, **chacharera** NF (**a**) (*parlanchín*) chatterbox. (**b**) (*Méx: vendedor*) rag-and-bone man.

chache[*] NM oneself, me, the speaker; **el perjudicado es el** ~ the one that suffers is yours truly*.

chachi[*] [1] ADJ marvellous, smashing*, jolly good*; *chica* smashing*; **café del** ~ real good coffee*; **unos amigos** ~s real friends; **¡estás** ~! I think you're terrific!*

[2] ADV marvellously, jolly well*; **me fue** ~, **lo pasé** ~ I had a smashing time*; it went like a bomb*.

chachipé(n) = **chachi**.

chacho[*] NM (**a**) (*chico*) boy, lad. (**b**) (*CAm: gemelo*) twin. (**c**) (*Méx: criado*) servant.

chacina NF pork.

chacinería NF pork butcher's.

chacinero ADJ pork (*atr*); **industria chacinera** pigmeat industry.

chacó NM shako.

chacolí NM *chacolí*, sharp-tasting Basque wine.

chacolotear [1a] VI to clatter.

chacoloteo NM clatter(ing).

chacón NM Philippine lizard.

chacota NF noisy merriment, fun (and games), high jinks; **estar de** ~ to be in a joking mood; **echar algo a** ~, **hacer** ~ **de algo**, **tomar algo a** ~ to make fun of sth, take sth as a joke.

chacotear [1a] [1] VI to have fun, make merry.

[2] **chacotearse** VR: ~ **de algo** to make fun of sth, take sth as a joke.

chacoteo NM (*Cono Sur*) = **chacota**.

chacotería NF (*Cono Sur*) = **chacota**.

chacotero ADJ, **chacotón** ADJ (*Cono Sur*) fond of a laugh, merry.

chacra NF (*LAm*) (**a**) (*granja*) small farm, smallholding, market garden, truck farm (*US*); (*hacienda*) country estate; (*esp Cono Sur*) large orchard, fruit-farming estate; (*tierras*) cultivated land. (**b**) (*casa*) farmhouse. (**c**) (*productos*) farm produce.

chacuaco [1] ADJ (*Carib, Cono Sur*) coarse, rough; (*Carib*) clumsy.

[2] NM (*CAm: cigarro*) roughly-made cigar; (*CAm, Méx: colilla*) cigar stub.

Chad NM Chad.

chadiano, -a ADJ, NM/F Chadian.

chador NM chador.

chafa[*] ADJ (*Méx*) useless.

chafallar [1a] VT to botch, mend clumsily, make a mess of.

chafallo NM botched job.

chafalonía NF (*And*) worn-out gold jewellery.

chafalote [1] ADJ (*Cono Sur: ordinario*) common, vulgar.

[2] NM (**a**) = **chafarote**. (**b**) (*LAm*[*]) prick*.

chafar [1a] VT (**a**) (*aplastar*) to flatten; (*ajar etc*) to crumple; to ruffle, muss up; (*arrugar*) to crease; (*Culin*) *patatas* to mash; (*Med*) to lay out.

(**b**) ~ **a uno, dejar chafado a uno** to crush sb, floor sb; to cut sb short, shut sb up; to take sb down a peg; **quedó chafado** he was speechless.

(**c**) *negocio etc* to mess up, make a hash of, spoil; **le chafaron el negocio** they messed up the deal for him.

(**d**) (*Cono Sur: engañar*) to hoax, deceive.

chafardear [1a] VI to gossip.

chafardeo NM gossip.

chafarote NM (**a**) (*Hist*) cutlass; (*) sword; (*LAm*) machete. (**b**) (*CAm*[*]: *policía*) cop*.

chafarrinada NF spot, stain.

chafarrinar [1a] VT to blot, stain.

chafarrinón NM spot, stain; **echar un** ~ **a** (*fig*) to smear, slander.

chafir(r)o NM (*CAm, Méx*) knife.

chaflán NM (**a**) (*bisel*) bevel (surface), chamfer. (**b**) (*Aut*) street corner, road junction. (**c**) (*casa*) corner house.

chaflanar [1a] VT to bevel, chamfer.

chaflar[*] [1a] VT (*Chile*) to sack*, fire*.

chagra[1] [1] NF (*And*) = **chacra**.

[2] NM (*And*) peasant farmer.

chagra[2] NF (*Carib*) = **chaira**.

chagrín NM shagreen.

chagua NF (*And*) gang; system of gang labour.

chaguar [1i] VT (*Cono Sur*) *vaca* to milk; *ropa* to wring out.

cháguar NM (*And*) agave fibre, hemp; rope of agave fibre.

cháguara NF (*Cono Sur*) = **cháguar**.

chagüe NM (*CAm*) swamp, bog.

chagüite NM (*CAm, Méx*) (*pantano*) swamp; (*campo*) flooded field; (*bananal*) banana plantation.

chagüitear[*] [1a] VI (*CAm, Méx*) to chat, natter*.

chah NM Shah.

chai[*] NF bird*, dame*.

chai(ne) NM (*And, CAm*) shoeshine.

chainear [1a] VT (*CAm*) to shine, polish.

chaira NF (*de afilar*) steel; (*de zapatero*) shoemaker's knife; (*: cuchillo*) chiv*, knife.

chairar [1a] VT (*Cono Sur*) to sharpen.

chal NM shawl; ~ **de noche** evening wrap.

chala NF (**a**) (*And, Cono Sur: de maíz*) tender leaf of maize. (**b**) (*And, Cono Sur: dinero*) money, dough*; **pelar la** ~ **a uno** to fleece sb. (**c**) (*Cono Sur: zapato*) sandal.

chalado[*] [1] ADJ dotty*; cranky*; **¡estás** ~! are you mad?; **estar** ~ **por una** to be crazy about sb; **¡ven acá,** ~! come here, you idiot!

[2] NM, **chalada** NF crazy sort.

chaladura[*] NF crankiness*.

chalán NM (**a**) (*traficante*) dealer, huckster, (*esp*) horse dealer; (*pey*) shady businessman, shark*. (**b**) (*LAm*) horse-breaker.

chalana NF barge, lighter, wherry.

chalanear [1a] [1] VT (**a**) *persona* to haggle successfully with, beat down; *negocio* to handle cleverly, bring off.

(**b**) (*LAm*) *caballo* to break in, tame.

(**c**) (*Cono Sur*[*]: *acosar*) to pester.

(**d**) (*CAm: burlarse de*) to make fun of.

[2] VI to bargain shrewdly.

chalaneo NM, **chalanería** NF (*trato*) hard bargaining, horse trading; (*trampas*) trickery, deception.

chalaquear[*] [1a] (*CAm*) [1] VT to trick, con*.

[2] VI to chatter away, rabbit on*.

chalar[*] [1a] [1] VT to drive crazy, drive round the bend*.

[2] **chalarse** VR to go crazy, go off one's rocker*; ~ **por** to be crazy about.

chalchihuite NM (*Méx*) jade.

chale[*] NMF (*Méx pey*) Chink*.

chalé NM = **chalet**.

chalecito[*] NM (*frec*) second home, little place in the country, country retreat.

chaleco NM waistcoat, vest (*US*); (*Cono Sur*) sweater; ~ **antibalas** bulletproof vest, flakjacket; ~ **de fuerza** straitjacket; ~ **salvavidas** life jacket; **a** ~ (*CAm, Méx*) by hook or by crook; **quedar como** ~ **de**

mano (*Cono Sur*) to lose one's credibility; to disgrace o.s.

chalecón ① ADJ (*Méx*) tricky, deceitful.
② NM con man*.

chalequear [1a] VT (*Cono Sur, Méx*) to trick.

chalet [tʃaˈle] NM, PL **chalets** [tʃaˈles] (*de campo*) villa, cottage; (*de turista*) villa; (*de costa*) bungalow; (*de montaña*) chalet; (*de ciudad*) semi-detached house, detached house (with a garden); (*Golf etc*) clubhouse; ~ **adosado** semi-detached house.

chalina NF (a) (*corbata*) cravat(e), floppy bow tie. (b) (*esp LAm: chal*) small shawl, headscarf.

chalón NM (*LAm*) shawl, wrap.

chalona NF (*LAm*) dried salted mutton.

chalote NM shallot.

chalupa¹ NF launch, boat; ship's boat, lifeboat; (*And, Carib, Méx: canoa*) narrow canoe.

chalupa² NF (*Méx Culin*) stuffed tortilla.

chalupa³* ① ADJ crazy; **volver ~ a uno** to drive sb crazy.
② NM madman, crackpot.

chamaca NF (*Méx etc*) (*muchacha*) girl; (*novia*) girlfriend, sweetheart.

chamaco NM (*Méx etc*) (*muchacho*) boy, lad; (*novio*) boyfriend.

chamada NF (a) (*leña*) brushwood. (b) (*incendio*) brushwood fire; (*) smoke.

chamagoso* ADJ (*Méx*) (*mugriento*) filthy; (*chabacano*) crude, rough.

chamal NM (*Cono Sur*) tunic.

chamar* [1a] VTI to smoke.

chámara NF, **chamarasca** NF (*leña*) kindling, brushwood; (*incendio*) brush fire, blaze.

chamaril(l)ero NM secondhand dealer, junk dealer.

chamarra NF (a) sheepskin jacket; (*LAm: saco corto*) short jacket; (*Méx: saco*) jacket. (b) (*CAm, Carib: manta*) blanket, poncho. (c) (*CAm**: *engaño*) con*, swindle.

chamarrear* [1a] VT (*CAm*) to con*, swindle.

chamarrero NM (*Carib*) quack doctor.

chamarro NM (*CAm, Cono Sur, Méx*) (*manta*) coarse woollen blanket; (*serape*) poncho, woollen cape.

chamba¹ NF (a) (*And: tepe*) turf, sod.
(b) (*And: charca*) pond, pool; (*And: zanja*) ditch.
(c) (*CAm, Méx**: *trabajo*) work; job; (*negocio*) business; (*empleo*) occupation.
(d) (*Méx**) (*sueldo*) wages, pay; (*sueldo bajo*) low pay; (*chollo*) soft job*.
(e) (*Carib, Méx**) dough‡, bread‡ (*US*).

chamba² NF (*chiripa*) fluke, lucky break; **por ~** by a fluke.

chambeador* (*Méx*) ① ADJ hard-working.
② NM, **chambeadora** NF hard worker, slogger.

chambear [1a] (*Méx*) ① VT to exchange, swap, barter.
② VI to work; (*inútilmente*) to slave away.

chambelán NM chamberlain.

chamberga* NF coat.

chambergo NM (*Hist*) cocked hat; broad-brimmed soft hat; (*) coat.

chambero NM (*Méx*) draughtsman.

chambón* ① ADJ (a) (*torpe*) awkward, clumsy. (b) (*afortunado*) lucky, jammy‡. (c) (*desaseado*) slovenly.
② NM, **chambona** NF fluky player, lucky player; **hacer algo a la chambona** (*And*) to do sth in a rush.

chambonada NF (a) (*torpeza*) awkwardness, clumsiness. (b) (*chiripa*) fluke, stroke of luck, lucky shot. (c) (*plancha*) blunder.

chambonear [1a] VI (*esp LAm*) to have a stroke of luck, win (*etc*) by a fluke.

chamborote ADJ (*And, CAm*) long-nosed.

chambra¹ NF (*bata*) housecoat; (*blusa*) blouse; (*chaqueta*) loose jacket.

chambra² NF (*Carib*) din, hubbub.

chambra³ NF (*Carib*) machete, broad knife.

chambrana NF (*And, Carib*) row, uproar; brawl.

chambre‡ NM (*CAm*) tittle-tattle, gossip.

chambroso‡ ADJ (*CAm*) gossipy.

chamburgo NM (*And*) pool, stagnant water.

chamelicos NMPL (*And, Cono Sur: trastos*) lumber, junk; (*ropa*) old clothes.

chamiza NF (*de techo*) thatch, thatch palm; (*leña*) brushwood.

chamizo NM (a) (*árbol*) half-burned tree (o log *etc*). (b) (*casita*) thatched hut; (*chabola*) shack, slum; (*) den, joint‡. (c) (*mina*) illegal coalmine.

chamo*, **-a** NM/F (*LAm*) kid*, child.

chamorro ① ADJ *cabeza* shorn, close-cropped.
② NM: ~ **de cerdo** (*Méx*) leg of pork.

champa¹ NF (*LAm*) (a) (*tepe*) sod, turf; ball of earth (*left round roots*).
(b) (*greña*) mop of hair. (c) (*fig*) tangled mass.

champa² NF (*CAm, Méx*) roughly-built hut; tent.

champán NM champagne.

champanero ADJ champagne (*atr*).

champanizar [1f] VT *vino* to add a sparkle to.

Champaña NF Champagne.

champaña NM champagne.

champañazo NM (*Cono Sur etc*) champagne party.

champañero ADJ champagne (*atr*).

champi* NM = **champiñón**.

champiñón NM mushroom.

champú NM shampoo; ~ **anticaspa** anti-dandruff shampoo.

champudo ADJ (*LAm*) *pelo* dishevelled, messy; *persona* long-haired.

champurrado NM mixture of liquors, cocktail; (*Carib, Méx*) mixed drink (*of various ingredients*); (*Méx: de chocolate*) thick chocolate drink; (*fig*) mixture, mess.

champurrar [1a] VT *bebidas* to mix, make a cocktail of.

champurreado NM (a) (*Cono Sur Culin*) hastily-prepared dish; (*fig*) hash, botch. (b) = **champurrado**.

champurrear [1a] VT (*Carib*) (a) = **champurrar**. (b) = **chapurr(e)ar**.

chamuchina NF (a) (*LAm: turba*) rabble, mob; (*niños*) crowd of small children, mob of kids*. (b) (*And, Carib: jaleo*) row, shindy*. (c) (*LAm*) = **chamusquina**.

chamullar* [1a] ① VTI to speak, talk; to burble; **yo también chamullo el caló** I can talk slang too; **chamullaban en árabe** they were jabbering away in Arabic; **¿qué chamullas tú?** what are you burbling about?
② VI (*Cono Sur*) to cook up a story.

chamuscar [1g] ① VT (a) (*quemar*) to scorch, sear, singe. (b) (*Méx: vender*) to sell cheap.
② **chamuscarse** VR (a) to get scorched, singe. (b) (*And**) to fly off the handle*.

chamusquina NF (a) (*quemadura*) singeing, scorching.
(b) (*jaleo*) row, quarrel, shindy; **esto huele a ~** I can see there's trouble brewing, there's sth nasty coming.
(c) (*And, CAm**: *niños*) bunch of kids.

chan NM (*CAm*) local guide.

chanada* NF trick, swindle.

chanar‡ [1a] VT (*t VI*: ~ **de**) to understand.

chanca NF (a) (*And, Cono Sur: molienda*) grinding, crushing. (b) (*And, Cono Sur: paliza*) beating.

chancaca NF (a) (*CAm Culin*) maize cake, wheat cake. (b) (*And Med*) sore, ulcer. (c) (*LAm: azúcar*) brown sugar, honey mass, solidified molasses (*used in the preparation of chicha*).

chancadora NF (*LAm*) grinder, crusher.

chancar [1g] VT (a) (*LAm*) (*moler*) to grind, crush; (*pegar*) to beat; (*aporrear*) to beat up*; (*maltratar*) to ill-treat. (b) (*And, Cono Sur: chapucear*) to botch, bungle.

chance ① NM (*a veces NF*) (*LAm**) (a) (*oportunidad*) chance; prospects; **dale ~** let him have a go. (b) (*suerte*) good luck.
② CONJ (*Méx*) maybe, perhaps.

chancear [1a] VI *y* **chancearse** VR to joke, make jokes (*de* about); to fool about, play around (*con* with); **~se de uno** to make fun of sb.

chancero ADJ joking, merry, facetious; fond of a joke.

chancha NF (a) (*LAm Zool*) sow. (b) (*Cono Sur*) (*carro*) small wooden cart; (*: *bicicleta*) bike*. (c) (*And hum*) mouth; **hacer la ~** (*And, Cono Sur*) to play truant.

chanchada NF (*LAm*) dirty trick.

chánchamo NM (*Méx Culin*) tamale.

cháncharas máncharas: andar en ~ to beat about the bush.

chanchería NF (*LAm*) pork-butcher's shop.

chanchero NM (*LAm*) pork butcher.

chanchi* = **chachi**.

chanchito* NM: **mi ~** (*LAm*) my darling.

chancho ① ADJ (*LAm*) dirty, filthy.
② NM (a) (*LAm: cerdo*) pig, hog; (*carne*) pork; ~ **salvaje** wild boar.
(b) (*LAm: Ajedrez etc*) blocked piece.
(c) (*Cono Sur*) = **chancadora**.
(d) (*LAm fig*) **son como ~s** they're as thick as thieves; **hacerse el ~ rengo** to pretend not to notice; **quedar como ~** to come off badly.
(e) (*Cono Sur: de suelos*) floor polisher.

chanchono* NM lie.

chanchullero* ① ADJ crooked*, bent‡.
② NM crook*, twister.

chanchullo* NM fiddle*, wangle*; crooked deal*; piece of graft, dirty business; **andar en ~s** to be on the fiddle*, be engaged in sth shady.

chanciller NM = **canciller**.

chancillería NF chancery.

chancla NF (a) old shoe, broken shoe. (b) = **chancleta**.

chancleta ① NF (*zapatilla*) slipper; **tirar la ~** (*Cono Sur*) to have a good time. (b) (*LAm: bebé*) baby girl. (c) (*Carib Aut*) accelerator.
② NMF (‡) muggins‡, charlie‡.

chancletero ADJ (*And, Carib*), **chancletudo** ADJ (*And, Carib, Cono Sur*) (a) (*ordinario*) common, low-class. (b) (*desaseado*) scruffy.

chanclo NM (*zueco*) clog; (*de goma*) rubber overshoe, galosh.

chancón, -ona* NM/F (*And*) swot*.

chancro NM chancre.

chandal NM, **chándal** NM tracksuit.

chanelar* [1a] VT to catch on to, twig*.

chanfaina NF (a) (*Culin*) cheap stew. (b) (*And, CAm: enredo*) mess; (*chance*) lucky break.

chanfle¹: NM (*Cono Sur*) bobby*, cop*.

chanfle² NM (*Méx*) = **chaflán**.

chanflón ADJ misshapen; (*fig*) crude, coarse.

changa¹ NF (a) (*And, Cono Sur*) (*transporte*) (portering) job; (*chapuz*) odd job, occasional job. (b) (*And: propina*) tip, payment (to a porter).

changa² NF (*Carib*) joke.

changador NM (*And, Cono Sur*) (*cargador*) porter; (*factótum*) odd-job man; (*temporero*) casual worker.

changango NM (*Cono Sur*) small guitar.

changarro¹* NM (*Aut*) old car, jalopy.

changarro² NM (*Méx*) small shop.

changarse: [1h] VR to break (down), go wrong.

chango 1 ADJ (a) (*Méx: listo*) quick, sharp; alert; **¡ponte ~!** wake up!, get wise!*; watch out!
(b) (*Carib, Méx: juguetón*) mischievous, playful.
(c) (*Carib*) (*tonto*) silly, brainless; (*afectado*) affected.
(d) (*Cono Sur: molesto*) annoying.
(e) **la gente está changa** (*Méx etc*) there are lots of people. 2 NM, **changa³** NF (a) (*Méx Zool*) small monkey.
(b) (*Cono Sur, Méx*) (*niño*) child; (*criado*) young servant.
(c) (*Méx*:*) cunt:*.

changuear [1a] VI (*And, Carib, Méx*) = **chancear**.

changüí* NM (a) (*chiste*) joke. (b) (*estafa*) trick, swindle; **dar ~ a** to trick, swindle.

changurro NM crab.

chanquete NM whitebait.

chanta: NMF (*Cono Sur*) (*fanfarrón*) loudmouth*; (*que no cumple*) fraud.

chantaje NM blackmail(ing).

chantajear [1a] VT to blackmail.

chantajista NMF blackmailer.

chantar [1a] VT (a) *vestido etc* to put on.
(b) *objeto* to thrust, stick; to put.
(c) **~ algo a uno** to tell sb sth to his face.
(d) (*And, Cono Sur*) *objeto* to throw, chuck.
(e) (*And, Cono Sur*) *persona* to put, throw; **~ a uno en la calle** to throw sb out; **~ a uno en la cárcel** to put sb in jail.
(f) (*And, Cono Sur*) *golpe* to give, deal.
(g) (*Cono Sur*) (*abandonar*) to leave in the lurch; (*engañar*) to deceive, trick.

chantre NM (*Ecl*) precentor.

chanza NF joke; piece of tomfoolery, lark; **~s** jokes, banter; tomfoolery; **de ~, en ~** in fun, as a joke; **estar de ~** to be joking.

chañaca NF (*Cono Sur*) (a) (*Med*) itch, rash. (b) (*fig*) bad reputation.

chao¹ NM chow.

chao²* EXCL (*esp Cono Sur*) bye-bye!, so long!

chapa NF (a) (*metal*) plate, sheet; **~ acanalada, ~ ondulada** (sheet of) corrugated iron.
(b) (*madera*) board, panel, sheet; veneer; **madera de 3 ~s** 3-ply wood.
(c) (*disco etc*) small metal plate, disc, tally; (*ficha*) counter; check; (*cápsula*) bottle-top, cap; **~s** (*juego*) game of tossing coins; **~s** (*Cono Sur Fin*) small change; **~ de identidad** identity disc; **~ de matrícula, ~ de patente** (*Cono Sur*) licence plate; **estar sin ~*** to be broke*; **hacer ~s*** to be on the game*; **poner la ~** (*Cono Sur*) to be best at everything.
(d) (*LAm: cerradura*) lock; (*tirador*) door handle.
(e) (*carmín*) rouge; (*chapeta*) flush (on the cheeks).
(f) (*juicio*) good sense, prudence; **hombre de ~** sensible man.

chapado ADJ (a) *muebles, adornos* covered (o lined) with sheet metal (o veneer); **~ de roble** with an oak veneer, with an oak finish; **~ de oro** gold-plated.
(b) **~ a la antigua** (*fig*) old-fashioned, of the old school.

chapalear [1a] VI (a) (*persona*) to splash (about); (*agua*) to lap. (b) (*herraduras etc*) to clatter.

chapaleo NM (*V VI*) (a) splash(ing); lap(ping). (b) clatter(ing).

chapapote NM (*Méx*) = **chapopote**.

chapar¹ [1a] 1 VT (a) (*Téc*) to plate, cover (o line) with sheet metal (o veneer); *pared* to tile. (b) *observación etc* to throw out, come out with; **le chapó un 'no' como una casa** he gave him a flat 'no'. (c) (**: aprender*) to learn, memorize. (d) (*:: cerrar*) to shut, close. 2 VI (a) (*:*) (*Univ*) to swot*. (b) (*dormir*) to kip:, sleep.

chapar² [1a] VT (a) (*And: espiar*) to spy on.
(b) (*And*) (*atrapar*) to catch; (*alcanzar*) to catch up with, overtake; *objeto* to seize, grasp.
(c) (*besar*) to kiss.

chaparra¹ NF (*árbol*) kermes oak; (*maleza*) brush, scrub.

chaparrada NF = **chaparrón**.

chaparral NM thicket (of kermes oaks), chaparral.

chaparrear [1a] VI to pour in torrents.

chaparreras NFPL (*Méx*) leather chaps.

chaparro 1 ADJ squat, short and chubby.
2 NM (*Bot*) kermes oak, dwarf oak.
3 NM, **chaparra²** NF (*fig*) short chubby person; (*Méx*) child, kid*.

chaparrón NM downpour, cloudburst.

chapatal NM muddy place.

chape NM (*And, Cono Sur*) tress, pigtail.

chapear [1a] 1 VT (a) = **chapar¹**. (b) (*LAm Agr*) to weed. (c) **~ a uno** (*Carib*) to cut sb's throat.
2 VI (*LAm*) to clear the ground.

chapeau [tʃa'po] 1 EXCL bravo!, well done!
2 NM (a) **hacer ~** to take off one's hat (*ante* to). (b) (message of) appreciation, congratulations.

chapeo: NM titfer:, hat.

chapero: NM (*homosexual*) queer:; (*prostituto*) male prostitute, rent boy.

chapeta NF flush (on the cheeks).

chapetón (*LAm*) 1 ADJ awkward, clumsy.
2 NM Spaniard in America.

chapetonada NF (a) (*And*) (*Med*) illness caused by a change of climate; (*sarpullido*) rash.
(b) (*And, Cono Sur: torpeza*) awkwardness, clumsiness.
(c) (*Carib: aguacero*) sudden downpour.

chapín 1 ADJ (*LAm*) with crooked legs (o feet).
2 NM (a) (*zueco*) clog. (b) (*CAm hum*) Guatemalan.

chapinada NF (*CAm hum*) action typical of a Guatemalan, dirty trick.

chapiri: NM titfer:, hat.

chápiro* NM: **¡por vida del ~!, ¡voto al ~!** damn it!

chapisca NF (*CAm*) maize harvest.

chapista NM tinsmith; (*Aut*) car-body worker, panel-beater.

chapistería NF car-body works, panel-beating shop.

chapita* NF (*And*) cop*.

chapitel NM (*Arquit: de columna*) capital; (*de torre*) spire.

chapo¹ ADJ (*Méx*) short and chubby.

chapo² NM (*Méx Culin*) maize porridge.

chapó 1 INTERJ bravo!, well done!
2 NM: **hacer el ~** to take off one's hat (*ante* to).

chapodar [1a] VT (a) *árbol* to prune, trim. (b) (*fig*) to cut down, reduce.

chapola NF (*And*) butterfly.

chapolín NM pool (game).

chapo(po)te NM (*CAm, Carib, Méx*) (*pez*) pitch, tar; (*asfalto*) asphalt.

chapotear [1a] 1 VT (*lavar*) to sponge (down); (*humedecer*) to wet, moisten.
2 VI to splash about; to paddle; to dabble (one's hands).

chapoteo NM (a) (*limpieza con esponja*) sponging; moistening. (b) (*chapaleo*) splashing; paddling; dabbling.

chaptalizar [1f] VT to chaptalize, add sugar to.

chapucear [1a] VT (a) (*trabajo*) to botch, bungle, make a mess of; to do in a slapdash way. (b) (*Méx: estafar*) to swindle.

chapuceramente ADV roughly, crudely, shoddily; amateurishly; clumsily.

chapucería NF (a) (*cualidad*) shoddiness. (b) (*una ~*) botched job, shoddy piece of work, mess.

chapucero 1 ADJ *objeto* rough, crude, shoddy; *trabajo* bungled, slapdash; *persona* clumsy, bungling.
2 NM bungler, clumsy workman (*etc*); bungling amateur.

chapulín NM (*LAm*), **chapulú** NM (*CAm*) (a) (*langosta*) locust; (*cigarra*) cricket. (b) (*) child, kid*.

chapupa* NF: **me salió de pura ~** (*CAm*) it was pure luck, it was sheer fluke.

chapuro NM (*CAm*) asphalt.

chapurr(e)ar [1a] VT (a) *bebidas* to mix. (b) *idioma* to speak badly; **chapurrea el italiano** he speaks broken (o bad) Italian.

chapuz NM (a) (*chapuzón*) ducking; plunge, dive, dip. (b) = **chapuza**.

chapuza NF (a) (*chapucería*) botched job, shoddy piece of work, mess; (*trabajillo*) odd job, spare-time job; small job (done) about the house.
(b) (*Méx: estafa*) trick, swindle.

chapuzar [1f] 1 VT to duck, dip, plunge.
2 VI y **chapuzarse** VR to duck, dive.

chapuzas NM INVAR bungler, clumsy sort.

chapuzón NM (a) (*zambullida*) dip, swim; ducking; **darse un ~** to go for a dip. (b) (*de cápsula*) splashdown. (c) (*LAm**) cloudburst, downpour.

chaqué NM morning coat.

chaquet [tʃa'ke] NM, PL **chaquets** [tʃa'kes] = **chaqué**.

chaqueta NF (a) (*prenda*) jacket; **~ de cuero** leather jacket. (b) **cambiar la ~** = **chaquetear**. (c) **volarse la ~** (*CAm*:*) to toss off:*.

chaquetar [1a] (*Méx*), **chaquetear** [1a] 1 VT (:) to slag off:, criticize.
2 VI (*cambiar de política*) to change sides, be a turncoat, turn traitor; (*acobardarse*) to go back on one's word, chicken out*, rat*.

chaquete NM backgammon.

chaquetero, -a NM/F (Pol) turncoat; **es ~** he's always changing sides.

chaquetón NM long jacket, reefer, shooting jacket; (de mujer) three-quarter coat.

charada NF charade.

charadrio NM plover.

charaludo ADJ (Méx) thin.

charamusca NF (a) (LAm: t ~s) firewood, kindling. (b) (Méx: dulce) candy twist. (c) (Carib: alboroto) noise, row.

charanga NF (a) (Mús) brass band; band of street musicians; (Cono Sur Mil) cavalry band. (b) (LAm*: baile) informal dance, hop*.

charango NM (And, Cono Sur) a small five-stringed guitar.

charanguero ADJ = **chapucero 1**.

charape NM (Méx) type of pulque.

charca NF pond, pool.

charchina* NF (LAm) old crock, old banger‡.

charco NM pool, puddle; **cruzar el ~, pasar el ~** to cross the water, (esp) to cross the herring-pond (ie the Atlantic).

charcón¹ ADJ (And, Cono Sur) thin, skinny.

charcón² NM pool (in a river).

charcutería NF (a) (productos) cooked pork products. (b) (tienda) delicatessen.

charcutero, -a NM/F person who works in a 'charcutería'.

charla NF talk, chat; (pey) chatter; (Univ etc) talk; **~ radiofónica** radio talk; **~ literaria** literary talk, informal literary lecture; **es de ~ común** it's common knowledge.

charla-coloquio NF, PL **charlas-coloquio** talk (followed by debate).

charlado* NM: **echar un ~** to have a chat.

charlador ① ADJ talkative; gossipy.
② NM, **charladora** NF chatterbox; gossip.

charladuría NF (t ~s) small talk, chatter, gossip.

charlar [1a] VI to chat, talk (de about); (pey) to chatter, gossip.

charlatán ① ADJ talkative; gossipy.
② NM, **charlatana** NF (a) (hablador) chatterbox; (chismoso) gossip; (bocón) bigmouth‡, indiscreet talker. (b) (timador) (confidence) trickster; (vendedor) smooth-tongued salesman, clever (but untrustworthy) salesman, showman; (Med) quack, charlatan.

charlatanear [1a] VI to chatter away, babble on; (pey) to shoot one's mouth off*.

charlatanería NF (a) (locuacidad) talkativeness, garrulity. (b) (arte de vender etc) (clever) salesmanship; showmanship; (Med) quackery, charlatanism. (c) (jerga publicitaria) sales talk, patter; (palabrería) hot air.

charlatanismo NM = **charlatanería (a)**.

charlestón NM charleston.

charleta NMF (Cono Sur) chatterbox; gossip.

charli‡ NM 1000-peseta note.

charlista NMF speaker, lecturer.

Charlot NM Charlie Chaplin.

charlota NF type of frozen cream cake.

charlotada NF (Teat) gag; (Taur) mock bullfight.

charlotear [1a] VI to chatter, talk a lot.

charloteo NM chatter.

charnego, -a NM/F immigrant (esp Andalusian or Murcian in Catalonia).

charnela NF, **charneta** NF hinge.

charol NM (a) (barniz) varnish; (cuero) patent leather; **calzárselas de ~** (Cono Sur) to make a packet*; **darse ~*** to swank*, brag. (b) (LAm: bandeja) tray.

charola NF (a) (LAm: bandeja) tray. (b) **~s** (CAm*: ojos) eyes.

charolado ADJ polished, shiny.

charolar [1a] VT to varnish, japan.

charolés ADJ, NM Charolais.

charpa NF (CAm Mil) pistol belt, sword belt; (Med) sling.

charquear [1a] VT (LAm) (a) carne to dry, jerk. (b) persona to carve up, slash, wound severely; to beat (up)*.

charquecillo NM (And Culin) dried salted fish.

charqui NM (LAm: carne) dried beef, jerked meat; (Cono Sur) (frutas) dried fruit, (legumbres) dried vegetables; **hacer ~ a uno** (fig) = **charquear (b)**.

charquicán NM (Cono Sur Culin) dish of dried meat and vegetables.

charra NF (a) (prov: Salamanca) peasant woman; (fig) low-class woman, coarse woman. (b) (CAm: sombrero) broad-brimmed hat. (c) (And: grano) itch, pimple. (d) (CAm*‡) prick‡‡, tool‡‡.

charrada NF (a) (dicho, acto) coarse thing, piece of bad breeding; example of bad taste.
(b) (adorno) flashy ornament, vulgar adornment; (objeto) tastelessly decorated object.
(c) (cualidad) coarseness, bad breeding; bad taste; tawdriness, gaudiness.
(d) (Mús) country dance.

charral NM (CAm) scrub, scrubland.

charramasca NF (CAm) firewood, kindling.

charrán¹ NM (Orn) tern.

charrán² NM rascal, villain.

charranada NF dirty trick.

charrar‡ [1a] VI (hablar) to talk, burble; (soplar) to blab.

charrasca NF (††) trailing sword; (And, Cono Sur, Méx) knife, razor.

charrasquear [1a] VT (a) (Méx: apuñalar) to knife, stab. (b) (And, CAm, Carib: rasguear) to strum.

charré NM trap, dog-cart.

charrería NF (Méx) horsemanship.

charretera NF (Mil etc) epaulette; shoulder flash; (Cos) shoulder pad.

charro ① ADJ (a) persona rustic; coarse, vulgar, ill-bred.
(b) vestido etc loud, gaudy; objeto flashy, showy; over-ornamented, decorated in bad taste.
(c) (salmantino) Salamancan.
(d) (mejicano) Mexican.
(e) (Méx) costumbre picturesque, quaint; traditional; see also CONJUNTO MARIACHI.
(f) (Méx) jinete skilled in horsemanship.
② NM (a) (prov: Salamanca) peasant.
(b) (pey) rustic, boor, coarse individual; flashy sort, overdressed individual.
(c) (Méx) (vaquero) horseman, cowboy; (mejicano) typical Mexican.
(d) (Méx: sombrero) wide-brimmed hat.
(e) (Méx Pol*) corrupt union boss.

charrúa ADJ, NMF (Cono Sur) Uruguayan.

chart, PL charts (Bolsa) ① NM (gráfico) (stock) market forecast.
② NMF (analista) market analyst.

chárter ① ATR: **vuelo ~** charter flight.
② NM, PL **chárters** ['tʃarter] charter (flight).

chartista ① ADJ (stock) market (atr).
② NMF market analyst.

chasca NF (a) (maleza) brushwood. (b) (LAm: pelo) mop of hair, tangled hair; tangle.

chascar [1g] ① VT (a) lengua etc to click; dedos to snap; látigo to crack; grava etc to crunch. (b) comida to gobble, gulp down.
② VI to click, snap; to crack; to crunch.

chascarrillo NM funny story.

chasco¹ ADJ (And, Cono Sur) pelo etc thick and crinkly, coarse.

chasco² NM (a) (desilusión) disappointment; failure, let-down; **dar un ~ a uno** to disappoint sb; **llevarse (un) ~** to be disappointed, suffer a let-down; **¡vaya ~ que me llevé!** what a let-down!
(b) (broma) trick, joke; prank; **dar ~ a uno** to pull sb's leg*; **dar un ~ a uno** to play a trick on sb.

chascón ADJ (And, Cono Sur) (a) pelo dishevelled, matted, entangled; persona dishevelled. (b) (torpe) slow, clumsy.

chasis NM INVAR (Aut etc) chassis; (Fot) plateholder; **quedarse en el ~*** to be terribly thin.

chasque NM (LAm) = **chasqui**.

chasquear¹ [1a] VT (a) (decepcionar) (t dejar chasqueado) to disappoint, let down; (faltar a) to fail, break one's promise to.
(b) (engañar) to play a trick on, make a fool of.

chasquear² [1a] ① VT = **chascar 1**; (And, CAm) freno to champ.
② VI = **chascar 2**; (madera etc) to creak; to crack, crackle; **~ con la lengua** to click one's tongue.
③ **chasquearse** VR (And*) to make a mess of things, mess things up*.

chasqui NM (LAm Hist) messenger, courier.

chasquido NM click; snap; crack; crunch; creak, crackle.

chasquilla NF (LAm) fringe of hair.

chata NF (a) (Med) bedpan. (b) (Náut) lighter, barge, transport. (c) (Cono Sur: Aut) lorry, truck. (d) (*: escopeta) sawn-off shotgun.

chatarra NF scrap iron, junk; (*: dinero) coppers, small change; (Mil hum) gongs*, medals; **vender para ~** to sell for scrap.

chatarrería NF scrapyard, scrap merchant's, junkyard (US).

chatarrero NM scrap dealer, scrap merchant, junkman (US).

chatear* [1a] VI to go drinking, have a few drinks.

chateo* NM drinking expedition; **ir de ~** = **chatear**.

chati‡ NF girl, bird‡; **¡oye ~!** hey, beautiful!*

chato ① ADJ (a) nariz flat, snub; persona snub-nosed; (*) dear, love; **¡oye, chata!*** hey, beautiful!*
(b) objeto flattened, blunt; barca etc flat; torre etc low, squat.
(c) (Carib, Cono Sur: pobre) mean, wretched.
(d) **dejar ~ a uno** (LAm) (anonadar) to crush sb; (avergonzar) to embarrass sb; (Méx: estafar) to swindle sb; **quedarse ~ con algo** to appropriate sth.
② NM (small) wine glass; glass (of wine); **tomarse unos ~s** to have a few drinks.

chatón NM large mounted stone.

chatre ADJ (And, Cono Sur) smartly-dressed; **está hecho un ~** he's looking very smart.

chatungo* ADJ = **chato**; **¡eh, ~!** hey, lad!; **¡oye, chatunga!** hey, beautiful*!

chau* INTERJ (*Cono Sur*) so long!

chaucha [1] ADJ INVAR (**a**) (*And, Cono Sur: Agr etc*) papa early; (*inmaduro*) unripe, not fully grown; *nacimiento* premature; *mujer* who gives birth prematurely.
(**b**) (*Cono Sur*) (*malo*) poor-quality; (*soso*) insipid, tasteless, characterless; (*de mal gusto*) in poor taste.
[2] NF (**a**) (*LAm: papa*) early potato, small potato; (*And, Cono Sur: judía*) string bean; (*And: comida*) food (*gen*); **pelar la ~** (*And, Cono Sur*) to brandish (o use) one's knife.
(**b**) (*And, Cono Sur: moneda*) 20-cent coin; (any) small coin; (*And, Cono Sur: dinero*) dough*; (*pequeña cantidad*) small amount; **le cayó la ~** the penny dropped.
(**c**) **~s**‡ (*Cono Sur*) peanuts*, trifles.

chauchau‡ NM (*And, Cono Sur*) grub‡, chow‡.

chauchera NF (*And, Cono Sur*) purse, pocket-book (*US*).

chauchero NM (*Cono Sur*) errand boy; odd-job man; poorly-paid worker.

chaufa NF (*LAm*) chop suey.

chauvinismo NM chauvinism.

chauvinista [1] ADJ chauvinist(ic).
[2] NMF chauvinist.

chava¹‡ NM = **chaval**.

chava²‡ NF (*CAm, Méx*) lass, girl.

chaval* NM lad, boy, kid*; **mi ~** my bloke‡, my boyfriend; **estar hecho un ~** to feel (o look) very young again; **es un ~** he's only a kid (still)*.

chavala* NF girl, kid*; **mi ~** my bird‡, my girlfriend.

chavalería* NF young people, kids*.

chavalo NM (*CAm*) (*golfo*) street urchin; (*chico*) boy.

chavalongo NM (*Cono Sur: fiebre*) fever; (*insolación*) sunstroke; (*modorra*) drowsiness, drowsy feeling.

chavea* NMF kid*, youngster.

chaveta [1] NF cotter, cotter pin; (*And, Méx*) broad bladed knife; **perder la ~*** (*loco*) to go off one's rocker‡, (*indignado*) go through the roof*; **perder la ~ por una chica** to go crazy about a girl.
[2] ADJ INVAR: **estar ~**‡ to be nuts‡.

chavetear [1a] VT (*And, Carib*) to knife.

chavo¹‡ NM five pesetas; **no tener un ~, estar sin un ~** to be stony-broke*, be stone-broke* (*US*).

chavo²* NM (*CAm, Méx*) bloke‡, guy*.

chavó* NM kid*, boy.

chayote NM chayote, fruit of the *chayotera*.

chayotera NF chayote (plant).

che¹ NF the (name of the) letter *ch*.

che² INTERJ oh dear!; (*Cono Sur*) hey!, hi!, I say!; (*CAm*) who cares!, so what?

checa¹ NF (**a**) (*policía*) secret police. (**b**) (*central*) secret police headquarters; (‡) nick‡, jail.

checar [1g] VT (*Méx etc*) = **chequear**.

cheche NM (*Carib*) bully, braggart.

chechear [1a] VT (*Cono Sur*) = **vosear**.

chécheres NMPL (*And, CAm*) things, gear; junk, lumber.

chechón ADJ (*Méx*) spoilt, pampered.

checo, -a² [1] ADJ, NM/F Czech.
[2] NM (*Ling*) Czech.

checoslovaco, -a ADJ, NM/F Czechoslovakian.

Checoslovaquia NF Czechoslovakia.

chef NM, PL **chefs** chef.

cheira NF = **chaira**.

Chejov NM Chekhov.

chele ADJ (*CAm*) fair, blond(e).

chelear [1a] VT (*CAm*) to whiten, whitewash.

cheli‡ NM (**a**) (*tío*) bloke‡, guy*; (*amigo*) boyfriend; **ven acá, ~** come here, man. (**b**) (*Ling*) *Cheli* jargon, Madrid slang of 1970s.

chelín NM (*Fin*) shilling.

chelista NMF cellist.

chelo¹ NM (**a**) (*Mús*) cello. (**b**) (*persona*) cellist.

chelo² ADJ (*Méx*) fair, blond(e).

chepa NF hump.

cheposo [1] ADJ hunchbacked.
[2] NM, **cheposa** NF hunchback.

▼ **cheque** NM cheque, check (*US*); **~ abierto** open cheque; **~ en blanco** blank cheque; **~ caducado** stale cheque; **~ de compensación** clearing cheque; **~ cruzado** crossed cheque; **~ en descubierto** (*Méx*), **~ sin fondos, ~ sin provisión** bad cheque; **~ al portador** bearer cheque, cheque payable to bearer; **~ de viaje, ~ de viajero** traveller's cheque; **pagar mediante ~** to pay by cheque.

chequear [1a] VT (*esp LAm*) *cuenta, documento, salud etc* to check; *persona* to check (up) on; (*investigar*) to investigate, examine; (*CAm, Carib*) *cheque* to issue, write; to issue a cheque for; (*And, CAm, Carib*) *equipaje* to register, check in; (*And: apuntar*) to note down, record,

register; (*Méx: Aut*) to service, overhaul, check.

chequeo NM (*esp LAm*) check; checking-up; (*Med*) check-up; (*Aut*) service, overhaul(ing).

chequera NF (*LAm*) chequebook.

cherife NM (*LAm*) sheriff (*US*).

cherna NF wreck fish.

chero* NM (*CAm*) pal*, mate, buddy (*US*).

cheruto NM cheroot.

cherva NF castor oil plant.

cheurón NM (*Her*) chevron.

chévere* [1] ADJ (*And, Carib, Méx*) smashing*, super*.
[2] NM (*Carib*) bully, braggart.

chevió NM, **cheviot** NM cheviot.

chibola NF (*CAm*) (**a**) (*refresco*) fizzy drink, pop*. (**b**) = **chibolo**. (**c**) (*canica*) marble.

chibolo NM (*And, CAm*) bump, swelling; wen.

chic [1] ADJ INVAR chic, smart, elegant.
[2] NM elegance; composure.

chica¹ NF (*joven*) girl; (*criada*) maid, servant; **~ de alterne** bar-girl, bar-room hostess; **~ de conjunto** chorus-girl.

chica² NF (*Cono Sur*) plug of chewing tobacco.

chicana¹ NF (*LAm*) chicanery.

chicanear [1a] [1] VT to trick, take in*, con*.
[2] VI (*LAm*) to use trickery, be cunning.

chicanería NF (*LAm*) chicanery.

chicanero ADJ (**a**) (*LAm: astuto*) tricky, crafty. (**b**) (*And: tacaño*) mean.

chicano [1] ADJ Chicano, Mexican-American.
[2] NM, **chicana²** NF Chicano, Mexican immigrant in the USA.

chicar* [1g] VI (*And*) to booze*, drink.

chicarrón [1] ADJ strapping, sturdy.
[2] NM, **chicarrona** NF strapping lad; sturdy lass.

chicato* ADJ (*Cono Sur*) short-sighted.

chicha¹ NF (**a**) (*bebida*) chicha, maize liquor, corn liquor (*US*); **~ de uva** (*And, Cono Sur*) unfermented grape juice; **estas cosas están como ~** (*And*) there are hundreds (o any number) of these things; **no es ni ~ ni limonada** it's neither one thing nor the other, it's neither fish nor fowl; **sacar la ~ a uno** to make sb sweat blood; **sacar la ~ a algo** to squeeze the last drop out of sth*.
(**b**) (*: And, CAm: berrinche*) rage, bad temper; **estar de ~** to be in a bad mood.

┌─── **CHICHA** ───┐

ⓘ **Chicha** *is a strong alcoholic drink made from fermented maize and produced in Peru, where it is associated with ceremonial and ritual occasions. It is now an element of what is known as* **chicha** *culture, a dynamic blend of traditional Indian and modern imported styles and fashions created out of the migration of the rural poor to major cities.* **Chicha** *music has become the most popular music in Peru. It combines the traditional Andean* **huayno** *with tropical, Afro-Hispanic music and electronic instruments.*

chicha² NF (*And*) thick-soled shoe.

chicha³* NF meat; **de ~ y nabo*** insignificant; **tener poca(s) ~(s)** to be slim; (*pey*) to be skinny.

chicha⁴ ADJ (*Náut*): **calma ~** dead calm.

chícharo NM pea, chickpea.

chicharra NF (**a**) (*Ent*) harvest bug, cicada; **es como ~ en verano** it's nasty, it's unpleasant; **canta la ~** it's terribly hot.
(**b**) (*: habladora*) chatterbox.
(**c**) (*: Elec*) bell, buzzer; (*Telec*) bug*, bugging device*.
(**d**) (*CAm, Carib: chicharrón*) crackling (of pork).
(**e**) (‡: *droga*) reefer‡.
(**f**) (‡: *monedero*) purse.

chicharrero¹ NM oven, hot place; (*fig*) suffocating heat.

chicharrero² [1] ADJ of Tenerife.
[2] NM, **chicharrera** NF native (o inhabitant) of Tenerife; **los ~s** the people of Tenerife.

chicharro NM horse-mackerel.

chicharrón NM (**a**) (*Culin*) crackling (of pork); piece of burnt meat; **estar hecho un ~** (*Culin*) to be burnt to a cinder; (*persona*) to be as red as a lobster.
(**b**) (*fig*) sunburnt person.
(**c**) (*Carib: adulador*) flatterer.

chiche [1] ADJ Y ADV (*CAm*) easy, simple; easily; **está ~** it's a cinch‡.
[2] NM (**a**) (*LAm Anat*) breast, teat.
(**b**) (*LAm*) (*objeto*) precious thing, delightful object; (*joya*) fancy jewel, trinket; (*juguete*) small toy; (*persona fiable*) trustworthy person; (*inteligente*) clever person; (*pulcro*) well-dressed person; (*sitio elegante*) elegant place, nice room (*etc*).
[3] NF (*Méx*) nursemaid.

chichear [1a] VTI to hiss.

chicheo NM hiss, hissing.

➤ LENGUA Y USO: **cheque → 47.5**

chichera⁑ NF (*CAm*) jail, clink⁑.
chichería NF (*LAm*) *chicha* tavern; *chicha* factory.
chichero NM (*LAm*) *chicha* vendor (*o* maker).
chichi ① NM (⁑⁑) cunt⁑⁑.
　② NF (*Méx*) (**a**) (*teta*) teat. (**b**) (*niñera*) nursemaid.
chichicaste NM (*CAm*) (*Bot*) nettle; (*Med*) nettle rash.
chichigua NF (**a**) (*CAm, Méx: niñera*) nursemaid. (**b**) (*Carib: cometa*) kite. (**c**) (*Méx*) (*animal manso*) tame animal; (*hembra*) nursing animal. (**d**) (*Méx*⁑) pimp.
chicho NM (**a**) (*bucle*) curl, ringlet. (**b**) (*bigudí*) curler, roller.
chichón¹⁎ ADJ (**a**) (*Cono Sur: jovial*) merry, jovial. (**b**) (*CAm: fácil*) easy, straightforward; **está ~** it's a piece of cake⁎.
chichón² NM bump, lump, swelling.
chichonear⁎ [1a] VI (*Cono Sur*) to joke.
chichonera NF helmet.
chichus NM (*CAm*) flea.
chicle NM chewing gum; **~ de burbuja, ~ de globo** bubble gum.
chiclear [1a] VI (*CAm, Méx*) (**a**) (*cosechar*) to extract gum (*for chewing*). (**b**) (*mascar*) to chew gum.
chiclero NM (*Méx, CAm*) rubber tapper.
chico ① ADJ small, little, tiny; small-size(d); **¿tiene en ~?** do you have the smaller size?; **dejar ~ a uno** to put sb in the shade.
　② NM (**a**) (*persona*) boy; child, youngster, lad; (⁎: *en oración directa*) my boy⁎, old boy⁎, old man⁎; **es (un) buen ~** he's a good lad (*o* chap *o* fellow); **los ~s del equipo** the lads in the team; **los ~s de la oficina** the fellows at the office; **~ de la calle** street urchin; **~ de oficina, ~ de los recados** office-boy; **~ prodigio** child prodigy, (*Com etc*) whizz-kid; **como ~ con zapatos nuevos** as happy as a sandboy. (**b**) (*LAm Billar, Naipes etc*) game, round; first game.
chicolear⁎ [1a] ① VI (**a**) (*flirtear*) to flirt, murmur sweet nothings, say nice things. (**b**) (*And: divertirse*) to amuse o.s., have a good time; to do childish things.
　② **chicolearse** VR (*And*) to amuse o.s.
chicoleo NM (**a**) (⁎: *dicho*) compliment, flirtatious remark; **decir ~s** to say nice things. (**b**) (⁎: *acto*) flirting; **estar de ~** to be in a flirtatious mood. (**c**) (*And: cosa infantil*) childish thing; **no andemos con ~s** let's be serious.
chicolero ADJ flirtatious.
chicoria NF chicory.
chicota NF fine girl; (*pey*) big girl, hefty wench.
chicotazo NM (*LAm*) lash, swipe.
chicote NM (**a**) (⁎: *chico*) big chap⁎, fine lad. (**b**) (*Náut*) piece of rope, rope end; (*LAm*) whip, lash. (**c**) (⁎) (*cigarro*) cigar; (*colilla*) cigar stub.
chicotear [1a] ① VT (*LAm: azotar*) to whip, lash; (*LAm: pegar*) to beat up⁎; (*And: matar*) to kill.
　② VI (*LAm: cola etc*) to lash about.
chifa (*And*) ① ADJ (*pey*⁑) Chinky⁑, Chinese.
　② NM Chinese restaurant.
chifla NF (**a**) (*sonido*) hiss, hissing, whistling. (**b**) (*instrumento*) whistle.
chifladera⁎ NF (*CAm, Méx*) crazy idea.
chiflado⁎ ADJ ① daft, barmy⁑; cranky⁎, crackpot; **estar ~ con, estar ~ por** to be crazy about.
　② NM, **chiflada** NF nut⁑, crank⁎, crackpot.
chifladura NF (**a**) = **chifla**. (**b**) (⁎: *locura*) daftness, craziness. (**c**) (⁎) (*una ~*) whim, fad, mania; crazy idea, wild scheme; **su ~ es el ajedrez** his mania is chess, he is crazy about chess; **ese amor no es más que una ~** what he calls love is just a foolish infatuation.
chiflar¹ [1a] ① VT (**a**) *actor, obra etc* to hiss, boo, whistle at; *silbato* to blow. (**b**) (⁎: *beber*) to drink, knock back⁎. (**c**) (⁎: *encantar*) to entrance, captivate; to drive crazy; **me chifla ese conjunto** I rave about that group⁎, I think that group is smashing⁎; **me chiflan los helados** I just adore ice cream; **a mí no me chiflan los eslobodios** I don't exactly go overboard for the Slobodians⁎; **esa chica le chifla** (*o* **tiene chiflado**) he's crazy about that girl.
　② VI to whistle, hiss; (*CAm, Méx: aves*) to sing.
　③ **chiflarse** VR (**a**) (⁎: *pirrarse*) to go barmy⁑, go crazy; **~ con, ~ por** to be (*o* go) crazy about. (**b**) **chiflárselas** (*CAm*⁑) to peg out⁑, kick the bucket⁑.
chiflar² VT (*Téc*) *cuero* to pare, pare down.
chiflato NM whistle.
chifle NM (**a**) (*silbo*) whistle; (*de ave*) call, bird call. (**b**) (*Hist, t CAm, Carib*) powder horn, powder flask.
chiflete NM whistle.
chiflido NM whistle, shrill sound; hiss.
chiflón NM (**a**) (*And, Cono Sur: viento*) draught, blast (of air); (*CAm, Méx*) gale. (**b**) (*CAm, Carib, Cono Sur: de río*) rapids, violent current; (*CAm*) water-

fall; (*Méx: caz*) flume, race; (*Méx: tobera*) nozzle.
chiguín, -ina⁎ NM/F (*CAm*) kid⁎.
chihuahua NM chihuahua.
chiíta ADJ, NMF Shi'ite.
chilaba NF (d)jellabah.
chilacayote NM (*LAm*) gourd.
chilango (*Méx*) ① ADJ of Mexico City.
　② NM, **chilanga** NF native (*o* inhabitant) of Mexico City.
chilco NM (*Chile*) wild fuchsia.
Chile NM Chile.
chile NM (**a**) (*Bot, Culin*) chili, red pepper. (**b**) (*CAm*⁎: *broma*) joke.
chilear⁎ [1a] VI (*CAm*) to tell jokes.
chilena¹ NF overhead kick, scissors kick.
chilenismo NM chilenism, word (*o* phrase *etc*) peculiar to Chile.
chileno, -a², chileño, -a ADJ, NM/F Chilean.
chilicote NM (*And, Cono Sur: Ent*) cricket.
chilindrón NM: **al ~** cooked with tomatoes and peppers.
chilla¹ NF thin board; weatherboard, clapboard (*US*).
chilla² NF (*Cono Sur*) fox.
chilla³ NF (*Méx*) (**a**) (*Teat*) gods, gallery. (**b**) (⁎: *pobreza*) poverty; **estar en la ~** to be flat broke⁎.
chilla⁴ NF (*Caza*) decoy, call.
chillador ADJ howling, screeching, screaming; blaring; squealing; creaking.
chillante ADJ (**a**) = **chillador**. (**b**) (*fig*) = **chillón** (b).
chillar [1a] ① VI (**a**) (*animal salvaje, gato etc*) to howl; (*ratón*) to squeak; (*cerdo*) to squeal; (*ave*) to screech, squawk; (*persona*) to yell; to shriek, scream; (*Caza*) to call; (*radio*) to blare; (*frenos*) to screech, squeal; (*puerta*) to creak; **~ a uno** to yell at sb, scream at sb. (**b**) (*colores*) to scream, be loud, clash. (**c**) (*LAm: fig: protestar*) to shout, protest; **no ~** (*Carib, Cono Sur: callarse*) to keep one's mouth shut, not say a word; (*CAm, Carib: informar*) to squeal⁑, turn informer; **el cochino chilló** (*Carib, Méx*) they (*etc*) let the cat out of the bag⁎. (**d**) (*LAm: llorar*) to sob.
　② **chillarse** VR (**a**) (*LAm: quejarse*) to complain (*con* to), protest (*con* to). (**b**) (*And, Carib, Méx*⁎) (*enojarse*) to get cross; (*ofenderse*) to take offence, get into a huff. (**c**) (*CAm: sofocarse*) to get embarrassed.
chillería NF row, hubbub.
chillido NM (*V* VI) howl; squeak; squeal; screech; squawk; yell, shriek, scream; blare; creak.
chillo NM (**a**) (*CAm: deuda*) debt. (**b**) (*Carib: muchedumbre*) rabble, mob. (**c**) (*And*) (*ira*) anger; (*protesta*) loud protest.
chillón¹ ① ADJ (**a**) *persona* loud, shrill, noisy; *sonido, voz* shrill, strident; harsh; piercing. (**b**) *color* loud, gaudy, lurid. (**c**) (*LAm*⁎: *quejumbroso*) moaning, whingeing⁎.
　② NM, **chillona** NF (*LAm*) (**a**) (*quejón*) moaner, whiner. (**b**) (*gritón*) loudmouth⁎.
chillón² NM (*Téc*) small nail, panel pin, finishing nail (*US*).
chillonamente ADV loudly, shrilly; stridently; piercingly.
chilpayate⁎, **-a** NM/F (*Méx*) kid⁎, youngster.
chilposo ADJ (*Cono Sur*) ragged, tattered.
chimal NM (*Méx*) dishevelled hair, mop of hair.
chimar [1a] VT (**a**) (*CAm: arañar*) to scratch. (**b**) (*CAm, Méx: molestar*) to annoy, bother. (**c**) (*CAm*⁎) to fuck⁑⁑, screw⁑⁑.
chimba¹ NF (*And, Cono Sur: orilla*) opposite bank (of a river); (*Cono Sur: barrio*) poor quarter (*on other side of river*); (*And: vado*) ford.
chimba² NF (*And*) pigtail.
chimbar [1a] VT (*And*) *río* to ford.
chimbe NM = **chimba¹**.
chimbero ADJ (*Cono Sur*) (*de chimba*) slum (*atr*); (*grosero*) coarse, rough.
chimbo ① ADJ (**a**) (*And, Carib: gastado*) worn-out, wasted, old. (**b**) (*And*) *cheque* bad.
　② NM (*And*) piece of meat.
chimenea NF (**a**) (*de edificio etc*) chimney; (*Náut etc*) funnel; smokestack; (*Min*) shaft; (*Alpinismo*) chimney; **~ de aire** air shaft. (**b**) (*hogar*) hearth, fireplace; **~ (francesa)** fireplace, mantelpiece; chimney piece. (**c**) (⁑: *cabeza*) bonce⁑, head.
chimichurri NM barbecue sauce.
chimiscolear⁎ [1a] VT (*Méx*) (*chismear*) to gossip; (*curiosear*) to poke (*o* go poking) one's nose in⁎.
chimiscolero, -a NM/F (*Méx*) gossip, busybody.
chimpancé NM chimpanzee.
chimpín NM (*And*) brandy, liquor.
chimuelo ADJ (*LAm*) toothless.
China NF China.
china¹ NF (**a**) (*Culin etc*) china; chinaware; porcelain. (**b**) (*seda*) China silk.

china² NF **(a)** (*Geol*) pebble; (*juego*) guessing game played with pebbles; (*de droga*) block; **poner ~s** to put obstacles in the way; **le tocó la ~** he had bad luck; he carried the can*. **(b)** (*And*: *trompo*) spinning-top.

china³ NF **(a)** (*LAm*: *india*) (Indian) woman, (half-breed) girl; (*And, CAm, Cono Sur*: *niñera*) nursemaid; (*And, Cono Sur*: *criada*) servant girl; (*LAm*: *amante*) mistress, concubine; (*And*: *señorita*) elegant young lady. **(b)** (*LAm Téc*) fan, blower.

china⁴ NF (*Carib, Méx*: *naranja*) orange.

chinaca: NF: **la ~** (*Méx*) the plebs*, the proles.

chinado: ADJ crazy.

chinaloa: NF (*Méx*) heroin, smack*.

chinampa NF (*Méx*) floating garden.

chinar: [1a] VT to carve up*, slash.

chinarro NM large pebble, stone.

chinazo NM blow from a stone; **le tocó el ~** he had bad luck; he carried the can*.

chinchada NF (*Cono Sur*) tug-of-war.

chinchal NM (*Carib*) tobacco stall; small shop.

chinchar* [1a] **[1]** VT to pester, bother, annoy; to upset; **me chincha tener que** + *infin* it upsets me to have to + *infin*. **[2]** **chincharse** VR to get cross, get upset; **¡chínchate!** get lost!*; **¡para que te chinches!** so there!; and you can lump it!*; **¡y que se chinchen los demás!** and the rest can go chase themselves!*

chincharrero NM (*And*) fishing boat.

chinche **[1]** NF **(a)** (*Ent*) bug, (*esp*) bedbug; **caer (o morir) como ~s** to die like flies. **(b)** (*chincheta*) drawing pin, thumbtack (*US*). **(c)** (*Cono Sur*: *rabieta*) pique, irritation. **[2]** NMF (*fig*) nuisance; annoying person, pest, bore; (*And, CAm*) naughty child.

chincheta NF drawing pin, thumbtack (*US*).

chinchetear [1a] VT to pin up.

chinchibí NM (*And, CAm, Cono Sur*), **chinchibirra** NF (*Cono Sur*) ginger beer.

chinchilla NF chinchilla.

chinchín¹, chin-chín **[1]** NM **(a)** street music, tinny music. **(b)** (*CAm*: *sonajero*) baby's rattle. **[2]** INTERJ (*para brindar*) cheers!

chinchín² NM (*Carib*) drizzle.

chinchón NM anisette.

chinchona* NF quinine.

chinchorrería* NF **(a)** (*cualidad*) fussiness; critical nature, disrespectful manner; impertinence. **(b)** (*chisme*) piece of gossip; (*cuento*) malicious tale.

chinchorrero* ADJ **(a)** (*exigente*) fussy (about details); (*criticón*) critical, disrespectful; nit-picking*; (*fresco*) impertinent. **(b)** (*chismoso*) gossipy; (*rencoroso*) malicious.

chinchorro NM **(a)** (*red*) net, dragnet, trawl. **(b)** (*bote*) rowing boat, dinghy. **(c)** (*LAm*: *hamaca*) hammock; (*vivienda*) poor tenement; (*Carib*: *tienda*) little shop.

chinchoso ADJ **(a)** (*con chinches*) full of bugs. **(b)** = **chinchorrero**. **(c)** (*pesado*) tiresome, annoying; boring. **(d)** (*And, Carib*: *quisquilloso*) touchy, irritable.

chinchudo* ADJ: **estar ~** (*Cono Sur*) to be in a huff.

chinchulines NMPL (*Cono Sur*) tripe.

chindar: [1a] VT to chuck out.

chinear [1a] **[1]** VT (*CAm*) *niño* to carry in one's arms; to care for; (*pey*) to spoil. **[2]** VI (*Cono Sur*) to have an affair with a half-breed girl.

chinel: NM guard.

chinela NF (*zapatilla*) slipper, mule; (*zueco*) clog.

chinero¹ NM china cupboard.

chinero² ADJ (*And, Cono Sur*) fond of the (half-breed) girls.

chinesco ADJ Chinese.

chinetero ADJ (*Cono Sur*) = **chinero²**.

chinga NF **(a)** (*CAm, Carib*: *colilla*) fag-end*, cigar stub; (*fig*) drop, small amount; **una ~ de agua** a drop of water. **(b)** (*Carib*: *borrachera*) drunkenness. **(c)** (*Méx*) beating-up.

chingada: NF (*CAm, Méx*) (*acto sexual*) fuck*, screw*; (*molestia*) bloody nuisance*.

chingadazo* NM (*Méx*) bash*, punch.

chingado: ADJ (*CAm, Méx*) lousy*, bloody*.

chingadura NF (*Cono Sur*) failure.

chingana NF **(a)** (*And, Cono Sur*: *local*) dive*, tavern; (*de baile*) cheap dance-hall. **(b)** (*Cono Sur*: *fiesta*) wild party.

chinganear [1a] VI (*And, Cono Sur*) to go on the town, live it up*.

chinganero (*And, Cono Sur*) **[1]** ADJ fond of living it up*, wildly social. **[2]** NM, **chinganera** NF owner of a *chingana*.

chingar [1h] **[1]** VT **(a)** (*CAm*) *animal* to dock, cut off the tail of. **(b)** (*LAm*: *joder*) to fuck*, screw*; **hijo de la chingada** bastard*, son of a bitch* (*US*); **¡chinga tu madre!** fuck off!*.

(c) (*: Méx etc*) (*fastidiar*) to annoy, upset; (*arruinar*) to fuck up*; **estar chingado** to be cross, be upset; **¡no chingues!** don't mess me around!*

(d) (*Cono Sur*) *tiro* to aim badly, miss with; *tentativa* to fail in.

(e) (*Carib*) to carry on one's shoulder.

(f) (*Méx*: *robar*) to nick*, pinch*.

[2] VI **(a)** (*beber*) to drink too much.

(b) (*LAm*: *joder*) to fuck*, screw*.

(c) (*CAm*: *contar chistes*) to joke.

(d) (*Méx*: *ganar*) to win.

[3] **chingarse** VR **(a)** (*: emborracharse*) to get tight*.

(b) (*LAm*: *fracasar*) to fail, fall through, come to nothing; **la fiesta se chingó** the party was a failure (*o* a flop*); **el cohete se chingó** the rocket failed to go off, the rocket was a dud*.

chingo **[1]** ADJ **(a)** (*CAm*) *vestido* short; *cuchillo* blunt; *animal* docked, tailless; *persona* in one's underclothes, bare. **(b)** (*And, Carib*: *chico*) small. **(c)** (*CAm, Carib*) *persona* snub-nosed; *nariz* flat, snub. **(d)** **estar ~ por algo** (*Carib*) (*loco por*) to be crazy about sth; (*desear*) to be dying for sth. **[2]** NM **(a)** (*And*: *potro*) colt. **(b)** (*And, CAm*: *barca*) small boat. **(c)** **~s** (*CAm*) underclothes. **(d)** **un ~ de** (*Méx**) lots of, loads of. **[3]** EXCL (*LAm*:*) fuck it!*

chingón* NM (*Méx*) big shot*, top man, boss.

chingue **[1]** ADJ (*Cono Sur*) stinking, repulsive. **[2]** NM (*Cono Sur*) skunk.

chinguear [1a] VT *etc* (*CAm*) = **chingar**.

chinguirito NM (*Carib, Méx*: *licor*) rough liquor, firewater; (*And, Carib*: *trago*) swig (of liquor)*.

chinita¹ NF small stone, pebble; **poner ~s a uno** (*fig*) to make trouble for sb.

chinita² NF (*Cono Sur*: *Ent*) ladybird.

chinito NM, **chinita** NF **(a)** (*Cono Sur*: *criado*) servant. **(b)** (*LAm*: *en oración directa*) dear, dearest. **(c)** (*And, Carib, Cono Sur*: *indio*) Indian boy, Indian girl.

chino¹ **[1]** ADJ Chinese. **[2]** NM, **china⁵** NF Chinese; (*M t*) Chinaman. **[3]** NM **(a)** (*Ling*) Chinese; (*fig*) Greek, double Dutch*; **ni que hablara en ~ ...** I couldn't have understood less even if he'd been talking Chinese. **(b)** (*Culin*) Chinese restaurant.

chino² NM (*Geol*) pebble, stone.

chino³ **[1]** ADJ **(a)** (*CAm*: *calvo*) bald, hairless. **(b)** (*Méx*) *pelo* curly, kinky; *persona* curly-haired. **(c)** (*CAm, Carib*: *furioso*) angry, furious; **estar ~** to be angry; **estar ~ por algo** to be crazy about sth. **(d)** (*LAm*: *joven*) young. **[2]** NM **(a)** (*LAm*: *mestizo*) half-breed; (*Cono Sur, Carib*: *indio*) Indian; (*And*: *t ~* **cholo**) offspring of Indian and Negress; (*Carib*: *hijo de mulato y negra*) offspring of mulatto and Negress; (*And, Carib, Cono Sur*: *criado*) servant; (*And*: *golfo*) street urchin; (*LAm*: *en oración directa*) dear, dearest; **quedar como un ~** (*Carib, Cono Sur*) to come off badly; **trabajar como un ~** (*Carib, Cono Sur*) to work like a slave. **(b)** (*And, CAm*: *cerdo*) pig. **(c)** (*rizos*) **~s** curls. **(d)** (*CAm, Carib*: *enojo*) anger; **le salió el ~** he got angry; **tener un ~** to be angry.

chino⁴ NM (*Culin*) mincer, grinder; mixer, blender.

chinólogo, -a NM/F expert in Chinese affairs, Sinologist; (*hum*) China watcher.

chinorri: NF bird*, chick*.

chip NM, PL **chips** [tʃip] **(a)** (*Inform*) chip; **~ de memoria** memory chip; **~ de silicio** silicon chip. **(b)** (*Culin*) crisp. **(c)** (*Golf*) chip (shot).

chipe **[1]** ADJ (*CAm*) **(a)** (*enfermizo*) weak, sickly. **(b)** (*llorón*) whining, snivelling. **[2]** NMF (*And, CAm, Méx*) baby of the family.

chipé(n): **[1]** ADJ (*t de ~*) super*, smashing*. **[2]** ADV marvellously, really well; **comer de ~** to have a super meal*. **[3]** NF: **la ~** the truth.

chipear [1a] **[1]** VT (*CAm*) to bother, pester. **[2]** VI (*And, CAm*) to moan, whine.

chipi ADJ *etc* = **chipe**.

chipiar* [1a] VT (*CAm*) to bother, pester.

chipichipi NM (*prov, LAm*) continuous drizzle, mist.

chipichusca* NF whore.

chipil* ADJ (*Méx*) sad, gloomy.

chipión* NM (*CAm*) telling-off*.

chipirón NM small cuttlefish.

chipotear [1a] VT (*CAm*) to slap.

Chipre NF Cyprus.

chipriota, chipriote **[1]** ADJ Cyprian, Cypriot.

2 NMF Cypriot.

chiquear [1a] **1** VT (*Carib, Méx*) (*mimar*) to spoil, indulge; (*dar coba a*) to flatter, suck up to*.

2 chiquearse VR (a) (*Méx: mimarse*) to be spoiled.

(b) (*CAm: contonearse*) to swagger along.

chiqueo NM (a) ~s (*Carib, Méx*) flattery, toadying. (b) (*CAm: contoneo*) swagger.

chiquero NM (*pocilga: t fig*) pigsty; (*Taur*) bull pen; (*Cono Sur*) hen run.

chiquilicuatro* NM, **chiquilicuatre*** NM nobody, insignificant person; **es un ~** he's a nobody.

chiquilín NM (*CAm, Cono Sur, Méx*) tiny tot, small boy.

chiquillada NF (a) childish prank; childish thing (to do); **eso son ~s** that's kid's stuff*, that's for children. (b) (*LAm*) kids*, youngsters.

chiquillería NF: **una ~** a crowd of youngsters, a mob of kids*; **llevar la ~** to take the kids*.

chiquillo, -a NM/F kid*, youngster, child.

chiquirín NM (*CAm Ent*) cricket.

chiquirritín ADJ, **chiquirrito** ADJ small, tiny, wee.

chiquitear [1a] VI (a) (*jugar*) to play like a child. (b) (*: beber*) to tipple.

chiquitín **1** ADJ very small, tiny.

2 NM, **chiquitina** NF small child, tiny tot.

chiquito **1** ADJ very small, tiny.

2 NM, **chiquita** NF kid*, youngster; **andarse en chiquitas** to beat about the bush, fuss about details.

3 NM (a) small glass of wine. (b) (*Cono Sur*): **un ~** a bit, a little; **¡espera un ~!** wait a moment!

chiquitura NF (a) (*CAm: nimiedad*) small thing; insignificant detail. (b) (*CAm*) = **chiquillada**.

chira NF (a) (*And: andrajo*) rag, tatter. (b) (*CAm: llaga*) wound, sore.

chirajos NMPL (a) (*CAm: trastos*) lumber, junk. (b) (*And: andrajos*) rags, tatters.

chirajoso ADJ (*CAm*) ragged, tattered.

chircal NM (*And*) brickworks, tileworks.

chiri: NM joint:.

chiribita NF (a) (*chispa*) spark; **echar ~s, estar que echa ~s** to be furious, blow one's top; **le hacían ~s los ojos** her eyes sparkled, her eyes lit up.

(b) ~s* (*Med*) spots before the eyes.

(c) (*Bot*) daisy.

chiribitil NM attic, garret; den; cubbyhole; (*pey*) poky little room, hole.

chiribito NM poker.

chirigota NF joke; fun; **fue motivo de ~** it got a laugh, it led to some amusement; **hacer de uno una ~** to poke fun at sb.

chirigotero ADJ full of jokes, facetious.

chirimbolo NM thingummyjig*; strange object, odd-looking implement; ~s (*equipo*) things, gear, equipment; (*trastos*) lumber, junk; (*Culin*) kitchen things.

chirimía NF (peasant-type) oboe, flageolet, shawm.

chirimiri NM drizzle.

chirimoya NF (a) (*Bot*) custard apple. (b) (*: cabeza*) nut:, head.

chirimoyo* NM (*Cono Sur*) dud cheque*.

chirinada NF (a) (*Cono Sur: fracaso*) failure, disaster. (b) = **chirinola**.

chiringuito NM small shop, stall; open air restaurant, open air drinks stall; bar; night club.

chirinola NF (a) (*riña*) fight, scrap*; (*discusión*) heated discussion; (*conversación*) lengthy conversation, lively talk; **pasar la tarde de ~** to spend the afternoon deep in conversation.

(b) (*nimiedad*) trifle, triviality, unimportant thing.

(c) (*juego*) skittles.

chiripa NF (*Billar*) lucky break; (*fig*) lucky event, fluke, stroke of luck; **de ~, por ~** by a fluke, by chance.

chiripá NM (*And, Cono Sur*) kind of blanket worn as trousers; **gente de ~** country people, peasants.

chiripero **1** ADJ lucky, fluky.

2 NM lucky sort.

chirís* NMF (*CAm*) kid*, child.

chirivía NF (a) (*Bot*) parsnip. (b) (*Orn*) wagtail.

chirivisco NM (*CAm*) firewood, kindling.

chirla[1] NF mussel, clam.

chirla²: NF armed hold-up.

chirlata* NF whore.

chirle ADJ (a) (*sopa etc*) watery, wishy-washy*. (b) (*fig*) flat, dull, wishy-washy*; **poeta ~** mere versifier, uninspired poet.

chirlo NM gash, slash (in the face); long scar.

chirola: NF (*CAm, Carib*), **chirona** NF jug:, jail; **estar en ~** to be in jug:.

chiros NMPL (*And*) rags, tatters.

chiroso ADJ (*And, CAm*) ragged, tattered.

chirota NF (*CAm*) tough woman.

chirote* ADJ (*And*) daft*.

chirri: NM joint:.

chirriado ADJ (*And*) (*gracioso*) witty; (*alegre*) merry, jovial.

chirriar [1b] VI (a) (*grillo etc*) to chirp, sing; (*pájaro*) to chirp, cheep; to screech, squawk; (*rueda, gozne, puerta*) to creak, squeak; (*frenos*) to screech, squeal; (*al freír*) to hiss, sizzle; (*persona*) to sing (o play) out of tune.

(b) (*And: tiritar*) to shiver (with cold *etc*).

(c) (*And*: ir de juerga) to go on a spree.

chirrido NM (*V vi*) shrill sound, high-pitched unpleasant sound; chirp(ing); screech(ing); squawk(ing); creak(ing); squeak(ing); squeal(ing); sizzle, sizzling.

chirrión NM (a) (*carro*) tumbrel. (b) (*And, CAm, Méx: látigo*) whip. (c) (*CAm: sarta*) string, line. (d) (*CAm: charla*) chat, conversation (*esp* between lovers).

chirrionar [1a] VT (*And, Méx*) to whip, lash.

chirrisco ADJ (a) (*CAm, Carib: diminuto*) very small, tiny. (b) (*Méx*) **mujer ~** flirtatious; **viejo ~** dirty old man.

chirucas NFPL canvas mountain boots.

chirumen* NM nous*, savvy*.

chirusa* NF (*Cono Sur: niña*) girl, kid*; (*mujer*) poor woman.

chis INTERJ (*pidiendo silencio*) sh!; (*llamando*) hey!, psst!; (*LAm: asco*) ugh!

chischís NM (*And, CAm, Carib*) drizzle.

chiscón NM shack, hovel, slum.

chisgarabís* NM meddler, nosey-parker*.

chisguete* NM swig*, drink.

chisme NM (a) (*Téc*) gadget, contrivance, jigger*; ~s things, gear, tackle.

(b) (*fig: objeto*) thing, whatnot*, thingummyjig*; **dáme el ~ ese** give me that whatsit, please*; ~s (*fig*) paraphernalia, things, odds and ends.

(c) (*fig: habladuría*) piece of gossip, tale; ~s gossip, tittletattle, tales; **no me vengas con esos ~s** don't bring those tales to me, I don't want to hear your tittle-tattle.

chismear [1a] VI to gossip, tell tales, spread scandal.

chismería NF, **chismerío** NM (*Carib, Cono Sur*) gossip, tittle-tattle, scandal.

chismero ADJ Y N = **chismoso**.

chismografía NF gossip.

chismorrear [1a] VI = **chismear**.

chismorreo NM = **chismería**.

chismoso **1** ADJ gossiping, scandalmongering.

2 NM, **chismosa** NF talebearer, scandalmonger.

chispa NF (a) (*centella*) spark (*t Elec*); (*fig*) sparkle, gleam; **echar ~s*, estar que echa ~s*** to be hopping mad*.

(b) (*gota*) drop (*esp* of rain); ~s sprinkling (of rain); **caen ~s** there are a few drops falling.

(c) (*hoja*) flake; small particle, (*esp*) small diamond.

(d) (*fig: pizca*) bit, tiny amount; **ni ~** not the least bit, nothing at all; **eso no tiene (ni) ~ de gracia** that's not in the least bit funny; **si tuviera una ~ de inteligencia** if he had an atom of intelligence.

chisparse* [1a] VR (a) (*And: emborracharse*) to get tight*. (b) (*CAm, Méx: huir*) to run away, slip off.

chispazo NM (a) spark (*t fig*); **primeros ~s** (*fig*) first signs, opening shots, intimations. (b) (*fig*) = **chisme** (c). (c) (*: bebida*) swig*.

chispeante ADJ (*fig*) sparkling, scintillating.

chispear [1a] **1** VI (a) to spark (*t Elec*).

(b) (*fig*) to sparkle, scintillate.

(c) (*Met*) to drizzle, spot with rain.

(d) (*And*) to gossip, spread scandal.

2 chispearse VR (*Carib, Cono Sur*) to get drunk.

chispero¹ **1** ADJ (*And, Carib*) gossiping, scandalmongering.

2 NM (*CAm*) (††) lighter; (*Aut*) spark(ing) plug.

chispero²* **1** ADJ of low-class Madrid.

2 NM, **chispera** NF low-class inhabitant of Madrid.

chispita* NF: **una ~ de vino** a drop of wine.

chisporrotear [1a] VI to throw out sparks; (*esp Culin: aceite etc*) to hiss, splutter; (*jamón etc*) to sizzle; (*madera*) to crackle.

chisporroteo NM (*de aceite*) hissing, spluttering; (*de carne*) sizzling; (*de madera*) crackling.

chisquero NM pocket lighter.

chist INTERJ = **chis**.

chistada NF bad joke.

chistar [1a] VI to speak, say something; **no ~** not to say a word; **lo aceptó sin ~** he took it without a word; **nadie chistó** nobody spoke up, nobody answered back.

chiste NM joke, funny story; (*en periódico etc*) cartoon; **~ goma** shaggy-dog story; **~ verde** blue joke, dirty story; **caer en el ~** to get the point of the story, get it; **dar en el ~** to guess right; **hacer ~ de algo, tomar algo a ~** to take sth as a joke; **¡aquello tiene ~!** (*iró*) I suppose you think that's funny?; **no veo el ~** I don't get it; what's funny about that?

chistera NF (a) (*Pesca*) fish basket; (*Dep*) long curved variety of pelota racquet. **(b)** (*: *sombrero*) top hat, topper*; **~ de encantador** magician's hat.

chistosamente ADV funnily, amusingly; wittily.

chistoso [1] ADJ funny, amusing; witty.

[2] NM, **chistosa** NF wit, amusing person.

chistu NM (Basque) flute.

chistulari NM (Basque) flute player, flautist.

chita[1]: **a la ~ callando** quietly; unobtrusively; (*pey*) on the quiet, on the sly.

chita[2] NF **(a)** (*Anat*) anklebone; (*juego*) boys' game played with an anklebone; **dar en la ~** to hit the nail on the head; **no se me da una ~**, (**no**) **me importa una ~** I don't care two hoots (*de* about).

(b) (*Méx*) (*saco*) net bag; (*dinero*) money; (*ahorros*) small savings, nest egg.

chiticalla• NMF quiet sort; (*fig*) clam.

chiticallando = **chita**[1].

chito, chitón INTERJ sh!

chiva [1] NF **(a)** (*Agr, Zool*) kid; (*LAm*) (*cabra*) goat, nanny-goat; (*oveja*) sheep; **estar como una ~** to be crazy.

(b) (*LAm: barba*) goatee (beard).

(c) (*And, CAm*) (*autobús*) bus; (*coche*) car.

(d) (*CAm: manta*) blanket, bedcover; **~s** bedclothes.

(e) (*Carib, Cono Sur: niña*) naughty little girl; (*CAm, Cono Sur: marimacho*) mannish woman; (*And, Carib, Cono Sur: vividora*) immoral woman.

(f) (*CAm, Cono Sur: rabieta*) rage, tantrum.

(g) (*Carib: mochila*) knapsack.

(h) **~s** (*Méx*•) junk.

(i) (*Cono Sur*•) fib, tall story; **meter una ~** to cook up a story.

(j) (*Carib*•: *delator*) grass‡, informer.

[2] ADJ (*CAm*•: *despabilado*) alert, sharp.

[3] EXCL (*CAm*•) look out!, careful!

chivar [1a] (*prov, LAm*) [1] VT (*fastidiar*) to annoy, upset; (*estafar*) to swindle.

[2] **chivarse** VR **(a)** (*enojarse*) to get annoyed. **(b)** (‡) = **chivatear** (**a**).

chivata‡ NF **(a)** (*linterna*) torch. **(b)** (*pluma*) fountain-pen.

chivatazo‡ NM tip-off; **dar ~** to inform, give a tip-off.

chivatear [1a] [1] VI **(a)** (‡: *soplar*) to grass‡ (*contra* on), inform (*contra* on); (‡) to blow the gaff‡.

(b) (*And, Cono Sur*) (*gritar*) to shout, make a hullabaloo; (*saltar*) to jump about; (*retozar*) to indulge in horse-play, have a noisy free-for-all.

(c) (*Carib: impresionar*) to create a big impression.

[2] **chivatearse** VR (*Carib*) to get scared.

chivato NM **(a)** (*Agr, Zool*) kid.

(b) (*: soplón*) stool-pigeon*, informer; (*de fábrica etc*) time-keeper.

(c) (*LAm: niño*) child, kid*.

(d) (*And: pillo*) rascal, villain.

(e) (*And: aprendiz*) apprentice, mate.

(f) (*Carib*) outstanding individual.

(g) (*Cono Sur: aguardiente*) cheap liquor, firewater.

(h) (*Aut*) indicator (light).

(i) (*busca*) pager, beeper.

chivearse• [1a] VR (*CAm*) to get embarrassed.

chivera NF (*And, CAm*) goatee (beard).

chivero NM **(a)** (*And: conductor*) busdriver. **(b)** (*And: matón*) brawler. **(c)** (*Carib: intrigante*) intriguer.

chiviroso• ADJ (*CAm*) outgoing, extrovert.

chivo [1] NM **(a)** (*Agr, Zool*) kid; goat; billy goat; **~ expiatorio** scapegoat; **esto huele a ~** (*Carib, Cono Sur*) this smells suspicious, there's something fishy about this•.

(b) (*CAm: dados*) dice; (*juego*) game of dice.

(c) (*Carib: estafa*) fraud; (*intriga*) plot, intrigue; (*Com: acto*) smuggling; illegal trading; (*géneros*) contraband, smuggled goods.

(d) (*And, CAm, Carib, Cono Sur*) rage, fit of anger; **comer ~** (*And, Carib*), **ponerse como ~** (*CAm, Carib*) to get furious.

(e) (*Méx*) (*jornal*) day's wages; (*anticipo*) advance; (*: soborno*) backhander•.

(f) (*Carib: golpe*) punch, blow.

(g) (*And, CAm: niño*) naughty boy, scamp.

(h) (*CAm*•: *guatemalteco*) Guatemalan.

(i) (*CAm*‡: *chulo*) pimp.

(j) (‡: *maricón*) poofter‡.

[2] ADJ (*CAm*•) **(a)** (*guatemalteco*) Guatemalan.

(b) **andas bien ~** you're looking very smart.

chivón (*Carib*) [1] ADJ annoying, irritating.

[2] NM, **chivona** NF bore.

chocante ADJ **(a)** (*sorprendente*) startling, striking; (*raro*) odd, strange; (*notable*) noteworthy; **es ~ que ...** it is odd that ..., it is surprising that ...; it is noteworthy that ...; **lo ~ es que ...** the odd thing about it is that ...

(b) (*escandaloso*) shocking, scandalous.

(c) (*esp LAm*) (*pesado*) tiresome, tedious, annoying; (*fresco*) cheeky, impertinent; (*repugnante*) disgusting, repulsive; (*antipático*) unpleasant.

chocantería NF (*LAm*) **(a)** (*descaro*) impertinence. **(b)** (*chiste*) coarse joke.

chocar [1g] [1] VT **(a)** (*asombrar*) to shock; to startle, surprise; **me choca que no lo hayan hecho** I am surprised that they haven't done it; **ello me chocó bastante** it gave me rather a jolt; it did surprise me rather.

(b) *vasos* to clink; *mano* to shake; **¡chócala!**• put it there!•, shake (on it)!; **~ la mano con uno** to shake hands with sb; **~ los cinco**• to shake on it•.

(c) (*Méx: asquear*) to disgust; **me choca su actitud** I can't stand his attitude, his attitude makes me sick•.

[2] VI **(a)** (*sorprender*) to shock; to be surprising, be startling, be odd; **no es de ~** it's not all that surprising.

(b) (*Aut etc*) to collide, crash; (*vasos*) to clink; (*platos*) to clatter; (*Mil*) to clash; **~ con** to collide with, crash into, smash against; to hit, strike; **el buque chocó con una mina** the ship struck a mine; **el balón chocó con el poste** the ball crashed into the post; **por fin chocó con el jefe** finally he fell out with (o clashed with) the boss; **esta teoría choca con dificultades** this theory runs into (o up against) difficulties.

[3] **chocarse** VR (*Méx Aut*) to have a crash.

chocarrear [1a] VI **(a)** (*tontear*) to clown, act the fool. **(b)** (*contar chistes*) to tell rude jokes.

chocarrería NF **(a)** (*cualidad*) coarseness, vulgarity; scurrility; clownishness. **(b)** (*una ~*: *chiste*) coarse joke, dirty story; (*acción*) clownish act.

chocarrero ADJ (*grosero*) coarse, vulgar, rude; (*escandaloso*) scurrilous; (*de payaso*) clownish.

chocha[1] NF (*t ~ perdiz*) woodcock.

chochada‡‡ NF **(a)** (‡‡) cunt‡‡. **(b)** (*CAm*•: *nimiedad*) triviality; **~s** bits and pieces.

chochaperdiz NF woodcock.

chochear [1a] VI **(a)** (*ser senil*) to dodder, be doddery, be senile; to be in one's dotage. **(b)** (*fig*) to be soft, go all sentimental.

chochecientos• ADJ PL umpteen•.

chochera NF, **chochez** NF **(a)** (*vejez*) dotage; senility; second childhood.

(b) (*una ~*) silly thing; sentimental act.

(c) (*And, Cono Sur: preferido*) favourite, pet; **tener ~ por una** to dote on sb, be crazy about sb.

chochín NM **(a)** (*Orn*) wren. **(b)** (‡: *amiga*) bird‡, girlfriend.

chochita NF wren.

chocho[1] [1] ADJ **(a)** (*senil*) doddering, doddery, senile.

(b) (*fig*) soft, doting, sentimental; **estar ~ por** to dote on, be soft about.

(c) (*Cono Sur: alegre*) happy.

(d) (*CAm*•: *nicaragüense*) Nicaraguan.

[2] NM, **chocha**[2] NF **(a)** (*: drogadicto*) drug addict.

(b) (*CAm*•: *nicaragüense*) Nicaraguan.

[3] EXCL (*CAm*•) no kidding!•, really?

chocho[2] NM cinnamon sweet; **~s** sweets, candies (*US*).

chocho[3]‡‡ NM (*Anat*) cunt‡‡.

chocho[4]• NM (*lío*) rumpus•, shindy•.

chochoca‡ NF (*CAm*) nut‡, head.

chocholear [1a] VT (*And*) to spoil, pamper.

chock NM (*And, Carib Aut*) choke.

choclo[1] NM clog; sandal; overshoe; (*Méx*) low-heeled shoe; **meter el ~** (*Méx*) to put one's foot in it.

choclo[2] NM **(a)** (*LAm Agr*) ear of (tender) maize, cob of sweet corn; (*Culin*) (*gen*) corn on the cob; (*guisado*) Indian maize stew.

(b) **~s** (*Cono Sur*) children's arms, children's legs.

(c) **un ~ de** (*And fig*) a group of, a lot of.

(d) (*Cono Sur*) (*dificultad*) difficulty, trouble; (*molestia*) annoyance; (*carga*) burden, task.

choclón NM (*Cono Sur*) crowd, mob.

choco[1] (*And, Cono Sur*) [1] ADJ curly, curly-haired.

[2] NM poodle.

choco[2] ADJ (*And, Cono Sur*) (*rojo*) dark red; (*chocolate*) chocolate-coloured; (*moreno*) swarthy, dark.

choco[3] [1] ADJ (*CAm, Cono Sur, Méx: manco*) one-armed; (*cojo*) one-legged; (*tuerto*) one-eyed; (*Cono Sur: rabón*) tailless.

[2] NM **(a)** (*Cono Sur: cabo*) stump. **(b)** (*And: chistera*) top hat. **(c)** (*Méx*‡‡) cunt‡‡.

choco[4] NM (*Zool*) cuttlefish.

choco[5]‡ NM (*droga*) = **chocolate** (**c**).

chocolatada NF hot chocolate drink, cocoa.

chocolate [1] ADJ (*LAm*) chocolate-coloured; dark red.

[2] NM **(a)** (*de comer*) chocolate; (*de beber*) drinking chocolate, cocoa; **~ con leche** milk chocolate; **~ sin leche**, **~ negro** plain chocolate.

(b) (*LAm**: *hum*) blood; **dar a uno agua de su propio ~** (*Méx**) to give sb a taste of his own medicine; **sacar el ~ a uno** to make sb's nose bleed.

(c) (‡: *hachís*) hash*, pot‡; **darle al ~** to be hooked on drugs.

chocolatera NF **(a)** (*recipiente*) chocolate pot. **(b)** (*: *vehículo viejo*) old thing, piece of junk; (*Aut*) old crock; (*Náut*) hulk.

chocolatería NF chocolate factory; *café specializing in serving drinking chocolate.*

chocolatero ⃞1 ADJ fond of chocolate.
⃞2 NM **(a)** (*And*: *chcolatera*) chocolate pot. **(b)** (*Carib, Méx*: *viento*) strong northerly wind.

chocolatina NF **(a)** chocolate. **(b)** (‡) 100 pesetas.

chocolear [1a] (*And*) ⃞1 VT to dock, cut off the tail of.
⃞2 VI to get depressed.

chófer NM, **chofer** NM, **choferesa** NF (*LAm*) driver; motorist; (*empleado*) chauffeur.

cholada NF (*And*: *pey*) action typical of a *cholo*.

cholar [1a] VT to nick‡, pinch*.

cholería NF (*And*), **cholerío** NM (*And*) group of *cholos*.

cholga NF (*LAm*) mussel, clam.

cholla NF **(a)** (‡: *cabeza*) nut‡, head; (*fig*) nous*, gumption*. **(b)** (*CAm*: *herida*) wound, sore. **(c)** (*And, CAm*: *pereza*) laziness, slowness.

chollo‡ NM **(a)** (*Com*) bargain, snip*; (*prebenda*) plum, soft job; **¡qué ~!** what luck!; **es un ~** it's a doddle*, it's a cinch‡. **(b)** (*amorío*) love-affair.

cholludo ADJ (*And, CAm*) lazy, slow.

cholo ⃞1 ADJ **(a)** (*LAm*) half-breed, mestizo (*y V* **2**).
(b) (*Cono Sur*: *cobarde*) cowardly.
⃞2 NM, **chola** NF **(a)** (*LAm*) (*mestizo*) half-breed, mestizo; (any) dark-skinned person; (*CAm*: *indio*) half-civilized Indian; (*Cono Sur*: *indio*) Indian.
(b) (*LAm hum*: *peruano*) Peruvian.
(c) (*Cono Sur*: *cobarde*) coward.
(d) (*And, Carib*: *en oración directa*) darling, honey (*US*).

chomba NF (*Cono Sur*) = **chompa**.

chompa NF (*LAm*) jumper, sweater.

chompipe NM (*CAm*) turkey.

chonchón NM (*Cono Sur*) lamp.

chonco (*CAm*) ⃞1 ADJ = **choco³**.
⃞2 NM stump.

chongo NM **(a)** (*Cono Sur*: *cuchillo*) blunt knife, worn-out knife. **(b)** (*Carib*: *caballo*) old horse. **(c)** **~s** (*CAm, Méx*) (*trenzas*) pigtails, tresses; (*moño*) bun.

chonta NF (*And*) palm shoots.

chontal ADJ **(a)** (*CAm*) *indio* wild, uncivilized; (*rebelde*) rebellious; (*revoltoso*) unruly. **(b)** (*And, CAm, Carib*: *inculto*) uncivilized; (*grosero*) rough, coarse; (*Carib*: *de habla inculta*) rough-spoken.

chop NM (*LAm*) tankard, mug.

chopa* NF jacket.

chopazo* NM (*Cono Sur*), **chope*** NM (*Cono Sur*) punch, bash*.

chopera NF poplar grove.

chopería NF (*Cono Sur*) bar.

chopito NM baby squid.

chopo NM **(a)** (*Bot*) black poplar; **~ de Italia, ~ lombardo** Lombardy poplar.
(b) (*: *Mil*) gun; **cargar con el ~** (*fig*) to join up, do one's military service.

choque NM **(a)** (*impacto*) impact; (*de vehículo en movimiento*) jolt, jar; (*de explosión*) blast, shock wave.
(b) (*ruido*) crash; (*de platos etc*) clatter; (*de vasos*) clink.
(c) (*Aut, Ferro etc*) crash, smash; collision; **~ de frente, ~ frontal** head-on collision; **~ de trenes** rail smash, rail accident.
(d) **~ eléctrico** (*Elec*) electric shock.
(e) (*Med*) shock.
(f) (*Mil y fig*) clash; conflict; **entrar en ~** to clash; **estar en abierto ~ con** to conflict openly with.

choquezuela NF kneecap.

chorar‡ [1a] VT *casa* to burgle; *objeto* to rip off‡.

chorba‡ NF bird‡, girlfriend.

chorbo‡ NM **(a)** (*novio*) boyfriend; (*tío*) bloke‡, guy*. **(b)** (*coime*) pimp.

chorcha NF **(a)** (*Méx*) (*fiesta*) noisy party; **una ~ de amigos** a group of friends (out for a good time).
(b) (*CAm Orn*) crest, comb.
(c) (*CAm Med*) goitre.
(d) (*CAm*‡: *clítoris*) clit‡, clitoris.

chorchero ADJ (*Méx*) party-loving.

chorchi‡ NM soldier.

chorear [1a] ⃞1 VT (‡) **(a) me chorea** it gets up my nose‡; **estar choreado** to be miffed*, be upset. **(b)** (*robar*) to pinch*, nick‡.
⃞2 VI (*Cono Sur*) to grumble, complain.

choreo* NM (*Cono Sur*) grouse*, complaint.

chori NM **(a)** (*cuchillo*) chiv‡, knife. **(b)** (*ladrón*) thief.

choricear‡ [1a] VT to rip off‡, lift*.

choricería‡ NF crookedness*, corruption.

choricero‡ NM crook*.

chorizada NF swindle, con*; theft.

chorizar‡ [1f] VT to nick‡, rip off‡.

chorizo ⃞1 ADJ (‡) lousy‡, bloody awful‡.
⃞2 NM **(a)** (*Culin*) hard pork sausage, salami.
(b) (*Circo*) balancing pole.
(c) (‡‡: *Anat*) prick‡‡.
(d) (*And, Cono Sur Culin*) rump steak.
(e) (*And, Cono Sur Arquit*) mixture of clay and straw used in plastering.
(f) (‡) (*matón*) thug, lout; (*ladrón*) small-time crook*; (*carterista*) pickpocket.
(g) (*And*: *idiota*) idiot.
(h) (*Carib pey*) mulatto.

chorlitejo NM, **chorlito** NM (*Orn*) plover.

chorlo NM, **chorla** NF (*And, CAm, Carib*) great-great-grandchild.

choro¹ NM **(a)** (*persona*) thief, burglar. **(b)** (*Ling*) thieves' slang.

choro² NM (*And, Cono Sur*: *Zool*) mussel.

chorote NM **(a)** (*bebida*) (*Carib, Méx*) drinking chocolate (with brown sugar); (*And*) thick drinking chocolate.
(b) (*Carib*) (any) thick drink; (*bebida aguada*) watery drink; (*café*) coffee.
(c) (*And*: *chocolatera*) unglazed chocolate pot.

chorra NF **(a)** (‡) luck, jam‡; **¡qué ~ tiene!** look at that for jam!‡ **(b)** (*Cono Sur*) underworld slang. **(c)** (‡‡: *Anat*) prick‡‡. **(d)** **de ~‡** (ADV) by chance. **(e)** (‡: *idiota*) idiot.

chorrada NF **(a)** (*de leche etc*) extra drop; bonus; **dar algo con ~** to give sth and a bit extra. **(b)** (*adorno*) unnecessary adornment; (*detalle*) superfluous detail. **(c)** (*: *dicho*) stupid remark; **~s** nonsense, drivel. **(d)** (*objeto*) knick-knack. **(e)** (‡‡: *meados*) piss‡‡; **echar la ~** to have a piss‡‡.

chorrar‡ [1a] VT = **chorar**.

chorrear [1a] ⃞1 VT **(a)** (*: *regañar*) to tick off*, dress down*.
(b) (*And*: *mojar*) to soak.
(c) (*Cono Sur*‡) to rip off‡.
⃞2 VI **(a)** (*salir a chorros*) to gush (forth), spout (out), spirt; (*gotear*) to drip, trickle; **~ de sudor** to run with sweat; **la ropa chorrea todavía** his clothes are still wringing wet.
(b) (*fig*) to trickle (in, away *etc*); **chorrean todavía las solicitudes** the applications are still trickling in.
⃞3 **chorrearse** VR: **~ algo** (*And*) to pinch sth*.

chorreo NM **(a)** (*de agua*) gushing; spouting; dripping; trickling.
(b) (*fig*) constant drain (on resources *etc*).
(c) (‡: *reprimenda*) ticking-off*, dressing-down*.
(d) **~ mental‡** nonsense, rubbish.

chorreón NM cascade.

chorrera NF **(a)** (*pico*) spout; (*canal*) channel, runlet.
(b) (*señal*) mark (left by dripping water *etc*).
(c) (*de río*) rapids.
(d) **~s** (*Cos*) frill, lace adornment.
(e) (*LAm fig*) string, stream, lot; **una ~ de** a whole string of, a lot of.
(f) (*Carib**: *regañada*) ticking-off*.
(g) *V* **jamón**.

chorrero ADJ jammy‡, lucky.

chorretada NF **(a)** (*chorro*) spirt, squirt, jet. **(b)** = **chorrada** (a).

chorretón NM **(a)** (*chorro*): **echa un buen ~ de aceite** put plenty of oil on it. **(b)** (*mancha*) dribble.

chorrillo NM (*fig*) constant stream, steady trickle.

chorro NM **(a)** (*de agua etc*) jet; spirt, squirt, stream; dribble, trickle; **beber a ~** to drink a jet of wine (from a wineskin); **llover a ~s** to pour; **salir a ~s** to gush forth, come spirting out.
(b) (*Téc*) jet, blast; (*Aer*) jet; **~ de arena** sandblast; **~ de vapor** steam jet; **avión a ~** jet plane; **motor a ~** jet engine; **con propulsión a ~** jet-propelled.
(c) (*fig*) stream; **un ~ de palabras** a stream of words, a torrent of words; **un ~ de gente** (*Méx*) lots of people; **un ~ de voz** a verbal blast, an awfully loud voice; **a ~s** in plenty, in abundance; **hablar a ~s** to talk nineteen to the dozen; **soltar el ~** to burst out laughing; to produce a torrent of insults (*etc*).
(d) (‡: *suerte*) jam‡, luck; **¡qué ~ tiene!** look at that for jam!‡
(e) (*And*: *de látigo*) strand (of a whip).
(f) (*CAm*: *grifo*) tap, faucet.
(g) (*Carib**: *reprimenda*) ticking-off*.
(h) (*Cono Sur**: *ladrón*) thief, pickpocket.

chorva *etc* = **chorba** *etc*.

chota¹ NMF (*parásito*) hanger-on; (*pelotillero*) creep‡, toady; (*de cárcel*) trusty.

chota² NF: **la ~** (*Méx*) the fuzz‡.

chotacabras NM INVAR nightjar.

chotear [1a] ⃞1 VT **(a)** (*LAm*: *burlarse de*) to make fun of.

(b) (*And: mimar*) to spoil, pamper.
(c) (*CAm*) *sospechoso* to shadow, tail.
[2] **chotearse** VR **(a)** (*bromear*) to joke, take things as a joke; **~ de** to make fun of, ridicule. **(b)** (‡) to cough‡, inform.
choteo NM joking, amusement.
chotis NM INVAR **(a)** schottische. **(b)** *traditional dance of Madrid.* **(c) ser más agarrado que un ~*** to be tight-fisted.
choto¹ [1] ADJ (*CAm*) abundant, plentiful; **estar ~ de** to be full of, be loaded with; **de ~** free, for nothing.
[2] NM (*cabrito*) kid; (*ternero*) calf.
choto²‡ (*Cono Sur*) [1] NM **(a)** (*pene*) prick‡, cock‡. **(b) viejo ~** stupid old git‡.
[2] ADJ (*de poco valor*) crummy‡; (*viejo*) clapped-out*.
chotuno ADJ *cabrito, ternero* sucking, very young; *cordero* weakly; **oler a ~** to smell bad.
chova NF crow, rook; **~ piquirroja** chough.
chovinismo NM *etc* = **chauvinismo** *etc*.
chow-chow ['tʃautʃau] NM, PL **chow-chow** chow.
choza NF hut, shack.
chozno NM, **chozna** NF great-great-great-grandchild.
chrisma ['krisma] NF, **christma(s)** ['krisma] NM, PL **christmas** ['krismas] Christmas card.
chubasco NM **(a)** (*Met*) shower, squall. **(b)** (*fig*) setback; bad patch; **aguantar el ~** (*fig*) to weather the storm.
chubascoso ADJ squally, stormy.
chubasquero NM **(a)** (*hule*) oilskins; (*gabardina*) light raincoat; anorak. **(b)** (‡: *hum*) French letter.
chucán ADJ (*CAm*) (*bufón*) buffoonish; (*grosero*) coarse, rude.
chúcaro ADJ (*LAm*) *animal* wild, untamed; *persona* shy.
chucear [1a] VT (*LAm*) to prick, goad.
chucha NF **(a)** (*Zool*) dog, bitch; **¡~!** down! **(b)** (*: novia*) sweetheart. **(c)** (*And: Zool*) opossum. **(d)** (*And: olor*) body odour. **(e)** (*And: juego*) hide-and-seek. **(f)** (*And, Cono Sur*‡: *Anat*) cunt‡. **(g)** (‡: *Fin*) one peseta.
chuchada NF (*CAm*) trick, swindle.
chuchear¹ [1a] VI to hunt, trap, fowl.
chuchear² [1a] VI = **cuchichear**.
chuchería NF **(a)** (*adorno*) trinket, bit of jewellery, knick-knack. **(b)** (*bocado*) titbit, dainty morsel; (*dulce*) sweet.
chuchito NM = **chucho 2(i)**.
chucho [1] ADJ **(a)** (*And*) *fruta* soft, watery; *persona* wrinkled.
(b) (*CAm: tacaño*) mean.
(c) (*Méx: chismoso*) gossipy.
[2] NM **(a)** (*Zool*) hound, mongrel, mutt‡; **¡~!** down boy!
(b) (*: novio*) sweetheart.
(c) (*Carib: Ferro*) switch; siding.
(d) (*Carib: látigo*) rawhide whip.
(e) (*Cono Sur*: *cárcel*) jail.
(f) (*LAm*) (*escalofrío*) shakes, shivers; (*fiebre*) fever; **entrarle a uno el ~*** to get the jitters*.
(g) (*CAm*: *ostentoso*) spiv*.
(h) (*LAm*‡) joint‡, reefer‡.
(i) (*And, CAm, Méx Culin*) tamale.
chuchoca* NF (*Cono Sur*): **estar en la ~** to be in the thick of it, be where the action is.
chuchumeca NF (*And, Cono Sur*) whore.
chuchumeco NM **(a)** (*tacaño*) mean person, skinflint.
(b) (*Cono Sur*: *enfermizo*) sickly person; (*enano*) dwarf, runt; (*derrochador*) wastrel; (*And*: *viejo*) old dodderer.
(c) (*And, Carib*) toff*, dude* (*US*).
(d) (*Carib*: *idiota*) idiot.
chuchurrío* ADJ **(a)** *flor, planta* wilted. **(b)** *persona* down.
chuco ADJ (*And, CAm, Méx*) *pescado etc* high, off; (*CAm*: *asqueroso*) disgusting, filthy.
chucrú NM, **chucrut** NM sauerkraut.
chueca NF **(a)** (*Bot*) stump.
(b) (*Anat*) rounded bone; round head of a bone.
(c) (*fig*) practical joke, hoax, prank; **gastar una ~ a uno** to play a joke on sb.
chueco ADJ **(a)** (*LAm*: *patizambo*) knock-kneed; (*And, Cono Sur*: *patituerto*) pigeon-toed; (*And*: *cojo*) lame; (*Méx*: *manco*) one-armed, (*con una sola pierna*) one-legged; (*CAm, Carib, Cono Sur, Méx*: *torcido*) crooked, twisted, bent; (*corrupto*) bent‡, crooked*; (*Méx*: *zurdo*) left-handed; **un negocio ~** a crooked deal*.
(b) (*Méx*: *de mala vida*) loose-living; (*sospechoso*) suspicious.
chufa NF **(a)** (*Bot*) chufa, tiger nut. **(b)** (*: puñetazo*) bash*, punch. **(c)** (‡: *Fin*) one peseta.
chufeta NF = **chufleta**.
chufla NF joke, merry quip; mockery, derision; **a ~** jokingly; **tomar algo a ~** to take sth as a joke.
chuflarse [1a] VR to joke, make jokes; to take things as a joke.
chuflay NM (*Cono Sur*) punch (*drink*).

chufleta NF joke, merry quip; taunt.
chufletear [1a] VI (*bromear*) to joke, make jokes; (*mofarse*) to jeer, make taunting remarks.
chuico NM (*Cono Sur*) carafe.
chula NF **(a)** (*madrileña*) woman from the back streets (of Madrid), low-class woman, coarse woman. **(b)** (*charra*) loud wench, flashy female, brassy girl. **(c)** (*LAm*: *novia*) girlfriend.
chulada NF **(a)** (*grosería*) coarse thing; (*cosa graciosa*) funny thing; (*truco*) mean trick.
(b) = **chulería (a)**.
chulángano‡ NM roughneck‡, tough*.
chulapa NF Madrid girl in traditional dress.
chulear* [1a] [1] VT to pinch*, nick‡.
[2] VI to brag, talk big*, show off.
[3] **chulearse** VR: **~ de** to take the mickey out of‡.
chulería NF **(a)** (*cualidad: encanto*) natural charm, winning ways; (*pey: ordinariez*) commonness, vulgarity; (*pey: ostentación*) flashiness; flamboyant manner.
(b) (*la ~*) the *chulos* (collectively, as a group).
(c) (*una ~*) = **chulada (a)**.
chulesco ADJ = **chulo 1**.
chuleta [1] NF **(a)** (*Culin*) chop, cutlet; **~ de puerco** pork chop; **~ de ternera** veal chop.
(b) (*Cos*) insert, piece let in; (*Téc*) filling.
(c) (*: golpe*) punch, bash*.
(d) (*: Univ*) crib*, trot (*US*); (*TV*) autocue, teleprompter.
(e) **~s** (*patillas*) side-whiskers.
(f) (*: persona*) (*elegante*) toff*; (*fresco*) cheeky individual*; (*agresivo*) pushy person*; (*fachendón*) show-off*, swank*.
(g) (*: Golf*) divot.
[2] NM (*) = **chulo 3 (b)**.
[3] ADJ INVAR (*) cheeky*, saucy; pushy*.
chuletada NF barbecue.
chuletón NM large steak, T-bone steak.
chulillo NM (*And*) tradesman's assistant.
chulleco ADJ (*Cono Sur*) twisted, crooked.
chullo NM (*And*) woollen hat.
chulo [1] ADJ **(a)** (*gracioso*) amusing; (*encantador*) charming, attractive, winning.
(b) *aspecto* smart, showy, attractive; (*pey*) flashy, vulgar, gaudy.
(c) *aire, porte* proud; *paso* jaunty, swaggering; **con el sombrero a lo ~** with his hat at a rakish angle; **iba muy ~** he walked with a swagger, he swaggered along.
(d) (*) *comportamiento* bold, free from servility, outspoken; (*pey: fresco*) overbold, fresh*; (*impertinente*) pert, saucy; (*revoltoso*) obstreperous; (*agresivo*) truculent; **se puso en plan ~*** he got stroppy*; **no te pongas ~ conmigo** don't get fresh with me*.
(e) *carácter* slick; rascally, villainous.
(f) (*And, CAm, Méx*) (*bonito*) pretty; (*elegante*) attractive, elegant, graceful.
(g) (*: muy bueno*) brilliant*, super*.
[2] ADV (*CAm*, *Méx*) well; **jugar ~** to play well.
[3] NM **(a)** *typical working-class Madrilenian* (≈ *Cockney*); easy-going sort, free-and-easy person.
(b) (*pey: gandul*) spiv*, layabout, ne'er-do-well; (*matón*) tough guy*, lout; (*bribón*) villain, rascal; **~ (de putas)** pimp, pander.
(c) (*Taur*) bullfighter's assistant.
(d) (*And Orn*) turkey buzzard.
chulón ADJ (*CAm*) naked.
chuma NF (*And, Cono Sur*) drunkenness.
chumacera NF (*Mec*) ball bearing, journal bearing; (*Náut*) rowlock, oarlock (*US*).
chumado* ADJ (*And*) drunk, tight*.
chumarse [1a] VR (*And*) to get drunk.
chumbar [1a] VT **(a)** (*Cono Sur: perro*) to attack, go for; **¡chúmbale!** at him, boy! **(b)** (*And: fusilar*) to shoot. **(c)** (*And*) *bebé* to swaddle.
chumbe NM (*LAm*) sash.
chumbera NF, **chumbimba** NF (*LAm*) prickly pear.
chumbo¹ NM **(a)** (*Bot*) prickly pear (*fruit*); V **higo**. **(b)** (*And*‡) prick‡.
chumbo² NM (*Cono Sur*) shot, pellet.
chumeco NM (*CAm*) apprentice.
chuminada* NF **(a)** (*tontería*) silly thing, piece of nonsense. **(b)** (*detalle*) petty detail.
chumino‡ NM cunt‡.
chumpa NF (*CAm*) jacket.
chumpi NM (*And*) = **chumbe**.
chumpipe NM (*CAm*) turkey.
chumpipear [1a] VI (*CAm*) to wander about.
chunche* NM (*CAm*) whatsit*, thingumabob*.
chuncho (*And*) [1] ADJ (*salvaje*) savage; (*inculto*) uncivilized; (*tímido*) bashful, shy.
[2] NM, **chuncha** NF savage Indian.

chunco ADJ (*And*, *CAm*) = **choco**[3].

chuneco*, **-a** ADJ, NM/F (*CAm*) Jamaican.

chunga* NF joke; fun, banter; **contar ~s** to crack jokes*; **estar de ~** to be in a merry mood; **decir algo de ~** to say sth banteringly; **tomar las cosas en ~** to take things as a joke.

chungo: ADJ (*malo*) bad, rottten; (*desagradable*) nasty; (*feo*) ugly; (*dudoso*) dicey*, dodgy*; (*falso*) *billete* dud*; (*enfermo*) poorly, under the weather.

chungón* NM, **chungona*** NF joker, tease.

chunguearse* [1a] VR to gag, crack jokes*, be in a merry mood; to banter; **~ de uno** to have a bit of fun with sb, make fun of sb.

chuño NM (*LAm*) potato starch, dried potato.

chupa[1]* NF: **poner a uno como ~ de dómine** to give sb a tremendous ticking off*; to shower insults on sb; **en la prensa le pusieron como ~ de dómine** they gave him a tremendous pasting in the press*.

chupa[2] NF (a) (*LAm: embriaguez*) drunkenness. (b) (*CAm: bolsa*) bag. (c) (:) (*chaleco*) waistcoat; (*chaqueta*) leather jacket.

chupachupa [1] NMF (:) sucker:.
[2] NF lollipop.

chupa-chups* NM INVAR lollipop.

chupada NF suck; (*de pipa etc*) pull, puff; (*de bebida*) sip; **~s** sucking, suction; **dar ~s a la pipa** to puff away at one's pipe; **se cree la última ~ del mate*** (*Cono Sur*) he thinks he's the cat's pyjamas*.

chupadero* NM (*Argentina: 1975-81*) secret military prison.

chupado [1] ADJ (a) *persona* skinny, gaunt; emaciated; **~ de cara** with a gaunt face, lantern-jawed.
(b) *falda* tight.
(c) **estar ~** (*LAm**) to be drunk.
(d) **está ~:** it's dead easy*, it's a cinch:.
[2] NM (*Cono Sur*: desaparecido*) missing person.

chupador NM (a) (*aro*) teething ring; (*de biberón*) teat. (b) (*LAm: borracho*) drunkard. (c) (*LAm: fumador*) smoker.

chupaflor NM (*CAm*, *Carib*) hummingbird.

chupagasolina* [1] ADJ INVAR gas-guzzling*, heavy on petrol.
[2] NM INVAR gas-guzzler*.

chupalla NF (*Cono Sur*, *Méx*) straw hat.

chupamangas: NM INVAR (*And*, *Cono Sur*), **chupamedias**: NM INVAR (*And*, *Cono Sur*) creep:, bootlicker*.

chupamirto NM (*Carib*, *Méx*) hummingbird.

chupandina* NF (*Cono Sur*) boozy party*.

chupar [1a] [1] VT (a) (*gen*) to suck; (*sacar*) to suck out, suck up; (*absorber*) to absorb, take in, take up; *bebida* to sip; *esencia etc* to extract; *pecho*, *caramelo etc* to suck; *pipa etc* to suck, smoke, puff at; *sello* to lick, moisten (with one's tongue).
(b) (*LAm: fumar*) to smoke.
(c) (*: *beber*) to drink (*esp* to excess), knock back*.
(d) (*fig*) to milk; to sap; **le chupan el dinero** they are milking him (of his money); **el trabajo le chupa la salud** his work is undermining his health.
(e) (*LAm*: aguantar*) to put up with, take.
(f) **~ la pelota** (*Fútbol*) to be greedy with the ball, not to pass the ball.
[2] VI (a) to suck.
(b) (*LAm*: beber*) to booze*.
(c) (*LAm: fumar*) to smoke.
[3] **chuparse** VR (a) (*) **¡chúpate ésa!** put that in your pipe and smoke it!*
(b) **~ el dedo** to suck one's finger; V t **dedo**.
(c) **~ un insulto** (*LAm*) to put up with an insult, swallow an insult.
(d) (*Med*) to waste away, decline, get thin.

chupasangres NM INVAR (*fig*) bloodsucker.

chupatintas NM INVAR penpusher; petty clerk, minor bureaucrat; (*) toady, creep:.

chupe NM (*LAm: sopa*) a typical spicy soup; (*cocido*) stew; (*Cono Sur: tapa*) snack.

chupeta NF (*Náut*) roundhouse.

chupete NM (a) (*aro etc*) dummy, pacifier (*US*); (*de biberón*) teat; (*LAm: piruli*) lollipop. (b) (*LAm: chupada*) suck. (c) **de ~** V **rechupete**.

chupetear [1a] VT to suck.

chupetón NM suck.

chupi* [1] ADJ super*, brilliant*.
[2] ADV: **pasarlo ~** to have a great time*.

chupinazo NM (a) loud bang. (b) (*Dep*) hard kick, fierce shot.

chupinudo* ADJ = **chupi**.

chupo NM (a) (*LAm Med*) boil. (b) (*And: biberón*) baby's bottle.

chupón NM (a) (*Bot*) sucker.
(b) (*: *persona*) sponger*, hanger-on, parasite; swindler.
(c) (*dulce*) lollipop, sucking sweet; **~ de caramelo** toffee apple.
(d) (*Fútbol*) greedy player.
(e) (*LAm*) dummy, pacifier (*US*); (*biberón*) baby's bottle; (*Méx*) teat.
(f) (*And*, *Carib: de pipa etc*) puff, pull.

(g) (*And Med*) boil.

chupóptero* NM rich layabout; bloodsucker.

churdón NM (*fruta*) raspberry; (*planta*) raspberry cane; (*jarabe*) raspberry syrup, raspberry paste.

churi: NM chiv:, knife.

churo[1] ADJ (*And*, *Cono Sur*) handsome, attractive.

churo[2] NM (a) (*And Mús*) coiled wind instrument. (b) (*And: escalera*) spiral staircase. (c) (*And: rizo*) curl. (d) (*And:: cárcel*) nick:, jail.

churra[1] NF (*And*, *Cono Sur*) girl.

churra[2] NF (*suerte*) luck, jam:.

churrasco NM (*LAm: barbacoa*) barbecue, barbecued meat; (*LAm*) steak; (*Cono Sur: filete*) steak.

churrasquear [1a] VI (*Cono Sur*) to eat steak.

churrasquería NF barbecue stall.

churre[1] NF thick grease; filth.

churre[2] NM (*And*) bloke:, guy* (*US*).

churrería NF fritter stall.

churrero [1] ADJ (:) lucky, jammy:.
[2] NM, **churrera** NF fritter maker, fritter seller.

churrete NM grease spot, dirty mark.

churretear [1a] VT (*LAm*) to spot, stain, dirty.

churretón NM dribble.

churrias* NFPL (*And*, *CAm*, *Carib*) diarrhoea.

churriento ADJ (a) (*mugriento*) greasy; filthy. (b) (*LAm Med*) loose.

churrigueresco ADJ (a) (*Arquit*) Churrigueresque (*lavishly ornamented*). (b) (*fig*) excessively ornate, flowery; flashy.

churro [1] ADJ *lana* coarse; *oveja* coarse-wooled.
[2] NM (a) (*Culin*) fritter; **venderse como ~s** to sell like hot cakes.
(b) (*: *chapuza*) botch, mess; **el dibujo ha salido un ~** the sketch came out all wrong, he messed up the drawing.
(c) (*: *chiripa*) fluke.
(d) (*Anat*:) prick::.
(e) **Juan es un ~** (*And*, *Cono Sur**) Juan is dishy*.
(f) (*Méx**) bad film.

┌─── **CHURROS** ───────────────────────────┐

i **Churros**, long fritters made with flour and water, are popular in much of Spain and are often eaten with thick hot chocolate either for breakfast or as a snack. In Madrid, they eat a thicker variety of **churro** called a **porra**.

└──┘

churrullero ADJ talkative, gossipy.

churruscar [1g] [1] VT to burn, scorch.
[2] **churruscarse** VR to burn, scorch.

churrusco[1] NM burnt toast.

churrusco[2] ADJ (*And*, *CAm*) *pelo* kinky, curly.

churumbel* NM (*niño*) kid*, brat; (*tío*) bloke:, guy*.

churumbela NF (a) (*Mús*) flageolet. (b) (*LAm: para mate*) maté cup; (*And: pipa*) short-stemmed pipe. (c) (*And: preocupación*) worry, care.

churumen* NM nous*, savvy*.

chus: **no decir ~ ni mus** not to say a word.

chuscada NF funny remark, joke; (*pey*) coarse joke.

chusco ADJ (a) (*gracioso*) funny, droll; *persona* coarse but amusing; *suceso* oddly amusing. (b) (*And*) *perro* mongrel; *caballo etc* ordinary; *persona* coarse, ill-mannered.

chuse NM (*And*) blanket.

chusma NF rabble, mob, riffraff.

chusmaje NM (*LAm*) = **chusma**.

chuspa NF (*LAm*) bag, pouch.

chusquero* NM (*Mil*) ranker.

chut NM (a) (*Dep*) shot (at goal). (b) (:: *droga*) shot*, fix:.

chuta[1]: NF (a) (*jeringuilla*) needle. (b) = **chut** (b).

chuta[2]: EXCL: **¡~!** (*Cono Sur*) good God!, good heavens!

chutador(a) NM/F (*Dep*) shooter.

chutar [1a] [1] VI (a) (*Dep*) to shoot (at goal).
(b) **está que chuta*** (*persona*) he's hopping mad*; (*comida*) it's scalding hot.
(c) (*: *ir bien*) to go well; **esto va que chuta** it's going fine*; **y va que chuta** and he'll be perfectly happy; and that's more than enough.
[2] **chutarse** VR to give o.s. a shot* (of drugs), shoot up:.

chutazo* NM fierce drive, fierce shot (at goal).

chute[1]: NM = **chut** (b).

chute[2]* ADJ (*Cono Sur*) spruce, natty*.

chuzar [1f] VT (*And*) to prick; to sting, hurt.

chuzo [1] NM (a) (*Mil*, *Hist*) pike; (*bastón*) spiked stick, metal-tipped stick; (*aguijón*) prick, goad; (*Cono Sur: zapapico*) pickaxe; (*Carib*, *Cono Sur: látigo*) whip; (*CAm Orn*) beak; (*CAm: de alacrán*) sting; **aunque caigan ~s** whatever the weather, (*fig*) come what may; **echar ~s** (*fig*) to brag; **llover a ~s** to rain cats and dogs, rain in torrents; **nevar a ~s** to snow heavily.
(b) (*And*) shoe.

(c) (**:**: *Anat*) prick**:**.

[2] ADJ (*CAm**) pelo lank.

chuzón ADJ **(a)** (*astuto*) wily, sharp, cunning. **(b)** (*gracioso*) witty, amusing.

chuzonada NF piece of tomfoolery, piece of buffoonery.

C.I. NM ABR *de* **coeficiente de inteligencia** (*o* **intelectual**) intelligence quotient, IQ.

cía NF hip bone.

Cía. NF ABR *de* **Compañía** Company, Co.

cianhídrico ADJ hydrocyanic.

cianotipia NF, **cianotipo** NM blueprint.

cianuro NM cyanide; **~ potásico, ~ de potasio** potassium cyanide.

ciar [1c] VI **(a)** (*ir hacia atrás*) to go backwards; (*Náut*) to go astern, back water. **(b)** (*fig: volverse atrás*) to back down, back out.

ciática NF sciatica.

ciático ADJ sciatic.

cibercafé NM cybercafe.

ciberespacial ADJ cyberspace (*atr*).

ciberespacio NM cyberspace.

cibernauta NMF cybernaut.

cibernética NF cybernetics.

cibernético ADJ cybernetic.

ciberpunk NM cyberpunk.

cibersexo NM cybersex.

cicatear [1a] VI to be stingy, be mean.

cicatería NF stinginess, meanness.

cicatero [1] ADJ stingy, mean.

    [2] NM, **cicatera** NF miser, skinflint; (*) pickpocket.

cicatriz NF scar (*t fig*).

cicatrización NF healing.

cicatrizar [1f] [1] VT to heal.

    [2] **cicatrizarse** VR to heal (up), form a scar.

Cicerón NM Cicero.

cicerone NM guide, cicerone.

ciceroniano ADJ Ciceronian.

ciclamato NM cyclamate.

ciclamen NM, **ciclamino** NM cyclamen.

cíclico ADJ cyclic(al).

ciclismo NM cycling; (*Dep*) cycle racing; **~ en ruta** road racing.

ciclista [1] ADJ cycle (*atr*), cycling (*atr*); **vuelta ~** cycle race.

    [2] NMF cyclist.

ciclo NM cycle; (*Liter*) cycle; (*de conferencias etc*) course, series, programme; (*LAm: Univ*) year, course; **~ circadiano** circadian cycle; **~ de instrucción** instruction cycle; **~ del nitrógeno** nitrogen cycle; **~ vital** life-cycle.

ciclo-cross NM cyclo-cross.

ciclomoto(r) NM moped, autocycle.

ciclón NM cyclone.

cíclope NM Cyclops.

ciclópeo ADJ gigantic, colossal.

ciclorama NM cyclorama.

ciclostilado ADJ cyclostyled.

ciclostilar [1a] VT to cyclostyle.

ciclostil(o) NM cyclostyle.

ciclotrón NM cyclotron.

cicloturismo NM touring by bicycle.

cicloturista NMF cycling tourist, touring cyclist.

-cico, -cica (*a veces t* -ecico, -ecica) V Aspects of Word Formation in Spanish 2.

cicuta NF hemlock.

cidiano ADJ relating to the Cid; **estudios ~s** Cid studies.

cidra NF citron.

cidracayote NM (*LAm*) gourd, calabash.

cidro NM citron (tree).

ciega NF blind woman.

ciego [1] ADJ **(a)** (*gen*) blind; (*cegado*) blinded; **a ciegas** blindly; **andar a ciegas, caminar a ciegas** to grope one's way; **volar a ciegas** to fly blind; **jugar a la ciega** (*Ajedrez*) to play blindfold; **quedar ~** to go blind; **quedó ~ después de la explosión** he was blinded in the explosion; **más ~ que un topo** as blind as a bat; **tan ~ el uno como el otro** it's a case of the blind leading the blind. **(b)** (*fig*) blind; **~ a, ~ para** blind to; **~ de ira** blind with rage; **con una fe ciega** with a blind faith, with an unquestioning faith; **a ciegas** blindly; heedlessly, thoughtlessly. **(c)** (**:**) **estar ~** (*borracho*) to be canned**:**, (*drogado*) to be high**:**; **ponerse ~** to get high**:** (*de* on). **(d)** (*Arquit*) blind; **tubo etc** blocked, stopped up, choked.

    [2] NM **(a)** (*gen: persona*) blind man, blind person; **los ~s** the blind, blind people.

    (b) (*Cono Sur Cartas*) player who holds bad cards.

    (c) (*Carib: claro de bosque*) forest clearing.

    (d) (**:**) junkie**:**.

cielito NM **(a)** (*Mús*) Argentinian folk dance. **(b)** (*palabra cariñosa*) my love, sweetheart.

cielo NM **(a)** (*gen*) sky; (*Astron*) sky, heavens, firmament; **~ aborregado** mackerel sky; **~ encopetado** overcast sky; **~ máximo** (*Aer*) ceiling; **a ~ abierto, a ~ raso** in the open air; **mina a ~ abierto** opencast mine; **a ~ descubierto** in the open; **se le juntaron el ~ con la tierra** (*LAm*) he lost his nerve; **mover ~s y tierra para** + *infin* to move heaven and earth to + *infin*; **querer tapar el ~ con las manos** to try to hide sth obvious; **se vino el ~ abajo** it rained cats and dogs, the heavens opened.

    (b) (*Arquit: t* **~ raso**) ceiling; (*de boca*) roof; (*de cama*) canopy; (*CAm: Aut*) roof.

    (c) (*Rel*) heaven; **¡~s!** good heavens!; **esto clama al ~** this cries out to heaven (*to be reformed etc*); **estar en el séptimo ~** to be in seventh heaven; **ganar el ~** to win salvation; **ir al ~** to go to heaven; **poner a uno en el ~** (*o* **en los cielos,** (*LAm*) **por los cielos**) to praise sb to the skies; **tomar el ~ con las manos** to be asking for trouble, be over-optimistic; **ver el ~ abierto** to see one's way out of a difficulty; to see one's chance; V **llover.**

    (d) (*palabra cariñosa*) my love, sweetheart.

    (e) (*) **el jefe es un ~** the boss is a dear, the boss is sheer heaven*.

ciempiés NM INVAR centipede.

cien[1] ADJ (*apócape de ciento, delante n*) **(a)** (*gen*) a hundred, one hundred; **~ mil** a hundred thousand; **las últimas ~ páginas** the last hundred pages; **estar a ~*** to be highly excited; **me pone a ~*** (*enoja*) it sends me up the wall*; (*encandila*) it makes me feel randy*. **(b)** **10 por ~** ten per cent; **~ por ~** a hundred per cent (*t fig*); **es español ~ por ~** he's Spanish through and through, he's Spanish to the core; **lo apoyo ~ por ~** I support it a hundred per cent, I support it wholeheartedly; **estar hasta el ~** (*And*) to be on one's last legs.

    CIEN, CIENTO   ver también las entradas

- La traducción de *cien(to)* puede ser *a hundred* o *one hundred*:
    Tengo que escribir cien páginas
    I've got to write a o *one hundred pages*
    Murió a la edad de ciento veinte años
    He died at the age of a o *one hundred and twenty*

    Sin embargo, hay que utilizar siempre one hundred:
- cuando *cien(to)* va detrás de otra cifra:
    El curso cuesta dos mil ciento noventa libras
    The course costs two thousand one hundred and ninety pounds
- cuando se quiere precisar que se trata de *cien(to)* y no de doscientos, *etc*:
    I said "one hundred" not "two hundred"
    Para otros usos y ejemplos ver las entradas cien *y* ciento.

---

cien[2] NM bog**:**, lavatory.

ciénaga NF marsh, bog, swamp.

ciencia NF science; (*sentido antiguo*) knowledge, learning, scholarship, erudition; **hombre de ~** scientist; **~ de la alimentación** food science; **~s económicas** economics; **~s empresariales** business studies; **~s físicas** physical science; **~s forestales** forestry; **~ del hogar** domestic science, home economics (*US*); **~s naturales** natural sciences; **~s ocultas** occult sciences; **~s políticas** political science, politics; **~ social** social science; **~s de la vida** life sciences; **a ~ y paciencia de uno** with sb's knowledge and agreement, with sb's connivance; **saber algo a ~ cierta** to know sth for certain (*o* for a fact).

ciencia-ficción NF science fiction.

Cienciología NF Scientology.

cieno NM (*lodo*) mud, mire; (*de río*) silt, ooze; (*limo*) slime.

cienoso ADJ muddy, miry; slimy.

científicamente ADV scientifically.

cientificidad NF scientific nature.

científico [1] ADJ scientific.

    [2] NM, **científica** NF scientist; **~ social** social scientist.

cientifismo NM scientific spirit.

cientista NMF (*LAm*) scientist.

ciento ADJ Y NM a hundred, one hundred; **~ veinte** a hundred and twenty; **en su año ~** in its hundredth year; **15 por ~** 15 per cent; **las calles están al ~ por ~ de su capacidad** the streets are at full capacity, the streets can hold no more traffic; **estar al ~ por ~** (*Dep etc*) to be on top form; **hay un 5 por ~ de descuento** there is a 5 per cent discount; **por ~s** in hundreds, by the hundred; **de ~ en boca** tiny, insignificant; **dar ~ y raya al más pintado** to be a match for anyone; **había ~ y la madre** there were far too many; and even that was still too many; *ver también* CIEN, CIENTO

cierne NM blossoming, budding; **en ~(s)** (*Bot*) in blossom; (*fig*) in its infancy; **es un ajedrecista en ~s** he's a budding chessplayer, he's a future chess champion.

cierra etc V **cerrar.**

cierre NM (**a**) (*acto*) closing, shutting; locking; (*Com etc*) closing, (*final*) closing-down; (*Rad, TV*) close-down; (*de fábrica*) shutdown; **~ centralizado** central locking; **~ de dirección** steering lock; **~ de los dueños**, **~ patronal** lockout.
(**b**) (*dispositivo*) closing device, locking device; snap fastener; (*de vestido*) fastener; (*de cinturón*) buckle, clasp; (*de libro*) clasp; (*de puerta*) catch; (*de tienda*) shutter, blind; (*Aut*) choke; **~ de cremallera**, **~ relámpago** (*And, Cono Sur*) zip (fastener), zipper; **~ hidráulico** water seal; **~ metálico** roll shutter, metal blind; **echar el ~‡** to shut one's trap‡.
(**c**) **de ~** closing; **precios de ~** (*Fin*) closing prices.

cierrecler NM (*Chile*) zip (fastener), zipper (*esp US*).

cierro NM (**a**) = **cierre**. (**b**) (*Cono Sur: muro*) wall; (*sobre*) envelope.

ciertamente ADV certainly, surely; **no era ~ de los más inteligentes** he was certainly not one of the brightest.

▼ **cierto** ADJ (**a**) (*seguro*) sure, certain; *promesa etc* positive, definite; **¡~!** certainly!; **~, ...** granted, ...; **por ~** certainly; by the way; **por ~ que no era el único** and moreover he was not the only one, and what is more he wasn't the only one; **no, por ~** certainly not; **¡sí, por ~!** yes of course!; **es ~** it is true, it is correct; that's it; **¿no es ~?** isn't that so?; **¿es ~ eso?** it that really so?; **es ~ que ...** it is certain that ..., it is true that ...; **lo ~ es que ...** the fact is that ...; **lo único ~ es que ...** the only sure thing is that ...; **estar ~** to be sure; **¿estás ~?** are you sure?; **estar ~ de** + *infin* to be certain to + *infin*; **estar en lo ~** to be right; **saber algo de ~** to know sth for certain.
(**b**) (*en concreto*) a certain; **~s** some, certain; **~ día de mayo** one day in May; **cierta persona que yo conozco** a certain person I know; *V* **cada** etc.

cierva NF hind.

ciervo NM deer; stag; (*Culin*) venison; **~ común** red deer; **~ volante** stag beetle.

cierzo NM north wind.

CIF NM (*Esp*) ABR de **Cédula de Identificación Fiscal** company tax code.

cifra NF (**a**) (*número*) number, numeral; **~ arábiga** Arabic numeral; **~ romana** Roman numeral; **en ~s redondeadas** in round numbers; **escribirlo en ~s y palabras** to write it down in figures and in words.
(**b**) (*cantidad*) number, quantity, amount; sum; **~ global** lump sum; **~ de ventas** sales figures, turnover; **la ~ de este año es elevada** the quantity this year is large; **la ~ de los muertos** the number of dead.
(**c**) (*clave*) code, cipher; **en ~** in code; (*fig*) mysteriously, enigmatically.
(**d**) (*abreviatura*) abbreviation; (*monograma*) monogram; (*resumen*) abridgement, summary; **en ~** in brief, briefly, concisely; in a shortened form.

cifradamente ADV (**a**) (*con clave*) in code. (**b**) (*resumiendo*) in brief, in a shortened form.

cifrado 1 ADJ coded, in code.
2 NM (en)coding, ciphering.

cifrar [1a] 1 VT (**a**) *mensaje* to code, write in code; (*Ling*) to encode; (*fig*) to abridge, summarize; to abbreviate. (**b**) *esperanzas* to place, concentrate (*en* on). (**c**) (*calcular*) to reckon; **una duración cifrada en miles de años** a duration reckoned in thousands of years.
2 **cifrarse** VR: **todas las esperanzas se cifran en él** all hopes are centred on him.

cigala NF Norway lobster.

cigarra NF cicada.

cigarral NM (*Toledo*) *country house on the banks of the Tagus*.

cigarrera NF (**a**) (*estuche*) cigar case. (**b**) (*obrera*) cigar maker; (*vendedora*) cigar seller.

cigarrería NF (*LAm*) (*tienda*) tobacconist's (shop); (*fábrica*) tobacco factory.

cigarrero NM (*obrero*) cigar maker; (*vendedor*) cigar-seller.

cigarrillo NM cigarette.

cigarro NM cigar (*t* **~ puro**); cigarette (*t* **~ de papel**); **~ habano** Havana cigar.

cigoto NM zygote.

ciguato ADJ (**a**) (*Carib, Méx: simple*) simple, stupid. (**b**) (*Carib, Méx: pálido*) pale, anaemic.

cigüeña NF (**a**) (*Orn*) stork. (**b**) (*Mec: manivela*) crank, handle; (*cabrestante*) winch, capstan. (**c**) (*CAm Mús*) barrel organ. (**d**) (*Carib Ferro*) bogie, bogy. (**e**) **la ~‡** the fuzz‡.

cigüeñal NM crankshaft.

CIJ NF ABR de **Comisión Internacional de Juristas** International Commission of Jurists, ICJ.

cija NF sheep shed; hayloft.

cilampa NF (*CAm*) drizzle.

cilampear [1a] VI (*CAm*) to drizzle.

cilantro NM (*Bot, Culin*) coriander.

cilicio NM hair shirt; spiked belt (*o* chain *etc*) worn by penitents.

cilindrada NF cylinder capacity.

cilindradora NF steamroller, road roller.

cilindraje NM cylinder capacity.

cilindrar [1a] VT to roll, roll flat.

cilíndrico ADJ cylindrical.

cilindrín‡ NM fag‡, cigarette.

cilindro NM (*Mat, Téc*) cylinder; (*de máquina de escribir*) roller; (*) top hat; (*Méx*) barrel-organ; **~ de caminos**, **~ compresor** steamroller, roadroller.

cilla NF (**a**) (*granero*) tithe barn, granary. (**b**) (*diezmo*) tithe.

cima NF (*de árbol*) top; (*de montaña*) top, peak, summit; (*fig*) summit, height; (*fig*) completion; **dar ~ a** to complete, crown with success, carry out successfully.

cimarra NF: **hacer ~** (*Cono Sur*) to play truant.

cimarrón 1 ADJ (**a**) (*LAm Bot, Zool*) wild, untamed; (*fig: inculto*) rough, uncouth; (*vago*) lazy; **negro ~** (*Hist*) runaway slave, fugitive slave.
(**b**) (*Cono Sur*) *maté* bitter, unsweetened.
2 NM (*Cono Sur*) unsweetened maté.
3 NM, **cimarrona** NF (*Hist*) runaway slave, maroon.

cimarronear [1a] VI (*LAm: esclavo*) to run away.

cimba NF (**a**) (*And: cuerda*) plaited rope of hard leather. (**b**) (*And: trenza*) pigtail. (**c**) (*And: escala*) rope ladder.

címbalo NM cymbal.

cimbel NM (**a**) (*señuelo*) decoy (*t* fig). (**b**) (**‡**) prick‡.

cimbor(r)io NM (*Arquit*) dome; base of a dome; (*Min*) roof.

cimbrar [1a] VT (**a**) (*agitar*) to shake, swish, swing; (*curvar*) to bend.
(**b**) **~ a uno*** to clout sb (with a stick); **le cimbró de un porrazo** he clouted him with his stick.

cimbreante ADJ swaying.

cimbrear [1a] 1 VT = **cimbrar**.
2 **cimbrearse** VR (**a**) to sway, swing; to shake; to bend; **~ al viento** to sway in the wind.
(**b**) (*persona*) to walk gracefully.

cimbreño ADJ pliant, flexible; *talle* willowy, lithe.

cimbreo NM swaying, swinging; shaking; bending.

cimbrón NM (*And, CAm, Cono Sur: sacudida*) shudder; (*And*) sharp pain; (*Cono Sur, Méx: espadazo*) blow with the flat of a sword; (*LAm: de lazo etc*) crack; (*LAm: tirón*) jerk, yank, tug.

cimbronada NF (*And, Cono Sur, Méx*), **cimbronazo** NM (*And, Cono Sur, Méx*) = **cimbrón**; (*Carib: terremoto*) earthquake.

cimentación NF (**a**) (*cimientos*) foundation. (**b**) (*acto*) laying of foundations.

cimentar [1j] VT (**a**) (*Arquit*) to lay the foundations of (*o* for); (*fig: fundar*) to found, establish. (**b**) *oro* to refine. (**c**) (*fig: reforzar*) to strengthen, cement.

cimera NF crest (*t* Her).

cimero ADJ top, topmost, uppermost; (*fig*) crowning, finest.

cimiento NM foundation, groundwork; (*fig*) basis, source; **~s** (*Arquit*) foundations; **abrir los ~s** to dig the foundations; **echar los ~s de** to lay the foundations for.

cimitarra NF scimitar.

cimpa NF (*And*) = **cimba**.

cinabrio NM cinnabar.

cinc NM zinc.

cincel NM chisel.

cincelado NM chiselling; engraving.

cincelador NM (**a**) (*persona*) sculptor; engraver; stone cutter. (**b**) (*herramienta*) (chipping) chisel, chipping hammer.

cincelar [1a] VT (**a**) to chisel; to carve, engrave, cut. (**b**) (*fig*) to be precise about, make more precise; to go into fine details about.

cincha NF (**a**) (*de caballo*) girth, saddle strap; **a revienta ~s** at breakneck speed; hurriedly; (*LAm: con renuencia*) reluctantly.
(**b**) (*Cos: para sillas*) webbing.
(**c**) **tener ~** (*And*) to have a strain of Negro (*o* Indian) blood.

cinchada NF (*Cono Sur, Méx*) tug-of-war.

cinchar [1a] 1 VT *caballo* to girth, secure the girth of; (*Téc*) to band, hoop, secure with hoops.
2 VI (*Cono Sur**) (*trabajar*) to work hard; **~ por** (*apoyar*) to root (*o* shout) for.

cincho NM (*faja*) sash, belt, girdle; (*aro*) iron hoop, metal band; (*CAm, Carib, Méx*) = **cincha (a)**.

cinchona NF (*LAm*) quinine bark.

cinco 1 ADJ five; (*fecha*) fifth; (*Univ*) five (*the pass mark*); **las ~** five o'clock; **estar sin ~***, **no tener ni ~*** to be broke*; **no estar en sus ~*** to be off one's rocker‡; **le dije cuántas son ~** I told him a thing or two; **saber cuántas son ~** to know what's what, know a thing or two; **tener los ~ muy listos*** to be light-fingered; **¡vengan esos ~!*** shake (on it)!*
2 NM (**a**) (*número*) five.
(**b**) (*And, CAm, Carib: guitarra*) 5-stringed guitar.
(**c**) (*: Méx: trasero*) bottom, backside*.
(**d**) (*CAm, Méx: moneda*) 5 peso piece.

cincuenta ADJ fifty; fiftieth; **los (años) ~** the fifties; **cantar las ~ a uno** to haul sb over the coals.

cincuentañero 1 ADJ fiftyish, about fifty.

2 NM, **cincuentañera** NF person of about fifty, person in his (o her) fifties.

cincuentavo ADJ, NM fiftieth.

cincuentena NF fifty, about fifty.

cincuentenario NM 50th anniversary.

cincuenteno ADJ fiftieth.

cincuentón **1** ADJ fifty-year-old, fiftyish. **2** NM, **cincuentona** NF person of about fifty.

cine NM (a) (*gen y como arte*) cinema; film(s), movies (*US*); **unos muebles** (*etc*) **de ~*** posh furniture* (*etc*), luxurious furniture; **el ~ español actual** the present-day Spanish cinema; **~ de arte y ensayo** arts cinema; **~ en colores** colour films; **~ hablado, ~ sonoro** talkies; **~ mudo** silent films; **~ de terror** horror movies; **hacer ~** to make films, be engaged in film work, be working for the cinema. (b) (*edificio*) cinema, movie theater (*US*); **~ de verano** open-air cinema; **ir al ~** to go to the cinema, go to the pictures, go to the movies (*US*).

cine... PREF cine...

cineasta NMF (*entusiasta*) film fan, movie fan (*US*); (*experto*) film buff*; (*crítico*) film critic; (*creador*) film maker, director.

cine-club NM, PL **cine-clubs** (*para pronunciación V* **club**) cine club, film society.

cinefilia NF love of the cinema.

cinéfilo, -a NM/F film fan, movie fan (*US*); film buff*.

cinegética NF hunting, the chase.

cinegético ADJ hunting (*atr*), of the chase.

cinema NM cinema.

cinemateca NF film library, film archive.

cinemático ADJ cinematic.

cinematografía NF films, film-making, cinematography.

cinematografiar [1a] VT to film.

cinematográfico ADJ cine-..., film (*atr*); cinematographic.

cinematógrafo NM (a) (*cine*) cinema. (b) (*aparato*) cine projector, film projector.

cineración NF incineration.

cinerama NM cinerama.

cinerario ADJ (a) *urna* cinerary. (b) = **ceniciento**.

cinéreo ADJ ashy; ash-grey, ashen.

cineteca NF (*LAm*) film archive.

cinética NF kinetics.

cinético ADJ kinetic.

cingalés, -esa **1** ADJ, NM/F Singhalese. **2** NM (*Ling*) Singhalese.

cíngaro **1** ADJ gipsy. **2** NM, **cíngara** NF gipsy (*esp* Hungarian).

cinguería NF (*Cono Sur: obra*) sheet-metal work; (*taller*) sheet-metal shop.

cinguero NM (*Cono Sur*) sheet-metal worker.

cínicamente ADV (a) (*con cinismo*) cynically. (b) (*sinvergonzadamente*) brazenly, shamelessly, impudently; in an unprincipled way.

cínico **1** ADJ (a) (*escéptico*) cynical. (b) (*descarado*) brazen, shameless, impudent; unprincipled. **2** NM (a) (*gen*) cynic. (b) (*sinvergüenza*) brazen individual; unprincipled person.

cinismo NM (a) (*gen*) cynicism. (b) (*desvergüenza*) brazenness, shamelessness, effrontery, impudence; lack of principle; **¡qué ~!** what a nerve!*

cinofilia NF (a) dog-fancying, dog-breeding. (b) (*personas*) dog-fanciers, dog-breeders.

cinólogo, -a NM/F canine expert.

cinta NF (a) (*tira*) band, strip; tape; (*Cos*) ribbon, tape; (*Téc*) surveyor's tape; (*Cine*) film; reel; (*de grabación*) tape; **~ adhesiva** adhesive tape; **~ aisladora, ~ aislante, ~ de aislar** (*CAm, Méx*) insulating tape; **~ de cotizaciones, ~ de teleimpresor** ticker tape; **~ de freno** brake lining; **~ de goma** rubber band; **~ de llegada** (*Dep*) (finishing) tape; **~ para máquina de escribir** typewriter ribbon; **~ magnética** magnetic tape, recording tape; **~ magnetofónica** audio tape; **~ de corto metraje** short (film); **~ de largo metraje** full-length film; **~ de medir** (*LAm*), **~ métrica** tape measure; **~ de pelo** hairband; **~ perforada** punched tape; **~ de producción** assembly belt; **~ simbólica** ceremonial tape; **~ transbordadora** travelator, people mover; **~ transportadora, ~ de transporte** conveyor belt; **~ de vídeo** videotape; **~ virgen** blank tape. (b) (*Arquit*) fillet, scroll. (c) (*de acera*) kerb; (*de habitación*) tile skirting. (d) (*LAm: lata*) tin, can. (e) **~s** (*Méx*) shoelaces.

cinteado ADJ beribboned.

cintero NM (a) (*de mujer*) girdle. (b) (*cuerda*) rope.

cintillo NM (a) (*de sombrero*) hatband; (*LAm: para pelo*) hairband. (b) (*anillo*) small ring with jewels. (c) (*Tip*) heading, collective heading. (d) (*Carib: bordillo*) kerb.

cinto NM (*Mil*) belt, girdle, sash; **~ negro** black belt; **armas de ~** side arms.

cintura NF (a) (*Anat*) waist; waistline; **~ de avispa** wasp waist; **~ de castidad** chastity belt; **de la ~ (para) arriba** from the waist up; **tener poca ~** to have a slim waist. (b) (*faja*) girdle; **meter a uno en ~** to bring (o keep) sb under control, keep sb under; to make sb see reason.

cinturilla NF waistband.

cinturón NM (a) (*ceñidor*) belt; girdle; (†) sword belt; **~ de salvamento, ~ salvavidas** lifebelt; **~ de seguridad** safety belt; **apretarse el ~** to tighten one's belt. (b) (*fig: zona*) belt, zone; **el ~ industrial de Madrid** the Madrid industrial belt; **~ de miseria** (*Méx*) slum area; **~ verde** green belt. (c) (*Aut: carretera; t ~ de circunvalación, ~ de ronda*) ringroad, beltway (*US*).

ciña, ciñendo *etc* V **ceñir**.

CIP [θip] **1** NF ABR de **Comisión Internacional de Paz**. **2** NM (*Madrid*) ABR de **Club Internacional de Prensa**.

cipayo NM (a) (*Brit Mil Hist*) sepoy. (b) (*Cono Sur Pol*) politician in the service of foreign commerce.

cipe NM sickly baby.

cipo NM (*monumento*) memorial stone; (*mojón*) milestone, signpost.

cipote **1** ADJ (a) (*And, Carib: estúpido*) stupid, thick*. (b) (*CAm: rechoncho*) plump, chubby. **2** NM (a) (*CAm, Carib: chico*) lad, youngster; urchin. (b) (*CAm: maza*) Indian club. (c) (*: *idiota*) chump*, blockhead. (d) (*: *And*) **~ de chica** smashing girl*; **~ de película** splendid film. (e) (‡: *barriga*) belly, guts. (f) (⁎) prick⁎.

cipotear [1a] VT to screw⁎.

ciprés NM cypress (tree).

cipresal NM cypress grove.

CIR [θir] NM ABR de **Centro de Instrucción de Reclutas**.

circadiano ADJ circadian.

circense ADJ circus (*atr*), of the circus.

circo NM (a) (*recinto*) circus, amphitheatre. (b) (*función*) circus.

circonio NM zirconium.

circuir [3g] VT to encircle, surround.

circuitería NF circuitry.

circuito NM circuit; circumference, distance round (*the outside*); (*viaje*) tour; (*Elec etc*) circuit; (*Dep*) lap; **~ en bucle** loop; **~ cerrado** closed circuit, loop; **~ cerrado de TV, ~ interno de TV, TV por ~ cerrado** closed-circuit TV; **corto ~** short circuit; **~ impreso** printed circuit; **~ integrado** integrated circuit; **~ lógico** logical circuit; **~ urbano** city circuit, town circuit.

circulación NF (a) (*gen: t Fin, Med*) circulation; (*fig*) circulation; propagation; **~ fiduciaria** paper money, paper currency; **~ sanguínea, ~ de la sangre** circulation of the blood; **estar fuera de ~** to be out of circulation, be no longer current; **poner algo en ~** to issue sth, put sth into circulation. (b) (*Aut*) traffic; movement of traffic; **~ rodada** vehicular traffic, wheeled traffic; **'cerrado a la ~ rodada'** 'closed to vehicles'; **la ~ es por la derecha** they drive on the right; **calle de gran ~** busy street, street much used by traffic; **'~ única'** (*Méx*) 'one way (traffic)'.

circulante ADJ *biblioteca* lending, circulating.

circular **1** ADJ circular, round; *billete* return, round-trip (*atr*); *viaje* round; *carta* circular. **2** NF circular. **3** [1a] VT to circulate; to pass round, send round; to put into circulation. **4** VI (a) (*gen*) to circulate (*t Fin, Med*); (*Fin*) to be in circulation; **hacer ~ una carta** to circulate a letter, send round a letter. (b) (*personas*) to move about, walk around (*por* in); **¡circulen!** move along!; **hacer ~ a la gente** to move people along. (c) (*Aut*) to drive; **~ por la izquierda** (*regla de país*) to drive on the left, (*en calle etc*) to keep to the left; **hacer ~ los coches** to keep the cars moving. (d) (*transporte*) to run; **no circula los domingos** it does not run on Sundays; **circula entre A y B** it runs between A and B, it operates between A and B.

circularidad NF circularity.

circulatorio ADJ (a) circulatory. (b) (*Aut*) traffic (*atr*); **colapso ~** traffic jam, stoppage of traffic.

círculo NM (a) (*Mat etc*) circle; **~ de giro, ~ de viraje** turning circle; **~ máximo** great circle; **~ polar antártico** Antarctic Circle; **~ polar ártico** Arctic Circle; **~ vicioso** vicious circle (*t fig*). (b) (*anillo etc*) circle, ring, band. (c) (*grupo*) circle, club, group; (*casino*) clubhouse; (*And, Cono Sur*) social gathering; (*Pol*) political group, faction. (d) (*fig: campo*) scope, compass, extent.

circun... PREF circum...

circuncidar [1a] VT (a) (*Med*) to circumcise. (b) (*fig: restringir*) to curtail; to moderate.
circuncisión NF circumcision.
circunciso [1] ADJ circumcised.
[2] NM (*Hist*) Jew, Moor.
circundante ADJ surrounding.
circundar [1a] VT to surround.
circunferencia NF circumference.
circunferir [3i] VT to circumscribe.
circunflejo NM circumflex.
circunlocución NF, **circunloquio** NM circumlocution, roundabout expression.
circunnavegación NF circumnavigation.
circunnavegar [1a] VT to sail round, circumnavigate.
circunscribir [3a: PTP **circunscrito**] [1] VT to circumscribe; (*fig*) to circumscribe, limit, restrict (*a* to).
[2] **circunscribirse** VR (*fig*) to limit o.s., confine o.s. (*a* to).
circunscripción NF (*de territorio*) division, subdivision; (*Parl*) constituency, electoral district.
circunspección NF circumspection, caution, prudence.
circunspecto ADJ circumspect, cautious, prudent; deliberate; *palabras* carefully chosen, guarded.
circunstancia NF circumstance; **~s agravantes** aggravating circumstances; **~s atenuantes** extenuating circumstances; mitigating circumstances; **en las ~s** in (*o* under) the circumstances; **en las ~s actuales** in the present state of things, under present conditions; **las ~s cambian los casos** circumstances alter cases; *V* **altura**.
circunstanciado ADJ detailed, circumstantial.
circunstancial ADJ (a) (*gen*) circumstantial. (b) *arreglo etc* makeshift, emergency (*atr*); *caso etc* incidental; **mi estancia en Lima era ~** I just happened to be in Lima.
circunstante [1] ADJ (a) (*que rodea*) surrounding. (b) *persona* present.
[2] NMF onlooker, bystander; **los ~s** those present.
circunvalación NF: **carretera de ~** bypass, ring road.
circunvecino ADJ adjacent, neighbouring, surrounding.
cirial NM (*Ecl*) processional candlestick.
cirílico ADJ, NM Cyrillic.
cirio NM (a) (*Ecl*) (wax) candle. (b) (*) row, shindy*; **montar un ~** to kick up a row (*a uno* with sb).
cirquero, -a NM/F (*Méx*) circus performer, acrobat; circus impresario.
cirro NM cirrus.
cirrocúmulo NM cirrocumulus.
cirrosis NF cirrhosis; **~ hepática** cirrhosis of the liver.
cirrostrato NM cirrostratus.
ciruela NF plum; **~ claudia, ~ verdal** greengage; **~ damascena** damson; **~ pasa** prune.
ciruelo NM (a) (*Bot*) plum tree. (b) (*) dolt, idiot.
cirugía NF surgery; **~ estética** cosmetic surgery; **~ plástica** plastic surgery.
ciruja NMF (*Cono Sur*) tramp.
cirujano, -a NM/F surgeon; **~ plástico** plastic surgeon.
ciscar [1g] [1] VT (a) (*ensuciar*) to dirty, soil, mess up.
(b) (*Carib, Méx: avergonzar*) to shame, put down.
(c) (*Carib, Méx: meterse con*) to provoke, needle*.
[2] **ciscarse** VR (a) (*defecar*) to soil o.s.; to do one's business*; **los que se ciscan en las teorías** those who thumb their noses at theories; **¡me cisco en todo!** blast it!*
(b) (*Carib, Méx: avergonzarse*) to feel ashamed.
(c) (*Carib, Méx: ofenderse*) to get upset, take offence.
cisco NM (a) (*carbón*) coaldust, slack; **hacer algo ~** to tear sth to bits, shatter sth; **estar hecho ~*** to be a wreck, be all in.
(b) (*: riña*) row, shindy*; **armar un ~, meter ~** to kick up a row, make trouble.
(c) (*Méx: miedo*) fear, fright.
ciscón ADJ (*Carib, Méx*) touchy.
Cisjordania NF West Bank.
cisjordano ADJ West Bank (*atr*).
cisma NM (a) (*Ecl*) schism; (*Pol etc*) split; (*fig*) discord, disagreement.
(b) (*And: remilgo*) prudery, over-niceness. (*And: chismes*) gossip.
cismático ADJ (a) (*Ecl*) schismatic(al); (*fig*) troublemaking, fractious, dissident. (b) (*And: remilgado*) prudish, overnice; finicky. (c) (*And*) gossipy.
cisne NM (a) (*Orn*) swan. (b) (*Cono Sur: borla*) powder puff.
Císter NM Cistercian Order.
cisterciense ADJ, NM Cistercian.
cisterna NF cistern; tank; reservoir.
cistitis NF cystitis.
cita NF (a) (*compromiso*) appointment, engagement; (*encuentro*) meeting; (*lugar*) place of meeting, rendez-vous; (*de amantes*) meeting, (*con amigo o amiga*) date; **~ a ciegas** blind date; **~ espacial** rendez-vous in space, space link-up; **acudir a una ~** to keep an appointment, turn up for an appointment; **se dieron (una) ~ para las 8** they

agreed to meet at 8; **aquí los mejores atletas se han dado ~** the best athletes are gathered here; **las cualidades que se dan ~ en ella** the qualities which come together in her; **faltar a una ~** to miss an appointment, break an appointment, not turn up for a date; **tener una ~ con uno** to have an appointment with sb, have a date with sb.
(b) (*Liter etc*) quotation (*de* from); reference; (*acto*) citation; **con largas ~s probatorias** with long quotations in support.
citable ADJ quotable.
citación NF (a) (*Liter etc*) quotation. (b) (*Jur*) summons, citation; **~ judicial** summons, subpoena; **~ a licitadores** invitation to bidders, invitation of tenders.
citadino, -a NM/F (*LAm*) city-dweller.
citado ADJ aforementioned; **en el ~ país** in the aforementioned country, in this country; in the country in question.
citar [1a] [1] VT (a) *persona* to make an appointment with; to make a date with; **la cité para las 9** I arranged to meet her at 9; **la cité para delante de Correos** I arranged to meet her in front of the post office; **¿está Vd citado?** have you an appointment?, is he *etc* expecting you?
(b) (*Jur*) to call, summon; **tiene facultades para ~ testigos** he has the power to call witnesses.
(c) (*Taur*) to incite, provoke, stir up; to call out to.
(d) (*Liter etc*) to quote, cite (*de* from).
[2] **citarse** VR: **~ con uno** to arrange to meet sb (*para las 7* at 7); **citémonos para delante del estadio** let's meet outside the stadium.
cítara NF zither.
-cito, -cita (*a veces t* **-ecito, -ecita**) *V* **Aspects of Word Formation in Spanish 2.**
citología NF (a) (*análisis*) smear test. (b) (*Bio*) cytology.
citotóxico ADJ cytotoxic.
citrato NM citrate.
cítrico [1] ADJ citric.
[2] **~s** NMPL citrus fruits.
citrícola ADJ citrus (*atr*).
citrón NM lemon.
CiU NM (*Pol: Cataluña*) ABR *de* **Convergència i Unió.**
ciudad NF city, town; **C~ del Cabo** Cape Town; **~ colmena, ~ dormitorio** commuter suburb, dormitory town; **C~ Condal** Barcelona; **C~ Encantada** Cuenca; **C~ Eterna** Eternal City (*Rome*); **C~ Imperial** (*Hist de España*) Toledo; **~ perdida** (*Méx*) slum area, shantytown; **C~ del Turia** Valencia; **C~ del Vaticano** Vatican City; **es el mejor café de la ~** it's the best café in town; **hoy vamos a la ~** we're going to (*o* into, up to) town today.
ciudadanía NF (a) (*habitantes*) citizens, citizenry.
(b) (*status*) citizenship; **~ de honor** freedom of a city; **derechos de ~** citizen's rights, rights of citizenship.
ciudadano [1] ADJ civic, city (*atr*); **el orgullo ~** civic pride.
[2] NM, **ciudadana** NF (a) (*habitante*) city dweller, townsman.
(b) (*Pol etc*) citizen; **~s** townsfolk, townspeople; inhabitants; **el ~ a pie** the man in the street; **~ de honor** freeman of city; **~ del mundo** citizen of the world; **~s de segunda clase** second-class citizens, under-privileged persons; **~ de la tercera edad** senior citizen.
ciudadela NF (a) (*Mil*) citadel, fortress. (b) (*LAm: casa pobre*) tenement block.
ciudad-estado NF, PL **ciudades-estado** city-state.
ciudadrealeño [1] ADJ of Ciudad Real.
[2] NM, **ciudadrealeña** NF native (*o* inhabitant) of Ciudad Real; **los ~s** the people of Ciudad Real.
civeta NF civet cat.
civeto NM civet.
cívico [1] ADJ civic; domestic; (*fig*) public-spirited, patriotic.
[2] NM (a) (*LAm*) policeman. (b) (*Cono Sur: vaso*) large glass of beer.
civil [1] ADJ (a) (*Pol etc*) civil; **derechos ~es** civil rights; **guerra ~** civil war; **casarse por lo ~** to have a civil wedding, get married in a registry office (*or equivalent*).
(b) (*Mil*) **población ~** civilian population.
(c) (*fig: cortés*) civil, courteous, polite.
[2] NM (a) Civil Guard.
(b) (*en lenguaje de militares*) civilian.
civilidad NF civility, courtesy, politeness.
civilización NF civilization.
civilizado ADJ civilized.
civilizador ADJ *influencia etc* civilizing.
civilizar [1f] [1] VT to civilize.
[2] **civilizarse** VR to become civilized.
civilizatorio ADJ civilizing.
civismo NM public spirit; community spirit; patriotism.
cizalla NF (a) (*gen* **~s** PL: *herramienta*) wire-cutters, metal shears. (b) (*virutas*) shavings, metal clippings.
cizaña NF (a) (*Bot*) darnel; (*Bib*) tares.
(b) (*fig: discordia*) discord; **sembrar ~** to sow discord (*entre* among).

(c) (*fig: vicio*) vice, corruption, harmful influence.

cizañar [1a] VT to sow discord among.

cizañear VT = **cizañar**.

cizañero, -a NM/F troublemaker, mischief-maker.

cl. ABR *de* **centilitro** centilitre, cl. .

clac ⊡ NM, PL **claques** opera hat; cocked hat.
⊡ NF = **claque**.

clamar [1a] ⊡ VT (*liter*) *justicia, venganza* to cry out for; *inocencia* to proclaim.
⊡ VI to cry out, clamour; ~ **contra** to cry out against, protest vociferously against; ~ **por** to clamour for, demand vociferously; **esto clama al cielo** this cries out to heaven (to be reformed *etc*).

clamor NM **(a)** (*grito*) cry, shout; (*ruido*) noise, clamour. **(b)** (*de campana*) tolling, knell. **(c)** (*fig: protesta*) clamour, outcry, protest.

clamorear [1a] ⊡ VT = **clamar 1**.
⊡ VI (*campana*) to toll.

clamoreo NM **(a)** (*griterío*) clamour(ing), (prolonged) shouting. **(b)** (*fig: protestas*) sustained outcry, vociferous protests; ~**s de protesta** vigorous protests.

clamorosamente ADV noisily, loudly, clamorously.

clamoroso ADJ **(a)** (*ruidoso*) noisy, loud, clamorous; screaming, shrieking. **(b)** (*fig*) *éxito* resounding, enormous.

clan NM clan; (*fig*) faction, group.

clandestinamente ADV secretly, clandestinely; by stealth, stealthily.

clandestinidad NF secrecy; secret nature; **en la** ~ in secrecy; **movimiento en la** ~ (*Pol*) underground movement; **pasar a la** ~ to go into hiding (o underground).

clandestinista NM (*LAm*) bootlegger.

clandestino ⊡ ADJ (*gen*) secret, clandestine; stealthy; (*Pol*) *actividad etc* clandestine, underground; *agente* secret, undercover; *boda* secret; *runaway*; **andar** ~ (*LAm Pol*) to be underground, operate under cover.
⊡ NMPL: ~**s** (*And*) shacks.

clánico ADJ clannish, clan (*atr*).

claque NF claque.

claqué NM tap-dancing.

claqueta NF (*Cine*) clapperboard.

clara NF **(a)** (*de huevo*) white of an egg. **(b)** (*en cabeza*) bald spot; (*de paño*) bare patch, thin place. **(c)** (*Met*) bright interval.

claraboya NF skylight.

claramente ADV **(a)** (*lit*) brightly; clearly. **(b)** (*fig*) clearly, plainly.

clarea NF white wine with cinnamon, sugar and spices added.

clarear [1a] ⊡ VT **(a)** (*gen*) to brighten; to light up; *color* to make lighter.
(b) (*fig*) to clarify, make clear(er).
(c) (*Méx: atravesar*) to go right through, penetrate; ~ **a uno** to put a bullet through sb.
⊡ VI **(a)** (*Met*) to clear up, brighten up.
(b) (*día*) to dawn, break; to grow light.
⊡ **clarearse** VR **(a)** (*paño*) to be transparent, let the light through.
(b) (*: revelar*) to give the game away.

clareo: NM: **darse un** ~ (*pasear*) to take a stroll; (*irse*) to hoof it*.

clarete NM mixture of red and white wine.

claridad NF **(a)** (*luz*) brightness; light.
(b) (*fig*) clearness, clarity; **lo explicó todo con mucha** ~ he explained it all very clearly.
(c) ~**es** sharp remarks, unpleasant remarks; home truths.

claridoso ADJ (*CAm, Méx*) blunt, plain-spoken.

clarificación NF **(a)** (*lit*) illumination, lighting (up). **(b)** (*fig*) clarification.

clarificador ADJ illuminating, enlightening; explanatory.

clarificante ⊡ ADJ = **clarificador**.
⊡ NM clarifier, clarifying agent.

clarificar [1g] VT **(a)** (*iluminar*) to illuminate, light (up); to brighten.
(b) *líquido* to clarify; to refine, purify.
(c) (*fig: explicar*) to clarify.

clarín NM **(a)** (*Mús*) bugle; (*de órgano*) clarion. **(b)** (*persona*) bugler. **(c)** (*LAm: Bot*) sweet pea.

clarinada* NF uncalled-for remark.

clarinazo NM (*fig*) trumpet call.

clarinero NM clarion player.

clarinete ⊡ NM (*instrumento*) clarinet.
⊡ NMF (*persona*) clarinettist.

clarinetista NMF clarinettist.

clarión NM chalk, white crayon.

clarisa ⊡ ADJ: **monja** ~ = **2**.
⊡ NF nun of the Order of St Clare.

clarividencia NF **(a)** (*lit*) clairvoyance. **(b)** (*fig: previsión*) far-sightedness; (*discernimiento*) discernment; (*intuición*) intuition.

clarividente ⊡ ADJ far-sighted, far-seeing; discerning; gifted with intuition.
⊡ NMF clairvoyant(e).

▼ **claro** ⊡ ADJ **(a)** *día, luz, ojos etc* bright; *cuarto* light, bright, well-lit.
(b) *agua* clear, transparent; *cristal, sonido, voz* clear.
(c) *cerveza, color* light; **verde** ~ light green; **una tela verde** ~ a light-green cloth.
(d) *contorno, letra etc* clear, distinct; bold; **tan** ~ **como la luz del día** as plain as a pikestaff; **tan** ~ **como el agua, más** ~ **que el sol** as clear as daylight.
(e) (*en consistencia*) *líquido* thin; *té etc* weak; *pelo* thin, sparse.
▼ **(f)** *explicación, lenguaje, prueba etc* clear; plain, evident; **todo queda muy** ~ it's all very clear; **¡~!** naturally!, of course!; (*esp LAm*) yes of course!, please do!; **¡pues ~!** I quite agree with you!; **¡~ que sí!** yes of course!; **¡~ que no!** of course not!; ~ **que no es verdad** of course it isn't true; **está** ~ **que** ... it is plain that ..., it is obvious that ...; **a las ~as** clearly, plainly; openly.
(g) (*fig*) (*ilustre*) famous, illustrious; (*noble*) noble.
⊡ ADV clearly; **hablar** ~ (*fig*) to speak plainly, speak bluntly.
⊡ NM **(a)** **poner** (*o* **sacar**) **algo en** ~ to explain sth, clear up sth, clarify sth; (*LAm: t* **pasar algo en** ~) to copy sth out; **no sacamos nada en** ~ we couldn't get anything definite; there were no concrete decisions.
(b) **pasar la noche en** ~ to have a sleepless night.
(c) **tener** ~ (*LAm**) to have class.
(d) **de** ~ **en** ~ (*obviamente*) obviously, plainly; (*toda la noche*) from dusk to dawn; **velar de** ~ **en** ~ to lie awake all night.
(e) (*abertura*) opening; (*brecha, espacio*) gap, break, space; (*en bosque*) opening, clearing, glade; (*en tráfico etc*) gap, break; (*en pelo*) bald patch.
(f) (*Arquit*) light, window; skylight.
(g) (*Arte*) highlight; light tone.
(h) (*Met*) break in the clouds; (*CAm*) bright interval.
(i) (*Carib Culin*) guava jelly.
(j) (*Carib: bebida*) sugar-cane brandy.
(k) ~ **de luna** moonlight.
(l) ~ **de huevo** (*LAm*) eggwhite.

claroscuro NM chiaroscuro.

clase ⊡ NF **(a)** (*gen*) class; kind, sort; **con toda** ~ **de** with all kinds of, with every sort of, with all manner of; **gente de toda** ~ people of every kind, all sorts of people; **de esta** ~ of this kind; **de otra** ~ of another sort; **de una misma** ~ of the same kind; **de primera** ~ first-class; **os deseo toda** ~ **de felicidades** I wish you every kind of happiness.
(b) (*transportes, vehículos*) class; **primera** ~ first class; ~ **de cámara,** ~ **intermedia** (*Náut*) cabin class; ~ **económica** economy class; ~ **preferente** club class; ~ **turista** tourist class.
(c) (*lección etc*) (*Escol*) class; (*Univ*) lecture, class; ~ **de conducción,** ~ **de conducir** driving lesson; ~ **de geografía** geography class, geography lesson; ~ **nocturna** evening class; ~**s particulares** private classes, private lessons; **dar** ~**s** to teach; (*Univ*) to lecture; **dar** ~**s con uno** to take lessons from sb, study with sb; **ella da** ~**s de italiano** she gives Italian lessons; **faltar a** ~ to miss class, not go to class; **fumarse la** ~**, soplarse la** ~ to play truant.
(d) (*aula*) (*Escol*) classroom; (*Univ*) lecture room.
(e) (*Pol*) class; ~ **alta** upper class; ~ **baja** lower class(es); ~ **media** middle class(es); ~ **media-alta** upper-middle class; ~ **media-baja** lower-middle class; ~ **obrera** working class; **de la** ~ **obrera** working-class (*atr*); ~**s pasivas** pensioners; ~ **política** politicians; **las** ~**s poseyentes** the property-owning classes; **las** ~**s pudientes** the well-to-do, the moneyed classes; **ser de la** ~ (*Carib: euf*) to belong to the black race, be a half-breed.
(f) ~**s de tropa** (*Mil*) non-commissioned officers.
(g) **la** ~ **médica** the medical profession.
⊡ NM: **un primera** ~ a first-class person, an outstanding person.
⊡ ADJ (*And**) first-rate, classy*.

clásicas NFPL (*Univ*) classics.

clasicismo NM classicism.

clásico ⊡ ADJ **(a)** (*Arte etc*) classical.
(b) (*fig*) classic; (*destacado*) outstanding, remarkable; *coche etc* vintage; *institución* traditional, typical; *costumbre* time-honoured; **le dio el** ~ **saludo** he gave him the time-honoured salute; **es la clásica plazuela española** it is a typical Spanish square.
⊡ NM **(a)** (*obra etc*) classic.
(b) (*persona*) classicist.

clasificable ADJ classifiable.

clasificación NF classification; (*Correos*) sorting; (*Dep*) table, league; (*Náut*) rating; ~ **nacional del disco** ≃ top twenty, record hit parade.

clasificador NM **(a)** (*persona*) classifier. **(b)** (*mueble*) filing cabinet; ~ **de cartas** letter file. **(c)** (*aparato*) collator.

clasificar [1g] ⊡ VT (*gen*) to classify (*en la B* under B); (*Com etc*) to grade, rate, class; *cartas* to sort.
⊡ **clasificarse** VR **(a)** (*Dep*) to win a place; to occupy a position; **Meca se clasificó después de la Ceca** Meca came after Ceca, Meca finished after Ceca; **¿dónde se clasificó el equipo local?** where did

the home team come?
(b) (*Dep*) to qualify; **no se clasificó el equipo para la final** the team did not qualify for the final.

CLÁSICO	ver también la entrada

¿"Classic" o "classical"?

Hay que tener en cuenta que el adjetivo *clásico* se puede traducir por *classic* o por *classical*:

- Se traduce por *classic* cuando el sustantivo al que acompaña reúne todas las características propias de su especie o cuando nos referimos a películas, libros, *etc* de una calidad extraordinaria:

  Es el clásico ejemplo de niño mimado
  He's a classic example of a spoilt child
  ...una de las historias de detectives clásicas de esa época...
  ...one of the classic detective stories of that time...

- Se traduce por *classical* cuando *clásico* hace referencia a la música clásica o a asuntos relacionados con las civilizaciones griega y romana:

  Cuanta más música clásica escucho más me gusta
  The more classical music I listen to the more I enjoy it
  El Partenón es uno de los ejemplos más significativos de la arquitectura clásica
  The Parthenon is one of the most significant examples of classical architecture

Para otros usos y ejemplos ver la entrada.

---

clasificatoria NF qualifying round; (*Atletismo*) heat.
clasificatorio ADJ *fase, prueba* qualifying; **tabla clasificatoria** league table.
clasismo NM class feelings; class-consciousness; class structure.
clasista ADJ (*Pol*) class (*atr*); class-conscious; (*pey*) snobbish.
claudia NF greengage.
claudicación NF giving way, abandonment of one's principles, shirking one's duty, backing down; **~ moral** failure of moral duty.
claudicar [1g] VI **(a)** (*cojear*) to limp. **(b)** (*fig*) (*engañar*) to act deceitfully; (*hacerlo mal*) to bungle it; (*vacilar*) to waver, stall. **(c)** (*fig: cejar*) to give way, abandon one's principles, shirk one's duty, back down; **no podemos ~ de nuestro pasado** we cannot deny our past, we cannot break free from our past.
Claudio NM Claudius.
claustral NMF (*Univ*) member of the Senate.
claustro NM **(a)** (*Ecl etc*) cloister. **(b)** (*Univ*) staff, faculty (*US*); (*como asamblea*) staff meeting; senate. **(c)** **~ materno** (*Anat*) womb.
claustrofobia NF claustrophobia.
claustrofóbico ADJ claustrophobic.
cláusula NF clause.
clausura NF **(a)** (*acto*) closing, closure; (*ceremonia*) formal closing, closing ceremony; **discurso de ~** closing speech. **(b)** (*Ecl*) monastic life; cloister; inner recess, sanctuary; **convento de ~** enclosed convent, enclosed monastery. **(c)** (*Méx Jur*) closing down, suspension of business.
clausurar [1a] VT **(a)** (*gen*) to close, bring to a close; (*Parl etc*) to adjourn, close. **(b)** (*LAm*) *casa etc* to close (up). **(c)** (*Méx Jur*) to close (down).
clava NF club, cudgel.
clavada NF **(a)** (*salto*) dive. **(b)** (‡) **pegar una ~ a uno** to rip sb off‡, overcharge sb.
clavadista NM/F (*CAm, Méx*) diver.
clavado [1] ADJ **(a)** (*asegurado con clavo*) nailed; (*fijado*) stuck fast, firmly fixed; **quedó ~ en la pared** it stuck in the wall, it remained fixed in the wall; **estamos ~s** we're stuck.
(b) (*mueble*) studded with nails.
(c) *vestido* just right, exactly fitting.
(d) dejar a uno ~ to leave sb speechless; **quedó ~** he was dumbfounded.
(e) a las 5 clavadas at 5 sharp, at 5 on the dot.
(f) es Domingo ~ he's the living image of Domingo; **está ~ a su padre** (*LAm*) he's the spitting image of his father.
(g) ¡~! exactly!, precisely!
[2] NM dive; **dar un ~** to dive, take a dive.
clavar [1a] [1] VT **(a)** *clavo* to knock in, drive in, bang in; (*fijar*) to fasten, fix; to pin; *tablas etc* to nail together, nail up; *puñal, cuchillo etc* to stick, thrust (*en* into), bury (*en* in); *cañón* to spike; **~ un anuncio a (o en) la puerta** to nail an announcement to the door.
(b) *joya* to set, mount.
(c) *ojos, vista*, to fix (*en* on), rivet (*en* to).
(d) (‡: *estafar*) to cheat, twist‡; **me clavaron 50 dólares** they stung me for 50 dollars‡.
(e) (⁎) to fuck⁑.
[2] **clavarse** VR **(a)** (*clavo etc*) to penetrate, go in.
(b) ~ una astilla en el dedo to get a splinter in one's finger; **~ una**

---

espina to prick o.s. on a thorn; **se clavó el cuchillo en el pecho** he thrust the knife into his chest.
(c) (*fig: equivocarse*) to be mistaken.
(d) clavársela to get drunk.
(e) ~ algo (*Méx‡*) to pocket sth, nick sth‡.
(f) (*Mex: Dep*) to dive.
clave [1] NF **(a)** (*de cifra, clasificación*) key; (*cifra*) code; **la ~ del problema** the key to the problem.
(b) (*Ajedrez*) key move.
(c) (*Mús*) clef; **~ de fa** bass clef; **~ de sol** treble clef; **en ~ de humor** in a humorous tone, on a humorous note.
(d) (*Arquit*) keystone.
[2] NM (*Mús*) harpsichord.
[3] *como* ADJ INVAR key (*atr*); **cuestión ~** key question; **posición ~** key position.
clavecín NM spinet.
clavel NM carnation; **no tener un ~⁎** to be broke⁎.
clavellina NF pink.
clavelón NM marigold; African marigold.
clavero NM (*Bot*) clove tree.
claveteado NM studs, studding.
clavetear [1a] VT **(a)** *puerta etc* to stud, decorate with studs. **(b)** *cordón etc* to put a metal tip on, tag. **(c)** (*fig*) *trato etc* to clinch, close, wind up.
clavicémbalo NM clavicembalo, harpsichord.
clavicordio NM clavichord.
clavícula NF collar bone, clavicle.
clavidista NMF (*Méx Dep*) diver.
clavija NF peg, dowel, pin; pintle; (*Mús*) peg; (*Elec*) plug; **~ hendida, ~ de dos patas** split pin, cotter pin; **apretar las ~s a uno⁎** to put the screws on sb⁎.
clavijero NM **(a)** (*Mús*) pegbox. **(b)** (*percha*) clothes hooks *pl*.
clavillo NM **(a)** (*t* **clavito** NM) small nail, brad, tack; **~ (de tijeras)** pin, rivet. **(b)** (*Bot*) clove.
clavo NM **(a)** (*Téc*) nail; tack; stud; spike; **~ romano** brass-headed nail; **~ de rosca** screw; **de ~ pasado** (*obvio*) obvious, undeniable; (*fácil*) easy; (*anticuado*) outworn, out-of-date; **verdad de ~ pasado** platitude, truism; **agarrarse a un ~ ardiendo** to clutch at a straw; **no da (o pega) ni ~** he doesn't do a stroke; **dar en el ~** (*fig*) to hit the nail on the head; **entrar de ~** to squeeze in; **estar como un ~** to be terribly thin; **llegar como un ~** to arrive on the dot; **meter a uno en ~** (*And, CAm, Cono Sur*) to put sb on the spot; **meter algo de ~** to squeeze sth in; **está que parte ~s** he's furious; **remachar el ~** (*fig*) to make matters worse; **ni un ~!⁎** not a sausage!⁎
(b) (*Bot*) clove.
(c) (*Med: callo*) corn; (*costra*) scab.
(d) (*Med: dolor*) migraine, severe headache; sharp pain; (*de borracho*) hangover⁎; (*fig*) anguish, acute distress.
(e) (*CAm, Méx Min*) rich vein of ore.
(f) (*And, Cono Sur*) (*cosa desagradable*) unpleasant thing; (*situación*) nasty situation; (*Com*) unsaleable article.
(g) (*CAm, Méx: problema*) problem, snag.
claxon NM, PL **claxons** ['klakson] o **cláxones** (*Aut*) horn, hooter; **tocar el ~** to sound one's horn, hoot.
claxonar [1a] VI (*Aut*) to sound one's horn, hoot.
claxonazo NM (*Aut*) hoot, toot (on the horn).
clemátide NF clematis.
clemencia NF mercy, clemency; leniency.
clemente ADJ merciful, clement; lenient.
clementina NF tangerine.
Cleopatra NF Cleopatra.
cleptomanía NF kleptomania.
cleptómano, -a NM/F kleptomaniac.
clerecía NF **(a)** (*clericato*) priesthood. **(b)** (*personas*) clergy.
clergyman [klerxi'man] ADJ INVAR: **traje ~** modernized form of priest's attire (*adopted in Spain 1962*).
clerical [1] ADJ clerical.
[2] NM (*CAm, Carib*) clergyman, minister.
clericalismo NM clericalism.
clericato NM, **clericatura** NF priesthood.
clericó NM (*Cono Sur*) mulled wine.
clérigo NM (*católico*) priest; (*anglicano*) clergyman, priest; (*otro*) minister.
clero NM clergy.
clic NM click.
cliché NM **(a)** (*Tip*) cliché, stereotype plate. **(b)** (*Liter*) cliché; = **clisé**.
cliente NMF (*t* **clienta** NF) (*Com*) client, customer; (*Jur*) client; (*Med*) patient.
clientela NF (*Com*) clients, clientèle, customers; (*Med*) practice; patients.
clientelismo NM patronage system.
clima NM climate; (*fig*) atmosphere, climate; **~ artificial** (*LAm*) air-

conditioning.
climatérico ADJ climacteric.
climático ADJ climatic.
climatización NF air-conditioning.
climatizado ADJ air-conditioned.
climatizador NM air-conditioner.
climatología NF (*ciencia*) climatology; (*tiempo*) weather.
climatológico ADJ climatological.
climatólogo, -a NM/F climatologist.
clímax ['klimas] NM INVAR climax.
clinch [klinʃ] NM, **clincha** NF (*LAm*) clinch.
clínica NF (a) (*lugar*) clinic; private hospital, nursing-home; teaching hospital; doctor's surgery; **~ de alergias** allergy clinic; **~ de reposo** convalescent home. (b) (*Univ*) clinical training.
clínicamente ADV clinically; **~ muerto** clinically dead.
clínico ADJ clinical.
clip NM, PL **clips** [klis] (*para papeles*) paper-clip; (*de pelo*) clip; (*de pantalón*) trouser-clip; (*joya*) clip; (*de vídeo*) videoclip; (*LAm*) earring.
clipe NM = **clip**.
clíper NM (*Náut*) clipper.
clisar [1a] VT to stereotype, stencil.
clisé NM (a) (*Tip*) cliché, stereotype plate; (*Fot*) plate. (b) (*Liter*) cliché.
clisos; NMPL peepers;, eyes.
clitoridectomía NF clitoridectomy.
clítoris NM clitoris.
clo NM cluck; **hacer ~** to cluck.
cloaca NF sewer (*t fig*); drain.
cloacal ADJ (a) **sistema ~** sewage system. (b) *chiste etc* lavatorial.
cloche NM (*CAm, Carib: Aut*) clutch.
clon NM clone.
clonación NF, **clonado** NM, **clonaje** NM cloning.
clonar [1a] VT to clone.
clónico [1] ADJ clonal, cloned; identical.
[2] NM (*Inform*) clone.
cloquear [1a] VI to cluck.
cloqueo NM clucking.
cloración NF chlorination.
clorador NM chlorinator.
cloral NM chloral.
clorar [1a] VT to chlorinate.
clorhídrico ADJ hydrochloric.
clorinar [1a] VT to chlorinate.
clorinda NF (*Cono Sur*) bleach.
cloro NM chlorine.
clorofila NF chlorophyl(l).
clorofluorocarbono NM chlorofluorocarbon.
cloroformar [1a] VT (*Carib, Cono Sur, Méx*), **cloroformizar** [1f] VT to chloroform.
cloroformo NM chloroform.
cloruro NM chloride; **~ de cal** chloride of lime; **~ cálcico** calcium chloride; **~ de hidrógeno** hydrogen chloride; **~ de polivinilo** polyvinyl chloride.
closet [klo'se] NM (*LAm*) built-in cupboard (o wardrobe).
clown [klawn] NM, PL **clowns** [klawn] clown.
clownesco ADJ clownish.
club [klu o kluß] NM, PL **clubs** o **clubes** [klus o 'klußes] club; **~ campestre** country club; **~ de fans** fan-club; **~ de golf** golf club; **~ náutico** yacht club; **~ nocturno** night-club.
clubista NMF club member.
clueca NF broody hen.
clueco ADJ (a) *gallina* broody. (b) (*Cono Sur: enfermizo*) sickly, weak. (c) (*Carib*: *engreído*) stuck-up*.
cluniacense ADJ, NM Cluniac.
clutch NM (*Méx Aut*) clutch.
cm¹ ABR *de* **centímetro** centimetre, cm.
cm² ABR *de* **centímetros cuadrados** square centimetres, sq. cm.
cm³ ABR *de* **centímetros cúbicos** cubic centimetres, c.c.
CMCC NF ABR *de* **Comunidad y Mercado Común del Caribe** Caribbean Community and Common Market, CARICOM.
CN NF ABR *de* **Carretera Nacional** ≈ 'A' road.
CNA NM (a) ABR *de* **Congreso Nacional Africano** African National Congress, ANC. (b) (*Esp*) ABR *de* **Comité Nacional de Árbitros** *refereeing body*.
CNEA NF (*Argentina*) ABR *de* **Comisión Nacional de Energía Atómica**.
CNI NF (*Chile*) ABR *de* **Central Nacional de Informaciones** *Chilean secret police*.
CNMV NF ABR *de* **Comisión Nacional del Mercado de Valores**.
CNT NF (a) (*Esp*) ABR *de* **Confederación Nacional del Trabajo**. (b) (*Colombia, Guatemala, Méx, Uruguay*) ABR *de* **Confederación Nacional de Trabajadores**. (c) (*Chile*) ABR *de* Comando Nacional de Trabajadores.
co... PREF CO...

coa NF (a) (*CAm, Carib, Méx: Agr*) (*para cavar*) long-handled narrow spade; (*para sembrar*) pointed stick for sowing seed. (b) (*Cono Sur: argot*) underworld slang.
coacción NF coercion, compulsion; duress.
coaccionador ADJ constraining, compelling.
coaccionar [1a] VT to coerce, compel, put great pressure on.
coactivo ADJ coercive; compelling.
coacusado, -a NM/F co-defendant.
coadjutor(a) NM/F assistant, coadjutor.
coadjuvar [1a] VT (*t VI ~ a*) *persona* to help, assist; *obra* to help in, contribute to.
coagulación NF coagulation; clotting; curdling.
coagulante NM coagulant.
coagular [1a] [1] VT to coagulate; *sangre* to clot, congeal; *leche* to curdle.
[2] **coagularse** VR to coagulate; to clot, congeal; to curdle.
coágulo NM coagulated mass, coagulum; clot; congealed lump; **~ sanguíneo** blood clot.
coalescente ADJ coalescent.
coalición NF coalition; **gobierno de ~** coalition government.
coalicionarse [1a] VR to form a coalition.
coaligado [1] ADJ: **estar ~s** to be allied.
[2] NM, **coaligada** NF ally; (*Pol*) coalition partner.
coaligarse [1h] VR to make common cause (*con* with).
coartada NF alibi.
coartar [1a] VT to limit, restrict.
coaseguro NM coinsurance.
coatí NM coati.
coautor(a) NM/F co-author.
coaxial ADJ coaxial.
coba* NF (a) (*mentirilla*) fib; (*truco*) neat trick. (b) (*jabón*) soft soap*; (*halagos*) cajolery; **dar ~ a uno** to soap sb up*, soft-soap sb*, play up to sb.
cobalto NM cobalt.
cobarde [1] ADJ cowardly; fainthearted, timid.
[2] NMF coward.
cobardear [1a] VI to be a coward, show cowardice, act in a cowardly way.
cobardía NF cowardliness; faintheartedness, timidity.
cobardón NM shameful coward, great coward.
cobaya NF, **cobayo** NM guinea-pig (*t fig*).
cobayismo NM use of animals (*o humans*) in medical experiments.
cobertera NF (a) (*tapa*) lid, cover. (b) (*Bot*) white water lily. (c) (*alcahueta*) procuress.
cobertizo NM (*edificio*) shed, outhouse, lean-to; (*refugio*) shelter; (*pasillo*) covered passage; **~ de aviación** hangar; **~ de coche** carport.
cobertor NM bedspread, coverlet.
cobertura NF (a) (*que cubre*) cover, covering. (b) (*cobertor*) bedspread. (c) (*por periódico etc*) coverage; **~ aérea** air cover; **~ informativa** news coverage; **~ del seguro** insurance cover.
cobija NF (a) (*Arquit*) coping tile, imbrex. (b) (*LAm*) (*de vestir*) poncho; (*manta*) blanket; **~s** bedclothes; **pegársele a uno las ~s** to oversleep. (c) (*Carib: techo*) roof of palm leaves).
cobijar [1a] [1] VT (a) (*cubrir*) to cover (up), close in. (b) (*proteger*) to protect, shelter; (*acoger*) to take in, give shelter to, (*pey*) harbour. (c) (*And, Carib: techar*) to thatch, roof with palms. [2] **cobijarse** VR to take shelter.
cobijo NM (a) (*lit*) shelter, lodging. (b) (*fig*) cover.
cobista* [1] ADJ soapy*, smarmy*.
[2] NM soapy individual*, smarmy sort*.
cobo NM (*Carib*) (a) (*Zool*) sea snail. (b) (*persona*) unsociable person, shy person; **ser un ~** to be shy, be withdrawn.
cobra¹ NF (*Zool*) cobra.
cobra² NF (*Caza*) retrieval.
cobrable ADJ, **cobradero** ADJ (a) (*que puede cobrarse*) retrievable. (b) (*Com*) *precio* chargeable; *suma* recoverable.
cobrador NM (a) (*Com*) collector. (b) (*de autobús etc*) conductor. (c) (*perro*) retriever.
cobradora NF conductress.
cobranza NF (a) = **cobro**. (b) (*Caza*) retrieval.
cobrar [1a] [1] VT (a) *cosa perdida* to recover; (*Caza*) to retrieve, fetch, bring back; *cuerda* to take in, pull in; *palos* to get, receive; **¡vas a ~!*** you'll cop it!*; **el accidente cobró la vida de 50 personas** the accident took the lives of 50 people.
(b) *precio* to charge; **cobran 200 dólares por componerlo** they charge 200 dollars to repair it; **¿me cobra, por favor?** how much do I owe you?, how much is that please?; **me han cobrado demasiado** they've charged me too much, they've overcharged me.
(c) *suma* to collect, receive; *cheque* to cash; *sueldo* to earn; to draw, get, collect; **¿cuánto cobras al año?** how much do you get a year?, how much do they pay you a year?; **fue a la oficina a ~ el sueldo**

he went to the office to get his wages; **cantidades por ~** sums receivable; **cuenta por ~** unpaid bill.

(d) ~ a uno (*LAm*) to press sb for payment.

(e) ~ carnes to put on weight.

(f) *crédito, fama etc* to get, acquire, gain; *valor* to summon up, muster; *fuerzas* to gather; **~ cariño a uno** to take a liking to sb, grow fond of sb; **~ fama de** to acquire a reputation as (*o* for being).

[2] VI **(a)** (*Fin*) to draw one's pay, get one's wages; to collect one's salary; **cobra los viernes** he gets paid on Fridays; **te pagaré en cuanto cobre** I'll pay you when I get my wages; **vino el lechero a ~** the milkman came for his money, the milkman came to be paid.

(b) ~ al número llamado (*Telec*) to reverse the charges, call collect (*US*).

[3] **cobrarse** VR **(a)** (*Med*) to recover, get well; to come to.

(b) ~ de una pérdida to make up for a loss.

cobre NM **(a)** (*metal*) copper.

(b) (*Culin*) copper pans, kitchen utensils.

(c) (*Mús*) brass (*t* **~s**); **batir(se) el ~** to work hard, work with a will; to hustle; (*en discusión*) to get worked up; **batirse el ~ por** + *infin* to go all out to + *infin*.

(d) (*LAm: moneda*) cent, small copper coin.

(e) (*LAm*) **enseñar el ~** to show one's true colours.

cobreado ADJ copperplated.

cobreño ADJ copper (*atr*), coppery.

cobrero NM coppersmith.

cobrizo ADJ coppery.

cobro NM **(a)** (*acto*) recovery, retrieval.

(b) (*Fin*) collection; payment; **cargo por ~** collection charge; **deuda de ~ difícil** debt that is hard to collect; **~ a la entrega** collect on delivery; **~ de morosos** debt collection; **~ revertido automático** automatic reverse-charge dialling; **llamar a ~ revertido** to reverse the charges, call collect (*US*), call toll-free (*US*); **poner al** (*o* **en**) **~** to make payable; *factura* to send out.

(c) (*lugar seguro*) safe place; **poner algo en ~** to put sth in a safe place, put sth out of harm's way; **ponerse en ~** to take refuge, get to safety.

coca¹ NF **(a)** (*: cabeza*) head, nut‡. **(b)** (‡: *golpe*) rap on the nut‡. **(c)** (*de pelo*) bun, coil. **(d)** (*en cuerda*) kink.

coca² NF **(a)** (*LAm Bot*) (*árbol*) coca tree (*o* bush); (*hojas*) coca leaves; (*cocaína*) cocaine. **(b) de ~** (*Méx*) free, gratis.

┌─ **COCA** ─────────────────────────────┐

In Peru, Colombia and Bolivia, the leaves of the Erythroxylon coca plant have traditionally been chewed as a mild stimulant and for a variety of medicinal purposes. As such, they are sold quite legally in street markets. Since coca is also the raw material for cocaine, peasant farmers in remote areas grow it to sell it to the illegal drugs trade. Cartels in Cali and Medellín control most of the processing, shipment and distribution of cocaine and retain most of the profits. The cocaine industry brings few benefits to the vast majority of Latin Americans and the power struggle between the drug barons and government is responsible for widespread violence.

└──────────────────────────────────────┘

coca³* NF Coke* ®, Coca-Cola ®.

cocacho NM (*And, Cono Sur*) tap on the head.

cocacolo, -a NM/F (*And*) frivolous teenager, idle young person.

cocacolonización NF (*hum*) americanization.

cocada NF **(a)** (*CAm*) (*Culin*) sweet coconut; (*viaje*) length of a journey.

(b) (*And Aut*) tyre grip.

cocaína NF cocaine.

cocaínico ADJ cocaine (*atr*).

cocainomanía NF addiction to cocaine.

cocainómano, -a NM/F cocaine addict.

cocal NM (*LAm*) coconut plantation.

cocción NF **(a)** (*Culin*) (*acto*) cooking; (*duración*) cooking time; **~ al vapor** steam cooking, steaming. **(b)** (*Téc*) baking, firing.

cóccix NM INVAR COCCYX.

cocear [1a] VTI to kick; (*fig*) to kick (*contra* against), resist.

cocer [2b *y* 2h] [1] VT **(a)** (*Culin*: *gen*) to cook; (*hervir*) to boil; (*al horno*) to bake.

(b) (*Téc*) *ladrillos etc* to bake, fire.

[2] VI (*gen*) to cook; (*hervir*) to boil; (*burbujear*) to bubble, seethe; (*vino*) to ferment.

[3] **cocerse** VR **(a)** (*fig*: *sufrir*) to suffer intensely, be in great pain. **(b)** (‡) to get plastered‡. **(c)** (*) **no está a lo que se cuece** he's not with it*; **¿qué se cuece por ahí?** what's cooking?*

cocha¹ NF (*And, Cono Sur*) (*charca*) pool; (*pantano*) swamp; (*laguna*) lagoon.

cochambre NMF (*mugre*) muck, filth; (*papeles*) litter; (*objeto*) filthy thing, disgusting object; (*fig*) muck, rubbish; **caer en la ~** (*fig*) to sink very low.

cochambroso ADJ filthy, nauseating, stinking; (*fig*) vile.

cochayuyo NM (*And, Cono Sur*) seaweed.

cochazo* NM whacking great car*.

coche¹ NM **(a)** (*Aut*) car, motorcar, automobile (*US*); **~ ambulancia** ambulance; **~ de alquiler** taxi, cab; hire car; **~ blindado** armoured car; **~ de bomberos** fire-engine; **~ de carreras** racing car; **~ celular** prison van, patrol wagon (*US*); **~ de cortesía** courtesy car; **~ chocón, ~ de choque** dodgem car; **~ deportivo** sports car; **~ de época** vintage car; **~ fúnebre, ~ mortuorio** hearse; **~ de grúa** breakdown van, tow truck; **~ K** unmarked police-car; **~ de línea** long-distance taxi; **~ de ocasión, ~ usado** used car, second-hand car; **~ de punto** taxi; **~ radio-patrulla** radio patrol-car; **~ de serie** standard model, production model; **~ de turismo** saloon car, sedan (*US*); tourer; **~ zeta** Z-car; **ir en ~** to go by car; to drive, motor; **ir en el ~ de San Francisco** (*o* **Fernando**) to go on Shank's pony, ride Shank's mare.

(b) (*Ferro*) coach, car, carriage; **~ directo** through carriage; **~ de equipajes** luggage-van, baggage car (*US*); **~ de viajeros** passenger coach.

(c) (*Hist*) coach, carriage.

(d) (*Méx*: *taxi*) taxi, cab.

coche² NM (*CAm, Méx*) pig, hog; pork; **~ de monte** wild pig (*o* boar).

coche-bomba NM, PL **coches-bomba** car-bomb.

coche-cabina NM, PL **coches-cabina** bubble-car.

coche-cama NM, PL **coches-cama** sleeping car, sleeper.

cochecillo NM small carriage (*etc*); **~ de inválido** invalid carriage.

cochecito NM pram, perambulator, baby carriage (*US*); **~ de golf** golf buggy; **~ de niño** go-cart.

coche-comedor NM, PL **coches-comedor** dining-car, restaurant car.

coche-correo NM, PL **coches-correo** (*Ferro*) mail-van, mobile sorting-office.

coche-cuba NM, PL **coches-cuba** tank lorry, water wagon.

coche-habitación NM, PL **coches-habitación** caravan, trailer.

cochemonte NM (*CAm Zool*) wild pig, wild boar.

coche-patrulla NM, PL **coches-patrulla** patrol-car.

cochera NF **(a)** (*de carruajes*) coach house; **~ de alquiler** livery stable.

(b) (*Aut*) garage, carport. **(c)** (*Ferro*) engine-shed; **~ de tranvías** tram shed, tram depot.

cocherada NF (*Méx*) coarse (*o* vulgar) expression.

coche-restaurante NM, PL **coches-restaurante** dining-car, restaurant car.

cochero [1] ADJ: **puerta cochera** carriage entrance.

[2] NM coachman; **~ de punto** cabman, cabby*; **hablar (en) ~** (*Méx*) to swear, use obscene language.

cocherón NM (*Ferro*) engine-shed, locomotive depot.

coche-salón NM, PL **coches-salón** (*Ferro*) saloon coach.

coche-vivienda NM, PL **coches-vivienda** caravan, trailer, camper.

cochina NF SOW.

cochinada NF **(a)** (*cualidad*) filth, filthiness.

(b) (*objeto*) filthy object, dirty thing.

(c) (*acto etc*) beastly thing (to do); filthy act, filthy word; (*canallada*) dirty trick; **eso fue una ~** that was a beastly thing to do; **hacer una ~ a uno** to play a dirty trick on sb.

Cochinchina* NF = **Conchinchina**.

cochinear* [1a] VI to wallow in filth.

cochinería NF = **cochinada**.

cochinilla NF **(a)** (*Zool*) woodlouse.

(b) (*Ent, colorante*) cochineal.

(c) de ~ (*Carib, Méx*) trivial, unimportant.

cochinillo NM piglet, sucking-pig.

cochino [1] ADJ **(a)** (*sucio*) filthy, dirty.

(b) (*fig*: *miserable*) filthy, rotten*, measly*; **esta vida cochina** this wretched life.

[2] NM **(a)** (*lit*) pig; **~ de leche** sucking-pig; **~ montés** wild pig.

(b) (*fig*: *bestia*) hog; swine; filthy person; **realmente es un ~** he really is a swine.

cochiquera NF, **cochitril** NM pigsty (*t fig*).

cocho* (*LAm*) [1] ADJ old, past it.

[2] NM, **cocha²** NF old man, old woman.

cochón, -ona‡ NM/F (*hombre*) poof‡, queer‡; (*mujer*) dyke‡.

cochoso ADJ (*And*) filthy.

cochura NF **(a)** (*acto*) = **cocción**. **(b)** (*hornada*) batch of loaves (*o* cakes, bricks *etc*).

cocido [1] ADJ **(a)** (*Culin*) boiled, cooked; **bien ~** well done.

(b) (*perito*) skilled, experienced; **estar ~ en** to be skilled at, be expert at.

(c) estar ~‡ to be plastered‡, be drunk.

[2] NM stew (*in Spain: of meat, bacon, chickpeas etc*); **ganarse el ~** to earn one's living; to eke out a living.

cociente NM quotient; **~ intelectual** intelligence quotient.

cocina NF **(a)** (*cuarto*) kitchen; **de ~** kitchen (*atr*); **~ integral** fitted kitchen.

(b) (*aparato*) stove, cooker; **~ económica** cooker, range; **~ eléctrica** electric cooker; **~ a gas**, **~ de gas** gas stove, gas cooker; **~ de petróleo** oil stove.

(c) (*arte*) cooking, cookery; cuisine; **alta ~** haute cuisine; **~ casera** plain cooking, homely cooking; **nueva ~** nouvelle cuisine; **la ~ valenciana** Valencian cooking, the Valencian cuisine; **libro de ~** cookery book, cookbook (*US*).

cocinada NF (*LAm*) (period of) cooking, cooking time.

cocinado NM cooking.

cocinar [1a] **1** VT to cook.
  2 VI **(a)** (*lit*) to cook, do the cooking. **(b)** (*fig*) to meddle.

cocinero, -a NM/F cook.

cocinilla NF **(a)** (*cuarto*) small kitchen, kitchenette. **(b)** (*aparato*) small cooker; (*infiernillo*) spirit stove; (*escalfador*) chafing dish.

cocker ['koker] NM cocker (spaniel).

coco¹ NM (*Med*) coccus; (*Ent*) grub, maggot.

coco² NM **(a)** (*duende*) bogeyman; **parece un ~** he's an ugly devil; **¡que viene el ~!** the bogeyman will get you!
  (b) (*mueca*) face, grimace; **hacer ~s a uno** to make faces at sb, (*amantes*) to make eyes at sb; to coax sb, wheedle sb.

coco³ **1** NM **(a)** (*Bot: nuez*) coconut; (*árbol*) coconut palm.
  (b) (*hum**) (*cabeza*) noddle*; (*cerebro*) brain; (*inteligencia*) brains; **comer el ~ a uno** to brainwash sb, pull the wool over sb's eyes; **comerse el ~** to think hard; to worry; **me estoy comiendo el ~** I'm trying to think; **estar hasta el ~*** to be utterly fed up*; **lavar el ~ a uno** to brainwash sb.
  (c) (*LAm: vasija*) cup (*etc*) made from a coconut shell.
  (d) (*And: sombrero*) derby, bowler (hat).
  (e) (*And, Cono Sur: tela*) percale.
  (f) **cortarse el cabello a ~** (*And*) to have one's head shaved.
  (g) **~s** (*And Naipes*) diamonds.
  (h) (*Cono Sur*) **~s** (♠) balls♠; **hinchar los ~s a uno♠** to get up sb's nose♠.
  2 ADJ (*Carib*) **(a)** (*duro*) hard, strong.
  (b) (*testarudo*) obstinate.

cococha NF (*de bacalao etc*) barbel.

cocodrilo NM crocodile.

cocoliche NM (*Cono Sur: argot*) pidgin Spanish; (*italiano*) Italian.

cócona NF (*Carib*) tip.

coconote NM (*Méx*) child; chubby child; squat person.

cócora NMF **(a)** (*: *pesado*) bore. **(b)** (*Cono Sur: machaca*) conceited person, pest.

cocoroco ADJ (*Cono Sur*) (*engreído*) vain, stuck-up*; (*descarado*) insolent, cheeky*.

cocorota♠ NF bonce♠, head.

cocoso ADJ maggoty, worm-eaten.

cocotal NM coconut grove, coconut plantation.

cocotero NM coconut palm.

cóctel ['koktel *o* 'kotel] NM, PL **coctels** *o* **cócteles (a)** (*bebida*) cocktail; **~ de frutas** fruit cocktail; **~ de gambas** prawn cocktail; **~ Mólotov** Molotov cocktail.
  (b) (*fiesta*) cocktail party; **ofrecer un ~ en honor de uno** to hold a cocktail party in sb's honour.

coctelera NF cocktail shaker.

cocuyo NM (*LAm*) firefly; (*Aut*) rear light.

cod. NM ABR *de* **código** code.

coda NF **(a)** (*Mús*) coda. **(b)** (*Téc*) wedge.

codal NM **(a)** (*Bot*) layered vine shoot. **(b)** (*Arquit*) strut, prop.

codaste NM stern post.

codazo NM **(a)** (*golpe*) jab, poke, nudge (with one's elbow). **(b)** (*Méx: consejo*) tip-off.

codeador ADJ (*And, Cono Sur*) whingeing, demanding.

codear [1a] **1** VT **(a)** (*empujar con el codo*) to elbow, nudge, jostle.
  (b) (*And, Cono Sur: insistir*) **~ a uno** to keep on at sb, pester sb.
  2 VI **(a)** to elbow, jostle; **abrirse paso codeando** to elbow one's way through.
  (b) (*) (*And, Cono Sur*) to sponge*, live by sponging*.
  3 codearse VR: **~ con** to hobnob with, rub shoulders with.

codeína NF codeine.

codeo* NM (*And: sablazo*) sponging*; (*insistencia*) pestering.

codera NF elbow patch; elbow guard.

codeso NM laburnum.

códice NM manuscript, codex.

codicia NF greed, covetousness; **~ de** greed for, lust for.

codiciable ADJ covetable, desirable; enviable.

codiciado ADJ widely desired; much in demand; sought-after, coveted; **obtuvo el ~ título** he won the coveted title.

codiciar [1b] VT to covet.

codicilo NM codicil.

codiciosamente ADV greedily, covetously.

codicioso ADJ greedy, covetous; **estoy ~ de verte** I am very eager to see you.

codificación NF codification; **~ de barras** bar coding.

codificado NM: **el programa se emitirá en ~** the programme will be encrypted.

codificador NM encoder.

codificar [1g] VT to codify; (*TV*) to encrypt, scramble.

código NM **(a)** (*Jur etc*) code; law, statute; (*reglas*) rules, set of rules; **~ de (la) circulación** highway code; **~ civil** civil code; **~ de leyes** law code, statute book; **~ militar** articles of war; **~ penal** penal code, criminal code.
  (b) (*Inform, Telec etc*) code; **mensaje en ~** message in code, coded message; **~ barrado**, **~ de barras** bar-code; **~ binario** binary code; **~ de colores** colour code; **~ hexadecimal** hexadecimal code; **~ legible por máquina** machine-readable code; **~ máquina** machine code; **~ postal** postcode; **~ de señales** signal code; **~ territorial** area code.

codillo NM (*Zool*) elbow; top joint of the foreleg; upper foreleg; (*Bot*) stump (of a branch); (*Téc*) elbow (joint), bend; angle iron; **~ de cerdo** (*Méx Culin*) pig's trotter.

codirigir [3c] VT (*TV, Cine*) to co-direct.

codo¹ NM **(a)** (*Anat*) elbow; **~ del tenista** tennis elbow; **~ a ~** (*como N*) rivalry, intense competition; needle match; close-run result; **comerse los ~s de hambre** to be utterly destitute; **dar con el ~ a uno**, **dar de(l) ~ a uno** to nudge sb; **empinar el ~** to booze*, drink; **hablar por los ~s** to talk too much, talk nineteen to the dozen; **llevar a uno ~ con ~** to frogmarch sb along, drag sb along with his hands tied behind his back; (*fig*) to arrest sb; **mentir por los ~s** to tell huge lies; **morderse el ~** (*Cono Sur, Méx*) to restrain o.s., bite one's lip; **romperse los ~s*** to swot*; **ser del ~**, **ser duro de ~** to be mean; **trabajar ~ con ~** to work side by side.
  (b) (*Téc*) elbow (joint), bend; angle iron.
  (c) (*fig*) elbow grease; **hacer más ~s** to put more elbow grease into it; **sacó la oposición a base de ~s** he won the post by sheer hard work; **apretar los ~s** (*estudiar*) to work hard.

codo²* ADJ (*Méx*) mean, stingy.

codorniz NF quail.

COE NM ABR *de* **Comité Olímpico Español** Spanish Olympic Committee.

coedición NF (*libro*) joint publication; (*acto*) joint publishing.

coeditar [1a] VT to publish jointly.

coeducación NF coeducation.

coeducacional ADJ coeducational.

coeficiente NM coefficient; **~ aerodinámico**, **~ de penetración aerodinámica** drag factor; **~ de caja** cash deposit requirement; **~ intelectual**, **~ de inteligencia**, **~ mental** intelligence quotient.

coercer [2b] VT to coerce, constrain; to restrain.

coerción NF coercion, constraint; restraint.

coercitivamente ADV forcibly.

coercitivo ADJ coercive, forcible.

coestrella NF co-star.

coetáneo, -a ADJ, NM/F contemporary (*con* with).

coevo ADJ coeval.

coexistencia NF coexistence; **~ pacífica** peaceful coexistence.

coexistente ADJ coexistent.

coexistir [3a] VI to coexist (*con* with).

cofa NF (*Náut*) top; **~ mayor** maintop.

cofabricar [1g] VT to manufacture jointly.

cofia NF (*de enfermera, criada etc*) cap, white cap; (††) coif; bonnet.

cofinanciación NF joint financing.

cofinanciar [1b] VT to finance jointly.

cofrade NM member (of a brotherhood), brother.

cofradía NF brotherhood, fraternity; guild, association; (*de ladrones etc*) gang; *see also* SEMANA SANTA .

cofre NM chest; case (for jewels *etc*); (*Méx Aut*) bonnet.

cofrecito NM casket.

cofundador(a) NM/F co-founder.

cogedero **1** ADJ *fruto* ripe, ready to be picked.
  2 NM handle.

cogedor NM small shovel, ash shovel; dustpan.

coger [2c] **1** VT **(a)** (*agarrar*) *mango, objeto etc* to take hold of, catch hold of; to seize, grasp; to hold on to; *pelota etc* to catch; *objeto caído* to pick up; *vestido etc* to gather up, hold up; *libro etc* to pick up, take up; *herramienta* (*fig*) to hold, use; **~ a uno de la mano** to take sb by the hand; **ir cogidos de la mano** to go hand-in-hand; (*amantes*) to go along holding hands; **no ha cogido un fusil en la vida** he's never held a gun in his life.
  (b) (*robar*) to take, pinch*; **me coge siempre las cerillas** he always takes my matches; **en la aduana le cogieron una radio** they found a radio on him in the customs, they confiscated a radio from him in the customs.
  (c) *flor, fruto etc* to pick, pluck; (*cosechar*) to harvest; to gather, collect.
  (d) *persona etc* to catch; (*Jur*) to arrest; (*Mil*) to take prisoner; *prisionero* to take, capture; *animal* to catch, capture, trap; *pez* to catch;

competidor etc to catch (up with); **¡por fin te he cogido!** caught you at last!; **~ un buen marido** to catch o.s. (o get, acquire) a good husband; **~ a uno en una mentira** to catch sb in a lie; **la noche nos cogió todavía en el mar** the night caught us still at sea; **la guerra nos cogió en Francia** the war caught us in France; **antes que nos coja la noche** before night overtakes us (o comes down on us); **~ a uno en la hora tonta, ~ a uno detrás de la puerta** to catch sb at a disadvantage; **~ in fraganti** to catch red-handed; **~ de nuevas a uno** to take sb by surprise; *V t* **desprevenido** etc.

(**e**) (toro) to gore; to toss; (coche) to knock down, run over.

(**f**) **~ los dedos en la puerta** to catch one's fingers in the door.

(**g**) propina etc to take, accept; trabajo to take on; noticia etc to take, receive; **cogió la noticia sin interés** he received the news without interest.

(**h**) (emprender) curso, período, trabajo etc to begin on; **cogí la conferencia a mitad** I joined the discussion halfway through.

(**i**) (obtener) to get, obtain, acquire; **he cogido el billete del avión** I've got my air ticket; **cógeme un puesto en la cola** get me a place in the queue; **acabo de ~ una cocinera nueva** I've got a new cook.

(**j**) enfermedad, resfriado etc to catch; polvo to gather, collect; hábito to get, get into, catch, acquire; **el niño cogió sarampión** the child got (o caught) measles; **los perros cogen pulgas** dogs get fleas; **ha cogido la manía de las quinielas** he's caught the pools craze.

(**k**) (emoción) to take; **~ cariño a** to take a liking to; **~ celos a** to become jealous of; **~ aversión a** to take a strong dislike to.

(**l**) sentido to get, understand; palabra hablada to catch; radio to pick up, get; frase, giro to pick up; acento to catch, acquire; técnica to pick up, learn; **con esta radio cogemos Praga** with this set we can get Prague.

(**m**) (apuntar) notas etc to take down; **le cogieron el discurso taquigráficamente** they took his speech down in shorthand.

(**n**) (escoger) to choose, pick; **has cogido un mal momento** you've picked a bad time.

(**o**) medio de transporte to take, catch, go by; **vamos a ~ el tren** let's take the train.

(**p**) (recipiente) to hold, take; área to cover, extend over, take up.

(**q**) (LAm‡) to lay‡, screw‡.

2 VI (**a**) (Bot) to take, strike.

(**b**) (caber) to fit, go, have room; **aquí no coge** it doesn't fit in here, there's no room for it here.

(**c**) **cogió y se fue*** he just upped and went*.

(**d**) (LAm‡) to fuck‡, screw‡.

3 cogerse VR (**a**) (gen) to catch; **~ los dedos en la puerta** to catch one's fingers in the door; **~ a uno** to cling tight to sb, press close against sb.

(**b**) **~ algo*** to steal sth, pinch sth*.

(**c**) **~ con uno** (Carib) to get on (well) with sb; **~ en algo** to get involved in sth; to get used to sth.

cogestión NF co-partnership (in industry etc), worker participation.

cogida NF (**a**) (Agr) gathering, picking; harvesting; (Pesca) catch. (**b**) (Taur) goring, tossing; **tener una ~** to be gored, be tossed. (**c**) (‡) (dose of) pox*.

cogido NM (Cos) fold, gather, tuck.

cogienda NF (**a**) (And, Carib) = **cogida** (a); (Mil) forced enlistment. (**b**) (Méx‡) fucking‡, screwing‡.

cognado ADJ, NM cognate.

cognición NF cognition.

cognitividad NF cognition.

cognitivo ADJ, **cognoscitivo** ADJ cognitive.

cogollo NM (**a**) (de planta) shoot, sprout; (de lechuga, col) heart; (de árbol) top; (LAm: de caña de azúcar) top of sugar cane.

(**b**) (fig: lo mejor) best part, cream; **el ~ de la sociedad** the cream of society.

(**c**) (fig: núcleo) centre, core, nucleus.

(**d**) (Carib: sombrero) straw hat.

cogorza‡ NF: **pescar una ~** to get blotto‡, get very drunk.

cogotazo NM blow on the back of the neck; (Boxeo etc) rabbit punch.

cogote NM back of the neck, nape; scruff of the neck; **de ~** (Cono Sur) animal fat; **carne de ~** (Cono Sur) rubbish, trash; **coger a uno por el ~** to take sb by the scruff of the neck; **estar hasta el ~** (Carib) to have had it up to here; **ponérselas en el ~** (CAm‡) to beat it*.

cogotudo‡ **1** ADJ (And, Cono Sur) well-heeled*, filthy rich*; (Carib) powerful in politics; **es un ~** he's got pull, he's got friends in high places.

2 NM (LAm) self-made man, parvenu.

coguionista NMF co-scriptwriter.

cogujada NF woodlark.

cogulla NF (hood of) monk's habit.

cohabitación NF cohabitation; (Pol) coexistence.

cohabitar [1a] VI to live together, cohabit (t pey); (Pol) to coexist.

cohechar [1a] VT to bribe, offer a bribe to.

cohecho NM bribe, bribery.

coheredera NF coheiress.

coheredero NM coheir, joint heir.

coherencia NF coherence; (Fís etc) cohesion.

coherente ADJ coherent; logical; right; **no sería ~ cumplir con sus órdenes** there is no sense in following his orders; **~ con** in line with, in tune with.

coherentemente ADV (**a**) coherently. (**b**) **A ~ con B** A together with B, A in conjunction with B.

cohesión NF cohesion.

cohesionado ADJ united, unified; solid.

cohesionador ADJ: **elemento ~** unifying force.

cohesionar [1a] VT to unite, draw together.

cohesivo ADJ cohesive.

cohete **1** NM (**a**) (gen) rocket; **~ espacial** (space) rocket; **~ luminoso, ~ de señales** flare, star shell, distress signal.

(**b**) (CAm, Méx: pistola) pistol.

(**c**) (Méx: mecha) blasting fuse.

(**d**) **al ~** (And, Cono Sur) without rhyme or reason.

2 ADJ (CAm, Méx) drunk, tight*.

cohetería NF rocketry.

cohibición NF restraint; inhibition.

cohibido ADJ restrained, restricted; (de temperamento) inhibited, full of inhibitions; shy, timid, self-conscious; ill at ease; **sentirse ~** to feel shy, feel embarrassed.

cohibir [3a] **1** VT (refrenar) to restrain, check, restrict; (Med etc) to inhibit; (incomodar) to make uneasy, make shy, embarrass.

2 cohibirse VR (**a**) (refrenarse) to restrain o.s.

(**b**) (sentirse cohibido) to feel inhibited; to get uneasy, to become shy, feel embarrassed.

cohombro NM cucumber.

cohonestar [1a] VT (**a**) (justificar) to explain away, whitewash, make appear reasonable. (**b**) dos cualidades etc to blend, harmonize, reconcile.

cohorte NF cohort.

COI NM ABR de **Comité Olímpico Internacional** International Olympic Committee, IOC.

coima NF (**a**) (concubina) concubine; (puta) whore. (**b**) (‡: en el juego) rake-off*. (**c**) (*: And, Cono Sur: soborno) bribe; (acto) bribing, bribery.

coimacracia* NF (Perú) rule of graft, corruption.

coime NM (**a**) (chulo) pimp, ponce. (**b**) (en el juego) gambling operator. (**c**) (And: camarero) waiter.

coimero ADJ (*: And, Cono Sur) easily bribed, brib(e)able, bent‡.

coincidencia NF (**a**) (gen) coincidence. (**b**) (acuerdo) agreement; **en ~ con** in agreement with.

coincidente ADJ coincidental.

coincidentemente ADV coincidentally.

▼ **coincidir** [3a] VI (**a**) (sucesos) to coincide (con with). (**b**) (personas) to coincide, agree; **todos coinciden en que ...** everybody agrees that ...

cointérprete NMF fellow actor.

coinversión NF joint investment.

coipo NM, **coipu** NM (LAm) coypu.

coito NM intercourse, coitus.

cojan etc V **coger**.

cojear [1a] VI (**a**) (persona: al andar) to limp, hobble (along); (estado) to be lame (de in); (mueble) to wobble, rock, be rocky; **cojean del mismo pie** they both have the same faults; **sabemos de qué pie cojea** we know his weak spots (o weaknesses).

(**b**) (fig: equivocarse) to slip up, be at fault (de in); (moralmente) to deviate from virtue.

cojera NF lameness; limp.

cojijo NM (**a**) (Ent) bug, small insect. (**b**) (fig) peeve*, grudge, grumble.

cojijoso ADJ peevish, cross, grumpy.

cojín NM (**a**) (almohadilla) cushion. (**b**) (‡: euf) = **cojón**.

cojinete NM (**a**) (cojín) small cushion, pad.

(**b**) (Mec) **~ a bolas, ~ de bolas** ball-bearing; **~ de rodillos** roller-bearing.

(**c**) (Ferro etc) chair.

(**d**) **~s** (And, Carib, Méx) saddlebags.

cojinillos NMPL (CAm, Méx) saddlebags.

cojo **1** ADJ (**a**) persona lame; crippled; limping; mueble wobbly, rocky; **~ de un pie** lame in one foot.

(**b**) (fig) lame, weak, shaky; **el verso queda ~** the line is defective; **la frase está coja** the sentence is incomplete; **el ~ echa la culpa al empedrado** (Cono Sur) a bad workman blames his tools.

2 NM, **coja** NF lame person, cripple.

cojón‡ NM (**a**) (Anat) ball‡; **¡cojones!** (rechazo) balls!‡; (sorpresa) bugger me!‡; **¡y un ~!, ¡por los cojones!** no way!*, not on your life!; **¡olé sus cojones!** good for him!; **una película de ~** a tremendous film*, a smashing film*; **¿qué cojones haces aquí?** what the bloody hell are you doing here!‡; **me lo paso por los cojones** I just laugh at it; **tocar los cojones a uno** (fig) to get up sb's nose‡.

(**b**) **cojones** (fig) guts; **es un tío con cojones** he's got guts; he's a good sort; **es un tipo sin cojones** he's a gutless individual*; **hace falta tener cojones** you've got to have guts; **hacer algo por cojones** to do sth by hook or by crook, do sth at all costs; **tienes que hacerlo por los cojones** you've bloody well got to do it‡; **echar cojones a una situación** to face resolutely up to a situation.

(c) (*como* ADV) **hace un frío de cojones** it's bloody cold‡; **me importa un ~** I don't give a damn; **sabe un ~** he knows a hell of a lot; **vale un ~** it's worth a hell of a lot.

cojonudamente‡ ADV marvellously, splendidly.

cojonudo‡ ADJ (a) (*físicamente*) strong; (*moralmente*) brave; tough; full of guts. (b) (*grande*) huge, colossal; very important; (*destacado*) outstanding. (c) (*soberbio*) marvellous, splendid; smashing*; **un tío ~** a great bloke‡; **una hembra cojonuda** a smashing bird‡; **¡qué ~!** great stuff!* (d) (*gracioso*) very funny, highly amusing. (e) (*LAm: holgazán*) lazy, slow; (*tonto*) stupid.

cojudear‡ [1a] (*LAm*) ① VT to con*, swindle.
② VI to mess about.

cojudez‡ NF silly thing, piece of stupidity; **¡déjate de cojudeces!** stop your nonsense!

cojudo ① ADJ (a) (*Agr*) *animal* entire, not castrated; used for stud purposes. (b) (*And*‡: *ingenuo*) gullible; **hacerse el ~** to act dumb.
② NM, **cojuda** NF (*Méx*) Simple Simon.

cok [kok] NM, **coke** ['koke] NM (*LAm*) coke.

col NF cabbage; **~es de Bruselas** (Brussels) sprouts; **~ rizada** curly kale; **~ roja** red cabbage; **~ de Saboya** savoy; **entre ~ y ~, lechuga** a change is a good thing, variety is the spice of life.

col, col.ª NF ABR *de* **columna** column, col.

cola¹ NF (a) (*Aer, Astron, Orn, Zool*) tail.
(b) (*de frac*) tail; (*de vestido*) train; **~ de caballo** (*pelo*) pony-tail.
(c) (*posición*) end, last place, bottom; tail end; (*silla*) end seat; **estar a la ~ de la clase** to be (at the) bottom of the class; **venir a la ~** to come last, come at the back; **estar arrimado a la ~** (*Pol*) to be a reactionary; **vagón de ~** last truck, rear coach.
(d) (*línea etc*) queue, line; (*Inform*) queue; **~ de impresión** print(ing) queue; **~ de trabajos** job queue; **guardar ~, hacer ~** to queue (up), line up; **¡a la ~!, ¡haga Vd ~!** get in the queue!
(e) (*Téc*) **~ de milano** dovetail; **~ de pato** dovetail.
(f) (*fig*) consequence(s); aftermath; **tener ~, traer ~** to have grave consequences.
(g) (‡) prick‡.
(h) (*LAm Aut*) lift; **pedir ~** to ask for a lift.
(i) (*Cono Sur**: *trasero*) bum‡, bottom.

cola² NF (a) (*pegamento*) glue, gum; (*Arte*) size; **~ de contacto** glue; **~ de pescado** fish glue; isinglass; **~ de retal** size; **pintura a la ~** distemper, (*Arte*) tempera; **comer ~** (*Cono Sur*) to be let down, be disappointed; **eso no pega ni con ~** that has nothing whatsoever to do with it; that's utter rubbish.
(b) (*And: bebida*) fizzy drink; **~ de naranja** orangeade.

cola³* NF Coke* ®, Coca-Cola ®.

colaboración NF (a) (*acto*) collaboration; **escrito en ~** written in collaboration.
(b) (*en periódico etc*) contribution (*a, en* to); article; (*de congreso*) paper, communication.

colaboracionismo NM (*Pol*) collaboration.

colaboracionista NMF (*Pol*) collaborator, collaborationist.

colaborador(a) NM/F collaborator, helper, co-worker; (*Liter etc*) contributor.

colaborar [1a] VI (a) to collaborate; to help, assist; **~ con uno en un trabajo** to collaborate with sb on a piece of work.
(b) **~ a, ~ en** (*Liter etc*) to contribute (articles) to, write for.

colaborativo ADJ collaborative.

colación NF (a) (*comparación*) collation, comparison; **sacar a ~** to mention, bring up; to air; (*pey*) to drag in, drag up; **traer algo a ~** to adduce sth as proof.
(b) (*Culin*) collation (*t Ecl*); light meal, snack; buffet meal; reception, wedding breakfast; (*LAm: dulce*) sweet.

colacionar [1a] VT to collate, compare.

colada¹ NF (a) (*acto, ropa*) wash, washing; **día de ~** washing day; **tender la ~** to hang out the washing; **todo saldrá en la ~** it will all come out in the wash. (b) (*Quím*) bleach, lye. (c) (*Agr*) sheep run, cattle run; (*Geog*) defile.

coladera NF (a) (*Culin*) strainer. (b) (*Méx: alcantarilla*) sewer.

coladero NM, **colador** NM strainer; colander.

coladicto, -a NM/F glue-sniffer.

colado ① ADJ (a) (*molde*) metal cast. (b) **aire ~** draught. (c) **estar ~*** to be in love.
② NM, **colada²** NF intruder; uninvited guest, gatecrasher.

colador NM sieve.

coladura NF (a) (*acto*) straining. (b) **~s** grounds, dregs. (c) (*) absurdity, piece of nonsense; blunder, clanger‡.

colágeno NM collagen.

colapsar [1a] ① VT (a) (*derribar*) to overthrow, cause to collapse. (b)

(*Aut etc*) to jam, bring to a halt, block; to disrupt; *puerta etc* to jam, block.
② VI y **colapsarse** VR to collapse, go to pieces.

colapso NM (a) (*Med*) collapse; breakdown; **~ nervioso** nervous breakdown. (b) (*fig*) collapse; breakdown; stoppage; ruin, destruction. (c) (*Aut etc*) jam, blockage; disruption.

colar [1l] ① VT (a) *café, legumbres etc* to strain (off); to filter; *metal* to cast, pour.
(b) *ropa* to bleach.
(c) (*pasar*) **~ algo por un sitio** to slip sth through a place, squeeze sth past a place; **~ unos géneros por la aduana** to slip goods through the customs.
(d) (*fig: pasar*) **~ algo a uno** to foist sth off on sb, palm sth off on sb; **~ una moneda** to pass a (false) coin; **~ una noticia a uno** to make sb believe a (false) piece of news; **¡a mí no me la cuelas!** I'm not going to swallow that!, don't give me that stuff!
(e) (*Méx: taladrar*) to drive, bore.
(f) **~la**‡‡ to screw‡‡.
② VI (a) (*líquido*) to ooze, seep (through), filter (through), percolate; (*aire*) to get in (*por* through).
(b) (*pasar*) to pass; **no cuela*** I'm not swallowing that; **y si cuela, cuela** if they swallow that they'll swallow anything; **esa noticia es demasiado sospechosa para ~** that news item is too suspect to pass.
(c) (*: *beber*) to booze*, tipple.
③ **colarse** VR (a) (*pasar*) to slip in, slip past, squeeze in; (*en cola*) to jump the queue; (*en reunión etc*) to slip in, sneak in, get in unobserved; (*en fiesta*) to gatecrash; **la moto se cuela por entre la circulación** the motorcycle slips through the traffic; **se ha colado algún indeseable** some undesirable has slipped in.
(b) (*: *meter la pata*) to blunder, slip up; to put one's foot in it, drop a clanger‡.
(c) **~ la a una**‡‡ to screw sb‡‡.

colateral ADJ collateral.

colca NF (*And*) (*troje*) barn, granary; (*almacén*) storeroom; (*ático*) attic store, loft.

colcha NF bedspread, counterpane.

colchón NM (a) mattress; **~ de aire** airbed; (*Téc*) air-cushion; **~ de muelles** spring mattress, interior sprung mattress; **~ neumático** airbed; **~ de plumas** feather-bed; **~ de seguridad** padding, padded protection; (*fig*) buffer; buffer zone; **servir de ~ a** (*fig*) to act as a buffer for. (b) (*Fin: precio*) floor price, reserve price; (*fondos*) reserve fund.

colchoneta NF (*Dep*) mat.

colcrén NM cold cream.

cole* NM = **colegio (a)**.

colear [1a] ① VT (a) (*Taur*) *toro* to throw by twisting the tail.
(b) (*And: regañar*) to vex, nag, harass.
(c) (*CAm: seguir*) to tail, follow.
② VI (a) **el perro colea** the dog wags its tail.
(b) (*fig*) **el asunto todavía colea** the affair is still not settled; **estar vivito y coleando** to be alive and kicking.
(c) (*CAm, Carib: edad*) **colea en los 50** he's close on 50, he's knocking on 50.
③ **colearse** VR (*Carib*) (a) (*Aut*) to skid (out of control).
(b) (*huésped*) to arrive unexpectedly (*o* uninvited).

colección NF collection; **es de ~** (*Méx*) it's a collector's item.

coleccionable ① ADJ collectable, which can be collected.
② NM (*objeto*) collectable; (*prensa*) pull-out section.

coleccionador(a) NM/F collector.

coleccionar [1a] VTI to collect.

coleccionismo NM collecting.

coleccionista NMF collector.

colecta NF (a) (*recaudación*) collection (for charity). (b) (*Ecl*) collect.

colectar [1a] VT *impuestos etc* to collect.

colecticio ADJ (a) (*Mil*) raw, untrained. (b) **tomo ~** omnibus edition, collected works.

colectivamente ADV collectively.

colectivero NM (*Cono Sur*) bus driver.

colectividad NF (a) (*gen*) collectivity; (*grupo*) group as a whole, community. (b) (*Pol*) collective ownership.

colectivización NF collectivization.

colectivizar [1f] VT to collectivize.

colectivo ① ADJ collective (*t Ling*); **acción colectiva** joint action, group action, communal action.
② NM (a) group, grouping, body; (*Pol*) collective. (b) (*And, Cono Sur, Méx: autobús*) (small) bus, minibus; (*And: taxi*) taxi.

colector NM (a) (*persona*) collector. (b) (*Elec*) collector; (*Mec*) sump; trap, container; (*albañal*) sewer.

colega NMF colleague; (*) pal*, mate, buddy; (*en oración directa*) man*.

colegiado ① ADJ (a) collegiate; **decisión colegiada** decision voted on by members. (b) (*LAm*) qualified.

2 NM, **colegiada** NF (*Med*) doctor; (*Dep*) referee.
colegial 1 ADJ (**a**) (*Escol*) school (*atr*), college (*atr*). (**b**) (*Ecl*) collegiate. (**c**) (*Méx: inexperto*) raw, green*, inexperienced. 2 NM schoolboy; (*fig*) inexperienced person, callow youth.
colegiala NF schoolgirl.
colegialidad NF (**a**) (*cuerpo*) college; collegiate membership. (**b**) (*cualidad*) collegiality; corporate feeling.
colegiarse [1b] VR to become a member of one's professional association; to form a professional association.
colegiata NF collegiate church.
colegiatura NF (*Méx*) school fees, university fees.
colegio NM (**a**) (*escuela*) school; ~ (**de párvulos**) kindergarten, primary school; ~ **de internos** boarding school; ~ **de monjas** convent school; ~ **de pago** fee-paying school; **¡comó se ve que tú no fuiste a ~s de pago!** where were you brung up?*; ~ **privado** private school; **ir al ~** to go to school.
(**b**) (*Univ*) college; ~ **mayor** (*Hist*) college (*p.ej. of Salamanca or Oxford*); (*moderno*) hall of residence.
(**c**) (*otros*) ~ **de abogados** bar association; **C~ de Cardenales** College of Cardinals; ~ **electoral** polling-station; (*p.ej. US Pol*) electoral college; ~ **de médicos** medical association.

┌─ COLEGIO ──────────────── ver también la entrada ─┐

Uso del artículo
A la hora de traducir expresiones como *al colegio/a la escuela* o *en el colegio/en la escuela, desde el colegio/desde la escuela etc,* hemos de tener en cuenta el motivo por el que alguien acude al recinto o está allí:
- Se traduce *al colegio/a la escuela* por *to school, en el colegio* o *en la escuela* por *at school* y *desde el colegio* o *desde la escuela* por *from school* cuando alguien va o está allí en calidad de alumno:
  El primer día que fui al colegio me pasé toda la mañana llorando
  The first day I went to school I spent the whole morning crying
  Juan todavía está en el colegio. Lo han castigado
  Juan's still at school. He's been given a detention
- Se traduce *al colegio/a la escuela* por *to the school, en el colegio/en la escuela* por *at the school* y *desde el colegio/desde la escuela* por *from the school* cuando alguien va o está en el centro por otros motivos:
  Ayer fueron mis padres al colegio para hablar con el director
  Yesterday my parents went to the school to talk to the headmaster
  Podemos quedar en el colegio y luego ir a tomar algo
  We can meet at the school and then go for a drink
  Para otros usos y ejemplos ver la entrada.
└───┘

---

colegir [3c y 3k] VT (**a**) (*reunir*) to collect, gather. (**b**) (*deducir*) to infer, gather, conclude (*de from*); **de lo cual colijo que ...** from which I gather that ...
coleóptero NM beetle.
cólera 1 NF (**a**) (*ira*) anger, rage; **descargar la ~ en** to vent one's anger on; **montar en ~** to get angry.
(**b**) (*Anat*) bile.
2 NM (*Med*) cholera.
colérico ADJ (*furioso*) angry, furious, irate; (*de temperamento*) irascible, bad-tempered.
colero NM (*Cono Sur*) top hat.
colesterol NM cholesterol.
coleta NF (**a**) (*pelo*) pigtail; **gente de ~** bullfighters, bullfighting people; **cortarse la ~** to quit the ring, give up bullfighting; (*fig*) to quit, give it all up, retire; **me cortaré la ~ si ...*** I'll eat my hat if ...
(**b**) (*: idea adicional*) postscript, afterthought.
coletazo NM (**a**) (*Zool etc*) lash, blow with the tail; **está dando los últimos ~s** (*fig*) it's on its last legs.
(**b**) (*de vehículo*) sway, swaying movement; **dar ~s** to sway about.
(**c**) (*fig*) sting in the tail; unexpected after-effect; **un ~ de la memoria** a trick of the memory.
coletero NM scrunchy.
coletilla NF *filler phrase or cliched phrase added at the end of sentences.*
coleto NM (**a**) (*Hist*) doublet, jerkin.
(**b**) (*: uno mismo*) body; oneself; **decir para su ~** to say to o.s.; **echarse algo al ~** (*comer*) to eat sth right up; (*beber*) to drink sth down; **echarse un libro al ~** to read a book right through, devour a book.
(**c**) (*Carib: fregasuelos*) mop.
colgadero NM hook, hanger, peg.
colgadizo 1 ADJ hanging, loose.
2 NM (*cobertizo*) lean-to shed; (*Carib: techo*) flat roof.
colgado ADJ, PTP (**a**) (*dudoso*) uncertain, doubtful.
(**b**) **dejar ~ a uno** to let sb down, fail sb; **quedarse ~** to be disappointed; **quedar ~ en una cita** to be stood up on a date*; **antes le veré ~ que ...** I'll see him damned before ...
(**c**) (*) **estar ~** to have withdrawal pains (from drugs); (*Fin*) to be

broke*; **¡estás ~!*** rubbish!, get away!*; **quedar ~** to get hooked (on drugs)*.
colgadura NF (*t* ~s) hangings, drapery; (*tapiz*) tapestry; **~s de cama** bed hangings, bed curtains.
colgajo NM (**a**) (*trapo*) rag, tatter, shred. (**b**) (*Bot*) bunch (*of grapes, hung to dry*). (**c**) (*Med*) flap of flesh.
colgante 1 ADJ hanging; droopy, floppy; dangling; **puente ~** suspension bridge.
2 NM (**a**) (*joya*) drop, pendant, earring; (*Carib, Cono Sur: de reloj*) watch chain.
(**b**) (*Arquit*) festoon.
(**c**) (*pelo*) ~s fringe.
(**d**) **~s** balls*.
colgar [1h y 1l] 1 VT (**a**) *cuadro etc* to hang (up) (*de from, en on*); *persona* to hang; *bandera, colada etc* to hang out; **~ los hábitos** (*fig*) to leave the priesthood; **~ los libros** (*etc*) to abandon one's studies (*etc*).
(**b**) *pared* to decorate with hangings, drape (*de with*).
(**c**) (*atribuir*) to attribute, impute (*a to*); **~ la culpa a uno** to pin the blame on sb.
(**d**) (*Univ*) to fail, flunk*.
2 VI to hang, be suspended (*de on, from*); (*orejas etc*) to hang down, droop, dangle; (*Telec*) to hang up, ring off.
3 **colgarse** VR (**a**) (*) to get high* (on drugs). (**b**) (*Cono Sur*) to plug illegally into the mains, steal electricity.

┌─ COLGAR ──────────────── ver también la entrada ─┐

¿"Hanged" o "hung"?
- Cuando *colgar* significa *ahorcar, hang* es un verbo regular y *hanged* es tanto el pasado como el participio:
  Le colgaron al amanecer
  He was hanged at dawn
- En el resto de los casos *hang* es irregular, y *hung* es la forma tanto de pasado como de participio:
  He colgado el cuadro en mi habitación
  I've hung the picture in my room
  Para otros usos y ejemplos ver la entrada.
└───┘

---

colibrí NM hummingbird.
cólico NM (*Med*) colic.
colicuar [1d] 1 VT to melt, dissolve; to fuse.
2 **colicuarse** VR to melt, dissolve, liquefy.
colifato* (*Cono Sur*) 1 ADJ nuts*, crazy.
2 NM madman, nutcase*.
coliflor NF cauliflower.
coligado 1 ADJ allied, coalition (*atr*); **estar ~s** to be allied, be in league.
2 NM ally, confederate.
coligarse [1h] VR to unite, join together, make common cause (*con* with).
coliguacho NM (*Cono Sur*) horsefly.
colilla NF fag-end*; butt, stub; **ser una ~*** to be past it, be all washed up*.
colimba* (*Cono Sur Mil*) 1 NM conscript.
2 NF military service; **hacer la ~** to do military service.
colimbo¹ NM (*Orn*) diver.
colimbo² NM (*Cono Sur*) recruit, conscript.
colín NM (*Carib*) machete, cane knife.
colina NF hill.
colinabo NM kohlrabi.
colindante ADJ adjacent, adjoining, neighbouring.
colindar [1a] VI to adjoin, be adjacent; **~ con** to adjoin, be adjacent to, border on.
colirio NM eye-drops.
colirrojo NM redstart.
colís NM (*And*) machete, cane knife.
Coliseo NM Coliseum.
colisión NF (*Aut etc*) collision; crash, smash; **~ de frente, ~ frontal** head-on collision. (**b**) (*fig*) clash.
colisionar [1a] VI to collide; **~ con, ~ contra** to collide with; (*fig*) to clash with, conflict with.
colista 1 NM (*Dep*) bottom club (in the league).
2 NMF person who stands in a queue.
colita¹ NF (*LAm Aut*) lift; **hacer ~** to hitchhike, thumb a lift.
colita²* NF willy*.
colitis NF colitis.
collado NM (**a**) (*colina*) hill, height; hillock. (**b**) (*puerto*) mountain pass.
collage [ko'laːʒ] NM (*Arte*) collage.
collalba NF (*Orn*) wheatear.
collar NM (**a**) (*adorno*) necklace; (*cuentas*) (string of) beads; (*insignia*) chain (of office); (*de perro*) (dog) collar; (*Orn, Zool etc*) collar, ruff; ~

de perlas pearl necklace.
(b) (*Mec*) collar, ring.
(c) **~ de fuerza** stranglehold.
collarín NM surgical collar.
colleja NF dandelion; campion.
collera NF **(a)** horse-collar. **(b)** **~s** (*LAm*) cufflinks.
collie ['koli] NM collie.
collín NM (*CAm*), **collines** NM (*And*) cane knife, machete.
colmado ☐1 ADJ abundant, copious; full (*de* of), overflowing (*de* with); heaped (*de* with); **una cucharada colmada** one heaped spoonful; **una tarde colmada de incidentes** an afternoon (more than) full of incident.
☐2 NM cheap seafood restaurant; (*Cataluña*) grocer's shop; (*Andalucía*) retail wine shop.
colmar [1a] VT **(a)** *vaso etc* to fill to the brim, fill right up, fill to overflowing (de *with*); *plato* to heap (de *with*).
(b) (*fig*) *esperanzas etc* to fulfil, more than satisfy, realize completely.
(c) (*fig*) **~ a uno de honores** to shower honours upon sb; **~ a uno de alabanzas** to heap praises on sb; **~ a uno de favores** to lavish favours on sb, overwhelm sb with favours.
colmatación NF silting.
colmena NF **(a)** (*lugar*) beehive; (*fig*) hive. **(b)** (*Méx: insecto*) bee; bees.
colmenar NM apiary.
colmenero, -a NM/F beekeeper.
colmillo NM **(a)** (*Anat*) eye tooth, canine (tooth); (*Zool*) fang; (*de elefante, morsa etc*) tusk.
(b) (*fig*) **enseñar los ~s** to show one's teeth; **escupir por el ~** to talk big, brag; **tener ~s** (*Méx*) to be long in the tooth*; **tener el ~ torcido** to be an old fox; **¡ya tengo ~s!** (*Méx*) you can't fool me!
colmillón NM (*LAm*) greed.
colmilludo ADJ **(a)** (*lit*) having big teeth (*o* fangs *etc*). **(b)** (*fig*) sharp, alert.
colmo NM (*fig*) height, summit, extreme; **el ~ de la elegancia** the height of elegance; **el ~ de lo absurdo** the height of absurdity; **a ~** in plenty, in abundance; **con ~** heaped, to overflowing; **para ~ de desgracias** to make matters worse, to cap it all; **¡es el ~!** it's the limit!, it's the last straw!; **sería el ~ si ...** it would be the last straw if ...
colocación NF **(a)** (*acto*) placing; positioning; collocation; (*Com*) investment. **(b)** (*empleo*) job, place, situation; **no encuentro ~** I can't find a job. **(c)** (*situación*) place, position.
colocado ADJ: **apostar para ~** to back (a horse) for a place; **estar ~‡** (*drogado*) to be high (on drugs)‡, (*borracho*) to be smashed‡.
colocar [1g] ☐1 VT **(a)** (*gen*) to place, put, position; (*ordenar*) to arrange; *tropas etc* to position, station; (*esp LAm*) to put away, put back; **~ la quilla de un buque** to lay down a ship; **~ un satélite en órbita** to put (*o* place) a satellite in orbit.
(b) *persona* to place (in a job), find a post for; *hija* to marry off.
(c) (*Com, Fin*) *mercancías, pedido* to place; *dinero* to place, invest; *empréstito* to float.
(d) **~ una historia a uno** to bore sb with the same old story; **~ una responsabilidad a uno** to saddle sb with a responsibility.
(e) (‡) to nick‡, arrest.
☐2 VI (‡): **es una sustancia que coloca** it's a substance that gets you high‡.
☐3 **colocarse** VR **(a)** (*gen*) to place o.s., station o.s.; (*Dep*) to be placed, get a place; **~ con** (*Ling*) to collocate with; **el equipo se ha colocado en quinto lugar** the team has climbed to fifth position; **el paro se coloca en 2 millones** unemployment reaches 2 million.
(b) (*obtener un puesto*) to get a job.
(c) (‡) to get high (*con* on)‡.
colocata‡ NMF (*borracho*) drunk*; (*drogado*) junkie*.
colocho (*CAm*) ☐1 ADJ curly(-haired).
☐2 **~s** NMPL (*rizos*) curls; (*virutas*) wood shavings.
colocolo NM (*Chile*) **(a)** (*gato montés*) wildcat. **(b)** (*monstruo*) mythical monster.
colocón‡ NM: **cogerse un ~** to get high‡, go on a trip‡.
colodrillo NM back of the neck.
colofón NM **(a)** (*Tip*) colophon. **(b)** (*fig*) culmination, climax.
colofonia NF rosin, colophony.
colombianismo NM colombianism, word (*o* phrase *etc*) peculiar to Colombia.
colombiano, -a ADJ, NM/F Colombian.
colombicultor(a) NM/F pigeon-breeder.
colombicultura NF pigeon-breeding.
colombino ADJ of Columbus, relating to Columbus.
colombofilia NF pigeon-fancying.
colombófilo, -a NM/F pigeon-fancier.
colon NM (*Anat*) colon.
Colón NM Columbus.
colón NM colon (*unit of currency of Costa Rica and El Salvador*).
Colonia NF Cologne.
colonia¹ NF **(a)** (*Bio, Pol etc*) colony; (*de ciudad*) (*barrio*) suburb;

(*residencial*) residential district; housing estate; **~ escolar, ~ de vacaciones, ~ de verano** summer camp for schoolchildren; **~ obrera** working-class housing scheme; **~ penal** penal settlement; **~ proletaria** shanty-town; **~ (veraniega)** holiday camp; **las antiguas ~s españolas** the former Spanish colonies; **la ~ norteamericana en Madrid** the Americans resident in Madrid, the American population of Madrid.
(b) (*Cos*) silk ribbon.
(c) (*Carib*) sugar-cane plantation.
colonia² NF eau-de-Cologne.
coloniaje NM (*LAm*) (*período*) colonial period; (*sistema*) system of colonial government; (*pey*) slavery, slave status.
colonial ADJ colonial; *alimentos, producto* overseas (*atr*), imported.
colonialismo NM colonialism.
colonialista ADJ, NMF colonialist.
colonización NF colonization; settlement.
colonizador ☐1 ADJ colonizing.
☐2 NM, **colonizadora** NF colonist, colonizer, settler; pioneer.
colonizar [1f] VT to colonize; to settle; (*Bio*) to inhabit, live in.
colono NM **(a)** (*Pol*) colonist, settler; colonial. **(b)** (*Agr*) tenant farmer. **(c)** (*Carib: de azúcar*) sugar planter. **(d)** (*And: indio*) Indian bound to an estate.
coloqueta‡ NF **(a)** (*detención*) arrest; **dar una ~ a** to nick‡, arrest. **(b)** (*redada*) police sweep. **(c)** = **colocata**.
coloquial ADJ colloquial, familiar.
coloquiante NMF speaker; person taking part in a discussion; **mi ~** the person I was (*etc*) talking to.
coloquiar [1b] VI to talk, discuss.
coloquio ☐1 NM (*conversación*) conversation, talk; (*congreso*) conference; (*científico etc*) colloquium; (*Liter*) dialogue.
☐2 ATR: **almuerzo ~** lunch with speakers and discussion; **charla ~** talk followed by a discussion; **mesa ~** round-table discussion.
color NM **(a)** (*gen*) colour; hue, shade; (*fig*) colour, colouring; **a ~, en ~es** *película* in colour, colour (*atr*); **a todo ~** in full colour; **gente de ~** coloured people; **huevos de ~** (*LAm*) brown eggs; **zapatos de ~** brown shoes; **subido de ~** blue, rude, scabrous; **so ~ de** under pretext of; **el suceso tuvo ~es trágicos** the event had its tragic aspect, the event had a sad side to it; **~ base** basic colour; **~ local** local colour; **~ muerto, ~ quebrado** dull colour; **~es pastel** pastel colours; **~ sólido** fast colour; **un vestido de ~ malva** a mauve(-coloured) dress; **un vino ~ fresa** a strawberry-coloured wine; **verlo todo ~ de rosa** to see everything through rose-coloured spectacles, be ridiculously optimistic; **cambiar de ~, mudar de ~** to change colour, turn pale; **ponerse de mil ~es** to colour up; **sacar los ~es a uno** to make sb blush; **le salieron** (*o* **subieron**) **los ~es** he blushed; **subírsele a uno el ~** (*Méx*) to blush; **hay ~*** it's O.K. here*, it's an O.K. scene*; **no hay ~*, no tienen ~*** there's no comparison, they're streets apart*; **eso no tiene ~*** that seems unlikely, that's not on*.
(b) (*Arte*) colour, paint; (*Téc*) dye, colouring matter; (*cosmético*) rouge.
(c) (*Naipes*) suit.
(d) **~es** (*Mil*) colours; **los ~es nacionales** the national colours, the national flag.
(e) (*) drug(s).
coloración NF coloration, colouring; (*Zool etc*) coloration, markings.
colorado ☐1 ADJ **(a)** (*gen*) coloured, (*esp*) red; *cara* rosy, ruddy; **poner ~ a uno** to make sb blush; **ponerse ~** to blush.
(b) (*fig: esp LAm*) *chiste* blue, rude, scabrous; *argumento* plausible.
☐2 NM **(a)** (‡: *dinero*) bread‡, money.
(b) (*Carib: enfermedad*) scarlet fever.
(c) **los C~s** Uruguayan political party.
coloradón, coloradote ADJ red-faced, ruddy.
colorante ☐1 ADJ colouring.
☐2 NM colouring (matter).
colorar [1a] VT (*gen*) to colour; (*teñir*) to dye, tint, stain; **~ algo de amarillo** to colour (*o* dye *etc*) sth yellow.
coloratura NF coloratura.
coloreado ☐1 ADJ coloured; tinted.
☐2 NM colouring; tinting.
colorear [1a] ☐1 VT **(a)** = **colorar**. **(b)** (*fig: justificar*) to excuse; to put in a favourable light; to gloss over, whitewash.
☐2 VI to redden, show red.
colorete NM rouge.
colorido NM colour(ing) (*t fig*); **~ local** local colour.
colorín ☐1 ADJ (*Cono Sur*) strawberry (*o* reddish) blond(e).
☐2 NM **(a)** (*gen* **colorines** PL) bright colour; **tener muchos colorines** to have vivid colours; **¡qué colorines tiene el niño!** what rosy cheeks the little fellow has!; **¡~ colorado!** hey presto!, abracadabra!, (*como n*) happy ending.
(b) (*Orn*) goldfinch.
(c) (*Med*) measles.
(d) (*revista*) magazine of love-stories.

colorir [3a; *defectivo*] 1 VT (a) (*gen*) to colour. (b) (*fig*) = **colorear** (b).
2 VI to take on a colour, colour up.
colorista 1 ADJ colouristic.
2 NMF colourist.
colosal ADJ colossal (*t fig*); *comida etc* splendid.
coloso NM (a) (*lit*) colossus; (*esp LAm*) **el ~ del norte** the United
States. (b) (*Cono Sur Aut*) trailer.
coludo ADJ (*Cono Sur*) long-tailed.
columbario NM columbarium.
Columbina NF Columbine.
columbrar [1a] VT (a) (*divisar*) to glimpse, spy, make out. (b) (*fig*) to
guess; *solución* to begin to see.
columna NF (a) (*Arquit*) column; pillar.
(b) (*Mil*) column; **~ blindada** armoured column; **quinta ~** fifth column; **~ volante** flying column.
(c) (*Anat*) **~ vertebral** spine, spinal column.
(d) (*Mec*) column; **~ de dirección** steering column.
(e) (*Tip*) column.
(f) (*fig: soporte*) pillar, support; **una ~ de la religión** a pillar of religion.
columnata NF colonnade.
columnista NMF columnist.
columpiar [1b] 1 VT to swing.
2 **columpiarse** VR (a) (*mecerse*) to swing; (*cuerpo etc*) to sway;
(*andear*) to waddle; (*pavonearse*) to swagger (along). (b) (*fig: oscilar*)
to swing to and fro, seesaw. (c) (**: meter la pata*) to drop a clanger‡.
columpio NM (*gen*) swing; (*LAm: mecedora*) rocking chair; **~
basculante, ~ de tabla** seesaw.
colusión NF collusion.
colza NF (*Bot*) rape, colza.
coma[1] NM (*Med*) coma.
coma[2] NF (*Tip*) comma; (*Mat*) (decimal) point; **~ flotante** floating
point; **sin faltar una ~** right down to the last detail, with complete
accuracy; **12,5** 12·5 (twelve point five).
comadre NF (a) (*madrina, madre*) kinswoman, *woman relative of
godparents.*
(b) (*vecina*) neighbour; (*amiga*) friend, crony; (*mujer de pueblo*) village
woman, peasant woman; (*chismosa*) gossip; **un grupo de ~s** a group
of gossips, a gathering of gossipy women.
(c) (*Med*) midwife.
(d) (*alcahueta*) go-between, procuress.
(e) (*‡: maricón*) pansy‡.
(f) (*prov*) en oración directa entre mujeres, no se traduce.
comadrear [1a] VI to gossip.
comadreja NF weasel.
comadreo NM, **comadrería** NF gossip; gossiping, chattering.
comadrona NF midwife.
comal NM (*CAm, Méx*) griddle.
comanche ADJ, NMF Comanche.
comandancia NF (a) (*mando*) command. (b) (*graduación*) rank of major. (c) (*cuartel*) commander's headquarters (*o* office). (d) (*zona*) area
under a commander's jurisdiction.
comandanta NF (a) (woman) commander; (*Mil*) (woman) major;
(*Hist*) major's wife. (b) (*Náut*) flagship.
comandante NM (a) (*jefe*) commandant, commander; **~ en jefe**
commander-in-chief; (*Méx*) **~ de policía** chief of police; **~ de vuelo**
pilot, captain; **segundo ~** copilot, second pilot. (b) (*graduación*) major.
comandar [1a] VT to command, lead.
comandita NF sleeping partnership, silent partnership (*US*).
comanditario ADJ: **socio ~** sleeping partner, silent partner (*US*).
comando NM (a) (*Mil: mando*) command; leadership; (*Téc*) control;
(*Inform*) command; **~ a distancia** remote control; **~ vocal** speech
command. (b) (*soldado, grupo*) commando; **~ de acción** active-
service unit; **~ de información** intelligence unit; **~ suicida** suicide
squad. (c) (*prenda*) duffel coat.
comarca NF region, area, part.
comarcal ADJ *carretera* local; *emisora* local, regional.
comarcano ADJ neighbouring, bordering.
comarcar [1g] VI to border (*con* on), be adjacent (*con* to).
comatoso ADJ comatose.
comba NF (a) (*curva*) bend; (*alabeo*) bulge, warp, sag. (b) (*cuerda*) skipping rope; **dar a la ~** to turn the skipping rope; **saltar a la ~** to skip.
(c) (*juego*) skipping. (d) **no pierde ~** he doesn't miss a trick.
combadura NF (*en carretera*) curve, camber; *V t* **comba** (a).
combar [1a] 1 VT to bend, curve.
2 **combarse** VR to bend, curve; to bulge, warp; to sag.
combate NM fight, combat, engagement; (*fig*) battle, struggle; **~
naval** naval battle, sea fight; **~ singular** single combat; **estar fuera
de ~** to be out of action (*t fig*); (*Boxeo*) to be knocked out; **poner a
uno fuera de ~** to put sb out of action; (*Boxeo*) to knock sb out;
ganar por fuera de ~ to win by a knockout.

combatiente NM combatant; **no ~** non-combatant.
combatir [1a] 1 VT (a) (*Mil*) to attack; (*fig*) *tendencia, propuesta etc* to
combat, fight, oppose; *mente* to assail, harass.
(b) (*olas, viento*) to beat upon.
2 VI y **combatirse** VR to fight, struggle (*con, contra* against).
combatividad NF fighting spirit, fight; (*pey*) aggressiveness.
combativo ADJ full of fight, spirited; (*pey*) aggressive, combative.
combazo NM (*Cono Sur*) punch.
combés NM (*Náut*) waist.
combi[1]* NF, **combinable** NF (*Aut*) multi-purpose van; (*LAm: bus*)
minibus.
combi[2]* NF (a) (*ardid*) fiddle*, wangle*. (b) (*prenda*) slip.
combinación NF (a) (*acto etc*) combination.
(b) (*Quím*) compound; (*bebida*) cocktail.
(c) (*Ferro etc*) connection; **hacer ~ con** to connect with.
(d) (*Mat, quinielas etc*) permutation; **~ métrica** (*Liter*) stanza form,
rhyme scheme.
(e) (*proyecto*) arrangement, set-up, scheme; plan; (*pey*) cunning
scheme, deep-laid plan.
(f) (*Cos*) slip; combination, combs*.
combinacional ADJ combinatory.
combinadamente ADV jointly (*con* with).
combinado NM (a) cocktail. (b) (*Cono Sur*) radiogram. (c) (*equipo*) selection.
combinar [1a] 1 VT (*gen*) to combine; to join, unite, put together;
colores etc to blend, mix, match; *proyecto* to devise, work out.
2 **combinarse** VR to combine; (*personas*) to get together, join together (*para + infin* to + *infin*); (*pey*) to form a ring, gang up, conspire; (*Méx: alternarse*) to take it in turns.
combinatoria NF (*Mat*) combinatorial analysis.
combinatorio ADJ combining; **posibilidades combinatorias** (possible) combinations.
combo 1 ADJ bent; bulging; warped.
2 NM (a) (*LAm: martillo*) sledgehammer. (b) (*And, Cono Sur*) (*golpe*)
slap; (*puñetazo*) punch.
combustible 1 ADJ combustible.
2 NM (a) (*gen*) fuel, combustible; **~ nuclear** nuclear fuel. (b) (*Méx:
gasolina*) petrol, gas (*US*).
combustión NF combustion; **~ espontánea** spontaneous combustion.
comebolas NM INVAR (*Carib*) simple soul, gullible individual.
comecocos* NM INVAR (a) (*manía*) obsession, mania; (*pasatiempo*) idle
pastime, absorbing but pointless activity; (*lavacerebros*) brainwashing
enthusiasm.
(b) (*preocupación*) nagging worry.
COMECON, Comecon NM ABR *de* **Council for Mutual Economic
Assistance** Comecon.
comedero 1 ADJ eatable, edible.
2 NM (a) (*Agr*) trough, manger; (*Orn etc*) feeding-box, feeder.
(b) (*comedor*) dining-room; (*de animal*) feeding place.
(c) (*Carib: prostíbulo*) brothel.
(d) (*And: sitio favorito*) haunt, hang-out*.
comedia NF (a) (*moderna*) comedy; (*Hist*) play, drama, *comedia*; **alta ~**
high comedy; **~ en un acto** one-act play; **~ de costumbres** comedy
of manners; **~ de capa y espada** cloak-and-dagger play; **~ de
enredos** comedy of intrigue; **~ negra** black comedy; **~ de situación**
situation comedy.
(b) (*fig*) farce; pretence; **hacer la ~** to make-believe, pretend.

┌─ **COMEDIA** ─┐

The Spanish **comedias** *written by dramatists of the Golden Age, or*
Edad de Oro, were five-act plays performed in open-air theatres. They
involved stock characters similar to those of the Italian Commedia
dell'Arte: a beautiful lady, her suitor, servants and go-betweens. In these
comedias, which were not always comical in nature, action and a moral
theme took precedence over character. Cloak and dagger episodes were built
around plots involving disguises and mistaken identity. They dealt
primarily with affairs of the nobility, while peasants were there to provide
comic relief or to enhance particular pastoral themes. One of the most
prolific comedia writers was Lope de Vega, who wrote on religious,
historical and social themes. Other major comedia writers were Pedro
Calderón de la Barca and Tirso de Molina, from whose pen came the figure
of the archetypal seducer, Don Juan, in **El Burlador de Sevilla y Convidado
de Piedra** *(1630).*

comedianta NF (a) (*actriz*) actress, comedienne. (b) (*pey: hipócrita*)
hypocrite.
comediante NM (a) (*actor*) actor. (b) (*pey: hipócrita*) hypocrite, humbug, fraud.
comedidamente ADV moderately; courteously; (*LAm*) obligingly.
comedido ADJ (*moderado*) moderate, restrained; (*cortés*) courteous;
(*LAm*) obliging.

comedieta NF light comedy.

comedimiento NM moderation, restraint; courtesy; (*LAm*) helpfulness.

comedio NM middle; interval.

comediógrafo, -a NM/F playwright.

comedirse [3k] VR (a) (*conducta*) to behave moderately, be restrained, restrain o.s.; to be courteous, answer (*etc*) politely.
(b) **~ a** (*LAm*) + *infin* to offer to + *infin*, volunteer to + *infin*.

comedón NM blackhead.

comedor 1 ADJ greedy, gluttonous.
2 NM (a) (*de casa*) dining-room; (*restaurante*) restaurant; (*LAm Ferro*) dining-car; **~ de beneficencia** soup kitchen.
(b) (*muebles*) dining-room suite.
3 NM, **comedora** NF glutton; **ser buen ~** to have a good appetite; **ser mal ~** to have a poor appetite, not eat much.

comedura* NF: **~ de coco** = comecocos.

comefuego NM (*Circo*) fire-eater.

comegente NM (*And, Carib*) glutton.

comehostias* NMF INVAR goody-goody*.

comején NM (a) (*Ent*) termite, white ant. (b) (*And: glotón*) glutton. (c) (*And: preocupación*) nagging worry, gnawing anxiety.

comelitona NF (*Méx*) = comilona.

comelón ADJ (*LAm*) = comilón.

comelona NF (*LAm*) = comilona.

comemierdas** NMF INVAR shit**.

comendador NM knight commander (*of a military order*).

comendatorio ADJ: **carta comendatoria** letter of recommendation.

comensal NMF (a) (*compañero*) fellow guest, diner; **habrá 13 ~es** there will be 13 to dinner; **me lo dijo mi ~** the man sitting next to me at dinner told me so; **mis ~es** those dining with me, those at table with me.
(b) (*And: en hotel*) guest.

comentador(a) NM/F commentator.

comentar [1a] VT (*hacer comentarios sobre*) to comment on; *teoría etc* to expound; (*) (*discutir*) to discuss; (*criticar*) to criticize, gossip about.

comentariar [1b] VT = comentar.

comentario NM (a) (*observación*) comment, remark, observation; **y ahora sin más ~** ... and now without further ado...; **'no hay ~s'** 'no comment'.
(b) (*Liter*) commentary.
(c) (*pey*) **~s** gossip, (nasty) talk, tittle-tattle; **dar lugar a ~s** to cause gossip; **hacer ~s** to gossip, pass (nasty) remarks.

comentarista NMF commentator (*t Rad*); **~ deportivo** sports commentator.

comento NM comment; (*Liter*) commentary; (*fig*) lie, pretence.

▼ **comenzar** [1f y 1j] VTI to begin, start, commence; **~ protestando** to begin by protesting; **~ a hacer algo** to begin to do sth, start to do sth, start doing sth; **~ con** to begin with; **~ por** to begin with; **~ por** + *infin* to begin by + *ger*.

comer [2a] 1 VT (a) (*gen*) to eat; **sin ~lo ni beberlo** (*fig*) without having (had) anything to do with it, without wishing to be involved; without intervening at all; **sin ~lo ni beberlo, yo** ... before I knew where I was, ...
(b) (*almorzar, cenar*) to eat (*o* have) for lunch (*o* dinner); **hoy comimos truchas** today we had trout for lunch (*o* dinner).
(c) (*Quím*) to eat away, eat into, corrode; (*Geol*) to swallow up, erode; **~ las uñas** to bite one's nails; **me come la pierna** my leg itches; **esto come las existencias** this devours (*o* uses up) the stocks.
(d) *color* to fade; **~ los colores a uno** to take away sb's colours.
(e) (*fig*) **le come la envidia** she is eaten up with envy.
(f) (*Ajedrez etc*) to take, capture.
2 VI (a) (*gen*) to eat; **~ de** to eat, partake of, have some of; **~ como una vaca** (*o* **fiera**) to eat like a horse; **no ~ ni dejar ~** to be a dog in the manger.
(b) (*tomar una comida*) to have a meal, eat; (*esp*) to have lunch; (*en algunas regiones*) to have dinner, have supper.
(c) (*fig*) **¡pero ~ y callar!** but I'd better say no more!; **el mismo que come y viste** the very same; **este pescado es de buen ~** this fish is good eating; **Juan es de buen ~** John eats anything, John has a hearty appetite; **no tienen qué ~** they don't have enough to live on.
(d) **~ a una** (*And***) to screw sb**.
3 **comerse** VR (a) (*gen*) to eat up; **se lo comió todo** he ate it all up; **está para ~la*** she looks a treat*.
(b) (*fig*) *recursos etc* to consume, devour, eat up.
(c) (*fig*) *pasaje etc* to skip; *consonante* to swallow, slur; **se come las palabras** he mumbles; **tiene muchos nombres y se come el García** she has lots of names and drops the García.
(d) (*locuciones*) **~ a uno por pies** to take sb in completely; **se comen unos a otros** they're at daggers drawn.
(e) (*) **se comió tres atracos** he confessed to three hold-ups.

comerciabilidad NF marketability, saleability.

comerciable ADJ (a) (*Com*) marketable, saleable; **valores ~s** marketable securities. (b) (*fig*) sociable.

comercial 1 ADJ commercial; business (*atr*), trading (*atr*); **barrio ~** business quarter, shopping district; **centro ~** business centre.
2 NM (*TV*) commercial.

comercializable ADJ marketable, saleable.

comercialización NF (a) (*proceso*) commercialization. (b) (*marquetín*) marketing.

comercializar [1f] VT (a) (*gen*) to commercialize. (b) *producto* to market.

comercialmente ADV commercially.

comerciante NMF (*t comercianta* NF) trader, dealer, merchant; **~ al por mayor** wholesaler; **~ al por menor** retailer.

comerciar [1b] VI (*dos personas*) to have dealings; (*dos países*) to trade; **~ con** (*t ~ en*) *mercancías* to deal in, handle; *persona* to do business with, have dealings with; *país* trade with.

comercio NM (a) (*gen*) commerce; trade; business; **~ de, ~ en** trade in, traffic in; dealings in; **el ~ español** Spanish trade; **~ de esclavos** slave trade; **~ de exportación** export trade; **~ exterior** foreign trade, overseas trade; **~ de importación** import trade; **~ interior** home trade.
(b) (*personas etc colectivamente*) business interests, business world; big business.
(c) (*tienda*) shop, store (*US*).
(d) (*fig*) intercourse; dealings, contacts (*con* with); **~ sexual** sexual intercourse; **~ social** social intercourse, social contacts.
(e) (*: *comida*) grub*.

comestible 1 ADJ eatable; *hongo etc* edible.
2 NM (a) (*alimento*) foodstuff, comestible; **~s** foods, foodstuffs.
(b) (*Com*) **~s** groceries, provisions; **tienda de ~s** grocer's (shop), grocery (*US*).

cometa¹ NM (a) (*Astron*) comet. (b) (*) sweetener*, backhander*.

cometa² NF kite; **~ delta, ~ voladora** (*And*) hang-glider.

cometer [2a] VT (a) *crimen etc* to commit; *error* to make, commit. (b) *tarea etc* to entrust, commit (*a* to). (c) (*Ling*) *figura retórica* to use, employ.

cometido NM task, assignment; commitment.

comezón NF (a) (*lit*) itch, itching; (*de calor etc*) tingle, tingling sensation; **siento ~ en el brazo** my arm itches; my arm tingles. (b) (*fig*) itch (*por* for); **sentir ~ de** + *infin* to feel an itch to + *infin*.

comi* NF = comisaría (a).

comible ADJ eatable, (just) fit to eat.

Comibol NF (*Bolivia*) ABR *de* **Corporación Minera de Bolivia**.

cómic ['komik] NM, PL **cómics** ['komik] comic.

cómica NF (*comic*) actress; comedienne.

comicastro NM ham (actor)*.

comicidad NF humour, comedy, comicalness.

comicios NMPL elections, voting.

cómico 1 ADJ (a) (*gracioso*) comical, funny, amusing. (b) (*Teat*) comedy (*atr*), comic (*atr*).
2 NM (*comic*) actor; comedian.

┌─ CÓMICO ─────────────────────────────┐

¿"Comic" o "comical"? | *ver también la entrada*

El adjetivo *cómico* se puede traducir por *comic* y *comical*, pero éstos no son intercambiables.

Comic

• Algo que es *cómico* porque se hace o se dice con la intención de hacer reír a la gente se traduce al inglés por *comic*:
  El efecto cómico se consigue poniéndose ropa que te queda grande
  Comic effect is achieved by wearing clothes that are too big

• *Cómico* también se traduce por *comic* para describir algo perteneciente o relativo a la comedia:
  ...un actor cómico...
  ...a comic actor...
  NOTA: Hay que tener en cuenta que en este caso *comic* nunca funciona como atributo.

Comical

• *Cómico* se traduce por *comical* para describir algo o a alguien que resulta gracioso o absurdo (a menudo porque es raro o inesperado):
  Su gesto rozaba lo cómico
  Her expression was almost comical
  Hay algo en él ligeramente cómico
  There is something slightly comical about him
  Para otros usos y ejemplos ver la entrada.

└──────────────────────────────────────┘

comida NF (a) (*gen*) food; **~ basura** junk food; **~ para perros** dogfood; **~ rápida** fast food.
(b) (*acto*) eating; (*una ~*) meal; (*esp*) lunch, dinner; (*LAm*) supper,

evening meal, dinner; **~ de coco*** brainwashing; **~ corrida** (*LAm*) fixed-price menu; **bendecir la ~** to say grace.
(c) (*en pensión etc*) board, keep; **~ y casa** board and lodging; **'C~s y camas'** (*letrero*) 'Rooms and Meals'.

comidilla NF **(a)** (*pasatiempo*) pastime, special interest. **(b) ser la ~ de la ciudad** (*etc*) to be the talk of the town.

comido ADJ Y PTP **(a) estar ~** to have had lunch (*etc*); **vengo ~** I've had lunch (before coming). **(b) es ~ por servido** it doesn't pay, it's not worth while.

comience NM (*And*) = **comienzo.**

comienzo NM beginning, start; (*de proyecto etc*) birth, inception; (*Med etc*) onset; **al ~** at the start, at first; **en los ~s de este siglo** at the beginning of this century; **dar ~ a un acto** to begin a ceremony; **dar ~ a una carrera** to start a race (off).

comillas NFPL quotation marks, inverted commas, quotes (*US*); **en ~, entre ~** in inverted commas, in quotes (*US*).

comilón 1 ADJ greedy.
2 NM, **comilona**[1] NF big eater, glutton.

comilona[2]* NF spread*, blow-out‡, feast.

cominero 1 ADJ fussy.
2 NM, **cominera** NF fusspot*, fussy person, milksop.

comino NM cumin, cumin seed; **no vale un ~** it's not worth tuppence; **no se me da un ~, (no) me importa un ~** I don't care two hoots (*de* about).

comiquero ADJ comic.

comisaría NF **(a)** (*policía*) police station. **(b)** (*Mil*) administrative office; (*Náut*) purser's office.

comisariado NM **(a)** commission. **(b)** (*Pol*) commissary.

comisariato NM administrative office.

comisario, -a NM/F commissioner; (*Mil*) administrative officer, service corps officer; (*Náut*) purser; (*de hipódromo*) steward; (*de exposición*) organizer; (*Pol*) commissar; **~ de carreras** course steward; **~ europeo** European commissioner; **~ parlamentario** parliamentary commissioner, ombudsman; **~ de policía** police superintendent, commissioner of police; **alto ~** high commissioner.

comiscar [1g] VT to nibble from time to time (at).

comisión NF **(a)** (*cometido*) assignment, task, commission; mission. **(b)** (*Parl etc: junta*) committee; board, commission; (*Com, Fin*) board; **~ de encuesta** fact-finding committee, board of inquiry; **C~ Europea** European Commission; **~ mixta** joint committee; mixed commission; **Comisiones Obreras** Workers' Unions; **~ permanente** standing committee; **~ planificadora** planning board; **~ de seguimiento** watchdog committee.
(c) (*Com: pago*) commission; **~ porcentual** percentage commission (*sobre* on); **~ sobre las ventas** sales commission; **a ~** on a commission basis.
(d) (*acto*) commission; (*de atentado*) perpetration; **pecado de ~** sin of commission.
(e) ~ de servicio(s) secondment; leave of absence.

comisionado, -a NM/F commissioner; (*Parl etc*) committee member; (*Com, Fin*) board member.

comisionar [1a] VT to commission.

comisionista NMF commission agent, person working on a commission basis.

comiso NM (*Jur*) **(a)** (*acto*) seizure, confiscation. **(b)** (*géneros*) confiscated goods.

comisquear [1a] VT = **comiscar.**

comistrajo NM bad meal, awful food; (*fig*) mess, hotchpotch.

comisura NF join; corner, angle; (*Anat*) commissure; **~ de los labios** corner of the mouth.

comité NM committee; **~ de dirección** steering committee; **~ ejecutivo** executive board; **~ de empresa** works committee, shop stewards' committee; **C~ de No Intervención** Non-Intervention Committee; **~ de redacción** drafting committee; editorial committee.

comitiva NF suite, retinue; train; procession; **~ fúnebre** cortège, funeral procession.

como 1 ADV (*semejanza*) as, like; (*por ejemplo*) such as; as it were; (*más o menos*) about, approximately; **es ~ un pez** it's like a fish; **hay peces, ~ truchas y salmones** there are fish, such as trout and salmon; **juega ~ yo** he plays like I do; **toca ~ canta** she plays in much the same way as she sings, her playing is like her singing; **asistió ~ espectador** he attended as a spectator; **lo dice ~ juez** he says it (in his capacity) as a judge; **~ éste hay pocos** there are few like this; **vale más ~ poeta** he is better as a poet; **libre ~ estaba** free as he was; **la manera ~ sucedió** the way (in which) it happened; **había ~ cincuenta** there were about fifty; **vino ~ a las dos** (*LAm*) he came at about two o'clock; **sentía una ~ tristeza** she felt a sort of sadness; **fue así ~ comenzó la cosa** that was how the thing began, the thing started in that way; **tuvo resultados ~ no se habían conocido antes** it had results such as had never been known before; **pues tocar, ~ tocar, no sabe** if you mean really

play, well, he doesn't.
2 CONJ **(a)** (+ *indic: ya que*) as, since; **~ no tenía dinero** as (*o* since, because) I had no money; **~ que ...** because ..., since ...; seeing that ...; it looks as if ...; **hacía ~ que no nos veía** he pretended not to see us.
(b) (+ *indic: en cuanto*) as soon as; **así ~ nos vio lanzó un grito** as soon as he saw us he shouted.
(c) (+ *subj*) **~ si** ... as if ...
(d) (+ *subj: a menos que*) if, unless; provided that; **~ no lo haga en seguida** unless he does it at once; **~ sea** as the case may be; **~ no sea para** + *infin* unless it be to + *infin*, except to + *infin*; **~ vengas tarde no comerás** (*LAm*) if you come late you won't eat; **¡~ lo pierdas!** mind you don't lose it!, there'll be hell to pay if you lose it!; *V* **así, pronto, querer** *etc.*

cómo 1 ADV *interrog* how?; why?, how is it that ...?; **¿~ lo hace?** how does he do it?; **¿~ son?** what are they like?, what do they look like?; **¿~ están mis nietos?** how are my grandchildren?; **¿~ estás?** how are you?; **¿~ es de alto?** how tall is it?, what height is it?; **¿a ~ son las peras?** how much are the pears?; **¿~ así?, ~ es eso?** how can that be?, how come?*; **¿~ no?** why not?; what do you mean?; **no sé ~ hacerlo** I don't know how to do it; **no veo ~** I don't see how; **no había ~ alcanzarlo** there was no way of reaching it.
2 INTERJ *etc*: **¿~?** (*no entiendo*) I beg your pardon?, what?, eh?; (*sorpresa*) what was that?; (*enojo*) how dare you!; **¡y ~!** and how!, not half!*; **¡~ no!** (*esp LAm*) certainly!, of course!, with pleasure!; **¿~ no?** why not?; **¿~ 4 libros?** how do you mean, 4 books?; **¿~ qué no?** I don't see why not; what do you mean, 'no'?
3 NM: **el por qué y el ~ de** the whys and wherefores of.

cómoda NF chest of drawers; bureau.

cómodamente ADV comfortably; conveniently.

comodidad NF **(a)** (*gen*) comfort; comfortableness; convenience; **pensar en su propia ~** to consider one's own convenience; **venga a su ~** come at your convenience; **vivir con ~** to live in comfort.
(b) ~es comforts, amenities, pleasant things; facilities; **~es de la vida** good things of life.
(c) ~es (*LAm Com*) commodities, goods.

comodín 1 ADJ (*And, Carib, Méx*) = **comodón.**
2 NM **(a)** (*Naipes*) joker. **(b)** (*Mec etc*) useful gadget. **(c)** (*excusa*) pretext, regular excuse, standby. **(d)** (*Ling*) catch-all, useful vague word, all-purpose word (*o* phrase *etc*). **(e)** (*Inform*) wild card.

cómodo ADJ **(a)** (*silla etc*) comfortable; *cuarto* comfortable; cosy, snug, comfy*; *objeto* convenient. handy; *arreglo* convenient; *trabajo, tarea* agreeable.
(b) *persona* comfortable; **así estarás más ~** you'll be more comfortable this way; **ponerse ~** to make o.s. comfortable.
(c) (*satisfecho*) smug.

comodón ADJ (*regalón*) comfort-loving; (*pasivo*) easy-going, liking a quiet life; (*mimado*) spoiled, spoilt; **es muy ~** he'll do anything for a quiet life.

comodonería NF love of comfort; liking for a quiet life.

comodoro NM commodore.

comoquiera CONJ (*liter*) **(a) ~ que ...** (+ *indic*) since ..., in view of the fact that .... **(b) ~ que ...** (+ *subj*) in whatever way ...; **~ que sea eso** however that may be, in whatever way that may be.

comp. ABR *de* **compárese** compare, cp.

compa* NM **(a)** (*Pol*) comrade. **(b)** (*amigo*) pal*, mate.

compacidad NF compactness.

compact NM, PL **compacts** (*t ~ disc*) compact disc.

compactación NF compacting, compression.

compactadora NF compacter.

compactar [1a] VT to compact, press together (*o* down *etc*), compress.

compacto 1 ADJ compact; dense; *líneas, hilos, tipo etc* close.
2 NM (*Elec etc*) compact disc; (*Mús*) compact hi-fi system.

compadecer [2d] 1 VT to pity, be sorry for; to sympathize with.
2 **compadecerse** VR: **~ con** to harmonize with, blend with; to agree with, fit, square with; **~ de = 1.**

compadrada NF (*Cono Sur*) cheek, insolence.

compadrazgo NM **(a)** (*condición*) kinship, *relationship through one's godparents.* **(b)** (*esp LAm: amistad*) close friendship.

compadre NM **(a)** (*padrino*) godfather *o* father (*with respect to each other*). **(b)** (*: *amigo*) (*esp LAm*) friend, pal*, buddy (*esp US*); (*prov: en oración directa*) friend. **(c)** (*Cono Sur*) (*jactancioso*) braggart; (*engreído*) show-off*; (*matón*) bully*.

compadrear [1a] VI **(a)** (*: *ser amigos*) to be pals*. **(b)** (*Cono Sur: jactarse*) to brag, show off; (*presumir*) to put on airs; (*amenazar*) to give threatening looks.

compadreo NM (*LAm*) companionship; close contact.

compadrito NM (*LAm*) = **compadre (c).**

compagable ADJ compatible; **motivos difícilmente ~s** motives which it is hard to reconcile.

compaginación NF (*Cine*) continuity.

compaginar [1a] ☐ VT (a) (*ordenar*) to arrange, put in order.
(b) (*Tip*) to make up.
(c) ~ **A con B** to reconcile A with B, bring A into line with B, adjust A and B.
☐ **compaginarse** VR to agree, tally; ~ **con** to agree with, tally with, square with; (*colores*) to blend with; **no se compagina esa conducta con su carácter** such conduct does not fit in with (o square with) his character.

compañerismo NM comradeship, fellowship; companionship; (*Dep etc*) team spirit.

compañero, -a NM/F (a) (*gen*) companion; partner (*t Naipes, Dep*); mate; ~ **de armas** comrade-in-arms; ~ **de baile** dancing-partner; ~ **de cama** bedfellow; ~ **de candidatura** running mate; ~ **de clase** schoolmate, classmate; ~ **de cuarto** roommate; ~ **de infortunio** companion in misfortune; ~ **de juego** playmate; ~ **de piso** flatmate; ~ **de rancho** messmate; ~ **de trabajo** workmate; ~ **de viaje** fellow traveller (*t fig*); **es un ~ divertido** he's good company.
(b) **dos calcetines que no son ~s** two socks which do not match, two socks which do not make up a pair; **¿dónde está el ~ de éste?** where is the one that goes with this?, where is the other one (of the pair)?

compañía NF (a) (*gen*) company; **hacer ~ a uno** to keep sb company; **andar en malas ~s, frecuentar malas ~s** to keep bad company, have unsavoury companions.
(b) (*Com, Ecl, Teat etc*) company; **C~ de Jesús** Society of Jesus; **Pérez y C~** Perez and Company; ~ **de bandera** national company; ~ **inversionista** investment trust; ~ **naviera** shipping company; ~ **pública** public company; ~ **de seguros** insurance company; ~ **tenedora** holding company.

comparabilidad NF comparability.

comparable ADJ comparable (*a, con* to, with).

▼ **comparación** NF comparison; **en ~ con** in comparison with, beside; **es superior a toda ~, no tiene ~** it is beyond compare, it is incomparable.

▼ **comparado** ADJ (a) ~ **con** compared with, in comparison with, beside. (b) *estudio etc* comparative.

▼ **comparar** [1a] VT to compare (*a, con* to, with); to liken (*con* to).

comparativo ADJ, NM (*Ling*) comparative.

comparecencia NF (*Jur*) appearance (in court); **su no ~** his non-appearance.

comparecer [2d] VI (*Jur*) to appear (in court); ~ **ante un juez** to appear before a judge.

comparecimiento NM = **comparecencia**.

comparencia NF (*Cono Sur*) = **comparecencia**.

comparendo NM (*Jur*) summons; subpoena.

comparsa ☐ NF (*de carnaval etc*) group, procession; masquerade; **la ~** (*Teat*) the extras.
☐ NMF (*Teat*) extra, supernumerary; (*Carib: bailadores*) dance team.

comparsería NF (*Teat*) extras, supernumeraries.

compartible ADJ which can be shared; *opinión* acceptable, readily shared.

compartimentación NF compartmentalization.

compartimentado ADJ compartmentalized.

compartim(i)ento NM (a) (*acto*) division, sharing; distribution.
(b) (*Náut, Ferro etc*) compartment; ~ **de carga** (*Aer*) hold; ~ **estanco** watertight compartment.

▼ **compartir** [3a] VT to divide (up), share (out); *opinión, responsabilidad etc* to share (*con* with); **no comparto ese criterio** I do not share that view.

compás NM (a) (*Mús*) measure, time; (*ritmo*) beat, rhythm; (*división*) bar; ~ **de 2 por 4** 2/4 time; ~ **de vals** waltz time; **a ~** in time; **al ~ de la música** in time to the music; **martillar a ~** to hammer rhythmically; **fuera de ~** off beat; **llevar el ~** to beat time, keep time; **perder el ~** to lose the beat; **entraron a los compases de un vals** they came in to the strains of a waltz; **mantenemos el ~ de espera** we are still waiting.
(b) (*Mat etc: t ~ de puntas*) compasses, pair of compasses.
(c) (*Náut etc*) compass.

compasado ADJ measured, moderate.

compasar [1a] VT (a) (*Mat*) to measure (with a compass). (b) *gastos, tiempo* to adjust. (c) (*Mús*) to divide into bars.

compasión NF pity, compassion; sympathy; **¡por ~!** for pity's sake!; **mover a uno a ~** to move sb to pity; **tener ~ de** to feel sorry for, take pity on; **tener pronta ~** to be quick to pity, be easily moved to pity.

compasivamente ADV compassionately; pityingly; sympathetically, understandingly.

compasividad NF = **compasión**.

compasivo ADJ compassionate, full of pity; sympathetic, understanding.

compata⁚ NMF = **compañero**.

compatibilidad NF compatibility.

compatibilización NF harmonization.

compatibilizar [1f] VT to harmonize, reconcile, bring into line, make compatible (*con* with).

compatible ADJ compatible (*con* with).

compatriota NMF compatriot, fellow countryman, fellow countrywoman.

compeler [2a] VT to compel; ~ **a uno a** + *infin* to compel sb to + *infin*.

compendiar [1b] VT to abridge, condense, summarize.

compendio NM abridgement, condensed version; summary, abstract; compendium; **en ~** briefly, in brief.

compendiosamente ADV briefly, succinctly.

compendioso ADJ condensed, abridged; brief, succinct.

compenetración NF (*fig*) mutual understanding, fellow feeling, natural sympathy; mutual influence.

compenetrarse [1a] VR (*Quím etc*) to interpenetrate, fuse.
(b) (*fig*) to (come to) share each other's feelings; to undergo mutual influence; ~ **de** to share the feeling of; to enter into the spirit of; to absorb, take in, become permeated by, undergo the pervasive influence of.

compensación NF (a) (*gen*) compensation; (*Jur*) redress, compensation; **en ~** in exchange, as compensation; ~ **por despido** severance pay, redundancy payment. (b) (*Fin*) clearing; **cámara de ~** clearing house.

compensador ADJ compensating, compensatory.

compensar [1a] VT *persona* to compensate (*de* for); *pérdida* to compensate for, make up (for); *error etc* to redeem, make amends for; (*Mec etc*) to balance, adjust, equalize; **le compensaron con 100 dólares por los cristales rotos** they gave him 100 dollars' compensation for the broken windows.

compensatoriamente ADV by way of compensation.

compensatorio ADJ compensatory.

competencia NF (a) (*rivalidad*) competition (*t Com*); rivalry; competitiveness; ~ **desleal** unfair competition; ~ **leal** fair trading; **a ~** vying with each other, as rivals; **en ~ con** in competition with; **estar en ~** to be in competition; **hacer ~ con** to compete against.
(b) (*aptitud*) competence (*t Jur*); aptitude; adequacy; suitability.
(c) (*esfera*) domain, field, province; **y otras cosas de su ~** and other things which concern him, and other things for which he is responsible; **no es de mi ~** that is not my responsibility; that is not (in) my field; **es de la ~ de ...** (*decisión*) it is at the discretion of ...
(d) (*Pol*) ~s powers; **~s transferidas a las comunidades autónomas** powers transferred to the autonomous regions.

competente ADJ (a) (*Jur*) competent; proper, appropriate; **esto se elevará al ministerio ~** this will be sent to the appropriate ministry.
(b) (*apto*) competent; fit, adequate, suitable; **de fuente ~** from a reliable source; **ser ~ para un cargo** to be suitable for a post.
(c) *suma etc* adequate, proper.

competentemente ADV (a) (*apropiadamente*) appropriately. (b) (*suficientemente*) competently; adequately, suitably.

competer [2a] VI: ~ **a** to be the responsibility of, fall to; **le compete castigarlos** it is his job to punish them, it is up to him to punish them.

competición NF competition (*t Dep*); contest.

competido ADJ *carrera etc* hard-fought, close-run.

competidor ☐ ADJ competing, rival.
☐ NM, **competidora** NF competitor (*t Com*); rival (*a* for); opponent; (*TV etc*) contestant.

competir [3k] VI (a) (*gen*) to compete (*t Com, Dep; con* against, with; *en* in; *para* for).
(b) ~ **con** (*fig*) to rival, vie with; **los dos cuadros compiten en belleza** the two pictures vie with each other in beauty; **en cuanto a resistencia A no compite con B** A cannot compete with B for stamina.

competitivamente ADV competitively.

competitividad NF competitiveness.

competitivo ADJ competitive.

compilación NF compilation.

compilador(a) ☐ NM/F (*persona*) compiler.
☐ NM (*Inform*) compiler; ~ **incremental** incremental compiler.

compilar [1a] VT to compile.

compincharse [1a] VR to band together, team up.

compinche NM pal*, chum*, buddy (*esp US*); **estar ~s** to be in cahoots (*con* with)*.

compita* NMF (*Nicaragua*) freedom fighter; (: *como apelativo*) comrade*.

complacencia NF (a) (*placer*) pleasure, satisfaction.
(b) (*agrado*) willingness; **lo hizo con ~** he did it gladly.
(c) (*indulgencia*) indulgence, indulgent attitude; **tiene excesivas ~s con los empleados** he is too indulgent towards his employees.
(d) (*LAm: autosatisfacción*) complacency.

▶ LENGUA Y USO: **comparación** → 32.1, 32.3, 32.5, 53.5   **comparado: a** → 32.1, 53.5   **comparar** → 32.1, 32.4, 32.5, 53.5   **compartir** → 38.1

▼ **complacer** [2w] ① VT *persona* to please; *cliente etc* to help, oblige; *déspota* to humour; *deseo etc* to gratify, indulge; **nos complace que sea así** we are glad it is so; **¿en qué puedo ~le?** (*Com etc*) can I help you?, what can I do for you?

▼② **complacerse** VR: **~ en** + *infin* to be pleased (*o* glad) to + *infin*; to take pleasure in + *ger*; **el Banco se complace en comunicar a su clientela que ...** the Bank is glad to tell its clients that ...

complacido ADJ pleased, satisfied; **me miró complacida** she gave me a grateful look; **quedamos ~s de la visita** we were pleased with our visit.

complaciente ADJ (a) *persona* kind, obliging, helpful; *mirada etc* cheerful; **ser ~ con** to be helpful to, be well-disposed towards. (b) *marido* complaisant.

complejidad NF complexity.

complejo ① ADJ complex.
② NM (a) (*Psic*) complex; **~ de culpa**, **~ de culpabilidad** guilt complex; **~ de Edipo** Oedipus complex; **~ de inferioridad** inferiority complex; **~ persecutorio** persecution complex. (b) (*Téc*) complex; **~ deportivo** sports complex, sports hall; **~ industrial** industrial complex.

complementar [1a] VT to complement; to complete, make up, round off.

complementariamente ADV in addition (*a* to), additionally.

complementariedad NF complementarity.

complementario ADJ complementary; **visita complementaria** follow-up visit.

complemento NM (a) (*Mat etc*) complement.
(b) (*Ling*) complement, object; **~ directo** direct object; **~ indirecto** indirect object.
(c) (*esencial*) essential part, natural concomitant; **el vino es un ~ de la buena comida** wine is an essential concomitant to good food.
(d) (*culminación*) culmination; rounding-off, perfection; **sería el ~ de su felicidad** it would complete her happiness, it would be a crowning happiness to her.
(e) **~s** (*Aut*, **~ de mujer** *etc*) accessories.
(f) (*Cine*) short, supporting feature.
(g) **oficial de ~** (*Mil*) reserve officer.
(h) (*pago*) **~ de destino** extra allowance (attached to a post); **~ salarial**, **~ de sueldo** bonus, extra pay; **~ por peligrosidad** danger money.

completa NF (*Carib Culin*) full (cheap) meal.

completamente ADV completely.

completar [1a] VT (*gen*) to complete; to round off, make up; to perfect; *pérdida* to make good; (*acabar, terminar*) to complete, finish.

completas NFPL (*Ecl*) compline.

completez NF completeness.

completo ① ADJ (a) (*gen*) complete; (*acabado*) perfect, rounded, finished; *busca etc* thorough; *pensión, precio etc* inclusive, all-in; *comida* with all the trimmings; **por ~** completely, utterly; **fue un ~ fracaso** it was a complete (*o* total, utter) failure.
(b) *vehículo* full (up).
② NM (a) **en la sesión estuvo el ~** all members were present at the meeting.
(b) (*Cono Sur Culin*) hot dog.

complexión NF (a) (*constitución*) constitution, make-up; (*temperamento*) temperament. (b) (*Anat*) build; **un hombre de ~ fuerte** a well-built man. (c) (*LAm: tez*) complexion.

complexionado ADJ: **bien ~** strong, tough, robust; **mal ~** weak, frail.

complexional ADJ constitutional; temperamental.

complicación NF complication, complexity; **una persona sin ~** an uncomplicated person; **han surgido complicaciones** complications have arisen.

complicado ADJ complicated, complex; *fractura etc* complex; *decoración etc* elaborate; *método* complicated, involved, intricate.

complicar [1g] ① VT (a) (*gen*) to complicate.
(b) *persona* to involve (*en* in).
② **complicarse** VR (a) (*gen*) to get complicated.
(b) **~ en un asunto** to get involved (*o* entangled) in a matter.
(c) **~ la vida** to make things difficult for o.s., make life difficult for o.s.

cómplice NMF accomplice.

complicidad NF complicity, involvement (*en* in).

complió NM, PL **complós**, **complot** [kom'plo] NM, PL **complots** [kom'plo] plot; conspiracy; intrigue.

complotado, -a NM/F plotter, conspirator.

complotar [1a] VI to plot, conspire.

complutense ADJ of Alcalá de Henares.

componedor(a) NM/F: **~ de huesos** bonesetter.

componenda NF (a) (*acuerdo*) compromise; (provisional) settlement, (temporary) arrangement. (b) (*pey*) shady deal.

componente ① ADJ component, constituent.

② NM (*Quím etc*) component; (*de bebida etc*) ingredient; (*Mec*) part, component; **~s lógicos** (*Inform*) software; **un viento de ~ norte** a northerly wind.

componer [2q] ① VT (a) *colección etc* to make up, put together, compose.
(b) (*elementos*) to compose, constitute, make up; *número* to make up; **componen el jurado 12 personas** 12 persons make up the jury, the jury consists of 12 persons.
(c) (*Liter, Mús etc*) to compose, write.
(d) (*Tip*) to set (up), compose.
(e) *bebida, comida* to prepare.
(f) *objeto roto* to mend, repair, fix; to overhaul; *hueso* to set; (*Med*) *estómago etc* to settle; to strengthen; *espíritu* to quieten, soothe; *abuso* to set to rights, correct.
(g) *riña* to settle, compose, resolve; *diferencias* to reconcile; *personas* to reconcile.
(h) (*asear*) to arrange; to tidy up, polish up, adorn; *persona* to dress up, deck out.
(i) (*Cono Sur, Méx: castrar*) to doctor*, neuter.
(j) (*And: hechizar*) to bewitch.
② **componerse** VR (a) **~ de** to consist of, be composed of, be made up of; **se compone de 6 partes** it consists of 6 parts.
(b) (*mujer etc*) to dress up; to tidy o.s. up; (*maquillarse*) to make up.
(c) **~ con uno** to come to terms with sb, reach an agreement with sb.
(d) **componérselas** to manage, get along; to find a way; **componérselas para** + *infin* to manage to + *infin*, contrive to + *infin*; **¡allá se las componga!*** that's his funeral!*
(e) (*LAm Med*) to recover, get better; **las cosas se compondrán** everything will be all right.

componible ADJ (a) *objeto roto* repairable; worth mending. (b) (*que se puede conciliar*) reconcilable; capable of settlement.

comportable ADJ bearable.

comportamental ADJ behavioural.

comportamiento NM behaviour, conduct; (*Mec etc*) performance.

comportar [1a] ① VT (a) (*aguantar*) to bear, endure, put up with.
(b) (*acarrear*) to involve, carry with it; to mean; **ello no comporta obligación alguna** it carries no obligation.
(c) (*And, Cono Sur: causar*) to entail, bring with it.
② **comportarse** VR to behave; to comport o.s., conduct o.s.; **~ como es debido** to behave properly.

comporte NM (a) = **comportamiento.** (b) (*porte*) bearing, carriage.

composición NF (a) (*en muchos sentidos, t Liter, Mús*) composition; (*Univ*) essay; **~ de lugar** stocktaking; **hacer una ~ de lugar** to take stock (of one's situation).
(b) (*de riña*) settlement; (*de personas*) reconciliation; **~ procesal** (*Jur*) out-of-court settlement.
(c) (*arreglo*) arrangement.
(d) (*acuerdo*) agreement.
(e) (*cualidad*) composure.
(f) (*Tip*) typesetting; **~ por ordenador** computer typesetting.

compositor(a) NM/F (a) (*Mús*) composer. (b) (*Tip*) compositor. (c) (*Cono Sur: curandero*) quack doctor, bonesetter.

compost ['kompos] NM compost.

compostación NF, **compostaje** NM composting.

compostelano ① ADJ of Santiago de Compostela.
② NM, **compostelana** NF native (*o* inhabitant) of Santiago de Compostela; **los ~s** the people of Santiago de Compostela.

compostura NF (a) (*constitución*) composition; structure; make-up.
(b) (*Mec etc*) mending, repair, repairing; overhauling; **estar en ~** to be undergoing repairs.
(c) (*Culin*) condiment, seasoning.
(d) (*arreglo*) arrangement; tidying, polishing, adornment.
(e) (*acuerdo*) arrangement, agreement; settlement.
(f) (*cualidad*) (*serenidad*) composure; (*discreción*) discretion, good sense; (*modestia*) modesty; **perder la ~** to lose one's composure.

compota NF stewed fruit, preserve, compote; **~ de manzanas** (*etc*) stewed apples (*etc*).

compotera NF dessert dish.

compra NF (a) (*acto*) purchase, buying; **~ al contado** cash purchase; **~ a crédito** buying on credit; **~ a plazos** hire purchase; **ir de ~s, ir a la ~** to go shopping, shop; **hacer la ~** to do the shopping.
(b) (*artículo*) purchase; **~s** purchases, shopping; **es una buena ~** it's a good buy.

comprador(a) NM/F buyer, purchaser; (*en tienda*) shopper, customer; **~ principal** head buyer.

comprar [1a] VT (a) (*gen*) to buy, purchase (*a, de* from); **~ al contado** to pay cash for; **~ al fiado** to buy on credit; **~ a plazos**, **~ a cuotas** (*LAm*) to buy on hire purchase, pay for in instalments.
(b) (*fig*) to buy off, bribe; to win over, secure the allegiance of.

compraventa NF (a) (*acto*) buying and selling, dealing; (*negocio de ~*) second-hand shop. (b) (*Jur*) contract of sale.

➤ LENGUA Y USO: **complacer: 1 → 46.5 2 → 51.1, 51.2**

comprender [2a] VTI (a) (*incluir*) to comprise, include; (*abarcar*) to take in; (*extenderse a*) to extend to; (*consistir en*) to consist of; **servicio no comprendido** service not included; **todo comprendido** everything included, all in.
(b) (*entender*) to understand; to see; to realize; **~ que ...** to understand that ..., see that ...; to realize that ...; **¿comprendes?** see?, understand?; **¡comprendido!** all right!, sure!; agreed!; **¡ya comprendo!** I see!, now I get it!; **no comprendo cómo** I don't see how; **comprendo su actitud** I understand his attitude; **cuando comprendió que no iba a ayudarle** when he realized (*o* saw) I was not going to help him; **compréndase bien que ...** let it be clearly understood that ...; **compréndanme Vds** let's be clear about this; **hacerse ~** to make o.s. understood.
▼ **comprensible** ADJ understandable, comprehensible (*para* to); **no es ~ que ...** it is incomprehensible that ..., I (*etc*) cannot understand how ...
comprensiblemente ADV understandably.
comprensión NF (a) (*lo inclusivo*) comprehensiveness, inclusiveness; inclusion.
(b) (*acto, facultad*) understanding, comprehension; grasp; **ejercicio de ~ auditiva** listening comprehension test.
(c) (*emoción*) understanding (attitude); sympathy, tolerance, kindness.
comprensivo ADJ (a) (*inclusivo*) comprehensive, inclusive; all-embracing; **un bloque ~ de 50 viviendas** a block containing 50 flats.
(b) *persona, actitud* understanding; sympathetic, tolerant, kindly.
compresa NF compress; **~ higiénica** sanitary towel, sanitary napkin (*US*).
compresibilidad NF compressibility.
compresible ADJ compressible.
compresión NF compression.
compresor NM compressor.
comprimible ADJ compressible.
comprimido ① ADJ compressed.
② NM (*Med*) pill, tablet; **~ para dormir** sleeping pill.
comprimir [3a] ① VT (a) (*gen*) to compress (*t Téc*; *en* into); (*prensar*) to squeeze (down *etc*), press (down *etc*); (*condensar*) to condense.
(b) (*fig*) to control, restrain; *lágrimas* to keep back.
② **comprimirse** VR (*fig*) to control o.s., contain o.s.; **tuve que comprimirme para no reír** I had to keep myself from laughing; **tendremos que comprimirnos** (*Fin*) we shall have to restrict ourselves.
comprobable ADJ verifiable, capable of being checked; **un alegato fácilmente ~** an allegation which is easy to check.
comprobación NF checking, verification; proof; **en ~ de ello** in proof whereof, as proof of what I (*etc*) say; **de difícil ~** hard to check, difficult to prove.
comprobador NM tester; **~ de lámparas** valve tester.
comprobante ① ADJ: **documento ~** supporting document; **documentos ~s de ello** documents in proof thereof.
② NM proof, supporting document; (*Com*) receipt, voucher.
comprobar [1l] VT (a) (*averiguar*) to check, verify; (*probar*) to prove; (*demostrar*) to confirm, show; **~ que ...** to check that ...; to show that ..., establish that ...; **~ si ...** to check whether ...
(b) (*Mec etc*) to check, test.
comprometedor ADJ compromising.
comprometer [2a] ① VT (a) *persona* to compromise; to embarrass, put in an awkward situation; *cómplice etc* to involve, implicate; **aquellas cartas le comprometieron** those letters compromised him.
(b) (*arriesgar*) to risk; (*poner en peligro*) to endanger, imperil, jeopardize; **~ la reputación** to risk one's reputation; **~ la neutralidad del país** to imperil one's country's neutrality.
(c) **~ a uno a algo** to hold sb to sth, pin sb down to sth; **~ a uno a** + *infin* to force sb to + *infin*, make sb feel obliged to + *infin*.
(d) (*Com, Jur*) to agree formally; *habitación, plaza etc* to book, reserve.
② **comprometerse** VR (a) (*gen*) to compromise o.s.; to get involved (*en* in).
(b) **~ a** + *infin* to undertake to + *infin*, promise to + *infin*, engage to + *infin*; **se compromete a todo** he'll say yes to anything.
comprometido ADJ (a) *situación etc* awkward, embarrassing.
(b) *escritor etc* engagé, engaged, committed; **no ~** uncommitted.
(c) **estar ~** to be engaged; to be involved; to be at stake; **estar ~ para** + *infin* to be engaged to + *infin*.
compromisario, -a NM/F convention delegate.
▼ **compromiso** NM (a) (*obligación*) obligation; commitment; (*promesa*) undertaking, pledge, promise; (*cita*) engagement, date; (*Pol etc*) engagement; **por ~** out of a sense of duty; **libre de ~, sin ~** without obligation; **adquirir un ~ de** + *infin* to commit o.s. to + *infin*, take on an obligation for + *ger*; **atender** (*o* **cumplir**) **sus ~s** to meet one's obligations; **hacer honor a sus ~s** to honour one's pledges; **tener muchos ~s** to have many commitments; **¿tienes ~ para esta noche?** have you anything on this evening?, are you booked up tonight?

▼ (b) (*acuerdo*) agreement; **~ histórico** epoch-making deal; **~ matrimonial** engagement (to marry); **~ verbal** verbal agreement, gentlemen's agreement.
(c) (*aprieto*) awkward situation, jam, fix; predicament; **estar en un fuerte ~** to be in a real difficulty; **poner a uno en un ~** to place sb in an embarrassing situation; **poner a uno en el ~ de** + *infin* to put sb in the position of + *ger*; **salir de un ~** to get out of a difficulty.
(d) (*transacción*) compromise.
compuerta NF (*de canal*) sluice, floodgate; (*en puerta etc*) hatch; (*Inform*) gate.
compuesto ① PTP *de* **componer**; **estar ~ de** to be composed of, consist of, be made up of.
② ADJ (a) (*Quím, Ling, Mat, interés etc*) compound; *flor, material* composite.
(b) *persona etc* elegant, dressed up; tidy, neat.
(c) (*fig*) composed, calm.
③ NM (a) (*t Quím*) compound; preparation; composite material; **~ químico** chemical compound.
(b) (*Ling*) compound (word).
compulsa NF (a) (*acto*) checking, comparison. (b) (*Jur*) attested copy, certified true copy.
compulsar [1a] VT (a) (*comparar*) to collate, compare. (b) (*Jur*) to make an attested copy of.
compulsión NF compulsion.
compulsivamente ADV compulsively.
compulsivo ADJ compulsory; compulsive.
compulsorio ADJ (*LAm*) compulsory.
compunción NF (*arrepentimiento*) compunction, regret, remorse; (*compasión*) pity; (*tristeza*) sorrow.
compungido ADJ remorseful, contrite, sorry; sad, sorrowful.
compungir [3c] ① VT to make remorseful, arouse feelings of contrition in.
② **compungirse** VR (*arrepentirse*) to feel remorseful (*por* about, because of), feel sorry (*por* for); (*entristecerse*) to feel sad, be sorrowful.
compurgar [1h] VT (*And, Cono Sur, Méx*) *ofensa* to purge; (*Méx Jur*) *pena* to serve out.
computación NF = **cómputo**.
computacional ADJ computational.
computador NM, **computadora** NF computer; **~ central** mainframe computer; **~ digital** digital computer; **~ de (sobre)mesa** desktop computer.
computadorización NF computerization.
computadorizado ADJ computerized.
computadorizar [1f] VT to computerize.
computar [1a] VT to calculate, compute, reckon (*en* at).
computerización NF computerization.
computerizado ADJ computerized.
computerizar [1f] VT to computerize.
computista NMF computer user.
cómputo NM (*cálculo*) calculation, computation, reckoning; (*Méx: suma*) total; **según nuestros ~s** according to our calculations.
comulgante NMF communicant.
comulgar [1h] ① VT to administer communion to.
② VI (a) (*Ecl*) to take communion, receive communion. (b) **~ con** to like, accept, agree with; to sympathize with; to share; **hay varias cosas con las que ella no comulga** there are several things she doesn't agree with.
comulgatorio NM communion rail, altar rail.
común ① ADJ (a) (*gen*) common (*a* to); (*conjunto*) joint; (*público*) public, belonging to all, held in common; *género, fosa etc* common; *sala, baño* communal; **los intereses comunes** common interests; **de ~ con** in common with; **en ~** in common; joint, mutual; **hacer algo en ~** to do sth jointly (*o* together); **tener algo en ~ con uno** to have sth in common with sb.
(b) *distribución etc* common; *costumbre, opinión* common, widespread, general; **es costumbre muy ~** it is a very widespread custom; **la planta es ~ en la provincia** the plant is common in the province.
(c) *cualidad* common, ordinary; **fuera de lo ~** out of the ordinary; **por lo ~** generally.
② NM (a) **el ~** the community, the people (at large); **bienes del ~** communal property, public property.
(b) **el ~ de las gentes** most people, the common run of people.
(c) (*wáter*) toilet.
(d) **los Comunes** (*Brit Pol*) the Commons.
(e) **Comunes** (*Escol*) subjects taken in common during first two years of the *bachillerato* course.
comuna NF (a) (*comunidad*) commune. (b) (*LAm: municipio*) municipality, town council.
comunacho, -a NM/F (*Cono Sur: pey*) commie*.
comunal ADJ communal; community (*atr*).
comunalmente ADV communally; as a community.

➤ LENGUA Y USO: **compresible** → 53.6   **compromiso**: b → 51.2, 52.2

comunicable ADJ (a) *noticias etc* communicable, that can be communicated. (b) *persona* approachable; sociable.

comunicación NF (a) (*gen*) communication; contact; **las comunicaciones están rotas** communications are broken; **no hemos tenido más ~ con él** we have had no further contact with him, we have heard nothing further from him.
(b) (*mensaje*) message; (*informe*) report; (*de congreso etc*) paper.
(c) (*Telec*) connection, contact; **póngame en ~ con el Sr Q** please put me through to Mr Q.
(d) (*Liter*) rhetorical question.
(e) **no hay ~ entre los dos pueblos** (*Méx: camino*) there's no way of getting from one town to the other.

comunicacional ADJ communication (*atr*); of communication, for communication.

comunicado [1] ADJ *cuartos* connected, interconnecting.
[2] NM communiqué; **~ final** final communiqué; **~ a la prensa** press-release.

comunicador(a) NM/F communicator.

comunicante NMF correspondent, letter-writer; informant; (*de congreso*) speaker.

▼ **comunicar** [1g] [1] VT (a) *información* to communicate, tell, pass on (*a* to); *noticia* to convey, tell (*a* to); *mensaje* to give, pass (*a* to); *enfermedad etc* to carry; to give (*a* to); *costumbre* to transmit, pass on; *legado etc* to pass on (*a* to), bestow (*a* on); *temor etc* to communicate (*a* to); **nos comunicó su miedo** he affected us with his fear, his fear infected us.
(b) *cuartos, lagos etc* to connect, join, open a way between; **cuartos comunicados** connecting rooms.
(c) **¿me comunica con el Sr Gomez?** (*Telec*) may I speak to Mr Gomez?
[2] VI (a) (*informar*) to send a report (*de* from); **comunican desde Lisboa que ...** it is reported from Lisbon that ...
(b) (*Telec*) **estar comunicando** to be engaged, be busy (*US*).
(c) (*Arquit*) **~ con** to connect with; to open into.
[3] **comunicarse** VR (a) (*personas*) to communicate (with each other); to be in touch, correspond; **nos comunicamos nuestras impresiones** we exchanged impressions.
(b) (*noticia, enfermedad etc*) to pass, be transmitted; **el miedo se comunicó a todos** the fear affected everybody.
(c) (*Arquit*) to be connected, lead into each other, intercommunicate.
(d) (*Ferro etc*) **la colonia está bien comunicada por tren** the development has good train services; **pueblos bien comunicados** towns having good communications.

comunicatividad NF communicativeness; powers of communication.

comunicativo ADJ (a) *persona* communicative; approachable, sociable. (b) *risa etc* infectious.

comunicología NF communication theory.

comunicólogo, -a NM/F communication theorist.

comunidad NF (a) (*gen*) community; (*sociedad*) society, corporation; (*Ecl*) community; (*And*) commune (of free Indians); **C~ Europea** European Community; **C~ Europea del Carbón y del Acero** European Coal and Steel Community; **C~ Británica de Naciones** British Commonwealth; **~ autónoma** (*Esp*) autonomous region; **~ lingüística** speech community; **~ de vecinos** residents' association; **de ~, en ~** jointly, together, in common. (b) (*: de piso*) service charge, charge for communal services.

┌─────────────────────────┐
│ **COMUNIDAD AUTÓNOMA** │
└─────────────────────────┘

ⓘ *In Spain the* **comunidades autónomas** *are any of the 19 administrative regions consisting of one or more provinces and having political powers devolved from Madrid, as stipulated by the 1978 Constitution. They have their own democratically elected parliaments, form their own cabinets and legislate and execute policies in certain areas such as housing, infrastructure, environment, health and education, though Madrid still retains jurisdiction for all matters affecting the country as a whole, such as defence, foreign affairs and justice. The* **Comunidades Autónomas** *are: Andalucía, Aragón, Asturias, Islas Baleares, Canarias, Cantabria, Castilla y León, Castilla-La Mancha, Cataluña, Extremadura, Galicia, Madrid, Murcia, Navarra, País Vasco, La Rioja, Comunidad Valenciana, Ceuta, and Melilla.*

The term **Comunidades Históricas** *refers to Galicia, Catalonia and the Basque Country, which for reasons of history and language consider themselves to some extent separate from the rest of Spain. They were given a measure of independence by the Second Republic (1931-1936), only to have it revoked by Franco in 1939. With the transition to democracy, these groups were the most vociferous and successful in their demand for home rule, partly because they already had experience of federalism and had established a precedent with autonomous institutions like the Catalan* **Generalitat.**

comunión NF communion.

comunismo NM communism.

comunista [1] ADJ communist(ic).
[2] NMF communist; **~ libertario** libertarian communist.

comunitariamente ADV communally.

comunitario [1] ADJ (a) (*gen*) community (*atr*); communal. (b) (*CE*) Community (*atr*), (of the) Common Market.
[2] NM member nation (of the EC).

comunizar [1f] VT to communize.

comúnmente ADV commonly; usually, generally; frequently.

con PREP (a) (*gen*) with; **atado ~ cuerda** tied with string; **~ su ayuda** with his help; **andar ~ muletas** to walk on (o with) crutches; **me escribo ~ ella** I write to her; **¡~ lo difícil que es todo esto!** what with all this being so difficult; **once ~ siete** eleven point seven (*11.7*); **un dólar ~ cincuenta** one dollar fifty cents; **murió ~ 60 años** she died at the age of 60.
(b) (*a pesar de*) in spite of; **~ tantas dificultades, no se descorazonó** in spite of all the difficulties he was not discouraged; **~ ser su madre, le odia** even though she is his mother she hates him.
(c) (*t para ~*) to, towards; **amable ~ todos** kind to everybody; **ser insolente ~ el jefe** to be disrespectful to the leader.
(d) (+ *infin*) **~ llegar tan tarde** (by) arriving so late; **~ confesarlo se libró del castigo** by owning up he escaped punishment; **~ decirle que no voy** when I tell you I'm not going; **~ llegar a las 6 estará bien** if you come at 6 it will be all right.
(e) **~ que** (+ *indic*) and so, so then; whereupon; **¿~ que Vd es el jefe?** so you're the boss?; **~ que fuimos a la cama** and so we went to bed.
(f) **~ que** (+ *subj*) by; if; providing that.

CONADEP [ko'naðep] NF (*Argentina Pol*) ABR de **Comisión Nacional sobre la Desaparición de Personas.**

Conasupo NF (*Méx*) ABR de **Compañía Nacional de Subsistencias Populares** *government buying and selling organization for subsidized food, clothes and furniture.*

conato NM attempt; endeavour, effort (*de* + *infin* to + *infin*); **~ de robo** attempted robbery; **hacer un ~ de** + *infin* to make an attempt to + *infin*; **poner ~ en algo** to put an effort into a task.

concatenación NF concatenation, linking; **~ de circunstancias** chain of circumstances.

concatenar [1a] VT to link together, concatenate.

concavidad NF concavity, hollow, cavity.

cóncavo [1] ADJ concave; hollow.
[2] NM hollow, cavity.

concebible ADJ conceivable, thinkable; **no es ~ que ...** it is unthinkable that ...

concebir [3k] [1] VT (*gen*) to conceive; to imagine; (*comprender*) to understand; **~ esperanzas** to nourish hopes; to become hopeful; **~ una antipatía hacia** (*o por*) to take a dislike to; **no concibo que ...** I cannot understand how (*o why*) ...
[2] VI (*Bio*) to conceive, become pregnant.

conceder [2a] VT (*gen*) to concede, grant, admit; *honor* to confer, bestow (*a* on); *atención etc* to pay; *descuento* to allow; *premio* to award (*a* to).

concejal(a) NM/F town councillor.

concejalía NF post of town councillor; seat on the town council.

concejil ADJ relating to a town council; municipal, public.

concejo NM council; **~ (municipal)** town council.

concelebrar [1a] VT to concelebrate.

concentración NF (a) (*gen*) concentration; (*Pol etc*) gathering, meeting, rally; (*Dep*) team meeting, team briefing. (b) **~ escolar** rural school at centre of a catchment area. (c) (*LAm Com*) merger.

concentrado [1] ADJ concentrated.
[2] NM (a) (*Culin etc*) extract, concentrate; **~ de carne** meat extract. (b) (*Pol*) demonstrator.

concentrar [1a] [1] VT to concentrate (*en un lugar* in a place, *en una escena* on a scene).
[2] **concentrarse** VR (a) (*Mil etc*) to gather (together), assemble. (b) **~ a** + *infin* (*fig*) to concentrate on + *ger*; **el interés se concentra en esta lucha** the interest is centred on this fight.

concéntrico ADJ concentric.

concepción NF (a) (*Bio etc*) conception; **la Inmaculada C~** the Immaculate Conception. (b) (*facultad*) understanding. (c) (*idea*) conception, idea.

conceptismo NM conceptism (*witty, allusive and involved style, esp 17th century*); *see also* CULTERANISMO, CONCEPTISMO.

conceptista [1] ADJ witty, allusive and involved.
[2] NMF writer in the style of *conceptismo*.

▼ **concepto** NM (a) (*idea*) concept, conception; idea, notion; thought; **un ~ grandioso** a bold conception, a bold plan; **formarse un ~ de algo** to get an idea of sth.
▼ (b) (*opinión*) view, opinion; judgement; **en mi ~** in my view; **formarse un ~ de uno** to form an opinion of sb; **¿qué ~ has**

formado de él? what do you think of him?; **tener buen ~ de uno, tener un buen ~ a uno** to think highly of sb.
(c) (*de narración etc*) heading, section; **bajo todos (los) ~s, por todos ~s** from every point of view; in every way, in every respect; **bajo ningún ~** in no way; **por dicho ~** for this reason; **en ~ de, por ~ de** as, by way of; under the heading of; **se le pagó esa cantidad por ~ de derechos** he was paid that amount as royalties; **deducciones por ~ de seguro** deductions for social security; **por ningún ~** in no way.
(d) (*Liter*) conceit.
conceptual ADJ conceptual.
conceptualización NF conceptualization.
conceptualizar [1f] VT to conceptualize.
conceptuar [1e] VT to think, judge, deem; **le conceptúo poco apto para eso** I think him unsuited for that; **~ a uno de** (o **como, por**) ... to regard sb as ..., deem sb to be ...; **no está bien conceptuado actualmente** he is not well thought of at present.
conceptuosamente ADV wittily; (*pey*) over-elaborately, in a mannered way.
conceptuoso ADJ witty, full of conceits; (*pey*) overelaborate, mannered.
concerniente ADJ: **~ a** concerning, relating to; **en lo ~ a** with regard to, as for.
concernir [3i; *defectivo*] VT to concern.
concertación NF **(a)** (*acto*) harmonizing; coordination; reconciliation; **~ social** social harmony; **política de ~** consensus politics. **(b)** (*pacto*) agreement, pact.
concertadamente ADV methodically, systematically; in an orderly fashion; harmoniously.
concertado ① ADJ **(a)** (*metódico*) methodical, systematic; (*ordenado*) orderly; (*armonioso*) harmonious. **(b)** (*Pol*) officially approved; state-assisted.
② NM, **concertada** NF (*And*) contract worker.
concertar [1j] ① VT **(a)** (*Mús*) to harmonize, bring into harmony; to tune (up).
(b) *esfuerzos* to coordinate; *diferencias* to adjust, bring into line, reconcile; *personas* to achieve agreement between; to reconcile; **~ a varias personas para que** ... to get various people to agree to + *infin*.
(c) (*acordar*) to agree to; *acuerdo, tratado* to conclude (*con* with); *trato, reunión etc* to arrange, fix up; *precio* to agree, fix (*en* at); **~ una venta en 20 dólares** to agree to sell sth for 20 dollars, agree to a sale price of 20 dollars; **hemos concertado el piso en sesenta mil pesetas** we have agreed to rent the flat for 60000 pesetas; **~ hacer algo** to agree to do sth.
② VI **(a)** (*Mús*) to harmonize, be in tune.
(b) (*fig*) to agree (*t Gram*).
③ **concertarse** VR **(a)** (*Mús etc*) to harmonize.
(b) (*personas*) to reach agreement, come to terms; **~ para** + *infin* (*pey*) to conspire together to + *infin*, act in concert to + *infin*.
concertina¹ NF (*instrumento*) concertina.
concertino, -a² NM/F (*persona*) first violin, leader (of the orchestra), concertmaster (*US*).
concertista NMF soloist, solo performer; **~ de guitarra** concert guitarist; **~ de piano** concert pianist.
concesión NF concession; grant(ing); allowance; award; (*Com*) concession.
concesionario, -a NM/F concessionaire, concessionary, licensee, authorized dealer; outlet; **~ exclusivo** sole agency, exclusive dealership.
concesivo ADJ concessive.
Concha NF *forma familiar de* **María de la Concepción.**
concha NF **(a)** (*Zool*) shell; shellfish, (*esp*) scallop, scallop shell; (*carey*) tortoiseshell; **~ de perla** (*And*) mother-of-pearl; **meterse en su ~** to retire into one's shell; **tener muchas ~s** to be very sharp, be a sly one; **tiene más ~s que un galápago** he's as slippery as an eel; *see also* CAMINO DE SANTIAGO .
(b) (*de porcelana*) flake, chip.
(c) (*Teat*) prompt box.
(d) (*And, Carib: descaro*) nerve, cheek*; **¡qué ~ la tuya!** you've got a nerve!
(e) (*And: pereza*) sloth, sluggishness.
(f) (*Anat: euf*) = **coño.**
(g) (*Carib: cartucho*) cartridge case.
(h) (*Carib: piel*) peel; (*corteza*) bark.
(i) **~ de su madre** (*Cono Sur*⁑) son of a bitch⁑, bastard⁑.
conchabado, -a NM/F (*LAm*) servant.
conchabar [1a] ① VT **(a)** (*mezclar*) to mix, blend.
(b) (*LAm*) *criado* to hire, engage, employ.
(c) (*And, Cono Sur: trocar*) to barter.
② **conchabarse** VR **(a)** (*confabularse*) to gang up (*contra* on), plot, conspire (*para* + *infin* to + *infin*); **los dos estaban conchabados** the

two were in cahoots*.
(b) (*LAm: colocarse, esp como criado*) to hire o.s. out, get a job (as a servant).
conchabo NM **(a)** (*LAm: contratación*) hiring, engagement; **oficina de ~** (*Cono Sur*) employment agency for domestics. **(b)** (*Cono Sur: permuta*) barter(ing).
cónchale INTERJ: **¡~!** (*Carib*) well!, goodness!
Conchinchina* NF: **estar en la ~** to be miles away, be on the other side of the world.
Conchita NF = **Concha.**
conchito NM (*And, Cono Sur*) youngest child, baby of the family.
concho¹ NM (*Carib*) taxi.
concho² (*CAm*) ① ADJ crude, vulgar.
② NM (*campesino*) peasant; (*pey*) rustic, country bumpkin.
concho³ NM (*LAm: t ~s*) (*poso*) dregs, sediment; (*residuo*) residue; (*sobras*) left-overs; **hasta el ~** to the very end; **irse al ~** (*Cono Sur*) to go down, go under, sink.
concho⁴ NM (*And, Cono Sur*) = **conchito.**
concho⁵ NM (*Anat: euf*) = **coño.**
conchudo ① ADJ (*And, Carib, Cono Sur*) sluggish, slow.
② NM, **conchuda** NF **(a)** (*And, Méx⁑: sinvergüenza*) shameless person, cheeky bastard⁑.
(b) (*LAm: persona terca*) stubborn person, pigheaded person.
conciencia NF **(a)** (*aspecto moral*) conscience; moral sense; conscientiousness; **~ doble** double personality; **a ~** conscientiously; **hecho a ~** solidly built, well built; **en ~** with a clear conscience; honestly, in truth; **te lo digo en ~** I say it with my hand on my heart; **obrar en ~** to act honourably; **con ~ limpia, con ~ tranquila** with a clear conscience; **ancho de ~** not overscrupulous; **anchura de ~** lack of scruple; **libertad de ~** freedom of worship; **hombre sin ~** unscrupulous person; **empezó a remorderle la ~** his conscience began to prick him; **tener mala ~, tener la ~ negra** to have a bad conscience; **tener la ~ tranquila** to have a clear conscience.
(b) (*conocimiento*) knowledge, awareness, consciousness; **~ de clase** class-consciousness; **a ~ de que** ... fully aware that ..., in the certain knowledge that ...; **tener plena ~ de** to be fully aware of; **tomar ~ de** to become aware of; **tomar ~ de que** ... to become aware that ...
concienciación NF arousal, awakening, (process of) becoming aware; conscience-raising.
concienciado ADJ politically aware, socially aware.
concienciar [1b] ① VT (*despertar*) to arouse, awaken, make aware; (*sensibilizar*) to raise the conscience of; (*condicionar*) to prepare (mentally); (*convencer*) to convince, persuade.
② **concienciarse** VR to be aroused (*de* to), become aware (*de* of); to convince o.s. (*de que* that).
concientización NF = **concienciación.**
concienzar [1f] VT = **concienciar.**
concienzudamente ADV conscientiously, painstakingly, thoroughly.
concienzudo ADJ conscientious, painstaking, thorough.
concierto NM **(a)** (*acuerdo*) concert, agreement; order; harmony; **de ~ con** in concert with; **quedar de ~ acerca de** to be in agreement with regard to.
(b) (*Mús: función*) concert; **~ de arias** song recital; **~ de cámara** chamber concert; **~ sinfónico** symphony concert.
(c) (*Mús: obra*) concerto.
conciliable ADJ reconcilable; **dos opiniones no fácilmente ~s** two opinions which it is not easy to reconcile.
conciliábulo NM secret meeting, secret discussion.
conciliación NF **(a)** (*acto*) conciliation; reconciliation. **(b)** (*afinidad*) affinity, similarity.
conciliador ① ADJ conciliatory.
② NM, **conciliadora** NF conciliator.
conciliar¹ [1b] ① VT **(a)** *enemigos etc* to reconcile; *actitudes etc* to harmonize, bring into line, blend.
(b) *respeto, antipatía etc* to win, gain; **~ el sueño** to (manage to) get to sleep.
② **conciliarse** VR = 1(b).
conciliar² ① ADJ (*Ecl*) of a council, council (*atr*), conciliar.
② NM council member.
conciliatorio ADJ conciliatory.
concilio NM (*Ecl*) council; **el Segundo C~ Vaticano** the Second Vatican Council.
concisamente ADV concisely, briefly, tersely.
concisión NF concision, conciseness, brevity.
conciso ADJ concise, brief, terse.
concitar [1a] VT **(a)** (*provocar*) to stir up, incite (*contra* against). **(b)** (*reunir*) to gather, assemble, bring together.
conciudadano, -a NM/F fellow citizen.
conclave NM, **cónclave** NM conclave.
▼ **concluir** [3g] ① VT **(a)** (*terminar*) to conclude, finish.
▼**(b)** (*deducir*) to infer, deduce; *consecuencia etc* to reach, arrive at.
② VI to end, conclude, finish; **~ de** + *infin* to finish + *ger*; **~ por** +

infin to end up by + *ger*; **~ con, ~ en, ~ por** *palabra etc* to end in; **todo ha concluido** it's all over; **¡vamos a ~ de una vez!** let's get it over.

3 concluirse VR to end, conclude.

▼ **conclusión** NF conclusion; **en ~** in conclusion, lastly, finally; **extraiga Vd las conclusiones oportunas** draw your own conclusions; **llegar a la ~ de que ...** to come to the conclusion that ...

concluyente ADJ conclusive; decisive; unanswerable.

concluyentemente ADV conclusively; decisively; unanswerably.

concolón NM (*LAm Culin*) scrapings.

concomerse* [2a] VR: **~ de envidia** to be green with envy; **~ de impaciencia** to be itching with impatience.

concomitante ADJ concomitant.

conconete NM (*Méx*) child, little one.

concordancia NF (a) (*cualidad*) concordance; harmony. (b) (*Ling*) concord, agreement. (c) (*Mús*) harmony. (d) **~s** (*Liter*) concordance.

concordante ADJ concordant.

concordar [1l] **1** VT to reconcile; to bring into line; (*Ling*) to make agree.

2 VI to agree (*con* with), tally (*con* with), correspond (*con* to); (*Ling*) to agree; **esto no concuerda con los hechos** this does not square with (o fit in with) the facts; **los dos concuerdan en sus gustos** the two agree in their tastes, the two have the same tastes.

concordato NM concordat.

concorde ADJ: **estar ~(s)** to be agreed, be in agreement; **estar ~ en** + *infin* to agree to + *infin*; **poner a dos personas ~s** to bring about agreement between two people.

concordia NF (a) (*armonía*) concord, harmony, agreement; conformity. (b) (*anillo*) double finger-ring. (c) **Línea de la C~** (*Cono Sur*) frontier between Chile and Peru.

concreción NF concretion; (*Med*) stone; **la falta de ~ del dominio español** (*Dep*) the failure of the Spaniards to turn their dominance into goals.

concretamente ADV particularly, specifically; exactly; to be exact; **~, ... in short ..., in a word ..., to cut a long story short ...; se refirió ~ a dos** he referred specifically to two; **no es ~ una fiesta** it's not exactly a party; **~ eran 39** to be exact there were 39.

concretar [1a] **1** VT (a) (*hacer más concreto*) to make concrete, make (more) specific; (*especificar*) to specify; *idea etc* to express in concrete terms; *problema, pega* to pinpoint, put one's finger on; (*reducir a lo esencial*) to reduce to essentials, boil down; **concreta sus esperanzas a ganar el premio** he is concentrating all his hopes on winning the prize; **concretemos, para ~** let us be more specific, let's come down to details; **vamos a ~ los puntos esenciales** let us sum up the essential points.

(b) *situación* to capitalize on, turn to advantage.

2 concretarse VR (a) (*gen*) to become (more) definite; **~ a** to come down specifically to.

(b) **~ a** + *infin* to limit o.s. to + *ger*, confine o.s. to + *ger*; to concentrate on + *ger*.

concretizar [1f] VT = **concretar**.

▼ **concreto 1** ADJ (*gen*) concrete; (*específico*) definite, actual, particular, specific; **en este caso ~** in this particular instance; **no me dijo ninguna hora concreta** he didn't tell me any definite (o particular) time; **en ~** to sum up; exactly, specifically; to be exact (o precise); **en ~ había 7** there were 7 to be exact; **no hay nada en ~** there's nothing you can put your finger on, there's nothing definite.

2 NM (a) (*gen*) concretion.

(b) (*LAm: hormigón*) concrete.

concubina NF concubine.

concubinato NM concubinage.

concúbito NM copulation.

conculcación NF infringement, violation.

conculcar [1g] VT to infringe (on); *ley* to break, violate.

concupiscencia NF (a) (*codicia*) greed, acquisitiveness. (b) (*lujuria*) lustfulness, concupiscence.

concupiscente ADJ (a) (*avaro*) greedy, acquisitive. (b) (*lujurioso*) lewd, lustful, concupiscent.

concurrencia NF (a) (*coincidencia etc*) concurrence; simultaneity, co-incidence.

(b) (*reunión*) crowd, gathering, assembly; (*público*) spectators, public, audience; (*asistencia*) attendance, turnout; **había una numerosa ~** there was a big attendance, there was a large crowd (present).

(c) (*Com*) competition.

concurrente 1 ADJ (a) *suceso etc* concurrent.

(b) (*Com etc*) competing.

2 NM (a) (*asistente*) person present, person attending; **~ al cine** cinemagoer, moviegoer (*US*); **los ~s** those present, those in the audience (*etc*).

(b) (*rival*) competitor.

concurrido ADJ *lugar* crowded; much frequented; *calle* busy, crowded; *función* popular, well-attended, full (of people).

concurrir [3a] VI (a) (*unirse: caminos etc*) to meet, come together (*en* at).

(b) (*reunirse: personas*) to meet, gather, assemble (*a* at, *en* in); **~ a un baile** to go to a dance, attend a dance; **~ a las urnas** to go to the polls; **concurren a la misma tertulia** they go to the same group.

(c) (*contribuir*) to contribute; **~ a la derrota** to contribute to the defeat; **~ al éxito de una empresa** to contribute to the success of an enterprise; **~ con su dinero** to contribute one's money; **~ en una empresa** to cooperate in an undertaking.

(d) (*cualidades etc*) to be found, be present; **concurren en ella muchas buenas cualidades** she has many good qualities.

(e) **~ en una opinión** to concur in an opinion, agree with an opinion.

(f) (*sucesos*) to coincide (*con* with).

(g) (*Com*) to compete; **~ a un mercado** to compete in a market.

(h) (*Dep etc*) to compete (*a* in), take part (*a* in).

concursado, -a NM/F (*Jur*) insolvent debtor, bankrupt.

concursante NMF competitor, contestant, participant.

concursar [1a] **1** VT (a) (*Jur*) to declare insolvent, declare bankrupt.

(b) (*competir*) to compete in, compete for; **va a ~ la vacante** he is going to compete for (o apply for) the vacancy.

2 VI to compete, participate.

concurso 1 NM (a) = **concurrencia**.

(b) **~ de acreedores** (*Jur*) meeting of creditors.

(c) (*coincidencia*) coincidence, concurrence.

(d) (*ayuda*) help, collaboration; support; cooperation; **con el ~ de** with the help of; **prestar su ~** to help, collaborate.

(e) (*Dep etc*) competition, contest; meeting, match, tournament; show; (*examen*) examination, open competition; **~ de belleza** beauty contest; **~ hípico** horse show, show-jumping contest; **~ de méritos** competition for posts; **~ de pastoreo** sheepdog trials; **~ radiofónico** radio quiz (show); **~ de redacción** essay competition; **~ de saltos** show-jumping contest; **precios sin ~s** competitive prices; unbeatable prices; **ganar un puesto por ~** to win a post in open competition.

(f) (*Com*) tender.

2 ATR: **corrida ~** bullfighting competition; **programa ~** TV game show; **cata ~** wine-tasting competition.

concurso-subasta NM, PL **concursos-subasta** competitive tendering.

concusión NF (a) (*Med*) concussion.

(b) (*Fin*) extortion.

concusionario, -a NM/F extortioner.

condado NM county; (*Hist*) earldom.

condal ADJ V **ciudad**.

conde NM earl, count; **el C~ Fernán González** Count Fernán González.

condecoración NF (*medalla etc*) decoration, medal; (*divisa*) badge; (*insignia*) insignia.

condecorar [1a] VT to decorate (*con* with).

condena NF (*Jur*) sentence; conviction; (*período*) term; **~ a perpetuidad, ~ de reclusión perpetua** life sentence, sentence of life imprisonment; **el año pasado hubo X ~s por embriaguez** last year there were X convictions for drunkenness; **cumplir una ~** to serve a sentence; **ser uno la ~ de otra** (*Méx: fig*) to be the bane of sb's life.

condenable ADJ condemnable; blameworthy.

condenación NF (a) (*gen*) condemnation; disapproval, censure; (*Ecl*) damnation; (*Jur*) = **condena**. (b) **¡~!** damn!, damnation!

condenadamente* ADV: **una mujer ~ lista** a darned clever woman*; **es un trabajo ~ duro** it's darned hard work*.

condenado 1 ADJ (a) (*gen*) condemned; (*Jur*) condemned, convicted; (*Ecl*) damned.

(b) (*fig*) doomed; **el buque ~** the doomed vessel; **una especie condenada a la extinción** a species doomed to extinction; **instituciones condenadas a desaparecer** institutions doomed to disappear.

(c) (*) *niño* mischievous, naughty.

(d) (*: *maldito*) damned, flaming‡, ruddy*; **aquel ~ teléfono** that ruddy telephone*.

(e) (*Cono Sur: listo*) clever; sharp.

2 NM, **condenada** NF (a) (*Jur*) convicted person, criminal; **el ~ a muerte** the condemned man.

(b) (*Ecl*) damned soul.

(c) **el ~ de mi tío*** that ruddy uncle of mine*.

▼ **condenar** [1a] **1** VT (a) (*gen*) to condemn.

(b) (*Jur*) to condemn, convict, sentence; to find guilty; **~ a uno a 3 meses de cárcel** to sentence sb to 3 months in jail, give sb a 3 month prison sentence; **~ a uno a una multa** to sentence sb to pay a fine; **~ a uno a presidio** to sentence sb to hard labour; **le condenaron por ladrón** they found him guilty of robbery.

(c) (*Ecl*) to damn.

➤ LENGUA Y USO: **conclusión** → 53.4   **concreto: 1** → 53.1   **condenar: 1a** → 41

(d) (*Arquit*) to block up, wall up.
(e) (*: *fastidiar*) to vex, annoy.
2 **condenarse** VR **(a)** (*confesar*) to confess (one's guilt), own up; (*reprocharse*) to blame o.s.
(b) (*Ecl*) to be damned.
(c) (*: *enfadarse*) to get cross, get worked up.
condenatorio ADJ condemnatory; **declaración condenatoria** statement of condemnation.
condensación NF condensation.
condensado ADJ condensed.
condensador NM condenser.
condensar [1a] 1 VT to condense.
2 **condensarse** VR to condense, become condensed.
condesa NF countess.
condescendencia NF helpfulness, willingness (to help); affability; acquiescence (*a* in); submissiveness; **aceptar algo por ~** to accept sth so as not to hurt feelings.
condescender [2g] VI to acquiesce, comply, agree, say yes; **~ a algo** to consent to sth, say yes to sth; **~ a los ruegos de uno** to agree to sb's requests; **~ a** + *infin* to deign to + *infin*; **~ en** + *infin* to agree to + *infin*.
condescendiente ADJ (*servicial*) helpful, willing (to help); obliging; (*amable*) kind; (*afable*) affable; (*conforme*) acquiescent; (*sumiso*) submissive.
condición NF **(a)** (*naturaleza*) nature, condition; (*temperamento*) temperament, character; **la ~ humana** the human condition; **de ~ perversa** of a perverse nature; **de ~ cruel** cruel-natured.
(b) (*clase*) social class, rank; (*status*) status, position; **persona de ~** person of rank; **de humilde ~** of lowly origin; **una boda de personas de distinta ~** a wedding between people of different social scale.
(c) (*cualidades*) **condiciones** qualities; **de excelentes condiciones** of splendid qualities; **ella no tiene condiciones para pintora** she is not cut out to be a painter.
(d) (*estado*) **condiciones** condition, state; **condiciones de trabajo** working conditions; **condiciones de vida, condiciones vitales** living conditions; **nuestras condiciones económicas** our economic circumstances; **estar en condiciones** (*Mec*) to be in working order; **el coche está en malas condiciones** the car is in a bad state; **no está en (buenas) condiciones** it's not in a fit state; **no estamos en condiciones de resolverlo** we are not able to resolve it; **no está en condiciones para** + *infin* it is not fit to + *infin*; **no estamos en condiciones para** + *infin* we are not in a position to + *infin*; **poner en condiciones** (*Mec*) to mend, repair, put right.
(e) (*Jur etc*) condition; term, provision, stipulation; **las condiciones del contrato** the terms of the contract; **condiciones de favor, condiciones favorables** concessionary terms; **~ previa** precondition; **~ sine qua non** essential condition; **a ~ de que ...** on condition that ..., provided that ...; **con esta ~** on this condition; **ayuda sin condiciones** help with no strings attached; **rendición sin condiciones** unconditional surrender; **rendirse sin condiciones** to surrender unconditionally.
condicionado ADJ conditioned.
condicional ADJ conditional (*t Ling*).
condicionalmente ADV conditionally.
condicionamiento NM conditioning.
condicionante NM determining factor, determinant.
condicionar [1a] VT **(a)** to condition; to determine; to prepare; *futuro* to shape, mould. **(b)** **X condiciona su apoyo a la retirada de Y** X makes his support conditional on the withdrawal of Y.
condigno ADJ proper, corresponding.
condimentación NF seasoning.
condimentar [1a] VT to flavour, season; to spice.
condimento NM seasoning, flavouring; dressing.
condiscípulo, -a NM/F fellow pupil, fellow student.
condolencia NF condolence, sympathy.
condolerse [2h] VR: **~ de, ~ por** to sympathize with, feel sorry for.
condominio NM **(a)** (*Jur*) joint ownership; condominium. **(b)** (*LAm: piso*) flat, apartment (*US*) (*owned by the occupant*).
condón NM condom, sheath.
condonación NF (*de deuda*) cancellation, forgiveness; (*de pena*) remission.
condonar [1a] VT *acto* to condone; *castigo* to remit; *deuda* to cancel, forgive; *criminal* to reprieve.
cóndor NM condor.
conducción NF **(a)** (*acto*) leading; guiding; management; transport(ation); conveyance; piping; (*Fís*) conduction.
(b) (*Aut*) drive; driving; **~ a derecha** right-hand drive; **coche de ~ interior** saloon car; **~ descuidada, ~ negligente** careless driving; **~ temeraria** reckless driving.
(c) (*Téc*) pipe; intake; outlet; **~ de agua** water pipe; **~ principal de agua** water main; **~ principal de gas** gas main.

conducente ADJ: **~ a** conducive to, leading to.
conducir [3n] 1 VT **(a)** *líquido etc* to take, convey; to pass; *carga* to take, transport, convey; **los cables conducen la electricidad** the cables carry the electricity.
(b) (*Aut etc*) to drive; to steer; **~ por la derecha** to drive on the right.
(c) *persona* to take, lead (*a* to); to guide, conduct (*a* to); **me condujeron por un pasillo** they led me along a passage.
(d) *negocio, asunto* to direct, manage, conduct; *ejército, grupo, sublevación etc* to lead.
2 VI **(a)** (*Aut*) to drive; **aprender a ~** to learn to drive.
(b) **~ a** (*fig*) to lead to; **esto ha de ~ al desastre** this is bound to lead to disaster; **¿a qué conduce?** what's the point?; **no conduce a ninguna parte** this is getting us nowhere.
3 **conducirse** VR to behave, conduct o.s.
conducta NF **(a)** (*de persona*) conduct, behaviour; **mala ~** misconduct, misbehaviour; **cambiar de ~** to mend one's ways.
(b) (*de negocio etc*) direction, management.
conductibilidad NF (*Fís*) conductivity.
conductismo NM behaviourism.
conductista ADJ, NMF behaviourist.
conductividad NF = **conductibilidad**.
conductivo ADJ conductive.
conducto NM **(a)** (*de agua etc*) pipe, tube, conduit; (*Anat*) duct, canal; **~s** (*Aut*) leads; **~ alimenticio** alimentary canal; **~ biliar** bile duct; **~ de desagüe** drain; **~ de humo** flue; **~ lacrimal** tear duct.
(b) (*fig*) agency; channel; (*persona*) agent, intermediary; **por ~ de** through, by means of; **por los ~s normales** through the usual channels.
conductor 1 ADJ **(a)** (*gen*) leading, guiding.
(b) (*Fís*) conductive.
2 NM (*Fís*) conductor; (*Elec*) lead; cable, flex; **no ~** non-conductor.
3 NM, **conductora** NF **(a)** (*jefe*) leader; (*guía*) guide; (*Dep*) leader.
(b) (*Aut*) driver; motorist; **aprendiz de ~, ~ novato** learner, learner-driver.
(c) (*LAm: Mús*) conductor; (*de autobús etc*) conductor, conductress.
conductual ADJ behavioural.
condueño, -a NM/F joint owner, part owner, co-owner.
conduje *etc* V **conducir**.
condumio * NM food, grub*.
conectable ADJ connectable (*a* to).
conectado ADJ (*Elec etc*) connected; **estar ~** (*aparato*) to be on; (*hilo etc*) to be live.
conectar [1a] 1 VT **(a)** (*Téc*) to connect (up); (*Elec, TV etc*) to connect (up); to switch on, plug in; (*Telec*) to put through, connect (*con* to); **~ un aparato a tierra** (*o* **con masa**) to earth (*o* ground *US*) a piece of apparatus.
(b) **~ a uno con otra persona** to put sb in touch with sb else; **yo les puedo ~** I can put you in touch (with one another); **le conectamos con Sevilla** (*Telec*) we're putting you through to Seville.
2 VI: **~ con** *persona* to communicate with; to form contacts with, enter into a relationship with; **~ con el espíritu europeo** to become imbued with the European spirit; **ellos conectan bien** they get on well, they have a good relationship; **ahora conectamos con Londres** (*TV*) now we're going over to London.
3 **conectarse** * VR to make a connection*, get drugs.
conectividad NF connectivity.
conectivo ADJ connective.
conector NM connector.
coneja NF doe rabbit.
conejar NM warren, burrow.
conejera NF **(a)** (*madriguera*) warren, burrow; (*jaula*) rabbit hutch. **(b)** (*: *tasca*) den, dive*.
conejillo NM young rabbit; bunny; **~ de Indias** guinea-pig.
conejita NF bunny girl.
conejito NM young rabbit; bunny; = **conejo** (c).
conejo 1 ADJ (*CAm*) flat, unsweetened; bitter, sour.
2 NM **(a)** (*Zool*) rabbit; **~ casero** tame rabbit, pet rabbit; **~ de monte, ~ silvestre** wild rabbit.
(b) (*CAm*) detective; **andar de ~** (*LAm*) to be (operating) under cover.
(c) (*: *Anat*) = **coño**.
(d) (*Mil*) recruit, squaddie*.
conejuna NF rabbit fur, coney.
conexión NF **(a)** (*Téc*) connection; plug; coupling; joint. **(b)** (*fig*) connection; relationship.
conexionarse [1a] VR to get in touch; to make connections, establish contacts.
conexo ADJ connected, related.
confabulación NF plot; intrigue; dubious scheme; (*Com*) ring.
confabularse [1a] VR to plot, conspire, scheme (*para* + *infin* to + *infin*); (*Com*) to form a ring.

confección NF (a) (*acto*) making; making-up, preparation; **~ de vestidos** dressmaking.
(b) (*arte*) workmanship, work; **traje de ~** ready-to-wear suit.
(c) (*artículo*) manufactured article, made-up article; (*Farm*) concoction, preparation; (*Cos*) ready-made garment (o suit *etc*); **es una ~ Pérez** it's a Pérez creation, it's a Pérez product.
confeccionado ADJ (*Cos*) ready-made, ready-to-wear.
confeccionador NM (*Prensa*) layout man.
confeccionar [1a] VT *lista etc* to make out; *informe* to prepare, write up; (*Cos*) to make (up); (*Farm*) to concoct, make up.
confeccionista NMF ready-made clothier.
confederación NF confederation, confederacy, league.
confederado, -a ADJ, NM/F confederate.
confederal ADJ federal.
confederarse [1a] VR to confederate, form a confederation.
conferencia NF (a) (*Pol etc*) conference, meeting; **~ cumbre** summit conference; **~ de desarme** disarmament conference; **~ episcopal** synod; **~ de prensa** press conference.
(b) (*oración*) lecture, address; **dar una ~** to give a lecture.
(c) (*Telec*) call; **~ a cobro revertido** reversed-charge call; **~ interurbana, ~ de larga distancia** long-distance call, trunk call; **~ de persona a persona** personal call; **tiene facilidad de ~ múltiple** it has a follow-on call facility.
(d) (*Inform*) conference; conferencing.
conferenciante NMF lecturer.
conferenciar [1b] VI to confer (*con* with); to be in conference.
conferencista NMF (*LAm*) lecturer.
conferir [3i] VT (a) *premio* to award (*a* to); *honor* to grant (*a* to), confer (*a* on), bestow (*a* on).
(b) (*fig*) *cualidad* to lend, give (*a* to); **los cuadros confieren dignidad al cuarto** the pictures give the room dignity.
(c) *documentos etc* to compare (*con* with).
confesante NM (*Hist*) penitent.
confesar [1j] ① VT (a) *error* to confess, admit, acknowledge; *crimen* to own up to; (*Ecl*) *pecado* to confess.
(b) (*Ecl*) *pecador* to confess, hear the confession of.
② VI y **confesarse** VR to confess, own up; (*Ecl*) to confess (*a, con* to), make one's confession; **~ de sus pecados** to confess one's sins; **¡que Dios nos coja confesados!** God help us!
confesión NF confession.
confesional ADJ (a) (*de la confesión*) confessional; **secreto ~** secrecy of confession. (b) (*de sectas*) confessional, denominational.
confes(i)onario NM confessional box.
confeso ① ADJ (a) (*Jur etc*) (self-)confessed. (b) (*Hist*) *judío* converted.
② NM (*Hist*) converted Jew; (*Ecl*) lay-brother.
confesor NM confessor.
confeti NM (*t* **~s**) confetti.
confiabilidad NF reliability, trustworthiness.
confiable ADJ reliable, trustworthy.
confiadamente ADV (a) (*con confianza*) trustingly. (b) (*tranquilamente*) confidently; self-confidently; hopefully. (c) (*de manera presumida*) conceitedly.
confiado ADJ (a) (*que confía*) trusting; (*crédulo*) unsuspecting, gullible.
(b) (*seguro de sí mismo*) confident; **~ en sí mismo** self-confident, self-reliant; **estar muy ~** to be excessively hopeful, nourish false hopes.
(c) (*vanidoso*) vain, conceited, presumptuous.
confianza NF (a) (*en otro*) trust (*en* in), reliance (*en* on); (*confiabilidad*) trustfulness; **~ mutua** mutual trust; **persona de (toda) ~** reliable person, trustworthy person; **puesto de ~** responsible post, post of responsibility; **recluso de ~** (prison) trusty; **él es de ~** he is all right, you can speak freely in front of him; **decir algo en ~** to say sth in confidence; **dicho sea en ~** let it be said in confidence (o strictly between ourselves); **defraudar la ~ de uno** to let sb down; **poner su ~ en** to put one's trust in.
(b) (*en sí mismo*) confidence; **~ en sí mismo** self-confidence; **con toda ~** with complete confidence, with every confidence, without hesitation; **estar lleno de ~** to be full of confidence; **infundir ~ a uno** to give sb confidence.
(c) (*vanidad*) vanity, conceit; presumption.
(d) (*intimidad*) intimacy, familiarity (*con* with); **amigo de ~** close friend, intimate friend; **reunión de ~** intimate gathering, informal gathering; **en tono de ~** in a confidential tone; **tener ~ con uno** to be on close terms with sb; **tratar a uno con ~** to treat sb without formality, not stand on ceremony with sb; **os ruego tratarme con toda ~** I ask you to treat me as one of yourselves.
(e) **~s** confidences; (*pey*) familiarities; **se toma demasiadas ~s** he is too familiar, he's too fresh, he takes too many liberties.
confianzudo ADJ (a) (*demasiado familiar*) overfamiliar, fresh. (b) (*LAm: entrometido*) meddlesome.
confiar [1c] ① VT: **~ algo a uno, ~ algo en uno** to entrust sth to sb, commit sth to the care of sb; **~ algo al azar** to leave sth to chance.

② VI to trust, be trusting; **~ en** to trust, trust in; to rely on, count on; **~ en el éxito de algo** to feel confident about the success of sth; **confiemos en Dios** let us trust in God; **~ en que ...** to trust that ...; to expect that ...
③ **confiarse** VR (a) **~ a algo** to entrust o.s. to sth.
(b) **~ a uno** (*fig*) to open one's heart to sb.
confidencia NF confidence, secret; confidential remark; (*a policía etc*) tip-off; **hacer ~s a uno** to tell secrets to sb, confide in sb.
confidencial ADJ confidential; secret.
confidencialidad NF confidentiality, confidential nature; secrecy; **en la más estricta ~** in the strictest confidence.
confidencialmente ADV confidentially; secretly.
confidente NM, **confidenta** NF (a) (*amigo*) confidant(e); intimate friend. (b) (*agente*) informer; secret agent; **~ policial** police informer.
configurabilidad NF configurability.
configuración NF shape, configuration; (*Inform*) configuration; **la ~ del futuro** the shape of things to come; **la ~ del terreno** the lie of the land.
configurar [1a] VT to shape, form, fashion.
confín NM (*gen* **confines** PL) (*límite*) limit, boundary; (*horizonte*) horizon; **confines** confines, limits (*t fig*); (*parte exterior*) remote part, outermost parts, edges.
confinamiento NM (*encierro*) confinement; (*destierro*) banishment, exiling.
confinar [1a] ① VT (*Jur etc*) to confine (*a, en* in); (*desterrar*) to banish, exile (*a* to); (*detener*) to arrest; (*encerrar*) to shut away.
② VI: **~ con** to border on (*t fig*).
③ **confinarse** VR to shut o.s. away.
▼ **confirmación** NF confirmation (*t Ecl*).
▼ **confirmar** [1a] VT (*gen*) to confirm (*t Ecl*); (*Jur*) to corroborate; (*apoyar*) to endorse, bear out, prove; **~ a uno de** (o **como, por**) to confirm sb as; **la excepción confirma la regla** the exception proves the rule.
confirmatorio ADJ confirmatory.
confiscación NF confiscation.
confiscar [1g] VT to confiscate.
confisgado ADJ (*CAm*) mischievous, naughty.
confitado ADJ: **fruta confitada** crystallized fruit.
confitar [1a] VT to preserve (in syrup); to candy; (*t fig*) to sweeten.
confite NM sweet, candy (*US*).
confitería NF (a) (*dulces*) confectionery, sweets, candies (*US*). (b) (*tienda*) confectioner's (shop), sweetshop, candy store (*US*); (*Cono Sur*) café; shop selling pastry *etc*.
confitero, -a NM/F confectioner.
confitura NF preserve; crystallized fruit; jam.
conflagración NF conflagration; (*fig*) flare-up, outbreak; **~ bélica** outbreak of war.
conflictividad NF (a) (*tensiones*) tensions and disputes; strains; potentiality for conflict; **~ laboral** industrial disputes, labour troubles; **~ social** social unrest. (b) (*cualidad*) controversial nature, debatable nature.
conflictivo ADJ *sociedad etc* troubled, filled with conflict; *sistema* unstable; *asunto* controversial; fraught with conflict; *situación* tense, troubled; *propuesta* likely to lead to a clash; **la edad conflictiva** the age of conflict; **punto ~** point at issue; controversial point, debatable point; **zona conflictiva** area of conflict, troubled region, trouble spot.
conflicto NM (a) (*Mil*) conflict; struggle; (*fig*) clash; **~ de intereses** clash of interests; **~ laboral** labour dispute. (b) (*fig*) difficulty, fix, jam; **estar en un ~** to be in a jam.
conflictual ADJ = **conflictivo**.
confluencia NF confluence.
confluente ① ADJ confluent.
② NM confluence.
confluir [3g] VI (*ríos etc*) to meet, join, come together; (*personas etc*) to gather, come together; to mass.
conformación NF shape, form, structure.
conformado ① ADJ (a) **bien ~** well-made, well-shaped. (b) (*sufrido*) patient, resigned, long-suffering.
② NM (*Téc*) moulding, shaping, forming
conformar [1a] ① VT (a) (*formar*) to shape, fashion; (*Téc*) to mould, shape, form.
(b) (*ajustar*) to adjust (*a* to), adapt (*a* to), bring into line (*a* with); *enemigos* to reconcile.
(c) (*constituir*) to constitute, make up.
② VI to agree (*con* with).
③ **conformarse** VR to conform; to resign o.s.; **~ con** *original* to conform to, agree with; *regla* to comply with, abide by, observe; *política etc* to adjust to, conform to, fall into line with; *situación difícil* to resign o.s. to, accept; **se conforma con cualquier cosa** he agrees to anything; he puts up with anything; **no me conformo con hacerlo así** I do not agree to doing it that way.
conforme ① ADJ (a) (*parecido*) alike, similar; **son muy ~s en todo**

► LENGUA Y USO: **confirmación** → 47.3 **confirmar** → 38.1, 47.3

they are very similar in every respect.

(b) (*que corresponde*) consistent (*a* with); **un premio ~ a sus méritos** a prize consistent with his merits, a reward in accordance with his merits.

(c) (*acorde*) agreed, in agreement; **¡~(s)!** agreed!, all right!; **estar ~s** to be agreed; **estamos ~s en el precio** we are agreed about the price; **estamos ~s en que ...** we agree that ...; **declararse ~ con algo** to consent to sth, acquiesce in sth; **por fin se mostró ~ con** finally he agreed.

(d) (*satisfecho*) satisfied, content (*con* with); resigned (*con* to); **no se quedó ~ con la propina** he was not satisfied with the tip.

2 PREP: **~ a** in conformity with, in accordance with; in keeping with; **~ a la muestra** as per sample; **lo hicieron ~ a sus instrucciones** they acted according to their instructions.

3 CONJ as; in proportion as; **todo sigue ~ estaba** everything is as it was; **~ lo iban sacando** (in proportion) as they were taking it out; **~ trabajas, así irás cobrando** you'll be paid in accordance with your work.

4 NM agreement; **dar el ~** to agree, give one's agreement.

conformidad NF **(a)** (*parecido*) similarity; correspondence; uniformity (*entre* between).

(b) (*acuerdo*) agreement; (*aprobación*) approval, consent; **de ~** by common consent; **de ~ con** in accordance with; **en ~** accordingly; **en ~ con** in compliance with; **no ~** nonconformity; disagreement; **dar su ~** to consent, give one's approval.

(c) (*resignación*) resignation (*con* to); forbearance; **soportar algo con ~** to bear sth with resignation, resign o.s. to putting up with sth.

conformismo NM conformism.

conformista ADJ, NMF conformist.

confort [kon'for(t)] NM, PL **conforts** [kon'for(t)] **(a)** (*gen*) comfort; **'todo ~'** (*anuncio*) 'all mod cons'. **(b)** (*Cono Sur euf: papel higiénico*) toilet paper.

confortabilidad NF comfort.

confortable **1** ADJ comfortable.

2 NM (*And*) sofa.

confortablemente ADV comfortably.

confortante ADJ **(a)** (*gen*) comforting. **(b)** (*Med*) invigorating, tonic.

confortar [1a] VT **(a)** (*gen*) to comfort, console; to encourage. **(b)** (*Med etc*) to strengthen, invigorate, act as a tonic to.

confortativo **1** ADJ **(a)** (*gen*) comforting, consoling; encouraging.

(b) (*Med etc*) invigorating, tonic.

2 NM **(a)** comfort, consolation; encouragement.

(b) (*Med etc*) tonic, restorative.

confraternidad NF fraternity, brotherhood.

confraternización NF fraternization.

confraternizar [1f] VI to fraternize (*con* with).

confrontación NF **(a)** (*gen*) confrontation; **~ nuclear** nuclear confrontation. **(b)** (*de textos*) comparison.

confrontar [1a] **1** VT **(a)** *peligro etc* to confront, face; to face up to.

(b) *dos personas* to bring face to face; **~ a uno con otro** to confront sb with sb else.

(c) *textos* to compare, collate.

2 VI to border (*con* on).

3 **confrontarse** VR: **~ con** to confront, face.

Confucio NM Confucius.

confundible ADJ: **fácilmente ~** easily mistaken (*con* for), easily confused (*con* with).

confundir [3a] **1** VT **(a)** (*borrar*) to blur, confuse.

(b) (*equivocar*) to mistake (*con* for), confuse (*con* with), mix up (*con* with); **confundimos el camino** we mistook our way, we got our route wrong; **ha confundido todos los sellos** he has mixed up (*o* jumbled up) all the stamps.

(c) (*mezclar*) to mix, mingle (*con* with).

(d) (*despistar*) to confound; to confuse, put off; to bewilder, perplex; *acusador etc* to put to shame; **~ a uno con atenciones** to bewilder (*o* overwhelm) sb with kindness.

(e) (*perder*) to lose; **me has confundido ese libro otra vez** you've lost that book of mine again.

2 **confundirse** VR **(a)** (*borrarse*) to become blurred, become confused.

(b) (*armarse un lío*) to get confused, get in a muddle; to get bewildered; to make a mistake; **Vd se ha confundido de número** you have the wrong number.

(c) (*mezclarse*) to mix; to blend, fuse; **se confundió con la multitud** he became lost in the crowd, he disappeared in the crowd; **los policías se confundieron con los manifestantes** the police mingled with the demonstrators.

confusamente ADV *recordar etc* in a confused way, confusedly; vaguely, hazily; *retirarse* in confusion, in disorder.

confusión NF confusion; **no hagamos confusiones** let's be clear about this, let's get this straight.

confusional ADJ: **estado ~** confused state, state of confusion.

confusionismo NM confusion; uncertainty; confused state; muddle-headedness; **sembrar el ~ y desconcierto** to spread alarm and despondency.

confusionista **1** ADJ muddle-headed; given to creating confusion.

2 NMF muddle-headed person; person given to creating confusion.

confuso ADJ (*gen*) confused; mixed up, jumbled up, in disorder; *recuerdo* confused, vague, hazy; *imagen* blurred, cloudy; **estar ~** to be confused, be bewildered; to be embarrassed.

confutar [1a] VT to confute.

conga NF (*Mús*) conga.

congal NM (*Méx*) brothel.

congelación NF **(a)** (*acto*) freezing; congealing; **~ de imagen** (*de vídeo*) freeze-frame. **(b)** (*Med*) frostbite. **(c)** (*Fin etc*) freeze, freezing; **~ de créditos** credit freeze; **~ de salarios** wage freeze.

congelado ADJ **(a)** *carne etc* frozen, chilled; *grasa* congealed. **(b)** (*Med*) frostbitten. **(c)** (*Fin etc*) frozen, blocked.

congelador NM **(a)** (*electrodoméstico*) deep freeze, freezer; freezing unit, ice compartment; **~ horizontal** chest freezer; **~ vertical** cabinet freezer. **(b)** (*Náut*) frozen-food vessel; ship for freezing fish.

congeladora NF deep freeze, freezer.

congelar [1a] **1** VT **(a)** *carne, agua etc* to freeze; *sangre, grasa* to congeal; *imagen de vídeo* to freeze.

(b) (*Med*) to freeze, affect with frostbite.

(c) (*Fin etc*) to freeze, block; *proceso etc* to suspend, freeze.

2 **congelarse** VR **(a)** (*gen*) to freeze, become frozen; to congeal.

(b) (*Med*) to get frostbitten.

congénere NM fellow, person (*etc*) of the same sort; **el criminal y sus ~s** the criminal and others like him, the criminal and people of that sort.

congeniar [1b] VI to get on (well; *con* with); **congeniamos con los dos hermanos** we hit it off with the two brothers.

congenital ADJ (*LAm*), **congénito** ADJ congenital.

congénitamente ADV congenitally.

congénito ADJ congenital.

congestión NF congestion.

congestionado ADJ **(a)** (*gen*) congested. **(b)** (*Med*) congested, (*esp*) chesty; *cara* flushed, red.

congestionamiento NM (*Carib Aut*) traffic jam.

congestionar [1a] **1** VT to congest, produce congestion in.

2 **congestionarse** VR to become congested; **se le congestionó la cara** his face became flushed, he got red in the face.

conglomeración NF conglomeration.

conglomerado NM (*Geol, Téc*) conglomerate; (*fig*) conglomeration.

conglomerar [1a] **1** VT to conglomerate.

2 **conglomerarse** VR to conglomerate.

Congo NM: **el ~** the Congo; **¡vete al ~!** get lost!

congo NM (*LAm*) Negro.

congoja NF anguish, distress, grief.

congola NF (*And*) pipe.

congoleño, -a ADJ, NM/F Congolese.

congolés = **congoleño**.

congosto NM narrow pass, canyon.

congraciador ADJ ingratiating.

congraciamiento NM ingratiation; winning over.

congraciante ADJ ingratiating.

congraciar [1b] **1** VT to win over.

2 **congraciarse** VR to ingratiate o.s. (*con* with).

congratulaciones NFPL congratulations.

congratular [1a] **1** VT to congratulate (*por* on).

2 **congratularse** VR to congratulate o.s., be pleased; **de eso nos congratulamos** on that we congratulate ourselves, we are glad about that.

congregación NF (*asamblea*) gathering, assembly; (*sociedad*) brotherhood, guild; (*Ecl*) congregation; **la ~ de los fieles** the (Catholic) Church.

congregacionalista **1** ADJ congregational.

2 NMF congregationalist.

congregar [1h] **1** VT to bring together.

2 **congregarse** VR to gather, congregate.

congresal NMF (*LAm*) = **congresista**.

congresional ADJ congressional.

congresista NMF delegate, member (of a congress).

⎡ CONGRESO DE LOS DIPUTADOS ⎤

i The **Congreso de los Diputados**, the lower house in the Spanish Parliament, has 350 seats. Members (**diputados**) are elected by proportional representation for a maximum term of four years. The house itself chooses the prime minister (**Presidente del Gobierno**) by majority vote and he/she is invited in turn by the King to form the government.
⇨ See also CORTES GENERALES, SENADO

congreso NM congress; assembly, convention; conference; (*Pol*) parliament; **C~** Congress (US); **~ anual** annual conference; (Esp Pol) **C~ de los Diputados** ≃ House of Commons.

congresual ADJ congress (atr), of (the) congress; parliamentary, congressional; **reunión ~** meeting of parliament, meeting of Congress.

congrio NM conger (eel).

congruencia NF **(a)** (t Mat) congruence, congruity. **(b)** (oportunidad) suitability.

congruente ADJ, **congruo** ADJ **(a)** (t Mat) congruent, congruous (con with); in keeping (con with); related (con to). **(b)** (conveniente) suitable, fitting.

cónico ADJ conical; sección etc (Mat) conic.

conífera NF conifer.

conífero ADJ coniferous.

conjetura NF guess, conjecture, surmise; **por ~** by guesswork; **son meras ~s** it's just guesswork.

conjeturable ADJ that can be guessed at; **es ~ que ...** one may conjecture that ...

conjetural ADJ conjectural.

conjeturar [1a] VT to guess (at), conjecture, surmise (de, por from; que that).

conjugación NF conjugation.

conjugar [1h] **1** VT **(a)** (Ling) to conjugate.
(b) (reunir) to combine, bring together, fit together, blend; **la obra conjuga cualidades y defectos** the work has both qualities and defects; **es difícil ~ los deseos de los dos** it is difficult to fit their wishes together.
2 conjugarse VR **(a)** (Ling) to be conjugated.
(b) (unirse) to fit together, blend; to be as one, become indistinguishable.

conjunción NF conjunction.

conjuntado ADJ united, combined; in harmony.

conjuntamente ADV jointly, together; **~ con** together with.

conjuntar [1a] VT to unite, combine; to harmonize.

conjuntero, -a NM/F member of a musical group.

conjuntivitis NF conjunctivitis.

conjuntivo ADJ conjunctive.

conjunto **1** ADJ **(a)** (colaborativo) etc joint; united; (Mil) **operaciones conjuntas** combined operations.
(b) (afín) allied, related.
2 NM **(a)** (gen) whole; **en ~** as a whole, altogether; **en su ~** in its entirety; **foto de ~** group photo; **impresión de ~** overall impression; **vista de ~** all-embracing view; **formar un ~** to form a whole.
(b) (Cos) ensemble; costume; twin-set.
(c) (Mús) (de cámara etc) ensemble; (de pop) group; (Dep) team.
(d) (Teat) chorus.
(e) (Mec) unit, assembly.
(f) (Mat) set.

conjura NF, **conjuración** NF plot, conspiracy.

conjurado, -a NM/F plotter, conspirator.

conjurar [1a] **1** VT **(a)** demonio to conjure, to exorcise.
(b) peligro to stave off, ward off.
(c) pensamiento etc to rid o.s. of, get rid of.
(d) persona to entreat, beseech.
2 VI y **conjurarse** VR to plot, conspire (together).

conjuro NM **(a)** (ensalmo) incantation, conjuration, exorcism; spell; **al ~ de sus palabras** under the magical effect of his words. **(b)** (ruego) entreaty.

conllevar [1a] VT **(a)** sentido to convey, carry (with it); (acarrear) to imply, involve, to bring with it, bring in its wake.
(b) (aguantar) dolor to bear, suffer (patiently), live with; persona to bear, put up with; **~ las penas de otro** to help sb else to bear his troubles.

conmemoración NF commemoration.

conmemorar [1a] VT to commemorate.

conmemorativo ADJ commemorative; memorial (atr).

conmigo PRON with me; with myself; V consigo.

conmilitón NM fellow soldier.

conminación NF **(a)** (amenaza) threat. **(b)** (Méx Jur) judgement.

conminar [1a] VT **(a)** (amenazar) to threaten (con with). **(b)** **~ a uno a hacer algo** to warn sb (officially) to do sth, instruct sb to do sth. **(c)** (Méx: desafiar) to challenge.

conminatorio ADJ threatening, warning.

conmiseración NF pity, sympathy; commiseration.

conmoción NF **(a)** (Geol) shock; tremor, earthquake.
(b) **~ cerebral** (Med) concussion.
(c) (fig) shock; commotion, disturbance; upheaval; **una ~ social** a social upheaval; **producir una ~ desagradable a uno** to give sb a nasty shock.

conmocionado ADJ (Med) shocked, concussed.

conmocionar [1a] VT **(a)** (conmover) to move, affect deeply; (sacudir) to shake profoundly, cause an upheaval in. **(b)** (Med) to put into shock, concuss.

conmovedor ADJ touching, moving; poignant; exciting, stirring; disturbing.

conmovedoramente ADV touchingly, movingly.

conmover [2h] **1** VT **(a)** edificio etc to shake, disturb.
(b) (fig) to move, touch, stir, affect; to disturb, upset.
2 conmoverse VR **(a)** (Geol) to shake, be shaken.
(b) (fig) to be moved, be stirred.

conmuta NF (And, Cono Sur) change, alteration.

conmutación NF commutation; **~ de paquetes** packet-switching.

conmutador NM (Elec) switch; (LAm Telec) (centralita) switchboard; (central) telephone exchange.

conmutar [1a] VT **(a)** (trocar) to exchange (con, por for); (transformar) to convert (en into). **(b)** (Jur) to commute (en, por to).

connatural ADJ innate, inherent (a in).

connaturalizarse [1f] VR to become accustomed (con to); to become acclimatized, become acclimated (US) (con to).

connivencia NF collusion; connivance; **estar en ~ con** to be in collusion with.

connotación NF **(a)** (sentido) connotation. **(b)** (parentesco) distant relationship.

connotado ADJ (famoso) notable, famous; (destacado) outstanding.

connotar [1a] VT to connote.

cono NM cone; **el C~ Sur** = Argentina, Chile, Uruguay.

conocedor **1** ADJ expert, knowledgeable; **muy ~ de** very knowledgeable about.
2 NM, **conocedora** NF expert (de in), judge (de of); connoisseur (de of); **es buen ~ de ganado** he's a good judge of cattle.

conocencia NF (esp LAm) girlfriend, sweetheart.

conocer [2d] **1** VT **(a)** (gen) to know; (por primera vez) to meet; **~ a uno de vista** to know sb by sight; **le conozco ligeramente** I know him slightly; **conozco las dificultades** I know the difficulties; **la conocí en Sevilla** I met her in Seville; **conoce su oficio** he knows his job; **no conoce gran cosa de ciencias** he doesn't know much about science; **conocían la existencia de los documentos** they had known about the existence of the documents; **nunca llegué a ~la bien** I never got to know her very well; **no se le conoce tal defecto** she isn't known to have any such shortcoming; **~ a uno como su propia mano** to read sb like an open book; **le conozco de haber trabajado juntos** I know him from having worked with him; **dar a ~** to introduce, present; noticia etc to release (to the press etc); (filtrar) leak; **darse a ~** to make a name for o.s.; to make one's debut; **darse a ~ a uno** to make o.s. known to sb.
(b) (reconocer) to know, tell, recognize, distinguish (en, por by); **~ a uno por su modo de andar** to know sb by (o from) his walk; **él conoce cuáles son buenos** he knows (o can tell) which ones are good; **conocieron el peligro** they recognized the danger; **¿de qué le conoces?** how do you recognize him?; **no me conoce de nada** he doesn't know me from Adam.
(c) (Jur) causa to try, judge.
2 VI **(a)** **~ de** to know about.
(b) **~ de** (o **en**) **una causa** (Jur) to try a case.
3 conocerse VR **(a)** (persona) to know o.s.; to attain self-knowledge.
(b) (2 personas) to know each other; to get to know each other, meet, get acquainted; **se conocieron en un baile** they met at a dance.
(c) **se conoce que ...** it is clear that ...; it is known that ...; it is established that ...; it is recognized that ...; apparently ...; presumably ...

┌─ **CONOCER** ─────────────── **ver también la entrada** ─┐

• *Conocer*, aplicado a personas o cosas, se traduce generalmente por *know*:
   No conozco muy bien a su familia
   I don't know his family very well
   Nos conocemos desde que éramos pequeños
   We have known each other since we were little
   Conoce Manchester como la palma de la mano
   He knows Manchester like the back of his hand
• Sin embargo, cuando queremos indicar que se trata del primer encuentro, se debe utilizar *meet*:
   La conocí en una fiesta
   I (first) met her at a party
   ¿Conoces a Carmen? Ven que te la presento
   Have you met Carmen? Come and I'll introduce you
   Para otros usos y ejemplos ver la entrada.

└──────────────────────────────────────┘

conocible ADJ knowable.

conocido **1** ADJ known; well-known; (pey) notorious; famous, noted (por for); **un médico ~** a well-known doctor, a prominent doctor; **un hecho conocidísimo** a very well-known fact.
2 NM, **conocida** NF acquaintance.

conocimiento NM (a) (*gen*) knowledge; **para su ~ y archivo** for your information; **hablar con ~ de causa** to know what one is talking about, speak with full knowledge of the facts; **obrar con ~ de causa** to know what one is up to; **hacer ~ de un hecho** to learn a fact; **hacer ~ de un tema** to learn about a subject, become acquainted with a subject; **ha llegado a mi ~ que ...** it has come to my notice that ...; **poner algo en ~ a uno** to inform sb of sth; to bring sth to sb's attention; **tener ~ de** to know about, have knowledge of; **al tenerse ~ del suceso** as soon as the event became known; **venir en ~ de** to learn of, hear about.
▼(b) **~s** knowledge (*de* of); information (*de* about); **~s elementales** basic knowledge; **~s generales** general knowledge; **mis pocos ~s de filosofía** my small knowledge of philosophy.
(c) **~s** (*personas*) acquaintances.
(d) (*juicio*) good sense, understanding; **los niños no tienen ~** children have no sense.
(e) (*Med*) consciousness; **estar sin ~** to be unconscious; **perder el ~** to lose consciousness; **recobrar el ~** to regain consciousness.
(f) (*Náut*) bill of lading.
(g) (*Jur*) cognizance.

conorte NM (*LAm*) comfort.

conozca etc V **conocer**.

conque ① CONJ V **con 2**.
② NM (a) (*: condición*) condition, reservation; **~s** ifs and buts. (b) (*t* **conqué**: *LAm*: *dinero*) wherewithal, means.

conquense ① ADJ of Cuenca.
② NMF native (*o* inhabitant) of Cuenca; **los ~s** the people of Cuenca.

conquista NF conquest (*t fig*); **ir de ~** (*fig*) to be dressed up to kill.

conquistador ① ADJ conquering.
② NM (a) (*Mil etc*) conqueror; (*s. XVI*) conquistador. (b) (*seductor*) wolf*, ladykiller.

conquistar [1a] VT (a) (*Mil etc*) to conquer (*a* from); to overcome.
(b) (*fig*) *puesto etc* to win; *mercado* to win, open up; *persona* to win round, win over; *mujer* to win, succeed in attracting.

consabido ADJ (a) (*conocido*) well-known, familiar; (*usual*) usual; (*traído y llevado*) old, oft-repeated, timeworn. (b) (*susodicho*) above-mentioned.

consagración NF consecration, dedication.

consagrado ADJ (a) (*Rel*) consecrated (*a* to); dedicated (*a* to).
(b) (*fig*) time-honoured, hallowed, ritual, traditional; **según la expresión consagrada** in the time-honoured phrase; **principios ~s en la constitución** principles enshrined in the constitution; **un actor ~** an established actor.

consagrar [1a] ① VT (a) (*Rel*) to consecrate, hallow; to dedicate (*a* to); *emperador* to deify.
(b) (*fig*) *esfuerzo, tiempo, vida etc* to devote, dedicate (*a* to); to put in (*a* at); *monumento, placa* to put up, dedicate (*a* to).
(c) (*confirmar*) to confirm; **este triunfo le consagra como un cirujano excepcional** this success confirms him as (*o* shows him to be) a really exceptional surgeon.
② **consagrarse** VR: **~ a** to devote o.s. to.

consanguíneo ADJ related by blood, consanguineous.

consanguinidad NF blood relationship, consanguinity.

consciencia NF consciousness; awareness; realization; = **conciencia**.

consciente ① ADJ (a) (*gen*) conscious; **ser ~ de** to be conscious of, be aware of.
(b) (*Med*) **estar ~** to be conscious.
(c) (*Jur*) fully responsible for one's actions, aware of what one is doing.
(d) (*sensato*) sensible; balanced, responsible.
② NM conscious, conscious mind.

conscientemente ADV consciously.

conscripción NF conscription.

conscripto, -a NM/F conscript.

consecución NF obtaining, acquisition; attainment; (*Escol etc*) achievement; **de difícil ~** hard to obtain, difficult to get hold of; **les ayudó en la ~ de trabajo** he helped them in obtaining work; **para la ~ de estos objetos** for the attainment of these aims.

▼**consecuencia** NF (a) (*resultado*) consequence; outcome, result; (*conclusión*) deduction, conclusion; **a ~ de eso, en ~ de eso** as a result of that, as a consequence of that; **como ~, en ~** in consequence, accordingly; **aceptar las ~s** to take the consequences; **¡pues aténgase a las ~s!** then you'd better watch out!; **saqué la ~ de que ...** I gathered that ...; I drew the conclusion that ...; **no tuvo ~s** it had no ill effects, nothing bad happened as a result; **traer algo a ~** to bring sth up.
(b) (*importancia*) importance; **de ~** of importance, of some weight; **ser de ~** to be important.
(c) (*constancia*) consistency; **obrar con ~** to act consistently.
(d) (*esp LAm*: *honradez*) integrity.

consecuente ADJ (a) (*de acuerdo*) consistent (*con* with). (b) (*Filos*) con-

sequent. (c) (*importante*) important; **no demasiado ~** not very important. (d) **una persona ~** (*LAm*) an honourable person, a person of integrity.

consecuentemente ADV consistently.

consecutivo ADJ (*Ling etc*) consecutive.

conseguible ADJ obtainable; attainable.

conseguido ADJ successful.

conseguir [3d y 3k] VT (a) (*obtener*) to get, obtain, secure; to bring about; **~ + infin** to succeed in + *ger*, manage to + *infin*; **~ que uno haga algo** to manage to make sb do sth, get sb to do sth; **lo consigue como mi abuela** he has as much chance of getting it as the man in the moon.
(b) *fin etc* to attain, achieve.

conseja NF story, tale, legend; old wives' tale.

consejería NF (a) (*concejo*) council, commission. (b) (*Pol Esp*) ministry in a regional government.

consejero, -a NM/F adviser; consultant; member (of a board *etc*); (*de autonomía*) minister in a regional government; **~ delegado** managing director; **~ militar** military adviser; **~ de publicidad** advertising consultant.

consejillo NM inner cabinet, kitchen cabinet.

▼**consejo** NM (a) **un ~** a piece of advice; a hint; **su ~** his advice; **agradezco el ~** I am grateful for your advice; **pedir ~ a uno** to ask sb for advice, ask sb's advice; **~ pericial** expert advice; **~s** advice.
(b) (*Pol etc*) council; (*Com*) board; (*Jur*) tribunal; court; (*acto*) meeting (of a council *o* board *etc*); **~ de administración** board of directors; **~ asesor** advisory board; **~ de disciplina** disciplinary board; **~ escolar** school council; **C~ General del Poder Judicial** (*Esp*) governing body of the Spanish judiciary; **~ de guerra** court-martial; **~ de guerra sumarísimo** drumhead court-martial; **~ de ministros** cabinet; cabinet meeting; **~ de redacción** editorial board; **C~ de Seguridad** Security Council.

┌─ CONSEJO ─┐   ┌─ ver también la entrada ─┐

• Para traducir la palabra *consejo* al inglés, hemos de tener en cuenta que el sustantivo *advice* es incontable y lleva el verbo en singular:
  Te voy a dar un consejo
  Let me give you some advice
  Los consejos que me diste han sido muy útiles
  The advice you gave me has been very useful
  Actuó siguiendo los consejos de su abogado
  He acted on his lawyer's advice
• Cuando queremos referirnos a un *consejo* en particular o a un número determinado de consejos lo traducimos con la expresión *piece/pieces of advice* o a veces *bit/bits of advice*:
  Te voy a dar un consejo
  Let me give you a piece o *a bit of advice*
  Tengo dos buenos consejos para quien quiere vender su casa
  I have two useful pieces of advice for anyone selling their house
  Para otros usos y ejemplos ver la entrada.
---

consenso NM accord; assent; consensus.

consensuado ADJ *texto etc* agreed; established by consensus.

consensual ADJ agreed; **unión ~** common-law marriage.

consensuar [1e] VT to agree on, reach an agreement on, reach a consensus on.

consentido ADJ (a) *niño* spoiled, pampered. (b) *marido* complaisant.

consentidor ADJ *madre etc* indulgent; weak, compliant; *marido* complaisant.

▼**consentimiento** NM consent.

consentir [3i] ① VT (a) (*asentir a*) to consent to; (*permitir*) to allow, permit; (*tolerar*) to tolerate; **~ a uno + infin, ~ que uno + subj** to allow sb to + *infin*; **aquí no consienten hablar** they don't let you speak here; **¡eso no se puede ~!** we can't have (*o* allow) that.
(b) (*aceptar*) to admit; (*aguantar*) to bear, put up with; **la plataforma no consiente más peso** the platform will not bear any more weight; **el abrigo consiente un arreglo más** the overcoat will bear repairing once more.
(c) *niño* to pamper, spoil.
② VI to agree, consent, say yes (*en* to); to give in; **~ en hacer algo** to agree to + *infin*, consent to + *infin*.
③ **consentirse** VR to break, give (way); to split, crack (up *etc*).

conserje NM porter; doorman; caretaker; **~ automático** entry phone; **~ de noche** night porter.

conserjería NF porter's office.

conserva NF (a) (*acto*) preserving.
(b) (*alimentos*) preserved foods; preserve(s); (*mermelada*) jam; (*encurtido*) pickle; **~s alimenticias** tinned foods, canned goods; **~s de carne** canned meat; potted meat; **en ~** preserved; pickled; tinned, canned.
(c) (*Náut*) convoy; **navegar en (la) ~** to sail in convoy.

➤ LENGUA Y USO: **conocimiento:** b → 46.2   **consecuencia:** a → 44.1   **consejo:** a → 28.1, 29.2   **consentimiento** → 36.2

conservación NF conservation; preservation; (*Arquit etc*) maintenance, upkeep; **~ de la energía** energy conservation; **~ de la naturaleza** nature conservation; **~ refrigerada** cold storage; **~ de suelos** soil conservation; **gastos de ~** upkeep costs, maintenance expenses; **instinto de ~** instinct of self-preservation.

conservacionismo NM conservationism; nature conservation; conservation movement.

conservacionista ① ADJ conservationist; conservation (*atr*).
② NMF conservationist.

conservador ① ADJ (a) (*Culin etc*) preservative.
(b) (*Pol*) conservative.
② NM, **conservadora** NF (a) (*Pol*) conservative.
(b) (*de museo*) curator, keeper; **~ adjunto** assistant keeper.

conservadurismo NM (*Pol etc*) conservatism.

conservante NM preservative.

conservar [1a] ① VT (a) (*preservar*) *alimentos etc* to preserve; *carne* to tin, can; *recursos* to conserve; (*Arquit etc*) to preserve.
(b) (*guardar*) to keep, retain; (*mantener*) *costumbre* to keep up, maintain, retain; *propiedad etc* to keep up; *color, secreto, amigo etc* to keep; '**conserve su derecha**' (*Aut*) 'keep to the right'; **conservo varias cartas suyas** I have a few letters of his; **conserva todavía la señal** he still has (*o* bears) the mark.
② **conservarse** VR (a) (*costumbre etc*) to survive, remain, still exist; to be retained, be kept; (*durar*) to last out.
(b) (*persona*) to keep (well); to take good care of o.s.; **~ con** (*o* **en**) **salud** to keep well; **¡consérvese bien!** look after yourself!, I hope you keep well!

conservatismo NM conservatism.

conservativo ADJ preservative.

conservatorio NM (a) (*Mús*) conservatoire. (b) (*Cono Sur: invernáculo*) greenhouse. (c) (*Cono Sur: escuela*) private school.

conservero ADJ canning (*atr*); **la industria conservera** the canning industry.

considerable ADJ (*importante*) considerable; substantial; sizeable; (*digno de consideración*) worthy of consideration.

consideración NF (a) (*acto*) consideration; thought; reflexion; **está en ~** it is under consideration; **tomar en ~** to take into account, take into consideration.
(b) (*atención*) consideration; respect, regard; **en ~ a** considering, in consideration of; **por ~ a** out of regard for; **sin ~ a** irrespective of; without regard to; **hablar sin ~** to speak disrespectfully; **tratar a uno sin ~** to treat sb without consideration; **no le tengan Vds ninguna ~** don't give him any special treatment.
(c) (*respeto*) respect, esteem; **tengo una gran ~ por él** I hold him in high esteem; (*LAm: cartas*) '**de mi ~**', '**de nuestra ~**' 'Dear Sir'; **le saludo con mi más distinguida ~** Yours faithfully.
(d) **consideraciones** kindness; **tener consideraciones con uno** to be kind to sb.
(e) (*importancia*) importance; **una casa de cierta ~** a sizeable house; **una herida de ~** a serious wound; **de poca ~** unimportant, of no account; **no es de ~** it's not important.

consideradamente ADV considerately, kindly, thoughtfully.

considerado ADJ (a) (*respetado*) respected, esteemed; **bien ~** well-regarded; **mal ~** ill-regarded. (b) (*amable*) considerate, kind (*con* to), thoughtful.

considerando NM (*Jur*) word with which each item in a judgement begins ('whereas ...'); (*en sentido lato*) point, item, statement.

▼ **considerar** [1a] VT (a) (*pensar*) to consider; to think about, reflect on; **~ que ...** to consider that ..., think that ...; **bien considerado, eso es razonable** on reflection, that is reasonable.
(b) (*tener en cuenta*) to take into account; **considera que ...** bear in mind that ..., don't forget that ...
(c) (*juzgar*) to consider; to think, deem; **lo considero imposible** I consider it (to be) impossible; **le consideran como loco** they think him mad; **le consideran como futuro rey** they consider him to be a future king.
(d) (*respetar*) to esteem, respect; **~ poco a** to scorn, despise.
(e) (*tratar bien*) to be kind to, show consideration for.

consigna NF (a) (*orden*) order, instruction; (*Mil*) watchword; (*de campaña etc*) watchword, slogan, motto; catchword; **~s de un vuelo** operating instructions for a flight, operational orders for a flight.
(b) (*Ferro etc*) cloakroom, left-luggage office, checkroom (*US*); **~ automática** left-luggage locker.

consignación NF (a) (*envío*) consignment, shipment. (b) (*Fin*) appropriation; earmarked sum.

consignador(a) NM/F consignor.

consignar [1a] VT (a) (*Com*) to send, dispatch, remit (*a* to); to consign (*a* to); to deposit (*a* with).
(b) (*asignar*) to assign (*para* to, for), earmark (*para* for).
(c) (*registrar*) to record, register; to put, set down, state; **olvidé ~ mi nombre** I forgot to write my name in, I forgot to state my name; **el hecho no quedó consignado en ningún libro** the fact was not recorded (*o* set down) in any book.
(d) (*CAm, Méx: Jur*) to remand, hold for trial.

consignatario, -a NM/F (*Com*) consignee; (*Com*) agent; (*Jur*) assign(ee); (*de carta etc*) recipient, addressee.

consigo PRON (*él*) with him; (*ella*) with her; (*usted, ustedes*) with you; (*uno mismo*) with one(self) *etc*; **no lleva nada ~** he isn't taking anything with him, he's not carrying anything on him, he doesn't have anything on him; **hablaba ~** she was talking to herself; *V* **dar** *etc*.

consiguiente ADJ consequent (*a* upon); resulting; **por ~** and so, therefore, consequently.

consiguientemente ADV consequently, therefore.

consistencia NF consistence, consistency.

consistente ADJ (a) *conducta, teoría etc* consistent; *persona* (*LAm: consecuente*) consistent; *razón etc* sound, valid.
(b) *materia* solid, firm, tough, durable; *pasta etc* stiff, thick; substantial.
(c) **~ en** consisting of.

consistir [3a] VI: **~ en** (*LAm:* **~ de**) (a) (*componerse de*) to consist of; to be made of, be composed of; **¿en qué consiste?** what does it consist of?
(b) (*estribar en*) to lie in, be due to; **no consiste en eso la dificultad** the difficulty does not lie in that; **su atractivo consiste en su naturalidad** her charm lies in her naturalness; **si en mí solo consistiese** if it lay with me alone, if it depended entirely on me.

consistorial ADJ (*Ecl*) consistorial; *V* **casa**.

consistorio NM (*Ecl*) consistory; (*Pol*) town council; (*edificio*) town hall.

consocio NMF fellow member; (*Com*) co-partner, associate.

consola NF console table; (*Arquit, Inform, Mús*) console.

consolación NF consolation.

consolador ① ADJ consoling, comforting.
② NM, **consoladora** NF consoler, comforter.
③ NM (*aparato*) dildo.

consolar [1l] ① VT to console, comfort; **me consuela de no haber ido** it consoles me for not having gone.
② **consolarse** VR to console o.s.; to find consolation (*con* in), take comfort (*con* from).

consolatorio ADJ consolatory.

consolidación NF consolidation.

consolidar [1a] VT to consolidate, strengthen; *muro etc* to shore up; *deuda* to fund.

consomé NM consommé, clear soup.

consonancia NF (a) (*gen*) consonance, harmony; **en ~ con** in accordance with, in harmony with. (b) (*Liter*) (full) rhyme.

consonante ① ADJ (a) (*gen*) consonant, harmonious; consistent.
(b) (*Ling*) consonantal.
(c) (*Liter*) rhyming.
② NM (*Liter*) rhyme, rhyming word.
③ NF (*Ling*) consonant.

consonántico ADJ consonantal.

consonar [1l] VI (a) (*Mús y fig*) to be in harmony, harmonize. (b) (*Liter*) to rhyme (*con* with).

consorciarse [1b] VR to form a consortium, go into partnership.

consorcio NM (a) (*Com*) consortium; association, partnership; syndicate. (b) (*de circunstancias etc*) conjunction.

consorte NMF (a) (*esposo*) consort, spouse; **príncipe ~** prince consort.
(b) (*fig: compañero*) partner, companion. (c) (*Jur*) **~s** colitigants; (*pey*) partners in crime, accomplices.

conspicuo ADJ eminent, famous.

conspiración NF conspiracy.

conspirador(a) NM/F conspirator.

conspirar [1a] VI to conspire, plot (*con* with, *contra* against); **~ a + infin** to conspire to + *infin* (*t fig*).

conspirativo ADJ conspiratorial.

constancia NF (a) (*firmeza*) constancy; steadiness; firmness, steadfastness; loyalty.
(b) (*seguridad*) certainty; (*prueba*) proof, evidence; **no hay ~ de ello** there is no certainty of it; there is no record of it, it is not recorded; **dejar ~ de algo** to place sth on record; to show evidence of sth; **para que quede ~ de la fecha** in order to give proof of the date.
(c) (*LAm: comprobante*) documentary proof, written evidence; **dar ~** to give proof, provide evidence.

constante ① ADJ (a) *viento, esfuerzo etc* constant; unchanging; steady; *persona* firm, steadfast; *amigo* loyal, faithful, staunch.
(b) (*que continúa*) constant; continual; unending.
② NF (a) (*Mat, fig*) constant. (b) (*Med*) **~s vitales** essential life processes.

constantemente ADV constantly.

Constantino NM Constantine.

Constantinopla NF (*Hist*) Constantinople.

Constanza NF Constance.

constar [1a] VI (a) (*ser evidente*) ~ **de** to be clear from, be evident from; **consta que ...** it is clear that ..., it is a fact that ...; it is known that ...; **me consta que ...** I know for sure that ..., I have evidence that ...; **conste que yo no lo aprobé** let it be clearly understood that I did not approve it, I should like to point out that I did not approve it; **consta por ...** as is shown by ...; **que conste que lo hice por ti** believe me, I did it for your own good.
(b) (*existir etc*) to be on record, exist in recorded form; **no consta** (*libro etc*) not available; **no consta en el catálogo** it is not listed in the catalogue, it does not figure in the catalogue; **en el carnet no consta su edad** his age is not stated on the licence; **hacer ~** to record; to certify; **hacer ~ que ...** to reveal that ...; **y para que así conste ...** and for the record ...; **que conste: no estoy de acuerdo** for the record: I disagree; **que consten los hechos** let us put the record straight.
(c) ~ **de** to consist of, be composed of.
(d) (*Poét*) to scan.
constatable ADJ observable, evident; (easily) verifiable; **es ~ que ...** it can be observed that ...
constatación NF confirmation, verification; observation.
constatar [1a] VT (*comprobar*) to confirm, verify; to check (*que* that); (*demostrar*) to show, prove; (*observar*) to observe (*que* that), note (*que* that).
constelación NF constellation.
constelado ADJ starry, full of stars; (*fig*) bespangled (*de* with).
consternación NF consternation, dismay.
consternado ADJ: **estar ~, quedarse ~** to be dismayed, be shattered; to be aghast; **dejar ~ = consternar.**
consternar [1a] ① VT to dismay, shatter, shock.
② **consternarse** VR to be dismayed, be shattered; to be aghast.
constipación NF = **constipado 2.**
constipado ① ADJ: **estar ~** to have a cold.
② NM (*Med*) cold, catarrh; **coger un ~** to catch a cold.
constiparse [1a] VR to catch a cold.
constitución NF constitution.

┌─── *LA CONSTITUCIÓN ESPAÑOLA* ───┐

ⓘ *Since its first constitution of 1812, Spain has had no fewer than nine, including the current one, which brought stability to Spanish political life. Drawn up by the democratically elected **UCD** government, the **Constitución de 1978** symbolizes the spirit of reconciliation that prevailed during Spain's transition to democracy (1975-82), and has helped the country through a period of radical but peaceful change. The Constitution was ratified by Parliament on October 31, 1978 and approved by a referendum on December 6, finally receiving the royal assent on December 27, 1978. Apart from setting forth general principles on the nature of the Spanish state, it deals with such issues as the powers of the **comunidades autónomas** (regional governments), the role of the Crown in a parliamentary monarchy, and the status of Spain's different languages.*
⇨ *See also* COMUNIDAD AUTÓNOMA , LENGUAS COOFICIALES

---

constitucional ① ADJ constitutional.
② NMF constitutionalist.
constitucionalidad NF constitutionality.
constitucionalmente ADV constitutionally.
constituir [3g] ① VT (a) (*formar*) *familia, grupo, unidad etc* to constitute, form, make up; **lo constituyen 12 miembros** it consists of 12 members, it is made up of 12 members; **esa industria constituye su principal riqueza** that industry constitutes (*o* is *o* forms) its chief wealth.
(b) (*equivaler a*) to be; **eso no constituye estorbo** that isn't an obstacle; that doesn't amount to an obstacle; **para mí constituye un placer** for me it is a pleasure.
(c) (*crear*) to constitute, create, set up, establish; *colegio etc* to found; *beca etc* to institute, endow.
(d) (*hacer, erigir*) ~ **una nación en república** to make a country into a republic; ~ **una ciudad en capital** to make a city the capital; ~ **a uno en árbitro** to set sb up as arbiter; ~ **heredero a uno** to make sb one's heir; ~ **algo en principio** to erect sth into a principle, set sth up as a principle.
(e) (*forzar*) ~ **a uno en una obligación** to force sb into an obligation.
(f) *abogado* to brief, instruct.
② **constituirse** VR (a) ~ **en** (*o* **por**) **juez** to set o.s. up as a judge, constitute o.s. a judge.
(b) ~ **en un lugar** to present o.s. at a place, appear in person in a place; (*en orden*) report at a place.
constitutivo ① ADJ constitutive, essential; **acto ~ de delito** act constituting a crime.
② NM constituent element.
constituyente ADJ (*Pol*) constituent.
constreñir [3h y 3k] VT (a) (*limitar*) to restrict.

(b) ~ **a uno a hacer algo** to compel (*o* force, constrain) sb to do sth.
(c) (*Med*) *arteria* to constrict; *persona, vientre* to constipate.
constricción NF constriction.
construcción NF (a) (*gen*) construction; building; structure; ~ **de buques,** ~ **naval** shipbuilding; ~ **de carreteras** road building; **en ~, en vía de ~** under construction, in course of construction.
(b) (*Ling*) construction.
constructo NM construct.
constructivamente ADV constructively.
constructivismo NM constructivism.
constructivista ADJ, NMF constructivist.
constructivo ADJ constructive.
constructor ① ADJ building, construction (*atr*).
② NM builder (*t fig*); ~ **de buques,** ~ **naval** shipbuilder; ~ **cinematográfico** set designer, set builder.
constructora NF construction company.
construible ADJ *solar* suitable for building.
construir [3g] ① VT (a) (*gen*) to construct; to build, erect, put up. (b) (*Ling*) to construe.
② **construirse** VR (*Ling*) **este verbo se construye con 'en'** this verb takes 'en'; **aquí el verbo se construye con subjuntivo** here the verb goes into the subjunctive.
consuegra NF mother-in-law of one's son *o* daughter.
consuegro NM father-in-law of one's son *o* daughter.
consuelda NF comfrey.
consuelo NM consolation, solace, comfort; **llorar sin ~** to weep inconsolably; **premio de ~** consolation prize.
consuetudinario ADJ (a) (*usual*) habitual, customary; *borracho* hardened, confirmed. (b) **derecho ~** common law.
cónsul NM consul; ~ **general** consul-general.
consulado NM (*puesto*) consulship; (*oficina*) consulate.
consular ADJ consular.
consulta NF (a) (*acto*) consultation; ~ **popular** referendum.
(b) (*Med: consultorio*) consulting room; ~ **externa** outpatients department.
(c) (*Med: reconocimiento*) examination; **horas de ~** surgery hours; **la ~ es de 5 a 8** the surgery is from 5 to 8; **el doctor no pasa ~ a domicilio** the doctor does not make home visits.
(d) (*Hist*) opinion.
(e) **libro de ~, obra de ~** reference book, work of reference.
consultable ADJ: ~ **por todos** which can be consulted by anybody.
consultación NF consultation.
consultar [1a] VT (a) *persona* to consult (*acerca de, sobre* about, on); ~ **a un médico** to consult a doctor, see a doctor; **consultado si era cierto, contestó ...** asked if it was true, he replied ...
(b) *asunto* to discuss, raise, take up (*con* with); **lo consultaré con mi abogado** I will take the matter up with my lawyer, I will consult my lawyer about it.
(c) *libro* to consult, look up; *referencia, palabra* to look up; to hunt up, chase up.
consúlting [kon'sultin] NM, PL **consúltings** [kon'sultin] business consultancy.
consultivo ADJ consultative.
consultor(a) ① NM/F (*persona*) consultant.
② NM (*Inform*): ~ **de ortografía** spell(ing) checker.
③ NF consultancy (firm).
consultoría NF consultancy (firm); ~ **de dirección,** ~ **gerencial** management consultancy.
consultorio NM information bureau; (*Med*) surgery, consulting room; (*de revista: t* ~ **sentimental**) agony column, problem page; (*Rad*) programme of answers to listeners' queries.
consumación NF consummation; end; extinction.
consumado ① ADJ consummate, perfect; accomplished (*en* in); *bribón etc* thorough, out-and-out.
② NM (‡) (a) (*cosas robadas*) loot, swag*. (b) (*droga*) hash*.
consumar [1a] VT (a) (*acabar*) to complete, accomplish, carry out; *crimen* to commit; *asalto, robo* to carry out; *trato* to close, complete; *matrimonio* to consummate; (*Jur*) *condena* to carry out.
(b) (*And, CAm: hundir*) to submerge.
consumerismo NM = **consumismo.**
consumición NF (a) (*acto*) consumption. (b) (*en bar etc*) food *o* drink; ~ **mínima** minimum charge; **pagar la ~** to pay for what one has had.
consumido ADJ (a) *persona* skinny, wasted; *fruta etc* shrivelled, shrunken. (b) (*fig: tímido*) timid; fretful, easily upset; **tener ~ a uno** to keep sb in a nervous state.
consumidor(a) NM/F consumer; ~ **de drogas** drug-taker; **productos al ~** consumer products.
consumir [3a] ① VT (a) *comida* to consume, eat; *producto* to use, consume; *combustible* to burn, use, consume; (*en restaurante etc*) to take, have.

(b) *material* to wear away; *paciencia* to wear down; *contenido líquido* to dry up; *persona* to waste away, exhaust the energies of, wear out.
(c) *(fig)* **le consumen los celos** he is eaten up with jealousy; **ese deseo le consume** that desire is burning him up; **me consume su terquedad** his obstinacy is getting on my nerves.
(d) *(And, CAm: sumergir)* to submerge.
2 consumirse VR **(a)** *(fruta etc)* to shrink, shrivel (up), lose its substance; *(persona)* to waste away; *(sopa etc)* to boil down.
(b) *(con fuego)* to burn out, be consumed, be devoured; **se ha consumido la vela** the candle is finished.
(c) *(fig: quemarse)* to burn o.s. out; *(apenarse)* to pine away, mope *(de* because of*);* **~ de envidia** to be eaten up with jealousy; **~ de rabia** to fume with rage; **me consumo de verle así** it vexes me to see him like that.
consumismo NM *(tendencia)* consumerism; *(sociedad)* consumer society.
consumista 1 ADJ consumer *(atr)*, consumerist; **el sector ~** the consumer section.
2 NMF consumer.
consumo NM **(a)** *(gen)* consumption; **~ conspicuo, ~ ostentoso** conspicuous consumption; **~ de drogas** drug-taking; **fecha de ~ ferente** best-before date; **precios al ~** consumer prices; **sociedad de ~** consumer society. **(b)** **~s** *(Fin)* municipal tax on food.
consunción NF consumption.
consuno: de ~ ADV with one accord.
consustancial ADJ consubstantial; **ser ~ con** to be inseparable from, be all of a piece with.
contabilidad NF accounting, book-keeping; *(como profesión)* accountancy; *(letrero)* **'C~'** 'Accounts', 'Accounts Department'; **~ creativa** creative accountancy; **~ financiera** financial accounting; **~ de inflación** inflation accounting; **~ por partida doble, doble ~** book-keeping by double entry; **~ por partida simple** book-keeping by single entry.
contabilizable ADJ eligible for inclusion.
contabilización NF accounting, accountancy.
contabilizadora NF accounting machine, adding machine.
contabilizar [1f] VT **(a)** *(Fin)* to enter in the accounts; to tabulate. **(b)** *(fig)* to assess; to reckon with, take into account.
contable 1 ADJ countable.
2 NMF accountant, book-keeper.
contactar [1a] 1 VT = VI.
2 VI: **~ con** to contact, get in touch with.
contacto NM **(a)** *(gen)* contact *(t fig)*; touch; *(Aut)* ignition; **dar el ~** *(Aut)* to switch on (the ignition); **estar en ~ con** to be in touch with; **entrar en ~ con** to come into contact with; *(fig)* to get in touch with, enter into relations with; **poner a A en ~ con B** to put A in touch with B; **ponerse en ~ con** to get in touch with, contact; **lo hizo el municipio en ~ con el gobierno** the city did it in collaboration with the government.
(b) *(LAm: interruptor)* switch, contact breaker; *(Méx: enchufe)* plug.
contado 1 ADJ **(a)** **tiene los días ~s** his days are numbered.
(b) **~s** few, scarce; rare; **en contadas ocasiones** on rare occasions; **contadas veces** seldom, rarely; **son ~s los que ...** there are few who ...; **pero son contadísimos los que pueden** but those who can are very few and far between.
2 NM **(a)** *(Com)* **al ~, de ~** *(LAm)* for cash, cash down; **pago al ~** cash payment; **¡al ~!*** sure!, O.K.!*
(b) **por de ~** naturally, of course; **tomar algo por de ~** to take sth for granted.
(c) *(And: plazo)* instalment.
contador NM **(a)** *(Mat)* abacus, counting frame.
(b) *(de café)* counter.
(c) *(esp LAm Com: t* **contadora** NF*)* accountant, book-keeper; *(cajero)* cashier; *(Jur)* receiver; **~ de navío** purser.
(d) *(And: prestamista)* pawnbroker, moneylender.
(e) *(Téc)* meter; **~ de agua** water meter; **~ de aparcamiento** parking meter; **~ de electricidad** electricity meter; **~ de gas** gas meter; **~ Geiger** Geiger counter; **~ de revoluciones** tachometer; **~ de taxi** taximeter.
contaduría NF **(a)** *(como profesión)* accountancy. **(b)** *(oficina)* accountant's office; cashier's office; *(Teat)* box office; *(And)* pawnbroker's, pawnshop.
contagiar [1b] 1 VT **(a)** *enfermedad* to pass on, transmit, give *(a* to*);* to spread; *persona* to infect *(con* with*).*
(b) *(fig)* to infect, contaminate *(con* with*);* to corrupt.
2 contagiarse VR **(a)** *(Med: enfermedad)* to be contagious *(t fig)*; **el mal ejemplo se contagia** a bad example is contagious *(o* catching*);* **la anarquía se contagia a otros** anarchy spreads to others.
(b) *(persona)* to become infected *(de* with*);* *(fig)* to become infected, become tainted *(de* with*);* **se contagió de un amigo** he caught it from a friend.
contagio NM infection, contagion; *(fig)* contagion, corruption; taint.

contagioso ADJ *enfermedad* contagious, infectious, catching; *persona* infected, infectious; *(fig)* catching; corrupting.
contáiner NM container.
contaje NM count, counting.
contaminación NF **(a)** *(gen)* contamination; *(de texto)* corruption; *(Liter)* influence; **~ del aire, ~ atmosférica** air pollution, atmospheric pollution; **~ ambiental** environmental pollution. **(b)** *(fig)* taint, infection; defilement.
contaminador(a) NM/F polluter.
contaminante NM pollutant.
contaminar [1a] 1 VT **(a)** *(gen)* to contaminate; *aire, agua* to pollute; *ropa* to soil; *texto* to corrupt; *(Liter)* to influence, affect.
(b) *(fig)* to taint, infect; to defile; *(Ecl)* to profane.
2 contaminarse VR to be(come) contaminated *(con, de* with, by*).*
contante ADJ: **dinero ~ (y sonante)** cash, ready money.
contar [1l] 1 VT **(a)** *(Mat)* to count; to number off; *dinero etc* to count (up); *(incluir)* to include, count in; **cuenta 18 años** she is 18; **~ con los dedos** to count on one's fingers; **hay 9 kms a ~ desde aquí** it's 9 kms starting from here.
(b) *(considerar)* to count, reckon, consider; **al niño le cuentan por medio** they count the child as half; **le cuento entre mis amigos** I reckon him among my friends; **sin ~** not counting, not including; except for; not to mention; **sin ~ con que ...** leaving aside the fact that ...
(c) *(recordar)* to remember, bear in mind; **cuenta que es más fuerte que tú** don't forget he's stronger than you are.
(d) *(narrar)* to tell; **es muy largo de ~** it's a long story; **¡cuéntaselo a tu abuela!*** *(etc)* tell that to the marines!; **¡a quien se lo cuentas!*** you're telling me!; **¿a mí me lo cuentas?*** *(iró)* so what?; **ya me contarás** you tell me how you see things; **una obra que no te voy a ~*** an indescribably fine work.
2 VI (a) *(Mat)* to count, count up; **hay que ~ mucho para llegar con la paga al final del mes** we have to go carefully *(o* watch it) in order to get to the end of the month; **cuentan por dos** he counts for *(o* as) two.
(b) *(fig: importar)* to count, matter; **esos puntos no cuentan** those points don't count; **no cuenta para nada** he doesn't count at all; **unas pocas equivocaciones no cuentan** a few errors don't matter.
(c) *(fiarse)* **~ con** to rely on, count on, depend on; to have; **cuenta conmigo** trust me, you can rely on me; **contaban por segura su ayuda** they were relying absolutely on his help, they thought he was sure to help them; **cuenta con varias ventajas** it has a number of advantages; **no contábamos con eso** we had not bargained for that, that was unexpected.
3 contarse VR **(a)** *(incluirse)* to be counted; to be included, to figure *(entre* among*);* **se le cuenta entre los más famosos** he is reckoned among the most famous; **me cuento entre sus admiradores** I count myself among his admirers.
(b) *(narrarse)* to be told; **cuéntase que ...** it is said that ..., it is related that ...; **¿qué te cuentas?*** how's things?*; **cuenta y no acaba de hablar** he never stops talking.
contemplación NF **(a)** *(gen)* contemplation; meditation, reflexion.
(b) **contemplaciones** indulgence; leniency, gentle treatment; **no andarse con contemplaciones** not to stand on ceremony; **tener demasiadas contemplaciones con uno** to be too indulgent towards sb, be too soft on sb; **no tiene contemplaciones en eso** he makes no compromises with that sort of thing; **tratar a uno con contemplaciones** to treat sb leniently; to handle sb with kid gloves; **no me vengas con contemplaciones** don't come to me with excuses; **sin contemplaciones** without ceremony; without any explanation.
▼ **contemplar** [1a] 1 VT **(a)** *(mirar)* to look at, gaze at, watch, contemplate; *(fig)* to contemplate.
(b) *(tratar bien)* to show (extra) consideration for, treat (too) indulgently, be (too) lenient with.
(c) *(tomar en cuenta)* to take account of, deal with; **la ley contempla los casos siguientes** the law provides for the following cases.
▼ **(d)** **~ + infin** to contemplate +*ger,* plan to +*infin,* foresee the possibility of +*ger.*
2 VI *(Rel)* to meditate.
contemplativo ADJ **(a)** *vida etc* contemplative. **(b)** *(indulgente)* indulgent *(con* towards*).*
contemporáneo 1 ADJ contemporary; contemporaneous.
2 NM, **contemporánea** NF contemporary.
contemporización NF hedging, temporizing; *(Pol)* appeasement.
contemporizador 1 ADJ excessively compliant; temporizing; lacking firm principles.
2 NM, **contemporizadora** NF timeserver, compromiser; person who lacks firm principles.
contemporizar [1f] VI to be compliant, show o.s. ready to compromise; *(pey)* to lack firm principles; to temporize; **~ con uno** to hedge with sb; *(Pol)* to appease sb.
contención NF **(a)** *(Mil etc)* containing, containment; **operación de**

~ holding operation. (**b**) (*restricción*) restraint; **sin** ~ freely, without restraint. (**c**) (*rivalidad*) contention; rivalry. (**d**) (*Jur*) suit.

contencioso [1] ADJ (**a**) *asunto* contentious; *persona* argumentative, captious. (**b**) (*Jur*) litigious.
[2] NM (*disputa*) dispute; (*problema*) problem; (*punto conflictivo*) point of disagreement.

contender [2g] VI to contend (*con* with, *sobre* over); to compete, be rivals (*en* in); (*Mil etc*) to fight; ~ **en unas oposiciones** to take part in a competitive examination.

contendiente NMF contestant, contender.

contenedor NM container; (*Náut*) container ship; ~ **de escombros** (builder's) skip; ~ **del vidrio** bottlebank.

contenedorización NF (*Com*) containerization.

contener [2k] [1] VT (**a**) *contenido* to hold, contain.
(**b**) (*Mil etc*) to contain; *turba* to hold back; *rebeldes* to keep down, hold down; *caballo* to hold back, restrain; *respiración* to hold; *emoción* to keep back, choke back, bottle up; *enojo* to contain; *bostezo, risa* to smother; *tendencia* to check, restrain, curb.
(**c**) (*Cono Sur: significar*) to mean.
[2] **contenerse** VR to control o.s., restrain o.s., hold o.s. in check.

contenerización NF containerization.

contenerizar [1f] VT to containerize.

contenido [1] ADJ (**a**) *persona* restrained, controlled; moderate; equable. (**b**) *emoción* suppressed.
[2] NM contents; content.

contenta NF (*Com*) endorsement; (*Mil*) good-conduct certificate; (*LAm Jur*) release, acknowledgement.

contentadizo ADJ (*t bien* ~) easy to please; **mal** ~ hard to please.

contentamente ADV contentedly.

contentamiento NM contentment, satisfaction.

contentar [1a] [1] VT (**a**) (*gen*) to satisfy, content; to please, make happy.
(**b**) (*Com*) to endorse.
(**c**) ~ **a dos personas** (*LAm*) to reconcile two people.
[2] **contentarse** VR (**a**) ~ **con** to be contented with, be satisfied with; ~ **con** + *infin* to content o.s. with + *ger*; **se contenta con cualquier cosita** he's satisfied with anything, any little thing keeps him happy.
(**b**) (*LAm: reconciliarse*) to be (*o* become) reconciled (*con* with).

▼ **contento** [1] ADJ (*satisfecho*) contented, satisfied; (*alegre*) pleased; glad, happy; **estar** ~ **con** (*o* **de**) to be satisfied with, be happy about, be content with; **están** ~**s con el coche** they are pleased with the car; **no está** ~ **en su trabajo** he's not happy in his work; **viven muy** ~**s** they live very happily; **¿estás** ~**?** are you happy?; **estar tan** ~ **como unas castañuelas** to be as happy as a lark; **para dejar** (*o* **poner, tener**) **a uno** ~ in order to keep sb happy; **estar** (*o* **quedar**) ~ **de** + *infin* to be content to + *infin*; **estaría tan** ~ **de** + *infin* I would as soon + *infin*.
[2] NM (**a**) (*alegría*) contentment; joy, happiness; **a** ~ to one's satisfaction; **no caber en sí de** ~ to be overjoyed, be overwhelmed with joy.
(**b**) (*Jur*) release, discharge (of a debt).

contentura NF (*CAm, Carib*) = **contento 2**.

conteo NM count, counting; (*Méx Dep*) count.

contera NF (**a**) (*Téc*) (metal) tip, end; ferrule. (**b**) (*fig*) small extra, small addition. (**c**) **por** ~ to crown it all, as a final blow.

contertuliano NM, **contertulio** NM fellow member (*of a social set*); ~**s de café** café companions, people who regularly meet in a café, members of the same coffee set.

contesta NF (*LAm*) answer.

contestable ADJ questionable, debatable.

contestación NF (**a**) (*respuesta*) answer, reply; ~ **a la demanda** (*Jur*) defence plea; **mala** ~ sharp retort, piece of backchat; **dejar una carta sin** ~ to leave a letter unanswered. (**b**) (*Pol*) protest; **movimiento de** ~ protest movement, (*fig*) rebellion.

contestado ADJ contentious, controversial.

contestador [1] ADJ (*LAm*) cheeky, saucy.
[2] NM: ~ **automático** answering machine, Ansaphone ®.

contestar [1a] [1] VTI (**a**) (*gen*) to answer, reply; (*replicar*) to answer back; ~ **una pregunta** (*Univ etc*) to answer a question; ~ **una carta** to reply to a letter; ~ **el teléfono** to answer the telephone; ~ **a un saludo** to return a greeting, respond to a greeting; **contestó que sí** he replied that it was (*o* he would *etc*); **abstenerse de** ~ to make no reply; (*encuesta*) **un 7 por 100 se abstuvo de** ~ there were 7% 'don't knows'.
(**b**) (*Jur: t* ~ **con**) to corroborate, confirm.
[2] VI (**a**) (*Méx*) to chat, talk; to argue.
(**b**) (*Pol*) to protest.

contestatario [1] ADJ rebellious; non-conformist, anti-establishment; contentious; **movimiento** ~ protest movement.
[2] NM, **contestataria** NF rebel; non-conformist, person of anti-establishment views; protester.

contesto NM (*And, Cono Sur, Méx*††) answer, reply.

contestón* ADJ given to answering back, argumentative.

contexto NM (**a**) (*Liter etc*) context. (**b**) (*Téc*) web, tangle.

contextualizar [1f] VT to provide a context for, set in a context.

contextura NF (**a**) (*gen*) contexture. (**b**) (*Anat*) build, physique; constitution; make-up.

contienda NF contest; struggle, fight.

contigo PRON with you; (††, *to God*) with thee; *V* **consigo.**

contigüidad NF nearness, closeness, contiguity.

contiguo ADJ next; adjacent (*a* to); contiguous (*a* to), adjoining; **en un cuarto** ~ in an adjoining room.

continencia NF continence.

continental ADJ continental.

continentalidad NF continental nature.

continente [1] ADJ continent.
[2] NM (**a**) (*Geog*) continent; **el viejo** ~ Europe, the Old World.
(**b**) (*recipiente*) container.
(**c**) (*fig*) air, mien, bearing; **de** ~ **distinguido** with an air of distinction; **de** ~ **duro** harsh-looking.

contingencia NF contingency; risk; hazard, danger.

contingentación NF quota system.

contingentado ADJ subject to a quota system.

contingentar [1a] VT to make subject to quotas; to fix quotas for.

contingente [1] ADJ contingent.
[2] NM (**a**) (*Mil etc*) contingent. (**b**) = **contingencia**. (**c**) (*Com etc*) quota; ~ **de importación** import quota.

▼ **continuación** NF continuation; sequel; **a** ~ then, next; immediately after; later (on), subsequently; **según lo expuesto a** ~ as set out below, as follows; **a** ~ **de** after, following.

continuamente ADV continuously; continually, constantly.

continuar [1e] [1] VT to continue, go on with; to resume; to carry on (with); *carretera etc* to continue, prolong, extend.
[2] VI (**a**) (*ir adelante*) to continue; to go on, carry on; **'continuará'** (*serie de TV etc*) 'to be continued'; ~ **hablando** to continue talking, continue to talk, go on talking; **continúa lloviendo** it's still raining; **la puerta continúa cerrada** the door is still shut; **continuaba en Noruega** he was still in Norway; he remained in Norway; ~ **con su trabajo** to continue (*o* go on) with one's work; ~ **con salud** to keep in good health; ~ **en su puesto** to stay at one's job, carry on with one's work.
(**b**) (*prolongarse*) to continue; **la carretera continúa más allá de la frontera** the road continues (on) beyond the frontier.

continuidad NF continuity.

continuismo NM (*Pol*) politics of continuity; wish for everything to go on as before; maintenance of the status quo.

continuista NMF person who maintains the status quo; loyal successor (*de* to).

continuo [1] ADJ (**a**) (*no interrumpido*) continuous; (*Téc*) *correa etc* endless; (*Elec*) *corriente* direct; *V* **acto, sesión.**
(**b**) (*constante*) continual, constant; **sus continuas quejas** his continual complaints.
(**c**) **a la continua, (de)** ~ continually.
[2] NM (*t* **contínuum**) continuum.

contonearse [1a] VR (*hombre*) to swagger, strut; (*mujer*) to swing one's hips, walk with a waggle; to walk affectedly, show off as one walks.

contoneo NM swagger, strut; hip-swinging, waggle; affected gait.

contorcerse [2b *y* 2h] VR to writhe, twist.

contorno NM (**a**) (*perfil*) outline (*t Arte*); (*Geog*) contour; (*perímetro*) perimeter; (*forma*) form, shape; (*de moneda*) edge, rim; **en** ~ round about, all around.
(**b**) (*medida*) measurement round, distance round; ~ **de un árbol** girth of a tree, distance round a tree's trunk; **el** ~ **de cintura es de 26 pulgadas** her waist measurement is 26 inches.
(**c**) ~**s** environs, neighbourhood, surrounding area; **Caracas y sus** ~**s** Caracas and its environs; **en estos** ~**s** in these parts, hereabouts.

contorsión NF contortion.

contorsionarse [1a] VR to contort o.s.

contorsionista NMF contortionist.

▼ **contra** [1] ADV (**a**) against; **puntos en** ~ points against; **hablar en** ~ to speak against; **votar en** ~ to vote against; **opinar en** ~ to disagree, take the contrary view.
(**b**) **de** ~ (*LAm*) extra, over and above.
(**c**) (*LAm*) **en** ~ **nuestra** (*etc*), **en nuestra** ~ (*etc*) against us (*etc*).
[2] PREP (*gen*) against; (*enfrente*) opposite, facing; (*Com: giro*) on; **apoyar algo** ~ **la pared** to lean sth against the wall; **en** ~ **de** against; **hablar en** ~ **de un proyecto** to speak against a plan; **en** ~ **de lo que habíamos pensado** contrary to what we had thought; **ir en** ~ **de algo** to go against sth, run counter to sth.
[3] NM (**a**) con; *V* **pro.**
(**b**) (*Nicaragua*) counter-revolutionary, Contra (guerrilla).
[4] NF (**a**) (*Esgrima*) counter.
(**b**) (*pega*) trouble, snag; inconvenience.

(c) hacer la ~ to be consistently obstructive, persist in taking an opposite view; **llevar la ~ a uno** to oppose sb, contradict sb.
(d) (*LAm Med*) antidote.
(e) (*Bridge*) double.
(f) la ~ (*Nicaragua*) the Contras.
contra... PREF counter-..., contra...; cross-...; **~manifestación** counter-demonstration; **~propaganda** counter-propaganda.
contra(a)lmirante NM rear admiral.
contra(a)menaza NF counter-threat.
contra(a)rgumento NM counter-argument.
contra(a)tacar [1g] VTI to counter-attack.
contra(a)taque NM counter-attack.
contrabajista NMF double-bass player, contrabassist; (*de rock*) bass guitarist.
contrabajo NM **(a)** (*instrumento, músico*) double bass; (*rock*) bass guitar. **(b)** (*cantante, voz*) low bass, contrabasso.
contrabalancear [1a] VT to counterbalance.
contrabalanza NF counterbalance.
contrabandear [1a] VI to smuggle, live by smuggling.
contrabandista NMF smuggler; **~ de armas** gun-runner.
contrabando NM **(a)** (*acto*) smuggling; **~ de armas** gun-running. **(b)** (*mercancías*) contraband, smuggled goods; (*artículo*) prohibited article, banned item; **géneros de ~** smuggled goods; **amores de ~** (*fig*) clandestine love affair; **pasar** (*o* **introducir**) **algo de ~** to smuggle sth in, get sth in illegally.
contracampaña NF counter-campaign.
contracargo NM counter-charge.
contracarro ATR: **defensas ~** anti-tank defences.
contracción NF **(a)** (*gen*) contraction; shrinkage; wasting. **(b)** (*And: aplicación*) diligence, industry.
contracepción NF contraception.
contraceptivo ADJ, NM contraceptive.
contrachapado [1] ADJ: **madera contrachapada = 2.** [2] NM plywood.
contracifra NF key (to a code).
contracorriente NF cross-current; undercurrent; **ir a ~** to go against the current, go upstream; (*fig*) to go against the tide.
contráctil ADJ contractile.
contractual ADJ contractual.
contractualmente ADV contractually.
contractura NF muscular contraction.
contracubierta NF back cover (*of book*).
contracultura NF counter-culture; alternative society.
contracultural ADJ of the counter-culture, alternative.
contracurva NF (*Aut*) second bend, bend the other way.
contradecir [3o] VT to contradict.
contradicción NF contradiction; (*fig*) incompatibility; **~ de** (*o* **en los**) **términos** contradiction in terms; **espíritu de ~** contrariness; **A y B están en ~** A and B stand in contradiction to each other.
contradictorio ADJ contradictory.
contradique NM outer harbour wall.
contradón NM reciprocal gift.
contraejemplo NM counter-example.
contraempuje NM counter-thrust.
contraer [2o] [1] VT **(a)** (*encoger*) *materia, sustancia etc* to contract; to shrink, to make smaller (*o* tighter *etc*); *discurso, texto* to condense, shorten; **~ la frente** to wrinkle one's brow; **la humedad contrae las cuerdas** the damp makes the ropes tauten. **(b)** (*adquirir*) *deuda, obligación etc* to contract; *costumbre* to acquire, pick up, get into; *enfermedad* to contract, catch; **~ matrimonio** to marry (*con una sb*); **~ parentesco con** to become related to. **(c)** (*restringir*) to restrict, limit (*a* to); **contrae su teoría a ciertos puntos** he limits his theory to certain points. [2] **contraerse** VR **(a)** (*encogerse*) to contract; to shrink; to get smaller; to tighten, tauten. **(b) ~ a** to limit o.s. to.
contraespionaje NM counter-espionage, counter-intelligence.
contraetiqueta NF second label, label on the back (*of the bottle*).
contrafallar [1a] VT to overtrump.
contrafuerte NM (*Arquit*) buttress; (*Mil*) outwork; (*Geog*) spur; foothill; (*de zapato*) heel-pad, heel-stiffener.
contragambito NM counter-gambit.
contragolpe NM counter-blow; (*fig*) backlash, reaction, kickback; (*Dep*) counter-attack.
contragolpear [1a] VI to strike back.
contrahacer [2r] VT (*copiar*) to copy, imitate; *moneda* to counterfeit; *documento, prueba* to forge, fake; *libro* to pirate; *persona* to mimic, impersonate, do an impression of.
contrahaz NM (*de paño*) wrong side.
contrahecho ADJ **(a)** (*gen*) counterfeit; fake, faked, forged; spurious, pirated. **(b)** (*Anat*) hunchbacked, deformed.
contrahechura NF counterfeit; forgery, fake; pirated edition, spuri-

ous edition.
contraído ADJ **(a)** (*encogido*) contracted; shrunken, wasted. **(b)** (*And: trabajador*) diligent, industrious.
contraimagen NF mirror image; (*pey*) negative image.
contraincendios ATR: **aparato ~** fire-prevention apparatus, fire-alarm system.
contraindicación NF (*Med*) counter-indication.
contrainformación NF disinformation.
contrainforme NM counter-report.
contrainsurgencia NF counter-insurgency.
contrainteligencia NF counter-intelligence.
contrairritante NM counterirritant.
contralor NM (*real*) comptroller; (*LAm*) treasury inspector.
contraloría NF (*LAm*) treasury inspector's office; accounts office.
contralto [1] ADJ contralto. [2] NM counter tenor. [3] NF contralto.
contraluz NM view against the light; **a ~** against the light.
contramaestre NM (*Náut*) warrant officer; boatswain; (*Téc*) foreman.
contramandar [1a] VT to countermand.
contramandato NM counter-order.
contramanifestación NF counter-demonstration.
contramano: **a ~** ADV in the wrong direction, the wrong way; **eso queda a ~** that's in the other direction.
contramarcha NF **(a)** (*Mil*) countermarch. **(b)** (*Aut etc*) reverse; **dar ~** **(a)** to reverse, (*fig*) go into reverse.
contramarchar [1a] VI to countermarch.
contramatar [1a] [1] VT: **~ a uno** (*LAm*) to bang sb against the wall. [2] **contramatarse** VR **(a)** (*LAm*) to crash into sth, collide with sth. **(b) ~ de + infin** (*Méx*) to repent of (*o* regret) + ger.
contramedida NF counter-measure.
contranatural ADJ unnatural.
contraofensiva NF counter-offensive.
contraoferta NF counter-offer.
contraorden NF counter-order.
contrapartida NF **(a)** (*Com, Fin*) balancing entry. **(b)** (*fig*) compensation; counter-weight; **pero como ~ añade que ...** but in contrast she adds that ...; **como ~ de** as compensation for; as a counter-weight to; **dar algo de ~** to give sth in return (*de* for).
contrapelo: **a ~** ADV **(a) acariciar un gato a ~** to stroke a cat the wrong way. **(b)** (*fig*) **a ~** the wrong way; against the grain; **a ~ de** against, counter to; **todo lo hace a ~** he does everything the wrong way round; **intervino muy a ~** he spoke up in a most unfortunate way, he chose quite the wrong way in which to intervene.
contrapesar [1a] VT to counterbalance (*con* with); to counterweigh; (*fig*) to offset; to balance, compensate for.
contrapeso NM **(a)** (*lit*) counterpoise, counterweight; (*Com*) make-weight; (*Circo*) balancing pole. **(b)** (*fig*) counterweight.
contrapié: **a ~** ADV with the wrong foot; awkwardly.
contrapoder NM anti-establishment movement.
contraponer [2q] VT **(a)** *dos colores etc* to compare, set against each other. **(b) ~ A a B** to set up A against B, put up A as a barrier against B; **a esta idea ellos contraponen su teoría de que ...** against this idea they set up their theory that ...
contraportada NF inside cover (*of book*).
contraposición NF comparison; contrast, clash; **en ~ a** in contrast to; **pero en ~, ...** but on the other hand, ...
contraprestación NF compensation; consideration.
contraproducente ADJ self-defeating; counter-productive; **tener un resultado ~** to have a boomerang effect, boomerang; **es ~ +infin** it is worse than useless to +infin, it is a mistake to +infin.
contraproductivo ADJ counterproductive.
contraprogramación NF (*TV*) competitive programme scheduling.
contraprogramar [1a] VI (*TV*) to set competitive schedules.
contrapropuesta NF counter-proposal.
contrapuerta NF inner door; second door.
contrapuesto ADJ *intereses* conflicting, opposing.
contrapuntear [1a] VI (*And*) to compete in a verse duel; (*fig*) to compete.
contrapunteo NM (*And, Carib, Cono Sur: riña*) argument, quarrel; (*And, Cono Sur: liter* ††) improvised verse duel; (*And, Carib, Cono Sur: debate*) debate; **en ~** (*And*) in competition.
contrapuntístico ADJ contrapuntal; (*fig*) contrasting.
contrapunto NM **(a)** (*lit*) counterpoint. **(b)** (*LAm: concurso de poesía*) poetic competition with improvised verses; **de ~** in competition.
contrariado ADJ upset, annoyed, put out.
contrariamente ADV: **~ a lo que habíamos pensado** contrary to what we had thought.
contrariar [1c] VT **(a)** (*oponerse a*) to oppose, be opposed to, go against; (*contradecir*) to contradict; (*estorbar*) to impede, thwart. **(b)**

(*fastidiar*) to vex, upset, annoy.

contrariedad NF (**a**) (*obstáculo*) obstacle; (*desgracia*) setback, misfortune; (*pega*) snag, trouble.
(**b**) (*disgusto*) vexation, annoyance; **producir ~ a uno** to upset sb, cause annoyance to sb.
(**c**) (*oposición*) contrary nature; opposition.

▼ **contrario** ① ADJ (**a**) (*carácter*) opposed, different; **son ~s en sus aficiones** they have opposing tastes, they differ widely in tastes.
(**b**) *dirección, lado etc* opposite; **en sentido ~** the other way, in the other direction.
(**c**) *sentido* opposite (*de* to); **se ha interpretado en sentido ~ del que realmente tiene** it has been interpreted in the opposite sense to its true one.
(**d**) (*opuesto*) contrary (*a* to); harmful, damaging, hostile (*a* to); **~ a los intereses del país** contrary to the nation's interests.
(**e**) *viento etc* contrary; *fortuna* adverse.
(**f**) (*opinión*) opposed; **él es ~ a las reformas** he is opposed to the reforms, he is against the changes.
▼ (**g**) (*frases*) **al ~, por el ~** on the contrary; **al ~ de** unlike; **al ~ de lo que habíamos pensado** against what we had thought; **todo salió al ~ de lo que habíamos previsto** it all turned out differently from what we had expected; **lo ~** the opposite, the reverse; **de lo ~** otherwise; were it not so; **todo lo ~** quite the reverse; **llevar la contraria** to maintain an opposite point of view; to oppose sth systematically; **llevar la contraria a uno** to oppose sb, contradict sb.
② NM, **contraria** NF enemy, adversary; (*Dep, Jur etc*) opponent; **la contraria*** my other half, my old woman*.
③ NM obstacle, snag.

contrarreembolso NM cash on delivery.

Contrarreforma NF Counter-Reformation.

contrarreloj ① ADV against the clock.
② ATR: **prueba ~ = 3**.
③ NF time trial; race against the clock.

contrarréplica NF rejoinder.

contrarreplicar [1g] VI to answer back.

contrarrestar [1a] VT (**a**) (*compensar*) to counteract, offset, balance; *efectos* to counter, counteract. (**b**) *pelota* to return.

contrarrevolución NF counter-revolution.

contrarrevolucionario, -a ADJ, NM/F counter-revolutionary.

contrasentido NM (**a**) (*gen*) contradiction; (*falta de lógica*) illogicality; (*inconsecuencia*) inconsistency; (*disparate*) piece of nonsense; **aquí hay un ~** there is a contradiction here; **es un ~ que él actúe así** it doesn't make sense for him to act like that.
(**b**) (*Liter*) misinterpretation; mistranslation.

contraseña NF (**a**) (*gen*) countersign, secret mark; counter-mark; (*Mil etc*) watchword, password. (**b**) (*Teat:* **~ de salida**) pass-out ticket.

contrastar [1a] ① VT (**a**) (*resistir*) to resist.
(**b**) *metal* to assay; to hallmark; *medidas, pesas* to verify; *radio to* monitor; *hechos* to check, confirm, document.
② VI (**a**) (*hacer contraste*) to contrast, form a contrast (*con* with).
(**b**) **~ a, ~ con, ~ contra** (*resistir*) to resist; (*hacer frente a*) to face up to.

▼ **contraste** NM (**a**) (*gen*) contrast (*t TV*); **~ de pareceres** difference of opinion; **en ~ con** in contrast to; **por ~** in contrast; **hacer ~ con** to contrast with.
(**b**) (*Téc*) assay; verification; (**marca del**) **~** hallmark; (*oficina*) assay office.
(**c**) (*persona*) inspector of weights and measures; (*oficina*) weights and measures office.

contrata NF contract(ing).

contratación NF signing-up; hiring, contracting; (†) trade.

contratante NMF (*Com*) contractor; (*Jur*) contracting party.

contratar [1a] ① VT *mercancías etc* to contract for; to negotiate for; to sign a contract for; *trabajo* to put out to contract; *arriendo etc* to take on; *persona* to hire, engage; *jugador etc* to sign up.
② **contratarse** VR (*jugador etc*) to sign on; **~ para hacer algo** to contract to do sth.

contratenor NM counter-tenor.

contraterrorismo NM counter-terrorism; campaign against terrorism.

contraterrorista ADJ: **medidas ~s** measures against terrorism, anti-terrorist measures.

contratiempo NM (**a**) (*revés*) setback, reverse, contretemps; (*accidente*) mishap, accident. (**b**) (*Mús*) **a ~** offbeat, syncopated.

contratista NMF contractor; **~ de obras** building contractor, builder.

contrato NM contract (*de* for), agreement; **~ de arrendamiento** rental agreement; **~ basura** mickey-mouse contract; **~ bilateral** bilateral agreement; **~ de mantenimiento** maintenance contract, service agreement; **~ de sociedad** deed of partnership; **~ verbal** verbal agreement.

contratuerca NF locknut.

contravalor NM exchange value.

contravención NF contravention, infringement, violation.

contraveneno NM antidote (*de* to).

contravenir [3r] VT: **~ a** to contravene, infringe, violate.

contraventana NF shutter.

contrayendo V contraer.

contrayente NMF: **los ~s** the bride and groom.

contribución NF (**a**) (*gen*) contribution; **poner a ~** to make use of, put to use, draw upon.
(**b**) (*Fin*) tax; **contribuciones** taxes, taxation; **~ directa** direct tax; **~ municipal, ~ territorial urbana** rates; **exento de contribuciones** free of tax, tax-free, tax-exempt (*US*); **pagar las contribuciones** to pay one's taxes (o rates).

contribuidor(a) NM/F contributor.

contribuir [3g] VTI (**a**) (*gen*) to contribute (*a, para* to, towards); **~ con una cantidad** to contribute a sum; **~ al éxito de algo** to contribute to (o help towards) the success of sth; **~ a** + *infin* to help to + *infin*.
(**b**) (*Fin*) to pay (in taxes).

contribuyente NMF contributor; (*Fin*) taxpayer.

contrición NF contrition.

contrincante NM opponent, rival.

contristar [1a] ① VT to sadden.
② **contristarse** VR to grow sad, grieve.

contrito ADJ contrite.

control NM (**a**) (*gen*) control; **bajo ~** under control; **fuera de ~** out of control; **perder el ~** to lose control (of o.s.); **perder ~ de** to lose control of; **~ de alquileres** rent control; **~ armamentista** arms control; **~ de cambio** exchange control; **~ de la circulación** traffic control; point duty; **~ de costos** cost control; **~ de créditos** credit control; **~ de la demanda** demand management; **~ a distancia, ~ remoto** remote control; **~ de (la) natalidad** birth control; **~ de precios** price-control; **~ presupuestario** budget control; **~ de sí mismo** self-control; **~ de tonalidad** tone control; **~ de volumen** volume control.
(**b**) (*acto*) inspection, check, checking; (*Com, Fin*) audit(ing); (*Aut: de rallye*) checkpoint; (*de policía*) road-block; **~ antidoping** drug test, test for drugs; **~ de (la) calidad** quality control; **~ de carretera** checkpoint; **~ de frontera** frontier checkpoint; **~ nuclear** nuclear inspection; **~ de pasaportes** passport inspection; **montar un ~** to set up a roadblock.

controladamente ADV in a controlled way.

controlador(a) NM/F controller; (*LAm Ferro*) inspector, ticket-collector; **~ de estacionamiento** traffic warden; **~ (de tráfico) aéreo** air-traffic controller.

controlar [1a] VT (**a**) (*regir*) to control. (**b**) (*comprobar*) to inspect, check; (*vigilar*) to supervise; to keep an eye on; *conversación, radio etc* to monitor; (*Com, Fin*) to audit.

controversia NF controversy.

controversial ADJ controversial.

controvertible ADJ controversial; debatable, disputable.

controvertido ADJ controversial.

controvertir [3i] ① VT to dispute, question; to argue about.
② VI to argue.

contubernio NM (**a**) (*confabulación*) ring, conspiracy; (*connivencia*) collusion. (**b**) (*cohabitación*) cohabitation.

contumacia NF obstinacy, stubborn disobedience; contumaciousness; perversity; (*Jur*) contempt (of court); contumacy.

contumaz ADJ (**a**) (*terco*) obstinate, stubbornly disobedient; *perverso etc* wayward, perverse; (*bebedor*) inveterate, hardened, incorrigible; (*Jur*) guilty of contempt (of court); contumacious.
(**b**) (*Med*) disease-carrying, germ-laden.

contumazmente ADV obstinately; perversely; contumaciously.

contumelia NF contumely.

contumerioso ADJ (*CAm*) finicky, fussy.

contundencia NF forcefulness, power; conclusive nature; crushing nature; strictness, severity; toughness; aggressive nature.

contundente ADJ (**a**) *arma* offensive, for striking a blow with; **instrumento ~** blunt instrument.
(**b**) (*fig*) *argumento etc* forceful, convincing, powerful; *prueba* conclusive; *tono* forceful; *derrota etc* crushing, overwhelming; *arbitraje etc* strict, severe; *juego* tough, hard; aggressive; *efecto* severe.

contundir [3a] VT to bruise, contuse.

conturbar [1a] ① VT to trouble, dismay, perturb.
② **conturbarse** VR to be troubled, be dismayed, become perturbed.

contusión NF bruise, bruising, contusion.

contusionar [1a] VT to bruise; to hurt, damage.

contuso ADJ bruised.

conuco NM (*And, Carib*) smallholding, small farm.

conuquero NM (*And, Carib*) smallholder, farmer.

conurbación NF conurbation.

convalecencia NF convalescence.

convalecer [2d] VI to convalesce, get better (*de* after), recover (*de* from).

convaleciente ADJ, NMF convalescent.

convalidable ADJ which can be validated.

convalidación NF acceptance, recognition; validation; ratification, confirmation.

convalidar [1a] VT *título* to accept, recognize; to validate; *documento* to ratify, confirm.

convección NF convection.

convecino, -a NM/F (close) neighbour.

convectivo ADJ convective.

convector NM convector.

▼ **convencer** [2b] **1** VT to convince; to persuade; **~ a uno de que algo es mejor** to convince sb sth is better; **~ a uno para que haga algo** to persuade sb to do sth; **no me convence del todo** I'm not fully convinced; **no me convence ese tío** I don't really trust that chap.
2 VI to convince; **el argumento no convence** the argument does not convince (o is not convincing).
3 **convencerse** VR to become convinced; **¡convéncete!** believe you me!; I tell you it is so!; you'll have to get used to the idea!

convencido ADJ *pacifista, cristiano, católico* committed, convinced; **estar ~ de algo** to be convinced of sth, be certain of sth.

convencimiento NM **(a)** *(acto)* convincing; persuasion.
(b) *(certeza)* conviction, certainty; **llegar al ~ de** to become convinced of; **llevar algo al ~ de uno** to convince sb of sth; **tener el ~ de que ...** to be convinced that ...

convención NF convention; **C~ de Ginebra** Geneva Convention.

convencional ADJ conventional.

convencionalismo NM conventionalism.

convencionero ADJ *(And, Méx)* comfort-loving, self-indulgent.

convencionista NMF *(Méx) follower of Convención movement led by Zapata and Villa (1914-15).*

convenible ADJ **(a)** *(apropiado)* suitable; fitting; *precio* fair, reasonable.
(b) *persona* accommodating.

conveniencia NF **(a)** *(aptitud)* suitability, fitness; *(provecho)* usefulness, advantageousness; expediency; advisability; **a la primera ~** at one's earliest opportunity, when convenient; **ser de la ~ de uno** to suit sb; **atender a la propia ~** to think of how sth will affect one.
(b) **~s** conventions *(t ~s sociales)*; proprieties, decencies.
(c) *(acuerdo)* agreement.
(d) *(puesto)* domestic post, job as a servant.
(e) **~s** *(Fin) (propiedad)* property; *(renta)* income; *(de criado)* perquisites.

conveniente ADJ *(apto)* suitable; *(correcto)* fit, fitting, proper; *(provechoso)* useful, profitable, advantageous; *(oportuno)* expedient; *(aconsejable)* advisable; **nada ~** unsuitable; **no es ~ que ...** it is not advisable that ...; it is not desirable that ...; **sería ~ que ...** it would be a good thing if ..., it would be an advantage if ...; **creer** (o **estimar, juzgar**) **~** to think fit, see fit; **juzgar ~ + infin** to see fit to + *infin*, deem it wise to + *infin*.

convenio NM agreement, treaty, convenant; **~ colectivo** collective bargain, general wages agreement; **~ comercial** trade agreement; **~ salarial** wages agreement.

▼ **convenir** [3r] **1** VI **(a)** *(estar de acuerdo)* to agree *(con with, en about)*; **~ (en) hacer algo** to agree to do sth; **~ (en) que ...** to agree that ...; **'sueldo a ~'** *(anuncio)* 'salary to be agreed'.
▼**(b)** *(ser adecuado)* to suit, be suited to; to be suitable for; to be good for; **si le conviene** if it suits you; **no me conviene** it's not in my interest, it's not worth my while; **me conviene quedarme aquí** it is best for me to stay here; **él no te conviene para marido** he's not the husband for you; **lo que más le conviene es un reposo completo** the best thing for him is complete rest.
▼**(c)** *(impers)* **conviene + infin** it is as well to + *infin*; it is important to + *infin*; **conviene recordar que ...** it is as well to remember that ..., it is to be remembered that ...; **no conviene que se publique eso** it is not desirable that that should be published; **conviene a saber** namely, that is.
2 **convenirse** VR to agree, come to an agreement *(en on, about)*.

conventillero *(And, Cono Sur)* **1** ADJ gossipy.
2 NM, **conventillera** NF scandalmonger, gossip, telltale.

conventillo NM *(And, Cono Sur)* tenement, inner-city slum.

convento NM monastery; **~ (de monjas)** convent, nunnery.

conventual ADJ conventual.

convergencia NF **(a)** *(lit)* convergence. **(b)** *(fig)* common tendency, common direction; concurrence; **~ de izquierdas** *(Pol)* grouping (o coming together) of left-wing forces.

convergente ADJ **(a)** *(lit)* convergent, converging. **(b)** *(fig)* having a common tendency, tending in the same direction. **(c)** *(Pol)* of the Catalan party Convergència i Unió.

convergentemente ADV: **~ con** together with, jointly with.

converger [2c] VI, **convergir** [3c] VI **(a)** *(lit)* to converge *(en on)*.
(b) *(fig)* to have a common tendency, tend in the same direction

(con as); to concur, be in accord *(con* with); *(Pol etc)* to come together; **sus esfuerzos convergen a un fin común** their efforts have a common purpose, their efforts are directed towards the same objective.

conversa¹ NF *(esp LAm) (charla)* talk, chat; *(lisonjas)* smooth talk.

conversación NF conversation, talk; **cambiar de ~** to change the subject; **trabar ~ con uno** to get into conversation with sb.

conversacional ADJ *tono etc* conversational; *estilo* colloquial.

conversada NF *(LAm)* talk, chat.

conversador **1** ADJ *(LAm)* talkative, chatty.
2 NM, **conversadora** NF **(a)** *(persona locuaz)* conversationalist. **(b)** *(LAm: zalamero)* smooth talker.

conversar [1a] **1** VT **(a)** *(And, Cono Sur) (contar)* to tell, relate; *(informar)* to report. **(b)** *(Carib: ligar)* to chat up*.
2 VI **(a)** *(charlar)* to talk, converse. **(b)** *(Mil)* to wheel.

conversata NF *(Cono Sur)* talk, chat.

conversión NF **(a)** *(gen)* conversion. **(b)** *(Mil)* wheel.

converso **1** ADJ converted.
2 NM, **conversa²** NF convert; *(Hist: esp)* converted Jew(ess), converted Moor; *see also* RECONQUISTA .

conversón *(And)* **1** ADJ talkative, gossiping.
2 NM, **conversona** NF talkative person, gossip.

conversor NM *(Rad)* converter.

convertibilidad NF convertibility.

convertible ADJ convertible.

convertidor NM converter; **~ catalítico** catalytic converter.

convertir [3i] **1** VT **(a)** *(gen)* to convert *(t Ecl)*; to transform, turn *(en* into); *(Com, Elec, Téc)* to convert; *dinero* to convert, change *(en* into); **~ a uno al catolicismo** to convert sb to Catholicism.
(b) *ojos etc* to turn *(a* on).
2 **convertirse** VR to be converted, be transformed, be changed *(en* into); *(Ecl)* to be converted, convert *(a* to).

convexidad NF convexity.

convexo ADJ convex.

convicción NF conviction.

convicto **1** ADJ convicted, found guilty; condemned.
2 NM *(LAm)* convict.

convidada NF round *(esp* of drinks); **dar una ~, pagar una ~** to stand a round.

convidado, -a NM/F guest.

convidar [1a] **1** VT **(a)** *(lit)* to invite; **~ a uno a hacer algo** to invite sb to do sth; **~ a uno a una cerveza** to stand sb a beer, treat sb to a beer, invite sb to have a beer; **~ a uno con un café** to offer sb a cup of coffee.
(b) *(fig)* **~ a** to stir to, move to; **el ambiente convida a la meditación** the setting invites one to indulge in meditation, the atmosphere is conducive to meditation.
2 **convidarse*** VR **(a)** *(invitarse)* to invite o.s. along.
(b) *(ofrecerse)* to volunteer, offer one's services.

▼ **convincente** ADJ convincing.

convincentemente ADV convincingly.

convite NM **(a)** *(acto)* invitation. **(b)** *(función)* banquet, feast; treat; party; **~ a escote** Dutch treat.

convivencia NF **(a)** living together, life together; good fellowship, socializing; **'~ en familia'** *(anuncio)* 'living with a family', 'live as family'. **(b)** *(Pol)* coexistence.

convivencial ADJ social; communal; community *(atr)*.

conviviente NMF *(LAm)* live-in lover.

convivir [3a] VI to live together *(esp* amicably, in harmony); to share the same life; *(Pol)* to coexist; *(fig)* to exist side by side *(con* with).

convocación NF summoning, calling, convoking.

convocante NMF organizer; promoter.

convocar [1g] **1** VT to summon, call (together), convoke; *elecciones, huelga* to call.
2 VI: **~ a** to call for.

convocatoria NF **(a)** *(llamamiento)* summons, call (to a meeting); notice of a meeting; **'C~s para hoy'** *(Prensa)* 'Today's Meetings'; **~ de huelga** strike call; **~ de premio** announcement of a prize competition. **(b)** = **convocación**.

convólvulo NM convolvulus.

convoy NM **(a)** *(Náut)* convoy; *(Ferro)* train; (*) procession; retinue. **(b)** *(vinagrera)* cruet, cruet stand. **(c)** *(Carib: ensalada)* salad.

convoyar [1a] **1** VT **(a)** *(escoltar)* to convoy; to guard, escort. **(b)** *(Cono Sur: financiar)* to back, sponsor.
2 **convoyarse** VR *(Carib)* to connive together, plot.

convulsión NF convulsion; upheaval.

convulsionar [1a] VT *(Med)* to produce convulsions in; *(fig)* to convulse, cause an upheaval in.

convulsivo ADJ convulsive; disturbed, distraught.

convulso ADJ convulsed *(de* with).

conyugal ADJ conjugal; married.

conyugalidad NF married life.

▶ LENGUA Y USO: **convencer: 1** → 39.2, 43.1, 53.6 **convenir: 1b** → 28.1, 29.2 **1c** → 28.1 **convincente** → 53.4

cónyuge NMF spouse; partner; husband o wife; **~s** (*frec*) spouses; married couple, husband and wife.

cónyuges NMFPL spouses; married couple, husband and wife.

coña: NF (a) (*guasa*) humour, humorous tone, joking way; **en ~** as a joke, for a laugh; **¡ni de ~!** no way!*; **y esto no es ~** and this is no joke, and this is serious; **estar de ~** to be in a joking mood; **tomar algo a ~** to take sth as a joke. (b) (*molestia*) annoyance, bind*; **¡es la ~!** it's beyond a joke!

coñá = **coñac**.

coñac [koˈɲa] NM, PL **coñacs** [koˈɲas] brandy, cognac.

coñazo: NM (a) (*persona, cosa*) pain*; **ponerse ~** to get stroppy*. (b) **dar el ~** to be a real pain*.

coñe: EXCL = **coño** (b).

coñearse: [1a] VR to speak in a joking way, adopt a humorous tone; **~ de** to make fun of.

coñete: ADJ (*And, Cono Sur*) stingy, tightfisted.

coño NM (a) (✱ *Anat*) cunt✱✱.
(b) EXCL (✱) (*t* **¡qué ~!**: *enojo*) hell!, damn!, damn it all!; (*sorpresa*) well I'm damned!, Christ!; (*alegría*) **¡esto hay que celebrarlo, ~!** we jolly well must celebrate this!*; (*a persona*) **¡ayúdeme, ~!** help me, you idiot!; **¡por fin, ~!** and it was bloody well time!:
(c) (✱: *como adv*) **¿qué ~(s) haces ahí?** what in hell's name are you up to?*; **¿qué ~ te importa?** why the hell does it matter to you?
(d) (✱: *locuciones*) **¡ay, qué ~!** what a pain!*; **¡qué libro ni qué ~!** what bloody book!:; **que lo haga él ... ¡qué ~!** let him do it ... no way!*; **viven en el quinto ~** they live way out (in the sticks)*, they live at the back of beyond*.
(e) (*Cono Sur, Méx: español*) pejorative term applied to Spaniards.

cooficial ADJ: **dos lenguas ~es** two languages equally recognized as official.

cooficialidad NF: **la ~ de dos lenguas** the equal official status of two languages.

cooperación NF cooperation.

cooperador [1] ADJ cooperative; collaborating, participating.
[2] NM, **cooperadora** NF collaborator, co-worker.

cooperante NMF (overseas) voluntary worker.

cooperar [1a] VI to cooperate (*a, en* in; *con* with); **~ a** + *infin* to cooperate in + *ger*; **~ a un mismo fin** to work for a common aim, work together in a common cause; **~ en** to collaborate in, work together on, take part (together) in; **los factores que cooperaron al fracaso** the factors which together led to failure, the factors which contributed to the failure.

cooperativa NF cooperative, mutual association; **~ agrícola** agricultural cooperative; **~ de crédito** credit union.

cooperativismo NM cooperativism; (*como movimiento*) cooperative movement.

cooperativista NMF member of a cooperative.

cooperativización NF cooperativisation.

cooperativizar [1f] VT to cooperativize.

cooperativo ADJ cooperative.

cooptación NF cooption.

cooptar [1a] VT to coopt (*a* on to).

coordenada NF (*Mat*) coordinate.

coordinación NF coordination.

coordinado [1] ADJ coordinated; (*Mil*) *operación* combined.
[2] **~s** NMPL (*ropa*) separates.

coordinador(a)¹ NM/F coordinator.

coordinadora² NF coordinating committee.

coordinar [1a] VT to coordinate.

copa NF (a) (*vaso*) glass; (*poét*) goblet; (*Dep etc*) cup, trophy; **~ balón** brandy glass; **~ flauta** champagne glass; **C~ Mundial** World Cup; **llevar una ~ de más** to have (had) one over the eight; **irse de ~s, salir de ~s** to go out for a drink; **tomarse unas ~s** to have a drink or two.
(b) (*fig*) **~ de la amargura** cup of sorrow; **apurar la ~** to know the utmost depths of suffering.
(c) (*de sombrero*) crown; (*de árbol*) top.
(d) **~s** hearts; **la ~** the ace of hearts.
(e) (*And: conocedor*) connoisseur, judge of wine.
(f) (*And Aut*) hubcap.

copado ADJ *árbol* thick, with dense foliage.

copal NM (*CAm, Méx*) resin, incense.

copante NM (*CAm, Méx*) **~s** stepping stones.

copar [1a] VT (a) (*Mil*) to surround, cut off; (*fig*) to corner; **quedar copado en un trabajo** to get bogged down in a piece of work.
(b) (*Naipes: t ~ la banca*) to win (all the tricks), sweep the board; (*en el juego*) to go banco; (*Pol y fig*) to sweep the board, win hands down; *premio* to walk off with, collar*; **~ el mercado** to corner the market (*de* in).
(c) (*Méx: monopolizar*) to monopolize.

coparticipación NF joint participation (*en* in).

copartícipe NMF (*socio*) partner; (*Dep etc*) fellow participant, fellow competitor; (*condueño*) joint owner; (*colaborador*) collaborator (*en* in).

copazo* NM mixed drink of e.g. rum and Coke.

COPE NF ABR *de* **Cadena de Ondas Populares Españolas** *private radio station*.

copear [1a] VI (a) (✱: *beber*) to booze*, tipple; to go on a drinking spree. (b) (*Com*) to sell wine (*etc*) by the glass.

Copei NM (*Venezuela*) ABR *de* **Comité Organizador para Elecciones Independientes** *Christian Democrat party*.

Copenhague NM Copenhagen.

copeo* NM: **ir de ~** to go drinking.

Copérnico NM Copernicus.

copete NM (a) (*de persona*) tuft (of hair), quiff; (*de caballo*) forelock; (*Orn*) tuft, crest; (*de bebida*) head; **estar hasta el ~** (*Carib, Méx*) to be fed up to the back teeth*.
(b) (*fig*) pride, haughtiness; **de alto ~** aristocratic; important, socially prominent; **tener mucho ~** to be haughty, be stuck-up*.

copetín NM (*And, Cono Sur*) (*copa de licor*) glass of spirits; (*cóctel*) cocktail; (*aperitivo*) aperitif; (*vasito*) liqueur glass.

copetón ADJ (a) (*LAm*) = **copetudo** (a). (b) (✱) (*And*) **estar ~** to be tight*. (c) (*Carib*) cowardly.

copetudo ADJ (a) (*Orn etc*) tufted; crested. (b) (*fig: linajudo*) highborn, of noble birth, blue-blooded; (*engreído*) haughty, stuck-up*.

copia¹ NF (*gen*) copy; (*Arte*) copy; (*reproducción*) replica, reproduction; duplicate; **~ de calco, ~ al carbón, ~ carbónica** (*Cono Sur*) carbon copy; **~ certificada** certified copy; **~ fotostática** photostat; **~ impresa** (*Inform*) hard copy; **~ en limpio** fair copy; **~ de respaldo, ~ de seguridad** back-up document; back-up; **sacar una ~ de** to make a copy of.

copia² NF (*abundancia*) abundance, plenty; **con gran ~ de** with an abundance of, with a great deal of.

copiado NM copying.

copiador(a)¹ NM/F (a) (*persona*) copier, copyist. (b) (*libro*) letter-book.

copiadora² NF copying machine, photocopier.

copiante NMF copyist.

copiar [1b] VT to copy (*de* from); *estilo etc* to imitate; *dictado* to take down.

copichuela* NF social drink.

copihue NM (*Chile*) Chilean bell flower (*national symbol of Chile*).

copilotar [1a] VT (*Aut*) to be the co-driver of; (*Aer*) to copilot.

copiloto NMF (*Aut*) co-driver; (*Aer*) co-pilot.

copión*, -ona NM/F (*alumno*) cheat; (*imitador*) copycat*.

copiosamente ADV copiously, abundantly, plentifully.

copioso ADJ copious, abundant, plentiful.

copista NMF copyist.

copistería NF copy shop.

copita NF (small) glass; **una ~ de jerez** a glass of sherry; **tomarse unas ~s** to have a drink or two.

copla NF (a) (*Liter*) verse (*esp of 4 lines*); (*Mús*) popular song, folksong, ballad; **~s** verses, poetry; **~s de Calaínos** silly story (*etc*) with which sb irrelevantly interrupts; **~s de ciego** doggerel; **andar en ~s** to be the talk of the town; **es la misma ~** it's the same old story; **hacer ~s** to write verse; **no valen ~s** it's no use your arguing (*o* apologizing *etc*).
(b) (*CAm, Cono Sur: Téc*) pipe joint.

copo NM (a) (*de lino etc*) tuft, small bundle; **~ de algodón** cotton ball; **~s de avena** oatmeal, rolled oats; **~s de maíz tostado** cornflakes; **~ de nieve** snowflake.
(b) (*And, Carib: de árbol*) tree top.
(c) (*Cono Sur: nubes*) piled-up clouds.

copón* NM large cup; (*Rel*) pyx; **¡~!** hell's teeth!*; **y todo el ~** and all the rest, and all that stuff*; **un susto (etc) del ~** a tremendous fright* (*etc*).

coprocesador NM (*Inform*) co-processor.

coproducción NF (*Cine etc*) joint production.

coproducir [3n] VT (*Cine etc*) to co-produce, produce jointly.

copropiedad NF co-ownership.

copropietario, -a NM/F co-owner, joint owner.

copucha NF (*Cono Sur*) gossip.

copuchar [1a] VI (*Cono Sur*) to gossip.

copuchento ADJ (*Cono Sur*) lying.

copudo ADJ *árbol* bushy, thick.

cópula NF (a) (*Bio*) copulation; **~ carnal** copulation, sexual intercourse. (b) (*Ling*) conjunction; (*Gram*) copula.

copulador ADJ copulatory.

copular [1a] VI to copulate (*con* with).

copulativo ADJ (*Ling*) copulative.

coque NM coke.

coquear [1a] VI (*And, Cono Sur*) to chew coca.

coqueluche NF whooping cough.

coquero, -a NM/F cocaine addict.

coqueta [1] ADJ flirtatious, flighty, coquettish; vain.
[2] NF (a) (*persona*) flirt, coquette. (b) (*pan*) roll, small loaf. (c) (*mueble*) dressing table (with a full-length mirror).

coquetear [1a] vi to flirt (*con* with; *t fig*).
coqueteo NM, **coquetería** NF (a) (*cualidad*) flirtatiousness, flightiness, coquetry; flirtatious disposition; (*fig*) affection. (b) (*acto*) flirtation.
coqueto, coquetón ① ADJ (a) *vestido etc* smart, natty*, attractive. (b) *hombre* flirtatious; attractive (to women). (c) *mujer* = **coqueta 1**.
② NM ladykiller, wolf*.
coquilla NF (*Cono Sur*) shell.
coquitos NMPL: **hacer ~** to make faces (*a* at).
coracha NF (*esp LAm*) leather bag.
coraje NM (a) (*bríos*) fighting spirit; (*dureza*) toughness; (*valor*) courage; (*fortaleza*) fortitude. (b) (*enojo*) anger; **dar ~ a** to make angry, enrage.
corajina NF fit of temper, explosion of rage.
corajudo ADJ (a) (*animoso*) spirited; tough; bold; (*Cono Sur*: *valiente*) brave. (b) (*de genio vivo*) quick-tempered, peppery.
coral¹ (*Mús*) ① ADJ choral.
② NM chorale.
③ NF choir, choral group.
coral² NM (a) (*Zool*) coral. (b) (*serpiente*) coral snake.
coralina NF coralline.
coralino ADJ coral (*atr*), coralline.
corambre NF hides, skins.
Corán NM Koran.
corana NF (*And, Cono Sur*: *Hist*) sickle.
coránico ADJ Koranic.
coraza NF (a) (*Mil, Hist*) cuirass; (*fig*) breastplate, protection. (b) (*Náut*) armour-plating. (c) (*Zool*) shell. (d) (*Aut*) radiator cover.
corazón NM (a) (*Anat y fig*) heart; **de ~** willingly; **de todo ~** from the heart; **de buen ~** kind-hearted; **¡hijo de mí ~!** my precious child!; **revista del ~** magazine of love stories; **sección del ~ solitario** lonely hearts column; **duro de ~** hard-hearted; **sin ~** heartless; **con el ~ en la mano** frankly; sincerely; **estar enfermo del ~** to have heart trouble; **sí, mi ~** yes darling; **arrancar** (*o* **partir, romper**) **el ~ a uno** to break sb's heart; **no caberle a uno el ~ en el pecho** to be bursting with joy; to be the very soul of kindness; **le dio en el ~** she had a premonition; **encoger a uno el ~** to fill sb with fear (*o* dismay, pity); **llevar el ~ en la mano** to wear one's heart on one's sleeve; **meter a uno el ~ en un puño** (*o* **en la boca**) to give sb a scare; **tener el ~ en un puño** to have one's heart in one's mouth; **morir con el ~ destrozado** to die of a broken heart; **poner el ~ en algo** to set one's heart on sth; **no tener ~** to have no heart, be heartless; **tener el ~ para** + *infin* to have the heart to + *infin*; **no tener el ~ para algo** not to feel up to sth; *V* **íntimo** *etc*.
(b) (*Bot*) core.
(c) **corazones** (*Naipes*) hearts.
corazonada NF (a) (*pálpito*) presentiment, hunch. (b) (*impulso*) rash impulse, sudden impulse; (*acto*) impulsive act.
corazoncito* NM: **tener su ~** to have a heart.
corbata NF tie, necktie; cravat(e); **~ de lazo, ~ michi** (*And*) bow-tie; **~ de smoking** black tie.
corbatín NM bow tie.
corbeta NF corvette.
corca NF woodworm.
Córcega NF Corsica.
corcel NM steed, charger.
corcha NF (piece of) cork bark.
corchea NF (*Mús*) quaver.
corchero ADJ cork (*atr*); **industria corchera** cork industry.
corcheta NF (*Cos*) eye (*of hook and eye*).
corchete NM (a) (*Cos*) snap fastener; catch, clasp; hook and eye. (b) (*Tip*) **~s agudos** angled brackets < >; **~s rectos** square brackets [ ].
(c) (*Cono Sur*: *grapa*) staple.
corchetear [1a] VT (*Cono Sur*) to staple (together).
corchetera NF (*Cono Sur*) stapler.
corcho NM (*gen*) cork; (*corteza*) cork bark; (*estera*) cork mat; (*zueco*) cork-soled clog; (*Pesca*) float; **~ bornizo, ~ virgen** virgin cork; **sacar el ~** to draw the cork, uncork.
corcholata NF (*Méx*) metal bottle-top.
córcholis* EXCL good Lord!, dear me!
corchoso ADJ corklike, corky.
corcor NM (*CAm, Carib*) gurgle; **beber ~*** to swig*, knock it back*.
corcova NF (a) hump, hunchback. (b) (*And, Cono Sur*: *fiesta*) all night party.
corcovado ① ADJ hunchbacked.
② NM, **corcovada** NF hunchback.
corcovar [1a] VT to bend (over); to crook.
corcovear [1a] vi (a) to prance about, cut capers; (*caballo*) to buck, plunge. (b) (*And, Carib, Cono Sur*: *quejarse*) to grumble, grouse*. (c) (*Méx*: *tener miedo*) to be frightened, be afraid.
corcovo NM (a) (*brinco*) prance, caper; buck, plunge. (b) (*) crookedness*.

cordada NF (*Alpinismo*) team, roped team.
cordaje NM cordage; (*de raqueta*) strings; (*Náut*) rigging.
cordal NM hill range.
cordel NM cord, line; thin rope; **a ~** straight, in a straight line.
cordelería NF (a) (*cuerdas*) cordage, ropes; (*Náut*) rigging.
(b) (*fábrica*) ropeyard, ropeworks.
(c) (*arte*) cordmaking, ropemaking.
cordelero NM cordmaker, ropemaker.
cordería NF cordage, cords, ropes.
corderillo NM, **corderina** NF lambskin.
cordero, -a ① NM/F (a) (*Zool*) lamb; **~ asado** roast lamb; **C~ de Dios** Lamb of God; **~ lechal** young lamb; **¡no hay tales ~s!** it's nothing of the sort.
(b) (*fig*) meek and mild person.
② NM (*piel*) lambskin.
corderuna NF lambskin.
cordial ① ADJ (a) (*gen*) cordial; heartfelt, hearty. (b) (*Farm*) tonic, invigorating.
② NM cordial; tonic.
cordialidad NF warmth, cordiality.
cordialmente ADV cordially; heartily; (*en carta*) sincerely.
cordillera NF range, chain (*of mountains*).
cordillerano ADJ (*Cono Sur*) Andean.
cordita NF cordite.
Córdoba NF Cordova.
córdoba NM *standard monetary unit of Nicaragua*.
cordobán NM cordovan (*leather*).
cordobana: **andar a la ~** to go around stark naked.
cordobés ① ADJ Cordovan.
② NM, **cordobesa** NF Cordovan.
cordón NM (a) (*cuerda*) cord, string; (*Náut*: *de cable*) strand; (*de zapato*) lace; (*Mil*) braid; (*Elec*) flex, extension wire (*US*); **cordones** (*Mil*) aiguillettes; **lana de 3 cordones** 3-ply wool; **~ detonante** (*Cono Sur*) fuse.
(b) (*Anat*) cord; **~ umbilical** umbilical cord.
(c) (*Arquit*) cordon.
(d) (*Mil, de policía etc*) cordon; **~ sanitario** sanitary cordon, cordon sanitaire.
(e) (*Cono Sur*) kerb.
(f) **~ de cerros** (*And, Carib, Cono Sur*) chain of hills.
(g) (*And, Carib*: *licor*) liquor, brandy.
cordoncillo NM (*de tela*) rib; (*Cos*) braid, piping; (*de moneda*) milling, milled edge.
cordura NF good sense, prudence, wisdom; **con ~** sensibly, prudently, wisely.
Corea NF Korea; **~ del Norte** North Korea; **~ del Sur** South Korea.
coreano, -a ADJ, NM/F Korean.
corear [1a] ① VT to say in a chorus; *slogan* to shout (*in unison*), chant; (*Mús*) to sing in chorus, sing together; (*Mús*: *componer*) to compose choral music for; (*fig*) to chorus, echo parrot-fashion; **su opinión es coreada por ...** his opinion is echoed by ...
② VI to speak all together; (*Mús*) to sing all together, join in.
coreografía NF choreography.
coreografiar [1c] VT to choreograph.
coreográfico ADJ choreographic.
coreógrafo, -a NM/F choreographer.
Corfú NM Corfu.
coriana NF (*And*) blanket.
corifeo NM (a) (*Hist*) coryphaeus. (b) (*fig*) leader, spokesman.
corindón NM corundum.
corintio ADJ Corinthian.
Corinto N Corinth.
corinto ① ADJ INVAR maroon, purplish.
② NM maroon, purplish colour.
corista ① NMF (*Ecl*) chorister; (*Mús*) member of the chorus.
② NF (*Teat etc*) chorus girl.
coritatis* ADV: **estar en ~** to be in the buff*.
cormorán NM cormorant.
cornada NF butt, thrust (*with the horns*), goring; **dar una ~ a** to gore.
cornadura NF horns; (*de ciervo*) antlers.
cornalina NF cornelian, carnelian.
cornamenta NF horns; (*de ciervo*) antlers; (*hum*: *de marido*) cuckold's horns; **poner la ~ a uno** to cuckold sb.
cornamusa NF (*gaita*) bagpipe; (*cuerna*) hunting horn.
córnea NF cornea.
corneal ADJ corneal.
cornear [1a] VT to butt, gore.
corneja NF crow; rook; **~ negra** carrion crow; **~ calva** rook.
córneo ADJ horny, corneous.
córner ['korne] NM, PL **córners** ['korne *o* 'kornes] *o* **córneres** ['korneres]
(a) (*Dep*) corner, corner kick; **¡~!** (*INTERJ*) corner! (b) (*LAm*: *Boxeo*) cor-

ner.

cornerina NF cornelian, carnelian.

corneta ☐1 NF (*instrumento*) bugle; (*Carib: Aut*) horn; **~ acústica** ear trumpet; **~ de llaves** cornet; **~ de monte** hunting horn.
☐2 NMF (*persona*) bugler; cornet player.

cornetear [1a] VI (*Carib Aut*) to sound one's horn.

cornetín ☐1 NM (*instrumento*) cornet.
☐2 NMF (*persona*) cornet player.

cornetista NMF bugler.

corneto ADJ (*CAm*) bow-legged.

cornezuelo NM (*Bot*) ergot.

cornflaques NMPL, **cornflés** NMPL (*LAm*) cornflakes.

cornial ADJ horn-shaped.

córnico ☐1 ADJ Cornish.
☐2 NM (*Ling*) Cornish.

corniforme ADJ horn-shaped.

cornisa NF cornice; **la C~ Cantábrica** the Cantabrian coast.

cornisamento NM entablature.

corno NM (*Mús*) horn; **~ de caza** hunting horn; **~ inglés** cor anglais.

Cornualles NM Cornwall.

cornucopia NF (**a**) (*Mit etc*) cornucopia, horn of plenty. (**b**) (*espejo*) small ornamental mirror.

cornudo ☐1 ADJ (**a**) (*Zool*) horned; antlered. (**b**) *marido* cuckolded.
☐2 NM cuckold.

cornúpeta NM (*t* **cornúpeto** NM) (*Taur. liter*) bull; (*hum*) cuckold.

coro NM (**a**) (*Mús, Teat*) chorus; **una chica del ~** a girl from the chorus, a chorus girl; **cantar** (*etc*) **a ~s** to sing (*etc*) alternately; **decir algo a ~** to say sth in a chorus, say sth in unison; **aprender algo de ~** to learn sth by heart; to learn sth by rote; **hacer ~ de** (*o* **a**) **las palabras de uno** to echo sb's words.
(**b**) (*Mús, Ecl*) choir; **~ celestial** celestial choir, heavenly choir; **niño de ~** choirboy.
(**c**) (*Arquit*) choir.

corola NF corolla.

corolario NM corollary.

corona NF (**a**) (*de rey etc*) crown; coronet; (*aureola*) halo; **~ de espinas** crown of thorns; **~ de nieve** snowcap; **ceñirse la ~** to take the crown; **rey sin ~ de Eslobodia** uncrowned king of Slobodia.
(**b**) (*Astron*) corona; (*Met*) halo.
(**c**) (*t* **~ de flores**) garland; chaplet; **~ funeraria, ~ mortuoria** wreath.
(**d**) (*Anat*) crown (of the head), top of the head; (*de diente*) crown; (*Ecl*) tonsure.
(**e**) (*Fin*) crown.

coronación NF (**a**) (*de rey*) coronation. (**b**) (*fig*) crowning, completion. (**c**) (*Arquit*) = **coronamiento** (**b**). (**d**) (*Ajedrez*) queening.

coronamiento NM (**a**) (*fig*) crowning, completion. (**b**) (*Arquit*) crown, coping stone; top, ornamental finish.

coronar [1a] VT (**a**) *persona* to crown; **~ a uno** (**por**) **rey** to crown sb king.
(**b**) *edificio etc* to crown (**con, de** with); to top, cap.
(**c**) (*fig*) to crown; to complete, round off; **~ algo con éxito** to crown sth with success; **para ~lo** to crown it all.
(**d**) (*Ajedrez, Damas*) to queen.
(**e**) (*And, Carib, Cono Sur: poner los cuernos a*) to cuckold, make a cuckold of.

coronario ADJ coronary.

coronel NM colonel; **~ de aviación** group captain, colonel (*US*).

coronela NF (woman) colonel; (*Hist*) colonel's wife.

▼ **coronilla** NF crown, top of the head; **andar** (*o* **bailar, ir**) **de ~** to slog away, do one's utmost (to please sb); **dar de ~** to bump one's head; **estar hasta la ~** to be utterly fed up (*de* with).

coronta NF (*And, Cono Sur*) deseeded corncob.

corotear [1a] VI (*And*) to move house.

coroto NM (*And, CAm, Carib*) (**a**) (*vasija*) gourd, vessel. (**b**) **~s** gear, things; junk.

corpacho NM, **corpanchón** NM, **corpazo** NM (*) carcass*, fat body*.

corpiño NM bodice; (*Cono Sur*) brassière, bra.

corporación NF corporation; association; (*Com, Fin*) corporation, company.

corporal ADJ corporal, bodily; **ejercicio ~** physical exercise; **higiene ~** personal hygiene.

corporativismo NM corporate nature; corporate spirit.

corporativo ADJ corporate.

corporeidad NF corporeal nature.

corporeizar [1f] ☐1 VT (*encarnar*) to embody.
☐2 VI (*aparecer*) to materialize, turn up.
☐3 **corporeizarse** VR (*tomar cuerpo*) to take shape.

corpóreo ADJ corporeal, bodily.

corpulencia NF burliness, heavy build; stoutness, massiveness; **cayó con toda su ~** he fell with his full weight.

corpulento ADJ *persona* burly, heavily-built; *árbol etc* stout, solid, massive.

Corpus NM Corpus Christi.

corpus NM INVAR corpus, body.

corpúsculo NM corpuscle.

corral NM (*Agr*) yard, farmyard; stockyard, cattlepen, corral (*US*); (*de niño*) playpen; (*Carib*) small cattle farm; (††) open-air theatre; **~ de abasto** (*Cono Sur*) slaughterhouse; **~ de carbonera** coal dump, coalyard; **~ de madera** timberyard; **~ de vacas*** slum; **~ de vecindad** tenement; **hacer ~es** to play truant.

corralillo NM, **corralito** NM playpen.

corralón NM large yard; (*Cono Sur: maderería*) timberyard, woodyard; (*And*) vacant site, vacant lot (*US*).

correa NF (**a**) (*gen*) strap; leather strap, thong; belt (*t Téc*); (*traílla*) leash; (*ronzal*) tether; **~ para afilar navaja** razor strop; **~ de seguridad** safety belt; **~ sin fin** endless belt; **~ de transmisión** driving belt, drive; **~ transportadora, ~ de transporte** conveyor belt; **~ de ventilador** (*Aut etc*) fan-belt; **besar la ~** to eat humble pie.
(**b**) (*cualidad*) give, stretch, elasticity; **tener ~** to be able to put up with a lot, know how to take it, be long-suffering.

correaje NM belts, straps; (*Téc*) belting.

correalizador(a) NM/F (*TV, Cine*) co-director.

correcalles NF INVAR streetwalker.

corrección NF (**a**) (*acto*) correction; adjustment; **~ de pruebas** (*Tip*) proofreading, proof-correction.
(**b**) (*reprimenda*) rebuke, reprimand; (*castigo*) punishment.
(**c**) (*cualidad*) correctness; courtesy, politeness; good manners; propriety.

correccional NM reformatory.

correcorre NM (*Carib*) headlong rush, stampede.

correctamente ADV (**a**) (*exactamente*) correctly; accurately; aright. (**b**) (*regularmente*) regularly. (**c**) (*decentemente*) correctly, politely; properly, fittingly.

correctivo ADJ, NM corrective.

▼ **correcto** ADJ (**a**) *solución etc* correct; accurate; right; **¡~!** right!, O.K.!*
(**b**) *rasgos etc* regular, well-formed.
(**c**) *persona* correct; courteous, polite, well-mannered; *conducta* courteous, correct; *vestido* correct, proper, fitting; **estuvo muy ~ conmigo** he was very polite to me.

corrector(a) ☐1 NM/F (*Tip*) proofreader; (*Prensa*) **~ de estilo** copy editor.
☐2 NM (**a**) (*líquido*) correcting fluid. (**b**) (*Inform*) **~ ortográfico** spell(ing) checker. (**c**) (*de dientes*) brace.

corredera NF (**a**) (*Téc*) slide; track, rail, runner; slide valve; (*abrochador*) zip, zipper (*US*); **puerta de ~** sliding door.
(**b**) (*Náut*) log.
(**c**) (*Téc: de molino*) upper millstone.
(**d**) (*Ent*) cockroach.
(**e**) (*Dep*) racetrack.
(**f**) (*Cono Sur: rápidos*) rapids.

corredero NM (**a**) (*Méx Dep*) racetrack. (**b**) (*And: lecho de río*) old riverbed.

corredizo ADJ *puerta etc* sliding; *grúa* travelling; *nudo* running, slip (*atr*).

corredor(a) ☐1 NM/F (**a**) (*Dep*) runner; athlete; **~ automovilista** racing driver, racing motorist; **~ ciclista** racing cyclist; **~ de cortas distancias** sprinter; **~ de fondo, ~ de larga distancia** long-distance runner; **~ de pista** track athlete.
(**b**) (*Com*) agent, broker; (*: *coime*) procurer, pimp; **~ de bienes raíces, ~ de propiedades** (*Cono Sur*) estate agent, real-estate broker (*US*); **~ de bodas** matchmaker; **~ de bolsa** stockbroker; **~ de casas** house agent; **~ de comercio** business agent; **~ de fincas rurales** land agent; **~ de oreja** gossip.
(**c**) (*Mil*) scout; (††) raider.
☐2 NM corridor, passage; **~ de popa** (*Náut*) stern gallery.

correduría NF brokerage.

corregible ADJ which can be corrected.

corregidor NM (*Hist*) chief magistrate; mayor.

corregidora NF (*Hist*) wife of the chief magistrate; mayoress.

corregir [3c y 3k] ☐1 VT (**a**) (*gen*) to correct; to put right, adjust; (*repasar*) to revise, look over; *pruebas* to correct, read.
(**b**) (*reprender*) to rebuke, reprimand; (*castigar*) to punish.
☐2 **corregirse** VR (*persona*) to reform, mend one's ways; **~ de su terquedad** to stop being obstinate.

correlación NF correlation.

correlacionar [1a] VT to correlate.

correlativo ADJ, NM correlative.

correligionario, -a NM/F (*Ecl*) co-religionist, person of the same faith; (*Pol*) fellow supporter, sympathizer, like-minded person.

correlón ADJ (**a**) (*LAm: corredor*) fast, good at running. (**b**) (*CAm, Méx: cobarde*) cowardly.

correntada NF (*Cono Sur*) rapids, strong current.

correntón ⓵ ADJ (a) (*activo*) busy, active. (b) (*bromista*) jokey, jolly, fond of a lark.
⓶ NM (*And, Carib*) strong current.

correntoso ADJ (*LAm*) *río* fast-flowing, rapid; in flood, in spate; *agua* torrential.

correo NM (a) (*persona*) courier; (*cartero*) postman, mailman (*US*); (⁑) drug-pusher; **~ de gabinete** (*Pol*) Queen's Messenger, diplomatic courier (*US*).
(b) (*Correos*) post, mail; **~ aéreo** airmail; **~ certificado** registered post; **~ electrónico** electronic mail; **~ de primera clase** first-class mail; **~ urgente** special delivery; **echar al ~**, **poner en el ~** to post, mail (*esp US*); **llevar algo al ~** to take sth to the post; **¿ha llegado el ~?** has the post come?; **a vuelta de ~** by return (of post); **por ~** by post, through the post.
(c) (*oficina*) **~s** post office; **Administración General de C~s** General Post Office; **ir a ~s, pasar por ~s** to go to the post office.
(d) **el ~s** (*Ferro*) the mail train, the slow train.

correosidad NF toughness, leatheriness; flexibility.

correoso ADJ (*duro*) tough, leathery; (*flexible*) flexible.

correr [2a] ⓵ VT (a) *terreno, distancia* to traverse, cover, travel over; to pass over; **ha corrido medio mundo** he's been round half the world.
(b) (*Mil: Hist*) to overrun; to raid, invade; to lay waste.
(c) *objeto* to push along; *silla* to pull up, draw up; *cerrojo* to shoot, slide, draw; *llave* to turn; *cortina, velo* to draw; *botones etc* to move; *vela* to unfurl; *nudo* to undo, untie; *balanza* to tip.
(d) *caballo* to race, run; *toro* to fight; *presa* to chase, hunt, pursue.
(e) *riesgo* to run; *aventura* to have; *suerte* to suffer, undergo.
(f) *colores* to make run.
(g) (*Com*) to auction.
(h) *persona* (*t* **dejar corrido**) to embarrass, put to shame, cover with confusion.
(i) **~ la clase*** to cut class, play hooky.
(j) **~la*** to live it up*; to have one's fling; to go on a spree.
(k) **~ a uno*** (*CAm, Carib, Méx*) to throw sb out.
(l) (⁑) to screw⁑.
⓶ VI (a) (*gen*) to run; to hurry, rush; **corrió a decírselo** he ran to tell him, he hastened to tell him; **~ a la perdición** to rush headlong to disaster; **¡corre!** hurry!, hurry up!; **¡no corras tanto!** don't run so hard!, not so fast!; **~ a todo ~** to run as hard as one can; **~ como un galgo** (*o* gamo) to run like a hare; **echar a ~** to start to run, break into a run; to run off; **dejar ~ las cosas** to let things run on, let matters ride, let things take their course.
(b) (*agua, electricidad etc*) to run, flow; (*aire*) to flow, go, pass; (*grifo*) to run; (*fuente*) to play; (*Cono Sur: viento*) to blow; (*coche*) to go fast; **el río corre muy crecido** the river is running very high; **corre mucho viento** it's very windy, there's a strong wind blowing; **dejar ~ la sangre** to let the blood flow.
(c) (*tiempo*) to pass (quickly), elapse; (*período*) to run, extend, stretch; **el tiempo corre** time is passing, time presses; **el mes que corre** the present month, the current month; **durante lo que corre del año** during the year so far.
(d) (*dinero etc*) to pass, be valid, be acceptable; (*rumor*) to circulate, go round; (*creencia*) to be commonly held.
(e) (*Geog etc*) to run; **las montañas corren del este al oeste** the mountains run from east to west.
(f) (*sueldo etc*) to be payable; **su sueldo correrá desde el primer día del mes** his salary will be payable from the first of the month.
(g) **~ con la casa** to run the house, manage the house; **~ con los gastos** to pay (*o* meet, bear) the expenses; **él corre con eso** he is responsible for that, that is in his charge; **esto corre por tu cuenta** (*fig*) that's your problem.
(h) **~ a, ~ por** (*Com*) to sell at.
⓷ **correrse** VR (a) (*moverse: objeto*) to slide, move along; (*lastre, carga*) to shift; (*persona*) to move (up); **se ha corrido unos centímetros el tablero** the board has moved a few centimetres; **córrete un poco hacia este lado** move a bit this way.
(b) (*excederse*) to go too far, let o.s. go; **no te vayas a ~ en la propina** don't overdo it on the tip.
(c) (*colores*) to run; (*hielo etc*) to melt; (*vela*) to gutter; (*tinta*) to spread, make a blot.
(d) (*sofocarse*) to blush, to get embarrassed; (*aturdirse*) to become confused.
(e) **~ una juerga** *etc*: V **juerga**.
(f) (*CAm, Carib, Méx: huir*) to take flight, run away; (*acobardarse*) to get scared, take fright.
(g) (⁑) to come⁑, have an orgasm.

correría NF (*Mil*) raid, foray; (*fig*) trip, excursion; **~s** (*fig*) trips, travels.

correspondencia NF (a) (*gen*) correspondence.
(b) (*cartas*) correspondence, letters; (*Correos*) post, mail; **~ entrante** incoming mail; **~ particular** private correspondence; **curso por ~** correspondence course; **entrar en ~ con uno** to enter into corre-

spondence with sb; **estar en ~ con uno** to be in correspondence with sb.
(c) (*enlaces*) communications, contact; (*Ferro etc*) connection (*con* with); (*Arquit*) communication, communicating passage.
(d) (*acuerdo*) agreement; (*armonía*) harmony; (*agradecimiento*) gratitude; (*de palabras*) equivalence; (*de afecto etc*) return; **mis ofertas no tuvieron ~** my offers met with no response; **yo esperaba más ~** I had expected a greater response.

▼ **corresponder** [2a] ⓵ VI (a) (*Mat etc*) to correspond (*a* to, *con* with); to tally (*con* with); **no corresponde con sus principios** it does not fit in (*o* accord) with his principles.
(b) (*convenir*) to be suitable, be fitting, be right; to belong; **~ a** (*color, mueble etc*) to match; to fit, fit in with, go with; **ese libro no corresponde aquí** that book doesn't belong here; **la llave corresponde a esta cerradura** the key fits this lock; **todavía no corresponde hacerlo** it is still not the right time to do it; **el resultado no ha correspondido a nuestras esperanzas** the result did not come up to our expectations; **con una gravedad que corresponde a su importancia** with a gravity which befits its importance.
(c) (*ser para*) **~ a** to fall to the lot of, be the share of; **le dieron lo que le correspondía** they gave him his share; **correspondieron 100 ptas a cada uno** everyone got 100 ptas (as his share), each one's share amounted to 100 ptas.
(d) (*incumbir*) **~ a** (*deber etc*) to concern; to rest with, devolve upon; **'a quien corresponda'** 'to whom it may concern'; **me corresponde hacerlo** it is my job to do it, it is my business to do it; **no me corresponde criticarle** it is not for me to criticize him; **me corresponde jugar a mí** it's my turn to play.
(e) (*contestar*) to respond, reply; **~ a cariño** to return, reciprocate; *favor* to repay; **~ dignamente a** to make a fitting reply; **ella le correspondió con una corbata** she gave him a tie in return; **pero ella le correspondió con desprecio** but she responded scornfully, but all she gave in return was disdain; **nunca podré ~ a tanta generosidad** I can never adequately repay such generosity; **un amor no correspondido** an unrequited love, a love which was never returned.
(f) (*Ferro etc*) to connect (*con* with).
(g) (*Arquit*) to communicate (*con* with).
⓶ **corresponderse** VR (a) (*gen*) to correspond; (*armonizar*) to agree, be in harmony (*con* with); (*personas*) to have mutual affection (*etc*), have regard for one another; (*colores etc*) to match, go together.
(b) (*Correos*) to correspond (*con* with).

correspondiente ⓵ ADJ (*que corresponde*) corresponding (*a* to); (*apropiado*) appropriate; *palabra* equivalent; (*respectivo*) respective.
⓶ NMF (*de academia etc*) corresponding member.

corresponsabilidad NF joint responsibility.

corresponsable ADJ jointly responsible (*de* for).

corresponsal NMF (newspaper) correspondent; **~ de guerra** war correspondent.

corretaje NM brokerage.

corretear [1a] ⓵ VT (a) (*LAm: acosar*) to pursue, harass.
(b) (*CAm: ahuyentar*) to scare off.
(c) (*Cono Sur Com*) to sell on behalf of, act for.
(d) (*Cono Sur*) *trabajo* to hurry along, push*.
⓶ VI (a) (*ir de prisa*) to run about, rush around.
(b) (*vagar*) to loiter, hang about the streets.

correteo NM: **andar en ~s** (*CAm*) to rush about.

corretero, -a NM/F busy person, gadabout.

correve(i)dile NM (a) (*acusique*) tell-tale; (*chismoso*) gossip. (b) (*coime*) pimp.

corrida NF (a) (*acto*) run, dash, sprint; **dar una ~** to make a dash; **decir algo de ~** to rattle off sth from memory; **en una ~** in an instant.
(b) **~ (de toros)** (*Taur*) bullfight; **tener ~ de toros (en casa)** to have a big family row.
(c) (*Carib, Cono Sur: fiesta*) party, rave-up⁑.
(d) (*Cono Sur: fila*) row, line, file.
(e) (*Méx: recorrido*) run, journey.
(f) (*Geol*) outcrop.
(g) (⁑) orgasm.

corrido ⓵ ADJ (a) (*seguido*) **tres noches corridas** three nights running; **hasta muy corrida la noche** far into the night.
(b) *peso etc* extra (large); **un kilo ~** a good kilo, a kilo and a bit more.
(c) (*Arquit etc*) continuous.
(d) (*avergonzado*) abashed, sheepish; (*confuso*) confused; (*sofocado*) embarrassed; **~ de vergüenza** covered with shame.
(e) (*perito*) experienced (in the wicked ways of the world), wise, sharp, knowing; **es una mujer corrida** she's a woman who has been around.
(f) *estilo* fluent, confident; **decir algo de ~** to rattle sth off; **lo sabía de ~** he knew it all right through, he could say it all from memory.

➤ LENGUA Y USO: **corresponder: 1a → 32.4**

(g) *fiesta* excellent, splendid.
2 NM **(a)** (*And, Méx: balada*) ballad.
(b) (*And: fugitivo*) fugitive from justice.

| CORRIDO |

ℹ️ **Corridos** *are Mexican ballads, usually sung by a solo voice and accompanied on the guitar. Traditionally they were used to narrate important events to semi-literate communities, and favourite themes include the Mexican Revolution and Mexican migration to the USA. The* **corrido** *is similar in form to the Spanish* **romance** *from which it derives, but deals with the common people's struggle for justice, rather than the chivalrous deeds of the aristocracy.*

---

corriente 1 ADJ **(a)** *agua* running; *estilo* flowing, fluent, easy, smooth; *dinero etc* current, valid, accepted; *cuenta, publicación, año etc* current; *interés, noticia* topical; **el año ~** the current year, the present year.
(b) (*normal*) ordinary, normal, common, everyday; standard; **~ y moliente** ordinary, run-of-the-mill; **lo ~ es no pintarlo** the usual thing is not to paint it; **aquí es ~ ver eso** it's common to see that here, that is a common sight here; **es una chica ~** she's an ordinary sort of girl.
(c) (*en regla*) in order; **tiene ~ la documentación** his papers are in order; **todo está ~ para la partida** everything is fixed up for your departure.
(d) **ir** (o **estar**) **~ en los pagos** to be up to date in one's payments.
2 NM **(a)** (*mes*) current month; **el 9 del ~** the 9th of the current month, the 9th inst.
(b) **al ~** punctually, on time; up-to-date.
(c) **estar al ~ de** to be informed about, be aware of, be well up with; **mantenerse al ~** to keep up to date (*de* with); **tener a uno al ~ de** to keep sb informed about, keep sb in touch with; **téngame al ~** keep me informed.
3 NF **(a)** (*de agua*) current; stream, flow; **C~ del Golfo** Gulf Stream; **C~ de Humboldt** Humboldt Current; **~ de lava** stream of lava; **~ sanguínea** bloodstream; **~ submarina** undercurrent.
(b) **~ de aire** draught; **~ de aire caliente** flow of warm air; **~ en chorro** jet stream; **~ térmica** thermal.
(c) (*Elec*) current; **~ alterna** alternating current; **~ continua, ~ directa** direct current; **el hilo está con ~** the wire is live.
(d) (*tendencia*) course; tendency; drift; **dejarse llevar de la ~** to drift along, follow the crowd; **las ~s modernas del arte** modern trends in art; **una fuerte ~ innovadora** a strong innovating tendency.
corrientemente ADV usually, normally.
corrillero, -a NM/F idler, person with time to gossip.
corrillo NM huddle, knot of people, small group; (*fig*) clique, coterie.
corrimiento NM **(a)** (*Geol*) slipping, sliding; **~ de tierras** landslide.
(b) (*Med*) discharge; (*Carib, Cono Sur*) rheumatism; (*And*) tooth abscess.
(c) (*fig*) embarrassment; shyness, sheepishness.
(d) (*Inform*) scrolling.
corrincho NM **(a)** (*muchedumbre*) mob. **(b)** (*And: jaleo*) uproar, row. **(c)** (*And: emoción*) excitement; (*prisa*) haste.
corro NM **(a)** (*de gente*) ring, circle; huddle, knot (of people); (*Fin*) round enclosure (in the stock exchange); **la gente hizo ~** the people formed a ring.
(b) (*juego*) ring-a-ring-a-roses; **los niños cantan esto en ~** the children sing this in a ring.
(c) (*espacio*) circular space; **hacer ~** to make room, leave a circular space.
(d) (*trozo*) small area, part, piece (of a surface); (*Agr*) plot, small field, patch.
corroboración NF corroboration.
▼ **corroborar** [1a] VT to corroborate.
corroborativo ADJ corroborative.
corroer [2a] 1 VT to corrode; (*Geol*) to erode; (*fig*) to corrode, eat away, eat up; **le corroen los celos** he is eaten up with jealousy.
2 **corroerse** VR to corrode, become corroded.
corromper [2a] 1 VT **(a)** (*pudrir*) *madera etc* to rot; *alimentos* to turn bad; (*arruinar*) to spoil, ruin, cause damage to.
(b) (*fig*) *costumbres, lengua, joven etc* to corrupt, pervert; *placeres* to spoil; *juez, oficial* to bribe.
(c) (*enviciar*) to seduce, debauch, dishonour.
(d) (*: enojar*) to vex, annoy.
2 VI (*) to smell bad.
3 **corromperse** VR **(a)** (*lit*) to rot; to go bad, deteriorate; to be spoiled.
(b) (*fig*) to become corrupted, become perverted.
corrompido ADJ **(a)** rotten, putrid. **(b)** (*fig*) corrupted, corrupt; depraved, degenerate, perverted.
corroncha NF (*And, CAm*) crust, scale.
corroncho ADJ **(a)** (*Carib: torpe*) slow, sluggish. **(b)** (*And*) *persona* diffi-

cult, prickly.
corronchoso ADJ (*And, CAm, Carib*) (*burdo*) rough, coarse; (*escamoso*) crusty, scaly.
corrongo ADJ (*CAm, Carib: excelente*) first-rate, splendid; (*encantador*) charming, attractive.
corrosión NF corrosion; rust; (*Geol*) erosion.
corrosivo ADJ corrosive; (*fig*) ruinous, disastrous.
corrte. ABR *de* **corriente, de los corrientes** instant, inst.
corrugación NF contraction, shrinkage.
corrupción NF **(a)** (*pudrición*) rot, decay; (*hedor*) stink, stench.
(b) (*fig*) corruption; perversion; (*de texto*) corruption; (*Jur*) corruption; (*soborno*) graft, bribery; (*Jur*) seduction; **en el gobierno existe mucha ~** there is a lot of corruption in the government.
corruptela NF **(a)** (*gen*) corruption. **(b)** (*una ~*) corrupt practice, abuse.
corruptible ADJ **(a)** *persona* corruptible, bribable. **(b)** *alimentos etc* perishable.
corrupto ADJ corrupt.
corruptor 1 ADJ corrupting.
2 NM, **corruptora** NF corrupter, perverter.
corsario NM privateer, corsair.
corsé NM corset; (*fig*) straitjacket.
corso¹, -a ADJ, NM/F Corsican.
corso² NM (*Náut: Hist*) privateering, piratical enterprise.
corta NF felling, cutting.
cortaalambres NM INVAR wire-cutters.
cortabolsas NM INVAR pickpocket.
cortacésped NM lawnmower.
cortacircuitos NM INVAR circuit breaker.
cortacorriente NM switch.
cortacutícula NF cuticle scissors.
cortada NF **(a)** (*LAm: corte*) cut, slash; (*zanja*) trench; (*atajo*) short cut.
(b) (*de pan etc*) slice. **(c)** (*Tenis*) stroke giving backspin.
cortadillo NM **(a)** (*vaso*) small glass, small tumbler. **(b)** (*azúcar*) lump of sugar. **(c)** (*: ligue*) affair.
cortado 1 ADJ **(a)** (*gen*) cut; clipped; **~ a pico** steep, sheer, precipitous.
(b) *leche* sour.
(c) *estilo* abrupt; disjointed.
(d) (*avergonzado*) shamed, shamefaced; (*tímido*) shy; (*confuso*) confused; (*sofocado*) embarrassed.
(e) **estar ~** (*: Cono Sur*) to be broke*.
(f) **tener** (o **sentir**) **el cuerpo ~** (*Méx*) to feel off colour.
2 NM **(a)** (*café*) coffee with a little milk.
(b) (*Ballet*) caper, leap.
cortador 1 ADJ cutting.
2 NM **(a)** (*t Téc*) cutter; **~ de cristal** glass cutter.
(b) (*Cos*) cutter.
cortadora NF cutter, cutting-machine; slicer; **~ de césped** lawnmower.
cortadura NF **(a)** (*acto*) cut, cutting.
(b) (*corte*) cut; slash, slit; (*borde*) cut edge.
(c) (*Geog*) narrow pass, defile.
(d) **~s** cuttings, clippings; (*de periódico*) newspaper cuttings, newspaper clippings (*US*).
cortafrío NM cold chisel.
cortafuego(s) NM (INVAR) firebreak, fire-lane (*US*).
cortahuevos NM INVAR egg-slicer.
cortahumedades NM INVAR damp course.
cortalápices NM INVAR pencil sharpener.
cortante 1 ADJ **(a)** (*gen*) cutting, sharp. **(b)** *viento* cutting, biting; *frío* bitter.
2 NM (*trinchador*) cleaver, chopper.
cortapapel NM (*LAm*), **cortapapeles** NM INVAR paper knife; (*Téc*) paper cutter, guillotine.
cortapicos NM INVAR earwig.
cortapisa NF **(a)** (*restricción*) restriction, limitation (attached to a concession), condition (attached to a gift); **sin ~s** without strings attached.
(b) (*pega*) snag, obstacle; **se pone ~s para sí mismo** he makes obstacles for himself; **hablar sin ~s** to talk freely.
(c) (*gracia*) charm, wit.
cortaplumas NM INVAR **(a)** penknife. **(b)** (*Ent*) earwig.
cortapuros NM INVAR cigar-cutter.
cortar [1a] 1 VT **(a)** (*gen*) to cut; to hack, chop, slash; *pelo* to cut, clip, trim; *rama, miembro, cabeza etc* to cut off; *garganta* to cut, slit; *árbol* to cut down, fell; *carne* to carve, cut up; *disco, tela* to cut; *recorte, dibujo, vestido* to cut out; **~ por la mitad** to cut down the middle.
(b) (*Mat*) to intersect, cut; (*Geog*) to cut, cut across; **esa línea corta la provincia en dos** that line cuts the province in two.
(c) (*Dep*) *pelota* to cut, slice, spin.

➤ LENGUA Y USO: corroborar → 38.1

(d) *aire, agua etc* to cut through.
(e) (*frío*) *piel* to chap, crack, split.
(f) (*Cartas*) to cut.
(g) *comunicación, enemigo, retirada etc* to cut off; (*interrumpir*) *carretera, puente etc* to cut; *agua etc* to cut off, turn off, shut off; (*Elec*) to switch off; *incendio etc* to prevent the spread of; **la carretera está cortada** the road is cut; **quedaron cortados por la nieve** they were cut off by snow.
(h) (*abreviar*) *carta, oración etc* to cut short, stop, bring to a close; *persona* to interrupt; *conversación* to interrupt, cut into, break into.
(i) (*suprimir*) *pasaje, detalle etc* to cut out, remove, suppress.
(j) (*) *droga* to cut, adulterate, dilute.
2 VI (a) (*gen*) to cut; **este cuchillo no corta** this knife doesn't cut; *V* **sano** *etc.*
(b) (*Cartas*) to cut.
(c) (*viento*) to be biting; **hace un viento que corta** there's a bitter wind.
(d) ~ **con el pasado** to (make a) break with the past; **ha cortado con su novia** (*LAm*) he's finished with his girlfriend, he and his girlfriend have broken up.
(e) **¡corta!*** get away!*
(f) (*Rad*) **¡corto!** over!; **¡corto y cierro!** over and out!
3 **cortarse** VR (a) ~ **el pelo** to have one's hair cut; **si no acepta, me la corto** if he doesn't accept, I'll eat my hat.
(b) (*manos*) to get chapped; (*tela*) to split, come apart.
(c) (*leche*) to curdle, turn, turn sour.
(d) (*fig*) to become embarrassed, get confused, become tongue-tied; **no se corta** he isn't shy, he isn't backward in coming forward.
(e) (*: Cono Sur*) (*separarse*) to become separated (from the others), get left behind; (*irse*) to clear off*; (*en trato etc*) to get left out; ~ **solo** to go off on one's own.
(f) (*: Cono Sur: morir*) to die.
(g) (*And, Carib, Méx Med*) to shiver, get the shivers.
(h) (*Cono Sur: caballo*) to be out of breath.
cortauñas NM INVAR nail clippers.
cortavidrios NM INVAR glass cutter.
cortavientos NM INVAR windbreak.
corte¹ NM (a) (*acto*) cut, cutting; (*Cos*) cutting out; (*de árboles*) cutting, felling; (*Cine*) cutting; (*Golf*) cut; (*: de droga*) cut; ~ **de carretera** closing of a road; ~ **de digestión** stomach cramp; ~ **de pelo** haircut; ~ **a lo garçon** Eton crop, shingle; **dar** ~ **a** to sharpen, put an edge on.
(b) (*señal*) cut.
(c) (*Tip etc*) cut, deletion; **el censor lo dejó sin** ~**s** the censor did not cut it, the censor did not delete anything.
(d) (*Elec etc*) cut; failure; (*Aut: en carretera*) block; ~ **de corriente**, ~ **de fluido eléctrico** power cut; power failure; **hay** ~ **de agua** the water has been cut off (o turned off).
(e) (*Téc*) section; ~ **transversal** cross section; ~ **vertical** vertical section.
(f) (*Min*) stint.
(g) (*Cos: trozo*) piece, length; ~ **de vestido** dress length.
(h) (*Cos: arte*) tailoring; dressmaking; (*estilo*) cut, style; **un traje de** ~ **muy moderno** a suit of very modern cut; **academia de** ~ **(y confección)** dressmaking school; ~ **de mangas** *obscene sign equivalent to two fingers*; **hacer un** ~ **de mangas a uno** to give sb the two fingers (sign); **programa de** ~ **liberal** programme with liberal leanings.
(i) (*Tip: de libro*) edge; **con** ~**s dorados** with gilt edges.
(j) (*Mús, de disco*) short item, individual piece; (*TV*) ~ **publicitario** commercial break.
(k) **darse** ~**s** (*Cono Sur*) to put on airs.
(l) (*: susto*) start, surprise.
(m) (*: desaire*) snub, rebuff; **¡qué** ~**!** that's one in the eye!; **no le dé** ~ don't be shy, don't be reticent.
(n) (*: réplica*) sharp answer.
corte² NF (a) (*real*) (royal) court.
(b) (*ciudad*) capital (city); **La C~** Madrid.
(c) (*séquito*) suite, retinue.
(d) **C~s** (*Generales*) (*Pol*) Spanish parliament; **C~s de Castilla y León** Regional Assembly of Castile and León; **C~s Constituyentes** constituent assembly, constitution-making body.
(e) **hacer la** ~ **a una** to woo sb, court sb.
(f) (*LAm: tribunal*) law court; **C~ Suprema** Supreme Court.

CORTES GENERALES

ⓘ *The Spanish parliament consists of a lower house, the* **Congreso de los Diputados** *and an upper house, the* **Senado***. Members of the lower house are called* **diputados** *and members of the* **Senado** *are* **senadores**.
⇨ *See also* CONGRESO DE LOS DIPUTADOS , SENADO

---

cortedad NF (a) (*de tamaño*) shortness, smallness; (*de tiempo*) brevity; ~ **de vista** shortsightedness.

(b) (*t* ~ **de ánimo**) bashfulness, timidity, shyness; diffidence.
(c) (*t* ~ **de alcances**) stupidity.
cortejar [1a] VT to court, woo (*t fig*).
cortejo NM (a) (*séquito*) entourage, suite, retinue.
(b) (*desfile*) procession; solemn gathering; ~ **fúnebre** funeral procession; ~ **nupcial** wedding procession, wedding party.
(c) (*de amante*) wooing, courting; courtship.
(d) (*persona*) lover, beau.
cortés ADJ (a) (*atento*) courteous, polite; gracious. (b) **amor** ~ courtly love.
cortesana NF courtesan.
cortesanía NF politeness; good manners.
cortesano 1 ADJ of the court; courtly; court (*atr*); **ceremonias cortesanas** court ceremony.
2 NM courtier.
cortesía NF (a) (*cualidad*) courtesy, politeness; graciousness; **visita de** ~ formal visit, courtesy call; **entrada de** ~ free ticket, complimentary ticket; **días de** ~ (*Com*) days of grace; **por** ~ as a courtesy.
(b) (*etiqueta*) social etiquette; **la** ~ **pide que ...** etiquette demands that ...
(c) (*regalo*) present, gift.
(d) (*título*) title.
(e) (*reverencia*) bow; curtsy; **hacer una** ~ **a** to bow to; to curtsy to.
(f) (*en carta*) concluding formula.
cortésmente ADV courteously, politely; graciously.
córtex NM cortex.
corteza NF (a) (*de árbol*) bark; (*de fruta*) peel, skin, rind; (*Anat, Bot*) cortex; (*de pan*) crust; (*de queso*) rind; ~ **cerebral** cerebral cortex; **añadir una** ~ **de limón** to add a bit of lemon peel.
(b) (*fig: exterior*) outside, outward appearance; hide, exterior.
(c) (*fig: grosería*) roughness, coarseness.
corticoide NM corticoid.
cortijo NM farm, farmhouse.
cortina NF curtain; screen, flap; ~ **de ducha** shower curtain; ~ **de fuego** artillery barrage; ~ **de hierro** (*Pol*) iron curtain; ~ **de humo** smoke screen (*t fig*); ~ **de tienda** tent flap; ~ **musical** (*Cono Sur: TV etc*) musical interlude; **correr la** ~ (*fig*) to draw a veil over sth; **descorrer la** ~ (*fig*) to draw back the veil.
cortinado NM (*Cono Sur*) curtains.
cortinilla NF lace curtain; thin curtain.
cortisona NF cortisone.
corto 1 ADJ (a) (*espacio*) short; (*tiempo*) brief, short; (*Com, Rad*) short; (*demasiado* ~) too short; **parece** ~ it looks too short; **a la corta o a la larga** sooner or later; **el vestido le ha quedado corto** the dress has got too short for her; **el niño va todavía de** ~ the child is still wearing short trousers (*etc*); **el toro quedó** ~ the bull stopped short (in its charge).
(b) (*provisión etc*) scant, scanty; inadequate; defective; *ración etc* small; ~ **de oído** hard of hearing; ~ **de resuello** short of breath, short-winded; ~ **de vista** shortsighted; **pongamos 50 ptas y me quedo** ~ let's say 50 ptas and that's an underestimate; **se quedó corta en la comida** she did not provide enough food, she underestimated the food that would be needed; **esta ley se queda corta** this law does not go far enough, this law is less than fully satisfactory.
(c) (*t* ~ **de ánimos**) bashful, timid, shy; socially backward; tongue-tied; **quedarse** ~ to say less than one should say, not say nearly enough; **ni** ~ **ni perezoso, él ...** not to be outdone, he ...; without a moment's delay, he ...; without thinking twice, he ...
(d) (*t* ~ **de alcances**) dim*, not very bright; **es más** ~ **que las mangas de un chaleco*** he's as thick as two short planks*.
2 NM (a) (*Cine*) short.
(b) (*caña*) small glass (of beer).
cortocircuitar [1a] VT to short-circuit.
cortocircuito NM short-circuit; **poner(se) en** ~ to short-circuit.
cortometraje NM (*Cine*) short.
cortón¹ NM (*Ent*) mole cricket.
cortón²* ADJ (a) (*tímido*) bashful, timid. (b) **es muy** ~ (*CAm*) he's always interrupting.
cortopunzante ADJ (*Cono Sur*) sharp.
Coruña NF: **La** ~ Corunna.
coruñés 1 ADJ of Corunna.
2 NM, **coruñesa** NF native (o inhabitant) of Corunna; **los coruñeses** the people of Corunna.
corva NF back of the knee.
corvadura NF curve, curvature; bend.
corvejón NM (*de caballo*) hock; (*de gallo*) spur.
corveta 1 ADJ (*CAm*) bow-legged.
2 NF curvet, prance.
corvetear [1a] VI to curvet, prance.
corvina NF sea bass, croaker.
corvo ADJ curved; bent.
corza NF doe.

corzo NM roe deer, roebuck.

cosa NF **(a)** (gen) thing; matter; **hay una ~ que no me gusta** there is something I don't like; **alguna ~** something; **¿alguna ~ más?** anything else?; **20 kilos o ~ así** 20 kilos or thereabouts; **ni ~ que le parezca** nor anything like it; **otra ~** anything else, something else; **ésa es otra ~** that's another matter (altogether); **no me queda otra ~** I have no alternative; **poca ~** nothing much; **es poca ~, no es gran ~** it's not important; it isn't up to much; **como si tal ~** as if nothing (out of the ordinary) had happened; as cool as you please; **y ~s así** and suchlike; **así las ~s ...** at this point ...; **la ~ es que ...** the trouble is that ...; **no es ~ que lo dejes todo** there's no reason for you to give it all up; **no sea ~ que ...** lest ..., in case ...; **tal como están las ~s** as things stand; **¡no hay tal ~!** nothing of the sort!; **¡vaya una ~!** well!; **¡lo que son las ~s!** just imagine!; fancy that!; **las ~s van mejor** things are going better; **pasa cada ~** anything can happen; **como quien no quiere la ~** tentatively; unobtrusively, surreptitiously; **decir una ~ por otra** (euf) to lie; **decir cuatro ~s a uno** to give sb a piece of one's mind.

(b) (con adj etc) **es ~ de nunca acabar** there's no end to it; **no es ~ de broma** (o risa) it's no laughing matter; **~(s) de comer** eatables, food; **es ~ distinta** that's another matter; **~ dura, ~ fuerte** tough business, hard thing to bear; **~s de escribir** writing things, writing materials; **es ~ fácil** it's easy; **es ~ fina*** it's top-quality gear*; **¿has visto ~ igual?** did you ever see the like?; **es ~ perdida** he's a dead loss; **~ rara** strange thing; **¡qué ~ más rara!** how strange!, most odd!; **y, ~ rara, nadie lo vio** and, oddly enough, nobody saw it; **es ~ de ver** it's worth seeing, one must see it; **le explicó las ~s de la vida** she told her the facts of life, she told her about the birds and the bees; **ésa es ~ vieja** that's stale, that's old history; **las ~s de palacio van despacio** (fig) it all takes time, the mills of God grind slowly.

(c) (asunto) affair, business; **ésa es ~ tuya** that's your affair, that's up to you.

(d) (idea) **~s** odd ideas, wild notions; **¡~s de España!** that's typical of Spain!, what else can you expect in Spain!; **¡~s de muchachos!** boys will be boys!; **¡son ~s de Juan!** that's typical of John!, that's John all over!; **¡qué ~s dices!** (hum) what dreadful things you say!; **¡tienes unas ~s!** the things you say!

(e) (cantidad) **~ de 8 días** about a week; **en ~ de 10 minutos** in about 10 minutes; **es ~ de unas 4 horas** it takes about 4 hours.

(f) (‡: droga) hash*.

(g) (LAm: como conj) **~ que: camina lento, ~ que no te canses** walk slowly so that you don't get tired (o so as not to get tired); **no le digas nada, ~ que no se ofenda** don't say anything to him, that way he won't get offended.

cosaco [1] ADJ Cossack.

[2] NM, **cosaca** NF **(a)** Cossack. **(b)** (Cono Sur) mounted policeman.

coscacho NM (And, Cono Sur) rap on the head.

coscarana NF cracknel.

coscarse* [1g] VR to catch on, get it*.

coscoja NF kermes oak.

coscolino ADJ **(a)** (Méx) (malhumorado) peevish, touchy; **niño** naughty. **(b)** (moralmente) of loose morals.

coscorrón NM **(a)** (lit) bump on the head. **(b)** (fig) setback, disappointment, knock.

coscurro NM hard crust (of bread).

cosecha NF (gen) crop, harvest (t fig); (acto) harvesting, gathering; (época) harvest, harvest time; (producto) crop, yield; **la ~ de 1992** (vino) the 1992 vintage; **de ~ propia** legumbres etc home-grown, home-produced; **cosas de su propia ~** (fig) things of one's own invention, things out of one's own head; **no añadas nada de tu ~** don't add anything that you've made up.

cosechado NM harvesting.

cosechadora NF combine-harvester.

cosechar [1a] VT **(a)** (gen) to harvest, gather (in); (frutas) to pick; cereales to cut, reap; (cultivar) to grow, cultivate; **aquí no cosechan sino patatas** the only thing they grow here is potatoes. **(b)** (fig) to reap, reap the reward of; admiración etc to win; **no cosechó sino disgustos** all he got was troubles.

cosechero, -a NM/F harvester, reaper; picker.

cosechón NM bumper crop.

coseno NM cosine.

coser [2a] [1] VT **(a)** (Cos) to sew (up); to stitch (up); botón etc to sew on, stitch on; (Med) to stitch (up). **(b)** (fig) to unite, join closely (con to). **(c)** **es cosa de ~ y cantar** it's straightforward; it's plain sailing; it's a cinch‡. **(d)** **~ a uno a balazos** to riddle sb with bullets; **~ a uno a puñaladas** to stab sb repeatedly, carve sb up; **le encontraron cosido a puñaladas** they found him covered with stab wounds.

[2] VI to sew.

[3] **coserse** VR: **~ con uno** to become closely attached to sb.

cosher ADJ INVAR kosher.

cosiaca NF (LAm) small thing, trifle.

cosido NM sewing, needlework.

cosificación NF reification.

cosificar [1g] VT to reify.

cosignatario, -a NM/F cosignatory.

cosijoso ADJ **(a)** (CAm, Méx: molesto) bothersome, annoying. **(b)** (CAm, Méx: displicente) peevish, irritable.

cosmética NF cosmetics.

cosmético ADJ, NM cosmetic.

cosmetizar VT to improve the appearance of.

cosmetólogo, -a NM/F cosmetician.

cósmico ADJ cosmic.

cosmódromo NM space-station.

cosmogonía NF cosmogony.

cosmografía NF cosmography.

cosmógrafo, -a NM/F cosmographer.

cosmología NF cosmology.

cosmonauta NMF cosmonaut, spaceman, spacewoman.

cosmopolita ADJ, NMF cosmopolitan.

cosmos NM cosmos.

cosmovisión NF world view.

coso¹ NM (ruedo) arena, enclosure; (esp) bullring.

coso² NM (Ent) deathwatch beetle, woodworm.

coso³ NM (hum) = **cosa.**

cospel NM (Téc) planchet, blank (for a coin).

cosquillar [1a] VT to tickle.

cosquillas NFPL tickling (sensation); ticklishness; **buscar las ~ a uno** to tease sb, try to stir sb up; **me hace ~** it tickles; **hacer ~ a uno** to tickle sb; (fig) to tickle sb's curiosity; **siento ~ en el pie** my foot tickles; **tener ~** to be ticklish; **no sufre ~, tiene malas ~** he's touchy, he can't take a joke.

cosquillear [1a] VT to tickle (t fig).

cosquilleo NM tickling (sensation).

cosquilloso ADJ **(a)** (lit) ticklish. **(b)** (fig) touchy, easily offended.

costa¹ NF (Fin) cost, price; **~s** (Jur) costs; **a ~** (Com) at cost; **a ~ de** at the expense of; **a toda ~** at any price; **a ~ de lo que sea** cost what it may; **condenar a uno en ~s** (Jur) to order sb to pay the costs.

costa² NF (Geog) **(a)** coast; coastline; shore, seashore; **~ afuera** offshore.

(b) (Cono Sur: de río) riverbank, lake-side.

(c) **C~ Azul** Côte d'Azur; **C~ de Marfil** Ivory Coast; **C~ de Oro** Gold Coast.

(d) **C~ Blanca** coast near Almería; **C~ Brava** coast north of Barcelona; **C~ Clara** coast near Valencia; **C~ Dorada** coast near Tarragona; **C~ del Sol** coast west of Málaga.

costabravense ADJ of the Costa Brava.

costado NM **(a)** (Anat, Náut, de objeto) side; (Mil) flank; **de ~ moverse** sideways; tumbarse on one's side; **neumáticos de ~ blanco** white-walled tyres.

(b) (Méx: Ferro) platform.

(c) **~s** ancestors, ancestry; **español por los 4 ~s** Spanish on both sides of the family; (fig) thoroughly Spanish, wholly Spanish, Spanish through and through; **es un gandul por los 4 ~s** he's an absolute idler.

costal NM sack, bag; **estar hecho un ~ de huesos** to be all skin and bone.

costalada NF = **costalazo.**

costalar [1a] VI (Cono Sur) to roll over; to fall on one's side (o back).

costalazo NM heavy fall; **darse (o pegarse) un ~** to come a cropper, take a knock.

costanera NF **(a)** (costado) side, flank. **(b)** (cuesta) slope. **(c)** (Cono Sur: muelle) jetty; promenade, paved area beside the sea (o river). **(d)** (Carib: alrededor de un pantano) firm ground (surrounding a swamp). **(e)** **~s** (Arquit) rafters.

costanero ADJ **(a)** sloping; steep. **(b)** (Náut) coastal.

▼ **costar** [1l] VTI (Com, Fin) **(a)** (gen) to cost; **¿cuánto cuesta?** how much does it cost?, (en tienda) how much is it?; **¿cuesta mucho?** is it expensive?

(b) (fig) to cost (dear, dearly); **cuesta poco** it's easy; **cuesta mucho** it's difficult; **cueste lo que cueste** cost what it may; **le ha costado caro** it has cost him dear; **eso me ha costado reñir con él** doing that has meant my falling out with him, I did that only at the cost of quarrelling with him; **es un trabajo que cuesta unos minutos** it's a job which takes a few minutes; **me costó Dios y ayuda terminarlo** I had a terrible job to finish it; V **trabajo** etc.

▼ **(c)** **~ + infin** to find it hard to + infin, have a job to + infin; **me cuesta hablar alemán** I find it difficult to speak German, I have trouble speaking German; **me cuesta creerlo** I find that hard to believe.

costarricense = **costarriqueño.**

costarriqueñismo NM word (o phrase etc) peculiar to Costa Rica.

---

costarriqueño, -a ADJ, NM/F Costa Rican.
costasoleño ADJ of the Costa del Sol.
coste NM cost, price; expense; ~ **humano** human cost, cost in human terms; **~s laborales unitarios** unitary labour costs; V t **costo**.
costear[1] [1a] VT (*Fin*) to pay for, defray the cost of; to endow; (*Rad, TV etc*) to back, sponsor; **costea los estudios a su sobrino** he is paying for his nephew's education; **no lo podemos ~** we can't afford it.
costear[2] [1a] [1] VT (*Náut*) to sail along the coast of; (*fig*) to skirt, go along the edge of; to pass close to.
   [2] **costearse** VR (*Cono Sur**) to traipse around*.
costear[3] [1a] VT (*Cono Sur*) ganado to pasture.
coste-eficacia NM cost-efficiency.
costeño [1] ADJ coastal.
   [2] NM, **costeña** NF (*LAm*) coastal dweller.
costera NF (a) (*de paquete etc*) side. (b) (*Geog*) slope. (c) (*Náut*) coast; (*Pesca*) fishing season.
costero ADJ coastal; *barco, comercio* coasting.
costilla NF (a) (*Anat, Náut*) rib.
   (b) (*carne*) chop; ~ **de cerdo** pork chop, pork cutlet.
   (c) **~s*** back, shoulders; **todo carga sobre mis ~s** I get all the burdens, everything is put on my back; **medir las ~s a uno** to beat sb.
   (d) (*hum: esposa*) wife, better half.
costilludo ADJ broad-shouldered, strapping.
costipado ADJ, NM = **constipado**.
costo NM (a) (*Fin*) cost; ~ **directo** direct cost; ~ **efectivo** actual cost; ~ **de expedición** shipping charges; **~s de fabricación** manufacturing costs; **~s de funcionamiento** running costs; **~, seguro y flete** (*csf*) cost, insurance and freight (*cif*); ~ **de (la) vida** cost of living; **el ~ de salarios de la industria** the industry's wages bill.
   (b) (*LAm: esfuerzo*) trouble, effort; **hacerse el ~ de hacer algo** (*Cono Sur*) to take the trouble (o make the effort) to do sth.
   (c) (**:** *drogas*) hash*.
costosamente ADV expensively.
costoso ADJ costly, expensive.
costra NF (*corteza*) crust; (*Med*) scab; (*de vela*) snuff.
costroso ADJ crusty; incrusted; (*Med*) scabby.
costumbre NF custom, habit; **~s** customs, ways, (*fig*) morals; **las ~s de esta provincia** the customs of this province; **persona de buenas ~s** respectable person, decent person; **de ~** (ADJ) usual; (ADV) usually; **como de ~** as usual; **más que de ~** more than usual; **he perdido la ~** I have got out of the habit, (*Dep etc*) I'm out of practice; **tener la ~ de** + *infin*, **tener por ~** + *infin* to be in the habit of + *ger*; **novela de ~s** novel of (local) customs and manners.
costumbrismo NM *literary genre of (local) customs and manners.*

┌─── COSTUMBRISMO ───┐

ⓘ *Costumbrismo is a literary genre which emerged in Spain in the 1830s. It concentrated on a detailed depiction of social and regional traditions and customs and often contrasted them with the changes brought by industrial development. Among the most noted writers of this movement were Fernán Caballero, Pedro Antonio de Alarcón, Juan Valera, and José María de Pereda.*

---

costumbrista [1] ADJ *novela etc* of (local) customs and manners.
   [2] NMF writer about (local) customs and manners, author with a strong regional flavour.
costura NF (a) (*Cos, Náut*) seam; **sin ~** seamless; **sentar las ~s** to press the seams; **sentar las ~ a uno*** to give sb a hiding*.
   (b) (*arte, labor*) sewing; needlework; (*confección*) dressmaking; **alta ~** haute couture, high fashion, fashion designing; **la ~ italiana** Italian fashions, the Italian fashion trade.
costur(e)ar [1a] VTI (*LAm*) = **coser**.
costurera NF dressmaker, seamstress.
costurero NM (*caja*) sewing box, sewing case; (*cuarto*) sewing room.
cota[1] NF (a) (*Hist*) tabard; doublet; ~ **de malla** coat of mail. (b) (*Carib: blusa*) blouse.
cota[2] NF (a) = **cuota**. (b) (*Geog*) height above sea level; (*fig*) height, level; standard; **misil de baja ~** low-flying missile; **volar a baja ~** to fly low. (c) (*cifra*) number, figure.
cotarro NM (a) (*Hist*) night shelter for tramps *etc*; **alborotar el ~** to stir up trouble; **andar** (o **ir**) **de ~ en ~** to wander about, gad about; **dirigir el ~** to be the boss. (b) (*Cono Sur**) mate, pal*.
coteja NF (*And, CAm*) equal, match.
cotejar [1a] VT (a) (*comparar*) to compare, collate; to check. (b) (*And, Carib: arreglar*) to arrange.
cotejo [1] ADJ (*LAm*) similar, same.
   [2] NM (a) (*comparación*) comparison, collation; check. (b) (*Dep*) match, game.
cotelé NM (*Cono Sur*) corduroy.
cotense NM (*And, Cono Sur, Méx*), **cotensia** NF (*And, Cono Sur*), **cotensio** NM (*Cono Sur*) coarse hemp fabric.
coterna NF (*And*) broad hat.

coterráneo [1] ADJ from the same country.
   [2] NM, **coterránea** NF compatriot, fellow-countryman, fellow-countrywoman.
cotí NM ticking.
cotidianeidad NF daily nature, routine character; ordinariness.
cotidiano ADJ daily.
cotiledón NM cotyledon.
cotilla NMF busybody, gossip.
cotillear [1a] VI to gossip.
cotilleo NM gossip(ing).
cotillero NM, **cotillera** NF = **cotilla**.
cotillón NM ≈ New Year's Eve party.
cotín NM (*Dep*) backhand shot.
cotitular NMF joint owner.
cotiza NF (*And, Carib*) sandal.
cotización NF (a) (*Fin*) quotation, price; ~ **de apertura** opening price; ~ **de cierre**, ~ **de clausura** closing price. (b) (*de miembro*) dues, subscription. (c) (*impuestos*) assessment (for tax); taxation. (d) (*cambio*) exchange rate.
cotizado ADJ in demand, popular, sought-after; (*fig*) valued, esteemed.
cotizante NMF contributor; paid-up member.
cotizar [1f] [1] VT (a) (*Fin*) *acción* to quote, price (*en* at).
   (b) *cuota* to fix; *suscripción, contribución* to pay.
   (c) (*Carib, Cono Sur: tasar*) to value (*en* at).
   (d) (*Cono Sur: prorratear*) to share out proportionally.
   (e) (*And, Carib: vender*) to sell.
   [2] VI (a) (*miembro*) to pay one's dues, pay one's subscription. (b) (*Fin*) to be quoted; **la sociedad cotiza ahora en Bolsa** the company is now quoted on the Stock Exchange.
   [3] **cotizarse** VR (a) (*Com, Fin*) ~ **a** to sell at, sell for, fetch, stand at; (*Bolsa*) to stand at, be quoted at; **estos tomates son los que más se cotizan** these tomatoes are the ones which fetch the highest price.
   (b) (*fig*) to be valued, be esteemed; **tales conocimientos se cotizan mucho** such knowledge is highly valued.
coto[1] NM (a) (*Agr*) enclosure, enclosed pasture; (*Caza*) preserve; reserve; ~ **de caza** game preserve; ~ **cerrado** (*fig*) closed shop; ~ **redondo** large estate.
   (b) (*mojón*) boundary stone; (*fig*) limit; **poner ~ a** to put a stop to; to bring under control.
   (c) (*Com*) price-fixing agreement.
   (d) (*Bridge*) rubber.
coto[2] NM (*LAm Med*) goitre.
cotón NM (a) (*tela*) printed cotton, cotton fabric. (b) (*LAm: camisa*) shirt; (*Méx: camiseta*) vest, undervest (*US*); (*Méx: blusa*) blouse.
cotona NF (a) (*LAm*) (*camisa*) strongly-made shirt; (*Cono Sur*) camisole; vest, undervest (*US*); (*And, CAm, Carib: blusa*) blouse. (b) (*Méx: cazadora*) suede jacket. (c) (*Carib: camisón*) child's nightdress.
cotonete NM (*Méx: Med etc*) cotton bud.
cotorina NF (*Méx*) jerkin.
cotorra NF (a) (*Orn: loro*) parrot, cockatoo; (*urraca*) magpie. (b) (*: parlanchina*) windbag, chatterbox. (c) (*Méx*: *orinal*) chamberpot. (d) (*Méx**:**) (*puta*) whore, slag**:**; (*vagina*) cunt**:**.
cotorrear [1a] VI to chatter, gabble.
cotorreo NM (a) (*plática*) chatter, gabble. (b) (*Méx*: *diversión*) fun, good time.
cotorrera NF female parrot; = **cotorra** (a), (b).
cotorro* ADJ (*Méx*) (*platicón*) chatty, talkative; (*alborotado*) loud, noisy.
cototo NM (*Cono Sur*) bump, bruise (on the head).
cotudo ADJ (a) (*peludo*) hairy, cottony. (b) (*LAm Med*) suffering from goitre. (c) (*And: tonto*) stupid.
cotufa NF (a) (*Bot*) Jerusalem artichoke. (b) **~s** (*LAm*) popcorn.
coturno NM buskin; **de alto ~** (*fig*) lofty, elevated.
COU [kow] NM (*Esp*) ABR *de* **Curso de Orientación Universitaria**.

┌─── COU ───┐

ⓘ *Spanish 17-year-olds who had successfully completed BUP, non-vocational secondary education, used to go on to do the Curso de Orientación Universitaria, a preparatory one-year course for the university entrance examinations (selectividad). Nowadays academically oriented 16-year-olds go on to do the 2-year Bachillerato once they have completed ESO.*
⇨ *See also* BUP , ESO

---

coulis NM (*carne*) broth; (*fruta*) syrup.
covacha NF (a) (*cueva*) small cave. (b) (*And, Carib, Cono Sur: trastera*) lumber room. (c) (*CAm, Carib: bohío*) hut. (d) (*And: puesto*) vegetable stall. (e) (*Carib: perrera*) kennel.
covachuela NF (*fig*) hovel.
covadera NF (*And, Cono Sur*) guano deposit.
cover* NM (*Prensa*) cover story; (*Mús*) cover version.
covin NM, **covín** NM (*Cono Sur*) popcorn.
coxcojilla NF, **coxcojita** NF hopscotch.

coxis NM INVAR coccyx.

coy NM (*Náut*) hammock; (*And, Carib*) cradle, cot.

coyón* ADJ (*Méx*) cowardly.

coyotaje* NM (*Méx: Com, Fin*) speculation.

coyote NM (a) (*Zool*) coyote, prairie wolf.
(b) (*: *Méx: astuto*) astute person; (*guía*) guide of illegal immigrants (to USA); (*Com, Fin*) speculator, dealer in shares (*etc*); (*intermediario*) middleman, (*pey*) fixer*; (*sablista*) con man*; (*encubridor*) fence*.
(c) (*: *Méx: hijo*) youngest child.

coyotear [1a] VI (*CAm, Méx*) (a) (*ser listo*) to be smart, be clever. (b) (*Com, Fin*) to deal (*o* speculate) in shares.

coyunda NF (a) (*CAm*) (*correa*) strap; (*dogal*) tether, halter; (*tralla*) lash. (b) (*hum*) yoke (of marriage).

coyuntura NF (a) (*Anat*) joint.
(b) (*fig*) (*momento*) moment, juncture, occasion; (*oportunidad*) opportunity; (*momento favorable*) favourable moment; (*tendencia*) trend; (*situación*) situation; **~ crítica** critical moment; turning point; **la ~ política** the political situation; **esperar una ~ favorable** to await a favourable moment.

coyuntural ADJ relating to the (present) moment (*o* situation *etc*); **datos ~es** relevant data; **medidas ~es** immediately relevant measures; **solución ~** ad hoc solution.

coyunturalismo NM (*Pol etc*) opportunism.

coyunturalmente ADV in an opportunistic way, responding to the demands of the moment; in the circumstances of the moment.

coz NF (a) (*con pie*) kick; **dar coces, dar de coces a** to kick; **dar coces contra el aguijón** to kick against the pricks; **tirar coces** to lash out (*t fig*).
(b) (*de arma: movimiento*) kick; (*de agua*) backward flow.
(c) (*de arma: parte*) butt.
(d) (*fig*) insult, rude remark; **tratar a uno a coces** to be rude to sb, treat sb like dirt.

CP (*Esp*) NF (a) ABR *de* **Caja Postal.** (b) (*Com*) ABR *de* **contestación pagada** reply paid, RP. (c) (*LAm*) ABR *de* **casilla postal** post-office box, POB.

C.P.A. NF ABR *de* **Caja Postal de Ahorros** ≈ Post Office Savings Bank.

CPN NM (*Esp*) ABR *de* **Cuerpo de la Policía Nacional.**

CPS NMPL ABR *de* **caracteres por segundo** characters per second, cps.

crac¹ NM (*t* **crack**) (a) (*Com, Fin*) failure, crash; bankruptcy; **~ financiero** financial crash; **el ~ del 29** the 1929 Stock Exchange crash. (b) (*fig*) crack-up.

crac² INTERJ snap!, crack!; **hizo ¡~! y se abrió** it went crack! and it opened out.

crac³* NMF (*t* **crack**) (*persona*) star player, star performer; (*caballo*) best horse, champion horse.

crack⁑ NM (*droga*) crack⁑.

crampón NM crampon.

cranear* [1a] VT (*Cono Sur*) to dream up.

cráneo NM skull, cranium; **ir de ~*** (*en aprieto*) to be in a tough spot; **voy de ~*** (*me va mal*) everything's going wrong for me, (*me presionan*) I'm rushed off my feet; **ir de ~ con uno*** to be on bad terms with sb; **va de ~ si hace eso*** he's got another think coming if he does that*; **esto me lleva** (*o* **trae**) **de ~*** this is driving me crazy.

crápula ① NF drunkenness; (*fig*) dissipation. ② NM (*) rake.

crapuloso ADJ drunken, (*fig*) dissipated.

craquear [1a] VT (*Quím*) to crack.

craqueo NM (*Quím*) cracking.

crasitud NF fatness.

craso ADJ (a) *persona* fat. (b) *líquido* greasy, thick. (c) (*fig*) *error* gross, crass, stupid. (d) (*And, Cono Sur*) *persona* coarse.

cráter NM crater.

crawl [krol] NM crawl.

crayón NM crayon, chalk.

crayota NF (*And*) crayon.

creación NF creation; **campaña de ~ de imagen** image-building campaign.

creacionismo NM creationism.

creacionista NMF creationist.

creador ① ADJ creative. ② NM, **creadora** NF creator; inventor, originator; **el C~** the Creator.

crear [1a] VT (*gen*) to create; *oficial* to make; (*inventar*) to invent, originate; (*fundar*) to found, establish, institute.

creatividad NF creativity.

creativo ① ADJ creative.
② NM, **creativa** NF: **~ de publicidad** copywriter.

crece NM O F (*Cono Sur*) = **crecida.**

crecepelo(s) NM hair-restorer.

crecer [2d] ① VI (*gen*) to grow; to increase; (*precio, río*) to rise; (*días*) to get longer; (*luna*) to wax; **dejar ~ la barba** to grow a beard, let one's beard grow.
② **crecerse** VR (a) (*Cos*) 'se crece un punto' 'increase by one

stitch'.
(b) (*cobrar ánimo*) to grow bolder, acquire greater confidence; (*pey*) to get conceited, have an exaggerated sense of one's importance.

creces NFPL (a) (*aumento*) increase.
(b) (*Cos*) room to let out; **para los niños se hace la ropa con ~** children's clothes are made to be let out.
(c) **con ~** amply, fully; (*fig*) with a vengeance; **pagar a uno con ~** to more than repay one's debt; **devolver algo con ~** to return sth with interest; **había cumplido su obligación con ~** he had amply carried out his obligation.

crecida NF (*de río*) rise; spate, flood.

crecido ADJ (a) *persona, planta etc* full-grown; grown-up; **ya eres ~ para eso** you're too big for that now.
(b) *número, proporción* large.
(c) **estar ~** (*río*) to be in flood.
(d) (*fig*) vain, conceited.

creciente ① ADJ growing; increasing; rising; **luna ~** crescent moon, waxing moon; *V* **cuarto.**
② NM crescent.
③ NF (a) (*de río*) flood; **~ del mar** high tide, flood tide.
(b) (*luna*) crescent moon.

crecientemente ADV increasingly.

crecimiento NM growth; increase; rise; (*Fin*) rise in value, appreciation; **~ cero** zero growth; **~ negativo** negative growth.

credencial ① ADJ accrediting; *V* **carta.**
② NF document confirming appointment (in civil service); **~es** letters of credence.

▼ **credibilidad** NF credibility.

crediticio ADJ (*Fin*) credit (*atr*).

crédito NM (a) (*fe*) credit; belief; credence; **dar ~ a** to believe (in), credit; **apenas daba ~ a sus oídos** he could scarcely believe his ears.
(b) (*buena fama*) credit; authority, standing, reputation; **persona (digna) de ~** reliable person; **tiene ~ de muy escrupuloso** he has the reputation of being thoroughly honest.
(c) (*Com, Fin*) credit; loan; **a ~** on credit; **~ de aceptación** acceptance credit; **~ bancario** bank credit; **~ diferido** deferred credit; **~ a la exportación** export credit; **~ hipotecario** mortgage loan; **~ puente** bridging loan; **~ de vivienda** mortgage; **abrir un ~ a** to open a credit for.
(d) (*Cine, TV*) **~s** credits.

credo NM creed; credo; **en un ~, en menos que se canta un ~** in next to no time.

credulidad NF credulity.

crédulo ADJ credulous.

creederas NFPL: **tiene buenas ~** he's terribly gullible, he'll swallow anything.

creencia NF belief (*en* in); **en la ~ de que ...** in the belief that ...

creencial ADJ relating to belief; ideological.

▼ **creer** [2e] ① VT (a) (*gen*) to think, believe; **~ que ...** to think that ..., believe that ...; **creo que sí, lo creo** I think so; **creo que no, no creo** I don't think so; **¡ya lo creo!** I should think so!, rather!; of course!; **¡ya lo creo que está roto!** I should jolly well say it's broken!; **créame** believe me, take my word for it; **no se vaya Vd a ~ que ...** don't go thinking that ...; **es difícil, no creas** it's hard enough, I'm telling you.
(b) (*considerar*) to think, deem, consider; **no le creo tan culpable** I don't think him so much to blame; **creo de él que es sincero** I consider him to be sincere; **lo creo de mi deber** I consider it (to be) my duty.
② VI: **~ en** to believe in.
③ **creerse** VR (a) (*gen*) to believe o.s. (to be), consider o.s. (to be); **se cree muy astuto** he thinks he's pretty clever; **¿quién se cree que es?** who do you think you are?; **~ alguien** to give o.s. airs; **¿qué se ha creído?** who does he think he is?; **se lo tiene muy creído*** he's very conceited, he's full of himself.
(b) **no me lo creo** I don't believe it; **se cree todo lo que le dicen** he swallows everything he's told; **¿(que) te crees tú eso?*** that's what you think!*; **¡no te lo creas ni tú!*** come off it!*; **se lo tiene creído*** he fancies himself; **hace falta que yo me lo crea** I still have to be convinced.

creíble ADJ believable, credible; **¿es ~ que ...?** is it conceivable that ...?

creíblemente ADV credibly.

creído ADJ (a) (*crédulo*) gullible, trusting; foolishly optimistic. (b) (*engreído*) vain, conceited.

crema NF (a) (*de leche*) cream; (*Culin*) cream; custard; **~ agria** sour cream; **~ batida** whipped cream; **un coche color ~** a cream-coloured car; **~ inglesa** custard; **~ pastelera** confectioner's cream (*o* custard); **dejar la ~*** (*Cono Sur*) to make a hash of things*; to put one's foot in it.
(b) (*cosmético*) cold cream, facecream; **~ de afeitar** shaving cream; **~ antiarrugas** anti-wrinkle cream; **~ base** foundation cream; **~ de be-

▶ LENGUA Y USO: **credibilidad** → 53.6   **creer: 1a** → 33.2, 53.5

lleza beauty-cream; **~ bronceadora** suntan cream; **~ capilar** haircream; **~ dental** toothpaste; **~ depilatoria** hair-remover; **~ hidratante**, **~ humectante** moisturizing cream; **~ de limpiar** cleansing cream; **~ de manos** handcream.
(c) **~ para el calzado** shoe polish.
(d) (*fig*) cream, best; **la ~ de la sociedad** the cream of society.
cremación NF cremation; incineration.
cremallera NF (a) (*t cierre de* ~) zip fastener, zipper (*US*); **echar la ~**: to shut one's trap**:**. (b) (*Téc*) rack; **~ y piñón** rack and pinion.
crematístico ADJ financial, economic.
crematorio ☐1 ADJ: **horno ~** = NM.
☐2 NM crematorium; (*de basura*) incinerator.
crémor NM (*t ~ tártaro*) cream of tartar.
cremosidad NF creaminess.
cremoso ADJ creamy.
crencha NF (*de pelo*) parting.
creosota NF creosote.
crep[1] NM, **crepa** NF (*LAm: Culin*) pancake, crêpe.
crep[2] NM, **crepé** NM crêpe.
crepar: [1a] VI (*Cono Sur*) to peg out**:**, kick the bucket**:**.
crepería NF pancake bar.
crepitación NF crackling; sizzling.
crepitar [1a] VI (*leño etc*) to crackle; (*jamón*) to sizzle.
crepuscular ADJ twilight, crepuscular; **luz ~** twilight.
crepúsculo NM twilight, dusk.
cresa NF maggot; larva; (*de abeja*) eggs of the queen bee.
crescendo NM crescendo.
Creso NM Croesus.
crespo ☐1 ADJ (a) *pelo* curly; kinky; *hoja etc* curled.
(b) *estilo* involved, tortuous.
(c) *persona* cross, angry.
☐2 NM hair, head of hair; (*esp Carib: bucle*) curl, ringlet.
crespón NM crape, crêpe.
cresta NF (a) (*Orn*) crest, comb; tuft. (b) (*peluca*) wig, toupée. (c) (*de ola*) crest. (d) (*Geog*) crest, ridge; summit.
crestería NF (*Arquit*) crenellations, battlements.
crestomatía NF anthology, collection of texts.
crestón NM (a) (*Mil*) crest (of helmet). (b) (*Min*) outcrop.
Creta NF Crete.
creta NF chalk.
cretáceo ADJ cretaceous.
cretense ADJ, NMF Cretan.
cretinada NF silly thing, stupid act.
cretinez NF stupidity.
cretinismo NM cretinism.
cretino ☐1 ADJ cretinous (*t fig*).
☐2 NM, **cretina** NF cretin (*t fig*).
cretona NF cretonne, chintz.
cretoso ADJ chalky.
creyendo *etc V* **creer**.
creyente NMF believer; **no ~** non-believer, unbeliever.
CRI NF ABR *de* **Cruz Roja Internacional** International Red Cross.
cría NF (a) (*acto*) rearing, keeping, breeding; **~ caballar** horse breeding; **~ de ganado** cattle breeding, stock raising; **~ de peces** fish farming; **hembra de ~** breeding female.
(b) (*animal*) baby animal, young creature; (*conjunto*) young; litter, brood.
criada NF servant, maid; **~ por horas** hourly-paid woman, daily (woman); **~ para todo** maid of all work, servant with general duties.
criadero NM (a) (*Bot*) nursery.
(b) (*Zool*) breeding ground, breeding place; **~ de ostras** oyster bed; **~ de peces** fish hatchery, fish farm.
(c) (*Geol*) vein, seam.
criadilla NF (a) (*patata*) potato, tuber; **~(s) de tierra** truffles. (b) (*pan*) small loaf, roll. (c) **~s** (*Culin*) bull's testicles; (**:**) balls**:**.
criado ☐1 ADJ bred, reared, brought up; **bien ~** well-bred; **mal ~** *V* **malcriado**.
☐2 NM (a) (*sirviente*) servant. (b) (*Naipes*) jack, knave.
criador NM (a) (*Agr etc*) breeder. (b) **el C~** (*Rel*) the Creator.
criajo, -a[*] NM/F wretched child, urchin; spotty herbert*.
criandera NF (*LAm*) nursemaid, wet-nurse.
crianza NF (a) (*Agr etc*) rearing, keeping, breeding. (b) (*Med*) lactation.
(c) (*de vino*) ageing, maturing. (d) (*fig*) breeding; **mala ~** bad breeding, lack of breeding; **sin ~** ill-bred.

───── CRIANZA ─────

i *Quality Spanish wine is often graded* **Crianza**, **Reserva** *or* **Gran Reserva** *according to the length of bottle-ageing and barrel-ageing it has undergone.* **Crianza** *wines are in their third year, reds having spent at least twelve months in cask and whites six.*
⇨ *See also* RESERVA

criar [1c] ☐1 VT (a) *bebé, hijuelos* to suckle, feed; **~ a los pechos** to breast-feed, nurse.
(b) *plantas* to grow; to tend, cultivate.
(c) *animales* to rear, raise; to keep, breed; to fatten.
(d) (*tierra etc*) to bear, grow, produce; **esta tierra no cría hierba** this land does not grow grass, this soil is not suitable for grass; **los perros crían pulgas** dogs have (*o* get) fleas; **~ carnes** to put on weight; **está criando pelo** he's getting some hair, his hair is growing.
(e) *niños* to bring up, raise; to educate; *V* **algodón**.
(f) *vino* to age, mature.
(g) (*fig*) *esperanzas etc* to foster, nourish, nurture.
☐2 VI (*animal*) to have young, produce.
☐3 **criarse** VR to grow (up); **se criaron juntos** they were brought up together, they grew up together; **~ en buena cuna** (*o* **en buenos pañales**) to be born with a silver spoon in one's mouth.
criatura NF (a) (*ser criado*) creature (*t fig*); being.
(b) (*niño*) infant, baby, small child; **¡~! look out!**; I say, do be careful!; **todavía es una ~** she's still very young, she's only a child still; **¡no seas ~!** be your age!; **hacer una ~ a una** to get a girl in the family way*.
criba NF (a) (*instrumento*) sieve, screen. (b) (*acto: fig*) sifting, selection; screening; **hacer una ~** (*fig*) to sort out the sheep from the goats.
cribar [1a] VT (a) to sieve, sift, screen. (b) (*fig*) to sift, select; to screen.
cric NM (*Mec*) jack.
Crimea NF Crimea.
crimen NM crime (*esp murder*); **~ de guerra** war crime; **~ organizado** organized crime; **~ pasional** crime of passion; **~ de sangre** violent crime.
criminal ☐1 ADJ criminal; of murder, murderous.
☐2 NMF criminal (*esp murderer*); **~ de guerra** war criminal.
criminalidad NF (a) (*gen*) criminality; guilt. (b) (*índice*) crime rate.
criminalista NMF (a) (*Univ*) criminologist. (b) (*Jur*) criminal lawyer.
criminalística NF criminology; study of the criminal, study of crime.
criminalizar [1f] VT: **~ un acto** to make an act a criminal offence.
criminógeno ADJ conducive to crime, encouraging criminal tendencies.
criminología NF criminology.
criminólogo, a NM/F criminologist.
crin NF horsehair; (*t ~es*) mane.
crinolina NF crinoline.
crinudo ADJ (*LAm*) *caballo* long-maned.
crío* NM kid*, child; (*pey*) brat.
criogénico ADJ cryogenic.
criogenizar [1f] VT to freeze cryogenically.
criollaje NM (*LAm*) Creoles (*collectively*); peasantry.
criollo ☐1 ADJ (a) (*gen*) Creole.
(b) (*LAm*) (*natural*) native (to America), indigenous; national; (*de origen español*) of Spanish extraction.
☐2 NM, **criolla** NF (a) Creole.
(b) (*LAm*) native (of America), native American; person of Spanish extraction.
(c) (*And: cobarde*) coward.
criosfera NF cryosphere.
cripta NF crypt.
críptico ADJ cryptic.
cripto... PREF crypto...
criptocomunista NMF crypto-communist.
criptografía NF cryptography.
criptográfico ADJ cryptographic(al).
criptógrafo, -a NM/F cryptographer.
criptograma NM cryptogram.
criptología NF cryptology.
críquet NM cricket.
crisálida NF chrysalis.
crisalidar [1a] VI to pupate.
crisantemo NM chrysanthemum.
crisis NF INVAR crisis; **~ de los cuarenta** midlife crisis; **~ económica** economic crisis; **~ de la energía**, **~ energética** energy crisis; **~ de identidad** identity crisis; **~ nerviosa** nervous breakdown; **~ de la vivienda** housing shortage; **hacer ~** to be in crisis; **llegar a la ~** to reach crisis point, come to a head.
crisma[1] NF (a) (*Ecl*) chrism, holy oil. (b) (**:** *cabeza*) nut**:**, head; **romper la ~ a uno** to knock sb's block off**:**.
crisma[2] ☐1 NM (*a veces* F; *t ~s*) Christmas card.
☐2 NF (*Méx*) Christmas present.
crismón NM *monogram of Christ*.
crisol NM crucible; (*fig*) melting pot.
crispación NF (*fig*) tension, nervousness; increase of tension; outrageous nature; **una escena de absoluta ~** an utterly shattering scene.
crispado ADJ tense, on edge.
crispante ADJ infuriating; outrageous; shattering.
crispar [1a] ☐1 VT (a) *músculo* to cause to twitch (*o* contract); *nervios*

to set on edge; **con el rostro crispado por la ira** with his face contorted with anger; **tengo los nervios crispados** my nerves are all on edge; **eso me crispa los nervios** that gets on my nerves; that jars (o grates) on me.

(b) ~ **a uno*** to annoy sb intensely, get on sb's nerves.

[2] **crisparse** VR (*músculo*) to twitch, contract; (*cara*) to contract; (*nervios*) to get all on edge; (*situación*) to become tense, get tenser.

crispetas NFPL (*And*) popcorn.

cristal NM **(a)** (*Quím*) crystal (*t fig*); ~ **líquido** liquid crystal; ~ **de roca** rock crystal.

(b) (*vidrio*) glass; **un** ~ a pane of glass, a sheet of glass; ~**es** (*frec*) window(s); ~ **ahumado** smoked glass; ~ **antibalas** bullet-proof glass; ~ **de aumento** lens, magnifying glass; ~ **cilindrado** plate glass; ~**es emplomados** leaded lights; ~ **hilado** fibreglass; ~ **inastillable** splinterproof glass; ~ **de patente** (*Náut*) bull's-eye; ~ **de seguridad** safety glass; ~ **soplado** blown glass; ~ **tallado** cut glass; **de** ~ glass (*atr*); **puerta de** ~**es** glass door.

(c) (*espejo*) glass, mirror.

cristalera NF (large) window.

cristalería NF **(a)** (*arte*) glasswork; glass making. **(b)** (*fábrica*) glassworks; (*tienda*) glassware shop. **(c)** (*vasos*) glasses (*collectively*), glassware.

cristalero NM (*Cono Sur*) glass cabinet.

cristalinamente ADV transparently.

cristalino ADJ (*Fís*) crystalline; (*fig*) clear, limpid, translucent; transparent.

cristalizar [1f] [1] VTI to crystallize.

[2] **cristalizarse** VR to crystallize.

cristalografía NF crystallography.

cristalógrafo, -a NM/F crystallographer.

cristero, -a NM/F (*Méx: Hist*) Catholic militant.

cristianamente ADV in a Christian way; **morir** ~ to die as a Christian, to die like a good Christian.

cristianar [1a] VT **(a)** (*bautizar*) to christen, baptize. **(b)** *vino* to water.

cristiandad NF Christendom; Christianity.

cristianismo NM Christianity.

cristianizar [1f] VT to Christianize.

cristiano [1] ADJ **(a)** (*Rel*) Christian.

(b) *vino* ~ watered wine.

(c) (*LAm: ingenuo*) simple-minded.

[2] NM, **cristiana** NF Christian; ~ **nuevo** (*Hist*) convert to Christianity; ~ **viejo** (*Hist*) Christian with no Jewish or Moslem blood.

[3] NM **(a)** (*persona*) person, (*living*) soul; **eso lo sabe cualquier** ~ any idiot knows that; **eso no hay** ~ **que lo entienda** that is beyond anyone's comprehension; **no hay** ~ **que lo sepa** there's nobody can tell that; **este** ~***** yours truly*.

(b) (*Ling*) ordinary language, (*esp*) Spanish; **hablar en** ~ to speak straightforwardly, make sense with what one says; ≈ to speak the Queen's (o King's) English.

Cristo NM Christ; **el año 41 antes de** ~ 41 BC; **el año 80 después de** ~ AD 80; **con el** ~ **en la boca** (*CAm**) with one's heart in one's mouth; **armar** ~***** to raise Cain; **donde** ~ **dio las tres voces***, **donde** ~ **perdió la gorra*** at the back of beyond*; in the middle of nowhere; **¡ni** ~ **que lo fundó!** don't you believe it!; **ni** ~ **ni nadie** nobody at all; **no había ni** ~ there wasn't a soul; **eso no lo sabe ni** ~ nobody knows that; **todo** ~ every mortal soul, every man Jack; **ir hecho un** ~***** to be a sight; **poner a uno como un** ~***** to give sb a dressing-down*; to heap abuse on sb.

cristo NM crucifix.

Cristóbal NM Christopher.

criterio NM **(a)** (*norma*) criterion; yardstick, standard of judgement; **por cualquier** ~ by any standard.

(b) (*enfoque*) viewpoint, attitude, approach; **depende del** ~ **de cada uno** it depends on the individual viewpoint; **lo mira con otro** ~ he looks at it from a different point of view; **hace falta tener un** ~ **más maduro** one needs a more mature approach.

(c) (*juicio*) discernment, discrimination; **lo dejo a su** ~ I leave it to your discretion; **tiene buen** ~ his taste is admirable.

(d) (*opinión*) view, opinion; **en mi** ~ in my opinion; **cambiar de** ~ to change one's mind; **no comparto ese** ~ I do not share that view; **formar un** ~ **sobre** to form an opinion of.

criterioso* ADJ (*Cono Sur*) level-headed, sensible.

crítica¹ NF **(a)** (*gen*) criticism; ~ **literaria** literary criticism; ~ **teatral** dramatic criticism.

(b) (*una* ~) criticism; (*reseña*) review, notice, critique; (*pey*) criticism; (*chismes*) gossip.

criticable ADJ: **no es** ~ **que se te oponga** you can't blame him for standing against you.

criticador [1] ADJ critical.

[2] NM, **criticadora** NF critic.

criticar [1g] VT to criticize.

criticastro, -a NM/F hack critic, ignorant critic.

criticidad NF critical nature; **fase de** ~ critical phase.

crítico [1] ADJ critical.

[2] NM, **crítica²** NF critic; ~ **de cine**, ~ **cinematográfico** film critic; ~ **literario** literary critic.

criticón [1] ADJ hypercritical, overcritical, faultfinding.

[2] NM, **criticona** NF carping critic, faultfinder.

critiquizar [1f] VT to be overcritical of, indulge in petty criticism of.

CRM NM ABR **de Certificado de regulación monetaria**.

Croacia NF Croatia.

croar [1a] VI to croak.

croata ADJ, NMF Croat(ian).

croché NM (*Cos*) crochet(work); **hacer** ~ to crochet.

crochet [kro'tʃe] NM **(a)** (*Cos*) = **croché**. **(b)** (*Boxeo*) hook.

crocitar [1a] VI to crow, caw.

croissant [krwa'zan] NM, PL **croissants** croissant.

croissantería [krwazante'ria] NF croissant shop.

crol NM (*Natación*) crawl.

cromado [1] ADJ chromium-plated; chrome.

[2] NM chromium plating; chrome.

cromático ADJ chromatic.

cromatografía NF chromatography.

cromatograma NM chromatogram.

cromo NM **(a)** (*Quím*) chromium; chrome. **(b)** (*Tip*) religious card; chromolithograph; (*cheap*) coloured print, chromo (*US*).

cromosoma NM chromosome.

cromosomático ADJ, **cromosómico** ADJ chromosomal.

cromoterapia NF chromotherapy, colour therapy.

crónica NF **(a)** (*Hist*) chronicle; **C~s** (*Biblia*) Chronicles; (*fig*) chronicle, account.

(b) (*en periódico*) news report; feature, article; ~ **deportiva** sports page; ~ **literaria** literary page; ~ **de sociedad** society column, gossip column; '**C~ de sucesos**' 'News in Brief'.

crónico ADJ (*Med y fig*) chronic; *vicio* ingrained.

cronificar [1g] [1] VT (*Prensa*) to chronicle.

[2] VI (*Med*) to become chronic.

[3] **cronificarse** VR (*Med*) to become chronic.

cronista NMF **(a)** (*Hist*) chronicler. **(b)** (*de periódico*) reporter, feature writer, columnist; ~ **deportivo** sports writer; ~ **de radio** radio commentator.

crono* [1] NM **(a)** (*reloj*) stopwatch. **(b)** (*tiempo*) recorded time.

[2] NF time-trial.

cronografista NMF (*Cono Sur*) timekeeper.

cronograma NM (*Cono Sur*) timetable, (*fig*) schedule.

cronología NF chronology.

cronológicamente ADV chronologically, in chronological order.

cronológico ADJ chronological.

cronometrada NF (*Dep*) time-trial.

cronometrador(a) NM/F timekeeper.

cronometraje NM timing.

cronometrar [1a] VT to time.

cronómetro NM (*Téc etc*) chronometer; (*Dep*) stopwatch.

croquet [kro'ke] NM croquet.

croqueta NF croquette, (*aprox*) rissole.

croquis NM INVAR sketch.

cross [kros] NM INVAR cross-country race; cross-country running.

crostón NM crouton.

crótalo NM **(a)** (*Zool*) rattlesnake. **(b)** ~**s** (*Mús: liter*) castanets.

croto* NM (*Cono Sur*) bum, layabout*.

cruasán NM croissant.

cruce NM **(a)** (*acto*) crossing; (*Aer*) ~ **incontrolado** air-miss, near miss.

(b) (*Mat etc*) (point of) intersection.

(c) (*Aut etc*) crossing, intersection; ~ **de carreteras** crossroads; ~ **giratorio** roundabout, traffic circle (*US*); ~ **a nivel** level crossing, grade crossing (*US*); ~ **de peatones** pedestrian crossing, crosswalk (*US*).

(d) (*Telec*) crossing of lines; **hay un** ~ **en las líneas** the wires are crossed.

(e) (*Bio*) cross, crossing.

(f) (*Ling*) cross, mutual interference.

crucerista NMF cruise passenger.

crucero NM **(a)** (*Mil*) cruiser; ~ **de batalla** battle cruiser; ~ **pesado** heavy cruiser.

(b) (*Náut*) cruise; ~ **de recreo** pleasure cruise.

(c) (*Ecl*) transept.

(d) (*Téc*) crosspiece.

(e) (*Aut etc*) crossroads; crossing; (*Ferro*) crossing.

(f) (*Ecl: persona*) crossbearer.

(g) (*Astron*) **C~** (*Austral*) Southern Cross.

(h) (*misil*) cruise missile.

cruceta NF **(a)** (*Téc*) crosspiece; (*Náut*) crosstree. **(b)** (*Mec*) crosshead.

(c) (*Cono Sur: torniquete*) turnstile.

crucial ADJ crucial.

crucificar [1g] VT to crucify; (*fig*) to torment, torture; to mortify.
crucifijo NM crucifix.
crucifixión NF crucifixion.
cruciforme ADJ cruciform.
crucigrama NM crossword (puzzle).
crucigramista NMF crossword enthusiast.
cruda* NF (*LAm*) hangover*.
crudelísimo ADJ (*liter: superl de* **cruel**) most cruel, terribly cruel.
crudeza NF (a) (*Culin*) (*de carne*) rawness; (*de frutas*) unripeness. (b) (*de comida*) indigestibility. (c) (*de agua*) hardness. (d) (*rigor*) bleakness, harshness. (e) (*aspereza*) crudity, crudeness, coarseness. (f) (*comida*) undigested food (in the stomach).
crudo ① ADJ (a) *carne* raw; (*Culin*) half-cooked, underdone, raw; *legumbres* green, uncooked; *fruta etc* unripe.
(b) *alimentos* hard to digest; **lo tendrán ~ si piensan que ...** they'll have a tough time of it if they think that ...
(c) *agua* hard.
(d) (*Téc*) untreated; *seda* raw; *lino* unbleached.
(e) *tiempo* raw, bleak, harsh.
(f) (*liter*) cruel, merciless.
(g) *frase, tema etc* crude, coarse; overrealistic.
② NM (a) (*petróleo*) crude (oil).
(b) (*LAm: tela*) coarse cloth, sackcloth.
(c) (*Méx*: resaca*) hangover*.
cruel ADJ cruel (*con, para* to).
crueldad NF cruelty.
cruelmente ADV cruelly.
cruento ADJ (*liter*) bloody, gory.
crujía NF (*Arquit*) corridor, gallery; bay; (*Med*) ward; (*Náut*) midship gangway; (*de cárcel*) wing; **pasar ~** to have a tough time of it.
crujido NM rustle; creak; crack; crunch; grinding, gnashing; chattering; crackle.
crujiente ADJ rustling; creaking; crunchy; grinding; crackling.
crujir [3a] VI (*hojas, seda, papel*) to rustle; (*madera, mueble, rama*) to creak; (*articulación, hueso*) to crack; (*grava etc*) to crunch; (*dientes*) to grind, gnash; to chatter; (*objeto que arde*) to crackle; **hacer ~ los nudillos** to crack one's knuckles.
crupier NM croupier.
crustáceo NM crustacean.
cruz NF (a) (*gen*) cross; **~ gamada** swastika; **~ de hierro** iron cross; **~ de Malta** Maltese Cross; **~ de mayo** (*LAm*), **C~ del Sur** Southern Cross; **C~ Roja** Red Cross; **¡~ y raya!** that's quite enough!, no more!; **en ~** cross-shaped; crosswise; **con los brazos en ~** with arms crossed; **por éstas que son cruces** by all that is holy; **cargar la ~** (*Méx**) to have a hangover; **firmar con una ~** to make one's mark; **hacerse cruces** to cross o.s.; (*fig*) to show one's surprise; **hacerse cruces de que ...** to be astonished that ...; **quedar en ~** to be in an agonising situation.
(b) (*de espada*) hilt; (*de ancla*) crown; (*de moneda*) tails; (*Tip*) dagger; (*Zool*) withers.
(c) (*fig*) cross, burden; **cada uno lleva su ~** each of us has his cross to bear.
cruza NF (*Cono Sur*) (a) (*Agr*) second ploughing. (b) (*Bio*) cross, crossing; hybrid.
cruzada NF crusade; **La C~** (*in official Spanish usage up to 1975*) the Civil War of 1936-39.
cruzadilla NF (*CAm*) level crossing, grade crossing (*US*).
cruzado ① ADJ (a) *brazos, cheque etc* crossed. (b) (*Cos*) double-breasted. (c) (*Zool*) crossbred, hybrid. (d) (*And**) hopping mad*, furious.
② NM (*Hist*) crusader.
cruzador(a)* NM/F (*Méx*) shoplifter.
cruzamiento NM (a) (*Bio*) crossing. (b) (*Ferro*) crossover.
cruzar [1f] ① VT (a) (*gen*) to cross; to cut across, intersect; *cheque* to cross; **~ un palo sobre otro** to place a stick across another; **~ algo sobre una superficie** to pass (o draw) sth across a surface; **~ el lago a nado** to swim across the lake.
(b) (*Náut*) to cruise.
(c) (*Bio*) to cross.
(d) **~ la espada con uno** to cross swords with sb; **~ palabras con uno** to have words with sb; **~ a uno con una condecoración** to invest sb with a decoration.
(e) *dinero* to put, stake.
(f) (*Agr, esp LAm*) to plough a second time.
(g) (*And, Cono Sur: atacar*) to fight, attack.
② **cruzarse** VR (a) (*caminos, líneas etc*) to cross, cross each other; to intersect.
(b) **~ de brazos** V **brazo**.
(c) (*personas*) to pass each other; **~ con uno en la calle** to pass sb in the street.
(d) **~ con uno** (*And, Cono Sur*) to fight sb, attack sb.
(e) **nuestras cartas se cruzaron** our letters crossed (in the post).

CSD NM (*Esp*) ABR *de* **Consejo Superior de Deportes** ≃ *Sports Council*.
c.s.f. ABR *de* **coste, seguro, y flete** cost, insurance, and freight, c.i.f.
CSIC [θe'sik] NM (*Esp*) ABR *de* **Consejo Superior de Investigaciones Científicas**.
CSN NM (*Esp*) ABR *de* **Consejo de Seguridad Nuclear** *nuclear safety council*.
CSP NM (*Esp*) ABR *de* **Cuerpo Superior de Policía**.
cta., c.^{ta} ABR *de* **cuenta** account, a/c.
cta. cte. ABR *de* **cuenta corriente** current account, C/A.
cta. cto. ABR *de* **carta de crédito** letter of credit, L/C.
ctdad. ABR *de* **cantidad** quantity, qty.
cte. ABR *de* **corriente, de los corrientes** of the present month, instant, inst.
CTM NF (*Méx*) ABR *de* **Confederación de Trabajadores de México**.
CTNE NF ABR *de* **Compañía Telefónica Nacional de España** ≃ *British Telecom*.
ctra. ABR *de* **carretera**.
CTV NF (*Venezuela*) ABR *de* **Confederación de Trabajadores de Venezuela**.
cu NF the (name of the) letter q.
c/u ABR *de* **cada uno** each, ea.
cuacar [1g] VT (*And, Carib, Cono Sur*): **no me cuaca** (*no quiero*) I don't want to; (*no me cuadra*) it doesn't suit me; **no me cuaca aquel muchacho** I don't like that boy.
cuácara NF (*And: levita*) frock coat; (*Cono Sur: blusa*) workman's blouse.
cuacho (*CAm*) = **cuate**.
cuaco* NM (a) (*Carib, Méx*) (*caballo*) nag. (b) (*bolsista*) bag snatcher.
cuaderna NF (*Náut*) timber; rib, frame.
cuadernillo NM quinternion; (*Ecl*) liturgical calendar; **~ de sellos** book of stamps.
cuadernito NM notebook.
cuaderno NM notebook; (*Escol etc*) exercise book; folder; (*) pack of cards; (*Náut*) **~ de bitácora**, **~ de trabajo** logbook; **C~ de Cortes** (*Hist*) official parliamentary record.
cuadra NF (a) (*Agr*) stable; **~ de carreras** racing stable.
(b) (*de hospital etc*) ward.
(c) (*Mil*) hut.
(d) (*sala*) hall, large room; (*And*) reception room.
(e) (*LAm: manzana*) block (of houses), city block.
(f) (*And: casa etc*) small rural property (*near a town*).
(g) (*medida: And, Cono Sur*) = *125.50 metres*, (*And, CAm, Carib, Cono Sur*) = *83.5 metres*.
cuadrada NF (*Mús*) breve.
cuadrado ① ADJ (a) (*Mat etc*) square; **tenerlos ~s*** to be real tough*.
(b) *diseño* with squares, chequered.
(c) *persona* broad, square-shouldered.
(d) (*Carib, Cono Sur: grosero*) coarse, rude.
(e) (*And: elegante*) graceful, elegant.
② NM (a) (*forma, t Mat*) square.
(b) (*regla*) (parallel) rule(r).
(c) (*Téc*) die.
(d) (*Cos*) gusset.
(e) (*Tip*) quadrat.
(f) (*Carib, Cono Sur*: persona*) boor, oaf.
Cuadragésima NF Quadragesima.
cuadragésimo ADJ fortieth.
cuadrangular ADJ quadrangular.
cuadrángulo ADJ quadrangular.
cuadrante NM (a) (*Mat, Náut*) quadrant. (b) (*de instrumento, radio*) dial; (*de reloj*) face; **~ (solar)** sundial.
cuadrar [1a] ① VT (a) (*Mat*) to square.
(b) (*Téc etc*) to square (off), make square.
(c) *papel* V **cuadricular**.
(d) (*fig*) to please; to suit; **si le cuadra** if it suits you.
(e) (*And Aut*) to park.
② VI (a) **~ con** to square with, tally with, fit, correspond to; to match; to suit, go with.
(b) **~ + infin** (*Cono Sur*) to be ready to + *infin*.
③ **cuadrarse** VR (a) **~** to square up, square one's shoulders; (*Mil*) to stand to attention.
(b) (*fig*) to dig one's heels in, refuse to budge; to take a firm line.
(c) **~ con uno** to become very solemn towards sb, adopt a coldly official attitude towards sb.
(d) (*Carib*: enriquecerse*) to make one's pile*; (*tener éxito*) to come out on top.
cuadratín NM (*Tip*) quadrat, quad, space.
cuadratura NF quadrature.
cuadrícula NF squares (ruled on paper *etc*); criss-cross pattern; (*de mapa*) grid.
cuadriculado ADJ = **cuadricular 1**; **papel ~** squared paper.
cuadricular ① ADJ *papel* ruled in squares, divided into squares; squared; *tela* chequered.

2 [1a] VT to rule squares on, divide into squares.
cuadrilátero **1** ADJ quadrilateral, four-sided.
   2 NM (*Mat, Arquit*) quadrilateral; (*Boxeo*) ring.
cuadrilla NF (*grupo*) party, group; (*pandilla*) band; gang; (*Mil*) squad; (††) armed patrol; (*de obreros*) gang, squad, team; shift; (*Taur*) cuadrilla, team of bullfighters; **~ de demolición** demolition squad; **~ de noche** night shift, night squad.
cuadrillazo NM (*And, Cono Sur*) gang attack.
cuadrillero NM group leader; chief; gang leader; (*pey, esp And, Cono Sur*) hooligan.
cuadrilongo **1** ADJ oblong.
   2 NM oblong.
cuadringentésimo ADJ four hundredth.
cuadripartido ADJ quadripartite.
cuadrito NM (*Culin etc*) cube; **cortar en ~s** to dice.
cuadrivio NM quadrivium.
cuadro **1** NM (a) (*Mat*) square; **2 metros en ~** 2 metres square; **diseño a ~s** chequered pattern, check (pattern), checked pattern (*US*); **un vestido de ~s** a check suit; **~s escoceses** tartan (pattern).
   (b) (*Arquit, Téc*) frame; **~ de bicicleta** bicycle frame; **~ de ventana** window frame.
   (c) (*Arte*) picture, painting; **dos ~s de Velázquez** two Velazquez paintings.
   (d) (*Teat*) scene (*t fig*); (*TV*) picture; **~ vivo** tableau; **fue un ~*** it was some scene*, it was really quite dramatic; **fue un ~ desgarrador** it was a heart-breaking scene (o picture).
   (e) (*Liter*) description, picture; **~ de costumbres** description of (regional) customs, scene of local colour.
   (f) (*Agr, Hort*) bed; patch; plot.
   (g) (*Elec etc*) panel; **~ de conexión manual** (*Telec*), **~ de conmutadores** (*Elec*), **~ de distribución** (*Elec*) switchboard; **~ de instrumentos** instrument panel; (*Aut*) dashboard; **~ de mandos** control panel.
   (h) (*Mil*) square (formation); **formar el ~** (*fig*) to close ranks.
   (i) (*t* **~ sinóptico**) table, chart, diagram.
   (j) (*personas*) cadre; staff, establishment of officials (*etc*); (*Dep*) team; (*Pol: de partido*) executive.
   (k) (*Med*) set of symptoms; **el paciente presentaba un cuadro vírico** the patient showed all the signs of a virus.
   (l) (*Cono Sur: matadero*) slaughterhouse.
   (m) (*Cono Sur: bragas*) knickers.
   (n) (*And: pizarra*) blackboard.
   2 ATR: **programa ~** general programme, framework programme.
cuadrúpedo NM quadruped; four-footed animal.
cuádruple ADJ quadruple; fourfold.
cuadruplicado ADJ quadruplicate; **por ~** in quadruplicate.
cuadruplicar [1g] **1** VT to quadruple; **las pérdidas cuadruplican las del año pasado** losses are four times last year's.
   2 cuadruplicarse VR to quadruple.
cuádruplo ADJ, NM quadruple.
cuajada NF curd; cottage cheese; cheese tart.
cuajado **1** ADJ (a) (*gen*) curdled, set, coagulated, congealed.
   (b) **~ de** (*fig*) full of, filled with; covered with; **una situación cuajada de peligros** a situation fraught with dangers; **un texto ~ de problemas** a text bristling with problems; **una corona cuajada de joyas** a crown covered with jewels.
   (c) **estar ~** (*asombrarse*) (*fig*) to be dumbfounded.
   (d) **quedarse ~** (*fig: dormido*) to fall asleep.
   2 NM: **~ de limón** lemon curd.
cuajaleche NM (a) (*Culin*) cheese rennet. (b) (*Bot*) bedstraw.
cuajar [1a] **1** VT (a) (*espesar*) to thicken; *leche* to curdle; *sangre etc* to congeal, coagulate, clot; *grasa* to congeal; *gelatina etc* to set.
   (b) (*cubrir*) to cover, adorn (excessively; *de* with); (*llenar*) to fill (*de* with); **cuajó el tablero de cifras** he covered the board with figures.
   2 VI (a) (*semilla etc*) to set; (*nieve*) to lie; V **3**.
   (b) (*fig*) to become set, become firm, become established; to jell; (*proyecto etc*) to take shape; to come off, work; (*resultado*) to materialize; (*propuesta, moción*) to be received, be acceptable; **el noviazgo no cuajó** the engagement did not work, the engagement was not a success; **los eslobodios no cuajan con los ruritanios** the Slobodians don't get on with (o don't hit it off with) the Ruritanians.
   (c) (*Méx: charlar*) to chat.
   3 cuajarse VR (a) (*espesarse*) to thicken; to curdle; to congeal, coagulate; to set.
   (b) **~ de** (*fig*) to fill with, fill up with; to become crowded with.
   (c) (*fig*) to go fast asleep.
cuajarón NM clot.
cuajo NM (a) (*Culin*) rennet; **~ en polvo** powdered rennet.
   (b) (*fig*) phlegm, calmness; **tiene mucho ~** he's very phlegmatic.
   (c) **coger un ~*** to cry one's eyes out; V *t* **llorar**.
   (d) **arrancar algo de ~** to tear sth out by its roots; **arrancar una puerta de ~** to wrench a door out of its frame; **extirpar un vicio de**

~ to eradicate a vice completely.
   (e) (*Méx*: charla*) chat; chatter.
   (f) (*Méx*: mentirilla*) fib.
   (g) (*Méx*: proyecto*) pipe-dream.
   (h) (*Méx*: en escuela*) playtime.
cual **1** ADJ (*liter*) such as, of the kind (that); (*Jur*) said, aforementioned; **los ~es bienes** the said property, which property; **las ceremonias fueron ~es convenían a su importancia** the ceremonies were such as befitted his importance.
   2 PRON (a) **cada ~** each one, everyone; **allá cada ~** every man to his own taste; **cada ~ con su cada cuala*** like with like.
   (b) (*relativo*) **el ~** (*etc*) which; who; whom; **ese edificio, el ~ se construyó en el siglo XV** that building, which was built in the 15th century; **un policía, el ~ me puso una multa** a policeman, who gave me a fine.
   (c) **lo ~** (*relativo*) which; a fact which; **se rieron mucho, lo ~ me disgustó** they laughed a lot, which upset me; **con lo ~** at which, whereupon; **por lo ~** (and) so, and because of this, on account of which; whereby.
   3 ADV Y CONJ: + *noun* like, as; + *verb* (just) as; **brillaba ~ estrella** it shone like a star; **~ ... tal** (o **así**) **...** like ... like ...; (*verbo*) just as ..., so ...; **~ el padre, tal el hijo** like father like son; **~ el otro, tal éste** this one is just like the other, this one is as bad (*etc*) as the other; **~ llega el día tras la noche** just as day follows night; **~ si ...** as if ...; V **tal**.
cuál **1** PRON INTERROG (a) which (one)?; **¿~ quieres?** which (one) do you want?; **¿~ es el que dices?** which one are you talking about?; **tú ¿a ~ colegio vas?** (*Méx*) which school do you go to?; **si es tan malo A, ¿~ debe ser B?** if A is so bad, what must B be like?; **ignora ~ será el resultado** he does not know what the outcome will be. (b) (*locuciones*) **son a ~ más gandul** each is as idle as the other; **una serie de coches a ~ más rápido** a series of cars each faster than the last (o outdoing each other in speed); **gritar a ~ más** to see who can shout the loudest; **~ más, ~ menos** some more, some less.
   2 EXCL: **¡~ no sería mi asombro!** how surprised I was!; **¡~ gritan esos malditos!** how those wretched people shout!
   3 ADJ INTERROG (*LAm*) which?; **¿~ libro dices?** which book do you mean?; **¿~es carros?** which cars?; **¿a ~ colegio vas?** which school do you go to?
cualidad NF (*gen*) quality; (*atributo*) attribute, trait, characteristic; (*Filos, Fís etc*) property; **tiene buenas ~es** he has good qualities.
cualificado ADJ (a) *obrero* skilled, qualified; **obrero no ~** unskilled worker. (b) **estar ~ para** + *infin* to be entitled to + *infin*. (c) V **calificado**.
cualitativamente ADV qualitatively.
cualitativo ADJ qualitative.
cualquier(a), PL **cualesquier(a)** **1** ADJ (a) (*gen*) any; any ... you care to name (o like to mention *etc*); **~ hombre de los de aquí** any man from these parts; **en ~ momento** at any time; **en ~ sitio donde lo busques** in whatever place you look for it, whichever place you look for it in; **con ~ resultado que sea** with whatever result it may be.
   (b) **hay ~ cantidad** (*LAm*) there's a large quantity, there's any amount.
   (c) (*tras n*) any; **ella no es una mujer ~** she's not just any woman, she's not just an ordinary woman.
   2 PRON **cualquiera**, PL **cualesquiera** (a) (*gen*) anybody; whoever; whichever; **¡así ~!** anybody could manage that!; big deal!*; **te lo diría ~** anyone would tell you the same; **~ puede hacer eso** anybody can do that; **¡~ lo sabe!** who knows?; **yo me contento con ~** I am happy with any (o either); I don't mind either (of the two).
   (b) **~ que sea** whoever he is; whichever it is.
   (c) **es un ~** he's a nobody; **yo no me caso con un ~** I'm not marrying just anybody.
   (d) **una ~*** a whore, a slut.
cuan ADV (*liter*): **tan estúpidos ~ criminales** as much stupid as they are criminal.
cuán ADV how; **¡~ agradable fue todo eso!** how delightful it all was!
cuando **1** ADV Y CONJ (a) (*tiempo*) when; **~ nos veamos** when we meet again; **~ iba allí le veía** whenever I went there I saw him; **ven ~ quieras** come when(ever) you like; **me acuerdo de ~ ...** I remember the time when ...; **lo dejaremos para ~ estés mejor** we'll leave it until you're better; **de ~ en ~** from time to time; V **cada**.
   (b) (*condicional, causal*) if, even if, although; since, when; **~ lo dice él, será verdad** if he says so, it must be true; **~ no sea así** even if it is not so; **~ más** at (the) most; **~ menos** at least; **~ mucho** at (the) most; **~ no** if not, otherwise; **¡~ no!** (*LAm*) of course!, naturally!; **~ nos convida a cenar, de seguro comeremos bien** since he's inviting us, we're sure to eat well; V **aun** etc.
   2 PREP at the time of; **eso fue ~ la guerra** that was during the war; **ocurrió ~ la boda** it happened at the same time as the wedding; **~ niño** as a child, when I (*etc*) was a child.

cuándo ADV Y CONJ INTERROG when; ¿~ **lo perdiste?** when did you lose it?; **no sé ~ será** I don't know when it will be; ¿**de ~ acá?** since when?; (*fig*) how come?; ¿**desde ~ es esto así?** how long has it been like this?; ~ **con A, ~ con B** sometimes with A, sometimes with B.

cuandoquiera CONJ: ~ **que ...** whenever ...

cuantía NF (*cantidad*) quantity, amount; (*alcance*) extent; (*importancia*) importance; **de mayor ~** first-rate; important; **de menor ~, de poca ~** second-rate; unimportant, of little account; **se ignora la ~ de las pérdidas** the extent of the losses is not known.

cuántico ADJ: **teoría cuántica** quantum theory.

cuantificable ADJ quantifiable.

cuantificación NF quantifying; **hacer una ~ de** to quantify.

cuantificador NM quantifier.

cuantificar [1g] VT to quantify.

cuantimás: ~ **que** CONJ all the more so because ...

cuantioso ADJ (*grande*) large, substantial; (*abundante*) abundant; (*numeroso*) numerous; (*importante*) considerable; *pérdida* heavy, grave.

cuantitativamente ADV quantitatively.

cuantitativo ADJ quantitative.

cuanto ① ADJ all that, as much as, whatever; **daremos ~s créditos se precisen** we will give all the credits that may be necessary, we will give whatever credits are needed; ~**s hombres la ven la quieren** all the men that see her fall in love with her; **unos ~s libros** a few books, some books; ~**s más haya tantas más comidas habrá que preparar** the more there are the more meals will have to be cooked. ② PRON all that (which), as much as; ~**s** all those that, as many as; **tiene ~ desea** he has all (that) he wants; **toma ~ quieras** take all you want, take as much as you want; ~**s más, mejor** the more the merrier. ③ ADV Y CONJ (a) **en ~** inasmuch as; **él, en ~ erudito, ...** he, as a scholar, ...; **en ~** (CONJ) as soon as, immediately, directly; **en ~ lo supe me fui** as soon as I heard it I left; **en ~ a** as for, as to, with regard to; **en ~ que ...** insofar as ...; **por ~** and so, hence; because; inasmuch as, in that ...
(b) ~ **más** at least; ~ **más difícil parezca** the more difficult it may seem, however difficult it seems; ~ **más trabaja menos gana** the more he works the less he earns; ~ **más que resultó ser mujer** all the more so because it turned out to be a woman; *V* **antes** *etc.*

cuánto ADJ, PRON Y ADV ① EXCL (a) (+ *verbo*) ¡~ **has crecido!** how you've grown!; ¡~ **trabajas!** how hard you work!; ¡~ **has gastado!** what a lot you've spent!; ¡~ **me alegro!** I'm so glad!
(b) (+ N) ¡**cuanta gente!** what a lot of people!; ¡~ **tiempo perdido!** what a lot of time wasted!, the time you've wasted!; *V* **bueno.**
② INTERROG (*sing*) how much?; ¿~ **has gastado?** how much have you spent?; ¿~ (**tiempo**)? how long?; ¿~ **durará esto?** how long will this last?; ¿~ **hay de aquí a Bilbao?** how far is it from here to Bilbao?; ¿**a ~ estamos?** (*Dep*) what's the score?; ¿**a ~ están las peras?** how much are (the) pears?; **le dije ~ la quería** I told her how much I loved her; *V* **cada, cinco.**
(b) (PL) ¿~**s?** how many?; ¿**cuantas personas había?** how many people were there?; ¿**a ~s estamos?** what's the date?
(c) **el señor no sé ~s** Mr So-and-So; **el señor Anastasio no sé ~s** Mr Anastasius Something.

CUÁNTO ___ *ver también la entrada*

¿Cuánto tiempo?
- Cuando se habla de la duración de algo, *cuánto (tiempo)* se traduce al inglés por *how long* y se utiliza el pretérito perfecto cuando la acción comenzó en el pasado y continúa todavía:
  ¿Cuánto tiempo llevas esperando?
  How long have you been waiting?
  ¿Cuánto hace que nos conocemos?
  How long have we known each other?
- En otros contextos, no debe utilizarse el pretérito perfecto:
  ¿Cuánto tardasteis en llegar a Barcelona?
  How long did it take you to get to Barcelona?
  ¿Cuánto dura la película?
  How long is the film?
  Para otros usos y ejemplos ver la entrada.

---

cuaquerismo NM Quakerism.

cuáquero, -a ADJ, NM/F Quaker.

cuarcita NF quartzite.

cuarenta ADJ forty; fortieth; **ésas son otras ~** (*And, Cono Sur*) that's a different story; **los (años) ~** the forties; '**Los ~ principales**' (*Rad*) ≃ 'the Top Forty' (*Spanish hit parade*); **los ~ rugientes** the Roaring Forties; **cantar las ~ a uno** to tell sb a few home truths; **hasta el ~ de mayo no te quites el sayo** ne'er cast a clout till May be out.

cuarentañero ① ADJ fortyish, about forty.
② NM, **cuarentañera** NF person of about forty, person in his (o her) forties.

cuarentavo ① ADJ fortieth; **la cuarentava parte** a fortieth.

② NM fortieth.

cuarentena NF (a) (*gen*) forty; about forty. (b) (*Ecl*) Lent. (c) (*Med*) quarantine; **poner en ~** (*fig*) *persona* to send to Coventry, *asunto* to suspend judgement on.

cuarentón ① ADJ forty-year old, fortyish.
② NM, **cuarentona** NF person of about forty.

cuaresma NF Lent; *see also* CARNAVAL.

cuaresmal ADJ Lenten.

cuark NM, PL **cuarks** quark.

cuarta NF (a) (*Mat*) quarter, fourth, fourth part.
(b) (*de mano*) span.
(c) (*Náut*) point (of the compass).
(d) (*LAm: látigo*) whip, riding crop.
(e) (*Cono Sur Agr*) extra pair of oxen.
(f) (*) **andar de la ~ al pértigo** (*Cono Sur*), **vivir a la ~** (*Cono Sur, Méx*) to be on the bread line.

cuartago NM pony.

cuartazos* NM INVAR fat person, lump*.

cuartear [1a] ① VT (a) (*dividir*) to quarter; to divide up, cut up; *carne* to quarter, joint.
(b) *carretera* to zigzag up.
(c) (*Náut*) ~ **la aguja** to box the compass.
(d) (*Carib, Méx: azotar*) to whip, beat.
② VI (a) (*Naipes*) to make a fourth (player), make up a four.
(b) (*Taur*) to dodge, step aside, swerve.
③ **cuartearse** VR (a) (*superficie*) to crack, split.
(b) (*Taur*) to dodge, step aside.
(c) (*Méx: desdecirse*) to go back on one's word.

cuartel NM (a) (*cuarta parte*) quarter, fourth part; (*de ciudad*) quarter, district.
(b) (*Her*) quarter.
(c) (*Hort*) bed.
(d) (*Mil*) barracks; ~**es** quarters; ~ **de bomberos** fire station; ~ **general** headquarters; ~**es de invierno** winter quarters; **vida de ~** army life, service life; **estar de ~** to be on half-pay.
(e) **guerra sin ~** war without mercy; **lucha sin ~** (*fig*) a fight with no holds barred; **dar ~ a** to support, encourage; **no dar ~** to give no quarter, show no mercy; **no hubo ~ para los revoltosos** no mercy was shown to the rioters.

cuartelada NF, **cuartelazo** NM military uprising, mutiny, coup, putsch.

cuartelero ① ADJ barracks (*atr*).
② NM (*And*) waiter.

cuartelillo NM police-station; fire station.

cuartería NF (*Carib, Cono Sur*) bunkhouse (*on a ranch*).

cuarterón NM (a) (*peso*) quarter; quarter pound. (b) (*Arquit*) door panel. (c) (*LAm*) quadroon.

cuarteta NF quatrain.

cuarteto NM (a) (*Mús*) quartet(te). (b) (*Liter*) quatrain.

cuartil NM quartile.

cuartilla NF (a) (*hoja*) sheet (of paper); ~**s** (*Tip*) manuscript, copy; (*apuntes*) notes, jottings. (b) (*de caballo*) pastern. (c) (*cuarta parte*) fourth part (*of a measure*).

cuarto ① ADJ fourth.
② NM (a) (*cuarta parte*) quarter, fourth part; (*abrigo*) **tres ~s** three-quarter length coat; ~ **de final** quarter finals; ~ **de hora** quarter of an hour; **las 6 y ~** a quarter past 6; **las 7 menos ~** a quarter to seven; **tardó tres ~s de hora** he took three-quarters of an hour; ~ **de luna** quarter of the moon; ~ **creciente** first quarter; ~ **menguante** last quarter.
(b) (*de carne*) joint; ~**s** (*de animal*) legs, limbs; ~ **trasero** hind-quarters, (*Culin*) rump.
(c) (*Tip*) quarto; **libro en ~** quarto volume.
(d) (*Fin*) an ancient coin; ~**s*** money, brass*; **de tres al ~** worthless, third-rate, tuppenny-ha'penny; **por 5 ~s** for a song; ¡**qué coche ni qué ocho ~s!** car, my foot!; **es hombre de muchos ~s** he's got pots of money*; **estar sin un ~, no tener un ~** to be broke*; **dar un ~ al pregonero** to tell everyone one's private business.
(e) (*Arquit*) (*gen*) room; rooms; (*piso*) small flat; (*Cono Sur*) bedroom; ~ **de aseo**, ~ **de baño** bathroom; ~ **de desahogo**, ~ **trastero** lumber room; ~ **de descanso** rest room; ~ **de estar** living room; ~ **de juego** playroom; ~ **de los niños** nursery; ~ **oscuro** (*Fot*) darkroom; **poner ~** to set up house; **poner ~ a la querida** to set one's mistress up in a little place.
(f) (*servidumbre*) household, establishment of servants.
(g) (*Mil*) watch; **estar de ~** to be on duty.

cuartofinalista NMF quarter-finalist.

cuartón NM plank.

cuartones NMPL dressed timber, beams, planks.

cuartucho NM hovel; poky little room.

cuarzo NM quartz.

cuás* NM (*Méx*) bosom pal*.

cuásar NM quasar.

cuasi ADV (*liter*) = **casi.**

cuasi- ... PREFIX quasi- ...

cuate (*And, CAm, Méx*) [1] ADJ twin.
[2] NM (a) (*gemelo*) twin. (b) (*amigo*) pal*, buddy (*esp US*). (c) (*escopeta*) double-barrelled gun.
[3] NF girl.

cuaternario ADJ, NM quaternary.

cuatre(re)ar [1a] [1] VT (*Cono Sur*) *ganado* to rustle, steal.
[2] VI (*Cono Sur*) to act treacherously.

cuatrero [1] ADJ (*CAm*) treacherous, disloyal.
[2] NM (*Cono Sur*) (*de ganado*) cattle rustler; (*de caballos*) horse thief.

cuatrienal ADJ four-year (*atr*); four-yearly, quadrennial.

cuatrifónico ADJ quadraphonic.

cuatrillizo NM, **cuatrilliza** NF quadruplet.

cuatrimestral ADJ four-monthly, every four months.

cuatrimestralmente ADV every four months.

cuatrimestre NM four-month period.

cuatrimotor [1] ADJ four-engined.
[2] NM four-engined plane.

cuatriplicado ADJ quadruplicate; **por ~** in quadruplicate.

cuatro [1] ADJ (a) (*gen*) four; (*fecha*) fourth; **las ~** four o'clock.
(b) **más de ~** (*fig*) quite a few, rather a lot; **sólo había ~ muebles** there were only a few sticks of furniture; **había ~ gatos** there was hardly a soul; **cayeron ~ gotas** a few drops fell.
[2] NM (a) four.
(b) (*And, Carib: Mús*) four-stringed guitar.
(c) (*Méx: trampa*) trick, fraud; (*error*) blunder.
(d) (*Aut*) ~ ~ four-wheel drive vehicle.

cuatrocientos ADJ four hundred.

cuatrojos* NMF INVAR person who wears glasses.

cuba¹ NF (a) (*tonel*) cask, barrel; (*tina*) tub; vat; (*Ferro*) tank car; **~ para el agua de lluvia** rainwater butt; **~ de riego** water wagon, street sprinkler.
(b) (*: *gordo*) pot-bellied person.
(c) (*: *borracho*) drunkard, boozer‡; **estar hecho una ~** to be as drunk as a lord.

cuba² NM (*And*) youngest child.

cubaje NM (*LAm*) volume, contents.

cuba-libre NM, PL **cubas-libres** o **cuba-libres** drink of rum and Coca Cola.

cubanismo NM cubanism, word (*o phrase etc*) peculiar to Cuba.

cubano, -a ADJ, NM/F Cuban.

cubata* NM = **cuba-libre.**

cubero NM cooper.

cubertería NF cutlery; (*Com*) table wares.

cubeta NF (*tonel*) keg, small cask; (*balde*) pail; (*Quím, Fot*) tray; (*de termómetro*) bulb; **~ de siembra** seed box.

cubicaje NM (*Aut*) cylinder capacity.

cubicar [1g] VT (a) (*Mat*) to cube. (b) (*Fís*) to determine the volume of.

cúbico ADJ cubic; **metro ~** cubic metre; **raíz cúbica** cube root.

cubículo NM cubicle.

cubierta NF (a) (*gen*) cover, covering; (*Tip*) paper cover, jacket; (*Arquit*) roof; (*Téc*) casing; (*Aut: capó*) bonnet, hood (*US*); (*Aut etc: neumático*) tyre, outer cover; (*Correos*) envelope; **~ de cama** coverlet; **~ sin cámara** tubeless tyre; **~ de lona** tarpaulin, canvas; **bajo esta ~** (*Correos*) under the same cover, enclosed herewith; **bajo ~ separada** (*Correos*) under separate cover.
(b) (*Náut*) deck; **~ de aterrizaje, ~ de botes** boat-deck; **~ de paseo** promenade deck; **~ del sol** sun deck; **~ de vuelo** flightdeck.
(c) (*And, Méx: funda*) sheath.
(d) (*fig*) cover, pretext.

cubierto [1] PTP *de* **cubrir** *y adj:* (a) (*gen*) covered; *cielo* overcast; *persona* with a hat, wearing a hat; **no ~** *cheque* bad, unbacked; **poco ~** *neumático* threadbare, worn.
(b) **la vacante está ya cubierta** the place has already been filled.
[2] NM (a) **a ~, bajo ~** under cover; **a ~ de** safe from, out of the way of; **ponerse a ~** to take cover, shelter (*de* from).
(b) (*en mesa*) place (at table), place setting; knife, fork and spoon, set of cutlery; (*comida*) meal; meal at a fixed charge; **~s** cutlery; **~ de 8000 pesetas** 8000-peseta meal; **precio del ~** cover charge.

cubil NM den, lair.

cubilete NM (a) (*Culin: cuenco*) basin, bowl; (*molde*) mould; (*copa*) goblet. (b) (*en juegos*) cup; (*de dados*) dice box. (c) (*LAm: intriga*) intrigue.
(d) (*LAm*) (*chistera*) top hat; (*hongo*) bowler hat.

cubiletear [1a] VI (a) (*en el juego*) to shake the dice box. (b) (*fig*) to intrigue, scheme.

cubiletero, -a NM/F conjurer.

cubismo NM cubism.

cubista ADJ, NMF cubist.

cubitera NF ice-tray.

cubito NM (a) (*de niño*) bucket, beach pail. (b) **~ de caldo** stock cube;

~ de hielo ice-cube.

cúbito NM ulna.

cubo NM (a) (*Mat*) cube; **~ de Rubik** Rubik cube.
(b) (*balde*) bucket, pail; (*tina*) tub; **~ de (la) basura** dustbin, ashcan (*US*); **~ para el carbón** coal scuttle; **llover a ~s** to rain cats and dogs, rain in torrents.
(c) (*de reloj*) barrel, drum.
(d) (*de rueda*) hub.
(e) (*caz*) millpond.
(f) (*Arqui*) round turret.

cuboflash NM (*Fot*) flashcube.

cubrebocas NM INVAR (*Med*) mask.

cubrebotones NM INVAR button-cover.

cubrecama NM coverlet, bedspread.

cubrecorsé NM camisole.

cubremesa NF table cover.

cubreobjetos NM INVAR (*Bio etc*) slide cover.

cubrerradiadores NM INVAR wooden cover for radiator.

cubretetera NM, **cubreteteras** NM INVAR tea cosy, tea cozy (*US*).

cubrir [3a; PTP **cubierto**] [1] VT (a) (*gen*) to cover (in, over, up; *con, de* with); (*Arquit*) to roof, put a roof over; *fuego* to make up, bank up; **lo cubrieron los aguas** the waters closed over it; **el agua casi me cubría** the water almost covered me, I was almost out of my depth; **no te metas donde te cubra el agua** don't go out of your depth.
(b) (*Dep, Mil*) to cover; to protect, defend; **~ su retirada** to cover one's retreat.
(c) (*disimular etc*) to cover; to hide, conceal, cloak; **cubre su tristeza con una falsa alegría** she covers up her sadness with a false cheerfulness.
(d) (*llenar*) **~ a uno de improperios** to shower insults on sb, shower sb with insults; **~ a uno de alabanzas** to heap praises on sb; **~ a uno de atenciones** to overwhelm sb with kindnesses; **~ a uno de oprobio** to cover sb in shame; **~ a uno de besos** to smother sb with kisses.
(e) *proteger* to cover, protect; to cover up for.
(f) *distancia* to cover, travel, do; **~ 80 kms en una hora** to cover 80 kms in an hour.
(g) *vacante* to fill.
(h) (*Bio*) to cover, mate with; (‡‡) to screw ‡‡.
(i) (*Fin etc*) *gastos, necesidades* to meet, cover; *déficit, préstamo etc* to cover; *deuda* to repay; **esto cubre todas nuestras necesidades** this meets all our needs; **ello apenas cubre los gastos** this scarcely covers the expenses.
(j) (*Periodismo*) *suceso* to cover.
[2] **cubrirse** VR (a) (*persona*) to cover o.s.; (*ponerse el sombrero*) to put on one's hat.
(b) **~ de gloria** (*fig*) to cover o.s. with glory.
(c) **~ contra un riesgo** to cover (o protect) o.s. against a risk; **~ contra una posibilidad** to take precautions against an eventuality.
(d) (*Met*) to become overcast.

cuca NF (a) (*jugador*) compulsive gambler. (b) **~s** sweets, candy (*US*); titbits; confectionery. (c) (‡: *Fin*) one peseta. (d) (*CAm*‡‡) cunt‡‡. (e) (*: *cucaracha*) cockroach.

cucambé NM (*And*) hide-and-seek.

cucamente ADV shrewdly; slyly, craftily.

cucamonas* NFPL (*palabras*) sweet nothings; (*caricias*) caresses; (*magreo*) fondling, petting*; **ella me hizo ~** she gave me a come-hither look.

cucaña NF (a) (*) (*prebenda*) plum*, soft job*; (*ganga*) bargain; (*chollo*) cinch*, easy thing. (b) (*de feria etc*) greasy pole.

cucañero, -a* NM/F shrewd person, fly sort; hanger-on.

cucar [1g] VT (a) (*guiñar*) to wink. (b) (*burlarse*) to deride, poke fun at.
(c) (*LAm: instar*) to urge on, incite, provoke.

cucaracha [1] NF (a) (*Ent*) cockroach. (b) (*Méx** *Aut*) old crock. (c) (‡: *droga*) roach‡. (d) (*Inform*) chip.
[2] NM (*) priest.

cucarachero NM (*And, Carib: parásito*) parasite, hanger-on; (*And: adulador*) flatterer, creep‡.

cuchara NF (a) (*gen*) spoon; scoop; (*cucharón*) ladle; (*Téc*) scoop; (*balde*) bucket; dipper; **~ de café** coffee spoon, (*equivalente a*) teaspoon; **~ de sopa, ~ sopera** soup spoon, (*como medida*) tablespoon; **militar de ~*** officer who has risen from the ranks, ranker; **meter su ~** (*en conversación*) to butt in; (*en asunto*) to meddle, shove one's oar in; **meter algo a uno con ~** to have a hard job getting sb to understand sth; **despacharse** (*o* **servirse**) **con la ~ grande** (*esp LAm*) to give o.s. a big helping, (*fig*) look after Number One; **soplar ~*** to eat; **soplar ~ caliente*** to eat well.
(b) (*LAm: paleta*) flat trowel; **albañil de ~** skilled bricklayer.
(c) (*CAm, Carib, Cono Sur: puchero*) pout; **hacer ~** to pout.
(d) (*Méx: carterista*) pickpocket.

cucharada NF spoonful; **~ de café** teaspoonful; **~ rasada** level spoonful; **~ de sopa, ~ sopera** tablespoonful.

cucharadita NF teaspoonful.

cucharear [1a] VT (*Culin*) to spoon out, ladle out; (*Agr*) to pitch, pitchfork.

cucharetear [1a] VI (a) (*lit*) to stir (with a spoon). (b) (*fig*) to meddle.

cucharilla NF (a) (*t* **cucharita**, **~ de café**, **~ de té**) small spoon, teaspoon. (b) (*Pesca*) spoon. (c) (*Golf*) wedge.

cucharón NM (*Culin*) ladle; (*Téc*) scoop, bucket; **tener el ~ por el mango** to be the boss, be in control.

cuche NM (*CAm*), **cuchí** NM (*And*) pig.

cuché NM art paper.

cuchi* (*Perú*) [1] INTERJ *call to a pig.*
[2] NM piggy.

cuchichear [1a] VI to whisper (*a* to).

cuchicheo NM whispering.

cuchilear* [1a] VT (*LAm*) to egg on.

cuchilla NF (a) (*Culin*) (large, kitchen) knife; (*de carnicero*) chopper, cleaver; (*Téc*) blade; (*de patín*) blade; (*LAm*: *cortaplumas*) penknife; **~ de afeitar** razor blade.
(b) (*Geog*) ridge, crest; (*LAm*: *colinas*) line of low hills; (*Carib*: *cumbre*) mountain top.

cuchillada NF (a) (*herida*) slash, cut, gash, knife wound; **~ de cien reales** long gash, severe wound; **dar ~** (*Teat**) to make a hit.
(b) (*Cos*) slash.
(c) **~s** (*fig*) fight, brawl.

cuchillazo NM (*LAm*) = **cuchillada** (a).

cuchillería NF (a) (*cubiertos*) cutlery. (b) (*tienda*) cutler's (shop).

cuchillero [1] ADJ (*LAm*) quarrelsome, fond of brawling.
[2] NM cutler.

cuchillo NM (a) (*gen*) knife; **~ de caza**, **~ de monte** hunting knife; **~ de cocina** kitchen knife; **~ del pan** breadknife; **~ de trinchar** carving knife; **pasar a ~** to put to the sword; **remover el ~ en la llaga** to turn the knife in the wound.
(b) (*Arquit*: *t* **~ de armadura**) upright, support.
(c) **~ de aire** sharp draught, cold draught.
(d) (*de jabalí etc*) fang, tusk.
(e) (*Cos*) gore.

cuchipanda* NF feed*, beano‡.

cuchitril NM (a) (*Agr*) pigsty. (b) (*fig*) hovel; pigsty; den, hole.

cucho¹ NM (a) (*CAm*: *jorobado*) hunchback; (*Méx*: *manco*) limbless person. (b) (*Cono Sur*: *gato*) puss. (c) (*And*) = **cuchitril** (b).

cucho²* ADJ (*Méx*) gloomy, depressed.

cuchuche NM: **ir a ~** (*CAm*) to ride piggyback.

cuchuflé NM (*Carib*) = **cuchuflí**.

cuchufleta* NF (a) (*broma*) joke, crack*. (b) (*Méx*: *baratija*) trinket, trifle.

cuchuflí* NM (*Carib*) uncomfortable place; (*celda*) cell.

cuchugos NMPL (*And*, *Carib*) saddlebags.

cuchumbo NM (*CAm*) (*embudo*) funnel; (*balde*) bucket, pail; (*de dados*) dice box; (*juego*) game of dice.

cuclillas ADV: **en ~** squatting, crouching; **ponerse en ~**, **sentarse en ~** to squat, sit on one's heels.

cuclillo NM (a) (*Orn*) cuckoo. (b) (*) cuckold.

cuco [1] ADJ (a) (*astuto*) shrewd; sly, crafty.
(b) (*mono*) pretty; cute; dainty.
[2] NM (a) (*Orn*) cuckoo.
(b) (*Ent*) grub, caterpillar.
(c) (*: *jugador*) gambler.
(d) **hacer ~ a uno** (*Méx*) to poke fun at sb.
(e) (*Cono Sur**: *sabelotodo*) smart guy*, wise guy*.
(f) (*Carib*‡) cunt‡‡.
(g) (*And*, *Cono Sur*: *fantasma*) bogeyman.

cucú NM (*grito*) cuckoo.

cucuche (*CAm*): **ir a ~** to ride astride.

cucufato* NM (*And*, *Cono Sur*) (*hipócrita*) hypocrite; (*mojigato*) prude; (*loco*) nut‡.

cuculí NM (*And*, *Cono Sur*) wood pigeon.

cucur(r)ucú INTERJ, NM (*LAm*) cockadoodledoo.

cucurucho NM (a) (*papel*) paper cone, cornet; (*Aut*) cone. (b) (*Ecl etc*) hooded garment; pointed hat. (c) (*And*, *CAm*, *Carib*: *cumbre*) top, summit, apex. (d) (*Carib*: *cuchitril*) hovel, shack.

cueca NF (*Cono Sur*) handkerchief dance.

cuelga NF (a) (*acto*) hanging (of fruit *etc* to dry); (*racimo*) bunch (of drying fruit *etc*). (b) (*regalo*) birthday present. (c) (*And*, *Cono Sur*: *Geog*) fall (in the level of a stream *etc*).

cuelgacapas NM INVAR (*percha*) coat hanger; (*mueble*) hallstand.

cuelgue‡ NM (a) **tener un ~** (*Fin*) to be broke*; (*confuso*) to be all at sea, be in a bad way; (*drogas*) to need a fix‡. (b) **¡qué ~!** how awful!, how embarrassing!

cuellicorto ADJ short-necked.

cuellilargo ADJ long-necked.

cuello NM (a) (*Anat*) neck; **~ de botella** (*fig*) bottleneck; **~ del útero**, **~ uterino** cervix, neck of the womb; **apostar el ~***, **jugarse el ~*** to

stick one's neck out; **te cortaré el ~** I'll slit your throat; **erguir el ~** to be haughty; **levantar el ~** to get on one's feet again (*fig*).
(b) (*prenda*) collar; **~ alto** high collar; **de ~ blanco** white-collar (*atr*); **~ blando** soft collar; **~ de cisne** polo neck, turtleneck (*US*); **~ de pajarita** wing collar; **~ postizo**, **~ de quita y pon** detachable collar; **~ de recambio** spare collar.

cuenca NF (a) (*hueco*) hollow; (*Anat*) eye socket.
(b) (*Hist*) wooden bowl, begging bowl.
(c) (*Geog*) bowl, deep valley; (*de río*) basin, catchment area; **la ~ del Ebro** the Ebro basin; **~ hullera**, **~ minera** coalfield.

cuenco NM (a) (*concavidad*) hollow; (*de cuchara*) bowl; **~ de la mano** hollow of the hand.
(b) (*recipiente*) earthenware bowl, wooden bowl.

▼ **cuenta** NF (a) (*Mat*) count, counting; calculation; (*esp fig*) reckoning; (*Boxeo*) count; **~ de la vieja** counting on one's fingers; **~ atrás**, **~ al revés** countdown; **a esa ~** at that rate; **por la ~** apparently, as far as one can tell; **beber más de la ~** to have too much to drink, have one over the eight; **caer en la ~** to catch on (*de* to), see the point (*de* of); **habida ~ de eso** bearing that in mind; **hacer algo con su ~ y razón** to be fully aware of what one is doing; **perder la ~ de** to lose count of; **tener** (*o* **tomar**) **en ~** to bear in mind, take into account; **es otra cosa a tener en ~** that's another thing to be borne in mind.
(b) (*Com*, *Fin*: *en banco*) account; **~ de ahorros** savings account; **~** (**de ahorro**) **vivienda** homebuyer's savings account; **~ de amortización** depreciation account; **~ bancaria**, **~ de banco** bank account; **~ de caja** cash account; **~ de compensación** clearing account; **~ corriente** current account; **~ de crédito** loan account; **~ de depósitos** deposit account; **~ de diversos** sundries account; **~ de gastos** expense account; **~ indistinta**, **~ en participación** joint account; **~ de pérdidas y ganancias** profit and loss account; **~ personal** personal account; **~ a plazo** (**fijo**) fixed-term account; **~ presupuestaria** budget account; **abrir una ~** to open an account; **a** (**buena**) **~** on account; **tomar un coche a ~** to take a car in part payment; **abonar una cantidad en ~ a uno** to credit a sum to sb's account; **cargar una cantidad en ~ a uno** to charge a sum to sb's account.

▼ (c) (*Com*, *Fin*: *factura*) account, bill; (*en restaurante etc*) bill; (*fig*) check, tally; **la ~ del sastre** the tailor's bill; **~ pendiente** unpaid bill, outstanding account; **la ~ es la ~** business is business; **ajustar** (*o* **liquidar**) **una ~** to settle an account; **echar las ~s** to reckon up; **hacer las ~s de la lechera** to indulge in wishful thinking, count one's chickens before they are hatched; **llevar la ~ de** to keep an account; **pasar la ~** to send the bill; **presentar las ~s del Gran Capitán** to make excessive demands; **sale más a ~** it's more economical; **vivir a ~ de** to live at the expense of.
(d) (*fig*: *de disputa etc*) account; **ajustar ~s** to settle up (*con* with); **ajustar ~s con uno** to settle a score with sb; **le ajusté las ~s*** I told him where to get off*; **voy a ajustar ~s con él** I'm going to have it out with him; **arreglar las ~s a uno*** (*Méx*) to punish sb; **¡vamos a ~s!** let's get down to business!; **tener ~s pendientes con uno** to have a matter to settle with sb.
(e) (*fig*: *relato*) account; (*informe*) report, statement; **en resumidas ~s** in short, in a nutshell; all in all; **dar ~ de** to give an account of, report on; **dar ~ a uno de sus actos** to account to sb for one's actions; **no tiene que dar ~s a nadie** he's not answerable to anyone; **dar ~ de una botella** to finish off a bottle, put paid to a bottle; **dar buena ~ de sí** to give a good account of o.s.; to give as good as one gets; **darse ~ de** to realize (*que* that); **hay que darse ~ de que ...** one must not forget that ...; **¡date ~!** just fancy!; **sin darse ~** without realizing it, without noticing; **exigir** (*o* **pedir**) **~s a uno** to call sb to account, bring sb to book; **haz ~ de que no voy** (*esp LAm*) just imagine I'm not going; **rendir ~s a uno** to report to sb; **salir de ~s** to be about to give birth (*de* to).
(f) (*fig*: *asunto*) affair, business; **ésa es ~ mía** that's my affair, that's up to me; **~ de ~ y riesgo de uno** at one's own risk; **por ~ propia**, **por su propia ~** on one's own account, for o.s.; **por mi ~** in my opinion; as for me; **eso corre de** (*o* **por**) **mi ~** that's my affair; **éste corre por mi ~** (*bebidas etc*) this one's on me; **no querer ~s con uno** to want nothing to do with sb; to want no trouble with sb; *V* **apañar** *etc*.
(g) (*proyectos*) **~s** plans; **echar ~s** to reflect, take stock; **echar ~ de + infin** to plan to + *infin*; **le salieron fallidas las ~s** his plans went wrong.
(h) (*fig*: *importancia*) importance; **de** (**mucha**) **~** important; **no tiene ~ + infin** there is no point in + *ger*.
(i) (*fig*: *beneficio*) benefit; **por la ~ que le tiene** because it is to his benefit; **no trae ~ hacerlo** it is not profitable to do it; **me sale más a ~** it suits me better; **no tiene ~** there's no point in it.
(j) (*Rel*) bead.
(k) (*: *Med*) period, curse (of Eve).

cuentacorrentista NMF depositor.

cuentacuentos NMF INVAR storyteller.

► LENGUA Y USO: **cuenta:** c → 47.5

cuentagotas NM INVAR (*Med*) dropper; **a ~** (*fig*) drop by drop, bit by bit.

cuentakilómetros NM INVAR (*distancia*) *equivalente a* milometer; (*velocidad*) speedometer.

cuentarrevoluciones NM INVAR tachometer.

cuente *etc* V **contar**.

cuentear [1a] **1** VT (**a**) (*And*) (*pretender*) to court; (*felicitar*) to compliment. (**b**) (*Méx**) to kid*, have on. **2** VI (*CAm*) to gossip.

cuenterete NM (*CAm*) (*chisme*) piece of gossip; (*cuento*) tall story, tale.

cuentero* NM (*Cono Sur*) confidence trickster, con man*.

cuentista NMF (**a**) (*narrador*) storyteller; (*Liter*) short-story writer. (**b**) (*chismoso*) gossip; (*soplón*) telltale. (**c**) (*persona afectada*) affected person, person with a theatrical manner; (*presumido*) conceited person, bigmouth‡. (**d**) (*Cono Sur: estafador*) con man*.

cuentística NF (genre of) the short story.

cuento¹ NM (**a**) (*relato*) story, tale; (*Liter*) short story; (*chiste*) funny story, joke; **~ de hadas** fairy-tale; **~ de la lechera** (piece of) wishful thinking; **~ del tío** (*And, Cono Sur*) confidence trick, confidence game (*US*); **~ de viejas** old wives' tale; **es un ~ largo** it's a long story; **esto es mucho ~** this is terribly tedious; **es el ~ de nunca acabar** it's an endless business; **aplicarse el ~** to take note; **estar en el ~** to be in the picture, be fully informed; **ir a uno con el ~** to go off and tell sb; **va de ~ que ...** the story goes that ..., it is said that ...; **traer algo a ~** to mention sth, bring sth up; (*pey*) to drag sth in; **eso no viene a ~** that's off the point, that's irrelevant; **vivir del ~** to live by one's wits. (**b**) **sin ~** countless. (**c**) (*fábula*) story, tale; (*mentira*) fib; (*pretexto*) pretext; **¡puro ~!** a likely story!; **~ chino** tall story; **¡déjese de ~s!** stop beating about the bush!, get on with it!; **se me hace ~** (*Cono Sur*) I don't believe it, come off it!*; **tener más ~ que siete viejas** (*etc*) to be given to fibbing. (**d**) (*problemas*) **~s** trouble, difficulties; (*trastornos*) upsets; **han tenido no se qué ~s entre ellos** they've had some upset among themselves; **no quiero ~s con él** I don't want any trouble with him. (**e**) (*jaleo*) fuss; (*exageración*) exaggeration; (*palabrería*) hot air, mere words; **tiene mucho ~** he makes a lot of fuss (about nothing), he exaggerates everything so.

cuento² NM (*punta*) point, tip; ferrule.

cuera NF (**a**) (*LAm: piel*) hide; (*correa*) leather strap. (**b**) (*Méx: chaqueta*) leather jacket. (**c**) **~s** (*CAm*) leggings. (**d**) (*And, CAm, Carib: paliza*) flogging.

cuerazo NM (*LAm*) lashing.

cuerda NF (**a**) (*de atar*) rope; (*delgada*) string, cord; (*de perro*) lead; (*Pesca*) fishing line; (*Agrimen*) measuring tape; **~ arrojadiza** lasso; **~ floja** tightrope; **~ de plomada** plumbline; **~ de presidiarios** (*Hist*) chain gang; **~ de salvamento**, **~ salvavidas** lifeline; **~ de tendedero**, **~ para tender la ropa** clothesline; **aflojar la ~** (*fig*) to ease up; **apretar la ~** (*fig*) to tighten up; **bailar en la ~ floja** to keep in with both parties; **estar en** (*o* **contra**) **las ~s** (*fig*) to be on the ropes, be up against it; **estirar la ~** (*fig*) to go too far, overdo it; **poner a uno contra las ~s** (*fig*) to put sb up against the ropes, put sb in a tight spot; **son de la misma ~** they're all as bad as each other; **bajo ~**, **por debajo de ~** in an underhand way, by stealth, on the side; behind the scenes. (**b**) (*de reloj*) spring; (*Mec*) clockwork mechanism; **dar ~ al reloj** to wind up one's watch; **dar ~ a uno** to encourage sb (to talk); **un coche de ~** a clockwork car. (**c**) (*Mec: fig*) energy; **aún le queda ~** he's still got some steam left in him; **no le duró mucho la ~** he didn't keep it up long; **tienen ~ para rato** they've something to keep them going, (*esp*) they've a lot to talk about. (**d**) (*Mús*) string, cord; **~ de arco** bowstring; **~ de tripa** catgut; **estar en su ~** (*LAm*) to be in one's element; **estar con ~** (*LAm*) to be ready and willing. (**e**) (*Mús: fig*) vocal range. (**f**) (*Anat*) cord; tendon; **~ espinal** spinal cord; **~s vocales** vocal chords. (**g**) (*Mat*) chord.

cuerdamente ADV (**a**) (*sensatamente*) sanely. (**b**) (*prudentemente*) wisely, sensibly, prudently.

cuerdo ADJ (**a**) *persona* sane. (**b**) *acción etc* wise, sensible, prudent.

cuereada NF (*LAm*) beating, tanning*.

cuerear [1a] VT (**a**) (*LAm*) *animal* to skin, flay. (**b**) (*LAm*) *persona* to whip, beat. (**c**) **~ a uno** (*Carib, Cono Sur: regañar*) to tear a strip off sb.

cuerito: de ~ a ~ ADV (*LAm*) from end to end.

cueriza NF (*LAm*) beating, tanning*.

cuerna NF (**a**) (*Zool*) horns; (*de ciervo*) antlers. (**b**) (*para beber*) drinking horn. (**c**) (*Mús*) rustic horn, hunting horn.

cuerno NM (**a**) (*Zool*) horn; (*de ciervo*) antler; **~ de la abundancia** cornucopia, horn of plenty; **el C~ de Africa** the Horn of Africa; **estar en los ~s** (**del toro**) to be in danger; to be in a jam; **poner a uno en los ~s** (**del toro**) to place sb at risk; to get sb into a fix; **poner los ~s a uno** to cuckold sb; **oler** (*o* **saber**) **a ~ quemado** to be suspicious; to leave a nasty taste in one's mouth; **esto me sabe a ~ quemado** this upsets me, this makes my blood boil. (**b**) (*) (*locuciones*) **¡~(s)!** gosh!*, blimey!‡; **¡(y) un ~!** my foot!; **irse al ~** (*negocio*) to fail, fall through; (*persona*) to go to the dogs; **¡que se vaya al ~!** he can go to hell!; **¡vete al ~!** go to hell!, get lost!‡; **mandar a uno al ~** to tell sb to go to hell; **mandar algo al ~** to consign sth to hell; **romperse los ~s** to work one's butt off*; **¡así te rompas los ~s!** I hope you break your neck! (**c**) (*Culin*) roll, croissant. (**d**) (*Mil*) wing. (**e**) (*Mús*) horn; **~ alpino** alpenhorn.

cuero NM (**a**) (*Zool*) skin, hide; (*de conejo etc*) pelt; (*Dep*) ball, leather*; (*Téc, materia etc*) leather; **~ adobado** tanned skin; **~ cabelludo** scalp; **~ charolado** patent leather; **andar en ~s*** to go about stark naked; **dejar a uno en ~s** (*fig*) to rob sb of everything. (**b**) (*odre*) wineskin; (‡) toper, old soak‡; **estar hecho un ~** to be as drunk as a lord. (**c**) (*de grifo*) washer. (**d**) (*LAm: látigo*) whip; **arrimar** (*o* **dar** *etc*) **el ~ a uno** to give sb a beating. (**e**) (*And, Carib*‡: *puta*) whore; (*And: solterona*) old maid; (*Carib*‡: *vieja*) old bag‡; (*And, Méx**: *amante*) mistress. (**f**) (*CAm, Carib**: *descaro*) cheek*, nerve*. (**g**) (‡: *cartera*) wallet.

cuerpada* NF: **tiene buena ~** (*Cono Sur*) she's got a good body.

cuerpazo* NM huge frame, mighty bulk.

cuerpear [1a] VI (*Cono Sur*) to dodge.

cuerpo NM (**a**) (*Anat etc*) body; (*tipo*) figure; (*talle*) build; (*cadáver*) corpse; (*Dep*) length; **combate ~ a ~** hand-to-hand fight; **luchar ~ a ~** to fight hand-to-hand; **~ del delito** corpus delicti; **de ~ entero** *espejo, cuadro* full-length; *bribón etc* thoroughgoing, out-and-out; true, real; *vino* full-bodied; **coche de dos ~s** hatchback (car); **coche de tres ~s** three-box car; **a ~ limpio** unarmed; **de medio ~** half-length; **en ~ y alma** fully; **un vino de mucho ~** a full-bodied wine; **dar con el ~ en tierra** to fall down; **echar el ~ atrás** to lean suddenly backwards; **estar de ~ presente** to lie in state; **ganar por 4 ~s** to win by 4 lengths; **ganar por medio ~** to win by half a length; **hacer del ~** to relieve o.s.; **hurtar el ~** to dodge, move (one's body) out of the way; **ir a ~**, **ir en ~** to go without a coat; **vivir a ~ de rey** to live like a king. (**b**) (*corporación etc*) body; corporation; **~ estatal** public body; **~ legislativo** legislative body. (**c**) (*Jur etc*) **~ de doctrina** body of teaching; **~ de leyes** body of laws. (**d**) (*personas*) body; brigade; force; (*Mil*) corps; **~ de baile** corps de ballet; **~ de bomberos** fire-brigade, fire department (*US*); **~ diplomático** diplomatic corps; **~ de ejército** army corps; **~ electoral** electorate; **~ de intendencia** service corps; **~ de sanidad** medical corps. (**e**) (*Quím*) body, substance; **~ compuesto** compound; **~ simple** element; **~ extraño** foreign body. (**f**) (*Astron*) body. (**g**) (*Anat: tronco*) trunk; (*fig*) main part; mass, bulk; **el ~ de un libro** the main part of a book, the book proper; **dar ~ a un líquido** to thicken a liquid; **tomar ~** to swell, get bigger; (*proyecto etc*) to take shape. (**h**) (*de edificio*) wing; part; (*de mueble*) part, section; (*de cohete*) stage. (**i**) (*Cos*) bodice. (**j**) (*Tip: de letra*) point; **negritas del ~ 6** 6-point black. (**k**) (*de papel etc*) thickness. (**l**) (*Liter*) volume; **una biblioteca de 50 mil ~s** a library of 50,000 books. (**m**) (‡: *en oración directa*) man*, brother*. (**n**) **este ~*** yours truly*, I myself.

cuerudo ADJ (**a**) (*LAm*) *caballo* slow, sluggish; lazy. (**b**) (*LAm*) *persona* annoying. (**c**) (*Cono Sur: valiente*) brave, tough. (**d**) (*CAm, Carib: descarado*) impudent, cheeky*.

cuervo NM raven; crow; **~ marino** cormorant.

cuesco NM (**a**) (*Bot*) stone. (**b**) (*Mec*) millstone (*of oil mill*). (**c**) (*) punch, bash*. (**d**) (‡: *pedo*) loud fart‡‡.

cuesta NF (**a**) (*pendiente*) slope; (*en carretera etc*) hill; **~ abajo** downhill; **ir ~ abajo** (*fig*) to decline, go downhill; **~ arriba** uphill; **se me hace ~ arriba + infin** I find it hard to + infin; **~ de enero** *period of financial stringency following Christmas spending*; **hemos vencido la ~ ya** we're over the hump now; we're more than halfway. (**b**) **a ~s** on one's back; **echar algo a ~s** to put sth on one's back; (*fig*) to take on the burden of sth; **lleva también eso a ~s** he has the additional burden of that.

cuestación NF charity collection; flag day.

cueste *etc* V **costar**.

▼ **cuestión** NF (a) (*asunto*) matter, question, issue; (*Mat etc*) problem; **~ batallona** vexed question; **~ clave** key question; **~ de confianza** (*Parl*) vote of confidence; **~ madre** chief problem; **~ candente**, **palpitante** burning question; **~ de orden** (*Parl*) point of order; **~ de principio** point of principle; **la cosa en ~** the matter at issue, the thing in question; **en ~ de** about, concerning; **es ~ de** it is a matter of; **eso es otra ~** that's another matter; **otra ~ sería si** ... it would be different if ...; **llamar a uno a la ~** (*Parl*) to call sb to order.

(b) (*disputa*) quarrel, dispute; (*dificultad*) trouble; complication; **hay ~ sobre si** ... there's an argument about whether ...; **la ~ es que** ... the trouble is that ...; **no quiero cuestiones con los empleados** I don't want trouble with the staff; **no tengamos ~** let's not have an argument about it, let's not have a fuss about it.

(c) (‡: *dinero*) dough‡, money.

cuestionable ADJ questionable.

cuestionador ADJ questioning.

cuestionamiento NM questioning.

cuestionar [1a] **1** VT to question, dispute, argue about.

2 cuestionarse VR: **~ algo** (*preguntarse*) to ask o.s. sth; (*poner en duda*) to question sth.

cuestionario NM questionnaire; (*Escol, Univ etc*) question paper.

cuestor¹ NM (*Hist*) quaestor.

cuestor², **cuestora** NM/F charity collector.

cuete **1** ADJ (*Méx*) drunk.

2 NM (a) (*And, CAm, Méx: pistola*) pistol. (b) (*CAm, Méx*) = **cohete**. (c) (*Méx: embriaguez*) drunkenness. (d) (*Méx Culin*) steak.

cuetearse [1a] VR (*And*) (a) to go off, explode. (b) (‡) to kick the bucket‡.

cueva NF (a) (*caverna*) cave; (*de vino, en casa etc*) cellar, vault; **~ de ladrones** den of thieves. (b) (*Cono Sur*‡) cunt‡‡; **tener ~** ‡ to be lucky.

cuévano NM pannier, deep basket.

cuezo*** NM: **meter el ~** to drop a clanger‡, put one's foot in it.

cui NM (*LAm*) guinea-pig.

cuica NF (*And*) earthworm.

cuico **1** ADJ (*And*) thin; (*Carib*) rachitic, feeble.

2 NM (a) (*Cono Sur: forastero*) foreigner, outsider. (b) (*And, Cono Sur: pey: boliviano*) Bolivian. (c) (*Carib: mejicano*) Mexican. (d) (*Méx: policía*) policeman.

cuidadero, -a NM/F (*Zool*) keeper.

▼ **cuidado** **1** ADJ *aspecto etc* soigné, elegant.

▼ **2** NM (a) (*preocupación*) care, worry, concern; solicitude; **dar ~** to cause concern; **estar con ~** to be anxious, be worried; **estar de ~** to be gravely ill, be in a bad way; **enfermar de ~** to fall seriously ill; **¡no haya ~!**, **¡pierda Vd ~!** don't worry!; (*LAm*) don't mention it!; **eso me trae** (o **tiene**) **sin ~** I'm not worried about that; I couldn't care less.

▼ (b) (*atención*) care, carefulness; **¡~!** careful!, look out!, watch out!; (*letrero*) 'Caution'; **~s intensivos** intensive care; **¡~ con el paquete!** careful with the parcel!; **¡~ con el perro!** beware of the dog!; **¡~ con los rateros!** watch out for pickpockets!; **¡~ con perderlo!** mind you don't lose it!; **andarse con ~** to go carefully, watch out; **de ~** serious; worrying; threatening; **él es de ~** he's a man to be wary of; (*Méx*) he's hard to please; **poner mucho ~ en algo** to take great care over sth; **tener ~** to be careful, take care; **tener ~ con** to be careful of, watch out for, beware of; **hay que tener ~ con él** you have to handle him carefully; **¡ten ~!** careful!

(c) (*asunto*) care; affair; business, concern; **¡allá ~s!** let others worry about that!, that's their funeral!*; **'al ~ del Sr A'** (*Correos*) 'care of Mr A'; **eso no es ~ mío**, **eso no corre de mí** that's not my concern; **lo dejo a su ~** I leave it to you; **está al ~ de la computadora** he's in charge of the computer; **los niños están al ~ de la abuela** the children are in their grandmother's charge.

cuidador NM (*Boxeo*) second; (*de caballos etc*) trainer; **~ de campo** groundsman.

cuidadora NF (*Méx*) nursemaid, nanny.

cuidadosamente ADV (a) carefully. (b) anxiously; solicitously. (c) cautiously.

cuidadoso ADJ (a) (*atento*) careful (*con* about, with). (b) (*solícito*) anxious, concerned (*de, por* about); solicitous (*de* for). (c) (*prudente*) careful, cautious.

cuidar [1a] **1** VT (a) (*gen*) to take care of, look after; to pay attention to; **ella cuida a los niños** she looks after the children, she minds the children; **no cuidan la casa** they don't look after the house.

(b) (*Med*) to look after, care for.

2 VI (a) **~ de** to take care of, look after; **~ de una obligación** to attend to a duty; **~ de que** ... to take care that ..., see (to it) that ...; **cuidó de que todo saliera bien** he ensured that everything should go smoothly; **cuide de que no pase nadie** see that nobody gets in; **que cuide que no le pase lo mismo** let him beware lest the same thing happens to him; **cuide de no caer** take care not to fall.

(b) **cuida con esa gente** be wary of those people.

3 cuidarse VR (a) to look after o.s. (*t Med*); (*pey*) to look after Number One; **¡cuídate!** (*adiós*) take care!; **ella ha dejado de ~** she's let herself go.

(b) **~ de algo** to worry about sth; **~ de + infin** to be careful to + *infin*; **no se cuida del qué dirán** she doesn't worry about what people will think.

(c) **~ muy bien de + infin** to take good care not to + *infin*.

cuido NM care, minding; **para su ~**, **en su ~** for your own good.

cuita NF (a) (*preocupación*) worry, trouble; (*pena*) grief, affliction; (*civil, doméstico*) strife; **contar sus ~s a uno** to tell sb one's troubles. (b) (*CAm*) excrement; birdlime.

cuitado ADJ (a) (*preocupado*) worried, troubled; wretched. (b) (*tímido*) timid.

cuitlacoche NM (*Méx*) mushroom.

cuja NF (a) bedstead. (b) (*CAm, Méx*) envelope.

cujinillos NMPL (*Gaut, Méx*) saddlebags.

culada‡ NF: **darse una ~** to drop a clanger‡.

culamen‡ NM bottom.

culandrón‡ NM queer‡.

culantrillo NM (*Bot*) maidenhair.

culantro NM coriander.

culata NF (a) (*de fusil*) butt; (*de cañón*) breech; (*de cilindro*) head. (b) (*Zool*) haunch, hindquarters; (‡: *de persona*) backside, bottom. (c) (*LAm: de casa*) side; rear, back, back part. (d) (*Cono Sur: cobertizo*) hut, shelter.

culatazo NM kick, recoil.

culé* NMF supporter of Barcelona Football Club.

culear **1** VT (*And, Cono Sur, Méx*‡‡) to fuck‡‡.

2 VI (a) (‡: *mover el culo*) to waggle one's bottom. (b) (*And, Cono Sur, Méx*‡‡) to fuck‡‡.

culebra NF (a) (*Zool*) snake; **~ de cascabel** rattlesnake; **hacer ~** to zigzag, stagger along.

(b) (*Mec*) worm (*of a still*).

(c) (‡: *alboroto*) disturbance, disorder.

(d) (*And: cuenta*) debt, bill.

(e) (*Méx*) waterspout.

(f) (*Méx: manga*) hosepipe.

culebrear [1a] VI (a) (*culebra etc*) to wriggle (along); (*camino*) to zigzag; (*río etc*) to wind, meander. (b) (*Carib*) to stall, hedge.

culebreo NM wriggling; zigzag; winding, meandering.

culebrina NF (a) (*Hist*) culverin. (b) (*Met*) forked lightning.

culebrón* NM soap-opera*.

culeco ADJ (a) (*LAm*) *gallina* broody.

(b) (*LAm*) *persona* home-loving.

(c) **estar ~** (*And, Carib, Cono Sur*) to be head over heels in love.

(d) **estar ~ con algo** (*And, CAm, Carib, Méx**) (*satisfecho*) to be very pleased about sth, be over the moon about sth; (*orgulloso*) to be very proud of sth.

culera NF seat (of the trousers).

culeras* NMF INVAR coward.

culero **1** ADJ lazy.

2 NM (a) (*pañal*) nappy, diaper (*US*). (b) (*Méx: cobarde*) coward; sissy. (c) (*CAm*‡: *maricón*) poof‡, queer‡.

3 NM (*), **culera** NF drug courier, drug smuggler.

culí NM coolie.

culibajo ADJ short, dumpy.

culigordo* ADJ big-bottomed, broad in the beam*.

culillera NF (*CAm*), **culillo** NM (a) (*And, CAm, Carib**: *miedo*) fear, fright. (b) **tener ~** (*Carib**) to be in a hurry.

culín NM cider glass.

culinario ADJ culinary, cooking (*atr*).

culipandear [1a] VI y **culipandearse** VR (*Carib*) to stall, hedge.

culmen **1** NM: **el ~ de la ignorancia** the height of ignorance; (*persona*) the epitome of ignorance; **el ~ de su carrera** the crowning moment of his career; **llegar a su ~** to reach its height.

2 ADJ: **el momento ~** the crowning moment.

culminación NF culmination.

culminante ADJ *punto etc* highest, topmost, culminating; *momento* culminating; (*fig*) outstanding.

culminar [1a] **1** VT *objetivo etc* to reach, attain; *acuerdo* to conclude, put the finishing touches to; *tarea, carrera etc* to finish.

2 VI to reach its highest point, reach a peak; to culminate (*en* in).

culo NM (a) (‡: **~en regiones de LAm*) bottom, backside, arse‡‡, ass (*US*‡‡); (*ano*) anus, arsehole‡‡; **dar a uno un puntapié en el ~** to kick sb's backside, (*fig*) to boot sb out; **dejar a uno (con el) ~ al aire** to leave sb stranded; **ser un ~ de mal asiento** to be restless, be fidgety; to chop and change, keep changing one's job (*etc*); **confunde el ~ con las témporas** he can't tell his arse from his elbow‡; **¡que te den por (el) ~!**‡‡ get stuffed!‡‡; **ir con el ~ a rastras** to be in a jam*; (*Fin*) to be on one's beam ends; **ir de ~*** (*persona*) to be overloaded with work; (*precio etc*) to slide, collapse; **hacer que uno vaya de ~***

► LENGUA Y USO: **cuestión: a** → 53.1, 53.2 **cuidado: 2a** → 34.5 **2b** → 29.2, 29.3

to make sb work terribly hard; **la ciudad va de ~** the city is going downhill; **les mandó a tomar por ~⁞** he told them to get stuffed⁞.
(b) (⁙: *de recipiente etc*) bottom; **ser ~ de vaso** to be false, be a fake.

culón ADJ = **culigordo**.

culote NM culotte(s).

▼ **culpa** NF **(a)** (*gen*) fault; blame; (*Jur etc*) guilt; **por ~ de** through the fault of; through the negligence of; **no le alcanza ~** no blame attaches to him; **echar la ~ a uno** to blame sb (*de* for); **tener la ~ to** be to blame (*de* for); **nadie tiene la ~** nobody is to blame; **tú tienes la ~** it's your fault; **la ~ fue de los frenos** the brakes were to blame; **es ~ suya** it's his fault.
(b) (*pecado*) sin, offence; **pagar las ~s ajenas** to pay for sb else's sins.

culpabilidad NF guilt.

culpabilizar [1f] VT = **culpar**.

culpable ⓵ ADJ **(a) la persona ~** the person to blame, the person at fault; (*Jur*) the guilty person, the culprit; **acusarse ~** (*LAm*), **confesarse ~** to plead guilty; **declarar ~ a uno** to find sb guilty.
(b) *acto* to be condemned, be blameworthy; **es ~ no hacerlo** it is criminal not to do it; **con descuido ~** with culpable negligence.
⓶ NMF culprit; (*Jur etc*) offender, guilty party.

culpado ⓵ ADJ guilty.
⓶ NM, **culpada** NF culprit; (*Jur*) the accused.

culpar [1a] VT (*acusar*) to blame, accuse; (*condenar*) to condemn; **~ a uno de algo** to blame sb for sth; **~ a uno de descuidado** to blame sb for being careless, accuse sb of carelessness.

cultamente ADV in a cultured way, in a refined tone (*etc*); elegantly; (*pey*) affectedly, in an affected way.

culteranismo NM (*Liter*) latinized, precious and highly metaphorical style (*esp 17th century*).

┌─── **CULTERANISMO, CONCEPTISMO** ───┐

ⓘ *Culteranismo* and *conceptismo* were opposing literary fashions which developed in the early 17th century in Spain. Luis de Góngora was the main exponent of **culteranismo**, also known as **gongorismo**. His poetry was very learned in style, full of metaphor, classical allusions, neologisms and deliberate syntactic playfulness. By contrast, **conceptismo**, as championed by Francisco de Quevedo, meant very precise, economic and rational language with complex ideas presented in a simple and succinct style. Góngora, who was much vilified in his time, and not only by Quevedo, found posthumous favour with generations of modern Spanish poets, most notably the **Generación del 27**.
⇨ *See also* ▢ GENERACIÓN DEL 27/98 ▢

culterano (*Liter*) ⓵ ADJ latinized, precious and highly metaphorical.
⓶ NM, **culterana** NF writer in the style of *culteranismo*.

cultismo NM (*Ling*) learned word.

cultista ADJ learned.

cultivable ADJ cultivable.

cultivado ADJ *campo, superficie* cultivated; *persona* cultured, cultivated; *perla* cultured.

cultivador(a)¹ NM/F farmer, grower; (*de cultivo concreto*) grower; **~ de vino** winegrower; **~ de café** coffee grower, coffee planter.

cultivador² NM (*Agr*) cultivator.

cultivar [1a] VT **(a)** *tierra* to cultivate, work, till; *cultivo etc* to grow; (*Bio*) to culture.
(b) (*fig*) *arte, estudio etc* to cultivate; *talento etc* to develop; *memoria* to develop, improve; *amistad* to cultivate.

cultivo NM **(a)** (*acto*) cultivation, growing.
(b) (*cosecha*) crop; **el ~ principal de la región** the chief crop of the area; **rotación de ~s** rotation of crops.
(c) (*Bio*) culture.

culto ⓵ ADJ **(a)** *persona* cultivated, cultured, refined; educated; elegant; (*pey*) affected.
(b) (*Ling*) learned; **palabra culta** learned word.
⓶ NM worship; cult (*a* of); (*Ecl*) divine service, worship; **~ a la personalidad** personality cult; **rendir ~ a** to worship; (*fig*) to pay homage to, pay tribute to.

cultrún NM (*Cono Sur Mús*) drum.

cultura NF culture; refinement; education; elegance; **~ física** physical culture; **~ de masas**, **~ popular** popular culture; **persona de ~** cultured person; educated person; **no tiene ~** he has no manners, he doesn't know how to behave.

cultural ADJ cultural.

culturalmente ADV culturally.

culturismo NM body-building.

culturista NMF body-builder.

culturización NF education, enlightenment.

culturizar [1f] ⓵ VT to educate, enlighten.
⓶ **culturizarse** VR to educate o.s., improve one's mind.

cuma NF **(a)** (*CAm: cuchillo*) long knife, curved *machete*. **(b)** (*And: mujer*) old crone, gossip.

cumbancha NF (*Carib*) spree, drinking bout.

cumbia NF (*And*) (*música*) Colombian dance music; (*baile*) popular Colombian dance.

cúmbila NM (*Carib*) pal⁙, buddy (*esp US*).

cumbo NM **(a)** (*CAm*) (*chistera*) top hat; (*hongo*) bowler hat. **(b)** (*CAm: taza*) narrow-mouthed cup.

cumbre ⓵ NF summit, top; (*fig*) top, height, pinnacle, (*Pol*) summit, summit meeting; **conferencia (en la) ~** summit conference; **está en la ~ de su poderío** he is at the height of his power; **hacer ~** to make it to the top, reach the summit.
⓶ ATR: top-level; outstanding, most important; **conferencia ~** summit conference; **momento ~** greatest moment; culminating point; **es su libro ~** it is his most important book.

cume NM, **cumiche** NM (*CAm*) baby of the family.

cumpa⁙ NM (*LAm*) pal⁙, buddy (*esp US*).

cumpleañero NM, **cumpleañera** NF (*LAm*) person celebrating a birthday, person whose birthday it is.

▼ **cumpleaños** NM INVAR birthday; **~ del matrimonio** (*LAm*) wedding anniversary.

cumplido ⓵ ADJ **(a)** (*perfecto*) complete, perfect; full; **un ~ caballero** a perfect gentleman, a real gentleman.
(b) (*Cos etc*) full, extra large.
(c) *comida etc* large, plentiful.
(d) (*cortés*) courteous, correct; formal (in manner); (*pey*) stiff, ceremonious.
(e) **tiene 60 años ~s** he is 60 (years old).
(f) (*LAm*) punctual.
⓶ NM compliment; courtesy; **visita de ~** formal visit, courtesy call; **por ~** as a compliment; out of politeness, as a matter of courtesy; **¡sin ~s!** no ceremony, please!; make yourself at home!; **andarse con ~s, estar de ~, usar ~s** to stand on ceremony, be formal; **cambiar los ~s de etiqueta** to exchange formal courtesies; **he venido por ~** I came out of a sense of duty.

cumplidor ADJ reliable, trustworthy.

cumplimentar [1a] VT **(a)** (*visitas*) to pay one's respects to, pay a courtesy call on; (*felicitar*) to congratulate (*por* on). **(b)** *orden etc* to carry out; *deber* to perform, do. **(c)** *formulario etc* to complete, fill in.

cumplimentero ADJ formal, ceremonious; effusive.

cumplimiento NM **(a)** (*acto*) fulfilment; completion; performance; **falta de ~** non-fulfilment; non-compliance; **dar ~ a** to fulfil. **(b)** = **cumplido 2**.

cumplir [3a] ⓵ VT **(a)** *promesa, deseo, contrato, amenaza etc* to carry out, fulfil; *condición* to comply with; (*Naipes*) *contrato* to make; *ley etc* to observe, obey; *ambición* to fulfil, realize.
(b) *condena* to serve; *condena de muerte* to carry out.
(c) *años etc* to reach, attain, complete; **hoy cumple 8 años** she's 8 today; **cuando cumpla los 21 años** when you're 21, when you reach the age of 21; **¿cuándo cumples años?** when is your birthday?; **¡que los cumplas muy felices!** many happy returns (of the day)!
⓶ VI **(a)** (*plazo*) to end, expire; (*pago*) to fall due.
(b) (*Mil*) to finish one's military service.
(c) (*hacer su deber*) to do one's duty, carry out one's task, do what is required of one; (⁙) to do one's marital duty; **sólo por ~** as a matter of form, as a mere formality.
(d) **~ con = 1 (a)**; **~ con uno** to do one's duty by sb; **~ con la iglesia** to fulfil one's religious obligations; **~ por uno** to act on sb's behalf.
(e) **le cumple hacerlo** it behoves him to do it, it is up to him to do it; **no le cumple** + *infin* it is not his place to + *infin*.
⓷ **cumplirse** VR **(a)** (*plan etc*) to be fulfilled, come true.
(b) (*plazo*) to expire, end, be up.
(c) **se obedece pero no se cumple** the letter of the law is observed but not its spirit.

cumquibus NM (††, *hum*): **el ~** the wherewithal, the cash.

cumucho NM (*Cono Sur*) **(a)** (*multitud*) gathering, mob, crowd. **(b)** (*cabaña*) hut, hovel.

cumulativo ADJ cumulative.

cúmulo NM **(a)** (*montón*) pile, heap; accumulation; (*fig*) pile, lot. **(b)** (*Met*) cumulus.

cumulonimbo NM cumulonimbus.

cuna NF **(a)** (*camita*) cradle; cot; **~ portátil** carrycot.
(b) (*asilo*) home, foundling hospital.
(c) (*fig: familia*) family, stock, birth; **de ~ humilde** of humble origin; **criarse en buena ~** to be born with a silver spoon in one's mouth.
(d) (*fig: nacimiento*) birthplace; **~ del famoso poeta** the birthplace of the famous poet.
(e) (*juego*) **~s** cat's-cradle.

cundir [3a] VI **(a)** (*extenderse*) to spread; (*fig*) to spread, expand, increase; (*fig y pey*) to be rampant, be rife; **cunde el rumor que ...** there's a rumour going round that ...; **¡que no cunda el pánico!** don't panic!

(b) (*arroz etc*) to swell, expand; (*rendir*) to produce a good (*etc*) quantity, give good (*etc*) results; **hoy no me ha cundido el trabajo** work did not go well for me today; **¿te cunde?** how's it going?; **no me cunde** I'm not making any headway.

cunear [1a] **1** VT to rock, cradle.

2 cunearse VR to rock, sway; (*al andar*) to swing along, walk with a roll.

cuneco NM (*Carib*) baby of the family.

cuneiforme ADJ cuneiform.

cuneta NF **(a)** ditch, gutter; **A deja a B en la ~** A leaves B standing, A leaves B far behind; **quedarse en la ~** (*fig*) to get left behind, miss the bus*. **(b)** (*CAm, Méx: de acera*) kerb.

cunicultura NF rabbit breeding.

cuña NF **(a)** (*Téc*) wedge; (*de rueda*) chock; (*Tip*) quoin.

(b) meter ~ to sow discord.

(c) (*LAm*: *pez gordo*) big shot*, influential person.

(d) (*: palanca*) influence, pull; **tener ~s** to have pull, have influence.

(e) (*CAm, Carib: Aut*) two-seater car.

(f) (*Rad, TV*) spot, slot; (*Prensa*) space-filler, brief item; **~ publicitaria** commercial.

cuñada NF sister-in-law.

cuñadismo* NM nepotism, old boy network.

cuñado NM brother-in-law.

cuñete NM keg.

cuño NM **(a)** (*Téc*) stamp, die-stamp; **de nuevo ~** *persona* new-fledged; *palabra* newly-coined. **(b)** (*fig*) stamp, mark; official stamp.

cuota NF **(a)** (*proporción*) quota; share; **~ de inmigración** immigration quota; **~ de mercado** market share, share of the market; **~ de pantalla** quota of screen time; **~ patronal** employer's contribution (to national insurance). **(b)** (*derechos*) fee, dues; **~ de enseñanza** school fees; **~ de entrada** entry fee, admission fee; **~ del gremio** union dues; **~ de socio** membership fee. **(c)** (*impuesto*) tax. **(d)** (*LAm*) (*mensualidad etc*) instalment, payment; **vender a ~s** to sell on credit, give credit terms for.

cuotidiano ADJ = **cotidiano.**

cupaje NM blending (of wines).

cupe *etc* V **caber.**

cupé NM (*Aut*) coupé.

Cupido NM Cupid.

cupiera *etc* V **caber.**

cuplé NM pop song, light lyric.

cupletista NF cabaret singer.

cupo NM **(a)** (*proporción*) quota; share; **~ de azúcar** sugar quota; **~ de importación** import quota, trade quota. **(b)** (*Méx: capacidad*) space, room, capacity; (*And, Carib, Méx*) empty seat, vacancy; **no hay ~** there's no room; **'no hay ~'** (*Teat*) 'house full', 'sold out'.

cupolino NM hubcap.

cupón NM coupon; (*Com*) trading stamp; **~ de (los) ciegos** ticket for the lottery for the blind; **~ de dividendos** dividend voucher; **~ de franqueo** (o **respuesta**) **internacional** international reply coupon; **~ de interés** interest warrant; **~ obsequio** gift-coupon; **~ de racionamiento** ration coupon; **~ de regalo** gift-coupon.

cuponazo* NM lottery.

cuprero ADJ (*Cono Sur*) copper (*atr*).

cúpula NF **(a)** (*Arquit*) dome, cupola. **(b)** (*Náut*) turret. **(c)** (*Bot*) husk, shell. **(d)** (*Pol*) party leadership, leading members; (*Com, Fin*) top management.

cuquería NF craftiness.

cura¹ NM **(a)** (*Ecl*) priest; father; **~ obrero** worker priest; **~ párroco** parish priest; **sí, señor** ~ yes, father. **(b)** (*: yo mismo*) I, myself; **este ~** yours truly*; **no se ofrece este ~** this poor devil isn't volunteering.

cura² NF **(a)** (*Med*) cure, healing; treatment; remedy; **primera ~** first aid; **~ de reposo**, **de sueño** rest cure; **~ de urgencia** emergency treatment, first aid; **tiene ~** it can be cured, it is curable; **no tiene ~*** there's no remedy, it's quite hopeless.

(b) ~ de almas (*Ecl*) cure of souls.

curable ADJ curable.

curaca NF **(a)** (*And*: *ama*) priest's housekeeper. **(b)** (*And: cacique*) Indian chief, Indian native authority.

curación NF cure, healing; treatment; **primera ~** first aid.

curadillo NM **(a)** (*Culin*) dried cod. **(b)** (*Téc*) bleached linen.

curado 1 ADJ **(a)** (*Téc*) cured; hardened; tanned, prepared. **(b)** (*And, Cono Sur**: *borracho*) drunk, tight*.

2 NM (*Culin*) curing.

curador(a) NM/F healer; **~ por fe** faith-healer.

curalotodo NM cure-all.

curanderismo NM folk medicine; (*pey*) quack medicine, quackery.

curandero NM quack; bonesetter.

curar [1a] **1** VT **(a)** (*Med*) *persona, enfermedad* to cure (*de* of); *herida* to treat, dress; (*con droga etc*) to treat (*con* with).

(b) (*fig*) *mal* to remedy, put right.

(c) *carne, pescado* to cure, salt; *piel* to tan; *paño* to bleach; *madera* to season.

2 VI (*Med*) to get well (*de* after), recover (*de* from).

3 curarse VR **(a)** (*Med*) to recover, get better; (*t* **curarse en salud**) (*herida etc*) to heal up; (*persona*) to be on a cure, go for a cure.

(b) ~ de to take notice of, heed; (*enfermo etc*) to look after.

(c) (*And, Cono Sur*: emborracharse*) to get drunk, get tight*; (*Méx*: para reponerse*) to take a drink to sober up.

curare NM curare, curari.

curasao NM curaçao.

curativo ADJ curative.

curato NM curacy, parish.

curazao NM curaçao.

curca¹ NF (*And, Cono Sur*) hump.

curco (*And, Cono Sur*) **1** ADJ hunchbacked.

2 NM, **curca²** NF hunchback.

curcuncho 1 ADJ **(a)** (*LAm: jorobado*) hunchbacked. **(b)** (*And**) (*hastiado*) fed up*; (*molesto*) annoyed.

2 NM, **curcuncha** NF (*LAm*) hunchback.

curda 1 NM (***) drunk*, sot.

2 NF (***) drunkenness; **agarrar una ~** to get tight*; **estar (con la) ~**, **estar en ~** (*Cono Sur*) to be tight*.

cureña NF gun carriage; **a ~ rasa** out in the open, exposed to the elements.

curia NF **(a)** (*Ecl*: *t* **~ romana**) Curia, papal Curia. **(b)** (*Jur*) the Bar, the legal profession.

curiana NF cockroach.

curiara NF (*Carib*) dug-out canoe.

curiche* NM (*Cono Sur*) Negro.

curiosamente ADV **(a)** (*extrañamente*) curiously; oddly. **(b)** (*pulcramente*) neatly, cleanly.

curiosear [1a] **1** VT (*mirar*) to glance at, look over; (*visitar*) to look round; (*husmear*) to nose out.

2 VI to look round, wander round; to poke about, nose about; (*pey*) to snoop, pry; **~ por las tiendas** to wander round the shops; **~ por los escaparates** to go window-shopping.

curiosidad NF **(a)** (*gen*) curiosity; (*pey*) inquisitiveness; **despertar la ~ de uno** to arouse sb's curiosity; **la ~ de noticias me llevó allí** the quest for news took me there; **tenemos ~ de saber si ...** we are curious to know if ...; **estar muerto de ~** to be dying of curiosity.

(b) (*objeto*) curiosity; curio; **~es** sights, attractions; **visitar las ~es** to see the sights.

(c) (*aseo*) neatness, cleanliness.

(d) (*cuidado*) care(fulness), conscientiousness.

curioso 1 ADJ **(a)** (*persona*) curious; eager; (*pey*) inquisitive; **~ de noticias** eager for news; **estar ~ por** + *infin* to be curious to + *infin*, be eager to + *infin*.

(b) *acto, objeto etc* curious, odd; quaint; **¡qué ~!** how curious!, how odd!

(c) (*aseado*) neat, clean, tidy.

(d) (*cuidadoso*) careful, conscientious.

(e) (***) queer*.

2 NM, **curiosa** NF bystander, spectator, onlooker; (*pey*) busybody; **los ~s de la literatura** those interested in literature.

curiosón, -ona NM/F busybody.

curita NF (*LAm*) (sticking) plaster.

currante* NMF worker, labourer.

currar* [1a] VI, **currelar*** [1a] VI to work.

curre* NM, **currele*** NM, **currelo*** NM work; job; activity.

curricular ADJ curriculum (*atr*).

currículo NM curriculum.

▼ **curriculum, currículum** NM (*t* **~ vitae**) curriculum vitae.

currinche NM **(a)** (*Tip*) apprentice journalist, cub reporter. **(b)** (**: persona insignificante*) little man, nonentity.

currito* NM working man, working bloke*.

Curro NM *forma familiar de* **Francisco.**

curro* 1 ADJ **(a)** (*elegante*) smart; (*ostentoso*) showy, flashy. **(b)** (*presumido*) cocky, brashly confident.

2 NM (***) **(a)** (*trabajo*) work; job. **(b)** (*golpe*) bash*, punch; (*golpes*) bashing*, beating; **dar un ~ a uno** to beat sb up*.

curroadicto, -a* NM/F workaholic.

currusco* NM hard crust (*at the end of French bread*).

currutaco* 1 ADJ **(a)** (*ostentoso*) loud, showy, flashy.

(b) (*LAm: bajito*) short, squat.

2 NM **(a)** (†: *petimetre*) toff*, dandy.

(b) (*hombrecito*) insignificant little man.

(c) ~s (*CAm*) diarrhoea.

curry ['kuri] NM curry.

cursante NMF (*LAm*) student.

cursar [1a] **1** VT **(a)** *mensaje* to send, dispatch; *orden* to send out; *solicitud* to pass on, dispatch, deal with.

➤ LENGUA Y USO: **curriculum** → 46.2

(b) *asignatura* to study; *curso* to take, attend.
(c) *sitio* to frequent.
[2] VI: **el mes que cursa** the present month.
cursi [1] ADJ (*de mal gusto*) in bad taste, vulgar; (*pretencioso*) pretentious; (*ostentoso*) loud, showy, flashy; (*esnob*) posh*, genteel; pseudo-refined; (*afectado*) affected.
[2] NMF = **cursilón**.
cursilería NF (*V adj* **1**) bad taste, vulgarity; pretentiousness; loudness, showiness, flashiness; poshness*, gentility, pseudo-refinement; affectation.
cursillista NMF member (of a course).
cursillo NM short course; short series (of lectures).
cursilón, -ona NM/F (*V adj* **1**) common but pretentious person; flashy type; posh sort*, genteel individual; affected person.
cursiva NF (*Tip*) italics; (*escritura*) cursive writing.
cursivo ADJ *escritura* cursive; (*Tip*) italic.
curso NM **(a)** (*de río etc*) course; direction; flow; **~ de agua, ~ fluvial** watercourse.
(b) (*Astron*) course.
(c) (*fig*) course; **el ~ de la enfermedad** the course of the disease, the progress of the disease; **dejar que las cosas sigan su ~** to let matters take their course; **en el ~ de la vida** in the course of a lifetime; **en el ~ de la semana** in the course of the week; **el proceso está en ~** the process is going on, the process is under way; **el año en ~** the current year, the present year; **trabajo en ~** work in progress.
(d) (*Jur*) **moneda de ~ legal** legal tender.
(e) dar ~ a una solicitud to deal with an application; **dar ~ a su indignación** to give vent to one's indignation, express one's indignation; **dar ~ al llanto** to let one's tears flow.
(f) (*Escol, Univ: personas*) year; **~ escolar** school year; **~ lectivo** academic year; **los del segundo ~** those in the second year, the second years.
(g) (*Escol, Univ: asignatura*) course; subject; **he perdido 2 ~s** I failed 2 subjects, I have to repeat 2 subjects; **~ acelerado** crash course; **~ de actualización** refresher course; **~ de base** foundation course; **~ por correspondencia** correspondence course; **~ intensivo** intensive course, crash course; **~ de secretaria** secretarial course.
cursor NM (*Téc*) slide; (*Inform*) cursor.
curtido [1] ADJ **(a)** *cuero* tanned; *piel* hardened, leathery; *cara* (*al sol: t* **~ a la intemperie**) tanned, weather-beaten.
(b) estar ~ en (*fig*) to be expert at, be skilled in; *sufrimientos* to be inured to.
[2] NM **(a)** (*acto*) tanning.
(b) (*cuero*) tanned leather, tanned hides.
curtidor NM tanner.
curtiduría NF, **curtiembre** NF (*LAm*) tannery.
curtir [3a] [1] VT **(a)** *cuero* to tan.
(b) *cara etc* to tan, bronze.
(c) (*avezar*) to harden, inure.
[2] **curtirse** VR **(a)** (*al sol*) to become tanned, become bronzed; (*a la intemperie*) to get weather-beaten.
(b) (*avezarse*) to become inured.
(c) (*LAm*) (*ensuciarse*) to get o.s. dirty; to dirty one's clothes.
curva NF curve; (*Mat*) graph, curve; (*Aut etc*) curve, bend; **~ de la felicidad** paunch, beer-belly; **~ de indiferencia** indifference curve; **~ de nivel** contour line.
curvar [1a] [1] VT *material* to bend; *labios* to curl.
[2] **curvarse** VR *material* to bow; *estante* to sag, bend; *madera* to warp.

curvatura NF curvature.
curvilíneo ADJ curved, curvilinear.
curvo ADJ **(a)** (*gen*) curved; crooked, bent. **(b)** (*And: estevado*) bow-legged. **(c)** (*Carib: zurdo*) left-handed.
cusca NF **(a) hacer la ~ a uno*** to play a dirty trick on sb; to harm sb, damage sb's interests.
(b) (*CAm: coqueta*) flirt.
(c) (*Méx: puta*) whore, slut.
cuscha NF (*CAm*) liquor, rum.
cuscurrante ADJ crunchy, crisp.
cuscurro NM crouton.
cuscús NM couscous.
cusma NF (*And*) sleeveless shirt, tunic.
cuspa NF (*And Agr*) weeding.
cuspar [1a] VT (*And Agr*) to weed.
cúspide NF **(a)** (*Anat: de diente*) cusp. **(b)** (*Geog*) summit, peak; tip, apex; (*fig*) top, pinnacle. **(c)** (*Mat*) apex.
cusqui* NF = **cusca (a)**.
custodia NF **(a)** care, safekeeping, custody (*t Jur*); (*policial*) police protection; **~ preventiva** protective custody; **bajo la ~ de** in the care (*o* custody) of. **(b)** (*Ecl*) monstrance.
custodiar [1b] VT to keep, take care of, look after; to guard, watch over.
custodio NM guardian, keeper, custodian; *V* **ángel**.
cususa NF (*CAm*) home-made liquor (*o* rum).
cutacha NF (*LAm*) = **cuma**.
cutama NF (*Cono Sur*) bag, sack.
cutáneo ADJ cutaneous, skin (*atr*).
cutaras NFPL (*CAm, Carib, Méx*), **cutarras** NFPL (*CAm*) sandals, rough shoes.
cúter NM (*Náut*) cutter.
cutí NM ticking.
cutícula NF cuticle.
cutis NM skin, complexion.
cuto ADJ **(a)** (*And, CAm*) (*tullido*) maimed, crippled; (*desdentado*) toothless; *objeto* damaged, spoiled. **(b)** (*And: corto*) short.
cutre* ADJ (*tacaño*) mean, stingy; (*grosero*) vulgar, coarse; tasteless; *lugar* squalid, shabby; **un sitio ~** a dive*, a hole*.
cutrería* NF meanness, stinginess; vulgarity, coarseness; squalidness, shabbiness; **me parece una ~** I think it's utterly tasteless.
cutter ['kuter] NM, PL **cutters** (*de carpintero*) Stanley knife ®, razor knife (*US*); (*para papel*) artist's scalpel.
cuy NM (*LAm*) guinea-pig.
cuya NF (*Carib, Cono Sur*) gourd, drinking vessel.
cuyano*, -a ADJ, NM/F (*Chile*) Argentinian.
cuyo [1] REL ADJ **(a)** (*gen*) whose; of whom, of which; **la señora en cuya casa nos hospedábamos** the lady in whose house we were staying; **el asunto ~s detalles conoces** the matter of which you know the details, the matter whose details you know about.
(b) en ~ caso in which case; **por cuya razón** for which reason, and for this reason.
[2] NM (*) lover.
cuz: ¡~ ~! INTERJ (*a perro*) here boy!
cuzqueño [1] ADJ of Cuzco.
[2] NM, **cuzqueña** NF native (*o* inhabitant) of Cuzco; **los ~s** the people of Cuzco.
C.V. NMPL ABR *de* **caballos de vapor** horsepower, h.p.
C y F ABR *de* **coste y flete** cost and freight, CAF, C and F.
czar *etc* = **zar** *etc*.

CH

Words beginning "ch" are now listed at the appropriate alphabetical position under letter C.

Las palabras que empiezan por "ch" aparecen ahora bajo la letra C en su correspondiente orden alfabético.

D

D, d [de] NF (*letra*) D, d.

D. (**a**) (*Fin*) ABR *de* **debe** debit side. (**b**) ABR *de* **Don** Esquire, Esq; *see also* DON/DOÑA . (**c**) ABR *de* **diciembre** December, Dec.

Da., D.ª ABR *de* **Doña.**

dable ADJ possible, feasible, practicable; **no es ~ hacerlo** it is not possible to do it; **en lo que sea ~** as far as possible, as far as is feasible.

dabuti ‡ ⊡ ADJ (*gracioso*) funny, killing; (*estupendo*) super*, smashing*.
⊡ ADV: **pasarlo ~** to have a great time*.

DAC NF ABR *de* **división acorazada** armoured division.

daca INTERJ hand it over!; **en ~ las pajas** in a jiffy; **andar al ~ y toma** to argue back and forth, bicker.

dacrón NM dacron.

dactilar ADJ finger (*atr*); **huella ~, impresión ~** fingerprint.

dactílico ADJ dactylic.

dáctilo NM dactyl.

dactilografía NF typing.

dactilografiar [1c] VT to type.

dactilógrafo, -a NM/F typist.

dactilograma NM (*Méx*) fingerprint.

dadá NF, **dadaísmo** NM dadaism.

dadista NM (*Méx*) gambler.

dadito NM (*Culin*) small cube; **cortar en ~s** to dice.

dádiva NF gift, present; (*fig*) sop.

dadivosidad NF generosity, lavishness with gifts.

dadivoso ADJ generous, open-handed, lavish with gifts.

dado¹ NM (**a**) (*en juegos*) die, dice; **~s dice**; **el ~ está tirado** the die is cast. (**b**) (*Arquit*) dado. (**c**) (*Mec*) block. (**d**) (*Culin*) cube; **cortar a ~s** to dice.

▼ **dado²** PTP *de* **dar** (**a**) **en un caso ~** in a given case; **dada su corta edad** in view of his youth; **dadas estas circunstancias** since these circumstances exist, in view of these circumstances.
(**b**) **ser ~ a** to be given to; **es muy ~ a discutir** he is much given to arguing.
▼ (**c**) **~ que ...** (*como conj*) provided that ..., so long as ...; given that ..., granted that ...

dador(a) NM/F (*gen*) giver, donor; (*de carta*) bearer; (*Naipes*) dealer; (*Com*) drawer; **~ de sangre** blood donor.

Dafne NF Daphne.

daga NF dagger, stiletto; (*Carib*) machete.

dagazo NM (*Carib, Méx*) stab wound.

daguerrotipo NM daguerrotype.

daifa NF mistress, concubine; prostitute.

daiquiri NM daiquiri.

dalia NF dahlia.

Dalila NF Delilah.

daliniano ADJ Daliesque.

dallar [1a] VT to scythe, mow with a scythe.

dalle NM scythe.

Dalmacia NF Dalmatia.

dálmata NMF dalmatian (dog).

daltónic ADJ colour-blind.

daltonismo NM colour blindness.

dama NF (**a**) (*gen*) lady; (*noble*) lady, gentlewoman; (*amante*) mistress, lover; concubine; **¡D~s y caballeros!** (*esp LAm*) Ladies and gentlemen!; **el poeta y su ~** the poet and his lady, the poet and his mistress; **primera ~** (*Teat*) leading lady; (*Pol*) first lady (*US*), president's wife; **~ de compañía** (*LAm*) (lady) companion; **~ de hierro** Iron Lady; **~ de honor** (*real*) lady-in-waiting; (*en boda*) bridesmaid, maid of honour; **~ joven** (*Teat*) ingénue; **~ regidora** carnival queen.
(**b**) (*Naipes, Ajedrez*) queen; (*Damas*) king.
(**c**) **~s** (*juego*) draughts, checkers (*US*).

damajuana NF, **damasana** NF (*LAm*) demijohn.

Damasco NM Damascus.

damasco NM (**a**) (*tela*) damask. (**b**) (*Bot*) damson; (*LAm: fruta*) apricot; (*árbol*) apricot tree.

damasquinado NM (*Téc*) damascene (work).

damasquinar [1a] VT (*Téc*) to damascene, damask.

damasquino ADJ (*Téc*) damask; damascene.

damero NM (*tablero*) draughtboard; (*crucigrama*) type of crossword.

damesana NF (*LAm*) demijohn.

damisela NF (*Hist*) damsel; (*pey*) courtesan, prostitute.

damita NF (*CAm*) young lady.

damnificar [1g] VT (*herir*) to injure, harm; (*dejar incapacitado*) to disable; (*perjudicar*) to harm the interests of; **los damnificados** (*en accidente etc*) the victims, those affected, those who have suffered loss.

Damocles NM Damocles.

dandi, dandy ⊡ NM dandy, fop.
⊡ ATR: **estilo ~** dandy style.

dandismo NM foppishness, foppish ways; extreme elegance.

danés ⊡ ADJ Danish.
⊡ NM, **danesa** NF (**a**) (*persona*) Dane. (**b**) (*perro*) Great Dane.
⊡ NM (*Ling*) Danish.

Daniel NM Daniel.

danone* NM police-car.

danta NF (*And, CAm, Méx*) tapir; (*anta*) elk, moose.

dantesco ADJ (**a**) (*liter*) of Dante, relating to Dante. (**b**) (*fig*) Dantesque; horrific, weird, macabre; hellish, infernal.

dantzari [dan'sari] NM Basque folk-dancer.

Danubio NM Danube.

danza NF (**a**) (*gen*) dancing; (*una ~*) dance; **~ de aparamiento** courtship dance, mating display; **~ contemporánea** contemporary dance; **~ de espadas** sword dance; **~ guerrera** war dance; **~ macabra, ~ de la muerte** dance of death, danse macabre; **~ de salón** ballroom dancing; **~ de los siete velos** dance of the seven veils; **~ del vientre** belly-dance.
(**b**) (*: *asunto*) shady affair, suspect deal; mess; **meterse en la ~** to get caught up in a shady affair.
(**c**) (*: *jaleo*) row, rumpus*; **armar una ~** to kick up a row; **no metas los perros en ~** let sleeping dogs lie.

danzante NM, **danzanta** NF (**a**) (*bailarín*) dancer. (**b**) (*: *persona activa*) hustler, live wire, person who is always on the go; (*pey*) busybody. (**c**) (*casquivano*) scatterbrain.

danzar [1f] ⊡ VT to dance.
⊡ VI (**a**) (*bailar*) to dance (*t fig*). (**b**) (*: *entrometerse*) to meddle; to butt in, shove one's oar in.

danzarín, -ina NM/F (**a**) (*bailarín*) dancer; artistic dancer, professional dancer; **~ del vientre** belly-dancer. (**b**) = **danzante** (**b**) *y* (**c**).

dañado ADJ (**a**) (*gen*) damaged; *fruta etc* spoiled; bad. (**b**) (*fig*) bad, wicked, evil.

dañar [1a] ⊡ VT *objeto* to damage; *persona* to harm, hurt; (*estropear*) to spoil.
⊡ **dañarse** VR to get damaged, get hurt; to spoil, to rot, go bad; (*Med*) to hurt o.s., do o.s. harm.

dañinear [1a] VT (**a**) (*Cono Sur*) = **dañar**. (**b**) (*Cono Sur: robar*) to steal.

dañino ⊡ ADJ harmful; damaging; injurious; **animales ~s** vermin, pests, injurious creatures.
⊡ NM (*Cono Sur*) thief.

daño NM (**a**) (*gen*) damage; hurt, harm, injury; **en ~ de** to the detriment of; **por mi ~** to my cost; **hacer ~ a** to damage, harm; (*Med*) to hurt, injure; *estómago* to upset; **no hace ~** it doesn't hurt; **el ajo me hace ~** garlic disagrees with me; **hacerse ~** to hurt o.s., do o.s. an injury; **se hizo ~ en el pie** he hurt his foot.
(**b**) (*Med*) trouble; **los médicos no saben dónde está el ~** the doctors cannot tell where the trouble is.
(**c**) (*Jur*) **~s y perjuicios** damages; **graves ~s corporales** grievous

bodily harm.

(**d**) (*LAm: maleficio*) spell, curse.

dañoso ADJ harmful, bad, injurious; **~ para** harmful to, bad for.

DAO NM ABR *de* **diseño asistido por ordenador** computer-aided design, CAD.

▼ **dar** [1q] **1** VT (**a**) (*gen*) to give; *objeto* to give, hand, pass (*a* to); *recado* to give, deliver; *aviso* to give; *permiso* to give, grant, concede; *ejemplo* to set; *paso* to take; *paseo* to take, go for; *golpe* to give, deal, fetch, strike; *paliza* to give; *grito* to give, utter; *suspiro* to fetch, heave; *batalla* to fight; *examen* to sit, take; *olor* to give off; **ir dando cuerda** to pay out a rope, let out a rope; **~ los buenos días a uno** to wish (*o* bid) sb good-day; **~ de comer a uno** to give sb sth to eat; **nos daban garbanzos** they gave us chickpeas (to eat); **a mí no me la das*** you can't fool me; **lo que cada uno puede ~ de sí** what each one can contribute; **ahí me las den todas** that won't bother me, I can cope with everything; **el cálculo dio 99** the sum worked out at 99; **el atleta dio positivo en el control antidoping** the athlete's drug test proved positive; **por si vienen mal dadas** in case of emergency, (*ahorrar etc*) for a rainy day.

(**b**) *cosecha, beneficio etc* to yield, bear, produce, give; **dan un 7 por 100 de interés** they yield 7% interest, they bear interest at 7%.

(**c**) (*Naipes*) to deal.

(**d**) *impresión* to give, cause, produce; *placer* to give; *compasión* to cause, excite, arouse; **le dio un fuerte dolor de costado** he felt a sharp pain in his side.

(**e**) (*Teat etc*) to do, perform, put on; (*Cine*) to show, put on, screen.

(**f**) (*hora*) to strike; **el reloj dio las 3** the clock struck 3; **han dado las 4, son las 4 dadas** it's past 4 o'clock.

(**g**) **~ como, ~ por** to consider, regard, assume; **lo dio como cierto** he regarded it as certain, he considered it definite; **lo daba por bien empleado** he considered it well spent; **lo podremos ~ por terminado** we shall be able to consider it finished.

(**h**) **~ de barniz a** to varnish; **~ de jalbegue a** to whitewash.

(**i**) **~ a uno de puñetazos** to punch sb.

(**j**) **~la de** to brag of being; to set o.s. up as; **la da de poeta** he tries to make out he's a poet.

(**k**) **¡dale!** (*Boxeo etc*) hit him!; (*dando caza*) after him!; (*Dep etc*) come on!; get on with it!; (*iró*) just look at him!, what an idiot!; **¡y dale!** there he goes again!; **¡dale que dale!** you do carry on so!, stop harping on it; **estoy dale que dale a este problema** I've been bashing away at this problem*; **la vecina está dale que dale al piano** our neighbour is pounding away on her piano; **~le al vicio** to be on drugs.

▼ (**l**) **lo mismo da** it's all the same, it makes no difference; **lo mismo me da, me da igual** it's all the same to me; **¡qué más da!** what does it matter!; never mind!; **¡qué más da un sitio que otro!** surely one place is as good as another!

(**m**) *para muchas locuciones, V el sustantivo p.ej.* **caza, grito, paseo;** *o verbo, p.ej.* **conocer, entender** *etc.*

2 VI (**a**) (*gen*) to give; **a quien dan no escoge** beggars can't be choosers.

(**b**) **~ a** (*ventana*) to look out on, look on to, overlook; (*casa*) to face, face towards; **~ sobre** to overlook.

(**c**) **~ a la bomba** to pump, work the pump.

(**d**) **~ con** *persona etc* to meet, run into, find; *idea, solución etc* to hit on; **~ con algo en el suelo** to knock sth to the ground, drop sth; **el barco dio con el puente** the ship crashed into (*o* struck) the bridge; **no doy con el nombre** I can't think of the name.

(**e**) **~ consigo en** to end up in, land in; **dio consigo en la cárcel** he ended up in jail.

(**f**) **~ contra** to hit (against), knock against, bang into.

(**g**) **~ de cabeza** to fall on one's head; **~ de narices** to fall flat on one's face; **~ de narices contra la puerta** to bang one's face on the door.

(**h**) **~ en** + *infin* to take to + *ger*, get into the habit of + *ger*; **han dado en llamarle Boko** they've taken to calling him Boko.

(**i**) **~ en** *suelo etc* to hit, strike; *blanco* to hit, land on; *solución* to hit on; *error* to fall into; *chiste* to catch on to, see, get the point of; **~ en ello** to see the point, get it; **el sol le daba en la cara** the sun was shining straight into her face.

(**j**) **le da por** + *infin* he takes it into his head to + *infin*, he decides to + *infin*; he persists in + *ger*; **le ha dado por no venir a clase** he has begun to cut classes; **al chico le daba por dormirse en clase** the boy was apt to go to sleep in class; **les dio por venir a vernos** they took it into their heads to come and see us; **la casa que a uno le dio por llamar 'Miramar'** the house that sb had the bright idea of calling 'Miramar'.

(**k**) **~ tras uno** to pursue sb vigorously, set off after sb.

(**l**) **~ de sí** (*tela etc*) to give, stretch; (*Agr etc*) to bear heavily, yield well, produce a lot.

3 **darse** VR (**a**) (*entregarse*) to surrender, give in; to give o.s. up (*a* to).

(**b**) **~ a** (*dedicarse*) to take to; to devote o.s. to; (*pey*) to abandon o.s. to; **~ a la bebida** to take to drink; **~ a creer que ...** to take to thinking that ...

(**c**) (*suceso*) to happen; **si se da el caso** if that happens.

(**d**) (*Bio etc*) to exist, occur, be found; **la planta no se da en el sur** the plant is not found in the south.

(**e**) (*Agr*) to grow, come up; **el cultivo se da bien este año** the crop is coming on well this year.

(**f**) **~ por** to consider o.s. (as); **~ por ofendido** to take offence; **~ por perdido** to give o.s. up for lost; **~ por vencido** to give up, acknowledge defeat.

(**g**) **~las de** to pose as, fancy o.s. as; **nunca me las di de experto** I never claimed to be an expert.

(**h**) **no se me da mal** I'm not doing too badly; **se le dan muy bien las matemáticas** she's pretty good at maths, maths comes easily to her.

(**i**) **no se me da un bledo** (*o* **higo, rábano** *etc*) I don't care two hoots (*de* about).

(**j**) (*) **dársela (con queso) a uno** to fool sb, put one over on sb*; **se la da a su marido** she's unfaithful to her husband.

(**k**) *para otras locuciones V el sustantivo, p.ej.* **prisa, tono;** *o verbo, p.ej.* **conocer.**

Dardanelos NMPL Dardanelles.

dardo NM dart, shaft; (*juego*) **~s** darts.

dares* NMPL: **~ y tomares** arguments, bickering; **andar en ~ y tomares con uno** to bicker with sb, squabble with sb.

Darío NM Darius.

dársena NF (**a**) (*Náut*) dock; basin, inner harbour; **~ de marea** tidal basin. (**b**) (*Aut*) bus shelter.

darviniano, darwiniano ADJ Darwinian.

darvinismo, darwinismo NM Darwinism.

darvinista, darwinista **1** ADJ Darwinist; Darwinian.

2 NMF Darwinist.

data NF (**a**) (*gen*) date; **es de larga ~** it is old-established, it goes back a long way. (**b**) (*de cuenta*) item.

datable ADJ datable, that can be dated.

datación NF date, dating; **de difícil ~** hard to date.

datáfono NM dataphone.

datar [1a] **1** VT to date, put a date on.

2 VI: **~ de** to date from, date back to; **esto data de muy atrás** this dates back a long time, this goes a long way back.

datero* NM (*Cono Sur*) tipster.

dátil NM (**a**) (*Bot*) date; (‡) **~es** dabs‡, fingers. (**b**) (*Zool*) date mussel.

datilera NF date palm.

dativo NM dative.

dato NM (*gen*) fact, datum, piece of information; **un ~ interesante** an interesting fact; **~s** data, facts, information; **otro ~ que tener en cuenta es ...** another thing to bear in mind is ...; **no tenemos todos los ~s** we do not have all the facts; **~s de entrada** input data; **~s estadísticos** statistical information, statistical data, statistics; **~s personales** personal particulars, details about o.s.; **~ de salida** output data.

David NM David.

dB NM ABR *de* **decibelio** decibel, dB.

DC NF (*Pol*) ABR *de* **Democracia Cristiana.**

dcha. ABR *de* **derecha** (right hand, r.h.).

d. de J.C. ADV ABR *de* **después de Jesucristo** Anno Domini, in the year of our Lord, AD.

DDT NM ABR *de* **diclorodifeniltricloroetano** dichlorodiphenyltrichloroethane, DDT.

de PREP (**a**) (*posesión*) of; **el coche ~ mi amigo** the car of my friend, my friend's car; **los coches ~ mis amigos** my friends' cars; **es ~ ellos** it's theirs; **la señora ~ Pérez** Mrs Pérez; **el interés del préstamo** the interest on the loan.

(**b**) (*superlativo*) in; **el peor alumno ~ la clase** the worst pupil in the class; **es el coche más caro del mercado** it's the dearest car on the market.

(**c**) (*valor*) **una moneda ~ a 5 pesos** a 5-peso coin; **un pan ~ a libra** a pound loaf.

(**d**) (*origen, distancia*) from; **es ~ Calatayud** she's from Calatayud; **Dolores no es ~ aquí** Dolores is not from these parts; **los ~ Madrid son los mejores** those from Madrid are the best, the Madrid ones are the best; **~ A a B hay 5 kms** it is 5 kms from A to B; **ir ~ A a Z** to go from A to Z; **altura del suelo** height above ground; **~ esto se deduce que ...** from this one deduces that ...; **tiene 3 hijos ~ su primera mujer** he has 3 children by his first wife; **el camino ~ Elche** the Elche road, the road to Elche.

(**e**) (*aposición*) of; **la ciudad ~ Caracas** the city of Caracas.

(**f**) (*partitivo*) of; **uno ~ nosotros** one of us.

(**g**) (*números*) **3 ~ cada 4** 3 in every 4, 3 out of every 4.

(**h**) (*tema*) **una clase ~ francés** a French class; **un libro ~ biología** a biology book, a book about (*o* on) biology; **no sé nada ~ él** I don't

know anything about (o of, concerning) him; **hablaba ~ política** he was talking about politics.
(i) (*materia*) of; **una cadena ~ oro** a chain of gold, a gold(en) chain.
(j) (*contenido*) of; **una tacita ~ café** a cup of coffee.
(k) (*edad*) of; **un chico ~ 15 años** a boy of 15, a 15-year old boy.
(l) (*profesión*) by; **es abogado ~ profesión** he's a lawyer by profession.
(m) (*autoría*) by, of; **un libro ~ Cela** a book by Cela, a book of Cela's.
(n) (*finalidad*) **goma ~ mascar** chewing gum; **máquina ~ coser** sewing machine.
(o) (*que funciona con*) **cocina ~ gas** gas stove; **este modelo es ~ electricidad** this model works on electricity, this is an electric model.
(p) (*manera, estilo*) in; **amueblado ~ roble** furnished in oak; **vestido ~ azul** dressed in blue; **pintado ~ negro** painted (in) black; **~ puerta en puerta** from door to door; **iban entrando ~ 2 en 2** they came in 2 by 2; **bajó la escalera ~ 4 en 4** he came down 4 stairs at a time; **~ más en más** more and more.
(q) (*medio*) at, in, with; **~ un salto** at one bound, with one jump; **~ un trago** at a gulp, in one swallow.
(r) (*motivo*) with; **estar loco ~ contento** to be crazy with joy; **saltar ~ alegría** to jump for joy; **morir ~ hambre** to die of (o from) starvation, starve to death; **estar enfermo ~ gripe** to be ill with flu; **no poder moverse ~ miedo** to be unable to move for (o with) fright; **~ puro cansado** out of sheer tiredness.
(s) (*respecto de*) in; **mejor ~ salud** in better health, better in health; **paralizado ~ las dos piernas** paralysed in both legs.
(t) (*descriptivo*) with; **la niña ~ pelo largo** the girl with long hair; **ese tío del sombrero** that chap with (o in) the hat.
(u) (*en calidad de*) as; **~ niño** as a child; when a child; **'el gran actor, ~ Segismundo'** (*pie de foto*) 'the great actor as Segismundo'.
(v) (*agente*) by; **una persona amada ~ todos** a person loved by all, a person beloved of all.
(w) (*hora*) at, in, by; **a las 7 ~ la mañana** at 7 o'clock, at 7 a.m.; **muy ~ mañana** very early in the morning; **~ día** by day, during the day(time); **~ noche** at night, by night, in the night time.
(x) (*condicional*) if; **~ resultar esto así** if this turns out to be true; **~ no poder encontrarlo** if we can't find it; **~ no ser así** if it were not so, were it not so.
(y) (*tras más, menos*) than; **más ~ 7** more than 7.
(z) (*giros*) **aquel burro ~ ministro** that ass of a minister; **el pobre ~ Pedro** poor old Peter; **el bueno ~ Juan** good old John; *para otras locuciones, V el sustantivo, p.ej.* **pie, prisa.**

dé *V* **dar.**

deambulador NM walking frame, zimmer ®.
deambular [1a] VI to saunter, stroll, wander (*por* along, about, in, through).
deambulatorio NM (*Ecl*) ambulatory.
deán NM (*Ecl*) dean.
debacle NF débâcle, disaster.
debajo [1] ADV (*t por ~*) underneath, below; on the underside.
[2] **~ de** PREP under; below, beneath; **~ de la mesa** under the table, underneath the table; **por ~ de** under; below.
▼ **debate** NM debate (*t Parl*); discussion, argument; **estar a ~** to be under debate; **poner un tema a ~** to raise an issue for discussion.
▼ **debatir¹** [3a] VT to debate (*t Parl*); to discuss, argue about.
debatir² [3a] VI *y* **debatirse** VR (*luchar*) to struggle; (*forcejar*) to writhe; to flail about; **~se entre la vida y la muerte** to be fighting for life.
debe NM debit, debit side (*of account*); **~ y haber** debit and credit; **asentar algo al ~ de uno** to debit sth to sb.
debelador(a) NM/F conqueror.
debelar [1a] VT to conquer.
▼ **deber** [2a] [1] VT to owe; **me debes 5 dólares** you owe me 5 dollars; **¿qué le debo?** (*bares, tiendas*) how much is it?; what's the damage?*; **el respeto que todos deben a la patria** the respect which everybody owes to his country; **esto lo debe a influencia francesa** he owes this to French influence.
▼ [2] VI (a) (*obligación*) **debo hacerlo** I must do it, I have to do it; I ought to do it; **no debes comer tanto** you shouldn't eat so much; **debiera ir** he ought to go, he should go; **deberá cambiarse cada mes** (*instrucción*) it should be changed every month; **debíamos partir ayer** we were to have left yesterday; **he debido perderlo** I must have lost it; **hubieras debido traerlo** you ought to have brought it, you should have brought it.
(b) (*suposición*) **debe de ser así** it must be like that; that must be it; **debe de hacer mucho frío allí** it must be pretty cold then; **debe de ser brasileño** he must be a Brazilian; **no debe de ser muy caro** it can't be very dear; **debe de haber ido** he must have gone; **debió de perderlo** he must have lost it.
[3] **deberse** VR: **~ a** to be owing to, be due to, be on account of; **se debe al mal tiempo** it's on account of the bad weather; **se debe a**

que no hay carbón it is because (of the fact that) there's no coal; **puede ~ a que ...** it may be because ...; **¿a qué se debe esto?** what is the explanation of this?, why is this?
[4] NM (a) (*obligación*) duty, obligation; **~ ciudadano** civic duty; **últimos ~es** last rites; **cumplir con un ~** to perform a duty, carry out a duty.
(b) (*Fin*) debt.
(c) **~es** (*Escol*) homework; task, assignment.
debidamente ADV properly, as one should (o as it should be *etc*); in due form, duly; **si te conduces ~** if you behave properly; **un documento ~ redactado** a properly drawn up document.
▼ **debido** ADJ (a) (*correcto*) proper, due, just; (*justo*) right, correct; **en debida forma** duly, in due form; **con el ~ respeto** with (all) due respect; **como es ~, según es ~** as is (only) proper, as is right; **un padre como es ~ no haría eso** a true father would not do that.
▼ (b) **~ a** owing to, due to, because of; **~ a ello** because of this; **~ a la falta de agua** because of the water shortage; **~ a que no hay plátanos** because (of the fact that) there are no bananas.
débil [1] ADJ (*gen*) weak; (*físicamente*) weak, feeble, frail; *salud* poor; *carácter* weak; *esfuerzo etc* feeble; half-hearted; *grito* faint, feeble, weak; *luz* dim, wan, weak; **~ mental** mentally deficient.
[2] NMF: **~ mental** mental deficient; *V* **económicamente.**
▼ **debilidad** NF (a) (*gen*) weakness; feebleness; faintness; dimness; **~ senil** senility, senile decay.
▼ (b) (*una ~*) weakness; **tener una ~ por el chocolate** to have a weakness for chocolate; **tener una ~ por uno** to have a soft spot for sb.
debilitación NF weakening, debilitation, enfeeblement.
debilitador ADJ, **debilitante** ADJ debilitating.
debilitamiento NM = **debilitación.**
debilitar [1a] [1] VT to weaken, debilitate; *resistencia etc* to weaken, impair, lower.
[2] **debilitarse** VR to grow weak(er), weaken.
débilmente ADV weakly; feebly; half-heartedly; faintly; dimly, wanly.
debitar [1a] VT to debit.
débito NM (a) (*Com*) debit; debt. (b) **~ conyugal** conjugal duty, marital duty. (c) **~s varios** (*de hotel*) (*LAm*) sundries.
debocar* [1g] VTI (*LAm*) to vomit, throw up.
Débora NF Deborah.
debú NM, **debut** [de'βu] NM, PL **~s** [de'βus] début.
debutante [1] ADJ inexperienced, novice; **jugador ~** player appearing for the first time.
[2] NMF (*t* **debutanta** *f*) (*en sociedad*) debutante; (*Dep*) new player, new cap.
debutar [1a] VI to make one's début.
década NF (*decenio*) decade; (*serie*) set of ten, series of ten.
decadencia NF decadence, decline, decay; **estar en franca ~** to be in full decline.
decadente ADJ decadent; effete.
decaer [2n] VI (a) (*gen*) to decay, decline; (*esfuerzo*) to flag, weaken; (*moda*) to wane; (*negocio*) to fall off; (*en salud*) to decline, sink, fail; **~ (de ánimo)** to lose heart; **ella ha decaído en belleza** her beauty is not what it was; **decayó de poderío** his power declined.
(b) (*Náut*) to drift, drift off course.
decagramo NM decagram.
decaído ADJ (*fig: desanimado*) downcast, crestfallen; **estar ~** to be down.
decaimiento NM decay; decline; weakening, weakness; warning; falling-off; **~ (de ánimo)** discouragement, depression.
decalaje NM time-lag, shift of time; gap, interval, discrepancy.
decalitro NM decalitre, decaliter (*US*).
decálogo NM decalogue.
decámetro NM decametre, decameter (*US*).
decana NF doyenne.
decanato NM deanship; deanery.
decano NM (a) (*Univ etc*) dean. (b) (*de grupo, de prensa etc*) doyen, senior member.
decantación NF leaning, tendency, movement (*hacia* towards).
decantamiento NM preference; (*ideológico*) leaning.
decantar¹ [1a] VT (*liter*) to praise, laud; **el tan decantado edificio** (*iró*) this building which has been so effusively praised.
decantar² [1a] [1] VT *vino etc* to decant; to pour off; *sedimento* to leave behind, form, deposit.
[2] **decantarse** VR: **~ hacia** to move towards, evolve in the direction of; to lean towards, tend towards; **~ por algo** (o **uno**) to show preference for sth (o sb).
decapado NM scaling.
decapitar [1a] VT to behead, decapitate.
decasílabo [1] ADJ decasyllabic, ten-syllable.
[2] NM decasyllable.
decatlón NM decathlon.
deceleración NF deceleration.

---

decena NF ten; about ten; **~s** (*Mat*) tens; **una ~ de barcos** about ten ships, some ten ships; **~s de miles de españoles** tens of thousands of Spaniards; **contar por ~s** to count in tens; **vender por ~s** to sell in tens.

decenal ADJ decennial; **plan ~** ten-year plan.

decencia NF (*V ADJ*) (**a**) decency; seemliness, decorum; respectability; modesty; **faltar a la ~** to offend against decency (*o* propriety). (**b**) cleanness, tidiness.

decenio NM decade.

decente ADJ (**a**) (*gen*) decent; (*correcto*) seemly, proper; (*honrado*) respectable; (*modesto*) modest. (**b**) (*aseado*) clean, tidy.

decentemente ADV (*V ADJ*) (**a**) decently; properly; respectably; modestly. (**b**) tidily.

decepción NF disappointment.

decepcionado ADJ disappointed; **estar ~ con algo** to be disappointed with sth.

decepcionante ADJ disappointing.

decepcionar [1a] VT to disappoint.

decesado, -a NM/F (*LAm*) deceased person.

deceso NM (*esp LAm*) passing, death; fatality.

dechado NM (*Cos*) model, example, epitome; **es un ~ de virtudes** she's a paragon of virtue; **no es ningún ~ de perfección** it isn't a model of perfection.

decibel NM, **decibelio** NM decibel.

decibélico ADJ loud, noisy.

decible ADJ expressible; communicable; **eso no es ~** that cannot be expressed, there are no words to say it.

decididamente ADV decidedly.

▼ **decidido** ADJ decided, determined; resolute; emphatic; **de carácter ~** firm, strong-willed.

▼ **decidir** [3a] **1** VT (**a**) *persona* to decide, persuade, convince; **esto le decidió a dejarlo** this decided him to give it up; **esto por fin le decidió** this finally made his mind up (for him). (**b**) *cuestión, resultado* to decide, settle, resolve.

▼**2** VI to decide (*de, en* about); **~ + infin** to decide to + *infin*; **~ en favor de uno** to decide in sb's favour; **~ sobre cuál conviene más** to decide which is more suitable.

3 **decidirse** VR to decide, make up one's mind (*a + infin* to + *infin*); **~ por** to decide on, settle on, choose.

decidor **1** ADJ (**a**) (*gracioso*) witty, amusing, racy. (**b**) (*elocuente*) fluent, eloquent. **2** NM (**a**) (*chistoso*) wit, witty talker. (**b**) (*narrador*) fluent speaker, eloquent speaker.

decil NM decile.

decilitro NM decilitre, deciliter (*US*).

décima NF (**a**) (*Mat*) tenth; tenth part (*esp* of a lottery ticket). (**b**) (*Ecl*) tithe. (**c**) (*Liter Hist*) a ten-line stanza. (**d**) **tiene sólo unas ~s de fiebre** (*Med*) he's only got a slight fever.

decimación NF decimation.

decimal **1** ADJ decimal. **2** NM decimal. **3** NF: **~ periódica** recurring decimal.

decimalización NF decimalization.

decimalizar [1f] VT to decimalize.

decímetro NM decimetre, decimeter (*US*).

décimo **1** ADJ tenth. **2** (**a**) NM tenth. (**b**) (*t* **~ de lotería**) ≈ lottery ticket; *see also* LOTERÍA PRIMITIVA, LOTERÍA NACIONAL , EL GORDO .

decimoctavo ADJ eighteenth.

decimocuarto ADJ fourteenth.

decimonónicamente ADV in the style of the 19th century.

decimonónico ADJ (*hum o pey*) nineteenth-century (*atr*); Victorian; (*fig*) outdated, antiquated.

decimonono ADJ, **decimonoveno** ADJ nineteenth.

decimoprimero ADJ eleventh.

decimoquinto ADJ fifteenth.

decimosegundo ADJ twelfth.

decimoséptimo ADJ seventeenth.

decimosexto ADJ sixteenth.

decimotercio ADJ, **decimotercero** ADJ thirteenth.

decir **1** [3o] VTI (**a**) (*gen*) to say; to tell; (*texto*) to say, read; *buenaventura* to tell; *mentira* to tell; *verdad* to speak, tell; *misa* to say; *disparates etc* to talk; (***) to ask; **le dije cuántos había** I asked him how many there were; **no dijo nada** he said nothing; **¿quién te lo dijo?** who told you?; **dicen que ...** they say that ..., people say that ...; **~ a uno que se calle** to tell sb to be quiet; **nos dijo que fuéramos** he told us to go.
(**b**) (*locuciones: gen*) **¿digo algo?** have I said sth?; **eso digo** that's what I say; that's just what I'm saying; **¡digo, digo!** hey!, say!; just listen to this!; now wait a minute!; **digo ...** (*Méx*) well, er ...; **había 8, digo 9** there were 8, (no) I mean 9; **pero digo mal 'decadente'** but I am wrong to say (*o* to call them *etc*) 'decadent'; **pero dice mal**

but he is wrong; **y dice bien** and he is right; **como aquel que dice** so to speak; **no lo digo por ti** I'm not referring to you, I'm not getting at you; **~ que no** to say no; **~ que sí** to say yes; **~ para sí, ~ entre sí** to say to o.s.; **~ digo donde dijo Diego** to take back what one said earlier; **como quien dice, como si dijéramos** so to speak; in a way, more or less; **como quien no dice nada** quite casually; as though it wasn't important; **¿cómo has dicho?** what did you say?, pardon?; **decía** (*después de interrupción*) as I was saying; **¿decía Vd?** you were saying?; **¿cómo diríamos?** how shall I put it?; **¡si te lo digo yo!** of course it's true!; **¡lo que he dicho!** I stand by what I said!; **¡quién lo diría!** would you believe it!; did you ever?*; **me dijo de todo*** he called me all the names under the sun.
(**c**) (*locuciones con infin*) **es ~** that is to say; **es mucho ~, ya es ~** that's saying a lot, that's a big claim to make; **me permito ~ que ...** I submit that ..., I venture to say that ...; **querer ~** to mean; **¿qué quiere ~ 'spatha'?** what does 'spatha' mean?; **¿qué quiere Vd ~ con eso?** what do you mean by that?; **dar que ~ (a la gente)** to make people talk, set the tongues wagging; **no sé qué ~** I don't know what to say; **no hay más que ~** there's no more to be said about it; **no hay que ~ que ..., ni que ~ tiene que ...** it goes without saying that ...; **no hay para qué ~** of course ...; **~ por ~** to talk for talking's sake; **o por mejor ~** or rather; **por ~lo así** so to speak.
(**d**) (*locuciones con futuro*) **dirás aquel otro** you must mean that other one; **ya me dirás** you tell me your side of it, you tell me how you see things; **Vd dirá** it's for you to say; (*al preparar bebida*) how much do you like?, say when*; **ello dirá** the event will show; **el qué dirán** public opinion, what people will say; **pero no quiso por el qué dirán** but she didn't want to because of what people might say; **el maldito 'qué dirán'** the curse of concern for what people will think.
(**e**) (*locuciones con subjuntivo*) (*Telec*) **¡diga!, ¡dígame!** hullo?; **dicho sea de paso ...** by the way ..., and I (*etc*) might add that ...; **digan lo que digan** whatever they (may) say; let them say what they please; **digámoslo así** so to speak; for want of a better word; **¡no me digas!** you don't say!; well I'm blowed!*; come off it!*; so what's new?*; **¡y que lo digas!** you can say that again!; **no es que yo lo diga, pero ...** it's not because I say so, but ...; **y no digamos de ...** not to mention ...; **no estuvo muy cortés, que digamos** actually he wasn't all that polite, he wasn't what you could call polite; **no es un pintor, que digamos** he's not what you could really call a painter; **es, digamos, un comerciante** he's a sort of dealer, he's a dealer ... for want of a better word; **no es muy guapa que digamos** she's not really that pretty.
(**f**) (*locuciones con ptp*) **mejor dicho** rather; I mean ...; **no es para dicho** it's not fit to be told; **¡lo dicho dicho!** I stand by what I said!; **¡dicho y hecho!** no sooner said than done!; **dicho sea de paso ...** by the way ..., and I (*etc*) might add that ...; **¡haberlo dicho!** you might have told me!; **tragarse lo dicho** to eat one's words; **dicho de otra manera ...** in other words ...
(**g**) (*mostrar, indicar*) to show, indicate, reveal; **su cara dice lo que es** his face shows him up for what he is; **una situación que tan mal dice de nuestro gobierno** a situation which shows our government up in such a bad light.
(**h**) (*: *nombrar*) to call; **al niño le dicen Anastasio** they call the child Anastasio.
(**i**) (*convenir*) to suit; **~ con** to go with, match; **el vestido le dice bien** the dress suits her (nicely); **el color dice bien con su cutis** the colour goes with (*o* suits, harmonizes with) her complexion.

2 **decirse** VR (**a**) **yo sé lo que me digo** I know what I'm talking about; I know what I'm up to.
(**b**) (*llamarse*) to be called, be named; **esta plaza se dice de la Revolución** this is called Revolution Square; **¿cómo se dice en inglés 'cursi'?** what's the English for 'cursi'?, how do you say 'cursi' in English?
(**c**) **se dice** it is said, they say, people say; the story goes ...; **se me ha dicho que ...** I have been told that ...; **no se diría eso ahora** that could not be said nowadays; **y no se diga ...** not to mention ...; **no se diga que ...** never let it be said that ...; **se diría que no está** she doesn't seem to be here; **eso se dice en seguida** that's easier said than done.
(**d**) **hablar portugués, lo que se dice hablar, no sé** I can't really talk Portuguese, I don't speak Portuguese at all well; **esto es lo que se dice un queso** this is a real cheese, this is what you really call a cheese.

3 NM (*refrán etc*) saying; (*gracia*) witty remark; **es un ~** it's just a phrase; if I may use the expression ...; I was only thinking aloud; **a ~ de todos** by all accounts; **al ~ de X** according to X; as X has it, as X would have it.

decisión NF (**a**) (*una ~*) decision; (*Jur*) judgement; **~ por mayoría** majority decision; **forzar una ~** to force the issue; **tomar una ~** to make (*o* take) a decision. (**b**) (*cualidad*) decisiveness; determination, resolution.

decisivo ADJ decisive; *argumento, consideración* over-riding.

► LENGUA Y USO: **decidido** → 35.2   **decidir: 2** → 35.2

┌─ **DECIR** ──────────── *ver también la entrada* ─┐

¿"Say" o "tell"?

● *Decir* se puede traducir por *say* o por *tell*. Por regla general, *say* simplemente *dice* y *tell informa* u *ordena* hacer algo.

● *Decir* generalmente se traduce por *say* en estilo directo. Normalmente no lleva un complemento de persona pero si se menciona a quién se está dirigiendo el hablante, el complemento de persona tiene que ir precedido por la preposición *to*:

    "Ya son las tres", dije.
    "It's already three o'clock", I said
    "¡Qué tiempo más malo!". Eso fue lo único que me dijo
    "The weather is awful!". That's all he said to me

● En estilo indirecto, *decir* se puede traducir por *say* cuando simplemente se cuenta lo que alguien ha dicho. Si *say* lleva complemento de persona, éste se coloca después del complemento directo:

    Dijo que se tenía que marchar
    He said he had to leave
    Me dijo algo que no entendí
    He said something to me that I didn't understand

● *Decir* se traduce por *tell* cuando se *informa* o se *ordena* hacer algo. Suele llevar un objeto de persona sin la preposición *to*:

    Me dijo que tenía una entrevista de trabajo
    He told me he had a job interview
    ¡Te he dicho que no lo toques!
    I've told you not to touch it!

● Hay algunos usos idiomáticos en los que *decir* se traduce por *tell* aunque no lleva complemento de persona. Por ejemplo: *to tell the truth* (decir la verdad) y *to tell a lie* (decir una mentira).

Otros verbos

● Si *decir* va acompañado de un calificativo en español, a menudo se puede traducir al inglés por otros verbos que no sean *say* o *tell*:

    "Lo he perdido todo", dijo entre sollozos
    "I've lost everything," she sobbed
    Dijo con voz ronca algo sobre necesitar un médico
    He croaked something about needing a doctor
    Para otros usos y ejemplos ver la entrada.

└──┘

decisorio ① ADJ: **poderes ~s** decision-making powers; **proceso ~** decision-making process.
  ② NM (*Méx Jur*) judgment, verdict.
declamación NF (**a**) (*acto*) declamation; recital, recitation; (*cualidad*) delivery. (**b**) (*pey*) ranting.
declamador(a) NM/F (**a**) (*orador*) orator; reciter. (**b**) (*pey*) ranter.
declamar [1a] ① VT to declaim; *versos etc* to recite.
  ② VI (**a**) (*gen*) to speak out, hold forth (*contra* against). (**b**) (*pey*) to rant, carry on.
declamatorio ADJ declamatory; (*pey*) ranting.
declaración NF (**a**) (*gen*) declaration; (*afirmación*) pronouncement, statement; (*explicación*) explanation; (*de amor*) proposal (of marriage); **~ conjunta** joint communiqué, joint declaration; **~ de derechos** (*Pol*) bill of rights; **~ de impuestos**, **~ de ingresos**, **~ de renta** income-tax return.
  (**b**) (*Naipes*) bid.
  (**c**) (*Jur*) statement; evidence; **~ de culpabilidad** confession of guilt; **~ inmediata** (*Méx*) verbal statement; **~ jurada** sworn statement, affidavit; **prestar ~** to make a statement; to give evidence; **tomar la ~ a uno** to take a statement from sb.
declaradamente ADV confessedly, frankly.
declarado ADJ confessed, declared.
declarante NMF (**a**) (*Jur*) deponent. (**b**) (*Naipes*) bidder, declarer.
declarar [1a] ① VT (**a**) (*gen*) to declare, state (*que* that); (*explicar*) to explain, expound; (*en aduana*) to declare; *guerra* to declare (*a* on).
  (**b**) (*Naipes*) to bid; **~ 2 picos** to bid 2 spades.
  (**c**) (*Jur*) to find; **~ culpable a uno** to find sb guilty.
  ② VI (**a**) (*gen*) to declare; **según él mismo declara** as he himself declares.
  (**b**) (*Naipes*) to bid, declare; **declaró menos de lo que tenía** he underbid.
  (**c**) (*Jur*) to make a statement; to testify, give evidence.
  ③ **declararse** VR (**a**) (*gen*) to declare o.s.; to make one's opinion (*o* position *etc*) known; **~ a una joven** to say to a girl that one loves her; (*más formal*) to propose to a girl; **~ por** to come out in favour of, declare one's support for, side with.
  (**b**) **~ culpable** (*Jur*) to plead guilty; **~ inocente** to plead not guilty.
  (**c**) (*epidemia, incendio, guerra etc*) to break out.
declaratoria (*Jur*) ① ADJ declaratory.
  ② NF declaration.

declinable ADJ declinable.
declinación NF (**a**) (*gen*) decline, falling-off; decay. (**b**) (*Astron, Náut*) declination. (**c**) (*Ling*) declension.
▼ **declinar** [1a] ① VT (**a**) (*gen*) to decline, refuse; (*Jur*) to reject; **~ hacer algo** to decline to do sth.
  (**b**) (*Ling*) to decline; to inflect.
  ② VI (**a**) (*decaer*) to decline, fall off, fall away; to decay; to deteriorate; (*día*) to draw to a close.
  (**b**) (*terreno*) to slope (away, down).
  (**c**) (*Ling*) to decline.
declive NM (**a**) (*gen*) slope, incline, declivity; pitch; (*Ferro*) gradient; **tierra en ~** sloping ground, land on a slope; **estar en ~** to slope.
  (**b**) (fig: *Fin etc*) (*t* **~ económico**) slump.
decocción NF decoction.
decodificador NM = **descodificador**.
decodificar *etc* = **descodificar** *etc*.
decolaje NM (*LAm Aer*) takeoff.
decolar [1l] VI (*LAm Aer*) to take off.
decolorado ADJ discoloured.
decolorante NM bleaching agent.
decolorar [1a] ① VT to discolour, affect the colour of.
  ② **decolorarse** VR to get discoloured, lose colour.
decomisar [1a] VT to seize, confiscate.
decomiso NM seizure, confiscation.
decongestionante NM decongestant.
deconstrucción NF deconstruction.
decoración NF (**a**) (*gen*) decoration; **~ de escaparate** window display; **~ de escaparates** window dressing; **~ del hogar**, **~ de interiores** interior decorating; interior design. (**b**) (*Teat*) scenery, set, décor.
decorado NM (*Cine, Teat*) scenery, set, décor.
decorador(a) NM/F decorator; interior designer; (*Cine, TV*) set designer.
decorar[1] [1a] VT (*adornar*) to decorate, adorn (*de* with).
decorar[2] [1a] VT (*aprender*) to learn, memorize; to learn by heart; (*recitar*) to chorus.
decorativo ADJ decorative, ornamental.
decoro NM (**a**) (*gen*) decorum, propriety, decency; proprieties; **~ virginal** maidenly modesty. (**b**) (*honor*) honour, respect.
decorosamente ADV decorously.
decoroso ADJ decorous, proper, decent; seemly; modest.
decrecer [2d] VI to decrease, diminish; (*inundación, agua*) to go down; (*días*) to get shorter, draw in.
decreciente ADJ decreasing, diminishing.
decrecimiento NM, **decremento** NM decrease, diminution; fall; shortening.
decrépito ADJ decrepit.
decrepitud NF decrepitude.
decretar [1a] ① VT (**a**) (*ordenar*) to decree, order, ordain; **~ que ... to** decree that ...
  (**b**) *premio* to award (*a* to); *penalti* to award.
  (**c**) (*Méx*) *dividendo* to declare.
  ② VI (*Jur*) to deliver a judgment.
decreto NM decree, order; (*Parl*) act; **real ~** royal decree; **por real ~*** compulsorily, willy-nilly.
decreto-ley NM, PL **decretos-leyes** decree law, order in council (*Brit*).
decúbito NM (*Med*): **~ prono** prone position; **~ supino** supine position; **úlcera de ~** bedsore.
decuplar [1a] VT, **decuplicar** [1g] VT to multiply tenfold, increase tenfold.
décuplo ① ADJ tenfold.
  ② NM: **es el ~ de lo que era** it is ten times what it was, it has increased tenfold.
decurso NM (*liter*): **en el ~ de los años** over the years; **en el ~ del tiempo** in the course of time.
dedada NF thimbleful; (*fig*) very small quantity, very modest amount; (*de mermelada etc*) spot, dab, drop; (*de rapé*) pinch; **dar una ~ de miel a uno** (*fig*) to give sb a crumb of comfort.
dedal NM (**a**) (*Cos*) thimble. (**b**) (*fig*) thimbleful.
dedalera NF foxglove.
dédalo NM (**a**) (*gen*) labyrinth. (**b**) (*fig*) tangle, mess.
dedazo NM fingermark.
dedicación NF (**a**) (*gen*) dedication; (*fig*) dedication, devotion (*a* to); **las profesiones de ~ humanitaria** the caring professions.
  (**b**) (*Ecl*) consecration.
  (**c**) (*en régimen de*) **~ exclusiva** (*o* **plena**), **trabajar con ~ plena** to work full-time; '**~ plena**' (*anuncio*) 'full-time'.
dedicado ADJ (*Inform*) dedicated.
dedicar [1g] ① VT (**a**) (*gen*) to dedicate (*a* to); (*Ecl*) to consecrate; *libro* to dedicate (*a* to); *ejemplar* to autograph, inscribe, write in.
  (**b**) *esfuerzo, tiempo* to devote, give (*a* to); **dedico un día a la semana**

a pescar I spend one day a week fishing; **tengo que ~ mucho tiempo a eso** I have to give a lot of time to that.
[2] **dedicarse** VR: **~ a** to devote o.s. to; to go in for, take up; **~ a +** *infin* to devote o.s. to + *ger*; **se dedicó a la cerámica** he devoted himself to pottery, he took up pottery; **¿a qué se dedica Vd?** what do you do?; what's your line?, what business are you in?; **¡dedícate a lo tuyo!** mind your own business!

dedicatoria NF inscription, dedication.

dedicatorio ADJ dedicatory.

dedil NM fingerstall.

dedillo NM: **saber algo al ~** to have sth at one's fingertips; **saber una lección al ~** to have a lesson off pat; **dijo la lista al ~** he rattled off the list with complete accuracy.

dedismo* NM arbitrary selection, arbitrary nomination.

dedo NM (a) finger; **~ (del pie)** toe; **~ anular** ring finger; **~ auricular, ~ meñique** little finger; **~ (del) corazón, ~ cordial** middle finger; **~ chico** little toe; **~ gordo** big toe; **~ índice** index finger, forefinger; **~ (en) martillo** hammer-toe; **~ pulgar** thumb; **comerse** (o **morderse**) **los ~s** to get very impatient; **contar con los ~s** to count on one's fingers; **cruzar los ~s** to cross one's fingers, keep one's fingers crossed; **chuparse los ~s** to eat with relish; (*fig*) to smack one's lips; to rub one's hands; **no se chupa el ~** he's no fool; he doesn't waste any time; **dale un ~ y se toma hasta el codo** give him an inch and he'll take a yard; **se le escapó de entre los ~s** it slipped through his fingers; **hacer ~*, ir al ~*** (*LAm*), **tirar ~** (*LAm*) to thumb a lift*, hitch-hike; **hacer ~s** (*Mús*) to practise, do scales; **no se mama el ~** he's pretty smart; **meter el ~ en la boca a uno** to try to get sb to talk; **no se mueve un ~** (*fig*) he won't lift a finger; **pillarse los ~s** (*fig*) to get caught red-handed; to burn one's fingers; **poner el ~ en** to put one's finger on, pinpoint, identify precisely; **poner el ~ en la llaga** to put one's finger on the spot; **señalar algo con el ~** to point the finger of scorn at sth; **no se ven los ~s de la mano** it's pitch-dark; **viajar a ~*** to hitch-hike; **vine a ~** I hitched here*, I hitch-hiked here.
(b) (*fig*) spot, bit, drop; (*como medida*) finger; finger's breadth; **¡dos ~s nada más!** (*de bebida*) just a tiny drop!; **estar a dos ~s de** to be within an inch of, be within an ace of; to be on the verge of; **no tiene dos ~s de frente** he's pretty dim; he's a lout.
(c) (*fig*) (system of) arbitrary selection (o appointment *etc*); **entrar a ~** to get in (o get a job) by pulling strings.

dedocracia* NF arbitrary exercise of power; system of arbitrary appointment.

deducción NF (a) (*gen*) deduction; inference. (b) (*suma etc*) deduction.

deducible ADJ (a) (*gen*) deducible, inferable (*de* from); **según es fácilmente ~** as may readily be deduced. (b) (*Fin etc*) deductible; (*por razones impositivas*) allowable, deductible (*US*).

▼ **deducir** [3n] VT (a) (*razonar*) to deduce, infer (*de* from); *fórmula* to deduce, derive. (b) *suma etc* to deduct; **deducidos los gastos** less charges.

deductivo ADJ deductive.

defalcar [1g] VT = **desfalcar**.

defecación NF defecation.

defecar [1g] VI to defecate.

defección NF defection, desertion.

defectible ADJ fallible, imperfect; faulty.

defectivo ADJ defective (*t Ling*).

defecto NM (*gen*) fault, defect, flaw; (*Elec, Téc*) fault; (*en fabricación, argumento*) flaw; (*moral*) shortcoming, failure; **~ físico** physical defect; **~ de fonación, ~ del habla, ~ de la palabra** speech defect, impediment; **en ~ de** for lack of, for want of; **A, o en su ~, B** A, or failing him, B; **por ~** (*Inform*) default.

defectuosamente ADV defectively, faultily.

defectuoso ADJ defective, faulty.

defender [2g] [1] VT (*gen*) to defend (*contra* against, *de* from); to protect; (*Jur*) to defend; *causa* to champion, uphold; **para ~los contra el frío** in order to protect them from the cold.
[2] **defenderse** VR (a) to defend o.s. (*contra* against, *de* from); **~ bien** to resist firmly; to give a good account of o.s.
(b) (*fig*) **me defiendo en inglés** I can manage in English, I can get along in English, I can keep going in English; **'¿qué tal?' ... 'hombre, nos defendemos'** 'how are things?' ... 'we're managing'; **gana poco pero se defiende** she doesn't earn much but she manages (o gets by); **~ como un gato** o **panza arriba** to fight tooth and nail.

defendible ADJ defensible; that can be defended.

defendido, -a NM/F (*Jur*): **mi ~** my client.

defenestración NF (*hum*) abrupt dismissal, sudden removal; sudden expulsion.

defenestrar [1a] VT (*hum*) to dismiss abruptly, remove suddenly; to expel suddenly.

defensa [1] NF (a) (*gen*) defence (*t Ajedrez, Jur, Dep*); protection, shelter; **~ contra, ~ de** defence against; **~ pasiva** civil defence; **~ personal** self-defence; **~ en profundidad** defence in depth; **en ~ propia** in self-defence.
(b) (*Náut*) fender; (*Dep*) shinpad, leg-pad; (*Méx Aut*) bumper, fender (*US*); **~s** (*Taur*) horns.
(c) **~s** (*Mil etc*) defences, defensive works; **~s costeras** coastal defences; **~ marítima** (*Cono Sur*) sea-wall, coast defence.
[2] NM (*Dep*) defender; back, fullback; **~ escoba, ~ libre** sweeper.

defensiva NF defensive; **estar a la ~** to be on the defensive.

defensivo [1] ADJ defensive; **política ~** defence policy.
[2] NM defence, safeguard.

defenso NM (*Méx Jur*) defendant.

defensor(a) NM/F defender; protector; (*de causa*) champion, upholder; (*de teoría*) proponent; (*Jur: t* **abogado ~**) defending counsel; **~ del pueblo** parliamentary commissioner, ombudsman.

deferencia NF deference; **por ~ hacia** out of deference to.

deferente ADJ deferential.

deferir [3k] [1] VT (*Jur*) to refer, relegate (*a* to).
[2] VI: **~ a** to defer to.

deficiencia NF deficiency, shortcoming, defect (*de* in, of); **~ mental, ~ psíquico** mental deficiency; **~ visual** visual handicap.

deficiente [1] ADJ deficient, wanting (*en* in); defective; (*mentalmente*) retarded, handicapped.
[2] NMF: **~ mental, ~ psíquico** mental defective; **~ visual** visually handicapped person.

déficit NM (a) (*Com, Fin*) deficit; **~ comercial** trade deficit; **~ exterior** balance of payments deficit, trade deficit; **~ por cuenta corriente** deficit on current account; **~ presupuestario** budget(ary) deficit. (b) (*fig*) lack, shortage; shortfall.

deficitario ADJ (a) (*Fin*) deficit (*atr*); *cuenta* in deficit, showing a deficit; *empresa, operación* loss-making. (b) **ser ~ en** to be short of, be lacking in.

definible ADJ definable, that can be defined.

definición NF definition; **por ~** by definition.

definido ADJ (a) (*gen*) (*t Ling*) definite; **bien ~** well defined, clearly defined; **~ por el usuario** (*Inform*) user defined. (b) *carácter* tough, manly.

definir [3a] VT (*gen*) to define; (*aclarar*) to clarify, explain; (*decidir*) to determine, establish.

definitivamente ADV definitively, finally.

▼ **definitivo** ADJ definitive; final, ultimate; **en definitiva** (*de una vez*) definitively; (*finalmente*) finally, once and for all; (*en resumen*) in short; in the last analysis.

definitorio ADJ defining, distinctive.

deflación NF deflation.

deflacionar [1a] VT to deflate.

deflacionario ADJ, **deflacionista** ADJ deflationary.

deflactación NF (*Cono Sur*) deflation.

deflactar [1a] VT (*Cono Sur*) to deflate.

deflector NM (*Téc*) baffle, baffle plate.

defoliación NF defoliation.

defoliante NM defoliant.

defoliar [1b] VT to defoliate.

deforestar *etc* = **desforestar** *etc*.

deformación NF deformation; (*Rad etc*) distortion; (*Mec*) strain; (*de madera etc*) warping.

deformante ADJ: **espejo ~** distorting mirror.

deformar [1a] [1] VT (*gen*) to deform; to disfigure; (*Rad etc*) to distort; (*Mec*) to strain; *madera etc* to warp, push out of shape.
[2] **deformarse** VR to become deformed; to get distorted; to warp, get out of shape, lose shape.

deforme ADJ deformed, misshapen; ugly; abnormal.

deformidad NF (a) (*lit*) deformity, malformation; abnormality. (b) (*fig*) (moral) shortcoming.

defraudación NF (*V VT*) (a) defrauding; deceit; **~ fiscal, ~ de impuestos** tax evasion. (b) dashing, disappointment.

defraudador(a) NM/F fraudster*.

defraudar [1a] VT (a) *acreedores* to cheat, defraud; to deceive; *amigos* to let down; **~ impuestos** to evade taxes, fiddle one's income tax*. (b) *esperanzas* to dash, disappoint, frustrate. (c) (*Fís*) *luz* to intercept, cut off.

defraudatorio ADJ fraudulent.

defuera ADV (*t* **por ~**) outwardly, on the outside.

defunción NF decease, demise.

defuncionar: [1a] VT to do in:.

DEG NMPL ABR *de* **derechos especiales de giro** special drawing rights, SDR.

degeneración NF (a) (*acto*) degeneration (*en* into). (b) (*estado*) (moral) degeneracy.

degenerado [1] ADJ degenerate.
[2] NM degenerate, degenerate type.

degenerar [1a] VI (*gen*) to degenerate (*en* into); (*decaer*) to decline,

➤ LENGUA Y USO: **deducir: a** → 53.4   **definitivo** → 53.4

decay; (*empeorar*) to get worse, get more serious; **la manifestación degeneró en una sangrienta revuelta** the demonstration degenerated into a bloody riot.

degenerativo ADJ degenerative.

deglución NF swallowing.

deglutir [3a] VTI to swallow.

degollación NF throat cutting; (*Jur*) beheading, execution; (*sentido más amplio*) massacre, slaughter; **D~ de los Inocentes** Slaughter of the Innocents.

degolladero NM (**a**) (*Anat*) throat, neck, throttle.
(**b**) (*Hist*) scaffold, block (for executions); **ir al ~** (*fig*) to expose o.s. to mortal danger, (*hum*) put one's head in the lion's mouth.
(**c**) (*matadero*) slaughterhouse.

degollador NM (*Hist*) executioner.

degollar [1m] VT (**a**) (*cortar la garganta de*) to cut (*o* slit) the throat of; (*decapitar*) to behead, decapitate; (*Taur*) to kill badly, butcher; (*fig*) to massacre, slaughter.
(**b**) (*fig: destruir*) to destroy; *comedia etc* to murder, make nonsense of; *papel* to make a dreadful hash of.
(**c**) (*Cos*) to cut low in the neck.

degradación NF (**a**) (*gen*) degradation; humiliation. (**b**) (*Mil etc*) demotion, reduction in rank. (**c**) (*Geol*) impoverishment; (*de calidad*) worsening, decline.

degradante ADJ degrading.

degradar [1a] **1** VT (**a**) (*gen*) to degrade, debase; (*humillar*) to humiliate.
(**b**) (*Mil etc*) to demote, reduce in rank.
(**c**) *suelo* to impoverish; *calidad* to lower, make worse, cause to decline.
2 degradarse VR to demean o.s.

degüello NM (**a**) = **degollación**; **entrar a ~ en una ciudad** to put the people of a city to the sword, give no quarter to the inhabitants of a town; **tirarse a ~ contra** to lash out against.
(**b**) (*de arma*) shaft, neck, narrow part.

degustación NF tasting, sampling; drinking; eating, consumption.

degustar [1a] VT (*probar*) to taste, sample; (*beber*) to drink, take; (*comer*) to eat, consume.

dehesa NF pasture, meadow; pastureland, range; (*finca*) estate.

deíctico ADJ, NM deictic.

deidad NF deity; divinity; **~ pagana** pagan god, pagan deity.

deificación NF deification; apotheosis (*t fig*).

deificar [1g] VT (**a**) (*Rel, t fig*) to deify; to apotheosize. (**b**) (*fig: ensalzar*) to exalt, over-praise, put on a pedestal.

deísmo NM deism.

deísta **1** ADJ deistic(al).
2 NMF deist.

deixis NF INVAR deixis.

dejación NF (**a**) (*Jur*) abandonment, relinquishment. (**b**) (*And, CAm: descuido*) carelessness.

dejada NF (*Tenis*) let.

dejadez NF (*V ADJ*) (**a**) untidiness, slovenliness; abandon. (**b**) carelessness, negligence, neglect, slackness; laziness; supineness, lack of willpower.

dejado ADJ (**a**) (*desaliñado*) untidy, slovenly; abandoned; unkempt.
(**b**) (*descuidado*) careless, negligent, slack; (*vago*) lazy.
(**c**) (*triste*) dejected.
(**d**) **~ de la mano de Dios** (*fig*) godforsaken; beyond all hope of redemption.

dejamiento NM = **dejación** (a); = **dejadez.**

▼**dejar** [1a] **1** VT (**a**) (*gen*) to leave; (*omitir*) to forget, leave out; (*abandonar*) to leave, abandon, desert, forsake; (*prestar*) to lend; *esfuerzo, trabajo etc* to give up, stop, abandon; *pasajero* to put down, set down; to drop; (*Com*) *balance etc* to show, leave; *beneficio* to produce, yield; *aparte* to leave aside; **~ atrás** to leave behind, outstrip, out-distance; (*fig*) to surpass; **~ a uno muy atrás** to leave sb far behind; **~ algo para mañana** to leave sth till tomorrow, postpone (*o* put off) sth till tomorrow; **~ algo para después** to leave sth till later; **lo dejamos por muy difícil** we gave it up because it was too hard; **lo dejamos por imposible** we gave it up as (being) impossible; **así que lo dejamos** so we gave it up; **¡deja eso!** stop that!, drop that!, chuck it!; **te lo dejo en la conserjería** I'll leave it for you at the porter's office; **~ así las cosas** to leave things as they are; **dejémoslo así** let's leave it at that; **como dejo dicho** as I have said; **deja escritas 3 novelas** he left 3 novels which he had written; he left 3 finished novels; **deja mucho que desear** it leaves a lot to be desired; **¿me dejas 10 dólares?** can I borrow 10 dollars, can you lend me 10 dollars?; **¿me dejas el auto?** can you (*o* will you) let me have the car?

▼(**b**) (*permitir*) to let, allow; **quiero pero no me dejan** I want to but they won't let me; **~ a uno** + *infin* to let sb + *infin*, allow sb to + *infin*; **~ a uno entrar** to let sb in; **~ a uno pasar** to let sb in (*o* through, past *etc*); **~ a uno salir** to let sb out; **~ que las cosas vayan**

de **mal en peor** to let things go from bad to worse; **~ que se enfríe** (*instrucción*) leave till cold; *V* **caer, mano** (c) *etc.*
2 VI: **~ de** + *infin* (**a**) (*terminar de*) to stop + *ger*, leave off + *ger*, give up + *ger*; **dejó de cantar** she stopped singing; **cuando deje de llover** when it stops raining, when the rain stops; **no puedo ~ de fumar** I can't give up smoking; *V* **existir** *etc.*
(**b**) (*no cumplir*) to fail to + *infin*, neglect to + *infin*; **no dejes de visitarles** don't fail to visit them, on no account neglect to pay them a visit.
(**c**) (*no poder menos de*) **no puedo ~ de asombrarme** I cannot but be amazed, I cannot help being astonished; **no puedo ~ de pensar que ...** I can't help thinking that ...; **no deja de ser algo raro** all the same it's rather odd; **eso no deja de tener gracia** it's not without its amusing side; **yo había dejado de oírle tocar desde hacía 5 años** I had not heard him play for 5 years.
3 dejarse VR (**a**) (*abandonarse*) to neglect o.s., let o.s. go, get slovenly.
(**b**) **~ de** + *infin* (*permitirse*) to allow o.s. to be + *ptp*, let o.s. be + *PTP*; **~ persuadir** to allow o.s. to be persuaded; **no se dejó engañar** he was not to be deceived; **se dejó decir que ...** he let it slip that ...; **se dejó oír una débil voz** a weak voice made itself heard (*o* could be heard); *V* **vencer** *etc.*
(**c**) **~ de** + *infin* (*terminar*) to stop + *ger*; **¡déjate de eso!** stop that!, cut it out!; *V* **broma.**

┌─ **DEJAR** ──────────── **ver también la entrada** ─┐

Dejar en el sentido de prestar se puede traducir al inglés empleando **borrow** o **lend**. *Borrow* se usa cuando el sujeto es quien pide (significa tomar prestado) y *lend* cuando el sujeto es quien da (significa dejar prestado):
   ¿Me dejas tus botas de esquiar?
   Can I borrow your ski boots? o *Can you lend me your ski boots?*
   ¿Me podrías dejar tu reloj?
   Could I borrow o *Could you lend me your watch?*
! *Borrow* y *lend* no se utilizan normalmente con cosas que no pueden trasladarse de un sitio a otro:
   ¿Me dejas tu apartamento este fin de semana?
   Can I use your flat this weekend?
   Para otros usos y ejemplos ver la entrada.

└──────────────────────────────┘

deje NM = **dejo** (c).

dejo NM (**a**) (*sabor*) aftertaste, tang; **tiene un ~ raro** it leaves an odd taste.
(**b**) (*fig*) touch, smack, tang, flavour.
(**c**) (*Ling*) accent, trace of accent, special inflection.

del = **de** + **el.**

Del. ABR **de Delegación** district office.

delación NF accusation; denunciation.

delantal NM apron; **~ de cuero** leather apron; **~ de niña** pinafore.

delante **1** ADV (**a**) (*t por ~*) in front; ahead; opposite; **la parte de ~** the front part; **la casa no tiene nada ~** the house has nothing opposite; **estando otros ...** with others present; in the presence of others; **abierto por ~** open in front; **¡las damas por ~!** ladies first!; **entrar al puerto (con) la popa ~** to enter harbour stern first; **tenemos todavía 4 horas por ~** we still have 4 hours in front of us; we still have 4 hours to go.
(**b**) (*LAm*) **~ nuestro** (*etc*), **en nuestro ~** (*etc*) in front of us (*etc*).
2 ~ de PREP in front of, before; ahead of.

delantera NF (**a**) (*de casa, vestido*) front, front part; (*Teat*) front row; front row seat; (*Dep*) forward line.
(**b**) (*fig: ventaja*) advantage, lead; **llevar la ~** to lead, be in the lead; **llevar la ~ a uno** to be ahead of sb; **coger la ~ a uno** to get ahead of sb; to get a start on sb; **sacar la ~ a uno** to steal a march on sb; **tomar la ~** to take the lead.
(**c**) (*Anat*) knockers, tits.
(**d**) **~s** (*calzones*) chaps; (*mono*) overalls.

delantero **1** ADJ *parte, fila, rueda etc* front; *pata* front, fore; (*Dep*) *línea, posición* forward; (*en progreso etc*) first, foremost.
2 NM (*Dep*) forward; **~ centro** centre-forward; **~ extremo** outside forward, wing forward; **~ interior** inside forward.

delatar [1a] VT (**a**) (*gen*) to denounce, inform against, accuse; to betray.
(**b**) (*fig*) to reveal, betray.

delator(a) NM/F informer, accuser; betrayer.

delco NM (*Aut*) distributor.

delectación NF delight, delectation.

delegación NF (**a**) (*acto*) delegation; **~ de poderes** (*Parl*) devolution.
(**b**) (*cuerpo*) delegation; **~ comercial** trade mission; **la ~ fue a cumplimentar al Ministro** the delegation went to pay its respects to the minister.
(**c**) (*Com etc*) local office, branch; (*estatal*) office of a government department; (*comisaría*) police station; **~ de Hacienda** local tax office.

► LENGUA Y USO: **dejar: 1b** → 36.1, 36.3

delegado, -a NM/F delegate; (*Com*) agent, representative; **~ del Gobierno** (*Esp*) representative of central government (attached to each autonomous region); **~ sindical** shop-steward.

delegar [1h] VT to delegate (*a* to).

deleitable ADJ enjoyable, delightful, delectable.

deleitación NF, **deleitamiento** NM delectation.

deleitar [1a] ① VT to delight, charm.
② **deleitarse** VR: **~ con, ~ en** to delight in, take pleasure in; **~ en** + *infin* to delight in + *ger*.

deleite NM delight, pleasure; joy; **~s** delights.

deleitosamente ADV delightfully; deliciously.

deleitoso ADJ delightful, pleasing; delicious.

deletéreo ADJ deleterious.

deletrear [1a] VT (a) *apellido, nombre etc* to spell (out). (b) (*fig*) to decipher, interpret. (c) (*Cono Sur: escudriñar*) to observe in great detail, look minutely at.

deletreo NM (a) spelling, spelling-out. (b) (*fig*) decipherment, interpretation.

deleznable ADJ (a) *materia* fragile, brittle; crumbly; unstable; *superficie etc* slippery. (b) (*fig*) frail; *argumento etc* weak; (*efímero*) fleeting, ephemeral; insubstantial.

délfico ADJ Delphic.

delfín[1] NM (*Zool*) dolphin.

delfín[2] NM (*Pol*) heir apparent, designated successor.

delfinario NM dolphinarium.

Delfos N Delphi.

delgadez NF (a) (*flaqueza*) thinness; slimness. (b) (*delicadeza*) delicateness; tenuousness. (c) (*agudeza*) sharpness, cleverness.

delgado ① ADJ (a) (*gen*) thin; (*flaco*) thin; (*esbelto*) slim, slender; slight; **~ como un fideo** as thin as a rake.
(b) (*fig: delicado*) delicate; (*tenue*) light, tenuous.
(c) (*fig*) *tierra* poor, exhausted.
(d) (*fig: agudo*) sharp, clever.
(e) (*Méx: aguado*) weak, thin, watery.
② ADV V **hilar**.

deliberación NF deliberation.

deliberadamente ADV deliberately.

deliberado ADJ deliberate.

deliberar [1a] ① VT (a) to debate, discuss. (b) **~** + *infin* to decide to + *infin*.
② VI to deliberate (*sobre* on), discuss (*si* whether).

deliberativo ADJ deliberative.

delicadamente ADJ delicately.

delicadez NF (a) = **delicadeza**. (b) (*debilidad*) weakness. (c) (*sensibilidad excesiva*) hypersensitiveness, touchiness, susceptibility.

delicadeza NF (*V* ADJ) (a) delicacy; sensitivity; daintiness; thinness; frailness; refinement.
(b) touchiness, hypersensitiveness; fastidiousness; squeamishness; tactfulness; subtlety; **falta de ~** tactlessness; **¡qué ~!** how charming of you!

delicado ADJ (a) (*gen*) delicate; dainty; *máquina etc* delicate, sensitive; *tela* thin; slender, frail; *salud* delicate; *color* soft, delicate; *plato, rasgos* dainty; *gusto* refined, exquisite; *distinción* nice, delicate, subtle; *situación* (*difícil*) delicate, tricky; (*violento*) embarrassing; *punto* tender, sensitive; sore; **está ~ del estómago** he has a delicate stomach.
(b) *carácter* (*difícil*) demanding; hard to please; (*quisquilloso*) touchy, hypersensitive; (*exigente*) fastidious; (*remilgado*) squeamish; (*escrupuloso*) (over)scrupulous; (*discreto*) tactful; (*atento*) considerate; *mente* subtle; keen; **es muy ~ en el comer** he's very choosy about food; **es muy ~ para la limpieza** he's very particular about cleanliness.

delicia NF delight; delightfulness; **el país es una ~** the country is delightful; **tiene un jardín que es una ~** he has a delightful garden; **un libro que ha hecho las ~s de muchos niños** a book which has been the delight of many children.

deliciosamente ADJ delightfully; deliciously.

delicioso ADJ delightful; (*al gusto*) delicious.

delictivo ADJ criminal.

Delilá NF Delilah.

delimitación NF delimitation.

delimitar [1a] VT to delimit.

delincuencia NF delinquency, criminality; **~ de guante blanco** white-collar crime; **~ juvenil, ~ de menores** juvenile delinquency; **~ menor** petty crime; **cifras de la ~** figures of crimes committed, incidence of criminality.

delincuencial ADJ criminal.

delincuente ① ADJ delinquent; criminal; guilty.
② NMF delinquent, criminal, offender; guilty person; **~ sin antecedentes penales** first offender; **~ común** common criminal; **~ de guante blanco** white-collar criminal; **~ habitual** hardened criminal; **~ juvenil** juvenile delinquent.

delineación NF, **delineamiento** NM delineation.

delineador NM eyeliner.

delineante NM draughtsman.

delinear [1a] VT to delineate; to outline; to draw.

delinquimiento NM delinquency; guilt.

delinquir [3e] VI to commit an offence; to offend, transgress.

deliquio NM swoon, fainting fit.

delirante ADJ (a) (*Med*) delirious; light-headed; raving. (b) (*) *chiste etc* deliciously funny; *idea* crazy.

delirantemente ADV deliriously.

delirar [1a] VI to be delirious, rave; (*fig*) to rave, rant, talk nonsense; **¡tú deliras!*** you must be mad!

delirio NM (a) (*Med y fig*) delirium; ravings, wanderings; (*palabras*) nonsense, nonsensical talk.
(b) (*frenesí*) frenzy; (*manía*) mania; **~ de grandezas** megalomania; **~ de persecución** persecution mania.
(c) (*) **con ~** madly; **me gusta con ~** I'm crazy about it; **¡fue el ~!** it was great!*; **cuando acabó de hablar fue el ~** when he finished speaking there were scenes of wild enthusiasm.

delírium NM: **~ tremens** delirium tremens.

delito NM (a) (*gen*) crime, offence; **~ de mayor cuantía** felony; **~ de menor cuantía** misdemeanour; **~ fiscal** tax offence; **~ menor** minor offence; **~ contra la propiedad** crime against property; **~ de sangre** violent crime, crime involving bloodshed. (b) (*fig*) misdeed, wicked act, offence.

delta ① NM (*Geog*) delta.
② NF (*letra*) delta.

deltaplano NM (a) (*aparato*) hang-glider. (b) (*deporte*) hang-gliding.

deltoideo ADJ, NM deltoid.

deludir [3a] VT to delude.

delusorio ADJ delusive.

demacración NF emaciation.

demacrado ADJ emaciated, wasted away.

demacrarse [1a] VR to become emaciated, waste away.

demagogia NF demagogy, demagoguery.

demagógico ADJ demagogic.

demagogismo NM demagogy, demagoguery.

demagogo NM demagogue.

demanda NF (a) (*solicitud*) demand, request (*de* for); (*pregunta*) inquiry; (*reivindicación*) claim; (*petición*) petition; **~ de extradición** request for extradition; **~ final** final demand; **~ de pago** demand for payment; **~ del Santo Grial** quest for the Holy Grail; **escribir en ~ de ayuda** to write asking for help; **ir en ~ de** to go in search of, go looking for; **partir en ~ de** to go off in search of; **morir en la ~** to die in the attempt.
(b) (*Teat*) call.
(c) (*Com*) demand; **hay mucha ~ de cerillas** matches are in great demand; **tener ~** to be in demand; **ese producto no tiene ~** there is no demand for that product.
(d) (*Elec*) load; **~ máxima** peak load.
(e) (*Jur*) action, lawsuit; **~ civil** private prosecution; **~ judicial** legal action; **entablar ~** to bring an action, take legal proceedings, sue; **presentar ~ de divorcio** to sue for divorce, take divorce proceedings.

demandado, -a NM/F defendant; (*en divorcio*) respondent.

demandante NMF claimant; (*Jur*) plaintiff; **~ de empleo** job seeker.

demandar [1a] VT (a) (*gen*) to demand, ask for, request; to claim; to petition.
(b) (*Jur*) to sue, file a suit against, start proceedings against; **demandó al periódico por calumnia** he sued the paper for libel; **~ a uno por daños y perjuicios** to sue sb for damages; **ser demandado por libelo** to be sued for libel.

demaquillador NM make-up remover.

demarcación NF (a) demarcation; **línea de ~** demarcation line. (b) (*Dep*) position.

demarcar [1g] VT to demarcate.

demarraje NM spurt, break, dash.

demarrar [1a] VI to spurt, break away, make a dash.

demás ① ADJ: **los ~ libros** the other books, the rest of the books, the remaining books; **y ~ gente de ese tipo** and other people of that sort.
② PRON: **lo ~** the rest (of it); **los ~, las ~** the others, the rest (of them); **por lo ~** for the rest, as to the rest; otherwise; furthermore, moreover.
③ ADV = **además; por ~** moreover; in vain; **y ~** etcetera, and so on; **V más (estar de más)**.

demasía NF (a) (*exceso*) excess, surplus; superfluity; **con ~, en ~** too much, excessively. (b) (*fig: atropello*) excess, outrage, wicked thing; (*tuerto*) wrong; (*ofensa*) affront. (c) (*fig: temeridad*) boldness; (*impertinencia*) insolence.

demasiado ① ADJ (a) (*gen*) too much; (*excesivo*) overmuch, excessive; **eso es ~** that's too much; **con ~ cuidado** with excessive care; **hace ~ calor** it's too hot; **¡esto es ~!** this is too much!, that's the limit;

¡qué ~! great!, marvellous!
(b) **~s** too many.
2 ADV too; too much, excessively; (*LAm*) a lot, a great deal; **comer ~** to eat too much; **es ~ pesado para levantar** it is too heavy to lift; **~ lo sé** I know it only too well.

┌─ *DEMASIADO* ──────────────── *ver también la entrada* ─┐

¿"Too", "too much" o "too many"?

- *Demasiado* se traduce por *too* delante de *adjetivos* y *adverbios*:
  Hace demasiado calor
  It's too hot
  Hace un día demasiado bueno para quedarse trabajando en casa
  It's too nice a day to stay at home working
  Hablas demasiado deprisa
  You talk too quickly
- Se traduce por *too much* cuando *demasiado* describe o se refiere a nombres *incontables* y como complemento de verbos:
  Le he echado demasiada agua a las patatas
  I've put too much water in the potatoes
  Creo que he comido demasiado
  I think I've eaten too much
  Habla demasiado
  He talks too much
  NOTA: Cuando acompaña a un verbo de tiempo *demasiado* suele traducirse como *too long*:
  Ha tardado demasiado en acabar la tesis
  He's taken too long to finish his thesis

Too many
- Se traduce por *too many* cuando *demasiado* precede a nombres *contables* en *plural*:
  Tiene demasiadas preocupaciones
  She has too many worries
  Para otros usos y ejemplos ver la entrada.

└───┘

demasié: **1** ADJ, ADV = **demasiado**.
2 NM: **es un ~** it's way over the top.
demediar [1b] **1** VT to divide in half.
2 VI to be divided in half.
demencia NF madness, insanity, dementia; **~ senil** senile dementia.
demencial ADJ mad, crazy, demented.
dementar [1a] **1** VT to drive mad.
2 dementarse VR to go mad, become demented.
demente **1** ADJ mad, insane, demented.
2 NMF mad person, lunatic.
demérito NM **(a)** (*defecto*) demerit, fault; disadvantage. **(b)** (*indignidad*) unworthiness. **(c)** (*LAm: menosprecio*) contempt.
demeritorio ADJ undeserving, unworthy.
demo* NMF (*Chile*) Christian Democrat.
democracia NF democracy; **~ parlamentaria** parliamentary democracy; **~ popular** people's democracy.
demócrata NMF democrat.
democratacristiano, -a ADJ, NM/F Christian Democrat.
democráticamente ADV democratically.
democrático ADJ democratic.
democratización NF democratization.
democratizador ADJ democratizing.
democratizar [1f] VT to democratize.
democristiano, -a ADJ, NM/F Christian Democrat.
demodé* ADJ out of fashion.
demografía NF demography.
demográficamente ADV demographically.
demográfico ADJ demographic; population (*atr*); **la explosión demográfica** the population explosion.
demógrafo, a NM/F demographer.
demoledor ADJ (*fig*) *argumento etc* powerful, overwhelming; *ataque, efecto* shattering, devastating.
demoledoramente ADV overwhelmingly.
demoler [2h] VT **(a)** (*gen*) to demolish; pull down. **(b)** (*fig*) to demolish.
demolición NF demolition.
demonche NM (*euf*) = **demonio**.
demoniaco, demoníaco ADJ demoniacal, demonic.
demonio NM **(a)** (*gen*) devil; demon; evil spirit; **~ familiar** familiar spirit.
(b) (*fig*) **ese ~ de sereno** that devil of a night watchman; **como el ~** like the devil; **ir como el ~** to go like the devil, go hell for leather; **esto pesa como el ~** this is devilish heavy; **¡vete al ~!** go to hell!; **¡vaya con mil ~s!** go to blazes!; **¡que se lo lleve el ~!** to hell with it!; the devil take it!; **tener el ~ en el cuerpo** to be always on the go, have the devil in one; **esto sabe a ~(s)** this tastes awful; **un ruido de todos los ~s** a devil of a noise.

(c) (EXCL *etc*) **¡~!, ¡qué ~!** (*ira*) hell!, confound it!; (*exasperación*) hang it all!; (*sorpresa*) good heavens!; what the devil ...?; the devil it is!; **¿qué ~s será?** what the devil can that be?; **¡qué príncipe ni qué ~s!** prince my foot!; **¿dónde ~ lo habré dejado?** where the devil can I have left it?
demonología NF demonology.
demontre NM (*euf*) = **demonio**.
demora NF **(a)** delay; **sin ~** without delay. **(b)** (*Náut*) bearing.
demorar [1a] **1** VT to delay; to hold up, hold back.
2 VI **(a)** (*quedarse*) to stay on, linger on; (*tardar*) to delay, waste time; **no demores!** don't be long! **(b)** **~ en** + *infin* (*LAm*) V **3**.
3 demorarse VR = **2**; **¿cuántos días se demora para ir allá?** (*LAm*) how many days does it take to get there?; **~ en** + *infin* (*esp LAm*) to take a long time to + *infin*, be slow in + *ger*.
demorón ADJ (*And, Cono Sur*) = **demoroso**.
demoroso ADJ (*Cono Sur*) (*lento*) slow, lazy; (*moroso*) late, overdue; **ser ~ en** + *infin* to take a long time to + *infin*, be slow in + *ger*.
demos V **dar**.
demoscopia NF public opinion research.
demoscópico ADJ: **sondeo ~** public opinion survey, survey of public opinion.
Demóstenes NM Demosthenes.
demostrable ADJ demonstrable, that can be demonstrated.
demostración NF demonstration, show, display; gesture; (*Mat*) proof; **~ de cariño** show of affection; **~ de cólera** display of anger; **~ comercial** commercial display, trade exhibition.
▼ **demostrar** [1l] VT to demonstrate, show; to show off; to prove; **~ cómo se hace algo** to demonstrate how sth is done; **~ que ...** to show that ..., prove that ...; **Vd no puede ~me nada** you can't prove anything against me.
demostrativo ADJ, NM demonstrative.
demótico ADJ demotic.
demudación NF change, alteration (of countenance).
demudado ADJ *rostro* pale.
demudar [1a] **1** VT *rostro* to change, alter.
2 demudarse VR **(a)** (*gen*) to change, alter.
(b) (*fig*: *perder color*) to change colour, change countenance; (*alterarse*) to look upset, show one's distress; **sin ~** without a flicker of emotion; **continuó sin ~** he went on quite unaffected (*o* unabashed).
den V **dar**.
denante(s) ADV (*LAm*) earlier, a while ago; in past times.
dendrocronología NF dendrochronology.
denegación NF refusal; rejection; denial.
denegar [1h y 1k] VT (*rechazar*) to refuse; to reject; (*negar*) to deny; (*Jur*) *apelación* to reject, refuse to allow.
dengoso ADJ affected; prudish; dainty, finicky.
dengue NM **(a)** (*afectación*) affectation; (*coquetería*) coyness; (*remilgo*) prudery; (*delicadeza*) daintiness, finickiness; (*And*: *contoneo*) wiggle; **hacer ~s** to act coyly, simper; to be finicky; **no me vengas con esos ~s** I don't want to hear your silly complaints.
(b) (*Med*) dengue, breakbone fever.
denguero ADJ = **dengoso**.
denier NM denier.
denigración NF denigration.
denigrante ADJ insulting; degrading.
denigrar [1a] VT (*difamar*) to denigrate, revile, run down; (*injuriar*) to insult.
denigratorio ADJ denigratory; insulting; **campaña denigratoria** campaign of denigration, smear campaign.
denodadamente ADV boldly, dauntlessly, intrepidly; **luchar ~** to fight bravely.
denodado ADJ bold, dauntless, intrepid, brave.
denominación NF **(a)** (*acto*) naming. **(b)** (*nombre*) name, designation; denomination; **moneda de baja ~** (*LAm*) low value coin; **~ social** (*Méx*) firm's official name.

┌─ *DENOMINACIÓN DE ORIGEN* ─────────────┐

ⓘ *The **Denominación de Origen**, abbreviated to D.O., is a prestigious product classification which is awarded to food products such as wines, cheeses, sausages and hams that are produced in designated Spanish regions according to stringent production criteria. D.O. labels serve as a guarantee of quality.*

└───┘

denominado ADJ named, called; so-called.
denominador NM denominator; **~ común** (*Mat*) common denominator; (*fig*) staple, constant feature.
denominar [1a] VT to name, call, designate.
denostar [1l] VT to insult, revile, abuse; to condemn.
denotación NF (*Ling, Filos*) denotation.
denotar [1a] VT (*significar*) to denote; (*indicar*) to indicate, show; (*expresar*) to express.

▶ LENGUA Y USO: **demostrar** → 53.3, 53.4

densamente ADV densely; compactly; thickly; solidly.

densidad NF density; compactness; thickness; heaviness, dryness; solidity; (*Inform*) density; (*Inform: de caracteres*) pitch; ~ **de grabación** recording density; ~ **de población** density of population.

denso ADJ (*gen*) dense; compact; *humo, líquido etc* thick; *libro, lectura, discurso* heavy, substantial, solid; **el argumento es algo** ~ (*pey*) the reasoning is somewhat confused.

dentado 1 ADJ having teeth; *rueda* cogged, toothed; *filo* jagged; *sello* perforated; (*Bot*) dentate.
2 NM (*de sello*) perforation.

dentadura NF set of teeth, teeth (*collectively*); denture; ~ **artificial, ~ postiza** false teeth, denture(s); **tener mala** ~ to have bad teeth.

dental ADJ, NF dental.

dentamen* NM teeth.

dentar [1j] 1 VT to put teeth on, furnish with teeth; *filo* to make jagged; (*Téc*) to indent; *sello* to perforate; **sello sin** ~ imperforate stamp.
2 VI to teethe, cut one's teeth.

dentellada NF (a) (*mordisco*) bite, nip; **partir algo a** ~s to sever sth with one's teeth. (b) (*señal*) tooth mark.

dentellar [1a] VI (*dientes*) to chatter; **estaba dentellando** his teeth were chattering; **el susto le hizo** ~ the fright made his teeth chatter.

dentellear [1a] VT to bite, nibble (at), sink one's teeth into.

dentera NF (a) (*gen*) the shivers, the shudders; **dar** ~ **a uno** to set sb's teeth on edge, give sb the shivers.
(b) (*fig: envidia*) envy, jealousy; (*deseo*) great desire; **dar** ~ **a uno** to make sb jealous; to make one's mouth water; **le da** ~ **que hagan fiestas al niño** it makes him jealous when they make a fuss of the baby.

dentición NF (a) (*acto*) teething; **estar con la** ~ to be teething. (b) (*Anat*) dentition; ~ **de leche** milk teeth.

dentífrico 1 ADJ tooth (*atr*); **pasta dentífrica** toothpaste.
2 NM dentifrice, toothpaste.

dentilargo ADJ long-toothed.

dentina NF dentin(e), ivory.

dentista NMF dentist.

dentistería NF (*And, Carib*) (a) (*clínica*) dentist's, dental clinic. (b) (*ciencia*) dentistry.

dentística NF (*Cono Sur*) dentistry.

dentón ADJ large-toothed, buck-toothed, toothy.

dentradera NF (*And*), **dentrera** NF (*And*) housemaid.

dentro 1 ADV (*estar*) inside; indoors; *sentir etc* inwardly, inside; **allí** ~ in there; **de** ~, **desde** ~ from inside; **por** ~ inside, on the inside, in the interior; **meter algo para** ~ to push sth in; **vamos** ~ let's go in(side).
2 ~ **de** PREP (a) (*estar*) in, inside, within; ~ **de la casa** inside the house.
(b) (*meter etc*) into, inside; **lo metió** ~ **del cajón** he put it into the drawer.
(c) (*tiempo*) within, inside; ~ **de 3 meses** inside 3 months, within 3 months; ~ **de poco** shortly; soon after.
(d) ~ **de lo posible** as far as one (*etc*) can, as far as is possible; **eso no cabe** ~ **de lo posible** that does not come within the bounds of possibility.

dentrodera NF (*And*) servant.

denudación NF denudation.

denudar [1a] VT to denude (*de* of); to lay bare.

denuedo NM boldness, daring; bravery.

denuesto NM insult; **llenar a uno de** ~s to heap insults on sb.

denuncia NF report; denunciation; (*a policía*) complaint; (*Jur etc*) accusation; ~ **de accidente** report of an accident; ~ **falsa** false accusation; **hacer una** ~, **poner una** ~ to make an official complaint (to the police *etc*).

denunciable ADJ *crimen* indictable, punishable.

denunciación NF denunciation; accusation.

denunciador(a) NM/F, **denunciante** NMF accuser; informer; **el** ~ **del accidente** the person who reported the accident.

denunciar [1b] VT *delito etc* to report (*a* to); (*proclamar*) to proclaim, announce; (*presagiar*) to foretell; (*Jur etc*) to denounce (*a* to), accuse (*a* before), inform against; (*pey*) to betray, give away (*a* to); *tratado* to denounce; (*indicar*) to denote, indicate, reveal; ~ **que ...** to report that ...; **denunciaron los precios abusivos a las autoridades** they reported the exorbitant prices to the authorities; **el accidente fue denunciado a la policía** the accident was reported to the police; **esto denunciaba la presencia del gas** this betrayed the presence of gas, this indicated the presence of gas.

denuncio NM (*LAm*) = **denuncia**.

deontología NF deontology; (*profesional*) (professional) ethics *pl*.

Dep. (a) ABR *de* **Departamento** Department, Dept. (b) (*Com*) ABR *de* **Depósito** deposit.

D.E.P. ABR *de* **descanse en paz** may he rest in peace, R.I.P.

deparar [1a] VT to provide, furnish with; to present, offer; **nos deparó la ocasión para ...** it gave us a chance to ...; **los placeres**

que el viaje nos deparó the pleasures which the trip afforded us; **pero también nos deparó la solución** but it also furnished us with the solution; **¡Dios te la depare buena!** and the best of luck! (*iró*).

departamental ADJ departmental.

departamento NM (a) (*gen*) department, section; office; bureau; ~ **jurídico** legal department; ~ **de visados** visa section.
(b) (*de caja etc*) compartment.
(c) (*Ferro etc*) compartment; ~ **de fumadores** smoking compartment; ~ **de no fumadores** non-smoking compartment; ~ **de primera** first-class compartment.
(d) (*esp Cono Sur, Méx: piso*) flat, apartment.
(e) (*LAm: distrito*) department, administrative district, province.

departir [1a] VI to talk, converse (*con* with, *de* about).

depauperación NF (a) impoverishment. (b) (*Med*) weakening, exhaustion.

depauperar [1a] VT (a) to impoverish. (b) (*Med*) to weaken, deplete, exhaust.

dependencia NF (a) (*gen*) dependence (*de* on); reliance (*de* on); ~ **psicológica** psychological dependency.
(b) (*parentesco*) relationship, kinship.
(c) (*Pol etc*) dependency.
(d) (*Com: sección*) section, office; (*sucursal*) branch office.
(e) (*Arquit: cuarto*) room; (*anejo*) outbuilding, outhouse; ~ **policial** police premises; **permanecer en** ~s **policiales** to remain in police custody.
(f) (*Com etc: plantilla*) personnel, sales staff, employees.
(g) ~s accessories.

▼ **depender** [2a] VI (a) (*gen*) to depend; ~ **de** to depend on; (*contar con*) to rely on; **depende** it (all) depends; **depende de lo que haga él** it depends on what he does; **todo depende de que él esté listo** it all turns on his being ready; **no depende de mí** it does not rest with me; **todos dependemos de ti** we are all relying on you. (b) ~ **de** *autoridad* to be (*o* come) under, be answerable to; **el museo depende de otro ministerio** the museum is run by another ministry.

dependienta NF salesgirl, saleswoman, shop assistant.

dependiente 1 ADJ dependent (*de* on).
2 NM (*empleado*) employee; (*oficinista*) clerk; (*de tienda*) salesman, shop assistant, salesperson (*US*).

depilación NF, **depilado** NM depilation.

depilador 1 ADJ: **crema** ~a hair remover, depilatory cream.
2 NM hair remover, depilatory.

depiladora NF hair remover (*machine*).

depilar [1a] VT to depilate, remove the hair from; *cejas* to pluck.

depilatorio 1 ADJ depilatory.
2 NM depilatory, hair remover.

deplorable ADJ deplorable; lamentable, regrettable.

deplorar [1a] VT to deplore, regret; to condemn; **lo deploro** I greatly deplore it, I'm extremely sorry.

deponente 1 ADJ (a) (*Ling*) deponent. (b) **persona** ~ (*Jur*) = **2**.
2 NMF (*Jur*) deponent, person making a statement.

deponer [2q] 1 VT (a) (*dejar*) to lay down; to lay aside; (*quitar*) to remove, take down; *armas* to lay down.
(b) *rey* to depose; *gobernante* to oust, overthrow; *ministro* to remove from office.
2 VI (a) (*Jur*) to give evidence, make a statement.
(b) (*CAm, Méx: vomitar*) to vomit.

deportación NF deportation.

deportar [1a] VT to deport.

deporte NM sport; game; outdoor recreation; ~s **acuáticos** water sports; ~ **blanco** winter sports, (*esp*) skiing; ~ **de competición** competitive sport; ~ **de exhibición** show event; ~ **hípico** horse-riding; ~s **de invierno** winter sports; ~ **náutico** water sports; yachting; ~ **del remo** rowing; ~ **de la vela** sailing; **el fútbol es un** ~ football is a game; **es muy aficionado a los** ~s he is very fond of sport.

deportista 1 ADJ sports (*atr*); sporting; **el público** ~ the sporting public.
2 NM (*jugador*) sportsman; (*aficionado*) sporting man, sports fan.
3 NF sportswoman.

deportivamente ADV (a) sportingly; in a good spirit. (b) **hablando** ~ in sport, in sporting terms.

deportividad NF sportsmanship.

deportivo 1 ADJ (a) *club, periódico etc* sports (*atr*). (b) *actitud, conducta etc* sporting, sportsmanlike. (c) (*pey*) casual, breezy, (too) free-and-easy.
2 NM (a) (*Aut*) sports car. (b) ~s (*zapatos*) sports shoes, trainers. (c) (*Prensa*) sports paper.

deposición NF (a) (*acto*) deposition, removal. (b) (*afirmación*) assertion, affirmation; (*Jur*) deposition, evidence, statement (c) **hacer sus deposiciones** (*euf*) to defecate.

depositador(a) NM/F, **depositante** NMF (*Com, Fin*) depositor.

depositar [1a] 1 VT (*gen*) to deposit; (*poner*) to place; (*poner aparte*) to lay aside; (*guardar*) to put away, store, put into store; (*confiar*) to en-

➤ LENGUA Y USO: **depender: a → 52.6**

trust (*en* to), confide (*en* to).

2 depositarse VR (*heces*) to settle.

depositaría NF depository; (*Fin etc*) trust.

depositario, -a NM/F depository, trustee; receiver; (*de secreto etc*) repository.

depósito NM (a) (*Quím etc*) deposit; sediment; (*Geol, Min*) deposit.
(b) (*Com, Fin: dinero*) deposit; ~ **bancario** bank deposit; ~ **a plazo** (**fijo**) fixed-term deposit; **dejar una cantidad en** ~ to leave a sum as a deposit.
(c) (*Com etc: almacén*) store, storehouse, warehouse; depot; (*de objetos perdidos*) pound; (*Mil*) depot; (*vertedero*) dump; ~ **de aduana** customs warehouse; ~ **afianzado** bonded warehouse; ~ **de alimentación** (*Inform*) feeder bin; ~ **de basura** rubbish dump, tip; ~ **de cadáveres** mortuary, morgue; ~ **de carbón** coal tip; ~ **de equipajes** cloakroom; ~ **de libros** book stack; ~ **de locomotoras** engine shed; ~ **de maderas** timber yard; ~ **de municiones** ammunition dump.
(d) (*de líquidos*) tank; (*de wáter*) cistern; (*alberca*) reservoir; ~ **de agua** water tank, cistern; reservoir; ~ **de combustible** fuel tank; ~ **de gasolina** petrol tank.

depravación NF depravity, depravation, corruption.

depravado ADJ depraved, corrupt.

depravar [1a] **1** VT to deprave, corrupt.
2 depravarse VR to become depraved.

depre* **1** ADJ: **estar** ~ to be feeling down.
2 NF depression; **tiene la** ~ she's feeling a bit down.

depreciación NF depreciation; ~ **acelerada** accelerated depreciation; ~ **acumulada** accumulated depreciation.

depreciar [1b] **1** VT to depreciate, reduce the value of.
2 depreciarse VR to depreciate, lose value.

depredación NF depredation; outrage, excess; pillage; (*Bio*) predation.

depredador NM (*Bio*) predator.

depredar [1a] VT to pillage; to commit outrages against; (*Bio*) to be predatory on, take as its prey.

depresión NF (a) (*Geog etc*) depression; hollow; (*de horizonte etc*) dip; (*en muro*) recess, niche.
(b) (*acto*) lowering; (*baja*) drop, fall (*de* in); ~ **del mercurio** fall in temperature (*o* pressure).
(c) (*Met*) depression.
(d) (*Econ*) depression, slump, recession.
(e) (*mental*) depression; ~ **nerviosa** nervous depression; ~ **posparto** postnatal depression.

depresivo, -a ADJ, NM/F depressive.

deprimente **1** ADJ depressing.
2 NM depressant.

deprimido ADJ depressed.

deprimir [3a] **1** VT (a) (*físicamente*) to depress, press down; to flatten.
(b) (*mentalmente etc*) to depress.
(c) *nivel etc* to lower, reduce.
(d) (*fig: humillar*) to humiliate; (*despreciar*) to belittle, disparage.
2 deprimirse VR to get depressed.

deprisa ADV fast, quickly; **¡~!** quick!; ~ **y corriendo** in a rush.

depuración NF (a) (*gen*) purification; cleansing. (b) (*Pol etc*) purge.
(c) (*Inform*) debugging.

depurado ADJ *estilo* pure, refined.

depurador NM water purifier.

depuradora NF purifying plant; water-treatment plant; ~ **de aguas residuales** sewage farm.

depurar [1a] VT (a) (*gen*) to purify; to cleanse, purge. (b) (*Pol etc*) to purge. (c) (*Inform*) to debug. (d) (*Carib**) *empleado* to fire*.

depurativo NM blood tonic.

dequeísmo NM tendency to use 'de que' in place of 'que' (*eg* 'pienso de que').

der., der.º ADJ ABR *de* **derecho** right, r.

derby ['derbi] NM, PL **derbys** local derby.

derecha NF (a) (*mano*) right hand; (*lado*) right side, right-hand side; **estar a la** ~ **de** to be on the right; **torcer a la** ~ to turn (to the) right; **conducción a** ~ right-hand drive; **el poste de la** ~ the post on the right; **seguir por la** ~ to keep (to the) right.
(b) (*Pol*) right; **es de** ~**s** she's on the right, she has right-wing views.
(c) **a** ~**s** rightly, aright; justly; **si le entiendo a** ~**s** if I understand you rightly.

derechamente ADV (a) (*gen*) straight, directly. (b) (*fig*) properly, rightly.

derechazo NM (*Boxeo*) right; (*Tenis*) forehand drive; (*Taur*) *a right-handed pass with the cape*.

derechismo NM right-wing outlook (*o* tendencies *etc*).

derechista (*Pol*) **1** ADJ rightist, right-wing.
2 NMF rightist, right-winger.

derechización NF drift towards the right.

derechizar [1f] **1** VT *partido* to lead towards the right.

2 derechizarse VR to move to the right, become right-wing.

derecho **1** ADJ (a) (*mano*) right; *lado* right hand.
(b) (*recto*) straight; (*vertical*) upright, erect, standing; **más** ~ **que una vela** as straight as a die; **poner algo** ~ to stand sth upright.
(c) (*LAm: con suerte*) lucky.
(d) (*LAm: honrado*) honest, straight.
2 ADV (a) (*de manera recta*) straight, directly; (*verticalmente*) upright.
(b) (*directamente*) straight, directly; **ir** ~ **a** to go straight to; **siga** ~ carry (*o* go) straight on.
3 NM (a) (*lado, cara*) right side.
(b) (*gen*) right; (*título*) claim, title; (*privilegio*) privilege, exemption; ~ **de antena** broadcasting rights; ~**s de autor** author's copyright; ~**s cinematográficos** film rights; ~**s civiles** civil rights; ~ **divino** divine right; ~ **a domicilio** right of abode; ~**s humanos** human rights; ~**s de la mujer** women's rights; ~ **de paso**, ~ **de tránsito** right of way; ~ **de propiedad literaria** copyright; ~ **de réplica** right of reply; ~ **de retención** (*Com*) lien; ~ **de reunión** right of assembly; ~ **de visita** right of search; ~ **de votar**, ~ **al voto** right to vote, franchise; **con** ~ rightly, justly; **con** ~ **a** with a right to, with entitlement to; **por** ~ **propio** in his own right; **según** ~ by right(s); **'reservados todos los** ~**s'** 'all rights reserved', 'copyright'; **¡no hay** ~**!** it's not fair!; it's an outrage!; **'se reserva el** ~ **de entrada'** 'the management reserves the right to exclude certain persons'; **tener** ~ **a** to have a right to, be entitled to; **tener** ~ **a** + *infin* to have a right to + infin.
(c) (*Jur*) law; justice; ~ **civil** civil law; ~ **de compañías**, ~ **de sociedades** company law; ~ **comunitario** Community law; ~ **laboral**, ~ **del trabajo** labour law; ~ **mercantil** commercial law; ~ **penal** criminal law; ~ **político** constitutional law; ~ **tributario** tax law; **Facultad de D**~ Faculty of Law; **estudiante de** ~ law student; **propietario en** ~ legal owner; **lo que manda el** ~ **en este caso** what justice demands in this case.
(d) (*Fin*) due(s); fee(s); tax(es); (*de libro, petróleo etc*) royalties; (*profesional*) fee(s); **franco de** ~**s** duty-free; **sujeto a** ~**s** subject to duty, dutiable; ~**s de aduana**, ~**s arancelarios** customs duty; ~ **de asesoría**, ~ **de consulta** consulting fees; ~**s de autor** royalties; ~ **de enganche** (*Telec*) connection charge; ~**s de entrada** import duties; ~**s de exportación** export duty; ~**s de matrícula** registration fee; ~**s de peaje** toll; ~ **preferente** preferential duty; ~**s de puerto** harbour dues; ~**s reales** death duties.

derechohabiente NMF rightful claimant.

derechura NF (a) (*franqueza*) straightness; directness; **hablar en** ~ to speak plainly, talk straight; **hacer algo en** ~ to do sth right away.
(b) (*justicia*) rightness, justice.
(c) (*And, CAm: suerte*) (good) luck.

deriva NF (*Náut*) drift; leeway; (*apartamiento*) deviation; ~ **continental**, ~ **de los continentes** continental drift; **buque a la** ~ ship adrift, drifting ship; **ir a la** ~ to drift, be adrift.

derivación NF (a) (*gen*) derivation; (*origen*) origin, source. (b) (*Ling: etimología*) etymology, derivation; (*composición*) word formation; compounding; (*palabra*) derivative; ~ **regresiva** back-formation. (c) (*Elec*) shunt; en ~ shunt (*atr*); **hacer una** ~ **en un alambre** to tap a wire. (d) (*de río etc*) diversion; tapping.

derivado **1** ADJ derived; derivative (*t Ling*).
2 NM (a) derivative (*t Ling*). (b) (*Quím etc*) by-product; ~ **cárnico** meat product; ~ **lácteo** milk product; ~ **del petróleo** oil product.

derivar [1a] **1** VT (a) to derive (*t Ling*; *de* from).
(b) *agua, conversación etc* to direct, divert; *río* to tap; (*Elec*) to shunt.
2 VI (a) (*Ling etc*) ~ **de** to derive from, be derived from.
(b) (*Náut*) to drift; ~ **en** (*fig*) to lead to, end up as; (*pey*) to drift into, degenerate into; ~ **hacia** to incline towards.
3 derivarse VR (a) (*Ling*) = **2** (a).
(b) ~ **de** (*resultar*) to stem from, arise from.

derivativo ADJ, NM derivative.

dermatología NF dermatology.

dermatólogo, -a NM/F dermatologist.

dérmico ADJ skin (*atr*); **enfermedad dérmica** skin disease.

dermohidratante NM skin moisturizer.

dermoprotector **1** ADJ skin (*atr*).
2 NM skin protector.

derogación NF repeal, abolition.

derogar [1h] VT to repeal, abolish.

derrabar [1a] VT to dock, cut off the tail of.

derrabe NM rock-fall; cave-in.

derrama NF (*reparto*) apportionment of (local) tax; (*sobretasa*) special levy; (*tasación*) valuation, rating; (*vale*) credit voucher; (*dividendo*) interim dividend payment.

derramadero NM spillway; ~ **de basura** rubbish dump.

derramamiento NM (a) (*gen*) spilling; shedding; overflowing; ~ **de sangre** bloodshed. (b) (*esparcimiento*) scattering, spreading. (c) (*fig*) squandering, wasting, lavishing.

derramar [1a] **1** VT (a) (*por accidente*) *líquido* to spill; (*verter*) to pour out, pour away; *lágrimas* to weep, shed; *sangre* to shed; *luz* to shed, cast; **~ una taza de café** to spill a cup of coffee.

(b) (*esparcir*) to scatter, spread (about); *favores* to scatter, lavish, pour out; *chismes, noticias* to spread.

(c) *impuestos* to apportion.

(d) (*fig*) to squander, waste.

2 derramarse VR **(a)** (*líquido etc*) to spill; to pour out, overflow, run over, flow out; (*pluma, vasija*) to leak; **llenar una taza hasta ~** to fill a cup to overflowing.

(b) (*esparcirse*) to spread, scatter, be scattered; **la multitud se derramó por todos lados** the crowd scattered in all directions.

derrame NM **(a)** (*acto*) = **derramamiento**.

(b) (*cantidad*) loss; (*salida*) overflow; outflow; (*pérdida*) leakage; waste. **(c)** (*Med*) discharge; excess of liquid present in the body; (*de sangre*) haemorrhage; **~ cerebral** brain haemorrhage; **~ sinovial** water on the knee.

derrapada NF, **derrapaje** NM, **derrapamiento** NM skid, skidding.

derrapante ADJ: **'camino ~'** (*Méx*) 'slippery road'.

derrapar [1a] **1** VI (*Aut*) to skid.

2 derraparse VR (*Méx*) **(a)** (*patinar*) to slip. **(b) ~ por uno*** to be mad about sb*.

derrape NM **(a)** (*Aut*) skid. **(b)** (*Carib*: alboroto*) uproar, shindy*.

derredor: al ~ (de), en ~ (de) ADV Y PREP around, about; **en su ~** round about him.

derrelicto NM (*Náut*) derelict.

derrengado ADJ **(a)** (*torcido*) bent, twisted, crooked. **(b)** (*lisiado*) crippled, lame; **estar ~** (*fig*) to ache all over; to be footsore; **dejar ~ a uno** (*fig*) to wear sb out.

derrengante ADJ exhausting, crippling.

derrengar [1h] VT **(a)** (*torcer*) to bend, twist, make crooked. **(b) ~ a uno** to break sb's back, cripple sb; (*fig*) to wear sb out.

derrepente NM (*CAm*): **en un ~** = **de repente**.

derretido ADJ **(a)** *metal* melted; molten; *nieve* thawed. **(b) estar ~ por una*** to be crazy about sb.

derretimiento NM **(a)** (*gen*) melting; thawing. **(b)** (*fig: derroche*) squandering. **(c)** (*fig: pasión*) mad passion, burning love.

derretir [3k] **1** VT **(a)** *metal* to melt; to liquefy; *helado etc* to melt; *nieve* to thaw.

(b) (*fig*) to squander, throw away.

(c) (*) (*aburrir*) to bore to tears; (*irritar*) to exasperate.

2 derretirse VR **(a)** (*fundirse*) to melt; to run, liquefy.

(b) (*fig*) to be very susceptible to love, fall in love easily; **~ por una** to be crazy about sb.

(c) (*: *sulfurarse*) to get worked up, fret and fume.

(d) (*: *mostrarse sensible*) to come over very sentimental; to go all weak at the knees.

derribar [1a] **1** VT **(a)** *edificio* to knock down, pull down, demolish; *barrera* to tear down; *puerta* to batter down.

(b) *persona* to knock down; to floor, lay out; *luchador* to floor, throw.

(c) (*Aer*) to shoot down, bring down; **fue derribado sobre el Canal** he was shot down over the Channel.

(d) (*Caza*) to shoot, bag, bring down.

(e) *gobierno etc* to bring down, overthrow, topple.

(f) (*fig*) *pasión* to subdue.

2 derribarse VR **(a)** (*caer al suelo*) to fall down, collapse.

(b) (*tirarse al suelo*) to throw o.s. down, hurl o.s. to the ground; to prostrate o.s.

derribo NM **(a)** (*de edificio*) knocking down, demolition. **(b)** (*Lucha*) throw. **(c)** (*Aer*) shooting down; destruction. **(d)** (*Pol*) overthrow. **(e) ~s** rubble, debris.

derrisco NM (*Carib*) gorge, ravine.

derrocadero NM cliff, precipice, steep place.

derrocamiento NM **(a)** (*derrumbamiento*) flinging down, throwing down. **(b)** (*demolición*) demolition. **(c)** (*derribo*) overthrow, toppling; ousting.

derrocar [1g] **1** VT **(a)** *objeto, persona* to fling down, hurl down.

(b) *edificio etc* to knock down, demolish.

(c) *gobierno* to overthrow, topple; *ministro etc* to oust (*de* from).

2 derrocarse VR: **~ por un precipicio** to throw o.s. over a cliff.

derrochador 1 ADJ spendthrift.

2 NM **derrochadora** NF spendthrift, wastrel.

derrochar [1a] VT **(a)** *dinero etc* to squander, waste; to lavish, pour out. **(b) ~ salud** to be bursting with health; **~ mal genio** to be excessively bad-tempered.

derroche NM **(a)** (*despilfarro*) squandering, waste; lavish expenditure; (*exceso*) extravagance; **con un formidable ~ de recursos** with a lavish use of resources; **no se puede tolerar tal ~** such extravagance is not to be tolerated.

(b) (*gran cantidad*) abundance, excess; **con un ~ de buen gusto** with a fine display of good taste.

derrochón = **derrochador**.

derrota[1] NF **(a)** (*camino*) road, route, track. **(b)** (*Náut*) course.

derrota[2] NF (*Dep, Mil etc*) defeat; rout; débâcle, disaster; **sufrir una grave ~** to suffer a serious defeat, (*en proyecto etc*) to suffer a grave setback.

derrotado ADJ **(a)** (*vencido*) defeated; *equipo* defeated, beaten, losing. **(b)** *ropa, persona* shabby; **un actor ~** a shabby old actor, a down-and-out actor.

derrotar [1a] **1** VT **(a)** (*Mil*) to defeat; to rout, put to flight; *equipo etc* to defeat, beat. **(b)** *ropa* to tear, ruin; (*fig*) *salud* to ruin.

2 derrotarse VR (*delincuente*) to cough‡, sing‡; **~ de uno** to grass on sb‡.

derrotero NM **(a)** (*Náut*) course; (*fig*) course, plan of action; **tomar otro ~** (*fig*) to adopt a different course. **(b)** (*Carib: tesoro*) hidden treasure.

derrotismo NM defeatism.

derrotista ADJ, NMF defeatist.

derruir [3g] VT to demolish, tear down.

derrumbadero NM **(a)** (*precipicio*) cliff, precipice, steep place. **(b)** (*fig: peligro*) danger, hazard; pitfall.

derrumbamiento NM **(a)** (*caída*) plunge, headlong fall.

(b) (*demolición*) demolition; (*desplome*) collapse; fall, cave-in; **~ de piedras** fall of rocks; **~ de tierra** landslide.

(c) (*fig*) collapse, ruin, destruction; (*de precio*) sharp fall, collapse.

derrumbar [1a] **1** VT **(a)** *objeto, persona* to fling down, hurl down; to throw headlong.

(b) *edificio etc* to knock down, demolish.

(c) (*volcar*) to upset, overturn.

2 derrumbarse VR **(a)** (*persona etc*) to fling o.s., hurl o.s. (headlong; *por* down, over); to fall headlong.

(b) (*edificio etc*) to collapse, fall down, tumble down; (*techo*) to fall in, cave in.

(c) (*fig: esperanzas etc*) to collapse, be ruined; **se han derrumbado los precios** prices have tumbled; the bottom has fallen out of the market.

derrumbe NM **(a)** = **derrumbadero**. **(b)** = **derrumbamiento**.

derviche NM dervish.

des... PREF de..., des...; un...; *p.ej.* **descolonización** decolonization; **desmilitarizado** demilitarized; **desempleo** unemployment; **desfavorable** unfavourable; **desgana** unwillingness.

desabastecido ADJ: **estar ~ de** to be out of (supplies of); **nos cogió ~s de gasolina** it caught us without petrol.

desabastecimiento NM shortage, scarcity.

desabillé NM deshabille.

desabolladura NF (*esp LAm: Aut*) panel beating.

desabollar [1a] VT to knock the dents out of.

desabonarse [1a] VR to stop subscribing, cancel one's subscription.

desabono NM **(a)** (*acto*) cancellation of one's subscription. **(b)** (*fig*) discredit; **hablar en ~ de uno** to say damaging things about sb, speak ill of sb.

desaborido ADJ *comida* insipid, tasteless; *persona* dull.

desabotonar [1a] **1** VT to unbutton, undo.

2 VI (*Bot*) to open, blossom.

3 desabotonarse VR to come undone.

desabrido ADJ **(a)** *comida* tasteless, insipid, flat.

(b) *tiempo* unpleasant.

(c) *persona* surly, rude, disagreeable; *tono etc* harsh, rough; *respuesta etc* sharp; *debate* bitter, acrimonious.

desabrigado ADJ **(a)** (*sin abrigo*) too lightly dressed, without adequate clothing. **(b)** (*fig*) unprotected, exposed; defenceless.

desabrigar [1h] **1** VT **(a)** (*desarropar*) to remove the clothing of; to leave bare, uncover.

(b) (*fig*) to leave without shelter, deprive of protection.

2 desabrigarse VR to take off one's (outer) clothing; to leave o.s. bare, uncover o.s.; **~ en la cama** to throw off one's bedcovers.

desabrigo NM **(a)** (*acto*) uncovering. **(b)** (*estado*) bareness; exposure; lack of clothing (*o* covers). **(c)** (*fig*) unprotectedness; poverty, destitution.

desabrimiento NM **(a)** (*de comida*) tastelessness, insipidness.

(b) (*disgusto*) unpleasantness.

(c) (*hosquedad*) surliness, rudeness; harshness; sharpness; acrimony; **contestar con ~** to answer sharply.

(d) (*fig*) depression, lowness of spirits; uneasy feeling.

desabrir [3a] VT **(a)** *comida* to give a nasty taste to. **(b)** (*fig*) to embitter; to torment.

desabrochar [1a] **1** VT **(a)** *ropa* to undo, unfasten, unbutton; *persona* to loosen the clothing of.

(b) (*fig*) to uncover, expose.

2 desabrocharse VR (*fig*) to pour one's heart out (*con* to).

desaburrirse [3a] VR (*LAm*) to enjoy o.s., have a good time.

desacatador ADJ disrespectful, insulting.

desacatar [1a] VT *persona* to be disrespectful to, behave insultingly towards; *orden* to disobey; *norma* to be out of line with, not comply with.

desacato NM disrespect; insulting behaviour; (*Jur etc*) contempt, act of contempt; **~ a la autoridad, ~ a la justicia** contempt (of court).

desaceleración NF deceleration, slowing down, slowdown; (*Econ*) downturn, reduction.

desacelerar [1a] ☐ VT to slow down.

☐ VI to decelerate, slow down; (*Econ*) to slow down, decline.

desacertadamente ADV mistakenly, erroneously, wrongly; unwisely, injudiciously.

desacertado ADJ *opinión etc* mistaken, erroneous, wrong; *medida etc* unwise, injudicious.

desacertar [1j] VI to be mistaken, be wrong; to get it wrong; to act unwisely.

desachavar* [1a] VI (*Cono Sur*) to spill the beans*.

desacierto NM (*error*) mistake, miscalculation, error; miss; (*dicho*) unfortunate remark (*etc*); **fue uno de muchos ~s suyos** it was one of his many errors; **ha sido un ~ elegir tal sitio** it was a mistake to choose such a place.

desacomedido ADJ (*And*) unhelpful, obstructive.

desacomodado ADJ (a) *criado* unemployed, out of a job. (b) (*pobre*) badly off. (c) (*incómodo*) awkward, troublesome, inconvenient.

desacomodar [1a] ☐ VT (a) *criado* to discharge. (b) (*incomodar*) to put out, inconvenience.

☐ **desacomodarse** VR to lose one's post.

desacompasado ADJ = **descompasado**.

desaconsejable ADJ inadvisable.

desaconsejado ADJ ill-advised.

desaconsejar [1a] VT *persona* to dissuade, advise against; *proyecto etc* to advise against; to disapprove of; **los rigores del viaje desaconsejaron esa decisión** the rigours of the journey made that decision seem inadvisable (*o* wrong).

desacoplable ADJ detachable, removable.

desacoplar [1a] VT (*Elec*) to disconnect; (*Mec*) to take apart, uncouple.

desacordar [1l] ☐ VT to put out of tune.

☐ **desacordarse** VR (a) (*Mús*) to get out of tune. (b) (*olvidar*) to be forgetful; **~ de algo** to forget sth.

desacorde ADJ (a) (*Mús*) discordant. (b) (*fig*) discordant, incongruous.

desacostumbrado ADJ unusual; unaccustomed.

desacostumbrar [1a] ☐ VT: **~ a uno de** to break sb of the habit of, wean sb away from.

☐ **desacostumbrarse** VR: **~ de** to break o.s. of the habit of.

desacralizar [1f] VT to demystify.

desacreditado ADJ discredited.

desacreditar [1a] ☐ VT (a) (*desprestigiar*) to discredit, damage the reputation of, bring into disrepute. (b) (*denigrar*) to cry down, disparage, run down.

☐ **desacreditarse** VR to become discredited.

desactivación NF defusing, making safe; **~ de bombas** bomb disposal.

desactivador NM bomb-disposal officer.

desactivar [1a] VT *bomba* to defuse, make safe, render harmless; *alarma* to deactivate, neutralize.

desactualizado ADJ out of date.

▼ **desacuerdo** NM (a) (*discrepancia*) discord, disagreement; **~ amistoso** agreement to differ; **estar en ~** to be out of keeping (*con* with), be at variance (*con* with); **la corbata está en ~ con la camisa** the tie does not go with the shirt. (b) (*error*) error, blunder. (c) (*desmemoria*) forgetfulness.

desadaptación NF maladjustment.

desadaptado, -a ADJ, NM/F = **inadaptado**.

desadeudarse [1a] VR to get out of debt.

desadorno NM bareness, lack of ornamentation.

desadvertido ADJ careless.

desadvertir [3i] VT (*no ver*) to fail to notice; (*desatender*) to disregard.

desafecto ☐ ADJ disaffected; hostile; **elementos ~s al régimen** those hostile to the régime, those out of sympathy with the régime.

☐ NM disaffection; ill-will, dislike; hostility.

desaferrar [1k *o* 1a] ☐ VT (a) (*soltar*) to loosen, unfasten. (b) **~ a uno** to make sb change his mind, dissuade sb (from a strongly held opinion *etc*). (c) **~ el áncora** (*Náut*) = **2**.

☐ VI to weigh anchor.

desafiador ☐ ADJ defiant; challenging.

☐ NM, **desafiadora** NF challenger.

desafiante ADJ challenging; *actitud etc* defiant.

desafiar [1c] VT (a) *persona etc* to challenge; **~ a uno a** + *infin* to challenge sb to + *infin*, dare sb to + *infin*. (b) *peligro* to defy; to face, face up to. (c) (*fig: competir*) to challenge, compete with, measure up to.

desaficionarse [1a] VR: **~ de** to come to dislike, take a dislike to.

desafilado ADJ blunt.

desafilar [1a] ☐ VT to blunt, dull.

☐ **desafilarse** VR to get blunt.

desafiliarse [1b] VR to disaffiliate (*de* from).

desafinadamente ADV *cantar etc* out of tune, off key.

desafinado ADJ flat, out of tune.

desafinar [1a] VI (a) (*Mús*) to be (*o* play, sing) out of tune; to go out of tune. (b) (*fig*) to speak out of turn.

desafío NM (a) (*gen*) challenge; (*combate*) duel. (b) (*fig*) challenge; defiance; competition, rivalry; **es un ~ a todos nosotros** it is a challenge to us all.

desaforadamente ADV (a) *comportarse etc* outrageously. (b) *gritar* at the top of one's voice.

desaforado ADJ (a) *persona* lawless, violent, disorderly; *comportamiento* outrageous; **es un ~** he's a violent sort, he's dangerously excitable. (b) (*enorme*) great, huge; *grito* mighty, ear-splitting.

desaforarse [1l] VR to behave in an outrageous way, act violently; to get worked up, lose control.

desafortunadamente ADV unfortunately.

desafortunado ADJ (a) (*desgraciado*) unfortunate, unlucky. (b) (*no oportuno*) inopportune, untimely; (*desacertado*) unwise.

desafuero NM outrage, excess.

desagraciado ADJ graceless, unattractive; unsightly.

desagradable ADJ disagreeable, unpleasant; **ser ~ con uno** to be rude to sb.

desagradablemente ADV unpleasantly.

▼ **desagradar** [1a] ☐ VT to displease; to bother, upset; **me desagrada ese olor** I don't like that smell; **me desagrada tener que hacerlo** I dislike having to do it.

☐ VI to be unpleasant.

desagradecido ADJ ungrateful.

desagradecimiento NM ingratitude.

desagrado NM displeasure; dislike; dissatisfaction; **hacer algo con ~** to do sth with distaste, do sth unwillingly.

desagraviar [1b] ☐ VT (a) *persona* to make amends to; (*compensar*) to indemnify; (*disculparse con*) to apologize to. (b) *ofensa etc* to make amends for, put right.

☐ **desagraviarse** VR to get one's own back; to exact an apology; to restore one's honour.

desagravio NM amends; compensation, indemnification, satisfaction; **en ~** as amends for.

desagregación NF disintegration.

desagregar [1h] ☐ VT to disintegrate.

☐ **desagregarse** VR to disintegrate.

desaguadero NM (a) drain (*t fig; de* on). (b) (*Méx**) lavatory, loo*.

desaguar [1i] ☐ VT (a) *líquido* to drain, empty, run off. (b) (*fig*) to squander. (c) (*And: enjuagar*) to rinse (out).

☐ VI (a) (*líquido*) to drain away, drain off. (b) (*río*) **~ en** to drain into, flow into.

desagüe NM (a) (*acto*) drainage, draining. (b) (*canal*) drainage channel; (*tubo*) drainpipe; (*salida*) outlet, drain; **tubo de ~** drainpipe, waste pipe.

desaguisado ☐ ADJ illegal.

☐ NM offence, outrage.

desahogadamente ADV comfortably.

desahogado ☐ ADJ (a) *vestido, casa etc* roomy, large. (b) *espacio* clear, free, unencumbered. (c) *situación, vida* comfortable; *persona* comfortably off, in easy circumstances. (d) (*descarado*) brazen, impudent, fresh*; **el tan ~ se lo comió todo** he was brazen enough to eat it all up.

☐ NM, **desahogada** NF brazen person, shameless individual.

desahogar [1h] ☐ VT (a) *dolor etc* to ease, relieve; *ira* to vent (*en* on). (b) *persona* to console.

☐ **desahogarse** VR (a) (*reponerse*) to recover; to make things more comfortable for o.s.; (*relajarse*) to take it easy, relax. (b) (*librarse*) to get out of a difficulty (*o* debt *etc*). (c) (*desfogarse*) to relieve one's feelings; to let off steam, let o.s. go; (*hablar francamente*) to speak one's mind frankly; (*confesarse*) to confess, get sth off one's chest; **~ con uno** to pour one's heart out to sb.

desahogo NM (a) (*comodidad*) comfort, ease; comfortable circumstances; **vivir con ~** to be comfortably off. (b) (*alivio*) relief; recovery; **es un ~ de tantas cosas malas** it's an outlet for so many unpleasant things, it's a way of getting rid of so many bad things. (c) (*libertad*) freedom; (*pey*) excessive freedom, brazenness, impudence; **expresarse con cierto ~** to express o.s. with a certain freedom, feel free to say what one really thinks.

desahuciado ADJ *caso* hopeless.

desahuciar [1b] ☐ VT (a) *inquilino* to evict, eject; *empleado* to oust, remove, get out; (*Cono Sur: despedir*) to dismiss. (b) (*quitar esperanza a*) to deprive of hope, kill the hopes of; *enfermo*

to give up hope for, declare past recovery; *plan etc* to give up as a lost cause; **con esa decisión le desahuciaron definitivamente** by that decision they finally put an end to his hopes.
[2] **desahuciarse** VR to lose all hope.

desahucio NM eviction, ejection; (*Cono Sur: despido*) dismissal.

desairado ADJ **(a)** (*menospreciado*) spurned; disregarded. **(b)** (*sin éxito*) unsuccessful; **quedar ~** to be unsuccessful, come off badly. **(c)** (*desgarbado*) unattractive; graceless.

desairar [1a] VT *persona* to slight, snub; *asunto* to disregard; to rebuff; **lo haré por no ~** I'll do it rather than cause offence.

desaire NM **(a)** (*menosprecio*) slight, snub; (*desacato*) act of disrespect; (*repulsa*) rebuff; **fue un ~ sin precedentes** it was an unprecedented snub; **dar** (o **hacer**) **un ~ a uno** to rebuff sb, offend sb; **¿me vas a hacer ese ~?** (*acerca de invitación*) I won't take no for an answer!; **sufrir un ~** to suffer a rebuff; **no lo tomes a ~** don't be offended. **(b)** (*falta de garbo*) unattractiveness, gracelessness, lack of charm.

desajustado ADJ ill-adjusted, poorly adjusted.

desajustar [1a] [1] VT to disarrange, disturb the order of.
[2] **desajustarse** VR **(a)** (*estropearse*) to get out of order; (*Mec*) to break down. **(b)** (*reñir*) to disagree, fall out.

desajuste NM **(a)** (*falta de orden*) disorder, disarrangement; (*Mec*) breakdown. **(b)** (*desequilibrio*) imbalance, lack of balance. **(c)** (*desacuerdo*) disagreement.

desalación NF desalination.

desalado¹ ADJ (*apresurado*) hasty; (*impaciente*) impatient; (*ansioso*) eager; anxious.

desalado² ADJ desalted.

desaladora NF desalination plant.

desalar¹ [1a] VT to remove the salt from; *agua salada* to desalinate.

desalar² [1a] [1] VT to clip the wings of.
[2] **desalarse** VR **(a)** (*correr*) to rush, hasten along. **(b)** (*anhelar*) to long, yearn; **~ por** + *infin* to long to + *infin*; to be keen to + *infin*.

desalentador ADJ discouraging.

desalentar [1j] [1] VT **(a)** **~ a uno** to make sb breathless, make sb gasp for breath.
(b) (*fig*) to discourage.
[2] **desalentarse** VR to get discouraged, lose heart.

desaliento NM (*fig*) discouragement; depression, dejection; dismay.

desalinización NF desalination.

desalinizador ADJ: **planta ~a** desalination plant.

desalinizar [1f] VT to desalinate.

desaliñado ADJ **(a)** (*desaseado*) slovenly, dirty, down-at-heel; (*raído*) shabby; (*desordenado*) untidy, unkempt, dishevelled. **(b)** (*negligente*) careless, slipshod, slovenly.

desaliño NM **(a)** (*desarreglo*) slovenliness, dirtiness; shabbiness; untidiness; dishevelled state. **(b)** (*descuido*) carelessness.

desalmado ADJ cruel, heartless.

desalmarse [1a] VR: **~ por** to long for, crave (for).

desalojamiento NM (*V* VT (*a*), (*c*)) **(a)** ejection, ousting, removal; dislodging. **(b)** evacuation; abandonment; clearing.

desalojar [1a] [1] VT **(a)** *ocupante* to eject, oust, remove (*from* de); to dislodge (*t Mil*; *de* from); to clear out; *inquilino* to evict.
(b) *contenido, gas etc* to dislodge, remove, expel.
(c) *sitio* to evacuate; to abandon, move out of, move away from; **~ un tribunal de público** to clear a court, to clear the public from a court; **las tropas han desalojado el pueblo** the troops have moved out of the village; **la policía desalojó el local** the police cleared people out of the place.
[2] VI to move out.

desalojo NM ejection, removal; evacuation; abandonment; clearance.

desalquilado ADJ vacant, untenanted.

desalquilar [1a] [1] VT to vacate, move out of.
[2] **desalquilarse** VR to become vacant.

desalterar [1a] [1] VT to assuage, calm; to quieten down.
[2] **desalterarse** VR to calm down, quieten down.

desamar [1a] VT to cease to love; to dislike, detest.

desamarrar [1a] VT to untie; (*Náut*) to cast off.

desamarre NM untying; (*Náut*) casting-off.

desambiguar [1i] VT to disambiguate.

desamor NM coldness, indifference; dislike; enmity.

desamorado ADJ cold-hearted.

desamortización NF (*Jur*) disentailment; (*Hist Esp*) sale of Church lands.

desamortizar [1f] VT to disentail.

desamparado ADJ **(a)** *niño etc* helpless, defenceless; abandoned; **los niños ~s de la ciudad** the city's waifs and strays; **sentirse ~** to feel helpless.
(b) *lugar* (*expuesto*) exposed.
(c) *lugar* (*desierto*) lonely, deserted.

desamparar [1a] VT **(a)** *persona* to desert, abandon, leave helpless; to forsake. **(b)** *sitio* to leave, abandon; to leave defenceless. **(c)** *actividad* to cease, abandon; to lose interest in.

desamparo NM **(a)** (*acto*) desertion, abandonment. **(b)** (*estado*) helplessness; defencelessness, lack of protection. **(c)** (*cesación*) cessation; loss of interest (*de* in).

desamueblado ADJ unfurnished; empty, with the furniture removed.

desamueblar [1a] VT to remove the furniture from, clear the furniture out of.

desandar [1p] VT: **~ lo andado**, **~ el camino** to retrace one's steps, go back the way one has come; **no se puede ~ lo andado** one cannot undo what has been done.

desangelado ADJ *persona* charmless, dull, unattractive; *cosa* dull, insipid; *flat*; played-out; *lugar* empty, lifeless.

desangramiento NM bleeding; **morir de ~** to bleed to death.

desangrar [1a] [1] VT **(a)** *persona* to bleed; *lago* to drain. **(b)** (*fig*) to impoverish, bleed white.
[2] **desangrarse** VR to lose a lot of blood.

desangre NM (*LAm*) bleeding, loss of blood.

desanidar [1a] [1] VT to oust, dislodge.
[2] VI to fly, begin to fly, leave the nest.

desanimado [1] ADJ **(a)** (*desalentado*) downhearted, dispirited, dejected. **(b)** (*soso*) dull, lifeless, flat; **fue una fiesta de lo más ~** it was a terribly dull party.
[2] NM, **desanimada** NF dropout (from the labour market).

desanimante ADJ discouraging.

desanimar [1a] [1] VT to discourage; to depress, sadden.
[2] **desanimarse** VR to get discouraged, lose heart; **no hay que ~** we must not lose heart, we must keep our spirits up.

desánimo NM **(a)** (*desaliento*) despondency, depression, dejection. **(b)** (*flojedad*) dullness, lifelessness.

desanudar [1a] VT to untie, unknot; to disentangle; **~ la voz** to manage to speak again, find one's voice.

desapacible ADJ (*gen*) unpleasant, disagreeable; *sonido* sharp, jangling; nasty; discordant; *tono* harsh, rough; *sabor* unpleasant, sharp; *discusión* bitter, bad-tempered; *persona* surly, unpleasant.

desaparcar [1g] VI to drive off.

desaparecer [2d] [1] VT (*esp LAm*) to cause to disappear, eliminate.
[2] VI to disappear, vanish; to drop out of sight; (*efecto*) to wear off; (*euf*) to pass away.

desaparecido [1] ADJ (*gen*) missing; *especie* extinct; **el libro ~** the missing book; **uno de los animales ~s** one of the extinct animals; **3 siguen ~s** 3 are still missing.
[2] NM, **desaparecida** NF missing person; (*LAm: secuestrado*) kidnap victim, kidnapped person; (*detenido*) person improperly arrested, victim of arbitrary arrest; **los ~s** the missing, those missing; **número de muertos, heridos y ~s** the number of dead, wounded and missing.

┌─ **LOS DESAPARECIDOS** ─┐

ⓘ *Los desaparecidos is the name given to those who disappeared during the military dictatorships in Argentina, Chile, Uruguay and Brazil in the 1970s. Thousands of people were taken from their homes, schools and places of work and never seen again. Few of "the disappeared" were ever found alive, although a certain number of bodies were recovered in mass graves. Families of the victims joined forces to form pressure groups like Argentina's* Madres y Abuelas de la Plaza de Mayo, *but although some managed to identify and recover the bodies of their relatives, the perpetrators were rarely brought to justice.*

desaparejar [1a] VT **(a)** (*gen*) to unharness, unhitch. **(b)** (*Náut*) to unrig.

desaparición NF disappearance; extinction.

desapasionadamente ADV dispassionately, impartially.

desapasionado ADJ dispassionate, impartial.

desapego NM **(a)** (*frialdad*) coolness, indifference (*a* towards); (*distancia*) alienation, detachment (*a* from). **(b)** (*ecuanimidad*) detachment, impartiality.

desapercibido ADJ **(a)** (*no visto*) unnoticed; **marcharse ~** to slip away (unseen); **pasar ~** to go unnoticed. **(b)** (*desprevenido*) unprepared.

desaplicación NF slackness, laziness.

desaplicado ADJ slack, lazy.

desapoderado ADJ *acción, movimiento* headlong, precipitate; *pasión etc* wild, violent, uncontrollable; *avidez etc* excessive; *orgullo* overweening.

desapoderar [1a] VT to deprive of authority; to dispossess (*de* of).

desapolillarse [1a] VR (*fig*) to get rid of the cobwebs.

desaprender [2a] VT to forget; to unlearn.

desaprensión NF unscrupulousness, lack of scruple.

desaprensivamente ADV unscrupulously.

desaprensivo ADJ unscrupulous.

desapretar [1j] VT to loosen, slacken, undo.

desaprobación NF disapproval; condemnation; rejection.

desaprobar [1l] VT (*no aprobar*) to disapprove of; (*condenar*) to frown on, condemn; *solicitud etc* to reject, dismiss.

desaprobatorio ADJ disapproving.

desapropiarse [1b] VR: ~ **de** to divest o.s. of, surrender, give up.

desaprovechado ADJ (a) (*improductivo*) unproductive, unprofitable; (*no satisfactorio*) below expectations. (b) *estudiante etc* slow, backward; slack. (c) *oportunidad* wasted.

desaprovechamiento NM waste.

desaprovechar [1a] ① VT to fail to take advantage of, not use, waste; *oportunidad* to waste, miss.
② VI to lose ground, slip back.

desarbolado ADJ *paisaje* treeless; stripped of trees.

desarbolar [1a] VT to dismast.

desarmable ADJ: **mesa** ~ fold-away table.

desarmador NM (*de fusil*) trigger; (*LAm*) screwdriver.

desarmante ADJ disarming.

desarmar [1a] ① VT (a) (*Mil*) to disarm.
(b) (*Mec*) to take apart, take to pieces, dismantle; to strip down; *remos* to ship; *barco* to lay up; *barrera* to remove, take down.
(c) (*fig*) *persona* to disarm; *ira* to calm, appease.
② VI to disarm.

desarme NM disarmament; ~ **arancelario** removal of tariff barriers; ~ **industrial** removal of trade tariffs, lifting of protectionist barriers; ~ **unilateral** unilateral disarmament.

desarraigado ADJ *persona* rootless, without roots.

desarraigar [1h] VT (a) *árbol* to uproot, root out, dig up. (b) (*fig*) to root out, eradicate; to extirpate; *persona* to uproot; to banish, expel.

desarraigo NM (*fig*) eradication; extirpation; uprooting; banishment, expulsion.

desarrajar [1a] VT (*LAm*) to break open, force the lock of.

desarrapado ADJ = **desharrapado.**

desarrebujar [1a] VT (a) (*desenredar*) to untangle; (*descubrir*) to uncover. (b) (*fig*) to clarify, elucidate.

desarreglado ADJ (a) (*Mec etc*) out of order; *estómago etc* upset; *cuarto etc* untidy, in disorder.
(b) *conducta* disorderly; *aspecto* slovenly, untidy; *hábitos* irregular; unsystematic; (*en comer etc*) immoderate.

desarreglar [1a] ① VT (*gen*) to disarrange; *proyectos etc* to disturb, mess up, upset; (*Mec*) to put out of order; **el viento le desarregló el peinado** the wind made a mess of her hairdo; **no desarregles la cama** don't mess up your bed.
② **desarreglarse** VR to get disarranged, get untidy; (*Mec*) to get out of order, break down.

desarreglo NM disorder, confusion, chaos; untidiness; irregularity; (*Mec*) trouble; (*Med*) upset; **para evitar los ~s estomacales** in order to avoid stomach upsets; **viven en el mayor ~** they live in complete chaos.

desarrimado* NM loner, lone wolf.

desarrimar [1a] VT (a) to move away, separate. (b) *persona* to dissuade.

desarrollado ADJ (*t bien ~*) well-developed.

desarrollar [1a] ① VT (a) *rollo* to unroll, unwind; *mapa etc* to unfold, open (out).
(b) *abreviatura, ecuación* to expand.
(c) (*fig*) to develop; to evolve; *teoría, tema etc* to explain, expound; *trabajo* to carry out.
(d) (*Mec*) **el motor desarrolla 30 caballos** the engine develops 30 hp.
② **desarrollarse** VR (a) (*gen*) to unroll, unwind; (*desplegarse*) to open (out).
(b) (*fig*) to develop; to evolve; (*historia etc*) to unfold; (*suceso, reunión etc*) to take place; **la industria se desarrolla rápidamente** the industry is developing rapidly; **la acción se desarrolla en Roma** (*Cine etc*) the scene is set in Rome, the action takes place in Rome.

desarrollismo NM policy of economic development; unimpeded development.

desarrollo NM (a) development; evolution; unfolding; expansion; growth; (*de juego*) run; ~ **en línea** ribbon development; **en ~ de** in the course of; during the development of; **un país en (vías de)** ~ a developing country; **la industria está en pleno** ~ the industry is making rapid growth, the industry is expanding steadily; **el niño tiene mucho ~ para su edad** the child is overdeveloped for his age.
(b) (*de bicicleta*) gear.

desarropado ADJ: **estar** ~ (*en la cama*) to have lost the covers; (*fig*) to be exposed.

desarroparse [1a] VR to undress; to uncover o.s.; (*en la cama*) to sleep without any bed coverings; **todavía el tiempo no es para** ~ it's not yet weather for leaving off any clothes.

desarrugar [1h] VT to smooth (out), remove the wrinkles from.

desarticulación NF taking to pieces; separation; dislocation; breaking up.

desarticulado ADJ disjointed.

desarticular [1a] VT (*desmontar*) to take apart, take to pieces; to separate; *huesos* to put out, dislocate; *pandilla* to break up; ~ **un grupo terrorista** to put a terrorist group out of action.

desarzonar [1a] VT *jinete* to throw, unsaddle.

desaseado ADJ (*sucio*) slovenly, dirty; (*desaliñado*) untidy, unkempt, messy; (*raído*) shabby.

desasear [1a] VT to dirty, soil; to mess up.

desaseo NM slovenliness, dirtiness; untidiness; messiness; shabbiness.

desasimiento NM (a) (*acto*) loosening, undoing; release. (b) (*fig*) detachment (*de* from), disinterest; (*pey*) indifference (*de* to), remoteness (*de* from).

desasir [3a, *pero presente como* **salir**] ① VT to loosen, undo, let go.
② **desasirse** VR (a) (*gen*) to extricate o.s. (*de* from), get clear (*de* of).
(b) ~ **de** (*ceder*) to let go, give up; (*deshacerse de*) to rid o.s. of, free o.s. of; to get rid of.

desasistir [3a] VT to desert, abandon; to neglect.

desasnar [1a] VT (*civilizar*) to civilize, improve, knock the corners off; (*instruir*) to make less stupid.

desasosegado ADJ uneasy, anxious; restless.

desasosegador ADJ, **desasosegante** ADJ disturbing, upsetting.

desasosegar [1h y 1j] ① VT to disturb, perturb, make uneasy; to make restless.
② **desasosegarse** VR to become uneasy, get perturbed; to become restless.

desasosiego NM disquiet, uneasiness, anxiety; restlessness; (*Pol etc*) unrest.

desastrado ADJ (a) (*sucio*) dirty; (*harapiento*) shabby, ragged. (b) (*desgraciado*) unlucky; wretched.

desastre NM disaster; **¡un ~!** (*hum*) what a calamity!; how awful!; **la boda fue un** ~ the wedding was a disaster; **la función fue un** ~ the show was a shambles.

desastroso ADJ disastrous, calamitous.

desatado ADJ (*fig*) wild, violent, uncontrolled.

desatar [1a] ① VT (a) *nudo* to untie, undo, unfasten; *cuerda* to loosen, slacken; *pieza* to detach, separate; *perro* to unleash; (*Quím*) to dissolve.
(b) (*fig*) *pasión, represión etc* to unleash.
(c) (*fig*) *misterio* to solve, clear up, unravel.
② **desatarse** VR (a) (*cuerda*) to come untied, come undone, unfasten itself; to work loose; (*perro etc*) to break away, break loose.
(b) ~ **de un compromiso** to get out of an agreement.
(c) (*fig: tormenta etc*) to break, burst; (*motín*) to break out; (*entusiasmo*) to break all bounds; (*desastre*) to fall (*sobre* on); ~ **en injurias** to let rip with a torrent of abuse.
(d) (*fig: persona*) to get worked up, lose self-control; to talk wildly; to go too far, forget o.s.

desatascador NM plunger.

desatascar [1g] VT (a) *carro etc* to pull out of the mud; ~ **a uno** (*fig*) to get sb out of a jam. (b) *tubo etc* to clear, free, unblock.

desatención NF (a) (*distracción*) inattention; neglect; absent-mindedness. (b) (*descortesía*) discourtesy.

desatender [2g] VT to disregard, pay no attention to; to ignore; *deber* to neglect; *persona* to slight, offend.

desatentado ADJ (a) (*irreflexivo*) thoughtless, rash, ill-advised; (*poco sensato*) unwise, foolish. (b) (*excesivo*) excessive, extreme, out of all proportion.

desatento ADJ (a) (*descuidado*) heedless, careless; (*negligente*) neglectful; (*distraído*) inattentive. (b) (*descortés*) discourteous, unmannerly (*con* to).

desatierre NM (*LAm*) slag heap.

desatinadamente ADV foolishly; wildly, recklessly.

desatinado ADJ silly, foolish; wild, reckless.

desatinar [1a] ① VT to perplex, bewilder.
② VI (*obrar*) to act foolishly; (*hablar*) to talk nonsense, rave; (*ponerse nervioso*) to get rattled, begin to act wildly.

desatino NM (a) (*cualidad*) foolishness, folly, silliness; tactlessness. (b) (*acto etc*) silly thing, foolish act; (*error*) blunder, mistake; **~s** nonsense; **¡qué ~!** how silly!, what rubbish!; **un libro lleno de ~s** a book stuffed with nonsense; **cometer un** ~ to make a blunder.

desatochar [1a] VT (*Cono Sur*) *tráfico* to clear.

desatornillador NM (*LAm*) screwdriver.

desatornillar [1a] VT to unscrew.

desatracar [1g] VTI (*Náut*) to cast off.

desatraillar [1a] VT to unleash, let off the lead.

desatrancar [1g] VT (a) *puerta* to unbar, unbolt. (b) *caño etc* to clear, unblock; *pozo* to clean out.

desatraque NM casting-off.

desatufarse [1a] VR (a) to get some fresh air. (b) (*fig*) to calm down.

desautorización NF (a) discrediting; disapproval; repudiation. (b) denial.

desautorizado ADJ (*no aprobado*) unauthorized; (*no oficial*) unofficial; (*no justificado*) unwarranted.

desautorizar [1f] VT (a) *oficial etc* to deprive of authority, declare without authority; (*desacreditar*) to discredit; (*desaprobar*) to disapprove of; (*rechazar*) to disown, repudiate. (b) *noticia* to deny, issue a denial of.

desavenencia NF (*desacuerdo*) disagreement; (*tirantez*) friction, unpleasantness; (*riña*) rift, quarrel.

desavenido ADJ (*incompatible*) incompatible; (*opuestos*) contrary, opposing; (*reñidos*) in disagreement; **ellos están ~s** they are at odds, they disagree.

desavenir [3r] ① VT to cause a rift between, make trouble between; to split, break the unity of.
② **desavenirse** VR to disagree (*con* with), fall out (*con* with).

desaventajado ADJ (*inferior*) inferior; (*desfavorable*) unfavourable, disadvantageous.

desavisado ADJ unwary; uninformed.

desayunado PTP: **estar ~** to have had breakfast.

desayunar [1a] ① VT (a) to have for breakfast, breakfast on. (b) **vengo desayunado** I've had breakfast.
② VI *y* **desayunarse** VR to breakfast, have breakfast; **~ con** to have for breakfast, breakfast on; **ahora me desayuno de ello** this is the first I've heard of it.

desayuno NM breakfast; **~ a la inglesa**, **~ británico** English breakfast; **~ continental** continental breakfast; **~ de trabajo** working breakfast.

desazón NF (a) (*insipidez*) tastelessness, lack of flavour.
(b) (*de tierra*) poorness.
(c) (*Med*) discomfort, indisposition, slight trouble.
(d) (*fig*) (*molestia*) annoyance, displeasure; (*frustración*) frustration; (*inquietud*) uneasiness.

desazonante ADJ annoying, upsetting.

desazonar [1a] ① VT (a) *comida* to make tasteless, take the flavour out of.
(b) (*fig*) (*molestar*) to annoy, upset, displease; (*inquietar*) to worry, cause anxiety to.
② **desazonarse** VR (a) (*Med*) to feel off-colour, be out of sorts.
(b) (*fig*) to be annoyed; to worry, be anxious.

desbancar [1g] ① VT (a) (*Naipes*) *banca* to bust*; *persona* to take the bank from.
(b) (*fig*) to displace, oust, dislodge; to cut out, supplant (in sb's affections); **el corredor fue desbancado por el pelotón a 5 km de la meta** the group overtook the leader 5 kms from the tape.
② VI (*Naipes*) to go bust*.

desbandada NF rush (to get away); **hubo una ~ general de turistas** there was a mass exodus of tourists, masses of tourists suddenly left; **cuando empezó a llover hubo una ~ general** when it started to rain everyone rushed for shelter; **a la ~** in disorder; helter-skelter; **retirarse a la ~** to retreat in disorder, make a disorderly retreat.

desbandar* [1a] VT (*Carib*) *empleado* to fire*.

desbandarse [1a] VR (a) (*Mil*) to disband. (b) (*fig*) to flee in disorder; to go off in all directions, disperse in confusion.

desbande* NM (*Cono Sur*) rush (to get away).

desbarajustar [1a] VT to throw into confusion.

desbarajuste NM confusion, chaos, disorder.

desbaratamiento NM, **desbarate** NM, **desbarato** NM (a) (*destrucción*) ruin, destruction, foiling, thwarting; disruption; debunking.
(b) (*Mil*) rout.
(c) squandering.

desbaratar [1a] ① VT (a) (*arruinar*) to ruin, spoil, destroy; to mess up; *plan etc* to foil, thwart, frustrate; *sistema* to disrupt, cause chaos in; *teoría* to make nonsense of, debunk.
(b) (*Mil*) to throw into confusion, rout.
(c) *fortuna* to squander.
(d) (*Mec*) to take to pieces.
② VI to rave, talk nonsense.
③ **desbaratarse** VR (a) (*Mec*) to get out of order, develop a defect.
(b) (*persona*) to fly off the handle*, go off the deep end*; to become unbalanced.

desbarbar [1a] ① VT (a) (*) *persona* to shave; *papel* to trim (the edges of); *planta* to cut back, trim (off).
② **desbarbarse** VR (*) to shave.

desbarrancadero NM (*LAm*) precipice.

desbarrancar [1g] ① VT (a) (*LAm*) to fling over a precipice. (b) (*And*, *Carib*: *arruinar*) to ruin; (*And**: *aplastar*) to crush.
② **desbarrancarse** VR (a) (*LAm*) to fall over a precipice. (b) (*) to come down in the world.

desbarrar [1a] VI to talk rubbish; to be very wide of the mark.

desbastación NF = **desbaste**.

desbastar [1a] ① VT (a) (*Téc*) to rough-hew; to plane (down), smooth (down).

(b) (*fig*) to take the rough edges off; (*refinar*) to refine, polish; *recluta etc* to knock the corners off, lick into shape.
② **desbastarse** VR (*fig*) to acquire some polish.

desbaste NM (a) (*Téc*) planing, smoothing. (b) (*fig*) polishing, refinement; licking into shape.

desbeber⁑ [2a] VI to piss⁑.

desbloquear [1a] VT (a) (*Mil*) to break the blockade of. (b) (*Com*, *Fin*) to unfreeze, unblock. (c) *caño etc* to unblock, free; *tráfico* to free, get moving; *negociación* to break a stalemate in, secure progress in.

desbloqueo NM unfreezing, unblocking, freeing.

desbocado ADJ (a) *taza* chipped.
(b) *cañon* wide-mouthed.
(c) *caballo* runaway.
(d) *herramienta* worn, defective, damaged.
(e) *persona* foul-mouthed, foul-spoken.
(f) (*LAm*) *líquido* overflowing.

desbocar [1g] ① VT *taza* to chip.
② VI: **~ en** (*río*) to run into, flow into; (*calle*) to open into, come out into.
③ **desbocarse** VR (a) (*caballo*) to bolt, run away; (*multitud*) to rush off, run riot, get out of control.
(b) (*persona*) to start to swear, let out a stream of insults.

desbolado⁑ ADJ (*Cono Sur*) disorganized.

desbole⁑ NM (*Cono Sur*) (*desorden*) mess, mix-up; (*alboroto*) row, racket.

desbordamiento NM (a) (*gen*) overflowing, flooding; spilling. (b) (*fig*) eruption, outburst; **un tremendo ~ de entusiasmo** a great upsurge of enthusiasm. (c) (*Inform*) overflow.

desbordante ADJ overflowing; (*fig*) overwhelming, excessive.

desbordar [1a] ① VT to pass, go beyond; to exceed, surpass; **desbordaron las líneas enemigas** they burst through the enemy lines; **el proyecto desborda los límites señalados** the plan goes well beyond the limits which were set; **esto desborda mi tolerancia** this is more than I can tolerate.
② VI *y* **desbordarse** VR (a) (*río*) to overflow, flood, burst its banks; (*líquido*) to overflow, spill (over).
(b) (*entusiasmo etc*) to erupt, burst forth.
(c) (*persona*) to give free rein to one's feelings; (*pasarse*) to get carried away, go over the top; (*pey*) to fly off the handle*, lose one's self-control; **~(se) de alegría** to be bursting with happiness.

desborde NM (*Cono Sur*) = **desbordamiento**.

desbraguetado* ADJ: **estar ~** to be broke*.

desbravador NM horse-breaker.

desbravar [1a] ① VT to break in, tame.
② VI *y* **desbravarse** VR (a) (*animal*) to get less wild, grow less fierce.
(b) (*corriente etc*) to lose its strength, diminish in force.
(c) (*licor*) to lose its strength.

desbrozadora NF weeding machine.

desbrozar [1f] VT *camino etc* to clear (of rubbish); *tierra* to clear, clear the undergrowth from; *cosecha* to weed, keep clear of weeds.

desburocratizar [1f] VT to make less bureaucratic.

descabal ADJ, **descabalado** ADJ incomplete.

descabalgar [1h] ① VT (*fig*) to unseat, remove from office.
② VI to dismount.

descabellado ADJ (*fig*) wild, crazy, preposterous.

descabellar [1a] VT (a) *persona* to dishevel; to ruffle, rumple. (b) *toro* to kill with a thrust in the neck, administer the coup de grâce to.

descabello NM (*Taur*) final thrust, coup de grâce.

descabezado ADJ (a) (*lit*) headless. (b) (*fig*) wild, crazy, light-headed.

descabezar [1f] ① VT (a) *persona etc* to behead, cut the head off; *árbol* to lop, poll, cut the top off; *planta* to top.
(b) (*fig*) *dificultad* to begin to get over, get over the worst part of, surmount.
② **descabezarse** VR (a) (*Bot*) to shed the grain.
(b) (*persona*) to rack one's brains.

descachalandrado* ADJ (*And*) shabby, scruffy.

descachalandrarse* [1a] VR (*And*) to dress carelessly.

descachar [1a] VT (*And*, *Carib*, *Cono Sur*) to de-horn.

descacharrado ADJ (*CAm*) dirty, slovenly.

descacharrante* ADJ hilarious.

descacharrar* [1a] ① VT to bust.
② **descacharrarse** VR to break down.

descachimbarse* [1a] VI (*CAm*) to fall flat on one's face, come a cropper*.

descafeinado ADJ decaffeinated; (*fig*) diluted, watered-down.

descafeinar [1a] VT to decaffeinate; (*fig*) to dilute, water down.

descalabrado ADJ: **salir ~** to come out the loser (*de* in), come off badly.

descalabrar [1a] ① VT (a) (*romper*) to smash, damage; *persona* to hit, hurt, (*esp*) to hit on the head.
(b) (*fig*) to harm, damage, injure; to attack the character of.
② **descalabrarse** VR to hurt one's head, give o.s. a bang on the head.

descalabro NM (*revés*) blow, setback; (*desastre*) disaster, misfortune; (*daño*) damage; (*Mil*) defeat; ~ **electoral** electoral setback, disaster at the polls.

descalcificación NF (*Med*) lack of calcium, calcium deficiency.

descalificación NF discrediting; rejection, relegation to oblivion; dismissal; (*Dep*) disqualification; ~ **global** general rejection, downright condemnation.

descalificar [1g] VT to discredit; to write off, reject, relegate to oblivion; to dismiss (the views of); (*Dep*) to disqualify.

descalzar [1f] ①VT (**a**) *zapato* to take off.
(**b**) ~ **a uno** to take off sb's shoes (*etc*); **A no vale para ~ a B** A can't hold a candle to B.
(**c**) *rueda* to remove the chocks from.
(**d**) (*fig: minar*) to dig under, undermine.
② **descalzarse** VR (**a**) to take off one's shoes (*etc*); ~ **los guantes** to take off one's gloves.
(**b**) (*caballo*) to cast a shoe.

descalzo ADJ (**a**) (*con pies desnudos*) barefoot(ed); (*sin zapatos*) shoeless; (*sin medias*) stockingless; **estar ~, estar con los pies ~s** to be barefooted, have one's shoes off, have no shoes (*etc*) on; **ir ~** to go barefooted.
(**b**) (*Ecl*) discalced.
(**c**) (*fig*) destitute; **su padre le dejó ~** his father left him without a bean.

descamarse [1a] VR to flake off, scale off; (*Med*) to desquamate.

descambiar* [1b] VT to swap, change back; (*Com*) to exchange.

descambio NM swap, change back; (*Com*) exchange.

descaminado ADJ (**a**) **andar ~, ir ~** to be on the wrong road.
(**b**) (*fig*) mistaken; misguided; ill-advised; **ir ~** to be on the wrong track; **andar ~** to be mistaken in (*o* about); **en eso no andas muy ~** you're not far wrong there.

descaminar [1a] ①VT (**a**) *persona* to misdirect, give wrong directions to, put on the wrong road; (*fig*) to mislead, lead astray.
(**b**) *mercancías* to seize as contraband.
(**c**) (*LAm*) to hold up.
② **descaminarse** VR to get lost, go the wrong way; (*fig*) to go astray.

descamisado ①ADJ (*fig*) ragged, shabby; wretched.
② NM ragamuffin; down-and-out; poor devil, wretch; (*Argentina Pol*) Peronist.

descamisar [1a] VT (**a**) *persona* to strip the shirt off; *fruta* to peel. (**b**) (*fig*) to ruin; (*en el juego*) to fleece.

descampado NM open space, piece of empty ground; open field; **comer al ~** to eat in the open air; **vivir en ~** to live in open country; **se fue a vivir en ~** he went off to live in the wilds.

descansadero NM stopping place, resting place.

descansado ADJ (**a**) *persona* rested, refreshed. (**b**) *sitio etc* restful; *vida etc* tranquil, unworried, free from care.

descansapié NM pedal, footrest.

descansar [1a] ①VT (**a**) (*apoyar*) to rest, support, lean (*sobre* on).
(**b**) (*aliviar*) to rest; **esto descansa la vista más** this rests one's eyes better.
(**c**) (*ayudar*) to help, give a hand to.
(**d**) ~ **sus penas en uno** to tell one's troubles to sb, confide in sb about one's troubles.
② VI (**a**) (*persona*) to rest; to take a rest, have a break (*de* from); (*dormir*) to sleep, lie down; (*cadáver*) to lie, rest; **necesito ~ un rato** I need to rest a bit; **podemos ~ aquí** we can rest here; ~ **en paz** to rest in peace; **no descansé en todo el día** I didn't have a moment's rest all day; **¡descanse Vd!** don't worry!; **¡que Vd descanse!, ¡descanse bien!** sleep well!
(**b**) (*Agr*) to lie fallow.
(**c**) ~ **en** (*Arquit*) to rest on, be supported by.
(**d**) ~ **en** (*fig*) to rely on; to trust in; **el argumento descansa sobre los siguientes hechos** the argument is based on the following facts.
③ **descansarse** VR: ~ **en uno** to rely on sb, count on sb; to confide in sb.

descansillo NM (*Arquit*) landing.

descanso NM (**a**) (*gen*) rest; repose; (*alivio etc*) relief; (*período*) rest, break; ~ **maternal, ~ de maternidad** maternity leave; **tomarse unos días de ~** to take a few days' rest; **trabajar sin ~** to work without a break; **es un ~ saber que no estás solo** it's a relief to know you are not alone.
(**b**) (*Dep*) interval, half-time; (*Teat*) interval.
(**c**) (*Téc*) (*apoyo*) rest, support; (*banco*) bench; (*escuadra*) bracket; ~ **de cabeza** headrest.
(**d**) (*Arquit*) landing.

descañonar [1a] VT (**a**) *gallina* to pluck. (**b**) *cara* to shave against the grain; to shave close. (**c**) (*Naipes) to fleece, clean out*.

descapachar [1a] VT (*And*) *maíz* to husk.

descapiruzar [1f] VT (*And*) to rumple the hair of.

descapitalización NF under-capitalization.

descapitalizado ADJ undercapitalized.

descapotable ADJ, NM (*Aut*) convertible.

descapsulador NM bottle-opener.

descaradamente ADV shamelessly, brazenly; cheekily, saucily; blatantly.

descarado ADJ (*desvergonzado*) shameless, brazen, barefaced; (*insolente*) cheeky, saucy; (*patente*) blatant.

descararse [1a] VR to behave impudently, be insolent, be cheeky (*con* to); ~ **a pedir algo** to have the nerve to ask for sth.

descarburar [1a] VT to decarbonize.

descarga NF (**a**) (*Náut etc*) unloading; clearing; ~ **de aduana** customs clearance.
(**b**) (*Mil*) firing, discharge; ~ (*cerrada*) volley; **como una ~** suddenly, unexpectedly.
(**c**) (*Elec*) discharge.

descargadero NM wharf.

descargado ADJ empty, unloaded; *pila* flat.

descargador NM unloader; (*de puerto*) docker, stevedore.

descargar [1h] ①VT (**a**) *barco, carro etc* to unload; to empty; (*Inform*) to download.
(**b**) *cañón* to fire, discharge, shoot; to unload; ~ **un golpe en uno** to let fly a blow at sb, deal sb a blow; ~ **golpes sobre la mesa** to beat the table, rain blows on the table; ~ **un golpe contra la censura** to strike a blow against censorship.
(**c**) (*Elec*) to discharge; *pila* to flatten, run down, exhaust.
(**d**) *vientre* to evacuate.
(**e**) (*nube*) *granizo etc* to send down, let fall.
(**f**) *ira etc* to vent (*en, sobre* on).
(**g**) *conciencia* to ease, relieve; *corazón* to unburden.
(**h**) (*Com*) *letra* to take up.
(**i**) *persona* to relieve, release (*de una obligación* from an obligation); to free (*de una deuda* from a debt); (*Jur etc*) to clear, acquit (*de* of).
② VI (**a**) ~ **en** (*río*) to run into, flow into; (*calle*) to open into, come out into.
(**b**) (*Elec*) to discharge.
(**c**) (*tormenta*) to burst, break.
③ **descargarse** VR (**a**) (*gen*) to unburden o.s., disburden o.s.; ~ **de algo** to get rid of sth; ~ **con** (*o* **en**) **uno de algo** to unload sth on to sb.
(**b**) (*Jur etc*) to clear o.s., vindicate o.s. (*de* of).
(**c**) (*dimitir*) to resign.

descargo NM (**a**) (*descargue*) unloading; emptying.
(**b**) (*de deuda*) discharge.
(**c**) (*Com*) receipt, voucher.
(**d**) ~ **de una obligación** release from an obligation; ~ **de una acusación** acquittal on a charge.
(**e**) (*Jur: t ~s, pliego de ~s*) evidence, depositions (in favour of the defendant); answers, rebuttals; (*fig*) excuses, piece of special pleading; **testigo de ~** witness for the defence.

descargue NM unloading; emptying.

descarnado ADJ (*flaco*) thin, lean, scrawny; emaciated; (*cadavérico*) cadaverous; (*fig*) bare; *estilo, descripción* raw, harsh.

descarnador NM (*de dientes*) dental scraper; (*de uñas*) cuticle remover.

descarnar [1a] ①VT (**a**) *hueso* to remove the flesh from; *piel* to scrape the flesh from.
(**b**) (*fig*) to eat away, corrode, wear down.
② **descarnarse** VR to lose flesh, get thin.

descaro NM shamelessness, brazenness; cheek*, sauce*, nerve*; blatancy; **tuvo el ~ de decirme que ...** he had the nerve to tell me that ...; **¡qué ~!** what cheek!*, what a nerve!*

descarozado ADJ (*Cono Sur*) *fruta* dried.

descarriar [1c] ①VT (**a**) (*descaminar*) to misdirect, put on the wrong road.
(**b**) (*fig*) to lead astray; **ser una oveja descarriada** to be like a lost sheep.
(**c**) *animal* to separate from the herd, single out.
② **descarriarse** VR (**a**) (*persona*) to lose one's way; (*animal*) to stray, get separated (from the herd).
(**b**) (*fig*) to err, go astray.

descarrilamiento NM derailment.

descarrilar [1a] VI (*t* **descarrilarse** VR (*LAm*)) (**a**) (*Ferro*) to be derailed, run off the rails, jump the track.
(**b**) (*fig*) to get off the track, wander from the point.

descarrilo NM derailment.

descartable ADJ that can be done without, dispensable; (*Inform*) temporary.

▼ **descartar** [1a] ①VT (*gen*) to discard (*t Naipes*); (*poner a un lado*) to put aside, lay aside; (*rechazar*) to reject; *posibilidad etc* to rule out.
② **descartarse** VR (**a**) (*Naipes*) (*t ~ de*) to discard.
(**b**) ~ **de** to excuse o.s. from; to shun, shirk, evade.

descarte NM (**a**) (*Naipes*) discard. (**b**) (*acto*) discarding, rejection, ruling out; **por ~** by a process of elimination. (c) (*fig*) excuse; shirking, evasion.

descasar [1a] VT (a) to annul the marriage of. (b) (*fig*) (*separar*) to separate; (*desordenar*) to disarrange, upset the arrangement of.

descascar [1g] ☐ VT *fruta* to peel; *nuez, huevo* to shell; *árbol* to remove the bark from.

☐ **descascarse** VR (a) to smash to pieces, come apart. (b) (*) to bluster.

descascarar [1a] ☐ VT (a) *fruta* to peel; *nuez, huevo* to shell, take the shell off.

(b) (*And*) *animal* to flay, skin.

(c) (*And fig*) to dishonour.

☐ **descascararse** VR to peel (off), scale (off); to chip off.

descascarillar [1a] ☐ VT *vasija etc* to chip; *arroz* to husk.

☐ **descascarillarse** VR *vajilla* to get chipped; *pintura* to flake; **las paredes estaban descascarilladas** the paint had flaked off the walls.

descastado ADJ (a) (*intocable*) that has lost caste, untouchable; *palabra etc* improper. (b) (*enajenado*) alienated from one's family; (*frío*) cold, indifferent (to affection).

descaste NM culling.

descatalogado ADJ *libro* out-of-print, unlisted; *disco* unlisted; *producto* discontinued.

descaudalado ADJ penniless.

descelerar [1a] VI *etc* = **desacelerar** *etc.*

descendedero NM ramp.

descendencia NF (a) (*origen*) descent, origin. (b) (*personas*) offspring, descendants; **morir sin dejar ~** to die without issue, leave no children.

descendente ADJ (a) descending, downward; downward-sloping; *cantidad* diminishing; **tren ~** down train. (b) (*Inform*) top-down.

descender [2g] ☐ VT (a) (*bajar*) to lower, let down; *maleta etc* to get down, lift down, take down.

(b) *escalera etc* to go down, descend.

☐ VI (a) (*ir abajo*) to descend, come down, go down; (*de categoría*) to be demoted; (*Dep*) to be relegated.

(b) (*fiebre, nivel, temperatura etc*) to drop, fall, go down (**en un 5 por cien** by 5%).

(c) (*líquido*) to run, flow.

(d) (*cortina etc*) to hang.

(e) (*persona, fuerza*) to fail, get weak, decay; **~ de** (*o* **en**) **energía** to suffer a loss of energy.

(f) **~ a** (*fig*) to stoop to, lower o.s. to.

(g) **~ de** to descend from, be descended from; to be derived from; **~ de linaje de reyes** to come from a line of kings; **la tribu desciende de la región central** the tribe comes from the central region; the tribe originated in the central region; **de esa palabra descienden otras muchas** many other words derive from that one.

descendiente NMF descendant.

descendimiento NM descent; lowering; **el D~ de la Cruz** the Descent from the Cross.

descenso NM (a) (*acto*) descent; going down; (*de categoría*) demotion; (*de fiebre, temperatura etc*) drop, fall; (*de producción*) downturn; (*Dep en liga*) relegation; (*esquí*) downhill race; (*de calidad*) decline, falling-off; **las cifras han experimentado un brusco ~** the figures show a sharp fall; **hay un ~ de calidad** there is a falling-off in quality.

(b) (*Min etc*) collapse, subsidence.

(c) (*Med*) rupture; **~ del útero** prolapse, fallen womb.

(d) (*pendiente*) slope, drop, descent; **el ~ hacia el río** the descent to the river, the slope down to the river.

descentración NF maladjustment.

descentrado ADJ (a) (*lit*) off-centre.

(b) (*fig*) out of focus; wrongly adjusted, maladjusted; **parece que el problema está ~** the problem seems to be out of focus, it seems that the question has not been properly stated; **todavía está algo ~** he is still somewhat out of touch, he is still not properly adjusted (to the situation).

descentralización NF decentralization.

descentralizar [1f] VT to decentralize.

descentrar [1a] VT to decentre.

desceñir [3h *y* 31] VT to loosen; to undo, unfasten.

descepar [1a] VT (a) (*Agr*) to uproot, pull up by the roots. (b) (*fig*) to extirpate, eradicate.

descercar [1g] VT (a) (*Agr*) to remove the fence (*o* wall) round. (b) (*Mil*) *city* to relieve, raise the siege of.

descerco NM (*Mil*) relief.

descerebrado ADJ brainless, mindless.

descerrajar [1a] VT (a) *puerta etc* to force the lock of; *cerradura* to break open, force. (b) *disparo* to let off, fire (*a* at).

descervigar [1h] VT to break the neck of.

deschachar* [1a] VT (*CAm*) to sack*, fire*.

deschalar [1a] VT (*And, Cono Sur*) *maíz* to husk.

deschapar [1a] VT (*LAm*) *cerradura* to break.

descifrable ADJ decipherable.

descifrador(a) NM/F decipherer; decoder; **el ~ del misterio** the man who solved the mystery.

descifrar [1a] VT *escritura* to decipher, (manage to) read; *mensaje* to decode; *problema* to puzzle out, figure out; *misterio* to solve, crack.

descinchar [1a] VT *caballo* to loosen the girths of.

desclasado ADJ who has gone from one social class to another.

desclasificación NF (*Dep*) disqualification.

desclasificar [1g] VT (*Dep*) to disqualify.

desclavar [1a] VT to pull out the nails from, unnail.

descobijar [1a] VT to uncover, leave exposed.

descocado* ADJ = **descarado**; *chica* brazen, forward.

descocarse* [1g] VR = **descararse**.

descochollado ADJ (*Cono Sur*) (a) (*harapiento*) ragged, shabby. (b) (*malo*) wicked. (c) (*de mal genio*) ill-tempered.

descoco* NM = **descaro**.

descodificación NF decoding; (*TV*) unscrambling, descrambling.

descodificador NM decoder.

descodificar [1g] VT to decode; (*TV*) to unscramble, descramble.

descoger [2c] VT to spread out, unfold.

descojonación: NF: **¡(es la) ~!** it's the absolute bloody end!:.

descojonado: ADJ (a) (*cansado*) knackered*, (dead) beat*. (b) (*estropeado*) bust*, knackered*.

descojonante: ADJ (a) (*gracioso*) wildly funny. (b) (*impresionante*) immensely impressive.

descojonarse: [1a] VR (a) (*reír*) to die laughing. (b) (*matarse: t ~* **vivo**) to kill o.s., do o.s. in:.

descojono: NM: **fue un ~, ¡qué ~!** (*situación graciosa*) what a bloody riot!*; **¡esto es un ~!** (*desastre*) what a bloody shambles!*.

descolada NF (*Méx*) snub, rebuff.

descolar [1a] VT (a) *animal* to dock, cut the tail off. (b) (*CAm: despedir*) to fire, sack. (c) (*Méx: desairar*) to snub, slight.

descolgado, -a NM/F backslider.

descolgar [1h *y* 1l] ☐ VT (a) (*gen*) to take down, get down; (*desenganchar*) to unhook; *cuerda etc* to lower, let down; *teléfono* to pick up.

☐ **descolgarse** VR (a) (*bajar*) to let o.s. down (**con** by, **de** from), lower o.s.; to come down, descend, climb down; **~ por una pared** to climb down a wall; **quedar descolgado** (*fig*) to be left behind.

(b) (*fig: persona*) to turn up unexpectedly, drop by; (*Met*) to come on suddenly, set in unexpectedly.

(c) **~ con una cifra** to come up with a figure; **~ con una estupidez** to come out with a silly remark, blurt out sth silly.

descollante ADJ outstanding.

descollar [1l] VI to stand out, be outstanding; **descuella entre los demás** he stands out among the others; **la obra que más descuella de las suyas** his most outstanding work; **la iglesia descuella sobre los demás edificios** the church stands out above (*o* towers over) the other buildings.

descolocado ADJ *criado* out of a place; *objeto* misplaced; *cosa, lugar* untidy; **sentirse ~** to feel out of place.

descolocar [1g] VT to mess up.

descolón NM (*Méx*) snub, rebuff.

descolonización NF decolonization.

descolonizar [1f] VT to decolonize.

descoloramiento NM discolo(u)ration.

descolorar [1a] VT = **decolorar**.

descolorido ADJ (a) (*gen*) discoloured, faded; pale. (b) (*fig*) colourless.

descombrar [1a] VT to clear (of obstacles), disencumber.

descomedidamente ADV (a) (*excesivamente*) excessively. (b) (*groseramente*) rudely, insolently, disrespectfully.

descomedido ADJ (a) (*excesivo*) excessive, immoderate. (b) *persona* rude, insolent, disrespectful (*con* to, towards).

descomedimiento NM rudeness, insolence, disrespect.

descomedirse [31] VR to be rude, be disrespectful (*con* to, towards).

descompaginar [1a] VT to disarrange, disorganize, mess up.

descompasadamente ADV excessively, disproportionately.

descompasado ADJ excessive, disproportionate, out of all proportion; **a una hora descompasada** at an unearthly hour; **de tamaño ~** of disproportionate size, extra big.

descompasarse [1a] VR = **descomedirse**.

descompensar [1a] VT to unbalance.

descompletar [1a] VT (*LAm*) to make incomplete, impair the completeness of; *serie, conjunto* to break, ruin.

descomponer [2q] ☐ VT (a) (*gen*) to separate into its constituent parts; (*analizar*) to break down, split up; (*Quím*) to separate into its elements; *masa, unidad etc* to split up, break down; *argumento* to break down, analyse, reduce to a series of points; (*Mat*) to break down.

(b) *materia orgánica* to rot, decompose.

(c) (*Mec*) to break; to put out of order; to tamper with, mess up; *facciones* to distort; *estómago etc* to upset; **~ el peinado a una** to mess up sb's hair.

(d) *orden etc* to disarrange, disturb, upset; *calma* to ruffle, disturb; ~ **los planes de uno** to upset sb's plans, mess up sb's plans.

(e) *persona* to shake up, give a jolt to; to put out; to anger, provoke.

(f) *dos personas* to cause a rift between, set at odds.

2 descomponerse VR **(a)** *(pudrirse)* to rot, decompose.

(b) *(Mec)* to break down, get out of order, develop a fault; *(estómago)* to get upset; *(tiempo)* to break up, change for the worse; *(Cono Sur: vomitar)* to be sick, throw up; *(Cono Sur: llorar)* to burst into tears; ~ **el brazo** *(And)* to put one's arm out of joint.

(c) *(enojarse)* to lose one's temper, get worked up; ~ **con uno** to fall out with sb.

(d) se le descompuso la cara her face fell (*o* dropped).

descomponible ADJ separable, detachable.

descomposición NF **(a)** *(gen)* splitting up, breakdown; *(Quím)* decomposition; *(LAm Aut)* breakdown; ~ **estadística** statistical breakdown.

(b) *(putrefacción)* rotting, decomposition.

(c) ~ **de vientre** *(Med)* stomach upset, diarrhoea.

(d) *(fig)* discomposure.

descompostura NF **(a)** *(Mec etc)* breakdown, fault, trouble; bad working order; *(LAm Elec)* fault, failure; *(desorden)* disorder; *(desorganización)* disorganization; *(desaseo)* untidiness, slovenliness.

(b) *(fig: de cara)* discomposure.

(c) *(fig: descaro)* brazenness, forwardness.

(d) *(And: dislocación)* dislocation.

descompresión NF decompression.

descomprometido ADJ lacking in commitment, uncommitted.

descompuesto ADJ **(a)** *(Mec etc)* broken, out of order, faulty; *cara, facciones* twisted, distorted; *roca* loose; *sistema etc* disordered, disorganized, chaotic; *cuarto* untidy; *aspecto* slovenly; **estar** ~ *(esp LAm Aut)* to be broken down.

(b) *(fig: enojado)* angry; **ponerse** ~ to get angry, get worked up, lose one's composure.

(c) *(fig: descarado)* brazen, forward; rude.

(d) estar ~ *(LAm*: borracho)* to be tipsy.

descomunal ADJ huge, enormous, colossal.

desconcentración NF **(a)** *(Pol etc)* decentralization, breaking-up. **(b)** *(defecto)* lack of concentration.

desconcentrar [1a] **1** VT **(a)** *persona* to distract. **(b)** *industria etc* to decentralize, break up, distribute over a wider area.

2 desconcentrarse VR to get distracted.

desconceptuado ADJ discredited; not well thought-of, ill-reputed.

desconceptuar [1e] VT to discredit.

desconcertado ADJ: **estar** (*o* **quedar**) ~ *(fig)* to be disconcerted, be taken aback; to be bewildered.

desconcertador ADJ, **desconcertante** ADJ disconcerting, upsetting; embarrassing; baffling, bewildering, puzzling.

desconcertar [1j] **1** VT **(a)** *(Mec etc)* to put out of order, damage; *(Anat)* to dislocate; *orden* to disarrange, disturb; *plan* to upset, dislocate, throw out of gear.

(b) *persona (incomodar)* to disconcert, upset, put out; *(azorar)* to embarrass; *(problema etc)* to baffle, bewilder, puzzle.

2 desconcertarse VR **(a)** *(Mec etc)* to get out of order, develop a fault; *(Anat)* to get out of joint, be dislocated.

(b) *(persona)* to be disconcerted, be upset, be put out; to get embarrassed; to be bewildered; **siguió sin** ~ he went on quite unruffled; **esto basta para que se desconcierte el más sosegado** this would get even the calmest of people worked up.

desconchabar [1a] VT *(LAm)* to dislocate.

desconchado NM *(de pared)* place where plaster *(etc)* has broken away; *(de vasija)* chip.

desconchar [1a] **1** VT to strip off, peel off; to chip off.

2 desconcharse VR to peel off, flake off; to chip.

desconcierto NM **(a)** *(Mec etc)* disorder, trouble; *(daño)* damage; *(desarreglo)* disarrangement, disturbance, chaos.

(b) *(fig)* *(inquietud)* uneasiness; *(desorientación)* uncertainty; *(azoramiento)* embarrassment; *(perplejidad)* bewilderment; **contribuye al** ~ **de la juventud** it increases young people's bewilderment; **sembrar el** ~ **en el partido** to sow confusion in the party, create discord in the party; **hay un** ~ **fundamental** there is a basic disagreement.

desconectado ADJ **(a)** *(Elec)* disconnected, switched off; *(Inform)* off-line. **(b)** *persona:* **estar** ~ **de** *(sociedad, entorno)* to be cut off from; *(actualidad)* to be out of touch with.

desconectar [1a] **1** VT *(Mec)* to disconnect; to uncouple; *(Elec)* to disconnect; *radio, televisor* to switch off, turn off.

2 VI *(de una conversación)* to switch off.

desconfiado ADJ distrustful, suspicious *(de* of).

desconfianza NF distrust, mistrust, lack of confidence; **voto de** ~ vote of no confidence.

desconfiar [1c] VI to be distrustful; to lack confidence; ~ **de** to distrust, mistrust, suspect; to have no confidence in; **desconfío de ello**

I doubt it; **desconfíe de las imitaciones** *(Com)* beware of imitations; **desconfía de sus posibilidades** he has no faith in his potential; **desconfío de que llegue a tiempo** I doubt if he will get here in time, I cannot be sure that he will arrive in time.

desconformar [1a] VI *y* **desconformarse** VR **(a)** *(disentir)* to disagree, dissent.

(b) se desconforman they do not get on well together; they are not suited to each other.

desconforme ADJ = **disconforme**.

descongelación NF *(Aer)* de-icing; *(de salarios)* freeing, unfreezing.

descongelado NM defrosting.

descongelar [1a] VT *nevera (Culin)* to defrost; *(Aer)* to de-ice; *salarios* to free, unfreeze.

descongestión NF relief, relieving; **una política de** ~ a policy of relieving population pressure in the cities.

descongestionante NM decongestant.

descongestionar [1a] VT to relieve; *cabeza* to clear; *ciudad etc* to make less crowded, relieve the population pressure in; *calle* to relieve the traffic problems of, make less crowded.

desconocer [2d] VT **(a)** *(ignorar)* not to know, be ignorant of, be unfamiliar with; *(no estar enterado de)* to be unaware of; *(no recordar)* to fail to remember; **desconocen los principios fundamentales** they are ignorant of the basic principles; **no desconozco que ...** I am not unaware that ...

(b) *(no reconocer)* not to recognize; *(fingir no conocer)* to pretend not to know; *(no hacer caso a)* to ignore, disregard.

(c) *(rechazar)* to disown, repudiate; **pero el poeta desconoció la obra** but the poet disowned the work.

desconocido **1** ADJ **(a)** *(gen)* unknown, not known *(de, para* to); *(poco familiar)* strange, unfamiliar; *(no reconocido)* unrecognized; **lo** ~ the unknown; **por razones desconocidas** for reasons which are not known (to us *etc*); **el triunfo de un atleta** ~ the success of an unknown athlete.

(b) *(cambiado)* much changed; **está** ~ he is much altered, he is hardly recognizable.

(c) *(ingrato)* ungrateful.

2 NM, **desconocida** NF *(persona no conocida)* stranger; unknown person; *(recién llegado)* newcomer.

desconocimiento NM **(a)** *(ignorancia)* ignorance. **(b)** *(rechazo)* disregard, repudiation. **(c)** *(ingratitud)* ingratitude.

desconsideración NF inconsiderateness, thoughtlessness.

desconsideradamente ADV inconsiderately, thoughtlessly.

desconsiderado ADJ inconsiderate, thoughtless.

desconsoladamente ADV disconsolately; inconsolably.

desconsolado ADJ disconsolate; inconsolable; *cara* sad, woebegone.

desconsolador ADJ distressing, grievous.

desconsolar [1m] **1** VT to distress, grieve.

2 desconsolarse VR to be grieved; to despair, lose hope.

desconstrucción NF deconstruction.

desconsuelo NM affliction, distress, grief; sadness; despair; **con** ~ sadly, despairingly.

descontado ADJ: **por** ~ of course, naturally; **eso lo podemos dar por** ~ we can take that for granted, we can assume that; we can rely on that; **por** ~ **que** *(como conj)* of course ...

descontaminación NF decontamination.

descontaminar [1a] VT to decontaminate.

descontar [1m] VT **(a)** *(deducir)* to take away; *(Com)* to discount, deduct. **(b)** *(dar por sentado)* to discount; to assume, take for granted. **(c)** *(contar atrás)* to count down.

descontentadizo ADJ hard to please; restless, unsettled.

descontentar [1a] VT to displease.

descontento **1** ADJ dissatisfied, discontented *(de* with); disgruntled *(de* about, at); **estar** ~ **de** to be dissatisfied with, be unhappy about.

2 NM **(a)** *(insatisfacción)* dissatisfaction, displeasure; disgruntlement. **(b)** *(Pol etc)* discontent, unrest; ~ **social** social unrest; **hay mucho** ~ there is a lot of unrest.

3 NM, **descontenta** NF *(Méx)* malcontent.

descontextualización NF decontextualization.

descontextualizar [1f] VT to decontextualize, take out of context.

descontinuación NF discontinuation.

descontinuar [1e] VT to discontinue.

descontrol NM decontrol; lack of control, loss of control.

descontroladamente ADV in an uncontrolled way.

descontrolado ADJ **(a)** *(desordenado)* wild, undisciplined, out of control; **desarrollo** ~ uncontrolled development; **elementos** ~s wild elements, *(Pol)* rebellious factions. **(b)** *(LAm: perturbado)* upset, irritated.

descontrolarse [1a] VR **(a)** *(perder control)* to lose control, get out of control, go wild. **(b)** *(*: enojarse)* to blow one's top*, go up the wall*.

desconvenir [3s] VI **(a)** *(personas)* to disagree *(con* with).

(b) *(no corresponder)* to be incongruous; not to fit, not match; *(diferir)* to differ *(con* from).

(c) *(no convenir)* to be inconvenient; to be unsuitable.

desconvocación NF calling-off, cancellation.
desconvocar [1g] VT *huelga, reunión* to call off, cancel.
desconvocatoria NF calling-off, (notice of) cancellation.
descoordinación NF lack of coordination; disorganization.
descoque NM = descaro.
descorazonador ADJ discouraging, disheartening.
descorazonamiento NM discouragement; dejection, depression.
descorazonar [1a] ① VT to discourage, dishearten.
  ② **descorazonarse** VR to get discouraged, lose heart.
descorbatado ADJ tieless.
descorchador NM (a) (*persona*) bark stripper. (b) (*sacacorchos*) corkscrew.
descorchar [1a] VT (a) *árbol* to remove the bark from; to strip. (b) *botella* to uncork, draw the cork of, open. (c) *arca etc* to force, break open.
descorche NM uncorking, opening (of a bottle).
descornar [1m] ① VT to de-horn, poll.
  ② **descornarse** VR (*fig*) (*trabajar*) to slog away, work like a slave; (*pensar*) to rack one's brains; (*: caer*) to have a nasty fall, break one's head.
descorrer [2a] VT *cortina, cerrojo* to draw back.
descortés ADJ discourteous, rude, impolite.
descortesía NF discourtesy, rudeness, impoliteness.
descortésmente ADV discourteously, rudely, impolitely.
descortezar [1f] VT (a) *árbol* to strip the bark from, remove the bark of; *pan* to cut the crust off; *fruta etc* to peel.
  (b) (*fig*) to polish up a bit, knock the corners off.
descoser [2a] ① VT (a) (*Cos*) *puntos* to unstitch, unpick; (*romper*) to rip, tear.
  (b) (*separar*) to separate, part; V **labio**.
  ② **descoserse** VR (a) (*Cos*) to come apart (at the seam), burst, tear.
  (b) (*: revelar un secreto*) to blurt out a secret, let the cat out of the bag.
  (c) (*: ventosear*) to fart*.
  (d) ~ **de risa** to split one's sides with laughing, die laughing.
descosido ① ADJ (a) (*Cos*) unstitched, torn; (*raído*) shabby.
  (b) (*fig*) *narración etc* disconnected, disjointed, chaotic.
  (c) *persona, habla etc* wild, immoderate; (*hablador*) talkative; (*indiscreto*) big-mouthed*, indiscreet, blabbing.
  ② NM (a) (*Cos*) open seam; (*rasgón*) rip, tear.
  (b) **obrar como un** ~ to act wildly; **beber como un** ~ to drink an awful lot; **comer como un** ~ to eat to excess, stuff o.s.; **gastar como un** ~ to spend money wildly; **estudiar** (*etc*) **como un** ~ to study (*etc*) like mad.
descotado ADJ (*LAm*) = escotado.
descoyuntado ADJ (a) (*Anat*) dislocated, out of joint. (b) *narración etc* incoherent, disjointed, chaotic.
descoyuntar [1a] ① VT (a) (*Anat*) to dislocate, put out of joint.
  (b) (*fig*) *persona* (*cansar*) to tire out; (*molestar*) to bother; to weary, annoy.
  (c) *hechos etc* to twist, force the sense of, adapt improperly.
  ② **descoyuntarse** VR (a) (*Anat*) ~ **un hueso** to put a bone out of joint; **los huesos se descoyuntaron** the bones became dislocated.
  (b) ~ **de risa** to split one's sides with laughing, die laughing; ~ **a cortesías** to overdo the courtesies, be exaggeratedly polite.
descrecer [2d] VI to decrease.
descrédito NM discredit; disrepute; **caer en** ~ to fall into disrepute; **ir en** ~ **de** to be to the discredit of, damage the reputation of.
descreencia NF (*esp LAm*) unbelief.
descreer [2e] ① VT to disbelieve; to place no faith in.
  ② VI (*Rel*) to lose one's faith.
descreído ① ADJ unbelieving; (*pey: ateo*) godless.
  ② NM, **descreída** NF unbeliever.
descreimiento NM unbelief.
descremado ADJ *leche* skimmed, low-fat.
descremar [1a] VT *leche* to skim.
describir [3a; PTP **descrito**] VT to describe.
descripción NF description; **supera a toda** ~ it is beyond description, it is indescribable.
descriptible ADJ describable.
descriptivo ADJ descriptive.
descrismar [1a] ① VT: ~ **a uno** to bash sb on the head*; **¡o eso o te descrismo!** either that or I'll bash you!*.
  ② **descrismarse** VR (a) (*trabajar*) to slave away; (*pensar*) to rack one's brains.
  (b) (*enojarse*) to blow one's top*.
descrispar [1a] VT to take the tension out of.
descrito PTP *de* **describir**; **no es para** ~ it is indescribable, it beggars description.
descruzar [1f] VT *piernas* to uncross.
descuadre NM error (*on balance sheet*).
descuajar [1a] VT (a) *masa, sólido* to melt, dissolve.

(b) (*Bot*) to uproot, pull up by the root; *objeto* to pull out, tear from its place.
  (c) (*fig: extirpar*) to eradicate.
  (d) (*fig: desanimar*) to dishearten.
descuajaringado* ADJ (*LAm*), **descuajeringado*** ADJ (*LAm*) (*destartalado*) broken-down; dilapidated; (*desaliñado*) scruffy, shabby.
descuajaringante* ADJ side-splitting.
descuajaringar* [1a] ① VT (*And*) to smash to bits (*o* pieces).
  ② **descuajaringarse** VR (a) (*Anat*) to come apart; (*cansarse*) to become exhausted; ~ **de risa** to split one's sides with laughing, die laughing; **es para** ~ it's enough to make you die laughing.
  (b) (*LAm: deshacerse*) to fall to bits.
descuartizamiento NM (a) (*de animal*) carving up, cutting up. (b) (*Hist*) quartering.
descuartizar [1f] VT (a) *animal* to carve up, cut up. (b) *persona* (*Hist*) to quarter; (*fig*) to tear apart; **ni que me descuarticen** not even if they tear me apart.
descubierta NF (a) (*Mil*) reconnoitring, patrolling. (b) **a la** ~ openly; in the open.
descubierto ① PTP *de* **descubrir**.
  ② ADJ (a) *situación* open, exposed; (*Mil*) under fire; *cuerpo* bare, uncovered; *cabeza* bare; *persona* bareheaded, hatless; *coche* open; *campo* open, bare, treeless.
  (b) **al** ~ in the open; exposed; in full view; **poner algo al** ~ to lay sth bare, expose sth to view; **quedar al** ~ to be exposed; to be manifest, be obvious.
  ③ NM (*Com: en cuenta*) deficit; (*saldo deudor*) overdraft; *empréstito etc* unbacked; **a** ~, **al** ~ short; **vender al** ~ to sell short; **estar en** ~ to be overdrawn; **girar en** ~ to overdraw.
descubretalentos NMF INVAR = cazatalentos.
descubridero NM look-out post.
descubridor ① NM (*Mil*) scout.
  ② NM, **descubridora** NF discoverer.
descubrimiento NM discovery; detection; disclosure, revelation; unveiling.
descubrir [3a; PTP **descubierto**] ① VT (a) *país, remedio etc* to discover; *criminal, fraude etc* to find, detect, spot; (*revelar*) to bring to light; to unearth, uncover; *petróleo etc* to find, strike; *solución etc* to discover, ascertain, learn.
  (b) (*divisar*) to see, make out, glimpse; **apenas lo descubría entre las nubes** I could just see it among the clouds.
  (c) *estatua, placa etc* to unveil.
  (d) (*poner al descubierto*) to expose to view; (*revelar*) to show, reveal, disclose; (*Naipes*) to lay down; ~ **el estómago** to uncover one's stomach, bare one's stomach; ~ **la cabeza** to bare one's head; ~ **sus intenciones** to reveal one's intentions; ~ **su pecho a uno** to open one's heart to sb; **le descubrió su escritura** his writing gave him away, his writing betrayed him; **fue la criada la que les descubrió a la policía** it was the servant who gave them away to the police.
  ② **descubrirse** VR (a) (*mostrarse*) to reveal o.s., show o.s.; to disclose one's whereabouts; (*verse*) to come into sight.
  (b) (*quitarse el sombrero*) to take off one's hat; (*al saludar*) to raise one's hat (in greeting).
  (c) ~ **a uno**, ~ **con uno** to confess to sb, pour one's heart out to sb.
  (d) (*salir a luz*) to come out, come to light.
descuelgue NM removal, taking out; exception; opting out.
descuento NM discount; rebate, reduction; **a** ~ below par; **al** ~, **con** ~ a discount; ~ **por pago al contado** discount for cash payment; ~ **por no declaración de siniestro** no claims bonus.
descuerar [1a] VT (*Cono Sur*) (a) (*desollar*) to flay, skin. (b) (*fig: infamar*) to defame; (*) to tear to pieces, tick off*.
descuernar [1a] VT (*And, CAm, Carib*) to de-horn.
descueve* ADJ (*Cono Sur*) great*, fantastic*.
descuidadamente ADV (a) (*gen*) carelessly; (*negligentemente*) slackly, negligently; forgetfully. (b) (*desaliñadamente*) untidily; in a slovenly way.
descuidado ADJ (a) (*sin cuidado*) careless; (*negligente*) slack, negligent; (*olvidadizo*) forgetful.
  (b) *aspecto etc* untidy, slovenly; unkempt.
  (c) (*desprevenido*) unprepared; off guard; **coger** (*o* **pillar** *etc*) **a uno** ~ to catch sb off his guard.
  (d) (*tranquilo*) easy in one's mind, without worries; nonchalant, carefree; **puedes estar** ~ you needn't worry.
  (e) (*abandonado*) neglected; **con aspecto de niños** ~**s** with the look of neglected children; **tener algo** ~ to neglect sth.
descuidar [1a] ① VT *deber etc* to neglect; *consejo* to disregard; (*olvidar*) to overlook; **ha descuidado mucho su negocio** he has neglected his business a lot.
  ② VI *y* **descuidarse** VR (a) (*no hacer caso*) to be careless, be negligent; to get careless; (*sentirse seguro*) to feel safe, drop one's guard; **en cuanto me descuide él me lo roba** the moment I drop my guard (*o* cease to watch out) he'll steal it from me; **a poco que te**

descuides te cobran el doble you've got to watch them all the time or they'll charge you double; **a poco que te descuides ya no está** before you know where you are it's gone.
(b) (*no preocuparse*) not to worry; **¡descuida!** don't worry!, it's all right!, you can forget about that!; **~se de algo** not to bother about sth; **~se de hacer algo** not to bother to do sth, neglect to do sth.
(c) (*abandonarse*) to let o.s. go, stop taking care of o.s.

descuidero, -a NM/F sneak thief.

descuido NM (a) (*gen*) carelessness; slackness; negligence; forgetfulness; **al ~** nonchalantly; **al menor ~** if your (*etc*) attention wanders for a moment; **con ~** thoughtlessly, without thinking.
(b) (*desaseo*) untidiness, slovenliness.
(c) (*un ~*) oversight; mistake, slip; **en un ~** (*LAm*) when least expected; **por ~** by an oversight, inadvertently.

desculpabilizar [1f] VT to exonerate, free from blame.

desculturización NF cultural impoverishment.

desde 1 PREP (a) (*lugar etc*) from; **~ Burgos hay 30 km** it's 30 km from Burgos; **~ abajo** from below; **~ arriba** from (up) above; **~ lejos** from afar, from a long way off; **~ A hasta M** from A to M.
(b) (*tiempo*) from; since; **~ ahora** from now on; **~ entonces** since then; **~ el siglo XV para acá** from the 15th century onward; **~ 1960 no existe** it ceased to exist in 1960, it went out of existence in 1960; **~ el martes** since Tuesday, after Tuesday; **~ el 4 hasta el 16** from the 4th to the 16th; **llueve ~ hace 3 días** it's been raining for 3 days; **~ hace 2 años no le vemos** we haven't seen him for 2 years, we haven't seen him these last 2 years; **¿~ cuándo es esto así?** how long has it been like this?
(c) **~ niño** since childhood, since I (*etc*) was a child.
2 **~ que** CONJ since; **~ que llovió** since it rained; **~ que puedo recordar** ever since I can remember, (for) as long as I can remember.

┌─ DESDE ─────────────────── *ver también la entrada* ─┐

Expresiones temporales

En expresiones temporales, *desde* puede traducirse por *since, from* o, en combinación con *hace/hacía* por *for*.

- *Desde (que)* se traduce por *since* siempre que se especifique a partir de cuándo comenzó una acción o un estado que sigue desarrollándose en el presente o en el momento en que se habla:

  Llevo aquí de vacaciones desde el viernes
  I have been here on holiday since Friday
  No come mejillones desde que sufrió aquella intoxicación alimenticia
  He hasn't eaten mussels since he had that bout of food poisoning
  Dijo que no la había visto desde la guerra
  He said he hadn't seen her since the war

  ! Hay que tener en cuenta que en casos como éstos cuando se trata de algo que comienza en el pasado y sigue en el presente, el inglés hace uso del *pretérito perfecto* (en sus formas simple o progresiva).

- Traducimos *desde* por *from* cuando *desde* simplemente indica el momento en el que empezó la acción cuando la oración indica el final de la acción o se implica, de algún modo, que ésta ya ha terminado:

  Y desde aquel día el rey no volvió a hablar del asunto
  And from that day on(wards), the king never spoke about the subject again

- La construcción *desde … hasta* se traduce por *from … until* o por *from … to*:

  Trabajamos desde las nueve de la mañana hasta las cinco de la tarde
  We work from nine in the morning until o to five in the afternoon
  Tendrás que pagar el alquiler desde julio hasta octubre
  You will have to pay rent from July until o to October

- *Desde hace* y *desde hacía* se traducen por *for* ya que van seguidos de una cantidad de tiempo:

  Estoy esperando desde hace más de una hora
  I have been waiting for over an hour
  No se había sentido tan feliz desde hacía años
  He hadn't felt so happy for years

- En oraciones interrogativas, *desde cuándo* se traduce por *how long*. En este tipo de preguntas, el inglés utiliza el pretérito perfecto para referirse a algo que empezó en el pasado y continúa en el presente:

  ¿Desde cuándo os conocéis?
  How long have you known each other?

  Para otros usos y ejemplos ver la entrada.

└──┘

desdecir [3p] 1 VI: **~ de (a)** (*ser indigno de*) to be unworthy of, be below the standard set by; (*no convenir a*) to be unbecoming to; **desdice de su patria** he is unworthy of his country; **esta novela no**

desdice de las otras this novel is well up to the standard of the others, this novel is not inferior to the others.
(b) (*no ir bien con*) to clash with, not match, not suit; **la corbata desdice del traje** the tie does not go with the suit.
2 **desdecirse** VR to retract, withdraw; to go back on what one has said; **~ de algo** to go back on sth, take back sth one has said; **~ de una promesa** to go back on a promise.

desdén NM scorn, disdain; **al ~** carelessly, nonchalantly.

desdentado ADJ toothless.

desdeñable ADJ contemptible; **una cantidad nada ~** a far from negligible amount.

desdeñar [1a] 1 VT to scorn, disdain; to turn up one's nose at; to despise.
2 **desdeñarse** VR: **~ de** + *infin* to scorn to + *infin*, not deign to + *infin*.

desdeñosamente ADV scornfully, disdainfully; contemptuously.

desdeñoso ADJ scornful, disdainful; contemptuous.

desdibujado ADJ *contorno etc* blurred; (*nada claro*) unclear; (*descolorado*) faded.

desdibujar [1a] 1 VT to blur (the outlines of).
2 **desdibujarse** VR to blur, get blurred, fade (away); **el recuerdo se ha desdibujado** the memory has become blurred.

desdicha NF (a) (*gen*) unhappiness, wretchedness; misfortune; misery. (b) (*una ~*) misfortune, calamity. (c) (*: persona etc inútil*) dead loss.

desdichadamente ADV unhappily; unluckily, unfortunately.

desdichado 1 ADJ (a) (*infeliz*) unhappy; (*desgraciado*) unlucky; unfortunate; wretched; **¡qué ~ soy!** how wretched I am!
(b) (*aciago*) unlucky, ill-fated; **fue un día ~** it was an unlucky day.
2 NM, **desdichada** NF poor devil, wretch.

desdicho PTP *de* **desdecir**.

desdinerar [1a] 1 VT to impoverish.
2 **desdinerarse**[*] VR to cough up[*], fork out[*].

desdoblado ADJ (*fig*) *personalidad* split; *carretera* two-lane.

desdoblamiento NM (a) (*de carreteras*) widening. (b) (*Escol: de grupos*) breaking down, reduction. (c) (*explicación*) explanation, clarification. (d) **~ de la personalidad** split personality.

desdoblar [1a] 1 VT (a) (*desplegar*) to unfold, spread out; *alambre etc* to untwist, straighten; (*desmontar*) to take apart.
(b) (*Quím*) to break down (*en* into).
(c) (*fig*) to double, divide, make two of; to split; *carretera* to widen; **~ un cargo** to split the functions of a post.
(d) *tema* to expand (up)on, explain.
2 **desdoblarse** VR (a) to divide, split into two.
(b) **~ sobre un tema** to expand upon a topic.

desdoble NM (*Fin*) reorganization of capital.

desdorar [1a] VT to tarnish (*t fig*).

desdoro NM (*fig*) blot, blemish, stigma, dishonour; **consideran un ~ trabajar** they think it dishonourable to work; **es un ~ para todos** it is a blot on us all; **hablar en ~ de uno** to speak disparagingly of sb, discredit sb by what one says.

desdramatizar [1f] VT to take the drama out of; to lower the tension of; *crisis* to defuse.

deseabilidad NF desirability.

deseable ADJ desirable.

▼ **desear** [1a] VT to want, desire, wish (for); **os deseo toda clase de éxito** I wish you every success; **¿qué desea la señora?** (*Com etc*) what can I do for you, madam?; **desearía más tiempo** I should like more time; **estoy deseando que esto termine** I wish this would end; **~ + *infin*** to want to + *infin*, wish to + *infin*; V **dejar.**

desecación NF desiccation; draining.

desecado ADJ *fruta etc* dried.

desecar [1g] 1 VT (*gen*) to dry up, desiccate; *estanque, terreno* to drain.
2 **desecarse** VR to dry up.

desecha NF (*And*) = **desecho.**

desechable ADJ disposable, throwaway; **la oferta no es ~** the offer is not to be lightly turned down; **envases ~s** non-returnable empties; **variable ~** temporary variable.

desechar [1a] VT (a) *basura* to throw out; *objeto inútil* to scrap, get rid of, jettison; *ropa* to cast off.
(b) *consejo, miedo, escrúpulo* to cast aside; *petición, oferta* to reject; *idea, plan* to drop, discard.
(c) (*subestimar*) to underrate, underestimate; (*menospreciar*) to think little of.
(d) (*censurar*) to censure, reprove.
(e) *llave* to turn.

desecho NM (a) (*t ~s: residuo*) residue; (*basura*) waste, rubbish; (*hierro etc*) scrap, junk; (*carne*) offal; (*barcia*) chaff; **~ de hierro, hierro de ~** scrap iron; **~s radiactivos** radioactive waste; **producto de ~** waste product; **vestidos de ~** cast-off clothing.
(b) **el ~ de la sociedad** the scum of society, the dregs of society.
(c) **ese tío es un ~[*]** that fellow is a disaster, that chap is a dead

loss.

(d) (*desprecio*) contempt, scorn; low opinion.

(e) (*LAm*) (*atajo*) short cut; (*desvío*) detour; (*sendero*) path, temporary road.

desegregación NF desegregation.

desegregar [1h] VT to desegregate.

desellar [1a] VT to unseal, open.

desembalaje NM unpacking.

desembalar [1a] VT to unpack.

desembanastar [1a] ① VT **(a)** (*sacar*) to unpack; to take out (of a basket); (*) *espada* to draw. **(b)** (*fig*) *secreto* to blurt out.

② **desembanastarse** VR **(a)** (*animal*) to break out.

(b) (*bajar*) to alight.

desembarazado ADJ **(a)** *camino etc* clear, free, open; (*sin carga*) unburdened, light. **(b)** (*fig*) free and easy, free of commitments; nonchalant; ~ **de trabas** free, unrestrained.

desembarazar [1f] ① VT **(a)** *camino etc* to clear, free (*de* of); ~ **un cuarto de trastos** to clear a room of furniture.

(b) *lugar, piso* to vacate, leave free, leave empty.

(c) ~ **a uno de algo** to rid sb of sth.

(d) (*And, Carib, Cono Sur* ††: *dar a luz a*) to give birth to.

② **desembarazarse** VR: ~ **de algo** to get rid of sth, free o.s. of sth.

desembarazo NM **(a)** (*acto*) clearing, freeing, disencumbrance; unburdening.

(b) (*And, Carib, Cono Sur: parto*) birth, delivery.

(c) (*desenfado*) freedom; (*naturalidad*) ease, naturalness; (*libertad*) lack of restraint; **hablar con** ~ to talk easily, talk freely.

desembarcadero NM quay, landing stage, pier.

desembarcar [1g] ① VT *personas* to land, put ashore; *mercancías* to land, unload.

② VI **y desembarcarse** VR **(a)** (*Náut*) to land, go ashore, disembark; (*Aer*) to leave, disembark.

(b) (*esp LAm*: *bajar*) to alight (*de* from), get out (*de* of).

(c) **estar para** ~* to be about to give birth.

desembarco NM (*Arquit, Náut*) landing.

desembargar [1h] VT to free; (*Jur*) to remove the embargo on, remove the impediments from.

desembarque NM landing; unloading.

desembarrancar [1g] VT *barco* to refloat, get off.

desembarrar [1a] VT to clear of mud, remove the silt from.

desembaular [1a] VT **(a)** *equipaje* to unpack; to take out, get out (of a trunk); (*fig*) to empty. **(b)** (*fig*) to unburden o.s. of.

desembocadero NM, **desembocadura** NF (*gen*) outlet, exit; (*de río*) mouth; (*de alcantarilla*) outfall; (*de calle*) opening, end.

desembocar [1a] VI: ~ **en (a)** (*río*) to flow into, run into, empty into; (*calle*) to meet, join, run into, lead into.

(b) (*fig*) to end in, result in, produce; **esto desembocó en una tragedia** this ended in tragedy, this led to tragedy.

desembolsar [1a] VT (*pagar*) to pay out; (*gastar*) to lay out.

desembolso NM payment; disbursement; outlay, expenditure; ~ **de capital** capital outlay; ~ **inicial** deposit, down payment; **cubrir ~s** to cover expenses.

desembozar [1f] VT to unmask (*t fig*), uncover.

desembragar [1h] ① VT (*Mec*) to disengage, disconnect; *embrague* to release, let out.

② VI (*Aut*) to declutch, let out the clutch.

desembrague NM disengagement; (*Aut*: *acto*) declutching; (*pieza*) clutch release.

desembravecer [2d] ① VT to tame; (*fig*) to calm, pacify.

② **desembravecerse** VR to calm down.

desembriagar [1h] ① VT to sober up.

② **desembriagarse** VR to sober up.

desembrollar [1a] VT to unravel, disentangle.

desembuchar [1a] ① VT to disgorge; (*fig*) to tell, reveal, let out.

② VI (*fig*) to reveal a secret, spill the beans*; **¡desembucha!** out with it!

③ **desembucharse** VR (*Cono Sur*) to be sick.

desemejante ADJ dissimilar, unlike; **A es** ~ **de B** A is unlike B, A is different from B.

desemejanza NF dissimilarity.

desemejar [1a] ① VT to alter (the appearance of), change (for the worse); to disfigure.

② VI to be dissimilar, look different, not look alike.

desempacar [1g] VT to unpack.

desempacharse [1a] VR **(a)** **se desempachó** (*Med*) he got over his sick feeling; his stomach settled down (after its upset).

(b) (*fig*) to cease to feel shy, stop feeling awkward.

desempacho NM ease, confidence; unconcern; (*pey*) forwardness.

desempadronarse [1a] VR (*Méx*) to do o.s. in*, commit suicide.

desempantanar VT to clear up, resolve.

desempañador NM (*Aut*) demister.

desempañar [1a] VT *cristal* to clean, demist.

desempapelar [1a] VT *paquete* to unwrap; *pared* to remove (o strip) the (wall)paper from.

desempaquetar [1a] VT to unpack, unwrap.

desempatar [1a] VI to break a tie; **volvieron a jugar para** ~ they held a play-off (to resolve the earlier tie).

desempate NM (*Fútbol etc*) play-off (to resolve an earlier tie), decider; (*Tenis*) tie break(er); ~ **a penaltis** penalty shoot-out.

desempedrar [1j] VT *calle* to take up the paving stones of; **ir desempedrando la calle** (*fig*) to dash along the street.

desempeñar [1a] ① VT **(a)** *propiedad empeñada* to redeem, recover, get out of pawn.

(b) ~ **a uno** to get sb out of debt, pay sb's debts; (*fig*) to get sb out of a jam.

(c) *cargo* to hold, fill, occupy; *deber, función* to perform, discharge; (*Teat y fig*) *papel* to play.

② **desempeñarse** VR **(a)** (*Fin*) to get out of debt; (*fig*) to get o.s. out of a jam.

(b) ~ **como** (*LAm*) to act as, play as.

desempeño NM **(a)** (*de lo empeñado*) redeeming, redemption.

(b) (*de deudas*) payment.

(c) (*cargo*) occupation; performance, discharge; (*Teat y fig*) performance, acting, showing; **un** ~ **meritorio** a worthy performance; **una mujer de mucho** ~ a most active and able woman.

desempleada NF unemployed woman.

desempleado ① ADJ unemployed, out of work.

② NM unemployed man.

desempleo NM **(a)** unemployment. **(b)** (*pago*) unemployment benefit; **cobrar el** ~ to draw unemployment benefit.

desempolvar [1a] VT to dust, remove the dust from.

desencadenamiento NM (*fig*) unleashing; bursting; ~ **de hostilidades** outbreak of hostilities.

desencadenante ① ADJ: **los factores ~s del accidente** the factors which caused (o contributed to, triggered off) the accident.

② NM cause, trigger.

desencadenar [1a] ① VT **(a)** (*quitar las cadenas de*) to unchain; *perro etc* to unleash, let loose.

(b) (*fig*) to unleash; to cause, start, set off.

② **desencadenarse** VR **(a)** (*soltarse*) to break loose, free o.s.

(b) (*fig*: *tormenta etc*) to burst; (*guerra*) to break out; **se desencadenaron los aplausos** a storm of clapping broke out; **se desencadenó una violenta reacción** a violent reaction was produced.

desencajado ADJ *cara* twisted, contorted; *ojos* wild.

desencajar [1a] ① VT **(a)** *hueso* to throw out of joint; (*Anat*) to dislocate.

(b) (*Mec*) to disconnect, disengage, put out of gear.

② **desencajarse** VR (*cara*) to become distorted (with fear); (*ojos*) to look wild.

desencajonar [1a] VT to unpack.

desencallar [1a] VT *barco* to refloat, get off.

desencaminado ADJ headed in the wrong direction, misguided.

desencantar [1a] VT to disillusion, disenchant.

desencanto NM disillusion(ment), disenchantment.

desencapotarse [1a] VR *cielo* to clear (up).

desenchufar [1a] ① VT to disconnect, unplug.

② **desenchufarse*** VR (*hum*) to relax, unwind, switch off.

desencoger [2c] ① VT (*extender*) to spread out; (*alisar*) to smooth out, straighten out.

② **desencogerse** VR (*fig*) to lose one's timidity.

desencolarse [1a] VR to come unstuck.

desenconar [1a] ① VT **(a)** *inflamación* to reduce.

(b) (*fig*) to calm down, soothe.

② **desenconarse** VR **(a)** (*inflamación*) to grow less, abate.

(b) (*fig*: *odio*) to die down, abate; (*persona*) to calm down.

desencontrarse [1n] VR (*grupo etc*) to become separated, get split up; to fail to meet up.

desencorvar [1a] VT to unbend, straighten (out).

desencuadernar [1a] ① VT to unbind.

② **desencuadernarse** VR to come unbound.

desencuadrado ADJ (*Fot*) off centre.

desencuentro NM failure to meet up; (*fig*) mix-up.

desendeudar [1a] VI (*LAm*) to pay one's debts, get out of the red.

desenfadaderas NFPL: **tener buenas** ~ to be unflappable, be slow to anger; to be good at getting out of jams.

desenfadado ADJ **(a)** *aire, carácter etc* free, uninhibited; (*despreocupado*) free-and-easy; carefree; unabashed; (*desenvuelto*) self-confident; (*pey*) forward, disrespectful; *ropa etc* casual, unconventional.

(b) *espacio* free, unencumbered; ample.

desenfadar [1a] ① VT to pacify, calm down.

② **desenfadarse** VR to calm down.

desenfado NM freedom, lack of inhibition; free-and-easy manner;

self-confidence; (*pey*) forwardness, disrespect.

desenfocado ADJ out of focus; (*intencionado*) in soft focus.

desenfocar [1g] ① VT (*Fot*) imagen to blur; *instrumento* to put out of focus.
② **desenfocarse** VR (*Fot*) to go out of focus.

desenfoque NM lack of focus, state of being out of focus; (*intencionado*) soft focus.

desenfrenadamente ADV wildly, in an uncontrolled way; immoderately; licentiously.

desenfrenado ADJ (*descontrolado*) wild, uncontrolled; (*excesivo*) immoderate; *pasión etc* unbridled, licentious.

desenfrenarse [1a] VR (a) (*persona etc*) to give free rein to one's passions, let one's feelings run wild, lose all self-control; (*multitud*) to run riot, rampage.
(b) (*tormenta*) to burst; (*viento*) to rage.

desenfreno NM wildness; lack of self-control; lack of moderation; licentiousness.

desenfundar* [1a] VI to flash*, expose o.s.

desenganchar [1a] ① VT (*gen*) to unhook, undo, unfasten; (*Ferro*) to uncouple; (*Mec*) to disengage; *caballo* to unhitch.
② **desengancharse*** VR to come off drugs, free o.s. from drug addiction; ~ **de** hábito to give up, kick*.

desengañado ADJ (a) (*decepcionado*) disillusioned. (b) (*And, Cono Sur*: *feo*) terribly ugly.

desengañar [1a] ① VT (*desilusionar*) to disillusion; (*decepcionar*) to disappoint; (*hacer ver claro*) to disabuse (*de* about, of); **es mejor no ~la** it is best not to disillusion her; it is best not to destroy her hopes.
② **desengañarse** VR (a) (*desilusionarse*) to become disillusioned (*de* about); (*decepcionarse*) to be disappointed.
(b) (*ver claro*) to see the light, come down to earth, see things as they really are; **¡desengáñate!** don't you believe it!, don't go deceiving yourself!; make no mistake!

desengaño NM (a) (*desilusión*) disillusion(ment); disappointment; **sufrir un ~ amoroso** to be disappointed in love, have an unhappy love affair; **te enseñarán los ~s** the disillusioning experiences (of life) will teach you.
(b) (*reproche*) admonition, reproof; home truth.

desengranar [1a] VT to disengage.

desengrasado ADJ (a) *máquina* rusty, needing oil; (*fig*) rusty. (b) (*Culin*) fat-free.

desengrasar [1a] VT to degrease, remove the grease from; to scour.

desenhebrar VT to unthread.

desenjaular [1a] VT (a) (*gen*) to take out of a cage; to release from a cage. (b) (*) *preso* to let out of jail.

desenlace NM outcome; (*Liter*) ending; dénouement; ~ **fatal**, ~ **trágico** tragic ending; ~ **feliz** happy ending.

desenlatar [1a] VT (*LAm*) lata to open.

desenlazar [1f] ① VT (a) (*desatar*) to untie, unlace, undo.
(b) (*fig*) problema to solve; *asunto* to unravel.
② **desenlazarse** VR (a) (*desatarse*) to come undone.
(b) (*Liter*) to end, turn out.

desenmarañar [1a] VT to disentangle, unravel (*t fig*).

desenmascarar [1a] VT (*fig*) to unmask, expose.

desenojar [1a] VT to soothe, appease, calm down.

desenredar [1a] ① VT to unravel; to straighten out; to resolve, clear up.
② **desenredarse** VR (*fig*) to get out of a jam*; ~ **de** to get out of, extricate o.s. from.

desenredo NM (a) (*acto*) unravelling, disentanglement. (b) (*Liter*) dénouement.

desenrollar [1a] ① VT to unroll, unwind.
② **desenrollarse** VR to unroll, unwind; to get unrolled.

desenroscar [1g] VT to unscrew; to unwind.

desensibilizar [1f] VT to desensitize.

desensillar [1a] VT to unsaddle.

desentablar [1a] (*fig*) ① VT (*deshacer*) to break up.
② **desentablarse** VR: **una discusión se desentabló** a row broke out.

desentenderse [2g] VR: ~ **de** (a) (*fingir ignorar*) to affect ignorance of, pretend not to know about.
(b) (*repudiar etc*) to wash one's hands of; to repudiate; to have nothing to do with; **se ha desentendido de todo eso** he has ceased to take any part in that, he has withdrawn completely from that.

desentendido ADJ: **hacerse el ~** to pay no attention; to pretend not to be interested (*o* to hear *etc*); **no te hagas el ~** don't pretend you haven't heard.

desentendimiento NM: **su ~ sobre el asunto** his refusal to have anything to do with the matter.

desenterrar [1j] VT (a) *cadáver* to exhume, disinter. (b) (*fig*) to unearth, dig up, rake up.

desentonado ADJ (a) (*Mús*) out of tune. (b) *color* clashing, not matching.

desentonar [1a] ① VI (a) (*Mús*) to be out of tune.
(b) (*fig*) to be out of tune (*con* with); (*colores*) to clash (*con* with), not match; **para no ~** so as to do the right thing, so as to fall into line.
② **desentonarse** VR (*fig*) to behave rudely, speak disrespectfully, raise one's voice angrily.

desentono NM (*fig*: *cualidad*) rudeness, disrespect; (*tono*) rude (*o* angry) tone of voice.

desentorpecer [2d] VT (a) *pierna etc* to stretch, loosen up. (b) (*) *persona* to polish up.

desentramparse* [1a] VR to get out of the red*.

desentrañar [1a] VT (a) (*destripar*) to disembowel; to eviscerate. (b) (*fig*) misterio to puzzle out, get to the bottom of, unravel; *significado* to puzzle out, work out.

desentrenado ADJ *jugador* out of practice; off form; *soldado* untrained.

desentumecer [2d] VT to free from numbness, restore the feeling to, get the feeling back into; *pierna* to stretch; (*Dep*) músculos to loosen up.

desenvainar [1a] VT (a) *espada* to draw, unsheathe; *guisantes* to shell; *garras* to show, put out. (b) (*fig*) to show, reveal, expose.

desenvoltura NF ease, naturalness; confidence; free-and-easy manner; (*al hablar*) fluency, facility; (*pey*) forwardness, brazenness.

desenvolver [2h; PTP **desenvuelto**] VT (a) *paquete etc* to unwrap; *rollo* to unwind, unroll; *lana etc* to disentangle, unravel.
(b) *teoría etc* to develop; to expound, explain, set out.

desenvolvimiento NM development; exposition.

desenvuelto ADJ (*natural*) easy, natural; (*confiado*) confident; (*despreocupado*) free-and-easy; *habla* fluent, easy; (*pey*) forward, brazen.

desenyugar [1h] VT (*LAm*), **desenyuntar** [1a] VT (*LAm*) to unyoke.

▼ **deseo** NM wish, desire; **el ~ de** the desire for; **el ~ de** + *infin* the desire to + *infin*; ~ **de saber** thirst for knowledge; **buen ~** good intentions; **arder en ~s de algo** to yearn for sth; **se cumplieron sus ~s** his wishes were fulfilled; **tener ~ de, venir en ~ de** to want, yearn for.

deseoso ADJ: ~ **de** anxious for, desirous of; **estar ~ de** + *infin* to be anxious to + *infin*, be eager to + *infin*.

desequilibrado ADJ (a) (*gen*) unbalanced; badly balanced, out of true; (*desigual*) one-sided, lop-sided. (b) (*Med*) (mentally) unbalanced.

desequilibrar [1a] VT to unbalance; to overbalance, throw off balance.

desequilibrio NM (a) (*gen*) disequilibrium; unbalance, lack of balance; (*fig*) imbalance. (b) (*Med*) unbalanced mental condition, instability, psychological disorder.

deserción NF desertion; defection.

desertar [1a] VI to desert; ~ **de** (*Mil etc*) to desert; ~ **del hogar** to abandon one's home, leave home; ~ **de sus deberes** to neglect one's duties; ~ **de una tertulia** to stop going to a gathering.

desértico ADJ arid, desert-like; (*vacío*) deserted.

desertificar [1g] VT = **desertizar**.

desertización NF (process of) turning land into a desert; blighting; (*fig*) depopulation.

desertizar [1f] VT to turn into a desert; to blight; (*fig*) to depopulate.

desertor(a) NM/F (*Mil*) deserter; (*Pol*) defector.

deservicio NM disservice.

desescalada NF de-escalation.

desescalar [1a] VTI to de-escalate.

desescamar [1a] VT to descale.

desescarchador NM (*Mec*) defroster.

desescolarización NF lack of schooling.

desescolarizado ADJ: **niños ~s** children deprived of schooling.

desescombrar [1a] VT to clear up, clear of rubbish (*o* debris *etc*), clean up; *cadáver etc* to dig out, extract.

desescombro NM clearing-up, clean-up.

desespañolizar [1f] VT to weaken the Spanish nature of; *persona* to cause to become less Spanish, wean away from Spanish habits (*etc*).

desesperación NF (a) (*gen*) despair, desperation; **con ~** despairingly.
(b) (*fig*) fury; **nadar con ~** to swim furiously.
(c) (*una ~*) infuriating thing; **es una ~** it's maddening; it's unbearable; **es una ~ tener que ...** it's infuriating to have to ...

desesperadamente ADV desperately, despairingly; hopelessly.

desesperado ① ADJ (a) *persona* desperate, despairing; in despair; *caso, situación* hopeless; **estar ~ de** to have despaired of, have no hope of.
(b) *esfuerzo etc* furious, frenzied.
② NM: **como un ~** like mad.
③ NF: **hacer algo a la desesperada** to do sth as a last hope, try a final desperate solution.

desesperante ADJ (*enloquecedor*) maddening, infuriating; (*desesperado*) hopeless.

desesperanza NF despair.

➤ LENGUA Y USO: **deseo** → 35.5

desesperanzar [1f] **1** VT to deprive of hope.
2 desesperanzarse VR to lose hope, despair.
desesperar [1a] **1** VT to deprive of hope, drive to despair; (*) to drive to distraction, drive crazy.
2 VI to despair (*de* of), lose hope; ~ **de** + *infin* to give up all hope of + *ger*.
3 desesperarse VR to despair, lose hope; to get desperate.
desespero NM (*esp LAm*) despair, desperation.
desespinar [1a] VT *pescado* to fillet, bone.
desestabilización NF destabilization; subversion.
desestabilizador ADJ *campaña, influencia* destabilizing; *elemento, grupo* subversive.
desestabilizar [1f] VT to destabilize; to subvert.
desestancar [1g] VT *producto* to remove the state monopoly from, allow a free market in.
desestiba NF (*Náut*) unloading.
desestibar [1a] VT (*Náut*) to unload.
desestimable ADJ insignificant.
desestimar [1a] VT **(a)** (*menospreciar*) to have a low opinion of; to scorn, belittle, disparage. **(b)** *demanda, moción etc* to reject.
desestímulo NM disincentive.
desestructurado ADJ badly structured; disorganized; **familia desestructurada** broken home.
desexilio NM (*LAm*) return from exile, return home.
desfachatado* ADJ brazen, impudent, barefaced; cheeky*.
desfachatez* NF **(a)** (*cualidad*) brazenness, impudence; cheek*, nerve*. **(b) una ~** a piece of cheek*, an impudent remark.
desfalcador(a) NM/F embezzler.
desfalcar [1g] VT to embezzle.
desfalco NM embezzlement.
desfallecer [2d] **1** VT to weaken.
2 VI to get weak, weaken; to faint; (*voz*) to fail, falter; ~ **de ánimo** to lose heart.
desfallecido ADJ weak; faint.
desfallecimiento NM weakness; faintness.
desfasado ADJ (*Mec*) out of phase, badly adjusted; (*fig*) out of step; behind the times, antiquated; **estar ~** (*Aer*) to be suffering from jetlag.
desfasar [1a] VT (*Elec*) to change the phase of; (*fig*) to put out of phase, unbalance, upset.
desfase NM being out of phase; imbalance; gap, difference; lack of precise correspondence, failure to correspond; maladjustment; (*Aer*) jetlag; **hay un ~ entre A y B** A and B are out of phase.
desfavorable ADJ unfavourable.
desfavorablemente ADV unfavourably.
desfavorecer [2d] VT **(a)** *persona, causa* to cease to favour, withdraw support from. **(b)** (*ropa*) to be unbecoming to, not suit, not look well on.
desfavorecido ADJ underprivileged.
desfibradora NF shredder, shredding machine.
desfibrar [1a] VT *papel* to shred.
desfibrilador NM defibrillator.
desfiguración NF, **desfiguramiento** NM disfigurement, disfiguration; defacement; alteration; distortion, misrepresentation; (*Fot etc*) blurring; (*Rad*) distortion.
desfigurado ADJ (*gen*) disfigured; deformed; *sentido etc* distorted; twisted; *contorno* (*t Fot*) blurred; (*Rad*) distorted.
desfigurar [1a] VT *cara* to disfigure; *cuerpo* to deform; *cuadro, monumento etc* to deface; *contorno* (*t Fot*) to blur; *voz* to alter, disguise; *sentido* to distort, twist; to cloud; *suceso* to misrepresent, distort the truth of, alter the details of; **una cicatriz le desfigura la cara** a scar disfigures his face; **la niebla lo desfigura todo** the fog alters everything, the fog makes everything look strange.
desfiladero NM defile, pass; gorge.
desfilar [1a] VI to parade; to march past; to file by, file out (*etc*), file past; **desfilaron ante el general** they paraded before the general, they marched past the general.
desfile NM (*gen*) procession; (*Mil*) parade, march-past; ~ **aéreo** flypast; ~ **de modas**, ~ **de modelos** fashion show, fashion parade; ~ **naval** naval review; ~ **de promoción** (*Mil*) passing-out parade; ~ **de la victoria** victory parade.
desfiscalización NF exemption from tax.
desfiscalizar [1f] VT to exempt from taxation.
desfloración NF **(a)** deflowering, defloration. **(b)** tarnishing, messing-up, destruction of the fine appearance of.
desflorar [1a] VT **(a)** *mujer* to deflower.
(b) (*arruinar*) to tarnish, mess up, destroy the fine appearance of.
(c) ~ **un asunto** to touch briefly on a matter, treat a matter no more than superficially, skim over a matter.
desfogar [1h] **1** VT (*fig*) *cólera* to vent (*con, en* on).
2 VI (*Náut: tormenta*) to burst.
3 desfogarse VR (*fig*) to vent one's anger; to let o.s. go, let off

steam.
desfogue NM (*fig*) venting.
desfondado ADJ (*Fin*) bankrupt.
desfondar [1a] **1** VT **(a)** to knock the bottom out of, stave in (*t Náut*). **(b)** (*Agr*) to plough deeply.
2 desfondarse VR (*fig*) to go to pieces, have the bottom fall out of one's life.
desforestación NF deforestation.
desforestar [1a] VT to deforest.
desformatear [1a] VT to unformat.
desgaire NM **(a)** (*desaseo etc*) slovenliness, carelessness.
(b) (*descuido afectado*) nonchalance, affected carelessness; (*desdén*) scornful attitude, disdain.
(c) vestido al ~ dressed in a slovenly way; **hacer algo al ~** to do sth with a scornful air; **mirar a uno al ~** to sneer at sb, look scornfully at sb.
desgajado ADJ separated, unconnected.
desgajar [1a] **1** VT **(a)** *rama* to tear off, break off, split off.
(b) ~ **a uno de** to tear sb away from.
2 desgajarse VR **(a)** (*rama*) to come off, break off, split away.
(b) ~ **de** (*persona*) to tear o.s. away from.
desgalichado ADJ *movimiento etc* clumsy, awkward; *vestido* shabby, slovenly, sloppy; *persona* down-at-heel, unprepossessing.
desgana NF **(a)** (*para comer*) lack of appetite, loss of appetite.
(b) (*fig*) unwillingness, disinclination, reluctance; **su ~ para hacerlo** his unwillingness to do it; **hacer algo a ~** to do sth reluctantly.
(c) (*Med*) weakness, faintness.
desganadamente ADV without much interest, in a desultory fashion; without enthusiasm, reluctantly.
desganado ADJ: **estar ~, sentirse ~** to have no appetite, not be hungry, be off one's food.
desganarse [1a] VR **(a)** (*perder el apetito*) to lose one's appetite. **(b)** (*fig*) to lose interest, get bored, get fed up.
desgano NM = **desgana**.
desgañitarse [1a] VR to bawl, shout; to scream o.s. hoarse.
desgarbado ADJ (*movimiento*) clumsy, ungainly, gawky; graceless; (*aspecto*) slovenly, uncouth.
desgarbo NM clumsiness; gracelessness; slovenliness.
desgarrado ADJ **(a)** *ropa* torn; tattered, in tatters. **(b)** (*fig: descarado*) shameless, barefaced, brazen. **(c)** (*fig: vicioso*) licentious.
desgarrador ADJ *escena etc* heartbreaking, heartrending; *emoción* uncontrollable; *grito* piercing.
desgarramiento NM **(a)** (*de tela*) tearing, ripping; (*de sociedad, país*) upheaval.
desgarrar [1a] VT **(a)** *tela* to tear, rip (up), rend. **(b)** (*fig*) to shatter, crush; *corazón* to break. **(c)** (*LAm*) *flema* to cough up.
desgarro NM **(a)** (*rasgón*) tear, rip, rent; (*acto*) tearing apart, split; break-up. **(b)** (*fig: descaro*) impudence, brazenness, effrontery; (*de mujer*) forwardness. **(c)** (*fig: jactancia*) boastfulness. **(d)** (*LAm: flema*) phlegm. **(e)** (*Cono Sur Med*) sprain.
desgarrón NM big tear.
desgastar [1a] **1** VT **(a)** (*gen*) to wear away, wear down; (*Geol*) to erode, weather; *cuerda etc* to chafe, fray; *metal* to corrode, eat away, eat into; ~ **la ropa** to wear one's clothes out.
(b) (*fig*) to spoil, ruin.
2 desgastarse VR **(a)** (*gen*) to wear away; to erode; to chafe, fray; to corrode; to get worn out.
(b) (*Med*) to get weak, decline; to wear o.s. out.
desgaste NM **(a)** (*gen*) wear; wear and tear; erosion; chafing; fraying; corrosion; **aumenta el ~ del motor** it increases wear on the engine; **debido al ~ de su ropa** because his clothes were so worn.
(b) (*desperdicio*) waste, loss; slow wasting; (*Mil*) attrition; (*Med*) weakening, decline; ~ **económico** drain on one's resources; ~ **natural** natural wastage; **guerra de ~** war of attrition.
desglaciación NF thaw.
desglobar [1a] VT *cifras etc* to break down, analyse, split up.
desglosable ADJ separable, detachable; *cifras etc* which can be broken down.
desglosar [1a] VT to separate, remove, detach; (*fig*) *cifras etc* to break down.
desglose NM breakdown.
desgobernado ADJ uncontrollable, undisciplined; *niño* wild.
desgobernar [1j] VT **(a)** (*Pol*) to misgovern, misrule; *asunto* to mismanage, handle badly, make a mess of. **(b)** (*Anat*) to dislocate.
desgobierno NM **(a)** (*Pol*) misgovernment, misrule; mismanagement, bad handling. **(b)** (*Anat*) dislocation.
desgolletar [1a] VT *botella* to knock the neck off.
desgoznar [1a] **1** VT **(a)** *puerta* to take off its hinges, unhinge.
(b) (*quitar goznes de*) to take the hinges off.
2 desgoznarse VR **(a)** (*persona*) to get wild, lose control; to go off the rails.
(b) (*plan etc*) to be thrown out of gear.

desgrabar [1a] VT *cinta* to wipe (clean).

desgracia NF **(a)** (*infortunio*) misfortune; (*percance*) mishap; accident; (*mala suerte*) (piece of) bad luck; setback; **por ~** unfortunately; **¡qué ~!** what a misfortune!; what bad luck!; **estar en ~** to be unfortunate, suffer constant setbacks; **en el accidente no hay que lamentar ~s personales** there were no casualties in the accident; **la familia ha tenido una serie de ~s** the family has had a series of misfortunes. **(b)** (*falta de favor*) disgrace; disfavour; **caer en (la) ~ to fall from grace, fall into disgrace.**

desgraciadamente ADV unfortunately, unluckily; **¡~!** more's the pity!, alas!

desgraciado ① ADJ **(a)** (*sin suerte*) unlucky, unfortunate; luckless, hapless; wretched; (*infeliz*) unhappy, miserable; **una elección desgraciada** an unfortunate choice; **~ en sus amores** unlucky in love; **~ en el juego** unlucky at cards; **era ~ en su matrimonio** he was unhappy in his marriage; **una vida desgraciada** a wretched life, a life of misery; **¡qué ~ estoy!** how wretched I am!; **¡~ de ti si lo haces!** you'd better not!, it'll be the worse for you if you do!
(b) (*aciago*) ill-fated, unlucky; **ese día ~** that ill-fated day.
(c) (*desgarbado*) graceless, ugly, lacking charm; unappealing.
(d) (*desagradable*) unpleasant.
(e) (*LAm*) rotten, wretched.
② NM, **desgraciada** NF wretch, poor devil, unfortunate; **lo tiene aquel ~** that wretched creature has got it; **la hizo una desgraciada** he put her in the family way.

desgraciar [1b] ① VT **(a)** (*estropear*) to spoil, ruin (the appearance of).
(b) (*ofender*) to displease.
② **desgraciarse** VR **(a)** (*estropearse*) to spoil, be ruined, suffer damage; (*plan etc*) to fall through, collapse, fail to mature; **se le desgració el niño antes de nacer** she had a miscarriage, she lost the baby.
(b) **~ con uno** to fall out with sb; to lose sb's favour.

desgranar [1a] ① VT **(a)** (*gen*) to remove the grain (*o pips etc*) from; *trigo* to thresh; *guisantes* to shell; **~ un racimo** to pick the grapes from a bunch.
(b) **~ las cuentas del rosario** to tell one's beads.
(c) **~ imprecaciones** to let fly with a string of curses; **~ mentiras** to come out with a string of lies.
(d) (*fig: separar*) to sort out, distinguish between.
(e) (*fig*) *sentido* to spell out.
② **desgranarse** VR **(a)** (*Bot*) to fall; (*trigo*) to shed its grain; (*otra planta*) to drop its seeds.
(b) (*cuentas*) to come apart.

desgrasado ADJ (*Culin*) fat-free.

desgrasar [1a] VT = **desengrasar.**

desgravable ADJ tax-deductible, allowable against tax.

desgravación NF: **~ fiscal, ~ de impuestos** tax relief; tax deduction; **~ (de impuestos) personal** personal tax relief, personal allowance.

desgravar [1a] VT (*reducir*) *producto* to reduce the tax (*o duty etc*) on; (*exentar*) to exempt from tax; **la ley les desgrava estas compras** the law allows them tax relief on these purchases.

desgreñado ADJ dishevelled, tousled.

desgreñar [1a] VT to dishevel, rumple, tousle.

desgreño* NM (*And, Cono Sur*) untidiness; (*fig: desorden*) disorder, disarray; (*fig: descuido*) carelessness.

desguace NM **(a)** (*acto*) breaking up; scrapping; stripping. **(b)** (*parque*) scrapyard, breaker's yard.

desguarnecer [2d] VT **(a)** (*Téc*) to strip down; to remove the accessories (*o trimmings etc*) from; *instrumento* to dismantle, put out of action; **~ un barco de velas** to remove the sails from a boat.
(b) *caballo* to unharness.
(c) (*Mil*) *ciudad* to abandon, remove the garrison from; *fortaleza* to dismantle (the fortifications of).

desguarnecido ADJ **(a)** (*gen*) bare, shorn of trimmings (*etc*). **(b)** *ciudad* undefended, unprotected; *flanco* exposed.

desguazar [1f] VT **(a)** *madera* to dress, rough-hew. **(b)** *barco* to break up, scrap; *coche etc* to strip, scrap.

desgubernamentalizar [1f] VT to remove from government control.

deshabilitar [1a] VT to disable.

deshabillé NM negligee.

deshabitado ADJ uninhabited; deserted; empty, vacant.

deshabitar [1a] VT to move out of, leave empty; to desert, quit.

deshabituación NF losing the habit, breaking of the habit; conquering of one's addiction; (*Med*) treatment for drug dependency.

deshabituar [1e] ① VT: **~ a uno de la droga** to break sb of the drug habit, wean sb away from his addiction.
② **deshabituarse** VR to lose the habit; **~ de la droga** to break o.s. of the drug habit, conquer one's drug addiction.

deshacer [2s] ① VT (*gen*) to undo, unmake; (*arruinar*) to spoil, ruin, damage, destroy; (*Mec etc*) to take apart; to pull to pieces; *res, carne* to cut up, carve up; *barco* to break up; *cama* to unmake, pull to pieces; *paquete* to undo, unpack, unwrap; *maleta* to unpack; *nudo* to undo, untie; *costura* to unpick; *metal etc* to wear down, wear away; *hielo etc* to melt, dissolve; *vista* to harm, damage; *persona, economía etc* to shatter; *enemigo* to shatter, rout, put to flight; *contrario* to defeat; *tratado etc* to break, violate; *agravio* to right; **~ algo en agua** to dissolve sth in water; **la lluvia deshizo el techo** the rain damaged the roof; **~ un brazo contra algo** to hurt one's arm on sth; **~ el camino** to go back over one's route, retrace one's steps.
② **deshacerse** VR **(a)** (*desatarse*) to come undone; (*arruinarse*) to be spoiled, get damaged; (*descomponerse*) to come apart; to fall to pieces; to break up; (*nudo*) to come untied; (*hielo*) to melt, dissolve; (*ejército etc*) to be shattered, disintegrate; (*desaparecer*) to vanish; **se deshizo la pierna al caer** he hurt his leg when he fell; **se deshizo como el humo** it vanished into thin air, it vanished like smoke; **se deshace trabajando** he works excessively hard; **cuando se deshizo la reunión** when the meeting broke up.
(b) (*Med*) to get weak, grow feeble; to waste away.
(c) (*fig: afligirse*) to grieve; to pine; (*impacientarse*) to get impatient, get worked up.
(d) **~ de algo** to get rid of sth; (*Com etc*) to dump sth, unload sth; **no quiero deshacerme de eso** I don't want to part with that; **logramos deshacernos de él** we managed to get rid of him.
(e) **~ en lágrimas** to burst into tears; **~ en elogios de uno** to shower praises on sb; **~ en cumplidos** to pay lavish compliments, come out with extravagant courtesies; to overdo the politeness.
(f) **~ por los melocotones** to be crazy about peaches, adore peaches; **~ por hacer algo** to strive to do sth, struggle to do sth; **~ por complacer a uno** to do one's utmost to please sb.

desharrapado ① ADJ ragged, tattered, shabby.
② NM, **desharrapada** NF: **los ~s de la sociedad** (*fig*) society's outcasts.

deshebillar [1a] VT to unbuckle.

deshebrar [1a] VT to unpick.

deshechizar [1f] VT to remove the spell from, disenchant.

deshecho ① PTP *de* **deshacer.**
② ADJ **(a)** (*gen*) undone; *lazo, nudo* untied; (*roto*) broken, smashed, in pieces; (*despedazado*) shattered; **tener un brazo ~** to have a badly injured arm; **estar ~*** to be worn out.
(b) (*Med*) *persona* weak, emaciated; *salud* broken.
(c) (*fig*) *tormenta* violent.
(d) (*Cono Sur: desaliñado*) untidy.
③ NM (*And, Carib, Cono Sur*) short cut.

deshelador NM (*Aer*) de-icer.

deshelar [1j] ① VT to thaw, melt; (*Téc*) to defrost; (*Aer*) to de-ice.
② VI *y* **deshelarse** VR to thaw, melt; (*Met*) to thaw.

desherbaje NM weeding.

desherbar [1j] VT to weed.

desheredado, -a NM/F: **los ~s** the dispossessed.

desheredar [1a] VT to disinherit.

desherrarse [1k] VR (*caballo*) to cast a shoe.

deshidratación NF dehydration.

deshidratado ADJ dehydrated.

deshidratar [1a] VT to dehydrate.

deshielo NM thaw; **~ diplomático** diplomatic thaw.

deshierbe NM weeding.

deshilachado ADJ shabby; worn, frayed.

deshilachar [1a] ① VT to pull threads out of; to wear, fray.
② **deshilacharse** VR to get worn, fray.

deshilada NF: **a la ~ (a)** (*Mil*) in single file. **(b)** (*fig*) secretly, stealthily.

deshilado NM (*Cos*) openwork.

deshilar [1a] ① VT (*Cos*) to unravel; *carne* to shred.
② VI to get thin.
③ **deshilarse** VR to get worn, fray, come apart.

deshilvanado ADJ (*fig*) disjointed, disconnected, incoherent.

deshilvanar [1a] VT (*Cos*) to untack, take the stitches out of.

deshinchar [1a] ① VT **(a)** *neumático* to deflate, let down; *hinchazón* to reduce (the swelling of).
(b) (*fig*) *ira* to give vent to.
② **deshincharse** VR **(a)** (*neumático*) to go flat; (*hinchazón*) to go down.
(b) (*) to get down off one's high horse*.

deshipotecar [1g] VT *propiedad* to pay off the mortgage on.

deshojado ADJ *rama etc* leafless; *flor* stripped of its petals.

deshojar [1a] ① VT **(a)** *árbol* to strip the leaves off; (*Quím*) to defoliate; *flor* to pull the petals off.
(b) (*LAm*) *maíz* to husk; *fruta* to peel; *libro* to tear the pages out of.
② **deshojarse** VR to lose its leaves (*etc*).

deshollejar [1a] VT *uvas etc* to peel, skin.

deshollinador NM (chimney) sweep.

deshollinar [1a] VT **(a)** *chimenea* to sweep. **(b)** (*fig*) to take a close look at.

deshonestamente ADV (V ADJ) (a) indecently, lewdly. (b) dishonestly.

deshonestidad NF (V ADJ) (a) indecency, impropriety, lewdness. (b) dishonesty.

deshonesto ADJ (a) (*indecente*) indecent, improper, lewd. (b) (*no honrado*) dishonest.

deshonor NM (a) (*gen*) dishonour, disgrace. (b) (*un ~*) insult, affront (*de* to); **no es un ~ trabajar** it is no disgrace to work.

deshonorar [1a] VT (a) (*deshonrar*) to dishonour, disgrace; (*ser indigno de*) to be unworthy of. (b) (*despedir*) to dismiss, deprive of office (*o title etc*).

deshonra NF (a) (*gen*) dishonour, disgrace; shame; **lo tiene a ~** he thinks it shameful, he considers it beneath him; **tienen a ~ trabajar** they think it beneath them to work. (b) (*una ~*) shameful act.

deshonrabuenos NMF INVAR (a) (*calumniador*) backbiter. (b) (*oveja negra*) black sheep (of the family).

deshonrar [1a] VT (a) *gen*) to dishonour, disgrace, bring disgrace on. (b) (*afrontar*) to insult. (c) *mujer* to seduce, ruin.

deshonroso ADJ dishonourable, disgraceful, ignominious.

deshora: a ~ ADV at the wrong time; at an inconvenient time; **llegar a ~** to come unexpectedly; **acostarse a ~** to go to bed at some unearthly hour; **hacer algo a ~** to do sth at the wrong moment, mistime sth.

deshuesado ADJ *carne* boned; *fruta* stoned.

deshuesar [1a] VT *carne* to bone; *fruta* to stone.

deshuevarse⁇ [1a] VR *etc* = **descojonarse** *etc.*

deshumanización NF dehumanization.

deshumanizador ADJ, **deshumanizante** ADJ dehumanizing.

deshumanizar [1f] VT to dehumanize.

deshumedecerse [2d] VR to dry up, lose its moisture.

desideologizado ADJ non-ideological, free of ideological considerations.

desiderátum NM, PL **desiderátums** *o* **desiderata** desideratum; ideal, thing ideally required (*o* desired); observable lack; list of books (*etc*) to be bought.

desidia NF (a) (*pereza*) laziness, idleness. (b) (*desaseo*) neglect; slovenliness, carelessness.

desidioso ADJ (a) (*perezoso*) lazy, idle. (b) (*descuidado*) neglected; slovenly, careless.

desierto [1] ADJ (a) *isla, región etc* desert; *paisaje* empty, bleak, desolate; *casa etc* empty, deserted; **la calle estaba desierta** the street was deserted.
(b) **declarar ~ un premio** to declare that a prize will not be awarded (for lack of good candidates *etc*); **declarar desiertas unas oposiciones** to declare a competition void.
[2] NM desert; wilderness; **clamar en el ~, predicar en el ~** to be a voice crying in the wilderness.

designación NF (a) (*acto*) designation, appointment. (b) (*nombre*) designation, name.

designar [1a] VT (*gen*) to designate, appoint, name; (*escoger*) to select; *fecha, lugar etc* to name, fix, decide on.

designio NM plan, design.

desigual ADJ (a) (*no igual*) unequal, different; *lucha etc* unequal; *trato* unfair, inequitable.
(b) *tiempo etc* variable, changeable; *carácter* unpredictable.
(c) *terreno, escritura etc* uneven; irregular; *borde* rough.

desigualar [1a] VT *flequillo* to make uneven; *poderes, capacidades* to unbalance.

desigualdad NF (a) (*Econ, Pol*) inequality. (b) (*de carácter, tiempo*) variableness, changeableness; unpredictability. (c) (*de escritura*) unevenness; irregularity; (*de terreno*) roughness.

desilusión NF disillusion(ment), disappointment; **caer en la ~** to get disillusioned; **sufrir una ~** to suffer a disappointment.

desilusionante ADJ disillusioning, disappointing.

desilusionar [1a] [1] VT (*desengañar*) to disillusion; (*decepcionar*) to disappoint, let down.
[2] **desilusionarse** VR to get disillusioned, lose one's illusions; to be disappointed; to have one's hopes destroyed.

desimantar [1a] VT to demagnetize.

desincentivar [1a] VT to act as a disincentive to, discourage.

desincentivo NM disincentive.

desincrustante ADJ: **agente ~** descaling agent; **producto ~** descaling product.

desincrustar [1a] VT to descale.

desinencia NF (*Ling*) ending.

desinfección NF disinfection.

desinfectado NM disinfection.

desinfectante NM disinfectant.

desinfectar [1a] VT to disinfect.

desinfestar [1a] VT to decontaminate.

desinflación NF deflation.

desinflado ADJ *neumático* flat.

desinflar [1a] [1] VT to deflate, let the air out of.
[2] **desinflarse** VR (*neumático*) to go down, go flat.

desinformación NF (a) (*información engañosa*) disinformation, misleading information, black propaganda. (b) (*ignorancia*) ignorance, lack of information.

desinformado ADJ uninformed.

desinformador [1] ADJ *noticia* false, calculated to deceive.
[2] NM, **desinformadora** NF spreader of disinformation.

desinformar [1a] VT to misinform.

desinformativo ADJ misleading, false.

desinhibición NF lack of inhibition(s).

desinhibido ADJ uninhibited.

desinhibir [3a] [1] VT to free from inhibitions.
[2] **desinhibirse** VR to lose one's inhibitions.

desinsectación NF protection against insect pests; **la ~ de un jardín** freeing a garden of insect pests.

desinsectar [1a] VT to clear of insects.

desintegrable ADJ fissile.

desintegración NF disintegration; **~ nuclear** nuclear fission; **la ~ del átomo** the splitting of the atom.

desintegrar [1a] [1] VT to disintegrate; *átomo* to split, smash.
[2] **desintegrarse** VR to disintegrate; to split, be smashed.

desinterés NM disinterestedness, impartiality; unselfishness, generosity.

desinteresado ADJ (*imparcial*) disinterested, impartial; (*altruista*) unselfish, generous.

desinteresarse [1a] VR (a) (*perder interés*) to lose interest (*de* in). (b) **~ de** (*desentenderse*) to have nothing to do with.

desintoxicación NF curing of poisoning; curing of drug addiction.

desintoxicar [1g] [1] VT to cure of poisoning; to cure of drug addiction (*o* alcoholism).
[2] **desintoxicarse** VR to undergo treatment for drug addiction (*o* alcoholism).

desinversión NF disinvestment.

desinvertir [3i] VI to disinvest.

desistimiento NM (a) (*gen*) desisting. (b) (*Jur*) waiver.

desistir [3a] VI (a) (*gen*) to stop, desist; **~ de algo** to desist from sth; **~ de** + *infin* to desist from + *ger*, stop + *ger*.
(b) **~ de un derecho** (*Jur*) to waive a right.

desjarretar [1a] VT *animal* to hamstring; (*Med*) to weaken, debilitate.

desjuntar [1a] VT (*separar*) to separate, take apart; (*dividir*) to divide.

deslavado ADJ (a) (*gen*) half-washed. (b) (*fig*) brazen, barefaced. (c) = **deslavazado.**

deslavar [1a] VT (a) (*lavar a medias*) to half-wash, wash superficially; (*quitar lavando*) to wash away. (b) (*debilitar*) to weaken; (*desteñir*) to fade.

deslavazado ADJ (a) (*lacio*) soft, weak, limp; drooping; *persona* limp. (b) (*desteñido*) faded, washed-out, pale; (*fig*) colourless; unsubstantial. (c) (*fig*) *habla etc* disjointed, incoherent.

deslave NM (*Méx*) landslide, rockfall.

desleal ADJ disloyal (*a, con* to); (*Com*) *competencia* unfair; *juego* foul, dirty.

deslealmente ADV disloyally; unfairly.

deslealtad NF disloyalty; unfairness.

deslegalizar [1f] VT to outlaw, criminalize.

deslegitimar [1a] VT to discredit, undermine.

desleído ADJ (a) (*disuelto*) dissolved; diluted. (b) (*fig*) *idea etc* weak, woolly.

desleír [3m] [1] VT *sólido* to dissolve; *líquido* to dilute, thin; to make weaker.
[2] **desleírse** VR to dissolve; to become diluted; to get weaker.

deslenguado ADJ foul-mouthed.

deslenguarse [1i] VR (*decir demasiado*) to shoot one's mouth off, talk too much, be too free in what one says; (*descaradamente*) to speak insolently; (*obscenamente*) to pour out obscenities.

desliar [1c] [1] VT to untie, undo.
[2] **desliarse** VR to come undone.

desligado ADJ (a) (*suelto*) loose, free; unfastened. (b) (*fig*) separate, detached; **vive ~ de todo** he lives detached from everything, he lives in a world of his own.

desligamiento NM (*fig*) detachment (*de* from).

desligar [1h] [1] VT (a) (*desatar*) to untie, undo, unfasten; to unbind; (*desenredar*) to extricate (*de* from).
(b) (*fig: separar*) to separate, detach; to consider separately; **~ el primer aspecto del segundo** to separate the first aspect from the second.
(c) (*fig: aclarar*) to unravel, disentangle, clarify.
(d) (*fig: absolver*) to absolve, free (*de* from); (*eximir*) to excuse, exempt (*de* from); **~ a uno de una promesa** to release sb from a promise.
[2] **desligarse** VR to come undone, get unfastened; (*persona*) to extricate o.s. (*de* from).

deslindable ADJ definable.
deslindar [1a] VT (a) *terreno* to mark out, fix the limits (o boundaries) of. (b) (*fig*) to define, clarify.
deslinde NM (a) (*acto*) demarcation, fixing of limits (o boundaries). (b) (*fig*) definition.
desliz NM (a) (*gen*) slip, slide; (*Aut*) skid.
(b) (*fig*) slip; lapse; indiscretion; ~ **freudiano** Freudian slip; ~ **de lengua** slip of the tongue; **los deslices de la juventud** the indiscretions of youth, the minor sins of youth.
deslizadero NM (a) (*gen*) slide; (*sitio*) slippery spot. (b) (*Téc*) chute, slide.
deslizadizo ADJ slippery.
deslizador NM (a) (*de niño*) scooter. (b) (*Náut*) small speedboat. (c) (*Dep*) surfboard, aquaplane, water ski. (d) (*de patín*) runner, skid.
deslizamiento NM slide, sliding, slipping; (*Aut*) skid; ~ (**suave**) glide; ~ **salarial** (upward) drift of wages; ~ **de tierra** landslide.
deslizante ADJ sliding.
deslizar [1f] ⊡ VT (a) (*gen*) to slide, slip (*en* into, *por* along, through); ~ **una mesa por el suelo** to slide a table along the floor; ~ **la mano por la pierna de una** to run (o slide) one's hand up (o along) sb's leg.
(b) ~ **una propina a uno** to slip sb a tip; ~ **una observación** to slip a remark in; to let slip a remark.
⊡ **deslizarse** VR (a) (*por accidente*) to slip (*en* on, up on), slide (*por* along); (*Aut*) to skid.
(b) (*secreto*) to slip out; (*error*) to slip in, creep in.
(c) (*movimiento: culebra etc*) to slide, glide, slither; (*barca*) to glide; (*agua*) to go (gently), pass, flow gently; (*tiempo*) to pass, glide past; (*persona*) to slip away, slip off; to slip in; ~ **en un cuarto** to slip into a room; ~ **en una fiesta** to slip unnoticed into a party; **el agua se desliza mansamente** the water flows along gently; **la anguila se deslizó entre mis manos** the eel slipped away between my fingers; **el insecto se deslizó fuera del agujero** the insect wriggled out of the hole.
(d) (*equivocarse*) to slip up, blunder; (*moralmente*) to go wrong morally, get into bad ways, backslide.
deslomar [1a] ⊡ VT to break the back of; (*fig*) to wear out, exhaust utterly; ~ **a uno a garrotazos** to beat sb mercilessly.
⊡ **deslomarse** VR (*fig*) to get worn out; to work one's guts out.
deslucido ADJ (a) (*deslustrado*) tarnished; (*viejo*) worn out, old and useless.
(b) (*sin vida*) flat, dull, lifeless; *actuación* undistinguished, characterless; **hizo un papel** ~ he was dull in the part; **el jugador estuvo muy** ~ the player was far from his best form, he played in a very lifeless way.
(c) (*desgarbado*) graceless, inelegant, awkward.
(d) **quedó muy** ~ he did very badly, he made a very poor showing.
deslucimiento NM (V ADJ) (a) tarnished state; useless condition.
(b) flatness, dullness, lifelessness; (*Teat*) lack of character.
(c) gracelessness, inelegance.
(d) poor showing, bad performance.
deslucir [3f] ⊡ VT (a) (*deslustrar*) to tarnish; (*estropear*) to damage, spoil, ruin; to impair the splendour of, diminish the attractiveness of, dull; **la lluvia deslució el acto** the rain ruined the ceremony.
(b) *persona* to discredit, damage the standing of.
⊡ **deslucirse** VR (*fig*) to do badly, make a poor showing.
deslumbrador ADJ (a) (*lit*) dazzling, brilliant; glaring. (b) (*fig*) dazzling; puzzling, confusing, bewildering.
deslumbramiento NM (a) (*brillo*) glare, dazzle; brilliance. (b) (*fig*) confusion; bewilderment.
deslumbrante ADJ dazzling.
deslumbrar [1a] VT (a) (*con luz*) to dazzle; (*cegar*) to blind.
(b) (*fig*) (*impresionar*) to dazzle; (*dejar perplejo*) to puzzle, confuse, bewilder; (*aturdir*) to daze; **deslumbró a todos con su oratoria** he captivated everyone with his ora tory, he gave a dazzling oratorical display.
deslustrado ADJ (a) *vidrio* frosted, ground; *loza* unglazed. (b) (*esp fig*) dull, lustreless; tarnished.
deslustrar [1a] VT (a) *vidrio* to frost; *loza, paño* to remove the glaze from. (b) (*esp fig*) to dull, tarnish (the brilliance of), dim (the lustre of). (c) (*fig*) *reputación etc* to sully, stain, tarnish.
deslustre NM (a) (*de vidrio*) frosting; (*de loza, paño*) removal of glaze. (b) (*de muebles, adornos*) tarnishing; dullness, dimness. (c) (*fig*) stigma, stain; disgrace.
deslustroso ADJ (a) unbecoming, unsuitable. (b) (*fig*) disgraceful.
desmadejamiento NM enervation, weakness.
desmadejar [1a] ⊡ VT to enervate, weaken, take it out of.
⊡ **desmadejarse** VR to weaken; to go floppy, loll.
desmadrado ADJ (a) (*desenfrenado*) unruly, rebellious; (*desinhibido*) uninhibited; outrageous; (*excéntrico*) far out*.
(b) (*confuso*) confused; disoriented, lost.
desmadrarse [1a] VR (*rebelarse*) to rebel; (*descontrolarse*) to get out of

control, go too far, run to excess, run wild; (*divertirse*) to let one's hair down; (*excederse*) to go over the top; (*perder dignidad*) to lose one's dignity; ~ **por uno** to fall madly in love with sb; **los gastos se han desmadrado** costs have gone right over the top.
desmadre NM (a) (*exceso*) excess; excess of emotion; (*descontrol*) loss of control; loss of dignity; (*conducta*) outrageous behaviour; (*en cifras*) sudden leap, excessive rise; boom; **¡es el ~!** it's the end!; **esto va de ~ total** this is really getting out of hand.
(b) (*confusión*) chaos, confusion; mess; (*ultraje*) outrage.
(c) (*: juerga*) wild party, rave-up*.
desmalezar [1f] VT (*LAm*) to weed.
desmallar [1a] ⊡ VT *puntos* to pull out; *media* to make a ladder (o run) in.
⊡ **desmallarse** VR (*media*) to ladder.
desmamar [1a] VT to wean.
desmán[1] NM (*exceso*) excess, outrage; (*mala conducta*) piece of bad behaviour; (*abuso*) abuse (of authority); **cometer un** ~ to commit an outrage (*contra* on).
desmán[2] NM (*Zool*) muskrat.
desmanchar [1a] ⊡ VT (*LAm*) to clean, remove the spots (o stains etc) from.
⊡ **desmancharse*** VR (*And, CAm*) (a) (*salir de prisa*) to bolt out; (*retirarse*) to withdraw.
(b) (*Agr*) to stray from the herd.
desmandado ADJ (a) *persona* unruly, unbridled; wild; uncontrollable, out of hand; obstreperous. (b) *animal* stray; *caballo* runaway.
desmandarse [1a] VR (a) (*descontrolarse*) to get out of hand, run wild, go out of control; (*portarse mal*) to be obstreperous, behave badly; (*descararse*) to be insolent.
(b) (*animal*) to break loose; (*caballo*) to bolt, run away.
desmano: **a** ~ ADV V **contramano**.
desmanotado ADJ clumsy, awkward.
desmantelación NF dismantling.
desmantelamiento NM (a) (*acto*) dismantling; abandonment. (b) (*estado*) dilapidation.
desmantelar [1a] ⊡ VT (*Mil etc*) to dismantle, raze; *máquina* to strip down; *andamio etc* to take down; *pared* to strip; *casa etc* to strip of its contents, leave bare; *pandilla* to break up; *organización* to disband; to remove the threat of, put an end to; (*Náut*) to unmast, unrig; (*fig*) to abandon, forsake.
⊡ **desmantelarse** VR (*casa etc*) to fall into disrepair, become dilapidated.
desmaña NF (V ADJ) clumsiness, awkwardness; slowness, helplessness; unpractical nature.
desmañado ADJ (*torpe*) clumsy, awkward; (*lerdo*) slow, helpless; (*poco práctico*) unpractical.
desmaquillador NM, **desmaquillante** NM make-up remover.
desmaquillarse [1a] VR to remove one's make-up.
desmarcado ADJ (*Dep*) unmarked.
desmarcar [1g] ⊡ VT to disassociate (*de* from).
⊡ **desmarcarse** VR (*Dep*) to shake off one's attacker, avoid an opponent, get clear; (*fig*) to step out of line; to distance oneself (*de* from), set down the differences (*de* from).
desmasificar VT *cárceles, hospitales* to reduce overcrowding in; ~ **la universidad** to reduce student numbers.
desmayado ADJ (a) (*Med*) unconscious. (b) (*fig*) weak, faint; languid; *carácter etc* dull, lacklustre, colourless. (c) *color* pale, dull.
desmayar [1a] ⊡ VI (*persona*) to lose heart, get discouraged, get depressed; (*esfuerzo etc*) to falter, flag.
⊡ **desmayarse** VR (a) (*Med*) to faint (away), swoon.
(b) (*planta etc*) to droop low, trail.
desmayo NM (a) (*Med: acto*) faint, fainting fit, swoon; (*estado*) unconsciousness; **salír del** ~ to come to, come round; **sufrir un** ~ to have a fainting fit, faint.
(b) (*de voz*) faltering, flagging; (*de ánimo*) dejection, depression; (*del cuerpo en general*) languidness, limpness, limp feeling, listlessness; **tenía un** ~ **en todo el cuerpo** he felt limp all over; **las ramas caen con** ~ the branches droop low, the branches trail; **hablar con** ~ to talk in a small voice, speak falteringly.
desmedido ADJ (*gen*) excessive, disproportionate, out of all proportion; *ambición, orgullo* boundless, overweening; *dolor etc* exaggerated.
desmedirse [3k] VR to forget o.s., go too far.
desmedrado ADJ (a) (*estropeado*) impaired; reduced; in decline. (b) (*Med*) puny, feeble.
desmedrar [1a] ⊡ VT (*perjudicar*) to impair; (*reducir*) to reduce; (*estropear*) to spoil, ruin, affect badly.
⊡ VI **y desmedrarse** VR (a) (*decaer*) to fall off, decline; to go downhill; (*deteriorarse*) to deteriorate.
(b) (*Med*) to get weak; to get thin; (*niño*) to be sickly, waste away; (*Bot*) to grow poorly, do badly.
desmedro NM (a) (*gen*) impairment; (*reducción*) reduction; (*decaimiento*) decline, deterioration. (b) (*Med*) weakness, emaciation,

thinness.

desmejora NF, **desmejoramiento** NM = **desmedro** (a), (b).

desmejorado ADJ: **queda muy desmejorada** she's lost her looks, she's not as attractive as she used to be; (*Med*) she's not looking at all well.

desmejorar [1a] ☐ VT (a) (*perjudicar*) to impair, spoil, damage; to cause to deteriorate.
(b) (*Med*) to weaken, affect the health of.
② **desmejorarse** VR (a) to be impaired, be spoiled; (*decaer*) to decline, deteriorate, go downhill.
(b) (*persona*) to lose one's looks, look less attractive; (*Med*) to lose one's health, suffer, waste away.

desmelenado ☐ ADJ dishevelled, tousled.
② NM, **desmelenada** NF long-haired lout.

desmelenar [1a] ☐ VT to dishevel, tousle the hair of.
② VR **desmelenarse*** (a) (*asearse*) to spruce up, pull one's socks up.
(b) (*obrar*) to sail into action.
(c) (*ir de juerga*) to let one's hair down.

desmelene* NM excess; informality; **¡es el ~!** it's sheer chaos!; it's way over the top!*

desmembración NF dismemberment, break-up.

desmembrar [1j] VT to dismember, separate, break up.

desmemoria NF poor memory, forgetfulness.

desmemoriado ADJ forgetful, absent-minded.

desmemoriarse [1b] VR to grow forgetful, become absent-minded.

desmentida NF denial; **dar una ~ a** to deny, give the lie to.

desmentido NM = **desmentida**.

desmentimiento NM denial; refutation.

desmentir [3i] ☐ VT *acusación* to deny, refute, give the lie to; *rumor* to deny, scotch, scout; *teoría etc* to refute, explode; to contradict; *carácter, orígenes etc* to belie, not fit in with, be unworthy of; **~ rotundamente una acusación** to deny a charge flatly.
② VI to be out of line, not fit; **~ de** to belie, clash with, be unworthy of.
③ **desmentirse** VR (*contradecirse*) to contradict o.s.; (*desdecirse*) to go back on one's word.

desmenuzable ADJ crumbly, crumbling; flaky; friable.

desmenuzar [1f] ☐ VT (a) *pan etc* to crumble (up), break into small pieces; *carne* to chop, shred, mince; *queso* to grate.
(b) (*fig*) to examine minutely, take a close look at.
② **desmenuzarse** VR to crumble (up), break up.

desmerecedor(a) NM/F undeserving person.

desmerecer [2d] ☐ VT to be unworthy of.
② VI (a) (*deteriorarse*) to deteriorate, go off, be less good; (*perder valor*) to lose value.
(b) **~ de** to compare unfavourably with, not be comparable to, not live up to; **ésta no desmerece de sus otras películas** this is in no way inferior to his other films, this is every bit as good as his earlier films.

desmesura NF (a) (*exceso*) excess, enormity; (*desproporción*) disproportion; extra size. (b) (*falta de moderación*) lack of moderation.

desmesuradamente ADV disproportionately, excessively; enormously; **abrir ~ la boca** to open one's mouth extra wide.

desmesurado ADJ (a) (*excesivo*) disproportionate, excessive, inordinate; (*enorme*) enormous; *ambición etc* boundless; *dimensiones* extra big, unduly large, much too big.
(b) (*descarado*) insolent, impudent.

desmesurarse [1a] VR to become insolent, forget o.s., lose all restraint.

desmigajar [1a] VT, **desmigar** [1h] VT to crumble.

desmilitarización NF demilitarization.

desmilitarizado ADJ demilitarized.

desmilitarizar [1f] VT to demilitarize.

desmineralizado ADJ (*fig*) *actuación etc* lifeless, lacklustre; *persona* run down.

desmineralizar VT to demineralize.

desmirriado ADJ (*débil*) weak, sickly; (*flaco*) thin, weedy*.

desmitificación NF demythologizing.

desmitificador ADJ demythologizing.

desmitificar [1g] VT to demythologize.

desmochar [1a] VT *árbol* to lop, cut off the top of; to pollard; *defensas* to slight; *cuernos* to cut off the points of; *texto etc* to cut, hack about, mutilate.

desmoche NM (a) (*de árbol*) lopping, pollarding.
(b) (*) general slaughter, mowing down, mass removal; **hubo un ~ en el primer examen** there was a mass slaughter of candidates in the first exam.

desmocho NM lopped branches, cuttings.

desmodular [1a] VT (*Rad etc*) *mensaje* to scramble.

desmolado ADJ toothless.

desmoldar [1a] VT (*Culin*) to remove from its mould.

desmonetizar [1f] VT (a) (*Fin*) to demonetize. (b) (*Cono Sur: desvalorizar*) to devalue.

desmontable ☐ ADJ detachable; sectional, in sections, which takes apart; collapsible; that takes down.
② NM tyre lever.

desmontaje NM dismantling, stripping down; demolition.

desmontar [1a] ☐ VT (a) (*Mec*) to dismantle, strip down; to take apart, take to pieces; (*Arquit*) to knock down, demolish; *escopeta* to uncock; *tienda* to take down; *artillería enemiga* to silence, knock out; *vela* to take down.
(b) *terreno* to level; to clear of trees (*etc*); *árbol* to fell; *basura* to clear away.
(c) *jinete* to throw, unseat, unhorse; **~ a uno de un vehículo** to help sb down from a vehicle.
② VI y **desmontarse** VR to dismount, alight (*de* from).

desmonte NM (a) (*acto*) levelling; clearing; clearing away, removal; **los trabajos exigirán el ~ de X metros cúbicos** the work will necessitate the removal of X cubic metres.
(b) (*terreno*) levelled ground; (*montón*) heap of soil extracted.
(c) (*Ferro*) cutting, cut (*US*).
(d) (*madera*) felled timber.

desmoralización NF demoralization.

desmoralizado ADJ demoralized.

desmoralizador ADJ demoralizing.

desmoralizar [1f] ☐ VT *ejército etc* to demoralize; *costumbres etc* to corrupt.
② **desmoralizarse** VR to lose heart, get discouraged.

desmoronadizo ADJ crumbling; rickety; dilapidated.

desmoronado ADJ tumbledown, ruinous, dilapidated.

desmoronamiento NM crumbling, dilapidation, decay; collapse (*t fig*).

desmoronar [1a] ☐ VT to wear away, destroy little by little; (*fig*) to erode, affect, make inroads into.
② **desmoronarse** VR (*Geol etc*) to crumble, fall apart; (*casa etc*) to get dilapidated, fall into disrepair; (*ladrillos etc*) to fall, come down, collapse; (*fig*) to decline, decay.

desmotivación NF lack of motivation.

desmotivado ADJ unmotivated, lacking motivation.

desmotivar [1a] VT to discourage.

desmovilización NF (a) (*Mil*) demobilization. (b) demoralization.

desmovilizar [1f] VT (a) (*Mil*) to demobilize. (b) (*desanimar*) to demoralize.

desmultiplicar [1g] VT (*Mec*) to gear down.

desnacionalización NF denationalization.

desnacionalizado ADJ (a) *industria etc* denationalized. (b) *persona* stateless.

desnacionalizar [1f] VT to denationalize.

desnarigada NF (*hum*): **la ~** the skull.

desnarigado ADJ flat-nosed; snub-nosed.

desnatado ADJ *leche* skimmed, low-fat (*atr*).

desnatar [1a] VT *leche* to skim, take the cream off; *metal fundido* to remove the scum from; (*fig*) to take the cream off; **leche sin ~** whole milk.

desnaturalizado ADJ (a) (*Quím*) denatured. (b) *persona etc* unnatural; cruel, inhuman.

desnaturalizar [1f] ☐ VT (a) (*Quím*) to denature.
(b) (*fig*) to denaturalize, alter the fundamental nature of; (*pervertir*) to pervert, corrupt; *texto etc* to distort; *sentido* to misrepresent, twist.
② **desnaturalizarse** VR to give up one's nationality; to become stateless.

desnivel NM (a) (*desigualdad*) unevenness; (*tierra alta*) high ground; (*tierra baja*) low ground. (b) (*fig*) inequality, difference, gap; lack of adjustment (*entre* between).

desnivelado ADJ (a) *terreno* uneven. (b) (*fig*) unbalanced, badly adjusted, unequal.

desnivelar [1a] VT (a) *terreno* to make uneven. (b) (*fig*) to unbalance, upset the balance of, create imbalance in.

desnucar [1g] ☐ VT to break the neck of; to fell, poleaxe.
② **desnucarse** VR to break one's neck.

desnuclearización NF nuclear disarmament, denuclearization.

desnuclearizar [1f] VT to denuclearize; **región desnuclearizada** nuclear-free area.

desnudar [1a] ☐ VT (a) (*gen*; *t Bot, fig*; *de* of) to strip; *persona* to strip, undress; *brazo etc* to bare; *espada* to draw; (*Geol*) to denude; *objeto, monumento etc* to lay bare, uncover, remove the coverings from.
(b) (*fig*) to ruin, break; (*) *jugador* to fleece.
② **desnudarse** VR (a) (*persona*) to undress, get undressed; to strip (off); **~ hasta la cintura** to strip to the waist.
(b) **~ de algo** to get rid of sth, cast sth aside; **el árbol se está desnudando de sus hojas** the tree is shedding (*o* losing) its leaves.

desnudez NF (a) (*de persona*) nudity, nakedness. (b) (*fig*) bareness.

desnudismo NM nudism.

desnudista NMF nudist.

desnudo [1] ADJ (a) *cuerpo* naked, nude; unclothed; bare; *brazo, árbol etc* bare; *landscape* bare, flat, featureless; **en las paredes desnudas** on the bare walls; **la ciudad quedó desnuda** the town was flattened; **cavar con las manos desnudas** to dig with one's bare hands.
(b) (*fig*) *estilo etc* bare, unadorned; *verdad* naked, plain, unvarnished; **estar ~ de** to be devoid of, be bereft of, be without.
(c) (*fig: pobre*) penniless; **y ahora están ~s** and now all they've got is what they stand up in; **quedarse ~** to be ruined, be bankrupt.
[2] NM (a) nudity, nakedness; (*Arte*) nude; **~ integral** full-frontal nudity; **la retrató al ~** he painted her in the nude; **llevaba los hombros al ~** her shoulders were bare, she was bare-shouldered.
(b) **poner algo al ~** (*fig*) to lay sth bare.

desnutrición NF malnutrition, undernourishment.

desnutrido ADJ undernourished.

desobedecer [2d] VTI to disobey.

desobediencia NF disobedience; **~ civil** civil disobedience.

desobediente ADJ disobedient.

desobstruir [3g] VT to unblock, unstop, clear.

desocupación NF (a) (*tiempo libre*) leisure; (*pey*) idleness. (b) (*Econ*) unemployment.

desocupado ADJ (a) *espacio, silla etc* empty, vacant, unoccupied.
(b) *tiempo* spare, free; leisure (*atr*).
(c) *persona* free, not busy; at leisure; (*pey*) idle; (*Econ*) unemployed.

desocupar [1a] [1] VT (a) *casa etc* to vacate, move out of; to leave empty; *recipiente* to empty.
(b) *contenido* to remove, take out.
[2] VI (*) to shit**.
[3] **desocuparse** VR (a) **~ de un puesto** to give up one's job.
(b) (*Carib, Cono Sur*) to give birth.

desodorante NM deodorant.

desodorizar [1f] VT to deodorize.

desoír [3p] VT to ignore, disregard; to turn a deaf ear to.

desojarse [1a] VR to strain one's eyes.

desolación NF (a) (*gen*) desolation. (b) (*fig*) grief, distress.

desolado ADJ (a) (*gen*) desolate. (b) (*fig*) sad, distressed, disconsolate; **estoy ~ por aquello** I'm terribly grieved about that.

desolador ADJ (*doloroso*) distressing, grievous; *paisaje* bleak, cheerless; *epidemia etc* devastating.

desolar [1a] [1] VT to lay waste, ruin, desolate.
[2] **desolarse** VR to grieve, be distressed, be disconsolate.

desolidarizarse [1f] VR: **~ de** to dissociate o.s. from.

desolladero NM slaughterhouse.

desollado ADJ (*) brazen, barefaced.

desollador NM (a) (*Ind*) skinner; (*fig*) extortioner, robber. (b) (*Orn*) shrike.

desolladura NF (a) (*acto*) skinning, flaying. (b) (*Med*) graze, abrasion; bruise. (c) (*fig*) extortion, piece of robbery.

desollar [1l] VT (a) (*gen*) to skin, flay.
(b) **~ vivo a uno** (*fig*) (*hacer pagar*) to fleece sb, make sb pay through the nose; (*criticar*) to flay sb verbally, criticize sb unmercifully.

desopinar [1a] VT to denigrate.

desorbitado ADJ (a) (*excesivo*) disproportionate, excessive; *precio* exorbitant; *pretensión etc* exaggerated. (b) **con los ojos ~s** wild-eyed, pop-eyed, with bulging eyes.

desorbitante ADJ excessive, overwhelming.

desorbitar [1a] [1] VT (a) (*exagerar*) to carry to extremes; to exaggerate.
(b) **~ un asunto** to misinterpret a matter, get a matter out of perspective, take an unbalanced view of a matter.
[2] **desorbitarse** VR (*persona*) to go to extremes, lose one's sense of proportion; (*asunto etc*) to get out of hand.

desorden NM (a) (*gen*) disorder; confusion; turmoil; disarray; (*Pol*) disorder; **en ~** in confusion, in disorder; **poner las cosas en ~** to upset things, confuse things.
(b) (*un ~*) mess, litter, confusion.
(c) (*fig*) irregular life; loose living.
(d) **desórdenes** (*Pol etc*) disorders; (*excesos*) excesses.

desordenadamente ADV (V ADJ) (a) untidily; in disorder, in a mess.
(b) in a disorderly fashion; irregularly; unmethodically; wildly; lawlessly.

desordenado ADJ (a) *cuarto etc* untidy, in disorder; *objetos* disordered, confused, in a mess.
(b) *conducta* disorderly; *vida* irregular; *carácter* unmethodical; *niño etc* wild, unruly; *país* lawless, unsettled.

desordenar [1a] VT (a) *pelo etc* to disarrange, mess up; *cuarto* to mess up, make a mess of; (*causar confusión en*) to throw into confusion. (b) (*Mec etc*) to put out of order.

desorejado ADJ (a) (*And, Carib, Cono Sur: sin mangos*) without handles.
(b) (*And*) (*duro de oído*) hard of hearing; (*Mús*) tone deaf; **hacerse el ~*** to turn a deaf ear.
(c) (*fig*) (*degradado*) abject, degraded; (*disoluto*) dissolute.

(d) (*Carib: pródigo*) lavish; wasteful.
(e) (*CAm: tonto*) silly.

desorganización NF disorganization, disruption.

desorganizar [1f] VT to disorganize, disrupt.

desorientado ADJ disoriented, disorientated.

desorientamiento NM, **desorientación** NF disorientation.

desorientar [1a] [1] VT: **~ a uno** to direct sb wrongly, to make sb lose his way; to disorient sb (*t fig*); **el nuevo cruce me desorientó** the new junction made me lose my bearings.
[2] **desorientarse** VR (a) (*despistarse*) to lose one's way, lose one's bearings.
(b) (*fig*) to go wrong, go astray, get off the track; to get confused, become disorientated.

desovar [1l] VI (*pez*) to spawn; (*insecto, anfibio etc*) to lay eggs.

desove NM spawning; egg-laying.

desovillar [1a] VT (a) *lana* to unravel, unwind; to disentangle. (b) (*fig*) to unravel, clarify.

desoxidar [1a] VT to remove the rust from; (*Quím*) to deoxidize.

despabiladeras NFPL snuffers; **unas ~** a pair of snuffers.

despabilado ADJ (a) (*despierto*) wide-awake. (b) (*fig*) wide-awake; (*alerta*) alert, watchful; (*listo*) quick, sharp.

despabilar [1a] [1] VT (a) *vela* to snuff; *lámpara, mecha* to trim.
(b) (*fig*) *ingenio* to sharpen; *persona* to wake up; to sharpen the wits of, liven up, brighten up.
(c) (*fig*) *fortuna* to squander rapidly; *comida* to dispatch; *asunto* to get through quickly.
(d) (*: *robar*) to pinch*.
(e) (‡: *matar*) **~ a uno** to do sb in‡.
[2] VI y **despabilarse** VR (a) (*gen*) to wake up; (*fig*) to look lively, get a move on; **¡despabílate!** get a move on!, jump to it!
(b) (*CAm, Carib, Cono Sur: marcharse*) to vanish; (*escaparse*) to slip away, slope off*.

despachaderas NFPL (a) (*respuesta*) surly retort, unfriendly answer.
(b) (*inteligencia*) resourcefulness, quickness of mind; (*sentido práctico*) business sense, practical know-how; **tener buenas ~** to be practical, be on the ball; to be good at getting rid of fools.
(c) (*descaro*) brazenness, insolence.

despachado ADJ (a) (*inteligente*) resourceful, quick; businesslike; practical; **ir bien ~ de** to be well off for, be well provided with. (b) (*descarado*) brazen, insolent.

despachador [1] ADJ prompt, quick.
[2] NM, **despachadora** NF (a) (*empleado*) quick worker. (b) **~ de equipaje** baggage handler.

despachante NM (*Cono Sur*) clerk; customs agent.

despachar [1a] [1] VT (a) (*hacer*) *tarea* to complete; *negocio* to do, complete, dispatch, settle, transact; *correspondencia* to deal with, attend to; *tema etc* to deal with; to polish off, knock off; *problema* to settle; **~ asuntos con el gerente** to do business with the manager, settle matters with the manager; **medio capítulo llevo despachado ya** I've already knocked off half a chapter.
(b) (*) *comida etc* to dispatch, put away*; *bebida** to knock back*.
(c) *billete etc* to issue.
(d) (*enviar*) *mercancías* to send, dispatch, mail (*a* to).
(e) (*acelerar*) to expedite, hurry along.
(f) (*enviar*) *persona* to send away, send off; to send packing; *empleado* to fire*, sack*.
(g) (*Com*) *géneros* to sell, deal in; *cliente* to attend to; **en seguida le despacho** I'll attend to you at once.
(h) (*Cono Sur*) *equipaje* to register.
[2] VI (a) (*Com*) to do business; to serve; (*Pol etc*) **~ con uno** to meet sb, consult sb, have an interview with sb; **no despacha los domingos** he doesn't do business on Sundays, he's not in on Sundays; **¿quién despacha?** is anybody serving?
(b) (*terminar*) to finish things off, get things settled; (*decidirse*) to come to a decision; **¡despacha de una vez!** settle it once and for all!, make up your mind!
(c) (*acelerarse*) to hurry up, get on with it; **¡despacha!** get on with it!
[3] **despacharse** VR (a) (*terminar*) to finish off; **suelo despacharme a las 5** I finish at 5, I knock off at 5*; **~ de algo** to finish sth off; to get rid of sth, get clear of sth.
(b) (*darse prisa*) to hurry (up).
(c) **~ a su gusto con uno** to say what one really thinks to sb, speak very plainly to sb.
(d) **~ con el cucharón*** to help o.s. to the biggest (*o* best) portion; (*fig*) to look after Number One.

despachero, -a NM/F (*Chile*) shopkeeper.

despacho NM (a) (*acto*) dispatch; sending (out); (*de negocio*) dispatch, handling, settling; **~ aduanal**, **~ de aduanas** customs clearance.
(b) (*cualidad*) resourcefulness, quickness of mind; business sense; promptness, energy, efficiency; **tener buen ~** to be very efficient, be on top of one's job.

(c) (*Com: venta*) sale (of goods); **géneros sin ~** unsaleable goods; **tener buen ~** to find a ready sale, be in good demand.

(d) (*mensaje*) message; (*Mil, diplomático*) dispatch; **~ telegráfico** telegram.

(e) (*Com, Pol etc: oficina*) office; (*en casa*) study; **~ de billetes**, **~ de boletos** (*LAm*) booking-office; **~ de localidades** box-office; **~ de telégrafos** telegraph office.

(f) (*Com: tienda*) shop; depot; (*Cono Sur*) general store; small village shop.

(g) (*muebles*) set of office furniture.

(h) **~ de oficial** (*Mil*) commission.

(i) (*Pol etc*) meeting, consultation, interview (*con* with).

despachurrar [1a] VT **(a)** (*aplastar*) to squash, crush; to squelch; (*Culin*) to mash.

(b) *cuento* to mangle, make a dreadful mess of.

(c) *persona* to crush, flatten, floor.

despacio ⊡ ADV **(a)** (*lentamente*) slowly; (*sin esforzar*) gently; (*poco a poco*) gradually; **¡~!** gently!, not so fast!, easy there!

(b) (*LAm*) *hablar* softly, in a low voice.

⊡ NM (*LAm*) **(a)** (*retraso*) delay; (*lentitud*) slowness.

(b) (*táctica*) delaying tactic.

despaciosamente ADV (*LAm*) slowly.

despacioso ADJ slow, deliberate; sluggish; phlegmatic.

despacito ADV **(a)** (*lentamente*) very slowly, very gently; **¡~!** easy does it! **(b)** (*dulcemente*) softly.

despampanante* ADJ stunning.

despampanar [1a] ⊡ VT **(a)** *vid* to prune, trim.

(b) (*: *asombrar*) to shatter, stun, bowl over.

⊡ VI (*) to blow one's top*, give vent to one's feelings; to speak out freely.

⊡ **despampanarse** VR (*) to give o.s. a nasty knock.

despancar [1g] VT (*And*) *maíz* to husk.

despanzurrar [1a] ⊡ VT to squash.

⊡ **despanzurrarse** VR to get squashed (*contra* against).

desparasitar [1a] VT to delouse.

desparejado ADJ, **desparejo** ADJ odd, unpaired; **son ~s** they're odd, they don't match.

desparpajar [1a] ⊡ VT **(a)** (*desmontar*) to take apart carelessly; (*estropear*) to botch, bungle, spoil, mess up.

(b) (*CAm, Méx: dispersar*) to scatter, disperse.

⊡ VI to talk wildly, rant, rave.

⊡ **desparpajarse** VR **(a)** = VI.

(b) (*CAm, Carib: despertarse*) to wake up.

desparpajo NM **(a)** (*desenvoltura*) ease of manner, self-confidence; (*naturalidad*) naturalness; (*simpatía*) charm; (*labia*) glibness; (*descaro*) nerve*, pertness, impudence.

(b) (*inteligencia*) savoir-faire, practical know-how; sharpness, quickness of mind; (*presencia de ánimo*) presence of mind.

(c) (*CAm: desorden*) disorder, muddle.

(d) (*And: comentario*) flippant remark.

desparramado ADJ scattered; wide, open.

desparramar [1a] ⊡ VT **(a)** (*esparcir*) to scatter, spread (*por* over); *líquido etc* to spill; *partes* to separate.

(b) *fortuna* to squander; *atención* to spread too widely, fail to concentrate.

⊡ **desparramarse** VR **(a)** to scatter, spread out; to spill, be spilt; (*animales*) to bolt, stampede.

(b) (*: *pasarlo bomba*) to have a whale of a time*.

desparrame* NM confusion, disorder; lack of control.

desparramo NM **(a)** (*Carib, Cono Sur*) (*acto*) scattering, spreading; dispersal; (*el vertir*) spilling; (*fuga*) rush, stampede. **(b)** (*Cono Sur: desorden*) confusion, disorder.

despatarrado ADJ: **quedar ~** **(a)** (*lit*) to have one's legs wide apart.

(b) (*fig*) to be dumbfounded; to be scared to death.

despatarrante* ADJ side-splitting.

despatarrar [1a] ⊡ VT (*fig*) (*aturdir*) to amaze, dumbfound; (*asustar*) to scare to death.

⊡ **despatarrarse** VR **(a)** (*abrir las piernas*) to open one's legs wide; (*en suelo etc*) to do the splits; (*al caer*) to fall with one's legs spread wide.

(b) (*fig*) to be amazed, be dumbfounded; to be scared to death.

(c) (*) **~ de risa** to split one's sides laughing.

despatriar [1b] VT (*And, Carib*) to exile.

despavorido ADJ: **estar ~** to be utterly terrified.

despe* NF tag, 'he'; **dar la ~** to play tag.

despeado ADJ footsore, weary.

despearse [1a] VR to get footsore, get utterly weary.

despechado ADJ angry, indignant; spiteful.

despechar [1a] ⊡ VT **(a)** (*provocar*) to anger, enrage; (*causar pena a*) to spite; (*hacer desesperar*) to drive to despair.

(b) (*) *niño* to wean.

⊡ **despecharse** VR to get angry; to fret; to despair.

despecho NM **(a)** (*ojeriza*) spite, rancour; (*desesperación*) despair; **de puro ~, por ~** out of (sheer) spite.

(b) **a ~ de** in spite of, despite; in defiance of.

(c) (*de niño*) weaning.

despechugado ADJ *persona* with one's collar open, with one's shirt front undone; bare-chested; *camisa* open-necked, open at the neck.

despechugarse [1h] VR to open one's collar, unbutton one's shirt at the neck; to bare one's chest (o breast); to unbutton one's shirt down the front.

despectivamente ADV contemptuously, scornfully; in derogatory terms; (*Ling*) pejoratively.

despectivo ADJ contemptuous, scornful; derogatory; (*Ling*) pejorative.

despedazar [1f] VT **(a)** (*romper*) to tear apart, tear to pieces; (*cortar*) to cut into bits; (*hacer trizas*) to lacerate, mangle, cut to shreds. **(b)** (*fig*) *corazón* to break; *honor* to ruin.

despedida NF **(a)** (*adiós*) farewell; leave-taking; (*antes de viaje*) send-off; (*despido*) dismissal, sacking*; **cena de ~** farewell dinner; **función de ~** (*Teat*) farewell performance; **regalo de ~** parting gift; **~ de soltera** hen night; **~ de soltero** stag party.

(b) (*ceremonia*) farewell ceremony.

(c) (*Liter etc*) envoi; (*Mús*) final verse; (*en carta*) closing formula, closing phrases, ending.

(d) (*Inform*) log off, log out.

despedir [3k] ⊡ VT **(a)** *invitado, amigo* to see off; *visita* to see out; (*decir adiós a*) to say goodbye to; *cliente etc* to show out; **fuimos a ~le a la estación** we went to see him off at the station.

(b) *empleado etc* to dismiss, sack*, discharge; *pesado* to get rid of, send away; *inquilino* to evict; to give notice to.

(c) **~ algo de sí** to get rid of sth; **~ un pensamiento de sí** to put a thought out of one's mind, banish a thought from one's mind.

(d) (*arrojar*) *objeto* to hurl, fling; to project; *flecha etc* to fire; *mísil* to launch; *chorro etc* to send up; *jinete* to throw; *olor etc* to give off, give out, emit, throw off; *calor* to give out; *zumo etc* to release, allow to come out; **~ el espíritu** to give up the ghost.

⊡ **despedirse** VR (*decir adiós*) to say goodbye, take one's leave; (*dejar un empleo*) to give up one's job, leave (one's work); **se despidieron** they said goodbye to each other; **~ de uno** to say goodbye to sb, take one's leave of sb; (*en estación etc*) to see sb off; **¡ya puedes despedirte de ese dinero!** you can say goodbye to that money!

despegado ⊡ ADJ **(a)** (*separado*) detached, loose. **(b)** *persona* cold, indifferent, unconcerned.

⊡ NM: **es un ~** he has cut himself off from his family, he has kept no roots.

despegar [1h] ⊡ VT (*cosa pegada*) to unglue, unstick; (*separar*) to detach, loosen; *sobre* to open; **sin ~ los labios** without uttering a word.

⊡ VI (*Aer*) to take off (*t fig*); (*cohete*) to lift off, blast off.

⊡ **despegarse** VR **(a)** (*desprenderse*) to come loose, come unstuck; (*objeto*) to come apart.

(b) (*persona*) to become alienated, become detached (*de* from); **~ de los amigos** to break with one's friends; **~ del mundo** to withdraw from the world, renounce worldly things.

(c) **~ de*** not to go well with.

despego NM = **desapego**.

despegue NM **(a)** (*Aer, tb fig*) take-off; (*de cohete*) lift-off, blast-off; **~ corto** short take-off; **~ vertical** vertical take-off. **(b)** **~ industrial** (*fig*) industrial renewal.

despeinado ⊡ ADJ dishevelled, tousled; unkempt.

⊡ NM tousled hair-style.

despeinar [1a] VT ⊡ *pelo, persona* to tousle, ruffle; *peinado* to mess up, muss.

⊡ **despeinarse** VR (*fig*) to make a great effort, get really involved.

despejable ADJ explicable; **difícilmente ~** hard to explain.

despejado ADJ **(a)** *camino, espacio* clear, free, unobstructed, open; *frente* clear; *cuarto etc* unencumbered, spacious.

(b) *cielo* cloudless, clear.

(c) (*persona: estar*) wide-awake; (*Med*) free of fever; lucid.

(d) (*persona: ser*) sharp, bright, smart.

despejar [1a] ⊡ VT **(a)** *espacio etc* to clear, disencumber, free from obstructions; **los bomberos despejaron el teatro** the firemen cleared the theatre (of people); **los guardias obligaron a ~ el tribunal** the police ordered the court to be cleared, the police ordered people to leave the court; **¡despejen!** move along!; everybody out!

(b) (*Dep*) *balón* to clear.

(c) *misterio* to clear up, clarify, resolve; (*Mat*) *incógnita* to find.

⊡ VI **(a)** (*Dep*) to clear (the ball).

(b) (*Met*) to clear.

⊡ **despejarse** VR **(a)** (*Met*) to clear, clear up; (*misterio etc*) to become clearer.

(b) (*persona*) (*animarse*) to liven o.s. up; (*sentirse mejor*) to feel better, feel brighter; (*despejar la cabeza*) to clear one's head.

(c) (*persona: relajarse*) to relax, amuse o.s.

(d) (*persona: en temperamento*) to become more self-assured, gain in confidence.

despeje NM (a) (*Dep*) clearance. (b) (*de mente*) clarity, clearness of mind.

despejo NM brightness; self-confidence, ease of manner; fluency.

despellejar [1a] VT (a) to skin, flay. (b) (*fig: criticar*) to flay, criticize unmercifully. (c) (*: arruinar*) ~ **a uno** to fleece sb.

despelotado* ADJ half-naked, scantily clad; (*LAm*) disorganized.

despelotar* [1a] [1] VT to strip, undress.
[2] **despelotarse** VR (a) to strip (off), undress. (b) ~ **de risa** to laugh fit to bust*.

despelote* NM (a) (*estado*) nudity, nakedness; (*acto*) strip.
(b) (*Carib: juerga*) big spree, grand evening out.
(c) (*Cono Sur* (*alboroto*) row, racket; (*desorden*) mess, mix-up.
(d) **se ha comprado un coche que es un ~** (*Cono Sur*) he's bought a fantastic car*.
(e) **¡qué ~!, ¡vaya ~!** what a laugh!

despeluchado ADJ dishevelled, tousled.

despeluchar [1a] VT to dishevel, tousle.

despeluz(n)ar [1f] [1] VT (a) *pelo* to dishevel, tousle, rumple.
(b) ~ **a uno** (*fig*) to horrify sb, make sb's hair stand on end.
(c) (*Carib: arruinar*) to ruin, leave penniless.
[2] **despeluz(n)arse** VR (a) (*pelo*) to stand on end.
(b) (*persona*) to be horrified.

despenalización NF legalization; decriminalization.

despenalizar [1f] VT to legalize; to decriminalize.

despenar [1a] VT (a) (*consolar*) to console. (b) (*: matar*) to do in*, kill.

despendedor ADJ extravagant.

despendolado* ADJ uninhibited, unrestrained, free and easy, wild.

despendole* NM lack of inhibitions, lack of restraint; wildness.

despensa NF (a) (*armario*) pantry, larder; food store; (*Náut*) store-room. (b) (*provisión*) stock of food.

despensero NM butler, steward; (*Náut*) storekeeper.

despeñadero NM (a) (*Geog*) cliff, precipice. (b) (*fig*) risk, danger.

despeñadizo ADJ dangerously steep, sheer, precipitous.

despeñar [1a] [1] VT to fling down, hurl from a height, throw over a cliff.
[2] **despeñarse** VR (a) (*tirarse al suelo*) to hurl o.s. down, throw o.s. over a cliff; (*caer*) to fall headlong.
(b) ~ **en el vicio** to plunge into vice.

despeño NM fall, drop; (*fig*) failure, collapse.

despepitar [1a] [1] VT to remove the pips (*etc*) from.
[2] **despepitarse** VR (a) (*gritar*) to bawl, shriek (one's head off), shout o.s. hoarse; (*obrar*) to rave, act wildly; **salir despepitado*** to rush out, go rushing out.
(b) ~ **por algo** to long for sth, go overboard for sth*; ~ **por** + *infin* to long to + *infin*.

despercudir [3a] VT (a) (*limpiar*) to clean, wash. (b) (*LAm: fig*) *persona* to liven up, wake up, ginger up.

desperdiciado ADJ wasteful.

desperdiciador(a) ADJ, NM/F spendthrift.

desperdiciar [1b] VT *fortuna etc* to waste, squander, fritter away; *tiempo* to waste; *oportunidad* to throw away.

desperdicio NM (a) (*acto*) waste; wasting; squandering.
(b) ~**s** (*basura*) rubbish, refuse; (*restos*) scraps, left-overs; (*residuos*) waste; (*Bio, Téc*) waste products; ~**s de algodón** cotton waste; ~**s de cocina** kitchen scraps; ~**s de hierro** scrap iron, junk.
(c) **el cerdo es un animal que no tiene ~** nothing from a pig is wasted, everything from a pig can be used; **el muchacho no tiene ~** he's a fine lad; **el libro no tiene ~** the book is excellent from start to finish.

desperdigado ADJ scattered.

desperdigar [1h] [1] VT (*esparcir*) to scatter, separate, disperse; *energías etc* to spread too widely, dissipate.
[2] **desperdigarse** VR to scatter, separate.

desperezarse [1f] VR to stretch (o.s.).

desperezo NM stretch.

desperfecto NM flaw, blemish, imperfection; slight damage; **sufrió algunos ~s en el accidente** it suffered slight damage in the accident.

despernado ADJ footsore, weary.

despersonalizar [1f] VT to depersonalize.

despertador NM (a) (*reloj*) alarm clock; ~ **de viaje** travelling clock.
(b) (*persona*) knocker-up. (c) (*fig*) warning.

despertamiento NM awakening, revival, rebirth.

despertar [1j] [1] VT (a) *persona etc* to wake (up), awaken.
(b) (*fig*) *esperanzas etc* to awaken, raise, arouse; *memoria* to awaken, revive, recall; *sentimientos* to arouse, stir up.
[2] VI **y despertarse** VR to wake up, awaken; ~ **a la realidad** to wake up to reality.
[3] NM: **el ~ religioso** the religious awakening; **el ~ de la primavera** the awakening of spring.

despestañarse [1a] VR (*Cono Sur*) (a) (*desojarse*) to strain one's eyes.

(b) (*fig*) to burn the midnight oil, swot*.

despiadadamente ADV cruelly; mercilessly, relentlessly; heartlessly.

despiadado ADJ cruel; merciless, relentless; heartless.

despicarse [1g] VR to get even, get one's revenge.

despichar [1a] [1] VT (*And, Carib, Cono Sur*) (*aplastar*) to crush, flatten; (*fig*) to crush.
[2] VI (*:*) to kick the bucket*.

despido NM (a) (*acto*) dismissal; ~ **arbitrario**, ~ **improcedente** wrongful dismissal; ~ **colectivo** wholesale redundancies, large-scale dismissals; ~ **disciplinario** dismissal on disciplinary grounds; ~ **forzoso** compulsory redundancy; ~ **incentivado** voluntary redundancy; ~ **libre** right to hire and fire. (b) (*pago*) severance pay, redundancy payment.

despiece NM (a) (*de res*) quartering, carving-up. (b) (*Prensa*) comment, personal note.

despierto ADJ (a) (*gen*) awake. (b) (*fig*) wide-awake; sharp; alert, watchful.

despiezar [1f] VT to break up, split up; *res* to quarter, carve up.

despilfarrado ADJ (a) *derrochador* extravagant, wasteful, spendthrift.
(b) *desaseado* ragged, shabby.

despilfarrador [1] ADJ = **despilfarrado**.
[2] NM, **despilfarradora** NF spendthrift.

despilfarrar [1a] VT to waste, squander.

despilfarro NM (a) (*acto*) wasting, squandering. (b) (*cualidad*) extravagance, wastefulness. (c) (*desaseo*) shabbiness, slovenliness, ragged state.

despintar [1a] [1] VT (a) (*quitar pintura a*) to take the paint off.
(b) (*fig*) *cuento etc* to alter, distort; to spoil.
(c) **no ~ a uno** (*And, Carib, Cono Sur*) not to let sb out of one's sight.
[2] VI: **éste no despinta de su casta** he is no different from the rest of his family.
[3] **despintarse** VR (a) (*con la lluvia etc*) to wash off; (*desteñirse*) to fade, lose its colour; (*LAm: maquillaje*) to run, get smudged.
(b) ~ **algo** (*fig*) to forget sth, wipe sth from one's mind; **no se me despinta que ...** I never forget that ...; I remember vividly that ...

despiojar [1a] VT (a) (*lit*) to delouse. (b) ~ **a uno** (*fig*) to rescue sb from the gutter.

despiole* NM (*Cono Sur*) = **despelote**.

despiporrante* ADJ killingly funny.

despiporre(n)* NM wild disturbance; mayhem; **¡fue el ~!** it was something out of this world!, it was just about the end!; **esto es el ~** this is the limit!

despique NM satisfaction, revenge.

despistado [1] ADJ (a) (*ser*) vague, absent-minded; unpractical; hopeless.
(b) (*estar*) confused, out of touch, all at sea; off the beam*; **ando muy ~ con todo esto** I'm terribly muddled about all this.
[2] NM, **despistada** NF absent-minded person, vague individual; unpractical type; **es un ~** he's hopeless, he hasn't a clue; **hacerse el ~** to pretend not to understand.

despistaje NM (*Med*) early detection, early diagnosis.

despistar [1a] [1] VT (a) (*Caza*) to throw off the track (o scent).
(b) (*fig*) to put off the scent; to mislead, muddle; **esa pregunta está hecha para ~** that question is designed to mislead people.
(c) (*: robar*) to nick*, rip off*.
(d) (*Med*) to detect (early), diagnose at an early stage.
[2] **despistarse** VR (*fig*) to go wrong, take the wrong route (o turning *etc*); to get confused.

despiste NM (a) (*Aut etc*) swerve.
(b) (*error*) mistake, slip.
(c) (*cualidad*) absent-mindedness; (*estado*) muddle, confusion, bewilderment; **¡qué ~ tienes!** you're a bright one!, what a clot you are!*; **tiene un terrible ~** he's terribly absent-minded; he's hopelessly unpractical; he's hopeless, he hasn't a clue.

desplacer [1] [2w] VT to displease.
[2] NM displeasure.

desplanchar [1a] [1] VT *ropa* to crease, crumple.
[2] **desplancharse** VR to crease, crumple.

desplantador NM trowel.

desplantar [1a] VT (a) *planta* to pull up, uproot, take up. (b) *objeto* to move out of vertical, tilt, put out of plumb.

desplante NM (a) (*en baile etc*) wrong stance.
(b) (*dicho*) bold statement, outspoken remark; (*pey*) impudent remark, cutting remark (*etc*); (*LAm*: disparate*) crazy idea; **dar un ~** to interrupt sb rudely; **me dio un ~** (*asombrar*) he left me stunned; **ella me hizo un ~** (*LAm**) she stood me up*.
(c) (*descaro*) insolence, lack of respect.

desplazado [1] ADJ (a) *objeto* displaced, wrongly placed, offcentre.
(b) *persona* badly adjusted; out of one's depth, out of one's element; (*Pol*) displaced; **sentirse un poco ~** to feel rather out of place.
[2] NM, **desplazada** NF misfit; ill-adjusted person; outsider; (*Pol*) displaced person.

desplazamiento NM **(a)** (*acto*) displacement, movement; (*de casa*) removal; ~ **continental** continental drift; ~ **de tierras** landslip; **puede telefonear en pleno** ~ you can phone while on the move. **(b)** (*Náut*) displacement. **(c)** (*viaje*) journey, trip; (*salida*) outing; **reside en Madrid aunque con frecuentes ~s** she lives in Madrid but is often away. **(d)** (*de opinión, votos etc*) shift, swing. **(e)** (*Inform*) scroll(ing); ~ **hacia abajo** scroll down; ~ **hacia arriba** scroll up.

desplazar [1f] 1 VT **(a)** *objeto* to displace, move; to transport. **(b)** (*Náut, Fís*) to displace. **(c)** *persona etc* to displace, supplant, take the place of. **(d)** (*Inform*) to scroll. 2 **desplazarse** VR **(a)** (*objeto*) to move, shift. **(b)** (*persona, vehículo*) to go, travel; (*partir*) to move away, move out; **tiene que ~ todos los días 25 kms** he has to travel 25 kms every day; **el avión se desplaza a más de 1500 kph** the aircraft travels at more than 1500 kph. **(c)** (*opinión, votos etc*) to shift, swing; **se ha desplazado un 4 por 100 de los votos** there has been a swing of 4% in the voting.

desplegable 1 ADJ: **menú ~** pull-down menu. 2 NM folder, brochure; (*Prensa*) centrefold.

desplegar [1h y 1j] 1 VT **(a)** *mapa etc* to unfold, open (out), spread (out); *alas* to spread, open; *velas* to unfurl; (*Mil etc*) to deploy; (*Inform*) to display. **(b)** (*fig*) *energías etc* to put forth, use, display; *recursos* to deploy. **(c)** (*fig*) *misterio* to clarify, elucidate. 2 **desplegarse** VR (*flor etc*) to open (out), unfold; to spread (out); (*Mil etc*) to deploy.

despliegue NM **(a)** (*acto*) unfolding, opening; (*Mil etc*) deployment. **(b)** (*fig*) display, manifestation, show, exhibition; (*Inform*) display.

desplomarse [1a] VR **(a)** (*inclinarse*) to lean, tilt, get out of vertical; (*combarse*) to bulge, warp. **(b)** (*derrumbarse*) to collapse, tumble down, come crashing down; to topple over; (*precio etc*) to slump, tumble; (*gobierno, sistema*) to collapse; (*Aer*) to make a pancake landing; (*persona*) to collapse, crumple up; **se ha desplomado el techo** the ceiling has fallen in, the ceiling has collapsed; **¡se desploma el cielo!** it's incredible!; **caer desplomado** to collapse, drop dead.

desplome NM **(a)** (*acto*) leaning, tilting; fall, collapse; slump; (*Aer*) pancake landing; (*Fin*) collapse. **(b)** (*Arquit, Geol etc*) overhang, projecting part; (*Alpinismo*) overhang.

desplomo NM = **desplome (b)**.

desplumar [1a] 1 VT **(a)** *ave* to pluck. **(b)** (*: estafar*) to fleece, skin*. 2 **desplumarse** VR to moult.

despoblación NF depopulation; ~ **rural**, ~ **del campo** rural depopulation, drift from the land.

despoblado 1 ADJ unpopulated, deserted; (*fig*) desolate. 2 NM deserted spot, uninhabited place; wilderness.

despoblar [1m] 1 VT to depopulate; to reduce the population of, clear people out of; to lay waste; ~ **una zona de árboles** to clear an area of trees. 2 **despoblarse** VR to become depopulated, lose its population.

despojar [1a] 1 VT: ~ **de** to strip of, clear of, leave bare of; (*fig*) to divest of, denude of; (*Jur*) to dispossess of, deprive of; **habían despojado la casa de muebles** they had stripped the house of furniture, they had cleared all the furniture out of the house; **verse despojado de su autoridad** to find o.s. stripped of one's authority. 2 **despojarse** VR (*desnudarse*) to undress; ~ **de ropa** to take off, remove, strip off; *hojas etc* to shed; *poderes etc* to divest o.s. of, relinquish, give up; *prejuicio* to get rid of, free o.s. from.

despojo NM **(a)** (*acto*) spoliation, despoilment; plundering. **(b)** (*Mil etc*) plunder, loot, spoils. **(c)** ~**s** (*residuo*) waste, (*restos*) left-overs, scraps; (*de animal*) offal; (*Arquit*) rubble; secondhand building materials, usable waste; (*Geol*) debris; ~**s de hierro** scrap iron; ~**s mortales** mortal remains.

despolitización NF depoliticization.

despolitizar [1f] VT to depoliticize.

despolvorear [1a] VT to dust.

desportillado ADJ **(a)** *taza, plato* chipped. **(b)** (*en malas condiciones*) *coche* battered; *piso* dingy.

desportilladura NF chip; nick.

desportillar [1a] 1 VT to chip, nick. 2 **desportillarse** VR to chip, chip off.

desposado ADJ newly-wed, recently married; **los ~s** the bridal couple, the newly-weds.

desposar [1a] 1 VT (*cura*) *pareja* to marry. 2 **desposarse** VR **(a)** (*una persona*) to become engaged (*con* to); to get married (*con* to). **(b)** (*dos personas*) to get engaged; to marry, get married.

desposeer [2e] 1 VT to dispossess (*de* of); to oust (*de un puesto* from a post); ~ **a uno de su autoridad** to remove sb's authority, strip sb of his authority. 2 **desposeerse** VR: ~ **de algo** to give sth up, relinquish sth, divest o.s. of sth.

desposeído, -a NM/F: **los ~s** the deprived, those in want, the have-nots.

desposeimiento NM dispossession; ousting.

desposorios NMPL (*esponsales*) engagement, betrothal; (*boda*) marriage (ceremony).

déspota NMF despot; ~ **ilustrado** enlightened despot.

despóticamente ADV despotically.

despótico ADJ despotic.

despotismo NM despotism; ~ **ilustrado** enlightened despotism.

despotorrarse* [1a] VR to laugh o.s. silly*.

despotricar [1g] VI to rave, rant, carry on (*contra* about).

despreciable ADJ (*moralmente*) despicable, contemptible; (*en calidad*) worthless, trashy, valueless; (*en cantidad*) negligible; **una suma nada** ~ a far from negligible amount.

despreciar [1b] 1 VT (*desdeñar*) to scorn, despise, look down on; *oferta* to spurn, reject; (*ofender*) to slight; (*subestimar*) to underestimate, underrate; ~ **los peligros** to scorn the dangers; ~ **una oferta** to reject an offer; **no hay que ~ tal posibilidad** one should not underestimate such a possibility. 2 **despreciarse** VR: ~ **de** + *infin* to think it beneath o.s. to + *infin*, not deign to + *infin*.

despreciativamente ADV scornfully, contemptuously; in a derogatory way; cynically.

despreciativo ADJ scornful, contemptuous; *dicho etc* derogatory.

desprecintar [1a] VT to unseal.

desprecio NM **(a)** (*desdén*) scorn, contempt, disdain; disparaging attitude; **lo miró con ~** he looked at it contemptuously. **(b)** (*ofensa*) slight, snub; **le hicieron el ~ de no acudir** they snubbed him by not coming.

desprender [2a] 1 VT **(a)** (*soltar*) to unfasten, loosen; (*separar*) to detach, separate. **(b)** *gas etc* to give off; *piel etc* to shed. 2 **desprenderse** VR **(a)** (*pieza*) to become detached, work loose, fall off; to fly off. **(b)** ~ **de un estorbo** to extricate o.s. from a difficulty, get free of a difficulty; **la serpiente se desprende de la piel** the snake sheds its skin. **(c)** ~ **de algo** to give sth up, part with sth; to get rid of sth; to deprive o.s. of sth; **se desprendió de sus joyas** she parted with her jewels; **tendremos que desprendernos del coche** we shall have to get rid of the car; **se desprendió de su autoridad** he relinquished his authority. **(d)** (*gas etc*) to be given off, issue; **de la pared se desprende humedad** there is damp coming from the wall. **(e)** (*sentido etc*) ~ **de** to follow from; to be deduced from; to be implied by; to be clear from; **se desprende que ...** one gathers that ...; **se desprende de esta declaración que ...** it is clear from this statement that ...; **por fin se desprendió que ...** finally it transpired that ...

desprendido ADJ **(a)** *pieza* loose, detached; unfastened. **(b)** (*fig*) disinterested; generous.

desprendimiento NM **(a)** (*acto*) loosening, detachment; unfastening; ~ **de matriz** prolapse; ~ **de retina** detachment of the retina; ~ **de tierra(s)** landslide. **(b)** (*de gas etc*) release, emission; (*de piel etc*) shedding. **(c)** (*fig*) disinterestedness; generosity.

despreocupación NF (*V ADJ*) **(a)** unconcern; carefree nature; nonchalance, casualness. **(b)** unconventional outlook (*o* style *etc*); (*pey*) sloppiness, slovenliness. **(c)** impartiality. **(d)** (*Rel*) indifference, apathy; broad-mindedness. **(e)** looseness.

despreocupadamente ADV unconcernedly; in a carefree manner; nonchalantly.

despreocupado ADJ **(a)** (*sin preocupación*) unworried, unconcerned; (*tranquilo*) carefree; (*natural*) nonchalant, casual; free and easy. **(b)** (*en vestir etc*) unconventional, casual; (*pey*) careless, sloppy, slovenly. **(c)** (*imparcial*) unbiassed, impartial. **(d)** (*Rel*) (*indiferente*) indifferent, apathetic; (*tolerante*) broad-minded. **(e)** *mujer* loose.

despreocupamiento NM lack of interest, apathy.

despreocuparse [1a] VR not to worry.

despresar [1a] VT (*Cono Sur*) *ave etc* to cut up, carve up.

desprestigiar [1b] 1 VT (*criticar*) to disparage, run down; (*tachar*) to smear; (*rebajar*) to lower the prestige of, reduce the status of; (*desacreditar*) to discredit; (*aplebeyar*) to cheapen. 2 **desprestigiarse** VR to lose (one's) prestige; to lose caste; to cheapen o.s.

desprestigio NM disparagement; discredit; loss of prestige (*o caste,* standing); unpopularity; **campaña de ~** smear campaign; **esas cosas que van en ~ nuestro** those things which are to our discredit, those things which harm our reputation.

desprevención NF unreadiness, unpreparedness; lack of foresight.

desprevenido ADJ unready, unprepared; **coger a uno ~** to catch sb unawares, catch sb off his guard, take sb by surprise.

desprivatizar [1f] VT to take into public ownership.

desprogramar [1a] VT to deprogramme.

desprolijo* ADJ (*Argentina*) untidy, sloppy*.

desproporción NF disproportion, lack of proportion.

desproporcionadamente ADV disproportionately.

desproporcionado ADJ disproportionate, out of proportion.

despropósito NM absurdity, silly thing (to say), piece of nonsense; **~s** nonsense.

desprotección NF lack of (legal) protection; vulnerability, defencelessness; (*Inform*) deprotection.

desprotegido ADJ unprotected, vulnerable, defenceless; **los ~s** (*frec*) the poor and needy.

desproveer [2a, PTP **desprovisto** *y* **desproveído**] VT: **~ a uno de algo** to deprive sb of sth.

desprovisto ADJ: **~ de** devoid of, bereft of, without; **estar ~ de** to lack, be lacking in, be devoid of; **estar ~ de medios** to be without means; **un libro no ~ de méritos** a book not without merit.

después [1] ADV (a) (*tiempo*) (*gen*) afterwards, later; (*desde entonces*) since, since then; (*luego*) next; **un año ~** a year later; **años ~** years later; **¿qué pasó ~?** what happened then?; **poco ~** soon after, shortly after.
(b) (*orden*) next, after; **¿y ~?** and what comes next?; **nuestra casa viene ~** and then our house is next.
[2] **~ de** PREP (a) (*tiempo*) after; since; **~ de esa fecha** (*pasado*) since that date; (*futuro*) from that date, after that date; **~ de verlo** after seeing it; **no ~ de 1998** not later than 1998; **~ de descubierta la isla** after the discovery of the island, after the island had been discovered.
(b) (*orden*) next (to); **mi nombre está ~ del tuyo** my name comes next to yours; my name comes after yours; **es el primero ~ de éste** it's the next one after this.
[3]: **~ (de) que** CONJ after; **~ (de) que lo escribí** after (o since) I wrote it, after writing it.

despuesito* ADV (*Méx*) right away, in just a moment.

despulgar [1h] = **espulgar**.

despuntado ADJ blunt.

despuntar [1a] [1] VT to blunt, dull (the point o edge of).
[2] VI (a) (*Bot*) to sprout, bud, begin to show.
(b) (*alba*) to break, appear; (*día*) to dawn.
(c) (*persona etc*) (*descollar*) to excel, stand out; (*brillar*) to shine, sparkle; to show intelligence; **~ de agudo** to have a sparkling wit; **despunta en matemáticas** he shines at maths; **despunta por su talento** her talent shines out, her talent is outstanding.

desquiciado ADJ (*fig*) deranged, unhinged.

desquiciamiento NM (a) upsetting, disturbance, turning upside down. (b) (*turbación*) unhinging; mental unbalance; hysteria.

desquiciante ADJ maddening; disturbing, unsettling.

desquiciar [1b] VT (a) (*puerta*) to unhinge, take off its hinges.
(b) (*fig: descomponer*) to upset, disturb, turn upside down, make a mess of.
(c) *persona* (*turbar*) to disturb, upset; (*volver loco*) to unhinge, affect seriously, unbalance; (*enojar*) to anger, provoke.
(d) *persona* (*expulsar*) to oust, lever out.

desquicio NM (*CAm, Cono Sur*) confusion, disorder.

desquitar [1a] [1] VT *pérdida* to make good, make up.
[2] **desquitarse** VR (*obtener satisfacción*) VR to obtain satisfaction; (*Com, Fin*) to recover a debt, get one's money back; (*fig*) to get even (*con* with), get one's own back (*con* on); **~ de una pérdida** to make up for a loss, compensate o.s. for a loss; **~ de una mala pasada** to get one's own back for a dirty trick (played on one).

desquite NM (*satisfacción*) satisfaction; (*recompensa*) compensation for a loss, recovery of a debt; (*venganza*) revenge, retaliation; (*Dep, t* **partido de ~**) return match; **tomar el ~** to have one's revenge, get one's own back; **tomar el ~ de algo** to make up for sth.

desratización NF: **campaña de ~** anti-rodent campaign.

desratizador ADJ anti-rodent.

desratizar [1f] VT to clear of rats.

desrazonable ADJ unreasonable.

desregulación NF deregulation.

desregular [1a] VT to free, deregulate, remove controls from.

desrielar [1a] (*LAm*) [1] VT to derail.
[2] **desrielarse** VR to run off the rails, jump the track, be derailed.

desriñonar [1a] = **deslomar**.

desrizador NM, **desrizante** NM hair straightener.

desrizar [1f] VT *pelo* to straighten.

Dest. ABR *de* **destinatario** addressee; (*Com*) payee.

destacadamente ADV notably, outstandingly.

destacado ADJ notable, outstanding, distinguished; important.

destacamento NM (*Mil*) detachment; **~ de desembarco** (*Naút*) landing party.

destacar [1g] [1] VT (a) (*Arte etc*) to make stand out; (*fig*) to emphasize, show up, point up, bring out; to throw into relief; **quiero ~ que ...** I wish to emphasize that ...; **sirve para ~ su belleza** it serves to enhance her beauty, it serves to show up her beauty.
(b) (*Mil*) to detach, detail, assign.
(c) (*Inform*) to highlight.
[2] VI *y* **destacarse** VR (a) to stand out; **~se contra**, **~se en**, **~se sobre** to stand out against, be outlined against, be silhouetted against; **~se como un pegote** to stick out like a sore thumb.
(b) (*fig*) to stand out, be outstanding, be exceptional.

destajar [1a] VT (a) (*Naipes*) to cut. (b) (*And, CAm, Méx*) *res* to cut up.
(c) *trabajo etc* to contract for, agree conditions for; to do as piecework.

destajero, -a NM/F, **destajista** NMF pieceworker.

destajo NM (a) (*gen*) piecework; contract work; (*un ~*) job; stint; **a ~** by the job; (*fig*) eagerly, keenly; energetically; **trabajar a ~** to do piecework, be on piecework; **trabajo a ~** piecework; **hablar a ~*** to talk nineteen to the dozen.
(b) **a ~** (*Cono Sur*) by guesswork.
(c) **~ de esquí** ski-lift pass.

destapador NM (*LAm*) bottle opener.

destapamiento NM (*Méx: Pol*) *announcement of official PRI party presidential candidate.*

destapar [1a] [1] VT (*descubrir*) to uncover; *botella* to open, uncork; *caja* to open, take the lid off; *recipiente* to take the lid off, raise the lid of; (*fig*) to reveal, uncover.
[2] VI (*Méx: echar a correr*) to break into a run.
[3] **destaparse** VR (a) to get uncovered; (*persona*) to undress, strip off.
(b) (*fig*) (*causar sorpresa*) to cause surprise, do sth unexpected; (*mostrar su carácter*) to show o.s. in one's true character; **se destapó metiéndose monja** she astounded everyone by becoming a nun.
(c) (*fig: hablar*) to speak frankly, come into the open; **~ con uno** to unbosom o.s. to sb.
(d) (*fig: perder los estribos*) to let fly, lose control.

destape NM (a) (*de persona: estado*) state of undress, nudity; display of flesh; (*acto*) undressing, stripping off; **~ integral** full-frontal nudity. (b) (*fig*) permissiveness; (*Pol*) process (o period *etc*) of liberalization; **el ~ español** the process of liberalization in Spain (*from 1975*).

destaponar [1a] VT to uncork.

destartalado ADJ *cuarto etc* untidy, in disorder; *casa etc* large and rambling; ruinous, tumbledown, dilapidated; *vehículo etc* rickety, shaky.

destazar [1f] VT to cut up.

destechar [1a] VT to unroof, take the roof off.

destejar [1a] VT (a) *techo* to remove the tiles from. (b) (*fig*) to leave unprotected.

destejer [2d] VT (a) (*deshacer*) to undo, unravel; *labor de punto* to take the stitches out of. (b) (*fig*) to upset; to interfere with the progress of; *V* **tejer**.

destellante ADJ sparkling.

destellar [1a] VI to sparkle, flash; to glint, gleam.

destello NM (a) (*gen*) sparkle; flash; glint, gleam; wink(ing).
(b) (*Téc*) signal light, winking light.
(c) (*fig*) atom, particle; **no tiene un ~ de verdad** there's not an atom of truth in it.
(d) **~s** (*fig*) glimmer; **tiene a veces ~s de inteligencia** he sometimes shows a glimmer (o glimmerings) of intelligence.

destemplado ADJ (a) (*Mús*) *instrumento* out of tune; *voz* harsh, unpleasant.
(b) (*Arte*) inharmonious, badly blended, ill-matched.
(c) *pulso* irregular.
(d) (*Med*) indisposed, out of sorts; feverish.
(e) *carácter, ademán etc* ill-tempered; *actitud* ill-judged, intemperate, harsh.
(f) (*Met*) unpleasant.

destemplanza NF (a) (*Mús*) tunelessness; harshness, unpleasantness.
(b) (*Arte*) lack of harmony.
(c) (*irregularidad*) irregularity.
(d) (*Med*) indisposition; (*fiebre*) feverish condition.
(e) (*actitud*) intemperance, harshness.
(f) (*Met*) unpleasantness, inclemency.
(g) (*una ~*) sharp remark, harsh comment.

destemplar [1a] [1] VT (a) (*Mús*) to untune, put out of tune, upset the pitch of.
(b) (*fig*) to upset, disturb (the order of); to disconcert.

2 **destemplarse** VR (a) (*Mús*) to get out of tune, lose its pitch.
(b) (*fig*) to get out of order; (*persona*) to get upset, get worked up; (*pulso*) to become irregular; (*Med*) to become indisposed, get out of sorts.
(c) **con eso me destemplo** (*LAm*) that sets my teeth on edge, that gives me the shivers.

destemple NM (a) (*gen*) = **destemplanza**. (b) (*de metal*) lack of temper, poorly-tempered nature.

destensar [1a] VT to slacken, loosen.

desteñido ADJ faded, discoloured.

desteñir [3k] **1** VT to fade, discolour, take the colour out of.
2 VI y **desteñirse** VR (a) (*perder color*) to fade, lose colour, discolour.
(b) (*colores de tela*) to run; **'esta tela no destiñe'** 'this fabric will not run'.

desternillante* ADJ hilarious, very funny.

desternillarse* [1a] VR: ~ **de risa** to split one's sides with laughing, die laughing.

desternille* NM laughter, hilarity.

desterrado, -a NM/F exile; outlaw; (*esp fig*) outcast.

desterrar [1j] VT (a) (*exiliar*) to exile, banish.
(b) (*fig*) to banish; to dismiss, put aside; ~ **una sospecha** to banish a suspicion from one's mind; ~ **el uso de las armas de fuego** to banish firearms, prohibit the use of firearms.
(c) (*Agr, Min*) to remove the soil from.

destetar [1a] **1** VT to wean.
2 **destetarse** VR (a) (*niño*) to be weaned; ~ **con el vino** (*fig*) to have been brought up on wine. (b) (⁑: *mujer*) to show her tits⁑.

destete NM weaning.

destiempo NM: **a** ~ at the wrong time, at an inopportune moment.

destierro NM (a) (*exilio*) exile; banishment; **vivir en el** ~ to live in exile. (b) (*fig*) wilderness; remote spot.

destilación NF distillation.

destiladera NF still, distilling vessel; (*LAm*) filter.

destilado NM distillation.

destilador NM (a) (*aparato*) still. (b) (*persona*) distiller.

destilar [1a] **1** VT (a) *alcohol* to distil; *sangre etc* to exude, ooze.
(b) (*fig*) to exude, ooze; to reveal; **la carta destilaba odio** the letter exuded hatred; **es una orden que destila crueldad** it is an order which is steeped in cruelty.
2 VI (*gotear*) to drip, fall (drop by drop); (*rezumar*) to ooze (out); (*filtrarse*) to filter through.

destilatorio NM (*aparato*); still; (*fábrica*) distillery.

destilería NF distillery; ~ **de petróleo** oil refinery.

destinar [1a] VT (a) (*gen*) to destine (*a, para* for, to); (*asignar*) to assign (*a* to); (*encaminar*) to design (*a* for); (*dirigir*) to intend, mean (*a, para* for); *fondos etc* to set aside, earmark (*a* for); **me habían destinado una habitación elegante** they had assigned me an elegant room; **le destinan al sacerdocio** they intend him for the priesthood; **fabricantes de aviones destinados a Eslobodia** makers of aircraft destined for (o for use in) Slobodia; **una carta que viene destinada a ti** a letter for you, a letter addressed to you; (*Náut etc*) **ir destinado a** to be bound for; **estar destinado a** + *infin* to be destined to + *infin*.
(b) *persona* to appoint, assign (*a* to); (*Mil etc*) to post (*a* to); to station (*en* in); **le han destinado a Lima** they have appointed him to Lima.

destinatario, -a NM/F addressee.

destino NM (a) (*suerte*) destiny, fate; **es mi** ~ **no encontrarlo** I am fated not to find it; **el** ~ **lo quiso así** it was destiny, fate willed it thus; **rige los** ~**s del país** he rules the country's fate, the fate of the country is in his hands.
(b) (*de viajero, barco etc*) destination; **'a franquear en** ~' 'postage will be paid by the addressee'; **van con** ~ **a Londres** they are going to London; (*Náut*) they are bound for London; **salir con** ~ **a** to leave for; **¿cuál es el** ~ **de este cuadro?** what is the destination of this picture?, where is this picture for?
(c) (*puesto*) job, post, position; (*Mil*) posting; (*de funcionario*) placement; ~ **público** public appointment; **buscarse un** ~ **de cartero** to look for a job as a postman; **¿qué** ~ **tienes?** where have you been placed?
(d) (*uso*) use, utility; **dar** ~ **a algo** to put sth to good use, find a use for sth.

destitución NF dismissal, removal.

destituido ADJ: ~ **de** devoid of, bereft of, lacking (in).

destituir [3g] VT (a) *persona* to dismiss, remove, sack* (*de* from); *ministro etc* to remove from office; **le destituyeron por inmoral** they sacked him for immorality*.
(b) ~ **a uno de algo** to deprive sb of sth.

destorcer [2b y 2h] **1** VT *cuerda etc* to untwist, take the twists out of; *alambre etc* to straighten.
2 **destorcerse** VR (*Náut*) to get off course.

destornillado* ADJ crazy, potty*.

destornillador NM (a) (*herramienta*) (t **destornilladora** NF) screw-

driver. (b) (*: *bebida*) screwdriver* (*cocktail of vodka and orange juice*).

destornillar [1a] **1** VT to unscrew.
2 **destornillarse** VR (a) (*fig*) to behave wildly; (*) to go crazy. (b) (*LAm*) = **desternillarse.** (c) (*Méx**: *rabiar*) to burble on, rave.

destrabar [1a] VT (*gen*) to loosen, detach; *prisionero etc* to unfetter, take the shackles off.

destral NM small hatchet.

destreza NF skill, dexterity; cleverness; handiness; ~**s lingüísticas** linguistic skills.

destripacuentos NM INVAR interrupter, person who butts in.

destripador NM (*fig*) butcher; murderer.

destripar [1a] VT (a) *animal* to gut, draw, paunch; *persona* to disembowel; to cut open the belly of, slash the stomach of.
(b) (*fig*) to mangle, crush; *cuento* to spoil (by interrupting and telling its ending).

destripaterrones NM INVAR poor labourer; (*) clodhopper.

destrocar* [1g y 1l] VT to swap, change back.

destronamiento NM dethronement; (*fig*) overthrow.

destronar [1a] VT to dethrone; (*fig*) to overthrow.

destroncar [1g] VT (a) *árbol* to chop off, lop (the top off); (*Cono Sur, Méx*) *planta* to uproot.
(b) *persona* to maim, mutilate; (*fig*) to tire out, exhaust; *caballo* to wear out.
(c) (*fig*) *proyecto etc* to ruin; *desarrollo* to harm, damage, dislocate; *discurso etc* to interrupt.

destrozado ADJ smashed, shattered, ruined.

destrozar [1f] VT (a) (*romper*) to smash, shatter, ruin; to break up, break to pieces; to destroy; *ropa, zapatos* to ruin; (*Mil*) *ejército, enemigo* to smash; *carne* to mangle, lacerate, tear; *nervios* to shatter; *recursos etc* to squander, dissipate.
(b) (*fig*) *persona* to ruin; to shatter; *vida etc* to ruin; *corazón* to break; ~ **la armonía** to ruin the harmony; ~ **a uno en una discusión** to crush sb in an argument; **le ha destrozado el que no quisiera casarse con él** he was shattered when she wouldn't marry him, her refusal to marry him broke him up.

destrozo NM (*gen*) destruction; (*Mil*) smashing, annihilation, rout; (*de personas*) massacre; ~**s** damage, havoc, ravages; **causar** ~**s en** to create havoc in, cause great damage to, ravage.

destrozón ADJ: **un niño** ~ a child who is hard on his clothes; **la criada es muy destrozona** the servant is a terrible one for breaking things.

destrucción NF destruction; ~ **de empleo** job losses *pl*.

destructible ADJ destructible.

destructividad NF destructiveness.

destructivo ADJ destructive.

destructor **1** ADJ destructive.
2 NM (*Náut*) destroyer.

destruible ADJ destructible.

destruir [3g] **1** VT (*gen*) to destroy; (*arruinar*) to ruin, wreck; (*dañar*) to damage; *equilibrio etc* to destroy, upset; *recursos* to squander; *proyectos* to ruin.
2 **destruirse** VR (*Mat*) to cancel (each other) out.

desubicado ADJ (*Cono Sur*) tactless, silly.

desubicar [1g] VT (*LAm*) to disorientate, confuse, put off.

desudar [1a] VT to wipe the sweat off.

desuellacaras NM INVAR (a) (*barbero*) clumsy barber. (b) (*bribón*) rogue, villain.

desuello NM (a) (*acto*) skinning, flaying. (b) (*descaro*) brazenness, insolence. (c) (*: *robo*) extortion; **¡es un** ~**!** it's daylight robbery!

desuncir [3b] VT to unyoke.

desunión NF (a) (*acto*) separation; disconnection. (b) (*estado*) disunity; rift.

desunir [3a] VT (a) (*separar*) to separate, sever, detach. (b) (*fig*) to cause a rift between.

desuñarse [1a] VR (a) (*trabajar*) to work one's fingers to the bone (*por* + *infin* to + *infin*). (b) (*fig*) to be always up to mischief; **se desuña por el juego** he's an inveterate gambler.

desurbanización NF relief of city overcrowding, dispersal of city population(s) (to satellite towns).

desusado ADJ (a) (*anticuado*) obsolete, antiquated, out of date.
(b) **esa palabra está desusada de los buenos escritores** that word is no longer in use among good writers.
(c) (*insólito*) unwonted, unusual.

desusar [1a] **1** VT to stop using, discontinue the use of, give up.
2 **desusarse** VR to go out of use, become obsolete.

desuso NM disuse; **caer en** ~ to fall into disuse, become obsolete; **una expresión caída en** ~ an obsolete expression; **dejar algo en** ~ to cease to use sth, discontinue the use of sth.

desvaído ADJ (a) *color* pale, dull, washed-out.
(b) *contorno* ill-defined, vague, blurred.
(c) *persona* (*de carácter*) weak, characterless; *personalidad* flat, dull.
(d) *talla* gangling, lanky.

desvainar [1a] VT *guisantes etc* to shell.

desvalido ADJ helpless; destitute; (*Pol*) underprivileged; **los ~s** the helpless, (*Pol*) the underprivileged; **niños ~s** waifs and strays, abandoned children.

desvalijamiento NM robbing, robbery; rifling; burgling.

desvalijar [1a] VT (*gen*) to rob, plunder; *cajón, maleta etc* to ransack, rifle; *casa, tienda* to burgle, burglarize (*US*), break into, rob.

desvalimiento NM helplessness; destitution, great need.

desvalorar [1a] VT to devaluate; *moneda* to devalue.

desvalorización NF devaluation.

desvalorizar [1f] VT to devalue.

desván NM (*ático*) loft, attic; garret; (*trastera*) lumber room.

desvanecer [2d] **1** VT (a) (*gen*) to cause to vanish, make disappear; *humo etc* to dissipate.
(b) *duda etc* to dispel; *pensamiento, memoria* to banish, dismiss.
(c) *color* to tone down; *contorno* to blur; (*Fot*) to mask.
(d) *persona* to make conceited; **el dinero le ha desvanecido** the money has gone to his head.
2 desvanecerse VR (a) (*desaparecer*) to vanish, disappear.
(b) (*duda etc*) to vanish, be dispelled.
(c) (*Quím etc*) to evaporate; to dissolve, melt away, disappear.
(d) (*Med*) to faint (away).
(e) (*sonido, t Rad*) to fade (away), fade out.

desvanecido ADJ (a) (*Med*) faint; giddy, dizzy; **caer ~** to fall in a faint. (b) (*fig*) (*engreído*) vain; (*orgulloso*) proud, haughty.

desvanecimiento NM (a) (*gen*) vanishing, disappearance; dissipation, dispelling.
(b) (*de contornos*) blurring; (*Fot*) masking.
(c) (*Quím*) evaporation; melting.
(d) (*Med*) fainting fit, swoon; dizzy spell, attack of giddiness.
(e) (*Rad etc*) fading.
(f) (*fig*) vanity; pride, haughtiness.

desvarar [1a] VT to refloat.

desvariar [1c] VI (a) (*Med*) to be delirious. (b) (*fig*) to rave, talk nonsense.

desvarío NM (a) (*Med*) delirium; raving. (b) (*fig*) (*disparate*) absurdity; (*noción*) extravagant notion, strange notion; (*capricho*) whim; **~s** ravings, ramblings.

desvede NM ending of the close season.

desvelado ADJ (a) (*lit*) sleepless, wakeful; **estar ~** to be awake, be unable to get to sleep. (b) (*fig*) watchful, vigilant.

desvelar [1a] **1** VT (a) *persona* to keep awake; **el café me desvela** coffee keeps me awake.
(b) *misterio* to solve, explain; *lo oculto* to reveal, unveil.
2 desvelarse VR (a) (*estar sin dormir*) to stay awake, keep awake; (*no poder dormir*) to go without sleep, have a sleepless night.
(b) (*fig*) to be watchful, be vigilant, keep one's eyes open; **~ por algo** to be anxious about sth, be much concerned about sth; to take great care over sth; **~ por** + *infin* to do everything possible to + *infin*; **se desvela porque no nos falte nada** she works hard so that we should not go short of anything.

desvelo NM (a) (*falta de sueño*) lack of sleep; (*insomnio*) sleeplessness, insomnia.
(b) (*fig*) watchfulness, vigilance.
(c) **~s** PL (*fig*) (*preocupación*) anxiety, care, concern; (*esfuerzo*) effort, hard work; **gracias a sus ~s** thanks to his efforts.

desvencijado ADJ ramshackle, rickety, broken-down.

desvencijar [1a] **1** VT (a) (*romper*) to break; (*soltar*) to loosen, weaken.
(b) *persona* to weaken, exhaust.
2 desvencijarse VR (a) (*deshacerse*) to come apart, fall to pieces, break; to become disjointed.
(b) (*Med*) to rupture o.s.

desventaja NF disadvantage; handicap, liability; **estar en ~ con respecto a otros** to be at a disadvantage compared with others.

desventajado ADJ disadvantaged.

desventajosamente ADV disadvantageously, unfavourably.

desventajoso ADJ disadvantageous, unfavourable.

desventura NF misfortune.

desventuradamente ADV unfortunately.

desventurado **1** ADJ (a) (*desgraciado*) unfortunate, unlucky; ill-fated.
(b) (*infeliz*) miserable, wretched; unhappy; **¡qué ~ estoy!** how wretched I am!
(c) (*tímido*) timid, shy.
(d) (*tacaño*) mean.
2 NM, **desventurada** NF wretch, unfortunate; **algún ~** some poor devil.

desvergonzado **1** ADJ shameless; impudent, brazen; unblushing.
2 NM, **desvergonzada** NF shameless person.

desvergonzarse [1f y 1l] VR (a) (*perder la vergüenza*) to lose all sense of shame.
(b) (*insolentarse*) to be impudent, be insolent (*con* to); to behave in a shameless way (*con* to).
(c) **~ a pedir algo** to have the nerve to ask for sth, dare to ask for sth.

desvergüenza NF shamelessness; brazenness, effrontery, impudence; **esto es una ~** this is disgraceful, this is shameful; **¡qué ~!** how shocking!; what a nerve!*, the effrontery of it!; **tener la ~ de** + *infin* to have the impudence (o nerve*) to + *infin*.

desvertebración NF dislocation; disruption.

desvertebrado ADJ lacking cohesion, disorganized.

desvertebrar [1a] VT (*fig*) to dislocate; to disturb, disrupt, upset, throw off balance; *pandilla etc* to break up.

desvestir [3k] **1** VT to undress.
2 desvestirse VR to undress.

desviación NF (a) (*acto*) deviation (*de* from); deviance; deflection (*de* from), departure (*de* from); (*Mec, Fís, de brújula*) deviation; **~ estándar, ~ normal** standard deviation; **es una ~ de sus principios** it is a deviation (o departure) from his principles.
(b) (*Pol, Psic*) deviation.
(c) (*Aut etc*) (*rodeo*) detour; diversion; (*circunvalación*) bypass, ring road; **~ de la circulación** traffic diversion.

desviacionismo NM deviationism.

desviacionista ADJ, NMF deviationist.

desviadero NM (*Ferro*) siding.

desviado ADJ (a) (*oblicuo*) oblique; deflected; deviant. (b) *lugar* remote, off the beaten track; **~ de** remote from, away from.

desviar [1c] **1** VT (a) (*físicamente*) to turn aside; to deflect, divert (*de* from); *flecha etc* to deflect; *balón* to deflect, glance; *golpe* to parry, ward off, deflect; *pregunta* to parry; *ojos* to avert, turn away; (*Aut*) to divert, re-route (*por* through); (*Ferro*) to switch (into a siding), shunt; **~ el cauce de un río** to alter the course of a river.
(b) (*fig*) to turn aside (*de* from); **le desviaron de su propósito** they dissuaded him from his intention; **~ a uno de su vocación** to turn sb from his (true) vocation; **~ a uno de su pensamiento** to sidetrack sb from his theme; **~ a uno de las malas compañías** to wean sb away from evil company; **~ a uno del buen camino** to lead sb astray.
2 desviarse VR (*persona etc*) to turn aside, turn away, deviate (*de* from); (*camino*) to branch off, leave; (*Náut*) to sheer off; (*Náut*) to go off course; (*Aut*) to turn off; to swerve; **~ de un tema** to digress from a theme; to wander from the point.

desvincular [1a] **1** VT to detach (*de* from); *finca* to disentail.
2 desvincularse VR: **~ con, ~ de** to break (one's links) with, sever one's connections with; to get free of.

desvío NM (a) (*acto*) deflection, deviation (*de* from); (*Aut etc*) swerve.
(b) (*Aut etc: rodeo*) diversion, detour (*US*); (*circunvalación*) bypass; (*Ferro*) siding.
(c) (*fig*) coldness, indifference; dislike.

desvirgar [1h] VT (a) *virgen* to deflower. (b) (*) = **estrenar**.

desvirtuar [1e] **1** VT (*afectar mal*) to impair, spoil; to detract from, adversely affect the quality of; (*cancelar*) to counteract, cancel, nullify the effect of.
2 desvirtuarse VR to spoil, go off, decline in quality.

desvitalizado ADJ dull, lifeless.

desvitalizar [1f] VT to drain the life from.

desvivirse [3a] VR: **~ por algo** to crave sth, yearn for sth, long for sth; to be crazy about sth; **~ por los amigos** to do one's utmost for one's friends, live only to help one's friends; **~ por** + *infin* to be very eager to + *infin*; to do one's best to + *infin*, go out of one's way to + *infin*; **se desvivió por ayudarme** she did everything possible to help me.

desyerba NF, **desyerbo** NM (*LAm*) weeding.

desyerbar [1a] VT = **desherbar**.

detal(l): al ~ ADV retail.

detalladamente ADV in detail.

detallado ADJ detailed.

detallar [1a] VT (a) (*especificar*) to detail, list in detail, specify, itemize.
(b) *cuento etc* to tell in detail. (c) (*Com*) to sell retail.

detalle NM (a) (*gen*) detail, particular; item; **~s de publicación** publication details; **esto es el ~** this is the key to it, this is the secret; **al ~** in detail; **con todo ~, con todos los ~s** in detail, with full details; with full particulars; **en ~** in detail; **hasta en sus menores ~s** down to the last detail; **para más ~s vea ...** for further details see ...; **no pierde ~** he misses nothing, he doesn't miss a trick; **me observaba sin perder ~** he was watching me very closely, he watched my every move.
(b) (*fig: atención*) token (of appreciation), gesture; (*regalo*) gift; **¡qué ~!** how sweet of you!, what a nice gesture!; **tiene muchos ~s** he is very considerate; **es el primer ~ que te veo en mucho tiempo** it's the first sign of consideration I've had from you for a long time.
(c) **al ~** (*Com*) retail (ADJ, ADV); **vender al ~** to sell retail; **comercio al ~** retail trade.

(d) (*estado de cuenta*) statement; (*factura*) bill.

detallismo NM attention to detail, care for the details.

detallista [1] ADJ retail; **comercio ~** retail trade.
[2] NMF retailer, retail trader.

detalloso* ADJ kind, thoughtful.

detección NF detection.

detectable ADJ detectable.

detectar [1a] VT to detect.

detective NMF detective; **~ de la casa** house detective; **~ privado** private detective.

detectivesco ADJ detective (*atr*); investigative; **dotes detectivescas** gifts as a detective.

detector NM (*Náut, Tec etc*) detector; **~ de humo** smoke-detector; **~ de incendios** fire-detector; **~ de mentiras** lie-detector; **~ de metales** metal-detector; **~ de minas** mine-detector.

detención NF **(a)** (*acción*) stopping; (*estancamiento*) stoppage, holdup; (*retraso*) delay; **~ de juego** (*Dep*) stoppage of play; **una ~ de 15 minutos** a 15-minute delay.
(b) (*Jur*) arrest, detention; **~ cautelar, ~ preventiva** preventive detention; **~ domiciliaria** house-arrest; **~ ilegal** unlawful detention, wrongful arrest; **~ sin procesamiento** imprisonment without trial.
(c) (*cualidad*) = **detenimiento**.

detener [2k] [1] VT **(a)** (*parar*) *persona, balón, vehículo, epidemia* (*etc*) to stop; (*retrasar*) to hold up, check, delay; **~ el progreso de** to hold up the progress of; **no quiero ~te** I don't want to delay you; **me detuvo en la calle** he stopped me in the street, he accosted me in the street.
(b) (*retener*) to keep, hold back, retain; *respiración* to hold.
(c) (*Jur*) to arrest, detain.
[2] **detenerse** VR to stop; to pause; to delay, linger; **se detuvo a mirarlo** he stopped to look at it; **¡no te detengas!** don't hang about!, don't delay!; **se detiene mucho en eso** he's taking a long time over that.

detenidamente ADV carefully, thoroughly; at great length.

detenido [1] ADJ **(a)** (*Jur*) arrested, under arrest.
(b) *narración etc* detailed; *examen* lengthy, thorough; careful; (*pey*) slow, dilatory.
(c) (*fig*: *tímido*) timid.
(d) (*fig*: *tacaño*) mean, niggardly.
[2] NM, **detenida** NF person under arrest; detainee.

detenimiento NM care, thoroughness; **con ~** carefully, thoroughly.

detentar [1a] VT **(a)** *puesto, récord, título* to hold. **(b)** (*pey*) *título* to hold unlawfully; *puesto etc* to occupy unlawfully.

detentor(a) NM/F (*Dep*) holder; **~ de marca** record holder; **~ de trofeo** cup holder, champion.

detergente ADJ, NM detergent.

deterger [2c] VT to clean, clean of grease; *herida* to clean; (*Culin etc*) to clean with detergent.

deteriorado ADJ spoiled, damaged; worn; *géneros* shopsoiled, damaged.

deteriorar [1a] [1] VT (*estropear*) to spoil, damage; to worsen, make worse; to impair; (*Mec etc*) to cause wear on, cause wear and tear to.
[2] **deteriorarse** VR to deteriorate, spoil; to get damaged; to get worse; (*Mec etc*) to wear, get worn.

deterioro NM deterioration; impairment; damage; worsening; (*Mec etc*) wear, wear and tear; **en caso de ~ de las mercancías** should the goods be damaged in any way; **sin ~ de sus derechos** without any loss of rights, without any impairment of his rights.

determinable ADJ determinable; **fácilmente ~** easy to determine.

determinación NF **(a)** (*acto*) determination; decision; **tomar una ~** to take a decision. **(b)** (*cualidad*) determination, resolution.

determinado ADJ **(a)** (*preciso*) fixed, set, certain; **un día ~** on a certain day; on a given day; **en momentos ~s** at certain times; **hay ~s límites** there are fixed limits; **no hay ningún tema ~** there is no particular theme, there is no set subject.
(b) (*Mat*) determinate; (*Ling*) *artículo* definite.
(c) *persona* determined, resolute; purposeful.

determinante ADJ, NM determinant.

determinar [1a] [1] VT **(a)** (*decidir*) to determine, fix, settle; *fecha, precio etc* to fix; *daños, contribución etc* to determine, assess; *rumbo* to fix, decide, shape; **~ el peso de algo** to determine (o calculate, work out, fix) the weight of sth; **el reglamento determina que ...** the rule lays it down that ..., the rule states that ...; **'por ~'** (*anuncio*) 'to be arranged'.
(b) (*provocar*) to cause, bring about; **aquello determinó la caída del gobierno** that brought about the fall of the government.
(c) *persona* to decide, make up the mind of; **esto le determinó** this decided him; **~ a uno a hacer algo** to determine sb to do sth, lead sb to do sth.
[2] **determinarse** VR to decide, make up one's mind; **¿te has determinado?** have you made up your mind?; **~ a hacer algo** to decide to do sth, determine to do sth; **no se determina a mar-**

charse he can't make up his mind to go.

determinativo [1] ADJ determinative.
[2] NM (*Ling*) determiner.

determinismo NM determinism.

determinista ADJ deterministic.

detersión NF cleansing.

detestable ADJ detestable; odious, hateful; damnable.

detestablemente ADV detestably.

detestación NF detestation, hatred, loathing.

▼ **detestar** [1a] VT to detest, hate, loathe.

detonación NF detonation; report, explosion, bang.

detonador NM detonator.

detonante [1] ADJ **(a)** explosive. **(b)** (*) stunning, shattering.
[2] NM explosive; (*fig*) trigger (*de* for).

detonar [1a] VI to detonate, explode, go off.

detracción NF detraction, disparagement; knocking‡; slander; vilification.

detractor [1] ADJ disparaging; slanderous.
[2] NM, **detractora** NF detractor; (*Pol etc*) knocker*; slanderer.

detraer [2o] VT **(a)** (*quitar*) to remove, separate, take away. **(b)** (*desviar*) to turn aside. **(c)** (*denigrar*) to disparage; (*Pol etc*) to knock‡; (*difamar*) to slander; (*vilipendiar*) to vilify.

detrás [1] ADV **(a)** behind; at the back, in the rear; **~ la foto lleva una dedicatoria** the photo has a dedication on the back; **salir de ~** to come out from behind; **por ~** behind; **atacar a uno por ~** to attack sb from behind; **los coches de ~** the cars at the back, the cars in the rear.
(b) (*LAm*) **~ mío** (*etc*) behind me (*etc*).
[2] **~ de** PREP behind, back of (*US*); **por ~ de uno** (*fig*) behind sb's back; **salir de ~ de un árbol** to come out from behind a tree.

detrasito* ADV (*LAm*) behind.

detrimente ADJ detrimental.

detrimento NM (*daño*) harm, damage; (*de intereses etc*) detriment; **en ~ de** to the detriment of; **lo hizo sin ~ de su dignidad** he did it without detriment to (o loss of) his dignity.

detrito NM, **detritus** NM (*Geol etc*) detritus; debris.

detuve *etc* V **detener**.

deuda NF **(a)** (*gen*) indebtedness, debt; **estar en ~** to be in debt, owe (*por* for); **estar en ~ con uno** to be in debt to sb, (*fig*) to be indebted to sb.
(b) (*una ~*) debt; **~ a corto plazo** short-term debt; **~ a largo plazo** long-term debt; **~ exterior, ~ externa** foreign debt; **~ incobrable, ~ morosa** bad debt; **~ pública** national debt, public debt; **~ sin respaldo** unsecured debt; **una ~ de gratitud** a debt of gratitude; **contraer ~s** to contract debts, get into debt; **estar lleno de ~s** to be heavily in debt, be burdened with debts.
(c) (*Ecl*) **perdónanos nuestras ~s** forgive us our trespasses.

deudo NM relative.

deudor [1] ADJ **(a)** **saldo ~** debit balance, adverse balance.
(b) **le soy muy ~** I am greatly indebted to you.
[2] NM, **deudora** NF debtor; **~ moroso** slow payer, defaulter.

deuterio NM (*Quím*) deuterium.

devalar [1a] VI (*Náut*) to drift off course.

devaluación NF (*Fin*) devaluation.

devaluar [1e] VT (*Fin*) to devalue.

devaluatorio ADJ: **tendencia devaluatoria** tendency to depreciate, tendency to lose value.

devanadera NF (*Cos*) reel, spool; winding frame.

devanado NM (*Elec*) winding.

devanador NM (*Cos*) reel, spool, bobbin.

devanar [1a] [1] VT to wind; (*araña, gusano*) to spin.
[2] **devanarse** VR **(a)** **~ los sesos** to rack one's brains.
(b) (*CAm, Carib, Méx*) **~ de dolor** to double up with pain; **~ de risa** to double up with laughter.

devanear [1a] VI to rave, talk nonsense.

devaneo NM **(a)** (*Med*) delirium; (*fig*: *disparates*) ravings, nonsense, absurd talk. **(b)** (*fruslería*) time-wasting pastime, idle pursuit. **(c)** (*amorío*) affair, flirtation.

devastación NF devastation.

devastador ADJ devastating (*t fig*).

devastadoramente ADV devastatingly.

devastar [1a] VT to devastate.

devengar [1h] VT *sueldo* to earn; to draw, receive; *interés* to earn, bear, accrue; **interés devengado** accrued interest, earned interest.

devengo NM amount earned; **~s** income.

devenir [3r] [1] VI to develop into, become, evolve into; **~ en** to develop into, become, turn into, change into.
[2] NM evolution, process of development, (slow) change, transformation; **una nación en perpetuo ~** a nation in a constant process of development, a nation which is changing all the time.

devoción NF **(a)** (*Rel etc*: *cualidad*) devotion; devoutness, piety; **con ~** devoutly; piously; **la ~ a esta imagen** the cult of this image, the

➤ LENGUA Y USO: **detestar** → 34.3

veneration for this image.

(b) (*gen*) devotion (*a* to); attachment (*a* to); liking, affection (*a* for); **sienten ~ por su general** they feel devotion to their general, they are devoted to their general; **estar a la ~ de uno** to be completely under sb's thumb; **tener gran ~ a uno** to be wholly devoted to sb; **tener por ~** + *infin* to be in the habit of + *ger*.

(c) (*Ecl*: *acto*) devotion, prayer; religious observance; *V* **santo**.

devocional ADJ devotional.

devocionario NM prayerbook.

devolución NF (*gen*) return; (*Dep*) return; (*Com*) repayment, refund; **~ de derechos** (*Fin*) drawback; **pidió la ~ de los libros** he asked for the books to be given back, he asked for the return of the books; **'no se admiten devoluciones'** 'no refunds will be given', 'money cannot be refunded'.

devolver [2h; PTP **devuelto**] ① VT **(a)** (*gen*) to return; to give back, send back; to hand back; *pelota, golpe* to return; (*Com*) to repay, refund; (*) to throw up, vomit; *favor etc* to return; **~ una carta al remitente** to return a letter to the sender; **~ un florero a su sitio** to put a vase back in its place; **~ mal por bien** to return ill for good; **el espejo devuelve la imagen** the mirror sends back (*o* reflects) the image; **~ la salud a uno** to give sb back his health, restore sb to health; **esto nos devuelve al problema de los recursos** this brings us back to the problem of resources.

(b) *salud, vista etc* to restore; **han devuelto el castillo a su antiguo esplendor** they have restored the castle to its former glory.

② **devolverse** VR (*LAm*) to return, come back, go back.

devorador ADJ devouring; **fuego ~** all-consuming fire; **hambre ~a** ravenous hunger; **una mujer ~a de hombres** a man-eating woman.

devorar [1a] VT **(a)** (*gen*) to devour; (*comer*) to eat up, gobble up.

(b) (*fig*) (*gen*) to devour; (*agotar*) to consume, use up; *fortuna* to run through; **este coche devora los kilómetros** this car eats up the miles; **lo devoraba con los ojos** she was eyeing it greedily; **todo lo devoró el fuego** the fire consumed everything; **devora las novelas de amores** she laps up love stories, she devours love stories; **le devoran los celos** he is consumed with jealousy; **los chicos devoran el calzado** the kids are terribly hard on their shoes.

devotamente ADV devoutly.

devoto ① ADJ **(a)** (*Rel*) devout; pious; **ser muy ~ de un santo** to have a special devotion to a saint; **ser ~ de la Virgen del puño** to be tight-fisted.

(b) **obra devota** (*Rel*) devotional work, work of devotion.

(c) *amigo etc* devoted; **su ~ amigo** your devoted friend; **es ~ de ese café** he is much attached to that café.

② NM, **devota** NF **(a)** (*Rel*) devout person; (*en iglesia*) worshipper; **los ~s** the faithful; (*en iglesia*) the worshippers, the congregation.

(b) (*fig*) devotee, votary; admirer; **la estrella y sus ~s** the star and her admirers (*o* fans); **los ~s del ajedrez** devotees of chess.

devuelto PTP *V* **devolver**.

devuelva *etc V* **devolver**.

dextrosa NF dextrose.

deyección NF (*t* **deyecciones**) excrement; (*Med*) motion; (*Geol*) debris; (*de volcán*) lava.

deyectar [1a] VT (*Geol*) to deposit, leave, lay down.

DF NM (*Méx*) ABR *de* **Distrito Federal** Federal District.

Dg. ABR *de* **decagramo** decagram.

dg. ABR *de* **decigramo** decigram, dg.

D.G. **(a)** NF ABR *de* **Dirección General**. **(b)** NM ABR *de* **Director General** director-general, DG.

DGS NF **(a)** ABR *de* **Dirección General de Seguridad**. **(b)** ABR *de* **Dirección General de Sanidad**.

DGT NF **(a)** ABR *de* **Dirección General de Tráfico**. **(b)** ABR *de* **Dirección General de Turismo**.

dha., dho ABR *de* **dicha, dicho** aforesaid.

di *etc V* **dar, decir**.

día NM **(a)** (*gen*) day; **el ~ 2 de mayo** (on) the second of May; **ocho ~s** week; **quince ~s** fortnight; **cuatro ~s** (*fig*) a couple of days, a few days, a day or two; **¿qué ~ es?** what's the date today?; **hace buen ~** it's a fine day, it's fine today; **¡buenos ~s!**, (*Cono Sur*) **buen ~!** good morning!, good day!; **dar los buenos ~s a uno** to wish (*o* bid) sb good day; **dar los ~s a uno** to wish sb many happy returns of the day (*birthday o saint's day*); **~ y noche** night and day; **parece que no pasan por ti los ~s** you don't look a day older; **no tener más que el ~ y la noche** to be utterly poor.

(b) (*frases con artículo, adj etc*) **el ~ de hoy** today; **el ~ de mañana** tomorrow; (*fig*) at some future date; **el mejor ~** some fine day, any old day; **el ~ menos pensado** when you least expect it; **un ~ de éstos** one of these days; **un ~ sí y otro no, ~ (de) por medio** (*LAm*) every other day; **en días alternate days; ~ tras ~** day after day; **algún ~** some day, sometime; **cada ~** each day, every day; **¡cualquier ~!** (*iró*) not on your life!; **cualquier ~ viene** (*iró*) some fine day he'll turn up; **otro ~** some other day, some other time; **dejémoslo para otro ~** let's leave it for the moment; **¡tal ~ hará un año!*** a fat lot I care!*;

todos los ~s every day, daily; **no es cosa de todos los ~s** it's not an everyday thing; **todo el santo ~** the whole livelong day; the whole blessed day; *V* **hoy**.

(c) (*locuciones con prep*) **~ a ~** day in day out; **el ~ a ~** day-to-day routine; **a ~s** at times, once in a while; **a los pocos ~s** within a few days, after a few days, a few days later; **al otro ~** (on) the following day; **al ~ siguiente** on the following day; **7 veces al ~** 7 times a day, 7 times daily; **estar al ~** to be up to date; (*en la moda etc*) to be trendy; **quien quiera estar al ~ en estos estudios, lea ...** if anybody wants to keep up to date in these matters, he should read ...; **está al ~ vestir así** it's the thing to dress like that; **poner al ~** *diario* to enter up, write up; *libro mayor* to write up; **vivir al ~** to live from hand to mouth; **de ~ en ~** from day to day; **ese problema es ya de ~s** that's an old problem; **pollitos de un ~** day-old chicks; **los estilos del ~** fashionable styles, up-to-date styles, trendy styles*; **en ~s de Dios** (*o* **del mundo** *o* **de la vida**) never; **en los ~s de Victoria** in Victoria's day, in Victoria's times; **en su ~** in due time; **¡hasta otro ~!** so long!

(d) (*locuciones con adj etc*) **~ de asueto** day off; **~ de ayuno** fast day; **~ azul** (*Ferro*) cheap ticket day; **~ de la banderita** flag day; **~ de boda** wedding day; **cien ~s** (*Pol etc*) hundred days, honeymoon period; **~ de diario, ~ de entresemana, ~ entre semana** weekday; **D~ de los Difuntos** All Souls' Day; **~ de los enamorados** St Valentine's Day (*14 February*); **~ del espectador** *day each week when cinemas are discounted;* **~ feriado** holiday, day off; **~ festivo, ~ de fiesta** holiday; **~ franco** (*Mil*) day's leave; (*Com*) **~s de gracia** days of grace, days (allowed) to pay; **~ hábil** working day; **D~ de la Hispanidad** Columbus Day (*12 October*); **~ inhábil** non-working day; **~ de inocentes** (*28 December*) ≃ All Fools' Day, April Fools' Day (*1 April*); **~ del Juicio** (*Final*) Judgement Day; **estaremos aquí hasta el ~ del Juicio** we'll be here till Kingdom come; **~ laborable** working day, weekday; **~ lectivo** (*Escol*) working day, teaching day; **~ libre** free day, day off; **~ de la Madre** Mother's Day (*in Spain, 8 December*); **~ malo, ~ nulo** off day; **D~ de los Muertos** All Souls Day; **~ de paga** payday; **~ de puertas abiertas** open day; **D~ de la Raza** Columbus Day (*12 October*); **D~ de Reyes** Epiphany (*6 January);* **~ señalado** special day, red-letter day; **~ de trabajo, ~ útil** working day, weekday; **~ de tribunales** court day; **~ de vigilia** day of abstinence; *V* **anunciación, año** *etc; see also* DÍA DE LOS (SANTOS) INOCENTES , REYES, DÍA DE .

(e) (*horas de luz*) daytime; (*luz*) daylight; **antes del ~** before dawn; **de ~** by day, during the day(time); **en pleno ~** in broad daylight.

diabetes NF diabetes.

diabético, -a ADJ, NM/F diabetic.

diabla NF, **diablesa** NF she-devil; **a la diabla** carelessly, any old how*.

diablillo* NM imp, monkey.

diablo NM **(a)** (*demonio*) devil; fiend; **ése es el ~** that's the devil of it; **ahí será el ~** there'll be the devil to pay; **donde el ~ perdió el poncho** (*Cono Sur*) in some godforsaken spot.

(b) (*fig*) devil; fiend; **pobre ~** poor devil; **algún pobre ~ de cartero** some poor devil of a postman; *para muchas frases, V* **demonio**.

(c) **~s azules** (*LAm*) blue devils, delirium tremens.

(d) (*Cono Sur: carro*) heavy oxcart.

diablura NF devilry, devilment; prank; **~s** mischief, monkey tricks.

diabólicamente ADV diabolically, fiendishly.

diabólico ADJ diabolical, devilish, fiendish.

diábolo NM diabolo.

diacho* NM (*euf*) = **diablo**.

diaconato NM deaconry, diaconate.

diaconía NF (*distrito*) deaconry; (*casa*) deacon's house.

diaconisa NF deaconess.

diácono NM deacon.

diacrítico ADJ diacritic(al); **signo ~** diacritic, diacritical mark.

diacrónico ADJ diachronic.

Diada NF Catalan national day.

┌─ **DIADA NACIONAL DE CATALUNYA** ─────────────────┐

ⓘ *The* **Diada**, *or Catalonia's national day, is celebrated on 11 September to commemorate the fall of Barcelona to the Borbon Philip V in 1714 at the end of the War of the Spanish Succession. Prior to this Catalonia had enjoyed a high degree of autonomy which it lost, along with its government, the* **Generalitat**. *For the* **Diada** *streets and balconies all over Catalonia are decked out with the Catalan flag with its four red stripes on a gold background.*

└──┘

diadema NF (*gen*) diadem; (*corona*) crown; (*joya*) tiara.

diafanidad NF transparency; filminess; sheerness; limpidity.

diáfano ADJ **(a)** (*gen*) diaphanous, transparent; filmy; *medias, tela* sheer; *agua* limpid, crystal-clear. **(b)** (*iluminado*) bright, well-lit. **(c)** *argumento etc* clear; **es ~ que ...** it is clear that ...

diafragma NM diaphragm.

diagnosis NF INVAR diagnosis.

diagnóstica NF diagnostics.
diagnosticar [1g] VT to diagnose.
diagnóstico ① ADJ diagnostic.
   ② NM diagnosis; ~ **precoz** early diagnosis.
diagonal ADJ, NF diagonal.
diagonalmente ADV diagonally.
diagrama NM diagram; ~ **de barras** bar chart; ~ **de bloques** block diagram; ~ **circular** pie chart; ~ **de dispersión** scatter diagram; ~ **de flujo** flowchart.
dial NM (*Aut, Rad etc*) dial.
dialectal ADJ dialectal, dialect (*atr*).
dialectalismo NM **(a)** (*carácter*) dialectal nature, dialectalism; **un texto lleno de** ~ a text of a strongly dialectal character.
   (b) (*palabra etc*) dialectalism, dialect word (*o phrase etc*).
dialéctica NF dialectic(s).
dialécticamente ADV dialectically.
dialéctico ADJ dialectical.
dialecto NM dialect.
dialectología NF dialectology.
dialectólogo, -a NM/F dialectologist.
diálisis NF dialysis.
dialogado ADJ; **solución** *o* **salida dialogada** negotiated settlement.
dialogante ① ADJ open, open-minded, willing to discuss; approachable.
   ② NMF interlocutor; participant (in a discussion); **mi** ~ the person I was (*etc*) talking to.
dialogar [1h] ① VT to set down (*o compose etc*) as a dialogue, write in dialogue form.
   ② VI to talk, converse; ~ **con** to engage in a dialogue with.
diálogo NM dialogue; ~ **para besugos** fatuous exchange; ~ **norte-sur** north-south dialogue; ~ **de sordos** dialogue of the deaf.
diamante NM **(a)** (*joya*) diamond; ~ **en bruto** uncut diamond; (*fig*) **ser un** ~ **en bruto** to be a rough diamond; ~ **falso** paste; ~ **de imitación** imitation diamond. **(b)** ~**s** (*Naipes*) diamonds.
diamantífero ADJ diamond-bearing.
diamantino ADJ diamond-like, adamantine; glittering.
diamantista NMF (*Téc*) diamond cutter; (*Com*) diamond merchant.
diametral ADJ diametrical.
diametralmente ADV diametrically; ~ **opuesto a** diametrically opposed to.
diámetro NM diameter; ~ **de giro** (*Aut*) turning circle; **faros de gran** ~ wide-angle headlights.
Diana NF Diana.
diana NF **(a)** (*Mil*) reveille.
   (b) (*de blanco*) centre, bull's-eye; **dar en la** ~, **hacer** ~ to get a bull's-eye.
   (c) (*juego*) dartboard.
diantre* NM (*euf*) = **diablo**; **¡~!** oh hell!; **los había como un** ~ (*Cono Sur*) there were the devil of a lot of them, there were loads of them.
diapasón NM **(a)** (*Mús*) diapason; normal standard pitch; range, scale.
   (b) (*de violín etc*) fingerboard.
   (c) ~ **normal** tuning fork.
   (d) (*fig: de voz*) tone; **bajar el** ~ to lower one's voice; **subir el** ~ to raise one's voice.
diapositiva NF (*Fot*) slide, transparency; (*de vidrio*) lantern slide; ~ **en color** colour slide.
diariamente ADV daily, every day.
diariero NM (*Argentina*) paperboy.
diario ① ADJ daily; everyday; day-to-day; **100 dólares** ~**s** 100 dollars a day.
   ② ADV (*LAm*) daily, every day.
   ③ NM **(a)** (*periódico*) newspaper, daily; (*libro diario*) diary; (*Com*) daybook; ~ **de a bordo**, ~ **de navegación** log-book; ~ **hablado** (*Rad etc*) news, news bulletin; ~ **de escritorio** desk diary; ~ **dominical** Sunday paper; ~ **matinal**, ~ **de la mañana** morning paper; ~ **de la noche**, ~ **vespertino** evening paper; ~ **de sesiones** (*Parl*) parliamentary report, report of proceedings in Parliament.
   (b) (*Fin*) daily expenses.
   (c) **a** ~ daily; **de** ~, **para** ~ for everyday use; **nuestro mantel de** ~ our tablecloth for everyday (use), our ordinary tablecloth.
diarismo NM (*LAm*) journalism.
diarista NMF **(a)** (*de libro diario*) diarist. **(b)** (*LAm: de periódico*) newspaper owner (*o publisher*).
diarrea NF diarrhoea.
diarrucho* NM (*LAm*) rag*; **los** ~**s** the gutter press.
diáspora NF (*Hist*) diaspora; (*fig*) dispersal, migration.
diatónico ADJ diatonic.
diatriba NF diatribe, tirade.
dibujante NMF **(a)** (*Arte*) sketcher; cartoonist. **(b)** (*Téc*) draughtsman; (*de modas*) designer; ~ **de publicidad** commercial artist.
dibujar [1a] ① VT **(a)** (*Arte*) to draw, sketch.

(b) (*Téc*) to design.
   (c) (*fig*) to sketch (in words), describe, depict.
   ② **dibujarse** VR **(a)** (*perfilarse*) to be outlined (*contra* against); to loom, show up.
   (b) (*emoción etc*) to show, appear; **el sufrimiento se dibujaba en su cara** suffering showed in his face.
dibujo NM **(a)** (*gen*) drawing; sketching; art of design; ~ **mecánico** mechanical drawing.
   (b) (*un* ~) drawing, sketch (*t fig*); (*en periódico etc*) cartoon; (*caricatura*) caricature; ~ **animado**, ~**s animados** cartoon (film); ~ **al carbón** charcoal drawing; ~ **al natural**, ~ **del natural** drawing from life; ~ (**hecho**) **a pulso** freehand drawing.
   (c) (*Téc*) design; pattern; ~ **escocés** tartan (design); **un papel con** ~ **a rayas** a wallpaper with a striped pattern; **sedas con** ~**s de última novedad** silks with the latest patterns (*o designs*).
dic., dic.ᵉ ABR *de* **diciembre** December, Dec.
dicción NF **(a)** (*gen*) diction; style. **(b)** (*una* ~) word; expression.
diccionario NM dictionary; ~ **de bolsillo** pocket dictionary; ~ **bilingüe** bilingual dictionary; ~ **geográfico** gazetteer.
diccionarista NMF lexicographer, dictionary maker.
dicha NF **(a)** (*felicidad*) happiness; **para completar su** ~ to complete her happiness.
   (b) (*una* ~) happy thing, happy event; **es una** ~ **poder** ... it is a happy thing to be able to ...
   (c) (*suerte*) luck, good luck; **por** ~ by chance, fortunately.
dicharachería NF wittiness, raciness; slanginess; saltiness.
dicharachero ① ADJ (*gracioso*) witty, racy, sparkling; (*que usa argot*) slangy; (*de fuerte sabor*) salty.
   ② NM witty person, racy talker, sparkling conversationalist; slangy sort; salty individual.
dicharacho NM coarse remark, rude thing (to say).
dicho ① PTP *de* **decir**.
   ② ADJ (*este*) said; (*susodicho*) above-mentioned, aforementioned; ~**s animales** the said animals; **en** ~ **país** in this country, in this same country; **las avispas propiamente dichas** true wasps, wasps in the strict sense; *V t* **decir**.
   ③ NM (*proverbio*) saying, proverb; (*lugar común*) tag; (*ocurrencia*) bright remark, witty observation; (*insulto*) insult; ~ **gordo** rude remark; **del** ~ **al hecho hay gran trecho** talking is not the same as actually doing; there's many a slip 'twixt cup and lip; **es un** ~ it's just a saying; **tomarse los** ~**s** to exchange promises of marriage.
dichosamente ADV luckily, fortunately.
dichoso ADJ **(a)** (*feliz*) happy; **hacer** ~ **a uno** to make sb happy; **me siento** ~ **de** + *infin* I feel happy to + *infin*.
   (b) (*afortunado*) lucky, fortunate; **¡~s los ojos!** nice to see you!
   (c) (*) blessed; **¡aquel** ~ **coche!** that blessed car!
diciembre NM December.
diciendo *etc V* **decir**.
dicotomía NF dichotomy.
dictablanda NF (*hum*) kindly dictatorship, benevolent despotism.
dictado NM **(a)** (*gen*) dictation; **escribir al** ~ to take dictation; **escribir algo al** ~ to take sth down (as it is dictated).
   (b) ~**s** (*fig*) dictates; **los** ~**s de la conciencia** the dictates of conscience.
   (c) (*título*) honorific title, title of honour.
dictador(a) NM/F dictator.
dictadura NF dictatorship.
dictáfono ® NM Dictaphone ®.
dictamen NM (*opinión*) opinion, dictum; (*juicio*) judgement; (*informe*) report; (*Jur*) legal opinion; ~ **contable** (*Méx*) auditor's report; ~ **facultativo** (*Med*) medical report; **emitir un** ~ to issue a report; **tomar** ~ **de** to consult with.
dictaminar [1a] ① VT *sentencia* to pass.
   ② VI to pass judgement, give an opinion (*en* on).
dictar [1a] ① VT **(a)** *carta etc* to dictate (*a* to).
   (b) *sentencia* to pass, pronounce; *decreto etc* to issue.
   (c) (*indicar*) to suggest, say, dictate; **lo que dicta el sentido común** what common sense suggests.
   (d) (*LAm*) *clase* to give; *conferencia* to deliver, give; ~ **las noticias** (*Rad, TV*) to read the news.
   ② VI: ~ **a su secretaria** to dictate to one's secretary.
dictatorial ADJ, **dictatorio** ADJ dictatorial.
dicterio NM insult, taunt.
didáctica NF didactics; **departamento de** ~ (*Univ*) education department.
didacticismo NM didacticism.
didáctico ADJ didactic.
didactismo NM didacticism.
Dido NF Dido.
diecinueve ADJ nineteen; (*fecha*) nineteenth.
dieciochesco ADJ eighteenth-century (*atr*).
dieciocho ADJ eighteen; (*fecha*) eighteenth.

dieciochoañero, -a ADJ, NM/F eighteen-year-old.

dieciséis ADJ sixteen; (*fecha*) sixteenth.

diecisiete ADJ seventeen; (*fecha*) seventeenth.

Diego NM James.

dieldrina NF dieldrin.

diente NM (**a**) (*Anat*) tooth; (*Zool*) tusk; fang; **~ canino** canine (tooth); **~ cariado** decayed tooth, bad tooth; **~ incisivo** incisor; **~ de leche** milk tooth; **~ molar** molar; **~s postizos** false teeth; **de ~s afuera** (*fig*) as mere lip service, without meaning it; **decir algo para ~s afuera** to say one thing and mean another, pay lip service; **más cerca están mis ~s que mis parientes** charity begins at home; **daba ~ con ~** his teeth were chattering; he was trembling like a leaf, he was all of a shiver; **enseñar los ~s** (*fig*) to show one's claws, turn nasty; **estar a ~** to be ravenous; **hablar entre ~s** to mumble, mutter; **hincar el ~ en** to sink one's teeth into, bite into; **hincar el ~ en uno** (*fig*) to get one's knife into sb; **nunca pude hincar el ~ a ese libro** I could never get my teeth into that book; **pelar el ~** (*LAm*) (*coquetear*) to flirt; (*reír*) to giggle flirtatiously; **poner a uno los ~s largos** to make sb green with envy, make sb jealous **tener buen ~** to be a hearty eater.

(**b**) (*Mec*) cog; (*de hebilla*) tongue; (*de peine, sierra etc*) tooth.

(**c**) (*Bot*) **~ de ajo** clove of garlic; **~ de león** dandelion.

diera *etc* V **dar**.

diéresis NF diaeresis.

dieron V **dar**.

diesel ADJ, NM (PL **diesel**) (*Aut*) diesel(-engined car); (**motor**) **~** diesel engine; **tren ~** diesel train.

dieseléctrico ADJ diesel-electric.

diestra NF right hand.

diestramente ADV (**a**) (*hábilmente*) skilfully; dexterously; deftly. (**b**) (*astutamente*) shrewdly; (*pey*) cunningly.

diestro ① ADJ (**a**) (*derecho*) right; (*Her*) dexter; **a ~ y siniestro** wildly, at random, all over the place; **repartir golpes a ~ y siniestro** to lash out wildly, throw out punches right and left.

(**b**) (*hábil*) skilful; dexterous; handy, deft.

(**c**) (*listo*) shrewd, clever; (*pey*) cunning. ② NM (**a**) (*Taur*) matador, bullfighter.

(**b**) (*espadachín*) expert swordsman; (*esgrimidor*) expert fencer.

(**c**) (*correa*) bridle, halter.

(**d**) (*Dep*) right-hander.

dieta NF (**a**) (*Med*) diet; **~ láctea** milk diet; **~ mediterránea** Mediterranean diet; **estar a ~** to diet, be on a diet. (**b**) (*Pol*) diet, assembly.

(**c**) **~s** subsistence allowance, expense allowance; **~ de asistencia** attendance allowance. (**d**) (*And: guiso*) stew.

dietario NM engagement book.

dietética[1] NF dietetics.

dietético ① ADJ (**a**) dietetic, dietary. (**b**) **restaurante ~** restaurant for people on a diet.

② NM, **dietética**[2] NF dietician.

dietista NMF, **dietólogo, -a** NM/F dietician.

diez[1] ① ADJ ten; (*fecha*) tenth; **las ~** ten o'clock; **hacer las ~ de últimas** to scoop the pool, sweep the board; (*fig*) to queer one's own pitch, damage one's own cause.

② NM ten; **un ~ para Pérez** ten out of ten for Pérez.

diez[2]⁑ NM *euf de* **Dios**, *en locuciones*; V **cagar 3** (**b**).

diezmar [1a] VT to decimate (*t fig*).

diezmillo NM (*Méx*) sirloin steak.

diezmo NM tithe.

difamación NF slander, defamation (*de* of); libel (*de* on).

difamador ① ADJ slanderous, defamatory, libellous.

② NM, **difamadora** NF slanderer; defamer; scandalmonger.

difamar [1a] VT (*Jur*) to slander, defame; (*esp por escrito*) to libel; (*fig*) to slander, malign.

difamatorio ADJ slanderous, defamatory, libellous.

▼ **diferencia** NF difference; **~ de edades** difference in ages; **a ~ de** unlike; in contrast to; as distinguished from; **con corta ~, con poca ~** more or less; **hacer ~ entre** to make a distinction between; **partir la ~** to split the difference; **partir la ~ con uno** (*fig*) to meet sb halfway, agree to compromise; **va de A a Z** there's a big difference between A and Z; **no veo ~ de A a Z** I see no difference between A and Z; I see nothing to choose between A and Z.

diferenciable ADJ distinguishable.

diferenciación NF differentiation.

diferenciador ADJ distinguishing.

diferencial ① ADJ differential (*t Mat*); distinctive; *impuesto etc* discriminatory.

② NF (*Mat*) differential.

③ NM (*a veces t* F) (*Aut*) differential.

▼ **diferenciar** [1b] ① VT (**a**) (*distinguir*) to differentiate between; to make a difference between; **~ A de B** to separate A from B, distinguish between A and B.

(**b**) (*Mat*) to differentiate.

(**c**) (*variar*) to vary (the use of), alter the function of.

② VI to differ (*de* from), be in disagreement (*de* with; *en* about, over).

③ **diferenciarse** VR (**a**) (*ser distinto*) to differ, be different (*de* from); to be distinctive, be distinguished; **no se diferencian en nada** they do not differ at all; **se diferencian en que ...** they differ in that ...

(**b**) (*destacar*) to distinguish o.s., stand out.

diferendo NM difference, disagreement.

diferente ADJ (**a**) (*gen*) different; **~ a algo, ~ de algo** different from sth, unlike sth. (**b**) **~s** several, various; **por ~s razones** for various reasons.

diferentemente ADV differently.

diferido ADJ: **emisión diferida, emisión en ~** (*Rad, TV*) recorded programme, repeat broadcast.

diferir [3i] ① VT to defer, postpone, put off; to hold over; (*Jur*) *sentencia* to reserve.

② VI to differ, be different (*de* from, *en* in).

▼ **difícil** ADJ (**a**) (*gen*) difficult, hard; awkward; **~ de vencer** hard to beat, difficult to overcome; **encuentro ~ decidir si ...** I find it hard to decide whether ..., I find difficulty in deciding whether ...; **se hizo un silencio ~** there was an awkward (*o* embarrassing) silence; **creo que lo tiene ~** I think he's got a tough job on.

(**b**) (*poco probable*) unlikely; **es ~ que ...** it is unlikely that ..., it is doubtful whether ...; **es ~ que venga** she's not likely to come.

(**c**) (*de carácter*) difficult; (*rebelde*) unruly, rebellious; (*inconformista*) non-conformist; **es un hombre ~** he's a difficult man.

(**d**) (*) *cara* odd, ugly.

difícilmente ADV with difficulty; hardly; **~ se podrá hacer** it can hardly be done; **aquí ~ va a haber para todos** there's hardly going to be enough of this for everybody; **~ se alcanza eso** that is not likely to be reached.

dificultad NF (*gen*) difficulty; (*problema*) trouble; (*objeción*) objection; **sin ~ alguna** without the least difficulty; **la ~ es que ...** the difficulty is that ..., the trouble is that ...; **no hay ~ para aceptar que ...** there is no difficulty about accepting that ...; **ha tenido ~es con la policía** he's been in trouble with the police; **tuvieron algunas ~es para llegar a casa** they had some trouble getting home; **poner ~es** to raise objections; to create obstacles; **me pusieron ~es para darme el pasaporte** they made it awkward for me to get a passport.

dificultar [1a] VT (**a**) *camino, tráfico etc* to obstruct, impede, hinder; (*obstaculizar*) to put obstacles in the way of; (*afectar*) to interfere with, hold up; to render difficult; **las restricciones dificultan el comercio** the restrictions hinder trade, the restrictions make trade difficult.

(**b**) **~ que** + *subj* to make it unlikely that ...; (*persona*) to think (*o* consider) it unlikely that ...

dificultoso ADJ (**a**) (*difícil*) difficult, hard; awkward, troublesome. (**b**) (*) *cara* odd, ugly. (**c**) *persona* difficult, awkward, full of silly objections.

difracción NF diffraction.

difractar [1a] VT to diffract.

difteria NF diphtheria.

difuminadamente ADV sketchily.

difuminado ADJ *voz* slurred, husky; *representación* sketchy, vague, barely outlined.

difuminar [1a] ① VT *dibujo* to blur.

② **difuminarse** VR (**a**) **~ en** to shade into. (**b**) (*fig*) to fade away; to evaporate.

difumino NM stump.

difundir [3a] ① VT *color, luz* to diffuse; *noticia* to spread, disseminate; to divulge, circulate; (*Rad*) to broadcast, transmit; *gas etc* to give off, give out, emit; **~ la alegría** to spread happiness, radiate happiness.

② **difundirse** VR to spread (out); to become diffused.

difunto ① ADJ dead, deceased; **el ~ ministro** the late minister.

② NM, **difunta** NF dead person, deceased person; **la familia del ~** the family of the deceased; **Día de (los) D~s** All Souls' Day; *see also* DÍA DE LOS MUERTOS .

difusión NF (**a**) (*acto*) diffusion; spread(ing), dissemination; divulging, circulation; (*Prensa*) circulation, readership figures; **diario de ~ nacional** newspaper distributed nationally, newspaper having a nation-wide distribution. (**b**) (*cualidad*) diffuseness.

difuso ADJ (**a**) *luz* diffused; *conocimiento etc* widespread, widely extended. (**b**) *estilo etc* diffuse, wordy, discursive.

difusor NM blow-drier.

diga *etc* V **decir**.

digerible ADJ digestible.

digerir [3i] VT (**a**) *comida* to digest; (*tragar*) to swallow.

(**b**) (*Quím*) to digest, absorb, dissolve.

(**c**) (*fig*) *opiniones etc* to digest, absorb, assimilate; to ponder, think over; (*en locuciones negativas*) to swallow, stomach; **no puedo ~ a ese tío** I can't stand that chap.

digestible ADJ digestible.

digestión NF digestion.
digestivo ADJ digestive.
digesto M (*Jur etc*) digest.
digitación NF (*Mús*) fingering.
digital ① ADJ (a) digital; finger (*atr*); **impresión ~** fingerprint. (b) (*hum*) V **dedo (a dedo)**.
② NF (*Bot*) foxglove; (*droga*) digitalis.
digitalizador NM digitizer.
digitalizar [1f] VT to digitalize.
digitalmente ADV (a) digitally. (b) (*hum*) V **dedo (a dedo)**.
dígito NM digit; **~ binario** binary digit; **~ de control** check digit.
diglosia NF diglossia.
dignación NF condescension.
dignamente ADV (a) (*gen*) worthily; fittingly, properly, appropriately. (b) (*honradamente*) honourably. (c) (*con dignidad*) with dignity, in a dignified way. (d) (*decentemente*) decently.
dignarse [1a] VR: **~ + infin** (a) (*condescender*) to deign to + infin, condescend to + infin.
(b) (*fórmulas*) please ...; **dígnese venir a esta oficina** please (be so good as to) come to this office.
dignatario, -a NM/F dignitary.
dignidad NF (a) (*cualidad*) dignity; honour; self-respect; **herir la ~ de uno** to offend sb's self-respect.
(b) (*puesto*) post, office; (*categoría*) rank; **tiene ~ de ministro** he has the rank of a minister.
(c) (*persona*) dignitary, worthy.
dignificante ADJ dignifying.
dignificar [1g] VT to dignify.
digno ADJ (a) (*merecedor*) worthy; (*conveniente*) fitting; proper, appropriate; **~ de** worthy of, deserving; **~ de elogio** praiseworthy; **~ de toda alabanza** thoroughly praiseworthy, highly commendable; **~ de mención** worth a mention, worth mentioning; **un ~ castigo** a fitting punishment; **es ~ de nuestra admiración** it deserves our admiration; **es ~ de verse** it is worth seeing.
(b) (*honrado*) etc worthy, upright, honourable.
(c) (*grave*) dignified.
(d) (*decoroso*) decent; **viviendas dignas para los obreros** decent homes for the workers.
digresión NF digression.
dije¹ *etc* V **decir**.
dije² ① NM (a) (*medallón*) medallion; (*relicario*) locket; (*amuleto*) amulet, charm; (*pey*) trinket. (b) (*fig*) gem, treasure, person of sterling qualities. (c) **~s*** boasting, bravado.
② ADJ (*Cono Sur*) (a) (*guapo*) good-looking. (b) (*encantador*) nice, sweet, charming.
dilación NF delay; **sin ~** without delay, forthwith; **esto no admite ~** this must suffer no delay, this is most urgent.
dilapidación NF squandering, waste.
dilapidar [1a] VT to squander, waste.
dilatación NF (a) (*gen*) dilation; expansion (*t Fís*), enlargement, widening, stretching; protraction, prolongation. (b) (*fig*) calm, calm dignity.
dilatado ADJ *pupila* dilated; (*extenso*) vast, extensive, spacious; (*numeroso*) numerous; *período* long-drawn-out; *discurso etc* long-winded, discursive.
dilatar [1a] ① VT (a) *pupila* to dilate; *metal* to expand; (*ampliar*) to enlarge, widen; (*extender*) to stretch, extend; *fama etc* to spread.
(b) (*en tiempo*) to protract, prolong, stretch out.
(c) *diferir* to delay, put off.
② VI (*Méx*) to be delayed, be late.
③ **dilatarse** VR (a) to dilate; to expand (*t Fís*); to stretch, extend; to spread; **la llanura se dilata hasta el horizonte** the plain spreads (*o* extends, rolls) right to the horizon; **el valle se dilata en aquella parte** the valley widens (*o* spreads out) at that point.
(b) (*al hablar*) to be long-winded, be discursive; **~ en, ~ sobre** to expatiate on; to linger over, take one's time over.
(c) (*LAm: demorarse*) to delay, be slow; (*tren etc*) to be late; **~ en + infin** to take a long time to + infin, be slow to + infin.
dilatorias NFPL procrastination; delaying tactics; **andar en ~ con uno, traer a uno en ~** to use delaying tactics with sb, hedge with sb; **no me vengas con ~** don't hedge with me.
dilatorio ADJ delaying, dilatory.
dildo NM dildo.
dilección NF affection.
dilema NM dilemma; **estar en un ~** to be in a dilemma.
diletante NMF dilettante.
diligencia NF (a) (*cualidad*) diligence, care; assiduity; speed, dispatch.
(b) (*negocio*) piece of business; (*encargo*) errand, job, mission; **hacer ~s** to do business; **hacer una ~** to run an errand, go on an errand; (‡) to do one's business‡; **hacer las ~s de costumbre** to take the usual steps; **practicar sus ~s** to make every possible effort, do one's utmost (**para + infin** to + infin).

(c) (*Jur*) **~s** formalities; inquiries; steps (of an investigation *etc*); **~s judiciales** judicial proceedings; **~s previas** inquiries; **instruir ~s** to start proceedings.
(d) (*Hist*) stagecoach.
diligenciado NM, **diligenciamiento** NM processing.
diligenciar [1b] VT *asunto* to see about, deal with; to further, get moving; *documento, solicitud* to process, deal with.
diligente ADJ (*aplicado*) diligent; (*asiduo*) industrious, assiduous; (*pronto*) quick, speedy, prompt; **un alumno poco ~** a slack pupil, a lazy pupil.
diligentemente ADV diligently; industriously; assiduously; speedily.
dilucidar [1a] VT to elucidate, explain, clarify; *caso, misterio etc* to solve, clear up; *concurso* to decide, determine.
dilución NF dilution.
diluido ADJ dilute; diluted, weak; watered-down.
diluir [3g] VT to dilute; to water down, weaken; (*fig*) to water down.
diluvial ADJ torrential.
diluviar [1b] VI to pour with rain, rain in torrents.
diluvio NM deluge, flood (*t fig*); **el D~** the Flood; **un ~ de cartas** a deluge of letters; **¡fue el ~!** it was chaos!; **¡esto es el ~!** what a mess!
dimanar [1a] VI to flow; (*fig*) **~ de** to arise from, spring from, stem from.
dimensión NF (a) (*Mat*) dimension (*t fig*); size; **cuarta ~** fourth dimension; **de grandes dimensiones** of great size, of large dimensions; **tomar las dimensiones de** to take the measurements of.
(b) (*fig: cualidad de persona*) stature, standing; **un matemático de ~ universal** a mathematician of world stature.
dimensionado NM measuring; assessment.
dimes NMPL: **~ y diretes** (*riñas*) bickering, squabbling; (*chismes*) gossip; (*intriga*) petty intrigue; **andar en ~ y diretes con uno** to bicker (*o* squabble) with sb.
diminutivo ADJ, NM diminutive.
diminuto ADJ (a) (*pequeño*) tiny, minute, exceedingly small; miniature. (b) (*imperfecto*) defective, imperfect.
dimisión NF resignation; **presentar la ~** to send in (*o* tender *o* submit) one's resignation.
dimisionar [1a] = **dimitir**.
dimisionario, -a NM/F person resigning, person who has resigned.
dimitente ① ADJ resigning, outgoing, retiring; **el presidente ~** the outgoing chairman, the retiring chairman.
② NMF person resigning.
dimitir [3a] ① VT (a) *cargo* to resign; to give up, relinquish; **~ la jefatura del partido** to resign (from) the party leadership. (b) *persona* to dismiss, sack*.
② VI to resign (**de** from).
dimos V **dar**.
din* NM dough‡; **el ~ y el don** money and rank, dough and dukedom‡.
DINA NF (*Chile*) ABR de **Dirección de Inteligencia Nacional** *Chilean secret police (until 1977).*
Dinamarca NF Denmark.
dinamarqués = **danés**.
dinámica NF (**la ~**) dynamics; (**una ~**) dynamic; **~ de grupo** group dynamics.
dinamicidad NF dynamism.
dinámico ADJ dynamic.
dinamismo NM dynamism.
dinamita NF dynamite.
dinamitar [1a] VT to dynamite.
dinamitazo NM dynamite explosion; dynamiting.
dinamizador ADJ revitalizing.
dinamizar [1f] VT to invigorate, put (new) energy into; to stir into action.
dínamo NF, **dinamo** NF (*a veces m en LAm*) dynamo.
dinastía NF dynasty.
dinástico ADJ dynastic.
dinerada NF, **dineral** NM fortune, mint of money; **habrá costado un dineral** it must have cost a fortune.
dinerario ADJ money (*atr*); **aportación no dineraria** non-cash contribution.
dinerillo* NM small amount of money; pocket money, pin money; **tiene sus ~s** she's got a bit of money (put by).
dinero NM (*gen*) money; (*de país, período etc*) currency, coinage, money; **persona de ~** moneyed person, wealthy person; **es hombre de ~** he is a man of means; **¿cuánto es en ~ americano?** how much is that in American money?; **~ de bolsillo** pocket-money; **~ en caja** cash in hand; **~ por callar** hush money*; **~ caliente** hot money; **~ contante** cash; **~ contante y sonante** cash, ready money; **~ de curso legal** legal tender; **~ negro, ~ sucio** undeclared earnings; money proceeding from crime; **~ (de) plástico** plastic money; **los ~s del sacristán cantando se vienen y cantando se van** easy come easy go; **el ~ malo echa fuera al bueno** bad money drives out good;

el ~ lo puede todo, el ~ puede mucho money can do anything, money talks; **andar mal de ~** to be badly off, be in financial difficulties; **el negocio no da ~** the business does not pay, the business is not profitable, the business is not a paying proposition; **ganar ~ a espuertas** (o **a porrillo**) to make money hand over fist.

dingui NM dinghy.

dinosaurio [1] NM dinosaur.
[2] ADJ dinosaurian; **un coche ~** a car from the Stone Age.

dintel NM lintel; (*LAm*) threshold.

diñar [1a] VT to give; **~la** to kick the bucket*; **diñársela a uno** to swindle sb.

dio V dar.

diocesano ADJ diocesan.

diócesi(s) NF, PL **diócesis** diocese.

diodo NM diode.

dionisíaco ADJ, **dionisíaco** ADJ Dionysian.

Dionisio NM Denis; (*clásico*) Dionysius.

dioptría NF (*ojos, gafas*) dioptre; **~s** gradation.

Dios NM (a) (*Rel*) God; **~ delante** with God's help; **~ mediante** God willing, D.V.; **a ~ gracias** thank heaven; **a la buena de ~** at random; thoughtlessly, without preparation; trusting to luck; any old how*; **a la de ~** (**es Cristo**)* rashly; **una de ~ es Cristo*** an almighty row*; **armar la de ~ es Cristo*** to raise hell, cause a tremendous fuss; **esto clama a ~** this cries out to heaven (to be reformed *etc*); **~ los cría y ellos se juntan** birds of a feather flock together; **dar a ~ lo que es de ~ y al César lo que es del César** render unto Caesar that which is Caesar's and unto God that which is God's; **lo hace como ~ le da a entender** he does it as best he can, he does it according to his lights; **como ~ manda** as is proper; properly, well; **si ~ quiere** God willing, D.V.; **donde ~ pasó de largo** a godforsaken spot; **cuando ~ quiera** all in God's good time; **a ~ rogando y con el mazo dando** trust in God but keep your powder dry; **~ sabe** God knows; **sólo ~ sabe** God alone knows; **sabe ~ que no quería ofender** God knows I did not intend to cause offence; **vaya con ~** goodbye; (*ceremonioso*) may God be with you; (*iró*) and good riddance, and the best of luck; **le vino ~ a ver** he struck lucky, he had a stroke of luck.
(b) (EXCL) **¡~ mío!** good gracious!, good heavens!; well!; **¡por ~!** for God's sake!; — **pero ¡por ~!** may I smoke? — please do!; **¡~ le ampare!, ¡~ le asista!, ¡~ te la depare buena!** (*iró*) I hope it keeps fine for you!, and the best of luck!; **¡~ le ayude!** (*al estornudar*) bless you!; **¡~ te bendiga!** God bless you!; **¡~ me libre!** Heaven forbid!; **¡líbreme ~ de ...!** Heaven forbid that I ...!; **¡plegue a ~!** please God!; **¡no lo quiera ~!** God forbid!; **¡válgame ~!** bless my soul!; **¡vaya por ~!** well I never!, I ask you!; **¡vive ~!** good God!

dios NM (a) god; idol; **los ~es paganos** the pagan gods. (b) (*) **como todo ~** like any guy; **no hay ~ que entienda eso** nobody can understand that; **no había ni ~** there wasn't a soul.

diosa NF goddess.

dióxido NM dioxide; **~ de carbono** carbon dioxide; **~ de nitrógeno** nitrogen dioxide.

dioxina NF dioxin.

Dip. ABR *de* **Diputación** ≈ County Council, CC.

diploma NM diploma.

diplomacia NF diplomacy; **~ de cañoneras** gunboat diplomacy.

diplomado [1] ADJ qualified, trained, having a diploma.
[2] NM, **diplomada** NF qualified person, holder of a diploma.

diplomarse [1a] VR (*esp LAm*) to graduate (from college *etc*).

diplomática[1] NF (a) (*Hist, Jur*) diplomatics. (b) (*Pol: cuerpo*) diplomatic corps; (*carrera*) diplomatic career, (career in the) foreign service.

diplomáticamente ADV diplomatically.

diplomático [1] ADJ diplomatic.
[2] NM, **diplomática**[2] NF diplomat; (*fig*) diplomatist.

diplomatura NF diploma course, course leading to a diploma; *see also* LICENCIATURA.

dipsomanía NF dipsomania.

dipsomaníaco, -a NM/F, **dipsómano, -a** NM/F dipsomaniac.

díptero NM fly.

díptico NM diptych; (*Com*) folder, brochure, leaflet.

diptongar [1h] VTI to diphthongize.

diptongo NM diphthong.

diputación NF (a) (*gen*) deputation, delegation; (*Admin*) committee; **~ permanente** (*Parl*) standing committee.
(b) **D~ General** (*Aragón, Rioja*) regional government; **~ provincial** (*personas*) ≈ county council; (*oficina*) ≈ county council offices.

diputado, -a NM/F delegate, representative; (*Parl*) deputy, member of parliament, representative (*US*); **~ a Cortes** (*Esp*) parliamentary deputy, member of the Spanish *Cortes*; **el ~ por Guadalajara** the member for Guadalajara; **~ provincial** ≈ member of a county council; *see also* CONGRESO DE LOS DIPUTADOS .

diputar [1a] VT (*delegar*) to delegate, depute; (*autorizar*) to empower.

dique NM (a) (*marítimo*) dike, sea wall; (*muelle*) jetty, mole; (*rompeolas*)

breakwater; (*dársena*) dock; **~ de contención** dam; **~ flotante** floating dock; **~ seco** dry dock; **estar en el ~** (*fig*) to be out of action; (**hacer**) **entrar en ~** to dock.
(b) (*fig*) check; barrier; **es un ~ contra la expansión** it is a barrier to expansion; **poner un ~ a** to check, restrain.

diquelar [1a] VT (a) (*ver*) to see; (*mirar*) to look at, watch; (*vigilar*) to watch over, keep an eye on. (b) (*comprender*) to twig*, catch on to.

Dir. (a) ABR *de* **dirección**. (b) ABR *de* **director** director, dir.

dire* NMF = **director, directora**.

diré *etc* V **decir**.

dirección NF (a) (*gen: sentido*) direction; way; (*fig: tendencia*) course, trend; **~ del viento** wind direction; **con ~ norte** in a northerly direction; **con ~ a, en ~ a, en la ~ de** in the direction of; towards; **'~ prohibida'** (*Aut*) 'no entry', 'no thoroughfare'; **calle de ~ obligatoria, calle de ~ única** one-way street; (*Aut: de autopista*) **~ este** eastbound; **~ oeste** westbound; **calle de 2 direcciones** street with two-way traffic; **conmutador de 2 direcciones** two-way switch; **cambiar de ~** to change direction; **¿podría Vd indicarme la ~ ...?** could you please direct me to ...?; **salir con ~ a** to leave for, depart for; to go off in the direction of; **salir con ~ desconocida** to leave for an unknown destination.
(b) (*acto: gobierno etc*) direction; guidance; control; (*Com etc*) running, management; (*Pol*) leadership; **~ colectiva, ~ colegiada** collective leadership; **~ empresarial** business management; **~ escénica, ~ de escena** stage management; **bajo la ~ de** under the direction of; **asumir la ~, tomar la ~** to take (over) control; **me han confiado la ~ de la obra** I have been put in charge of the work; **la revista de su digna ~** the journal which you edit.
(c) (*personal*) management; (*junta*) board of directors; (*Pol*) leadership; **habrá cambios en la ~ del partido** there will be changes in the party leadership, there will be changes among the party's top people.
(d) (*puesto*) directorship; post of manager; (*de colegio*) headship; (*de periódico*) editorship; (*Mús*) conductorship.
(e) (*Aut etc*) steering; **~ asistida** power steering; **de ~** steering (*atr*).
(f) (*oficina*) (head) office, administrative office; **D~ General de Turismo** State Tourist Office; **D~ General de Seguridad** State Security Office (o Service); **~ provincial** provincial office of a government department.
(g) (*Correos, Inform*) address; **~ comercial** business address; **~ del remitente** return address; **ponga claramente su ~** write your address clearly.

direccional [1] ADJ directional.
[2] **~es** NMPL indicator lights.

direccionamiento NM (*Inform*) addressing.

direccionar [1a] VT (*Inform*) to address; to operate.

directa NF (*Aut*) top gear.

directamente ADV directly.

directiva NF board of directors; governing body.

directivo [1] ADJ *junta etc* managing, governing; directorial; *función* managerial, administrative; *clase* managerial, executive.
[2] NM (a) (*Com etc*) manager, executive; **un congreso de los ~s de la industria** a conference of executives from the industry.
(b) (*norma*) directive; guideline.

directo [1] ADJ (a) (*gen*) direct; *línea* straight; (*inmediato*) immediate; *acción, manera, traducción etc* direct.
(b) (*Ferro etc*) through, non-stop; (*Aer*) non-stop.
(c) (*TV*) *programa, vista* live; **entrevista en ~** live interview, interview broadcast live; **transmitir en ~** to broadcast live.
[2] NM (*Boxeo*) straight punch; (*Tenis*) forehand shot (o drive *etc*).

director [1] ADJ (F: **directriz**) leading; controlling; guiding; = **directivo**.
[2] NM director; (*Com etc*) director; manager, executive; (*Cine, TV*) director; (*Mús*) conductor; (*de colegio*) headmaster; principal; (*de escuela normal etc*) principal; (*Univ*) (*de colegio*) master; (*de residencia*) warden; (*de cárcel*) governor; (*de periódico*) editor; (*de Academia*) president; **~ adjunto** assistant manager; **~ de cine** film director; **~ comercial, ~ de márketing** marketing manager; **~ ejecutivo** executive director; **~ de empresa** company director; **~ de escena** stage manager; producer; **~ espiritual** father confessor; **~ de exportación** export manager; **~ de finanzas** financial director; **~ de funeraria** undertaker, funeral director, mortician (*US*); **~ general** general manager; **~ gerente** managing director; **~ de hotel** hotel manager; **~ de interiores** (*TV*) studio director; **~ de orquesta** conductor; **~ de personal** personnel manager; **~ de promoción** development officer; **~ de tesis** thesis supervisor, research supervisor; **~ de ventas** sales manager.

directora NF director; (*Com etc*) director; manageress (V t **director**); (*de colegio*) headmistress; principal; (*Univ*) (*de colegio*) mistress, (*de residencia*) warden.

directorial ADJ (*Com etc*) managing, executive; directorial; **clase ~** managers, management, executive class.

directorio NM (a) (*norma*) directive, instructions.

(b) (*junta*) directors, board of directors, directorate.
(c) (*libro*) directory; **~ de teléfonos** (*Méx*) telephone directory.
(d) (*Inform*) directory; **~ principal** root directory.
directriz ① ADJ F *V* **director 1.**
　② NF guideline, instruction, directive.
dirigencia NF leadership.
dirigente ① ADJ leading.
　② NM (*Pol etc*) leader.
dirigible ① ADJ (*Aer*) dirigible; (*Náut*) navigable, capable of being steered.
　② NM dirigible.
dirigido ADJ *misil* guided.
dirigir [3c] ① VT **(a)** (*gen*) to direct (*a, hacia* at, to, towards); *acusación* to level (*a* at), make (*a* against); *carta, observación, pregunta, protesta* to address (*a* to); *libro* to dedicate (*a* to); *mirada* to direct (*a* towards), turn (*a* on); *manga* to play, turn (*a* on); *cañón, telescopio etc* to aim, point (*a* at).
(b) (*Com etc*) *empresa* to manage; to run, operate; *expedición, partido, rebelión* to lead, head; *periódico, serie etc* to edit; *tesis, trabajo etc* to direct, supervise; *juego* to control, referee.
(c) (*guiar*) *persona* to direct; to guide, advise (*en* about, in); *curso de acción* to direct, shape; *esfuerzos* to direct (*a* towards), concentrate (*a* on).
(d) (*Aut, Náut*) to steer; (*Aut*) to drive.
(e) (*Mús*) to conduct.
(f) (*Cine, Teat*) to produce, direct.
　② **dirigirse** VR: **~ a (a)** (*ir hacia*) to go to, make one's way to; to head for; to turn towards; (*Náut etc*) to steer for, head for; **~ hacia** to head for.
(b) (*fig: hablar a*) to speak to, address; to approach; **~ a uno solicitando algo** to apply to sb for sth; **se dirigió a mí en la calle** he spoke to me in the street; he accosted me in the street; (*anuncio*) **'diríjase a ...'** 'apply to ...', 'write to ...'
dirigismo NM management, control; dirigisme, interventionism; **~ estatal** state control.
dirigista ADJ, NMF interventionist.
dirimente ADJ *argumento etc* decisive; *voto* casting; *opinión, decisión* (*en competición etc*) final.
dirimir [3a] VT **(a)** *contrato, matrimonio etc* to dissolve, annul, declare void. **(b)** *disputa* to settle.
discada NF (*LAm*) collection of records.
discado NM (*Telec*) dialling; **~ directo** direct dialling.
discapacidad NF disability, (physical) handicap.
discapacitado ① ADJ incapacitated, (physically) handicapped, disabled.
　② NM, **discapacitada** NF handicapped person, disabled person.
discapacitar [1a] VT to incapacitate, handicap.
discar [1g] VTI (*Telec*) to dial.
discernidor ADJ discerning, discriminating.
discernimiento NM discernment, discrimination; judgement; **edad de ~** years of discretion.
discernir [3i] ① VT **(a)** (*distinguir*) to discern, distinguish; **~ A de B** to distinguish A from B.
(b) (*Jur*) *tutor* to appoint.
(c) (*esp LAm*) *premio etc* to award (*a* to), confer (*a* on).
　② VI: **~ entre** to distinguish between, discriminate between.
disciplina NF **(a)** (*gen*) discipline; **~ férrea** iron discipline; **~ de voto** party discipline, party whip; **romper la ~ de voto** to vote against one's party. **(b)** (*azote*: *t* **~s**) whip, scourge. **(c)** **~ inglesa** (*hum*) beating, flagellation.
disciplinante NMF (*Rel*) flagellant, penitent.
disciplinar [1a] VT **(a)** (*gen*) to discipline. **(b)** (*entrenar*) to school, train; (*Mil*) to drill, train. **(c)** (*azotar*) to whip, scourge.
disciplinario ADJ disciplinary.
discipulado NM **(a)** (*Rel*) discipleship. **(b)** (*personas*) pupils, student body.
discípulo, -a NM/F pupil, student; (*Rel*) disciple; (*Filos etc*) follower.
discjockey [dis'jokei] NMF disc jockey.
disco[1] NM **(a)** (*gen*) disk, disc; (*Dep*) discus; (*Ferro*) signal; (*Aut*) traffic-light; (*Telec*) dial; (*Mús etc*) gramophone record, phonograph record (*US*); **~ compacto** compact disc; **~ de duración extendida** extended-play record (*EP*); **~ de larga duración, ~ microsurco** long-playing record (*LP*); **~ de freno** brake disc; **~ giratorio** turntable; **~ de marcar** (*Telec*) dial; **~ de oro** golden disc; **~ de platino** platinum disc; **~ rojo** red traffic-light; **~ sencillo** single; **~ volante** flying saucer; **cambiar de ~** (*fig*) to change one's tune.
(b) (*Inform*) disk; **~ de arranque** boot disk; **~ de cabeza fija** fixed-head disk; **~ duro, ~ fijo** hard disk; **~ flexible** floppy disk; **~ magnético** magnetic disk; **~ óptico** optical disk; **~ rígido** hard disk; **~ virtual** RAM disk.
(c) (***) boring affair; boring speech; tedious tale; **es un ~** it's a bore, it's so boring; **nos soltó el ~ una vez más** he told us the whole

dreary tale again.
disco[2] NF (*sala de baile*) disco.
discóbolo, -a NM/F discus thrower.
discografía NF **(a)** (*gen*) records; (*discos*) collection of records; **la ~ de Eccles** the complete recordings of Eccles. **(b)** (*compañía*) record company.
discográfica NF record company.
discográfico ADJ record (*atr*); **casa discográfica** record company; **el momento ~ actual** the present state of the record industry.
díscolo ADJ uncontrollable, unruly; rebellious; *niño* mischievous; **~ a** resistant to.
disconforme ADJ differing; **estar ~** to be in disagreement (*con* with), not agree.
disconformidad NF disagreement.
discontinuidad NF lack of continuity, discontinuity.
discontinuo ADJ discontinuous.
discordancia NF discord (*t fig*).
discordante ADJ discordant (*t fig*).
discordar [1l] VI **(a)** (*Mús*) to be out of tune. **(b)** (*personas etc*) to disagree (*de* with), differ (*de* from); (*opiniones, colores etc*) to clash.
discorde ADJ **(a)** (*Mús*) *sonido* discordant, unharmonious; *instrumento* out of tune.
(b) (*fig*) discordant, differing; clashing; **estar ~s** (*personas*) to disagree, be in disagreement (*de* with).
discordia NF discord, disagreement.
discoteca NF **(a)** (*colección*) record library, record collection.
(b) (*sala de baile*) discothèque, disco.
(c) (*LAm*) record shop.
discotequero ① ADJ disco (*atr*), discothèque (*atr*).
　② NM, **discotequera** NF frequenter of discothèques.
discreción NF **(a)** (*cualidad*) discretion, tact, good sense; discrimination; prudence; wisdom, sagacity, shrewdness.
(b) (*secreto*) secrecy.
(c) (*gracia*) wit; (*ocurrencia*) witticism.
(d) a ~ at one's discretion; **añadir azúcar a ~** (*Culin*) add sugar to taste; **comer a ~** to eat as much as one likes; **con vino a ~** with as much wine as one wants; **rendirse a ~** to surrender unconditionally.
discrecional ADJ *poder* discretionary; (*de opción*) optional, not prescribed, within one's judgement; **parada ~** request stop.
discrecionalidad NF discretional nature.
discrepancia NF (*diferencia*) discrepancy; divergence; (*desacuerdo etc*) disagreement.
discrepante ADJ divergent; dissenting; **hubo varias voces ~s** there were some dissenting voices, some were not in agreement.
discrepar [1a] VI to differ (*de* from), disagree (*de* with); **discrepamos en varios puntos** we disagree on a number of points; **discrepo de esa opinión** I disagree with that view.
discretamente ADV **(a)** (*diplomáticamente*) discreetly, tactfully, sensibly; (*con discriminación*) with discrimination; (*prudentemente*) prudently, shrewdly. **(b)** (*sobriamente*) soberly; (*en silencio*) quietly; (*modestamente*) unobtrusively.
discretear [1a] VI to try to be clever, be frightfully witty.
discreto ADJ **(a)** (*diplomático etc*) discreet, tactful, sensible; (*discernidor*) discriminating; (*sagaz*) prudent, wise, sagacious; shrewd.
(b) *vestido etc* sober, sensible; *color* quiet, sober; *posición etc* unobtrusive; *advertencia* discreet, gentle, tactful.
(c) (*mediano*) fair, middling, reasonable; **de inteligencia discreta** of reasonable intelligence, reasonably intelligent; **le daremos un plazo ~** we'll allow him a reasonable time; **la película es discreta** the film is quite good.
(d) (*Fís etc*) discreet.
discriminación NF **(a)** discrimination (*contra* against); **~ positiva** positive discrimination, affirmative action; **~ racial** racial discrimination; **~ sexual** sex discrimination. **(b)** (*descuido*) neglect.
discriminado ADJ: **sentirse ~** to feel that one has been unfairly treated, feel one has been discriminated against.
discriminador NM discriminator.
discriminar [1a] VT to discriminate against; to treat unfairly; *dos cosas* to differentiate between.
discriminatoriamente ADV unfairly, in a biased way.
discriminatorio ADJ discriminatory; unfair, biased.
▼ **disculpa** NF excuse; plea; apology.
disculpable ADJ excusable, pardonable.
▼ **disculpar** [1a] ① VT (*perdonar*) to excuse, pardon, forgive; to exonerate (*de falta* from blame); **¡disculpa!, ¡discúlpenme!** I'm sorry!; **disculpa el que venga tarde** forgive me for coming late; **le disculpan sus pocos años** his youth is an excuse, his youth provides an excuse; **te ruego ~me con el anfitrión** please make my apologies to the host.
　② **disculparse** VR to excuse o.s. (*de* from); to apologize (*por* + *infin* for + *ger*); **~ con uno por haber hecho algo** to apologize to sb for

➤ LENGUA Y USO: **disculpa** → 45.1 **disculpar: 1** → 45.1

having done sth.

disculpativo ADJ apologetic.

discurrideras* NFPL wits, brains.

discurrir [3a] **1** VT to invent, think up, contrive; **esos chicos no discurren nada bueno** these lads must be cooking up sth nasty, these lads are up to no good.
2 VI **(a)** (*recorrer*) to roam, wander (*por* about, along).
(b) (*río*) to flow.
(c) (*tiempo*) to pass, flow by; (*vida, período, sesión*) to go, pass, be spent; **la sesión discurrió sin novedad** the meeting went off quietly; **el verano discurrió sin grandes calores** the summer passed without great heat.
(d) (*meditar*) to think, reason, meditate (*en* about, on); (*hablar*) to speak, discourse (*sobre* about, on); **discurre poco, discurre menos que un mosquito** he just never thinks.

discursear [1a] VI to speechify.

discursivo ADJ discursive.

discurso NM **(a)** (*oración*) speech, address, discourse; **~ de clausura** closing speech; **~ directo** direct speech; **~ indirecto** indirect speech; **~ de informe** (*Jur*) summing-up, address to the jury; **~ programático** ≃ Speech from the Throne, Queen's Speech; **~ referido** reported speech; **pronunciar un ~, dictar un ~** (*LAm*) to make (o deliver) a speech.
(b) (*tratado*) treatise.
(c) (*habla*) speech, faculty of speech.
(d) (*mental*) reasoning power, mental powers.
(e) (*tiempo*) period; passing, passage; **en el ~ del tiempo** with the passage of time; **en el ~ de 4 generaciones** in the space of 4 generations.

discusión NF (*diálogo*) discussion; (*riña*) argument; **~ de grupo, ~ en grupo** group discussion; **eso no admite ~** there can be no argument about that; **estar en ~** to be under discussion; **tener una ~** to have an argument.

discutibilidad NF debatable nature.

▸ **discutible** ADJ debatable; disputed; arguable; **es ~ si ...** it is debatable whether ...; **de mérito algo ~** of somewhat dubious worth.

discutido ADJ much-discussed; controversial; **discutidísimo** highly controversial.

discutidor ADJ argumentative, disputatious.

▸ **discutir** [3a] **1** VT (*debatir*) to discuss, debate, talk over; *precio etc* to argue about; (*contradecir*) to contradict, argue against, object to; **~ a uno lo que uno está diciendo** to contradict what sb is saying.
2 VI (*dialogar*) to discuss, talk; (*disputar*) to argue (*de, sobre* about, over); **~ de política** to argue about politics, talk politics; **¡no discutas!** don't argue!

discutón* ADJ argumentative; quarrelsome.

disecar [1g] VT **(a)** (*Med y fig*) to dissect. **(b)** (*para museo etc*) *animal* to stuff; *planta* to preserve, mount; *flor etc* to dry, press.

disección NF (*V v*) **(a)** dissection. **(b)** stuffing; preservation, mounting.

diseccionar [1a] VT (*fig*) to dissect, analyse.

diseminación NF dissemination, spread(ing), scattering; **~ nuclear** spread of nuclear weapons.

diseminar [1a] VT to disseminate, spread, scatter.

disensión NF dissension.

disentería NF dysentery.

disentimiento NM dissent, disagreement.

disentir [3k] VI to dissent (*de* from), disagree (*de* with).

diseñador(a) NM/F (*Téc, TV etc*) designer; **~ gráfico** commercial artist; **~ de moda(s)** fashion-designer, dress-designer.

diseñar [1a] VT (*Téc etc*) to design; (*Arte*) to draw, sketch; to outline.

diseño NM (*Téc etc*) design; (*Arte*) drawing, sketch; (*Cos etc*) pattern, design; (*con palabras*) sketch, outline; **el D~ Divino** the Divine Plan; **~ gráfico** graphic design; **~ industrial** industrial design; **~ asistido por ordenador** computer-assisted design; **camisa de ~** designer shirt.

disertación NF dissertation, disquisition, discourse.

disertar [1a] VI to speak, discourse; **~ acerca de, ~ sobre** to discourse upon, expound on, speak about; **~ largamente** to speak at length.

disfavor NM disfavour.

disforme ADJ (*mal hecho*) ill-proportioned, badly-proportioned; (*monstruoso*) monstrous, huge; (*feo*) ugly.

disforzado* ADJ (*And*) **(a)** (*santurrón*) prim, prudish. **(b)** (*descarado*) cheeky*.

disfraz NM **(a)** (*gen*) disguise; (*máscara*) mask; (*traje*) fancy dress; (*fig*) pretext, blind (*de* for); **baile de disfraces** fancy-dress ball; **bajo el ~ de** in the guise of; under the cloak of.
(b) **ser un ~*** to be out of place; to look all wrong.

disfrazado ADJ: **~ de** disguised as; in the guise of; **ir ~ de duque** to be made up like a duke; to masquerade as a duke.

disfrazar [1f] **1** VT (*gen*) to disguise; (*ocultar*) to cover up, mask, conceal, cloak; **~ a uno de lavandera** to disguise sb as a washerwoman,

make sb up as a washerwoman.
2 **disfrazarse** VR: **~ de** to disguise o.s. as, make o.s. up as.

▼ **disfrutar** [1a] **1** VT to enjoy; to make use of, have the benefit of. **2**
▼ VI **(a)** (*gozar*) to enjoy o.s., have a good time; **¡cómo disfruto!** I'm enjoying this!, this is the life!; **¡que disfrutes!** have a good time!; **~ como un enano** to have a great time, enjoy o.s. hugely; **~ con algo** to enjoy sth, benefit from sth; **siempre disfruto con los libros así** I always enjoy books of that sort.
(b) **~ de** to enjoy; to have, possess; **~ de buena salud** to enjoy good health; **disfruta de las rentas de su finca** he enjoys (o has) the income from his estate.

disfrute NM enjoyment; use; possession.

disfuerzo NM (*And*) **(a)** (*descaro*) impudence, effrontery. **(b)** (*remilgo*) prudishness. **(c)** **~s** threats, bravado.

disfunción NF malfunction, difficulty; defect.

disfuncionalidad NF malfunction.

disgregación NF disintegration; break(ing)-up; separation; dispersal.

disgregar [1h] **1** VT to disintegrate; to break up; to separate (*de* from); to sever (*de* from); *manifestantes* to disperse.
2 **disgregarse** VR to disintegrate; to break up (*en* into).

disgresión NF digression.

disgustar [1a] **1** VT (*molestar*) to annoy, upset, displease; (*ofender*) to offend; **es un olor que me disgusta** it's a smell which upsets me; **me disgusta tener que repetirlo** it annoys me to have to repeat it, I don't like having to repeat it; **comprendí que le disgustaba mi presencia** I realized that my presence annoyed him; **estaba muy disgustado con el asunto** he was very upset about the affair.
2 **disgustarse** VR **(a)** (*enfadarse*) to be annoyed, get upset (*con, de* about); (*ofenderse*) to be displeased, be offended, feel hurt (*con, de* about); **~ de algo** to get bored with sth, get fed up with sth.
(b) (*2 personas*) to fall out; **~ con uno** to fall out with sb.

disgusto NM **(a)** (*enfado*) annoyance, displeasure; vexation; (*dolor*) grief, chagrin, sorrow; (*repugnancia*) repugnance; (*aburrimiento*) boredom; **a ~** unwillingly, against one's will; **con gran ~ mío** much to my annoyance.
(b) (*un ~*) (*dificultad*) trouble, bother, difficulty; (*percance*) unpleasant experience; (*desgracia*) misfortune; (*golpe*) blow, shock; **reírse de los ~s del prójimo** to laugh at a fellow man's troubles (o misfortunes); **me causó un gran ~** it was a great blow to me; it upset me very much; **dar un ~ a uno** to upset sb; **nunca nos dio un ~** he never gave us any trouble; **llevarse un ~** to be upset; **han de sobrevenir ~s** there's trouble ahead; **matar a uno a ~s** to wear sb out with burdens, heap troubles on sb; **sentirse a ~** (*Méx*) to feel (o be) ill at ease (o uncomfortable).
(c) (*riña*) quarrel, upset; **tener un ~ con uno** to have a quarrel with sb, fall out with sb.

disidencia NF dissidence, disagreement; (*Ecl*) dissent.

disidente **1** ADJ dissident; dissenting.
2 NMF dissident person (o element etc); (*Ecl*) dissenter, nonconformist.

disidir [3a] VI to dissent.

disílabo **1** ADJ disyllabic.
2 NM disyllable.

disímil ADJ not alike, dissimilar.

disimilación NF dissimilation.

disimulación NF dissimulation; furtiveness; cunning.

disimuladamente ADV furtively; cunningly, slyly; covertly.

disimulado ADJ (*solapado*) furtive; underhand; (*taimado*) cunning, sly; (*oculto*) covert; **hacerse el ~** to dissemble; to pretend not to notice (*etc*); **hacer la disimulada** to feign ignorance.

disimular [1a] **1** VT **(a)** (*ocultar*) to hide; (*fig*) to hide, cloak, disguise; *emoción, intención etc* to conceal.
(b) (*disculpar*) to excuse; (*pasar por alto*) to condone, overlook; (*tolerar*) to tolerate; *ofensa etc* to pass off; *persona etc* to be lenient to, behave tolerantly towards; **te ruego ~ la indiscreción** please pardon the liberty; **disimula mi atrevimiento** forgive me if I have been too bold.
2 VI to dissemble, pretend.

disimulo NM **(a)** (*fingimiento*) dissimulation; furtiveness; craftiness; **con ~** cunningly, craftily. **(b)** (*tolerancia*) indulgence, tolerance.

disimulón* ADJ furtive, shady.

disipación NF dissipation.

disipado ADJ **(a)** (*disoluto*) dissipated; rakish, raffish. **(b)** (*derrochador*) extravagant, spendthrift.

disipador NM spendthrift.

disipar [1a] **1** VT **(a)** *niebla etc* to drive away, cause to disappear, dispel.
(b) *duda etc* to dispel, remove; *esperanza* to destroy.
(c) *dinero* to squander, fritter away (*en* on).
2 **disiparse** VR **(a)** (*humo etc*) to vanish; to evaporate.
(b) (*duda etc*) to be dispelled, vanish.

disjunto ADJ separate, discrete.

▶ LENGUA Y USO: **discutible** → 53.6   **discutir: 1** → 53.6   **disfrutar: 2a** → 34.2

diskette NM floppy disk.
dislate NM absurdity, silly thing; **~s** nonsense.
dislexia NF dyslexia.
disléxico, -a ADJ, NM/F dyslexic.
dislocación NF (*gen*) dislocation; (*Med*) dislocation, sprain; (*Geol*) slip, fault.
dislocado ADJ (*fig*) unsettled, restless.
dislocar [1g] VT to dislocate; to sprain.
disloque* NM (**a**) **es el ~** it's the limit, it's the last straw; **fue el ~** (*hum*) it was the great moment, it was the crowning touch. (**b**) confusion; maladjustment; inappropriateness.
disminución NF (**a**) diminution, decrease (*de* of), fall (*de* in); **proceso de ~ de réditos** law of diminishing returns; **continuar sin ~** to continue unchecked, continue unabated; **ir en ~** to diminish, be on the decrease. (**b**) (*Med*) handicap.
disminuido [1] ADJ (*Med*) crippled, handicapped.
   [2] NM, **disminuida** NF (*Med*) cripple, handicapped person; **~ físico** physically-handicapped person; **~ psíquico** mentally-handicapped person.
disminuir [3g] VTI to diminish, decrease, lessen.
Disneylandia NF Disneyland (*t fig*).
disociable ADJ separable.
disociación NF dissociation.
disociar [1b] [1] VT to dissociate, separate (*de* from).
   [2] **disociarse** VR to dissociate o.s. (*de* from).
disoluble ADJ dissoluble, soluble.
disolución NF (**a**) (*acto*) dissolution (*t Parl*). (**b**) (*Quím*) solution; **~ de goma** rubber solution. (**c**) (*Com*) liquidation. (**d**) (*moral*) dissoluteness, dissipation.
disoluto ADJ dissolute, dissipated.
disolvente NM solvent, thinner.
disolver [2h; PTP **disuelto**] [1] VT (**a**) (*gen*) to dissolve; (*fundir*) to melt (down).
   (**b**) *contrato, matrimonio* to dissolve; (*Parl*) to dissolve; *manifestación etc* to break up; (*Mil*) to disband.
   [2] **disolverse** VR (**a**) (*fundirse*) to dissolve, melt.
   (**b**) (*Com*) to be dissolved, go into liquidation; (*Parl*) to dissolve.
disonancia NF (**a**) (*Mús*) dissonance. (**b**) (*fig*) discord, disharmony; **hacer ~ con** to be out of harmony with.
disonante ADJ (**a**) (*Mús*) dissonant, discordant. (**b**) (*fig*) discordant.
disonar [1l] VI (**a**) (*Mús*) to be discordant, be out of harmony, be out of tune; (*palabra etc*) to sound wrong; **no me disuena** it is not unfamiliar to me.
   (**b**) (*fig: no armonizar*) to lack harmony; (*estar en desacuerdo*) to disagree; **~ con** to be out of keeping with, clash with.
dísono ADJ discordant.
dispar ADJ unlike, different, disparate.
disparada NF (*LAm*) sudden flight, stampede, wild rush; **ir a la ~** to go at full speed; **irse a la ~** to be off like a shot; **de una ~** (*Cono Sur*) in a trice, instantly; **tomar la ~‡** (*Cono Sur*) to beat it*.
disparadero NM trigger, trigger mechanism; **poner a uno en el ~** to drive sb to distraction, make sb resort to violence.
disparado ADJ (**a**) **entrar ~** to shoot in; **salir ~** to shoot out, be off like a shot; **ir ~** to go like mad, go hell for leather. (**b**) (*Carib‡*) randy*, horny‡.
disparador [1] ADJ (*Méx*) lavish.
   [2] NM (*Mil etc*) trigger; (*Fot, Téc*) release; (*de reloj*) escapement; **~ de bombas** bomb release.
disparar [1a] [1] VT (**a**) *cañon, cohete etc* to shoot, fire (*a, contra* at); *piedra* to throw, hurl, let fly (*contra* at); (*Dep*) *balón* to shoot (*a* at, *en* into).
   (**b**) *consumo, precio* to cause to shoot up, increase excessively.
   [2] VI (**a**) (*tirar*) to shoot, fire; **¡disparad!** fire!; **~ a una distancia de 5 metros** to fire at a range of 5 metres; **~ a matar** to shoot to kill.
   (**b**) = **dispararse**.
   (**c**) (*Méx*: gastar dinero*) to spend lavishly.
   [3] **dispararse** VR (**a**) (*cañon*) to go off; (*pestillo etc*) to be released.
   (**b**) (*persona*) to rush off, dash away; V **disparado**.
   (**c**) (*caballo etc*) to bolt; (*consumo, precios*) to shoot up.
   (**d**) (*enfadarse*) to lose control, blow one's top*; **¡no te dispares!** take it easy!
disparatadamente ADV absurdly, nonsensically.
disparatado ADJ absurd, crazy, nonsensical.
disparatar [1a] VI (*hablar*) to talk nonsense; (*hacer*) to do something silly, blunder.
disparate NM (**a**) (*dicho*) foolish remark, (*idea*) silly idea; (*acto*) absurd thing (to do); (*error*) blunder, crass mistake; **~s** nonsense; **¡no digas ~s!** don't talk nonsense!; **¡qué ~!** what rubbish!, how absurd!; **hiciste un ~ protestando** it was silly of you to complain.
   (**b**) **reírse un ~** to laugh a lot; **costar un ~** to cost a fortune.
   (**c**) (*Arquit*) folly.
disparidad NF disparity.

disparo NM (**a**) (*tiro*) shot; report; (*de cohete*) firing; (*Dep*) shot; **~s** shots, shooting, exchange of shots; **~ de advertencia, ~ de amonestación, ~ de intimidación** warning shot, (*Náut*) shot across the bows; **~ inicial** (*de cohete*) blast-off.
   (**b**) (*Mec*) release, trip.
   (**c**) (*fig*) = **disparate**.
dispendiador ADJ free-spending, big-spending.
dispendio NM waste; extravagance.
dispendioso ADJ expensive.
dispensa NF exemption, excusal (*de* from); (*Ecl*) dispensation.
dispensabilidad NF dispensable nature.
dispensable ADJ dispensable.
dispensación NF dispensation.
dispensador NM dispenser.
dispensadora NF: **~ de monedas** change machine.
dispensar [1a] [1] VT (**a**) (*dar, repartir*) to dispense; to give out, distribute; *honor* to give, grant; *atención* to pay; *ayuda* to give; *acogida etc* to give, accord.
   (**b**) (*eximir*) to excuse, exempt (*de* from); *persona, falta etc* to excuse, pardon; **¡Vd dispense!, ¡dispénseme Vd!** I beg your pardon!, do forgive me!; **~ a uno de una obligación** to excuse sb (from) an obligation; **me dispensaron la multa, me dispensaron del pago de la multa** they excused me (from payment of) the fine; **~ a uno de + infin** to excuse sb from + *ger*, relieve sb of the need to + *infin*; **~ que uno + subj** to excuse sb for + *ger*; **así el cuerpo queda dispensado de ese esfuerzo** thus the body is freed from that effort (*o* relieved of that effort).
   [2] **dispensarse** VR: **no puedo dispensarme de esa obligación** I cannot escape that duty.
dispensario NM dispensary; clinic.
dispepsia NF dyspepsia.
dispéptico ADJ dyspeptic.
dispersar [1a] [1] VT to disperse, scatter; (*Mil*) to rout; *manifestación etc* to break up, disperse.
   [2] **dispersarse** VR to disperse, scatter; to break up.
dispersión NF dispersion, dispersal; (*Fís*) dispersion.
disperso ADJ scattered; dispersed; sparse; (*Mil*) separated, straggling.
displicencia NF (**a**) (*mal humor*) peevishness, bad temper. (**b**) (*desgana*) lack of enthusiasm; indifference.
displicente ADJ (**a**) (*malhumorado*) disagreeable, peevish, bad-tempered; fretful. (**b**) (*poco entusiasta*) unenthusiastic, lukewarm; (*indiferente*) indifferent.
disponer [2q] [1] VT (**a**) (*arreglar*) to arrange, dispose; to lay out; (*ordenar*) to put in order; (*alinear*)to line up.
   (**b**) (*preparar*) to prepare, get ready.
   (**c**) (*mandar*) to order, decide; (*Med*) *régimen etc* to order; **~ que ...** to order that ..., arrange that ..., provide that ...; **la ley dispone que ...** the law provides that ...
   [2] VI: **~ de** (**a**) (*tener*) to have, own; to have available, have at one's disposal; (*utilizar*) to make use of, avail o.s. of; **dispone de 2 coches** he has 2 cars; **disponemos de poco tiempo** we have very little time (at our disposal).
   (**b**) (*utilizar*) to dispose of (as one wishes); **no puede ~ de esos bienes** she cannot dispose of those properties.
   [3] **disponerse** VR: **~ a + infin, ~ para + infin** to prepare to + *infin*, get ready to + *infin*.
disponibilidad NF (**a**) (*gen*) availability; **empleado en ~** unposted employee, employee available for posting. (**b**) **~es** resources, means; **~es líquidas** available liquid assets.
disponible ADJ available; on hand, spare; *renta* disposable.
disposición NF (**a**) (*arreglo*) arrangement, disposition; order; layout (*t Arquit, Inform*).
   (**b**) (*ley etc*) order; (*cláusula*) provision, disposition; (*condición*) stipulation; **pasar a ~ judicial** to be taken into custody; **~ transitoria** temporary provision; **según las disposiciones del código** according to the provisions of the statute; **última ~** last will and testament.
   (**c**) **disposiciones** (*preparativos*) preparations (*para* for); (*medidas*) steps, measures; **tomar sus disposiciones** to make one's preparations, take steps.
   (**d**) (*disponibilidad*) disposal; **a la ~ de** at the disposal of; **a la ~ de Vd, a su ~** at your service; **tener algo a su ~** to have sth at one's disposal, have sth available.
   (**e**) (*posición*) position; **estar en ~ de + infin** to be ready to + *infin*, be in a position to + *infin*.
   (**f**) (*temperamento*) disposition, temperament; (*talento*) aptitude (*para* for); turn of mind; **~ de ánimo** attitude of mind; **no tener ~ para** to have no aptitude for.
dispositivo NM (**a**) (*Mec*) device, mechanism; appliance; contrivance; gadget; **~ de alimentación** hopper; storage device; **~ de arranque** starting mechanism; **~ intrauterino** intrauterine device; **~ periférico** peripheral device; **~ de seguridad** safety catch, safety device; (*fig*) security measure.

(b) (*Mil etc*) force, deployment; **~ de seguridad** security force.

dispuesto ADJ Y PTP **(a)** (*arreglado*) arranged, disposed; **~ según ciertos principios** arranged according to certain principles; **bien ~** (*Arquit*) well designed, well laid out.
(b) (*persona*) **bien ~** well-disposed (*hacia* towards); **mal ~** ill-disposed; (*Med*) ill, indisposed.
(c) **estar ~ a** + *infin* to be prepared to + *infin*; **estar poco ~ a** + *infin* to be reluctant to + *infin*.
(d) (*listo*) bright, clever, go-ahead.
(e) **bien ~** handsome.

disputa NF dispute; argument; controversy; **~ electoral** electoral contest, election; **los asuntos en ~** the matters in dispute, the matters at issue; **sin ~** undoubted(ly), beyond dispute.

disputable ADJ disputable, debatable.

disputado ADJ *partido* close, tough, hard fought.

disputador ☐1☐ ADJ disputatious, argumentative.
☐2☐ NM, **disputadora** NF disputant.

disputar [1a] ☐1☐ VT **(a)** *asunto* to dispute, question, challenge; to debate.
(b) *posesión* to fight for, contend for; *partido* to play.
☐2☐ VI **(a)** (*discutir*) to debate, argue (*con* with; *de, sobre* about).
(b) **~ con uno por un premio** to contend with sb for a prize.
☐3☐ **disputarse** VR: **~ un premio** to contend for a prize; **~ la posesión de** to fight over (*o* for) the possession of.

disque: NM: **darse ~** (*Cono Sur*) to fancy o.s.*

disquería NF (*Carib*) record shop.

disquero ADJ record (*atr*).

disqueta NF (*LAm*), **disquete** NM (*Inform*) floppy disk, diskette.

disquetera NF disk drive.

disquisición NF **(a)** (*análisis*) disquisition. **(b)** **disquisiciones** irrelevancies, comments on the side.

Dist. (a) ABR *de* **distancia** distance, dist. **(b)** ABR *de* **Distrito** district, dist.

distancia NF (*gen*) distance; (*de tiempo etc*) interval; (*disparidad*) gap, difference, disparity; **~ de despegue** (*Aer*) length of takeoff; **~ focal** focal distance, focal length; **~ de parada** braking distance; **~ de seguridad** (*Aut*) safe distance; **~ del suelo, ~ sobre el suelo** (*Aut etc*) height off the ground, clearance; **a ~** (ADV) at a distance; (ADJ) remote; **a gran ~, a larga ~** long-distance (*atr*); **ganó X, con Y a 2 golpes de ~** X won, with Y 2 strokes behind; **mantener a uno a ~** to keep sb at a distance; keep sb at arm's length; **mantenerse a ~** to keep one's distance; (*fig*) to hold back, remain aloof; **ganar ~s** to get ahead, make progress; **marcar ~s** to be far ahead; **cada cierta ~** every so often, at intervals; **guardar las ~s** to keep one's distance, maintain proper (social) distinctions; **salvando las ~s** recognizing that the cases are not precisely the same.

distanciado ADJ **(a)** (*remoto*) remote (*de* from); (*aislado*) widely separated, isolated; *carácter* remote, detached.
(b) (*fig*) far apart; **estamos algo ~s** we are not particularly close; **ella está distanciada de su familia** she has grown apart from her family, she has no close ties with her family; **estamos muy ~s en ideas** our ideas are poles apart.

distanciador ADJ: **efecto ~** distancing effect.

distanciamiento NM **(a)** (*acto*) spacing out. **(b)** (*estado*) remoteness, isolation; (*fig*) distance, lack of close links (*entre* between); **~ generacional** generation gap. **(c)** (*Teat etc*) distancing effect.

distanciar [1b] ☐1☐ VT **(a)** *objetos* to space out, separate; to put further apart.
(b) *rival* to outdistance.
(c) *personas* to cause a rift between.
☐2☐ **distanciarse** VR **(a)** **~ de un rival** to get ahead of a rival.
(b) (*dos personas*) to fall out, become estranged; to become (more) remote from each other.

distante ADJ **(a)** (*lejano*) distant; (*remoto*) far-off, remote; **~ de 10 kms** 10 kms away. **(b)** (*fig*) distant.

distar [1a] VI **(a)** **dista 5 kms de aquí** it is 5 kms from here; **dista mucho** it's a long way away; **¿dista mucho?** is it far?, how far is it?
(b) **dista mucho de la verdad** it's very far from the truth, it's a long way off the truth; **disto mucho de aprobarlo** I am far from approving of it.

distender [2g] VT to distend; to stretch.

distendido ADJ distended; relaxed; **ambiente ~** relaxed atmosphere.

distensión NF distension; stretching; relaxation; (*Pol*) détente; (*Med*) strain; **~ muscular** muscular strain.

distensivo ADJ conciliatory.

dístico NM distich.

distinción NF **(a)** (*diferencia*) distinction, difference; differentness; **a ~ de** unlike, in contrast to; **sin ~** indiscriminately; all together, mixed; **obrar sin ~** to act arbitrarily, act blindly; **sin ~ de personas** without respect to persons, without regard for the differences (of rank *etc*) between people; **sin ~ de edades** irrespective of differences of age; **sin ~ de raza** without distinction of race; **hacer una ~ entre** to

make a distinction between, differentiate between; **hacer ~ con uno** to show sb special consideration.
(b) (*honor*) distinction, honour; **~ honorífica** honour.
(c) (*elegancia*) elegance, refinement.

distingo NM (*salvedad*) reservation; (*distinción*) subtle distinction; (*objeción*) (petty) objection; **aquí hago un ~** here I must make a reservation.

distinguible ADJ distinguishable.

distinguido ADJ **(a)** (*gen*) distinguished; (*conocido*) prominent, well-known. **(b)** (*elegante*) elegant, refined; (*culto*) gentlemanly, ladylike, cultured. **(c)** **'D~ Señor'** (*LAm*) 'Dear Sir'.

distinguir [3d] ☐1☐ VT **(a)** (*lograr ver*) to distinguish, discern, make out; (*reconocer*) to recognize.
(b) (*diferenciar*) to distinguish (*de* from, *entre* between), tell (*de* from); **no distingo cuál es el mío** I can't tell which is mine; **lo sabría ~ entre cien iguales** I would know it anywhere.
(c) (*separar*) to distinguish, separate, single out; **aquí distingo dos aspectos** here I distinguish two aspects.
(d) (*señalar*) to mark, stamp, distinguish; **lo distinguen con una señal especial** they mark it with a special sign.
(e) (*señalar: fig*) to single out, mark out (for special treatment); (*honrar*) to honour, bestow an honour on; **amigo etc** to have a special regard for; **me distingue con su amistad** he honours me with his friendship.
☐2☐ VI: **no ~** to have no critical sense, be undiscriminating; **es un hombre que sabe ~** he is a discerning (*o* discriminating) person.
☐3☐ **distinguirse** VR **(a)** (*diferenciarse*) to be distinguished (*de* from), differ (*de* from); to stand out (*de* from); **~ por su calidad** to stand out by reason of its quality.
(b) (*destacar*) to distinguish o.s.

distintivo ☐1☐ ADJ distinctive; *señal etc* distinguishing.
☐2☐ NM badge, emblem; (*fig*) distinguishing mark, characteristic, typical feature.

distinto ADJ **(a)** (*claro*) clear, distinct, plain; (*definido*) well-defined.
(b) (*diferente*) different, distinct (*a, de* from); **son muy ~s** they are very different.
(c) **~s** several, various; **hay distintas opiniones sobre eso** there are various opinions about that.

distorsión NF **(a)** (*Anat*) sprain. **(b)** (*Rad etc*) distortion.

distorsionador ADJ, **distorsionante** ADJ distorting.

distorsionar [1a] VT to distort.

distracción NF **(a)** (*recreo*) distraction; amusement, relaxation; (*pasatiempo*) hobby, pastime; **es mi ~ favorita** it's my favourite amusement; **lo hace como ~ nada más** he only does it as a hobby.
(b) (*despiste*) absence of mind, forgetfulness; (*falta de atención*) heedlessness; **por ~** through sheer forgetfulness, absent-mindedly.
(c) (*error, olvido*) slip, blunder, oversight; **fue una ~ mía** it was an oversight on my part.
(d) (*moral*) loose living, dissipation.

distraer [2o] ☐1☐ VT **(a)** *atención etc* to distract, divert, lead away (*de* from); (*moralmente*) to lead astray; **~ a uno para robarle algo** to distract sb's attention so as to steal sth from him; **~ a uno de su dolor** to take sb's mind off his grief; **~ a uno de su razonamiento** to divert sb from his train of thought.
(b) (*entretener*) to amuse, relax, entertain; **la música me distrae** music relaxes me, I find music relaxing.
(c) (*Fin*) to embezzle, divert to one's own use.
☐2☐ VI to be relaxing; **el pescar distrae** fishing is a relaxation.
☐3☐ **distraerse** VR **(a)** (*entretenerse*) to amuse o.s., entertain o.s.; to relax; **me distraigo pescando** I relax when I fish, I find fishing relaxing; **no me opongo a que se distraiga honestamente** I don't mind her having a little innocent amusement.
(b) (*despistarse*) to be (*o* get) absent-minded; to cease to pay attention; **me distraje un momento** I allowed my attention to wander for a moment; **~ de** to forget about, be inattentive to.

distraídamente ADV (*V ADJ*) **(a)** absent-mindedly; unobservantly; (*pey*) inattentively; slackly. **(b)** idly, casually.

distraído ☐1☐ ADJ **(a)** *persona* (*despistado*) absent-minded; (*poco práctico*) vague, dreamy, unpractical; (*que no se fija*) unobservant; (*pey*) inattentive; slack, lackadaisical; **iba yo algo ~** I was rather absorbed in other things, I was not taking much notice.
(b) *aire, mirada etc* absent-minded; idle, casual; **con aire ~** idly, casually, in a casual manner; **me miró distraída** she gave me a casual glance.
(c) *divertido etc* amusing, entertaining.
(d) *vida* dissolute.
(e) (*Cono Sur, Méx*) (*desaliñado*) slovenly, untidy, shabby.
(f) (*Méx**: *chiflado*) crazy.
☐2☐ NM: **hacerse el ~** (*fingir no ver*) to pretend not to notice; (*fingir no tener interés*) to pretend not to be interested.

distribución NF **(a)** (*acto*) distribution; giving-out; sending out; (*Correos*) sorting; delivery; **~ de premios** prize giving.

(b) (*Estadística etc*) distribution; incidence; **la ~ de los impuestos** the incidence of taxes.

(c) (*estado*) distribution, arrangement; (*Arquit*) layout, ground plan.

(d) (*Mec*) timing gears.

distribuido ADJ: **una casa bien distribuida** a well-designed house.

distribuidor [1] NM **(a)** (*persona*) distributor; (*Com*) dealer, agent, stockist; **~ automático** (*Com*) (automatic) vending machine, slot machine.

(b) (*Aut*) distributor.

(c) (*LAm Aut*) motorway exit.

[2] NM, **distribuidora¹** NF (*persona*) distributor; (*Com*) dealer, agent, stockist.

distribuidora² NF (*Agr*) spreader.

distribuir [3g] VT **(a)** (*gen*) to distribute; *prospectos etc* to hand out; to give out; (*circular*) to send out, send round; *cartas* (*clasificar*) to sort; *cartas* (*entregar*), *leche* to deliver; *tareas etc* to allocate; *premios* to give out, award; (*Téc*) to spread; *carga etc* to stow, arrange; *peso* to distribute (equally *etc*).

(b) (*Arquit*) to design, plan, lay out.

distributivo ADJ distributive.

distrito NM (*gen*) district, region, zone; (*Pol*) administrative area; (*Jur*) circuit; **~ electoral** constituency, ward, electoral area; precinct (*US*); **~ postal** postal district.

distrofia NF: **~ muscular** (progressive) muscular dystrophy.

disturbio NM **(a)** (*gen*) disturbance; (*desorden*) riot, commotion; **los ~s** the disturbances, the troubles. **(b)** (*Téc*) disturbance; **~ aerodinámico** (*Aer*) wash, slipstream.

disuadir [3a] VT to dissuade, deter, discourage (*de* from); **~ a uno de** + *infin* to dissuade sb from + *ger*.

disuasión NF dissuasion; (*Mil etc*) deterrent force; deterrent action; **~ nuclear** nuclear deterrent; *V* **fuerza**.

disuasivo ADJ discouraging; dissuasive; (*Mil*) deterrent.

disuasorio ADJ (*Mil*) deterrent; *V* **fuerza**.

disuelto PTP *de* **disolver**.

disyuntiva NF **(a)** (*opción*) alternative, choice. **(b)** (*apuro*) dilemma; crisis.

disyuntivo ADJ disjunctive.

disyuntor NM (*Elec*) circuit breaker.

dita¹ NF **(a)** (*garantía*) surety; (*fianza*) security, bond. **(b)** (*And*: *empréstito*) loan at a high rate of interest; (*LAm*: *deuda*) small debt.

dita² NF (*Carib*) dish, cup, pot.

ditirambo NM dithyramb.

DIU ['diu] NM ABR *de* **dispositivo intrauterino** intrauterine device, IUD.

diurético ADJ, NM diuretic.

diurno ADJ diurnal, day (*atr*), daytime (*atr*).

diva NF prima donna, diva.

divagación NF digression; **divagaciones** wanderings, ramblings.

divagador ADJ rambling, discursive.

divagar [1h] VI to digress; to wander, ramble; **¡no ~!** get on with it!, come to the point!

divagatorio ADJ digressive.

diván NM divan, sofa; (*de psiquiatra*) couch.

diver* ADJ = **divertido**.

divergencia NF divergence.

divergente ADJ divergent; contrary, opposite.

divergir [3c] VI **(a)** (*líneas*) to diverge. **(b)** (*opiniones etc*) to differ, be opposed, clash; (*dos personas*) to differ, disagree.

diversidad NF diversity, variety.

diversificación NF diversification.

diversificado ADJ diversified; **ciclo ~** (*Venezuela Educ*) upper secondary education.

diversificador ADJ diversifying.

diversificar [1g] [1] VT to diversify.

[2] **diversificarse** VR to diversify.

diversión NF **(a)** (*recreo*) amusement, entertainment; recreation; (*pasatiempo*) hobby, pastime; **diversiones de salón** parlour games, indoor games. **(b)** (*Mil*) diversion.

diverso ADJ [1] **(a)** (*variado*) diverse.

(b) (*distinto*) different (*de* from); other; **se trata de ~ asunto** it's about a different (*o* another) matter.

(c) **~s** several, various; some; sundry; **está en ~s libros** it figures in several books.

[2] **~s** NMPL (*Com*) sundries, miscellaneous (items).

divertido ADJ **(a)** *libro etc* entertaining, amusing; funny; enjoyable; *chiste* funny, *persona* funny, amusing, witty; **la fiesta fue muy divertida** the party was great fun.

(b) (*iró*) **¡estoy ~!** you kill me!*; **¡estamos ~s!** how terribly amusing! (I don't think).

(c) **estar ~** (*LAm**) to be tight*.

divertimento NM divertimento.

divertimiento NM **(a)** amusement, entertainment. **(b)** diversion (*t Mil*).

divertir [3i] [1] VT **(a)** (*entretener*) to amuse, entertain.

(b) *atención* to divert, distract (the attention of).

[2] **divertirse** VR to amuse o.s.; to have a good time; **la juventud moderna no quiere más que ~** all modern youth wants to do is have a good time; **~ haciendo algo** to amuse o.s. doing sth; **~ con el amor de uno** to toy with sb's affections; **¡que os divirtáis!** have a good time!

┌─ DIVERTIDO ─────────────────────── ver también la entrada ─┐

¿"Funny o fun"?

• *Divertido* sólo se puede traducir por *funny* si nos hace reír:
Acabo de ver una obra muy divertida
I've just seen a very funny play

• Cuando hablamos de una actividad o situación *divertida* (en el sentido de entretenida y agradable), a menudo se la puede describir en inglés como *fun*:
Me gusta jugar al escondite. Es muy divertido
I like playing hide and seek. It's great fun

! *Fun* es un sustantivo incontable por lo tanto, al contrario que *funny*, no puede ir acompañado de adverbios como *very*. Se suele acompañar de *great*, *good* y *a lot of*.
Para otros usos y ejemplos ver la entrada.

└──┘

dividendo NM dividend; **~s por acción** earnings per share; **~ a cuenta** interim dividend; **~ final** final dividend.

dividir [3a] [1] VT (*gen*) to divide (up); to split (up), separate; (*repartir*) to share out, distribute; (*Mat*) to divide; **~ 12 entre 4** to divide 12 among 4; **~ 12 por 4** to divide 12 by 4; **~ algo en 5 partes** to divide sth into 5 parts; **~ algo por mitad** to divide sth into two, halve sth; **~ algo por la mitad** to divide sth down the middle; **divide y vencerás** divide and rule.

[2] **dividirse** VR (*persona*: *fig*) to be in two places at the same time.

divierta* NF (*CAm*) village dance, hop*.

divieso NM (*Med*) boil.

divinamente ADV divinely (*t fig*); **lo pasamos ~** we had a wonderful time.

divinidad NF **(a)** (*esencia divina*) divinity.

(b) (*una ~*) divinity; godhead; deity; **~ marina** sea god; **~ pagana** pagan god(dess), pagan divinity; **la D~** the Deity.

(c) (*fig*: *mujer*) goddess, beauty, beautiful woman; (*objeto*) precious thing, lovely object.

divinizar [1f] VT to deify; (*fig*) to exalt, extol.

divino [1] ADJ **(a)** divine. **(b)** (*fig*) divine, wonderful; (*) great*, brill*.

[2] ADV **pasarlo ~*** to have a smashing time*.

divirtiendo *etc V* **divertir**.

divisa NF **(a)** (*distintivo*) emblem, badge; (*Her*) device, motto. **(b)** **~s** (*Fin*) foreign exchange; **~s fuertes** hard currency; **control de ~s** exchange control.

divisar [1a] VT to make out, spy, descry.

divisibilidad NF divisibility.

divisible ADJ divisible.

división NF **(a)** (*Dep, Mat, Mil etc*) division; **primera ~**, **~ de honor** first division. **(b)** (*acto*) division; (*Pol*: *de partido*) split; (*de país*) partition: (*en familia, entre amigos*) split; discord, strife.

divisional ADJ divisional.

divisionismo NM divisiveness.

divisionista ADJ divisive.

divisivo ADJ divisive.

divismo NM **(a)** (*sistema*) star system. **(b)** (*temperamento*) artistic temperament, star temperament.

divisor NM (*Mat*) divisor; **máximo común ~** highest common factor.

divisoria NF dividing line; (*Geog*) divide; **~ de aguas** watershed; **~ continental** continental divide.

divisorio ADJ dividing; divisive; **línea divisoria de las aguas** watershed.

divo* NM (*pey*) movie star.

divorciado [1] ADJ **(a)** divorced. **(b)** **las opiniones están divorciadas** (*fig*) opinions are divided.

[2] NM, **divorciada** NF divorcee.

divorciar [1b] [1] VT **(a)** to divorce. **(b)** (*fig*) to divorce, separate (*de* from).

[2] **divorciarse** to get divorced, get a divorce (*de* from).

divorcio NM **(a)** (*gen*) divorce. **(b)** (*fig*) separation; division, split; **existe un ~ entre A y B** there is a great discrepancy between A and B.

divorcista NMF pro-divorce campaigner.

divulgación NF spreading, circulation; dissemination; popularizing; (*pey*) disclosure.

divulgar [1h] [1] VT to spread, circulate, publish; to disseminate; to popularize; (*pey*) to divulge, disclose, let out.

[2] **divulgarse** VR (*secreto*) to leak out; (*rumor etc*) to get about, become known.

divulgativo ADJ, **divulgatorio** ADJ popularizing; informative.

diz (†† *forma de* **dice**; *LAm*): ~ **que** ... they say that ..., it is said that ...; apparently ...; supposedly ...

dizque* ADV (*LAm*) apparently, supposedly; ~ **vendrán hoy** they're supposed to be coming today.

D.J.C. = **d. de J.C.**

dl. ABR *de* **decilitro** decilitre, dl.

Dls, dls NMPL (*LAm*) ABR *de* **dólares.**

DM ABR *de* **Deutschmark, marco alemán** Deutschmark, DM.

Dm. (a) ABR *de* **decámetro** decametre. (b) ABR *de* **decimal** decimal.

dm. ABR *de* **decímetro** decimetre, dm.

D.m. ABR *de* **Dios mediante** Deo volente, DV.

D.N. NF ABR *de* **Delegación Nacional.**

DNI NM ABR *de* **documento nacional de identidad.**

Dña. = **Dª**; *see also* DON/DOÑA .

do NM (*Mús*) do, C; ~ **mayor** C major; ~ **de pecho** high C; **dar el ~ de pecho** to give one's all, do one's very best.

D.O. ABR *de* **denominación de origen** denomination of origin; *see also* DENOMINACIÓN DE ORIGEN .

döberman NM Doberman.

dobladillar [1a] VT to hem.

dobladillo NM (*de vestido*) hem; (*de pantalón*) turn-up(s), cuff(s) (*US*).

doblado ADJ (a) (*Cos etc*) double; doubled over, folded. (b) (*Anat*) stocky, thickset. (c) *terreno* rough. (d) (*fig*) sly, deceitful.

doblador*1 NM (*CAm*) roll-your-own*, hand-rolled cigarette.

doblador2, -a NM/F (*Cine*) dubber.

dobladura NF fold, crease.

doblaje NM (*Cine*) dubbing.

doblamiento NM folding, creasing.

doblar [1a] **1** VT (a) (*gen*) to double; ~ **el sueldo a uno** to double sb's salary; **te doblo en edad, te doblo la edad** I'm twice your age. (b) *tela, papel etc* to fold (up, over), crease; *dobladillo* to turn up; *página* to turn down; *cabeza, rodilla etc* to bend; (*Méx: abalear*) to shoot down; ~ **a uno a palos** to give sb a beating. (c) *esquina* to turn, round, go round; *cabo* (*Náut*) to round; (*Aut*) to overtake; (*en carrera*) to lap. (d) *película* to dub. (e) ~ **dos papeles** (*Teat*) to take two parts. (f) (*Bridge*) to double; *apuesta etc* to double. (g) (*Dep: marcar*) to mark.

2 VI (a) (*torcer*) to turn (*a la izquierda* to the left). (b) (*campana*) to toll (*a muerto, por uno* for a death). (c) (‡) to peg out‡, die.

3 **doblarse** VR (a) (*cantidad etc*) to double. (b) (*plegarse*) to fold (up), crease; to bend, buckle. (c) (*fig*) to give in, yield (*a* to).

doble **1** ADJ (a) (*gen*) double; *flor, puerta, sentido etc* double; *control, nacionalidad etc* dual; *fondo* false; *tela* double, extra thick; *cuerda* thick, stout; ~ **o nada** double or quits; ~ **agente** double agent; ~ **cara** (ADJ) double-sided; ~ **densidad** (ADJ) double-density; ~ **espacio** double spacing; **calle de ~ sentido** (*Aut*) two-way road. (b) (*fig*) insincere; two-faced, deceitful.

2 NM (a) (*cantidad*) double (quantity); **el ~** twice the quantity, twice the amount; twice as much; **apostar ~ contra sencillo** to bet two to one; **hoy gana el ~** today he earns double, today he earns twice as much; **su sueldo es el ~ del mío** his salary is twice mine; **un ~ de whiskey** a double whisky; **un ~ de cerveza** a big glass of beer. (b) (*Cos etc*) fold, crease. (c) (*de campana*) toll, tolling; knell. (d) (*Tenis etc*) ~**s** doubles; ~**s** (**de**) **damas** ladies' doubles; ~**s de caballeros, ~s masculinos** men's doubles; ~**s mixtos** mixed doubles. (e) (*Bridge*) double; ~ **de castigo** penalty double; ~ **de llamada** asking double. (f) (‡: *de cárcel*) prison governor.

3 NMF (*Cine*) double, stand-in; **ser el ~ de uno** (*fig*) to be sb's double.

doblegar [1h] **1** VT (a) (*doblar*) to fold, crease; to bend. (b) *arma* to brandish. (c) (*fig*) to persuade, sway; ~ **a uno** to force sb to abandon his course (*o* change his ways *etc*), make sb give in.

2 **doblegarse** VR (*fig*) to yield, give in.

doblemente ADV (a) (*gen*) doubly. (b) (*fig*) insincerely; deceitfully.

doblete NM (*Ling*) doublet.

doblez **1** NM (*pliegue*) fold, crease; (*dobladillo: de vestido*) hem; (*de pantalón*) turn-up(s), cuff(s) (*US*).

2 NF insincerity; double-dealing, deceitfulness, duplicity.

doblista NMF doubles player.

doblón NM (*Hist*) doubloon; ~ **de a ocho** piece of eight.

doc. (a) ABR *de* **docena** dozen, doz. (b) ABR *de* **documento** document, doc.

doce **1** ADJ twelve; (*fecha*) twelfth; **las ~** twelve o'clock; **los ~ the** Twelve (member-countries of EC).

2 NM twelve.

doceavo **1** ADJ twelfth.

2 NM twelfth; **en ~** (*Tip*) in duodecimo.

docena NF dozen; ~ **del fraile** baker's dozen; **a ~s** by the dozen, in great numbers; **por ~(s)** by the dozen, in dozens.

docencia NF teaching.

doceno ADJ twelfth.

docente **1** ADJ educational; teaching (*atr*); **centro ~** teaching institution; **personal ~** teaching staff, academic staff; **personal no ~** non-academic staff.

2 NMF teacher.

dócil ADJ docile; obedient; gentle, mild.

docilidad NF docility; obedience; gentleness; mildness.

dócilmente ADV in a docile way; obediently; gently, mildly.

doctamente ADV learnedly.

docto **1** ADJ learned, erudite; scholarly.

2 NM, **docta** NF scholar; learned person.

doctor NM (*Med, Univ*) doctor; (*Ecl*) father, saint; ~ **en derecho** doctor of laws; ~**es tiene la Iglesia** there are plenty of people well able to pass an opinion (on that).

doctora NF (*Med*) (woman) doctor; (*Univ*) doctor; (*) bluestocking.

doctorado NM doctorate; **estudiante de ~** research student.

doctoral ADJ (a) doctoral. (b) (*hum*) learned, pompous.

doctorando, -a NM/F PhD student.

doctorar [1a] **1** VT to confer a doctor's degree on.

2 **doctorarse** VR to take one's doctor's degree (*o* doctorate).

doctrina NF (*gen*) doctrine; (*erudición*) learning; (*enseñanza*) teaching; (*en escuela*) catechism, religious instruction.

doctrinal ADJ doctrinal.

doctrinar [1a] VT to teach.

doctrinario, -a ADJ, NM/F doctrinaire.

doctrinero NM (*LAm*) parish priest (*among Indians*).

docudrama NM docudrama, dramatized documentary.

documentación NF (a) (*gen*) documentation. (b) (*papeles*) papers, documents; ~ **del barco** ship's papers; **la ~, por favor** your papers, please. (c) (*Prensa*) reference section.

documentadamente ADV in a well-informed way; citing documents in evidence.

documentado ADJ (a) *libro, trabajo* documented, researched; **un libro bien ~** a well documented (*o* researched) book. (b) *persona*: **no voy ~** I don't have my papers with me.

documental ADJ, NM documentary.

documentalista NMF (*que hace documentales*) documentary maker; (*que trabaja en los archivos*) archivist.

documentar [1a] **1** VT to document, establish with documentary evidence.

2 **documentarse** VR to get the necessary information, do one's homework.

documento NM document (*t Inform*); paper; record; certificate; (*Jur*) exhibit; ~**s del coche** papers relating to one's car; ~**s de envío** dispatch documents; ~ **justificativo** voucher, certificate; supporting document; ~ **nacional de identidad** identity card; ~ **secretísimo** top-secret document; ~ **de trabajo** working paper; **los ~s, por favor** your papers, please.

┌─ **DOCUMENTO NACIONAL DE IDENTIDAD** ─┐

i *The Spanish **Documento Nacional de Identidad** is a laminated plastic ID card which is renewable every 10 years. All Spanish nationals over the age of 14 are required to carry this card, which has their photo, fingerprints and personal details, at all times, and must be able to produce it to the police on request. As a legal document it is commonly used as proof of identity, for instance when opening a bank account, and it can be used instead of a passport for travelling around the EU. In Spain it is commonly known as the **DNI**, or else **carnet (de identidad)**. In Latin America a similar card is called the **cédula (de identidad)**.*

dodecafónico ADJ dodecaphonic.

dodecafonismo NM twelve-note system.

dodecágono NM dodecagon.

dodo NM, **dodó** NM dodo.

dodotis NM INVAR nappy, diaper (*US*).

dogal NM (*de animal*) halter; (*de verdugo*) hangman's noose; **estar con el ~ al cuello** (*o* **a la garganta**) to be in an awful jam*.

dogma NM dogma.

dogmáticamente ADV dogmatically.

dogmático ADJ dogmatic.

dogmatismo NM dogmatism.

dogmatizador(a) NM/F dogmatist.

dogmatizar [1f] VI to dogmatize.

dogo NM (*t perro ~*) bulldog; ~ **alemán** Great Dane.

dola* NF = **pídola.**

dolamas NFPL, **dolames** NFPL (*Vet*) hidden defects (*of a horse*); (*LAm*

††) chronic illness.

dólar NM dollar; **gente montada en el ~*** filthy rich people*.

dolencia NF (*achaque*) ailment, complaint, affliction; (*dolor*) ache; (*fig*) ailment, ill; **la ~ de la economía** the ills of the economy.

doler [2i] ① VTI (a) (*Med*) to hurt, pain; to ache; **me duele el brazo** my arm hurts, my arm aches; **me duele el estómago** I have a pain in my stomach, my stomach aches, I've got stomachache; **¿dónde te duele?** where does it hurt (you)?; **¿duele mucho?** does it hurt much?; **no me ha dolido nada** it didn't hurt at all.
(b) (*fig*) to grieve, distress; **le duele aún la pérdida** the loss still grieves him, he still feels the loss; **no me duele el dinero** I don't mind about the money, the money doesn't bother me; **a cualquiera le dolería verlo** it would grieve anyone to see it; **¡ahí (le) duele!** that's the whole point!, you've put your finger on it!
② **dolerse** VR (a) (*afligirse*) to grieve (*de* about, for), feel sorry (*de* about, for); **~ de** to regret; to repent (of); *persona* to feel sorry for, pity; **¡duélete de mí!** pity me!; show some sympathy for me!; **se duele de que no le visitéis** he complains that you don't go to see him; **~ de los pecados** to repent (of) one's sins.
(b) (*quejarse*) to complain; to moan, groan; **lo sufre todo sin ~** he puts up with everything without complaining.

dolido ADJ: **estar ~** (*fig*) to be distressed, be upset.

doliente ① ADJ (a) (*Med*) suffering, ill; aching.
(b) (*triste*) sad, sorrowful; (*por una muerte*) grieving, mourning; **la familia ~** the bereaved family, the sorrowing relatives.
② NMF (a) (*Med*) sufferer, sick person; patient.
(b) bereaved person; (*en entierro*) mourner.

dolmen NM dolmen.

dolo NM fraud, deceit; **sin ~** openly, honestly.

dolomía NF **dolomita** NF dolomite.

▼ **dolor** NM (a) pain; ache; pang; **~ de cabeza** headache; **con ~ de mi corazón** with an ache in my heart; **~ de espalda**, **~ lumbar** backache; **~ de estómago** stomachache; **~ de muelas** toothache; **~ de oídos** earache; **~es del parto** labour pains; **~es de posparto** afterpains; **~ sordo** dull ache; **estar con mucho ~**, **tener mucho ~** to be in great pain; **estar con ~es** (*mujer*) to feel the labour pains beginning.
▼ (b) (*fig*) grief, sorrow; affliction, distress; regret; **le causa mucho ~** it causes him great distress, it is a great grief to him; **con ~ te lo digo** it grieves me to say it to you; **es un ~** it's a shame, it's a pity.

dolorido ADJ (a) (*Med*) sore, tender, aching; **la parte dolorida** the part which hurts, the part where the pain is.
(b) (*fig*) *persona* distressed; grieving, grief-stricken.
(c) *tono* plaintive, sad, pained.

Dolorosa NF: **la ~** the Madonna, Our Lady of Sorrow.

dolorosa NF (*hum*) bill, check (*US*) (*in a restaurant*).

dolorosamente ADV (a) (*Med*) painfully. (b) (*fig*) painfully, grievously, distressingly.

doloroso ADJ (a) (*Med*) painful. (b) (*fig*) painful, grievous, distressing.

doloso ADJ fraudulent, deceitful.

dom. ABR *de* **domingo** Sunday, Sun.

doma NF (a) (*de animal*) taming; (*adiestramiento*) training; (*de caballo*) breaking-in. (b) (*fig*) mastering, controlling.

domable ADJ tamable; controllable.

domador(a) NM/F trainer; tamer; **~ de caballos** horse-breaker.

domadura NF = **doma**.

domar [1a] VT (a) (*amansar*) to tame; (*adiestrar*) to train; *caballo etc* to break in. (b) (*fig*) to master, control; (*reprimir*) to repress.

domeñar [1a] VT = **domar**.

domesticación NF domestication; taming.

domesticado ADJ tame; pet; **un tejón ~** a tame badger, a pet badger.

domesticar [1g] ① VT to tame, domesticate; to make a pet of.
② **domesticarse** VR to become tame, become domesticated.

domesticidad NF (a) (*cualidad*) domesticity, homeliness; (*ambiente*) homely atmosphere.
(b) (*de animal*) (state of being in) captivity; **el lobo no vive bien en ~** the wolf does not live happily in captivity, the wolf does not take to captivity.

doméstico ① ADJ (a) *vida etc* domestic; home (*atr*), family (*atr*); **economía doméstica** home economy, housekeeping, home economics (*US*); **gastos ~s** household expenses, housekeeping expenditure; **faenas domésticas** housework.
(b) *animal* tame, pet.
② NM, **doméstica** NF servant, domestic.

Domiciano NM Domitian.

domiciliación NF (*Fin*) automatic payment (through a bank), direct debiting.

domiciliado ADJ (a) **~ en Valencia** resident in Valencia. (b) *pago* by direct debit.

domiciliar [1b] ① VT (a) (*dar un domicilio a*) to domicile, establish; to house. (b) (*Méx*) *carta* to address. (c) (*Com*) *activo* to place. (d) **~ su cuenta** (*o cobro, nómina, pago*) to give the number of one's account (for automatic payment), authorize direct debiting of one's account.
② **domiciliarse** VR to establish o.s., take up (one's) residence.

domiciliario ADJ domiciliary; home (*atr*); house (*atr*); **arresto ~** house arrest; **asistencia domiciliaria** home help.

domicilio NM home; (*en lenguaje oficial*) domicile, residence, abode; (*en formulario*) home address; **~ conyugal** conjugal home; **~ particular** private residence; **~ social** (*Com*) registered office, head office; **a ~** (*Dep*) at home; **servicio a ~** delivery service; **ventas a ~** door-to-door selling; **trabajar a ~** to work at home, do outwork; **sin ~ fijo** of no fixed abode.

dominación NF (a) (*gen*) domination; dominance; rule, sway. (b) (*Mil*) high ground, commanding position.

dominador ADJ (a) *papel etc* dominating, controlling. (b) *carácter* domineering.

dominante ADJ (a) (*gen*) dominant (*t Mús*), predominant; **la tendencia ~** the dominant tendency, the ruling tendency; **el viento ~** the prevailing wind; **la consideración ~** the overriding consideration.
(b) *carácter* domineering; masterful; *amor etc* possessive.

dominar [1a] ① VT (a) (*gen*) to dominate; to rule (over); hold sway over; *adversario* to overpower; *barca, caballo, nervios etc* to control, bring under control; *epidemia, incendio* to check, bring under control; *rebelión* to put down, suppress, subdue; *pasión* to control, master; *dolor etc* to get over; **le domina la envidia** he is ruled by envy, his ruling passion is envy.
(b) *materia* to have a good grasp of; *lengua* to know well, be fluent in, have a good command of; **domina 7 idiomas** he knows 7 languages well.
(c) (*edificio etc*) to dominate, tower above (*o over*), look down on.
② VI (*edificio etc*) to dominate; (*color, rasgo etc*) to stand out; (*opinión, viento, tendencia etc*) to predominate, prevail.
③ **dominarse** VR to control o.s.

dómine NM (*Hist*) schoolmaster; (*hum*) pedant.

domingas‡ NFPL boobs‡.

Domingo NM Dominic.

domingo NM Sunday; **D~ de Cuasimodo** Low Sunday; **D~ de Ramos** Palm Sunday; **D~ de la Pasión** Passion Sunday; **D~ de Resurrección** Easter Sunday; **hacer ~** to take a day off, make a day into a holiday.

dominguejo NM (*And, Cono Sur: espantapájaros*) scarecrow.

dominguero ① ADJ Sunday (*atr*); **pintor ~** Sunday painter; **traje ~** Sunday clothes, Sunday suit.
② NM **dominguera** NF Sunday excursionist; Sunday visitor; (*Aut*) Sunday driver; (*) rotten driver*.

Dominica NF Dominica.

dominical ① ADJ Sunday (*atr*); **periódico ~** Sunday newspaper.
② NM Sunday supplement.

dominicanismo NM word (*o phrase etc*) peculiar to the Dominican Republic.

dominicano ① ADJ (*Ecl y Pol*) Dominican.
② NM (*Ecl*) Dominican.
③ NM, **dominicana** NF (*Pol*) Dominican.

dominico NM (*Ecl*), **dominíco** NM (*LAm*) Dominican.

dominio NM (a) (*gen*) dominion; (*autoridad*) power, sway, authority (*sobre over*); (*supremacía*) ascendancy, supremacy; (*control*) hold, grip (*de on*); (*de lengua*) command (*de of*), fluency (*de in*); **~ público** public property, national property; **la noticia es del ~ público** the news is widely known, the news is common knowledge; **~ de (*o sobre*) sí mismo** self-control; **¡qué ~ tiene!** isn't he good (at it)?; **tiene el ~ de la situación** he is in control of the situation.
(b) (*tierra*) domain; (*Pol*) dominion.
(c) (*fig*) subject, discipline; field (of study), domain.

dominó NM (a) domino; **un ~** a domino; a set of dominoes; **juego de ~** dominoes. (b) (‡) French letter.

dom.º ABR *de* **domingo** Sunday, Sun.

domo NM (*Méx*) skylight.

domótica NF home automation.

domótico ADJ automated, smart*.

┌─── **DON/DOÑA** ───┐

*ⓘ A courtesy title, **don/doña** placed before the first name of an older or more senior man/woman is a way of showing them your respect when talking to them or about them. E.g. "¿Podría hablar con **don César Roca**?", "Buenos días **doña Alicia**. ¿Qué tal su viaje?" Although now becoming rarer, in Spain **Don** and **Doña**, often abbreviated to **D.** and **Dña.**, are commonly used before full names on official documents and contracts. In formal correspondence, they are used in combination with **Sr., Sra.** and **Srta.**, e.g. **Sr. D. Bernardo Esplugas Martín, Sra. Dña. Ana Rodríguez.***

don¹ NM: **D~** (*en sobre*) ≃ Esquire; *en otros casos no se traduce directamente, p.ej.* **soy alumno de ~ Ramón** I am one of Menéndez

Pidal's students; **el rey ~ Pedro** King Peter; *V t* **Juan, Señor 1(c).**

don² NM **(a)** (*regalo*) gift; present.

(b) (*fig: talento*) gift; knack; aptitude, talent (*de* for); **tiene un ~ especial** he has a special gift; **~ de acierto** happy knack (of doing things well); intuition; **~ de gentes** personal charm, human touch; **tener ~ de gentes** to have a way with people, have the human touch, know how to handle people; **~ de lenguas** gift for languages; **~ de mando** (qualities of) leadership, (*Mil*) generalship; **~ de palabra** gift of oratory, fluency.

dona NF (*Cono Sur*) gift; legacy; **~s** (*Méx*) trousseau.

donación NF donation; (*Jur*) gift; **~ de sangre** donation of blood.

donada NF lay sister.

donado NM lay brother.

donador(a) NM/F donor.

donaire NM **(a)** (*ingenio*) charm, wit, cleverness. **(b)** (*elegancia*) grace(fulness). **(c)** (*un ~*) witticism; **dice muchos ~s** he's terribly witty.

donante NMF donor; **~ de órganos** organ donor; **~ de sangre** blood-donor.

donar [1a] VT to donate; to grant, bestow.

donativo NM donation, contribution.

doncel NM (*Hist*) page; young nobleman, young squire.

doncella NF **(a)** (*criada*) maid, lady's maid, maidservant. **(b)** (*virgen*) virgin; (*Hist y liter*) maid, maiden.

doncellez NF **(a)** (*estado*) virginity, maidenhood. **(b)** (*Anat*) maidenhead.

donde 1 REL ADV **(a)** (*gen*) where; (*fig*) wherein; in which; **el sitio ~ lo encontré** the place where I found it; **a ~** to where, to which; **fue a ~ estaban** he went to (the place) where they were; **es a ~ vamos nosotros** that's where we're going; **de ~** from where; from which, out of which; **el país de ~ vienen** the country they come from; **la caja de ~ lo sacó** the box from which he took it, the box he took it out of; **en ~** where; in which; **por ~** through which; (*fig*) whereby; **no hay por ~ cogerle** there's no way to catch him.

(b) (*Cono Sur: ya que*) as, since.

2 PREP **(a)** **es allí ~ el farol** it's where the lamp-post is, it's over there by the lamp-post.

(b) (*LAm: en casa de*) at the house (*etc*) of; **están cenando ~ mi mamá** they are dining at my mother's (house); **está ~ el médico** she's at the doctor's.

dónde INTERROG ADV **(a)** where?; **¿~ lo dejaste?** where did you leave it?; **¿a ~ vas?** where are you going (to)?; **¿de ~ vienes?** where have you come from?; **¿en ~?** where?; **¿por ~?** where?, whereabouts?; **which way?**; why?, for what reason?; **¿por ~ se va al estadio?** which way to the stadium?, how do I get to the stadium?

(b) (*indirecto*) where; **no sé ~ lo puse** I don't know where I put it.

(c) (*LAm: ¿cómo?*) how?

dondequiera 1 ADV anywhere; **por ~** everywhere, all over the place.

2 CONJ anywhere, wherever; **~ que lo busques** wherever you look for it.

donjuán NM wolf*, womanizer.

donjuanismo NM wolfishness*, womanizing.

donosamente ADV (*liter*) wittily, amusingly.

donoso ADJ (*liter*) witty, amusing; (*iró*) fine; **¡donosa idea!** (*iró*) highly amusing I'm sure!

Donosti(a) NF San Sebastián.

donostiarra 1 ADJ of San Sebastián.

2 NMF native (*o* inhabitant) of San Sebastián; **los ~s** the people of San Sebastián.

Don Quijote NM Don Quixote.

donus NM INVAR, **donut** NM, PL **donuts** doughnut, donut (*US*).

doña NF *antepuesto al nombre de pila no se traduce;* **~ Victoria Benito** Mrs Victoria Benito; *see also* DON/DOÑA .

dopado 1 ADJ doped, doped-up*.

2 NM (*t* **dopaje** NM) doping, drugging.

dopar [1a] 1 VT to dope, drug.

2 **doparse** VR to take drugs.

doping ['dopin] NM doping, drugging; administering (*o* use) of a drug.

dopingar [1h] VT to dope, drug.

doquier ADV (†† *o liter*) = **dondequiera**; **por ~** all over, everywhere; all over the place.

doradito ADJ (*Culin*) light brown.

dorado 1 ADJ golden; (*Téc*) gilt, gilded; gold-plated; **los ~s 60** the golden sixties.

2 NM **(a)** (*Téc*) gilding, gilt. **(b)** (*Pez*) dorado.

doradura NF gilding.

dorar [1a] VT **(a)** (*Téc*) to gild; (*Culin*) to brown, cook lightly. **(b)** (*fig*) to gild; to palliate, make more palatable, put a gloss on; **~ la píldora** to sweeten the pill.

dorífora NF Colorado beetle.

dormida NF (*LAm*) nap; **echarse una ~** to have a nap.

dormidera NF **(a)** (*Bot*) (opium) poppy. **(b)** **tener buenas ~s** to get off to sleep easily.

dormidero NM (*de ganado*) sleeping place; (*de gallinas*) roost.

dormido ADJ **(a)** (*durmiendo*) asleep; **estar ~** to be asleep; **estar medio ~** to be half asleep. **(b)** (*con sueño*) sleepy. **(c)** (*aletargado*) *pueblo, valle* sleepy.

dormilón 1 ADJ sleepy; much given to sleeping.

2 NM, **dormilona¹** NF sleepyhead; (*pey*) sleepy sort, lazy sort, lie-a-bed.

3 **dormilona²** NF **(a)** (*silla*) reclining chair. **(b)** (*Carib: camisón*) nightdress, nightgown.

dormir [3j] 1 VT **(a)** **~ la siesta** to have one's afternoon nap, have a doze, have a siesta.

(b) **~la*** to sleep it off; **~ la mona*** to sleep off a hangover*.

(c) **~ a uno** to send sb to sleep, make sb go to sleep; (*anestesiar*) to put sb to sleep; **Delius me duerme de maravilla** Delius is marvellous for sending me to sleep.

2 VI (*gen*) to sleep; (*pasar la noche*) to stay overnight, spend the night; **~ como un lirón** (*o* **tronco, poste** etc) to sleep like a log; **~ como un santo** (*o* **bendito**) to sleep peacefully, be fast asleep; **~ a pierna suelta** (*o* **tendida**) to sleep soundly, sleep the sleep of the just; **~ con uno** to sleep with sb; **quedarse dormido** to go to sleep, drop off; **durmiendo se me pasó la hora** the time went by while I slept, I overslept.

3 **dormirse** VR **(a)** (*persona*) to go to sleep, fall asleep.

(b) (*pierna etc*) to go to sleep, get numb.

dormirela* NF nap, snooze.

dormirlas NM hide-and-seek.

dormitar [1a] VI to doze, snooze*.

dormitorio 1 NM **(a)** (*alcoba*) bedroom; (*de colegio etc*) dormitory. **(b)** (*muebles*) bedroom suite. **(c)** (*Méx Ferro*) couchette.

2 ATR *V* **barrio, ciudad.**

dornillo NM wooden bowl; (*Agr*) small trough.

Dorotea NF Dorothy.

dorsal 1 ADJ dorsal; back (*atr*).

2 NM (*Dep*) number (worn on player's back).

3 NF ridge.

dorsalmente ADV dorsally; *flotar* on one's back.

dorso NM back (*t fig*); **escribir algo al ~** to write sth on the back; **'véase al ~'** 'see other side'; 'please turn over' (*PTO*).

dos 1 ADJ **(a)** (*gen*) two; (*fecha*) second; **las ~** two o'clock; **~ a ~** two against two; **~ por ~ son 4** two times two makes 4; **a cada ~ por tres** in rapid succession, continually; intermittently; **de ~ en ~** in twos, two by two; **cortar algo en ~** to cut sth in (to) two; **como ése no hay ~** they don't come any better than that.

(b) **los ~** the two of them, both (of them); **es para los ~** it's for both of you; **para entre los ~** (strictly) between you and me.

2 NM two; **en un ~ por tres** in no time at all; **coger el ~ː** to beat it*.

dos-caballos NM INVAR (*Aut*) deux-chevaux, 2 CV.

doscientos ADJ two hundred.

dosel NM canopy.

doselera NF valance.

dosificación NF dosage.

dosificador NM dispenser.

dosificar [1g] VT *medicina* to measure out, put up in doses; *ingredientes* to measure out, mix in proportion; **~ las fuerzas** to save one's strength; **el ministro ha dosificado sus aparicones** the minister has chosen his appearances carefully.

dosis NF INVAR **(a)** (*Med*) dose; dosage, amount, quantity. **(b)** (*fig*) dose; admixture; **con buena ~ de vanidad** with a good proportion of vanity.

dos piezas NM INVAR two-piece.

dos(s)ier NM, PL **dos(s)iers** [dosi'er] dossier.

dotación NF **(a)** (*acto, dinero*) endowment; **~ del premio** amount of the prize.

(b) (*plantilla*) staff, establishment, personnel; (*Náut*) crew, complement; (*de coche-patrulla etc*) crew, occupants; **una ~ del parque de bomberos** a squad of firemen; **la ~ es insuficiente** the staff is inadequate, we are under-staffed.

dotacional ADJ: **suelo ~** non-residential land.

dotado ADJ **(a)** *persona* gifted; **los niños excepcionalmente ~s** exceptionally gifted children; **bien ~** highly talented, well-equipped for life. **(b)** **~ de** *persona* endowed with; *máquina etc* equipped with, fitted with, possessing.

dotar [1a] VT **(a)** *mujer* to endow (*con* with), give a dowry to; **la dotó muy bien** he gave her a good dowry; **la dotó con** (*o* **en**) **un millón** he gave her a million as a dowry.

(b) (*fig*) to endow (*con, de* with); **la naturaleza le dotó de buenas cualidades** nature endowed him with good qualities.

(c) (*destinar bienes a*) to endow; (*destinar fondos a*) to provide funds for, assign money to; (*fijar el sueldo de*) to fix a salary for; (*asignar per-*

sonas *a*) to provide staff (*etc*) for; **son necesarias X pesetas para ~ estos puestos de enseñanza** X pesetas are needed to pay for these teaching posts; **la Academia ha dotado 2 premios** the Academy has established (*o* set aside funds for) 2 prizes.
(d) (*Mec etc*) to supply, fit, provide (*de* with); **~ un avión de todos los adelantos modernos** to equip a plane with all the latest devices.
(e) *barco etc* to man (*de* with); *laboratorio, oficina etc* to staff (*de* with).

DOS | **ver también la entrada**

El uso de "both"
Los dos con el sentido de *ambos* se traduce por *both*, pero el lugar que ocupa en la oración y la construcción en la que se usa depende de varios factores:

Como sujeto de "be" o un verbo auxiliar/modal
● Con nombre sólo:
  Las dos hermanas son cantantes
  Both (of the) sisters are singers ◊ *The sisters are both singers*
  Los dos castillos fueron construidos en el siglo XVIII
  Both (of the) castles were built in the 18th century ◊ *The castles were both built in the 18th century*
● Con nombre y demostrativo/posesivo:
  Estos dos niños son huérfanos
  Both (of) these children are orphans ◊ *These children are both orphans*
  Mis dos hijos han emigrado
  Both (of) my sons have emigrated ◊ *My sons have both emigrated*
● Sin nombre:
  Los dos son jóvenes
  Both of them are young ◊ *They're both young*
  Los dos sabemos esquiar
  Both of us can ski ◊ *We can both ski*

Como sujeto de otro verbo
● Con nombre sólo:
  Los dos chicos quieren estudiar medicina
  Both (of the) boys want to study medicine ◊ *The boys both want to study medicine*
● Con nombre y demostrativo/posesivo:
  Mis dos tíos viven solos
  Both (of) my uncles live alone ◊ *My uncles both live alone*
● Sin nombre:
  Los dos beben más de la cuenta
  Both of them o *They both drink too much*

Como objeto de un verbo o preposición
  Los hemos invitado a los dos
  We've invited both of them o *them both*
  Los dos me tenéis harta
  I'm fed up with both of you o *you both*
  NOTA: Cuando *los dos* no puede substituirse por *ambos*, se traduce por *the two* + NOMBRE EN PLURAL O *the two of us/you/them*:
  ¿Tienes los dos libros que te dejé?
  Have you got the two books (that) I lent you?
  Para otros usos y ejemplos ver la entrada.

---

dote *gen* NF **(a)** (*de mujer*) dowry, marriage portion; **con un millón de ~** with a dowry of a million.
(b) (*fig*) **~s** gifts, talents, aptitude; **tiene excelentes ~s** she has great gifts; **~s de adherencia** (*Aut*) road-holding qualities; **~s de mando** (qualities of) leadership.
dovela NF keystone, voussoir.
doy V dar.
dozavo = doceavo.
Dpto. ABR *de* **Departamento** department, dept.
Dr. ABR *de* **doctor** Doctor, Dr.
Dra. ABR *de* **doctora** Doctor, Dr.
dracma [1] NF (*Farm*) drachm, dram.
  [2] NM O NF (*Fin*) drachma.
draconiano ADJ draconian.
DRAE NM ABR *de* **Diccionario de la Real Academia Española.**
draga NF dredge; (*barco*) dredger.
dragado NM dredging.
dragaminas NM INVAR minesweeper.
dragar [1h] VT to dredge; *minas* to sweep.
drago NM dragon tree.
dragomán NM dragoman.
dragón NM **(a)** (*Zool*) dragon. **(b)** (*Mil*) dragoon. **(c)** (*Bot*) snapdragon.
dragona NF **(a)** (*Mil*) shoulder knot, epaulette. **(b)** (*And, Cono Sur, Méx: de espada*) guard. **(c)** (*Méx: capa*) hooded cloak.
dragoncillo NM (*Bot*) tarragon.
dragonear [1a] [1] VT (*Cono Sur*: †: *cortejar*) to court, woo.
  [2] VI (*LAm: jactarse*) to boast, brag; **~ de** to boast of being; (*Cono Sur: fingir ser*) to pretend to be, pass o.s. off as.

drama NM drama (*t fig*).
dramática NF drama, dramatic art.
dramáticamente ADV dramatically.
dramaticidad NF dramatic quality.
dramático ADJ [1] dramatic (*t fig*).
  [2] NM dramatist; (*tragic*) actor.
dramatismo NM drama, dramatic quality.
dramatizar [1f] VT to dramatize.
dramaturgia NF drama, theatre art; play-writing.
dramaturgo NMF (*t* **dramaturga** NF) dramatist, playwright.
dramón* NM (*hum*) strong drama, melodrama; **¡qué ~!** what a scene!
drapeado [1] ADJ draped.
  [2] NM drape.
Draque NM Drake.
drásticamente ADV drastically.
drástico ADJ drastic.
drenaje NM (*esp Agr, Med*) drainage.
drenar [1a] VT to drain; (*Fin*) to remove, syphon off.
Dresde NM Dresden.
driblar [1a] VTI (*Dep*) to dribble; **~ a uno** to dribble past sb.
drible NM (*Dep*) dribble; dribbling.
dril NM duck, drill.
drive NM [draif] (*Golf*) drive.
driza NF halyard.
droga NF **(a)** (*Med, Farm*) drug; medicine; (*pey*) drug; (*en carreras de caballos etc*) dope; **la ~** (*como problema*) drugs; **~ blanda** soft drug; **~ de diseño** designer drug; **~ dura** hard drug; **~ milagrosa** wonder drug; **el peligro de las ~s** the drug menace.
(b) (*) (*engaño*) trick, hoax; (*truco*) stratagem; (*mentira*) fib.
(c) (*) (*molestia*) nuisance; **es (mucha)** ~ it's a dreadful nuisance.
(d) (*And, Cono Sur, Méx*: *deuda*) debt; bad debt; **hacer ~** (*endeudarse*) to get into debt; (*no pagar*) to refuse to pay up, duck a bill.
(e) (*Com*) drug on the market, unsaleable article.
(f) **mandar a uno a la ~** (*CAm, Carib*) to tell sb to go to hell.
drogadicción NF drug addiction.
drogadicto, -a NM/F drug addict.
drogado NM drugging; drug taking; (*de caballo*) doping.
drogar [1h] [1] VT to drug; *caballo* to dope.
  [2] **drogarse** VR to drug o.s., take drugs.
drogata‡ NMF druggy‡.
drogodelincuencia NF drug-related crime.
drogodelincuente NMF drug addict (*who finances his habit through petty crime*).
drogodependencia NF dependence on drugs, drug addiction.
drogodependiente NMF person dependent on drugs, drug addict.
drogota‡ NMF druggy‡.
droguería NF store where cleaning materials are sold.
droguero NM **(a)** (*tendero*) druggist; owner of a 'droguería'; (* *pey*) drug pusher. **(b)** (*: *estafador*) cheat, crook*. **(c)** (*And, Cono Sur, Méx*: *moroso*) slow payer, defaulter.
drogui* NM (*Cono Sur*) **(a)** (*bebida*) liquor, alcohol. **(b)** (*borracho*) drunkard.
droguista NM = droguero.
dromedario NM **(a)** (*Zool*) dromedary. **(b)** (*Méx*) tailor.
dromeo NM emu.
dropar [1a] VT (*Golf*) to drop.
druida NM druid.
drupa NF drupe.
DSE NF ABR *de* **Dirección de la Seguridad del Estado.**
Dto., D.to ABR *de* **descuento** discount.
Dtor. ABR *de* **Director** Director, Dir.
Dtora. ABR *de* **Directora** Director, Dir.
dual ADJ dual (*t Gram*).
dualidad NF **(a)** (*gen*) duality. **(b)** (*Cono Sur Pol*) tied vote, indecisive election.
dualismo NM dualism.
dubitativamente ADV doubtfully, hesitantly.
dubitativo ADJ doubtful; uncertain, hesitant.
Dublín NM Dublin.
dublinés [1] ADJ Dublin (*atr*).
  [2] NM, **dublinesa** NF Dubliner.
ducado NM **(a)** (*territorio*) duchy, dukedom. **(b)** (*Fin*) ducat.
ducal ADJ ducal.
ducentésimo ADJ two hundredth.
ducha NF shower, shower bath; (*Med*) douche; **~ escocesa** alternately hot and cold shower; **~ (de) teléfono** shower with a detachable head; **tomarse una ~** to have a shower, shower o.s.; **dar una ~ de agua fría a un proyecto** (*fig*) to pour cold water on a plan.
duchar [1a] [1] VT (*Med*) to douche.
  [2] **ducharse** VR to have a shower, shower o.s.
ducho ADJ expert, skilled; **~ en** well versed in, experienced in; skilled at, adept at.

duco NM thick paint, lacquer; **pintar al ~** to lacquer, spray (with paint).

dúctil ADJ **(a)** (*lit*) ductile. **(b)** (*fig*) flexible, yielding; easy to handle.

ductilidad NF ductility.

▼ **duda** NF (*gen*) doubt; (*recelo*) misgiving; (*indecisión*) indecision; (*suspense*) suspense; **fuera de toda ~** beyond all doubt; **sin ~** undoubtedly, certainly; **¡sin ~!** of course!; **sin ~ alguna** without a shadow of a doubt; **le acometieron ~s** he was assailed by doubts, he began to have doubts; **ello constituye una ~ importante** this is a big question mark, it's a big if; **no cabe ~** there is no doubt about it; **no cabe ~ de que ...** there can be no doubt that ...; **¿qué ~ cabe** (o **coge)?** is sth bothering you?; **no te quepa ~** make no mistake about it, get this straight; **para desvanecer toda ~** in order to dispel all uncertainty; **queda la ~ en pie** the doubt remains; **surge una ~** a question arises; **estar en ~** to be in doubt; **poner algo en ~** to cast doubt on sth, call sth in question; **sacar a uno de ~s** to settle sb's doubts.

▼ **dudar** [1a] **[1]** VT to doubt; **no lo dudo** I don't doubt it; **a no ~lo** undoubtedly.

  ▼**[2]** VI **(a)** (*gen*) to doubt, be in doubt; **~ acerca de** to be uncertain about; **~ de** to doubt; to question; to mistrust; **no dudo de su talento** I don't question his talent; **~ entre A y B** to hesitate between A and B; **~ que ..., ~ si ...** to doubt whether; **dudo que sea capaz de hacerlo** I doubt whether he will be capable of doing it. **(b)** **~ en + infin** to hesitate to + *infin*.

dudosamente ADV doubtfully, uncertainly; **~ eficaz** of doubtful efficacy.

▼ **dudoso** ADJ **(a)** (*incierto*) doubtful, dubious, uncertain; *punto debatable*; *resultado* unclear, indecisive. **(b)** (*vacilante*) hesitant, undecided. **(c)** (*moralmente*) dubious, suspect.

duela NF stave.

duele *etc* V **doler**.

duelista NM duellist.

duelo[1] NM (*Mil*) duel; **batirse en ~** to fight a duel.

duelo[2] NM **(a)** (*dolor*) grief, sorrow; bereavement; **~s** sufferings, hardships; **sin ~** unrestrainedly; **gastar sin ~** to spend lavishly; **pegar a uno sin ~** to beat sb mercilessly. **(b)** (*luto etc*) mourning; (*personas*) mourners, party of mourners.

duende NM **(a)** (*elfo*) imp, goblin, elf; (*fantasma*) ghost; (*niño*) mischievous child; (*bromista*) prankster; **~ de imprenta** printer's devil. **(b)** **tener ~** (*tener encanto*) to have charm, have magic, have a special appeal; (*preocuparse*) to be preoccupied. **(c)** (*Inform*) bug.

duendecillo NM (*Aer etc*) gremlin, jinx (*US*).

dueña NF **(a)** (*de negocio etc*) owner, proprietress; (*de pensión*) landlady; **~ de la casa** mistress of the house, lady of the house. **(b)** (*Hist: dama*) lady; (*dama vieja*) matron; (*compañera*) duenna, companion. **(c)** (*fig*) mistress; **la marina era ~ de los mares** the navy was mistress of the seas.

dueño NM (*propietario*) owner, proprietor; (*de pensión*) landlord; (*amo*) master; (*empresario*) employer; **organismo de los ~s** (*Com etc*) employers' organization; **ser ~ de** to own, be the owner of, possess; **ser ~ de la baila, ser ~ de la situación** to be the master of the situation, have the situation in hand; **ser ~ de sí mismo** to be self-possessed, have self-control; **ser muy ~ de sí** to be very much in control of o.s.; **es Vd muy ~, es Vd ~ de mi casa** you're very welcome; **ser ~ de + infin** to be free to + *infin*; **ser muy ~ de + infin** to be amply entitled to + *infin*; **cambiar de ~** to change hands; **hacerse ~ de** to take over, take possession of; to acquire.

duerma *etc* V **dormir**.

duermevela* NF nap, snooze*.

Duero NM Douro.

dueto NM short duet.

dula NF common land, common pasture.

dulcamara NF nightshade.

dulce **[1]** ADJ (*gen*) sweet; *agua* fresh; *metal* soft; *sonido, voz* soft; *carácter* gentle, sweet, mild; *clima* mild; **un instrumento ~** a sweet-sounding instrument; a mellow instrument; **con el acento ~ del país** with the soft accent of the region; **más ~ que el almíbar** (o **azúcar** *etc*) sweeter than honey. **[2]** ADV gently, softly; **habla muy ~** she speaks very softly. **[3]** NM **(a)** (*gen*) sweet, candy (*US*); **~s** sweets; **~ de almíbar** preserved fruit; **melocotón en ~** preserved peaches; **a nadie le amarga un ~** nobody says no to a bit of luck. **(b)** (*And, CAm, Carib: azúcar*) (brown) sugar. **(c)** (*And: paleta*) lollipop.

dulcémele NM dulcimer.

dulcemente ADV sweetly; softly; gently, mildly.

dulcería NF confectioner's, sweetshop, candy store (*US*).

dulcificante NM sweetener.

dulcificar [1g] **[1]** VT **(a)** *comida* to sweeten. **(b)** (*fig*) to soften, make more gentle; to play down; to make more pleasant, make more tolerable.

[2] dulcificarse VR to moderate, become milder; (*tiempo*) to turn mild.

dulzarrón ADJ, **dulzón** ADJ **(a)** (*demasiado dulce*) sickly-sweet, too sugary. **(b)** (*fig*) cloying, sickening.

dulzonería NF **(a)** sickly-sweetness. **(b)** cloying nature.

dulzor NM sweetness.

dulzura NF sweetness; softness; gentleness; mildness; **con ~** sweetly, softly.

dumón*: **vivir a la gran ~** to live the life of Riley.

dúmper ['dumper] NM, PL **dúmpers** dumper.

dumping ['dumpin] NM (*Com*) dumping; **hacer ~** to dump goods.

duna NF dune.

dundeco* ADJ (*And, CAm*) silly, stupid.

dundera* NF (*And, CAm*) silliness, stupidity.

dundo* ADJ (*And, CAm*) = **dundeco**.

Dunquerque NM Dunkirk.

dúo NM duet, duo.

duodecimal ADJ duodecimal.

duodécimo ADJ twelfth.

duodenal ADJ duodenal.

duodeno NM duodenum.

dup., dpdo ABR *de* **duplicado** duplicated, bis.

dúplex NM INVAR **(a)** (*piso*) split-level flat, maisonette; (*casa*) semi-detached house. **(b)** (*Telec*) link up. **(c)** (*Inform*) duplex; **~ integral** full duplex.

duplicación NF duplication.

duplicado **[1]** ADJ duplicate; **número 14 ~** (ABR **dpdo**) No. 14A. **[2]** NM duplicate; **por ~** in duplicate.

duplicar [1g] **[1]** VT (*copiar*) to duplicate; (*repetir*) to repeat; *cantidad, cifra* to double; **las pérdidas duplican las de 1995** the losses are twice (o double) what they were in 1995. **[2] duplicarse** VR to double.

duplicidad NF duplicity, deceitfulness.

duplo ADJ double; **12 es ~ de 6** 12 is twice 6.

duque NM **(a)** duke. **(b)** (*Orn*) **gran ~** eagle owl.

duquesa NF duchess.

durabilidad NF durability.

durable ADJ durable, lasting.

duración NF duration; period, length of time; (*Aut, Mec etc*) life; **~ media de la vida** average life span; **de larga ~** *enfermedad etc* long-lasting, lengthy; *desempleo etc* long-term; *disco* long-playing.

duradero ADJ **(a)** *ropa, tela etc* hard-wearing, tough, durable. **(b)** *paz, efecto etc* lasting, permanent.

duralex ® NM INVAR Duralex ®.

┌───┐
│ ▭ **DURANTE** ▭   ▭ **ver también la entrada** ▭ │

Para traducir *durante* tenemos que diferenciar si hace referencia a cuándo ocurre la acción o a cuánto dura.

¿Cuándo ocurre la acción?

- Traducimos *durante* por *during* si nos referimos al intervalo de tiempo en que ocurre la acción, cuando la referencia temporal la indica un suceso o actividad determinados:

  Se conocieron durante la guerra
  They met during the war
  Se puso enferma durante una visita a Madrid
  She became ill during a visit to Madrid
  La bomba hizo explosión durante la entrega de premios
  The bomb went off during the prize-giving ceremony

- También se traduce por *during* cuando la referencia temporal viene indicada por un período de tiempo concreto:

  El tráfico es peor durante el verano
  The traffic is worse during the summer
  Durante los años treinta la economía se hallaba en dificultades
  The economy was in difficulties during the 1930s

  NOTA: Si se trata de una acción progresiva, o que continúa o que se repite durante todo el período de tiempo que se indica, es preferible traducir *durante* por *over*:

  La situación ha empeorado durante los últimos años
  The situation has worsened over the last few years
  Durante el fin de semana el actor ha sido visto en varias ocasiones
  There have been several sightings of the actor over the weekend

¿Cuánto dura la acción?

- Si nos referimos a la duración de la acción, *durante* se traduce generalmente por *for*:

  Llevo sufriendo dolores de cabeza durante más de treinta años
  I've been having headaches for more than 30 years
  Fue periodista durante cuatro años
  He was a journalist for four years
  Para otros usos y ejemplos ver la entrada.
└───┘

---

duramente ADV (*fig*) harshly; cruelly, callously.

durante PREP during; **~ todo el reinado** during the whole reign, right through the reign; **~ muchos años** for many years; **habló ~ una hora** he spoke for an hour.

durar [1a] VI (*período etc*) to last, go on, continue; (*efecto, memoria etc*) to survive, endure, remain; (*ropa etc*) to last, wear (well); **duró 5 años** it lasted 5 years, it went on for 5 years; **no va a ~ mucho más** it won't go on much longer, it'll soon be over.

duraznero NM peach-tree.

durazno NM (*fruta*) peach; (*árbol*) peach-tree.

Durero NM Dürer.

durex ® NM **(a)** (*Méx: cinta*) Sellotape ®, sticky tape. **(b)** (*LAm: preservativo*) Durex ®, sheath, condom.

dureza NF **(a)** (*gen*) hardness, toughness; (*rigidez*) stiffness; (*Dep*) rough play.
(b) (*aspereza*) harshness; callousness; roughness.
(c) **~ de oído** hardness of hearing; **~ de vientre** constipation.
(d) (*Med*) hard patch, callosity.

durmiente ① ADJ sleeping.
② NMF **(a)** (*gen*) sleeper; **La bella ~** (**del bosque**) Sleeping Beauty.
(b) (*Pol*) covert supporter.
③ NM (*Ferro*) sleeper, tie (*US*).

duro ① ADJ **(a)** (*gen*) hard; tough; *pan* stale, old; *carne, legumbres etc*

tough; *cuello* stiff; *puerta, articulación, mecanismo* stiff; *golpe* hard, heavy; *viento* strong; *luz, agua, sonido,* hard; **más ~ que una piedra** (*etc*) as hard as nails; **más ~ que un mendrugo** as tough as old boots; **tomar las duras con las maduras** to take the rough with the smooth.
(b) *carácter, clima, prueba etc* tough; *actitud, política* tough, harsh, hard; (*cruel*) cruel, callous; *juego* hard, rough, physical; (*Pol*) hawkish; *estilo etc* harsh; **ser ~ con uno** to be tough with (*o* on) sb, adopt a tough attitude to sb.
(c) **~ de mollera** (*lerdo*) dense, dim; (*terco*) pigheaded; **~ de oído** hard of hearing, (*Mús*) tone deaf; **es muy ~ de pelar** (*o* roer) it's a tough job, it's a hard nut to crack.
(d) **estar ~** (*: *Méx, Cono Sur*) to be drunk.
② ADV hard; **trabajar ~** to work hard; **pega ~** he's got a fierce punch.
③ NM (*moneda*) 5-peseta coin; **¡y que te den dos ~s!**‡ and you can get knotted!‡; **estar sin un ~*** to be broke*; **¡lo que faltaba para el ~!*** it's the last straw!; **allí venden ~s a tres pesetas** they're giving it away there.
④ NM, **dura** NF (*Pol*) hard-liner; hawk.

dux NM doge.

DYA NF ABR *de* **Detente y Ayuda** *Spanish highway assistance organization.*

E

E, e [e] NF (*letra*) E, e.

E ABR *de* **este** east, E.

e CONJ (*delante de* i~ *e* hi~, *pero no* hie~) and; *V* **t y.**

e/ (*Com*) ABR *de* **envío** shipment, shpt.

-e *V* Aspects of Word Formation in Spanish 2.

EA ☐1 NM (*Esp Mil*) ABR *de* **Ejército del Aire.**
☐2 NF ABR *de* **Eusko Alkartasuna** *Basque Nationalist political party.*

ea INTERJ hey!; come on!; ¡~ **pues!** well then!; let's see!; ¡~, **andamos!** come on, let's go!

EAU NMPL ABR *de* **Emiratos Árabes Unidos** United Arab Emirates, UAE.

ebanista NM cabinetmaker, carpenter.

ebanistería NF (a) (*oficio*) cabinetmaking; woodwork, carpentry. (b) (*taller*) cabinetmaker's (shop), carpenter's (shop).

ébano NM ebony.

ebonita NF ebonite.

ebriedad NF intoxication.

ebrio ADJ (a) intoxicated, drunk. (b) (*fig*) blind (*de* with); ~ **de alegría** drunk with happiness, beside o.s. with joy.

ebullición NF (a) boiling; **punto de** ~ boiling point; **entrar en** ~ to begin to boil, come to the boil.
(b) (*fig: movimiento*) movement, activity; (*estado cambiante*) state of flux; (*agitación*) ferment; **la juventud está en** ~ young people are in a state of ferment; **llevar un asunto a** ~ to bring a matter to the boil.

ebúrneo ADJ (*liter*) ivory, like ivory.

eccehomo NM poor wretch; **estar hecho un** ~ to be in a sorry state.

eccema NM eczema.

ECG NM ABR *de* **electrocardiograma** electrocardiogram, ECG.

echacuervos NM INVAR (a) (*chulo*) pimp. (b) (*tramposo*) cheat, impostor.

echada NF (a) throw, cast; pitch, shy; (*de moneda etc*) toss. (b) (*Méx*) boast; bluff.

echadizo ☐1 ADJ (a) *persona* spying, sent to spy.
(b) *propaganda* secretly spread; *carta* circulated in a clandestine way.
(c) *material* waste.
☐2 NM, **echadiza** NF spy.

echado ADJ Y PTP (a) **estar** ~ to lie, be lying (down).
(b) (*CAm, Carib: económicamente*) well-placed, in a good position.
(c) (*CAm*: *perezoso*) lazy.
(d) (*And*: *engreído*) stuck-up*, toffee-nosed*; **está** ~ **pa'lante*** (= **para adelante**) he's very pushy*; he's got a nerve*; **está** ~ **p'atrás** (= **para atrás**) he's very shy.

echador ☐1 ADJ boastful, bragging.
☐2 NM (a) (*presumido*) boaster, braggart. (b) (*forzudo*) bouncer*.

echadora NF: ~ **de cartas** fortune-teller.

echamiento NM throwing *etc*; *V* **echada.**

echao⁑ ADJ = **echado** (d).

echar [1a] ☐1 VT (a) (*gen*) to throw; to cast, fling, pitch, toss; *áncora, anzuelo* to cast; *moneda* to toss; *mirada* to cast, give; *suertes* to cast, draw; *dados* to throw.
(b) (*Culin etc*) to put in, add; ~ **un poco de azúcar al líquido** add a little sugar to the liquid; ~ **carbón a la lumbre** to put coal on the fire.
(c) (*servir*) *vino etc* to pour out; *comida* to serve (out); **échame agua** give me some water, pour me some water.
(d) (*despedir*) to emit, send forth, discharge; *gas* to give off, give out; *sangre* to lose, shed; *cartas* to deal; *maldiciones* to mutter.
(e) (*expulsar*) *persona* to eject, throw out, chuck out; to turn out; *empleado* to dismiss, fire*; (*de club etc*) to expel; *basura* to throw away, throw out; (*Náut*) to jettison; *piel* to slough; ~ **algo de sí** to throw sth off, get rid of sth; **cuando protesté me echaron** when I protested they threw me out; **¡que le echen fuera!** chuck him out!
(f) *pelo etc* to grow, begin to grow, begin to have; *dientes* to cut;

(*Bot*) *hojas etc* to put forth, sprout.
(g) *llave* to turn; *cerrojo* to shoot; *pestillo* to slide, work.
(h) (*empujar*) to move, push; ~ **a uno a un lado** to push sb aside; ~ **atrás a la multitud** to push the crowd back; ~ **el cuerpo atrás** to lean suddenly backwards.
(i) ~ **abajo** to demolish, pull down; (*fig*) to overthrow.
(j) *discurso* to give, make, deliver; *reprimenda* to give; *decreto* to issue.
(k) *carta* to post, put in the post, mail.
(l) *impuesto* to lay, impose (*a* on).
(m) (*achacar*) to attribute, ascribe (*a* to); (*pey*) to impute (*a* to); *culpa* to lay (*a* on).
(n) (*Carib, Cono Sur*) *animal* to urge on.
(o) (*otras locuciones*) *cuenta* to make up, balance; *freno* to apply, put on; *cigarrillo* to have, smoke; *fortuna* to tell; *cimientos* to lay; *raíz* to strike; *partida* to have, play; (*) *obra, película* to put on; **¿qué echan?** what's showing?, what's on?
(p) **~la de** to pose as, give o.s. the airs of, claim to be.
(q) (**Méx*) ~ **encima algo** (*asumir*) to take responsibility for sth; ~ **encima a uno** to alienate sb, turn sb against one.
(r) ~ **a uno por delante** (*CAm*: culpar*) to put the blame on sb.
☐2 VI (a) ~ **por una dirección** to go in a direction, turn in a direction; ~ **por una calle** to go down a street; **echemos por aquí** let's go this way; **¡echa para adelante!** lead on!; **es un olor que echa para atrás*** it's a smell that knocks you back*.
(b) ~ **a** + *infin* to begin to + *infin*, start + *ger*; ~ **a reír** to start laughing, burst out laughing; ~ **a correr** to start to run, break into a run; to run off; *V* **ver** *etc*.
(c) ~ **a faltar** (*Méx*) to miss.
☐3 **echarse** VR (a) ~ **un pitillo** to have a smoke; ~ **una novia** to get o.s. a girlfriend; ~ **una siestecita** to have a doze; ~ **un trago** to have a drink.
(b) (*lanzarse*) to throw o.s., fling o.s.; ~ **atrás** to throw o.s. back(wards); ~ **en brazos de uno** to throw o.s. into sb's arms; ~ **por un precipicio** to throw o.s. over a cliff; ~ **sobre uno** to hurl o.s. at sb, rush at sb; to fall on sb.
(c) (*tumbarse*) to lie down; to stretch out; **se echó en el suelo** he lay down on the floor.
(d) (*viento*) to slacken, drop.
(e) ~ **a** + *infin* = **2** (b).
(f) **echárselas de** (*jactarse*) to brag of, boast of; (*fingir*) to pose as.
(g) (*Méx*) ~ **encima a uno** (*asumir*) to take responsibility for sth; ~ **encima a uno** to alienate sb, turn sb against one.
(h) (*Méx⁑: matar*) ~ **a** to bump off⁑.

echarpe NM scarf, shawl.

echazón NF (a) (*acto*) throwing. (b) (*Náut*) jettison, jetsam.

echón, -ona¹* NM/F (*Carib, Méx*) braggart, swank*; poseur; **¡qué ~!** isn't he full of himself!*

echona² NF (*Cono Sur*) small sickle, reaping hook.

eclecticismo NM eclecticism.

ecléctico, -a ADJ, NM/F eclectic.

eclesial ADJ ecclesiastic(al), church (*atr*).

eclesiástico ☐1 ADJ ecclesiastic(al), church (*atr*).
☐2 NM clergyman, priest, ecclesiastic.

eclipsamiento NM eclipse.

eclipsar [1a] VT to eclipse; (*fig*) to eclipse, outshine, overshadow.

eclipse NM eclipse (*t fig*); ~ **lunar** eclipse of the moon; ~ **solar** eclipse of the sun.

eclíptica NF ecliptic.

eclíptico ADJ ecliptic.

eclisa NF (*Ferro*) fishplate.

eclosión NF (a) bloom, blooming; **hacer** ~ (*fig*) to bloom, blossom (forth). (b) (*Ent*) hatching, emerging; **hacer** ~ to hatch, emerge.

eclosionar [1a] VI (*Ent*) to hatch, emerge.

eco NM **(a)** (*gen*) echo; **hacer ~** to echo, awaken an echo.
(b) (*fig*) echo; response; **despertar un ~, encontrar un ~** to produce a response (*en* from), awaken an echo (*en* in); **la llamada no encontró ~** the call produced no response, the call had no effect; **hacer ~** to fit, correspond; to make an impression; **hacerse ~ de una opinión** to echo an opinion; **tener ~** to catch on, arouse interest.
eco... PREF eco...
ecoauditor(a) NMF environmental auditor, eco-auditor.
ecoauditoría NF environmental audit, eco-audit.
ecobolsa NF refill bag.
ecocardiograma NM echocardiogram.
ecoclimático ADJ ecoclimatic.
ecodesarrollo NM sustainable development.
ecoequilibrio NM ecobalance.
ecoetiqueta NF ecolabel.
ecografía NF (*imagen*) ultrasound scan; (*técnica*) ultrasound scanning.
ecógrafo NM ultrasound scanner.
ecolecuá INTERJ (*LAm*) exactly!, that's it!
ecología NF ecology.
ecológicamente ADV ecologically.
ecológico ADJ ecological; *producto etc* environment-friendly; *cultivo* organic, organically-grown.
ecologismo NM conservation(ism); environmentalism.
ecologista [1] ADJ conservation (*atr*); environmental.
[2] NMF conservationist; environmentalist.
ecologizar [1f] VT to make environmentally aware.
ecólogo, -a NM/F ecologist.
ecómetro NM echo-sounder.
economato NM cooperative store; cut-price store; company store; (*Mil*) ≃ NAAFI shop, PX (*US*).
econometría NF econometrics.
econométrico ADJ econometric.
economía NF **(a)** (*gen*) economy; **~ dirigida** planned economy; **~ doméstica** home economy, housekeeping, home economics (*US*); **~ de pleno empleo, ~ de empleo completo** full-employment economy; **~ de guerra** war economy; **~ de libre empresa, ~ de libre mercado** free-market economy; **~ de mercado** market economy; **~ mixta** mixed economy; **~ negra** black economy; **~ oculta, ~ subterránea, ~ sumergida** underground economy, black economy; **~ política** political economy; **~ de subsistencia** subsistence economy.
(b) (*ahorro*) economy, saving; **~ de escala** economy of scale; **hacer ~s** to make economies, economize, save.
(c) (*cualidad*) economy, thrift, thriftiness.
(d) (*estudio*) economics.
(e) (**Ministerio de**) **E~ (y Hacienda)** Ministry of Finance.
económicamente ADV economically; **los ~ débiles** (*euf*) the poor; **los ~ fuertes** (*euf*) the well-off, the wealthy.
economicidad NF **(a)** (*gen*) economic nature (*o* working *etc*). **(b)** (*rentabilidad*) economic viability, profitability.
económico ADJ **(a)** (*Com, Fin*) economic; *año etc* fiscal, financial.
(b) (*barato*) economical, inexpensive; cheap; **edición económica** cheap edition, popular edition.
(c) *persona* economical, thrifty; (*pey*) miserly.

| ECONÓMICO | **| ver también la entrada |**

¿"Economic" o "economical"?
• El adjetivo *económico* se traduce por *economic* cuando se refiere al comercio o las finanzas:
  China ha vivido cinco años de reformas económicas
  China has lived through five years of economic reforms
  ...el ritmo del crecimiento económico...
  ...the pace of economic growth...
• *Económico* se traduce por *economical* cuando se usa para describir algo que presenta una buena relación calidad-precio:
  Resulta más económico tener un coche de gasoil
  It is more economical to have a diesel-engined car
  NOTA: *Economic* se puede usar en inglés para traducir *rentable*:
  Mantendremos las tarifas altas para que el servicio resulte rentable
  We shall keep the fares high to make the service economic
  Para otros usos y ejemplos ver la entrada.

---

economista NMF economist; (*de banco etc*) accountant.
economizar [1f] [1] VT to economize (on), save; **~ tiempo** to save time.
[2] VI to economize, save; to save up; (*pey*) to be miserly, skimp, pinch.
ecónomo, -a NM/F trustee, guardian; (*Ecl*) ecclesiastical administrator.
ecopacifismo NM eco-pacifism.
ecopacifista ADJ, NMF eco-pacifist.
ecoproducto NM eco-friendly product, environmentally-friendly product.

ecosensible ADJ ecosensitive.
ecosistema NM ecosystem.
ecosond(e)ador NM echo-sounder.
ecotasa NF green tax, eco-tax.
ecotipo NM ecotype.
ecoturismo NM ecotourism.
ecoturístico ADJ ecotourism (*atr*).
ectópico ADJ ectopic.
ectoplasma NM ectoplasm.
ecu NM ecu.
ecuación NF equation; **~ cuadrática, ~ de segundo grado** quadratic equation; **~ diferencial** differential equation.
Ecuador NM: **el ~** Ecuador.
ecuador NM equator.
ecualizador NM equalizer.
ecualizar [1f] VT to equalize.
ecuánime ADJ *carácter* level-headed, equable; *humor, estado* calm, composed; *juicio etc* impartial.
ecuanimidad NF equanimity, level-headedness; calmness, composure; impartiality.
ecuatoguineano [1] ADJ of (*o* from) Equatorial Guinea.
[2] NM, **ecuatoguineana** NF native (*o* inhabitant) from Equatorial Guinea.
ecuatoreñismo NM, **ecuatorianismo** NM, word (*o* phrase *etc*) peculiar to Ecuador.
ecuatorial ADJ equatorial.
ecuatoriano, -a ADJ, NMF Ecuador(i)an.
ecuestre ADJ equestrian.
ecuménico ADJ ecumenical.
ecumenismo NM ecumenicism.
eczema NM = **eccema**.
ed. ABR *de* **edición** edition, ed.
edad NF **(a)** (*de persona*) age; **¿qué ~ tiene?** what age is he?, how old is he?; **a la ~ de 8 años, en ~ de 8 años** at the age of 8; **de ~** elderly; **de corta ~** young, of tender years; **de ~ madura, de mediana ~** middle-aged; **avanzado de ~, de ~ avanzada** advanced in years; **a una ~ avanzada** at an advanced age, late in life; **mayor ~** majority; **ser mayor de ~** to be of age, be adult; **llegar a mayor ~, cumplir la mayoría de ~** to come of age; **menor ~** minority; **ser menor de ~** to be under age; **el instrumento es como una guitarra menor de ~** the instrument is like a young (*o* undersized, underdeveloped) guitar; **~ adulta** adult age; manhood, womanhood; **llegar a la ~ adulta** to reach manhood (*etc*); **~ crítica** change of life; **~ escolar** school age; **~ escolar obligatoria** compulsory school attendance age; **la ~ ingrata** the awkward age (*13-16*); **~ de jubilación** retirement age; **~ límite** age-limit; **~ mental** mental age; **la ~ del pato, la ~ del pavo, la ~ del chivateo** (*LAm*) the tender years, the green years; the awkward age; **~ penal** age of legal responsibility; **tercera ~** third age; **persona de la tercera ~** senior citizen; **~ tierna** tender years; **~ viril** manhood; prime of life; **ella no aparenta la ~ que tiene** she doesn't look her age; **¿qué ~ le das?** how old do you think she is?; **A le saca mucha ~ a B** A is much older than B.
(b) (*Hist*) age, period; **por aquella ~** at that time; **~ de oro** golden age; **~ moderna** modern period, modern times; **E~ de(l) Bronce** Bronze Age; **E~ de(l) Hierro** Iron Age; **E~ Media** Middle Ages; **E~ de (la) Piedra** Stone Age.
edafología NF pedology, study of soils.
edecán NM aide-de-camp.
edema NM oedema.
Edén NM Eden, Paradise; **es un ~** it's a garden of Eden, it's an earthly paradise.
edible ADJ (*LAm*) edible.
edición NF **(a)** (*acto*) publication, issue; (*industria*) publishing; (*Inform*) editing; **~ en pantalla** on-line editing; **~ de sobremesa** desktop publishing; **el mundo de la ~** the publishing world.
(b) (*libro etc: nueva versión*) edition; (*reimpresión*) reprint; **~ aérea** airmail edition; **~ de bolsillo** pocket edition; **~ económica** cheap edition, popular edition; **~ extraordinaria** special edition; late-night final; **~ de la mañana** morning edition; **~ numerada** numbered edition; **~ príncipe** first edition; **~ semanal** weekly edition; **~ viva** edition in print, available edition; **en ~ de** edited by; **'al cerrar la ~'** 'stop-press'; **ser la segunda ~ de uno** to be the very image of sb.
(c) **Ediciones Ramírez** (*Com*) Ramírez Publications.
(d) (*fig*) event, occasion; **es la tercera ~ de este festival** this is the third occasion on which this festival has been held.
edicto NM edict, proclamation.
edificabilidad NF suitability for building; development potential.
edificable ADJ: **terreno ~** building land, land available for building.
edificación NF **(a)** (*Arquit*) construction, building. **(b)** (*fig*) edification.
edificante ADJ edifying; improving; uplifting, ennobling; **una escena poco ~** an unedifying spectacle.

edificar [1g] VT **(a)** (*Arquit*) to build, construct. **(b)** (*fig*) to edify; to improve; to uplift, ennoble.

edificio NM building; edifice; (*fig*) edifice, structure; **~ de apartamentos** block of flats; **~ inteligente** smart building, intelligent building; **~ de oficinas** office block.

edil NMF (*España: alcalde*) mayor; (*concejal*) town councillor; (*dignatario*) civic dignitary; (*Hist*) aedile.

Edimburgo NM Edinburgh.

Edipo NM Oedipus.

editable ADJ editable.

editaje NM editing.

editar [1a] VT **(a)** (*publicar*) to publish. **(b)** (*corregir*) to edit, correct. **(c)** *texto* to edit (*t Inform*).

editor 1 ADJ publishing (*atr*); **casa ~a** publishing house.
  2 NM, **editora** NF **(a)** (*de libros, periódicos etc*) publisher. **(b)** (*redactor*) editor, compiler; (*TV*) editor. **(c)** (*LAm: de periódico*) newspaper editor.
  3 NM (*Inform*): **~ de pantalla** screen editor; **~ de texto** text editor.

editorial 1 ADJ **(a)** publishing (*atr*); **casa ~** publishing house. **(b)** *función, política etc* editorial.
  2 NM leading article, editorial.
  3 NF publishing house.

editorialista NMF leader-writer.

editorializar [1f] VI to write editorials; **el periódico editorializa contra ...** the paper argues editorially against ...; **el diario editorializa ...** the paper says in its editorial ...

Edo. (*Méx*) ABR *de* Estado.

edredón NM eiderdown; feather pillow; duvet.

Eduardo NM Edward.

educabilidad NF educability.

educable ADJ educable, teachable.

educación NF **(a)** (*gen*) education; training; upbringing; **~ de adultos** adult education; **~ compensatoria** remedial teaching; **~ especial** special education; **~ física** physical education; **~ preescolar** pre-school education, nursery education; **~ primaria** primary education; **~ sanitaria** health education; **~ sexual** sex education; **~ de la voz** elocution lessons, voice training.
  (b) (*modales*) (good) manners, (good) breeding; (*cortesía*) politeness, civility; **falta ~, mala ~** bad manners, incivility; **es de mala ~ escupir** it's bad manners to spit, it's ill-mannered to spit; **es de mala ~ comportarse así** it's rude to behave like that; **es una persona sin ~** he's a badly-bred person, he's an ill-mannered individual; **¡qué falta de ~!** how rude!; **¡habla con más ~!** don't be so rude!, be more civil!; **no tener ~** to lack breeding, lack good manners.
  (c) (**Ministerio de**) **E~** (**y Ciencia**) Ministry of Education (and Science).

educacional ADJ educational.

educacionista NMF education(al)ist.

educado ADJ (*de buenos modales*) well-mannered, polite; nicely behaved; (*culto*) cultivated, cultured; **mal ~** ill-mannered, unmannerly; rude.

educador(a) NM/F educator, teacher.

educando, -a NM/F pupil.

educar [1g] VT (*gen*) to educate; (*entrenar*) to train; (*hijos*) to raise, bring up; *voz* to train.

educativo ADJ educative; educational; **política educativa** education(al) policy.

edulcoración NF (*Farm*) sweetening.

edulcorante NM sweetener.

edulcorar [1a] VT (*Farm*) to sweeten.

EE ABR *de* **Euskadiko Ezkerra** *Basque political party.*

EEB NF ABR *de* encefalopatía espongiforme bovina bovine spongiform encephalopathy, BSE.

EE.UU. NMPL ABR *de* Estados Unidos MPL United States, US, USA.

efectismo NM straining after effect; sensationalism.

efectista 1 ADJ strained; sensational.
  2 NMF strainer after effect; sensationalist.

efectivamente ADV really; in fact; (*como respuesta*) exactly, precisely, just so; sure enough.

efectividad NF effectiveness.

efectivo 1 ADJ **(a)** (*eficaz*) effective; **hacer algo ~** to make sth effective, carry sth out; to put sth into effect; **hacer ~ un cheque** to cash a cheque.
  (b) (*verdadero*) actual, real; **el poder ~ está en manos de X** the real power is in X's hands.
  (c) *empleo* regular, permanent, established.
  2 NM **(a)** cash; specie; **con 50 libras en ~** with £50 in cash; **y 3 premios en ~** and 3 cash prizes; **~ en caja, ~ en existencia** cash in hand.
  (b) **~s** (*Mil etc*) forces, troops; establishment.

efecto NM **(a)** (*consecuencia*) effect; **~ bumerán** boomerang effect; **~ dominó** domino effect; **~ embudo** funnel effect; **~s especiales** spe-

cial effects; **~ (de) invernadero** greenhouse effect; **~ secundario** side effect; **~s sonoros** sound effects; **~ útil** (*Mec*) efficiency, output; **~ visuales** (*TV*) visual effects; **hacer ~** (*medicina*) to take effect; **hacer ~, surtir ~** to have the desired effect; to work; to tell (*en on*); (*idea etc*) to get across, have an impact; **llevar a ~, poner en ~** to put into effect, carry out; **tener ~** (*entrar en vigor*) to take effect; (*suceso etc*) to take place; **en ~** in effect; in fact, really; (*como respuesta*) yes indeed, precisely.
  (b) (*resultado*) result; **tener por ~** to have as a result (*o* consequence).
  (c) (*finalidad*) purpose, end; **a este ~, a estos ~s, a tal ~** to this end; **a cuyo ~** to which end; **a mis ~s** for my purposes; **a ~s fiscales** for tax purposes; **a ~s policiales** so far as the police are concerned; **a ~s de máxima seguridad** in order to ensure the tightest security; **al ~ de que** + *subj* in order that ...; **a ~s de** + *infin* with a view to + *ger*, with the object of + *ger*; **construido al ~** (specially) built for the purpose.
  (d) (*impresión*) effect, impression, impact; **hacer ~** to make an impression; **me hace el ~ de que ...** it gives me the impression that ...
  (e) (*de pelota*) spin; **dar ~ a una pelota** to put some spin on a ball; **lanzar una pelota con ~** to throw a ball so that it spins (*o* swerves).
  (f) **~s** bills, securities; **~s bancarios** bankable bills; **~s a cobrar** bills receivable; **~s descontados** bills discounted; **~s a pagar** bills payable.
  (g) (*bienes*) **~s** effects, goods; things; (*Fin*) assets; (*Com*) goods, articles, merchandise; **~s de consumo** consumer goods; **~s de escritorio** writing materials; **~s personales** personal effects.

efectuación NF accomplishment; bringing about.

efectuar [1e] VT to effect, carry out, bring about; *plan, reparación* to carry out; *mejoría, parada, visita, gira, baza etc* to make; *censo* to take.

efeméride NF event (remembered on its anniversary); **~s** (*en periódico*) list of the day's anniversaries; (*título*) *equivalente a* '50 years (*etc*) ago today'.

efervescencia NF **(a)** effervescence; fizziness; **entrar en ~, estar en ~** to effervesce. **(b)** (*fig*) (*alboroto*) commotion, agitation; (*alegría*) high spirits, effervescence.

efervescente ADJ **(a)** (*gen*) effervescent; (*gaseoso*) fizzy, bubbly. **(b)** (*fig*) effervescent; high-spirited, bubbling.

eficacia NF **(a)** (*fuerza*) efficacy, effectiveness. **(b)** (*eficiencia*) efficiency.

eficaz ADJ **(a)** (*efectivo*) efficacious, effective. **(b)** (*eficiente*) efficient.

eficazmente ADV **(a)** (*con efecto*) efficaciously, effectively; tellingly. **(b)** (*eficientemente*) efficiently.

eficiencia NF efficiency.

eficiente ADJ efficient.

eficientemente ADV efficiently.

efigie NF effigy.

efímera NF mayfly.

efímero ADJ ephemeral, fleeting, short-lived.

eflorescente ADJ efflorescent.

efluvio NM (*emanación*) outpour, outflow; **tiene un ~ de simpatía** (*fig*) there's something nice about him.

efugio NM subterfuge, evasion.

efusión NF **(a)** (*derramamiento*) outpouring; shedding; **~ de sangre** bloodshed, shedding of blood.
  (b) (*fig*) (*acto*) effusion, outpouring; (*cualidad*) warmth, effusiveness; (*pey*) gush, gushing manner; **con ~** effusively; **efusiones amorosas** amorous excesses.

efusividad NF effusiveness.

efusivo ADJ effusive; *gracias* effusive, warm; *manera* effusive, (*pey*) gushing; **mis más efusivas gracias** my warmest thanks.

EGB NF ABR *de* **Educación General Básica** (*from age 6 to 14*).

┌─ EGB ───

ⓘ *Spanish schoolchildren between the ages of 6 and 14 studied EGB (Educación General Básica). Children started the primer ciclo when they were 6 and moved on to the segundo ciclo at 11, to complete it at around 14. Anyone wanting to stay on at school after this needed to obtain the school leaving certificate Graduado Escolar. Now children start EP (Educación Primaria) at 6 and move onto ESO (Educación Secundaria Obligatoria) at 12.*

⇨ *See also* EP - EDUCACIÓN PRIMARIA , ESO

Egeo NM: **el (Mar) ~** the Aegean Sea.

égida NF aegis, protection; **bajo la ~ de** under the aegis of.

egipcio, -a ADJ, NM/F Egyptian.

Egipto NM Egypt.

egiptología NF Egyptology.

eglantina NF eglantine.

eglefino NM haddock.

égloga NF eclogue.

ego NM ego.

egocéntrico ADJ egocentric, self-centred.

egocentrismo NM egocentrism.

egocentrista NMF egocentric, self-centred person.

egoísmo NM egoism; selfishness.

egoísta [1] ADJ egoistical; selfish.

[2] NMF egoist, selfish person.

egoístamente ADV egoistically; selfishly.

egoistón* ADJ rather selfish.

ególatra [1] ADJ egotistical.

[2] NMF egotist.

egolatría NF egotism.

egotismo NM egotism.

egotista [1] ADJ egotistic(al).

[2] NMF egotist.

egregio ADJ eminent, distinguished.

egresado, -a NM/F (*LAm*) graduate.

egresar [1a] VI (*LAm*) (a) (*irse*) to go out, go away, leave; **~ de** to go away from, leave; to emerge from. (b) (*Univ*) to graduate, take one's degree.

egreso NM (*LAm*) (a) (*acto*) departure, leaving, going away. (b) (*salida*) exit. (c) (*Univ*) graduation. (d) (*Fin*) outgoings, expenditure.

eh INTERJ hey!, hi!; I say!

eider NM eider, eider duck.

Eire NM Eire.

ej. ABR *de* **ejemplo** example, ex.

eje NM (a) (*Geog, Mat*) axis; **partir a uno por el ~*** to muck up sb's plans*; to cause a lot of trouble for sb; to do a mischief.

(b) (*Mec: de rueda*) axle; **~ delantero** front axle; **~ trasero** rear axle.

(c) (*Mec: de máquina*) shaft, spindle; **~ de balancín** rocker shaft; **~ del cigüeñal** crankshaft; **~ de la hélice** propeller shaft; **~ de impulsión, ~ motor** drive shaft.

(d) (*Pol*) axis; **las fuerzas del E~** the Axis forces.

(e) (*fig*) (*centro*) hinge, hub; (*núcleo*) essential part, crux, core; (*idea*) central idea, main idea.

(f) **~ vial** (*Méx Aut*) urban motorway.

ejecución NF (a) (*gen*) execution, performance, carrying out; fulfilment; enforcement; **poner en ~** to carry out, carry into effect.

(b) (*Jur*) attachment, distraint.

(c) (*Mús*) performance, rendition.

(d) (*muerte*) execution; **~ sumaria** summary execution.

ejecutable ADJ feasible, practicable; **legalmente ~** legally enforceable.

ejecutante [1] NMF (*Mús*) performer.

[2] NM (*Jur*) distrainer.

ejecutar [1a] VT (a) *orden etc* to execute, carry out; *deseos* to perform, fulfil; *hecho* to execute.

(b) (*Jur*) to attach, distrain on.

(c) (*Mús*) to perform, render, play.

(d) (*matar*) to execute.

(e) (*Inform*) to run.

ejecutiva¹ NF (*Pol etc*) executive (body); executive committee.

ejecutivo [1] ADJ (a) *función, poder* executive.

(b) *demanda etc* pressing, insistent; *negocio* urgent, immediate.

[2] NM, **ejecutiva²** NF (*Com*) executive; **~ de cuentas** account executive; **~ de ventas** sales executive.

[3] NM (*Pol*) **el E~** the Executive.

ejecutor NM (*t ~ testamentario*) executor.

ejecutoria NF (a) (*diploma*) letters patent of nobility; (*fig*) pedigree.

(b) (*Jur*) final judgement.

ejem INTERJ hem! (*cough*).

ejemplar [1] ADJ exemplary; model.

[2] NM (a) (*ejemplo*) example; (*Zool etc*) specimen, example; (*de libro*) copy; (*de revista*) number, issue; **~ de firma** specimen signature; **~ gratuito** free copy; **~ obsequio, ~ de regalo** complimentary copy.

(b) (*precedente*) example, model, precedent; **sin ~** unprecedented.

ejemplaridad NF exemplariness.

ejemplarizador ADJ, **ejemplarizante** ADJ exemplary; warning, intended to serve as a warning.

ejemplarizar [1f] VT (*esp LAm*) to set an example to; to exemplify, demonstrate by example, set an example of.

ejemplarmente ADV *actuar* in exemplary fashion; **castigar ~ a uno** to make an example of sb.

ejemplificar [1g] VT to exemplify, illustrate, be illustrative of.

▼ **ejemplo** NM (*gen*) example, instance; (*lección*) object lesson; (*precedente*) precedent, parallel; **por ~** for example, for instance; **sin ~** unprecedented, unparalleled; **dar ~** to set an example; **tomar algo por ~** to take sth as an example.

ejercer [2b] [1] VT (*gen*) to exercise; *influencia* to exert, use, bring to bear; *poder* to exercise, wield; *profesión* to practise; *negocio etc* to manage, conduct, run; *función* to perform.

[2] VI to practise (*de as*); to be in office, hold office.

ejercicio NM (a) (*gen*) exercise; (*práctica*) practice, drill; (*Mil*) exercise, drill, training; (*Escol*) exercise, test; **~ acrobático** (*Aer*) stunt; **~ anti-**

aéreo air-raid drill; **~ de calentamiento** warm-up exercise; **~ de castigo** (*Escol*) imposition; **~ de comprensión lectora** reading comprehension test; **~ de defensa contra incendios** fire-drill; **~s espirituales** (*Rel*) retreat; **~s gimnásticos** gymnastic exercises; **~ práctico** (*examen*) practical; **~ de tiro** target practice; **hacer ~s** to do exercises; to take exercise; (*Mil*) to drill, train.

(b) (*de cargo*) tenure; **abogado en ~** practising lawyer.

(c) (*Com, Fin*) fiscal year; financial year; business year; **~ fiscal** tax year; **durante el ~ actual** during the current financial year.

ejerciente ADJ practising.

ejercitación NF (*de la mente, los músculos*) exercising; (*de un idioma*) practice.

ejercitar [1a] [1] VT to exercise; *profesión* to practise; *tropas* to drill, train.

[2] **ejercitarse** VR to exercise; to practise; (*Mil*) to drill, train.

ejército NM army; **miembros de los 3 ~s** members of the forces (*o* Services); **~ de ocupación** army of occupation; **~ permanente** standing army; **E~ de Salvación** Salvation Army; **E~ de Tierra** Army; **estar en el ~** to be in the army.

ejidal ADJ (*Méx*) communal land (*atr*); *terreno* communal.

ejidatario, -a NM/F (*Méx*) holder of a share in communal lands.

ejido NM ≃ common, communal land.

-ejo, -eja V Aspects of Word Formation in Spanish 2.

ejote NM (*CAm, Méx*) string bean.

el¹ ART DEF M, **la** F the; *no se traduce en los casos siguientes* **La India** India; **en el México de hoy** in present-day Mexico; **me gusta el fútbol** I like football; **está en la cárcel** he's in jail; **el General Prim** General Prim; **¿qué manda la señora?** what would madam like?; **a las ocho** at eight o'clock; **a los quince días** after a fortnight; **el tío ese** that chap; **el hacerlo fue un error** doing it was a mistake, it was a mistake to do it.

el² PRON DEM **mi libro y ~ de Vd** my book and yours; **este jugador y ~ de la camisa azul** this player and the one in the blue shirt; **~ de Pepe es mejor** Joe's is better; **y ~ de todos los demás** and that of everybody else, and everybody else's.

el³: ~ que PRON REL (*t* **la que, los que, las que**) he who, whoever; the one(s) that; **el que quiera, que lo haga** whoever wants to can get on with it; **los que hacen eso son tontos** those who do so are foolish; **el que compramos no vale** the one we bought is no good; **a los que mencionamos añádase éste** add this one to those we mentioned.

él PRON PERS M (a) (*sujeto: persona*) he; (*cosa*) it.

(b) (*tras prep: persona*) him; (*cosa*) it; **esto es para ~** this is for him; **vamos sin ~** let's go without him.

(c) (*tras de: persona*) his; (*cosa*) its; **mis libros y los de ~** my books and his; **todo eso es de ~** all that is his, all that belongs to him.

elaboración NF elaboration; manufacture, production; working; **~ de presupuestos** (*Com*) budgeting.

elaborar [1a] VT *materia prima* to elaborate; *producto* to make, manufacture, produce; to prepare; *metal, madera etc* to work; *plan etc* to work on, work out.

elación NF (a) (*orgullo*) haughtiness, pride. (b) (*generosidad*) generosity. (c) (*de estilo*) pomposity. (d) (*LAm: alegría*) elation.

elasticidad NF (a) (*gen*) elasticity; spring, sponginess; give. (b) (*fig*) elasticity; (*moral*) resilience.

elástico [1] ADJ (a) (*gen*) elastic; flexible; *superficie etc* springy. (b) (*fig*) elastic; (*moralmente*) resilient.

[2] NM elastic.

ELE, E/LE ['ele] NM ABR *de* **español como lengua extranjera** Spanish as a foreign language.

elección NF (a) (*selección*) choice, selection; (*opción*) option; **una ~ acertada** a sensible choice; **su patria de ~** his chosen country; **no queda otra ~** there is no alternative.

(b) (*Pol etc*) election (*a* for); **elecciones autonómicas** regional election; **~ complementaria, elecciones parciales** by-election; **elecciones generales** general election; **elecciones legislativas** parliamentary election; **elecciones municipales** council elections; **elecciones primarias** primary election.

eleccionario ADJ (*LAm*) electoral, election (*atr*).

electivo ADJ elective.

electo ADJ elect; **el presidente ~** the president-elect.

elector(a) NM/F elector; voter.

electorado NM electorate; voters.

electoral ADJ electoral; **potencia ~** voting power, power in terms of votes.

electoralismo NM electioneering; vote-catching.

electoralista ADJ electioneering (*atr*); vote-catching (*atr*).

electoralmente ADV electorally; in terms of winning votes.

electorista ADJ election (*atr*).

eléctrica NF electricity company.

electricidad NF electricity; **~ estática** static electricity.

electricista NMF electrician.

eléctrico ADJ electric; electrical.

| ELÉCTRICO | ver también la entrada |

¿"Electric" o "electrical"?

- El adjetivo *eléctrico* se traduce por *electric* cuando nos referimos a un aparato en particular o a la luz eléctrica:
  Siempre duermo con una manta eléctrica
  I always sleep with an electric blanket
  ...una estufa eléctrica...
  ...an electric heater...
  ...la invención de la luz eléctrica...
  ...the invention of electric light...
- En cambio, si hablamos de aparatos eléctricos en general o de la electricidad generada por un organismo vivo, se traduce por *electrical*:
  ...aparatos eléctricos...
  ...electrical appliances...
  ...componentes eléctricos...
  ...electrical components...
  ...la actividad eléctrica en el cerebro...
  ...electrical activity in the brain...
  Eso ha ocurrido a consecuencia de un fallo eléctrico
  That was caused by an electrical fault

---

electrificación NF electrification.
electrificar [1g] VT to electrify.
electrizante ADJ electrifying (*t fig*).
electrizar [1f] VT to electrify (*t fig*); **su discurso electrizó al público** his speech electrified his listeners.
electro... PREF electro...
electrocardiograma NM electrocardiogram.
electrochapado ADJ electroplated.
electrochoque NM electroshock.
electroconvulsivo ADJ electroconvulsive.
electrocución NF electrocution.
electrocutar [1a] VT to electrocute.
electrodinámica NF electrodynamics.
electrodo NM, **eléctrodo** NM electrode.
electrodoméstico [1] ADJ: **aparato ~ = 2.**
  [2] NM (home electrical) appliance; **~s de línea blanca** white goods.
electroencefalograma NM electroencephalogram.
electroimán NM electromagnet.
electrólisis NF electrolysis.
electromagnético ADJ electromagnetic.
electromagnetismo NM electromagnetism.
electromotor NM electric motor.
electrón NM electron.
electrónica NF electronics; **~ de consumo** consumer electronics; **~ de precisión** precision electronics.
electrónico ADJ electronic; *microscopio* electron (*atr*).
electronuclear ADJ: **central ~** nuclear power station; **programa ~** nuclear power programme.
electroshock NM = **electrochoque**.
electrotecnia NF electrical engineering.
electrotécnico, -a NM/F electrical engineer.
electrotermo NM immersion heater.
electrotren NM express electric train.
elefante NM, **elefanta** NF elephant; **~ blanco** white elephant; **como un ~ en una cacharrería** like a bull in a china shop.
elefantino ADJ elephantine.
elegancia NF elegance; gracefulness; stylishness, smartness; tastefulness; polish.
elegante ADJ (*gen*) elegant; graceful; *vestido, fiesta, tienda etc* stylish, fashionable, smart; *sociedad* fashionable, elegant; *decoración etc* tasteful; *frase etc* elegant, well-turned, polished; **no es ~ gritar** it's rude to shout, it's not dignified to shout.
elegantemente ADV elegantly; gracefully; stylishly, fashionably, smartly; tastefully; in a polished way.
elegantoso ADJ (*LAm*) = **elegante**.
elegía NF elegy.
elegiaco ADJ, **elegíaco** ADJ elegiac.
elegibilidad NF eligibility.
elegible ADJ eligible.
elegido ADJ (a) (*selecto*) chosen, selected. (b) (*Pol etc*) elect, elected.
elegir [3c y 3k] VT (a) (*escoger*) to choose, select; to opt for; **café con bizcochos a ~** coffee with a choice of cakes; **a ~ entre 5 tipos** there are 5 sorts to choose from; **hablará en francés o italiano, a ~** he will talk in French or Italian, as you (*etc*) prefer; **te toca a ti ~** the choice is yours, it's up to you to choose.
  (b) (*Pol etc*) to elect.
elementado ADJ (*And, Cono Sur: aturdido*) bewildered; (*bobo*) silly, stupid.

elemental ADJ elementary; elemental, fundamental; **eso es ~** that's elementary.
elementarse [1a] VR (*Cono Sur*) to get bewildered.
elemento NM (a) (*gen*) element; **los cuatro ~s** the four elements; **estar en su ~** to be in one's element.
  (b) (*Quím etc*) element; (*fig*) ingredient, constituent (part); (*de situación*) element, factor; **~s** material, ingredients; **~s de juicio** data, facts (on which to base a judgement).
  (c) (*Elec*) element; (*de pila*) cell.
  (d) (*persona*) person, individual; (*LAm*: *tipo*) chap*, guy* (*US*); **vino a verle un ~** someone came to see you; **dos ~s distinguidos** two distinguished individuals.
  (e) (*And, Carib, Cono Sur: imbécil*) dimwit*, ass*.
  (f) (*Carib: tipo raro*) odd person, eccentric.
  (g) (*Esp pey*) undesirable (person), suspicious individual.
  (h) **~s** (*de una materia*) elements, rudiments, first principles.
Elena NF Helen.
elenco NM (*lista*) catalogue, list; (*And, Cono Sur: personal*) staff, team; (*esp LAm Cine, Teat*) cast.
elepé NM long-playing record.
elevación NF (a) (*acto*) elevation (*a* to), raising, lifting; (*Ecl*) elevation; (*de precio, tipo etc*) rise.
  (b) (*Geog etc*) elevation, height, altitude.
  (c) (*de estilo, mente etc*) elevation; (*de persona*) exaltation, loftiness; (*pey*) conceit, pride.
  (d) (*éxtasis*) rapture.
elevadamente ADV loftily, sublimely.
elevado [1] ADJ (a) (*alto*) elevated, raised; high, lofty; *edificio* high, tall; *precio, tipo etc* high; *puesto* exalted, high; **a precios elevadísimos** at terribly high prices.
  (b) *estilo, pensamiento etc* elevated, lofty, noble; grand, sublime; **de pensamientos ~s** of noble thoughts, high-minded.
  [2] NM (*Carib Ferro*) overhead railway; (*Carib Aut*) flyover.
elevador NM elevator, hoist; (*LAm: ascensor*) lift, elevator (*US*); **~ de granos** (grain) elevator; **~ de tensión, ~ de voltaje** (*Elec*) booster.
elevadorista NMF (*Méx*) lift operator.
elevalunas NM INVAR (*Aut*) electric windows.
elevar [1a] [1] VT (a) (*alzar*) to raise, lift (up), elevate; *precio, tipo* to raise, put up; *producción* to step up; (*Elec*) to boost; (*Mat*) to raise (*a una potencia* to a power); *persona* to promote; to exalt; *estilo* to raise the tone of; **~ los pensamientos a Dios** to raise one's thoughts to God.
  (b) *informe etc* to present, submit (*a* to); **el comité elevará un informe al ministro** the committee will report to the minister.
  [2] **elevarse** VR (a) (*alzarse*) to rise, go up; (*edificio etc*) to rise, soar, tower; **la cantidad se eleva a ...** the quantity amounts to ...; **los precios se han elevado mucho** prices have risen a lot.
  (b) (*extasiarse*) to be transported, go into a rapture.
  (c) (*pey*) to get conceited, become overbearing.
Elías NM Elijah.
elidir [3a] [1] VT to elide.
  [2] **elidirse** VR to elide, be elided.
elija *etc* V **elegir**.
eliminable ADJ dispensable.
eliminación NF elimination; removal; (*Dep: t ~ progresiva*) knockout.
eliminar [1a] [1] VT (*gen*) to eliminate; to remove; *necesidad etc* to remove, obviate; *residuos* to get rid of; (*Dep*) to eliminate, knock out; (*matar*) to eliminate, do away with.
  [2] **eliminarse** VR (a) (*Dep*) to play an eliminating round. (b) (*Méx*) to go away.
eliminatoria NF (*Dep: vuelta*) heat, preliminary round, qualifying round; (*competición*) knockout competition.
elipse NF (*Mat*) ellipse.
elipsis NF INVAR (*Ling*) ellipsis.
elíptico ADJ elliptic(al).
Elíseo[1] NM (*Biblia*) Elishah.
Elíseo[2] NM (*clásico*) Elysium.
elisión NF elision.
elite [e'lite] NF, **élite** ['elite] NF élite.
elitismo NM elitism.
elitista ADJ, NMF elitist.
elixir NM elixir; **~ de la (eterna) juventud** elixir of life.
ella PRON PERS F (a) (*sujeto: persona*) she; (*cosa*) it.
  (b) (*tras prep: persona*) her; (*cosa*) it; **estuve con ~** I was with her; **no podemos sin ~** without her we can't.
  (c) (*tras de: persona*) hers; (*cosa*) its; **mi sombrero y el de ~** my hat and hers; **nada de esto es de ~** none of this is hers, none of this belongs to her.
ellas V **ellos**.
ello PRON *'neutro'* (a) (*gen*) it; this business, that whole affair; **~ es difícil** it's awkward; **~ no me gusta** I don't like it; **todo ~ se acabó**

the whole thing is over and done with; **no tiene fuerzas para ~** he is not strong enough for it.

(b) (*locuciones*) **~ es que ...** the fact is that ...; **por ~ no quiero** that's why I don't want to; **es por ~ que ...** (*LAm*) that is why ...; **luego será ~** there'll be trouble later; **~ dirá** the event will show; **¡a por ~!** here goes!; **¡aquí fue ~!** and then it started, and that was it.

(c) (*Psic*) id.

ellos PRON PERS MPL, **ellas** PRON PERS FPL **(a)** (*sujeto*) they. **(b)** (*tras prep*) them. **(c)** (*tras de*) theirs; V **él, ella.**

ELN NM (*Bolivia, Colombia*) ABR *de* **Ejército de Liberación Nacional.**

elocución NF elocution.

elocuencia NF eloquence.

elocuente ADJ eloquent; (*fig*) telling; significant; **un dato ~** a significant fact, a fact which speaks for itself.

elocuentemente ADV eloquently.

elogiable ADJ praiseworthy.

elogiar [1b] VT to praise, eulogize (*liter*).

elogio NM praise, eulogy; tribute; **queda por encima de todo ~** it's beyond praise; **hacer ~ de** to praise, extol; to pay (a) tribute to; **hizo un caluroso ~ del héroe** he paid a warm tribute to the hero, he was warm in his praise of the hero.

elogiosamente ADV eulogistically; very favourably, with warm approval; **comentó ~ sus cualidades** he spoke very favourably of his qualities.

elogioso ADJ eulogistic; highly favourable, warmly approving; **en términos ~s** in highly favourable terms.

elotada NF (*CAm, Méx*) (*Agr*) ears of maize (*collectively*).

elote NM (*CAm, Méx*) (*mazorca*) corncob; (*maíz*) maize, corn (*US*), sweet corn; **coger a uno asando ~s** to catch sb red-handed; **pagar los ~s*** to carry the can*.

elotear [1a] VI (*CAm, Méx: maíz*) to come into ear.

El Salvador NM El Salvador.

elucidación NF elucidation.

elucidar [1a] VT to elucidate.

elucubración NF lucubration.

elucubrar [1a] VI to lucubrate.

eludible ADJ avoidable.

eludir [3a] VT to elude, evade, avoid, escape.

elusivo ADJ (*LAm*) evasive, tricky.

E.M. ABR *de* **Estado Mayor** General Staff, GS.

Em.ª ABR *de* **Eminencia** Eminence.

emanación NF emanation; (*olor*) smell.

emanar [1a] VI: **~ de** to emanate from, come from, originate in.

emancipación NF emancipation; freeing.

emancipado ADJ emancipated; independent, free.

emancipar [1a] ① VT to emancipate; to free. ② **emanciparse** VR to become emancipated (*de* from); to become independent (*de* of); to free o.s. (*de* from).

emascular [1a] VT to castrate, emasculate.

embadurnar [1a] VT to daub, bedaub, smear (*de* with).

embaidor NM cheat, swindler.

embaimiento NM imposture, trick, swindle; deceit.

embaír [3a: *defectivo*] VT to swindle, cheat.

embajada NF **(a)** (*edificio*) embassy. **(b)** (*cargo*) ambassadorship. **(c)** (*fig*) errand, message. **(d)** (*pey*) unwelcome proposal, silly suggestion.

embajador NM ambassador (*en* in, *cerca de* to); **~ itinerante, ~ volante** roving ambassador, ambassador at large; **~ político** politically-appointed ambassador.

embajadora NF (*oficial*) (woman) ambassador; (*esposa*) ambassador's wife.

embajatorio ADJ ambassadorial.

embalado ① ADJ (‡) **(a)** (*sexualmente*) randy*. **(b)** (*Carib*: drogado*) high‡. ② NM packing, packaging.

embalador(a) NM/F packer.

embaladura NF (*LAm*), **embalaje** NM packing.

embalar [1a] ① VT to pack, parcel up, wrap; *mercancías pesadas* to crate, bale. ② VI **(a)** (*Dep*) to sprint, make a dash; (*Aut*) to step on it*. **(b)** (*Carib: huir*) to run off, escape. ③ **embalarse** VR **(a)** (*correr*) to rush off; to go hell for leather; (*Aut*) to race along; (*hablar*) to talk nineteen to the dozen; **el orador estaba embalándose** the speaker was in full flow. **(b)** (*: *ponerse cachondo*) to get randy*.

embaldosado NM tiled floor, tiling.

embaldosar [1a] VT to tile, pave with tiles.

embalsadero NM boggy place.

embalsado NM (*Cono Sur*) mass of floating water weeds.

embalsamar [1a] VT to embalm.

embalsar [1a] ① VT **(a)** *agua* to dam, dam up; to retain, collect; **este mes se han embalsado X m³** this month reservoir stocks have gone up by X cubic metres.

(b) (*Náut*) to sling, hoist. ② VI (*And: cruzar*) to cross a river (*etc*).

embalse NM **(a)** (*acto*) damming. **(b)** (*presa*) dam; (*lago*) reservoir.

embanastar [1a] VT to put into a basket; (*fig*) to jam in, overcrowd.

embancarse [1g] VR (*And, Cono Sur*) to silt up, become blocked by silt.

embanderar [1a] VT to deck with flags; **embanderado** beflagged, decked with flags.

embanquetado NM (*LAm*) pavement(s), sidewalk(s) (*US*).

embanquetar [1a] VT (*LAm*) to provide with pavements o sidewalks (*US*).

embarazada ① ADJ pregnant; **dejar ~ a una** to get a girl pregnant, put a girl in the family way; **estar ~ de 4 meses** to be 4 months pregnant. ② NF pregnant woman, expectant mother.

embarazar [1f] VT **(a)** (*estorbar*) to obstruct, hamper, hinder. **(b)** *mujer* to make pregnant, put in the family way.

embarazo NM **(a)** (*estorbo*) obstacle, obstruction, hindrance. **(b)** (*de mujer*) pregnancy; **~ no deseado, ~ involuntario** unwanted pregnancy; **~ nervioso** phantom pregnancy; **durante el ~** during pregnancy; **interrumpir el ~** to terminate a pregnancy.

embarazosamente ADV awkwardly, inconveniently; embarrassingly.

embarazoso ADJ (*molesto*) awkward, inconvenient, troublesome; (*violento*) embarrassing.

embarcación NF **(a)** (*barco*) boat, craft, (small) vessel; **~ de arrastre** trawler; **~ auxiliar** tender; **~ de cabotaje** coasting vessel; **~ fueraborda** motorboat; **~ pesquera** fishing boat; **~ de recreo** pleasure boat; **~ de vela** sailing boat. **(b)** (*acto*) embarkation.

embarcadero NM **(a)** pier, landing stage, jetty. **(b)** (*LAm Ferro*) goods station; (*andén*) platform; (*corral*) cattle pen (attached to a railway station).

embarcar [1g] ① VT **(a)** *personas* to embark, put on board; *carga* to ship, get on board, stow. **(b)** **~ a uno en una empresa** to involve sb in an enterprise. **(c)** (*LAm**) **~ a uno** to set sb up*. **(d)** (*Carib*: engañar*) to con*. ② **embarcarse** VR **(a)** (*pasajero*) to embark, go on board; (*marinero*) to sign on, join a ship; **~ para** to sail for. **(b)** (*LAm Ferro etc*) to get on, get in; **se embarcó en el autobús** he got on the bus, he boarded the bus. **(c)** **~ en un asunto** to get involved in a matter.

embarco NM embarcation.

embargar [1h] VT **(a)** (*estorbar*) to impede, hinder; (*frenar*) to restrain, put a check on. **(b)** *sentidos* to blunt, confuse, paralyse, overpower. **(c)** (*Jur*) to seize, impound, distrain upon.

▼ **embargo** NM **(a)** (*Jur*) seizure, distraint; (*Com etc*) embargo; **sin ~** still, however, none the less; **sin ~ de** despite the fact that. **(b)** (*Med*) indigestion.

embarnizar [1f] VT to varnish.

embarque NM **(a)** embarkation; shipment, loading. **(b)** (*Carib**) melodrama; emotional affair.

embarrada* NF (*LAm*) blunder.

embarrado ADJ *calle etc* muddy.

embarradura NF smear, daub.

embarrancamiento NM running aground; beaching, stranding.

embarrancar [1g] ① VTI **(a)** (*Náut*) to run aground. **(b)** (*Aut etc*) to run into a ditch. ② **embarrancarse** VR **(a)** (*Náut*) to run aground; **quedar embarrancado** (*ballena etc*) to be beached, be stranded. **(b)** (*Aut etc*) to run into a ditch; to get stuck; (*fig*) to get bogged down.

embarrar [1a] ① VT **(a)** (*manchar*) to smear, bedaub (*de* with); (*enfangar*) to splash with mud. **(b)** (*LAm*) *pared* to cover with mud; to plaster. **(c)** **~ a uno** (*CAm, Méx**) to set sb up*. **(d)** **~ a uno** (*Carib, Cono Sur*) to smear sb, damage sb's standing. ② VI (*Cono Sur*) to make a mess of things. ③ **embarrarse** VR (*Carib: niño*) to dirty o.s.

embarrialarse [1a] VR **(a)** (*CAm: enfangarse*) to get covered with mud. **(b)** (*CAm Aut*) to get stuck. **(c)** (*CAm, Carib*: enredarse*) to get o.s. in a mess.

embarullador ADJ bungling.

embarullar [1a] VT to bungle, mess up.

embastar [1a] VT to baste, stitch, tack.

embaste NM basting, stitching, tacking.

embate NM **(a)** (*Mil etc*) sudden attack; brunt of the attack. **(b)** (*de olas*) dashing, breaking, beating; violence. **(c)** **~s de la fortuna** (*fig*) blows of fate.

embaucador(a) NM/F (*estafador*) trickster, swindler; (*impostor*) impostor; (*farsante*) humbug.

embaucamiento NM swindle, swindling; humbug.

embaucar [1g] VT to trick, swindle; to fool, lead up the garden path.

embaular VT (a) to pack (into a trunk). (b) (*) *comida* to tuck away*, stuff o.s. with, guzzle; *bebida* to sink*, knock back*. (c) (*Carib*) to clean out.

embazar [1f] ⬚1 VT (a) (*teñir*) to dye brown.
(b) (*fig: pasmar*) to astound, amaze.
(c) (*fig: estorbar*) to hinder.
⬚2 VI to be dumbfounded, stand amazed.
⬚3 **embazarse** VR to get tired, get bored; to have had enough.

embebecer [2d] ⬚1 VT to fascinate.
⬚2 **embebecerse** VR to be fascinated, be lost in wonder; to be dumbfounded.

embebecimiento NM (a) (*fascinación*) absorption, fascination; (*encanto*) enchantment. (b) (*asombro*) astonishment, wonderment.

embeber [2a] ⬚1 VT (a) (*absorber*) to absorb, soak up; (*saturar*) to saturate, soak.
(b) (*Cos*) to take in, gather in.
(c) (*fig: absorber*) to imbibe; (*meter*) to insert, introduce (*en* into); (*abarcar*) to contain, incorporate, comprise.
⬚2 VI (*tela*) to shrink.
⬚3 **embeberse** VR (a) *lectura, tema etc* to be absorbed, become engrossed (*en* in); to be enraptured, be enchanted (*en* with).
(b) ~ **de** to imbibe, soak o.s. in, become well versed in.

embelecar [1g] VT to deceive, cheat.

embeleco NM, **embelequería** NF (*And, Carib, Cono Sur*) deceit, fraud.

embelequero ADJ (a) (*LAm: aspaventero*) given to making a great fuss, highly emotional. (b) (*And, Carib: tramposo*) shifty. (c) (*Carib: frívolo*) frivolous, silly.

embelesado ADJ spellbound, enraptured.

embelesador ADJ enchanting, entrancing.

embelesar [1a] ⬚1 VT to enchant, entrance, enrapture.
⬚2 **embelesarse** VR to be enchanted, be enraptured.

embeleso NM (a) (*encanto*) enchantment, rapture, delight. (b) (*en oración directa*) sweetheart, my love.

embellecedor NM (*Aut: tapacubos*) hubcap; (: *adorno*) trim; ~**es laterales** 'go-faster' stripes.

embellecer [2d] VT to embellish, beautify.

embellecimiento NM embellishment.

embestida NF (a) (*ataque*) assault, onrush, onslaught; (*de toro etc*) charge, rush. (b) (*fig*) importunate demand.

embestir [3k] ⬚1 VT (a) (*agredir*) to assault, attack, assail; (*lanzarse sobre*) to rush at (*o* upon); (*toro etc*) to charge; (*Aut*) to hit, collide with, crash into.
(b) ~ **a uno** (*fig*) to pester sb for a loan.
⬚2 VI to attack; to rush, charge; ~ **con**, ~ **contra** to rush upon; (*toro etc*) to charge down on.

embetunar [1a] VT *superficie* to tar (over), pitch; *zapatos* to black.

embicar [1g] VT (a) (*Cono Sur*) *barco* to head straight for land. (b) (*Carib*) to insert. (c) (*Méx*) to turn upside down, upturn.

embicharse [1a] VR (*Cono Sur*) to become wormy, get maggoty.

embiste NM (*Carib*) = **embestida**.

emblandecer [2d] ⬚1 VT to soften; (*fig*) to mollify.
⬚2 **emblandecerse** VR to soften, get soft; (*fig*) to relent.

emblanquecer [2d] ⬚1 VT to whiten; to bleach.
⬚2 **emblanquecerse** VR to whiten, turn white; to bleach.

emblema NM emblem.

emblemático ADJ emblematic.

embobamiento NM amazement; fascination.

embobar [1a] ⬚1 VT (*asombrar*) to amaze; (*fascinar*) to fascinate; **esa niña me emboba*** that girl is driving me crazy.
⬚2 **embobarse** VR to be amazed, stand agape (*con, de, en* at); to be fascinated (*con, de, en* by); **reírse embobado** to laugh like mad.

embobecer [2d] ⬚1 VT to make silly.
⬚2 **embobecerse** VR to get silly.

embocadura NF (a) narrow entrance; (*de río*) mouth; (*Náut*) passage, narrows.
(b) (*Mús*) mouthpiece; (*de cigarrillo etc*) tip; (*de freno*) bit.
(c) (*de vino*) taste, flavour.
(d) (*Teat*) proscenium arch.

embocar [1g] ⬚1 VT (a) ~ **algo** to put sth into sb's mouth; ~ **una cosa en un agujero** to insert sth into a hole; ~ **la comida** to cram one's food, wolf one's food; ~ **la pelota** (*Golf*) to hole the ball; (*Billar etc*) to pocket the ball, pot the ball.
(b) ~ **un negocio** to undertake a piece of business.
(c) ~ **algo a uno** (*fig*) to put one over on sb, hoax sb with sth; **le embocaron la especie** they got him to swallow the tale.
⬚2 VI (*Golf*) to hole out.

embochinchar [1a] VT (*LAm*) to throw into confusion, create chaos in.

emboinado ADJ wearing a beret.

embolado NM (a) bull with wooden balls on its horns. (b) (*Teat*) bit part, minor role. (c) (*: *truco*)) trick. (d) (*: *aprieto*) jam*, difficulty; **meter a uno en un** ~ to put sb in a difficult position, put sb in a tight spot.

embolador(a) NM/F (*And*) bootblack.

embolar [1a] VT (a) *cuernos* to tip with wooden balls. (b) (*And*) *zapatos* to black, shine. (c) (*CAm, Méx: emborrachar*) to make drunk.

embolia NF (*Med*) clot; embolism; ~ **cerebral** clot on the brain.

embolismar* [1a] VT to gossip about; to make mischief for.

embolismo NM (a) (*lío*) muddle, mess, confusion. (b) (*chismes*) gossip, backbiting. (c) (*engaño*) hoax, trick.

émbolo NM plunger; (*Mec*) piston.

embolsar [1a] VT, **embolsicar** (*LAm*) [1g] VT to pocket, put into one's pocket; *dinero, recaudación etc* to pocket, collect, take in; (*Billar*) to pot.

embolsillar [1a] VT: ~ **las manos** to put one's hands in one's pockets.

embonar [1a] VT (a) (*Carib, Cono Sur, Méx*) *tierra* to manure.
(b) (*fig*) to improve.
(c) (*Náut*) to sheathe; (*And, Méx*) *cuerda* to join (the ends of).
(d) **le embona el sombrero** (*And, Carib, Méx*) the hat suits him, the hat looks well on him.

emboque NM (a) tight passage, squeezing through. (b) (*) trick, hoax.

emboquillado ADJ *cigarrillo* tipped.

emboquillar [1a] VT (a) *cigarrillo* to tip. (b) (*Cono Sur Arquit*) to point, repoint.

emborrachar [1a] ⬚1 VT to intoxicate, make drunk; to get drunk.
⬚2 **emborracharse** VR to get drunk (*con, de* on).

emborrar [1a] VT (a) (*rellenar*) to stuff, pad, wad (*de* with). (b) (*) *comida* to cram, wolf.

emborrascarse [1g] VR (a) (*Met*) to get stormy. (b) (*fig*) to get cross, get worked up. (c) (*Com: negocio*) to fail, do badly. (d) (*CAm, Cono Sur, Méx: vena*) to peter out.

emborronar [1a] ⬚1 VT (*manchar*) to blot, make blots on; (*escribir*) to scribble on.
⬚2 VI to make blots; to scribble.

emboscada NF ambush; **tender una** ~ **a** to lay an ambush for.

emboscarse [1g] VR to lie in ambush; to hide away (in the woods); **estaban emboscados cerca del camino** they were in ambush near the road.

embotado ADJ dull, blunt (*t fig*).

embotamiento NM (a) (*acto*) dulling, blunting (*t fig*). (b) (*estado*) dullness, bluntness (*t fig*).

embotar [1a] VT (a) *objeto* to dull, blunt. (b) (*fig*) *sentidos* to dull, blunt; (*debilitar*) to weaken, enervate.

embotellado ⬚1 ADJ bottled; *discurso etc* prepared (beforehand).
⬚2 NM bottling.

embotellador(a) NM/F bottler.

embotellamiento NM (a) (*Aut*) traffic jam. (b) (*lugar*) bottleneck (*t fig*).

embotellar [1a] ⬚1 VT (a) (*gen*) to bottle.
(b) (*Mil etc*) to bottle up.
(c) (*Escol etc*) to mug up*, swot up*.
(d) (*Carib*) *discurso* to prepare beforehand, memorize.
⬚2 **embotellarse** VR (a) (*Aut*) to get into a jam, get jammed.
(b) (*Carib*) to learn a speech off by heart.

emboticarse [1g] VR (*Cono Sur, Méx*) to stuff o.s. with medicines.

embotijar [1a] ⬚1 VT to put into jars; to keep in jars.
⬚2 **embotijarse** VR (a) (*hincharse*) to swell up. (b) (*fig*: encolerizarse*) to fly into a passion.

embovedar [1a] VT to arch, vault.

embozadamente ADV covertly, stealthily.

embozado ADJ (a) (*cubierto*) muffled up (to the eyes). (b) (*fig*) covert, stealthy.

embozalar [1a] VT (*Cono Sur*) to muzzle.

embozar [1f] ⬚1 VT (a) (*de ropa*) to muffle (up), wrap (up). (b) (*fig*) to cloak, disguise, conceal.
⬚2 **embozarse** VR to muffle o.s. up (*con, de* in).

embozo NM (a) (*de la cara*) muffler; top (*o* fold) of the cape; mask, covering of the face; **quitarse el** ~ (*fig*) to drop the mask, end the play-acting.
(b) (*de sábana*) turndown.
(c) (*fig*) (*astucia*) cunning; (*encubrimiento*) concealment; **sin** ~ frankly, openly.

embragar [1h] ⬚1 VT (*Aut, Mec*) to engage; *piezas* to connect, couple; (*Náut*) to sling.
⬚2 VI (*Aut etc*) to put the clutch in.

embrague NM (*Aut, Mec*) clutch; **le patina el** ~* he's not right up top*.

embravecer [2d] ⬚1 VT to enrage, infuriate.
⬚2 VI (*Bot*) to flourish, grow strongly.

3 embravecerse VR **(a)** (*mar*) to get rough.
(b) (*persona*) to get furious.
embravecido ADJ **(a)** *mar* rough; *viento etc* wild. **(b)** *persona* furious, enraged.
embravecimiento NM rage, fury.
embrear [1a] VT to tar, cover with tar; to cover with pitch.
embretar [1a] **1** VT (*LAm*) *ganado* to pen, corral.
2 VI (*Cono Sur*) (*asfixiarse*) to suffocate; (*ahogarse*) to drown.
embriagado ADJ **(a)** (*borracho*) drunk, inebriated *frm*. **(b)** (*fig*) ~ **de éxito** drunk with success; ~ **de poder** power-crazed.
embriagador ADJ *olor* intoxicating; *vino etc* heady, strong.
embriagar [1h] **1** VT **(a)** (*emborrachar*) to make drunk, intoxicate; to get drunk. **(b)** (*fig*) to enrapture, delight, intoxicate.
2 embriagarse VR to get drunk.
embriaguez NF **(a)** (*gen*) drunkenness, intoxication. **(b)** (*fig*) rapture, delight, intoxication.
embridar [1a] VT **(a)** *caballo* to bridle, put a bridle on. **(b)** (*fig*) to check, restrain.
embriología NF embryology.
embriólogo, -a NM/F embryologist.
embrión NM embryo; **en** ~ in embryo.
embrionario ADJ embryonic.
embriónico ADJ embryonic.
embrocación NF embrocation.
embrocar [1g] **1** VT **(a)** (*Cos*) *hilo* to wind (on to a bobbin); *zapatos* to tack.
(b) *líquido* to pour from one container into another.
(c) (*volcar*) to turn upside down, invert.
2 embrocarse VR: ~ **un vestido** (*Méx*) to put a dress on over one's head.
embrollante ADJ muddling, confusing.
embrollar [1a] **1** VT *asunto* to muddle, confuse, complicate; to mess up; *personas* to involve, embroil (*en* in).
2 embrollarse VR to get into a muddle, get into a mess; ~ **en un asunto** to get involved in a matter.
embrollista NM (*And, CAm, Cono Sur*) = **embrollón**.
embrollo NM (*confusión*) muddle, tangle, confusion; (*aprieto*) fix, jam, entanglement; (*fraude*) fraud, trick.
embrollón, -ona NM/F troublemaker, mischief-maker.
embromado ADJ (*LAm*) **(a)** annoying; difficult. **(b) estar** ~ to be in a fix; to be having a tough time; (*Med*) to be in a bad way; (*Fin*) to be in financial trouble; (*con prisa*) to be in a hurry.
embromar [1a] **1** VT **(a)** (*tomar el pelo a*) to tease, make fun of, rag.
(b) (*engatusar*) to wheedle, cajole.
(c) (*engañar*) to hoodwink.
(d) (*LAm: molestar*) to annoy, vex; (*perjudicar*) to harm, set back; (*salud etc*) to affect badly.
2 embromarse VR (*LAm*) (*enojarse*) to get cross; (*aburrirse*) to get bored.
embroncar* (*esp LAm*) **1** VT (*enfadar*) to drive mad.
2 embroncarse VR (*enfadarse*) to get mad.
embrujado ADJ *persona* bewitched; *casa, lugar* haunted; **una casa embrujada** a haunted house.
embrujar [1a] VT *persona* to bewitch, put a spell on; *casa, lugar* to haunt; **la casa está embrujada** the house is haunted.
embrujo NM (*acto*) bewitching. **(b)** (*maldición*) curse. **(c)** (*ensalmo*) spell, charm; **el** ~ **de la Alhambra** the enchantment (o magic) of the Alhambra.
embrutecer [2d] **1** VT to brutalize, deprave; to coarsen.
2 embrutecerse VR to become brutalized, get depraved; to coarsen.
embuchacarse [1g] VR: ~ **algo** (*CAm, Méx*) to pocket sth; (*) to pocket sth, pinch sth*.
embuchado NM **(a)** (*Culin*) sausage. **(b)** (*: *pretexto*) pretext, blind; (*Pol*) electoral fraud; (*Teat*) gag.
embuchar [1a] VT **(a)** (*Culin*) to stuff with minced meat. **(b)** (*) *comida* to wolf, bolt.
embudar [1a] VT **(a)** (*Téc*) to fit with a funnel, put a funnel into. **(b)** (*fig*) to trick.
embudo NM **(a)** (*para líquidos*) funnel; (*And, Méx: tolva*) hopper. **(b)** (*fig: fraude*) trick, fraud; V **ley. (c)** (*fig: Aut etc*) bottleneck.
embullar [1a] (*And, CAm, Carib*) **1** VT **(a)** (*excitar*) to excite, disturb.
(b) *enemigo* to put to flight.
2 embullarse VR **(a)** (*excitarse*) to get excited, get worked up; to become tense.
(b) (*divertirse*) to revel, have a good time.
embullo NM (*CAm, Carib*) (*ruido*) noise, excitement, bustle; (*juerga*) revelry.
emburujar [1a] **1** VT **(a)** (*mezclar*) to jumble together, jumble up; (*amontonar*) to pile up; *hilo etc* to tangle up.
(b) (*And: desconcertar*) to bewilder.
2 emburujarse VR (*And, Carib, Méx*) to wrap o.s. up.

emburujo NM (*Carib*) ruse, trick.
embuste NM **(a)** (*trampa*) trick, fraud, imposture; (*mentira*) lie, (*hum*) fib, story. **(b)** ~**s** trinkets.
embustería NF trickery, deceit; lying.
embustero **1** ADJ **(a)** (*engañador*) deceitful, rascally.
(b) persona embustera (*Cono Sur*) person who cannot spell properly.
(c) (*CAm: altanero*) haughty.
2 NM, **embustera** NF (*estafador*) cheat; (*impostor*) impostor; (*mentiroso*) liar, (*hum*) fibber, storyteller; (*hipócrita*) hypocrite; **¡~!** (*hum*) you rascal!
embute¹* NM: **de** ~ smashing*, brilliant*.
embute²* NM (*Méx*) bribe*.
embutido NM **(a)** (*Culin*) sausage. **(b)** (*Téc*) inlay, inlaid work, marquetry. **(c)** (*Carib, Cono Sur, Méx: encaje*) strip of lace.
embutir [3a] **1** VT **(a)** (*meter*) to insert (*en* into); (*atiborrar*) to pack tight, stuff, cram (*de* with, *en* into); (*) *comida* to cram, scoff*; ~ **algo a uno** to make sb swallow sth; **estar embutido*** to be safely tucked away*, be in hiding; **ella estuvo embutida en un vestido apretadísimo** she had been poured into a terribly close-fitting dress.
(b) (*Téc*) to inlay; *metal* to hammer, work.
2 embutirse* VR to stuff o.s. (*de* with)*.
eme* NF (*euf*) = **mierda.**
emergencia NF **(a)** (*acto*) emergence; appearance. **(b)** (*urgencia*) emergency; **de** ~ emergency (*atr*).
emergente ADJ **(a)** (*consiguiente*) resultant, consequent. **(b)** *nación* emergent.
emerger [2c] VI to emerge; to appear; (*submarino*) to surface.
emeritense **1** ADJ of Mérida.
2 NMF native (o inhabitant) of Mérida; **los** ~**s** the people of Mérida.
emérito ADJ emeritus.
emético ADJ, NM emetic.
emigración NF emigration; migration.
emigrado, -a NM/F emigrant; (*Pol etc*) emigré(e).
emigrante ADJ, NMF emigrant.
emigrar [1a] VI to emigrate; to migrate.
Emilia NF Emily.
emilianense ADJ of San Millán de la Cogolla.
eminencia NF **(a)** (*Geog*) (*altura*) height, eminence; (*lo alto*) loftiness. **(b)** (*fig*) eminence; prominence. **(c)** (*títulos*) **Su E~** His Eminence; **Vuestra E~** Your Eminence.
eminente ADJ **(a)** (*alto*) high, lofty. **(b)** (*fig*) eminent, distinguished; prominent.
eminentemente ADV eminently, especially.
emir NM emir.
emirato NM emirate.
emisario NM emissary.
emisión NF **(a)** (*gen*) emission; (*Fin etc*) issue; (*Inform*) output; ~ **de valores** (*Bolsa*) flotation.
(b) (*Rad, TV: acto*) broadcasting; (*programa*) broadcast, programme; ~ **deportiva** sports programme; ~ **publicitaria** commercial, advertising spot.
emisor **1** ADJ: **banco** ~ issuing bank.
2 NM **(a)** (*Rad, TV*) transmitter. **(b)** (*Fin*) issuing company.
emisora NF radio station; broadcasting station; ~ **comercial** commercial radio station; ~ **de onda corta** shortwave radio station; ~ **pirata** pirate radio station.
emisor-receptor NM (*portátil*) walkie-talkie, transmitting and receiving set, transceiver.
emitir [3a] VT **(a)** *gas, sonido etc* to emit, give off, give out.
(b) *bonos, dinero, sellos etc* to issue; *dinero falso* to put into circulation, utter; *préstamo* to float, launch.
(c) *opinión* to express; *veredicto* to return, issue, give; *voto* to give, cast.
(d) (*Rad, TV*) to broadcast; *señal* to send out.
emoción NF **(a)** (*gen*) emotion; (*sentimiento*) feeling; **sentir una honda** ~ to feel a deep emotion; **nos comunica una** ~ **de nostalgia** it gives us a nostalgic feeling.
(b) (*excitación*) excitement; thrill; (*tensión*) tension, suspense; **¡qué ~!** how exciting!; **al abrirlo sentí gran** ~ I felt very excited on opening it; **la** ~ **de la película no disminuye** the excitement (o tension) of the film does not flag.
emocionado ADJ deeply moved, deeply stirred.
emocional ADJ emotional.
emocionante ADJ exciting, thrilling; touching, moving; stirring.
emocionar [1a] **1** VT (*excitar*) to excite, thrill; (*conmover*) to touch, move; to stir.
2 emocionarse VR to get excited, be thrilled; to be moved, to be stirred; **¡no te emociones tanto!** don't get so excited!, don't get so worked up!
emoliente ADJ, NM emollient.
emolumento NM emolument.

emotividad NF emotive nature.

emotivo ADJ emotive.

empacada NF (LAm) (a) (de caballo) balk, shy. (b) (fig) obstinacy.

empacado NM baling.

empacadora NF (a) (Agr) baler, baling machine. (b) **~ de carne** (Méx) meat-packing factory.

empacar [1g] ☐1☐ VT (gen) to bale, crate, pack up; (Agr) to bale; (LAm) to pack; (And, Méx) to package.

☐2☐ VI (Méx: hacer las maletas) to pack.

☐3☐ **empacarse** VR (a) (confundirse) to get rattled, get confused.

(b) (LAm: caballo) to balk, shy; (fig) to be obstinate, get stubborn.

empachado ADJ (a) clogged; (Náut) overloaded; estómago upset, uncomfortable. (b) (avergonzado) embarrassed. (c) (torpe) awkward, clumsy.

empachar [1a] ☐1☐ VT (a) (obstruir) to stop up, clog; (Náut) to overload; (Med) estómago to upset, make uncomfortable; persona to give indigestion to.

(b) (estorbar) to impede, hinder; (incomodar) to embarrass.

☐2☐ **empacharse** VR (a) to get stopped up, get clogged; (Med) to get indigestion, have indigestion.

(b) (avergonzarse) to get embarrassed, feel awkward; to become bashful.

empacho NM (a) (estorbo) hindrance, obstacle.

(b) (Med) surfeited feeling, indigestion.

(c) (fig) embarrassment; awkwardness, awkward feeling; bashfulness; **sin ~** without ceremony; unconcernedly; **no tener ~ en** + infin to have no objection to + ger.

empachoso ADJ (a) comida cloying, indigestible. (b) (fig) embarrassing. (c) niños tiresome.

empadronamiento NM (a) (censo) census; register. (b) (acto) census-taking; registration.

empadronar [1a] ☐1☐ VT población to take a census of; votante to register, enter on a register.

☐2☐ **empadronarse** VR to register (for electoral purposes).

empajar [1a] VT to cover (o fill etc) with straw; (And, Cono Sur) to thatch.

empalagar [1h] ☐1☐ VT (a) (suj: comida) to pall on. (b) (fig) to pall on, bore; to sicken.

☐2☐ VI to pall.

☐3☐ **empalagarse** VR to get surfeited (de with).

empalago NM (a) (empacho) cloying, palling. (b) (aburrimiento) boredom; (asco) disgust.

empalagoso ADJ (a) (empachoso) cloying; comida sickeningly sweet, over-rich. (b) (fig) boring, wearisome; trying.

empalar [1a] ☐1☐ VT to impale.

☐2☐ **empalarse** VR (And, Cono Sur) to dig one's heels in.

empalidecer [2d] VI = **palidecer**.

empalizada NF fence; (Mil etc) palisade, stockade.

empalmar [1a] ☐1☐ VT (a) (juntar) to join, connect; cuerdas to splice. (b) (fig) to combine, put together.

☐2☐ VI (Ferro etc: líneas) to join, meet, come together; (trenes) to connect (con with).

☐3☐ **empalmarse*** VR to get randy*.

empalme NM (a) (Téc) joint, connection, union; splice; (Elec) junction-box. (b) (combinación) combination. (c) (de carreteras, líneas) junction; (de trenes) connection. (d) (*ːↄ) hard-on*ↄ, erection.

empamparse [1a] VR (LAm) (a) (desorientarse) to get lost on the pampas; to get disorientated, lose one's way. (b) (fig) to be amazed, stand agape.

empanada NF (a) (Culin) ≃ (meat) pie, patty. (b) (*: timo) fraud, piece of shady business*. (c) **~ mental*** confusion.

empanadilla NF patty, small pie.

empanado ADJ (Culin) done (o rolled etc) in breadcrumbs, breaded.

empanar [1a] VT (a) (Culin) to do (o roll etc) in breadcrumbs; to roll in pastry. (b) (Agr) to sow with wheat.

empantanado ADJ flooded, swampy.

empantanamiento NM (fig) stagnation.

empantanar [1a] ☐1☐ VT (a) (inundar) to flood, swamp.

(b) (fig) to obstruct; to bog down.

☐2☐ **empantanarse** VR (a) (inundarse) to be flooded, get swamped.

(b) (fig) to be obstructed, be held up; **~ en un asunto** to get bogged down in a matter.

empañado ADJ ventana etc misty, steamy, steamed-up; contorno dim, blurred; superficie tarnished; voz faint, unsteady; honor tarnished.

empañar [1a] ☐1☐ VT (a) bebé to put a nappy o diaper (US) on.

(b) ventana etc to mist, steam up; contorno to dim, blur; superficie, honor to tarnish.

☐2☐ **empañarse** VR (a) (gafas etc) to film over, get misty; to cloud over; (voz) to falter.

(b) (fig) to become sad, get gloomy.

empañetar [1a] VT (LAm) to plaster; to whitewash.

empapar [1a] ☐1☐ VT (a) (mojar) to soak, saturate, drench; to steep (t

fig; de, en in).

(b) (absorber) to soak up, absorb.

☐2☐ **empaparse** VR (a) to soak.

(b) **~ de** to soak up, soak in.

(c) **~ de, ~ en** (fig) to steep o.s. in; to become imbued with.

empapelado NM papering, paperhanging.

empapelador(a) NM/F paperhanger.

empapelar [1a] VT (a) objeto to wrap in paper; caja to paper, line with paper; cuarto, pared to paper. (b) **~ a uno** (Jur) to lay a charge against sb; (*) to do sb*, (fig) to throw the book at sb.

empapuzar [1f] VT to stuff with food.

empaque NM (a) (acto) packing. (b) (*: aspecto) look, appearance; (aire) manner. (c) (fig) solemnness, pomposity. (d) (LAm*: descaro) nerve*, cheek*. (e) (Méx) washer, gasket.

empaquetado ☐1☐ ADJ pre-packed.

☐2☐ NM packaging.

empaquetador(a) NM/F packer.

empaquetadura NF packing; filling; (Mec) gasket.

empaquetamiento NM packaging.

empaquetar [1a] VT (a) to pack; to pack up, parcel up; (Com) to package. (b) (conservar) buque etc to mothball. (c) (Mil*) to punish.

emparamarse [1a] VR (And, Carib) (mojarse) to get soaked; (entumecerse) to get numb with cold; (morir) to die of cold, freeze to death.

emparar* [1a] (And) ☐1☐ VT to catch.

☐2☐ **empararse** VR (a) (sonrojarse) to blush. (b) **~ de** to mock.

emparedado NM sandwich.

emparedar [1a] VT to immure, confine.

emparejamiento NM (Biol) pairing, mating; (Psiq) pair-bonding.

emparejar [1a] ☐1☐ VT (a) dos casas to pair, match. (b) (nivelar) to level, make level; to make flush; (igualar) to even up.

☐2☐ VI (a) (llegar a la altura de) to catch up (con with), come abreast (con of). (b) (ser igual) to be even (con with).

☐3☐ **emparejarse** VR to pair off.

emparentado ADJ related (by marriage) (con to).

emparentar [1j] VI to become related by marriage (con to); **~ con una familia** to marry into a family.

emparrado NM trained vine; vine arbour.

emparrandarse* [1a] VR (LAm) to go on a binge*.

empastado ADJ (a) (Tip) clothbound, bound. (b) diente filled.

empastar [1a] ☐1☐ VT (a) (engomar) to paste.

(b) (Tip) to bind in boards, bind in stiff covers, bind in cloth.

(c) diente to fill, stop.

(d) (LAm Agr) to convert into pasture land.

☐2☐ **empastarse** VR (Cono Sur: ganado) to get bloated.

empaste NM (a) (de diente) filling. (b) (Tip) binding.

empatar [1a] ☐1☐ VT (a) (LAm: juntar) to join, connect, tie firmly together.

(b) (Carib: acosar) to bother, harass.

(c) (Cono Sur) tiempo to waste.

☐2☐ VI (juego) to draw, tie; (carrera) to tie, have a dead heat; (en voto) to tie; **los equipos empataron** (o **quedaban empatados**) **a 2** the teams drew 2-all; **los tres equipos quedan empatados a puntos** the three teams are level on points (in the league table).

empate NM (a) (Dep) draw, tie; dead heat; **un ~ a 0** a 0-0 draw, a goalless draw. (b) (LAm: junta) joint, connection.

empatía NF empathy.

empatizar [1f] VI (t **empatizarse**) to empathize (con with).

empavado* ADJ (Carib) unlucky, jinxed*.

empavar* [1a] VT (Carib) to put a jinx on*, bring bad luck to.

empavesado NM bunting.

empavesar [1a] VT to deck, adorn; barco to dress.

empavonar [1a] ☐1☐ VT (a) (Téc) acero to blue. (b) (LAm Mec) to grease, cover with grease.

☐2☐ **empavonarse** VR (CAm) to dress up.

empecatado ADJ (a) (incorregible) incorrigible; (astuto) wily, fiendish. (b) (malhadado) ill-fated. (c) (maldito) damned, cursed.

empecinadamente ADV stubbornly, pigheadedly.

empecinado ADJ stubborn, pigheaded.

empecinamiento NM stubbornness, pigheadedness.

empecinarse [1a] VR to be stubborn, dig one's heels in; **~ en algo** to be stubborn (o dig one's heels in) about sth; **~ en** + infin to persist in, insist on + ger.

empedarse* [1a] VR (Cono Sur, Méx) to get drunk, get sloshed*.

empedernido ADJ (a) persona heartless; obdurate; corazón flinty, stony.

(b) (en un vicio) hardened, inveterate; **un fumador ~** a strongly addicted smoker, a smoker firmly set in the habit; **un pecador ~** an unregenerate sinner.

empedernir [3a: defectivo] ☐1☐ VT to harden.

☐2☐ **empedernirse** VR (a) to harden; to petrify. (b) (fig) to harden one's heart, resolve to be tough.

empedrado [1] ADJ *superficie* paved; (*fig*) pitted (*de* with); *cara* pockmarked; *color* dappled, flecked; *cielo* cloud-flecked.
[2] NM (*pavimento*) paving; (*CAm: calle*) cobbled street.
empedrar [1j] VT to pave.
empegado NM tarpaulin.
empeine NM (a) (*Anat*) groin; (*de pie, zapato*) instep. (b) (*Bot*) cotton flower. (c) ~s (*Med*) ringworm.
empella NF (a) (*de zapatero*) vamp; (*de zapato*) uppers. (b) (*LAm: manteca de cerdo*) lard.
empellar [1a] VT to push, shove, jostle.
empellón NM push, shove; **mover a empellones** to shove, move by pushing; **abrirse paso a empellones** to get through by shoving, push one's way rudely through, push roughly past; **dar empellones** to shove, jostle.
empelotado ADJ (a) (*And, Carib, Cono Sur, Méx: desnudo*) naked, stripped. (b) (*Méx: enamorado*) in love.
empelotar [1a] [1] VT (a) (*desnudar*) to undress, strip to the skin. (b) (*LAm Mec*) to strip down, dismantle, take to pieces.
[2] **empelotarse*** VR (a) (*aturdirse*) to get muddled. (b) (*: meterse en un lío*) to get into a row. (c) (*: desnudarse*) to strip naked, strip off. (d) (*Carib, Méx: enamorarse*) to fall head over heels in love (*con* with).
empelucado ADJ bewigged.
empenachado ADJ plumed; (*fig*) pretentious, extravagant; baroque.
empenachar [1a] VT to adorn with plumes.
empeñado ADJ (a) *objeto* pawned.
(b) **estar ~ hasta los ojos** to be deeply in debt.
(c) *persona* determined; **estar ~ en + *infin*** to be determined to + *infin*, be completely set on + *ger*.
(d) *discusión* bitter, heated.
empeñar [1a] [1] VT (a) *objeto* to pawn, pledge.
(b) *palabra* to pledge, give; *persona* to engage, compel.
(c) *batalla* to join; *riña* to start, engage in.
[2] **empeñarse** VR (a) (*prometer*) to bind o.s., pledge o.s.
(b) (*endeudarse*) to get into debt.
(c) ~ **en algo** to insist on sth; to persist in sth; ~ **en + *infin*** to be determined to + *infin*, be set on + *ger*; to insist on + *ger*; **se empeña en que es así** he insists that it is so.
(d) ~ **en una lucha** to engage in a fight; ~ **en una discusión** to get involved in a heated argument.
(e) ~ **por uno** to intercede for sb, intervene on sb's behalf.
empeñero, -a NM/F (*Méx*) pawnbroker, moneylender.
empeño NM (a) (*objeto*) pledge.
(b) (*promesa*) obligation, undertaking.
(c) (*resolución*) determination; (*insistencia*) insistence; **su ~ en hacerlo** his determination to do it; his insistence on doing it; **con ~** with determination; insistently; eagerly, keenly; **tener ~ en + *infin*** to be bent on + *ger*, be eager to + *infin*.
(d) (*tienda*) pawnshop; moneylender's.
empeñoso ADJ (*LAm*) persevering, diligent.
empeoramiento NM deterioration, worsening.
empeorar [1a] [1] VT to make worse, worsen; to impair.
[2] VI y **empeorarse** VR to get worse, worsen, deteriorate.
empequeñecedor ADJ belittling.
empequeñecer [2d] VT (a) (*disminuir*) to dwarf, make (seem) smaller. (b) (*fig*) to minimize; to belittle.
empequeñecimiento NM belittling.
emperador NM (a) emperor. (b) (*Carib: pez*) swordfish.
emperatriz NF empress.
emperejilarse [1a] VR to dress up, doll o.s. up*.
empericarse* [1g] VR (a) (*And: emborracharse*) to get drunk. (b) (*Carib, Méx: ruborizarse*) to blush.
emperifollar [1a] [1] VT to adorn, deck; *persona* to doll up.
[2] **emperifollarse** VR to dress up, doll o.s. up*.
empernar [1j] VT to bolt, secure with a bolt; to fit a bolt to.
empero CONJ († *y liter*) but; yet, however; **estaba muy cansado, no se sentó ~** he was very tired, nonetheless he didn't sit down.
emperramiento NM stubbornness.
emperrarse [1a] VR to get stubborn, be obstinate; ~ **en algo** to be stubborn about sth; to persist in sth.
emperro NM (*prov, And*) (*terquedad*) stubbornness; (*rabieta*) fit of temper.
empertigar [1h] VT (*Cono Sur*) *caballo* to hitch up.
empezar [1f *y* 1j] VTI to begin, start; ~ **a + *infin*** to start to + *infin*; ~ **por + *infin*, ~ + *ger*** to begin by + *ger*, start by + *ger*; **empezó diciendo que ...** he began by saying that ...; **bueno, para ~** well, to start with; **¡no empieces!** don't start on that (all over again)!
empicotar [1a] VT to pillory.
empiece *etc* V **empezar**.
empiezo NM (*And, CAm, Cono Sur*) = **comienzo**.
empilchar [1a] [1] VT (*Cono Sur*) *caballo* to saddle; (*) *persona* to keep in clothes.

[2] **empilcharse*** VR (*Cono Sur*) to dress up, get dolled up*.
empilonar [1a] VT (*And, Carib*) to pile up.
empinada NF (*Aer*) steep climb, zoom upward.
empinado ADJ (a) *cuesta* steep; *edificio* high, lofty. (b) (*fig*) proud; stiff.
empinar [1a] [1] VT (a) (*alzar*) to raise, lift; (*botella*) to tip up; V **codo**. (b) (*enderezar*) to straighten.
[2] VI (*: beber*) to drink, booze*.
[3] **empinarse** VR (a) (*persona*) to stand on tiptoe; (*caballo*) to rear up; (*edificio*) to tower, soar; (*Aer*) to climb steeply, zoom upwards. (b) (*And, Cono Sur: comer en exceso*) to overeat.
empingorotado* ADJ stuck-up*.
empipada* NF (*And, Cono Sur*) blow-out*.
empiparse [1a] VR: ~ **algo** (*And, Cono Sur*) (*comer*) to stuff o.s. with sth, (*beber*) drink sth down.
empírico [1] ADJ empiric(al).
[2] NM, **empírica** NF empiricist.
empirismo NM empiricism.
empitonar [1a] VT (*Taur*) to gore, impale (on the horns of the bull).
empizarrado NM slate roof.
empizarrar [1a] VT to roof with slates, slate.
emplantillar [1a] VT (a) (*And, Carib, Cono Sur*) *zapatos* to put insoles into. (b) (*And, Cono Sur*) *pared* to fill with rubble.
emplastar [1a] VT (a) (*Med*) to put a plaster on, poultice. (b) *cara* to make up, paint. (c) *trato* to block.
emplasto NM (a) (*Med*) plaster, poultice. (b) (*fig: expediente*) makeshift arrangement. (c) (*débil*) weakling; (*inadaptado*) misfit, useless individual. (d) (*: pesado*) bore, tedious person, wet*.
emplazamiento NM (a) (*Jur*) summons; summoning. (b) (*sitio*) site, location; (*Mil*) (gun) emplacement.
emplazar [1f] VT (a) (*llamar*) to summon, convene; (*Jur*) to summons; to subpoena; ~ **a uno para el jueves** to give sb an appointment for Thursday. (b) (*ubicar*) to site, locate, place; *misil* to site, station; *estatua etc* to set up, erect. (c) ~ **a uno a hacer algo** to call on sb to do sth.
empleado, -a NM/F employee; (*esp*) clerk, office worker, clerical worker; (*LAm*) domestic servant; ~ **bancario, ~ de banco** bank clerk; ~ **de confianza** confidential clerk; ~ **de correos** post-office worker; ~ **de cuello y corbata** (*Cono Sur*) white-collar worker; ~ **de finca urbana** porter, concierge; **empleada de hogar** servant, maid; ~ **de pompas fúnebres** undertaker's assistant, mortician's assistant (*US*); ~ **público** civil servant; ~ **de ventanilla** booking office clerk, counter clerk.
empleador(a) NM/F employer.
emplear [1a] [1] VT *herramienta, palabra etc* to use, employ; *persona* to employ; to give a job to, engage, hire; *tiempo* to occupy, spend; to put in; *dinero* to invest; ~ **mal** to misuse; ~ **mal el tiempo** to waste time; **¡le está bien empleado!** it serves him right!
[2] **emplearse** VR to be used, be employed; ~ **haciendo algo** to occupy o.s. doing sth; ~ **a fondo** to make a great effort, do one's utmost; **¡bien se te emplea!** it serves you right!
▼ **empleo** NM (a) (*gen*) use, employment; occupation, spending; (*Com*) investment; '**modo de ~**' (*en etiqueta*) 'instructions for use'; **el ~ de esa palabra es censurable** the use of that word is to be condemned.
(b) (*trabajo*) employment, work; ~ **comunitario** community work; ~ **juvenil** youth employment; **pleno ~** full employment.
▼(c) (*puesto*) job, employment, post; **buscar un ~** to look for a job; **estar sin ~** to be unemployed, be out of a job; '**solicitan ~**' (*encabezamiento*) 'situations wanted'; **suspender a uno de ~ y sueldo** to suspend sb without pay.
emplomadura NF leading; lead covering, lead lining; (*Cono Sur: de diente*) filling.
emplomar [1a] VT *vidriera etc* to lead; (*revestir etc*) to cover (*o* line, weight *etc*) with lead; (*precintar*) to seal with lead; (*Cono Sur*) *diente* to fill.
emplumar [1a] [1] VT (a) (*gen*) to adorn with feathers; (*castigo*) to tar and feather; **¡que me emplumen si ...!** I'll eat my hat if ...!
(b) (*: estafar*) to swindle, con*.
(c) (*: detener*) to nick*, arrest.
(d) ~ **algo a uno*** to spring sth on sb.
(e) (*CAm*: *zurrar*) to beat up*, thrash.
(f) (*Carib*) *empleado* to fire*.
(g) ~**las** (*And, Cono Sur*) to run away.
[2] VI (a) (*ave*) to grow feathers.
(b) (*LAm*: *huir*) to run away, take to one's heels.
[3] **emplumarse** VR: **emplumárselas** (*And, Cono Sur*: *huir*) to run away.
emplumecer [2d] VI to grow feathers.
empobrecer [2d] [1] VT to impoverish.
[2] **empobrecerse** VR to become poor, become impoverished.
empobrecimiento NM impoverishment.

▶ LENGUA Y USO: **empleo: c → 46.1**

empollada* NF: **darse** (o **pegarse**) **una ~** to swot*, cram.
empollar [1a] **1** VT **(a)** *huevos* to incubate, sit on; to hatch.
 (b) (*Univ etc**) *asignatura* to swot up*.
 2 VI **(a)** (*gallina*) to sit, brood.
 (b) (*insectos*) to breed.
 (c) (*Univ etc**) to swot*, cram.
empolle* NM swotting*, cramming; **¡tiene un ~!** he's been working really hard, he really knows his stuff*.
empollón*, -ona NM/F (*Univ etc*) swot*, bookworm.
empolvado ADJ *sustancia* powdery; *superficie* dusty.
empolvar [1a] **1** VT *cara* to powder; *superficie* to cover with dust, make dusty.
 2 empolvarse VR **(a)** (*persona*) to powder o.s., powder one's face, put powder on; (*superficie*) to get dusty, gather dust.
 (b) (*Méx: perder la práctica*) to get rusty, get out of practice.
 (c) (*Carib: huir*) to run away.
emponchado ADJ **(a)** (*LAm: vestido de poncho*) wearing a poncho, covered with a poncho. **(b)** (*And, Cono Sur*) (*sospechoso*) suspicious; (*taimado*) crafty, sharp.
emponcharse [1a] VR to put on one's poncho, wrap o.s. up in one's poncho.
emponzoñamiento NM poisoning.
emponzoñar [1a] VT to poison; (*fig*) to poison; to taint, corrupt.
emporcar [1g y 1l] VT to soil, dirty, foul.
emporio NM emporium, mart, trading centre; (*LAm*) department store.
emporrado; ADJ: **estar ~** to be high (on drugs);.
emporroso ADJ (*CAm, Carib*) annoying, irritating.
empotrable **1** ADJ fitted, built-in.
 2 NM fitted unit, built-in unit.
empotrado ADJ *armario etc* built-in; (*Mec*) fixed, integral.
empotrar [1a] **1** VT to embed, fix; *armario etc* to build in.
 2 empotrarse VR: **el coche se empotró en la tienda** the car embedded itself in the shop; **los vagones se empotraron uno en otro** the carriages telescoped together.
empotrerar [1a] VT **(a)** (*LAm*) *ganado* to pasture, put out to pasture. **(b)** (*Carib, Cono Sur*) *tierra* to convert into fenced pasture, enclose.
empozarse [1f] VR (*And, Cono Sur*) to form pools.
emprendedor **1** ADJ enterprising; go-ahead, pushy, aggressive.
 2 NM (*Fin*) entrepreneur.
emprender [2a] VT **(a)** *trabajo etc* to undertake; *problema etc* to take on, tackle; *viaje* to begin on, embark on; **~ marcha a** to set out for; **~ el regreso** to go back, return; to begin the homeward journey; **~ la retirada** to begin to retreat.
 (b) **~la** to start, set out; **~la con uno** to tackle sb about a matter, have it out with sb; to attack sb; to have a row with sb; **la emprendieron con el árbitro a botellazos** they attacked the referee by throwing bottles at him.
empreñador* ADJ irksome, vexatious.
empreñar [1a] **1** VT **(a)** *mujer* to make pregnant; *animal* to impregnate, mate with. **(b)** (*: *fastidiar*) to rile*, irk, vex.
 2 empreñarse VR to become pregnant.
empresa NF **(a)** (*espíritu etc*) enterprise; **~ libre, libre ~** free enterprise; **~ privada** private enterprise.
 (b) (*Com, Fin*) enterprise, undertaking, venture; company, concern; (*patrón*) employer; **~ colectiva** joint venture; **~ fantasma** dummy company; **~ filial** affiliated company; **~ fletadora** shipping company; **~ funeraria** undertaker's; **~ matriz** parent company; **~ particular** private company; **pequeñas y medianas ~s** small and medium-sized companies; **~ pública** public sector company; **~ de seguridad** security company; **~ de servicios públicos** public utility company; **~ de trabajo temporal** temp recruitment agency.
 (c) (*esp Teat*) management; **la ~ lamenta que ...** the management regrets that ...
empresariado NM business (world); managers (*collectively*), management.
empresarial ADJ owners', managers'; *función, clase etc* managerial; **estudios ~es** business studies, management studies; **sector ~** business sector.
empresariales NFPL business studies.
empresario NM (*Fin*) businessman; (*patrón*) employer; (*Téc*) manager; (*Mús, de ópera etc*) impresario; (*Boxeo*) promoter; (*Com*) contractor; **~ de pompas fúnebres** undertaker, mortician (*US*); **~ de transporte** (*Cono Sur*) shipping agent; **pequeño ~** small businessman.
empresología NF business consultancy.
empresólogo, -a NM/F business consultant.
emprestar* [1a] VT to borrow; (*prestar*) to lend.
empréstito NM (public) loan; **~ de guerra** war loan.
empufado* ADJ: **estar ~** to be in debt, be in the red.
empujada NF (*And, CAm*) push, shove.
empujadora NF: **~ frontal, ~ niveladora** bulldozer.
empujar [1a] **1** VT **(a)** (*gen*) to push, shove; to push, thrust (*en into*);

(*Mec*) to drive, move, propel; *bicicleta* to push, wheel; *botón* to press; **'empujad'** (*en puerta etc*) 'push'; **~ el botón a fondo** to press the button down hard; **¡no empujen!** stop pushing!, don't shove.
 (b) (*) *persona* to sack*, give the push to*.
 2 VI (*fig*) to intrigue, work behind the scenes (*para + infin* to + *infin*).
empujaterrones NM INVAR bulldozer.
empujatierra NF bulldozer.
empuje NM **(a)** (*gen*) pressure; (*Mec, Fís*) thrust.
 (b) (*un ~*) push, shove.
 (c) (*fig*) push, drive; **le falta ~** he hasn't got any go to him, he lacks drive; **en un espíritu de ~** in a thrustful spirit.
empujón NM push, shove; dig, poke, jab; **abrirse paso a empujones** to shove (o elbow) one's way through, get through by pushing; **avanzar a empujones** to go forward by fits and starts, jerk forward; **trabajar a empujones** to work intermittently.
empulgueras NFPL thumbscrew.
empuntar [1a] **1** VT **(a)** to put a point on. **(b)** **~las** (*And*) to run away.
 2 empuntarse VR (*Carib*) (*empecinarse*) to dig one's heels in; (*caminar*) to walk on tiptoe.
empuñadura NF **(a)** (*de espada*) hilt; (*de herramienta*) grip, handle. **(b)** (*de cuento*) start, traditional opening.
empuñar [1a] VT **(a)** (*coger*) to grasp, clutch, grip, take (firm) hold of; (*Cono Sur*) *puño* to clench. **(b)** (*fig*) **~ las armas** to take up arms; **~ el bastón** (*fig*) to take command. **(c)** (*And: dar un puñetazo a*) to punch, hit with one's fist.
empupar [1a] VI (*LAm*) to pupate.
empurar; [1a] VT (*Mil*) to punish.
empurrarse* [1a] VR (*CAm*) (*enojarse*) to get angry; (*hacer pucheros*) to pout.
E.M.T. NF (*Esp*) ABR *de* **Empresa Municipal de Transportes.**
emú NM emu.
emulación NF (*gen, Inform*) emulation.
emulador **1** ADJ emulous (*de of*).
 2 NM, **emuladora** NF rival.
emular [1a] **1** VT to emulate, rival.
 2 VI: **~ con** = VT.
emulgente NM emulsifier.
émulo **1** ADJ emulous.
 2 NM, **émula** NF rival, competitor.
emulsión NF emulsion.
emulsionante NM emulsifier.
emulsionar [1a] VT to emulsify.
EN NF (*Esp*) ABR *de* **Editora Nacional.**
en PREP **(a)** (*lugar*) in; on; at; **está ~ el cajón** it's in the drawer; **meter algo ~ el bolsillo** to put sth in (o into) one's pocket; **no entra ~ el agujero** it won't go into the hole; **está ~ el suelo** it's on the floor; **está ~ Argentina** he's in Argentina; **está ~ Santiago** he's in Santiago; **está ~ algún lugar de la Mancha** he's at some place in la Mancha; **~ casa** at home; **te esperé ~ la estación** I waited for you at the station; **sentarse ~ la mesa** to sit down at table; **trabaja ~ la tienda** she works in the shop; **ir de puerta ~ puerta** to go from door to door; **'curvas peligrosas ~ 2 kilómetros'** 'Dangerous bends 2 kilometres ahead'.
 (b) (*tiempo*) in; on; **~ 1605** in 1605; **~ el siglo X** in the 10th century; **~ la mañana** (*LAm*) in the morning; **~ la mañana del desastre** (*LAm*) on the morning of the disaster; **~ aquella ocasión** on that occasion; **lo terminaron ~ 3 semanas** they finished it in 3 weeks.
 (c) (*precio*) at, for; **lo vendió ~ 5 dólares** he sold it at (o for) 5 dollars; **vendió la casa ~ 11 millones** she sold the house for 11 millions.
 (d) (*proporción*) by; **reducir algo ~ una tercera parte** to reduce sth by a third; **ha aumentado ~ un 20 por cien** it has increased by 20%.
 (e) (*medio*) **le conocí ~ el andar** I recognized him by his walk; **ir ~ avión** to go by plane, go by air; **vine ~ el autobús** I came by bus, I came in the bus.
 (f) **Hugo ~ Segismundo** (*Cine, Teat*) Hugo as (o in the role of) Segismundo.
 (g) (*con ger.* ††, *prov*) **~ viéndole se lo dije** the moment I saw him I told him; **~ viéndole se lo diré** the moment I see him I'll tell him, as soon as I see him I'll tell him.
 (h) (*con infin*) **fue el último ~ hacerlo** he was the last to do it.
enaceitar [1a] VT (*Cono Sur*) to oil.
ENAGAS, Enagas [ena'γas] NF ABR *de* **Empresa Nacional del Gas.**
enagua NF, *gen* **~s** PL petticoat; underskirt.
enaguazar [1f] VT to flood.
enajenación NF, **enajenamiento** NM **(a)** (*Jur etc*) alienation; transfer; **enajenación forzosa** expropriation.
 (b) (*entre amigos*) estrangement.
 (c) (*despiste*) absentmindedness; (*éxtasis*) rapture, trance; (*Psic*) alienation; **~ mental** mental derangement.

EN   *ver también la entrada*

Como preposición de lugar, *en* se traduce normalmente por *on*, *in* o *at*. La elección de una de estas tres preposiciones depende a menudo de cómo percibe el hablante la relación espacial. He aquí unas líneas generales:

- Se traduce por *on* cuando *en* equivale a *encima de* o nos referimos a algo que se percibe como una superficie o una línea, por ejemplo una mesa, una carretera, *etc*:

  "¿Has visto mi vestido?" - "Está en la tabla de planchar"
  "Have you seen my dress?" - "It's on the ironing-board"
  Estaban tumbados en la playa
  They were lying on the beach
  Está construyendo una casa en la colina
  He's building a house on the hill
  ...un pueblo en la costa oeste...
  ...a village on the west coast...
  La gasolinera está en la carretera que va a Motril
  The petrol station is on the road to Motril
  Dibujó un león en la hoja de papel
  He drew a lion on the piece of paper
  Tiene un grano en la nariz
  He has a spot on his nose
  Lo vi en la tele
  I saw him on TV

- Se usa *in* cuando equivale a *dentro de* o cuando nos referimos a un espacio que se percibe como limitado (calle, montañas, etc):

  Tus gafas están en mi bolso
  Your glasses are in my bag
  Tienes una pestaña en el ojo
  You've got an eyelash in your eye
  Lo leí en un libro
  I read it in a book
  Se han comprado un chalet en la sierra
  They've bought a chalet in the mountains
  Viven en la calle de Serrano
  They live in the Calle de Serrano

- Lo traducimos por *at* para referirnos a un edificio cuando hablamos de la actividad que normalmente se realiza en él o cuando *en* indica un lugar concreto. También se traduce por *at* cuando en la dirección incluimos el número o el nombre de la casa:

  ¿Por qué no comemos en el restaurante de tu hermano?
  Why don't we have lunch at your brother's restaurant?
  Voy a pasar el día en el museo
  I'm going to spend the day at the museum
  Te espero en la parada del autobús
  I'll meet you at the bus-stop
  Vivimos en la calle Dale nº 12
  We live at 12 Dale Street
  Para otros usos y ejemplos ver la entrada.

enajenar [1a] **1** VT **(a)** (*Jur*) *bienes* to alienate, transfer; *derechos* to dispose of.
(b) *persona* to alienate, estrange.
(c) (*fig*: *extasiar*) to enrapture, carry away; (*volver loco*) to drive mad.
2 enajenarse VR **(a)** ~ **algo** to deprive o.s. of sth; ~ **las simpatías** to alienate people, make o.s. disliked.
(b) (*amigos*) to become estranged.
(c) (*extasiarse*) to be enraptured, get carried away.
enaltecer [2d] VT to exalt; to praise, extol.
enamoradizo ADJ (*gen*) amorous, that falls in love easily.
enamorado 1 ADJ **(a)** (*gen*) in love, lovesick. **(b) estar** ~ to be in love (*de* with). **(c)** (*Carib, Cono Sur*) = **enamoradizo**.
2 NM, **enamorada** NF lover.
enamoramiento NM falling in love.
enamorar [1a] **1** VT to inspire love in, win the love of; **por fin la enamoró** eventually he got her to fall in love with him.
2 enamorarse VR to fall in love (*de* with).
enamoricarse [1g] VR, **enamoriscarse** [1g] VR to be just a bit in love (*de* with).
enancar [1g] **1** VT: ~ **a uno** (*LAm*) to put sb on the crupper (of one's horse).
2 VI (*Cono Sur: seguir*) to follow, be a consequence (*a* of).
3 enancarse VR **(a)** (*LAm*) to get up on the crupper, ride behind.
(b) (*Méx: caballo*) to rear up.
enanez NF dwarfishness; (*fig*) stunted nature.
enangostar [1a] **1** VT to narrow.
2 enangostarse VR to narrow, get narrower.
enanismo NM (*Med*) dwarfism.
enanito, -a NM/F dwarf.
enano 1 ADJ dwarf, small, tiny; stunted.

2 NM dwarf; midget; (*pey*) runt.
enantes ADV (*And*) = **denante(s)**.
enarbolar [1a] **1** VT *bandera etc* to hoist, raise; *pancarta etc* to hang up, hang out; *espada etc* to flourish.
2 enarbolarse VR **(a)** (*persona*) to get angry.
(b) (*caballo*) to rear up.
enarcar [1g] VT **(a)** *tonel* to hoop, put a hoop on.
(b) *cejas* to raise, arch; *lomo* to arch; *pecho* to throw out.
enardecer [2d] **1** VT to fire, inflame; to fill with enthusiasm.
2 enardecerse VR **(a)** (*Med*) to become inflamed. **(b)** (*fig*) to get excited, get enthusiastic (*por* about); to blaze, be afire (*de* with).
enarenar [1a] **1** VT to sand, cover with sand.
2 enarenarse VR (*Náut*) to run aground.
enastado ADJ horned; antlered, with antlers.
encabalgamiento NM (*Liter*) enjambement.
encabestrar [1a] **1** VT **(a)** *caballo* to put a halter on; to lead by a halter. **(b)** (*fig*) to induce, persuade; to dominate.
2 encabestrarse VR (*LAm*) to dig one's heels in.
encabezado 1 ADJ *vino* fortified.
2 NM **(a)** (*Méx Prensa, Tip*) heading; headline. **(b)** (*Carib: capataz*) foreman.
encabezamiento NM **(a)** (*de apartado*) heading; (*de periódico*) headline; rubric; (*preámbulo*) opening words, preamble; (*Com*) bill head, letterhead. **(b)** (*registro*) roll, register.
encabezar [1f] VT **(a)** *movimiento, revolución etc* to lead, head.
(b) *liga, lista etc* to head, be at the top of, come first in.
(c) *papel, documento* to put a heading to; *artículo, dibujo* to head, entitle.
(d) *población etc* to register (for tax purposes *etc*).
(e) *vino* to fortify.
encabrestarse VR (*LAm*) = **emperrarse**.
encabritamiento* NM fit of bad temper; anger.
encabritar [1a] **1** VT (*) to rile*, upset.
2 encabritarse VR **(a)** (*caballo*) to rear up. **(b)** (*: enfadarse*) to get riled*, get cross.
encabronar* [1a] **1** VT to rile*, upset.
2 encabronarse VR to get riled*, get cross.
encabuyar [1a] VT (*And, Carib*) to tie up.
encachado ADJ (*Cono Sur*) appealing, attractive.
encachar [1a] **1** VT (*Cono Sur*) *cabeza* to lower.
2 VI (*Méx*) to make a conquest.
encachilarse [1a] VR (*Cono Sur*) to get furious.
encachimbado* ADJ: **está** ~ (*CAm*) he's livid, he's hopping mad*.
encachimbarse* [1a] VR (*CAm*) to fly off the handle*, lose one's temper.
encachorrarse* [1a] VR (*And*) (*enojarse*) to get angry, fly off the handle*; (*Carib, Cono Sur*) (*empecinarse*) to turn obstinate.
encadenación NF, **encadenamiento** NM **(a)** chaining (together).
(b) (*fig*) linking, connection, concatenation.
encadenado NM (*Cine*) fade, dissolve.
encadenar [1a] **1** VT **(a)** (*atar*) to chain (together); *prisionero etc* to put chains on, fetter, shackle. **(b)** (*fig: inmovilizar*) to shackle, paralyze, immobilize; **los negocios le encadenan al escritorio** business ties him to his desk. **(c)** (*fig: unir*) to connect, link.
2 (*Cine*) to fade in; ~ **a** to fade to.
encajable ADJ (*fig*) feasible; manageable.
encajadura NF **(a)** (*acto*) insertion, filling. **(b)** (*hueco*) socket; (*ranura*) groove; (*armazón*) frame.
encajar [1a] **1** VT **(a)** (*ajustar*) to insert, fit (*en* into); (*meter*) to push in, thrust in, force in; *máquina etc* to house, encase; *piezas* to join, fit together, fit into each other; (*Dep*) *gol* to net, score; to let in, concede.
(b) *comentario, cuenta etc* to get in, put in, intrude; *insinuación* to drop.
(c) ~ **algo a uno** to palm sth off on sb, foist sth off on sb; ~ **una historia a uno** to force sb to listen to a (disagreeable) story.
(d) (*) *golpe* to give, deal, fetch (*a* to).
(e) (*: lanzar*) to chuck (*a* at); *insultos* to hurl.
(f) (*aguantar*) to put up with, not flinch under, resist; **sabe** ~ **los golpes** he can take the punches, (*fig*) he can take a lot of stick; **sabes** ~ **una broma** you know how to take a joke.
2 VI **(a)** to fit; to fit well (*o* properly).
(b) (*fig*) to fit, match, correspond; to be appropriate; **esto no encaja con lo que dijo antes** this does not square with what he said before.
3 encajarse VR **(a)** (*: meterse con dificultad*) to squeeze (o.s.) in; (*fig*) to intrude, gatecrash; ~ **en una reunión** to intrude upon a meeting; ~ **en una fiesta** to crash a party*.
(b) (*: interrumpir*) to butt in.
(c) ~ **una chaqueta** to put on a jacket.
(d) (*LAm Aut*) to get stuck.
encaje NM **(a)** (*acto*) insertion, fitting; fitting together, joining.

(b) (*hueco*) socket, cavity; (*ranura*) groove; (*armazón*) frame; (*Mec*) housing; **aquí la violencia no tiene ~** there is no place for violence here.

(c) (*taracea*) inlay, inlaid work, mosaic; (*Cos*) lace; **~ de aplicación** appliqué (work); **~ de bolillos** (*lit*) handmade lace; (*fig*) juggling act, delicate manoeuvre.

(d) (*Fin*) reserve, stock; **~ de oro** gold reserve.

encajera NF lacemaker.

encajetillar [1a] VT (*Méx*) to pack in boxes, box.

encajonado NM cofferdam.

encajonar [1a] ☐1 VT **(a)** (*poner en caja*) to box (up), put in a box, crate, pack (in a box); (*Mec*) to box in, encase.

(b) *río* to confine (between banks), canalize.

(c) (*meter con dificultad*) to squeeze in, squeeze through.

☐2 **encajonarse** VR (*río*) to run through a narrow place, narrow.

encajoso: NM (*LAm*) creep:, toady.

encalabrinar [1a] ☐1 VT **(a)** (*Med*) to make dizzy, make giddy.

(b) **~ a uno** to get sb worked up; to fluster sb.

(c) **~ a una*** to attract a girl, click with a girl*, get a girl to show an interest.

☐2 **encalabrinarse*** VR **(a)** (*empeñarse*) to get an obsession, get the bit between one's teeth; to dig one's heels in.

(b) **~ de una** to get infatuated with a girl; **X anda encalabrinado con Z** X is mad keen on Z*.

encaladura NF **(a)** (*blanqueo*) whitewash(ing). **(b)** (*Agr*) liming.

encalambrarse [1a] VR (*LAm*) to get cramp; (*del frío*) to get stiff with cold.

encalamocar [1g] ☐1 VT (*And, Carib*) **(a)** (*emborrachar*) to make drunk.

(b) (*aturdir*) to confuse, bewilder.

☐2 **encalamocarse** VR (*And, Carib*) **(a)** to get drunk.

(b) to get confused, get bewildered.

encalar [1a] VT **(a)** *pared* to whitewash. **(b)** (*Agr*) to lime.

encalatarse [1a] VR (*And*) **(a)** (*desnudarse*) to strip naked. **(b)** (*fig*) to be ruined.

encalladero NM shoal, sandbank.

encalladura NF stranding, running aground.

encallar [1a] VI **(a)** (*Náut*) to run aground, run ashore, get stranded (*en on*). **(b)** (*fig*) to fail; (*en negociación etc*) to get stuck, get bogged down. **(c)** (*mecanismo*) to jam, stick, get stuck.

encallecer [2d] VI y **encallecerse** VR to harden, form corns.

encallecido ADJ hardened.

encalmada NF period of calm.

encalmado ADJ **(a)** (*Náut*) becalmed. **(b)** (*Com, Fin*) quiet, slack, dull.

encalmarse [1a] VR to be becalmed.

encalomarse: [1a] VR to hide.

encalvecer [2d] VI to go bald.

encamar [1a] ☐1 VT **(a)** (*CAm, Méx: hospitalizar*) to take to hospital, hospitalize.

(b) (*Carib*) *animal* to litter, bed down; (*Méx*) *niño etc* to put to bed.

☐2 **encamarse** VR **(a)** (*persona*) to take to one's bed; **~ con una** (*And, Cono Sur*) to go to bed with sb, sleep with sb; **estar encamado** to be confined to bed.

(b) (*cosecha etc*) to be laid, be flattened.

(c) (*animal*) to crouch, hide.

encamburarse [1a] VR (*Carib*) to make good, (*esp*) achieve public office.

encame NM den, lair; hiding-place.

encamillado, -a NM/F (*CAm, Méx*) stretcher case.

encaminamiento NM (*Inform*) routing.

encaminar [1a] ☐1 VT **(a)** *persona* to guide, direct, set on the right road (*a to*); **pude ~le** I was able to tell him the way to go.

(b) *vehículo, expedición etc* to route (*por via*); (*Inform*) to route.

(c) *atención, energía etc* to direct (*a towards*); **el proyecto está encaminado a + infin** the plan is directed towards + *ger*, the plan is designed to + *infin*.

☐2 **encaminarse** VR **(a)** **~ a** (*lit*) to set out for, make for, take the road to.

(b) **~ a** (*fig*) to be directed towards, be intended for.

encamotado ADJ: **estar ~** (*LAm*) to be in love (*de with*).

encamotarse* [1a] VR (*LAm*) to fall madly in love (*de with*).

encampanado ADJ bell-shaped.

encampanar [1a] ☐1 VT **(a)** (*And, Carib: encumbrar*) to raise, raise on high.

(b) (*And, Carib, Méx*: abandonar*) to leave in the lurch, leave in a jam.

(c) **~ a uno a** (*Carib*) to send sb to.

(d) (*Méx: agitar*) to excite, agitate.

☐2 **encampanarse** VR **(a)** (*LAm: jactarse*) to boast, brag.

(b) (*And*: enamorarse*) to fall in love.

(c) (*Méx*: meterse en un lío*) to get into a jam*.

(d) (*Carib*) to go off to a remote spot.

(e) (*And*: complicarse*) to become difficult, get complicated.

encanado*, -a NM/F (*And*) prisoner.

encanalar [1a] VT, **encanalizar** [1f] VT to pipe; to channel, canalize.

encanallarse [1a] VR to degrade o.s.; to become coarse, acquire coarse habits.

encanar: [1a] VT (*And, Cono Sur*) to throw into jail.

encandecer [2d] VT to make white-hot.

encandelar [1a] VT (*Carib*) to annoy, irritate.

encandelillar [1a] VT (*LAm*) to dazzle; to bewilder.

encandellar [1a] VT (*And*) *fuego* to fan.

encandiladera NF procuress; madame.

encandilado ADJ high, erect.

encandiladora NF procuress; madame.

encandilar [1a] ☐1 VT **(a)** (*deslumbrar*) to dazzle.

(b) *lumbre* to stir, poke.

(c) (*fig: aturdir*) to daze, bewilder.

(d) (*fig*) *emoción* to kindle, stimulate, excite; *deseo* to arouse, stir; **~ a una** to arouse a woman, make a woman feel randy*.

(e) (*And, Carib: privar de sueño*) to deprive of sleep.

☐2 **encandilarse** VR **(a)** (*ojos*) to glitter, sparkle, look unnaturally bright.

(b) (*persona*) to get excited, become emotional; (*sexualmente*) to become aroused, feel randy*.

(c) (*And, Carib*) (*asustarse*) to get scared; (*Carib, Méx*) (*enfadarse*) to get angry.

encanecer [2d] VI y **encanecerse** VR **(a)** (*pelo*) to go grey; (*persona*) to go grey, look old. **(b)** (*fig*) to go mouldy.

encanijado ADJ weak, puny.

encanijarse [1a] VR to grow weak, become emaciated, begin to look ill.

encanillar [1a] VT to wind (on to a spool).

▼**encantado** ADJ **(a)** (*hechizado*) bewitched; haunted; *sitio* romantic, bewitching; (*fig*) *casa* rambling.

▼**(b)** (*contento*) delighted, pleased, charmed; **¡~!** (*presentación*) how do you do!, pleased to meet you; **estoy ~ de conocerle** I'm delighted to meet you; **yo, ~** it's all right with me.

(c) (*distraído*) absent-minded, daydreaming; **parecer estar ~** to seem to be in a trance.

encantador ☐1 ADJ charming, delightful, lovely, enchanting.

☐2 NM, **encantadora** NF magician, enchanter; **~ de serpientes** snake-charmer.

encantadoramente ADV charmingly, delightfully.

encantamiento NM enchantment.

▼**encantar** [1a] VT **(a)** (*hechizar*) to bewitch, cast a spell on (*o over*).

▼**(b)** (*gustar*) to charm, delight, enchant, captivate, fascinate; **nos encanta la casa** we are delighted with the house, we are charmed with the house; **pero pronto dejó de ~nos** but we soon stopped liking it.

encanto NM **(a)** charm, spell, enchantment; **como por ~** as if by magic; (*fig*) in a flash, instantly.

(b) (*fig*) charm; enchantment, delight; **la playa es un ~** the beach is delightful, the beach is marvellous; **el niño es un ~** the child is a little treasure; **¡qué ~ de jardín!** what a lovely garden!

(c) (*palabra cariñosa*) sweetheart, my love; **¡oye, ~!*** (*piropo*) hullo gorgeous!* .

encañada NF ravine.

encañado NM conduit, pipe.

encañar [1a] ☐1 VT **(a)** *agua* to pipe. **(b)** *planta* to stake, prop up. **(c)** *terreno* to drain. **(d)** *seda* to wind (on to a spool).

☐2 VI (*planta*) to form a stalk.

encañonar [1a] ☐1 VT **(a)** *agua* to pipe. **(b)** (:: *atracar*) to stick up:, hold up; to cover (with a gun).

☐2 VI (*ave*) to grow feathers.

encapado ADJ cloaked, wearing a cloak.

encapotado ADJ **(a)** (*vestido de capa*) cloaked, wearing a cloak. **(b)** *cielo* cloudy, overcast.

encapotar [1a] ☐1 VT to cover with a cloak.

☐2 **encapotarse** VR **(a)** (*ponerse la capa*) to put on one's cloak; to wrap up.

(b) (*fig*) to frown.

(c) (*Met*) to become cloudy, cloud over, become overcast.

encaprichamiento NM whim.

encapricharse [1a] VR to persist in one's foolishness; to dig one's heels in, insist on having one's way; **~ con** to take a fancy to, get infatuated with.

encapuchado ADJ hooded.

encapuchar [1a] VT: **~ un pozo de petróleo** to cap an oil-well.

encarado ADJ: **bien ~** good-looking, with nice features; **mal ~** ill-favoured, plain; (*LAm*) wicked-looking, with criminal features.

encaramar [1a] ☐1 VT **(a)** (*alzar*) to raise, lift up.

(b) (*alabar*) to praise, extol.

(c) (*And, CAm: avergonzar*) to embarrass, cause to blush.

$\boxed{2}$ **encaramarse** VR **(a)** (*ponerse arriba*) to perch, sit up high; (*en carrera*) to rise high; ~ **a** to climb (up, on to), get to the top of.

(b) (*And, CAm*) to get embarrassed, blush.

encarapitarse [1a] VR (*And, Carib*) = **encaramarse (a)**.

encarar [1a] $\boxed{1}$ VT **(a)** *arma* to aim, point.

(b) *problema etc* to face (up to), confront.

(c) *dos cosas* to bring face to face.

$\boxed{2}$ VI (*Cono Sur*) to fall sick.

$\boxed{3}$ **encararse** VR: ~ **a**, ~ **con** to face, confront, come face to face with; **tendrá que ~ con los electores** he will have to face the electorate; **se encaró en seguida con el problema** he immediately faced up to the problem.

encarcelación NF, **encarcelamiento** NM imprisonment.

encarcelar [1a] VT to imprison, jail.

encarecer [2d] $\boxed{1}$ VT **(a)** (*Com*) to put up the price of, make more expensive.

(b) (*alabar*) to praise, extol; *persona* to recommend; *política etc* to recommend (*a* to), urge (*a* on); *dificultad etc* to stress, emphasize; to exaggerate; **le encarezco que ...** I urge you to + *infin*.

$\boxed{2}$ VI y **encarecerse** VR (*Com*) to get dearer, rise in price.

encarecidamente ADV insistently, earnestly, strongly.

encarecimiento NM **(a)** (*Com*) rise in price, price increase.

(b) (*elogio*) extolling; stressing, emphasizing; exaggeration, overrating; **con ~** insistently, earnestly, strongly.

encargado $\boxed{1}$ ADJ: **el empleado ~ de estos géneros** the employee in charge of these stocks.

$\boxed{2}$ NM, **encargada** NF (*agente*) agent, representative; (*responsable*) person in charge; ~ **de campo** groundsman; ~ **de curso** lecturer in charge; ~ **de mostrador** counter clerk; ~ **de negocios** (*Pol*) chargé d'affaires; (*And, Méx*) agent; ~ **de obra** foreman, site manager; ~ **de prensa** press officer; ~ **de la recepción** receptionist; ~ **de relaciones públicas** public relations officer; ~ **de seguridad** security officer; **encargada de vestuario** (*Teat*) wardrobe mistress; ~ **de vestuario** (*Cine, TV*) costume designer.

▼ **encargar** [1h] $\boxed{1}$ VT (*confiar*) to entrust; (*ordenar*) to charge, commission; (*aconsejar*) to urge, recommend, advise; (*pedir*) to ask for; (*Com*) to order; ~ **algo a uno** to entrust sth to sb; to put sb in charge of sth; ~ **un deber a uno** to charge sb with a duty.

$\boxed{2}$ **encargarse** VR: ~ **de algo** to take charge of sth; to take sth over; to look after sth, see about sth, attend to sth; **no había queso, pues las ratas se habían encargado de ello** there was no cheese, the rats had seen to that (o had made sure of that); ~ **de** + *infin* to see about + *ger*, attend to the matter of + *ger*; to undertake to + *infin*.

encargo NM **(a)** (*cometido*) assignment, job; (*puesto*) post; (*orden*) charge, commission; (*responsabilidad*) responsibility; **hacer ~s** to run errands; **tener ~ de** + *infin* to have the job of + *ger*, have the responsibility of + *ger*.

(b) (*petición*) order, request; (*Com*) order (*de* for); **cancelar el ~ de** to cancel the order for, stop the delivery of; **el cuadro fue de ~** the picture was commissioned.

(c) **estar de ~** (*Carib, Cono Sur*) to be in the family way.

(d) **traer a uno de ~** (*Méx**) to pester sb.

encargue NM (*Cono Sur*) = **encargo**.

encariñado ADJ: **estar ~ con** to be fond of, be attached to.

encariñarse [1a] VR: ~ **con** to grow fond of, get attached to.

Encarna NF *forma familiar de* **Encarnación**.

encarnación NF incarnation; embodiment.

encarnadino ADJ incarnadine.

encarnado ADJ **(a)** *diablo* incarnate. **(b)** *color* red, blood-red; flesh-coloured; *tez* ruddy, (*pey*) florid; **ponerse ~** to blush red.

encarnadura NF: **tiene buena ~** his skin heals quickly.

encarnar [1a] $\boxed{1}$ VT **(a)** (*personificar*) to embody, personify; (*Teat*) to embody, represent; **Iago encarna el odio** Iago is hatred personified.

(b) *anzuelo* to bait.

$\boxed{2}$ VI **(a)** to take on bodily form; (*Rel etc*) to become incarnate.

(b) (*Med*) to heal (over).

(c) *arma* to enter the flesh, penetrate the body.

encarnecer [2d] VI to put on flesh.

encarnizadamente ADV (*fig*) bloodily, bitterly, fiercely.

encarnizado ADJ **(a)** *herida etc* red, inflamed; *ojo* bloodshot. **(b)** *lucha* bloody; bitter, fierce.

encarnizamiento NM rage, fury; bitterness, ferocity.

encarnizar [1f] $\boxed{1}$ VT (*fig*) to enrage, infuriate; to make cruel.

$\boxed{2}$ **encarnizarse** VR **(a)** ~ **en** to gorge on; to become greedy for.

(b) (*fig*) to get furious; to fight fiercely; ~ **con**, ~ **en** to be cruel to, treat cruelly.

encaro NM **(a)** (*mirada*) stare, staring, gaze. **(b)** (*puntería*) aim(ing). **(c)** (*Hist*) blunderbuss.

encarpetar [1a] VT to file away; to pigeonhole; (*LAm*) *plan etc* to shelve, bury.

encarrilamiento NM (*fig*) rectification; correction; direction, guiding.

encarrilar [1a] VT **(a)** *tren* to put back on the rails.

(b) (*fig*) to put on the right track, start off again on the right lines; (*corregir*) to correct; (*dirigir*) to direct, guide.

(c) **ir encarrilado** to be on the right lines, be doing nicely; (*pey*) to be in a rut.

encarrujar [1a] VT (*Cono Sur Cos*) to ruffle, frill.

encartado, -a NM/F (*Jur*) accused, defendant.

encartar [1a] VT **(a)** (*gen*) to enroll, register, enter (on a list); (*Jur*) to summon. **(b)** *criminal* to outlaw.

encarte NM (*Tip*) insert, inset.

encartonar [1a] VT to cover with cardboard; (*Tip*) to bind in boards.

encartuchar [1a] VT (*LAm*) *papel* to make a cone of, roll up into a cone.

encasar [1a] VT *hueso* to set.

encasillado $\boxed{1}$ ADJ *actor* type-cast.

$\boxed{2}$ NM (set of) pigeonholes.

encasillamiento NM **(a)** piegonholing; sorting, classification. **(b)** (*Teat etc*) type-casting.

encasillar [1a] VT **(a)** (*poner en casillas*) to pigeonhole; (*clasificar*) to sort out, classify; (*archivar*) to file. **(b)** (*Teat etc*) to type-cast.

encasquetar [1a] VT **(a)** *sombrero* to pull on, pull down tight, jam on.

(b) ~ **una idea a uno** to get an idea firmly fixed in sb's mind. **(c)** (*Teat*) to typecast. **(d)** ~ **algo a uno*** to foist sth on sb.

encasquillador NM (*LAm*) blacksmith.

encasquillar [1a] $\boxed{1}$ VT **(a)** (*poner casquillos a*) to put a tip on.

(b) (*LAm*) *caballo* to shoe.

(c) (*: *incriminar*) to frame*.

$\boxed{2}$ **encasquillarse** VR **(a)** (*bala, revólver*) to jam.

(b) (*And*: *en discurso etc*) to get stuck, dry up*.

(c) (*Carib*: *asustarse*) to get scared.

(d) (*Carib**: *vacilar*) to waver.

encastillado ADJ **(a)** (*Arquit*) castellated. **(b)** (*fig*) haughty; stubborn.

encastillar [1a] $\boxed{1}$ VT to fortify, defend with castles.

$\boxed{2}$ **encastillarse** VR **(a)** (*Mil*) to take to the hills; (*Hist*) to shut o.s. up in a castle. **(b)** (*fig*) to refuse to yield; ~ **en un principio** to stick to a principle, refuse to give up a principle.

encatrado NM (*Cono Sur*) hurdle.

encatrinarse [1a] VR (*Méx*) to dress up.

encauchado NM (*And, Carib*) (*tela*) rubberized cloth; (*capa*) waterproof cape.

encauchar [1a] VT to rubberize, waterproof.

encausado, -a NM/F (*Jur*) accused, defendant.

encausamiento NM prosecution.

encausar [1a] VT to prosecute, sue; to put on trial.

encauzar [1f] VT **(a)** *agua* to channel.

(b) (*fig*) to channel, direct, guide; **las protestas se pueden ~ a fines buenos** the protests can be directed towards good objectives, the protests can be guided into useful channels.

encefalitis NF encephalitis; ~ (**letárgica**) sleeping sickness.

encefalograma NM encephalogram.

encefalomielitis NF: ~ **miálgica** myalgic encephalomyelitis.

encefalopatía NF: ~ **espongiforme bovina** bovine spongiform encephalopathy.

enceguecer [2d] (*LAm*) $\boxed{1}$ VT to blind.

$\boxed{2}$ VI y **enceguecerse** VR to go blind.

encelar [1a] $\boxed{1}$ VT to make jealous.

$\boxed{2}$ **encelarse** VR **(a)** (*persona*) to become jealous. **(b)** (*Zool*) to rut, be on heat.

encenagado ADJ **(a)** (*enfangado*) muddy, mud-stained. **(b)** (*fig*) sunk in vice, depraved.

encenagarse [1h] VR **(a)** to get muddy. **(b)** (*fig*) to wallow in vice, get depraved.

encendedor NM **(a)** (*mechero*) lighter; ~ (**de cigarrillos**) cigarette lighter; ~ **de cocina**, ~ **de(l) gas** gas lighter. **(b)** (*persona*) lamplighter.

encender [2g] $\boxed{1}$ VT **(a)** (*gen*) to light; (*pegar fuego a*) to set fire to, ignite; to kindle; *fósforo* to strike, light; *luz, radio* to turn on, switch on, put on; *gas* to light, turn on; (*Inform*) to switch on.

(b) (*fig*) to kindle, inflame; to stir up, provoke.

(c) (*Carib*) (*azotar*) to beat; (*castigar*) to punish.

$\boxed{2}$ **encenderse** VR **(a)** (*fuego*) to catch, catch fire, ignite; (*llama*) to burn up, flare up; **¿cuándo se encienden las luces?** when is lighting-up time?

(b) (*fig: persona*) to get excited; to flare up.

(c) (*fig: cara*) to blush, get red.

encendida* NF (*Carib*) (*paliza*) beating; (*reprimenda*) telling-off*.

encendidamente ADV passionately, ardently.

encendido $\boxed{1}$ ADJ **(a)** **estar ~** to be alight, be on fire, be burning; (*luz*) to be on.

(b) *color* glowing (*de* with); fiery.

(c) *cara* red (*de* with); inflamed (*de* with).

[2] NM (*Aut*) ignition; (*de la luz*) switching on.

encendimiento NM **(a)** burning, kindling. **(b)** (*fig: pasión*) passion, ardour; (*ansia*) eagerness; (*intensidad*) intensity.

encenizar [1f] VT to cover with ashes.

encentar [1j] VT to begin to use; *pan etc* to cut the first slice from.

encerado [1] ADJ waxed; waxy, wax-coloured.

[2] NM oilcloth; (*Náut*) tarpaulin. **(c)** (*Escol etc*) blackboard.

encerador(a) NM/F polisher, polishing machine; **~ de piso** floor polisher.

encerar [1a] VT to wax; *piso* to wax, polish.

encercamiento NM (*LAm*) encirclement.

encercar [1g] VT (*LAm*) = **cercar**.

encerotar [1a] VT *hilo* to wax.

encerradero NM fold, pen.

encerrar [1j] [1] VT **(a)** (*gen*) to shut in, shut up; (*con llave*) to lock in, lock up; (*cercar*) to enclose; (*confinar*) to confine, hem in.

(b) (*abarcar*) to include, contain, comprise; **el libro encierra profundas verdades** the book contains deep truths.

(c) (*implicar*) to involve, imply.

[2] **encerrarse** VR **(a)** to shut o.s. up, lock o.s. in; to go into seclusion; **se encerró en su cuarto** she shut herself in her room; **~ en el silencio** to maintain a total silence.

(b) (*Méx*: *ser hosco*) to be stand-offish.

encerrona* NF (*Escol*) detention; (*protesta*) sit-in; **preparar a uno una ~** (*fig*) to put sb in a tight spot.

encespedar [1a] VT to turf.

encestar [1a] VI (*Dep*) to score (a basket).

enceste NM (*Dep*) basket.

enchalecar [1g] VT (*fig*) to place in a strait-jacket.

enchapado NM plating; veneer.

enchapar [1a] VT **(a)** (*con metal*) to plate, overlay (with metal); (*con madera*) to veneer. **(b)** (*Méx*) *puerta* to fit locks to.

enchaquetarse [1a] VR **(a)** (*And, Carib: ponerse la chaqueta*) to put one's jacket on. **(b)** (*And: vestirse de etiqueta*) to dress up.

encharcada NF pool, puddle.

encharcado ADJ still, stagnant.

encharcar [1g] [1] VT to swamp, flood; to cover with puddles, turn into pools.

[2] **encharcarse** VR **(a)** (*tierra*) to swamp, get flooded, get covered with puddles.

(b) (*agua*) to form puddles, form a pool; to become stagnant.

(c) (*LAm: enfangarse*) to get muddy.

(d) (*Cono Sur: atascarse*) to get stuck in a puddle.

(e) **~ en los vicios** (*fig*) to wallow in vice.

encharralarse [1a] VR (*CAm*) to make an ambush, lie in ambush.

enchastrar* [1a] VT (*Cono Sur*) to dirty, cover in muck.

enchauchado* ADJ (*Cono Sur*) well-heeled.

enchicharse* [1a] VR **(a)** (*LAm: emborracharse*) to get drunk. **(b)** (*And, CAm: enfadarse*) to get angry, lose control.

enchilada NF (*CAm, Méx*) stuffed tortilla.

enchilado [1] ADJ **(a)** (*CAm, Méx Culin*) seasoned with chili; (*picante*) spicy, hot. **(b)** (*Méx: color*) bright red.

[2] NM (*Carib, Méx*) stew with chili sauce.

enchilar [1a] [1] VT **(a)** (*CAm, Méx Culin*) to season with chili. **(b)** (*fig*) (*CAm, Méx: molestar*) to annoy, vex; (*CAm: decepcionar*) to disappoint.

[2] VI (*CAm, Méx*) to sting, burn.

[3] **enchilarse** VR (*Méx*) to go red in the face; (*fig*) to fly into a rage.

enchiloso ADJ (*CAm, Méx*) *sabor* hot.

enchilotarse* [1a] VR (*Cono Sur*) to get cross.

enchinar [1a] [1] VT (*Méx*) *pelo* to curl, perm.

[2] **enchinarse** VR: **~ el cuerpo** to get gooseflesh; to get scared.

enchinchar [1a] [1] VT **(a)** (*CAm, Carib, Méx: molestar*) to put out, bother. **(b)** (*Méx: persona*) to cause to waste time; *asunto* to delay. **(c)** (*Cono Sur, Méx*: *enojar*) to rile*, annoy.

[2] **enchincharse** VR **(a)** (*And, CAm, Carib, Méx: infestarse*) to get infested with bugs. **(b)** (*Cono Sur*: *enfadarse*) to get bad-tempered.

enchiquerar [1a] VT (*LAm*) to pen, corral.

enchironar* [1a] VT to jug*, jail.

enchisparse* [1a] VR (*LAm*) to get tight*.

enchisterado ADJ top-hatted, with a top hat on.

enchivarse* [1a] VR (*And*) to fly into a rage.

enchufable ADJ which plugs in, plug-in (*atr*).

enchufado, -a* NM/F (*influyente*) well-connected person, person with pull; (*cobista*) creep*; (*en escuela*) teacher's pet.

enchufar [1a] [1] VT **(a)** (*Téc etc*) to join, connect, fit together, fit in; to telescope together; (*Elec*) to plug in. **(b)** (*Com, Fin*) to merge. **(c)** (*) = **2.**

[2] **enchufarse*** VR (*puesto*) to wangle o.s. a job (*etc*)*, get a cushy job*; (*relacionarse bien*) to get in with the right people*.

enchufe NM **(a)** (*Téc etc*: *unión*) joint, connection; (*manguito*) sleeve; (*encaje*) socket.

(b) (*Elec*) (*clavija*) plug; (*toma*) point, socket; **~ múltiple** adaptor.

(c) (*: influencia*) connection, useful contact; **tiene un ~ en el ministerio** he's got a contact in the ministry, he can pull wires at the ministry; **hay que tener ~s** you've got to have contacts; **lo hizo por ~** he pulled strings to do it.

(d) (*: puesto*) soft job*, cushy job*.

enchufismo* NM (system of getting things done by) wirepulling*, use of contacts to obtain favours; old-boy network.

enchufista* NM wirepuller*, contact man, person who uses the old-boy network.

encía NF (*Anat*) gum.

encíclica NF encyclical.

enciclopedia NF encyclopaedia.

enciclopédico ADJ encyclopaedic.

encielar [1a] VT (*CAm, Cono Sur*) to roof, put a roof on.

encienda *etc* V **encender**.

encierra NF (*Cono Sur*) **(a)** (*acto*) penning (of cattle, for slaughter). **(b)** (*pasto*) winter pasture.

encierras V **encerrar**.

encierre NM (*Carib*) penning (of cattle, for slaughter).

encierro NM **(a)** (*acto*) shutting-in, shutting-up, locking, closing; confinement; (*de manifestantes*) sit-in; (*en fábrica*) work-in; sit-down strike.

(b) (*cercado*) enclosure; (*cárcel*) prison, lock-up; (*Agr*) pen; (*Taur*) bull-pen.

(c) (*Taur*) penning (of bulls), corralling; *see also* SANFERMINES .

encima [1] ADV **(a)** (*lugar*) above, over; overhead; at the top; on top; **por ~** over, overhead; **muy por ~** (*fig*) very superficially, very hastily; **ponlo ~ y no debajo** put it over and not under, put it on top and not underneath; **el avión pasó ~** the plane passed over.

(b) (*fig*) **echarse algo ~** to take sth upon o.s.; **quitarse algo de ~** to get rid of sth; to cast sth off, shake sth off; **se me vino ~** it fell on top of me; **la guerra está ~** war is upon us, war is imminent; **no llevo tabaco ~** I haven't any tobacco on me, I don't carry tobacco; **¿tienes un duro ~?** do you have a *duro* about you?; **¿tienes cambio ~?** have you any change on you?; **tienes bastante ~** you've got enough to worry about.

(c) (*fig: además*) besides; **y otras muchas cosas ~** and a lot else besides, and much else in addition; **de ~** (*LAm*) into the bargain; **y ~ no me dio las gracias** and on top of all that he didn't even thank me; **no viniste y ~ no me llamaste** you didn't come and on top of that you didn't ring me.

(d) (*Cono Sur*) **~ nuestro** (*etc*) above us (*etc*).

[2] **~ de** PREP **(a)** (*lugar*) above, over; on; on top of; **por ~ de** over; **pasó ~ de nuestras cabezas** it passed over our heads.

(b) (*fig*) besides, in addition to; over and above, in preference to; **y luego ~ de todo eso** and then in addition to all that, and then on top of all that; **han preferido la cantidad por ~ de la calidad** they have preferred quantity to quality.

encimar [1a] (*And, Cono Sur*) [1] VT **(a)** (*: añadir*) to throw in, add on; **le encimaron el sueldo** they gave him a bonus on top of his wages. **(b)** (*Dep*) to mark.

[2] VI (*Naipes*) to add a new stake.

encime NM (*And*) bonus, extra.

encimera NF worktop; top, surface.

encimero ADJ top, upper.

encina NF ilex, holm oak, evergreen oak.

encinar NM holm-oak wood.

encinta ADJ pregnant; (*Zool*) with young; **mujer ~** pregnant woman, expectant mother; **dejar a una ~** to make a woman pregnant.

encintado NM kerb.

encizañar [1a] [1] VT to sow discord among, create trouble among.

[2] VI to sow discord, cause trouble.

enclaustrar [1a] VT to cloister; (*fig*) to hide away.

enclavar [1a] [1] VT **(a)** (*clavar*) to nail; (*traspasar*) to pierce, transfix.

(b) (*empotrar*) to embed, set; *edificio etc* to set, place; **las ruinas están enclavadas en un valle** the ruins are set in a valley, the ruins have a valley as their setting.

(c) (*: estafar*) to swindle.

[2] **enclavarse** VR to interlock.

enclave NM enclave; **~ regional de gobierno** regional seat of government.

enclavijar [1a] VT to peg, pin; to join.

enclencle ADJ (*LAm*) terribly thin.

enclenco ADJ (*And, Carib*), **enclenque** ADJ weak, weakly, sickly.

enclítica NF enclitic.

enclítico ADJ enclitic.

enclocar [1g y 1l] VI, **encloquecer** [2d] VI to go broody.

encobar [1a] VI y **encobarse** VR (*gallina*) to sit, brood.

encocorante* ADJ annoying, maddening.

encocorar* [1a] [1] VT to annoy, enrage, madden.

[2] **encocorarse** VR **(a)** (*enojarse*) to get cross, get mad. **(b)** (*Carib:*

sospechar) to get suspicious. (**c**) (*Cono Sur**) to put on airs.

encofrado NM (*Téc*) form, plank mould.

encofrador, -a NM/F (*Constr*) shutterer.

encofrar [1a] VT to plank, timber.

encoger [2c] ⊡ VT (**a**) (*contraer*) to shrink, contract, shorten.

(**b**) (*fig*) to intimidate, scare, discourage.

② **encogerse** VR (**a**) (*contraerse*) to shrink, contract; to shrivel up.

(**b**) ~ **de hombros** to shrug one's shoulders.

(**c**) (*fig: acobardarse*) to cringe; (*desalentarse*) to get discouraged, get disheartened; (*ser tímido*) to be shy, be timid.

encogidamente ADV (*fig*) shyly, timidly, bashfully.

encogido ADJ (**a**) (*contraído*) shrunken; shrivelled. (**b**) (*fig*) shy, timid, bashful.

encogimiento NM (**a**) (*contracción*) shrinking, contraction; shrinkage.

(**b**) ~ **de hombros** shrug (of the shoulders). (**c**) (*fig*) shyness, timidity, bashfulness.

encogollado* ADJ (*Cono Sur*) stuck-up*, snobbish.

encogollarse [1a] VR (*Cono Sur*) to get conceited, be haughty.

encohetarse* [1a] VR (*And, CAm*) to get furious.

encojar [1a] ⊡ VT to lame, cripple.

② **encojarse** VR to go lame; (*) to pretend to be ill.

encojonarse*‡ [1a] VR (*CAm*) to fly off the handle*, explode.

encolar [1a] VT (*engomar*) to glue, gum, paste; (*aprestar*) to size; (*pegar*) to stick down, stick together.

encolerizar [1f] ⊡ VT to anger, provoke.

② **encolerizarse** VR to get angry.

encomendar [1j] ⊡ VT to entrust, commend (*a* to, to the charge of).

② **encomendarse** VR: ~ **a** to entrust o.s. to, put one's trust in.

encomendería NF (*And*) grocer's, grocery store.

encomendero NM (**a**) (*And*) grocer; (*Carib*) wholesale meat supplier.

(**b**) (*LAm Hist*) holder of an *encomienda*.

encomiable ADJ laudable, praiseworthy.

encomiar [1b] VT to praise, extol, pay tribute to.

encomienda NF (**a**) (*Hist Mil*) command (of a military order); (*en LAm*) *encomienda* (*land and inhabitants granted to a conquistador*).

(**b**) (*encargo*) charge, commission.

(**c**) (*protección*) protection; patronage.

(**d**) (*elogio*) praise, tribute, commendation.

(**e**) (*LAm Correos*) parcel; parcel post; ~ **contra reembolso** parcel sent cash on delivery.

(**f**) ~**s** regards, respects.

┌─ **ENCOMIENDA** ─┐

ⓘ The **encomienda** *was a repressive system fixing the Spanish conquistadors' entitlement to labour and tribute from Indian communities. Although the Indians theoretically remained free subjects of the Spanish Crown, in practice they were enslaved to the* **encomenderos** *(those having* **encomienda** *rights). One of its most celebrated opponents was the Dominican friar and former* **encomendero** *Fray Bartolomé de Las Casas (1474-1566). In 1542, in response to protests from the Church, and fearful of the growing power of the* **encomenderos**, *Charles V brought in laws aimed at phasing out the system. The Spanish settlers rebelled, but the Crown held fast to the central principle that* **encomienda** *rights should not be hereditary.*

---

encomio NM praise, eulogy, tribute.

encomioso ADJ (*LAm*) laudatory, eulogistic.

enconadamente ADV (*fig*) angrily, bitterly.

enconado ADJ (**a**) (*Med*) inflamed, angry; sore. (**b**) (*fig: airado*) angry, bitter. (**c**) (*fig: fervoroso*) ardent, fervent.

enconar [1a] ⊡ VT (**a**) (*Med*) to inflame; to make sore.

(**b**) (*fig*) to anger, irritate, provoke.

(**c**) (*Carib, Méx*: ratear*) to pilfer.

② **enconarse** VR (**a**) (*Med*) to become inflamed; to fester.

(**b**) (*fig: persona*) to get angry, get irritated; (*agravio*) to fester, rankle.

enconcharse [1a] VR (*LAm*) (*psicológicamente*) to go into one's shell; (*físicamente*) to retire into seclusion.

encono NM (**a**) (*rencor*) rancour, spite(fulness); ill-feeling, bad blood.

(**b**) (*And, Cono Sur: Med*) inflammation, soreness.

enconoso ADJ (**a**) (*Med*) inflamed, sore. (**b**) (*fig*) resentful, rancorous, malevolent. (**c**) (*LAm*) *planta* noxious, poisonous.

encontradizo ADJ met by chance; **hacerse el** ~ to contrive an apparently chance meeting, manage to bump into sb.

encontrado ADJ contrary, conflicting, hostile; opposed; **las posiciones siguen encontradas** their positions are still poles apart.

encontrar [1l] ⊡ VT (**a**) (*hallar*) to find; **lo encontró bastante fácil** he found it pretty easy; **¿qué tal lo encuentras?** how do you find it?; **no lo encuentro en ninguna parte** I can't find it anywhere; **no sé lo que le encuentran** I don't know what they see in her.

(**b**) (*topar*) to meet, encounter, run into; ~ **dificultades** to encounter difficulties, run into trouble.

② **encontrarse** VR (**a**) (*personas*) to meet, meet each other; ~ **con uno** to meet sb, run across sb, encounter sb; ~ **con un obstáculo** to run into an obstacle, encounter an obstacle; **me encontré con que no tenía gasolina** I found I was out of petrol; I was faced with the fact that I had no petrol.

(**b**) (*vehículos etc*) to crash, collide; (*opiniones etc*) to clash, conflict, come into collision.

(**c**) (*estar*) to be, be situated, be located, stand; **se encuentra en la plaza principal** it is in the main square; **¿dónde se encuentra el cine?** where is the cinema?

(**d**) (*hallarse*) to find o.s., be; **se encuentra enferma** she is ill; **¿cómo te encuentras ahora?** how are you now?, how do you feel now?, how do you find yourself now?; **me encontré sin coche** I found myself without a car; **en este momento no se encuentra** she's not in at the moment.

encontrón NM, **encontronazo** NM collision, crash, smash.

encoñamiento‡ NM infatuation; whim.

encoñar‡ [1a] ⊡ VT (**a**) (*alentar*) to lead on, draw on, raise (false) hopes in. (**b**) (*enojar*) to upset.

② **encoñarse** VR: ~ **de** to fall madly in love with, take a great fancy to.

encopetado ADJ (**a**) (*noble*) of noble birth; blue-blooded. (**b**) (*fig*) (*altanero*) haughty, high and mighty; (*presumido*) conceited; (*de buen tono*) posh*, grand.

encopetarse [1a] VR to get conceited, give o.s. airs.

encorajar [1a] ⊡ VT (**a**) (*animar*) to encourage, put heart into. (**b**) (*inflamar*) to inflame.

② **encorajarse** VR to fly into a rage.

encorajinar [1a] ⊡ VT (**a**) (*LAm*) = **encorajar**. (**b**) (*Méx: enfadar*) to anger, irritate.

② **encorajinarse** VR (*Cono Sur: trato*) to fail, go awry.

encorar [1l] VT to cover with leather.

encorbatado ADJ wearing a tie.

encorchado NM (**a**) corking. (**b**) hiving.

encorchar [1a] VT (**a**) *botella* to cork. (**b**) *abejas* to hive.

encordado NM (**a**) (*Cono Sur Mús*) (*cuerdas*) strings; (*guitarra*) guitar. (**b**) (*Boxeo*) ring.

encordar [1l] ⊡ VT (**a**) (*Mús etc*) to string, fit strings to. (**b**) (*atar*) to bind, tie, lash (with ropes); to rope together. (**c**) *espacio, zona* to rope off.

② **encordarse** VR (*alpinistas*) to rope themselves together, rope up.

encordelar [1a] VT to tie (with string).

encornado ADJ: **un toro bien** ~ a bull with good horns.

encornadura NF horns.

encornar [1l] VT to gore.

encornudar [1a] VT to cuckold.

encorralar [1a] VT to pen, corral.

encorsetar [1a] VT (*fig*) to confine, put into a straitjacket.

encorvada NF stoop, bend; **hacer la** ~* to malinger, pretend to be ill.

encorvado ADJ curved, bent; stooping; crooked.

encorvadura NF curve, curving, curvature; bend; crookedness.

encorvar [1a] ⊡ VT (**a**) to bend, curve; (*hacia abajo*) to bend (down, over); (*en forma de gancho*) to hook; (*torcer*) to make crooked.

② **encorvarse** VR (**a**) (*inclinarse*) to bend (down, over), stoop.

(**b**) (*combarse*) to sag, warp; (*torcerse*) to buckle.

encrespado ADJ *pelo* curly; *mar* choppy.

encrespador NM curling tongs.

encrespar [1a] ⊡ VT (**a**) *pelo* to curl, frizzle; *plumas* to ruffle; *mar* to make rough, produce waves on.

(**b**) (*fig*) to anger, irritate.

② **encresparse** VR (**a**) to curl; to ripple; to get rough.

(**b**) (*fig*) to get cross, get irritated.

encrestado ADJ haughty.

encrucijada NF crossroads; intersection, junction; **estamos en la** ~ (*fig*) we are at the crossroads; we are at the parting of the ways; **poner a uno en la** ~ (*fig*) to put sb on the spot.

encuadernación NF (**a**) binding; ~ **en cuero**, ~ **en piel** leather binding; ~ **en pasta** hardback (binding); ~ **en rústica** paperback (binding). (**b**) (*taller*) bindery, binder's.

encuadernador(a) NM/F bookbinder.

encuadernar [1a] VT to bind (*en* in); to cover; **libro sin** ~ unbound book.

encuadrable ADJ: ~ **en** that can be placed in, that can be included in.

encuadramiento NM (*acto*) framing; (*fig*) frame, framework.

encuadrar [1a] ⊡ VT (**a**) (*poner cuadro a*) to frame, put in a frame, make a frame for.

(**b**) (*encajar*) to fit, insert (*en* into).

(**c**) (*fig*) to contain, comprise.

(**d**) (*LAm: resumir*) to summarize, give a synthesis of.

② VI (*Cono Sur*) to fit, square (*con* with).

encuadre NM (*Fot etc*) setting, background, frame; (*fig*) setting.

encuartar [1a] (*Méx*) [1] VT *ganado* to tie up, rope.
  [2] **encuartarse** VR (a) (*animal*) to shy, balk; to get caught in its straps (*etc*).
  (b) (*fig*) to get involved, get bogged down (*en* in).
  (c) (*interrumpir*) to butt in.
encuartelar [1a] VT (*LAm*) to billet, put in barracks.
encubierta NF fraud.
encubierto ADJ (*oculto*) hidden, concealed; (*turbio*) underhand; (*secreto*) undercover; *crítica* veiled.
encubridor [1] ADJ concealing.
  [2] NM, **encubridora** NF harbourer; receiver of stolen goods; (*Jur*) accessory after the fact, abettor.
encubrimiento NM concealment, hiding; receiving of stolen goods; (*Jur*) complicity, abetment; **se le acusó de ~** he was charged with being an accessory after the fact.
encubrir [3a; PTP **encubierto**] VT (*ocultar*) to conceal, hide, cover (up), cloak; *criminal, sospechoso* to harbour, shelter; *crimen* to conceal; (*ayudar*) to abet, be an accomplice in.
encucurucharse* [1a] VR (*And, CAm*) to get up on top, reach the top.
encuentro NM (a) meeting; encounter; **~ de escritores** (small) congress of writers; **~ de inteligencias** meeting of minds; **un ~ fortuito** a chance meeting; **su primer ~ con la policía** his first encounter with the police; **ir** (*o* **salir**) **al ~ de uno** to go to meet sb; **ir al ~ de lo desconocido** to go out to face the unknown.
  (b) (*Mil*) encounter; skirmish, action, fight.
  (c) (*Dep*) meeting, match, game; **~ de ida** away game; **~ de vuelta** return match.
  (d) (*Aut etc*) collision, smash, crash; (*de opiniones etc*) clash; **llevarse a uno de ~** (*Carib, Méx***) (*derrotar*) to crush sb; (*arruinar*) to drag sb down to disaster; **llevarse todo de ~** (*Carib***) to ride roughshod over everyone.
encuerada NF (*Carib, Méx*) = **encuerista**.
encuerado ADJ (*Carib, Méx*) (*harapiento*) ragged; (*desnudo*) nude, naked.
encuerar [1a] [1] VT (*Carib, Cono Sur, Méx*) (a) (*desnudar*) to strip (naked).
  (b) (*fig***) to skin, fleece.
  [2] **encuerarse** VR (a) (*Carib, Cono Sur, Méx*: *desnudarse*) to strip off, get undressed.
  (b) (*Carib*: *vivir juntos*) to live together.
encueratriz* NF (*Méx*) = **encuerista**.
encuerista* NF (*Carib, Méx*) striptease artiste, stripper.
encuesta NF (a) (*Jur*) inquiry, investigation; probe (*de* into); inquest (*fig*); **~ judicial** post-mortem, coroner's inquest.
  (b) (*sondeo*) public-opinion poll; survey, inquiry; quiz; **E~ Gallup** Gallup Poll; **~ por teléfono** telephone poll.
encuestador(a) NM/F pollster.
encuestar [1a] VT to poll, take a poll of; **el 69 por 100 de los encuestados** 69% of those polled.
encuetarse: [1a] VR (*CAm*) to fly off the handle*, lose one's temper.
encuitarse [1a] VR (a) (*afligirse*) to grieve. (b) (*And*: *endeudarse*) to get into debt.
encujado NM (*Carib*) framework, lattice.
enculebrarse: [1a] VR (*CAm*) to fly off the handle*, lose one's temper.
enculecarse [1g] VR (*LAm*) to go broody.
encumbrado ADJ (a) *torre etc* lofty, towering, high. (b) *persona* exalted, eminent. (c) (*pey*) high and mighty, haughty.
encumbramiento NM (a) (*acto*) raising, elevation. (b) (*altura*) height, loftiness; (*fig*) exaltation, eminence. (c) (*fig*) haughtiness.
encumbrar [1a] [1] VT (a) (*alzar*) to raise, elevate.
  (b) *persona* to elevate, exalt (*a* to); (*fig*) to extol.
  [2] **encumbrarse** VR (a) (*torre etc*) to rise, soar, tower.
  (b) **~ sobre** (*fig*) to tower over, be far superior to.
  (c) (*fig*: *pey*) to be proud, be haughty.
encurdelarse: [1a] VR (*Cono Sur*) to get sloshed*.
encurrucarse* [1g] VR (*LAm*) (*de cuclillas*) to squat, crouch; (*ovillarse*) to curl up (in a ball).
encurtidos NMPL pickles; appetizers, savouries.
encurtir [3a] VT to pickle.
ende ADV (†† *o liter*): **por ~** hence, therefore.
endeble ADJ (*Med*) feeble, weak, frail; (*fig*) feeble, flimsy.
endeblez NF feebleness, weakness, frailty; flimsiness.
endecasílabo [1] ADJ hendecasyllabic.
  [2] NM hendecasyllable.
endecha NF lament, dirge.
endecharse [1a] VR to grieve, mourn.
endémico ADJ endemic; (*fig*) rife, chronic.
endemoniado ADJ (a) (*poseído*) possessed of the devil. (b) (*fig*: *endiablado*) devilish, fiendish; (*perverso*) perverse; (*furioso*) furious, wild.
endemoniar [1b] [1] VT (a) (*endiablar*) to bedevil. (b) (*: provocar*) to rile*, anger.

  [2] **endemoniarse** VR to get riled*.
endenantes* ADV (*LAm*) a short time back; earlier, before.
endentar [1j] VTI (*Mec*) to engage, mesh (*con* with).
endentecer [2d] VI to teethe, cut one's teeth.
enderezado ADJ appropriate; favourable, opportune.
enderezar [1f] [1] VT (a) (*poner derecho*) to straighten, straighten out (*o* up); (*destorcer*) to unbend.
  (b) (*poner vertical*) to set upright, stand vertically; (*Náut*) to right; *vehículo etc* to stand the right way up, put back on its wheels (*etc*), straighten up.
  (c) (*fig*: *arreglar*) to put in order, set to rights.
  (d) (*fig*) (*dirigir*) to direct; to manage; (*dedicar*) to address, dedicate (*a* to); **las medidas están enderezadas a** (*o* **para**) **corregirlo** the measures are designed to correct it.
  [2] **enderezarse** VR (a) (*ponerse recto*) to straighten up, stand up straight, draw o.s. up; (*Náut*) to right itself; (*Aer*) to flatten out.
  (b) **~ a un lugar** to set out for a place.
  (c) **~ a** + *infin* to take steps to + *infin*, prepare to + *infin*; (*medida etc*) to be designed to + *infin*.
ENDESA, Endesa [en'desa] NF ABR *de* **Empresa Nacional de Electricidad, Sociedad Anónima**.
endespués ADV (*And, Carib*) = **después**.
endeudamiento NM indebtedness, (extent of) debt.
endeudarse [1a] VR to get into debt (*con* with); **~ con uno** (*fig*) to become indebted to sb.
endeveras ADV (*LAm*) = **de veras**.
endiabladamente* ADV: **~ difícil** devilish(ly) difficult.
endiablado ADJ (a) (*diabólico*) devilish, diabolical, fiendish.
  (b) (*hum*) impish, mischievous, wicked.
  (c) (*feo*) ugly.
  (d) (*enojado*) furious, angry.
  (e) (*LAm*) *camino etc* difficult, dangerous; *asunto* complicated, tricky.
endiablar [1a] [1] VT (a) (*endemoniar*) to bedevil, bewitch. (b) (*: corromper*) to pervert, corrupt.
  [2] **endiablarse** VR to get furious.
endibia NF endive.
endija NF (*LAm*) = **rendija**.
endilgar* [1h] VT (a) (*enviar*) to send, direct; (*encaminar*) to guide.
  (b) *golpe* to fetch.
  (c) **~ algo a uno** to spring sth on sb; to unload sth on to sb; **~ un sermón a uno** to give sb a lecture, ram a sermon down sb's throat; **le han endilgado el mote de enchufado** they've labelled him a creep:.
endiñar [1a] VT (a) (*) *golpe* to fetch. (b) **~la:** to put it in:.
endiosado ADJ stuck-up*, conceited; high and mighty.
endiosamiento NM (a) (*engreimiento*) vanity, conceit; haughtiness.
  (b) (*ensimismamiento*) absorption.
endiosar [1a] [1] VT to deify; (*fig*) to make a god out of.
  [2] **endiosarse** VR (a) (*engreírse*) to get conceited, give o.s. airs; to be high and mighty.
  (b) **~ en algo** to be(come) absorbed in sth.
enditarse [1a] VR (*And, CAm*) to get into debt.
endocrina NF endocrine.
endocrino ADJ endocrine.
endodoncia NF endodontics.
endogamia NF inbreeding; **engendrado por ~** inbred.
endógeno ADJ endogenous.
endomingado ADJ all dressed up, in one's Sunday best.
endomingarse [1h] VR to dress up, put on one's Sunday best.
endomorfina NF endomorphine.
endomorfo NM endomorph.
endorfina NF endorphine.
endorsar [1a] VT (a) (*CAm, Carib*) = **endosar**. (b) (*fig*) to endorse, support, back; to confirm.
endosante NMF endorser.
endosar [1a] VT (a) *cheque etc* to endorse.
  (b) **~ algo a uno*** to lumber sb with sth*, make sb put up with sth; to unload sth on to sb.
endosatario, -a NM/F endorsee.
endoso NM endorsement; **sin ~** unendorsed.
endriago NM fabulous monster, dragon.
endrina NF sloe.
endrino NM blackthorn, sloe.
endrogarse* [1h] VR (*And, Méx*) to get into debt.
endulzante NM sweetening, sweetener.
endulzar [1f] VT (a) to sweeten. (b) (*fig*) to sweeten; to soften, mitigate.
endurecer [2d] [1] VT (a) to harden, make hard; to toughen; to stiffen; *lodo etc* to harden, cake, set.
  (b) (*fig*) to toughen, inure; *ley etc* to toughen up, make tougher; **~ a uno a los peligros** to inure sb to dangers.
  [2] **endurecerse** VR (a) to harden, get hard; to stiffen; (*lodo etc*) to

cake, set, set firm; (*Fin: precio*) to harden.

(**b**) (*fig*) to become cruel, become hard-hearted.

(**c**) ~ **a los peligros** to become inured to danger, inure o.s. to danger.

endurecido ADJ (**a**) (*duro*) hard; (*fuerte*) tough; (*rígido*) stiff; *lodo etc* hardened, caked, set.

(**b**) (*fig*) hardy, tough; ~ **a** inured to, used to.

(**c**) (*fig: pey*) cruel, callous, hard-hearted; obdurate.

endurecimiento NM (**a**) (*acto*) hardening; stiffening; setting; ~ **de las arterias** hardening of the arteries.

(**b**) (*estado*) hardness; toughness; stiffness; firmness.

(**c**) (*fig*) cruelty, callousness, hard-heartedness; obduracy.

ENE ABR *de* **estenordeste** east-north-east, ENE.

ene NF the (name of the) letter N; **supongamos que hay ~ objetos** let us suppose there are X objects.

ene. ABR *de* **enero** January, Jan.

enea NF = **anea**.

Eneas NM Aeneas.

enebro NM juniper.

Eneida NF Aeneid.

enema NF enema.

enemiga¹ NF enmity, hostility; ill-will.

enemigo [1] ADJ enemy, hostile; unfriendly; **ser ~ de** (*fig*) to dislike, be hostile to; (*tendencia etc*) to be inimical to; **una actitud enemiga de todo progreso** an attitude inimical to all progress.

[2] NM, **enemiga²** NF enemy; foe, adversary, opponent; **el E~, el ~ malo** the devil; ~ **infiltrado**, ~ **interior** enemy within; **pasarse al ~** to go over to the enemy.

enemistad NF enmity.

enemistar [1a] [1] VT to make enemies of, cause a rift between, set at odds.

[2] **enemistarse** VR to become enemies; ~ **con uno** to become an enemy of sb; to fall out with sb, become estranged from sb.

energético ADJ (**a**) (*Tec*) energy (*atr*), fuel (*atr*), power (*atr*); **la crisis energética** the energy crisis. (**b**) (*LAm*) = **enérgico**.

energía NF (**a**) (*gen*) energy; (*vigor*) vigour, drive; (*empuje*) push, go; **obrar con ~** to act energetically; **reaccionar con ~** to react vigorously.

(**b**) (*Téc*) power; energy; (*Elec*) power, energy, current; ~(**s**) **alternativa(s)** alternative energy; ~ **atómica** atomic energy; ~ **eólica** wind power; ~ **hidráulica** water power; ~ **nuclear** nuclear power; ~ **renovable** renewable energy; ~ **solar** solar energy.

enérgicamente ADV energetically; vigorously; forcefully; emphatically; strenuously; boldly.

enérgico ADJ energetic; *persona* energetic, vigorous; *manera* forceful, forthright; vital; pushful; *ademán, habla, tono* emphatic, forceful; *esfuerzo* determined, vigorous; *ejercicio* strenuous; *campaña* vigorous, forceful, high-pressure; *golpe* bold; *medida* bold; *ataque* vigorous, strong; **ponerse ~ con uno** to get tough with sb.

energizar [1f] VT to energize.

energúmeno, -a NM/F person possessed of the devil; (*fig*) (*demonio*) demon; (*loco*) wild person, madman; (*gritón*) loud and irascible person; (*Pol etc*) fanatic, extremist; **ponerse como un ~** to get mad.

enero NM January.

enervador ADJ, **enervante** ADJ enervating.

enervar [1a] [1] VT (**a**) (*debilitar*) to enervate. (**b**) (*provocar*) to anger, upset.

[2] **enervarse** VR to get cross, get upset.

enésimo ADJ (**a**) (*Mat*) n^{th}; **elevado a la enésima potencia** raised to the nth power, (*fig*) to the nth degree. (**b**) (*fig*) umpteenth*; **por enésima vez** for the umpteenth time*.

enfadadizo ADJ irritable, crotchety.

enfadado ADJ annoyed, angry.

enfadar [1a] [1] VT (**a**) (*enojar*) to anger, irritate, annoy; (*ofender*) to offend.

(**b**) (*LAm: aburrir*) to bore.

[2] **enfadarse** VR (**a**) (*enojarse*) to get angry, get cross, get annoyed (*con* with, *de* about, at); **no te enfades** don't be cross; don't be offended; **de nada sirve enfadarte** it's no good getting cross.

(**b**) (*LAm: aburrirse*) to be bored, get bored.

enfado NM (**a**) (*enojo*) annoyance, irritation, anger. (**b**) (*molestia*) trouble, bother.

enfadoso ADJ annoying, vexatious; irksome, tedious.

enfajillar [1a] VT (*CAm, Méx Correos*) to put a wrapper on.

enfangado ADJ (**a**) *terreno, persona* muddy. (**b**) (*fig*) *ideal* muddied.

enfangar [1h] [1] VT to cover with mud.

[2] **enfangarse** VR (**a**) (*enlodarse*) to get muddy, get covered in mud; to sink into the mud.

(**b**) (*fig*) to dirty one's hands, get involved in dirty work; ~ **en los vicios** to wallow in vice.

enfardado NM baling.

enfardadora NF (*Agr etc*) baler, baling machine.

enfardar [1a] VT to bale.

énfasis NM INVAR (**a**) emphasis; stress; **hablar con ~** to speak emphatically; to speak ponderously.

(**b**) (*fig*) emphasis; **poner el ~ en** to put the emphasis on, stress.

enfático ADJ emphatic; positive; *discurso* heavy, pompous, ponderous; **dijo ~** he said emphatically.

enfatizar [1f] [1] VT to emphasize, stress.

[2] VI: ~ **en** = VT.

enfebrecidamente ADV feverishly.

enfebrecido ADJ feverish.

enfermar [1a] [1] VT to make ill, cause illness in.

[2] VI to fall ill, be taken ill (*de* with); ~ **del corazón** to develop heart trouble.

[3] **enfermarse** VR (*LAm*) = VI.

enfermedad NF (**a**) (*indisposición*) illness; sickness; **durante esta ~** during this illness; **ausentarse por ~** to be away ill, be away sick.

(**b**) (*una ~*) illness, disease; (*fig*) disease, malady, ill; **una ~ muy peligrosa** a very dangerous disease; ~ **de Alzheimer** Alzheimer's disease; ~ **contagiosa** contagious disease; ~ **de declaración obligatoria** notifiable disease; ~ **degenerativa** degenerative disease; ~ **de la descompresión** decompression sickness; ~ **hereditaria** hereditary disease; ~ **holandesa del olmo** Dutch elm disease; ~ **del legionario** legionnaire's disease; ~ **de la piel** skin disease, skin infection; ~ **profesional** occupational disease; ~ **del sueño** sleeping sickness; ~ **terminal** terminal illness; ~ **transmisible** contagious disease; ~ **de transmisión sexual** sexually transmitted disease; ~ **venérea** venereal disease; ~ **por virus** virus disease; **contagiar a uno con una ~**, **pegar una ~ a uno** to give sb a disease.

ENFERMEDAD	*ver también la entrada*

¿"Illness" o "disease"?

Enfermedad tiene dos traducciones principales en inglés: *illness* y *disease*.

- Lo traducimos por *illness* cuando no concretamos la enfermedad de la que se trata, y también cuando se refiere al tiempo que una persona está enferma:

  Su enfermedad no le permite llevar una vida normal

  Her illness prevents her from living a normal life

  Adelgazó mucho durante su enfermedad

  She lost a lot of weight during her illness

- Lo traducimos por *disease* cuando nos referimos a una enfermedad infecciosa, a una enfermedad en concreto o a un tipo específico de enfermedad:

  Este tipo de enfermedad venérea es muy común

  This type of venereal disease is very common

  ...mineros que sufren de enfermedades de pulmón...

  ...miners suffering from lung diseases...

  Para otros usos y ejemplos ver la entrada.

---

enfermera NF nurse; ~ **ambulante** visiting nurse; ~ **jefa** matron.

enfermería NF infirmary; sanatorium; (*de colegio etc*) sick-bay; (*Taur*) hospital, medical section.

enfermero NM male nurse; (*Mil*) medical orderly.

enfermizo ADJ sickly, weak, unhealthy; infirm; *mente* morbid, unhealthy.

enfermo [1] ADJ (**a**) ill, sick, unwell; sickly; ~ **de amor** lovesick; ~ **del chape**, ~ **del mate** (*Cono Sur*) crazy; **caer ~, ponerse ~** to fall ill (*de* with); **estar ~ de gravedad, estar ~ de peligro** to be seriously ill, be dangerously ill.

(**b**) **estar ~** (*Cono Sur‡*) to be in jug‡, be in jail.

(**c**) (*Cono Sur*) **es ~ de malo** it's terribly bad; **es ~ de loca** she's clean crazy*.

[2] NM, **enferma** NF patient; invalid, sick person; ~ **terminal** terminal patient, terminally ill person.

enfermoso ADJ (*LAm*) = **enfermizo**.

enfervorizado ADJ ecstatic.

enfervorizar [1f] VT to arouse, arouse fervour in.

enfeudar [1a] VT (*Hist*) to enfief; ~ **a uno de una propiedad** to grant sb (the freehold of) a property.

enfiestarse* [1a] VR (*LAm*) to have a good time, enjoy o.s.

enfilada NF enfilade.

enfilar [1a] VT (**a**) (*Mil*) to enfilade.

(**b**) (*alinear*) to line up, put in a row; *cuentas* to thread.

(**c**) *rumbo* to direct, bear.

(**d**) *calle etc* to go straight along (*o* down *etc*); **el piloto trató de ~ la pista** the pilot tried to line the aircraft up with the runway.

enfisema NM emphysema.

enflaquecer [2d] [1] VT to make thin; to weaken, sap the strength of.

[2] VI **o enflaquecerse** VR (**a**) (*adelgazarse*) to get thin, lose weight.

(**b**) (*fig: esfuerzo etc*) to flag, weaken; (*persona*) to lose heart.

enflaquecido ADJ thin, extenuated.

enflaquecimiento NM (**a**) (*adelgazamiento*) loss of weight; emaciation. **(b)** (*fig*) weakening.

enflatarse* [1a] VR **(a)** (*CAm, Carib: entristecerse*) to sulk, be grumpy*. **(b)** (*Carib, Méx: enfadarse*) to fly off the handle*.

enflautada* NF (*And, CAm*) blunder.

enflautado ADJ pompous.

enflautar [1a] VT: **~ algo a uno** (*And, CAm, Méx*) to unload sth on to sb.

enfocar [1g] ①VT **(a)** (*Fot etc*) to focus (*a, sobre* on). **(b)** *problema etc* to approach, consider, look at; to size up; **podemos ~ este problema de tres maneras** we can approach this problem in three ways; **no me gusta su modo de ~ la cuestión** I do not like his approach to the question. ②VI y **enfocarse** VR to focus (*a, sobre* on).

enfollonado* ADJ muddled, confused.

enfollonarse* [1a] VR to get muddled, get all mixed up.

enfoque NM **(a)** (*Fot etc*) focus; focusing. **(b)** (*fig*) grasp; approach.

enfoscar [1g] ①VT to fill with mortar. ②**enfoscarse** VR **(a)** (*estar de mal humor*) to sulk, be sullen. **(b)** **~ en** to get absorbed in, get up to the eyes in. **(c)** (*cielo*) to cloud over.

enfrascar [1g] ①VT to bottle. ②**enfrascarse** VR: **~ en un libro** to bury o.s. in a book, become absorbed in a book; **~ en su laboratorio** to bury (*o* hide) o.s. away in one's laboratory; **~ en un problema** get deeply involved in a problem.

enfrenar [1a] VT **(a)** *caballo* to bridle; (*Mec*) to brake, slow, halt. **(b)** (*fig*) to curb, restrain.

enfrentado ADJ *posiciones* conflicting; *opiniones* opposing.

enfrentamiento NM clash, confrontation.

enfrentar [1a] ①VT **(a)** (*carear*) to put face to face. **(b)** *problema etc* to face, confront. ②VI to face. ③**enfrentarse** VR: **~ con** to face, face up to, confront; to stand up to; (*Dep*) to meet, play against; **hay que ~ con el peligro** one must face up to the danger, one must face the danger squarely.

enfrente ①ADV **(a)** opposite; in front, facing; (*fig*) in opposition; **la casa de ~** the house opposite, the house across the street; **sus amigos estaban ~** (*fig*) his friends were against it. **(b)** (*Cono Sur*) **~ mío** (*etc*) opposite me (*etc*), in front of me (*etc*). ②**~ de** PREP opposite (to), facing; (*fig*) opposed to, against.

enfriadera NF cooling jar; bottle cooler.

enfriadero NM cold storage, cold room.

enfriado NM cooling, chilling.

enfriador NM cooler, cooling plant.

enfriamiento NM **(a)** (*acción*) cooling; (*Econ etc*) cooling-down; (*refrigeración*) refrigeration. **(b)** (*Med*) cold, chill.

enfriar [1c] ①VT **(a)** (*helar*) to cool, chill; (*fig*) to cool down, take the heat out of; (*Econ etc*) to cool down. **(b)** (*LAm‡: matar*) to bump off‡. ②**enfriarse** VR **(a)** (*gen*) to cool, cool down, cool off; **déjelo hasta que se enfríe** leave it till it gets cool, leave it to cool down. **(b)** (*fig*) to cool off, grow cold.

enfrijolarse [1a] VR (*Méx*) to get messed up.

enfullinarse [1a] VR (*Cono Sur*) to get angry.

enfundar [1a] VT **(a)** *espada* to sheathe; *instrumento etc* to put away*, put in its case; **una señora enfundada en visón** a lady swathed in mink. **(b)** (*llenar*) to fill, stuff (*de* with). **(c)** (*) *comida* to scoff*.

enfurecer [2d] ①VT to enrage, madden. ②**enfurecerse** VR **(a)** to get furious, fly into a rage. **(b)** (*mar*) to get rough.

enfurruñarse* [1a] VR **(a)** to sulk, get sulky. **(b)** (*cielo*) to cloud over.

engaitar* [1a] VT: **~ a uno** to wheedle sb, talk sb round.

engajado ADJ (*And*) curly.

engalanar [1a] ①VT to adorn, deck (*de* with). ②**engalanarse** VR to adorn o.s.; to dress up, deck o.s. out.

engallado ADJ (*arrogante*) arrogant, haughty; (*confiado*) confident; (*jactancioso*) boastful.

engallinar [1a] VT (*LAm*) to cow, intimidate.

enganchado, -a* NM/F drug-addict.

enganchar [1a] ①VT **(a)** (*con gancho*) to hook; to hitch; to hang up; *caballo* to harness; *caballa, carro* to hitch up; (*Mec*) to couple, connect; (*Ferro*) to couple (up); **~la‡** to get canned‡. **(b)** (*fig: atraer*) to inveigle, ensnare; to rope in; *marido** to hook, land; (*cautivar*) to hook; **los programas que más enganchan** the programmes which get most people hooked. **(c)** (*Mil*) to recruit; to persuade to join up, lure into military service; (*Méx*) *trabajadores* to contract. ②**engancharse** VR **(a)** (*prenderse*) to get hooked up, catch (*en* on); (*Mec*) to engage (*en* with). **(b)** (*Mil*) to enlist, join up, sign on. **(c)** **~ a drogas** to get hooked on drugs*, become addicted to drugs; **estar enganchado*** to be hooked on drugs.

enganche NM **(a)** (*acto*) hooking (up); hitching; coupling, connection; (*Telec*) connection. **(b)** (*gancho*) hook, hooking device; (*Mec*) coupling, connection; (*Ferro*) coupling. **(c)** (*Mil*) recruitment, enlistment; (*pago*) bounty. **(d)** (*Méx: fianza*) deposit, down payment. **(e)** (*Carib: trabajo*) job; engagement. **(f)** (*Telec*) connection charge.

enganchón NM tear.

engañabobos NM INVAR **(a)** (*persona*) trickster. **(b)** (*trampa*) trick, trap.

engañadizo ADJ gullible.

engañador ①ADJ deceiving, cheating; deceptive. ②NM, **engañadora** NF cheat, deceiver, impostor.

engañapichanga NF (*And, Cono Sur*) trick, fraud, hoax.

engañar [1a] ①VT (*embaucar*) to deceive; to cheat, trick, swindle, fool; (*despistar*) to mislead; (*con esperanzas etc*) to beguile, delude; *hambre* to stay; *tiempo* to kill, while away; **a mí no me engaña nadie** you can't fool me; **logró ~ al inspector** he managed to trick the inspector; **engaña a su marido** she's unfaithful to her husband. ②VI to be deceptive; **las apariencias engañan** appearances are deceptive. ③**engañarse** VR to deceive o.s.; to be wrong, be mistaken; to delude o.s.; **en eso te engañas** you're wrong there; **se engaña con falsas esperanzas** she deludes herself with false hopes; **no te engañes, no te dejes ~** don't go deceiving yourself.

engañifa* NF trick, swindle.

engañito NM (*Cono Sur*) small gift, token.

engaño NM **(a)** (*cualidad*) deceit; (*trampa*) deception; fraud, trick, swindle; (*cosa fingida*) sham; (*decepción*) delusion; (*de pesca*) lure; **todo es ~** it's all a sham; **aquí no hay ~** there is no attempt to deceive anybody here, it's all on the level*; **llamar a ~** to protest that one has been cheated; **que nadie llame a ~** let nobody say he wasn't warned. **(b)** (*malentendido*) mistake, misunderstanding; **no haya ~** let there be no mistake about it; **padecer ~** to labour under a misunderstanding. **(c)** **~s** wiles, tricks. **(d)** (*Cono Sur: regalo*) small gift, token.

engañosamente ADV deceitfully, dishonestly; deceptively; misleadingly, wrongly.

engañoso ADJ *persona etc* deceitful, dishonest; *apariencia* deceptive; *consejo etc* misleading, wrong.

engañufla* NF trick*, swindle.

engarabitarse [1a] VR **(a)** (*subir*) to climb, shin up. **(b)** (*padecer frío*) to get stiff with cold. **(c)** (*And*) to grow weak, get thin.

engaratusar [1a] VT (*And, CAm, Méx*) = **engatusar**.

engarce NM **(a)** (*de joya*) setting, mount. **(b)** (*fig*) linking, connection. **(c)** (*And*: *jaleo*) row, shindy*.

engaripolarse* [1a] VR (*Carib*) to doll o.s. up*.

engarrotarse [1a] VR (*LAm*) to get stiff, go numb.

engarruñarse* [1a] VR (*And, CAm, Méx*) = **engurruñarse**.

engarzar [1f] ①VT **(a)** *joya* to set, mount; *cuentas* to thread; *pelo* to curl. **(b)** (*fig*) to link, connect. **(c)** (*And*: *enganchar*) to hook (up). ②**engarzarse** VR (*Cono Sur*) to get tangled, get stuck.

engastar [1a] VT to set, mount.

engaste NM setting, mount.

engatado ADJ thievish.

engatusar* [1a] VT to coax, wheedle, soft-soap*; **~ a uno para que haga algo** to coax sb into doing sth.

engendrar [1a] VT **(a)** (*Bio*) to beget, breed; to have as offspring. **(b)** (*Mat*) to generate. **(c)** (*fig*) to breed, cause, engender.

engendro NM **(a)** (*Bio*) foetus; (*pey*) malformed creature, abortion; freak. **(b)** (*fig*) abortion, monstrosity; (*chapuza*) bungled job; (*proyecto*) idiotic scheme, impossible plan; (*idea*) brain-child; **el proyecto es el ~ del ministro** the plan is some brain-child of the minister. **(c)** (*: feo*) terribly ugly person. **(d)** **mal ~, ~ del diablo*** bad lot, no-good lout* (*US*).

engerido* ADJ (*And: alicaído*) down, glum.

engerirse* [3k] VR (*And*) to grow sad.

engestarse [1a] VR (*Méx*) to make a wry face.

englobar [1a] VT **(a)** (*abarcar*) to include, comprise. **(b)** (*unir*) to lump together, put all together. **(c)** (*) **estar englobado** to be tight*.

engodo NM (*Carib*) bait.

engolado ADJ haughty.

engolfarse [1a] VR **(a)** (*Náut*) to sail out to sea, lose sight of land. **(b)** **~ en** (*fig*) to get deeply involved in; to plunge into, become deeply absorbed in; to launch out into.

engolletarse [1a] VR to give o.s. airs.

engolondrinarse [1a] VR **(a)** (*envanecerse*) to get conceited. **(b)**

(*amorosamente*) to have a flirtation.

engolosinar [1a] ☐1 VT to tempt, entice.
☐2 **engolosinarse** VR: ~ **con** to grow fond of.

engomado ADJ gummed.

engomar [1a] VT to gum, glue, stick.

engominar [1a] VT *pelo* to put hair-cream on; **iba todo engominado** his hair was all smarmed down.

engorda NF (a) (*And, Cono Sur: Agr: acto*) fattening (up). (b) (*Cono Sur: ganado*) fattened animals (*collectively*).

engordante ADJ fattening.

engordar [1a] ☐1 VT (a) to fatten (up). (b) (*fig*) *número* to swell, increase.
☐2 VI (a) (*ponerse gordo*) to get fat; to fill out, put on weight; (*Agr*) to fatten. (b) (*: enriquecerse*) to get rich.

engorde NM fattening (up).

engorrar [1a] VT (*Méx, Carib*) to annoy.

engorro NM bother, nuisance.

engorroso ADJ bothersome, vexatious, trying; cumbersome, awkward.

engrampador NM (*LAm*) stapler.

engrampar [1a] VT (*LAm*) to clip together, staple.

engranaje NM (*un* ~) gear; (*conjunto*) gears, gearing; (*engrane*) mesh; (*dientes*) gear teeth; ~ **de distribución** timing gear.

engranar [1a] ☐1 VT to gear; to put into gear; ~ **con** to gear into, engage.
☐2 VI to interlock; (*Mec*) to engage (*con una rueda* a wheel), mesh (*con* with); **A engrana con B** A is in gear with B; **A y B están engranados** A and B are in mesh.
☐3 **engranarse** VR (*Cono Sur, Méx Mec*) to seize up, get locked, jam.

engrandecer [2d] VT (a) to enlarge, magnify. (b) (*fig*) (*ensalzar*) to extol, magnify; to exalt; (*exagerar*) to exaggerate.

engrandecimiento NM (a) enlargement. (b) exaltation; aggrandizement; exaggeration.

engrane NM (a) mesh, meshing. (b) (*Cono Sur, Méx Mec*) seizing, jamming.

engrasación NF greasing, lubrication.

engrasado NM greasing, lubrication.

engrasador NM (*aceitera*) greaser, lubricator; (*punto*) grease point; (*Aut*) grease nipple; (*recipiente*) grease cup; ~ **de compresión, ~ de pistón** grease gun.

engrasamiento NM greasing, lubrication.

engrasar [1a] VT (a) (*Mec*) to grease, lubricate, oil. (b) (*manchar*) to make greasy, stain with grease. (c) (*Agr*) to manure. (d) (*: sobornar*) to bribe.

engrase NM (a) greasing, lubrication. (b) (*) bribe.

engreído ADJ (a) vain, conceited, stuck-up*. (b) (*LAm: afectuoso*) affectionate; (*mimado*) spoiled.

engreimiento NM vanity, conceit.

engreír [3k] ☐1 VT (a) (*envanecer*) to make vain, make conceited. (b) (*: dar coba a*) to butter up*, flatter. (c) (*LAm*) *niño* to spoil, pamper.
☐2 **engreírse** VR (a) to get conceited. (b) (*LAm*) to get spoiled, be pampered. (c) (*LAm*) ~ **a**, ~ **con** to grow fond of.

engrifarse [1a] VR (a) (*And*) to get haughty. (b) (*Méx*) to get cross. (c) (‡) to get high on drugs‡.

engrillar [1a] ☐1 VT (a) to shackle; to handcuff. (b) (*And, Carib*) to trick.
☐2 **engrillarse** VR (a) (*Carib: caballo*) to lower its head. (b) (*Carib: engreírse*) to get conceited. (c) (*And, CAm*) to get into debt.

engringolarse [1a] VR (*Carib*) to doll o.s. up.

engriparse [1a] VR to catch the flu.

engrosar [1l] ☐1 VT to enlarge; *cantidad* to increase, swell; to thicken.
☐2 VI to get fat.
☐3 **engrosarse** VR to increase, swell, expand.

engrudar [1a] VT to paste.

engrudo NM paste.

engrupido ADJ (*Cono Sur*) (a) (*engreído*) stuck-up*, conceited. (b) (*de mucha labia*) smooth-talking.

engrupidor NM (*Cono Sur*) smooth talker; con man*.

engrupir [3a] (*Cono Sur*) ☐1 VT (*engañar*) to con*.
☐2 VI to blarney one's way in.
☐3 **engruparse** VR to be conned*; (*engreírse*) to get conceited, put on airs.

enguacharse [1a] VR (*And*) to coarsen, get coarse.

enguadar [1a] VT (*Carib*) = **engatusar**.

engualichar [1a] VT (*Cono Sur*) (a) (*embrujar*) to bewitch (with a potion). (b) *amante* to rule, tyrannize.

enguandos NMPL (*And*) knick-knacks.

enguantado ADJ gloved, wearing a glove.

enguantarse [1a] VR to put one's gloves on.

enguaracarse [1g] VR (*CAm*) to hide o.s. away.

enguaraparse [1a] VR (*CAm*) to ferment.

enguarrado* ADJ filthy, dirty.

enguarrar* [1a] VT to make filthy, make dirty.

enguasimar [1a] VT (*Carib*) to hang.

enguayabado* ADJ: **está** ~ (*And, Carib*) he's got a hangover*, he's hung over*.

enguijarrado NM cobbles.

enguijarrar [1a] VT to cobble.

enguirnaldar [1a] VT to garland, wreathe (*de, con* with); (*fig*) to wreathe.

engullir [3a y 3h] VT to gobble, bolt, gulp (down); to devour.

engurrioso* ADJ jealous, envious.

engurruñarse [1a] VR to get sad, grow gloomy.

enharinar [1a] VT (*Culin*) to flour.

enhebrado NM threading.

enhebrar [1a] VT to thread.

enhestar [1j] ☐1 VT (a) (*erigir*) to erect; (*poner vertical*) to set upright. (b) (*alzar*) to hoist (up), raise (on high).
☐2 **enhestarse** VR (a) to straighten up, stand up straight. (b) to rise high.

enhiesto ADJ (a) (*derecho*) erect, straight, upright. (b) *bandera etc* raised; (*alto*) lofty, towering.

enhilar [1a] VT (a) *aguja* to thread. (b) (*fig*) to arrange, put in order.

▼ **enhorabuena** ☐1 NF congratulations; ¡~! congratulations!, and the best of luck!; **dar la ~ a uno** to congratulate sb, wish sb well; **estar de ~** to be in luck, be on to a good thing.
☐2 ADV: ¡~! all right!; well and good; ~ **que** ... thank heavens that ...

enhoramala INTERJ: ¡~! good riddance!; ¡**vete** ~! go to the devil!

enhorquetarse [1a] VR (*Carib, Cono Sur, Méx*) to sit astride.

enhuerar [1a] VT to addle.

enigma NM enigma; puzzle; mystery.

enigmáticamente ADV enigmatically.

enigmático ADJ enigmatic; puzzling; mysterious.

enjabonado NM, **enjabonadura** NF soaping, lathering.

enjabonar [1a] VT (a) to soap; to lather. (b) (*: dar coba a*) to soap up*, soft-soap*. (c) (*: reprender*) to tick off*.

enjaezar [1f] VT to harness, saddle up.

enjalbegado NM, **enjalbegadura** NF whitewashing.

enjalbegar [1h] VT *pared* to whitewash; *cara* to paint, make up.

enjambrar [1a] ☐1 VT to hive.
☐2 VI to swarm.

enjambre NM swarm (*t fig*).

enjaranarse [1a] VR (*CAm*) to get into debt.

enjarciar [1b] VT (*Náut*) to rig.

enjaretado NM grating, grille.

enjaretar [1a] ☐1 VT (a) (*: recitar*) to reel off, spout. (b) (*) **me enjaretó la tarea de** ... he lumbered me with the task of ...* (c) (*hacer de prisa*) to rush, rush through. (d) (*Cono Sur, Méx*) to slip in.
☐2 **enjaretarse** VR: ~ **la carrera** to shape one's career, mould one's career.

enjaular [1a] VT to cage, put in a cage; to coop up, pen in; (*) to jail, lock up.

enjertar [1a] VT = **injertar**.

enjetado‡ ADJ (*Cono Sur, Méx*) cross-looking, scowling.

enjetarse‡ [1a] VR (*Cono Sur, Méx*) (*enojarse*) to get cross; (*hacer muecas*) to scowl.

enjoyado ADJ bejewelled, set with jewels.

enjoyar [1a] VT to adorn with jewels, set with precious stones; to set precious stones in; (*fig*) to bejewel, adorn, embellish.

enjuagadientes NM INVAR mouthwash.

enjuagado NM rinsing.

enjuagar [1h] VT to rinse, rinse out; to wash out, swill out.

enjuague NM (a) (*líquido*) mouthwash. (b) (*acto*) rinse, rinsing; washing, swilling. (c) (*fig*) scheme, intrigue.

enjugamanos NM INVAR (*LAm*) towel.

enjugar [1h] VT (a) to wipe (off), wipe the moisture from; to dry; **~se la frente** to wipe one's brow, mop one's brow. (b) *déficit, deuda* to wipe out.

enjuiciamiento NM (a) (*acto*) judgement. (b) (*Jur*) ~ **civil** lawsuit, civil suit; ~ **criminal** trial, criminal prosecution.

enjuiciar [1b] VT (a) (*juzgar*) to judge, pass judgement on; (*examinar*) to examine. (b) (*Jur: acusar*) to indict; (*procesar*) to prosecute, try; (*sentenciar*) to sentence.

enjundia NF (a) animal fat, grease. (b) (*fig*) substance; strength, drive, vigour; essence, character.

enjundioso ADJ (a) fat. (b) (*fig*) substantial, solid, meaty.

enjuto ADJ (a) (*seco*) dry; dried; *V* **pie**. (b) (*marchito*) shrivelled up; wizened. (c) (*flaco*) lean, skinny, spare; *economía etc* lean (and fit).

enlabiar* [1b] VT to blarney, bamboozle*, take in.

enlabio NM blarney, honeyed words, plausible talk.

▼ **enlace** NM (a) (*vinculación*) link, tie-up, connection; (*vínculo*) bond;

(*relación*) relationship; (*Quím, Elec*) linkage; (*Mil etc*) liaison; (*Ferro*) connection; (*matrimonio*) marriage, union; (*encuentro*) meeting, rendezvous; **~ fijo** fixed link; **el ~ de A con B** the marriage of A and B; **~ de datos** (*Inform*) data line; **el ~ de las dos familias** the linking of the two families by marriage; **los buques no lograron efectuar el ~ en el punto indicado** the ships did not manage to rendezvous at the spot indicated; **~ telefónico** telephone link-up.

(**b**) (*persona*) link, go-between; **~ sindical** shop steward.

enladrillado NM brick paving.

enladrillar [1a] VT to pave with bricks.

enlardar [1a] VT (*Culin*) to baste.

enlatado [1] ADJ canned, tinned; (*Mús*) canned.
[2] NM canning, tinning.

enlatar [1a] VT (**a**) to can, tin. (**b**) (*grabar*) to record; (*TV*) to pre-record.

enlazar [1f] [1] VT (**a**) to link, connect; to tie (together), bind (together); to knit together.
(**b**) (*LAm*) to lasso.
[2] VI (*Ferro etc*) to connect (*con* with).
[3] **enlazarse** VR to link (up), be linked; to be connected; to join; to interlock; to entwine; (*novios*) to marry, get married; (*familias*) to become linked by marriage (*con* to).

enlentecimiento NM slowing-down.

enlistar [1a] VT (*CAm, Carib, Méx*) = **alistar**.

enllavar [1a] VT (*CAm*) to lock up.

enlodar [1a], **enlodazar** [1f] [1] VT (**a**) to muddy, cover in mud. (**b**) (*fig*) to besmirch, stain; to smear, defame.
[2] **enlodarse** VR, **enlodazarse** VR to get muddy.

enloquecedor ADJ maddening; *dolor de cabeza* splitting; *dolor* excruciating.

enloquecedoramente ADV maddeningly; excruciatingly.

enloquecer [2d] [1] VT to drive mad; (*fig*) to madden, drive crazy.
[2] VI y **enloquecerse** VR to go mad, go out of one's mind.

enloquecimiento NM madness.

enlosado NM flagstone pavement, tiled pavement.

enlosar [1a] VT to pave (with flagstones o tiles).

enlozado ADJ (*LAm*) enamelled, glazed.

enlozar [1f] VT (*LAm*) to enamel, glaze.

enlucido NM plaster.

enlucidor NM plasterer.

enlucir [3f] VT *pared* to plaster; *metal* to polish.

enlutado ADJ *persona* in mourning, wearing mourning; *ciudad etc* stricken.

enlutar [1a] [1] VT (**a**) *persona* to put into mourning; to dress in mourning.
(**b**) *vestido etc* to put crêpe on; to put a symbol of mourning on.
(**c**) *ciudad, país etc* to plunge into mourning; (*fig*) to sadden, grieve; **el accidente enlutó a la ciudad entera** the accident plunged the whole town into mourning.
(**d**) (*fig*) to darken.
[2] **enlutarse** VR to go into mourning, dress in mourning.

enmacetar [1a] VT *planta* to pot (up), put in a pot.

enmaderado ADJ timbered; boarded.

enmaderamiento NM timbering; boarding.

enmaderar [1a] VT to timber; to board (up).

enmadrado ADJ: **está ~** he's a mummy's boy*, he's tied to his mother's apron strings.

enmalezarse [1f] VR (*And, Carib, Cono Sur*) to get overgrown, get covered in scrub.

enmaniguarse [1i] VR (*Carib*) (**a**) (*tierra*) to get overgrown with trees, turn into jungle. (**b**) (*: persona*) to go native.

enmantecar [1g] VT (*Culin*) to grease, butter.

enmarañado ADJ (**a**) *pelo* tousled, tangled. (**b**) *asunto* messy, complicated.

enmarañar [1a] [1] VT (**a**) to tangle (up), entangle.
(**b**) (*fig: asunto*) to complicate, make more involved; *tarea* to make a mess of; *persona* to confuse, perplex; **sólo logró ~ más el asunto** he only managed to make a still worse mess of the matter, he only succeeded in complicating things further.
[2] **enmarañarse** VR (**a**) to get tangled (up), become entangled.
(**b**) (*fig*) to get more involved; to get into a mess; to get confused; **~ en un asunto** to get entangled in an affair.
(**c**) (*cielo*) to darken, cloud over.

enmarcado NM (*marco*) frame; (*acto*) framing.

enmarcar [1g] [1] VT (**a**) *cuadro* to frame. (**b**) (*fig*) to fit into a framework, set in a framework; to provide the setting for, act as a background to.
[2] **enmarcarse** VR: **~ en** to place o.s. in (the context of).

enmarillecerse [2d] VR to turn yellow; to turn pale.

enmascarada NF masked woman.

enmascarado NM masked man.

enmascaramiento NM masking, disguising.

enmascarar [1a] [1] VT (**a**) to mask (*t Inform*). (**b**) (*fig*) to mask, disguise.
[2] **enmascararse** VR (**a**) to put on a mask. (**b**) **~ de** (*fig*) to masquerade as.

enmedallado ADJ bemedalled.

enmendación NF emendation, correction.

enmendar [1j] [1] VT (**a**) *texto* to emend, correct; *ley, constitución etc* to amend.
(**b**) (*moralmente*) to reform.
(**c**) *pérdida* to make good, compensate for.
[2] **enmendarse** VR to reform, mend one's ways.

enmicado NM (*Méx*) plastic cover(ing).

enmicar [1g] VT (*Méx*) *documento* to cover in plastic, seal in plastic.

enmienda NF (**a**) emendation; correction; (*Jur, Pol etc*) amendment; **~ a la totalidad** motion for the rejection of a bill. (**b**) reform. (**c**) compensation, indemnity.

enmohecer [2d] [1] VT (**a**) *metal* to rust. (**b**) (*Bot etc*) to make mouldy.
[2] **enmohecerse** VR (**a**) to rust, get rusty. (**b**) (*Bot etc*) to get mouldy.

enmohecido ADJ (**a**) rusty, rust-covered. (**b**) mouldy, mildewed.

enmonarse [1a] VR (**a**) (*droga*) to get cold turkey*, suffer withdrawal symptoms. (**b**) (*LAm*) to get tight*.

enmontarse [1a] VR (*And, CAm, Carib*) to get overgrown, revert to scrub.

enmoquetado ADJ carpeted.

enmoquetador NM carpet-layer.

enmoquetar [1a] VT to carpet.

enmudecer [2d] [1] VT to silence.
[2] **enmudecerse** VR (*callarse*) to be silent; to remain silent, say nothing; (*hacerse mudo*) to become dumb; (*no poder hablar*) to lose one's voice.

enmugrar [1a] VT (*And, Cono Sur, Méx*), **enmugrecer** [2d] VT, **enmugrentar** [1a] VT (*Cono Sur*) to soil, dirty.

ennegrecer [2d] [1] VT (*poner negro*) to blacken; (*teñir*) to dye black; (*oscurecer*) to darken, obscure.
[2] VI y **ennegrecerse** VR to turn black; to get dark, darken.

ennoblecer [2d] VT (**a**) to ennoble. (**b**) (*fig*) to embellish, adorn; to dignify.

ennoblecimiento NM ennoblement.

ennoviarse* [1b] VR to get engaged.

en.º ABR *de* **enero** January, Jan.

enofilia NF oenophilia, liking for wines; expertness in wines.

enófilo, -a NM/F oenophile, lover of wines; wine expert.

enojada NF (*Carib, Méx*) (fit of) anger.

enojadizo ADJ irritable, peevish, short-tempered.

enojado ADJ angry, cross; **dijo ~** he said angrily.

enojar [1a] [1] VT to anger; to upset, annoy, vex.
[2] **enojarse** VR to get angry, lose one's temper; to get annoyed, get cross (*con, contra* with; *de* at, about); **¡no te enojes!** (*preocuparse*) don't bother!, don't trouble yourself!; (*enfadarse*) don't be (o get) angry.

enojo NM (**a**) (*ira*) anger; (*irritación*) annoyance, vexation; **decir con ~** to say angrily.
(**b**) **de prontos ~s, de repentinos ~s** quick-tempered; **tener prontos (o repentinos) ~s** to be quick to anger, be easily upset.
(**c**) **~s** troubles, trials.

enojón ADJ (*And, Cono Sur, Méx*) = **enojadizo.**

enojoso ADJ irritating, annoying.

enología NF oenology, science of wine(-making).

enólogo, -a NM/F oenologist, wine expert; wine-grower.

enorgullecer [2d] [1] VT to fill with pride.
[2] **enorgullecerse** VR to be proud, swell with pride; **~ de** to be proud of, pride o.s. on.

enorme ADJ (**a**) enormous, huge, vast; tremendous. (**b**) (*fig*) heinous, monstrous. (**c**) (*) killing, marvellous; **cuando remeda al profe es ~** when he takes off the teacher he's killing.

enormemente ADV enormously, vastly; tremendously.

enormidad NF (**a**) (*inmensidad*) enormousness; hugeness.
(**b**) (*fig: de crimen etc*) heinousness, monstrousness, enormity.
(**c**) (*acto etc*) wicked thing, monstrous thing.
(**d**) (*) **me gustó una ~** I liked it enormously.

enoteca NF wine-cellar, collection of wines.

ENP NF, **ENPETROL** [enpe'trol] NF ABR *de* **Empresa Nacional del Petróleo.**

enqué* NM: **lo traeré si encuentro ~** (*And*) I'll bring it if I can find something to put it in (o a bag for it).

enquistamiento NM (*fig*) sealing off, shutting off, enclosure.

enquistar [1a] [1] VT (*fig*) to seal off, shut off, enclose.
[2] **enquistarse** VR (*Med*) to develop a cyst.

enrabiar [1b] [1] VT to enrage.
[2] **enrabiarse** VR to get enraged.

enrabietarse [1a] VR to throw a tantrum, get very cross.

enrachado ADJ lucky; enjoying a run of luck.

enraizado ADJ *tradición* well established, long-standing; *idea, prejuicio* deep-seated, deeply rooted.

enraizar [1f] VI to take root.

enramada NF (a) arbour, bower. (b) (*Cono Sur: cobertizo*) cover (*etc*) made of branches.

enramar [1a] **1** VT to cover with branches.
2 VI (*Cono Sur*) to come into leaf.

enranciarse [1b] VR to go rancid, get stale.

enrarecer [2d] **1** VT (a) *aire etc* to rarefy. (b) (*hacer que escasee*) to make scarce, cause to become rare.
2 enrarecerse VR (a) (*aire*) to become rarefied, get thin. (b) (*escasear*) to become scarce, grow rare. (c) (*relaciones*) to deteriorate, become tense.

enrarecido ADJ (a) rarefied. (b) *relaciones* tense, difficult.

enrarecimiento NM (a) rarefaction; thinness. (b) scarceness, rareness. (c) deterioration; tension.

enrastrojarse [1a] VR (*LAm*) to get covered in scrub.

enrazado ADJ (*And*) *persona* half-breed; *animal* crossbred.

enrazar [1f] VT (*And*) to mix (racially); *animales* to crossbreed.

enredadera NF (*Bot*) climbing plant, creeper; ~ (**de campo**) bindweed.

enredador **1** ADJ trouble-making, mischief-making; *niño* naughty.
2 NM, **enredadora** NF (*chismoso*) gossip; (*entrometido*) busybody, meddler; (*subversivo*) troublemaker, mischief-maker.

enredar [1a] **1** VT (a) *animal etc* to net, catch in a net. (b) *trampa* to set. (c) (*entrelazar*) to intertwine, interweave; (*pey*) to entangle, tangle (up). (d) *asunto* to confuse, complicate; *tarea* to make a mess of. (e) (*comprometer*) *persona* to embroil, involve, implicate (*en* in). (f) *dos personas* to sow discord among (o between); ~ **a A con B** to sow discord between A and B, embroil A with B. (g) (*engañar*) *persona* to deceive.
2 VI (*niño etc*) to get up to mischief, cause trouble; ~ **con** to mess about with.
3 enredarse VR (a) (*enmarañarse*) to get entangled, get tangled (up); ~ **en** (*cuerda etc*) to catch on, (*Náut*) foul. (b) (*asunto*) to get complicated; to get into a mess. (c) (*persona*) to get entangled (*con* with), get involved (*con* with); **no te enredes** don't you get mixed up in this, keep out of this mess; **se enredó con una estudiante** he got involved with a student, he had an affair with a student; ~ **de** (o **en**) **palabras** to get involved in an argument.

enredista (*LAm*) = **enredador**.

enredo NM (a) (*de lana etc*) tangle. (b) (*fig:* *lío*) tangle, entanglement; (*amorío*) love affair; (*confusión*) mess, confusion, mix-up; (*de detalles etc*) maze, tangle. (c) (*apuro*) jam, difficult situation. (d) (*envolvimiento*) embroilment, involvement. (e) (*Teat*) plot. (f) ~**s** (*intrigas*) intrigues; (*mentiras*) mischief, mischievous lies; **comedia de** ~(**s**) comedy of intrigue.

enredoso ADJ (a) tangled, complicated; tricky. (b) (*Méx*) = **enredador 1**.

enrejado NM (*reja*) grating, grille; (*de ventana*) lattice; (*de jardín*) trellis; (*Cos*) openwork; (*verja*) fence, railings; (*de jaula*) bars; ~ **de alambre** wire netting (fence).

enrejar [1a] VT (a) to fix a grating to, put a grating on; to fence, put railings round. (b) (*LAm*) *caballo* to put a halter on. (c) (*Méx: zurcir*) to darn, patch.

enrejillado NM small-mesh grille.

ENRESA, Enresa [en'resa] NF ABR de **Empresa Nacional de Residuos Nucleares.**

enrevesado ADJ complicated, intricate.

enrielar [1a] VT (a) (*Téc*) to make into ingots. (b) (*LAm: poner rieles en*) to lay rails on. (c) (*LAm*) *tren* to put on the tracks, set on the rails; (*fig*) to put on the right track.

Enrique NM Henry.

enriquecer [2d] **1** VT to make rich, enrich.
2 enriquecerse VR to get rich; to prosper; (*pey*) to enrich o.s.; ~ **a costa ajena** to do well at other people's expense.

enriquecido ADJ *producto* enriched.

enriquecimiento NM enrichment.

enriscado ADJ craggy, rocky.

enristrar [1a] VT (a) *ajos* to string, make a string of, put on a string. (b) (*fig*) *dificultad* to straighten out, iron out. (c) *lugar* to go straight to.

enrizar [1f] VT to curl.
2 enrizarse VR to curl.

enrocar [1g] VI (*Ajedrez*) to castle.

enrojecer [2d] **1** VT (*volver rojo*) to redden, turn red; *persona* to make blush; *metal* to make red-hot.
2 VI y **enrojecerse** VR to blush, redden; to go red (with anger); to get red-hot.

enrojecimiento NM reddening; blushing, blush.

enrolar [1a] (*LAm*) **1** VT to enrol, sign on, sign up; (*Mil*) to enlist.
2 enrolarse VR to enrol, sign on; (*Mil*) to enlist, join up; (*Dep*) to enter (*en* for).

enrollable ADJ that rolls up, roll-up (*atr*); **persiana** ~ slatted shutter.

enrollado* **1** ADJ: **un tío muy** ~ a thoroughly turned-on guy*.
2 NM, **enrollada** NF fan, enthusiast.

enrollamiento NM (a) rolling up; (*Elec*) coiling. (b) (*) event, happening; festival.

enrollante* ADJ smashing*, super*; fascinating.

enrollar [1a] **1** VT (a) to roll (up), wind (up); *cuerda* to coil. (b) (*: *atraer*) to turn on*; **a mí no me enrolla eso** that doesn't turn me on*, **a mí no me enrolla eso** that doesn't turn me on*, I don't dig that*.
2 enrollarse VR (a) (*al explicarse*) to go on a long time, jabber on, explain (*etc*) at great length; **cuando se enrolla no hay quien lo pare** when he gets going there's no stopping him. (b) **se enrollaron*** they paired off, they started going around together; ~ **con uno** to get involved with sb; (*como amante*) to get off with sb*, make it with sb*t*; ~ **bien con uno** to get on well with sb, hit it off with sb; ~ **en** to get involved in. (c) (*) to get with it*, get turned on*, get into the swing of things.

enrolle* NM boring event, bad scene*, pain*.

enronquecer [2d] **1** VT to make hoarse.
2 VI y **enronquecerse** VR to get hoarse, grow hoarse.

enronquecido ADJ hoarse.

enroque NM (*Ajedrez*) castling.

enroscado ADJ (a) coiled; twisted; kinky. (b) (*And*) angry.

enroscadura NF coil; twist; kink.

enroscar [1g] **1** VT (a) (*arrollar*) to coil (round), wind; (*torcer*) to twist, twine; (*en espiral*) to curl (up). (b) *tornillo* to screw in. (c) (*rodear*) to wreathe (*de* in).
2 enroscarse VR to coil, wind; to twist, twine; to curl (up); ~ **alrededor de un árbol** to twine round a tree.

enrostrar [1a] VT (*LAm*) to reproach.

enrulado ADJ (*Cono Sur*) curly.

enrular [1a] VT (*And, Cono Sur*) to curl.

enrumbar* VI (*LAm*) to go, set off.

ensacar [1g] VT to sack, bag, put into bags.

ensaimada NF *light, spiral-shaped pastry typical of Mallorca.*

ensalada NF (a) (*Culin*) salad; ~ **de col** coleslaw; ~ **de frutas** fruit salad; ~ **de patatas** potato salad. (b) (*fig*) hotchpotch, unholy mixture; mix-up; medley; (*Aut*) traffic jam; ~ **de tiros*** shoot-out, shooting.

ensaladera NF salad-bowl, salad-dish.

ensaladilla NF (a) ≃ Russian salad. (b) (*And, Carib*††: *sátira*) lampoon, satirical verse.

ensalmado ADJ (*LAm*) magic.

ensalmador NM quack, bonesetter.

ensalmar [1a] VT *hueso* to set; *enfermedad* to cure by spells, treat by quack remedies.

ensalme NM (*And*) spell, incantation.

ensalmo NM spell, charm, incantation; (*Med*) quack remedy, quack treatment (using spells); (**como**) **por** ~ as if by magic.

ensalzable ADJ praiseworthy, meritorious.

ensalzamiento NM exaltation; extolling.

ensalzar [1f] VT to exalt; to praise, extol.

ensamblado NM (*Aut etc*) assembly.

ensamblador(a) **1** NM/F (a) joiner; fitter.
2 NM (*Inform*) assembler.

ensambladura NF (a) (*gen*) joinery; assembling. (b) (*Téc*) joint; ~ **de inglete** mitre joint.

ensamblaje NM (a) (*Téc*) assembly; docking, link-up; **planta de** ~ assembly plant. (b) (*Inform*) assembly language.

ensamblar [1a] VT (*Téc*) to join; to assemble; *astronaves* to dock, link up.

ensanchar [1a] **1** VT to enlarge, widen, extend; to stretch; to expand; (*Cos*) to enlarge, let out.
2 ensancharse VR (a) to get wider, spread, expand; to stretch. (b) (*fig*) to give o.s. airs.

ensanche NM enlargement, widening, extension; expansion; stretch(ing); (*de ciudad*) extension, new suburb, suburban development; (*Cos*) extra piece, room to let out.

ensangrentado ADJ bloodstained; bloody, gory.

ensangrentar [1j] **1** VT to stain with blood, cover in blood.
2 ensangrentarse VR (*fig*) to get angry; ~ **con,** ~ **contra** to be cruel to, treat cruelly, be vindictive towards.

ensañado ADJ furious; cruel, merciless.

ensañamiento NM rage; fury; cruelty, barbarity.

ensañar [1a] **1** VT to enrage.

2 **ensañarse** VR: ~ **con**, ~ **en** to vent one's anger on; to delight in tormenting, take a sadistic pleasure in the sufferings of.

ensarnarse [1a] VR (*CAm, Cono Sur, Méx*) to get mangy.

ensartada* NF: **pegarse una** ~ (*And*) to be very disappointed, feel let down.

ensartador NM (*Cono Sur*) roasting spit.

ensartar [1a] **1** VT (a) *cuentas etc* to string; *aguja* to thread; *carne* to spit.

(b) (*fig*) to string together; to link; *disculpas etc* to reel off, trot out, rattle off.

2 **ensartarse*** VR (a) (*And, Carib*) to get into a jam*.

(b) (*Cono Sur: salir mal*) to mess things up.

ensarte* NM (*And*) disappointment, let-down.

ensayar [1a] **1** VT (a) (*probar*) to test, try, try out.

(b) *metal* to assay.

(c) (*Mús, Teat*) to rehearse.

2 **ensayarse** VR to practise; to rehearse; ~ **a** + *infin* to practise + *ger.*

ensaye NM assay.

ensayista NMF essayist.

ensayística NF essays, essay-writing; genre of the essay.

ensayístico ADJ essay (*atr*); **obra ensayística** essays, work in essay form.

ensayo NM (a) (*prueba*) test, trial; (*experimento*) experiment; (*intento*) attempt; (*ejercicio*) practice, exercise; ~ **clínico** clinical trial; ~ **nuclear** nuclear test; **de** ~ tentative; practice (*atr*); experimental; **pedido de** ~ (*Com*) trial order; **viaje de** ~ trial run; **vuelo de** ~ test flight; **hacer algo a modo de** ~ to do sth as an experiment, do sth to try it out; **hacer** ~**s** to practise (*en* on), train.

(b) (*de metal*) assay.

(c) (*Liter, Escol etc*) essay.

(d) (*Mús, Teat*) rehearsal; ~ **general** dress rehearsal.

(e) (*Rugby*) try.

ensebado ADJ greased, greasy.

enseguida ADV V **seguida** (b).

enselvado ADJ wooded.

ensenada NF (a) inlet, cove; creek. (b) (*Cono Sur*) small fenced pasture.

enseña NF ensign, standard.

enseñado ADJ trained; informed; educated; **bien** ~ *perro* housetrained.

enseñante **1** ADJ teaching.

2 NMF teacher.

enseñanza NF (a) (*gen: acto*) education; (*acto, profesión*) teaching; instruction, training; schooling; tuition; **primera** ~, ~ **primaria** elementary education; **segunda** ~, ~ **secundaria** secondary education; ~ **superior** higher education; ~ **universitaria** university education; ~ **de los niños atrasados** remedial teaching, teaching of backward children; ~ **para ambos sexos** coeducation; ~ **a distancia** distance learning; ~ **asistida por ordenador** computer-assisted learning; ~ **general básica** education course in Spain from 6 to 14; ~ **programada** programmed learning.

(b) (*doctrina*) teaching, doctrine; **la** ~ **de la Iglesia** the teaching of the Church.

enseñar [1a] **1** VT (a) *persona* to teach, instruct, train; to educate; *asignatura* to teach; ~ **a uno a hacer algo** to teach sb (how) to do sth, train sb to do sth; to show sb how to do sth.

(b) (*mostrar*) to show; (*señalar*) to point out; **nos enseñó el museo** he showed us (over) the museum; **te enseñaré mis aguafuertes** I'll show you my etchings; **esto nos enseña las dificultades** this reveals the difficulties to us.

2 **enseñarse** VR (a) (*LAm*) to learn; ~ **a hacer algo** to learn (how) to do sth.

(b) (*esp LAm*) to accustom o.s., become inured (*a* to); **no me enseño aquí** I can't get used to it here, I can't settle down here.

enseñorearse [1a] VR: ~ **de** to take possession of, take over; (*fig*) to overlook, dominate.

enseres NMPL (*efectos personales*) goods and chattels; (*avíos*) things, gear, tackle, equipment; ~ **domésticos** household goods; ~ **eléctricos** electrical applicances.

enseriarse [1b] VR (*And, CAm, Carib*) to look serious.

ENSIDESA, Ensidesa NF (*Esp Com*) ABR *de* **Empresa Nacional Siderúrgica, Sociedad Anónima.**

ensilado NM ensilage; ~ **de patatas** potato clamp.

ensiladora NF silo.

ensilar [1a] VT to store in a silo.

ensillar [1a] VT to saddle (up), put a saddle on.

ensimismamiento NM (a) absorption; reverie. (b) (*LAm*) conceit.

ensimismarse [1a] VR (a) to be(come) lost in thought, go into a reverie. (b) (*LAm*: engreírse*) to get conceited.

ensoberbecer [2d] **1** VT to make proud.

2 **ensoberbecerse** VR (a) to become proud, become arrogant. (b) (*mar*) to get rough.

ensobrar VT *carta* to put in an envelope; (*Inform*) *fichero* to attach.

ensombrecer [2d] **1** VT (a) to darken, cast a shadow over. (b) (*fig*) to overshadow, put in the shade.

2 **ensombrecerse** VR (a) to darken, get dark.

(b) (*fig*) to get gloomy.

ensombrerado ADJ with a hat, wearing a hat.

ensoñación NF fantasy, fancy, dream; **¡ni por ~!** not a bit of it!, never!

ensoñador **1** ADJ dreamy.

2 NM, **ensoñadora** NF dreamer.

ensopar [1a] **1** VT *galleta etc* to dip, dunk; (*LAm*) to soak, drench; to saturate.

2 **ensoparse** VR (*LAm*) to get soaked.

ensordecedor ADJ deafening.

ensordecer [2d] **1** VT *persona* to deafen; *ruido* to muffle.

2 VI to go deaf; (*fig*) to pretend not to hear, pretend to be deaf.

ensortijado ADJ (*pelo*) in ringlets.

ensortijar [1a] **1** VT (a) *pelo* to curl, put curls into. (b) *nariz* to ring, fix a ring in.

2 **ensortijarse** VR to curl.

ensuciamiento NM soiling, dirtying.

ensuciar [1b] **1** VT (a) to soil, dirty; to foul; to mess up, make a mess of.

(b) (*fig*) to defile, pollute.

2 **ensuciarse** VR to get dirty; (*niño*) to soil o.s.

ensueño NM (a) dream, fantasy, illusion; reverie; **de** ~ dream-like; other-wordly; **una cocina de** ~ a dream kitchen, a kitchen of one's dreams; **mundo de** ~ dream world, world of fantasy; **¡ni por ~!** not a bit of it!, never!

(b) ~**s** visions, fantasies.

entabicar [1g] VT (*LAm*) to partition off.

entablado NM boarding, planking; wooden flooring.

entabladura NF boarding, planking.

entablar [1a] **1** VT (a) *suelo etc* to board (in, up), plank, cover with boards.

(b) (*Ajedrez*) *trebejos* to set up.

(c) (*Med*) to splint, put in a splint.

(d) *conversación etc* to start, strike up; *contrato* to enter into; *proceso* to begin, file, bring; *reclamación* to file, put in.

2 VI (a) (*LAm Ajedrez*) to draw.

(b) (*And †: fanfarronear*) to boast.

3 **entablarse** VR (a) (*viento*) to settle. (b) (*Méx*) to take place.

entable NM (a) (*tablas*) boarding, planking.

(b) (*Ajedrez*) position.

(c) (*LAm: organización*) order, arrangement, disposition.

(d) (*And: empresa nueva*) new business; (*And: de terrenos vírgenes*) breaking, opening up.

entablillar [1a] VT (*Med*) to splint, put in a splint; **con el brazo entablillado** with his arm in a splint.

entalegar [1h] VT (a) to bag, put in a bag. (b) (*fig*) to hoard, stash away. (c) (**:**) to jug**:**, jail.

entallado ADJ (*Cos*) waisted, with a waist.

entallador(a) NM/F sculptor; engraver.

entalladura NF (a) (*arte, objeto*) sculpture, carving; engraving. (b) (*corte*) slot, notch, cut, groove.

entallar [1a] **1** VT (a) (*esculpir*) to sculpt, carve; (*grabar*) to engrave; ~ **el nombre en un árbol** to carve one's name on a tree.

(b) (*hacer un corte en*) to notch, cut a slot in, cut a groove in.

(c) (*Cos*) to cut, tailor.

2 VI to fit (well); **traje que entalla bien** a suit that fits well, a well-cut suit.

entallecer [2d] VI y **entallecerse** VR to shoot, sprout.

entapizado **1** ADJ (a) upholstered (*de* with); hung (*de* with); covered (*de* with).

(b) (*Bot*) overgrown (*de* with).

2 NM (*Méx*) wall-coverings, tapestries.

entapizar [1f] VT (a) *mueble* to upholster (*de* with, in); *pared* to hang with tapestries; *butaca etc* to cover with fabric; (*Cono Sur*) *suelo* to carpet.

(b) (*Bot*) to grow over, cover, spread over.

entarascar [1g] **1** VT to dress up, doll up.

2 **entarascarse** VR to dress up, doll up.

entarimado NM (a) (*tablas*) floorboarding, roof boarding; (*taracea*) inlaid floor; ~ (**de hojas quebradas** o **de maderas finas**) parquet.

(b) (*estrado*) dais, stage, platform.

entarimar [1a] VT to board, plank; to put an inlaid floor on (o over).

entarugado NM block flooring, block paving.

ente NM (a) entity, being; (*Pol etc*) body, organization; **el E~** (*esp*) the Spanish state TV and radio; ~ **moral** (*Méx*) non-profit-making organization; **~ gubernamental, ~ oficial** official entity, official body; **~ público** public body, public corporation. **(b)** (*) fellow, chap*; odd sort.

entecarse [1g] VR (*Cono Sur*) to be stubborn.

entechar [1a] VT (*LAm*) to roof.

enteco ADJ weak, sickly, frail.

entediarse [1b] VR to get bored.

entejar [1a] VT (*LAm*) to tile.

enteje NM (*LAm*) tiling.

Entel NF ABR *de* **Empresa Nacional de Telecomunicaciones**.

entelar [1a] VT *pared* to cover with hangings.

entelequia NF (*Fil*) entelechy; (*fig: plan etc*) pipe-dream, pie in the sky.

entelerido ADJ **(a)** (*frío*) shivering with cold; (*atemorizado*) shaking with fright. **(b)** (*LAm: débil*) weak, sickly, frail. **(c)** (*LAm: acongojado*) distressed, upset.

entenada NF stepdaughter.

entenado NM stepson; stepchild.

entendederas* NFPL brains; **ser corto de ~, tener malas ~** to be pretty dim, be slow on the uptake; **sus ~ no llegan a más*** he has a brain the size of a pea*, he's bird-brained*.

entendedor(a) NM/F understanding person; **al buen ~, pocas palabras** (**le bastan**) a word to the wise is sufficient; enough said!

entender [2g] **1** VTI **(a)** (*comprender*) to understand; (*darse cuenta*) to realize, grasp; to comprehend; **¿entiendes?** (do you) understand?, do you get me?; **no le entiendo** I don't understand you; **lo que es ~, entiendo** I understand it as far as anybody can understand it; **no entiendo palabra** it's Greek to me; **no entendió jota** (*o* **una patata** *etc*) he didn't understand a word of it; **a mi ~** to my way of thinking, in my opinion; **~ mal** to misunderstand; **dar a ~ que ...** to give to understand that ..., imply that ...; **según él da a ~** according to what he says, as he implies; **hacer ~ algo a uno** to make sb understand sth, put sth across to sb; **hacerse ~** to make o.s. understood, get across (*por* to); **lograr ~** to manage to grasp; to get the hang of.
(b) (*querer decir*) to intend, mean; **¿qué entiendes con eso?** what do you mean by that?
(c) (*creer*) to think, believe; to infer; **entiendo que es ilegal** I feel it is illegal, to my mind it's illegal; **¿debo ~ que lo niegas?** am I to understand that you deny it?
(d) (*oír*) to hear.
2 VI **(a)** **~ de** to be an expert on, be good at, know all about; **~ de carpintería** to know all about carpentry, be an expert carpenter; **yo no entiendo de vinos** I'm no judge of wines; **ella no entiende de coches** she's hopeless with cars.
(b) **~ en** to deal with, be concerned with, have to do with; to be familiar with; **~ en un asunto** (*juez etc*) to have the authority to handle a matter, be in charge of an affair.
(c) **~ por** (*perro*) to answer to the name of.
3 **entenderse** VR **(a)** (*comprenderse*) to be understood; to be meant; **¿qué se entiende por estas palabras?** what is meant by these words?; **¿cómo se entiende que ...?** how can one understand that ...?; **how can one grasp that ...?; se entiende que ...** it is understood that ...; **eso se entiende** that is understood.
(b) (*tener razones*) to know what one is about; **yo me entiendo** I know what I'm up to; I have my reasons; **~ con algo** to know how to deal with sth.
(c) (*2 personas*) to understand each other; to get along (well) together; to have a (secret) understanding; **digamos, para entendernos, que ...** let us say, so that there should be no misunderstanding, that ...; **~ con uno** to come to an arrangement with sb, fix things with sb; **~ con una mujer** to have an affair with a woman; **entendérselas con uno** to face up to sb; to have it out with sb.
(d) **en caso de duda ~ con el cajero** in case of doubt see the cashier; **eso no se entiende conmigo** that doesn't concern me, that has nothing to do with me.

entendido **1** ADJ **(a)** understood; agreed; **¡~!** agreed!; **bien ~ que ...** on the understanding that ...; **no darse por ~** to pretend not to understand; **tenemos ~ que ...** we understand that ...; **según tenemos ~** as far as we can gather.
(b) *persona* (*experto*) expert; (*perito*) skilled, trained; (*sabio*) wise; knowing; (*informado*) well-informed; **ser ~ en** to be versed in, be skilled at.
2 NM, **entendida** NF knowledgeable person; expert; connoisseur; **según el juicio de los ~s** in the opinion of those who know, according to the experts; **el whisk(e)y de los ~s** the connoisseur's whisky.

entendimiento NM **(a)** (*comprensión*) understanding; grasp, comprehension.
(b) (*inteligencia*) mind, intellect, understanding; **de ~ poco lucido** of limited understanding.
(c) (*juicio*) judgement.

entenebrecer [2d] **1** VT **(a)** to darken, obscure.

(b) (*fig*) to fog, cloud, obscure; **esto entenebrece más el asunto** this fogs the issue still more.
2 **entenebrecerse** VR to get dark.

entente NF (*a veces* M) entente.

enteradillo, -a* NM/F little know-all, smarty*.

enterado **1** ADJ **(a)** knowledgeable; well-informed; **estar ~** to be informed, be in the know; **estar ~ de** to know about, be aware of; **estar ~ de que ...** to know that ..., be aware that ...; **no darse por ~** to pretend not to understand, not take the hint; (*declaración*) **quedo ~ de que ...** I understand that ...
(b) (*Cono Sur**) conceited, stuck-up*.
2 NM, **enterada*** NF know-all.

enteramente ADV entirely, completely; quite.

enterar [1a] **1** VT **(a)** to inform (*de* about, of), acquaint (*de* with), tell (*de* about).
(b) (*LAm*) *dinero* to pay, hand over; *deuda* to pay off; (*And, Cono Sur, Méx*) *cantidad* to make up, complete, round off.
2 VI **(a)** (*LAm: reponerse*) to get better, get well.
(b) (*Cono Sur*) to let the days go by.
3 **enterarse** VR **(a)** to find out, get to know; **~ de** to find out about, learn of, hear of, get to know about; **¿te enteras?** do you hear?; do you understand?, do you get it?; **¡entérate!, ¡entérese!** listen!, get this!*; **¡estás que no te enteras!** you just don't pay attention!; **seguir sin ~** to remain ignorant, remain in the dark; **para que te enteres ...** I'd have you know ...; **ya me voy enterando** I'm beginning to understand; **es así pero no se han enterado** it is so, but they haven't realized it yet.
(b) (*LAm: recobrar lo perdido*) to recoup one's losses.

entercado* ADJ: **~ en hacer algo** (*LAm*) determined to do sth, dead set on doing sth.

entereza NF **(a)** entirety; completeness; perfection.
(b) (*fig*) integrity; decency, honesty; strength of mind; fortitude; firmness.
(c) (*fig*) strictness, severity.

entérico ADJ enteric.

enteritis NF enteritis.

enterito NM (*Argentina*) boilersuit.

enterizo ADJ in one piece.

enternecedor ADJ affecting, touching, moving.

enternecer [2d] **1** VT to soften; to affect, touch, move (to pity).
2 **enternecerse** VR to relent; to be affected, be touched, be moved (to pity); to feel tender.

entero **1** ADJ **(a)** (*gen*) entire, complete; whole; **la cantidad entera** the whole sum, the complete sum; **por el mundo ~** over the whole world; **con entera satisfacción** with complete satisfaction; **por ~** wholly, completely, fully; **el reloj da las enteras** the clock strikes the hours.
(b) (*Mat*) whole, integral.
(c) (*Bio*) not castrated.
(d) (*fig: honrado*) upright, honest; (*firme*) resolute, firm.
(e) (*fig: fuerte*) sound; robust; *tela etc* strong, thick.
(f) (*And, CAm, Carib**): (*fig: en olvido*) identical, similar; **está ~ a su papá** he's just like his dad*, he's the spitting image of his dad*.
2 NM **(a)** (*Mat*) integer, whole number.
(b) (*Com, Fin*) point; **las acciones han subido dos ~s** the shares have gone up two points.
(c) (*LAm: pago*) payment.
(d) (*Cono Sur: Fin*) balance.

enteropostal NM pre-stamped postcard, letter-card.

enterradero NM (*Cono Sur*) burial ground.

enterrado ADJ buried; *uña* ingrowing.

enterrador NM gravedigger.

enterramiento NM burial, interment.

enterrar [1a] VT **(a)** to bury, inter. **(b)** (*LAm*) *navaja etc* to bury (*en* in), thrust (*en* into). **(c)** (*fig: en olvido*) to bury, forget.

enterratorio NM (*Cono Sur*) (*cementerio*) Indian burial ground; (*restos*) archaeological remains, site of archaeological interest.

entesar [1j] VT to stretch, tauten.

entibiar [1b] **1** VT **(a)** to cool; to take the chill off. **(b)** (*fig*) to cool (down).
2 **entibiarse** VR **(a)** to become lukewarm, cool down. **(b)** (*fig*) to cool off.

entibo NM (*Arquit*) buttress; (*Min*) prop.

entidad NF **(a)** entity; (*Pol etc*) body, organization; (*Com, Fin*) firm, concern, company; **~ bancaria** bank; **~ crediticia** credit company; **~ financiera** financial institution. **(b)** importance; solidity, solid reputation; **de ~** of importance, of consequence; **de menor ~** less important, not so large; **el equipo tiene mucha ~** the team has a very solid reputation.

entienda *etc* V **entender**.

entierrar* [1a] VT (*Chile*) to make dirty.

entierro NM **(a)** (*acto*) burial, interment. **(b)** (*funeral*) funeral; **asistir al**

~ to go to the funeral. **(c)** (*tumba*) grave. **(d)** (*LAm Arqueol*) (buried) treasure; treasure-trove; *see also* CARNAVAL .

entintar [1a] VT *tampón* to ink; *blanco* to ink in; (*manchar*) to stain with ink.

entizar [1f] VT (*LAm Billar*) *taco* to chalk.

entoldado NM awning(s).

entoldar [1a] **1** VT **(a)** (*cubrir con toldo*) to put an awning over, fit with an awning. **(b)** (*decorar*) to decorate (with hangings). **2 entoldarse** VR **(a)** (*Met*) to cloud over, become overcast. **(b)** (*emoción, alegría*) to be dimmed. **(c)** (*persona*) to give o.s. airs.

entomología NF entomology.

entomólogo, -a NM/F entomologist.

entonación NF **(a)** (*Ling*) intonation. **(b)** (*fig*) conceit.

entonado ADJ **(a)** (*Mús*) toned; harmonious; in tune. **(b)** (*fig: engreído*) conceited; (*orgulloso*) haughty, arrogant, stiff. **(c)** (*fig: en forma*) lively, in good form.

entonar [1a] **1** VT **(a)** (*Mús*) *canción etc* to intone; *voz* to modulate; to sing in tune; *nota* to give, pitch, set; *órgano* to blow. **(b)** (*fig*) *alabanzas* to sound. **(c)** (*Arte, Fot*) to tone. **(d)** (*Med*) to tone up. **(e)** (*fig: vigorizar*) to liven up, enliven, invigorate. **2** VI **(a)** (*Mús*) to intone; to be in tune (*con* with). **(b)** (*fig*) to be in tune (*con* with), harmonize (*con* with). **3 entonarse** VR to give o.s. airs.

entonces ADV **(a)** (*tiempo*) then; at that time; **desde ~** since then; **en aquel ~** at that time; **hasta ~** up till then; **las costumbres de ~** the customs of the time; **el ~ embajador de Eslobodia** the Slobodian ambassador at the time; **fue ~ que ...** it was then that ... that was when ... **(b)** (*concesivo*) and so; then; **pues ~** well then; **¿~ cómo no viniste?** then why didn't you come?; **¡y ~!** (*Carib, Cono Sur*) why of course!

entonelar [1a] VT to put into barrels (*o* casks).

entongado* ADJ (*And*) cross, riled*.

entongar [1h] VT **(a)** to pile up, pile in layers. **(b)** (*And: enojar*) to anger.

entono NM **(a)** (*Mús*) intonation, intoning; being in tune, singing in tune. **(b)** (*fig*) conceit; haughtiness.

entontecedor ADJ stupefying.

entontecer [2d] **1** VT to make silly. **2** VI *y* **entontecerse** VR to get silly.

entorchado NM **(a)** gold braid, silver braid. **(b)** (*Mús*) bass string.

entorchar [1a] VT **(a)** to twist (up). **(b)** to braid.

entornacional ADJ environmental.

entornado ADJ half-closed; ajar.

entornar [1a] VT **(a)** *ojos* to half-close; to screw up; *puerta* to half-close, leave ajar. **(b)** (*volcar*) to upset, tip over.

entorno NM **(a)** setting, milieu, ambience; environment; climate; scene; **el ~ cultural** the cultural scene; **~ natural** natural environment; **~ social** social setting. **(b)** (*Inform*) environment; **~ gráfico** graphics environment; **~ de programación** programming environment; **~ de red(es)** network environment; **~ de trabajo** work(ing) environment.

entorpecer [2d] VT **(a)** (*entendimiento*) to dull, benumb, stupefy; (*aletargar*) to make torpid, make lethargic. **(b)** (*estorbar*) to obstruct, hinder; *planes etc* to set back; *movimiento, tráfico* to slow down, slow up; *trabajo* to hinder, delay.

entorpecimiento NM **(a)** stupefaction; numbness; torpor, lethargy. **(b)** obstruction; obstacle, drawback; delay, slowing-up.

entrabar [1a] VT (*And*) = **trabar**.

entrada NF **(a)** (*lugar*) entrance (*de* to), way in (*de* to); (*puerta*) gate, gateway; (*acceso*) access; (*Min*) entrance, adit; (*pórtico*) porch, doorway; (*hall*) entrance hall; (*de cueva, túnel*) mouth; (*de pelo*) place where the hair is thinning; **tiene ~s** he's got a receding hairline, he's losing his hair. **(b)** (*Mec*) inlet, intake; **~ de aire** air intake. **(c)** (*acto*) entry, entrance (*en* into); admission (*en* into); right of entry; **la ~ de las tropas en 1940** the entry of the troops in 1940; **la ~ de turistas este año** this year's influx of tourists; **~ en bolsa** launch(ing) on the stock exchange; **~ en escena** (*Teat*) entrance; **~ en vigor** coming into effect; **~ en una casa** entrée to a house, privilege of entry to a house; **~ a viva fuerza** forced entry; **'~ gratis'** 'admission free'; **'prohibida la ~'** 'no entry', 'no admission', 'keep out'; **su ~ en la Academia** his admission to the Academy; **la ~ de la palabra en el diccionario** the admission of the word into the dictionary, the acceptance of the word for the dictionary; **dar ~ a** to admit; **hacer su ~** to make one's entry, make a formal entry. **(d)** (*Teat etc: billete*) ticket; **~ de favor, ~ de regalo** complimentary ticket. **(e)** (*Teat etc: público*) house, audience; (*Dep*) gate, crowd; **~ floja** thin

audience; **gran ~, ~ llena** full house; **hubo poca ~** there was a small audience. **(f)** (*Teat, Fin*) receipts, takings; (*Dep*) gate money. **(g)** (*principio: de discurso, libro etc*) beginning; (*Prensa*) lead-in, opening paragraph; **la ~ de la primavera** the start of spring; **de ~** right away, from the start; as a start, for a start; **de primera ~** at first sight; **~ en materia** introduction. **(h)** (*Culin*) entrée; (*LAm*) first course. **(i)** (*Béisbol*) innings, inning (*US*). **(j)** (*Com*) entry; (*de catálogo etc*) entry: (*de diccionario*) entry, headword. **(k)** (*Carib, Méx: ataque*) attack, onslaught; assault. **(l)** (*Carib, Méx: paliza*) beating. **(m)** (*Fin: desembolso inicial*) down payment, deposit; (*de club*) entrance fee; (*al alquilar piso*) deposit, key money; **'sin ~'** 'no down payment'. **(n)** (*Cono Sur Fin*) income; **~s** receipts, takings; income; **~s brutas** gross receipts; **~s familiares** family income; **~s y salidas** income and expenditure. **(o)** (*Inform*) input; **~ de datos** data entry, data input; **~ inmediata** immediate access; **~ de trabajos a distancia** remote job entry. **(p)** (*Ftbl*) tackle (*a* on); **~ violenta** hard tackle.

entradilla NF (*Prensa*) lead-in, opening paragraph.

entrado ADJ **(a)** **~ en años** elderly, advanced in years. **(b)** **hasta muy entrada la noche** until late at night; on into the small hours; **hasta bien ~ mayo** until well on into May. **(c)** (*Cono Sur*) meddling, officious.

entrador ADJ **(a)** (*LAm: valiente*) brave; spirited; (*enérgico*) energetic; (*emprendedor*) enterprising. **(b)** (*Cono Sur: entrometido*) meddling, officious. **(c)** (*LAm: simpático*) charming, likeable, attractive. **(d)** (*And, Carib, Méx: mujeriego*) amorously inclined. **(e)** (*CAm: coqueta*) flirtatious.

entramado NM (*Arquit*) truss; timber framework; (*de puente*) framework; span; (*fig*) network.

entrambos ADJ PL (*liter*) both.

entrampar [1a] **1** VT **(a)** to trap, catch, snare; (*fig*) to snare, trick. **(b)** (*fig*) to mess up, make a mess of. **(c)** (*Com*) to burden with debts. **2 entramparse** VR (*fig*) **(a)** to get into a mess, get tangled up. **(b)** (*Com*) to get into debt.

entrante **1** ADJ **(a)** next, coming; **la semana ~** next week. **(b)** *persona* new, incoming. **2** NM **(a)** (*Geog*) inlet. **(b)** **~s y salientes** people coming to and leaving a house (*etc*). **(c)** (*Culin*) starter.

entraña NF **(a)** (*fig*) core, root, essential part; **esto es la ~ del problema** this is the real core of the problem. **(b)** **de mala ~** malicious; evil-minded. **(c)** **~s** (*Anat*) entrails; insides; bowels; (*fig: lo esencial*) core, innermost parts; (*fig: sentimientos*) heart, feelings; (*temperamento*) disposition; **en las ~s de la tierra** in the bowels of the earth; **¡hijo de mis ~s!** my precious child!; **arrancar las ~s a uno** (*fig*) to break sb's heart; **dar hasta las ~s** to give one's all; (*fig*) to put all one has into it, make a great effort; **echar las ~s** (*fig*) to throw up*; **no tener ~s** (*fig*) to be heartless, lack all feelings.

entrañabilidad NF **(a)** closeness, intimacy. **(b)** beloved quality. **(c)** charm, winning nature.

entrañable ADJ **(a)** *amigo* close, intimate; *paisaje etc* beloved, dearly loved. **(b)** (*afectuoso*) affectionate; (*simpático*) charming, winning. **(c)** *afecto, amistad* deep.

entrañablemente ADV *amar etc* dearly, deeply.

entrañar [1a] **1** VT **(a)** to bury deep. **(b)** (*fig: contener*) to contain, carry within; (*acarrear*) to entail, mean. **2 entrañarse** VR **(a)** to become deeply attached (*con* to). **(b)** **~ en** to reach to the bottom of, reach to the very heart of.

entrañudo ADJ (*Cono Sur*) **(a)** (*valiente*) brave, daring. **(b)** (*cruel*) cruel, heartless.

entrar [1a] **1** VT **(a)** *objeto* to introduce; *persona* to bring in, show in; (*Inform*) to access, enter; **mañana van a ~ el carbón** they'll bring the coal in tomorrow; **no sabe ~ el coche en el garaje** she can't get the car into the garage. **(b)** (*abordar*) to get at, approach; (*Dep*) to tackle; **sabe ~ a la gente** he knows how to approach (*o* tackle) people. **(c)** (*Mil*) to attack; to invade; to capture, enter. **2** VI **(a)** to go in, come in, enter; **Juan entró tercero** (*Dep*) John came in third; **~ a** (*LAm*), **~ en** to go into, come into, enter; (*fig*) to enter into; **~ bien** to be fitting, be appropriate; to be relevant; **~ a puerto** to enter port, put into port; **el enchufe entra en esa toma** the plug goes into (*o* fits into) that point; **el paquete no entra en el saco** the parcel won't go into the bag; **~ en una profesión** to adopt a profession, take up a profession; **~ en una sociedad** to join a society, become a member of a society, be admitted to a society; **el río**

entra en el lago the river flows into the lake; **~ en el número de** to be one of, count among, be reckoned among; **~ en detalles** to go into details; **eso no entra en nuestros planes** that does not enter into our plans; **no ~ ni salir en un asunto** to play no part in a matter; **eso entra de lleno en ...** that comes right into the category of ...; **estar entrada en copas** to be in one's cups; **entra por una sexta parte** he gets a sixth, his share is one sixth; **le entraron deseos de** + *infin* he felt a sudden urge to + *infin*.

(b) (*año etc*) to begin; (*marea, viento*) to rise; **el año que entra** next year.

(c) (*ropa*) to fit, be big enough for; **estos zapatos no me entran** those shoes don't fit.

(d) ese tío no me entra I can't bear that fellow, I can't get on with that chap; **no me entra la lógica** I can't get the hang of logic; **no le entra a la gente que ...** people can't get it into their heads that ...

(e) ~ a + *infin* to begin to + *infin*.

ENTRAR   *ver también la entrada*

Para precisar la manera de entrar
Entrar (*en*) por regla general se suele traducir por *come in* (*to*) o por *go in* (*to*), según la dirección del movimiento (hacia o en dirección contraria al hablante), pero, *come* y *go* se pueden substituir por otros verbos de movimiento si la frase en español explica la forma en que se entra:
  Entró cojeando en Urgencias
  He limped into Casualty
  Acabo de ver a un ratón entrar corriendo en ese agujero
  I've just seen a mouse running into that hole
Para otros usos y ejemplos ver la entrada.

---

entrazado* ADJ (*Cono Sur*) **(a)** *persona* (*vestido*) **mal ~** shabby, ragged; **bien ~** well-dressed, natty*. **(b)** *persona* (*expresión*) **mal ~** nasty-looking; **bien ~** pleasant-looking.

entre PREP **(a)** (*dos cosas*) between; (*más de dos cosas*) among, amongst; (*en medio de*) in the midst of; (*dentro de*) within, inside; **~ tú y yo** between the two of us; **~ esto y lo otro** what with this and that; **~ azul y verde** midway between blue and green, of some colour between blue and green; **había ~ todos 12 personas** there were 12 people in all (*o* all told); **~ los que conozco es el mejor** it's the best of those that I know; **de ~** out of, from among; **por ~** through; between; **decir ~ sí** to say to o.s.

(b) (*LAm*) **~ más tiene más quiere** the more he gets the more he wants.

entre... PREF inter...
entreabierto ADJ half-open; ajar.
entreabrir [3a; PTP **entreabierto**] VT to half-open, open halfway; to leave ajar.
entreacto NM interval, entr'acte.
entreayudarse [1a] VR to help one another, be of mutual assistance.
entrecano ADJ greyish, greying.
entrecejo NM space between the eyebrows; frown; **arrugar el ~, fruncir el ~** to frown, wrinkle one's brow.
entrecerrar [1j] VT (*CAm, Méx*) to half-close, close halfway; *puerta* to leave ajar.
entrechocar [1g] **1** VI (*dientes*) to chatter.
  2 entrechocarse VR to collide, crash; to clash.
entrecó NM sirloin steak.
entrecoger [2c] VT **(a)** to catch, intercept; to seize. **(b)** (*fig*) to press, compel; to corner.
entrecomillado **1** ADJ in inverted commas, in quotes.
  2 NM inverted commas, quotes.
entrecomillar [1a] VT to place in inverted commas, put inverted commas round.
entrecoro NM chancel.
entrecortadamente ADV in a laboured way; falteringly, hesitatingly.
entrecortado ADJ *respiración* laboured; *habla* faltering, hesitant, confused; **en voz entrecortada** in a faltering voice, in a voice choked with emotion.
entrecortar [1a] VT **(a)** (*cortar*) to cut into, partially cut, cut halfway through.
  (b) (*interrumpir*) to cut off, interrupt (from time to time); *voz* to cause to falter, choke from time to time.
entrecot NM sirloin steak.
entrecruzar [1f] **1** VT **(a)** to interlace, interweave. **(b)** (*Bio*) to cross, interbreed.
  2 entrecruzarse VR (*Bio*) to interbreed.
entrecubierta NF (*t ~s*) between-decks.
entredicho NM **(a)** prohibition, ban, interdict; (*Jur*) injunction; **estar en ~** (*prohibido*) to be under a ban, be banned; (*discutible*) to be questionable, be debatable; **levantar el ~ a** to raise the ban on; **poner algo en ~** (*prohibir*) to place a ban on sth; (*dudar*) to call sth into

question, query sth, cast doubt on sth; (*comprometer*) to jeopardize sth, endanger sth.

(b) (*Cono Sur: ruptura*) break-up, split.
(c) (*And*) alarm bell.
entredós NM **(a)** (*Cos*) insertion, panel. **(b)** (*mueble*) cabinet, dresser.
entrefino ADJ medium, medium-quality.
entrefuerte ADJ (*LAm*) *tabaco* medium strong.
▼ **entrega** NF **(a)** (*acto*) delivery; handing over, surrender; (*Correos*) post, delivery; (*Dep*) pass; **'~ a domicilio'** 'we deliver'; **~ contra pago, ~ contra reembolso** cash on delivery, COD; **~ en fecha futura** forward delivery; **pagadero a la ~** payable on delivery; **hacer ~ de** to hand over (formally), present.
  (b) (*de novela etc*) part, instalment; (*de revista etc*) part, number, fascicule.
  (c) (*cualidad*) commitment; dedication; enthusiasm.
entregado ADJ committed, devoted; **~ a** absorbed in; **~ en** committed to.
entregar [1h] **1** VT to deliver; (*dar*) to hand, give; *carta, pedido* to hand over, hand in; (*rendir*) to surrender; (*ceder*) to give up, part with; **~ algo a un abogado** to refer sth to a lawyer, place a matter in a lawyer's hands; **~la⁎** to kick the bucket⁎; **no quiso entregármelo** he refused to hand it over to me.
  2 entregarse VR **(a)** (*Mil etc*) to surrender, give in, submit; **se entregó a la policía** he gave himself up to the police.
  (b) ~ a (*dedicarse*) *carrera etc* to devote o.s. to; (*pey*) to give o.s. up to, abandon o.s. to, indulge in; **~ a estudiar** to devote o.s. to studying.
  (c) ~ de to take possession of.
entreguerras: el período de ~ the inter-war period, the period between the wars (*ie 1918-39*).
entreguismo NM (*apaciguamiento*) (policy of) appeasement; (*derrotismo*) defeatism; (*oportunismo*) opportunism; (*traición*) betrayal, selling-out.
entrelazado ADJ entwined, interlaced; criss-crossed (*de* with); interlocking.
entrelazar [1f] **1** VT to entwine, interlace, interweave; to interlock.
  2 entrelazarse VR to entwine, interlace; to interlock.
entrelistado ADJ striped.
entrelucir [3f] VI **(a)** (*verse*) to show through. **(b)** (*relucir*) to gleam, shine dimly.
entremás **1** ADV (*And, Méx: además*) moreover; (*en especial*) especially.
  2 CONJ **~ lo pienso, más convencido estoy** the more I think about it the more convinced (*o* the surer) I am.
entremedias **1** ADV in between, halfway; in the meantime.
  2 ~ de PREP between; among.
entremedio NM (*LAm*) interval, intermission.
entremés NM **(a)** (*Teat Hist*) interlude, short farce. **(b)** (*Culin*) side dish; **~ salado** savoury; **entremeses** hors d'oeuvres.

ENTREMÉS

ⓘ An *entremés* is a short farce used as an entertaining interval between the first and second act of a *comedia*. It is thought that the *entremés* (derived from the Italian *intermezzo*) was first performed on the Spanish stage in the 16th century and derives from the influential Italian **Commedia dell'Arte**. Often using slapstick, stock characters and situations, *entremeses* had enormous audience appeal and were written by such distinguished writers as Miguel de Cervantes.

---

entremesera NF tray for hors d'oeuvres.
entremeter [2a] VT to insert, put in; to put between.
entremeterse *etc* = **entrometerse** *etc*.
entremezclar [1a] **1** VT to intermingle; **entremezclado de** interspersed with.
  2 entremezclarse VR to intermingle.
entrenador **1** NM (*Aer*) trainer, training plane.
  2 NM, **entrenadora** NF (*Dep*) trainer, coach.
entrenamiento NM training, coaching.
entrenar [1a] **1** VT (*Dep*) to train, coach; *caballo* to exercise; **estar entrenado** (*futbolista etc*) to be in training, be fit.
  2 entrenarse VR to train.
entreno NM (*acto*) training; (*período*) training session.
entreoír [3q] VT to half-hear, hear indistinctly.
entrepágina NF centrefold.
entrepaño NM **(a)** (*muro*) (stretch of) wall. **(b)** (*panel*) door panel; (*anaquel*) shelf.
entrepierna NF (*t ~s*) crotch, crutch; **pasar algo por la ~⁎** to reject sth totally; to feel utter contempt for sth.
entreplanta NF mezzanine.
entrepuente NM between-decks; steerage.
entrerrejado ADJ interwoven, criss-crossed.
entrerrenglonar [1a] VT to interline, write between the lines of.
entresacar [1g] VT (*seleccionar*) to pick out, select; (*cribar*) to sift; *pelo,*

➤ LENGUA Y USO: **entrega: a → 47.2, 47.3**

plantas etc to thin out.

entresemana NF (*LAm*) midweek; working days of the week; **de ~** midweek *(atr)*; **cualquier día de ~** any day midweek (*o* in the middle of the week).

entresijo NM (**a**) (*Anat*) mesentery.
(**b**) (*fig: secreto*) secret, mystery; (*parte oculta*) hidden aspect; (*pega*) difficulty, snag; **esto tiene muchos ~s** this is very complicated, this has its ins and outs; **él tiene sus ~s** he's a deep one.

entresuelo NM mezzanine, entresol; (*Teat*) dress circle.

entretanto [1] ADJ meanwhile, meantime.
[2] NM meantime; **en el ~** in the meantime.

entretecho NM (*Cono Sur*) attic, garret.

entretejer [2a] VT to interweave; to intertwine, entwine; (*fig*) to interweave, insert, put in.

entretejido NM interweaving.

entretela NF (**a**) (*Cos*) interlining. (**b**) **~s** inmost being; heartstrings.

entretelar [1a] VT to interline.

entretelón NM thick curtain, heavy curtain.

entretención NF (*Méx*) entertainment, amusement.

entretener [2l] [1] VT (**a**) (*divertir*) to entertain, amuse; (*distraer*) to distract.
(**b**) (*demorar*) to delay; (*detener*) to hold up, detain, keep waiting; to keep occupied; (*tener suspenso*) to keep in suspense; **nos entretuvo en conversación** he engaged us in conversation; he kept us talking; **~ a los acreedores** to keep one's creditors at bay, hold off one's creditors; **pues no te entretengo más** then I won't keep you any longer.
(**c**) *hambre* to kill, stave off; *dolor* to allay; *tiempo* to while away.
(**d**) (*Mec etc*) to maintain.
[2] **entretenerse** VR (**a**) (*divertirse*) to amuse o.s.; (*pasar el rato*) to while away the time.
(**b**) (*tardar*) to delay; to loiter (on the way); **¡no te entretengas!** don't hang about!, don't loiter on the way!

entretenida NF (**a**) mistress; kept woman.
(**b**) **dar** (**con**) **la ~ a uno** to hold sb off with vague promises, hedge with sb, stall sb; to keep sb talking.

entretenido [1] ADJ entertaining, amusing.
[2] NM (*) gigolo, toyboy*.

entretenimiento NM (**a**) entertainment, amusement; diversion, distraction; recreation; **es un ~ nada más** it's just an amusement.
(**b**) (*Mec etc*) upkeep, maintenance; **sólo necesita un ~ mínimo** it only needs minimum maintenance.

entretiempo NM period between seasons; (*primavera*) spring; (*otoño*) autumn.

entrever [2u] VT (**a**) to glimpse, catch a glimpse of; to see indistinctly, make out sth of. (**b**) (*fig*) to guess, suspect (sth of).

entreverado ADJ mixed; patchy; *tocino* streaky.

entreverar [1a] [1] VT to mix, intermingle; to mix up.
[2] **entreverarse** VR (**a**) to intermix, be intermingled.
(**b**) (*Cono Sur*) to mingle; to get tangled, get mixed up.

entrevero NM (**a**) (*LAm*) mix-up; jumble. (**b**) (*And, Cono Sur*) (*desorden*) confusion, disorder; (*riña*) brawl; (*Mil*) confused cavalry skirmish.

entrevía NF (*Ferro*) gauge; **~ angosta** narrow gauge; **de ~ angosta** narrow-gauge *(atr)*; **~ normal** standard gauge.

▼ **entrevista** NF interview; meeting; **celebrar** (*o* **tener**) **una ~ con** to have an interview with, hold a meeting with; **hacer una ~ a** to interview.

entrevistado, -a NM/F interviewee, person being interviewed.

entrevistador(a) NM/F interviewer.

entrevistar [1a] [1] VT to interview.
[2] **entrevistarse** VR to have an interview, meet; **~ con** to interview, meet, have an interview with; **el ministro se entrevistó con la reina ayer** the minister saw the queen yesterday.

entripado NM (*secreto*) ghastly secret; (*ira*) concealed anger, suppressed rage.

entripar [1a] [1] VT (**a**) (*And**: *enfurecer*) to enrage, madden.
(**b**) (*Carib, Méx*: *mojar*) to soak.
(**c**) (*Méx*‡: *embarazar*) to put in the family way, put in the club.
[2] **entriparse** VR (**a**) (*And*) to get cross, get upset.
(**b**) (*Carib, Méx*) to get soaked.

▼ **entristecer** [2d] [1] VT to sadden, grieve.
[2] **entristecerse** VR to grow sad, grieve.

entrometerse [2a] VR to meddle, interfere (*en* in, with), intrude.

entrometido [1] ADJ meddlesome, interfering.
[2] NM, **entrometida** NF busybody, meddler; intruder.

entromparse [1a] VR (**a**) (*: *emborracharse*) to get very drunk, get tight*. (**b**) (*LAm*: *enojarse*) to fly off the handle*.

entrón ADJ (**a**) (*And*) meddlesome, daring. (**b**) (*Méx*) spirited, daring. (**c**) (*Méx*: *coqueta*) flirtatious.

entroncar [1g] [1] VT to connect, establish a relationship between.
[2] VI (**a**) (*tener parentesco*) to be related, be connected (*con* to, with).
(**b**) (*Ferro*) to connect (*con* with).

entronización NF (**a**) enthronement. (**b**) (*fig*) exaltation.

entronizar [1f] VT (**a**) to enthrone. (**b**) (*fig*) to exalt.

entronque NM (**a**) relationship, connection, link. (**b**) (*Aut, Ferro*) junction.

entropía NF entropy.

entruchada NF (**a**) (*: *trampa*) trap, trick. (**b**) (*Cono Sur**) (*discusión*) slanging match*; (*conversación*) intimate conversation.

entruchar [1a] [1] VT (*) to lure, decoy, lead by the nose.
[2] **entrucharse** VR (*Méx*) to stick one's nose into other people's affairs.

entuerto NM (**a**) wrong, injustice. (**b**) **~s** (*Med*) afterpains.

entumecer [2d] [1] VT to numb, benumb.
[2] **entumecerse** VR (**a**) (*miembro*) to get numb, go to sleep. (**b**) (*río*) to swell, rise; (*mar*) to surge.

entumecido ADJ numb, stiff.

entumecimiento NM numbness, stiffness.

entumido ADJ (**a**) (*LAm*) numb, stiff. (**b**) (*And, Méx*: *tímido*) timid.

enturbiar [1b] [1] VT (**a**) *agua* to muddy; to disturb, make cloudy.
(**b**) (*fig*) *asunto* to fog, confuse; *mente, persona* to derange, unhinge.
[2] **enturbiarse** VR (**a**) to get muddy; to become cloudy.
(**b**) (*fig*) to get confused, become obscured; to become deranged.

enturcado‡ ADJ (*CAm*) *persona* hopping mad*, livid; **un problema ~** a knotty problem.

entusiasmante ADV thrilling, exciting.

▼ **entusiasmar** [1a] [1] VT (*gen*) to fill with enthusiasm; to fire, excite; (*encantar*) to delight, please a great deal; **no me entusiasma mucho la idea** I'm not very keen on the idea.
▼[2] **entusiasmarse** VR to get enthusiastic, get excited (*con, por* about); **~ con, ~ por** to be keen on, rave about, be delighted with; **se ha quedado entusiasmada con el vestido** she was delighted with the dress, she raved about the dress.

entusiasmo NM enthusiasm (*por* for); **con ~** enthusiastically; keenly.

entusiasta [1] ADJ enthusiastic; keen (*de* on); zealous (*de* for).
[2] NMF enthusiast; fan, follower, supporter; admirer.

entusiástico ADJ enthusiastic.

enumeración NF enumeration; count, reckoning.

enumerar [1a] VT (*nombrar*) to enumerate; (*contar*) to count, reckon up.

enunciación NF enunciation; statement, declaration.

enunciado NM (**a**) (*principio*) principle. (**b**) (*Prensa*) heading.

enunciar [1b] VT to enunciate; to state, declare.

enuresis NF enuresis, bedwetting.

envagonar VT (*LAm*) *mercancías* to load into a railway truck.

envainar [1a] [1] VT (**a**) to sheathe, put in a sheath; **¡enváinala!**‡ shut your trap!‡. (**b**) (*And*: *molestar*) to vex, annoy.
[2] VI (*And*) to succumb.
[3] **envainarse** VR (**a**) (*And, Carib**) to get into trouble; **estar envainado** to be in a jam*. (**b**) **envainársela*** to take back what one has said, back down.

envalentonamiento NM boldness; (*pey*) Dutch courage; bravado.

envalentonar [1a] [1] VT to embolden; (*pey*) to fill with Dutch courage.
[2] **envalentonarse** VR to take courage, become bolder; (*pey*) to strut, brag; to put on a bold front.

envanecer [2d] [1] VT to make conceited.
[2] **envanecerse** VR to grow vain, get conceited, give o.s. airs; to swell with pride (*con, de* at).

envanecido ADJ conceited, stuck-up*.

envanecimiento NM conceit, vanity.

envarado ADJ rigid, stiff.

envaramiento NM (*Méx*) numbness, stiffness.

envarar [1a] [1] VT (*And: Agr*) to stake.
[2] **envararse** VR (*Méx*) to be numb, become stiff.

envasado NM packing, packaging.

envasador(a) NM/F packer.

envasar [1a] [1] VT (**a**) (*en paquete*) to pack, wrap; to package; (*en botella*) to bottle; (*en lata*) to can, tin; (*en tonel*) to barrel; (*en saco*) to sack, bag.
(**b**) (*) *vino* to knock back*, put away*.
(**c**) (*esp LAm*) **~ un puñal en uno** to plunge a dagger into sb, bury a dagger in sb.
[2] VI (*) to tipple, knock it back*.

envase NM (**a**) (*acto*) packing, wrapping; packaging; bottling; canning.
(**b**) (*recipiente*) container; (*papel*) package, wrapping; (*botella*) bottle; (*botella vacía*) empty; (*lata*) can, tin; (*tonel*) barrel; (*saco*) bag; **~ de hojalata** tin can; **~ de vidrio** glass container; **precio con ~** price including packing; **géneros sin ~** unpackaged goods; **~s a devolver** returnable empties.

envasijar [1a] VT (*LAm*) = **envasar**.

envedijarse [1a] VR (**a**) to get tangled (up). (**b**) (*personas*) to come to blows.

envegarse [1h] VR (*Cono Sur*) to get swampy, turn into a swamp.

envejecer [2d] **1** VT to age, make (seem) old.

2 VI *y* **envejecerse** VR (a) (*persona*) to age, get old, grow old; to look old; **en 2 años ha envejecido mucho** he's got very old these last two years.
(b) (*objeto*) to become old-fashioned, become antiquated, get out-of-date.

envejecido ADJ old, aged; old-looking; **está muy ~** he looks terribly old.

envejecimiento NM ageing.

envelar [1a] VI (*Cono Sur Náut*) to hoist the sails; (*t* **~las**) to run away.

envenenador(a) NM/F poisoner.

envenenamiento NM poisoning.

envenenar [1a] **1** VT to poison; (*fig*) to poison, embitter.

2 **envenenarse** VR to poison o.s., take poison.

enverdecer [2r] VI to turn green.

enveredar [1a] VI: **~ hacia** to head for, make a beeline for.

envergadura NF (a) expanse, spread, extent; (*Náut*) breadth, beam; (*Aer*: *t* **~ de alas**) wingspan; (*Ent, Orn*) span, wingspan; (*de boxeador*) reach.
(b) (*fig*) scope, compass; magnitude; **un programa de gran ~** a programme of considerable scope, a far-reaching programme; **una operación de cierta ~** an operation of some magnitude; an operation of some size; **la obra es de ~** the plan is ambitious.

envés NM (*de tela*) back, wrong side; (*de espada*) back, flat; (*Anat**) back.

enviado, -a NM/F envoy; **~ especial** (*Periodismo*) special correspondent.

▼ **enviar** [1c] VT to send; **~ a uno a hacer algo** to send sb to do sth; **~ a uno a una misión** to send sb on a mission; **~ por el médico** to send for the doctor, fetch the doctor.

enviciador(a) NM/F (*LAm*) drug-pusher.

enviciar [1b] **1** VT to corrupt; (*fig*) to vitiate.

2 **enviciarse** VR to get corrupted; **~ con**, **~ en** to become addicted to.

envidar [1a] VTI (*Naipes*) to bid; **~ en falso** to bluff.

envidia NF envy, jealousy; desire; bad feeling; **es pura ~** it's sheer envy; **tener ~ a** to envy.

envidiable ADJ enviable.

envidiar [1b] VT to envy; to desire, covet; **~ algo a uno** to envy sb sth, begrudge sb sth; **A no tiene nada que ~ a B** A is at least as good as B, A is quite up to the standard of B.

envidioso ADJ envious, jealous; covetous.

envilecer [2d] **1** VT to debase, degrade.

2 **envilecerse** VR to degrade o.s., lower o.s.; to grovel, crawl.

envilecimiento NM degradation, debasement.

envinado ADJ (*Cono Sur*) drunk.

▼ **envío** NM (a) (*acto*) sending, dispatch; (*en barco*) shipment; **gastos de ~** (cost of) postage and packing, transport charges; **~ de segundo curso** second-class mail; **~ de datos** data transmission; **~ a domicilio** home delivery (service); **~ contra reembolso** cash on delivery, COD.
(b) (*mercancías*) consignment, lot, (*Náut*) shipment; (*dinero*) remittance.

envión NM push, shove.

envite NM (a) (*apuesta*) stake; side bet. (b) (*oferta*) offer, bid; invitation. (c) (*empuje*) push, shove; **al primer ~** right away, from the very start.

enviudar [1a] VI to become a widow(er), be widowed; **~ de su primera mujer** to lose one's first wife; **enviudó 3 veces** she lost three husbands.

envoltijo NM, **envoltorio** NM bundle, package; *V* **envoltura**.

envoltura NF (*gen*) cover; (*papel*) wrapper, wrapping; (*Mec etc*) case, casing; sheath; (*Aer, Bot etc*) envelope; **~s** baby-clothes.

envolvedero NM, **envolvedor** NM cover; wrapper, wrapping; envelope.

envolvente ADJ (a) (*que rodea*) surrounding; (*Mil*) **movimiento** encircling, enveloping; **asiento ~** bucket seat. (b) (*fig*) comprehensive. (c) (*Carib, Cono Sur*) fascinating, intriguing.

envolver [2h; PTP **envuelto**] **1** VT (a) (*con papel etc*) to wrap (up), pack (up), tie up, do up; (*con ropa*) to wrap, swathe, cover; to envelop, enfold; to muffle (up); **envuelto en una capa** wrapped in a cloak, muffled up in a cloak; **dos paquetes envueltos en papel** two parcels wrapped in paper; **¿quiere que se lo envuelva?** shall I wrap it (up) for you?
(b) (*Mil*) to encircle, surround.
(c) (*fig*) to imply, involve; *persona* to involve, implicate (*en* in); **son elogios que envuelven una censura** it is praise which implies blame.

2 **envolverse** VR (a) to wrap o.s. up (*en* in).
(b) (*fig*) to become involved (*en* in).

envolvimiento NM (a) wrapping; envelopment. (b) (*Mil*) encircle-

ment. (c) (*fig*) involvement.

envuelto PTP *de* **envolver**.

enyerbar [1a] **1** VT (*And, Cono Sur, Méx*: *hechizar*) to bewitch.

2 **enyerbarse** VR (a) (*LAm*: *campo etc*) to get covered with grass.
(b) (*Carib*: *trato*) to fail.
(c) (*CAm, Méx*: *envenenarse*) to poison o.s.
(d) (*Méx*: *enamorarse*) to fall madly in love.
(e) (*Carib**: *complicarse*) to get complicated.

enyesado NM, **enyesadura** NF plastering; (*Med*) plaster cast.

enyesar [1a] VT (a) to plaster. (b) (*Med*) to put in a plaster cast.

enyeyado* ADJ (*Carib*) gloomy, depressed.

enyugar [1h] VT to yoke.

enyuntar [1a] VT (*LAm*) to put together, join.

enzacatarse [1a] VR (*CAm, Méx*) to get covered with grass.

enzarzar [1f] **1** VT (*fig*) to involve (in a dispute), entangle, embroil.

2 **enzarzarse** VR to get involved in a dispute; to get o.s. into trouble; **~ a golpes** to come to blows; **~ en una discusión** to get involved in an argument.

enzima NF enzyme.

enzocar [1g] VT (*Cono Sur*) to insert, put in, fit in.

-eo *V* Aspects of Word Formation in Spanish 2.

EOI NF ABR *de* **Escuela Oficial de Idiomas**; *see also* ESCUELA OFICIAL DE IDIOMAS .

eólico ADJ wind (*atr*); **energía eólica** wind power.

eón NM aeon.

EP NF (*Esp*) ABR *de* **Educación Primaria** *primary education for 6 to 12 year olds*.

┌─── **EP - EDUCACIÓN PRIMARIA** ───┐

Following the implementation of the 1990 Spanish education reform law, LOGSE, primary education was renamed **Educación Primaria** *and divided into two* ciclos *or stages:* **primer ciclo** *for 6- to 9-year olds, and* **segundo ciclo** *for 9- to 12-year olds.*
⇨ *See also* ESO , LOGSE
└────────────────────┘

epa*, épale* INTERJ (*LAm*) hey!; wow!*

epatante* ADJ amazing, astonishing; startling, dazzling.

epatar* [1a] VT (*asombrar*) to amaze, astonish; (*deslumbrar*) to startle, dazzle.

epazote NM (*Méx*) herb tea.

E.P.D. ABR *de* **en paz descanse** may he rest in peace, R.I.P.

epi... PREF epi...

épica NF epic.

epiceno ADJ (*Ling*) epicene.

epicentro NM epicentre.

épico ADJ epic.

epicureísmo NM, **epicurismo** NM epicureanism.

epicúreo, -a ADJ, NM/F epicurean.

epidemia NF epidemic.

epidémico ADJ epidemic.

epidérmico ADJ skin (*atr*); (*fig*) superficial, skin-deep.

epidermis NF epidermis.

Epifanía NF Epiphany.

epiglotis NF epiglottis.

epígrafe NM epigraph; (*inscripción*) inscription; (*encabezamiento*) title, headline; (*pie*) caption; (*lema*) motto.

epigrafía NF epigraphy.

epigrama NM epigram.

epigramático ADJ epigrammatic(al).

epilepsia NF epilepsy.

epiléptico, -a ADJ, NM/F epileptic.

epilogar [1h] VT to sum up; to round off, provide a conclusion to.

epílogo NM epilogue.

episcopado NM (a) (*oficio*) bishopric. (b) (*período*) episcopate. (c) (*obispos*) bishops (*collectively*), episcopacy.

episcopal ADJ episcopal.

episcopalista ADJ, NMF Episcopalian.

episódico ADJ episodic.

episodio NM episode; incident; (*entrega etc*) episode, instalment, part.

epistemología NF epistemology.

epístola NF epistle.

epistolar ADJ epistolary.

epistolario NM collected letters.

epitafio NM epitaph.

epitelial ADJ epithelial.

epíteto NM epithet.

epitomar [1a] VT to condense, abridge; to summarize.

epítome NM epitome, summary, abstract, résumé; compendium.

EPL NM (*Colombia*) ABR *de* **Ejército Popular de Liberación**.

época NF (a) (*gen*) period, time; age, epoch; spell; **la ~ de Carlos III** the age of Charles III; **en la ~ de Carlos III** in Charles III's time; **en aquella ~** at that time, in that period; **~ dorada** golden age; **~**

glacial ice-age; **~ de la serpiente de mar** (*hum*) silly season; **muebles de ~** period furniture; **coche de ~** vintage car; **drama de ~** costume drama; **un Picasso de primera ~** an early (period) Picasso; **la ~ azul del pintor** the painter's blue period; **con decoraciones de ~** with period set; **anticiparse** (*o* **adelantarse**) **a su ~** to be ahead of one's time; **formar ~, hacer ~** to be epoch-making, be a landmark; **el invento hace ~** it's an epoch-making discovery; **eso hizo ~ en nuestra historia** that was a landmark in our history; **todos tenemos ~s así** we all go through spells like that.
(**b**) (*del año*) season; time; **~ del año** season of the year, time of year; **~ de celo** mating season; **~ de lluvias** rainy season; **~ monzónica** monsoon season; **~ de** (**la**) **sequía** dry season.

epopeya NF epic (*t fig*).

epopéyico ADJ epic.

EPS NM (*Nicaragua*) ABR de **Ejército Popular Sandinista**.

equi... PREF equi...

equidad NF equity; justice, fairness, impartiality; (*de precio etc*) reasonableness.

equidistante ADJ equidistant.

equilátero ADJ equilateral.

equilibradamente ADV in a balanced way.

equilibrado [1] ADJ balanced.
[2] NM: **~ de ruedas** wheel-balancing.

equilibrar [1a] [1] VT (**a**) to balance; to poise. (**b**) (*fig*) to balance; to adjust, redress; *presupuesto* to balance.
[2] **equilibrarse** VR to balance (o.s.; *en* on).

equilibrio NM (**a**) balance, equilibrium; **perder el ~** to lose one's balance. (**b**) (*fig*) balance; (*social etc*) poise; **~ de fuerzas, ~ de poderes, ~ político** balance of power; **~ del terror** balance of terror.

equilibrista NMF (**a**) tightrope walker; acrobat. (**b**) (*LAm*) politician of shifting allegiance.

equino [1] ADJ equine, horse (*atr*).
[2] NM (**a**) (*caballo*) horse; (**carne** *f* **de**) **~** horsemeat. (**b**) (*de mar*) sea urchin.

equinoccial ADJ equinoctial.

equinoccio NM equinox; **~ otoñal** autumnal equinox; **~ vernal** vernal equinox.

equipaje NM (**a**) (**el ~**) luggage, baggage (*US*); (**un ~**) piece of luggage, piece of baggage (*US*); (*avíos*) equipment, outfit, kit; **~ de mano** hand-luggage; **facturar el ~** to register one's luggage; **hacer el ~** to pack, do the packing.
(**b**) (*Náut*) crew.

equipal NM (*Méx*) leather chair.

equipamiento NM equipment.

equipar [1a] VT to equip, furnish, fit up (*con, de* with); (*Náut*) to fit out.

equiparable ADJ comparable (*con* to, with); applicable (*con* to).

equiparación NF comparison.

equiparar [1a] [1] VT (*igualar*) to put on the same level, consider equal; (*comparar*) to compare (*con* with).
[2] **equipararse** VR: **~ con** to be on a level with, rank equally with.

equipazo* NM crack team.

equipo NM (**a**) (*conjunto de cosas*) equipment; outfit, kit; (*avíos*) gear, tackle; (*industrial*) plant; (*de turbinas etc*) set; **el ~ de la fábrica está bastante anticuado** the factory plant is pretty antiquated; **~ de alpinismo** climbing kit; **~ de boda** wedding outfit; **~ de caza** hunting gear; **~ cinematográfico móvil** mobile film unit; **~ de conversión** conversion kit; **~ físico** hardware; **~ de fumador** smoker's outfit, smoker's accessories; **~ lógico** software; **~ luminoso** lighting; **~ de música** Hi-Fi, music centre; **~ de novia** trousseau; **~ de oficina** office furniture; **~ de primeros auxilios** first-aid kit; **~ de reparaciones** repair kit; **~ rodante** rolling stock; **~ de sonido** sound system; public-address system.
(**b**) (*personas*) team; gang; (*tanda*) shift; **~ de cámara** camera crew; **~ de desactivación de explosivos** bomb-disposal unit; **~ de día** day shift; **~ médico** medical team, medical unit; **~ de rescate, ~ de socorro** rescue team.
(**c**) (*Dep*) team; side; **~ de casa** home team; **~ de fuera** away team; **~ de fútbol** football team; **~ de relevos** relay team; **~ titular** first team, A team; **~ visitante** visiting team; **los ~s formaron así ...** the teams lined up as follows ...

equis NF (**a**) the (name of the) letter *x*; **pongamos que cuesta ~ dólares** let us suppose it costs X dollars; **averiguar la ~** to find the value of X; **tenía que hacer ~ cosas*** I had to do any amount of things.
(**b**) (*And, CAm**) **estar en la ~** (*flaco*) to be all skin and bones; (*sin dinero*) to be broke*.

equitación NF (**a**) (*acto*) riding; **escuela de ~** riding school. (**b**) (*arte*) horsemanship.

equitativamente ADV equitably, fairly; reasonably.

equitativo ADJ equitable, fair; reasonable; **trato ~** fair deal, square deal.

equivalencia NF equivalence.

▼ **equivalente** [1] ADJ equivalent (*a* to).
[2] NM equivalent.

equivaler [2q] VI to be equivalent, be equal; **~ a** to be equivalent to, be equal to; to rank as, rank with, be on a level with.

equivocación NF (*error*) mistake, error; (*olvido*) oversight; (*malentendido*) misunderstanding; **por ~** by mistake, in error; mistakenly; **ha sido por ~** it was a mistake.

equivocadamente ADV mistakenly, wrongly.

equivocado ADJ wrong, mistaken; *afecto, confianza etc* misplaced; **estás ~** you are mistaken.

▼ **equivocar** [1g] [1] VT to mistake; **~ A con B** to mistake A for B; **~ el camino** to take the wrong road, go the wrong way; **~ el golpe, ~ el tiro** to miss.
▼ [2] **equivocarse** VR to be wrong, be mistaken; to make a mistake; **pero se equivocó** but he was wrong; **A puede ~ con B** A can be mistaken for B; **~ de casa** to go to the wrong house; **~ de camino** to take the wrong road; **~ en una elección** to make a wrong choice, choose wrongly.

equívoco [1] ADJ (**a**) equivocal, ambiguous. (**b**) (*LAm*) mistaken.
[2] NM (**a**) (*ambigüedad*) equivocation, ambiguity; quibble. (**b**) (*juego de palabras*) pun, wordplay, play on words; (*doble sentido*) double meaning. (**c**) (*LAm*) mistake.

equivoquista NMF quibbler; punster.

era¹ *etc* V **ser.**

era² NF era, age; **~ atómica** atomic age; **~ cristiana, ~ de Cristo** Christian era; **~ espacial** space age; **~ española, ~ hispánica** Spanish Era (*from 38 B.C.*); **~ glacial** ice-age.

era³ NF (*Agr*) threshing floor; (*Hort*) bed, plot, patch.

erais, éramos V **ser.**

erario NM exchequer, treasury; public funds, public finance.

-eras V **Aspects of Word Formation in Spanish 2.**

erasmismo NM Erasmism.

erasmista ADJ, NMF Erasmist.

Erasmo NM Erasmus.

ERC NF ABR de **Esquerra Republicana de Catalunya** *Catalan left-wing party*.

erección NF (*acto*) erection, raising; (*fig*) establishment, foundation; (*Anat*) erection.

ereccionarse [1a] VR to become erect.

eremita NM hermit; recluse.

eremitismo NM living like a hermit, hermit's way of life.

eres V **ser.**

ergio NM erg.

ergonomía NF ergonomics.

ergonómico ADJ ergonomic.

ergonomista NMF ergonomist.

erguido ADJ (**a**) erect, straight. (**b**) (*fig*) proud.

erguir [3m] [1] VT (**a**) (*alzar*) to raise, lift; **~ la cabeza** (*fig*) to hold one's head high.
(**b**) (*enderezar*) to straighten.
[2] **erguirse** VR (**a**) to straighten up, stand up straight, sit up straight.
(**b**) (*fig*) to swell with pride.

-ería V **Aspects of Word Formation in Spanish 2.**

erial [1] ADJ uncultivated, untilled.
[2] NM uncultivated land; piece of waste ground.

erigir [3c] [1] VT (**a**) to erect, raise, build.
(**b**) (*fig*) to establish, found.
(**c**) **~ a uno en algo** to set sb up as sth.
[2] **erigirse** VR: **~ en algo** to set o.s. up as sth.

erisipela NF erysipelas.

erizado ADJ (**a**) bristly; **~ de espinas** covered with thorns, with prickles all over. (**b**) **~ de problemas** bristling with problems.

erizar [1f] [1] VT (**a**) **el gato erizó el pelo** the cat bristled, the cat's hair stood on end. (**b**) *asunto* to complicate, surround with difficulties.
[2] **erizarse** VR (*pelo*) to bristle, stand on end.

erizo NM (**a**) (*Zool*) hedgehog; **~ de mar, ~ marino** sea urchin. (**b**) (*Bot*) burr; prickly husk. (**c**) (***) surly individual, grumpy sort*; prickly person.

ermita NF hermitage.

ermitaño NM (**a**) hermit. (**b**) (*Zool*) hermit crab.

Ernesto NM Ernest.

-ero V **Aspects of Word Formation in Spanish 2.**

erogación NF (**a**) distribution. (**b**) (*Cono Sur, Méx: gastos*) expenditure; outlay; (*And, Carib: contribución*) contribution.

erogar [1h] VT (**a**) *bienes* to distribute. (**b**) (*Cono Sur*) to pay; *deuda* to settle; (*And, Cono Sur: contribuir*) to contribute; (*Méx: gastar*) to spend, lay out.

erógeno ADJ erogenous.

Eros NM Eros.

erosión NF (*Geol etc*) erosion; (*Med*) graze; **causar ~ en** to erode.

erosionable ADJ subject to erosion; **un suelo fácilmente ~** a soil which is easily eroded.
erosionante ADJ erosive.
erosionar [1a] [1] VT to erode.
   [2] **erosionarse** VR to erode, be eroded.
erosivo ADJ erosive.
erótica NF: **la ~ del poder** the thrill of power.
erótico ADJ erotic; *poesía etc* love *(atr)*; **el género ~** the genre of love poetry.
erotismo NM eroticism.
erotizar [1a] [1] VT to eroticize; to stimulate.
   [2] **erotizarse** VR to be (sexually) stimulated.
erotomanía NF (pathological) eroticism.
erotómano ADJ (pathologically) erotic.
ERP NM *(Argentina, El Salvador)* ABR de **Ejército Revolucionario del Pueblo.**
errabundear [1a] VI to wander, rove.
errabundeo NM wanderings.
errabundo ADJ wandering, roving.
erradamente ADV mistakenly.
erradicación NF eradication.
erradicar [1g] VT to eradicate.
erradizo ADJ wandering, roving.
errado ADJ mistaken, wrong; wide of the mark; unwise.
errante ADJ **(a)** wandering, roving; itinerant; nomadic; *animal* lost, stray. **(b)** *(fig)* errant; **el marido ~** the errant husband.
errar [1k] [1] VT *tiro* to miss with, aim badly; *blanco* to miss; *vocación etc* to miss, mistake; **~ el camino** to lose one's way.
   [2] VI **(a)** *(vagar)* to wander, rove; to roam about.
   (b) = VR.
   [3] **errarse** VR *(equivocarse)* to err, go astray, be mistaken; **~ es humano, de los hombres es ~** to err is human.
errata NF misprint, erratum, printer's error; **es ~ por 'poder'** it's a misprint for 'poder'.
errático ADJ erratic.
erratismo NM wandering tendencies, tendency to wander; erratic movement.
erre NF the (name of the) letter *r, rr;* **~ que ~** stubbornly, pigheadedly.
erróneamente ADV mistakenly, erroneously; falsely.
erróneo ADJ mistaken, erroneous; false, untrue.
▼ **error** NM *(gen)* error, mistake; *(defecto)* fault; *(de teoría etc)* fallacy; *(Inform)* bug; **~ de copia** clerical error; **~ de escritura** *(Inform)* write error; **~ freudiano** Freudian slip; **~ de imprenta, ~ tipográfico** misprint, printer's error; **~ judicial** miscarriage of justice; **~ de lectura** *(Inform)* read error; **~ de máquina** typing error; **~ de pluma** clerical error; **por ~** by mistake, in error; **caer en un ~** to fall into error; **salvo ~ u omisión** errors and omissions excepted.
ERT (a) NMPL *(Esp)* ABR de **Explosivos Río Tinto. (b)** NM *(Argentina)* ABR de **Ente de Radiotelevisión.**
ertzaina [er'tʃaina] [1] NMF member of the Basque police force, policeman, policewoman.
   [2] NF: **E~** Basque police force.
Ertzaintza [er'tʃaintʃa] NF Basque police force.

   ⎡ **ERTZAINTZA** ⎤

  ⓘ *The Ertzaintza is the Basque autonomous police force, recognizable by its distinctive uniform of red sweater, red beret and white truncheon. Madrid has devolved certain policing responsibilities to the Basque government (as well as to Catalonia) but the national police forces, **Policía Nacional** and **Guardia Civil**, continue to have a role as well.*

eructación NF belch.
eructar [1a] VI to belch.
eructo NM belch.
erudición NF erudition, learning, scholarship.
eruditamente ADV learnedly.
erudito [1] ADJ erudite, learned, scholarly.
   [2] NM, **erudita** NF scholar; savant; learned person; **los ~s en esta materia** those who are expert in this subject, those who really know about this subject; **~ a la violeta** pundit, pseudo-intellectual, soi-disant expert.
erupción NF **(a)** *(Geol)* eruption; **~ solar** solar flare; **estar en ~** to be erupting; **entrar en ~** to (begin to) erupt.
   (b) *(Med: t ~* **cutánea)** rash, eruption.
   (c) *(fig)* eruption; outbreak, explosion; outburst.
eruptivo ADJ eruptive.
es *V* ser.
esa, ésa *etc V* ese, ése.
Esaú NM Esau.
esbeltez NF slimness, slenderness; litheness; gracefulness.
esbelto ADJ slim, slender; lithe, willowy; graceful.

esbirro NM **(a)** *(ayudante)* henchman, minion; *(sicario)* killer; *(Carib*: soplón) grass*; informer. **(b)** *(Hist)* bailiff, constable.
esbozar [1f] VT to sketch, outline; **~ una sonrisa** to smile wanly, force a smile.
esbozo NM sketch, outline.
escabechado NM pickling, marinating.
escabechar [1a] VT **(a)** *(Culin)* to pickle, souse, marinate. **(b)** *pelo* to dye. **(c)** (*) to do in*; carve up*. **(d)** *(Univ*)* to plough*.
escabeche NM **(a)** *(de escabechar)* (liquid) pickle, brine, *(salsa)* sauce of vinegar, oil, garlic etc. **(b)** *(pescado)* soused fish.
escabechina NF slaughter; *(fig)* destruction, slaughter; ravages; **hacer una ~*** to wreak havoc.
escabel NM low stool, footstool.
escabinado NM jury of lay people and judges.
escabiosa NF scabious.
escabioso ADJ scabby; mangy.
escabro NM *(Vet)* sheep scab, scabs; *(Bot)* scab.
escabrosamente ADV *(fig)* riskily, salaciously.
escabrosidad NF *(V* ADJ**) (a)** roughness, ruggedness; unevenness. **(b)** harshness. **(c)** toughness, difficulty. **(d)** riskiness, salaciousness.
escabroso ADJ **(a)** *terreno* rough, rugged; *superficie* uneven. **(b)** *(fig) sonido etc* harsh. **(c)** *problema etc* tough, difficult, thorny. **(d)** *chiste etc* risky, risqué, blue.
escabuche NM weeding hoe.
escabullarse [1a] VR *(LAm)*, **escabullirse** [3h] VR to slip away, slip off, clear out; to make o.s. scarce; **~ por** to slip through.
escachalandrado* ADJ *(And, CAm)* slovenly.
escacharrar* [1] VT to bust*.
   [2] **escacharrarse** VR to break.
escachifollarse* [1a] VR to break, smash, come to bits.
escafandra NF diving suit; **~ autónoma** scuba suit; **~ espacial** space-suit.
escafandrismo NM underwater fishing; deep-sea diving.
escafandrista NMF underwater fisherman; deep-sea diver.
escala NF **(a)** ladder; **~ de cuerda, ~ de viento** *(Náut)* rope ladder.
   (b) *(Mat, Mús y fig)* scale; *(de colores, velocidades etc)* range; **~ (de) Beaufort** Beaufort scale; **~ móvil** sliding scale; *(salarial)* index-linked automatic wage review; **~ de la popularidad** popularity chart, *(Mús)* hit parade; **~ de Richter** Richter scale; **~ de sueldos** salary scale; **modelo a ~** scale model; **el dibujo no está a ~** the drawing is not to scale; **a (o en) pequeña ~** on a small scale; **a (o en) ~ nacional** on a national scale; **una investigación a ~ nacional** a nation-wide inquiry, a countrywide investigation; **en gran(de) ~** on a large scale, in a big way; **un plan en gran ~** a large-scale plan; **reproducir según ~** to reproduce to scale.
   (c) *(parada)* stopping place; *(Náut)* port of call; intermediate stop, stopover; **~ técnica** *(Aer)* refuelling stop; **vuelo sin ~s** non-stop flight; **hacer ~ en** to stop at, make an intermediate stop at, *(Náut)* to call at, put in at.
escalabrar [1a] VT = descalabrar.
escalada NF **(a)** *(Alpinismo etc)* climb; climbing, scaling; **~ en rocas** rock-climbing. **(b)** *(Mil, Pol)* escalation; boom, increase.
escalador(a) NM/F **(a)** *(alpinista)* climber; mountaineer; **~ en rocas** rock climber. **(b)** *(ladrón)* burglar, housebreaker.
escalafón NM **(a)** *(de personas)* roll, list, register; *(plantilla)* list of officials, establishment; *(de promoción)* promotion ladder; **seguir el ~** to work one's way up.
   (b) *(de sueldos)* salary scale, wage scale.
   (c) *(fig)* table, chart; **en esta industria España ocupa el tercer lugar en el ~ mundial** Spain occupies third place in the world table for this industry.
escalamiento NM **(a)** = escalada. **(b)** *(Méx Jur)* burglary, housebreaking.
escálamo NM thole, tholepin.
escalante ADJ escalating; **la crisis ~** the escalating crisis.
escalar [1a] [1] VT **(a)** *montaña etc* to climb, scale; **~ puestos** *(fig)* to move up.
   (b) *casa* to burgle, burglarize *(US)*, break into, force an entry into.
   (c) *(Inform: reducir)* to scale down; *(aumentar)* to scale up.
   [2] VI **(a)** to climb; *(fig)* to climb the social ladder, rise, get on.
   (b) *(Náut)* to call, put in *(en* at).
   (c) *(Mil, Pol)* to escalate.
Escalda NM Scheldt.
escaldado ADJ **(a)** wary, fly, cautious. **(b)** *mujer* loose.
escaldadura NF **(a)** scald, scalding. **(b)** chafing.
escaldar [1a] [1] VT **(a)** *(quemar)* to scald. **(b)** *(rozar)* to chafe, rub. **(c)** *metal* to make red-hot.
   [2] **escaldarse** VR **(a)** to get scalded, scald o.s. **(b)** to chafe.
escalera NF **(a)** *(de casa)* stairs, staircase, stairway; *(escala)* ladder; *(escalinata)* steps, flight of steps; *(de camión, carro)* tailboard; **~ de caracol** spiral staircase, winding staircase; **~ de cuerda, ~ de nudos** rope ladder; **~ doble, ~ de mano, ~ de pintor, ~ de tijera** steps,

➤ LENGUA Y USO: **error → 39.1, 45.2**

stepladder; **~ de incendios** fire-escape; **~ mecánica, ~ móvil, ~ rodante** escalator, moving staircase; **~ de servicio** service stairs, backstairs.

(**b**) (*Naipes*) run, sequence.

escalerilla NF small ladder; low step; (*Náut*) gangway, companionway; (*Aer*) steps.

escalfador NM chafing dish.

escalfar [1a] VT (**a**) *huevo* to poach. (**b**) (*Méx: desfalcar*) to embezzle.

escalilla NF (**a**) (*Téc*) calibrated scale. (**b**) (*de ascenso*) promotion ladder.

escalinata NF steps, flight of steps; outside staircase.

escalofriado ADJ: **estar ~** to feel chilly, feel shivery, feel hot-and-cold.

escalofriante ADJ bloodcurdling, hair-raising; chilling, frightening.

escalofriarse [1c] VR (**a**) to feel chilly, get the shivers, feel hot-and-cold by turns. (**b**) to shiver with fright, get a cold shiver of fright.

escalofrío NM (**a**) (*Med*) chill, feverish chill. (**b**) **~s** (*fig*) shivers; shivery fright.

escalón NM (**a**) (*peldaño*) step, stair; (*de escalera de mano*) rung; tread; (*de cohete*) stage; **~ de hielo** ice step.

(**b**) (*fig*) stage, grade; (*hacia el éxito etc*) ladder; rung, stepping stone.

(**c**) (*Mil*) echelon.

escalonadamente ADV step by step, in a series of steps.

escalonar [1a] VT to spread out at intervals; (*Mil etc*) to echelon; *tierra* to terrace, cut in a series of steps; *horas, producción etc* to stagger; (*Med*) *dosis* to regulate; *novedad* to phase in.

escalope NM escalope; **~ de ternera** escalope of veal.

escalopín NM fillet.

escalpar [1a] VT to scalp.

escalpelo NM scalpel.

escama NF (**a**) (*Bot, Pez etc*) scale; (*de jabón etc*) flake; (*de pintura*) flake; **~s de jabón, jabón en ~s** soapflakes. (**b**) (*fig*) resentment, grudge; suspicion. (**c**) (*Méx**) cocaine.

escamado ADJ (**a**) wary, cautious. (**b**) (*Cono Sur: harto*) wearied, cloyed.

escamar [1a] **1** VT (**a**) to scale, remove the scales from.

(**b**) (*fig*) to make wary, create distrust in, shake the confidence of; **eso me escama** that makes me suspicious, that sounds ominous to me.

2 escamarse VR (**a**) to scale (off), flake off.

(**b**) (*fig*) to get wary, become suspicious; to smell a rat; **y luego se escamó** and after that he was on his guard.

escamocha* NF (*Méx*) left-overs.

escamón ADJ wary, distrustful; apprehensive.

escamondar [1a] VT to prune; (*fig*) to prune, trim.

escamoso ADJ *pez* scaly; *sustancia* flaky.

escamoteable ADJ retractable.

escamoteador(a) NM/F (**a**) conjurer, juggler. (**b**) (*pey*) swindler.

escamotear [1a] VT (**a**) (*hacer desaparecer*) to whisk away, whisk out of sight, snatch away, make vanish; *naipe* to palm; (*Téc*) to retract.

(**b**) (*) to lift*.

(**c**) (*fig*) *dificultad etc* to shirk, disregard.

escamoteo NM (**a**) (*destreza*) sleight of hand; (*ilusionismo*) conjuring; (*de naipe*) palming.

(**b**) (*un ~*) conjuring trick.

(**c**) (*) lifting*; swindling; (*un ~*) swindle.

(**d**) shirking.

escampar [1a] **1** VT to clear out.

2 VI (**a**) (*cielo*) to clear; (*lluvia*) to stop; (*tiempo*) to clear up, stop raining.

(**b**) (*Carib, Méx: de la lluvia*) to shelter from the rain.

(**c**) (*LAm**) to clear off*.

escampavía NF revenue cutter.

escanciador NM wine waiter; (*Hist*) cupbearer.

escanciar [1b] **1** VT (*liter*) *vino* to pour (out), serve; *vaso* to drain.

2 VI to drink a lot of wine, make merry on wine.

escandalera* NF row, uproar.

escandalizante ADJ scandalous, shocking.

escandalizar [1f] **1** VT to scandalize, shock.

2 VI to make a fuss, kick up a row.

3 escandalizarse VR to be shocked (*de* at, by), be scandalized; to be offended (*de* at, by); **se escandalizó ante la pintura** he threw up his hands in horror at the picture.

escandallo NM (**a**) (*Náut*) lead. (**b**) (*Com: etiqueta*) price tag; (*acto*) pricing. (**c**) (*Com: prueba*) sampling.

escándalo NM (**a**) (*gen*) scandal; outrage; **un resultado de ~** a scandalous result, (*fig*) a great result, an outstanding result; **¡qué ~!** what a scandal!

(**b**) (*alboroto*) row, uproar, commotion, fuss; **armar un ~** to make a scene, cause an uproar.

(**c**) (*asombro*) sense of shock; astonishment; **llamar a ~** to cause astonishment, be a shock.

escandalosa NF (**a**) (*Náut*) topsail. (**b**) (*And: tulipán*) tulip. (**c**) **echar la ~** to fly off the handle, curse and swear.

escandalosamente ADV scandalously, shockingly, outrageously; flagrantly; licentiously.

escandaloso ADJ (*gen*) scandalous, shocking, outrageous; *crimen etc* flagrant; *vida* scandalous; disorderly, licentious; *risa* uproarious, hearty; *niño* noisy; uncontrollable, undisciplined; *color* (*And*) loud.

Escandinavia NF Scandinavia.

escandinavo, -a ADJ, NM/F Scandinavian.

escandir [3a] VT *versos* to scan.

escaneado NM scanning.

escanear [1a] VT to scan.

escaneo NM scanning.

escáner NM (**a**) (*aparato*) scanner. (**b**) (*imagen*) scan; **hacerse un ~** to have a scan.

escansión NF scansion.

escantillón NM pattern, template.

escaño NM bench; settle; (*Parl*) seat.

escapada NF (**a**) (*huida*) escape, flight; **en una ~** in a jiffy; **haré la comida en una ~** I'll get the meal right away; **¿puedes comprarme tabaco en una ~?** can you slip out and get me some cigarettes?

(**b**) (*Dep*) breakaway.

(**c**) (*viaje*) flying visit, quick trip; **hice una ~ a la capital** I made a flying visit to the capital.

(**d**) (*pey*) escapade.

escapado ADJ, ADV at top speed, in a rush; **irse ~** to rush off, be off like a shot; **se volvió ~** he rushed back; **tengo que volverme ~ a la tienda** I must get back double-quick to the shop; **lo harán ~s** they'll do it like a shot.

escapar [1a] **1** VT *caballo* to ride hard, drive hard.

2 VI (**a**) to escape, flee, run away; **~ a uno** to escape from sb; **~ de la cárcel** to escape from prison; **escapó de mis manos** it escaped from my hands, it eluded my grasp.

(**b**) (*Dep*) to break away.

(**c**) **no escapa a los estudiantes que tienen que aplicarse más** the students are well aware that they need to buckle down more.

3 escaparse VR (**a**) (*persona*) to escape, flee, run away, get away; **~ con algo** to make off with sth; **~ de morir** to miss death narrowly; **~ por un pelo, ~ en una tabla** to have a narrow escape, have a close shave.

(**b**) (*gas etc*) to leak, leak out, escape.

(**c**) (*detalle, noticia etc*) **se me escapa** it eludes me, it escapes me; **se me escapa su nombre** his name escapes me; **se le escapó la fecha de la reunión** he let the date of the meeting slip out, he unintentionally revealed the date of the meeting; **ese detalle se me había escapado** that detail had escaped my notice; **no se me escapa que ...** I am perfectly aware that ...

escaparate NM (**a**) (*de tienda*) shop window; (*vitrina*) showcase, display case; (*fig*) showcase; **ir de ~s, mirar ~s** to go window-shopping.

(**b**) (*LAm: armario*) wardrobe. (**c**) (‡) tits‡, bosom.

escaparatismo NM window-dressing.

escaparatista NMF window dresser.

escapatoria NF (**a**) escape, flight; getaway; (*) secret trip; **~ del trabajo** escape from work. (**b**) (*fig*) let-out, way out, loophole; excuse, pretext.

escape NM (**a**) (*huida*) escape, flight, getaway; **a ~** at full speed; in a great hurry; **salir a ~** to rush out.

(**b**) (*de gas etc*) leak, leakage, escape.

(**c**) (*Téc*) exhaust; **gases de ~** exhaust (fumes); **tubo de ~** exhaust (pipe).

(**d**) (*Mec*) escapement.

escapismo NM escapism.

escapista ADJ, NMF escapist.

escápula NF scapula, shoulder blade.

escapulario NM scapular(y).

escaque NM (*de tablero*) square; **~s** (*Hist*) chess.

escaqueado ADJ checked, chequered.

escaquearse* [1a] VR (*rajarse*) to duck out; (*gandulear*) to shirk, skive‡; (*negar la responsabilidad*) to pass the buck*; (*irse*) to slope off*.

escara NF (*Med*) crust, slough.

escarabajas NFPL firewood, kindling.

escarabajear [1a] **1** VT (*) to bother, worry.

2 VI (**a**) (*arrastrarse*) to crawl; (*agitarse*) to wriggle, squirm. (**b**) (*garabatear*) to scrawl, scribble.

escarabajo NM (**a**) (*Ent*) beetle; **~ de Colorado, ~ de la patata** Colorado beetle. (**b**) (*Téc*) flaw. (**c**) (*: *persona*) dwarf, runt. (**d**) **~s** (*: *garabatos*) scrawl, scribble. (**e**) (*Aut*) Beetle.

escaramujo NM (**a**) (*Bot*) wild rose, dog rose, briar; (*fruto*) hip. (**b**) (*Zool*) goose barnacle. (**c**) (*Carib: mal de ojo*) spell, curse.

escaramuza NF (**a**) (*Mil*) skirmish, brush. (**b**) (*fig*) brush; squabble.

escaramuzar [1f] VI to skirmish.

escarapela NF (**a**) cockade, rosette. (**b**) (*) brawl, shindy*.

escarapelar [1a] 　1　 VT (a) (*LAm: descascarar*) to scrape off, scale off, chip off.
(b) (*And: arrugar*) to crumple, rumple, muss.
　2　 VI (a) (*reñir*) to wrangle, quarrel.
(b) = VR.
　3　 **escarapelarse** VR (a) (*LAm: descascararse*) to peel off, flake off.
(b) (*And, Méx: temblar*) to go weak at the knees, tremble all over.

escarbadientes NM INVAR toothpick.

escarbador NM scraper.

escarbar [1a] 　1　 VT (a) *tierra* to scratch; *fuego* to poke; *dientes, oreja* to pick, clean.
(b) (*fig*) to inquire into, investigate, delve into; (*pey*) to pry into; to rake around in (o among).
　2　 VI (a) to scratch.
(b) ~ **en** = 1 (b).

escarcear [1a] VI (*Carib, Cono Sur*) to prance.

escarcela NF (*Caza*) pouch, bag.

escarceos NMPL (a) (*de caballo*) nervous movement; prance; (*fig*) amateur effort.
(b) (*olas*) small waves.
(c) ~ **amorosos** amorous posturings, amorous attitudinizing; love affairs.

escarcha NF frost, hoarfrost.

escarchado ADJ (a) covered in hoarfrost, frosted. (b) *fruta* crystallized.

escarchar [1a] 　1　 VT (a) to frost, cover in hoarfrost.
(b) (*Culin*) *tarta* to ice; *fruta* to crystallize (in liqueur).
(c) (*Cos*) to embroider with silver (o gold).
　2　 VI: **escarcha** there is a frost, it's frosty, it's freezing.

escarchilla NF (*And, Carib*) hail.

escarcho NM (red) gurnard.

escarda NF (a) (*acto*) weeding, hoeing; (*fig*) weeding out. (b) (*herramiento*) weeding hoe.

escardador NM weeding hoe.

escardadura NF weeding, hoeing.

escardar [1a] VT (a) to weed, weed out. (b) (*fig*) to weed out.

escardillo NM weeding hoe.

escariador NM reamer.

escariar [1b] VT to ream.

escarificación NF (*Agr, Med*) scarification.

escarificador NM scarifier.

escarificar [1g] VT to scarify.

escarlata 　1　 ADJ INVAR scarlet.
　2　 NM (*color*) scarlet.
　3　 NF (a) (*tela*) scarlet cloth. (b) (*Med*) scarlet fever.

escarlatina NF scarlet fever.

escarmenar [1a] VT (a) *lana* to comb. (b) (*fig*) to punish; ~ **algo a uno*** to swindle sb out of sth.

escarmentado ADJ wary, cautious.

escarmentar [1j] 　1　 VT to punish severely, teach a lesson to.
　2　 VI to learn one's lesson; **yo escarmenté y no lo volví a hacer** I learned my lesson and never did it again; **¡para que escarmientes!** that'll teach you!; ~ **en cabeza ajena** to learn by someone else's mistakes.

escarmiento NM (*castigo*) punishment; (*aviso*) lesson, warning, example; **para ~ de los malhechores** as a lesson to wrongdoers; **que esto te sirva de ~** let this be a lesson (o warning) to you.

escarnecedor 　1　 ADJ mocking.
　2　 NM, **escarnecedora** NF scoffer, mocker.

escarnecer [2d] VT to scoff at, mock, ridicule.

escarnio NM jibe, taunt; derision, ridicule.

escarola NF (a) (*Bot*) endive. (b) (*Méx Cos*) ruff, flounce.

escarolar [1a] VT (*Cos*) to frill, flounce; to curl.

escarpa NF (a) slope; (*Geog, Mil*) scarp, escarpment. (b) (*Méx*) pavement.

escarpado ADJ steep, sheer; craggy.

escarpadura NF = **escarpa** (a).

escarpar [1a] VT (a) (*Geog etc*) to escarp. (b) (*Téc*) to rasp.

escarpia NF spike; meat hook; (*Téc*) tenterhook.

escarpín NM (*zapatilla*) pump, slipper; (*calcetín*) extra sock, outer sock; (*de niña*) ankle sock.

escarrancharse* [1a] VR to do the splits.

escasamente ADV (a) scantily, sparingly; meagrely. (b) (*apenas*) scarcely, hardly, barely.

escasear [1a] 　1　 VT to be sparing with, give out in small amounts, skimp.
　2　 VI to be scarce, get scarce; to be in short supply; to fall short; to diminish.

escasez NF (a) (*falta*) scarcity, shortage, lack; (*pobreza*) poverty, want; ~ **de dinero** lack of money, shortage of funds; **vivir con ~** to live in poverty. (b) (*tacañería*) meanness, stinginess.

escaso ADJ (a) (*gen*) scarce; scant, scanty; limited; slight; *ración* mea-

gre, skimpy; *cosecha, público* thin, sparse; *posibilidad* slim, slender, small; *recursos* slender; *dinero* scarce, tight; *provisión* small, short, insufficient; *visibilidad* poor; ~ **de población** thinly populated; ~ **de recursos naturales** poor in natural resources; **andar ~ de dinero** to be short of money, be in need of money; **estar ~ de víveres** to be short of food supplies; **con escasa compasión** with scant pity; **su inteligencia es escasa** his intelligence is slight, his intelligence is limited.
(b) (*muy justo*) bare; **hay 2 toneladas escasas** there are barely 2 tons; **tiene 15 años ~s** he's barely 15, he's hardly 15; **ganar por una cabeza escasa** to win by a short head.
(c) (*tacaño*) mean, stingy; sparing.

escatimar [1a] VT (*reducir*) to curtail, cut down; (*dar poco de*) to give grudgingly, skimp, stint; to be sparing of; **no ~ esfuerzo para** + *infin* to spare no effort to + *infin*; **no escatimaba sus alabanzas de ...** he was unstinting in his praise of ..., he did not stint his praise of ...

escatimoso ADJ (a) (*tacaño*) sparing, scrimpy, mean. (b) (*taimado*) sly.

escatología¹ NF (*Rel*) eschatology.

escatología² NF scatology.

escatológico¹ ADJ (*Rel*) eschatological.

escatológico² ADJ scatological.

escay NM imitation leather.

escayola NF (*Med etc*) plaster.

escayolado NM plastering.

escayolar [1a] VT to put in plaster; **con la pierna escayolada** with his leg in plaster; **tener el cuello escayolado** to have one's neck in plaster.

escena NF (a) (*gen*) scene; **una ~ conmovedora** a touching scene; **con ~s de la revolución** with scenes from the revolution; ~ **muda** by-play; ~ **retrospectiva** (*Cine*) flashback.
(b) (*Teat: escenario*) stage; **entrar en ~** to enter, come on; **poner en ~** to stage, put on, perform.

escenario NM (a) (*Teat*) stage; setting; scenery; **en el ~** on (the) stage.
(b) (*Cine*) scenario; continuity.
(c) (*fig*) scene, scenario; setting; **el ~ del crimen** the scene of the crime; **fue ~ de un motín** it was the scene of a riot; **desapareció del ~ político** he disappeared from the political scene; **la ceremonia tuvo por ~ X** the ceremony was set in X, the ceremony had X as its setting.

escénico ADJ scenic.

escenificación NF staging; dramatization.

escenificar [1g] VT *comedia* to stage; *novela etc* to dramatize, make a stage version of; *suceso histórico* to re-enact, reproduce.

escenografía NF scenography; stage design.

escenógrafo, -a NM/F theatrical designer, designer of sets; scene painter.

escenotecnia NF staging, stagecraft.

escepticismo NM scepticism.

escéptico 　1　 ADJ sceptical.
　2　 NM, **escéptica** NF sceptic; doubter.

Escila NF Scylla; ~ **y Caribdis** Scylla and Charybdis.

escindible ADJ fissionable.

escindir [3a] 　1　 VT to split; **el partido está escindido** the party is split.
　2　 **escindirse** VR (*partido etc*) to split (*en* into); (*facción*) to split off.

Escipión NM Scipio.

escisión NF (a) scission; fission; split; (*Med*) excision; ~ **nuclear** nuclear fission. (b) (*fig*) split, division.

escisionismo NM (*Pol*) tendency to split into factions.

escisionista ADJ: **tendencia ~** breakaway tendency, tendency to split (off).

esclarecedor ADJ *explicación* illuminating.

esclarecer [2d] 　1　 VT (a) to light up, illuminate. (b) (*fig: explicar*) to explain, elucidate, shed light on; *crimen* to clear up. (c) (*fig: instruir*) to enlighten. (d) (*fig: ennoblecer*) to ennoble.
　2　 VI to dawn.

esclarecido ADJ illustrious, distinguished.

esclarecimiento NM (a) illumination. (b) explanation, elucidation, clarification. (c) enlightenment. (d) ennoblement.

esclava NF (a) slave; (*fig*) slave, drudge; ~ **blanca** white slave. (b) (*pulsera*) slave bangle, bracelet.

esclavatura NF (*LAm Hist*) (a) (*personas*) slaves (*collectively*). (b) (*período*) period of slavery. (c) (*esclavitud*) slavery.

esclavina NF short cloak, cape, tippet.

esclavismo NM = **esclavitud**.

esclavitud NF slavery, servitude, bondage.

esclavización NF enslavement.

esclavizar [1f] VT to enslave.

esclavo NM slave; **ser ~ del tabaco** to be a slave to tobacco; **vender a uno como ~** to sell sb into slavery.

esclerosis NF (a) sclerosis; ~ **múltiple** multiple sclerosis. (b) (*fig*) fossilization, stagnation.

esclerotizado ADJ (*fig*) fossilized, stagnant.

esclerotizar [1f] VT (*fig*) to make stagnant.

esclusa NF lock, sluice; floodgate; **~ de aire** airlock.

esclusero NM lock keeper.

-esco V Aspects of Word Formation in Spanish 2.

escoba ① NF (a) broom; brush; **~ mecánica** carpet-sweeper; **esto no vende una ~** this is a dead loss. (b) (*Bot*) broom. ② NM (*Dep*) sweeper.

escobada NF brush, sweep.

escobar [1a] VT to sweep, sweep out.

escobazo NM (a) (*golpe*) blow with a broom. (b) (*barrido*) quick sweep; **dar un ~** to have a quick sweep-up; **echar a uno a ~s** to kick sb out.

escobilla NF (a) small broom, brush; whisk; (*Aut*) windscreen wiper; **~ de dientes** (*And*) toothbrush. (b) (*Aut, Elec*) brush. (c) (*Bot*) teasel.

escobillar [1a] ① VI (*LAm*) to tap one's feet on the floor. ② VT (*And*) (*cepillar*) to brush; (*restregar*) to scrub.

escobillón NM swab.

escobón NM (*escoba*) large broom, long-handled broom; (*bruza*) scrubbing brush; (*algodón etc*) swab.

escocedor ADJ painful, hurtful.

escocedura NF = escozor.

escocer [2b y 2h] ① VT to annoy, hurt. ② VI to smart, sting; to feel a burning pain; **esto escuece en la lengua, esto me escuece la lengua** it makes my tongue smart. ③ **escocerse** VR to chafe, get chafed.

escocés ① ADJ Scotch, Scots, Scottish; *dibujo* tartan (*atr*). ② NM (a) (*persona*) Scot, Scotsman. (b) (*whisky*) Scotch; **~ de malta** malt whisky. ③ NM (*Ling*) Scots.

escocesa NF Scot, Scotswoman.

Escocia NF Scotland.

escocido ADJ: **el niño está ~, el niño tiene el culito ~** the baby has a nappy rash.

escoda NF stonecutter's hammer.

escofina NF rasp, file.

escofinar [1a] VT to rasp, file.

escogedor NM (*Agr etc*) riddle.

escogencia NF (*And, Carib*) choice.

escoger [2c] VTI to choose (*entre* between), select, pick (out); (*por voto*) to elect; **puestos a ~, ellos ...** faced with the choice, they ...

escogido ADJ (a) chosen, selected; (*en calidad*) choice, select; *obras* selected. (b) **ser muy ~** to be choosy; fussy (*para, con* about).

escogimiento NM choice, selection.

escolanía NF (*centro*) schola cantorum; (*niños*) choirboys pl.

escolano NM choirboy.

escolar ① ADJ scholastic; school (*atr*); **año ~** school year. ② NM schoolboy, pupil. ③ NF schoolgirl, pupil.

escolaridad NF schooling; **~ obligatoria** compulsory schooling, compulsory attendance at school; **el porcentaje de ~ es elevado** the proportion of those in school is high.

escolarización NF schooling; school attendance; enrolment in school.

escolarizar [1f] VT to enrol in school, send to school; to provide with schooling; **niños sin ~** children not in school, children receiving no schooling.

escolástica NF, **escolasticismo** NM scholasticism.

escolástico ① ADJ scholastic. ② NM scholastic, schoolman.

escoleta NF (*Méx*) (a) (*banda*) amateur band. (b) (*ensayo*) rehearsal, practice (of an amateur band). (c) (*lección de baile*) dancing lesson.

escollar [1a] VI (a) (*And, Cono Sur Náut*) to hit a reef, strike a rock. (b) (*Cono Sur: empresa*) to fail, come unstuck.

escollera NF breakwater, jetty.

escollo NM (a) reef, rock. (b) (*fig: problema etc*) pitfall; (*obstáculo*) stumbling block; (*peligro oculto*) hidden danger; **los muchos ~s del inglés** the many pitfalls of English.

escolopendra NF (*Zool*) centipede.

escolta ① NF escort; **dar ~ a** to escort, accompany. ② NMF (*persona*) escort; (*guardaespaldas*) bodyguard; (*de ministro etc*) minder*.

escoltar [1a] VT (*gen*) to escort; (*proteger*) to guard, protect; (*acompañar*) to attend, accompany; (*Náut*) to escort, convoy.

escombrar [1a] VT to clear out, clean out, clear of rubbish.

escombrera NF tip, dump, rubbish heap; (*Min*) slag heap.

escombro¹ NM (*Pez*) mackerel.

escombro² NM (*frec* **~s** PL) rubbish; debris, wreckage, rubble; (*Min*) waste, slag.

escondedero NM hiding place.

escondeloro NM (*CAm*) hide-and-seek.

esconder [2a] ① VT to hide, conceal (*de* from). ② **esconderse** VR to hide (*de* from); to hide o.s., conceal o.s.; to be hidden; to lurk.

escondida(s) NF(PL) (a) **hacer algo a ~s** to do sth secretly, do sth by stealth; **hacer algo a ~s de uno** to do sth behind sb's back. (b) (*LAm*) hide-and-seek; **jugar a (las) ~** to play hide-and-seek.

escondido(s) NM(PL) (*LAm*) hide-and-seek.

escondite NM (a) (*escondrijo*) hiding place; (*Caza, Orn*) hide. (b) (*juego*) hide-and-seek; **jugar al ~ con** (*fig*) to play hide-and-seek with.

escondrijo NM hiding place, hideout; (*fig*) nook.

escoñado NM has-been.

escoñar [1a] ① VT (*dañar*) to smash up, break, shatter; (*matar*) to do in*; (*arruinar*) to smash, ruin, destroy. ② **escoñarse** VR (a) (*persona*) to hurt o.s.; **estoy escoñado** I'm knackered*; **~ de risa** to laugh o.s. silly*. (b) (*Mec*) to break, get broken; to have a breakdown. (c) (*proyecto etc*) to fail.

escopeta NF (a) shotgun; **~ de aire comprimido** airgun; **~ de cañones recortados, ~ recortada** sawn-off shotgun; **~ paralela, ~ de dos cañones, ~ de tiro doble** double-barrelled gun; **~ de perdigones, ~ de postas** shotgun; **~ de viento** airgun. (b) (⁑) prick⁑.

escopetado ADJ = escopeteado.

escopetazo NM (a) (*disparo*) gunshot; (*herida*) gunshot wound. (b) (*fig*) bad news; blow; bombshell. (c) **dar un ~⁑** to have a screw⁑.

escopeteado ADJ: **salir ~** to be off like a shot; **voy ~** I'm in a terrible rush; **ella hablaba escopeteada** her words came in a torrent, her words came pouring out.

escopetear [1a] ① VT (a) to shoot at (with a shotgun). (b) (*Méx**) to get at, have a dig at*. ② VI (*Carib*) to answer irritably. ③ **escopetearse** VR: **se escopetearon en el bosque** they shot at each other in the wood; **se escopetean a injurias** they shower one another with insults, they heap insults upon each other.

escopeteo NM (a) (*disparos*) shooting, volley of shots. (b) (*de injurias, cumplimientos etc*) shower, lively exchange.

escopetero NM gunsmith; (*Mil*) rifleman.

escoplear [1a] VT to chisel.

escoplo NM chisel.

escor NM (*LAm*) score.

escora NF (*Náut*) (a) (*línea*) level line, load line. (b) (*apoyo*) prop, shore. (c) (*inclinación*) list; **con una ~ de 30 grados** with a thirty-degree list.

escoración NF, **escorada** NF (a) (*Náut*) list (*a, hacia* to). (b) (*fig*) leaning, inclination.

escorar [1a] (*Náut*) ① VT to shore up. ② VI (a) (*Náut*) to list, heel (over); **~ a babor** to list to port. (b) (*fig*) **~ a, ~ hacia** to lean towards, be inclined towards.

escorbútico ADJ scorbutic.

escorbuto NM scurvy.

escorchar [1a] VT (a) to flay, skin. (b) (*Cono Sur: fastidiar*) to bother, annoy.

escoria NF (a) (*Metal*) slag, dross; **~ básica** basic slag. (b) (*fig*) scum, dregs; **la ~ de la humanidad** the scum of humanity.

escorial NM (*industrial*) dump, slag heap, tip; (*Geol*) bed of lava, deposit of volcanic ash.

escorpena NF, **escorpina** NF scorpion fish.

Escorpio NM Scorpio.

escorpión NM scorpion; **E~** (*Zodíaco*) Scorpio.

escorrentía NF (*Agr*) run-off (*of chemicals etc*); (*torrente*) rush, torrent; (*derrame*) overflow; **~ superficial** surface run-off.

escorzar [1f] VT to foreshorten.

escorzo NM foreshortening.

escota NF (*Náut: cabo*) sheet.

escotado ① ADJ *vestido* low-cut, low-necked, cut low, décolleté. ② NM = escotadura.

escotadura NF (a) (*Cos*) low neck(line). (b) (*Teat*) large trap door. (c) (*hueco*) recess; (*corte*) notch.

escotar [1a] ① VT (a) (*Cos*) to cut out, cut to fit; to cut low in front. (b) *río etc* to draw water from. ② VI to pay one's share.

escotch NM (*LAm*) sticky tape.

escote NM (a) (*Cos*) low neck; décolletage; cleavage; **~ en pico, ~ en V** V-neck; **~ profundo** plunging neckline. (b) (*Fin*) share; **ir a ~, pagar a ~** to share the expenses, go fifty-fifty, (*pareja*) to go Dutch.

escotilla NF (*Náut etc*) hatch, hatchway; (*fig*) floodgates; **atrancar las ~s** (*fig*) to batten down the hatches.

escotillón NM trap door.

escozor NM (a) smart, sting; burning pain. (b) (*fig*) grief, heartache.

escriba NM scribe.

escribanía NF (a) (*mueble*) writing desk; writing case. (b) (*enseres*) writing materials; inkstand. (c) (*Jur: cargo*) clerkship; (*oficina*) clerk's office, (*Hist*) notary's office.

escribano NM (**a**) court clerk; lawyer's clerk; (*Hist*) notary; ~ **municipal** town clerk. (**b**) (*Orn*) bunting; ~ **cerillo** yellowhammer.

escribiente NM copyist, amanuensis; clerk.

▼ **escribir** [3a; PTP **escrito**] ☐ VTI (**a**) to write; ~ **a mano** to write in longhand; to write out; ~ **a máquina** to type; **el que esto escribe** the present writer; (*Prensa etc*) this correspondent.
(**b**) (*ortografiar*) to spell; **'voy' se escribe con 'v'** 'voy' is spelled with a 'v'; **¿cómo se escribe eso?** how is that spelled?, how do you spell that?
☐ **escribirse** VR (**a**) to write to each other.
(**b**) ~ **con** to correspond with, write to.

escrito ☐ PTP *de* **escribir**.
☐ ADJ (*en forma escrita*) written; (*dicho*) said, stated; **lo arriba ~** what has been said above.
☐ NM writing, document; text; manuscript; (*Jur*) brief; ~**s** (*Liter etc*) writings, works; **por ~** in writing; in black and white; **acuerdo por ~** written agreement, agreement in writing; **poner algo por ~** to commit sth to paper; to write sth down, get sth down in writing; **tomar algo por ~** to write sth down, take sth down in writing.

escritor(a) NM/F writer; ~ **de material publicitario** copywriter; ~ **satírico** satirist, satirical writer.

escritorio NM (**a**) (*mueble*) desk, bureau; writing case; **de ~** (*frec*) desktop (*atr*). (**b**) (*despacho*) office.

escritorzuelo, -a NM/F hack (writer), scribbler.

escritura NF (**a**) (*acto, arte*) writing.
(**b**) (*de nación*) writing, script; alphabet; (*de persona*) writing, handwriting; **tiene malísima ~** her writing is terrible; **no acierto a leer su ~** I can't read his writing; ~ **aérea** skywriting; ~ **automática** automatic writing; ~ **corrida**, ~ **normal** longhand; ~ **china** Chinese writing, Chinese script; ~ **fonética** phonetic script; ~ **a máquina** typing.
(**c**) **Sagrada E~** (Holy) Scripture.
(**d**) (*Jur*) deed; document, instrument; ~ **de aprendizaje** indenture; ~ **de propiedad** title deed; ~ **de seguro** insurance certificate; ~ **de traspaso** conveyance, deed of transfer.

escriturado ADJ *capital etc* registered.

escriturar [1a] VT (**a**) (*Jur*) *documentos* to execute by deed, formalize legally; *aprendiz* to indenture. (**b**) (*Teat etc*) to book, engage, sign up.

escriturario ADJ, **escriturístico** ADJ scriptural.

escrófula NF scrofula.

escrofuloso ADJ scrofulous.

escroto NM scrotum.

escrupulizar [1f] VT to scruple, hesitate; **no ~ en** + *infin* not to scruple to + *infin*.

escrúpulo NM (**a**) (*duda*) scruple; doubt, hesitation; **falta de ~s** unscrupulousness; **sin ~** unscrupulous; **no hizo ~ de** + *infin* he did not scruple to + *infin*, he did not hesitate to + *infin*.
(**b**) (*cualidad*) scrupulousness.
(**c**) (*Farm*) scruple.

escrupulosamente ADV scrupulously; exactly, precisely.

escrupulosidad NF scrupulousness; exactness, preciseness.

escrupuloso ADJ scrupulous; exact, particular, precise.

escrutador ☐ ADJ *mirada etc* searching, penetrating.
☐ NM, **escrutadora** NF (*Pol*) returning officer, scrutineer; inspector of election returns; (*Parl*) teller.

escrutar [1a] VT (**a**) (*examinar*) to scrutinize, examine. (**b**) *votos* to count.

escrutinio NM (**a**) scrutiny, examination, inspection. (**b**) (*Pol: cuenta*) count, counting (of votes); (*votación*) voting, ballot.

escuadra NF (**a**) (*Téc*) carpenter's square, draughtsman's square; bracket, angle iron; ~ **de delineante** set square; **a ~** square, at right angles; **fuera de ~** out of true.
(**b**) (*Mil*) squad; (*Náut*) squadron; (*de coches etc*) fleet; ~ **de demolición** demolition squad; ~ **de fusilamiento** firing squad.
(**c**) (*And: pistola*) pistol.
(**d**) (*LAm Dep*) team.

escuadrar [1a] VT (*Téc*) to square.

escuadrilla NF (*Aer*) squadron.

escuadrón NM (*Aer*) squadron; (*Mil*) squadron, troop; ~ **de la muerte** death squad, murder squad; ~ **volante** flying squad.

escualidez NF (**a**) paleness, weakness, emaciation; skinniness, scragginess. (**b**) squalor, filth.

escuálido ADJ (**a**) (*débil*) pale, weak, emaciated; (*flaco*) skinny, scraggy. (**b**) (*sucio*) squalid, filthy.

escualo NM dogfish.

escucha ☐ NF (**a**) (*acto*) listening; listening-in; (*Rad*) monitoring; ~**s telefónicas** telephone tapping; **estar a la ~** to listen in; **estar de ~** to spy, eavesdrop.
(**b**) (*Ecl*) chaperon.
☐ NM (*Mil*) scout; (*Rad*) monitor (*person*); listener.

escuchar [1a] ☐ VT to listen to; (*LAm*) to hear; *consejo etc* to listen to, heed, pay attention to; *aplausos, avisos etc* to receive.
☐ VI to listen.
☐ **escucharse** VR to hear; **le gusta ~** he likes the sound of his own voice.

escuchimizado* ADJ skinny; **estar ~** to be (all) skin and bones.

escucho NM (*And*) whispered secret.

escuchón ADJ (*And*) prying, inquisitive.

escudar [1a] ☐ VT to shield; (*fig*) to shield, protect, defend.
☐ **escudarse** VR to shield o.s., protect o.s.

escudería NF motor-racing team.

escudero NM (*Hist*) squire; page.

escudete NM (**a**) (*Her, Hist*) escutcheon. (**b**) (*Cos*) gusset. (**c**) (*Bot*) white water lily.

escudilla NF bowl, basin.

escudo NM shield (*t fig*); ~ **de armas** (*Her*) coat of arms; ~ **humano** human shield; ~ **térmico** heat shield.

escudriñar [1a] VT (*investigar*) to inquire into, investigate; (*examinar*) to examine, scan, scrutinize.

escuela NF (**a**) school; ~ **de artes y oficios** technical school, trade school; ~ **automovilista** driving school; ~ **de baile** school of dancing; ballet school; ~ **de cine** film school; ~ **de comercio** business school, school of business studies; ~ **elemental**, ~ **primaria**, ~ **de primera enseñanza** primary school; ~ **de enfermería** nursing college; ~ **de equitación**, ~ **hípica** riding school; ~ **de formación profesional** polytechnic; ~ **de hogar** domestic science college; ~ **infantil** primary school; ~ **laboral** technical school; trade school; ~ **naval** naval academy; ~ **nocturna** night school; ~ **normal** training college, college of education; ~ **de pago** fee-paying school; ~ **particular**, ~ **privada** private school; ~ **de párvulos** infant(s') school, kindergarten; ~ **pública** state school; ~ **unitaria** school having one teacher; ~ **de verano** summer school; **abandonar la ~** to drop out of school; **estar en la ~** to be at school; **ir a la ~** to go to school; **soplarse la ~** to play truant.
(**b**) (*Arte, de pensamiento etc*) school; **la ~ catalana** the Catalan school; **gente de la vieja ~** people of the old school; **crear ~** to create a following; **formarse en una ~ dura** to learn in a tough school; *ver también* [COLEGIO].

ESCUELA OFICIAL DE IDIOMAS

ⓘ *The Escuelas Oficiales de Idiomas are state-run language schools which offer tuition in a wide range of foreign languages, particularly English and French. Examinations are also open to external candidates and the final qualification, after 5 years' study, the **Certificado de la Escuela Oficial de Idiomas** is recognized all over Spain.*

---

escuelante NMF (**a**) (*Méx*) country schoolteacher. (**b**) (*And: alumno*) schoolboy, schoolgirl.

escuelero ☐ ADJ (*LAm*) school (*atr*).
☐ NM (*And, Carib, Cono Sur: pey: maestro*) schoolmaster.
☐ NM, **escuelera** NF (*And*) (*alumno*) schoolboy, schoolgirl; (*: *estudioso*) swot*.

escuerzo NM (**a**) (*Zool*) toad. (**b**) (*fig*) wretched creature, runt; pitiful object, scarecrow.

escuetamente ADV plainly; baldly, without frills.

escueto ADJ plain, unadorned, bare; bald; *mensaje etc* short, abrupt, succinct.

escuincle* NM (*Méx*) (*chico*) kid*; (*animal*) runt.

esculcar [1g] VT (*LAm*) to search.

esculpir [3a] VT to sculpt, sculpture; to carve, engrave; *inscripción* to cut.

esculque NM (*LAm*) body search.

escultismo NM = **escutismo**.

escultor NM sculptor.

escultora NF sculptress.

escultórico ADJ sculptural.

escultura NF sculpture, carving; ~ **en madera** wood carving.

escultural ADJ sculptural; (*fig*) *talla etc* statuesque.

escupe* NM (*Prensa*) scoop.

escupidera NF (**a**) spittoon, cuspidor (*US*). (**b**) (*LAm: euf*) chamberpot; **pedir la ~** to get scared; to give in, give o.s. up.

escupidor NM (**a**) (*persona*) spitter. (**b**) (*And, Carib: recipiente*) spittoon. (**c**) (*And: estera*) round mat, doormat.

escupir [3a] VTI (**a**) *sangre* to spit; *comida etc* to spit out; ~ **a uno** to spit at sb; ~ **a la cara a uno** to spit in sb's face; ~ **en el suelo** to spit on the ground; **ser de medio ~*** to be as common as dirt.
(**b**) (*fig*) *palabra* to spit, spit out, fling (*a* at); *llamas etc* to spit, belch, give out; to throw off, fling off, cast aside; ~ **a** to scoff at.
(**c**) (‡: *confesar*) to cough‡, sing‡.
(**d**) (‡: *pagar*) to cough up*.

escupitajo* NM spit.

escurana NF (*LAm*) darkness; (*cielo*) overcast sky, threatening sky.

escurialense ADJ of (*o* from) El Escorial.

escurreplatos NM INVAR plate rack.

escurreverduras NM INVAR colander, strainer.

► LENGUA Y USO: **escribir: 1a** → 48.1, 48.2

escurribanda NF **(a)** (*Med: de vientre*) looseness, diarrhoea. **(b)** (*Med: de úlcera*) running. **(c)** (*fuga*) escape; (*fig*) loophole, way out. **(d)** (*paliza*) thrashing.

escurridera NF draining board.

escurrideras NFPL (*Méx, CAm*) = **escurriduras**.

escurridero NM draining board, drainboard (*US*).

escurridizo ADJ **(a)** *superficie* slippery; *objeto* difficult to hold; *nudo* running; *idea* elusive; **hacerse ~** to slip away, vanish. **(b)** *carácter* slippery.

escurrido ADJ **(a)** (*delgado*) *mujer* narrow-hipped, slightly built; wearing a tight-fitting skirt. **(b)** (*And, Carib, Méx*) (*avergonzado*) abashed, ashamed; (*tímido*) shy.

escurridor NM (*de ropa*) wringer; **~ (de loza)** plate rack; (*Culin*) colander, strainer; (*Fot*) drying rack.

escurriduras NFPL (*heces*) dregs; (*gotas*) drops.

escurrir [3a] **1** VT *ropa* to wring (out); *platos, líquido* to drain; *sustancia* to press dry, squeeze dry; V **bulto.**
  2 VI **(a)** (*líquido*) to drip, trickle; to ooze; (*objeto*) to slip, slide. **(b)** (*superficie*) to be slippery.
  3 escurrirse VR **(a)** (*líquido*) to drip, trickle; to ooze; (*objeto*) to slip, slide; **se me escurrió de entre las manos** it slipped out of my hands.
  (b) (*platos*) to drain; (*Culin*) to drain, strain; **'se escurre bien'** (*receta*) 'drain well'.
  (c) (*observación etc*) to slip out.
  (d) (*persona etc*) to slip away, sneak off; to glide away.
  (e) (*excederse*) to go too far; **se escurrió en la reprimenda** she laid it on with a very heavy hand; **se escurrió en la propina** his tip was much too generous.
  (f) (⁎⁎) to come⁎⁎.

escúter NM (motor) scooter.

escutismo NM scouting (movement), boy scouts.

esdrújulo **1** ADJ having dactylic stress, accented on the antepenult. **2** NM word having dactylic stress, word accented on the antepenult (*p.ej.* **mísero**).

ESE ABR *de* **estesudeste** east-south-east, ESE.

ese¹ NF **(a)** the (name of the) letter *s*. **(b)** (*pieza etc*) S-shaped part (o link *etc*); **hacer ~s** (*camino*) to zigzag, twist and turn; (*borracho*) to reel about, stagger along.

ese² ADJ DEM M, **esa** F that; **esos** ADJ DEM MPL, **esas** FPL those.

ése PRON DEM M, **ésa** F that; that one; the former; **ésos** PRON DEM MPL, **ésas** FPL those; the former; **en ésa** in your town; **... y cosas de ésas** ... and suchlike; **ni por ésas** on no account, under no circumstances; **¡no me salgas ahora con ésas!** don't bring all that up again!; **no es una chica de ésas** she's not one of those, she's not that kind of a girl.

esencia NF essence; (*de problema etc*) heart, core; **quinta ~** quintessence; **en ~** in essence.

esencial ADJ essential; chief, main; **lo ~** the essential thing, the main thing; **cosa no ~** non-essential thing, inessential.

esfagno NM sphagnum.

esfera NF **(a)** (*Geog, Mat etc*) sphere; globe; **~ celeste** celestial sphere; **~ impresora** (*Tip*) golfball; **en forma de ~** spherical, globular.
  (b) (*Téc*) dial; (*de reloj*) face, dial.
  (c) (*fig*) sphere; plane, field; **~ de acción** scope; field of action; range; **~ de actividad** sphere of activity; **~ de influencia** sphere of influence.

esférico **1** ADJ spherical. **2** NM (*Dep*) ball, football.

esferográfica NF (*Carib*) ballpoint pen.

esferoide NM spheroid.

esfinge NF **(a)** sphinx; **ser como una ~** to be expressionless; to have one's lips sealed. **(b)** (*Ent*) hawk moth.

esfínter NM sphincter.

esforzadamente ADV vigorously, energetically; enterprisingly; bravely.

esforzado ADJ (*fuerte*) vigorous, energetic, strong; (*duro*) tough; (*emprendedor*) enterprising; (*valiente*) brave, valiant.

esforzar [1f y 1m] **1** VT **(a)** (*fortalecer*) to strengthen; to invigorate.
  (b) (*animar*) to encourage, raise the spirits of.
  2 esforzarse VR to exert o.s., make an effort; to strain; **hay que ~ más** you must try harder, you must put more effort into it; **~ en +** *infin*, **~ por +** *infin* to struggle to + *infin*, strive to + *infin*.

esfuerzo NM **(a)** (*gen*) effort, endeavour; exertion; (*imaginación*) effort, stretch; **sin ~** effortlessly, without strain; **no perdonar ~s para +** *infin* to spare no effort to + *infin*; **bien vale el ~** it's well worth the effort.
  (b) (*Mec*) stress.
  (c) (*valentía*) courage, spirit; (*vigor*) vigour; **con ~** with spirit.

esfumar [1a] **1** VT (*Arte*) to shade (in); to tone down, soften.
  2 esfumarse VR **(a)** (*esperanzas etc*) to fade away, melt away.
  (b) (*persona*) to vanish, make o.s. scarce; **¡esfúmate!⁎** get lost!⁎

esfumino NM (*Arte*) stump.

esgrima NF (*Dep: como arte*) fencing; (*Mil: arte*) swordsmanship.

esgrimidor **1** NM (*Mil*) swordsman. **2** NM, **esgrimidora** NF (*Dep*) fencer.

esgrimir [3a] **1** VT *espada* to wield; to brandish; (*fig*) *argumento etc* to use; to brandish, flourish, fling about; **~ que ...** to argue that ..., maintain that ...
  2 VI to fence.

esgrimista NMF (*LAm*) fencer.

esguazar [1f] VT to ford.

esguince NM **(a)** (*movimiento*) swerve, dodge, avoiding action; **dar un ~** to swerve, duck, dodge.
  (b) (*Med*) sprain.
  (c) (*ceño*) scowl, frown; (*mirada*) scornful look.
  (d) (*fig: de intriga etc*) twist; **un ~ ingenioso** an ingenious twist.

eskay NM imitation leather.

eslabón NM (*de cadena*) link (*t fig*); (*chaira*) steel; (*Náut, Téc*) shackle; **~ giratorio** swivel; **~ perdido** missing link.

eslabonar [1a] VT to link (together, up), join; (*fig*) to link, interlink, connect, knit together.

eslálom NM, **eslalon** NM = **slalom.**

eslavo **1** ADJ Slav, Slavonic. **2** NM, **eslava** NF Slav. **3** NM (*Ling*) Slavonic.

eslinga NF (*Náut*) sling.

eslingar [1h] VT (*Náut*) to sling.

eslip NM, PL **eslips** = **slip.**

eslogan NM = **slogan.**

eslomar [1a] VT = **deslomar.**

eslora NF (*Náut*) length; **tiene 250 m de ~** she is 250 m in length.

eslovaco **1** ADJ Slovak(ian). **2** NM, **eslovaca** NF Slovak.

Eslovaquia NF Slovakia.

Eslovenia NF Slovenia.

esloveno, -a ADJ, NM/F Slovene.

esmaltar [1a] VT **(a)** *metal* to enamel; *uñas* to varnish, paint. **(b)** (*fig*) to embellish, beautify, adorn (with a variety of colours).

esmalte NM **(a)** (*Anat, Téc*) enamel; enamelwork, smalt; **~ de uñas** nail-varnish, nail-polish. **(b)** (*fig*) lustre.

esmeradamente ADV carefully, neatly; elegantly.

esmerado ADJ **(a)** *trabajo* careful, neat; polished, elegant. **(b)** *persona* careful, painstaking, conscientious.

esmeralda NF emerald.

esmerar [1a] **1** VT to polish, brighten up.
  2 esmerarse VR to take great pains (*en* over), exercise great care (*en* in), do one's best; to shine, do well; **~ en +** *infin* to take great pains to + *infin*, go to great trouble to + *infin*.

esmerejón NM merlin.

esmeril NM emery.

esmeriladora NF lapping machine, emery wheel.

esmerilar [1a] VT to polish with emery.

esmero NM care, carefulness; neatness; polish, elegance; refinement; **con el mayor ~** with the greatest care; **poner ~ en algo** to take great care over sth.

Esmirna N Smyrna.

esmirriado ADJ = **desmirriado.**

esmoladera NF grindstone.

esmoquin NM dinner-jacket, tuxedo (*US*).

esnifada⁎ NF sniff; snort⁎.

esnifar⁎ [1a] VT *colas etc* to sniff; *cocaína* to snort⁎.

esnife⁎ NM sniff.

esnob **1** ADJ (⁎) INVAR *persona* snobbish; *coche, restaurante etc* posh⁎, de luxe, swish⁎. **2** NMF, PL **esnobs** [ez'noß] snob.

esnobear⁎ [1a] VT to snub, cold-shoulder.

esnobismo NM snobbery, snobbishness.

esnobista ADJ snobbish.

ESO NF (*Esp*) ABR *de* **Educación Secundaria Obligatoria** *secondary education for 12 to 16 year olds.*

  | ESO |

🛈 *As a consequence of the 1990 education reform law,* **LOGSE,** *secondary education in Spain is now divided into two stages. The first stage,* **ESO,** *or* **Educación Secundaria Obligatoria,** *is for 12- to 16-year-olds. It is free and compulsory and includes both vocational and academic subjects. Students are awarded the* **Título de Graduado en Educación Secundaria** *on successful completion at age 16 and can leave school at this point. If they choose to continue their education they go on to the second stage, which consists of either the academically orientated* **Bachillerato** *or the vocational* **Formación Profesional Específica.**
⇨ *See also* | LOGSE |

eso PRON DEM *'neutro'* that; that thing, that affair, that matter; ~ **no me gusta** I don't like that; **¿qué es ~?** what's that?; ~ **de su coche** that business about his car; ~ **de no tener dinero el colegio** that story about the college having no money; ~ **de que los cerdos volarán algún día** the idea that pigs will fly one day; **¿qué es ~ de que ...?** what's all this about ...?; **¡~!** that's right!; **¡~ a ellos!** that's their look-out!; ~ **es** that's it, that's right; that's just it; **no es ~** that's not the reason; **¡no es ~!** hardly!; **nada de ~** nothing of the kind, far from it; **¡nada de ~!** not a bit of it!; **¿no es ~?** isn't that so?; **¿y ~?** why? how so?*; ~ **sí** yes; naturally, of course; ~ **digo yo** I quite agree; *(respondiendo a pregunta)* that's what I'd like to know; **el coche es viejo, ~ sí** the car is certainly old, to be sure the car is old; **a ~ de las 2** at about 2 o'clock, round about 2; **antes de ~** before that; **después de ~** after that; **en ~** thereupon, at that point; **por ~** therefore, and so; **por ~ no vine** that's why I didn't come; **es por ~ que no vino** that's why she didn't come; **y ~ que llovía** in spite of the fact that it was raining; bearing in mind that it was raining.

esófago NM oesophagus, gullet.

Esopo NM Aesop.

esotérico ADJ esoteric.

esoterismo NM *(culto)* cult of the esoteric; *(como género)* esoterics; *(carácter)* esoteric nature.

esp. ABR *de* **español** Spanish, Sp., Span.

espabilada[1]* NF *(And)* blink; **en una ~** in a jiffy*.

espabilado[1] ADJ *persona* bright.
[2] NM, **espabilada**[2] NF clever dick*, smart alec*.

espabilar [1a] [1] VT (a) *vela* to snuff; V **despabilar**.
(b) (‡: *robar*) to nick‡.
(c) (‡: *matar*) to do in‡.
[2] VI *(And)* to blink.
[3] **espabilarse** VR to wake up; *(fig)* to look lively, get a move on; to pull one's socks up; **¡espabílate!** get a move on!; jump to it!; **¡espabilado!** *(iró)* wake up!, you're a bright one!

espachurrar [1a] VT to squash, flatten.

espaciadamente ADV: **la revista saldrá más ~** the journal will come out less frequently (*o* at longer intervals).

espaciado NM *(Tip, Inform)* spacing.

espaciador NM spacing key, spacing bar.

espacial ADJ (a) *(Mat etc)* spatial. (b) space *(atr)*; **programa ~** space programme; **viajes ~es** space travel.

espaciar [1b] [1] VT (*t Tip*) to space (out); to spread, expand; *noticia* to spread; *pago* to spread out, stagger.
[2] **espaciarse** VR (a) *(hablando)* to expatiate, spread o.s.; ~ **en un tema** to enlarge on a subject, expatiate on a subject.
(b) *(esparcirse)* to relax, take one's ease; *(estar de juerga)* to make merry.

espacio NM (a) *(gen)* space; room; distance; period, interval; ~ **aéreo** air space; ~ **amortiguador** buffer zone; ~ **libre** room, clear space; ~ **de maniobra** room for manoeuvre; ~ **muerto** clearance; ~ **natural** open space; ~ **vital** living space, *(Pol)* lebensraum; **en el ~ de una hora** in the space of one hour; **en el ~ de 3 generaciones** in the space of 3 generations, over 3 generations; **por ~ de** during, for; **por ~ de 3 años** over 3 years; **ocupa mucho ~** it takes up a lot of room.
(b) *(Aer, Geog)* space; **exploración del ~** space exploration; ~ **estelar**, ~ **exterior**, ~ **extraterrestre** outer space.
(c) *(tardanza)* delay, slowness.
(d) *(Tip, Inform)* space; spacing; **a un ~** single-spaced; **a dos ~s, a doble ~** double-spaced.
(e) *(Mús)* interval.
(f) *(Rad, TV)* short programme, item; spot, slot; ~ **informativo** newscast; ~ **publicitario** advertising spot, commercial.

espacioso ADJ (a) *cuarto etc* spacious, roomy, big; capacious. (b) *movimiento* slow, deliberate.

espaciotemporal ADJ spatio-temporal.

espada [1] NF (a) *(arma)* sword; (‡) picklock; **estar entre la ~ y la pared** to be between the devil and the deep blue sea; **estar hecho una ~** to be as thin as a rake; **poner a ~** to put to the sword.
(b) ~**s** *(Naipes)* spades.
(c) *(persona)* swordsman.
[2] NM *(Taur)* matador.

espadachín NM skilled swordsman; *(pey)* bully, thug.

espadaña NF (a) *(Bot)* bullrush. (b) *(Arquit)* steeple, belfry.

espadarte NM swordfish.

espadazo NM sword thrust, slash with a sword.

espadero NM swordsmith.

espadilla NF *(remo)* scull (oar).

espadín NM (a) *(espada)* dress sword, ceremonial sword. (b) *(de espadista)* picklock. (c) *(Pez: t* **espadines**) whitebait.

espadista‡ NM burglar, lock-picker.

espadón NM (a) broadsword. (b) *(hum*)* big shot*, top person; *(Mil)* brass hat*.

espaguetis NMPL spaghetti.

espalda NF (a) (*t* ~**s**) back, shoulder(s); **a ~s de uno** behind sb's back; **a ~s (vueltas)** treacherously; **eso ha quedado ya a la ~** that's all behind us now; **atar las manos a la ~** to tie sb's hands behind his back; **echar algo a las ~s** to forget about sth; **tiene 40 años de eso a las ~s** he has 40 years of that behind him; ~ **con ~** back to back; **de ~s** from behind; **dar de ~s** to fall on one's back; **estar de ~s** to be on one's back; **estar de ~s a** *(fig)* to ignore, pay no heed to; **de ~s a la marcha** facing backwards, with one's back to the engine *(etc)*; **volverse de ~s a** to turn one's back on (*t fig*); **fue muerto por la ~** he was killed from behind; **cubrir las ~s** *(fig)* to cover o.s., protect o.s.; **dar la ~ a la pared** to have one's back to the wall; **echar algo sobre las ~s** to take sth on, take charge of sth; **tener guardadas las ~s** to have influential friends; **volver la ~** to turn away; *(pey)* to turn tail; **volver las ~s a uno** to give sb the cold shoulder, cold-shoulder sb.
(b) *(Natación)* backstroke.
(c) *(And: destino)* fate, destiny; star.
(d) ~ **mojada** *(Méx*)* wetback.

espaldar NM (a) *(de silla)* back. (b) *(Hort)* trellis, espalier. (c) ~**es** wall hangings.

espaldarazo NM slap on the back; pat on the back; *(Hist)* accolade.

espaldera NF trellis, espalier.

espaldero NM *(Carib)* bodyguard, henchman.

espaldilla NF *(Anat)* shoulder blade; *(Méx Culin)* shoulder of pork.

espantá* NF = **espantada**.

espantable ADJ = **espantoso**.

espantada NF (a) *(miedo)* sudden scare, sudden fear; **dar la ~** to bolt.
(b) *(huida)* stampede, panic.

espantadizo ADJ shy, timid, easily scared (off).

espantado ADJ frightened, scared, terrified; *(LAm)* sick with fear.

espantador ADJ (a) *(espantoso)* frightening. (b) *(And, CAm, Cono Sur)* = **espantadizo**.

espantajo NM (a) *(lit)* scarecrow. (b) *(fig)* scarecrow; sight, fright; bogey, bogeyman.

espantamoscas NM INVAR fly-swat.

espantapájaros NM INVAR scarecrow.

espantar [1a] [1] VT *(asustar)* to frighten, scare; *(ahuyentar)* to frighten off, scare away; *(horrorizar)* to appal, horrify.
[2] **espantarse** VR (a) *(asustarse)* to get frightened, get scared (*de* at, of); to be appalled; *(asombrarse)* to be amazed, be astonished (*de* at).
(b) *(Carib: sospechar)* to get suspicious.

espanto NM (a) *(miedo)* fright, terror; *(consternación)* consternation, dismay; *(asombro)* amazement, astonishment.
(b) *(amenaza)* threat, menace.
(c) *(LAm: fantasma)* ghost.
(d) (*) **¡qué ~!** how awful!; goodness!; **es un coche de ~** it's a smashing car*, it's a tremendous car*; **hace un frío de ~** it's terribly cold.

espantosamente ADV frightfully; terrifyingly; shockingly; amazingly.

espantosidad NF *(And)* terror, fear.

espantoso ADJ frightful, dreadful; terrifying; shocking; appalling; amazing.

España NF Spain; **las ~s** *(hum*)* Spain; **Nueva ~** *(Hist)* New Spain (*ie* Mexico); **la ~ de pandereta** *(pey)* touristy Spain, pseudo-romantic Spain, picturesque Spain.

español [1] ADJ Spanish.
[2] NM, **española**[1] NF Spaniard; **los ~es** the Spaniards, the Spanish.
[3] NM *(Ling)* Spanish; ~ **antiguo** Old Spanish; ~ **medieval** Medieval Spanish; ~ **moderno** Modern Spanish.

española[2] NF *(Méx)* spanner.

españolada NF typically Spanish product (*o* feature *etc*) (*t pey*).

españolidad NF *(carácter español)* Spanishness; *(patriotismo)* Spanish patriotism; *(sentimientos nacionales)* Spanish national feelings.

españolísimo ADJ *superl* typically Spanish, unmistakably Spanish, Spanish to the core; terribly Spanish.

españolismo NM (a) *(amor a lo español)* love of Spain, love of things Spanish; *(tendencia a españolizarse)* tendency to adopt Spanish ways *(etc)*.
(b) *(carácter)* Spanishness; Spanish nature, essentially Spanish character.
(c) *(Ling)* hispanicism, word (*o* phrase *etc*) borrowed from Spanish.

españolista [1] ADJ centralist, unionist (as opposed to regionalist).
[2] NMF member (*o* supporter) of a Madrid-based party.

españolito* NM ordinary Spaniard, man in the Spanish street; **algún ~** some poor little Spaniard; **cada ~ de a pie** each poor little Spaniard that there is.

españolizar [1f] [1] VT to make Spanish, hispanicize; to give a Spanish flavour (*o* colouring *etc*) to.
[2] **españolizarse** VR to adopt Spanish ways *(etc)*; to acquire a Spanish flavour *(etc)*; *(pey)* to affect Spanish ways; **se españolizó por completo** he became completely Spanish.

esparadrapo NM sticking plaster; adhesive tape.

esparaván NM (**a**) (*Orn*) sparrowhawk. (**b**) (*Vet*) spavin.

esparavel NM (casting) net.

esparceta NF sainfoin.

esparcido ADJ (**a**) (*desparramado*) scattered; (*extendido*) widespread. (**b**) (*fig*: *alegre*) merry, jolly, cheerful; (*franco*) open, frank.

esparcimiento NM (**a**) (*gen*) spreading, scattering. (**b**) (*fig*: *descanso*) relaxation; (*recreo*) amusement, diversion; recreation. (**c**) (*fig*) (*alegría*) cheerfulness; (*franqueza*) openness, frankness.

esparcir [3b] **1** VT (**a**) (*desparramar*) to spread, scatter; (*sembrar*) to sow; (*divulgar*) to disseminate.
(**b**) (*fig*) to amuse, divert.
2 esparcirse VR (**a**) (*desparramarse*) to spread (out), scatter, be scattered.
(**b**) (*fig*) (*relajarse*) to relax; (*distraerse*) to amuse o.s.

espárrago NM asparagus; **~ triguero** wild asparagus; **estar hecho un ~** to be as thin as a rake; **¡ve a freír ~s!*** go to hell!; **mandar a uno a freír ~s*** to tell sb to go to hell.

esparraguera NF asparagus plant.

esparrancado ADJ (with legs) wide apart, (with legs) spread far apart.

esparrancarse [1g] VR to spread one's legs (wide apart); to do the splits; **~ sobre algo** to straddle sth.

Esparta N Sparta.

espartal NM esparto field.

espartano, -a ADJ, NM/F Spartan.

esparteña NF = **alpargata**.

espartillo NM (*LAm*) esparto (grass).

espartizal NM esparto field.

esparto NM esparto (grass); **estar como el ~** to be all dried up.

Espasa NM: **ser el ~*** to be a walking encyclopedia.

espasmo NM spasm.

espasmódicamente ADV spasmodically.

espasmódico ADJ spasmodic.

espasticidad NF spasticity.

espástico, -a ADJ, NM/F spastic.

espatarrarse* [1a] VR = **esparrancarse**.

espato NM (*Geol*) spar; **~ de Islandia** Iceland spar.

espátula NF (**a**) (*Med*) spatula; (*Arte*) palette knife; (*Arquit*) putty knife; **estar hecho una ~** to be as thin as a rake. (**b**) (*Orn*) spoonbill.

especia NF spice.

especiado ADJ spiced, spicy.

especial **1** ADJ (**a**) special, especial; **en ~** especially, particularly. (**b**) *persona* particular, fussy (*en* about).
2 NF (*Méx Com*) special offer.
3 NM (*Méx Teat*) show.

especialidad NF speciality, specialty; special branch, special field (of study *etc*), line; **no es de mi ~** it's not in my line.

especialista NMF (**a**) (*gen*) specialist. (**b**) (*Cine etc*) stuntman, stuntwoman.

especialización NF specialization.

especializado ADJ specialized; *obrero* skilled, trained; **mano de obra especializada** skilled labour.

especializarse [1f] VR to specialize (*en* in).

especialmente ADV (e)specially, particularly.

especiar [1b] VT to spice.

especie NF (**a**) (*Bio*) species; **~ amenazada**, **~ en peligro** endangered species; **~ protegida** protected species.
(**b**) (*clase*) kind, sort; **de otra ~** of another kind.
(**c**) (*asunto*) matter; (*idea*) idea, notion; (*noticia*) rumour piece of false news; (*observación*) remark; (*pretexto*) pretext; **con la ~ de que ...** on the pretext that ...; **corre la ~ de que ...** there is a rumour about that ...; **soltar una ~** to fly a kite.
(**d**) **en ~** in kind; **pagar en ~** to pay in kind.

especiero NM spice rack.

especificación NF specification.

específicamente ADV specifically.

especificar [1g] VT to specify; to particularize; to list, itemize.

específico **1** ADJ specific.
2 NM (*Med*) specific; patent medicine.

especifidad NF specific nature, specificity.

espécimen NM, PL **especímenes** specimen.

especioso ADJ specious, plausible; deceitful.

espectacular ADJ spectacular.

espectacularidad NF spectacular nature; showiness.

espectacularmente ADV spectacularly, in spectacular fashion.

espectáculo **1** NM spectacle; sight; (*Teat etc*) show; function, performance; **~ de variedades** variety show; **~ de luz y sonido** son et lumière show; **dar un ~** to make a scene; to create a stir.
2 ATR: **atletismo ~** athletics on the grand scale; **cine ~** epic films; **fútbol ~** soccer presented as show-biz; **programa ~** TV variety show; **restaurante ~** restaurant with a floor-show.

espectador(a) NM/F spectator; onlooker, looker-on; **los ~es** the spectators; (*Teat etc*) the audience.

espectral ADJ (**a**) (*Fís*) spectral;. (**b**) (*fig*) ghostly; unearthly.

espectro NM (**a**) (*Fís*) spectrum (*t fig*); **de amplio ~** wide-ranging, covering a broad spectrum. (**b**) (*fantasma*) spectre, ghost; (*fig*) spectre; **el ~ del hambre** the spectre of famine.

espectrógrafo NM spectrograph.

espectrograma NM spectrogram.

espectrometría NF spectrometry.

espectrómetro NM spectrometer.

espectroscopia NF spectroscopy.

espectroscopio NM spectroscope.

especulación NF (**a**) (*gen*) speculation; (*meditación*) contemplation, meditation. (**b**) (*Com, Fin*) speculation; venture; **~ bursátil** speculation on the stock exchange; **~ inmobiliaria** property speculation.

especulador(a) NM/F speculator.

especular¹ [1a] **1** VT (*examinar*) to examine, inspect; (*meditar sobre*) to speculate about, reflect on, contemplate.
2 VI (**a**) to speculate, meditate.
(**b**) (*Com, Fin*) to speculate (*en, sobre* in, on).

especular² [1a] VT (*LAm*) to ruffle the hair of.

especulativo ADJ speculative.

espéculo NM (*Med*) speculum.

espejado ADJ glossy, bright, shining, mirror-like.

espejeante ADJ gleaming, glistening.

espejear [1a] VI to shine (like a mirror), gleam, glimmer, glint.

espejeras NFPL (*Carib*) chafing, chafed patch.

espejismo NM (**a**) (*gen*) mirage. (**b**) (*fig*) mirage, illusion; (piece of) wishful thinking, (piece of) wish fulfilment.

espejito NM small mirror; handbag mirror.

espejo NM (**a**) (*gen*) mirror, looking-glass; **~ de cortesía** courtesy mirror; **~ de cuerpo entero** full-length mirror, pier glass; **~ retrovisor**, **~ de retrovisión** driving mirror, rear-view mirror; **mirarse al** (*o* **en el**) **~** to look at o.s. in the mirror.
(**b**) (*Zool*) white patch.
(**c**) (*fig*) mirror, reflection; model; **un ~ de caballería** a model of chivalry.

espejoso ADJ = **espejado**.

espejuelo NM small looking-glass; **~s** lenses, spectacles.

espeleoarqueología NF cave archaeology.

espeleobuceo NM cave diving.

espeleología NF speleology, potholing, caving.

espeleólogo, -a NM/F speleologist, potholer, caver.

espelta NF (*Bot*) spelt.

espelunca NF (*liter*) cave.

espeluznante ADJ hair-raising, horrifying, bloodcurdling; lurid.

espeluzno NM (*Méx*) = **escalofrío**.

▼ **espera** NF (**a**) (*período*) wait, period of waiting; waiting; delay; **en ~ de** waiting for; expecting; **en ~ de su contestación** awaiting your reply; **estar a la ~ de una carta** to be expecting a letter; **la cosa no tiene ~** the matter brooks no delay, the affair is most urgent.
(**b**) (*Jur*) stay, respite.
(**c**) (*cualidad*) patience.

esperable ADJ to be hoped for; to be expected.

esperado ADJ (**a**) (*previsto*) *resultados* expected. (**b**) (*deseado*) **el acontecimiento más ~ del año** the most keenly anticipated event of the year.

esperantista NMF Esperantist.

esperanto NM Esperanto.

esperanza NF hope; expectation; prospect; **un jugador de ~s** a promising player, a player of promise; (**gran**) **~ blanca** great white hope; **~ de vida** life expectancy; **¡qué ~!** (*LAm*) some hope!; not on your life!; **con la ~ de que ...** in the hope that ...; **hay pocas ~s de que venga** there is little prospect of his coming; **no daba ~s de permitirlo** he held out no prospect of allowing it, he gave no hope of allowing it; **tener ~s de** to have hopes of; **tener la ~ puesta en** to pin one's faith to; to set one's heart on.

esperanzador ADJ hopeful, encouraging; promising.

esperanzadoramente ADV encouragingly; promisingly.

esperanzar [1f] VT to give hope to, buoy up with hope.

▼ **esperar** [1a] **1** VT (**a**) (*tener esperanza de*) to hope; to expect (*de* of); **no esperaba yo menos, no se podía ~ menos** it was the least that could be expected; **no esperaba menos de Vd** I expected nothing less of you, I hoped for nothing less from you; **~ que** + *subj* to hope that ...; **espero que sea así** I hope it is so, I hope it will be so; **espero que te haya gustado** I hope you liked it; **espero que vengas** I hope you'll come.
(**b**) (*aguardar*) to wait for, await; *bebé, visita etc* to expect; **~ el avión** to wait for the plane; **espero la llamada en cualquier momento** I expect his call at any moment; **ir a ~ a uno** to go and meet sb; **no me esperes después de las 7** don't wait for me after 7; **~ algo como el agua de mayo** to await sth with eager anticipation; **un lío**

de aquí te espero* a tremendous row*, the father and mother of a row*.

▼ ② VI (a) (*tener esperanza*) to hope; to expect; ~ + *infin* to hope to + *infin*; ~ **a que** + *subj* to expect that ...; ~ **en uno** to put one's hopes (*o* trust) in sb; ~ **en Dios** to trust in God; ~ **desesperando** to hope against hope.

(b) (*aguardar*) to wait; to stay; **esperaré aquí** I'll wait here; **¡espera un momento!** wait a moment!, just a minute!; ~ **que salga uno** to wait for sb to come out; ~ **a** (*o* **hasta**) **que uno haga algo** to wait for sb to do sth, wait until sb does sth; **hacer** ~ **a uno** to make sb wait, keep sb waiting; **espera y verás** wait and see.

③ **esperarse** VR: **como podía** ~ as might have been expected, as was to be expected; **no fue tan bueno como se esperaba** it was not so good as was hoped, it did not come up to expectations; **se espera que todo esté listo** it is hoped that all will be ready.

┌───┐
│ ┌───────────┐   ┌──────────────────────┐ │
│ │ ESPERAR   │   *ver también la entrada* │
│ └───────────┘   └──────────────────────┘ │

Esperar tiene en inglés varias traducciones, entre las que se encuentran *expect, hope, wait (for)* y *await*.

- Se traduce por *hope* cuando deseamos que algo suceda, pero no estamos seguros de si ocurrirá o no:

  Espero mucho que no se enfade mucho conmigo
  I hope (that) she won't be very annoyed with me
  Después de terminar la carrera espero conseguir un buen trabajo
  I hope to get a good job when I finish university

- Traducimos *esperar* por *expect* cuando estamos muy seguros de que algo va a suceder o cuando hay una razón lógica para que algo suceda:

  Espero aprobar porque el examen me salió muy bien
  I expect to pass o *I expect I'll pass because the exam went very well*
  Ha resultado mejor de lo que esperábamos
  It was better than we expected
  Está esperando un niño
  She's expecting (a baby)

- Se traduce por *wait (for)* cuando *esperar* se refiere al hecho de aguardar la llegada de alguien o de un suceso:

  Hice el examen hace dos meses y todavía estoy esperando los resultados
  I took the exam two months ago and I'm still waiting for the results
  La esperó media hora y después se fue a casa
  He waited half an hour for her and then went home

- El verbo *await* es un verbo de uso similar a *wait for*, aunque no requiere el uso de la preposición y no es muy corriente en inglés moderno:

  Esperaban ansiosamente la llegada del Rey
  They eagerly awaited the arrival of the King
  Para otros usos y ejemplos ver la entrada.
└───┘

esperma ① NM (*Bio*) sperm; ~ **de ballena** spermaceti.
② NF (*LAm: vela*) candle.

espermaceti NM spermaceti.

espermatozoide NM, **espermatozoo** NM spermatozoon.

espermicida NM spermicide.

espermio NM sperm.

espernancarse [1g] VR (*LAm*) = **esparrancarse**.

esperón NM (*Carib*) long wait.

esperpéntico ADJ (a) (*absurdo*) absurd, nonsensical. (b) (*grotesco*) grotesque, exaggerated; caricaturesque; macabre.

esperpentización NF presentation in an absurd (*o* grotesque *etc*) manner; caricaturing.

esperpentizar [1f] VT to present in an absurd (*o* grotesque *etc*) way; to caricature.

esperpento NM (a) (*persona*) fright, sight; scarecrow. (b) (*disparate*) absurdity, (piece of) nonsense. (c) (*cuento*) macabre story, grotesque tale. (d) (*Teat*) play which focuses on the grotesque.

┌───┐
│ ┌───────────────┐ │
│ │ ESPERPENTO   │ │
│ └───────────────┘ │

ⓘ *Esperpento is a type of theatre developed by Ramón del Valle-Inclán (1869-1936) focusing on characters whose physical and psychological characteristics have been deliberately deformed and warped to the point where they become grotesque caricatures. Valle-Inclán used this* **esperpento** *as a vehicle for social and political satire.*
└───┘

espesamente ADV thickly; densely.

espesante NM thickener, thickening agent.

espesar [1a] ① VT (a) *líquido etc* to thicken; to make dense(r). (b) *tejido* to weave tighter; to knit tighter.
② **espesarse** VR to thicken, get thicker, get denser; to coagulate, solidify.

espeso ADJ (a) (*gen*) thick; *bosque* dense; *nieve* deep; *pasta etc* stiff; *líquido* thick, heavy. (b) (*sucio*) dirty, untidy.

espesor NM thickness; density; (*de nieve*) depth; **tiene medio metro de** ~ it is half a metre thick.

espesura NF (a) (*espesor*) thickness; density; **en la** ~ **de la selva** in the depths of the jungle. (b) (*Bot*) thicket, overgrown place; **se refugiaron en las** ~**s serranas** they took refuge in the mountain fastnesses. (c) (*suciedad*) dirtiness, untidiness.

espeta‡ NM COP*.

espetar [1a] ① VT (a) (*atravesar*) to transfix, pierce, run through; *carne* to skewer, spit; *persona* to run through. (b) (*fig*) *orden* to rap out; *lección, sermón* to read; *pregunta* to fire; ~ **algo a uno** to broach a subject (unexpectedly) with sb, spring sth on sb.
② **espetarse** VR (a) (*ponerse cómodo*) to steady o.s., settle o.s. (b) (*envanecerse*) to get on one's high horse.

espetera‡ NF tits‡, bosom.

espetón NM (a) (*broqueta*) skewer, spit; (*clavija*) large pin, iron pin; (*atizador*) poker. (b) (*pinchazo*) jab, poke.

espía ① NMF spy.
② ATR: **avión** ~ spy plane; **buque** ~ spy ship; **satélite** ~ spy satellite.

espiantar* [1a] ① VT (*Cono Sur: robar*) to pinch*.
② VI y **espiantarse** VR (*Cono Sur*) to scram*, beat it*.

espiar [1c] ① VT (a) (*vigilar*) to spy on; to keep (a) watch on. (b) (*CAm, Cono Sur: mirar*) to look at, see, watch.
② VI to spy.

espicha NF (*Asturias*) cider party.

espichar¹ [1a] ① VT (a) (*pinchar*) to prick. (b) (*Cono Sur*: entregar*) to hand over reluctantly, relinquish. (c) (*And, Cono Sur Téc*) to put a tap on. (d) ~**la(s)**‡ = **2**.
② VI (‡) to peg out‡.
③ **espicharse** VR (a) (*And: neumático*) to go flat. (b) (*Carib, Méx: enflaquecerse*) to get thin. (c) (*CAm: asustarse*) to get scared.

espichar² [1a] VI (*LAm: pronunciar un discurso*) to make a speech; to speechify.

espiche¹ NM spike; peg.

espiche² NM (*LAm*) speech.

espidómetro NM (*LAm*) speedometer.

espiedo NM (*Cono Sur Culin*) spit.

espiga NF (a) (*Bot*) (*de trigo*) ear; (*de flores*) spike. (b) (*Téc*) spigot; (*clavija*) tenon, dowel, peg; (*de pestillo etc*) shaft; (*de cuchillo, herramienta*) tang. (c) (*badajo*) clapper. (d) (*Mil*) fuse. (e) (*Náut*) masthead.

espigadera NF gleaner.

espigado ADJ (a) (*Bot*) ripe; ready to seed. (b) *persona* tall, tall and slim, lanky; **¡tan** ~**!** how he's shot up!

espigador(a) NM/F gleaner.

espigar [1h] ① VT (a) (*Agr*) to glean (*t fig*); (*fig*) *fruta etc* to look closely at, scrutinize; *libro etc* to consult. (b) (*Téc*) to pin, peg, dowel.
② VI (a) (*trigo*) to form ears, come into ear; (*flor*) to run to seed. (b) = **3**.
③ **espigarse** VR to get very tall, shoot up.

espigón NM (a) (*Bot*) ear; spike. (b) (*Zool*) sting. (c) (*de herramienta*) sharp point, spike. (d) (*Náut*) breakwater, groyne.

espigueo NM gleaning.

espiguero NM (*Méx*) granary.

espiguilla NF herring-bone pattern.

espín NM porcupine.

espina NF (a) (*Bot*) thorn, prickle; (*astilla*) splinter; **mala** ~ spite, resentment, ill-will; **estar en** ~**s** to be on tenterhooks, be all on edge; **me da mala** ~ it worries me, it makes me suspicious; it gives me a bad impression; **sacarse la** ~ (*fig*) to pay off an old score, get even; **sacarse la** ~ **de una dificultad** to master a problem, overcome a longstanding difficulty. (b) (*de pez*) bone. (c) (*Anat*: *t* ~ **dorsal**) spine; ~ **bífida** spina bifida; **doblar la** ~ to bend over. (d) (*fig*) doubt, worry, suspicion.

espinaca NF spinach.

espinal ADJ spinal.

espinaquer NM spinnaker.

espinar ① [1a] VT (a) (*punzar*) to prick. (b) (*fig*) to sting, hurt, nettle.
② **espinarse** VR to prick o.s.
③ NM (a) (*Bot*) thicket, thornbrake, thorny place. (b) (*fig*) difficulty.

espinazo NM spine, backbone; **doblar el** ~ (*fig*) to knuckle under.

espineta NF (*Mús*) spinet.

espingarda NF (a) (*Hist*) (kind of) cannon; Moorish musket. (b) (*: *chica*) lanky girl.

espinglés NM (*hum*) Spanglish.

espinilla NF (a) (*Anat*) shin, shinbone. (b) (*Med*) blackhead.
espinillera NF shinpad, shin guard (*US*).
espinita NF (*fig*) irritation.
espino NM (t ~ **albar**, ~ **blanco**) hawthorn; ~ **cerval** buckthorn; ~ **negro** blackthorn, sloe.
espinoso ① ADJ (a) *planta* thorny, prickly; *pez* bony, spiny. (b) (*fig*) thorny, knotty, difficult.
② NM stickleback.
espinudo ADJ (*LAm*) = **espinoso 1**.
espión NM spy.
espionaje NM spying, espionage; ~ **industrial** industrial espionage; **novela de** ~ spy story.
espíquer NM (*Téc*) speaker.
espira NF (*Mat etc*) spiral; (*Zool*) whorl, ring; (*de espiral, hélice*) turn.
espiráculo NM blow-hole; spiracle.
espiral ① ADJ spiral; winding; (*Téc*) helical; corkscrew (*atr*), corkscrew-shaped.
② NF spiral; corkscrew (shape); (*anticonceptiva*) intra-uterine coil; (*Téc*) whorl; (*de reloj*) hairspring; (*de humo etc*) spiral, wreath; (*Dep*) corkscrew dive; **la** ~ **inflacionista** the inflationary spiral; **dar vueltas en** ~ to spiral (up *etc*); **el humo subía en** ~ the smoke went spiralling up.
espiralado ADJ spiral.
espirar [1a] ① VT *aire etc* to breathe out, exhale; *olor* to give off, give out.
② VI to breathe; to breathe out, exhale.
espirea NF spiraea.
espiritado ADJ (*fig*) like a wraith, ghost-like.
espiritismo NM spiritualism.
espiritista ① ADJ spiritualist(ic).
② NMF spiritualist.
espirituoso ADJ (a) *licor* spirituous. (b) *persona* spirited, lively.
espíritu NM (a) (*gen*) spirit; ~ **de cuerpo** esprit de corps; ~ **de equipo** team spirit; ~ **guerrero**, ~ **de lucha** fighting spirit; **en la letra y en el** ~ in the letter and in the spirit; **pobre de** ~ poor in spirit; **levantar el** ~ **de uno** to raise sb's spirits.
(b) (*mente*) mind; (*inteligencia*) intelligence; (*talento*) turn of mind; **con** ~ **amplio** with an open mind; in a generous spirit; **de** ~ **crítico** of a critical turn of mind.
(c) (*Rel*) spirit, soul; **E~ Santo** Holy Ghost; **dar el** ~, **rendir el** ~ to give up the ghost.
(d) (*fantasma*) spirit, ghost; ~ **maligno** evil spirit.
(e) (*alcohol*) spirits, liquor; ~ **de vino** spirits of wine.
espiritual ① ADJ (a) (*Rel etc*) spiritual. (b) (*fantasmal*) unworldly; ghostly. (c) (*And, Cono Sur: gracioso*) gay, witty.
② NM (*Negro*) spiritual.
espiritualidad NF spirituality.
espiritualismo NM spiritualism.
espiritualista ① ADJ spiritualistic.
② NMF spiritualist.
espiritualización NF spiritualization.
espiritualizar [1f] VT to spiritualize.
espiritualmente ADV spiritually.
espirituoso ADJ = **espiritoso**.
espita NF (a) tap, faucet (*US*), cock, spigot; ~ **de entrada del gas** gastap; **abrir la** ~ **de las lágrimas** (*hum*) to weep buckets*. (b) (*) drunkard, soak‡. (c) (‡‡) prick‡‡.
espitar [1a] VT to tap, broach.
espitoso‡ ADJ (*eufórico*) hyper.
espléndidamente ADV (*V ADJ*) (a) splendidly, magnificently, grandly. (b) lavishly; generously; '**gratificaré** ~' 'there will be a generous reward'.
esplendidez NF (*V ADJ*) (a) splendour; magnificence, grandeur; pomp. (b) lavishness; generosity.
espléndido ADJ (a) (*magnífico*) splendid; magnificent, grand. (b) (*generoso*) lavish; liberal, generous.
esplendor NM splendour; magnificence, grandeur; brilliance.
esplendoroso ADJ magnificent; brilliant, radiant.
esplénico ADJ splenetic.
espliego NM lavender.
esplín NM melancholy, depression, the blues.
espolada NF (a) (*espolazo*) prick with a spur. (b) ~ **de vino** swig of wine*.
espolazo NM prick with a spur.
espolear [1a] VT (a) *caballo* to spur (on). (b) (*fig*) to spur on, stimulate; to stir up, enliven.
espoleta NF (a) (*Mil*) fuse; ~ **de tiempo** time-fuse. (b) (*Anat*) wishbone.
espolón ① NM (a) (*Zool: de gallo*) spur; (*de caballo*) fetlock.
(b) (*Geog*) spur (of a mountain range).
(c) (*Náut: proa*) stem; (*para atacar*) ram.
(d) (*Náut: malecón*) sea wall, dike, jetty; (*de puente*) cutwater; (*Arquit*) buttress.
(e) (*paseo*) promenade.
(f) (*Med*) chilblain.
② ADJ (*And*) sharp, astute.
espolvoreador NM (*Culin*) dredge.
espolvorear [1a] VT to dust, sprinkle (*de* with); **espolvoree X sobre la superficie** dust X on the surface, dust the surface with X.
espondeo NM spondee.
espongiforme ADJ (*Med*) spongiform.
esponja NF (a) (*gen*) sponge; ~ **de baño** bath sponge; **arrojar la** ~ (*fig*) to throw in the towel; **beber como una** ~ to drink like a fish; **pasemos la** ~ **por todo aquello** let's forget all about it.
(b) (*: gorrón*) sponger*.
(c) (*Cono Sur, Méx‡*) old soak‡, boozer*, lush‡ (*US*).
esponjado ADJ (a) (*lit*) spongy; fluffy. (b) (*fig*) puffed up, pompous.
esponjar [1a] ① VT to make spongy; *lana etc* to fluff up, make fluffy.
② **esponjarse** VR (a) (*lit*) to become spongy; to fluff up, become fluffy.
(b) (*fig: rebosar salud*) to glow with health; (*tener aspecto próspero*) to look prosperous.
(c) (*fig: engreírse*) to be puffed up, swell with conceit.
esponjera NF sponge bag, make-up bag.
esponjosidad NF sponginess; sogginess.
esponjoso ADJ *materia* spongy; porous; *tierra* soggy, waterlogged.
esponsales NMPL betrothal.
esponsor NM, **espónsor** NM (*Com, Dep etc*) sponsor.
esponsorizar [1f] VT to sponsor.
espontáneamente ADV spontaneously.
espontanearse [1a] VR (*confesar*) to own up; (*hablar francamente*) to speak frankly; (*abrir su pecho*) to unbosom o.s. (*con* to).
espontaneidad NF spontaneity.
espontaneísmo NM amateurish enthusiasm, enthusiasm without experience.
espontáneo ① ADJ spontaneous; impromptu, unprepared.
② NM (*Taur*) intruder, spectator who rushes into the ring and attempts to take part; (*bombero*) volunteer fireman.
espora NF spore.
esporádicamente ADV sporadically; in a desultory way.
esporádico ADJ sporadic; desultory.
esportillo NM basket, pannier.
esportivo ADJ (*LAm*) sporty.
esportón NM large basket; **a esportones** in vast quantities, by the ton.
esposa NF (a) (*mujer*) wife. (b) ~**s** handcuffs; manacles; **poner las** ~**s a uno** to handcuff sb.
esposar [1a] VT to handcuff.
esposo NM husband; **los** ~**s** husband and wife, the couple.
espray NM = **spray**.
esprín NM (*CAm*) interior sprung mattress.
esprint NM etc = **sprint** etc.
esprinter NMF, PL **esprinters**, **esprínter** NMF, PL **esprínters** sprinter.
espuela NF (a) (t *fig*) spur; ~ **de caballero** (*Bot*) larkspur.
(b) (*And: de mujer*) feminine charm; coquettishness.
(c) (*And Com*) skill in business, acumen.
(d) (*: bebida*) last drink, one for the road*.
espueleado ADJ (*And, Carib*) tested, tried.
espuelear [1a] VT (a) (*LAm: espolear*) to spur, spur on. (b) (*And, Carib: probar*) to test, try out.
espuelón ADJ (*And*) sharp, astute.
espuerta NF basket, pannier; **a** ~**s** in vast quantities, by the ton.
espulgar [1h] VT (a) (*quitar las pulgas a*) to delouse, rid of fleas, get the lice (o fleas) out of. (b) (*fig*) to go through with a fine tooth comb.
espuma NF (*sobre agua*) foam, spray; (*sobre olas*) surf; (*sobre cerveza*) froth, head; (*de jabón*) lather; (*residuos*) floating waste, surface scum; ~ **de baño** bubble-bath; ~ **de caucho**, ~ **de látex** foam rubber; ~ **de mar** (*fig*) meerschaum; **crecer como la** ~ to flourish like the green bay tree; **echar** ~ to foam, froth.
espumadera NF, **espumador** NM (*Culin*) whisk; (*LAm Culin etc*) skimmer, skimming ladle; (*de atomizador*) nozzle.
espumajear [1a] VI to foam at the mouth.
espumajo NM froth, foam (*at the mouth*).
espumajoso ADJ frothy, foamy.
espumar [1a] ① VT to skim off.
② VI to froth, foam; (*vino*) to sparkle.
espumarajo NM froth, foam (*at the mouth*); **echar** ~**s (de rabia)** to foam with rage, splutter with rage.
espumear [1a] VI to foam.
espumilla NF (*And, CAm*) meringue.
espumillón NM tinsel.
espumoso ADJ frothy, foamy; foaming; *vino* sparkling.
espúreo ADJ, **espurio** ADJ spurious; adulterated; *niño* illegitimate,

bastard.

esputar [1a] VTI to spit (out), hawk (up).

esputo NM spit, spittle, (*Med*) sputum.

esqueje NM (*Hort*) slip, cutting.

esquela NF (a) (*nota*) note; short letter; ~ **amorosa** love letter, billet doux. (b) (*anuncio*) notice, announcement; ~ (**de defunción**), ~ (**mortuoria**) death notice, announcement of death.

esquelético ADJ skeletal; (*) thin, skinny.

esqueleto NM (a) (*Anat*) skeleton; **menear el ~*** to shake a hoof*, dance; **tumbar el ~** to hit the hay*, go to bed.
(b) (*fig*) skeleton; bare bones (of a matter); framework; (*LAm: borrador*) rough draft, outline, preliminary plan; **en ~** unfinished, incomplete.
(c) (*And, CAm, Méx: formulario*) blank, form.

esquema NM (a) (*diagrama*) diagram, plan; (*proyecto*) scheme; (*esbozo*) sketch, outline. (b) (*Filos*) schema.

esquemático ADJ schematic; diagrammatic.

esquematizar [1f] VT to outline.

esquí NM, PL **~s** (a) (*objeto*) ski. (b) (*Dep*) skiing; ~ **acuático**, ~ **náutico** water-skiing; surfriding; ~ **alpino** alpine skiing; ~ **de fondo**, ~ **de travesía** cross-country skiing; **hacer ~** to go skiing.

esquiable ADJ: **pista ~** slope suitable for skiing, slope that can be skiied on.

esquiador(a) NM/F skier; ~ **acuático**, ~ **náutico** water-skier; surfrider.

esquiar [1c] VI to ski.

esquife NM skiff.

esquijama NM winter pyjamas *pl*.

esquila[1] NF (*campanilla*) small bell, handbell; cowbell.

esquila[2] NF, **esquilado** NM (*Agr*) shearing.

esquilador NM shearer.

esquilar [1a] VT to shear; to clip, crop.

esquileo NM shearing.

esquilimoso ADJ fastidious, finicky.

esquilmamiento NM (*de tierra*) impoverishment; (*de recursos*) exhaustion.

esquilmar [1a] VT (a) *cosecha* to harvest. (b) *tierra* (*t fig*) to exhaust, impoverish.

esquilmo NM harvest, crop; yield.

Esquilo NM Aeschylus.

esquimal [1] ADJ, NM/F Eskimo.
[2] NM (*Ling*) Eskimo.

esquina NF (a) (*gen*) corner (*t Dep*); **doblar la ~** to turn the corner; (*Cono Sur*: *morir*) to die; **sacar de ~** to take a corner-kick; **la tienda de la ~** the corner shop. (b) (*LAm: tienda*) corner shop, village store. (c) (*) **la ~** the game*, prostitution.

esquinado ADJ (a) (*que tiene esquinas*) having corners; sharp-cornered. (b) (*LAm*) *mueble* standing in a corner, corner (*atr*). (c) *pelota* swerving, with a spin on it; **tiro ~** low shot into the corner of the net. (d) (*fig*) *persona* (*antipático*) unpleasant; (*difícil*) awkward, prickly; (*malévolo*) malicious; *noticia etc* malicious, ill-intentioned, designed to cause trouble.

esquinar [1a] [1] VT (a) (*hacer esquina*) to form a corner with; to be on the corner of.
(b) *madera etc* to square (off).
(c) (*LAm: meter*) to put in a corner.
(d) *pelota* to swerve, slice.
(e) *personas* to set at odds.
[2] VI: ~ **con** to form a corner with; to be on the corner of.
[3] **esquinarse** VR (a) (*pelearse*) to quarrel (*con* with), fall out (*con* with).
(b) (*estar resentido*) to get a chip on one's shoulder.

esquinazo NM (a) (*: esquina*) corner. (b) (*Cono Sur*: *serenata*) serenade. (c) **dar ~ a uno** to dodge sb, give sb the slip, shake sb off.

esquinera NF (a) (*) whore. (b) (*LAm*) corner cupboard.

esquinero [1] ADJ corner (*atr*); **farol ~** corner lamppost, lamppost on the corner; **café ~** corner café.
[2] NM (*) idler, layabout.

esquirla NF splinter.

esquirol NM blackleg, scab*, strikebreaker, fink (*US*).

esquirolada NF strike-breaking action, work of a scab.

esquirolaje NM, **esquirolismo** NM blacklegging, strikebreaking.

esquisto NM schist.

esquites NMPL (*CAm, Méx*) popcorn.

esquivada NF (*LAm*) dodge, evasion.

esquivar [1a] [1] VT to avoid, shun; to elude, dodge, side-step; ~ **el contacto con uno** to avoid meeting sb; ~ **un golpe** to dodge a blow; ~ + **infin** to avoid + *ger*, be chary of + *ger*, be shy of + *ger*.
[2] **esquivarse** VR to withdraw, stand back, shy away; to dodge.

esquivez NF shyness, reserve, aloofness; unsociability; elusiveness; evasiveness.

esquivo ADJ (*tímido*) shy, reserved, aloof; (*hurano*) unsociable; (*difícil de encontrar*) elusive; (*evasivo*) evasive.

esquizo* ADJ, NM schizo*.

esquizofrenia NF schizophrenia.

esquizofrénico, -a ADJ, NM/F schizophrenic.

esquizoide ADJ, NM/F schizoid.

esta, ésta *etc* V **este, éste**.

está V **estar**.

estabilidad NF stability.

estabilización NF stabilization.

estabilizador NM stabilizer; (*Aut*) anti-roll bar; ~ **de cola** tailplane, rudder.

estabilizante [1] ADJ stabilizing.
[2] NM stabilizer.

estabilizar [1f] [1] VT to stabilize; to make stable, steady; *precios* to stabilize, peg.
[2] **estabilizarse** VR to become stable, become stabilized; (*en la vida*) to settle down.

estable ADJ (*firme*) stable, steady; firm; (*habitual*) regular.

establecer [2d] [1] VT (*gen*) to establish; (*fundar*) to set up, found, institute; *colonos* to settle; *alegato* to justify, substantiate; *récord* to set (up); *domicilio* to take up, establish; **la ley establece que** ... the law provides that ...
[2] **establecerse** VR to establish o.s., settle; (*Com*) to set up in business, start a business; to open an office, open a branch.

establecimiento NM (a) (*acto*) establishment, setting-up, founding; institution; settlement.
(b) (*local*) establishment; (*Cono Sur*) plant, works; ~ **central** head office; ~ **comercial** commercial establishment, business house; (*bar*) bar; (*tienda*) shop.
(c) (*Jur*) statute, ordinance.

establero NM stableboy, groom.

establo NM (a) cowshed, stall; (*esp LAm: granero*) barn; **~s de Augias** Augean stables. (b) (*Carib: garaje*) garage.

estaca NF (a) (*poste*) stake, post, paling; (*de tienda etc*) peg; (*palo*) cudgel, stick; **plantar la ~**** to have a crap**.
(b) (*Agr*) cutting.
(c) (*And, Cono Sur: espuela*) spur.
(d) (*And, Cono Sur: Min*) mining claim, mining property.
(e) **arrancar la ~** (*Méx*) to champ at the bit, strain at the leash.
(f) (*Carib*) (*indirecta*) hint; (*pulla*) taunt.

estacada NF (a) (*cerca*) fence, fencing; (*Mil*) palisade, stockade; (*LAm: malecón*) dike; **dejar a uno en la ~** (*fig*) to leave sb in the lurch; **estar** (*o* **quedar**) **en la ~** (*fig*) to be in a jam, be left in the lurch; to fail disastrously.
(b) (*LAm: herida*) jab, prick.

estacar [1g] [1] VT (a) *tierra, propiedad etc* to stake (out, off), mark with stakes; to fence with stakes; (*LAm*) to stretch by fastening to stakes.
(b) *animal* to tie to a post.
(c) (*Carib: herir*) to wound, prick.
(d) (*And, Carib: engañar*) to deceive.
[2] **estacarse** VR (a) (*quedarse inmóvil*) to stand rooted to the spot, stand stiff as a pole.
(b) ~ **un pie** (*And, CAm, Carib*) to prick o.s. in the foot, hurt one's foot.

estacha NF (*Náut*) line, mooring rope.

estación NF (a) (*gen*) station; (*de vacaciones*) (holiday) resort; ~ **balnearia** spa; ~ **ballenera** whaling station; ~ **biológica** biological research station; ~ **de bombeo** pumping-station; ~ **cabecera**, ~ **de cabeza** terminus; ~ **carbonera** coaling station; ~ **clasificadora** marshalling yard; ~ **de contenedores** container terminal; ~ **cósmica**, ~ **espacial** space-station; ~ **depuradora** water purifying plant; ~ **emisora** broadcasting station; ~ **de empalme**, ~ **de enlace** junction; ~ **de escucha** listening-post; ~ **de esquí** ski resort; ~ **de ferrocarril** railway station; ~ **de fuerza** power station; ~ **de gasolina** petrol station; ~ **invernal**, ~ **de invierno** winter sports resort; ~ **marítima** ferry terminal; ~ **de mercancías** goods station; ~ **meteorológica** weather station; ~ **orbital** orbiting space-station; ~ **de peaje** line of toll booths, toll plaza (*US*); ~ **purificadora de aguas residuales** sewage works, sewage farm; ~ **de rastreo**, ~ **de seguimiento** tracking station; ~ **de servicio** service station; ~ **de televisión** television station; ~ **termal** spa; ~ **terminal** terminus; ~ **de trabajo** (*Inform*) workstation; ~ **transformadora** substation; ~ **transmisora** transmitter; ~ **de trasbordo** junction; ~ **veraniega** summer resort.
(b) **Estaciones del vía crucis** (*Ecl*) Stations of the Cross; Maundy Thursday devotions; **correr las estaciones*** to go on a pub-crawl*.
(c) (*temporada*) season; ~ **de (las) lluvias** rainy reason; ~ **muerta** off season, dead season; ~ **de plantar** planting season.

estacional ADJ seasonal.

estacionalidad NF seasonal nature; seasonal variation.

estacionalmente ADV seasonally; according to the season.

estacionamiento NM (a) stationing, placing. (b) (*Aut*) (*acto*) parking; (*sitio*) car-park; ~ **limitado** restricted parking.

estacionar [1a] [1] VT to station, place; (*Aut*) to park.

estacionarse [2] VR to station o.s.; (*Aut*) to park; to remain stationary, be parked.

estacionario ADJ stationary; motionless; (*Med*) stable; (*Com, Fin*) slack.

estacionómetro NM (*Méx*) parking meter.

estacón NM (*LAm*) prick, jab.

estada NF (*LAm*) stay.

estadía NF (a) (*Com*) demurrage. (b) (*Náut*) stay in port. (c) (*LAm*) (*estancia*) stay; (*duración*) length of stay.

estadillo NM count, survey; inventory.

estadio NM (a) (*fase*) stage, phase. (b) (*Mat*) furlong. (c) (*Dep*) stadium.

estadista NM (a) (*Pol*) statesman. (b) (*Mat*) statistician.

estadística¹ NF (a) (*gen*) statistics; official return(s). (b) (*una ~*) figure, statistic.

estadísticamente ADV statistically.

estadístico [1] ADJ statistical.
[2] NM, **estadística²** NF statistician.

estadizo ADJ *comida* not quite fresh, stale, off.

estado NM (a) (*gen*) state, condition; **~ de alarma**, **~ de alerta**, **~ de atención** state of alert; **~ de ánimo** state of mind; **~ de emergencia**, **~ de excepción** state of emergency; **~ de gracia** (*fig*) honeymoon period; **~ de guerra** state of war; **~ de sitio** state of siege; **~ sólido** solid state; **estar en ~** (*interesante*), **estar en ~ de buena esperanza** to be pregnant, be expecting, be in the family way; **estar en buen ~** to be in good condition; to be in good order, be in working order; **estar en malísimo ~** to be in a terrible condition; **quedar en ~** to become pregnant.
(b) (*status*) status; rank, class; **~ civil** marital status; **el ~ matrimonial** the married state.
(c) (*Pol Hist*) estate; **~ llano** third estate, commoners; **tercer ~** third estate.
(d) (*Mil*) **~ mayor** staff; **~ mayor general** general staff.
(e) (*Pol*) state; **las fuerzas del E~** the forces of the state; **~ asistencial**, **~ benefactor**, **~ de(l) bienestar**, **~ de previsión** welfare state; **~ colchón**, **~ tapón** buffer state; **~ de derecho** state ruled by law, constitutional state; **~ policíaco**, **~ policial** police state; **hombre de ~** statesman.
(f) (*lista*) list (of employees).
(g) (*Com, Fin*) (*resumen*) summary; (*informe*) report, statement; **~ de contabilidad** (*Méx*) balance-sheet; **~ de cuenta(s)** statement of account, bank statement; **~ financiero** financial statement; **~ de pérdidas y ganancias** profit and loss account; **~ de reconciliación** reconciliation statement.

estado-ciudad NM, PL **estados-ciudad** city-state.

estado-nación NM, PL **estados-nación** nation-state.

Estados Unidos NMPL United States (of America).

estadounidense [1] ADJ United States (*atr*), American.
[2] NMF United States citizen (*etc*), American.

estafa NF swindle, trick; (*Com, Fin*) racket, ramp*, fraud.

estafador(a) NM/F swindler, trickster; (*Com, Fin*) swindler; racketeer.

estafar [1a] VT to swindle, defraud, twist*; **~ algo a uno** to swindle sth out of sb, defraud sb of sth.

estafermo NM (a) (*Hist*) quintain, dummy target. (b) (*: idiota*) twit*, idiot.

estafeta NF (a) (*Correos*) post; **~ diplomática** diplomatic post. (b) (*oficina*) (sub) post-office. (c) (*persona*) courier (*t nm*); (*LAm*) drug courier.

estafetero NM postmaster, post-office clerk.

estafilococo NM staphylococcus.

estagnación NF (*CAm, Carib*) = **estancamiento**.

estaje NM (*CAm*) piecework.

estajear [1a] VT (*CAm*) to do as piecework; to discuss rates and conditions for.

estajero, -a NM/F (*CAm*) pieceworker.

estalactita NF stalactite.

estalagmita NF stalagmite.

estaliniano ADJ Stalinist.

estalinismo NM Stalinism.

estalinista ADJ, NMF Stalinist.

estallar [1a] VI (*bomba etc*) to burst, explode, go off; (*volcán*) to erupt; (*neumático*) to burst; (*vidrio etc*) to shatter; (*látigo*) to crack; (*epidemia*) to break out; (*motín*) to break out, flare up; **~ en llanto** to burst into tears; **el parabrisas estalló en pedazos** the windscreen shattered; **cuando estalló la guerra** when the war broke out; **hacer ~** to set off; (*fig*) to spark off, start.

estallido NM explosion, report; crash, crack; (*fig*) outbreak; **el gran ~** the big bang.

estambre NM (a) (*tela*) worsted, woollen yarn. (b) (*Bot*) stamen.

Estambul NM Istanbul.

estamento NM (*Pol*) estate; (*cuerpo*) body; (*estrato*) stratum, layer, level; (*clase*) class.

estameña NF serge.

estampa NF (a) (*huella*) imprint; footprint, track.
(b) (*Tip: imagen*) print, engraving; (*en libro*) picture; (*fig*) vignette.
(c) (*fig: aspecto*) stamp; appearance, aspect; **de buena ~** decent-looking; **de ~ poco agradable** of disagreeable appearance, unpleasant-looking; **ser la propia ~ de uno** to be the very image of sb.
(d) (*imprenta: arte*) printing; (*máquina*) printing press; **dar un libro a la ~** to publish a book.

estampación NF (*acto*) printing; engraving; (*fileteado*) tooling.

estampado [1] ADJ *tela* printed; *vestido* print.
[2] NM (a) (*impresión*) printing; stamping. (b) (*vestido*) print (dress), cotton print.

estampar [1a] VT (*imprimir*) to print; (*marcar*) to stamp; (*grabar*) to engrave; (*filetear*) to tool; *beso* to plant, place (*en* on); (*fig*) to stamp, imprint (*en* on); **quedaba estampado en la memoria** it was stamped on one's memory.

estampía: de ~ ADV suddenly, without warning, unexpectedly.

estampida NF (a) (*Agr, Zool: esp LAm*) stampede. (b) **de ~ V estampía**. (c) = **estampido**.

estampido NM report; detonation; bang, boom, crash; **~ sónico** sonic boom.

estampilla NF (a) (*sello*) stamp, seal; rubber stamp. (b) (*LAm Correos*) stamp.

estampillado NM (*LAm*) stamp duty.

estampillar [1a] VT to rubber-stamp.

estampita NF (a) (*Rel*) small religious picture. (b) (*) con trick*.

están V **estar**.

estancado ADJ (a) *agua* stagnant. (b) (*fig*) static; **estar ~** to be held up, be blocked, be at a standstill; to be deadlocked.

estancamiento NM (a) (*de agua*) stagnancy, stagnation. (b) (*fig*) stagnation; blockage, stoppage, suspension; deadlock.

estancar [1g] [1] VT (a) *agua* to hold up, hold back, stem.
(b) (*fig*) *progreso* to stem, block, check, hold up; *negocio* to stop, suspend; *negociación* to bring to a standstill; to deadlock; (*Com*) to monopolize, establish a monopoly in; (*pey*) to corner.
[2] **estancarse** VR (a) (*agua*) to stagnate, become stagnant; to be held back.
(b) (*fig*) to stagnate.

estancia NF (a) (*permanencia*) stay. (b) (*domicilio*) dwelling, abode; (*cuarto*) living room. (c) (*LAm: de ganado*) farm, cattle ranch; country estate; (*Carib: quinta pequeña*) small farm, smallholding. (d) (*Poét*) stanza.

estanciera NF (*Cono Sur*) station wagon.

estanciero NM (*LAm*) farmer, rancher.

estanco [1] ADJ watertight; **~ al aire** airtight.
[2] NM state monopoly; government store where monopoly goods are sold, (*esp*) tobacconist's (shop), cigar store (*US*); (*And: bodega*) liquor store.

┌─── **ESTANCO** ───

ⓘ *In Spain, an **estanco** is a government-licensed tobacconist's, recognizable by the brown and yellow "T" logo of the state tobacco monopoly, **Tabacalera S.A.**, which regulates the entire tobacco industry. Tobacco can also be bought at bars and restaurants and **quioscos**, but at a higher price. As well as tobacco products the **estanco** sells stamps, papel timbrado (official forms) and coupons for the **quiniela** or football pools.*
⇨ *See also* QUINIELA

---

estand NM = **stand**.

estándar ADJ, NM standard.

estandar(d)ización NF standardization.

estandar(d)izado ADJ standardized.

estandar(d)izar [1f] VT to standardize.

estandarte NM banner, standard; **~ real** royal standard.

estanflación NF stagflation.

estánnico ADJ stannic.

estanque NM (a) pool, pond, small lake; (*Agr etc*) tank, reservoir; **~ de juegos**, **~ para chapotear** paddling-pool. (b) (*Cono Sur*) (petrol-) tank.

estanqueidad NF (*al agua*) watertightness; (*al aire*) air tightness.

estanquero, -a NM/F tobacconist.

estanquillo NM (a) (*Méx*) booth, kiosk, stall. (b) = **estanco**.

estante NM (a) (*mueble*) rack, stand; piece of furniture with shelves; **~** (*para libros*) bookcase. (b) (*LAm: soporte*) prop.

estantería NF shelving, shelves.

estantigua NF apparition; (*) fright, sight, scarecrow.

estantillo NM (*And, Carib*) prop, support.

estañar [1a] VT (*Téc*) to tin; to solder.

estaño NM tin; **~ para soldar** solder.

estaquear [1a] VT (*LAm*) *pieles* to stretch on stakes.

estaquilla NF (*de madera*) peg; pin; (*clavo*) spike, long nail; (*de tienda*) tent peg.

estaquillar [1a] VT to pin, peg (down, out), fasten with pegs.

estar [1o] **1** VI **(a)** (gen) to be; (hallarse) to stand, be found; (estar en casa) to be in, be at home; (permanecer) to stay, remain, keep; (asistir) to be present (en at); **el monumento está en el mercado** the monument is (o stands) in the market; **¿está?** is he in?; **la señora no está madam** is not in, madam is not at home; **está fuera** she's away; she's out of town, she's on a trip; **para eso estamos** that's why we're here, that's why we've come; (respondiendo a gracias) it's the least we can do; **¿cómo está?** how is he?; **está mucho mejor** he's much better; **¿cómo estamos?** how do we stand?; (Dep) what's the score?; **aquí no se puede ~** it's intolerable here; it's too hot (o cold o dangerous etc) here; **el día que estuve a verlo** the day I went to see it.
(b) (+ ADJ) to be; **está enfermo** he is ill; **ahora está vacío** now it's empty; **¡qué elegante estás!** how smart you're looking!; **está más viejo** he looks older, he seems older.
(c) (comprensión) **¿está Vd?** do you get it?, understand?; (acuerdo) **¿estamos?** are we agreed?, right?, OK?*
(d) (estar listo) to be ready; **en seguida está** it'll be ready in a moment; **dos vueltas más y ya está** two more turns and that's it, two more turns and it's done; **ya estoy** I'm ready; I'm all done, I'm finished; **¡ya estamos!** that's it!; (enfadado) that's enough!, I'll not listen to any more!
(e) (+ ger) to be; **estaba corriendo** he was running; **me está molestando** he's annoying me; **está siendo preparado** it is being prepared; **nos estamos engañando** we are deceiving ourselves.
(f) (+ PTP) to be; **está envuelto en papel** it is wrapped in paper; **para las 5 estará terminado** it will be finished for 5 o'clock.
(g) (fecha) **estamos a 5 de mayo** it is the 5th of May, today is the 5th of May; **¿a cuántos estamos?** what's the date?
(h) (precio etc) **~ a** to be, sell at, stand at; (récord) to stand at; **las uvas están a 50 pesetas** grapes are at 50 pesetas; **el récord anterior estaba a** (o **en**) **33 minutos** the previous record stood at 33 minutes.
(i) **~ a lo que resulte** to stand by the result.
(j) **~ con la gripe** to have flu, be down with flu; **estuvo con la enfermedad durante 2 años** she suffered from the disease for 2 years.
(k) **~ de vacaciones** to be (away) on holiday; **~ de paseo** to be out for a walk; **~ de uniforme** to be in uniform; **~ de viaje** to be travelling, be on a trip.
(l) **está de jefe** he is acting as head, he is the acting head; **está de camarero** he's working as a waiter.
(m) **estoy así de nervioso** I'm so nervous, I'm that nervous.
(n) **~ en** (causar) to be the cause of; **en eso está** that's the reason, that must be the motive.
(o) **~ en algo** (involucrado) to be involved in sth, be mixed up in sth; **en ello estamos** we're doing all we can.
(p) **no está en él hacerlo** it is not in his power to do it; **no está en sí** she's not in her right mind.
(q) **~ en que ...** (persona) to believe that ..., understand that ...; to be sure that ...; **el problema está en que ...** the problem lies in the fact that ...
(r) **~ para** + infin to be about to + infin, be on the point of + ger.
(s) **~ para** + N to be in the mood for + n.
(t) **~ por** política to be in favour of; persona to back, support, side with.
(u) **~ por** + infin to be half inclined to + infin, have half a mind to + infin; **yo estoy por dejarlo** I vote (o say) we leave it; **está por llover** (LAm) it's about to rain.
(v) **está todavía por hacer** it remains to be done, it is still to be done; **la historia de aquello está por escribir** the history of that is still to be written.
(w) **está que rabia** he's hopping mad, he's furious.
(x) **están sin vender** they remain unsold, they have not been sold.
(y) **~ sobre sí** to have o.s. under control; to be puffed up with conceit; V **bien 1** (a), **mal 1** (a), **más 1** (e) y muchos sustantivos.
2 estarse VR **(a)** refuerza el sentido del vi: **se estaba muriendo** he was (gradually, at that moment) dying.
(b) (quedarse) to stay, remain; **~ tranquilamente en casa** to stay quietly at home.
(c) **¡estáte quieto!** keep still!, stop fidgeting!; behave yourself!
(d) **se está bien aquí** it's nice here.

estarcido NM stencil, stencilled sketch.

estarcir [3b] VT to stencil.

estaribel NM nick‡, prison.

estárter NM = **stárter**.

estás V estar.

estatal ADJ state (atr); (Esp frec) national, nationwide.

estatalismo NM state ownership.

estatalista **1** ADJ (Esp) national, nationwide.

2 NMF member of a nationwide party.

estatalización NF nationalization, taking into public ownership.

estatalizar [1f] VT to nationalize; take into public ownership.

estática NF statics.

estático ADJ **(a)** static. **(b)** = **extático**.

estatificación NF nationalization, taking into public ownership.

estatificado ADJ nationalized, publicly-owned.

estatificar [1g] VT to nationalize; take into public ownership.

estatismo NM **(a)** stillness, motionlessness. **(b)** (Pol) state control.

estatización NF nationalization, taking into public ownership.

estatizar [1f] VT to nationalize, take into public ownership.

estator NM (Elec, Mat) stator.

estatua NF statue.

estatuaria NF statuary (art).

estatuario ADJ statuesque.

estatuilla NF statuette, figure, figurine.

estatuir [3g] VT **(a)** (ordenar) to establish, enact, ordain. **(b)** (probar) to prove.

estatura NF stature, height; **de regular ~** of average height; **un hombre de 1,80m de ~** a man 1.80m in height.

estatus NM INVAR status.

estatutario ADJ statutory.

estatuto NM (Jur) statute; (de ciudad etc) by-law; (de comité etc) rule, standing rule; **E~ de Autonomía** (Esp Pol) statute of autonomy.

estay NM (Náut) stay.

este¹ (Geog) **1** ADJ parte east, eastern; dirección easterly; viento east, easterly.

2 NM **(a)** (Geog) east; **los países del E~** the countries of the East (of Europe); **en la parte del ~** in the eastern part; **al ~ de Toledo** to the east of Toledo, on the east side of Toledo; **eso cae más hacia el ~** that lies further (to the) east.
(b) (viento) east wind.

este² ADJ DEM M, **esta** F this; **estos** ADJ DEM MPL, **estas** FPL these.

éste PRON DEM M, **esta** F **(a)** this; this one; the latter; **éstos** PRON DEM MPL, **éstas** FPL these; the latter; **en ésta** in this town (from where I am writing); **jurar por éstas** to swear by all that is holy. **(b)** (LAm*) **este ...*** er ...*, um ...*

esté V estar.

estearina NF **(a)** (Quím) stearin. **(b)** (LAm: vela) candle.

esteatita NF soapstone.

Esteban NM Stephen.

estecolado NM, **estercoladura** NF, **estercolamiento** NM manuring; muck-spreading.

estela NF **(a)** (Náut) wake; (Aer) trail; **~ de condensación, ~ de humo** vapour trail.
(b) (fig) trail; **el discurso dejó larga ~ de comentarios** the speech caused a great deal of comment.
(c) (Arquit) stele, stela.

estelar ADJ **(a)** (Astron) stellar, sidereal. **(b)** (Teat etc) star (atr); **cargo ~** star role; **combate ~** (Boxeo) star bout, star contest; **función ~** all-star show.

estemple NM pit prop.

estén V estar.

esténcil NM (LAm) stencil.

estenografía NF shorthand, stenography.

estenografiar [1c] VT to take down in shorthand.

estenográfico ADJ shorthand (atr).

estenógrafo, -a NM/F shorthand writer, stenographer.

estenotipia NF shorthand typing.

estenotipista NMF shorthand typist.

estentóreamente ADV in a stentorian voice.

estentóreo ADJ voz stentorian, booming; sonido strident.

estepa NF **(a)** (Geog) steppe. **(b)** (Bot) rockrose.

estepario ADJ steppe (atr).

estera NF mat, matting; **~ de baño** bathmat.

esteral NM (Cono Sur) swamp, marsh.

esterar [1a] **1** VT to cover with a mat, put a mat on (o over).

2 VI (*) to put on one's winter clothes (ahead of time).

estercolar [1a] VT to manure.

estercolero NM manure heap, dunghill.

estéreo NM stereo.

estéreo... PREF stereo...

estereofonía NF stereophony.

estereofónico ADJ stereophonic, stereo.

estereoscópico ADJ stereoscopic.

estereoscopio NM stereoscope.

estereotipación NF stereotyping.

estereotipado ADJ stereotyped.

estereotipar [1a] VT to stereotype.

estereotipo NM stereotype.

esterero NM: **quedar en el ~** (Carib*) to be on one's uppers*.

estéril ADJ **(a)** terreno sterile, barren. **(b)** (fig) esfuerzo etc vain, futile, unproductive.

esterilidad NF (a) (*de terreno*) sterility, barrenness. (b) (*fig*) futility, uselessness.

esterilización NF sterilization.

esterilizar [1f] VT to sterilize.

esterilla NF (a) (*alfombrilla*) small mat; straw mat. (b) (*materia*) matting; (*LAm*) wickerwork, rush matting; **silla de ~** rush chair, wicker chair; **~ de alambre** wire mesh. (c) (*Cos*) gold (o silver) braid.

estérilmente ADV (*fig*) vainly, uselessly, fruitlessly.

esterlina ADJ: **libra ~** pound sterling.

esternón NM breastbone, sternum.

estero¹ NM matting.

estero² NM (a) (*estuario*) estuary; tideland; inlet. (b) (*Cono Sur: pantano*) swamp, marsh. (c) (*Cono Sur, And: arroyo*) brook. (d) **estar en el ~** (*Carib**) to be in a fix*.

esteroide NM steroid; **~ anabólico, ~ anabolizante** anabolic steroid.

estertor NM death rattle.

estertoroso ADJ stertorous.

estés V estar.

esteta NMF aesthete.

estética NF aesthetics; aesthetic doctrine, aesthetic outlook.

esteticién NF beautician, beauty specialist.

esteticismo NM aestheticism.

esteticista NMF beauty consultant, beauty specialist.

estético ADJ aesthetic.

estetoscopio NM stethoscope.

esteva NF plough handle.

estevado ADJ bow-legged, bandy-legged.

estiaje NM low water.

estiba NF (a) (*Mil Hist*) rammer. (b) (*Náut*) stowage; **mudar la ~ to** shift the cargo about. (c) (*Náut: acto*) loading. (d) (‡) beating up*, bashing*.

estibado NM stowage.

estibador ① ADJ: **empresa estibadora** shipping company. ② NM stevedore.

estibar [1a] VT (a) (*Náut: meter*) to stow, put; (*cargar*) to load; (*almacenar*) to house, store. (b) *lana etc* to pack tight, compress.

estiércol NM dung, manure; **~ de caballo** horse manure; **~ líquido** liquid manure.

Estigia NM Styx.

estigio ADJ Stygian.

estigma NM (a) (*lit, fig*) stigma; (*marca*) mark, brand; (*marca de nacimiento*) birthmark; (*Rel: t* **~s** PL) stigmata. (b) (*Bot*) stigma.

estigmatizar [1f] VT to stigmatize.

estilar [1a] ① VT (a) *documento* to draw up (in due form). (b) (*usar*) to use, be in the habit of using; to wear, adopt. ② VI y **estilarse** VR to be in fashion, be used, be worn; **ya no se estila la chistera** top hats aren't in fashion any more; **~ + infin** to be customary to + infin.

estilete NM (*arma*) stiletto; (*de tocadiscos*) stylus.

estilismo NM fashion design(ing).

estilista NMF (*Liter etc*) stylist; (*Téc*) designer; (*de vestidos*) dress stylist, fashion designer.

estilística NF stylistics.

estilístico ADJ stylistic.

estilización NF (*Téc*) styling.

estilizado ADJ stylized.

estilizar [1f] ① VT to stylize; (*Téc*) to design, style. ② VI to cut a dash, show off.

estilo NM (a) (*gen*) style; manner; fashion; **el ~ oscuro del escritor** the writer's obscure style; **~ directo** (*Ling*) direct speech; **~ indirecto libre** free indirect style; **~ de vida** life-style; way of life; **el ~ de vida británico** the British way of life; **un comedor ~ Luis XV** a dining-room suite in Louis XV style; **un andar ~ oso** a gait like a bear's; **una casa ~ Tudor** a Tudor-style house; **al ~ de** in the style of; after the manner of; **al ~ antiguo** in the old style; **algo por el ~** something of the sort, that sort of thing; something along these lines; **los dictadores y otros por el ~** dictators and others of that sort, dictators and suchlike; **no tenemos nada por ese ~** we have nothing in that line. (b) (*Natación*) stroke; **~ (libre)** freestyle; **~ (de) pecho** breast-stroke. (c) (*pluma: Téc*) stylus; (*de reloj de sol*) gnomon, needle. (d) (*Bot*) style.

estilográfica NF fountain-pen.

estiloso ADJ stylish.

estima NF (a) (*aprecio*) esteem, respect; **tener a uno en gran ~ to** hold sb in high esteem. (b) (*Náut*) dead reckoning; **a ~ by** dead reckoning.

estimable ADJ (a) (*gen*) estimable, esteemed; reputable; **su ~ carta** (*Com*) your esteemed letter. (b) *cantidad etc* considerable.

estimación NF (a) (*acto*) estimation; (*evaluación*) valuation; (*pronóstico*)

forecast. (b) estimate, estimation; valuation. (c) (*aprecio*) esteem, regard; **~ propia** self-esteem.

estimado ADJ esteemed, respected; **'E~ Señor ...'** 'Dear Sir ...'.

estimador, -a NM/F (*Com*) estimator.

estimar [1a] ① VT (a) (*evaluar*) to estimate; to appraise; (*calibrar*) to gauge; (*calcular*) reckon, compute; **~ algo en mil pesetas** to value sth at a thousand pesetas. (b) **~ que ...** to think that ..., reckon that ... (c) (*apreciar*) to esteem, respect; **~ a uno en mucho** to have a high regard for sb; **~ a uno en poco** to have a low opinion of sb; **se lo estimo mucho** I am much indebted to you for it. ② **estimarse** VR (a) (*evaluarse*) to be estimated (*en* at), be valued (*en* at). (b) **¡se estima!** thanks very much!, I appreciate it! (c) (*uno mismo*) to have a good opinion of o.s.; **si se estima no hará tal cosa** if he has any self-respect he'll do nothing of the sort.

estimativamente ADV roughly, by guesswork.

estimativo ADJ rough, approximate.

estimulación NF stimulation.

estimulante ① ADJ stimulating. ② NM stimulant.

estimular [1a] VT (*gen*) to stimulate; to encourage, excite, incite, prompt; *apetito* to stimulate; *debate etc* to promote; *esfuerzo, industria* to encourage, boost.

estímulo NM stimulus, stimulation; encouragement; inducement, incentive.

estío NM summer.

estipendiar [1b] VT to pay a stipend to.

estipendiario ADJ, NM stipendiary.

estipendio NM (*sueldo*) stipend; salary; (*derechos*) fee.

estíptico ① ADJ (a) (*Med*) styptic. (b) (*estreñido*) constipated. (c) (*fig*) mean, miserly. ② NM styptic.

estipulación NF stipulation, condition, proviso.

estipular [1a] VT to stipulate.

estirada NF (*Dep*) dive, stretch.

estirado ① ADJ (a) stretched, extended; stretched tight; (*alambre*) drawn. (b) (*fig*) (*tieso*) stiff, starchy; (*pomposo*) pompous; (*Cono Sur: engreído*) vain, stuck-up*. (c) (*fig: tacaño*) tight-fisted. ② NM (*de vidrio*) drawing; (*de pelo*) straightening; **~ de (la) piel** face-lift, cosmetic surgery.

estirador NM (*Téc*) stretcher.

estirajar* [1a] = estirar.

estiraje NM stretching.

estiramiento NM: **~ facial** face-lift.

estirar [1a] ① VT (a) (*extender*) to stretch, pull out, draw out; to extend; (*Téc*) *alambre etc* to draw; *oído* to prick up; *cuello* to stretch, crane; *ropa* to iron lightly, run the iron over. (b) (*demasiado*) to overstretch, strain. (c) (*fig*) *discurso etc* to spin out, stretch out; *dinero* to eke out. (d) (*And*: matar*) to kill, shoot. (e) (*And ††: azotar*) to flog. (f) (*Cono Sur, Méx: tirar*) to pull, tug at. ② **estirarse** VR (a) (*alargarse*) to stretch. (b) (*Dep*) **el equipo se estiró** the team moved upfield; **el jugador se estiró por la banda** the player ran up the touchline.

estirón NM (a) (*tirón*) pull, tug, jerk. (b) (*crecimiento*) spurt, sudden growth; **dar un ~** to shoot up.

estironear [1a] VT (*Cono Sur*) to pull hard at, tug sharply at.

estirpe NF stock, lineage; race; **de la ~ regia** of royal stock, of the blood royal.

estítico = estíptico.

estitiquez NF (*LAm*) constipation.

estival ADJ summer (*atr*); summery.

esto PRON DEM *'neutro'* this; this thing, this affair, this matter; **~ es difícil** this is difficult; **todo ~ es inútil** all this is useless; **~ es, ...** that is (to say), ...; **~ de la boda** this business about the wedding; **antes de ~** before this; **con ~** herewith; whereupon; **durante ~** in the meantime, while this was going on; **en ~** at this point; **por ~** for this reason; **¿qué es ~?** what's all this?; **y esto ¿qué es?** whatever is this?; **~ ...** (*vacilando*) er ..., um ...

estocada NF (a) (*golpe*) stab, thrust; lunge; (*herida*) stab wound; (*Taur etc*) death blow, (*final*) thrust. (b) (*fig*) sharp retort.

Estocolmo NM Stockholm.

estofa NF (a) (*tela*) quilting, quilted material. (b) (*fig*) quality, class; **de baja ~** poor-quality, *persona* low-class.

estofado ① ADJ (a) (*Culin*) stewed. (b) (*Cos*) quilted. ② NM stew, hotpot.

estofar [1a] VT (a) (*Culin*) to stew. (b) (*Cos*) to quilt.

estoicidad NF stoicism.

estoicismo NM stoicism.

estoico ① ADJ stoic(al).

2 NM stoic.

estola NF stole; ~ **de visón** mink cape.

estolidez NF stupidity.

estólido ADJ stupid.

estomacal 1 ADJ stomachic; stomach (atr); **trastorno** ~ stomach upset.

2 NM stomachic.

estomagante ADJ (a) comida indigestible. (b) (*: molesto) upsetting, annoying; revolting.

estomagar [1h] VT (a) (Med) to give indigestion to, upset. (b) (fig) to upset, annoy.

estómago NM stomach; **dolor de** ~ stomach ache; **revolver el** ~ **a uno** to revolt sb, make sb's stomach turn over; (fig) to upset sb, annoy sb; **tener buen** ~ (fig) to be thick-skinned; to have an elastic conscience, be none too scrupulous.

estomatólogo, -a NM/F dentist.

Estonia NF Estonia.

estonio, -a 1 ADJ, NM/F Estonian.

2 NM (Ling) Estonian.

estopa NF (a) (del cáñamo) tow; (harpillera) burlap; (Náut) oakum; (Carib) cotton waste. (b) **largar** (etc) ~ **a:** to bash*, hit.

estopero NM (Méx Aut) oil seal.

estoperol NM (a) (mecha) tow, wick. (b) (And: tachuela) brass tack. (c) (And: sartén) frying pan.

estopilla NF cheesecloth.

estoque NM (a) (espada) rapier, sword; **estar hecho un** ~ to be as thin as a rake. (b) (Bot) gladiolus.

estoquear [1a] VT to stab, run through.

estorbar [1a] 1 VT (obstaculizar) to hinder, obstruct, impede, be (o get) in the way of; (dificultar) to interfere with; (molestar) to bother, disturb, upset.

2 VI to be in the way.

estorbo NM hindrance, obstruction, impediment, obstacle; drag; nuisance; **no hay** ~ **para que se haga** there is no obstacle (o bar, impediment) to its being done; **el mayor** ~ **es el director** the biggest obstacle is the headmaster.

estornino NM starling.

estornudar [1a] VI to sneeze.

estornudo NM sneeze.

estoy etc V **estar**.

estrábico ADJ persona wall-eyed; ojo squinting, strabismic.

estrabismo NM squint, strabismus.

Estrabón NM Strabo.

estrada NF (a) (carretera) road, highway; **batir la** ~ (Mil) to reconnoitre. (b) (And: Agr) section of a rubber plantation (150 trees).

estrado NM stage, platform; dais; (Mús) bandstand; (Hist) drawing room; ~s law courts; ~ **del testigo** witness stand; **citar a uno para** ~s to subpoena sb.

estrafalario ADJ (a) (excéntrico) odd, outlandish, eccentric. (b) ropa slovenly, sloppy.

estragado ADJ (arruinado) ruined; (corrompido) corrupted, spoiled, perverted; (depravado) depraved; (descuidado) slovenly, careless, disorderly.

estragante ADJ damaging, destructive.

estragar [1h] VT to ruin; gusto etc to corrupt, spoil, pervert; to deprave.

estrago NM ruin, destruction; corruption, perversion; ~s havoc, destruction, ravages; ~s (Jur) criminal damage; **los** ~s **del tiempo** the ravages of time; **hacer** ~s **en** (o **entre**) to play havoc with, wreak havoc among.

estragón NM (Bot, Culin) tarragon.

estramador NM (Méx) comb.

estrambólico ADJ (LAm), **estrambótico** ADJ odd, outlandish, eccentric.

estrambote NM (Poét) extra lines, extra verses, addition.

estrangis* ADV: **de** ~ secretly, on the quiet.

estrangul NM (Mús) mouthpiece.

estrangulación NF strangulation.

estrangulado ADJ (Med) strangulated.

estrangulador NM (a) (persona) strangler. (b) (Mec) throttle; (Aut etc) choke.

estrangulamiento NM (Aut) narrow stretch of road, bottleneck.

estrangular [1a] VT (a) persona to strangle. (b) (Med) to strangulate. (c) (Mec) to throttle; to choke.

estranji ADV = **estrangis**.

estranqui* NMF = **extranjero**.

estraperlear* [1a] VI to deal in black-market goods.

estraperlista 1 ADJ black-market (atr).

2 NMF blackmarketeer.

estraperlo NM black market; **comprar algo en el** ~, **comprar algo de** ~ to buy sth on the black market.

estrapontín NM (Aut) back seat; side seat, extra seat.

Estrasburgo NM Strasbourg.

estratagema NF stratagem.

estratega NMF strategist; V t **gabinete**.

estrategia NF strategy; generalship; ~ **de la tensión** destabilizing campaign.

estratégico ADJ strategic(al).

estratificación NF stratification.

estratificado ADJ stratified; madera laminated.

estratificar [1g] 1 VT to stratify.

2 **estratificarse** VR to stratify, be stratified.

estratigrafía NF stratigraphy.

estratigráfico ADJ stratigraphic.

estrato NM (a) (gen) stratum, layer. (b) (nube) stratus.

estratocúmulo NM stratocumulus.

estratosfera NF stratosphere.

estratosférico ADJ stratospheric.

estraza NF rag; **papel de** ~ brown paper, wrapping paper.

estrechamente ADV (a) (apretadamente) narrowly; tightly. (b) (austeramente) austerely. (c) (íntimamente) closely, intimately. (d) (severamente) strictly, rigidly; meanly; narrow-mindedly.

estrechamiento NM (a) (de valle, calle) narrowing. (b) (de lazos) tightening, closening.

estrechar [1a] 1 VT (a) (hacer estrecho) to narrow; ropa to make smaller, reduce, take in; amistad etc to draw tighter.

(b) (apretar) to squeeze; persona to hug, embrace, enfold in one's arms; mano to grasp, clasp; to shake.

(c) (fig) enemigo to press hard.

(d) (fig: presionar) to compel, constrain, bring pressure to bear on.

2 **estrecharse** VR (a) (encogerse) to narrow, get narrow; to tighten, get tighter; ~ **en** to squeeze into.

(b) (dos personas) to embrace (one another), hug.

(c) **se estrecharon la mano** they shook hands.

(d) (amistad etc) to become closer, become more intimate; ~ **con uno** to get very friendly with sb.

(e) ~ (**en los gastos**) (Fin) to stint o.s., economize, cut down on expenditure.

estrechez NF (a) (angostura) narrowness, tightness; (falta de espacio) cramped nature, smallness, lack of room.

(b) (Fin) want; financial stringency; ~ **del dinero** tightness of money, shortage of money; **estrecheces** financial difficulties, financial straits; **vivir con** ~ to live in straitened circumstances.

(c) (de amistad) closeness, intimacy.

(d) (rigidez) strictness, rigidity; (austeridad) austerity; ~ **de conciencia** small-mindedness; ~ **de miras** narrow-mindedness.

estrecho 1 ADJ (a) (angosto) narrow; tight; cuarto cramped, small; falda etc tight; pantalón tight, narrow, close-fitting; **estos zapatos me están muy** ~s these shoes are too small for me, these shoes pinch my feet.

(b) dinero etc tight, short; vida austere.

(c) relación etc close, intimate; amistad close.

(d) actitud, prohibición strict, rigid; carácter austere; (pey) mean, mean-spirited; (t ~ **de conciencia**) small-minded; (t ~ **de miras**) narrow-minded; insular, parochial; **es muy estrecha** she's very strait-laced; **hacerse el** ~ **con uno** to be mean to sb, be difficult with sb; **¡no te hagas la estrecha!** don't be so coy!

2 NM (a) (Geog) strait(s); narrows, channel; **E~ de Gibraltar** Straits of Gibraltar.

(b) (*: aprieto) fix*, jam*, predicament; **al** ~ by force, under compulsion; **poner a uno en el** ~ **de** + infin to force sb into a position of having to + infin.

estrechura NF (a) = **estrechez**. (b) = **estrecho** 2.

estregadera NF (a) (bruza) scrubbing brush; (fregasuelos) floor mop. (b) (de puerta) door scraper, boot scraper.

estregar [1h y 1j] VT (frotar) to rub; (rasear) to scrape; (con cepillo) to scrub, scour.

estrella 1 NF (a) (Astron y fig) star; ~ **de Belén** star of Bethlehem; ~ **de David** Star of David; ~ **fija** fixed star; ~ **fugaz** shooting star; ~ **de guía** guiding star; ~ **de mar** starfish; ~ **de neutrones**, ~ **neutrónica** neutron star; ~ **del norte** north star; ~ **polar** polar star; ~ **de rabo** comet; ~ **vespertina** evening star; **creer en su buena** ~ to believe in one's lucky star; **nacer con** ~ to be born under a lucky star, be born lucky; **poner a uno sobre las** ~s to praise sb to the skies; **tener (buena)** ~ to be lucky; **tener mala** ~ to be unlucky; **ver las** ~s (fig) to see stars.

(b) (Tip) asterisk, star; **un hotel (de) cinco** ~s a five-star hotel.

(c) (Zool) blaze, white patch.

(d) (Mil) star, pip.

(e) (Cine, Teat etc) star; ~ **del cine** movie star, film star; **ser la** ~ to star, be the star.

2 ATR star (atr); **atracción** ~ star attraction.

estrelladera NF (Culin etc) slice.

estrellado ADJ (a) (con estrellas) starred; (de forma de estrella) star-shaped; *cielo* starry, full of stars; *vestido* spangled. **(b)** *(roto)* smashed, shattered. **(c)** *(Culin) huevo* fried.

estrellamar NF starfish.

estrellar [1a] 1 VT **(a)** *(decorar)* to star, spangle, cover with stars. **(b)** *(romper)* to smash, shatter; to dash to pieces, smash to pieces; **lo estrelló contra la pared** he smashed it against the wall; **estrelló el balón en el poste** he crashed the ball into the goal-post; **la corriente amenazaba con ~ el barco contra las rocas** the current threatened to dash the boat on to the rocks. **(c)** *huevo* to fry. 2 **estrellarse** VR to smash, shatter, crash *(contra* against); to be dashed to pieces; **~ contra** to crash into; **~ con una dificultad** to come right up against a difficulty.

estrellato NM stardom.

estrellón NM **(a)** *(fig) (estrella)* star, large star; *(fuegos artificiales)* star firework. **(b)** *(esp LAm) (Aer)* crash; *(Aut)* crash, smash, collision.

estremecedor ADJ alarming, disturbing, shattering.

estremecer [2d] 1 VT *(t fig)* to shake. 2 **estremecerse** VR *(edificio etc)* to shake, vibrate, tremble; *(persona: miedo)* to tremble *(ante* at, *de* with); *(horror)* to shiver, shudder *(de* with); *(emoción)* to tingle, tremble, thrill *(de* with); *(frío)* to shiver *(de* with).

estremecido ADJ shaking, trembling *(de* with).

estremecimiento NM, **estremezón** NM **(a)** *(V VR) (And, Carib)* tremor, vibration; shiver, shudder; shaking, trembling; tingling. **(b)** *(And, Carib: de tierra)* tremor.

estrena NF **(a)** *(regalo)* good-luck gift, token; **~s** *(de Navidad)* Christmas presents. **(b)** = **estreno.**

estrenar [1a] 1 VT **(a)** to use for the first time; *ropa* to wear *(o* put on *etc)* for the first time, show off for the first time. **(b)** *(Cine)* to give its première, show for the first time; to release, put on release; *(Teat)* to perform for the first time, give a first performance to. 2 VI **(a)** *(Teat)* **aquí estrenan mucho** they stage a lot of premières here, they put on a lot of new plays here. **(b)** *(Carib Com)* to make a down payment. 3 **estrenarse** VR **(a)** *(persona)* to make one's début, appear for the first time; (*) to start to do some work; **no se estrena** he hasn't done a hand's turn. **(b)** *(Cine)* to have its première, be shown for the first time; *(Teat)* to open, have its first night; to be performed for the first time. **(c)** *(Com)* to make the first sale of the day. **(d)** (*) to cough up*, pay up.

estrenista NMF *(Teat)* first-nighter.

estreno NM **(a)** first use; first appearance; **fue cuando el ~ del coche nuevo** it was when we went out in the new car for the first time. **(b)** *(de persona)* début, first appearance; **¡mal ~!** what a wretched start! **(c)** *(Cine)* première; release; *(Teat)* first night, first performance; **~ general** general release; **riguroso ~** world première. **(d)** *(Carib)* down payment, deposit.

estrenque NM stout esparto rope.

estrenuo ADJ vigorous, energetic; enterprising.

estreñido ADJ constipated, costive.

estreñimiento NM constipation.

estreñir [3h y 3k] 1 VT to constipate, bind. 2 **estreñirse** VR to get constipated.

estrepitarse [1a] VR *(Carib)* to kick up a fuss, make a scene.

estrépito NM noise, racket, row; tremendous din; fuss; **reírse con ~** to laugh uproariously.

estrepitosamente ADV noisily; loudly, deafeningly; rowdily, boisterously.

estrepitoso ADJ noisy; loud, deafening; *fiesta, persona etc* rowdy, boisterous; **con aplausos ~s** with loud applause.

estreptococo NM streptococcus.

estreptomicina NF streptomycin.

estrés NM stress.

estresado 1 ADJ stressed; **estar ~** to be under stress. 2 NM, **estresada** NF stress sufferer.

estresante ADJ stressful.

estresar [1a] VT to cause stress to, put stress on.

estría NF groove; *(Arquit)* flute, fluting; *(Anat)* stretchmark; *(Bio, Geol etc)* striation.

estriado 1 ADJ grooved; *(Arquit)* fluted; *(Anat)* stretchmarked *(Bio, Geol etc)* striate, striated. 2 NM grooving; fluting; striation.

estriar [1c] VT to groove, make a groove in; to flute; to striate.

estribación NF *(Geog etc)* spur; **estribaciones** spurs, foothills.

estribar [1a] VI: **~ en** to rest on, be supported by; *(fig)* to rest on, be based on; **la dificultad estriba en el texto** the difficulty lies in the text, the difficulty stems from the text; **su prosperidad estriba en esta industria** their prosperity is based on *(o* derives from) this in-

dustry.

estribera NF **(a)** *(estribo)* stirrup; *(de moto)* footrest. **(b)** *(LAm: cincha)* girth, saddle strap.

estriberón NM stepping stone.

estribillo NM *(Liter)* refrain; *(Mús)* chorus; *(fig)* pet word, pet phrase; **¡siempre (con) el mismo ~!** the same old story!

estribo NM **(a)** *(de jinete)* stirrup; *(Aut etc)* running board, step, footboard; *(apoyapié)* footrest; **perder los ~s** *(fig)* to fly off the handle*, lose one's temper; to get hot under the collar; to lose one's head; **tomar algo para el ~, tomar la del ~** *(And, Cono Sur) (jinete)* to drink a stirrup cup; *(gen)* to have one for the road*. **(b)** *(Téc)* brace, bracket, stay. **(c)** *(Arquit)* buttress; *(de puente)* pier, support. **(d)** *(Geog)* spur. **(e)** *(fig)* basis, foundation.

estribor NM starboard.

estricnina NF strychnine.

estricote NM: **andar al ~** *(Carib*)* to live a wild life.

estrictamente ADV strictly; severely.

estrictez NF *(LAm)* strictness; severity.

estricto ADJ strict; severe.

estridencia NF stridency; raucousness; **llevaba ropa cara pero sin ~s** she was expensively but not loudly dressed.

estridente ADJ *ruido* strident, raucous, unpleasant-sounding; jangling; *color* loud.

estridentemente ADV stridently, raucously; loudly.

estridor NM stridency; raucousness; screech.

estrillar [1a] VI *(And, Cono Sur)* to get cross.

estrillo NM *(And, Cono Sur)* bad temper, annoyance.

estriptís* NM, **estriptise*** NM *(And)* striptease.

estriptisero*, -a NM/F *(And)* stripper*, striptease artist.

estriptista* NF stripper*.

estro NM **(a)** *(inspiración)* inspiration. **(b)** *(Med, Vet)* oestrus.

estrofa NF verse, stanza, strophe.

estrófico ADJ strophic; composed in stanzas.

estrógeno NM oestrogen.

estroncio NM strontium; **~ 90** strontium 90.

estropajo NM **(a)** *(de fregar)* scourer, scouring pad, scrubber; *(trapo)* dishcloth; *(fregasuelos)* swab, mop; **~ de acero** steel wool; **poner a uno como un ~** to shower insults on sb; to make sb feel a heel; **servir de ~** to be exploited, be used to do the dirty work. **(b)** *(basura)* dirt, rubbish; *(objeto inútil)* worthless object; *(persona)* dead loss.

estropajoso ADJ **(a)** *carne etc* tough, leathery, gristly. **(b)** *habla* stammering; indistinct. **(c)** *persona (desaseado)* slovenly; scruffy; *(vil)* mean, despicable. **(d)** *pelo* straw-like.

estropeado ADJ damaged, spoiled; ruined; crumpled, torn; *persona* maimed, crippled; **está muy estropeada** she looks older than she is.

estropear [1a] 1 VT *comida, cosecha* to damage, spoil; to ruin; *proyecto, vida* to mess up, make a mess of; *tela* to crumple, tear; *persona* to maim, cripple, hurt; *texto etc* to mangle; *sentido* to pervert, distort. 2 **estropearse** VR to get damaged; to spoil, go bad; to deteriorate; *(plan etc)* to fail.

estropiciar* [1b] VT to trash*, wreck.

estropicio* NM **(a)** *(rotura)* breakage, smashing, smash-up. **(b)** *(efectos)* harmful effects, damaging results; **ese alimento es responsable de muchos ~s** that foodstuff can have very harmful effects. **(c)** *(fig)* rumpus*, row, fuss; turmoil.

estructura NF *(gen)* structure; *(armazón)* frame, framework; *(orden)* arrangement; *(liter)* structure; plot; **~ atómica** atomic structure; **~ del poder** power structure; **~ profunda** deep structure; **~ salarial** pay structure.

estructuración NF structure; structuring.

estructural ADJ structural.

estructuralismo NM structuralism.

estructuralista ADJ, NMF structuralist.

estructuralmente ADV structurally.

estructurar [1a] VT to construct; to arrange, organize.

estruendo NM **(a)** *(ruido)* noise, clamour, din; crash, clatter, racket; thunder. **(b)** *(fig: alboroto)* uproar, turmoil, confusion. **(c)** *(fig: pompa)* pomp, ostentation.

estruendosamente ADV noisily, uproariously; loudly, obstreperously.

estruendoso ADJ noisy; uproarious; *persona* loud, obstreperous.

estrujado NM *(de uvas)* pressing.

estrujadura NF squeeze, press(ing).

estrujar [1a] 1 VT *(exprimir)* to squeeze; *(apretar)* to press, crush; *(machacar)* to bruise, mash; *(fig)* to drain, bleed white. 2 **estrujarse** VR: **~ la mollera*** to rack one's brains.

estrujón NM squeeze, press; pressing, crushing; *(Agr)* final pressing of grapes; (*) crush, jam.

Estuardo NM Stuart.

estuario NM estuary.

estucado [1] ADJ (a) *papel* coated. (b) *pared* plastered, stuccoed.
[2] NM stucco, stucco work.

estucar [1g] VT to stucco, plaster.

estuche NM (a) (*caja*) box, case, container; (*vaina*) sheath; ~ **de afeites** vanity case; ~ **de aseo** toilet case; ~ **de cigarros** cigar-case; ~ **de costura** sewing basket; ~ **de cubiertos** canteen of cutlery; ~ **de herramientas** toolbox; ~ **de joyas** jewel-box.
(b) **ser un ~*** to be a handyman, be a useful chap*.

estuchero* NM (*Méx*) safebreaker.

estuco NM stucco, plaster.

estudiado ADJ (*fig*) studied, elaborate; (*pey*) *persona* affected; *estilo* recherché.

estudiantado NM students (*collectively*), student body.

estudiante NMF (*t* **estudianta***NF) student; ~ **de derecho** law student; ~ **de medicina** medical student; ~ **de ruso** student of Russian.

estudiantil ADJ student (*atr*); **vida** ~ student life; **los problemas ~es** student problems, problems of students, problems relating to students.

estudiantina NF student music group, student band; *see also* TUNA.

estudiantino ADJ student (*atr*); **a la estudiantina** like a student, in the manner of students.

estudiar [1b] [1] VTI to study; to work; to think about, think over, ponder; ~ **para abogado** to study to become a lawyer, study law; **tengo que ir a** ~ I must go and work; **estudia todo el día en la biblioteca** he works all day in the library; **lo estudiaré** I'll think about it.
[2] **estudiarse** VR: **se está estudiando** it is under consideration.

estudio NM (a) (*gen*) study; (*encuesta*) research; survey; (*investigación*) investigation; (*proyecto*) plan, design (*de* for); (*planificación*) planning; ~**s** (*educación*) schooling, education; (*investigaciones*) work, studies, researches; **le pagaron los ~s** they paid for his schooling, they paid for his education; **hizo sus ~s en París** he studied in Paris; **se fue a Suiza para completar sus ~s** she went to Switzerland to finish her education; **los ~s de Menéndez Pidal sobre la épica española** Menéndez Pidal's work on Spanish epic; **los últimos ~s de lingüística** the latest work in linguistics, recent research in linguistics; **publicó un** ~ **sobre Bécquer** he published a study of Bécquer; ~ **de campo** field study; ~**s empresariales** business studies; ~**s del mercado**, ~ **de mercados** market research; ~ **de las posibilidades**, ~ **de viabilidad** feasibility study; ~**s de tiempo y movimiento** time and motion study; **estar en** ~ to be under consideration.
(b) (*cuarto en casa*) study; (*piso*) bedsitter, one-room flat; studio flat.
(c) (*Arte, Cine, Rad etc: sala*) studio; ~ **de cine**, ~ **cinematográfico** film studio; ~ **de diseños** design studio; ~ **de grabación** recording studio; ~ **radiofónico** broadcasting studio; ~ **de registro de sonidos** sound-recording studio; ~ **de televisión** television studio.
(d) (*Arte: cuadro etc*) study.
(e) (*Mús: composición*) study, étude.
(f) (*Cono Sur: de abogado etc*) office.
(g) (*erudición*) learning; **un hombre de mucho** ~ a man of great learning.

estudiosamente ADV studiously.

estudioso [1] ADJ studious; bookish.
[2] **estudiosa** NF student, scholar.

estufa NF (a) (*calentador*) stove, heater; (*LAm*) cooker; ~ **eléctrica** electric fire; ~ **de gas** gas fire; ~ **de petróleo** oil stove. (b) (*Agr*) hothouse; **criar a uno en** ~ (*fig: horno*) to pamper sb.

estufilla NF (a) (*brasero*) small stove, brazier. (b) (*manguito*) muff.

estulticia NF (*liter*) stupidity, foolishness.

estultificar [1g] VT (*CAm*): ~ **a uno** to make sb look stupid, make sb out to be a fool.

estulto ADJ (*liter*) stupid, foolish.

estupa* [1] NF drug squad.
[2] NM member of the drug squad.

estupefacción NF stupefaction.

estupefaciente [1] ADJ stupifying; narcotic; **sustancia** ~ = 2.
[2] NM narcotic, drug.

estupefacto ADJ astonished, speechless, thunderstruck; **me miró** ~ he looked at me in amazement; **dejar a uno** ~ to leave sb speechless.

estupendamente ADV stupendously; (*) marvellously, wonderfully, terrifically*; **estoy** ~ (*salud*) I feel great; **le salió** ~ he did it very well.

▼ **estupendo** ADJ stupendous; (*) marvellous, wonderful, terrific*, great*; **¡~!** that's great!*, splendid!; **tiene un coche** ~ he's got a marvellous car; **hay chicas estupendas** there are some smashing girls*;

es ~ **para tocar la trompeta** he's great on the trumpet*.

estúpidamente ADV stupidly.

estupidez NF (a) (*cualidad*) stupidity, silliness. (b) (*acto*) stupid thing, piece of stupidity; **fue una** ~ **mía** it was a silly mistake of mine; **cometer una** ~ to do something silly.

estupidizador ADJ stupefying.

estúpido ADJ stupid, silly.

estupor NM (a) (*Med etc*) stupor. (b) (*fig*) astonishment, amazement.

estuprar [1a] VT to rape.

estupro NM rape.

estuque NM stucco.

estuquería NF stuccoing, stucco work.

esturión NM sturgeon.

estuve *etc* V estar.

esvástica NF swastika.

ET NM (*Esp Mil*) ABR de **Ejército de Tierra**.

ETA ['eta] NF (*Esp Pol*) ABR de **Euskadi Ta Askatasuna = Patria Vasca y Libertad**; ~ **p-m** ABR de **ETA político-militar**.

-eta V Aspects of Word Formation in Spanish 2.

etano NM (*Quím*) ethane.

etanol NM ethanol.

etapa NF (a) (*de viaje etc*) stage; (*Dep*) stage, leg; lap; (*Mil*) stopping place; **a cortas ~s, a pequeñas ~s** in easy stages; **hacer** ~ **en** to break one's journey at; **quemar ~s** to make rapid progress.
(b) (*de cohete*) stage; **cohete de 3 ~s** 3-stage rocket.
(c) (*Mil*) food ration (*for stage of a march*).
(d) (*fig*) stage, phase; **en la segunda** ~ **del plan** in the second phase of the plan; **una adquisición proyectada por ~s** a phased takeover; **desarrollo por ~s** phased development, development in stages; **lo haremos por ~s** we'll do it in stages, we'll do it gradually.

etario ADJ age (*atr*); **grupo** ~ age group.

etarra [1] ADJ of ETA.
[2] NMF member of ETA; V ETA.

etc. ABR de etcétera.

etcétera ADV etcetera, *etc;* **gatos y perros** ~, ~ cats and dogs and so on, cats and dogs and what have you; **y un largo** ~ and a lot more besides, and much much more; **y un largo** ~ **de autores** and many more authors besides.

-ete V Aspects of Word Formation in Spanish 2.

éter NM ether.

etéreo ADJ ethereal (*t fig*).

eternamente ADV eternally, everlastingly.

eternidad NF eternity.

eternizar [1f] [1] VT to etern(al)ize, perpetuate; to make everlasting; (*pey*) to drag out, prolong endlessly.
[2] **eternizarse** VR (*pey*) to be interminable; ~ **en** to take hours over, take all day over; to dwell endlessly on; ~ **haciendo algo** to be very slow doing sth.

eterno ADJ eternal, everlasting.

ethos ['etos] NM ethos.

ética NF ethics; ~ **profesional** professional ethics.

ético¹ ADJ ethical.

ético² ADJ (*Med*: = **héctico, hético**) consumptive; (*fig*) frail.

eticoso* ADJ (*And*) fussy, finicky.

etileno NM (*Quím*) ethylene.

etílico ADJ *alcohol* ethyl (*atr*); **en estado** ~ intoxicated; **intoxicación etílica** alcohol poisoning.

etilo NM ethyl.

étimo NM etymon.

etimología NF etymology.

etimológico ADJ etymological.

etiología NF etiology, aetiology.

etíope, etiope ADJ, NMF Ethiopian.

Etiopía NF Ethiopia.

etiquencia NF (*Carib, Méx Med*) consumption.

etiqueta NF (a) (*formalismo*) etiquette; formality; **de** ~ formal, full-dress (*atr*); **baile de** ~ ball, dress ball, formal dance; **ir de** ~ to wear evening dress; (*invitación*) **'vestir de ~'** 'dress: formal'.
(b) (*rótulo*) ticket, label, tag; ~ **del precio** price-tag.

etiquetación NF, **etiquetado** NM, **etiquetaje** NM labelling.

etiquetadora NF labelling machine.

etiquetar [1a] VT to label.

etiquetero ADJ formal, ceremonious, punctilious; stiff, prim.

etnia NF ethnic group; race.

etnicidad NF ethnicity.

étnico ADJ ethnic.

etnocéntrico ADJ ethnocentric.

etnocentrismo NM ethnocentrism.

etnografía NF ethnography.

etnográfico ADJ ethnographic.

etnología NF ethnology.

etnológico ADJ ethnological.

etnomusicología NF ethnomusicology.
etrusco, -a [1] ADJ, NM/F Etruscan.
[2] NM (*Ling*) Etruscan.
ETS (**a**) NF (*Med*) ABR *de* **enfermedad de transmisión sexual** sexually transmitted disease, STD.
(**b**) (*Esp*) ABR *de* **Escuelas Técnicas Superiores.**
ETT NF (*Esp*) ABR *de* **Empresa de Trabajo Temporal** temp recruitment agency.
EUA NMPL (*LAm*) ABR *de* **Estados Unidos de América** United States of America, USA.
eucaliptal NM, **eucaliptar** NM eucalyptus plantation.
eucalipto NM eucalyptus, gum-tree.
Eucaristía NF Eucharist.
eucarístico ADJ eucharistic.
Euclides NM Euclid.
euclidiano ADJ Euclidean.
eufemismo NM euphemism.
eufemístico ADJ euphemistic.
eufonía NF euphony.
eufónico ADJ euphonic, euphonious.
euforia NF euphoria; exuberance, elation.
eufórico ADJ euphoric; exuberant.
euforizante ADJ: **droga** ~ drug that produces euphoria.
euforizar [1f] [1] VT to produce euphoria in, exhilarate.
[2] **euforizarse** VR to become exhilarated.
Eufrates NM Euphrates.
eugenesia NF eugenics.
eugenésico ADJ eugenic.
Eugenio NM Eugene.
eugenismo NM eugenics.
eunuco NM eunuch.
eurasiático, -a ADJ, NM/F Eurasian.
eureka EXCL eureka!
Eurídice NF Eurydice.
Eurípedes NM Euripides.
eurítmica NF eurhythmics.
euro NM (**a**)(*moneda*) euro. (**b**) (*liter*) east wind.
euro... PREF Euro...
eurobonos NMPL Eurobonds.
Eurocámara NF Euro Parliament, European Parliament.
eurocheque NM Eurocheque.
eurocomisario, -a NM/F Euro-commissioner.
eurocomunismo NM Eurocommunism.
eurocomunista ADJ, NMF Eurocommunist.
euroconector NM SCART connector, Euroconnector.
eurócrata NMF Eurocrat.
Eurocrédito NM Eurocredit.
eurodiputado, -a NM/F Euro MP, member of the European Parliament.
eurodivisa NF Eurocurrency.
eurodólar NM Eurodollar.
euroescéptico, -a ADJ, NM/F Eurosceptic.
eurofanático ADJ fanatically pro-European.
eurófilo, -a ADJ, NM/F Europhile.
eurófobo, -a ADJ, NM/F Europhobe.
eurofuncionario, -a NM/F EU official.
euromercado NM Euromarket.
euromisil NM short-range nuclear missile.
Europa NF Europe.
europarlamentario, -a NM/F member of the European Parliament.
europarlamento NM European Parliament.
europeidad NF Europeanness; Europe-mindedness; European character.
europeísmo NM Europeanism.
europeísta [1] ADJ pro-European; European-minded.
[2] NMF pro-European; European-minded person.
europeización NF Europeanization.
ºeuropeizante ADJ (*LAm*) = **europeísta.**
europeizar [1f] [1] VT to Europeanize.
[2] **europeizarse** VR to become Europeanized.
europeo, -a ADJ, NM/F European.
Eurovisión NF Eurovision.
éuscaro ADJ, NM = **euskera** *etc.*
Euskadi NM Basque Country; ~ **norte** Pays Basque (*France*).
euskaldún [1] ADJ Basque; (*Ling*) Basque-speaking.
[2] NM, **euskalduna** NF Basque speaker.
euskaldunización NF conversion to Basque norms; (*Ling*) conversion to Basque, process of making people (*etc*) Basque-speaking.
euskaldunizar [1f] VT to convert to Basque norms; (*Ling*) to convert to Basque, make Basque-speaking.
euskera, eusquera, eusquero [1] ADJ Basque.
[2] NM (*Ling*) Basque; ~ **batua** standard Basque.

┌─ **EUSKERA** ─────────────────────────┐

Spoken by over half a million people in the Western Pyrenees, Basque, which is a non-Indo-European language, has been one of Spain's **lenguas cooficiales** *(along with* **catalán** *and* **gallego**) *since 1982. Originally spoken also in Burgos and the Eastern Pyrenees, it began to lose ground to Castilian from the 13th century onwards. Under Franco its use was prohibited in the media, but it began to experience a revival in the 1950s through semi-clandestine Basque-language schools called* **ikastolas**. *In 1968 the Academy of the Basque Language created a standardized form called* **euskera batua**, *an attempt to homogenize several divergent dialects. Nowadays there is Basque-language radio and television, and under the autonomous government the teaching of the language has become a cornerstone of educational policy.*
⇨*See also* **LENGUAS COOFICIALES**

└──────────────────────────────────────┘

eutanasia NF euthanasia, mercy killing.
Eva NF Eve.
evacuación NF (**a**) (*acto*) evacuation. (**b**) (*Téc*) waste; exhaust. (**c**) (*Med*) evacuation, bowel movement.
evacuado, -a NM/F evacuee.
evacuar [1d] VT (**a**) (*gen*) to evacuate; to move out of, leave empty, vacate; *ciudad, población* to evacuate; *recipiente* to empty; (*Med*) *llaga* to drain.
(**b**) ~ **el vientre** to have a movement of the bowels.
(**c**) *deber* to fulfil; *consulta* to carry out, undertake; *negocio* to transact; *trato* to conclude.
(**d**) (*Jur*) *dictamen* to issue.
evacuatorio NM public lavatory.
evadido, -a NM/F fugitive, escaped prisoner.
evadir [3a] [1] VT (**a**) to evade, avoid. (**b**) *dinero etc* to pass, get away with. [2] **evadirse** VR (**a**) to escape; to break out, slip away. (**b**) (*LAm⁕*) to trip⁕.
evaluación NF (**a**) (*gen*) evaluation; assessment; appraisal; refereeing. (**b**) (*Escol*) report, assessment; ~ **continua** continuous assessment; ~ **por pares** peer review.
evaluador(a) NM/F assessor; appraiser; referee.
evaluar [1e] VT to evaluate, assess; *personal* to appraise; *artículo* to referee.
evaluativo ADJ evaluative.
evanescente ADJ evanescent.
evangélico ADJ evangelic(al).
evangelio NM gospel; **el E~ según San Juan** the Gospel according to St John; **se aceptan sus ideas como el** ~ his ideas are accepted as gospel truth; **dice como el** ~ he speaks the gospel truth.
evangelismo NM evangelism; revivalism.
Evangelista ADJ: **San Juan** ~ St John the Evangelist.
evangelista NMF (**a**) (*Rel*) gospeller; revivalist; member of an Evangelical church; **los cuatro ~s** the four evangelists. (**b**) (*Méx*) scribe.
evangelizador(a) NM/F evangelist.
evangelizar [1f] VT to evangelize.
evaporación NF evaporation.
evaporar [1a] [1] VT to evaporate. [2] **evaporarse** VR to evaporate; (*fig*) to vanish.
evaporizar [1f] [1] VT to vaporize. [2] **evaporizarse** VR to vaporize.
evasión NF escape, flight; (*fig*) evasion, escapism; **lectura de** ~ light reading, escapist literature; ~ **de capitales** flight of capital; ~ **fiscal,** ~ **de impuestos,** ~ **tributaria** tax evasion.
evasionario ADJ (*Liter*) escapist.
evasionismo NM escapism.
evasiva NF evasion; (*escapatoria*) loophole, way out; (*pretexto*) excuse; **viene con sus ~s** he avoids a straight answer.
evasivo ADJ evasive, non-committal, ambiguous.
evento NM (**a**) (*incidente*) unforeseen happening; contingency; eventuality; **a todo** ~ whatever happens, in any event.
(**b**) (*acontecimiento*) event; (*Dep*) sporting fixture; (*fiesta etc*) social event.
eventual [1] ADJ (**a**) (*casual*) fortuitous; (*posible*) possible; conditional upon circumstances. (**b**) *obrero, trabajo* temporary, casual; *oficial etc* acting; *solución* stopgap, temporary. (**c**) (*LAm*) eventual.
[2] NMF temporary worker.
eventualidad NF (**a**) (*casualidad*) eventuality; contingency; **en esa** ~ in that eventuality. (**b**) (*trabajo*) casual employment.
eventualmente ADV (**a**) (*accidentalmente*) by chance, fortuitously. (**b**) (*posiblemente*) possibly, depending upon circumstances; **algún número de la revista se publicará** ~ special issues of the journal will be published from time to time. (**c**) (*LAm: por fin*) eventually.
Everest NM: **el** ~ (Mount) Everest.
evidencia NF (**a**) (*pruebas*) evidence, proof; **poner en** ~ (*hacer claro*) to make clear; (*demostrar*) to show, demonstrate; (*fig*) to make a fool of, make a laughing stock of; **ponerse en** ~ to put o.s. forward; **dejar** (*o* **poner**) **a uno en** ~ to put sb in an embarrassing position, show sb

up in a bad light. (**b**) (*cualidad*) obviousness.

evidencial ADJ tangible, visible.

evidenciar [1b] VT to prove, show, demonstrate; to make evident; **~ de modo inconfundible** to give clear proof of, prove unmistakably.

evidente ADJ obvious, clear, evident; **¡~!** naturally!, obviously!

evidentemente ADV obviously, clearly, evidently.

evitable ADJ avoidable, preventable; **un accidente fácilmente ~** an accident which could easily be avoided.

evitación NF avoidance, prevention; **~ de accidentes** accident prevention.

evitar [1a] VT (*gen*) to avoid; (*precaver*) to prevent; *peligro etc* to avoid, escape; *molestia* to save, spare; *tentación etc* to shun; **para ~ tales dificultades** in order to avoid such difficulties; **para ~se trabajo** in order to save o.s. trouble; **no lo lograrán si puedo ~lo** they won't get away with that if I can help it; **~ hacer algo** to avoid doing sth; to be chary of doing sth.

evocación NF evocation; invocation.

evocador ADJ evocative; reminiscent (*de* of).

evocar [1g] VT to evoke, call forth, conjure up; *espíritu etc* to invoke, call up.

evocativo ADJ (*LAm*) evocative.

evolución NF (**a**) (*Bio*) evolution. (**b**) (*fig*) evolution, change, development; (*Med*) progress. (**c**) (*Mil etc*) manoeuvre; (*movimiento*) movement.

evolucionar [1a] VI (**a**) (*Bio*) to evolve. (**b**) (*fig*) to evolve, change, develop; (*Med etc*) to progress. (**c**) (*Mil*) to manoeuvre, wheel; (*Aer*) to manoeuvre, circle, wheel.

evolucionista ADJ evolutionist.

evolutivo ADJ evolutionary.

ex [1] PREF ex-; former, late; **~ secretario** ex-secretary, former secretary; **la ~ querida de** the former mistress of, the ex-mistress of, the one-time mistress of.

[2] NMF: **mi ~*** my ex* (husband *o* wife); **un ~ del equipo** an ex-member of the team, a former member of the team.

exabrupto NM (*hum: ataque*) broadside; sudden attack; (*interjección*) interjection; (*observación*) sharp remark.

exacción NF (**a**) (*acto*) exaction, extortion. (**b**) (*suma etc*) demand; levy.

exacerbación NF exacerbation.

exacerbante ADJ (*LAm*) irritating, provoking; (*fig*) aggravating.

exacerbar [1a] VT to irritate, provoke; (*fig*) to aggravate, exacerbate.

▼ **exactamente** ADV exactly; accurately; precisely; punctually; correctly.

exactitud NF exactness; accuracy; precision; punctuality; correctness.

exacto ADJ (*gen*) exact; (*acertado*) accurate; (*preciso*) precise; (*puntual*) punctual; (*correcto*) right, correct; **¡~!** exactly!, quite right!; that's just what I say!; **eso no es del todo ~** that's not quite right.

exageración NF exaggeration.

exageradamente ADV in an exaggerated way; excessively, exorbitantly; over-demonstratively, theatrically; intensely; fulsomely; oddly.

exagerado ADJ *pretensión etc* exaggerated; *relato* highly-coloured; *precio etc* excessive, exorbitant, steep; *persona* over-demonstrative, theatrical, given to extravagant gestures; (*de fuertes emociones*) intense; *elogio* fulsome; (*en vestir*) over-dressed, dressy; (*raro*) peculiar, odd.

exageradura NF (*Carib*) exaggeration.

▼ **exagerar** [1a] [1] VT (*gen*) to exaggerate; to overdo, overstate, make too much of; (*aumentar*) to enlarge upon.

▼ [2] VI to exaggerate; (*pey*) to overdo it, overdo things; **creo que eso sería** I think that would be going a bit far.

exaltación NF (**a**) (*ensalzamiento*) exaltation. (**b**) (*sobreexcitación*) overexcitement; elation; excitability, intenseness; hotheadedness; passion, impassioned nature. (**c**) (*Pol*) extremism.

exaltado [1] ADJ (**a**) (*elevado*) exalted.
(**b**) *estado, humor* over-excited, worked up; elated; *carácter* excitable, intense; (*fanático*) hot-headed; *discurso etc* impassioned.
(**c**) (*Pol*) extreme, far out.
[2] NM, **exaltada** NF (*fanático*) hothead; (*Pol*) extremist, far-out person; (*loco*) mad person, deranged person.

exaltante ADJ exciting; uplifting.

exaltar [1a] [1] VT (**a**) (*elevar*) to exalt; to elevate, raise (*a* to).
(**b**) (*fig: elogiar*) to extol, praise.
(**c**) (*emocionar*) *persona* to excite, carry away, work up; *emoción* to intensify; *imaginación* to fire.
[2] **exaltarse** VR (*persona*) to get excited, get worked up; to get carried away (*con* by); (*en discusión*) to get heated; (*emoción*) to run high, become very intense; **¡no te exaltes!** don't get so worked up!

exalumno, -a NM/F (*LAm: Univ*) graduate; former student; alumnus, alumna (*US*).

examen NM (*gen*) examination; exam; (*encuesta*) inquiry (*de* into); (*inspección*) inspection; **~ de acceso, ~ de admisión, ~ de ingreso** entrance examination; **~ de conductor** driving test; **~ de**

consecución achievement test; **~ eliminatorio** qualifying examination; **~ de fin de curso** final examination, finals; **~ ocular** visual inspection; **~ oral** oral examination; **~ de suficiencia** proficiency test; **~ tipo test** multiple-choice test; **presentarse a un ~** to enter (*o* go in for, sit) an examination.

examinado, -a NM/F examinee, candidate.

examinador(a) NM/F examiner.

examinando, -a NM/F examinee, candidate.

▼ **examinar** [1a] [1] VT (*gen*) (*t Med, Escol, Univ etc*) to examine; (*poner a prueba*) to test; (*inspeccionar*) to inspect, look through, go over; (*indagar*) to inquire into, investigate, look into; *problema* to examine, consider.
[2] **examinarse** VR to take an examination, be examined (*en* in; *de* for the degree of); **~ de doctor** to take one's doctoral examination.

exangüe ADJ bloodless; anaemic; (*fig*) weak.

exánime ADJ lifeless; (*fig*) weak, exhausted, lifeless; **caer ~** to fall in a faint.

exasperación NF exasperation.

exasperador ADJ, **exasperante** ADJ exasperating, infuriating.

exasperar [1a] [1] VT to exasperate, infuriate.
[2] **exasperarse** VR to get exasperated, lose patience.

Exc.ª ABR *de* **Excelencia** Excellency.

excarcelación NF release (from prison).

excarcelado, -a NM/F ex-prisoner, former prisoner.

excarcelar [1a] VT to release (from prison).

excavación NF excavation.

excavador(a)¹ NM/F (*persona*) excavator, digger.

excavadora² NF (*Mec*) digger, power shovel.

excavar [1a] VT to excavate, dig (out); to hollow out.

excedencia NF leave of absence, leave without pay; **~ por maternidad** maternity leave; **~ primada** voluntary severance; **~ voluntaria** voluntary retirement; **pedir la ~** to ask for leave of absence.

excedentario ADJ surplus.

excedente [1] ADJ excess, surplus; excessive; *trabajador* redundant.
[2] NM excess, surplus; **~ empresarial** profit margin; **~ laboral** surplus (of) labour, overmanning.
[3] NMF person on leave of absence; **~ forzoso** person on compulsory leave of absence.

exceder [2a] [1] VT (*superar*) to exceed, surpass; (*sobrepasar*) to pass, outdo, excel; (*en importancia etc*) to transcend.
[2] VI: **~ de** to exceed, surpass.
[3] **excederse** VR (**a**) (*gen*) to excel o.s.
(**b**) (*pey*) to overreach o.s.; to go too far, go to extremes; **~ en sus funciones** to exceed one's duty.
(**c**) **~ de** to exceed, surpass; **no ~ de lo corriente** to be no more than average.

excelencia NF (**a**) excellence; superiority, superior quality; **por ~** par excellence. (**b**) **su E~** his Excellency; **sí, E~** yes, your Excellency.

excelente ADJ excellent; superior.

excelentemente ADV excellently.

excelso ADJ lofty, exalted, sublime.

excentricidad NF eccentricity.

excéntrico, -a ADJ, NM/F eccentric.

excepción NF exception; **~ de la regla** exception to the rule; **la ~ confirma la regla** the exception proves the rule; **un libro de ~** an exceptional book; **a ~ de, ~ hecha de** with the exception of, except for; **hacer una ~** to make an exception; *V* **estado.**

excepcional ADJ exceptional.

excepcionalidad NF exceptional nature.

excepcionalmente ADV exceptionally; as an exception.

excepto PREP except (for), excepting.

exceptuar [1e] VT to except, exclude, leave out of account; (*Jur etc*) to exempt.

excesivamente ADV excessively; unreasonably, unduly.

excesivo ADJ (*gen*) excessive; (*indebido*) unreasonable, undue; over-, *p.ej.* **con generosidad excesiva** over-generously, with excessive generosity.

exceso NM (**a**) (*gen*) excess; (*de comida*) surfeit; (*Com, Fin*) surplus; **~ de equipaje** excess luggage, excess baggage (*US*); **~ de mano de obra, ~ de plantillas** overmanning, overstaffing; **~ de peso** excess weight; **debido al ~ de peso** because of the extra weight; **me detuvieron por ~ de velocidad** they arrested me for speeding, they booked me for exceeding the speed limit; **en ~, por ~** excessively, to excess; **cuidadoso en ~** excessively careful, too careful; **una cantidad en ~ de X toneladas** a quantity in excess of (*o* over) X tons; **generoso hasta el ~** generous to a fault; **beber en ~** to drink to excess; **llevar algo al ~** to carry sth to excess, overdo sth.
(**b**) (*fig*) excess; **los ~s de la revolución** the excesses of the revolution.

excipiente NM (*Farm*) excipient.

excisión NF (*Med*) excision.

➤ LENGUA Y USO: **exactamente** → 38.1   **exagerar: 2** → 53.1   **examinar: 1** → 53.1, 53.2, 53.4

excitabilidad NF excitability.

excitable ADJ excitable; highly-strung, high-strung (*US*), nervy; temperamental.

excitación NF (**a**) (*acto*) exciting, inciting; (*estado*) excitement. (**b**) (*Elec*) excitation.

excitante [1] ADJ (**a**) (*emocionante*) exciting. (**b**) (*Med*) stimulating. [2] NM stimulant.

excitar [1a] [1] VT (**a**) (*gen*) to excite; *emoción* to excite, arouse, stir up; *duda, esperanza* to raise.
(**b**) (*incitar*) to incite, urge on; **~ al pueblo a la rebelión** to incite the populace to rebellion; **~ a uno a hacer algo** to urge sb to do sth.
(**c**) (*Elec*) to excite, energize.
[2] **excitarse** VR to get excited, get worked up.

exclamación NF exclamation; cry.

exclamar [1a] [1] VT to exclaim; to cry out.
[2] **exclamarse** VR to complain (*contra* about), protest (*contra* against).

exclamativo ADJ (**a**) exclamatory. (**b**) *ropa* loud.

exclamatorio ADJ exclamatory.

exclaustración NF (*Ecl*) secularization; expulsion (*of monks or nuns*).

exclaustrada NF secularized nun; expelled nun; ex-nun.

exclaustrado (*Ecl*) [1] ADJ secularized; expelled (from the order).
[2] NM secularized monk; expelled monk; ex-monk.

➤ **excluir** [3g] VT to exclude (*from de*); to shut out; *solución* to reject; *posibilidad etc* to exclude, rule out, preclude.

exclusión NF exclusion; **con ~ de** excluding, to the exclusion of.

exclusiva NF (**a**) (*Com*) sole right, sole agency; **tener la ~ de un producto** to have the sole right to sell a product, be the sole agents for a product.
(**b**) (*Periodismo*) exclusive interview (*o story etc*); exclusive news release; (*pisotón*) scoop.
(**c**) (*negativa*) rejection (*for a post etc*).
(**d**) **trabajar en ~ para** to work exclusively for.

exclusivamente ADV exclusively.

exclusive ADV exclusively; exclusive of, not counting; **hasta el primero de enero ~** till the first of January exclusive.

exclusividad NF (**a**) (*cualidad*) exclusiveness; clannishness; snobbery.
(**b**) (*Com*) = **exclusiva** (**a**).

exclusivista ADJ *club etc* exclusive, select; *grupo* clannish; *actitud* snobbish.

exclusivo ADJ exclusive; sole; (*horas de trabajo*) full-time.

excluyente ADJ (*LAm*) *clase, club etc* exclusive.

excluyentemente ADV exclusively.

Excma., Excmo. ABR *de* **Excelentísima, Excelentísimo** (*courtesy title*).

excombatiente NM exserviceman, veteran (*US*).

excomulgado [1] ADJ (**a**) (*Ecl*) excommunicated. (**b**) (*: maldito*) blessed*, cursed.
[2] NM, **excomulgada** NF excommunicated person.

excomulgar [1h] VT (**a**) (*Ecl*) to excommunicate. (**b**) (*fig*) to ban, banish; (*: maldecir*) to curse.

excomunión NF excommunication.

excoriación NF graze; chafing.

excoriar [1b] [1] VT (*despellejar*) to skin, flay; (*raspar*) to graze, take the skin off; (*rozar*) to chafe.
[2] **excoriarse** VR to graze o.s., skin o.s.

excrecencia NF excrescence.

excreción NF excretion.

excremento NM excrement, excreta.

excretar [1a] VT to excrete.

exculpación NF exoneration; (*Jur*) acquittal.

exculpar [1a] [1] VT to exonerate, exculpate; (*Jur*) to acquit (*de* of).
[2] **exculparse** VR to exonerate o.s.

exculpatorio ADJ: **declaración exculpatoria** statement of innocence.

excursión NF excursion, outing, trip; (*Mil*) raid, incursion; **~ campestre** picnic; **~ de caza** hunting trip; **~ a pie** walk, hike, ramble; **ir de ~** to go (off) on a trip, go on an outing.

excursionar [1a] VI to go on a trip, have an outing.

excursionismo NM going on trips; sightseeing; walking, hiking, rambling.

excursionista NMF (*turista*) tourist; sightseer; (*en excursión de un solo día*) day-tripper; (*por campo, montaña*) hiker, rambler.

excurso NM, **excursus** NM INVAR excursus.

➤ **excusa** NF excuse; apology; **buscar ~** to look for an excuse; **presentar sus ~s** to make one's excuses, excuse o.s.; **presentar ~s de su país** to make excuses for one's country.

excusabaraja NF hamper, basket with a lid.

excusable ADJ excusable, pardonable.

excusado [1] ADJ (**a**) (*inútil*) unnecessary, superfluous; **~ es decir que ...** needless to say ..., I (*etc*) need scarcely say that ...; **pensar en lo ~** to think of something which is quite out of the question.
(**b**) **estar ~ de** to be exempt from.
(**c**) (*privado*) reserved, private; *entrada* concealed.
[2] NM lavatory, toilet.

excusar [1a] [1] VT (**a**) (*disculpar*) to excuse; **~ a A con B** to tell B that A begs to be excused, to present A's apologies to B.
(**b**) (*eximir*) to exempt (*de* from).
(**c**) (*evitar*) to avoid, prevent; **así excusamos disgustos** this way we avoid difficulties; **podemos ~ lo otro** we can forget about the rest of it, we don't have to bother with the rest.
(**d**) **~ + *infin*** not to have to + *infin*; to save the trouble of + *ger*; **excusamos decirle que ...** we don't have to tell you that ...; **por eso excuso escribirte más largo** so I can save myself the trouble of writing at greater length.
[2] **excusarse** VR to excuse o.s.; to apologize (*de* for); **~ de + *infin*** to decline to + *infin*; to apologize for not being able to + *infin*; **~ de haber hecho algo** to apologize for having done sth.

execrable ADJ execrable.

execración NF execration.

execrar [1a] VT to execrate, loathe, abominate.

exégesis NF exegesis.

exención NF exemption (*de* from); immunity, freedom (*de* from); **~ contributiva, ~ de impuestos** tax exemption, tax allowance.

exencionar [1a] VT = **exentar**.

exentar [1a] VT to exempt (*de* from); to excuse (*de* from).

exento ADJ (**a**) (*libre*) exempt (*de* from); free (*de* from, of); **~ de alquileres** rent-free; **~ de derechos** duty-free; **~ de impuestos** tax-free, tax-exempt (*US*), free of tax; **un libro ~ de interés** a book devoid of interest; **estar ~ de cuidados** to be free of worries; **una expedición no exenta de peligros** an expedition not without (its) dangers.
(**b**) *lugar etc* unobstructed, open.
(**c**) (*Arquit*) free-standing.

exequias NFPL funeral rites, obsequies.

exfoliación NF exfoliation.

exfoliador NM (*Cono Sur*) tear-off pad, loose-leaf notebook.

exfoliante NM exfoliant.

exfoliar [1b] VT to exfoliate.

exhalación NF (**a**) (*acto*) exhalation; (*vapor*) fumes, vapour. (**b**) (*Astron*) shooting star; **como una ~** at top speed, like lightning.

exhalar [1a] [1] VT *aire etc* to exhale, breathe out; *gas etc* to emit, give off, give out; *suspiro* to breathe, heave; *gemido* to utter.
[2] **exhalarse** VR (*jadear*) to breathe hard; (*darse prisa*) to hurry, run.

exhaustivamente ADV exhaustively; thoroughly; comprehensively.

exhaustividad NF exhaustiveness; thoroughness.

exhaustivo ADJ exhaustive; thorough; comprehensive.

exhausto ADJ exhausted.

exheredar [1a] VT to disinherit.

exhibición NF exhibition, display, show; (*Cine*) showing; **~ aérea** flying display; **~ de escaparate** window display; **~ folklórica** folk festival, display of folk-dancing (*etc*); **la pobre ~ del equipo** the team's poor showing; **una impresionante ~ de fuerza** an impressive show of strength.

exhibicionismo NM (**a**) exhibitionism. (**b**) (*sexual*) indecent exposure, flashing*.

exhibicionista [1] ADJ exhibitionist.
[2] NMF (**a**) exhibitionist. (**b**) (*sexual*: *m*) flasher:.

exhibidor NM display case.

exhibir [3a] [1] VT (**a**) to exhibit, display, show; *pasaporte* to show; *película* to show, screen; (*mostrar con orgullo*) to show off. (**b**) (*Méx*) to pay in cash.
[2] **exhibirse** VR (**a**) to show o.s. (**b**) (*sexualmente*) to expose o.s., flash*.

exhortación NF exhortation.

exhortar [1a] VT to exhort (*a* + *infin* to + *infin*).

exhumación NF exhumation, disinterment.

exhumar [1a] VT to exhume, disinter.

exigencia NF (**a**) (*requerimiento*) demand, requirement; exigency; **según las ~s de la situación** as the situation requires; **tener muchas ~s** to be very demanding.
(**b**) (*Carib*: *petición*) request.
(**c**) (*CAm*: *escasez*) need, lack.

exigente ADJ demanding, exacting, exigent; particular; *profesor* strict; **ser ~ con uno** to be hard on sb; **es muy ~ en la limpieza** she is very particular about cleanliness.

exigir [3c] VT (**a**) *contribución etc* to exact, levy (*a* from).
(**b**) (*requerir*) to demand, require (*a* of, from); to call for, ask for (*a* from); to insist on; **~ el pago** to demand payment; **esto exige mucho cuidado** this needs a lot of care; **exigirá mucho dinero** it will require (*o* need, take) a lot of money; **ello no exige comentario** it does not call for any comment, comment on it would be superfluous; **exija recibo** insist on getting a receipt; **exige mucho** he's very demanding.
(**c**) (*Carib*) *cosa* to ask for, request; *persona* to beg, plead with, entreat.

➤ LENGUA Y USO: **excluir** → 53.4 **excusa** → 45.2

exiguo ADJ meagre, small, scanty, exiguous.
exilado [1] ADJ exiled, in exile.
[2] NM, **exilada** NF exile.
exilar [1a] [1] VT to exile.
[2] **exilarse** VR to go into exile; to exile o.s.
exiliado = **exilado**.
exiliar VT = **exilar**.
exilio NM exile; **estar en el ~, vivir en el ~** to be in exile; **gobierno en el ~** government in exile.
eximente NM excuse; justification; reason for being exempt.
eximio ADJ *persona* distinguished, eminent.
eximir [3a] [1] VT to exempt (*de* from); to free, excuse (*de* from); **esto me exime de toda obligación con él** this frees me from any obligation to him.
[2] **eximirse** VR: **~ de** + *infin* to excuse o.s. from + *ger*; to free o.s. from having to + *infin*.
existencia NF **(a)** (*vida*) existence; being; life; **lucha por la ~** struggle for survival; **amargar la ~ a uno** to make sb's life a misery; **quitarse la ~** (*euf*) to do away with o.s., commit suicide.
(b) (*t ~s: Com*) stock; goods; **nuestras ~s de carbón** our coal stocks, our stock(s) of coal; **estar en ~** to be in stock; **liquidar ~s** to clear stock; **tener en ~** to have in stock.
existencial ADJ existential.
existencialismo NM existentialism.
existencialista ADJ, NMF existentialist.
existencialmente ADV existentially.
existente ADJ **(a)** existing; in being, in existence; actual; *texto etc* extant; surviving; **la situación ~** the existing (*o* present) situation. **(b)** (*Com*) in stock.
existir [3a] VI to exist, be; **dejar de ~** to pass out of existence, come to an end; (*morir: euf*) to pass away; **esta sociedad existe desde hace 90 años** the company has been in existence for 90 years, the company was founded 90 years ago; **no existe tal cosa** there's no such thing.
exitazo NM great success; (*Mús, Teat etc*) smash hit.
éxito NM **(a)** (*resultado*) result, outcome; **buen ~** happy outcome, success; **con buen ~** successfully; **tener buen ~** to succeed, be successful; **tener mal ~** to have an unfortunate outcome, fail, be unsuccessful.
(b) (*logro*) success; **con ~** successfully; **tener ~ en** to be successful in; to make a success of; **el hombre de ~** the successful man; **es una chica de mucho ~** she's a girl who has lots of success (with the men).
(c) (*Mús, Teat, t fig*) success, hit; **~ editorial, ~ de librería** best-seller; **~ de taquilla** box-office success, successful play; **~ de venta(s)** best-seller; **~ clamoroso, ~ fulminante, ~ rotundo** huge success, overwhelming success; (*Mús etc*) hit song, smash hit; **los mejores ~s de ...** the greatest hits of ...
exitosamente ADV successfully.
exitoso ADJ successful.
éxodo NM exodus; **el ~ rural** the depopulation of the countryside, the drift from the land.
ex oficio ADJ, ADV ex officio.
exoneración NF **(a)** exoneration; freeing, relief. **(b)** dismissal.
exonerar [1a] VT **(a)** (*de culpa etc*) to exonerate; to exempt (*de un impuesto* from a tax); **~ a uno de un deber** to free sb from a duty, relieve sb of a duty; **le exoneraron de sus condecoraciones** they stripped him of his decorations.
(b) *empleado* to dismiss.
(c) **~ el vientre** to have a movement of the bowels.
exorbitancia NF exorbitance.
exorbitante ADJ exorbitant.
exorcismo NM exorcism.
exorcista [1] ADJ: **prácticas ~s** rites designed to secure exorcism.
[2] NMF exorcist.
exorcizar [1f] VT to exorcise.
exordio NM exordium; preface, preamble, introduction.
exornar [1a] VT to adorn, embellish (*de* with).
exosto NM (*LAm Aut*) exhaust.
exótica* NF (*Méx*) stripper*, striptease artist.
exótico ADJ exotic.
exotismo NM exoticism; taste for the exotic.
expandible ADJ expansible.
expandir [3a] [1] VT (*gen*) to expand; *ropa* to spread out; (*Com etc*) to expand, enlarge; (*fig*) to expand, extend, spread; *noticia* to spread; **~ el mercado de un producto** to expand the market for a product; **~ la afición a la lectura** to spread a love of reading; **en caracteres expandidos** (*Tip, Inform*) double width.
[2] **expandirse** VR to expand; to extend, spread.
expansible ADJ expansible; that can be expanded (*o* extended *etc*).
expansión NF **(a)** (*gen*) expansion; enlargement; extension; spread(ing); **la ~ económica** economic growth; **la ~ industrial** industrial expansion.
(b) (*fig: relajación*) relaxation; pleasure.
(c) (*fig: efusión*) expansiveness.
expansionar [1a] [1] VT *mercado etc* to expand.
[2] **expansionarse** VR **(a)** to expand.
(b) (*fig: relajarse*) to relax.
(c) (*fig: desahogarse*) to unbosom o.s., open one's heart (*con* to).
expansionismo NM (*Pol etc*) expansionism.
expansionista ADJ (*Pol etc*) expansionist.
expansividad NF expansiveness.
expansivo ADJ **(a)** (*gen*) expansive. **(b)** (*fig*) expansive, affable; communicative.
expatriación NF expatriation; exile.
expatriado, -a NM/F expatriate; exile.
expatriarse [1b *o* 1c] VR to emigrate, leave one's country; (*Pol etc*) to go into exile.
expectación NF (*esperanza*) expectation, expectancy, anticipation; (*ansia*) eagerness; (*ilusión*) excitement; **la ~ crece de un momento a otro** the excitement is growing every moment.
expectante ADJ expectant; eager; excited.
expectativa NF expectation; hope, prospect; **~ de vida** life expectancy; **estar a la ~** to wait and see (what will happen); **estar a la ~ de algo** to look out for sth, be on the watch for sth.
expectorar [1a] VTI to expectorate.
expedición NF **(a)** (*t Geog, Mil etc*) expedition; (*Dep*) away fixture; **~ de salvamento** rescue expedition; **~ militar** military expedition.
(b) (*Com etc*) shipment, shipping; **gastos de ~** shipping charges.
(c) (*prontitud*) speed, dispatch.
expedicionario ADJ expeditionary.
expedidor NM shipper, shipping agent.
expedientar [1a] VT (*investigar*) to make a file on, draw up a dossier on; (*censurar*) to censure, reprimand; (*expulsar*) to expel; *médico etc* to strike off the register; (*despedir*) to dismiss.
expediente NM **(a)** (*medio*) expedient; means; device, make-shift; **recurrir al ~ de** + *infin* to resort to the device of + *ger*.
(b) (*Jur*) action, proceedings; records of a case; **~ disciplinario** disciplinary proceedings; **~ judicial** legal proceedings; **~ de regulación de empleo** procedure for issuing notices of dismissal; **abrir ~, incoar ~** to start proceedings; **instruir un ~** to collect all the documents.
(c) (*historial*) record; (*dossier*) dossier; (*ficha*) file; **~ académico** student's record, pupil's record card, transcript (*US*); **~ personal** personal file; **~ policíaco** police dossier.
(d) (*despido*) dismissal.
(e) **cubrir el ~** to do just enough to keep out of trouble.
expedienteo NM bureaucracy, red tape.
expedir [3k] VT *mercancías etc* to send, ship off, forward; *documento* to draw up; to make out, issue; *orden, pasaporte, billete etc* to issue; *negocio* to deal with, dispatch.
expeditar [1a] VT (*LAm*) to expedite, hurry along; (*concluir*) to conclude.
expeditivo ADJ expeditious; prompt, efficient.
expedito ADJ **(a)** (*pronto*) expeditious, prompt, speedy. **(b)** *camino* clear, unobstructed, free; **dejar ~ el camino para** to clear the way for. **(c)** (*LAm: fácil*) easy.
expeler [2a] VT to expel, eject.
expendedor [1] NM, **expendedora** NF (*persona: al detalle*) dealer, retailer; (*agente*) agent; (*de tabaco*) tobacconist; (*Teat*) ticket agent; **~ de billetes** ticket clerk, booking clerk; **~ de moneda falsa** distributor of counterfeit money.
[2] NM ticket machine; **~ automático** vending machine; **~ automático de bebidas** drink vending machine.
expendeduría NF retail shop, (*esp*) tobacconist's (shop), cigar store (*US*).
expender [2a] VT **(a)** *dinero* to expend, spend.
(b) *moneda falsa* to utter; to pass, circulate.
(c) *mercancías* to sell (retail); to be an agent for, sell on commission; to deal in.
(d) (*Jur*) **~ de moneda falsa** issuing false coin, passing false coin.
expendio NM **(a)** (*gasto*) expense, outlay.
(b) (*LAm: tienda*) small shop; **~ de boletos** (*Méx*) ticket office.
(c) (*acto: And, Cono Sur, Méx*) retailing, retail selling.
(d) (*Jur*) **~ de moneda falsa** issuing false coin, passing false coin.
expensar [1a] VT (*LAm*) to defray the costs of.
expensas NFPL expenses; (*Jur*) costs; **a ~ de** at the expense of (*t fig*); at the mercy of, subject to; **a mis ~** at my expense.
▼ **experiencia** NF **(a)** experience; **~ laboral** work experience; **una triste ~** a sad experience; **aprender por la ~** to learn by experience; **intercambiar ~s** to swap stories; **saber algo por ~** to know sth from experience.
(b) (*experimento etc*) experiment (*en* on); **~ clínica** clinical trial; **~ piloto** pilot scheme.

► LENGUA Y USO: **experiencia: a → 46.2**

experienciar [1b] VT = **experimentar**.
experimentación NF experimentation.
experimentado ADJ experienced.
experimental ADJ experimental.
experimentalmente ADV experimentally.
experimentar [1a] ☐1 VT (a) (*Téc etc*) to test, try out; to experiment with; **el nuevo fármaco está siendo experimentado** the new drug is being tested, experiments with the new drug are going on; **están experimentando un nuevo helicóptero** they are testing a new helicopter.
(b) (*sufrir*) *cambio etc* to experience, undergo, go through; *deterioro, pérdida* to suffer; *aumento* to show; *emoción* to feel; **las cifras han experimentado un aumento de un 5 por 100** the figures show an increase of 5%; **no experimenté ninguna sensación nueva** I felt no new sensation.
☐2 VI to experiment (*con* with, *en* on).
experimento NM experiment (*con* with, *en* on); **como ~** as an experiment, by way of experiment; **hacer ~s** to experiment (*con* with, *en* on).
experticia NF (*LAm*) expertise.
expertización NF expert assessment.
expertizar [1f] VT to appraise as an expert, give an expert assessment of.
experto ☐1 ADJ expert; skilled, experienced; seasoned; knowledgeable.
☐2 NM, **experta** NF expert.
expiación NF expiation, atonement.
expiar [1c] VT to expiate, atone for.
expiatorio ADJ expiatory.
expiración NF expiration.
expirar [1a] VI to expire.
explanación NF (a) (*Téc*) levelling. (b) (*fig*) explanation, elucidation.
explanada NF (*plataforma*) raised area, terrace, platform; (*zona nivelada*) levelled area; (*paseo*) esplanade; (*Mil*) glacis; **~ de ensillado** saddling enclosure.
explanar [1a] VT (a) (*Ferro, Téc etc*) to level, grade. (b) (*fig*) to unfold; to explain, elucidate.
explayar [1a] ☐1 VT to extend, expand, enlarge.
☐2 **explayarse** VR (a) (*extender*) to extend, spread; to open out, unfold.
(b) (*fig: relajarse*) to relax, take it easy; to take an outing.
(c) (*fig: en discurso etc*) to speak at length; to spread o.s.; **~ a su gusto** to talk one's head off, talk to one's heart's content; **~ con uno** to unbosom o.s. to sb, confide in sb.
explicable ADJ explicable, explainable, that can be explained; **cosas no fácilmente ~s** things not easily explained, things not easy to explain.
explicación NF (a) explanation; reason (*de* for); **sin dar explicaciones** without giving any reason. (b) (*Univ etc*) lecture, class.
explicaderas NFPL: **tener buenas ~** to be good at explaining things (away); (*pey*) to be plausible.
explicar [1g] ☐1 VT (*gen*) to explain; *teoría etc* to expound; *curso* to lecture on, teach; *materia* to lecture in; *clase* to give, deliver.
☐2 **explicarse** VR (a) to explain (o.s.); **se explica con claridad** he states things clearly; **¡explíquese Vd!** explain yourself!; **explíquese con la mayor brevedad** please be as brief as possible; **se explica de acuerdo con las nuevas teorías** he follows the latest theories.
(b) **~ algo** to understand sth; **no me lo explico** I can't understand it, I can't make it out.
(c) (*ser explicable*) to be explained; **esto no se explica fácilmente** this cannot be explained (away) easily.
(d) (*: pagar*) to cough up*, pay.

┌───┐
│ **│ EXPLICAR │**   *ver también la entrada* │
│   │
│ • Cuando *explicar* lleva objeto directo e indirecto, el orden en in-   │
│   glés es normalmente *explain* + OBJETO DIRECTO + *to* + OBJETO INDIRECTO: │
│   ¿Puedes explicarme eso?   │
│   *Can you explain that to me?*   │
│   Ya se lo he explicado a mi familia   │
│   *I've already explained it to my family*   │
│   Os explicaré la situación   │
│   *I will explain the situation to you*   │
│ • Sin embargo, si el objeto directo es una construcción más com-   │
│   pleja, en inglés se sigue el mismo orden que en español, sin   │
│   olvidar el uso de la preposición *to*:   │
│   ¿Puedes explicarme por qué no viniste ni llamaste ayer?   │
│   *Can you explain to me why you didn't come or phone yesterday?*   │
│   *Para otros usos y ejemplos ver la entrada.*   │
└───┘

explicativo ADJ, **explicatorio** ADJ explanatory.
explícitamente ADV explicitly.
explicitar [1a] VT (*declarar*) to state, assert, make explicit; (*aclarar*) to

clarify; **~ que ...** to make clear that ...
explícito ADJ explicit.
exploración NF exploration; (*Mil*) reconnaissance, scouting; (*Radar etc*) scanning; **~ física** (*Med*) physical examination; **~ submarina** underwater exploration; (*como deporte*) skin-diving.
explorador NM (a) (*Geog etc*) explorer; pioneer; (*Mil*) scout; (*niño*) **~** (boy) scout. (b) (*Med*) probe; (*Radar etc*) scanner; **~ láser** laser scanner.
exploradora NF girl guide, girl scout (*US*).
explorar [1a] ☐1 VT (*Geog etc*) to explore; to pioneer, open up; (*Med*) to probe; (*Radar etc*) to scan.
☐2 VI to explore; (*Mil*) to scout, reconnoitre.
exploratorio ADJ exploratory.
explosión NF (a) explosion; blast; **~ controlada** controlled explosion; **~ por simpatía** secondary explosion; **motor de ~** internal combustion engine; **teoría de la gran ~** big bang theory; **hacer ~** to explode.
(b) (*fig*) explosion, outburst; **una ~ de cólera** an explosion of anger; **~ demográfica** population explosion.
explosionar [1a] VTI to explode, blow up.
explosiva NF (*Ling*) plosive (consonant).
explosivo ☐1 ADJ (a) (*gen, t fig*) explosive. (b) (*Ling*) plosive.
☐2 NM explosive; **alto ~, ~ detonante, ~ de gran potencia** high explosive; **~ plástico** plastic explosive; **~ de ruido** stun grenade.
explotable ADJ exploitable, that can be exploited.
explotación NF exploitation; running, operation; (*Min etc*) working; **~ agrícola** farm; **~ a cielo abierto** opencast working, opencast mining; **~ forestal** forestry; **en ~** in operation; **gastos de ~** operating costs, operating expenses.
explotador ☐1 ADJ exploitative.
☐2 NM, **explotadora** NF exploiter.
explotar [1a] ☐1 VT (a) (*gen*) to exploit; *fábrica etc* to run, operate; *mina, veta* to work; *recursos* to exploit, tap; to harness.
(b) (*pey*) *obreros* to exploit; *situación* to exploit, make capital out of.
(c) (*Mil etc*) to explode.
☐2 VI (*Mil etc*) to explode; to go off; **explotaron 2 bombas** 2 bombs exploded; **cayó sin ~** it fell but did not go off, it landed without going off.
expoliación NF pillaging, sacking.
expoliar [1b] VT (a) to pillage, sack. (b) (*desposeer*) to dispossess.
expolio NM (a) pillaging, sacking. (b) **armar un ~** to cause a hullaballoo*.
exponencial ADJ exponential.
exponente ☐1 NMF (*persona*) exponent.
☐2 NM (a) (*Mat*) index, exponent.
(b) (*LAm: ejemplo*) model, (prime) example; **el tabaco cubano es ~ de calidad** Cuban tobacco is the best of its kind.
exponer [2q] ☐1 VT (a) (*gen, Ecl, Fot*) to expose; *cuadro etc* to show, exhibit, put on show; *cartel* to display, put up.
(b) *vida* to risk.
(c) *niño* to abandon.
(d) *argumento* to expound; *idea* to explain, unfold; *hechos* to set out, set forth, state; (*Jur*) *acusación* to bring.
☐2 VI (*pintor*) to exhibit, hold an exhibition.
☐3 **exponerse** VR: **~ a** to expose o.s. to, lay o.s. open to; **~ a + *infin*** to run the risk of + *ger*.
exportable ADJ exportable.
exportación NF (a) (*acto*) export, exportation; **~ en pie** live export.
(b) (*artículo*) export, exported article; (*mercancías*) exports; **géneros de ~** exports, exported goods; **comercio de ~** export trade.
exportador(a) NM/F exporter; shipper.
exportar [1a] VT to export.
exposición NF (a) (*acto*) exposing, exposure; display; (*Fot*) exposure; (*de cuadro etc*) showing.
(b) (*de hechos etc*) statement, exposition; (*petición*) petition, claim; **~ de motivos** (*Jur*) explanatory preamble.
(c) (*Arte etc*) show, exhibition; (*Com*) show, fair; **~ canina** dog show; **~ itinerante** travelling show; **~ de modas** fashion show; **~ universal** world fair.
exposímetro NM (*Fot*) exposure meter.
expósito ☐1 ADJ: **niño ~** = **2**.
☐2 NM, **expósita** NF foundling.
expositor(a) ☐1 NM/F (*persona*: *Arte etc*) exhibitor; (*de teoría*) exponent.
☐2 NM (*vitrina*) showcase, display case; (*puesto*) sales stand.
exprés NM (a) (*LAm*) express train. (b) (*Méx*) black coffee.
expresado ADJ above-mentioned; **según las cifras expresadas** according to these figures, according to the figures I (*etc*) have already quoted, according to the figures given earlier.
expresamente ADV expressly; on purpose, deliberately; clearly, plainly; **no lo dijo ~** he didn't say so in so many words.
expresar [1a] ☐1 VT (*gen*) to express; to voice; (*redactar*) to word,

phrase, put; (*declarar*) to state, set forth; (*citar*) to quote; **expresa las opiniones de todos** he is voicing the opinions of us all; **estaba expresado de otro modo** it was worded differently; **el papel no lo expresa** the paper doesn't say so; **Vd deberá ~ el número del giro postal** you should quote (*o* give, state) the number of the postal order.

2 **expresarse** VR (a) (*persona*) to express o.s.; **no se expresa bien** he doesn't express himself well.

(b) (*cifra, dato*) to be stated; **el número no se expresa** the number is not given, the number is not stated; **como abajo se expresa** as is stated below.

expresión NF (a) (*acto*) expression; **~ corporal** self-expression through movement; **esta ~ de nuestro agradecimiento** this expression of our gratitude.

(b) (*Ling*) expression; **~ familiar** colloquialism, conversational expression; **la ~ es poco clara** the expression is not very clear.

(c) **expresiones** (††) greetings, regards.

expresionismo NM expressionism.

expresionista ADJ, NMF expressionist.

expresivamente ADV (a) (*gen*) expressively. (b) (*cariñosamente*) tenderly, affectionately, warmly.

expresividad NF expressiveness.

expresivo ADJ (a) (*gen*) expressive. (b) (*afectuoso*) tender, affectionate, warm.

expreso 1 ADJ (a) (*explícito*) express; (*exacto*) specific, clear, exact.

(b) *tren etc* fast; **carta (por) ~** special delivery letter.

2 NM (a) (*persona*) special messenger; **mandar algo por ~** to send sth by express (delivery).

(b) (*Ferro etc*) fast train.

(c) (*Carib: autobús*) long-distance coach.

exprimelimones NM INVAR lemon-squeezer.

exprimidera NF squeezer.

exprimidor NM squeezer; **~ de limones** lemon-squeezer.

exprimir [3a] VT (a) *fruta etc* to squeeze; *zumo* to squeeze out, press out, express; *ropa* to wring out, squeeze dry; *limón etc* to squeeze.

(b) **~ a uno** to exploit sb.

ex profeso ADV on purpose.

expropiación NF expropriation; commandeering; **~ forzosa** compulsory purchase; **orden de ~** compulsory purchase order.

expropiar [1b] VT to expropriate; to commandeer.

expuesto 1 PTP *de* exponer; **según lo arriba ~** according to what has been stated (*o* set out, said) above.

2 ADJ (a) *sitio etc* exposed; dangerous.

(b) *cuadro etc* on show, on display, on view; **los artículos ~s en el escaparate** the goods displayed in the window.

(c) **estar ~ a** to be exposed to, be open to; to be liable to.

expugnar [1a] VT to take by storm.

expulsar [1a] VT to expel (*de* from), eject (*de* from), turn out (*de* of); *jugador* to send off; **~ a uno a puntapiés** to kick sb out.

expulsión NF expulsion, ejection; (*Dep*) sending-off; (*Econ*) crowding out effect.

expulsor 1 ADJ: **asiento ~** (*Aer*) ejector seat.

2 NM (*Téc*) ejector.

expurgar [1h] VT to expurgate.

expurgatorio ADJ expurgatory; **índice ~** (*Ecl*) Index.

exquisitamente ADV (*V* ADJ) (a) exquisitely; deliciously, delightfully; excellently. (b) (*pey*) affectedly.

exquisitez NF (a) exquisiteness; excellence. (b) (*pey*) affectation.

exquisito ADJ (a) (*excelente*) exquisite; delicious, delightful; excellent. (b) *persona* (*afectado*) affected; (*melindroso*) choosy*, finicky.

Ext. (a) ABR *de* **Exterior** external, ext. (b) ABR *de* **Extensión** extension, ext.

extasiado ADJ in ecstasies, in raptures; **quedarse ~ ante/con** to be mesmerized by.

extasiar [1c] 1 VT to entrance, enrapture, captivate.

2 **extasiarse** VR to become entranced; to go into ecstasies, rhapsodize (*ante* over, about).

éxtasis NM INVAR (a) ecstasy; rapture; (*de médium etc*) trance; **estar en el ~** to be in ecstasy. (b) (*: droga*) ecstasy*, E*.

extático ADJ ecstatic, rapturous; **lo miró ~** he looked at it ecstatically.

extemporal ADJ, **extemporáneo** ADJ *lluvia etc* unseasonable; *viaje* untimely.

extender [2g] 1 VT (a) (*gen*) to extend; (*ampliar*) to enlarge, make bigger; to prolong; to stretch (out), expand; *mapa, tela etc* to spread (out), open (out); to lay out; *cartas* to lay down; *crema de belleza, mantequilla* to spread; *pila* to spread out; *guerra* to extend, widen, escalate; *conocimiento* to extend, spread (*a* to); *brazo, mano* to stretch out.

(b) *documento* to draw up; to write out; *cheque* to draw, make out; *recibo* to make out; *certificado* to issue.

2 **extenderse** VR (a) (*en el espacio*) to extend; to stretch (out); to spread (out); to be, lie; **delante de nosotros se extendía la mar** be-

fore us the sea stretched away, the sea lay spread out before us; **sus terrenos se extienden sobre muchos kilómetros** his lands spread over many miles; **no se extiende más al oeste** it does not go any further west.

(b) (*espacio: fig*) to range, extend; **las posibilidades se extienden de A a Z** the possibilities range from A to Z.

(c) (*en el tiempo*) to extend, last (*a* to, till; *de* from).

(d) (*fig: conocimiento, costumbre*) to spread, extend; (*guerra*) to escalate, widen, broaden; **su venganza se extendió hasta matar a las mujeres** in his vengeance he even killed the women; **la epidemia se extendió rápidamente** the epidemic spread rapidly.

(e) (*cantidad*) **~ a** to amount to, reach, go as high as; (*tamaño*) to run to; **el libro se extiende a 400 páginas** the book runs to 400 pages.

(f) (*fig: en discurso*) to spread o.s.; **~ sobre un tema** to enlarge on a subject.

extendido ADJ (a) *tela etc* spread out, open; extended; *brazos* outstretched, spread wide.

(b) *costumbre etc* widespread; prevalent, (*pey*) rife, rampant; *conocimiento* widespread.

extensamente ADV (a) *viajar, leer* extensively, widely. (b) *tratar* fully, in full, with full details.

extensible ADJ extending, extensible, extendable; **un período ~ a 3 meses** a period which can be extended to three months.

extensión NF (a) (*acto*) extension; stretching; spreading; **~ de plazo** (*Com*) extension; **por ~** by extension.

(b) (*dimensiones*) extent, size; spaciousness; **un solar de mayor ~** a site of greater size, a site of larger area.

(c) (*de mar, tierra*) expanse, stretch; **por toda la ~ del paisaje** over the whole (expanse) of the countryside.

(d) (*de tiempo*) length, duration; span.

(e) (*Mús*) range, compass.

(f) (*fig: de conocimientos etc*) extent, range; (*de sentidos*) range; (*de plan, programa*) scope.

(g) (*Telec*) extension.

(h) **~ de cable** (*Elec*) extension lead.

(i) **E~ Agraria** agricultural advisory service; **E~ Universitaria** extramural studies.

extensivo ADJ extensive; **hacer ~ a** to extend to, apply to, make applicable to; **la crítica se hizo extensiva a toda la ciudad** the criticism applied to the whole city.

extenso ADJ (a) (*grande*) extensive; vast; *cuarto etc* big, broad, spacious; *imperio* far-flung.

(b) *conocimiento etc* widespread; *informe, narración* full; **en ~, por ~** in full, with full particulars, at length.

extensor NM chest expander.

extenuación NF emaciation, weakness; exhaustion.

extenuado ADJ emaciated, wasted, weak; exhausted.

extenuar [1e] 1 VT to emaciate, weaken; to exhaust.

2 **extenuarse** VR to become emaciated, waste away; to get weak.

exterior 1 ADJ (a) (*gen*) exterior, external; outer; *aspecto* outward; *cuarto* outside, outward-facing.

(b) *deuda, relaciones* foreign; **asuntos ~es** foreign affairs; **comercio ~** foreign trade, overseas trade.

2 NM (a) (*parte, de casa etc*) exterior, outside; (*aspecto*) outward appearance; **al ~, por el ~** on the outside; outwardly; (*carreras*) **avanzar por el ~** to come up on the outside; **de ~ poco agradable** of unprepossessing appearance; **con el ~ pintado de azul** with the outside painted blue; **rodar en ~es** to film on location.

(b) (*países extranjeros*) foreign parts; **así aquí como en el ~** both here and abroad; **noticias del ~** foreign news, overseas news, news from abroad; **comercio con el ~** foreign trade, overseas trade.

(c) (*Dep*) wing, wing-forward, winger; **~ derecho** outside-right; **~ izquierdo** outside-left.

(d) **E~es** (*Pol*) (Ministry of) Foreign Affairs.

exterioridad NF (a) (*apariencia*) outward appearance, externals. (b) **~es** (*fig*) pomp, show; formalities.

exteriorización NF externalization, exteriorization.

exteriorizar [1f] VT (*expresar*) to express outwardly; (*mostrar*) to show, reveal.

exteriormente ADV outwardly.

exterminación NF extermination.

exterminar [1a] VT to exterminate.

exterminio NM extermination.

externamente ADV externally; outwardly.

externo 1 ADJ external, outside; outward.

2 NM, **externa** NF day pupil.

extinción NF extinction.

extinguido ADJ (a) **estar ~** (*incendio*) to be out, be extinguished. (b) *animal, volcán* extinct.

extinguir [3d] 1 VT (a) *incendio etc* to extinguish, put out; *sublevación* to put down.

(**b**) (*Bio*) to exterminate, wipe out.
(**c**) *deuda etc* to wipe out.
(**d**) ~ **una sentencia** (*Jur*) to serve a sentence.
[2] **extinguirse** VR (**a**) (*fuego*) to go out.
(**b**) (*Bio*) to die out, become extinct.
extinto ADJ (**a**) extinct. (**b**) (*Cono Sur, Méx: euf*) dead, deceased.
extintor NM (*t* ~ **de incendios**) fire extinguisher; ~ **de espuma** foam extinguisher.
extirpación NF (**a**) extirpation, eradication. (**b**) (*Med*) removal.
extirpar [1a] VT (**a**) to extirpate, eradicate, root out.
(**b**) (*Med*) to remove (surgically), take out.
extorno NM (*Com*) rebate.
extorsión NF (**a**) (*Fin etc*) extortion, exaction; (*chantaje*) blackmail. (**b**) (*molestia*) inconvenience.
extorsionador(a) NM/F extortioner; (*chantajista*) blackmailer.
extorsionar [1a] VT (**a**) (*usurpar*) to extort, extract (*de* from). (**b**) (*fig*) to pester, bother.
extorsionista NMF (*Méx*) extortionist, blackmailer.
extra¹ [1] ADJ INVAR extra; **vino** ~ high-quality wine; **gasolina** ~ high-octane petrol; ~ **de** in addition to, on top of.
[2] NM (**a**) (*de menú, cuenta*) extra; (*de pago*) bonus. (**b**) (*Tip*) extra, special edition, special supplement.
[3] NMF (*Cine*) extra.
extra²... PREF extra...
extraacadémico ADJ non-university (*atr*), (taking place) outside the university.
extracción NF extraction; (*de lotería*) draw.
extracomunitario ADJ: **países** ~**s** countries outside the European Community.
extraconstitucional ADJ unconstitutional.
extraconyugal ADJ extramarital, adulterous.
extracorto ADJ *onda* ultra-short.
extractar [1a] VT (**a**) to make extracts from. (**b**) (*resumir*) to abridge, summarize.
extracto NM (**a**) (*Quím etc*) extract. (**b**) (*Liter*) abstract, summary. (**c**) ~ **de cuenta** (*Fin*) statement (of account), bank statement.
extractor NM extractor; ~ **de humos** extractor fan.
extracurricular ADJ extracurricular, outside the curriculum.
extradeportivo ADJ unrelated to sport; (*antideportivo*) unsporting.
extradición NF extradition; **crimen sujeto a** ~ extraditable offence.
extradicionar [1a] VT to extradite.
extradir [3a] VT to extradite.
extraditable [1] ADJ subject to extradition.
[2] NMF person subject to extradition.
extraditar [1a] VT to extradite.
extraer [2o] VT to extract (*t Mat, Med, Min*), take out, pull out.
extraescolar ADJ: **actividad** ~ out-of-school activity.
extrafino ADJ superfine.
extraíble ADJ removable, detachable.
extrajudicial ADJ extrajudicial, out of court.
extrajudicialmente ADV out of court.
extrajurídico ADJ outside the law.
extralargo ADJ king-size.
extralimitación NF abuse (of authority).
extralimitarse [1a] VR to go too far, exceed (*o abuse*) one's authority; to go beyond what is proper, overstep the mark.
extramarital ADJ extramarital.
extramatrimonial ADJ *relaciones* extramarital; **hijo** ~ child born outside marriage (*o* wedlock).
extramuros [1] ADV outside the city; (*liter*) without (*liter*).
[2] PREP: ~ **de** outside.
extranjería NF alien status, status of foreigners; **ley de** ~ law on aliens.
extranjerismo NM foreign word (*o phrase etc*).
extranjerizante ADJ tending to favour foreign ways (*etc*); *palabra* foreign-looking, foreign-sounding.
extranjero [1] ADJ foreign; alien.
[2] NM, **extranjera** NF foreigner; alien.
[3] NM foreign country; foreign lands; **cosas del** ~ things from abroad; foreign things; **estar en el** ~ to be abroad, be overseas, be in foreign parts; **ir al** ~ to go abroad; **pasó 6 años en el** ~ he spent 6 years abroad; **no me siento a gusto en el** ~ I don't feel at ease abroad.
extranjis*: de ~ ADV (**a**) (*súbitamente*) unexpectedly. (**b**) (*secretamente*) secretly, on the sly.
extrañamente ADV strangely, oddly.
extrañamiento NM (**a**) (*enajenación*) estrangement (*de* from). (**b**) = **extrañeza**. (**c**) (*Jur* ††) banishment.
extrañar [1a] [1] VT (**a**) (*asombrar*) to find strange, find odd, wonder at; **extrañaba la falta de autobuses** she found the absence of buses strange; **me extrañaba que no hubieras venido** I was surprised that you had not come; **apenas es de** ~ **que ...** it is hardly surprising

that ...; **eso me extraña** that surprises me, that puzzles me, I find that odd; **me extraña su conducta** I am surprised at your behaviour.
(**b**) (*LAm: echar de menos*) to miss; to feel the lack of, regret the absence of; to yearn for.
(**c**) (*Jur*) to deport, send away; (††) to banish.
[2] **extrañarse** VR (**a**) (*asombrarse*) to be amazed, be surprised (*de* at); (*maravillarse*) to marvel (*de* at); ~ **de que ...** to be surprised that ...; to marvel that ...
(**b**) (*negarse*) to refuse.
(**c**) (*amigos*) to become estranged, grow apart.
extrañeza NF (**a**) (*rareza*) strangeness, oddness, oddity.
(**b**) (*asombro*) surprise, amazement; (*inquietud*) uneasiness; **me miró con** ~ he looked at me in surprise.
(**c**) (*de amigos*) estrangement, alienation.
extraño [1] ADJ (**a**) (*raro*) strange, odd, queer; singular; **es muy** ~ it's very odd; **¡cosa extraña!** how strange!, how odd!; **parece** ~ **que ...** it seems strange that ...
(**b**) (*ajeno*) extraneous (*a* to); **cosas extrañas a las que tratamos** things unconnected with those we handle.
(**c**) (*extranjero*) foreign.
[2] NM, **extraña** NF foreigner.
extrañoso ADJ (*And*) surprised.
extraoficial ADJ unofficial; informal.
extraoficialmente ADV unofficially; informally.
extraordinaria NF (*paga*) Christmas bonus.
extraordinariamente ADV extraordinarily.
extraordinario [1] ADJ (*gen*) extraordinary; (*insólito*) unusual; (*destacado*) outstanding; *descuento, edición, número etc* special; *cobro* extra, supplementary; **por sus servicios** ~**s** for his outstanding services; **no tiene nada de** ~ there's nothing special about it.
[2] NM (**a**) (*de menú*) special dish, extra dish.
(**b**) (*de periódico*) special issue.
extraparlamentario ADJ (taking place) outside parliament.
extrapeninsular ADJ outside Iberia, relating to areas outside the Peninsula.
extraplanetario ADJ other-worldly.
extraplano ADJ super-slim.
extraplomado ADJ overhanging.
extraplomo NM overhang.
extrapolable ADJ comparable.
extrapolación NF extrapolation.
extrapolar [1a] VT to extrapolate.
extrarradio NM (*de ciudad*) outer parts, outlying area.
extrasensorial ADJ extrasensory.
extratasa NF surcharge, extra charge.
extraterrenal ADJ (*LAm*), **extraterreno** ADJ (*LAm*) extraterrestrial, from another planet.
extraterrestre [1] ADJ extraterrestrial.
[2] NMF extraterrestrial being.
extraterritorial ADJ extraterritorial.
extravagancia NF (**a**) (*cualidad*) extravagance; outlandishness; oddness, strangeness. (**b**) (*una* ~) (*capricho*) whim; (*rareza*) vagary, peculiarity; ~**s** nonsense; **tiene sus** ~**s** he has his oddities.
extravagante ADJ extravagant; (*estrafalario*) outlandish, eccentric; (*raro*) odd, strange, nonsensical.
extravagantemente ADV extravagantly; eccentrically; oddly, strangely; nonsensically.
extravasarse [1a] VR to leak out, flow out; (*sangre*) to ooze out.
extravertido = **extrovertido**.
extraviado ADJ lost; missing; *animal* lost, stray.
extraviar [1c] [1] VT (**a**) *persona* to mislead, misdirect; to lead astray.
(**b**) *objeto* to lose, mislay, misplace.
(**c**) *dinero* (*pey*) to embezzle.
[2] **extraviarse** VR (**a**) (*persona*) to lose one's way, get lost; (*animal*) to stray, wander; (*carta*) to go astray, get lost in the post, miscarry.
(**b**) (*moralmente*) to go astray, err, fall into evil ways.
extravío NM (**a**) (*pérdida*) loss, misplacement, mislaying; straying; wandering; (*fig*) deviation (*from* de). (**b**) (*fig: moral*) misconduct, erring, evil ways.
extremadamente ADV extremely, exceedingly; extraordinarily.
extremado ADJ (*gen*) extreme; (*intenso*) intense; (*muy bueno*) extremely good; (*muy malo*) extremely bad; **frío** ~ extreme cold; **con extremada delicadeza** with extraordinary delicacy.
Extremadura NF Estremadura.
extremar [1a] [1] VT to carry to extremes; to force the sense of, stretch the application of; to overdo; **sin** ~ **el sentimentalismo** without overdoing the sentimentality; **el dictador extrema sus incendiarios discursos** the dictator is making even more inflammatory speeches, the dictator is being still more outrageous in his inflammatory speeches.
[2] **extremarse** VR to do one's utmost, exert o.s. to the full, make

every effort (*en* + *infin* to + *infin*).

extremaunción NF extreme unction.

extremeño, -a ADJ, NM/F Extremaduran.

extremidad NF **(a)** (*punta*) end, tip, extremity; (*borde*) edge, outermost part. **(b)** ~**es** (*Anat*) extremities.

extremismo NM extremism.

extremista ADJ, NMF extremist.

extremo ☐1 ADJ **(a)** (*lugar*) extreme, last; end (*atr*); (*más remoto*) far, furthest, outer, outermost.
(b) (*en orden*) last.
(c) (*fig*) extreme; utmost; critical, desperate; **en caso** ~ as a last resort, in an extreme case.
☐2 NM **(a)** (*cabo, límite*) end; extremity; ~ **muerto** dead end; **pasar de un** ~ **a otro** to go from one end to the other, (*fig*) go from one extreme to the other.
(b) (*fig: punto más alto*) highest point, highest degree; (*punto más bajo*) lowest point; (*punto más remoto*) extreme; **al** ~ **de, hasta el** ~ **de** to the point of; **con** ~, **en** ~ in the extreme; **en último** ~ as a last resort; in the final analysis; **por** ~ extremely; **hacer** ~**s** to gush, behave effusively; **quedó reducido al** ~ **de ir a pie** he was reduced to (the extreme of) going on foot; **los** ~**s se tocan** extremes meet.
(c) (*fig: asunto*) point, matter, question; **los** ~**s de la declaración** the detailed content of the statement; **ese** ~ **no se tocó en la discusión** that point was not dealt with in the discussion.
(d) (*fig: cuidado*) great care.
(e) (*Dep*) wing; (*persona*) wing-forward, winger; ~ **derecho** outside-right; ~ **izquierdo** outside-left.

Extremo Oriente NM Far East.

extremoso ADJ (*persona*) gushing, effusive; (*vehemente*) vehement, extreme in his (*etc*) attitudes (*o reactions*).

extrínseco ADJ extrinsic.

extroversión NF extroversion.

extrovertido ☐1 ADJ extrovert; outgoing.
☐2 NM, **extrovertida** NF extrovert.

exuberancia NF **(a)** (*gen*) exuberance. **(b)** (*Bot*) luxuriance, lushness. **(c)** (*de tipo*) fullness, buxomness.

exuberante ADJ **(a)** (*gen*) exuberant. **(b)** (*Bot*) luxuriant, lush. **(c)** *tipo etc* full, buxom, well-covered.

exudación NF exudation.

exudar [1a] ☐1 VT to exude, ooze (*de* from).
☐2 VI to exude, ooze out.

exultación NF exultation.

exultante ADJ elated, overjoyed; ~ **de felicidad** flushed with happiness.

exultar [1a] VI to exult.

exvoto NM votive offering.

eyaculación NF (*Med*) ejaculation; ~ **precoz** premature ejaculation.

eyacular [1a] VTI (*Med*) to ejaculate.

eyectable ADJ: **asiento** ~ ejector seat.

eyectarse [1a] VR (*Aer*) to eject.

eyector NM (*Téc*) ejector.

-ez *V* **Aspects of Word Formation in Spanish 2**.

Ezequiel NM Ezekiel.

EZLN NM (*Méx*) ABR *de* **Ejército Zapatista de Liberación Nacional**.

F

F, f [efe] NF (*letra*) F, f.

F **(a)** ABR de **fuerza** force; **un viento F8** a force 8 wind. **(b)** ABR de **febrero** February, Feb.; **el 23-F** the 23rd February (*date of the Tejero coup, 1981*).

┌─ **23-F** ───┐

23-F *refers to the attempted coup d'état carried out in the* **Cortes** *on 23 February 1981 by a group of* **Guardias Civiles** *led by Lt. Colonel Antonio Tejero and supported by certain sectors of the army. Members of the Spanish Parliament were held hostage overnight, the national TV station - TVE - was taken over by the military and forced to broadcast nothing but military music and, in some big cities, the army took up positions on the streets. In his role as Supreme Commander of the Armed Forces King Juan Carlos defused the situation by reassuring army commanders that the coup did not have his backing and by pledging his support for democracy. The rebels surrendered the following morning.*

f.ª (*Com*) ABR de **factura** Invoice, Inv.

fa NM (*Mús*) F; **~ mayor** F major.

f.a.b. ABR de **franco a bordo** free on board, f.o.b.

fabada NF (*Asturias*) rich stew of beans, pork etc.

fabe NF broad bean.

fabla NF **(a)** (*Hist*) pseudo-archaic style. **(b) ~ aragonesa** Aragonese dialect.

fábrica NF **(a)** (*Téc*) factory; works, plant; mill; (*And: alambique*) still, distillery; **~ de armas** arms factory, ordnance factory; **~ de cerveza** brewery; **~ de conservas** canning plant; **~ experimental** pilot plant; **~ de gas** gasworks; **~ de moneda** mint; **~ de papel** paper-mill; **~ de vidrio** glassworks; **marca de ~** trademark; **precio en ~** price ex-factory, price ex-works.
(b) (*acto*) manufacture, making.
(c) (*origen*) make; **de ~ alemana** of German make, German-made.
(d) (*Arquit*) building, structure; fabric; masonry.

fabricación NF manufacture, making, production; make; **~ asistida por ordenador** computer-assisted manufacturing; **~ de coches** car manufacture; **~ de tejas** tile making; **de ~ casera** home-made; **de ~ nacional** made in Spain (*o* Britain *etc*); **de ~ propia** made on the premises, our own make; **~ en serie** mass production; **estar en ~** to be in production.

fabricante NMF manufacturer; maker; (*industrial*) factory owner, mill owner.

fabricar [1g] VT **(a)** (*producir*) to manufacture, make; to put together; (*Arquit*) to build, construct; **~ en serie** to mass-produce.
(b) (*fig: pey*) to fabricate, invent; *documento* to fabricate, falsify; *mentira* to concoct.

fabril ADJ manufacturing, industrial.

fabriquero NM **(a)** = **fabricante**. **(b)** (*Ecl*) churchwarden. **(c)** (*Méx: destilador*) distillery operator (in a sugar mill).

fábula NF **(a)** (*Liter etc*) fable; myth; tale.
(b) (*Liter: argumento*) story, plot, action.
(c) (*rumor*) rumour; (*chisme*) piece of gossip; (*mentira*) fib.
(d) (*persona*) talk of the town; laughing-stock.
(e) (*) **un negocio de ~** a splendid piece of business; **es una cosa de ~** it's fabulous*.

fabulación NF **(a)** (*creación*) invention; **capacidad de ~** inventiveness. **(b)** (*historia*) invention.

fabulador [1] ADJ story-telling.
[2] NM, **fabuladora** NF story-teller.

fabular [1a] [1] VT *historia* to make up.
[2] VI: **~ sobre algo** to write a story about sth.

fabulario NM collection of fables.

fabulista NMF writer of fables.

fabulosamente ADV fabulously.

fabuloso ADJ **(a)** (*gen*) fabulous; (*mítico*) mythical; imaginary, fictitious. **(b)** (*: estupendo*) fabulous*, fantastic*; **es francamente ~** it's just fabulous*.

FACA ['faka] NM (*Esp*) ABR de **Futuro avión de combate y ataque.**

facción NF **(a)** (*Pol*) faction; (*pey*) breakaway group; hostile group, group of troublemakers.
(b) (*Anat*) feature; **de facciones irregulares** with irregular features.
(c) (*Mil*) routine duty; **estar de ~** to be on duty.

faccioso [1] ADJ factious; hostile; rebellious, seditious.
[2] NM, **facciosa** NF rebel; hostile person, troublemaker.

faceta NF facet (*t fig*).

faceto* ADJ (*Méx*) cocksure, arrogant.

facha¹ [1] NF **(a)** (*) (*aspecto*) look, appearance; (*cara*) face; (*persona*) sight, object; **~ a** face to face; **estar hecho una ~** to look a sight, look terrible; **tiene ~ de poli** he looks like a copper*; **tiene ~ de buena gente** he looks OK*. **(b) ponerse en ~** (*Náut*) to lie to.
[2] NMF (*) posh person*.
[3] ADJ INVAR (*) posh*, classy*.

facha²* NMF (*fascista*) reactionary, fascist.

fachada NF **(a)** (*Arquit*) façade, front; (*medida etc*) frontage; **con ~ al parque** looking towards the park, overlooking the park; **con 15 metros de ~** with a frontage of 15 metres.
(b) (*Tip*) title page.
(c) (*fig*) façade, outward show; **no tiene más que ~** it's all just show with him; **tener mucha ~** to be all show and no substance.
(d) (*: cara*) mug*, face.

fachado* ADJ: **bien ~** good-looking; **mal ~** ugly, plain.

fachenda* [1] NF swank*, conceit.
[2] NM swank*, show-off*.

fachendear* [1a] VI to swank*, show off.

fachendista*, **fachendón***, **fachendoso***, **fachento*** (*CAm*) [1] ADJ swanky*, conceited; snooty*.
[2] NM swank*, show-off*.

fachendoso* [1] ADJ swanky, conceited.
[2] NM, **fachendosa** NF show-off.

fachinal NM (*Cono Sur*), swamp, swampy place.

fachoso ADJ **(a)** (*LAm*) = **fachendista**. **(b)** (*raro*) ridiculous, odd-looking. **(c)** (*And, Cono Sur*: *elegante*) elegant, natty*.

facial [1] ADJ facial; **valor ~** face value.
[2] NM facial.

fácil [1] ADJ **(a)** (*gen*) easy; (*sencillo*) simple, straightforward; **~ para el usuario**, **~ de usar** easy to use, (*Inform*) user-friendly; **es ~ ver que ...** it is easy to see that ...; **~ de hacer** easy to do.
(b) *estilo etc* easy, fluent; ready; (*pey*) facile, too easy; glib.
(c) *persona* docile, compliant; *mujer* easy, loose.
(d) es ~ que venga he may well come; **no veo muy ~ que ...** I don't think it is at all likely that ...; **es ~ que proteste** she is liable to protest.
[2] ADV (*) = **fácilmente**.

facilidad NF **(a)** (*gen*) ease, easiness, facility; simplicity, straightforwardness; **con la mayor ~** with the greatest ease.
(b) (*Ling*) fluency; **~ de palabra** fluency in speech, readiness with which one talks.
(c) (*docilidad*) docility, compliant nature.
(d) ~es facilities; **~es de crédito** credit facilities; '**~es de pago**' 'easy payment terms'; **las ~es del puerto** the port facilities; **me dieron todas las ~es** they gave me every facility.

facilitar [1a] VT **(a)** (*hacer fácil*) to facilitate, make easy; (*agilizar*) to expedite.
(b) (*proporcionar*) to provide, furnish, supply; *documento* to issue; **¿quién facilitó el dinero?** who provided the money?; **me facilitó un coche** he supplied me with a car, he provided a car.
(c) ~ algo (*Cono Sur*) to make sth out to be easier than it really is,

play down the difficulty of sth.

fácilmente ADV easily; readily; simply, straightforwardly.

facilón ADJ very easy.

facilonería NF taking the easy way out, recourse to simple solutions.

facilongo* ADJ: **es ~** (*And*) it's a piece of cake*.

facineroso [1] ADJ criminal; wicked, villainous.

[2] NM, **facinerosa** NF criminal; wicked person.

facistol [1] ADJ (**a**) (*And, Carib: descarado*) insolent.

(**b**) **es tan ~** (*Carib*) he's full of tricks, he loves playing jokes on people.

(**c**) (*Carib: pedante*) pedantic.

[2] NM (**a**) (*Ecl*) lectern.

(**b**) (*And, Carib*) (*descarado*) insolent person; (*jactancioso*) braggart.

facistolería NF (*And, Carib, Méx*) insolence; boastfulness, conceit.

facochero NM warthog.

facón NM (*Cono Sur*) long knife, gaucho knife; *see also* GAUCHO .

facsímil(e) ADJ, NM facsimile.

factibilidad NF feasibility; practicality; **estudio de ~** feasibility study.

factible ADJ feasible; workable, practical; **es ~ que lo haga** she might do it.

fácticamente ADV really, actually, in fact.

facticio ADJ artificial, factitious.

fáctico ADJ real, actual; **los poderes ~s** the powers that be.

factor NM (**a**) (*Mat*) factor.

(**b**) (*elemento*) factor, element; **~ determinante** determining factor; **~ humano** human factor; **~ Rh** rhesus factor; **~ de seguridad** safety factor; **~ sorpresa** element of surprise; **el ~ suerte** the luck factor, the element of chance; **~ tiempo** time factor; **es un nuevo ~ de la situación** it is a new factor in the situation.

(**c**) (*Com*: *t* **factora** NF) agent, factor; commission merchant.

(**d**) (*Ferro*: *t* **factora** NF) freight clerk.

factoría NF (**a**) (*Com*) trading post; agency. (**b**) (*LAm: fábrica*) factory; (*And: fundición*) foundry.

factorización NF factoring.

factótum NM (**a**) (*empleado*) factotum; jack-of-all-trades. (**b**) (*pey*) busybody.

factual ADJ factual; based on fact(s), consisting of facts.

▼ **factura** NF (**a**) (*Com*) bill, invoice; **~ proforma, ~ simulada** pro forma (invoice); **según ~** as per invoice; **pasar ~, presentar ~** to send an invoice, send the bill (*t fig*); (*) to cash in. (**b**) (*Cono Sur*) bun, cake.

facturación NF (**a**) (*Com*: *acto*) invoicing. (**b**) (*Com*: *ventas*) sales (collectively), turnover. (**c**) (*Aer*) check(ing)-in; (*Ferro*) registration.

facturar [1a] VT (**a**) (*Com*) *géneros* to invoice; *persona* to bill. (**b**) (*Com*) **la compañía facturó X pesetas en 1995** the company turned over (o had a turnover of) X pesetas in 1995. (**c**) (*Ferro*) *equipaje* to register, check (*US*); (*Aer*) to check in.

facultad NF (**a**) (*gen*) faculty.

(**b**) (*autoridad*) power, authority; (*permiso*) permission; **tener la ~ de + infin** to have the power to *+ infin*; **tener ~(es) para + infin** to be authorized to *+ infin*.

(**c**) (*de mente*) **~es** faculties, powers; **~es del alma, ~es mentales** mental powers.

(**d**) (*Univ*) faculty, school; **F~ de Filosofía y Letras** Faculty of Arts; **F~ de Derecho** Faculty of Law; **está en la ~** he's at the university; **quedarse a comer en la ~** to lunch at the university.

facultar [1a] VT to authorize, empower; **~ a uno para hacer algo** to empower sb to do sth.

facultativo [1] ADJ (**a**) (*de opción*) optional.

(**b**) (*Univ*) faculty (*atr*).

(**c**) (*profesional*) professional; (*Med*) *dictamen etc* medical.

[2] NM, **facultativa** NF doctor, practitioner.

facundia NF eloquence.

facundo ADJ eloquent.

FAD NM (*Esp*) ABR *de* **Fondo de Ayuda al Desarrollo** development aid fund.

faena NF (**a**) (*trabajo*) task, job, piece of work; duty; (*) tough job, sweat*, fag*; (*Mil*) fatigue; (*LAm*) obligatory work, compulsory labour; (*CAm, Carib, Mex*: *horas extraordinarias*) extra work, overtime; **~ doméstica** housework; **~s** (*de casa*) chores; **esto es una ~** this is a tough one, this is a real sweat*; **estar de ~** to be at work; **estar en plena ~** to be hard at work; **tener mucha ~** to be terribly busy.

(**b**) (*: *t* **mala ~**) dirty trick; **hacer una ~ a uno** to play a dirty trick on sb; **¡menuda ~ la que me hizo!** a fine thing he did to me!

(**c**) (*Taur*) play with the cape; performance; **hizo una ~ maravillosa** he gave a splendid performance (with the cape).

(**d**) (*Cono Sur*) (*obreros*) gang of workers; (*local*) working place.

faenar [1a] [1] VT (**a**) *ganado* to slaughter. (**b**) (*Cono Sur*) *madera* to cut, work.

[2] VI (**a**) (*Cono Sur*: *trabajar*) to work, labour. (**b**) (*pescador*) to fish, work.

faenero NM (*Cono Sur*) farmhand, farm worker.

fafarechero (*LAm**) [1] ADJ swanky*, conceited.

[2] NM swank*, show-off*.

fagocitar [1a] VT (*fig*) to absorb, gobble up.

fagocito NM phagocyte.

fagot [1] NM (*instrumento*) bassoon.

[2] NMF bassoonist.

failear [1a] VT (*CAm, Cono Sur*) to file.

fain ADJ (*CAm*) fine.

fainada NF (*Carib*), **fainera** NF (*CAm*) silly thing, foolish act.

faíno ADJ (*Carib*) rude; coarse, rough.

faisán NM pheasant.

faisanaje NM hanging (of game).

faite (*LAm*) [1] ADJ tough, strong.

[2] NM (**a**) (*luchador*) tough man, good fighter. (**b**) (*pey*) quarrelsome sort, brawler.

faitear* [1a] VI (*LAm*) to brawl.

faja NF (**a**) (*tira de tela*) strip, band; (*prenda*) sash, belt; (*de mujer*) girdle, corset; (*Mil*) sash; (*Med*) bandage, support; (*And Aut*) fanbelt; **~ pantalón** panty girdle.

(**b**) (*Correos*) wrapper (*t* **~ postal**).

(**c**) (*Geog*) strip, belt, zone; **una estrecha ~ de terreno** a narrow strip of land.

(**d**) (*Aut*) lane.

(**e**) (*Rad, TV*) channel.

(**f**) (*Arquit*) band, fascia.

(**g**) (*Méx Tip*) label, title (on spine of book).

fajada NF (**a**) (*Carib: ataque*) attack, rush. (**b**) (*Cono Sur*: paliza*) beating. (**c**) (*Carib: decepción*) disappointment.

fajador(a)* NM/F grafter*, hard worker.

fajar [1a] [1] VT (**a**) (*envolver*) to wrap; to swathe; (*vendar*) to bandage; (*Correos*) to wrap up, put a wrapper on.

(**b**) (*LAm: atacar*) to attack, lay into*; (*golpear*) to bash*, beat; to thrash; *mujer* to try to seduce.

(**c**) **¡que lo fajen!** (*Cono Sur, Méx*⁎) tell him to wrap up!*

[2] VI: **~ con uno*** to go for sb, lay into sb*.

[3] **fajarse** VR (**a**) (*ponerse una faja*) to put on one's belt (*o sash etc*).

(**b**) (*LAm: pelear*) to come to blows; to fight, bash each other*; **los boxeadores se fajaron duro** the boxers really laid into each other*.

(**c**) **~ a una*⁎** to fuck sb*⁎.

fajilla NF (*de periódicos, revistas, impresos*) seal, address label; (*Cono Sur Correos*) wrapper.

fajín NM (*Mil*) sash.

fajina NF (**a**) (*Agr*) shock, pile, rick.

(**b**) (*leña*) kindling, brushwood, faggots.

(**c**) (*Mil*) bugle call, (*esp*) call to mess.

(**d**) (*Cono Sur: trabajo*) task, job (to be done quickly); hard work; **tenemos mucha ~** we've a lot to do, we've a tough job on here.

(**e**) (*Carib: horas extraordinarias*) extra work, overtime.

(**f**) (*Cono Sur*) **ropa de ~** working clothes; **uniforme de ~** ordinary uniform.

fajo NM (**a**) (*papeles*) bundle, sheaf; (*billetes*) roll, wad. (**b**) (*de bebé*) **~s** baby clothes. (**c**) (*Méx: golpe*) blow. (**d**) (*LAm*: trago*) swig (of liquor)*. (**e**) (*Méx: cinturón*) belt.

falacia NF (**a**) (*engaño*) deceit, fraud; (*error*) fallacy, error. (**b**) (*cualidad*) deceitfulness.

falange NF (**a**) (*Mil*) phalanx; **la F~** (*Pol*) the Falange. (**b**) (*Anat*) phalange.

ⓘ ┌─ *FALANGE ESPAÑOLA* ─────────────────────────┐

*Founded in 1933 by José Antonio Primo de Rivera, son of the dictator Miguel Primo de Rivera, the **Falange Española** was a sort of paramilitary fascist party. It grew rapidly in the early months of the Spanish Civil War, particularly after its leader was executed by the Republicans. Franco later merged the **Falange** with the **Carlistas** to form the **Falange Española Tradicionalista de las Juntas de Ofensiva Nacional-Sindicalista**. After the Civil War, the **FET de las JONS** was the only legally political party permitted in Franco's Spain. The **Falange** is still in existence.*

└──┘

falangista ADJ, NMF Falangist.

falaz ADJ *persona* deceitful; treacherous; *doctrina etc* fallacious; *aspecto etc* deceptive, misleading.

falca NF (**a**) (*And, Carib, Méx: transbordador*) river ferryboat. (**b**) (*And: alambique*) small still.

falciforme ADJ sickle-shaped.

falda NF (**a**) (*prenda*) skirt; (*Cos*) flap, fold; **~ escocesa** kilt; **~ pantalón** culotte, divided skirt; **~ de tablas, ~ tableada** pleated skirt; **estar cosido a las ~s de su madre** to be tied to mother's apron strings; **estar cosido a las ~s de su mujer** to be dominated by one's wife; **haberse criado bajo las ~s de mamá** to have led a very sheltered life.

(**b**) (*Anat*) lap; **sentarse en la ~ de una** to sit on sb's lap.

(**c**) (*: *mujer*) bird⁎, dame*; **ser muy aficionado a ~s** to be fond of the ladies; **es asunto de ~s** there's a woman in it somewhere.

➤ LENGUA Y USO: **factura: a →** 47.5

(d) (*Geog*) slope, hillside; foot, bottom (of a slope); **a la ~ de la montaña** at the foot of the mountain.
(e) (*de sombrero*) brim.
(f) (*Culin*) brisket.
(g) (*de camilla*) table cover.
faldear [1a] VT *montaña* to skirt.
faldellín NM **(a)** (*falda*) short skirt; (*enagua*) underskirt. **(b)** (*Carib: de bautizo*) christening robe.
faldero ADJ: **perro ~** lap-dog; **hombre ~** ladies' man; **es muy ~** he's a great one for the ladies.
faldicorto ADJ short-skirted.
faldilla NF (*Aut*) apron, skirt; flap.
faldillas NFPL coat-tails.
faldón NM **(a)** (*de vestido*) tail, skirt; coat-tails; (*Cos*) flap; (*de bebé*) long dress. **(b)** (*Arquit*) gable. **(c)** (*Aut*) apron, skirt.
falena NF moth.
falencia NF **(a)** (*error*) error, misstatement. **(b)** (*LAm: bancarrota*) bankruptcy.
falibilidad NF fallibility.
falible ADJ fallible.
fálico ADJ phallic.
falla NF **(a)** (*fallo*) fault, defect; failure; (*LAm: escasez*) lack, shortage; (*LAm: error*) oversight; (*LAm: defecto moral*) failure to keep one's promises; **~ en caja** cash shortage; **géneros que tienen ~s** (*Com*) defective goods, seconds.
(b) (*Geol*) fault.
(c) (*Mec*) failure, breakdown; **~ de encendido** (*Aut*) ignition fault; **~ de tiro** (*Mil*) misfire.
(d) (*And Naipes*) void.
fallada NF (*Naipes*) ruff, trumping.
fallar [1a] ① VT **(a)** (*Naipes*) to ruff, trump.
(b) (*Jur*) to pronounce sentence on; *premio* to award, decide (on).
(c) (*errar*) to miss; **~ el blanco** to miss the target.
② VI **(a)** (*cosecha, freno, memoria etc*) to fail; (*plan*) to go wrong, miscarry; (*tiro*) to miss, go astray; (*apoyo, cuerda etc*) to break, snap, give way; (*piernas*) to give way; (*fusil*) to misfire, fail to go off; (*motor*) to miss; **~ a uno** to fail sb, let sb down; **algo le falla a X** there's sth up with X; **algo falló en sus planes** sth went wrong with his plans; **le falló el corazón** his heart failed; **no falla nunca** it never fails.
(b) (*faltar*) to be missing, be lacking.
(c) (*Jur*) to pronounce sentence, pass judgement.
(d) (*Naipes*) to ruff, trump (in).
Fallas NFPL (*Valencia*) celebration of the feast of St Joseph.

┌─ ▐*FALLAS*▐ ───┐
*In the week of 19 March (the feast of San José), Valencia honours its patron saint with a spectacular fiesta called **las Fallas**. **Fallas** is the name given to the huge papier-mâché, cardboard and wooden sculptures depicting politicians and other well-known public figures which, amidst a deafening display of fireworks, are put on bonfires and set alight by members of competing groups, or **falleros**, who will have spent the previous year creating and building them. Only the sculpture which is voted best escapes the flames.*
└──┘

falleba NF door (o window) catch, espagnolette.
▼ **fallecer** [2d] VI **(a)** (*morir*) to pass away, die. **(b)** (*caducar*) to end, run out, expire.
fallecido ① ADJ late.
② NM, **fallecida** NF deceased, person who has lately died.
▼ **fallecimiento** NM death, demise, passing.
fallera¹ NF *woman who takes part in the 'Fallas' parade*; **~ mayor** Fallas queen.
fallero¹ ① ADJ of (o relating to) the 'Fallas'.
② NM, **fallera²** NF maker of 'Fallas'.
fallero² ADJ (*Cono Sur*) slack (about work), work-shy.
fallido ① ADJ **(a)** *esfuerzo etc* unsuccessful; *esperanza* disappointed; (*Mec, Mil etc*) dud; *deuda* bad, uncollectable.
(b) (*Com*) bankrupt.
② NM, **fallida** NF bankrupt.
fallir [3a] VI **(a)** (*fallar*) to fail. **(b)** (*caducar*) to end, run out, expire. **(c)** (*Carib: quebrar*) to go bankrupt.
▼ **fallo** ① ADJ **(a)** (*Naipes*) **estar ~** to be out of a suit; **estar ~ de** (*Naipes*) to be out of, have a void in; (*Méx*) to lack, be without.
(b) (*Cono Sur: fatuo*) fatuous; stupid.
▼② NM **(a)** (*defecto*) shortcoming, defect; (*Mec*) failure, trouble, breakdown; (*Inform*) bug; (*Med*) failure; (*Dep*) mistake, tactical error, mix-up; **debido a un ~ de los frenos** because of a brake failure; **~ cardíaco, ~ de corazón** heart failure; **~ de diseño** design fault; **~ humano** human error.
(b) (*Naipes*) void; **tener un ~ a corazones** to have a void in hearts.
(c) (*Jur etc*) sentence, verdict; decision, ruling; findings; **recurrir el ~** to appeal against the verdict.

fallón* ADJ unreliable, given to making mistakes; shaky; bungling.
fallutería NF (*Cono Sur*) **(a)** untrustworthiness. **(b)** hypocrisy.
falluto* ADJ (*Cono Sur*) **(a)** (*fracasado*) unsuccessful, failed. **(b)** (*poco fiable*) untrustworthy. **(c)** (*hipócrita*) two-faced, hypocritical.
FALN NFPL (*Venezuela*) ABR de **Fuerzas Armadas de Liberación Nacional**.
falo NM phallus.
falocracia* NF male domination, male chauvinism.
falócrata NM male chauvinist pig.
falocrático ADJ male chauvinist (*atr*); **actitud falocrática** male chauvinist attitude.
falopa‡ NF (*Cono Sur*) hard drugs.
falopearse‡ [1a] VR (*Cono Sur*) to take drugs, be a junkie‡.
falopero, -a‡ NM/F (*Cono Sur*) junkie‡.
falsamente ADV falsely; unsoundly, mistakenly; insincerely, dishonestly.
falsario, -a NM/F **(a)** (*mentiroso*) falsifier; liar. **(b)** (*falseador*) forger, counterfeiter.
falseable ADJ: **fácilmente ~** easy to forge, readily forged.
falseador(a) NM/F forger, counterfeiter.
falsear [1a] ① VT (*falsificar*) to falsify; *firma etc* to forge, counterfeit, fake; *moneda* to counterfeit; *cifras, voto* to fiddle (with), juggle with; *cerradura* to pick; (*Téc*) to bevel.
② VI **(a)** (*ceder*) to buckle, sag, give way; (*fig*) to flag, slacken. **(b)** (*Mús*) to be out of tune.
falsedad NF **(a)** (*gen*) falseness; falsity; unsoundness; hollowness, insincerity; dishonesty; treachery, deceit. **(b)** (*una ~*) falsehood.
falsete NM **(a)** (*Téc*) plug, bung. **(b)** (*Mús*) falsetto. **(c)** (*And**) hypocrite.
falsía NF falseness, duplicity.
falsificación NF **(a)** (*acto*) falsification, forging. **(b)** (*objeto*) forgery; fabrication.
falsificador(a) NM/F forger, counterfeiter.
falsificar [1g] VT (*gen*) to falsify; *moneda* to counterfeit; *cuadro, sello etc* to forge, fake; *elección etc* to rig, fiddle (with), juggle with.
falsilla NF guide (*in copying*).
falso ① ADJ **(a)** to false; *moneda* false, counterfeit, bad, dud*; *cuadro, sello etc* forged, fake; bogus, sham; *joya* imitation (*atr*); *caballo, mula* vicious; *declaración* false; *opinión, teoría* unsound; mistaken; *testimonio* false, untrue; perjured; *persona* hollow, insincere; dishonest; *amigo* false, treacherous.
(b) **en ~** falsely; without proper support; **coger a uno en ~** to catch sb in a lie; **jurar en ~** to commit perjury; **dar un paso en ~** to step on something that is not there, trip; (*fig*) to take a false step.
② NM (*CAm, Méx*) false evidence.
▼ **falta** NF **(a)** (*carencia*) lack, want, need; (*ausencia*) absence; (*escasez*) shortage; (*Jur*) default; non-, *p.ej.* **~ de asistencia** non-attendance; **~ de pago** non-payment; **a ~ de** (PREP) failing; **a ~ de, por ~ de** for want of, for lack of; **~ de dinero** shortage of money; **~ de peso** short weight; **~ de respeto** lack of respect, disrespect; **~ de seriedad** frivolity; irresponsibility; **echar algo en ~** to miss sth; **hacer ~** to be lacking, be wanting; to be missed; **el hombre que hace ~** the right man, the man we (*etc*) want; **eso me hace (mucha) ~** I need it (badly); **me hizo Vd mucha ~** I missed you a lot; **aquí no haces ~** you are not needed here; **¡~ hacía!** and about time too!; **hacer ~ + infin** to be necessary to + infin; **hace ~ pintarlo** sb ought to paint it, it needs painting; **poner ~ a uno** (*Escol*) to mark sb absent, put sb down as absent.
(b) (*fallo*) failure, shortcoming; (*culpa*) fault; (*error*) mistake; (*fechoría*) misdeed; (*de fabricación etc*) flaw, defect, fault; (*Mec*) trouble; **~ de ortografía** spelling mistake; **~ garrafal** stupid mistake; gross blunder; **sin ~** without fail; **sacar ~s a uno** to point out sb's defects.
(c) (*Jur*) misdemeanour; (*Dep*) foul, infringement; (*Tenis*) fault; **cometer una ~ contra uno** to commit a foul on sb, foul sb.
faltar [1a] ① VT (*Carib, Cono Sur, Méx: al respeto*) to be rude to, show disrespect for.
② VI **(a)** (*ser necesario*) to be lacking, be wanting; **le falta dinero** he lacks money, he needs money; **no le faltan buenas cualidades** he is not lacking in good qualities; **nos falta tiempo para hacerlo** we lack the time to do it, we are short of time to do it, we haven't the time to do it; **lo que falta son libros** what is lacking is books.
(b) (*estar ausente*) to be absent, be missing (*de* from); **faltaron 3 de la reunión** there were 3 missing (o absent) from the meeting; **~ a clase** to miss class, not go to class; **~ a una cita** to miss an appointment, break an appointment, not turn up for a date; **~ al trabajo** to stay away from work; **¿falta algo?** is anything missing?; **faltan 9** there are 9 missing, we are 9 short; **no falta quien opina que ...** there are some who think that ...; **en 8 años no he faltado ni una sola vez** I've not missed once in 8 years.
(c) (*Mec etc: fallar*) to fail, go wrong, break down.
(d) (*ser infiel a*) **~ a principio** to be false to; *persona* to fail; to offend; **~ a la decencia** to offend against decency; **~ a una promesa** to break

a promise, go back on one's word; **~ al respeto** to be disrespectful (*a* to); **~ a la verdad** to lie, be untruthful; **~ en los pagos** to default on one's payments.
(e) ~ en hacer algo to fail to do sth; **no faltaré en comunicárselo** I shall not fail to tell him.
(f) (*cantidad, tiempo etc*) **faltan pocos minutos para el comienzo** it's only a few minutes to go to the start; **faltan 3 semanas para las elecciones** there are 3 weeks to go to the election, the election is 3 weeks off; **falta poco para las 8** it's nearly 8 o'clock, it's getting on for 8 o'clock; **faltan 5 para las 8** (*LAm*) it's five to eight; **falta mucho todavía** there's plenty of time yet; **¿falta mucho?** is there long to go?; **falta poco para terminar** it's almost over; it's almost finished; **le faltaba poco para decírselo** she was about to tell him; **falta todavía por hacer** it remains to be done, it is still to be done.
(g) (*locuciones*) **¡no faltaba más!** (*no hay de qué*) don't mention it!; (*naturalmente*) of course, naturally; (*¡ni hablar!*) certainly not!, no way!*; (*¡es el colmo!*) it's the limit!, it's the last straw!; **¡lo que faltaba!, ¡es lo único que faltaba!** that's the very end!, it's all I *etc* needed!; **¡no faltaría más!** (*naturalmente*) of course, naturally; (*¡es el colmo!*) it's the limit!, it's the last straw!
(h) (*esp LAm: ser grosero*) to be rude, be disrespectful.
falto ADJ **(a)** (*deficiente*) short, deficient, lacking; **estar ~ de** to be short of; *cualidad etc* to be wanting in, be lacking in; **estar ~ de personal** to be short-handed.
(b) (*moralmente*) poor, wretched, mean.
(c) (*And: fatuo*) fatuous, vain.
faltón ADJ **(a)** (*negligente*) remiss, neglectful, unreliable; (*LAm: vago*) slack (about work), work-shy. **(b)** (*Andalucía, Carib: irrespetuoso*) disrespectful, rude.
faltoso ADJ **(a)** (*CAm, Méx*) = **faltón (a). (b)** (*CAm, Méx: irrespetuoso*) disrespectful. **(c)** (*And: discutidor*) quarrelsome.
faltriquera NF (*bolsillo*) pocket, pouch; (*de reloj*) fob, watch pocket; (*bolso*) handbag; **rascarse la ~** (*fig*) to dig into one's pocket.
falúa NF launch; tender.
fama NF **(a)** (*renombre*) fame; (*reputación*) reputation, repute; **mala ~** bad reputation; notoriety; **de mala ~** of ill fame; **el libro que le dio ~** the book which made him famous, the book which made his name; **tener ~ de gran cazador** to have the reputation of being a great hunter, be known as a great hunter; **tiene ~ de poco escrupuloso** he is thought to be unscrupulous.
(b) (*rumor*) report, rumour; **corre la ~ de que** ... it is rumoured that ...
famélico ADJ starving, famished; **los ~s** the starving.
familia NF **(a)** family; (*los que viven en una misma casa*) household; **~ nuclear** nuclear family; **~ numerosa** large family; **~ política** relatives by marriage, in-laws; **de buena ~** of good family; **tener mucha ~** to have lots of children; **ser como de la ~** to be one of the family; **eso viene de ~** that runs in the family; **acordarse de la ~ de uno*** to insult sb at length; **sentirse como en ~** to feel thoroughly at home.
(b) (*And, Carib, Méx: pariente*) relative; **él es ~** he's family, he's a relative.
(c) (*Tip*) fount.
familiar ☐1 ADJ **(a)** (*de la familia*) family (*atr*); **los lazos ~es** the family bond, the ties of blood; **subsidio ~** family allowance; **dioses ~es** household gods.
(b) (*conocido*) familiar (*a* to).
(c) (*fig*) (*casero*) homely, domestic; (*sin ceremonia*) informal; (*llano*) plain, ordinary; (*Ling*) colloquial, familiar; **estilo ~** familiar.
☐2 NMF (*pariente*) relative, relation; (*de casa*) member of the household; (*amigo*) intimate friend, close acquaintance.
familiaridad NF familiarity (*con* with); homeliness; informality; **~es** familiarities.
familiarizar [1f] ☐1 VT to familiarize, acquaint (*con* with).
☐2 **familiarizarse** VR: **~ con** to familiarize o.s. with, make o.s. familiar with, get to know.
famosillo ☐1 ADJ well-known in limited circles.
☐2 NM, **famosilla** NF minor celebrity.
famoso ☐1 ADJ **(a)** famous (*por* for). **(b)** (*: estupendo*) famous, great*, splendid.
☐2 NM, **famosa** NF famous person, celebrity; **los ~s** the famous.
fan NMF, PL **fans** (*Cine, Mús etc*) fan.
fanal NM **(a)** (*faro*) lighthouse; (*harbour*) beacon; (*linterna*) lantern; (*Aut*) headlight. **(b)** (*campana*) bell glass; (*pantalla*) (glass) lampshade.
fanaticada NF (*Carib*) fans.
fanático ☐1 ADJ fanatical.
☐2 NM, **fanática** NF fanatic; bigot; (*Cine, Dep etc*) fan, supporter, admirer; **es un ~ del aeromodelismo** he's mad about model aeroplanes; **los ~s de la estrella** the star's fans, the star's admirers.
fanatismo NM fanaticism; bigotry; enthusiasm.
fanatizar [1f] VT to arouse fanaticism in.
fancine NM = **fanzine.**

fandango NM **(a)** (*Mús*) fandango. **(b)** (*: jaleo*) row, shindy*; **se armó un ~** there was a great row. **(c)** (*LAm*: *fiesta*) rowdy party, booze-up*.
fandanguear [1a] VI (*Cono Sur*) to live it up*.
fané ADJ (*LAm*) (*arrugado*) messed-up, crumpled, rumpled; (*cursi*) vulgar; **estar ~** (*persona*) to be in a terrible state.
faneca NF (*Pez*) a species of flatfish.
fanega NF **(a)** *grain measure* (= *Spain 1.58 bushels, Méx 2.57 bushels, Cono Sur 3.89 bushels*). **(b)** *land measure* (= *Spain 1.59 acres, Carib 1.73 acres*).
fanfarrear [1a] VI = **fanfarronear.**
fanfarria NF **(a)** (*jactancia*) bluster, bravado, bragging. **(b)** (*Mús*) fanfare.
fanfarrón ☐1 ADJ blustering, boastful; flashy.
☐2 NM blusterer, braggart; bully; flashy type.
fanfarronada NF bluster, bravado, swagger; bluff.
fanfarronear [1a] VI to bluster, boast, swagger; to rant; to talk big*, bluff.
fanfarronería NF blustering, boasting, bragging; ranting; big talk, bluffing.
fangal NM bog; quagmire, muddy place.
fango NM mud, mire; slush; (*fig*) mire, dirt.
fangoso ADJ muddy, miry; slushy.
fanguero ☐1 ADJ (*Cono Sur*) *animal, jugador* suited to heavy going.
☐2 NM (*Carib, Méx*) = **fango, fangal.**
fantasear [1a] VI to fantasize, daydream, let one's imagination run free.
fantaseo NM fantasizing, dreaming, imagining.
fantasía NF **(a)** (*facultad*) fantasy, imagination, fancy; **es obra de la ~** it is a work of the imagination; **dejar correr la ~** to let one's imagination roam.
(b) (*Arte, Liter etc*) fantasy; fantastic tale; work of the imagination; (*Mús*) fantasia.
(c) (*capricho*) whim, fancy.
(d) (*afectación*) conceit, vanity, airs.
(e) (*Com*) **de ~** fancy; **joyas de ~** imitation jewellery.
fantasioso* ADJ **(a)** (*engreído*) vain, conceited, stuck-up*; **¡fantasiosa!** you vain thing! **(b)** (*soñador*) dreamy.
fantasma ☐1 NM **(a)** (*lit*) ghost, phantom, apparition. **(b)** (*: presumido*) show-off*, stuck-up person*; (*: fanfarrón*) boaster, braggart; **¡no seas ~!** stop showing off! **(c)** (*TV*) ghost image. **(d)** (*Esp* *Fin*) 5000 pesetas.
☐2 ATR ghost, phantom (*atr*); **buque ~** ghost ship; **ciudad ~** ghost city; **compañía ~** dummy company; **un lugar ~** an imaginary place.
fantasmada* NF bluster, bravado; empty show.
fantasmagoría NF phantasmagoria.
fantasmagórico ADJ phantasmagoric.
fantasmal ADJ ghostly; phantom (*atr*).
fantasmear* [1a] VI to show off, put on a display.
fantasmón ☐1 ADJ bigheaded*, stuck up*.
☐2 NM, **fantasmona** NF bighead*, swank*.
fantásticamente ADV fantastically; weirdly; fancifully.
fantástico ☐1 ADJ **(a)** (*gen*) fantastic; (*extraño*) weird, unreal; (*caprichoso*) fanciful, whimsical. **(b)** (*vanidoso*) vain. **(c)** (*: estupendo*) fantastic. **(d)** (*Cono Sur: jactancioso*) bragging, swaggering.
☐2 EXCL fantastic!*, great!*, terrific!*
fantoche ☐1 NM **(a)** (*muñeco*) puppet, marionette. **(b)** (*: persona*) (*mediocre*) mediocrity, nonentity; (*presumido*) braggart, loud-mouth*.
☐2 ATR puppet (*atr*); **régimen ~** puppet régime.
fantochesco ADJ puppet-like.
fantomático ADJ shadowy, mysterious, imaginary.
fanzine NM fanzine.
FAO ['faw] NF **(a)** ABR *de* **Organización de las Naciones Unidas para la Agricultura y la Alimentación** Food and Agriculture Organization of the United Nations, FAO. **(b)** ABR *de* **fabricación asistida por ordenador** computer-assisted manufacture, CAM.
faquín NM porter, errand-boy.
faquir NM fakir.
farabute* NM (*Cono Sur*) (*pícaro*) rogue; (*poco cumplidor*) untrustworthy person; (*pobre diablo*) poor wretch.
faralá NM flounce, frill; **~s** (*pey*) frills, buttons and bows.
farallón NM (*Geog*) steep rock, cliff; headland; bluff; (*Geol*) outcrop; (*Cono Sur*) rocky peak.
faramalla* NF **(a)** (*labia*) blarney, humbug, claptrap*; (*Com etc*) patter, spiel.
(b) (*impostura*) empty show, sham.
(c) (*Cono Sur: jactancia*) bragging, boasting.
faramallear [1a] VI (*Cono Sur, Méx*) to brag, boast.
faramallero ADJ (*Cono Sur*) bragging, boastful.
farándula NF **(a)** (*Teat: Hist*) troupe of strolling players; **el mundo de la ~** the theatre world.
(b) (*) (*labia*) humbug, claptrap*; (*mentiras*) pack of lies; (*trampa*) confidence trick, confidence game (*US*), swindle; (*chisme*) wicked

gossip.

faranduleo NM trickery.

farandulero [1] ADJ (*LAm*) = **farolero.**
[2] NM, **farandulera** NF (a) (*Teat: Hist*) strolling player. (b) (*timador*) confidence trickster, con man, swindler, rogue.

Faraón NM Pharaoh.

faraónico ADJ Pharaonic.

faraute NM (a) (††) herald. (b) (*: entrometido*) busybody.

FARC NFPL (*Colombia*) ABR de **Fuerzas Armadas Revolucionarias de Colombia.**

fardada* NF show, display; piece of showmanship; **ese cuadro es una ~** that picture is something to really boast about; **¡vaya ~!** that's really great!*; **pegarse una ~** to swank*, show off.

fardar* [1a] VI (a) (*objeto*) to be classy*; **es un coche que farda mucho** it's a car with a lot of class. (b) (*persona*) to show off, put on a display; **~ bien** to dress nattily*. (c) (*jactarse*) to boast, shoot a line*; **fardaba de sus amigas** he boasted about his girlfriends.

farde* NM (a) tone, class. (b) showing-off, display. (c) boasting, swanking*.

fardel NM (a) (*talega*) bag, knapsack; ragbag. (b) (*bulto*) bundle.

fardo NM bundle; bale, pack; (*fig*) burden.

fardón* [1] ADJ (a) (*precioso*) nice, lovely, great*. (b) (*de clase*) classy*, posh*. (c) (*elegante*) natty*, nattily dressed*. (d) (*vanidoso*) stuck-up*, swanky*.
[2] NM swank*, show-off*.

farero NM lighthouse-keeper.

farfulla* [1] NF (a) (*tartamudez*) splutter(ing); jabber(ing). (b) (*LAm: jactancia*) bragging, boasting.
[2] NMF jabberer, gabbler.

farfullador ADJ spluttering; jabbering; gabbling.

farfullar [1a] [1] VT to do hastily, botch, scamp.
[2] VI to splutter; to jabber, gabble.

farfulleo NM spluttering; jabbering, gabbling.

farfullero* ADJ (a) = **farfullador.** (b) (*LAm*) = **fanfarrón.**

farináceo ADJ starchy, farinaceous.

faringe NF pharynx.

faringitis NF pharyngitis.

fariña NF (*And, Cono Sur*) coarse manioc flour.

fario NM: **mal ~** bad luck.

farisaico ADJ Pharisaic(al), hypocritical; smug.

fariseo NM Pharisee, hypocrite; smug sort.

farmacéutico [1] ADJ pharmaceutical.
[2] NM, **farmacéutica** NF chemist, pharmacist.

farmacia NF (a) (*ciencia*) pharmacy. (b) (*tienda*) chemist's (shop), drugstore (*US*); **~ de guardia** all-night chemist's.

fármaco NM medicament, medicine.

farmacodependencia NF dependence on drugs.

farmacología NF pharmacology.

farmacológico ADJ pharmacological.

farmacólogo, -a NM/F pharmacologist.

farmacopea NF pharmacopoeia.

faro [1] NM (a) (*Náut*) (*torre*) lighthouse; (*señal*) beacon; **~ aéreo** air beacon.
(b) (*Náut: luz*) light, lantern; (*Aut*) headlamp, headlight; **~ antiniebla** foglamp; **~ lateral** sidelight; **~ piloto, ~ trasero** rear light, tail light; **~ de marcha atrás** reversing light; V t **luz** (d). (c) **~s‡** peepers‡, eyes.
[2] (*) como ADJ: **idea ~** bright idea, brilliant idea.

farol NM (a) (*linterna*) lantern, lamp; (*Ferro*) headlamp; **~ de calle, ~ público** street lamp; **~ de viento** hurricane lamp; **¡adelante con los ~es!** press on regardless!; (*LAm*) if they don't like it they can lump it!*
(b) (*farola*) lamppost; (*Gimnasia*) handstand.
(c) (*envase*) wrapping of tobacco packet.
(d) **~es** (*LAm**) eyes.
(e) (*And, Cono Sur: ventana*) bay window, glassed-in balcony.
(f) (*: ostentación*) swank*; **echarse un ~, marcarse un ~** to shoot a line*, swank*, brag; **tiene mucho ~** he's terribly swanky*.
(g) (*) (*mentira*) lie, fib; (*Naipes etc*) bluff, piece of bluff; **echarse un ~, tirarse un ~** to tell a fib, (*Naipes etc*) to bluff.
(h) **hacer de ~*** to play gooseberry.

farola NF street lamp; lamppost.

faroladas* NFPL showing-off, boasting.

farolazo* NM (*CAm, Méx*) swig of liquor*.

farolear* [1a] VI to swank*, strut around; to brag.

farolero [1] *ADJ vain, stuck-up*.
[2] NM (a) lamp-maker; lamplighter. (b) (*) braggart, loud-mouth*.

farolillo NM (a) (*Elec*) fairy-light, Chinese lantern; **~ rojo** (*fig*) back marker, team (*etc*) in last place. (b) (*Bot*) Canterbury bell.

farra¹ NF (*pez*) salmon trout.

farra² NF (a) (*juerga*) spree, party, carousal; **ir de ~** to go on a spree.
(b) (*mofa*) mockery, teasing; **tomar a uno para la ~** to pull sb's leg.

fárrago NM medley, hotchpotch.

farragoso ADJ cumbersome; *discurso etc* involved, dense.

farrear [1a] [1] VI to make merry.
[2] **farrearse** VR (a) **~ de uno** to tease sb. (b) **~ el dinero** to spend one's money on drink.

farrero [1] ADJ (*And, Cono Sur*) merry; fun-loving.
[2] NM, **farrera** NF reveller.

farrista ADJ (*Cono Sur*) (*borracho*) dissipated, hard-drinking; (*juerguista*) boisterous, rowdy.

farruco* ADJ pig-headed; **estar** (o **ponerse**) **~** to get aggressive.

farruto ADJ (*And*) sickly, weak.

farsa¹ NF (a) (*Teat*) farce; (*pey*) bad play, crude play. (b) (*fig*) humbug, sham, masquerade.

farsa² NF (*Culin*) stuffing.

farsante* NM humbug, fraud, pseud*.

farsear [1a] VI (*CAm*) to joke.

farsesco ADJ farcical.

FAS NFPL ABR de **Fuerzas Armadas** armed forces.

fas: **por ~ o por nefas** by hook or by crook, rightly or wrongly; at any cost.

fascículo NM fascicule, part, instalment.

fascinación NF fascination.

fascinador ADJ fascinating.

fascinar [1a] VTI (*gen*) to fascinate; to captivate; (*hechizar*) to bewitch; (*aojar*) cast the evil eye on.

fascismo NM fascism.

fascista ADJ, NMF fascist.

fase NF (a) phase, stage; (*Dep*) half; **~ terminal** terminal phase; **estar en ~ ascendente** to be on one's way up; to be on a winning run; **estar fuera de ~** to be out of phase. (b) (*Astron, Bio, Elec*) phase. (c) (*de cohete*) stage.

faso* NM (*Cono Sur*) cigarette, fag‡.

fastidiado* ADJ (*estropeado*) ruined, bust*; **ando ~ del estómago, tengo el estómago ~** I've got a queasy stomach.

fastidiar [1b] [1] VT (a) (*molestar*) to annoy, bother, vex; (*aburrir*) to bore; (*dar asco a*) to upset, disgust, sicken, irk; **eso me fastidia terriblemente** it annoys me no end; it upsets me terribly; **¡no fastidies!** you can't mean it!, you're kidding!; **¡no me fastidies!** stop bothering me!
(b) (*dañar*) to harm, damage.
[2] **fastidiarse** VR (a) (*enojarse*) to get cross; (*aburrirse*) to get bored; **¡a ~!*, ¡fastídiate!*** get lost!‡; **¡que se fastidie!*** tell him to go to blazes!; that's his funeral!*; **¡para que te fastidies!*** so there!*
(b) (*hacerse daño*) to harm o.s., do o.s. an injury.
(c) (*aguantarse*) to put up with it.

fastidio NM (a) (*molestia*) annoyance, bother, nuisance; **¡qué ~!** what a nuisance! (b) (*aburrimiento*) boredom. (c) (*asco*) disgust, repugnance.

fastidioso ADJ (a) (*molesto*) annoying, bothersome, vexing; (*aburrido*) tedious, tiresome, boring; irksome; (*asqueroso*) sickening. (b) (*LAm: quisquilloso*) fastidious.

fasto NM (a) (*pompa*) pomp, pageantry. (b) **~s** (*Liter*) annals.

fastuosamente ADV magnificently, splendidly; lavishly; pompously.

fastuoso ADJ magnificent, splendid; lavish; pompous.

fatal [1] ADJ (a) (*mortal*) fatal; (*malhadado*) ill-fated, disastrous.
(b) (*irrevocable*) irrevocable; (*inevitable*) unavoidable, fated.
(c) (*: horrible*) awful, ghastly*, rotten*; **tiene un inglés ~** he speaks awful English; **la obra estuvo ~*** the play was rotten*.
[2] ADV (*) awfully, terribly (badly); **lo pasaron ~** they had a terrible time (of it); **canta ~** she sings terribly!.

fatalidad NF (a) (*destino*) fate; fatality. (b) (*desdicha*) mischance, misfortune, ill-luck.

fatalismo NM fatalism.

fatalista [1] ADJ fatalistic.
[2] NMF fatalist.

fatalizarse [1f] VR (a) (*And: cometer un delito*) to commit a grave crime.
(b) (*Cono Sur: sufrir herida*) to be seriously wounded; (*And: sufrir desgracia*) to suffer a series of misfortunes (as a punishment for a wrong committed).

fatalmente ADV (*V ADJ*) (a) fatally; disastrously. (b) unavoidably, irremediably.

fatídicamente ADV (*V ADJ*) (a) prophetically. (b) fatefully, ominously.

fatídico ADJ (a) (*profético*) prophetic. (b) (*de mal agüero*) fateful, ominous.

fatiga NF (a) (*cansancio*) fatigue, weariness; **~ cerebral** mental fatigue. (b) (*Téc*) fatigue; **~ del metal** metal fatigue. (c) **~s** hardships, troubles, toils.

fatigabilidad NF tendency to tire easily.

fatigadamente ADV with difficulty, wearily.

fatigar [1h] [1] VT (a) (*cansar*) to tire, weary, fatigue. (b) (*molestar*) to annoy.
[2] **fatigarse** VR to tire, get tired, grow weary; **~ de andar** to wear

o.s. out walking.

fatigosamente ADV painfully, with difficulty.

fatigoso ADJ **(a)** (*que cansa*) tiring, exhausting, fatiguing. **(b)** (*Med*) laboured, difficult; **respiración fatigosa** laboured breathing. **(c)** (*molesto*) trying, tiresome.

fato* NM (*Cono Sur*) **(a)** (*negocio*) shady deal. **(b)** (*amorío*) love affair.

fatuidad NF (*V* ADJ) **(a)** fatuity, foolishness, inanity. **(b)** conceit.

fatuo ADJ **(a)** (*necio*) fatuous, foolish, inane. **(b)** (*vanidoso*) conceited; *V* **fuego.**

fauces NFPL (*Anat*) fauces, gullet; (*LAm: colmillos*) tusks, teeth; (*fig: boca*) jaws, maw.

faul NM (*Méx: Dep*) foul.

faulear [1a] VT (*Méx: Dep*) to foul.

fauna NF fauna.

faunístico ADJ faunal; **riqueza faunística** wealth of the fauna.

fauno NM faun.

Fausto NM Faust.

fausto ☐1 ADJ lucky, fortunate; auspicious.
☐2 NM splendour, pomp, magnificence.

fautor(a) NM/F accomplice, helper; instigator.

▼ **favor** NM **(a)** (*ayuda, servicio*) favour, service, good turn, kindness; **~es** (*de mujer*) favours; **entrada de ~** complimentary ticket; **es de ~** it's complimentary, it's free; **por ~** please; **no es ~, no hay ~** (*contestando a 'por favor'*) think nothing of it, it's no trouble; **haga el ~ de esperar** please wait, kindly wait; **haga el ~ de no fumar** please be so good as to refrain from smoking; **¿me haces el ~ de pasar la sal?** would you please pass the salt?, would you be so kind as to pass the salt?; **~ que me haces** you're very kind, it's good of you; **si hace ~** (*LAm*) if you don't mind; **¡está para hacerle un ~!*** she's really something!*; **~ de venir puntualmente** (*LAm*) please be punctual.
(b) (*gracia*) favour, good graces; **estar en ~** to be in favour; **gozar de ~ cerca de uno** to be in favour with sb.
(c) (*apoyo*) protection, support; **gracias al ~ del rey** thanks to the king's protection.
(d) (*símbolo*) favour; token; (*regalo*) gift.
(e) **a ~ de** in favour of; on behalf of; (*Com*) to the order of; **a ~ de la marea** helped by the tide, taking advantage of the tide; **a ~ de la noche** under the cover of night, helped by the darkness.

▼ **favorable** ADJ favourable; auspicious; advantageous.

favorablemente ADV favourably; auspiciously; advantageously.

favorecedor ADJ *vestido etc* becoming; *relato, retrato* flattering.

favorecer [2d] VT **(a)** (*gen*) to favour; (*amparar*) to help, protect; (*tratar bien*) to treat favourably; (*fortuna*) to favour, smile on. **(b)** (*vestido*) to become, flatter, look well on; (*relato, retrato*) to flatter.

favorecido ADJ favoured; **trato de nación más favorecida** most-favoured nation treatment.

favoritismo NM favouritism.

favorito, -a ADJ, NM/F favourite (*t Dep*).

fax NM fax, fax machine.

faxear [1a] VT to fax, send by fax.

faxteléfono NM phone/fax (machine).

fayuca NF (*Méx*) smuggling.

fayuquear [1a] VT (*Méx*) to smuggle.

fayuquero, -a NM/F (*Cono Sur*) travelling salesman, travelling saleswoman; (*Méx*) seller of smuggled goods.

fayuto ADJ (*Cono Sur*) = **falluto.**

faz NF **(a)** (*liter, fig*) face; front; aspect; **~ a** face to face; **~ de la tierra** face of the earth. **(b)** (*de moneda*) obverse.

FC, f.c. ABR de **ferrocarril** railway, Rly.

Fco. ABR de **Francisco.**

Fdez ABR de **Fernández.**

Fdo. (*en correspondencia*) ABR de **firmado** Signed.

FE NF (*Hist*) ABR de **Falange Española.**

fe NF **(a)** (*Rel*) faith (*en* in); **la ~ católica** the Catholic faith.
(b) (*confianza*) faith, belief; reliance; **de buena ~** in good faith; (*Jur*) bona fide; **obrar de buena ~** to act in good faith; **mala ~** bad faith; **a ~ mía, por mi ~** (††) by my faith, upon my honour; **dar ~ a, prestar ~ a** to believe, credit, place reliance on; **tener ~ en** to have faith in, believe in.
(c) (*palabra*) assurance; **a ~** in truth; **en ~ de lo cual** in witness whereof; **dar ~ de** to testify to, bear witness to; **de eso doy ~** I'll swear to that.
(d) (*lealtad*) fidelity, loyalty.
(e) (*certificado*) certificate; **~ de bautismo** certificate of baptism; **~ de erratas** errata; **~ de vida** document proving that a person is still alive.

FEA NF **(a)** (*Aut*) ABR de **Federación Española de Automovilismo.**
(b) (*Dep*) ABR de **Federación Española de Atletismo.**
(c) (*Hist*) ABR de **Falange Española Auténtica.**

fea NF ugly woman, plain girl; **ser la ~ del baile** to be a wallflower; **me tocó la ~ del baile** (*fig*) I got the short straw.

fealdad NF ugliness, hideousness.

feamente ADJ hideously.

feb., feb.º ABR de **febrero** February, Feb.

feble ADJ feeble, weak.

Febo NM Phoebus.

febrero NM February.

febril ADJ **(a)** (*Med*) fevered, feverish. **(b)** (*fig*) feverish, hectic.

febrilmente ADV (*fig*) feverishly, hectically.

fecal ADJ faecal; **aguas ~es** sewage.

fecha NF **(a)** date; **~ de caducidad** (*de billete etc*) expiry date; **~ de caducidad, ~ de consumo preferente** sell-by date; **~ de emisión** date of issue; **~ de entrega** delivery date; **~ límite** deadline; **~ de nacimiento** date of birth; **~ tope** closing date, last date; **a la ~** to date; at that time; **de larga ~** (*Fin*) long-dated; **a partir de esta ~** from today, starting from today; **a 30 días ~** (*Com*) at 30 days' sight; **con ~ del 15 de agosto** dated the 15th of August; **con ~ adelantada** *cheque* post-dated; **en alguna ~ futura** at some future date; **en ~ próxima** soon, at an early date; **hasta la ~** to date, so far; **manuscrito sin ~** undated manuscript; **pasarse de ~** (*Com*) to pass the sell-by date.
(b) (*: *día*) **unas ~s de descanso** a few days' rest; **dentro de breves ~s** soon; **hace unas ~s** a few days ago; **para estas ~s** by this time; **por estas ~s** now, about now; at this time of year.

fechable ADJ datable (*en* to).

fechado NM dating.

fechador NM date-stamp.

fechar [1a] VT to date.

fechoría NF misdeed, villainy.

FECOM NM ABR de **Fondo Europeo de Cooperación Monetaria** European Monetary Cooperation Fund, EMCF.

fécula NF starch; **~ de papa** (*LAm*) potato flour.

feculento ADJ starchy.

fecundación NF fertilization; **~ artificial** artificial insemination; **~ in vitro** in vitro fertilization.

fecundar [1a] VT to fertilize; **~ por fertilización cruzada** to cross-fertilize.

fecundidad NF **(a)** (*gen*) fertility; fecundity. **(b)** (*fig*) fruitfulness, productiveness.

fecundizar [1f] VT to fertilize.

fecundo ADJ **(a)** (*Bio etc*) fertile; fecund; prolific.
(b) (*fig*) fruitful; (*copioso*) copious, abundant; (*productivo*) productive; **~ de palabras** fluent, eloquent; **~ en** fruitful of, productive of; **una época muy fecunda en buenos poetas** a period abounding in good poets, a period in which good poets abounded; **un libro ~ en ideas** a book full of ideas.

FED NM ABR de **Fondo Europeo de Desarrollo** European Development Fund, EDF.

FEDER NM ABR de **Fondo Europeo de Desarrollo Regional** European Regional Development Fund, ERDF.

federación NF federation.

federal ADJ federal.

federalismo NM federalism.

federalista NMF federalist.

federalizar [1f] VT to federate, federalize.

federar [1a] ☐1 VT to federate.
☐2 **federarse** VR **(a)** (*Pol*) to federate. **(b)** (*hacerse socio*) to become a member.

federativo ADJ federative.

Federico NM Frederick.

feérico ADJ fairy (*atr*).

FEF NF ABR de **Federación Española de Fútbol.**

féferes NMPL (*LAm*) junk, lumber; things (in general), thingummyjigs*.

fehaciente ADJ reliable, authentic; irrefutable.

fehacientemente ADV reliably; irrefutably.

feíllo* ADJ a bit plain, rather unattractive.

FE-JONS [fe'xons] NF (*Hist*) ABR de **Falange Española de las Juntas de Ofensiva Nacional Sindicalista.**

felación NF fellatio.

feldespato NM felspar.

feliciano⁂ NM: **echar un ~** to have a screw⁂.

▼ **felicidad** NF **(a)** (*alegría*) happiness.
(b) **viajamos con toda ~** all went well on the journey.
▼**(c)** **~es** best wishes, congratulations; **os deseo toda clase de ~es** I wish you every kind of happiness; **¡~es!** best wishes!; happy birthday! (*etc*); **¡mis ~es!** congratulations!

▼ **felicitación** NF congratulation; (*Mil*) commendation; **~ de Navidad** Christmas greetings, (*tarjeta*) Christmas card.

▼ **felicitar** [1a] VT to congratulate (*a uno por algo* sb on sth); **¡te felicito!** congratulations!; **~ la Navidad** (*etc*) **a uno** to wish sb a happy Christmas (*etc*).

feligrés NM, **feligresa** NF parishioner.

feligresía NF parish; parishioners (*collectively*).

felino ADJ feline, catlike.

Felipe NM Philip.

felipismo NM *policies and following of Felipe González (Spanish prime minister from 1982 to 1996)*.

felipista [1] ADJ *related to Felipe González or his policies*; **la mayoría ~** the pro-Felipe González majority.
[2] NMF supporter of Felipe González.

➤ **feliz** ADJ (a) (*gen*) happy; **¡~ año nuevo!** happy new year!; **¡~ viaje!** bon voyage!; **y vivieron felices, fueron felices y comieron perdices** and they lived happily ever after.
(b) *frase etc* felicitous, happy, exactly right.
(c) (*afortunado*) lucky, fortunate; successful; **la cosa tuvo un fin ~** the affair had a successful outcome, the affair turned out well; **no ha sido ~ con sus biógrafos** she has not been lucky with her biographers.

felizmente ADV (*V ADJ*) (a) happily. (b) felicitously. (c) luckily, fortunately; successfully.

felón [1] ADJ wicked, treacherous.
[2] NM, **felona** NF wicked person, villain.

felonía NF (*LAm*) felony, crime.

felpa NF (a) plush. (b) (*: tunda*) hiding*; (*reprimenda*) dressing-down*.

felpar [1a] VT to cover with plush; (*fig*) to carpet (*de* with).

felpeada NF (*Cono Sur, Méx*) dressing-down*.

felpear [1a] VT (*Cono Sur, Méx*) (*regañar*) to dress down*; (*azotar*) to beat, thrash.

felpilla NF chenille, candlewick.

felpudo [1] ADJ plush, plushy.
[2] NM doormat.

femenil ADJ (a) feminine, womanly. (b) (*CAm, Méx*) women's (*atr*); **equipo ~** women's team.

femenino [1] ADJ feminine; *sexo* female; **deporte ~** sport for women; **equipo ~** women's team; **del género ~** of the feminine gender.
[2] NM (*Ling*) feminine.

FEMENINO	ver también la entrada

Femenino se puede traducir al inglés por *female* o *feminine*.
- *Femenino* se traduce por *female* cuando nos referimos al hecho de ser del sexo femenino (en oposición al sexo masculino):
  Este tipo de enfermedad es más común entre la población femenina
  This type of disease is more common among the female population
- Se traduce por *feminine* para referirse a las cualidades y características que tradicionalmente se han relacionado con la mujer:
  Tiene una forma muy femenina de vestir
  She dresses in a very feminine way
- También se emplea *feminine* en el ámbito gramatical:
  La palabra "mar" puede llevar tanto artículo femenino como masculino.
  The word "mar" can take both feminine and masculine articles
  Para otros usos y ejemplos ver la entrada.

---

fémina NF (*hum o pey*) woman, female.

feminidad NF femininity.

feminismo NM feminism.

feminista NMF feminist.

FEMP NF ABR *de* Federación Española de Municipios y Provincias.

fémur NM femur.

fenecer [2d] [1] VT to finish, conclude, close.
[2] VI (a) (*terminar*) to come to an end, cease. (b) (*euf*) to pass away, die; to perish.

fenecimiento NM (a) (*fin*) end, conclusion, close. (b) (*euf*) passing, demise.

Fenicia NF Phoenicia.

fenicio, -a ADJ, NM/F Phoenician.

fénico ADJ carbolic.

fénix NM phoenix; (*fig*) marvel; **el F~ de los ingenios** the Prince of Wits, the genius of our times (*Lope de Vega*).

fenol NM phenol, carbolic acid.

fenomenal ADJ (a) phenomenal. (b) (*: estupendo*) tremendous*, terrific*.

fenomenalmente ADV terrifically (well)*.

fenómeno [1] NM (a) phenomenon; (*fig*) freak, accident. (b) **Pedro es un ~** Peter is a genius, Peter is altogether exceptional.
[2] ADJ (*) great*, marvellous; **una chica fenómena** a smashing girl*; **¡él estuvo ~!** he was great!*; he was the tops!*
[3] ADV (*) **lo hemos pasado ~** we had a terrific time; **le va ~** he's getting on tremendously well*.

feo [1] ADJ (a) *aspecto* ugly; hideous, unsightly; **más ~ que Picio, más ~ que un grajo** (*etc*) as ugly as sin; **me tocó bailar con la más fea** (*fig*) I got the short straw.

(b) (*desagradable*) *olor etc* bad, nasty; *jugada* dirty, foul; *tiempo* nasty, awful, foul; *situación* nasty; ugly; **es una costumbre fea** it's a nasty habit; **eso es muy ~** that's nasty, that's not nice; **él me puso el problema ~** he made me see the difficulties of the problem; **esto se está poniendo ~** this is beginning to look bad, I don't like the look of this; **hace ~ comerse las uñas en público** it's not done (o it's bad-mannered) to bite your nails in public.
(c) (*LAm*) (*asqueroso*) disgusting, foul; (*de olor*) foul-smelling; (*de sabor*) foul-tasting.
[2] NM insult, slight; **hacer un ~ a uno** to insult sb, offend sb; **¿me vas a hacer ese ~?** but you can't refuse!
[3] ADV (*LAm*) bad, badly; **oler ~** to smell bad, have a nasty smell; **cantar ~** to sing terribly.

FEOGA NM ABR *de* Fondo Europeo de Orientación y de Garantía Agrícola European Agricultural Guidance and Guarantee Fund, EAGGF.

feón ADJ (*LAm*) ugly; **medio ~** rather ugly.

feote ADJ terribly ugly.

feracidad NF fertility, productivity.

feralla NF scrap metal.

feraz ADJ fertile, productive.

féretro NM coffin, casket (*US*); bier.

feri NM (*LAm*) = ferryboat.

feria NF (a) (*Com etc*) fair, market; (*Agr*) agricultural show; (*carnaval*) carnival; (*LAm: mercado*) village market, weekly market; **la F~ de Sevilla** the Seville Fair, the Seville Carnival; **~ agrícola** agricultural show; **~ de ganado** cattle-show; **~ de libros** book-fair; **~ de muestras** trade show, trade exhibition; **~ de vanidades** empty show, inane spectacle; **irle a uno como en ~** (*Méx*) to go very badly.
(b) (*descanso*) holiday; rest, rest day.
(c) (*Méx Fin*) change; (*CAm: propina*) tip.

feriado [1] ADJ: **día ~** holiday, day off; **día medio ~** half-holiday, half-day off.
[2] NM (*LAm*) bank holiday (*Brit*), public holiday.

ferial [1] ADJ fair (*atr*), fairground (*atr*); **recinto ~** fairground; exhibition area.
[2] NM fair, market; fairground.

feriante NMF (a) (*vendedor*) stallholder, trader; (*de espectáculos*) showman. (b) fair-goer.

feriar [1b] [1] VT (a) (*comerciar*) to buy, sell (in a market, at a fair); to trade, exchange; (*Méx*) *dinero* to change. (b) (*And: vender barato*) to sell cheap.
[2] VI to take time off, take a break.

ferino ADJ savage, wild; **tos ferina** whooping cough.

fermata NF (*Mús*) run.

fermentación NF fermentation.

fermentado [1] ADJ fermented.
[2] NM fermentation.

fermentar [1a] VI to ferment; **hacer ~** to ferment, cause fermentation in.

fermento NM (a) (*acto*) ferment. (b) (*sustancia*) leaven, leavening.

fermio NM (*Quím*) fermium.

Fernán NM, **Fernando** NM Ferdinand; **te lo han puesto como a ~ VII** they've given it to you on a plate.

ferocidad NF fierceness, ferocity, savageness; cruelty.

ferocísimo ADJ (*superl*) *de* feroz.

Feroe NF: **Islas** FPL **~** Faroe Islands, the Faroes.

feromona NF pheromone.

feroz ADJ (a) fierce, ferocious, savage; cruel. (b) (*LAm: feo*) ugly.

ferozmente ADV fiercely, ferociously, savagely; cruelly.

férreo ADJ (a) (*gen*) iron; (*Quím*) ferrous; **metal no ~** non-ferrous metal. (b) (*Ferro*) rail (*atr*); **vía férrea** railway. (c) (*fig*) iron; hard, rigid, tough; **con voluntad férrea** with an iron will, with a will of iron.

ferrería NF ironworks, foundry.

ferretería NF (a) (*objetos*) ironmongery, hardware. (b) (*tienda*) ironmonger's (shop), hardware store. (c) = ferrería.

ferretero, -a NM/F ironmonger, hardware dealer.

férrico ADJ ferric.

ferroaleación NF ferro-alloy.

ferrobús NM (*Ferro*) diesel car.

ferrocarril NM railway, railroad (*US*); **~ de cercanías** suburban rail network; **~ de cremallera** rack railway; **~ elevado** elevated railway, overhead railway; **~ funicular** funicular (railway); **~ subterráneo** underground railway; **~ de vía estrecha** narrow-gauge railway; **~ de vía única** single-track railway; **por ~** by rail, by train; **de ~** railway (*atr*), railroad (*atr*: US), rail (*atr*).

ferrocarrilero (*LAm*) [1] ADJ railway (*atr*), railroad (*atr*: US), rail (*atr*).
[2] NM railway, railroad (*US*).
[3] NM, **ferrocarrilera** NF (*LAm: trabajador*) railway worker.

ferroprusiato NM (*Arquit, Téc*) blueprint.

ferroso ADJ ferrous; **metal no ~** non-ferrous metal.

ferrotipo NM (*Fot*) tintype.

ferroviario ① ADJ railway *(atr)*, railroad *(atr: US)*, rail *(atr)*.
② NM railwayman.
ferry ['feri] NM ferry.
ferry boat [feri'βot] NM *(LAm)* ferryboat, railway ferry, train-ferry.
fértil ADJ fertile, fruitful, productive; rich *(en* in); *imaginación etc* fertile.
fertilidad NF fertility; fruitfulness; richness.
fertilización NF fertilization; **~ cruzada** cross-fertilization.
fertilizante NM fertilizer.
fertilizar [1f] VT to fertilize; to make fruitful; to enrich.
férula NF **(a)** *(vara)* ferule, birch, rod.
(b) *(Med)* splint.
(c) *(fig)* rule, domination; **vivir bajo la ~ de un tirano** to live under the harsh rule *(o* jackboot) of a tyrant.
férvido ADJ fervid, ardent.
ferviente ADJ fervent.
fervor NM fervour, ardour, passion.
fervorosamente ADV fervently, ardently, passionately.
fervoroso ADJ fervent, ardent, passionate.
festejar [1a] VT **(a)** *persona* to feast, wine and dine; to throw a party for; to entertain; to fête.
(b) *aniversario, ocasión etc* to celebrate.
(c) *mujer* to woo, court.
(d) *(LAm: azotar)* to thrash.
festejo NM **(a)** *(fiesta)* feast; entertainment; *(And)* revelry; **~ nupcial** wedding reception. **(b)** *(celebración)* celebration; **~s** public festivities, rejoicings; **hacer ~s a uno** to make a great fuss of sb. **(c)** *(cortejo)* wooing, courtship.
festín NM feast, banquet.
festinar [1a] VT **(a)** *(CAm)* *(agasajar)* to feast, wine and dine; *(entretener)* to entertain. **(b)** *(LAm: arruinar)* to mess up, ruin (by being overhasty). **(c)** *(LAm: acelerar)* to hurry along, speed up.
festival NM festival.
festivalero ① ADJ festival *(atr)*.
② NM, **festivalera** NF festival-goer.
festivamente ADV wittily, facetiously, humorously; jovially.
festividad NF **(a)** *(actos)* festivity, merrymaking. **(b)** *(Ecl)* feast, festivity; holiday. **(c)** *(gracia)* wit, humour; *(alegría)* joviality.
festivo ADJ **(a)** *(alegre)* festive, merry, gay. **(b)** **día ~** holiday. **(c)** *(gracioso)* witty, facetious, humorous; jovial; *(Liter etc)* humorous, comic, burlesque.
festón NM *(Cos)* festoon, scallop; *(de flores)* garland.
festonear [1a] VT to festoon, scallop; to garland.
FET [fet] NF **(a)** *(Dep)* ABR *de* **Federación Española de Tenis**.
(b) : **~ de las JONS** ABR *de* **Falange Española Tradicionalista de las Juntas de Ofensiva Nacional-Socialista**.
fetal ADJ foetal.
fetén* ① ADJ INVAR **(a)** *(auténtico)* real, authentic.
(b) *(estupendo)* smashing*, super*; **una chica ~** a smashing girl*.
② ADV splendidly, marvellously.
③ NF **(a)** **de ~** *(estupendo)* smashing*, super*; **ser la ~ (y la chipén)** to be smashing*.
(b) *(verdad)* truth; **ser la ~** to be gospel truth.
fetiche NM fetish; *(fig)* mumbo-jumbo, rigmarole.
fetichismo NM fetishism.
fetichista ① ADJ fetishistic.
② NMF fetishist.
fetidez NF smelliness, rankness.
fétido ADJ foul-smelling, stinking, rank.
feto NM **(a)** *(Bio)* foetus. **(b)** *(*: monstruo)* abortion, monster; *(chica)* plain girl, ugly girl.
feúcho* ADJ plain, homely *(US)*.
feudal ADJ feudal.
feudalismo NM feudalism.
feudo NM **(a)** *(Hist)* fief; manor. **(b)** **~ franco** *(Jur)* freehold.
feúra NF *(LAm)* **(a)** *(gen)* ugliness. **(b)** *(una ~)* ugly person, ugly thing.
FEVE ['feβe] NF ABR *de* **Ferrocarriles Españoles de Vía Estrecha**.
fez NM fez.
FF, f.f. ABR *de* **franco (en) fábrica**; **precio ~** price ex-factory.
FFAA ABR *de* **Fuerzas Armadas** armed forces.
FFCC ABR *de* **Ferrocarriles**.
FGD NM ABR *de* **Fondo de Garantía de Depósitos**.
fha. ABR *de* **fecha** date, d.
fiabilidad NF reliability, trustworthiness; credibility.
fiable ADJ reliable, trustworthy; credible.
fiaca: NF *(Cono Sur)* laziness, apathy.
fiado NM **(a)** **al ~** on trust, *(Com)* on credit. **(b)** **en ~** *(Jur)* on bail.
fiador ① NM, **fiadora** NF *(Jur: persona)* surety, guarantor; *(Com)* sponsor, backer; **salir ~ por uno** to go bail for sb, stand security for sb.
② NM **(a)** *(Mec)* catch, fastener, pawl, trigger; *(de revólver)* safety catch; *(de cerradura)* tumbler; *(de ventana)* fastener, bolt.
(b) *(*: trasero)* bottom, backside.
(c) *(And, Cono Sur: de perro)* muzzle; *(And, Cono Sur: de casco)* chinstrap.

fiambre ① ADJ **(a)** *(Culin)* cold, served cold.
(b) *(*) noticia etc* old, stale.
② NM **(a)** *(Culin)* cold meat, cold food; cold lunch, buffet lunch; **~s** cold meats, cold cuts *(US)*.
(b) *(Méx Culin)* pork, avocado and chili dish.
(c) *(*: cadáver)* corpse, stiff‡; **el pobre está ~** the poor chap is stone dead, the poor fellow is cold meat now*.
(d) *(*: noticia)* (piece of) stale news.
(e) *(*: chiste)* corny joke*, chestnut*.
(f) *(Cono Sur: fiesta)* lifeless party, cold affair.
fiambrera NF **(a)** *(canasto)* lunch basket, dinner pail *(US)*. **(b)** *(Cono Sur: fresquera)* meat safe; icebox.
fiambrería NF *(LAm)* delicatessen.
fianza NF **(a)** *(garantía)* surety, security, bond; *(señal)* deposit; **bajo ~** *(Jur)* on bail; **~ de aduana** customs bond; **~ de averías** average bond; **~ carcelera** bail. **(b)** *(persona)* surety, guarantor.
fiar [1c] ① VT **(a)** *(gen)* to entrust, confide *(a* to).
(b) *(Fin etc)* to guarantee, vouch for; to stand security for; *(Jur)* to go bail for.
(c) *(Com: a crédito)* to sell on credit; *(LAm)* to buy on credit.
② VI to trust *(en* in); **ser de ~** to be reliable, be trustworthy.
③ **fiarse** VR: **~ de uno** to trust sb; to rely on sb, depend on sb; to confide in sb; **me fié completamente de ti** I trusted in you completely; **no me fío de él** I don't trust him; **nos fiamos de Vd para conseguirlo** we rely on you to get it; *(en tienda)* **'no se fía'** 'no credit given'.
fiasco NM fiasco.
fíat NM, PL **fíats** official sanction, fiat; consent, blessing.
fibra NF **(a)** *(gen)* fibre; **~ acrílica** acrylic fibre; **~ de amianto** asbestos fibre; **~ artificial** man-made fibre; **~ de carbono** carbon fibre; **~ dietética** dietary fibre; **~ ocular** ocular fibre; **~ sintética** synthetic fibre; **~ de vidrio** fibre-glass.
(b) *(en madera)* grain; *(Min)* vein.
(c) *(fig)* vigour, toughness; sinews; **~s del corazón** heartstrings; **despertar la ~ sensible** to strike a sympathetic cord, awaken a sympathetic response.
fibravidrio NM fibre-glass.
fibrina NF fibrin.
fibroóptica NF fibre optics.
fibrosis NF fibrosis; **~ cística** cystic fibrosis.
fibrositis NF fibrositis.
fibroso ADJ fibrous.
fíbula NF *(Hist)* fibula, brooch.
ficción ① NF **(a)** fiction; *(pey)* invention, fabrication. **(b)** *(Liter)* fiction; **~ científica** science-fiction; **obras de no ~** non-fiction books.
② ATR fictitious, make-believe; mock; **historia ~** (piece of) historical fiction, fictionalized history; **reportaje ~** dramatized documentary.
ficcioso *(Cono Sur)* ① ADJ bluffing; false, double-dealing.
② NM bluffer; double-dealer.
ficha NF **(a)** *(Telec etc)* token; *(en juegos)* token, counter, marker; *(póquer)* chip; *(Com, Fin)* token, tally; **~ del dominó** domino; **~ de silicio** silicon chip; **mover ~** *(fig)* to make a move.
(b) *(tarjeta)* card; index card, record-card, catalogue card; *(en hotel)* registration form; **~ antropométrica** card recording personal particulars; **~ perforada** punched card; **~ policíaca** police record, police dossier; **~ técnica** *(TV etc)* (list of) credits.
(c) *(CAm, Carib, Cono Sur ††)* 5-cent piece; *(CAm*: moneda)* coin.
(d) *(Méx: de botella)* flat bottle cap.
(e) *(And, Carib: t mala ~)* rogue, villain.
(f) *(Dep)* signing-on fee.
fichaje NM **(a)** *(Dep)* signing (up); *(Fin)* signing-on fee. **(b)** **nuevos ~s** *(Pol)* new members, new supporters.
fichar [1a] ① VT **(a)** *ficha* to file, index.
(b) *persona* to file the personal particulars of; *dato* to record, enter (on a card etc); **está fichado** he's got a (police) record; **le tenemos fichado** we have his record, *(fig)* we've got him taped*, we know all about him.
(c) *dominó* to play.
(d) *(Dep etc)* to sign up, sign on *(en un club* for a club, with a team).
(e) *(Carib: engañar)* to swindle.
② VI **(a)** *(Dep etc)* to sign up, sign on; *(en fábrica etc)* to clock in.
(b) *(And: morir)* to die.
fichero NM card-index; filing-cabinet; *(Inform)* file; **~ de datos** datafile; **~ fotográfico de delincuentes** photographic records of criminals, rogues' gallery; **~ indexado** index file; **~ informático** computer file.
ficticio ADJ fictitious; imaginary; *(pey)* fabricated.
ficus NM INVAR *(Bot)* rubber plant.
FIDA NM ABR *de* **Fondo Internacional de Desarrollo Agrícola** International Fund for Agricultural Development, IFAD.
fidedigno ADJ reliable, trustworthy.

fideería NF (*LAm*) pasta factory.

fideicomisario [1] ADJ trust (*atr*); **banco ~** trust company.

  [2] NM, **fideicomisaria** NF trustee.

  [3] NM trust.

fideicomiso NM trust.

fidelería NF (*LAm*) pasta factory.

fidelidad NF (a) (*lealtad*) fidelity, loyalty (*a* to).

  (b) (*exactitud*) accuracy.

  (c) **alta ~** (*Rad*) high fidelity; **de alta ~** high-fidelity (*atr*), hi-fi.

fidelísimo ADJ (*superl*) *de* **fiel**.

fideo NM (a) **~s** (*Culin*) noodles, spaghetti. (b) (*: persona*) beanpole*.

fiduciario [1] ADJ fiduciary.

  [2] NM, **fiduciaria** NF fiduciary, trustee.

fiebre NF (a) (*Med*) fever; **~ aftosa** foot-and-mouth disease; **~ amarilla** yellow fever; **~ entérica** enteric fever; **~ glandular** glandular fever; **~ del heno** hay fever; **~ palúdica** malaria; **~ porcina** swine fever; **~ reumática** rheumatic fever; **~ tifoidea** typhoid; **tener ~** to have a (high) temperature, be feverish; to have fever, be in a fever.

  (b) (*fig*) fever; feverish excitement, fevered atmosphere; **la ~ del juego** the gambling fever; **~ del oro** gold fever; gold-rush.

  (c) (*Cono Sur*: *taimado*) slippery customer*.

fiel [1] ADJ (a) (*gen*) faithful, loyal; (*fiable*) honest, reliable, trustworthy; **seguir siendo ~ a** to remain loyal to, remain true to.

  (b) *relación, traducción etc* accurate, exact, faithful.

  [2] **los ~es** (*Ecl*) NMPL the faithful.

  [3] NM (a) (*persona*) inspector of weights and measures.

  (b) (*Téc*) needle, pointer.

fielmente ADV (a) (*gen*) faithfully, loyally; reliably. (b) (*exactamente*) accurately, exactly.

fieltro NM (a) (*tela*) felt. (b) (*objeto*) felt, piece of felt; felt rug; felt hat.

fiera [1] NF (a) wild beast, wild animal; (*Taur*) bull.

  (b) **~ sarda** (*And*) expert, top man.

  [2] NMF (*fig*) fiend; virago, dragon; (*en buen sentido*) ball of fire, highly energetic person; **como una ~ enjaulada** like a caged tiger; **es un ~ para el trabajo** he's a demon for work; **es una ~ para el deporte** he's a fiend for sport, he's a sports fiend; **estar hecho una ~** to be wild, be furious; **ella entró hecha una ~** she came in absolutely furious.

fierecilla NF (*fig*) shrew.

fiereza NF (a) (*ferocidad*) fierceness; ferocity; cruelty; frightfulness. (b) (*fealdad*) ugly deformity.

fiero [1] ADJ (a) (*feroz*) fierce, ferocious; (*Zool*) wild, fierce; (*cruel*) cruel; (*horroroso*) frightful. (b) (*: feo*) ugly.

  [2] **~s** NMPL threats, boasts; **echar ~s, hacer ~s** to utter threats, bluster, brag.

fierro NM (a) (*LAm*: *gen*) iron; (*Agr*) marking-iron, brand; (*Cono Sur*: *cuchillo*) knife; (*Cono Sur*: *Aut*) accelerator; (*Cono Sur**: *arma*) gun, weapon. (b) **~s** (*Méx*: *fig*) money; (*LAm*: *resortes*) springs.

▼ **fiesta** NF (a) (*en casa etc*) party, entertainment; social gathering; celebration; (*de ciudad etc*) festival, fête; **~s** public festivities, public rejoicings; **~ de armas** (*Hist*) tournament; **la ~ brava, la ~ nacional** (*Taur*) bullfighting; **~ de disfraces** fancy-dress party; **organizar una ~ en honor de uno** to give a party in sb's honour; **¡se acabó la ~!** (*fig*) drop it!, that's enough of that!, joke over!; **aguar la ~** to spoil the fun, be a spoilsport; to spoil the party; **la noticia del accidente nos aguó la ~ a todos** news of the accident put a real dampener on us all; **estar en ~s** to be en fête; **para coronar la ~, por fin de ~** to round it all off, as a finishing touch; **no sabe de qué va la ~** he hasn't a clue; **¡tengamos la ~ en paz!** none of that!; cut it out!

▼ (b) (*Ecl*) feast, feast day; holiday; **~s** holidays; **~s*** (*esp*) Christmas festivities, Christmas season; **~ de la banderita** flag day; **~ cívica, ~ laboral** public holiday; **~ fija, ~ inmoble** immovable feast; **~ de guardar, ~ de precepto** day of obligation, holiday; **F~ de la Hispanidad, F~ de la Raza** Columbus Day; **~ movible, ~ móvil** movable feast; **~ nacional** public holiday, bank holiday; **F~ del Trabajo** Labour Day; **mañana es ~** it's a holiday tomorrow; **la ~ del santo** the saint's feast, the saint's day; **celebrar la ~, guardar la ~** to observe the feast (*de* of); **hacer ~** to take a day off.

  (c) (*juerga*) merrymaking, festivities, fun and games; **la ~ continuó hasta muy tarde** the festivities went on very late; **estar de ~s** to be in high good humour; **¡estás de ~!** you're joking!; **no estoy para ~s** I'm in no mood for jokes.

  (d) **~s** (*palabras*) endearments; soothing words, flattering words; (*caricias*) caresses; **hacer ~s a** to caress, fondle; (*perro*) to fawn on; (*fig*) to make a great fuss of.

┌─── **FIESTAS** ───

ⓘ *There are a fixed number of public holidays in the Spanish calendar but some dates vary locally. National public holidays include* **Navidad** *(25 Dec),* **Reyes** *(6 Jan), the* **Día de los Trabajadores** *(1 May), the* **Día de la Hispanidad/del Pilar** *(12 Oct) and the* **Día de la Constitución** *(6 Dec). Additionally, each autonomous region and town has at its discretion a*

small number of public holidays that usually coincide with local traditions like a patron saint's day or other celebrations such as **Carnaval**. *Thus there is a holiday in Madrid for* **San Isidro**, *the city's patron saint, and one in Catalonia for* **Sant Jordi**, *who is the patron saint of the region.*

---

fiestero ADJ gay; fun-loving, pleasure-seeking; fond of parties.

fiestorro* NM (*hum*) grand party, big party.

FIFA NF ABR *de* **Fédération Internationale de Football Association** FIFA.

fifí † NM (*LAm*) playboy, young man about town.

fifiriche ADJ (*CAm, Méx*) weak, sickly.

figón NM cheap restaurant.

figulino ADJ clay (*atr*); **arcilla figulina** potter's clay.

figura [1] NF (a) (*gen, Arte etc*) figure; shape, form; image; **de ~ entera** full-length; **~ de nieve** snowman.

  (b) (*persona*) figure; **una ~ destacada** an outstanding figure; **~ del partido** man of the match; **~ de culto** cult figure; **las principales ~s del partido** the chief figures in the party; **cuando uno es ~** when one is a famous person; **hacer ~** to cut a figure.

  (c) (††) countenance; **hacer ~s** to make faces.

  (d) (*Mat etc, Tip*) figure, drawing, diagram; **~ celeste** horoscope.

  (e) (*Ling*) figure; **~ retórica** rhetorical figure, figure of speech.

  (f) (*Teat*: *personaje*) character, role; **en la ~ de** in the role of.

  (g) (*Teat*: *títere*) marionette.

  (h) (*Naipes*) picture card, court card; (*Ajedrez*) piece, man.

  (i) (*Baile, Patinaje*) figure.

  (j) (*Mús*) note.

  [2] NM: **ser un ~** to be a big name, be somebody.

figuración NF (a) (*imaginación*) **eso son figuraciones tuyas** it's just your imagination, you're imagining things. (b) (*Cine*) extras.

figuradamente ADV figuratively.

figurado ADJ figurative.

figurante NM, **figuranta** NF (a) (*Teat*) extra, walker-on, super-(numerary). (b) (*fig*) figurehead.

▼ **figurar** [1a] [1] VT to figure, shape, form; to represent.

  [2] VI (a) (*incluirse*) to figure (*como* as, *entre* among), appear; **los nombres no figuran aquí** the names do not appear here.

  (b) (*fig*) to show off, cut a dash; **todo se debe al afán de ~** it's all due to the urge to cut a dash, it's the urge to be somebody that causes it all.

▼ [3] **figurarse** VR to suppose; to expect; to imagine, fancy; to figure (*US*); **¡figúrate!, ¡figúrese!** just think!, just imagine!; **¡figúrate lo que sería con dos!** imagine what it would be like with two of them!; **ya me lo figuraba** I thought as much; **me figuro que es caro** I fancy it's dear, I imagine it's dear; **¿qué te figuras que me preguntó ayer?** what do you think he asked me yesterday?; **no te vayas a figurar que ...** don't go thinking that ...

figurativismo NM representational art.

figurativo ADJ figurative; *arte* representational.

figurilla NF figurine.

figurín NM fashion plate; model; dummy; (*Teat*) design for a costume.

figurinismo NM (*Teat*) costume design.

figurinista NMF (*Teat*) costume designer.

figurón NM (a) (*gen*) grotesque figure, huge figure; **~ de proa** figurehead. (b) (*: presumido*) pretentious nobody; pompous ass*.

figuroso ADJ (*Cono Sur, Méx*) showy, loud.

fija NF (a) (*Téc*) hinge; (*Arquit*) trowel.

  (b) (*And, Cono Sur*: *Carreras*) favourite; **es una ~** (*Cono Sur*) it's a cert*; **ésa es la ~** that's for sure; **ésta es la ~** it's a sure thing.

fijación NF (a) (*acto*) fixing; securing; fastening; sticking (on); posting; establishing. (b) (*Med*) fixation. (c) (*de esquí*) binding, harness.

fijador NM (a) (*Fot*) fixer; fixing bath. (b) **~ para el pelo** hair lotion, haircream.

fijamente ADV firmly, steadily, securely; fixedly; **mirar ~ a uno** to stare at sb, look hard at sb.

fijapelo NM hair lotion, haircream.

fijar [1a] [1] VT (a) (*gen*) to fix; (*clavar*) to secure, fasten (on, down *etc*); *sello etc* to affix, stick (on), paste on, glue on; *cartel* to post, stick, put up; *pelo* to set; (*Fot*) to fix; *residencia* to take up, establish; *ojos* to fix (*en* on); *atención* to focus, fix (*en* on).

  (b) (*fig*: *determinar*) to settle (on), decide, determine; *fecha, hora, precio etc* to fix, set; **la fecha no se puede ~ con precisión** the date cannot exactly be determined; **hemos fijado una hora** we have fixed a time, we have agreed on a time.

  (c) (*) *persona* to catch (the attention of), draw, pull.

  [2] **fijarse** VR (a) (*establecerse*) to become fixed, get set; to settle, lodge; to establish o.s.; **el dolor se ha fijado en la pierna** the pain has settled in the leg.

  (b) (*prestar atención*) to notice, pay attention; **lo malo es que no se fija** the trouble is he doesn't pay attention; **el debería fijarse más en lo que dice** he ought to be more careful about what he says; **no**

me había fijado I hadn't noticed; **fíjese bien** pay close attention, watch this carefully; **¡fíjate!** fancy that!, just imagine!; **¿te fijas?** (*: esp LAm) see what I mean?*
(c) **~ en algo** to notice sth, observe sth, pay attention to sth; (*mirar*) to stare at sth; **~ en un detalle** to seize upon a detail; **¡fíjense en los precios!** just look at these prices!; **se fijó en mí en seguida** he fixed on me at once; **~ en** + *infin* to be intent on + *ger*.

fijasellos NM INVAR stamp hinge.

fijativo NM fixative.

fijeza NF firmness, stability; constancy; fixity; **mirar con ~ a uno** to stare at sb, look hard at sb.

fijo ① ADJ (a) (*gen*) fixed; (*firme*) firm, steady, stable, secure; *estrella, fecha, precio etc* fixed; *mirada* fixed, steady; *color* fast; *cliente* regular; **de ~** certainly, for sure.
(b) *propósito etc* fixed, firm.
(c) *plantilla* permanent, established; *novio* regular, steady.
② EXCL: **¡~!** quite right!

fil NM: **~ derecho** leapfrog.

fila NF (a) (*gen*) row, line; (*en marcha*) file; (*Dep, Teat etc*) row, tier (of seats); (*cola*) queue; **una ~ de coches** a line of cars; **~ cero** row of seats for VIPs; **~ india** single file, Indian file; **una chaqueta de dos ~s** a double-breasted jacket; **en ~** in a row; in a line; **en ~ de a uno, en ~ india** in single file; **aparcar en doble ~** to double-park; **ponerse en ~** to line up, get into line; (*fig*) **salir de la ~** to step out of line.
(b) (*Mil*) rank; (*fig*) **las ~s** the ranks; **los eslobodios de ~s** the rank-and-file Slobodians; **¡en ~s!** fall in!; (*fig*) **apretar las ~s** to close ranks; **cerrar ~s** to close ranks (*t fig*); **estar en ~s** to be with the colours, be on active service; **formar ~s** to form up, fall in; **llamar a uno a ~s** to call sb up, call sb to the colours; **romper ~s** to fall out, dismiss; **¡rompan ~s!** dismiss!; **romper las ~s** to break ranks.
(c) (*: antipatía*) dislike, antipathy; **el jefe le tiene ~** the boss has it in for him*.
(d) (*CAm: cumbre*) peak, summit.

filacteria NF phylactery.

Filadelfia N Philadelphia.

filamento NM filament.

filamentoso ADJ filamentous; sinewy.

filantropía NF philanthropy.

filantrópico ADJ philanthropic.

filantropismo NM philanthropy.

filántropo NM, **filántropa** NF philanthropist.

filar* [1a] VT (a) (*calar*) to size up, rumble*. (b) (*observar*) to notice, spot, take note of.

filarmónica NF philharmonic (orchestra).

filarmónico ADJ philharmonic.

filatelia NF (a) (*gen*) philately, stamp collecting. (b) (*tienda*) stamp shop, stamp dealer's.

filatélico ① ADJ philatelic; stamp (*atr*).
② NM, **filatélica** NF stamp dealer.

filatelista NMF philatelist, stamp collector.

filático ADJ (*And*) *caballo* vicious; *persona* (*travieso*) mischievous; (*taimado*) crafty; (*grosero*) rude.

filete NM (a) (*Arquit*) fillet.
(b) (*Mec: de tornillo*) thread, worm; (*de brida*) snaffle (-bit).
(c) (*Culin: carne*) fillet, tenderloin, steak; (*pescado*) fillet; **darse el ~*** to neck*, pet*; **darse el ~ con*** to feel*, touch up*.
(d) (*Cos*) narrow hem.
(e) (*Tip*) fillet.

fileteado NM filleting.

filetear [1a] VT to fillet; to cut into strips.

filetón NM fillet steak.

filfa* NF (a) (*fraude*) fraud, hoax; piece of humbug. (b) (*falsificación*) fake. (c) (*rumor*) rumour, canard.

fili* NM pocket; **~ de la buena** breast pocket (of a jacket).

filiación NF (a) (*relación*) filiation; (*de ideas etc*) connection, relationship. (b) (*señas*) personal description; characteristics, particulars. (c) (*Pol*) affiliation.

filial ① ADJ filial; (*Com*) subsidiary, affiliated; (*Dep*) sister (*atr*).
② NF (*Com*) subsidiary, affiliated company.
③ NM (*Dep*) sister club.

filibusterismo NM (*piratería*) buccaneering; (*Parl*) filibustering.

filibustero NM (a) (*bucanero*) buccaneer, freebooter. (b) (*fig*) rogue.

filiforme ADJ thread-like; *persona* (*hum*) skinny.

filigrana NF (a) (*Téc*) filigree; filigree work; (*Tip*) watermark. (b) (*Dep etc*) delicate move, clever piece of play; **~s** (*fig*) elegant play, fancy footwork.

filípica NF harangue, tirade, philippic.

Filipinas NFPL: **las (Islas) ~** the Philippines.

filipino ① ADJ Philippine.
② NM, **filipina** NF Philippine, Filipino.

filisteísmo NM Philistinism.

filisteo ① ADJ Philistine.
② NM (a) (*Hist, fig*) Philistine. (b) (*fig*) big man, giant.

film NM, PL **films** [film] film; picture, movie (*US*).

filmación NF (a) (*acto*) filming, shooting. (b) **filmaciones** footage.

filmador NM film-maker.

filmadora NF (*estudio*) film studio; (*aparato*) film camera.

filmar [1a] VT to film, shoot.

filme NM = **film**.

fílmico ADJ film (*atr*), movie (*atr*: US); screen (*atr*); **su carrera fílmica** her film career, her career in films; **obras teatrales y fílmicas** theatrical and screen works, works for stage and screen.

filmina NF (*Fot: diapositiva*) slide, transparency; (*película*) filmstrip, short film; (*de microscopio*) slide.

filmografía NF (a) (*estudio*) study of the film; **la ~ de la estrella** the star's film history, the star's screen history. (b) (*filmes*) films (*collectively*); **la ~ del Oeste** the history of the Western, films (*collectively*) about the West, the West on the screen.

filmología NF science of film-making, art of film-making.

filmoteca NF film library, film archive.

filo¹ NM (a) (*de herramienta etc*) edge; cutting edge, blade; (*línea*) dividing-line; (*cresta*) ridge; **~ de la navaja** (*fig*) razor's edge; **~ del viento** (*Náut*) direction of the wind; **de doble ~, de dos ~s** double-edged (*t fig*); **al ~ de las 12** at 12 precisely; **por ~** exactly; **de ~** (*And*) resolutely; **dar (un) ~ a, sacar el ~ a** to sharpen, put an edge on; **dar ~ a** (*fig: And*) to tell off, (*Carib*) to wound with a knife; **herir a uno por los mismos ~s** to pay sb back in his own coin; **pasar al ~ de la espada** to put to the sword.
(b) (*CAm, Méx: hambre*) hunger; **tener ~*** to be starving, be ravenous.
(c) (*Cono Sur*: cuento) tale, tall story.
(d) (*Cono Sur*: pretendiente) suitor; (*novia*) girlfriend; (*cortejo*) courtship.

filo² NM (*Bio*) phylum.

filo³*: NM con-man's accomplice*.

filo... PREF philo..., pro..., *p.ej.* **filosoviético** pro-Soviet; **filo-terrorista** sympathetic to terrorism.

-filo SUF -phile, *p.ej.* **francófilo** NM, **francófila** NF francophile.

filocomunismo NM pro-communist feeling(s); fellow-travelling.

filocomunista ① ADJ pro-communist; with communist leanings, fellow-travelling.
② NMF pro-communist; fellow traveller.

filología NF philology.

filológico ADJ philological.

filólogo, -a NM/F philologist.

filomela NF, **filomena** NF (*poét*) nightingale.

filón NM (*Min*) seam, vein, lode; (*fig*) rich seam, gold-mine.

filongo NM (*Cono Sur*) girlfriend (of inferior social status).

filosa*: NF (a) (*navaja*) chiv*, knife. (b) (*cera*) mug*, face.

filoso ADJ (a) (*CAm, Cono Sur, Méx*) sharp. (b) (*Cono Sur*) **él es ~** he's sharp, he's really on the ball; **estar ~ en algo** to be well up on sth. (c) (*CAm*) hungry.

filosofal ADJ: **piedra ~** philosopher's stone.

filosofar [1a] VI to philosophize.

filosofía NF philosophy; **~ de la ciencia** philosophy of science; **~ moral** moral philosophy; **~ natural** natural philosophy; **~ de la vida** philosophy of life.

filosófico ADJ philosophic(al).

filósofo, -a NM/F philosopher.

filosoviético ADJ pro-Soviet.

filote NM (*And*) ear of green maize; maize silk; **estar en ~** (*niño*) to begin to grow hair.

filotear [1a] VI (*And: maíz*) to come into ear, begin to ripen; (*niño*) to grow hair.

filoxera NF phylloxera.

filtración NF (a) (*Téc*) filtration; seepage, leakage, loss. (b) (*información*) leak(age), leaking.

filtrado ① ADJ (a) *información* leaked. (b) (*) **estoy ~** (*Cono Sur*) I'm whacked*.
② NM filtering; screening.

filtrador ① ADJ filtering.
② NM filter.

filtraje NM filtering; screening.

filtrar [1a] ① VT (a) (*Téc*) to filter; (*fig*) to screen.
(b) *información etc* to leak (*a* to).
② VI y **filtrarse** VR (a) (*gen*) to filter; **~ por** to filter through; to percolate (through); to seep through, leak through.
(b) (*fig: dinero etc*) to dwindle, disappear bit by bit.

filtro NM (a) (*Téc*) filter; screen; (*en carretera, de policía*) checkpoint, roadblock; **~ de aceite** oil-filter; **~ de aire** air-filter; **cigarrillo con ~** filter-tipped cigarette.
(b) (*Hist*) love-potion, philtre.

filudo ADJ (*LAm*) sharp.

filván NM feather-edge; (*de papel*) deckle edge; (*de cuchillo*) burr.

fimbria NF (*Cos*) border, hem.

▼ **fin** NM **(a)** (*final*) end; ending; conclusion; '~ **de la cita**' 'end of quote', 'unquote'; **función de ~ de curso** end-of-year party; ~ **de fichero** end-of-file; ~ **de fiesta** (*Teat*) grand finale; ~ **de semana** weekend; **a ~es del mes** at (o about) the end of the month; **hacia ~es del siglo** towards the end of the century; **al ~** finally, in the end; **al ~ y al cabo** at long last; in the end; after all, when all is said and done; **en ~, por ~** finally, at last; in short; **en ~** (*fig*) well, well then; **¡en ~!** so that's that!, what next?; **pero en ~, ...** but still, ...; **en ~ de cuentas** in the last analysis; **sin ~** (ADV) endlessly; (ADJ: *t Téc*) endless; **correa sin ~** endless belt; **un sin ~** *V* **sinfín**; **dar ~ a un discurso** to end a speech, close a speech; **llegar a ~ de mes** (*fig*) to make ends meet; to hold out; **llevar algo a buen ~** to carry sth through to a successful conclusion; **poner ~ a** to stop, put a stop to.
(b) (*objetivo*) aim, purpose, objective; scope; **los ~es de este estudio** the aims of this study; the scope of this study; **a ~ de** + *infin* in order to + *infin*, so as to + *infin*; **a ~ de que ...** in order that
▼ ..., so that ...; **a tal ~** with this aim in view; con el ~ de + *infin* with the purpose of + *ger*; con ~es deshonestos with an immoral purpose.

Fina NF *forma familiar de* **Josefina.**

finado [1] ADJ late, deceased; **el ~ presidente** the late president.
[2] NM, **finada** NF deceased.
[3] NM (*Téc*) finishing.

final [1] ADJ final, last; ultimate; eventual.
[2] NM end; conclusion; (*Liter etc*) ending; (*Mús*) finale; ~ **feliz** happy ending; **al ~ de la calle** at the end of the street; **por ~** finally.
[3] NF (*Dep etc*) final; ~ **de consolación** play-off among losers (for third place *etc*).

finalidad NF **(a)** (*propósito*) object, purpose, intention; **la ~ de este libro** the aim of this book; **¿qué ~ tendrá todo esto?** what can be the purpose of all this?; **perseguir algo como ~** to set sth as one's goal.
(b) (*Filos etc*) finality.

finalista NMF finalist.

finalización NF ending, conclusion.

finalizar [1f] [1] VT (*gen*) to end, finish; **dar algo por finalizado** to consider sth finished; ~ **la sesión** (*Inform*) to log out (o log off).
[2] VI y **finalizarse** VR to end, finish, conclude.

finalmente ADV finally, lastly.

finamente ADV politely; elegantly; acutely, shrewdly; subtly; delicately.

finamiento NM decease, demise, passing.

financiador(a) NM/F financial backer.

financiamiento NM, **financiación** NF financing.

financiar [1b] VT to finance.

financiero [1] ADJ financial; **los medios ~s** the financial means; **el mundo ~** the financial world, the world of finance.
[2] NM, **financiera** NF (*banquero*) financier.
[3] NF (*empresa*) finance company, finance house.

financista [1] ADJ financial.
[2] NMF (*LAm*) (*patrocinador*) financier; (*experto*) financial expert.

finanzas NFPL finances.

finar [1a] [1] VI to pass away, die.
[2] **finarse** VR to long, yearn (*por* for).

finca NF **(a)** (*propiedad etc*) property; land, real estate; ~ **raíz** (*And*) real estate; ~ **urbana** town property.
(b) (*casa etc*) country estate, country house; (*LAm*) farm; (*minifundio*) small rural holding; (*de ganado*) ranch; ~ **azucarera** sugar plantation; ~ **cafetera** coffee plantation; ~ **de experimentación** experimental farm; **cazar en ~ ajena** to poach (on sb else's property); **penetrar en ~ ajena** to trespass (on sb else's property); **tienen una ~ en Guadalajara** they have a country house (o property, estate) in Guadalajara; **pasan un mes en su ~** they're spending a month at their country place.

fincar [1g] [1] VT (*Carib*) to till, cultivate.
[2] VI: ~ **en** (*And, Méx*) to consist of, comprise.

finchado* ADJ stuck-up*, conceited.

fincharse* [1a] VR to get conceited.

finde* NM weekend.

finés = **finlandés.**

fineza NF **(a)** (*calidad*) fineness, excellence; purity; select quality.
(b) (*de modales*) refinement; elegance.
(c) (*acto*) kindness, favour; courtesy, nice thing (to say o do *etc*); (*cumplido*) compliment; (*regalo*) small gift, token.

fingar: [1h] VT to nick:, swipe:.

finger ['finger] NM, PL **fingers** (*Aer*) (telescopic) passenger walkway.

fingidamente ADV feignedly; in a sham way; as a piece of make-believe.

fingido ADJ feigned, false; fake, sham; mock; make-believe; **nombre ~** false name, assumed name.

fingimiento NM pretence; simulation, feigning.

fingir [3c] [1] VT to sham, fake; to invent; to simulate; ~ **desinterés** to feign disinterest, pretend not to be interested; ~ **mucha humildad** to pretend to be very humble; **lo habrán fingido** I expect they invented it, I expect they faked it up.
[2] VI to pretend, feign; ~ **dormir** to pretend to be asleep, to feign sleep.
[3] **fingirse** VR: ~ **un sabio** to pretend to be an expert; ~ **dormido** to pretend to be asleep.

finiquitar [1a] VT *cuenta* to settle and close, balance up; (*) *asunto* to conclude, finish off, wind up.

finiquito NM (*Com, Fin*) settlement.

finisecular ADJ fin-de-siècle (*atr*).

finito ADJ finite.

finlandés [1] ADJ Finnish.
[2] NM, **finlandesa** NF Finn.
[3] NM (*Ling*) Finnish.

Finlandia NF Finland.

finlandización NF neutralization and subordination (of one country to another).

finlandizar [1f] VT *país* to neutralize and subordinate.

fino [1] ADJ **(a)** (*de buena calidad*) fine, excellent; pure; *fruta, vino etc* choice, quality (*atr*); *tabaco etc* select; *jerez* fino, dry; (*Min*) refined; **oro ~** pure gold, refined gold.
(b) (*delgado*) thin; *persona* slender, slight; *tela* thin, delicate, sheer; *capa etc* thin.
(c) *punta* sharp.
(d) (*cortés*) *persona* polite, well-bred, refined; *modales* refined, cultured; *cumplido etc* elegant, well-turned; **ponerse ~** to turn on the charm.
(e) *inteligencia* shrewd, acute, penetrating; *gusto* fine, discriminating; *oído* sharp, acute.
(f) (*sutil*) *distinción etc* fine, subtle, delicate; *ironía* subtle.
[2] NM dry sherry, fino sherry.

finolis ADJ INVAR affected.

finquero NM (*LAm*) farmer.

finta NF feint; **hacer ~s** to feint, spar.

fintar [1a] VI, **fintear** [1a] VI to feint, spar.

finura NF **(a)** (*calidad de fino*) fineness, excellence; purity; choiceness, high quality.
(b) (*cortesía*) politeness, courtesy; refinement; elegance; **¡qué ~!** what refinement!, how charming!
(c) (*astucia*) shrewdness, acuteness.
(d) (*sutileza*) subtlety, delicacy.

fiñe ADJ (*Carib*) small, weak, sickly.

fiordo NM fiord.

FIP [fip] NF (*Esp*) ABR *de* **Formación Intensiva Profesional.**

fique NM (*And, Méx, Carib*) (*fibra*) henequen; fibre; (*cuerda*) rope, cord.

F.I.R. [fir] NM (*Esp*) ABR *de* **farmacéutico interno residente.**

firma NF **(a)** (*gen*) signature; (*acto*) signing; **es de mi ~** I signed that; **6 novelas de su ~** 6 novels of his, 6 novels which he has written; ~ **de libros** book-signing session.
(b) (*Com, Fin*) firm, company, concern.

firmamento NM firmament.

firmante [1] ADJ signatory (*de* to).
[2] NMF signatory; **el abajo ~** the undersigned; **el último ~** the last person signing (o to sign).

firmar [1a] VTI to sign; **firmado y lacrado, firmado y sellado** signed and sealed.

firme [1] ADJ **(a)** (*gen*) firm; (*estable*) steady, secure, stable; (*duro*) hard; (*sólido*) solid, compact; *color* fast; *resistencia etc* firm; resolute; **estar en lo ~** to be in the right; to be positive; **mantenerse ~** to hold one's ground, not give way.
(b) (*Com, Fin*) *mercado* steady; *precio* firm, stable.
(c) *persona* staunch, steadfast, resolute.
(d) (*Mil*) **¡~s!** attention!; **estar en posición de ~s** to stand at attention; **poner ~s a un pelotón** to bring a squad to attention; **ponerse ~(s)** to come to attention.
(e) **de ~** firmly, strongly; steadily; **batir de ~** to strike hard; **resistir de ~** to resist strongly; **trabajar de ~** to work hard, work solidly.
(f) (*Com*) **oferta en ~** firm offer; **pedido en ~** firm order.
[2] ADV hard; **pegar ~** to hit hard; **trabajar ~** to work hard.
[3] NM roadbed, road foundation layer; road surface; '~ **ondulado**' 'uneven surface'; '~ **provisional**' 'temporary surface'.

firmemente ADV **(a)** firmly; securely, solidly. **(b)** (*lealmente*) staunchly, steadfastly.

firmeza NF **(a)** firmness; steadiness, stability; solidity, compactness. **(b)** (*Com, Fin*) steadiness. **(c)** (*moral*) firmness; steadfastness, resolution.

firmita* NF (mere) signature; **echar una ~** to sign on the dotted line (*t fig*); **¿me echas una ~?** would you sign here, please?

firuletes* NMPL (*LAm*) (*objetos*) knick-knacks; (*al bailar*) gyrations, con-

---

tortions.

fiscal [1] ADJ (*económico*) fiscal, financial; (*relativo a impuestos*) tax (*atr*); **año** ~ fiscal year, financial year.
[2] NMF (*t* **fiscala** NF) (a) (*Jur*) public prosecutor, district attorney (*US*); ~ **general de Estado** attorney-general.
(b) (*: entrometido*) busybody, meddler.

fiscalía NF office of the public prosecutor.

fiscalidad NF taxation; tax system, tax regulations.

fiscalista ADJ: **abogado** ~ lawyer specializing in tax affairs.

fiscalizar [1f] VT (a) (*controlar*) to control, oversee, inspect (officially). (b) (*fig*) to criticize, find fault with. (c) (*: entrometerse*) to pry into, meddle with.

fiscalmente ADV fiscally; from a tax point of view, taxation-wise.

fisco NM treasury, exchequer; **declarar algo al** ~ to declare sth for tax purposes.

fisga NF (a) (*de pesca*) fish spear; (*CAm: Taur*) banderilla. (b) (*fig*) banter, chaff; **hacer** ~ **a uno** to tease sb, banter sb.

fisgar [1h] [1] VT (a) *pez* to spear, harpoon. (b) (*fig*) to pry into, spy on.
[2] VI (a) (*fisgonear*) to pry, snoop*, spy. (b) (*mofarse*) to mock, scoff, jeer.

fisgón [1] ADJ (a) (*curioso*) snooping*, prying, nosey*. (b) (*guasón*) bantering, teasing; (*mofador*) mocking.
[2] NM, **fisgona** NF (a) snooper*, nosey-parker*. (b) banterer, tease; mocker.

fisgonear* [1a] VT to be always prying into, spy continually on.

fisgoneo* NM constant prying; chronic nosiness.

física¹ NF physics; ~ **de alta(s) energía(s)** high-energy physics; ~ **cuántica** quantum physics; ~ **del estado sólido** solid-state physics; ~ **nuclear** nuclear physics; ~ **de partículas** particle physics.

físicamente ADV physically.

físico [1] ADJ (a) physical.
(b) (*Carib, Méx*) (*melindroso*) finicky; (*afectado*) affected.
[2] NM, **física²** NF physicist; (*Med: ††*) physician; ~ **nuclear** nuclear physicist.
[3] NM (*Anat*) physique; (*aspecto*) appearance, looks; **de** ~ **regular** ordinary-looking.

físil ADJ fissile.

fisiología NF physiology.

fisiológico ADJ physiological.

fisiólogo NM, **fisióloga** NF physiologist.

fisión NF fission; ~ **nuclear** nuclear fission.

fisionable ADJ fissionable.

fisionarse [1a] VR to undergo fission, split.

fisioterapeuta NMF physiotherapist.

fisioterapia NF physiotherapy.

fisioterapista NMF physiotherapist.

fiso: NM (*LAm: cara*) mug:, dial:.

fisonomía NF (a) (*cara*) physiognomy, face; features. (b) **la** ~ **de la ciudad** the appearance of the city.

fisonomista NMF: **ser buen** ~ to have a good memory for faces.

fistol NM (*Méx*) tiepin.

fístula NF fistule.

fisura NF fissure; crack; (*Med*) fissure, hairline fracture.

fitobiología NF phytobiology, plant breeding.

fitocultura NF plant breeding.

fitófago [1] ADJ plant-eating.
[2] NM, **fitófaga** NF plant-eater.

fitopatología NF phytopathology, plant pathology.

fitoplancton NM phytoplankton.

fitoquímica NF phytochemistry.

fitosanitario [1] ADJ *productos, industria, problemas* phytosanitary.
[2] NM pesticide.

FIV NF ABR *de* **fecundación in vitro** in vitro fertilization, IVF.

flac(c)idez NF flaccidity; softness, flabbiness.

flác(c)ido ADJ flaccid; soft, flabby.

flaco [1] ADJ (a) (*Anat*) thin, skinny, lean; (*And*) slim; **ponerse** ~ to get thin. (b) (*fig*) weak, feeble; *memoria* bad, short; *lado, punto* weak; *año* lean; (*LAm*) *tierra* barren.
[2] NM weakness, weak spot, failing.
[3] NF: **la F~** (*Méx*) Death; **acompañar a la** ~ to pass away.

flacón ADJ (*Carib, Cono Sur*) very thin.

flacuchento ADJ (*LAm*) very thin.

flacura NF (a) (*delgadez*) thinness, skinniness. (b) (*debilidad*) weakness, feebleness.

flagelación NF flagellation, whipping.

flagelar [1a] VT (a) (*azotar*) to flagellate, whip, scourge. (b) (*fig*) to flay, criticize severely.

flagelo NM (a) (*azote*) whip, scourge. (b) (*fig*) scourge, calamity.

flagrante ADJ flagrant; **en** ~ in the act, red-handed.

flama NF (a) (*Méx: llama*) flame. (b) (*destello*) glitter. (c) (*calor*) stifling heat.

flamante ADJ (a) (*lit*) brilliant, flaming. (b) (*fig: nuevo*) brand-new; (*lujoso*) luxurious, high-class; (*estupendo*) superb.

flam(b)eado ADJ flambé.

flamear [1a] [1] VI (a) to flame, blaze (up). (b) (*Náut: vela*) to flap; (*bandera*) to flutter.
[2] VT (*Culin*) to flambé.

flamenco¹ NM (*Orn*) flamingo.

flamenco² [1] ADJ (a) (*Geog*) Flemish.
(b) (*Mús etc*) Andalusian gipsy (*atr*); **cante** ~ flamenco (*Andalusian gipsy singing*).
(c) (*pey*) flashy, vulgar, gaudy.
(d) **ponerse** ~* (*engreído*) to get cocky*; (*satisfecho*) to get on one's high horse; (*chulo*) to become obstreperous, turn nasty.
(e) (*CAm, Carib, Méx*) = **flaco**.
[2] NM, **flamenca** NF Fleming; **los** ~**s** the Flemings, the Flemish.
[3] NM (a) flamenco (*Andalusian gipsy singing and dancing*).
(b) (*Ling*) Flemish.

flamencología NF study of flamenco music and dance.

flamencólogo, -a NM/F student of flamenco music and dance.

flamenquilla NF marigold.

flamígero ADJ: **estilo gótico** ~ flamboyant Gothic style.

flámula NF streamer.

flan NM caramel cream; **estar hecho** (*o* **estar como**) **un** ~ to shake like a jelly.

flanco NM (a) (*Anat*) side, flank. (b) (*Mil*) flank; **coger a uno por el** ~ to catch sb off guard.

Flandes NM Flanders.

flanear* [1a] VI to stroll, saunter.

flanecito NM dumpling.

flanera NF ≃ jelly mould, ≃ jelly mold (*US*).

flanín NM caramel cream.

flanquear [1a] VT (a) (*gen*) to flank. (b) (*Mil*) to outflank.

flaquear [1a] VI to weaken, grow weak; (*esfuerzo*) to slacken, flag; (*madera etc*) to give way; (*salud*) to decline, get worse; (*moralmente*) to lose heart, become dispirited.

flaquencia NF (*LAm*) = **flacura**.

flaqueza NF (a) (*cualidad*) thinness, leanness; weakness, feebleness, frailty; **la** ~ **de su memoria** his poor memory; **la** ~ **humana** human frailty.
(b) (*una* ~) failing, weakness; **las** ~**s de la carne** the frailties to which the flesh is heir.

flaquísimo ADJ (*superl*) *de* **flaco**.

flash [flas] NM, PL **flashes** *o* **flashs** [flas] (a) (*noticia*) newsflash. (b) (*Fot*) flash, flashlight; **con** ~ by flashlight. (c) (*: *) surprise, strong impression, shattering experience; **¡qué** ~! how awful (for you)!

flashback ['flasβak] NM, PL **flashbacks** flashback.

flato NM (a) (*Med*) flatulence, wind; stitch. (b) (*LAm: depresión*) gloom, depression; (*And, Carib, CAm: temor*) fear, apprehension.

flatoso ADJ (a) (*Med*) flatulent, windy. (b) (*Carib: deprimido*) gloomy, depressed; (*CAm, Carib: aprensivo*) apprehensive.

flatulencia NF flatulence.

flatulento ADJ flatulent.

flatuoso ADJ flatulent, windy.

flauta [1] NF (a) (*instrumento*) († ~ **travesera**) flute; ~ (**dulce**) recorder; **estar hecho una** ~ to be as thin as a rake; **por fortuna sonó la** ~* it was a lucky coincidence.
(b) (*LAm*) **de la gran** ~* terrific*, tremendous*; **hijo de la gran** ~: son of a bitch:, bastard:.
[2] NMF (*persona*) flautist, flute player.
[3] (*) INTERJ (*And, Cono Sur*) **¡~ la** ~! gosh!*; **¡la gran** ~! my God!; **¡por la** ~! (*Cono Sur*) oh dear!

flautín [1] NM (*instrumento*) piccolo.
[2] NMF (*persona*) piccolo player.

flautista NMF flautist, flute player; **el** ~ **de Hamelin** the Pied Piper of Hamelin.

flavina NF flavin.

flebitis NF phlebitis.

flecha [1] NF (a) arrow; dart; (*And*) sling; (*Méx Aut*) axle; (*de billar*) cue rest; ~ **de mar** squid; ~ **de dirección** (*Aut*) trafficator; **como una** ~ like an arrow, like a shot; **con alas en** ~ swept-wing, with swept-back wings; **subida en** ~ sharp rise; **subir en** ~ to rise sharply.
(b) (*Cono Sur*: *coqueta*) flirt.
[2] NM (*: Hist*) member of the Falangist youth movement.

flechado* ADV: **salir** ~ to shoot off.

flechar [1a] VT (a) *arco* to draw, stretch.
(b) (*herir etc*) to wound (*o* kill) with an arrow, shoot (with an arrow).
(c) (*) *mujer* to make a hit with, sweep off her feet.
(d) (*Cono Sur: picar*) to prick (*esp* with a goad); (*sol*) to burn, scorch.

flechazo NM (a) (*acto*) arrow shot, bowshot; (*herida*) arrow wound; (*And*) slingshot.
(b) (*: amor*) love at first sight; **con nosotros fue el** ~ with us it was

love at first sight.
(c) (*: *revelación*) sudden illumination, revelation; **aquello fue el ~** then it hit me, that was the moment of illumination.

flechero NM archer, bowman; arrow maker.

fleco NM (*pelo*) fringe, fringe curls; (*Cos*) tassel; **~(s)** frayed edge (of cloth); **~s** (*fig*) loose ends.

flejar [1a] VT **(a)** (*esp LAm*) secure with metal strips. **(b)** (*Méx*) *paquete* to pack.

fleje NM iron hoop, metal band.

flema NF **(a)** (*Med*) phlegm. **(b)** (*fig*) imperturbability; impassiveness; sangfroid.

flemático ADJ phlegmatic, matter-of-fact, unruffled.

flemón NM gumboil.

flemudo ADJ slow, sluggish.

flequetería NF (*And*) cheating, swindling.

flequetero ADJ (*And*) tricky, dishonest.

flequillo NM fringe.

Flesinga NM Flushing.

fleta NF (*And, Carib*) **(a)** (*fricción*) rub, rubbing. **(b)** (*paliza*) thrashing.

fletado* ADJ **(a)** (*CAm*) sharp, clever. **(b)** (*Carib, Méx**) **salir ~*** to be off like a shot.

fletador ⟨1⟩ ADJ shipping (*atr*), freighting (*atr*).
⟨2⟩ NM shipper, freighter.

fletamento NM, **fletamiento** NM (*Méx*) charter, chartering; **contrato de ~** chartering agreement.

fletán NM (*t ~ negro*) Greenland halibut.

fletar [1a] ⟨1⟩ VT **(a)** *avión, barco* to charter; to load, freight.
(b) (*LAm*) *vehículo etc* to hire.
(c) (*And, Cono Sur*) *insultos* to let fly, utter; *golpe* to deal.
(d) (*Cono Sur**) (*despedir*) to fire*, sack*; (*expulsar*) to chuck out, remove by force.
⟨2⟩ **fletarse** VR **(a)** (*) (*And, Carib, Méx: largarse*) to get out, beat it*; to slip away, get away unseen; (*Cono Sur: colarse*) to gatecrash.
(b) (*CAm*: enojarse*) to be annoyed, get cross.
(c) (*Cono Sur*) '*se fleta*' (*letrero*) 'to let'.

flete NM **(a)** (*alquiler*) charter; **vuelo ~** charter flight.
(b) (*carga*) freight, cargo; **salir sin ~s** (*And, Carib*) to leave in a hurry, be off like a shot.
(c) (*gastos*) freightage; (*LAm: de transporte*) transport charges, carriage; (*LAm: gen*) hire, hire charge, hiring fee; **~ por cobrar** freight forward; **~ pagado** advance freight.
(d) (*And, Cono Sur*) (*caballo*) fast horse; (*de carreras*) racehorse; (*Cono Sur: rocín*) old nag.
(e) (*And: amante*) lover, companion.
(f) (‡: *prostitución*) prostitution, the game*.
(g) echarse un ~ ‡‡ to have a screw‡‡.

fletera NF (*Carib*) prostitute.

fletero ⟨1⟩ ADJ **(a)** (*LAm: chárter*) charter (*atr*); freight (*atr*); **avión ~** charter plane.
(b) (*LAm: de alquiler*) hired, for hire; **camión ~** lorry for hire.
⟨2⟩ NM **(a)** (*LAm*) (*transportista*) owner of vehicles for hire; owner of a transport business; (*recaudador*) collector of transport charges.
(b) (*And, Guat: mozo*) porter.

flexibilidad NF flexibility; suppleness, pliability; compliant nature; **~ laboral, ~ de plantillas** (*euf*) freedom to 'restructure'.

flexibilización NF (*de actitud, control*) relaxation; **~ del mercado laboral** (*o del trabajo*) *relaxation of laws relating to terms of employment*; **~ de plantillas** downsizing.

flexibilizar [1f] VT to make (more) flexible; to adjust, adapt.

flexible ⟨1⟩ ADJ flexible; soft, supple, pliable; *sombrero* soft; *persona* open-minded, open to argument; (*pey*) compliant.
⟨2⟩ NM **(a)** (*sombrero*) soft hat. **(b)** (*Elec*) flex, cord, wire.

flexión NF **(a)** (*gen*) flexion; (*ejercicio*) press-up. **(b)** (*Ling*) inflexion.

flexional ADJ flexional, inflected.

flexionar [1a] VT to bend; *músculo* to flex.

flexo NM adjustable table-lamp.

flipado‡, -a NM/F drop-out.

flipante‡ ADJ **(a)** cool‡; great*, smashing*. **(b)** (*pasmoso*) amazing.

flipar‡ [1a] ⟨1⟩ VT **(a)** (*gustar*) to turn on*, send*; **esto me flipa** this really sends me, I just adore this.
(b) (*pasmar*) to amaze, knock sideways.
⟨2⟩ VI **(a)** (*desmadrarse*) to freak out‡; (*volverse loco*) to go round the twist*; (*drogarse, emborracharse*) to get stoned‡.
(b) (*pasarlo bien*) to have a great time*; **~ con algo** (*disfrutar*) to enjoy sth, rave about sth*; (*pasmarse*) to be amazed at sth; **~ por algo** to be mad keen on (*o* to get *etc*) sth; to be dying for sth.
(c) (*ser atractivo*) to be very attractive, be really gorgeous.
⟨3⟩ **fliparse** VR to get excited, get carried away (*con, por* by); V *t* **2.**

flipe‡ NM **(a)** (*experiencia*) amazing experience, startling revelation.
(b) (*droga*) high‡; trip‡.

flipper ['fliper] NM pinball machine; **jugar a ~** to play pinball.

flirt* NM, PL **flirts** [flir] **(a)** (*persona*) sweetheart; boyfriend, girlfriend;

la estrella vino con su ~ del momento the star came with her current boyfriend.
(b) (*amorío*) flirtation, (light-hearted) affair; **A tuvo un ~ con B** A had a brief affair with B.

flirteador(a) NM/F flirt.

flirtear* [1a] VI to flirt (*con* with), have a light-hearted affair (*con* with).

flirteo* NM **(a)** (*gen*) flirting. **(b)** (*un ~*) flirtation, (light-hearted) affair.

FLN NM (*Pol: Esp, Perú, Venezuela*) ABR *de* **Frente de Liberación Nacional.**

flojamente ADV **(a)** (*sueltamente*) loosely, slackly; limply. **(b)** (*débilmente*) weakly, feebly; (*ligeramente*) lightly.

flojear [1a] VI to weaken; to slacken, ease up.

flojedad NF (*V* ADJ) **(a)** looseness, slackness; limpness.
(b) weakness, feebleness; lightness.
(c) limpness, flaccidity.
(d) poor quality.
(e) slackness, laxity, negligence.

flojel NM (*de tela*) nap; (*Orn*) down.

flojera NF **(a)** (*) = flojedad. **(b)** (*LAm: pereza*) laziness; **me da ~ (hacerlo)** I can't be bothered (doing it).

flojito ADJ (*gen*) = flojo; *viento* very light, slack.

flojo ADJ **(a)** *cuerda etc* loose, slack; limp; *tuerca etc* loose; **me la trae floja‡** it leaves me stone-cold; **la tengo floja‡** I'm not bothered; **a mí me la trae floja la política** I don't give a damn about politics.
(b) *esfuerzo* weak, feeble; *viento* light.
(c) *carne etc* soft, limp, flaccid.
(d) *té, vino etc* weak; *obra literaria etc* poor, thin, weak, feeble.
(e) *estudiante etc* poor, weak; *actitud* slack, lax.
(f) *precio* low, weak; *mercado* slack, dull.
(g) (*LAm*) (*vago*) lazy; (*tímido*) timid, cowardly.

floppy ['flopi] NM, PL **floppys** floppy disk.

flor ⟨1⟩ NF **(a)** (*Bot*) flower, blossom, bloom; **~ de mano** artificial flower; **~ de nieve** snowdrop; **~ de (la) Pascua** poinsettia; **~ del sol** sunflower; **~ somnífera** (*LAm*) opium poppy; **en ~** in flower, in bloom; **en plena ~** in full bloom; **hijos como una ~** lovely children; **de ~** (*Carib*) very good, splendid; **no es ~ de un día** this is no mere flash in the pan; **ser una ~ de estufa** to be very delicate; **¡ni ~es!*** no way!*
(b) (*de ciruela etc*) bloom.
(c) (*de cuero*) grain.
(d) (*fig*) flower, best part, cream; **~ de azúcar** icing-sugar; **~ de harina** finest flour; **la ~ y nata de la sociedad** the cream of society, the pick of society; **es la ~ de la canela** it's the very best; **en la ~ de la edad** in the flower of one's youth; **en la ~ de la vida** in the prime of life.
(e) (*Téc*) surface; **a ~ de** level with, on a level with; flush with; on the surface of; **a ~ del agua** at water level, close to the surface of the water; (*barca*) awash; **a ~ de cuño** in mint condition; **tiene el humorismo a ~ de piel** his humour is always ready to break out, his wit is never far below the surface; **los odios salen a ~ de piel** hatred comes out into the open, hatred comes to the surface; **ajustado a ~** flush.
(f) (*piropo*) compliment, nice thing (to say); **decir** (*o* **echar**) **~es a una** to pay pretty compliments to a girl, flirt with a girl.
(g) ~es (*Cono Sur*) popcorn.
(h) (*LAm*) *p.ej.* **~ de caballo** splendid horse, great horse; **~ de alegre** very cheerful.
⟨2⟩ ADJ (*LAm*) splendid, excellent.

flora NF flora.

floración NF flowering; bloom.

floral ADJ floral.

florar [1a] VI to flower, bloom.

florcita NF (*LAm*) little flower.

floreado ADJ **(a)** *tela* flowery, flowered. **(b)** *pan* of the finest flour, top-quality. **(c)** (*Mús*) elaborate, with flourishes.

florear [1a] ⟨1⟩ VT **(a)** *tela etc* to adorn with flowers, add a flowery design to.
(b) *harina* to sift.
(c) *naipes* to stack.
(d) (*fig: adular*) to flatter.
⟨2⟩ VI **(a)** (*LAm Bot*) to flower, bloom.
(b) (*Mús*) to play a flourish, play elaborate variations; (*Esgrima*) to flourish.
(c) (*piropear*) to indulge in flowery compliments, flatter.
⟨3⟩ **florearse** VR (*LAm*) to show off; to perform brilliantly.

florecer [2d] VI **(a)** (*Bot*) to flower, bloom. **(b)** (*fig*) to flourish, thrive; to flower.

floreciente ADJ **(a)** (*Bot*) in flower, flowering, blooming. **(b)** (*fig*) flourishing, thriving.

florecimiento NM **(a)** (*Bot*) flowering, blooming. **(b)** (*fig*) flourishing, thriving; flowering.

Florencia NF Florence.
florentino [1] ADJ Florentine, of Florence.
[2] NM, **florentina** NF Florentine.
floreo NM (a) (*Esgrima, Mús*) flourish. (b) (*gracia*) witty but insubstantial talk; (*cumplido*) compliment, nicely-turned phrase; **andarse con ~s** to beat about the bush.
florería NF (*LAm*) florist's (shop).
florero [1] NM, **florera** NF florist; (street) flower-seller.
[2] NM (a) (*recipiente*) vase; (*fig*) ornament. (b) (*Arte*) flower painting. (c) (*persona*) flatterer; specialist in elegant compliments.
florescencia NF florescence.
floresta NF (a) (*bosque*) wood, grove; (*claro*) glade; (*lugar atractivo*) beauty spot; (*escena rural*) charming rural scene; (*And: bosque*) forest, jungle. (b) (*Liter*) anthology.
florete NM (*Esgrima*) foil.
floretear [1a] VT to decorate with flowers.
floretista NMF (*LAm*) fencer.
florícola ADJ: **el sector ~** the flower-growing sector.
floricultor(a) NM/F flower-grower.
floricultura NF flower-growing.
florido ADJ (a) *campo etc* flowery, full of flowers; *árbol etc* in bloom, in flower. (b) (*fig*) choice, select. (c) *estilo* flowery, florid.
florilegio NM anthology.
florín NM florin; (*holandés*) guilder.
floriona NF (*And*) = **fanfarrón**.
floripón NM (*LAm*), **floripondio** NM (*LAm*) (a) (*Cos etc*) big flower. (b) (*Liter*) rhetorical flourish, extravagant figure. (c) (‡) effeminate person, pansy‡. (d) (*And Bot*) lily of the valley.
florista NMF florist.
floristería NF florist's (shop).
floristero [1] ADJ florist (*atr*).
[2] NM, **floristera** NF florist.
florístico ADJ botanical; floral.
floritura NF flourish.
florón NM (a) (*Bot*) big flower. (b) (*Arquit*) fleuron, rosette. (c) (*Tip*) fleuron.
flota NF (a) (*Náut*) fleet; shipping; **~ de altura** deep-sea fishing fleet; **~ de bajura** inshore fishing fleet; **~ mercante** merchant marine; **la ~ española** the Spanish fleet.
(b) (*Aer, Aut*) fleet.
(c) (*And etc: autobús*) long-distance bus, inter-city bus.
(d) (*LAm: muchedumbre*) lot, crowd, heap; **una ~ de** a lot of, a crowd of.
(e) (*And, CAm: jactancia*) boasting, bluster; **echar ~s** (*And, CAm, Carib*) to brag.
flotación NF floating, flotation; *V* **línea**.
flotador NM (*gen*) float; (*de cisterna*) ballcock; (*de niño*) rubber ring, float.
flotante [1] ADJ (*gen*) floating; *pieza* loose, hanging loose; **de coma ~** (*Inform*) floating point.
[2] NM (*And*) braggart.
flotar [1a] VI (a) (*gen*) to float. (b) (*pieza etc*) to hang, hang loose; (*bandera etc*) to flutter; **~ en el aire** to float in the air; to hover; (*pelo etc*) **~ al viento** to stream in the wind. (c) (*Fin*) to float.
flote NM: **estar a ~** to be afloat; **poner a ~** to float, set afloat; (*t sacar a ~*) to refloat, raise; (*fig: revelar*) to bring into the open; (*fig: Econ etc*) to make viable, restore to profitability; **ponerse a ~** (*fig*) to get back on one's feet, get out of a jam; **sostenerse a ~** to keep afloat.
flotilla NF flotilla, fleet of small ships; line of vessels being towed, string of barges; (*de taxis, camiones etc*) fleet.
flou [flo] NM soft focus (effect).
flox [flos] NM phlox.
FLS NM (*Pol: Nicaragua*) ABR *de* **Frente de Liberación Sandinista**.
fluctuación NF (a) (*gen*) fluctuation; **las fluctuaciones de la moda** the fluctuations of fashion, the ups and downs of fashion. (b) (*indecisión*) uncertainty, hesitation.
fluctuante ADJ fluctuating; *población* floating.
fluctuar [1e] VI (a) (*gen*) to fluctuate. (b) (*vacilar*) to waver, hesitate.
fluente ADJ fluid, flowing.
fluidez NF (a) (*gen*) fluidity. (b) (*fig*) fluency, smoothness.
fluido, flúido [1] ADJ (a) (*Téc*) fluid; **la circulación es bastante fluida** traffic is moving quite freely. (b) (*fig*) *lenguaje* fluent; *estilo* smooth, free-flowing.
[2] NM (a) (*líquido*) fluid; **~s del cuerpo** body fluids. (b) (*Elec*) current, power; **cortar el ~** to cut off the electricity.
fluir [3g] VI to flow, run.
flujo NM (a) (*gen*) flow; stream; flux; (*Náut*) flow, rising tide, incoming tide; (*de votantes*) swing; **~ de caja**, **~ de fondos** cash-flow; **~ de consciencia** stream of consciousness; **~ y reflujo** ebb and flood, (*fig*) ebb and flow.
(b) (*Med*) (*vaginal*) (vaginal) discharge; **~ sanguíneo** blood flow, flow of blood; **~ de vientre** diarrhoea.

flujograma NM flow chart.
fluminense (*LAm*) [1] ADJ of Río de Janeiro.
[2] NMF native (o inhabitant) of Río de Janeiro; **los ~s** the people of Río de Janeiro.
flúor NM fluoride.
fluoración NF fluoridation.
fluorescencia NF fluorescence.
fluorescente ADJ fluorescent.
fluorización NF fluoridation.
fluorizar [1f] VT to fluoridate.
fluoruro NM fluoride.
flus NM (*And, Carib*) suit of clothes.
flute NF champagne glass.
fluvial ADJ fluvial, river (*atr*); *pez* river (*atr*), freshwater (*atr*).
flux [flus] NM INVAR (a) (*Naipes*) flush; **~ real** royal flush.
(b) (*CAm*: *suerte*) stroke of luck.
(c) (*And, Carib*: *traje*) suit of clothes.
(d) (*Méx*) **estar a ~**, **quedarse a ~** not to have a bean‡; **hacer ~** to blow all one's money‡.
FM NF ABR *de* **Frecuencia Modulada** frequency modulation, FM.
FMI NM ABR *de* **Fondo Monetario Internacional** International Monetary Fund, IMF.
FMLN NM (*El Salvador*) ABR *de* **Frente Farabundo Martí de Liberación Nacional**.
FN [1] NM ABR *de* **Frente Nacional**.
[2] NF (*Esp: Hist*) ABR *de* **Fuerza Nueva**.
FNAS NM (*Esp*) ABR *de* **Fondo Nacional de Asistencia Social**.
FNMT NF (*Esp*) ABR *de* **Fábrica Nacional de Moneda y Timbre**.
FNPT NM (*Esp*) ABR *de* **Fondo Nacional de Protección del Trabajo**.
f.º, fol. ABR *de* **folio** folio, fo., fol.
fobia NF phobia.
-fobia SUF -phobia, *p.ej.* **agorafobia** NF agoraphobia.
fóbico ADJ phobic.
-fobo SUF -phobe, *p.ej.* **francófobo, -a** NM/F francophobe.
foca NF (a) (*Zool*) seal; **~ de trompa** sea elephant. (b) (‡: *persona fea*) ugly lump‡. (c) (‡: *dormilón*) lie-abed, lazy individual.
focal ADJ focal.
focalizar [1f] VT *objeto* to focus on, get into focus; *atención etc* to focus.
focha NF coot.
foche ADJ smelly, pongy‡.
foco NM (a) (*Mat, Med, Fís etc*) focus; (*centro*) focal point, centre; (*de calor, luz*) source; (*de incendio*) seat; **estar fuera de ~** to be out of focus.
(b) (*Elec*) floodlight; (*Aut*) headlight; (*Teat etc*: *t* **~ direccional**) spotlight; (*LAm*: *de lámpara etc*) electric light bulb; (*LAm*: *de calle*) street light.
(c) (*fig*) centre, focal point.
fodolí ADJ meddlesome.
fodongo ADJ (*Méx*) (*sucio*) filthy; (*vago*) lazy, bone-idle.
foete NM = **fuete**.
fofadal NM (*Cono Sur*) bog, quagmire.
fofera NF, **fofez** NF flabbiness.
fofo ADJ (a) (*esponjoso*) soft, spongy; porous; fluffy; *carnes* flabby. (b) (‡: *rechoncho*) fat, plump.
fofoscientos ADJ umpteen; **fofoscientas mil pesetas** umpteen thousand pesetas.
fogaje NM (a) (*LAm*) (*calor*) scorching heat; (*bochorno*) sultry weather. (b) (*Carib, Méx*) (*sarpullido*) heat rash; (*rubor*) blush; (*fig*) fluster. (c) (*And*: *fuego*) fire, blaze.
fogarada NF, **fogarata** NF (*Cono Sur*), **fogata** NF blaze, bonfire.
fogón NM (a) (*Culin*) stove, kitchen range; (*Ferro*) firebox; (*Náut*) galley. (b) (*de cañón, máquina*) vent. (c) (*CAm, Cono Sur*) (*fuego*) fire, bonfire; (*hogar*) hearth.
fogonazo NM (a) (*estallido*) flash, explosion. (b) (*Méx*: *carajillo*) coffee with spirits added.
fogonero NM (a) (*Náut*) stoker. (b) (*Ferro*) fireman, stoker. (c) (*And*: *chófer*) chauffeur.
fogosidad NF spirit, mettle; fire, dash, verve; fieriness, friskiness.
fogoso ADJ spirited, mettlesome; fiery, ardent; *caballo* fiery, frisky.
fogueado ADJ (a) (*LAm*: *perito*) expert, experienced. (b) (*And*: *cansado*) weary.
foguear [1a] (*LAm*) [1] VT to fire on.
[2] **foguearse** VR to have one's baptism of fire; to gain experience, become hardened.
fogueo NM: **bala de ~** blank cartridge.
foguerear [1a] VT (*Carib, Cono Sur*) *maleza* to burn off; *fogata* to set light to.
foguista NM (*Cono Sur*) = **fogonero**.
foie-gras [fwa'gras] NM INVAR foie gras.
foil NM (*Méx Culin*) foil.
foja[1] NM coot.

foja² NF (*LAm*) = **hoja**; **~ de servicios** record.
fol. ABR *de* **folio** folio, fol.
folclore *etc* = **folklore.**
folder NM, **fólder** NM (*LAm*) folder.
folgo NM foot muff.
foliación NF (a) (*Bot*) foliation. (b) (*Tip*) foliation, page numbering.
foliar [1b] VT to foliate, number the pages of; **páginas sin ~** unnumbered pages.
folículo NM follicle.
folio NM (a) (*gen*) folio; (*hoja*) leaf, sheet; (*Tip*) running title, page heading; **al primer ~** (*fig*) from the very start, at a glance; **en ~** in folio; **libro en ~** folio (book). (b) (*tamaño de papel*) A4-size (paper); **doble ~** A3-size (paper). (c) (*And*) (*dádiva*) tip; (*de bautismo*) money given as christening present.
folk ADJ INVAR, NM folk.
folklore NM (a) folklore. (b) (*) row, shindy*; **se armó un ~** there was a row.
folklórico [1] ADJ (a) folklore (*atr*); folk (*atr*), popular, traditional; **es muy ~** it's very quaint, it's full of local colour; it is rich in historical interest. (b) (*pey*) frivolous, unserious; overblown; laughable.
[2] NM, **folklórica** NF (a) (*Mus*) folk singer. (b) (*pey*) clown, figure of fun.
folklorista [1] ADJ folklore (*atr*).
[2] NMF folklorist, specialist in folklore, student of folklore.
folklorizar [1f] [1] VT to give a popular (o folksy) character to.
[2] **folklorizarse** VR to acquire popular (o folksy) features.
follá: NF: **tener mala ~** to be thoroughly nasty.
follada: NF fuck:.
follado NM (*And*) petticoat.
follador: [1] ADJ fond of screwing:.
[2] NM fornicator.
follaje¹ NM (a) (*Bot*) foliage, leaves; (*Arte*) leaf motif. (b) (*fig*) excessive ornamentation; bombast, verbiage, waffle*.
follaje²: NM fucking:, screwing:.
follar [1m] [1] VT (a) (*Téc*) to blow (on) with bellows. (b) (:) to fuck:.
(c) (:) to bother, annoy; to harm.
[2] VI (:) to fuck:.
[3] **follarse** VR (a) (:: *echar un pedo*) to fart silently:. (b) (:: *joder*) to fuck:; **se la folló** he screwed her:. (c) **me lo voy a follar vivo:** I'll have his guts for garters:.
folletería NF leaflets.
folletín NM newspaper serial; (*TV*) soap-opera, TV serial; (*Rad*) radio serial.

| FOLLETÍN |

Folletines were originally popular serialized stories that appeared in newspapers and magazines in the 19th and early 20th centuries, often before being published as novels. They usually covered familiar themes such as unrequited love, adultery and family relationships. Nowadays, the word folletín can refer to radio or TV serials and soaps, radionovelas or telenovelas, and people even use folletín figuratively to talk about any long-running story or intrigue.

folletinesco ADJ make-believe, romantic, improbable.
folletinista NMF pulp writer.
folletista NMF pamphleteer.
folleto NM pamphlet; folder, brochure, leaflet; **~ informativo** information leaflet.
follín* NM (*Cono Sur*) bad-tempered individual.
follisca NF (*And*) (*lío*) confusion, shindy; (*riña*) brawl.
follón [1] ADJ (a) (*perezoso*) lazy, slack.
(b) (*arrogante*) arrogant, puffed-up; (*fanfarrón*) blustering.
(c) (*cobarde*) cowardly.
(d) (*CAm vestido*) roomy, loose.
[2] NM (a) (*Bot*) sucker.
(b) (*persona*) good-for-nothing, layabout; conceited person.
(c) (*cohete*) noiseless rocket; (:) silent fart:.
(d) (*: jaleo*) rumpus*, row, shindy*; (*lío*) mess, trouble; fuss; **armar un ~** to make a row, kick up a fuss.
(e) (*And: prenda*) petticoat.
(f) (*Carib: juerga de borrachera*) drinking bout.
follonarse: [1a] VR (*Cono Sur, Méx*) to fart silently:.
follonero* [1] ADJ *conducta* outrageous; provoking; *persona* rowdy, trouble-making, boisterous; rebellious.
[2] NM rowdy element, troublemaker; rebel.
fome* ADJ (*Cono Sur*) boring, dull.
fomentación NF (*Med*) fomentation, poultice.
fomentar [1a] VT (a) (*Med*) to foment; to warm.
(b) (*fig*) to promote, foster, encourage, foment; *odio, rebelión* to foment, stir up; *producción etc* to boost.
(c) (*Carib*) *negocio* to found, promote.
fomento NM (a) (*Med*) fomentation.

(b) (*fig*) promotion, fostering, encouragement, fomentation; **Ministerio de F~** (*Hist*) ministry responsible for public works, buildings etc.
fonador ADJ *sistema, aparato, órgano* speech (*atr*).
fonda NF (*Hist*) inn, tavern; (*restaurante*) small restaurant; (*pensión*) boarding-house; (*Ferro*) buffet; (*Cono Sur*) refreshment stall; (*LAm pey*) cheap restaurant.
fondeadero NM anchorage; berth.
fondeado ADJ (a) estar ~ (*Náut*) to be anchored, be at anchor. (b) (*LAm**) estar ~ to be in the money, be well heeled*; **quedar ~** (*Cono Sur**) to be broke*.
fondear [1a] [1] VT (a) (*Náut*) *profundidad* to sound; *barco* (*anclar*) to anchor; (*registrar*) to search; (*fig*) to examine thoroughly.
(b) (*Carib: violar*) to rape.
(c) (*CAm: financiar*) to provide with money, finance.
(d) (*Cono Sur*) to throw into the sea.
[2] VI to anchor, drop anchor.
[3] **fondearse** VR (a) (*LAm*: *enriquecerse*) to get rich; (*ahorrar*) to save for the future.
(b) (*LAm*: *emborracharse*) to get drunk.
fondero, -a NM/F (*LAm*) innkeeper; restaurant owner.
fondillos NMPL (a) (*del pantalón*) seat (*of trousers*). (b) (*LAm: Anat*) seat, bottom.
fondilludo, -a* NM/F (*LAm*): **es un ~** he's got a big backside.
fondista NMF (a) (*de fonda*) innkeeper; restaurant owner. (b) (*Dep*) long-distance runner.
fondo NM (a) (*de caja, mar etc*) bottom; (*de sala etc*) back, far end; (*en medidas*) depth; **doble ~, ~ falso** false bottom; **~ del mar** bottom of the sea, sea bed, sea floor; **a ~** (ADJ) thorough; (ADV) thoroughly; **una investigación a ~** a thorough investigation; **conocer algo a ~** to know sth thoroughly; **emplearse a ~** to do one's utmost, go all out; **al ~** (*de sala etc*) at the back, at the rear; **al ~ de** at the bottom of; at the back of; **de ~** (*Dep*) long-distance (*atr*), endurance (*atr*); **corredor de medio ~** middle-distance runner; **pruebas de medio ~** middle-distance events; **cuestión de ~** basic question; **el problema de ~** the fundamental problem, the underlying problem; **de bajo ~** shallow; flat; **en el ~** (*fig*) at bottom; basically; at heart; really; **en el ~ del corazón** deep down in one's heart; **sin ~** bottomless; **dar ~** to anchor; **echar un buque al ~** to sink a ship; to scuttle a ship; **irse al ~** to sink, founder, go to the bottom; **llegar al ~ de un misterio** to get to the bottom of a mystery; **tener poco ~** (*Med*) to be short-winded, quickly get out of breath; **tocar ~** to touch bottom (*t fig*).
(b) (*Arte*) background, ground; (*Cos*) ground; **se ve una casa en el ~** there is a house in the background.
(c) **bajos ~s sociales** dregs of society, underworld.
(d) (*Com, Fin*) fund; **~s** funds; money; finance; resources; **~ de amortización** sinking fund; **~s bloqueados** frozen assets; **~ de comercio** goodwill; **~ de compensación** compensation fund; **~ consolidado** consolidated fund; **~ de empréstitos** loan fund; **~ de huelga** strike fund; **~ para imprevistos** contingency fund; **~ mutualista** mutual fund; **~ de previsión** provident fund; **cheque sin ~s** bad cheque; **estar sin ~s** to have no money, be broke*; **a ~ perdido** (ADV) without security, (ADJ) unsecured, non-repayable; **subvención a ~ perdido** capital grant; **invertir a ~ perdido** to invest without hope of recovering one's money; **reunir ~s** to get money together, raise funds.
(e) (*fig: reservas*) fund, supply, reservoir; **tiene un ~ de alegría** he has a fund of cheerfulness; **tiene un ~ de energías** he has reserves of energy.
(f) (*fig: carácter*) nature, disposition; **de ~ jovial** of cheery disposition; **tener buen ~** to be good at heart.
(g) (*And: finca*) country estate.
(h) (*LAm: prenda*) petticoat; **medio ~** slip.
fondón* ADJ big-bottomed*, broad in the beam*; weighty, fat.
fondongo NM (*Carib Anat*) bottom.
fonducha NF (*And*) = **fonducho.**
fonducho NM cheap restaurant.
fonema NM phoneme.
fonémico ADJ phonemic.
fonética NF phonetics.
fonético ADJ phonetic.
fonetista NMF phonetician.
foniatra NMF speech therapist.
foniatría NF speech therapy.
fónico ADJ phonic.
fono NM (a) (*Cono Sur Telec*) (*auricular*) earpiece; (*número*) telephone number. (b) (*Ling*) phone.
fonobuzón NM voice mail.
fonocaptor NM (*de tocadiscos*) pick-up.
fonógrafo NM gramophone, phonograph (*US*).
fonología NF phonology.
fonológico ADJ phonological.
fonoteca NF record library, sound archive.

fonta* NM (*Pol*) = **fontanero**.
fontanal NM, **fontanar** NM spring.
fontanería NF (a) (*arte*) plumbing. (b) (*tienda*) plumber's shop.
fontanero NM plumber; (* *Pol*) back-room boy; investigator of leaks.
footing ['futin] NM jogging; **hacer ~** to jog, go jogging.
F.O.P. [fop] NFPL (*Esp*) ABR *de* **Fuerzas del Orden Público** forces of law and order, security forces.
foque NM jib.
foquillos NMPL fairy-lights.
foquismo NM (*LAm Pol*) theory of guerrilla war advocated by Che Guevara and Fidel Castro.
forajido NM outlaw, bandit; desperado.
foral ADJ relative to the *fueros*, pertaining to the privileges of a town (o region); statutory.
foramen NM (*Méx*) hole.
foráneo ADJ foreign; (from) outside.
forasta* NMF = **forastero**.
forastero [1] ADJ alien, strange; (from) outside; exotic.
[2] NM, **forastera** NF stranger; outsider; visitor; person from another part.
forcej(e)ar [1a] VI to struggle, wrestle; to make violent efforts; to flounder about.
forcej(e)o NM struggle; violent efforts; floundering.
forcejudo ADV tough, strong, powerful.
fórceps NM INVAR forceps.
forcito NM (*LAm*) little Ford (*vehicle*).
forense [1] ADJ forensic, legal; *V* **médico**.
[2] NMF pathologist.
forestación NF afforestation.
forestal ADJ forest (*atr*); woodland (*atr*), tree (*atr*); **cubierta ~** tree cover; *V* **repoblación** *etc*.
forestalista NMF owner of a woodland.
forestar [1a] VT (*LAm*) to afforest.
forfait [for'fe] NM (a) (*ausencia*) absence, non-appearance; (*retirada*) withdrawal, scratching; **declararse ~** to withdraw; **ganar por ~** to win by default; **hacer ~** to fail to show up.
(b) (*precio*) flat rate, fixed price; (*Esquí etc*) all-in charge.
fori\| NM hankie*, handkerchief.
forito NM (*LAm*) = **fotingo**.
forja NF (a) (*fragua*) forge; (*fundición*) foundry. (b) (*acto*) forging.
forjado ADJ *hierro* wrought.
forjar [1a] VT (a) *hierro etc* to forge, shape, beat (into shape).
(b) (*formar*) to forge, shape, make; **~ un plan** to make a plan, hammer out a plan; **tratamos de ~ un estado moderno** we are trying to build a modern state.
(c) (*pey*) to invent, think up, concoct; to forge.
forma NF (a) (*gen*) form, shape; **de ~ triangular** of triangular shape, triangular in shape; **en ~ de U** U-shaped, shaped like a U.
(b) (*Téc*) mould; block, pattern; (*de sombrero*) hatter's block; (*de zapatero*) last.
(c) (*Dep etc*) form; (*Med*) fitness; **estar en ~** to be in (good) form; to be fit; (*) to be in the mood (for sex); **estar en baja ~** to be off form; to be going through a bad spell; **estar en plena ~** to be on top form, be on the top of one's form; **mantenerse en ~** to keep fit; **ponerse en ~** to get fit.
(d) (*modo*) way, means, method; **la única ~ de hacerlo es ...** the only way to do it is ...; **no hubo ~ de convencerle** there was no means of persuading him, it was impossible to persuade him; **~ de pago** (*Com*) manner of payment, method of payment; **~ de ser** character, temperament; **de esta ~** in this way; **de (tal) ~ que ... so** that ...; in such a way that ...; so much so that ...; **de todas ~s** at any rate, in any case, anyway; **en debida ~** duly, in due form; **ver la ~ de** + infin to see one's way to + infin o ger.
(e) ~s social forms, conventions; **buenas ~s** good manners; **por la(s) ~(s)** for form's sake, as a matter of form; **cubrir las ~s, guardar las ~s** to keep up appearances.
(f) (*fórmula*) formula; **es pura ~** it's just for form's sake, it's a mere formality.
(g) (*Tip*) forme, form (*US*); *ver también* ⌐MANERA, FORMA, MODO⌐.
formación NF (a) (*gen*) formation. (b) (*Geol*) formation. (c) (*educación*) training, education; **~ laboral**, **~ ocupacional** occupational training; **~ profesional** vocational training; **~ sexual** sex education; **sin la debida ~ en la investigación** without the proper research training.
formado ADJ formed; grown; **bien ~** nicely-shaped, well-formed; **hombre (ya) ~** grown man.
formal ADJ (a) (*rel a la forma*) formal.
(b) (*serio*) serious; official; *declaración, promesa etc* formal, express, definite; *aire* serious, earnest, inspiring confidence; *persona (de fiar)* reliable, dependable; businesslike; steady, stable; (*grave*) dignified; (*puntual*) punctual; (*en edad*) adult, grown-up; *niño* well-behaved; **es una persona muy ~** he is a perfectly reliable sort; **¿has sido ~?** (*a ni-*

ño) did you behave yourself?; **¡estáte ~!** behave yourself!; **siempre estuvo muy ~ conmigo** he was always very correct towards me, he always treated me very properly.
(c) (*And: afable*) affable, pleasant.
(d) *vestido etc* formal.
formaldehído NM formaldehyde.
formaleta NF (*And, CAm, Méx*) bird trap.
formalidad NF (a) (*requisito*) form, formality; established practice; **son las ~es de costumbre** these are the usual formalities; **es pura ~** it's a pure formality, it's just a matter of form; **hay muchas ~es** there are a lot of formalities, there's a lot of red tape.
(b) (*seriedad*) seriousness; formal nature, express character; earnestness; reliability, dependable nature; steadiness, stability; (*de niño*) good behaviour; **hablar con ~** to speak in earnest; **¡niños, ~!** kids, behave yourselves!*; **¡señores, un poco de ~!** gentlemen, let's be serious!
formalina NF formalin(e).
formalismo NM (a) (*Liter*) formalism. (b) (*pey*) conventionalism; (*burocrático etc*) red tape, useless formalities.
formalista [1] ADJ (a) (*Liter*) formalist. (b) (*pey*) conventional, rigid.
[2] NMF (a) (*Liter*) formalist. (b) (*pey*) stickler for the regulations.
formalito* ADJ prim and proper.
formalizar [1f] [1] VT to formalize; to formulate, draw up; to put in order, give proper form to, regularize; **~ el noviazgo**, **~ sus relaciones** to become formally engaged.
[2] **formalizarse** VR (a) (*relación*) to acquire a proper form, get on to a proper footing; (*situación*) to be regularized.
(b) (*ponerse serio*) to grow serious.
(c) (*ofenderse*) to take offence.
formalote* ADJ stiff, serious.
formar [1a] [1] VT (a) (*gen*) to form, shape, fashion, make; *plan etc* to make, lay; *existenciar, reserva* to build up.
(b) (*integrar*) to form, make up, constitute; **está formado por** it is formed by, it is made up of.
(c) (*educar*) to train, educate.
(d) (*Mil*) to form up, parade.
[2] VI (*Mil*) to form up, fall in; (*Dep*) to line up; **¡a ~!** (*Mil*) fall in!; **los equipos formaron así:** ... the line-up of the teams was: ...
[3] **formarse** VR (a) (*gen*) to form; to take form, begin to form; (*desarrollarse*) to shape, develop.
(b) (*educarse*) to be trained, be educated; **se formó en la escuela de Praga** he was trained in the Prague school.
(c) (*Mil*) to form up, fall in, get into line; (*Dep*) to line up; **¡fórmense!** fall in line!; **el equipo se formó sin González** the team lined up without Gonzalez; the team left out Gonzalez at the start.
(d) **~ una opinión** to form an opinion; **¿qué impresión se ha formado?** what impression have you formed?
formateado NM formatting.
formatear [1a] VT to format.
formateo NM formatting.
formativo ADJ formative.
formato NM (*Inform, Tip*) format; (*tamaño de papel*) size; **papel (de) holandesa** (*aprox*) foolscap; **periódico de ~ reducido** tabloid newspaper; **~ fijo** fixed format; **~ libre** free format; **~ de registro** record format; **¿de qué ~ lo quiere?** what size do you want?
formica NF Formica ®.
fórmico ADJ: **ácido ~** formic acid.
formidable ADJ (a) (*terrible*) formidable, redoubtable; (*enorme*) huge; forbidding. (b) (*: *estupendo*) terrific*, tremendous*; **¡~!** that's great!*, splendid!
formón NM chisel.
Formosa NF: **(la Isla de) ~** (*Hist*) Formosa.
fórmula NF (*Quím, Mat, fig*) formula; (*Med etc*) prescription; **~ mágica** magic formula; **una ~ para conseguir el éxito** a formula to ensure success; **por pura ~** just for form's sake, purely as a matter of form.
formulación NF formulation; **~ de datos** data capture.
formulaico ADJ formulaic.
formular [1a] VT to formulate; to draw up, make out; *pregunta* to frame, pose; *protesta* to make, lodge; *reivindicación* to file, put in.
formulario [1] ADJ routine, ritual; formulaic.
[2] NM (a) (*fórmulas*) (*t Farm*) formulary, collection of formulae. (b) (*hoja*) form, blank; **~ de inscripción**, **~ de solicitud** application form; registration form; **~ de pedido** order blank, order form; **llenar un ~** to fill in a form.
formulismo NM red tape; useless formalities.
fornicación NF fornication.
fornicador, fornicario [1] ADJ fornicating.
[2] NM fornicator; adulterer.
fornicar [1g] VI to fornicate.
fornicio NM fornication.
fornido ADJ well-built, strapping, hefty.
fornitura NF (*CAm, Carib*) furniture.

foro NM (a) (*reunión*) forum, (open) meeting; (*Hist*) forum. (b) (*Jur*) court of justice; (*fig*) bar, legal profession; **el F~** (*Esp*) Madrid. (c) (*Teat*) back of the stage, upstage area.

forofada* NF fans, supporters (*collectively*).

forofismo NM (volume of) support.

forofo, -a* NM/F fan, supporter.

FORPPA NM ABR *de* **Fondo de Ordenación y Regulación de Precios y Productos Agrarios**.

FORPRONU NF ABR *de* **Fuerza(s) de Protección de las Naciones Unidas** United Nations Protection Force, UNPROFOR.

forrado ADJ (a) (*Cos etc*) lined; **~ de nilón** lined with nylon; **un libro ~ de pergamino** a book bound in parchment; **un coche ~ de ...** a car upholstered in ...
(b) (*: rico*) well heeled*, moneyed.

forraje NM (a) (*pienso*) forage, fodder. (b) (*acto*) foraging. (c) (*: mezcolanza*) hotchpotch, mixture.

forrajear [1a] VI to forage.

forrapelotas: NMF INVAR (a) (*caradura*) rotter*, berk:. (b) (*tonto*) idiot.

forrar [1a] ▢1 VT (*Cos etc*) to line (*de* with); to pad; *libro* to cover (*de* with); *coche* to upholster; (*Téc*) to line, face, cover; *cisterna, tubo* to lag.
▢2 **forrarse** VR (a) (*: enriquecerse*) to line one's pockets; to make one's pile*.
(b) (*: de comida*) to stuff o.s. (*de* with)*.
(c) (*CAm, Méx: proveerse*) to stock up (*de* with).

forro NM (a) (*Cos*) lining; padding; (*Tip*) cover, dust-cover, jacket; (*Náut*) sheathing; (*Téc*) lining; facing, sheathing; (*Aut*) upholstery; (*Cono Sur Aut*) tyre; **~ polar** fleece, Polartec ®; **con ~ de piel** with a fur lining, fur-lined; **~ de freno** brake lining; **ni por el ~** not in the slightest; **limpiar el ~ a uno** (*LAm:*) to bump sb off:.
(b) (*Cono Sur*: *preservativo*) rubber:, sheath.
(c) (*Carib: timo*) swindle, fraud.
(d) (*Cono Sur: talento*) aptitude.

forsitia NF forsythia.

fortacho NM (*Cono Sur*) strongly-built car, good car; (*pey*) old car, old crock.

fortachón* ADJ strong, tough.

fortalecer [2d] ▢1 VT (a) (*gen*) to strengthen; (*Mil*) to fortify.
(b) (*moralmente*) to encourage; *moral* to stiffen; **~ a uno en una opinión** to encourage sb in a belief.
▢2 **fortalecerse** VR (a) (*gen*) to fortify o.s. (*con* with).
(b) (*opinión etc*) to become stronger.

fortalecimiento NM (a) (*gen*) strengthening; fortification, fortifying.
(b) (*fig*) encouragement; stiffening.

fortaleza NF (a) (*Mil*) fortress, stronghold. (b) (*cualidad*) strength, toughness, vigour; (*moral*) fortitude, resolution. (c) (*Cono Sur, Méx:* *olor*) stench, pong:.

fortificación NF fortification.

fortificar [1g] VI to fortify; (*fig*) to strengthen.

fortín NM (small) fort; pillbox, bunker, blockhouse.

fortísimo ADJ SUPERL *de* **fuerte**; (*Mús*) fortissimo.

fortuitamente ADV fortuitously; accidentally; by chance, by coincidence.

fortuito ADJ fortuitous; accidental; chance (*atr*).

fortuna NF (a) (*gen*) fortune; chance; (*suerte*) (good) luck; **mala ~** misfortune; **por ~** luckily, fortunately; **pista de ~** emergency airstrip, improvised airstrip; **hacer ~** to be a success, make a hit; **tener la ~ de +** *infin* to have the good fortune to + *infin*; **probar ~** to try one's luck, have a shot.
(b) (*Náut*) storm; **correr ~** to go through a storm, experience a storm.
(c) (*Fin*) fortune; wealth.

fortunón* NM vast fortune, pile*.

fórum NM = **foro**.

forúnculo NM boil.

forzadamente ADV forcibly, by force; **sonreír ~** to force a smile; **reírse ~** to laugh in a forced way.

forzado ADJ forced; compulsory; **sonrisa forzada** forced smile; *V* **trabajo**.

forzar [1f *y* 1m] VT (a) (*obligar*) to force, compel, make; **~ a uno a hacer algo** to force sb to do sth, make sb do sth.
(b) *puerta etc* to force, break down, break open; *cerradura* to force, pick; *casa* to break into, enter by force, force a way into; *bloqueo* to run; (*Mil*) to storm, take; to force a passage through; *mujer* to ravish, rape.
(c) *ojos etc* to strain.

forzosamente ADV necessarily; inescapably; compulsorily; **tiene ~ que ser así** it must necessarily be so; **tuvieron ~ que venderlo** they had no choice but to sell it.

forzoso ADJ (*necesario*) necessary; (*inevitable*) inescapable, unavoidable; (*obligatorio*) compulsory; *aterrizaje etc* forced; **es ~ que ...** it is inevitable that ...; **le fue ~ hacerlo** he was forced to do it, he had no choice but to do it.

forzudo ▢1 ADJ strong, tough, brawny.
▢2 NM (*de circo*) strong man; (*pey*) thug, tough*; tough guy.

fosa NF (a) (*gen*) pit; (*sepultura*) grave; **~ atlántica** Atlantic trench; **~ común** common grave; **~ fecal, ~ séptica** septic tank; **~ marina, ~ oceánica** deep trough in the ocean bed.
(b) (*Anat*) fossa, fosse; cavity; **~s nasales** nasal cavities.
(c) (*fig*) chasm, wide gap.

fosar [1a] VT to dig a ditch (*o* trench *etc*) round.

fosco ADJ (a) *pelo* wild, disordered. (b) = **hosco**.

fosfatina* NF: **estar hecho ~** to be worn out, be shattered*.

fosfato NM phosphate.

fosforecer [2d] VI to phosphoresce, glow.

fosforera NF (a) (*cajita*) matchbox. (b) (*fábrica*) match factory.

fosforescencia NF phosphorescence.

fosforescente ADJ phosphorescent.

fosfórico ADJ phosphoric.

fosforito* ADJ INVAR fluorescent, garish.

fósforo NM (a) (*Quím*) phosphorus.
(b) (*cerilla*) match; (*And: cápsula fulminante*) percussion cap.
(c) (*Méx: carajillo*) coffee laced with brandy.
(d) **tener ~** (*Cono Sur*) to be shrewd, be sharp.
(e) (*CAm: exaltado*) hothead.
(f) (*CAm*: *pelirrojo*) redhead.

fosforoso ADJ phosphorous.

fosgeno NM phosgene.

fósil ▢1 ADJ fossil, fossilized.
▢2 NM (a) (*Geol*) fossil. (b) (*) (*chocho*) old crock, old dodderer; (*carroza*) old square*.

fosilizado ADJ fossilized.

fosilizarse [1f] VR to fossilize, become fossilized.

foso NM pit, hole; ditch, trench; (*Teat*) pit (*below stage*); (*Mil*) moat, fosse; entrenchment, defensive ditch; **~ de agua** (*Dep*) water jump; **~ generacional** generation gap; **~ de reconocimiento** (*Aut*) inspection pit; **irse al ~, venirse al ~** (*Teat*) to flop*, fail.

fotingo NM (*LAm*) old car, old crock.

foto NF photo; snap, snapshot; **~ aérea** aerial photograph; **~ de carnet** passport(-size) photograph; **~ de conjunto** group photo; **~ fija** still, still photograph; **~ robot** quick photo; booth for quick photography; **sacar una ~, tomar una ~** to take a photo (*de* of); **ella saca buena ~** she photographs well.

foto... PREF photo...

fotoacabado NM photo-finishing.

fotocalco NM photoprint.

fotocomponedora NF photocomposer.

fotocomposición NF filmsetting, photosetting (*US*), photocomposition.

fotocompositora NF filmsetting machine, photosetting machine (*US*).

fotoconductor NM photoconductor.

fotocontrol NM photocontrol; **resultado comprobado por ~** photo-finish.

fotocopia NF (a) (*una ~*) photocopy, print. (b) (*acto*) photocopying.

fotocopiadora NF photocopier.

fotocopiar [1b] VT to photocopy.

fotocopista NMF photocopier.

fotocopistería NF copy shop.

fotocromía NF colour photography.

fotoeléctrico ADJ photoelectric.

fotoenvejecimiento NM photo-ageing.

foto-finish, foto finish [foto'finis] NF INVAR photo-finish.

fotogenia NF photogenic qualities; **es de una ~ maravillosa** she's wonderfully photogenic.

fotogénico ADJ photogenic.

fotograbado NM photogravure, photoengraving.

fotografía NF (a) (*gen*) photography; **~ aérea** aerial photography; **~ en colores** colour photography.
(b) (*una ~*) photograph; **~ en colores** colour photograph; **~ al flash, ~ al magnesio** flashlight photograph; **~ instantánea** snapshot; '**~ de X'** (*pie de foto*) 'photographed by X'; **hacer una ~ de** to take a photograph of, photograph; *V t* **foto**.

fotografiar [1c] ▢1 VT to photograph.
▢2 VI to come out well in photographs.

fotográficamente ADV photographically; **le reconocieron ~** they recognized him through photographs.

fotográfico ADJ photographic.

fotógrafo, -a NM/F photographer; **~ aficionado** amateur photographer; **~ ambulante, ~ callejero** street photographer; **~ de estudio** portrait photographer; **~ de prensa** press photographer.

fotograma NM (*Cine*) shot, still.

fotogrametría NF: **~ aérea** aerial photography, mapmaking from the air.

fotomatón NM (a) (*quiosco*) photograph booth. (b) (*: foto*) passport-type photo.

fotómetro NM exposure meter, light meter, photometer.

fotomodelo NF photographic model.

fotomontaje NM photomontage.

fotón NM photon.

fotonoticia NF photographic reportage.

fotonovela NF romance (o crime story etc) illustrated with photos.

fotoperiodismo NM photojournalism.

fotoperiodista NMF photojournalist.

fotoprotección NF UV protection.

fotoprotector [1] ADJ UV protective.
[2] NM UV protectorant.

fotoquímico ADJ photochemical.

foto-robot NF, PL **foto-robots** Photofit picture ®.

fotorreceptor ADJ photoreceptor.

fotorreportaje NM report (with photographs).

fotorrobot NF, PL **fotorrobots** = foto-robot.

fotosensible ADJ photosensitive.

fotosensor NM photosensor.

fotosíntesis NF photosynthesis.

fotostatar [1a] VT to photostat.

fotostato NM photostat.

fototeca NF collection of photographs, photographic library.

fototopografía NF = fotogrametría.

fototropismo NM phototropism.

fotovoltaico ADJ photovoltaic.

fotuto NM (LAm Aut) horn.

foul [faul] [1] INTERJ (Dep) foul!
[2] NM (LAm) foul.

foulard [fu'lar] NM (de mujer) (head)scarf; (de hombre) cravate.

fox [fos] NM, PL **fox** [fos] foxtrot.

FP (a) NF (Esp Escol, Com) ABR de **Formación Profesional** technical education. **(b)** NM (Pol) ABR de **Frente Popular** Popular Front; see also PSOE.

FPA NF (Argentina, Esp: Escol, Com) ABR de **Formación Profesional Acelerada.**

FPLP NM ABR de **Frente Popular para la Liberación de Palestina** Popular Front for the Liberation of Palestine, PFLP.

FPMR NM (Chile) ABR de **Frente Patriótico Manuel Rodríguez.**

Fr. ABR de **Fray** Friar, Fr.

frac NM, PL **~s o fraques** dress coat, tails.

fracasado [1] ADJ failed; unsuccessful.
[2] NM, **fracasada** NF failure, person who is a failure.

fracasar [1a] [1] VT (LAm) to mess up, make a mess of.
[2] VI to fail, be unsuccessful; (plan etc) to fail, come to grief, fall through.

fracaso NM failure; fiasco; collapse, breakdown; **~ escolar** school drop-out; failure in end-of-year exams; **~ sentimental** disappointment in love, disastrous love affair; **el ~ de las negociaciones** the failure of the negotiations, the breakdown of the talks; **es un ~ total** it's a complete disaster; **ir a un ~** to court disaster.

fracción NF **(a)** (Mat) fraction; **~ decimal** fraction.
(b) (parte) fraction, part, fragment.
(c) (Pol etc) faction, splinter group.
(d) (acto) division, breaking-up (en into).

fraccionado ADJ: **pago ~** payment by instalments.

fraccionadora NF (Méx) estate agent, realtor (US).

fraccionalismo NM (Pol) tendency to form splinter-groups.

fraccionamiento NM **(a)** (gen) division; breaking-up (en into). **(b)** (Méx Constr) ≃ housing estate.

fraccionar [1a] VT to divide, break up, split up (en into).

fraccionario ADJ fractional; dinero small, in small units; **'Se ruega moneda fraccionaria'** 'Please tender exact fare'.

fractura NF fracture, break (t Med); **~ complicada** compound fracture.

fracturar [1a] [1] VT to fracture, break.
[2] **fracturarse** VR to fracture, break.

fragancia NF fragrance, sweet smell, perfume.

fragante ADJ **(a)** (gen) fragrant, sweet-smelling, scented. **(b)** = flagrante.

fraganti V in fraganti.

fragata NF frigate.

frágil ADJ fragile, frail; (Com) breakable; (fig) frail, delicate.

fragilidad NF fragility, frailty; (fig) frailty, delicacy.

fragmentación NF fragmentation.

fragmentadamente ADV: **pagar ~** to pay in instalments.

fragmentado ADJ fragmented.

fragmentar [1a] [1] VT (gen) to fragment; (en trozos etc) to break up, divide up.
[2] **fragmentarse** VR to fragment; (en trozos etc) to break up, divide up.

fragmentariedad NF fragmentary nature.

fragmentario ADJ fragmentary.

fragmento NM fragment; piece, bit.

fragor NM din, clamour, noise; uproar; crash, clash; (de máquina, río) roar.

fragoroso ADJ deafening, thunderous.

fragosidad NF **(a)** (cualidad) roughness, unevenness; difficult nature; denseness. **(b)** (una ~) rough spot; rough road.

fragoso ADJ rough, uneven; terreno difficult; bosque dense, overgrown.

fragua NF forge.

fraguado NM **(a)** (de metal) forging. **(b)** (de hormigón etc) hardening, setting.

fraguar [1i] [1] VT **(a)** hierro etc to forge. **(b)** (fig) to hatch, concoct; to plot.
[2] VI (hormigón etc) to harden, set.
[3] **fraguarse** VR (tormenta) to blow up; (fig) to blow up, be brewing, be in the offing.

fraile NM **(a)** (Rel) friar; monk; (pey) (any) priest; **~ descalzo** discalced friar; **~ mendicante** mendicant friar (gen Franciscan); **~ de misa y olla** ignorant friar, simple-minded friar; **~ predicador** friar preacher. **(b)** (Carib: bagazo) bagasse, residue of sugar cane.

frailecillo NM (Orn) puffin.

frailería NF friars (collectively); monks (collectively); (pey) priests.

frailesco ADJ, **frailuno** ADJ (pey) monkish.

frambuesa NF raspberry.

frambuesero NM, **frambueso** NM raspberry cane.

francachela* NF (comida) spread*, big feed*; (juerga) spree, binge*.

francachón ADJ (LAm: pey) too direct, too outspoken.

francamente ADV **(a)** (hablar etc) frankly, openly, forthrightly.
(b) (realmente) frankly; really, definitely; **~ no lo sé** frankly I don't know, I really don't know; **eso está ~ mal** that is definitely wrong; **es una obra ~ divertida** it's a really funny play.

francés [1] ADJ French; **a la francesa** in the French manner (o style etc); **despedirse a la francesa** to take French leave.
[2] NM **(a)** (persona) Frenchman. **(b)** (Ling) French. **(c)** (‡) blow job‡.

francesa NF Frenchwoman.

francesilla NF **(a)** (Bot) buttercup. **(b)** (Culin) roll.

franchute NM, **franchuta** NF (pey) Frenchy*, Frog‡.

Francia NF France.

fráncico [1] ADJ Frankish.
[2] NM (Ling) Frankish.

francio NM (Quím) francium.

Francisca NF Frances.

franciscano ADJ, NM Franciscan.

Francisco NM Francis.

francmasón NM (free)mason.

francmasonería NF (free)masonry.

franco[1] (Hist) [1] ADJ Frankish.
[2] NM Frank.

franco[2] (Fin) franc.

franco[3] ADJ **(a)** (directo) frank, open, forthright, candid; (familiar) familiar; free; intimate; (patente) clear, evident; **si he de ser ~** frankly, to tell the truth; **seré ~ contigo** I will be frank with you, I will be plain with you; **son francas imposibilidades** they are plain impossibilities, they are downright impossible; **estar en franca rebeldía** to be in open rebellion; **estar en franca decadencia** to be in full decline.
(b) (Com etc) free, gratis; exempt; camino etc free, open; puerto etc free; **~ a bordo** free on board; **~ de derechos** duty-free; **precio ~ (en) fábrica** price ex-factory, price ex-works; **~ de porte** (Com) carriage-free, (Correos) post-free; **~ sobre vagón** free on rail; **mantener mesa franca** to keep open house.
(c) **~ de servicio** (Mil) off-duty; **estar de ~** (Cono Sur) to be off duty, be on leave.

franco... PREF franco...

francocanadiense ADJ, NMF French-Canadian.

francófilo, -a NM/F francophile.

francófobo [1] ADJ francophobe, francophobic.
[2] NM, **francófoba** NF francophobe.

francófono [1] ADJ French-speaking.
[2] NM, **francófona** NF French speaker.

franco-hispano ADJ Franco-Spanish.

francote ADJ outspoken, blunt, bluff.

francotirador NM **(a)** (Mil) sniper, sharpshooter. **(b)** (periodista etc) freelance.

franela NF **(a)** (tela) flannel. **(b)** (LAm: ropa interior) vest, undershirt (US); (camiseta) T-shirt.

franelear‡ [1a] VI to pet*.

frangollar [1a] [1] VT **(a)** (chapucear) to bungle, botch, rush. **(b)** (Cono Sur) granos to grind.
[2] VI (And) to dissemble.

frangollero ADJ (And, Cono Sur) bungling.

frangollo NM **(a)** (Culin) crushed and boiled corn, wheat porridge; (Carib: dulce) sweet made from mashed bananas; (Cono Sur: locro) meat and maize stew.

(b) (*LAm Orn*) birdseed.

(c) (*Méx*) (*lío*) muddle, mess; (*mezcla*) mixture.

frangollón (*LAm*) ⓵ ADJ bungling.

⓶ NM, **frangollona** NF bungler.

franja NF **(a)** (*Cos*) fringe, border, trimming; braid.

(b) (*zona*) fringe, strip, band; **~ de tierra** strip of land; **la F~ de Gaza** the Gaza Strip.

franj(e)ar [1a] VT to fringe, trim (*de* with).

franqueadora NF (*Correos*: *t máquina ~*) franking machine.

franquear [1a] ⓵ VT **(a)** *esclavo* to free, liberate; *contribuyente etc* to free, exempt (*de* from).

(b) *derecho etc* to grant, allow, concede (*a* to); **~ la entrada a** to give free entry to.

(c) *camino etc* to clear, open.

(d) *río etc* to cross; *obstáculo* to negotiate, overcome, get round.

(e) (*Correos*) to frank, stamp; to pay postage on; **una carta franqueada** a post-paid letter, a letter with the postage paid on it; **una carta insuficientemente franqueada** a letter with insufficient postage.

⓶ **franquearse** VR: **~ a uno, ~ con uno** to unbosom o.s. to sb, have a heart-to-heart talk with sb.

franqueo NM postage; franking; **con ~ insuficiente** with insufficient postage, with postage underpaid.

franqueza NF frankness, openness, forthrightness, candidness; familiarity; freedom, intimacy; **con ~** frankly; **lo digo con toda ~** I say so quite frankly; **tengo suficiente ~ con él para discrepar** I am on close enough terms with him to disagree.

franquía NF (*Náut*) searoom, room to manoeuvre.

franquicia NF **(a)** (*exención*) exemption (*de* from); **~ aduanera, ~ arancelaria** exemption from customs duties; **~ de equipaje** (*Aer*) free baggage allowance; **~ postal** privilege of franking letters. **(b)** (*Com*) franchise.

franquiciado, -a NM/F franchise-holder, franchisee.

franquiciador(a) NM/F franchisor.

franquiciamiento NM franchising.

franquiciar [1b] VT to franchise.

franquismo NM: **el ~** (*período*) the Franco years, the Franco period; (*política*) the Franco system, the Franco outlook; **bajo el ~** under Franco; **luchó contra el ~** he fought against Franco.

| FRANQUISMO |

ⓘ *Franquismo is the term used to refer both to the years when General Francisco Franco was the dictator of Spain (from the end of the* **Guerra Civil** *in 1939 to his death in 1975) and to his style of government. He was an authoritarian, right-wing dictator whose political philosophy included imposing traditional Catholic values and making Spain self-sufficient economically. Following a prolonged period of severe isolation from the international community, in the 1960s Spain gradually opened its doors to foreign investment and influence. This coincided with a rise in economic growth and internal political opposition. On his death, Spain became a democratic constitutional monarchy.*

---

franquista ⓵ ADJ pro-Franco; **tendencia ~** tendency to support Franco, pro-Franco tendency; **una familia muy ~** a strongly pro-Franco family, a family which strongly supported Franco.

⓶ NMF supporter of Franco.

FRAP NM **(a)** (*Esp*) ABR *de* **Frente Revolucionario Antifascista y Patriótico. (b)** (*Chile*) ABR *de* **Frente de Acción Popular.**

frasca NF **(a)** dry leaves, small twigs. **(b)** (*CAm, Méx*: *fiesta*) riotous party. **(c) pegarle a la ~*** to hit the bottle*.

frasco NM **(a)** flask, bottle; **~ de bolsillo** hip flask; **~ de campaña** (*LAm*) water bottle; **~ de perfume** scent bottle; **~ al vacío** vacuum flask; **¡chupa el ~!⁑, ¡toma del ~, (Carrrasco)!⁑** stone the crows!⁑ **(b)** (*medida*) liquid measure (*Carib = 2.44 litres, Cono Sur = 21.37 litres*).

frase NF **(a)** (*oración*) sentence; **~ compleja** complex sentence. **(b)** (*locución*) phrase, expression; (*cita*) quotation; **~ hecha** saying, proverb; idiom; (*pey*) cliché, stock phrase; **~ lapidaria** axiom; **diccionario de ~s** dictionary of quotations.

fraseo NM (*Mús*) phrasing.

fraseología NF **(a)** phraseology. **(b)** (*pey*) verbosity, verbiage.

Frasquita NF *forma familiar de* **Francisca.**

Frasquito NM *forma familiar de* **Francisco.**

fratás NM (plastering) trowel.

fraterna* NF ticking-off*.

fraternal ADJ brotherly, fraternal.

fraternidad NF brotherhood, fraternity; (*CAm, Carib*: *Univ*) fraternity.

fraternización NF fraternization.

fraternizar [1f] VI to fraternize.

fraterno ADJ brotherly, fraternal.

fratricida ⓵ ADJ fratricidal.

⓶ NMF fratricide (*person*).

fratricidio NM fratricide (*act*).

fraude NM **(a)** (*cualidad*) dishonesty, fraudulence. **(b)** (*acto*) fraud, swindle; deception; **~ fiscal** tax fraud; **por ~** by fraud, by false pretences.

fraudulencia NF fraudulence.

fraudulentamente ADV fraudulently, by fraud; dishonestly.

fraudulento ADJ fraudulent; dishonest, deceitful.

fray NM (*Ecl*) brother, friar.

frazada NF (*esp LAm*) blanket.

freático ADJ V **capa.**

frecuencia NF **(a)** frequency; **con ~** frequently, often. **(b)** (*Elec, Inform, Rad*) frequency; **alta ~** high frequency; **de alta ~** high-frequency (*atr*); **~ modulada** frequency modulation; **~ de red** mains frequency; **~ del reloj** clock speed.

frecuentador(a) NM/F frequenter.

frecuentar [1a] VT to frequent; to haunt.

frecuente ADJ **(a)** frequent; common; *costumbre etc* common, usual, prevalent. **(b)** (*Méx*: *familiar*) familiar, over-familiar; **andarse ~ con** to be on close terms with.

frecuentemente ADV frequently, often.

Fredemo NM (*Perú*) ABR *de* **Frente Democrático.**

freelance, free-lance [fri'lans] ADJ, NMF INVAR freelance.

fregada* NF (*CAm, Méx*) (*embrollo*) mess, muck-up*; (*problema*) snag; (*molestia*) nuisance, drag; **¡la ~!⁑** you don't say!, never!; **¡me lleva la ~!⁑** well, I'm blowed!*

fregadera* NF (*LAm*) nuisance, annoyance.

fregadero NM **(a)** (*recipiente*) (kitchen) sink. **(b)** (*pieza*) scullery. **(c)** (*CAm, Méx*: *molestia*) pain in the neck*.

fregado ⓵ ADJ (*) **(a)** (*LAm*: *molesto*) tiresome, annoying; (⁑: *puñetero*) bloody⁑, lousy⁑; (*Cono Sur*: *difícil*) difficult, problematic. **(b)** (*LAm*) *asunto* nasty, messy, dishonest. **(c)** (*LAm*: *tonto*) silly, stupid. **(d)** (*And, CAm, Méx*: *astuto*) cunning, sly. **(e)** (*And, CAm, Carib*) (*testarudo*) pigheaded; (*tenaz*) persistent. **(f)** (*Carib*: *fresco*) cheeky*, fresh*. **(g)** (*Méx*: *pobre*) poor.

⓶ NM **(a)** (*acto*) rubbing, scrubbing, scouring; (*de platos*) washing-up; **hacer el ~** to do the washing-up, wash up. **(b)** (*: lío*) mess, messy affair; (*: asunto turbio*) nasty affair, dishonest deal. **(c)** (*LAm*: *riña*) row, tiff; **tener un ~ con uno** to have a row with sb. **(d) dar un ~ a uno*** to give sb a dressing-down*. **(e) es un ~** (*And, Cono Sur*) he's a dead loss.

fregador NM **(a)** (*fregadero*) sink. **(b)** (*trapo*) dishcloth; scourer; mop.

fregadura NF = **fregado 2 (a).**

fregancia NF (*And*) = **fregada.**

fregandera NF (*Méx*) charwoman, cleaner.

fregantina NF (*And, Cono Sur*) = **fregada.**

fregar [1h y 1k] ⓵ VT **(a)** (*estregar*) to rub, scrub; to scour; *suelo* to mop, scrub; *platos* to wash (up). **(b)** (*LAm**) (*fastidiar*) to bother, annoy; (*acosar*) to worry, harass; (*arruinar*) to mess up, make a mess of; **¡no me friegues!** stop bothering me!, leave me alone! **(c)** (*Carib**) (*pegar*) to thrash; (*Dep*) to beat, thrash. **(d)** (*Cono Sur*⁑) to screw⁑.

⓶ **fregarse** VR (*CAm, Méx**: *malograrse*) to break down, go wrong.

fregasuelos NM INVAR mop.

fregazón* NM (*Cono Sur*) = **fregada.**

fregón* ADJ **(a)** (*And, CAm, Méx*: *molesto*) trying, tiresome, annoying. **(b)** (*LAm*: *tonto*) silly, stupid. **(c)** (*And, Carib*: *fresco*) brazen, fresh.

fregona NF **(a)** (*persona*) kitchen maid, dishwasher; (*pey*) skivvy; (*Carib*: *sinvergüenza*) shameless hussy. **(b)** (*: utensilio*) mop.

fregota⁑ NM waiter.

fregoteo* NM = **fregado 2 (a).**

freidera NF (*Carib*) frying-pan.

freidora NF frying-pan.

freiduría NF (*t ~ de pescado*) fried-fish shop.

freír [3m; PTP **frito**] ⓵ VT **(a)** (*Culin*) to fry; (*fig*: *sol*) to burn, fry; **al ~ será el reír** the proof of the pudding is in the eating. **(b)** (*fig*) (*molestar*) to annoy; (*atormentar*) to torment; (*acosar*) to harass; (*aburrir*) to bore; **~le a uno a preguntas** to bombard sb with questions. **(c)** (⁑: *matar*) to do in⁑.

⓶ **freírse** VR **(a)** (*Culin*) to fry, be frying; **~ de calor** to fry in the heat, be roasted. **(b) ~la a uno*** to have sb on.

fréjol NM = **fríjol.**

frenada NF, **frenaje** NM (*Aut*) braking.

frenado NM (*Aut*) braking.

frenar [1a] VT **(a)** (*Aut, Mec*) to brake; to put the brake on, apply the brake to. **(b)** (*fig*) to check, curb, restrain.

frenazo NM (*acto*) sudden braking; (*parada*) sudden halt; (*ruido*) squeal of brakes; **dar un ~** to brake suddenly, brake hard.

frenesí NM frenzy.

frenéticamente ADV frantically, frenziedly; furiously, wildly.

frenético ADJ frantic, frenzied; furious, wild.

frenillo NM: **tener ~** (*fig*) to have a speech defect.

freno NM (**a**) (*Aut, Mec etc*) brake; **~ de aire** airbrake; **~s de disco** disc brakes; **~ hidráulico** hydraulic brake; **~ de mano** handbrake; **~ de pedal** footbrake; **~ de tambor** drum brake; **poner el ~, echar los ~s** to put the brake(s) on, apply the brake(s); **¡echa el ~, Madaleno!**‡ put a sock in it!*; **soltar el ~** to release the brake.
(**b**) (*de caballo*) bit; bridle; **morder** (o **tascar**) **el ~** (*fig*) to restrain o.s., hold back.
(**c**) (*fig*) check, curb, restraint; **~s y contrapesos, ~s y equilibrios** (*Pol*) checks and balances; **poner ~ a** to curb, check; **poner ~ a las malas lenguas** to stop the gossip.
(**d**) (*Cono Sur: hambre*) hunger.

frenología NF phrenology.

frenólogo, -a NM/F phrenologist.

frenopático [1] ADJ psychiatric.
[2] NM (*Med*) mental home; (*: hum*) loony bin‡.

frentazo* NM (*Cono Sur, Méx*) rebuff, disappointment; **pegarse un ~** to come a cropper*.

▼ **frente** [1] NM (**a**) (*parte delantera*) front, front part; face; (*Arquit*) front, face, façade; **~ de arranque, ~ de trabajo** (*Min*) working face; **al ~** in front (*de* of); **al ~ de** (*fig*) in charge of, at the head of; **¡de ~** (*mar*)! forward march!, by the right quick march!; **ir de ~** to go forward; to face forwards; **chocar de ~** to crash head-on; **atacar de ~** to make a frontal attack; **mirar de ~** to look (straight) ahead; **viajar de ~ a la marcha** (*Ferro*) to travel facing the engine; **marchar 6 de ~** to march 6 abreast; **en ~** opposite; in front; **la casa de en ~** the house opposite; **estar ~ por ~ de** to be directly opposite; **hacer ~ a** to resist, stand up to, face; **hacer ~ a unos grandes gastos** to (have to) meet considerable expenses; **hacer ~ a un temporal** (*Náut*) to ride out a storm.
(**b**) (*Mil*) front; **~ de batalla** battle front, firing-line; **~ del oeste** western front; **cambiar de ~** to wheel.
(**c**) (*Pol*) front; **~ popular** popular front; **hacer ~ común con uno** to make common cause with sb.
(**d**) (*Met*) front; **~ cálido** warm front; **~ frío** cold front.
[2] NF forehead, brow; face; **~ a ~** face to face; **adornar la ~ a uno*** to cuckold sb; **arrugar la ~** to knit one's brow, frown; **llevarlo escrito en la ~** to make no effort to hide one's feelings.
▼ [3] PREP: **~ a** opposite (to), facing; in front of; (*fig*) as opposed to, as contrasted with.
[4] ADV (*Cono Sur*): **~ mío** (*etc*) opposite me (*etc*), in front of me (*etc*).

freo NM channel, strait.

fresa [1] NF (**a**) (*Bot*) (*fruta*) strawberry (*esp wild*); (*planta*) strawberry plant. (**b**) (*Téc*) milling cutter; (dentist's) drill.
[2] ADJ: **la gente ~** (*Méx**) the in crowd.

fresado NM (*Mec*) milling.

fresadora NF (*Mec*) milling machine; **~ de roscar** thread cutter.

fresal NM strawberry bed.

fresar [1a] VT (*Mec*) to mill.

fresca NF (**a**) (*aire*) fresh air, cool air; (*período*) cool part of the day; **tomar la ~** to get some fresh air, go out for a breath of air.
(**b**) (*descarada*) **decir cuatro ~s a uno*** to give sb a piece of one's mind.
(**c**) (***) (*descarada*) shameless woman, brazen woman; (*puta*) whore; **¡es una ~!** she's a hussy!, she's quite brazen!

frescachón ADJ (**a**) (*robusto*) glowing with health, ruddy; robust. (**b**) *niño* bouncing, healthy. (**c**) *mujer* buxom. (**d**) (*Náut*) *viento* fresh, stiff.

frescales NM INVAR cheeky rascal, rogue.

fresco [1] ADJ (**a**) (*gen*) fresh; (*nuevo*) new, recent; *pan* new; *huevo* new-laid; **cosas todavía frescas en la memoria** things still fresh in the memory.
(**b**) (*algo frío*) cool; **agua fresca** cold water; **bebida fresca** cool drink, cooling drink, cold drink; **hacer ~** (*Met*) to be cool, be fresh.
(**c**) *viento* fresh.
(**d**) *tela, vestido* light, thin.
(**e**) *tez* fresh, ruddy, healthy.
(**f**) (*sereno*) cool, calm, unabashed; **tan ~** quite unabashed, quite unconcerned; **me lo dijo tan ~** he said it to me as cool as you please; **estar más ~ que una lechuga** to be as cool as a cucumber.
(**g**) (**: descarado*) cool, fresh*; cheeky*, saucy; bad-mannered; **¡qué ~!** what cheek!*, what a nerve!*; **ponerse ~ con una** to get fresh with a girl*.
(**h**) **dejar ~ a uno** to disappoint sb; **quedarse ~** to be disappointed, feel cheated.
[2] NM (**a**) (*aire*) fresh air, cool air; **al ~** in the open air, out of doors; **tomar el ~** to get some fresh air, go for a stroll in the open; **¡vete a tomar el ~!*** get lost!‡; **me trae al ~** it leaves me cold.
(**b**) (*Arquit, Arte*) fresco; **pintar al ~** to paint in fresco.
(**c**) (**: sinvergüenza*) fresh guy* (*US*), shameless individual; bad-mannered person; **¡Vd es un ~!** you've got a nerve!*; mind your

manners!
(**d**) **echar ~ a uno** (*LAm*) to tell sb a few home truths.
(**e**) (*CAm: jugo*) fruit juice, fruit drink.

frescor NM freshness; coolness; **gozar del ~ nocturno** to enjoy the cool night air.

frescote ADJ blooming; buxom.

frescura NF (**a**) (*gen*) freshness; (*frío*) coolness; (*de tez*) freshness.
(**b**) (*serenidad*) coolness, calmness, unconcern; **con la mayor ~** with the greatest unconcern, completely unconcerned.
(**c**) (**: descaro*) cheek*, sauce*, nerve*; **¡qué ~!** what a nerve!*; **tiene la mar de ~** he's got the cheek of the devil*.
(**d**) (**: impertinencia*) impudent remark, cheeky thing (to say)*; **me dijo unas ~s** he said some cheeky things to me*.

fresia NF freesia.

fresnada NF ash grove.

fresno NM ash, ash tree.

fresón NM (*fruta*) strawberry (*esp cultivated*); (*planta*) strawberry plant.

fresquera NF meat safe; icebox.

fresquería NF (*LAm*) refreshment stall.

fresquito ADJ *viento* rather fresh; *V* **fresco**.

freudiano, -a ADJ, NM/F Freudian.

freza NF (**a**) (*huevos*) spawn; (*acto, estación*) spawning. (**b**) (*Zool*) dung, droppings.

frezadero NM spawning ground.

frezar [1f] VI to spawn.

friable ADJ friable.

frialdad NF (**a**) (*gen*) coldness, cold, chilliness. (**b**) (*fig*) coldness, coolness; indifference, unconcern. (**c**) (*Méx*) (*impotencia*) impotence; (*esterilidad*) sterility.

fríamente ADV (*fig*) coldly.

frían *V* **freír**.

frica NF (*Cono Sur*) beating.

fricandó NM, **fricasé** NM fricassee.

fricativa NF fricative.

fricativo ADJ fricative.

fricción NF rub, rubbing; (*Med*) massage; (*Mec*) friction; (*fig: Pol etc*) friction, trouble.

friccionar [1a] VT to rub; (*Med*) to rub, massage.

friega NF (**a**) (*gen*) rub, rubbing; (*Med*) massage.
(**b**) (*LAm*: molestia*) nuisance, annoyance; bother; (*lío*) fuss.
(**c**) (*LAm*: idiotez*) silliness, stupidity.
(**d**) (*And, Carib, Cono Sur*: paliza*) thrashing.
(**e**) (*And, Méx*: reprimenda*) ticking-off*.

friegaplatos NM INVAR (**a**) (*aparato*) dishwasher. (**b**) (*persona*) dishwasher, washer-up.

friegasuelos NM INVAR floor mop.

frígano NM caddis fly.

frigidaire NM of (*LAm*) refrigerator.

frigidez NF frigidity (*t Med*).

frígido ADJ frigid (*t Med*).

frigo* NM fridge, refrigerator.

frigorífico [1] ADJ refrigerating, cold-storage (*atr*); **camión ~** refrigerator lorry, refrigerator truck (*US*); **instalación frigorífica** cold-storage plant.
[2] NM refrigerator; (*Cono Sur*) cold-storage plant, meat-packing depot; (*Náut*) refrigerator ship.

frigorífico-congelador NM, PL **frigoríficos-congeladores** fridge-freezer.

frigorista NMF refrigeration engineer.

frijar‡ [1a] VI to have a screw‡.

fríjol NM, **frijol** NM (**a**) (*Bot*) kidney bean, French bean; **~ de café** coffee-bean; **~ de soja** soya bean.
(**b**) **~es** (*LAm: comida*) food (*in general*).
(**c**) (*Méx*: mofa*) taunt; **echar ~es** to blow one's own trumpet.
(**d**) **¡~es!** (*Carib*) certainly not!, not on your life!.
(**e**) (*And, Méx: cobarde*) coward; **ser como los ~es que al primer hervor se arrugan** to run at the first sign of trouble.
(**f**) (*Fin*‡) dough‡, money.

fringolear [1a] VT (*Cono Sur*) to thrash, beat.

frío [1] ADJ (**a**) (*gen*) cold; chilly; **más ~ que el hielo, ~ como un mármol** as cold as ice; **quedarse ~*** to peg out‡.
(**b**) *bala* spent.
(**c**) (*fig*) cold, unconcerned, unmoved, indifferent; *acogida* cool; **¡me deja Vd ~!** you amaze me!; **eso me deja ~** that leaves me cold.
[2] NM (**a**) cold; coldness; **¡qué ~!** isn't it cold!, how cold it is!; **hace ~** it's cold; **hace mucho ~** it's very cold; **coger ~** to catch cold; **pasar ~** to be cold, suffer cold; **tener ~** to be cold, feel cold; **no me da ni ~ ni calor** it's all the same to me; it leaves me cold; *V* **helador** etc.
(**b**) (*fig*) coldness, indifference.
(**c**) **~s** (*And, CAm, Méx*) (*fiebre*) intermittent fever; (*paludismo*) malaria.

friolento ADJ = **friolero**.

▶ LENGUA Y USO: **frente: 3 → 32.1**

friolera NF trifle, mere nothing.
friolero ADJ *persona* chilly, sensitive to cold, shivery.
friorizado ADJ deep-frozen.
frisa NF **(a)** *(tela)* frieze.
  (b) *(And, Cono Sur Cos)* nap (on cloth); *(Cono Sur: pelusa)* fluff; *(Carib: manta)* blanket; **sacar a uno la ~*** *(Cono Sur)* to tan sb's hide*; **sacar la ~ a algo*** *(Cono Sur)* to make the most of sth.
frisar [1a] **1** VT *tela* to frizz, rub.
  2 VI: **~ en** to border on, be close to; **frisa en los 50** she's close on 50, she's getting on for 50.
Frisia NF Friesland.
friso NM frieze; wainscot, dado.
fritada NF fry, fried dish.
fritanga NF **(a)** *(And, CAm: guiso)* ≃ hotpot, stew; *(Cono Sur, CAm: pey)* greasy food. **(b)** *(CAm: restaurante)* cheap restaurant. **(c)** *(Cono Sur*: molestia)* nuisance, pain in the neck*.
fritanguería NF *(Chile, Perú: tienda)* fried food shop; (: *puesto)* fried food stall.
fritar [1a] VT *(LAm)* to fry.
frito **1** ADJ **(a)** *(Culin)* fried.
  (b) **(*)** **tener ~ a uno, traer ~ a uno** *(acosar)* to worry sb to death; *(vencer)* to defeat sb; *(enojar)* to make sb cross; **ese hombre me trae ~** that chap bothers me all day long*, that chap makes me really cross*; **las matemáticas me traen ~** maths is getting me down, maths just defeats me.
  (c) *pelo* frizzy.
  (d) **dejar a uno ~‡** *(matar)* to do sb in‡; **estar ~‡** *(dormido)* to be kipping‡; *(muerto)* to be a goner‡; *(excitado)* to be really worked up; *(Carib, Cono Sur)* to be finished, be done for; **quedarse ~‡** *(dormirse)* to go out like a light; *(morir)* to snuff it‡.
  2 NM **(a)** *(plato)* fry, fried dish; **~s variados** mixed fry.
  (b) **a esa mujer le gusta el ~** *(Cono Sur‡)* she looks like hot stuff*.
  (c) *(en disco)* hiss, crackling sound.
fritura NF **(a)** *(plato frito)* fry, fried dish. **(b)** *(buñuelo)* fritter. **(c)** *(Telec)* interference, crackling.
frívolamente ADV frivolously.
frivolidad NF frivolity, frivolousness.
frivolité NM *(Cos)* tatting.
frivolizar [1f] VT to trivialize; to play down.
frívolo ADJ frivolous.
frivolón ADJ superficial, frothy, lightweight.
frízer NM *(Cono Sur)* freezer.
fronda NF frond; **~s** fronds; foliage, leaves.
frondís ADJ *(And)* dirty.
frondosidad NF leafiness; luxuriance.
frondoso ADJ leafy; luxuriant.
frontal **1** ADJ **(a)** frontal; *parte, posición* front; *(Inform)* front-end; **choque ~** head-on collision. **(b)** *rechazo etc* outright, forthright, total.
  2 NM front, front part.
frontalmente ADV frontally; **chocar ~** to collide head-on; **está situado ~** it is placed on the front; **se oponen ~** they are directly opposed.
frontera NF **(a)** frontier, border; *(zona)* frontier area, borderland *(t fig)*. **(b)** *(Arquit)* façade.
fronterizo ADJ *frontier (atr)*; border *(atr)*. **(b)** *(enfrente)* opposite, facing; **las casas fronterizas** the houses opposite; **el puente ~ con Eslobodia** the bridge bordering Slobodia.
frontero ADJ opposite, facing.
frontis NM *(Arquit)* façade.
frontispicio NM **(a)** *(Arquit)* façade; *(Tip)* frontispiece. **(b)** (‡: *cara)* clock‡, face.
frontón NM **(a)** *(Arquit)* pediment. **(b)** *(Dep)* pelota court; (main) wall of a pelota court.
frotación NF, **frotadura** NF, **frotamiento** NM rub, rubbing; *(Mec)* friction.
frotado NM rubbing.
frotar [1a] **1** VT to rub; *cerilla* to strike; **quitar algo frotando** to rub sth off.
  2 **frotarse** VR to rub, chafe; **~ las manos** to rub one's hands; **frotársela‡** to wank‡.
frote NM rub.
frotis NM: **~ cervical** cervical smear; **~ vaginal** vaginal smear.
fr(s). ABR *de* **franco(s)** franc(s), fr.
fructífero ADJ **(a)** *(Bot etc)* productive, fruit-bearing. **(b)** *(fig)* fruitful.
fructificación NF *(fig)* fruition.
fructificar [1g] VI **(a)** *(Bot)* to produce, yield a crop, bear fruit. **(b)** *(fig)* to yield a profit; to bear fruit; to come to fruition.
fructosa NF fructose.
fructuosamente ADV fruitfully.
fructuoso ADJ fruitful.
frufrú NM rustling.

frugal ADJ frugal; thrifty; parsimonious.
frugalidad NF frugality; thrift, thriftiness; parsimony.
frugalmente ADV frugally; thriftily; parsimoniously.
fruición NF enjoyment; satisfaction, delight; **~ maliciosa** malicious pleasure.
frunce NM pleat, tuck, gather, shirr.
fruncido **1** ADJ **(a)** *(gen)* contracted; *(Cos)* pleated, gathered; *frente* wrinkled, furrowed; *cara* frowning.
  (b) *(Cono Sur*)* *(remilgado)* prudish, demure; *(afectado)* affected.
  2 NM = **frunce**.
fruncimiento NM = **frunce**.
fruncir [3b] VT to contract, pucker; to ruffle; *(Cos)* to pleat, gather, shirr, put a tuck in; *frente* to wrinkle, knit; *labios* to purse; **V ceño** etc.
fruslería NF trifle, trinket; *(fig)* trifle, small thing, triviality.
frustración NF frustration.
frustrado ADJ *persona* frustrated; *intento, plan, atentado* failed; **delito de homicidio ~** attempted murder.
frustrante ADJ frustrating.
frustrar [1a] **1** VT to frustrate, thwart.
  2 **frustrarse** VR to be frustrated; *(plan etc)* to fail, miscarry.
frustre* NM = **frustración**.
fruta NF **(a)** fruit; **~s** *(Culin)* fruit; **~s confitadas** candied fruits; **~ de la pasión** passionfruit; **~ prohibida** forbidden fruit; **~ de sartén** fritter; **~ seca** dried fruit; **~ del tiempo** *(Culin)* seasonal fruit. **(b)** *(fig)* fruit, consequence.
frutal **1** ADJ fruit-bearing, fruit *(atr)*; **árbol ~ = 2**.
  2 NM fruit-tree.
frutar [1a] VI to fruit, bear fruit.
frutera NF fruit-dish, fruit-bowl.
frutería NF fruiterer's (shop), fruit shop.
frutero **1** ADJ fruit *(atr)*; **plato ~** fruit-dish.
  2 NM **(a)** *(persona)* fruiterer. **(b)** *(recipiente)* fruit-dish, fruit-bowl; basket of fruit.
fruticultor(a) NM/F fruit-farmer, fruit-grower.
fruticultura NF fruit-growing, fruit-farming.
frutilla NF *(LAm)* strawberry.
fruto NM **(a)** *(Bot)* fruit; **~ del árbol del pan** breadfruit; **~s del país** *(Cono Sur)* agricultural products; **dar ~** to fruit, bear fruit.
  (b) *(fig)* fruits; *(resultado)* result, consequence; *(beneficio)* profit, benefit; *(hijo etc)* offspring, child; **~ de bendición** legitimate offspring; **el ~ de esta unión** the offspring of this marriage; **dar ~** to bear fruit; **sacar ~ de** to profit from, derive benefit from.
frutosidad NF fruitiness, fruity flavour.
FSE NM ABR *de* **Fondo Social Europeo** European Social Fund, ESF.
FSLN NM *(Pol: Nicaragua)* ABR *de* **Frente Sandinista de Liberación Nacional**.
FSM NF ABR *de* **Federación Sindical Mundial** World Federation of Trade Unions, WFTU.
fu¹ INTERJ ugh!
fu²: **ni ~ ni fa** neither one thing nor the other.
fuácata* NF: **estar en la ~** *(Carib, Méx)* to be broke*.
fucha INTERJ *(Méx)*, **fuchi** INTERJ *(Méx)* yuk!, ugh!
fucilazo NM (flash of) sheet lightning.
fuco NM *(Bot)* wrack.
fucsia NF fuchsia.
fudiño ADJ *(Carib)* weak, sickly.
fudre‡ NM drunk*, old soak‡.
fue V **ser**; **ir**.
fuego NM **(a)** *(gen)* fire; conflagration; **~s artificiales** fireworks; **~ fatuo** will-o'-the-wisp; **apagar el ~** to put out the fire; **atizar el ~** to poke the fire; **encender un ~** to light a fire; **se declaró el ~** fire broke out; **echar ~ por los ojos** to glare, look daggers; **jugar con ~** *(fig)* to play with fire; **matar a uno a ~ lento** to worry sb to death; **pegar** (o **prender**) **~ a** to set fire to, set on fire; **poner un pueblo a ~ y sangre** to lay a village waste.
  (b) *(Culin: de gas)* burner, ring; *(Elec)* plate, hot plate; **una cocina a gas de 4 ~s** a gas cooker with 4 burners.
  (c) *(Culin: calor)* flame, heat; **a ~ suave, sobre un ~ bajo** on a low flame, on a low gas; **a ~ vivo** on a high flame, on a high gas; **hervir a ~ lento** to simmer.
  (d) *(Náut etc)* beacon, signal fire.
  (e) *(para cigarro)* light; **¿tienes ~?** have you got a light?; **le pedí ~** I asked him for a light.
  (f) *(Mil)* fire; firing; **¡~!** fire!; **¡alto el ~!** cease fire!; **~ de andanada** *(Náut)* broadside; **~ cruzado** crossfire; **~ graneado, ~ nutrido** heavy fire; **disparos con ~ real** shooting with live bullets; **abrir ~** to open fire; **hacer ~** to fire *(sobre* at, on); **romper el ~** to open fire.
  (g) *(Med)* rash, skin eruption; *(Méx: bucal)* mouth ulcer; **~ pérsico** shingles.
  (h) *(hogar)* hearth, home; **un pueblo de 50 ~s** a village of 50 houses (o families).
  (i) *(fig)* fire, ardour, passion; **apagar los ~s de uno** to damp down

sb's ardour; **atizar el ~** to add fuel to the flames, stir things up.

fueguear [1a] VT (*CAm*) to set fire to.

fueguino (*Cono Sur*) [1] ADJ of Tierra del Fuego.

[2] NM, **fueguina** NF native (o inhabitant) of Tierra del Fuego; **los ~s** the people of Tierra del Fuego.

fuel [fuel] NM, **fuel-oil** [fuel'oil] NM paraffin, kerosene.

fuelle NM (**a**) (*de soplar*) bellows; blower; (*Mús: de gaita*) bag; **~ de pie** footpump; **tener el ~ flojo**⁑ to fart⁑.

(**b**) (*Aut etc*) folding hood, folding top (*US*); (*Fot*) bellows; **~ quitasol** (*Fot*) hood.

(**c**) (*⁕: soplón*) telltale.

(**d**) (*fig*) vigour, force; inspiration.

fuelóleo NM = **fuel**.

fuente NF (**a**) (*manantial*) fountain, spring; **~ de beber** drinking fountain; **~ de río** source of a river; **~ de soda** (*LAm*) soda fountain, café; **~ termal** hot spring; **abrir la ~ de las lágrimas** (*hum*) to weep buckets.

(**b**) (*Culin*) (large) serving dish, platter; **~ de horno** oven dish.

(**c**) (*fig*) source; origin; **~ de alimentación** (*Elec*) power supply; **de ~ desconocida** from an unknown source; **de ~ fidedigna** from a reliable source; **~ de ingresos** source of income; **~ de suministro** source of supply.

(**d**) **~ de soda** (*Cono Sur*) snack bar, soda fountain (*US*).

fuer NM (*liter*): **a ~ de caballero** as a gentleman; **a ~ de hombre honrado** as an honest man.

fuera [1] ADV (**a**) (*situación*) outside; (*dirección*) out; **¡~!** get out!, off with you!; chuck him out!; **¡segundos ~!** (*Boxeo*) seconds out!; **'¡ruritanos ~!'** 'Ruritanians go home!'; **ir ~** to go out, go away, go outside; **con la camisa ~** with his shirt hanging out; **esta camisa se lleva ~** this shirt is worn outside, this shirt is not tucked in; **el perro tenía la lengua ~** the dog had his tongue hanging out; **la parte de ~** the outside part, the outer part; **desde ~** from outside; **por ~** (on the) outside; **los de ~** those from outside; strangers, newcomers.

(**b**) (*fuera del país*) abroad; **estar ~** (*persona*) to be out of town, be on a trip; to be away; to be abroad; **estuvo ~ 8 semanas** he was away for 8 weeks; **salir ~** to go abroad; **trabajar ~** to work away (from home).

(**c**) (*Dep: de juego*) **estar ~** to be out, be in touch; **poner ~** to put into touch; **tirar ~** to shoot wide.

(**d**) (*Dep: de casa*) away; **los de ~**, **el equipo de ~** the away team; **jugar ~** to play away.

[2] **~ de** (PREP) (**a**) (*lugar*) outside (of); out of; **estaba ~ de su jaula** it was outside (o out of) its cage; **esperamos ~ de la puerta** we waited outside the door; **~ de alcance** out of reach, beyond one's reach; **~ de moda** out of fashion; **estar ~ de sí** to be beside o.s.; V **combate** etc.

(**b**) (*fig*) in addition to, besides, beyond; **pero ~ de eso** but in addition to that; but aside from that; **todo ~ de eso** anything short of that.

[3] **~ de serie** NMF exceptional person.

fuera-borda NM INVAR, **fuerabordo** NM INVAR outboard engine, outboard motor; dinghy with an outboard engine.

fuereño, -a NM/F (*Méx*) outsider, incomer.

fuerino, -a NM/F (*Cono Sur*) stranger, non-resident.

fuero NM (**a**) (*carta municipal*) municipal charter; (*de región etc*) local (o regional etc) law-code; (*de grupo*) privilege, exemption; **a ~ according to law; ¿con qué ~?** by what right?; **de ~** de jure, in law.

(**b**) (*autoridad*) jurisdiction, authority; **el ~ no alcanza a tanto** his authority does not extend that far.

(**c**) **en nuestro ~ interno** inwardly, in our hearts.

┌─ **FUEROS** ─┐

ⓘ *Fueros were the charters granted to villages, towns and regions by Spanish monarchs in the Middle Ages and which established their rights and obligations. The fueros under which the Basques and Navarrese received certain privileges (some fiscal autonomy, their own local administration system and exemption from military service outside their province) became a political football in the 19th Century, being alternately abolished and restored depending on the interests of the monarch or administration in power. Today, Navarre is recognized in the Estado de las Autonomías as the Comunidad Foral de Navarra.*

fuerte [1] ADJ (*gen*) strong; tough, sturdy, robust; vigorous; solid; *argumento, defensa, fe, objeción etc* strong; *terreno* rough, difficult; *golpe* hard, heavy; *ruido* loud; *gastos, lluvia* heavy; *comida* heavy, big; *plato* main; rich; *curva* sharp; *sabor, té, vino etc* strong; *calor, dolor etc* intense, great, considerable; *crisis* grave; *ejercicio* strenuous; *rigor etc* excessive, extreme; **¡qué ~!** (*estupendo*) that's great!⁕; (*qué sorpresa*) well!, extraordinary!; **~ como un león** (o **roble** *etc*) as strong as a horse; **¡eso es un poco ~!** that's a bit much!; **eso es muy ~** that's a very serious thing to say; **hacerse ~ en una colina** to entrench o.s. on a hill, make a fortified position on a hill; **se hicieron ~s en la**

casa they prepared to defend the house; they barricaded themselves in the house; they made a stand in the house; **ser ~ en filosofía** to be strong in (o on) philosophy, be well up in philosophy.

[2] ADV strongly; *golpear* hard; *hablar, tocar* loud, loudly; **pegar ~ al enemigo** to hit the enemy hard; **toca muy ~** she plays very loud; **¡más ~!** (*a orador*) speak up!; **poner la radio más ~** to turn the radio up; **comer ~** to eat a big meal, eat too much.

[3] NM (**a**) (*Mil*) fort, strongpoint.

(**b**) (*Mús*) forte.

(**c**) (*fig*) forte, strong point; **el canto no es mi ~** singing is not my strong point.

fuertemente ADV strongly; loudly; intensely.

fuerza NF (**a**) (*gen*) strength; toughness, sturdiness; vigour; solidity; power; intensity; **~s** (*de persona*) strength; (*de argumento*) force, strength, effect; **un viento de ~ 6** a force 6 wind; **~ de voluntad** willpower; **a ~ de** by dint of, by force of; **a viva ~** by sheer strength, by main force; **entrada a viva ~** forced entry, **cobrar ~s** to recover one's strength; to gather strength; **hacer ~ de vela** to crowd on sail; **írsele a uno la ~ por la boca**⁕ to be all talk and no action, be all mouth⁕; **restar ~s a** to weaken; **sacar ~s de flaqueza** to make a supreme effort; to screw up one's courage; **no me siento con ~s para eso** I don't feel up to it; **tener ~s para** + *infin* to have the strength to + *infin*, be strong enough to + *infin*.

(**b**) (*Mec, Fís*) force; power; **~ de arrastre** pulling power; **~ ascensional** (*Aer*) buoyancy; **~ de brazos** manpower; **~ centrífuga** centrifugal force; **~ centrípeta** centripetal force; **~ de gravedad** force of gravity; **~ hidráulica** water power, hydraulic power; **~s del mercado** market forces; **~ motriz** motive power; (*fig*) driving force; **~ de sustentación** (*Aer*) lift.

(**c**) (*Elec*) power, current, energy; **han cortado la ~** they've cut off the power.

(**d**) (*obligación*) force, compulsion; (*presión*) pressure; **~ mayor** force majeure; act of God; **es una cosa de ~ mayor** it's a question of dire necessity; **a la ~, por ~** by force; willy-nilly, against one's will; under pressure, compulsively; perforce, of necessity; **por la ~ de la costumbre** (*fig*) out of habit; **en ~ de** by virtue of; **es ~ reconocer que ...** we must needs recognize that ..., it must be admitted that ...

(**e**) (*violencia*) force, violence; **~ bruta** brute force; **hacer ~ a una mujer** to rape a woman; **recurrir a la ~** to resort to force, use violence; **rendirse a la ~** to yield to superior force; **sin usar ~** without using force, without using violence.

(**f**) (*Mil etc*) force, forces; **~s aéreas** air force; **~s aliadas** allied forces; **~ de apoyo** back-up force; **~s armadas** armed forces; **~ de choque** storm-troops; (*fig*) spearhead; **~ de disuasión, ~ disuasoria, ~ disuasiva** deterrent; **~ expedicionaria** expeditionary force, task force; **~s de mar y de tierra** land and sea forces; **~s del orden (público)** forces of law and order; **~ de pacificación** peace-keeping force; **~ pública** police (force); **~s de seguridad** security forces; **~s terrestres** land forces; **~ de trabajo** workforce; **~ de ventas** sales force.

fuese V ser; ir.

fuetazo NM (*LAm*) lash.

fuete NM (*LAm*) whip; **dar ~ a** to whip.

fuetear [1a] VT (*LAm*) to whip.

fuga¹ NF (**a**) (*huida*) flight, escape; (*de amantes*) elopement; **~ hacia adelante** desperate fling, crazy attempt; **~ de capitales** flight of capital abroad; **~ de la cárcel** escape from prison, jailbreak; **le aplicaron la ley de ~** (*LAm*) he was shot while trying to escape; **apelar a la ~, darse a la ~, ponerse en ~** to flee, take to flight; **poner al enemigo en ~** to put the enemy to flight. (**b**) (*de gas etc*) leak, escape; **~ de cerebros** brain-drain. (**c**) (*fig*) ardour, impetuosity.

fuga² NF (*Mús*) fugue.

fugacidad NF fleetingness, transitory nature, brevity.

fugado NM escapee.

fugar [1h] VI (*LAm*) y **fugarse** VR (**a**) (*huir*) to flee, escape (*a* to); to run away (*con* with); (*amantes*) to elope (*con* with); **~ de la ley** to abscond from justice.

(**b**) (*gas etc*) to leak out, escape.

fugaz ADJ (**a**) *momento etc* fleeting, short-lived, transitory, brief. (**b**) (*esquivo*) elusive. (**c**) **estrella ~** shooting star.

fugazmente ADV fleetingly, briefly.

fugitivo [1] ADJ (**a**) (*que huye*) fugitive, fleeing. (**b**) = fugaz.

[2] NM, **fugitiva** NF fugitive.

fuguista NMF escaper, jailbreaker.

fui, fuimos etc V ser; V ir.

fuina NF marten.

ful¹ [1] ADJ (*And*) full, full up.

[2] NM (*And*) **marchar a todo ~** to work at full capacity.

ful²⁑ ADJ = fulastre.

ful³⁑ NF (*droga*) hash⁕.

fulana NF (**a**) **Doña F~** Mrs So-and-so, Mrs Blank. (**b**) (*⁕: puta*) tart⁑, whore.

fulaneo* NM whoring.

fulano NM so-and-so, what's-his-name; (*) bloke‡, guy*; **~ de tal, Don F~** Mr So-and-so, Mr Blank; Joe Soap, John Doe (*US*); **~, zutano y mengano** Tom, Dick and Harry; **me lo dijo ~** somebody told me; old what's-his-name told me; **no te vas a casar con un ~** you're not going to marry just anybody; **nombramos a ~ y ya está** we nominate some chap and that's that.

fular NM = **foulard**.

fulastre‡ ADJ (*falso*) false, sham; (*malo*) bad, rotten*.

fulbito NM five-a-side football.

fulcro NM fulcrum.

fulero ADJ (a) (*inútil*) useless; (*falso*) sham, bogus; (*pobremente hecho*) poor-quality, poorly made; nasty. (b) (*taimado*) tricky, sly. (c) (*torpe*) blundering, incompetent.

fulgente ADJ, **fúlgido** ADJ dazzling, bright, brilliant, radiant.

fulgir [3c] VI to glow, shine; to glitter.

fulgor NM brilliance, radiance, glow; (*fig*) splendour.

fulgurante ADJ (a) (*brillante*) bright, shining. (b) (*fig*) shattering, stunning.

fulgurar [1a] VI to shine, gleam, glow; to flash.

fulguroso ADJ bright, shining, gleaming; flashing.

fúlica NF coot.

fullerear* [1a] VI (*And*) to swank*.

fullería NF (a) (*Naipes etc: acto*) cheating, cardsharping; (*cualidad*) guile, low cunning. (b) (*trampas*) trickery. (c) (*And*: ostentación*) swankiness*, conceit.

fullero NM (a) (*Naipes etc*) cheat, card-sharper; (*criminal*) crook*; (*tramposo*) tricky individual. (b) (*And*: fachendón*) swank*, show-off*.

fullingue ADJ (*Cono Sur*) (a) *tabaco* inferior, poor-quality. (b) *niño* small, sickly.

fulmicotón NM gun-cotton.

fulminación NF fulmination.

fulminador ☐1 ADJ = **fulminante**.
☐2 NM, **fulminadora** NF fulminator (*de* against), thunderer (*de* against).

fulminante ☐1 ADJ (a) *polvo* fulminating; **cápsula ~** percussion cap. (b) (*Med*) fulminant; sudden; *V* **ataque** (b). (c) (*) *éxito etc* terrific*, tremendous*; **golpe ~** terrific blow*, smash hit; **tiro ~** (*Dep*) sizzling shot.
☐2 NM (*LAm: cápsula fulminante*) percussion cap.

fulminantemente ADV without warning; **despedir ~ a uno** to fire sb on the spot*.

fulminar [1a] ☐1 VT (a) (*gen*) to fulminate; *amenazas* to utter, thunder (*contra* against); **~ a uno con la mirada** to look daggers at sb. (b) (*con rayo*) to strike with lightning; **murió fulminado** he was killed by lightning.
☐2 VI to fulminate, explode.

fulo ADJ (a) (*CAm: rubio*) blond(e), fair. (b) (*Cono Sur*: furioso*) furious, hopping mad*.

fumada NF whiff of smoke, puff of smoke; (*LAm*) puff, pull.

fumadero NM smoking room; **~ de opio** opium den.

fumado‡ ADJ: **estar ~** to be stoned‡.

fumador(a) NM/F smoker; **gran ~** heavy smoker; **~ pasivo** passive smoker; **~ de pipa** pipe-smoker.

fumar [1a] ☐1 VTI to smoke; **'prohibido ~'** 'no smoking'; **zona de no ~** no-smoking area; **~ como una chimenea** to smoke like a chimney; **él fuma en pipa** he smokes a pipe; **está fumando su pipa** he is smoking his pipe; **¿puedo ~?, ¿se permite ~?** may I smoke?
☐2 **fumarse** VR (a) (*) *dinero* to dissipate, squander; *clase* to cut, miss. (b) (*Méx*: escaparse*) to vanish, slope off*. (c) **fumárselo a uno** (*LAm**) to outdo sb; **~ de uno** to trick sb, swindle sb. (d) **~ a una‡‡** to screw sb*‡.

fumarada NF (a) (*fumada*) puff of smoke. (b) (*en pipa*) pipeful.

fumata ☐1 NF (a) (‡) smoking session (of drugs). (b) (*Rel*) **~ blanca** white smoke; (*fig*) indication of success.
☐2 NMF (‡: *persona*) pot-smoker‡.
☐3 NM (‡: *cigarrillo*) fag‡, gasper‡.

fumeta: NMF pot-smoker‡.

fumeteo‡ NM pot-smoking‡.

fumigación NF fumigation: **~ aérea** crop-dusting, crop-spraying.

fumigar [1h] VT to fumigate; *cosecha* to dust, spray.

fumista NM (a) (*gandul*) idler, shirker. (b) (*Cono Sur: bromista*) joker, tease.

fumo NM (*Carib*) puff of smoke.

fumosidad NF smokiness.

fumoso ADJ smoky.

funambulesco ADJ grotesque, wildly extravagant.

funambulista NMF, **funámbulo, -a** NM/F tightrope walker.

funcia NF (*And, CAm, Cono Sur: hum*) = **función**.

función NF (a) (*gen*) function; (*de máquina*) functioning, operation; **en ~ de** according to, depending on.

(b) (*de puesto*) duties; **presidente en funciones** acting president; **entrar en funciones** to take up one's duties; **excederse en sus funciones** to exceed one's duty.
(c) (*Teat etc*) show, performance; entertainment; spectacle; **~ benéfica** charity performance; **~ de despedida** farewell performance; **~ de la tarde** matinée; **~ de títeres** puppet show; **~ taquillera** box-office success, big draw; **mañana no hay ~** there will be no performance tomorrow.
(d) **~ pública** civil service, civil servants (*collectively*).

funcional ADJ functional.

funcionalidad NF functional character; functionality, functioning.

funcionalismo NM functionalism.

funcionamiento NM (a) (*gen*) functioning, operation; (*Mec, Téc*) operation, working, running; performance; behaviour; **máquina en ~** machine in working order; **sociedad en ~** going concern; **entrar en ~** to come into operation; **poner en ~** to bring into operation, bring into service. (b) **cursillo en ~** in-service course; **formación en ~** in-service training.

funcionar [1a] VI (*gen*) to function; (*Mec, Téc*) to go, work, run; (*Aut etc*) to perform; to behave; (*idea, película etc*) to work, be a success; **'funcionando'** (*en anuncio etc*) 'in working order', 'in running order'; **'no funciona'** (*aviso*) 'out of order'; **hacer ~ una máquina** to operate a machine.

funcionariado NM civil service, bureaucracy.

funcionarial ADJ administrative; (*pey*) bureaucratic.

funcionario, -a NM/F official, functionary; employee; civil servant; (*de banco etc*) clerk; **~ aduanero** customs official; **~ penitenciario** prison official; **~ público** civil servant, official; clerk; (*de cárcel*) prison officer.

funda NF (a) (*gen*) case, cover, sheath; (*de disco*) sleeve, jacket; (*) French letter; **~ de almohada** pillowcase, pillowslip; **~ de pistola** holster; **~ protectora del disco** (*Inform*) disk-jacket; **~ sobaquera** shoulder holster. (b) (*bolsa*) small bag, holdall. (c) (*And: falda*) skirt.

fundación NF foundation.

fundadamente ADV with good reason, on good grounds.

fundado ADJ firm, well-founded, justified; **una pretensión mal fundada** an ill-founded claim.

fundador(a) NM/F founder.

▼ **fundamental** ADJ fundamental, basic; essential.

fundamentalismo NM fundamentalism.

fundamentalista ADJ, NMF fundamentalist.

fundamentalmente ADV fundamentally, basically; essentially.

fundamentar [1a] ☐1 VT (a) (*sentar los bases de*) to lay the foundations of. (b) (*fig*) *argumento etc* to base, found (*en* on).
☐2 **fundamentarse** VR: **~ en** to base o.s. on; to be based on.

fundamento NM (a) (*Arquit etc*) foundation(s).
(b) (*fig: base*) foundation, basis; groundwork; grounds, reason; **eso carece de ~** that is groundless, that is completely unjustified; **creencia sin ~** groundless belief, unfounded belief; **¿qué ~ tiene esta teoría?** what is the basis of this theory?, what is the basic justification for this theory.
(c) (*fig: moral*) reliability, trustworthiness.
(d) (*Téc*) weft, woof.
(e) **~s** (*fig*) fundamentals; basic essentials.

fundar [1a] ☐1 VT (a) (*gen*) to found; (*crear*) to institute, set up, establish; (*erigir*) to raise, erect; (*dotar*) to endow.
(b) *teoría etc* to base, found (*en* on).
☐2 **fundarse** VR (a) (*gen*) to be founded, be established.
(b) **~ en** to be founded on, be based on; to base o.s. on; **me fundo en los siguientes hechos** I base myself on the following facts.

fundente ☐1 ADJ melting.
☐2 NM (*Quím*) dissolvent; flux.

fundería NF foundry; **~ de hierro** iron foundry.

fundición NF (a) (*acto*) fusing, fusion; (*Téc*) smelting, founding; melting.
(b) (*fábrica*) foundry, forge, smelting plant; **~ de hierro** iron foundry.
(c) (*objeto*) cast-iron; casting; **~ de acero** steel casting.
(d) (*Tip*) fount, font (*esp US*).

fundido ☐1 ADJ (*LAm Com*) ruined, bankrupt.
☐2 NM (a) (*Cine*) dissolve, fading; **~ (de cierre)** fade-out. (b) **~ nuclear** (*Téc*) nuclear melt-down.

fundidor NM smelter, founder.

fundillo(s) NM(PL) (*LAm: de pantalón*) seat; (‡: *trasero*) seat*, bottom.

fundir [3a] ☐1 VT (a) (*fusionar*) to fuse (together); (*unir*) to join, unite. (b) (*Téc*) to melt (down), smelt; *nieve etc* to melt; (*Elec*) to fuse; *pieza* to found, cast; (*Com*) to merge. (c) (*: *arruinar*) to spoil, upset, ruin; (*LAm*) to ruin, bankrupt. (d) (‡) *dinero* to throw away, chuck around.
☐2 VI (*Cine*) to fade (*a* to).
☐3 **fundirse** VR (a) (*gen*) to fuse (together); to join, unite; (*colores, efectos etc*) to merge, blend (together).

➤ LENGUA Y USO: **fundamental** → 53.2, 53.5

(b) (*derretirse*) to melt (*t fig*); (*Elec: fusible, lámpara*) to blow, burn out.

(c) (*LAm: arruinarse*) to ruin oneself; to be ruined.

fundo NM (*LAm*) country property, estate; farm.

fundón NM (*And, Carib*) riding-habit.

fúnebre ADJ **(a)** *pompa etc* funeral (*atr*). **(b)** (*fig*) funereal; *sonido etc* mournful, lugubrious.

funeral ⬚1 ADJ funeral (*atr*).
⬚2 NM funeral; **~es** funeral, obsequies.

funerala NF: **marchar a la ~** to march with reversed arms; **ojo a la ~** black eye.

funeraria NF undertaker's, undertaker's establishment, funeral parlor (*US*); **director de ~** undertaker, funeral director, mortician (*US*).

funerario ADJ, **funéreo** ADJ funeral (*atr*); funereal.

funestamente ADV banefully; fatally, disastrously.

funestidad NF (*Méx*) calamity.

funesto ADJ ill-fated, unfortunate; baneful; fatal, disastrous (*para* for).

fungible ADJ (*Jur*) **bienes ~s** perishable goods.

fungicida NM fungicide.

fungiforme ADJ mushroom-shaped.

fungir [3c] VI (*CAm, Méx*) to act (*de* as); (*Carib*) to substitute, stand in (*a* for).

fungo NM (*Med*) fungus.

fungoideo ADJ fungoid.

fungoso ADJ fungous.

funguelar⁑ [1a] VI to pong⁑.

funicular NM funicular (railway).

fuñido ADJ **(a)** (*Carib*) (*pendenciero*) quarrelsome; (*insociable*) unsociable. **(b)** (*Carib: enfermizo*) weak, sickly, feeble.

fuñingue ADJ (*Cono Sur*) weak.

fuñir⁑ [3h] VT: **~la** to make a real mess of things, mess things up.

furcia* NF tart⁑, whore; **¡~!** you slut!

furgón NM wagon, van, truck; (*Ferro*) van; **~ blindado** armoured van; **~ celular** police van, prison van; **~ de cola** guard's-van; caboose (*US*); **~ de equipajes** luggage-van, baggage car (*US*); **~ funerario** hearse; **~ de mudanzas** removal van.

furgonada NF wagonload, vanload.

furgonero NM carter, vanman.

furgoneta NF (*Com*) van; transit van, pick-up truck (*US*); (*coche particular*) estate car; **~ de reparto** delivery van.

furia NF fury; rage, violence; **a la ~** (*Cono Sur*) at top speed; **ella salió como una ~, ella salió hecha una ~** she went out furiously (angry); **trabajar a toda ~** to work like fury.

furibundo ADJ furious; frenzied.

furiosamente ADV furiously; violently; frantically.

furioso ADJ furious; violent; frantic, raging; **estar ~** to be furious; **ponerse ~** to get furious.

furor NM **(a)** (*ira*) fury, rage; (*pasión*) frenzy; passion; **~ uterino** nymphomania; **dijo con ~** he said furiously. **(b)** (*fig*) rage, craze, furore; **hacer ~** to be all the rage; **tener ~ por** (*LAm*) to have a passion for.

furquina NF (*And*) short skirt.

furriel NM, **furrier** NM quartermaster.

furriña NF (*Méx*) anger.

furrular* [1a] VI to work.

furrús* NM switch, swap, change.

furrusca* NF (*And*) row, brawl.

furtivamente ADV furtively; in a clandestine way; slyly, stealthily.

furtivismo NM poaching, illegal hunting (*o* fishing).

furtivo ADJ furtive; clandestine; sly, stealthy; *edición* pirated; *V* **cazador.**

furular* [1a] VI to work.

furuminga NF (*Cono Sur*) intrigue, scheme, plot.

furúnculo NM (*Med*) boil.

fusa NF demisemiquaver, thirty-second note (*US*).

fusca⁑ NF, **fusco**⁑ NM rod⁑, gun.

fuselado ADJ streamlined.

fuselaje NM fuselage; **de ~ ancho** wide-bodied.

fusible NM fuse.

fusil NM rifle, gun; **~ de asalto** assault rifle; **~ de juguete** popgun, toy gun.

fusilamiento NM **(a)** shooting, execution. **(b)** (*) pinching*, plagiarism; (*de producto*) piracy, illegal copying.

fusilar [1a] VT **(a)** (*ejecutar*) to shoot, execute; (*Carib: matar*) to kill; (*Dep*) *gol* to shoot. **(b)** (*: *plagiar*) to pinch*, plagiarize; *producto* to pirate, copy illegally.

fusilazo NM rifle-shot.

fusilería NF gunfire, rifle-fire.

fusilero NM rifleman, fusilier.

fusión NF (*Fís etc*) fusion; (*unión*) joining, uniting; (*Inform*) merge; (*de metal etc*) melting; (*Com*) merger, amalgamation; **~ nuclear** nuclear fusion.

fusionamiento NM (*Com*) merger, amalgamation.

fusionar [1a] ⬚1 VT to fuse (together); (*Inform*) to merge; (*Com*) to merge, amalgamate.
⬚2 **fusionarse** VR to fuse; (*Com*) to merge, amalgamate.

fusta NF **(a)** (*látigo*) long whip; riding whip. **(b)** (*leña*) brushwood, twigs.

fustán NM **(a)** (*tela*) fustian. **(b)** (*LAm: enaguas*) petticoat, underskirt; (*And: falda*) skirt.

fuste NM **(a)** (*madera*) wood, timber; **de ~** wooden.
(b) (*de arma*) shaft; (*de columna, chimenea*) shaft; **de ~** (*fig*) important, of some consequence; **de poco ~** (*fig*) unimportant.
(c) (*silla*) saddle tree.
(d) (*CAm* Anat*) bottom.

fustigar [1h] VT **(a)** (*lit*) to whip, lash. **(b)** (*fig*) to upbraid, lash (with one's tongue).

futbito NM five-a-side football.

fútbol (*frec* **futbol** *en LAm*) NM football; **~ americano** American football; **~ asociación** association football, soccer.

futbolero ⬚1 ADJ football (*atr*); footballing (*atr*).
⬚2 NM, **futbolera** NF soccer supporter.

futbolín NM table football, bar football.

futbolista NMF footballer, football player.

futbolístico ADJ football (*atr*).

futbolmanía NF football mania.

fútbol-rugby NM rugby (*Brit*), American football (*US*).

fútbol-sala NM indoor football, seven-a-side football.

futearse [1a] VR (*And: fruta etc*) to go bad, rot.

futesa NF trifle, mere nothing; **~s** small talk, trivialities.

fútil ADJ trifling, trivial.

futileza NF (*Cono Sur*) trifle, bagatelle.

futilidad NF **(a)** (*gen*) triviality, trifling nature, unimportance. **(b)** (*una ~*) trifle.

futing ['futin] NM = **footing.**

futón NM futon.

futre NM (*LAm*) dandy, toff*, dude* (*US*).

futrería NF (*And, Cono Sur*) **(a)** (*conducta*) affected behaviour.
(b) (*grupo*) group of dandies, group of dudes* (*US*).
(c) (*querencia*) dude's hang-out* (*US*).

futura NF **(a)** (*Jur*) reversion. **(b)** (*: *novia*) fiancée.

futurible ⬚1 ADJ (*venidero*) forthcoming; (*potencial*) potential; (*probable*) likely; (*especulativo*) speculative; (*digno de ascenso*) promotion-worthy.
⬚2 NMF (*Pol*) potential minister; potential leader.
⬚3 NM hot tip, good bet; **es un ~ Olímpico** he's a good prospect for the Olympics.

futurismo NM futurism.

futurista ADJ, **futurístico** ADJ futuristic.

futuro ⬚1 ADJ future; **futura madre** mother-to-be; **los equipos más ~s son A y B** the teams with the best prospects are A and B.
⬚2 NM **(a)** future; **en el ~** in (the) future; **en un ~** some time in the future; **en un ~ próximo** in the very near future, very soon; **el ~ se presenta muy oscuro** the future looks bleak.
(b) (*Ling*) future, future tense.
(c) (*: *novio*) fiancé.
(d) **~s** (*Com*) futures.

futurología NF futurology.

futurólogo, -a NM/F futurologist.

G

G, g [xe] NF (*letra*) G, g.
g/ ABR *de giro* draft, money order.
gaba NMF (*Tejas: pey*) white American, Yankee.
gabacho [1] ADJ (a) (*Geog*) Pyrenean.
  (b) (*afrancesado*) frenchified.
  (c) **le salió gabacha la cosa** (*And, Méx**) it came to nothing, the affair was a failure.
  [2] NM, **gabacha¹** NF (a) (*Geog*) Pyrenean villager.
  (b) (*) (*pey*) Frenchy*, Froggy*; frenchified Spaniard; (*Tejas*) white American, Yankee; (*Méx*) (*any*) foreigner, outsider.
  [3] **gabacha²** NF (*CAm*) overall.
gabán NM overcoat, topcoat; (*Carib*) jacket.
gabanear [1a] [1] VT (*CAm*) to steal.
  [2] VI (*Méx*) to flee.
gabanero NM hall wardrobe.
gabarda NF wild rose.
gabardina¹ NF (*tela*) gabardine; (*prenda*) raincoat, mackintosh; **en ~** coated in batter.
gabardino, -a² NM/F (*Tejas: pey*) white American, Yankee.
gabarra NF barge, lighter, flatboat; **botar la ~*** to push the boat out*.
gabarrero NM bargee, bargeman, lighterman.
gabarro NM (a) (*de tela*) flaw, defect. (b) (*Vet*) (*de caballo*) tumour; (*de gallina*) pip. (c) (*fig*) (*error*) error, slip, miscalculation; (*pega*) snag; (*molestia*) annoyance.
gabear [1a] VT (*Carib*) to climb.
gabela NF (a) (*Hist*) tax, duty; (*fig*) burden. (b) (*And: ventaja*) advantage, profit.
gabinete NM (a) (*estudio*) study, library; (*cuarto de estar*) private sitting room; (*tocador*) boudoir; (*Jur, Med*) office; (*laboratorio*) laboratory; (*museo*) museum; (*Arte*) studio; (*And*) enclosed balcony; **~ de consulta** consulting-room; **~ de estrategia** (*Pol etc*) think-tank; **~ fiscal** tax advisory office; **~ de imagen** public relations office; **~ de lectura** reading room; **~ de prensa** press office; **~ de teléfono** (*Méx*) telephone booth; **estratega de ~** armchair strategist.
  (b) (*Pol*) cabinet; **~ fantasma, ~ en la sombra** shadow cabinet.
  (c) (*muebles*) suite of office furniture.
gablete NM gable.
Gabriel NM Gabriel.
gacel NM, **gacela** NF gazelle.
gaceta NF (a) (*boletín*) gazette, official journal; (*LAm: diario*) newspaper. (b) (*Carib**) (*chismoso*) gossip; (*soplón*) telltale.
gacetero, -a NM/F (a) (*periodista*) newswriter, journalist. (b) (*vendedor*) newspaper seller.
gacetilla NF (a) (*notas de sociedad*) gossip column; (*noticias*) section of local news, section of miscellaneous news items; **'G~'** (*título*) 'News in Brief'.
  (b) (*) gossip, scandalmonger; **ella es una ~ andando** (*o* **con dos patas**) she's a dreadful gossip.
gacetillero, -a NM/F newspaper reporter; gossip columnist; (*pey*) hack.
gacetista NMF gossip, scandalmonger.
gacha NF (a) thin paste; watery mass; mush; **~s** (*Culin*) pap; porridge; **~s de avena** oatmeal porridge; **se ha hecho unas ~s** it's got mushy, it's got soggy, (*fig*) she's turned all sentimental.
  (b) (*And, Carib: cerámica*) earthenware bowl.
gachí NF, PL **gachís** *o* **gachises** (a) (*mujer*) bird‡, dame* (*US*). (b) **ser del ~** to be one of the people, be common, be very ordinary.
gacho ADJ (a) (*rama*) bent down, turned downward; *cuerno* down-curved; *vaca* with down-curved horns; *sombrero* with down-turned brim; *orejas etc* drooping, floppy; **sombrero ~** slouch hat.
  (b) (*Méx*) (*desagradable*) unpleasant, disagreeable; (*sin suerte*) unlucky.
  (c) **ir a gachas** to go on all fours.
  (d) **a cabeza gacha** (*Cono Sur*) obediently.

gachó‡ NM, PL **gachós** chap*, bloke‡; **¡~!** brother!*
gachón* ADJ (*encantador*) nice, charming, sweet; *niño* spoilt; (‡) *mujer* sexy.
gachumbo NM (*LAm*) hollowed-out shell.
gachupín NM (*LAm*), **gachuzo** NM (*Méx*) (*pey*) (*any*) Spaniard.
gacilla NF (*CAm Cos*) clasp, hook and eye.
gaditano [1] ADJ of Cadiz.
  [2] NM, **gaditana** NF native (*o* inhabitant) of Cadiz; **los ~s** the people of Cadiz.
GAE NM (*Esp Mil*) ABR *de* **Grupo Aéreo Embarcado**.
gaélico [1] ADJ Gaelic.
  [2] NM, **gaélica** NF Gael.
  [3] NM (*Ling*) Gaelic.
gafa¹ NF (*grapa*) grapple; (*abrazadera*) clamp; **~s** glasses, spectacles; (*Aut etc*) goggles; **~s ahumadas** smoked glasses; **~s de aro** John Lennon glasses; **~s sin aros** rimless glasses; **~s de baño, ~s de bucear** diving goggles; **~s bifocales, ~s graduadas** bifocals; **~s de cerca, ~s de leer** reading glasses; **~s de esquiar** skiing goggles; **~s de media luna** half-moon glasses; **~s de motorista** motorcyclist's goggles; **~s negras** dark glasses; **~s protectoras** protective goggles; **~s de sol, ~s para sol** sunglasses; **~s submarinas** underwater goggles; *ver también* PANTALONES, ZAPATOS, GAFAS .
gafancia* NF propensity to attract bad luck; accident-proneness.
gafar [1a] VT (a) (*agarrar*) to hook, claw, latch on to. (b) (*: *traer mala suerte a*) to bring bad luck to, put a jinx on*; (*estropear*) to spoil, mess up; **la máquina parece gafada*** the machine is jinxed*, the machine seems to have a jinx on it*.
gafe* [1] ADJ: **ser ~** to have constant bad luck; to have a jinx*, be jinxed*.
  [2] NM (*) bad luck; jinx*.
gafete NM clasp, hook and eye.
gafitas NFPL granny glasses.
gafo [1] ADJ (a) (*LAm*) footsore, dog-tired; (*Méx**) numb; **estar ~** (*CAm**) to be broke*.
  (b) (*Carib*) (*: *no confiable*) unreliable, erratic; (‡: *bruto*) thick*.
  [2] NM, **gafa²** NF (*Carib*) idiot.
gafudo ADJ that wears glasses, with glasses.
gag [gax] NM, PL **gags** [gax] (*Teat etc*) gag.
gagá [1] ADJ: **estar ~** to be gaga*.
  [2] NMF old dodderer.
gago (*LAm**) [1] ADJ stammering, stuttering.
  [2] NM, **gaga** NF stammerer, stutterer.
gagoso ADJ (*And**) stammering, stuttering.
gaguear [1a] VI (*LAm**) to stammer, stutter.
gagueo NM (*LAm**) stammer(ing), stutter(ing).
gaguera NF (*LAm*) stammer, stutter, speech defect.
gaita [1] NF (a) (*Mús*) (*flauta*) flute, flageolet; (*organillo*) hurdy-gurdy; **~ (gallega)** bagpipe; **ser como una ~** to be dissatisfied, be very demanding; **estar de ~** to be merry; **templar ~s** to calm sb down, smooth things out.
  (b) (*: *cuello*) neck; **estirar la ~** to crane one's neck.
  (c) (*molestia*) bother, nuisance; (*trabajo*) tough job; **y toda esa ~*** and all that jazz*.
  (d) (*Venezuela*) folk music.
  (e) (*: *persona*) cheat, trickster.
  [2] NMF (*LAm: hum*) Galician, (*any*) Spaniard.
gaitero [1] ADJ (a) (*llamativo*) gaudy, flashy. (b) *persona* buffoonish.
  [2] NM, **gaitera** NF (bag)piper.
gaje NM (a) (*t* **~s** PL) emoluments; perquisite; (*fig*) reward, bonus; **~ del oficio** (*hum*) occupational hazards, occupational risks. (b) **en ~ de** (*LAm*) as a token of, as a sign of.
gajo NM (a) (*rama*) (torn-off) branch, bough; (*de uvas etc*) small cluster, bunch. (b) (*de naranja etc*) slice, segment, quarter. (c) (*de tenedor*)

point, prong; (*Geog*) spur. (**d**) (*And*) curl, ringlet.

GAL [gal] NMPL (*Esp*) ABR de **Grupos Antiterroristas de Liberación** *anti-ETA terrorist group.*

gal NMF member of GAL.

gala NF (**a**) (*traje de etiqueta*) full dress; best dress; court dress; **de ~ state** (*atr*), dress (*atr*), full-dress (*atr*); gala (*atr*); **estar de ~** to be in full dress; to be in one's best dress, be all dressed up; (*ciudad etc*) to be bedecked, be in festive mood.
(**b**) (*lujos*) **~s** finery, trappings; jewels, adornments; regalia; fine things; **~s de novia** bridal attire.
(**c**) (*fig*) (*elegancia*) elegance, gracefulness; (*pompa*) pomp, display; **hacer ~ de** to display, show off; to boast of, glory in; **tener algo a ~** to be proud of sth; **tener a ~ + infin** to be proud to + infin.
(**d**) (*fig*) (*lo más selecto*) cream, flower; (*orgullo*) pride, chief ornament; **es la ~ de la ciudad** it is the pride of the city.
(**e**) (*fig: especialidad*) speciality, special accomplishment.
(**f**) (*LAm*) (*regalo*) gift; (*propina*) tip.
(**g**) (*Mús*) gig, show, concert.
(**h**) (*espectáculo etc*) show; **~ benéfica** charity event.

galáctico ADJ galactic.

galafate NM expert thief, sly thief.

galaico ADJ Galician.

galán ① NM (**a**) (*joven*) handsome fellow, attractive young man; (*Don Juan*) ladies' man; (*Hist*) young gentleman, courtier.
(**b**) (*novio*) gallant, beau; (*pretendiente*) suitor.
(**c**) (*Teat*) male lead, chief male part; hero; **~ de cine** matinée idol; **joven ~** juvenile lead; **primer ~** leading man.
(**d**) (*mueble*) clothes-rack.
(**e**) (*CAm Bot*) night-flowering cactus.
② ADV (*LAm**) = **bien.**

galanamente ADV (*V ADJ* (**a**)) smartly, sprucely; elegantly, tastefully.

galanas NFPL (*CAm*): **echar ~** to boast, brag; **hacer ~** to do naughty things, be wicked.

galancete NM handsome young man; (*hum*) dapper little man; (*Teat*) male juvenile lead.

galancito NM juvenile lead.

galano ADJ (**a**) (*pulcro*) smart, spruce; (*elegante*) elegant, tasteful; (*gallardo*) gaily dressed. (**b**) (*Carib*) **vaca** mottled (*with red and white patches*).

galante ADJ (**a**) *hombre* gallant; (*atento*) charming, attentive (to women); (*cortés*) polite, urbane. (**b**) *mujer* flirtatious; (*pey*) wanton, free, licentious.

galantear [1a] VT (*cortejar*) to court, WOO; (*coquetear con*) to flirt with.

galantemente ADV (*V ADJ*) gallantly; charmingly, attentively; politely.

galanteo NM courting, courtship, wooing; flirting.

galantería NF (**a**) (*gen*) gallantry; attentiveness (to women); politeness, urbanity. (**b**) (*cumplido*) compliment; (*piropo*) charming thing (to say), gallantry.

galanto NM (*Bot*) snowdrop.

galanura NF prettiness; charm; elegance, tastefulness.

galápago NM (**a**) (*Zool*) tortoise. (**b**) (*Agr*) mouldboard. (**c**) (*Téc*) ingot, pig. (**d**) (*silla de montar*) light saddle; (*LAm*) sidesaddle.

Galápagos: Islas NFPL **~** Galapagos Islands.

galapagueño ① ADJ of (*o* from) the Galapagos (Islands).
② NM, **galapagueña** NF native (*o* inhabitant) of the Galapagos (Islands).

galardón NM (*liter*) reward, prize; award.

galardonado, -a NM/F prize-winner, award-winner.

galardonar [1a] VT (*liter*) to reward, recompense (*de* with); (*Liter*) *obra* to give a prize to; **obra galardonada por la Academia** work which won an Academy prize.

galaxia NF galaxy.

galbana* NF sloth, laziness; shiftlessness.

galbanoso* ADJ slothful, lazy; shiftless.

galdosiano ADJ relating to Benito Pérez Galdós; **estudios ~s** Galdós studies.

galdufo NM swine‡, villain.

galembo NM (*And, Carib*) turkey buzzard.

galena NF galena, galenite.

galeniano ADJ Galenic.

Galeno NM Galen; **g~** (*LAm: médico*) doctor.

galeón NM galleon.

galeote NM galley slave.

galera NF (**a**) (*Náut*) galley.
(**b**) (*carro*) (covered) wagon.
(**c**) (*Med*) hospital ward; (*Hist*) women's prison; (*CAm, Méx: cobertizo*) open shed; (*CAm*) slaughterhouse.
(**d**) (*LAm*) (*chistera*) top hat; (*fieltro*) felt hat; (*hongo*) bowler hat.
(**e**) (*Tip*) galley.

galerada NF (**a**) (*carga*) wagonload. (**b**) (*Tip*) galley proof.

galería NF (*gen*) gallery; (*pasillo*) passage, corridor; (*Min*) gallery;

(*balcón*) veranda(h); (*Arte*) gallery; (*And, Carib*) store; **~ de alimentación** food hall; **~ de arte** art gallery; **~ de columnas** colonnade; **~ de la muerte** death row; **~ de popa** (*Náut*) stern gallery; **~ secreta** secret passage; **~ de tiro** shooting gallery; **~ de viento** (*Aer*) wind-tunnel.

galerista NMF owner (*o* director) of an art gallery.

galerita NF crested lark.

galerna NF, **galerno** NM violent north-west wind (*on N coast of Spain*).

galerón NM (**a**) (*CAm*) shed; shed roof; (*Méx*) hall, large room. (**b**) (*Carib*) folk dance.

Gales NM Wales.

galés ① ADJ Welsh.
② NM, **galesa** NF Welshman, Welshwoman.
③ NM (*Ling*) Welsh.

galfaro NM (*Carib*) little rascal.

galga NF (**a**) (*Zool*) greyhound (bitch). (**b**) (*Geol*) boulder, rolling stone; (*Téc*) millstone (of an oil press). (**c**) (*Agr*) hub brake (on a cart). (**d**) (*Mec*) gauge.

galgo[1] NM greyhound; **~ afgano** Afghan; **~ ruso** borzoi, Russian wolfhound; **¡échale un ~!*** not a hope!, no way!*; **¡vaya Vd a espulgar un ~!*** go to blazes!*

galgo²* ADJ (*And*) sweet-toothed, fond of sweets.

galgón* ADJ (*And*) = **galgo².**

galguear* [1a] VI (*CAm, Cono Sur*) to be starving, be ravenous; to wander about looking for food.

Galia NF Gaul.

gálibo NM (*Téc*) gauge; (*luz*) warning light, flashing light.

galicano ADJ Gallic; (*Rel*) Gallican.

galiciano, -a ADJ, NM/F Galician.

galicismo NM gallicism.

gálico ① ADJ Gallic.
② NM syphilis.

galicoso, -a ADJ, NM/F syphilitic.

Galilea NF Galilee.

galillo NM (*Anat*) uvula.

galimatías NM INVAR rigmarole; gibberish, nonsense.

galla‡ NF (*Cono Sur*) bird‡, girl.

gallada NF (**a**) (*And, Cono Sur: baladronada*) boast. (**b**) **la ~** (*Cono Sur**: *chicos*) the lads, the boys; (*gente*) people.

gallardamente ADV (*V ADJ*) gracefully, elegantly; splendidly; bravely; gallantly, dashingly; nobly.

gallardear [1a] VI (*comportarse con elegancia*) to be elegant, be graceful, act with ease and grace; (*tener buen porte*) to bear o.s. well; (*pavonearse*) to strut.

gallardete NM pennant, streamer.

gallardía NF (*V ADJ*) gracefulness, elegance; fineness, splendidness; bravery; gallantry, dash; nobleness.

gallardo ADJ (*elegante*) graceful, elegant; (*magnífica*) fine, splendid; (*valiente*) brave; (*bizarro*) gallant, dashing; (*noble*) noble.

gallareta NF (*LAm*) South American coot; *V* **pato.**

gallear [1a] ① VT (*gallo*) to tread.
② VI (**a**) (*destacar*) to excel, stand out.
(**b**) (*descollar*) to put on airs, strut; (*envalentonarse*) to bully, chuck one's weight about; (*jactarse*) to brag; (*gritar*) to bluster, bawl.

gallego ① ADJ (**a**) Galician.
(**b**) (*LAm: pey*) Spanish (*gen used of immigrants*).
(**c**) (*) yellow, cowardly.
② NM, **gallega** NF (**a**) Galician.
(**b**) (*LAm: pey*) (any immigrant) Spaniard.
(**c**) (‡) free-loader*, sponger*.
(**d**) (*viento*) north-west wind.
③ NM (*Ling*) Galician.

ⓘ **GALLEGO**

Gallego, a romance language dating back to the 12th century and closely related to Portuguese, is spoken by 80-85% of the inhabitants of Galicia. During the Franco régime, the use of Galician and other minority national languages was prohibited in the media and in public institutions. It has enjoyed **lengua cooficial** *status alongside* **castellano** *since 1981. There are several dialects of the language and formal attempts to standardize them in the 1970's were unsuccessful. However, a standard form is now beginning to emerge naturally in the larger urban areas.*
⇨ *See also* LENGUAS COOFICIALES

---

galleguismo NM (**a**) (*Ling*) galleguism, word (*o* phrase *etc*) peculiar to Galicia.
(**b**) sense of the differentness of Galicia; (*Pol*) doctrine of (*o* belief in) Galician autonomy.

galleguista ① ADJ that supports (*etc*) Galician autonomy; **el movimiento ~** the movement for Galician autonomy; **la familia es muy ~** the family strongly supports Galician autonomy.

2 NMF supporter (*etc*) of Galician autonomy.

gallera NF (*LAm: palenque*) cockpit; (*And, CAm: gallinero*) coop (for gamecocks).

gallería NF (*Carib*) (a) (*palenque*) cockpit. (b) (*fig*) egotism, selfishness.

gallero **1** ADJ (*LAm*) fond of cockfighting.

2 NM (a) (*LAm*) (*responsable*) man in charge of gamecocks (*o cockfighting*); (*aficionado*) cockfighting enthusiast. (b) (*Cono Sur Ferro*) pilferer.

galleta NF (a) biscuit; cracker; cookie (*US*); wafer; (*Náut*) ship's biscuit, hardtack; (*Cono Sur*) coarse bread; **~ de perro** dog biscuit; **ir a toda ~*** to go full-speed.
(b) (*puñetazo*) bash*, punch, slap.
(c) (*Andes, Cono Sur*) gourd for drinking maté.
(d) (*Cono Sur*: bronca*) ticking-off*.
(e) (*Cono Sur**) **colgar la ~ a uno, dar la ~ a uno** (*despedir*) to sack sb*, to give sb the boot*; (*rechazar*) to give sb the brush-off*; (*no hacer caso a*) to give sb the cold shoulder; **le dieron una buena ~** they gave him a good ticking-off*; **hacerse una ~** to get in a mess.
(f) **~ del tráfico** (*Carib*) (*embotellamiento*) traffic jam; (*burla*) practical joke.
(g) **tener mucha ~** (*Méx*) to be very strong.

galletear* [1a] VT (*Cono Sur*) (a) (*despedir*) to sack*, fire*; (*reñir*) to tick off*. (b) (*golpear*) to bash*, belt*.

galletero NM (a) (*recipiente*) biscuit barrel, biscuit tin. (b) (*Cono Sur: persona*) quick-tempered person; argumentative sort, brawler.

gallina **1** NF (a) hen, fowl; **~ de agua** coot; **~ de bantam** bantam; **~ clueca** broody hen; **~ de Guinea** guinea fowl; **~ ponedora** laying hen, hen in lay; **acostarse con las ~s** to go to bed early; **andar como ~ clueca** (*Méx*) to be as pleased as Punch; **estar como ~ con huevos** to be very distrustful; **estar como ~ en corral ajeno** to have no freedom of movement; to be like a fish out of water; to be timid, be shy; **¡hasta que meen las ~s!*** pigs might fly!*; **la ~ de arriba ensucia la de abajo** (*LAm*) the underdog always suffers; **matar la ~ de los huevos de oro** to kill the goose that lays the golden eggs.
(b) **~ ciega** (*juego*) blind man's buff.
(c) **~ de mar** gurnard.
(d) **~ ciega** (*CAm, Carib: gusano*) white worm.
2 NMF (a) (*) coward.
(b) (*And: pey*) Peruvian.

gallinacera NF (*And*) bunch of Negroes.

gallinaza NF hen droppings.

gallinazo NM (*LAm*) turkey buzzard.

gallinería NF (a) (*gallinas*) flock of hens. (b) (*Com*) (*tienda*) poultry shop; (*mercado*) chicken market. (c) (*fig*) cowardice.

gallinero NM (a) (*criadero*) henhouse, coop; (*cesta*) poultry basket.
(b) (*persona*) chicken farmer; poulterer, poultry dealer.
(c) (*Teat*) gods, top gallery.
(d) (*confusión*) babel, hubbub; (*griterío*) noisy gathering; madhouse, bedlam.

gallineta NF (*Orn*) woodcock; coot; (*LAm*) guinea-fowl.

gallinilla NF: **~ de bantam** bantam.

gallipavo NM (a) (*Orn*) turkey. (b) (*Mús*) false note, squeak, squawk.

gallito **1** ADJ (*) cocky*, cocksure.
2 NM (a) (*Orn*) small cock. (b) (*fig*) rowdy, tough*, troublemaker; **el ~** (*del mundo*) the cock-o'-the-walk, the top dog. (c) (*And*) small arrow, dart.

gallo NM (a) (*Orn*) cock, cockerel, rooster; **~ lira** black grouse; **~ montés, ~ silvestre** capercaillie; **~ de combate, ~ de pelea, ~ de riña** gamecock, fighting cock; **al primer ~** (*Méx*) at midnight; **estar como ~ en corral** to be much esteemed, be well thought of; **en menos que canta un ~** in an instant; **otro ~ me cantara** that would be quite a different matter; **comer ~** (*And, CAm**) to suffer a setback; **ha comido ~** (*Méx*) he's in a fighting mood; **dormírsele a uno el ~** (*CAm**) to let an opportunity slip; **hay ~ tapado** (*LAm*) I smell a rat; **no me va nada en el ~** (*Méx**) it doesn't matter to me, it's no skin off my nose*; **levantar el ~** (*Carib, Méx**) to throw in the towel; **matar a uno el ~ en la mano** to floor sb (in an argument), shut sb up*; **pelar el ~** (*Méx**) to make tracks*.
(b) (*: *jefe*) boss; (*LAm*) expert, master; **yo he sido ~ para eso** I was a great one at that.
(c) **alzar el ~, levantar el ~** (*fig*) to put on airs, brag; to bawl, behave noisily; **tener mucho ~** to be cocky.
(d) (*Pesca*) cork float.
(e) (*Mús*) false note, squeak, squawk; **soltó un ~** his voice cracked.
(f) (*LAm**) (*flema*) phlegm, spit, spittle; (*escupitajo*) gob* of spit.
(g) (*And: flecha*) small arrow, dart.
(h) (*And, Cono Sur: de bomberos*) fire-engine, hose truck.
(i) (*Méx Mús*) street serenade.
(j) **vestirse de ~** (*Méx*) to wear old clothes.
(k) (*Cono Sur**) bloke*, guy*.
(l) (*Pez*) john dory.
(m) **~ pinto** (*CAm Culin*) rice and beans.

(n) (*LAm Dep*) shuttlecock.
(o) (*Boxeo*) bantamweight.

gallofero **1** ADJ idle, loafing; vagabond.
2 NM idler, loafer; tramp; beggar.

gallón* **1** ADJ (*Méx*) cocky*.
2 NM local boss.

gallote* **1** ADJ (*CAm, Méx*) cocky*.
2 NM (*CAm*) cop*.

galo **1** ADJ Gallic; (*moderno*) French.
2 NM, **gala** NF Gaul; (*moderno*) Frenchman, Frenchwoman.

galocha NF clog, patten.

galón¹ NM (a) braid; (*Mil*) stripe, chevron; **quitar los galones a uno** to take his stripes away from sb, demote sb; **la acción le valió 2 galones** the action got him a couple of stripes.

galón² NM (*medida*) gallon.

galonear [1a] VT to trim with braid.

galopada NF gallop.

galopante ADJ galloping (*t Med y fig*).

galopar [1a] VI to gallop; **echar a ~** to break into a gallop.

galope NM gallop; **a ~, al ~** (*LAm*), **de ~** at a gallop, (*fig*) in great haste, in a rush; **a ~ tendido** at full gallop; **alejarse a ~** to gallop off; **desfilar a ~** to gallop past; **llegar a ~** to gallop up; **medio ~** canter.

galopín NM (*pícaro*) ragamuffin, urchin; (*bribón*) scoundrel, rogue; (*sabelotodo*) smart Aleck*, clever Dick*; (*Náut*) cabin boy.

galpón NM (a) (*LAm*) (*cobertizo*) (large) shed, storehouse; (*Hist: para esclavos*) slaves' quarters; (*Aut*) garage. (b) (*And: tejar*) tileworks, pottery.

galucha NF (*LAm*) short gallop; (*Carib*) start of a gallop.

galuchar [1a] VI (*LAm*) to gallop.

galvánico ADJ galvanic.

galvanismo NM galvanism.

galvanizado ADJ galvanized.

galvanizar [1f] VT (*lit*) to galvanize, electroplate; (*fig*) to galvanize.

galvano NM (*Cono Sur: placa*) commemorative plaque.

galvanoplastia NF electroplating.

gama¹ NF (*Mús*) scale; (*fig*) range, scale, gamut; **una extensa ~ de colores** an extensive range of colours; **~ de frecuencias** frequency range; **~ de ondas** wave range; **~ sonora** sound range; **alto de ~, de ~ alta** in the top part of the range; **bajo de ~, de ~ baja** in the lower part of the range.

gama² NF (*letra*) gamma.

gama³ NF (*Zool*) doe (of fallow deer); **sentársele a uno la ~** (*Cono Sur*) to get discouraged.

gamarra NF (*CAm*) halter; **llevar a uno de la ~*** to lead sb by the nose.

gamba NF (a) (*Zool*) prawn. (b) (‡) 100 pesetas; **media ~** 50 pesetas. (c) (‡: *pierna*) leg; **meter la ~** to put one's foot in it.

gambado ADJ (*Carib*) knock-kneed.

gamberrada NF (*pey*) piece of hooliganism, loutish thing (to do); (*inocente*) lark*, rag*, piece of horseplay; **hacer ~s = gamberrear**.

gamberrear [1a] VI (*pey*) to go around causing trouble, act like a hooligan; to be a lout; (*gandulear*) to loaf; (*tontear*) to lark about*, horse around*.

gamberrismo NM hooliganism; loutishness.

gamberrístico ADJ loutish, ill-bred.

gamberro **1** ADJ (*pey*) ill-bred, loutish, rough; (*inocente*) boisterous, high-spirited.
2 NM (*pey*) lout, hooligan, troublemaker; roughneck*; boisterous youth, high-spirited lad; **hacer el ~*** to act like a hooligan; = **gamberrear**.

gambeta NF (a) (*de caballo*) prance, caper. (b) (*And, Cono Sur: esguince*) dodge, avoiding action; (*) dodge, pretext.

gambito NM gambit.

gambuza NF (*Náut*) store, storeroom.

gamella NF trough; washtub.

gameto NM gamete.

gamín* NM (*And*) street urchin.

gamma **1** NF (*letra*) gamma.
2 ADJ INVAR: **rayos ~** gamma rays.

gamo NM buck (of fallow deer).

gamonal NM (*And, CAm*) = **cacique**.

gamonalismo NM (*And, CAm*) = **caciquismo**.

gamulán NM (*Cono Sur*) sheepskin.

gamuza NF (a) (*Zool*) chamois. (b) (*piel*) chamois leather, wash leather; (*sacudidor*) duster.

▼ **gana** NF (*deseo*) desire, wish (*de* for); (*apetito*) appetite (*de* for); (*afán*) inclination, longing (*de* for); **¡las ~s!** you'll wish you had (agreed)!; **son ~s de joder‡** (*o molestar etc*) they're just trying to be awkward; **es ~** (*And, Carib, Méx*) it's a waste of time, there's no point; **~ tiene de coles quien besa al hortelano** it's just cupboard love; **donde hay ~ hay maña** where there's a will there's a way; **con ~s** (*CAm,*

Carib: de veras) really, truly; **con ~(s)** (*LAm**) with a will; **comer con ~** to eat heartily; **ser malo con ~** (*CAm, Carib*) to be thoroughly nasty; **hacer algo con ~s** to do sth willingly (*o* enthusiastically); **hacer algo sin ~s** to do sth reluctantly (*o* unwillingly); **de ~** (*And**) (*sin querer*) unintentionally; (*en broma*) as a joke, in fun; **de buena ~** willingly, readily; **¡de buena ~!** gladly!; **de mala ~** unwillingly, reluctantly, grudgingly; **hasta las ~s** (*Méx*) right up to the end; **me da la ~ de** + *infin* I feel like + *ger*, I want to + *infin*, I have an inclination to + *infin*; **esto da ~s de comerlo** it makes you want to eat it; **porque no me da la** (*real o* realísima) ~ because I don't (damned well) want to; **como te dé la ~** just as you wish; **le entran ~s de** + *infin* he begins to want to + *infin*, he feels the urge to + *infin*; **siempre hace su regalada ~** (*Méx**) he always goes his own sweet way; **pagar hasta las ~s*** to pay over the odds; **no me pega la ~** (*Méx**) I don't feel like it; **quedarse con las ~s** to fail, be disappointed; to have one's hopes dashed; **quitársele a uno las ~s de** to spoil one's appetite for; **tener ~*** to be in the mood; **tener ~s de** + *infin* to feel like + *ger*, have a mind to + *infin*; **tengo pocas ~s de** + *infin* I don't much feel like + *ger*; **tengo ~s de verte** I'm longing to see you.

ganadería NF (**a**) (*crianza*) cattle raising, stockbreeding; ranching. (**b**) (*estancia*) stock farm; (*rancho*) cattle ranch. (**c**) (*ganado*) cattle, livestock; (*raza*) strain, breed, race (of cattle).

ganadero [1] ADJ *animal* cattle (*atr*), stock (*atr*); cattle-raising (*atr*).
[2] NM (*persona*) stockbreeder, rancher (*US*); cattle dealer.

ganado NM (**a**) (*gen*) stock, livestock; (*esp LAm*) cattle; (*un ~*) herd, flock; **~ asnal, ~ asnar** donkeys; **~ caballar** horses; **~ cabrío** goats; **~ lanar, ~ ovejuno** sheep; **~ mayor** cattle, horses and mules; **~ menor** sheep, goats and pigs; **~ porcino** pigs; **~ vacuno** cattle.
(**b**) **un ~ de** (*LAm: fig*) a crowd of, a mob of.

ganador [1] ADJ winning, victorious; **el equipo ~** the winning team; **apostar a ~ y colocado** to back (a horse) each way, back for a win and a place.
[2] NM, **ganadora** NF winner; (*Fin*) earner; (*fig*) gainer, one who gains.

ganancia NF (**a**) (*beneficio*) gain; (*aumento*) increase; (*Com, Fin*) profit; **~s** earnings; profits, winnings; **~s y pérdidas** profit and loss; **~ bruta** gross profit; **~ líquida** net profit; **no le arriendo la ~** I don't envy him; **sacar ~ de** to draw profit from. (**b**) (*LAm: propina*) extra, bonus.

ganancial ADJ profit (*atr*).

ganancioso [1] ADJ (**a**) (*lucrativo*) gainful; profitable, lucrative. (**b**) (*triunfador*) winning; **salir ~** to be the winner.
[2] NM, **gananciosa** NF: **en esto el ~ es él** he'll come out of this better off.

ganapán NM (**a**) (*recadero*) messenger, porter. (**b**) (*temporero*) casual labourer; odd-job man. (**c**) (*patán*) lout, rough individual.

ganar [1a] [1] VT (**a**) (*adquirir*) to gain; (*lograr*) to get, acquire, obtain; (*Com, Fin*) to earn; (*interés*) to earn; to draw; *dinero* to earn, make; *premio* to win; **gana un sueldo** he earns a salary; **¿cuánto ganas al mes?** how much do you earn (*o* make) a month?; **ha ganado mucho dinero** she has made a great deal of money; **tierras ganadas al mar** land reclaimed from the sea, land won from the sea.
(**b**) (*Dep etc*) *carrera, partido*, to win; *punto* to score, win; *contrario* to beat; *rival* to outstrip, surpass, leave behind; **~ unas oposiciones para un puesto** to win a post by public competition; **A le ganó a B esta vez** A beat B this time; **no hay quien le gane** there's nobody who can beat him; **A le gana a B en pericia** A has more expert knowledge than B; **A le gana a B trabajando** A is a better worker than B; **A le ganó 5 duros a B** A won 5 duros from (*o* off) B.
(**c**) (*Mil*) *ciudad etc* to take, capture.
(**d**) (*alcanzar*) to reach; **~ la orilla** to reach the shore; **~ la orilla nadando** to swim to the shore.
(**e**) (*fig: conquistar*) to win over; *apoyo, partidarios* to win, get; **dejarse ~ por** to allow o.s. to be won over by; **no se deja ~ en ningún momento por la desesperación** he never gives way to despair.
[2] VI (**a**) (*Dep etc*) to win; to gain.
(**b**) (*fig*) to thrive, improve; (*prosperar*) to do well; **ha ganado mucho en salud** he has much improved in health; **saldrás ganando** you'll do well out of it.
(**c**) (*t ganarse; LAm*) to go off; to escape, take refuge; **~ a la cama** to go off to bed; **~ hasta la casa** to get to the house; **se ganó en la iglesia** he took refuge in the church; **el caballo ganó para el bosque** the horse moved off towards the wood, the horse made for the wood.
[3] **ganarse** VR: **~ la confianza de uno** to win sb's trust; **~ las antipatías de uno** to attract sb's dislike.

gancha: NF hash*, pot:.

ganchera NF (*Cono Sur*) matchmaker.

ganchero NM (*Cono Sur*) (*ayudante*) helper, assistant; (*factótum*) odd-job man.

ganchete NM: **mirar al ~** (*Carib**) to look out of the corner of one's eye (at); **ir de ~** (*LAm*) to go arm-in-arm.

ganchillo NM (**a**) small hook; (*Cos*) crochet hook. (**b**) (*labor*) crochet, crochet work; **hacer ~** to crochet.

ganchito ® NM *light potato snack*, ≃ Wotsit ® (*Brit*).

gancho NM (**a**) (*gen*) hook; (*colgador*) hanger; (*de árbol*) stump; (*Agr*) shepherd's crook; (*LAm: horquilla*) hairpin; (*CAm: imperdible*) safety pin; (*Boxeo*) hook; **~ a la cara** uppercut; **~ de carnicero** butcher's hook; **echar el ~ a** (*fig*) to hook, land, capture; **estar en ~s** (*LAm:*) to be hooked on drugs*.
(**b**) (*persona*) (*coime*) pimp, procurer; (*agente*) tout; (*cómplice*) mate, partner.
(**c**) (*: *atractivo*) appeal, attraction; drawing power; (*de slogan etc*) bite, pull; (*de mujer*) charm, attractiveness; **tiene muchísimo ~** she's very charming.
(**d**) (*And*) lady's saddle.
(**e**) (*LAm**) (*ayuda*) help; (*protección*) protection; **hacer ~** (*CAm, Cono Sur*) to lend a hand.

ganchoso ADJ, **ganchudo** ADJ hooked, curved.

gandalla: NMF (*Méx*) (*vagabundo*) tramp, bum (*US*); (*arribista*) upstart.

gandido ADJ (*And*) greedy.

gandinga NF (*Carib*) (**a**) (*Culin*) thick stew. (**b**) (*: *apatía*) sloth, apathy; **tener poca ~** to have no sense of shame.

gandola NF (*LAm*) articulated truck.

gandul [1] ADJ idle, lazy, slack; good-for-nothing.
[2] NM, **gandula**[1] NF idler, slacker; good-for-nothing.

gandula[2]* NF (*Jur*) law on vagrancy.

gandulear [1a] VI to idle, loaf, slack.

gandulería NF idleness, loafing, slackness.

gandulitis NF (*hum*) congenital laziness.

gane NM (*CAm Dep*) win, victory; **llevarse el ~, lograr el ~** to win.

ganga NF (**a**) (*Com*) bargain; **¡una verdadera ~!** a genuine bargain!; **precio de ~** bargain price, give away price. (**b**) (*fig*) (*extra*) extra, bonus; cheap acquisition; (*suerte*) windfall; (*cosa fácil*) cinch:, gift; **esto es una ~** this is a cinch:. (**c**) (*Méx*: *sarcasmo*) taunt, jeer.

Ganges NM: **el** (*Río*) **~** the Ganges.

ganglio NM ganglion; swelling; **~s:** tits:.

gangosear [1a] VI (*And, Cono Sur*) (**a**) (*pey**) to talk through one's nose, whine. (**b**) = **ganguear.**

gangoseo NM (*And, Cono Sur*) = **gangueo.**

gangoso ADJ *acento* nasal, twanging.

gangrena NF gangrene.

gangrenar [1a] [1] VT (**a**) (*Med*) to make gangrenous, cause gangrene in. (**b**) (*fig*) to infect, destroy.
[2] **gangrenarse** VR to become gangrenous.

gangrenoso ADJ gangrenous.

gán(g)ster [ˈganster] NM, PL **gán(g)sters** [ˈganster] gangster, gunman.

gan(g)sterismo [gansteˈrizmo] NM gangsterism.

ganguear [1a] VI to talk with a nasal accent, speak with a twang.

gangueo NM nasal accent, twang.

ganoso ADJ (**a**) (*afanoso*) anxious, keen; **~ de** + *infin* anxious to + *infin*, keen to + *infin*. (**b**) (*Cono Sur*) *caballo* spirited, fiery.

gansa NF (**a**) (*Orn*) goose. (**b**) (*) goose, silly girl.

gansada NF daft thing to do; lark*, caper.

gansear* [1a] VI play the fool, clown around.

ganso [1] NM (**a**) (*Orn*) goose, gander; **~ salvaje** wild goose. (**b**) (*) idiot, dimwit*, dolt; country bumpkin; **¡no seas ~!** don't be an idiot!; **hacer el ~** to play the fool.
[2] ADJ (*) (*grande*) huge, hefty; (*atractivo*) hunky*, dishy*.

gánster NM gangster.

Gante NM Ghent.

ganzúa [1] NF picklock, skeleton key.
[2] NMF (*ladrón*) burglar, thief; (*curioso*) inquisitive person, smeller out of secrets.

gañán NM farmhand, labourer.

gañido NM (*V v*) yelp, howl; croak; wheeze.

gañir [3h] VI (*perro*) to yelp, howl; (*pájaro*) to croak; (*persona*) to wheeze, talk hoarsely, croak.

gañón* NM, **gañote*** NM throat, gullet.

gapo: NM: **echar un ~** to gob:, spit.

GAR NM ABR *de* **Grupo Antiterrorista Rural.**

garabatear [1a] [1] VT to scribble, scrawl.
[2] VI (**a**) (*Mec*) to use a hook. (**b**) (*escribiendo*) to scribble, scrawl. (**c**) (*andar con rodeos*) to beat about the bush.

garabato NM (**a**) (*gancho*) hook; grapple, grapnel; (*Carib*) long forked pole; (*Náut*) grappling iron.
(**b**) (*en ejercicio de escritura*) pothook; **~s** scribble, scrawl.
(**c**) (*Carib**: *flaco*) beanpole*.
(**d**) (*Cono Sur*: *palabrota*) swearword; **echar ~s** to swear.
(**e**) = **gancho** (c).

garabina NF (**a**) (*And*: *bagatela*) trifle, bagatelle; cheap finery. (**b**) (*Carib*: *crisálida*) chrysalis.

garabito NM (**a**) (*de mercado*) market stall. (**b**) (*Cono Sur*) tramp, hobo (*US*).

garabullo: NM 5 pesetas.

garaje NM garage; **el ~ La Estrella** (*hum*) the street.

garajista NM (*dueño*) garage owner; (*trabajador*) garage man, garage attendant.

garambaina NF (**a**) (*adornos*) cheap finery, tawdry finery.
(**b**) (*carácter chillón*) gaudiness.
(**c**) **~s** (*muecas*) (affected) grimaces; (*ademanes*) absurd mannerisms; **¡déjate de ~s!** stop that silly simpering!
(**d**) **~s** (*garabatos*) scribble, scrawl.

garambetas NFPL (*Carib**) (**a**) = **garambaina** (**a**) y (**c**). (**b**) **hacer ~** to pull faces.

garandumba NF (*Cono Sur*) (**a**) (*Náut*) flatboat, flat river boat. (**b**) (*hum*) big woman.

garante [1] ADJ (*responsable*) guaranteeing, responsible.
[2] NMF (*Fin*) guarantor, surety.

▼ **garantía** NF (*gen*) guarantee; (*seguridad*) pledge, security; (*compromiso*) undertaking; (*Jur*) warranty; **bajo ~** under guarantee; **~s constitucionales** constitutional safeguards; **~ en efectivo** cash guarantee, surety; **~ escrita** express warranty; **~ implícita** implied warranty; **de máxima ~** absolutely guaranteed.

garantir [3a; *defectivo*] VT (**a**) to guarantee. (**b**) (*And, Carib, Cono Sur: asegurar*) to guarantee, assure; **le garanto** I assure you, I warrant you.

garantizadamente ADV genuinely, authentically.

garantizado ADJ guaranteed; (*fig*) genuine, authentic.

garantizar [1f] VT to guarantee, warrant; to vouch for.

garañón NM (**a**) (*asno*) stud jackass; (*LAm: semental*) stallion. (**b**) (*Cono Sur*) brothel keeper.

garapiña NF (**a**) (*Culin*) sugar icing, sugar coating. (**b**) (*LAm: bebida*) iced pineapple drink. (**c**) (*Méx: robo*) theft.

garapiñada NF sugar and almond sweet.

garapiñados NMPL sugared almonds.

garapiñar [1a] VT *helado etc* to freeze; *nata* to clot; *pastel* to ice, coat with sugar; *fruta* to candy.

garapiñera NF ice-cream freezer.

garapullo NM (*rehilete*) dart; (*Taur*) banderilla.

garata NF (*Carib**) fight, brawl.

garatusas NFPL: **hacer ~ a uno** to coax sb, wheedle sb.

garba NF (*Agr*) sheaf.

garbanzo NM (**a**) (*Bot*) chickpea; **ser el ~ negro** to be the black sheep of the family; **ganarse los ~s** to earn one's living.
(**b**) **de ~** ordinary, unpretentious, common; **gente de ~** humble folk, ordinary people.

garbear [1a] [1] VT (*: *robar*) to pinch*, swipe*.
[2] VI (**a**) (*afectar garbo*) to affect elegance, make a show, show o.s. off. (**b**) (*robar*) to steal (for a living). (**c**) = **3**.
[3] **garbearse** VR to get along, rub along.

garbeo NM affected elegance, show; **darse un ~*, pegarse un ~*** to go for a walk.

garbera NF (*Agr*) stook, shock.

garbí NM south-west wind (*Catalonia*).

garbillar [1a] VT (*Agr*) to sift, sieve; (*Min*) to sift, screen, riddle.

garbillo NM sieve; screen, riddle.

garbo NM (**a**) (*elegancia*) grace, elegance; (*porte*) graceful bearing, fine carriage; (*aire*) jauntiness, jaunty bearing; (*de mujer*) glamour, allure, attractiveness; (*de escrito etc*) style, stylishness; **andar con ~** to walk gracefully, carry o.s. well; **hacer algo con ~** to do sth with grace and ease (o with style); **¡qué ~!** isn't she lovely?
(**b**) (*largueza*) magnanimity, generosity.

garbosamente ADV (V ADJ) (**a**) gracefully, elegantly; jauntily; stylishly. (**b**) generously.

garboso ADJ (**a**) (*elegante*) graceful, elegant; *andar* jaunty; *escrito* stylish. (**b**) (*generoso*) magnanimous, generous.

garceta NF egret.

garciamarquiano ADJ of (o relating to) Gabriel García Márquez.

garcilla NF: **~ bueyera** cattle egret.

garçon: **con pelo a lo ~** with bobbed hair, with hair in a boyish style.

gardenia NF gardenia.

garduña[1] NF (*Zool*) marten.

garduño, -a[2] NM/F sneak thief.

garete NM: **estar al ~, ir al ~** to be adrift; (*fig*) to be all at sea.

garfa NF claw.

garfada NF clawing, scratching.

garfil* NM (*Méx*) cop*.

garfio NM hook; gaff; (*Téc*) grapple, grappling iron, claw; (*Alpinismo*) climbing iron.

gargá: NF = **garganta**.

gargajear [1a] VI to spit phlegm, hawk.

gargajo NM phlegm, sputum.

garganta NF (**a**) (*Anat*) throat, gullet; neck; **mojar la ~*** to wet one's whistle*; **le tengo atravesado en la ~** he sticks in my gullet; **tener**

el agua a la ~ to be in great danger.
(**b**) (*Anat: de pie*) instep.
(**c**) (*Mús*) singing voice; **tener buena ~** to have a good singing voice.
(**d**) (*de botella*) neck.
(**e**) (*Geog*) gorge, ravine; narrow pass.
(**f**) (*Arquit: de columna etc*) shaft.

gargantear [1a] VI (*Mús*) to warble, quaver, trill.

garganteo NM warble, quaver, trill.

gargantilla NF necklace.

gargantuesco ADJ gargantuan.

gárgara NF (*t* **~s** PL) gargle, gargling; **hacer ~** to gargle; **¡vaya Vd a hacer ~!** go to blazes!*; **mandar a uno a hacer ~*** to tell sb to go to hell.

gargarear [1a] VI (*And, CAm, Cono Sur*) to gargle.

gargarismo NM (**a**) (*líquido*) gargle, gargling solution. (**b**) (*acto*) gargle, gargling.

gargarizar [1f] VI to gargle.

gárgol NM (*Téc: ranura*) groove.

gárgola NF gargoyle.

garguero NM gullet; windpipe.

garifo ADJ (**a**) (*elegante*) spruce, elegant, natty*. (**b**) (*Cono Sur: astuto*) sharp. (**c**) (*And*: engreído*) stuck-up*. (**d**) (*CAm, And: hambriento*) hungry. (**e**) **estar ~** (*And*) to be broke*.

gariga NF (*Méx*) drizzle.

garita NF (*caseta*) cabin, hut, box; (*Mil*) sentry box; (*de camión etc*) cab; (*consejería*) porter's lodge; (*de vigilancia*) look-out post; (*: *WC*) water closet; (*LAm: de policía de tráfico*) stand, box; **~ de control** checkpoint; **~ de señales** signal-box.

garitea NF (*And*) river flatboat.

garitero, -a NM/F (*dueño*) keeper of a gaming house; (*jugador*) gambler.

garito NM (**a**) (*club*) nightclub, night spot; (*de juego*) gaming house, gambling-den. (**b**) (*ganancias*) winnings.

garla NF talk, chatter.

garlador [1] ADJ garrulous.
[2] NM, **garladora** NF chatterer, great talker.

garlito NM fish trap; (*fig*) snare, trap; **caer en el ~** to fall into the trap; **coger a uno en el ~** to catch sb in the act.

garlopa NF jack plane.

garnacha NF (**a**) (*Jur: Hist*) gown, robe. (**b**) (*persona*) judge. (**c**) (*Méx Culin*) tortilla with filling. (**d**) **a la ~** (*CAm**) violently; **¡ni de ~!** (*Carib**) not on your life! (**e**) (*vino*) garnacha (*a sweet wine made from purple grapes*).

garnachear [1a] VT (*Cono Sur: llevar ventaja a*) to have the edge over.

garnucho NM (*Méx*) tap, rap on the nose.

Garona NM Garonne.

garpar: [1a] VT (*Cono Sur*) to pay, fork out*.

garra NF (**a**) (*Zool*) claw; talon; (*mano: pey*) paw; (*Méx**) muscular strength; **echar la ~ a uno** to arrest sb, seize sb; **estar como una ~** (*And, Cono Sur*) to be as thin as a rake*.
(**b**) **~s** (*Zool*) claws, talons; (*fig*) clutches; **caer en las ~s de uno** to fall into sb's clutches.
(**c**) (*Téc*) claw, tooth, hook; (*Mec*) clutch; **~ de seguridad** safety clutch.
(**d**) (*) (*fig*) bite, penetration; (*Dep*) sharpness, edge; **esa canción no tiene ~** that song has no bite to it.
(**e**) (*LAm*) piece of old leather; **~s** (*Méx**) bits, pieces, scraps; **no hay cuero sin ~s** (*Méx**) you can't make an omelette without breaking eggs.
(**f**) (*And: bolsa*) leather bag.

garrafa NF (*de vino, licor*) carafe; (*LAm: bombona*) cylinder.

garrafal ADJ enormous, terrific; *error etc* monumental, terrible.

garrafón NM demijohn.

garrancha* NF (*espada*) sword; (*And: gancho*) hook.

garrapata NF (**a**) (*Zool*) tick. (**b**) (*Mil: hum*) disabled horse, useless horse.

garrapatear [1a] VI to scribble, scrawl.

garrapatero NM (*Orn*) cowbird, buffalo bird; (*LAm*) tick-eater.

garrapaticida NM (*LAm*) insecticide, tick-killing agent.

garrapato NM pothook; **~s** (*fig*) scribble, scrawl.

garrapiñada NF sugar-coated almond.

garrapiñado ADJ sugar-coated.

garrear [1a] (*Cono Sur*) [1] VT (**a**) *animal* to skin the feet of. (**b**) (*: *robar*) to pinch*.
[2] VI to sponge, live off other people.

garreo* NM: **es de puro ~** (*Cono Sur*) it's a piece of cake*.

garrete NM (*And, CAm, Cono Sur*) (*de caballo*) hock; (*de persona*) back of the knee.

garrido ADJ (**a**) (*elegante*) neat, elegant, smart. (**b**) (††: *bien parecido*) handsome; pretty.

garroba NF carob bean.

➤ LENGUA Y USO: **garantía** → 42.1

garrobo NM (*CAm*) (*iguana*) iguana; (*caimán*) small alligator.

garrocha NF (*Agr*) goad; (*Taur*) spear; (*LAm Dep*) vaulting pole.

garrón NM (*Orn*) spur; talon; (*Zool*) paw; heel; (*de carne*) shank; (*Cono Sur: de caballo*) hock; (*Bot*) snag, spur; **vivir de ~** (*Cono Sur*) = **garronear**.

garronear [1a] VI (*Cono Sur: vivir de gorra*) to sponge*, live off other people.

garrotazo NM blow with a stick (*o club etc*).

garrote NM (**a**) (*bastón*) stick, club, cudgel; **política del ~ y la zanahoria** the carrot-and-stick approach; **usar el gran ~** (*fig*) to use the big stick.
(**b**) (*Med*) tourniquet; (*Jur*) garrotte; **dar ~ a uno** to garrotte sb.
(**c**) (*Méx*) (*Aut*) brake; **darse ~*** to check o.s., hold o.s. back.

garrotear [1a] VT (*LAm*) to club, cudgel.

garrotero ⒈ ADJ (*Carib, Cono Sur**) stingy.
⒉ NM (**a**) (*Méx*) brakeman. (**b**) (*And, Cono Sur*) (*matón*) bully, tough*; (*pendenciero*) brawler, troublemaker. (**c**) (*Carib: prestamista*) money-lender.

garrotillo NM (**a**) (*Med*) croup. (**b**) (*Cono Sur: granizada*) summer hail.

garrucha NF pulley.

garrudo ADJ (**a**) (*Méx*) tough, muscular. (**b**) (*And*) *vaca* terribly thin.

garrulería NF chatter.

garrulidad NF garrulousness, talkativeness.

garrulo ⒈ ADJ (*bruto*) thick.
⒉ NM, **garrula** NF lout.

gárrulo ADJ *persona* garrulous, chattering, talkative; *pájaro* twittering; *agua* babbling, murmuring; *viento* noisy.

garúa NF (**a**) (*LAm: lloviznar*) drizzle. (**b**) (*Carib: alboroto*) row, din.

garuar [1e] VI (*LAm: lloviznar*) to drizzle; **¡qué le garúe fino!** I wish you luck!, I hope it keeps fine for you!

garubar [1a] VI (*Cono Sur*) = **garuar**.

garufa* NF: **ir de ~** (*Cono Sur*) to go on a spree.

garuga NF (*CAm, Cono Sur, Méx*) = **garúa.**

garugar [1h] VI (*Cono Sur*) = **garuar.**

garulla ⒈ NF (**a**) (*uvas*) loose grapes. (**b**) (*: gentío*) mob, rabble.
⒉ NMF (*) urchin, rascal.

garullada* NF mob, rabble.

garza¹ NF (*t ~ real*) heron; **~ imperial** purple heron.

garza² NF (*Cono Sur*) beer glass.

garzo ADJ (*liter*) *ojos* blue, bluish; *persona* blue-eyed.

garzón NM (*Cono Sur*) waiter.

garzona NF (*Cono Sur*) waitress.

gas NM (**a**) gas; (*vapores*) fumes; **~ del alumbrado** coalgas; **~ asfixiante, ~ tóxico** poison gas; **~ butano** butane; **~ de efecto invernadero** greenhouse gas; **~es de escape** exhaust (fumes); **~ hilarante** laughing-gas; **~ inerte** inert gas; **~ lacrimógeno** teargas; **~ licuado** (*Cono Sur*) Calor gas ⓡ; **~ mostaza** mustard-gas; **~ natural** natural gas; **~ nervioso** nerve-gas; **~ de los pantanos** marsh gas; **~ pobre** producer gas; **asfixiar con ~** to gas; **estar ~** (*CAm: hum*) to be head over heels in love.
(**b**) (*gasolina*) petrol, gas (*US*); **darle ~** to step on the gas*; **ir a todo ~** (*Aut, t fig*) to go flat out; **perder ~** (*fig*) to slow down, lose impetus.

gasa NF gauze; (*Med*) lint; (*luto*) crêpe; (*de pañal*) nappy-liner; **~ higiénica** sanitary towel.

Gascuña NF Gascony.

gaseado ADJ carbonated, aerated.

gasear [1a] VT to gas, kill with gas.

gaseosa NF mineral water; (*frec*) pop*, fizz, fizzy drink; **~ de limón** fizzy lemonade.

gaseoso ADJ gaseous; aerated, carbonated; gassy; *bebida* fizzy.

gásfiter NM, PL **gásfiters** (*Cono Sur*) plumber.

gasfitería NF (*And, Cono Sur*) plumber's (shop).

gasfitero, -a NM/F (*And, Cono Sur*) plumber.

gasificación NF (**a**) (*Quím*) gasification. (**b**) (*de ciudad*) supply of piped gas (*de to*).

gasista ⒈ ADJ gas (*atr*); **industria ~** gas industry.
⒉ NM gas fitter, gasman.

gasístico ADJ gas (*atr*).

gasoducto NM gas pipeline.

gasofa* NF juice*, petrol.

gas-oil [ga'soil] NM diesel oil.

gasóleo NM diesel oil; **~ B** red diesel.

gasolero NM diesel-powered car.

gasolina NF (**a**) (*Aut*) petrol, motor spirit, gasoline (*US*), gas (*US*); **~ de aviación** aviation spirit; **~ normal** two-star petrol; **~ súper** three-star petrol; **~ extra** four-star petrol; **~ sin plomo** unleaded petrol; **~ de alto octanaje** high-octane petrol; **echar ~*** to take a leak*; **repostar ~*** to have a drink.
(**b**) (*Carib: gasolinera*) petrol-station, gas station (*US*).

gasolinera NF (**a**) (*Náut*) motorboat. (**b**) (*Aut*) petrol-station, gas station (*US*).

gasolinero NM (*dueño*) owner of a filling-station; (*empleado*) petrol-pump attendant.

gasómetro NM gasometer.

gásquet NM, PL **gásquets** (*LAm*) gasket.

gastable ADJ expendable; dispensable.

gastado ADJ (**a**) (*usado*) spent; used up. (**b**) (*decaído*) worn out; *ropa* shabby, threadbare. (**c**) (*trillado*) hackneyed, trite; *chiste* old, corny*.

gastador ⒈ ADJ (*extravagante*) extravagant, lavish; (*disipador*) wasteful.
⒉ NM, **gastadora** NF (*derrochador*) spender; (*pey*) spendthrift.
⒊ NM (*Mil: Hist*) sapper, pioneer.

gastar [1a] ⒈ VT (**a**) *dinero, esfuerzo, tiempo* to spend; *dinero* to expend, lay out; **han gastado un dineral** they've spent a fortune.
(**b**) (*consumir*) to use up, consume.
(**c**) (*pey*) to waste; **~ palabras** to waste words, waste one's breath.
(**d**) (*Mec etc*) to wear away, wear down; *ropa, zapatos* to wear out; to spoil.
(**e**) (*vestir*) to have, wear, sport; (*usar*) to use; *coche etc* to have, own, run; **~ barba** to have a beard, wear a beard, sport a beard; **antes no gastaba gafas** he used not to wear glasses; **¿qué número (de zapatos) gasta Vd?** (*Esp*) what size (of shoes) do you take?
(**f**) *broma* to crack; *burla* to play (*a on*).
(**g**) **~las*** to act, behave; **todos sabemos cómo las gasta Juan** we all know how John carries on*.
⒉ VI to spend, spend money.
⒊ **gastarse** VR to become exhausted; to run out; to wear out; to waste, go to waste, spoil.

Gasteiz NM Vitoria.

gasto NM (**a**) (*acto*) spending, expenditure.
(**b**) (*cantidad*) amount spent, expenditure, expense; **supone un gran ~ para él** it means a considerable expense for him.
(**c**) (*consumo*) consumption, use.
(**d**) (*Mec etc*) wear.
(**e**) (*pey*) waste.
(**f**) (*de gas etc*) flow, rate of flow.
(**g**) (*Com, Fin*) **~s** expenses; charge(s), cost(s), rate(s); **~s de acarreo** transport charges, haulage; **~s de administración, ~s administrativos** administrative costs, overheads; **~s bancarios** bank charges; **~s comerciales** business expenses; **~s de comunidad, ~s de escalera** service charge; **~s de conservación, ~s de mantenimiento** upkeep costs, maintenance costs; **~s de correo** postal charges; **~s corrientes** running costs; **~s de defensa** (*Mil*) defence costs; **~s de desplazamiento** (*al mudarse*) removal expenses; (*de viaje*) travelling expenses; **~s de entrega** (*t ~s de envío*) delivery charge; **~s de envío** charge for post and packing; **~s de explotación** operating costs, operating expenses; **~s fijos** fixed charges; **~s de flete** freight charges; **~s generales** overheads; **~s menores (de caja)** petty cash; **~s del negocio** business expenses; **~ público** public expenditure; **~ de representación** entertainment allowance; **~s de servicio** service charge; **~s de viaje** travelling expenses; **cubrir ~s** to cover expenses; **meterse en ~s** to go to expense, incur expense; **pagar los ~s** to pay the expenses, foot the bill; **con todos los ~s pagados** with all expenses paid.

gastón¹* NM (*CAm: diarrea*) the runs*.

gastón²* ADJ free-spending.

gastoso ADJ extravagant, wasteful.

gástrico ADJ gastric.

gastritis NF gastritis.

gastroenteritis NF gastroenteritis.

gastronomía NF gastronomy.

gastronómico ADJ gastronomic.

gastrónomo, -a NM/F gastronome, gourmet.

gastroplastia NF gastroplasty.

gastrópodo NM gastropod.

gata NF (**a**) (*Zool*) cat, she-cat.
(**b**) (*: madrileña*) Madrid woman; (*Méx*) servant, maid; **~ de callejón** (*fig*) alley cat.
(**c**) (*Met*) hill cloud.
(**d**) (*And, Cono Sur*) crank, handle; (*Aut*) car jack.
(**e**) **a ~s** (*lit*) on all fours; (*And, Cono Sur**) barely, by the skin of one's teeth; **andar a ~s** to go on all fours; to creep, crawl; (*niño*) to crawl.
(**f**) (*) **echar la ~** (*CAm*), **soltar la ~** (*And*) to lift*, steal.
(**g**) **tener ~** (*agujetas*) to ache all over.

gatada NF (**a**) (*movimiento etc*) movement (*o act etc*) typical of a cat. (**b**) (*arañazos*) scratch, clawing. (**c**) (*trampa*) artful dodge, sly trick.

gatazo NM: **dar el ~** (*LAm**) to look younger than one is, not to show one's age.

gateado ⒈ ADJ (**a**) (*gatuno*) catlike, feline.
(**b**) *mármol* striped, veined.
⒉ NM (**a**) (*movimiento: gatear*) crawl, crawling; (*subir*) climb, climbing.

(b) (*arañazos*) scratch, clawing. **(c)** (*Carib*) hard veined wood (used in cabinet-making).

gateamiento NM = **gateado 2 (a)** y **(b)**.

gatear [1a] ① VT **(a)** (*arañar*) to scratch, claw. **(b)** (*) to pinch*, steal. **(c)** (*CAm, Méx: seducir*) to seduce. ② VI **(a)** (*trepar*) to climb, clamber (*por* up); (*andar a gatas*) to creep, crawl, go on all fours. **(b)** (*LAm*) to be on the prowl.

gateo NM crawling.

gatera ① NF **(a)** (*aficionada a gatos*) cat-lover. **(b)** (*apertura: Náut*) cat hole; (*de gato*) catflap. **(c)** (*And*) market woman, stallholder. ② NM (*) sneak thief.

gatería NF **(a)** (*gatos*) cats, collection of cats. **(b)** (*pandilla*) gang of louts. **(c)** (*cualidad*) false modesty.

gatero ① ADJ fond of cats. ② NM cat-lover; *V t* **gatera 1 (a)**.

gatillar [1a] VT to cock.

gatillero NM gunman, hitman.

gatillo NM **(a)** (*Mil*) trigger; (*Med*) dental forceps; (*Téc*) clamp. **(b)** (*Zool*) nape (of the neck). **(c)** (*) young thief, young pickpocket.

gatito, -a NM/F kitten; puss, pussy.

gato¹ NM **(a)** (*Zool*) cat, tomcat; ~ **de algalia** civet cat; ~ **de Angora** Angora cat; ~ **callejero** alley cat, stray cat; ~ **montés** wild cat; ~ **romano** tabby cat; ~ **siamés** Siamese cat; **'El ~ con botas'** 'Puss in Boots'; **¡es pa'l ~!** it's rubbish!; **no había más que cuatro ~s** there was hardly a soul; **de noche todos los ~s son pardos** at night all cats are grey; **dar a uno ~ por liebre** to take sb in*, pull the wool over sb's eyes, swindle sb; **el ~ escaldado del agua fría huye** once bitten twice shy; **aquí hay ~ encerrado** I smell a rat, there's sth fishy here*; **jugar al ~ y ratón con uno** to play a cat-and-mouse game with sb; **llevar el ~ al agua** to pull off sth difficult; **a ver quién se lleva el ~ al agua** let's see who can manage to come out on top; **pasar sobre algo como ~ sobre ascuas** to tread carefully round sth, pass gingerly over sth; **ser ~ viejo** to be an old hand. **(b)** (*Téc, Aut etc*) jack; (*torno*) clamp, vice; (*grapa*) grab; (*Méx: de arma*) trigger ~ **de tornillo** screw jack. **(c)** (*Fin*) money-bag. **(d)** (*) (*ladrón*) sneak thief, cat burglar; (*taimado*) slyboots*. **(e)** (*: madrileño*) native of Madrid. **(f)** (*Méx: criado*) servant. **(g)** (*CAm: músculo*) muscle. **(h)** (*Méx: propina*) tip. **(i)** (*Cono Sur: bolsa de agua*) hot-water bottle. **(j)** (*Cono Sur: baile*) Argentine folk dance.

gato² NM (*And*) open-air market, market place.

gatopardo NM ocelot.

GATT NM ABR *de* **General Agreement on Tariffs and Trade** GATT.

gatuno ADJ catlike, feline.

gatuperio NM **(a)** (*mezcla*) hotchpotch. **(b)** (*fraude*) fraud, piece of underhand dealing.

gaucano* NM (*Carib*) rum-based cocktail.

gaucha NF (*Cono Sur* †: *marimacho*) mannish woman.

gauchada NF (*Cono Sur*) **(a)** (*personas*) gauchos (*collectively*). **(b)** (*acto*) gaucho exploit, (*pey*) typical gaucho trick. **(c)** (*favor*) favour; good turn; helping hand; **hacer una ~ a uno*** to do sb a favour.

gauchaje NM (*Cono Sur*) gauchos (*collectively*); gathering of gauchos; (* *pey*) riffraff, rabble.

gauchear [1a] VI (*Cono Sur: vivir de gaucho*) to live as a gaucho.

gauchesco ADJ (*Cono Sur*) gaucho (*atr*); like a gaucho; of the gauchos; **vida gauchesca** gaucho life.

gaucho ① NM **(a)** (*LAm*) gaucho, cowboy. **(b)** (*Cono Sur: jinete*) good rider, expert horseman. **(c)** (*And: sombrero*) wide-brimmed straw hat. ② ADJ **(a)** gaucho (*atr*); of the gauchos. **(b)** (*LAm: pey*) coarse, rough; sly, tricky.

┌─ **GAUCHO** ─────────────────────────────────────┐

ⓘ *Gaucho is the name given to the men who rode the **Pampa**, the plains of Argentina, Uruguay and parts of southern Brazil, earning their living on cattle farms. Important parts of the **gaucho's** traditional costume include the **faja**, a sash worn round the waist, the **facón**, a sheath knife, and **boleadoras**, strips of leather weighted with stones at either end which were used somewhat like lassos to catch cattle. During the 19th century this vast **pampas** area was divided up into large ranches and the free-roaming lifestyle of the **gaucho** gradually disappeared. **Gauchos** were the inspiration for a tradition of **literatura gauchesca**, of which the most famous work is the two-part epic poem "Martín Fierro" written by the Argentine José Hernández between 1872 and 1879 and mourning the loss of the **gaucho** way of life and their persecution as outlaws.*

└──┘

gaudeamus* NM (*hum*) party, beano*.

gaulista ADJ, NMF Gaullist.

gavera NF (*LAm*) crate.

gaveta NF drawer, till; locker.

gavia NF **(a)** (*Náut*) (main) topsail. **(b)** (*Orn*) seagull. **(c)** (*Agr*) ditch.

gavilán NM **(a)** (*Orn*) sparrowhawk. **(b)** (*de plumilla*) nib. **(c)** (*de espada*) quillon. **(d)** (*CAm, Carib*) ingrowing nail.

gavilla NF **(a)** (*Agr*) sheaf. **(b)** (*) gang, band.

gavillero NM (*LAm*) gunman, trigger-man.

gaviota NF **(a)** (*Orn*) seagull, gull; ~ **argéntea** herring-gull. **(b)** (*Méx*: *hum*) flier.

gavota NF gavotte.

gay [gai] ① ADJ INVAR gay. ② NM, PL **gays** gay man, gay; **los ~s** the gays.

gaya NF **(a)** (*Orn*) magpie. **(b)** (*en tela*) coloured stripe.

gayo ADJ **(a)** (*alegre*) merry, gay; **gaya ciencia** art of poetry, art of the troubadours. **(b)** (*vistoso*) bright, showy.

gayola NF (*jaula*) cage; (*: cárcel*) jail.

gayumbos: NMPL (*pantalones*) pants, trousers; (*calzoncillos*) underpants.

gaza NF loop; (*Náut*) bend, bight.

gazafatón* NM = **gazapatón**.

gazapa* NF fib, lie.

gazapatón* NM (*error*) blunder, slip; (*disparate*) piece of nonsense.

gazapera NF **(a)** (*conejera*) rabbit hole, warren. **(b)** (* *fig*) den of thieves. **(c)** (*riña*) brawl, shindy*.

gazapo NM **(a)** (*Zool*) young rabbit. **(b)** (*taimado*) sly fellow; (*: ladrón*) cat burglar; (*LAm: mentiroso*) liar. **(c)** (*disparate*) blunder, bloomer*; (*mentira*) lie; (*Tip*) misprint; **cazar un ~** to spot a mistake. **(d)** (*Carib: estafa*) trick.

gazmoñada NF, **gazmoñería** NF (*V ADJ*) **(a)** hypocrisy, cant. **(b)** prudery, priggishness; sanctimoniousness.

gazmoñero, gazmoño ① ADJ **(a)** (*hipócrita*) hypocritical, canting. **(b)** (*remilgado*) prudish, priggish; strait-laced; (*beato*) sanctimonious. ② NM, **gazmoñera** NF, **gazmoña** NF **(a)** hypocrite. **(b)** prude, prig; sanctimonious person.

gaznápiro, -a NM/F dolt, simpleton.

gaznatada: NF (*CAm, Carib, Méx*) smack, slap.

gaznate NM **(a)** (*) gullet; windpipe, throttle; **remojar el ~*** to have a drink. **(b)** (*Méx*) (fruit) fritter.

gaznetón ① ADJ (*And, Méx*) loud-mouthed. ② NM, **gaznetona** NF loudmouth*.

gazpacho NM **(a)** gazpacho (*Andalusian cold soup*); **de ~ no hay empacho** one can never have too much of a good thing. **(b)** (*CAm*) (*bebida*) dregs; (*comida*) left-overs.

gazuza NF **(a)** (*) ravenous hunger. **(b)** (*CAm: alboroto*) din, row. **(c)** (*CAm:: chusma*) common people. **(d) es una ~** (*CAm**) she's a wily old bird.

GC NF ABR *de* **Guardia Civil**.

geco NM gecko.

géiser NM (*Geog*) geyser.

geisha ['geiʃa] NF geisha (girl).

gel NM, PL **gels** [gel] *o* **geles** gel.

gelatina NF gelatin(e), jelly; ~ **explosiva** gelignite.

gelatinoso ADJ **(a)** gelatinous. **(b)** (*And*) lazy, stolid.

gelidez NF chill, iciness.

gélido ADJ chill, icy.

gelificarse [1g] VR to gel, coagulate.

gelignita NF gelignite.

gema NF **(a)** (*joya*) gem, jewel. **(b)** (*Bot*) bud.

gemelo ① ADJ twin; **buque ~** sister ship; **hermanas gemelas** twin sisters. ② NM (*Náut*) sister ship. ③ NM, **gemela** NF twin; **G~s** (*Zodíaco*) Gemini; **~s idénticos** identical twins. ④ NMPL **(a)** (*Cos*) cufflinks. **(b)** **~s de campo** field glasses, binoculars; **~s de teatro** opera glasses.

gemido NM groan, moan; wail, howl.

gemidor ADJ groaning, moaning; wailing, howling.

Géminis NMPL (*Zodíaco*) Gemini.

gemiquear [1a] VI (*Cono Sur*) to whine.

gemiqueo NM (*Cono Sur*) whining.

gemir [31] VI (*quejarse*) to groan, moan; (*lamentarse*) to wail, howl; (*animal*) to whine; (*viento etc*) to moan, howl; (*fig*) to moan, lament; (*en cárcel*) to languish, rot; **'Sí' dijo gimiendo** 'Yes' he groaned.

gen NM gene.

gen. (*Ling*) **(a)** ABR *de* **género** gender, gen. **(b)** ABR *de* **genitivo** genitive, gen.

genciana NF gentian.

gendarme NM policeman, gendarme.

gendarmería NF police, gendarmerie.

gene NM gene.

genealogía NF (*ascendientes*) genealogy; (*árbol*) family tree; (*raza*) pedigree.

genealógico ADJ genealogical.

genealogista NMF genealogist.

generación NF **(a)** (*acto*) generation.
(b) (*grupo*) generation; **la ~ del 27/98** the generation of '27/'98; **las nuevas generaciones** the rising generation; **la quinta ~ de ordenadores** the fifth generation of computers.
(c) (*descendencia*) progeny, offspring; (*sucesión*) succession; (*cría*) brood.

┌─────────────────────────────┐
│ *GENERACIÓN DEL 27/DEL 98* │
└─────────────────────────────┘

ⓘ The **Generación del 27** is the collective name given to a group of writers and poets including Lorca, Alberti, Guillén, Cernuda and Aleixandre, who drew inspiration from earlier Spanish poets as well as from popular folk song and contemporary European art (Dadaism, Surrealism, Cubism). They particularly admired Góngora (1561 -1627) and it was their commemoration of the anniversary of his death that earned them the title **Generación del 27**.

The **Generación del 98** was the name coined by Azorín for a group of writers (Baroja, Machado, Unamuno, Maeztu, Ganivet, and himself, amongst others) who saw Spain's defeat in the Cuban American war of 1898 as the start of a decline in values. While not all the supposed members of the group accepted their inclusion in it, their work demonstrates shared themes, ideals, and concerns.

generacional ADJ generation (*atr*).

generacionalmente ADV in terms of generation(s).

generador ① ADJ generating.
② NM generator.

general ① ADJ general; (*amplio*) wide; (*común*) common, prevailing; (*pey*) rife; (*frecuente*) usual; **es ~ por toda España** it is common throughout Spain, it exists in the whole of Spain; **de distribución ~** of general distribution, generally distributed; **en ~, por lo ~** generally, as a general rule, in general; for the most part; **el mundo en ~** the world in general, the world at large.
② NM **(a)** (*Mil*) general; **~ de brigada** brigadier-general; **~ de división** major-general.
(b) (*Teat*) stalls.
③ NF (*Aut*) main road.
④ NFPL: **~es de la ley** prescribed personal questions.

generala NF **(a)** (*persona*) (woman) general; (*Hist*) general's wife. **(b)** (*llamamiento*) call to arms, general alert.

generalato NM **(a)** (*arte, puesto*) generalship. **(b)** (*personas*) generals (collectively). **(c)** (*Méx**: *madama*) madame, brothel keeper.

generalidad NF **(a)** generality; mass, majority; **la ~ de los hombres** the mass of ordinary people, the common run of men.
(b) (*vaguedad*) vague answer, generalization, general statement.
(c) **la G~** (*Pol*) = Generalitat.

generalísimo NM generalissimo, supreme commander; **el G~ Franco** General Franco.

generalista NMF general practitioner.

Generalitat NF: **la ~** (*Pol*) Catalan autonomous government.

┌─────────────────┐
│ *GENERALITAT* │
└─────────────────┘

ⓘ The **Generalitat** is the autonomous government of Catalonia. The name originally applied to the finance committee of the Catalan parliament, or Corts, in the early 13th century, but in 1932 was given to the partially devolved government granted to Catalonia under the Second Republic (1931-36). When its leader, Luis Companys, went on to proclaim the "Catalan State of the Spanish Federal Republic" in 1934, Madrid sent in the troops, and imprisoned members of the breakaway **Generalitat**. Catalan autonomy was restored under the Popular Front in 1936, but was abolished by Franco after the Civil War. Since his death the **Generalitat** has risen again under the 1978 Constitution and Catalonia now enjoys a considerable degree of autonomy from Madrid.
⇨ See also │ *LA CONSTITUCIÓN ESPAÑOLA* │

generalización NF **(a)** (*acto*) generalization. **(b)** (*de conflicto*) widening, escalation.

generalizado ADJ crisis, creencia widespread; **existe la creencia generalizada de que...** it is commonly (o widely) believed that...

generalizar [1f] ① VT **(a)** to generalize; to make more widely known, bring into general use.
(b) (*Mil: ampliar*) to widen, escalate, scale up.
② VI to generalize.
③ **generalizarse** VR **(a)** to become general, become universal; to become widely known (o used *etc*).
(b) (*Mil*) to widen, escalate.

generalmente ADV generally.

generar [1a] VT to generate.

generativismo NM generative grammar.

generativo ADJ generative.

genérico ADJ generic.

género NM **(a)** (*clase*) class, kind, type, sort; **~ humano** human race, mankind; **te deseo todo ~ de felicidades** I wish you all the happiness in the world.
(b) (*Bio*) genus.
(c) (*Arte, Liter*) genre; type; **~ chico** (genre of) comic one-act pieces; (*sainetes*) short farces; (*zarzuela*) zarzuela, Spanish operetta; **~ novelístico** novel genre, fiction; **pintor de ~** genre painter; **es todo un ~ de literatura** it is a whole type of literature.
(d) (*Ling*) gender.
(e) (*Com*) cloth, stuff, material; **~s** (*productos*) goods, merchandise; commodities; **~s de lino** linen goods; **~s de punto** knitwear, knitted goods; **le conozco el ~** I know his sort; I know all about him, I recognize the type.

generosamente ADV (*V ADJ*) generously; nobly, magnanimously.

generosidad NF **(a)** (*largueza*) generosity; nobility, magnanimity. **(b)** (*liter*) nobility; valour.

generoso ADJ **(a)** (*liberal*) generous (*con, para* to); (*noble*) noble, magnanimous.
(b) (*liter*) noble, highborn; gentlemanly; brave, valiant; **de sangre generosa** of noble blood; **en pecho ~** in a noble heart.
(c) vino rich, full-bodied.

genésico ADJ genetic.

Génesis NM (*Bíb*) Genesis.

génesis NF genesis.

genética NF genetics.

genéticamente ADV genetically.

geneticista NMF geneticist.

genético ADJ genetic.

genetista NMF geneticist.

genial ADJ **(a)** (*brillante*) inspired, brilliant, of genius; **escritor ~** writer of genius; **fue una idea ~** it was a brilliant idea; **¡eso fue ~!** it was marvellous!, it was wonderful!
(b) (*agradable*) pleasant, cheerful, genial; (*afable*) cordial, affable; (*divertido*) witty.
(c) (*propio*) in character, characteristic; (*singular*) individual; (*típico*) typical.

genialidad NF **(a)** (*genio*) genius. **(b)** (*una ~*) stroke of genius, brilliant idea; (*obra*) brilliant work; **eso fue una ~** that was a stroke of genius. **(c)** (*acción extravagante*) eccentricity.

genialmente ADV **(a)** (*con genio*) in an inspired way, brilliantly, with genius. **(b)** (*alegremente*) pleasantly, cheerfully.

genio NM **(a)** (*temperamento*) disposition, nature, character; **~ alegre** cheerful nature; **buen ~** good nature; **~ y figura (hasta la sepultura)** the leopard cannot change its spots; **de ~ franco** of an open nature; **mal ~** bad temper; evil disposition; **de mal ~** bad-tempered; ill-disposed; **estar de mal ~** to be in a bad temper; **~ vivo** quick temper, hot temper; **corto de ~** spiritless, timid; **llevar el ~ a uno** to humour sb; not to dare to contradict sb.
(b) (*mal carácter*) bad temper; **es una mujer de mucho ~** she's a quick-tempered woman; **tiene ~** he's temperamental; he has an uncertain temper, he's bad-tempered.
(c) (*talento*) genius; **¡eres un ~!** you're a genius!
(d) (*peculiaridad*) genius, special nature, peculiarities; **esto va en contra del ~ de la lengua** this goes against the genius of the language.
(e) (*Mit, Rel*) spirit; genie; **~ del mal** evil spirit; **~ tutelar** guardian spirit.

genioso ADJ (*CAm*) bad-tempered.

genista NF broom, genista.

genital ① ADJ genital.
② **~es** NMPL genitals, genital organs.

genitalidad NF sexual activity.

genitivo ① ADJ generative, reproductive.
② NM (*Ling*) genitive.

genocida NMF person accused (o guilty) of genocide.

genocidio NM genocide.

genoma NM, **genomio** NM genome.

Génova NF Genoa.

genovés, -esa ADJ, NM/F Genoese.

genoveva NF vintage car, classic car.

gental NM (*And*) lot, mass; **un ~ de gente** a mass of people.

gente NF **(a)** (*gen*) people, folk; (*nación*) race, nation; (*Mil*) men, troops, (*séquito*) followers, retinue; (**: *parientes*) relatives, folks, people; **el rey y su ~** the king and his retinue; **mi ~** my people, my folks; **son ~ inculta** they're rough people; **no me gusta esa ~** I don't like those people; **hay muy poca ~** there are very few people; **~ baja** lower classes, low-class people; **~ bien** upper-class people; nice people, respectable people; (*pey*) posh people*; smart set; **~ de bien** honest folk, decent people; **~ de capa parda** country folk; **~**

de color coloured people; **~ de la cuchilla** butchers; **~ gorda = ~ bien; ~ guapa** beautiful people; **~ de mar** seafaring men; **~ menuda** (*humildes*) small fry; humble folk; (*niños*) children, kids*, little people; **~ natural** (*CAm*) Indians, natives; **~ de paz** peace-loving people; **¡~ de paz!** (*Mil*) friend!; **~ de pelo** well-to-do people; **~ de medio pelo** people of limited means; **~ perdida** bad people; criminals; idlers, loafers; **~ de pluma** clerks, penpushers; **~ principal** nobility, gentry; **~ de tomuza** (*Carib*‡) Negroes, black people; **~ de trato** tradespeople; **de ~ en ~** from generation to generation; **hacer ~** to make a crowd.

(**b**) (*esp LAm*) upper-class people; nice people, respectable people; **ser ~** to be somebody, have social importance.

(**c**) (*LAm*) person; **había dos ~s** there were two people; **Carlos es buena ~** (*LAm**) o **muy ~** (*Cono Sur*) Carlos is a good sort.

gentecilla NF unimportant people; (*pey*) rabble, riffraff.

genterío NM (*CAm*) = **gentío**.

gentil ☐1 ADJ (**a**) (*elegante*) elegant, graceful, attractive; (*encantador*) charming; (*fino*) courteous; (*Méx*) kind, helpful.

(**b**) (*iró*) pretty, fine; **¡~ cumplido!** a fine compliment!

(**c**) (*Rel*) pagan, heathen; gentile.

☐2 NMF pagan, heathen; gentile.

gentileza NF (**a**) (*elegancia*) elegance, gracefulness; (*encanto*) charm; (*finura*) courtesy; '**por ~ de X**' 'by courtesy of X'. (**b**) (*boato*) show, splendour, ostentation. (**c**) (*bizarría*) dash, gallantry.

gentilhombre NM (*Hist: corte*) gentleman; **~ de cámara** gentleman-in-waiting.

gentilicio ☐1 ADJ: **nombre ~ = 2**.

☐2 NM name of the inhabitants of a country (*o region etc*).

gentilidad NF, **gentilismo** NM the pagan world; heathenism, paganism.

gentilmente ADV (**a**) (*con elegancia*) elegantly, gracefully, attractively; (*con encanto*) charmingly; (*con gracia*) prettily; (*cortésmente*) courteously. (**b**) (*iró*) prettily.

gentío NM crowd, throng; **había un ~** there were lots of people.

gentualla NF, **gentuza** NF rabble, mob; riffraff; **¡qué ~!** what a shower!‡

genuflexión NF genuflexion.

genuflexo ADJ (*Cono Sur*) servile, slavish.

genuinamente ADV genuinely; really, truly.

genuino ADJ (**a**) genuine; real, pure, true. (**b**) (*And**) smashing*, super*.

GEO ['xeo] NMPL (*Esp*) ABR *de* **Grupo Especial de Operaciones** *special police unit*.

geo NMF member of GEO.

geo... PREF geo...

geoambiental ADJ geoenvironmental.

geociencia NF geoscience.

geodemografía NF geodemography.

geodesía NF geodesy.

geodésico ADJ geodesic.

geoecología NF geoecology.

geoestacionario ADJ geostationary.

geoestadística ADJ geostatistics.

geoestrategia NF geostrategy.

geoestratégico ADJ geostrategic.

geofísica¹ NF geophysics.

geofísico ☐1 ADJ geophysical.

☐2 NM, **geofísica²** NF geophysicist.

Geofredo NM Geoffrey.

geografía NF (**a**) geography; **~ física** physical geography; **~ humana** human geography; **~ política** political geography. (**b**) (*país*) territory; country; **en toda la ~ nacional** all over the country; **recorrer la ~ nacional** to travel all over the country.

geográfico ADJ geographical.

geógrafo, -a NM/F geographer.

geohistoria NF, **geo-historia** NF geohistory.

geolingüística NF geolinguistics.

geología NF geology.

geológico ADJ geological.

geólogo, -a NM/F geologist.

geomagnético ADJ geomagnetic.

geometría NF geometry; **~ del espacio** solid geometry; **de ~ variable** (*Aer*) variable-geometry (*atr*).

geométrico ADJ geometric(al).

geomorfología NF geomorphology.

geopolítica NF geopolitics.

geopolítico ADJ geopolitical.

Georgia del Sur NF South Georgia.

georgiano ADJ Georgian.

geostacionario ADJ geostationary.

geotermal ADJ geothermal.

geranio NM geranium.

Gerardo NM Gerald, Gerard.

gerencia NF (**a**) (*dirección*) management. (**b**) (*cargo*) managership, post of manager. (**c**) (*oficina*) manager's office. (**d**) (*personas*) management, managers (*collectively*); **~ intermedia** middle management.

gerencial ADJ managerial.

gerenciar [1b] VT to manage.

gerente NMF manager, director; executive; **~ de fábrica** works manager.

geriatra NMF geriatrician.

geriatría NF geriatrics.

geriátrico, -a ☐1 ADJ, NM/F geriatric.

☐2 NM (*centro*) old people's home.

gerifalte NM (**a**) (*Orn*) gerfalcon. (**b**) (*fig*) important person; **estar** (*o* **vivir**) **como un ~** to live like a king.

germanesco ADJ: **palabra germanesca** a word from thieves' slang, cant word.

germanía NF thieves' slang.

germánico ADJ Germanic.

germanio NM germanium.

germanista NMF Germanist.

germanística NF German studies.

germano ☐1 ADJ Germanic; German.

☐2 NM, **germana** NF German.

germanófilo, -a NM/F germanophile.

germanófobo ☐1 ADJ germanophobe, germanophobic.

☐2 NM, **germanófoba** NF germanophobe.

germanófono ☐1 ADJ German-speaking.

☐2 NM, **germanófona** NF German speaker.

germanooccidental ADJ, NMF (*Hist*) West German.

germanooriental ADJ, NMF (*Hist*) East German.

germen NM (**a**) (*Bio, Med*) germ; **~ plasma** germ plasma; **~ de trigo** wheat germ. (**b**) (*fig*) germ, seed; source, origin; **el ~ de una idea** the germ of an idea.

germicida ☐1 ADJ germicidal.

☐2 NM germicide, germ killer.

germinación NF germination.

germinar [1a] VI to germinate; to sprout, shoot.

Gerona NF Gerona.

gerontocracia NF gerontocracy.

gerontología NF gerontology.

gerontólogo, -a NM/F gerontologist.

Gertrudis NF Gertrude.

gerundense ☐1 ADJ of Gerona.

☐2 NMF native (*o* inhabitant) of Gerona; **los ~s** the people of Gerona.

gerundiano ADJ bombastic.

gerundino NM gerundive (*Latin*).

gerundio NM gerund; **bebiendo, que es ~** drinking, and I do mean drinking; **andando, que es ~** get a move on — now!

gervasio NM (*And*) fellow, guy*; shrewd fellow.

gesta NF (**a**) (*hazaña*) heroic deed, epic achievement. (**b**) (*Liter: Hist*) epic, epic poem; *V t* **cantar**.

gestación NF gestation; **~ de alquiler** surrogate motherhood.

gestante ADJ: **mujer ~** pregnant woman, expectant mother.

Gestapo NF Gestapo.

gestar [1a] ☐1 VT (*Bio*) to gestate; (*fig*) to prepare, hatch.

☐2 **gestarse** VR (*Bio*) to gestate; (*fig*) to be in preparation, be brewing.

gestear [1a] VI (*hacer ademanes*) to gesture; (*hacer muecas*) to grimace.

gesticulación NF (**a**) (*ademán*) gesticulation. (**b**) (*mueca*) grimace, (wry) face.

gesticular [1a] VI (**a**) (*hacer ademanes*) to gesticulate, gesture. (**b**) (*hacer muecas*) to grimace, make a face.

gestión NF (**a**) (*Com etc*) management, conduct; **~ de datos** data management; **~ forestal** woodland management.

(**b**) (*negociación*) negotiation.

(**c**) (*medida*) measure, step; (*acción*) action; (*esfuerzo*) effort; (*operación*) operation; **gestiones** measures, steps; **hacer las gestiones necesarias para** + *infin* to take the necessary steps to + *infin*; **hacer las gestiones preliminares** to do the groundwork, make the first steps; **donde él tenía que realizar unas gestiones** where he had some business to transact; **el gobierno tendrá que hacer las primeras gestiones** the government will have to make the first move.

gestionable ADJ manageable; **difícilmente ~** difficult to manage.

gestionar [1a] VT (**a**) (*conducir*) to manage, conduct. (**b**) (*negociar*) to negotiate (for). (**c**) (*procurar*) to try to arrange, strive to bring about, work towards.

gesto NM (**a**) (*cara*) face; (*semblante*) expression on one's face; **estar de buen ~** to be in a good mood; **estar de mal ~** to be in a bad mood; **poner mal ~, torcer el ~** to make a (wry) face; to scowl, look cross.

(**b**) (*mueca*) grimace, (wry) face; scowl; **hacer ~s** to make faces (*a* at); **hacer un ~** to make a face; **hizo un ~ de asco** he looked disgusted; **hizo un ~ de extrañeza** he looked surprised.

(c) (ademán) gesture (t fig); (señal) sign; **hacer ~s** to make gestures (a to); **con un ~ de cansancio** with a weary gesture; **con un ~ generoso remitió la deuda** in a generous gesture he let him off the debt.

gestología NF study of body-language.
gestor ① ADJ managing.
② NM, **gestora¹** NF manager; promoter; business agent, representative; **~ de carteras** portfolio management.
gestora² NF committee of management.
gestoría NF agency (for undertaking business with government departments, insurance companies, etc).

┌─── **GESTORÍA** ───┐

🅘 In Spain gestorías are private agencies which specialize in dealing with legal and administrative work. For a fee they carry out the trámites involved in getting passports, work permits, car documentation, etc and liaise with the Inland Revenue (**Agencia Tributaria**), thereby saving their clients much inconvenience and queueing time.

gestual ADJ gestural; **lenguaje ~** body-language.
gestualidad NF body-language.
Getsemaní NM Gethsemane.
geyser NM geyser.
Ghana NF Ghana.
ghanés, -esa ADJ, NM/F Ghanaian.
ghetto NM ghetto.
giba NF **(a)** (lit) hump; hunchback. **(b)** (*) nuisance, bother.
gibado ADJ with a hump, hunchbacked.
gibar* [1a] ① VT **(a)** (molestar) to bother, annoy. **(b)** (embaucar) to put one over on*; (tomar la revancha) to get one's own back on; to do down*.
② **gibarse** VR to put up with it; **se van a ~** they'll have to lump it.
gibón NM gibbon.
giboso ADJ with a hump, hunchbacked.
Gibraltar NM Gibraltar.
gibraltareño ① ADJ of Gibraltar, Gibraltarian.
② NM, **gibraltareña** NF Gibraltarian, native (o inhabitant) of Gibraltar; **los ~s** the Gibraltarians, the people of Gibraltar.
gigabyte NM gigabyte.
giganta NF **(a)** giantess. **(b)** (Bot) sunflower.
gigante ① ADJ giant, gigantic.
② NM giant.
gigantesco ADJ gigantic, giant.
gigantez NF gigantic stature, vast size.
gigantismo NM (Med) gigantism, giantism.
gigantón, -ona ① NM/F giant carnival figure.
② NF (CAm: baile) folk dance with giant masks.
gigoló NM gigolo.
Gijón NM Gijón.
gijonés ① ADJ of Gijón.
② NM, **gijonesa** NF native (o inhabitant) of Gijón; **los gijoneses** the people of Gijón.
Gil NM Giles.
gil (Cono Sur) ① ADJ stupid, silly.
② NMF berk*, twit*.
gilar* [1a] VT to watch, keep tabs on.
gilda NF lollipop.
gili*, **gilí*** ① ADJ: **no seas ~** don't be such a prat* (o (US) jerk*.
② NMF prat*, jerk* (US).
gilipollada* NF = **gilipollez**.
gilipollas* ① ADJ INVAR **so seas ~** don't be such a dickhead*.
② NMF INVAR dickhead*, wanker*.
gilipollear* [1a] VI to piss about*.
gilipollesco* ADJ bloody stupid*, bloody idiotic*.
gilipollez* NF: **es una ~** it's bloody stupid*; **decir gilipolleces** to talk crap*.
gilipuertas* ADJ, NMF INVAR (euf) = **gili**.
gillet(t)e [xi'lete] NF (hoja) (any) razorblade; (maquinilla) safety razor.
gimnasia NF gymnastics; physical training; **~ aeróbica** aerobics; **~ deportiva** competitive gymnastics; **~ de mantenimiento** keep-fit exercises; **~ respiratoria** deep breathing; **~ rítmica** eurhythmics; **hacer ~** to do gymnastics, do physical training.
gimnasio NM gymnasium, gym; **~ múltiple** multigym.
gimnasta NMF gymnast.
gimnástica NF gymnastics.
gimnástico ADJ gymnastic.
gimotear [1a] VI (gemir) to whine, whimper; (lamentar) to wail; (niño: lloriquear) to snivel, grizzle.
gimoteo NM (gemido) whine, whining; (lamento) wailing; (lloriqueo) snivelling, grizzling.

gincana NF gymkhana.
Ginebra¹ NF (Geog) Geneva.
Ginebra² NF (Hist) Guinevere.
ginebra¹ NF gin.
ginebra²* NF bedlam, uproar, confusion.
ginecología NF gynaecology.
ginecológico ADJ gyn(a)ecological.
ginecólogo, -a NM/F gynaecologist.
ginesta NF (Bot) broom.
gineta NF genet.
gingival ADJ gum (atr), gingival.
gingivitis NF INVAR gingivitis.
ginkana NF gymkhana.
ginseng [jin'sen] NM ginseng.
gin-tonic [jin'tonik] NM, PL **gin-tonics** gin and tonic.
giña* NF (Carib) hatred.
Gioconda NF: **la ~** (the) Mona Lisa.
gira NF (Mús, Teat etc) tour; trip; **estar en ~** to be on tour; V t **jira**.
giradiscos NM INVAR record turntable.
girado, -a NM/F (Com) drawee.
girador(a) NM/F (Com) drawer.
giralda NF, **giraldilla** NF weathercock.
girante ADJ revolving, rotating.
girar [1a] ① VT **(a)** (dar vuelta a) to turn, turn round, rotate; (torcer) to twist; (revolver) to spin; **~ la manivela 2 veces** turn the crank twice.
(b) (volver) to swing, swivel; **~ la vista** to look round.
(c) (Com) to draw (a cargo de, contra on), issue.
② VI **(a)** (voltearse) to turn, turn round, go round; (dar vueltas) to rotate, revolve; (Mec) to spin, gyrate; (rodar) to wheel; (Dep: pelota) to spin; **~ hacia la derecha** to turn (to the) right, swing right; **gira a 1600 rpm** it rotates at 1600 rpm; **el satélite gira alrededor del mundo** the satellite circles the earth, the satellite revolves round the earth; **la conversación giraba en torno de las elecciones** the conversation turned on (o centred on) the election; **el número de asistentes giraba alrededor de 500 personas** there were about 500 people in the audience.
(b) (balancear) to swing (from side to side), swivel; (sobre gozne) to hinge; (en equilibrio) to pivot; **la puerta giró sobre sus goznes** the door swung on its hinges.
(c) (Com, Fin) to operate, do business; **la compañía gira bajo la razón social de X** the company operates under the name of X.
(d) (Com) to draw; **~ en descubierto** to overdraw.
(e) (Mús, Teat etc) to go on tour.
girasol NM sunflower.
giratorio ADJ (gen) revolving, rotatory; gyratory; escena, puerta etc revolving; puente swing (atr), swivel (atr); silla swivel (atr).
girl* NF (Teat) showgirl, chorus-girl; (Dep) junior player.
giro¹ NM **(a)** (vuelta) turn; (revolución) revolution, rotation; gyration; **hacer un ~** to turn, make a turn; **el coche dio un ~ brusco** the car swung away suddenly.
(b) (fig: de sucesos etc) (tendencia) trend, tendency, course; (cambio) switch, change, turn; **~ de 180 grados, ~ copernicano** U-turn, complete turnabout; **la cosa ha tomado un ~ favorable** the affair has taken a turn for the better; **la intriga tiene un ~ inesperado** the plot has an unexpected twist in it.
(c) (Ling) turn of phrase, expression.
(d) (Com) draft; bill of exchange; **~ bancario** bank giro, bank draft; **~ en descubierto** overdraft; **~ postal** money order, postal order; **~ postal internacional** international money order; **~ a la vista** sight draft.
giro² ADJ **(a)** (LAm) gallo with some yellow colouring. **(b)** (Carib: atolondrado) scatterbrained, thoughtless. **(c)** (CAm*: ebrio) drunk. **(d)** (Méx*: confiado) cocky, confident.
girocompás NM gyrocompass.
girola NF ambulatory.
Gironda NM Gironde.
giroscópico ADJ gyroscopic.
giroscopio NM, **giróscopo** NM gyroscope.
gis NM (LAm: tiza) chalk; (And: lápiz de pizarra) slate pencil. **(b)** (Méx: pulque, (any) colourless drink.
gitana NF gipsy; (de feria etc) fortuneteller.
gitanada NF **(a)** (acto) gipsy trick, mean trick. **(b)** (gen) wheedling, cajolery; humbug.
gitanear [1a] VT to wheedle, cajole.
gitanería NF **(a)** (gitanos) band of gipsies; gathering of gipsies. **(b)** (vida) gipsy (way of) life. **(c)** (dicho) gipsy saying. **(d)** (fig: gitanada) wheedling, cajolery.
gitanesco ADJ **(a)** gipsy (atr); gipsy-like. **(b)** (pey) wily, tricky.
gitano ① ADJ **(a)** gipsy (atr). **(b)** (fig: halagüeño) wheedling, cajoling; (zalamero) smooth, flattering. **(c)** (fig: taimado) wily, tricky, sly. **(d)** (*: sucio) dirty.
② NM gipsy; **vivir como ~s** to live from hand to mouth; **volvió he-**

cho un ~ he came back dirty all over.

glabro ADJ hairless.

glaciación NF glaciation.

glacial ADJ (a) glacial; *viento etc* icy, bitter, freezing. (b) *(fig)* icy, cold, stony.

glaciar NM glacier.

gladiador NM gladiator.

gladio NM, **gladiolo** NM, **gladíolo** NM gladiolus.

glamour [gla'mur] NM glamour.

glamo(u)roso ADJ glamorous.

glándula NF gland; **~ cerrada, ~ de secreción interna** ductless gland; **~ endocrina** endocrine gland; **~ pituitaria** pituitary (gland); **~ prostática** prostate (gland); **~ tiroides** thyroid (gland).

glandular ADJ glandular.

glas ADJ: **azúcar ~** icing-sugar.

glaseado ADJ glazed, glossy; *(Culin)* glacé, glazed.

glasear [1a] VT *papel etc* to glaze; *(Culin)* to glacé, glaze.

glásnost NF glasnost.

glauco ADJ *(liter)* glaucous, light green; *(esp LAm)* green.

glaucoma NM glaucoma.

gleba NF (a) clod. (b) *(Hist)* glebe.

glicerina NF glycerin(e).

glicina NF *(Bot)* wisteria.

global ADJ *(en conjunto)* global; *(completo)* total, complete, overall; *informe, investigación etc* full, searching, comprehensive; *suma* total, aggregate.

globalidad NF totality; **la ~ del problema** the problem as a whole; the problem in its widest sense; **en su ~** as a whole.

globalización NF making universal, world-wide extension.

globalizador ADJ comprehensive.

globalizante ADJ universalizing, world-wide.

globalizar [1f] VT (a) *(abarcar)* to encompass, include. (b) *(extender)* to make universal, extend world-wide.

globalmente ADV *considerar, examinar* as a whole; *(en total)* all in all.

globo NM (a) globe, sphere; **~s:** boobs:; **~ de luz** spherical lamp; **~ del ojo, ~ ocular** eyeball; **~ terráqueo** globe, schoolroom globe. (b) *(Aer)* **~ (aerostático)** balloon; **~ de aire caliente** hot-air balloon; **~ de barrera** barrage-balloon; **~ cautivo** captive balloon; **~ dirigible** dirigible; **~ meteorológico** weather balloon; **~ de protección** barrage-balloon. (c) (: *preservativo*) French letter. (d) **en ~** as a whole, all in all; *(Com)* in bulk; *(fig)* in broad outline only. (e) (:) **tener un ~** to be stoned:. (f) *(Tenis)* lob.

globoso ADJ, **globular** ADJ globular, spherical.

glóbulo NM (a) globule. (b) *(Anat)* corpuscle; **~ blanco** white corpuscle; **~ rojo** red corpuscle; **~ sanguíneo** blood cell.

gloria NF (a) *(fama)* glory; *(Rel)* eternal glory, heaven; *(fig)* glory; *(delicia)* delight; *(éxtasis)* bliss; **una vieja ~** a has-been, a great figure *(etc)* from the past; **el día es pura ~** it's a wonderful day; **¡sí, ~! yes, my love!; ¡por la ~ de mi madre!** by all that's holy!; **estar en su(s) ~(s)** to be in one's element, be in one's glory; **ganarse la ~** to go to heaven; **oler a ~** to smell divine; **saber a ~** to taste heavenly; **que santa ~ haya, Dios le tenga en su santa ~** God rest his soul. (b) (: *droga*) hash*, pot:.

gloriado NM *(And)* hot toddy.

gloriarse [1c] VR: **~ de algo** to boast of sth, be proud of sth; **~ en algo** to glory in sth, rejoice in sth.

glorieta NF (a) *(pérgola)* bower, arbour; *(cenador)* summerhouse. (b) *(Aut)* roundabout, traffic circle *(US)*; *(plaza redonda)* circus; *(cruce)* junction, intersection.

glorificación NF glorification.

glorificar [1g] 1 VT to glorify, extol, praise.
2 **glorificarse** VR: **~ de, ~ en** to boast of, be proud of, glory in.

gloriosamente ADV gloriously.

glorioso ADJ (a) glorious; *(Ecl) Santo* blessed, in glory; *memoria* blessed; **la Gloriosa** *(Ecl)* the Blessed Virgin; *(Hist)* the 1868 revolution *(in Spain)*. (b) *(pey)* proud, boastful.

glosa NF gloss; comment, note, annotation; *(And)* telling off.

glosar [1a] VT to gloss; to comment on, annotate; *(fig)* to put an unfavourable interpretation on, criticize.

glosario NM glossary.

glosopeda NF foot-and-mouth disease.

glotal ADJ, **glótico** ADJ glottal.

glotis NF INVAR glottis.

glotón 1 ADJ gluttonous, greedy.
2 NM, **glotona** NF glutton.
3 NM *(Zool)* wolverine.

glotonear [1a] VI to be greedy, be gluttonous.

glotonería NF gluttony, greediness.

glub INTERJ gulp!

glucosa NF glucose.

gluglú NM (a) *(de agua)* gurgle, gurgling; glug-glug; **hacer ~** to gurgle. (b) *(de pavo)* gobble, gobbling; **hacer ~** to gobble.

gluglutear [1a] VI *(pavo)* to gobble.

gluten NM gluten.

glúteo 1 ADJ *(Anat)* gluteal.
2 NM (a) *(músculo)* gluteal muscle. (b) **~s** *(nalgas)* buttocks, backside *sing.*

glutinoso ADJ glutinous.

GN NF *(Nicaragua, Venezuela)* ABR *de* **Guardia Nacional.**

gneis [neis] NM gneiss.

gnomo ['nomo] NM gnome.

gobelino NM Gobelin tapestry.

gobernabilidad NF governability; **llegar a un pacto de ~** to form a government with the support of minority parties.

gobernable ADJ (a) *(Pol)* governable; **un pueblo difícilmente ~** a people hard to govern, an unruly people. (b) *(Náut)* navigable, steerable.

gobernación NF (a) *(acto)* governing, government; **Ministerio de la G~** Ministry of the Interior, ≃ Home Office *(Brit)*, Department of the Interior *(US)*; **Ministro de la G~** *(Esp)* Minister of the Interior. (b) *(residencia)* governor's residence; *(oficina)* governor's office; *(Méx Pol)* Ministry of the Interior.

gobernador 1 ADJ governing, ruling.
2 NM, **gobernadora** NF governor, ruler; **~ civil** civil governor; **~ general** governor-general; **~ militar** military governor.

gobernalle NM rudder, helm.

gobernanta NF *(niñera)* governess; *(de hotel)* staff manageress, housekeeper.

gobernante 1 ADJ *(que gobierna)* ruling, governing.
2 NMF *(líder)* ruler, governor; *(político)* politician; *(en el poder)* person in power; *(fig)* self-appointed boss *(o leader etc)*.

gobernar [1j] 1 VT (a) *(Pol)* to govern, rule. (b) *(en general)* to govern; *(dirigir)* to guide, direct; *(controlar)* to control, manage, run; *(manejar)* to handle. (c) *(Náut)* to steer, sail.
2 VI (a) *(Pol)* to govern, rule; **~ mal** to misgovern. (b) *(Náut)* to handle, steer.

gobi: NF nick:, jail.

gobierno NM (a) *(Pol)* government; **~ autonómico, ~ autónomo** autonomous government; **~ central** central government; **~ de coalición** coalition government; **~ de concentración** government of national unity; **~ directo** direct rule; **~ fantasma** shadow cabinet; **~ en funciones, ~ de gestión, ~ interino, ~ de transición** caretaker government; **~ militar** military government. (b) *(en general)* guidance, direction; control, management, running; handling; **~ doméstico, ~ de la casa** housekeeping, running of the household; **para su ~** for your guidance, for your information; **servir de ~ a** to act as a guide to, serve as a norm for. (c) *(puesto)* governorship. (d) *(Náut)* steering; helm; **buen ~** navigability, good steering qualities; **de buen ~** navigable, easily steerable. (e) **mirar contra el ~** *(Cono Sur:)* to squint, be boss-eyed*.

gobio NM gudgeon.

gob.no ABR *de* **gobierno** government, govt.

goce NM enjoyment; possession.

gocho* NM pig.

godo 1 ADJ Gothic.
2 NM, **goda** NF (a) *(Hist)* Goth. (b) *(LAm pey: español)* Spaniard; *(Hist: primera parte del s. XIX)* loyalist; *(Pol moderna)* conservative, reactionary. (c) *(Canarias)* (peninsular) Spaniard.

Godofredo NM Godfrey.

gofio NM *(Canarias, LAm)* roasted maize meal *(often stirred into coffee)*.

gofre NM waffle.

gogó 1 NF go-go girl, go-go dancer.
2 **a ~** ADV in plenty, by the bucketful.

gol NM goal; **¡~!** goal!; **~ del empate** equalizer; **~ del honor** consolation goal; **meter un ~ a uno** *(fig)* to score a point against sb, outsmart sb, put one over on sb*.

gola NF (a) *(Anat)* throat, gullet. (b) *(Mil: Hist)* gorget; *(Cos: Hist)* ruff; *(Ecl)* clerical collar, dog-collar. (c) *(Arquit)* cyma, ogee.

golaverage NM goal-average.

golazo* NM great goal.

goleada NF quantity of goals, high score; **ganar por ~** to win by a lot of goals, thrash the opponents.

goleador 1 ADJ (a) **el equipo más ~** the team which has scored most goals. (b) **deseos ~es** goal-scoring intentions; **aumentó su cuenta goleadora** he improved his goal-scoring record.
2 NM, **goleadora** NF (goal) scorer; **el máximo ~ de la liga** the top goal scorer in the league.

golear [1a] **1** VT to score a goal against; **Eslobodia goleó a Ruritania por 13 a 0** Slobodia overwhelmed Ruritania by 13-0; **A fue goleado por B** A had a lot of goals scored against it by B; **el portero menos goleado** the keeper who has let in fewest goals; **el equipo más goleado** the team against which most goals have been scored. **2** VI to score (a goal).

goleta NF schooner.

golf NM (*juego*) golf; (*pista*) golf-course; (*club*) golf-club; (*chalet*) club-house; **~ miniatura** miniature golf(-course).

golfa* NF tart‡, whore.

golfada NF mischief, piece of hooliganism.

golfán NM water-lily.

golfante **1** ADJ loutish; delinquent, criminal. **2** NM oaf, lout; rascal.

golfear [1a] VI to loaf, idle; to live like a street urchin.

golferas* NM INVAR = **golfo²**.

golfería NF (a) (*golfos*) loafers (*collectively*); street urchins (*collectively*). (b) (*acto*) loafing, idling; (*estilo de vida*) life of idleness; life in the gutter. (c) (*trampa*) dirty trick.

golfillo NM urchin, street urchin.

golfismo NM golfing.

golfista NMF golfer.

golfístico ADJ golf (*atr*), golfing (*atr*).

golfo¹ NM (*Geog*) (a) (*bahía*) gulf, bay; **G~ de Méjico** Gulf of Mexico; **G~ Pérsico** Persian Gulf; **~ de Vizcaya** Bay of Biscay. (b) (*mar*) open sea.

golfo² NM urchin, street urchin; tramp; oaf, lout; loafer.

Gólgota NM Golgotha.

Goliat NM Goliath.

golilla NF (a) (*Cos: Hist*) ruff, gorget; magistrate's collar; (*And, Cono Sur*) neckcloth, neckerchief; **alzar ~** (*Méx*) to puff out one's chest; **andar de ~** (*And, Cono Sur**) to be dressed up to the nines. (b) (*LAm Orn*) collar, ruff. (c) (*Téc*) flange (of a pipe). (d) (*Carib: deuda*) debt. (e) (*Carib: trampa*) trick, ruse. (f) **de ~** (*CAm: gratis*) free, for nothing; (*Carib**: *por casualidad*) by chance, accidentally.

gollería NF (a) (*Culin: golosina*) dainty, titbit, delicacy; **pedir ~s** to ask too much. (b) (***) extra, special treat; (*Com etc*) perk*; **un empleo con muchas ~s** a job with lots of perks*.

golleroso ADJ affected; pernickety.

gollete NM (*Anat: garganta*) throat, neck; (*de botella*) neck; **estar hasta el ~*** to be fed up*; **beber a ~** to drink straight from the bottle.

golletero* NM (*LAm*) scrounger*.

golondrina NF (a) (*Orn*) swallow; **~ de mar** tern; **una ~ no hace verano** one swallow does not make a summer. (b) (*lancha*) motor-launch. (c) (*Cono Sur*) migrant worker. (d) (*Cono Sur Aut*) furniture van.

golondrino NM (a) (*vagabundo*) rolling stone, drifter; (*Mil*) deserter. (b) (*Med*) tumour under the armpit.

golondro* NM fancy, yen*, longing; **andar en ~s** to cherish foolish hopes; **campar de ~** to sponge*, live on other people.

golosina NF (a) (*manjar*) titbit, delicacy, dainty; (*dulce*) sweet. (b) (*bagatela*) bauble, knick-knack. (c) (*deseo*) desire, longing; (*antojo*) fancy. (d) (*gula*) sweet tooth, liking for sweet things; (*glotonería*) greed.

goloso ADJ (a) (*de lo dulce*) sweet-toothed, fond of dainties. (b) (*pey*) greedy. (c) (*apetitoso*) appetising, attractive.

golpazo NM heavy thump, whack.

golpe NM (a) (*gen*) (*impacto*) blow; hit, punch, knock; (*manotazo*) smack; (*encuentro*) bump; (*de remo etc*) stroke; (*de corazón*) beat, throb; (*de reloj etc*) tick; **se dio un ~ en la cabeza** he got a bump on his head, he banged his head; **A le dio a B un ~ en el pecho** A punched B on the chest; **A dio a B un ~ con un palo** A gave B a blow with his stick, A hit B with his stick; **~ aplastante** crushing blow, knockout blow; **~ bien dado** hit, well-aimed blow; **~ de gracia** (*t fig*); coup de grâce; **~ mortal** death blow; **arma de primer ~** first-strike weapon; **dar ~s en la puerta** to thump the door, pound (at, on) the door; **descargar ~s sobre uno** to rain blows on sb; **darse ~s de pecho** to beat one's breast; **no dar ~*** not to do a stroke, be bone-idle; **a ~ dado no hay quite** (*CAm**) what's done cannot be undone.
(b) (*Téc*) stroke; **~ de émbolo** piston stroke.
(c) (*Dep*) (*Boxeo*) blow, punch; (*Ftbl etc*) kick; (*Béisbol, Golf, Tenis etc*) hit, stroke, shot; **con un total de 280 ~s** (*Golf*) with a total of 280 strokes; **~ de acercamiento** (*Golf*) approach shot; **~ bajo** low blow, punch below the belt; (*fig*) dirty trick; **~ de castigo** (*Ftbl etc*) penalty kick; **~ franco, ~ libre** (*Ftbl*) free kick; **~ libre indirecto** indirect free kick; **~ de martillo** (*Tenis*) smash; **~ de penalidad** (*Golf*) penalty stroke; **~ de salida** (*Golf*) tee shot; **preparar el ~** (*Golf*) to address the ball.

(d) (*fig*: *desgracia etc*) blow, (hard) knock, misfortune; (*Med*) bruise; **ha sufrido un ~ duro** it was a hard knock for him.
(e) (*fig*: *choque*) shock, clash.
(f) (*fig*: *sorpresa*) surprise, astonishment.
(g) (*: *criminal*) job*; attack, holdup; **preparaba su primer ~** he was planning his first job*; **dieron un ~ en un banco** they did a bank job*.
(h) (*salida*) witticism, sally; **¡qué ~!** how very clever!, what a good one!
(i) (*Pol*) coup; **~ de estado** coup d'état; **~ de mano** rising; sudden attack; **~ de palacio** palace coup.
(j) (*fig*), **~ de agua** heavy fall of rain; **~ de calor** heat-stroke; **~ de efecto** coup de théâtre; **~ de fortuna** stroke of luck; **~ maestro** master stroke, stroke of genius; **~ de mar** heavy sea, surge; **~ de sol** sunstroke; **~ de suerte** stroke of luck; **~ de teatro** coup de théâtre; **~ de teléfono** telephone call; **~ de timón** change of direction; **~ de tos** fit of coughing; **~ de viento** gust of wind; **~ de vista** look, glance; **dar el ~** to come up with a telling phrase.
(k) (*locuciones con prep*) **a ~ seguro** with an assurance of success, without any risk; **ir a ~ de calcetín** (*o* **alpargata** *etc*)* to go on Shanks' pony; **a ~ de** by means of; **al ~** (*Carib*) instantly; **de ~** (**y porrazo**) suddenly, unexpectedly; **de un ~** at one stroke, in one go; outright; at a stretch; **abrir una puerta de ~** to fling open a door; **la puerta se abrió de ~** the door flew open; **cerrar una puerta de ~** to slam a door.
(l) (*fig*) (*multitud*) crowd, mass; (*abundancia*) abundance; **~ de gente** crowd of people.
(m) (*Mec*) spring lock; **de ~** spring (*atr*), p.ej. **pestillo de ~** spring bolt.
(n) (*Cos*) pocket flap; (*And*) facing.
(o) (*Méx*) sledgehammer.
(p) (*Carib**) swig*, slug* (of liquor).

golpeador NM (*CAm*) door knocker.

golpeadura NF = **golpeo**.

golpear [1a] **1** VT (*gen*) to strike, knock, hit; *superficie* to beat, pound (on, at); (*a puñetazos*) to punch; *mesa etc* to thump, bang; *alfombra etc* to beat; *puerta* to bang; (*suj: desastre natural*) to hit, strike; *abuso etc* to strike a blow against; (*suavemente*) to tap; **ha sido golpeado por la vida** life has treated him badly. **2** VI (*latir*) to throb, tick; (*Aut, Mec*) to knock; **el ~ de las olas** the buffeting of the waves, the pounding of the sea.

golpecito NM (light) blow, tap, rap; **dar ~s en** to tap (on), rap (on).

golpeo NM (*V v*) striking, knocking, hitting; beating, pounding; punching; thumping, banging; tapping; (*Aut, Mec*) knock, knocking.

golpetazo* NM: **darse un ~ contra algo** to bang into sth, crash into sth.

golpetear [1a] VTI to beat (repeatedly); (*martillar*) to knock, hammer, drum, tap; (*traquetear*) to rattle.

golpeteo NM (*V v*) beating; knocking, hammering, drumming, tapping; rattling.

golpismo NM tendency to military coups; coup d'état mentality; government by a clique installed by a military coup.

golpista **1** ADJ *tendencia etc*: V **golpismo**. **2** NMF participant in a coup d'état.

golpiza NF bash*, bashing*, beating-up*; **dar una ~ a uno** to bash sb*, beat sb up*.

goma NF (a) (*gen*) gum; rubber; (*Cos*) elastic; **~ arábiga** gum arabic; **~ espumosa** foam rubber; **~ de mascar** chewing gum; **~ de pegar** gum, glue. (b) (*una ~*) (*gomita*) rubber band, elastic band; length of elastic, piece of elastic; (*Aut*) tyre; (*: *preservativo*) French letter; (*LAm*) rubber overshoe; **~ de borrar** rubber, eraser; **~ de borrar de máquina** typewriter rubber. (c) **~ 2** plastic explosive. (d) (‡: *droga*) hash*, pot‡; (*LAm*) opium den. (e) (‡: *de policía*) truncheon. (f) **estar de ~** (*CAm**) to have a hangover*.

gomaespuma NF foam rubber.

gomal NM (*And*) rubber plantation.

Gomera NF: **la ~** Gomera.

gomero **1** ADJ gum (*atr*); rubber (*atr*). **2** NM (a) (*Bot: árbol*) gum-tree; rubber tree. (b) (*persona*) (*dueño*) rubber planter, rubber producer; (*obrero*) rubber-plantation worker.

gomina NF (*para hombres*) haircream; (*fijador*) (hair) gel.

gominola NF winegum.

gomita NF rubber band, elastic band.

Gomorra NF Gomorrah.

gomosidad NF gumminess, stickiness.

gomoso **1** ADJ gummy, sticky. **2** NM (†: *petimetre*) dandy.

gónada NF gonad.

góndola NF (*Náut*) gondola; (*Ferro*) goods wagon, freight truck (*US*);

(*Com*) gondola; (*And, Cono Sur*) bus; **~ de cable** cable-car; ski-lift; **~ del motor** (*Aer*) engine casing.

gondolero NM gondolier.

gong [gon], PL **gongs** [gon], **gongo** NM gong.

gongorino ADJ relating to Luis de Góngora; **estilo ~** Gongorine style; **estudios ~s** Góngora studies.

gongorismo NM Gongorism (*literary style pioneered by Luis de Góngora in the 17th century*); *see also* CULTERANISMO, CONCEPTISMO .

gonorrea NF gonorrhoea.

gorda* NF **(a)** (*mujer*) fat woman; (*Cono Sur, Méx: en oración directa*) darling.
 (b) (*Fin**) = **perra gorda; ni ~** absolutely nothing; **no tener ni ~** to be broke*; **no entiende ni ~** he doesn't understand a blind thing*.
 (c) **la G~** the 1868 revolution (*in Spain*); **se armó la ~*** there was a hell of a row, there was a tremendous fuss; **aquí se va a armar la ~*** there's going to be trouble; **ahora nos va a tocar la ~*** now we're for it.
 (d) (*Méx Culin*) thick tortilla.

gordal [1] ADJ fat, big, thick.
 [2] NM kind of large olive.

gordiflón* ADJ, **gordinflón*** ADJ podgy, chubby; **¡~!** fatty!*

gordito [1] ADJ chubby, plump.
 [2] NM, **gordita** NF chubby person, plump person.

gordo [1] ADJ **(a)** *persona* fat; stout, plump; *objeto* big; *hilo, tela etc* thick, coarse, rough; *hecho, suceso* important, big; *premio* first, big, main; **está más ~ que nunca** he's fatter than ever; **en mi vida las he visto más gordas** (*fig*) I've never been in a tougher spot; **fue el desastre más ~ de su historia** it was the biggest (o worst) disaster in their history; **hacer de lo ~*⁑** to have a crap⁑.
 (b) *comida, sustancia* fatty, greasy, oily.
 (c) *agua* hard.
 (d) (*) unpleasant; **ese tipo me cae ~** that chap gets on my nerves, I can't bear that fellow; **eso me cae ~** (*Méx⁑*) it gets right up my nose⁑; **lo más ~ fue ...** the most outrageous part was ...
 [2] ADV: **hablar ~*** to talk big*.
 [3] NM **(a)** (*persona*) fat man; **¡~!** fatty!*; (*Cono Sur, Méx: en oración directa*) darling.
 (b) (*Culin*) fat, suet.
 (c) (*: *premio*) first prize, big prize; jackpot; **ganar el ~** to win the big prize; **sacarse el ~** (*fig*) to bring home the bacon*.

┌─ **EL GORDO** ─┐

ⓘ *El Gordo, "the big one", refers to a large lottery jackpot, particularly the one offered in the Spanish Lotería Nacional at Christmas. The Sorteo Extraordinario de Navidad takes place on 22 December and the jackpot is worth several million pounds. Because of the cost of whole tickets people generally form syndicates so the prize is usually shared out between a number of people.*

⇨ *See also* LOTERÍA PRIMITIVA, LOTERÍA NACIONAL

gordolobo NM mullein.

gordura NF **(a)** (*obesidad*) fat, fatness; (*corpulencia*) corpulence, stoutness. **(b)** (*Culin: grasa*) grease, fat. **(c)** (*Carib, Cono Sur*: crema*) cream.

gorgojear [1a] VI = **gorjear**.

gorgojeo NM = **gorjeo**.

gorgojo NM **(a)** (*Ent*) grub; weevil. **(b)** (*fig*) dwarf, runt.

gorgón NM (*And*) concrete.

gorgoritear [1a] VI to trill, warble.

gorgorito NM trill, warble.

gorgorizar [1f] VI to trill, warble.

górgoro NM (*Méx*) bubble.

gorgotear [1a] VI to gurgle.

gorgoteo NM gurgle.

gorguera NF ruff; (*Mil Hist*) gorget.

gori* NM: **armar el ~** to make a row, kick up a fuss.

gorigori* NM wailing, keening.

gorila NM **(a)** (*Zool*) gorilla. **(b)** (*) (*matón*) tough, bruiser, thug; (*de club*) bouncer*; (*guardaespaldas*) henchman, minder*, bodyguard; strong-arm man. **(c)** (*LAm Pol*) reactionary; (*Mil*) senior officer.

gorilismo NM thuggery.

goriloide NM (*fig*) brute, thug.

gorja NF throat, gorge; **estar de ~*** to be very cheerful.

gorjear [1a] [1] VI to chirp, twitter, trill.
 [2] **gorjearse** VR (*niño*) to crow, gurgle, burble.

gorjeo NM (V v) chirping, twittering, trilling; crowing, gurgling, burbling.

gorobeto ADJ (*And*) twisted, bent, warped.

gorra [1] NF (peaked) cap; (*de bebé*) bonnet; (*Mil*) bearskin, busby; (*Univ*) cap; **~ de montar** riding cap; **~ de paño** cloth cap; **~ de punto** knitted cap; **~ de visera** peaked cap; **~ de yate** yachting cap; **pasar la ~** to pass the hat round; **pegar la ~*** to be unfaithful.
 [2] NMF (*) cadger, sponger*, parasite; **andar** (*o* **ir, vivir**) **de ~** to

cadge, sponge*, scrounge*, live at sb else's expense; **colarse de ~** to gatecrash; **comer de ~** to scrounge a meal*; **entrar de ~** to get in free; **sacar algo de ~** to scrounge sth*; **me** *etc* **vino de ~** (*CAm*: por suerte*) it was a stroke of luck, it came out of the blue.

gorrazo NM: **correr a uno a ~s** to run sb out of town.

gorrear [1a] [1] VT (*Cono Sur⁑*) to cuckold.
 [2] VI (*LAm*) to sponge*, live off others.

gorrero, -a NM/F **(a)** cap maker. **(b)** NM (*) = **gorra 2.**

gorrinada NF **(a)** (*cerdos*) (number of) pigs. **(b)** (*fig: mala pasada*) dirty trick.

gorrinera NF pigsty.

gorrinería NF **(a)** dirt. **(b)** (*fig: mala pasada*) dirty trick.

gorrino NM, **gorrina** NF **(a)** (*cochinito*) small pig, sucking-pig; (*cerdo*) hog; (*cerda*) sow. **(b)** (*fig*) dirty individual.

gorrión NM sparrow; **de ~** (*Carib*) = **de gorra.**

gorrista* NMF = **gorra 2.**

gorro NM cap; (*de mujer, niño*) bonnet; **~ de baño** bathing cap; **~ de caña** pith helmet; **~ de dormir** nightcap; **~ frigio** Phrygian cap, revolutionary cap; **~ de montaña** Balaclava (helmet); **~ de papel** paper hat; **~ de piel** fur hat; **estar hasta el ~ de*** to be fed up with*; **me hincha el ~⁑** he gets on my wick⁑; **poner el ~ a uno** to embarrass sb; (*Cono Sur, Méx⁑*) to be unfaithful to sb.

gorrón¹ NM **(a)** (*guijarro*) pebble; cobblestone. **(b)** (*Mec*) pivot, journal, gudgeon.

gorrón²* NM = **gorra 2.**

gorrona* NF tart⁑, whore.

gorronear* [1a] [1] VT to scrounge*; **~ algo a uno** to scrounge sth from sb*; **le gorronean los amigos** his friends scrounge off him*.
 [2] VI (*) to cadge, sponge*, scrounge*, live at sb else's expense.

gorroneo* NM cadging, scrounging*.

gorronería* NF **(a)** (*el sablear*) cadging, sponging. **(b)** (*And: avaricia*) avarice, greed.

gospel NM gospel music.

gota NF **(a)** (*gen*) drop; (*de sudor*) bead; (*de pintura*) blob; (*Med*) (*saline etc*) drip; **~s amargas** bitters; **~ a ~** drop by drop; (*fig*) in dribs and drabs; (NM: *Med*) drip, drip-feed; (*Agr*) trickle irrigation; **¡ni ~!** not a bit!; **caer a ~s** to drip; **parecerse como dos ~s de agua** to be as like as two peas; **unas ~s de coñac** a few drops of brandy; **la ~ que colma el vaso** the straw that breaks the camel's back, the last straw; **sudar la ~ gorda** to sweat blood; **no ver ~** not to see a thing.
 (b) (*Med*) gout; **~ caduca, ~ coral** epilepsy.
 (c) (*Met*) **~ fría** cold front.
 (d) **~ de leche** (*LAm: fig*) child welfare clinic, welfare food centre.

goteado ADJ speckled, spotted.

gotear [1a] VI (*destilar*) to drip, dribble; (*escurrir*) to trickle; (*salirse*) to leak; (*vela*) to gutter; (*Met*) to spit, rain lightly.

goteo NM (V v) dripping, dribbling; trickle, trickling; leak; (*Med*) drip.

gotera NF **(a)** (*gotas*) drip; trickle; (*agujero*) leak.
 (b) (*mancha*) mark left by dripping water, stain.
 (c) (*de colgadura*) valance.
 (d) (*Med*) chronic ailment; **estar lleno de ~s** to be full of aches and pains, feel a wreck.
 (e) **~s** (*LAm: afueras*) outskirts, environs.

gotero NM (*Med*) drip, drip-feed; (*LAm Med*) dropper.

goterón NM big raindrop.

gótico [1] ADJ Gothic; (*fig*) noble, illustrious.
 [2] NM (*Ling*) Gothic.

gotita NF droplet; **¡una ~ nada más!** (*al servir bebida*) just a drop!; **hubo dos ~s de lluvia** it rained a drop or two.

gotoso ADJ gouty.

gouache [gwaʃ] NM gouache.

gourmet [gur'me] NM, PL **gourmets** [gur'me] gourmet, connoisseur (of food).

goyesco ADJ **(a)** (*de Goya*) of Goya, pertaining to Goya. **(b)** **estilo artístico** Goy(a)esque, in the style of Goya, after the manner of Goya.

gozada* NF (great) pleasure, delight; **es una ~** it's a real joy.

gozar [1f] [1] VT **(a)** (*disfrutar*) to enjoy; (*poseer*) to have, possess.
 (b) (††) *mujer* to have, enjoy, seduce.
 [2] VI **(a)** (*divertirse*) to enjoy o.s., have a good time; **~ de** to enjoy; to have, possess; **~ de buena salud** to enjoy good health.
 (b) (⁑) to come⁑.
 [3] **gozarse** VR to enjoy o.s.; to rejoice; **~ en** + *infin* to enjoy + *ger*, take pleasure in + *ger*.

gozne NM hinge.

gozo NM **(a)** (*placer*) enjoyment, pleasure; (*complacencia*) delight; (*alegría*) joy, gladness, rejoicing; **es un ~ para los ojos** it's a joy to see, it's a sight for sore eyes; **¡mi ~ en el pozo!** I'm sunk!, it's all ruined!; **no caber** (*en sí*) **de ~** to be beside o.s. with joy, be overjoyed; **da ~ escucharle** it's a pleasure to listen to him.
 (b) **~s** (*Liter, Mús*) verses in honour of the Virgin.

gozosamente ADV joyfully, delightedly.

gozoso ADJ glad, joyful, delighted (*con, de* about).

gozque NM small yapping dog; (*cachorro*) puppy.

g.p. NM ABR *de* **giro postal** postal order, p.o., money order, m.o. (*US*).

gr. ABR *de* **gramos** grams, grammes, gr.

grabación NF recording; **~ en cinta**, **~ magnetofónica** tape-recording; **~ digital** digital recording.

grabado [1] ADJ *música etc* recorded; (*en cinta*) on tape.

[2] NM engraving, print; (*en libro*) illustration, picture, print; (*Inform*) writing; **~ al agua fuerte** etching; **~ al agua tinta** aquatint; **~ en cobre** o **en dulce** copperplate; **~ en madera** woodcut.

grabador [1] NM (*Elec*) tape-recorder.

[2] NM, **grabadora¹** NF (*persona*) engraver.

grabadora² NF (a) (*Téc*) graver, cutting tool. (b) (*Elec etc*) recorder; **~ de cassette**, **~ de cinta** (*LAm*) tape-recorder. (c) (*Com*) recording company.

grabadura NF (act of) engraving.

grabar [1a] VT (a) (*Arte*) to engrave; **~ al agua fuerte** to etch.

(b) (*en cinta, disco*) to record.

(c) (*fig*) to engrave, impress; **~ algo en el ánimo de uno** to impress sth on sb's mind; **la escena está grabada en mi memoria** the scene is engraved on my memory.

gracejada NF (*CAm, Méx*) stupid joke.

gracejo NM (a) (*chispa*) wit; (*encanto*) charm, gracefulness. (b) (*CAm, Méx: payaso*) clown.

▼ **gracia** NF (a) (*garbo*) grace, gracefulness; (*atractivo*) attractiveness; **sin ~** graceless, unattractive.

(b) (*favor*) favour, kindness; **de ~** free, gratis; **hacer a uno ~ de algo** to excuse sb sth, spare sb sth; **te hago ~ de los detalles** I'll spare you the details; **¡vaya ~ que me ha hecho!** (*iró*) some favour he's done me!

(c) (*benevolencia*) graciousness.

(d) (*agrado*) grace, good graces, favour; **caer de la ~ de uno** to lose sb's favour; **me cayó en ~** I took (a liking) to him.

(e) (*Jur*) pardon, mercy.

(f) (*chiste*) joke, witticism.

(g) (*humor*) humour, funniness; (*ingenio*) wit; (*sentido*) point (of a joke); **por ~** in fun, as a joke; **¡qué ~!** how funny!, (*iró*) what a nerve!*, the very idea!; **coger** (o **pescar**) **la ~** to see the point (of a joke); **ha dado en la ~ de decir que ...** he's taken to saying ..., he's taken it into his head to say ...; **ahí está la ~** that's what's so funny about it; **hacer ~ a uno** to amuse sb, strike sb as funny; **no nos hace ~** we are not amused; **no me hace ~ la idea** I'm not keen on the idea; **tener ~** to be funny, be amusing; **el tío tiene mucha ~ hablando*** the chap talks very amusingly*, the fellow is an amusing talker; **si lo haces se va la ~** if you do it it breaks the spell.

(h) (*) first name; **¿cómo es su ~, señorita?** what's your (first) name, miss?

(i) (*Rel*) grace; **~ de Dios** (*fig*) sunshine, fresh air; **por la G~ de Dios** (*en moneda etc*) by the grace of God; **estar en ~** (**de Dios**) to be in a state of grace.

(j) **en ~ a** for the sake of; on account of, because of; **en ~ a la brevedad** for brevity's sake, to be brief.

▼ (k) **~s** thanks; **¡~s!** (*aceptando*) thanks!, thank you!; (*negando*) no thanks!, thank you but no; **¡muchas ~s!**, **¡muchísimas ~s!** many thanks!, thanks very much!; **~s a Dios** thank heaven; **~s a la ayuda de otros** thanks to the help of others; **y ~s si no llegó a más** and we *etc* were lucky to get off so lightly; **~s a que ...** thanks to the fact that ..., because of the fact that ...; **toma eso, ¡y ~s!** take that and be thankful!; **con anticipadas ~s** thanking you in advance; **con repetidas ~s** thanking you again; **dar las ~s a uno por algo** to thank sb for sth.

(l) **las G~s** (*Mit*) the Three Graces.

graciable ADJ (a) (*benévolo*) gracious; (*afable*) affable. (b) *concesión etc* easily granted. (c) *pago* discretionary.

graciablemente ADV (a) graciously; affably. (b) *pagar* on a discretionary basis.

grácil ADJ (*garboso*) graceful; (*esbelto*) slender; (*fino*) small, delicate.

gracilidad NF gracefulness, grace.

graciosamente ADV (V ADJ) (a) gracefully; pleasingly, elegantly. (b) funnily, amusingly; wittily. (c) comically.

graciosidad NF (V ADJ) (a) grace, gracefulness; elegance; beauty. (b) funniness, amusing qualities; wittiness.

gracioso [1] ADJ (a) (*garboso*) graceful; (*atractivo*) pleasing, elegant.

(b) (*chistoso*) funny, amusing; (*ingenioso*) witty; **una situación muy graciosa** a very amusing situation; **¡qué ~!** how funny!; **es un tío de lo más ~** he's a most amusing chap; **lo ~ del caso es que ...** the funny thing about it is that ...

(c) (*gratuito*) free.

[2] NM (*Teat: Hist*) comic character, fool, funny man; **¡no se haga el ~!** don't try to be funny!

grada NF (a) (*peldaño*) step, stair; (*Ecl*) altar step; **~s** (flight of) steps.

(b) (*Dep, Teat etc*) tier, row (of seats).

(c) **~s** (*Náut*) slips, slipway; **~s de construcción** shipyard, ship-

building yard; **~ de lanzamiento** slipway.

(d) (*Agr*) harrow; **~ de disco** disk harrow; **~ de mano** hoe, cultivator.

(e) **~s** (*And, Cono Sur*) paved terrace (in front of a building).

gradación NF (a) (*progresión*) gradation; (*serie*) graded series. (b) (*Retórica*) climax; (*Ling*) comparison.

gradar [1a] VT (*Agr*) to harrow; to hoe.

gradería NF, **graderío** NM (a) (*escalón*) (flight of) steps. (b) (*Dep*) terrace, tiers; (*Teat*) rows (of seats); **~ cubierta** covered stand, grandstand.

grado NM (a) (*peldaño*) step.

(b) (*punto*) degree; (*etapa*) stage, step; (*medida*) measure; (*nivel*) rate; **quemaduras de primer ~** first-degree burns; **el ~ que ahora hemos alcanzado** the stage we have now reached; **está en el segundo ~ de elaboración** it is now in the second stage of production; **~ de velocidad** (rate of) speed; **es lo mismo pero en mayor ~** it's the same only more so; **de ~ en ~**, **por ~s** by degrees, gradually, step by step; **en sumo ~**, **en ~ superlativo** in the highest degree; in the extreme; vastly.

(c) (*calidad*) grade, quality; (*Mil*) rank; **de ~ superior** of superior quality.

(d) (*Escol*) class, year, grade (*US*).

(e) (*Univ*) degree; **~ universitario** university degree.

(f) (*Fís, Geog, Mat*) degree; **~ cero** zero; **~ de latitud** degree of latitude; **en un ángulo de 45 ~s** at an angle of 45 degrees; **la temperatura es de 40 ~s** the temperature is 40 degrees; **este vino es de 12 ~** this wine is 12 degrees proof.

(g) (*Ling*) degree (of comparison).

(h) (*de parentesco*) degree; **dentro de los ~s prohibidos** within the prohibited degrees.

(i) (*gana*) willingness; **de ~**, **de buen ~** willingly; **de mal ~**, **mal de mi ~** unwillingly; **de ~ o por fuerza** willy-nilly.

(j) **~s** (*Ecl*) minor orders.

graduable ADJ adjustable, that can be adjusted.

graduación NF (a) (*acto*) gradation, grading; (*Univ*) graduation.

(b) (*clasificación*) rating, grading; (*de bebida*) alcoholic strength, proof grading; **~ octánica** octane rating.

(c) (*Mil*) rank; **de alta ~** of high rank, high-ranking.

graduado, -a NM/F graduate; **~ escolar** certificate of success in EGB course (*age 14*), school-leaving certificate.

gradual ADJ gradual.

gradualidad NF gradualness.

gradualismo NM (*esp Pol*) gradualism.

gradualista ADJ, NMF gradualist.

gradualmente ADV gradually.

graduando, -a NM/F graduand.

graduar [1e] [1] VT (a) (*clasificar*) to grade, classify (*de, por* as); (*evaluar*) to appraise; (*medir*) to gauge, measure; (*Téc*) to calibrate; *vista* to test; *termómetro etc* to graduate.

(b) (*Univ*) to confer a degree on.

(c) (*Mil*) to confer a rank on, commission; **~ a uno de capitán** to confer the rank of captain on sb.

[2] **graduarse** VR (a) (*Univ*) to graduate, take one's degree; **~ de** to take the degree of.

(b) (*Mil*) to take a commission (*de* as).

GRAE NF ABR *de* **Gramática de la Real Academia Española.**

grafía NF (*Ling*) graph, signs representing the sound of a word; (*ortografía*) (way of) spelling; **se inclina por la ~ 'jira'** he prefers the spelling 'jira'.

gráfica NF (*Mat*) graph; (*diagrama*) diagram; **~ de fiebre**, **~ de temperatura** (*Med*) temperature chart.

graficación NF (a) (*Inform*) graphics. (b) (*Mat*) representation on a graph.

gráficamente ADV graphically.

gráfico [1] ADJ (a) graphic; *revista etc* pictorial, illustrated. (b) (*fig*) graphic, vivid, lively.

[2] NM (*t* **gráfica** NF) (*Mat etc*) graph; diagram; chart; (*Ferro etc*) timetable; **~s** (*Inform*) graphics; **~ de barras** bar graph; **~ de porción de pastel** pie-chart.

grafiosis NF Dutch elm disease.

grafismo NM (*Inform*) computer graphics; (*logotipo*) logo; (*escritura*) graphology; (*Arte*) graphic art.

grafista NMF (*Arte*) graphic artist; (*TV*) graphic designer.

grafiti NMPL graffiti.

grafito NM graphite, black lead.

grafología NF graphology.

grafólogo, -a NM/F graphologist.

gragea NF small coloured sweets; (*Med*) pill.

graja NF rook.

grajea NF (*And*) fine shot, birdshot.

grajear [1a] VI (*Orn*) to caw; (*bebé*) to gurgle.

grajiento ADJ (*LAm*) sweaty, smelly.

▶ LENGUA Y USO: **gracia: k** → 48.1, 49, 52.1, 52.4

grajilla NF jackdaw.

grajo NM (**a**) (*Orn*) rook. (**b**) (*LAm*) body odour, smell of sweat; underarm odour.

Gral. ABR *de* **General** General, Gen.

grama NF (*esp LAm*) grass; (*Carib**: *césped*) lawn.

gramaje NM weight (*of paper etc*).

gramática[1] NF (**a**) grammar; **~ generativa** generative grammar; **~ profunda** deep grammar; **~ transformacional** transformational grammar. (**b**) **~ parda** native wit, horse-sense; **andar a la ~** to look out for o.s.

gramatical ADJ grammatical.

gramático [1] ADJ grammatical.
[2] NM, **gramática**[2] NF grammarian.

gramil NM (*Téc*) gauge.

gramilla NF (*LAm: césped*) grass, lawn; turf.

gramillar NM (*Cono Sur*) meadow, grassland.

gramínea NF grass; (*LAm*) pulse.

gramo NM gramme, gram (*US*).

gramófono NM gramophone, phonograph (*US*).

gramola NF gramophone, phonograph (*US*); (*en café etc*) jukebox.

grampa NF (*LAm*) = **grapa**.

gran ADJ *V* **grande**.

grana[1] NF (*Bot*) (**a**) (*semilla*) small seed; **dar en ~** to go to seed, run to seed. (**b**) (*acto*) seeding; (*estación*) seeding time. (**c**) (*LAm: pasto*) grass; (*CAm, Méx: Dep*) turf.

grana[2] NF (*Zool etc*) cochineal; (*tinte*) kermes; (*color*) scarlet; (*tela*) scarlet cloth; **de ~** scarlet, bright red; **ponerse como la ~** to turn scarlet.

Granada NF (*Carib*) Grenada.

granada NF (**a**) (*Bot: fruta*) pomegranate. (**b**) (*Mil*) shell; grenade; **~ anticarro** anti-tank grenade; **~ detonadora** stun grenade; **~ fallida** dud shell; **~ de fragmentación** fragmentation grenade; **~ de humo** smoke-bomb; **~ lacrimógena** teargas grenade; **~ de mano** hand-grenade; **~ de metralla** shrapnel shell; **a prueba de ~** shellproof.

granadero NM (*Mil*) grenadier; **~s** (*Méx: policía*) riot police.

granadilla NF (*flor*) passionflower; (*fruta*) passion fruit.

granadino [1] ADJ of Granada.
[2] NM, **granadina** NF native (*o* inhabitant) of Granada; **los ~s** the people of Granada.

granado[1] NM (*Bot*) pomegranate tree.

granado[2] ADJ (**a**) (*selecto*) fine, choice, select; (*maduro*) mature; (*notable*) distinguished, illustrious; **lo más ~ de** the cream of, the pick of. (**b**) (*alto*) tall, full-grown.

granangular ADJ: **objetivo ~** wide-angle lens.

granar [1a] VI to seed, run to seed.

granate [1] NM garnet.
[2] ADJ INVAR deep red, dark crimson.

granazón NF seeding.

Gran Bretaña NF Great Britain.

grancanario [1] ADJ of Grand Canary.
[2] NM, **grancanaria** NF native (*o* inhabitant) of Grand Canary; **los ~s** the people of Grand Canary.

grande [1] ADJ (**gran** *delante de nmf sing*) (**a**) (*de tamaño*) big, large; (*de estatura*) big, tall; *número, velocidad etc* high, great; (*LAm: mayor*) *persona* old, elderly; **el gran Buenos Aires** greater Buenos Aires; **~ como una montaña** as big as a house; **en cantidades más ~s** in larger quantities; **hay una diferencia no muy ~** there is not a very big difference; **los zapatos le están (muy) ~s** the shoes are too big for her; **con gran placer** with great pleasure; **¿cómo es de ~?** how big is it?, what size is it?; **lo hace por lo ~** he does it in style.
(**b**) (*moralmente etc*) great; **un gran hombre** a great man; **fue una gran hazaña** it was a great achievement.
(**c**) (*impresionante*) grand, grandiose, impressive.
(**d**) **en ~** (*en conjunto*) as a whole; (*en gran escala*) on a large scale, on a grand scale, in a big way; **estar en ~** to be going strong; **pasarlo en ~*** to have a tremendous time*; **hacer algo en ~*** to do sth in style, make a splash doing sth*; **vivir en ~*** to live in style.
(**e**) **¡qué ~!** how funny!
[2] ADV (*Cono Sur**) much, a lot.
[3] NM (**a**) **los ~s** the great; **los ~s de la industria** the major companies in the industry; **uno de los ~s de la pantalla** one of the screen greats; **los siete ~s (bancos)** the Big Seven.
(**b**) **~ (de España)** grandee.
(**c**) (**‡**) 1000-peseta note; **3 de los ~s*** 3000 pesetas.
[4] NF (**a**) (*Cono Sur*) first prize, big prize (*in the lottery*).
(**b**) (*And, Cono Sur*) naughty thing, misdeed.
(**c**) (*And*‡) clink‡, jail.
[5] NMF (*LAm: adulto*) adult.

grandemente ADV greatly, extremely; **~ equivocado** greatly mistaken.

grandeza NF (**a**) (*gran tamaño*) bigness; size, magnitude.
(**b**) (*moral*) greatness.

(**c**) (*lo impresionante etc*) grandness, grandiose quality, impressiveness; grandeur, magnificence.
(**d**) (*rango*) status of grandee.
(**e**) (*personas*) grandees (*collectively*), nobility.

grandilocuencia NF grandiloquence.

grandilocuente ADJ (*LAm*) boastful, arrogant.

grandílocuo ADJ grandiloquent.

grandiosidad NF = **grandeza (c)**.

grandioso ADJ grand, impressive, magnificent; (*pey*) grandiose.

grandísimo ADJ SUPERL *de* **grande** (*hum, iró*) great big, huge; **un coche ~** a whacking great car*, a car and a half*; **¡~ tunante!** you old crook!

grandón ADJ solidly-built.

grandor NM size.

grandote ADJ great big, huge.

grandullón* ADJ overgrown, oversized.

grandulón ADJ (*And*) = **grandullón**.

grandura NF (*Cono Sur*) = **grandeza (b)** *y* (**c**).

granear [1a] VT (**a**) *semilla* to sow. (**b**) (*Arte*) to grain, stipple.

granel NM (*montón*) heap of corn; (*Com*) bulk commodity, commodity in bulk; **a ~** (*en abundancia*) in abundance; (*a montones*) by the score, by the ton; (*con profusión*) lavishly; (*al azar*) at random; (*Com*) in bulk, loose; in quantity; **vino a ~** wine in bulk, wine in the barrel.

granelero NM (*Náut*) bulk-carrier.

granero NM granary, barn; (*fig*) granary, corn-producing area.

granetario NM precision balance.

granete NM (*Téc*) punch.

granguiñolesco ADJ melodramatic, exaggerated.

granilla NF grain (*in cloth*).

granítico ADJ granitic, granite (*atr*).

granito[1] NM (*Geol*) granite.

granito[2] NM (*Agr etc*) small grain; granule; (*Med*) pimple.

granizada NF (**a**) (*Met*) hail, hailstorm. (**b**) (*fig*) hail; shower, volley; vast number; **una ~ de balas** a hail of bullets. (**c**) (*And, Cono Sur: bebida*) iced drink.

granizado NM iced drink; **~ de café** iced coffee.

granizal NM (*LAm*) hailstorm.

granizar [1f] VI to hail; (*fig*) to rain, shower.

granizo NM hail.

granja NF (*gen*) farm; (*cortijo*) farmhouse; (*lechería*) dairy; **~ avícola** chicken farm, poultry farm; **~ colectiva** collective farm; **~ escuela** educational farm; **~ marina** fish-farm.

granjear [1a] [1] VT to gain, earn; to win; (*And, Cono Sur: robar*) to steal.
[2] **granjearse** VR *afecto, antipatía etc* to win for o.s., gain for o.s.

granjería NF (**a**) (*Com, Fin*) profits, earnings; (*Agr*) farm earnings. (**b**) (*Agr*) farming, husbandry.

granjero NM farmer.

grano NM (**a**) (*Agr, Bot*) grain; (*semilla*) seed; (*baya*) berry; **~s** grain, corn, cereals; **~ de arroz** grain of rice; **~ de cacao** cocoa bean; **~ de café** coffee-bean; **~ de polen** pollen grain; **~ de sésamo** sesame seed; **~ de trigo** grain of wheat; **~s panificables** bread grains; **no es ~ de anís*** it isn't peanuts*, it's no small matter; **tomarlo con un ~ de sal** to take it with a pinch of salt; **ir al ~** to get to the point, get down to brass tacks; **¡vamos al ~!** let's get on with it!
(**b**) (*partícula*) particle, grain; (*punto*) speck; **~ de arena** grain of sand; **no es ~ de anís** (*o* **arena**) it's not just a small thing, you can't laugh this one off; **poner su ~ de arena** (*fig*) to make one's contribution.
(**c**) (*en madera, piedra etc*) grain; **de ~ fino** fine-grained; **de ~ gordo** coarse-grained.
(**d**) (*Med*) pimple, spot.
(**e**) (*Farm*) grain.
(**f**) (**‡**: *droga*) fix‡, shot*.

granoso ADJ granular; granulated; grainy.

granuja [1] NF loose grapes; grape seed.
[2] NM urchin, ragamuffin; rogue.

granujada NF dirty trick; **hacer una ~** to pull a fast one; **es una ~** it's a low-down thing to do.

granujería NF urchins (*collectively*), rogues (*collectively*).

granujiento ADJ, **granujoso** ADJ pimply, spotty.

granulación NF granulation.

granulado [1] ADJ granulated.
[2] NM: **~ vitamínico** vitamin powder.

granular[1] ADJ granular.

granular[2] [1a] [1] VT to granulate.
[2] **granularse** VR (**a**) to granulate, become granulated. (**b**) (*Med*) to break out in pimples, become spotty.

gránulo NM granule.

granuloso ADJ granular.

grapa[1] NF (*para papeles*) staple; clip, fastener; (*Mec*) dog, clamp;

(*Arquit*) cramp.

grapa² NF (*Cono Sur*) grape liquor, grappa.

grapadora NF stapler, stapling machine.

grapar [1a] VT *papeles* to staple.

GRAPO ['grapo] NMPL (*Esp Pol*) ABR *de* **Grupos de Resistencia Antifascista Primero de Octubre.**

grapo NMF member of GRAPO.

grasa ① NF (a) (*gen*) grease; (*Culin*) fat; (*sebo*) suet; **~ de ballena** blubber; **~ de pescado** fish oil; **~ saturada** saturated fat; **~ vegetal** vegetable fat; **alimentos bajos en ~s** low-fat foods.
(b) (*Aut, Mec*) oil; grease; **~ para ejes** axle grease.
(c) (*Anat*) fat, fattiness; **tener mucha ~** to be very fat.
(d) (*Méx*) shoe polish.
(e) (*pey*) grease, greasy dirt, filth.
(f) **~s** (*Min*) slag.
② ADJ (*Cono Sur*: *pey*) common.
③ NM: **es un ~** (*Cono Sur*) he's common.

grasiento ADJ (*grasoso*) greasy, oily; (*resbaladizo*) greasy, slippery; (*pey*) filthy.

graso ① ADJ fatty; greasy; *comida* oily.
② NM fattiness; greasiness; oiliness.

grasoso ADJ (*graso*) fatty; (*grasiento*) greasy.

grata NF (*Com*): **su ~ del 8** your letter of the 8th.

gratamente ADV pleasingly, pleasantly, agreeably; gratifyingly.

gratificación NF (a) (*Fin etc*) (*recompensa*) reward, recompense; (*propina*) tip; gratuity; (*de sueldo*) bonus (on wages); bounty. (b) (*esp LAm*) gratification, pleasure, satisfaction.

gratificador ADJ (*LAm*) gratifying; pleasurable, satisfying.

gratificante ADJ gratifying.

gratificar [1g] VT (a) (*Fin etc*) to reward, recompense; to tip, give a gratuity to; to give a bonus to, pay extra to; **'se gratificará'** 'a reward is offered'.
(b) (*satisfacer*) to gratify; (*contentar*) to give pleasure to, satisfy; *anhelo* to gratify, indulge.

gratinado ① ADJ au gratin.
② NM dish cooked au gratin.

gratinador NM overhead grill.

gratinar [1a] VT to cook au gratin.

gratis ADV gratis, free, for nothing; **'entrada ~'** 'admission free'; **de ~** (*LAm*) gratis.

gratitud NF gratitude.

grato ADJ (a) (*placentero*) pleasing, pleasant; (*agradable*) agreeable; (*satisfactorio*) welcome, gratifying; **una decisión muy grata para todos** a very welcome decision for everybody; **recibir una impresión grata** to get a pleasing impression; **nos es ~ informarle que ...** we are pleased to inform you that ...
(b) (*And, Cono Sur*: *agradecido*) grateful; **le estoy ~** (*frm*) I am most grateful to you.

gratuidad NF cost-free status.

gratuitamente ADV (a) (*gratis*) free, for nothing. (b) *comentar* gratuitously; *acusar* unfoundedly.

gratuito ADJ (a) (*gratis*) free, free of charge. (b) *observación etc* gratuitous, uncalled-for; *acusación* unfounded, unjustified.

gratulatorio ADJ congratulatory.

grava NF (*guijos*) gravel; (*piedra molida*) crushed stone; (*de carretera*) road metal.

gravable ADJ taxable, subject to tax.

gravamen NM (*carga*) burden, obligation; (*Jur*) lien, encumbrance; (*Fin*) tax, impost; **libre de ~** unencumbered, free from encumbrances; **~ bancario** banker's lien; **~ general** general lien; **~ del vendedor** vendor's lien.

gravar [1a] ① VT (*cargar*) to burden, encumber (*de* with); (*Jur*) *propiedad* to place a lien upon; (*Fin*) to assess for tax; **~ con impuestos** to burden with taxes; **~ un producto con un impuesto** to place a tax on a product; **los impuestos que gravan esta vivienda** the taxes to which this dwelling is subject; **el préstamo y el interés que se le grava** the loan and the interest charged upon it.
② **gravarse** VR (*LAm*) to get worse, become more serious.

gravativo ADJ burdensome.

grave ADJ (a) (*pesado*) heavy, weighty.
(b) (*fig*) (*serio*) grave, serious; (*espinoso*) critical; (*importante*) important, momentous; *pérdida etc* grave, severe, grievous; **un deber muy ~** a very grave duty; **la situación es ~** the situation is grave (o critical); **me es muy ~ tener que** + *infin* it is a very serious matter for me to + *infin*.
(c) (*de carácter*) serious, sedate, dignified; **y otros hombres ~s** and other worthy men.
(d) (*Med*) *enfermedad, estado,* grave serious; *herida* severe; **estar ~** to be seriously ill, be critically ill.
(e) (*Mús*) *nota, tono,* low, deep; *voz* deep.
(f) (*Ling*) *acento* grave; *palabra* paroxytone, stressed on the penulti-

mate syllable (*p.ej. padre, romance*).

gravedad NF (a) (*Fís*) gravity; **~ nula** zero gravity.
(b) (*fig*) gravity, seriousness; (*grandeza*) importance; (*severidad*) severity, grievousness.
(c) (*dignidad*) seriousness, dignity.
(d) (*Med*) gravity; **estar de ~** to be seriously ill, be dangerously ill; **estar herido de ~** to be severely injured (o wounded); **tiene heridas de ~** he has serious injuries; **parece que la lesión es sin ~** it seems that the injury is not serious.
(e) (*Mús*) depth.

gravemente ADV gravely, seriously; critically; severely, grievously; **habló ~** he spoke gravely; **estar ~ enfermo** to be critically ill.

gravera NF gravel bed, gravel pit.

gravidez NF pregnancy; **en estado de ~** pregnant.

grávido ADJ (a) (*embarazado*) pregnant; (*Zool*) with young, carrying young.
(b) (*fig*) full (*de* of), heavy (*de* with); **me sentí ~ de emociones** I was heavy with emotions, I was weighed down with emotions.

gravilla NF gravel.

gravitación NF gravitation.

gravitacional ADJ gravitational.

gravitante ADJ (*fig*) menacing.

gravitar [1a] VI (a) (*Fís*) to gravitate (*hacia* towards). (b) **~ sobre** to rest on; (*caer sobre*) to bear down on, weigh down on; (*fig*: *pesar sobre*) to be a burden to; to encumber.

gravitatorio ADJ gravitational.

gravoso ADJ (a) (*molesto*) burdensome, oppressive, onerous; **ser ~ a** to be a burden to, weigh on.
(b) (*Fin*) costly, expensive; *precio* extortionate.
(c) (*insufrible*) tiresome, vexatious.

graznar [1a] VI (*gen*) to squawk; (*cuervo*) to caw, croak; (*ganso*) to cackle; (*pato*) to quack; (*cantante*: *hum*) to croak.

graznido NM squawk; caw, croak; cackle; quack.

grébano NM (*Cono Sur*: *pey*) Italian, wop‡.

greca NF (*franja, orla*) border.

Grecia NF Greece.

greco (*liter*) = **griego.**

grecochipriota ADJ, NMF Greek-Cypriot.

greda NF (*Geol*) clay; (*Téc*) fuller's earth.

gredal NM claypit.

gredoso ADJ clayey.

green [grin] NM, PL **greens** [grin] (*Golf*) green.

gregario ① ADJ (a) gregarious; **instinto ~** herd instinct. (b) (*fig*) servile, slavish.
② NM (*Dep*) domestic.

gregarismo NM gregariousness.

gregoriano ADJ Gregorian; **canto ~** Gregorian chant.

Gregorio NM Gregory.

greguería NF (a) hubbub, uproar, hullabaloo. (b) (*Liter*) *brief, humorous and often mildly poetic comment or aphorism about life.*

grelos NMPL parsnip tops, turnip tops.

gremial ① ADJ (a) (*Hist*) guild (*atr*). (b) (*Pol*: *sindical*) trade-union (*atr*), trades-union (*atr*); (*LAm*) trade (*atr*).
② NMF (*miembro*) union member.

gremialista NMF trade unionist.

gremio NM (a) (*Hist*) guild, corporation, company. (b) (*Pol*: *sindicato*) union; **~ obrero, ~ de obreros** trade union, trades union. (c) **ella es del ~*** she's on the game*.

greña NF (a) (*t ~s*) (*cabellos revueltos*) shock of hair, mat (o mop) of hair, matted hair.
(b) (*fig*) tangle, entanglement; **andar a la ~** to bicker, squabble; **estar a la ~ con uno** to be at daggers drawn with sb.
(c) **en ~** (*Méx*) *seda* raw; *plata* unpolished; *azúcar* unrefined.

greñudo ADJ *pelo* tangled, matted; *persona* dishevelled.

gres NM (a) (*Geol*) potter's clay. (b) (*alfarería*) earthenware, stoneware.

gresca NF uproar, hubbub; row, shindy*; **andar a la ~** to row, brawl.

grey NF (*Ecl*) flock, congregation.

Grial NM: **Santo ~** Holy Grail.

griego ① ADJ Greek, Grecian.
② NM, **griega** NF (a) Greek.
(b) (*) cheat.
③ NM (*Ling*) (a) Greek; **~ antiguo** ancient Greek.
(b) (* *fig*) gibberish, double Dutch*; **para mí es ~** it's Greek to me; **hablar en ~*** to talk double Dutch*.
(c) (⁝) anal intercourse.

grieta NF fissure, crack; chink; crevice; chasm; (*de piel*) chap, crack; (*Pol etc*) rift.

grietarse [1a] VR = **agrietarse.**

grifa‡ ① NF hash*, pot‡, (*esp*) Moroccan marijuana.
② NMF (*Méx**) drug addict.

grifear‡ [1a] VI to smoke pot‡.

grifería¹ NF plumbing, fixtures, taps (*collectively*), faucets (*collectively*:

US).

grifería² NF (Carib‡) Negroes (collectively).

grifero NM (And) petrol-pump attendant.

grifo¹ NM **(a)** tap, faucet (US); cock; (Cono Sur) fire hydrant; **cerveza (servida) al ~** draught beer, beer on draught; **cerrar el ~** (fig) to turn off the tap, cut off the funds. **(b)** (LAm: surtidor de gasolina) petrol-pump; (And: gasolinera) petrol-station, gas station (US); (bar) dive‡; drink shop.

grifo²‡ ① ADJ **(a)** (Méx) (borracho) drunk, plastered‡; (drogado) high‡, doped up; (loco) nuts‡, crazy.
(b) (And: engreído) snobbish, stuck-up*.
② NM **(a)** (droga) pot‡, hash*.
(b) (drogado) marijuana addict, pot smoker‡.
(c) (borracho) drunkard.

grifo³ (Carib) ① ADJ **(a)** pelo curly, kinky. **(b)** persona (euf) coloured, black.
② NM **(a)** kinky hair. **(b)** (euf) Negro, coloured person.

grifo⁴ NM (Mit) griffin.

grifón NM (perro) griffon; (mítico) gryphon.

grifota‡ NMF pot-smoker‡.

grigallo NM blackcock.

grill [gril] NM (aparato) grill; (local) grillroom; **asar al ~** to grill.

grilla NF **(a)** (Ent) female cricket; **¡ésa es ~ (y no canta)!*** that's a likely story!; **dice la ~ que ...** (Méx) there's word going round that ... **(b)** (And: pleito) row, quarrel.

grillado‡ ADJ barmy‡.

grilladura‡ NF barminess‡.

grillera NF **(a)** (jaula) cage for crickets; (nido) cricket hole. **(b)** (fig) madhouse, bedlam. **(c)** (‡) police wagon.

grillete NM fetter, shackle.

grillo NM **(a)** (Ent) cricket; **~ cebollero, ~ real** mole cricket. **(b)** (Bot) shoot, sprout. **(c)** ~s (grilletes) fetters, shackles, irons; (*: esposas) handcuffs; (fig) shackles.

grilo‡ NM **(a)** (cárcel) nick‡, jail. **(b)** (bolsillo) pocket; **~ bueno** right-hand pocket.

grima NF **(a)** (asco), loathing, disgust; (aversión) aversion, reluctance; (inquietud) uneasiness; (molestia) annoyance, irritation, displeasure; **un dato de ~** a really shattering piece of information; **me da ~** it gets on my nerves, it gives me the shivers; it sickens me.
(b) **una ~ de licor** (Cono Sur) just a drop (of spirits).
(c) **en ~** (And) alone.

grimillón NM (Cono Sur) lot, heap.

grímpola NF pennant.

gringada‡ NF, **gringaje‡** NM (Cono Sur) dirty foreigners; (grupo) group of dirty foreigners.

gringo ① ADJ **(a)** (LAm) foreign (V 2).
(b) (LAm) lenguaje foreign, unintelligible.
(c) (And, Cono Sur) blond(e), fair.
② NM, **gringa** NF **(a)** (LAm) (extranjero) dirty foreigner; (†: británico) Briton, Anglo-Saxon; (norteamericano) North American, Yankee; (Cono Sur: italiano) Italian, wop‡.
(b) (And, Cono Sur: rubio) blond(e), fair-haired person.
③ NM (LAm*: Ling) gibberish, unintelligible speech; **hablar en ~** to talk double Dutch*.

┌─ **GRINGO** ──┐
ⓘ The word **gringo** is a derogatory term used in Latin America to refer to white English-speakers, usually Americans, especially in the context of alleged economic, cultural and political interference in Latin America. One rather fanciful theory traces its origin to the Mexican-American War of 1846-48 and the song "Green Grow the Rushes-oh", supposedly sung by the American troops. According to another theory it is a corruption of **griego** or "Greek", in the sense of anything foreign and unintelligible, as in the English expression "it's all Greek to me".
└──┘

gringolandia* NF (LAm: pey) the USA, Yankeedom*.

gringuería NF (LAm) group of gringos.

gripa NF (Méx) = **gripe**.

gripaje NM (Mec) seize-up.

gripal ADJ flu (atr).

gripar* [1a] VI to seize up.

gripazo NM attack of flu.

gripe* NF influenza, flu; **~ asiática** Asian flu; **~ del cerdo** swine fever.

griposo ADJ: **estar ~** to have flu.

gris ① ADJ grey; día, tiempo grey, dull; **~ carbón** charcoal grey; **~ ceniza** ash-grey; **~ marengo** (tela) dark grey; **~ perla** pearl-grey.
② NM **(a)** grey; **hace un ~** there's a cold wind. **(b)** (‡) cop*; **los ~es** the fuzz‡.

grisáceo ADJ greyish.

grisalla NF (Méx) rubbish; scrap metal.

grisma NF (Cono Sur) strand, shred, bit.

grisoso ADJ (LAm) greyish.

gristapo‡ NF (hum) police.

grisú NM firedamp.

grisura NF greyness; dullness.

grita NF uproar, hubbub; shouting; (Teat) catcalls, booing; **dar ~ a** to boo, hoot (at).

gritadera NF (LAm) loud shouting, clamour.

gritar [1a] VTI to shout, yell; to scream, shriek, cry out; (Teat etc) to hoot, boo; **¡no grites!** stop shouting!

gritería NF **(a)** = **griterío**. **(b)** (CAm Rel) festival of the Virgin.

griterío NM shouting, uproar, clamour.

grito NM **(a)** shout, yell; scream, shriek, cry; (Teat etc) hoot, boo; (Zool) cry, sound; (Orn) call, cry; **a ~s, a ~ herido, a ~ pelado, a voz en ~** at the top of one's voice; **dar ~s** to shout out, cry out; **llorar a ~s** to weep and wail; **poner el ~ en el cielo** to make a great fuss, scream blue murder*; **es el último ~** it's the very latest; **es el último ~ del lujo** it's the last word in luxury.
(b) (LAm) proclamation; **~ de independencia** proclamation of independence; **el ~ de Dolores** the proclamation of Mexican independence (1810).

gritón ADJ loud-mouthed; screaming, shouting.

gro NM grosgrain.

groenlandés ① ADJ Greenland (atr).
② NM, **groenlandesa** NF Greenlander.

Groenlandia NF Greenland.

groggy ['grogi] ADJ, **grogui** ADJ (Boxeo etc) groggy; (fig) shattered, shocked, in a state of shock.

groncho‡ NM (Cono Sur: pey) worker.

grosella NF (red)currant; **~ espinosa** gooseberry; **~ negra** blackcurrant; **~ colorada, ~ roja** redcurrant.

grosellero NM currant bush; **~ espinoso** gooseberry bush.

groseramente ADV (descortésmente) rudely, discourteously; (ordinariamente) coarsely, crudely, vulgarly, indelicately; (toscamente) roughly, loutishly; grossly, stupidly.

grosería NF **(a)** (gen) rudeness, discourtesy; (ordinariez) coarseness, crudeness, vulgarity; (tosquedad) roughness; (estupidez) stupidity.
(b) (observación etc) rude thing, coarse thing, vulgar remark (etc); (palabrota) swearword.

grosero ADJ (descortés) rude, discourteous; (ordinario) coarse, crude, vulgar; (indecente) indelicate; (maleducado) rough, loutish; error etc gross, stupid.

grosor NM thickness.

grosura NF fat, suet.

grotesca NF (Tip) sans serif.

grotescamente ADV grotesquely; bizarrely, absurdly.

grotesco ADJ grotesque; bizarre, absurd.

grúa NF (Téc) crane; derrick; (Aut) tow-truck, towing vehicle; break-down truck; **~ corredera, ~ corrediza, ~ móvil** travelling crane; **~ de pescante** jib crane; **~ (de) puente** gantry crane, overhead crane; **~ de torre** tower crane.

gruesa NF gross, twelve dozen.

grueso ① ADJ **(a)** (espeso) thick; (voluminoso) bulky, stout, massive, solid; (grande, pesado) big, heavy; persona stout, thickset; artillería, mar, heavy; intestino large; tronco etc thick, massive.
(b) tela etc coarse.
② NM **(a)** (calidad) thickness; (tamaño) bulkiness, bulk, size; (densidad) density.
(b) (parte principal) thick part; main part, major portion; (de multitud, tropas etc) main body, mass; **el ~ del pelotón** (Dep) the ruck of the runners; **va mezclado con el ~ del pasaje** he is mingling with the mass of the passengers.
(c) **en ~** (Com) in bulk.

grujidor NM glass cutter, glazier.

grulla¹ NF (Orn: t ~ común) crane.

grullo ① ADJ **(a)** (*) uncouth, rough.
(b) (Méx) sponging*, cadging.
(c) (CAm, Méx) caballo, mula grey.
② NM, **grulla²** NM bumpkin, yokel.
③ NM (Méx) grey (horse); (Cono Sur) big colt, large stallion.

grumete NM cabin boy, ship's boy.

grumo NM **(a)** (coágulo) clot, lump; (masa) dollop; (de sangre) clot; **~ de leche** curd. **(b)** (de uvas etc) bunch, cluster.

grumoso ADJ clotted; lumpy.

gruñido NM grunt, growl; snarl; (fig) grouse*, grumble; **dar ~s** = **gruñir**.

gruñidor ① ADJ grunting, growling; snarling; (fig) grumbling.
② NM, **gruñidora** NF (fig) grumbler.

gruñir [3h] VI to grunt, growl; to snarl; (fig) to grouse*, grumble; (puerta etc) to creak.

gruñón ① ADJ grumpy, grumbling.
② NM, **gruñona** NF grumbler.

grupa NF hindquarters, rump (of horse).

grupal ADJ group (atr).

grupalmente ADV in groups.

grupera NF (*de caballo*) pillion (seat); **ir en la ~** to sit behind the rider, be carried on the horse's rump.

grupi: NF groupie*.

grupín* NM (*Cono Sur*) crook*; embezzler; (*en subasta*) false bidder.

grupo NM **(a)** (*gen*) group; (*de árboles etc*) cluster, clump; (*Pol*) group; **~ avanzado** advance party; **~ (de) control** control group; **~ del dólar** dollar block; **~ de encuentro** encounter group; **~ de estafas** fraud squad; **~ de estupefacientes** drug squad; **~ de homicidios** murder squad; **~ de presión** pressure group; **~ de riesgo** high-risk group; **~ sanguíneo** blood-group; **~ testigo** control group; **~ de trabajo** working party; **discusión en ~** group discussion; **reunirse en ~s** to gather in groups; **reunirse en ~ en torno a** to gather round, cluster round.

(b) (*Elec, Téc etc*) unit, set, plant; assembly; **~ compresor** compressor unit; **~ dental** dentist's operating equipment; **~ electrógeno, ~ generador** generating set, power plant.

(c) (**:** *trampista*) con man's accomplice*; (*Cono Sur: trampa*) trick, con*.

grupúsculo NM (*Pol*) small group, splinter group.

gruta NF cavern, grotto.

Gta. (*Aut*) ABR *de* **glorieta** roundabout, traffic circle (*US*).

gua INTERJ (*LAm: inquietud*) oh dear!; (*sorpresa*) well!; (*desdén*) get away!*.

gua...: *para diversas palabras escritas así en LAm*, V t **hua...**

guabiroba NF (*Cono Sur*) dugout canoe.

guaca NF **(a)** (*LAm: tumba*) (Indian) tomb, funeral mound; (*tesoro*) buried treasure; (*riqueza*) wealth, money; (*de armas, droga*) cache; (*And, CAm, Carib, Méx: alcancía*) moneybox; **hacer ~** (*And, Carib, Méx:*) to make money, make one's pile*; **hacer su ~** (*Carib, Cono Sur*) to make hay while the sun shines.

(b) (*Carib*: reprimenda*) ticking-off*.

(c) (*Méx: escopeta*) double-barrelled shotgun.

(d) (*Carib Med*) large sore.

guacal NM (*LAm*) (*cajón*) wooden crate; (*calabaza*) gourd, vessel.

guacamarón NM (*Carib*) brave man.

guacamayo [1] ADJ (*Cono Sur*:* †) dressed garishly.

[2] NM **(a)** (*Orn*) macaw. **(b)** (*Carib: pey*) Spaniard.

guacamole NM (*Méx*) guacamole, avocado sauce.

guacamote NM (*Méx Bot*) yucca plant.

guacarnaco ADJ **(a)** (*And, Carib, Cono Sur*) silly, stupid. **(b)** (*Cono Sur*) long-legged.

guachada NF (*LAm*) dirty trick.

guachafita NF (*Carib*) **(a)** (*ruido*) hubbub, din; (*desorden*) disorder. **(b)** (*garito*) gambling joint:. **(c)** (*mofa*) mockery, jeering.

guachaje NM (*Cono Sur*) orphaned animal; group of calves separated from their mothers.

guachalomo NM (*Cono Sur*) sirloin steak.

guachapear [1a] [1] VT **(a)** *agua* to dabble in, splash about in.

(b) (*estropear*) to botch, mess up, bungle.

(c) (*Cono Sur**) to pinch*, borrow.

(d) (*And*) *maleza* to clear, cut.

[2] VI to rattle, clatter, bang about.

guachar [1a] VT (*Méx*) to watch.

guáchara* NF (*Carib*) lie.

guácharo NM (*CAm Orn*) nightingale.

guache*¹ NM (*And, Carib: persona rural*) rustic, peasant; (*pey*) layabout, loafer.

guache² NM (*Arte*) gouache.

guachicar(ro) NM (*Méx*) parking attendant.

guachimán NM (*LAm*) watchman.

guachinanga NF (*Carib*) wooden bar (on door *etc*).

guachinango [1] ADJ **(a)** (*And*: zalamero*) smooth; slimy. **(b)** (*Carib**) sharp, clever; smooth-tongued.

[2] NM **(a)** (*Carib: pey*) Mexican. **(b)** (*Carib: persona astuta*) clever person. **(c)** (*Ling*) Latin-American colloquial Spanish.

guacho [1] ADJ (*esp And, Cono Sur*) **(a)** *persona* (*sin casa*) homeless; *niño* abandoned; *animal* motherless.

(b) *zapato etc* odd.

(c) (*Méx:*) *capitalino*) of Mexico City.

[2] NM **(a)** (*Orn*) baby bird, chick.

(b) (*And, Cono Sur*) (*niño abandonado*) homeless child, abandoned child; (*huérfano*) orphan, foundling; (*bastardo*) illegitimate child, (*pey*) bastard; (*Agr*) motherless animal.

(c) (*Cono Sur, And*: *objeto*) odd one (of a pair).

(d) (*Méx:*) *capitalino*) person from Mexico City.

guadal NM (*And, Cono Sur*) sandy bog.

guadalajareño [1] ADJ of Guadalajara.

[2] NM, **guadalajarense** NF, **guadalajereña** NF native (*o* inhabitant) of Guadalajara; **los ~s** the people of Guadalajara.

guadaloso ADJ (*Cono Sur*) boggy.

Guadalquivir NM: **el** (*Río*) **~** the Guadalquivir.

guadamecí NM embossed leather.

guadaña NF scythe.

guadañadora NF mowing machine.

guadañar [1a] VT to scythe, mow.

guadañero NM mower.

guadaño NM (*Carib, Méx*) lighter, small harbour boat.

Guadiana NM: **el** (*Río*) **~** the Guadiana; **aparece y desaparece como el ~** it keeps coming and going; now you see it now you don't.

guadianesco ADJ sporadic, intermittent; will-o'-the-wisp-like.

guágara* NF: **echar ~** (*Méx*) to gossip, chew the fat.

guagua¹ NF (*Carib, Canarias*) bus.

guagua² [1] ADJ (*And*) small, little.

[2] NF (*a veces t* NM) **(a)** (*LAm: bebé*) baby. **(b)** (*bagatela*) trifle, small thing; **de ~** (*Carib, Méx*) free, for nothing.

guaguarear [1a] VI (*CAm, Méx*) to babble, chatter.

guaguatear [1a] VT (*CAm, Cono Sur*) to carry in one's arms.

guaguatera NF (*Cono Sur*) nurse.

guagüero (*Carib*) [1] ADJ **(a)** sponging*, parasitical. **(b)** bus (*atr*).

[2] NM, **guagüera** NF **(a)** bus-driver. **(b)** (*pey*) scrounger*, sponger*.

guai* ADJ = **guay**.

guaica NF (*Cono Sur: cuenta*) rosary bead; (*And: collar*) bead necklace.

guaico NM (*And*) (*hondonada*) hollow, dip; (*hoyo*) ravine; (*barranco*) hole, pit; (*avalancha*) avalanche; (*estercolero*) dung heap; (*basurero*) rubbish tip, garbage tip (*US*).

guaina [1] NF (*Cono Sur*) girl, young woman.

[2] NM (*And*) youth, young man.

guaino NM (*And, Cono Sur: Dep*) jockey.

guaipe NM (*LAm*) wiper, cloth, cotton waste.

guáiper NM (*CAm*) windscreen wiper, windshield wiper (*US*).

guaira NF (*a*) (*CAm Mús*) Indian flute. **(b)** (*And, Cono Sur*) earthenware smelting furnace (*for silver ore*).

guairana NF **(a)** (*And: de cal*) limekiln. **(b)** = **guaira**.

guairo NM (*Carib: Náut*) small coastal vessel.

guairuro NM (*And, CAm*) dried seed.

guajada NF (*Méx*) stupid thing.

guajalote (*Carib, Méx*) = **guajolote**.

guaje¹ [1] ADJ (*CAm, Méx*) silly, stupid; **hacer ~ a uno** to fool sb, take sb in*.

[2] NM **(a)** (*CAm, Méx Bot*) gourd, calabash, squash (*US*).

(b) (*CAm*: trasto*) old thing, piece of junk.

[3] NMF (*CAm*: tonto*) fool, idiot.

guaje², -a NM/F **(a)** (***) child. **(b)** (*Min*) mining apprentice.

guajear [1a] VI (*Méx*) to play the fool, be silly.

guajería NF (*Méx*) **(a)** (*estupidez*) idiocy, foolishness. **(b)** (*acto*) stupid thing, foolish act.

guajero, -a NM/F, **guajiro¹, -a** NM/F (*Carib*) (white) peasant; (*CAm*) countryman; outsider.

guajiro² NM (*Cuba*) peasant.

guajolote (*Méx*) [1] ADJ silly, stupid.

[2] NM **(a)** (*Orn*) turkey. **(b)** (***) fool, idiot, turkey (*US*).

gualda NF dyer's greenweed, reseda.

gualdo ADJ yellow, golden; V **bandera**.

gualdrapa NF **(a)** (*de caballo*) trappings. **(b)** (***) tatter, ragged end. **(c)** (*CAm:*) down-and-out, bum (*US*).

gualdrapear [1a] VI **(a)** (*Náut: vela*) to flap. **(b)** (*Carib: caballo*) to walk.

gualicho NM **(a)** (*And, Cono Sur:* ††: *diablo*) devil, evil spirit; (††: *maleficio*) evil spell. **(b)** (*Cono Sur: talismán*) talisman, good-luck charm.

guallipén NM (*Cono Sur*) fool, idiot.

Gualterio NM Walter.

guama NF **(a)** (*And, CAm, mentira*) lie. **(b)** (*And*) (*pie*) big foot; (*mano*) big hand. **(c)** (*And, Carib: desastre*) calamity, disaster.

guambito NM (*And*) kid*, boy.

guambra NMF (*And*) **(a)** young Indian. **(b)** child, baby; (**: amor*) sweetheart.

guamiza* NF (*Méx*) beating-up*.

guampa NF (*Carib, Cono Sur*) horn.

guampara NF (*Carib*) machete.

guámparo NM (*Cono Sur*) horn; drinking vessel.

guampudo ADJ (*And, Cono Sur*) horned.

guanábana NM **(a)** (*Bot*) custard apple. **(b)** (*And*) fool.

guanábano NM (*árbol*) soursop (tree).

guanacada NMF (*LAm*) simpleton, dimwit*; rustic.

guanaco [1] ADJ (*LAm*) (*tonto*) simple, silly; (*lento*) slow.

[2] NM **(a)** (*Zool*) guanaco.

(b) (*LAm*: tonto*) simpleton, dimwit* (*CAm**) bumpkin, country cousin.

(c) (*CAm*: pey: salvadoreño*) Salvadorean.

(d) (*Cono Sur*) water-cannon.

guanajada* NF (*Carib*) silly thing, foolish act.

guanajo, -a NM/F (*Carib*) **(a)** (*Orn*) turkey. **(b)** (***) fool, idiot.

guanay NM (*Cono Sur*) oarsman; longshoreman; (*fig*) tough man.

guanayerías* NFPL (*Carib*) silly actions.

guanche [1] ADJ Guanche.

[2] NMF Guanche (*original inhabitant of Canary Islands*).

guando NM (*And, Chile*) stretcher.

guanear [1a] [1] VT (a) (*And*) to fertilize with guano. (b) (*And*) to dirty, soil.

[2] VI (*LAm: animales*) to defecate.

guanera NF guano deposit.

guanero ADJ guano (*atr*), pertaining to guano.

guango* ADJ (*LAm*) andar loose, floppy.

guanín NM (*And, Carib, Cono Sur: Hist*) base gold.

guano[1] NM (a) guano; artificial manure; (*And, Cono Sur*) dung, manure. (b) (*Carib: hum*) money, brass; **meter ~** (*Carib*: fig*) to put one's back into it.

guano[2] NM (*Carib*) (*árbol*) palm tree; (*penca*) palm leaf.

guantada NF, **guantazo** NM slap.

guante NM (a) glove; **~ de boxeo** boxing-glove; **~ de cabritilla** kid glove; **~ de goma** rubber glove; **~s de terciopelo** (*fig*) kid gloves; **~ con puño** gauntlet; **tratamiento de ~ blanco** gentlemanly treatment; **crimen de ~ blanco** white-collar crime; **se ajusta como un ~** it fits like a glove; **me conviene como un ~** it suits me down to the ground; **ser como un ~** (*fig*) to be very meek and mild, be submissive; **arrojar el ~** to throw down the gauntlet; **echar un ~** to take a collection (*a beneficio de* for, on behalf of); **echar el ~ a uno** to catch hold of sb, seize sb; (*fig*) to catch sb out, come down on sb; **hacer ~s** to take up boxing; **recoger el ~** to take up the challenge.

(b) (*Cono Sur*) whip, cat-o'-nine-tails.

(c) **~s** (*gratificación*) tip, commission.

guantear [1a] VT (*Cono Sur*) to slap, smack.

guantelete NM gauntlet.

guantera NF (*Aut*) glove compartment.

guantería NF (a) (*tienda*) glove shop; (*fábrica*) glove factory. (b) (*fabricación*) glove making.

guantero, -a NM/F glover.

guantón NM (*LAm*) slap, hit, blow.

guañusco* ADJ (*Cono Sur*) (a) (*marchito*) withered, faded. (b) (*quemado*) burned, burned up.

guapear* [1a] [1] VI (a) (*ostentarse*) to cut a dash, dress flashily. (b) (*fanfarronear*) to bluster, swagger.

[2] VT (*And*) to urge on.

guaperas* INVAR [1] ADJ excessively good-looking.

[2] NM excessively good-looking youth; (*iró*) heart-throb*, dream-boy*.

guapetón [1] ADJ (a) good-looking, handsome; dashing; **guapetona** good-looking in a mature way, full-figured and very attractive. (b) (*pey*) flashy.

[2] NM bully, roughneck‡.

guapeza NF (a) (*atractivo*) good looks; prettiness, attractiveness. (b) (*elegancia*) smartness, elegance; (*pey: ostentación*) flashiness. (c) boldness, dash; (*pey: bravata*) bravado.

guapo [1] ADJ (a) (*atractivo*) good-looking; *chica* pretty, attractive; *hombre* handsome; **¡oye, guapa!** hey, beautiful!*

(b) (*elegante*) smart, elegant, well-dressed; (*pey*) flashy, overdressed; **¡hombre, qué ~ estás!** how smart you're looking!; **va de ~ por la vida** he goes through life with every confidence in his good looks.

(c) (*valiente*) bold, dashing; (*Carib*) brave; (*Cono Sur: duro*) tough; (*Cono Sur: sin escrúpulos*) unscrupulous.

(d) (‡: *increíble*) incredible; (*interesante*) interesting; (*encantador*) nice; (*guay*) ace*, brill‡.

[2] NM (a) (*amante*) lover, boyfriend.

(b) (*currutaco*) dandy; (*LAm: pey*) bully, tough guy* (*US*); (*fanfarrón*) braggart.

(c) (*CAm Cine*) male lead.

guaposo ADJ (*Carib*) bold, dashing.

guapucha* NF (*And*) cheating.

guapura* NF good looks *pl*.

guaquear [1a] VT (*And, CAm*) *tumba* to rob, sack (*in search of archaeological valuables*).

guaqueo NM (*And, CAm*) graverobbing.

guaquero, -a NM/F (*And, CAm*) graverobber.

guara NF (a) (*And*) lot, heap. (b) **~s** (*Cono Sur*) tricks, wiles.

guaraca NF (*And*) (*honda*) catapult, slingshot (*US*); (*cordel*) cord, string; (*para trompo*) whip.

guaracha NF (a) (*Carib*) (*canción*) popular song; (*baile*) folk dance.

(b) (*Carib**) (*alboroto*) din, racket; (*riña*) quarrel; (*juerga*) party, shindig*.

(c) (*Carib: banda*) street band.

(d) (*Carib*) joke.

(e) (*And*) litter, rough bed.

(f) **~s** (*CAm*) old shoes.

(g) (*CAm*) = **guarache**.

guarache NM (*Méx*) (a) (*chancleta*) sandal. (b) (*Aut*) patch.

guarachear* [1a] VI (*Carib*) to revel; (*fig*) to let one's hair down.

guaragua NF (a) **~s** (*And*) adornments, finery.

(b) (*CAm*: mentira*) lie.

(c) (*CAm*) liar, taleteller.

(d) (*And, Cono Sur*) rhythmical movement (*of the body in dancing*).

guaral NM (*And, Carib*) (*cuerda*) rope, cord; (*de trompo*) whip.

guarangada NF (*LAm*) rude remark.

guarango ADJ (a) (*And, Cono Sur*: grosero*) acto etc rude; *persona* uncouth. (b) (*And*) (*sucio*) dirty; (*harapiento*) ragged.

guaranguear* [1a] VI (*And, Cono Sur*) to be rude, be bad-mannered.

guaranguería* NF (*Cono Sur*) rudeness, uncouthness.

guaraní [1] ADJ, NMF Guaraní.

[2] NM (*Ling*) Guaraní.

┌─── **GUARANÍ** ───────────────────────────────┐
*Guaraní is an American Indian language of the **tupí-guaraní** family and is widely spoken in Paraguay, Brazil, Argentina and Bolivia. In Paraguay it is the majority language and has equal official status with Spanish, which is spoken mainly by non-Indians. In parts of southern Brazil, **tupí-guaraní** is the basis for a pidgin known as **Língua Geral**, now losing ground to Portuguese. From **guaraní** and its sister dialect **tupí** come words like "jaguar", "tapir", "toucan" and "tapioca".*
└───┘

guaranismo NM word (*o expression etc*) from Guaraní.

guarapazo NM (*And*) (a) (*de bebida*) shot*, slug*. (b) (*golpe*) blow, knock; (*caída*) hard fall.

guarapear [1a] VI y **guarapearse** VR (*And*) to drink sugar-cane liquor; (*Carib*: emborracharse*) to get tight*.

guarapo NM (*LAm*) sugar-cane liquor; palm wine; (*Carib*) watered-down drink; (*Carib*) fermented pineapple juice; **menear el ~** (*Carib*) to get a move on; **se le enfrió el ~** (*Carib*: †*) he lost the urge; **volver ~ algo** to tear sth up.

guarapón NM (*And, Cono Sur*) broad-brimmed hat.

guarda [1] NMF (*persona: gen*) guard; (*cuidador*) keeper, custodian; (*Cono Sur Ferro*) ticket collector; **~ de coto**, **~ forestal** forest ranger, gamekeeper, game warden; **~ fluvial**, **~ de pesca** water bailiff; **~ jurado** (*de empresa etc*) security guard; (*caza*) gamekeeper, game warden; **~ de dique** lock-keeper; **~ nocturno** night watchman.

[2] NF (a) (*acto*) guard, guarding; safekeeping; custody.

(b) (*de ley*) observance.

(c) (*de cerradura*) ward; (*de espada, máquina*) guard; (*Tip*) flyleaf, endpaper.

(d) (*Cono Sur: adorno*) trimming.

guarda(a)gujas NM INVAR (*Ferro*) pointsman, switchman (*US*).

guard(a)almacén NMF storekeeper.

guardabarrera [1] NMF (*Ferro: persona*) crossing keeper.

[2] NF (*paso*) level-crossing gate(s), grade-crossing gate(s) (*US*).

guardabarros NM INVAR mudguard, fender (*US*).

guardabosque(s) NM gamekeeper, game warden; ranger, forester.

guardabrisa NF (*Aut*) windscreen, windshield (*US*); (*de vela*) shade; (*Méx*) screen.

guardacabo NM (*Náut*) thimble.

guardacabras NMF INVAR goatherd.

guardacalor NM (*tea*) cosy, cover.

guardacamisa NF (*Carib*) vest, undershirt (*US*).

guardacantón NM roadside post, corner post.

guardacoches NMF INVAR parking attendant.

guardacostas NM INVAR coastguard vessel, revenue cutter.

guardador [1] ADJ (a) (*protector*) protective.

(b) (*de ley etc*) observant; scrupulous.

(c) (*pey*) mean, stingy.

[2] NM, **guardadora** NF (a) (*cuidador etc*) keeper; guardian; protector.

(b) (*de ley etc*) observer.

(c) (*pey*) mean person.

guardaespaldas NM INVAR bodyguard, henchman; minder*.

guardaesquinas* NMF INVAR layabout.

guardafango NM mudguard, fender (*US*).

guardafrenos NM INVAR guard, brakeman.

guardafuego NM (*alambrera*) fireguard; (*Náut: defensa*) fender.

guardagujas NM INVAR (*Ferro*) pointsman, switchman (*US*).

guardajoyas NM INVAR jewel case.

guardajurado, -a NM/F security guard.

guardalado NM railing, parapet.

guardalmacén NMF storekeeper.

guardalodos NM INVAR mudguard, fender (*US*).

guardamano NM guard (*of a sword*).

guardamechones NM INVAR locket.

guardameta NM goalkeeper.

guardamuebles NM INVAR furniture repository.

guardapapeles NM INVAR filing cabinet.

guardaparques NMF INVAR park ranger.

guardapelo NM locket.

guardapolvo NM (a) (*cubierta*) dust-cover, dust-sheet. (b) (*ropa*) dustcoat; (*mono*) overalls; (*abrigo*) outdoor coat. (c) (*de reloj*) inner lid.

guardapolvos⁝ NM INVAR (a) (*Anat*) cunt⁝. (b) (*goma*) rubber*.

guardapuerta NF (*puerta*) outer door, storm door; (*cortina*) door curtain, draught excluder.

guardapuntas NM INVAR top (*of pencil etc*).

guardar [1a] ① VT (a) (*cuidar*) to guard; (*proteger*) to watch over, protect, take care of, keep safe; (*preservar*) to maintain, preserve; *rebaño etc* to watch over, tend; **¡Dios guarde a la Reina!** God save the Queen!; **Dios os guarde** (††) may God be with you.
(b) (*retener*) to keep, hold, hold on to, retain; (*Inform*) to save; (*conservar*) to put away, put by, lay by, store away; (*ahorrar*) to save; **~ algo para sí** to keep sth for o.s.; **lo guardó en el bolsillo** he put it away in his pocket; **te lo puedes ~** you keep it, you can keep it; **guardo los sellos para mi hermano** I save the stamps for my brother; **guardo los mejores recuerdos** I have the nicest memories; **guárdame un asiento** save me a seat.
(c) *promesa, secreto* to keep.
(d) *mandamiento etc* to keep; *ley* to observe, respect.
(e) *respeto etc* to have, show (*a* for); *rencor etc* to bear, have (*a* for, towards); V **cama, silencio** etc.
② **guardarse** VR (a) (*precaverse*) to be on one's guard, look out for o.s.
(b) **~ de algo** (*evitar*) to avoid sth; (*cuidarse*) to look out for sth; (*abstenerse*) to refrain from sth; (*protegerse*) (*abstenerse*) to protect o.s. against sth; **~ de** + *infin* to be careful not to + *infin*; to refrain from + *ger*; to avoid + *ger*; to guard against + *ger*; **guárdate de no ofenderle** take care not to upset him; **¡ya te guardarás de hacerlo!** I bet you won't!; you wouldn't dare!
(c) **~la a uno** to have it in for sb, bear a grudge against sb.

guardarraya NF (*And, CAm, Carib*) boundary.

guardarropa ① NM (a) (*cuarto*) cloakroom, checkroom (*US*). (b) (*ropero*) wardrobe.
② NMF cloakroom attendant.

guardarropía NF (*Teat*) wardrobe; (*accesorios*) properties, props*; **de ~** make-believe, (*pey*) sham, fake.

guardatiempo(s) NM timekeeper.

guardatrén NM (*Cono Sur Ferro*) guard, brakeman.

guardavalla(s) NM (*LAm*) goalkeeper.

guardavía NM (*Ferro*) linesman.

guardavidas NM INVAR (*Cono Sur: de playa*) lifeguard.

guardavista NM visor, sunshade.

guardería NF: **~ infantil** crèche, day nursery, day-care centre.

guardés, -esa NM/F guard; (*de puerta*) doorman; (*de casa de campo*) gatekeeper.

guardia ① NF (a) (*gen*) custody, care; (*defensa*) defence, protection; (*Mil etc*) guarding; (*turno*) shift, spell of duty; **farmacia de ~** all-night chemist's; **médico de ~** doctor on call; **estar de ~** to be on guard, be on duty; to keep watch; **estar en ~ contra** to be on one's guard against; **hacer ~, montar (la) ~** to mount guard; **poner a uno en ~** to put sb on his guard.
(b) (*hombres*) guard; (*Mil*) guard; (*policía*) police; (*Náut*) watch; **~ de asalto** riot police; **G~ Civil** Civil Guard; **~ de corps** bodyguard; **~ de honor** guard of honour; **~s montadas** horse guards; **~ municipal, ~ urbana** municipal police; **~ real** household troops; **vieja ~** old guard; **relevar la ~** to change guard.
(c) (*Esgrima: posición*) guard; **aflojar** (o **bajar**) **la ~** to lower one's guard (*t fig*); **estar en ~** to be on guard.
② NMF (*policía*) (*hombre*) policeman; (*mujer*) policewoman; (*Mil*) guard, guardsman; **~s de asalto** riot police, (*Mil*) shock troops; **~ de la circulación, ~ de tráfico** traffic policeman; **~ civil** civil guard; **~ forestal** game warden, ranger; **~ jurado** security guard; **~ marina** midshipman; **~ municipal, ~ urbano** municipal policeman; **~ nocturno** night watchman.

GUARDIA CIVIL

ⓘ *The **Guardia Civil**, commonly referred to as **la Benemérita**, is the oldest of Spain's various police forces. A paramilitary force like the French **Gendarmerie**, it was set up in 1844 to combat banditry in rural areas, but was also used as an instrument of repression in the cities. Under Franco it was resented by many as an oppressive, reactionary force, and was especially hated in the Basque Country. With the return of democracy, Franco's despised **Policía Armada** were reformed as the **Policía Nacional**, and the present-day role of the **Guardia Civil** was redefined. They are mainly stationed in rural areas, and their duties include policing highways and frontiers and taking part in anti-terrorist operations. Their traditional tunics and capes have been replaced by a green uniform, and the famous black patent-leather three-cornered hats are now reserved for ceremonial occasions.*
⇨ *See also* POLICÍA

---

guardián, -ana NM/F guardian, custodian, keeper; warden; watchman; (*Zool*) keeper; **~ de parque** park keeper.

guardiero NM (*Carib*) watchman (*on an estate*).

guardilla NF attic, garret; attic room.

guardiola* NF piggy-bank, moneybox.

guardoso ADJ careful, thrifty; (*pey*) mean.

guare NM (*And*) punt pole.

guarearse* [1a] VR (*CAm*) to get tight*.

guarecer [2d] ① VT to protect, give shelter to, take in; to preserve.
② **guarecerse** VR to shelter, take refuge (*de* from).

guargüero NM (*LAm*) throat, throttle.

guari NM (*Cono Sur*) throat, throttle.

guaricha* NF (*And, CAm, Carib*) (*mujer*) woman; (*vieja*) old bag*.

guariche NM (*And*) = **guaricha**.

guaricho NM (*Carib*: †) young farm labourer.

guarida NF (*Zool*) den, lair, hideout; (*fig*) refuge, shelter; cover; (*de persona*) haunt, hideout.

guarismo NM figure, numeral.

guarnecer [2d] VT (a) (*proveer*) to equip, provide (*de* with); (*adornar*) to adorn, embellish, garnish (*de* with); (*Cos*) to trim, edge (*de* with); *frenos* to line; *pared* to plaster, stucco; *joya* to set, mount; *caballo* to harness; (*Téc*) to cover, protect, reinforce (*de* with).
(b) (*Mil*) to man, garrison; to be stationed in.

guarnecido NM (*de pared*) plaster, plastering; (*Aut*) upholstery.

guarnés NM (*Méx: para arneses*) harness room.

guarnición NF (a) (*acto*) equipment, provision; fitting; adorning, embellishing; (*Culin*) garnishing.
(b) (*adorno*) adornment; (*Cos*) trimming, edging, binding; (*de freno*) lining; (*de pared*) plastering; (*de joya*) setting, mount; (*de espada*) guard; (*Mec*) packing; (*Culin*) garnish.
(c) **guarniciones** (*de caballo*) harness; (*equipo*) gear; (*de casa*) fittings, fixtures; **guarniciones del alumbrado** light fittings.
(d) (*Mil*) garrison.

guarnicionar [1a] VT to garrison, man; to be stationed in.

guarnicionero NM harness maker; leather worker, craftsman in leather.

guaro NM (a) (*CAm*: licor*) liquor, spirits. (b) (*Orn*) small parrot.

guarola* NF (*CAm: coche*) old crock, old banger⁝.

guarolo ADJ (*Carib*) stubborn.

guarra NF (a) (*Zool*) sow; (*fig*) slut. (b) (⁝) punch, bash*.

guarrada NF, **guarrería** NF (*trampa*) dirty trick; (*dicho*) rotten thing (to say); (*indecencia*) indecent act, vulgar thing (to do).

guarrazo* NM (*golpe*) **darse** (o **pegarse**) **un ~** to take a thump*; (*en coche*) to have a smash.

guarrear [1a] VT to dirty, mess up.

guarreta* NF slut.

guarrindongo* ADJ = **guarro 1**.

guarro ① ADJ dirty, filthy.
② NM pig, hog; (*fig*) dirty person, slovenly person.

guarrusca NF (*And*) machete, big knife.

guarte INTERJ (††) look out!, take care!

guarura* NM (*Méx*) (*policía*) cop*; (*guardaespaldas*) bodyguard, minder*.

guasa¹ NF (a) (*broma*) joke; (*chanza*) joking, teasing, kidding*; **con ~, de ~** jokingly, in fun.
(b) (*sosería*) dullness, insipidness.
(c) (*Cono Sur*) peasant woman.
(d) (*CAm: suerte*) luck.

guasábara NF (*And, Carib*) (*Hist: de esclavos*) uprising; (††: *clamor*) clamour, uproar.

guasada⁝ NF (*Cono Sur: expresión*) obscenity.

guasamaco ADJ (*Cono Sur*) rough, coarse.

guasanga NF (a) (*And, Carib*) = **guasábara**; (*CAm: bulla*) uproar. (b) (*CAm: chiste*) joke.

guasca¹ NF (a) (*LAm*) leather strap, rawhide thong; (*And*) riding-whip, crop; **dar ~ a** (*LAm*) to whip, flog; (*Cono Sur*) to insist stubbornly on; (*And*) to wind up; **¡déle ~ no más!** (*Cono Sur*) keep at it!; **pisarse la ~** (*And, Cono Sur⁝*) to fall into the trap; **volverse ~** (*And*) to be full of longing.
(b) (*Cono Sur⁝*) prick⁝.

guasca² NF (*And*) mountain peak.

guascaro ADJ (*And*) impulsive.

guascazo NM (*LAm*) lash; blow, punch.

guasearse [1a] VR to joke, tease, kid*, rag.

guasería* NF (*And, Cono Sur*) obscenity.

guaserío NM (*Cono Sur*) rabble.

guaso ① ADJ (*And, Carib, Cono Sur*: grosero*) coarse, crude, rough; (*Cono Sur*) (*tímido*) shy; (*sencillo*) simple, unsophisticated.
② NM, **guasa²** NF (*And, Cono Sur: campesino*) peasant, countryman, countrywoman; (*vaquero*) cowboy; (*Cono Sur*: grosero*) uncouth person.
③ NM (*Carib*: parranda*) merrymaking, revelry.

guasón ① ADJ (a) (*gracioso*) witty, humorous; (*burlón*) joking; **dijo** …

he said jokingly, he said teasingly. **(b)** (*soso*) dull, insipid; (*aburrido*) boring. [2] NM, **guasona** NF **(a)** wag, wit; joker, tease. **(b)** tedious person, bore.

guasqueada NF (*Cono Sur*) lash; whipping, flogging.

guasquear [1a] VT (*Cono Sur**) to whip, flog.

guata¹ NF **(a)** (*And, Cono Sur**: *barriga*) paunch, belly; (*Cono Sur Culin*) tripe; **echar ~** (*Cono Sur**) to get fat. **(b)** (*Cono Sur*) warping, bulging.

guata² NF **(a)** (*algodón*) raw cotton; (*relleno*) padding; (*And*) twine, cord.
(b) (*Carib**) lie, fib.
(c) (*And**) inseparable friend, bosom buddy.

guata³ NMF (*And*) inhabitant of the interior.

guataca (*Carib*) [1] NF **(a)** (*Agr*) small hoe; wooden shovel. **(b)** (*Anat*) big ear.
[2] NMF creep‡, bootlicker*.

guataco ADJ **(a)** (*And*) Indian, native. **(b)** (*CAm, Méx**) chubby, plump.

guatal NM (*CAm*) hillock.

guate NM **(a)** (*CAm Agr*) maize plantation.
(b) (*: *serrano*) highlander; (*Carib**: *colombiano*) Colombian.
(c) (*And**) bosom buddy.

guateado ADJ quilted.

guatearse [1a] VR (*Cono Sur*) to warp, bulge.

Guatemala NF **(a)** Guatemala. **(b)** **salir de ~ y entrar en Guatepeor** to jump out of the frying pan into the fire.

guatemalteco [1] ADJ Guatemalan, of Guatemala.
[2] NM, **guatemalteca** NF Guatemalan.

guatemaltequismo NM word (*o phrase etc*) peculiar to Guatemala.

guateque NM party, celebration, binge*.

guatero NM (*Cono Sur*) hot-water bottle.

guatitas NFPL (*And, Cono Sur Culin*) tripe.

guato‡ NM (*LAm*) joint‡, reefer‡.

guatón ADJ (*Cono Sur**: *barrigón*) paunchy, pot-bellied; (*regordete*) plump; **sí, ~*** yes darling.

guatuso ADJ (*CAm*) blond(e), fair.

guau¹ [1] INTERJ *etc* bow-wow!
[2] NM bark.

guau² EXCL wow!*

guay* ADJ super*, great*, smashing*.

guaya NF (*Carib*) wire.

guayaba NF **(a)** (*Bot*) guava; (*jalea*) guava jelly. **(b)** (*fig y hum: LAm*) fib, lie; (*LAm: tobillo*) ankle; (*CAm: beso*) kiss; (*CAm‡: boca*) gob‡; **la ~** (*CAm Pol*) power.

guayabal NM grove of guava trees.

guayabear‡ [1a] [1] VT (*CAm*) to kiss.
[2] VI (*Carib, Cono Sur*) to lie, tell fibs.

guayabera NF (*LAm*) loose shirt with large pockets; lightweight jacket.

guayabero‡ ADJ (*Carib, Cono Sur*) lying, deceitful.

guayabo NM **(a)** (*Bot*) guava tree. **(b)** (*And*) (*pena*) grief, sorrow; (*murria*) nostalgia; (*And, Cono Sur**: *resaca*) hangover*. **(c)** (*: *guapa*) pretty girl, smasher‡; **está hecha un ~** (*atractiva*) she looks marvellous; (*joven*) she looks very young. **(d)** (*Méx‡‡*) cunt‡‡.

guayaca [1] ADJ (*Cono Sur*) slow, dull; simple-minded.
[2] NF (*LAm*) bag, purse.

guayacán NM lignum vitae.

Guayana NF Guyana; (*Hist*) Guiana; **~ Británica** British Guiana; **~ Francesa** French Guiana; **~ Holandesa** Dutch Guiana.

guayanés, -esa ADJ, NM/F Guyanese.

guayar [1a] VT (*Carib Culin*) to grate.

guayo NM (*Carib*) (*Culin*) grater; (*Mús**) bad street band.

guayuco* NM (*And, Carib*) loincloth.

guayunga NF (*And*) lot, heap.

gubernamental [1] ADJ government = (*atr*), governmental; (*de facción*) loyalist.
[2] NMF loyalist, government supporter; (*Mil*) government soldier.

gubernamentalización NF (increase in) government intervention (*o control*).

gubernativo ADJ governmental.

gubia NF gouge.

güe... (*prov, LAm*) *a veces se escriben así diversas palabras que empiezan* **hue...**; *p.ej. para* **güevón** V **huevón**.

guedeja NF long hair, lock; (*de león*) mane.

güegüecho [1] ADJ **(a)** (*And**) silly, stupid.
(b) (*CAm, Méx Med*) suffering from goitre.
[2] NM **(a)** (*LAm Med*) goitre.
(b) (*CAm Orn*) turkey.
(c) (*CAm**: *bohío*) hovel.

güeñi NM (*Cono Sur*) (*chico*) boy; (*criado*) servant.

guepardo NM cheetah.

güereque NM (*And Orn*) plover.

Guernesey NM Guernsey.

güero ADJ (*CAm, Méx*) *pelo, persona* blond(e), fair; *persona* (*de tez*) fair,

---

guerra NF **(a)** war; warfare; struggle, fight, conflict; **~ de agotamiento, ~ de desgaste** war of attrition; **~ atómica** atomic war(fare); **~ bacteriana, ~ bacteriológica** germ warfare; **~ biológica** biological warfare; **~ caliente** hot war, shooting war; **~ del catorce** Great War, First World War; **~ civil** civil war; **~ comercial** trade war; **~ convencional** conventional war; **~ fría** cold war; **~ de las galaxias** Star Wars; **~ de guerrillas** guerrilla warfare; **~ a muerte** war to the knife, war to the bitter end; **~ mundial** world war; **~ de nervios** war of nerves; **~ nuclear** nuclear war(fare); **~ de precios** price war; **~ psicológica** psychological warfare; **~ química** chemical warfare; **~ relámpago** blitzkrieg; **~ santa** holy war, crusade; **~ sucia** dirty war; **~ a tiros** shooting war, hot war; **~ de trincheras** trench warfare; **G~ de los Cien Años** Hundred Years' War; **G~ de los Treinta Años** Thirty Years' War; **G~ de la Independencia** (*LAm*) War of Independence; (*Esp*) Peninsular War; **G~ de Sucesión** War of Spanish Succession; **G~ del Transvaal** Boer War; **Primera G~ Mundial** First World War; **Segunda G~ Mundial** Second World War; **de ~** military; war (*atr*); **Ministerio de G~** Ministry of War, War Office (*Brit*), War Department (*US*); **estar en ~** to be at war (*con* with); **dar ~** to be annoying (*a* to), be a nuisance (*a* to), make trouble (*a* for); (*niño*) to carry on, make a great fuss; **dar ~ a uno** to rag sb; **declarar la ~** to declare war (*a* on); **hacer la ~** to wage war, make war (*a* on); **pedir** (*o querer*) **~** (*: *sexualmente*) to feel randy*. **(b)** (*juego*) (kind of) billiards.

┌─── **GUERRA CIVIL ESPAÑOLA** ───┐

ⓘ *Spain's political climate was extremely volatile in the 1930s, under the Second Republic, with various sectors of society all vying for power. The elections of February 1936 were won by a coalition of socialist and anarchist groups known as the* **Frente Popular** *or FP, and were followed by a period of strikes, uprisings and social disorder. On 18 July of that year, General Francisco Franco led a military coup. In the ensuing war Franco's side was known as the* **Nacionales** *and the government forces as the* **Republicanos***. Neither army was well-equipped, so foreign support was a decisive factor: the USSR sent aid to the Republicans and volunteers from all over Europe formed* **Brigadas Internacionales** *(International Brigades) to fight with them. Fascist Italy and Germany sent troops and weapons to Franco. The fighting was bitter and protracted, and the Nationalists' superior firepower finally triumphed. The war ended officially on 1 April 1939, when Franco proclaimed himself* **Jefe del Estado***, a position he held for the next 36 years.*
⇨ See also FRANQUISMO

guerrear [1a] VI to wage war, fight; (*fig*) to put up a fight, resist.

guerrera¹ NF trench coat; combat jacket; (*Mil*) military jacket.

guerrero [1] ADJ **(a)** (*belicoso*) fighting (*atr*); war (*atr*); **espíritu ~** fighting spirit.
(b) (*contrario*) warring.
(c) *carácter* warlike, martial; **un pueblo ~** a warlike people.
[2] NM, **guerrera²** NF warrior, soldier, fighter.
[3] NM (*Carib**) rum and vodka-based cocktail.

guerrilla NF **(a)** (*grupo*) guerrilla band; group of partisans; (*fuerzas*) guerrilla forces. **(b)** (*lucha*) guerrilla warfare.

guerrillear [1a] VI to wage guerrilla warfare; to fight as a guerrilla band.

guerrillero, -a NM/F guerrilla (fighter); partisan; irregular; **~ urbano** urban guerrilla.

guerrista ADJ combative, fighting.

güesear‡ [1a] VT (*CAm*) to wash.

gueto NM ghetto.

güevo NM: **a ~, de ~** (*Méx*) by hook or by crook.

güevón (*LAm*) = **huevón**.

güi... *para diversas palabras escritas así en LAm, V t* **hui...**

guía [1] NF **(a)** (*acto*) guidance, guiding; **~ vocacional** vocational guidance; **para que te sirva de ~** for your guidance.
(b) (*Tip*) guide, guidebook (*de* to); (*manual*) handbook; (*Telec etc*) directory; (*Inform*) prompt; **~ de campo** (*Bio*) field guide; **~ de carga** (*Ferro*) waybill; **~ de datos** data directory; **~ del ocio** 'what's on' booklet; **~ oficial de ferrocarriles** official railway guide, official timetable; **~ telefónica, ~ de teléfonos** telephone directory; **~ del turista** tourist's guide; **~ del viajero** traveller's guide.
(c) (*Mec*) guide; (*de bicicleta*) handlebars; (*caballo*) leader, front horse; **~s** reins; **~ sonora** (*Cine*) soundtrack.
[2] NMF (*persona*) guide; leader; adviser; (*de grupo de viajeros*) courier, guide.
[3] ATR guide (*atr*), guiding; **manual ~** guidebook; **cable ~** guiding wire, guiderope.

guiado NM guiding, guidance; (*de misil*) guiding, steering.

guiar [1c] [1] VT **(a)** (*gen*) to guide; (*dirigir*) to lead, direct; (*controlar*) to manage; (*orientar*) to advise.
(b) (*Aut etc*) to drive; (*Náut*) to steer; (*Aer*) to pilot.

(c) (*Bot*) to train.

[2] **guiarse** VR: ~ **por** to be guided by, be ruled by, go by.

güicoy NM (*CAm Bot*) courgette.

Guido NM Guy.

guija¹ NF (*piedra*) pebble; (*de camino*) cobble, cobblestone.

guija² NF (*Bot*) vetch.

guijarral NM stony place; (*en playa*) shingle, pebbles, pebbly part.

guijarro NM pebble; (*de camino*) cobble, cobblestone.

guijarroso ADJ *terreno* stony; *camino* cobbled; *playa* pebbly, shingly.

guijo NM **(a)** (*grava*) gravel; (*en playa*) shingle. **(b)** (*Carib, Méx*) shaft.

guil: NM 5-peseta coin.

güila¹ NF **(a)** (*Méx: puta*) whore. **(b)** (*CAm: trompito*) small spinning top.

güila²* NMF (*CAm*) kid*.

guili* NM bobby*, cop*.

güiliento ADJ (*Cono Sur*) ragged, tattered.

guillado: ADJ crazy.

guillame NM (*Téc*) rabbet plane.

guillarse [1a] VR **(a)** (*: *chiflarse*) to go round the twist*. **(b)** (:) (*t* **guillárselas:** *irse*) to beat it*. **(c) guillárselas:** (*morir*) to kick the bucket:.

Guillermo NM William.

guillotina NF guillotine; paper-cutter; **ventana de ~** sash window.

guillotinado NM guillotining.

guillotinar [1a] VT to guillotine.

güilo ADJ (*Méx*) maimed, crippled.

güincha NF (*And, Cono Sur*) **(a)** (*ribete*) narrow strip of cloth; (*cinta*) ribbon; (*para pelo*) hair ribbon. **(b)** (*Dep*: *meta*) tape, finishing-line; (*salida*) starting-line. **(c)** ¡las ~s! rubbish!, forget it!

güinche NM (*LAm*) winch, hoist; crane.

güinchero NM (*LAm*) winch operator; crane operator.

guinda NF **(a)** (*Bot*) mazzard cherry, morello cherry; **poner la ~ a la oferta** (*fig*) to top off the offer, add a final attraction to the offer; **poner ~s a la tarta** (*fig*) to put the icing on the cake; **ponerse como una ~** to turn scarlet.
(b) (*Náut*) height of masts.
(c) (*Carib*) guttering, spout.
(d) eso es una ~ (*Cono Sur:*) that's simple, it's a cinch:.
(e) ~s (*Cono Sur:*) balls:, bollocks:.

guindalejo NM (*And, Carib*) (*ropa vieja*) old clothes; (*trastos*) junk, lumber.

guindaleza NF hawser.

guindar [1a] [1] VT **(a)** to hoist, hang up (high); (*Carib: colgar*) to hang (up); (*: *ahorcar*) *criminal* to hang, string up*.
(b) (:) to win (against competition), land; (*robar*) to nick:.
[2] **guindarse*** VR to hang o.s.

guindaste NM (*CAm*) jib crane.

guinde: NM nicking:, thieving; **un ~** a job*.

guindilla [1] NF (*Bot, Culin*) hot pepper, red chili pepper.
[2] NM (*) bobby*, copper*.

guindo¹ NM mazzard (o morello) cherry-tree; **caer del ~*** to twig*, cotton on*.

guindo² NM (*CAm*) ravine.

guindola NF lifebuoy.

guindón: NM thief.

Guinea NF Guinea; ~ **Española** Spanish Guinea.

guinea¹ NF (*moneda*) guinea.

guineo¹ [1] ADJ Guinea(n), of Guinea.
[2] NM, **guinea²** NF Guinean.

guineo² NM (*LAm Bot*) banana.

guiña NF (*And, Carib*) bad luck; (*And*) witchcraft.

guiñada NF **(a)** wink; blink. **(b)** (*Aer, Náut*) yaw.

guiñapo NM **(a)** (*andrajo*) rag, tatter; **poner a uno como un ~** to shower insults on sb. **(b)** (*persona*) slovenly person; ragamuffin; rogue, reprobate.

guiñar [1a] [1] VT (*parpadear*) to wink; (*pestañear*) to blink.
[2] VI **(a)** to wink; to blink. **(b)** (*Aer, Náut*) to yaw.

guiño NM **(a)** (*parpadeo*) wink; (*mueca*) grimace, wry face; **hacer ~s a** to wink at, (*amantes*) to make eyes at. **(b)** (*Aer, Náut*) yaw.

guiñol NM art of the puppeteer, puppet theatre, Punch-and-Judy show.

guiñolista NMF puppeteer.

guión NM **(a)** (*Orn, persona*) leader.
(b) (*Tip*) hyphen, dash.
(c) (*Liter*) summary, outline; handout; explanatory text; (*Cine: texto*) script; (*Cine: traducción*) subtitle.
(d) (*bandera*) royal standard; (*Ecl*) processional cross, processional banner.
(e) ~ **de codornices** (*Orn*) corncrake.

guionista NMF (*Cine*) scriptwriter; writer of subtitles.

guionizar [1f] VT to script, write the script for.

guipar: [1a] VT **(a)** (*ver*) to see. **(b)** (*observar*) to spot; (*entender*) to cot-

ton on to*, catch on to.

güipil NM = **huipil**.

Guipúzcoa NF Guipúzcoa.

guipuzcoano [1] ADJ of Guipúzcoa.
[2] NM, **guipuzcoana** NF native (o inhabitant) of Guipúzcoa; **los ~s** the people of Guipúzcoa.

guiri [1] NM (*Hist*) Carlist soldier; (*) policeman; civil guard.
[2] NMF (:) (*extranjero*) foreigner; (*turista*) tourist.
[3] NM: **en el ~:** abroad, in foreign parts.

guirigay NM **(a)** (*Ling*) gibberish, jargon. **(b)** (*gritería*) hubbub, uproar; (*confusión*) chaos, confusion; **¡esto es un ~!** the place is like a bear garden!

guirizapa NF (*Carib*) quarrel, squabble.

guirlache NM (*turrón*) type of nougat.

guirnalda NF garland; (*de funeral*) wreath; (*Arte*) garland, floral motif.

güiro NM **(a)** (*LAm Bot*) bottle gourd.
(b) (*Carib Mús*) musical instrument made of a gourd.
(c) (*Carib:* *cabeza*) head, nut:.
(d) (*CAm: bebé*) small baby.
(e) (*Carib: mujerzuela*) loose woman.
(f) (*And: brote de maíz*) maize shoot.

güirro [1] ADJ (*LAm*) weak, sickly.
[2] NM (*CAm*) small baby.

guisa NF: **a ~ de** as, like, in the manner of; **de tal ~** in such a way (*que* that).

guisado NM stew.

guisador(a) NM/F, **guisandero, -a** NM/F cook.

guisante NM pea; ~ **de olor** sweet pea.

guisar [1a] VT **(a)** to prepare; to arrange. **(b)** (*Culin*) to cook; to stew.

güisingue NM (*And*) whip.

güisinguear [1a] VT (*And*) to whip.

guiso NM **(a)** cooked dish; (*esp LAm: guisado*) stew. **(b)** (*aliño*) seasoning.

guisote NM (*pey*) hash, poor-quality stew; (*mezcla*) concoction; (*comida*) grub:.

güisquería NF night-club.

güisqui NM whisky.

guita NF **(a)** twine; packthread. **(b)** (:) dough:.

güita NF (*Méx:*) dough:.

guitarra [1] NF (*instrumento*) guitar; ~ **baja** bass guitar; ~ **clásica** classical guitar; ~ **eléctrica** electrical guitar; **ser como ~ en un entierro** to be quite out of place, strike the wrong note; **chafar la ~ a uno** to queer sb's pitch.
[2] NMF (*person*) guitarist.

guitarrear [1a] VI to play the guitar, strum a guitar.

guitarreo NM strum(ming).

guitarrero, -a NM/F (electric) guitarist.

guitarrista NMF guitarist.

guitarrón NM **(a)** (*Méx Mús*) large guitar. **(b)** (*CAm: abeja*) bee.

güitos: NMPL balls:.

güizcal NM (*CAm Bot*) chayote.

gula NF greed, gluttony.

gulag [gu'lax] NM, PL **gulags** gulag.

gulash [gu'laʃ] NM INVAR goulash.

guloso ADJ greedy, gluttonous.

gulusmear [1a] VI to nibble titbits; to sniff the cooking; to snoop.

guma: NF hen.

gumarra* NM (*Méx*) cop*.

gurguciar [1b] [1] VT (*CAm*) to sniff at, sniff out.
[2] VI (*Méx*: gruñir*) to grunt, snort.

guri: NM (*policía*) copper*, bobby*; (*Mil*) soldier.

gurí NM, PL **gurís, guríes, o gurises** (*Cono Sur*) (†: *mestizo*) mestizo, Indian child, child of mixed race; (*: *muchacho*) boy, lad.

guripa: NM (*Mil*) soldier; (*policía*) cop*; (*pillo*) rascal, rogue; (*tonto*) berk:; (*sujeto*) bloke:, guy*.

gurisa NF (*Cono Sur*) (†: *mestiza*) Indian child, child of mixed race; (*: *chica*) girl, lass; (*: *esposa*) young wife.

gurrí NM (*LAm*) wild duck.

gurrumino [1] ADJ **(a)** (*débil*) weak, sickly; (*pequeño*) small, puny.
(b) *marido* complaisant, indulgent.
(c) (*And*) cowardly.
(d) (*CAm: listo*) clever, sharp.
[2] NM cuckold; complaisant husband, indulgent husband.
[3] NM, **gurrumina** NF **(a)** (*Méx: niño*) child.
(b) (*LAm*: persona astuta*) sharp customer*.
[4] NF (*And*: molestia*) bother, nuisance.

gur(r)upié NM **(a)** (*LAm: de garito*) croupier. **(b)** (*Carib, And: en subasta*) false bidder. **(c)** (*Carib*: amigo*) buddy (*esp US*), pal*.

gurú NM, **guru** NM, PL **gurús** guru.

gus NM (*And*) turkey buzzard.

gusa* NM (*a veces* F) (= **gusanillo**) hunger; **me anda el ~** I'm hungry; **tener ~** to be hungry.

gusanera NF (**a**) nest of maggots; breeding ground for maggots. (**b**) (*fig*) bunch, lot, crowd; **una ~ de chiquillos** a bunch of kids.

gusaniento ADJ maggoty, worm-eaten, grub-infested.

gusanillo NM (**a**) small maggot, small worm; **~ de la conciencia** (*fig*) prickings of conscience; **me anda el ~** I feel peckish*; **matar el ~** to have a snack, take the edge off one's appetite; to have a nip of liquor first thing in the morning.
(**b**) (*: *manía*) craze, obsession; **le entró el ~ de las motos** he was bitten by the motorbike craze.

gusano NM (**a**) maggot, grub, worm; (*de mariposa, polilla*) caterpillar; (*de tierra*) earthworm; **~ de luz** glow-worm; **~ de seda** silkworm; **criar ~s*** to be pushing up the daisies*; **matar el ~*** (*beber*) to have a drink, (*comer*) to have a bite to eat.
(**b**) (*fig*) worm, contemptible person; meek creature.
(**c**) (*Inform*) virus, worm.
(**d**) (*Cuba*: Pol*) traitor (*Cuban in self-imposed exile*).

gusanoso ADJ = **gusaniento**.

gusarapa NF, **gusarapo** NM tadpole; (*) bug.

gusgo ADJ (*Méx*) sweet-toothed.

gustación NF tasting, sampling.

gustado ADJ (*LAm*) esteemed, well-liked, popular.

▼ **gustar** [1a] 1 VT (**a**) to taste, try, sample. (**b**) (*Méx**) **gusto un café** I'd like a coffee.

2 VI (**a**) to please, be pleasing; **es una película que siempre gusta** it's a film which always pleases (o gives pleasure); **la comedia no gustó** the play was not a success, the play was not much liked; **mi número ya no gusta** my act isn't popular any more.

▼ (**b**) (*con complemento personal*) **me gusta el té** I like tea; **¿te gusta Méjico?** do you like Mexico?; **no le gusta que le llamen Pepe** he doesn't like to be called Joe; **no me gusta mucho** I don't like it much, I'm not very struck (on it); **me gusta como anda** I like the way she walks.
(**c**) (*fórmulas*) **¿gusta Vd?** would you like some?, may I offer you some?; **si Vd gusta** if you please, if you don't mind; **como Vd guste** as you wish.
(**d**) **~ de algo** to like sth, enjoy sth; **~ de + *infin*** to like to + *infin*, be fond of + *ger*, enjoy + *ger*.

gustazo* NM great pleasure; (*malsano*) unhealthy pleasure, nasty pleasure.

gustillo NM suggestion, touch, tang; aftertaste; **coger el ~ a algo** to get to like sth.

gustito NM sheer pleasure, honest enjoyment.

▼ **gusto** NM (**a**) (*sentido*) taste; **agregue azúcar al ~** add sugar to taste.
(**b**) (*sabor*) taste, flavour; **tiene un ~ amargo** it has a bitter taste, it tastes bitter.
(**c**) (*Arte etc*) taste; (*estilo*) style, fashion; **buen ~** good taste; **mal ~** bad taste; **de buen ~** in good taste; **es de un mal ~ extraordinario** it is in extraordinarily bad taste; **para mi ~** to my taste; **al ~ de hoy, según el ~ de hoy** in the taste of today; **ser persona de ~** to be a person of taste; **sobre ~s no hay disputa, de ~s no hay nada escrito** there's no accounting for tastes; **tiene ~ para vestir** she dresses elegantly, she has taste in dresses.
▼ (**d**) (*placer*) pleasure; **con mucho ~** with pleasure; (*con voluntad*) gladly, willingly; **con sumo ~** with the very greatest pleasure; **por ~** de for the sake of; **comer con ~** to eat heartily; **da ~ hacerlo** it's nice to do it; **dar ~ a uno** to gratify sb's wishes, do as sb wishes; **estar a ~** to be at ease, feel comfortable; to feel at home; **aquí me encuentro a ~** I like it here, I feel at home here; **acomodarse a su ~** to make o.s. comfortable, make o.s. at home; **es por ~ que siga allí** (*LAm*) you'll wait there in vain; **sentirse mal a ~** to feel ill at ease; **tengo los pies a ~ y calientes** my feet are nice and warm; **tener el ~ de + *ger*** to have the pleasure of + *ger*; **tener ~ en + *infin*** to be glad to + *infin*; **tomar el ~ a** to take a liking to.
(**e**) (*presentaciones*) **¡mucho ~!, ¡tanto ~!** how do you do?; pleased to meet you; **el ~ es mío** how do you do?; the pleasure is mine; **tengo mucho ~ en presentar al Sr X** allow me to introduce Mr X; **tengo mucho ~ en conocerle** I'm very pleased to meet you.
(**f**) (*agrado*) liking (*por* for); **al ~ de** to the liking of; **ser del ~ de uno** to be to sb's liking; **tener ~ por** to have a liking for, have an eye for; **tomar ~ a** to take a liking to.
(**g**) (*antojo*) whim, fancy; **a ~** at will, according to one's fancy.
(**h**) (*Cono Sur Com*) style, design, colour; range, assortment.

gustosamente ADV gladly, with pleasure.

gustoso ADJ (**a**) (*sabroso*) tasty, savoury, nice.
(**b**) (*agradable*) pleasant.
(**c**) (*con placer*) willing, glad; **lo hizo ~** he did it gladly, he did it with pleasure; **le ofrezco ~ una habitación de matrimonio** I am glad to be able to offer you a double room.

gutapercha NF gutta-percha.

gutifarra NF (*LAm*) = **butifarra**.

gutural ADJ guttural (*t Ling*); throaty.

Guyana NF Guyana.

guyanés, -esa ADJ, NM/F Guyanese.

Gzlez. ABR *de* **González**.

H

H, h ['atʃe] NF (*letra*) H, h.

H. (**a**) (*Fin*) ABR *de* **haber** credit, Cr. (**b**) ABR *de* **hectárea(s)** hectare(s). (**c**) (*Rel*) ABR *de* **Hermano** Brother, Br. (**d**) (*Quím*) ABR *de* **hidrógeno** hydrogen, H.

h. (**a**) ABR *de* **hacia** circa, about, c. (**b**) ABR *de* **hora(s)** hour(s), h, hr. (**c**) ABR *de* **habitantes** population, pop.

ha¹ V **haber.**

ha² INTERJ oh!

Ha. ABR *de* **hectárea** NF, **hectáreas** NFPL hectare, hectares.

haba NF (**a**) (*Bot*) (broad) bean; (*de café etc*) bean; **~ de las Indias** sweet pea; **~ de soja** soya bean; **son ~s contadas** we know all about that; it's a sure thing, it's a certainty; **en todas partes cuecen ~s** it's the same the whole world over.
(**b**) (*Vet*) tumour.
(**c**) (⁂) prick⁂.

Habana NF: **La ~** Havana.

habanera¹ NF (*Mús*) habanera.

habanero [1] ADJ of Havana.
[2] NM, **habanera²** NF native (*o* inhabitant) of Havana; **los ~s** the people of Havana.

habano [1] ADJ Y N = **habanero.**
[2] NM (*puro*) Havana cigar.

hábeas corpus NM hábeas corpus.

▼ **haber** [2j] [1] VT (**a**) (††: *tener*) to have, possess.
(**b**) (*liter: obtener*) to get; to catch, lay hands on; **lee cuantos libros puede ~** he reads all the books he can lay his hands on.
(**c**) (*Rel: fórmula*) **bien haya ...** blessed be ...; **X, que Dios haya** X, God rest his soul.
(**d**) (*Jur: fórmula*) **todos los inventos habidos y por ~** all inventions present and future, the present inventions and any others that may be made; **las bajas habidas y por ~** casualties suffered and still to be suffered.
(**e**) (*liter, periodismo*) **en el encuentro habido ayer** in the fight which occurred yesterday; **la baja de temperatura habida ayer** the fall in temperature recorded yesterday; **la lista de los caídos habidos** the list of casualties suffered.
[2] V AUX (**a**) (*en tiempos compuestos*) to have; **he comido** I have eaten; **lo hubiéramos hecho** we would have done it; **antes de ~lo visto** before seeing him, before having seen him; **de ~lo sabido** if I had known it.
▼(**b**) **~ de** + *infin*; **he de hacerlo** I have to do it, I am to do it, I must do it; **¿qué he de hacer?** what am I to do?; **¿qué ha de tenerlo?** why should he have it?, how could he possibly have it?; **ha de llegar hoy** he is due to arrive today; **ha de haberse perdido** it must have got lost; **han de ser las 9** it must be about 9 o'clock; **has de estar equivocado** (*LAm*) you must be mistaken; **los has de ver** (*LAm*) you'll see them.
[3] V IMPERS (**a**) (*gen*) **hay** there is, there are; **hay calefacción** there is heating; **hay tanto que hacer** there is so much to be done; **no hay plátanos** there are no bananas, we have no bananas; **no lo hay** there isn't any; **no hubo discusión** there was no discussion; **'mejores no hay'** (*Com: slogan*) 'none better!'; **¡hay gaseosa!** (*Com: pregón*) soft drinks!; **buen chico si los hay** a good lad if ever there was one; **¿habrá tiempo?** will there be time?; **¿hay puros?** have you any cigars?; **tomará lo que haya** he'll take whatever there is, he'll take whatever is going; **lo que hay es que ...** what's happening is that ..., it's like this ...; **hay sol** the sun is shining, it is sunny; **¿qué hay?** what's up?, what's the matter?, what goes on?; **¡no hay de qué!** don't mention it!, not at all!; **¿cuánto hay de aquí a Cuzco?** how far is it from here to Cuzco?; **¿qué hubo?** (*Méx*) hi!, how are you?
▼(**b**) **hay que** + *infin* it is necessary to + *infin*, one must + *infin*; **hay que trabajar** one has to work, everyone must work; **hay que** trabajar más (*to individual*) you must work harder; **hay que hacerlo** it has to be done; **¡había que verlo!** you should have seen it!; **hay que ser fuertes** we must be strong; **no hay que tomarlo a mal** there's no cause to take it badly, you mustn't get upset about it; **y no hay más que conformarse** there's nothing one can do but fall into line.
(**c**) (*tiempo*) **3 años ha** 3 years ago; **poco tiempo ha** a short time ago.
[4] **haberse** VR (**a**) (††) to behave, comport o.s.; **se ha habido con honradez** he has behaved honourably.
(**b**) **habérselas con uno** to be up against sb, have to do with sb, have to contend with sb; **tenemos que habérnoslas con un enemigo despiadado** we are up against a ruthless enemy; **¡allá te las hayas!** that's your affair!
[5] NM (*ingresos*) income, salary; (*sueldo*) pay, wages; (*Com*) assets; (*en balance*) credit side; **~es** assets, property, goods; **asentar algo al ~ de uno, pasar algo al ~ de uno** to credit sth to sb; **¿cuánto tenemos en el ~?** how much have we on the credit side? (*t fig*); **la autora tiene 6 libros en el ~** the author has 6 books behind her (*o* to her credit).

habichuela NF kidney bean; **ganarse las ~s** to earn one's living.

hábil ADJ (**a**) (*listo*) clever; (*diestro*) skilful; (*capaz*) able, capable, proficient; (*experto*) good, expert (*en* at); (*pey*) cunning, smart.
(**b**) **~ para** fit for.
(**c**) **día ~** working day.
(**d**) (*Jur*) competent.

habilidad NF (**a**) (*gen*) cleverness; skill; (*capacidad*) ability, proficiency; (*destreza*) expertness, expertise; (*pey*) cunning, smartness; **hombre de gran ~ política** a man of great political skill; **tener ~ manual** to be clever with one's hands.
(**b**) fitness (*para* for).
(**c**) (*Jur*) competence.

habilidoso ADJ capable, handy; (*esp pey*) clever, smart.

habilitación NF (**a**) (*título*) qualification, entitlement.
(**b**) (*de casa etc*) equipment, fitting out.
(**c**) (*Fin*) financing; (*Cono Sur Agr*) credit in kind; (*CAm, Méx**: *anticipo*) advance, sub*.
(**d**) (*Cono Sur: sociedad*) offer of a partnership to an employee.
(**e**) (*oficina*) paymaster's office.

habilitado NM paymaster.

habilitar [1a] VT (**a**) (*gen*) to qualify, entitle (*para que haga* to do); (*permitir*) to enable (*para que haga* to do); (*autorizar*) to empower, authorize (*para que haga* to do).
(**b**) *casa etc* to equip, fit out, set up; **las aulas están habilitadas con TV** the rooms are equipped with TV.
(**c**) (*Fin*) to finance; **~ a uno** (*Cono Sur Agr*) to make sb a loan in kind (with the next crop as security), give sb credit facilities; (*CAm, Méx**) to give sb an advance, sub* sb.
(**d**) (*Cono Sur Com*) to take into partnership.
(**e**) (*CAm Agr*) to cover, serve.
(**f**) (*Carib*) to annoy, bother.

hábilmente ADV cleverly; skilfully; ably, proficiently, expertly; (*pey*) cunningly, smartly.

habiloso ADJ (*Cono Sur*) = **habilidoso.**

habitabilidad NF habitability; (*de casa*) quality, condition.

habitable ADJ inhabitable, that can be lived in.

habitación NF (**a**) (*vivienda*) habitation; dwelling, abode; (*alquilado*) lodging(s), apartment; (*Bio*) habitat.
(**b**) (*cuarto*) room; **habitaciones (particulares)** rooms, suite; **~ de dos camas, ~ doble, ~ de matrimonio** double room; **~ individual** single room; **~ para invitado** guest-room.

habitacional ADJ (*LAm*) housing (*atr*).

habitáculo NM living space; (*Aut*) inside, interior.

habitado ADJ inhabited; lived-in; *satélite etc* manned, carrying a crew.

habitante [1] NMF (*gen*) inhabitant; (*vecino*) resident; (*inquilino*) occupant, tenant; **una ciudad de 10.000 ~s** a town of 10,000 inhabitants (*o* people), a town with a population of 10,000.

[2] NM (*hum: piojo*) louse; **tener ~s** to be lousy.

habitar [1a] [1] VT to inhabit, live in, dwell in; *casa etc* to occupy, be the occupant of.

[2] VI to live.

hábitat NM, PL **hábitats** habitat.

hábito NM (a) habit, custom; **una droga que conduce al ~ morboso** a habit-forming drug; **tener el ~ de** + *infin* to be in the habit of + *ger*.

(b) (*Ecl*) habit; **~ monástico** monastic habit; **ahorcar** (*o* **colgar**) **los ~s** to leave the priesthood; **tomar el ~** (*hombre*) to take holy orders, become a monk, (*mujer*) to take the veil, become a nun.

habituado, -a NM/F habitué(e).

habitual [1] ADJ habitual, customary, usual; *cliente, lector etc* regular; *criminal* hardened; *mentiroso* incorrigible; *pecado* besetting; **su restaurante ~** one's usual restaurant; **como lector ~ de esa revista** as a regular reader of your journal.

[2] NMF (*de bar etc*) habitué(e); (*de tienda*) regular customer.

habituar [1e] [1] VT to accustom (*a* to).

[2] **habituarse** VR: **~ a** to become accustomed to, get used to.

habla NF (a) (*facultad*) speech; **estar sin ~** to be speechless; **perder el ~** to become speechless.

(b) (*nacional etc*) language; (*regional*) dialect, speech; (*de clase, profesión etc*) talk, speech; (*Liter*) language, style; **de ~ francesa** French-speaking.

(c) (*acto*) talk; **¡García al ~!** (*Telec*) García speaking!; **estar al ~** to be in contact, be in touch; (*Náut*) to be within hailing distance; (*Telec*) to be on the line, be speaking (*con* to); **negar** (*o* **quitar**) **el ~ a uno** to stop speaking to sb, not be on speaking terms with sb; **ponerse al ~ con uno** to get into touch with sb.

hablachento ADJ (*Carib*) talkative.

hablada NF (a) (*Cono Sur*) speech.

(b) (*Méx: t ~s*): *fanfarronada*) boast.

(c) (*And**) scolding, telling-off*.

(d) (*CAm, Cono Sur, Méx*) (*indirecta*) hint, innuendo; (*chisme*) rumour, piece of gossip; **echar ~s** to drop hints, make innuendoes.

habladera NF (a) (*LAm*) talking, noise of talking. (b) (*Cono Sur, Méx*) = **habladuría**.

habladero NM (*Carib**) piece of gossip.

hablado [1] PTP *de* **hablar** spoken; **el lenguage ~** the spoken language.

[2] ADJ: **bien ~** nicely-spoken, well-spoken; **mal ~** coarse, rude; foul-mouthed.

hablador [1] ADJ (a) (*parlanchín*) talkative; chatty; voluble.

(b) (*chismoso*) gossipy, given to gossip.

(c) (*Méx*) (*jactancioso*) boastful; (*amenazador*) bullying.

(d) (*Carib, Méx**) (*mentiroso*) lying; (*gritón*) loud-mouthed.

[2] NM, **habladora** NF (a) talkative person, great talker, chatterbox. (b) gossip.

habladuría NF (*rumor*) rumour; (*injuria*) nasty remark, sarcastic remark; (*chisme*) idle chatter, piece of gossip; **~s** gossip, scandal.

hablanchín ADJ talkative, garrulous.

hablante [1] ADJ speaking.

[2] NMF speaker.

-hablante *en palabras compuestas, p.ej.* **castellanohablante** (ADJ) Castilian-speaking, (NMF) Castilian speaker.

hablantín ADJ = **hablanchín**.

hablantina NF (*And: sin sentido*) gibberish, meaningless torrent; (*And, Carib: cháchara*) empty talk, idle chatter; (*Carib: algarabía*) hubbub, din.

hablantino(so) ADJ (*And, Carib*) = **hablador** (a) *y* (b).

hablar [1a] [1] VT *lengua* to speak, talk; *tonterías etc* to talk; **habla bien el portugués** he speaks good Portuguese, he speaks Portuguese well; **~lo todo** to talk too much, give the game away; **y no hay más que ~** so there's no more to be said about it; **eso habrá que ~lo con X** you'll have to discuss that with X.

[2] VI to speak, talk (*a, con* to; *de* about, of); **que hable él** let him speak, let him have his say; **¡hable!, ¡puede ~!** (*Telec*) you're through!; **¿quién habla?** (*Telec*) who is it?, who's calling?; **¡quién fue a ~!** look who's talking!; **¡ni ~!** nonsense!; no fear!, not likely!; not a bit of it!; **de eso ni ~** that's out of the question, that's not on; **~ alto** to speak loudly, (*fig*) to speak out (frankly); **~ bajo** to talk quietly, speak in a low voice; **~ claro** (*fig*) to speak plainly, speak bluntly; **¡para que luego hablen de coches!** as if cars came into it!; **~ por ~** to talk just for talking's sake; **habla por sí mismo** it speaks for itself; **los datos hablan por sí solos** the facts speak for themselves; **el retrato está hablando** the portrait is a speaking likeness; **dar que ~ a la gente** to make people talk, cause people to gossip; **hacer ~ a uno** (*fig*) to make sb talk; **el vino hace ~** wine loosens people's

tongues.

[3] **hablarse** VR: **'se habla inglés'** 'English spoken here'; **en el Brasil se habla portugués** Portuguese is spoken in Brazil; **se habla de que van a comprarlo** there is talk of their buying it; **no se hablan** they are not on speaking terms, they don't speak; **¡no se hable más!** enough said!; that's settled!, there's an end to it!

┌─ HABLAR ─────────────────────── ver también la entrada ─┐

¿"Speak" o "talk"?

• Se traduce por *speak* cuando *hablar* tiene un sentido general, es decir, hace referencia a la emisión de sonidos articulados:

   Estaba tan conmocionado que no podía hablar
   He was so shocked that he was unable to speak
   Su padre antes tartamudeaba al hablar
   Her father used to stutter when he spoke

• También se emplea *speak* cuando nos referimos a la capacidad de *hablar* un idioma:

   Habla francés y alemán
   She speaks French and German

• Cuando *hablar* implica la participación de más de una persona, es decir, se trata de una conversación, una charla, o un comentario, entonces se traduce por *talk*.

   Es una de esas personas que no para de hablar
   He's one of those people who won't stop talking

• Para traducir la construcción *hablar con alguien* podemos utilizar *talk to* (*talk with* en el inglés de EE.UU.) o, si el uso es más formal, se puede emplear *speak to* (*speak with* en el inglés de EE.UU.):

   Vi a Manolo hablando animadamente con un grupo de turistas
   I saw Manolo talking o speaking animatedly to o with a group of tourists

• Si queremos especificar el idioma en que se desarrolla la conversación, se puede emplear tanto *talk* como *speak*, aunque éste último se usa en un lenguaje más formal:

   Me sorprendió bastante verla hablar en francés con tanta soltura
   I was surprised to see her talking o speaking (in) French so fluently
   Para otros usos y ejemplos ver la entrada.

└──┘

hablilla NF rumour, story; (piece of) gossip, tittle-tattle.

hablista NMF good speaker, elegant user of language; linguistically-conscious person.

habloteo NM incomprehensible talk.

habré *etc* V **haber**.

Habsburgo NM Hapsburg.

hacedero ADJ practicable, feasible.

hacedor(a) NM/F maker; **el** (**Supremo**) **H~** the Maker.

hacendado [1] ADJ landed, property-owning.

[2] NM landowner; gentleman farmer; (*LAm: de ganado*) rancher; (*Carib: de ingenio*) sugar-plantation owner.

hacendario ADJ (*Méx*) treasury (atr), budgetary.

hacendista NMF economist, financial expert.

hacendoso ADJ (*trabajador*) industrious, hard-working; (*ocupado*) busy, bustling.

hacer [2r] [1] VT (a) (*gen*) to make, create; (*Téc*) to make, manufacture; (*construir*) to build, construct; *vestido etc* to make; *obra de arte* to make; to fashion; (*Liter, Mús*) to compose; *dinero* to make, earn; *humo etc* to make, give off, emit, produce; *guerra* to fight, wage; **~ ~ algo** to have sth made; **~lo** (*euf*) to have sex, do it; **lo harán en la tele*** they'll show it on the telly*.

(b) (*preparar*) to make, prepare; *cama* to make; *comida* to make, prepare, get, cook; *maleta* to pack; *corbata* to tie; (*Com*) *balance* to strike; *apuesta* to lay; *objeción* to make, raise; *pregunta* to put, ask; *orden* to give; *discurso* to make, deliver; *visita* to pay; **~ la barba a uno** to shave sb (*V t* **barba¹**); **~ el pelo a una** to do sb's hair; **~ un recado** to run a message, go on an errand.

(c) (*causar*) to cause, make; *sombra* to cast; **el árbol hace sombra** the tree gives shade, the tree casts a shadow.

(d) (*dedicarse a*) **~ cine** to make films, be engaged in film work, be working for the cinema; **este año hace turismo en África** this year he's gone touring (*o* as a tourist) in Africa.

(e) (*efectuar etc*) to do; (*realizar*) to execute, perform, put into practice; (*Teat*) to do, perform; *milagro etc* to do, work, perform; **no sé qué ~** I don't know what to do; **haga lo que quiera** do as you please; **¿qué haces ahí?** what are you doing?, what are you up to?; **¿qué le vamos a ~?** what can we do about it?; isn't he awful?; **~ por ~** to do sth for the sake of doing it, do sth even though it is not necessary; **la ha hecho buena** (*iró*) a fine mess he's made of it; *V* **bien, mal** *etc*.

(f) (*sustituye a otro verbo*) to do; **él protestó y yo hice lo mismo** he protested and I did the same; **no viene como lo solía ~** he doesn't come as he used to (do).

(g) **~ algo pedazos** (*etc*): V **pedazo** *etc*.

(h) ~ **el malo** (*Teat*) to play the (part of the) villain, act the villain.

(i) (*pensar*) to imagine, think, assume; **yo le hacía más viejo** I thought he was older; **te hacíamos en el Perú** we thought you were in Peru, we assumed you were in Peru.

(j) me hizo con dinero (*proveer*) he provided me with money.

(k) (*acostumbrar*) to accustom, inure; ~ **el cuerpo al frío** to inure the body to cold, get the body used to cold.

(l) (+ *infin etc*) to make, force, oblige, compel; **les hice venir** I made them come; **nos hizo que fuésemos** he made us go; **yo haré que vengan** I'll see to it that they come; **hágale entrar** show him in, have him come in; **me lo hizo saber** he told me it, he informed me of it; ~ **construir una casa** to have a house built, get a house built; **hago lavar la ropa a una vecina** I have a neighbour (to) wash my clothes.

(m) (*Mat*) to make (up), amount to; **6 y 3 hacen 9** 6 and 3 make 9; **éste hace 100** this one makes 100.

(n) (*volver*) to make, turn, render, send; **el vino lo hizo borracho** the wine made him drunk; **la tinta lo hizo azul** the ink made (o turned) it blue; **esto lo hará más difícil** this will make (o render) it more difficult.

2 VI **(a)** (*comportarse*) to act, behave; (*fingir*) to pretend; ~ **como que ...**, ~ **como si ...** to act as if ...; ~ **uno como que no quiere** to be reluctant, seem not to want to; ~ **de** to act as, (*Teat*) to act, play the part of; ~ **el muerto** to pretend to be dead (*V t* **muerto**); ~ **el tonto** to act the fool, play the fool; **¡no le hagas!** (*Méx**) don't give me that!*

(b) dar que ~ to cause trouble; to make work; **daban que** ~ **a la policía** they gave the police trouble, they caused trouble to the police.

(c) ~ **para** + *infin*, ~ **por** + *infin* to try to + *infin*, make an effort to + *infin*.

(d) (*importar*) to be important, matter; **no le hace** (*LAm*) it doesn't matter, never mind; **¿te hace que vayamos a tomar unas copas?** how about a drink?, what say we go for a drink?

(e) (*convenir*) to be suitable, be fitting; **hace a todo** he's good for anything; **¿hace?** will it do?, is it all right?; OK?*; is it a deal?; **la llave hace a todas las puertas** the key fits (o does for) all the doors.

(f) ~ **bueno** (*Méx*) persona to make good.

3 V IMPERS **(a)** (*Met*) to be; *V* **calor, frío, tiempo** *etc*.

(b) (*LAm*) **hace sed** I'm thirsty; **hace sueño** I'm sleepy.

(c) (*tiempo*) ago; **hace 3 años** 3 years ago; **hace 2 años que se fue** he left 2 years ago, it's 2 years since he left; **desde hace 4 años** for (the last) 4 years; **está perdido desde hace 15 días** it's been lost for a fortnight; **hace poco** a short while back, a short time ago; **no hace mucho** not long ago; **hace de esto varios años** this has been going on for some years; **X, conocido hace mucho por sus cuadros** X, long known for his pictures; *V* **tiempo** *etc*.

4 hacerse VR (*efectuarse etc*) **(a)** to be made, be done *etc*; **se hará de ladrillos** it will be built of brick; **todavía no se ha hecho** it still has not been done; **¡eso no se hace!** that's not done!; **la respuesta no se hizo esperar** the answer was not slow in coming.

(b) ~ **cortesías** (*mutuamente*) to exchange courtesies.

(c) (*personal*) **se hizo cortar el pelo** she had her hair cut; **me hago confeccionar un traje** I'm having a suit made; ~ **un retrato, ~ retratar** to have one's portrait painted; ~ **afeitar** to have a shave, have o.s. shaved.

(d) (*llegar a ser*) to become; **se hicieron amigos** they became friends; ~ **enfermera** to become a nurse, take up nursing, go into nursing.

(e) (*fingirse*) to pretend; ~ **el sordo** to pretend not to hear, turn a deaf ear; ~ **el sueco** to pretend not to hear (o understand); to act dumb*, not let on*; ~ **el tonto** to act the fool, play the fool.

(f) (*volverse*) to become, grow, get; to turn (into), come to be; **esto se hace pesado** this is becoming tedious; **si las cosas se hacen difíciles** if things get difficult, if things turn awkward; ~ **grande** to grow tall, get tall; ~ **viejo** to grow old, get old; ~ **cristiano** to turn Christian, become a Christian, be converted to Christianity; **se me hace imposible trabajar** it's becoming impossible for me to work, I'm finding it impossible to work.

(g) ~ **a** + *infin* to get used to + *ger*, become accustomed to + *ger*; ~ **a una idea** to get used to an idea.

(h) se me hace que ... (*esp LAm*) I think that ..., it seems to me that ..., I get the impression that ...

(i) ~ **con algo** to get hold of sth; to take sth, appropriate sth; to confiscate sth; **logró** ~ **con una copia** he managed to get hold of a copy.

(j) ~ **de algo** (*Méx: obtener*) to get (hold of) sth.

(k) ~ **a un lado** to stand aside (*t fig*), move over; ~ **atrás** to move back, fall back; *para muchas locuciones, V el* ADJ *o* N.

hacha¹ NF **(a)** axe; chopper; hatchet; ~ **de armas** battle-axe.

(b) (*) genius; **¡eres un ~!** you're a genius!; **es un ~ para el bridge** he's a genius at bridge, he's a brilliant bridge-player.

(c) (*locuciones*) **de ~ y tiza** (*Cono Sur**) tough, virile; (*pey*) brawling;

de ~ (*Cono Sur*: ADV) unexpectedly, without warning; **dar con el** ~ **a uno** (*Cono Sur**) to tear a strip off sb*; **ser** ~ **para la ropa** (*Méx*) to be hard on one's clothes; **estar** ~ (*Méx*) to be ready; **estar con el** ~ (*Cono Sur**) to have a hangover*.

hacha² NF (*tea*) torch, firebrand; (*vela*) large candle; **como** ~ **de muerto** *luz* dim, weak.

hachador NM (*CAm*) woodman, lumberjack.

hachar [1a] VT (*LAm*) = **hachear**.

hachazo NM **(a)** (*golpe*) axe blow, stroke with an axe; hack, cut.

(b) (*LAm*) gash, open wound.

(c) (*And: de caballo*) bolt, dash.

hache NF the (name of the) letter *h*; **por** ~ **o por be** for one reason or another; **llámele Vd** ~ call it what you will; **volverse** ~**s y erres** (*And*), **volverse** ~**s y cúes** (*Cono Sur*) to come to nothing, fall through.

hachear [1a] **1** VT to hew, cut (down *etc*).
2 VI to wield an axe.

hachemita ADJ Hashemite, Jordanian.

hachero¹ NM woodman, lumberjack; (*Mil*) sapper.

hachero² NM torch stand, sconce.

hacheta NF adze; small axe, hatchet.

hachich NM, **hachís¹** NM hashish.

hachís² INTERJ atishoo!

hacho NM (*fuego*) beacon; (*colina etc*) beacon hill.

hachón NM (large) torch, firebrand.

hachuela NF = **hacheta**.

hacia PREP **(a)** (*lugar*) towards, in the direction of; (*cerca*) about, near; ~ **abajo** down, downwards; ~ **arriba** up, upwards; **ir** ~ **las montañas** to go towards the mountains; **eso está más** ~ **el este** that's further over to the east, that is more in an easterly direction; **vamos** ~ **allá** let's go in that direction, let's go over that way; **¿**~ **dónde vamos?** where are we going?

(b) (*tiempo*) about; ~ **mediodía** about noon, towards noon.

(c) (*actitud*) towards; **su hostilidad** ~ **la idea** his hostility towards the idea.

hacienda NF **(a)** (*finca*) property; country estate, large farm; (*LAm: de ganado*) (cattle) ranch; (*Carib: ingenio*) sugar plantation.

(b) (*Cono Sur*) cattle, livestock.

(c) ~ **pública** public finance; (**Ministerio de**) **H~** Treasury, Exchequer, Ministry of Finance.

(d) ~**s** household chores.

hacina NF pile, heap; (*Agr*) stack, rick.

hacinado ADJ crowded; **la gente estaba hacinada** people were crowded (o packed) together; **viven** ~**s** they live in overcrowded conditions.

hacinamiento NM heaping (up); (*Agr*) stacking; (*fig*) crowding, overcrowding; accumulation.

hacinar [1a] **1** VT (*amontonar*) to pile (up), heap (up); (*Agr*) to stack, put into a stack (o rick); (*fig*) to crowd, overcrowd; (*acumular*) to accumulate, amass; (*ahorrar*) to hoard.
2 hacinarse VR: ~ **en** (*fig: gente*) to be packed into.

hada NF fairy; ~ **buena** good fairy; ~ **madrina** fairy godmother; **cuento de** ~**s** fairy tale.

hado NM fate, destiny.

haga, hago *etc*: *V* **hacer**.

hágalo Vd mismo NM do-it-yourself.

hagiografía NF hagiography.

hagiógrafo, -a NM/F hagiographer.

haiga* NM big car, posh car*.

haiku [ˈhaiku] NM haiku.

Haití NM Haiti.

haitiano, -a ADJ, NM/F Haitian.

hala INTERJ **(a)** (*oye*) hi!, hoy! **(b)** (*vamos*) come on!, let's go! **(c)** (*anda*) get on with it!, hurry up! **(d)** (*Náut*) heave!; *V t* **jalar. (e) no quiero, ¡~!** I don't want to, so there! **(f)** (*sorpresa, admiración*) good heavens!

halaco NM (*CAm*) piece of junk, useless object.

halagador ADJ (*que agrada*) pleasing, gratifying; (*adulador*) flattering.

halagar [1h] VT **(a)** (*mostrar afecto*) to show affection to, make up to.

(b) (*agradar*) to please, gratify; (*atraer*) to allure, attract; **es una perspectiva que me halaga** it's a possibility which pleases me.

(c) (*lisonjear*) to flatter; to cajole.

halago NM **(a)** (*t* ~**s**: *V* VT **(b)**) pleasure, delight; gratification; allurement, attraction; **los** ~**s de la vida de campo** the attractions of country life, the blandishments of country life. **(b)** (*t* ~**s**: *lisonjas*) flattery; (*pey*) cajolery.

halagüeño ADJ (*agradable*) pleasing, gratifying; (*atraente*) alluring, attractive; *opinión, observación* flattering (*para* to); *perspectiva* promising, hopeful.

halar [1a] VT Y VI = **jalar**.

halcón NM **(a)** falcon, hawk; ~ **común, ~ peregrino** peregrine; ~ **abejero** honey buzzard. **(b)** (*fig*) hawk, hardliner; **los halcones y las palomas** the hawks and the doves. **(c)** (*Méx**) young thug of the ruling party.

halconería NF falconry, hawking.

halconero NM falconer.

halda NF **(a)** *(falda)* skirt; **de ~s o de mangas** at all costs, by hook or by crook. **(b)** *(arpillera)* sackcloth, coarse wrapping material.

hale INTERJ = **hala.**

haleche NM anchovy.

halibut [ali'ßu] NM, PL **halibuts** [ali'ßu] halibut.

hálito NM *(aliento)* breath; *(vapor)* vapour, exhalation; *(poét)* gentle breeze.

halitosis NF halitosis, bad breath.

hall [xol] NM, PL **halls** [xol] hall; *(Teat)* foyer; *(de hotel)* lounge, foyer.

hallaca NF *(Carib)* tamale.

hallador(a) NM/F finder.

hallar [1a] **1** VT *(gen)* to find; *(descubrir)* to discover; *(localizar)* to locate; *(averiguar)* to find out; *oposición etc* to meet with, run up against.
2 hallarse VR to be; to find o.s.; **se hallaba fuera** he was away at the time; **¿dónde se halla la catedral?** where is the cathedral?; **se halla sin dinero** he has no money, he finds himself out of money; **~ enfermo** to be ill; **~ mejor** to be better; **aquí me hallo a gusto** I'm all right here, I'm comfortable here; **no se hallaba a gusto en la fiesta** she felt out of place at the party; **no se halla bien con el nuevo jefe** he doesn't get on with the new boss; **~ con un obstáculo** to encounter an obstacle, be up against an obstacle; **se halla en todo** he's mixed up in everything.

hallazgo NM **(a)** *(acto)* finding, discovery.
(b) *(objeto)* find, thing found; **un ~ interesantísimo** a most interesting find.
(c) *(premio)* finder's reward; '**500 pesos de ~**' '500 pesos reward'.

halo NM halo, aura.

halogenado ADJ halogenated.

halógeno **1** ADJ halogenous, halogen *(atr)*; **lámpara halógena** halogen lamp.
2 NM halogen.

halón NM *(LAm)* = **jalón (c).**

haltera **1** NF dumb-bell; bar-bell; **~s** weights.
2 NMF weight-lifter.

halterofilia NF weight-lifting.

halterófilo, -a NM/F weight-lifter.

hamaca NF **(a)** hammock. **(b)** *(Cono Sur)* *(columpio)* swing; *(mecedora)* rocking chair; **~ plegable** deckchair.

hamacar [1g], **hamaquear** [1a] *(LAm)* **1** VT **(a)** to rock, swing. **(b)** **~ a uno** *(Méx*)* to keep sb on tenterhooks. **(c)** *(Carib)* to beat, ill-treat.
2 hamacarse, hamaquearse VR to rock (o.s.), swing.

hambre NF **(a)** *(gen)* hunger; *(de población entera)* famine; *(mortal)* starvation; **~ canina, ~ feroz, ~ de lobo** ravenous hunger; **estar con ~, padecer ~, pasar ~** to be hungry, go hungry, starve; **entretener el ~** to stave off hunger; **matar el ~** to satisfy one's hunger; **morir de ~** to die of (o from) starvation, starve to death; **hacer morir de ~** to starve to death; **tener ~** to be hungry; **tener mucha ~** to be very hungry; **vengo con mucha ~** I'm terribly hungry, I've got a vast appetite.
(b) *(fig)* hunger, keen desire, longing *(de* for); **tener ~ de** to hunger for, be hungry for.
(c) (‡: *sexual)* randiness*; **pasar ~, tener ~** to want it*.

hambreado ADJ *(LAm)* = **hambriento.**

hambreador NM *(And, Cono Sur)* monopolist; exploiter.

hambrear [1a] **1** VT to starve; *(fig: LAm)* to exploit.
2 VI to be hungry, be famished.

hambriento **1** ADJ **(a)** starving, hungry, famished.
(b) **~ de** *(fig)* starved of, hungry for, longing for.
(c) (‡: *sexual)* randy*.
2 NM, **hambrienta** NF starving person; **los ~s** the hungry, the starving.

hambrón* ADJ greedy.

hambruna NF *(And, Cono Sur)*, **hambrusia** NF *(Carib)* ravenous hunger; **tener ~** to be ravenously hungry, be starving.

Hamburgo NM Hamburg.

hamburguesa NF hamburger.

hamburguesera NF hamburger-maker.

hamburguesería NF hamburger restaurant.

hamo NM fish-hook.

hampa NF underworld, low life, criminal classes; *(Hist)* rogue's life, vagrancy; **gente del ~** people of the underworld, criminals, riffraff.

hampesco ADJ underworld *(atr)*, criminal.

hampón NM tough, rowdy, thug.

hámster NM, PL **hámsters** hamster.

han V **haber.**

hand [xan] NM *(CAm Dep)* handball.

hándbol ['xandbol] NM handball.

handbolista NMF handball player.

hándicap ['xandikap] NM, PL **hándicaps** handicap.

handicapar [xandika'par] [1a] VT to handicap.

handling ['xanlin] NM *(Aer)* handling (of baggage *etc*).

hangar NM *(Aer)* hangar.

Hanovre NM Hanover.

hápax NM INVAR hapax, nonce-word.

happening ['xapenin] NM, PL **happenings** *(Arte)* happening.

haragán **1** ADJ idle, lazy, good-for-nothing.
2 NM, **haragana** NF idler, layabout, good-for-nothing.
3 NM *(Carib: limpiapisos)* mop.
4 NF *(CAm*)* reclining chair.

haraganear [1a] VI to idle, waste one's time; to lounge about, loaf around.

haraganería NF idleness, laziness.

harakiri NM = **haraquiri.**

harapiento ADJ ragged, tattered, in rags.

harapo NM rag, tatter; **~s** *(Méx‡)* clothes, clobber‡; **estar hecho un ~** to go about in rags.

haraposo ADJ = **harapiento.**

haraquiri NM hara-kiri; **hacerse el ~** to commit hara-kiri.

hard [xar] NM hardware.

hardware ['xarwer] NM hardware.

haré *etc* V **hacer.**

harén NM harem.

harina NF **(a)** flour; meal; powder; **~ de arroz** ground rice; **~ de avena** oatmeal; **~ de fuerza, ~ para levadura** self-raising flour; **~ de huesos** bonemeal; **~ lacteada** malted milk; **~ de maíz** cornflour, corn meal; **~ de patata** potato flour; **~ de pescado** fish-meal; **~ de soja** soya flour; **~ de trigo** wheat flour; **eso es ~ de otro costal** that's another story, that's a horse of a different colour; **el coche se hizo ~** the car was smashed up; **meterse en ~** *(fig)* to get involved; **estar en ~s** *(And*)* to be broke*.
(b) *(And)* small piece; **una ~ de pan** a bit of bread.
(c) *(Carib‡)* money, dough‡.

harinear [1a] VI *(Carib)* to drizzle.

harineo NM *(Carib)* drizzle.

harinero **1** ADJ flour *(atr)*.
2 NM **(a)** *(persona)* flour merchant. **(b)** *(recipiente)* flour bin.

harinoso ADJ floury.

harnear [1a] VT *(And, Cono Sur, Méx)* to sieve, sift.

harnero NM sieve.

harpagón‡ ADJ *(And)* very thin, skinny.

harpillera NF sacking, sackcloth.

hartar [1a] **1** VT **(a)** to satiate, surfeit, glut, more than satisfy *(con, de* with).
(b) *(fig)* to weary, tire.
(c) **~ a uno de algo** *(fig)* to overwhelm sb with sth; **~ a uno de palos** to rain blows on sb.
(d) *(CAm: maldecir de)* to malign, slander.
2 hartarse VR **(a)** to eat one's fill *(con* of), gorge *(con* on), be satiated; **comer hasta ~** to eat to repletion; **~ de uvas** to stuff o.s. with grapes, eat too many grapes.
(b) *(fig)* to weary, get weary *(de* of); to get fed up *(de* with); **~ de reír** to laugh fit to burst; **no se hartaron de reír** they couldn't stop laughing.

hartazgo NM surfeit, satiety; repletion; glut; bellyful; **darse un ~** to eat to repletion, overeat; **darse un ~ de** to eat one's fill of; *(fig)* to give o.s. a bellyful of, have too much of.

▼ **harto** **1** ADJ **(a)** full *(de* of), satiated; glutted *(de* with).
▼**(b)** *(fig)* **estar ~ de** to be fed up with*, be tired of; **¡estamos ~s ya!** we're fed up!*, enough is enough!; **¡estoy ~ de decírtelo!** I'm fed up with telling you so!*
(c) *(LAm)* a lot of; much, many.
2 ADV *(liter en España, normal en LAm)* amply; very, quite; **una tarea ~ difícil** a very difficult task, a difficult enough task; **lo sé ~ bien** I know (it) all too well; **ha habido ~ accidentes** *(LAm)* there were a lot of accidents.

hartón **1** ADJ **(a)** *(CAm, Méx: glotón)* greedy, gluttonous. **(b)** *(Méx*)* *(estúpido)* stupid; *(molesto)* annoying.
2 NM *(And, Carib, Méx)* large banana.

hartura NF **(a)** surfeit; glut; *(abundancia)* abundance, plenty; **con ~** in abundance, in plenty. **(b)** *(de deseo)* full satisfaction, fulfilment.

has V **haber.**

has. ABR *de* **hectáreas** NFPL hectares.

hasídico ADJ Hassidic, Chassidic.

hasta **1** ADV even; **y ~ la pegó** and he even hit her; **~ en Valencia hiela a veces** even in Valencia it freezes sometimes.
2 PREP **(a)** *(lugar)* as far as; up to, down to; **lo llevó ~ la iglesia** he carried it as far as the church; **los árboles crecen ~ los 4.000 metros** the trees grow up to 4,000 metres.
(b) *(tiempo)* till, until; as late as; up to; **se quedará ~ el martes** she will stay till Tuesday; **siguió en pie ~ el siglo pasado** it stood until

(o up to, as late as) the last century; **no me levanto ~ las 9** I don't get up until (o before) 9 o'clock; **no iré ~ después de la reunión** I shan't go till after the meeting; *V* **luego, vista** *etc*.

(c) (*CAm, Méx*) not until; **~ mañana viene** he's not coming till tomorrow; **~ hoy lo conocí** I didn't meet him till today, I met him only today.

3 CONJ: **~ que** till, until; **~ que me lo des** until you give it to me.

┌─ HASTA ─┐ **ver también la entrada**

La preposición *hasta* tiene varias traducciones posibles, dependiendo de si se emplea en expresiones de tiempo o de lugar.

En expresiones de tiempo

● Generalmente se traduce por *till* o *until*. *Till* tiene un uso más informal que *until* y no suele ir al principio de la frase.

El paquete no me llegó hasta dos semanas después
The parcel did not arrive until o till two weeks later
Hasta entonces las cosas nos iban bien
Until then things were going well for us

● Además, *hasta* también se puede traducir por *to* en la construcción *desde ... hasta ...*:

Estoy aquí todos los días desde las ocho hasta las tres
I'm here everyday from eight until o till o to three
Te estuve esperando desde las once de la mañana hasta la una de la tarde
I was waiting for you from eleven in the morning until o till o to one in the afternoon

En expresiones de lugar

● Cuando usamos *hasta* en expresiones de lugar, podemos traducirlo por (*up/down*) *to* o por *as far as*:

Caminó hasta el borde del acantilado
He walked (up) to o as far as the edge of the cliff
¿Vamos hasta la orilla?
Shall we go down to the shore?
Ya anda solo hasta el sofá
He can already walk on his own as far as o (up) to the sofa

Para otros usos y ejemplos ver la entrada.

---

hastiador ADJ = **hastiante**.

hastial NM **(a)** (*Arquit*) gable end. **(b)** [*gen* xas'tjal] (‡) roughneck*, lout.

hastiante ADJ wearisome, boring; sickening.

hastiar [1c] **1** VT (*fastidiar*) to weary, bore; (*asquear*) to sicken, disgust.
2 hastiarse VR: **~ de** to tire of, get fed up with*.

hastío NM weariness; boredom; disgust, loathing.

hatajo NM lot, collection; **un ~ de pícaros** a bunch of rogues.

hatillo NM = **hato**.

hato NM **(a)** (*ropa*) clothes, set of clothing; (*enseres*) personal effects, possessions; **~ y garabato** (*And, Carib**) all that one has; **coger el ~, echar el ~ a cuestas, liar el ~** to pack up; to clear out; **menear el ~ a uno** to beat sb up*; **revolver el ~** to stir up trouble.
(b) (*víveres*) provisions.
(c) (*choza*) shepherd's hut; (*parada*) stopping place (of migratory flocks *etc*).
(d) (*Agr. animales*) flock, herd; (*gente*) group, crowd, collection; (*pey*) bunch, band, gang; (*de objetos, observaciones etc*) lot, collection.
(e) (*And, Carib*) cattle ranch.

Hawai NM (*t* **Islas ~**) Hawaii.

hawaiano, -a **1** ADJ, NM/F Hawaiian.
2 NF (*Cono Sur: chancleta*) flip-flop.

hay, haya *etc: V* **haber.**

Haya NF: **La ~** The Hague.

haya NF beech, beech tree.

hayaca NF (*And*) tamale; (*Carib*) stuffed cornmeal pasty.

hayal NM, **hayedo** NM beechwood.

hayo NM (*Bot*) coca; coca leaves.

hayuco NM beechnut; (*t* **~s**) beechnuts, beechmast.

haz¹ NM **(a)** (*lío*) bundle, bunch; (*Agr. de trigo*) sheaf; (*de paja*) truss; **haces** (*Hist Pol*) fasces.
(b) (*rayo, TV etc*) beam; **~ de electrones** electron beam; **~ láser** laser beam; **~ de luz** beam of light, pencil of light; **~ de partículas** particle beam.

haz² NF (*Anat: liter*) face; (*fig*) face, surface; (*de tela*) right side; **~ de la tierra** face of the earth; **de dos haces** two-faced.

haz³ *V* **hacer.**

haza NF small field, plot of arable land.

hazaña NF feat, exploit, deed, achievement; **las ~s del héroe** the hero's exploits, the hero's great deeds; **sería una ~** it would be a great thing to do, it would be a great achievement.

hazañería NF fuss, exaggerated show; histrionics.

hazañero ADJ *persona* dramatic, histrionic, given to making a great fuss; *acción* histrionic, exaggerated.

hazañoso ADJ *persona* heroic, gallant, dauntless; *acción* heroic, doughty.

hazmerreír NM laughing stock, joke.

HB NM (*Esp Pol*) ABR *de* **Herri Batasuna** *Basque political party*.

he¹ *V* **haber.**

he² ADV (*liter*): **~ aquí** here is, here are; this is, these are; (*más dramático*) behold; **¡heme aquí!, ¡héteme aquí!** here I am!; **¡helo aquí!** here it is!; **¡helos allí!** there they are!; **~ aquí la razón de que ...**, **~ aquí por qué ...** that is why ...; **~ aquí los resultados** these are the results, here you have the results.

heavy ['xeβi], PL **heavies**. **1** ADJ **(a)** *música, grupo* heavy metal. **(b)** (‡: *duro*) heavy‡.
2 NMF heavy metal fan.
3 NM (*música*) heavy metal.

hebdomadario ADJ, NM weekly.

hebilla NF buckle, clasp.

hebra NF (*Cos*) thread; piece of thread, length of thread; (*Bot etc*) fibre; strand; (*de gusano de seda*) thread; (*de madera*) grain; (*de metal*) vein, streak; (*fig*) thread (of the conversation); **~s** (*poét*) hair; **ni ~** (*And**) nothing; **tabaco de ~** loose tobacco; **de una ~** (*Cono Sur, Méx**) in one go; **pegar la ~** to start a conversation; to chatter, talk nineteen to the dozen; **no quedó ni ~ de comida** (*And**) there wasn't a scrap of food left; **se rompió la ~ entre los dos amigos** (*Méx**) the two friends fell out.

hebraico ADJ Hebraic.

hebraísta NMF Hebraist.

hebreo **1** ADJ (*Hist*) Hebrew; (*moderno*) Israeli.
2 NM, **hebrea** NF (*Hist*) Hebrew; (*moderno*) Israeli; (*pey**) usurer, extortioner; pawnbroker.
3 NM (*Ling*) Hebrew; **jurar en ~*** to blow one's top*.

Hébridas NFPL Hebrides.

hebroso ADJ fibrous; *carne* stringy.

hecatombe NF hecatomb; (*fig*) slaughter, butchery; **¡aquello fue la ~!** what a disaster that was!, you should have seen it!

heces NFPL *V* **hez.**

hechicera NF sorceress, enchantress, witch.

hechicería NF **(a)** (*gen*) sorcery, witchcraft. **(b)** (*una ~*) spell. **(c)** (*fig*) spell, enchantment, charm.

hechicero **1** ADJ magic(al); bewitching, enchanting.
2 NM wizard, sorcerer, enchanter; (*en África etc*) witch doctor.

hechizante ADJ enchanting, bewitching.

hechizar [1f] VT **(a)** to bewitch, cast a spell on. **(b)** (*fig*) to charm, enchant, fascinate; (*pey*) to bedevil.

hechizo **1** ADJ **(a)** (*falso*) artificial, false, fake.
(b) (*separable*) detachable, removable.
(c) (*Téc*) manufactured.
(d) (*And, Cono Sur, Méx*) home-made; (*Méx, And: pey*) home-made, rough and ready.
2 NM **(a)** (*gen*) magic, witchcraft; (*un ~*) magic spell, charm.
(b) (*fig*) magic, spell, enchantment; glamour; fascination; **~s** (*de mujer etc*) charms.

▼ **hecho** **1** (PTP *de* **hacer**) done; **¡~!** agreed!, it's a deal!; **a lo ~ pecho** we must make the best of it now; **lo ~ ~ está** what's done cannot be undone; **bien ~** well done; well made; *persona* well-proportioned; **¡bien ~!** well done!; **mal ~** badly done; poorly made; *persona* ill-proportioned; **él, ~ un ...** he, like a ...; **ella, hecha una furia, se lanzó ...** she hurled herself furiously ..., she threw herself in a fury ...; **estar ~ a** to be used to, be inured to; *V* **basilisco, fiera** *etc*.
2 ADJ **(a)** (*acabado*) complete, finished; *hombre, queso, vino etc* mature; perfect; (*Cos*) ready-made, ready-to-wear; made-up; **~ y derecho** complete, right and true, as it should be in every way; **un hombre ~ y derecho** a real man, every inch a man; *V* **frase.**
(b) (*Culin*) **muy ~** overdone, well-cooked; **no muy ~, poco ~** underdone, undercooked.
3 NM **(a)** (*acto*) deed, act, action; **~ de armas** feat of arms; **H~s de los Apóstoles** Acts of the Apostles; **~s que no palabras** deeds not words.
(b) (*realidad*) fact; (*factor*) factor; (*asunto*) matter; (*suceso*) event; **~ consumado** fait accompli; **esto es un ~** this is a fact; **el ~ es que ...** the fact is that ..., the position is that ...; **volvamos al ~** let's get
▼ back to the facts; **de ~** in fact, as a matter of fact; (*Pol etc*: ADJ Y ADV) de facto; **de ~ y de derecho** de facto and de jure; **en ~ de verdad** as a matter of solid fact.

hechor NM **(a)** (*LAm*) stud donkey. **(b)** (*Cono Sur*) = **malhechor.**

hechura NF **(a)** (*acto*) making, creation; **no tiene ~** it can't be done.
(b) (*objeto etc*) creation, product; **somos ~ de Dios** we are God's handiwork.
(c) (*forma*) form, shape; (*de persona*) build; (*de traje*) cut; **a ~ de** like, after the manner of; **tener ~s de algo** to show an aptitude for sth; **no tener uno ~** (*Cono Sur, Méx*) to be a dead loss.
(d) (*Cos*) making-up, confection; **~s** cost of making up; **de ~ sastre** tailor-made.

(e) (*Téc*) craftsmanship, workmanship; **de exquisita ~** of exquisite workmanship.

(f) (*fig*) creature, puppet; **él es una ~ del ministro** he is a creature of the minister.

hectárea NF hectare (= *2.471 acres*).

héctico ADJ consumptive.

hectogramo NM hectogramme, hectogram (*US*).

hectolitro NM hectolitre, hectoliter (*US*).

Héctor NM Hector.

heder [2g] VI **(a)** to stink, smell, reek (*a* of). **(b)** (*fig*) to annoy, be unbearable.

hediondez NF **(a)** (*olor*) stink, stench. **(b)** (*cosa*) stinking thing.

hediondo ADJ **(a)** (*maloliente*) stinking, foul-smelling, smelly. **(b)** (*sucio*) filthy; (*repugnante*) repulsive; (*obsceno*) obscene. **(c)** (*fig: inaguantable*) annoying, unbearable.

hedonismo NM hedonism.

hedonista [1] ADJ hedonistic.
[2] NMF hedonist.

hedor NM stink, stench, smell (*a* of).

hegemonía NF hegemony.

hégira NF hegira.

helada NF frost; freeze, freeze-up; **~ blanca** hoarfrost; **~ de madrugada** early-morning frost.

heladamente ADV (*fig*) icily.

heladera NF (*Cono Sur*) refrigerator, icebox (*US*).

heladería NF ice-cream stall, ice-cream parlour.

heladero [1] ADJ ice-cream (*atr*).
[2] NM (*And, Cono Sur*) ice-cream man.

helado [1] ADJ **(a)** frozen; freezing, icy; icebound. **(b)** (*fig*) chilly, icy, cold, disdainful. **(c)** **dejar ~ a uno** to dumbfound sb, shatter sb; **¡me dejas ~!** you amaze me!; **quedarse ~** to be scared stiff. **(d)** (*Carib Culin*) iced, frosted.
[2] NM ice cream.

helador ADJ *viento etc* icy, freezing; **hace un frío ~** it's icy cold, it's perishing cold.

heladora NF (*de nevera*) freezing unit, freezer; (*LAm*) refrigerator, icebox (*US*).

helaje NM (*And*) (*frío intenso*) intense cold; (*sensación*) chill.

helar [1j] [1] VT **(a)** (*Met*) to freeze; to ice (up); *líquido* to congeal, harden; *bebida etc* to ice, chill. **(b)** (*fig*) (*pasmar*) to dumbfound, shatter, amaze; (*desalentar*) to discourage; (*aterrar*) to scare to death.
[2] VI to freeze.
[3] **helarse** VR (*Met*) to freeze; to be frozen; (*Aer, Ferro etc*) to ice (up), freeze up: (*líquido*) to congeal, harden, set.

helecho NM bracken, fern.

Helena NF Helen.

helénico ADJ Hellenic, Greek.

heleno NM, **helena** NF Hellene, Greek.

Helesponto NM Hellespont.

hélice NF **(a)** spiral; (*Anat, Elec, Mat*) helix; **~ doble** double helix. **(b)** (*Aer*) propeller, airscrew; (*Náut*) propeller, screw.

helicoidal ADJ spiral, helicoidal, helical.

helicóptero NM helicopter; **~ artillado, ~ de ataque, ~ de combate** helicopter gunship; **~ fumigador** crop-spraying helicopter.

heliesquí NM heli-skiing.

helio NM helium.

helioesquí NM heli-skiing.

heliógrafo NM heliograph.

heliosfera NF heliosphere.

heliosismología NF helioseismology.

helioterapia NF heliotherapy, sunray treatment.

heliotipia NF heliotype.

heliotropo NM heliotrope.

helipuerto NM heliport.

helitransportar [1a] VT to transport by helicopter; (*Mil etc*) to helicopter (in).

helmántico ADJ (*Esp*) of Salamanca.

helvético, -a ADJ, NM/F Swiss.

hematíe NM red blood cell.

hematología NF haematology.

hematoma NM bruise.

hembra NF **(a)** (*Bot, Zool*) female; (*humana*) woman; (*pey*) female; **el armiño ~** the female stoat, the she-stoat; **el pájaro ~** the female bird, the hen bird; **una real ~** a fine figure of a woman; **5 hijos, esto es 2 varones y 3 ~s** 5 children, that is 2 boys and 3 girls. **(b)** (*Mec*) nut; **~ de terraja** die. **(c)** (*Cos*) eye.

hembraje NM (*LAm*) female flock, female herd; (*hum*) womenfolk.

hembrería* NF (*Carib, Méx*), **hembrerío*** NM gaggle of women, crowd of women.

hembrilla NF (*Mec*) nut; eyebolt.

hembrista NMF (*hum*) feminist.

hemerográfico ADJ newspaper (*atr*).

hemeroteca NF newspaper archive.

hemiciclo NM semicircular theatre; (*Parl*) chamber; floor.

hemiplejía NF hemiplegia; stroke.

hemisferio NM hemisphere.

hemistiquio NM hemistich.

hemodiálisis NF INVAR haemodialysis.

hemodonación NF donation of blood.

hemofilia NF haemophilia.

hemofílico, -a ADJ, NM/F haemophiliac.

hemoglobina NF haemoglobin.

hemograma NM haemogram.

hemorragia NF (*Med*) haemorrhage; bleeding, loss of blood; (*fig*) drain, loss; **~ cerebral** cerebral haemorrhage; **~ nasal** nosebleed; **morir por ~** to bleed to death.

hemorroides NFPL haemorrhoids, piles.

hemos V **haber**.

henal NM hayloft.

henar NM meadow, hayfield.

henchir [3h] [1] VT to fill (up), stuff, cram (*de* with).
[2] **henchirse** VR **(a)** to swell; (*persona*) to stuff o.s. (with food). **(b)** **~ de orgullo** to swell with pride.

Hendaya NF Hendaye.

hendedura NF crack, fissure, crevice; cleft, split, slit; (*Geol*) rift, fissure.

hender [2g] VT (*gen*) to crack; (*cortar*) to cleave, split, slit; *olas* to cleave, breast; (*abrirse paso*) to make one's way through; (*fig*) to split.

hendidura NF = **hendedura**.

hendija NF (*LAm*) crack, crevice.

hendir [3i] VT (*LAm*) = **hender**.

henequén NM (*LAm*) (*planta*) agave, henequen; (*fibra*) agave fibre, henequen.

henificación NF haymaking; tedding.

henificar [1g] VT to ted.

henil NM hayloft.

heniquén NM (*Carib, Méx*) = **henequén**.

heno NM hay.

heñir [3h y 3k] VT to knead.

hepático ADJ hepatic, liver (*atr*); **trasplante ~** liver transplant.

hepatitis NF hepatitis.

hepato... PREF hepato..., hepat...

heptagonal ADJ heptagonal.

heptágono NM heptagon.

heptámetro NM heptameter.

heptatlón NM heptathlon.

heráldica NF heraldry.

heráldico ADJ heraldic.

heraldo NM herald.

herales: NMPL pants, trousers.

herbáceo ADJ herbaceous.

herbaje NM **(a)** herbage; grass, pasture. **(b)** (*Náut*) coarse woollen cloth.

herbaj(e)ar [1a] [1] VT to graze, put out to pasture.
[2] VI to graze.

herbario [1] ADJ herbal.
[2] NM **(a)** (*colección*) herbarium, plant collection. **(b)** (*persona*) herbalist; (*botánico*) botanist.

herbazal NM grassland, pasture.

herbicida NM weed-killer; **~ selectivo** selective weed-killer.

herbívoro [1] ADJ herbivorous.
[2] NM herbivore.

herbodietética NF **(a)** **centro** (o **tienda**) **de ~** (*disciplina*) health food shop. **(b)** (*tienda*) health food shop.

herbodietético ADJ health food (*atr*).

herbolario [1] ADJ (*fig*) crazy, cracked.
[2] NM, **herbolaria** NF (*persona*) herbalist.
[3] NM (*tienda*) herbalist's (shop), health food shop.

herboristería NF herbalist's (shop).

herborizar [1f] VI to gather herbs, pick herbs; (*como coleccionista*) to botanize, collect plants.

herboso ADJ grassy.

hercio NM hertz.

hercúleo ADJ Herculean.

Hércules NM Hercules; **h~** (*de circo*) strong man; **es un ~** (*fig*) he's awfully strong.

heredabilidad NF inheritability.

heredable ADJ inheritable, that can be inherited.

heredad NF landed property; country estate, farm.

heredar [1a] VT **(a)** *propiedad* to inherit (*de* from); to be heir to. **(b)** *persona* to name as one's heir. **(c)** (*LAm*) to leave, bequeath (*a* to).

heredera NF heiress.

heredero NM heir (*de* to); inheritor (*de* of); ~ **forzoso** heir apparent; ~ **presunto** heir presumptive; sole heir, sole beneficiary; **príncipe** ~ crown prince; ~ **del trono** heir to the throne.

hereditario ADJ hereditary.

hereje [1] ADJ (a) (*Cono Sur*: *irrespetuoso*) disrespectful. (b) (*And, Carib*: *excesivo*) excessive; **un trabajo** ~* a heavy task.
[2] NMF heretic; ¡~!* you brute!

herejía NF (a) (*Rel y fig*) heresy. (b) (*fig*: *trampa*) dirty trick, low deed; (*injuria*) insult. (c) (*And, Méx*) silly remark, gaffe.

herencia NF (a) inheritance, estate, legacy; (*fig*) heritage. (b) (*Bio*) heredity.

hereque NM (*Carib Med*) skin disease; (*Bot*) a disease of coffee.

heresiarca NMF heresiarch, arch-heretic.

herético ADJ heretical.

herida NF (a) wound, injury. (b) (*fig*) wound, insult, outrage; **hurgar en la** ~ (*fig*) to reopen an old wound; **lamer las** ~**s** to lick one's wounds.

herido [1] ADJ (a) injured; hurt; (*Mil etc*) wounded.
(b) (*fig*) wounded, offended.
[2] NM (a) injured man; (*Mil*) wounded man; **los** ~**s** (*Mil*) the wounded; **el número de los** ~**s en el accidente** the number of people hurt in the accident, the number of casualties in the accident.
(b) (*Cono Sur*) ditch, channel.

herir [3i] VT (a) (*dañar*) to injure, hurt; (*Mil etc*) to wound; ~ **a uno en el brazo** to wound sb in the arm.
(b) (*golpear*) to beat, strike, hit; (*Mús*) to pluck, strike, play; (*sol*) to strike on; to beat down on; **un sonido me hirió el oído** a sound reached (o struck o offended) my ear; **es un color que hiere la vista** it's a colour which offends the eye.
(c) (*fig*) *corazón etc* to touch, move, sway.
(d) (*fig*: *ofender*) to offend, hurt.

hermafrodita ADJ, NM hermaphrodite.

hermana NF (a) sister; **media** ~ half-sister; **prima** ~ first cousin; ~ **gemela** twin sister; ~ **mayor** elder sister; ~ **política** sister-in-law.
(b) (*Ecl*) sister; ~ **lega** lay sister.
(c) (*una de par*) twin; other half (*of pair*), corresponding part.

hermanable ADJ (a) (*de hermano*) fraternal. (b) (*compatible*) compatible. (c) (*a tono etc*) matching, that can be matched.

hermanamiento NM: ~ **de ciudades** town-twinning.

hermanar [1a] VT (*para formar par*) to match, put together; (*unir*) to join; *ciudades* to twin; (*relacionar*) to relate; (*armonizar*) to harmonize, bring into harmony; (*Cono Sur*: *hacer pares*) to pair.

hermanastra NF stepsister.

hermanastro NM stepbrother.

hermandad NF (a) (*relación*) brotherhood; close relationship, intimacy. (b) (*grupo etc*) brotherhood, fraternity; sisterhood; **Santa H~** (*Hist*) rural police (*15th to 19th centuries*).

hermanita NF little sister; ~**s de la caridad** Little Sisters of Charity.

hermanito NM little brother.

hermano [1] ADJ similar; matched, matching; *barco* sister; **ciudades hermanas** twin towns.
[2] NM (a) brother; (*Bio*) sibling; **medio** ~ half-brother; **primo** ~ first cousin; ~ **carnal** full brother; ~ **gemelo** twin brother; ~ **de leche** foster-brother; ~ **mayor** elder brother, big brother; ~ **político** brother-in-law; **mis** ~**s** my brothers, my brothers and sisters; **el Gran H~ te vigila** Big Brother is watching you; **su** ~ **pequeño**‡ his willy‡.
(b) (*Ecl*) brother; ~**s** brothers, brethren.
(c) (*uno de par*) twin; other half (*of pair*), corresponding part.
(d) (*LAm*: *espectro*) ghost.

hermética NF Hermetic philosophy, hermetics.

herméticamente ADV hermetically.

hermeticidad NF hermetic nature, hermeticism.

hermético ADJ hermetic; airtight, watertight; (*fig*) self-contained; *persona* reserved, secretive; *teoría* watertight; *misterio* impenetrable.

hermetismo NM (*fig*) tight secrecy, close secrecy; silence, reserve; hermeticism.

hermetizar [1f] VT (*fig*) to seal off, close off.

hermosamente ADV beautifully; handsomely.

hermosear [1a] VT to beautify, embellish, adorn.

hermoso ADJ (a) (*bello*) beautiful, lovely; (*espléndido*) fine, splendid; (*abundante*) abundant, lavish; *hombre* handsome; **un día** ~ a fine day, a lovely day; **¡qué escena más hermosa!** what a lovely scene!; **seis** ~**s toros** six magnificent bulls.
(b) (*LAm*) large, robust; *persona* large, impressive, stout.

hermosura NF (a) (*gen*) beauty, loveliness; splendour; lavishness; handsomeness. (b) (*persona*) beauty, belle; (*en oración directa*) darling.

hernia NF rupture, hernia; ~ **discal** slipped disc; ~ **estrangulada** strangulated hernia.

herniarse [1b] VR to rupture o.s.

Herodes NM Herod; **hacer lo de** ~* to put up with it; **ir de** ~ **a Pilatos** to be driven from pillar to post.

héroe NM hero.

heroicamente ADV heroically.

heroicidad NF (a) (*cualidad*) heroism. (b) (*una* ~) heroic deed.

heroico ADJ heroic.

heroicocómico ADJ mock-heroic.

heroína¹ NF heroine.

heroína² NF (*Farm*) heroin.

heroinomanía NF heroin addiction.

heroinómano, -a NM/F heroin addict.

heroísmo NM heroism.

herpes NM o NFPL (*Med*) herpes, shingles; ~ **genital** genital herpes.

herrada NF (a) bucket. (b) (*And Agr*) branding.

herrador NM farrier, blacksmith.

herradura NF horseshoe; **camino de** ~ bridle path; **curva en** ~ (*Aut*) hairpin bend; **mostrar las** ~**s** (*fig*) to bolt, show a clean pair of heels.

herraje NM (a) ironwork, iron fittings. (b) (*Cono Sur*) horseshoe. (c) (*Méx*) silver harness fittings.

herramental NM toolkit, toolbag.

herramienta NF (a) (*gen*) tool; implement, appliance; (*equipo*) set of tools; (**‡**) tool‡; ~ **de filo** edge tool; ~ **de mano** hand tool; ~ **mecánica** power tool. (b) (*de toro*) horns; (*dientes*) teeth.

herranza NF (*And*) branding.

herrar [1j] VT (*Agr*) *caballo* to shoe; *ganado* to brand; (*Téc*) to bind with iron, trim with ironwork.

herrería NF (a) (*taller*) smithy, forge, blacksmith's (shop). (b) (*fábrica*) ironworks. (c) (*oficio*) blacksmith's trade, craft of the smith. (d) (*fig*) uproar, tumult.

herrerillo NM (*Orn*) tit.

herrero NM blacksmith, smith; ~ **de grueso** foundry worker.

herrete NM metal tip, ferrule, tag; (*LAm*) branding-iron, brand.

Herri Batasuna N *Basque pro-independence political party*.

herribatasuno [1] ADJ of Herri Batasuna.
[2] NMF member (o supporter) of Herri Batasuna.

herrumbre NF (a) rust. (b) (*Bot*) rust. (c) (*fig*) iron taste, taste of iron.

herrumbroso ADJ rusty.

hervederas* NFPL (*Carib*) heartburn, indigestion.

hervidero NM (a) (*acto*) boiling; bubbling, seething.
(b) (*manantial*) hot spring; bubbling spring.
(c) (*fig*) swarm, throng, crowd; **un** ~ **de gente** a swarm of people; **un** ~ **de disturbios** a hotbed of unrest.

hervido [1] PTP Y ADJ boiled.
[2] NM (a) (*acto*) boiling. (b) (*LAm*: *guiso*) stew.

hervidor NM kettle; boiler.

hervidora NF: ~ **de agua** water heater.

hervir [3i] [1] VT (*esp LAm*) to boil; to cook.
[2] VI (a) (*gen*) to boil; (*burbujear*) to bubble, seethe; (*mar etc*) to seethe, surge; ~ **a fuego lento** to simmer; **dejar de** ~ to stop boiling, go off the boil; **empezar a** ~ to begin to boil, come to the boil.
(b) (*fig*) ~ **de**, ~ **en** to swarm with, seethe with, teem with; **la cama hervía de pulgas** the bed was swarming with fleas.

hervor NM (a) (*acto*) boiling; seething; **alzar el** ~, **levantar el** ~ to come to the boil. (b) (*fig*) fire, fervour (of youth); passion; restlessness.

hervoroso ADJ (a) boiling, seething; *sol* burning. (b) (*fig*) = **fervoroso**.

heteo, -a ADJ, NM/F Hittite.

hetero* ADJ = **heterosexual**.

heterodoxia NF heterodoxy.

heterodoxo ADJ heterodox, unorthodox.

heterogeneidad NF heterogeneousness, heterogeneous nature.

heterogéneo ADJ heterogeneous.

heterónimo NM heteronym.

heterónomo ADJ heteronomous.

heterosexual ADJ, NMF heterosexual.

heterosexualidad NF heterosexuality.

heticarse [1g] VR (*Carib*) to contract tuberculosis.

hético ADJ consumptive.

hetiquencia NF (*Carib*) tuberculosis.

heurístico ADJ heuristic.

hexadecimal ADJ hexadecimal.

hexagonal ADJ hexagonal.

hexágono NM hexagon; **el** ~ (*Geog*) France.

hexámetro NM hexameter.

hez NF (*esp heces* PL) sediment, dregs; slops; (*Med*) faeces; (*de vino*) lees; (*fig*) dregs, scum; **la** ~ **de la sociedad** the scum of society.

hg. ABR *de* **hectogramos** hectogram(me)s, hg.

hiatal ADJ: **hernia** ~ hiatus hernia, hiatal hernia.

hiato NM (*Ling*) hiatus.

hibernación NF hibernation; **estar en** ~ (*fig*) to be dormant.

hibernal ADJ wintry, winter (*atr*).

hibernar [1a] VI to hibernate.

hibisco NM hibiscus.

hibridación NF, **hibridaje** NM hybridization.
hibridar [1a] VTI to hybridize.
hibridismo NM hybridism.
hibridizar [1f] VT (*Bio*) to hybridize; (*fig*) to lend a mixed appearance to, produce a hybrid appearance in.
híbrido, -a ADJ, NM/F hybrid.
hice *etc V* **hacer.**
hidalga NF noblewoman.
hidalgo ☐1 ADJ noble; illustrious; (*fig*) gentlemanly, honourable; generous.
   ☐2 NM (**a**) nobleman, hidalgo. (**b**) (*Méx Hist*) 10-peso gold coin.
hidalguía NF nobility; (*fig*) nobility, gentlemanliness, honourableness; generosity.
hideputa: NM = **hijodeputa.**
hidra NF hydra; **H~** (*Mit*) Hydra.
hidratación NF (*del organismo*) hydration; (*de la piel*) moisturizing.
hidratante ☐1 ADJ *crema* moisturizing.
   ☐2 NF moisturizing cream.
hidratar [1a] VT to hydrate; to moisturize.
hidrato NM hydrate; **~ de carbono** carbohydrate.
hidráulica NF hydraulics.
hidráulico ADJ hydraulic, water (*atr*); **fuerza hidráulica** water power, hydraulic power.
hídrico ADJ water (*atr*).
hidro... PREF hydro..., water-...
hidroala NF hydrofoil.
hidroavión NM seaplane, flying boat.
hidrocarburo NM hydrocarbon.
hidrocefalia NF (*Med*) hydrocephalus, water on the brain.
hidrodeslizador NM hovercraft.
hidrodinámica NF hydrodynamics.
hidroeléctrica NF hydroelectric power station.
hidroeléctrico ADJ hydroelectric.
hidroesfera NF hydrosphere.
hidrófilo ADJ absorbent.
hidrofobia NF hydrophobia; rabies.
hidrofóbico ADJ, **hidrófobo** ADJ hydrophobic.
hidrofoil NM hydrofoil.
hidrofuerza NF hydropower.
hidrófugo ADJ damp-proof, damp-resistant, water-repellent.
hidrógeno NM hydrogen.
hidrografía NF hydrography.
hidrólisis NF INVAR hydrolysis.
hidrolizar [1f] ☐1 VT to hydrolyze.
   ☐2 **hidrolizarse** VR to hydrolyze.
hidromasaje NM hydromassage.
hidropesía NF dropsy.
hidrópico ADJ dropsical.
hidroplano NM hydroplane.
hidroponia NF hydroponics, aquiculture.
hidropónico ADJ hydroponic.
hidrosfera NF hydrosphere.
hidrosoluble ADJ soluble in water, water-soluble.
hidroterapia NF hydrotherapy.
hidrovía NF waterway.
hidróxido NM hydroxide; **~ amónico** ammonium hydroxide.
hiedra NF ivy.
hiel NF (**a**) (*Anat*) gall, bile; **echar la ~*** to overwork, sweat one's guts out*.
   (**b**) (*fig*) gall, bitterness; **no tener ~** to be very sweet-tempered.
   (**c**) **~es** (*fig*) troubles, upsets.
hiela *V* **helar.**
hielera NF ice tray; (*CAm, Méx*) refrigerator.
hielo NM (**a**) ice; frost; **~ a la deriva, ~ flotante, ~ movedizo** drift ice; **~ picado** crushed ice; **~ seco** dry ice; **con ~** (*bebida*) with ice, on the rocks*; **romper el ~** (*fig*) to break the ice. (**b**) (*fig*) coldness, indifference; **ser más frío que el ~** to be as cold as ice.
hiena NF hyena; **hecho una ~** furious; **ponerse como una ~** to get furious.
hierático ADJ *figura* hieratic(al); *aspecto* stern, severe.
hieratismo NM hieratic attitude; solemnity, stateliness.
hierba NF grass; small plant; (*Med*) herb, medicinal plant; (:) pot:, hash*; **~s** grass, pasture; **mala ~** weed, (*fig*) evil influence; **~ artificial** artificial playing surface; **~ cana** groundsel; **~ gatera** catmint; **~ lombriguera** ragwort; **~ mate** maté; **~ mora** nightshade; **~ rastrera** cotton grass; **~ de San Juan** St John's-wort; **y otras ~s** (*fig*) and so forth, and suchlike; **a las finas ~s** cooked with herbs; **oír** (o **sentir, ver**) **crecer la ~** to be pretty smart; **pisar mala ~** to have bad luck.
hierbabuena NF mint.
hierbajo NM weed.
hierbajoso ADJ weedy, weed-infested.
hierbaluisa NF lemon verbena, aloysia.

hierra NF (*LAm*) branding.
hierro NM (**a**) (*metal*) iron; **~ acanalado** corrugated iron; **~ batido** wrought iron; **~ bruto** crude iron, pig iron; **~ colado** cast iron; **~ forjado** wrought iron; **~ de fundición, ~ fundido** cast iron; **~ en lingotes** pig iron; **~ ondulado** corrugated iron; **~ viejo** scrap iron, old iron; **a ~ candente batir de repente** strike while the iron is hot; **como el ~** like iron, tough, strong; **de ~** iron (*atr*); **llevar ~ a Vizcaya** to carry coals to Newcastle; **machacar en ~ frío** to beat one's head against a wall, flog a dead horse; **el que a ~ mata, a ~ muere** those that live by the sword die by the sword; **quitar ~ a** to minimize an issue, cut things down to their proper size.
   (**b**) (*objeto*) iron object; (*herramienta*) tool; (*de flecha etc*) head; (*Agr*) brand, branding-iron; (*Golf*) iron; (:) rod:; (*pistola*) gun; **~s** irons.
hi-fi [i'fi] NM, PL **hi-fis** hi-fi.
higa NF rude sign, obscene gesture (*with fist and thumb*); (*fig*) scorn, derision; **no da una ~*** he doesn't give a damn; **dar ~ a** to jeer at, mock.
hígado NM (**a**) (*Anat*) liver; **castigar el ~*** to drink a lot; **echar los ~s*** to sweat one's guts out*; **tener ~ de indio** (*CAm, Méx*) to be a disagreeable sort.
   (**b**) **~s** (*fig**) guts, pluck.
   (**c**) **ser un ~** (*CAm, Méx*:) to be a pain in the neck*.
higadoso ADJ: **ser ~** (*CAm, Méx*:) to be a pain in the neck*.
highball NM (*LAm*) cocktail.
higiene NF hygiene.
higiénico ADJ hygienic; sanitary.
higienización NF cleaning, cleansing.
higienizar [1f] ☐1 VT to clean up, cleanse.
   ☐2 **higienizarse** VR (*Cono Sur*) to wash, bath.
higo NM (**a**) (*Bot*) fig, green fig; **~ chumbo, ~ de tuna** prickly pear; **~ paso, ~ seco** dried fig; **de ~s a brevas** once in a blue moon; **ser un ~ mustio** to be weakly; to be off-colour; *V* **importar** *etc.*
   (**b**) (*Vet*) thrush.
   (**c**) (:) cunt:.
higuera NF fig tree; **~ chumba, ~ de tuna** prickly pear (cactus), Indian fig tree; **~ del infierno, ~ infernal** castor-oil plant; **caer de la ~** to come down to earth with a bump; **estar en la ~** to be naïve; to be at a loss, not know what to do; to be day-dreaming.
higuerilla NF (*Méx*) castor-oil plant.
hija NF daughter; child; (*en oración directa, frec no se traduce, p.ej.*) **~ no te lo puedo decir** I can't tell you; **~ política** daughter-in-law; *V t* **hijo.**
hijastra NF stepdaughter.
hijastro NM stepson.
hijo NM (**a**) son; child; **~s** (*frec*) children; sons and daughters; offspring, descendants; **sin ~s** childless, without children; **¿cuántos ~s tiene?** how many children has she?; **Pitt ~** Pitt the Younger, the younger Pitt; **Juan Pérez, ~** Juan Pérez Junior; **~ de bendición** legitimate child; **~ de la cuna** foundling; **~ de la chingada** (*Méx*:) bastard:, son of a bitch:; **~ de leche** foster child; **~ natural** illegitimate child; **~ político** son-in-law; **nombrar a uno ~ predilecto de la ciudad** to name sb a favourite son of the city; **~ pródigo** prodigal son; **el ~ de mi madre*** I (myself), yours truly*; **cada ~ de vecino** everyone, every mother's son; **como cada ~ de vecino** like everyone else, like the next man; **~ de puta:** bastard:, son of a bitch:; **ser ~ de sus obras** to be a self-made man; **ser (muy) ~ de papá** to be daddy's boy, be a spoiled child; to have led a very sheltered life; **entró en el negocio como ~ de papá** he just followed his father in the business (so it was easy for him); **hacer a una un ~** to get a girl pregnant; **hacer a uno un ~ macho** (*LAm*) to do sb harm.
   (**b**) (*en oración directa: a chico*) son, sonny*, my boy; (*a adulto*) man, old chap* (*pero frec no se traduce*); **¡~ de mi alma!, ¡~ de mis entrañas!** my precious child!; **¡híjo(le)!** (*Méx**) good God!
hijodeputa: NM, **hijoputa:** NM bastard:, son of a bitch:.
hijoputada: NF dirty trick.
hijoputesco: ADJ rotten*, dirty.
hijoputez: NF dirty trick.
hijuela NF (**a**) (*niña*) little girl; (*hijita*) small daughter.
   (**b**) (*filial*) offshoot, branch, dependency.
   (**c**) (*Jur*) estate of a deceased person; share, portion, inheritance; list of bequests.
   (**d**) (*And, Cono Sur*) plot of land.
   (**e**) (*Cos*) piece of material (*for widening a garment*).
   (**f**) (*Agr*) small irrigation channel.
   (**g**) (*Méx Min*) seam of ore.
hijuelo NM (**a**) (*niño*) little boy; (*hijito*) small son; **~s** small children, (*Zool*) young. (**b**) (*Bot*) shoot. (**c**) (*And: camino*) side road, minor road.
hijuemadre: EXCL: **¡~!** (*CAm*) bloody hell!:, Jesus Christ!:
hijueputa: EXCL: **¡~!** (*CAm*) bloody hell!:, Jesus Christ!:
hijuna: (*LAm*) INTERJ you bastard!:
hila NF (**a**) (*fila*) row, line; **a la ~** in a row, in single file. (**b**) (*cuerda*)

thin gut; ~s (*Med*) lint.

hilacha NF (*hilo*) loose thread, hanging thread; shred; fibre, filament; ~ **de vidrio** spun glass; ~s (*Med*) lint; **mostrar la ~** (*Cono Sur**) to show (o.s. in) one's true colours.

hilachento ADJ (*LAm*) ragged, tattered; frayed; shabby.

hilacho NM (**a**) = **hilacha**. (**b**) ~s (*Méx*) rags, tatters. (**c**) **dar vuelo al ~** (*Méx**) to have a wild time.

hilachudo ADJ (*Méx*) = **hilachento**.

hilada NF row, line; (*Arquit*) course.

hilado [1] ADJ Y PTP spun; **seda hilada** spun silk.
[2] NM (**a**) (*acto*) spinning. (**b**) (*hilo*) thread, yarn.

hilador NM spinner.

hiladora NF (**a**) (*persona*) spinner. (**b**) (*Téc*) spinning jenny.

hilandería NF (**a**) (*arte*) spinning. (**b**) (*fábrica*) spinning mill; ~ **de algodón** cotton mill.

hilandero NM, **hilandera** NF spinner.

hilangos NMPL (*And*) rags, tatters.

hilar [1a] VT (**a**) to spin (*t Zool*). (**b**) (*fig*) to reason, infer; ~ (**muy**) **delgado**, ~ **fino** to be very particular (*o* meticulous, demanding); (*pey*) to split hairs; ~ **delgado** (*Cono Sur: morir*) to be dying.

hilaracha NF = **hilacha**.

hilarante ADJ hilarious; merry, mirthful; **gas ~** laughing gas.

hilaridad NF hilarity; merriment, mirth.

hilatura NF spinning.

hilaza NF yarn, coarse thread; **descubrir la ~** to show (o.s. in) one's true colours.

hilazón NF connection.

hilera NF (**a**) row, line; string; (*Mil etc*) rank, file; (*Arquit*) course; (*Agr*) row, drill. (**b**) (*Cos*) fine thread.

hilo NM (**a**) (*Cos etc*) thread, yarn; (*Bot etc*) fibre, filament; ~ **bramante** twine; ~ **de Escocia** lisle, strong cotton; ~ **de perlas** string of pearls; ~ **de zurcir** darning wool; **a ~** uninterruptedly, continuously; **coser al ~** to sew on the straight, sew with the weave; **dar mucho ~ que torcer** to cause a lot of trouble; **escapar con el ~ en una pata** (*Carib, Cono Sur**) to get out of a corner, wriggle out of a jam*; **colgar** (*o* **pender**) **de un ~** to hang by a thread; **contar algo del ~ al ovillo** to tell sth without omitting a single detail; **estar al ~** to be watchful, be on the look-out; **estar hecho un ~** to be as thin as a rake; **tela de ~** (*And, Carib*) linen cloth.
(**b**) (*de metal*) thin wire; (*Elec*) wire; flex; (*Telec*) line; ~ **directo** direct line, hot line; ~ **de tierra** earth wire, ground wire (*US*).
(**c**) (*de líquido etc*) thin line, thin stream, trickle; (*de gente*) thin line; ~ **dental** dental floss; ~ **de humo** thin line of smoke, plume of smoke; ~ **de música**, ~ **musical** piped music, muzak; **decir algo con un ~ de la voz** to say sth in a whisper; **irse tras el ~ de la gente** to follow the crowd.
(**d**) (*tela*) linen; **traje de ~** linen dress.
(**e**) (*fig: de conversación, discurso*) thread, theme; (*de vida*) course; (*de pensamiento*) train; ~ **conductor** connecting theme, principal theme; **coger el ~** to pick up the thread; (*en carrera etc*) to catch up; **perder el ~** to lose the thread; **seguir el ~** (*de razonamiento*) to follow, understand.

hilván NM tacking, basting; (*Cono Sur: hilo*) basting thread; (*Carib: dobladillo*) hem.

hilvanar [1a] VT (**a**) (*Cos*) to tack, baste. (**b**) (*fig: trabajo*) to do hurriedly; *construcción* to throw together, knock up hurriedly; **bien hilvanado** well done, well constructed.

Himalaya NM: **el ~**, **los montes ~** the Himalayas.

himalayo ADJ Himalayan.

himen NM hymen, maidenhead.

himeneo NM (**a**) (*liter*) nuptials (*liter*), wedding. (**b**) (*Poét*) epithalamium.

himnario NM hymnal, hymnbook.

himno NM hymn; ~ **nacional** national anthem.

hincada NF (**a**) (*Carib: hincadura*) thrust. (**b**) (*Cono Sur: cortesía*) genuflection. (**c**) (*Carib: dolor*) sharp pain, stabbing pain.

hincadura NF thrust, thrusting, driving.

hincapié NM: **hacer ~** to make a stand, take a firm stand; **hacer ~ en** to insist on; to dwell on, emphasize, make a special point of.

hincapilotes NM INVAR (*Cono Sur*) pile-driver.

hincar [1g] [1] VT (*meter*) to thrust (in), drive (in), push (in); *diente* to sink (*en into*); *pie etc* to set (firmly) (*en on*); ~**la*** to slog, work; **hincó la mirada en ella** he fixed his gaze on her, he stared at her fixedly; **hincó el bastón en el suelo** he stuck his stick in the ground, he thrust his stick into the ground; *V* **diente, rodilla**.
[2] **hincarse** VR: ~ **de rodillas** to kneel (down).

hincha [1] NF (**a**) ill will, animosity, bad blood; grudge; **uno de mis ~s** one of my pet hates*; **tener ~ a uno** to have a grudge against sb; **tomar ~ a uno** to take a dislike to sb.
(**b**) **¡qué ~!** (*Cono Sur**) what a bore!
[2] NMF (**a**) (*Dep etc*) fan, supporter, rooter (*US**); **los ~s del Madrid** the Madrid supporters.

(**b**) (*And**) pal*, chum*.

hinchable ADJ inflatable.

hinchabolas: NMF INVAR (*Cono Sur*) = **hinchapelotas**.

hinchada NF supporters, fans.

hinchado ADJ (**a**) swollen. (**b**) (:) **hinchada** pregnant; **dejar a una hinchada** to get a girl pregnant. (**c**) (*fig*) *persona* arrogant, vain; *estilo etc* pompous, high-flown, windy.

hinchador NM (**a**) ~ **de ruedas** tyre inflator. (**b**) (*Cono Sur:*) pest, bloody nuisance:.

hinchante: ADJ (**a**) (*molesto*) annoying, tiresome. (**b**) (*gracioso*) funny.

hinchapelotas: NMF INVAR: **es un ~** (*Cono Sur*) (*molesto*) he's a real pain in the neck*; (*aburrido*) he's a crashing bore.

hinchar [1a] [1] VT (**a**) to swell; to distend, enlarge; *neumático etc* to blow up, inflate, pump up; ~ **a una:** to get a girl pregnant.
(**b**) (*fig: exagerar*)) to exaggerate.
(**c**) (*Cono Sur:: molestar*) to annoy, upset; **me hincha todo el tiempo** he keeps on at me all the time.
[2] **hincharse** VR (**a**) to swell (up); to get distended; to stuff o.s. (*de* with).
(**b**) (*fig: engreírse*) to get conceited, become vain.
(**c**) (*: enriquecerse*) to make a pile*.
(**d**) ~ **a correr** (*etc*) to run (*etc*) hard, run (*etc*) about a lot; ~ **a reír** to laugh a lot, have a good laugh.

hinchazón NF (**a**) (*Med etc*) swelling; bump, lump.
(**b**) (*fig*) arrogance, vanity, conceit; (*de estilo etc*) pomposity, windiness.

hinco NM (*Cono Sur*) post, stake.

hindi NM Hindi.

hindú, -a ADJ, NM/F Hindu.

hinduismo NM Hinduism.

hiniesta NF (*Bot*) broom.

hinojo¹ NM (*Bot, Culin*) fennel.

hinojo² NM (*Anat*: ††) knee; **de ~s** on bended knee; **ponerse de ~s** to kneel (down), go down on one's knees.

hip INTERJ hic.

hipar [1a] [1] VI (**a**) to hiccup, hiccough.
(**b**) (*perro*) to pant; ~ **por algo** to long for sth, yearn for sth; ~ **por** + *infin* to long to + *infin*, yearn to + *infin*.
(**c**) (*fig*) to be worn out, be exhausted.
[2] VI [xi'par] to whine, whimper.

hipato* ADJ (*And*: *repleto*) full, swollen; (*And, Carib*: *pálido*) pale, anaemic; (*soso*) tasteless.

hipear [1a] VI (*Méx*) = **hipar**.

hiper* NM INVAR hypermarket.

hiper... PREF hyper...; (*) *p.ej.* **una cosa hipercara** a dreadfully expensive thing; **estoy hiperocupado** I'm up to my ears.

hiperacidez NF hyperacidity.

hiperactividad NF hyperactivity.

hiperactivo ADJ hyperactive.

hiperagudo ADJ abnormally acute.

hipérbaton NM, PL **hipérbatos** hyperbaton.

hipérbola NF hyperbola.

hipérbole NF hyperbole.

hiperbólico ADJ hyperbolic(al), exaggerated.

hipercorrección NF hypercorrection.

hipercrítico ADJ hypercritical; carping, censorious.

hiperexcitado ADJ over-excited.

hiperglucemia NF hyperglycaemia.

hiperinflación NF runaway inflation, hyperinflation.

hipermedia NM INVAR hypermedia.

hipermercado NM hypermarket.

hipermetropía NF, **hiperopía** NF long-sight, long-sightedness; **tener ~** to be long-sighted.

hipermillonario ADJ *acuerdo, ganancias* multi-million pound (*o* dollar *etc*).

hipernervioso ADJ excessively nervous, highly strung.

hiperrealismo NM Hyper-realism.

hipersensibilidad NF hypersensitivity; over-sensitiveness, touchiness.

hipersensible ADJ hypersensitive; over-sensitive, touchy.

hipersensitivo ADJ hypersensitive.

hipersónico ADJ supersonic.

hipertensión NF hypertension; ~ **arterial** high blood-pressure.

hipertenso [1] ADJ: **ser ~** to have high blood pressure.
[2] NM, **hipertensa** NF person with high blood pressure.

hipertexto NM hypertext.

hipertrofia NF hypertrophy.

hipervitaminosis NF INVAR hypervitaminosis.

hipiar [1b] VI (*Méx*) = **hipar**.

hípico ADJ horse (*atr*); equine.

hipido NM whine, whimper.

hipismo NM horse-racing.

hipnosis NF hypnosis.
hipnoterapia NF hypnotherapy.
hipnótico, -a ADJ, NM/F hypnotic.
hipnotismo NM hypnotism.
hipnotista NMF hypnotist.
hipnotizable ADJ susceptible to hypnosis.
hipnotizador ADJ hypnotizing.
hipnotizante NMF hypnotist.
hipnotizar [1f] VT to hypnotize, mesmerize.
hipo NM **(a)** hiccup(s), hiccough(s); **quitar el ~ a uno** to cure sb's hiccups, (fig) to take sb's breath away, be a shock to sb; **tener ~** to have hiccups.
  (b) (fig: deseo) longing, yearning; **tener ~ por** to long for, crave.
  (c) (fig) (asco) disgust; (rencor) grudge, ill will; **tener ~ con uno** to have a grudge against sb, have it in for sb.
hipo... PREF hypo...
hipoalergénico ADJ hypoallergenic.
hipocalórico ADJ low-calorie (atr).
hipocampo NM sea horse.
hipocondria, hipocondría NF hypochondria.
hipocondriaco, hipocondríaco [1] ADJ hypochondriac(al).
  [2] NM, **hipocondriaca, hipocondríaca** NF hypochondriac.
hipocorístico ADJ: **nombre ~** pet name, affectionate form of a name (p.ej. **Merche = Mercedes, Jim = James**).
Hipócrates NM Hippocrates.
hipocrático ADJ: **juramento ~** Hippocratic oath.
hipocresía NF hypocrisy.
hipócrita [1] ADJ hypocritical.
  [2] NMF hypocrite.
hipócritamente ADV hypocritically.
hipodérmico ADJ hypodermic.
hipódromo NM racetrack, racecourse; (Hist) hippodrome.
hipoglucemia NF hypoglycaemia.
hipónimo NM hyponym.
hipopótamo NM hippopotamus.
hiposulfito NM: **~ sódico** (Fot) hypo, sodium thiosulphate.
hipoteca NF mortgage; **~ dotal** endowment mortgage; **levantar una ~** to raise a mortgage; **redimir una ~** to pay off a mortgage.
hipotecar [1g] [1] VT to mortgage.
  [2] **hipotecarse** VR (fig) to commit o.s.
hipotecario ADJ mortgage (atr).
hipotensión NF low blood pressure.
hipotenso [1] ADJ: **ser ~** to have low blood pressure.
  [2] NM, **hipotensa** NF person with low blood pressure.
hipotensor ADJ hypotensive.
hipotenusa NF hypotenuse.
hipotermia NF hypothermia.
hipótesis NF INVAR hypothesis; supposition; theory, idea, notion.
hipotéticamente ADV hypothetically.
hipotético ADJ hypothetic(al).
hipotetizar [1f] VI to hypothesize.
hippie, hippy ['xipi] ADJ, NMF, PL **hippies** hippy.
hippioso* [xi'pjoso] [1] ADJ hippyish.
  [2] NM, **hippiosa** NF hippy type.
hippismo [xi'pismo] NM hippy movement; **los años del ~** the hippy years.
hiriente ADJ observación, tono wounding, cutting.
hirsutez NF hairiness.
hirsuto ADJ **(a)** hairy, hirsute; bristly. **(b)** (fig: brusco) brusque, gruff, rough.
hirvición* NF (And) abundance, multitude.
hirviendo (como ADJ) boiling.
hirviente ADJ boiling, seething.
hisca NF birdlime.
hisopear [1a] VT (Ecl) to sprinkle with holy water, asperse.
hisopo NM **(a)** (Ecl) sprinkler, aspergillum. **(b)** (Bot) hyssop. **(c)** (LAm: brocha) paintbrush; (Cono Sur: trapo)) dishcloth; (Cono Sur: de algodón) cotton bud.
hispalense ADJ, NMF Sevillian.
Híspalis N (liter) Seville.
Hispania NF (Hist) Hispania, Roman Spain.
hispánico ADJ Hispanic, Spanish.
hispanidad NF **(a)** (cualidad) Spanishness; Spanish quality, Spanish characteristics. **(b)** (Pol) Spanish world, Hispanic world; **Día de la H~** Columbus Day (12 October).

┌─ **DÍA DE LA HISPANIDAD** ─────────────────────┐

ⓘ *El Día de la Hispanidad, on 12 October, is a national holiday in Spain in honour of Colombus' arrival in the Americas. It is also a holiday in other Spanish-speaking countries where it is called the Día de la Raza.*

hispanismo NM **(a)** word (o phrase etc) peculiar to Spain; word (etc)
borrowed from Spanish, hispanicism.
  (b) (Univ etc) Hispanism, Hispanic studies; **el h~ holandés** Hispanic studies in Holland.
hispanista NMF (Univ etc) hispanist, Spanish scholar, student of Spain and Latin America.
hispanística NF Hispanic studies.
hispanizar [1f] VT to hispanicize.
hispano [1] ADJ Spanish, Hispanic; (en EE. UU.) Hispanic.
  [2] NM, **hispana** NF Spaniard; (en EE. UU.) Hispanic.
hispano-... PREF Hispano-..., Spanish-...; **pacto ~ruritano** Hispano-Ruritanian pact.
Hispanoamérica NF Spanish America, Latin America.
hispanoamericano [1] ADJ Spanish American, Latin American.
  [2] NM, **hispanoamericana** NF Spanish American, Latin American.
hispanoárabe ADJ Hispano-Arabic.
hispanófilo NM, **hispanófila** NF hispanophile.
hispanófobo NM, **hispanófoba** NF hispanophobe.
hispanohablante [1] ADJ Spanish-speaking.
  [2] NMF Spanish speaker.
hispanomarroquí ADJ Spanish-Moroccan.
hispanoparlante = **hispanohablante**.
hispinglés NM (hum) Spanglish.
histamínico ADJ histamine (atr).
histerectomía NF hysterectomy.
histeria NF hysteria.
histéricamente ADV hysterically.
histérico ADJ **(a)** personaje, novela hysterical; **paroxismo ~** hysterics.
  (b) (Cono Sur) queer‡.
histerismo NM hysteria; hysterics.
histerizarse [1f] VR to get hysterical, panic.
histograma NM histogram.
histología NF histology.
historia NF **(a)** (narración) story; (cuento) tale; **~s** (pey) tales, gossip; (Cono Sur: fig) mix-up, messy business; **la ~ es larga de contar** it's a long story; **dejarse de ~s** to come to the point, stop beating about the bush; **tener ~*** to be a long story; **no me vengas con ~s** don't give me that (one)*.
  (b) (~ humana etc) history; **en toda la ~ humana** in the whole of human history; **~ antigua** ancient history; **~ del arte** history of art, art history; **~ clínica** case-history; **~ natural** natural history; **H~ Sacra, H~ Sagrada** Biblical history, (en escuela) Scripture; **~ universal** world history; **es una mujer que tiene ~** she's a woman with a past; **ser de ~** to be famous, (pey) to be notorious; **pasar a la ~** to go down in (o to) history (como as); **picar en ~** to be a serious matter.
historiador(a) NM/F historian; chronicler, recorder.
historia-ficción NF historical novels pl.
historial [1] ADJ historical.
  [2] NM record; dossier; (Med: t **~ clínico**) case-history; **el brillante ~ del club** the club's brilliant record.
historiar [1b] VT **(a)** to tell the story of; to write the history of; to record, chronicle, write up. **(b)** (Arte etc) to paint, depict.
historicismo NM historicism.
historicista ADJ historicist.
histórico [1] ADJ **(a)** personaje, novela historical; (esp fig) historic. **(b)** miembro etc long-serving, original; long-established.
  [2] NM, **histórica** NF long-serving member, original member.

┌─ **HISTÓRICO** ─────────────── **ver también la entrada** ─┐

"¿Historical" o "historic"?
• Se traduce por *historical* cuando nos referimos a una persona o un hecho que pertenece a la historia o, si hablamos de una novela o película, que hace referencia a hechos del pasado:
  Fue una de las figuras históricas más importantes del siglo XIX
  He was one of the most important historical figures of the 19th century
  Las novelas históricas son mis preferidas
  I'm particularly keen on historical novels
• Se traduce por *historic* cuando nos referimos, o bien a hechos a los que se ha considerado decisivos en la historia, o bien a hechos a los que se considerará importantes en el futuro:
  Fue una decisión histórica
  It was a o an historic decision
  Ha sido una carrera histórica
  It has been a o an historic race

historiero ADJ (Cono Sur) gossipy.
historieta NF short story, tale; anecdote; (Tip) strip cartoon, comic strip.
historietista NMF strip cartoonist.
historificar [1g] VT to consign to the history books.
historiografía NF historiography, writing of history.
historiógrafo, -a NM/F historiographer.

histrión NM (*liter*) actor, player; (*pey*) playactor; buffoon.
histriónico ADJ histrionic.
histrionismo NM **(a)** (*Teat*) acting, art of acting. **(b)** (*fig*) histrionics. **(c)** (*actores*) actors (*collectively*), theatre people.
hita NF **(a)** (*Téc*) brad, headless nail. **(b)** = **hito**.
hitita ⌐1⌐ ADJ, NMF Hittite.
⌐2⌐ NM (*Ling*) Hittite.
hitleriano ADJ Hitlerian.
hito NM **(a)** boundary post, boundary mark; milestone; **~ kilométrico** kilometre stone.
(b) (*fig*) landmark, milestone; **es un ~ en nuestra historia** it is a landmark in our history; **esto marca un ~ histórico** this marks a historical milestone.
(c) (*Dep*) quoits.
(d) (*Mil*) target; (*fig*) aim, goal; **a ~** fixedly; **dar en el ~** to hit the nail on the head; **mudar de ~** to change one's tactics.
(e) mirar a uno de ~ en ~ to stare at sb.
hizo V **hacer**.
hl ABR de **hectolitro(s)** hectolitre(s), hl.
hm. ABR de **hectómetro(s)** hectometre(s), hm.
Hna(s) ABR de **Hermana(s)** Sister(s), Sr(s).
Hno(s) ABR de **Hermano(s)** Brother, Bro(s).
hobby ['xobi] NM, PL **hobbys** o **hobbies** ['xobis] hobby.
hocicada* NF: **darse una ~ en el suelo** to fall flat on one's face; **darse una ~ con la puerta** to bash one's face against the door*.
hocicar [1g] ⌐1⌐ VT (*cerdo*) to root among; (*persona etc*) to nuzzle.
⌐2⌐ VI **(a)** (*cerdo*) to root; (*persona*) to nuzzle; (*amantes*) to pet; **~ con, ~ en** to put one's nose against (o into *etc*).
(b) (*Náut*) to pitch.
(c) (*caer*) to fall on one's face.
(d) (*fig*) to run into trouble, come up against it.
hocico NM **(a)** (*Zool*) snout, muzzle, nose; (*de persona**: *nariz*) snout; (*cara*) face, mug‡; **caer** (o **dar**) **de ~s** to fall on one's face; **dar de ~s contra algo** to bump into sth, go slap into sth; **cerrar el ~‡** to shut one's trap‡; **estar de ~** to be in a bad mood; **meter el ~** to meddle, shove one's nose in.
(b) (*fig*) angry face, grimace; **poner ~** to show one's anger (o resentment) in one's expression; **torcer el ~** to make a (wry) face; to scowl, look cross.
hocicón ADJ (*And*) angry, cross.
hocicudo* ADJ (*And, Carib*) (*con mala cara*) scowling; (*de mal humor*) grumpy*.
hociquear [1a] VTI = **hocicar**.
hociquera NF (*And, Carib*) muzzle.
hockey ['oki o 'xoki] NM hockey (*t* **~ sobre césped, ~ sobre hierba**); **~ sobre hielo** ice-hockey.
hodierno ADJ daily, (*fig*) frequent.
hogaño ADV (†† o *liter*) this year; these days, nowadays.
hogar NM **(a)** fireplace, hearth; fireside; (*Téc*) furnace; (*Ferro*) firebox.
(b) (*fig*) home, house; (*vida familiar*) home life, family life; (*personas*) household; **artículos de ~** domestic goods; **~ de ancianos, ~ de jubilados, ~ de pensionistas** old folk's (o people's) home; **~ nacional judío** Jewish national home; **~ protegido** sheltered housing; **los (que han quedado) sin ~** the homeless, those left homeless; **no tienen ~** they have no home.
hogareño ADJ home (*atr*), family (*atr*); fireside (*atr*); **persona ~** home-loving, stay-at-home.
hogaza NF large loaf, cottage loaf.
hoguera NF **(a)** bonfire; blaze; **la casa estaba hecha una ~** the house was ablaze, the house was an inferno; *see also* [SAN JUAN] . **(b)** (*Hist*) stake; **morir en la ~** to die at the stake.
hoja NF **(a)** (*Bot*) leaf; petal; (*de hierba*) blade; **la ~** (*LAm‡*) pot‡, hash*; **~ de parra** (*fig*) figleaf; **de ~ ancha** broad-leaved; **de ~ caduca** deciduous; **de ~ perenne** evergreen.
(b) (*de papel*) leaf, sheet; (*Tip*) leaf, page; (*formulario etc*) sheet, form, document; **~ de cálculo, ~ electrónica** spreadsheet; **~ de cumplido** compliments slip; **~ de embalaje** packing-slip; **~ de guarda** flyleaf; **~ de inscripción** registration form; **~ de pedido** order form; **~ parroquial** parish magazine; **~ de reclamación** complaint form, form on which to make a complaint; **~ de ruta** waybill; **~ de servicio** record (of service); **~s sueltas** loose sheets, loose-leaf paper; **~ de trabajo** worksheet; **~ volandera, ~ volante** leaflet, handbill, pamphlet; **~ de vida** (*And*) curriculum vitae, CV; **doblar la ~** (*fig*) to change the subject; **volver la ~** to turn the page; (*fig: cambiar de tema*) to change the subject; (*fig*) to turn over a new leaf.
(c) (*de metal*) sheet; thin plate; (*de puerta*) leaf; (*de espada, patín*) blade; (*de vidrio*) sheet, pane; **~ de afeitar** razor blade; **~ de estaño** tinfoil; **~ de lata** tin, tinplate; **~ plegadiza** flap (*of table etc*); **~ de tocino** side of bacon, flitch.
hojalata NF tin, tinplate; (*Lam*) corrugated iron.
hojalatada NF (*Méx: Aut*) panel beating.
hojalatería NF **(a)** (*obra*) tinwork; sheet-metal work. **(b)** (*tienda*) tin-

smith's (shop). **(c)** (*LAm: objetos*) tinware.
hojalatería NM (*And, CAm, Méx*) tinware.
hojalatero NM tinsmith.
hojalda NF (*LAm*), **hojaldra** NF (*LAm*), **hojaldre** *gen* NM puff-pastry.
hojarasca NF **(a)** dead leaves, fallen leaves. **(b)** (*fig: basura*) rubbish, trash, worthless stuff; (*palabras*) empty verbiage, waffle.
hojear [1a] ⌐1⌐ VT to turn the pages of, leaf through; to skim through, glance through.
⌐2⌐ VI **(a)** (*Méx Bot*) to put out leaves.
(b) (*CAm, Méx: Agr*) to eat leaves.
(c) (*superficie*) to scale off, flake off.
hojerío NM (*CAm*) leaves, foliage.
hojoso ADJ leafy.
hojuela NF **(a)** (*Bot*) leaflet, little leaf.
(b) (*hoja delgada*) flake; (*de metal*) foil, thin sheet; **~ de estaño** tinfoil.
(c) (*Culin*) pancake; (*LAm*) ordinary fare, daily food; (*Carib, Méx: Culin*) puff pastry.
hola INTERJ (*saludo*) hullo!; (*sorpresa*) hullo!, hey!, I say!; (*Cono Sur Telec*) hullo?
holán NM **(a)** cambric, fine linen. **(b)** (*Méx*) flounce, frill.
Holanda NF Holland.
holandés ⌐1⌐ ADJ Dutch.
⌐2⌐ NM Dutchman; **el ~ errante** the Flying Dutchman; **los holandeses** the Dutch.
⌐3⌐ NM (*Ling*) Dutch.
holandesa NF **(a)** Dutchwoman. **(b)** (*Tip*) quarto sheet
holding ['xoldin] NM, PL **holdings** ['xoldin] holding company.
holgadamente ADV **(a)** loosely, comfortably; **caben ~** they fit in easily, they go in with room to spare.
(b) idly; in leisurely fashion.
(c) vivir ~ to live comfortably, live in luxury, be well off.
holgado ADJ **(a)** *ropa etc* loose, full, comfortable; roomy; baggy; *tipo* full; **demasiado ~** too big.
(b) (*sin trabajo*) idle, unoccupied, free; leisured.
(c) (*Fin*) comfortably off, well-to-do; **vida holgada** comfortable life, life of luxury.
holganza NF **(a)** idleness; (*descanso*) rest; (*ocio*) leisure, ease. **(b)** (*diversión*) amusement, enjoyment.
holgar [1h y 1l] ⌐1⌐ VI **(a)** (*descansar*) to rest, take one's ease, be at leisure; (*obrero etc*) to be idle, be out of work; (*objeto*) to lie unused.
(b) (*sobrar*) to be unnecessary, be superfluous; **huelga toda protesta** no protest is necessary, it is not necessary to protest; **huelga decir que ...** it goes without saying that ..., needless to say, ...
(c) = **2**; **huelgo de saberlo** I'm delighted to hear it.
⌐2⌐ **holgarse** VR to amuse o.s., enjoy o.s., have a good time; **~ con algo** to take pleasure in sth; **~ con una noticia** to be pleased about a piece of news; **~ de que ...** to be pleased that ..., be glad that ...
holgazán ⌐1⌐ ADJ idle, lazy, slack.
⌐2⌐ NM, **holgazana** NF idler, slacker, loafer; ne'er-do-well.
holgazanear [1a] VI to laze around, be idle, slack, loaf.
holgazanería NF idleness, laziness, slackness.
holgazanitis NF (*hum*) congenital laziness, work-shyness.
holgorio NM = **jolgorio**.
holgura NF **(a)** (*Cos etc*) looseness, fullness; roominess, bagginess; (*Mec*) play, free movement.
(b) (*ocio*) freedom, leisure; (*confort*) ease, comfort.
(c) (*goce*) enjoyment; (*alegría*) merriment, merrymaking.
(d) (*lujo*) comfortable living, luxury; **vivir con ~** to live well, live comfortably, live in luxury.
hollar [1l] VT **(a)** to tread, tread on; to trample down, trample underfoot. **(b)** (*fig*) to trample underfoot; to humiliate, humble.
hollejo NM (*Bot*) skin, peel.
hollín NM soot.
holliniento ADJ, **hollinoso** ADJ sooty, covered in soot.
holocausto NM (*Rel: Hist*) holocaust, burnt offering; (*fig*) sacrifice; (*fig: desastre*) holocaust; **el H~** the Holocaust; **~ nuclear** nuclear holocaust.
holografía NF (*ciencia*) holography; (*imagen*) holograph.
holograma NM hologram.
hombracho NM, **hombrachón** NM hulking great brute, big tough fellow.
hombrada NF manly deed, brave act.
hombradía NF manliness; courage, guts.
hombre ⌐1⌐ NM (*un ~*) man; (*gen*) man, mankind; **su ~** her man, her husband; **es otro ~** he's a changed man; **pobre ~** poor devil, (*pey*) poor fish, weak man; slow-witted chap; **es un pobre ~** he's a poor fish*; **está hecho un pobre ~** he's now a man to be pitied, he's a shadow of his former self; **una charla de ~ a ~** a man-to-man talk; **el ~ propone, pero Dios dispone** man proposes, God disposes; **ser muy ~** to be a real man, be pretty tough; **no me fastidien, pues sé ser muy ~** don't provoke me, because I can get tough; **desde que el**

~ es ~ always, since the year dot; **si lo compras, me haces un ~*** if you buy it, you'll be doing me a big favour; **¡~ al agua!, ¡~ al mar!** man overboard!; **~ de armas** man-at-arms; **~ de bien** honest man, good man; **~ blanco** white man; paleface; **~ bueno** (*Jur*) arbiter; **el ~ de** (**o en**) **la calle** the man in the street; **~ de las cavernas** caveman; **~ de confianza** right-hand man; **~ del día** man of the moment; **~ de empresa** businessman; **~ de estado** statesman; **~ fuerte de Ruritania** the strong man of Ruritania; **~ hecho** grown man; **~ de letras** man of letters; **~ de mar** seafaring man, seaman; **el ~ masa, el ~ medio, el ~ del montón** the average man, the ordinary man, the man in the street; **~ mundano** man-about-town; **~ de mundo** man of the world; **~ de negocios** businessman; **el abominable ~ de las nieves** the abominable snowman; **~ orquesta** one-man band; **~ de paja** stooge*, man of straw; **~ de pro, ~ de provecho** worthy man, honest man; **~ del tiempo** weatherman.

[2] NM (*elemento con guión*) p.ej.: **~-gol** striker who can score goals; **~-milagro** miracle-man; **~-mito** man who is a myth in his own lifetime; **~-mosca** trapeze artist; V **~-rana** *etc.*

[3] INTERJ (a) (*en oración directa*) old chap*, my boy, man (*pero frec no se traduce*); **sí ~** yes, yes of course.
(b) (*sorpresa*) well!, good heavens!, you don't say!
(c) (*compasión*) dear me!; yes I know!
(d) (*protesta*) come now!, but my dear fellow!, heavens man!

hombre-anuncio NM, PL **hombres-anuncio** sandwich man.

hombrear¹ [1a] VI (*joven*) to play the man, act grown-up; (*hombre*) to act tough, try to be somebody.

hombrear² [1a] [1] VT (a) to shoulder; to push with one's shoulder, put one's shoulder to.
(b) (*And, Cono Sur, Méx*) to help, lend a hand to.
[2] VI: **~ con uno** to try to keep up with sb, strive to equal sb.
[3] **hombrearse** VR = **2**.

hombrecillo NM (a) little man, little fellow. (b) (*Bot*) hop.

hombre-lobo NM, PL **hombres-lobo** werewolf.

hombre-masa NM INVAR ordinary man, man in the street.

hombre-mono NM, PL **hombres-mono** apeman.

hombrera NF (*tirante*) shoulder strap; (*almohadilla*) shoulder pad; (*Mil*) epaulette.

hombre-rana NM, PL **hombres-rana** frogman.

hombretón NM big strong fellow.

hombría NF manliness; **~ de bien** honesty, uprightness, worthiness.

hombrillo NM (*Carib Aut*) hard shoulder.

hombro NM shoulder; **~ a ~, ~ con ~** shoulder to shoulder; **¡armas al ~!, ¡sobre el ~ armas!** shoulder arms!; **arrimar el ~** to put one's shoulder to the wheel, lend a hand; **cargar algo sobre los ~s** to shoulder sth; **echar algo al ~** (*fig*) to shoulder sth, take sth upon o.s.; **encogerse de ~s** to shrug one's shoulders; **enderezar los ~s** to square one's shoulders, straighten up; **mirar a uno por encima del ~** to look down on sb; **poner el ~** (*Cono Sur fig*) to put one's shoulder to the wheel; **sacar a uno en ~s** to carry sb out on (their) shoulders; **el vencedor salió en ~s** the victor was carried out shoulder-high.

hombruno ADJ mannish, manlike.

homenaje [1] NM (a) (*Hist, Jur etc*) homage; allegiance; **rendir ~ a** to do (**o** pay, render) homage to, swear allegiance to.
(b) (*fig*) tribute, testimonial; **en ~ a** in honour of; in recognition of; **rendir ~ a, tributar ~ a** to pay a tribute to; **rendir el último ~** to pay one's last respects; **una cena** (**de**) **~ para don XY** a dinner in honour of don XY.
(c) (*LAm*) celebration; gathering (*in honour of sb*).
(d) (*LAm: regalo*) gift, favour.
[2] ATR: **una cena-~ para don XY** a dinner in honour of don XY; **un concierto-~ para el compositor** a concert in honour of the composer; **libro-~** homage volume; **partido-~** benefit match, testimonial game.

homenajeado, -a NM/F: **el ~** the person being honoured, the guest of honour.

homenajear [1a] VT to honour, pay tribute to.

homeópata NMF homeopath.

homeopatía NF homeopathy.

homeopático ADJ homeopathic.

homérico ADJ Homeric.

Homero NM Homer.

homicida [1] ADJ murderous, homicidal; **el arma ~** the murder weapon.
[2] NM murderer.
[3] NF murderess.

homicidio NM murder, homicide; manslaughter; **~ frustrado** attempted murder.

homilía NF homily.

homínido NM hominid.

homoerótico ADJ homo-erotic.

homofobia NF homophobia.

homofóbico ADJ homophobic.

homófobo [1] ADJ homophobic.
[2] NM, **homófoba** NF homophobe.

homogeneidad NF homogeneity.

homogeneización NF levelling (down), equalization, unification.

homogeneizante, homogeneizador [1] ADJ homogenizing; **una tendencia ~** a tendency for homogenization.
[2] NM homogenizer.

homogen(e)izar [1f] VT to homogenize; to level (down), equalize, unify.

homogéneo ADJ homogeneous.

homógrafo NM homonym, homograph.

homologable ADJ equivalent, comparable (*a, con* to).

homologación NF official approval, authorization, sanction(ing); (*de sueldos*) parity.

homologado ADJ officially approved, authorized.

homologar [1h] VT (a) (*coordinar*) to coordinate; (*estandarizar*) to bring into line, standardize. (b) (*comparar*) to compare. (c) (*aprobar*) to check and approve; to approve officially, authorize, sanction; *récord* to accept.

homólogo [1] ADJ equivalent (*de* to).
[2] NM, **homóloga** NF counterpart, equivalent, opposite number.

homónimo [1] ADJ homonymous.
[2] NM homonym; (*persona*) namesake.

homosexual ADJ, NMF homosexual.

homosexualidad NF, **homosexualismo** NM homosexuality.

honda NF sling; (*LAm*) catapult.

hondear¹ [1a] VT (*Náut*) (a) (*sondear*) to sound. (b) (*descargar*) to unload.

hondear² [1a] VT (*LAm*) to hit with a slingshot, kill with a sling; to hit with a catapult.

hondo [1] ADJ (a) (*gen*) deep; (*bajo*) low.
(b) (*Carib*) *río etc* swollen, high.
(c) (*fig*) profound, deep, heartfelt; **con ~ pesar** with deep regret, with profound sorrow.
[2] ADV: **respirar ~** to breathe deeply.
[3] NM depth(s); bottom.

hondón NM (a) (*de taza, valle etc*) bottom; (*de espuela*) footrest. (b) (*de aguja*) eye.

hondonada NF (a) (*vallecito*) hollow, coombe; (*hoyo*) dip, depression; (*barranco*) gully, ravine. (b) (*llano*) lowland.

hondura NF (a) (*medida*) depth; profundity. (b) (*lugar*) depth; deep place; **meterse en ~s** to get out of one's depth, get into deep water (*t fig*).

Honduras NF Honduras; **~ Británica** (*Hist*) British Honduras.

hondureñismo NM word (**o** phrase *etc*) peculiar to Honduras.

hondureño, -a ADJ, NM/F Honduran.

honestamente ADV (a) decently, properly, decorously. (b) modestly; purely. (c) fairly, justly, reasonably. (d) honourably; honestly, really, frankly.

honestidad NF (a) decency, decorum. (b) modesty; purity, chastity. (c) fairness, justice. (d) honourableness; honesty.

honesto ADJ (a) (*decente*) decent, proper, decorous. (b) (*modesto*) modest; (*casto*) pure, chaste. (c) (*justo*) fair, just, reasonable. (d) (*honrado*) honourable, honest.

hong kongés [1] ADJ Hong Kong (*atr*), of Hong Kong.
[2] NM, **hong kongesa** NF native (**o** inhabitant) of Hong Kong; **los hong kongeses** the people of Hong Kong.

hongo NM (a) (*Bot*) fungus; (*comestible*) mushroom; (*tóxico*) toadstool; **un enorme ~ de humo** an enormous mushroom of smoke; **crecen** (**o proliferan**) **como ~s** they grow like mushrooms. (b) (*sombrero*) bowler, bowler hat, derby (*US*).

Honolulú NM Honolulu.

honor NM honour; (*de mujer*) honour, virtue, good name; (*fig*) glory; **~es** (*Mil etc*) honours, honorary status (**o** rank); **~ profesional** professional etiquette; **en ~ a la verdad** to be fair, for the sake of truth; **en ~ de uno** in sb's honour; **13 puntos de ~es** (*Naipes*) 13 honours points; **hacer ~ a un compromiso** to honour a pledge; **hacer ~ a su firma** to honour one's signature; **hacer los ~es de la casa** to do the honours (of the house); **hacer los debidos ~es a una comida** to do full justice to a meal; **sepultar a uno con todos los ~es militares** to bury sb with full military honours; **tener el ~ de** + *infin* to have the honour to + *infin*, to be proud to + *infin*; **el poeta X, ~ de esta ciudad** the poet X in whom this city glories, the poet X who is this city's claim to fame.

honorabilidad NF (a) (*cualidad*) honourableness, honour; worthiness. (b) (*persona*) distinguished person.

honorable ADJ honourable, worthy.

honorario [1] ADJ honorary, honorific.
[2] NM honorarium; **~s** (*professional*) fees, charges.

honorífico ADJ honourable; honorific; **mención honorífica** honourable mention.

honra NF self-esteem, sense of personal honour, dignity; (*de mujer*) honour, virtue, good name; **~s fúnebres** last honours, funeral rites; **¡a mucha ~!** I'm honoured!, delighted!; **puritano, sí, y a bastante ~** I'm a puritan, certainly, and proud of it; **tener algo a mucha ~** to be proud of sth, consider sth an honour; **tener a mucha ~** + *infin* to be proud to + *infin*, deem it an honour to + *infin*; *V* **atentado.**

honradamente ADV honestly; honourably, uprightly.

honradez NF honesty; honourableness, uprightness, integrity.

honrado ADJ honest; honourable, upright; **hombre ~** honest man, decent man, honourable man.

honrar [1a] **1** VT **(a)** to honour, revere, respect; to do honour to. **(b)** (*Com etc*) to honour.
2 honrarse VR: **me honro con su amistad** I am honoured by his friendship; **~ de** + *infin* to be honoured to + *infin*, deem it an honour to + *infin*.

honrilla NF: **por la negra ~** out of concern for what people will say, out of a sense of shame; for the sake of appearances.

honrosamente ADV honourably.

honroso ADJ honourable; respectable, reputable; **es una profesión honrosa** it is an honourable profession, it is a respectable profession.

hontanar NM spring, group of springs.

hopa¹ NF cassock.

hopa² INTERJ **(a)** (*Cono Sur*: *¡deja!*) stop it!, that hurts! **(b)** (*And, CAm, Méx*: *saludo*) hullo!

hopo¹ ['xopo] NM (fox's) brush, tail.

hopo² INTERJ out!, get out!

hora NF **(a)** hour; (*tiempo*) time; **media ~** half an hour; **durante 2 ~s** for 2 hours; **esperamos ~s y ~s** we waited hours and hours; **en la ~ de su muerte** at the moment of his death, at the time of his death; **¿a qué ~?** at what time?; **¿qué ~ es?** what is the time?, what time is it?; **¡la ~!, ¡es la ~!** time's up!; **es ~ de** + *infin* it is time to + *infin*; **es ~ de irnos** it's time we went, it's time for us to go; **¡ya es (o va siendo) ~ de que ...!** it is high time that ...!; **¡ya era ~!** and about time too!; **no comer entre ~s** not to eat between meals.
(b) (*con adj o prep*) **a altas ~s, en las altas ~s** in the small hours, late at night; **~ de apertura** opening time; **a una ~ avanzada** at a late hour; **a buena ~** opportunely; **¡a buena ~, mangas verdes!** a fine time you choose to tell me that!, it's too late now!; **en buena ~** fortunately; safely; **~ cero** zero hour; **desde las cero ~s** from the start of the day, from midnight; **~ del cierre** closing time; **~ de comer** mealtime; **a la ~ de comer** at lunchtime; **~s de comercio, ~s comerciales** business hours; **~s de consulta** consulting hours; **~s extra, ~s extraordinarias** overtime; **~ H** zero hour; **¡~ inglesa!** on the dot; **~s de insolación** hours of sunshine; **~ insular** time in the Canary Islands; **~s lectivas** working time (in school); **~ legal** official time, standard time; **~s libres** free time, spare time; **~ local** local time; **en mala ~** unluckily; **~ media de Greenwich** Greenwich mean time; **~s muertas** dead period; **~ oficial** official time, standard time; **~s de oficina** business hours, office hours; **~ peninsular** time in mainland Spain; **a primera ~** first thing in the morning; **~ pico** (*LAm*), **~ punta** peak hour, rush hour; **~s punta** peak hours, rush hours; **~ de recreo** playtime; **dos ~s de reloj** two hours exactly; **~s suplementarias** overtime; **~ suprema** one's last hour, hour of death; **~s de trabajo** working hours; working day; **'última ~'** (*Prensa*) 'stop-press'; **a última ~** at the last moment; in the nick of time; at the eleventh hour; last thing at night; **noticias de última ~** last-minute news; **dejar las cosas hasta última ~** to leave things until the last moment; **~s valle** off-peak times; **~ de verano** summer time; **~s de vuelo** (*Aer*) flying time; (*experiencia*) experience; (*antigüedad*) seniority; **a la ~** punctually, on the dot; **a la ~ justa** on the stroke of time; **a estas ~s** now, at this time; **a la ~ de pagar** when it comes to paying; **antes de ~** too early; **fuera de ~s** out of hours, out of working hours; **por ~s** by the hour; **sueldo por ~** hourly wage; **trabajar por ~s** to be paid by the hour; to work part-time.
(c) (*con verbo*) **dar ~** to fix a time, offer an appointment; **dar la ~** to strike (the hour); **estar en sus ~s más bajas** to be at an all-time low, be at its (o one's) lowest ebb; **hacer ~s** (*extra*) to work overtime; **se le ha llegado la ~** her time has come; **poner el reloj en ~** to set one's watch, put one's watch right; **tener ~** to have an appointment; **no ver la ~ de algo** to be scarcely able to wait for sth, look forward impatiently to sth.
(d) (*Ecl*) **~s** book of hours; **~s canónicas** canonical hours.

horaciano ADJ Horatian.

Horacio NM Horace.

horadar [1a] VT to bore (through), pierce, drill, perforate; to tunnel (into).

hora-hombre NF, PL **horas-hombre** man-hour.

horario **1** ADJ hourly; hour (*atr*), time (*atr*).
2 NM (*de reloj*) hour hand; (*Aer, Ferro etc*; *t LAm*: *escuela*) timetable; **llegar a ~** (*LAm*) to arrive on time, be on schedule; **~ comercial** business hours; **~ flexible** flexitime; **puesto de ~ partido** job involving a split day; **~ de visitas** (*de hospital etc*) visiting hours, (*de médico*) doctor's surgery hours.

horca NF **(a)** (*de ejecución*) gallows, gibbet; **condenar a uno a la ~** to condemn sb to the gallows.
(b) (*Agr*) pitchfork; hayfork; manure fork.
(c) (*de ajos etc*) string.
(d) (*Carib*: *regalo*) birthday present, present given on one's saint's day.

horcadura NF fork (of a tree).

horcajadas: **a ~** ADV astride.

horcajadura NF (*Anat*) crotch.

horcajo NM **(a)** (*Agr*) yoke. **(b)** (*de árbol, río*) fork.

horcar [1g] VT (*LAm*) = **ahorcar.**

horchata NF tiger nut milk.

horchatería NF refreshment stall.

horcón NM **(a)** (*Agr*: *horca*)) pitchfork. **(b)** (*Agr*: *para frutales*) forked prop; (*LAm*: *para techo*) prop, support.

horda NF horde; (*fig*) gang.

hordiate NM barley water.

horero NM (*And, Méx*) hour hand.

horita ADV (*LAm*) = **ahorita.**

horizontal **1** ADJ horizontal.
2 NF **(a)** horizontal position; **tomar la ~** to stand upright. **(b)** (**‡**: *prostituta*) prostitute.

horizontalmente ADV horizontally.

horizonte NM horizon (*t fig*); (*t línea del ~*) skyline.

horma NF **(a)** (*Téc*) form, mould; **~ de sombrero** hat block; **~ (de calzado)** last, boot tree; **encontrar(se con) la ~ de su zapato** to meet one's match; to find just what one wanted, find the very thing. **(b)** (*muro*) dry-stone wall.

hormadoras NFPL (*And*) petticoat.

hormiga NF **(a)** (*Ent*) ant; **~ blanca** white ant; **~ león** ant lion; **~ obrera** worker ant; **~ roja** red ant.
(b) **~s** (*Med*) itch; pins and needles.
(c) **ser una ~** (*Cono Sur*) (*trabajador*) to be hard-working; (*ahorrativo*) to be thrifty.

hormigón NM concrete; **~ armado** reinforced concrete; **~ pretensado** pre-stressed concrete.

hormigonera NF concrete mixer.

hormigonero ADJ concrete (*atr*).

hormiguear [1a] VI **(a)** (*piel etc*) to itch; to have pins and needles; to have a feeling as though insects were crawling over one. **(b)** (*insectos*) to swarm, teem.

hormigueo NM **(a)** itch, itching; tingling, prickly feeling, pins and needles. **(b)** (*fig*) anxiety, uneasiness. **(c)** swarming.

hormiguero **1** ADJ ant-eating; **oso ~** anteater.
2 NM **(a)** (*Ent*) ants' nest, ant hill. **(b)** (*fig*) ant hill; swarm of people, place swarming with people.

hormiguillo NM = **hormigueo (a).**

hormiguita NF: **ser una ~** to be hardworking and thrifty.

hormona NF hormone; **~ de(l) crecimiento** growth hormone.

hormonal ADJ hormonal.

hormonarse [1a] VR to have hormone treatment.

hornacina NF (*vaulted*) niche.

hornada NF **(a)** batch (of loaves *etc*), baking. **(b)** (*fig*) batch, collection, crop.

hornalla NF (*Cono Sur*: *horno*) oven; (*de estufa*) hotplate, ring.

hornazo NM **(a)** batch (of cakes *etc*), baking. **(b)** (*pastel*) Easter cake.

horneado NM cooking (time), baking (time).

hornear [1a] **1** VT to cook, bake.
2 VI to bake, be a baker.

hornero, -a NM/F baker.

hornillo NM **(a)** (*Téc*) small furnace; (*Culin*) cooker, stove; portable stove; (*de pipa*) bowl; **~ eléctrico** hotplate; **~ de gas** gas ring. **(b)** (*Mil Hist*) mine.

horno NM (*Culin*) oven; (*Téc*) furnace; (*de alfarero*) kiln; (*de pipa*) bowl; **~ alto** blast furnace; **~ de cal** lime kiln; **~ crematorio** crematorium; **~ de fundición** smelting furnace; **~ de ladrillos** brick kiln; **~ (de) microondas** microwave oven; **resistente al ~** ovenproof; **asar al ~** to bake; **el ~ no está para bollos** this is the wrong moment, this is a bad time to ask; **meter un plato al ~ fuerte** to put a dish into a high oven.

horóscopo NM horoscope.

horqueta NF (*Agr*) pitchfork; (*Bot*) fork of a tree); (*LAm*) bend in the road.

horquetear [1a] **1** VT **(a)** (*Cono Sur*) oído to prick up; *persona* to listen suspiciously to. **(b)** (*Méx*) to sit astride, straddle.
2 VI (*LAm*) to grow branches, put out branches.

horquilla NF (*del pelo*) hairpin, hairclip; (*Agr*) pitchfork; (*de bicicleta*) fork; (*Mec*) yoke; (*Telec*) rest, cradle; (*de zanco*) footrest; **~ de cavar** garden fork; **~ de salarios** (*fig*) wage levels.

horrarse [1a] VR (*LAm Agr*) to abort.
horrendo ADJ horrible; hideous; dire, frightful.
hórreo NM (*prov*) (raised) granary.
horrible ADJ **(a)** horrible, dreadful, ghastly. **(b)** (*fig*) dreadful, nasty, terrible; **¡qué persona más ~!** what a dreadful man!; **la película es ~** the film is dreadful.
horriblemente ADV **(a)** horribly, dreadfully. **(b)** (*fig*) dreadfully, terribly.
horripilante ADJ hair-raising, horrifying; harrowing; grisly; creepy.
horripilar [1a] **1** VT: **~ a uno** to make sb's hair stand on end, horrify sb, give sb the creeps.
2 horripilarse VR to be horrified, be terrified; **era para ~** it was enough to make your hair stand on end.
horro ADJ **(a)** (*exento*) free, exempt, enfranchised; **~ de** bereft of, devoid of. **(b)** (*Bio*) sterile.
horror NM **(a)** (*gen*) horror, dread, terror (*a* of); abhorrence (*a* of); enormity; frightfulness; **¡qué ~!** how ghastly!*; isn't it dreadful?; well!, goodness!; **la fiesta ... ¡un ~!** the party was ghastly!*; **se dicen ~es de la cocina inglesa** awful things are said about English cooking; **tener ~ a algo** to have a horror of sth; **tener algo en ~** to detest sth, loathe sth.
(b) (*acto*) atrocity, terrible thing.
(c) (*: como adv*) **me gusta ~es** o **un ~** I like it awfully; **hoy he trabajado un ~** today I worked awfully hard; **se divirtieron ~es** they had a tremendous time*; **me duele ~es** it's frightfully painful, it hurts a lot; **ella sabe ~es** she knows a hell of a lot; **había ~es de gente** there were masses of people.
horrorizar [1f] **1** VT to horrify; to terrify, frighten.
2 horrorizarse VR to be horrified, be aghast.
horrorosamente ADV **(a)** horrifyingly; horribly, frightfully. **(b)** (*fig*) dreadfully, awfully.
horroroso ADJ **(a)** horrifying, terrifying; horrible, frightful. **(b)** (*fig*) ghastly*, dreadful, awful; (*feo*) hideous, ugly.
horrura NF filth, dirt; rubbish.
hortaliza NF **(a)** vegetable; **~s** vegetables, garden produce. **(b)** (*Méx*) vegetable garden.
hortelano NM gardener; market gardener; truck farmer (*US*).
hortensia NF hydrangea.
hortera **1** NF wooden bowl.
2 NM **(a)** shop-assistant, grocer's boy **(b)** (*fig*) (*inculto*) rough type, coarse person; (*ostentoso*) flashy type; (*palurdo*) bumpkin; (*fingido*) fraud, sham.
3 ADJ INVAR (*ordinario*) common, vulgar; crude, tasteless; (*ostentoso*) flashy.
horterada NF crude thing; coarse remark; vulgarity; **ese vestido es una ~** that dress is a disgrace; **los celos son una ~** it's vulgar to be jealous.
horterez NF coarseness, vulgarity.
horterismo NM fraud, sham, pretence.
horterizar [1f] VT to coarsen, cheapen, make vulgar.
hortícola **1** ADJ horticultural; garden (*atr*).
2 NMF = **horticultor(a)**.
horticultor(a) NM/F horticulturist; gardener; nurseryman.
horticultura NF horticulture; gardening.
horticulturista NMF horticulturalist, horticulturist.
hortofrutícola ADJ fruit and vegetable (*atr*).
hortofruticultura NF fruit and vegetable growing.
hosco ADJ **(a)** (*oscuro*) dark; (*lúgubre*) gloomy. **(b)** *persona* sullen; morose; grim.
hospedador NM (*Bio*) host.
hospedaje NM lodging; (cost of) board and lodging.
hospedar [1a] **1** VT to put up, lodge, give a room (*etc*) to; to receive as a guest, entertain.
2 hospedarse VR to stay, stop, put up, lodge (*con* with, *en* at).
hospedera NF hostess; innkeeper's wife.
hospedería NF **(a)** (*fonda*) hostelry, inn. **(b)** (*habitación*) guest room. **(c)** (*Ecl*) hospice, guest quarters.
hospedero NM host; innkeeper, landlord.
hospiciano, -a NM/F, **hospiciante** NMF (*LAm*) inmate of an orphanage, orphan.
hospicio NM poorhouse; orphanage; (*Cono Sur*) old people's home; (*Ecl*) hospice.
hospital NM hospital; infirmary; **~ de aislamiento, ~ de contagiosos** isolation hospital; **~ de campaña** field hospital; **~ de día** day hospital; **~ de (primera) sangre** field dressing station.
hospitalariamente ADV: **fue atendido ~** he was treated in hospital.
hospitalario ADJ **(a)** hospitable. **(b)** (*Med*) hospital (*atr*); **estancia hospitalaria** stay in hospital.
hospitalidad NF hospitality.
hospitalización NF hospitalization.
hospitalizar [1f] **1** VT to send (o take) to hospital, hospitalize; **quedó hospitalizado durante 3 meses** he spent 3 months in hospi-

tal.
2 hospitalizarse VR (*LAm*) to go into hospital.

┌───┐
│ **HOSPITAL**   *ver también la entrada* │
│   │
│ **Uso del artículo**   │
│ En inglés el uso del artículo delante de *hospital* depende del │
│ motivo por el que alguien haya acudido al centro hospitalario: │
│ • Se traduce *al hospital* por *to hospital*, *en el hospital* por *in hospital* │
│   y *desde el hospital* por *from hospital* cuando alguien está o va a ser │
│   ingresado allí: │
│   La llevaron con urgencia al hospital como consecuencia de un │
│   infarto   │
│   *She was rushed to hospital following a heart attack* │
│   Después del accidente estuvo tres meses en el hospital │
│   *Following the accident, she was in hospital for three months* │
│ • Se traduce *al hospital* por *to the hospital*, *en el hospital* por *at the* │
│   *hospital* y *desde el hospital* por *from the hospital* cuando alguien va │
│   o está allí por otros motivos. También se emplea el artículo │
│   cuando se trata de consultas externas: │
│   Este lunes tengo que ir al hospital para una revisión │
│   *I've got to go to the hospital on Monday for a check-up* │
│   Mi hermana trabaja en el hospital   │
│   *My sister works at the hospital*   │
│ *Para otros usos y ejemplos ver la entrada.*   │
└───┘

hosquedad NF sullenness; moroseness; grimness.
hostal NM boarding house, cheap hotel.
hostelería NF hotel trade, hotel business; **empresa de ~** catering company.
hostelero NM innkeeper, landlord.
hostería NF inn, hostelry; (*Cono Sur*) tourist hotel.
hostia NF **(a)** (*Ecl*) host, consecrated wafer.
(b) (*) (*golpe*) punch, bash*; (*choque*) bang, bash*, smash; **liarse a ~s** to get involved in a punch-up*; **le pegaron un par de ~s** they hit him twice.
(c) (*: lo mejor*) **es la ~** she's the tops*; she's incredible; **eso no quiere decir que yo sea la ~** that doesn't mean I'm anything special.
(d) (*) **¡~!, ¡~s!, ¡qué ~s!** (*sorpresa*) Christ almighty!*; (*fastidio*) damn it all!; (*negación*) get away!, never!; not a bit of it!; (*rechazo*) balls!*; **¿qué ~s quieres?** what the hell do you want?; **¡qué libros ni qué ~s!** books, nothing!*
(e) (*: locuciones*) **y toda la ~** and all the rest; **ese inspector de la ~** that bloody inspector*; **había un tráfico de la ~** the traffic was appalling; **una tormenta de la ~** a storm and a half*; **echar ~s** to shout blue murder*; to go up the wall*; **no entiendo ni ~** I don't understand a word of it; **estar de mala ~** to be in a bad mood; **hacer un par como unas ~s** to muck it all up*; **ir a toda ~** to go like the clappers*; **salió cagando ~s** he shot out like a bat out of hell; **tener mala ~** (*carácter*) to have a nasty streak; (*suerte*) to have rotten luck*; **no tiene media ~** he's no use at all.
hostiar [1b] VT (*) to bash*, sock*.
hostiazo NM bash*, sock*.
hostigamiento NM (*fig*) harassment.
hostigar [1h] VT **(a)** to lash, whip, scourge. **(b)** (*fig*) to harass, plague, pester; to bore. **(c)** (*LAm: comida*) to surfeit, cloy.
hostigoso ADJ (*And, Cono Sur*) *comida* sickly, cloying; *persona* annoying, tedious.
hostil ADJ hostile.
hostilidad NF **(a)** (*gen*) hostility. **(b)** (*acto*) hostile act; **romper las ~es** to start hostilities.
hostilizar [1f] VT (*Mil*) to harry, harass, worry.
hostión NM bash*, sock*.
hotel NM **(a)** (*Com*) hotel. **(b)** (*casa*) detached house, suburban house, villa. **(c)** (*: cárcel; t ~ del Estado, ~ rejas*) nick*; (*Mil*) glasshouse*.
(d) **~ garaje** (*Méx*), **~ alojamiento** (*Cono Sur*) *hotel where one pays by the hour.*
hotelería NF **(a)** (*hoteles*) hotels (*collectively*). **(b)** (*negocio*) hotel trade. **(c)** (*gerencia*) hotel management.
hotelero **1** ADJ hotel (*atr*); **la industria hotelera** the hotel trade.
2 NM, **hotelera** NF hotelkeeper, hotel manager, hotelier.
hotelito NM small house, (*esp*) cottage, vacation retreat, second home.
hoy ADV today; now, nowadays; **la juventud de ~** the youth of today; **en el correo de ~** in today's post; **~ día, ~ en día** nowadays; in this day and age; **~ por ~** at the present time, right now, as things stand (at present); **de ~ en ocho días, de ~ en una semana** today week, a week today; **de ~ en quince (días)** today fortnight, a fortnight today; **de ~ a mañana** any time now; **está para llegar de ~ a mañana** it might happen any day now; **de ~ en adelante** from now on, henceforward; **de ~ no pasa que le escriba** I'll write to him this very day; **desde ~** from now on, starting from now; **¡y**

hasta ~! and I've heard no more about it!, and that was the last I heard!; **por ~** for the present.

hoya NF (a) (*agujero*) pit, hole; (*tumba*) grave; **~ de arena** bunker. (b) (*Geog*) wide valley, plain (among hills); (*LAm*) riverbed, river basin. (c) (*Agr*) seedbed.

hoyada NF hollow, depression.

hoyador NM (*And, Carib*) dibber, seed drill.

hoyanco NM (*Carib, Méx: bache*) pothole, hole in the road.

hoyar [1a] VT (*CAm, Carib, Méx*) to make holes (*for sowing seeds*).

hoyito NM (*LAm*) dimple.

hoyo NM (a) (*agujero*) hole, pit; (*hueco*) hollow, cavity; (*tumba*) grave; **irse al ~*** (*Cono Sur*) to get into an awful jam*; to face ruin; **se cree el ~ del queque*** (*Cono Sur*) he thinks he's the cat's pyjamas. (b) (*Golf*) hole; **en el ~ 18** at the 18th hole. (c) (*Med*) pockmark.

hoyuelo NM dimple.

hoz NF (a) (*Agr*) sickle; **~ y martillo** hammer and sickle. (b) (*Geog*) defile, narrow pass, gorge. (c) **de ~ y coz** wildly, recklessly.

hozar [1f] VT (*suj: cerdo*) to root in, root among.

hs. ABR *de* **horas** hours, h., hrs.

hua...: *para diversas palabras escritas así en LAm, V t* **gua...**; *p.ej., para* **huaico** *V* **guaico**.

huaca NF *etc* = **guaca** *etc*.

huacalón ADJ (*Méx: de voz áspera*) gravel-voiced.

huacarear‡ [1a] VI (*LAm*) to throw up.

huacha NF (*And*) washer.

huachafería NF (*And*) (a) (*gente*) middle-class snobs, social climbers. (b) (*actitud*) snobbery, airs and graces.

huachafo (*And*) ①️ ADJ = **cursi**.
②️ NM, **huachafa** NF middle-class snob, social climber.
③️ NM (*Carib*) funny man, comic.

huacho ①️ NM (a) (*And*) section of a lottery ticket. (b) (*Méx**) common soldier. ②️ ADJ (*Méx*) = **guacho**.

huaco ①️ ADJ (*LAm: sin dientes*) toothless.
②️ NM (*And Hist*) ancient Peruvian pottery artefact.

huahua NF (*And, Méx*) = **guagua**.

huaica NF (*And*) bargain sale.

huaico NM (*And*) alluvium.

huaipe NM (*Chile*) cotton waste.

huáncar NM, **huáncara** NF (*And*) Indian drum.

huaquero, -a NM/F (*And*) = **guaquero**.

huaraca NF (*And*) = **guaraca**.

huarache NM (*Méx*) = **guarache**.

huáscar* NM (*Chile*) (police) water cannon truck.

huasicama NMF (*And*) Indian servant.

huasipungo NM (*And: Agr*) (Indian's) tied plot of land.

huaso NM/F (*Chile*) = **guaso 2**.

huasteca NF: **la H~** the region round the Gulf of Mexico.

huatal NM (*LAm*) hillock.

huave NMF (*Méx*) Huave Indian.

huayco‡ NM (*And*) paid thug.

huayno NM (*And*) (*ritmo*) traditional folk tune; (*canción*) traditional ballad; *see also* CHICHA .

hube *etc* *V* **haber.**

hucha NF (a) (*arca*) chest, bin; (*alcancía*) moneybox; **~ petitoria** charity collecting box. (b) (*fig: ahorros*) savings; **tener una buena ~** to have money laid by, have a good nest-egg.

hueca‡ NF pansy‡, queer‡.

hueco ①️ ADJ (a) (*gen*) hollow; (*vacío*) empty.
(b) (*blando*) soft, spongy.
(c) *sonido, voz* resonant, resounding, booming.
(d) *persona* conceited; *estilo* pompous, affected.
②️ NM (a) (*vacío*) hollow, cavity; (*agujero*) hole; (*brecha*) gap, opening; (*espacio*) empty space; (*en formulario*) blank; (*Arquit*) recess, window space; (*de escalera*) well; (*de ascensor*) shaft; (*: *vacante*) vacancy; **~ de la mano** hollow of the hand; **deja un ~ que será difícil llenar** he leaves a gap which it will be hard to fill.
(b) (*Méx‡*) queer‡, faggot‡ (*US*).

huecograbado NM (*Tip*) photogravure.

huela *etc* *V* **oler.**

huelán (*Cono Sur*) ADJ (a) (*inmaduro*) immature, not fully developed; *madera* unseasoned; *hierba* withered; *trigo* unripe. (b) **una persona huelana** a person who has come down in the world.

huelebraguetas* NM INVAR private eye*.

hueleguisos* NM INVAR (*And*) sponger*, scrounger*.

huelehuele* NMF (*Carib*) idiot.

huelga NF (a) (*descanso*) rest, repose; (*ocio*) leisure; idleness; (*recreo*) recreation.
(b) (*Pol etc*) strike; stoppage, walkout; **~ de brazos caídos** sit-down strike; **~ de celo** work-to-rule, go-slow; **~ general** general strike; **~ de hambre** hunger strike; **~ de hostigamiento** guerrilla strike; **~ patronal** lock out; **~ de reglamento** work-to-rule, go-slow; **~ relámpago** lightning strike; **~ salvaje** (*o* **descabellada**) wildcat

strike; **~ por solidaridad** sympathy strike; **los obreros en ~** the workers on strike, the striking workers; **estar en ~** to be on strike; **declarar la ~, declararse en ~, ir a la ~, ponerse en ~** to come out on strike, go on strike; to walk out.
(c) (*Mec*) play, free movement.

huelgo NM (a) (*aliento*) breath; **tomar ~** to take breath, pause. (b) (*espacio*) room, space; **entra con ~** it goes in easily, it goes in with room to spare. (c) (*Mec*) play, free movement.

huelguear [1a] VI (*And*) to strike, be on strike.

huelguismo NM strike mentality, readiness to strike.

huelguista NMF striker.

huelguístico ADJ strike (*atr*); **movimiento ~** wave of strikes; **el panorama ~** the strike scene.

huella NF (a) (*acto*) tread, treading.
(b) (*rastro*) trace, mark, sign, imprint; (*de pie*) footprint; footstep; (*de animal, coche etc*) track; **~ dactilar, ~ digital** fingerprint; **~ genética** genetic fingerprint; **sin dejar ~** without leaving a trace, leaving no sign; **seguir las ~s de uno** to follow in sb's footsteps.
(c) (*de escalera*) tread.

huellear [1a] VT (*And*) to track, follow the trail of.

huellero ADJ: **perro ~** (*And*) tracking dog.

huello NM condition of the ground *etc* (for walking); **camino de buen ~** good road for walking; **camino de mal ~** bad road for walking, badly-surfaced road.

Huelva NF Huelva.

huemul NM (*Cono Sur*) southern Andean deer.

huérfano ①️ ADJ (a) orphan, orphaned; (*fig*) unprotected, defenceless, uncared-for; **una niña huérfana de madre** a motherless child, a child that has lost her mother.
(b) **~ de** (*fig*) bereft of, short of, without.
②️ NM, **huérfana** NF orphan.

huero ADJ (a) *huevo* addled, rotten. (b) (*fig*) empty; (*estéril*) sterile; (*podrido*) rotten; dud; **un discurso ~** an empty speech. (c) (*CAm, Méx*) = **güero**.

huerta NF (a) vegetable garden, kitchen garden; (large) market garden, truck farm (*US*).
(b) (*esp Murcia, Valencia*) irrigated region, fertile irrigated area.
(c) (*And: de cacao*) cocoa plantation.

huertano ①️ ADJ of the 'huerta'.
②️ NM, **huertana** NF inhabitant of the 'huerta'; market gardener, farmer (of the 'huerta').

huertero, -a NM/F (*Cono Sur*) market gardener.

huerto NM (*de verduras*) kitchen garden; (*Com*) (small) market garden, truck garden (*US*); (*de frutales*) orchard; (*de casa pequeña*) back garden; **le llevaron al ~*** they put one over on him*, they led him up the garden path.

huesa NF grave.

huesear‡ [1a] VI (*LAm*) to beg.

huesecillo NM small bone.

hueserío NM (*And*) unsaleable merchandise.

huesillo NM (*And, Cono Sur*) sun-dried peach.

huesista* NMF (*Méx*) person with a soft job.

hueso NM (a) (*Anat*) bone; **~ de la alegría** funny bone; **un ~ duro de roer** a hard nut to crack, a tough assignment; **~ de la suerte** wishbone; **sin ~** boneless; **la sin ~*** the tongue; **darle a la sin ~*** to talk a lot; **irse de la sin ~, soltar la sin ~*** to shoot one's mouth off*; to let the cat out of the bag; **dar con sus ~s en la cárcel** to land (o end up) in jail; **no dejar ~ sano a uno** to pull sb to pieces; **estar en los ~s** to be nothing but skin and bone; **tener los ~s molidos** to be shattered, ache all over.
(b) (*Bot*) stone, pit (*US*); core.
(c) (*And*) unsaleable article.
(d) (*fig*) (*trabajo*) hard work, drudgery; (*obstáculo*) stumbling block.
(e) (*CAm, Méx Pol: sinecura*) government job, sinecure; (*puesto cómodo*) soft job.
(f) (*: *persona*) very strict person; **su profesor es un ~** her teacher is terribly strict.
(g) (*And*) mule; **ser ~** (*fig*) to be stingy.
(h) **~ colorado** (*Méx*) strong northerly wind.

huesoso ADJ bony; bone (*atr*).

huésped ①️ NM (a) (*invitado*) guest; (*en pensión etc*) lodger, boarder, resident. (b) (*anfitrión*) host. (c) (*Hist*) innkeeper, landlord.
②️ ATR: **ordenador ~** host computer; **hembra ~** host female.

huéspeda NF (a) (*invitada*) guest; (*en pensión etc*) lodger, boarder, resident. (b) (*anfitriona*) hostess. (c) (*Hist*) innkeeper's wife; **no contar con la ~** to reckon without one's host.

hueste NF (a) (†️†️) host, army. (b) (*muchedumbre*) crowd, mass; (*partidarios*) followers.

huesudo ADJ bony; big-boned, raw-boned.

hueva NF (a) (*de pez*) (hard) roe; **~s** eggs, spawn; **~ de lisa** (*Méx*) cod roe. (b) **~s** (*Cono Sur‡*) balls‡.

huevada NF (a) (*LAm*) nest of eggs, clutch of eggs; number of eggs.

(b) (*And, Cono Sur**) (*comentario*) (piece of) nonsense; (*acto*) stupid thing (to do); (*idea*) crazy idea; **~s** (*tonterías*) nonsense, rubbish. **(c)** **~s** (⁑) balls⁑⁑. **(d)** (⁑: *como adv*) **una ~** a hell of a lot; **se divirtió una ~** he had a tremendous time*.

huevear* [1a] VI (*Chile*) to mess about*.

huevera NF **(a)** eggcup. **(b)** (⁑: *suspensorio*) jockstrap.

huevería NF *shop that specializes in selling eggs.*

huevero ADJ egg (*atr*); **industria huevera** egg industry.

huevo NM **(a)** egg; **~ amelcochado** (*CAm*) (soft-)boiled egg; **~ en cáscara** (soft-)boiled egg; **~ a la copa** (*And, Cono Sur*) boiled egg; **~s de corral** free-range eggs; **~ crudo** raw egg; **~ duro** hard-boiled egg; **~ escalfado** poached egg; **~ a la escocesa** Scotch egg; **~ estrellado**, **~ frito**, **~ al plato** fried egg; **~ fresco** new-laid egg; **~ de gallina de pasto libre** free-range egg; **~ moreno** brown egg; **~ pasado por agua**, **~ tibio** (*And, CAm, Méx*) (soft-)boiled egg; **~ de Pascua** Easter egg; **~ de Paslama** (*CAm*) turtle's egg; **~ pericos** (*And*), **~ revueltos** scrambled eggs; **andar sobre ~s** to go very gingerly; **ser como el ~ de Colón** to be simple, be easy; **¡que te fríen un ~!** get knotted!⁑; **hacerle ~ a algo** (*CAm*⁑) to face up to sth; **pensar en los ~s del gallo** (*And, CAm*) to be in a daydream; **a ~** cheap; easy; **nos lo han puesto a ~** they've made it easy for us; **lo tenemos a ~** we've got it made, we've got it taped*.

(b) (⁑) ball⁑⁑, testicle; **¡un ~!** bollocks!⁑⁑, no way!*; **me costó un ~** (*precio*) it cost me an arm and a leg, it cost me a bomb*; **nos costó un ~ terminarlo** it was one hell of a job to finish it; we sweated blood to finish it; **tener ~s** to have guts, be tough; *para muchas locuciones, V* **cojón.**

(c) **un ~*** (*como adv*): **sufrí un ~** I suffered a lot; **le queremos un ~** we like him a lot; **sabe un ~ de vinos** he knows a lot about wine.

(d) (*CAm*) courage, guts, toughness.

(e) (*LAm*) (*vago*) idler, loafer; (*imbécil*) idiot; (*cobarde*) coward.

huevón⁑ (*LAm*) **[1]** ADJ **(a)** (*vago*) idle, lazy; (*tonto*) dim*, thick*; (*lento*) slow; (*cobarde*) chicken-livered, yellow.

(b) (*valiente*) brave, gutsy*.

[2] NM (*flojera*) laziness, idleness; (*torpeza*) slowness, dullness; (*cobardía*) cowardice.

[3] NM, **huevona** NF (*vago*) lazy sod⁑⁑, skiver⁑; (*imbécil*) idiot, berk⁑.

Hugo NM Hugh, Hugo.

hugonote, -a ADJ, NM/F Huguenot.

hui...: *para palabras que en LAm se escriben así V t* **gui..., güi...** *p.ej.* **huinche** *V* **güinche.**

huida¹ NF **(a)** flight, escape; **~ hacia adelante** relentless pursuit of the unattainable; **~ de capitales** flight of capital. **(b)** (*de caballo*) shy(ing), bolt(ing).

huidizo ADJ **(a)** *persona etc* shy; elusive. **(b)** *impresión etc* fleeting. **(c)** *frente* receding.

huido **[1]** ADJ **(a)** (*que ha huido*) fugitive, on the run; **un esclavo ~** a runaway slave. **(b)** (*tímido*) very shy, easily scared.

[2] NM, **huida²** NF fugitive.

huilas* NFPL (*Chile*) rags.

huile NM (*Méx*) roasting grill.

huilón ADJ (*And*) elusive.

huincha NF (*Cono Sur*) = **güincha.**

huipil NM (*CAm, Méx*) embroidered smock.

huir [3g] **[1]** VT to run away from, flee (from), escape (from); to avoid, shun.

[2] VI *y* **huirse** VR to run away, flee, escape; (*tiempo*) to fly; (*LAm*) to elope.

huira NF (*And, Cono Sur*) (*cuerda*) rope; (*cabestro*) halter, tether; **dar ~ a uno*** to thrash sb; **sacar las ~s a uno*** to beat sb up*.

huiro NM (*Cono Sur*) seaweed.

huisache **[1]** NMF (*CAm, Méx*: *leguleyo*) shyster lawyer.

[2] NM (*LAm*: *árbol*) acacia.

huisachear [1a] VI (*CAm, Méx*) **(a)** (*litigar*) to go to law, engage in litigation. **(b)** (*: *ejercer sin título*) to practise law without a qualification.

huisachería NF (*CAm, Méx*) **(a)** lawyer's tricks, legal intricacies. **(b)** practice of law without a qualification.

huisachero NM (*CAm, Méx*) **(a)** (*leguleyo*) shyster lawyer, unqualified lawyer. **(b)** (*Méx*: *plumífero*) scribbler, pen-pusher.

huitlacoche NM (*Méx Bot*) type of edible fungus.

huizache *etc* (*Méx*) = **huisache** *etc.*

hulado NM (*CAm*) (*tela*) oilskin, rubberized cloth; (*capa*) oilskin.

hula-hop [xula'xop] NM Hula-Hoop ®.

hular NM (*Méx*) rubber plantation.

hule¹ NM **(a)** (*goma*) rubber. **(b)** (*tela*) oilskin, oilcloth. **(c)** (*CAm, Méx*: *Bot*) rubber tree. **(d)** (*Méx**: *preservativo*) condom, sheath.

hule² NM (*Taur*) goring; row; **habrá ~** there's going to be trouble.

hulear [1a] VI (*CAm*) to extract rubber.

hulero **[1]** ADJ (*CAm*) rubber (*atr*).

[2] NM, **hulera** NF rubber tapper.

hulla NF coal, soft coal.

hullera NF colliery, coalmine.

hullero ADJ coal (*atr*).

huloso ADJ (*CAm*) rubbery, elastic.

humanamente ADV **(a)** (*en términos humanos*) humanly; in human terms. **(b)** (*con humanidad*) humanely.

humanar [1a] **[1]** VT to humanize.

[2] **humanarse** VR **(a)** to become more human; **~ a** + *infin* (*LAm*) to condescend to + *infin*.

(b) (*Rel: Cristo*) to become man.

humanidad NF **(a)** (*género humano*) humanity, mankind. **(b)** (*cualidad*) humanity, humaneness. **(c)** (*: *gordura*) corpulence. **(d)** **las ~es** the humanities.

humanismo NM humanism.

humanista NMF humanist.

humanístico ADJ humanistic.

humanitario **[1]** ADJ humanitarian; humane.

[2] NM, **humanitaria** NF humanitarian.

humanitarismo NM humanitarianism.

humanización NF humanization.

humanizador ADJ humanizing.

humanizar [1f] **[1]** VT to humanize, make more human.

[2] **humanizarse** VR to become more human.

humano **[1]** ADJ **(a)** (*relativo al humano*) human. **(b)** (*benévolo*) humane. **(c)** **ciencias humanas** humane learning, humanistic learning, humanities.

[2] NM human (being).

humanoide ADJ, NMF humanoid.

humarasca NF (*CAm*), **humareda** NF cloud of smoke.

humazo NM dense smoke, cloud of smoke; **dar ~ a uno** to get rid of sb.

humeante ADJ smoking, smoky; steaming.

humear [1a] **[1]** VT **(a)** (*And, Carib, Méx: fumigar*) to fumigate.

(b) (*Méx**: *golpear*) to beat, thrash.

[2] VI **(a)** (*humo*) to smoke, give out smoke; (*vapor*) to fume, steam, give off fumes.

(b) (*fig: memoria, rencor etc*) to be still alive, linger on.

(c) (*fig: presumir*) to give o.s. airs, be conceited.

humectador NM humidifier; humidor.

humectante ADJ moisturizing.

humectar [1a] VT = **humedecer.**

húmeda* NF: **la ~** the tongue.

humedad NF humidity; damp, dampness; moisture; **a prueba de ~** damp-proof; **sentir la ~** (*And, Carib**) to have to answer for one's actions.

humedal NM wetland.

humedecedor NM humidifier.

humedecer [2d] **[1]** VT to dampen, wet, moisten; to humidify.

[2] **humedecerse** VR to get damp, get wet; **se le humedecieron los ojos** his eyes filled with tears, tears came into his eyes.

húmedo ADJ humid; damp, wet; moist.

┌─ HÚMEDO ─┐

Para traducir el adjetivo *húmedo* en inglés hay que tener en cuenta la diferencia entre: *damp, moist, humid* y *wet*.

- Se traduce por *damp* cuando *húmedo* se utiliza para describir cosas que han estado mojadas y que todavía no se han secado del todo:
  No salgas con el pelo húmedo
  Don't go out with your hair damp
  ...el olor de la tierra húmeda...
  ...the smell of damp earth...
  Pásele un trapo húmedo
  Wipe it with a damp cloth

- Se traduce por *moist* cuando queremos sugerir que el hecho de que esté o sea *húmedo* le da un carácter agradable o atractivo.
  El pastel estaba húmedo y esponjoso
  The cake was moist and smooth
  Hay que mantener las raíces húmedas
  The roots must be kept moist

- En contextos científicos se traduce por *humid* cuando se refiere a condiciones atmosféricas:
  ...el clima caluroso y húmedo de Chipre...
  ...the hot and humid climate of Cyprus...

- También referido al tiempo atmosférico, pero en un lenguaje menos científico, lo traducimos por *wet* cuando se refiere a un tiempo lluvioso:
  Hemos tenido un verano muy húmedo
  It's been very wet this summer

---

humera NF **(a)** (*Carib*) cloud of smoke. **(b)** = **jumera.**

humero NM **(a)** chimney, smokestack; flue. **(b)** (*And*) cloud of smoke.

húmero NM humerus.

humidificar [1g] VT to wet; to dampen, moisten.

humildad NF (a) humbleness, humility; meekness. (b) humbleness; lowliness.

humilde ADJ (a) *carácter etc* humble; meek; *voz* small. (b) *clase etc* low, modest; lowly, lowborn, humble; **son gente ~** they are humble people, they are poor people.

humildemente ADV humbly; meekly.

humillación NF humiliation; humbling.

humillante ADJ humiliating; humbling; degrading.

humillar [1a] ☐1 VT to humiliate; to humble; *cabeza* to bow, bend; *enemigos, rebeldes etc* to crush.
☐2 **humillarse** VR to humble o.s.; **~ a** to bow to, bow down before; to grovel to.

humita NF (*And, Cono Sur*) (*tamal*) tamale; (*maíz molido*) ground maize, ground corn (US); **~s** *snack of meat and cornflour wrapped in a leaf.*

humo NM (a) (*gen*) smoke; (*gases*) fumes; (*vapor*) vapour, steam; **a ~ de pajas** thoughtlessly, heedlessly; **ni hablaba a ~ de pajas** nor was he talking idly; **quedó en ~ de pajas** it all came to nothing; **hacer ~, echar ~** to smoke; **lo que hace ~ es porque está ardiendo, donde se hace ~ es porque hay fuego** there's no smoke without fire; **hacerse ~, irse todo en ~** to go up in smoke; (*fig*) to disappear completely, vanish without trace; **írsele al ~ a uno** (*Cono Sur, Méx*) to jump sb*; **tomar la del ~**‡ to beat it*.
(b) **~s** (*fig: hogares*) homes, hearths.
(c) **~s** (*fig: presunción*) conceit, airs; **bajar los ~s a uno** to take sb down a peg; **darse ~s** to brag, swank*; **tener muchos ~s** to be terribly vain, have a big head; **tener ~s para + infin** to have the nerve to* + *infin*; **vender ~s** to brag, talk big*.

humor NM (a) mood, humour; temper, disposition; (*Med*) humour; **buen ~** good humour, good mood, high spirits; **estar de buen ~** to be in a good mood; **mal ~** bad mood, bad temper; **en un tono de mal ~** in an ill-tempered tone; **seguir el ~ a uno** to humour sb, go along with sb's mood.
(b) (*gracia*) humour; humorousness; **~ negro** black humour.

humorada NF (a) (*chiste*) joke, witticism, pleasantry. (b) (*capricho*) caprice, whim.

humorado ADJ: **bien ~** good-humoured, good-tempered; **mal ~** bad-tempered, cross, peevish.

humorismo NM humour; humorousness.

humorista NMF humorist.

humorísticamente ADV humorously, facetiously.

humorístico ADJ humorous, funny, facetious.

humoso ADJ smoky.

humus NM humus.

hundible ADJ sinkable.

hundido ADJ sunken; *ojos* deep-set, hollow.

hundimiento NM (a) (*gen*) sinking. (b) (*de edificio*) collapse, fall, ruin, destruction; (*de tierra*) cave-in, subsidence.

hundir [3a] ☐1 VT (a) (*gen*) to sink; (*sumergir*) to submerge, engulf.
(b) *edificio etc* to ruin, destroy, cause the collapse of; *plan etc* to sink, ruin; (*en debate*) to confound.
☐2 **hundirse** VR (a) (*Náut*) to sink; (*en arena, lodo etc*) to sink; (*nadador etc*) to plunge, go down.
(b) (*edificio etc*) to collapse, tumble (down), fall (down); (*tierra*) to cave in, subside.
(c) (*fig*) to be destroyed, be ruined; (*persona*) to collapse, break down; to disappear, vanish; **se hundió la economía** the economy collapsed; **se hundieron los precios** prices slumped; **se hundió en el estudio de la historia** he plunged into the study of history, he became absorbed in the study of history; **se hundió en la meditación** he became lost in meditation.

húngaro, -a ☐1 ADJ, NM/F Hungarian.
☐2 NM (*Ling*) Hungarian.

Hungría NF Hungary.

huno NM Hun.

huracán NM hurricane.

huracanado ADJ: **viento ~** hurricane wind, violent wind.

huraco NM (*LAm*) hole.

huraña NF (*timidez*) shyness; (*insociabilidad*) unsociableness; (*esquivez*) elusiveness.

huraño ADJ (*tímido*) shy; (*poco sociable*) unsociable; *animal* shy, elusive; (*salvaje*) wild.

hure NM (*And*) large pot.

hureque NM (*And*) = **huraco**.

hurgar [1h] ☐1 VT (a) to poke, jab; to stir (up); *fuego* to poke, rake.
(b) (*LAm*) = **hurguetear**.
(c) (*fig*) to stir up, excite, provoke.
☐2 VI: **~ en el bolsillo** to feel in one's pocket, rummage in one's pocket.
☐3 **hurgarse** VR (*t* **~ las narices**) to pick one's nose.

hurgón NM (a) (*de fuego*) poker, fire rake. (b) (*con arma*) thrust, stab.

hurgonada NF, **hurgonazo** NM poke, jab; poking, raking.

hurgonear [1a] VT *fuego* to poke, rake (out); *adversario etc* to thrust at, jab (at).

hurgonero NM poker, fire rake.

hurguete NM (*Cono Sur*) busybody, nosey-parker*.

hurguetear [1a] VT (*LAm: remover*) to finger, turn over, rummage (inquisitively) among; (*fisgonear*) to shove one's nose into*, pry into.

hurí NF houri.

hurón ☐1 ADJ (a) shy, unsociable.
(b) (*Cono Sur*: *glotón*) greedy.
☐2 NM (a) (*Zool*) ferret.
(b) (*fig*) shy person, unsociable person.
(c) (*fig: pey*) busybody, nosey-parker*, snooper.

huronear [1a] VT (*fig*) to ferret out; to pry into, shove one's nose into*.

huronera NF ferret hole; (*fig*) den, lair; hiding place.

hurra INTERJ hurray!, hurrah!

hurtadillas: a ~ ADV stealthily, by stealth, on the sly.

hurtar [1a] ☐1 VT (a) (*robar*) to steal; (*Liter etc*) to plagiarize, pinch*, lift*; **con esta maniobra pretenden ~ al país las elecciones** they are trying with this manoeuvre to deprive the country of (the chance of holding) elections.
(b) (*mar etc*) to eat away, erode, encroach on.
(c) **~ el cuerpo** to dodge, move (one's body) out of the way.
☐2 **hurtarse** VR (*retirarse*) to withdraw; (*irse*) to make off; (*no tomar parte*) to keep out of the way.

hurto NM (a) (*acto*) theft, robbery; (*gen*) thieving, robbery; (*Jur*) larceny; **a ~** stealthily, by stealth, on the sly. (b) (*cosa robada*) thing stolen, (piece of) stolen property, loot.

húsar NM hussar.

husillo NM (a) (*Mec*) spindle, shaft; (*de prensa etc*) screw, worm. (b) (*conducto*) drain.

husma NF snooping*; prying; **andar a la ~** to go snooping around*, go prying (*de* after, for).

husmear [1a] ☐1 VT (a) to scent, get wind of, sniff out. (b) (*fig*) to smell out; to nose into, pry into.
☐2 VI (*carne*) to (begin to) smell high, be smelly.

husmeo NM (a) scenting. (b) (*fig*) smelling-out; prying, snooping*.

husmo NM high smell, strong smell, gaminess; **estar al ~** to watch one's chance.

huso NM (a) (*Tec*) spindle; bobbin; (*de torno etc*) drum. (b) (*Cono Sur*) kneecap. (c) **~ horario** (*Geog*) time zone.

hutu ADJ, NMF Hutu.

huy INTERJ (*dolor*) ow!, ouch!; (*sorpresa*) well!; (*alivio*) phew!

huyente ADJ *frente* receding.

huyón (*LAm*) ☐1 ADJ (*cobarde*) cowardly; (*huraño*) shy, unsociable.
☐2 NM, **huyona** NF coward; shy person, unsociable person.

Hz ABR *de* **hertzio** hertz, Hz.

I

I, i [i] NF (*letra*) I, i; **~ griega** Y, y.
IA NF ABR *de* **inteligencia artificial** artificial intelligence, AI.
IAC NF ABR *de* **ingeniería asistida por computadora** computer-assisted engineering, CAE.
IAE NM (*Esp*) ABR *de* **Impuesto de** o **sobre Actividades Económicas** *tax on commercial and professional activities*.
-iano V Aspects of Word Formation in Spanish 2.
IAO NF ABR *de* **instrucción asistida por ordenador** computer-assisted instruction, CAI.
IB N (*Aer*) ABR *de* **Iberia, Líneas Aéreas de España, Sociedad Anónima**.
iba etc V ir.
Iberia NF Iberia.
ibérico ADJ Iberian; **la Península Ibérica** the Iberian Peninsula.
ibero, -a, íbero, -a ADJ, NM/F Iberian.
Iberoamérica NF Latin America.
iberoamericano, -a ADJ, NM/F Latin-American.
ibex NM INVAR ibex.
IBI NM (*Esp*) ABR *de* **Impuesto de** o **sobre Bienes Inmuebles** *rates, real estate tax (US)*.
íbice NM ibex.
ibicenco ① ADJ of Ibiza.
　② NM, **ibicenca** NF native (o inhabitant) of Ibiza; **los ~s** the people of Ibiza.
-ibilidad V Aspects of Word Formation in Spanish 2.
ibis NF INVAR ibis.
Ibiza NF Ibiza.
-ible V Aspects of Word Formation in Spanish 2.
ibón NM Pyrenean lake, tarn.
ícaro NM (*LAm Dep*) hang-glider.
ICE ['iθe] NM **(a)** (*Esp Escol*) ABR *de* **Instituto de Ciencias de la Educación. (b)** (*Esp Com*) ABR *de* **Instituto de Ciencias Económicas**.
iceberg NM ['iθeßer], PL **icebergs** ['iθeßer] iceberg.
ICEX ['iθeks] NM ABR *de* **Instituto de Comercio Exterior**.
ICH NM (*Esp*) ABR *de* **Instituto de Cultura Hispánica**.
ICI ['iθi] NM (*Esp*) ABR *de* **Instituto de Cooperación Iberoamericana**.
ICO (*Esp*) ABR *de* **Instituto de Crédito Oficial**.
-ico, -ica V Aspects of Word Formation in Spanish 2.
ICONA, Icona [i'kona] NM (*Esp*) ABR *de* **Instituto para la Conservación de la Naturaleza**.
icono NM ikon, icon.
iconoclasta ① ADJ iconoclastic.
　② NMF iconoclast.
iconoclas(t)ia NF iconoclasm.
iconografía NF iconography.
iconográfico ADJ iconographic.
ictericia NF jaundice.
ictio- PREF ichthyo-.
ictiofauna NF fish, fishes.
ICYT ['iθit] NM ABR *de* **Instituto de Información y Documentación sobre Ciencia y Tecnología**.
I + D ABR *de* **Investigación y Desarrollo** Research and Development, R & D.
id¹ NM id.
id² V ir.
íd. ABR *de* **ídem** ditto, do.
ida NF **(a)** (*partida*) going, departure; **~s y venidas** comings and goings; **en dos ~s y venidas** in an instant; **dejar las ~s por las venidas** to miss the boat; **(viaje de) ~** outward journey, trip out; **~ y vuelta** round trip; **partido de ~** away game (in two-match contest).
(b) (*Caza*) track, trail.
(c) (*fig*) rash act; rashness, hastiness.
IDCA ['iðka] NM ABR *de* **Instituto de Desarrollo Cooperativo en América**.

iddish ['idiʃ] NM Yiddish.
IDE NF ABR *de* **Iniciativa de Defensa Estratégica** Strategic Defence Initiative, SDI.
idea NF **(a)** (*noción*) idea, notion; **~ faro*, ~ genial, ~ luminosa** bright idea, brilliant idea; **~ fija** fixed idea, obsession, idée fixe; **~ fuerza** key idea, central idea; **~ monstruo*** fantastic idea; **una persona de mala ~** a malicious person, an evil-minded person; **¡ni ~!** I haven't a clue!, search me!*; **meterse una ~ en la cabeza** to get an idea into one's head; **no tengo la menor ~, no tengo la más remota ~** I haven't the faintest (o foggiest) idea; **no tenía la menor ~ de que ...** I had no idea that ...; **tiene ~s de bombero** he's all at sea, he hasn't a clue.
(b) (*impresión*) idea, opinion, estimate; **¿qué ~ tienes de él?** what impression do you have of him?; **darse una ~ de, hacerse una ~ de** to get an idea of, form an impression of.
(c) (*propósito*) idea, intention; **con la ~ de** + *infin* with the idea of + *ger*; **cambiar de ~, mudar de ~** to change one's mind; **hace falta que cambie de ~** he'll have to alter his outlook; he'll have to buck his ideas up*; **llevar ~ de** + *infin* to have the idea of + *ger*, intend to + *infin*.
(d) (*inventiva*) ingenuity, inventiveness.
ideación NF conception, thinking-out.
ideal ADJ, NM ideal.
idealismo NM idealism.
idealista ① ADJ idealistic.
　② NMF idealist.
idealización NF idealization.
idealizar [1f] VT to idealize.
idealmente ADV ideally.
idear [1a] VT to think up; to contrive, invent, devise; to plan, design.
ideario NM set of ideas; ideology; ideological formation.
ideático ADJ **(a)** (*LAm: excéntrico*) eccentric, odd. **(b)** (*CAm: inventivo*) ingenious, full of ideas.
IDEM ['iðem] NM (*Esp*) ABR *de* **Instituto de los Derechos de la Mujer**.
ídem ① PRON ditto, the same, idem.
　② NM: **ser un ~ de lienzo** to be another of the same sort, be tarred with the same brush; **y ella, ~ de lienzo** and she (did) the same.
idénticamente ADV identically.
idéntico ADJ identical; the same, the very same.
identidad NF identity; sameness, similarity; **~ corporativa** corporate identity.
identificable ADJ identifiable.
identificación NF identification; **~ errónea** mistaken identity.
identificador ① ADJ identifying.
　② NM identifier.
identificar [1g] ① VT to identify; to recognize, spot, pick out; **víctima sin ~** unidentified victim.
　② **identificarse** VR: **~ con** to identify (o.s.) with.
identificatorio ADJ identifying.
ideograma NM ideogram.
ideología NF ideology.
ideológicamente ADV ideologically.
ideológico ADJ ideological.
ideólogo, -a NM/F ideologue, ideologist.
ideoso ADJ (*Méx*) (*maniático*) obsessive; (*caprichoso*) wilful.
idílico ADJ idyllic.
idilio NM idyll; (*amor*) romance, love-affair.
idiolecto NM idiolect.
▼ **idioma** NM language; **los ~s de trabajo de la CE** the working languages of the European Community.
idiomaticidad NF idiomatic nature.
idiomático ADJ language (*atr*), linguistic; idiomatic.
idiosincrasia NF idiosyncrasy.

➤ LENGUA Y USO: **idioma** → 46.3

idiosincrásico ADJ idiosyncratic.
idiota [1] ADJ idiotic, stupid.
  [2] NMF idiot; ¡~! you idiot!
idiotez NF idiocy; **hablar idioteces** to talk rubbish.
idiotismo NM (a) (*Ling*) idiom, idiomatic expression. (b) (*ignorancia*) ignorance.
idiotizar [1f] VT (a) to reduce to a state of idiocy, make an idiot of; (*fig*) to stupefy. (b) **~ a uno** (*LAm**) to drive sb crazy.
IDO ['iðo] NM (*Esp*) ABR de **Instituto de Denominaciones de Origen.**
ido [1] ADJ (a) (*LAm*: despistado*) absent-minded.
  (b) (*LAm*: chiflado*) crazy; **estar ~** (**de la cabeza**) to be crazy.
  (c) **estar ~** (*CAm, Méx**) to be drunk.
  [2] NMPL: **los ~s** the dead, the departed.
idólatra [1] ADJ idolatrous.
  [2] NMF idolater, idolatress.
idolatrar [1a] VT to worship, adore; (*fig*) to idolize.
idolatría NF idolatry.
idolátrico ADJ idolatrous.
ídolo NM idol.
idoneidad NF suitability, fitness; (*capacidad*) aptitude, ability.
idoneizar [1f] VT to make suitable.
idóneo ADJ (*apropiado*) suitable, fit, fitting; (*Méx: genuino*) genuine.
idus NMPL ides.
IEE NM (a) (*Admin*) ABR de **Instituto Español de Emigración.** (b) (*Esp Com*) ABR de **Instituto de Estudios Económicos.**
IEI NM (*Esp*) ABR de **Instituto de Educación e Investigación.**
IEM NM (*Esp*) ABR de **Instituto de Enseñanza Media.**
iglesia NF church; **I~ Anglicana** Church of England, Anglican Church; **~ catedral** cathedral; **I~ Católica** Catholic Church; **~ colegial** collegiate church; **~ parroquial** parish church; **casarse por la ~** to get married in church, have a church wedding; **casarse por detrás de la ~** to set up house together; **cumplir con la ~** to fulfil one's religious obligations; **llevar a una a la ~** to lead sb to the altar; **¡con la ~ hemos topado!** now we're really up against it!

IGLESIA	ver también la entrada

Uso del artículo

En inglés el uso del artículo delante de *church* depende del motivo por el que alguien se encuentre en el edificio.
- Se traduce *a la iglesia* por *to church, en la iglesia* por *in church, desde la iglesia* por *from church, etc*, cuando alguien va o está allí para asistir al servicio religioso:
  Vamos a la iglesia todos los domingos
  We go to church every Sunday
- Se traduce *a la iglesia* por *to the church, en la iglesia* por *at the church* y *desde la iglesia* por *from the church, etc* cuando alguien va o está allí por otros motivos:
  Mi padre ha ido a la iglesia a arreglar las ventanas
  My father has gone to the church to fix the windows
  Para otros usos y ejemplos ver la entrada.

---

iglesiero* ADJ (*LAm*) churchy*, church-going.
iglú NM igloo.
IGN NM (*Esp, Honduras*) ABR de **Instituto Geográfico Nacional.**
Ignacio NM Ignatius.
ignaro ADJ ignorant.
ígneo ADJ igneous.
ignición NF ignition.
ignifugación NF fireproofing.
ignífugo ADJ fireproof, fire-resistant.
igniscible ADJ flammable, easy to ignite.
ignominia NF (a) (*gen*) ignominy, shame, disgrace. (b) (*acto*) disgraceful act.
ignominiosamente ADV ignominiously, shamefully.
ignominioso ADJ ignominious, shameful, disgraceful.
ignorado ADJ unknown; obscure, little-known.
ignorancia NF ignorance; **por ~** through ignorance.
ignorante [1] ADJ ignorant; uninformed.
  [2] NMF ignoramus.
ignorar [1a] VT (a) (*desconocer*) not to know, be ignorant of, be unaware of; **lo ignoro en absoluto** (o **por completo**) I don't know at all, I've no idea; **ignoramos su paradero** we don't know his whereabouts; **no ignoro que** ... I am fully aware that ..., of course I know that ...
  (b) (*no hacer caso a*) to ignore.
ignoto ADJ unknown; undiscovered.
igual [1] ADJ (a) (*gen*) equal (*a* to); (the) same; (*semejante*) alike, similar; **no vi nunca cosa ~** I never saw the like; **1 kilómetro es ~ a 1.000 metros** a kilometre is equal to 1,000 metres, a kilometre equals 1,000 metres; **A es ~ a B** A is like B, A is the same as B; **es ~** it makes no difference, it's all the same; **me es ~** it's all the same to me, I don't mind.

(b) (*llano*) even, level; (*constante*) uniform, constant, unvarying, unchanging; (*liso*) smooth; *temperatura* even; *clima* equable; **ir ~es** (*en carrera*) to be level, be even.
(c) **~ que** (*como* PREP) like, the same as; **A, ~ que B, no sabe** A, like B, doesn't know.
(d) **al ~ que** (*como* PREP *o* CONJ) like, just like; while, whereas; **Chile, al ~ que Argentina, estima que** ... Chile, (just) like Argentina, thinks that ...
  [2] ADV (a) **~ no sabe*** he may not know, maybe he doesn't know.
(b) (*LAm*) all the same, in spite of everything.
  [3] NMF equal; **al ~, por ~** equally, on an equal basis; **sin ~** without equal, matchless; **ser el ~ de** to be the equal of, be a match for; **no tener ~** to be unrivalled, have no equal; **alternar de ~ a ~** to be on an equal footing; **tratar a uno de ~ a ~** to treat sb as an equal.
  [4] NM (a) (*Mat*) equals sign, sign of equality.
(b) **~es** (*Guardia Civil*) Civil Guard.
iguala NF (a) equalization. (b) (*Com*) agreement; agreed fee.
igualación NF equalization; evening up, levelling; (*Mat*) equating.
igualada NF (*Dep: tanto*) equalizer, equalizing goal (*etc*); (*igualdad de puntos*) level score.
igualado ADJ (*CAm, Méx*) (*irrespetuoso*) cheeky; (*astuto*) sly.
igualar [1a] [1] VT (a) (*hacer igual*) to equalize, make equal; (*Mat*) to equate (*a* to); (*fig*) to compare, match (*a* with).
(b) (*allanar*) to level, level off, level up; to even, even out; (*alisar*) to smooth; (*fig*) to even out, adjust.
(c) (*Com*) to agree upon.
  [2] VI e **igualarse** VR (a) to be equal; **~ a, ~ con** to equal, be equal to, be the equal of.
(b) (*Dep*) to equalize, score the equalizer; to tie.
(c) (*Com*) to come to an agreement.
(d) (*CAm, Méx**) to be too familiar, be cheeky*.
igualatorio NM (*Med*) insurance group.
igualdad NF (a) (*gen*) equality; (*semejanza*) sameness; (*Mat*) equality; **~ de oportunidades** equality of opportunity; **~ de retribución** equal pay; **en ~ de condiciones** on the same conditions, on an equal basis, on a level footing.
(b) (*de superficie etc*) evenness, levelness; uniformity; smoothness; **~ de ánimo** equanimity.
igualitario ADJ egalitarian.
igualitarismo NM egalitarianism.
igualito ADJ (*diminutivo de* **igual**) (*esp LAm*) exactly the same, identical; **los dos están ~s** they're the spitting image of each other.
igualización NF equalization.
igualmente ADV (a) (*gen*) equally. (b) (*de modo uniforme*) evenly; uniformly. (c) (*también*) likewise, also. (d) (*respuesta a saludo etc*) the same to you.
iguana NF iguana.
IHS ABR de **Jesús** Jesus, IHS.
III NM (*Méx*) ABR de **Instituto Indigenista Interamericano.**
ijada NF (a) (*Anat*) flank, side, loin. (b) (*Med: dolor*) stitch, pain in the side; **esto tiene su ~** this has its weak side.
ijadear [1a] VI (*Zool*) to pant.
ijar NM flank, side.
ikastola NF Basque language school; *see also* EUSKERA .
ikurriña NF Basque national flag.
-il V Aspects of Word Formation in Spanish 2.
ilación NF inference; connection, relationship.
ILARI [i'lari] NM ABR de **Instituto Latinoamericano de Relaciones Internacionales.**
ilativo ADJ inferential; (*Ling*) illative.
ilegal ADJ illegal, unlawful.
ilegalidad NF illegality, unlawfulness.
ilegalización NF outlawing, banning.
ilegalizar [1f] VT to outlaw, declare illegal, ban.
ilegalmente ADV illegally, unlawfully.
ilegible ADJ illegible, unreadable.
ilegítimamente ADV illegitimately.
ilegitimar [1a] VT to make illegal.
ilegitimidad NF illegitimacy.
ilegitimizar [1f] VT = **ilegitimar.**
ilegítimo ADJ (a) (*gen*) illegitimate; (*ilegal*) unlawful. (b) (*falso*) false, spurious.
ilerdense [1] ADJ of Lérida.
  [2] NMF native (o inhabitant) of Lérida; **los ~s** the people of Lérida.
ileso ADJ unhurt, unharmed; untouched; **salió ~ del accidente** he came out of the accident unharmed, he got out of the accident unscathed; **los pasajeros resultaron ~s** the passengers were unhurt.
iletrado ADJ uncultured, illiterate.
Ilíada NF Iliad.
iliberal ADJ illiberal.
ilícitamente ADV illicitly, illegally, unlawfully.
ilicitano [1] ADJ of Elche.

[2] NM, **ilicitana** NF native (o inhabitant) of Elche; **los ~s** the people of Elche.

ilícito ADJ illicit, illegal, unlawful.

ilimitado ADJ unlimited, limitless, unbounded.

iliterato ADJ illiterate.

illanco NM (And) slow stream, quiet-flowing stream.

-illo, -illa V Aspects of Word Formation in Spanish 2.

Ilma., Ilmo. ABR de Ilustrísima, Ilustrísimo (courtesy title).

ilocalizable ADJ that cannot be found; unavailable; **ayer X seguía ~** X could still not be found yesterday; X was still unavailable yesterday.

ilógicamente ADV illogically.

ilógico ADJ illogical.

ILPES ['ilpes] NM ABR de Instituto Latinoamericano de Planificación Económica y Social.

ilu* NF = ilusión; **¡qué ~!** how thrilling!, how exciting!

iluminación NF (a) (gen) illumination, lighting; floodlighting; **~ indirecta** indirect lighting. (b) (fig) enlightenment.

iluminado [1] ADJ (a) illuminated, lighted, lit; (fig) enlightened. (b) **estar ~:** (borracho) to be lit up:; (drogado) to be high (on drugs):. [2] NM, **iluminada** NF visionary; illuminist; **los I~s** the Illuminati.

iluminador [1] ADJ illuminating. [2] NM, **iluminadora** NF illuminator.

iluminar [1a] VT (a) (alumbrar) to illuminate, light, light up; edificio etc to floodlight. (b) (fig) to enlighten.

iluminista NMF (Cine, TV) electrician, lighting engineer.

ilusión NF (a) (noción falsa) illusion; delusion; **~ óptica** optical illusion; **todo es ~** it's all an illusion. (b) (esperanza, sueño) (unfounded) hope, dream; piece of wishful thinking; hopefulness; **con ~** hopefully; **el hombre de sus ilusiones** the man of her dreams; **su ~ era comprarlo** her dream was to buy it, she dreamed of buying it; **forjarse ilusiones, hacerse ilusiones** to build up (false) hopes, deceive o.s. with false hopes, indulge in wishful thinking; **no te hagas ilusiones** don't get any false ideas, don't kid yourself*; **se hace la ~ de que ...** she fondly imagines that ...; **no me hago muchas ilusiones de que ...** I am not very hopeful that ...; **poner su ~ en algo** to pin one's hopes on sth; **tendió la mano con ~** she put her hand out hopefully. (c) (emoción) excitement, thrill; (entusiasmo) eagerness; (expectación) hopeful anticipation; **¡qué ~!** how thrilling!, how exciting!; **comer con ~** to eat eagerly; **trabajar con ~** to work with a will; **el viaje me hace mucha ~** I am so looking forward to the trip, I am getting very excited about the trip; **tu carta me hizo mucha ~** I was thrilled to get your letter; **me hace una gran ~ que ...** it gives me a thrill that ...; **tener ~ por** to look forward to.

ilusionadamente ADV with high hopes; excitedly.

ilusionado [1] ADJ hopeful; excited, eager; **el viaje me trae muy ~** I am so looking forward to the trip, I am getting very excited about the trip. [2] NM, **ilusionada** NF hopeful; **joven ~** young hopeful.

ilusionante ADJ exciting.

ilusionar [1a] [1] VT (*: engañar) to deceive; (alentar) to give false hopes to, encourage falsely. [2] **ilusionarse** VR to have unfounded hopes, indulge in wishful thinking; **no te ilusiones** don't get any false ideas.

ilusionismo NM conjuring, illusionism.

ilusionista NMF conjurer, illusionist.

iluso [1] ADJ easily deceived; deluded. [2] NM, **ilusa** NF dreamer, visionary; **¡~!** you're hopeful!

ilusorio ADJ illusory, deceptive, unreal; empty, ineffectual.

ilustración NF (a) (gen) illustration. (b) (Tip) illustration, picture, drawing. (c) (erudición) learning, erudition; enlightenment; **la I~** the Enlightenment, the Age of Enlightenment.

ilustrado ADJ (a) illustrated. (b) learned, erudite; enlightened.

ilustrador [1] ADJ illustrative; enlightening. [2] NM, **ilustradora** NF illustrator.

▼ **ilustrar** [1a] [1] VT (a) (gen) to illustrate. (b) (aclarar) to explain, elucidate, make clear. (c) (instruir) to instruct, enlighten. (d) (hacer famoso) to make famous, make illustrious. [2] **ilustrarse** VR (a) (instruirse) to acquire knowledge, become enlightened. (b) (hacerse famoso) to become famous.

ilustrativo ADJ illustrative.

ilustre ADJ illustrious, famous.

ilustrísimo ADJ most illustrious; **Su Ilustrísima** His Grace; His Lordship; **Vuestra Ilustrísima** Your Grace; Your Lordship.

IM NM ABR de Instituto de la Mujer.

IMAC [i'mak] NM ABR de Instituto de Mediación, Arbitraje y Conciliación ≃ Advisory, Conciliation and Arbitration Service, ACAS.

imagen NF (a) (gen) image; (idea) (mental) picture; (semejanza) likeness; **~ de marca** brand image; **~ pública** public image, public face; **cultivar la ~** to cultivate one's image; **ser la viva ~ de** to be the living image of; **hacer a uno a su ~** to make sb in one's own image. (b) (Ecl) image, statue; **quedar para vestir imágenes** to be an old maid. (c) (Prensa, TV) picture; **~ fantasma** ghost image; **~ fija** still (picture). (d) (Liter) image; **imágenes** (en conjunto) imagery.

imaginable ADJ imaginable, conceivable.

imaginación NF imagination; fancy; **ni por ~** on no account; **no se me pasó por la ~ que ...** it never even occurred to me that ...; **ella se deja llevar por la ~** she lets her imagination run away with her.

imaginar [1a] [1] VT (gen) to imagine; (visualizar) to visualize; (idear) to think up, invent; **cosas que nadie imagina** things that no-one imagines; **¿quién imaginó esto?** who thought this one up? [2] VI e **imaginarse** VR to imagine, fancy, suppose; to picture (to o.s.); **¡imagínate!** just imagine!, just fancy!; **imagínese que ...** suppose that ..., imagine that ...; **me imagino que ...** I suppose that ...; **me imagino que sí** I suppose so; **sí, me imagino** yes, I can imagine.

imaginaria NF (Mil) reserve guard, night guard.

imaginario ADJ imaginary.

imaginativa NF imagination, imaginativeness.

imaginativo ADJ imaginative.

imaginería NF (a) (Ecl) images, statues. (b) (Liter) imagery.

imaginero -a NM/F maker (o painter) of religious images.

imam NM, **imán**[1] NM (Rel) imam.

imán[2] NM (Téc) magnet (t fig); **~ de herradura** horseshoe magnet.

iman(t)ación NF magnetization.

iman(t)ar [1a] VT to magnetize.

imbatibilidad NF unbeatable character; (Dep) unbeaten record.

imbatible ADJ unbeatable.

imbatido ADJ unbeaten.

imbebible ADJ undrinkable.

imbécil [1] ADJ (a) (Med) imbecile, feeble-minded. (b) (fig) silly, stupid. [2] NMF (a) (Med) imbecile. (b) (fig) imbecile, idiot; **¡~!** you idiot!

imbecilidad NF (a) (Med) imbecility, feeble-mindedness. (b) (fig) silliness, stupidity, idiocy; **decir ~es** to say silly things.

imbecilizar [1f] VT to reduce to a state of idiocy; (fig) to stupefy.

imberbe ADJ beardless.

imbíbito ADJ (CAm, Méx) included (in the bill).

imbombera NF (Carib) pernicious anaemia.

imbombo NM (Carib) anaemic.

imbornal NM scupper; **irse por los ~es** (LAm*) to go off at a tangent.

imborrable ADJ ineffaceable, indelible; recuerdo etc unforgettable.

imbricación NF overlapping; interweaving, interdependence.

imbricado ADJ (LAm) (sobrepuesto) overlapping; asunto etc involved.

imbricar [1g] [1] VT to overlap; to interweave; **~ a uno*** to involve sb. [2] **imbricarse** VR to overlap; to be interwoven.

imbuir [3g] VT to imbue, infuse (de, en with); **imbuido de la cultura de** imbued with the culture of, full of the culture of.

imbunchar [1a] VT (Cono Sur) (a) (hechizar) to bewitch. (b) (estafar) to swindle, cheat.

imbunche NM (Cono Sur) (a) (hechizo) spell, piece of witchcraft; (brujo) sorcerer, wizard. (b) (confusión) mess; (lío) fuss, row.

IMCE ['imse] NM ABR de Instituto Mejicano de Comercio Exterior.

IMEC [i'mek] NF ABR de Instrucción Militar de la Escala de Complemento.

imitable ADJ imitable; to be imitated, worthy of imitation.

imitación NF (a) (gen) imitation; (parodia) mimicry; **a ~ de** in imitation of; **desconfíe de las imitaciones** beware of imitations. (b) **de ~** imitation (atr); **joyas de ~** imitation jewellery. (c) (Teat) imitation, impersonation.

imitador [1] ADJ imitative. [2] NM, **imitadora** NF imitator; follower; (Teat) imitator, impersonator; impressionist.

imitar [1a] VT (a) (gen) to imitate; (parodiar) to mimic, ape; (copiar) to follow. (b) (falsificar) to counterfeit.

imitativo ADJ imitative.

impaciencia NF impatience.

impacientar [1a] [1] VT to make impatient; to irritate, exasperate. [2] **impacientarse** VR to get impatient (ante, por about, at; con with), lose patience, get worked up; to fret; **~ por + infin** to be impatient to + infin.

impaciente ADJ impatient; anxious; fretful; **~ por empezar** impatient to start, keen to get going; **¡estoy ~!** I can't wait! (por + infin to + infin).

impacientemente ADV impatiently; anxiously; fretfully.

impactante ADJ (impresionante) striking, impressive; (contundente) shattering; (abrumador) crushing, overwhelming.

impactar [1a] [1] VT (impresionar) to impress, have an impact on; (gustar) to please, delight, be a hit with.

---

[2] VI to hit, strike; **~ en** to affect, have an effect on, influence.

[3] **impactarse** VR: **~ ante, ~ por** to be overawed by.

impacto NM **(a)** impact; (*repercusión*) incidence; (*Mil*) hit; (*LAm Boxeo*) punch, blow; **~ ambiental** environmental impact, environmental damage; **~ directo** direct hit; **~ político** political impact. **(b)** (*esp LAm: fig*) impression; shock.

impagable ADJ unpayable; (*fig*) priceless, inestimable.

impagado ADJ unpaid, still to be paid.

impagador(a) NM/F defaulter, non-payer.

impago (*LAm*) [1] ADJ unpaid, still to be paid.

[2] NM non-payment, failure to pay.

impajaritable ADJ (*Cono Sur*) necessary, imperative.

impalpable ADJ impalpable.

impar [1] ADJ **(a)** (*Mat*) odd; **los números ~es** the odd numbers. **(b)** (*fig*) unique, exceptional.

[2] NM odd number.

imparable ADJ (*Dep*) unstoppable.

imparablemente ADV unstoppably.

imparcial ADJ impartial, unbiassed, fair.

imparcialidad NF impartiality, lack of bias, fairness.

imparcialmente ADV impartially, fairly.

impartible ADJ indivisible, that cannot be shared out.

impartición NF teaching.

impartir [3a] VT *instrucción etc* to impart, give, convey; *orden* to give.

impase [im'pas] NM o NF **(a)** (*atascamiento*) impasse. **(b)** (*Bridge*) finesse; **hacer el ~ a uno** to finesse against sb.

impasibilidad NF impassiveness, impassivity; **los precios siguen bajando ante la ~ del gobierno** the government remains unmoved (*o* impassive) despite the continual fall in prices.

impasible ADJ impassive, unmoved.

impávidamente ADV (*V ADJ*) **(a)** intrepidly; dauntlessly. **(b)** (*LAm*) cheekily.

impavidez NF (*V ADJ*) **(a)** intrepidity; dauntlessness. **(b)** (*LAm*) cheek, cheekiness.

impávido ADJ **(a)** (*valiente*) intrepid; (*impasible*) dauntless, undaunted. **(b)** (*LAm: insolente*) cheeky.

IMPE ['impe] NM (*Esp*) ABR *de* **Instituto de la Mediana y Pequeña Empresa.**

impecable ADJ impeccable, faultless.

impecablemente ADV impeccably, faultlessly.

impedido [1] ADJ crippled, disabled, handicapped; **estar ~ para algo** to be unfit for sth.

[2] NM, **impedida** NF cripple, handicapped person.

impedimenta NF (*Mil*) impedimenta (*pl*).

impedimento NM **(a)** (*obstáculo*) impediment (*t Jur*), obstacle, hindrance. **(b)** (*Med*) disability, handicap; **~ del habla** speech impediment.

impedir [3k] VT **(a)** (*dificultar*) to impede, obstruct, hinder, hamper; (*disuadir*) to deter; **~ el tráfico** to block the traffic, obstruct the traffic.

(b) (*prohibir*) to stop, prevent; (*frustrar*) to thwart; **~ algo a uno** to keep sb from doing sth, to make sth impossible for sb; **~ a uno hacer algo, ~ que uno haga algo** to stop sb doing sth, prevent sb (from) doing sth; **me veo impedido para ayudar** I find it impossible for me to help; **esto no impide que ...** this does not alter the fact that ...; **lo que no se puede ~** what cannot be prevented.

impeditivo ADJ preventive.

impeler [2a] VT **(a)** (*Mec*) to drive, propel. **(b)** (*fig*) to drive, impel; to urge; **~ a uno a hacer algo** to drive sb to do sth; to urge sb to do sth; **impelido por la necesidad** impelled by necessity.

impenetrabilidad NF impenetrability.

impenetrable ADJ impenetrable (*t fig*); impervious; (*fig*) obscure, incomprehensible.

impenitencia NF impenitence.

impenitente ADJ impenitent, unrepentant.

▼ **impensable** ADJ unthinkable.

impensadamente ADV **(a)** unexpectedly. **(b)** at random, by chance. **(c)** (*sin querer*) inadvertently; unintentionally.

impensado ADJ **(a)** (*imprevisto*) unexpected, unforeseen. **(b)** (*casual*) random, chance (*atr*).

impepinable* ADJ certain, inevitable, undeniable.

impepinablemente* ADV inevitably; **~ se le olvida** he's sure to forget, he always forgets.

imperante ADJ ruling (*t Com*), prevailing.

imperar [1a] VI **(a)** (*reinar*) to rule, reign; (*mandar*) to be in command. **(b)** (*fig*) (*prevalecer*) to reign, prevail; (*precio etc*) to be in force, be current.

imperativamente ADV **(a)** imperatively. **(b)** *decir etc* imperiously, in a commanding tone.

imperatividad NF imperative nature; compulsory character.

imperativo [1] ADJ **(a)** (*gen*) imperative (*t Ling*). **(b)** *tono etc* imperious, commanding.

[2] NM **(a)** (*necesidad etc*) imperative; need; essential task; **~ categórico** moral imperative. **(b)** (*Ling*) imperative (mood).

imperceptibilidad NF imperceptibility.

imperceptible ADJ imperceptible, undiscernible.

imperceptiblemente ADV imperceptibly.

imperdible NM safety pin.

imperdonable ADJ unpardonable, unforgivable, inexcusable.

imperdonablemente ADV unpardonably, inexcusably.

imperecedero ADJ imperishable, undying; (*fig*) immortal.

imperfección NF imperfection; flaw, fault, blemish.

imperfeccionar VT (*Cono Sur*) to spoil.

imperfectamente ADV imperfectly.

imperfecto [1] ADJ **(a)** *objeto etc* imperfect, faulty. **(b)** *tarea* unfinished, incomplete. **(c)** (*Ling*) imperfect.

[2] NM (*Ling*) imperfect (tense).

imperial [1] ADJ imperial.

[2] NF (*de autobús*) top, upper deck.

imperialismo NM imperialism.

imperialista [1] ADJ imperialist(ic).

[2] NMF imperialist.

imperialmente ADV imperially.

impericia NF unskilfulness; lack of experience, inexperience; **a prueba de ~** foolproof.

imperio NM **(a)** empire; **I~ Español** Spanish Empire; **vale un ~, vale siete ~s** it's worth a fortune. **(b)** (*autoridad*) rule, authority; sway; **el ~ de la ley** the rule of law. **(c)** (*fig*) haughtiness, pride.

imperiosamente ADV (*V ADJ*) **(a)** imperiously. **(b)** urgently; imperatively, overridingly.

imperiosidad NF pressing necessity, overriding need.

imperioso ADJ **(a)** *porte, tono etc* imperious; lordly. **(b)** (*urgente*) urgent; imperative, overriding; **necesidad imperiosa** absolute necessity, pressing need.

imperito ADJ (*inhábil*) inexpert, unskilled; (*inexperto*) inexperienced; (*torpe*) clumsy.

impermanente ADV impermanent.

impermeabilidad NF impermeability, imperviousness.

impermeabilización NF waterproofing; (*Aut*) undersealing.

impermeabilizar [1f] VT to waterproof, make waterproof; (*Aut*) to underseal; *frontera etc* to seal off.

impermeable [1] ADJ impermeable, impervious (*a* to); waterproof.

[2] NM **(a)** (*prenda de vestir*) raincoat, mackintosh, mac. **(b)** (‡: *preservativo*) French letter.

impersonal ADJ impersonal.

impersonalidad NF impersonality.

impersonalismo NM impersonality; (*LAm*) disinterestedness.

impersonalmente ADV impersonally.

impertérrito ADJ unafraid, unshaken, undaunted, fearless.

impertinencia NF **(a)** (*irrelevancia*) irrelevance. **(b)** (*insistencia*) fussiness; peevishness. **(c)** (*insolencia*) impertinence; intrusion.

impertinente [1] ADJ **(a)** (*irrelevante*) irrelevant, not pertinent; (*fuera de lugar*) uncalled for. **(b)** (*quisquilloso*) touchy, fussy; (*malhumorado*) peevish. **(c)** (*insolente*) impertinent; (*intruso*) intrusive.

[2] **~s** NMPL lorgnette.

impertinentemente ADV (*V ADJ* **(a), (c)**) **(a)** irrelevantly. **(b)** impertinently.

imperturbable ADJ imperturbable; (*sereno*) unruffled, unflappable; (*impasible*) impassive.

imperturbablemente ADV imperturbably; impassively.

imperturbado ADJ unperturbed.

impétigo NM impetigo.

impetrar [1a] VT **(a)** (*rogar*) to beg for, beseech. **(b)** (*obtener*) to obtain, win.

ímpetu NM **(a)** (*gen*) impetus, impulse; (*Mec*) momentum. **(b)** (*acometida*) rush, onrush. **(c)** (*prisa*) haste; (*violencia*) violence; (*impetuosidad*) impetuosity.

impetuosamente ADV impetuously, impulsively; violently; hastily.

impetuosidad NF impetuousness, impulsiveness; violence; haste, hastiness.

impetuoso ADJ *persona* impetuous, impulsive; headstrong; *torrente etc* rushing, violent; *acto* hasty, impetuous.

impiadoso ADJ (*LAm*) impious.

impiedad NF impiety, ungodliness.

impío ADJ impious, ungodly.

implacable ADJ implacable, relentless, inexorable.

implacablemente ADV implacably, relentlessly, inexorably.

implantable ADJ that can be implanted.

implantación NF implantation; introduction.

implantar [1a] VT to implant; *costumbre etc* to introduce.

implante NM implant.

implementar [1a] (*LAm*) [1] VT to implement.

[2] VI to help, give aid.

implemento NM (*LAm*) means; tool, implement; (*Agr: esp LAm*) implement.

implicación NF (a) (*contradicción*) contradiction (in terms). (b) (*complicidad*) involvement, implication, complicity. (c) (*significado*) implication.

implicancia NF (*LAm*) implication.

implicar [1g] VT (a) (*involucrar*) to implicate, involve; **las partes implicadas** the parties concerned. (b) (*significar*) to imply; **esto no implica que ...** this does not imply that ..., this does not mean that ...

implícitamente ADV implicitly.

implícito ADJ implicit, implied.

imploración NF supplication, entreaty.

implorante ADJ imploring.

implorar [1a] VT to implore, beg, beseech.

implosionar [1a] VI to implode.

implotar [1a] VI to implode.

implume ADJ featherless; unfledged.

impolítico ADJ (a) (*imprudente*) impolitic, imprudent, tactless, undiplomatic. (b) (*descortés*) impolite.

impoluto ADJ unpolluted, pure.

imponderable ⓵ ADJ imponderable; (*fig*) priceless. ⓶ **~s** NMPL imponderables.

imponencia NF (*LAm*) imposing character, impressiveness; stateliness, grandness.

imponente ⓵ ADJ (a) imposing, impressive; stately, grand. (b) (*) terrific*, tremendous*, smashing*. ⓶ NMF (*Fin*) depositor.

imponer [2q] ⓵ VT (a) (*gen*) to impose; (*Tip*) to impose; *obligación, pena, silencio etc* to impose (*a* on); *carga* to lay, thrust (*a* upon); *tarea* to set; *impuesto* to put, impose (*a, sobre* on); (*Ecl*) *manos* to lay. (b) *obediencia etc* to exact (*a* from), demand (*a* from); *respeto* to command (*a* from); *miedo etc* to inspire (*a* in). (c) (*achacar*) to impute falsely (*a* to). (d) (*instruir*) to inform, instruct (*en* in). (e) (*Fin*) deposit.
⓶ **imponerse** VR (a) **~ un deber** to assume a duty, take on a duty. (b) (*hacerse obedecer*) to assert o.s., get one's way; **~ a** to dominate, impose one's authority on, exact obedience from. (c) (*prevalecer*) to prevail (*a* over); (*costumbre*) to grow up; **~ a** (*Dep*) to get the better of; **se impondrá el buen sentido** good sense will prevail. (d) (*ser inevitable*) to be necessary, to impose itself; **la conclusión se impone** the conclusion is inescapable. (e) **~ de** (*instruirse*) to acquaint o.s. with, inform o.s. about. (f) (*Méx*: *acostumbrarse*) to get accustomed (*a* + *infin* to + *infin*).

imponible ADJ (*Fin*) taxable, subject to tax; *importación* dutiable, subject to duty; **no ~** free of tax, tax-free, tax-exempt (*US*).

impopular ADJ unpopular.

impopularidad NF unpopularity.

importación NF (a) (*acto*) importation, importing; **artículo de ~** imported article; **comercio de ~** import trade. (b) (*artículo*) import; imports.

importador(a) NM/F importer.

importancia NF importance; significance, weight; size, magnitude; **de cierta ~** of some importance; **sin ~** unimportant, insignificant, minor; **carecer de ~** to be unimportant; **conceder** (*o* **dar**) **mucha ~ a** to attach great importance to, make much of, put the emphasis on; **no dar ~ a** to consider unimportant; to make light of; **darse ~** to give o.s. airs; **restar ~ a** to diminish the importance of; to play down, make light of; **no tiene ~** it's nothing, it's not important.

▼ **importante** ADJ (a) (*gen*) important; significant, weighty, momentous; **lo ~ es ...**, **lo más ~ es ...** the main thing is ...; **poco ~** unimportant. (b) *cantidad, pérdida* considerable, sizeable; *sala etc* magnificent, imposing; *capa* thick; *retraso* serious.

importantizarse [1f] VR (*Carib*) to give o.s. airs.

importar¹ [1a] VT (*Com*) to import (*a, en* into; *de* from).

▼ **importar²** [1a] ⓵ VT (a) (*Fin*) to amount to; to cost, be worth; **la cuenta importa 500 pesos** the bill amounts to 500 pesos; **el libro importa 50 dólares** the book costs 50 dollars. (b) (*implicar*) to involve, imply, carry with it.
▼ ⓶ VI to be important, be of consequence, matter; **~ a** to concern; **esto importa mucho** this is very important; **no importa** it doesn't matter; **¡no importa!** never mind!; **¿qué importa?** what does it matter?, what difference does it make?; who cares?; **y a ti ¿qué te importa?** and what business is it of yours?; **¡a ti no te importa!** it's nothing to do with you!; **no le importa** he doesn't care, it doesn't bother him; **(no) me importa un bledo** (*o* **higo** *etc*) I don't care two hoots (*de* about); **¿te importa prestármelo?** would you mind lending it to me?; **no le importa conducir todo el día** he doesn't mind driving all day; **'no importa precio'** 'cost no object'; **lo comprará a no importa que precio** he'll buy it at any price, he'll buy it regardless of the price; **iremos no importa el tiempo que haga** we'll go

whatever the weather.

importe NM amount; (*coste*) value, cost; (*total*) total; **~ total** final total, grand total; **hasta el ~ de** up to the amount of; **por ~ de** to the value of; **el ~ de esta factura** the amount of this bill.

importunación NF pestering; **~ sexual** sexual harassment.

importunar [1a] VT to importune, bother, pester.

importunidad NF (a) (*acto*) importunity, pestering. (b) (*efecto*) annoyance, nuisance.

importuno ADJ (a) (*molesto*) importunate, troublesome, annoying. (b) (*inoportuno*) inopportune, ill-timed.

imposibilidad NF (a) impossibility. (b) **mi ~ para + infin** my inability to + *infin*.

imposibilitado ADJ (a) (*Med*) disabled, crippled; (*Fin*) helpless, without means. (b) **estar ~ para + infin**, **verse ~ para** *o* **de + infin** to be unable to + *infin*, be prevented from + *ger*.

imposibilitar [1a] VT (a) (*Med*) to disable; (*incapacitar*) to make unfit, incapacitate (*para* for). (b) (*impedir*) to make impossible, preclude, prevent; **esto me imposibilita hacerlo** this makes it impossible for me to do it, this prevents me from doing it.

▼ **imposible** ⓵ ADJ (a) (*gen*) impossible; (*inaguantable*) intolerable, unbearable; **es ~** it's impossible, it's out of the question; **es ~ de predecir** it's impossible to forecast; **hacer lo ~** to do one's utmost (*para + infin* to + *infin*); **¡parece ~!** I don't believe it! (b) *persona* difficult, awkward, impossible. (c) (*LAm*) (*descuidado*) slovenly, dirty; (*repugnante*) repulsive. ⓶ NM the impossible; impossible thing.

imposición NF (a) (*gen*) imposition. (b) (*Com, Fin*) tax, impost, imposition; **~ directa** direct taxation. (c) (*Tip*) imposition. (d) (*Fin*) deposit; **~ a plazo** (**fijo**) fixed-term deposit; **efectuar una ~** to make a deposit; to deposit money. (e) **~ de manos** (*Ecl*) laying-on of hands.

impositiva NF (*LAm*) tax office.

impositivamente ADV for tax purposes, with regard to taxation.

impositivo ADJ (a) (*Fin*) tax (*atr*); **sistema ~** taxation, tax system. (b) (*And, Cono Sur*) (*autoritario*) authoritative, domineering; (*imperativo*) imperative.

impositor(a) NM/F (*Fin*) depositor.

impostergable ADJ that cannot be delayed; ineluctable; **una cita ~** an appointment that cannot be put off.

impostor(a) NM/F (a) (*charlatán*) impostor, fraud. (b) (*calumniador*) slanderer.

impostura NF (a) (*fraude*) imposture, fraud; sham. (b) (*calumnia*) aspersion, slur, slander.

impotable ADJ undrinkable.

impotencia NF (a) (*gen*) impotence, powerlessness, helplessness. (b) (*Med*) impotence.

impotente ADJ (a) (*gen*) impotent, powerless, helpless. (b) (*Med*) impotent.

impracticabilidad NF impracticability.

impracticable ADJ (a) (*gen*) impracticable, unworkable. (b) *carretera* impassable, unusable.

imprecación NF imprecation, curse.

imprecar [1g] VT to curse.

imprecisable ADJ indeterminable.

imprecisión NF lack of precision, vagueness.

impreciso ADJ imprecise, vague.

impredecibilidad NF unpredictability.

impredecible ADJ unpredictable.

impregnación NF impregnation.

impregnar [1a] VT to impregnate (*de* with); to saturate (*de* with); (*fig*) to pervade.

impremeditado ADJ unpremeditated.

imprenta NF (a) (*arte*) printing, art of printing. (b) (*aparato*) press; (*taller*) printer's, printing house, printing office. (c) (*letra*) print; letterpress. (d) (*impresos*) printed matter.

imprentar [1a] VT (a) (*Cono Sur Cos*) to put a permanent crease into. (b) (*LAm*) to mark.

impreparado ADJ unprepared.

imprescindible ADJ essential, indispensable, vital; **cosas ~s** essential things, things one cannot do without; **es ~ que ...** it is essential that ..., it is imperative that ...

impresentable ADJ unpresentable; *acto* disgraceful; *persona* disreputable; **Juan es ~** you can't take John anywhere.

▼ **impresión** NF (a) (*gen*) impression; (*huella*) imprint; **~ dactilar**, **~ digital** fingerprint. (b) (*Tip: gen*) printing; (*letra*) print; (*tirada*) edition, impression, issue; **quinta ~** fifth impression; **una ~ de 5.000 ejemplares** an edition of 5,000 copies; **~ en color(es)** colour printing. (c) (*Fot*) print. (d) (*Inform*) printout.

➤ LENGUA Y USO: **importante: a** → 53   **importar: 2** → 31, 34.5, 36.1   **imposible: 1a** → 39, 43, 52.5

▼(e) (*fig*) impression; (*desagradable*) shock; **cambiar impresiones** to exchange impressions, compare notes; **da la ~ de** + *infin* it gives the impression of + *ger*; **formarse una ~ de** to get an idea of; **hacer buena ~** to make a good impression, impress; **no me hizo buena ~** I was not impressed (with it); **su muerte me causó una gran ~** her death was a great shock to me; **¿qué ~ te produjo?** how did it impress you?, what impression did it make on you?; **tener la ~ de que ...** to have the impression that ...; **¡estabas de ~!*** you were great!*; **esto le caerá de ~*** this will surely impress you.

(f) (*Bio, Psic*) imprinting.

impresionable ADJ impressionable.

impresionado ADJ (a) (*gen*) impressed. (b) (*Fot*) exposed; **excesivamente ~** overexposed.

impresionante ADJ (*gen*) impressive; (*espectacular*) striking; (*conmovedor*) moving, affecting; (*espantoso*) awesome, frightening.

impresionar [1a] ① VT (a) *disco* to cut; (*Fot*) to expose; **película sin ~** unexposed film.
(b) (*fig*) to impress, strike; to move, affect; to shock; **me impresionó mucho** it greatly impressed me; **no se deja fácilmente ~** he is not easily impressed.
② VI to impress, make an impression; **lo hace sólo para ~** he just does it to impress.
③ **impresionarse** VR to be impressed; to be moved, be affected.

impresionismo NM impressionism.

impresionista ① ADJ impressionist(ic).
② NM impressionist.

impreso ① ADJ printed.
② NM (a) (*artículo*) printed paper; (*libro*) printed book (*etc*). (b) (*formulario*) form; **~ de afiliación, ~ de solicitud** application form. (c) **~s** printed matter.

impresor NM printer.

impresora NF (*Inform*) printer; **~ (de) calidad carta** letter-quality printer; **~ de chorro de tinta** ink-jet printer; **~ de impacto** impact printer; **~ de no impacto** non-impact printer; **~ (por) láser** laser printer; **~ de línea** line-printer; **~ de margarita** daisy-wheel printer; **~ matricial, ~ de matriz de puntos** dot-matrix printer; **~ en paralelo** parallel printer.

imprevisibilidad NF unpredictability.

imprevisible ADJ unforeseeable.

imprevisión NF improvidence; lack of foresight; thoughtlessness.

imprevisor ADJ improvident; lacking foresight; thoughtless, happy-go-lucky.

imprevisto ① ADJ unforeseen, unexpected.
② NM (*t* **~s**) incidentals, unforeseen expense; contingencies; **si no surgen ~s** (*o* **un ~**) if nothing unexpected occurs.

imprimar [1a] VT (*Arte*) to prime.

imprimátur NM imprimatur.

imprimible ADJ printable.

imprimir [3a; PTP **impreso**] VT (a) (*gen*) to imprint, impress, stamp (a, en *on*; *t fig*). (b) (*Tip*) to print. (c) (*Bio, Psic*) to imprint (a *on*).

improbabilidad NF improbability, unlikelihood.

improbable ADJ improbable, unlikely.

improbar [1b] VT (*Carib*) to fail to approve, not approve.

improbidad NF dishonesty.

ímprobo ADJ (a) (*poco honrado*) dishonest, corrupt. (b) *tarea* arduous, thankless, tough; *esfuerzo etc* tremendous, awful, strenuous.

improcedencia NF (*V ADJ*) (a) wrongness; inappropriateness, inapplicability; irrelevancy. (b) (*Jur*) inadmissibility.

improcedente ADJ (a) (*incorrecto*) wrong, not right; (*inadecuado*) inappropriate, inapplicable; irrelevant. (b) (*Jur*) unfounded, inadmissible; out of order; **despido ~** unfair dismissal.

improductividad NF unproductiveness.

improductivo ADJ unproductive; non-productive.

impronta NF stamp, impress, impression; (*fig*) stamp, mark.

impronunciable ADJ unpronounceable.

improperio NM insult, taunt.

impropiamente ADV improperly; inappropriately, unsuitably.

impropicio ADJ inauspicious, unpropitious.

impropiedad NF (a) (*gen*) inappropriateness, unsuitability. (b) (*Ling*) impropriety, infelicity (of language).

impropio ADJ improper (*t Mat, Ling*); inappropriate, unsuitable; **~ de, ~ para** inappropriate for; unbecoming to; foreign to.

improrrogable ADJ *fecha* that cannot be extended.

impróvidamente ADV improvidently.

impróvido ADJ improvident.

improvisación NF improvisation; extemporization; (*Mús*) impromptu; (*Teat*) ad-lib.

improvisadamente ADV: **hacer algo ~** to improvise sth.

improvisado ADJ improvised; *reparación* makeshift; (*Mús etc*) extempore, impromptu.

improvisamente ADV unexpectedly, suddenly.

improvisar [1a] VTI to improvise; to extemporize; (*Mús*) to extempo-

rize; (*Teat*) to ad-lib; **~ una comida** to rustle up a meal*.

improviso ADJ (a) (*imprevisto*) unexpected, unforeseen. (b) **al ~, de ~** unexpectedly, suddenly; on the spur of the moment; **en un ~** (*And*: de golpe*) suddenly, without warning; **hablar de ~** to speak extempore, speak unprepared; **tocar de ~** to play impromptu.

improvisto ADJ unexpected, unforeseen; **de ~** unexpectedly, suddenly.

imprudencia (*V ADJ*) NF imprudence; rashness; indiscretion; carelessness; **~ temeraria** criminal negligence; **ser acusado de conducir con ~ temeraria** to be charged with dangerous driving.

imprudente ADJ (*precipitado*) unwise, imprudent, rash; (*indiscreto*) indiscreet; (*descuidado*) careless.

imprudentemente ADV unwisely, imprudently; rashly; carelessly.

Impte ABR *de* **Importe** amount, amt.

impúber ADJ not having reached puberty, immature.

impublicable ADJ unprintable.

impudencia NF shamelessness, brazenness.

impudente ADJ shameless, brazen.

impúdicamente ADV immodestly, shamelessly; (*obscenamente*) lewdly; lecherously.

impudicia NF immodesty, shamelessness; (*obscenidad*) lewdness; lechery.

impúdico ADJ immodest, shameless; (*obsceno*) lewd; lecherous.

impudor NM = **impudicia**.

impuesto ① PTP *de* **imponer**; **estar ~ de, quedar ~ de** to be informed about; **estar ~ en** to be well versed in.
② NM tax; duty, levy (*sobre on*); **~s** taxes, (*como sistema*) taxation; **libre de ~s** tax-free; duty-free; **sujeto a ~** taxable, dutiable; **~ de** *o* **sobre actividades económicas** tax on commercial and professional activities; **~ sobre apuestas** betting tax; **~ sobre los bienes heredados, ~ sobre herencias, ~ sobre las sucesiones** estate duty; **~ sobre el capital** capital levy; **~ directo** direct tax; **~ sobre espectáculos** entertainments tax; **~ de plusvalía** capital gains tax; **~ sobre la propiedad** property tax; **~ de radicación** property tax; **~ sobre la renta** income tax; **~ revolucionario** protection money paid to terrorists; **~ sobre la riqueza** wealth tax; **~ sobre sociedades** corporation tax; **~ del timbre** stamp duty; **~ sobre el valor añadido (IVA)** value-added tax (VAT); **~ de venta** sales tax, purchase tax.

impugnación NF challenge, contestation.

impugnar [1a] VT to oppose, contest, challenge; *teoría etc* to impugn, refute.

impulsador NM (*Aer*) booster.

impulsar [1a] VT to stimulate, promote; to drive; *V* **impeler**.

impulsión NF (a) (*gen*) impulsion; (*Mec*) propulsion, drive; **~ por correa** belt drive. (b) (*fig*) impulse.

impulsividad NF impulsiveness.

impulsivo ADJ impulsive; **compra impulsiva** impulse buying.

impulso NM (a) (*gen*) impulse; (*Mec*) drive, thrust; (*empuje*) impetus, momentum.
(b) (*fig*) impulse; stimulus, urge; **los ~s del corazón** the promptings of the heart; **~ sexual** sexual urge, sex drive; **a ~s del miedo** driven on by fear; **no resisto al ~ de decir que ...** I can't resist saying that ...

impulsor ① ADJ drive (*atr*), driving.
② NM (*Mec*) drive; (*Aer*) booster.
③ NM, **impulsora** NF (*persona*) promoter, instigator.

impune ADJ unpunished.

impunemente ADV with impunity.

impunidad NF impunity.

impuntual ADJ unpunctual.

impuntualidad NF unpunctuality.

impureza NF (a) (*gen*) impurity. (b) (*fig*) unchastity, lewdness.

impurificar [1g] VT (a) (*adulterar*) to adulterate, make impure. (b) (*fig: corromper*) to corrupt, defile.

impuro ADJ (a) (*gen*) impure. (b) (*fig*) impure, unchaste, lewd.

imputable ADJ: **fracasos que son ~s a** failures which can be attributed to, failures which are attributable to.

imputación NF imputation, charge.

imputar [1a] VT: **~ a** to impute to, attribute to, charge with; **los hechos que se les imputan** the acts with which they are charged.

imputrescible ADJ rot-proof; (*pey*) non-biodegradable.

in* ADJ INVAR in*; fashionable, up-to-date, state-of-the-art; **es el estilo más ~** this is the really in style*; **lo ~ es hablar de ...** the in thing is to talk about ...; **lo que llevan los más ~** what people who are really with it are wearing*.

-ín, -ina *V* Aspects of Word Formation in Spanish 2.

inabarcable ADJ vast, extensive.

inabordable ADJ unapproachable.

inacabable ADJ endless, interminable.

inacabablemente ADV endlessly, interminably.

inacabado ADJ unfinished; *problema* unresolved.

inaccesibilidad NF inaccessibility.

► LENGUA Y USO: **impresión: e → 33.2**

inaccesible ADJ inaccessible.
inacción NF inaction; inactivity, idleness; drift.
inacentuado ADJ unaccented, unstressed.
inaceptabilidad NF unacceptability.
▼ **inaceptable** ADJ unacceptable.
inactividad NF inactivity; laziness, idleness; (*Com, Fin*) dullness.
inactivo ADJ inactive; lazy, idle; (*Com, Fin*) dull.
inactual ADJ lacking present validity, no longer applicable; old-fashioned, out-of-date.
inadaptable ADJ unadaptable.
inadaptación NF maladjustment; failure of adjustment, failure to adjust (*a* to).
inadaptado ⬜1 ADJ maladjusted, who fails to adjust (*a* to).
⬜2 NM, **inadaptada** NF misfit; person who fails to adjust.
inadecuación NF inadequacy; unsuitability, inappropriateness.
inadecuado ADJ inadequate; unsuitable, inappropriate.
inadmisibilidad NF inadmissibility, unacceptable nature.
inadmisible ADJ inadmissible, unacceptable.
inadvertencia NF **(a)** (*gen*) inadvertence; **por ~** inadvertently, through inadvertence. **(b)** (*una ~*) oversight, slip.
inadvertidamente ADV inadvertently.
inadvertido ADJ **(a)** (*despistado*) unobservant, inattentive; (*descuidado*) careless. **(b)** (*no visto*) unnoticed, unobserved; **pasar ~** to escape notice, slip by.
inafectado ADJ unaffected.
inagotabilidad NF inexhaustibility; tireless nature.
inagotable ADJ inexhaustible, tireless.
inaguantable ADJ intolerable, unbearable.
inaguantablemente ADV intolerably, unbearably.
inajenable ADJ inalienable; not transferable.
inalámbrico ADJ wireless; (*Telec*) cordless.
in albis ADV: **quedarse ~** (*no saber*) not to know a thing; to be left in the dark; (*fracasar*) to get nothing for one's trouble, achieve nothing.
inalcanzable ADJ unattainable.
inalienable ADJ inalienable; not transferable.
inalterabilidad NF inalterability, unchangingness; immutability.
inalterable ADJ unalterable, unchanging; immutable; *cara* impassive; *color* fast; *lustre etc* permanent.
inalterado ADJ unchanged, unaltered.
inamistoso ADJ unfriendly.
inamovible ADJ fixed, immovable; undetachable.
inanición NF starvation, (*Med*) inanition; **morir de ~** to die of starvation.
inanidad NF inanity.
inanimado ADJ inanimate.
inánime ADJ lifeless.
INAP [i'nap] NM (*Esp*) ABR *de* **Instituto Nacional de la Administración Pública.**
inapagable ADJ unquenchable; inextinguishable.
inapeable ADJ **(a)** (*oscuro*) incomprehensible. **(b)** (*terco*) obstinate, stubborn.
inapelabilidad NF finality, unappealable nature.
inapelable ADJ (*Jur*) unappealable, not open to appeal; (*fig*) inevitable, irremediable; **las decisiones de los jueces serán ~s** the judges' decisions will be final.
inapercibido ADJ unperceived.
inapetencia NF lack of appetite, loss of appetite.
inapetente ADJ: **estar ~** to be suffering from loss of appetite.
inaplazable ADJ which cannot be postponed, pressing, urgent.
inaplicable ADJ inapplicable, not applicable.
inaplicado ADJ slack, lazy.
inapreciable ADJ **(a)** *diferencia etc* imperceptible. **(b)** (*de valor*) invaluable, inestimable.
inaprensible ADJ indefinite, hard to pin down; hard to grasp.
inaptitud NF unsuitability.
inapto ADJ unsuited (*para* to).
inarmónico ADJ unharmonious, unmusical.
inarrugable ADJ crease-resistant, which does not crease.
inarticulado ADJ inarticulate.
inasequible ADJ unattainable, out of reach; unobtainable.
inasistencia NF absence, failure to attend.
inastillable ADJ *cristal* shatterproof.
inasumible ADJ unacceptable.
inatacable ADJ unassailable.
inatención NF inattention, lack of attention (*a* to).
inatento ADJ inattentive.
inaudible ADJ inaudible.
inaudito ADJ unheard-of; unprecedented; outrageous.
inauguración NF inauguration; opening; unveiling; (*Com*) setting up; (*fig: fiesta*) house-warming party; **~ privada** (*Arte*) private viewing.

inaugural ADJ inaugural; opening; *viaje etc* maiden.
inaugurar [1a] VT to inaugurate; *canal, puente, exposición etc* to open (formally); *estatua etc* to unveil.
inautenticidad NF lack of authenticity.
inauténtico ADJ not genuine, false.
INB NM (*Esp Escol*) ABR *de* **Instituto Nacional de Bachillerato.**
INBAD [im'bað] NM (*Esp*) ABR *de* **Instituto Nacional de Bachillerato a Distancia.**
INC NM **(a)** (*Esp*) ABR *de* **Instituto Nacional de Colonización** (*land settlement institute*). **(b)** (*Esp Com*) ABR *de* **Instituto Nacional de Consumo.**
inc. ABR *de* **inclusive** inclusive, inc.
inca NMF Inca.
incachable* ADJ (*LAm*) useless.
INCAE NM ABR *de* **Instituto Centroamericano de Administración de Empresas.**
incaico ADJ Inca (*atr*).
incalculable ADJ incalculable.
incalificable ADJ indescribable, unspeakable.
incalificablemente ADV indescribably, unspeakably.
incanato NM (*And Hist*) (*época*) Inca period; (*reinado*) reign of an Inca.
incandescencia NF incandescence; white heat; glow.
incandescente ADJ **(a)** incandescent; white hot; glowing. **(b)** *mirada* burning, passionate.
incansable ADJ tireless, untiring, unflagging.
incansablemente ADV tirelessly, untiringly.
incapacidad NF incapacity; unfitness (*para* por); inadequacy, incompetence; **~ laboral** sick-leave; **~ laboral transitoria** short sick-leave; **su ~ para** + *infin* his inability to + *infin*.
incapacitación NF: **proceso de ~ presidencial** impeachment of a president.
incapacitado ADJ **(a)** incapacitated; unfitted (*para* for). **(b)** (*Méx: minusválido*) disabled, handicapped.
incapacitante ADJ incapacitating.
incapacitar [1a] VT to incapacitate, render unfit, handicap (*para* for); (*Jur etc*) to disqualify (*para* for).
▼ **incapaz** ADJ **(a)** (*gen*) incapable (*de* of); (*no apto*) unfit; (*inadecuado*) inadequate, incompetent; (*Jur*) incompetent; **~ de** + *infin* unable to + *infin*. **(b)** (*CAm, Méx*) *niño* trying, difficult.
incapturable ADJ unattainable.
incardinar [1a] VT to include (as an integral part).
incario NM (*And*) Inca period.
incasable ADJ unmarriageable.
incásico ADJ (*LAm*) Inca (*atr*).
incatalogable ADJ indefinable; off-beat; **persona ~** person who refuses to be pigeon-holed.
incautación NF seizure, confiscation.
incautamente ADV unwarily, incautiously.
incautarse [1a] VR: **~ de** to seize, confiscate, impound; to take possession of.
incauto ADJ unwary, incautious; gullible.
incendiar [1b] ⬜1 VT to set on fire, set fire to, set alight; (*fig*) to kindle, inflame.
⬜2 **incendiarse** VR to catch fire.
incendiario ⬜1 ADJ **(a)** incendiary. **(b)** (*fig*) inflammatory.
⬜2 NM, **incendiaria** NF fire-raiser, pyromaniac; incendiary; **~ de la guerra** warmonger.
incendiarismo NM pyromania.
incendio NM fire; conflagration; **~ forestal** forest fire; **~ intencionado, ~ malicioso, ~ provocado** arson, fire-raising; **echar** (*o* **hablar**) **~s de uno** (*And, Cono Sur*) to sling mud at sb.
incensar [1j] VT (*Ecl*) to cense, incense; (*fig*) to flatter.
incensario NM censer.
incentivación NF **(a)** motivation. **(b)** (*Fin*) incentive scheme; productivity bonus.
incentivar [1a] VT to encourage, stimulate, provide incentives for; **baja incentivada** voluntary severance.
incentivo NM incentive; **~ fiscal** tax incentive; **baja por ~** voluntary severance.
incertidumbre NF uncertainty, doubt.
incesable ADJ, **incesante** ADJ incessant, unceasing.
incesantemente ADV incessantly, unceasingly.
incesto NM incest.
incestuoso ADJ incestuous.
incidencia NF **(a)** (*Mat etc*) incidence. **(b)** (*suceso*) incident. **(c)** (*impacto*) effect, impact; **la huelga tuvo escasa ~** the strike was not widely supported, the strike had little impact.
incidentado ADJ unruly, riotous, turbulent.
incidental ADJ incidental.
incidente ⬜1 ADJ incidental.
⬜2 NM incident.
incidentemente ADV incidentally.

➤ LENGUA Y USO: **inaceptable** → 41   **incapaz: a** → 43.4

incidir [3a] **1** VT (*Med*) to incise, cut.

2 VI (a) **~ en** (*cargar en*) to fall upon; (*afectar*) to influence, affect, impinge on; **~ en un error** to fall into error; **el impuesto incide más en ellos** the tax falls most heavily on them, the tax affects them worst; **la familia ha incidido fuertemente en la historia** the family has influenced history a lot, the family has made itself strongly felt in history.

(b) **~ en un tema** to touch upon a subject.

incienso NM (*Ecl*) incense; (*Bib*) frankincense; (*fig*) flattery.

inciertamente ADV uncertainly.

incierto ADJ uncertain, doubtful; inconstant.

incineración NF incineration; **~ (de cadáveres)** cremation.

incinerador NM, **incineradora** NF incinerator.

incinerar [1a] VT to incinerate, burn; *cadáver* to cremate.

incipiente ADJ incipient.

incircunciso ADJ uncircumcised.

incisión NF incision.

incisividad NF incisiveness.

incisivo **1** ADJ sharp, cutting; (*fig*) incisive.

2 NM incisor.

inciso NM (a) (*Ling*) clause, sentence; comma. (b) (*Tip*) subsection. (c) (*observación*) parenthetical comment, aside. (d) (*conversación*) interjection, interruption.

incitación NF incitement; provocation.

incitante ADJ provoking, provocative, inviting.

incitar [1a] VT to incite, rouse, spur on; **~ a uno a hacer algo** to urge sb to do sth; **~ a uno contra otro** to incite sb against another person.

incívico **1** ADJ antisocial.

2 NM, **incívica** NF antisocial person.

incivil ADJ uncivil, rude.

incivilidad NF incivility, rudeness; **una ~** an incivility, a piece of rudeness.

incivilizado ADJ uncivilized.

incivismo NM antisocial behaviour (*o* outlook *etc*).

inclasificable ADJ unclassifiable, nondescript.

inclemencia NF harshness, severity, inclemency; **la ~ del tiempo** the inclemency of the weather; **dejar algo a la ~** to leave sth exposed to wind and weather.

inclemente ADJ harsh, severe, inclement.

inclinación NF (a) (*gen*) inclination; (*pendiente*) slope, incline; (*Náut*) pitch, tilt; (*de cuerpo*) stoop; **~ lateral** (*Aer*) bank; **a una ~ de 45 grados** at an inclination of 45 degrees.

(b) (*reverencia*) bow; (*de cabeza*) nod.

(c) (*fig*) inclination, leaning, propensity; **de malas inclinaciones** evilly inclined; **tener ~ hacia la poesía** to have a penchant for poetry.

inclinado ADJ (a) (*en ángulo*) inclined, sloping, leaning, slanting; *plano* inclined.

(b) **estar ~ a** + *infin* (*esp LAm*: *fig*) to be inclined to + *infin*.

inclinar [1a] **1** VT (a) (*gen*) to incline; (*sesgar*) to slope, slant, tilt; (*cabeza*: *afirmando*) to incline, bend, nod; (*bajar*) to bow.

(b) **~ a uno a hacer algo** (*fig*) to induce sb to do sth; to persuade sb to do sth.

2 VI: **~ a uno** to take after sb, resemble sb.

3 **inclinarse** VR (a) (*estar inclinado*) to incline; to slope, slant, tilt, be inclined.

(b) (*encorvarse*) to stoop, bend; (*hacer reverencia*) to bow; **~ a favor de** to be in favour of, support; **~ ante** (*fig*) to bow to, bow down before.

(c) **~ a uno** (*parecerse*) to take after sb, resemble sb.

(d) **~ a hacer algo** to be inclined to do sth, tend to do sth; **me inclino a decir que ...** I am inclined to say that ...

ínclito ADJ illustrious, renowned.

incluir [3g] VT to include; to comprise, contain; to incorporate; (*en carta*) to enclose; **todo incluido** (*Com*) inclusive terms; all found, all-in.

inclusa NF foundling hospital.

inclusero, -a NM/F foundling.

inclusión NF inclusion; **con ~ de** including.

inclusivamente ADV inclusive, inclusively.

inclusive ADV inclusive, inclusively; **hasta el próximo domingo ~** up to and including next Sunday.

inclusivo ADJ inclusive.

incluso **1** ADJ included; enclosed.

2 ADV even; **~ la pegó** he even hit her; **todos nos empezamos a reír, ~ el profesor** we all started to laugh, even the lecturer.

incoación NF inception.

incoar [1a] VT to start, initiate.

incobrable ADJ irrecoverable; *deuda* bad.

incógnita NF (*Mat*) unknown quantity; (*fig*) unknown quantity; unknown factor; hidden motive; mystery; **queda en pie la ~ sobre su**

influencia there is still a question-mark over his influence.

incógnito **1** ADJ unknown.

2 NM incognito; **viajar de ~** to travel incognito.

incognoscible ADJ unknowable.

incoherencia NF incoherence; disconnectedness.

incoherente ADJ incoherent; disconnected.

incoloro ADJ colourless; *barniz etc* clear.

incólume ADJ safe; unhurt, unharmed, unscathed; **salir ~ del accidente** to emerge unscathed from the accident.

incombustible ADJ incombustible, fire-resisting; fireproof.

incomible ADJ uneatable, inedible.

incómodamente ADV inconveniently; uncomfortably.

incomodar [1a] **1** VT to inconvenience, trouble, put out.

2 **incomodarse** VR (a) (*tomarse molestia*) to put o.s. out, take trouble; **¡no se incomode!** don't bother!, don't trouble yourself!

(b) (*enfadarse*) to get cross, get annoyed (*con* with); **~ con** to fall out with; **estar incomodado con** to be cross with; to be at odds with.

incomodidad NF (a) (*inoportunidad*) inconvenience; (*falta de comodidad*) discomfort, uncomfortableness. (b) (*fastidio*) annoyance, irritation.

incomodo NM = **incomodidad (b)**.

incómodo **1** ADJ (*inoportuno*) inconvenient; (*nada cómodo*) uncomfortable; (*molesto*) tiresome, annoying; **un bulto ~** an awkward package, a cumbersome package; **una casa incómoda** an inconvenient house; **sentirse ~** to feel uncomfortable, feel ill-at-ease; **estar ~ con uno** (*Cono Sur*) to be fed up with sb*, be cross with sb.

2 NM (*LAm*) = **incomodidad (b)**.

incomparable ADJ incomparable, matchless.

incomparablemente ADV incomparably.

incomparecencia NF failure to appear (in court *etc*), non-appearance.

incomparecimiento NM: **pleito perdido por ~** suit lost by default (*o* failure to appear); undefended suit.

incompasivo ADJ unsympathetic; pitiless.

incompatibilidad NF incompatibility; **~ de intereses** conflict of interests; **ley de ~es** law against the holding of multiple posts.

incompatibilizar [1f] VT to make incompatible, render incompatible.

incompatible ADJ incompatible.

incompetencia NF incompetence.

incompetente ADJ incompetent.

incompletamente ADV incompletely.

incompleto ADJ incomplete, unfinished.

incomprendido **1** ADJ *persona* misunderstood; not appreciated.

2 NM, **incomprendida** NF misunderstood person; person who is not appreciated.

incomprensibilidad NF incomprehensibility.

incomprensible ADJ incomprehensible.

incomprensión NF incomprehension, lack of understanding; lack of appreciation.

incomprobable ADJ unprovable.

incomunicación NF isolation; lack of communication; (*Jur*) solitary confinement; **ello permite la ~ de los detenidos** it allows those detained to be held incommunicado.

incomunicado ADJ isolated, cut off; (*Jur*) in solitary confinement, incommunicado.

incomunicar [1g] **1** VT to cut off the communications of, leave without communications; to cut off, isolate; (*Jur*) to put into solitary confinement; **~ un detenido** to refuse a prisoner access to a lawyer.

2 **incomunicarse** VR to isolate o.s., withdraw from society.

inconcebible ADJ inconceivable, unthinkable.

inconcebiblemente ADV inconceivably.

inconciliable ADJ irreconcilable.

inconcluso ADJ unfinished, incomplete.

inconcluyente ADJ inconclusive.

inconcreción NF vagueness.

inconcreto ADJ vague.

inconcuso ADJ indisputable, undeniable, incontroverible.

▼ **incondicional** **1** ADJ (a) (*gen*) unconditional; *fe* implicit, complete, unquestioning; *apoyo* wholehearted; *afirmación* unqualified; *amigo, partidario etc* staunch, stalwart.

(b) (*LAm**: *pey*) servile, fawning.

2 NMF (a) (*partidario*) stalwart, staunch supporter (*etc*); (*pey*) diehard, hardliner.

(b) (*LAm**: *pey*) toady, yes-man*.

incondicionalidad NF unconditional support; unquestioning loyalty.

incondicionalismo NM (*LAm*) toadyism, servility.

incondicionalmente ADV unconditionally, unreservedly; implicitly, unquestioningly; wholeheartedly; staunchly.

inconexión NF disconnectedness; incongruity.

inconexo ADJ unconnected; (*desarticulado*) disconnected, disjointed;

➤ LENGUA Y USO: **incondicional: 1a → 38.1**

(*no relacionado*) unrelated; (*incongruo*) incongruous.

inconfesable ADJ which cannot be told (o confessed); shameful, disgraceful.

inconfeso ADJ *reo* who does not confess; **homosexual ~** closet homosexual.

inconforme ADJ nonconformist; **estar** (*o* **mostrarse**) **~ con algo** (*CAm*) to disagree with sth.

inconformismo NM nonconformism.

inconformista ADJ, NMF nonconformist.

inconfundible ADJ unmistakable.

inconfundiblemente ADV unmistakably.

incongruencia NF incongruity.

incongruente ADJ, **incongruo** ADJ incongruous.

inconmensurable ADJ immeasurable, vast; incommensurate; fantastic.

inconmovible ADJ unshakeable.

inconmutable ADJ immutable.

inconocible ADJ unknowable; (*LAm*: *irreconocible*) unrecognizable; **lo ~** the unknowable.

inconquistable ADJ unconquerable; (*fig*) inconquerable, unyielding.

inconsciencia NF (**a**) (*Med*) unconsciousness. (**b**) (*fig*: *ignorancia*) unawareness. (**c**) (*fig*: *irreflexión*) thoughtlessness; recklessness.

inconsciente [1] ADJ (**a**) (*Med*) unconscious; **lo ~** the unconscious; **le encontraron ~** they found him unconscious.
(**b**) (*fig*: *ignorante*) unconscious, unaware (*de* of); oblivious (*de* to); (*sin saber*) unwitting.
(**c**) (*fig*: *irreflexivo*) thoughtless, reckless, carefree; **es más ~ que malo** he's thoughtless rather than wicked; **son gente ~** they're thoughtless people.
[2] NM unconscious; **el ~ colectivo** the collective unconscious.

inconscientemente ADV (**a**) (*sin saber*) unconsciously; unawares, unwittingly. (**b**) (*sin pensar*) thoughtlessly; recklessly; in a carefree manner.

inconsecuencia NF inconsistency; inconsequence.

inconsecuente ADJ inconsistent; inconsequent, inconsequential.

inconsideración NF inconsiderateness, thoughtlessness; rashness, haste.

inconsideradamente ADV inconsiderately, thoughtlessly; rashly, hastily.

inconsiderado ADJ inconsiderate, thoughtless; rash, hasty.

inconsistencia NF lack of firmness; unevenness; weakness; looseness; flimsiness.

inconsistente ADJ (*poco sólido*) lacking firmness, not solid; (*irregular*) uneven; *argumento* weak; *tierra etc* loose; *tela* flimsy, thin; (*Culin*) lumpy.

inconsolable ADJ inconsolable.

inconstancia NF inconstancy; unsteadiness; fickleness.

inconstante ADJ (*gen*) inconstant, changeable; (*poco firme*) unsteady; (*caprichoso*) fickle.

inconstantemente ADV inconstantly; unsteadily; in a fickle way.

inconstitucional ADJ unconstitutional.

inconstitucionalidad NF unconstitutional nature.

inconstitucionalmente ADV unconstitutionally.

inconsumible ADJ unfit for consumption.

incontable ADJ countless, innumerable.

incontaminante ADJ non-polluting.

incontenible ADJ uncontrollable, unstoppable, uncontainable.

incontestable ADJ unanswerable; undeniable, unchallengeable, indisputable.

incontestablemente ADV unanswerably; undeniably, indisputably.

incontestado ADJ unanswered; unchallenged, unquestioned; undisputed.

incontinencia NF incontinence (*t Med*).

incontinente [1] ADJ incontinent (*t Med*).
[2] ADV = **incontinenti**.

incontinenti ADV at once, instantly, forthwith.

incontrastable ADJ *dificultad* insuperable; *argumento* unanswerable; *persona* unshakeable, unyielding.

incontrolable ADJ uncontrollable.

incontrolablemente ADV uncontrollably.

incontrolado [1] ADJ uncontrolled; unauthorized; violent, wild.
[2] NM, **incontrolada** NF violent person; (*esp*) policeman (*etc*) who acts outside the law; (*Pol*) strong-arm man, bully-boy.

incontrovertible ADJ incontrovertible, indisputable.

incontrovertido ADJ undisputed.

inconveniencia NF (**a**) (*gen*) unsuitability, inappropriateness; inadvisability; inconvenience. (**b**) (*descortesía*) impoliteness. (**c**) (*incorrección*) impropriety, wrongness. (**d**) (*disparate*) silly remark, tactless remark; (*acto*) improper thing to do (*etc*), wrong thing to do (*etc*).

inconveniente [1] ADJ (**a**) (*impropio*) unsuitable, inappropriate; (*no aconsejable*) inadvisable; (*inoportuno*) inconvenient.
(**b**) (*descortés*) impolite.

(**c**) (*incorrecto*) improper, wrong.
▼[2] NM (*dificultad*) obstacle, difficulty; (*desventaja*) disadvantage, drawback; (*objeción*) objection; **el ~ es que ...** the trouble is that ..., the difficulty is that ...; **no hay ~ en +** *infin*, **no hay ~ para +** *infin* there is no objection to + *ger*; there will be no difficulty about + *ger*; **poner un ~** to raise an objection; **no tengo ~** I have no objection, I don't mind; **¿tienes algún ~ en venir?** do you mind coming?; **no veo ~** I see no objection, I see no difficulty.

inconvertibilidad NF inconvertibility.

inconvertible ADJ inconvertible.

incordiante* [1] ADJ annoying, bothersome, irksome.
[2] NMF troublemaker.

incordiar* [1b] VT to bother, annoy; **¡déjate de ~!** stop bothering me!; **¡no incordies!** stop it!, behave yourself!

incordio* NM nuisance.

incorporación NF incorporation, embodiment; inclusion; involvement; (*a filas*) enlisting, enlistment.

incorporado ADJ (*Téc*) built-in; **con antena incorporada** with built-in aerial.

incorporal ADJ = **incorpóreo.**

incorporar [1a] [1] VT (**a**) (*gen*) to incorporate (*a, con, en* into, in); to embody (*a, con, en* in); (*incluir*) to include (*a* in); (*involucrar*) to involve (*a* in, with); (*Culin*) to mix (in) (*a* with), add (*a* to); **X incorpora al personaje de Z** (*Teat etc*) X plays the part of Z; **~ a filas** (*Mil*) to call up, enlist.
(**b**) **~ a uno** to make sb sit up (in bed), help sb to sit up.
[2] **incorporarse** VR (**a**) (*cuando se está acostado*) to sit up, raise o.s.; **~ en la cama** to sit up in bed.
(**b**) **~ a** *regimiento, sociedad etc* to join; **~ a filas** (*Mil*) to join up, enlist; **~ al trabajo** to go to work, report for work.

incorpóreo ADJ incorporeal, bodiless; intangible.

incorrección NF (**a**) (*de datos*) incorrectness, inaccuracy.
(**b**) (*irregularidad*) irregularity.
(**c**) (*descortesía*) discourtesy; piece of bad manners, gaffe; impropriety; **cometer una ~** to commit a faux pas.
(**d**) (*Ling*) mistake.

incorrectamente ADV (*V* ADJ (**a**), (**c**)) (**a**) incorrectly, inaccurately, wrongly. (**b**) discourteously; improperly.

incorrecto ADJ (**a**) *cálculo, dato etc* incorrect, inaccurate, wrong.
(**b**) *facciones* irregular, odd.
(**c**) *conducta* discourteous, bad-mannered; improper; **ser ~ con una** to take liberties with sb.

incorregible ADJ incorrigible.

incorrosible ADJ rustproof.

incorruptible ADJ incorruptible.

incorrupto ADJ (**a**) *cuerpo* incorrupt; uncorrupted. (**b**) (*fig*) pure, chaste, undefiled.

incredibilidad NF incredibility.

incredulidad NF incredulity, unbelief.

incrédulo [1] ADJ incredulous, unbelieving, sceptical.
[2] NM, **incrédula** NF unbeliever, sceptic.

increíble ADJ incredible, unbelievable; **es ~ que ...** it is unbelievable that ...

increíblemente ADV incredibly, unbelievably.

incremental ADJ incremental.

incrementar [1a] [1] VT to increase; to promote.
[2] **incrementarse** VR to increase.

incremento NM increment; increase, rise, addition; growth; **~ salarial** pay increase, rise in wages; **~ de temperatura** rise in temperature; **tomar ~** to increase.

increpación NF severe reprimand, upbraiding.

increpar [1a] VT to reprimand severely, upbraid.

in crescendo [1] ADV: **ir ~** to increase, intensify, spiral upwards.
[2] NM increase, upward spiral.

incriminación NF accusation.

incriminar [1a] VT (**a**) (*Jur*) *persona* to accuse; *actividad* to make a crime of, consider criminal. (**b**) *falta etc* to magnify. (**c**) *artículos etc* to obtain illegally.

incruento ADJ bloodless.

incrúspido* ADJ (*LAm*) clumsy; ham-fisted.

incrustación NF (**a**) (*gen*) incrustation; (*fig*) grafting. (**b**) (*Arte*) inlay, inlaid work.

incrustar [1a] [1] VT to incrust (*de* with); (*de joyas etc*) to inlay (*de* with); (*fig*) to graft (*en* on to), introduce (*en* into); **una espada incrustada de joyas** a sword encrusted with jewels.
[2] **incrustarse** VR: **~ en** (*bomba etc*) to lodge in, embed itself in; **se le ha incrustado esta idea en la mente** he's got this idea firmly fixed in his head.

incuantificable ADJ unquantifiable.

incubación NF incubation.

incubadora NF incubator.

incubar [1a] [1] VT to incubate; to hatch (*t fig*).

▶ LENGUA Y USO: **inconveniente: 2 → 28.1, 36.1, 36.2, 38.1, 53.4**

2 incubarse VR to incubate.

íncubo NM incubus; nightmare.

incuestionable ADJ unquestionable, unchallengeable.

incuestionablemente ADV unquestionably.

inculcar [1g] **1** VT to instil, inculcate (*en* in, into).

2 inculcarse VR to be obstinate.

inculpable ADJ blameless, guiltless.

inculpación NF charge, accusation.

inculpado, -a NM/F accused person; **el ~** the accused, the defendant.

inculpar [1a] VT to charge (*de* with), accuse (*de* of); to blame (*de* for); **los crímenes que se le inculpan** the crimes with which he is charged.

incultamente ADV in an uncultured way; uncouthly.

incultivable ADJ uncultivable, unworkable.

inculto ADJ **(a)** (*Agr*) uncultivated, unworked, untilled; **dejar un terreno ~** to leave land uncultivated. **(b)** (*fig*) uncultured; uncivilized; uncouth.

incultura NF lack of culture; uncouthness.

incumbencia NF obligation, duty, concern; **no es de mi ~** it is not my job, it's not my province.

incumbir [3a] VI: **~ a** to be incumbent upon; **no me incumbe a mí** it's not my job, it is no concern of mine; **le incumbe hacerlo** it is his business to do it; it behoves him to do it, it's his duty to do it.

incumplible ADJ unattainable.

incumplido ADJ unfulfilled.

incumplimiento NM non-fulfilment; non-completion; **~ de contrato** breach of contract; **~ de promesa matrimonial** breach of promise; **por ~** by default.

incumplir [3a] VT *regla* to break, disobey, fail to observe; *promesa* to break, fail to keep.

incunable NM incunable, incunabulum; **~s** incunabula.

incurable 1 ADJ (*Med*) incurable; (*fig*) hopeless, irremediable.

2 NMF incurable.

incuria NF negligence; carelessness, shiftlessness; **por ~** through negligence.

incurrir [3a] VI: **~ en** *error* to fall into; *crimen etc* to commit; *deuda, ira, odio etc* to incur; *desastre etc* to bring on o.s., become a victim of.

incursión NF raid, incursion, attack; **~ aérea** air-raid.

incursionar [1a] **1** VT = **2.**

2 VI: **~ en** to make a raid into, penetrate into; **~ en un tema** to tackle a subject, broach a subject.

indagación NF investigation, inquiry.

indagador(a) NM/F investigator (*de* into, of), inquirer (*de* into).

indagar [1h] VT (*examinar*) to investigate, inquire into; (*averiguar*) to find out, ascertain.

indagatorio 1 ADJ investigatory.

2 indagatoria NF (*Méx*) investigation, inquiry.

indebidamente ADV unduly; improperly; illegally, wrongfully.

indebido ADJ undue; improper; illegal, wrongful.

indecencia NF **(a)** (*gen*) indecency; (*obscenidad*) obscenity. **(b)** (*porquería*) filth; wretchedness. **(c)** (*acto*) indecent act; (*palabra*) indecent thing.

indecente ADJ **(a)** (*gen*) indecent, improper; (*obsceno*) obscene; **¡~!** you brute!

(b) (*asqueroso*) filthy; (*despreciable*) miserable, wretched; (*vil*) low, mean; **algún empleadillo ~** some wretched clerk; **un cuchitril ~** a miserable pigsty of a place; **la calle está ~ de lodo*** the street is terribly muddy; **es una persona ~** he's a low sort, he's a mean character.

indecentemente ADV **(a)** indecently; obscenely. **(b)** miserably, wretchedly.

indecible ADJ unspeakable, unutterable; indescribable; **sufrir lo ~** to suffer terribly.

indeciblemente ADV unspeakably, unutterably; indescribably.

indecisión NF indecision, hesitation; indecisiveness.

indeciso 1 ADJ **(a)** *persona* undecided; hesitant, irresolute; vague. **(b)** *resultado etc* indecisive.

2 NM, **indecisa** NF (*Pol*) undecided voter; (*en encuesta*) don't-know.

indeclarable ADJ undeclarable.

indeclinable ADJ **(a)** (*Ling*) indeclinable. **(b)** (*inevitable*) unavoidable.

indecoro NM unseemliness, indecorum; indelicacy.

indecorosamente ADV indecorously, unbecomingly; indelicately.

indecoroso ADJ unseemly, indecorous, unbecoming; indelicate.

indefectible ADJ unfailing, infallible.

indefectiblemente ADV unfailingly, infallibly.

indefendible ADJ indefensible.

indefensión NF defencelessness.

indefenso ADJ defenceless, helpless.

indefinible ADJ indefinable; inexpressible.

indefinición NF lack of definition; absence of clarity, vagueness.

indefinidamente ADV indefinitely.

indefinido ADJ indefinite; undefined, vague; (*Ling*) indefinite; **por**

tiempo ~ for an indefinite time, indefinitely.

indeformable ADJ rigid, crush-proof; that keeps its shape.

indeleble ADJ indelible.

indelicadeza NF indelicacy.

indelicado ADJ indelicate, unscrupulous.

indemne ADJ undamaged; *persona* unharmed, unhurt.

indemnidad NF immunity, indemnity.

indemnizable ADJ that can be indemnified, recoverable.

indemnización NF **(a)** (*acto*) indemnification.

(b) (*pago*) indemnity, compensation; **indemnizaciones** (*p.ej. 1918*) reparations; **~ de despido** severance pay; **~ por enfermedad** sick pay; **pagó un dólar de ~** he paid a dollar in damages (*o* in compensation).

indemnizar [1f] VT to indemnify (*de* against, for), compensate (*de* for).

indemnizatorio ADJ compensatory.

indemostrable ADJ indemonstrable.

independencia NF independence; **con ~ de** independent of (*que* whether), irrespective of (*que* whether).

independentismo NM independence movement.

independentista ADJ, NMF = **independista.**

independiente 1 ADJ independent; self-sufficient, self-contained; (*Inform*) stand-alone; **hacerse ~** to become independent.

2 NMF independent.

independientemente ADV independently; **~ de que vengan más personas** irrespective (*o* regardless) of whether more people come.

independista 1 ADJ independence (*atr*).

2 NMF supporter of a movement for independence.

independizar [1f] **1** VT to emancipate, free; to make independent, grant independence to.

2 independizarse VR to become free, become independent (*de* of).

indesarraigable ADJ ineradicable.

indescifrable ADJ undecipherable, indecipherable; *misterio* impenetrable.

indescriptible ADJ indescribable.

indescriptiblemente ADV indescribably.

indeseable 1 ADJ undesirable.

2 NMF undesirable (person); **es un ~** he's an unsavoury sort, he's beyond the pale.

indeseado ADJ unwanted.

indesligable ADJ inseparable (*de* from).

indesmallable ADJ *media etc* ladderproof, which does not ladder, runproof.

indesmayable ADJ unfaltering.

indesmentible ADJ undeniable.

indespegable ADJ that will not come unstuck.

indestructible ADJ indestructible.

indetectable ADJ undetectable.

indeterminación NF (*al hablar*) vagueness; (*sobre el futuro*) uncertainty, unpredictability; **principio de ~** (*Phys*) uncertainty principle.

indeterminado ADJ **(a)** (*gen*) indeterminate; *resultado* inconclusive; (*incierto*) vague; (*Ling*) indefinite. **(b)** *persona* irresolute.

indexación NF indexation; (*Fin*) index-linking; (*Inform*) indexing.

indexado ADJ (*Fin*) index-linked.

indexar [1a] VT (*Fin*) to index-link.

India NF: **la ~** India; **las ~s** the Indies; **~s Occidentales** West Indies; **~s Orientales** East Indies.

indiada NF **(a)** (*LAm: reunión etc*) group of Indians, crowd of Indians; (*Cono Sur: pey*) mob. **(b)** (*LAm: acto etc*) typically Indian thing to do (*o* say *etc*).

indiana NF printed calico.

indiano 1 ADJ (Spanish-)American.

2 NM (*Hist*) Spaniard returning rich from America, equivalent to nabob; **~ de hilo negro** miser.

indicación NF **(a)** (*señal*) indication, sign; (*Med: síntoma*) sign, symptom.

(b) (*sugerencia*) hint, suggestion; **por ~ de** at the suggestion of; **aprovechó la ~** he took the hint; **seguiré sus indicaciones** I will follow your suggestion, I will do what you say.

(c) (*dato*) piece of information; (*Téc: de termómetro etc*) reading.

(d) indicaciones (*Com*) instructions, directions; **indicaciones para el empleo** instructions for use.

indicado ADJ right, suitable, proper; obvious; likely; **el sitio más ~** the most obvious place; **una elección indicada** an obvious choice; **es el más ~ para el puesto** he is the most suitable man for the job, he is the best man for the job; **eso es lo más ~** that's the best thing; **tú eres el menos ~ para hacerlo** you're the last person to do it, you're the least suitable person to do it.

indicador NM (*gen*) indicator; (*Téc*) gauge, meter, dial; (*aguja*) hand, pointer; **~ de carretera** roadsign; **~ de dirección** (*Aut*) indicator, trafficator; **~ económico** economic indicator; **~ de encendido** (*In-*

form) power-on indicator; **~ de velocidades** speedometer.

indicar [1g] VT (**a**) (*Téc etc*) to indicate, show; to register, record; (*termómetro etc*) to read.
(**b**) (*señalar*) to indicate, point out, point to; (*mostrar*) to show; (*sugerir*) to suggest, hint, intimate; **me indicó que ...** he told me that ..., he suggested to me that ...

indicativo ① ADJ indicative (*t Ling*).
② NM (**a**) (*Ling*) indicative. (**b**) (*Rad*) call sign; **~ de nacionalidad** (*Aut*) national identification plate.

índice NM (**a**) (*Tip etc*) index; (*catálogo*) (library) catalogue; **~ de materias** table of contents.
(**b**) (*Mat etc*) index; ratio, rate; **~ de audiencia** (*TV*) audience ratings; **~ de compresión** (*Mec*) compression ratio; **~ del coste de (la) vida** cost-of-living index; **~ de deuda** debt ratio; **~ Dow Jones** Dow Jones index; **~ expurgatorio** (*Ecl*) Index; **~ de mortalidad** death rate; **~ de natalidad** birth-rate; **~ de ocupación** occupancy rate (of hotel rooms *etc*); **~ de participación** (*Pol*) electoral turnout; **~ de precios al consumo** retail price index; **~ de vida** expectation of life, life expectancy.
(**c**) (*Téc: aguja*) pointer, needle, hand; (*de reloj*) hand.
(**d**) (*Anat*) index finger, forefinger.

indiciación NF indexing; (*Fin*) index-linking.

indiciario ADJ: **prueba indiciaria** circumstantial proof.

indicio NM (**a**) (*gen*) indication, sign; token; (*Jur etc*) piece of evidence, clue (*de* to); (*vestigio*) trace, vestige; **es ~ de** it is an indication of, it is a sign of; **no hay el menor ~ de él** there isn't the faintest sign of him, there isn't the least trace of him; **dar ~s de sorpresa** to show surprise, evince surprise.
(**b**) **~s** (*Jur*) circumstantial evidence.

indiferencia NF indifference; apathy, lack of interest.

indiferente ADJ (**a**) (*gen*) indifferent (*a* to), unconcerned (*a* about); (*apático*) apathetic, uninterested.
(**b**) (*fig*) indifferent, immaterial; **me es ~** it is immaterial to me, it makes no difference to me.

indiferentemente ADV indifferently.

indiferentismo NM indifference; apathy; (*Rel*) scepticism, indifferentism.

indígena ① ADJ indigenous (*de* to), native (*de* to); (*LAm*) Indian.
② NMF native; (*LAm*) Indian.

indigencia NF poverty, destitution, indigence.

indigenismo NM (**a**) (*Ling*) word (*o* phrase *etc*) borrowed from a native language. (**b**) (*LAm Pol*) indigenism, pro-Indian political movement.

indigenista ① ADJ: **propaganda ~** pro-Indian propaganda, propaganda for the Indian cause.
② NMF supporter of the Indian cause.

indigente ① ADJ destitute, poverty-stricken, indigent.
② NMF poor person.

indigerible ADJ undigestible.

indigestar [1a] ① VT to cause indigestion to.
② **indigestarse** VR (**a**) (*persona*) to get indigestion, have indigestion.
(**b**) (*comida*) to cause indigestion, be indigestible; **esa carne se me indigestó** that meat gave me indigestion, I couldn't digest that meat.
(**c**) (*fig*) to be insufferable; **se me indigesta ese tío** I can't stand that fellow.
(**d**) (*LAm: inquietarse*) to get worried, get alarmed.

indigestible ADJ indigestible.

indigestión NF indigestion.

indigesto ADJ undigested; indigestible, hard to digest; (*fig*) muddled, turgid, badly thought-out.

indignación NF indignation, anger; **descargar la ~ sobre** to vent one's spleen on, take out one's anger on.

indignado ADJ indignant, angry (*con, contra* with; *por* at, about).

indignamente ADV (**a**) (*no merecedor*) unworthily. (**b**) (*merecedor de desprecio*) contemptibly, meanly.

indignante ADJ outrageous, infuriating, unworthy, humiliating.

indignar [1a] ① VT to anger, make indignant; to provoke, stir up.
② **indignarse** VR to get angry, get indignant; **~ con uno** to get indignant with sb; **¡es para ~!** it's infuriating!; **~ por algo** to get indignant about sth, get angry about sth.

indignidad NF (**a**) (*cualidad*) unworthiness. (**b**) (*acto*) unworthy act; (*ofensa*) indignity, insult; **sufrir la ~ de** + *infin* to suffer the indignity of + *ger*.

indigno ADJ (**a**) (*sin mérito*) unworthy (*de* of). (**b**) (*vil*) contemptible, mean, low.

índigo NM indigo.

indino ADJ (**a**) (*insolente*) cheeky*. (**b**) (*And, Carib*: *tacaño*) mean, stingy.

indio ① ADJ (**a**) *persona* Indian.
(**b**) (*azul*) blue.

② NM, **india** NF (**a**) Indian (*of India, of West Indies, of America*).
(**b**) **hacer el ~** to play the fool; to make a silly mistake; **le salió el ~** (*CAm, Cono Sur*) he behaved like a boor; **se le subió el ~** (*Cono Sur*) he flew off the handle*; **ser el ~ gorrón*** to live by scrounging*.
(**c**) **~ viejo** (*CAm, Méx Culin*) stewed meat with maize and herbs.

indirecta NF hint; insinuation, innuendo; **~ del padre Cobos** broad hint; **soltar una ~** to drop a hint, make an insinuation.

indirectamente ADV indirectly.

indirecto ADJ indirect; roundabout.

indiscernible ADJ indiscernible.

indisciplina NF indiscipline, lack of discipline; insubordination.

indisciplinado ADJ undisciplined; lax.

indisciplinarse [1a] VR to get out of control.

indiscreción NF (*gen*) indiscretion; (*falta social*) tactless thing (to do), tactless remark (*etc*), gaffe; **..., si no es ~ ...**, if you don't mind my saying ...; **cometió la ~ de** + *infin* he committed the indiscretion of + *ger*, he was so tactless as to + *infin*.

indiscretamente ADV indiscreetly; tactlessly.

indiscreto ADJ indiscreet; tactless.

indiscriminadamente ADV indiscriminately.

indiscriminado ADJ indiscriminate.

indisculpable ADJ inexcusable, unforgivable.

▼ **indiscutible** ADJ indisputable, unquestionable.

▼ **indiscutiblemente** ADV indisputably, unquestionably.

indisimulable ADJ that cannot be disguised.

indisimulado ADJ undisguised.

indisociable ADJ inseparable (*de* from).

indisolubilidad NF indissolubility.

indisoluble ADJ indissoluble; inseparable.

indisolublemente ADV indissolubly; inseparably.

▼ **indispensable** ADJ indispensable, essential.

indisponer [2q] ① VT (**a**) *plan etc* to spoil, upset.
(**b**) (*Med*) to upset, make ill, make unfit.
(**c**) **~ a uno con otro** to set sb against another person, prejudice sb against another person.
② **indisponerse** VR (**a**) (*Med*) to become ill, fall ill.
(**b**) **~ con uno** to fall out with sb.

indisponible ADJ not available, unavailable.

indisposición NF (**a**) (*Med*) indisposition, slight illness. (**b**) (*desgana*) disinclination, unwillingness.

indispuesto ADJ (**a**) (*Med*) indisposed, unwell, slightly ill; **sentirse ~** to feel slightly ill, feel queer. (**b**) (*sin ganas*) disinclined, unwilling.

indisputable ADJ indisputable, unquestioned; unchallenged.

indistinción NF (**a**) (*gen*) indistinctness; vagueness. (**b**) (*falta de discriminación*) lack of discrimination. (**c**) (*igualdad*) lack of distinction, sameness, identity.

indistinguible ADJ indistinguishable (*de* from).

indistintamente ADV (*V ADJ*) (**a**) indistinctly; vaguely. (**b**) without distinction, indiscriminately. (**c**) **pueden firmar ~** either (joint holder of the account *etc*) may sign.

indistinto ADJ (**a**) (*poco claro*) indistinct; vague; (*borroso*) faint, dim. (**b**) (*indiscriminado*) indiscriminate.

individua* NF (*pey*) woman, female.

individual ① ADJ (**a**) (*gen*) individual; (*particular*) peculiar, special; *cama, habitación* single.
(**b**) (*And, Cono Sur*: *idéntico*) identical; **A es ~ a B** A is the spitting image of B.
② NM (*Dep*) singles, singles match; **~ femenino** women's singles; **~ masculino** men's singles.

individualidad NF individuality.

individualismo NM individualism.

individualista ① ADJ individualistic.
② NMF individualist.

individualizar [1f] VT to individualize.

individualmente ADV individually.

individuar [1e] VT to individualize.

individuo ① ADJ individual.
② NM (**a**) individual; (*pey*) individual, chap, fellow; **el ~ en cuestión** the person in question; **él cuida bien de su ~*** he knows how to look after Number One. (**b**) (*de sociedad*) member, fellow.

indivisibilidad NF indivisibility.

indivisible ADJ indivisible.

indiviso ADJ undivided.

indización NF indexation; (*Fin*) index-linking; (*Inform*) indexing.

indizado ADJ (*Fin*) index-linked.

indizar [1f] VT to index; (*Fin*) to index-link.

INDO NM (*Com*) ABR *de* **Instituto Nacional de Denominaciones de Origen**.

Indo NM (*Geog*) Indus.

indo, -a ADJ, NM/F Indian, Hindu.

indo... PREF Indo...

Indochina NF: **la ~** Indochina.

➤ LENGUA Y USO: **indiscutible** → 42.1   **indiscutiblemente** → 53.6   **indispensable** → 37.1

indócil ADJ unmanageable, headstrong; disobedient.

indocilidad NF unmanageableness, headstrong character; disobedience.

indocto ADJ ignorant, unlearned.

indoctrinar [1a] VT (*LAm*) to indoctrinate.

indocumentado [1] ADJ without identifying documents, who carries no identity papers.

[2] NM, **indocumentada** NF person who carries no identity papers; (*Méx etc*) illegal immigrant; (*hum*) ignoramus.

indoeuropeo, -a [1] ADJ, NM/F Indo-European.

[2] NM (*Ling*) Indo-European.

índole NF (a) (*naturaleza*) nature; character, disposition. (b) (*clase*) class, kind, sort; **cosas de esta ~** things of this kind.

indolencia NF indolence, laziness; listlessness.

indolente ADJ indolent, lazy; listless.

indoloro ADJ painless.

indomable ADJ *espíritu etc* indomitable; *animal* untameable; (*fig*) unmanageable, uncontrollable.

indomado ADJ wild, untamed.

indomesticable ADJ untameable.

indomiciliado ADJ homeless.

indómito ADJ = **indomable**.

Indonesia NF Indonesia.

indonesio, -a ADJ, NM/F Indonesian.

indormia* NF (*And, Carib*) trick, wangle*, wheeze*.

Indostán NM Hindustan.

indostanés, -esa ADJ, NM/F Hindustani.

indostaní NM (*Ling*) Hindustani.

indostánico [1] ADJ Hindustani.

[2] NM (*Ling*) Hindustani.

indotado ADJ without a dowry.

indte. ABR *de* **indistintamente.**

Indubán [indu'ban] NM (*Esp Fin*) ABR *de* **Banco de Financiación Industrial.**

indubitable ADJ indubitable, undoubted, certain.

indubitablemente ADV indubitably, undoubtedly.

inducción NF (a) (*Elec, Filos*) induction; **por ~** by induction, inductively. (b) (*persuasión*) inducement, persuasion.

inducido NM (*Elec*) armature.

inducir [3n] VT (a) (*Elec*) to induce; (*Filos*) to infer.

(b) (*persuadir*) to induce, persuade; **~ a uno a hacer algo** to induce sb to do sth; **~ a uno en el** (*o* **al**) **error** to lead sb into error.

inductivo ADJ inductive; **pregunta inductiva** leading question.

inductor(a) [1] NM/F instigator.

[2] NM (*Elec, Bio*) inductor.

▼ **indudable** ADJ undoubted, indubitable; unquestionable; **es ~ que ...** there is no doubt that ...

indudablemente ADV undoubtedly, doubtless; unquestionably.

indulgencia NF (a) (*gen*) indulgence; forbearance; **proceder sin ~ contra** to proceed ruthlessly against.

(b) (*Ecl*) indulgence; **~ plenaria** plenary indulgence.

indulgente ADJ indulgent, lenient (*con* towards).

indulgentemente ADV indulgently, leniently.

indultar [1a] [1] VT (a) (*Jur*) to pardon, reprieve (*de* from).

(b) (*eximir*) to exempt, excuse (*de* from).

[2] **indultarse** VR (a) (*And: entrometerse*) to meddle, pry.

(b) (*Carib**) to get o.s. out of a jam*.

indulto NM (a) (*Jur*) pardon, reprieve. (b) (*exención*) exemption, excusal.

indumentaria NF (a) (*ropa*) clothing, apparel, dress. (b) (*estudio*) (history of) costume.

indumentario ADJ clothing (*atr*); **elegancia indumentaria** elegance of dress, sartorial elegance.

indumento NM clothing, apparel, dress.

industria NF (a) (*Com etc*) industry; **~ algodonera** cotton industry; **~ artesanal** *o* **doméstica** cottage industry; **~ del automóvil** car industry, automobile industry (*US*); **~ básica** basic industry; **~ casera** cottage industry; **~s con chimeneas** smokestack industries; **~ ligera** light industry; **~ militar** weapons industry, defence industry; **~ pesada** heavy industry; **~ primaria** extractive industry; **~ secundaria** manufacturing industry; **~ siderúrgica** iron and steel industry; **~ terciaria** service industry.

(b) (*dedicación*) industry, industriousness.

(c) (*maña*) ingenuity, skill, expertise; **de ~** on purpose.

industrial [1] ADJ (a) (*de la industria*) industrial. (b) (*no casero*) factory-made, industrially produced; (*fig*) large, massive; large-scale.

[2] NMF industrialist, manufacturer.

industrialismo NM industrialism.

industrialista NM/F (*LAm*) industrialist.

industrialización NF industrialization.

industrializar [1f] [1] VT to industrialize.

[2] **industrializarse** VR to become industrialized.

industriarse [1b] VR to manage, find a way; **~ para** + *infin* to manage to + *infin*, contrive to + *infin*.

industriosamente ADV (a) industriously. (b) skilfully, resourcefully.

industrioso ADJ (a) (*trabajador*) industrious. (b) (*mañoso*) skilful, resourceful, versatile, handy.

INE ['ine] NM (*Esp*) ABR *de* **Instituto Nacional de Estadística.**

inédito ADJ (a) (*Liter*) unpublished; **un texto rigurosamente ~** a text never published previously in any form.

(b) (*fig*) new; not known hitherto, hitherto unheard-of; **una experiencia inédita** a completely new experience.

ineducable ADJ ineducable.

ineducado ADJ (a) (*sin instrucción*) uneducated. (b) (*maleducado*) ill-bred, bad-mannered, uncouth.

INEF [i'nef] NM ABR *de* **Instituto Nacional de Educación Física.**

inefable ADJ indescribable, inexpressible, ineffable.

inefectivo ADJ (*LAm*) ineffective.

ineficacia NF (a) (*de medida*) ineffectiveness. (b) (*de proceso*) inefficiency.

ineficaz ADJ (*V* N) (a) ineffective, ineffectual. (b) inefficient.

ineficazmente ADV (*V* N) (a) ineffectively, ineffectually. (b) inefficiently.

ineficiencia NF inefficiency.

ineficiente ADJ inefficient.

inelástico ADJ inelastic.

inelegancia NF inelegance, lack of elegance.

inelegante ADJ inelegant.

inelegantemente ADV inelegantly.

inelegibilidad NF ineligibility.

inelegible ADJ ineligible.

ineluctable ADJ, **ineludible** ADJ unavoidable, inescapable; **elemento ~** essential element.

INEM [i'nem] NM (a) (*Esp*) ABR *de* **Instituto Nacional de Empleo.** (b) (*Esp*) ABR *de* **Instituto Nacional de Enseñanza Media.**

INEN [i'nen] NM (*Méx*) ABR *de* **Instituto Nacional de Energía Nuclear.**

inenarrable ADJ inexpressible.

inencogible ADJ unshrinkable, non-shrink, which will not shrink.

inencontrable ADJ unobtainable.

inencontrolable ADJ that cannot be found, impossible to find; extremely scarce.

inepcia NF (a) (*gen*) ineptitude, incompetence; stupidity. (b) (*impropiedad*) unsuitability. (c) (*necedad*) silly thing (to say *etc*); **decir ~s** to talk rubbish.

ineptitud NF (*V* **inepcia**) (a) ineptitude, incompetence. (b) unsuitability.

inepto ADJ (a) (*incompetente*) inept, incompetent; stupid; **~ de toda ineptitud** utterly incompetent. (b) (*no apto*) unsuited (*para* to), unsuitable (*para* for).

inequívoco ADJ unequivocal, unambiguous; unmistakable.

inercia NF (a) (*Fís*) inertia. (b) (*fig*) passivity; sluggishness, slowness.

inerme ADJ unarmed; defenceless, unprotected.

inerte ADJ (a) (*Fís*) inert. (b) (*fig*) passive, inactive; sluggish, slow.

Inés NF Agnes.

inescamoteable ADJ that cannot be got rid of, unavoidable.

inescrupuloso ADJ unscrupulous.

inescrutabilidad NF inscrutability.

inescrutable ADJ inscrutable.

inespecífico ADJ unspecific, non-specific.

inesperadamente ADV unexpectedly; without warning, suddenly.

inesperado ADJ unexpected, unforeseen; sudden.

inesquivable ADJ unavoidable.

inestabilidad NF instability, unsteadiness.

inestabilizar [1f] [1] VT to destabilize.

[2] **inestabilizarse** VR to become unstable.

inestable ADJ unstable, unsteady.

inestimable ADJ inestimable, invaluable.

inevitabilidad NF inevitability.

▼ **inevitable** ADJ inevitable, unavoidable.

inevitablemente ADV inevitably, unavoidably.

inexactitud NF inaccuracy; incorrectness.

inexacto ADJ inaccurate; incorrect, untrue; **esto es ~** this is not so, this is incorrect.

inexcusable ADJ (a) (*imperdonable*) inexcusable, unforgivable. (b) (*inevitable*) necessary, unavoidable, inevitable; **una visita ~** a trip which must not be missed, an absolutely essential visit.

inexcusablemente ADV inexcusably, unforgivably; **el depósito será devuelto ~ si ...** the deposit will be returned as a matter of obligation if ...

inexhausto ADJ inexhaustible, unending.

inexistencia NF non-existence.

inexistente ADJ non-existent; which no longer exists, defunct.

inexorabilidad NF inexorability.

inexorable ADJ inexorable.

inexorablemente ADV inexorably.
inexperiencia NF inexperience; unskilfulness, lack of skill.
inexperimentado ADJ inexperienced.
inexperto ADJ inexperienced; unskilled, inexpert.
inexplicable ADJ inexplicable, unaccountable.
inexplicablemente ADV inexplicably, unaccountably.
inexplicado ADJ unexplained.
inexplorado ADJ unexplored; *mar etc* uncharted.
inexplotado ADJ unexploited, unused.
inexportable ADJ that cannot be exported.
inexpresable ADJ inexpressible.
inexpresividad NF inexpressiveness; flatness, woodenness.
inexpresivo ADJ inexpressive; dull, flat, wooden.
inexpuesto ADJ (*Fot*) unexposed.
inexpugnabilidad NF impregnability.
inexpugnable ADJ (a) (*Mil*) impregnable. (b) (*fig*) firm, unyielding, unshakeable.
inextinguible ADJ inextinguishable, unquenchable.
inextirpable ADJ ineradicable.
in extremis ADV: **estar ~** to be at death's door, be at one's last gasp.
inextricable ADJ inextricable; *bosque etc* impenetrable.
infalibilidad NF infallibility; certainty **~ pontificia** papal infallibility.
infalible ADJ infallible; certain, sure; foolproof; *puntería* unerring.
infaliblemente ADV infallibly; surely; unerringly.
infaltable ADJ (*LAm*) not to be missed.
infamación NF defamation.
infamador ①ADJ defamatory, slanderous.
 ②NM, **infamadora** NF slanderer.
infamante ADJ (*injurioso*) offensive, rude; (*difamatorio*) slanderous; *pena etc* shameful, degrading.
infamar [1a] VT to dishonour, discredit; to defame, slander.
infamatorio ADJ defamatory, slanderous.
infame ①ADJ infamous, odious, vile; *tarea* terrible, thankless; **esto es ~** this is montrous, this is infamous.
 ②NMF vile person, villain.
infamia NF infamy; disgrace.
infancia NF (a) (*edad*) infancy, childhood; (*fig*) infancy. (b) (*niños*) children.
infanta NF (a) (*niña*) infant. (b) (*princesa*) infanta, princess.
infante NM (a) (*niño*) infant. (b) (*príncipe*) infante, prince; (*Mil: Hist*) infantryman; **~ de marina** marine.
infantería NF infantry; **~ de marina** marines.
infanticida NMF infanticide (*person*), child-killer.
infanticidio NM infanticide (*act*); (‡) liking for young girls.
infantil ADJ (a) (*de niño*) infant; child's, children's; **libros ~es** children's books; (de) **tamaño ~** child's size; **para el uso ~** for children (to use). (b) (*inocente*) childlike, innocent; (*pey*) infantile, childish.
infantilada* NF: **es una ~** it's such a childish thing to do.
infantilismo NM infantilism.
infantiloide ADJ childish, puerile.
infanzón NM, **infanzona** NF (*Hist*) *member of the lowest rank of the nobility*.
infartante* ADJ heart-stopping*.
infarto NM (a) **~ (de miocardio)** heart attack. (b) **de ~** (*fig*) heart-stopping.
infatigable ADJ tireless, untiring.
infatigablemente ADV tirelessly, untiringly.
infatuación NF vanity, conceit.
infatuar [1d] VT to make conceited.
 ②**infatuarse** VR to get conceited (*con* about).
infausto ADJ unlucky; ill-starred, ill-fated.
INFE ['infe] NM ABR *de* **Instituto de Fomento de las Exportaciones**.
infección NF infection.
infecciosidad NF infectiousness.
infeccioso ADJ, **infectante** ADJ infectious.
infectar [1a] ① VT (a) (*gen*) to infect. (b) (*contaminar*) to contaminate, corrupt; (*pervertir*) to pervert.
 ②**infectarse** VR to become infected (*de* with; *t fig*).
infecto ADJ infected (*de* with); foul; corrupt, tainted.
infectocontagioso ADJ transmittable, infectious.
infecundidad NF infertility; sterility, barrenness.
infecundo ADJ infertile; sterile, barren; **la época infecunda de la mujer** the woman's infertile period.
infelicidad NF unhappiness; misfortune.
infeliz ①ADJ (a) (*desgraciado*) unhappy; (*desdichado*) unfortunate, miserable, wretched; *tentativa etc* unsuccessful.
 (b) (*bonachón*) simple, kind-hearted, good-natured; (*pey*) gullible.
 (c) (*Cono Sur, Méx**: *nimio*) trifling, insignificant.
 ②NMF (a) (*desgraciado*) wretch, poor devil.
 (b) (*inocentón*) simpleton.
infelizmente ADV unhappily.

infelizón* NM, **infelizote*** NM = **infeliz 2 (a)**.
inferencia NF inference; **por ~** by inference.
inferible ADJ inferable.
▼**inferior** ① ADJ (a) (*situación*) lower (*a* than); **la parte ~** the lower part; **el lado ~** the underside, the side underneath; **el Egipto ~** lower Egypt.
 ▼(b) (*calidad, rango*) inferior (*a* to), lower (*a* than); **de calidad ~** of inferior quality; **no ser ~ a nadie** to be inferior to none; **le es ~ en talento** he is inferior to him in talent.
 (c) (*Mat*) lower; **cualquier número ~ a 9** any number under 9, any number below 9, any number less than 9; **una cantidad ~** a lesser quantity.
 ②NMF inferior, subordinate; (*pey*) underling.
inferioridad NF inferiority; **en ~ de condiciones** on less good conditions.
inferir [3i] VT (a) (*deducir*) to infer, deduce; **~ una cosa de** (o *por*) **otra** to infer one thing from another.
 (b) *herida* to inflict (*a, en* on); *daños* to cause; *insulto* to offer (*a* to).
infernáculo NM hopscotch.
infernal ADJ infernal; (*fig*) infernal, hellish, devilish.
infernillo NM (*t ~ de alcohol*) spirit lamp, spirit stove; **~ campestre** camp stove; **~ de gasolina** petrol stove.
infértil ADJ infertile.
infestación NF infestation.
infestado ADJ: **~ de** *parásitos, gérmenes* infested with; (*fig*) *mendigos, turistas* crawling with; **~ de cucarachas** cockroach-infested.
infestante ADJ invasive, pervasive.
infestar [1a] VT (a) (*infectar*) to infect; (*insectos etc*) to infest; (*invadir*) to overrun, invade. (b) (*fig*) to harass, beset.
infibulación NF infibulation.
infibulado ADJ infibulated.
inficionar [1a] VT = **infectar**.
infidelidad NF (a) (*adulterio*) infidelity, unfaithfulness; **~ conyugal** marital infidelity. (b) (*Ecl*) unbelief, lack of faith. (c) (*Ecl: personas*) unbelievers, infidels.
infidencia NF (a) (*cualidad*) disloyalty, faithlessness; treason. (b) (*acto*) disloyal act; breach of trust.
infiel ①ADJ (a) (*desleal*) unfaithful, disloyal (*a, con, para* to); **fue ~ a su mujer** he was unfaithful to his wife.
 (b) (*Ecl*) unbelieving, infidel.
 (c) *informe etc* inaccurate; **la memoria le fue ~** his memory failed him.
 ②NMF (*Ecl*) unbeliever, infidel.
infielmente ADV (*V ADJ*) (a) unfaithfully, disloyally. (b) inaccurately.
infiernillo NM = **infernillo**.
infierno NM (a) hell.
 (b) (*fig y en locuciones*) hell, inferno; hades; **¡anda al ~!** go to hell!; **está en el quinto ~** it's at the back of beyond, it's right off the map; **mandar a uno al quinto ~** (o **a los quintos ~s**) to tell sb to go to hell.
infijo NM infix.
infiltración NF infiltration.
infiltrado, -a NM/F infiltrator.
infiltrar [1a] ① VT to infiltrate (*en* into); (*fig*) to inculcate (*en* in).
 ②**infiltrarse** VR to infiltrate (*t fig*; *en* into), filter (*en* in, through); to percolate.
ínfimo ADJ lowest; (*fig*) very poor, of very poor quality; vile, mean; least; **a precios ~s** at very low prices, at ridiculously low prices.
infinidad NF (a) (*Mat etc*) infinity.
 (b) (*fig*) great quantity, enormous number; **~ de** an infinity of, vast numbers of; **durante una ~ de días** for days on end; **~ de veces** countless times; **hay ~ de personas que ...** there are great numbers of people who ...
infinitamente ADV infinitely.
infinitesimal ADJ infinitesimal.
infinitivo ①ADJ infinitive.
 ②NM infinitive (mood).
infinito ①ADJ (a) (*Mat etc*) infinite.
 (b) (*fig*) infinite; boundless, limitless, endless; **hasta lo ~** ad infinitum.
 ②ADV infinitely, immensely; **se lo agradezco ~** I'm enormously grateful to you (for it).
 ③NM (*Mat*) infinity; **el ~** (*Filos etc*) the infinite.
infinitud NF infinitude.
inflable ADJ inflatable.
inflación NF (a) (*gen, t Econ*) inflation; (*hinchazón*) swelling. (b) (*fig*) pride, conceit.
inflacionario ADJ inflationary.
inflacionismo NM (*Econ*) inflation, inflationism.
inflacionista ADJ inflationary.
inflado NM inflating, pumping up.
inflador NM (*LAm*) bicycle pump.

► LENGUA Y USO: **inferior: 1b** → 32.3

inflagaitas* NMF INVAR twit*.
inflamabilidad NF inflammability.
inflamable ADJ inflammable, flammable.
inflamación NF (a) (*combustión*) ignition, combustion. (b) (*Med*) inflammation.
inflamar [1a] [1] VT (a) (*lit*) to set on fire, ignite.
(b) (*Med*) to inflame.
(c) (*fig*) to inflame, excite, arouse.
[2] **inflamarse** VR (a) to catch fire, flame up, ignite; **se inflama fácilmente** it is highly inflammable.
(b) (*Med*) to become inflamed.
(c) (*fig*) to become inflamed (*de, en* with), get excited.
inflamatorio ADJ inflammatory.
inflapollas: NM INVAR berk:, wimp:.
inflar [1a] [1] VT (a) (*hinchar*) to inflate, blow up, pump air into.
(b) (*fig*) to inflate, exaggerate; to make conceited.
(c) (*Cono Sur*) to heed, pay attention to.
(d) (*Econ*) to reinflate.
[2] VI (*Méx**) to booze*, drink.
[3] **inflarse** VR (a) to swell.
(b) (*fig*) to get conceited, get puffed up.
inflatorio ADJ inflationary.
inflexibilidad NF inflexibility; unyielding nature.
inflexible ADJ inflexible; unbending, unyielding; **~ a los ruegos** unmoved by appeals, unresponsive to appeals; **regla ~** strict rule, hard-and-fast rule.
inflexión NF inflexion.
infligir [3c] VT to inflict (*a* on).
influencia NF influence (*sobre* on); **bajo la ~ de** under the influence of.
influenciable ADJ impressionable, easily influenced.
influenciar [1b] VT to influence.
influenza NF influenza.
influir [3g] [1] VT to influence; **A, influido por B ...** A, influenced by B ...
[2] VI (a) to have influence, carry weight, have pull (*con* with); **es hombre que influye** he's a man of influence, he's a man who carries weight.
(b) **~ en, ~ sobre** to influence, affect, have an influence on; to have a hand in.
influjo NM influence (*sobre* on).
influyente ADJ influential.
infografía NF computer graphics.
▼ **información** NF (a) (*gen*) information; (*noticias*) news; (*Mil*) intelligence; (*Inform*) data; **una ~** a piece of information, a piece of news; **~ caliente** hot tip; **~ secreta** secret information, classified information.
(b) (*informe*) report, account; (*referencia*) reference, testimonial; (*apartado de periódico*) section; **~ de crédito** credit report; **~ deportiva** sports section, sporting page; **~ extranjera** news from abroad, foreign news; **~ periodística** newspaper report.
(c) (*Jur*) legal proceedings; judicial inquiry, investigation; **abrir una ~** to begin proceedings.
informado ADJ informed.
informador(a) NM/F (*gen*) informant; **~ (de policía)** informer; **~ gráfico** reporter, pressman; photojournalist; **~ turístico** tourist guide; **los ~es (de la Prensa** *etc*) (the representatives of) the media.
informal ADJ (a) (*pey: incorrecto*) irregular, incorrect; *conducta etc* bad, unmannerly; (*poco usual*) unconventional.
(b) (*pey*) *persona* (*poco fiable*) unreliable, untrustworthy; shifty; (*incapaz*) unbusinesslike, disorganized; (*maleducado*) offhand, bad-mannered; (*frívolo*) frivolous.
(c) (*no oficial*) informal; **conversación ~** informal talk; **lenguaje ~** informal language, non-official language.
informalidad NF (*V ADJ*) (a) irregularity, incorrectness; unmannerliness; unconventionality.
(b) unreliability, untrustworthiness, shiftiness; unbusinesslike nature; offhandedness, bad manners; frivolity, levity.
(c) informality, non-official nature.
informalmente ADV (*V ADJ*) (a) irregularly; badly; unconventionally.
(b) unreliably; shiftily; in an unbusinesslike way; offhandedly; frivolously. (c) informally, unofficially.
informante NMF informant.
▼ **informar** [1a] [1] VT (a) (*enterar*) to inform, tell (*de* of, *sobre* about); to announce (*que* that); **quedo informado de que ...** I understand that ....
(b) (*dar forma a*) to form, shape.
[2] VI (a) (*gen*) to report (*acerca de, de* on); **el profesor informará de su descubrimiento** the professor will report on his discovery.
(b) (*Jur: abogado*) to plead.
(c) (*Jur: delator*) to inform (*contra* against), lay information (*contra* against).

[3] **informarse** VR to find out, inform o.s.; **~ de** to find out about, acquaint o.s. with, inquire into; **~ sobre algo** to gather information about sth.
informática¹ NF information science, computer science, informatics, computing; **~ gráfica** computer graphics.
informático [1] ADJ computer (*atr*); **centro ~** computer centre; **servicios ~s** computer services.
[2] NM, **informática²** NF computer scientist; computer programmer.
informatividad NF informativity, informative nature.
informativo [1] ADJ (a) (*gen*) informative; news (*atr*); **un folleto ~** a booklet of information, an explanatory booklet; **programa ~** (*TV etc*) news programme. (b) *comité etc* consultative, advisory.
[2] NM (*Rad, TV*) news programme.
informatización NF computerization.
informatizar [1f] VT to computerize.
informe¹ ADJ shapeless.
informe² NM (a) (*declaración*) report, statement; announcement; (*Parl*) report, white paper; **~ forense** coroner's report; **~ de prensa** press release; **el ~ del ministro** the minister's statement.
(b) (*dato*) piece of information; **~s** information; data, particulars, references; **según mis ~s** according to my information; **dar ~s sobre** to give information about; **pedir ~s** to ask for information, make inquiries (*a* of, *sobre* about); **tomar ~s** to gather information.
(c) (*Jur*) plea; **~ forense**, **~ jurídico** pleading.
infortunado ADJ unfortunate, unlucky.
infortunio NM misfortune, ill luck; mishap.
infra... PREF infra..., under...
infraalimentación NF undernourishment.
infra(a)limentado ADJ underfed, undernourished.
infracción NF infraction, infringement (*de* of); breach (*de* of); (*Aut etc*) offence (*de* against); **~ de contrato** breach of contract.
infractor(a) NM/F offender (*de* against).
infradesarrollado ADJ under-developed.
infradesarrollo NM under-development.
infradotado [1] ADJ short of resources, insufficiently supplied; understaffed.
[2] NM, **infradotada** NF subnormal person.
infra(e)scrito [1] ADJ undersigned; undermentioned.
[2] NM, **infra(e)scrita** NF: **el ~** the undersigned; (*LAm: hum*) the present speaker, I myself.
infraestimación NF underestimate.
infraestimar [1a] VT to underestimate.
infra(e)structura NF infrastructure.
in fraganti ADV: **coger a uno ~** to catch sb red-handed.
infrahumano ADJ subhuman.
infraliteratura NF pulp fiction.
inframundo NM underworld.
infrangible ADJ unbreakable.
infranqueable ADJ impassable; (*fig*) unsurmountable.
infrarrojo ADJ infrared.
infrautilización NF under-use.
infrautilizado ADJ underused; *recursos* untapped.
infrautilizar [1f] VT to under-use.
infravaloración NF undervaluing; underestimate.
infravalorar [1a] VT to undervalue; to underestimate.
infravaluar [1e] VT to underestimate; to play down.
infraviviendas NFPL sub-standard housing.
infrecuencia NF infrequency.
infrecuente ADJ infrequent.
infringir [3c] VT to infringe, break, contravene.
infructuosamente ADV fruitlessly, unsuccessfully; unprofitably.
infructuoso ADJ fruitless, unsuccessful; unprofitable.
ínfulas NFPL (*vanidad*) conceit; (*disparates*) pretentious nonsense; **darse ~** to put on airs, get on one's high horse; **tener (muchas) ~ de** to fancy o.s. as.
infumable ADJ (a) (*gen*) unsmokable. (b) (*fig: insoportable*) unbearable, intolerable.
infundado ADJ unfounded, baseless, groundless.
infundia* NF (*LAm*) fat.
infundio* NM fairy tale, lie; malicious story.
infundir [3a] VT (a) (*gen*) to infuse (*a, en* into).
(b) (*fig*) to instil (*a, en* into); **~ ánimo a uno** to encourage sb; **~ miedo a uno** to scare sb, frighten sb, fill sb with fear; **~ un espíritu nuevo a un club** to inject new life into a club, put new life into a club.
infusión NF infusion; **~ de hierbas** herbal tea.
infuso ADJ: **ciencia infusa** instinct, intuition; **saber algo por ciencia infusa** to know sth instinctively.
Ing. ABR *de* **ingeniero, ingeniera** engineer.
ingeniar [1a] [1] VT to devise, think up, contrive.
[2] **ingeniarse** VR to manage, find a way, get along; **~ con algo** to manage with sth, make do with sth; **~ (o ingeniárselas) para + infin**

► LENGUA Y USO: **información: a → 48.3   informar: 1a → 48.3** to manage to + *infin,* contrive to + *infin.*

ingeniería NF engineering; **~ civil** civil engineering; **~ de control** control engineering; **~ eléctrica** electrical engineering; **~ genética** genetic engineering; **~ química** chemical engineering; **~ de sistemas** systems engineering; **~ social** social engineering.

ingeniero, -a NM/F **(a)** engineer (*t Mil, Náut*); **~ agrónomo** agronomist, agricultural expert; **~ de caminos, canales y puertos** civil engineer; **~ forestal, ~ de montes** forestry expert; **~ de mantenimiento** maintenance engineer; **~ de minas** mining engineer; **~ naval** shipbuilder, naval architect; **~ pecuario** veterinary surgeon; **~ químico** chemical engineer; **~ de sonido** sound engineer; **~ de vuelo** flight engineer.
(b) (*LAm Univ, frec*) graduate; **el I~ Pérez** Dr Pérez.

ingenio NM **(a)** (*inventiva*) ingenuity, inventiveness; (*talento*) talent; creativeness; (*agudeza*) wit, wits; **aguzar el ~** to sharpen one's wits.
(b) (*persona*) clever person, talented person; (*Hist*) wit.
(c) (*Mec*) apparatus, engine, machine, device; (*Mil*) device; **~ nuclear** nuclear device.
(d) (*Téc*) mill, plant; (*And: de acero*) foundry, steel works; **~ (de azúcar), ~ azucarero** sugar mill, sugar refinery.

ingeniosamente ADV **(a)** ingeniously, cleverly. **(b)** wittily.

ingeniosidad NF **(a)** (*maña*) ingenuity, ingeniousness, cleverness, resourcefulness. **(b)** (*una ~*) clever idea. **(c)** (*agudeza*) wittiness.

ingenioso ADJ **(a)** (*mañoso*) ingenious, clever, resourceful. **(b)** (*agudo*) witty.

ingénito ADJ innate, inborn.

ingente ADJ huge, enormous.

ingenuamente ADV ingenuously, naïvely; with candour; simply, unaffectedly.

ingenuidad NF ingenuousness, naïveté; candour; simplicity.

▼ **ingenuo** ADJ ingenuous, candid; simple, unaffected.

ingerido* ADJ (*Méx*) (*enfermo*) ill, under the weather; (*abatido*) downcast.

ingerir [3i] VT to swallow; to ingest, consume, take in; **el automovilista había ingerido 3 litros de alcohol** the motorist had drunk 3 litres of alcohol.

ingesta NF ingestion, intake.

ingestión NF swallowing; ingestion.

Inglaterra NF England; (*en sentido no estricto frec*) Great Britain, United Kingdom; **la batalla de ~** the Battle of Britain (*1940*).

ingle NF groin.

inglés [1] ADJ English; (*en sentido no estricto frec*) British.
[2] NM Englishman; Briton, Britisher (*US*); **los ingleses** the English, the British.
[3] NM (*Ling*) English.

inglesa NF Englishwoman; Briton, Britisher (*US*); **montar a la ~** to ride sidesaddle.

inglesismo NM anglicism.

inglete NM angle of 45°; (*ensambladura*) mitre joint.

ingobernabilidad NF uncontrollable nature; (*Pol*) ungovernable nature.

ingobernable ADJ uncontrollable, unmanageable; (*Pol*) ungovernable.

ingratitud NF ingratitude.

ingrato ADJ **(a)** *persona* ungrateful; **¡~!** you wretch! **(b)** *sabor* unpleasant, disagreeable; *tarea etc* thankless, unrewarding.

ingravidez NF weightlessness.

ingrávido ADJ weightless; very light.

ingrediente NM ingredient; **~s** (*Cono Sur*) hors d'oeuvres (*on the bar counter*).

ingresado, -a NM/F (*Univ etc*) entrant, new student.

ingresar [1a] [1] VT **(a)** *dinero* to deposit, pay in; *ganancias* to receive, take in; **~ dinero en una cuenta** to pay money into an account.
(b) **~ al hijo en un colegio** to get one's son into a school; **la cárcel donde X está ingresado** the prison in which X is being held.
(c) **~ a uno** (*Med*) to admit sb (as a patient); **X continúa ingresado en el hospital** X is still in hospital.
[2] VI to come in, enter; **~ en** (*LAm:* **a**) **una sociedad** to join a club, become a member of a club, be admitted to a society; **~ en la Academia** to be admitted to the Academy, be received into the Academy; **~ en el ejército** to join the army, join up; **~ en el hospital** to be admitted to hospital; **pero ingresó cadáver** but he was dead on arrival (at hospital).
[3] **ingresarse** VR (*Méx*) to join, become a member; (*Méx: Mil*) to join up.

ingreso NM **(a)** (*acto*) entry (*en* into), joining; admission (*en* to); **su ~ en la Academia** his admission to the Academy; **examen de ~** entrance examination.
(b) (*Com*) entry; deposit; sum received; **~ gravable** taxable income.
(c) **~s** (*Fin: renta*) income; revenue; receipts, takings; **~s accesorios** additional earnings, earnings on the side; fringe benefits; **~s anuales** annual income; **~s brutos** gross receipts; **~s devengados**

earned income; **~s ocasionales** casual earnings; **vivir con arreglo a los ~s** to live within one's income.

íngrimo ADJ (*LAm*) all alone.

inguandia NF (*And*) fib, tale.

inguinal ADJ inguinal, groin (*atr*).

INH NM ABR *de* **Instituto Nacional de Hidrocarburos.**

inhábil ADJ **(a)** (*torpe*) unskilful, inexpert, clumsy; (*incompetente*) incompetent. **(b)** (*no apto*) unfit (*para* for, *para + infin* to + *infin*). **(c)** **día ~** non-working day.

inhabilidad NF (*V ADJ*) **(a)** unskilfulness; clumsiness; incompetence. **(b)** unfitness (*para* for).

inhabilitación NF **(a)** (*Pol Jur*) disqualification; *V* **nota. (b)** (*Med*) disablement.

inhabilitar [1a] VT **(a)** (*Pol Jur*) to disqualify (*para + infin* from + *ger*); to bar (from office). **(b)** (*Med*) to disable; to render unfit (*para* for).

inhabitable ADJ uninhabitable.

inhabitado ADJ uninhabited.

inhabituado ADJ unaccustomed (*a* to).

inhabitual ADJ unusual, out of the ordinary, exceptional.

inhalación NF inhalation; **~ de colas** glue-sniffing.

inhalador NM (*Med*) inhaler.

inhalante NM inhalant.

inhalar [1a] VT to inhale; *colas* to sniff.

inherente ADJ inherent (*a* in); **la función ~ a un oficio** the function pertaining to a post, the duties attached to an office.

inhibición NF inhibition.

inhibidor [1] ADJ inhibiting.
[2] NM inhibitor; **~ del apetito** appetite depressant; **~ del crecimiento** growth inhibitor.

inhibir [3a] [1] VT to inhibit; (*Jur*) to restrain, stay.
[2] **inhibirse** VR to keep out (*de* of), to stay away (*de* from); to refrain (*de* from).

inhibitorio ADJ inhibitory.

inhospitalario ADJ inhospitable; (*fig*) bleak, cheerless, uninviting.

inhospitalidad NF inhospitality.

inhóspito ADJ inhospitable.

inhumación NF burial, inhumation.

inhumanamente ADV inhumanly.

inhumanidad NF inhumanity.

inhumano ADJ inhuman; (*Cono Sur*) dirty, disgusting.

inhumar [1a] VT to bury, inter.

INI ['ini] NM **(a)** (*Esp Com*) ABR *de* **Instituto Nacional de Industria. (b)** (*Chile*) ABR *de* **Instituto Nacional de Investigaciones.**

INIA NM **(a)** (*Esp Agr*) ABR *de* **Instituto Nacional de Investigación Agraria. (b)** (*Méx*) ABR *de* **Instituto Nacional de Investigaciones Agrícolas.**

iniciación NF initiation; beginning.

iniciado [1] ADJ initiate(d).
[2] NM, **iniciada** NF initiate.

iniciador(a) [1] NM/F initiator, starter; pioneer.
[2] NM (*de bomba*) primer, priming device.

inicial [1] ADJ initial.
[2] NF **(a)** initial. **(b)** (*Carib*) deposit, down payment.

inicializar [1f] VT to initialize.

iniciar [1b] VT **(a)** to initiate (*en* into); **~ a uno en un secreto** to let sb into a secret. **(b)** (*comenzar*) to begin, start, initiate; (*originar*) to originate, set on foot; (*fundar*) to pioneer; **~ la sesión** (*Inform*) to log in (*o* on).

iniciático ADJ **(a)** initial. **(b)** **ritos ~s** initiation rites.

iniciativa NF initiative, enterprise; (*liderazgo*) lead, leadership; **~s** initiatives; (*propósitos*) plans, intentions; **~ de paz** peace initiative; **~ privada** private enterprise; **bajo su ~** on his initiative; **por ~ propia** on one's own initiative; **carecer de ~** to lack initiative; **tomar la ~** to take the initiative.

inicio NM start, beginning.

inicuamente ADV wickedly, iniquitously.

inicuo ADJ wicked, iniquitous.

indentificable ADJ unidentifiable.

inidentificado ADJ unidentified.

inigualable ADJ unsurpassable.

inigualado ADJ unequalled.

inimaginable ADJ unimaginable, inconceivable, incredible.

inimitable ADJ inimitable.

ininflamable ADJ non-flammable, fire-resistant.

ininteligente ADJ unintelligent.

ininteligibilidad NF unintelligibility.

ininteligible ADJ unintelligible.

ininterrumpidamente ADV uninterruptedly; continuously, without a break; steadily.

ininterrumpido ADJ uninterrupted; continuous, without a break; steady; prolonged, sustained.

iniquidad NF wickedness, iniquity; injustice.

in itinere ADV: **siniestros ~** accidents which happen on one's way to or from work.
injerencia NF interference, meddling (*en* in).
injerir [3i] **1** VT to insert, introduce (*en* into); (*Agr*) to graft (*en* on, on to).
　2 injerirse VR to interfere, meddle (*en* in).
injertar [1a] VT (*Agr, Med*) to graft (*en* on, on to); (*fig*) to graft.
injerto NM **(a)** (*acto*) grafting. **(b)** (*Agr, Med*) graft; **~ de piel** skin graft.
injuria NF **(a)** (*insulto*) insult, offence, affront (*para* to); (*injusticia*) outrage, injustice; **~s** insults, abuse; **llenar a uno de ~s** to heap abuse on sb. **(b)** (*liter*) damage; **las ~s del tiempo††** the ravages of time.
injuriar [1b] VT **(a)** (*gen*) to insult, abuse, revile; to wrong. **(b)** (*liter: dañar*) to injure, damage, harm.
injuriosamente ADV (*V* ADJ) **(a)** insultingly, offensively; outrageously. **(b)** harmfully.
injurioso ADJ **(a)** (*ofensivo*) insulting, offensive; outrageous. **(b)** (*dañoso*) harmful, damaging.
injustamente ADV unjustly, unfairly; wrongfully.
injusticia NF injustice; unfairness; **una gran ~** a terrible injustice; **con ~** unjustly.
injustificable ADJ unjustifiable.
injustificadamente ADV unjustifiably.
injustificado ADJ unjustified, unwarranted.
injusto ADJ unjust, unfair; wrong, wrongful; **ser ~ con uno** to be unjust to sb.
INLE ['inle] NM ABR *de* **Instituto Nacional del Libro Español.**
inllevable ADJ unbearable, intolerable.
inmaculado ADJ immaculate.
inmadurez NF immaturity.
inmaduro ADJ *individuo* immature; *fruta* unripe.
inmancable ADJ (*And, Carib*) unfailing, infallible.
inmanejable ADJ unmanageable.
inmanencia NF immanence.
inmanente ADJ immanent; inherent (*a* in).
inmarcesible ADJ, **inmarchitable** ADJ imperishable, undying, unfading.
inmaterial ADJ immaterial.
INME ['inme] NM ABR *de* **Instituto Nacional de Moneda Extranjera.**
inmediaciones NFPL neighbourhood, surroundings, environs; immediate area; **en las ~ de** in the neighbourhood of.
inmediata* NF: **la ~** the natural thing, the first thing.
inmediatamente **1** ADV immediately, at once.
　2 PREP: **~ de recibido** on being received.
inmediatez NF immediacy.
inmediato ADJ **(a)** (*tiempo*) immediate; prompt; **de ~** immediately, promptly; **en lo ~** in the near future. **(b)** (*lugar*) immediate, next; adjoining; **~ a** close to, next to.
inmejorable ADJ unsurpassable; that cannot be bettered; **~s recomendaciones** excellent references; **precios ~s** unbeatable prices; **de calidad ~** of the very best quality.
inmejorablemente ADV in a way that could not be bettered; **portarse ~** to behave perfectly.
inmemorable ADJ, **inmemorial** ADJ immemorial.
inmensamente ADV immensely, vastly.
inmensidad NF immensity, hugeness, vastness.
inmenso ADJ immense, huge, vast; **sentir una tristeza inmensa** to be terribly sad.
inmensurable ADJ immeasurable.
inmerecidamente ADV undeservedly.
inmerecido ADJ, **inmérito** ADJ undeserved; uncalled-for.
inmergir [3c] VT to immerse.
inmersión NF immersion; (*de buzo etc*) dive, plunge; (*pesca submarina*) skin-diving, underwater fishing.
inmerso ADJ immersed (*en* in); **~ en sus meditaciones** deep in thought.
inmigración NF immigration.
inmigrado, -a NM/F immigrant.
inmigrante ADJ, NMF immigrant.
inmigrar [1a] VI to immigrate.
inminencia NF imminence.
inminente ADJ imminent, impending.
inmiscuirse [3g] VR to interfere, meddle (*en* in).
inmisericorde ADJ insensitive, hard-hearted, pitiless.
inmisericordioso ADJ merciless.
inmobiliaria¹ NF construction company, builder(s); property company.
inmobiliario **1** ADJ real-estate (*atr*), property (*atr*); **venta inmobiliaria** property sale.
　2 NM, **inmobiliaria²** NF property developer.
inmoble ADJ **(a)** (*inmóvil*) immovable; motionless. **(b)** (*fig*) unmoved, unshaken.
inmoderación NF (*Cono Sur*) excess.

inmoderadamente ADV immoderately, excessively.
inmoderado ADJ immoderate, excessive.
inmodestamente ADV immodestly.
inmodestia NF immodesty.
inmodesto ADJ immodest.
inmodificable ADJ that cannot be modified.
inmolación NF sacrifice.
inmolar [1a] VT to immolate.
inmoral ADJ immoral; unethical.
inmoralidad NF immorality; unethical nature.
inmortal ADJ, NMF immortal.
inmortalidad NF immortality.
inmortalizar [1f] VT to immortalize.
inmotivación NF lack of motivation.
inmotivado ADJ motiveless, unmotivated, without motive.
inmoto ADJ unmoved.
inmovible ADJ immovable.
inmóvil ADJ **(a)** (*inamovible*) immovable; immobile; (*sin mover*) motionless, still; **quedar ~** to remain (*o* be, stand *etc*) motionless; (*vehículo etc*) to remain stationary. **(b)** (*fig*) steadfast, unshaken.
inmovilidad NF immovability; immobility; stillness.
inmovilismo NM (*fig*) stagnation; resistance to change; do-nothing policy; idleness, lack of activity; (*Pol*) ultraconservatism.
inmovilista ADJ stagnant; resistant to change; idle, inactive; (*Pol*) ultraconservative; *see also* APERTURISMO .
inmovilización NF immobilization; stopping, paralysing; **~ de coches** (*Méx*) traffic-jam.
inmovilizado NM capital assets, fixed assets.
inmovilizar [1f] VT to immobilize; to stop, paralyse, bring to a standstill; (*Fin*) *capital* to tie up, lock up.
inmueble **1** ADJ: **bienes ~s** real estate, landed property.
　2 NM property; building; **~s** real estate, landed property.
inmundicia NF filth, dirt; nastiness; **~s** filth, rubbish; **esto es una ~** this is absolutely disgraceful.
inmundo ADJ filthy, dirty; foul, nasty.
inmune ADJ **(a)** (*Med*) immune (*contra* against, to). **(b)** (*fig*) exempt, free (*de* from).
inmunidad NF **(a)** (*gen, Med*) immunity; **~ diplomática** diplomatic immunity; **~ parlamentaria** parliamentary immunity. **(b)** (*fisco*) exemption.
inmunitario ADJ: **sistema ~** immune system.
inmunización NF immunization.
inmunizar [1f] VT to immunize.
inmunodefensivo ADJ: **sistema ~** immune defence system.
inmunodeficiencia NF immunodeficiency.
inmunodeprimido ADJ immunodeficient.
inmunología NF immunology.
inmunológico ADJ immune (*atr*); **sistema ~** immune system.
inmunólogo, -a NM/F immunologist.
inmunorrespuesta NF immune response.
inmunosupresivo ADJ immunosuppressive.
inmunosupresor **1** ADJ immunosuppressive.
　2 NM immunosuppressant.
inmunoterapia NF immunotherapy.
inmutabilidad NF immutability.
inmutable ADJ immutable, changeless.
inmutarse [1a] VR to change countenance, turn pale, lose one's self-possession; **se inmutó** his face fell, he seemed disappointed; **no ~** to keep a stiff upper lip, not turn a hair; **siguió sin ~** he carried on unperturbed, he showed no sign of what he was feeling.
innato ADJ innate, inborn; inbred.
innatural ADJ unnatural.
innavegable ADJ *río etc* unnavigable; *barco* unseaworthy.
innecesariamente ADV unnecessarily.
innecesario ADJ unnecessary.
▼ **innegable** ADJ undeniable.
innegociable ADJ non-negotiable.
innoble ADJ ignoble.
innocuo ADJ innocuous, harmless.
innombrable ADJ unmentionable.
innominado ADJ nameless, unnamed.
innovación NF (*acto*) innovation; (*novedad*) innovation, novelty, new thing.
innovador **1** ADJ innovative, innovatory.
　2 NM, **innovadora** NF innovator.
innovar [1a] **1** VT to introduce.
　2 VI to innovate, introduce something new.
innovativo ADJ innovative, innovatory.
innumerable ADJ, **innúmero** ADJ innumerable, countless.
inobediencia NF disobedience.
inobediente ADJ disobedient.
inobjetable ADJ unobjectionable; (*inatacable*) unassailable, unim-

peachable; impeccable.

inobservado ADJ unobserved.

inobservancia NF non-observance (*de* of); disregard (*de* for); neglect; (*de ley*) violation, breaking (*de* of).

inocencia NF innocence.

Inocencio NM (*papa*) Innocent.

inocentada NF (**a**) (*dicho*) naïve remark, simple-minded thing; (*error*) blunder. (**b**) (*trastada*) practical joke, April Fool joke; hoax; *see also* DÍA DE LOS (SANTOS) INOCENTES .

inocente¹ ① ADJ (**a**) (*sin culpa*) innocent (*de* of); (*sin malicia*) harmless.

(**b**) (*ingenuo*) simple, naïve.

② NMF (**a**) (*gen*) innocent, innocent person.

(**b**) (*bobo*) simple soul, naïve person.

DÍA DE LOS (SANTOS) INOCENTES
---

28 December, **el día de los (Santos) Inocentes,** *is when the Catholic Church in Spain commemorates the New Testament story of King Herod's slaughter of the innocent children of Judaea. Like our April Fools' Day, Spaniards play practical jokes or* **inocentadas** *on each other. A typical example is sticking a* **monigote,** *a cut-out paper figure, on someone's back. Whenever someone falls for a trick, the practical joker cries out* **"Inocente!"**

inocente² NM (**a**) (*And, Cono Sur*) avocado pear. (**b**) (*And*) masquerade.

inocentemente ADV innocently.

inocentón ① ADJ simple, naïve, gullible.

② NM, **inocentona** NF simple soul, naïve person.

inocuidad NF innocuousness, harmlessness.

inoculación NF inoculation.

inocular [1a] VT (**a**) (*Med*) to inoculate (*contra* against, *de* with). (**b**) (*fig*) to corrupt, contaminate (*de* with).

inocuo ADJ = **innocuo.**

inodoro ① ADJ odourless, having no smell.

② NM lavatory, toilet; **~ químico** chemical closet.

inofensivo ADJ inoffensive, harmless.

inoficioso* ADJ (*LAm*) useless.

inolvidable ADJ unforgettable.

inolvidablemente ADV unforgettably.

inope ADJ impecunious, indigent.

inoperable ADJ (*CAm, Cono Sur, Méx Med*) inoperable.

inoperancia NF (*V ADJ*) (**a**) inoperative character; unworkable nature; ineffectiveness, impotence. (**b**) (*LAm*) uselessness, fruitlessness.

inoperante ADJ (**a**) *plan* inoperative; unworkable; ineffective, impotent. (**b**) (*LAm*) (*inútil*) useless, fruitless, unproductive; (*inactivo*) inactive, out of use.

inopia NF indigence, poverty; **estar en la ~** (*fig: no saber*) to be in the dark, have no idea; (*estar despistado*) to be dreaming, be far away.

inopinadamente ADV unexpectedly.

inopinado ADJ unexpected.

inoportunamente ADV (*V ADJ*) (**a**) inopportunely, at the wrong time. (**b**) inconveniently; inappropriately.

inoportunidad NF (*V ADJ*) (**a**) inopportuneness, untimeliness. (**b**) inconvenience; inexpediency; inappropriateness.

inoportuno ADJ (**a**) (*intempestivo*) inopportune, untimely, ill-timed. (**b**) (*molesto*) inconvenient; (*imprudente*) inexpedient; (*no apto*) inappropriate.

inorgánico ADJ inorganic.

inoxidable ADJ rustless, rustproof; *acero* stainless.

inquebrantable ADJ (**a**) unbreakable. (**b**) (*fig*) unshakeable, unyielding, unswerving.

inquietador ADJ = **inquietante.**

inquietamente ADV (**a**) (*con ansiedad*) anxiously, uneasily. (**b**) (*agitadamente*) restlessly.

inquietante ADJ worrying, disturbing.

inquietar [1a] ① VT to worry, disturb, trouble, upset; to torment.

② **inquietarse** VR to worry, get worried, upset o.s.; **¡no te inquietes!** don't worry!

inquieto ADJ (**a**) (*preocupado*) anxious, worried, uneasy; **estar ~ por** to be anxious about, be worried about. (**b**) (*agitado*) restless, unsettled.

inquietud NF (*V ADJ*) (**a**) anxiety, worry, uneasiness, disquiet. (**b**) restlessness.

inquilinaje NM (**a**) (*Cono Sur*) = **inquilinato.** (**b**) (*Méx*) tenants.

inquilinato NM (**a**) (*gen*) tenancy; (*Jur*) lease, leasehold. (**b**) (*alquiler*) rent; (**impuesto de**) **~** rates. (**c**) (*Cono Sur*) tenement house, slum.

inquilino, -a NM/F (*arrendatario*) tenant; lessee; (*Cono Sur Agr*) tenant farmer.

inquina NF dislike, aversion; ill will, spite; **tener ~ a uno** to have a grudge against sb, have one's knife in sb.

inquiridor ① ADJ inquiring.

② NM, **inquiridora** NF inquirer; investigator.

inquiriente NMF inquirer.

inquirir [3i] ① VT to enquire into, investigate, look into.

② VT to inquire.

inquisición NF inquiry, investigation; **la I~** the Inquisition.

inquisidor NM inquisitor.

inquisitivo ADJ inquisitive, curious; *mirada* prying.

inquisitorial ADJ inquisitorial.

inrayable ADJ scratch-proof.

inri NM shame; (mental) suffering; **para más** (o **mayor**) **~** to make matters worse; to drive the point home; **hacer el ~** to do something ridiculous, make oneself look silly.

insaciable ADJ insatiable.

insaciablemente ADV insatiably.

insalubre ADJ unhealthy, insalubrious; insanitary.

insalubridad NF unhealthiness.

INSALUD, Insalud ['insa'luð] NM (*Esp*) ABR *de* **Instituto Nacional de la Salud.**

insalvable ADJ *obstáculo* insuperable.

insanable ADJ incurable.

insania NF insanity.

insano ADJ (**a**) (*loco*) insane, mad. (**b**) (*malsano*) unhealthy.

insatisfacción NF dissatisfaction.

insatisfactorio ADJ unsatisfactory.

insatisfecho ADJ unsatisfied; dissatisfied.

insaturado ADJ unsaturated.

inscribir [3a; PTP **inscrito**] ① VT (*grabar*) to inscribe (*t Mat*); (*poner en lista*) to list, enter (on a list); (*matricular*) to enrol; (*registrar*) to register, record.

② **inscribirse** VR to enrol, register.

inscripción NF (**a**) (*acto*) inscription; enrolment; registering, recording. (**b**) (*texto*) inscription; lettering.

inscrito PTP *de* **inscribir.**

insecticida NM insecticide.

insectívoro ADJ insectivorous.

insecto NM insect.

inseguridad NF unsafeness; insecurity; unsteadiness; uncertainty; **~ ciudadana** lack of safety in the streets, decline in law and order.

inseguro ADJ (*peligroso*) unsafe; insecure; *paso etc* unsteady; (*incierto*) uncertain.

inseminación NF insemination; **~ artificial** artificial insemination.

inseminar [1a] VT to inseminate, fertilize.

insensatez NF folly, foolishness, stupidity.

insensato ADJ senseless, foolish, stupid.

insensibilidad NF (**a**) (*gen*) insensitivity; lack of feeling; (*indiferencia*) callousness. (**b**) (*Med*) insensibility, unconsciousness; numbness.

insensibilizar [1f] VT to render insensitive, make callous; (*Téc*) to desensitize.

insensible ADJ (**a**) *persona* insensitive (*a* to); unfeeling; callous. (**b**) (*imperceptible*) imperceptible. (**c**) (*Med*) insensible, unconscious; *miembro* numb, without feeling.

insensiblemente ADV (*V ADJ*) (**a**) insensitively; unfeelingly. (**b**) imperceptibly.

inseparable ADJ inseparable.

inseparablemente ADV inseparably.

insepulto ADJ unburied; without burial.

inserción NF insertion.

INSERSO, Inserso ['in'serso] NM (*Esp*) ABR *de* **Instituto Nacional de Servicios Sociales.**

insertable ADJ plug-in.

insertar [1a] VT to insert.

inserto ① ADJ: **problemas en los que está ~ el gobierno** problems with which the government finds itself involved.

② NM insert.

inservible ADJ useless; unusable.

insidia NF (**a**) (*trampa*) snare, trap. (**b**) (*acto*) malicious act. (**c**) (*cualidad*) maliciousness.

insidiosamente ADV insidiously; treacherously.

insidioso ADJ insidious; treacherous.

insigne ADJ distinguished; notable, famous.

insignia NF (**a**) (*señal*) badge, device, emblem; decoration. (**b**) (*bandera*) flag, banner; (*Náut*) pennant. (**c**) **~s** insignia.

insignificancia NF insignificance, trifle.

insignificante ADJ insignificant; trivial, tiny, petty.

insinceridad NF insincerity.

insincero ADJ insincere.

insinuación NF insinuation.

insinuador ADJ insinuating.

insinuante ADJ (**a**) (*que insinúa*) insinuating; (*atrevido*) forward, suggestive. (**b**) (*zalamero*) ingratiating. (**c**) (*taimado*) cunning, crafty.

insinuar [1e] ① VT (**a**) to insinuate, hint at, imply; **~ que ...** to hint that ..., imply that ...

(**b**) **~ una observación** to slip in a comment.

② **insinuarse** VR (**a**) **~ con uno** to ingratiate o.s. with sb.

(**b**) **~ en** to worm one's way into, creep into, slip into; **~ en el**

ánimo de uno to work one's way gradually into sb's mind. **(c)** (*atreverse*) to drop (suggestive) hints, make (suggestive) advances; **~ a una mujer** to make advances to a woman.

insipidez NF insipidness, tastelessness; (*fig*) dullness, flatness.

insípido ADJ insipid, tasteless; (*fig*) dull, flat, tedious.

insistencia NF insistence (*en* on); persistence; **a ~ de** at the insistence of; **con ~ machacona** with wearisome insistence.

insistente ADJ insistent; persistent.

insistentemente ADV insistently; persistently.

▼ **insistir** [3a] VI to insist; to persist; **~ en algo** to insist on sth; to stress sth, emphasize sth; **~ en una idea** to press an idea; **~ en hacer algo** to insist on doing sth; **~ en que se haga algo** to insist that sth should be done; **~ en que algo es así** to insist that sth is so.

in situ ADV in situ; on the spot.

insobornable ADJ incorruptible.

insociabilidad NF unsociability.

insociable ADJ unsociable.

insolación NF **(a)** (*Met*) sunshine; **horas de ~** hours of sunshine; **la ~ media diaria es de ...** the daily sunshine average is ... **(b)** (*pey*) exposure (to the sun); (*Med*) sunstroke; **darse** (o **coger**) **una ~** to get sunstroke.

insolar [1a] ① VT to expose to the sun, put in the sun. ② **insolarse** VR (*Med*) to get sunstroke.

insoldable ADJ (*Esp: fig*) irremediable; unmendable.

insolencia NF **(a)** (*descaro*) insolence, effrontery. **(b)** (*acto*) piece of rudeness, rude thing.

insolentarse [1a] VR to be insolent (*con* to), become insolent.

insolente ADJ **(a)** (*descarado*) insolent, rude; unblushing. **(b)** (*altivo*) haughty, contemptuous.

insolentemente ADV (*V* ADJ) **(a)** insolently, rudely; unblushingly. **(b)** haughtily, contemptuously.

insolidaridad NF lack of solidarity; lack of brotherly feelings.

insolidario ADJ unsupportive, uncooperative; self-interested; **hacerse ~ de** to dissociate o.s. from, declare o.s. out of sympathy with.

insolidarizarse [1f] VR: **~ con** to dissociate oneself from.

insólitamente ADV unusually, unwontedly.

insólito ADJ unusual, unwonted.

insolubilidad NF insolubility.

insoluble ADJ insoluble.

insolvencia NF insolvency, bankruptcy.

insolvente ADJ insolvent, bankrupt.

insomne ① ADJ sleepless. ② NMF insomniac.

insomnio NM sleeplessness, insomnia.

insondable ADJ bottomless; (*fig*) unfathomable, impenetrable, inscrutable.

insonorización NF soundproofing.

insonorizado ADJ soundproof; **estar ~** to be soundproofed.

insonorizar [1f] VT to soundproof.

insonoro ADJ noiseless, soundless.

insoportable ADJ unbearable, intolerable.

insoportablemente ADV unbearably, intolerably.

insoria NF (*Carib*) insignificant thing; **una ~** a minimal amount.

insoslayable ADJ *problema etc* unavoidable, which cannot be got round.

insoslayablemente ADV unavoidably.

insospechable ADJ beyond suspicion.

insospechado ADJ unsuspected.

▼ **insostenible** ADJ untenable.

inspección NF inspection, examination; check; survey; **~ ocular** visual examination; **~ técnica de vehículos** ≃ MOT test.

inspeccionar [1a] VT (*examinar*) to inspect, examine; (*controlar*) to check; to survey; (*supervisar*) to supervise.

inspector(a) NM/F inspector; superintendent, supervisor; (*Cono Sur: de bus*) conductor; **~ de aduanas** customs officer; **~ de enseñanza** school inspector; **~ de Hacienda** tax inspector.

inspectorado NM inspectorate.

inspiración NF **(a)** (*gen*) inspiration. **(b)** (*Med*) inhalation.

inspirado ADJ inspired.

inspirador ① ADJ inspiring; inspirational. ② NM, **inspiradora** NF inspirer; creator, originator.

inspirar [1a] ① VT **(a)** (*gen*) to inspire; **~ algo a uno** to inspire sb with sth; to inspire sth in sb. **(b)** (*Med*) to inhale, breathe in. ② **inspirarse** VR: **~ en** to be inspired by, find inspiration in, draw inspiration from.

inspirativo ADJ inspiring; inspirational.

INSS NM (*Esp*) ABR de **Instituto Nacional de Seguridad Social**.

Inst., Instº ABR de **Instituto**.

instable ADJ = **inestable**.

instalación NF **(a)** (*acto*) installation, instalment. **(b)** (*equipo*) installation; fittings, equipment; (*Téc*) plant; **~ de fuerza** power plant;

instalaciones deportivas sports facilities; **instalaciones portuarias** harbour installations; **instalaciones recreativas** recreational facilities; **~ sanitaria** sanitation, plumbing.

instalador NM installer; fitter; **~ eléctrico** electrician.

instalar [1a] ① VT to install; to set up, erect, fit up, lay on. ② **instalarse** VR to install o.s., establish o.s., settle (down).

instancia NF **(a)** (*solicitud*) request; application; (*Jur*) petition; **a ~(s) de** at the request of; **pedir algo con ~** to demand sth insistently, demand sth urgently. **(b)** (*formulario*) application form. **(c)** **en última ~** in the last analysis, **de prima ~** first of all. **(d)** (*Pol etc*) authority; agency; **~s del poder** (*fig*) corridors of power.

instantánea NF **(a)** (*Fot*) snap, snapshot. **(b)** (‡) tart‡, whore.

instantáneamente ADV instantaneously, instantly.

instantáneo ADJ instantaneous, instant; **café ~** instant coffee.

instante NM instant, moment; **al ~** instantly, at once; **(a) cada ~** every single moment, all the time; **en un ~** in a flash; **por ~s** incessantly, all the time; **hace un ~** a moment ago.

instantemente ADV insistently, urgently.

instar [1a] ① VT to urge, press; **~ a uno a hacer algo, ~ a uno para que haga algo** to urge sb to do sth. ② VI to be urgent, be pressing.

instauración NF (*V v*) **(a)** restoration, renewal. **(b)** establishment, setting-up.

instaurar [1a] VT **(a)** (*renovar*) to restore, renew. **(b)** (*fundar*) to establish, set up (again).

instigación NF instigation; **a ~ de** at the instigation of.

instigador(a) NM/F instigator; **~ de un delito** instigator of a crime, (*Jur*) accessory before the fact.

instigar [1h] VT to instigate; to abet; **~ a uno a hacer algo** to incite sb to do sth, urge sb to do sth, induce sb to do sth.

instilar [1a] VT to instil (*a, en* into).

instintivamente ADV instinctively.

instintivo ADJ instinctive.

instinto NM instinct; impulse, urge; **~ asesino, ~ de matar** killer instinct; **~ sexual** sexual urge, sexual desire; **~ de supervivencia** instinct for survival, survival instinct; **por ~** by instinct, instinctively.

institución NF **(a)** (*acto*) institution, establishment. **(b)** (*organismo*) institution; establishment; **~ benéfica, ~ de beneficencia** charitable organization, charitable foundation; **~ pública** public institution, public body. **(c)** **instituciones** (*bases*) principles.

institucional ADJ institutional.

institucionalizado ADJ institutionalized.

institucionalizar [1f] ① VT to institutionalize. ② **institucionalizarse** VR to become institutionalized.

instituir [3g] VT to institute, establish; to found, set up.

instituto NM **(a)** (*gen*) institute, institution; **los ~s armados** the army, the military; **~ de belleza** (*Esp*) beauty parlour; **el benemérito ~** the Civil Guard; **~ financiero** financial institution. **(b)** (*Esp Educ: t ~ nacional de bachillerato*) secondary school, high school (*US*). **(c)** (*regla*) principle, rule; (*Ecl*) rule.

institutriz NF governess.

instrucción NF **(a)** (*gen*) instruction; education, teaching; (*Mil etc*) training, drill; (*Dep*) coaching, training; **~ primaria** primary education; **~ programada** programmed teaching; **~ pública** state education. **(b)** (*conocimientos*) knowledge, learning, instruction; **tener poca ~ en** to have little knowledge of, know little about. **(c)** (*Jur*) (institution of) proceedings. **(d)** (*Inform*) statement; instruction, command. **(e)** **instrucciones** (*órdenes*) instructions, orders, direction; **de acuerdo con sus instrucciones** in accordance with your instructions; **instrucciones para el uso** directions for use; **instrucciones de funcionamiento** operating instructions.

instructivo ADJ instructive; illuminating, enlightening; *película etc* educational.

instructor(a) NM/F **(a)** instructor, teacher; (*Dep*) coach, trainer; **~ de vuelo** flight instructor. **(b)** **~ de diligencias** (*Jur*) judge appointed to look into a case.

instruido ADJ well-educated; well-informed.

instruir [3g] ① VT **(a)** to instruct, teach (*de, en, sobre* in, about); to educate; (*Mil etc*) to train, drill; (*Dep*) to coach, train. **(b)** (*Jur*) *proceso* to prepare, draw up; to investigate. ② **instruirse** VR to learn, teach o.s. (*de, en, sobre* about).

instrumentación NF orchestration, scoring.

instrumental ① ADJ instrumental. ② NM instruments, set of instruments.

instrumentalista NMF instrumentalist.

instrumentalización NF exploitation.

instrumentalizar [1f] VT **(a)** (*llevar a cabo*) to carry out. **(b)** **~ a uno** to use sb as a tool, make cynical use of sb; to exploit sb, manipulate sb.

instrumentar [1a] VT **(a)** (*Mús*) to score, orchestrate; **está instru-**

► LENGUA Y USO: **insistir** → 35.4   **insostenible** → 53.3

mentado para ... it is scored for ... **(b)** (*fig*) *campaña* to orchestrate. **(c)** (*fig: manipular*) to manipulate.

instrumentista NMF **(a)** (*Mús*) instrumentalist; (*fabricante*) instrument maker; **~ de cuerda** string player. **(b)** (*Med*) theatre nurse. **(c)** (*Mec*) machinist.

instrumento NM **(a)** (*gen*) instrument; (*herramienta*) tool, implement; (✵) tool✲; **~ auditivo** listening device; **~s científicos** scientific instruments; **~s de mando** (*Aer etc*) controls; **~ de precisión** precision instrument; **~s quirúrgicos** surgical instruments; **~s topográficos** surveying instruments; **volar por ~s** to fly on instruments.
(b) (*Mús*) instrument; **~ de batería**, **~ de percusión** percussion instrument; **~ de cuerda** stringed instrument; **~ musical**, **~ músico** musical instrument; **~ de tecla** keyboard instrument; **~ de viento** wind instrument.
(c) (*fig*) instrument, tool; **fue solamente el ~ del dictador** he was merely the dictator's tool, he was just a tool in the dictator's hands.
(d) (*Jur*) deed, legal document, instrument; **~ de venta** bill of sale.

insubordinación NF insubordination; turbulence, unruliness.

insubordinado ADJ insubordinate; turbulent, rebellious, unruly.

insubordinar [1a] **1** VT to stir up, rouse to rebellion.
2 insubordinarse VR to become unruly; to rebel.

insubsanable ADJ *problema* insoluble.

insubstituible ADJ = **insustituible**.

insudar [1a] VI (*liter*) to toil away.

insuficiencia NF **(a)** insufficiency, inadequacy; lack, shortage; **~ de franqueo** underpaid postage; **debido a la ~ de personal** through shortage of staff.
(b) incompetence.
(c) (*Med*) **~ cardíaca** heart failure, **~ renal** kidney failure.

insuficiente ADJ **(a)** (*inadecuado*) insufficient, inadequate. **(b)** *persona* incompetent.

insuficientemente ADV insufficiently, inadequately.

insuflar [1a] VT to breathe into, introduce by blowing.

insufrible ADJ unbearable, insufferable.

insufriblemente ADV unbearably, insufferably.

insular ADJ insular.

insularidad NF insularity.

insulina NF insulin.

insulsez NF **(a)** (*insipidez*) tastelessness, insipidity. **(b)** (*fig*) flatness, dullness.

insulso ADJ **(a)** (*insípido*) tasteless, insipid. **(b)** (*fig*) flat, dull.

insultante ADJ insulting; abusive.

insultar [1a] VT to insult.

insulto NM **(a)** (*ofensa*) insult (*para* to). **(b)** (*Méx*✲: *indigestión*) belly-ache, stomach-ache.

insumergible ADJ unsinkable.

insumisión NF rebelliousness; (*esp*) refusal to do military service.

insumiso **1** ADJ unsubmissive, rebellious.
2 NM (*esp*) man who refuses to do military service.

┌─── **INSUMISO** ───
│ ⓘ *In Spain most men are required to do national service. If they object on conscientious grounds, they are legally entitled to opt to do the longer community-based alternative,* **Prestación Social Sustitutoria (PSS)**. *Those who refuse to do either form of service are called* **insumisos**. *Many* **insumisos** *argue that the discrimination against men inherent in the system is unconstitutional and the exploitation, as they see it, of unpaid labour is unlawful. Penalties for* **insumisión** *(refusal to do either form of service) can be severe, and may include prison sentences.*
│ ⇨ *See also* MILI , PRESTACIÓN SOCIAL SUSTITUTORIA
└───

insumo NM **(a)** (*LAm*) consumption. **(b)** (*Cono Sur*) ingredient, component. **(c)** **~s** (*Econ*) input, materials.

insuperable ADJ insuperable, unsurmountable; *calidad* unsurpassable.

insuperado ADJ unsurpassed.

insurgencia NF **(a)** (*acto*) rebellion, uprising. **(b)** (*fuerzas*) insurgent forces.

insurgente ADJ, NMF insurgent.

insurrección NF revolt, insurrection.

insurreccional ADJ insurrectional.

insurreccionar [1a] **1** VT to rouse to revolt, incite to rebel.
2 insurreccionarse VR to rebel, rise in revolt.

insurrecto, -a ADJ, NM/F rebel, insurgent.

insustancial ADJ unsubstantial.

insustituible ADJ irreplaceable.

INTA NM **(a)** (*Esp Aer*) ABR *de* **Instituto Nacional de Técnica Aeroespacial**. **(b)** (*Argentina Agr*) ABR *de* **Instituto Nacional de Tecnología Agropecuaria**. **(c)** (*Guatemala*) ABR *de* **Instituto Nacional de Transformación Agraria**.

intachable ADJ irreproachable; faultless, perfect.

intacto ADJ untouched; whole, intact, undamaged; pure.

intangible ADJ intangible, impalpable.

integérrimo ADJ *superl de* **íntegro**.

integración NF integration; **~ a muy gran escala** very large-scale integration; **~ racial** racial integration.

integrado ADJ **(a)** (*entero*) integrated; in one piece, all of a piece; *sociedad* integrated. **(b)** **un grupo ~ por** a group made up of, a group consisting of.

integrador ADJ: **política ~a** policy of integration, integrationist policy; **proceso ~** process of integration.

integral **1** ADJ **(a)** integral; (*Mec etc*) built-in; (*Mat*) integral; *cereal* wholegrain; *pan* wholemeal. **(b)** (✲) total, complete; **un idiota ~** an utter fool.
2 NF (*Mat*) integral; integral sign.

íntegramente ADV **(a)** wholly, entirely, completely. **(b)** (*fig*) uprightly, with integrity.

integrante **1** ADJ integral; **una parte ~ de** an integral part of.
2 NMF member; **los ~s del conjunto** the members of the group.

integrar [1a] VT **(a)** (*formar*) to make up, compose, form; **y los que integran el otro grupo** and those who make up the other group. **(b)** (*Mat y fig*) to integrate. **(c)** (*Fin*) to repay, reimburse; (*And, Cono Sur, Méx*: *pagar*) to hand over, pay up.

integridad NF **(a)** (*entereza*) wholeness, completeness; **~ física** physical wellbeing; **en su ~** in its entirety. **(b)** (*fig: honradez*) uprightness, integrity. **(c)** (*Jur*) **delito contra la ~ de la persona** crime against the person; **peligró su ~ física** he was nearly hurt, he came close to suffering personal injury. **(d)** (*fig: virginidad*) virginity.

integrismo NM reaction; entrenched traditionalism; fundamentalism.

integrista **1** ADJ reactionary; traditionalist; fundamentalist.
2 NMF reactionary; traditionalist; fundamentalist.

íntegro ADJ **(a)** whole, entire, complete; integral; **la cantidad íntegra** the whole sum, the sum in full; **versión íntegra** (*Liter*) unabridged version; **en versión íntegra de Pérez** in Pérez's edition of the complete text.
(b) (*fig*) honest, upright.

integumento NM integument.

intelectiva NF intellect, mental faculty.

intelecto NM intellect; understanding; brains.

intelectual ADJ, NMF intellectual.

intelectuala✲ NF (*hum*) bluestocking.

intelectualidad NF **(a)** (*cualidad*) intellectuality; intellectual character. **(b)** (*personas*) intelligentsia, intellectual people, intellectuals.

intelectualmente ADV intellectually.

intelectualoide ADJ, NMF pseudo-intellectual.

inteligencia NF **(a)** (*intelecto etc*) intelligence; mind, wits, understanding; ability; (*Inform*) intelligence; **~ artificial** artificial intelligence; **~ máquina** machine intelligence; **de mediocre ~** of mediocre intelligence; **una persona de fina ~** a person with a sharp mind.
(b) (*comprensión*) understanding; **la buena ~ entre los pueblos** good understanding between peoples.
(c) (*Mil etc*) intelligence.
(d) (*pey*) secret agreement, collusion.
(e) (*personas*) intelligentsia.

inteligente ADJ **(a)** (*gen*) intelligent; (*listo*) clever, brainy, talented. **(b)** (*hábil*) skilful; (*experto*) skilled, trained (*en* in). **(c)** (*Inform*) intelligent; *misil* smart.

inteligentemente ADV intelligently.

inteligibilidad NF intelligibility.

inteligible ADJ intelligible.

inteligiblemente ADV intelligibly.

intemperancia NF intemperance, excess.

intemperante ADJ intemperate, excessive.

intemperie NF inclemency (of the weather); bad weather, rough weather; **estar a la ~** to be out in the open, be exposed to wind and weather, be at the mercy of the elements; **aguantar la ~** to put up with wind and weather; **una cara curtida a la ~** a face tanned by wind and weather.

intempestivamente ADV in an untimely way, at a bad time; unseasonably.

intempestivo ADJ untimely, ill-timed; unseasonable.

intemporal ADJ timeless.

▼ **intención** NF intention; purpose; plan; **mis intenciones** my intentions, my plans; **~ delictiva** criminal intent; **intenciones delictivas** criminal intentions; **segunda ~** duplicity, underhandedness; ulterior motive; **~ de voto** voting intention; **con ~** deliberately; **con (segunda)** meaningfully; with a second meaning, implying sth else; (*pey*) nastily; **dicho con ~** said deliberately, said provocatively; **con la ~ de** + *infin* with the idea of + *ger*, intending to + *infin*; **de ~** on purpose; **aceptar las intenciones de uno** to accept sb's advances, respond to sb's advances; **curar a uno de primera ~** to give sb first aid; **sin hacer la menor ~ de** + *infin* without making the least move to + *infin*; **tener la ~ de** + *infin* to intend to + *infin*, mean to + *infin*.

intencionadamente ADV (*V* ADJ) (**a**) meaningfully; nastily. (**b**) deliberately.

intencionado ADJ (**a**) (*significativo*) meaningful. (**b**) (*deliberado*) deliberate. (**c**) **bien ~** well-meaning; **mal ~** ill-disposed, hostile, unkind; malicious.

intencional ADJ intentional, deliberate.

intencionalidad NF (**a**) (*propósito*) purpose, intention; motivation; **la ~ del incendio** the fact that the fire was deliberately started. (**b**) **una pregunta cargada de ~** a loaded question, a question full of implications.

intencionalmente ADV intentionally.

intendencia NF (**a**) (*dirección*) management, administration. (**b**) (*oficina*) manager's office. (**c**) (*Mil: t* **cuerpo de ~**) ≃ service corps, quartermaster corps (*US*). (**d**) (*Cono Sur*) (*alcaldía*) mayoralty; (*cargo de gobernador*) governorship.

intendente NM (**a**) (*gerente*) manager. (**b**) **~ de ejército** quartermaster-general. (**c**) (*Cono Sur*) (*alcalde*) mayor; (*gobernador*) governor; (*Méx*) police inspector.

intensamente ADV intensely; powerfully, strongly; vividly, profoundly.

intensar [1a] **1** VT to intensify. **2 intensarse** VR to intensify.

intensidad NF intensity; power, strength; vividness; deepness; (*Elec, Téc*) strength.

intensificación NF intensification.

intensificar [1g] VT to intensify.

intensión NF intensity, intenseness.

intensivamente ADV intensively.

intensivo ADJ intensive.

intenso ADJ (*gen*) intense; *emoción, sentimiento* intense, powerful, strong; *impresión* vivid, profound; *bronceado* deep; *color* deep, intense; (*Elec etc*) strong.

intentar [1a] VT (**a**) (*probar*) to try, attempt; **~ algo** to have a go at sth, try sth; **~ + infin** to try to + *infin*, attempt to + *infin*, endeavour to + *infin*. (**b**) (*proponerse*) to mean, intend (*con* by); **~ + infin** to mean to + *infin*.

intento NM (**a**) (*propósito*) intention, intent, purpose; **al ~ de** + *infin* (*Cono Sur*) with the aim of + *ger*; **de ~** on purpose. (**b**) (*tentativa*) attempt; **~ fracasado** failed attempt, unsuccessful attempt; **~ de suicidio** attempted suicide; **acusado de ~ de violación** charged with attempted rape.

intentona NF foolhardy attempt, wild attempt; (*Pol*) putsch, rising.

inter... PREF inter...

ínter NM (*And, Cono Sur Rel*) curate.

interacción NF interaction, interplay.

interaccionar [1a] VI to interact (*con* with; *t Inform*).

interactivo ADJ interactive.

interactuación NF interaction.

interactuar [1e] VI to interact (*con* with; *t Inform*).

interamericano ADJ inter-American.

interandino ADJ inter-Andean, concerning areas on both sides of the Andes.

interanual ADJ: **promedio ~** year-on-year average; **variación ~** variation from year to year.

interbancario ADJ inter-bank (*atr*).

interbibliotecario ADJ inter-library (*atr*); **préstamo ~** inter-library loan.

intercalación NF intercalation, insertion; (*Inform*) merging.

intercalar [1a] VT to intercalate, insert; (*Inform*) to merge.

intercambiable ADJ interchangeable.

intercambiar [1b] VT to change over, interchange; *prisioneros, revistas etc* to exchange; *sellos etc* to exchange, swap.

intercambio NM interchange; exchange; swap, swapping.

interceder [2a] VI to intercede; **~ con A por B** to intercede with A on B's behalf, to plead with A for B.

intercentros ADJ INVAR: **comité ~** joint committee (*with representatives from all the different workplaces*).

interceptación NF interception; stoppage, holdup.

interceptar [1a] VT to intercept, cut off; *tráfico* to stop, hold up.

interceptor NM (**a**) interceptor. (**b**) (*Mec*) trap; separator.

intercesión NF intercession; mediation.

intercesor(a) NM/F interceder.

interclasista ADJ inter-class, which crosses class barriers; classless.

inter-club ADJ *partido* inter-club, between two clubs.

intercomunicación NF intercommunication.

intercomunicador NM intercom.

intercomunicar [1g] VT to link.

intercomunión NF intercommunion.

interconectar [1a] VT to interconnect.

interconectividad NF interconnectivity.

interconexión NF interconnection.

interconfesional ADJ interdenominational.

interconsonántico ADJ interconsonantal.

intercontinental ADJ intercontinental.

intercultural ADJ intercultural.

interdecir [3o] VT to forbid, prohibit.

interdepartamental ADJ interdepartmental.

interdependencia NF interdependence.

interdependiente ADJ interdependent.

interdicción NF prohibition, interdiction.

interdicto NM prohibition, ban, interdict.

interdisciplinariedad NF interdisciplinary nature.

interdisciplinar(io) ADJ interdisciplinary.

▼ **interés** NM (**a**) (*gen*) interest; concern; **con gran ~** with great interest; **de gran ~** of great interest, very interesting; **su ~ en, su ~ por** his interest in; his concern for; **poner ~ en** to take an interest in; **sentir ~ por** to be interested in, feel an interest in; **no tiene ~** it has no interest. (**b**) (*participación*) interest, share, part; **intereses** interests, affairs; **~ controlador** controlling interest; **los intereses españoles en África** Spanish interests in Africa; **intereses creados** vested interests; **en ~ de** in the interest of; **en ~ de la higiene** in the interest of hygiene, for the sake of cleanliness; **fomentar los intereses de uno** to promote sb's interests. (**c**) (*pey*) self-interest; selfishness, egotism; **todo es cuestión de ~** it's all a matter of self-interest. (**d**) (*Com, Fin*) interest; **con ~ de 9 por cien, con un ~ del 9 por cien** at an interest of 9%; **~ compuesto** compound interest; **~ devengado** accrued interest, earned interest; **~ simple** simple interest; **dar a ~** to lend at interest; **devengar intereses** to bear interest; **intereses por cobrar** interest receivable; **intereses por pagar** interest payable; **poner a ~** to put out at interest, invest.

interesadamente ADV (*V* ADJ) in a biassed way; selfishly.

interesado **1** ADJ (**a**) (*gen*) interested; concerned; **estar ~ en** to be interested in, have an interest in; **la compañía está interesada en comprarlo** the company is interested in buying it. (**b**) (*parcial*) biassed, prejudiced; **actuar de una manera interesada** to act in a biassed way. (**c**) (*egoísta*) selfish, self-seeking; having an ulterior motive; mercenary. **2** NM, **interesada** NF (**a**) person concerned, interested party; **los ~s** those interested, those concerned. (**b**) (*firmante*) the undersigned, the applicant.

▼ **interesante** ADJ (*de interés*) interesting; (*útil*) useful, convenient; (*provechoso*) profitable, valuable; *precio, sueldo etc* attractive; **hacerse el** (*o* **la**) **~** to try to attract attention.

interesar [1a] **1** VT (**a**) (*tener interés en*) to interest, be of interest to; to appeal to; **¿te interesa el fútbol?** are you interested in football?; **no me interesan los toros** I'm not interested in bullfighting, bullfighting does not appeal to me; **la propuesta no nos interesa** the proposal is of no interest to us. (**b**) (*captar el interés de*) to interest (*in* en); **logré ~le en mi idea** I succeeded in interesting him in my idea. (**c**) (*afectar*) to concern, involve; **el asunto interesa a todos** the matter concerns everybody; **a quien interese, a quien pueda ~** to whom it may concern. (**d**) (*Med*) to affect, involve; **la lesión interesa la región lumbar** the injury affects the lumbar region. (**e**) **el portador interesa 100 pesetas en ...** the bearer has a stake of 100 pesetas in ... (*lottery ticket*). **2** VI to be of interest; to be important; **la idea no interesó** the idea was of no interest, the idea did not interest anybody. **3 interesarse** VR to be interested, take an interest (*en, por* in); **~ en una empresa** to participate in an enterprise, concern o.s. with an enterprise; **~ por** to ask after, inquire about.

interestatal ADJ inter-state.

interestelar ADJ interstellar.

interétnico ADJ interracial.

interface NM (*a veces* F), **interfase** NF interface; **~ de serie** serial interface.

interfaz NF interface.

interfecto **1** ADJ killed, murdered. **2** NM, **interfecta** NF (**a**) murdered person, murder victim. (**b**) (*) person in question, punter*.

interferencia NF (**a**) (*Fís, Rad*) interference, (*con intención*) jamming; (*Inform*) glitch. (**b**) (*injerencia*) interference (*en* in); **no ~** non-interference.

interferir [3i] **1** VT (**a**) (*Fís, Rad*) to interfere with, (*con intención*) jam. (**b**) (*injerirse en*) to interfere with, upset, affect; **su acción ha interferido nuestras operaciones** his action has interfered with our operations.

► LENGUA Y USO: **interés** → 35.4   **interesante** → 53.6

2 VI to interfere (*en* in, with).

3 interferirse VR to interfere (*en* in, with); **no está en posición de ~ en el conflicto** he is in no position to interfere in the conflict.

interferón NM interferon.

interfijo NM infix.

interfono NM intercom, interphone.

intergeneracional ADJ between generations.

intergubernamental ADJ inter-governmental, between governments.

ínterin **1** ADV meanwhile.

2 CONJ while; until.

3 NM (PL **intérines**) (**a**) (*tiempo*) interim; **en el ~** in the interim, in the meantime. (**b**) (*en un puesto*) temporary incumbency.

interinamente ADV (**a**) (*entretanto*) in the interim, meanwhile. (**b**) (*temporalmente*) temporarily, as a temporary holder of the post (*etc*), as a stopgap.

interinar [1a] VT *puesto* to occupy temporarily, occupy in an acting capacity.

interinato NM (**a**) (*Cono Sur: temporaneidad*) temporary nature. (**b**) (*Cono Sur: período*) period of temporary occupation of a post. (**c**) (*CAm Med*) residence, internship (*US*).

interinidad NF temporary nature; provisional status; **una situación de ~** a temporary state.

interino **1** ADJ (**a**) provisional, temporary, interim; **informe ~** interim report, progress report. (**b**) *persona* acting.

2 NM, **interina** NF temporary holder of a post, acting official (*etc*); stopgap, stand-in; (*Ecl, Med*) locum, locum tenens.

3 NF (*criada*) non-resident maid.

interior **1** ADJ (*gen*) interior, inner, inside; *pensamiento etc* inward, inner; *comercio, política* domestic, internal; (*Geog*) inland, inner; **habitación ~** room without a view; **en la parte ~** inside, on the inside; **pista ~** (*Dep*) inside track; *V* **ropa** *etc*.

2 NM (**a**) (*gen*) interior, inside; (*parte*) inner part; (*Cine*) interior. (**b**) (*fig*) mind, soul; **en su ~** in one's heart, deep inside one; **dije para mi ~** I said to myself. (**c**) (*Geog*) interior; **Ministerio del I~** Ministry of the Interior, Home Office (*Brit*), Department of the Interior (*US*). (**d**) (*Dep*) inside-forward; **~ derecho** inside-right; **~ izquierdo** inside-left. (**e**) **~es** (*Anat*) insides. (**f**) (*LAm: prenda*) underpants.

interioridad NF (**a**) inwardness; (*fig*) inner being; (*pensamientos*) innermost thoughts; **en su ~, sabe que ...** (*CAm*) in his heart he knows that ..., deep down he knows that ... (**b**) **~es** family secrets, private affairs; inner history, secret goings-on; ins and outs; **explicó las ~es de la lucha** he explained the inner history of the struggle; **desconocen las ~es del mercado** they don't know all the ins and outs of the market.

interiorismo NM interior decoration, interior design.

interiorista NMF interior decorator, interior designer.

interiorizar [1f] VT (**a**) (*Psic*) to internalize. (**b**) (*LAm*) to look into, investigate closely.

2 interiorizarse VR: **~ algo** to familiarize o.s. with sth.

interiormente ADV internally, inwardly; **lo que pasa ~** what goes on inside.

interjección NF interjection.

interlínea NF (*Inform*) line feed.

interlineado NM space (*o* writing) between the lines.

interlineal ADJ interlinear.

interlinear [1a] VT (**a**) (*gen*) to interline, write (*o* print *etc*) between the lines. (**b**) (*Tip*) to space, lead.

interlocutor(a) NM/F speaker, interlocutor; **mi ~** the person I was speaking to, the person who spoke to me; **~ válido** official negotiator; official spokesman.

intérlope **1** ADJ (*Méx: fraudulento*) fraudulent.

2 NM (*Com*) interloper, unauthorized trader.

interludio NM interlude.

intermediación NF mediation; (*Fin*) brokerage.

intermediario **1** ADJ (**a**) (*gen*) intermediary. (**b**) (*mediador*) mediating.

2 NM, **intermediaria** NF (**a**) (*gen*) intermediary, go-between; negotiator; (*Com*) middleman. (**b**) (*árbitro*) mediator.

intermedio **1** ADJ (**a**) *etapa* intermediate, halfway (*entre* between). (**b**) *tiempo* intervening; **el período ~** the intervening period, the period between.

2 NM (**a**) interval (*t Teat*); (*Parl*) recess. (**b**) **por ~ de** (*LAm*) through, by means of.

intermezzo [inter'metso] NM intermezzo.

interminable ADJ endless, interminable.

interminablemente ADV endlessly, interminably.

interministerial ADJ interministerial.

intermisión NF intermission.

intermitencia NF intermittence.

intermitente **1** ADJ intermittent.

2 NM (*Aut*) directional light, flashing light, indicator; (*Inform*) indicator light.

internación NF internment.

internacional **1** ADJ international.

2 NF: **I~** Internationale.

internacionalidad NF international nature; international standing.

internacionalismo NM internationalism.

internacionalista ADJ, NMF internationalist.

internacionalizar [1f] VT to internationalize.

internacionalmente ADV internationally.

internada¹ NF (*Dep*) run towards goal.

internado, -a² **1** NM/F (*Mil etc*) internee.

2 NM (**a**) (*colegio*) boarding-school; (*acto*) boarding. (**b**) (*alumnos*) boarders.

internalización NF internalization.

internalizar [1f] VT to internalize.

internamente ADV internally.

internamiento NM (**a**) (*Pol*) internment. (**b**) (*Med*) admission (to hospital).

internar [1a] **1** VT (**a**) (*Mil*) to intern; (*Med*) to admit (*en* to); **~ a uno en un manicomio** to put sb into a psychiatric hospital, commit sb to a psychiatric hospital. (**b**) (*enviar tierra adentro*) to send inland.

2 internarse VR (**a**) (*avanzar*) to advance (deeply); to penetrate; **el jugador se interna** the player goes deep into the opponent's half. (**b**) (*avanzar*) **~ en** to go into, go deeply into, penetrate into; **se internó en el edificio** he went into the building, he disappeared into the building; **~ en un país** to go into the interior of a country. (**c**) **~ en un estudio** to go deeply into a subject, study a subject in depth.

internauta NMF Net user, Internet user.

Internet, internet NM *o* NF Internet.

interno **1** ADJ internal, interior; inside; **criada interna** live-in servant, servant who lives in; **la política interna** internal politics, domestic politics; **por vía interna** (*Med*) internally.

2 NM, **interna** NF (**a**) (*alumno*) boarder. (**b**) (*preso*) inmate, prisoner, convict.

3 NM (*Cono Sur Telec*) extension.

interparlamentario ADJ interparliamentary.

interpelación NF appeal, plea, interpellation.

interpelante NMF (*Parl etc*) questioner.

interpelar [1a] VT (**a**) (*impetrar*) to implore, beseech; to interpellate; to beg for the aid of. (**b**) (*dirigirse a*) to address, speak to; (*Parl etc*) to ask for explanations, question formally.

interpersonal ADJ interpersonal.

interplanetario ADJ interplanetary.

Interpol NF Interpol.

interpolación NF interpolation.

interpolar [1a] VT (**a**) to interpolate. (**b**) to interrupt briefly.

interponer [2q] **1** VT (**a**) (*insertar*) to interpose, put in, insert. (**b**) (*Jur*) *apelación* to lodge, put in. (**c**) (*en discurso*) to interpose, interject.

2 interponerse VR to intervene.

interposición NF (**a**) (*inserción*) insertion. (**b**) (*Jur*) lodging, formulation. (**c**) (*en discurso*) interjection.

interpretable ADJ interpretable.

interpretación NF (**a**) (*gen*) interpretation; **mala ~** misinterpretation, misunderstanding. (**b**) (*traducción*) interpretation, translation; **~ simultánea** simultaneous translation. (**c**) (*Mús*) rendition, performance; interpretation; **~ en directo** live performance. (**d**) (*Teat*) performance; playing.

interpretar [1a] VT (**a**) (*gen*) to interpret; **~ mal** to misinterpret, misunderstand, misconstrue. (**b**) (*Ling*) to interpret, translate; **~ del chino al ruso** to translate (*o* interpret) from Chinese into Russian. (**c**) (*Mús*) to render, perform; to interpret; (*Teat*) *obra* to perform; *papel* to play.

interpretativo ADJ interpretative.

intérprete NMF (**a**) (*Ling*) interpreter, translator. (**b**) (*Mús*) performer; exponent; artist(e). (**c**) (*Inform*) interpreter.

interprofesional ADJ *V* **salario**.

interprovincial NM (*And*) long-distance bus, coach.

interracial ADJ interracial.

interregno NM interregnum; (*LAm*) interval, intervening period; **en el ~** in the meantime.

interrelación NF interrelation.

interrelacionado ADJ interrelated.

interrelacionar [1a] VT to interrelate.

interrogación NF (**a**) (*de policía etc*) interrogation. (**b**) (*pregunta*) ques-

tion; (*Inform*) inquiry. (**c**) (*signo*) question-mark.
interrogador(a) NM/F interrogator; questioner.
▼ **interrogante** [1] ADJ questioning.
  [2] NMF (*persona*) interrogator; questioner.
▼ [3] NF (*a veces* NM; *signo*) question-mark; (*fig*) question-mark, query; (*pregunta*) question, query.
interrogar [1h] VT to question, interrogate; (*Jur*) to examine.
interrogativo ADJ, NM interrogative.
interrogatorio NM (**a**) (*gen*) questioning; (*Mil*) debriefing; (*Jur*) examination. (**b**) (*cuestionario*) questionnaire.
interrumpir [3a] VT (*gen*) to interrupt; *vacaciones etc* to interrupt, cut short; *electricidad, servicio* to cut off; *tráfico etc* to block, hold up; (*Elec: apagar*) to switch off; (*Inform*) to abort; *embarazo* to terminate.
interrupción NF interruption; break; stoppage, holdup; disturbance; (*de embarazo*) termination.
interruptor NM (*Elec*) switch; ~ **de dos direcciones** two-way switch; ~ **con regulador de intensidad** dimmer switch; ~ **de seguridad** safety switch.
intersecarse [1g] VR to intersect.
intersección NF intersection; (*Aut*) intersection, crossing, junction.
intersticio NM (*gen*) interstice; (*grieta*) crack; (*intervalo*) interval, gap; (*Mec*) clearance.
intertanto (*LAm*) [1] ADV meanwhile.
  [2] CONJ: ~ **que él llegue** until he comes, while we wait for him to come.
  [3] NM: **en el** ~ in the meantime.
intertextualidad NF intertextuality.
intertítulo NM caption, subtitle.
interurbano [1] ADJ inter-city; (*Telec*) long-distance, trunk (*atr*).
  [2] NM (*CAm: colectivo*) inter-city taxi.
intervalo NM, **intérvalo** NM (*tiempo*) interval; break; (*Mús*) interval; (*espacio*) gap; **a ~s** at intervals; intermittently; every now and then.
intervención NF (**a**) (*control*) supervision, control; (*LAm: de sindicato*) government takeover.
  (**b**) (*Com*) audit, auditing.
  (**c**) (*Med*) operation; ~ **quirúrgica** surgical operation.
  (**d**) (*Telec*) tapping.
  (**e**) (*participación*) intervention (*en* in); participation (*en* in), contribution (*en* to); **su ~ en la discusión** his contribution to the discussion; **la política de no ~** the policy of non-intervention, the non-intervention policy.
intervencionista ADJ interventionist; **no ~** (*Com*) non-interventionist, laissez-faire.
intervenir [3r] [1] VT (**a**) (*controlar*) to supervise, control; (*LAm*) *sindicato* to instal government appointees in, take over the control of.
  (**b**) (*Com*) to audit.
  (**c**) (*Med*) to operate on.
  (**d**) (*Telec*) to tap, bug*.
  (**e**) (*Jur*) to confiscate, seize.
  [2] VI (**a**) (*tomar parte*) to intervene (*en* in); to take part, participate (*en* in); to contribute (*en* to); **no intervino en el debate** he did not take part in the debate, he did not contribute to the debate; **él no intervino en la decisión** he did not have a hand in the decision; **una reyerta en la que intervino X** a brawl in which X was involved.
  (**b**) (*interceder*) to intercede; (*mediar*) to mediate; ~ **por uno** to intercede for sb.
interventor(a) NM/F inspector, supervisor; (*Com: t* ~ **de cuentas**) auditor.
interviniente NMF participant.
interviú NF (*a veces* NM), **interview** NF interview; **hacer una ~ a uno** to interview sb.
interviu(v)ador(a) NM/F interviewer.
interviu(v)ar [1a] VT to interview, have an interview with.
intestado ADJ intestate.
intestinal ADJ intestinal.
intestino [1] ADJ internal; domestic, civil.
  [2] NM intestine; gut; ~ **ciego** caecum; ~ **delgado** small intestine; ~ **grueso** large intestine.
inti NM (*And Fin*) Peruvian national currency.
Intifada NF, **intifada** NF Intifada.
intimación NF intimation, announcement, notification.
íntimamente ADV intimately.
intimar [1a] [1] VT (*notificar*) to intimate, announce, notify (*a* to); (*ordenar*) to order, require (*que* that).
  [2] VI *y* **intimarse** VR to become intimate, become friendly (*con* with); **ahora intiman mucho** they're very friendly now.
intimidación NF intimidation; *V* **disparo**.
intimidad NF (**a**) (*amistad etc*) intimacy, familiarity; **disfrutar de la ~ de uno** to be on close terms with sb, enjoy sb's confidence; **entrar en ~ con uno** to become friendly with sb.

(**b**) (*vida privada*) privacy, private life; **conocido en la ~ como X** known in private life as X; **la ceremonia se celebró en la ~** the wedding took place privately, it was a quiet wedding.
  (**c**) **~es** PL (*Anat*) private parts.
intimidador ADJ intimidating.
intimidar [1a] [1] VT to intimidate, overawe; to bully, scare.
  [2] **intimidarse** VR to be intimidated, be overawed; to get scared.
intimidatorio ADJ intimidating.
intimista ADJ intimate, private.
íntimo ADJ intimate; *relación* intimate, close; *pensamientos* inner, innermost; *vida etc* private; **una boda íntima** a quiet wedding, a private wedding; **es ~ amigo mío** he is a close friend of mine; **en lo más ~ de su corazón** in one's heart of hearts.
intitular [1a] VT to entitle, call.
intocable [1] ADJ untouchable; (*fig*) sacrosanct.
  [2] NMF untouchable.
▼ **intolerable** ADJ intolerable, unbearable.
intolerancia NF intolerance; narrow-mindedness, bigotry.
intolerante ADJ intolerant (*con, para* of); narrow-minded, bigoted (*en* about).
intonso ADJ (**a**) *persona* with long hair, unshorn, shaggy. (**b**) *libro* (with edges) untrimmed. (**c**) (*grosero*) boorish.
intoxicación NF (**a**) poisoning; ~ **alimenticia** food poisoning; ~ **etílica** alcohol poisoning, (*euf*) drunken state. (**b**) (*Pol*) disinformation, black propaganda.
intoxicador [1] ADJ (**a**) intoxicating. (**b**) (*Pol*) misleading, deceptive.
  [2] NM, **intoxicadora** NF spreader of disinformation, black propagandist.
intoxicar [1g] VT (**a**) to poison. (**b**) (*Pol*) to mislead, disinform.
intra... PREF intra...
intracomunitario ADJ within the European Community.
intraducible ADJ untranslatable.
intragable ADJ unpalatable; (*fig*) unpalatable; intolerable, unacceptable.
intramatrimonial ADJ: **agresión ~** violence within a marriage, violence between husband and wife.
intramuros ADV within the city, within the walls.
intranquilidad NF worry, uneasiness, disquiet, anxiety.
intranquilizar [1f] [1] VT to worry, disquiet, make uneasy.
  [2] **intranquilizarse** VR to get worried, feel uneasy, be anxious.
intranquilo ADJ worried, uneasy, anxious; restless.
intra(n)scendencia NF unimportance, insignificance.
intra(n)scendente ADJ unimportant, insignificant.
intranscribible ADJ unprintable.
intransferible ADJ untransferable, not transferable.
intransigencia NF intransigence; uncompromising attitude, intolerance.
intransigente ADJ intransigent; uncompromising, intolerant; unyielding; diehard.
intransitable ADJ impassable.
intransitivo ADJ intransitive.
intratable ADJ *problema* intractable; awkward, tough; *persona* unsociable; difficult, impossible; **¡son ~s!** they're impossible!
intrauterino ADJ intrauterine.
intravenoso ADJ intravenous.
intrépidamente ADV intrepidly, dauntlessly, fearlessly.
intrepidez NF intrepidity, fearlessness.
intrépido ADJ intrepid, dauntless, fearless.
intricado ADJ = **intrincado**.
intriga NF intrigue; plot, scheme; (*Teat*) plot; ~ **secundaria** subplot.
intrigante [1] ADJ (**a**) (*pey*) intriguing, scheming. (**b**) (*interesante*) intriguing, interesting, puzzling.
  [2] NMF intriguer.
intrigar [1h] [1] VT (**a**) to intrigue, interest, puzzle.
  (**b**) (*LAm*) *asunto* to conduct in a surprising way.
  [2] VI to intrigue, scheme, plot.
  [3] **intrigarse** VR (*LAm*) to be intrigued, be puzzled.
intrincadamente ADV (*V* ADJ) (**a**) densely, impenetrably. (**b**) (*fig*) intricately.
intrincado ADJ (**a**) (*impenetrable*) dense, impenetrable; tangled. (**b**) (*fig: complicado*) intricate; involved, complicated.
intrincar [1g] VT to entangle; to confuse, complicate.
intríngulis* NM INVAR (*motivo*) ulterior motive; (*pega*) hidden snag, catch; (*misterio*) puzzle, mystery.
intrínsecamente ADV intrinsically; inherently.
intrínseco ADJ intrinsic; inherent.
intro... PREF intro...
▼ **introducción** NF introduction; insertion; creation; (*libro*) foreword; (*Inform*) input.
introducir [3n] [1] VT (*gen*) to introduce; *visita etc* to bring in, show in; *objeto* to insert, introduce, put in; *discordia etc* to create, sow, cause; (*Inform*) to input, enter.

▶ LENGUA Y USO: **interrogante: 3** → 53.6   **intolerable** → 34.3   **introducción** → 53.1

2 introducirse VR (a) (*meterse*) to get in, slip in, gain access (*en to*); (*fig*) to insinuate o.s., worm one's way (*en* into).
(b) (*fig: entrometerse*) to interfere, meddle.
introductor ADJ introductory.
introductorio ADJ introductory.
introito NM (*Teat*) prologue; (*Ecl*) introit.
intromisión NF (a) (*inserción*) introduction, insertion. (b) (*pey*) interference, meddling.
introspección NF introspection.
introspectivo ADJ introspective.
introversión NF introversion.
introvertido 1 ADJ introvert, introverted; inward-looking.
2 NM, **introvertida** NF introvert.
intrusión NF intrusion; (*Jur*) trespass; ~ **informática** hacking, computer piracy.
intrusismo NM infiltration.
intruso 1 ADJ intrusive.
2 NM, **intrusa** NF (*gen*) intruder, interloper; (*forastero*) outsider; (*en fiesta etc*) gatecrasher; (*Jur*) trespasser; (*Mil, Pol*) infiltrator; ~ **informático** hacker, computer pirate.
intuible ADJ that can be intuited.
intuición NF intuition; **por** ~ by intuition, intuitively.
intuir [3g] 1 VT to know by intuition; to intuit; to sense, feel, have an intuition of.
2 **intuirse** VR: **eso se intuye** that can be guessed; **se intuye que ...** one can tell intuitively that ..., one can guess that ...; you can feel that ...; **el hombre se intuye observado** the man realizes he is under observation.
intuitivamente ADV intuitively.
intuitivo ADJ intuitive.
intumescencia NF swelling.
intumescente ADJ intumescent, swollen.
inuit ADJ, NMF Inuit.
inundación NF flood, flooding.
inundadizo ADJ (*LAm*) liable to flooding.
inundar [1a] VT to flood, inundate, swamp (*t fig; de, en* with); ~ **el mercado de un producto** to flood the market with a product; **quedamos inundados de ofertas** we are swamped with offers; **la lluvia inundó la campiña** the rain flooded the countryside, the rain left the countryside under water.
inusitado ADJ unusual, unwonted, rare.
inusual ADJ unusual.
inusualmente ADV unusually.
inútil ADJ (*gen*) useless; *tentativa etc* vain, fruitless; *esfuerzo* vain; **todo es** ~ nothing is any use; **es** ~ **que Vd proteste** it is useless for you to protest, it's no good your protesting.
inutilidad NF uselessness.
inutilizable ADJ unusable, unfit for use.
inutilización NF disablement; spoiling; cancellation.
inutilizar [1f] 1 VT (*gen*) to make useless, render useless; *barco etc* to disable, put out of action; (*estropear*) to spoil, ruin; *esfuerzo etc* to nullify; *sello* to cancel.
2 **inutilizarse** VR to become useless; to be disabled; to be spoiled.
inútilmente ADV uselessly; vainly, fruitlessly.
INV NM (*Esp*) ABR *de* **Instituto Nacional de la Vivienda.**
invadeable ADJ unfordable; (*fig*) impassable; (*fig*) unsurmountable.
invadir [3a] VT (a) (*Mil etc*) to invade; to overrun; **la turba invadió las calles** the mob poured out on to the streets. (b) (*fig*) *derechos etc* to encroach upon.
invalidación NF invalidation.
invalidante ADJ disabling, incapacitating.
invalidar [1a] VT to invalidate, nullify.
invalidez NF (a) (*Med*) disablement; unfitness; disability; ~ **permanente** permanent disability. (b) (*Jur*) invalidity, nullity.
inválido 1 ADJ (a) (*Med*) invalid, disabled; unfit.
(b) (*Jur etc*) invalid, null and void; **declarar inválida una elección** to declare an election invalid.
2 NM, **inválida** NF (*Med*) invalid.
3 NM (*Mil: Med*) disabled soldier, wounded soldier; pensioner.
invaluable ADJ (*LAm*) invaluable.
invariable ADJ invariable.
invariablemente ADV invariably.
invariancia NF invariability, lack of variation.
invasión NF (a) (*gen*) invasion (*t Med*); attack. (b) (*fig*) encroachment (*de* on); inroad (*de* into).
invasor 1 ADJ invading.
2 NM, **invasora** NF invader, attacker.
invectiva NF invective; **una** ~ a piece of invective, a tirade.
invectivar [1a] VT to inveigh against; to heap abuse upon.
invencibilidad NF invincibility.
invencible ADJ invincible; *obstáculo* unsurmountable, insuperable; **La I~** the Armada (*1588*).

invenciblemente ADV invincibly; insuperably.
invención NF (*invento*) invention; (*descubrimiento*) discovery, finding; (*pey*) fabrication; (*Poét etc*) fiction, tale, fable.
invendible ADJ unsaleable, unmarketable.
invendido 1 ADJ unsold.
2 NM unsold item.
inventar [1a] VT to invent; (*idear*) to devise; (*pey*) to make up, fabricate, concoct.
inventariado NM detailed account.
inventariar [1b] VT to inventory, make an inventory of.
inventario NM inventory; stocktaking; ~ **continuo** continuous inventory; **hacer** ~ **de** to make an inventory of, take stock of.
inventiva NF inventiveness; ingenuity, resourcefulness.
inventivo ADJ inventive; ingenious, resourceful.
invento NM invention; ~ **del tebeo*** silly idea.
inventor(a) NM/F inventor.
inverificable ADJ unverifiable.
invernáculo NM = **invernadero** (a).
invernada NF (a) (*estación*) winter season.
(b) (*etapa invernal*) wintering; (*hibernación*) hibernation.
(c) (*And, Cono Sur: pasto*) winter pasture.
(d) (*Carib: tempestad*) heavy rainstorm.
invernadero NM (a) greenhouse, hothouse; conservatory. (b) (*LAm*) winter pasture.
invernal ADJ wintry, winter (*atr*).
invernante 1 ADJ over-wintering.
2 NM (*Orn*) over-wintering species, winter visitor.
invernar [1j] VI to winter, spend the winter; (*Zool*) to hibernate.
invernazo* NM (*Carib*) rainy season (*July to September*).
inverne NM (*LAm*) winter pasturing; winter fattening.
invernizo ADJ wintry, winter (*atr*).
inverosímil ADJ unlikely, improbable; implausible.
inverosimilitud NF unlikeliness, improbability; implausibility.
inversamente ADV inversely; **e** ~ and vice versa.
inversión NF (a) (*gen*) inversion; reversal; (*Aut, Mec*) reversing; ~ **de marcha** reversing, backing; ~ **sexual** homosexuality; ~ **térmica** temperature inversion.
(b) (*Com, Fin*) investment (*en* in); ~ **de capital(es)** capital investment.
inversionista NMF (*Com, Fin*) investor.
inverso ADJ inverse, inverted; reverse, contrary; *cara* reverse; **a la inversa** inversely, the other way round; (*fig*) vice versa; on the contrary.
inversor 1 ADJ investment (*atr*).
2 NM, **inversora** NF investor; ~ **financiero** investments manager; ~ **inmobiliario** property investor; ~ **institucional** institutional investor.
invertebrado ADJ, NM invertebrate.
invertido 1 ADJ (a) (*volcado*) inverted; (*al revés*) reversed; **escritura invertida** mirror writing. (b) (*Bio*) homosexual.
2 NM, **invertida** NF homosexual.
invertir [3i] VT (a) (*volcar*) to invert, turn upside down; (*poner al revés*) to reverse, put the other way round; (*cambiar el orden de*) to change over, change the order of; (*Aut, Mec*) to reverse; (*Mat*) to invert.
(b) *esfuerzo, tiempo* to spend, put in (*en* on); **invirtieron 5 días en el viaje** they spent 5 days on the journey.
(c) (*Com, Fin*) to invest (*en* in).
investidura NF investiture; (*Parl*) vote of confidence (in the prime minister).
investigación NF (a) (*indagación*) investigation; inquiry (*de* into); ~ **policíaca** police investigation. (b) (*Univ etc*) research, research work (*de* in, into); ~ **básica** basic research; ~ **y desarrollo** research and development; ~ **operativa** operational research.
investigador 1 ADJ investigative; research (*atr*); **capacidad ~a** research ability, ability in research.
2 NM, **investigadora** NF (a) investigator; ~ **privado** private detective. (b) (*Univ etc*) research worker, researcher; (*de doctorado*) research student.
investigar [1h] VT (a) (*indagar*) to investigate; to inquire into, look into. (b) (*Univ etc*) to do research into, do research work on.
investir [3k] VT: ~ **a uno con el título de doctor** to confer the title of doctor on sb.
inveterado ADJ inveterate; *criminal* confirmed, hardened; *hábito* deep-seated, well-established.
inviabilidad NF impossibility, non-viability; invalidity.
inviable ADJ impossible, non-viable; *reclamación* invalid.
invicto ADJ unconquered, unbeaten.
invidencia NF sightlessness.
invidente 1 ADJ sightless, blind.
2 NMF sightless person, blind person.
invierno NM (a) winter, wintertime; ~ **nuclear** nuclear winter. (b) (*And, CAm, Carib: meses de lluvia*) rainy season. (c) (*Carib: aguacero*)

heavy shower.

inviolabilidad NF inviolability; **~ parlamentaria** parliamentary immunity.

inviolable ADJ inviolable.

inviolado ADJ inviolate.

invisibilidad NF invisibility.

invisible [1] ADJ invisible.

[2] NM (*And, Cono Sur*) hairpin.

▼ **invitación** NF invitation (*a* to); **a ~ de** at the invitation of.

invitado, -a ADJ, NM/F guest; **~ de honor** guest of honour; **estrella invitada** guest star.

▼ **invitar** [1a] VT to invite; **~ a uno a hacer algo** to invite sb to do sth; to call on sb to do sth; **invito yo** it's on me, be my guest; **hoy invito a café** today I'll buy the coffee, today I'll stand coffees all round; **nos invitó a cenar fuera** she took us out for a meal; **dio las gracias a los que le habían invitado** he thanked his hosts.

in vitro ADJ, ADV in vitro; **fecundación (o fertilización) in vitro** in vitro fertilization.

invocación NF invocation.

invocar [1g] VT (a) (*llamar en ayuda*) to invoke, call on; **~ la ley** to invoke the law. (b) (*rogar*) to beg for, implore; **~ la ayuda de** to beg for the help of. (c) (*Inform*) to call.

involución NF (*Pol*) regression, reaction, turning back.

involucionismo NM (*Pol*) reaction; reactionary forces.

involucionista (*Pol*) [1] ADJ regressive, reactionary.

[2] NMF reactionary.

involucración NF, **involucramiento** NM involvement.

involucrar [1a] [1] VT (a) (*implicar*) to involve; **~ a uno en algo** to involve sb in sth; **andar involucrado en** to be mixed up in.

(b) (*mezclar*) to jumble up, mix up; **lo tiene todo involucrado** he's got it all mixed up.

[2] **involucrarse** VR to meddle, interfere (*en* in); to get involved (*en* in); **las personas involucradas en el caso** the people involved in the affair, the persons concerned in the matter.

involuntariamente ADV involuntarily; unintentionally.

involuntario ADJ involuntary; *ofensa etc* unintentional.

involutivo ADJ (*Pol*) reactionary.

invulnerabilidad NF invulnerability.

invulnerable ADJ invulnerable.

inyección NF injection, shot*, jab*; (*Fin, Mec*) injection; **hacerse (o ponerse) una ~** to give o.s. an injection.

inyectable NM serum, vaccine; injection.

inyectado ADJ: **ojos ~s (en sangre)** bloodshot eyes.

inyectar [1a] [1] VT to inject (*en* into); **~ algo en uno** to inject sb with sth.

[2] **inyectarse** VR to give oneself an injection, shoot up⁑.

inyector NM injector; (*Téc*) nozzle.

ion NM ion.

iónico ADJ (*Quím*) ionic.

ionizador NM (negative) ionizer.

ionizar [1f] VT to ionize.

ionosfera NF ionosphere.

IORTV NM ABR *de* **Instituto Oficial de Radiodifusión y Televisión**.

iota NF iota.

IPC NM ABR *de* **índice de precios al consumidor** (*o* **consumo**) retail price index, RPI.

ipecacuana NF ipecacuanha.

ipomea NF (*Bot*) morning glory.

IPPV NM ABR *de* **Instituto para la Promoción Pública de la Vivienda**.

ir [3s] [1] VI (a) (*gen*) to go; to move; to travel; (*en pie*) to go, walk; (*en coche etc*) to go, drive; (*en bicicleta, caballo etc*) to go, ride; **~ a Quito** to go to Quito; **este camino va a Huesca** this road goes to Huesca, this is the road to Huesca; **~ hacia Sevilla** to go towards Seville, go in the direction of Seville; **~ hasta León** to go as far as Seville; **fui en coche** I went by car, I drove; **fui en tren** I went by train, I went by rail; **~ despacio** to go slow(ly); **~ con tiento** to go carefully, go cautiously; **vaya donde vaya, encontrará ...** wherever you go, you will find ...; **ya ha ido*** you've had it*; **¡voy!** I'm coming!, I'll be with you in a moment!; **¡ahora voy!** I'll be right there!; **¡vamos!** let's go! (*V t* (**k**)); **¿quién va?** (*Mil etc*) who goes there?; **~ por leña** to fetch wood, go and fetch wood, go for wood; **voy por el médico** I'll (go and) fetch the doctor, I'll call the doctor; **~ tras una chica** to chase (after) a girl.

(b) (*locuciones*) **~ con uno** to agree with sb; **~ de mal en peor** to go from bad to worse, get worse; **esto va de veras** this is serious; I'm in earnest; **es el no va más*** it's the very last word, it's the latest thing; **en lo que va de año** so far this year; **a eso voy** I'm coming to that; **a lo que iba** as I was saying; **si vamos a eso** for that matter, as for that; **~ a lo suyo** to go one's own way; (*pey*) to act selfishly, think only of o.s.; **va para 5 años que entré en la Universidad** it's getting on for five years since I started University; **va para los 40** he's going on for 40, he's knocking on 40; **va para viejo** he's get-

ting old; **con éste van 30** that makes 30; **~ y marcharse: fue y se marchó** (*Méx*) he just upped and left*; **¡que le vaya bien!** (*LAm*) goodbye!; **le va al Cruz Azul** (*Méx Dep*) he supports Cruz Azul.

(c) (*progresar*) to go; (*Med*) to be, go, get along; **¿cómo va eso?** how are things going?; **¿cómo te va?** how goes it?; **¿cómo va el ensayo?** how are you getting on with the essay?; **no me va bien el inglés** I'm not doing very well with English; **el enfermo va mejor** the patient is better, the patient is getting along nicely.

(d) (*diferencia*) **va mucho de A a B** there's a lot of difference between A and B, A is very different from B; **¡lo que va del padre al hijo!** what a difference there is between father and son!; **de 7 a 9 van 2** 7 from 9 leaves 2.

(e) **eso no va por ti** (*intención*) I wasn't referring to you, that wasn't meant for you; it's not your fault.

(f) (*importar*) **va mucho en esto** a lot depends on it; **¿qué te va en ello?** what does it matter to you?; **no le va la vida en esto** it's not as though his life depends on it; **ni le va ni le viene** it's nothing to do with him, he's not concerned, he doesn't care.

(g) (*apuestas*) **van 5 dólares a que no lo haces** I bet 5 dollars that you won't do it; **¿cuánto va?** how much do you bet?

(h) **va para ingeniero** (*carrera etc*) he's going to become an engineer, he's going into engineering.

(i) (*Naipes*) to lead; to go.

(j) (*ropa*) to suit, become; **¿me va bien esto?** does this suit me?; **no le va bien el sombrero** the hat doesn't suit her.

(k) (INTERJ *etc*) **¡vaya!** (*sorpresa*) well!, there!, I say!; (*enfado*) damn!; **¡vaya coche!** what a car!, there's a car for you!, that's some car!; **¡vaya susto que me pegué!** what a fright I got!; **¡vaya, vaya!** well I'm blowed!*; come now!; **¡vamos!** well!; **vamos, no es difícil** come now, it's not difficult; **una chica, vamos, una mujer** a girl, well ... a woman; **¡qué va!** rubbish!; nonsense!; **es molesto, pero ¡vamos!** it's a nuisance, but there it is; **¡vaya por Pepe!** (*Esp*) here's to Joe!

(l) (*en tiempos continuos*) **iba anocheciendo** it was getting dark; **iban fumando** they were smoking; **voy comprendiendo que ...** I am beginning to see that ..., I am in the process of learning that ...

(m) (*con PTP*) **iba cansado** he was tired; **van escritas 3 cartas** that's 3 letters I've written; **va vendido todo** everything has been sold.

(n) (**~ a** + *infin*) **voy a hacerlo** I'm going to do it; **vamos a hacerlo** we are going to do it; let's do it; **fui a verle** I went to see him, I went and saw him; **¿no irá a soplar?⁑** I hope he's not going to split on us*; **no vaya a ser que** + *subj* lest he should + *infin*, in case he should + *infin*; **¿cómo lo iba a tener?** how could he have had it?; **¡no lo va a saber!** of course he knows!; *V* hacer.

(o) (**~ de** + N): **el país va de democracia** the country is in a democratic mood; **Pérez va de presidente** Pérez is all set for the presidency; **sabe de qué va 'el rollo'** she knows what 'el rollo' is; **¿de qué vas?** what are you on about?*; **la película va de sexo** the film is all sex; **la que va de negro** the girl in black; *para locuciones de* **~ de** + *sustantivo V el sustantivo, p.ej.* **campo, etiqueta**.

[2] **irse** VR (a) **por aquí se va a Jaca** this is the way to Jaca; **¿por dónde se va al aeropuerto?** which way to the airport?

(b) (*marcharse*) to go away, leave, depart; **se fueron** they went, they went off, they left; **es hora de irnos** it's time we went, it's time for us to go; **¡vete!** go away!, get out!; **¡vete ya!** off with you!; **¡no te vayas!** don't go!; **¡vámonos!** let's go!; (*Ferro etc*) all aboard!; **~ de algo** to discard sth; **me voy de con Vd** (*CAm*) I'm leaving you.

(c) (*resbalar*) to slip, lose one's balance; (*muro etc*) to give way; *V* **mano, pie** *etc*.

(d) (*recipiente*) to leak; to overflow; (*contenido*) to leak out, overflow, ooze out; to evaporate; **se fue el vino** the wine was lost; **el neumático se va** the tyre is losing air.

(e) (*morir. euf*) to be dying; to die; **se nos va el amo** the master is dying; **se nos fue hace 3 años** he departed from us 3 years ago, he passed away 3 years ago.

(f) (⁑: *echar un pedo*) to fart⁑.

(g) (⁑: *eyacular*) to come⁑.

ira NF (*lit*) anger, rage, wrath (*liter*); (*de viento etc*) fury, violence.

iracundia NF ire; irascibility.

iracundo ADJ irate; irascible.

Irak NM Iraq.

irakí = **iraquí**.

Irán NM: (**el**) **~** Iran.

iranés = **iraní**.

iraní [1] ADJ, NMF Iranian, Persian.

[2] NM (*Ling*) Iranian, Persian, Farsi.

iranio (*Hist*) = **iraní**.

Iraq NM Iraq.

iraquí ADJ, NMF Iraqui.

irascibilidad NF irascibility.

irascible ADJ irascible.

irguiendo *etc V* **erguir**.

iribú NM (*Argentina*) turkey buzzard.

▶ LENGUA Y USO: **invitación** → 52.1, 52.4   **invitar** → 52.1, 52.4

iridiscente ADJ iridescent.
iridología NF iridology.
iris NM (*Met*) rainbow; (*Anat*) iris; **hacer un ~** (*LAm**) to wink.
irisación NF iridescence.
irisado ADJ iridescent.
irisar [1a] VI to be iridescent, iridesce.
Irlanda NF Ireland; **~ del Norte** Northern Ireland, Ulster.
irlandés ① ADJ Irish.
　② NM Irishman; **los irlandeses** the Irish.
　③ NM (*Ling*) Irish.
irlandesa NF Irishwoman.
ironía NF irony; **con ~** ironically.
irónicamente ADV ironically.
irónico ADJ ironical.
ironizar [1f] ① VT to ridicule.
　② VI to speak ironically; "...", ironizó Z "...", said Z ironically.
IRPF NM (*Esp*) ABR *de* **impuesto sobre la renta de las personas físicas** (personal income-tax).
irracional ① ADJ irrational; unreasoning; **ser ~** brute, brute creature.
　② NM brute, brute creature.
irracionalidad NF irrationality; unreasonableness.
irracionalmente ADV irrationally; unreasonably, unreasoningly.
irradiación NF irradiation.
irradiar [1b] VT to irradiate, radiate.
irrayable ADJ scratch-proof.
irrazonable ADJ unreasonable.
irreal ADJ unreal.
irrealidad NF unreality.
irrealista ADJ unrealistic.
irrealizable ADJ unrealizable; *plan* unworkable; impossible to carry out; *meta etc* unattainable.
irrebatible ADJ unanswerable, irrefutable, unassailable.
irrechazable ADJ irresistible.
irrecomendable ADJ inadvisable.
irreconciliable ADJ irreconcilable; inconsistent, incompatible.
irreconocible ADJ unrecognizable.
irrecuperable ADJ irrecoverable, irretrievable.
irrecurrible ADJ: **la decisión es ~** there is no appeal against this decision.
irrecusable ADJ unimpeachable.
irredento ADJ unrepentant, inveterate.
irredimible ADJ irredeemable.
irreducible ADJ (**a**) *mínimo* irreducible. (**b**) *diferencias* irreconcilable, incompatible.
irreductible ADJ *defensor etc* uncompromising, unyielding; (*pey*) hidebound, bigoted.
irreembolsable ADJ *depósito* non-returnable.
irreemplazable ADJ irreplaceable.
irreflexión NF thoughtlessness; rashness, impetuosity.
irreflexivamente ADV thoughtlessly, unthinkingly; rashly.
irreflexivo ADJ thoughtless, unthinking; rash, impetuous; *acto* rash, ill-considered.
irreformable ADJ unreformable.
irrefrenable ADJ *violencia etc* unrestrained, unbridled, uncontrollable; *persona* irrepressible; unmanageable; *deseo, fuerza* unstoppable.
irrefutable ADJ irrefutable, unanswerable.
irregular ADJ irregular; abnormal.
irregularidad NF irregularity; abnormality.
irregularmente ADV irregularly; abnormally.
irrelevante ADJ irrelevant.
irreligioso ADJ irreligious; ungodly.
irrellenable ADJ *botella, encendedor* disposable.
irremediable ADJ irremediable; incurable; hopeless.
irremediablemente ADV irremediably; incurably; hopelessly.
irremisible ADJ *falta* unpardonable; *pérdida* irretrievable.
irremisiblemente ADV unpardonably; **~ perdido** irretrievably lost, lost beyond hope of recovery.
irremontable ADJ *barrera* insurmountable.
irremunerado ADJ unremunerated.
irrentable ADJ unprofitable.
irrenunciable ADJ: **una aspiración ~** an aspiration which can never be given up.
irreparable ADJ irreparable.
irreparablemente ADV irreparably.
irrepetible ADJ one-and-only, unique.
irreprensible ADJ irreproachable.
irreprimible ADJ irrepressible.
irreprochable ADJ irreproachable.
irreproducible ADJ that cannot be reproduced, unrepeatable.
irresistible ADJ irresistible; (*pey*) unbearable, insufferable; (*demasiado fuerte*) impossibly strong.
irresistiblemente ADV irresistibly.

irresoluble ADJ unsolvable; unresolved.
irresolución NF irresolution, hesitation, undecidedness.
irresoluto ADJ (**a**) *carácter* irresolute, hesitant, undecided. (**b**) *problema* unresolved.
irrespetar [1a] VT (*LAm*) *persona* to show disrespect to, be disrespectful towards; *norma, ley* to break, disrespect.
irrespeto NM (*LAm*): **~ a uno** disrespect for sb; **~ a una ley** disrespect for the law, breaking of a law.
irrespetuosamente ADV disrespectfully.
irrespetuoso ADJ disrespectful.
irrespirable ADJ unbreathable.
irresponsabilidad NF irresponsibility.
irresponsable ADJ irresponsible.
irrestricto ADJ (*LAm*) *apoyo etc* unconditional.
irresuelto ADJ = **irresoluto** (**a**).
irreverencia NF irreverence; disrespect.
irreverente ADJ irreverent; disrespectful.
irreversible ADJ irreversible.
irrevocable ADJ irrevocable, irreversible.
irrevocablemente ADV irrevocably.
irrigación NF irrigation.
irrigador NM sprinkler.
irrigar [1h] VT to irrigate.
irrisible ADJ laughable, absurd; *precio* absurdly low, bargain (*atr*).
irrisión NF (**a**) (*mofa*) derision, ridicule. (**b**) (*persona*) laughing stock.
irrisorio ADJ derisory, ridiculous, absurd; *precio* absurdly low, bargain (*atr*).
irritabilidad NF irritability.
irritable ADJ irritable.
irritación NF irritation.
irritador ADJ irritating.
irritante ① ADJ irritating.
　② NM irritant.
irritar [1a] ① VT (**a**) (*gen*) to irritate, anger, exasperate. (**b**) (*fig*) to stir up, inflame. (**c**) (*Med*) to irritate, inflame.
　② **irritarse** VR to get angry, lose one's temper (*de* about, at, with).
irrompible ADJ unbreakable.
irrumpir [3a] VI: **~ en** to burst into, rush into; to invade.
irrupción NF irruption; inrush; invasion.
IRTP NM (*Esp*) ABR *de* **impuesto sobre el rendimiento del trabajo personal** ≈ pay-as-you-earn, PAYE.
IRYDA [i'riða] NM ABR *de* **Instituto para la Reforma y el Desarrollo Agrario**.
Isaac NM Isaac.
Isabel NF Isabel, Elizabeth; (*reinas de Inglaterra*) Elizabeth.
isabelino ADJ: **la España isabelina** Isabelline Spain, the Spain of Isabel (II); **la Inglaterra isabelina** Elizabethan England, the England of Elizabeth.
Isabelita NF Betty; Bess, Bessie; Liz.
Isaías NM Isaiah.
iscocoro‡ NM (*CAm pey*) Indian.
ISDE NM (*Esp Com*) ABR *de* **Instituto Superior de Dirección de Empresas**.
Iseo NF Iseult, Isolde.
Isías NM Isaiah.
isidrada NF, **isidros** NMPL celebration of St Isidore (*patron saint of Madrid*).
-ísimo *V* Aspects of Word Formation in Spanish 2.
Isla NF: **~s Británicas** British Isles; **~ de Francia** Mauritius; *para otros nombres, V el segundo elemento.*
isla NF (**a**) (*Geog*) island; isle. (**b**) (*Arquit*) block; (*Aut*) traffic island. (**c**) (*Méx: árboles*) isolated clump of trees. (**d**) (*Méx: istmo*) spit of land.
Islam NM Islam.
islámico ADJ Islamic.
islamismo NM (*Rel*) Islam; (*integrismo*) Islamic fundamentalism.
islamista ADJ, NMF Islamist, Islamic fundamentalist.
islamización NF Islamization.
islamizar [1f] VT to Islamize, convert to Islam.
islandés ① ADJ Icelandic.
　② NM, **islandesa** NF Icelander.
　③ NM (*Ling*) Icelandic.
Islandia NF Iceland.
islándico ADJ Icelandic.
isleño ① ADJ island (*atr*).
　② NM, **isleña** NF islander.
isleta NF islet.
islote NM small island, rocky isle.
ismo NM ism.
-ismo *V* Aspects of Word Formation in Spanish 2.
iso... PREF iso...

isobara, isóbara NF isobar.
isoca NF (*Cono Sur*) caterpillar.
isohispa NF contour line.
Isolde NF Iseult, Isolde.
isométrica NF isometrics, isometric exercises.
isométrico ADJ isometric.
isósceles ADJ: **triángulo ~** isosceles triangle.
isoterma NF isotherm.
isotérmico ADJ insulated; isothermal.
isotónico ADJ isotonic.
isótopo NM isotope.
Israel NM Israel.
israelí ADJ, NMF Israeli.
israelita ADJ, NMF Israelite.
-ista *V* Aspects of Word Formation in Spanish 2.
istmeño [1] ADJ of the Isthmus, (*frec*) Panamanian.
   [2] NM, **istmeña** NF native (*o* inhabitant) of the Isthmus, (*frec*) Panamanian.
istmo NM isthmus; neck; **~ de Panamá** Isthmus of Panama; **el I~** (*Méx*) the isthmus of Tehuantepec.
itacate NM (*Méx*) food, provisions.
Italia NF Italy.
italianismo NM italianism, word (*o* phrase *etc*) borrowed from Italian.
italiano, -a [1] ADJ, NM/F Italian.
   [2] NM (*Ling*) Italian.
itálica NF: **en ~** in italics.
ITE ['ite] NM (*Esp Hist*) ABR *de* impuesto de tráfico de empresas.
ítem [1] NM item.
   [2] ADV also, moreover.
itemizar [1f] VT (*LAm*) to itemize, specify; to divide into sections.
iterar [1a] VT to repeat.
iterativo ADJ iterative.
itinerante ADJ itinerant, roving, travelling; *embajador* roving, at large.
itinerario NM itinerary, route; (*Méx Ferro*) timetable.
-itis *V* Aspects of Word Formation in Spanish 2.
-ito, -ita *V* Aspects of Word Formation in Spanish 2.
ITV NF (*Esp*) ABR *de* **Inspección Técnica de Vehículos** ≃ Ministry of Transport Test Certificate, MOT.
IU NF ABR *de* **Izquierda Unida** *Spanish coalition of left-wing parties.*

| IU |
---

*ⓘ The Spanish political party **Izquierda Unida** was established in April 1986 as a coalition party uniting a number of existing left-wing parties including the Spanish Communist Party. It began as a civic platform campaigning against Spain's membership of NATO but now constitutes one of the main national parties, alongside the **PSOE** (Socialists) and the centre-right **Partido Popular** (Popular Party).*

---

i/v ABR *de* **ida y vuelta** return.
IVA ['iβa] NM (*Esp*) ABR *de* **impuesto sobre el valor añadido** value-added tax, VAT.
Ivan NM Ivan; **~ el Terrible** Ivan the Terrible.
IVP NM ABR *de* **Instituto Venezolano de Petroquímica**.
ixtle NM (*Méx*) fibre.
I. y D. NF ABR *de* **Investigación y Desarrollo** Research and Development, R and D.
iza: NF whore.
izada NF (*LAm*) raising, lifting.
izado NM: **~ de la bandera** raising the flag.
-izante *V* Aspects of Word Formation in Spanish 2.
izar [1f] VT (*Náut*) to hoist, haul up; *bandera* to raise, hoist, run up; **la bandera está izada** the flag is flying.
izcuinche NM (*Méx*) (**a**) (*perro*) mangy dog, mongrel. (**b**) (*niño*) ragged child, urchin.
izda, izq.ª ABR *de* **izquierda**.
izdo, izq, izq.º ABR *de* **izquierdo**.
-izo *V* Aspects of Word Formation in Spanish 2.
izquierda NF (**a**) (*mano*) left hand; (*lado*) left side, left-hand side; **estar a la ~ de** to be on the left of; **torcer a la ~** to turn (to the) left; **conducción por la ~** (*Aut*) left-hand drive; **el árbol de la ~** the tree on the left; **seguir por la ~** to keep (to the) left. (**b**) (*Pol*) left; **I~ Unida** (*Esp*) coalition of left-wing parties.
izquierdismo NM left-wing outlook (*o* tendencies *etc*), leftism.
izquierdista [1] ADJ leftist, left-wing.
   [2] NMF leftist, left-winger.
izquierdo ADJ (**a**) (*gen*) left; left-hand. (**b**) (*zurdo*) left-handed. (**c**) (*fig*) crooked, twisted.
izquierdoso* (*pey*) [1] ADJ leftish.
   [2] NM, **izquierdosa** NF lefty*.

J

J, j ['xota] NF (*letra*) J, j.

ja¹ INTERJ ha!

ja²⁑ NF (*mujer*) wife; (*amante*) bird⁑.

jaba NF **(a)** (*LAm: cesto*) straw basket; (*caja*) crate.
(b) (*Carib*) beggar's bag; (*) poverty; **llevar (o tener) algo en ~** (*fig*) to have sth up one's sleeve; **no poder ver a otro con ~ grande*** to envy sb; **soltar la ~** to go up in the world, acquire polish; **tomar la ~** to be reduced to begging.
(c) (*LAm Bot*) = **haba.**

jabado ADJ **(a)** (*Carib, Méx*) white with brown patches. **(b)** (*indeciso*) hesitant, undecided.

jabalí NM wild boar; **~ verrugoso** warthog.

jabalina NF **(a)** (*Zool*) wild sow, female wild boar. **(b)** (*Dep*) javelin.

jabato ① ADJ **(a)** (*valiente*) brave, bold. **(b)** (*Carib, Méx*) (*grosero*) rude, gruff; (*malhumorado*) ill-tempered.
② NM **(a)** young wild boar; **portarse como un ~** to be very brave. **(b)** (*) tough guy*.

jábega NF **(a)** (*red*) dragnet. **(b)** (*barco*) fishing smack.

jabón NM **(a)** soap; (*un ~*) piece of soap, bar of soap; **~ de afeitar** shaving soap; **~ en escama** soapflakes; **~ líquido** liquid soap; **~ de olor, ~ de tocador** toilet soap; **~ en polvo** soap powder; **~ de sastre** French chalk; **no es lo mismo ~ que hilo negro** (*And, Carib*) they're as different as chalk from cheese.
(b) (*: adulación*) soft soap*, flattery; **dar ~ a uno** to soft-soap sb*.
(c) **dar un ~ a uno** (⁑: *reprimenda*) to tell sb off*.
(d) **hacer ~** to laze around.
(e) (*Carib, Cono Sur, Méx: susto*) fright, scare; **agarrarse un ~** to get a fright.

jabonada NF (*LAm*) = **jabonadura.**

jabonado NM **(a)** (*acto*) soaping. **(b)** (*ropa*) wash, laundry. **(c)** (*: bronca*) ticking-off*.

jabonadura NF **(a)** (*acto*) soaping. **(b)** **~s** (*espuma*) lather, soapsuds.
(c) (*) telling-off*; **dar una ~ a uno** to tell sb off*.

jabonar [1a] VT **(a)** (*gen*) to soap; *ropa* to wash; *barba* to soap, lather.
(b) (*) to tell off*, dress down*.

jaboncillo NM (*piece of*) toilet soap; **~ de sastre** French chalk.

jabonera NF soapdish.

jabonería NF soap factory.

jabonete NM piece of toilet soap.

jabonoso ADJ soapy.

jabuco NM (*Carib*) (*caja*) large basket, big crate; (*bolsa*) bag; **dar ~ a uno** to snub sb, give sb the cold shoulder.

jaca NF **(a)** pony, cob, small horse; (*yegua*) mare; (*Carib*) gelding. **(b)** (⁑) bird⁑, dame*.

jacal NM (*CAm, Carib, Méx*) shack, hut; **al ~ viejo no le faltan goteras** old age is bound to have its problems; **no tiene ~ donde meterse** he's without a roof over his head.

jacalear* [1a] VI (*Méx*) to wander about gossiping.

jacalón NM (*Méx*) (*cobertizo*) shed; (*casucha*) shack, hovel; (*Teat**) flea-pit*.

jácara NF **(a)** (*Liter: Hist*) comic ballad of low life; (*Mús: Hist*) a merry dance; (*personas*) band of night revellers; **estar de ~** to be very merry.
(b) (*: cuento*) fib, story; hoax.
(c) (*: molestia*) annoyance.

jacarandá NM o F jacaranda.

jacarandoso ADJ (*alegre*) merry, jolly; lively; (*airoso*) spirited, stylish.

jacaré NM (*LAm*) alligator.

jacarear [1a] VI **(a)** (*cantar por la calle*) to sing in the streets at nights, (*dar serenata*) to go serenading. **(b)** (*fig*) (*armar un lío*) to cause a commotion; (*insultar*) to be rude, make offensive remarks.

jacarero ① ADJ merry, fun-loving.
② NM amusing person, wag.

jácena NF (*Téc*) summer.

jachís NM = **hachís.**

jachudo ADJ (*And*) strong, tough; obstinate.

jacinto NM (*Bot*) hyacinth; (*Min*) hyacinth, jacinth.

jaco NM **(a)** small horse, young horse; (*pey*) nag, hack. **(b)** (⁑) horse⁑, heroin.

jacobeo ADJ **(a)** (*Ecl*) of St James; **la devoción jacobea** the devotion to St James, the cult of St James. **(b)** (*Geog*) of Santiago de Compostela; **la ruta jacobea** the pilgrims' road to Santiago.

jacobino, -a ADJ, NM/F Jacobin.

Jacobo NM Jacob.

jactancia NF boasting, bragging; boastfulness.

jactanciosamente ADV boastfully.

jactancioso ADJ boastful.

jactarse [1a] VR to boast, brag; **~ de** to boast about, boast of; **~ de +** *infin* to boast of + *ger.*

jacuzzi ® [ja'kuzi] NM, PL **jacuzzis** Jacuzzi ®.

jade NM (*Min*) jade.

jadeante ADJ panting, gasping, breathless.

jadear [1a] VI to pant, gasp for breath, puff and blow.

jadeo NM panting, gasping, puffing and blowing.

jaez NM **(a)** harness, piece of harness; **jaeces** trappings. **(b)** (*fig*) kind, sort; **y gente de ese ~** and people of that sort.

jaguar NM jaguar.

jagüel NM, **jagüey** NM (*LAm*) pool; (*pozo*) well, cistern.

jai⁑ NF bird⁑, dame*.

jai alai NM pelota.

jaiba ① NF **(a)** (*LAm: cangrejo*) crab.
(b) (*And: boca*) mouth; **abrir la ~** to show o.s. greedy for money.
② NMF (*Carib, Méx**) sharp customer*.

jáibol NM (*LAm*) highball (*US*).

jaibón * ADJ (*CAm*) stuck-up*, pretentious, snobbish.

jáilaif (*LAm*) ① ADJ high-life (*atr*).
② NF high life.

jailoso ADJ (*And*) well-bred; (*pey*) stuck-up*, pretentious, snobbish.

Jaime NM James; **hacer el Jaimito*** to horse around*.

jalada NF (*Méx*) **(a)** (*tirón*) pull, tug, heave. **(b)** (*reprimenda*) ticking-off*. **(c)** (*And Univ*) failure.

jaladera NF (*Méx*) handle.

jalador NM (*LAm*) door-handle.

jalamecate* NM (*LAm*) toady, creep⁑.

jalapeño NM (*Méx*) (kind of) chili.

jalar [1a] ① VT **(a)** (*LAm: tirar de*) to pull, haul; (*Náut*) to heave; (*LAm Pol*) to draw, attract, win.
(b) (*LAm: trabajar mucho*) to work hard at.
(c) (*And, Carib**: hacer*) to make, do, perform.
(d) (*) to guzzle.
(e) (*Méx*: *dar aventón a*) to pick up, give a lift to.
(f) (*LAm**: conquistar*) to pull.
(g) **eso le jala** (*Méx**) she's big on that*, she's a fan of that.
② VI **(a)** (*LAm: tirar*) to pull; **~ de** to pull at, tug at.
(b) (*LAm: trabajar*) to work hard.
(c) (*LAm: irse*) to go, go off, clear out*; **~ para su casa** to clear off home.
(d) (*And⁑ Univ*) to flunk⁑, fail.
(e) (*CAm, Méx**: amantes*) to be courting.
(f) (*Méx: exagerar*) to exaggerate.
(g) (⁑: *correr*) to run.
(h) (*Méx: tener influencia*) to have pull.
(i) (*And⁑: fumar marijuana*) to smoke dope⁑.
③ **jalarse** VR **(a)** (*CAm**: amantes*) to be courting.
(b) (*LAm: emborracharse*) to get drunk.
(c) = VI **(c).**

(d) (**∵**: *masturbarse*) to wank**∵**.

jalbegar [1h] VT to whitewash; *cara* (**∗**) to make up, paint.

jalbegue NM whitewash; whitewashing; (**∗**) make-up, paint.

jalde ADJ, **jaldo** ADJ bright yellow.

jalea NF jelly; **~ de guayaba** guava jelly; **~ real** royal jelly; **hacerse una ~∶** to be madly in love; (*pey*) to be a creep**∶**.

jalear [1a] **1** VT (a) (*perro*) to urge on; *bailarina* to encourage (by shouting and clapping). (b) (*Méx*: *burlarse*) to jeer at.
2 VI (*Méx*) to have a high old time*.

jaleo NM (a) (*juerga*) spree, binge*; **estar de ~** to make merry, have a good time.
((b) (*ruido*) row, racket, uproar; (*confusión*) hassle, fuss; **armar un ~** to kick up a row; **se armó un tremendo ~** there was a hell of a row; **¡qué ~!** what a mess!, what a hassle!*
(c) (*Caza*) hallooing.
(d) (*Mús*) shouting and clapping (*to encourage dancers*).

jaleoso ADJ noisy, rowdy, boisterous.

jalisco¹∶ ADJ (*CAm, Méx*) plastered**∶**.

jalisco² NM (*CAm, Méx*) straw hat.

jallo (*Méx*) (*ostentoso*) showy, flashy; (*quisquilloso*) touchy.

jalón NM (a) (*poste*) stake, pole; (*de agrimensor*) surveying rod.
(b) (*fig*) (*etapa*) stage; (*hito*) landmark, milestone; **esto marca un ~ en ...** this is a milestone in ...
(c) (*LAm*) pull, tug; (**∶**: *robo*) snatch*; **hacer algo de un ~** (*Méx*) to do sth in one go.
(d) (*LAm*: *distancia*) distance, stretch; **hay un buen ~** it's a good way.
(e) (*CAm, Méx*∗: *trago*) swig*, drink.
(f) (*CAm*: *amante*) lover, sweetheart; (*pretendiente*) suitor.

jalona NF (*CAm*) flirt, flighty girl.

jalonamiento NM staking out, marking out.

jalonar [1a] VT to stake out, mark out; (*fig*) to mark; **el camino está jalonado por plazas fuertes** the route is marked out by a series of strongholds, a line of strongholds marks the route.

jalonazo NM (*CAm, Méx*) pull, tug.

jalonear [1a] **1** VT (*Méx*) to pull at, yank out.
2 VI (a) (*CAm, Méx*: *tirar*) to pull, tug. (b) (*CAm, Méx*∗: *regatear*) to haggle.

jalonero∶ NM bag-snatcher.

jalufa∶ NF hunger; **pasar ~, tener ~** to be hungry.

Jamaica NF Jamaica.

jamaica¹ NF (*CAm, Méx*) jumble sale, charity sale (*US*).

jamaica² NF (*Carib, Méx Bot*) hibiscus.

jamaicano, -a, jamaiquino, -a (*LAm*) ADJ, NM/F Jamaican.

jamancia∶ NF (a) (*comida*) grub**∶**. (b) (*hambre*) hunger; **pasar ~, tener ~** to be hungry.

jamar∶ [1a] **1** VI to eat, stuff oneself.
2 jamarse VR: **se lo jamó todo** he scoffed the lot*.

jamás ADV never; (not) ever; **¿se vio ~ tal cosa?** did you ever see such a thing?; **¡~!** never!; **¡~ de los jamases!** never in your life!; *V* **nunca** etc.

jamba¹ NF jamb; **~ de puerta** jamb, door post.

jamba²∶ NF bird**∶**, dame*.

jambado∗ ADJ (*Méx*) greedy, gluttonous; **estar ~** to be feeling overfull.

jambarse∗ [1a] VR (*CAm, Méx*) to stuff o.s.

jambo∶ NM bloke**∶**, geezer**∶**.

jamelgo NM wretched horse, nag, jade.

jamón **1** NM (a) (*gen*) ham; **~ (en) dulce, ~ (de) York** boiled ham; **~ serrano** cured ham; **¡y un ~ (con chorreras)!∗** get away!*, my foot!*; **you're hopeful!, you want jam on it!∗**
(b) (*Carib*: *ganga*) bargain.
(c) (*Carib*: *conflicto*) difficulty.
2 ADJ (**∗**) *persona* dishy*, attractive; **un plato que está ~** a delicious meal.

jamona NF buxom (middle-aged) woman.

jampa NF (*And, Méx*: *umbral*) threshold; (*puerta*) doorway.

jámparo NM (*And*) canoe, small boat.

jamurar∗ [1a] VT (*And*) to rinse.

jan NM (*Carib Agr*) seed drill; **ensartarse en los ~es** to get involved in an unprofitable piece of business.

jandinga∶ NF (*Carib*) grub**∶**.

janearse [1a] VR (*Carib*) (a) to leap into the saddle. (b) (**∗**: *pararse*) to come to a complete stop.

jangada¹ NF (*Náut*) raft.

jangada² NF (*disparate*) stupid remark; (*trampa*) dirty trick.

Jano NM Janus.

janpa NF = **jampa**.

Japón NM: **el ~** Japan.

japonés, -esa **1** ADJ, NM/F Japanese.
2 NM (*Ling*) Japanese.

jaque NM (a) (*Ajedrez*) check; **¡~ (al rey)!** check!; **~ continuo** continuous check; **~ mate** checkmate; **¡~ de aquí!** get out of here!; **dar ~ a**

to check; **dar ~ mate a** to checkmate, mate; **tener en ~** to check; (*fig*: *amenazar*) to hold a threat over; (*fig*: *mantener a raya*) to keep in check, hold at bay; (*fig*: *acosar*) to harass, worry.
(b) (**∗**: *matón*) bully, braggart.

jaquear [1a] VT (*Ajedrez*) to check; (*Mil y fig*) to harass; **quedar jaqueado** to be rendered powerless.

jaqueca NF (*severe*) headache, migraine; (*Cono Sur*: *resaca*) hangover; **dar ~ a** (*fig*: *aburrir*) to bore; (*fig*: *acosar*) to bother, pester.

jaquetón∗ NM bully, braggart.

jáquima NF (a) (*LAm*: *de caballo*) headstall. (b) (*CAm, Méx*∗) drunkenness, drunken state.

jaquimón NM (*LAm*) headstall, halter.

jara¹ NF (a) (*Bot*) rock rose, cistus; (*mata*) clump, thicket. (b) (*dardo*) dart, arrow. (c) **la ~** (*Méx*∗) the cops*.

jara² NF (*And*) halt, rest.

jarabe NM (a) (*syrup*) sweet drink; **~ de arce** maple syrup; **~ de palo∗** beating; **~ de pico** (*fig*) mere words, blarney; **~ para** (o **contra**) **la tos** cough syrup, cough mixture; **dar ~ a uno∗** to butter sb up.
(b) (*Méx*) *a popular dance*.

jaral NM (a) (*maleza*) ground covered with *jaras*, scrub; thicket. (b) (*fig*) difficult affair, thorny question.

jaramago NM hedge mustard.

jarana NF (a) (*juerga*) spree, binge*; (*lío*) rumpus, row; **andar de ~** to carouse; to lark about, have a high old time; **ir de ~** to go on the spree.
(b) (*trampa*) trick, deceit; (*LAm*) joke, practical joke, hoax; (*And*) fib; **la ~ sale a la cara** (*CAm*) a hoax can have a boomerang effect.
(c) (*And, Carib, Méx*: *baile*) folk dance; (*Carib*: *banda*) dance band.
(d) (*Mús Méx*) small guitar.
(e) (*Fin CAm*) debt.

jaranear [1a] **1** VT (*And, CAm*) to cheat, swindle.
2 VI (a) (*divertirse*) to lark about, have a high old time. (b) (*CAm*: *endeudarse*) to get into debt.

jaranero ADJ (a) (*de juerguista*) merry, roistering, rowdy. (b) (*CAm*: *tramposo*) deceitful, tricky.

jaranista ADJ (*LAm*) = **jaranero** (a).

jarano NM (*Méx*) broad hat, sombrero.

jarcha NF kharja.

jarcia NF (a) (*de pesca*) tackle, fishing tackle; (*Náut*: *t* **~s**) ropes, rigging; (*Carib, Méx*: *cuerda*) rope (*made from agave fibre*).
(b) (*CAm, Méx Bot*) agave.
(c) (*montón*) heap, mess.

jardín NM garden, flower garden; **~ alpestre, ~ rocoso** rock garden; **~ botánico** botanical garden; **~ de (la) infancia, ~ de infantes** (*LAm*) kindergarten, nursery school; **~ de rosas** (*fig*) bed of roses; **~ zoológico** zoo.

jardinaje NM (*LAm*) gardening.

jardinera NF (a) (*persona*) (woman) gardener.
(b) (*de balcón*) window box.
(c) (*Cono Sur*: *carrito*) handcart, barrow.
(d) (*And*: *saco*) jacket; (*Cono Sur*: *mono*) overalls.

jardinería NF gardening.

jardinero NM (a) (*gen*) gardener. (b) (*Cono Sur*: *de niño*) rompers.

jarea NF (*Méx*) hunger, keen appetite.

jarear [1a] VI (*And*) to halt, stop for a rest.

jarearse [1a] VR (*Méx*) (a) (*hambrear*) to be dying of hunger. (b) (*huir*) to flee.

jareta NF (a) (*Cos*) casing; (*red*) netting; (*Náut*) cable, rope. (b) (*CAm, Cono Sur*: *de pantalón*) trouser flies. (c) (*Carib*: *contratiempo*) snag, setback.

jarete NM (*Carib*) paddle.

jari∗ NM row, racket.

jarifo ADJ (*liter*) elegant, showy, spruce.

jaripeo∗ NM (*Méx*) horse show.

jaro NM arum lily.

jarope NM syrup; (**∗**) brew, concoction, nasty drink; **resultó un ~ poco agradable** it was a bitter pill to swallow.

jarra NF jar, pitcher; (*para leche*) churn; (*para cerveza*) mug, tankard; **de ~s, en ~s** with arms akimbo.

jarrada NF (*LAm*) jarful, jugful.

jarrete NM (*Anat*) back of the knee; (*de caballo*) hock; (*And*) heel.

jarro NM jug, pitcher; **echar un ~ de agua fría a una idea** to pour cold water on an idea; **caer como un ~ de agua fría** to come as a complete shock.

jarrón NM vase; (*Arquit*) urn.

jartón∗ ADJ (*CAm, Méx*) greedy, gluttonous.

Jartum NM, **Jartún** NM Khartoum.

jaspe NM jasper.

jaspeado ADJ mottled, speckled, marbled; streaked.

jaspear [1a] **1** VT to speckle, marble; to streak.
2 jaspearse∗ VR (*Carib*) to get cross.

jato NM (a) (*ternero*) calf.

(b) (*Carib: perro*) stray dog, mongrel.
(c) (*Méx: carga*) load.
(d) (*And: silla de montar*) saddle.
(e) (*LAm*) = **hato**.

jauja NF **(a)** (*t* J~) promised land, earthly paradise; **¡esto es ~!** this is the life!; **¿estamos aquí o en ~?** where do you think you are?; **vivir en ~** to live in luxury, have a marvellous life.
(b) (*Cono Sur•: chisme*) rumour, tale.

jaula NF (*gen*) cage; (*Min*) cage; (*de embalaje etc*) crate; (*de loco*) cell; (•: *tienda*) lock-up; (*Aut*) lock-up garage; (*Méx• Ferro*) cattle-truck; (*Carib*) Black Maria, police wagon (*US*); **hacer ~** (*Méx*) to dig one's heels in.

jauría NF pack of hounds.
Java NF Java.
java• NF (*Carib*) trick.
Javier NM Xavier.
jay: NF = **jai**.
jayán NM **(a)** big strong man; (*pey*) hulking great brute, tough guy•.
(b) (*CAm•: grosero*) foul-mouthed person.
jayares: NMPL bread:, money.
jáyaro• ADJ (*And*) rough, uncouth.
jazmín NM jasmine; **~ del Cabo**, **~ de la India** gardenia.
jazz [jaθ *o* jas] NM jazz.
jazzista ① ADJ jazz (*atr*); jazzy.
   ② NMF jazz player.
jazzístico ADJ jazz (*atr*).
J.C. ABR *de* **Jesu Cristo** Jesus Christ, J.C.
jeans ['jins] NMPL jeans.
jebe NM **(a)** (*LAm*) (*Bot*) rubber plant; (*goma*) rubber; (*elástico*) elastic.
(b) (*porra*) club, cudgel; **llevar ~** to suffer a lot. **(c)** (:: *trasero*) arse::.
(d) (*And:: preservativo*) French letter.
jebero NM (*LAm*) rubber-plantation worker.
jeep [jip] NM jeep.
jefa NF **(a)** (woman) head, (woman) boss; manager(ess); (*líder*) leader; **~ de sastrería** (*Teat*) wardrobe mistress. **(b)** (•: *mujer mandona*) bossy woman.
jefatura NF **(a)** (*liderato*) leadership; chieftainship; **bajo la ~ de** under the leadership of; **dimitir la ~ del partido** to resign the party leadership.
(b) (*sede*) headquarters; central office; **~ de policía** police headquarters.
(c) (*Carib: registro*) registry office.
jefazo• NM big shot•, big noise•.
jefe NMF (*V t* **jefa**) **(a)** (*gen*) chief, head, boss; (*líder*) leader; (*gerente*) manager; (*Mil*) field officer, officer in command; **~ de almacén** warehouse manager; **~ de bomberos** fire officer; **~ de cabina** (*Aer*) chief steward; **~ de camareros** head waiter; **~ civil** (*Carib*) registrar; **~ de cocina** chef; **~ de estación** station master; **~ de estado** head of state, chief of state; **~ de estado mayor** chief of staff; **~ de estudios** (*Escol*) deputy head; **~ de filas** (*Pol*) party leader; **~ de máquinas** (*Náut*) chief engineer; **~ de márketing** marketing manager; **~ de los mozos** head groom; **~ de obras** project manager; site manager; **~ de personal** personnel manager; **~ de pista** ringmaster; **~ de plató** (*Cine, TV*) floor-manager; **~ político** (*LAm Pol*) second-in-command to local politician; **~ de protocolo** chief of protocol; **~ de realización** (*Cine, TV*) production manager; **~ de redacción** editor-in-chief; **~ supremo** commander-in-chief; **~ de taller** foreman; **~ de tren** guard, conductor (*US*); **~ de ventas** sales manager; **comandante en ~** commander-in-chief; **¡oiga ~!** hey, mate!•; **¡sí, (mi) ~!** (*esp LAm*) yes, sir!, yes, boss! (*US*); **ser el ~** (*fig*) to be the boss.
(b) (*de tribu*) chief.
Jehová NM Jehovah.
jején NM **(a)** (*Zool*) mosquito; gnat; **sabe donde el ~ puso el huevo** (*Carib*) he's pretty smart.
(b) (*And, Méx•: montón*) heaps•, masses; **un ~ de cosas** a lot of things.
(c) (*Méx•: multitud*) mob.
jelenque• NM (*Méx*) din, racket.
jemeres NMPL: **los ~ rojos** the Khmer Rouge.
jemiquear [1a] VI (*Cono Sur*) = **jeremiquear**.
JEN [xen] NF (*Esp*) ABR *de* **Junta de Energía Nuclear** Nuclear Energy Authority.
jengibre NM ginger.
jenízaro ① ADJ mixed, hybrid.
   ② NM (*Hist*) janissary.
Jenofonte NM Xenophon.
jeque NM sheik(h).
jeremías• NMF INVAR moaner•, whinger•.
jerarca NM chief, leader; important person; (*pey*) big shot•.
jerarquía NF hierarchy; (high) rank; **una persona de ~** a high-ranking person.
jerárquico ADJ hierarchic(al).
jerarquización NF hierarchical structuring; arranging in order (of

importance).
jerarquizado ADJ hierarchical.
jerarquizar [1f] VT *organismo* to give a hierarchical structure to; *elementos* to arrange in order (of importance).
jeremiada NF jeremiad.
Jeremías NM Jeremy; (*Bib*) Jeremiah.
jeremiquear [1a] VI (*LAm*) (*lloriquear*) to snivel, whimper; (*regañar*) to nag.
Jerez NF: **~ de la Frontera** Jerez.
jerez NM sherry.

> ⓘ **Jerez** is a specific term for the fortified white wine from the *denominación de origen* area around Jerez de la Frontera in Andalusia. There are many varieties, which are not always equivalent to the sherries sold in Britain. The name given to each variety depends on the exact conditions of manufacture, such as the amount of yeast mould which is allowed to grow on the surface of the wine, and the blending process. The main types are: **fino** (very dry and pale), **amontillado** (dry, with a nutty flavour) and **oloroso** (darker colour, full flavour). A special type of fino called **manzanilla** (literally, "camomile tea") is produced only in the town of Sanlúcar de Barrameda, where the sea air is supposed to give it a salty tang.
> ⇨ *See also* DENOMINACIÓN DE ORIGEN , SOLERA

jerezano ① ADJ of Jerez.
   ② NM, **jerezana** NF native (*o* inhabitant) of Jerez; **los ~s** the people of Jerez.
jerga¹ NF coarse cloth, sackcloth; (*LAm: manta de caballo*) horse blanket; (*And*) coarse cloak; (*Méx*) floor cloth.
jerga² NF jargon; slang, cant; gibberish; **~ de germanía** thieves' cant; **~ informática** computer jargon; **~ publicitaria** sales talk, salesman's patter.
jergal ADJ jargon (*atr*); slang (*atr*), cant (*atr*).
jergón NM **(a)** palliasse, straw mattress. **(b)** (•: *vestido*) ill-fitting garment. **(c)** (•: *persona*) awkward-looking person, oaf.
jeribeque NM: **hacer ~s** to make faces, grimace.
Jericó NM Jericho.
jerigonza NF **(a)** = **jerga²**. **(b)** (*estupidez*) silly thing, piece of folly.
jeringa NF **(a)** (*gen*) syringe; **~ de engrase** grease-gun; **~ de un solo uso** throw-away syringe. **(b)** (*LAm•: persona*) pest, nuisance.
jeringador ADJ (*LAm*) annoying, bothersome.
jeringar [1h] ① VT **(a)** to syringe; to inject; to squirt. **(b)** (:: *molestar*) to annoy, bother, plague; **¡no jeringues!** stop mucking about!; **¡nos ha jeringado!** he's done it on us!•
   ② **jeringarse•** VR to put up with it; **¡que se jeringue!** he can lump it!•
jeringazo NM syringing; injection; squirt.
jeringón• ① ADJ (*LAm*) = **jeringador**.
   ② NM, **jeringona** NF (*LAm*) pest, nuisance.
jeringuear [1a] VT (*LAm*) = **jeringar** (b).
jeringuilla¹ NF mock orange, syringa.
jeringuilla² NF: **~ hipodérmica** (*Med*) syringe.
Jerjes NM Xerxes.
jeró: NM clock:, mug:.
jeroglífico ① ADJ hieroglyphic.
   ② NM hieroglyph(ic); (*fig*) puzzle.
Jerónimo NM Jerome.
jerónimo¹ ADJ, NM (*Ecl*) Hieronymite.
jerónimo² NM: **sin ~ de duda** (*LAm: hum*) without a shadow of doubt.
jersé NM, **jersei** NM, **jersey** [xer'sei] NM, PL **jerseis**, **jerseys** [xer'seis] jersey, sweater, pullover; jumper; (*LAm: tela*) jersey.
Jerusalén NM Jerusalem.
jeruza: NF (*CAm*) clink:, jail.
Jesucristo NM Jesus Christ.
jesuita ① ADJ (*Ecl*) Jesuit; (*fig*) Jesuitic(al).
   ② NM (*Ecl*) Jesuit; (*fig*) hypocrite, sly person.
jesuítico ADJ Jesuitic(al).
Jesús NM Jesus; **¡~!** good heavens!; (*al estornudar*) bless you!; **en un (decir) ~** in an instant, before one can say Jack Robinson; **morir sin decir ~** to die very suddenly.
jet [jet], PL **jets** [jet] ① NM (*Aer*) jet, jet plane.
   ② NF jet-set.
jeta ① NF **(a)** (*Anat*) thick lips.
(b) (*Zool*) snout; (•: *cara*) mug:, dial:; **estirar la ~** (*Cono Sur:*) to kick the bucket:; **te romperé la ~** I'll smash your mug in:.
(c) (•: *ceño*) frown, scowl, disagreeable expression; **poner ~** to frown, scowl.
(d) (•: *descaro*) cheek•, nerve•; **¡qué ~ tiene!** he's got a nerve!; **lo hace por la ~** he gets away with it by sheer cheek.
   ② NM (•) swine, bastard:.

jetazo* NM bash*, punch.
jetear [1a] VI (*Cono Sur*) to eat at someone else's expense.
jetón ADJ, **jetudo** ADJ **(a)** thick-lipped. **(b)** (*Cono Sur*) stupid.
Jezabel NF Jezebel.
JHS ABR *de* **Jesús** Jesus, IHS.
ji INTERJ ¡~, ~, ~! ha ha!; (*iró*) tee hee!
jibarear [1a] VI (*Carib*) to flirt.
jíbaro [1] ADJ (*Carib, Méx*) (*rústico*) country (*atr*), rustic; (*huraño*) sullen.
　[2] NM, **jíbara** NF (*Carib, Méx*) peasant.
　[3] NM **(a)** (*CAm*: *traficante*) (drug) dealer.
　(b) (*Carib*: *animal*) wild animal.
jibia [1] NF (*Zool*) cuttlefish.
　[2] NM (‡) queer‡, poof‡.
jícama NF (*CAm, Méx*) edible tuber.
jícara NF **(a)** (*tacita*) small cup (for drinking-chocolate *etc*).
　(b) (*CAm, Méx*) (*calabaza, vasija*) gourd, calabash; (*Méx**: *calva*) pate;
　bailar la ~ a uno* to soft-soap sb*; **sacar la ~ a uno** to shower sb
　with attentions.
jicarazo NM (cup of) poison, poisonous drink; (*CAm, Méx*) cupful.
jícaro NM (*CAm, Méx*) **(a)** (*Bot*) calabash tree. **(b)** (*plato*) bowl.
jicarón ADJ (*CAm*) big-headed.
jicarudo ADJ (*Méx**) broad-faced, broad-browed.
jiche NM (*CAm, Méx*) tendon, sinew.
jicote NM (*CAm, Méx*) wasp.
jicotera NF (*CAm, Méx*) (*nido*) wasps' nest; (*zumbido*) buzzing of wasps;
　armar una ~ to kick up a row.
jiennense [1] ADJ of Jaén.
　[2] NMF native (o inhabitant) of Jaén; **los ~s** the people of Jaén.
jifero [1] ADJ (*) filthy.
　[2] NM **(a)** (*matarife*) slaughterer, butcher. **(b)** (*cuchillo*) butcher's knife.
jifia NF swordfish.
jijona NM soft nougat (*made in Jijona*); *see also* [TURRÓN].
jilguero NM goldfinch; **¡mi ~!*** my angel!
jilibioso* ADJ (*Cono Sur*) (*lloroso*) weepy, tearful; (*delicado*) finicky, hard
　to please; *caballo* nervous.
jilipollas‡ ADJ, NMF INVAR = **gilipollas**.
jilote NM (*CAm, Méx*) (*elote*) green ear of maize; (*maíz verde*) young
　maize, young corn (*US*).
jilotear [1a] VI (*CAm, Méx*) to come into ear.
jimagua (*Carib*) [1] ADJ twin; identical.
　[2] NMF twin.
jimba NF **(a)** (*And*: *trenza*) pigtail, plait; (*Méx*: *bambú*) bamboo. **(b)**
　(*Méx**: *borrachera*) drunkenness.
jimbal NM (*Méx*) bamboo thicket.
jimbito NM (*CAm*) (*avispa*) small wasp; (*nido*) wasps' nest.
jimbo ADJ (*Méx*) drunk.
jimeno‡ NM (*Méx*) cop*.
jimio NM = **simio**.
jinaiste* NM (*Méx*) bunch of kids.
jincar* [1g] VT (*CAm*) to spike.
jindama* NF fear, funk*.
jindarse [1a] VR: **se lo jindó todo** he scoffed the lot*.
jineta¹ NF **(a)** (*esp LAm*) horsewoman, rider. **(b) a la ~** with short stir-
　rups.
jineta² NF (*Zool*) genet.
jinete NM horseman, rider; (*Mil*) cavalryman.
jinetear [1a] [1] VT **(a)** (*LAm*) (*domar*) to break in; (*montar*) to ride; **~ la**
　burra (*CAm*) to go the whole hog, stake everything.
　(b) (*Méx**) *fondos* to misappropriate.
　[2] VI to ride around, show off one's horsemanship.
　[3] **jinetearse** VR **(a)** (*And, Méx*) (*no caer*) to stay in the saddle; (*) to
　hang on, keep going.
　(b) (*And*: *ser presumido*) to be vain.
jingoísmo NM jingoism.
jingoísta [1] ADJ jingoistic.
　[2] NMF jingoist, jingo.
jiote NM (*CAm, Méx*: *Med*) impetigo.
jipa NF (*And*) straw hat.
jipar* [1a] VT: **le tengo jipado** I've got him taped*, I've got him all
　sized up.
jipatera NF (*And, Carib, Méx*), **jipatez** NF (*Carib, Méx*) paleness, wan-
　ness.
jipato ADJ (*LAm*) (*pálido*) pale, wan; (*enclenque*) sickly, frail; (*soso*) taste-
　less.
jipe NM (*And, Méx*), **jipi¹** NM straw hat.
jipi² NMF hippy.
jipijapa [1] NF (*paja*) straw for weaving.
　[2] NM (*sombrero*) straw hat.
jipioso (a) ADJ, NM/F = **hippioso**.
jipismo NM = **hippismo**.
jira¹ NF (*de tela*) strip.
jira² NF excursion, outing; picnic (*t* **~ campestre**); **ir de ~** to go on an

outing, go for a picnic; *V t* **gira.**
jirafa NF **(a)** (*Zool*) giraffe. **(b)** (*Téc*) jib, arm, boom.
jiribilla NF (*Méx*) spin, turn; **tener ~** (*Carib*) to have its awkward
　points; (*persona*) to be anxious.
jirimiquear [1a] VI (*LAm*) = **jeremiquear**.
jirón NM **(a)** (*andrajo*) rag, shred, tatter; **en jirones** in shreds; **hacer**
　algo jirones to tear sth to shreds.
　(b) (*fig*) bit, shred.
　(c) (*And*: *calle*) street.
jit* [xit] NM, PL **jits** [xit] (*LAm*) hit.
jitazo NM (*Méx*) hit, blow; (*Dep*) hit, stroke.
jitomate NM (*Méx*) tomato.
jiu-jitsu NM jiu-jitsu.
JJ.OO. NMPL ABR *de* **Juegos Olímpicos** Olympic Games.
jo* INTERJ **(a)** ¡~! (*sorpresa*) well I'm blowed!*; (*alivio*) phew!; (*saludo*)
　hey*, hi*; ¡~, ~! (*risa*) ha ha!, ho ho! **(b)** (*euf*) = **joder** *etc*.
Job NM Job.
jobar* INTERJ God!
jobo NM **(a)** (*CAm, Méx*: *Bot*) cedar (tree). **(b)** (*CAm**: *aguardiente*) spirits.
jockey ['joki] NM, PL **jockeys** ['jokis] jockey; (*LAm*) jockey cap.
joco ADJ **(a)** (*CAm, Méx*: *amargo*) sharp, sour, bitter. **(b)** (*And*: *hueco*)
　hollow.
jocolote* NM (*CAm*) hut, shack.
jocoque NM (*Méx*) sour cream.
jocosamente ADV humorously, comically.
jocoserio ADJ seriocomic.
jocosidad NF humour; jokiness; (*una ~*) joke.
jocoso ADJ humorous, comic, jocular, jokey.
joda‡ NF (*LAm*) **(a)** (*molestia*) annoyance; bother; (*daño*) harm;
　(*dificultad*) trouble. **(b)** (*broma*) joke; **lo dijo en ~** he said it as a joke;
　estar de ~ to have a booze-up‡.
jodedera‡ NF screwing‡.
joder‡ [2a] [1] VT **(a)** (*Esp*) to fuck‡, screw‡; ¡~! (*enfado*) damn it!,
　damnation!; (*sorpresa*) well I'm damned!
　(b) (‡*fig*) (*fastidiar*) to annoy, upset; (*dañar*) to harm, spoil; to dam-
　age; (*acosar*) to pester; (*estropear*) to mess up; **esto me jode** I'm fed
　up with this*; **esta ciudad está jodida** this town is all screwed up*‡;
　son ganas de ~ they're just trying to be awkward; **¡no me jodas!**
　(*no fastidies*) stop bothering me!; (*rechazo*) come off it!, tell us anoth-
　er!; (*no te creo*) you're joking!
　(c) (‡: *robar*) to pinch*, steal; **alguien le jodió el puesto** sb pinched
　the job from him.
　[2] VI to fuck‡, screw‡.
　[3] **joderse** VR **(a)** ¡que te jodas! get stuffed!‡; **¡hay que ~!** this is
　the end!, to hell with it all!
　(b) (*fracasar*) to flop; (*estropearse*) to get spoiled, get messed up; **se**
　jodió todo everything was spoiled; **se ha jodido la función** the
　show was a failure.
jodido‡ ADJ **(a)** (*difícil*) awkward, difficult, tough; **es un libro ~** it's a
　very difficult book; ¡~! sod it!‡
　(b) estoy ~ (*cansado*) I'm worn out, I'm shagged‡.
　(c) (*condenado*) bloody‡‡; **ni una jodida peseta** not one bloody pe-
　seta‡.
　(d) todo está ~ (*estropeado*) it's all cocked up‡.
　(e) (*LAm*) *persona* (*egoísta*) selfish; (*malo*) evil, wicked; (*quisquilloso*)
　awkward, prickly; (*zalamero*) smarmy, oily.
jodienda‡ NF (*Cono Sur, Méx*) fucking nuisance‡‡.
jodón‡ ADJ (*LAm*) **(a)** (*molesto*) bloody annoying‡; **es tan ~** (*bromista*)
　he loves arsing about‡‡. **(b)** (*tramposo*) slippery.
jodontón‡ ADJ randy*, oversexed.
jofaina NF washbasin.
jogging ['joɣin] NM **(a)** (*Dep*) jogging; **hacer ~** to jog. **(b)** (*Cono Sur*)
　jogging suit.
jojoba NF jojoba.
jojoto (*Carib*) [1] ADJ *fruta* (*manchado*) bruised; (*inmaduro*) green,
　underripe; *maíz* soft, tender.
　[2] NM ear of maize.
jol NM hall, lobby.
jolgórico ADJ riotous, hilarious; rowdy.
jolgorio NM **(a)** (*juerga*) fun, merriment; high jinks; revelry; rowdi-
　ness. **(b)** (*un ~*) spree, binge*; lark*; **ir de ~** to go on a binge*.
jolín*, jolines* INTERJ sugar!*
jolinche ADJ **jolino** ADJ (*Méx*) short-tailed, bob-tailed.
jolón NM (*Méx*) (*avispa*) wasp; (*avispero*) wasps' nest.
jolongo NM **(a)** (*Carib*) shoulder-bag. **(b)** (*) problem.
jolote NM (*CAm, Méx*) turkey.
joma NF (*Méx*) hump.
jomb(e)ado ADJ (*Méx*) hunchbacked.
Jonás NM Jonah.
Jonatás NM Jonathan.
jónico ADJ Ionic.
jonja NF (*Cono Sur*) mimicry.

jonjear [1a] VT (*Cono Sur*) to tease, make fun of.
jonjolear* [1a] VT (*And*) to spoil.
jonrón NM (*LAm Dep*) home run.
jonronear [1a] VI (*LAm Dep*) to make a home run.
JONS [xons] NFPL (*Esp Hist*) ABR *de* **Juntas de Ofensiva Nacional Sindicalista.**
jopé✲ INTERJ COR!✲
jopo[1] = **hopo**[2].
jopo[2] NM = **hopo**[1].
jora NF (*LAm*) *maize specially prepared for making high-grade chicha.*
Jordán NM Jordan (*river*); **ir al ~** (*fig*) to be rejuvenated.
Jordania NF Jordan (*country*).
jordano, -a ADJ, NM/F Jordanian.
jorga* NF (*And*) gang.
Jorge NM George.
jorgón NM (*And*) lot, abundance.
jorguín NM sorcerer, wizard.
jorguina NF sorceress, witch.
jorguinería NF sorcery, witchcraft.
jornada NF (**a**) (*viaje*) day's journey; (*etapa*) stage (of a journey); **a largas ~s** (*Mil*) by forced marches; **al fin de la ~** at the end.
(**b**) (*día de trabajo*) working day; (*horas*) hours of work; (*turno*) shift; (*fig*) lifetime, span of life; **~ de 8 horas** 8-hour day; **~ anual** working days in the year; **~ inglesa** five-day week; **~ laboral** (*semana*) working week; (*anual*) working year; **~ legal** maximum legal working hours; **~ de lucha** day of action; **~ partida** split shift; **~ de puertas abiertas** open day; **~ de reflexión** (*Pol*) day before election (*on which campaigning is banned*); **~ semanal** working week; **hay ~ limitada en la industria** there is short-time working in the industry; **trabajar en ~s reducidas** to work short-time.
(**c**) (*Mil*) expedition; **la ~ de Orán** the expedition against Oran.
(**d**) (*Univ etc*) congress, conference; **J~s Cervantinas** Conference on Cervantes, Cervantes Conference.
(**e**) (*Teat Hist*) act.
(**f**) (*Cono Sur: sueldo*) day's wage.
jornadista NMF (*Univ etc*) conference member, delegate.
jornal NM (*sueldo*) (day's) wage; (*trabajo*) day's work; **~ mínimo** minimum wage; **política de ~es y precios** prices and incomes policy; **trabajar a ~** to work for a day wage, be paid by the day.
jornalero NM (day) labourer.
joro NM (*Carib*) small basket.
joroba [1] NF (**a**) (*Anat*) hump, hunched back. (**b**) (*fig*) nuisance, bother, annoyance.
[2] NMF hunchback.
jorobado [1] ADJ hunchbacked.
[2] NM, **jorobada** NF hunchback.
jorobar* [1a] [1] VT (**a**) (*fastidiar*) to annoy, pester, bother; **esto me joroba** I'm fed up with this*, this gives me the hump*; **¡no me jorobes!** stop bothering me!
(**b**) (*estropear*) to break, smash; to mess up.
[2] **jorobarse** VR (**a**) (*enfadarse*) to get cross, get worked up; (*cansarse*) to get fed up*.
(**b**) (*aguantar*) to put up with it; **pues ¡que se jorobe!** well, he can lump it!*
(**c**) (*fracasar*) to fail, go down the drain; to spoil, be spoiled.
(**d**) (*romperse*) to break, smash, be damaged.
(**e**) **¡~!** (EXCL) hell!, well I'm damned!; **¡hay que ~!** to hell with it!
jorobeta NF (*Cono Sur*) nuisance.
jorobón ADJ (*LAm*) annoying.
joronche* NM (*Méx*) hunchback.
jorongo NM (*Méx*) poncho.
joropo NM (*Carib*) *a popular dance.*
jorro NM (*Carib*) poor-quality cigarette.
jorungo* ADJ (*Carib: molesto*) annoying, irritating.
José NM Joseph.
Josefina NF Josephine.
Josué NM Joshua.
jota[1] NF (**a**) (*letra*) the (name of the) letter *j*.
(**b**) (*fig*) jot, iota; **no entendió ni ~** he didn't understand a word of it; **sin faltar una ~** to a T, with complete accuracy, just as it should be; **no sabe ni ~** he hasn't a clue (*de about*).
jota[2] NF (*And, Cono Sur Orn*) vulture.
jota[3] NF *Spanish dance and tune* (*esp Aragonese*).
jota[4] NF (*Naipes*) knave, jack.
jote NM (*Cono Sur*) (**a**) (*Orn*) buzzard; (*cometa*) large kite. (**b**) (*desagradecido*) ungrateful person; (✲: *cura*) priest.
joto [1] ADJ (*Méx*) effeminate.
[2] NM (**a**) (*And*) bundle. (**b**) (*Méx*✲) queer✲.
jovata* NF (*Cono Sur*) old woman.
jovato* NM (*Cono Sur*) old man.
joven [1] ADJ young; *aspecto etc* youthful.
[2] NM (**a**) young man, youth; **los jóvenes** young people, youth, the

young; **¡eh, ~!** I say, young man!
(**b**) (*Cono Sur*) waiter.
[3] NF young woman, young lady, girl.
jovencito, -a NM/F youngster.
jovial ADJ jolly, cheerful, jovial.
jovialidad NF jolliness, cheerfulness, joviality.
jovialmente ADV in a jolly way, cheerfully, jovially.
joya NF (**a**) (*gen*) jewel, gem, piece of jewellery; **~ de familia** heirloom.
(**b**) **~s** jewels, jewellery; (*de novia*) trousseau; **~s de fantasía**, **~s de imitación** imitation jewellery.
(**c**) (*fig*) gem, treasure, precious thing; (*persona*) gem, treasure.
joyería NF (**a**) (*joyas*) jewellery, jewels. (**b**) (*tienda*) jeweller's (shop).
joyero NM (**a**) (*persona*) jeweller. (**b**) (*estuche*) jewel case.
Jruschov NM Khrushchev.
juagar [1h] VT (*And*) = **enjuagar.**
Juan NM John; **don ~** don John, don Juan; (*Mús*) Don Giovanni; **San ~ Bautista** St John the Baptist; **San ~ Evangelista** St John the Evangelist; **San ~ de la Cruz** St John of the Cross; **el Papa ~ Pablo II** Pope John Paul II; **un buen ~** a simple soul, a good-natured fool; **~ Lanas**, **~ Vainas** (*CAm: pey*) simpleton; (*marido*) henpecked husband; **~ Palomo** (*solitario*) lone wolf, loner; (*egoísta*) person who looks after Number One; **~ Zoquete** rustic, idiot.
juan NM (*And, Méx*) common soldier.
Juana NF Joan, Jean, Jane; **~ de Arco** Joan of Arc.
juana NF (**a**) (*And: prostituta*) whore. (**b**) (*Méx**) marijuana. (**c**) (*CAm**) cop*.
juancarlismo NM support for King Juan Carlos I.
juancarlista [1] ADJ of (o relating to) King Juan Carlos I; **ser ~** to be a supporter of King Juan Carlos I.
[2] NMF supporter of King Juan Carlos I.
juancho NM (*And*) boyfriend, lover.
juanete NM (**a**) (*Med*) bunion; (*pómulo*) prominent cheekbone; (*del pie*) ball of the foot. (**b**) (*Náut*) topgallant sail. (**c**) (*And, CAm: cadera*) hip.
juanillo* NM (*And, Cono Sur*) bribe.
juapao NM (*Carib*) beating, thrashing.
jubilación NF (**a**) (*acto, estado*) retirement; **~ anticipada**, **~ prematura** early retirement; **~ forzosa** compulsory retirement; **~ voluntaria** voluntary retirement. (**b**) (*pago*) pension, retirement pension.
jubilado [1] ADJ (**a**) retired. (**b**) (*And, Carib**: *sagaz*) wise. (**c**) (*And**: *lerdo*) thick*, slow-witted.
[2] NM, **jubilada** NF retired person, pensioner.
jubilar [1a] [1] VT (**a**) *persona* to pension off, retire.
(**b**) (*fig*) *persona* to shunt aside, put out to grass; *objeto* to discard, get rid of, cast aside; to banish, relegate.
[2] VI to rejoice.
[3] **jubilarse** VR (**a**) to retire, take one's pension.
(**b**) (*CAm: hacer novillos*) to play truant.
(**c**) (*Carib**: *ponerse listo*) to gain experience.
(**d**) (*And**: *deteriorar*) to deteriorate, go downhill; (*enloquecer*) to lose one's head.
jubileo NM (**a**) (*Rel*) jubilee; **por ~** once in a lifetime. (**b**) (*) comings and goings.
júbilo NM joy, jubilation, rejoicing; **con ~** joyfully, with jubilation.
jubiloso ADJ jubilant.
jubón NM (*de hombre*) doublet, jerkin, close-fitting jacket; (*de mujer*) bodice.
jud NM (*CAm Aut*) bonnet, hood (*US*).
Judá NM Judah.
judaico ADJ Jewish, Judaic.
judaísmo NM Judaism.
judaizante [1] ADJ Judaizing.
[2] NMF Judaizer.
Judas NM Judas; (*fig*) traitor, betrayer.
judas NM (**a**) (*LAm: en puerta*) peephole. (**b**) (*Méx: figura de papel*) figure burnt on Easter bonfires. (**c**) (*Cono Sur**) snooper*.
Judea NF Judea.
judeo-español ADJ, NM Judeo-Spanish.
judería NF (**a**) (*barrio*) Jewish quarter, ghetto. (**b**) (*judíos*) Jewry. (**c**) (*CAm, Méx**: *travesura*) prank.
judía NF (**a**) (*Jewess*, Jewish woman. (**b**) (*Bot*) kidney bean; **~ blanca** haricot bean; **~ colorada**, **~ escarlata**, **~ de España**, **~ negra** runner bean; **~ de Lima**, **~ de la peladilla** Lima bean; **~ pinta** pinto bean; **~ verde** French bean, green bean.
judiada NF (**a**) (*acto cruel*) cruel act, cruel thing. (**b**) (*Fin*) extortion.
judicatura NF (**a**) (*jueces*) judicature. (**b**) (*cargo*) judgeship, office of judge.
judicial ADJ judicial; **recurrir a la vía ~** to go to law, have recourse to the law.
judío [1] ADJ Jewish.
[2] NM Jew.

Judit NF Judith.

judo NM judo.

judoca NMF, **judoka** NMF judoist, judoka.

juego¹ etc (verbo) V **jugar**.

juego² NM **(a)** (gen, acto) play, playing; (Dep) sport; (diversión) fun, amusement; **los niños en el ~** children at play; **~ doble** double-dealing; **~ duro** rough play; **~ limpio** fair play; **~ de roles** role-playing; **~ sucio** foul play, dirty play; **el balón está en ~** the ball is in play; **hay diversos intereses en ~** there are various interests concerned; **entrar en ~** (persona) to take a hand; (factor) to come into play; **poner algo en ~** to set sth in motion, bring sth into play; **estar fuera de ~** (persona) to be offside; (balón) to be out, be out of play; **por ~** in fun, for fun.

(b) (recreo: un ~) game, sport; **es solamente un ~** it's only a game; **~s atléticos** (athletic) sports; **~ de azar** game of chance; **~ de las bochas** bowls; **~ de (las) bolas** American skittles; **~ de las bolitas, ~ de las canicas** marbles; **~ de bolos** ninepins, skittles, tenpin bowling; **~ de cartas** card game; **~ de la cuna** cat's cradle; **~ de damas** draughts, checkers (US); **~ de destreza** game of skill; **~ educativo** educational game; **~s infantiles** children's games; **~s malabares** juggling; **~ de manos** conjuring trick; **~s de manos** conjuring; **~ de mesa** table game; **~ de naipes** card game; **J~s Olímpicos** Olympic Games; **J~s Olímpicos de invierno** Winter Olympics; **~ de palabras** pun, play on words; **~ de prendas** (game of) forfeits; **~ de rol** role-playing game; **~ de salón, ~ de sociedad** parlour game, party game; **~ del tejo** hopscotch.

(c) (~ terminado) (complete o finished) game; (Tenis) game; (Bridge) rubber; **~, set y partido** game, set and match.

(d) (fig) game; **le conozco el ~, le veo el ~** I know his little game, I know what he's up to; **seguirle el ~ a alguien** to play along with sb.

(e) (con apuestas) gambling, gaming; **el ~ es un vicio** gambling is a vice; **lo perdió todo en el ~** he lost the lot gambling; **lo que está en ~** what is at stake; **¡hagan ~!** place your bets!

(f) (Mec) play, movement; **estar en ~** to be in gear, be in mesh.

(g) (luz etc) play; **el ~ de luces sobre el agua** the play of light on the water; **el ~ de los colores** the interplay of the colours.

(h) (pista) pitch, court; **en el ~ de pelota** on the pelota court.

(i) (conjunto) set; (vajilla) set, service; (muebles) suite; (herramientas etc) set, kit, outfit; (cartas) hand; pack; **~ de bolas** (Mec) ball bearing, set of ball bearings; **~ de café** coffee set; **~ de campanas** peal of bells; **~ de caracteres** character set; **~ de comedor** dining-room suite; **~ de mesa** dinner service; **~ de programas** suite of programmes; **una falda a ~ con un jersey** a skirt with a jersey to match; a skirt which goes with a jersey; **con falda a ~** with matching skirt, with skirt to match; **hacen ~** they match, they go well together.

juepucha INTERJ (Cono Sur) well I'm damned!

juerga* NF binge*, spree, carousal; good time; **correr las grandes ~s** to live it up*; **¡vaya ~ que nos vamos a correr con ellas!** what a time we'll have with them!; **ir de ~** to go on a spree, go out for a good time.

juergata* NF = **juerga**.

juerguearse* [1a] VR to live it up*.

juerguista* NMF reveller.

juev. ABR de **jueves** Thursday, Thur(s).

jueves NM INVAR Thursday; **J~ Santo** Maundy Thursday; **no es cosa del otro ~** it's nothing to write home about.

juez NMF (t **jueza** NF) **(a)** (Jur) judge (t fig); **Jueces** (Bíb) Book of Judges; **~ árbitro** arbitrator, referee; **~ de diligencias, ~ de instrucción, ~ instructor** examining magistrate; **~ municipal** magistrate.

(b) (Dep) judge; **~ de banda, ~ lateral, ~ de línea** (Fútbol etc) linesman, (Rugby) touch judge; **~ de llegada, ~ de meta, ~ de raya** (Cono Sur) judge; **~ de salida** starter; **~ de silla** (Tenis) umpire.

jugable ADJ playable, suitable for playing.

jugada NF **(a)** (gen) play; playing.

(b) (una ~) piece of play; (Ajedrez etc) move; (golpe) stroke, shot; (echada) throw; **una bonita ~** a pretty piece of play, a pretty shot; **con dos ~s más** in two more moves; **hacer una ~** to make a move, make a shot (etc); **~ limpia** fair play; **~ de pizarra** textbook move.

(c) (mala) **~** bad turn, dirty trick; **hacer una mala ~ a uno** to play sb a dirty trick.

(d) (Méx) dodge.

jugado ADJ (And) expert, skilled.

jugador(a) NM/F player; (de apuestas) gambler; **~ de bolsa** speculator, gambler on the stock exchange; **~ de fútbol** footballer, football player; **~ de manos** juggler, conjurer; **capitán no ~** non-playing captain.

jugar [1h y 1n] **1** VT **(a)** carta, papel, truco etc to play; **¡me la han jugado!*** they've done it on me!*

(b) (apostar) to gamble, stake; **~ 5 dólares a una carta** to stake (o put) 5 dollars on a card; **lo jugó todo** he gambled it all away.

(c) arma to handle, wield.

2 VI **(a)** (gen) to play (con with, contra against); **~ limpio** to play fair, play the game; **~ sucio** to play unfairly, indulge in dirty play; **yo no juego** I don't play, I can't play; **~ al tenis** to play tennis; **~ al ajedrez** to play chess; **la niña juega a ser madre** the little girl plays at being mother; **~ con** (pey) to play about with; (manosear) to finger, handle, mess up; (fig) to toy with, trifle with; **solamente está jugando contigo** he's just trifling with you, he's just having a game with you; **un coche de ~** a toy car, a model car; **de a jugando** (Cono Sur*) two-facedly; **de jugando** (Carib*) in fun, for fun.

(b) (hacer una jugada) to play, make a move; **¿quién juega?** whose move is it?, whose turn is it?, who's to play next?

(c) (apostar) to gamble; (Fin) to speculate, gamble; V **bolsa** etc.

(d) (LAm Mec) to have room to move about.

(e) (hacer juego) to match, go together.

3 **jugarse** VR **(a)** to gamble (away), risk; **se jugó 500 dólares** he staked 500 dollars; **esto es ~ la vida** this means risking one's life; **jugárselo todo, ~ el todo por el todo** to stake one's all, (fig) go to extremes, go the whole hog.

(b) **jugársela*** to be unfaithful.

(c) **el partido se juega hoy** (Dep) the match is being played today.

jugarreta NF **(a)** (jugada) bad move, poor piece of play. **(b)** (trampa) dirty trick; **hacer una ~ a uno** to play a dirty trick on sb.

juglar NM (Hist) minstrel, jongleur; juggler, tumbler, entertainer.

juglaresco ADJ (Hist) **arte ~** art of the minstrel(s); **estilo ~** minstrel style, popular style.

juglaría NF (Hist) minstrelsy, art of the minstrel(s).

jugo NM **(a)** (Bot etc) juice; sap; (de carne) juice; gravy; **~s digestivos** digestive juices; **~ de naranja** orange juice; **~ de muñeca** elbow grease.

(b) (fig) essence, substance, pith; **sacar el ~ a uno** to get the most out of sb, to pick sb's brains.

jugosidad NF **(a)** (suculencia) juiciness, succulence. **(b)** (fig) substantial nature, pithiness.

jugoso ADJ **(a)** (suculento) juicy, succulent.

(b) (fig) substantial, pithy; meaty, full of good stuff, full of solid sense; (rentable) profitable; **un discurso ~** a solid sort of speech, a speech full of good things.

jugué, juguemos etc V **jugar**.

juguera NF (Cono Sur) liquidizer, blender.

juguete NM **(a)** (de niño) toy; **~ educativo** educational toy; **un cañón de ~** a toy gun.

(b) (fig) toy, plaything; **fue el ~ de las olas** it was the plaything of the waves.

(c) (chiste) joke.

(d) (Teat) skit, sketch.

juguetear [1a] VI to play, romp, sport; **~ con** to play with, sport with.

jugueteo NM playing, romping.

juguetería NF **(a)** (negocio) toy trade, toy business. **(b)** (tienda) toyshop.

juguetero ADJ toy (atr).

juguetón ADJ playful; frisky, frolicsome.

juicio NM **(a)** (facultad) judgement, reason.

(b) (razón) sanity, reason; (buen sentido) good sense, prudence, wisdom; **asentar el ~** to come to one's senses, return to sanity; **lo dejo a su ~** I leave it to your discretion, I leave it to you to decide; **estar en su (cabal) ~** to be in one's right mind; **estar fuera de ~** to be out of one's mind; **perder el ~** to lose one's reason, go mad; **no tener ~** to lack common sense; **¿se te ha vuelto el ~?** are you mad?, have you gone out of your mind?

(c) (opinión) opinion; **~ de valor** value judgement; **a mi ~** in my opinion, to my mind.

(d) (Jur: proceso) trial; **~ con** (o por) **jurado** trial by jury; **~ de Dios** trial by ordeal; **pedir a uno en ~** to sue sb.

(e) (Jur: veredicto) verdict, judgement; **J~ Final** Last Judgement; **~ en rebeldía** judgement by default.

(f) (Jur: pena) punishment; **~ público** public punishment, carrying out of a sentence in public.

juicioso ADJ judicious, wise, prudent, sensible.

juilipío NM (And) sparrow.

juilón* ADJ (Méx) yellow.

JUJEM [xu'xem] NF (Esp Mil) ABR de **Junta de Jefes del Estado Mayor**.

jul. ABR de **julio** July, Jul.

jula* NM **(a)** (marica) queer*. **(b)** (idiota) twit*, berk*.

julai* NM poofter*.

julandra* NM, **julandrón*** NM queer*.

julepe NM **(a)** julep.

(b) (*: reprimenda) telling-off*, dressing-down*.

(c) (LAm*: susto) scare, fright; **irse de ~, salir de ~** (And) to run away in terror.

(d) (Carib, Méx*: trabajo) bind*.

(e) meter un ~ (*And*) to hurry on, speed up.

(f) (*Naipes*) a card game.

julepear* [1a] [1] VT **(a)** (*Cono Sur: asustar*) to scare, terrify.

(b) (*Méx: cansar*) to wear out, tire out.

(c) (*And: apresurar*) to hurry along, speed up.

[2] **julepearse** VR (*Cono Sur*) (*asustarse*) to get scared; (*estar atento*) to smell danger.

julia* NF (*Méx*) Black Maria, paddy wagon* (*US*).

Julián NM, **Juliano** NM Julian.

juliana NF julienne; **cortar en ~** to cut into thin shreds, cut into julienne strips.

Julieta NF Juliet.

Julio NM Julius; **~ César** Julius Caesar.

julio NM **(a)** July. **(b)** (†) 100-peseta note.

juma* NF (*LAm*) drunkenness, drunken state.

jumadera* NF (*Méx*) **(a)** (*borrachera*) drunkenness, drunken state. **(b)** (*humareda*) cloud of smoke.

jumado* ADJ (*LAm*) drunk, tight*.

jumar: [1a] VI to pong:, stink.

jumarse* [1a] VR (*LAm*) to get drunk.

jumatán* NM (*Carib*) drunkard.

jumazo: NM (*Carib*) fag:.

jumbo NM jumbo, jumbo jet.

jumeado* ADJ (*And*) drunk, tight*.

jumelar: [1a] VI to pong:, stink.

jumento NM donkey; beast of burden; (*fig*) dolt.

jumo ADJ (*LAm*) drunk.

jun. ABR *de* **junio** June, Jun.

junar: [1a] [1] VT (*ver*) to see; (*mirar*) to watch.

[2] VI (*Cono Sur*) to keep a look-out.

juncal [1] ADJ **(a)** (*Bot*) rushy, reedy. **(b)** (*fig*) willowy, lissom.

[2] NM = **juncar**.

juncar NM ground covered in rushes; reed bed.

juncia NF sedge.

junco¹ NM (*Bot*) rush, reed; (*CAm*) rattan; **~ de Indias** rattan.

junco² NM (*Náut*) junk.

juncoso ADJ **(a)** (*Bot*) rushy, reedy, reed-like. **(b)** *lugar* covered in rushes.

jungla NF jungle; **~ de asfalto** concrete jungle.

junguiano, -a ADJ, NM/F Jungian.

junio NM June.

junior NMF, PL **juniors** (*Dep*) junior.

júnior NM, PL **juniores** **(a)** (*Ecl*) novice monk, junior novice. **(b)** (*Cono Sur*) office-boy.

Juno NF Juno.

junquera NF rush; bulrush.

junquillo NM **(a)** (*Bot*) jonquil; reed. **(b)** (*bastón*) rattan; (*madera*) strip of light wood. **(c)** (*Carib, Méx*) gold necklace.

junta NF **(a)** (*asamblea*) meeting, assembly; (*sesión*) session; **~ de acreedores** meeting of creditors; **~ general** general meeting; **~ general de accionistas** annual general meeting (of shareholders); **~ general extraordinaria** special general meeting; **celebrar ~** to hold a meeting; to sit.

(b) (*consejo*) board, council, committee; (*Com, Fin*) board; **la ~ de la asociación** the committee of the association; **~ directiva** board of management; executive committee; **~ de gobierno** governing body; **~ de portavoces** (*Parl*) House business committee.

(c) (*punto de unión*) junction, (point of) union.

(d) (*Téc*) (*acoplamiento*) joint; coupling; **~ cardán, ~ universal** universal joint.

(e) (*Téc: arandela*) washer, gasket.

(f) (*Pol*) junta; **~ militar** military junta.

juntadero NM (*Cono Sur*) meeting place.

juntamente ADV **(a) hacer algo ~** to do sth together; to do sth at the same time.

(b) A ~ con B A together with B; **ella y yo ~** she and I together, she and I jointly.

juntar [1a] [1] VT **(a)** (*unir*) to join, unite; (*montar*) to assemble, put together; (*acumular*) to collect, gather (together), amass; *dinero* to collect, raise.

(b) *puerta* to pull to, push to.

[2] **juntarse** VR **(a)** (*unirse*) to join, come together; (*gente*) to meet, assemble, gather (together); **~ con uno** to join sb; to meet (up with) sb; to associate with sb; **se juntaron para oírle** they assembled to hear him, they came together to hear him; **se juntó con ellos en la estación** he met them at the station, he joined them at the station.

(b) (*Zool*) to mate, copulate.

(c) (*personas: euf*) to live together.

juntillo *etc* V **pie**.

junto [1] ADJ **(a)** joined, united; together; **fuimos ~s** we went together; **tenía los ojos muy ~s** his eyes were very close together; **vivir ~s** to live together.

(b) **~s** (*LAm*: ambos*) both.

[2] ADV **(a)** near, close; together; **(de) por ~, en ~** in all, all together; (*Com*) wholesale; **demasiado ~** too close; **muy ~** very close, very near; **ocurrió todo ~** it happened all at once.

(b) (*LAm*) **~ suyo** (*etc*) with him (*etc*), together with him (*etc*).

[3] PREP: **~ a** near (to), close to, next to; **~ con** together with.

juntura NF join, junction; (*Anat*) joint; (*Téc*) seam; (*Téc*) joint, coupling.

jupa NF (*CAm, Méx*) gourd; (:) head, nut:.

jupata: NF jacket.

jupiarse [1b] VR (*CAm*) to get drunk.

júpiter NM Jupiter.

jura¹ NF oath, pledge; **~ de la bandera** (taking the) oath of loyalty (*o* allegiance).

jura² [1] NM (*CAm, Carib*) cop*. [2] NF: **la ~** the cops*, the fuzz:.

juraco* NM (*CAm*) hole.

jurado [1] ADJ (*en profesión*) qualified, chartered.

[2] NM **(a)** (*cuerpo: Jur*) jury; (*en concurso, TV etc*) panel (of judges). **(b)** (*persona: Jur*) juror, juryman; (*en concurso etc*) member of a panel.

juramentar [1a] [1] VT to swear in, administer the oath to.

[2] **juramentarse** VR to be sworn in, take the oath.

juramento NM **(a)** (*promesa*) oath; **~ de fidelidad** oath of loyalty; **~ hipocrático** Hippocratic oath; **bajo ~** on oath; **prestar ~** to take the oath (*sobre* on); **tomar ~ a uno** to swear sb in, administer the oath to sb.

(b) (*palabrota*) oath, swearword, curse; **decir ~s a uno** to swear at sb.

jurar [1a] [1] VTI to swear; **~ decir la verdad** to swear to tell the truth; **le juro a Vd que ...** I swear to you that ...; **¡no jures!** don't swear!; **~ como un carretero** to swear like a trooper; **~ en falso** to commit perjury.

[2] **jurarse** VR: **jurárselas a uno** to have it in for sb.

jurdós: NM bread:, money.

jurel NM **(a)** horse mackerel. **(b) coger ~*** to get a fright.

jurero, -a NM/F (*And, Cono Sur*) perjurer, false witness.

jurgo NM, **jurgonera** NF (*And*) = **jorga**.

jurídico ADJ juridical; legal; **departamento ~** (*Com*) legal department.

jurisdicción NF **(a)** (*gen*) jurisdiction. **(b)** (*distrito*) district, administrative area.

jurisdiccional ADJ: **aguas ~es** territorial waters.

jurispericia NF jurisprudence.

jurisperito, -a NM/F jurist, legal expert.

jurisprudencia NF jurisprudence, (study of the) law.

jurista NMF jurist, lawyer.

juro NM (*derecho*) right of perpetual ownership; (*pago*) annuity, pension; **a ~** (*And, Carib*), **de ~** certainly.

justa NF (*Hist*) joust, tournament; (*fig*) contest.

justamente ADV **(a)** (*con justicia*) justly, fairly.

(b) (*precisamente*) just, precisely, exactly; **¡~!** precisely!; that's just it!; **de eso se trata ~** that's just the point, that's exactly the point; **son ~ las que no están en venta** they are precisely the ones which are not for sale.

justar [1a] VI to joust, tilt.

justicia NF **(a)** (*gen*) justice; (*equidad*) fairness, equity, rightness; (*derecho*) right; **~ catalana** summary justice; **~ gratuita** legal aid; **~ poética** poetic justice; **~ social** social justice; **de ~** justly, deservedly; **lo estimo de ~** I think it right; **es de ~ añadir que ...** it is only right to add that ...; **en ~** by rights; **hacer ~ a** to do justice to; **hacerse ~ por sí mismo, tomarse la ~ por su mano** to take the law into one's own hands.

(b) (*persona*) policeman; representative of authority; **~s y ladrones** cops and robbers*.

justiciable ADJ **(a)** (*procesable*) actionable. **(b)** *decisión* subject to review by a court; subject to arbitration.

justicialismo NM (*Argentina*) *political movement founded by Perón; see also* PERONISMO .

justicieramente ADV justly.

justiciero ADJ (strictly) just, righteous.

justificable ADJ justifiable.

▼ **justificación** NF justification; **~ automática** (*Inform*) automatic justification.

justificado ADJ (*gen, t Tip*) justified; **no ~** unjustified.

justificante NM voucher; receipt; supporting document, evidence in support.

justificar [1g] VT (*gen*) to justify; (*probar*) to verify, substantiate; *sospechoso* to clear (*de* of), vindicate.

justificativo ADJ: **documento ~** voucher, certificate; supporting document.

justillo NM jerkin.

justipreciar [1b] VT to evaluate, appraise.

justiprecio NM evaluation, appraisal.

▼ **justo** [1] ADJ **(a)** (*correcto*) just, fair, right; **una decisión justa** a just de-

cision; **los ~s** the righteous; **pagan ~s por pecadores** the innocent often pay for the guilty; **me parece muy ~** it seems perfectly fair to me; **más de lo ~** more than is proper, more than usual.
(b) (*exacto*) exact, correct; **el peso ~** the correct weight; **¡~!** that's it!, correct!, right!
(c) *ropa* tight; **el traje me viene muy ~** the suit is rather tight for me, the suit is a very tight fit.
2 ADV **(a)** (*con justicia*) justly.
▼**(b)** (*exactamente*) right; **vino ~ a tiempo** he came just in time; **llegaste en ~** you just made it; **llegar con las justas** to arrive just on time.
(c) (*con dificultad*) tightly; **tener ~ para vivir** to have just enough to live on; **vivir muy ~** to be hard up*, have only just enough to live on.
jute NM (*CAm*) edible snail.
juvenil ADJ youthful; **equipo ~** (*Dep*) youth team, junior team; **obra ~** youthful work, early work; **en los años ~es** in one's early years, in one's youth; **de aspecto ~** young-looking, youthful in appearance.
juventud NF **(a)** (*época*) youth; early life.
(b) (*jóvenes*) young people; **la ~ de hoy** young people today, today's youth; **J~es Comunistas** (*etc*) Young Communists (*etc*); **~ no conoce virtud** boys will be boys.
juyungo, -a* NM/F (*And*) Negro.
juzgado NM court, tribunal; **~ de primera instancia** court of first instance, low-level court; **esto es** (**asunto**) **de ~ de guardia** (*fig*) this is an absolute outrage.
juzgar [1h] VTI to judge; **~ mal** to misjudge; **júzguelo Vd mismo** see for yourself, form your own judgement; **lo juzgo mi deber** I consider it my duty, I deem it my duty; **juzgue Vd mi sorpresa** imagine my surprise; **~ de** to judge of, pass judgement on, appraise; **a ~ por** to judge by, judging by; **a ~ por lo que hemos visto** to judge by (*o* from) what we have seen.
juzgón ADJ (*CAm, Méx*) hypercritical, carping.

K

K NM **(a)** ABR *de* **kilobyte** kilobyte, K. **(b)** **vehículo K** unmarked police car.

K, k [ka] NF (*letra*) K, k.

kabuki NM kabuki.

kafkiano ADJ Kafkaesque.

káiser NM Kaiser.

kaki NM (*LAm*) khaki.

kamikaze NM kamikaze.

Kampuchea NF Kampuchea.

kampucheano, -a ADJ, NM/F Kampuchean.

kaperuj NM (*And*) embroidered shawl.

kaput* [ka'pu] ADJ kaput*; **hacer ~** to go kaput*, go phut*.

karaoke NM karaoke.

kárate NM, **karate** NM karate.

karateca NMF, **karateka** NMF karate expert, karateka.

karma NM karma.

kárting ['kartin] NM go-carting.

KAS NF ABR *de* **Koordinadora Abertzale Sozialista** *Basque nationalist umbrella group.*

Katar NM Qatar.

katiuska ①ADJ (*Esp*): **botas ~s** rubber boots.
　②NF rubber boot.

kayac NM, **kayak** NM kayak.

kazajo, -a ①ADJ, NMF Kazak(h).
　②NM (*Ling*) Kazak(h).

Kazajstán NM Kazakhstan.

k/c. ABR *de* **kilociclos** kilocycles, klc.

kebab NM, PL **kebabs** kebab.

kéfir NM (*And*) type of yoghurt.

Kenia NF Kenya.

keniano, -a ADJ, NM/F Kenyan.

keniata = **keniano.**

kepi(s) NM (*LAm*) kepi.

kermes NM, **kermesse** NM charity fair, bazaar.

kerosén NM, **kerosene** NM, **kerosín** NM (*CAm*), **kerosina** NF (*CAm*), kerosene, paraffin.

ketchup ['ketʃap, 'ketʃup] NM ketchup.

keynesiano, -a ADJ, NM/F Keynesian.

kg. ABR *de* **kilogramo(s)** kilogram(s), kg.

KHz ABR *de* **kilohercio** kilohertz, KHz.

kibutz [ki'βuts] NM, PL **kibutzim, kibutz** kibbutz.

kiki‡ NM joint‡, reefer‡.

kiko NM *snack of salted, toasted maize.*

kikongo NM Kikongo.

kilate NM = **quilate.**

kilo ① NM **(a)** kilo. **(b)** (‡) one million pesetas.
　② *como* ADV (*) a lot, a great deal.

kilobyte ['kiloβait] NM kilobyte.

kilocaloría NF kilocalorie.

kilociclo NM kilocycle.

kilogramo NM kilogramme, kilogram (*US*).

kilohercio NM kilohertz.

kilolitro NM kilolitre, kiloliter (*US*).

kilometraje NM **(a)** distance (*o* rate *etc*) in kilometres, mileage. **(b)** (*Fin*) ≃ mileage allowance.

kilometrar [1a] VT to measure (in kilometres).

kilométrico ① ADJ **(a)** (*gen*) kilometric; **billete ~** runabout ticket, mileage book. **(b)** (*) very long; **palabra kilométrica** very long word, multisyllabic word.
　② NM = **billete ~.**

┌─────────────────────────┐
│ **KILOS, METROS, AÑOS** │
└─────────────────────────┘

En inglés cuando la unidad de medida precede al nombre como adjetivo compuesto, debe escribirse en singular y unida por un guión al número correspondiente. En el resto de los casos se emplea en plural, como en español:

Una caja de bombones de dos kilos/La caja de bombones pesa dos kilos

A two-kilo box of chocolates/The box of chocolates weighs two kilos

Una regla de 20 cms/La regla mide 20 cms

A 20-centimetre ruler/The ruler is 20 centimetres long

Un muchacho de quince años/El muchacho tiene quince años

A fifteen-year-old boy/The boy is fifteen years old

kilómetro NM kilometre, kilometer (*US*); **~ cero** (*fig*) starting-point; central point; *ver también* KILOS, METROS, AÑOS .

kiloocteto NM kilobyte.

kilopondio NM kilopound.

kilotón NM kiloton.

kilovatio NM kilowatt.

kilovatio-hora NM, PL **kilovatios-hora** kilowatt hour.

kimona NF (*Carib, Méx*), **kimono** NM (*Cono Sur*) kimono.

kínder NM (*LAm*), **kindergarten** NM (*LAm*) kindergarten.

kinesiología NF kinesiology.

kión NM (*And*) ginger.

kiosco NM = **quiosco.**

kiosquero, -a NMF = **quiosquero.**

Kirguizistán NM Kyrgyzstan.

kit NM, PL **kits** kit.

kitsch [kitʃ] ADJ INVAR, NM kitsch.

kiwi NM **(a)** (*Orn*) kiwi. **(b)** (*fruta*) kiwi fruit.

klínex NM INVAR tissue, Kleenex ®.

km. ABR *de* **kilómetro** kilometre, km.

km/h. ABR *de* **kilómetros por hora** kilometres per hour, km/h.

knock-out ['nokau] NM, **K.O.** [kaw] NM knockout; knockout blow; **dejar a uno ~, poner a uno ~** to knock sb out, give sb a knockout blow; (*fig*) to put sb out of action, leave sb stretched out cold.

kodak [ko'ðak] NF, PL **kodaks** [ko'ðak] small camera.

kohl NM kohl (*eyeliner*).

koljós NM, PL **koljoses, koljoz** NM [kol'xos], PL **koljozi** kolkhoz.

k.p.h. ABR *de* **kilómetros por hora** kilometre(s) per hour, km/h.

k.p.l. ABR *de* **kilómetros por litro** ≃ miles per gallon, ≃ mpg.

krausismo NM *philosophy and doctrine of K.C.F. Krause.*

krausista ① ADJ Krausist, of Krause.
　② NMF follower of Krause.

kuchen NM (*Chile*) fruit tart.

Kurdistán NM Kurdistan.

kurdo ① ADJ kurdish.
　② NM, **kurda** NF Kurd.
　③ NM (*Ling*) Kurdish.

Kuwait NM Kuwait.

kuwaití ADJ, NMF Kuwaiti.

kv. ABR *de* **kilovatio, kilovatios** kilowatt, kilowatts, kw.

kv/h. ABR *de* **kilovatios-hora** kilowatt hours, kw/h.

L

L, l ['ele] NF (*letra*) L, l.
l. (a) ABR *de* **litro(s)** litre(s), l. (b) (*Liter*) ABR *de* **libro** book, bk. (c) (*Jur*) ABR *de* **ley** law.
L/ ABR *de* **Letra** letter.
l/100 km ABR *de* **litros por 100 kilómetros** litres per 100 kilometres; ≈ miles per gallon, mpg.
la¹ ART DEF F the (*para ejemplos de uso, V* **el¹**).
la² PRON (*persona*) her; (*Vd*) you; (*cosa*) it.
la³ PRON DEM: **mi casa y ~ de Vd** my house and yours; **esta chica y ~ del sombrero verde** this girl and the one in the green hat; **~ de Pedro es mejor** Peter's is better; **y ~ de todos los demás** and that of everybody else; **~ de Rodríguez** Mrs Rodríguez; **¡~ de goles que marcó!** what a lot of goals he scored!; **¡~ de veces que se equivoca!** how often he's wrong!; **ir a ~ de Pepe** to go to Pepe's place.
la⁴: **~ que** PRON REL: *V* **el³ que**.
la⁵ NM (*Mús*) A; **~ menor** A minor.
laberintero ADJ (*Méx*) = **laberintoso**.
laberíntico ADJ labyrinthine; *casa etc* rambling.
laberinto NM (a) labyrinth, maze; (*fig*) maze, tangle. (b) (*LAm*: *gritério*) row, racket.
laberintoso ADJ (*Méx*) (*ruidoso*) rowdy, brawling; (*chismoso*) gossipy.
labia NF fluency, blarney; (*pey*) glibness; **tener mucha ~** to have the gift of the gab*, be terribly persuasive.
labial ADJ, NF labial.
labihendido ADJ harelipped.
labio NM (*Anat*) lip; (*de vasija etc*) lip, edge, rim; (*fig*) tongue; **~s lips**, mouth; **~ inferior** lower lip; **~ superior** upper lip; **~ leporino** harelip; **lamerse los ~s** to lick one's lips; **no morderse los ~s** to be outspoken, pull no punches; **no descoser los ~s** to keep one's mouth shut; **sin despegar los ~s** without uttering a word; **es muy valiente de ~s para afuera** he comes over brave enough, outwardly he seems brave.
labiodental ADJ labiodental.
labiolectura NF, **labiología** NF lip-reading.
labiosear [1a] VT (*CAm*) to flatter.
labiosidad* NF (*And, CAm*) flattery.
labioso ADJ (*LAm*) (*hablador*) talkative; (*lisonjero*) flattering; (*persuasivo*) persuasive, glib; (*taimado*) sly.
labor NF (a) (*trabajo*) labour, work; (*una ~*) job, task, piece of work; **'sus ~es'** (*censo etc*) 'housewife'; **~ de chinos** tedious task; **~ de equipo** teamwork.
(b) (*Agr*) (*cultivo*) farm work, cultivation; (*arada*) ploughing.
(c) (*CAm, Carib*) small farm, smallholding.
(d) (*Cos*) needlework, sewing; (*bordado*) embroidery; (*punto*) knitting; **una ~** a piece of needlework (*etc*); **~ de aguja**, **~es femeninas** needlework; **~ de ganchillo** crochet, crocheting.
(e) **~es** (*Min*) workings.
laborable ADJ workable; arable; *V* **día**.
laboral ADJ labour (*atr*); technical; *V* **escuela** *etc*.
laboralista ADJ labour (*atr*); **abogado ~** labour lawyer.
laboralmente ADV: **~ productivo** productive in terms of work; **~, estoy en paro** so far as work goes, I'm unemployed.
laborar [1a] ① VT (*Agr*) to work, till.
② VI (a) (*CAm**) to work. (b) (*pey*) to scheme, plot.
laboratorio NM laboratory; **~ espacial** space laboratory; **~ de idiomas** language laboratory.
laborear [1a] VT to work (*t Min*); (*Agr*) to work, till.
laboreo NM (*Agr*) working, cultivation, tilling; (*Min*) working.
laborero NM (*And, Cono Sur*) foreman.
laboriosamente ADV industriously; painstakingly; with great difficulty.
laboriosidad NF (a) (*trabajo*) industry; painstaking skill. (b) (*pesadez*) laboriousness.

laborioso ADJ (a) *persona* hard-working, industrious, painstaking. (b) *trabajo* tough, hard, laborious, difficult.
laborismo NM (*LAm*) labour movement, workers' movement; (*Brit*) Labour Party, Labour Movement.
laborista ① ADJ (*Brit*) Labour (*atr*); **Partido L~** Labour Party; **miembro ~** Labour member.
② NMF (a) (*CAm*) small farmer, smallholder.
(b) (*Brit Pol*) Labour Party member, supporter of the Labour Party; Labour member of parliament.
laborterapia NF work-therapy.
labra NF carving, working, cutting.
labradío ADJ arable.
labrado ① ADJ worked; *metal* wrought; *madera etc* carved; *tela* patterned, embroidered.
② NM cultivated field; **~s** cultivated land.
Labrador NM (*Geog*) Labrador.
labrador NM (a) (*granjero*) farmer; (*labriego*) farm labourer; (*arador*) ploughman; (*campesino*) peasant; (*Méx*) lumberjack. (b) (*perro*) Labrador.
labradora NF peasant (woman).
labrantín NM small farmer.
labrantío ADJ arable.
labranza NF (a) (*cultivo*) farming; cultivation. (b) (*granja*) farm; (*tierras*) farmland.
labrar [1a] VT to work; to fashion, shape; *metal* to work; *madera etc* to carve; (*CAm, Méx*) *árbol* to fell and smooth; *tierra* to work, farm, till; *tela* to embroider; (*fig*) to cause, bring about.
labriego, -a NM/F farmhand, labourer; peasant.
laburante* NM (*Cono Sur*) worker.
laburar* [1a] VI (*Cono Sur*) to work.
laburno NM laburnum.
laburo* NM (*Cono Sur*) (*trabajo*) work; (*puesto*) job; **¡qué ~!*** what a job!
laca NF (a) (*t* **goma ~**) shellac; (*barniz*) lacquer; (*de pelo*) hair-spray; (*color*) lake; **~ de uñas**, **~ para uñas** nail polish, nail varnish. (b) (*Cono Sur*) = **lacra**.
lacado NM lacquer.
lacar [1g] VT to lacquer.
lacayo NM footman; (*fig*) lackey.
laceada NF (*Cono Sur*) whipping.
lacear [1a] VT (a) (*adornar*) to beribbon, adorn with bows; (*atar*) to tie with a bow; (*CAm, Méx*) *carga* to tie on firmly, strap securely.
(b) (*Cono Sur*: *zurrar*) to whip.
(c) (*Caza*) (*coger*) to snare, trap; (*ojear*) to beat, drive; (*LAm*) to lasso.
laceración NF laceration; (*fig*) damage, spoiling.
lacerante ADJ (*fig*) wounding, hurtful.
lacerar [1a] VT to lacerate, tear, mangle; (*fig*) to damage, spoil.
lacería NF (*pobreza*) poverty, want; (*sufrimiento*) distress, wretchedness; (*trabajo*) toil.
lacero, -a NM/F dog-catcher.
lacha NF (*honor*) sense of honour; (*vergüenza*) sense of shame; (*valentía*) guts.
lachear* [1a] VT (*Cono Sur*) to chat up*.
lacho* NM (*Cono Sur*) lover.
laciar [1b] VT (*LAm*) *pelo rizado* to straighten.
Lacio NM Latium.
lacio ADJ (*Bot*) withered, faded; *pelo* lank, straight; *movimiento etc* limp, languid.
lacón NM shoulder of pork.
lacónicamente ADV laconically, tersely.
lacónico ADJ laconic, terse.
laconismo NM laconic style (*o manner etc*), terseness.
lacra NF (a) (*Med*) mark, trace, scar; (*LAm*: *llaga*) sore, ulcer.
(b) (*fig*) blot, blemish; **la prostitución es una ~ social** prostitution

is a blot on society, prostitution is a disgrace to society.

lacrar¹ [1a] **1** VT **(a)** (*Med*) to injure the health of; to infect, strike (with a disease).

(b) (*fig*) to injure, harm, cause damage (*o* loss) to.

2 lacrarse VR: ~ **con algo** to suffer harm (*o* damage, loss *etc*) from sth; ~ **con el trabajo excesivo** to harm o.s. through overwork.

lacrar² [1a] VT to seal (*with sealing wax*).

lacre **1** ADJ (*LAm*) bright red.

2 NM sealing wax.

lacrimógeno ADJ **(a)** tear-producing; **gas** ~ teargas. **(b)** (*fig*) tearful, highly sentimental; weepy*; **canción lacrimógena, comedia lacrimógena** tear-jerker*.

lacrimoso ADJ tearful, lachrymose.

lacrosse [la'kros] NF lacrosse.

lactación NF, **lactancia** NF lactation; breast-feeding.

lactante ADJ: **mujer** ~ nursing mother.

lactar [1a] **1** VT to breast-feed, nurse, to feed on milk.

2 VI to suckle; to feed on milk.

lácteo ADJ lacteal, milk (*atr*); **producto** dairy (*atr*); (*fig*) milky, lacteous.

láctico ADJ lactic.

lacto-ovo-vegetariano, -a ADJ, NM/F lacto-ovo-vegetarian.

lactosa NF lactose.

lactosuero NM whey, buttermilk.

lacustre ADJ lake (*atr*), lacustrine; (*LAm*) marshy.

ladeado ADJ **(a)** (*inclinado*) tilted, leaning, inclined.

(b) (*Cono Sur: descuidado*) slovenly.

(c) (*Cono Sur: taimado*) crooked*.

(d) (*Cono Sur*) **andar** ~ to be in a bad temper; **andar** ~ **con uno** to be in a huff with sb.

ladear [1a] **1** VT **(a)** (*inclinar*) to tilt, tip; to incline (to one side); (*Aer*) to bank, turn; *cabeza* to tilt, put on one side.

(b) *montaña etc* to skirt, go round the side of.

2 VI **(a)** (*inclinarse*) to tilt, tip, lean.

(b) (*apartarse*) to turn aside, turn off.

3 ladearse VR **(a)** (*inclinarse*) to lean, incline (*t fig*: *a* towards); (*Aer*) to bank, turn; **se ladea al otro partido** he leans towards the other party.

(b) ~ **con** to be equal to, be even with.

(c) (*Cono Sur: enamorarse*) to fall in love (*con* with).

ladeo NM **(a)** (*inclinación*) tilting, inclination, leaning; (*Aer*) banking, turning. **(b)** (*fig*) inclination.

ladera NF slope, hillside.

ladero **1** ADJ side (*atr*), lateral.

2 NM (*Cono Sur*) backer.

ladilla NF crab louse; **¡qué ~!** (*Carib*) what a pain!*

ladillento ADJ (*CAm, Méx*) lousy.

ladillo NM (*Prensa*) subhead, subtitle.

ladinazo ADJ (*Cono Sur*) cunning, shrewd.

ladino **1** ADJ **(a)** (*taimado*) cunning, wily; (*astuto*) smart, shrewd.

(b) (*LAm*) *indio* Spanish-speaking.

(c) (*CAm, Méx*) half-breed, mestizo; (*blanco*) non-Indian, white, of Spanish descent.

(d) (*LAm: adulador*) smooth-tongued, smarmy*.

(e) (*Méx*) *voz* high-pitched, fluty.

2 NM, **ladina** NF (*a*) (*LAm*) Spanish-speaking Indian.

(b) (*CAm, Méx*) half-breed, mestizo; (*blanco*) non-Indian, white.

3 NM (*Ling*) Ladin (*Rhaeto-Romance dialect*); (*de sefardíes*) Ladino, Sephardic, Judeo-Spanish.

lado NM **(a)** (*gen*) side; ~ **débil** weak spot; ~ **izquierdo** left(-hand) side; **de ~ a ~** side by side; **al ~** near, at hand; **al ~ de** by the side of, beside; **estuvo a mi ~** she was at my side, she was beside me; **al otro ~ de la calle** on the other side of the street, across the street; **llevar algo al otro ~ del río** to carry sth across (*o* over) the river; **al ~ de aquello, esto no es nada** beside (*o* in comparison with) that, this is nothing; **la casa de al ~** the house next door; **viven al ~ de nosotros** they live next door to us; **estar de un ~ para otro** to be up and down; **ir de un ~ a otro** to go to and fro, walk up and down; **poner algo de ~** to put sth on its side; **por el ~ del mar** towards the sea, on the sea side; **por el ~ de Madrid** in the direction of Madrid; **salieron corriendo cada uno por su ~** they all ran off in different directions; **por todos ~s** on all sides, all round; **por un ~ ...**, **por otro ...** on the one hand ..., on the other ...; **dar a uno de ~** to disregard sb, be unconcerned about sb; **me da de ~** I don't care; **dejar a un ~** to skip, omit, pass over; to leave aside; **echar a un ~** to cast aside; **hacer ~** to make room (*a* for); **hacerse a un ~** to stand aside (*t fig*), move over; **mirar de (medio) ~** to look askance at; to steal a glance at; to look at out of the corner of one's eye; **poner a un ~** to put aside.

(b) (*Mil*) flank.

(c) (*Dep*) end; **cambiar de ~** to change ends.

(d) (*genealógico*) side; **por el ~ de la madre** on the mother's side.

(e) (*Pol etc*) side; faction; **ponerse al ~ de uno** to side with sb.

(f) (*favor*) favour, protection; **tener buenos ~s** to have good connections.

ladrar [1a] VI (*perro*) to bark; (*tripas*) to rumble; **está que ladra*** he's hopping mad*; **ladran, luego andamos** you can tell it's having some effect; **esta semana estoy ladrando** (*Carib*) I'm flat broke this week*.

ladrería NF (*And, Carib, Méx*), **ladrerío** NM (*Méx*) barking.

ladrido NM bark, barking; (*fig*) slander, scandal.

ladrillado NM (*de ladrillos*) brick floor; (*de azulejos*) tile floor.

ladrillar **1** NM brickworks.

2 VT to brick, pave with bricks.

ladrillazo NM: **dar un ~ a uno** to throw a brick at sb.

ladriller(í)a NF (*LAm*) brickworks.

ladrillo NM (*gen*) brick; (*azulejo*) tile; (*de chocolate*) block; ~ **de fuego**, ~ **refractario** firebrick; ~ **ventilador** air-brick.

ladrón **1** ADJ thieving.

2 NM, **ladrona** NF thief; ~ **de corazones** ladykiller; ~ **de guante blanco** white-collar criminal; **¡al ~!** stop thief!

3 NM (*Elec*) adaptor, multiple plug.

ladronera NF (*a*) (*guarida*) den of thieves. **(b)** (*acto*) robbery, theft.

lagaña NF = **legaña**.

lagar NM (*de vino*) winepress; (*de aceite*) oil press.

lagarta NF (*a*) (*Zool*) lizard. **(b)** (*Ent*) gipsy moth; ~ **falsa** lackey moth. **(c)** (*mujer*) sly woman; **¡~!** you bitch!‡

lagartear [1a] VT (*a*) (*Cono Sur*: *inmovilizar*) to pinion, pin down. **(b)** (*And*: *falsear*) to fiddle*, wangle*.

lagartera NF lizard hole.

lagartija NF (*a*) (*Zool*) (small) lizard, wall lizard. **(b)** (*Méx*): *salvavidas*) lifeguard. **(c)** (*ejercicio*) press-up.

lagarto NM (*a*) (*Zool*) lizard; (*LAm*: *t* ~ **de Indias**) alligator; **¡~, ~!** (*toca madera*) touch wood!; (*And, Méx*: *Dios nos libre*) God forbid! **(b)** (*persona*) sly fellow, fox. **(c)** (*CAm, Méx*: *codicioso*) get-rich-quick type*; (*And*: *sableador*) scrounger*, sponger*; (*And*: *especulador*) profiteer. **(d)** (*Méx*: *astuto*) sharp customer, smart operator.

lagartón ADJ (*CAm, Méx*) (*codicioso*) greedy; (*listo*) sharp, shrewd; (*taimado*) sly.

lago NM lake; **los Grandes L~s** the Great Lakes.

Lagos N Lagos.

lágrima NF tear; (*gota*) drop; **~s de cocodrilo** crocodile tears; **~s de don Pedro** (*Cono Sur*) June rains; **beberse las ~s** to hold back one's tears; **derramar una lagrimita** (*iró*) to shed a tear; **deshacerse en ~s** to burst into tears; **llorar a ~ viva** to sob one's heart out, cry uncontrollably; **nadie soltará una ~ por eso** nobody is going to shed a tear over that.

lagrimal NM corner of the eye.

lagrimar [1a] VI to cry.

lagrimear [1a] VI (*persona*) to shed tears easily, be tearful; (*ojos*) to water, fill with tears.

lagrimilla NF (*Cono Sur*) unfermented grape juice.

lagrimoso ADJ *persona* lachrymose, tearful; *ojos* watery.

laguna NF (*a*) (*Geog*) pool; (*de atolón*) lagoon. **(b)** (*Liter etc*) gap, lacuna; (*en escritos, conocimientos*) gap, blank; (*en proceso*) hiatus, gap, break.

lagunajo NM, **lagunato** NM (*Carib*) (*estanco*) pool, pond; (*charco*) puddle.

lagunoso ADJ marshy, swampy.

laicado NM laity.

laical ADJ lay.

laicidad NF (*LAm*), **laicismo** NM laicism (*doctrine of the independence of the state etc from church interference*).

laicizar [1f] VT to laicize.

laico **1** ADJ lay.

2 NM layman.

laísmo NM *use of* **la** *and* **las** *as indirect objects*; *see also* LEÍSMO, LOÍSMO, LAÍSMO.

laísta **1** ADJ *that uses* **la** *and* **las** *as indirect objects*.

2 NMF *user of* **la** *and* **las** *as indirect objects*.

laja¹ NF (*a*) (*CAm, Cono Sur*) (*piedra*) sandstone; (*roca*) rock. **(b)** (*And*) (*lugar*) steep ground.

laja² NF (*And*) fine rope.

laja³‡ NF (*chica*) bird‡, dame*.

Lalo NM (*LAm*) *forma familiar de* **Eduardo.**

lama¹ NF (*a*) mud, slime, ooze. **(b)** (*And, Méx*: *moho*) mould, mildew; (*Méx*: *musgo*) moss.

lama² NM (*Rel*) lama.

lama³ NF (*de persiana*) slat.

lama⁴ NM (*tejido*) lamé.

lambada NF lambada.

lambarear* [1a] VI (*Carib*) to wander aimlessly about.

lambeculo‡ NMF (*Cono Sur, Méx*) creep‡.

lambeladrillos* NM INVAR (*And*) hypocrite.

lambeplatos* NMF INVAR (*LAm*) (a) (*lameculos*) bootlicker*. **(b)** (*pobre* *hombre*) poor wretch.

lamber [2a] VT (*LAm*) (**a**) = **lamer**. (**b**) (*) to fawn on, toady to, suck up to*.

lambeta: NMF (*Cono Sur*) creep:, bootlicker*.

lambetada NF (*Carib, Cono Sur, Méx*) (**a**) (*lit*) lick. (**b**) (* *fig*) (*acto*) grovelling; (*adulación*) soft-soaping*.

lambetazo NM (*LAm*) (*lit*) lick. (**b**) = **lambetada**.

lambetear [1a] VT (*LAm*) (**a**) (*lit*) to lick; to lick greedily, lick noisily. (**b**) (*) to suck up to*.

lambiche ADJ (*Méx*) = **lambiscón**.

lambida NF (*LAm*) lick.

lambido* ADJ (*LAm*) (*desvergonzado*) cheeky*; (*presumido*) cocky*, cocksure.

lambioche* ADJ (*Méx*) servile, fawning.

lambiscón ADJ (*And, Méx*) (**a**) (*glotón*) greedy, gluttonous. (**b**) = **lambioche**.

lambisconear [1a] (*LAm*) [1] VT (**a**) (*lit*) to lick. (**b**) (*) to suck up to*. [2] VI (*) to creep*, crawl.

lambisconería NF (*LAm*) (**a**) (*: *gula*) greediness, gluttony. (**b**) (:: *adulación*) fawning, grovelling. (**c**) (:: *presunción*) cockiness*.

lambisquear [1a] (*And, Méx*) = **lambisconear**.

lambón ADJ (*LAm*) = **lambioche**.

lambraña NMF (*And*) wretch.

lambrijo* ADJ (*Méx*) skinny.

lambrusquear [1a] VT (*Cono Sur, Méx*) to lick.

lambuzo ADJ (*And, Carib, Méx*) (**a**) (*glotón*) greedy, gluttonous. (**b**) (*desvergonzado*) shameless, brazen.

lamé NM lamé.

lameculismo: NM bootlicking*, toadyism.

lameculos: NMF INVAR bootlicker*, toady.

lamedura NF lick, licking.

lamentable ADJ regrettable; lamentable; pitiful; **es ~ que ...** it is regrettable that ...

lamentablemente ADV regrettably; (*LAm*) unfortunately.

lamentación NF lamentation; sorrow.

▼ **lamentar** [1a] [1] VT to be sorry about, regret; *pérdida etc* to lament, bemoan, bewail; *muerte* to mourn; **~ que ...** to be sorry that ..., regret that ...; **lamentamos mucho que ...** we very much regret that ...; **lamento lo que pasó** I'm sorry about what happened; **no hay que ~ víctimas** fortunately there were no casualties.
[2] **lamentarse** VR to lament, wail, moan (*de, por* about, over); (*por muerte*) to mourn (*de, por* over); (*quejarse*) to complain (*de, por* about).

lamento NM lament; moan, wail; **~s** lamentation.

lamentoso ADJ (**a**) = **lamentable**. (**b**) plaintive.

lameplatos NMF INVAR (**a**) (*lit*) person who eats scraps. (**b**) (*Méx**) (*adulón*) toady; (*parásito*) scrounger*; (*inútil*) disaster.

lamer [2a] [1] VT to lick; (*olas*) to lap, lap against; (*pasar rozando*) to graze.
[2] **lamerse:** VR: **un problema** (*etc*) **que no se lame** a bloody great problem: (*etc*).

lametada NF lick; (*de ola*) lap.

lametazo NM lick; (*del sol*) touch, caress.

lamido ADJ (**a**) (*flaco*) very thin, emaciated; (*pálido*) pale. (**b**) (*afectado*) prim, affected.

lámina¹ NF (*de metal, vidrio, etc*) sheet; (*Metal, Fot, Tip*) plate; (*Inform*) chip; (*en libro etc*) plate, illustration, picture; (*grabado*) engraving; **~s de acero** steel in sheets, sheet steel; **~ de queso** slice of cheese; **~ de silicio** silicon wafer.

lámina² NMF (*And*) rogue, rascal.

laminado ADJ (**a**) (*gen*) laminate(d). (**b**) (*Téc*) sheet (*atr*), rolled; **cobre ~** sheet copper, rolled copper.

laminador NM rolling mill.

laminar [1a] VT to laminate; (*Téc*) to roll; (*fig*) to smash, destroy.

lamiscar [1g] VT to lick greedily, lick noisily.

lampa NF (*And: de mineros*) pick.

lampacear [1a] VT (*CAm*) *piso etc* to mop.

lampalague NF (**a**) (*Cono Sur: serpiente*) boa constrictor. (**b**) (*Cono Sur: fig*) glutton.

lampancia* NF ravenous hunger.

lampante* NMF beggar.

lampar* [1a] VI to live on the streets.

lámpara [1] NF (*gen*) lamp, light; (*bombilla*) bulb; (*Rad*) valve, tube (*US*); **~s** (*LAm: ojos*) eyes; **~ de Aladino** Aladdin's lamp; **~ de alcohol** spirit lamp; **~ de arco** arc-lamp; **~ de bolsillo** torch, flashlight; **~ bronceador** sunlamp; **~ de cuarzo** quartz lamp; **~ de escritorio** desk-lamp; **~ flexo** adjustable table-lamp; **~ de lectura** reading lamp; **~ de mesa** table-lamp; **~ de pared** wall light; **~ de pie** standard lamp; **~ de señales** signalling lamp; **~ de sol artificial**, **~ solar ultravioleta** sun-ray lamp; **~ de soldar** blowlamp, blowtorch; **~ de techo** overhead lamp; **atizar la ~*** to fill up the glasses; **quebrar la ~** (*Carib**) to ruin everything, blow it:.

[2] NMF (*Carib*) (*ladrón*) thief; (*estafador*) con man*.

lamparazo NM flash of light.

lamparilla NF (**a**) (*lámpara*) small lamp; nightlight. (**b**) (*Bot*) aspen.

lamparín NM (*Cono Sur: vela*) candle; (*And: quinqué*) paraffin lamp.

lámparo ADJ (*And*) penniless, broke*.

lamparón NM (**a**) (*Med*) scrofula. (**b**) (*mancha*) large grease spot.

lampazo¹ NM (*Bot*) burdock.

lampazo² NM (**a**) (*Náut*) swab; (*LAm: estropajo*) floor mop. (**b**) (*And, Carib: azotamiento*) whipping.

lampear [1a] VT (*And*) (*con pala*) to shovel; (*con azada*) to hoe.

lampiño ADJ hairless; *muchacho* beardless.

lampión NM lantern.

lampista NM plumber.

lampistería NF electrical shop.

lampón¹ ADJ (*And*) starving, hungry.

lampón² NM (*And*) (*pala*) spade; (*azada*) hoe.

lamprea NF (**a**) (*Pez*) lamprey. (**b**) (*Carib*) sore, ulcer.

lamprear [1a] VT (*CAm*) to whip.

lana¹ NF (**a**) (*gen*) wool; (*vellón*) fleece; (*tela*) woollen cloth; **~s** (*: *hum*) long hair, locks; **~ de acero** steel wool; **~ para labores** knitting wool; **~ virgen** pure new wool; **de ~, hecho de ~** wool (*atr*), woollen; **ir por ~ y volver trasquilado** to get more than one bargained for.
(**b**) (*And, Méx*:: *dinero*) dough:, money.
(**c**) (*CAm**: *estafador*) swindler.

lana² NF (*CAm*) = **lama¹** (**b**).

lanar ADJ wool (*atr*), wool-bearing; **ganado ~** sheep.

lance NM (**a**) (*de red etc*) throw, cast.
(**b**) (*peces*) catch, quantity of fish caught.
(**c**) (*jugada etc*) stroke, move, piece of play.
(**d**) (*suceso*) incident, event, occurrence; (*episodio*) episode; (*accidente*) chance, accident; **~ de fortuna** stroke of luck; **~ de honor** affair of honour, duel; **el libro tiene pocos ~s emocionantes** the book is dull, not much happens in the book; **tirarse a un ~** (*Cono Sur*) to take a chance.
(**e**) (*momento*) critical moment, difficult moment.
(**f**) (*riña*) row, quarrel.
(**g**) (*Cono Sur: agachada*) duck, dodge; **sacar ~** to dodge, duck away.
(**h**) (*Cono Sur Arquit*) section, range; **casa de 3 ~s** house in 3 sections.
(**i**) (*Com*) **de ~** secondhand; cheap; **libros de ~** secondhand books; **comprar algo de ~** to buy sth secondhand, buy sth cheap.

lancear [1a] VT to spear.

lancero [1] NM (*Mil*) lancer; **~s** (*Mús*) lancers.
[2] NMF (*Cono Sur**: *soñador*) dreamer, blind optimist.

lanceta NF (**a**) (*Med etc*) lancet; **abrir con ~** to lance. (**b**) (*LAm: aguijada*) goad; (*de insecto*) sting.

lancha¹ NF (**a**) (*Náut*) launch; (small) boat; lighter, barge; **~ (automóvil)** motor-launch, motorboat; **~ cañonera** gunboat; **~ de carga** lighter, barge; **~ de carreras** speedboat; **~ de desembarco** landing-craft; **~ fuera borda** outboard dinghy; **~ inflable** rubber dinghy; **~ motora** motorboat, speedboat; **~ neumática** rubber dinghy; **~ patrullera** patrol-boat; **~ de pesca** fishing-boat; **~ rápida** speedboat; **~ de salvamento**, **~ salvavidas**, **~ de socorro** lifeboat; **~ torpedera** torpedo boat.
(**b**) (*Cono Sur**) police car.

lancha² NF (*And*) mist, fog; (hoar)frost.

lanchaje NM (*Méx*) ferry charges.

lanchar [1a] VI († *And*) (*encapotarse*) to become overcast; (*helar*) to freeze.

lanchero NM (**a**) boatman; lighterman, bargee. (**b**) (*Carib*) Cuban refugee.

lanchón NM lighter, barge; **~ de desembarco** landing-craft.

lancinante ADJ *dolor* piercing.

lancinar [1a] VT to lance, pierce.

Landas NFPL: **las ~** the Landes.

landó NM (**a**) landau. (**b**) (*And Mús*) Peruvian folk music.

landre NF: **¡mala ~ te coma!** curse you!

lanería NF (**a**) (*géneros*) woollen goods. (**b**) (*tienda*) wool shop.

lanero [1] ADJ wool (*atr*); woollen; **la industria lanera** the wool industry.
[2] NM (**a**) (*persona*) woolman, wool dealer. (**b**) (*almacén*) wool warehouse.

lángara: NMF (*Méx*) creep:.

lángaro ADJ (**a**) (*CAm: vago*) vagrant, wandering, idle; (*And, Méx: hambriento*) starving, poverty-stricken; (*Méx: malo*) wicked; (*taimado*) sly, untrustworthy. (**b**) (*CAm: larguirucho*) lanky.

langarucho ADJ (*CAm, Méx*), **langarote** ADJ (*And*) lanky.

langosta NF (**a**) (*de mar*) lobster; (*de río*) crayfish. (**b**) (*Ent*) locust.

langostera NF lobster pot.

langostín NM, **langostino** NM prawn.

langostinero ADJ: **barco ~** prawn-fishing boat.

---

languceta ADJ (*Cono Sur*), **languciento** ADJ (*Cono Sur, Méx*), **langucio** ADJ (*Cono Sur*) (*hambriento*) starving; (*enclenque*) sickly.

lánguidamente ADV languidly; weakly, listlessly.

languidecer [2d] VI to languish, pine (away).

languidez NF languor, lassitude; listlessness.

lánguido ADJ languid; weak, listless, drooping.

languso ADJ (*Méx*) (**a**) (*taimado*) sly, shrewd. (**b**) (*larguirucho*) lanky.

lanilla NF (*flojel*) nap; (*tela*) thin flannel cloth.

lanolina NF lanolin(e).

lanoso ADJ woolly, fleecy.

lanudo ADJ (**a**) (*lanoso*) woolly, fleecy. (**b**) (*And, Carib: maleducado*) rustic, uncouth. (**c**) (*Carib, Méx*: *rico*) well off.

lanza [1] NF (**a**) (*Mil*) lance, spear; **estar ~ en ristre** to be ready for action; **medir ~s** to cross swords; **romper ~s por** to stick up for; **ser una ~** to be pretty sharp; (*Méx*) to be sly, be a rogue.
(**b**) (*de carro*) pole.
(**c**) (*de manguera*) nozzle.
[2] NM (*LAm**: *estafador*) shark*; (*Cono Sur*: *tironista*) bag-snatcher; (*ratero*) pickpocket.

lanzabengalas NM INVAR flare.

lanzabombas NM INVAR (*Aer*) bomb-release; (*Mil*) trench mortar.

lanzacohetes NM INVAR rocket-launcher; **~ múltiple** multiple rocket-launcher.

lanzada NF spear thrust; spear wound.

lanzadera NF shuttle; **~ espacial** space-shuttle; **~ de misiles** missile-launcher.

lanzadestellos NM INVAR (*Aut*) flashing light.

lanzado* ADJ (**a**) (*ser*) forward, brazen; impudent; confident with women. (**b**) (*estar*) randy*, in the mood.

lanzador NM (**a**) (*t* **lanzadora** NF: *gen*) thrower; (*Béisbol*) pitcher; **~ de cuchillos** knife-thrower; **~ de jabalina** javelin-thrower; **~ de martillo** hammer-thrower; **~ de peso** shot-putter. (**b**) (*t* **lanzadora** NF: *Com, Fin*) promoter. (**c**) (*Mil: de cohetes etc*) launcher; (*Aer*) launch vehicle.

lanzaespumas NM INVAR foam sprayer.

lanzagranadas NM INVAR grenade-launcher, mortar.

lanzallamas NM INVAR flamethrower.

lanzamiento NM (**a**) (*acto*) throw, cast; throwing, casting, hurling; (*Aer*) drop (*by parachute*), jump, descent; **~ de disco** discus-throwing, the discus; **~ de martillo** hammer-throwing, the hammer; **~ de pesos** putting the shot, shot-putting.
(**b**) (*Aer, Náut*) launch, launching.
(**c**) (*Com, Fin*) launching; promotion; **~ publicitario** launching of an advertising campaign; **oferta de ~** promotional offer.
(**d**) (*Jur*) dispossession, eviction.

lanzaminas NM INVAR minelayer.

lanzamisiles NM INVAR missile-launcher.

lanzar [1f] [1] VT (**a**) (*gen*) to throw, cast; (*con violencia*) fling, hurl; (*Dep*) *pelota* to pitch, bowl (*a at, to*); *pesa* to put; (*Aer*) to drop (*by parachute*); (*Med*) to bring up, throw up, vomit; *desafío* to throw out, throw down; *crítica* to hurl.
(**b**) *grito* to give, utter; *mirada* to give, cast (*a at*).
(**c**) (*Náut*) to launch.
(**d**) (*Bot*) *hojas etc* to put forth.
(**e**) (*Com, Fin*) to launch, promote.
(**f**) (*Jur*) to dispossess, evict.
[2] **lanzarse** VR (**a**) (*gen*) to throw o.s., hurl o.s., fling o.s. (*a, en* into; *sobre* on); to rush (*sobre* at, on), fly (*sobre* at); (*Aer*) to jump (*by parachute*), bale out; **se lanzó a la pelea** he rushed into the fray; **se lanzó al río** he jumped into the river, he dived into the river.
(**b**) **~ a** (*fig*) to launch into; to embark upon, undertake.

Lanzarote NM (**a**) (*persona*) Lancelot. (**b**) (*isla*) Lanzarote.

lanzaroteño [1] ADJ of Lanzarote.
[2] NM, **lanzaroteña** NF native (*o* inhabitant) of Lanzarote; **los ~s** the people of Lanzarote.

lanzatorpedos NM INVAR torpedo tube.

laña NF clamp; rivet.

lañar [1a] VT (**a**) (*Téc*) to clamp (together); to rivet. (**b**) (‡: *robar*) to nick‡, steal.

Laos NM Laos.

laosiano, -a ADJ, NM/F Laotian.

lapa NF (**a**) (*Zool*) limpet. (**b**) (*persona*) nuisance, pest. (**c**) (*And, Cono Sur Bot*) half gourd (*used as bowl etc*). (**d**) (*And: sombrero*) large flat-topped hat.

lapalada NF (*Méx*) drizzle.

laparoscopia NF laparoscopy.

laparoscópico ADJ laparoscopic.

lape ADJ (*Cono Sur*) (**a**) (*enredado*) matted. (**b**) *baile etc* merry, lively.

lapicera NF (*Cono Sur*) = **lapicero**.

lapicero NM (**a**) (*lápiz*) propelling pencil; **~ hemostático** styptic pencil.
(**b**) (*LAm*) (*plumafuente*) fountain-pen; (*bolígrafo*) ball-point pen, Biro ®.

(**c**) (‡‡) prick‡‡.

lápida NF stone, stone tablet, memorial tablet; **~ conmemorativa** commemorative tablet; **~ mortuoria** headstone, gravestone; **~ mural** tablet let into a wall; **~ sepulcral** tombstone.

lapidar [1a] VT (**a**) to stone, throw stones at; to stone to death. (**b**) (*And, CAm*) *joya* to cut.

lapidario [1] ADJ lapidary; **frase lapidaria** immortal phrase.
[2] NM, **lapidaria** NF lapidary.

lapislázuli NM lapis lazuli.

lápiz NM (**a**) (*gen*) pencil; crayon; **~ de carbón** charcoal pencil; **~ de carmín**, **~ labial**, **~ de labios** lipstick; **~ de cejas** eyebrow pencil; **~ electrónico**, **~ de luz**, **~ óptico** light pen; **~ lector** data pen; **~ negro** (*en la censura*) blue pencil; **~ de ojos** eyeliner; **~ a pasta** (*Cono Sur*) ball-point pen; **~ (de) plomo** lead pencil; **escribir algo a** (*o con*) **~** to write sth in pencil; **está añadido a ~** it is added in pencil; it is pencilled in; **meter ~ a** to sign.
(**b**) (*Min*) blacklead, graphite.

lapo NM (**a**) (*: *golpe*) bash*, swipe; **de un ~** (*And*) at one go. (**b**) (*And, Carib*: *trago*) swig*. (**c**) (*Carib: inocente*) simple soul.

lapón, -ona NM/F Lapp, Laplander.

Laponia NF Lapland.

lapso NM lapse; **~ de tiempo** interval of time, passage of time; **en un ~ de 5 días** in (the space of) five days.

lapsus NM INVAR lapse, mistake; **~ calami** slip of the pen; **~ freudiano** Freudian slip; **~ linguae** slip of the tongue; **~ de memoria** lapse of memory.

laqueado ADJ lacquered; varnished.

laquear [1a] VT to lacquer; *uñas* to varnish, paint.

LAR [lar] NF (*Esp Jur*) ABR de **Ley de Arrendamientos Rústicos.**

lard(e)ar [1a] VT to lard, baste.

lardo NM lard, animal fat.

lardoso ADJ lardy, fatty; greasy.

larga NF (*Dep*) length; **nadar 20 ~s** to swim 20 lengths (*V t* **largo 1** (*f*)).

largada NF (*Dep*) start.

largamente ADV (**a**) (*de tiempo*) for a long time; *narrar* at length, fully; **conversamos ~** we talked at length, we had a long conversation.
(**b**) *vivir* comfortably, at ease.
(**c**) *compensar, tratar etc* generously.

largar [1h] [1] VT (**a**) (*soltar*) to let go, let loose, release; (*aflojar*) to loosen, slacken; *cuerda* to let out, pay out; *bandera, vela* to unfurl; *barca* to launch, put out; *persona (despedir)* to sack*, fire*, (*expulsar*) to throw out.
(**b**) *golpe* to give, fetch, deal.
(**c**) *insulto etc* to let fly; *exclamación, suspiro etc* to let out.
(**d**) (*decir*) **nos largó ese rollo de ...** he gave us that spiel* about ...; **le largó una tremenda bronca** she gave him a good ticking-off*; **les largó todo un discurso** he gave them a whole speech.
(**e**) (*And**: *lanzar*) to throw, hurl.
(**f**) (*And**: *entregar*) to hand over.
[2] VI (‡) to speak, talk; to prattle on.
[3] **largarse** VR (**a**) (*) to beat it*, hop it*; to quit; **¡lárgate!** clear off!*.
(**b**) (*Náut*) to set sail, start out.
(**c**) (*LAm: empezar*) to start, begin; **~ a** + *infin* to start to + *infin*.

largavistas NM INVAR (*Cono Sur*) binoculars.

largo [1] ADJ (**a**) (*distancia, medida*) long; (*tiempo*) long, lengthy; (*demasiado* **~**) too long; **parece ~** it looks too long; **de pelo ~** long-haired; **~ de uñas** light-fingered, thieving; **~s años** long years, many years; **~ y tendido** (*como* ADV) at great length; **no es bastante ~** it's not long enough; **es muy ~ de contar** it's a long story.
(**b**) **¡~ (de aquí)!***, clear off!*, get out!
(**c**) (*con de*) **estar de ~** to be in a long dress; **ponerse de ~** to put on grown-up clothes, dress as an adult (*for the first time*); (*fig*) to come out (in society); **pasar de ~** to pass by, go by (*without stopping*); **dejar pasar a uno de ~** to give sb a wide berth; **seguir de ~** (*LAm**) (*no parar*) to keep on going; (*pasar de lado*) to pass by; **este problema viene de ~** this problem started way back, this problem has been with us a long time.
(**d**) (*con lo*) **a lo más ~** at the most; **a lo ~** *poner* lengthways; *contar* at great length, lengthily; *ver etc* in the distance, far off; **a lo ~ de** along; alongside; (*tiempo*) all through, throughout; **a lo ~ del río** along the river; **a lo ~ del túnel** throughout the tunnel; **a lo ~ y a lo ancho de** throughout the length and breadth of.
(**e**) (*cantidad*) full, good; **tardó media hora larga** he took a good (*o* full) half-hour; **los aventajó en un minuto ~** he beat them by a full minute; **le costó 50 dólares ~s** it cost him all of 50 dollars, it cost him a good 50 dollars; **una dama sesentañera larga** a lady well on in her sixties.
(**f**) (*larga*) **a la larga** in the long run; eventually, in the end; **a la larga o a la corta** sooner or later; **dar largas a un asunto** to delay a

matter, put off making a decision about a matter; **me dio largas con una promesa** she put me off with a promise; **saberla larga** to be shrewd; to know one's way about.

(g) (*generoso*) generous; lavish; **tirar de ~** to spend lavishly.

(h) (*copioso*) abundant, copious; *cosecha* heavy.

(i) (*astuto*) sharp, shrewd; quick.

(j) (*Náut*) *cuerda* loose, slack.

[2] NM **(a)** (*gen*) length; **el ~ de las faldas** the length of skirts; **tiene 9 metros de ~** it is 9 metres long; **¿cuánto tiene de ~?** how long is it?; **he nadado 4 ~s** I've swum four lengths (of the pool).

(b) (*Mús*) largo.

(c) (*Cine**) = **largometraje**.

largometraje NM full-length film, feature film.

largón NM spy, informer.

largona NF **(a)** (*And, Cono Sur: demora*) delay. **(b) darse una ~** (*Cono Sur**) to take a rest; **dar ~s a algo** (*And**) to keep putting sth off.

largor NM length.

largucho ADJ (*LAm*) lanky.

larguero [1] ADJ **(a)** (*Cono Sur**) (*largo*) long, lengthy; *discurso* wordy, long-drawn-out; *persona* slow, slow-working; (*Dep*) trained for long-distance running.

(b) (*Cono Sur**) (*generoso*) generous; lavish; (*copioso*) abundant, copious.

[2] NM (*Arquit*) beam, support; (*de puerta*) jamb; (*Dep*) crossbar; (*de cama*) bolster.

largueza NF largesse, generosity.

larguirucho ADJ lanky, gangling.

larguísimo ADJ (*superl*) *de* **largo**.

largura NF length.

largurucho ADJ (*LAm*) lanky, gangling.

lárice NM larch.

laringe NF larynx.

laringitis NF laryngitis.

larva NF larva; grub, maggot.

larvado ADJ hidden, latent; embryonic; gradually evolving; **permanecer ~** to be latent, remain dormant.

las ART DEF FPL *etc*: V **los**.

lasaña NF lasagne, lasagna.

lasca NF chip, stone chips; (*de comida*) slice.

lascadura NF (*Méx*) (*rozadura*) graze, abrasion; (*herida*) injury.

lascar [1g] [1] VT **(a)** (*Náut*) to slacken. **(b)** (*Méx*) *piel* to graze, bruise; *piedra* to chip, chip off.

[2] VI (*Méx*) to chip off, flake off.

lascivamente ADV lewdly, lasciviously; lustfully; (*fig*) playfully, wantonly.

lascivia NF lewdness, lasciviousness; lust, lustfulness; (*fig*) playfulness.

lascivo ADJ lewd, lascivious; lustful; (*fig*) playful, wanton.

láser NM laser.

laser disc, laserdisc NM INVAR laser disc.

lasérico ADJ laser (*atr*).

laserterapia NF laser therapy.

lasitud NF lassitude, weariness.

laso ADJ (*liter: cansado*) weary; (*débil*) weak; (*lánguido*) limp, slack, languid.

▼ **lástima** NF **(a)** (*sentimiento*) pity; compassion; shame; **¡qué ~!** what a pity!, what a shame!, that's too bad!; **¡qué ~ de hombre!** isn't he pitiful?; **es una ~** it's a shame; **es ~ que ...** it's a pity that ..., it's too bad that ...; **dar ~** to be pitiful, rouse to pity; **eso me da mucha ~** I feel very sorry about that; **es una película que da ~** it's a pathetic film; (*pey*) it's a pathetically bad film; **todos me dan ~** I feel sorry for them all.

(b) (*objeto*) pitiful object; (*escena*) pitiful sight; **estar hecho una ~** to be a sorry sight, be in a dreadful state.

(c) (*queja*) complaint, tale of woe.

lastimada NF (*CAm, Méx*) = **lastimadura**.

lastimador ADJ harmful, injurious.

lastimadura NF (*LAm*) (*herida*) wound, injury; (*moretón*) bruise.

lastimar [1a] [1] VT **(a)** (*lesionar*) to hurt, harm, injure; (*herir*) to wound; (*magullar*) to bruise.

(b) (*ofender*) to offend, distress.

(c) (*apiadarse de*) to pity, sympathize with, feel pity for.

(d) (*apiadar*) to move to pity.

[2] **lastimarse** VR **(a)** to hurt o.s., injure o.s.; **se lastimó el brazo** he hurt his arm.

(b) ~ de (*quejarse*) to complain about; (*apiadarse*) to feel sorry for, pity.

lastimero ADJ **(a)** (*dañoso*) harmful, injurious. **(b)** = **lastimoso**.

lastimón NM (*LAm*) = **lastimadura**.

lastimosamente ADV pitifully, pathetically.

lastimoso ADJ piteous, pitiful, pathetic.

lastrante ADJ (*fig*) burdensome.

lastrar [1a] VT to ballast; (*fig*) to burden, weigh down.

lastre NM **(a)** (*Téc*) ballast; **en ~** (*Náut*) in ballast. **(b)** (*fig: carga*) ballast; dead weight, useless load. **(c)** (*juicio*) good sense, steadiness, balance. **(d)** (*Cono Sur*‡: *comida*) grub‡.

lata NF **(a)** (*metal*) tinplate; (*envase*) tin, can; (*And: comida*) food, daily ration; **~ petitoria** collecting tin (*for charity*); **sardinas en ~** tinned sardines, canned sardines; **sonar a ~** (*Mús etc*) to sound tinny.

(b) (*) nuisance, drag, bind*; **es una ~ tener que ...** it's a nuisance having to ...; **¡vaya una ~!**, **¡qué ~!** what a nuisance!; **dar ~** (*And, CAm*: parlotear*) to babble on; (*And*: insistir*) to nag, go on; **dar ~ a** (*Carib*) to condemn, censure; **dar la ~** to be a nuisance, be annoying, be boring; **dar la ~ a uno** to annoy sb.

(c) (*madera*) lath.

(d) (‡: *dinero*) dough‡; **estar sin ~s, estar en la(s) ~(s)** (*And, CAm*) to be penniless, be broke*.

(e) (*Aut*‡) **un cuatro ~s** an old banger‡.

(f) (*LAm*: persona*) drag.

latazo* NM nuisance, bore, bind*.

latear* [1a] VI (*LAm*) **(a)** (*dar la lata*) to be a nuisance, be annoying. **(b)** (*hablar*) to talk a lot, chatter away pointlessly. **(c)** (*LAm**) to pet*.

lateazo* NM (*LAm*) petting*.

latente ADJ **(a)** (*gen*) latent. **(b)** (*LAm: vivo*) alive, intense, vigorous; *memoria* fresh, alive.

lateral [1] ADJ lateral, side (*atr*).

[2] NM **(a)** (*Teat*) wings, side of the stage. **(b)** (*Dep*) wing(er).

lateralmente ADV laterally; sideways.

latería NF (*CAm*) tinplate; (*Carib, Cono Sur*) tinsmith's workshop; tinworks.

laterío NM (*Méx*) tinned goods, canned goods.

latero NM (*LAm*) **(a)** (*Téc*) tinsmith. **(b)** (*) bore, drag.

látex NM latex.

latido NM **(a)** (*de corazón*) beat, beating; throb, throbbing; palpitation. **(b)** (*de perro*) bark, yelp.

latifundio NM large estate.

latifundista NMF important landowner, owner of a large estate.

latigazo NM **(a)** (*golpe*) lash; (*chasquido*) crack (of a whip). **(b)** (*fig: reprimenda*) harsh reproof; verbal lashing. **(c)** (*: *trago*) swig*, swallow. **(d) dar un ~**‡ to have a screw‡.

látigo NM **(a)** whip; (*And, CAm: latigazo*) crack (of a whip). **(b)** (*Cono Sur: Dep*) finishing post, finishing line; **salir al ~** to complete a task. **(c)** (*And, Cono Sur: jinete*) horseman, rider.

latigudo ADJ (*LAm*) leathery.

latigueada NF (*And, CAm, Cono Sur*) whipping, thrashing.

latiguear [1a] VT (*And, CAm, Cono Sur*) to whip, thrash.

latiguera NF (*And*) whipping, thrashing.

latiguillo NM cliché, overworked phrase, well-worn maxim.

latín NM **(a)** (*Ling*) Latin; **bajo ~** Low Latin; **~ clásico** Classical Latin; **~ tardío** Late Latin; **~ vulgar** Vulgar Latin; **saber (mucho) ~*** to be pretty sharp. **(b) latines** Latin tags.

latinajo NM dog Latin, bad Latin; **~s** Latin tags.

latinidad NF latinity.

latinismo NM latinism.

latinista NMF latinist.

latinización NF latinization.

latinizar [1f] VTI to latinize.

latino [1] ADJ Latin; (*LAm*) Latin-American.

[2] NM, **latina** NF Latin; (*LAm*) Latin-American; **te cantan los cinco ~s**‡ your feet smell.

Latinoamérica NF Latin America.

latinoamericano, -a ADJ, NM/F Latin-American.

latir [3a] [1] VT (*And, Méx**) **me late que todo saldrá bien** something tells me that everything will turn out all right.

[2] VI **(a)** (*corazón*) to beat, throb, palpitate. **(b)** (*perro*) to bark, yelp.

latitud NF (*Geog y fig*) latitude; (*extensión*) breadth; (*área*) area, extent.

latitudinal ADJ latitudinal.

LATN NF (*Paraguay Aer*) ABR *de* **Líneas Aéreas de Transporte Nacional**.

lato ADJ broad, wide, extensive; *sentido* broad.

latón NM **(a)** (*metal*) brass. **(b)** (*Cono Sur*) big tin, large tin container; (*And: balde*) tin bucket.

latoso* [1] ADJ annoying, tiresome; boring.

[2] NM, **latosa** NF bore, drag.

latrocinio NM robbery, theft.

Latvia NF Latvia.

latvio, -a [1] ADJ, NM/F Latvian.

[2] NM (*Ling*) Latvian, Lettish.

LAU NF **(a)** (*Esp Jur*) ABR *de* **Ley de Autonomía Universitaria**. **(b)** (*Esp Jur*) ABR *de* **Ley de Arrendamientos Urbanos**.

lauca NF (*Cono Sur*) baldness, loss of hair.

laucadura NF (*Cono Sur*) baldness.

laucar [1g] VT (*Cono Sur*) to fleece, shear, remove the hair (*o* wool) from.

laucha NF **(a)** (*Cono Sur*) (*Zool*) mouse; (*: *flacón*) weed*; (‡: *viejo verde*) dirty old man. **(b)** (*And*) expert; **ser una ~, ser una lauchita** (*Cono*

Sur) to be very sharp, be quick; **aguaitar la ~, catear la ~** (*Cono Sur*) to bide one's time.

lauco ADJ (*Cono Sur*) bald, hairless.

laúd NM (*Mús*) lute.

laudable ADJ laudable, praiseworthy.

laudablemente ADV laudably, in a praiseworthy way.

láudano NM laudanum.

laudatorio ADJ laudatory.

laudo NM (*Jur*) award, decision, finding; arbitration (award); **~ de obligado cumplimiento** binding decision.

laureado ① ADJ *persona* honoured, distinguished, famous; *obra* prize-winning.

  ② NM, **laureada** NF laureate; (*premiado*) prizewinner.

laurear [1a] VT to crown with laurel; (*fig*) to honour, reward.

laurel NM laurel; (*fig*) laurels; (*premio*) honour, reward; (**hojas de**) **~** (*Culin*) bay (leaves); **~ cerezo** cherry-laurel; **descansar** (*o dormirse*) **sobre sus ~es** to rest on one's laurels.

laurencio NM (*Quím*) lawrencium.

lauréola NF (a) (*gen*) laurel wreath, crown of laurel; halo. (b) (*Bot*) daphne.

lauro NM laurel; (*fig*) laurels; glory, fame.

Lausana NF Lausanne.

lava¹ NF (*Geol*) lava.

lava² NF (*Min*) washing; **camisa de ~ y pon** drip-dry shirt.

lavable ADJ washable.

lavabo NM (a) (*jofaina*) washbasin; washstand. (b) (*retrete*) lavatory, toilet (*Brit*), washroom (*US*).

lavacara NF (*And*) washbasin.

lavacaras• NMF INVAR toady, creep‡.

lavacoches ① NMF INVAR (*persona*) car washer.

  ② NM INVAR (*máquina*) car wash.

lavada NF (*LAm*) wash, washing.

lavadero NM (a) (*lavandería*) laundry, wash-house; (*de río*) washing place; (*Cono Sur: de casa*) utility room. (b) (*LAm*) gold-bearing sands (*in river*).

lavado NM (a) (*acto*) wash, washing; **~ de bonos** bond-washing; **~ de cabeza** shampoo; **~ de cara** (*fig*) clean-up; facelift; **~ de cerebro** brainwashing; **campaña de ~ de imagen** image-saving campaign; **~ en seco** dry cleaning; **le hicieron un ~ de estómago** he had his stomach pumped. (b) (*ropa*) wash, laundry. (c) (*Arte*) wash.

lavador NM (a) (*Cono Sur: fregadero*) washbasin. (b) (*Cono Sur: excusado*) lavatory, toilet (*Brit*), washroom (*US*).

lavadora NF (a) (*de ropa*) washing machine; **~ de coches** car-wash; **~ de platos** dish-washer. (b) (*And: persona*) laundress, washerwoman.

lavadura NF (a) (*acto*) washing. (b) (*agua*) dirty water.

lavafaros NM INVAR headlamp wiper.

lavafrutas NM INVAR finger bowl.

lavagallos NM (*And, Carib*) firewater.

lavaje NM (*Cono Sur*) (a) = **lavadura**. (b) (*Med*) enema.

lavaluneta NM rear window washer.

lavamanos NM INVAR washbasin.

lavanda NF (*Bot*) lavender; (*agua*) lavender water.

lavandera NF (a) laundress, washerwoman. (b) (*Orn*) wagtail.

lavandería NF laundry; **~ automática** launderette.

lavandero NM launderer, laundryman.

lavandina NF (*Cono Sur*) bleach.

lavándula NF lavender.

lavaojos NM INVAR eye bath.

lavaparabrisas NM INVAR windscreen washer, windshield washer (*US*).

lavaplatos NM INVAR (a) (*aparato*) dishwasher. (b) (*persona*) dish-washer, washer-up. (c) (*Cono Sur, Méx: fregadero*) sink.

lavar [1a] ① VT (a) to wash; (•) *dinero* to launder•; **~ y marcar** *pelo* to shampoo and set; **tejanos lavados a la piedra** stonewashed jeans; **~ en seco** to dry-clean; **~ la cabeza** to wash one's hair.

  (b) (*fig*) to wipe away; to wipe out.

  ② **lavarse** VR to wash, have a wash; **~ las manos** to wash one's hands; (*fig*) to wash one's hands of it.

lavarropas NM INVAR washing machine.

lavasecadora NF washer-dryer.

lavaseco NM (*Chile*) drycleaner's (shop).

lavativa NF (a) (*Med*) enema. (b) (*fig*) nuisance, bother, bore.

lavatorio NM (a) washstand. (b) (*LAm*) lavatory, washroom (*US*). (c) (*Med*) lotion.

lavavajillas NM INVAR (*aparato*) dishwasher; (*líquido*) washing-up liquid.

lavazas NFPL dishwater, dirty water, slops.

lavoteo• NM quick wash, cat-lick•.

laxante ADJ, NM laxative.

laxar [1a] VT to ease, relax, slacken; *vientre* to loosen.

laxativo ADJ laxative.

laxitud NF laxity, slackness.

laxo ADJ lax, slack.

laya NF (a) (*pala*) spade; **~ de puntas** (garden) fork. (b) (*liter*) kind, sort; **de esta ~** of this kind.

lazada NF bow, knot.

lazar [1f] ① VT to lasso, rope.

  ② VI (*CAm: tren*) to connect.

lazareto NM (*Hist*) leper hospital, isolation hospital.

lazariento ADJ (*CAm, Cono Sur, Méx*) leprous.

lazarillo NM blind man's guide.

lazarino ① ADJ leprous.

  ② NM, **lazarina** NF leper.

Lázaro NM Lazarus.

lazo NM (a) (*gen*) bow, knot; loop; (*Agr*) lasso, lariat; **~ corredizo** slip-knot; **~ de zapato** bootlace.

  (b) (*Caza*) snare, trap (*t fig*); **caer en el ~** to fall into the trap; **tender un ~ a uno** to set a trap for sb.

  (c) (*Aut*) bend, loop.

  (d) (*fig: vínculo*) link, bond, tie; **los ~s culturales entre A y B** cultural ties between A and B; **los ~s familiares** the family bond, the ties of blood.

LBE NF (*Esp Jur*) ABR *de* **Ley Básica de Empleo.**

L/C NF ABR *de* **Letra de Crédito** bill of exchange, B/E.

Lda., Ldo. ABR *de* **Licenciada, Licenciado.**

le PRON PERS (a) (*ac*) him; (*Vd*) you; **no le veo** I don't see him; **¿le ayudo?** shall I help you?

  (b) (*dativo*) (to) him, (to) her, (to) it; (*Vd*) (to) you; **le hablé** I spoke to him, I spoke to her; **quiero darle esto** I want to give you this; **le he comprado esto** I bought this for you; **uno de los mejores papeles que le hayamos visto** one of the best performances we have seen from him; **no se le conoce otra obra** no other work of his is known.

lea‡ NF tart‡, whore.

leal ADJ loyal, faithful, trustworthy; *competencia* fair.

lealmente ADV loyally, faithfully.

lealtad NF loyalty, fidelity; trustworthiness; **~ de marca** brand loyalty, loyalty to a brand.

leandra‡ NF one peseta.

Leandro NM Leander.

leasing ['lizin] NM leasing; **~ operativo** operational lease.

lebrato NM leveret.

lebrel NM greyhound.

lebrillo NM earthenware bowl.

lebrón• ADJ (*Méx*) (a) (*listo*) sharp, wide-awake. (b) (*arrogante*) boastful, insolent. (c) (*taimado*) sly; evil-minded.

LEC [lek] NF (*Esp Jur*) ABR *de* **Ley de Enjuiciamiento Civil.**

lección NF (a) lesson (*t Ecl*); (*Escuela*) lesson, class, (*Univ*) lecture, class; (*fig*) warning, example; **~ magistral** (*Mús*) master class; **~ particular** private lesson; **~ práctica** object-lesson (*de* in); **dar lecciones** to teach, give lessons; **dar una ~ a uno** (*fig*) to teach sb a lesson; **saberse la ~**• to know what the score is•; **¡que te sirva de ~!** let that be a lesson to you!; **tomar ~** to have a lesson.

  (b) (*Liter: de MS etc*) reading.

lecha NF milt, (soft) roe.

lechada NF (a) (*cal*) whitewash; (*pasta*) paste; grout; (*pulpa*) pulp. (b) (*LAm*) milking. (c) (‡) spunk‡, semen.

lechal ① ADJ sucking; **cordero ~** baby lamb, young lamb.

  ② NM milk (*fig*), milky juice.

lechar [1a] VT (a) (*LAm: ordeñar*) to milk; (*And, CAm: amamantar*) to suckle. (b) (*CAm, Méx: blanquear*) to whitewash.

lechazo¹ NM young lamb.

lechazo²‡ NM (*golpe*) bash•, swipe; (*choque*) bash•, bang.

leche NF (a) (*gen*) milk; **~ completa, ~ entera** unskimmed milk; **~ condensada** condensed milk; **~ descremada, ~ desnatada** skim(med) milk; **~ sin desnatar** (*Esp*) whole milk; **~ de larga duración, ~ de larga vida** long-life milk; **~ evaporada** evaporated milk; **~ de magnesia** milk of magnesia; **~ materna** mother's milk; **~ merengada** milkshake flavoured with cinnamon; **~ paste(u)-rizada** pasteurized milk; **~ en polvo** powdered milk; **~ semides-natada** semi-skimmed milk; **estar con** (*o* **tener**) **la ~ en los labios** (*fig*) to be young and inexperienced, be wet behind the ears.

  (b) (*Bot*) milk, milky juice; (*And*) rubber; (*Carib*) rubber tree.

  (c) (‡: *semen*) semen, spunk‡; **un tío de mala ~** a nasty sort, an evil person; a disagreeable chap•; **estar de mala ~** to feel pissed off‡, be in a foul temper; **poner a uno de mala ~** to annoy sb, make sb cross; **tener mala ~** to be vindictive, be nasty; **hay mucha mala ~ entre ellos** there's a lot of bad blood between them; **aquí hay mucha mala ~** there's a lot of ill-feeling here.

  (d) (•: *suerte*) good luck; **estar con ~, estar de ~, tener ~** to be lucky; **¡qué ~ tienes!** you lucky devil!

  (e) (•: *golpe*) bash•, swipe; (*choque*) bash•, bang; **darse una ~** (*fig*) to come a cropper•.

  (f) (•: *molestia*) bore, pain•; **¡es la ~!** it's such a pain!

  (g) (‡: *otras locuciones*) **¡~!** hell!, hell's teeth!; **¡~s!** no way!•, get

away!; ¿qué ~s quieres? what the hell do you want?; **muchos vinos**
(*etc*) **y mucha ~** lots of wines (*etc*) and all that jazz*; **¡qué coche ni**
qué ~! car my foot!*; **no entiende ni ~s** he doesn't understand a
bloody thing‡; **echar ~s** to go up the wall*; **salió echando** (*o*
cagando⁕) **~s** he went like a bat out of hell*; **ir a toda ~** to scorch
along*; **cantando es la ~** when she sings she's a bloody marvel‡,
(*pey*) when she sings she's bloody awful‡.

lecheada NF (*Cono Sur*) = **lechada**.
lechear [1a] VT (*LAm*) to milk.
lechecillas NFPL sweetbreads.
lechera NF **(a)** (*persona*) milkmaid, dairymaid. **(b)** (*recipiente*) milk can,
milk churn. **(c)** (*LAm*) cow. **(d)** (*) police-car.
lechería NF **(a)** (*edificio*) dairy, creamery; (*And, Cono Sur*) milking parlour. **(b)** (*Cono Sur: vacas*) cows, herd. **(c)** (*And, Méx: tacañería*) meanness.
lecherita NF milk jug.
lechero ① ADJ **(a)** (*gen*) milk (*atr*); dairy (*atr*); **ganado ~** dairy herd;
producción lechera milk production; *V* **vaca.**
(b) (*LAm: con suerte*) lucky.
(c) (*Méx*: *tacaño*) mean, stingy.
(d) (*Carib*: *codicioso*) greedy, grasping.
② NM (*de granja*) dairyman; (*repartidor*) milkman.
lechigada NF litter, brood; (*fig*) gang.
lecho NM **(a)** (*cama*) bed; couch; (*Agr*) bedding; **~ de enfermo**
sickbed; **~ de muerte, ~ mortuorio** deathbed; **~ de rosas** (*fig*) bed
of roses. **(b)** (*de río*) bed; bottom, floor; (*Geol*) layer; **~ del mar, ~**
marino sea-bed; **~ de roca** bedrock.
lechón NM **(a)** (*lit*) piglet, sucking-pig. **(b)** (*fig*) pig, filthy person.
lechona NF **(a)** (*lit*) sow. **(b)** (*fig*) pig, sow; slob*.
lechoncillo NM piglet, sucking-pig.
lechosa NF (*LAm*) papaya (*fruit*).
lechosidad NF milkiness.
lechoso ADJ **(a)** (*líquido*) milky. **(b)** (‡: *suertudo*) jammy‡, lucky.
lechucear [1a] VI (*And*) to be on night duty.
lechucero NM (*And*) **(a)** (*obrero*) nightshift worker; (*taxista*) night driver. **(b)** (*taxi*) night taxi.
lechudo ADJ (*LAm*) lucky.
lechuga NF **(a)** (*Bot*) lettuce; **~ Cos, ~ francesa, ~ orejona** (*Méx*) cos
lettuce. **(b)** (*Cos*) frill, flounce. **(c)** (*Esp‡*) 1000-peseta note; (*Carib*)
banknote. **(d)** (*: euf*) = **leche** (c).
lechuguilla NF (*Cos*) frill, flounce, ruff.
lechuguino NM **(a)** (*Bot*) young lettuce. **(b)** (‡) toff*, dude (*US*).
lechuza NF **(a)** (*Orn*) barn owl; **~ común** barn owl. **(b)** (*Cono Sur, Méx: albi-*
no) albino, light blond(e). **(c)** (*Carib, Méx: puta*) whore.
lechuzo* NM **(a)** (*feo*) ugly devil*. **(b)** (*lerdo*) dimwit*.
leco‡ ADJ (*Méx*) nuts‡, round the bend‡.
lectivo ADJ school (*atr*); *V* **año, día** *etc.*
lectoescritura NF reading and writing.
lector ① ADJ: **el público ~** the reading public.
② NM, **lectora** NF **(a)** (*lit*) reader; **~ de cartas** card-reader, fortune-
teller. **(b)** (*Colegio, Univ*) conversation assistant.
③ NM (*aparato*) reader; **~ de compact disc, ~ de discos compactos**
CD player, compact disc player; **~ de fichas** card reader; **~ óptico**
optical reader, optical scanner; **~ de tarjeta magnética** magnetic
card reader.
lectorado NM **(a)** (*de periódico etc*) readership. **(b)** (*Univ*) post of *lector*.
lectura NF reading; reading matter; (*Inform*) read-out; **una persona de**
mucha ~ a well-read person; **~ labial** lip-reading; **~ de marcas** (*In-*
form) mark sensing; **~ del pensamiento** mind-reading; **dar ~ a** to
read (publicly), deliver.
leer [2e] VTI to read; **~ en la boca** to lip-read; **~ entre líneas** to read
between the lines; **~ la mano a uno** to read sb's palm; **'al que**
leyere' 'to the reader'.
lefa⁕ NF spunk⁕, semen.
lega NF lay sister.
legación NF legation.
legado NM **(a)** (*enviado*) legate. **(b)** (*Jur*) legacy, bequest.
legajar VT (*And, Cono Sur, Méx*) to file.
legajo NM file, bundle (of papers).
legal ADJ **(a)** (*gen*) legal, lawful; *hora* standard. **(b)** *persona* trustworthy,
truthful; loyal, reliable; (*Jur*) clean*, with no police record; **tío ~***
good bloke‡. **(c)** (*And*: *excelente*) fine, marvellous.
legalidad NF legality, lawfulness.
legalista ADJ legalistic.
legalización NF legalization; authentication.
legalizar [1f] VT to legalize, make lawful; *documento* to authenticate.
legalmente ADV legally, lawfully.
légamo NM slime, mud, ooze; (*arcilla*) clay.
legamoso ADJ slimy, oozy; clayey.
legaña NF rheum, sleep.
legañoso ADJ bleary.
legar [1h] VT to bequeath (*t Jur, fig*), leave (*a* to).

legatario, -a NM/F legatee.
legendario ADJ legendary.
leggings ['leɣins] NMPL leggings.
legía* NM legionnaire, member of the Spanish Foreign Legion.
legibilidad NF legibility.
legible ADJ legible; **~ por máquina** machine-readable.
legiblemente ADV legibly.
legión NF legion; **L~ Extranjera** Foreign Legion; **la L~** (*esp*) the Spanish Foreign Legion; **son ~** they are legion; **el autor ~** (*Liter*) the
author whose name is legion, the collectivity of anonymous authors
(*of ballads etc*).
legionario ① ADJ legionary.
② NM legionary; legionnaire.
legionella NF legionnaire's disease.
legislación NF legislation.
legislador(a) NM/F legislator, lawmaker.
legislar [1a] VI to legislate.
legislativas NFPL parliamentary elections.
legislativo ADJ legislative.
legislatura NF (*Jur*) term; (*Pol*) session; period of office; **agotar la ~** to
serve out one's term of office; (*LAm: cuerpo*) legislature, legislative
body.
legista ① NMF jurist, legist.
② ADJ (*LAm*): **médico ~** forensic expert, criminal pathologist.
legítima* NF: **la ~** my better half.
legitimación NF legitimation.
legítimamente ADV legitimately, rightfully; justly; genuinely.
legitimar [1a] ① VT to legitimize; to legalize.
② **legitimarse** VR to establish one's identity; to establish one's title (*o claim etc*); **considerarse legitimado para** + *infin* to consider
o.s. entitled to + *infin*.
legitimidad NF legitimacy; justice; authenticity.
legitimista ADJ, NMF royalist.
legitimización NF legitimization.
legitimizar [1f] VT to legitimize.
legítimo ADJ (*gen*) legitimate, rightful; just; (*auténtico*) genuine,
authentic, real; (*Aut*) *repuestos* genuine.
lego ① ADJ **(a)** (*Ecl*) lay; secular. **(b)** (*fig*) ignorant, uninformed.
② NM layman; lay brother; (*fig*) layman; **los ~s** the laity.
legón NM hoe.
legrado NM (*Med*: *de útero*) D and C (*dilation and curettage*); (: *de hueso*)
scraping.
legua NF league; **eso se ve** (*o* **se nota**) **a la ~** you can tell it a mile
away.
leguaje NM **(a)** (*CAm: distancia*) distance in leagues. **(b)** (*And Parl:*
gastos de viaje) travelling expenses.
leguleyo NM pettifogging lawyer.
legumbre NF (*seca*) pulse; (*fresca*) vegetable.
leguminosa NF (*Bot*) pulse.
leguminoso ADJ leguminous.
lehendakari NM = **lendakari**.
leíble ADJ legible.
Leida, Leide NM Leyden.
leída NF (*LAm*) reading; **de una ~** in one reading, at one go; **dar una**
~ a* to read over.
leído ADJ (*iró*) *persona* well-read; **muy ~** (**y escribido**) pedantic, pretentious.
leísmo NM *use of* **le** *instead of* **lo** *and* **la** (*direct objects*).

┌─────────────────────────────────────┐
│ **LEÍSMO, LOÍSMO, LAÍSMO** │
└─────────────────────────────────────┘

ⓘ *These terms refer to the reversal of the standard distinction between*
direct and indirect object pronouns for people in Spanish. Normally
lo(s) and la(s) are the direct object pronouns (eg: **Lo/La vi ayer** *I saw him/*
her yesterday) and le(s) the indirect equivalents (eg: **Le di tu recado** *I gave*
him/her your message). **Leísmo** *involves replacing lo(s) and la(s) with le(s)*
(eg: **Le vi ayer***), while loísmo and laísmo mean using lo(s) and la(s) instead*
of le(s) (eg: **Lo/La di tu recado***). Whereas leísmo is relatively socially*
acceptable, loísmo and laísmo tend to be frowned upon.

leísta ① ADJ *that uses* **le** *instead of* **lo** *and* **la** (*direct objects*).
② NMF *user of* **le** *instead of* **lo** *and* **la.**
lejanía NF (*distancia*) distance, remoteness; (*lugar*) remote place.
lejano ADJ distant, remote, far-off.
Lejano Oriente NM Far East.
lejas ADJ PL: **de ~ tierras** of (*o* from) some distant land.
lejía¹ NF **(a)** (*gen*) bleach; lye. **(b)** (*) dressing-down*.
lejía² NM = **legía**.
lejísimos ADV (*superl*) *de* **lejos**.
lejos ① ADV far, far away, far off; **a lo ~** in the distance, far off; **de ~,**
desde ~ from afar, from a long way off; **más ~** further (off); **en eso**
no andaba muy ~ he wasn't far off the mark; **está muy ~** it's a
long way (away); **¿está ~?** is it far?; **eso queda demasiado ~** that's

too far (away); **ir ~** to go far (*t fig*); **para no ir más ~** (*fig*), **sin ir más ~** to take an obvious example; **eso viene de ~** (*fig*) that's been going on for a long time.

  [2] **~ de** PREP far from; **estoy muy ~ de pensar que ...** I am very far from thinking that ...

  [3] NM distant view; appearance from a distance; glimpse; (*Arte*) background; **tiene buen ~** it looks all right at a distance.

lejura NF (*And*) distance; **~s** (*Cono Sur*) remote place, remote area.

lele ADJ (*CAm, Cono Sur*), **lelo** ADJ silly, stupid; **quedarse ~** to be stunned.

lema NM motto, device; theme; (*Pol etc*) slogan, watchword.

lem(m)ing ['lemin] NM lemming.

lempira NM lempira (*Honduran unit of currency*).

lempo [1] ADJ (*And*) big, large.

  [2] NM (a) (*And*) bit, piece. (b) **un ~ de caballo** (*And*) a big horse.

lémur NM lemur.

lencería NF (a) (*telas*) linen, drapery; (*ropa interior*) lingerie. (b) (*tienda*) draper's (shop). (c) (*armario*) linen cupboard.

lencero, -a NM/F draper.

lendakari NM head of the Basque autonomous government.

lendroso ADJ lousy, infested with lice.

lengón ADJ (*And*) = **lenguón**.

lengua NF (a) (*Anat y fig*) tongue; **mala ~**, **~ larga** (*LAm*), **~ de trapo** (*LAm*), **~ viperina** gossip; **según las malas ~s ...** according to gossip ...; **de ~ en ~** from mouth to mouth; **andar en ~s** to be the talk of the town; **atar la ~ a uno** (*fig*) to silence sb; **beber con la ~** to lap up; **buscar la ~ a uno** to pick a quarrel with sb; **dar a la ~** to chatter, talk too much; **darse la ~*** to kiss passionately; **estar con la ~ fuera*** to be dead beat, be exhausted; **hacerse ~s de** to praise to the skies, rave about; **irse de la ~, írsele a uno la ~** to talk too much; to let the cat out of the bag; **morderse la ~** to hold one's tongue; to keep sth back; **no morderse la ~** not to mince one's words, not to pull one's punches; **nacer con la ~ fuera** to be born idle; **retener la ~** to hold one's tongue; **sacar la ~ a uno** to poke one's tongue out at sb; **soltar la ~*** to spill the beans*; **tener mucha ~*** to be cheeky*; **tirar de la ~ a uno** to draw sb out, make sb talk; to provoke sb; **se le trabó la ~** he began to stammer.

  (b) (*de campana*) clapper.

  (c) tierra (*Geog*) spit of land, tongue of land.

  (d) (*Ling*) language, tongue; (*Esp Escol*) Spanish language (as a school subject); **~ franca** lingua franca; **~ madre** parent language; **~ materna** mother tongue; first language; **~ minoritaria** minority language; **~ moderna** modern language; **~ muerta** dead language; **~ viva** living language; **hablar en ~** (*And*) to speak Quichua.

LENGUAS COOFICIALES

🛈 *Under the Spanish constitution* **catalán**, **euskera** *and* **gallego** *are* **lenguas oficiales** *and enjoy the same status as* **castellano** *in the autonomous regions in which they are spoken. These languages are also known as* **lenguas cooficiales** *to show they enjoy equal status with Spanish. The regional governments actively promote their use through the media and the education system.*

⇨ *See also* CATALÁN , EUSKERA , GALLEGO

---

lenguado NM sole, dab.

lenguaje NM (a) (*gen*) language; (faculty of) speech.

  (b) (*forma de hablar*) idiom, parlance, (mode of) speech; style; **~ comercial** business language; **~ del cuerpo** body-language; **~ de gestos**, **~ de las manos** sign language; **~ periodístico** newspaper language, journalese; **~ vulgar** common speech, ordinary speech; **en ~ llano** in plain English (*etc*).

  (c) (*Liter*) style, diction.

  (d) (*Inform*) language; **~ de alto nivel** high-level language; **~ de bajo nivel** low-level language; **~ ensamblador** assembly language; **~ fuente** source language; **~ informático**, **~ máquina** computer language; **~ objeto** target language; **~ de programación** program(m)ing language.

lenguaraz ADJ talkative; (*pey*) foul-mouthed.

lenguaz ADJ garrulous.

lengüeta NF (a) (*gen*) tab, small tongue; (*Téc, Mús, de zapato*) tongue; (*Anat*) epiglottis; (*de balanza etc*) needle, pointer; (*de flecha*) barb.

  (b) (*LAm*) (*hablador*) chatterbox; (*chismoso*) gossip.

  (c) (*LAm: cortapapeles*) paper knife.

  (d) (*LAm Cos*) fringe of a petticoat.

lengüetada NF lick.

lengüetazo NM (*LAm*) lick.

lengüetear [1a] [1] VT (*LAm*) to lick.

  [2] VI (*LAm*) to stick one's tongue out; (*Carib*) to jabber, chatter.

lengüeterías NFPL (*LAm*) gossip, tittle-tattle.

lengüetero ADJ (*Carib*) (*hablador*) garrulous; (*chismoso*) gossiping.

lengüicorto* ADJ shy, timid.

lengüilargo ADJ, **lengüisucio** ADJ (*Carib*) foul-mouthed.

lenguón (*LAm*) [1] ADJ (*hablador*) garrulous; (*franco*) outspoken; (*chismoso*) gossiping.

  [2] NM, **lenguona** NF gossip, talebearer.

lenidad NF lenience, softness.

Lenin NM Lenin.

Leningrado NM Leningrad.

leninismo NM Leninism.

leninista ADJ, NMF Leninist.

lenitivo [1] ADJ lenitive.

  [2] NM lenitive, palliative.

lenocinio NM pandering, procuring; (**casa de**) **~** brothel.

lentamente ADV slowly.

lente NF (*a veces* NM) lens; eyeglass; **~s** (*Hist, t Carib*) spectacles; **~ de aumento** magnifying glass; **~s de contacto**, **~s corneales** contact lenses; **~ de gran ángulo**, **~ granangular** wide-angle lens; **~ zoom** zoom-lens.

lenteja NF lentil; **ganarse las ~s** to earn one's bread and butter; **~s** lentil soup.

lentejuela NF spangle, sequin.

lentificar [1g] [1] VT to slow down.

  [2] **lentificarse** VR to slow down.

lentillas NFPL contact lenses.

lentitud NF slowness; **con ~** slowly.

lento ADJ slow.

lentorro* ADJ sluggish, slow.

leña NF (a) (*lit*) firewood; sticks, kindling; **~ de oveja** (*Cono Sur*) sheep droppings; **echar ~ al fuego** to add fuel to the flames; **llevar ~ al monte** to carry coals to Newcastle.

  (b) (*) thrashing; (*fig*) stick, punishment; **cargar de ~**, **dar ~ a**, **hartar de ~** to lay it on, thrash; **repartir ~** to dish out the punishment; **trincar ~** to sweat blood.

leñador NM woodcutter, woodman.

leñar [1a] VT (*Cono Sur, Méx*), **leñatear** [1a] VT (*And*) to make into firewood, cut up for firewood.

leñateo NM (*And, CAm*) woodpile.

leñatero NM (*Cono Sur*) woodcutter, woodman.

leñazo NM (*golpe*) bash*; blow with a stick; (*choque*) collision, bash*.

leñe NM (*euf*) = **leche** (c).

leñera NF woodshed.

leñero NM (a) (*comerciante*) dealer in wood. (b) (*depósito*) woodshed.

leño NM (a) (*tronco*) log; (*madera*) timber, wood, piece of wood; **hacer ~ del árbol caído** to kick sb when he's down. (b) (*) blockhead.

leñoso ADJ woody.

Leo NM (*Zodíaco*) Leo.

León NM (a) (*nombre*) Leon, Leo. (b) (*Geog*) León.

león NM (a) (*Zool*) lion (*t fig*); (*LAm*) puma; **L~** (*Zodíaco*) Leo; **~ marino** sea lion; **estar hecho un ~** to be furious; **ponerse como un ~** to get furious. (b) **leones** (**:** *dados*) loaded dice.

leona NF (a) (*Zool*) lioness. (b) (*Cono Sur*) confusion, mess, mix-up. (c) (*: portera*) porter, concierge. (d) (**:** *puta*) tart**:**.

leonado ADJ tawny.

leonera NF (a) (*jaula*) lion's cage; (*cueva etc*) lion's den.

  (b) (*: de juego*) gambling den, dive**:**; (*de niños*) glory hole*; (*para hobby*) hideout, hideaway; (*And, Cono Sur: celda*) communal prison cell; (*And*) noisy gathering.

leonés [1] ADJ Leonese; (*LAm*) from León.

  [2] NM, **leonesa** NF Leonese; (*LAm*) native (o inhabitant) of León.

  [3] NM (*Ling*) Leonese.

leonino ADJ (a) (*Poét*) leonine. (b) *contrato* one-sided, unfair.

Leonor NF Eleanor.

leontina NF watch chain.

leopardo NM leopard; **~ cazador** cheetah.

leopoldina NF fob, short watch chain.

leotardo NM (*t* **~s**) leotard, tights.

Lepe N: **ser más tonto que ~** to be a complete twit*; **ir donde las ~** (*Cono Sur*) to make a bloomer* (*in calculating*); **saber más que ~** to be pretty smart, have lots of savoir-faire.

leperada NF (*CAm, Méx*) (*en el habla*) coarse remark; (*acto*) dirty trick, rotten thing (to do)*.

lépero* [1] ADJ (a) (*CAm, Méx*) rough, uncouth; rude. (b) (*And*) **estar ~** to be broke*.

  [2] NM, **lépera** NF low-class person; guttersnipe.

leperusco ADJ (*Méx*) low-class, plebeian; (*pey*) rotten*, villainous.

lepidopterólogo, -a NM/F lepidopterist.

lepidópteros NMPL lepidoptera, butterflies and moths.

lepisma NF silverfish.

leporino ADJ leporine; hare-like; **labio ~** harelip.

lepra NF leprosy; **~ de montaña** (*LAm*) mountain leprosy, leishmaniasis.

leprosario NM (*Méx*), **leprosería** NF leper colony.

leproso [1] ADJ leprous.

  [2] NM, **leprosa** NF leper.

lerdear [1a] VI (*CAm*) to be slow (about doing things), do things unwillingly.

lerdera NF (*CAm*) = **lerdez**.

lerdez* NF, **lerdeza** NF (*CAm*) slowness; heaviness, dullness; slow-wittedness; clumsiness.

lerdo ADJ (*lento*) slow; (*pesado*) heavy, dull; (*de pocas luces*) slow-witted; (*torpe*) clumsy.

lerdura NF (*Cono Sur*) = **lerdez**.

lerén* NM (*And*) (*tipo*) bloke‡, guy*; (*de baja estatura*) midget.

leridano [1] ADJ of Lérida.

[2] NM, **leridana** NF native (*o* inhabitant) of Lérida; **los ~s** the people of Lérida.

les PRON PERS (a) (*ac*) them; (*Vds*) you. (b) (*dativo*) (to) them; (*Vds*) (to) you; *para ejemplos de uso,* V **le**.

lesa ADJ: **~ majestad** lese majesty; **crimen de ~ humanidad** crime against humanity; **acción de ~ patria** act of treachery to one's country.

lesbiana NF lesbian.

lesbianismo NM lesbianism.

lésbico ADJ lesbian.

lesbio ADJ lesbian.

lesera* NF (*And, Cono Sur: estupidez*) stupidity; (*tonterías*) nonsense.

lesión NF wound, lesion; injury (*t fig*); (*Jur*) **lesiones** assault and battery; **~ cerebral** brain-damage.

lesionado ADJ hurt, injured; *jugador* injured, unfit.

lesionar [1a] [1] VT (*dañar*) to hurt, injure; (*herir*) to wound.

[2] **lesionarse** VR to get hurt.

lesividad NF harmfulness.

lesivo ADJ harmful, damaging.

lesna NF awl.

leso ADJ (a) (*herido*) hurt; (*ofendido*) injured, offended. (b) (*And, Cono Sur**) simple, stupid; **no está para ~** (*Cono Sur*) he's not easily taken in; **hacer ~ a uno** (*Cono Sur*) to play a trick on sb; **hacerse el ~** to pretend not to know (*o* notice).

Lesoto NM Lesotho.

lesura NF (*Cono Sur*) stupidity.

letal ADJ deadly, lethal.

letalidad NF deadliness, lethal nature; **la enfermedad tiene una elevada ~** there is a high death-rate from this disease.

letanía NF (*Ecl*) litany; (*fig*) rigmarole; (*lista*) long list; (*recitado*) tedious recitation.

letárgico ADJ lethargic.

letargo NM lethargy.

Lete(o) NM Lethe.

letón, -ona [1] ADJ, NM/F Latvian.

[2] NM (*Ling*) Latvian, Lettish.

Letonia NF Latvia.

letra NF (a) (*Tip etc*) letter; **~ gótica** Gothic script, black letter; **~ de imprenta** print; **~ inicial** initial letter; **~ mayúscula** capital letter; **la ~ menuda, la ~ pequeña** the small print; **~ minúscula** small letter; **en ~s de molde** in print; in block letters; **~ muerta** dead letter; **~ negrilla** bold type, heavy type; **~ versal** capital letter; **~ versalita** small capital; **decir a una las cuatro ~s*** to call a woman a slut.

(b) (*fig*) letter, literal meaning; **a la ~** to the letter; **atarse a la ~** to stick to the literal meaning.

(c) (*escrito*) **~s** piece of writing; **poner unas** (*o* **dos**) **~s a uno** to drop sb a line.

(d) (*escritura*) writing, handwriting; **~ cursiva** cursive writing; **tiene buena ~** he writes a good hand; **tiene malísima ~** his writing is shocking.

(e) (*Com*) letter, bill, draft; (*plazo*) hire-purchase instalment; **~ abierta** letter of credit; **~ aceptada** accepted letter; **~ bancaria** banker's draft, bank draft; **~ de cambio** bill (of exchange), bank draft; **~ del Tesoro** Treasury bill; **~ a la vista** sight draft; **pagar a ~ vista** to pay on sight.

(f) (*Mús*) words, lyric.

(g) (*fig*) **~s** letters, learning; (*Univ*) Arts; **bellas ~s** belles lettres, literature; **~s humanas** humanities; **primeras ~s** elementary education, three Rs; **~s sagradas** Scripture.

(h) (*: *euf*) = **leche** (f).

letrado [1] ADJ learned; (*pey*) pedantic; **derecho a la asistencia letrada** right to have a lawyer present.

[2] NM, **letrada** NF (*t* **la letrado**) counsel, legal representative.

letrero NM (*anuncio*) sign, notice; (*cartel*) placard, poster; (*Com*) label; (*inscripción*) inscription; (*escrito*) words, (piece of) writing.

letrina NF latrine, privy; (*fig*) sewer, sump, filthy place; **el río es una ~** the river is an open sewer.

letrista NMF (*Mús*) lyricist, songwriter.

leucemia NF leukaemia.

leucémico, -a NM/F person suffering from leukaemia.

leucocito NM (*Med*) leucocyte.

leucoma NF leucoma.

leudar [1a] [1] VT to leaven.

[2] **leudarse** VR (*pan etc*) to rise.

leva NF (a) (*Náut*) weighing anchor.

(b) (*Mil*) levy.

(c) (*Mec*) lever; cam.

(d) (*And, CAm: estafa*) trick, swindle, ruse; **bajar la ~ a uno** (*And, Cono Sur*) to do sb a mischief; **caer de ~** (*CAm*) to play the fool; **echar ~s** (*: *And, Méx: jactarse*) to boast; (*And*: amenazar*) to bluster, utter threats; **encender la ~ a uno** (*Carib**) to give sb a good hiding*. (e) **ponerse la ~** (*And**) (*Escol*) to play truant; (*del trabajo*) to stay away from work; (*largarse*) to beat it*.

levadizo ADJ that can be raised; **puente ~** drawbridge.

levado NM raising; **sistema de ~** raising mechanism.

levadura NF (a) yeast, leaven; **~ de cerveza** brewer's yeast; **~ de panadero** baker's yeast; **~ en polvo** baking powder. (b) (*: *euf*) **mala ~** = **mala leche**.

levantada NF (*And*) upsurge.

levantado ADJ (*despierto*) up; **no me esperes ~** don't wait up for me.

levantador NM: **~ de pesas** weight-lifter.

levantamiento NM (a) (*lit*) raising, lifting; elevation; **~ del cadáver** removal of the body; **~ cartográfico** topographical survey, mapping; **~ de pesas** weight-lifting. (b) (*Pol*) rising, revolt.

levantamuertos* NM INVAR (*And Culin*) vegetable broth.

levantar [1a] [1] VT (a) (*gen*) to raise, lift (up); (*elevar*) to elevate; *objeto caído* to raise up, stand up; (*enderezar*) to straighten; (*recoger*) to pick up; (*Dep*) *pesa* to lift; (*Arquit*) to raise, build, erect; (*Med*) *bollo* to raise; *ejército* to raise, recruit; *censo* to take; *polvo* to raise; *caza* to flush, put up; *casa* to move, remove; *plano* to make, draw up; *sesión* to adjourn; *asedio* to raise; *tono, voz* to raise; **levantó la mano** he raised his hand, he put up his hand; **~ los ojos** to look up, raise one's eyes; **¡no levantes la voz!** keep your voice down!; **fue imposible ~lo** it was impossible to lift it.

(b) *mesa, mantel* to clear away; *campamento* to strike; *tienda* to take down.

(c) *prohibición* to raise, lift.

(d) (*fig*) *persona* to uplift, hearten, cheer up; *ánimos* to raise; (*Pol*) to rouse, stir up.

(e) (*) *dinero* to make, earn.

(f) (*And*‡) to nick‡, arrest.

(g) (*Cono Sur**) *amante* to pick up*.

[2] VI: **no levanta del suelo más de 1,40 m** she stands only 1.40 metres.

[3] **levantarse** VR (a) (*gen*) to rise; (*incorporarse*) to get up, stand up, rise to one's feet; to straighten up; **~** (**de la cama**) to get up, get out of bed; **~ en el pie izquierdo** (*And**) to get out of bed on the wrong side.

(b) (*niebla*) to lift; (*viento etc*) to rise.

(c) (*destacarse etc*) to stand up, stick up, stand out; **se levanta por encima de los demás edificios** it stands up higher than the other buildings.

(d) (*sesión*) to be adjourned; to conclude, be concluded.

(e) **~ con algo** to make off with sth.

(f) (*Pol*) to rise, revolt, rebel.

levantaválvulas NM INVAR valve tappet.

Levante NM (a) (*gen*) Levant; **el ~** the Levant, the (Near) East. (b) (*España*) east coast, south-east coast.

levante[1] NM (*Geog*) (a) (*este*) east. (b) (*viento*) east wind.

levante[2] NM (a) (*Carib Pol*) uprising.

(b) (*Carib: arreo*) driving of cattle.

(c) (*And: arrogancia*) arrogance, haughtiness.

(d) **dar** (*o* **pegar**) **un ~ a uno** (*Cono Sur**) to give sb a dressing-down*.

(e) (*Cono Sur*: encuentro*) pick-up*; **hacer un ~ a uno** to pick sb up*.

(f) **hacer un ~** (*Carib**) to fall in love.

levantino [1] ADJ (a) Levantine.

(b) (*de España*) of the eastern coast (*o* provinces *etc*) of Spain.

[2] NM, **levantina** NF (a) (*gen*) Levantine.

(b) (*de España*) native (*o* inhabitant) of the eastern provinces of Spain; **los ~s** the people of the east of Spain.

levantisco ADJ restless, turbulent.

levar [1a] [1] VT: **~ anclas** to weigh anchor.

[2] **levarse** VR to weigh anchor, set sail.

leve ADJ (*gen*) light; (*mínimo*) slight; (*poco importante*) trivial, small, unimportant; *una herida* a slight wound; **sin el más ~ optimismo** without the slightest optimism.

levedad NF lightness; (*fig*) levity.

levemente ADV lightly; slightly.

leviatán NM leviathan.

levita[1] NF frock coat.

levita[2] NM Levite.

levitación NF levitation.

levitar [1a] VI to levitate.

Levítico NM Leviticus.

lexema NM lexeme.

lexicalizador [1] ADJ lexicalizing.
[2] NM lexicalizer.

lexicalizar [1f] VT to lexicalize.

léxico [1] ADJ lexical.
[2] NM lexicon, dictionary; vocabulary; word list.

lexicografía NF lexicography.

lexicográfico ADJ lexicographical.

lexicógrafo, -a NM/F lexicographer.

lexicología NF lexicology.

lexicólogo, -a NM/F lexicologist.

lexicón NM lexicon.

ley NF **(a)** (*gen*) law; (*Parl*) act, bill, measure; (*Dep etc*) rule, law; ~ **de la calle** mob law, lynch law; ~ **cambiaria** currency exchange regulations; ~ **del embudo** unfair law; force majeure; ~ **no escrita** unwritten law; ~ **del más fuerte** (principle of) might is right; **se le aplicó la ~ de fugas** he was shot while trying to escape; ~ **fundamental,** ~ **orgánica** constitutional law; ~ **marcial** martial law; ~ **de Moisés** the Law (*Jewish*); ~ **natural** law of nature; ~ **seca** prohibition law; ~ **de la selva** law of the jungle; ~ **de la ventaja** (*Dep*) advantage rule; **a** ~ **de** on the word of; **de acuerdo con la** ~, **según la** ~ in accordance with the law; by law, in law; **con todas las de la** ~ properly; completely; **es la** ~ it's the law; **su palabra es** ~ his word is law; **está fuera de la** ~ he's outside the law; **un fuera de** ~ an outlaw; **está por encima de la** ~ he's above the law; **hecha la** ~ **hecha la trampa** every law has a loophole, laws are made to be broken; **recurrir a la** ~ to go to law.
(b) (*fig*) loyalty, devotion; **tener** ~ **a** to be devoted to; to have great respect for.
(c) (*Metal*) legal standard of fineness; **oro de** ~ standard gold; **bajo de** ~ base; **de buena** ~ (*fig*) genuine, reliable; **de mala** ~ (*fig*) base, disreputable; **en buena** ~ really; **entonces me toca esperar en buena** ~ then I really do have to wait.

leyenda NF **(a)** (*historia*) legend; **la** ~ **negra** the black legend. **(b)** (*Tip*) legend, inscription; key. **(c)** (*eslogan*) heading; footnote; slogan.

leyendo *etc* V **leer**.

leyente NMF reader.

leyista NM (*Carib*) pettifogging lawyer.

leyoso ADJ (*And*) cunning, sly; sophistical.

lezna NF awl.

lía NF (*LAm*) plaited esparto grass.

liana NF liana.

liante* NMF (*revoltoso*) trouble-maker; (*difícil*) problem person; (*timador*) con man*, swindler.

liar [1c] [1] VT **(a)** (*atar*) to tie, tie up, do up; to bind; (*envolver*) to wrap up; *cigarrillo* to roll; **estoy muy liado ahora** (*fig*) I'm tied up right now.
(b) (*fig) to confuse, embroil; **~la** to stir up trouble; to make a mess of things; **¡la liamos!*** we've cocked it up!‡, now we've done it!*
(c) **~las** (‡: *irse*) to beat it*; (*morir*) to peg out‡.
[2] **liarse** VR **(a)** (*gen*) to get tied up; to entwine.
(b) (*fig*) to get involved (*con* with), get embroiled (*con* in).
(c) (*: *amantes*) to get involved in an affair (*con* with), form a liaison (*con* with); **estar liado con** to live with.
(d) ~ **a hostias** (*o* **palos** *etc*) to start fighting, come to blows.

lib. ABR *de* **libro** book, bk.

libación NF libation; **libaciones** libations, potations.

libanés, -esa ADJ, NM/F Lebanese.

Líbano NM: **el** ~ the Lebanon.

libar [1a] [1] VT to suck; to sip; to taste.
[2] VI (*LAm**) to booze*, drink.

libelista NMF lampoonist, writer of lampoons.

libelo NM **(a)** (*sátira*) lampoon, satire (*contra* of). **(b)** (*Jur*) petition.

libélula NF dragonfly.

liberación NF liberation; release; ~ **de la mujer** women's liberation.

liberacionista* NF women's libber*.

liberada ADJ *mujer* liberated.

liberado [1] ADJ **(a)** (*Com, Fin*) paid-up, paid-in (*US*). **(b)** (*Pol*) full-time, paid; **miembro** ~ = **2.**
[2] NM, **liberada** NF (*Pol*) paid agent, full-time worker (of a trade-union *o* of a terrorist organization).

liberal [1] ADJ **(a)** (*Pol*) liberal. **(b)** *carácter* liberal, generous; lavish.
[2] NMF liberal.

liberalidad NF liberality, generosity, lavishness.

liberalismo NM liberalism.

liberalización NF liberalization.

liberalizador ADJ liberalizing.

liberalizar [1f] VT to liberalize; *mercado etc* to deregulate.

liberalmente ADV liberally, generously; lavishly.

liberar [1a] VT to free, liberate; ~ **a uno de una obligación** to release sb from a duty; ~ **a uno de una contribución** to exempt sb from a

tax; **estar liberado de servicios** to be free of duties.

Liberia NF Liberia.

liberiano, -a ADJ, NM/F Liberian.

líbero NM (*Dep*) sweeper.

libérrimo ADJ entirely free, absolutely free.

libertad NF liberty, freedom; (*pey*) licence; (*undue*) familiarity; '**¡~!**' (*slogan*) 'freedom!'; ~ **de cátedra** academic freedom, freedom to teach; **~es civiles** civil liberties; ~ **de comercio** free trade; ~ **de conciencia** freedom of thought; ~ **condicional,** ~ **vigilada** (*Jur*) probation; **estar en** ~ **condicional** (*o* **vigilada**) to be on probation; ~ **de cultos** freedom of worship, religious freedom; ~ **de empresa** free enterprise; ~ **bajo fianza** release on bail; ~ **de imprenta** freedom of the press; ~ **bajo palabra,** ~ **a prueba** parole; ~ **de (la) palabra** (*o* **de expresión**) freedom of speech; ~ **de prensa** freedom of the press; ~ **de voto** (*Parl*) free vote; **estar en** ~ to be free, be at liberty; **poner a uno en** ~ to set sb free, release sb, set sb at liberty; **tomarse una** ~ to take a liberty; **tomarse la** ~ **de** + *infin* to take the liberty of + *ger*, presume to + *infin*.

libertador [1] ADJ liberating.
[2] NM, **libertadora** NF liberator.

libertar [1a] VT (*gen*) to set free, liberate, release (*de* from); (*eximir*) to exempt, release (*de* from); (*salvar*) to save, deliver (*de* from); ~ **a uno de la muerte** to save sb from death.

libertario, -a ADJ, NM/F libertarian.

libertinaje NM licentiousness; profligacy.

libertino [1] ADJ **(a)** (*vicioso*) loose-living, rakish, profligate. **(b)** (*Rel Hist*) freethinking.
[2] NM **(a)** (*juerguista*) libertine, rake. **(b)** (*Rel Hist*) freethinker.

liberto [1] ADJ freed, liberated.
[2] NM, **liberta** NF freedman, freedwoman.

Libia NF Libya.

libídine NF lewdness, lasciviousness; libido.

libidinoso ADJ lustful, libidinous.

libido NF libido.

libio, -a ADJ, NM/F Libyan.

liborio* ADJ Cuban.

Libra NF (*Zodíaco*) Libra, the Scales.

libra NF **(a)** pound; ~ **esterlina** pound sterling. **(b)** (‡) 100 pesetas; **media** ~ 50 pesetas; *ver también* ⟨KILOS, METROS, AÑOS⟩.

libraco NM boring book, worthless book; old tome.

librado, -a NM/F (*Com*) drawee.

librador(a) NM/F (*Com*) drawer.

libramiento NM rescue, delivery (*de* from).

librante NMF (*Com*) drawer.

libranza NF **(a)** (*Com*) draft, bill of exchange; ~ **de correos** (*LAm*), ~ **postal** (*LAm*) money order. **(b)** (*de trabajador*) time off.

librar [1a] [1] VT **(a)** (*libertar*) to save, free, rescue, deliver (*de* from); (*Jur*) to exempt, free, release (*de* from); ~ **a uno de una obligación** to free sb from an obligation; **¡Dios me libre!** Heaven forbid!; **¡líbreme Dios de maldecir a nadie!** Heaven forbid that I should curse anyone!
(b) *confianza, esperanzas* to place (*en* in).
(c) *sentencia* to pass; *edicto etc* to issue; *secreto* to reveal.
(d) (*Com*) to draw; *cheque* to make out; ~ **a cargo de** to draw on.
(e) *batalla* to fight, wage; to join.
[2] VI **(a)** to give birth.
(b) ~ **bien** to fare well, succeed; ~ **mal** to fare badly, fail.
(c) (*tiempo*) **libro a las 3** I'm free at 3, I finish work at 3; **trabaja 6 horas y libra 2** he works 6 hours and has 2 hours off.
[3] **librarse** VR to free o.s., escape; ~ **de** to escape from, get out of; get away from; to get rid of; **de buena nos hemos librado** we did well to get out of that, we're well out of that.

libre [1] ADJ **(a)** (*gen*) free (*de* from, of); **¿estás ~?** are you free?; **esa plaza no está** ~ that seat is not free; **cada cual es** ~ **de hacer lo que quiera** everyone is free to do as he wishes; **por fin estamos ~s de él** at last we're rid of him; **estar** ~ **de servicio** to be off duty; ~ **de derechos** free of duty, duty-free; **al aire** ~ in the open air; **examinarse por** ~ to take one's exams as an independent candidate; **ahora funciono por** ~ now I'm on my own; **trabajar por** ~ to freelance, work on one's own account, work for o.s.
(b) (*pey*) free, outspoken; licentious, loose, immoral; **de vida** ~ loose-living, immoral.
(c) (*Dep*) free, free-style; **los 200 metros ~s** the 200 metre free-style race; **golpe** (*etc*) ~ free kick.
(d) ~ **a bordo** (*Com*) free on board.
[2] NM **(a)** (*Dep*: *golpe*) free kick; ~ **directo** direct free kick; ~ **indirecto** indirect free kick.
(b) (*Dep*: *persona*) sweeper.
(c) (*Méx*) taxi.

librea [1] NF livery, uniform.
[2] NM (*Cono Sur*) footman.

librecambio NM free trade.

librecambismo NM free-trade.
librecambista [1] ADJ free-trade (atr). [2] NM free-trader.
librepensador(a) NM/F freethinker.
librepensamiento NM freethinking.
librera[1] NF (Cono Sur) bookcase.
librería NF (a) (tienda) bookshop; ~ **anticuaria**, ~ **de antiguo** antiquarian bookshop; ~ **de ocasión**, ~ **de viejo** secondhand bookshop. (b) (estante) bookcase; (biblioteca) library. (c) (comercio) bookselling, book trade, book business.
librero[1], **-a**[2] NM/F (persona) bookseller; ~ **de viejo** secondhand bookseller.
librero[2] NM (Carib, Cono Sur, Méx: estante) bookcase.
libresco ADJ bookish.
libreta NF (a) notebook; (Com) account-book; (Cono Sur Aut) driving licence; ~ **de ahorros**, ~ **de banco**, ~ **de depósitos** bank-book, passbook; ~ **de direcciones** address-book; ~ **militar** (LAm) certificate of military service. (b) (pan) one-pound loaf.
librete NM booklet.
libretista NMF librettist.
libreto NM libretto; (LAm) film script.
libro NM book; ~ **de actas** minute book; ~ **de apuntes** notebook; ~ **blanco** (Parl) white paper; ~ **de bolsillo** paperback; ~ **de cabecera** bedside book; ~ **de caja** cashbook; ~ **de cálculos hechos** ready-reckoner; ~ **de cocina** cookery-book, cookbook (US); ~ **de consulta** reference book, work of reference; ~ **de cría** register of pedigrees; ~ **de cuentas**, ~ **de contabilidad** account-book; ~ **de cuentos** story-book; ~ **de cheques** chequebook; ~ **desplegable**, ~ **mágico**, ~ **móvil**, ~ **vivo** pop-up book; ~ **diario** journal; ~ **de direcciones** address-book; ~ **de encargos** order-book; ~ **escolar** (informe) school report; (de texto) schoolbook; ~ **de estilo** style-book; ~ **de familia** marriage certificate; ~ **genealógico** (Agr) herd-book; ~ **de hojas cambiables** loose-leaf book; ~ **de honor** distinguished visitors' book; ~ **de imágenes** picture-book; ~ **de lectura** reader; ~ **mayor** ledger; ~ **de orígenes** register of pedigrees; ~ **parroquial** parish register; ~ **de pedidos** order-book; ~ **de reclamaciones** complaints book; **l~ rojo** (Parl) white paper; ~ **en rústica** paperback (book); ~ **talonario** receipt book, book of tickets, book of counterfoils; ~ **de texto** textbook; ~ **verde** (Parl) green paper; ~ **de visitas** visitors' book; ~ **de vuelos** (Aer) logbook; **ahorcar los ~s, arrimar los ~s, colgar los ~s** (fig) to abandon one's studies; **cerrar los ~s** (Fin) to close the books; **no estar en el ~, no tener el ~** to be unaware of a matter, to be uninterested in a matter, have no intention of pursuing a matter; **hacer ~ nuevo** to turn over a new leaf; **llevar los ~s** (Fin) to keep the books.
librote NM big book, tome.
Lic. ABR de **Licenciado, Licenciada**.
licencia NF (a) (permiso) licence, permission; **sin mi ~** without my permission; **dar su ~** to give one's permission, grant permission. (b) (documento) licence, permit; ~ **de armas** gun licence; ~ **de caza** game licence, hunting permit; ~ **de conducir**, ~ **de conductor**, ~ **de manejar** (LAm) driving licence; ~ **fiscal** registration required by the Spanish Inland Revenue before someone can start up a business; ~ **de matrimonio** marriage licence; ~ **de obras** building permit; ~ **de piloto**, ~ **de vuelo** pilot's licence. (c) (Mil etc) leave (of absence); ~ **por enfermedad** sick leave; ~ **de maternidad** maternity leave; ~ **sin sueldo** leave without pay, unpaid leave; **estar de ~** to be on leave; **ir de ~** to go on leave. (d) (Mil: t ~ **absoluta**) discharge; ~ **honrosa** honourable discharge. (e) (moral) licence, licentiousness; ~ **poética** poetic licence. (f) (Univ Hist) degree.
licenciado, -a NM/F (a) (Univ) licenciate, bachelor; **L~ en Filosofía y Letras** ≃ Bachelor of Arts. (b) (LAm: abogado) lawyer (not translated as title before proper name).
licenciar [1b] [1] VT (a) (dar permiso para) to license, grant a permit or licence to. (b) (permitir) to permit, allow. (c) (Mil) to discharge. (d) (Univ) to confer a degree on. [2] **licenciarse** VR to graduate, take one's degree; ~ **en Derecho** to take a degree in Law.
licenciatario, -a NM/F licensee.
licenciatura NF (a) (título) degree, licentiate. (b) (acto) graduation. (c) (estudios) degree course, university degree.

LICENCIATURA

*Until recently most Spanish degree courses lasted 5 years. Students would be awarded a **diplomatura** (general degree) if they completed three years of study, and they would get their **licenciatura** (honours degree) after another two years. Now, under new **planes de estudio**, or curricula, **licenciaturas** take 4 years. The first two years are referred to as the **primer ciclo** and the final two years as the **segundo ciclo**.*

licencioso ADJ licentious.
liceo NM lyceum; (Cono Sur, Méx) secondary school.
licha‡ NF, **liche**‡ NF street.
lichi NM lychee.
líchigo NM (And) provisions, food.
licitación NF bidding (at auction).
licitador(a) NM/F bidder; (LAm) auctioneer.
licitar [1a] [1] VT (a) (en subasta: ofrecer) to bid for. (b) (LAm) to sell by auction. [2] VI to bid.
lícito ADJ (gen) lawful, legal, licit; (justo) fair, just; (permisible) permissible; **si es ~ preguntarlo** if one may ask.
licitud NF legality; fairness, justness; **la controversia sobre la ~ del aborto** the controversy about whether abortion should be permitted.
licor NM (a) (gen) liquid. (b) (alcohol) (alcoholic) liquor, spirits; (de frutas etc) liqueur.
licorera NF decanter.
licorería NF (LAm) distillery.
licorero NM (LAm) distiller.
licorista NM (fabricante) distiller; (comerciante) dealer in liquor, seller of liquor.
licoroso ADJ vino etc strong, of high alcoholic content.
licra ® NF Lycra ®.
licuación NF liquefaction; melting.
licuado NM: ~ **(de frutas)** (LAm) milk shake.
licuadora NF (Culin) blender, liquidizer.
licuar [1d] VT to liquefy, turn into liquid; nieve to melt.
licuefacción NF liquefaction.
lid NF (combate) fight, combat; (disputa) dispute, controversy; **en buena ~** in (a) fair fight, (fig) by fair means, fairly.
líder [1] ADJ top, leading, foremost; **marca ~** leading brand, brand leader. [2] NMF, PL **líders** o **líderes** leader; (Dep) leader, league leader, top club (etc).
liderar [1a] VT to lead; to head.
liderato NM, **liderazgo** NM leadership; (Dep) lead, leadership, top position.
lidia NF (a) (Taur) bullfight; bullfighting; **toro de ~** fighting bull. (b) (Méx: molestia) trouble, nuisance; **dar ~** to be trying, be a nuisance.
lidiador NM fighter; (Taur) bullfighter.
lidiar [1b] [1] VT toro to fight. [2] VI to fight (t fig; con, contra against, por for).
liebre NF (a) (Zool) hare; (fig) coward; **ser ~ corrida** (Méx*) to be an old hand; **coger una ~*** to come a cropper*; **levantar la ~** to blow the gaff‡. (b) (Dep) pacemaker. (c) (And, Cono Sur: bus) small bus.
Lieja NF Liège.
liencillo NM (LAm) thick cotton material.
liendre NF nit.
lienzo NM (a) (tela) linen; (Arte) canvas; (pañuelo) handkerchief; **un ~** a piece of linen (etc). (b) (Arquit: muro) wall; (fachada) face, front; (LAm) section (of fence etc); (Méx) corral, pen.
liftar [1a] VT pelota to loft.
lifting ['liftin] NM facelift (t fig); plastic surgery.
liga NF (a) (Pol etc) league. (b) (Cos) band; (prenda) suspender, garter. (c) (Metal) alloy; mixture. (d) (Bot) mistletoe. (e) (trampa viscosa) birdlime. (f) (CAm, Carib) binding; state of being bound. (g) (And*: amigo) bosom friend. (h) (*: persona) pick-up‡.
ligado NM (Mús) slur, tie; legato; (Tip) ligature.
ligadura NF (vínculo) bond, tie; (Náut) lashing; (Med) ligature; (Mús) ligature, legato.
ligamento NM ligament.
ligamiento NM bond, tie.
ligar [1h] [1] VT (a) (gen) to tie, bind; (Metal) to alloy; to mix; (Med) to put a ligature on, bind up; (Mús) to slur; (fig) to join, bind together; bebidas to mix; **estar ligado por contrato a** to be bound by contract to. (b) (*) chica etc to pick up*, get off with*. (c) (‡: conseguir) to get, lay hold of; (comprar) to buy; (robar) to nick‡; (detener) to nick‡. (d) (Carib Agr) to contract in advance for. [2] VI (a) (ir juntos) to mix (well), blend, go well together; **ligan A y B** (And, CAm) A and B get on well together. (b) (Carib, Méx*: tener suerte) to have a bit of luck, be lucky; **la cosa le ligó** (And, CAm) the affair went well for him. (c) (Carib, Méx: mirar) to look, stare. (d) **le ligó su deseo** (And, Carib*) her wish came true.

(e) **~ con una*** (*flirtear*) to flirt with sb; (*conocer*) to pick a girl up*; **salieron dispuestas a ~** they went out to try to pick up a man*; **han ligado A y Z** A and Z have paired up.
3 ligarse VR **(a)** (*unirse*) to unite, band together.
(b) (*fig*) to bind o.s., commit o.s.
(c) **~ con uno** (*Méx**) to get off with sb*.

ligazón NF **(a)** (*Náut*) rib, beam. **(b)** (*fig*) bond, tie, union.
ligeramente ADV **(a)** lightly. **(b)** *conocer etc* slightly. **(c)** *juzgar etc* hastily.
ligerear [1a] VI (*Cono Sur*) to walk fast, move quickly.
ligereza NF (*V ligero*) **(a)** lightness; thinness.
(b) swiftness, quickness, speed.
(c) agility, nimbleness.
(d) slightness.
(e) superficiality, shallowness; flippancy; frivolity; **obrar con ~** to act rashly, act thoughtlessly.
(f) **~ de espíritu** light-heartedness, gaiety.
(g) (*acto*) indiscretion.
ligero 1 ADJ **(a)** (*de poco peso*) light; *tela* light, lightweight, thin; *comida, sueño* light; *té* weak; **~ de ropa** lightly clad, scantily clad, not wearing much; **más ~ que un corcho** (*o una pluma etc*) as light as a feather.
(b) (*rápido*) swift, quick, rapid; **~ de dedos** light-fingered; **~ de pies** light-footed, quick; **más ~ que una bala** (*o el viento etc*) as quick as a flash.
(c) (*ágil*) agile, quick, nimble.
(d) (*modesto*) slight; **un ~ conocimiento** a slight acquaintance, a superficial acquaintance.
(e) *carácter* superficial, shallow, flippant; frivolous, flighty; **~ de cascos** scatterbrained, frivolous; **hacer algo a la ligera** to do sth quickly; to do sth without fuss; (*pey*) to do sth perfunctorily; **juzgar a la ligera** to judge hastily, jump to conclusions; **obrar de ~** to act rashly, act thoughtlessly.
2 ADV lightly; quickly, swiftly; **así andamos más ~** we go quicker like this.
light [laɪt] ADJ INVAR *tabaco* low-tar (*atr*); *comida* low in calories; *plan, política* diluted, watered-down, toned-down.
lignito NM lignite.
ligón¹ NM hoe.
ligón²* 1 ADJ **(a)** *persona* flirtatious; **es muy ~** he's a great one for the girls.
(b) *prenda* attractive; provocative, sexy.
(c) (*distinguido*) posh*, classy*.
2 NM womanizer, wolf*.
3 ligona NF: **es una ligona** she'll go with anybody, she's an easy lay‡.
ligoteo* NM = **ligue (a)**.
ligue* NM **(a)** (*acto: gen*) **se dedica mucho al ~** he's always after the women, he's always having affairs; **ir de ~** to go looking for partners. **(b)** (*acto: un ~*) pick-up*, date; affair. **(c)** (*persona*) pick-up*, date; (*chico*) boyfriend, bloke‡; (*chica*) girlfriend, bird‡.
liguero¹ NM suspender belt, garter belt (*US*).
liguero² ADJ (*Dep*) league (*atr*); **líder ~** league leader.
liguilla NF (*Dep*) section (*of competition*); group of teams which play off to determine promotion; small tournament.
ligur (*Hist*) **1** ADJ Ligurian.
2 NMF Ligur, Ligurian.
ligustro NM privet.
lija NF **(a)** (*Zool*) dogfish. **(b)** (*Téc*: *t papel de ~*) sandpaper; **~ esmeril** emery paper. **(c)** **darse ~** (*Carib**) to give o.s. airs.
lijadora NF sander, sanding machine.
lijar [1a] VT to sand, sandpaper.
lijoso* ADJ (*Carib*) vain, stuck-up*.
Lila NF Lille.
lila¹ NF (*Bot*) lilac.
lila²‡ NM twit*, wimp*; sucker‡.
lila³‡ NM 5,000 pesetas.
lilailas* NFPL tricks.
lile* ADJ (*Cono Sur*) weak, sickly.
liliche* NM (*CAm*) piece of junk.
liliputiense ADJ, NMF Lilliputian.
liliquear [1a] VI (*Cono Sur*) to tremble, shake.
Lima NF Lima.
lima¹ NF (*Bot*) lime, sweet-lime tree.
lima² NF (*Téc*) **(a)** (*herramienta*) file; **~ de uñas, ~ para las uñas** nail file. **(b)** (*acto*) filing, polishing. **(c)** (*fig*) polish, finish; **dar la última ~ a una obra** to give a work its final polish.
lima³‡ NF (*camisa*) shirt.
limadura NF **(a)** (*acto*) filing; polishing. **(b)** **~s** filings.
limar [1a] VT (*Téc*) to file, file down, file off; to smooth (over); (*fig: pulir*) to polish (up), put the final polish on; *diferencias* to smooth over, iron out.

limatón NM (*LAm*) crossbeam, roofbeam.
limaza NF slug.
limazo NM slime, sliminess.
limbo NM limbo; **estar en el ~** to be in limbo; (*fig*) to be distracted, be bewildered.
limeño 1 ADJ of Lima.
2 NM, **limeña** NF native (*o inhabitant*) of Lima; **los ~s** the people of Lima.
limero NM lime (tree).
limeta NF (*Cono Sur*) **(a)** (*frente*) broad brow, domed forehead; (*calvo*) bald head. **(b)** (*botella*) bottle.
liminar ADJ (*fig*) preliminary, introductory.
limitación NF limitation, restriction; **~ de velocidad** speed restriction; **sin ~** unlimited.
limitado ADJ **(a)** (*gen*) limited (*t Com*). **(b)** (*corto de luces*) slow-witted, dim.
▼ **limitar** [1a] **1** VT (*restringir*) to limit, restrict; (*reducir*) to cut down, reduce; **~ a uno a** + *infin* to limit sb to + *ger*, restrict sb to + *infin*.
2 VI: **~ con** to border on, be adjacent to, be bounded by.
▼ **3 limitarse** VR to limit o.s., restrict o.s.; **~ a** + *infin* to limit o.s. to + *infin*, confine o.s. to + *infin*.
limitativo ADJ, **limitatorio** ADJ limiting, restrictive.
límite 1 NM limit; end; (*Geog, Pol*) boundary, border; **~ de crédito** credit limit; **~ forestal** timber line, tree line; **~ de gastos** spending limit; **~ de velocidad** speed limit; **asciende a 100 como ~** it goes up to 100 at the most; **se celebrará en octubre como ~** it will be held in October at the latest; **sin ~s** limitless; **poner un ~ a** to set a limit to; (*fig*) to draw the line at; **no tener ~s** to have no limits, know no bounds.
2 ATR extreme, maximum; **caso ~** extreme case; **competición ~** out-and-out contest; **concentración ~** maximum concentration; **jornada ~** maximum possible working week; **sentencia ~** definitive ruling; **situaciones ~** extreme situations; **someter una máquina a pruebas ~** to test a machine to destruction.
limítrofe ADJ bordering, neighbouring.
limo NM **(a)** (*barro*) slime, mud. **(b)** (‡: *bolso*) handbag.
limón NM **(a)** (*Bot*) lemon; (*Carib*) lime. **(b)** **limones‡** tits‡.
limonada NF lemonade; **~ natural** lemon juice.
limonado ADJ lemon, lemon-coloured.
limonar NM lemon grove.
limonero NM lemon-tree.
limosina NF limousine.
limosna NF alms; charity; **¡una ~, señor!** can't you spare sth, sir?; **pedir ~** to beg; **vivir de ~** to live by begging, live on charity.
limosnear [1a] VI to beg, ask for alms.
limosnera¹ NF collecting tin (*for charity*).
limosnero 1 ADJ charitable.
2 NM **(a)** (*Hist*) almoner.
3 NM, **limosnera²** NF (*LAm*) beggar.
limoso ADJ slimy, muddy.
limpia 1 NF **(a)** (*acto de limpiar*) cleaning; (*CAm, Méx Agr*) weeding, cleaning, clearing; (*fig Pol etc*) clean-up, purge.
(b) (*And, Cono Sur, Méx**: *azotes*) beating.
2 NM (*) **(a)** (*persona*) bootblack. **(b)** (*Aut*) windscreen-wiper.
limpiabarros NM INVAR scraper; doormat.
limpiabotas NM INVAR bootblack.
limpiacabezales NM INVAR head-cleaner.
limpiachimeneas NM INVAR chimney-sweep.
limpiacoches NMF INVAR street car-washer.
limpiacristales NM INVAR **(a)** (*persona*) window-cleaner. **(b)** (*líquido*) window-cleaning fluid; (*trapo*) cleaning cloth. **(c)** (*Aut*) windscreen-wiper.
limpiada NF **(a)** (*LAm*) clean, clean-up. **(b)** (*Cono Sur: claro de bosque*) treeless area, bare ground; clearing in a wood.
limpiadientes NM INVAR toothpick.
limpiador(a) NMF cleaner.
limpiadura NF **(a)** (*acto de limpiar*) cleaning, cleaning-up. **(b)** **~s** dirt, dust, scourings.
limpiafaros NM INVAR headlamp wiper.
limpiahogares NM INVAR household cleaning fluid.
limpiahornos NM INVAR oven cleaner.
limpialuneta NM: **~ trasero** (*o posterior*) rear-screen wiper, rear wiper.
limpiamanos NM INVAR (*CAm, Méx*) hand towel.
limpiamente ADV cleanly; neatly; honestly; skilfully.
limpiametales NM INVAR metal-polish.
limpiamuebles NM INVAR furniture polish.
limpiaparabrisas NM INVAR windscreen-wiper, windshield wiper (*US*).
limpiapiés NM INVAR scraper; (*Méx: estera*) doormat.
limpiaplicador NM (*Méx*) cotton bud.
limpiaplumas NM INVAR penwiper.
limpiar [1b] **1** VT **(a)** (*gen*) to clean; to cleanse; (*enjugar*) to wipe,

wipe off, wipe clean; to wipe away; *zapatos* to shine, polish; (*Culin*) *conejo etc* to paunch; *pez* to gut; ~ **en seco** to dry-clean; ~ **las narices a un niño** to wipe a child's nose.
(b) (*fig*) to cleanse, purify, clean up; (*Mil etc*) to mop up; (*policía*) to clean up; (*Bot*) to prune, cut back.
(c) (**: en el juego*) to clean out*.
(d) (*‡: robar*) to nick‡.
(e) (*‡: matar*) to do in‡.
(f) (*Méx: pegar*) to hit, bash*, beat.
2 limpiarse VR to clean o.s.; to wipe o.s.; ~ **las narices** to wipe one's nose.
limpiaventanas NM INVAR (*líquido*) window-cleaner.
limpiavía NM (*LAm Ferro*) cowcatcher.
límpido ADJ limpid.
limpieza NF **(a)** (*acto*) clean; cleaning, cleansing; shine, shining, polishing; ~ **en seco** dry-cleaning; **hacer la** ~ to clean (up).
(b) (*acto: fig*) cleaning, cleaning-up; (*Mil*) mopping-up; (*de policía*) clean-up; ~ **étnica** ethnic cleansing.
(c) (*estado*) cleanness, cleanliness; ~ **de sangre** purity of blood, racial purity.
(d) (*cualidad*) purity; integrity, honesty; (*Dep etc*) fair play.
(e) hace las jugadas con mucha ~ he makes the moves with great skill (o very neatly).
limpio 1 ADJ **(a)** (*gen*) clean; (*ordenado*) neat, tidy; (*sangre*) pure; *agua etc* pure, clean; (*despejado*) clear; ~ **de** free from, clear of; **más** ~ **que el oro** (*etc*) as clean as can be.
(b) (*moralmente*) pure; (*honrado*) honest; *juego* fair, clean.
(c) (*Fin*) clear, net; **50 dólares de ganancia limpia** 50 dollars of clear profit.
(d) (*solo*) alone; **se defendieron a pedrada limpia** they defended themselves with stones alone; **lo hizo a clavo** ~ he simply nailed it together, he did it just using nails; **luchar a puñetazo** ~ to fight with bare fists.
(e) estar ~* not to know a single thing; **quedar(se)** ~ to be cleaned out*.
2 ADV *jugar* fair, clean.
3 NM **(a) en** ~ (*como* ADV) clearly; (*Fin*) clear, net; **copia en** ~ fair copy; **estar** (*o* **quedar**) **en** ~*, **estar** ~ **y soplado** (*And**) to be broke*; **poner algo en** ~ to make a fair copy of sth; **poner un texto en** ~ to tidy a text up, produce a final version of a text; **quedó en** ~ **que ...** it was clear that ...; **sacar algo en** ~ to make sense of sth; **no pude sacar nada en** ~ I couldn't make anything of it.
(b) (*Méx: claro de bosque*) treeless area, bare ground; clearing in a wood.
limpión NM **(a)** (*acto*) wipe, (quick) clean; **dar un** ~ **a algo** to give sth a wipe. **(b)** (*trapo*) cleaning rag, cleaning cloth; (*And, CAm, Carib*) dishcloth. **(c)** (*persona*) cleaner. **(d)** (*And**) ticking-off*.
limusina NF limousine.
lina NF (*Cono Sur*) **(a)** (*lana*) skein of coarse wool. **(b)** (*trenza*) pigtail, long hair.
linaje NM **(a)** (*familia*) lineage, family; **de** ~ **de reyes** descended from royalty, of royal descent; **de** ~ **honrado** of good parentage.
(b) ~**s** (*familias*) (local) nobility, noble families.
(c) (*clase*) class, kind; ~ **humano** mankind; **de otro** ~ of another kind.
linajudo ADJ highborn, noble, blue-blooded.
linar NM flax field.
linaza NF linseed.
lince 1 NM **(a)** (*Zool*) lynx; (*CAm, Méx*) wild cat; ~ **ibérico** pardal lynx, Spanish lynx.
(b) ser un ~ (*fig*) to be very observant, be sharp-eyed; to be shrewd.
(c) (*LAm*) sharpness, intelligence.
2 ADJ: **ojos** ~**s** sharp eyes; **es muy** ~ he's very observant, he's very sharp-eyed; he's pretty shrewd.
linchamiento NM lynching.
linchar [1a] VT to lynch.
linche NM (*And*) knapsack; ~**s** (*Méx*†: *alforjas*) saddlebags.
lindamente ADV **(a)** (*con elegancia*) prettily; daintily; elegantly. **(b)** (*iró*) well, jolly well*. **(c)** (*esp LAm*) excellently, marvellously, jolly well*.
lindante ADJ bordering (*con* on), adjoining, adjacent (*con* to).
lindar [1a] VI to adjoin, be adjacent; ~ **con** to border on, adjoin, be adjacent to; to extend to, be bounded by; (*Arquit*) to abut on.
linde NM *o* F boundary.
lindero 1 ADJ (*t* ~ **con**) adjoining, bordering.
2 NM edge, border; boundary.
lindeza NF **(a)** (*atractivo*) prettiness; (*finura*) daintiness; (*elegancia*) elegance.
(b) (*esp LAm*) (*amabilidad*) niceness; (*excelencia*) excellence, high quality.
(c) (*ocurrencia*) witticism.
(d) ~**s** pretty things; pretty ways, charming ways.

(e) ~**s** (*iró*) insults, abuse.
lindo 1 ADJ (*esp LAm*) **(a)** (*bonito*) pretty; (*exquisito*) exquisite, elegant, delicate; *hombre* good-looking.
(b) (*iró*) fine, pretty.
(c) (*precioso*) nice, lovely; (*excelente*) fine, excellent, first-rate, marvellous; **un** ~ **carro** a lovely car, a fine car; **un** ~ **partido** a first-rate game; **un** ~ **concierto** a marvellous concert; **de lo** ~ a lot, a great deal; wonderfully, marvellously, jolly well*; **es de** ~ (*LAm*) it's fine, it's marvellous.
2 ADV (*LAm*) nicely, well, marvellously; **baila** ~ she dances beautifully.
3 NM (*Hist*) fop.
lindura NF **(a)** (*Cono Sur: cualidad*) prettiness, loveliness; **está hecha una** ~* she looks very pretty.
(b) (*Carib, Cono Sur: persona*) ace, champion; expert; **ella es una** ~ **en el vestir** she's an expert on clothes.
(c) (*LAm: objeto*) precious thing, thing of beauty.
línea 1 NF **(a)** (*gen*) line; (*Elec*) line, cable; (*Telec etc*) line; (*Com, de géneros*) line; ~**s** (*Mil*) lines; ~ **aérea** (*Aer*) airline; (*Elec*) overhead cable; ~ **de alto el fuego** ceasefire line; ~ **de balón muerto** dead-ball line; ~ **de banda** sideline, touchline; ~ **de base** (*Agrimensura*) baseline; ~ **de batalla** line of battle, battle line; ~ **blanca** white goods; ~ **caliente** hot line; ~ **de cambio de fecha** international dateline; ~ **de medio campo**, ~ **de centro** halfway line; ~ **de carga** load-line; ~ **compartida** shared line; ~ **de conducción eléctrica** power line; ~ **delantera** forward line; ~ **derivada** (*Telec*) extension; ~ **discontinua** broken line; ~ **divisoria** dividing-line; (*Aut*) lane markings; ~ **de estado** (*Inform*) status line; ~ **exterior** (*Telec*) outside line; ~ **férrea** railway; ~ **de flotación** waterline; ~ **de fondo** (*Dep*) by-line; ~ **de fuego** firing-line; ~ **de gol** goal-line; ~ **lateral** sideline, touchline; ~ **de llegada** finishing-line; ~ **de meta** (*Fútbol etc*) goal-line; (*en carrera*) finishing-line; ~ **de montaje** assembly-line; production line; **primera** ~ front line; ~ **de puerta** goal-line; ~ **de puntos** dotted line; ~ **recta** straight line; ~ **roja** (*Telec*) hot line; ~ **de sangre** blood-line; ~ **de saque** baseline, service line; ~ **de situación** (*Inform*) status line; ~ **de alta tensión** high-tension cable; ~ **de tiro** line of fire; ~ **de toque** touchline; ~ **a trazos** broken line; ~ **de la vida** life line; **autobús de** ~ service bus, regular bus; **explicar algo a grandes** ~**s, explicar algo en sus** ~**s generales** to set sth out in broad outline, give the broad outline of sth; **de** ~ (*Mil*) regular, front-line, (*Náut*) of the line; **de primera** ~ first-rate, top-ranking; **en** ~ (*lit*) in (a) line, in a row; (*Inform*) on-line; **en** ~ **recta** in a straight line; **en toda la** ~ all along the line; **cerrar** ~**s** to close ranks; **leer entre** ~**s** to read between the lines; **fuera de** ~ (*Inform*) off-line; **poner unas** ~**s a uno** to drop a line to sb; **tirar una** ~ (*Arte*) to draw a line.
(b) (*talle*) figure; (*de barco etc*) lines, outline; **guardar** (*o* **conservar, mantener**) **la** ~ to keep one's figure (trim); **la** ~ **de 1902** the 1902 line, the fashion line of 1902.
(c) (*genealogía*) line (*t fig*); **en** ~ **directa** in an unbroken line; **es único en su** ~ it is unique in its line, it is the only one of its kind; **en esa** ~ **no tenemos nada** we have nothing in that line.
(d) (*moral, Pol etc*) line; ~ **de conducta** course of action; ~ **dura** (*Pol*) hard line; ~ **de partido** party line; **ser de** (*una o una sola*) ~ (*Carib, Cono Sur**) to be as straight as a die, be absolutely straight.
(e) (*‡: de droga*) dose, shot*; (*de cocaína*) line.
2 NM (*Dep*) linesman.
lineal ADJ linear; (*Inform*) on-line; **dibujo** ~ line drawing; **impuesto** ~ flat-rate tax; **aumento** ~ **de sueldos** across-the-board pay increase.
linealidad NF linearity.
lineamento NM lineament.
linear [1a] VT **(a)** (*gen*) to line, draw lines on. **(b)** (*Arte*) to sketch, outline.
linense 1 ADJ of La Línea.
2 NMF native (*o* inhabitant) of La Línea; **los** ~**s** the people of La Línea.
linfa NF lymph.
linfático ADJ lymphatic.
linfocito NM (*Med*) lymphocyte.
lingotazo* NM swig*, shot*.
lingote NM ingot.
lingüista NMF (*especialista en lenguas*) linguist, language specialist; (*en lingüística*) linguistician.
lingüística NF linguistics; ~ **computacional** computational linguistics.
lingüístico ADJ linguistic.
linier NM, PL **liniers** (*Dep*) linesman.
linimento NM liniment.
lino NM **(a)** (*Bot*) flax. **(b)** (*Carib, Cono Sur*) linseed. **(c)** (*tela fina*) linen; (*lona*) canvas; **géneros de** ~ linen goods.
linóleo NM lino, linoleum.
linón NM lawn (*fabric*).
linotipia NF, **linotipo** NM linotype.

linotipista NMF linotypist.

linterna NF lantern; lamp; (*And Aut*) headlight; **~s** (*LAm: ojos*) eyes; **~ eléctrica**, **~ de bolsillo**, **~ a pila** torch, flashlight; **~ mágica** magic lantern; **~ roja** (*fig*) back marker, team (*etc*) in last place.

linyera NM (*Cono Sur*) tramp, bum (*US*).

lío NM (a) (*gen*) bundle; (*paquete*) package, parcel; (*Cono Sur*) truss.
(b) (*) (*jaleo*) row, fuss; (*confusión*) mess, mix-up, confusion, muddle; (*aprieto*) jam; **ese ~ de los pasaportes** that fuss about the passports; **armar un ~** to make a fuss, kick up a row; to cause confusion; **se armó un tremendo ~** there was an almighty row*; **hacerse un ~** to get all mixed up, get into a muddle; **meterse en un ~** to get into a jam*; **tener ~s con el profesor** to have problems with the teacher.
(c) (*: amorío*) affair, liaison; **tener un ~ con una** to be having an affair with sb.
(d) (*chisme*) tale, piece of gossip; **no me venga con ~s** don't come telling tales to me, I don't want to know.

liofilizado ADJ freeze-dried.

Liorna NF (†) Leghorn.

lioso ADJ gossipy.

lipa NF (*Carib*) belly.

lipe NM (*LAm: t* **piedra ~**) vitriol; copper sulphate.

lipidia [1] NF (*CAm*) poverty.
[2] NMF (*Carib, Méx*) nuisance, pest.

lipidiar [1b] VT (*Carib, Méx*) to annoy, bother, pester.

lipidioso ADJ (*Carib, Méx*) (*impertinente*) cheeky; (*molesto*) annoying.

lipoaspiración NF liposuction.

lipocito NM fat-particle.

lipoescultura NF liposculpture.

lipólisis NF INVAR lipolysis.

lipón ADJ (*Carib*) fat, pot-bellied.

liposoma NM liposome.

liposucción NF liposuction.

lipotimia NF faint, black-out.

lique: NM kick; **dar el ~ a uno** to kick sb out; **dar el ~** to clear out*.

liquen NM lichen.

líquida NF (*Ling*) liquid.

▼**liquidación** NF (a) (*Quím*) liquefaction.
▼(b) (*Com, Fin*) liquidation; winding-up; (*de cuenta*) settlement; **~ forzosa**, **~ obligatoria** compulsory liquidation; **entrar en ~** to go into liquidation.
(c) (*t* **venta de ~**) sale, clearance sale; **~ por cierre del negocio** closing-down sale; **vender en ~** to sell up.
(d) (*Pol*) liquidation, elimination.
(e) (*Méx*) redundancy pay.
(f) **oficina** (o **sección**) **de ~** accounts section, payments office.

liquidador(a) NM/F liquidator.

liquidar [1a] [1] VT (a) (*Quím*) to liquefy.
(b) (*Com, Fin*) to liquidate; *cuenta* to settle; *negocio* to wind up; *deuda* to settle, pay off, clear; *existencias* to sell off, sell up, clear.
(c) (*Pol*) to liquidate, eliminate; (*LAm*: *matar*) to bump off:.
(d) (*LAm*: *destrozar*) to destroy, ruin, render useless.
(e) (*Méx*) *obreros* to dismiss, pay off.
[2] **liquidarse** VR (*Quím*) to liquefy.

liquidez NF liquidity, fluidity; (*Fin*) liquidity.

líquido [1] ADJ (a) (*gen*) liquid; fluid.
(b) (*Ling*) liquid.
(c) (*Com*) net; **ganancia líquida** net profit.
(d) (*LAm*) exact; accurate, right, correctly measured; **4 varas líquidas** exactly 4 yards.
[2] NM (a) (*gen*) liquid; fluid; **~ anticongelante** antifreeze; **~ de frenos** brake fluid.
(b) (*Fin*: *efectivo*) cash, ready money; (*Com, Fin*) net amount, net profit; **~ imponible** net taxable income.

liquiliqui NM (*Carib*) Venezuelan national dress.

lira NF (a) (*Mús*) lyre; (*Liter*) *a 5-line stanza popular in the 16th century*. (b) (*Fin*) lira.

lírica NF lyrical poetry, lyric.

lírico [1] ADJ (a) (*Liter*) lyric(al); (*Teat*) musical. (b) (*LAm*) *persona* full of idealistic plans; (*Cono Sur*) *plan* Utopian, fantastic.
[2] NM (*Cono Sur*) dreamer, Utopian.

lirio NM iris; **~ de los valles** lily of the valley.

lirismo NM (a) lyricism; lyrical feeling, sentimentality, (*pey*) gush, effusiveness. (b) (*LAm*: *sueños*) fantasy, dreams, Utopian ideals; (*cualidad*) dreaminess, fancifulness.

lirón NM dormouse; (*fig*) sleepyhead; **dormir como un ~** to sleep like a log.

lirondo V **mondo**.

lisamente ADV smoothly, evenly; **lisa y llanamente** plainly, in plain language.

Lisboa N Lisbon.

lisboeta [1] ADJ of Lisbon.
[2] NMF native (o inhabitant) of Lisbon; **los ~s** the people of Lisbon.

lisbonense, **lisbonés** = **lisboeta**.

lisérgico ADJ: **ácido ~** lysergic acid.

lisiado [1] ADJ (*gen*) injured, hurt; (*cojo*) lame, crippled.
[2] NM, **lisiada** NF cripple; **~ de guerra** wounded ex-service-man.

lisiar [1b] VT (*herir*) to injure (permanently), hurt (seriously); (*tullir*) to cripple, maim.

liso [1] ADJ (a) (*gen*) smooth, even; *pelo* straight; *mar* calm; *carrera* flat; *neumático* bald; **los 400 metros ~s** the 400-metres flat; **~ como la palma de la mano** as smooth as glass.
(b) (*fig*) plain, unadorned; **~ y llano** straightforward, simple; **la tiene lisa*** he's got it made*; *V t* **lisamente**.
(c) (*And, Méx*) fresh*, cheeky*; rude; **irse ~** (*Carib*) to leave without a word.
(d) (*: de poco pecho*) flat-chested.
[2] NM (*Cono Sur*) tall beer glass.
[3] **lisa** NF (a) (*Carib*: *cerveza*) beer. (b) (*And*: *pez*) mullet.

lisol NM lysol.

lisonja NF flattery.

lisonjear [1a] VT (a) (*halagar*) to flatter. (b) (*agradar*) to please, delight.

lisonjeramente ADV (*V* ADJ) (a) flatteringly; gratifyingly. (b) pleasingly, agreeably.

lisonjero [1] ADJ (a) (*halagüeño*) flattering; gratifying. (b) (*agradable*) pleasing, agreeable.
[2] NM, **lisonjera** NF flatterer.

lista NF (a) (*gen*) list; (*catálogo*) catalogue; (*Mil*) roll; roll call; (*en escuela*) roll, register; **~ de comidas** menu; **~ de correos** poste restante; **~ de direcciones** mailing list; **~ electoral** electoral roll, register of voters; **~ de encuentros** (*Dep*) fixture-list; **~ de espera** waiting-list; **~ de éxitos** (*Mús*) hit parade; **~ negra** blacklist; **~ de pagos** payroll; **~ de platos** menu; **~ de precios** price-list; **~ de premios** prize (o honours) list; **~ de raya** (*Méx*) payroll; **~ de tandas** duty roster, rota; **~ de vinos** winelist; **pasar ~** (*Mil*) to call the roll, (*Escol*) to call the register, call the roll.
(b) (*de tela*) strip; (*de papel*) slip.
(c) (*raya*) stripe; **tela a ~s** striped material.

listadillo NM (*And, Carib, Méx*) striped (white and blue) cotton cloth.

listado¹ [1] ADJ striped.
[2] NM (*And, Carib*) = **listadillo**.

listado² NM (a) (*Inform*) print-out; listing; **~ de alternativas** paged listing; **~ de comprobación** checklist; **~ paginado** paged listing. (b) (*Carib*) list.

listar [1a] VT to list, enter on a list.

listeria NF listeria.

listero, -a NM/F timekeeper, wages clerk.

listillo, -a NM/F know-all, smart Aleck*.

listín NM (*Telec*) telephone directory; list of numbers; (*Carib*) newspaper.

listo [1] ADJ (a) (*gen*) ready, prepared; **una pintura lista para usar** a ready-to-use paint; **un traje ~** (*Méx*) a ready-made suit; **el avión estará ~ para volar en 6 meses** the plane will be ready to fly in 6 months; **¿estás ~?** are you ready?; **todo está ~** everything is ready, everything is in order; **¡~ el pollo!** mission accomplished!
(b) **¡~!** (INTERJ) (*bien*) all right!, O.K.!*; (*estoy dispuesto*) ready!; (*se acabó*) that's the lot!; it's all over!
(c) *carácter* clever, smart, sharp, quick; **¡~!** (*iró*) wake up!, you're a bright one!; **es la mar de ~*** he's terribly clever; **ser más ~ que el hambre** to be as smart as they come; **dárselas de ~** to think o.s. very clever; **pasarse de ~** to be too clever by half.
(d) (*) **estoy ~** I'm done for, I'm finished; **¡estás ~!** no way!*, not likely!; **¡estamos ~s!** that's done it!*; **están** (o **van**) **~s si piensan eso** if they think that they've got another think coming*.
[2] NM (*) con man*.

listón NM (*Cos*) ribbon; (*de madera*) strip, lath; (*Dep: en salto de altura*) bar; (*de goma, metal etc*) strip; (*Arquit*) fillet; (*fig*) level, norm, standard; **~ de la pobreza** poverty line; **~ de los precios** level of prices; **bajar el ~** (*fig*) to make things too easy.

lisura NF (a) *superficie* smoothness, evenness; straightness; calmness.
(b) (*sinceridad*) plainness; sincerity; naïvety.
(c) (*LAm: descaro*) shamelessness, brazenness, impudence.
(d) (*LAm*: *dicho*) cheeky remark*, disrespectful thing (to say); (*And*) coarse remark, rude thing (to do o say).

lisurero ADJ (*And*), **lisuriento** ADJ (*And*) cheeky*.

litera NF (*Hist*) litter; (*cama*) bunk, bunk bed; (*Náut*) bunk, berth; (*Ferro*) couchette.

literal ADJ literal.

literalmente ADV literally (*t fig*).

literario ADJ literary.

literata NF woman writer, literary lady; (*pey*) blue-stocking.

literato NM man of letters, writer; **~s** (*frec*) literati.

literatura NF literature; **~ comparada** (study of) comparative literature; **~ de evasión** escapist literature; **~ gris**, **~ negra** promotional literature.

litigación NF litigation.

litigante NMF litigant.

litigar [1h] ⟦1⟧ VT to dispute at law; to fight.
⟦2⟧ VI (*Jur*) to go to law; to indulge in lawsuits; (*fig*) to argue, dispute.

litigio NM litigation; lawsuit; (*fig*) dispute; **en ~** at stake, in dispute; **el asunto en ~** the matter under debate.

litigioso ADJ litigious; contentious.

litio NM lithium.

litisexpensas NFPL (*Jur*) costs.

litografía NF (a) (*Arte*) lithography. (b) (*cuadro*) lithograph.

litografiar [1c] VT to lithograph.

litoral ⟦1⟧ ADJ coastal, littoral, seaboard (*atr*).
⟦2⟧ NM seaboard, littoral, coast.

litre NM (*Cono Sur*) rash.

litri⁕ ADJ affected, dandified.

litro¹ NM litre, liter (*US*); *ver también* ⟦KILOS, METROS, AÑOS⟧.

litro² NM (*Cono Sur*) coarse woollen cloth.

litrona⁕ NF litre bottle (of beer).

Lituania NF Lithuania.

lituano, -a ⟦1⟧ ADJ, NM/F Lithuanian.
⟦2⟧ NM (*Ling*) Lithuanian.

liturgia NF liturgy.

litúrgico ADJ liturgical.

livianamente ADV (*V* ADJ) (a) in a fickle way; frivolously; in a trivial way. (b) lewdly.

liviandad NF (*V* ADJ) (a) fickleness; frivolity, triviality. (b) lewdness. (c) (*LAm*) lightness.

liviano ⟦1⟧ ADJ (a) (*inconstante*) fickle; (*frívolo*) frivolous, trivial. (b) (*lascivo*) lewd. (c) (*LAm*) light.
⟦2⟧ **~s** NMPL lights, lungs.

lividez NF (a) lividness. (b) (*LAm*) paleness, pallor.

lívido ADJ (a) (*morado*) livid; (*amoratado*) black and blue. (b) (*pálido*) pale, pallid.

living ['lißin] NM, PL **livings** ['lißin] living-room, lounge.

lixiviar [1b] ⟦1⟧ VT to leach.
⟦2⟧ **lixiviarse** VR to leach.

liza NF (*Hist*) lists; (*fig*) contest.

Ll, ll NF former letter in the Spanish alphabet.

llacsa NF (*Cono Sur*) molten metal.

llaga NF (a) (*herida*) wound; (*úlcera*) ulcer, sore. (b) (*fig*) sore, affliction, torment; **las ~s de la guerra** the afflictions of war, the havoc of war; **renovar la ~** to open up an old wound.

llagar [1h] VT to wound, injure (*t fig*).

llalla NF (*Cono Sur*) = **yaya**.

llama¹ NF (*Zool*) llama.

llama² NF (a) (*gen*) flame; blaze; **~ piloto** pilot light (*on stove*); **~ solar** solar flare; **arder sin ~** to smoulder; **entregar algo a las ~s** to commit sth to the flames; **estallar en ~s** to burst into flames; **salir de las ~s y caer en las brasas** to jump out of the frying pan into the fire. (b) (*fig*) flame; passion, ardour.

▼ **llamada** NF (a) (*gen*) call; (*a la puerta*) (*golpe*) knock, (*timbrazo*) ring; (*Telec*) call; (*Mil*) call to arms; **~ de atención** warning; **~ a larga distancia**, **~ interurbana** long-distance call, trunk call; **~ internacional** international call; **~ local**, **~ urbana** local call; **~ al orden** call to order; **~ a procedimiento** (*Inform*) procedure call. (b) (*ademán*) signal, sign, gesture. (c) (*Tip*) reference mark. (d) (*Méx: cobardía*) cowardliness; timidity.

llamado ⟦1⟧ ADJ so-called.
⟦2⟧ NM (*LAm*) = **llamada**.

llamador NM (a) (*persona*) caller. (b) (*aldaba*) door-knocker; (*timbre*) bell; (*botón*) push-button.

llamamiento NM call; **~ a filas** call-up papers; **hacer un ~ a uno para que** + *subj* to call on sb to + *infin*.

▼ **llamar** [1a] ⟦1⟧ VT (a) (*nombrar*) to call, name; **le llamaron el Gordo** they called him Fatty; **¿cómo le van a ~?** what are they going to call him?; **el mal llamado problema** what has erroneously been called a problem.
▼ (b) (*hacer una llamada a*) to call; (*convocar*) to summon; (*invocar*) to invoke, call upon; (*con ademán*) to beckon; (*Telec*) to call, ring up, telephone (to); **¿quién me llama?** who's asking for me?; **que me llamen a las 7** please have them call me at 7; **le llamaron a palacio** they called (o summoned) him to the palace; **te llaman desde París** they're calling you from Paris; **~ a uno a hacer algo** to call on sb to do sth.
(c) (*atraer*) to draw, attract; *atención* to attract.
(d) **estar llamado a** + *infin* to be destined to + *infin*; **esto está llamado a ser de gran utilidad** this is destined to be very useful; **estaba llamado a fracasar** it was doomed to failure.
▼ ⟦2⟧ VI (a) (*gen*) to call; **¿quién llama?** who's calling?, who's that?; (*Telec*) who's calling?, who's that?; **'llama D de Dulcinea'** (*Aer etc*) 'this is D for Dulcinea (call-

ing)'; **~ por ayuda** to call for help.
(b) (*a la puerta*) (*golpe*) to knock, (*timbre*) ring; **~ a la puerta** to knock at the door; **¿quién llama?** who's there?

⟦3⟧ **llamarse** VR to be called, be named; **me llamo Mimi** my name is Mimi, they call me Mimi; **¿cómo te llamas?** what's your name?; **¿cómo se llama esto?**⁕ how much is this?, what's the damage?⁕; **¡eso sí que se llama cantar!** that's what you really call singing!; **¡eso sí que se llama hablar!** now you're talking!, that's more like it!; **¡como me llamo Rodríguez, que lo haré!** as sure as my name's Rodríguez, I'll do it!

llamarada NF flare-up, sudden blaze; (*en cara*) sudden flush; (*fig*) flare-up, outburst.

llamarón NM (*And, CAm, Cono Sur*) = **llamarada**.

llamativo ADJ gaudy, flashy, showy; *color* loud; **de modo ~** in such a way as to draw attention.

llame NM (*Cono Sur*) bird trap.

llameante ADJ blazing.

llamear [1a] VI to blaze, flame, flare.

llamón: ADJ (*Méx*) whining, whingeing⁕.

llampo NM (*And, Cono Sur*) ore, pulverized ore.

llana NF (a) (*Geog*) plain; flat ground. (b) (*Arquit*) mason's trowel.

llanada NF plain; flat ground.

llanamente ADV (*V* ADJ) (a) smoothly, evenly. (b) plainly, simply; clearly, straightforwardly; openly, frankly; *V* **lisamente**.

llanca NF (*And*) earthworm.

llanear [1a] VI (*Aut*) to cruise, coast along.

llanero NM, **llanera** NF plainsman, plainswoman; (*Carib: vaquero*) cowboy; **~ solitario** lone ranger.

llaneza NF (*fig*) plainness, simplicity; clearness, straightforwardness; naturalness; modesty; openness, frankness; informality.

llanito⁕, **-a** NM/F Gibraltarian.

llano ⟦1⟧ ADJ (a) *superficie* level, flat, smooth, even.
(b) (*fig*) (*sencillo*) plain, simple, unadorned; (*fácil*) clear, easy, straightforward; (*franco*) open, frank; **en lenguaje ~** in plain language; **a la llana** simply; openly, frankly; **decir algo por lo ~** to put matters bluntly, say things straight out; **de ~** openly.
⟦2⟧ NM plain, flat ground.

llanque NM (*And*) rustic sandal.

llanta¹ NF (*esp LAm*) tyre; (*borde*) rim; (*cámara de aire*) inner tube; (*Carib: anillo*) large finger-ring; **~s de aleación** alloy wheels; **~ de oruga** caterpillar track.

llanta² NF (*And*) sunshade, awning.

llantén NM plantain.

llantera⁕ NF = **llantina**.

llantería⁕ NF (*Cono Sur*) weeping and wailing.

llantina⁕ NF sobbing; **¡no empieces con la ~!** cut out the sob stuff!⁕

llanto NM weeping, crying; tears; (*fig*) lamentation; (*Liter*) dirge, funeral lament; **dejar el ~** to stop crying.

llanura NF (a) *superficie* flatness, smoothness, evenness. (b) (*Geog*) plain; prairie.

llapa NF = **yapa**.

llapango⁕ ADJ (*And*) barefoot.

llapingacho NM (*And*) ≈ cheese omelette.

llaretá NF (*And*) dried llama dung.

llauto NM (*And*) headband.

llave NF (a) (*de puerta*) key; (*Téc*) key; **~ de cambio** shift key; **~ de contacto**, **~ del contactor** (*Aut*) ignition key; **~s de la ciudad**, **~s de oro** (*fig*) freedom of the city; **~ espacial** spacing bar; **~ maestra** skeleton key, master key; **¡por las ~s de San Pedro!** by heaven!; **bajo ~**, **debajo de ~** under lock and key; **'~ en mano'** 'with vacant possession'; **cerrar una puerta con ~** to lock a door; **echar la ~** (a) to lock up; **guardar algo bajo siete ~s** to keep sth under lock and key.
(b) (*grifo*) tap, faucet (*US*); (*Elec*) switch; **~ de bola**, **~ de flotador** ballcock; **~ de cierre**, **~ de paso** stopcock.
(c) (*Mec*) spanner; **~ inglesa** adjustable spanner, (monkey-)wrench; **~ de ruedas** (**en cruz**) wheel brace.
(d) (*Mús*) stop, key.
(e) (*Tip*) bracket (|).
(f) (*lucha libre*) lock; (*de judo*) hold.
(g) (*de escopeta*) lock.
(h) (*Cono Sur: Arquit*) beam, joist.
(i) **~s** (*Méx Taur*) horns.

llavero NM (a) *objeto* key ring. (b) (*persona*: **t ~ de cárcel**) turnkey.

llavín NM latchkey.

llegada NF arrival, coming.

llegar [1h] ⟦1⟧ VT (*acercar*) to bring up, bring over, draw up; (*reunir*) to gather together.
⟦2⟧ VI (a) (*gen*) to arrive, come; **~ a** to arrive at, reach; **por fin llegamos** we're here at last; **avíseme cuando llegue** tell me when he comes; **hacer ~ una carta a** to send a letter to; **cuando llegue eso** when that happens; **le llegó el año pasado** (*LAm*) he died last year; **me llega** (*And*⁕) I don't give a damn; **~ a las manos** (*pelear*) to

---

➤ LENGUA Y USO: **llamada: a → 27.2, 27.3, 27.5** **llamar: 1b → 27.1, 27.4, 27.5, 27.6** **2a → 27.1, 27.2, 27.3, 27.4, 27.5, 27.7**

come to blows.

(b) *(fig)* to arrive, get to the top, triumph; to make it*.

(c) *(alcanzar)* to reach; *(bastar)* to be enough; *(sumar etc)* to amount to, equal, be equal to; **esta cuerda no llega** this rope won't reach, this rope isn't long enough; **las personas no llegan a 100** the people don't amount to 100, the people are fewer than 100; **el importe llega a 50 pesos** the total is 50 pesos; **con ese dinero no vas a ~** you won't have enough money; **el pobrecito no llega a Navidades** the poor chap won't last out *(o* live) till Christmas; **hacer ~ el dinero** to make one's money last out, eke out one's money; **hacer ~ el sueldo** to make both ends meet (on one's salary); **¡hasta allí podíamos ~!** that's the limit!, what a nerve!

(d) se nos hizo ~ que ... we were made to realize that ..., it was brought home to us that ...

(e) *(con verbo)* **~ a +** *infin* to reach the point of + *ger;* to manage to + *infin,* succeed in + *ger;* **por fin llegó a hacerlo** he managed to do it eventually; **llegué a creerlo** I even believed it; **~ a saber algo** to find sth out; to get wind of sth; **si llego a saberlo** if I had known it; **~ a ser +** ADJ *o* N to become + ADJ *o* N; **~ a ser el jefe** to become the boss; **el país llegará a ser una nulidad** the country will become a nonentity.

3 llegarse VR to come near, draw near, approach; **llégate más a mí** come closer to me; **llégate a mi casa mañana** drop round tomorrow.

| **LLEGAR** | *ver también la entrada* |

Llegar a

A la hora de traducir *llegar a* al inglés, tenemos que diferenciar entre *arrive in* y *arrive at.*

● Empleamos *arrive in* con países, ciudades, pueblos, *etc:*

Esperamos llegar a Italia el día 11 de junio
We expect to arrive in Italy on 11th June
Llegaremos a Córdoba dentro de dos horas
We'll be arriving in Cordoba in two hours' time

● En cambio, se traduce por *arrive at* cuando nos referimos a lugares más pequeños, como aeropuertos, estaciones, *etc.* La expresión *llegar a casa* es una excepción, ya que se traduce por *arrive/get home,* es decir, sin preposición.

Llegamos al aeropuerto con 4 horas de retraso
We arrived at the airport 4 hours late
Llegué a casa completamente agotada
I arrived home completely exhausted
Para otros usos y ejemplos ver la entrada.

---

lleísmo NM *pronunciation of Spanish 'y' as 'll'.*

llenador ADJ *(Cono Sur) comida* filling, satisfying.

llenar [1a] **1** VT **(a)** *(gen)* to fill *(de* with); *superficie etc* to cover *(de* with); *espacio, tiempo etc* to fill, occupy, take up *(de* with); *formulario* to fill in, fill up, fill out *(US).*

(b) *(cumplir) deber etc* to fulfil; *deseo* to satisfy; *requisitos* to meet, satisfy.

(c) *(fig)* **~ a uno de elogios** to heap praises on sb; **~ a uno de insultos** to heap insults on sb, revile sb.

2 llenarse VR **(a)** to fill, fill up *(de* with); (*) *comida* to stuff o.s. *(de* with); **la superficie se llenó de polvo** the surface got covered in dust.

(b) *(fig)* to get cross, lose patience.

llenazo* NM *(Teat, Dep: asientos ocupados)* full house; (: *entradas agotadas)* sellout; **hubo un ~ total en el estadio** the stadium was totally packed out.

llenazón NM *(Méx)* blown-out feeling, indigestion.

lleno **1** ADJ **(a)** full *(de* of), filled *(de* with); full up; **~ hasta el borde** brimful *(de* of); **estar ~ a reventar** to be full to bursting; **estar ~ de polvo** to be covered in dust; **estar ~ de sí mismo** to be full of o.s., be conceited; **de ~** fully, entirely; **le dio de ~ en la oreja** it hit him right on the ear; **dio de ~ consigo contra el muro** he went fair and square into the wall.

(b) *vino* strong, heady.

2 NM **(a)** *(abundancia)* abundance, plenty; *(perfección)* perfection.

(b) *(Teat)* full house, sellout.

(c) *(Astron)* full moon.

llevadero ADJ bearable, tolerable.

llevar [1a] **1** VT **(a)** *(gen)* to carry, take, transport, convey; **¿me llevas esta carta?** will you take this letter for me?; **yo llevaba la maleta** I was carrying the case; **es muy pesado para ~lo los dos** it's too heavy for the two of us to carry; **~ adelante** *plan etc* to carry forward, go on with; **~ a uno por delante** *(LAm Aut)* to run sb over; **comida para ~** food to take away, take-away food.

(b) *ropa etc* to wear; *objeto pequeño* to have, wear, carry (on one); *armas, nombre, título* to bear; **llevaba traje azul** he wore a blue suit; **llevaba puesto un sombrero raro** she had an odd hat on, she was wearing an odd hat; **no llevo dinero encima** *(o* **conmigo)** I have no

money on me, I have no money about me; **lleva un rótulo que dice ...** it has a label which says ...; **el libro lleva el título de ...** the book has the title of ..., the book is entitled ...; **el tren no lleva coche-comedor** the train has no dining car; **el avión no llevaba paracaídas** the plane had no parachutes, the plane was not carrying parachutes.

(c) *(con objeto personal)* to take *(a* to); to lead *(a* to); **este camino nos lleva a Bogotá** this road takes us to Bogotá; **le llevamos al teatro** we took him to the theatre; **~ a uno de la mano** to lead sb by the hand; **¿adónde me llevan Vds?** where are you taking me?; **me llevaron de suplente** they took me along as a substitute.

(d) *ruta* to follow, keep to; **¿qué dirección llevaba?** what direction was he going in?, what route was he following?

(e) *(apartar)* to carry off, take away, cut off; **el viento llevó una rama** the wind carried a branch away; **la bala le llevó dos dedos** the shot took off two of his fingers.

(f) *premio etc* to win, get, carry off.

(g) *precio* to charge; **¿cuánto me van a ~?** what are you going to charge me?

(h) *(Agr)* to bear, produce; *(Com, Fin)* to bear, carry; **no lleva fruto este año** it has no fruit this year; **los bonos llevan un 8 por cien de interés** the bonds bear interest at 8%.

(i) *vida* to lead; **~ una vida tranquila** to live a quiet life, lead a quiet life.

(j) *(soportar)* to bear, stand, put up with; **~ las desgracias con paciencia** to bear misfortunes patiently.

(k) *(tiempo)* to spend; **llevo 3 días aquí** I have been here for 3 days, I have so far spent 3 days here; **¿cuánto tiempo llevas aquí?** how long have you been here?; **el tren lleva una hora de retraso** the train is an hour late.

(l) *(como* V AUX) **llevo 3 meses buscándolo** I have been looking for it for 3 months; **lleva conseguidas muchas victorias** he has won many victories; **llevo estudiados 3 capítulos** I have studied 3 chapters, I have covered 3 chapters; **llevaba hecha la mitad** he had done half of it.

(m) *asunto, negocio etc* to conduct, direct, manage; **~ una finca** to manage an estate; **~ los libros** *(Com)* to keep the books; **~ la casa** to run the house *(V t* **casa**); **~ una materia** *(Méx)* to study a subject.

(n) *(exceder)* to exceed; **ella me lleva 2 años** she's 2 years older than I am; **él me lleva la cabeza** he's taller than me by a head; **les llevamos una gran ventaja** we have a great advantage over them.

(o) *(Mat)* to carry.

(p) *(inducir)* **~ a uno a creer que ...** to lead sb to think that ...; **esto me lleva a pensar que ...** this leads me to think that ...

(q) *(locuciones)* **la lleva hecha** he's got it all worked out; **lleva las de ganar** he holds all the winning cards, he looks like a winner; **llevar las de perder** to be fighting a losing battle; to look like losing; **~ lo mejor** to get the best of it; **~ lo peor** to get the worst of it; **no las lleva todas consigo** he's not at all sure of himself; **¡la que llevaba encima aquella noche!*** how drunk he was that night!

2 VI *(camino)* to go, lead; **esta carretera lleva a La Paz** this road goes to La Paz.

3 llevarse VR **(a)** *objeto, persona* to carry off, take away, remove; **se lo llevaron al cine** they took him off to the cinema; **se llevó mi máquina** he took my camera, he went off with my camera; **los ladrones se llevaron la caja** the thieves took the safe away; **¡que se lo lleve el diablo!** to hell with it!; **el pistolero se llevó 10.000 libras** the gunman got away with £10,000; **se llevó el primer premio** she carried off the first prize; **¡no lo toques o te la llevas!*** don't touch it or you'll live to regret it!

(b) **~ bien** to get on well (together); **no se lleva bien con el jefe** he doesn't get on *(o* along) with the boss.

(c) **~ a uno por delante** *(LAm)* to offend sb; to ride roughshod over sb.

(d) (*: *estar de moda)* to be in fashion, be in*.

lliclla NF *(And)* woollen shawl.

llicta NF *(And)* quinine paste.

llimo ADJ *(Cono Sur)* small-eared; earless.

llocalla NM *(And)* boy.

lloquena NF *(And)* fish spear, harpoon.

llora NF *(Carib)* wake.

llorado ADJ: **el ~ rey** the (late) lamented king; **un hombre no ~** an unlamented man.

llorar [1a] **1** VT to weep over, weep for, cry about; to bewail, lament; *muerte, pérdida* to mourn.

2 VI **(a)** *(persona)* to cry, weep; **¡no llores!** don't cry!; **~ a cuajo, ~ lágrima viva, ~ a moco y baba, ~ a moco tendido** to sob one's heart out, cry uncontrollably; **~ como una fuente** *(o* **criatura** *etc)** to weep buckets*; **el que no llora no mama** if you don't ask you don't get.

(b) *(ojos)* to water; *(grifo etc)* to drip.

(c) *(Cono Sur: quedar bien)* to suit, be becoming, look nice *(a* on).

(d) (*And, Carib, Cono Sur: quedar muy mal*) to be very unbecoming.

llorera* NF sobbing, fit of crying.

lloretas* NMF INVAR (*And, CAm*) crybaby.

llorica* [1] ADJ: **no seas ~** don't be such a crybaby*. [2] NMF crybaby*.

lloricón* ADJ *persona* weepy*, tearful; *film etc* tear-jerking*.

lloriquear [1a] VI to snivel, whimper.

lloriqueo NM snivelling, whimpering.

llorisquear [1a] VI (*Carib, Cono Sur*) *etc* = **lloriquear** *etc*.

lloro NM **(a)** crying, weeping; tears; wailing. **(b)** (*en grabación*) wow.

llorón [1] ADJ weeping, tearful; snivelling, whining; V **sauce**. [2] NM, **llorona¹** NF tearful person, weepy sort*; crybaby. [3] **llorona²** NF hired mourner; (*Méx*) ghost, soul in torment. [4] **lloronas** NFPL (*And, Cono Sur*) large spurs.

lloroso ADJ weeping, tearful; sad.

llovedera NF (*And, CAm, Carib*), **llovedero** NM (*Cono Sur*) (period of) continuous rain; (*época*) rainy season; (*tormenta*) rainstorm.

llovedizo ADJ **(a)** *techo* leaky. **(b)** *agua llovediza* rainwater.

llover [2h] VI **(a)** (*gen*) to rain; **llueve, está lloviendo** it is raining; **~ a cántaros, ~ a cubos, ~ a chuzos, ~ a mares, ~ a torrentes** to rain cats and dogs, rain in torrents; **como llovido (del cielo)** unexpectedly; **ser una cosa llovida del cielo** to come just right, be a godsend; **está llovido en la milpita*** (*Méx**) we're (*etc*) having a run of bad luck, we're (*etc*) going through a bad patch; **llueva o no** rain or shine, come what may; **mucho** (*o* **ya**) **ha llovido desde entonces** much water has flowed under the bridge since then; **¡como ahora llueve pepinos** (*o* **uvas**)! (*And*) rubbish!; **siempre que llueve escampa** (*Carib*) every cloud has a silver lining; V **mojado**. **(b)** (*fig*) to rain; **le llovieron regalos encima** gifts were rained on him, he was showered with gifts.

llovida NF (*LAm*) rain, shower.

llovido NM stowaway.

llovizna NF drizzle.

lloviznar [1a] VI to drizzle.

lloviznoso ADJ drizzly.

llueca NF broody hen.

lluqui ADJ (*And*) left-handed.

lluvia NF rain; shower; (*cantidad*) rainfall; (*insecticida etc*) spray; (*de balas, misiles*) hail, shower; (*de regadera*) rose; (*Cono Sur: ducha*) shower, shower bath; (*fig*) shower, mass, abundance; **día de ~** rainy day; **~ ácida** acid rain; **~ artificial** cloud seeding; **~ menuda** fine rain, drizzle; **~ de meteoros** meteor shower; **~s monzónicas** monsoon rains; **~ de oro** (*Bot*) laburnum; **~ radiactiva** radioactive fallout*; **~ torrencial** torrential rain; **una ~ de regalos** a shower of gifts; **la ~ cae sobre los buenos como sobre los malos** it rains on the just as well as on the unjust.

lluvioso ADJ rainy, wet.

lo¹ ART DEF '*neutro*' **(a) ~ bello** the beautiful, what is beautiful, that which is beautiful; **~ difícil** what is difficult; **~ difícil es que ...** the difficult thing about it is that ...; **quiero ~ justo** I want what is just; **defiendo ~ mío** I defend what is mine; **~ ocurrido** in view of what has happened; **~ insospechado del caso** what was unsuspected about the matter; **~ totalmente inesperado del descubrimiento** the completely unexpected nature of the discovery; **~ mejor de la película** the best part of the film, the best thing about the film; **sufre ~ indecible** she suffers terribly.

(b) (*estilo*) **construido a ~ campesino** built in peasant style; **viste a ~ americano** he dresses in the American style, he dresses like an American.

(c) (*cuán*) **no saben ~ aburrido que es** they don't know how boring it is; **me doy cuenta de ~ amables que ellas son** I realize how kind they are.

lo² PRON **(a)** (*persona*) him; (*cosa*) it; **~ tengo aquí** I have it here; **~ creo** I think so; **~ veo** I see; **~ sé** I know; **no ~ hay** there isn't any; **'¿anarquista?'** ... **'no ~ soy'** 'an anarchist?' ... 'I'm not'; **'¿estás cansado?'** ... **'~ estoy'** 'are you tired?' ... 'I am' (*o* 'yes'); **guapa sí que ~ es** she's certainly very pretty, I should jolly well say she's pretty*. **(b)** (*LAm*) = **le**.

lo³ PRON DEM: **~ de** that matter of, that business about; **~ de ayer** what happened yesterday; **~ de Rumasa** the Rumasa affair; **~ de no traer dinero** that business about not having any money.

lo⁴ PRON REL: **~ que (a)** what, that which; **~ que digo es ...** what I say is ...; **toma ~ que quieras** take what(ever) you want; **con ~ que él gana** with what he earns; **¡~ que sufre un hombre honrado!** what an honourable man has to suffer!; **~ que pasa es que ...**, **~ que hay es que ...** what's happening is that ..., it's like this ...; **empezó a tocar, ~ que le fastidió** she began to play, which made him cross.

(b) (*locuciones*) **~ que es eso** as for that; **¡~ que has tardado!** you've been a long time!; **¡~ que cuesta vivir!** isn't living expensive!; **¡~ que es saber lenguas!** isn't it wonderful to speak several languages!; **~ que se dice feo** really ugly; **~ que se dice un hombre** a real man; **¡~ que he dicho!** I stand by what I said!; **¡~ que ves!** can't you see?,

---

it's there for you to see!

(c) en ~ que ... *como conj* whilst ...

(d) (*LAm*) **a lo que ...** as soon as; **a lo que me vio me saludó** as soon as he saw me he said hullo.

loa NF **(a)** (*elogio*) praise. **(b)** (*Teat Hist*) prologue, playlet. **(c)** (*CAm, Méx*: regañada*) reproof.

loable ADJ praiseworthy, commendable, laudable.

loablemente ADV commendably.

LOAPA [lo'apa] NF (*Esp Jur*) ABR de **Ley Orgánica de Armonización del Proceso Autonómico.**

loar [1a] VT to praise.

lob NM lob.

loba NF **(a)** (*Zool*) she-wolf. **(b)** (*Agr*) ridge (between furrows). **(c)** (*: *prostituta*) whore. **(d)** (*LAm*) half-breed.

lobanillo NM wen, cyst.

lobato NM wolf cub.

lobby ['loßi] NM, PL **lobbys** ['loßi] lobby, pressure-group; **hacer ~** to lobby (*a favor de* for).

lobelia NF lobelia.

lobero ADJ: **perro ~** wolfhound.

lobezno NM wolf cub.

lobito NM (*Cono Sur: t ~ de río*) otter.

lobo [1] ADJ (*Cono Sur**) shy. [2] NM **(a)** wolf; **~ de mar** old salt, sea dog, (*Cono Sur*) seal; **~ marino** seal; **son ~s de una camada** they're birds of a feather; **arrojar a uno a los ~s** to throw sb to the wolves; **gritar ¡al ~!** to cry wolf; **pillar un ~***‡ to get plastered‡. **(b)** (*Méx**) traffic cop*. **(c)** (*LAm*) half-breed.

lobotomía NF lobotomy.

lóbrego ADJ dark, murky, gloomy.

lobreguez NF darkness, murk(iness), gloom(iness).

lóbulo NM lobe.

lobuno ADJ wolf (*atr*); wolfish, wolflike.

LOC NM (*Inform*) ABR de **lector óptico de caracteres** optical character reader, OCR.

loca NF **(a)** (*gen*) madwoman, lunatic. **(b)** (*Cono Sur*‡) whore. **(c) dar** (*o* **venir**) **a uno la ~** (*Cono Sur*) to get cross, get into a temper. **(d)** (‡) queer‡, fairy‡.

local [1] ADJ local; **equipo ~** home team. [2] NM (*gen*) place; (*sitio*) site, scene; rooms; (*Com etc*) premises *pl*; **~ comercial** business premises *pl*; (*sin ocupar*) shop unit.

localidad NF **(a)** (*gen*) locality; location; (*pueblo*) place, town, locality. **(b)** (*Teat*) seat, ticket; **sacar ~es** to get tickets; **'no hay ~es'** 'house full', 'sold out'.

localismo NM localism.

localizable ADJ: **fácilmente ~** easy to find; **difícilmente ~** hard to find; **el director no estaba ~** the director was not available.

localización NF location; placing, siting; finding.

localizado ADJ localized.

localizador NM pager, paging device, beeper.

localizar [1f] [1] VT **(a)** (*ubicar*) to locate; (*colocar*) to place, site; (*encontrar*) to find, track down; **el sitio donde se va a ~ la nueva industria** the place where the new industry is to be sited. **(b)** (*Med etc*) to localize. [2] **localizarse** VR **(a)** (*Méx: situarse*) to be located. **(b)** (*Med: dolor etc*) to be localized.

localmente ADV locally.

locamente ADV madly; wildly; **~ enamorado** madly in love.

locatario, -a NM/F (*LAm*) tenant, lessee.

locatis* NM INVAR madman, crackpot, crazy sort.

locería NF (*And*) (*loza fina*) china; (*loza*) pottery; (*Méx: vajilla*) crockery.

locero, -a NM/F (*And, CAm, Méx*) potter.

locha NF loach.

loche NM (*And: bermejo*) ginger colour.

locho ADJ (*And: bermejo*) ginger, reddish.

loción NF lotion; wash; **~ capilar, ~ para el cabello** hair restorer; **~ facial, ~ para después del afeitado** after-shave lotion.

loco¹ [1] ADJ **(a)** (*gen*) mad, crazy; (*fig*) wild, mad; **~ de atar, ~ perdido** *o* **de rematar** *o* **de remate** *o* **rematado** (*LAm*) raving mad, (as) mad as a hatter; **~ de verano** (*Cono Sur*) cracked, crazy; **~ lindo** (*Cono Sur*) mad in a nice sort of way; **más ~ que una cabra** as mad as a hatter; **andar ~ con algo** to be worried to death about sth; **ando ~ con el examen** the exam is driving me crazy; **estar ~ de alegría** to be mad with joy; **estar ~ por (una chica)** to be mad about (a girl); **estar ~ por hacer algo** to be mad keen to do sth; **está loca por la música**‡ she's an easy lay‡; **esto me tiene** (*o* **trae**) **~** it's driving me crazy; **no lo hago ni ~*** no way will I do that*; **poner ~ a uno*, volver ~ a uno** to drive sb mad; **volverse ~** to go mad; **esto es para volverse ~** it's maddening, it's enough to drive you mad; **estar para volverse ~** to be at one's wit's end.

(b) (*Mec*) loose, free.

(c) (*: *enorme*) huge, tremendous*; **un éxito ~** a huge success; **estoy con** (o **tengo**) **una prisa loca** I'm in a tremendous rush*; **he tenido una suerte loca** I've been fantastically lucky*; **una loquísima bailarina*** a fantastic dancer*.
[2] NM madman; lunatic, maniac; **correr como un ~** to run like mad; **gritar como un ~** to shout like a madman.
loco² NM (*Cono Sur Zool*) abalone.
locomoción NF **(a)** locomotion. **(b)** (*LAm*) transport; **~ colectiva** public transport.
locomotividad NF power of locomotion.
locomotor ADJ locomotor, locomotory; *aparato locomotor*.
locomotora NF **(a)** (*Ferro*) engine, locomotive; **~ de maniobras** shunting engine, switch engine (*US*). **(b)** (*fig*) driving force, engine, powerhouse.
locomóvil NF traction engine.
locrear [1a] VI (*LAm*) to eat, have a meal.
locro NM (*LAm*) meat and vegetable stew.
locuacidad NF talkativeness, loquacity.
locuaz ADJ talkative, loquacious, voluble.
locución NF **(a)** expression, idiom, phrase. **(b)** '**~**' (*TV*) 'voice', 'reader'.
locuelo* [1] ADJ daft, loony‡.
[2] NM, **locuela** NF loony‡, crackpot.
locumba (*And*) [1] NF grape liquor.
[2] ADJ INVAR (*: *loco*) nuts‡, crazy.
▼ **locura** NF **(a)** (*cualidad, estado*) madness, lunacy, insanity; **¡qué ~!** it's madness!, what lunacy!; **me gusta con ~*** I'm crazy about it; **es una casa de ~*** it's a smashing house*.
▼ **(b)** (*acto*) mad thing, crazy thing; **~s** folly; **es capaz de cometer cualquier ~** he is capable of any madness.
(c) (*manifestación*) explosion of joy, joyful celebration.
locutor(a) NM/F (*Rad*) announcer; (*comentarista*) commentator; (*TV*) newscaster, newsreader; (*de show*) compère; (*de desfile de modelos etc*) presenter; **~ de continuidad** (*TV, Rad*) linkman; **~ deportivo** sports commentator.
locutorio NM (*Ecl*) parlour; (*de cárcel*) visiting-room; (*Telec*) telephone box; **~ radiofónico** studio.
lodacero NM (*And*), **lodazal** NM muddy place, mudhole, quagmire.
LODE ['loðe] NF (*Esp Escol*) ABR de **Ley Orgánica del Derecho a la Educación**.
lodo NM mud, mire; sludge; **~s** (*Med*) mudbath.
lodoso ADJ muddy.
log ABR de **logaritmo** logarithm, log.
loga NF **(a)** (*CAm*) eulogy; (*: *iró*) **echar una ~ a uno** to tell sb off*. **(b)** (*Cono Sur*) ballad, short poem.
logaritmo NM logarithm.
logia NF **(a)** (*de masones etc*) lodge. **(b)** (*Arquit*) loggia.
lógica¹ NF logic; **~ booleana** Boolean logic; **~ simbólica** symbolic logic; **ser de una ~ aplastante** to be as clear as day, be crushingly obvious.
logical NM software.
▼ **lógicamente** ADV logically.
logicial NM software.
lógico [1] ADJ logical; natural, right, reasonable; (*Inform*) logic (*atr*); **¡~!** of course!; **es ~** it's only natural; **lo más ~ sería** + *infin* the most sensible thing would be to + *infin*; **es ~ que ...** it is natural that ..., it stands to reason that ...
[2] NM, **lógica²** NF logician.
logística NF logistics.
logístico ADJ logistic.
logo NM logo.
logopeda NMF speech therapist.
logopedia NF speech therapy.
logoprocesadora NF word processor.
logoterapeuta NMF speech therapist.
logoterapia NF speech therapy.
logotipo NM logo.
logradamente ADV successfully.
logrado ADJ successful.
lograr [1a] VT **(a)** (*conseguir*) to get, obtain; to achieve, attain; **por fin lo logró** eventually he achieved it, eventually he managed it; **logra cuanto quiere** he achieves whatever he wants; **¡no lo lograrán!** they shan't get away with it!
(b) **~ hacer algo** to manage to do sth, succeed in doing sth; **~ que uno haga algo** to (manage to) get sb to do sth, persuade sb to do sth.
lograr [1a] VI to lend money at interest, be a moneylender.
logrero NM **(a)** (*prestamista*) moneylender, (*pey*) profiteer. **(b)** (*LAm*) sponger, parasite.
logro NM **(a)** (*éxito*) achievement, attainment; success; **uno de sus mayores ~s** one of his greatest successes (o achievements). **(b)** (*Com, Fin*) profit; (*pey*) usury; **a ~** at (a high rate of) interest.

logroñés [1] ADJ of Logroño.
[2] NM, **logroñesa** NF native (o inhabitant) of Logroño; **los logroñeses** the people of Logroño.
LOGSE ['loɣse] NF ABR de **Ley Orgánica de Ordenación General del Sistema Educativo**.

┌─ LOGSE ─┐

ⓘ *Spain's **Ley de Ordenación General del Sistema Educativo** (1990) provided for a new educational system which began to be implemented in the 1991-92 academic year. Amongst other things, it raised the school-leaving age from 14 to 16 and introduced compulsory vocational training for all students. Religious education became optional and special-needs provision was incorporated into mainstream education. Following the implementation of the **LOGSE**, compulsory education is divided into **Educación Primaria (EP)** and **Educación Secundaria Obligatoria (ESO)**.*
⇨ *See also* EP , ESO

Loira NM Loire.
loísmo NM *use of* **lo** *instead of* **le** (*indirect object*) *see also* LEÍSMO, LOÍSMO, LAÍSMO .
loísta [1] ADJ *that uses* **lo** *instead of* **le** (*indirect object*).
[2] NMF *user of* **lo** *instead of* **le**.
Lola NF, **Lolita** NF *formas familiares de* **María de los Dolores**.
lola* NF (*Cono Sur*) girl, young woman.
lolailo*, -a NM/F *young Andalusian established in Barcelona*.
lolo* NM (*Cono Sur*) lad, youth, young man.
loma NF **(a)** hillock, low ridge. **(b)** (*Cono Sur*) **en la ~ del diablo** (o **del quinoto**) at the back of beyond*. **(c)** (*: *mano*) mitt‡, flipper‡.
lomada NF (*LAm*) = **loma**.
lomaje NM (*Cono Sur*) rolling hills *pl*.
lombarda¹ NF (*Agr*) red cabbage.
Lombardía NF Lombardy.
lombardo, -a² ADJ, NM/F Lombard.
lombriciento ADJ (*LAm*) suffering from worms.
lombriz NF worm, earthworm; **~ intestinal** (o **solitaria**) tapeworm; **~ de mar** lugworm.
lomería NF, **lomerío** NM (*CAm, Méx*) group of low hills, series of ridges.
lometón NM (*Carib, Méx*) isolated hillock.
lomillería NF (*Cono Sur*) **(a)** (*taller*) harness maker's; (*tienda*) harness shop. **(b)** (*equipo*) harness, harness accessories.
lomillero NM (*Cono Sur*) harness maker; harness seller.
lomillo NM (*Cos*) cross-stitch. **(b)** **~s** (*LAm*) pads (of a pack saddle).
lomo NM **(a)** (*Anat*) back; (*carne*) loin; **~s** ribs; **iba a ~s de una mula** he was riding a mule, he was mounted on a mule. **(b)** (*Agr*) balk, ridge. **(c)** (*de libro*) spine, back; (*de papel, tela*) fold.
lona¹ NF canvas; (*Náut*) sailcloth; (*Cono Sur, Méx*) sackcloth; (*fig: Dep*) **la ~** the canvas, the ring; **estar en la ~** (*And, Carib*) to be broke*.
lona²* ADJ INVAR (*Cono Sur*): **estar ~** to be knackered*, be worn out.
loncha NF = **lonja¹**.
lonchar [1a] (*LAm*) [1] VT to have for lunch.
[2] VI to have lunch, lunch.
lonche NM (*And*: *merienda*) tea, afternoon snack.
lonchera NF (*And*) lunch box.
lonchería NF (*LAm*) lunch counter, snack-bar.
loncho NM (*And*) bit, piece, slice.
londinense [1] ADJ London (*atr*), of London.
[2] NMF Londoner; **los ~s** the people of London, (the) Londoners.
Londres NM London.
londri NM (*LAm*) laundry.
loneta NF (*LAm*) canvas.
longa NF (*And*) Indian girl.
longanimidad NF (*liter*) forbearance.
longánimo ADJ (*liter*) forbearing.
longaniza NF **(a)** (*salchicha*) long pork sausage. **(b)** (*Cono Sur*: *serie*) string, series. **(c)** (*‡*) prick‡‡.
longevidad NF longevity.
longevo ADJ long-lived; **las mujeres son más longevas que los hombres** women live longer than men.
longitud NF **(a)** (*gen*) length; **~ de onda** wavelength. **(b)** (*Geog*) longitude. **(c)** (*Dep*: *salto*) long-jump.
longitudinal ADJ longitudinal.
longitudinalmente ADV longitudinally; lengthways.
longo NM (*And*) Indian youth.
longui(s)* NM: **hacerse el ~** to pretend not to know; to pretend not to be interested; to not let on*, keep mum.
lonja¹ NF **(a)** slice; (*de tocino*) rasher. **(b)** (*Cono Sur*) strip of leather; **sacar ~s a uno** to give sb a good thrashing.
lonja² NF (*Com*) **(a)** market, exchange; **~ de granos** corn exchange; **~ de pescado** fish market; **manipular la ~** to rig the market. **(b)** (*abacería*) grocer's (shop).
lonjear [1a] VT (*Cono Sur*) *persona* to give a good thrashing to.

lonjista NMF grocer.
lontananza NF (*Arte*) background; **en ~** far away, in the distance.
loor NM (*liter*) praise.
LOPJ NF (*Esp Jur*) ABR *de* **Ley Orgánica del Poder Judicial.**
loquear [1a] VI to play the fool; to make merry, have a high old time*.
loqueo NM (*Cono Sur*) uproar, hullaballoo.
loquera NF (a) (*manicomio*) madhouse, lunatic asylum. (b) (*LAm: locura*) madness.
loquería: NF (*And, Cono Sur*) madhouse, lunatic asylum.
loquero NM (a) (*persona*) nurse in an asylum. (b) **esta oficina es un ~** (*Cono Sur**) this office is a madhouse.
loquina NF (*And*) foolish thing, idiocy.
loquincho* ADJ (*Cono Sur*) crazy.
lora NF (a) (*LAm: Orn*) (female) parrot. (b) (*Cono Sur**) (*fea*) old boot:; (*habladora*) chatterbox. (c) (*And, Carib: herida*) severe wound, open wound.
lord [lor] NM, PL **lores** lord.
Lorena NF Lorraine.
Lorenzo NM Laurence, Lawrence.
lorna: ADJ INVAR (*Cono Sur*) daft, crackpot.
loro NM (a) (*Orn*) parrot.
(b) (*: arpía*) old bat*, old bag:.
(c) (*Cono Sur*) thieves' lookout man.
(d) (*Cono Sur Med*) bedpan.
(e) **sacar los ~s** (*Cono Sur**) to pick one's nose.
(f) (*Carib*) pointed and curved knife.
(g) (*) radio; transistor; radio-cassette; **estar al ~** (*alerta*) to be on the alert; (*informado*) to be on the ball, know the score*; **¡al ~!** watch out!; **está al ~ de lo que dice la gente** he's in touch with what people are saying.
lorquiano ADJ relating to Federico García Lorca; **estudios ~s** Lorca studies; **las influencias lorquianas** Lorca's influences.
los[1] ART DEF MPL, **las** FPL the; *para ejemplos de uso, V* **el**[1].
los[2], **las** PRON them; **¿los hay?** are there any?; **los hay** there are some.
los[3], **las** PRON DEM: **mis libros y los de Vd** my books and yours; **nuestros cines y los de París** our cinemas and those of Paris, our cinemas and the Paris ones; **las de Juan son verdes** John's are green; **una inocentada de las de niño pequeño** a practical joke typical of a small child, a practical joke such as a small child might play; **un bombardeo de los de cataclismo** a really shattering bombardment.
los[4], **las**: **los que, las que** PRON REL: *V* **el**[3] **que.**
losa NF (*stone*) slab, flagstone; **~ sepulcral** gravestone, tombstone.
losange NM diamond (shape); (*Mat*) rhomb; (*Her*) lozenge; (*Dep*) diamond.
loseta NF carpet square, carpet tile; floor tile.
lota NF burbot.
lote[1] NM (a) (*porción*) portion, share; (*Com etc*) lot; (*Inform*) batch; (*LAm: solar*) building site; (*LAm**) cache (*of drugs*).
(b) *medida*: (*Méx*) = *about 100 hectares*; (*Cono Sur*) = *about 400 hectares*.
(c) **al ~** (*Cono Sur**) any old how*; casually, carelessly.
(d) (:) affair; **darse** (o **pegarse**) **el ~ con una** to make it with a girl:.
lote[2]* NM (*Cono Sur*) idiot, clot:.
lotear [1a] VT (*Cono Sur*) to divide into lots.
lotería NF lottery; **~ primitiva** *weekly state-run lottery*; **le cayó la ~, le tocó la ~, se sacó la ~** (*LAm*) he won a big prize in the lottery; (*fig*) he struck lucky, he struck it rich; **jugar a la ~** to buy lottery tickets.

| LOTERÍA PRIMITIVA, LOTERÍA NACIONAL |

ⓘ *There are two state-run lotteries in Spain: the* **Lotería Primitiva** *and the* **Lotería Nacional***, with money raised going directly to the government. The* **Primitiva***, which is weekly, is similar to the British National Lottery in that players choose six numbers, including a bonus number, (***complementario***), out of a total of 49. There are also several other similar draws each week, for which players can buy a multiple-draw ticket called a* **bono-loto***. The* **Lotería Nacional** *works differently: people buy numbered tickets, which, if their number comes up, will entitle them to a share in the prize money with others who have the same numbered ticket. Whole numbers are quite costly, so people tend to buy either* **décimos** *or smaller* **participaciones***. Several dozen prizes are won in each of the ordinary weekly draws,* **sorteos ordinarios.** *Every year there are also a number of* **sorteos extraordinarios***, the most famous being the Christmas draw, or* **sorteo de Navidad***, and the* **sorteo del Niño** *at Epiphany.*
⇨ *See also* EL GORDO , ONCE

---

lotero, -a NM/F seller of lottery tickets.
lotificar [1g] VT (*CAm, Méx*), **lotizar** [1f] VT (*And*) to divide into lots.
loto[1] NM lotus.
loto[2] NF lottery.
Lovaina NF Louvain.
loza NF crockery; earthenware; **~ fina** china, chinaware.

lozanamente ADV (*V* ADJ) (a) luxuriantly; rankly; profusely; vigorously; in a lively fashion, in a sprightly way. (b) in a self-assured way; arrogantly.
lozanear [1a] VI (*Bot*) to flourish, do well, grow strongly; to grow profusely; (*persona*) to be full of life, be vigorous, flourish.
lozanía NF (*V adj*) (a) lushness, luxuriance; vigour; liveliness, sprightliness. (b) self-assurance; arrogance.
lozano ADJ (a) (*Bot*) lush, luxuriant; rank; profuse; *persona, animal* vigorous, lusty; lively, sprightly. (b) (*seguro de sí*) self-assured; (*arrogante*) arrogant.
LRA NF ABR *de* **Ley de Reforma Agraria.**
LRU NF ABR *de* **Ley de Reforma Universitaria.**
LSM ADJ ABR *de* **libre del servicio militar.**
lúa: NF one peseta.
lubina NF sea-bass.
lubricación NF lubrication.
lubricador [1] ADJ lubricating.
[2] NM lubricator.
lubricante [1] ADJ (a) (*Téc*) lubricant, lubricating. (b) (*) *persona* oily.
[2] NM lubricant.
lubricar [1g] VT to lubricate, oil, grease.
lubricidad NF (*V ADJ*) (a) slipperiness. (b) lewdness, lubricity.
lúbrico ADJ (a) (*resbaladizo*) slippery. (b) (*fig*) lewd, lubricious.
lubrificación NF lubrication.
lubrificante [1] ADJ lubricant, lubricating.
[2] NM lubricant.
lubrificar [1f] VT *etc* = **lubricar** *etc.*
Lucano NM Lucan.
Lucas NM Luke, Lucas; (*Ecl*) Luke.
lucas ADJ INVAR (*Méx*) crazy, cracked.
lucecitas NFPL (*esp*) fairy-lights.
lucense [1] ADJ of Lugo.
[2] NMF native (o inhabitant) of Lugo; **los ~s** the people of Lugo.
lucera NF skylight.
Lucerna NF Lucerne.
lucerna NF chandelier.
lucernario NM skylight.
lucero NM (a) (*Astron*) bright star, (*esp*) Venus; **~ del alba** morning star; **~ de la tarde, ~ vespertino** evening star. (b) (*fig*) brilliance, radiance.
Lucha NF *forma familiar de* **Luz, Lucía.**
lucha NF (a) fight, struggle (*por* for); conflict; contest, dispute; **~ armada** armed struggle; **~ de clases** class war; **~ contra la subversión** struggle against subversive elements.
(b) (*Dep*) **~ de la cuerda** tug-of-war; **~ grecorromana, ~ libre** (all-in) wrestling.
luchador(a) NM/F fighter; (*Dep*) wrestler; **~ por la libertad** freedom fighter.
luchar [1a] VI (a) (*gen*) to fight, struggle (*por algo* for sth; *por hacer* to do); **luchaba con los mandos** he was struggling (o wrestling) with the controls; **~ con uno, ~ contra uno** to fight (against) sb. (b) (*Dep*) to wrestle (*con* with).
luche NM (*Cono Sur*) (a) (*juego*) hopscotch. (b) (*Bot*) *an edible seaweed.*
Lucía NF Lucy.
lucidez NF (a) (*claridad*) lucidity, clarity. (b) (*CAm, Cono Sur: brillantez*) brilliance.
lucido ADJ (a) (*brillante*) splendid, brilliant; (*magnífico*) sumptuous, magnificent; (*elegante*) elegant; (*exitoso*) successful; **lucidísimo** brilliant, very clever.
(b) (*iró*) **estar ~, quedar(se) ~** to do splendidly (*iro*), make a mess of things; **¡estamos ~s!** a fine mess we're in!; **~s estaríamos si ...** a fine thing it would be (for us) if ...
lúcido ADJ lucid, clear.
luciente ADJ bright, shining, brilliant.
luciérnaga NF glow-worm.
Lucifer NM Lucifer.
lucimiento NM (*gen*) brilliance, lustre, splendour; (*ostentación*) show, ostentation; (*brío*) dash, verve; (*éxito*) success; **hacer algo con ~** to do sth outstandingly well, do sth very successfully.
lucio[1] NM (*Pez*) pike.
lucio[2] ADJ = **lúcido.**
lución NM slow-worm.
lucir [3f] [1] VT (a) (*iluminar*) to illuminate, light up.
(b) (*ostentar*) to show off, display; to sport; **~ las habilidades** to show off one's talents; **lucía traje nuevo** he was sporting a new suit.
[2] VI (a) to shine; to sparkle, glitter, gleam.
(b) (*fig*) to shine, be brilliant; to be a success; (*con ropa etc*) to look nice, cut a dash; (*hacer ostentación*) to show off; **no lucía en los estudios** he did not shine at his studies.
(c) (*LAm: parecer*) to look, seem; (**te**) **luce lindo** it looks nice (on you).
[3] **lucirse** VR (a) to dress up, dress elegantly.

(b) = VI (**b**).

(c) (*iró*) to make a fool of o.s., make a mess of things; **¡te has lucido!** a fine thing you've done! (*iro*), what a mess you've made!

lucrarse [1a] VR to do well out of a deal; (*pey*) to enrich o.s., feather one's nest.

lucrativo ADJ lucrative, profitable, remunerative; **institución no lucrativa** non-profitmaking institution.

Lucrecia NF Lucretia.

Lucrecio NM Lucretius.

lucro NM profit; **~s y daños** (*Fin*) profit and loss; *V* **ánimo**.

luctuoso ADJ mournful, sad, tragic.

lucubración NF lucubration.

lúcuma NF **(a)** (*Cono Sur*) (*fruta*) a pear-shaped fruit; (*berenjena*) aubergine, egg plant. **(b)** (**‡**: *cabeza*) head, nut**‡**. **(c)** **coger la ~** (*Carib**) (*enojarse*) to get mad*; (*afanarse*) to keep at it; **dar la ~** (*Méx**: *empeñarse*) to keep trying.

ludibrio NM mockery, derision.

lúdico ADJ (*liter*) ludic, playful.

ludir [3a] VT to rub (*con, contra* against).

ludoparque NM sports centre, sports complex.

ludópata ① ADJ addicted to gambling.

② NMF compulsive gambler, gambling addict.

ludopatía NF compulsive gambling, addiction to gambling.

ludoteca NF children's play-centre.

▼ **luego** ① ADV **(a)** (*gen*) then, next; (*pronto*) presently, soon; (*más tarde*) later (on), afterwards; (*en seguida*: *t Méx*) at once, instantly, immediately; (*CAm*: *después*) later; (*And, Carib, Cono Sur, Méx*: *de vez en cuando*) sometimes, from time to time; (*Cono Sur*: *ya*) already, earlier, previously; **~, ~** (*Méx**: *en seguida*) straightaway; **¿y ~?** what next?, what happened then?; **desde ~** naturally, of course; **desde ~ que no** of course not; **¡hasta ~!** see you later, so long!*; **¡para ~ es tarde!** (*lit*) later won't do; (*fig*) go on then, prove it!; **~ de eso** immediately after that; **~ de haberlo dicho** immediately after saying it.

(b) (*así que*) and so, therefore; consequently; **~ X vale 7** therefore X = 7.

② CONJ **~ que ...** (*tan pronto*) as soon as ...; (*LAm*: *después que*) after ...

lueguito ADV **(a)** (*CAm, Cono Sur, Méx*) at once, immediately. **(b)** (*CAm, Cono Sur, Méx*) nearby; **aquí ~** right here, near here.

luengo ADJ (††, *liter, t LAm*) long.

lúes NF syphilis.

▼ **lugar** NM **(a)** (*gen*) place, spot; (*posición*) position; **~ de encuentro(s)** meeting-place; **los Santos L~es** the Holy Places; **~ seguro** safe place; **~ al sol**, **~ bajo el sol** (*fig*) place in the sun; **el ~ del crimen** the scene of the crime; **una emisión de algún ~ de Europa** a broadcast from somewhere in Europe; **en ~ de** instead of, in place of; **en primer ~** in the first place, firstly; for one thing ...; **yo en su ~** if I were him; in his place, I ...; **en su ~, ¡descanso!** (*Mil*) stand easy!; **estar fuera de ~** to be out of place (*t fig*); **dejar a uno en mal ~** to let sb down, leave sb in the lurch; **devolver un libro a su ~** to put a book back (in its place); **ocupar el ~ de** to take the place of; **poner las cosas en su ~** (*fig*) to put things straight, put the record straight; **póngase en mi ~** put yourself in my place; **tener ~** to take place, happen, occur.

(b) (*espacio*) room, space; **¿hay ~?** is there any room?; **hacer ~ para** to make room for, make way for.

(c) (*pueblo*) village, town, place.

(d) (*razón*) reason (*para* for), cause; **no hay ~ para preocupaciones** there is no cause for concern, there is no need for worry.

(e) (*oportunidad*) opportunity; **si se me da el ~** if I have the chance; **dar ~ a** to give rise to, occasion; **dejar ~ a** to allow, permit of; **a como dé (o diera) ~** (*Méx*) somehow or other, whatever way it may be; at any cost, by all possible means.

(f) **~ común** commonplace, cliché, platitude.

lugareño ① ADJ **(a)** village (*atr*). **(b)** (*Méx*) local, regional; native.

② NM, **lugareña** NF villager.

lugarteniente NM deputy.

lugo NM (*And Zool*) ram.

lugre NM lugger.

lúgubre ADJ mournful, lugubrious, dismal.

luir [3g] VT (*Cono Sur*) (*arrugar*) to rumple, mess up; *cerámica* to polish.

Luis NM Louis.

Luisa NF Louise.

Luisiana NF Louisiana.

lujo NM **(a)** (*gen*) luxury; sumptuousness, lavishness; **~ asiático, ~ oriental** greatest possible luxury; **de ~** de luxe, luxury (*atr*); **vivir en el ~** to live in luxury. **(b)** (*fig*) profusion, wealth, abundance; **con ~ de fuerza** with an excessive show of force; **con todo ~ de detalles** with profuse details.

lujosamente ADV luxuriously; sumptuously, lavishly; ostentatiously; profusely.

lujoso ADJ luxurious; sumptuous, lavish; ostentatious; profuse.

lujuria NF lust, lechery; lewdness.

lujuriante ADJ **(a)** (*Bot*) luxuriant, lush. **(b)** (*lascivo*) lustful.

lujuriar [1b] VI to lust.

lujurioso ADJ lustful, lecherous; lewd, sensual.

lullir‡ [3h] VT (*And, CAm, Méx*) to rub (*con, contra* against, on).

lulo ① ADJ (*Cono Sur**) **(a)** *persona* lanky. **(b)** (*torpe*) dull, slow.

② NM **(a)** (*Cono Sur*) (*lío*) bundle; (*rizo*) kiss curl. **(b)** **~ del ojo** (*And*) eyeball; **al ~** (*Carib**) one after another.

lulú NM (*t* **~ de Pomerania**) Pomeranian, pom.

luma* NF (*Cono Sur*: *bastón*) police truncheon; (*reprimenda*) ticking-off*.

lumbago NM lumbago.

lumbalgia NF lumbago.

lumbar ADJ lumbar.

lumbre NF **(a)** (*fuego*) fire; **cerca de la ~** near the fire, at the fireside; **echar ~** to be furious.

(b) (*para cigarrillo*) light; **¿tienes ~?, ¿me das ~?** have you got a light?

(c) (*luz*) light; (*brillo*) brightness, brilliance, splendour; **~ del agua** surface of the water.

(d) (*Arquit*) light, opening (in a wall); skylight.

lumbrera NF **(a)** luminary; (*Arquit*) skylight.

(b) (*Mec*) vent, port; **~ de admisión** inlet; **~ de escape** exhaust vent.

(c) (*fig*) luminary, leading light, authority; **estaba rodeado de ~s literarias** he was surrounded by leading literary figures.

(d) (*Méx Taur, Teat*) box.

lumi‡ NF whore.

luminar NM luminary; = **lumbrera** (**c**).

luminaria NF sanctuary lamp; **~s** illuminations, lights.

luminescencia NF luminescence.

luminescente ADJ luminescent.

lumínico ADJ light (*atr*).

luminosidad NF **(a)** (*brillantez*) brightness (*t TV*), luminosity. **(b)** (*fig*) brightness, brilliance.

luminoso ① ADJ **(a)** (*brillante*) bright, luminous, shining; *letrero* illuminated. **(b)** (*fig*) *idea* bright, brilliant.

② NM (*Com*) neon sign; (*Dep*) electronic scoreboard.

luminotecnia NF lighting.

luminotécnico ADJ lighting (*atr*); **efectos ~s** lighting effects.

lumpen ① ADJ INVAR lumpen; **el Madrid ~** the Madrid underclass.

② NM INVAR underclass, lumpen.

lumpo NM lumpfish; **caviar de ~** lumpfish caviar.

luna NF **(a)** (*lit*) moon; **claro de ~** moonlight; **~ creciente** crescent moon, waxing moon; **~ llena** full moon; **media ~** half-moon, (*fig*) crescent; **~ menguante** waning moon; **~ nueva** new moon; **~ de miel** honeymoon; (*fig, Pol etc*) honeymoon (period); **estar de buena ~** to be in a good mood; **estar de mala ~** to be in a bad mood; **eso es hablar de la ~** that's nonsense; **quedarse a la ~ de Valencia** to be disappointed, be left in the lurch; **quedarse en la ~ de Paita** (*And**) to be struck dumb; **estar en la ~** to have one's head in the clouds; to be woolgathering.

(b) (*cristal*) plate glass; (*espejo*) mirror; (*de gafas*) lens; (*Aut etc*) window; pane; **~ térmica** (*Aut*) heated rear window.

lunar ① ADJ lunar.

② NM (*Anat*) mole, spot; (*fig*) defect, flaw, blemish; (*moral*) stain, blot; black spot; **~ postizo** beauty spot; **hay ~es en la prosperidad general** there are black spots in the general prosperity.

lunarejo ADJ (*LAm*) spotty, spotty-faced.

lunático, -a ADJ, NM/F lunatic.

lunch [lunʃ] NM, PL **lunchs** [lunʃ] lunch; midday snack; midday reception, cold buffet.

lunchería NF (*LAm*) = **lonchería**.

lunes NM INVAR Monday; **hacer San L~** (*LAm*) to stay away from work on Monday (*while nursing a hangover**); **no ocurre cada ~ y cada martes** it doesn't happen every day of the week.

luneta NF **(a)** (*de gafas*) lens, glass (of spectacles); (*Aut etc*) window; **~ trasera** rear window; **~ trasera térmica** heated rear window. **(b)** (*media luna*) half-moon shape, crescent. **(c)** (*Teat: Hist, Méx*) stall.

lunfa* NM (*Cono Sur*) thief.

lunfardismo NM (*Cono Sur*: *palabra*) slang word.

lunfardo NM (*Cono Sur Ling*) (*criminal*) thieves' slang, language of the underworld; (*argot*) slang (*in general*).

lupa NF lens, magnifying glass.

lupanar NM brothel.

Lupe NF *forma familiar de* **Guadalupe**.

lupia¹ NF **(a)** (*lobanillo*) wen, cyst. **(b)** (*And*; *t* **~s**) small amount of money; small change.

lupia²* NMF (*CAm*) quack.

lúpulo NM (*Bot*) hop, hops.

luquete NM (*Cono Sur*) (*Agr*) unploughed patch of land; (*calva*) bald patch; (*mancha*) grease spot.

lurio* ADJ (*Méx*) (*enamorado*) besotted; (*chiflado*) nutty**‡**.

lusitano ① ADJ Portuguese; (*Hist*) Lusitanian.

➤ LENGUA Y USO: **luego: 1a** → 39.1   **lugar: a** → 53.1, 53.2, 53.5

2 NM, **lusitana** NF Portuguese; (*Hist*) Lusitanian.

luso ADJ = lusitano.

lustrabotas NM INVAR (*LAm*) shoeshine boy.

lustrada NF (*LAm*) shoeshine.

lustrador NM (**a**) (*Téc*) polisher. (**b**) (*LAm*) shoeshine boy.

lustradora NF (**a**) (*Cono Sur Téc*) polisher. (**b**) (*LAm: lustrabotas*) shoeshine girl.

lustrar [1a] VT to shine, polish.

lustre NM (**a**) (*brillo*) polish, shine, gloss, lustre; **dar ~ a** to polish, put a shine on. (**b**) (*sustancia*) polish; **~ para calzado** shoe polish; **~ para metales** metal polish. (**c**) (*fig*) lustre, glory.

lustrín NM (*Cono Sur*) shoeshine parlour.

lustrina NF (**a**) (*Cono Sur*) shiny material of alpaca; (*And: tela*) silk cloth. (**b**) (*Cono Sur: betún*) shoe polish.

lustro NM lustrum, period of five years.

lustroso ADJ glossy, bright, shining.

lutencio NM (*Quím*) lutetium.

luteranismo NM Lutheranism.

luterano, -a ADJ, NM/F Lutheran.

Lutero NM Luther.

luto NM (**a**) (*gen*) mourning; (*duelo*) grief, sorrow; **medio ~** half-mourning; **~ riguroso** deep mourning; **estar de ~, llevar ~** to be in mourning (*por* for); **dejar el ~** to come out of mourning. (**b**) **~s** (*ropa*) mourning (clothes), crêpe.

luxación NF (*Med*) dislocation.

Luxemburgo NM Luxembourg.

luxemburgués 1 ADJ of (*o* from) Luxembourg.

2 NM, **luxemburguesa** NF native (*o* inhabitant) of Luxembourg.

▼ **luz** NF (**a**) (*gen*) light; (*de día*) daylight; **~ y sombra** light and shade; **la ~ del día** the light of day; **a la ~ del día** (*fig*) in the cold light of day; **como la ~ del día** as clear as daylight; **~ eléctrica** electric light; **~ de la luna** moonlight; **~ del sol, ~ solar** sunlight; **~ ultravioleta** ultraviolet light; **a la ~ de una vela** by the light of a candle; **a primera ~** at first light; **espectáculo de ~ y sonido** son et lumière show; **entre dos luces** at twilight; (**: borracho*) mellow, tipsy; **dar a ~** to give birth; **dar a ~ un niño** to give birth to a child; **dar a ~ un libro** to publish a book; **negar la ~ del día a uno** to concede absolutely nothing to sb; **quitar la ~ a uno** to stand in sb's light; **sacar a ~** to bring to light; *libro* to publish; **salir a ~** to come to light; (*libro*) to appear, come out, be published; **ver la ~ al final del túnel** to see light at the end of the tunnel.

(**b**) (*Elec**) electricity, electric current; **han cortado la ~** they've cut off the juice*.

▼ (**c**) (*fig*) light; **a la ~ de** in the light of; **a la ~ de un nuevo descubrimiento** in the light of a new discovery; **a todas luces** anyway; evidently; by any reckoning; **arrojar ~ sobre** to cast (*o* shed, throw) light on; **dar ~ verde a un proyecto** to give a plan the go-ahead; **estudiar algo a nueva ~** to study sth in a new light; **recibir ~ verde** to get the green light, get the go-ahead; **tuvo una larga experiencia de estar a la ~ de la publicidad** he had long experience of the limelight, he was used to being in the public eye.

(**d**) (*Elec etc*) light, lamp; **~ alta/baja** (*LAm Aut*) full-beam/dipped headlights; **~ antiniebla** foglamp; **luces de aterrizaje** (*Aer*) landing-lights; **~ de balización** (*Aer*) runway lights; **~ de Bengala** (*Mil*) flare, star-shell; (*LAm: fuego de artificio*) sparkler; **luces de carretera** full-beam headlights; **luces cortas** dipped headlights; **~ de cortesía** courtesy light; (*CAm*) sidelight; **~ de costado** sidelight; **luces de cruce** dipped headlights; **~ destelladora** winking light; **luces de detención, luces de freno** brake-lights; **luces de estacionamiento** parking lights; **~ de giro** direction indicator; **~ intermitente** winking light; **luces largas, luces intensas** (*LAm*) full-beam headlights, bright lights (*US*); **~ lateral** sidelight; **luces de navegación** navigation lights; **~ piloto, ~ de situación** sidelight, parking light; **luces de posición** sidelights; **~ relámpago** (*Fot*) flashlight; **~ roja** red light; **luces de tráfico** traffic-lights; **luces traseras** rear lights, tail lamps; **~ verde** green light; **dar ~ verde a** (*fig*) to give the green light to, give the go-ahead to; **~ vuelta** (*Méx*) direction indicator; **apagar la ~** to switch off (*o* put off, turn off) the light; **poner la ~, prender la ~** (*LAm*) to switch on (*o* put on, turn on) the light; **poner una lámpara a media ~** to dim a light; **hacer algo con ~ y taquígrafos** (*fig*) to do sth in the open; **reunirse sin ~ ni taquígrafos** (*fig*) to meet behind closed doors; to do something in a hole-in-the-corner way.

(**e**) (*Arquit etc*) light; window, opening; (*de puente*) space, span; (*Cono Sur: distancia*) distance between two objects; **~ al suelo** clearance (under a vehicle); **dar ~ a uno** (*Cono Sur Dep*) to give sb a start; **te doy 10 metros de ~** I'll give you 10 metres' start.

(**f**) (*fig*) **luces** enlightenment; intelligence; **corto de luces, de pocas luces** dim, stupid; **el siglo de las luces** the Age of Enlightenment (*18th century*).

(**g**) (*And**) dough*, money.

lycra ® NF Lycra ®.

Lyón NM Lyons.

Words beginning "ll" are now listed at the appropriate alphabetical position under letter L.

Las palabras que empiezan por "ll" aparecen ahora bajo la letra L en su correspondiente orden alfabético.

M

M, m ['eme] NF (*letra*) M, m.

M. (a) ABR *de* **Madrid. (b)** (*Ferro*) ABR *de* **Metropolitano** Metro. **(c)** (*Geog*) ABR *de* **Meridiano. (d)** ABR *de* **María.**

m. (a) ABR *de* **metro**(s) metre(s), m. **(b)** ABR *de* **minuto**(s) minute(s), m, min. **(c)** ABR *de* **masculino** masculine, masc., m.

m² ABR *de* **metros cuadrados** square metres, sq. m., m².

m³ ABR *de* **metros cúbicos** cubic metres, cu. m., m³.

M-19 NM (*Colombia Pol*) ABR *de* **Movimiento 19 de Abril.**

M.ª ABR *de* **María.**

maca¹ NF (*defecto*) flaw, defect; spot; (*en fruta*) bruise, blemish, bad patch.

maca² NF (*Carib*) parrot.

maca³; NM = **macarra.**

macabeo ① ADJ (*Hist*) Maccabean; *V t* **rollo.**
　② NM, **macabea** NF (*Hist*) Maccabee.

macabí NM **(a)** (*And*) shrewd person. **(b)** (*Carib*) bandit.

macabro ADJ macabre.

macaco ① ADJ **(a)** (*LAm**: *feo*) ugly. **(b)** (*CAm, Carib**: *tonto*) silly.
　② NM **(a)** (*Zool*) macaque. **(b)** (*Cono Sur**: *pey*) Brazilian. **(c)** (*Carib*) big shot*, bigwig. **(d)** (*Méx*) bogey.

macadamizar [1f] VT to macadamize.

macadán NM macadam.

macagua NF (*LAm*) macaw.

macana NF **(a)** (*LAm*) (*porra*) club, cudgel; (*de policía*) truncheon.
　(b) (*And, Cono Sur**) (*disparate*) stupid comment; (*mentira*) lie; **~s** (*Esp*) nonsense, rubbish.
　(c) (*Cono Sur**: *chapuza*) bad job, mess.
　(d) (*Cono Sur**: *charla*) long boring conversation; **¡qué ~!** what a bind!*
　(e) (*Carib*) **de ~** undoubtedly; **es de ~ que** ... of course ...

macanazo NM **(a)** (*Carib*) blow (with a club). **(b)** (*Cono Sur*) = **macana (b). (c)** (*molestia*) nuisance, bore.

macaneador* (*Cono Sur*) ① ADJ (*mañoso*) deceitful; (*poco fiable*) unreliable.
　② NM, **macaneadora** NF charlatan.

macanear [1a] ① VT **(a)** (*Carib: aporrear*) to beat, hit.
　(b) (*Carib*) to weed, clear of weeds.
　(c) (*Carib*) *asunto* to handle.
　② VI **(a)** (*And, Cono Sur**) to talk nonsense, talk rubbish; to exaggerate wildly, tell tall stories.
　(b) (*LAm**: *trabajar*) to work hard, keep one's nose to the grindstone.

macanero* ADJ (*And, Cono Sur*) given to talking nonsense, silly; given to telling tall stories.

macanudo ADJ **(a)** (*) smashing*, great*. **(b)** (*Cono Sur, Méx: abultado*) swollen, overlarge; (*Cono Sur**: *exagerado*) disproportionate. **(c)** (*And*) *persona* strong, tough; *trabajo* tough, difficult.

Macao NM Macao.

macaquear [1a] ① VT (*CAm*) to steal.
　② VI (*Cono Sur*) to make faces.

macarra; ① NM (*Esp: marica*) queer;; (*Esp: coime*) pimp; (*bruto*) lout, thug, bully-boy; (*mal vestido*) scruffily-dressed lad.
　② NF **(a)** (*acto*) brutal deed, loutish thing (to do). **(b)** (*porquería*) mess, filth; **esa camisa es una ~** that shirt looks a right mess*.

macarrada* NF piece of vulgarity; mess; filthy thing.

macarrón¹ NM **(a)** (*dulce*) macaroon. **(b)** **macarrones** (*pasta*) macaroni.

macarrón² NM (*Náut*) bulwark.

macarrónico ADJ macaronic.

macarse [1g] VR (*fruta*) to get bruised, (begin to) rot.

macear [1a] ① VT to hammer, pound.
　② VI **(a)** = **machacar 2. (b)** (*CAm**) to bet.

macedonia¹ NF: **~ de frutas** fruit salad.

macedonio, -a² ① ADJ, NM/F Macedonian.
　② NM (*Ling*) Macedonian.

maceración NF **(a)** (*Culin*) softening, soaking; maceration; **dejar en ~** to leave to soak. **(b)** (*fig*) mortification.

macerado NM maceration.

macerar [1a] ① VT to soften, soak, macerate.
　② **macerarse** VR to soften, soak, macerate; (*fig*) to mortify o.s.

macero NM macebearer.

maceta ① ADJ **(a)** (*And, Cono Sur**) slow, thick*; **ponerse ~** to get old.
　(b) (*Carib**) miserly.
　② NF **(a)** (*tiesto*) flowerpot; pot of flowers; (*Cono Sur: ramo*) bouquet, bunch of flowers.
　(b) (*martillo*) mallet, small hammer; stonecutter's hammer.
　(c) (*Méx**: *cabeza*) nut;; **ser duro de ~** (*And, Cono Sur**) to be pretty thick*.

macetero NM flowerpot stand (o holder); (*And, Carib, Cono Sur*) flowerpot.

macetón NM tub (*for plants*).

macha NF (*And, Carib*) mannish woman.

machaca ① NF (*aparato*) crusher, pounder.
　② NMF (*persona*) pest, bore.

machacadora NF crusher, pounder.

machacante ① ADJ insistent; monotonous.
　② NM (*Esp†*) 5 pesetas.

machacar [1g] ① VT **(a)** (*hacer polvo*) to crush, pound; (*moler*) to grind (up); (*aplastar*) to mash.
　(b) (*fig*) *objeto* to knock to bits; *enemigo* to maul, crush; (*en debate*) to crush, flatten, make mincemeat of; *precio* to slash.
　(c) (*: *Básquet*) to dunk, slam dunk.
　② VI **(a)** (*Esp: insistir*) to go on, keep on; to nag; **~ en un asunto** to keep on about a matter, harp on a matter; **¡no machaques!** don't go on so!, stop harping on it!; *V* **hierro.**
　(b) (*: *Univ etc*) to swot*.
　③ **machacarse** VR **(a)** **~ el verano*** to spend the summer swotting*. **(b)** **machacársela** (*Esp***) to wank**; **¡a mí me la machaco!** (*Esp;*) get away!, no way!

machacón ① ADJ (*pesado*) tiresome, wearisome; (*insistente*) insistent; (*monótono*) monotonous, repetitive; **con insistencia machacona** with wearisome insistence.
　② NM, **machacona** NF pest, bore.

machaconamente ADV tiresomely; insistently; monotonously, repetitively.

machaconeo NM insistence; monotony, repetitiveness.

machaconería NF = **machaconeo.**

machada NF **(a)** manly act, act of courage; heroic deed; (*pey*) piece of bravado. **(b)** **~s** nonsense; fooling around.

machado NM hatchet.

machamartillo: a ~ ADV: **creer a ~** to believe firmly, (*pey*) to believe blindly; **cumplir a ~** to carry out a task to the letter, perform a task down to the last detail; **eran cristianos a ~** they were absolutely convinced Christians.

machango ADJ (*Cono Sur*) tedious.

machaque* NM dunk, slam dunk.

machaquear [1a] VTI (*Méx*) = **machacar.**

machaqueo NM crushing, pounding.

machaquería NF tiresomeness; insistence, harping (on a subject); monotony.

macharse; [1a] VR (*Cono Sur*) to get drunk.

machetazo NM (*LAm*) **(a)** (*instrumento*) large machete. **(b)** (*golpe*) blow (o slash) with a machete.

machete¹ NM (*LAm*) machete, cane knife, big knife.

machete² ADJ mean, stingy.

machetear [1a] ① VT **(a)** (*LAm*) *caña etc* to cut down with a machete;

persona to slash (*o* wound, stab *etc*) with a machete. **(b)** (*And**: *vender barato*) to sell cheap. **2** VI **(a)** (*And*, *Méx*: *obstinarse*) to dig one's heels in. **(b)** (*Méx*) (*trabajar*) to hammer away; (*estudiante*) to plod on.

machetero NM **(a)** (*LAm Agr*) cane cutter. **(b)** (*Méx*: *cargador*) porter. **(c)** (*Carib*††) revolutionary; **~ de salón** armchair radical. **(d)** (*Méx Univ*) plodder. **(e)** (*Carib**: *soldado*) soldier.

machi NM, **machí** NM (*LAm*) medicine man.

machiega NF (*t* **abeja ~**) queen bee.

machihembrado NM (*Téc*) dovetail (joint).

machihembrar [1a] VT to dovetail.

machina NF **(a)** (*Mec*) crane, derrick; pile driver. **(b)** (*Carib*) merry-go-round.

machirulo (*Esp*) **1** ADJ tomboyish; mannish. **2** NM tomboy; mannish woman.

machismo NM machismo, masculinity; (*orgullo*) male pride, maleness; (*virilidad*) virility; (*pey*) male chauvinism.

machista **1** ADJ full of machismo, full of male pride, very masculine; (*pey*) male chauvinistic. **2** NM (*pey*) male chauvinist.

machito[1] NM (*Méx*) fried offal.

machito[2] NM: **estar montado** (*o* **subido**) **en el ~** to be well placed, be riding high.

macho **1** ADJ **(a)** (*Bio*) male; **la flor ~** the male flower; **una rata ~** a male rat.
(b) (*fig*) macho, masculine; strong, tough; **es muy ~** he's very tough.
(c) (*Mec*) male.
(d) (*) stupid.
(e) (*And**: *fantástico*) splendid, terrific*.
2 NM **(a)** (*Bio*) male; (*Zool*) mule; (*: *a persona, en oración directa*) man*, mate*, brother*; **~ cabrío** he-goat, billy-goat; **~ de varas** leading mule; (*fig*) person in charge; **atarse** (*o* **apretarse**) **los ~s** to pull out all the stops, make a great effort.
(b) (*Mec*) pin, peg; (*Elec*) pin; plug; (*Cos*) hook.
(c) (*Téc*) sledgehammer.
(d) (*Arquit*) buttress.
(e) (*fig: persona*) macho, tough guy (*US**), he-man*; (*pey*) idiot.
(f) **parar el ~ a uno** (*LAm*) to take the wind out of sb's sails.
(g) (*CAm**: *Mil*) US marine.
(h) (*Esp*†‡) 5 pesetas.

machón NM buttress.

machona NF (*And*, *Carib*, *Cono Sur*) (*mujer*) mannish woman; (*niña*) tomboy.

machorra‡ NF dyke‡, lesbian.

machota NF **(a)** (*mujer*) mannish woman. **(b)** (*Téc*) hammer, mallet; rammer. **(c) a la ~** (*And*, *Carib*) carelessly; (*CAm*) rudely, roughly.

machote NM **(a)** (*) tough guy (*US**), he-man*. **(b)** (*LAm*) (*borrador*) rough draft, sketch; (*modelo*) model; (*pauta*) pattern. **(c)** (*Méx*) blank form.

machucadura NF bruise.

machucar [1g] VT **(a)** (*hacer polvo*) to pound, crush; (*golpear*) to beat; (*abollar*) to dent; (*dañar*) to knock about, damage. **(b)** (*Med*) to bruise. **(c)** (*And*, *Carib*, *Méx*) *caballo* to tire out (*before a race*). **(d)** (*Carib*) *ropa* to rinse through.

machucho ADJ **(a)** (*mayor*) elderly, getting on in years. **(b)** (*prudente*) prudent; (*tranquilo*) sedate; (*juicioso*) sensible. **(c)** (*And*, *Méx**: *taimado*) cunning, sly, shrewd.

machucón NM (*LAm*) bruise.

macia NF = **macis**.

macicez NF massiveness; solidity; stoutness.

macilento ADJ wan, haggard; gaunt; emaciated.

macillo NM (*Mús*) hammer.

macis NF mace (*spice*).

maciza NF (*LAm*) chipboard.

macizamente ADJ massively; solidly; stoutly.

macizar [1f] VT to fill up, fill in, pack solid.

macizo **1** ADJ **(a)** (*grande*) massive; *neumático, oro, puerta etc* solid; (*bien hecho*) solidly made, stoutly made; *persona* solid, stoutly built; **de roble ~** of solid oak; **~ de gente** solid with people. **(b)** (*) *chica* smashing*.
2 ADV (*CAm*, *Méx*) quickly, fast.
3 NM **(a)** (*masa*) mass; (*trozo*) lump, chunk, solid piece; (*de plantas*) clump.
(b) (*Geog*) massif.
(c) (*Hort*) bed, plot.
(d) (*Aut*) solid tyre.
(e) (*Arquit*) stretch, section (of a wall).

macizorro* ADJ *hombre* hunky*; *mujer* well-stacked*.

maco‡ NM nick‡, prison; (*Mil*) glasshouse.

macollo NM bunch, cluster.

macramé NM macramé.

macro NF (*Inform*) macro.

macro... PREF macro...

macró NM pimp.

macrobiótico ADJ macrobiotic.

macrocefalía NF macrocephaly; (*fig*) top-heaviness.

macrocefálico ADJ macrocephalic; (*fig*) top-heavy.

macrocomando NM macro (command).

macroconcierto NM mega-gig.

macrocosmo(s) NM macrocosm.

macroeconomía NF macroeconomy.

macroeconómica NF macroeconomics.

macroeconómico ADJ macroeconomic.

macroestructura NF macrostructure.

macrófago NM macrophage.

macrofotografía NF macrophotography.

macromolecular ADJ macromolecular.

macroproyecto NM large-scale project.

macuache* ADJ (*Méx*) rough, coarse.

macuco **1** ADJ **(a)** (*And*, *Cono Sur**: *astuto*) crafty, cunning. **(b)** (*And*: *inútil*) old and useless. **(c)** (*And*, *Cono Sur*) (*grande*) big, great; (*demasiado grande*) overgrown. **2** NM (*And*, *Cono Sur**) overgrown boy, big lad.

macuenco ADJ **(a)** (*Carib**: *débil*) thin, weak, feeble. **(b)** (*Carib*: *inútil*) useless. **(c)** (*And*: *demasiado grande*) big; overgrown, extra large; (*) splendid, terrific*.

mácula NF **(a)** (*gen fig*) stain, spot, blemish; **~ solar** sunspot. **(b)** (*trampa*) trick, fraud.

macular [1a] VT to stain, spot.

macundales NMPL (*And*, *Carib*), **macundos** NMPL (*Carib*) (*trastos*) things, gear, junk; (*negocios*) affairs, business.

macutazo* NM rumour; hoax.

macuto NM **(a)** (*mochila*) knapsack; satchel. **(b)** (*Carib*) begging basket.

Madagascar NM Madagascar.

madalena NF fairy cake.

madaleno‡ NM secret policeman.

madama NF (*And*, *Cono Sur*), **madame** NF madame, brothel-keeper.

madeja **1** NF (*de lana*) skein, hank; (*de pelo*) mass, mop; **~ de nervios** bundle of nerves; **se está enredando la ~** the affair is getting complicated, the plot thickens. **2** NM (*persona*) layabout, idler.

Madera NF Madeira.

madera[1] NM Madeira (*wine*).

madera[2] NF **(a)** (*gen*) wood; (*Mús*) woodwind section (of the orchestra; *t* **~s**); **~ (de construcción** *etc*) timber; (*una* **~**) piece of wood; **la ~** (*Dep*) the woodwork; **~ contrachapada**, **~ (multi)laminada**, **~ terciada** plywood; **~ de deriva** driftwood; **~ dura** hardwood; **~ fósil** lignite; **de ~** wood, wooden; **¡toca ~!** touch wood!, knock on wood! (*US*).
(b) (*Zool*) horny part (*of hoof*).
(c) (*fig*) nature, temperament; aptitude; **tiene buena ~** there's a lot (of good) in him, he's made of solid stuff; **tiene ~ de futbolista** he'll make a footballer, he's got football in him.
(d) (‡) fuzz‡, police.

maderable ADJ: **árbol ~** tree useful for its wood; **bosque ~** wood containing useful timber.

maderaje NM, **maderamen** NM timber, wood; woodwork, timbering.

maderero **1** ADJ wood (*atr*), timber (*atr*); **industria maderera** timber industry; **productos ~s** wood products. **2** NM timber merchant; lumberman.

maderismo NM (*Méx Pol*) *reform movement led by Madero*.

maderista NMF (*Méx Pol*) supporter of Madero.

madero NM **(a)** (*viga*) beam; (*tronco*) log; (*trozo de madera*) (piece of) timber. **(b)** (*fig: Náut*) ship, vessel. **(c)** (*: *idiota*) oaf, blockhead. **(d)** (*Esp‡*: *policía*) cop‡.

Madona NF Madonna.

madrastra NF stepmother; (*fig*) unloving mother.

madraza* NF loving mother.

madrazo* NM (*Méx*) hefty blow*.

madre **1** ADJ **(a)** (*lit*) mother; **buque ~** mother ship; **lengua ~** parent language; **acequia ~** main channel; **alcantarilla ~** main sewer, principal sewer.
(b) **color ~** dominant colour, theme colour; **la cuestión ~** the chief problem, the central problem.
(c) (*LAm**) tremendous*, terrific*; **una regañada ~** one hell of a telling-off*.
2 NF **(a)** mother; (*orfanato etc*) matron; **~ adoptiva** foster-mother; **~ alquilada**, **~ de alquiler**, **~ portadora** surrogate mother; **~ biológica**, **~ genética** biological mother, true mother; **~ política** mother-in-law; **~ soltera** single mother; **~ trabajadora** working mother; **M~ de Dios** Mother of God; **¡M~ de Dios!** good heavens!;

futura ~ expectant mother; **su señora** ~ your mother; **sin** ~ motherless; **¡~ mía!** well!; oh dear!; **¡tu ~!⚒** up yours!⚒, get stuffed!⚒; **a toda** ~ (*LAm*⚒), **de la** ~ (*LAm*⚒) great*, terrific*; **ni ~*** not a thing; **ahí está la ~ del cordero** that's just the trouble; **mentar a la ~ a uno** to swear at sb; **él no tiene ~*** he's a real swine*; **esto no tiene ~*** this is the limit; *V* **ciento**.

(b) (*fig: de civilización etc*) origin, cradle.

(c) la ~ (*en juegos*) home.

(d) (*Anat*) womb.

(e) (*de río*) bed; **sacar de ~ a uno** to provoke sb, upset sb; **salirse de** ~ (*río*) to overflow, burst its banks; (*persona*) to lose all self-control; (*proceso etc*) to go beyond its normal limits.

(f) (*de vino etc*) dregs, lees; sediment.

(g) (*Agr*) main channel, main irrigation ditch; (*Téc*) main sewer.

(h) (*And*) dead skin, scab.

(i) (⚒) queer⚒.

madrejón NM (*Cono Sur Agr*) watercourse.

madreperla NF (*ostra*) pearl oyster; (*nácar*) mother-of-pearl; **~ de río** freshwater mussel.

madreselva NF honeysuckle; **~ siempreverde** Cape honeysuckle.

Madrid NM Madrid.

madridista ① ADJ of (o relating to) Real Madrid football club.

② NMF Real Madrid player (o supporter *etc*); **los ~s** Real Madrid.

madrigal NM madrigal.

madriguera NF **(a)** (*Zool*) den; burrow. **(b)** (*fig*) den.

madrileño ① ADJ of Madrid; **madrileñísimo** typical of Madrid, full of the character of Madrid; **la madrileñísima Cibeles** Cibeles Square which is so typical of Madrid, Cibeles Square which sums up so much of Madrid.

② NM, **madrileña** NF native (o inhabitant) of Madrid; **los ~s** the people of Madrid.

Madriles* NMPL: **Los** ~ Madrid.

madrina NF **(a)** (*en bautizo*) godmother; (*de empresa etc*) patron(ess), protectress; **~ de boda** ≈ bridesmaid.

(b) (*Arquit etc*) prop, shore; (*Téc*) brace.

(c) (*Agr*) lead mare.

(d) (*LAm*) tame animal (*used in breaking in or catching others*).

(e) (*Méx**) police informer.

madriza⚒ NF (*Méx*) bashing*, beating-up*.

madroño NM strawberry tree, arbutus.

madrugada NF early morning; dawn, daybreak; **levantarse de** ~ to get up early; **a las 4 de la** ~ at 4 o'clock in the morning, at 4 a.m.

madrugador ① ADJ early rising, who gets up early.

② NM, **madrugadora** NF early riser; (*fig*) early bird.

madrugar [1h] ① VT: **~ a uno** (*adelantarse a*) to forestall sb, get in ahead of sb; (*CAm*⚒: *matar*) to bump sb off⚒.

② VI **(a)** (*levantarse*) to get up early; to be an early riser; **a quien madruga, Dios le ayuda** God helps those who help themselves.

(b) (*fig*) to get ahead; to get in first (in replying *etc*); to jump the gun.

madrugón NM: **darse** (o **pegarse**) **un** ~ to get up terribly early.

maduración NF ripening; maturing.

madurar [1a] ① VT **(a)** *frutos* to ripen. **(b)** (*fig*) to mature; *plan etc* to think out.

② VI **(a)** (*frutos*) to ripen. **(b)** (*fig*) to mature.

③ **madurarse** VR to ripen.

madurez NF **(a)** (*lit*) ripeness. **(b)** (*fig*) maturity; mellowness; sageness, wisdom.

maduro ① ADJ **(a)** *fruta* ripe; **poco** ~ unripe, underripe.

(b) (*fig*) mature; mellow; **de edad madura** of mature years; **la cosa está madura para la reforma** the business is ripe for reform; **el divieso está** ~ the boil is about to burst.

② NM (*LAm*) plantain.

MAE NM (*Esp Pol*) ABR *de* **Ministerio de Asuntos Exteriores**.

maesa NF queen bee.

maestra NF **(a)** (*Escol*) teacher (*t fig*); **~ de escuela** schoolteacher. **(b)** (*Ent*) queen bee. **(c)** (*Arquit*) guide line.

maestranza NF **(a)** (*Mil*) arsenal, armoury; (*Náut*) naval dockyard. **(b)** (*personal*) staff of an arsenal (o dockyard). **(c)** (*LAm*) machine shop.

maestrazgo NM (*Hist*) office of grand master.

maestre NM (*Hist*) grand master (*of a military order*).

maestrear [1a] VT **(a)** (*dirigir*) to direct, manage. **(b)** (*Agr*) to prune.

maestría NF **(a)** (*dominio*) mastery; (*habilidad*) skill, expertise; **lo hizo con** ~ he did it very skilfully, he did it in a masterly fashion. **(b)** (*Univ*) master's degree.

maestro ① ADJ **(a)** (*genial*) masterly; (*experto*) skilled, expert.

(b) (*Téc*) main, principal; master (*atr*); **cloaca maestra** main sewer; **llave maestra** skeleton key, master key; **obra maestra** masterpiece; **viga maestra** main beam.

(c) (*Ent*) **abeja maestra** queen bee.

(d) *animal* trained; **halcón** ~ trained hawk.

② NM **(a)** (*gen*) master; (*profesor*) teacher; (*autoridad*) authority; **~ (de**

escuela) schoolteacher; (*Téc*) master craftsman; **el ~ de todos los medievalistas españoles** the greatest authority among the Spanish medievalists; **gran** ~ (*Ajedrez*) grand master; **beber en los grandes ~s** to absorb wisdom from the great teachers; **¿por dónde, ~?*** which way, squire?*

(b) (*aposición*) master ...; **~ albañil** mason, skilled building craftsman; **~ sastre** master tailor; **'Los ~s cantores'** 'The Mastersingers'.

(c) (*Mús*) maestro; **el ~ Falla** the great musician (o composer) Falla.

(d) ~ de armas, ~ de esgrima fencing master; **~ de ceremonias** master of ceremonies; **~ de cocina** chef; **~ de coros** choirmaster; **~ de maquillaje** make-up expert; **~ de obras** master builder; foreman, clerk of works.

(e) (*LAm: artesano*) skilled workman, craftsman; (*Cono Sur*) repairman; **~ de caminos** skilled road-construction man.

mafafa NF (*LAm*) marijuana.

mafia NF mafia, criminal gang, ring; **la M~** the Mafia.

mafioso NM mafioso, (*de la Mafia*) member of the Mafia; (*criminal: gen*) hood⚒, gangster.

Magallanes NM Magellan.

magancear [1a] VI (*And, Cono Sur*) to idle, loaf.

maganto ADJ **(a)** (*macilento*) wan, wasted. **(b)** (*preocupado*) worried; (*soso*) lifeless, dull.

maganza* NF (*And*) idleness, laziness.

maga(n)zón NM (*LAm*) idler, loafer.

maganzonería NF (*LAm*) = **maganza**.

magazine [maɣa'zin] NM (*Rad, TV*) magazine.

Magdalena NF Magdalen, Madeleine; **La** ~ Mary Magdalene; **m~** penitent woman; **llorar como una** ~ to cry one's eyes out.

magdalena NF fairy cake.

magenta NF magenta.

magia NF magic; **~ blanca** white magic; **~ negra** black magic; **por arte de** ~ (as if) by magic.

magiar ADJ, NMF Magyar.

mágico ADJ magic; magical.

⸋ MÁGICO

El adjetivo *mágico* se puede traducir por *magic* y *magical* aunque éstos no son intercambiables.

- *Mágico* se traduce por *magic* para hablar de cosas que se utilizan para hacer magia:

  Dijo las tres palabras mágicas y la mujer desapareció
  He said the three magic words and the woman disappeared
  Usó su varita mágica para convertir la calabaza en una carroza
  She used her magic wand to turn the pumpkin into a carriage

- Cuando describimos cualidades o acontecimientos de carácter sobrenatural, *mágico* se traduce por *magical*:

  Se encuentran explicaciones para lo que parece mágico
  Explanations are found for what seems magical
  Se creía que el hierro tenía propiedades mágicas
  Iron was believed to have magical powers

- Cuando *mágico* se usa en sentido figurado con el significado de extraordinario o con un encanto especial, se traduce al inglés por *magical*:

  Fue una noche mágica
  It was a magical evening

---

magín* NM fancy, imagination; mind; **todo eso salió de su** ~ it all came out of his own head.

magisterio NM **(a)** (*enseñanza*) teaching; (*profesión*) teaching profession; (*formación*) teachers' training; **dedicarse al** ~ to go in for teaching; **ejerció el** ~ **durante 40 años** he taught for 40 years.

(b) (*personas*) teachers (*collectively*).

(c) (*fig*) pompousness, pedantry.

(d) M~ (*CAm Univ*) Department of Education.

magistrado, -a NM/F magistrate; judge; **primer M~** (*LAm*) president, prime minister.

magistral ① ADJ **(a)** magisterial. **(b)** (*fig: genial*) masterly. **(c)** (*pey*) pompous, pedantic.

② NM (*reloj*) ~ master clock.

magistratura NF magistracy; judgeship; **alta** ~ (*fig*) highest authority; **~ de trabajo** industrial tribunal.

magma NM magma.

magnánimamente ADV magnanimously.

magnanimidad NF magnanimity.

magnánimo ADJ magnanimous.

magnate NM magnate; tycoon; (*Hist*) baron; **los ~s de la industria** the top people in industry, the big industrialists; **~ de la prensa** press baron, press lord.

magnavoz NM (*Méx*) loudspeaker.

magnesia NF magnesia.

magnesio NM (*Quím*) magnesium; (*Fot*) flash, flashlight.

magnéticamente ADV magnetically.

magnético ADJ magnetic.
magnetismo NM magnetism.
magnetizable ADJ magnetizable.
magnetizar [1f] VT to magnetize.
magneto NF magneto.
magnetofón NM (*Esp*), **magnetófono** NM (*Esp*) tape-recorder.
magnetofónico ADJ tape (*atr*), recording (*atr*); **cinta magnetofónica** recording tape.
magnetómetro NM magnetometer.
magnetoscopio NM video recorder.
magnetosfera NF magnetosphere.
magnicida NMF assassin (of an important person).
magnicidio NM assassination (of an important person).
magníficamente ADV splendidly, wonderfully, superbly, magnificently.
magnificar [1g] VT to praise, extol.
magnificencia NF (a) (*esplendor*) splendour, magnificence. (b) (*generosidad*) lavishness, generosity.
magnífico ADJ splendid, wonderful, superb, magnificent; **¡~!** splendid!, that's grand!; **~ rector** (*Esp Univ*) honourable Chancellor; **es un muchacho** ~ he's a fine boy; **tenemos un ~ profesor** we have a splendid teacher.
magnitud NF magnitude (*t Astron*); **de primera ~** (*Astron*) of the first magnitude.
magno ADJ (*liter*) great.
magnolia NF magnolia.
mago NM magician, wizard; *V* **rey**.
magra NF (a) (*de carne*) lean part (*of meat*). (b) (*lonja*) slice; rasher. (c) **¡~!**‡, not on your nelly!‡ (d) (*Esp‡: casa*) house.
magrear [1a] VT (*Esp*) to feel, touch up‡.
Magreb NM Maghrib.
magrebí ADJ, **magrebino** ADJ Maghribian.
magreo‡ NM (*Esp*) touching up‡.
magrez NF leanness.
magro ADJ (a) *persona* thin, lean. (b) *carne* lean; *queso* low-fat. (c) *tierra* poor, thin.
magrura NF leanness.
magua NF (*Carib*) disappointment; failure, setback.
maguarse* [1i] VR (*Carib*) (a) (*fiesta etc*) to be a flop*. (b) (*persona*) (*decepcionarse*) to suffer a disappointment; (*deprimirse*) to get depressed.
maguer (††, *liter*) 1 PREP in spite of, despite.
2 CONJ although.
maguey NM (*Bot*) maguey.
maguillo NM wild apple tree.
magulladura NF bruise.
magullamiento NM bruising.
magullar [1a] VT (*amoratar*) to bruise; (*dañar*) to hurt, damage; (*golpear*) to batter, bash*; (*And, Carib*) to crumple, rumple.
magullón NM (*LAm*) bruise.
Maguncia NF Mainz.
maharajá NM maharajah; **vivir como un ~** to live like a prince.
mahdi NM Mahdi.
Mahoma NM Mahomet, Muhammad.
mahometano, -a ADJ, NM/F Mahommedan.
mahometismo NM Mahommedanism.
mahonesa NF mayonnaise.
mai‡ NM joint‡.
maicena NF blancmange; (*LAm*) cornflour, corn starch (*US*).
maicero ADJ maize (*atr*), corn (*atr: US*).
maicillo NM (*Cono Sur*) gravel.
mailing ['mailin] NM, PL **mailings** ['mailin] mailshot.
maillot [ma'jot] NM (*Ciclismo*) jersey; **el ~ amarillo** the yellow jersey.
maitines NMPL matins.
maître ['metre] NM (*t ~ d'hôtel*) head waiter.
maíz NM (a) (*Agr*) maize, corn (*US*), sweet corn, Indian corn; **~ en la mazorca** corn on the cob. (b) **coger a uno asando ~** (*Carib*) to catch sb red-handed; **dar a uno ~ tostado** (*And*) to give sb their comeuppance.
maizal NM maize field, cornfield (*US*).
maizena NF (*LAm*) = **maicena**.
maizudo ADJ (*CAm*) rich, wealthy.
maja NF woman (*o* girl) of the people (*esp of Madrid*).
majada NF (a) (*corral*) sheepfold. (b) (*estiércol*) dung. (c) (*Cono Sur*) (*de ovejas*) flock of sheep; (*de chivos*) herd of goats.
majaderear [1a] VT (*LAm*) to bother, annoy.
majadería NF (a) (*tontería*) silliness; (*sin sentido*) absurdity. (b) (*una* ~) silly thing, absurdity; **~s** nonsense.
majadero 1 ADJ silly, stupid.
2 NM (a) (*tonto*) idiot, fool; **¡~!** you idiot! (b) (*Téc*) pestle. (c) (*Cos*) bobbin.
majador NM pestle.

majagranzas* INVAR = **majadero**.
majagua NF (*Carib*) (a) (*Dep*) baseball bat. (b) (*: *traje*) suit.
majar [1a] VT (a) (*aplastar*) to pound, crush, grind; to mash; (*Med*) to bruise. (b) (*) to bother, pester.
majara* ADJ INVAR, **majareta*** ADJ INVAR cracked, potty*.
maje 1 ADJ (*Méx‡*) gullible; **hacer ~ al marido** to cheat on one's husband.
2 NMF (*Méx‡*) sucker‡.
3 NM (*CAm**: *tipo*) bloke‡, guy*.
majestad NF majesty; stateliness; **Su M~** His (*o* Her) Majesty; **M~, Vuestra M~** Your Majesty.
majestuosamente ADV majestically.
majestuosidad NF majesty, stateliness.
majestuoso ADJ majestic, stately, imposing.
majete* 1 ADJ nice, likeable.
2 NM guy*, bloke‡; **¡jo, ~!** hey man!*
majeza NF (a) (*atractivo*) good looks, attractiveness; loveliness. (b) (*elegancia*) smartness, nattiness*; (*pey*) flashiness, gaudiness.
majo 1 ADJ (*Esp*) (a) (*agradable*) nice; (*guapa*) pretty, (*guapo*) attractive, handsome; (*precioso*) lovely.
(b) (*elegante*) smart, natty*; (*pey*) flashy, gaudy.
2 NM (a) toff*, masher‡††, sport* (*esp from the lower classes of Madrid, 19th century*); (*pey*) flashy sort; (*) *V* **majete**.
(b) (*pey*) lout, bully; **echársela de ~** to brag, give o.s. airs.
majong [ma'xon] NM mahjong.
majuela NF haw, hawthorn berry.
majuelo NM (a) (*vid*) young vine. (b) (*espino*) hawthorn.
mal 1 ADV (a) (*de mala manera*) badly; poorly; (*equivocadamente*) wrongly; (*apenas*) hardly, with difficulty; **¡~!** that's bad!, oh dear!; **lo hace muy ~** he does it very badly; **hace ~ en** + *infin* he is wrong to + *infin*, he is mistaken in + *ger*, it is unwise of him to + *infin*; **oigo ~** I don't hear well, I have difficulty in hearing; **ahora veo bastante ~** my sight is rather weak now; **huele ~** it smells bad; **sabe ~** it tastes nasty; **eso está ~** that's bad; that's wrong; **sentirse ~** to feel ill, feel bad; **está muy ~ escrito** it's very badly written; **lo hice lo menos ~ que pude** I did it as well as I could; **me entendió ~** he misunderstood me; **pero digo ~** but I am wrong to say ...; **~ puedo hablar yo de este asunto** I can hardly talk about this matter, I'm hardly the right person to talk about this.
(b) (*locuciones*) **~ que bien** somehow or other, by some means or other; **hacer algo ~ que bien** to do sth somehow; **ir de ~ en peor** to go from bad to worse, get worse; **¡menos ~!** that's a relief!; I'm glad to hear it; **menos ~ que** ... it's just as well that ..., it's a good job that ...
2 CONJ: **~ que le pese** however much he resents it, even though he hates the idea.
3 ADJ *V* **malo**.
4 NM (a) (*gen*) evil, wrong; **el bien y el ~** good and evil, right and wrong; **~ menor** lesser evil; **caer en el ~** to fall into evil ways; **combatir el ~** to fight against evil; **echar algo a ~** to despise sth; to waste sth, squander sth; **el ~ está en que** ... the trouble is ...; **estar a ~ con uno** to be on bad terms with sb; **no hay ~ que por bien no venga** it's an ill wind that blows nobody any good; it may be a blessing in disguise; **parar en ~** to come to a bad end.
(b) (*daño*) harm, hurt, damage; (*desgracia*) misfortune; **no le deseo ningún ~** I don't wish him any harm (*o* ill); **hacer ~ a uno** to do sb harm; **el ~ ya está hecho** the harm is done now; **no hay ningún ~** there's no harm done; **¡~ haya quien ...!** a curse on whoever ...!; **decir ~ de uno** to speak ill of sb, slander sb; **llevar** (*o* **tomar**) **algo a ~** to take sth amiss, be offended about sth.
(c) (*Med*) disease, illness; (*fig*) suffering; **~es** (*fig*) ills; **~ de altura** altitude sickness; **~ de amores** lovesickness; **~ caduco** epilepsy; **~ francés** (*Hist*) syphilis; **~ de mar** seasickness; **~ de ojo** evil eye; **~ de la tierra** homesickness; **los ~es de la economía** the things that are wrong with the economy; **dar ~ a uno** to make sb suffer; **darse ~** to torment o.s.
(d) (*LAm Med*) epileptic fit.
mala[1] NF bad luck.
mala[2] NF (*saco*) mailbag; (*correo*) mail, post.
malabar ADJ: **juegos ~es** juggling.
malabarismo NM (a) (*lit*) juggling, conjuring. (b) **~s** (*fig*) juggling; balancing act.
malabarista NMF juggler, conjurer.
malacate NM winch, capstan; (*CAm, Méx*: *huso*) spindle.
malaconsejado ADJ ill-advised.
malaconsejar [1a] VT to give bad advice to.
malacostumbrado ADJ (a) (*vicioso*) having bad habits, vicious. (b) (*mimado*) spoiled, pampered.
malacostumbrar [1a] VT: **~ a uno** (*CAm*) to get sb into bad habits.
malacrianza NF (*LAm*) = **malcriadez**.
malage NM = **malaje**.

malagradecido ADJ ungrateful.
malagueño [1] ADJ of Málaga.
[2] NM, **malagueña** NF native (o inhabitant) of Málaga; **los ~s** the people of Málaga.
Malaisia NF Malaysia.
malaje* NM (a) (mala sombra) malign influence; bad vibes*; (mala suerte) bad luck. (b) (sosería) dullness, lifelessness; lack of charm. (c) (persona: malévolo) swine*, rotter*; (soso) bore, pain*.
malamente ADV badly; poorly; wrongly; **estar ~ de dinero** to be badly off for money; **tenemos gasolina ~ para** + infin we hardly have enough petrol to + infin; **~ puede hacerse si ...** it can scarcely be done if ...
malandante ADJ unfortunate.
malandanza NF misfortune.
malandrín, -ina NM/F († o hum) scoundrel, rogue.
malandro; NM (Carib) scrounger*.
malanga [1] ADJ (Carib*) thick*.
[2] NF (CAm, Carib, Méx) tuber resembling a sweet potato.
malapata* NMF pest, nuisance; tedious individual; clumsy sort.
malapropismo NM malapropism.
malaria NF malaria.
Malasia NF Malaysia.
malasio, -a ADJ, NM/F Malaysian.
malasombra* NMF = **malapata**.
Malaui, Malawi NM Malawi.
malauiano, -a, malawiano, -a ADJ, NM/F Malawian.
malaúva* [1] ADJ mean, bad natured, miserable.
[2] NMF miserable sod;, grumpy bastard;.
malavenido ADJ: **estar ~s** to be in disagreement, be in conflict.
malaventura NF misfortune.
malaventurado ADJ unfortunate.
Malaya NF Malaya.
malaya INTERJ (LAm) damn!
malayo [1] ADJ Malay(an).
[2] NM, **malaya** NF Malay.
[3] NM (Ling) Malay.
Malaysia NF Malaysia.
malbaratar [1a] VT (Com) to sell off cheap, sell at a loss; (fig) to squander.
malcarado ADJ ugly, repulsive; fierce-looking, cross-looking.
malcasado ADJ (infeliz) unhappily married; (infiel) errant, unfaithful.
malcasarse [1a] VR to make an unhappy marriage.
malcomer [2a] VI to have a poor meal, eat badly.
malcontento [1] ADJ discontented.
[2] NM, **malcontenta** NF malcontent.
malcriadez NF (LAm) bad breeding, lack of breeding.
malcriado ADJ rude, bad-mannered, coarse.
malcriar [1c] VT niño to spoil, pamper.
maldad NF (a) (gen) evil, wickedness. (b) (una ~) wicked thing.
maldecir [aprox 3o] [1] VT (a) (con maldición) to curse. (b) (odiar) to loathe, detest.
[2] VI: **~ de** (a) (hablar mal de) to speak ill of; (difamar) to slander; (denigrar) to disparage, run down. (b) (quejarse) to curse, complain bitterly of.
maldiciendo etc V **maldecir**.
maldiciente [1] ADJ (quejumbroso) that speaks ill of everything, forever criticizing; (grosero) foul-mouthed.
[2] NMF grumbler, complainer; malcontent; slanderer.
maldición NF curse; **¡~!** curse it!, damn!; **parece que ha caído una ~ sobre este programa** there seems to be a curse on this programme.
maldiga, maldije etc V **maldecir**.
maldispuesto ADJ ill-disposed; (Med) ill, indisposed.
maldita NF (a) (lengua) tongue; **soltar la ~** (hablar mucho) to talk too much; (enojarse) to explode angrily, blow up. (b) (Carib) (llaga) sore, swelling; (picadura) insect bite.
malditismo NM aura of doom.
maldito [1] ADJ (a) (gen) damned (t Ecl), accursed.
(b) (*: condenado) damned; **¡~ sea!** damn it!; **ese ~ niño** that wretched child, that blessed child; **ese ~ libro** that damned book; **lo que me importa** I don't care a damn; **no le hace ~ el caso** he doesn't take a blind bit of notice*; **no le encuentro maldita la gracia** I don't find it in the least amusing; **no sabe maldita la cosa de ello** he knows damn-all about it;.
(c) (maligno) wicked.
(d) (Méx: taimado) crafty.
[2] NM (a) **el ~** the devil.
(b) (Teat) extra.
maldormir [3j] VI to sleep badly, sleep in fits and starts.
maleabilidad NF malleability.
maleable ADJ malleable.
maleado ADJ (LAm) corrupt.
maleante [1] ADJ wicked; villainous, rascally, unsavoury.

[2] NMF (malhechor) malefactor, unsavoury character, suspicious person; (vago) vagrant.
malear [1a] [1] VT to damage, spoil, harm; tierra to sour; (fig) to corrupt, pervert.
[2] **malearse** VR to spoil, be harmed; to be corrupted, get into evil ways, go to the bad.
malecón NM pier, jetty, mole.
maledicencia NF slander, scandal.
maledicente ADJ slanderous, scandalous.
maleducado ADJ ill-bred, bad-mannered.
maleducar [1g] VT niños to spoil.
maleficiar [1b] VT (a) (hechizar) to bewitch, cast an evil spell on. (b) (dañar) to harm, damage.
maleficio NM (hechizo) curse, spell; (brujería) witchcraft.
maléfico ADJ harmful, damaging, evil.
malejo* ADJ rather bad, pretty bad.
malencarado ADJ sour-faced.
malentendido NM misunderstanding.
malestar NM (a) (Med) discomfort; indisposition. (b) (fig) uneasiness, malaise; (Pol etc) unrest.
maleta¹* ADJ (a) (And, CAm, Carib, Méx) (travieso) naughty; mischievous; (malo) wicked. (b) (And, Cono Sur) (tonto) stupid; (inútil) useless. (c) (Cono Sur: astuto) sly. (d) (Cono Sur, Méx: vago) lazy. (e) (CAm, Méx: torpe) ham-fisted.
maleta² [1] NF (a) (gen) case, suitcase; travelling bag; **hacer la ~, hacer las ~s** to pack (up); **ya puede preparar la ~** he's on his way out, the skids are under him*.
(b) (Aut) boot, trunk (US).
(c) (CAm, Cono Sur) saddlebag.
(d) (And, CAm, Cono Sur) bundle of clothes.
(e) (And, Carib: joroba) hump.
[2] NM (*) bungler, clumsy novice; (Taur) clumsy bullfighter; (Dep) poor player, rabbit*; (Teat) ham*.
maletazo NM bump (with a suitcase).
maletera NF (a) (And, Méx) saddlebag. (b) (And Aut) boot, trunk (US). (c) (Cono Sur: cortabolsas) pickpocket.
maletero NM (a) (Aut) boot, trunk (US). (b) (cargador) porter. (c) (Cono Sur: cortabolsas) pickpocket.
maletilla NM (Taur) itinerant aspiring bullfighter.
maletín NM small case, bag; briefcase; satchel; **~ de excursiones** picnic case; **~ de grupa** saddlebag.
maletón ADJ (And) hunchbacked.
maletudo (And, Carib) [1] ADJ hunchbacked.
[2] NM, **maletuda** NF hunchback.
malevolencia NF malevolence, malice, spite, ill-will; **por ~** out of spite; **sin ~ para nadie** with malice toward none.
malevolente ADJ malevolent, malicious, spiteful.
malévolo ADJ malevolent, malicious, spiteful.
maleza NF (a) (Agr) weeds. (b) (monte bajo) scrub; undergrowth; (broza) brushwood; (matorral) thicket. (c) (Cono Sur Med) pus. (d) (CAm: enfermedad) sickness, illness.
malezal NM (a) (Carib, Cono Sur) mass of weeds. (b) (Cono Sur Med) pus.
malfamado ADJ notorious.
malformación NF malformation.
malformado ADJ malformed.
Malgache NM Malgache, Madagascar.
malgache [1] ADJ of Madagascar.
[2] NMF native (o inhabitant) of Madagascar.
malgastador [1] ADJ spendthrift, thriftless, wasteful.
[2] NM, **malgastadora** NF spendthrift.
malgastar [1a] VT dinero, recursos to waste, squander; esfuerzo, tiempo to waste; salud to ruin.
malgeniado ADJ, **malgenio(so)** ADJ (LAm) bad-tempered.
malhabido ADJ ganancia ill-gotten.
malhablado ADJ coarse, rude; foul-mouthed.
malhadado ADJ ill-fated, ill-starred.
malhaya INTERJ (LAm) damn!; **¡~ sea!** damn him! (etc).
malhecho [1] ADJ (*) ugly; misshapen.
[2] NM misdeed.
malhechor(a) NM/F malefactor, criminal, wrongdoer.
malherido ADJ badly injured, seriously wounded.
malhumorado ADJ bad-tempered, cross, tetchy.
mali; NM joint;.
malicia NF (a) (maldad) wickedness.
(b) (intención) evil intention; spite, malice, maliciousness; **lo dijo sin ~** he said it without any evil intention, he said it in all innocence.
(c) (carácter) viciousness, vicious nature; mischief, mischievous nature.
(d) (de mirada, chiste etc) roguishness, naughtiness, provocative nature; **contó un chiste con mucha ~** he told a very naughty story; **el niño tiene demasiada ~ para su edad** the kid is too knowing for his age*.

(e) (*astucia*) slyness, guile.

(f) ~s (*sospechas*) suspicions; **tengo mis ~s** I have my suspicions.

maliciarse [1b] VR to suspect, have one's suspicions; **ya me lo maliciaba** I thought as much, it's just what I suspected.

maliciosamente ADV (V ADJ) (a) wickedly. (b) spitefully, maliciously. (c) viciously; mischievously. (d) roguishly, naughtily, provocatively. (e) slyly.

malicioso ADJ (a) (*malo*) wicked, evil.

(b) (*malintencionado*) ill-intentioned; (*rencoroso*) spiteful, malicious.

(c) (*vicioso*) vicious; (*travieso*) mischievous.

(d) (*pícaro*) roguish, naughty, provocative; **una mirada maliciosa** a roguish look, a provocative glance.

(e) (*taimado*) sly, crafty.

malignidad NF (a) (*Med*) malignancy. (b) (*maldad*) evil nature, viciousness; (*daño*) harmfulness; (*rencor*) malice.

malignizarse [1f] VR *célula, tumor* to become malignant.

maligno [1] ADJ (a) (*Med*) malignant; pernicious. (b) *persona* evil, vicious; *influencia* evil, pernicious, harmful; *actitud, observación* malicious.

[2] NM: **el ~** the Evil One, the devil.

malinchismo NM (*Méx*) *tendency to favour things foreign*.

malinformar [1a] VT to misinform.

malintencionadamente ADV maliciously.

malintencionado ADJ ill-disposed, hostile, unkind; malicious.

malinterpretación NF misinterpretation, misunderstanding.

malinterpretar [1a] VT to misinterpret, misunderstand.

malísimamente ADV very badly, dreadfully, appallingly.

malísimo ADJ very bad, dreadful, appalling.

malito ADJ: **estar ~** to be in poor shape, be rather poorly.

malla NF (a) (*red*) mesh; network; **~ de alambre** wire mesh, wire netting; **hacer ~** to knit. (b) **las ~s** (*Dep*) the net. (c) (*Hist*) chain mail; (*Cono Sur*) swimsuit. (d) **~s** (*Teat etc*) tights.

mallo NM mallet.

Mallorca NF Majorca.

mallorquín, -ina [1] ADJ, NM/F Majorcan.

[2] NM (*Ling*) Majorcan.

malmandado ADJ (*desobediente*) disobedient; (*terco*) obstinate, bloody-minded‡.

malmedido NM (*Méx*) civil engineer.

malmirado ADJ (a) **estar ~** to be disliked. (b) (*desconsiderado*) thoughtless, inconsiderate.

malmodado‡ ADJ (*Carib, Méx*) (*hosco*) heavy-handed, rough; (*insolente*) rude, insolent.

malnacido* ADJ rotten*, awful.

malnutrición NF malnutrition.

malnutrido ADJ undernourished.

malo [1] ADJ (**mal** *delante de nm sing*) (a) (*gen*) bad; poor; wretched, dreadful; *olor etc* bad, nasty, unpleasant; *joya* false; *dedo, diente etc* bad, sore; *niño* bad, naughty, disobedient; **este papel es ~ para escribir** this paper is bad for writing; **ir por mal camino** to be on the wrong road; **¡no seas ~!** don't be naughty!, behave yourself!; that's a wicked thing to say.

(b) (*Med*) **estar ~** to be ill; **sentirse ~** to feel ill, feel bad; **me puse ~ de risa** I nearly died laughing.

(c) (*difícil*) hard, difficult; **es muy ~ de vencer** he's very hard to beat; **es un animal ~ de domesticar** it's a difficult animal to tame.

(d) (*locuciones*) **¡~!** oh dear!, that's bad!; **lo ~ es que ...** the trouble is that ...; **~ sería que no ganáramos** we're certain to win, I'd be surprised if we didn't win; **¿qué tiene de ~?** what's wrong with that?; **¿qué tiene de ~ comer helados en invierno?** what's wrong with eating ice cream in winter?; **a la mala** if the worst comes to the worst; (*And, Carib*: *a la fuerza*) by force, forcibly; (*Carib, Cono Sur, Méx*: *con doblez*) treacherously; **andar a malas con uno** to be on bad terms with sb; **los dos se pusieron a malas** the two fell out; **ponerse a malas con uno** to fall foul of sb, get on the wrong side of sb; **estar de malas** to be out of luck; to be in a bad mood; **venir de malas** to have evil intentions; **por las malas** by force, willy-nilly.

[2] NM (a) **el ~** (*Rel*) the Evil One, the devil.

(b) (*Teat*) villain; (*Cine*) bad guy, baddie*.

(c) (‡) **los ~s** the fuzz‡, the police.

[3] NF **mala³** spell of bad luck.

maloca NF (a) (*Cono Sur Hist*) Indian raid. (b) (*And*) village of uncivilized Indians.

malogrado ADJ (a) *plan etc* abortive; ill-fated; *esfuerzo etc* wasted. (b) *persona* who died before his time, who died early; **el ~ ministro** the late-lamented minister.

malograr [1a] [1] VT (*arruinar*) to spoil, upset, ruin; (*desperdiciar*) to waste.

[2] **malograrse** VR (a) (*plan etc*) to fail, miscarry, come to grief; (*decepcionar*) to fail to come up to expectations, not fulfil its early promise; (*And Aut, Mec*) to break down.

(b) (*persona*) to die before one's time, die early, come to an untime-

---

ly end.

malogro NM (a) (*fracaso*) failure; (*desperdicio*) waste. (b) (*muerte*) early death, untimely end.

maloliente ADJ stinking, smelly.

malón NM (a) (*Cono Sur Hist*) Indian raid. (b) (*LAm: persona*) tough, thug.

malpagar [1h] VT to pay badly, underpay.

malparado ADJ: **salir ~** to come off badly; **salir ~ de** to get the worst of.

malparar [1a] VT (*dañar*) to damage; (*estropear*) to harm, impair, wreck; (*maltratar*) to ill-treat.

malparido❖, -a NM/F son of a bitch❖, bastard❖.

malparir [3a] VT to have a miscarriage, miscarry.

malparto NM miscarriage.

malpensado ADJ nasty, evil-minded; **¡no seas ~!** don't be nasty!, don't be so horrid!*

malpensar [1j] VI: **~ de** to think ill of.

malqueda* NMF shifty sort, unreliable type.

malquerencia NF dislike.

malquerer [2t] VT to dislike.

malquerido ADJ unloved.

malquistar [1a] [1] VT: **~ a dos personas** to cause a rift between two people, set one person against another; **~ a A con B** to set A against B.

[2] **malquistarse** VR (a) (*persona*) **~ con uno** to incur the dislike of sb, become estranged from sb.

(b) (*2 personas*) to fall out, become estranged.

malquisto ADJ: **estar ~** to be disliked, be unpopular; **los dos están ~s** the two are estranged.

malrotar [1a] VT to squander.

malsano ADJ (a) *clima, atmósfera etc* unhealthy, bad. (b) (*Med*) sickly; *mente* sick, morbid.

malsín NM (*difamador*) slanderer; (*soplón*) informer, talebearer.

malsonante ADJ *palabra* nasty, rude, offensive.

malsufrido ADJ impatient.

Malta NF Malta.

malta NF malt.

malteada NF (*LAm*) malted milkshake.

malteado [1] ADJ malted.

[2] NM malting.

maltear [1a] VT to malt.

maltés, -esa [1] ADJ, NM/F Maltese.

[2] NM (*Ling*) Maltese.

maltirar [1a] VI to get by with difficulty, scrape a living.

maltón NM, **maltoncillo** NM (*LAm Zool*) young animal; (*niño*) child.

maltraer [2o] VT (a) (*injuriar*) to insult, abuse. (b) (*maltratar*) to ill-treat.

maltraído* ADJ (*And, Cono Sur*) shabby, untidy.

maltratado ADJ *bebé, mujer* battered.

maltratamiento NM = **maltrato**.

maltratar [1a] VT (a) *persona* to ill-treat, maltreat; *mujer, hijo* to batter; *objeto* to handle roughly, knock about, damage. (b) (*t ~ de palabra*) to abuse, insult.

maltrato NM (a) (*de persona*) ill-treatment, maltreatment; (*de objeto*) rough handling, damage; (*de bebé, mujer*) battering; **~ al niño** child abuse. (b) (*injurias*) abuse, insults.

maltrecho ADJ battered, damaged; injured; **dejar ~ a uno** to leave sb in a bad way.

malucho* ADJ (*Med*) poorly, under the weather.

malura* NF (*Cono Sur*) (*dolor*) pain, discomfort; (*malestar*) sickness, indisposition; **~ de estómago** stomach ache.

malva [1] ADJ INVAR mauve.

[2] NF mallow; **~ loca, ~ real, ~ rósea** hollyhock; **(de) color de ~** mauve; **criar ~s** (*Esp**) to be pushing up the daisies*; **ser como una ~** to be very meek and mild.

malvado [1] ADJ evil, wicked, villainous.

[2] NM villain.

malvaloca NF hollyhock.

malvarrosa NF hollyhock.

malvasía NF malmsey.

malvavisco NM (*Bot*) marshmallow.

malvender [2a] VT to sell off cheap, sell at a loss.

malversación NF embezzlement, misappropriation.

malversador(a) NM/F embezzler.

malversar [1a] VT (*Fin*) to embezzle, misappropriate; (*distorsionar*) to distort.

Malvinas: Islas NFPL **~** Falkland Isles.

malvinés [1] ADJ of the Falkland Islands.

[2] NM, **malvinesa** NF Falkland islander.

malviviente NMF (*Méx*) = **maleante**.

malvivir [3a] VI to live badly, live poorly; **malviven de lo que pueden** they get along as best they can.

malvón NM (*Cono Sur*) geranium.

mama NF (*Bio*) mammary gland; (*de mujer*) breast; (*de vaca etc*) udder.

mamá NF (a) (*) mummy*, mum*, mamma (*US**), mom (*US**). (b) (*LAm*) mother; **futura ~** expectant mother, mother-to-be; **~ grande, ~ señora** grandmother.

mamacallos NMF INVAR (*Esp*) useless person.

mamacita NF (*LAm*) (a) (*madre*) mum*. (b) (*apelativo*) ¡hola **~!** hello gorgeous* !

mamacona‡ NF (*And*) old lady.

mamada NF (a) (*chupada*) suck; (*leche*) milk; (*hora*) feeding time; (‡) blow job‡. (b) (*LAm**) (*cosa fácil*) cinch‡; (*prebenda*) soft job, sinecure; (*ganga*) bargain. (c) (*Cono Sur*: *borrachera*) drunkenness.

mamadera NF (*CAm, Cono Sur*: *tetilla*) rubber teat; (*LAm*: *biberón*) feeding-bottle; **~s**‡ boobs‡.

mamado‡ ADJ (a) (*LAm*: *borracho*) drunk. (b) (*Carib*: *tonto*) silly, stupid. (c) (*: fácil*); (*sencillo*) dead simple.

mamagrande NF (*Cono Sur, Méx*) grandmother.

mamaíta* NF = **mamá (a)**.

mamalón ADJ (*Carib*) idle; sponging.

mamamama* NF (*And*) grandma*.

mamandurria* NF (*prebenda*) cushy job‡; (*sueldo*) fat salary; (*gajes*) rich pickings.

mamantear [1a] VT (*LAm*) (a) (*mamar*) to nurse, feed, suckle. (b) (*fig*) to spoil, pamper.

mamaón NM (*Méx Culin*) tipsy cake.

mamar [1a] **1** VT (a) *leche, pecho* to suck.

(b) (*fig*) to absorb, assimilate; to acquire in infancy; **nació mamando el oficio** he was born to the trade.

(c) (*) *comida* to wolf, bolt; *recursos etc* to milk, suck dry; *fondos* to pocket (illegally); (*beber*) to booze*, drink; ¡**cómo la mamamos!** this is the life!, we never had it so good!

(d) (‡) to suck off‡.

2 VI (a) (*lit*) to suck; **dar de ~ a** to feed, suckle.

(b) (*: obtener gratis*) to get something for free*.

(c) ¡**no mames!** (*Méx*‡) come off it!*, don't give me that!*

(d) (*beber*) to booze*, drink.

3 mamarse* VR (a) *puesto, ventaja etc* to wangle*, fiddle*; (*conseguir*) to land, manage to get.

(b) **~ un susto** to give o.s. a scare.

(c) **~ a uno** (*madrugar a*) to get the better of sb; (*And, Cono Sur**: *engañar*) to cheat sb; (*CAm*‡: *matar*) to do sb in‡.

(d) (*: emborracharse*) to get tight*.

(e) (*And*) to go back on one's word.

mamario ADJ mammary.

mamarracha NF, **mamarracho** NM grotesque object, ridiculous sight; mess, botch; (*persona*) sight, object, scarecrow; (*Arte*) daub; **estaba hecha un ~** she looked a complete mess.

mamá-señora NF (*LAm*) grandmother.

mambo NM (*Mús*) mambo.

mamela* NF bribe, backhander*; (*por callar*) hush-money.

mameluca NF (*Cono Sur*) whore.

mameluco NM (a) (*Hist*) Mameluke. (b) (*LAm*) Brazilian mestizo, half-breed. (c) (*: idiota*) chump*, idiot. (d) (*LAm*: *t* **~s**) (*de niño*) rompers; (*de trabajo*) overalls.

mameo* NM: **cogerse un ~** to get plastered*, get smashed*.

mamerto, -a NM/F twit*, idiot.

mamey NM (*LAm*) mamey; **ser ~ colorado** (*Carib**) to be out of this world.

mameyal NM (*LAm*) mamey plantation.

mamífero **1** ADJ mammalian, mammal (*atr*).

2 NM mammal.

Mammón NM (*Bib, fig*) Mammon.

mamografía NF mammography.

mamola NF chuck under the chin; **dar** (o **hacer**) **la ~ a uno** to chuck sb under the chin; (‡) to make a sucker out of sb‡.

mamón **1** ADJ (a) *niño* small, baby, suckling.

(b) (*Méx**) (*bruto*) thick*; (*engreído*) cocky*.

2 NM (a) (*bebé*) small baby, baby still at the breast.

(b) (‡: *idiota*) berk‡, idiot.

(c) (‡: *gorrón*) scrounger*; (*indeseable*) rotter*, swine.

(d) (*Bot*) sucker, shoot.

(e) (*And, Cono Sur*) (*árbol*) papaya tree; (*fruta*) papaya.

(f) (*Cono Sur, Méx*) suck.

(g) (*CAm*) club, stick.

(h) (*Méx Culin*) soft spongecake.

mamonada‡ NF: **eso es una ~** that's bloody stupid‡.

mamoncete‡ NM (little) bastard‡.

mamonear [1a] VT (a) (*CAm*) to beat. (b) (*Carib*) (*aplazar*) to postpone; *tiempo* to waste.

mamotrético ADJ gigantic; unwieldy.

mamotreto NM (a) (*libro*) hefty tome, whacking great book*; (*fig*) monstrosity, vast useless object. (b) (*LAm**) (*aparato*) contraption;

(*bulto*) lump; (*coche viejo*) old crock, jalopy. (c) (*Méx*‡: *inútil*) dead loss.

mampara NF screen; partition.

mamparo NM (*Náut*) bulkhead.

mamplora‡ NM (*CAm*) queer‡.

mamporrera* NF madame, brothel-keeper.

mamporro* NM bash*, punch, clout; (*al caer*) bump; **atizar un ~ a uno** to give sb a swipe; **liarse a ~s con uno** to come to blows with sb.

mampostería NF masonry; (*sin labrar*) rubblework.

mampuesto NM (a) (*piedra*) rough stone. (b) (*muro*) wall, parapet. (c) (*LAm*) rest. (d) **de ~** spare, emergency (*atr*), extra.

mamúa‡ NF (*Cono Sur*) drunkenness.

mamut NM, PL **mamuts** mammoth.

mana NF (a) (*And, CAm*: *fuente*) spring, fountain. (b) (*LAm*) = **maná**.

maná NM manna.

manada NF (a) (*Zool*) herd, flock; (*de lobos*) pack; (*de leones*) pride. (b) crowd, mob; **a ~s, en ~** in a mob; in crowds.

manadero NM shepherd, herdsman, drover.

mánager ['manaʒer] NM, PL **mánagers** ['manaʒer] (*Dep, Teat etc*) manager.

managua **1** ADJ INVAR of Managua.

2 NMF native (o inhabitant) of Managua; **los ~s** the people of Managua.

manantial **1** ADJ: **agua ~** running water, flowing water.

2 NM (a) (*manantial*) spring, fountain; **~ termal** hot spring; **agua de ~** spring water. (b) (*fig*) source, origin; cause.

manantío ADJ running, flowing.

manar [1a] **1** VT to run with, flow with; **~ sangre** to run with blood; **la herida manaba sangre** blood flowed from the wound.

2 VI (a) (*líquido*) to run, flow (*de* from, *en* with); to pour out, stream, gush forth; to well up.

(b) (*fig*) to abound, be plentiful; **~ de** to spring from, flow from; **~ en** to flow with, abound in.

manatí NM manatee.

mánayer NM (*Dep*) manager.

manaza NF (a) (*mano*) great big hand; dirty hand. (b) **ser (un) ~s** to be clumsy.

manazo NM punch, slap.

mancar [1g] **1** VT (a) (*mutilar*) to maim, cripple. (b) (*Cono Sur*) **~ el tiro** to miss.

2 VI (*And**) (*Escol*) to fail; (*fracasar*) to blow it‡.

mancarrón NM (a) (*Cono Sur*: *caballo*) worn-out horse, nag. (b) (*And, Cono Sur*: *obrero*) disabled workman. (c) (*And, Cono Sur*: *presa*) small dam.

manceba NF lover, mistress; concubine.

mancebía NF (††: *burdel*) brothel.

mancebo NM (a) (*joven*) youth, young man. (b) (*soltero*) bachelor. (c) (*Com*) clerk; (*Farm*) assistant, dispenser.

mancera NF plough handle.

mancha NF (a) (*Zool etc*) spot, mark; speckle; (*en diseño*) spot, fleck; (*de suciedad*) spot, stain, mark; (*de tinta etc*) blot, smudge; (*Med*) spot; bruise, mark; (*vegetación etc*) patch, small area; (*Arte*) shading, shaded area; **~ de petróleo** oil slick; **~ solar** sunspot; **~s del sarampión** measles spots; **propagarse como una ~ de aceite** to spread like wildfire.

(b) (*fig*) stain, stigma; blemish, blot; **sin ~** unblemished.

(c) (*And, Carib*) cloud, swarm (*of locusts etc*); (*de gente*) swarm.

manchado ADJ *piel* spotty; *animal* spotted; dappled; pied; *papel etc* smudged, smudgy, covered with smudges (*etc*); **un abrigo ~ de barro** a coat stained (o bespattered) with mud.

manchar [1a] **1** VT (a) (*marcar*) to spot, mark; (*ensuciar*) to soil, dirty, stain; *tinta* to smudge.

(b) (*fig*) *honor etc* to stain, sully; *persona* to soil; **~ a otro** to smear sb else's reputation.

2 mancharse VR (a) (*ensuciarse*) to get dirty.

(b) (*fig*) to stain one's reputation; to dirty one's hands, soil o.s.

manchego **1** ADJ of La Mancha.

2 NM, **manchega** NF native (o inhabitant) of La Mancha; **los ~s** the people of La Mancha.

mancheta NF (*de libro*) blurb; (*de periódico*) masthead.

manchón[1] NM large stain, big spot (*etc*), patch; (*Bot*) patch of dense vegetation.

manchón[2] NM (*Cono Sur*) muff.

Manchuria NF Manchuria.

manchuriano, -a ADJ, NM/F Manchurian.

mancilla NF stain, blemish; **sin ~** unblemished, (*Rel*) immaculate, pure.

mancillar [1a] VT *honor* to stain, sully.

manco **1** ADJ (a) (*de una mano*) one-handed; (*de un brazo*) one-armed; (*sin brazos*) armless; (*tullido*) crippled, maimed, disabled; **~ de la izquierda** with a maimed left hand, lacking a left hand.

(b) (*fig*) defective, faulty.

(c) no ser ~ (*útil*) to be useful, be active; (*****: *largo de uñas*) to be light-fingered; (*sin escrúpulos*) to be quite unscrupulous; **A, jugador que tampoco es ~ A**, who is a pretty useful player; **no ser ~ en** not to be backward in, not be lacking in skill (*etc*) in.

2 NM, **manca** NF **(a)** (*tullido*) cripple, disabled person; (*de un brazo*) one-armed person; (*de una mano*) one-handed person.

(b) (*Cono Sur: caballo*) old horse, nag.

mancomún: de ~ ADV, *t* **mancomunadamente** ADV (*junto*) jointly, conjointly, together; (*de común acuerdo*) by common consent; **obrar de mancomún con uno** to act jointly with sb.

mancomunado ADJ joint, jointly held.

mancomunar [1a] 1 VT *personas* to unite, associate, bring together; *intereses* to combine; *recursos* to pool; (*Jur*) to make jointly responsible.

2 **mancomunarse** VR to unite, merge, combine, join together.

mancomunidad NF union, association; pool; community; (*Pol*) commonwealth; (*Jur*) joint responsibility; **la M~ Británica** the British Commonwealth.

mancornar [1l] VT **(a)** *toro* to seize by the horns; to hobble. **(b)** (*fig*) to join, couple.

mancornas NFPL (*LAm*), **mancuernas** NFPL (*Méx*), **mancuernillas** NFPL (*CAm, Méx*) cufflinks.

manda NF **(a)** (*legado*) bequest. **(b)** (*LAm*) religious vow.

mandadero NM messenger; errand boy, office boy.

mandado NM **(a)** (*orden*) order; (*recado*) commission, errand, job; **muchacho de ~s** errand boy, office boy; **hacer los ~s, ir a los ~s** to run errands. **(b)** (*****: *golpe*) bash*****, sock*****.

mandamás* NM INVAR big shot*****.

mandamiento NM **(a)** (*orden*) order, command. **(b)** (*Jur*) writ; warrant; **~ de entrada y registro** search warrant; **~ judicial** warrant; **~ de venir** summons. **(c)** (*Ecl*) commandment; **los diez ~s** the Ten Commandments.

mandanga NF **(a)** (*****: *cualidad*) calmness, self-possession. **(b)** (*****: *cuento*) tale, story; excuse; **¡no me vengas con ~s!*** who are you trying to kid?***** **(c)** (*****: *golpe*) bash*****. **(d)** (*****: *droga*) pot*****, hash*****.

mandanguero, -a* NM/F pot-smoker*****; dealer in pot*****.

mandar [1a] 1 VT **(a)** (*ordenar*) to order; **~ que ...** to order that ..., give orders that ...; **~ a uno hacer algo** to order sb to do sth; **~ hacer un traje** have a suit made, to order a suit; **~ reparar el coche** to have (*o* get) the car repaired; **~ llamar a uno** to send for sb; **~ salir a uno** to order sb out; **mándele sentarse** please ask him to take a seat.

(b) (*Com*) to order, ask for; **¿qué manda Vd?** what can I do for you?; **¿manda Vd algo más?** is there anything else?

(c) (*Mil etc*) to lead, command; *grupo* to be in charge of, lead, be the leader of.

(d) (*enviar*) to send; **le manda muchos recuerdos** he sends you warmest regards; **se lo mandaremos por correo** we'll send it to you by post, we'll post it to you.

(e) (*legar*) to bequeath.

(f) (*LAm*) (*echar*) to throw, hurl; (*tirar*) to throw away.

(g) (*LAm*) *golpe* to give, strike, fetch; *persona* to hit, punch.

(h) (*LAm*: *caballo*) to break in.

(i) (*Cono Sur Dep*) to start.

2 VI **(a)** (*ser el jefe*) to be in charge, be in command; to be in control; **¿quién manda aquí?** who's in charge here?; **aquí mando yo** I give the orders here, I'm the boss.

(b) (*dar órdenes*) to give the orders; **¡mande Vd!** at your service!; **¿mande?** pardon?, what did you say?; (*Méx*) yes sir? (*etc*), what can I do for you?; (*LAm: en restaurante*) what will you have?; **¡mande!** (*And, Méx*) I beg your pardon!; **~ por uno** to send for sb, fetch sb.

(c) (*pey*) to be bossy, boss people about.

3 **mandarse** VR **(a)** (*Med*) to get about by o.s., manage unaided.

(b) (*Arquit: cuartos*) to communicate (*con* with).

(c) (*Carib, Cono Sur*) (*irse*) to go away, slip away; (*desaparecer*) to disappear secretly.

(d) **~ algo** (*LAm******) (*comerse*) to scoff sth*****; (*beberse*) to knock sth back*****.

(e) **~ una sinfonía** (*Cono Sur: Mús*) to play (*o* perform) a symphony.

(f) (*LAm*) **mándese entrar** (*o* **pasar**) please come in; **~ cambiar**, **~ mudar** to go away, leave; (*****) to get out; **~ con uno** to be rude to sb, be bossy to sb.

mandarín NM (*lit*) mandarin; (*pey*) petty bureaucrat, jack-in-office; (*LAm*) little Hitler.

mandarina NF **(a)** (*Bot*) tangerine, mandarin (orange); **¡chúpate esa ~!** (*Esp******) get that!*****, hark at him! (*etc*). **(b)** (*Ling*) Mandarin.

mandarino NM mandarin (orange) tree.

mandatario NM **(a)** (*Jur*) agent, attorney. **(b)** (*Pol*) leader; political figure; **primer ~** head of state.

mandato NM **(a)** (*orden*) order; (*Jur*) writ, warrant; (*Inform*) command; **~ judicial** (search) warrant; **~ de prisión** warrant of arrest.

(b) (*Jur: poder*) power of attorney.

(c) (*Pol: gobierno*) mandate; **territorio bajo ~** mandated territory.

(d) (*Pol: período*) term (of office); period of rule; **durante su ~** during his term of office.

(e) (*Ecl*) maundy.

(f) **~ internacional** (*Correo*) international money order.

(g) (*de comisión*) terms of reference, brief; **pero eso no forma parte de mi ~** but that is not in my brief.

mandíbula NF jaw (*t Téc*), mandible; **reírse a ~ batiente** to laugh one's head off.

mandil NM (*de albañil*) (leather) apron; (*de mujer*) pinafore dress; (*Cono Sur*) horse-blanket.

mandilón NM **(a)** (*babi*) smock, pinafore dress. **(b)** (*overol*) overalls. **(c)** (*****) coward.

mandinga 1 ADJ **(a)** (*CAm, Cono Sur******: *afeminado*) effeminate. **(b)** (*Carib, Cono Sur: travieso*) impish, mischievous.

2 NM **(a)** (*LAm*) (*diablo*) devil; (*duende*) goblin; evil spirit. **(b)** (*And, Carib: negro*) Black.

mandioca NF cassava, tapioca, manioc.

mandiocal NM (*LAm*) cassava plot.

mando NM **(a)** (*Mil etc*) command; (*de país etc*) rule; control; authority; (*liderazgo*) leadership; **alto ~** high command; **~ supremo** commander-in-chief; **un oficial al ~ de un pelotón** an officer in command of a squad; **un pelotón al ~ de un oficial** a squad under the command of (*o* led by) an officer; **ejercer el ~, estar al ~, tener el ~** to be in command, be in control; **entregar el ~** to hand over command (*o* control).

(b) (*en carrera*) lead; **tomar el ~** to take the lead.

(c) **~s** (*personas*) leaders, leadership, top people.

(d) (*Mec*) drive; **~ a la izquierda** left-hand drive.

(e) (*Mec*) control; **~ a distancia, ~ remoto** remote control; **con ~ a distancia** remote-controlled; **~ por botón, ~ de teclado** push-button control; **palanca de ~** control lever, (*Aer*) joystick; **retrovisor de ~ interior** wing-mirror controlled from inside the car; **~ selector** control knob.

(f) **~s** (*Rad, Téc etc*) controls.

(g) (*Pol etc*) term of office.

mandoble NM **(a)** (*golpe*) two-handed blow, powerful blow (with a sword). **(b)** (*espada*) large sword, broadsword. **(c)** (*****) ticking-off*****.

mandolina NF mandolin(e).

mandón 1 ADJ bossy, domineering.

2 NM (*Cono Sur*) mine foreman; (*Dep*) starter.

mandonear* [1a] VT: **~ a uno** to boss sb around.

mandrágora NF mandrake.

mandria 1 ADJ worthless.

2 NM useless individual, weakling.

mandril¹ NM (*Zool*) mandrill.

mandril² NM (*Téc*) mandrel.

manduca* NF grub*****.

manducar* [1g] VT to scoff*****, stuff oneself with.

manducatoria* NF grub*****.

manea NF hobble.

maneador NM (*Cono Sur, Méx*) hobble; (*Cono Sur*) whip; (*Méx*) halter.

manear [1a] 1 VT to hobble.

2 **manearse** VR (*And, Méx*) to trip over one's own feet.

manecilla NF **(a)** (*Téc*) pointer, hand; (*de reloj*) hand; **~ grande** minute hand; **~ pequeña** hour hand. **(b)** (*de libro*) clasp.

maneco ADJ (*Carib, Cono Sur, Méx*) (*tullido*) maimed; (*de manos*) with deformed hands; (*de pies*) with deformed feet; (*patizambo*) knock-kneed.

manejabilidad NF manageability; handiness; manoeuvrability.

manejable ADJ manageable; *herramienta etc* handy, easy to use; (*Aer etc*) manoeuvrable.

manejador(a) NM/F (*Méx Aut*) driver, motorist.

manejar [1a] 1 VT **(a)** *caballo, herramienta, lengua etc* to handle; *máquina* to run, work, operate; *casa, empresa etc* to run, manage.

(b) *persona* to manage; to push around; **ella maneja a su marido** she manages her husband, she bosses her husband about.

(c) (*LAm Aut*) to drive.

2 VI **(a)** '**~ con cuidado**' 'handle with care'.

(b) (*LAm*) to drive.

3 **manejarse** VR **(a)** (*comportarse*) to act, behave.

(b) (*Esp: arreglárselas*) to manage; **se maneja bien con los chiquillos** she manages all right with the kids; **¿cómo te manejas para hacer eso?** how do you manage to do that?, how do you set about doing that?; **ya se manejarán** they'll manage, they'll find a way.

(c) (*Med*) to get about unaided.

manejo NM **(a)** (*acto*) handling; running, working, operation; management; (*de lengua*) command; **~ de crisis** crisis management; **~ a distancia** remote control; **~ doméstico, ~ de la casa** housekeeping, running the house; **una casa de fácil ~** an easily-run house, a house which is easy to run; **llevar todo el ~ de** to be in sole charge of; **tiene un buen ~ del alemán** she has a good command of German.

(b) (*seguridad*) confidence, ease of manner; (*perspicacia*) savoir-faire, shrewdness; **no tiene bastante ~** he's not sufficiently wide-awake.

(c) (*prontitud*) address, quickness, speed of action; **hay que ver el ~ que tiene la chica** you should see how quick the girl is.

(d) (*pey*) intrigue; stratagem; (*de cifras etc*) fiddling*; (*negocio turbio*) shady deal; **~s turbios** intrigues, underhand dealing.

(e) (*LAm Aut*) driving.

▼ **manera** NF **(a)** (*modo*) way, manner, fashion; **~ de obrar** way of going about things; conduct; **~ de ser** way of life; behaviour, manner (*of person*); **es su ~ de ser** that's the way she is; **no me gusta su ~ de ser** I don't like his way of doing things; **hay varias ~s de hacerlo** there are various ways of doing it; **no hay ~** there's no solution, there's nothing one can do; **no hay ~ con él** he's hopeless; **no hay ~ de** + *infin* there's no way of + *ger*; **no había ~ de persuadirle** there was no convincing him; **¡qué ~ de** + *infin*!, **¡vaya una ~ de** + *infin*! what a way to + *infin*!

▼ **(b)** (*locuciones con* PREP) **a la ~ de** in the manner of, after the fashion of; **siguen arando a la ~ de los abuelos** they still plough as their grandfathers did; **a mi ~ de ver** in my view, as I see it; **de esta ~** (in) this way, like this; **¡llovía de una ~!** it was just pouring!, you should have seen how it rained!; **de la ~ que sea** in whatever way you (*etc*) like; however he (*etc*) does it; **la pegó de mala ~** he hit her really hard; **le han estafado de mala ~** they really have cheated him, they've properly done him down; **de la misma ~** in the same way; **de otra ~** otherwise, if not; **de alguna ~** somehow; in a way; **de ninguna ~** by no means; **¡de ninguna ~!** certainly not!, never!; **de tal ~ que ...** in such a way that ...; to such a degree that ...; **de ~ que ...** so that ...; **¿de ~ que esto no le gusta?** so you don't like it?; **de todas ~s** at any rate; **en cierta ~** up to a point, to some degree; **en gran ~** in great measure; greatly, extremely; **sobre ~** exceedingly; *para otras locuciones V* **modo** (**a**) *y* (**b**).

(c) (*liter*) kind, sort; **es otra ~ de afirmación** it is another kind of affirmation; it is another method of saying yes; **que es otra ~ de valentía** which is another kind of courage.

(d) (*Arte, Liter etc*) manner, style; **la segunda ~ de Picasso** Picasso's second manner; **las dos ~s de Góngora** the two styles of Góngora.

(e) (*modales*) **~s** manners; **buenas ~s** good manners; **de ~s muy groseras** with very bad manners; **se lo dije con buenas ~s** I told him politely; **tener ~s** (*LAm*) to have good manners, be well-mannered.

MANERA, FORMA, MODO

De manera + ADJETIVO

- Cuando *de manera* + ADJETIVO añade información sobre una acción, la traducción más frecuente al inglés es un adverbio terminado en *-ly*. En inglés este tipo de adverbio es mucho más común que el equivalente *-mente* español:

  Todos estos cambios ocurren de manera natural
  All these changes happen naturally
  La Constitución prohíbe de manera expresa la especulación inmobiliaria
  The Constitution expressly forbids speculation in real estate

- *De manera* + ADJETIVO también se puede traducir por *in a* + ADJETIVO + *way* si no existe un adverbio terminado en *-ly* que equivalga al adjetivo:

  Se lo dijo de manera amistosa
  He said it to her in a friendly way

- En los casos en que se quiere hacer hincapié en la manera de hacer algo, se puede utilizar tanto un adverbio en *-ly* como la construcción *in a* + ADJETIVO + *way*, aunque ésta última posibilidad es más frecuente:

  Tienes que intentar comportarte de manera responsable
  You must try to behave responsibly or in a responsible way
  Ellos podrán ayudarte a manejar tu negocio de manera profesional
  They'll be able to help you run your business professionally or in a professional way

  Para otros usos y ejemplos ver las entradas manera, forma y modo.

---

maneta NF lever.

maneto ADJ (*And, CAm, Carib*) = **maneco.**

manflor(ita) NM (*LAm*) pansy, queer.

manga NF **(a)** (*Cos*) sleeve; **~ de camisa** shirtsleeve; **estar en ~s de camisa** to be in one's shirtsleeves; **sin ~s** sleeveless; **bajo ~** under the counter; **estar de ~** to be in league; **~ ancha** tolerance, tolerant attitude; lenience; broad-mindedness; **ser de ~ ancha, tener ~ ancha** to be easy-going, be overindulgent, be too lenient; to be broadminded; (*pey*) to be not overscrupulous; **andar ~ por hombro** to be a mess, be all over the place; **hacer ~s y capirotes de uno** to ignore sb completely; **pegar las ~s** to kick the bucket; **traer algo por la ~** to have something up one's sleeve.

(b) (*t* **~ de riego**) hose, hosepipe; **~ de incendios** fire hose.

(c) (*Culin*) cloth strainer.

(d) (*Aer*) windsock, windgauge; **~ de mariposas** butterfly-net.

(e) (*bolso*) travelling bag.

(f) (*Met*) cloudburst; **~ marina** waterspout; **~ de viento** whirlwind.

(g) (*Náut*) beam, breadth.

(h) (*Dep*) leg, round; (*de competición*) section; (*Tenis*) set; (*Bridge*) game; **~ clasificatoria** qualifying round; **~ de consolación** play-off among runners-up.

(i) (*LAm: multitud*) crowd, mob, swarm.

(j) (*LAm Agr*) corral entrance.

(k) (*CAm*) poncho, coarse blanket; **~ de agua** rain cape.

(l) (*And*) pasture.

(m) (*Méx*: *preservativo*) condom, sheath.

mangal NM (*LAm*) **(a)** = **manglar.** **(b)** (*Méx*: *trampa*) dirty trick. **(c)** (*And*: *plantío*) mango plantation.

mangana NF lasso, lariat.

mangancia NF **(a)** (*timo*) swindle, racket; (*ratería*) shoplifting; (*gorronería*) scrounging*. **(b)** (*cuento*) story, fib.

manganear [1a] **1** VT (*coger con lazo*) to lasso; (*CAm, Cono Sur*) (*saquear*) to pillage, plunder; (*: robar*) to pinch*, lift*. **2** VI (*Carib*) to loaf, hang about.

manganeso NM manganese.

manganeta NF (*LAm*), **manganilla** NF (*Méx*) disappearing trick; (*fig*) swindle, dodge, racket.

mangante **1** ADJ brazen. **2** NM (*mendigo*) beggar; (*gorrón*) scrounger*, freeloader*; (*ladrón*) thief; (*ratero*) shoplifter; (*vago*) loafer, layabout; (*caradura*) rotter*, villain.

manganzón ADJ (*LAm*) lazy.

mangar [1h] **1** VT **(a)** (*robar*) to pinch*, lift*. **(b)** (*mendigar*) to beg (for), scrounge*. **2** VI (*robar*) to pilfer; to shoplift; (*Cono Sur*) to scrounge*.

mangazón ADJ (*LAm*) lazy.

manglar NM mangrove swamp.

mangle NM mangrove.

mango[1] NM **(a)** (*Bot*) mango. **(b)** (*Cono Sur*) dough. **(c)** (*Méx*) good-looking lad.

mango[2] NM handle, haft; **~ de escoba** broomstick, (*Aer*) joystick; **~ de pluma** penholder.

mangón NM (*And*) (*prado*) pasture; (*estancia*) cattle ranch.

mangoneador NM **(a)** (*entrometido*) meddler, interfering sort; (*mandón*) bossy individual. **(b)** (*LAm*) corrupt official, grafter.

mangonear [1a] **1** VT **(a)** *persona* to manage, boss about.
(b) (*robar*) to pinch*, lift*.
(c) (*LAm: saquear*) to pillage, plunder.
2 VI **(a)** (*entrometerse*) to meddle, interfere (*en* in); (*interesarse*) to dabble (*en* in).
(b) (*ser mandón*) to boss people about; to run everything, take charge and insist on doing everything oneself.
(c) (*LAm*) to graft*, be on the fiddle*; (*Pol*) to fix things, fiddle the results*.

mangoneo NM **(a)** (*entrometimiento*) meddling, interference. **(b)** (*con personas*) bossing people about; personal dominance; brazenness. **(c)** (*LAm*) graft*, fiddling*; (*Pol*) fixing, fiddling of results*.

mangoneón, **mangonero** **1** ADJ meddlesome, interfering; bossy; brazen. **2** NM busybody; bossy individual; brazen sort.

mangosta NF mongoose.

manguear [1a] **1** VT (*Cono Sur, Méx*) *ganado* to drive; *caza* to beat, put up. **2** VI **(a)** (*And, Carib*: *gandulear*) to skive. **(b)** (*Cono Sur*: *sablear*) to scrounge money*.

mangueo NM thieving; scrounging*.

manguera NF **(a)** (*de riego*) hose, hosepipe; (*tubo*) pipe, tube; **~ antidisturbios** water-cannon; **~ de aspiración** suction pump; **~ de incendios** fire hose.
(b) (*And*) bicycle tyre, inner tube.
(c) (*Met*) waterspout.
(d) (*Cono Sur*) corral, yard.

mangui NM (*ladrón*) thief; small-time crook*; (*canalla*) villain, rotter*.

manguillo NM (*Méx*) penholder.

manguito NM **(a)** (*lit*) muff. **(b)** (*Téc*) sleeve; coupling; **~ incandescente** gas mantle.

mangurrina NF bash*, wallop*.

mangurrino ADJ rotten*, worthless.

manguta NM (*ladrón*) small-time thief; (*indeseable*) good-for-nothing.

mani NF demo*.

maní NM, PL **maníes** o **manises** **(a)** (*esp LAm*) peanut; groundnut plant. **(b)** (*Carib*) dough, money. **(c)** **¡~!** (*Cono Sur*) never!

manía NF **(a)** (*Med*) mania; **~ de grandezas** megalomania; **~ persecutoria** persecution mania.
(b) (*fig*) mania; (*moda*) rage, craze (*de* for); (*capricho*) whim, fad;

► LENGUA Y USO: **manera: b → 53.5**

(*peculiaridad*) peculiarity, oddity; **la ~ del fútbol** the soccer craze; **la ~ de la minifalda** the craze for miniskirts; **tiene ~s** he's rather odd, he has his little ways; **tiene la ~ de las motos** he's obsessed with motorbikes, he's bike-crazy*; **tiene la ~ de** + *infin* he has the (odd) habit of + *ger*; **ha dado en la ~ de salir sin abrigo** he's taken to going out without a coat.

(**c**) (*pey*) dislike; spite, ill will; **tener ~ a uno** to dislike sb; **el maestro me tiene ~** the teacher's got it in for me; **tiene ~ a los eslobodos** he can't stand the Slobodians.

maniabierto ADJ (*Carib*) lavish, generous.

maniaco, maníaco [1] ADJ maniac(al).

[2] NM, **maniaca** NF, **maníaca** NF maniac; **~ sexual** sex maniac.

maniacodepresivo [1] ADJ manic-depressive.

[2] NM, **maniacodepresiva** NF manic-depressive.

maniatar [1a] VT *persona* to tie the hands of; to handcuff; *animal* to hobble.

maniático [1] ADJ (**a**) (*lit*) maniacal; (*hum*) fanatical.

(**b**) (*fig*) (*chiflado*) crazy; (*excéntrico*) odd, eccentric, peculiar; cranky*; (*delicado*) fussy.

(**c**) (*terco*) stubborn.

[2] NM, **maniática** NF (**a**) (*lit*) maniac; (*hum*) fanatic; **~ de la ecología** ecology fanatic.

(**b**) (*fig*) maniac; odd individual, eccentric, crank*.

manicero, -a NM/F (*LAm*) peanut seller.

manicomio NM lunatic asylum, mental hospital.

manicura NF manicure.

manicuro, -a NM/F manicurist.

manida NF lair, den.

manido ADJ (**a**) *carne* high, gamy; smelly. (**b**) *tema etc* trite, stale.

manierismo NM (*Arte, Liter*) mannerism.

manierista ADJ, NMF mannerist.

manifa* NF demo, rally.

manifestación NF (**a**) (*de emoción etc*) manifestation; show; sign; **una gran ~ de entusiasmo** a great show of enthusiasm.

(**b**) (*declaración*) statement, declaration.

(**c**) (*Pol*) demonstration; mass meeting; rally.

(**d**) **~ de impuesto** (*Méx*) tax return.

manifestante NMF demonstrator.

▼ **manifestar** [1j] [1] VT (**a**) *emoción etc* to show, manifest, demonstrate, reveal.

▼ (**b**) *política etc* to state, declare; to express.

[2] **manifestarse** VR (**a**) (*emoción etc*) to show, be manifest; to become apparent; **~ en** to be evident in (*o* from), be revealed by, be shown by.

(**b**) (*Pol*) to demonstrate; to hold a mass meeting, hold a rally.

manifiesto [1] ADJ (*claro*) clear, manifest; (*patente*) evident, obvious; *error* glaring, obvious; *verdad* manifest; **poner algo de ~** to make sth clear; to disclose sth, reveal sth; **quiero poner de ~ que ...** I wish to state that ...; **quedar ~** to be plain, be clear.

[2] NM (**a**) (*Náut*) manifest.

(**b**) (*Pol*) manifesto.

manigua NF (*Carib, Méx*) (**a**) (*ciénaga*) swamp; (*maleza*) scrubland; (*selva*) jungle; (*fig*) countryside; **irse a la ~** (††) to take to the hills (in revolt). (**b**) **agarrar ~** (*Carib**) to get flustered.

manigual NM (*Carib*) = **manigua**.

manigueta NF (**a**) (*mango*) handle, haft; (*manivela*) crank; (*Cono Sur Aut*) starting handle. (**b**) (*maniota*) hobble.

manija NF (**a**) (*gen*) handle; (*And, Méx: de puerta*) door handle. (**b**) (*Mec*) clamp, collar; (*Ferro*) coupling. (**c**) (*Agr*) hobble. (**d**) (*Cono Sur: vaso*) mug, tankard. (**e**) (*Cono Sur Aut*) starting handle; **dar ~ a uno** to egg sb on.

Manila NF Manila.

manilargo ADJ (**a**) (*generoso*) open-handed. (**b**) (*LAm**) light-fingered, thievish.

manilense [1] ADJ of Manila.

[2] NMF native (*o* inhabitant) of Manila; **los ~s** the people of Manila.

manileño = **manilense**.

manilla NF (**a**) (*pulsera*) bracelet; **~s** (**de hierro**) handcuffs, manacles. (**b**) (*de reloj*) hand. (**c**) (*And, Méx*) door handle. (**d**) (*de tabaco etc*) bundle.

manillar NM handlebar(s).

maniobra NF (**a**) (*acto*) handling; manoeuvring; operation, control; (*Ferro*) shunting; **hacer ~s** to manoeuvre; (*Ferro*) to shunt.

(**b**) (*Náut: arte*) seamanship, (art of) navigation; handling.

(**c**) (*Náut: aparejo*) gear, rigging.

(**d**) **~s** (*Mil*) manoeuvres.

(**e**) (*fig*) manoeuvre, move; (*pey*) trick, stratagem; **~ dilatoria** delaying tactic; **mediante una hábil ~** by a clever move; **es una ~ para expulsar al jefe** it's a manoeuvre to get rid of the chief.

maniobrabilidad NF manoeuvrability; handling qualities.

maniobrable ADJ manoeuvrable; easy to handle.

maniobrar [1a] [1] VT to handle, operate; to manoeuvre; (*Ferro*) to

shunt.

[2] VI to manoeuvre (*t fig*).

maniota NF hobble.

manipulable ADJ (**a**) (*Téc*) operable, that can be operated. (**b**) *persona* easily influenced, readily manipulated.

manipulación NF manipulation.

manipulado NM handling.

manipulador(a) [1] NM/F manipulator; handler; **~ de alimentos** food-handler.

[2] NM (*Elec, Telec*) key, tapper.

manipular [1a] [1] VT to manipulate; to handle; (*pey*) to interfere with.

[2] VI: **~ con, ~ en** to manipulate.

manipulativo ADJ manipulative.

maniqueísmo NM (*Hist*) Manichenism; (*fig*) tendency to see things in black and white; **discutir sin ~s** to discuss without taking up extreme positions.

maniqueísta ADJ Manich(a)ean.

maniqueo [1] ADJ Manichean.

[2] NM, **maniquea** NF (*Hist*) Manichean; (*fig*) extremist; person who tends to see things in terms of black and white.

maniquí [1] NM (**a**) (*de sastre*) dummy, manikin; (*Esgrima etc*) dummy figure. (**b**) (*fig*) puppet.

[2] NF mannequin, model.

[3] NMF (*) poser*.

manir [3a] [1] VT *carne* to hang.

[2] **manirse** VR (*CAm*) to go off.

manirroto [1] ADJ lavish, extravagant, prodigal.

[2] NM spendthrift.

manisero NM (*LAm*) = **manicero**.

manisuelto [1] ADJ extravagant, spendthrift.

[2] NM, **manisuelta** NF spendthrift.

manita NF little hand; **~s de cerdo** (*etc*) trotters; **~s de plata** (*o de oro*) delicate hands, artistic hands, talented hands; **echar una ~ a uno** to lend sb a hand; **hacer ~s** (*amantes*) to hold hands (*con* with); **ser ~s** to be handy, be clever with one's hands.

manito¹ NM (*LAm*) pal*, buddy*; (*en oración directa*) mate*, chum*.

manito²* NM (*LAm*) = **manita**.

manivacío ADJ empty-handed.

manivela NF crank; **~ de arranque** starting handle.

manjar NM (**a**) (tasty) dish, special dish; **~ blanco** blancmange; **~ delicado, ~ exquisito** tasty morsel; **~ dulce** (*And*) fudge; **~ espiritual** food for the mind, spiritual sustenance. (**b**) (*CAm, Méx*) suit.

mano¹ NF (**a**) (*Anat*) hand; (*Zool*) foot, forefoot, paw; (*de elefante*) trunk; (*de ave*) foot, (*de halcón*) claws, talons; **~s de cerdo** pig's trotters.

(**b**) (*en locuciones, fig, gen*) hand; **~ derecha** (*fig*) right-hand man; **~ dura** harsh treatment, (*Pol*) tough policy; **Señor M~s Limpias** Mr Clean; (*Jur*) **~s muertas** mortmain; **~ de santo** sure remedy; **última ~** final touch, finishing touch; **~s de mantequilla, ~s de trapo** (*fig*) butterfingers; **¡~s a la obra!** let's get on with it!; **¡~s quietas!** hands off!, keep your hands to yourself!; **¡qué ~!** (*LAm: suerte*) what a stroke of luck!; **fue ~ de santo** it came just right, it was just what the doctor ordered; **¡~s fuera de Eslobodia!** (*slogan*) Hands off Slobodia!

(**c**) (*locuciones con* PREP) **a ~** by hand; **bordado a ~** hand-embroidered; **hecho a ~** handmade; **escribir a ~** to write in longhand, write out; **girar una manivela a ~** to turn a crank by hand; **mandar algo a ~** to send sth by hand; **estar a (la) ~** to be at hand, be on hand, be handy; to be within one's grasp; **¡eso está a la ~!** that's obvious!; **a ~ airada** violently; **robo a ~ armada** armed robbery; **a ~ salva** without risk; **estar (*o* quedar) a ~** (*LAm*) to be quits, be even; **a ~s llenas** lavishly, generously; **morir a ~s de** to die at the hands of; **llegó a mis ~s** it reached me, it came into my hands; **irse a las ~s** (*LAm*), **llegar a las ~s** to come to blows; **si a ~ viene** should the occasion arise; **votar a ~ alzada** to vote by a show of hands; **¡arriba las ~s!** hands up!; **bajo ~** in secret, behind the scenes; in an underhand way; **estar con una ~ adelante y otra atrás** to be broke; **coger a uno con las ~s en la masa** to catch sb red-handed, catch sb in the act; **de ~** hand (*atr*), *p.ej.* **equipaje de ~** hand-luggage; **los dos iban de la ~** the two were walking hand-in-hand; **llevar a uno de la ~** to lead sb by the hand; **de buena ~** on good authority; **de primera ~** (at) first-hand; **de segunda ~** (at) secondhand; **de ~s de** at the hands of; **recibir algo de ~s de uno** to receive sth from sb; **de ~s a boca** unexpectedly, suddenly; **vivir de la ~ a la boca** to live from hand to mouth; **dar de ~** to knock off*, stop working; **darse de ~s con uno** to come across sb; **dejar a uno de la ~** to abandon sb; **no pude dejar el libro de la ~** I couldn't put the book down; **ponerse de ~s** (*caballo*) to rear (up); **en ~s de** in the hands of, into the hands of; **carta en ~** letter delivered by hand; **ha hecho cuanto ha estado en su ~** he has done all in his power (*para* + *infin* to + *infin*); **traer un asunto entre ~s** to have a matter in hand; to have a matter on one's hands; **¡fuera las ~s!** hands off!, keep your hands to yourself!; **ganar por la ~ a uno** to beat sb to it; **tomarse la justicia por su ~** to take justice into one's own hands; **estar ~ sobre ~** to sit twiddling one's thumbs.

(**d**) (*locuciones con verbo*) **alzar la ~ a** (*o* **contra**) to raise one's hand against; **cargar la ~** to overdo it; to press too hard, be too exacting; (*Com*) to overcharge; (*Culin*) to put too much spice (*etc*) in; **dar una ~** (*LAm*) to lend a hand; **darse las ~s** to join hands; to shake hands on it; **echar una ~** to lend a hand (*a to*); **echar ~ a** to lay hands on; **echar ~ de** to make use of; to resort to; **estrechar la ~ a uno** to shake sb's hand; **se le fue la ~** his hand slipped (*t fig*); (*exagerar*) he overdid it; **llevarse las ~s a la cabeza** to throw one's hands in the air; **meter ~ a uno** to bring sb to book; **meter ~ a una*** (*hablando*) to make a pass at a girl*; (*tocando*) to (try to) touch up a girl‡; **no hay quien le meta ~** there's nobody to touch him; **meterle ~ a una cuestión** to take up a matter; to get a grasp on a problem; **pasar la ~ a uno** (*CAm*) to flatter sb, suck up to sb*; **pasar la ~ por la pared** (*Esp‡*) to have a feel‡; **sentar la ~ a uno** to beat sb; (*fig*) to bring sb to heel; (*Com*) to overcharge sb; **tener buena ~** to be lucky; to have the knack; **tener mala ~** to be clumsy, be awkward; **tener (mucha) ~ con** to have a way with; **tiene ~ izquierda con las mujeres** he's got a way with women; he knows what's what where women are concerned; **tener ~ para** to be clever at; **tener las ~s largas** to be light-fingered; **untar la ~ a uno** to grease sb's palm; **¡venga esa ~!** shake!, put it there!

(**e**) (*Dep*) handling, handball; **¡~!** handball!

(**f**) (*de reloj*) hand.

(**g**) (*de pintura*) coat; (*de jabón*) wash, soaping; **dar una ~ de jabón a la ropa** to give the clothes a soaping.

(**h**) (*Naipes etc*) hand; round; game; **echar una ~ de mus** to have a game (*o* hand) of *mus*; **ser ~, tener la ~** to lead; **soy ~** it's my lead.

(**i**) (*Mús*) scale.

(**j**) **~ de almirez, ~ de mortero** pestle.

(**k**) (*grupo*) lot, series; (*And, CAm, Cono Sur, Méx*) group of 5 (*o* 4, 6) things of the same kind; (*de plátanos*) bunch, hand; **una ~ de bofetadas** a series of punches; **una ~ de papel** a quire of paper.

(**l**) **~ de obra** labour, manpower; labour force; **~ de obra especializada** skilled labour.

(**m**) (*destreza*) skill, dexterity.

(**n**) (*personas*) **~s** hands, workmen; **contratar ~s** to sign up workmen.

(**o**) (*LAm*) (*desgracia*) misfortune, mishap; (*suceso imprevisto*) unexpected event.

(**p**) (*LAm Aut*) direction; **~ única** one-way street.

(**q**) **~ a ~** NM contest, struggle.

(**r**) **función ~s libres** hands-free function.

mano²* NM (*LAm: hermano*) pal*, buddy, chum*; (*en oración directa*) mate*, chum*.

manoizquierdoso ADJ knowing, cunning; sophisticated.

manojo NM handful, bunch; (*) bunch; (*Carib*) bundle of raw tobacco (*about 2 lbs*); **~ de hierba** tuft of grass; **~ de llaves** bunch of keys; **~ de pillos** bunch of rogues.

manola‡ NF needle, syringe.

manoletina NF (*Taur*) a kind of pass with the cape.

Manolo M forma familiar de **Manuel**.

manolo NM toff*, masher* (*esp Madrid: equivalent of cockney*).

manómetro NM pressure-gauge, manometer.

manopla NF (**a**) (*paño*) flannel, face-flannel. (**b**) (*guante*) mitten; (*Hist, Téc etc*) gauntlet; (*Culin*) oven-glove. (**c**) (*Carib, Cono Sur: puño de hierro*) knuckleduster. (**d**) (*Cono Sur: llave inglesa*) spanner.

manoseado ADJ (*fig*) hackneyed, well-worn.

manosear [1a] VT (**a**) (*tocar*) to handle, finger, touch; (*ajar*) to rumple, mess up; to paw*; (*jugar con*) to fiddle with, mess about with; (*LAm*) to feel up‡, touch up‡. (**b**) (*tema etc*) to overwork, repeat.

manoseo NM (**a**) handling, fingering, touching; rumpling; pawing*; (*LAm*) feeling up‡, touching up‡. (**b**) overworking, repetition.

manotada NF (**a**) (*golpe*) slap, smack. (**b**) (*And, Cono Sur, Méx*) handful, fistful.

manotazo NM slap, smack.

manoteador NM (*Cono Sur, Méx*) (**a**) (*ladrón*) thief; (*bolsista*) bagsnatcher; (*estafador*) fiddler*. (**b**) (*que hace ademanes*) gesticulator.

manotear [1a] [1] VT to slap, smack, cuff.
[2] VI to gesticulate, move (*o* use) one's hands.

manoteo NM (**a**) (*gestos*) gesticulation. (**b**) (*Méx*) (*robo*) theft, robbery; (*estafa*) fiddling*.

manque* CONJ (*esp LAm*) = **aunque**.

manquear [1a] VI to be maimed, be crippled; to pretend to be crippled; (*Cono Sur, Méx*) to limp.

manquedad NF, **manquera** NF (**a**) (*incapacidad*) disablement, crippled state, bodily incapacity. (**b**) (*fig*) defect.

mansalino ADJ (*Cono Sur*) huge; extraordinary; excellent.

mansalva: **a ~** ADV (*sin riesgo*) without risk, without any danger; (*a granel*) in abundance; (*en gran escala*) on a large scale; **le dispararon a ~** they shot at him with complete certainty of hitting him; **estar a ~ de** to be safe from.

mansamente ADV gently, mildly, meekly.

mansarda NF attic.

mansedumbre NF (**a**) (*de persona*) gentleness, meekness. (**b**) (*de animal*) tameness.

mansión NF (*esp LAm*) mansion.

manso [1] ADJ (**a**) *persona* gentle, mild, meek. (**b**) *animal* tame. (**c**) (*Cono Sur*) great, extraordinary.
[2] NM (*Esp‡*) mattress.

manta¹ NF (**a**) (*de cama*) blanket; (*chal*) shawl; **~ eléctrica** electric blanket; **~ de viaje** travelling rug; **a ~ (de Dios)** plentifully, abundantly; **a ~s** by the ton; **liarse la ~ a la cabeza** to decide to go the whole hog; to press on regardless; **tirar de la ~** to let the cat out of the bag, give the game away.
(**b**) (*And, Carib, Méx*) (*tela*) calico; (*poncho*) poncho.
(**c**) (*) hiding*.

manta²* (*Esp*) [1] ADJ bone-idle.
[2] NMF idler, slacker.
[3] NF idleness.

mantadril NM (*CAm*) denim.

mantear [1a] VT (**a**) (*lit*) to toss in a blanket. (**b**) (*Carib*) to ill-treat, abuse. (**c**) (*Carib*) to set on, beat up*.

manteca NF (**a**) (animal) fat; (*Cono Sur*) butter; **~ de cacahuete** peanut butter; **~ de cacao** cocoa butter; **~ de cerdo** lard; **~ de vaca** butter; **~ vegetal** vegetable fat.
(**b**) (‡) (*dinero*) dough‡, money; (*géneros*) goods.
(**c**) (*LAm‡*) hash*, marijuana.
(**d**) (*And*) servant, girl.

mantecada NF small cake, iced bun.

mantecado NM (*aprox: helado*) ice cream; (*pastel*) lardy cake.

mantecón* NM milksop, mollycoddle.

mantecoso [1] ADJ fat, greasy; lardy; buttery.
[2] NM (*Cono Sur*) cheese.

mantel NM tablecloth; (*Ecl*) altar cloth; **~ individual** place-mat; **una cena de ~ largo** (*Cono Sur*) a formal dinner; **levantar los ~es** to clear the table; **poner los ~es** to lay the table.

mantelería NF table linen.

mantelillo NM table runner.

mantelito NM doily.

mantención NF (*LAm*) = **manutención**.

mantenedor NM (*de certamen*) chairman, president; **~ de la familia** breadwinner.

▼ **mantener** [2k] [1] VT (**a**) (*Arquit, Téc etc*) to hold up, support; **~ algo en equilibrio** to keep sth balanced.
▼(**b**) *idea, opinión* to support, defend, maintain; *persona* to sustain, support; **mantenella y no emendalla** firm defence of a decision (*etc*).
(**c**) *fuego etc* to keep in, keep going; (*alimentar*) to sustain; **le mantiene la esperanza** he is sustained by hope, hope keeps him going.
(**d**) (*Fin*) to maintain, support.
(**e**) (*Mec etc*) to maintain, service.
(**f**) *costumbre, disciplina, relaciones etc* to keep up, maintain.
(**g**) **~ + ADJ** to keep + ADJ; **~ la comida caliente** to keep the food hot; 'Mantenga limpia España' 'Keep Spain clean'; 'mantenga su derecha' (*Aut*) 'keep to the right'.
[2] **mantenerse** VR (**a**) **se mantiene todavía en pie** it is still standing.
(**b**) **~ firme** to hold one's ground, not give way; **~ en vigor** to stand, remain in force; **~ en un puesto** to stay in one's job, keep one's post; **~ en contacto** to keep up one's contacts with.
(**c**) (*alimentarse*) to sustain o.s., subsist, keep going (*con, de* on); **se mantiene con leche** she keeps going on milk.

mantenibilidad NF ease of maintenance.

mantenido NM (*CAm, Méx*) (*chulo*) pimp; (*amante*) kept man, gigolo; (*gorrón*) sponger*, parasite.

mantenimiento NM maintenance (*t Aut, Mec*); (*Aut etc*) service, servicing; upkeep; support, sustenance; **clase de ~** keep-fit class.

manteo NM (*de hombre*) long cloak; (*de mujer*) full skirt.

mantequera NF (**a**) (*para batir*) churn. (**b**) (*de mesa*) butter dish.

mantequería NF (*lechería*) dairy, creamery; (*ultramarinos*) grocer's (shop).

mantequilla NF butter.

mantequillera NF butter-dish.

mantilla NF (**a**) (*de mujer*) mantilla; **~ de blonda, ~ de encajes** lace mantilla.
(**b**) (*de bebé*) **~s** baby clothes; **estar en ~s** (*persona*) to be terribly innocent; (*plan*) to be in the very early stages, be in its infancy; **dejar a uno en ~s** to leave sb in the dark.

▶ LENGUA Y USO: **mantener: 1b → 53.5**

mantillo NM humus, mould; mulch.

mantillón NM **(a)** (*CAm, Méx*) horse-blanket. **(b)** (*Méx**) (*amante: hombre*) kept man, (*mujer*) kept woman, mistress; (*parásito*) sponger.

mantis NF INVAR mantis; **~ religiosa** praying mantis.

manto NM **(a)** (*capa*) cloak; (*Ecl, Jur etc*) robe, gown. **(b)** (*Zool*) mantle. **(c)** (*Arquit*: *t ~* **de chimenea**) mantel. **(d)** (*Min*) layer, stratum. **(e)** (*fig*) cloak, mantle.

mantón NM shawl.

mantra NM mantra.

mantudo ADJ **(a)** *ave* with drooping wings. **(b)** (*CAm: disfrazado*) masked, in disguise.

manuable ADJ handy, easy to handle.

manual ⌐1¬ ADJ **(a)** (*lit*) manual, hand (*atr*); **habilidad ~** manual skill; **tener habilidad ~** to be clever with one's hands; **obrero ~** manual worker, worker who uses his hands; **trabajo ~** manual labour. **(b)** = **manuable**. ⌐2¬ NM manual, handbook, guide; **~ de estilo** stylebook; **~ de operación** instruction manual.

manualidad NF **(a)** (*arte*) manual craft; **~es** (*Escol*) handicraft. **(b)** (*objeto*) craft product.

manualmente ADV manually, by hand.

manubrio NM **(a)** (*manivela*) handle, crank; (*torno*) winch. **(b)** (*de bicicleta*) handlebar(s); (*LAm Aut*) steering-wheel. **(c)** (*Mús*) barrel-organ.

manudo ADJ (*LAm*) with big hands.

Manuel NM Emmanuel.

manuelita NF (*Carib*) rolled pancake.

manufactura NF **(a)** (*acto, producto*) manufacture. **(b)** (*fábrica*) factory.

manufacturado ADJ manufactured.

manufacturar [1a] VT to manufacture.

manufacturero ⌐1¬ ADJ manufacturing. ⌐2¬ NM (*LAm*) manufacturer. ⌐3¬ NM, **manufacturera** NF manufacturing company.

manumitir [3a] VT to manumit.

manú(s)⁑ NM (*Esp*) bloke⁑.

manuscrito ⌐1¬ ADJ handwritten, manuscript. ⌐2¬ NM manuscript; **~s del Mar Muerto** Dead Sea scrolls.

manutención NF **(a)** (*gen*) maintenance; (*sustento*) support; (*pensión*) keep, board. **(b)** (*Mec etc*) maintenance.

manyar⁑ [1a] VTI (*Carib, Cono Sur*) to eat.

manzana NF **(a)** apple; **~ ácida** cooking apple; **~ de la discordia** apple of discord, bone of contention; **~ de mesa** eating apple; **~ de sidra** cider apple; **~ silvestre** wild apple, crabapple.

manzanal NM **(a)** (*huerto*) apple orchard. **(b)** (*manzano*) apple tree.

manzanar NM apple orchard.

manzanilla NF **(a)** (*Bot*) camomile; camomile tea. **(b)** *a variety of small olive*. **(c)** (*jerez*) manzanilla, manzanilla sherry.

manzano NM apple tree.

maña NF **(a)** (*gen*) skill, dexterity; ingenuity; (*pey*) craft, guile; **con ~** craftily, slyly; **darse ~ para** + *infin* to contrive to + *infin*. **(b)** (*una ~*) trick, knack; (*malas*) **~s** evil ways, bad habits, vices; (*de niño etc*) naughty ways; **tiene ~ para hacerlo** he's got the knack of doing it; **es una ~ para conseguir algo** it's a trick (*o* ruse) to get sth. **(c)** (*And*) idleness; **hacer ~** to kill time. **(b)** **~ de Adán** (*LAm Anat*) Adam's apple. **(c)** (*Arquit: esp LAm*) block. **(d)** (*Cono Sur*) *land measure*, = *2.5 acres*; (*CAm*) *land measure*, = *1.75 acres*.

mañana ⌐1¬ ADV tomorrow; **~ por la ~** tomorrow morning; **¡hasta ~!** see you tomorrow!; **pasado ~** the day after tomorrow; **~ temprano** early tomorrow. ⌐2¬ NM future; **el ~ es incierto** the future is uncertain; **el día de ~** at some future time, in the future. ⌐3¬ NF **(a)** (*lit*) morning; tomorrow; **primera ~** period from 7 to 9 a.m.; **a la ~** in the morning; **a la ~ siguiente** (on) the following morning, the morning after; **a las 7 de la ~** at 7 o'clock, at 7 a.m.; **de ~, por la ~** in the morning; **muy de ~** very early in the morning; **en la ~ de hoy** this morning; **en la ~ de ayer** yesterday morning; **~ es otro día** there's a new day tomorrow. **(b)** **tomar** (*LAm: hacer*) **la ~*** to take a shot of liquor before breakfast.

mañanero ⌐1¬ ADJ early-rising, who gets up early. ⌐2¬ NM, **mañanera** NF early riser.

mañanita NF **(a)** (*madrugada*) early morning; **de ~** very early in the morning, at the crack of dawn. **(b)** (*chal*) bed jacket. **(c)** **~s** (*Méx*) serenade.

mañear [1a] ⌐1¬ VT to manage cleverly, contrive skilfully. ⌐2¬ VI to act shrewdly, go about things cunningly; (*pey*) to get up to one's tricks.

mañero ADJ **(a)** = **mañoso** (a). **(b)** (*Cono Sur*) *animal* vicious; obstinate; shy, nervous.

maño, -a ADJ, NM/F Aragonese.

mañosamente ADV cleverly, ingeniously, skilfully; (*pey*) craftily.

mañosear [1a] VI **(a)** (*And, Carib, Cono Sur*) = **mañear** 2. **(b)** (*And, Cono Sur, Méx: niño*) to be difficult, be finicky (*esp* about food).

mañoso ⌐1¬ ADJ **(a)** (*hábil*) clever, ingenious, skilful; (*pey*) sharp, crafty, wily. **(b)** (*And: perezoso*) lazy, indolent. **(c)** (*And, CAm, Cono Sur, Méx*) *animal* vicious; (*terco*) obstinate; (*tímido*) shy, nervous; (*And, Cono Sur, Méx*) difficult (*esp* about food). ⌐2¬ NM, **mañosa** NF (*CAm: ladrón*) thief.

maoísmo NM Maoism.

maoísta ADJ, NMF Maoist.

Mao Zedong NM Mao Tse-tung.

MAPA ['mapa] NM ABR *de* **Ministerio de Agricultura, Pesca y Alimentación**.

mapa NM map; **~ de carreteras** roadmap; **~ geológico** geological map; **~ hipsométrico** contour map; **~ meteorológico, ~ del tiempo** weather map; **~ mural** wall map; **~ en relieve** relief map; **el ~ político** the political scene; the political spectrum; **desaparecer del ~** to vanish off the face of the earth.

mapache NM rac(c)oon.

mapamundi NM **(a)** (*lit*) globe; world map. **(b)** (**: trasero*) bottom.

mapeado NM mapping.

mapeango ADJ, **mapiango** ADJ (*Carib, Méx*) useless, incompetent.

mapear [1a] VT (*Inform etc*) to map.

mapuche ⌐1¬ ADJ Araucanian. ⌐2¬ NMF Araucanian (Indian); *see also* |ARAUCANO| .

mapurito NM (*CAm*) skunk.

maque NM lacquer.

maquear [1a] ⌐1¬ VT to lacquer; **ir** (**bien**) **maqueado*** to be all dressed up. ⌐2¬ **maquearse** VR (***) to get ready (to go out), get dressed.

maqueta NF **(a)** model; (*a escala: Arquit*) scale model; (*Mús*) demo(nstration) tape. **(b)** (*libro*) dummy.

maquetación NF (*Prensa*) layout, design.

maquetar [1a] VT to lay out, design.

maquetear [1a] VT to lay out, design.

maquetista NMF model-maker.

maqueto NM (*pey*) immigrant worker (*in the Basque Country*).

maquiavélico ADJ Machiavellian.

Maquiavelo NM Machiavelli.

maquiladora NF (*Méx*) assembly plant.

maquilar [1a] VT (*Méx*) to assemble.

maquillador(a) NM/F (*Teat etc*) make-up artist.

maquillaje NM (*pintura*) make-up; (*acto*) making-up; **~ base, ~ de fondo** foundation make-up.

maquillar [1a] ⌐1¬ VT **(a)** to make up. **(b)** (***) *cifras, cuentas* to massage*. ⌐2¬ **maquillarse** VR to make up.

máquina NF **(a)** (*gen*) machine; (*Ferro*) engine, locomotive; (*Fot*) camera; (**: bicicleta*) bike; (*moto*) motorbike; (*Carib: coche*) car; taxi; (*de bar*) fruit-machine; **~ de afeitar** (*safety*) razor; **~ de afeitar eléctrica** electric razor, shaver; **~ de azar** gaming machine; **~ de calcular, ~ computadora** computer; **~ de contabilidad, ~ de sumar** adding-machine; **~ copiadora** copier, copying machine; **~ de coser** sewing machine; **~ de discos** jukebox; **~ electrónica, ~ tragaperras** fruit-machine, one-armed bandit; (*Com*) slot-machine; (*Mús*) jukebox; **~ de escribir** typewriter; **~ excavadora** mechanical digger; **~ expendedora** vending machine; **~ fotográfica** camera; **~ franqueadora, ~ de franquear** franking machine; **~ de lavar** washing machine; **~ ordeñadora** milking-machine; **~ para hacer punto, ~ de tricotar** knitting-machine; **~ picadora** mincer; **~ quitanieves** snowplough; **~ recreativa** game machine; **~ registradora** (*LAm*) cash-register; **~ tejedora** knitting-machine; **~ de vapor** steam engine; **a toda ~** full-speed, all-out; **hecho a ~** machine-made; *escrito* typed; **acabar a ~, coser** (*etc*) **a ~** to machine; **escribir a ~** to type; **entrar en ~** to go to press. **(b)** (*Arquit*) imposing building; edifice; structure. **(c)** (*fig*) (*maquinaria*) machinery, workings; scheme of things. **(d)** (*fig: proyecto*) plan, project.

maquinación NF machination, scheme, plot.

maquinador(a) NM/F schemer, plotter.

máquina-herramienta NF, PL **máquinas-herramientas** machine-tool.

maquinal ADJ (*fig*) mechanical, automatic.

maquinalmente ADV (*fig*) mechanically, automatically.

maquinar [1a] VTI to plot, machinate.

maquinaria NF **(a)** (*gen*) machinery; (*equipo*) plant; **~ agrícola** agricultural machinery, farm implements. **(b)** (*de reloj etc*) mechanism, works. **(c)** (*Pol*) machine.

maquinilla NF (*máquina pequeña*) small machine; (*torno*) winch;

(*tijeras*) clippers; **~ de afeitar** (safety) razor; **~ eléctrica** electric razor, shaver; **~ para liar cigarrillos** cigarette(-rolling) machine.

maquinista NM (*Ferro*) engine-driver, engineer (*US*); (*Náut etc*) engineer; (*Téc*) operator, machinist; (*Teat*) scene-shifter.

maquis NM INVAR resistance movement.

mar[1] NM Y F (a) (*gen*) sea; (*océano*) ocean; (*marea*) tide; **~ arbolada** heavy sea; **~ de fondo** groundswell; **~ gruesa** heavy sea; **~ llena** high tide; **~ rizada** choppy sea; **~ adentro, ~ afuera** out at sea, out to sea; **caer al ~** to fall into the sea, (*desde barco*) to fall overboard; **de alta ~** *barco* seagoing, ocean-going; *pesca* deepwater (*atr*); **en alta ~** on the high seas; **por ~** by sea, by boat; **arar en el ~** to labour in vain; **echar a la ~** to launch; **es hablar de la ~** it's all very vague; it's just a dream; **hacer un ~ con un vaso de agua** to make a mountain out of a molehill; **hacerse a la ~** to put to sea; to stand out to sea.

(b) **M~ Adriático** Adriatic Sea; **M~ de las Antillas, M~ Caribe** Caribbean Sea; **M~ Báltico** Baltic Sea; **M~ Caspio** Caspian Sea; **M~ Mediterráneo** Mediterranean Sea; **M~ Muerto** Dead Sea; **M~ Negro** Black Sea; **M~ del Norte** North Sea; **M~ Rojo** Red Sea.

(c) (*fig*) **un ~ de confusiones** a sea of confusion, a welter of confusion; **hay un ~ de diferencia** there's a world of difference.

(d) (*fig*) **estar hecho un ~ de lágrimas, llorar a ~es** to weep floods; **llover a ~es** to rain cats and dogs, rain in torrents.

(e) (*) **la ~** (*como ADV*) a lot; **la ~ de cosas** lots of things, no end of things, ever so many things; **es la ~ de tonto** he's no end of a fool; **es la ~ de guapa** she's awfully pretty; **está la ~ de contento** he's terribly happy.

mar[2] NF *euf de* **madre** (*in obscene expressions*).

mar[3] INTERJ (*Mil*) march!; *V* **frente** *etc*.

mar. ABR *de* **marzo** March, Mar.

mara: NF group of people, mob.

marabunta NF (a) (*de hormigas*) plague of ants. (b) (*fig*) (*daños*) havoc, ravages; (*multitud*) crowd.

maraca NF (a) (*Mús*) maraca, rattle. (b) (*Cono Sur: prostituta*) whore. (c) (*And, Carib: inútil*) dead loss.

maraco* NM (*Carib*) youngest child, baby of the family.

maracucho [1] ADJ of Maracaibo.
[2] NM, **maracucha** NF native (o inhabitant) of Maracaibo.

maracuyá NM passionfruit.

marajá NM = **maharajá**.

maraña NF (a) (*Bot*) thicket; tangle of plants. (b) (*de hilos etc*) tangle. (c) (*fig*) mess, tangle; jungle; puzzle. (d) (*: trampa*) trick, ruse. (e) (*And*) small tip.

marañero [1] ADJ scheming.
[2] NM, **marañera** NF schemer.

marañón NM (*Bot*) cashew.

maraquear* [1a] VT (*LAm*) to shake, rattle.

maraquero NM (*And, Carib*) maraca player.

marar: [1a] VT (a) (*matar*) to do in:. (b) (*pegar*) to bash*; to beat up*.

marasmo NM (a) (*Med*) wasting; atrophy. (b) (*fig*) paralysis, stagnation.

maratón NM (*a veces* F) marathon.

maratoniano [1] ADJ marathon.
[2] NM, **maratoniana** NF (*t* **maratonista** MF) marathon runner.

maravedí NM, PL **maravedís** o **maravedíes** old Spanish coin.

maravilla NF (a) (*objeto, asunto*) marvel, wonder; (*sentimiento*) wonderment; **las siete ~s del mundo** the seven wonders of the world; **hacer ~s** to work wonders; **ir a ~, ir a las mil ~s** to go wonderfully well, go extremely well; to go swimmingly; **lo hace a ~** he does it perfectly, he does it splendidly; **de ~** marvellous, wonderful; **por ~** for a wonder; by chance; very seldom.
(b) (*Bot*) marigold.

maravillar [1a] [1] VT to astonish, amaze.
[2] **maravillarse** VR to be astonished, be amazed (*con, de* at); **~ con, ~ de** to wonder at, marvel at.

maravillosamente ADV wonderfully, marvellously.

maravilloso ADJ wonderful, marvellous.

marbellí [1] ADJ of Marbella.
[2] NMF native (o inhabitant) of Marbella; **los ~es** the people of Marbella.

marbete NM (a) (*etiqueta*) label; tag, ticket, docket; **~ engomado** sticker. (b) (*Cos*) edge, border.

marca NF (a) (*gen*) mark; stamp; (*de nombre*) name tab; (*huella*) footprint, footmark; (*en papel*) watermark; (*Com*) trademark; (*Com*) make, brand; **~ de agua, ~ transparente** watermark; **~ comercial, ~ de fábrica** trademark; **~ de ley** hallmark; **~ de nacimiento** birthmark; **~ registrada** registered trademark; **de ~** excellent, outstanding; **de ~ mayor** absolutely outstanding; really big; **coches de 3 ~s distintas** cars of 3 different makes; **productos de varias ~s** various brands of products.
(b) (*Náut*) seamark; marker, buoy; landmark.
(c) (*Dep*) record; **batir la ~, mejorar la ~** to break the record; **esta-**

blecer una ~ to set up a record.
(d) (*Naipes*) bid.
(e) (*herramienta*) stamp.
(f) (*Hist*) march, frontier area; **la M~ Hispánica** the Spanish March (*Catalonia*).

marcable ADJ (*Naipes*) biddable.

marcación NF (a) (*Náut*) bearing. (b) (*Telec*) dialling; **~ automática** autodial.

marcadamente ADV markedly.

marcado [1] ADJ marked, strong, pronounced; distinct; **con ~ acento argentino** with a marked Argentinian accent.
[2] NM (a) (*de pelo*) set. (b) (*Agr*) branding. (c) (*pluma*) marker pen.

marcador NM (a) marker (*t Billar*); (*de libro*) bookmark; (*para escribir*) highlighter; **~ de caminos** roadsign. (b) (*Dep*) scoreboard; (*persona*) scorer; **~ electrónico** electronic scoreboard; **abrir el ~, inaugurar el ~** to open the scoring. (c) (*Telec*) dial.

marcaje NM (a) (*Dep*) marking; (*entrada*) tackle, tackling. (b) (*de criminal etc*) shadowing, following; **hacer ~ a uno** to shadow sb, tail sb.

marcapasos NM INVAR (*Med*) pacemaker.

▼ **marcar** [1g] [1] VT (a) (*gen*) to mark (*de* with); *ganado etc* to brand, stamp (*de* with); *tierra etc* to mark off, mark out; *ropa* to put one's name on, embroider a name on.
(b) (*fig*) (*indicar*) to mark, indicate, point to; (*cuadrante, termómetro etc*) to show, register, record, read, say; **las agujas marcan las 2** the hands point to 2 o'clock; **el tanteador marca 3 goles** the scoreboard shows 3 goals; **mi reloj marca la hora exacta** my watch is showing the exact time.
(c) *números etc* to keep a tally (o score) of, record; (*Dep*) *tanteo* to keep.
(d) (*Mús etc*) *paso* to mark; *compás* to beat, keep.
(e) (*Telec*) to dial.
(f) (*Naipes*) to bid.
(g) (*Dep*) *gol, tanto* to score (*t fig*); **~ un tanto en la discusión** to score a point in the argument.
(h) (*Dep*) *jugador contrario* to mark; (*Méx*) to tackle; *sospechoso* to shadow, tail.
(i) *tarea* to assign, set; *política* to lay down.
(j) (*Com*) to put a price on.
(k) (*Esp*) *pelo* to set, style.
[2] VI (a) (*Dep*) to score.
(b) (*Telec*) to dial.
(c) (*: jactarse*) to shoot a line*.
[3] **marcarse** VR (a) (*Náut*) to take one's bearings.
(b) (*Dep*) to score.
(c) (*) to make one's mark, stand out; **~ con relieve** to stand out in relief.
(d) **~ un rollo** (*etc*)* to go on at great length.
(e) (*pelo*) to have one's hair set (o styled).

marcha NF (a) (*Mil etc*) march; (*Pol etc*) (protest) march; **~ forzada** forced march; **~ del hambre** hunger march; **larga ~** (*Pol, fig*) long march; **a largas ~s** speedily; **a ~s forzadas** (*fig*) with all speed, as a matter of great urgency; **abrir la ~** to come first, be at the head of the procession (*etc*); **cerrar la ~** to come last, bring up the rear; **¡en ~!** (*Mil*) forward march!; (*fig*) let's go!, (*a otra persona*) get going!, get moving!; (*fig*) here goes!; **España es país en ~** Spain is a country on the move; **estar en ~** to be in motion, be going; (*Náut*) to be under way; (*fig*) to be on the move; **poner en ~** to start; (*fig*) to get going, set in motion, set on foot; **ponerse en ~** to start, get going; **comer sobre la ~** to eat as one goes along, eat along the way.
(b) (*Dep*) walk; (*excursión*) walk, hike; **~ atlética, ~ de competición** walk, walking race.
(c) (*velocidad*) speed; '**~ moderada**' (*Aut*) 'drive slowly'; **moderar la ~ de un coche** to slow a car down, reduce the speed of a car; **a toda ~** at full speed, at top speed; (*fig*) at full blast, full-blast.
(d) (*Mec*) running, working, functioning, operation; **apearse en ~** to get off while the bus (*etc*) is moving; (*:*) to withdraw; **estar en ~** to be working; to be in working order.
(e) (*Aut, Mec*) gear; speed; **~ adelante** forward gear; **~ atrás** reverse gear; **~ corta** low gear; **~ directa** top gear; **~ larga** high gear; **primera ~** first gear; **dar ~ atrás, poner en ~ atrás, invertir la ~** to reverse, put into reverse; **el coche tiene cinco ~s** the car has five gears.
(f) (*Mús*) march; **~ fúnebre** funeral march, dead march; **~ lenta** slow march; **~ nupcial** wedding march; **M~ Real** national anthem; **tiene mucha ~** it's got a good beat.
(g) (*fig*) (*progreso*) progress; (*avance*) march; (*rumbo*) trend, course; (*de huracán*) path, track; **la ~ de los acontecimientos** the march of events, the course of events; **coger la ~ de algo** to get into the way (o habit) of sth, get the hang of sth; **dar ~ atrás** to back down, back off; (*:*) to withdraw, practise coitus interruptus.
(h) (*: rollo*) **la ~** the scene, the action*; **me va la ~** I'm having a

➤ LENGUA Y USO: **marcar** → 27.1, 27.3

great time*; **no le va la** ~ he's not with it*; **pedir** ~ to be looking for the action; **la ciudad tiene mucha** ~ it's a very lively town, the town has a lot going on.
(i) (*) (*duende*) charm, magic, appeal; charisma; (*misterio*) mystery; (*inspiración*) inspiration; (*estilo*) style.
(j) (*Carib: de caballo*) slow trot.
(k) (*Méx Aut*) self-starter.
marchador(a) NM/F (*Dep*) walker.
marchamo NM label, tag; (*de aduana*) customs mark; (*fig*) stamp.
marchantaje NM (*LAm*) clients, clientèle.
marchante, -a NM/F (*a*) (*tratante*) dealer, merchant; (*LAm: ambulante*) pedlar. **(b)** (*LAm*: *cliente*) client, customer. **(c)** (*Carib*) trickster.
marchantía* NF (*CAm, Carib*) clients, clientèle.
marchar [1a] **1** VI **(a)** (*ir*) to go; (*viajar*) to move, travel; (*Mil*) to march.
(b) = marcharse; **¡marchando!** get moving!, on your way!
(c) (*Mec etc*) to go; to run, function, work; (*tren etc*) to run; **el motor no marcha** the engine isn't working, the engine won't work; **el motor marcha mal** the engine is running badly; ~ **en vacío** to tick over; **el reloj marcha atrasado** the watch is slow.
(d) (*fig*) to go, proceed; **todo marcha bien** everything is going well; **el proyecto marcha bien** the plan is coming along nicely; **el negocio no marcha** the business is getting nowhere, the deal is making no progress.
(e) (*Carib, Cono Sur: caballo*) to trot.
(f) (*Méx Mil*) to do military service.
2 marcharse VR to go (away), leave; ~ **a otro sitio** to go somewhere else, leave for another place; ~ **de la capital** to leave the capital; **¿os marcháis?** are you leaving?, must you go?; **con permiso me marcho** if you don't mind I must go.
marchista NMF (*protest*) marcher.
marchitar [1a] **1** VT to wither, fade, shrivel, dry up.
2 marchitarse VR **(a)** (*Bot*) to wither, fade, shrivel up. **(b)** (*fig*) to languish, fade away; to go into a decline.
marchitez NF withered state, faded condition.
marchito ADJ **(a)** (*lit*) withered, faded. **(b)** (*fig*) faded; in decline.
marchoso* **1** ADJ **(a)** (*moderno*) ultramodern; trendy, hip*. **(b)** (*animado*) lively, fast-living, turned-on*. **(c)** (*amigo de placeres*) fun-loving. **2** NMF go-getter.
Marcial NM Martial.
marcial ADJ *ley etc* martial; *poste, disciplina* military.
marcianitos NMPL (*juego*) space-invaders.
marciano, -a ADJ, NM/F Martian.
marco **1** NM **(a)** (*Arquit, Arte, de espejo etc*) frame; ~ **de chimenea** mantelpiece; ~ **para cuadro** picture-frame; ~ **de ventana** window-frame; **poner** ~ **a un cuadro** to frame a picture.
(b) (*Dep*) goalposts, goal.
(c) (*fig*) setting; **el paisaje ofreció un bello** ~ **para la fiesta** the countryside made a splendid setting for the festivity.
(d) (*fig: de plan etc*) framework.
(e) (*Fin*) mark.
(f) (*de pesos etc*) standard.
2 ATR: **acuerdo** ~ general framework of agreement; set of agreed guidelines; **ley** ~ framework law; **plan** ~ overall plan; **programa** ~ overall programme.
márcola NF (*prov*) pruning hook.
Marcos NM Mark.
marduga* NMF (*CAm*) tramp.
marea NF **(a)** (*lit*) tide; ~ **alta** high tide, high water; ~ **baja** low tide, low water; ~ **creciente** rising tide; ~ **menguante** ebb tide; ~ **muerta** neap tide; ~ **negra** oil spill, large oil slick; ~ **viva** spring tide.
(b) (*fig*) tide; **la** ~ **de la rebelión** the tide of revolt.
(c) (*brisa*) light sea breeze.
(d) (*llovizna*) drizzle; (*Cono Sur*) sea mist.
(e) (*período*) spell of duty at sea.
mareado ADJ: **estar** ~ **(a)** (*nauseado*) to feel sick; (*aturdido*) to feel dizzy; (*Náut*) to be (*o* feel) seasick. **(b)** (*: bebido*) to be a bit drunk.
mareaje NM **(a)** (*marinería*) navigation, seamanship. **(b)** (*rumbo*) ship's course.
marear [1a] **1** VT **(a)** (*Náut*) to sail, navigate.
(b) (*Med*) ~ **a uno** (*causar náuseas a*) to make sb feel sick; (*en mar*) to make sb seasick; (*aturdir*) to make sb feel dizzy.
(c) (*fig*) (*irritar*) to annoy, upset, disturb; (*cargar*) to burden with (useless) things to do.
(d) (*Carib, Méx*) to cheat.
2 marearse VR **(a)** (*Med*) to feel sick; to be (*o* get, feel) seasick; to feel dizzy, feel giddy; to feel faint.
(b) no te marees con esto don't bother your head about this.
(c) (*:*) to get a bit drunk; to be high*.
(d) (*Carib, Cono Sur: paño*) to fade.
marejada NF **(a)** (*Náut*) swell, heavy sea. **(b)** (*fig*) undercurrent (of unrest *etc*); wave, upsurge.

marejadilla NF slight swell.
maremagno NM, **mare mágnum** NM (*fig*) ocean, abundance; (*fig*) noisy confusion.
maremoto NM tidal wave.
marengo ADJ INVAR: **gris** ~ dark grey, dark gray (*US*).
mareo NM **(a)** (*Med*) (*náuseas*) sick feeling; (*en viaje*) travel sickness, (*en mar*) seasickness; (*aturdimiento*) dizziness, giddiness.
(b) (*fig*) (*irritación*) irritation; (*confusión*) confusion; (*nervios*) nervy state; (*aburrimiento*) boredom.
(c) (*lata*) nuisance, bore; **es un** ~ **tener que ...** it is a nuisance having to ...; **¡qué** ~ **de hombre!** what a bore that man is!
mareomotriz ADJ *energía* wave (*atr*), tidal (*atr*); **central** ~ tidal power station.
marfil NM **(a)** ivory. **(b)** (*LAm*) fine-toothed comb.
marfileño ADJ ivory, like ivory.
marga NF marl, loam.
margal NM marly patch; marlpit.
margarina NF margarine.
Margarita NF Margaret.
margarita NF **(a)** (*Zool: perla*) pearl; **echar ~s a los puercos** to cast pearls before swine.
(b) (*Zool: concha*) winkle.
(c) (*Bot*) daisy; **criar ~s*** to be pushing up the daisies*; **deshojar la** ~ (*vacilar*) to vacillate; (*juego*) to play 'she loves me, she loves me not'; **ir a coger ~s** to (*go to*) spend a penny*.
(d) (*Tip*) daisy-wheel.
(e) (*cóctel*) cocktail of tequila and fruit juice.
margen **1** NM **(a)** (*borde*) border, edge, fringe; (*de papel, Tip*) margin; **al** ~ in the margin.
(b) (*Liter*) marginal note.
(c) (*fig*) margin; (*intervalo*) gap, space; (*libertad de acción*) leeway; ~ **de beneficio**, ~ **de ganancia** profit margin; ~ **bruto** gross margin; ~ **comercial** mark-up; ~ **de credibilidad** credibility gap; ~ **de error** margin of (*o* for) error; ~ **de seguridad** safety margin; **hay un** ~ **de aproximación de 8 días** we allow a week each way; **le digo el número con un** ~ **de unos 20** I'm telling you the number, give or take about 20.
(d) (*fig*) **al** ~ **de** outside; apart from; **al** ~ **de lo que digas** despite what you may say; **dejar a uno al** ~ to leave sb out (in the cold); **mantenerse al** ~ to keep out, stand aside.
(e) (*fig*) occasion, opportunity; **dar** ~ **para** to give an opportunity for, give scope for.
2 NF (*de río etc*) bank.
marginación NF **(a)** (*acto*) exclusion, rejection. **(b)** (*estado*) isolation.
marginado **1** ADJ: **estar** ~, **quedar** ~ to be excluded, be left out; to be neglected; to be pushed aside; **sentirse** ~ to feel rejected.
2 NM, **marginada** NF outsider; outcast; drop-out; underprivileged person, poor person.
marginal ADJ marginal; (*fig*) *grupo etc* marginalized.
marginalidad NF state of being excluded (*o* rejected); state of being isolated.
marginalización NF marginalization; (*de minoría, pueblo*) exclusion.
marginalizar [1f] VT to marginalize; *minoría, pueblo* to exclude.
marginar [1a] **1** VT **(a)** *persona* to exclude, leave out, push aside; to reject; to isolate. **(b)** *página* to leave margins on. **(c)** *texto* to add marginal notes to, write marginal notes against.
2 marginarse VR to exclude oneself, isolate oneself.
margoso ADJ marly, loamy.
margullo NM (*Carib*) shoot, runner.
Mari NF *forma familiar de* **María**.
María NF Mary; ~ **Antonieta** Marie Antoinette; ~ **Estuardo** Mary Stuart; ~ **Magdalena** Mary Magdalene; **las tres ~s*** (*Colegio: Hist*) *religious, patriotic and physical training*.
maría¹ NF (*Esp: droga*) pot*, hash*.
maría² NF (*caja de caudales*) peter*, safe.
maría³* NF (*Escol*) unimportant subject; easy subject; (*fig*) soft option.
maría⁴* NF **(a)** (*pey*) housewife. **(b)** (*Méx*) migrant from the country into Mexico City.
mariachi (*Méx*) **1** NM (*música*) mariachi music; (*conjunto*) mariachi band.
2 NMF mariachi musician.

CONJUNTO MARIACHI

i   The **conjuntos mariachis**, bands of itinerant Mexican musicians, are mostly to be seen in the Plaza Garibaldi in Mexico City, wearing their traditional **charro** costumes: sequin-studded cowboy-style suits and wide-brimmed Mexican hats. Besides being a major tourist attraction, they provide music in the form of love songs for weddings, birthdays and **quinceañeras** (coming-out balls for Mexican girls who have reached their 15th birthday). The term **mariachi** is said to derive from the French word for wedding.

marial ADJ, **mariano** ADJ Marian.

marianismo NM Marianism.

maribén: NF (*Esp*) death.

marica ① NF (*Orn*) magpie.

② NM (**a**) (*) weak character; milksop, sissy*, mollycoddle. (**b**) (:) = maricón.

Maricastaña N: en los días de ~, en tiempos de ~ (*Esp*) way back, long ago; in the good old days.

maricón: NM queer:, pansy:; ¡~ el último! the last one's a sissy!*

mariconada: NF dirty trick.

mariconear: [1a] VI to act like a pansy:.

mariconeo: NM homosexual activities.

mariconera: NF (man's) handbag.

maridaje NM (**a**) (*vida*) conjugal life; (*unión*) marriage ties. (**b**) (*fig*) marriage, close association, intimate connection. (**c**) (*pey*) cohabitation; (*Pol etc*) unholy alliance.

maridar [1a] VT (**a**) (*combinar*) to combine, marry. (**b**) (*casar*) to marry.

marido NM husband.

marielito* NM (*Carib*) Cuban exile.

marihuana NF (*t* **mariguana, marijuana**) marijuana, cannabis, Indian hemp.

marijuanero ① ADJ marijuana (*atr*), cannabis (*atr*).

② NM (*cultivador*) cannabis grower; (*fumador*) marijuana smoker.

marimacha NF (*And*) = **marimacho**.

marimacho ① ADJ butch:, mannish.

② NF butch type:, mannish woman.

marimandón* ① ADJ nagging; overbearing, bossy.

② NM, **marimandona** NF bossy-boots.

marimba ① NF (**a**) (*Mús*) kind of drum; (*LAm*) marimba; (*Carib, Cono Sur*) out-of-tune instrument. (**b**) (*Cono Sur: paliza*) beating. (**c**) (*And Med*) large goitre.

② ADJ (*CAm, Carib*) cowardly.

marimoña NF buttercup.

marimorena NF (*Esp*) fuss, row, shindy*; **armar una ~** to kick up a row.

marina NF (**a**) (*Geog*) coast, coastal area.

(**b**) (*marinería*) seamanship; navigation; **término de ~** term from navigation, nautical term.

(**c**) (*barcos*) ships; **~ (de guerra)** navy; **la ~ española** the Spanish navy, the Spanish fleet; **~ mercante** merchant navy; **servir en la ~** to serve in the navy.

(**d**) (*Arte*) sea-piece, seascape.

(**e**) (*de yates*) marina, yachting harbour.

marinar [1a] VT (*Culin*) to marinade, marinate.

marinería NF (**a**) (*arte*) seamanship. (**b**) (*tripulación*) ship's crew; seamen, sailors (*collectively*).

marinero ① ADJ (**a**) = **marino**.

(**b**) *gente* sea (*atr*), seafaring.

(**c**) *barco* seaworthy.

(**d**) **a la marinera, a lo ~** in a seamanlike way; sailor-fashion.

② NM sailor, seaman; mariner, seafarer; **~ de agua dulce** landlubber; **~ de cubierta** deckhand; **~ de primera** able seaman.

③ **marinera** NF (*And*) (*baile*) Peruvian folkdance; (*música*) Peruvian folkmusic.

marinesco ADJ seamanly; **a la marinesca** in a seamanlike way; sailor-fashion.

marino ① ADJ sea (*atr*), marine; **pez ~** sea fish; **fauna marina** marine life, sea creatures.

② NM sailor, seaman; (*oficial*) Navy officer.

mariolatría NF mariolatry.

marioneta NF marionette, puppet; (*fig*) puppet; **régimen ~** puppet régime.

marionetista NMF puppeteer.

mariposa NF (**a**) (*Ent*) butterfly; **~ (nocturna)** moth; **~ de la col** cabbage-white (butterfly); **~ cabeza de muerte, ~ de calavera** death's-head moth.

(**b**) (*Natación*) butterfly stroke; **100 metros ~** 100 metres butterfly.

(**c**) (*And, CAm: juguete*) toy windmill.

(**d**) (*And*) blind-man's buff.

(**e**) (:: *gay*) pansy:, fairy:.

mariposear [1a] VI (**a**) (*revolotear*) to flutter about, flit to and fro. (**b**) (*fig: ser inconstante*) to be fickle, act capriciously; (*coquetear*) to flirt; **~ alrededor de uno** to dance attendance on sb, be constantly fluttering round sb.

mariposilla NF small moth, (*esp*) clothes-moth.

mariposo: NM gay, homosexual.

mariposón NM (**a**) (*: coqueto*) flirt, wolf*. (**b**) (:: *gay*) queer:, pansy:.

Mariquita NF *forma familiar de* **María.**

mariquita ① NF (**a**) (*Ent*) ladybird. (**b**) (*Orn*) parakeet. (**c**) (*Méx:*) hash*, pot:.

② NM (*) = **marica 2.**

marisabidilla NF know-all.

mariscada NF seafood dish.

mariscador(a) NM/F gatherer of shellfish.

mariscal NM (*Hist*) blacksmith, farrier; (*Hist: Mil*) major-general; **~ de campo** field-marshal.

mariscala NF (*woman*) marshal; (*Hist*) marshal's wife.

mariscar [1g] ① VT (:) to nick:, swipe:.

② VI to gather shellfish.

mariscos NMPL shellfish, seafood.

marisma NF marsh, swamp; mudflats.

marisqueo NM gathering shellfish, shellfishing.

marisquería NF shellfish bar, seafood restaurant.

marisquero ADJ shellfish (*atr*), seafood (*atr*); **barco ~** shellfishing boat.

marital ADJ marital.

maritatas NFPL (*Andalusia, LAm*), **maritates** NMPL (*CAm, Méx*) gear, tackle, tools; (*pey*) things, junk.

marítimo ADJ maritime; marine, sea (*atr*); *agente etc* shipping (*atr*); **ciudad marítima** seaside town, coastal town; **ruta marítima** ocean route, seaway, route by sea; **seguro ~** marine insurance.

maritornes NF INVAR (*criada*) sluttish servant; (*putilla*) wench, tart*.

marjal NM marsh, fen, bog.

márketing ['marketin] NM marketing; marketing technique(s); marketing campaign.

marmaja: NF (*Méx*) dough:, money.

marmellas: NFPL (*Esp*) tits:, breasts.

marmita NF (**a**) (*Culin*) pot; (*Mil*) mess tin; (*Méx*) kettle. (**b**) **~ de gigante** (*Geol*) pothole.

marmitón NM kitchen boy, scullion.

mármol NM marble; (*de cocina*) worktop; (*Culin*) chopping-block.

marmolejo NM small marble column.

marmolería NF: **~ funeraria** monumental masonry.

marmolista NMF monumental mason.

marmóreo ADJ marble; marmoreal.

marmosete NM (*Tip*) tailpiece, vignette.

marmota NF (**a**) (*Zool*) marmot; **~ de Alemania** hamster; **~ de América** woodchuck; **dormir como una ~** to sleep like a log. (**b**) (*fig*) sleepyhead. (**c**) (*: criada*) maid, servant.

maroma NF (**a**) (*cuerda*) rope. (**b**) (*LAm*) (*cuerda floja*) tightrope; (*actuación*) acrobatic performance; (*Carib*) circus. (**c**) (*LAm*) **~s** acrobatics, acrobatic stunts; **hacer ~s = maromear.**

maromear [1a] VI (*LAm*) (**a**) (*en cuerda floja*) to walk (on) a tightrope; to do acrobatic stunts.

(**b**) (*fig: política*) to change one's political allegiance, climb on the bandwaggon; to keep in with all parties, do a political balancing act.

maromero NM (*LAm*) (**a**) (*acróbata*) tightrope walker, acrobat. (**b**) (*fig: político*) clever politician, politician who manages to be on good terms with all parties.

maromo: NM (*Esp*) bloke:.

marona* NF: tiene 60 años y ~ (*Carib*) he's well over sixty.

marqués NM marquis.

marquesa NF marchioness.

marquesina NF (*cobertizo*) glass canopy, porch; (*techo*) glass roof, cantilever roof; (*Ferro*) roof, cab (*of locomotive*); (*de tienda de campaña*) flysheet; (*de parada*) bus-shelter.

marquetería NF marquetry, inlaid work.

márquetin NM marketing.

marquezote NM (*CAm*) sweet bread.

marquito NM slide mounting.

marrajo ① ADJ *toro* vicious, dangerous; *persona* sly.

② NM (**a**) (*Zool*) shark. (**b**) (*Méx: tacaño*) skinflint. (**c**) (*: candado*) padlock.

marramizar [1f] VI (*gato*) to howl, caterwaul.

marrana NF (**a**) (*Zool*) sow. (**b**) (*) slut.

marranada NF, **marranería** NF (**a**) (*gen*) filthiness. (**b**) (*acto*) filthy act; dirty trick, vile deed.

marrano ① ADJ filthy, dirty.

② NM (**a**) (*Zool*) pig, boar. (**b**) (*) swine*; dirty pig. (**c**) (*Hist*) Jew, converted Jew.

Marraquech NM, **Marraqués** NM Marrakesh.

marrar [1a] ① VT: **~ el tiro** to miss; **~ el golpe** to miss (with a blow).

② VI (**a**) (*gen*) to miss; (*fig*) to miss the mark. (**b**) (*fig: fallar*) to fail, miscarry, go astray; **no me marra una** everything's going well for me.

marras ADV (**a**) **de ~** old; long-standing; well-known, that you (*etc*) know all about; in question, aforementioned; **es el problema de ~** it's the same old problem; **volver a lo de ~** to go back over the same old stuff.

(**b**) **hace ~ que no le veo** (*And**) it's ages since I saw him.

marrazo NM (*pico*) mattock; (*cuchillo*) short machete; (*Méx*) bayonet.

marrocata: NF Moroccan hashish.
marrón [1] ADJ chestnut, brown; *zapatos* brown.
  [2] NM **(a)** (colour); brown.
  (b) (*Culin*) marron glacé.
  (c) (*LAm Hist*) maroon.
  (d) (*And*) curlpaper.
  (e) (*Carib*) coffee with milk.
  (f) (*Fin:*) 100-peseta note.
  (g) (*Jur**) (*acusación*) charge; (*condena*) sentence; **comerse un ~** to cough:, own up; **le pillaron de ~** they caught him red-handed; **le dieron 5 años de ~** they gave him 5 years' bird:.
  (h) (:: *policía*) cop*.
marroncito NM (*Carib*) coffee with milk.
marroquí [1] ADJ, NMF Moroccan.
  [2] NM (*Téc*) morocco (leather).
marroquinería NF **(a)** (*arte*) fine leatherwork. **(b)** (*artículos*) fine leather goods *pl*.
marrubio NM (*Bot*) horehound.
marrueco = **marroquí 1.**
Marruecos NM Morocco; **el ~ Español** (*Hist*) Spanish Morocco.
marrullería NF **(a)** (*cualidad*) smoothness, glibness, plausibility. **(b)** (*una ~*) plausible excuse; **~s** smooth approach, cajolery, wheedling.
marrullero [1] ADJ smooth, glib, plausible; cajoling, wheedling.
  [2] NM smooth type, plausible individual.
Marsella NF Marseilles.
Marsellesa NF Marseillaise.
marsopa NF porpoise.
marsupial ADJ, NM marsupial.
mart. ABR *de* **martes** Tuesday, Tue(s).
marta NF (*Zool*) (pine) marten; (*piel*) sable; **~ cebellina** sable.
martajar [1a] VT (*CAm, Méx*) **(a)** *maíz* to pound, grind. **(b)** **~ el español** to speak broken Spanish.
Marte NM Mars.
martellina NF sledgehammer.
martes NM INVAR Tuesday; **~ de carnaval, ~ de carnestolendas** Shrove Tuesday; **~ y trece** ≃ Friday 13th; *see also* [CARNAVAL] .

┌─ **MARTES Y TRECE** ──────────────────
│ *According to Spanish superstition Tuesday is an unlucky day, even more so if it falls on the 13th of the month. As the proverb goes, "En martes, ni te cases ni te embarques".*
└──────────────────────────────────

martiano (*Cuba: Pol*) [1] ADJ *supporting the ideas of José Martí.*
  [2] NM, **martiana** NF *supporter of José Martí.*
martillada NF hammer blow, blow with a hammer.
martillar [1a] VT **(a)** (*golpear con martillo*) to hammer; (*machacar*) to pound. **(b)** (*fig*) to worry, torment.
martillazo NM (heavy) blow with a hammer; **a ~s** by hammering; **formar algo a ~s** to hammer sth out (*o* into shape); **lograr algo a ~s** (*fig*) to succeed in doing sth by sheer force (*o* the hard way).
martilleante ADJ insistent, repetitious.
martillear [1a] [1] VT = **martillar.**
  [2] VI (*motor*) to knock.
martilleo NM hammering; pounding.
martillero, -a NM/F (*And, Carib*) auctioneer.
martillo NM **(a)** hammer (*t Dep*); (*de presidente etc*) gavel; **~ de hielo** ice-pick; **~ de madera** mallet; **~ mecánico** power hammer; **~ neumático** pneumatic drill, jackhammer (*US*); **~ de orejas, ~ sacaclavos** claw-hammer; **~ picador** pneumatic drill; **~ pilón** steam hammer.
  (b) (*Com*) auction-room.
  (c) (*Arquit*) projecting part, house (*etc*) that sticks out from the row; (*LAm*) wing (of a building).
  (d) (*fig: persona*) hammer, scourge.
Martín NM Martin; **San ~** St Martin, (*fiesta*) Martinmas, (*Agr*) season for slaughtering pigs; **a cada puerco le llega su San ~** (††) everyone comes to his day of reckoning; *V* **veranillo.**
martín NM: **~ pescador** kingfisher.
martinete NM drop hammer; pile driver; (*Mús*) hammer.
martingala* NF knack, trick; (*pey: LAm*) trick, fiddle*.
Martinica NF Martinique.
mártir NMF martyr.
martirio NM **(a)** (*Ecl*) martyrdom. **(b)** (*fig*) torture, torment.
martirizador ADJ (*fig*) agonizing, excruciating.
martirizar [1f] VT **(a)** (*Ecl*) to martyr. **(b)** (*fig*) to torture, torment.
martirologio NM martyrology.
Marucha NF, **Maruja** NF *formas familiares de* **María.**
marucha NF (*And*) rump steak.
maruja* NF (*pey*) housewife.
marujeo* NM chitchat, gossip.
marula NF (*Méx*) teat.
marullero ADJ = **marrullero.**

marusa NF (*Carib*) shoulder bag.
maruto NM (*Carib*) **(a)** (*Anat*) navel. **(b)** (*Med*) wart; bruise, welt.
marxismo NM Marxism.
marxista ADJ, NMF Marxist.
marzal ADJ March (*atr*), of March.
marzo NM March.
mas CONJ (*liter*) but.
más [1] ADV Y ADJ **(a)** (*comparaciones básicas*) (*comp*) more, (*superl*) most; **A es ~ difícil que B** A is more difficult than B, A is harder than B; **ella es la ~ guapa de todas** she is the prettiest of all; **él es el ~ inteligente** he is the most intelligent (one); **es el que sabe ~** he's the one who knows most; **tiene ~ dinero que yo** he has more money than I (do); **un libro de lo ~ divertido** a most amusing book, a highly amusing book; **es de lo ~ verde** it's as dirty as can be, it's as dirty as they come; **un hombre de lo ~ desaprensivo** a completely unscrupulous man.
  (b) (*ejemplos de uso con ciertos verbos*) **correr ~** to run faster; **durar ~** to last longer; **trabajar ~** to work harder; **ha viajado ~** he has travelled more (widely); **~ quiero + infin** I would rather + *infin*, I would prefer to + *infin*.
  (c) (*uso coloquial con adjs*) **¡qué perro ~ feo!** what an ugly dog!; **¡ya verán qué cena ~ rica!** you wait and see what a splendid supper it will be!; **¡es ~ bueno!** he's so kind!, he's ever so kind!
  (d) (*comparaciones de calidad y cantidad*) **~ de, ~ de lo que, ~ que** more than; **~ de 10** more than 10; **con ~ dinero de lo que creíamos** with more money than we thought; **no veo ~ solución que de ...** I see no other solution than to ... (*o* but to); **se trata de ~ voluntad ~ que de fuerza** it's more a question of will power than of strength, it's a matter of will power rather than of strength; **se estima en ~ de mil** it is reckoned at more than a thousand; **no ~ que ayer** only yesterday; **hace no ~ que 3 semanas** only 3 weeks ago, no longer than 3 weeks ago; **nadie lo sabe ~ que yo** nobody knows it better than I do.
  (e) (*otros usos, y locuciones con PREP*) **~ y ~** more and more; **~ o menos** more or less; **el que ~ y el que menos** every single one; the whole lot; **2 ~ 2 menos** give or take a couple; **los ~** most people; **los ~ de** most of, the majority of; **es ~ ...** furthermore ..., moreover ...; **a ~** in addition, besides; **y a ~** and moreover, and what is more; **a ~ de** in addition to, besides; **a lo ~** at most, at the most; **a las 8 a ~ tardar** at 8 o'clock at the latest; **está nevando a ~ y mejor** it really is snowing, it's snowing harder than ever; **la cosa no fue a ~** things did not get out of hand; **como el que ~** as well as anyone, as well as the next man; **llevaba 3 de ~** he was carrying 3 too many; **trae una manta de ~** bring an extra blanket; **estar de ~** to be unnecessary, be superfluous; **aquí yo estoy de ~** I'm not needed here, I'm de trop here, I'm in the way here; **unas copas no estarían de ~** a few drinks wouldn't do any harm; **está de ~ decir que ...** it is unnecessary to say that ...; **no estará por de ~ preguntar** there's no harm in asking; **de ~ en ~** more and more; **hasta no ~** to the utmost, to the limit; **nada ~** nothing else; **¡nada ~!** that's all!, that's the lot!; **¿nada ~?** anything else?; **ocurrió nada ~ iniciado el partido** it happened when the game had scarcely begun; **aparecen nada ~ terminado el invierno** they come when the winter is hardly over; **nada ~ llegar te llamo** I'll call you as soon as I arrive; **son 10 pesos nada ~** (*And, Méx*) it's only 10 pesos; **nada ~ que estoy muy cansado** (*And, Méx*) it's just that I'm very tired; **nadie ~ que tú** only you, nobody but you; **ni ~ ni menos** neither more nor less; just; **es un genio ni ~ ni menos** he's nothing more nor less than a genius, he's a real genius; **no ~ no more; habían llegado no ~** they had just arrived; **no ~ llegué me echaron** (*LAm*) no sooner had I arrived than they threw me out; **vengo no ~ a verlo** I've come just to see it; **así no ~** (*LAm*) just like that; **entre o pase no ~** please go in; **siéntese no ~** (*LAm*) do sit down; **sírvase no ~** (*LAm*) please help yourself; **pruébelo no ~** (*LAm*) just try it; **ayer no ~** (*LAm*) only yesterday; **¡espera no ~!** (*LAm*) just you wait!; **no trabaja ~** he no longer works, he doesn't work any more; **por ~ que se esfuerce** however much (*o* hard) he tries, no matter how (hard) he tries; **por ~ que quisiera ayudar** much as I should like to help; **¿qué ~?** what else?; what next?; **¿qué ~ da?** what difference does it make?; **sin ~ (ni ~)** without more ado; **todo lo ~** at most, at the most; *V* **allá, bien, cuento, nunca** *etc*.
  [2] CONJ and, plus; **2 ~ 3 son 5** 2 and 3 are 5, 2 plus 3 are 5; **con éstos ~ los que había antes** with these and (*o* together with) what there were before; **España ~ Portugal** Spain together with Portugal.
  [3] NM **(a)** (*Mat*) plus, plus sign.
  (b) **tiene sus ~ y sus menos** it has its good and bad points, there are things to be said on both sides.
masa¹ NF **(a)** (*Culin*) dough. **(b)** (*Cono Sur: pastelito*) small bun, teacake; (*And, Cono Sur*) puff-pastry; **~ quebrada** short pastry. **(c)** (*Arquit*) mortar, plaster.
masa² NF **(a)** (*Fís etc*) mass; (*fig*) mass; bulk; volume, quantity; **las ~s** the masses; **~ coral** choir; **~ crítica** critical mass; (*fig*) requisite num-

ber; **~ monetaria** money supply; **~ polar** polar icecap; **~ salarial** total wages bill; **en ~** (*gente*) en masse, in a body, all together; (*And, Cono Sur: en conjunto*) as a whole, altogether; **reunir(se) en ~** to mass; **llevar algo en la ~ de la sangre** to have sth in one's blood, have a natural inclination towards sth.

(**b**) (*Elec*) earth, ground (*US*); **conectar un aparato con ~** to earth a piece of apparatus, ground a piece of apparatus (*US*).

masacrar [1a] VT to massacre.

masacre NF (*a veces* M) massacre.

masacrear [1a] VT (*Carib*) to touch up*.

masada NF farm.

masadero NM farmer.

masaje NM massage; **dar ~ a** to massage; **hacerse dar ~s** to have o.s. massaged.

masajear [1a] VT to massage.

masajista [1] NM masseur.
　[2] NF masseuse.

masar* [1a] VT (*Dep*) to massage.

masato NM (*And, CAm*) *drink made from fermented maize or rice*; (*And: dulce de coco*) *coconut sweet*; (*And: de plátanos*) *banana custard*.

mascada NF (**a**) (*LAm: tabaco*) plug of chewing tobacco.

(**b**) (*And, CAm*) (*tesoro*) buried treasure; (*ahorros*) store of money, nest-egg; (*Cono Sur: ganancias*) illicit gains; (*: tajada*) rake-off*, cut.

(**c**) (*CAm: reprimenda*) rebuke.

(**d**) (*CAm, Méx: pañuelo*) silk handkerchief.

mascado* ADJ (*CAm*) creased, rumpled.

mascadura NF chewing.

mascar [1g] [1] VT (**a**) *comida* to chew. (**b**) (*) *palabras* to mumble, mutter. (**c**) **~ un asunto, dar mascado un asunto*** to explain a matter in very simple terms.
　[2] VI to chew; (*esp LAm*) to chew tobacco.

máscara [1] NF (**a**) (*lit*) mask; **~ antigás** gasmask; **~ para esgrima** fencing mask; **~ de oxígeno** (*Med*) oxygen mask; (*Aer etc*) breathing apparatus.

(**b**) **~s** (*Teat*) masque, masquerade.

(**c**) (*fig*) mask; disguise; **quitar la ~ a uno** to unmask sb; **quitarse la ~** to reveal o.s.

(**d**) (*rimel*) mascara.
　[2] NMF masked person.

mascarada NF (**a**) (*lit*) masque, masquerade. (**b**) (*fig*) masquerade; farce, charade.

mascarilla NF mask (*t Med*); (*vaciado*) plaster cast (of the face); (*maquillaje*) facepack; **~ de arcilla** mudpack; **~ mortuoria** death mask; **~ con oxígeno** oxygen mask.

mascarón NM large mask; **~ de proa** figurehead.

mascota NF mascot.

masculinidad NF masculinity, manliness.

masculinizador ADJ, **masculinizante** ADJ masculinizing.

masculinizar [1f] VT to make more masculine; (*Bio*) to masculinize.

masculino [1] ADJ (**a**) (*Bio*) male; *apariencia* masculine; **ropa masculina** men's clothing. (**b**) (*Ling*) masculine.
　[2] NM (*Ling*) masculine.

┌─ MASCULINO ──────── ver también la entrada ─┐

Masculino se traduce al inglés por *male* y *masculine*.

• *Masculino* se traduce por *male* cuando nos referimos a la condición masculina de los seres vivos (en oposición al sexo femenino):
　Un veinticinco por ciento de la población masculina sobrepasa ya el metro ochenta de estatura
　Twenty five per cent of the male population is now six foot or over

• Se traduce por *masculine* para referirse a las cualidades y características que tradicionalmente se han relacionado con los hombres:
　Una mujer tosca de rasgos más bien masculinos
　A rough woman with rather masculine features

• También se utiliza en el ámbito gramatical:
　Escribe cinco palabras españolas del género masculino que terminen en -e
　Write five masculine words in Spanish ending in -e
　Para otros usos y ejemplos ver la entrada.

---

mascullar [1a] VT to mumble, mutter.

masectomía NF mastectomy.

masera NF kneading trough.

masía NF (*Aragón, Catalonia*) farm.

masificación NF growth, extension; overcrowding; excessive quantity.

masificado ADJ overcrowded; overfull; overgrown, over-extended.

masificarse [1g] VR to get too big, become over-extended; to get overcrowded.

masilla NF (*para ventanas*) putty; (*para agujeros*) filler.

masillo NM (*Carib*) plaster.

masita NF (*LAm*) small bun, teacake, pastry.

masitero NM (*And, Carib, Cono Sur*) pastrycook, confectioner.

masivamente ADV massively; en masse, on a large scale.

masivo ADJ *ataque, dosis etc* massive; *evacuación etc* en masse, large-scale, general; *ejecución* mass (*atr*), wholesale; **reunión masiva** mass meeting.

masmediático ADJ mass-media (*atr*); **mucha atención masmediática** a lot of attention from the mass media.

masoca* [1] ADJ masochistic.
　[2] NMF masochist.

masocotudo ADJ (*And, Cono Sur*) = **amazacotado**.

masón NM (free)mason.

masonería NF (free)masonry.

masónico ADJ masonic.

masoquismo NM masochism.

masoquista [1] ADJ masochistic.
　[2] NMF masochist.

masoterapia NF massage (therapy).

mastate NM (*CAm, Méx*) loincloth.

mastectomía NF mastectomy.

mastelero NM topmast.

master [1] ADJ *copia* master.
　[2] NM, PL **masters** (**a**) (*Univ*) master's degree (*en* in); **M~ de Administración de Empresas** Master of Business Administration, MBA. (**b**) (*Cine, Mús*) master copy. (**c**) (*Dep*) masters' competition.

masticación NF mastication.

masticar [1g] VT to masticate, chew.

mástil NM (**a**) (*palo*) pole, post; (*sostén*) support; (*de bandera*) flagpole; (*Náut*) mast; (*Arquit*) upright; **~ de tienda** tent pole. (**b**) (*de guitarra*) neck. (**c**) (*de pluma*) shaft.

mastín NM mastiff; **~ danés** Great Dane; **~ del Pirineo** Pyrenean mountain dog.

mastique NM plaster; cement; putty.

mastitis NF mastitis.

masto NM (*Agr, Hort*) stock (*for grafting*).

mastodonte NM mastodon; (*) elephantine person (*u object etc*).

mastodóntico ADJ (*fig*) colossal, huge.

mastoides ADJ, NF mastoid.

mastuerzo NM (**a**) (*Bot*) cress; **~ (de agua)** watercress. (**b**) (*) dolt.

masturbación NF masturbation.

masturbarse [1a] VR to masturbate.

masturbatorio ADJ masturbatory.

Mat. ABR *de* **Matemáticas** mathematics, maths*.

mata NF (**a**) (*arbusto*) bush, shrub; (*esp LAm: cualquier planta*) plant; **~ de coco** (*Carib*) coconut palm; **~ de plátano** (*Carib*) banana tree; **~ rubia** kermes oak.

(**b**) (*ramita*) sprig; tuft, blade; (*raíz*) clump, root; (*ramo*) bunch.

(**c**) **~s** thicket, bushes; scrub.

(**d**) (*Agr*) field, plot; **~ de olivos** field of olive trees, olive grove.

(**e**) (*LAm: arboleda*) clump, group (of trees), grove; (*And: huerto*) orchard; (*Méx: matorral*) scrub; **~ de bananos** clump of banana trees, banana plantation.

(**f**) **~ de pelo** head of hair; mop of hair.

mataburros NM INVAR (*Carib, Cono Sur: hum*) dictionary.

matacaballo ADV: **a ~** at breakneck speed.

matacán NM (**a**) (*And, Carib*) fawn, young deer. (**b**) (*CAm*) calf.

matachín NM bully.

matadero NM (**a**) (*lit*) slaughterhouse, abattoir. (**b**) (*fig*) drudgery. (**c**) (*Méx, Cono Sur:*) brothel.

matador [1] ADJ (**a**) (*lit*) killing. (**b**) (*: ridículo*) ridiculous; absurd; **el vestido le está ~** the dress looks absurd on her.
　[2] NM, **matadora** NF killer.
　[3] NM (*Taur*) matador, bullfighter.

matadura NF (*Vet*) sore.

matafuego NM fire extinguisher.

matagigantes NM INVAR giant-killer.

matalahúga NF, **matalahúva** NF aniseed.

mátalas callando* NM smooth type, sly sort.

matalobos NM INVAR aconite, wolf's-bane.

matalón [1] ADJ *caballo* old, broken-down.
　[2] NM broken-down old horse, nag.

matalotaje NM (**a**) (*Náut*) ship's stores. (**b**) (*) jumble, mess.

matambre NM cold meat brawn.

matamoros NM INVAR swashbuckler, braggart.

matamoscas NM INVAR fly-swat; flypaper; flyspray.

matanza NF (**a**) (*lit*) slaughter, killing; (*Agr*) slaughtering, (*esp*) pig-killing; (*temporada*) slaughtering season; **~ sistemática** culling; (*fig*) slaughter, massacre, butchery.

(**b**) (*Carib: matadero*) slaughterhouse; (*And: tienda*) butcher's (shop); (*CAm: mercado*) meat market.

mataperrada NF (*And, Cono Sur*) prank; (*pey*) piece of hooliganism.

mataperrear* [1a] VI (*And, Cono Sur*) to wander the streets.
mataperros* NM INVAR urchin, hooligan.
matapolillas NM INVAR mothball.
matar [1a] ☐ VT (**a**) *persona* to kill; to slay; *animal* to slaughter; **~ a uno a disgustos** to make sb's life a misery; **así me maten ...** for the life of me ...; **que me maten si ...** I'll eat my hat if ...; believe me, I never ...; **~las callando** to do o.s. a lot of good on the quiet, go about things slyly; **se llevan a ~** they're at daggers drawn.
(**b**) (*fig*) *tiempo* to kill; *hambre* to stay; *polvo* to lay; *cal* to slake; *sello* to postmark, cancel; *ángulo, borde etc* to file down, smooth, round off; *color* to tone down; *violencia etc* to diminish, reduce.
(**c**) (*: *fastidiar*) to upset, annoy.
(**d**) (*: *aturdir*) to amaze, astound.
☐ VI (**a**) (*gen*) to kill; **no matarás** thou shalt not kill; **estar a ~ con uno** to be at daggers drawn with sb.
(**b**) (*Ajedrez*) to mate.
☐ **matarse** VR (**a**) (*suicidarse*) to kill o.s., commit suicide; (*en accidente*) to be killed, get killed.
(**b**) (*fig*) to wear o.s. out, kill o.s.; **~ a trabajar** to kill o.s. with work, overwork; **~ por** + *infin* to struggle to + *infin*, make a great effort to + *infin*.
matarife NM butcher, slaughterman; **~ de caballos** knacker.
matarratas NM INVAR rat poison; (*fig*) hooch*, bad liquor.
matasanos NM INVAR quack (doctor).
matasellado NM cancellation, postmark.
matasellar [1a] VT to cancel, postmark.
matasellos NM INVAR cancellation, postmark.
matasiete NM braggart, bully.
matasuegras NM INVAR streamer, blower (*toy*).
matasuelo NM: **darse un ~** (*And**) to come a cropper*.
matate NM (*CAm*) canvas bag.
matazón NM (*And, CAm, Carib*) = **matanza**.
match [maʃ] NM, PL **matchs** [maʃ] (*Dep*) match.
mate[1] ADJ dull, matt, unpolished.
mate[2] NM (*Ajedrez*) mate, checkmate; **dar ~ a** to mate, checkmate.
mate[3] NM (*LAm*) (**a**) (*bebida*) maté, Paraguayan tea (*herb and drink similar to tea*). (**b**) (*vasija*) gourd, drinking vessel; maté pot; **pegar ~** (*CAm*) to go crazy; **tener mucho ~** (*CAm*) to be sharp. (**c**) (*Cono Sur*‡) head, nut‡.
mate[4] NM (*Tenis*) smash.
matear[1] [1a] ☐ VT (*Agr*) to plant at regular intervals, sow in groups.
☐ VI (**a**) (*Bot*) to sprout (thickly). (**b**) (*Caza: perro*) to hunt among the bushes.
matear[2] [1a] VI (*LAm*) to drink maté.
matear[3] [1a] VT (*Cono Sur*) (**a**) (*Ajedrez*) to checkmate. (**b**) (*mezclar*) to mix.
matemáticamente ADV mathematically.
matemáticas NFPL mathematics; **~ aplicadas** applied mathematics; **~ puras** pure mathematics.
matemático ☐ ADJ mathematical; *cálculo* precise.
☐ NM, **matemática** NF mathematician.
Mateo NM Matthew.
materia NF (**a**) (*lit*) matter (*t Med, Fís*); material; stuff; **~ colorante** dyestuff; **~ gris** grey matter; **~ fecal** faeces; **~ prima** raw material; **~ vegetal** vegetable matter.
(**b**) (*Liter etc*) matter, subject matter; (*Univ etc*) subject; **índice de ~s** table of contents; **en ~ de** in the matter of, on the subject of; as regards; **entrar en ~** to begin on one's subject (after a preamble), get to the point; **será ~ de muchas discusiones** it will be the subject of a lot of argument, it will give rise to a lot of argument.
material ☐ ADJ (**a**) (*gen*) material.
(**b**) (*físico*) physical; **la presencia ~ de uno** sb's physical (*o* bodily) presence; **dolor ~** physical pain; **daños ~es** physical damage; damage to property.
(**c**) (*real*) real, true; (*literal*) literal; physical; **la imposibilidad ~ de ...** the physical impossibility of ...; **el autor ~ del hecho** the actual perpetrator of the deed.
☐ NM (**a**) (*gen*) material; **hecho de mal ~** made of bad material(s); **~ bélico, ~ de guerra** war material; **~ de construcción** building material; **~es de derribo** rubble; **~ de desecho** waste material; **~es plásticos** plastics, plastic materials.
(**b**) (*Téc*) equipment, plant; materials; **~es didácticos, ~ escolar** teaching materials, school equipment; **~ de envasado** packaging material; **~ fotográfico** photographic equipment; **~ informático** hardware; **~ de limpieza** cleaning materials; **~ móvil, ~ rodante** rolling-stock; **~ de oficina** stationery, office supplies; **el nuevo ~ de la fábrica** the new factory plant.
(**c**) (*Tip*) copy.
(**d**) (*: *de zapatos*) leather.
(**e**) **de ~** (*LAm*) made of bricks, brick-built.
materialidad NF material nature; outward appearance; literalness; substance; **percibe solamente la ~ del asunto** he sees only the

superficial aspects; **es menos la ~ del insulto que ...** it's not so much the insult itself as ...
materialismo NM materialism.
materialista ☐ ADJ materialist(ic).
☐ NMF materialist.
☐ NM (**a**) (*Méx: camionero*) lorry driver, truckdriver (*US*). (**b**) (*Méx: contratista*) building contractor.
materializable ADJ realizable, attainable.
materializar [1f] ☐ VT to materialize.
☐ **materializarse** VR to materialize.
materialmente ADV (**a**) (*gen*) materially; physically, in the physical sense.
(**b**) (*absolutamente*) absolutely; (*textualmente*) literally; **nos es ~ imposible** it is quite (*o* absolutely) impossible for us; **estaba ~ mojado** he was completely soaked.
maternal ☐ ADJ motherly; maternal.
☐ NM (*Carib*) nursery.
maternidad NF (**a**) (*lit*) motherhood, maternity. (**b**) (*t* **casa de ~**) maternity hospital.
materno ADJ (**a**) *lengua etc* mother (*atr*); *casa etc* mother's; **leche materna** mother's milk. (**b**) *parentesco* maternal; **abuelo ~** maternal grandfather, grandfather on the mother's side.
matero ADJ (*Cono Sur*) (**a**) (*de mate*) of maté, relating to maté. (**b**) *persona* fond of drinking maté.
mates* NFPL maths*, math* (*US*).
matete* NM (*Cono Sur*) (**a**) (*revoltijo*) mess, hash. (**b**) (*fig: riña*) quarrel, brawl. (**c**) (*fig: confusión*) confusion.
Matilde NF Mat(h)ilda.
matinal ADJ morning (*atr*).
matinée NM (**a**) (*Teat*) matinée. (**b**) (*And: fiesta infantil*) children's party.
matiz NM (**a**) (*de color*) shade, hue, tint. (**b**) (*de significado*) shade, nuance; (*de ironía etc*) touch.
matización NF (**a**) (*Arte*) blending. (**b**) (*teñido*) tingeing, tinting; (*fig*) variation; toning down; refinement, fine-tuning; clarification.
matizado ADJ: **~ de, ~ en** tinged with, touched with (*t fig*).
matizar [1f] VT (**a**) (*Arte*) to blend.
(**b**) *color* to tinge, tint (*de* with; *t fig*); *tono etc* to vary, introduce some variety into; *contraste, intensidad* to tone down; (*aclarar*) to make more precise, add precision to, fine-tune; to clarify; (*sutilizar*) to go into fine detail over, introduce subtle distinctions into; **~ que ...** to explain that ...; **se matizarán los cursos con deportes** classes will be interspersed with sports, there will be sports in addition to classes; **~ un discurso de ironía** to introduce ironical notes into a speech, give a speech an ironical slant.
matojal NM (*Carib*), **matojo** NM (*And, Carib, Méx*) = **matorral**.
matón NM bully, lout, thug.
matonismo NM bullying, loutishness; racketeering.
matonista NM bully, thug; (*en cárcel*) racketeer.
matorral NM thicket; brushwood, scrub.
matorro NM (*And*) = **matorral**.
matra NF (*Cono Sur*) horseblanket.
matraca ☐ NF (**a**) (*objeto*) rattle.
(**b**) (*) (*lata*) nuisance, bore; (*guasa*) chaff, banter; **dar ~ a uno** to pester sb, keep bothering sb; to banter sb.
(**c**) (*And*‡) hash*, pot‡.
(**d**) **~s** (*Escol*‡) maths*.
(**e**) (*Méx**: *metralleta*) machine-gun.
☐ NMF (*) nuisance, bore.
matraquear [1a] VT (**a**) (*hacer sonar*) to rattle. (**b**) (*) = **dar matraca a**.
matraz NM (*Quím*) flask.
matreraje NM (*Cono Sur*) banditry, brigandage.
matrero ☐ ADJ (**a**) (*astuto*) cunning, sly, knowing. (**b**) (*LAm*) suspicious, distrustful.
☐ NM (*LAm*) (*bandido*) bandit, brigand; (*fugitivo*) fugitive from justice; (*tramposo*) trickster.
matriarca NF matriarch.
matriarcado NM matriarchy.
matriarcal ADJ matriarchal.
matricería NF die-stamping.
matricida NMF matricide (*person*).
matricidio NM matricide (*act*).
matrícula NF (**a**) (*registro*) register, list, roll; (*Náut*) register.
(**b**) (*acto*) (*Náut*) registration; (*Univ*) registration, matriculation; **un buque de ~ extranjera** a foreign ship, a ship with foreign registration; **un barco con ~ de Bilbao** a boat registered in Bilbao; **~ de honor** first class with distinction (and remission of registration fee).
(**c**) (*licencia*) licence; (*Aut*) registration number; (*placa*) number-plate, licence plate; **~ de encargo** personalized number-plate.
matriculación NF registration; enrolment; licensing.
matricular [1a] ☐ VT to register; to enrol; to license.

2 **matricularse** VR to register; to enrol, sign on; ~ **en el curso de** ... to sign on for the course in ...

matrilineal ADJ matrilineal.

matrimonial ADJ matrimonial; **enlace** ~ link by marriage; **capitulaciones** ~**es** marriage settlement; **vida** ~ married life, conjugal life.

matrimonialista ADJ: **abogado** ~ lawyer specializing in matrimonial cases.

matrimoniar [1b] VI to marry, get married.

matrimonio NM **(a)** (*gen*) marriage, matrimony; married state; (*acto*) marriage; ~ **abierto** open marriage; ~ **canónico** canonical marriage; church wedding; ~ **civil** civil marriage; ~ **clandestino** secret marriage; ~ **consensual** common-law marriage; ~ **de conveniencia**, ~ **de interés** marriage of convenience; ~ **por la iglesia** church wedding; **contraer** ~ **(con)** to marry; **hacer uso del** ~ (*hum*) to make love; **hacer vida de** ~ to live together.
(b) (*personas*) couple, married couple; **el** ~ **García** the Garcías, Mr and Mrs García; **de** ~ *cama etc* double.

matritense = **madrileño**.

matriz 1 NF **(a)** (*Anat*) womb, uterus.
(b) (*Téc*) mould, die; (*Tip*) matrix; (*LAm*) stencil.
(c) (*Mat*) matrix; (*Inform*) array.
(d) (*de talonario etc*) stub, counterfoil.
(e) (*Jur*) original, master copy.
2 ATR: **casa** ~ (*Com etc*) head office; parent company; **convento** ~ (*Ecl*) parent house.

matrona NF **(a)** (*lit*) matron. **(b)** (*Esp Med*) midwife.

matronal ADJ matronly.

matungo: (*Carib, Cono Sur*) 1 ADJ old, worn-out.
2 NM (*caballo*) old horse, nag; (*persona*) beanpole*.

maturrango 1 ADJ (*Cono Sur*) clumsy, awkward; (*And, Cono Sur*) *jinete* poor, incompetent.
2 NM (*And, Cono Sur*) poor rider, incompetent horseman.

Matusalén NM Methuselah.

matute NM **(a)** (*acto*) smuggling, contraband; **de** ~ (*Com*) smuggled, contraband; (*como ADV*) secretly, stealthily; **introducir una idea de** ~ to bring in a (dangerous) notion from outside.
(b) (*géneros*) smuggled goods, contraband.
(c) (*casa de juego*) gambling den.

matuteo NM smuggling.

matutero NM smuggler.

matutino 1 ADJ morning (*atr*).
2 NM newspaper (published in the morning).

maula 1 ADJ (*LAm*) *animal* useless, vicious, lazy; (*Cono Sur, Méx*) *persona* good-for-nothing, unreliable; (*Cono Sur*) yellow.
2 NF **(a)** (*Cos*) remnant.
(b) (*objeto*) piece of junk, useless object; white elephant.
(c) (*: persona*) useless individual, dead loss.
(d) (*: trampa*) dirty trick, fraud.
3 NMF **(a)** (*vago*) idler, slacker.
(b) (*tramposo*) cheat, trickster; tricky individual; (*Fin*) bad payer.

maulería NF cunning, trickiness.

maulero NM **(a)** (*tramposo*) cheat, trickster; (*engañador*) smooth and deceitful type. **(b)** (*ilusionista*) conjurer.

maullar [1a] VI to mew, miaow.

maullido NM mew, miaow.

Mauricio[1] NM Maurice.

Mauricio[2] NM (*Geog*) Mauritius.

Mauritania NF Mauritania.

mauritano, -a ADJ, NM/F Mauritanian.

maurofilia NF (*Hist*) liking for Moors; liking for Moorish things.

maurofobia NF (*Hist*) dislike of Moors; dislike of Moorish things.

mausoleo NM mausoleum.

máx. ABR *de* **máximo** maximum, max.

maxi... PREF maxi...

maxiabrigo NM maxi-coat.

maxifalda NF maxiskirt.

maxilar 1 ADJ maxillary.
2 NM jaw, jawbone.

maxilofacial ADJ maxillofacial.

máxima[1] NF maxim.

máxima[2] NF (*Met*) highest temperature.

maximalismo NM going all out; (*Pol*) extremism, advocacy of extreme solutions.

maximalista 1 ADJ far-out, extreme.
2 NMF person who goes all out; (*Pol*) extremist, advocate of extreme solutions.

máxime ADV especially; principally; all the more so.

maximización NF maximization.

maximizar [1f] VT to maximize.

máximo 1 ADJ maximum; top; highest, greatest; **el** ~ **dirigente** the top leader; **el** ~ **premio** the highest award, the top prize; **su** ~

esfuerzo their greatest effort; **llegar al punto** ~ to reach the highest point; **es lo** ~ **en la moda juvenil:** it's the most in young people's fashions:.
2 NM maximum; **como** ~ at most, at the outside; **al** ~ to the maximum, to the utmost.

máximum NM maximum.

maxisencillo NM, **maxisingle** NM maxisingle, twelve-incher.

maxtate NM (*Méx*) straw basket.

may. ABR *de* **mayúscula(s)** capital(s), cap(s).

maya[1] NF **(a)** (*Bot*) daisy. **(b)** (*persona*) May Queen, Queen of the May.

maya[2] (*Hist*) 1 ADJ Mayan.
2 NMF Maya, Mayan.

mayal NM flail.

mayestático ADJ majestic; royal, regal; **el plural** ~ the royal 'we'.

mayo NM **(a)** (*mes*) May. **(b)** (*palo*) maypole.

mayólica NF (*And*) wall tile.

mayonesa NF mayonnaise.

mayor 1 ADJ **(a)** *parte etc* main, major, larger; **y otros animales** ~**es** and other larger animals.
(b) *altar, calle, misa etc* high; *plaza* main, principal; *mástil* main; V **colegio, libro** *etc*.
(c) (*Mús*) major.
(d) *persona (adulto)* grown up, adult; (*de edad*) of age; (*anciano*) elderly; **ser** ~ **de edad** to be of age, be adult; **hacerse** ~ to grow up.
(e) (*en rango etc*) head, chief; **montero** ~ head huntsman.
2 ADJ COMP **(a)** (*en tamaño*) bigger, larger, greater (*que* than).
(b) (*en edad*) older (*que* than), elder; (*en rango*) senior (*que* to).
3 ADJ SUPERL **(a)** (*en tamaño*) biggest, largest, greatest (*t fig*); **su** ~ **cuidado** his biggest worry; **su** ~ **enemigo** his greatest enemy; **hacer algo con el** ~ **cuidado** to do sth with the greatest care; **viven en la** ~ **miseria** they live in the greatest poverty.
(b) (*en edad*) oldest, eldest; (*en rango*) most senior.
4 NMF **(a)** (*en rango*) chief, boss, superior; (*en oficina*) chief clerk; (*LAm Mil*) major.
(b) (*adulto*) ~ **de edad** adult, person legally of age; ~**es** grown-ups, adults; elders (and betters); **eso es sólo para** ~**es** that's only for grown-ups; **¡más respeto con los** ~**es!** be more respectful to your elders (and betters)!
(c) (*antepasados*) ~**es** ancestors, forefathers.
(d) (*situación*) **llegar a** ~**es** to get out of hand, get out of control.
5 NM: **al por** ~ wholesale (*t fig*); **vender al por** ~ to sell wholesale; **repartir golpes al por** ~ to deal out punches wholesale, throw punches left and right.

mayoral NM (*Téc etc*) foreman, overseer, gaffer; (*Agr*) (*pastor*) head shepherd; (*mayordomo*) steward; farm manager; (*Hist*) coachman.

mayorazgo NM **(a)** (*institución*) primogeniture. **(b)** (*tierras*) entailed estate. **(c)** (*hijo*) eldest son, first-born.

mayorcito ADJ rather older, a bit more grown-up; **eres** ~ **ya** you're grown up, you're a big boy now; **ya eres un poco** ~ **para hacer eso** you're too old now to be doing that.

mayordomo NM (*de casa*) steward, butler; (*Náut*) steward; (*de hacienda*) steward; (*Cono Sur: capataz*) foreman; (*And: criado*) servant; (*LAm Rel*) patron (saint).

mayorear* [1a] VI (*CAm*) to be in charge, be the boss.

mayoreo NM (*Cono Sur, Méx*) wholesale (trade).

mayorete NF majorette.

▼ **mayoría** NF **(a)** (*gen*) majority; **la** ~ **de los españoles** the majority of Spaniards, most Spaniards; **en la** ~ **de los casos** in most cases; **en su** ~ in the main; ~ **absoluta** absolute majority; **la abrumadora** ~, **la inmensa** ~ the overwhelming majority, the vast majority; **por una** ~ **arrolladora** by an overwhelming majority; ~ **silenciosa** silent majority; ~ **simple** simple majority.
(b) (*Pol etc*) majority; **una** ~ **de las cuatro quintas partes** a four-fifths majority; **gobierno de la** ~ majority rule, majority government.
(c) ~ **de edad** majority, adult age; **cumplir** (*o* **llegar a**) **la** ~ **de edad** to come of age.

mayorista NMF wholesaler.

mayoritariamente ADV preponderantly, for the most part; (*al votar*) by a majority; **gente** ~ **joven** young people for the most part; **votar** ~ **por** to vote by a majority for.

mayoritario ADJ majority (*atr*); **gobierno** ~ majority government.

mayormente ADV (*principalmente*) chiefly, mainly; (*especialmente*) especially; (*tanto más*) all the more so; **no me interesa** ~ I'm not particularly interested.

mayúscula NF capital (letter); (*Tip*) upper case letter.

mayúsculo ADJ **(a)** *letra* capital. **(b)** (*fig*) big, tremendous; **un susto** ~ a big scare; **un error** ~ a tremendous mistake.

maza NF **(a)** (*Hist*) mace; war club; (*Dep*) bat; (*de polo*) stick, mallet; (*Mús*) drumstick; (*de taco de billar etc*) thick end; (*de cáñamo, lino*) brake; ~ **de fraga** drop hammer; ~ **de gimnasia** Indian club.
(b) (*) pest, bore.

(c) (*LAm*: *de rueda*) hub.
(d) (*And, Carib*: *de ingenio*) drum (of a sugar mill).
mazacote NM **(a)** (*gen*) hard mass; (*Culin*) dry doughy food; (*Arquit*) concrete; **el arroz se ha hecho un ~** the rice has gone lumpy, the rice has set like concrete.
(b) (*Arte, Liter etc*) crude piece of work; mess, hotchpotch.
(c) (*: *lata*) bore.
(d) (*Carib**) arse**.
mazacotudo ADJ = amazacotado.
mazada NF **(a)** (*golpe*) bash*, blow (with a club); **dar ~ a** (*fig*) to hurt, injure. **(b)** (*fig*) blow; **fue una ~ para él** it came as a blow to him.
mazamorra NF **(a)** (*LAm Culin*) maize, porridge; (*pey*) mush. **(b)** (*LAm*: *ampolla*) blister.
mazamorrero* (*And*) **1** ADJ of Lima.
2 NM, **mazamorrera** NF native (*o* inhabitant) of Lima; **los ~s** the people of Lima.
mazapán NM marzipan.
mazazo NM heavy blow.
mazmorra NF dungeon.
mazo NM **(a)** (*porra*) club; (*martillo*) mallet; (*de mortero*) pestle; (*Dep*) club, bat, (*de croquet*) mallet; (*Aragón*: *de campana*) clapper.
(b) (*manojo*) bunch, handful; (*lío*) bundle, packet; **~ de papeles** sheaf of papers, bundle of papers; **~ de naipes** pack of cards; **~ de billetes** wad of notes (*o* bills: *US*).
(c) (*: *lata*) bore.
mazorca NF **(a)** (*Bot*) spike; (*de maíz*) cob, ear; **~ de maíz** corncob; **maíz en la ~** corn on the cob.
(b) (*Téc*) spindle.
(c) (*Cono Sur Hist*) (*gobierno*) despotic government; (*banda*) political gang, terrorist gang.
mazota NF (*And, Méx*) = mazorca **(a)**.
mazote NM (*And, Méx*: *manotada*) handful; **de a ~** free.
Mb NM ABR *de* **megabyte** megabyte, Mb.
mb. ABR *de* **milibar(es)** millibar(s), mb.
Mbytes NMPL ABR *de* **megabytes** megabytes, Mbytes.
M.C. NM ABR *de* **Mercado Común** Common Market, C.M.
MCAC NM ABR *de* **Mercado Común de la América Central**.
MCCA NM ABR *de* **Mercado Común Centroamericano** Central American Common Market, CACM.
MCE NM (*Com*) ABR *de* **Mercado Común Europeo**.
MCI NM ABR *de* **Mercado Común Iberoamericano**.
MDP NM (*Chile*) ABR *de* **Movimiento Democrático Popular**.
me PRON PERS **(a)** (*ac*) me.
(b) (*dativo*) (to) me; **¡dámelo!** give it to me!; **~ lo compró** he bought it from me; he bought it for me; **~ rompí el brazo** I broke my arm.
(c) (*reflexivo*) (to) myself; **~ lavé** I washed, I washed myself; **~ retiro** I withdraw.
meada NF **(a)** (**: *orina*) piss**. **(b)** (*mancha*) mark (*o* stain *etc*) of urine. **(c)** (**: *dicho etc*) put-down*.
meadero* NM bog**, jakes**.
meado* ADJ **(a)** **esto está ~** it's a cinch**, it's dead easy. **(b)** (*Cono Sur*) **estar ~** to be canned**.
meados** NMPL piss**.
meaja NF crumb.
meandro NM meander.
meapilas **1** ADJ sanctimonious, holier-than-thou.
2 NMF INVAR sanctimonious person; goody-goody*.
mear** [1a] **1** VT **(a)** (*lit*) to piss on**. **(b)** (*Dep*) to beat easily, walk all over. **(c)** (*humillar*) to walk all over.
2 VI to piss**, have a piss**.
3 **mearse** VR to wet o.s.; **~ (de risa)** to piss o.s. laughing**.
MEC [mek] NM (*Esp*) ABR *de* **Ministerio de Educación y Ciencia**.
Meca NF: **La ~** Mecca.
meca NF (*And**) prostitute; **ser la ~** to be an ace.
mecachis INTERJ (*Esp*: *euf de* **¡me cago!**) *V* cagar.
mecánica¹ NF **(a)** (*gen*) mechanics; **~ de precisión** precision engineering. **(b)** (*mecanismo*) mechanism, works.
mecánicamente ADV mechanically.
mecanicista ADJ mechanistic.
mecánico **1** ADJ **(a)** (*gen*) mechanical; (*con motor*) power-driven, power-operated; (*de máquina*) machine (*atr*).
(b) *oficio etc* manual.
2 NM, **mecánica²** NF mechanic; (*operario*) machinist; (*ajustador*) fitter, repairman; (*Aut*) driver, chauffeur; (*Aer*) rigger, fitter; **~ de vuelo** flight engineer.
mecanismo NM **(a)** (*gen*) mechanism; works, machinery; gear; **~ de destrucción** destruct mechanism; **~ de dirección** steering gear; **lubricar el ~** (*fig*) to oil the wheels.
(b) (*movimiento*) action, movement.
(c) (*fig*) mechanism; machinery, structure; process; **~ de defensa** defence mechanism.
mecanización NF mechanization.

mecanizado ADJ mechanized.
mecanizar [1f] VT to mechanize.
mecano NM ® Meccano ®.
mecanografía NF typing, typewriting; **~ al tacto** touch-typing.
mecanografiado **1** ADJ typewritten, typescript.
2 NM typescript; typing.
mecanografiar [1c] VT to type.
mecanógrafo, -a NM/F typist.
mecapal NM (*CAm, Méx*) *headband used for attaching loads carried on one's back*.
mecapalero NM (*CAm, Méx*) porter.
mecatazo NM (*CAm*) **(a)** (*golpe*) lash, slash. **(b)** (*: *trago*) swig of liquor*.
mecate NM (*LAm*) **(a)** (*fibra*) strip of pita fibre; (*cuerda*) rope, string, cord; (*tosco*) twine; **¡es todo ~!** (*Méx**) it's terrific!*; **jalear el ~ a uno*** to suck up to sb*. **(b)** (*persona*) boor; (*: *pesado*) oaf.
mecateada NF (*CAm, Méx*) lashing, beating.
mecatear¹ [1a] **1** VT **(a)** (*CAm, Méx*) (*atar*) to tie up; (*azotar*) to lash, whip. **(b)** (*LAm**) to suck up to*.
2 **mecatearse** VR: **~, mecateárselas** (*Méx**) to run away, beat it*.
mecatear² [1a] VI (*And*) to eat cakes.
mecatero* NM (*LAm*) creep**, toady.
mecato NM (*And*) cakes, pastries.
mecedor **1** ADJ rocking; swinging.
2 NM **(a)** (*columpio*) swing. **(b)** (*CAm, Carib, Méx*: *asiento*) rocking-chair. **(c)** (*Carib*: *cuchara*) stirrer, spoon.
mecedora NF rocking-chair.
Mecenas NM Maecenas; **m~** (*fig*) patron.
mecenazgo NM patronage.
mecer [2b] **1** VT **(a)** *columpio* to swing; *cuna etc* to rock; *niño* to rock (to and fro), dandle; *rama etc* to sway, move to and fro.
(b) *líquido, recipiente* to stir, shake (up).
2 **mecerse** VR to swing; to rock (to and fro); to sway, move to and fro.
mecha NF **(a)** (*de vela*) wick; (*Mil etc*) fuse; **~ lenta** slow fuse; **~ tardía** time fuse; **aguantar (la) ~** (*fig*) to grin and bear it; **a toda ~** at full speed; **encender la ~** to stir up trouble; **tener mucha ~ para algo** to be good at sth, have a knack for sth.
(b) (*Esp Culin*) slice of bacon (*for larding*).
(c) (*pelo etc*) = mechón.
(d) (*And, Cono Sur*: *Téc*) bit (*of brace*).
(e) (*And, Carib**: *broma*) joke.
(f) (*Méx**: *miedo*) fear.
(g) (*: *ratería*) shoplifting.
(h) (*And*: *baratija*) trinket.
mechado ADJ: **~ de** full of.
mechar [1a] VT (*Culin*) to lard; to stuff.
mechero **1** NM **(a)** (*encendedor*) cigarette lighter; (*de cocina*) burner; jet; (*And, Cono Sur*) oil lamp; **~ Bunsen** Bunsen burner; **~ encendedor, ~ piloto** pilot light; **~ de gas** gas burner, gas jet, gas lighter.
(b) (*CAm, Méx*) mop of hair.
(c) (*Carib**: *bromista*) joker.
(d) (**) prick**.
2 NM, **mechera** NF (*: *persona*) shoplifter.
mechificar* [1g] VT (*And, Carib*) (*engañar*) to trick, deceive; (*mofarse de*) to mock.
mecho NM (*And, CAm*) (*vela*) candle; (*cabo*) candle end; (*candelero*) candlestick.
mechón NM (*de pelo*) tuft, lock; (*de hilos*) bundle.
mechudo ADJ (*CAm, Cono Sur*) tousled, unkempt.
meción NM (*CAm, Carib*) jerk, jolt.
meco* ADJ (*CAm, Méx*) (*salvaje*) uncivilized, wild; (*bruto*) thick*; (*ordinario*) crude.
medalla NF medal.
medallero NM (*Dep*) medal table.
medallista NMF medal designer; (*Dep*) medallist; **~ de bronce** bronze medallist; **~ de oro** gold medallist; **~ de plata** silver medallist.
medallón NM **(a)** (*medalla*) medallion. **(b)** (*relicario*) locket. **(c)** (*Culin*) round, slice.
médano NM, **medaño** NM sand dune; sandbank.
media NF **(a)** (*gen*) stocking; (*LAm*: *de hombre*) sock; **~ de malla** net stocking; **~ de nylon** nylon stocking; **~ pantalón, ~ panti** panty-hose, tights; **~s de red, ~s de rejilla** fishnet stockings; *ver también* PANTALONES, ZAPATOS, GAFAS .
(b) **de ~** knitting (*atr*); *punto* plain; **hacer ~** to knit.
(c) (*Dep*) half-back line.
(d) (*Mat*) mean; **~ aritmética** arithmetic mean; **~ ponderada** weighted average; **100 de ~ al día** 100 as a daily average, 100 each day on the average.
(e) **~ de cerveza** ½ litre bottle of beer.
mediación NF **(a)** (*intercesión*) mediation; intercession. **(b)** **por ~ de**

(*mediante*) through.

mediado ADJ (a) (*medio lleno*) half full; *proceso, trabajo* halfway through, half completed; **el local estaba ~** the place was half full; **mediada la tarde** halfway through the afternoon; **llevo ~ el trabajo** I am halfway through the job, I have completed half the work.

(b) (*de tiempo*) **a ~s de marzo** in the middle of March, halfway through March; **hacia ~s del siglo pasado** about the middle of last century.

mediador(a) NM/F mediator.

mediagua NF (*Cono Sur*) hut, shack.

medial ADJ medial.

medialuna NF croissant, breakfast roll.

mediana NF (*Aut*) central reservation, median (*US*).

medianamente ADV moderately, fairly; moderately well; **un trabajo ~ bueno** a moderately good piece of work; **quedó ~ en los exámenes** he did moderately well in the exams.

medianera NF (*And, Cono Sur*) party wall, dividing wall.

medianería NF (a) (*pared*) party wall. (b) (*Carib, Méx Com*) partnership; (*Agr*) share-cropping.

medianero 1 ADJ (a) *pared* party (*atr*), dividing; *valla* boundary (*atr*). (b) (*contiguo*) adjacent, next.
2 NM (a) (*de casa*) owner of the adjoining house (*o property etc*). (b) (*Carib, Méx Com*) partner; (*Agr*) share-cropper.

medianía NF (a) (*promedio*) average; (*punto medio*) halfway point; middling position; (*Econ*) moderate means, modest circumstances; (*en sociedad*) undistinguished social position.
(b) (*persona*) ordinary sort, mediocrity; **no pasa de ser una ~** he's no better than average, he's rather a mediocrity.
(c) (*Com*) middleman.

mediano ADJ (*regular*) middling, medium, average; *empresa etc* medium-sized; (*indiferente*) indifferent, undistinguished; (*euf*) mediocre, rather poor; **de tamaño ~** medium-sized; **de mediana edad** middle-aged; **es ~ de talento** he has average talent.

medianoche NF midnight.

▼ **mediante** PREP by means of, through, by; with the help of.

mediar [1b] VI (a) (*estar en medio*) to be in the middle; (*llegar a la mitad*) to get to the middle, get halfway; **entre A y B median 30 kms** it is 30 kms from A to B; **entre estas 2 casas median otras 3** there are 3 other houses between those 2; **media un abismo entre los dos gobiernos** there is a wide gap between the two governments; **entre los dos sucesos mediaron varios años** several years elapsed between the two events, there were some years between the two events; **mediaba el otoño** autumn was half over; **mediaba el mes de julio** it was halfway through July; **sin ~ palabra** directly.
(b) (*suceder*) to come up, happen; (*intervenir*) to intervene; (*existir*) to exist; **pero medió la muerte de su madre** but his mother's death intervened; **media el hecho de que ...** there is the fact that ... to be considered; **there is an obstacle in the fact that ...; median relaciones cordiales entre los dos** cordial relations exist between the two.
(c) (*interceder*) to mediate (*en* in, *entre* between), intervene; **~ con uno** to intercede with sb.

mediático ADJ *poder, cultura, estrella* media (*atr*).

mediatizar [1f] VT (a) (*estorbar*) to interfere with, obstruct; to affect adversely, influence for the worse. (b) (*Pol*) to annexe, take control of.

medible ADJ measurable; detectable, appreciable.

médica NF (woman) doctor.

medicación NF medication, treatment.

medicamente ADV medically.

medicamento NM medicine, drug; **~ de patente** patent medicine.

medicar [1g] 1 VT to medicate, give medicine to.
2 **medicarse** VR to take one's medicine.

medicastro NM (*pey*) quack (doctor).

medicina NF medicine; **~ alternativa** alternative (*o complementary*) medicine; **~ forense**, **~ legal** forensic medicine; **~ general** general practice; **~ preventiva** preventive medicine; **estudiante de ~** medical student.

medicinal ADJ medicinal.

medicinar [1a] 1 VT to treat, prescribe for.
2 **medicinarse** VR: **~ algo** to dose o.s. with sth.

medición NF measurement, measuring; **hacer mediciones** to take measurements.

médico 1 ADJ medical.
2 NMF doctor; medical practitioner, physician; **~ de cabecera** family doctor; **~ dentista** dental surgeon; **~ forense** forensic surgeon, expert in forensic medicine; (*Jur*) coroner; **~ general** general practitioner; **~ interno**, **~ residente** house physician, houseman, intern (*US*); **~ partero** obstetrician; **~ pediatra**, **~ puericultor** paediatrician.

medida NF (a) (*Mat*) measurement; (*acto*) measuring, measurement; **a la ~** in proportion; suitable; **el precio es a la ~ del tamaño** the price depends on the size; **hay uno a la ~ de sus necesidades** there is one to suit your needs; **no tenemos un sombrero a su ~** we don't have a hat in your size (*o to fit you*); **una caja a la ~** a specially made box, a box made for the purpose; **un traje a la ~, un traje hecho a la ~** a made-to-measure suit; **tiene una novia a la ~** he has a girl who is just right for him; **es una solución a la ~** it's a perfect solution; **a la ~ de mi deseo** just as I would have wished, exactly as I wanted (it); **a ~ de** in proportion to, in keeping with; **a ~ que ... as ...**; **a ~ que vaya bajando el agua** as the water goes down; **en cierta ~** up to a point, in a way; **en buena ~, en gran ~** to a great extent; **en la ~ de lo posible** as far as possible; **en la ~ en que esto sea verdad** insofar as this is true; **en no pequeña ~** in no small measure; **~s vitales** vital statistics; **tomar las ~s a uno** to measure sb, take sb's measurements; (*fig*) to size sb up; **tomar sus ~s** to size a situation up.
(b) (*sistema, recipiente etc*) measure; **pesas y ~s** weights and measures; **~ agraria** land measure; **~ para áridos** dry measure; **~ para líquidos** liquid measure; **esto colma la ~** (*fig*) this is the last straw; **con esto se colmó la ~ de la paciencia de su padre** this finally exhausted her father's patience.
(c) (*de camisa, zapato etc*) size, fitting; **ropa a sobre ~** (*Méx*) outsize clothing; **¿cuál es su ~?** (*LAm*) what size do you take?
(d) (*Liter*) (correct) scansion.
(e) (*fig: disposición*) measure, step, move; **~ cautelar** precautionary measure; **~ preventiva** preventive measure; **~ represiva** deterrent, check (*contra* to); **tomar ~s** to take steps (*para que* to ensure that).
(f) (*fig: moderación*) moderation, prudence; restraint; **sin ~** immoderately, in an unrestrained fashion.

medidor NM (*LAm*) meter; gauge; **~ de lluvia** rain gauge.

mediero, -a NM/F (*LAm*) share-cropper.

medieval ADJ medieval.

medievalismo NM medievalism.

medievalista NMF medievalist.

Medievo, medievo NM Middle Ages *pl*.

medio 1 ADJ (*mitad*) half (a).
(b) **media naranja** half an orange, a half orange; **media hora** half an hour; **nos queda media botella** we've half a bottle left; **media luna** half-moon, (*fig*) crescent; **~ luto** half-mourning; **media luz** half-light; **acudió media provincia** half the province turned up.
(c) *punto etc* mid, midway, middle; **clase media** middle class(es); **dedo ~** middle finger; **a media tarde** halfway through the afternoon.
(d) (*Mat*) mean, average; (*fig*) average; **el hombre ~** the average man, the ordinary man, the man in the street; *V* **término** *etc*.
(e) (*LAm: grande*) big, huge.
(f) **a medias** half; by halves; **está escrito a medias** it's half-written; **lo dejó hecho a medias** he left it half-done; **estoy satisfecho sólo a medias** I am only partly satisfied; **ir a medias** to go fifty-fifty (*con* with), divide the costs (*etc*) equally; **lo pagamos a medias** we share the cost; **verdad a medias** half-truth.
2 ADV (a) (*a medias*) half; **~ dormido** half asleep; **estar ~ borracho** to be half drunk; **está ~ escrito, está a ~ escribir** it is half-written; **eso no está ni ~ bien** that isn't at all right; **A ~ se ennovió con Z** A became half-engaged to Z.
(b) (*LAm: bastante*) quite, rather; **~ tonto** a bit of a fool; **fue ~ difícil** it was pretty hard; **~ se sonrió** she gave a half-smile.
3 NM (a) (*centro*) middle, centre; (*término medio*) halfway point (*etc*); (*Mat*) mean; **~ aritmético** arithmetical mean; **justo ~** happy medium, golden mean; fair compromise; **equivocarse de ~ a ~** to be completely wrong; **en ~** in the middle; in between; **en ~ de la plaza** in the middle of the square; **en ~ de tanta confusión** in the midst of such confusion; **la casa de en ~** the middle house; the house in between; **quitar algo de en ~** to remove sth; to get rid of sth, get sth out of the way; **quitarse de en ~** to get out of the way; to duck, dodge; to remove o.s.; **pasar por ~ de** to go through (the middle of); **tomar algo por el ~** to grasp sth round the middle; **por ~** in between; **hay dificultades de por ~** there are snags in the way; **habrá una falda de por ~** a woman probably comes into it somewhere; **meterse de por ~** to intervene; **día (de) por ~** (*LAm*) every other day.
(b) (*Dep*) half-back; **~ centro** centre-half; **~ de melé** (*Rugby*) scrum-half.
(c) (*Espiritismo*) medium.
(d) (*método*) means, way, method; medium; (*medida*) measure, expedient; **los ~s de comunicación, los ~s de difusión** the media; **~s de comunicación de masas** mass media; **~s informativos** news media; **~s de transporte** means of transport; **por ~ de** by means of, by, through; **por todos los ~s** by all possible means, in every possible way; **no hay ~ de conseguirlo** there is no way of getting it; **poner todos los ~s para + *infin*, no regatear ~ para + *infin*** to spare no effort to + *infin*.
(e) **~s** (*Econ, Fin*) means, resources.
(f) (*ambiente*) atmosphere; (*contorno*) milieu, ambience; environ-

ment; (*círculo*) circle; (*Bio*: *t ~* **ambiente**) environment; **~ de cultivo** culture medium; **en los ~s financieros** in financial circles; **encontrarse en su ~** to be in one's element.

medioambiental ADJ environmental.

medioambientalista NMF environmentalist.

medioambiente NM environment.

mediocampista NMF midfield player.

mediocampo NM midfield.

mediocre ADJ middling, average; (*pey*) mediocre, rather poor.

mediocridad NF middling quality; (*pey*) mediocrity; **es una ~** he's a nonentity, he's a dead loss.

mediodía NM (a) (*gen*) midday, noon; **a ~** at noon. (b) (*Geog*) south.

medioevo NM Middle Ages.

mediofondista NMF (*Dep*) middle-distance runner.

mediofondo NM (*Carib*) petticoat.

mediogrande ADJ medium large.

mediometraje NM medium-length film.

medioooeste NM Midwest.

medioooriental ADJ Middle East(ern).

Medio Oriente NM Middle East.

mediopensionista NMF day pupil (*who has lunch at school*).

mediopequeño ADJ medium small.

mediquillo NM (*pey*) quack (doctor).

medir [3k] **1** VT (a) (*gen*) to measure; *tierra* to survey, plot; **~ a millas, ~ por millas** to measure in miles; **~ a uno (con la vista:** *fig*) to size sb up.
(b) *posibilidad, proyecto etc* to weigh up.
(c) (*Liter*) *verso* to scan (properly).
2 VI (a) *objeto, persona* to measure, be; **la tela mide 90 cms** the cloth measures 90 cms; **el papel mide 20 cms de ancho** the paper is 20 cms wide; **ella mide 1,50 m** she is 1.50 m tall; **mide 88 cms de pecho** she is 88 cms round the chest, her bust measurement is 88 cms.
(b) (*Liter*) to scan (properly).
3 **medirse** VR (a) **~ con uno** to measure up to sb; to test o.s. against sb.
(b) (*fig*) to be moderate, act with restraint; (*Méx*: *no perder la calma*) to keep one's head.
(c) (*LAm*) (*Dep*) to play each other, meet; (*reñir*) to quarrel, come to blows.
(d) (*LAm*) *ropa* to try on.

meditabundo ADJ pensive, thoughtful.

meditación NF meditation; pondering; **~ trascendental** transcendental meditation; **meditaciones** meditations (*sobre* on).

meditar [1a] **1** VT to ponder, think over, meditate (on); *plan etc* to think out, work out, plan.
2 VI to ponder, think, meditate; to muse.

Mediterráneo NM Mediterranean; **descubrir el ~*** to reinvent the wheel, state the obvious.

mediterráneo ADJ Mediterranean; (*gen*) land-locked.

médium NMF, PL **médiums** medium.

mediúmnico ADJ: **sesión mediúmnica** session with a medium; **revelaciones mediúmnicas** revelations from a medium.

medo NM: **los ~s y los persas** the Medes and the Persians.

medra NF increase, growth; improvement; (*Econ etc*) prosperity.

medrar [1a] VI (*aumentarse*) to increase, grow; (*mejorar*) to improve, do well, do better; (*Econ etc*) to prosper, thrive, do well; (*animal, planta*) to grow, thrive; **¡medrados estamos!** (*iró*) a fine thing you've done!

medro NM = **medra**.

medroso ADJ fearful, timid, fainthearted.

medula NF, **médula** NF (a) (*Anat*) marrow; medulla; **~ espinal** spinal cord; **~ ósea** bone-marrow; **hasta la ~** (*fig*) to the core; through and through; **estoy convencido hasta la ~** I am profoundly convinced.
(b) (*Bot*) pith.
(c) (*fig*) essence; substance; pith.

medular ADJ (*fig*) central, fundamental, essential.

medusa NF jellyfish.

Mefistófeles NM Mephistopheles.

mefítico ADJ (*venenoso*) poisonous; (*hediondo*) foul-smelling.

mefitismo NM foul air; foul smells.

mega... PREF mega...

megabyte ['megabait] NM megabyte.

megaciclo NM megacycle.

megafonía NF public address system.

megáfono NM megaphone.

megahercio NM, **megaher(t)zio** NM megahertz.

megalítico ADJ megalithic.

megalito NM megalith.

megalomanía NF megalomania.

megalómano, -a NM/F megalomaniac.

megalópolis NF (*hum*) super-city.

megaocteto NM megabyte.

megatón NM megaton.

megavatio NM megawatt.

megavoltio NM megavolt.

meiga NF (*Galicia*) wise woman.

mejicanada NF typically Mexican thing.

mejicanismo NM mexicanism, word (*o phrase etc*) peculiar to Mexico.

mejicano, -a ADJ, NM/F Mexican.

Méjico NM Mexico.

mejido ADJ *huevo* beaten.

mejilla NF cheek.

mejillón NM mussel.

mejillonera NF mussel-bed.

mejillonero ADJ mussel (*atr*); **industria mejillonera** mussel industry.

▼ **mejor** **1** ADJ (a) (*comp*) better (*que* than).
(b) (*superl*) best; *oferta, postor* highest; **es el ~ de todos** he's the best of all; **lo ~** the best thing, the best part (*etc*); **lo ~ de la novela** the best part of the novel, the best thing about the novel; **lo ~ de la vida** the prime of life; **hice lo ~ que pude** I did the best I could, I did my best; **llevar lo ~** to get the best of it; **a lo ~, a la ~** (*LAm*) probably, maybe; with any luck; suddenly, when least expected; **'¿crees que lo hará?' ... 'a lo ~'** 'do you think he'll do it?' ... 'he may do', o 'maybe'.
▼ **2** ADV (a) (*comp*) better; **A canta ~ que B** A sings better than B; **~ quisiera + *infin*** I would rather + *infin*; **¡~!** good!, that's fine!; **~ que ~** better and better, all the better; **tanto ~** all the better, so much the better (*para* for); **está mucho ~** he's much better.
(b) (*superl*) best.
3 *como* CONJ (*esp LAm**) **~ me voy, ~ me vaya** I'd better go; **~ te vayas, ~ vete** you'd better go.

mejora NF (a) (*gen*) improvement; **~s** (*de casa etc*) improvements; alterations, repairs. (b) (*en subasta*) higher bid. (c) (*Méx Agr*) weeding.

mejorable ADJ improvable.

mejoramiento NM improvement.

mejorana NF marjoram.

▼ **mejorar** [1a] **1** VT (a) (*gen*) to improve, make better, ameliorate; (*Inform etc*) to upgrade; (*realzar*) to enhance; *postura* to raise; *oferta* to improve, increase; *récord* to break.
(b) **~ a** to be better than, be superior to.
▼ **2** VI y **mejorarse** VR (a) (*situación*) to improve, get better; (*Med*) to get better; (*Met*) to improve, clear up; (*Fin etc*) to do well, prosper; **los negocios mejoran** business is improving, business is picking up; **¡que se mejore!** get well soon!
(b) (*en subasta*) to raise one's bid.

mejorcito ADJ choice, select; **lo ~ del programa** the very best (item) in the programme; **lo ~ de la clientela** la crème de la crème among the customers.

mejoría NF improvement; recovery; **¡que siga la ~!** I hope the improvement continues.

mejunje NM (a) (*mezcla*) brew, mixture, concoction. (b) (*: *fraude*) fraud. (c) (*LAm***:*** *lío*) mess, mix-up.

melado **1** ADJ honey-coloured.
2 NM treacle, syrup; (*LAm: de caña*) cane syrup.

meladura NF (*Carib, Méx*) cane syrup.

melancolía NF melancholy, gloom(iness), sadness; (*Med*) melancholia.

melancólicamente ADV gloomily, sadly, in a melancholy way; wistfully.

melancólico ADJ (*triste*) melancholy, gloomy, sad; (*soñador*) dreamy, wistful.

melanésico ADJ Melanesian.

melanesio, -a ADJ, NM/F Melanesian.

melanina NF melanine.

melanismo NM melanism.

melanoma NM melanoma.

melarchía NF (*CAm*) = **melancolía**.

melaza NF (*t* **~s**) molasses; treacle.

melcocha NF (*melaza*) molasses; treacle; (*azúcar de cande*) candy, molasses toffee.

melcochado ADJ *fruta etc* candied; (*de color*) golden, honey-coloured.

melcocharse [1a] VR to thicken (*in boiling*).

mele* NM bash*, punch.

melé NF, **mêlée** [me'le] NF (*Rugby*) scrum; (*fig*) confusion, confused scene, imbroglio.

melena NF (*de hombre*) long hair; (*de mujer*) loose hair, flowing hair; (*pey*) mop of hair, bushy hair; (*cola de caballo*) ponytail; (*Zool*) mane; **andar a la ~** to pull one another's hair, (*fig*) to quarrel; **estar en ~** to have one's hair down.

melenas: NM INVAR, **melenero*** NM long-haired yob**:**.

melenudo ADJ long-haired.

melga NF (*Cono Sur, Méx*) plot of land prepared for sowing.

melifluo ADJ mellifluous, sweet.

melillense **1** ADJ of Melilla.

2 NMF native (o inhabitant) of Melilla; **los ~s** the people of Melilla.

melindre NM **(a)** (*Culin*) (*bollo*) sweet cake, iced bun; (*buñuelo*) honey fritter.
(b) ~s (*delicadeza*) daintiness, dainty ways; (*pey*) (*afectación*) affectation, affected ways; squeamishness; (*mojigatería*) prudery, prudishness; **gastar ~s = melindrear.**

melindrear [1a] VI to be affected, indulge in affectation; to be squeamish; to be prudish; to be excessively finicky, be terribly fussy.

melindroso ADJ affected; squeamish; prudish; finicky, fussy.

meliorativo ADJ ameliorative.

melisca NF (*Cono Sur*) gleaning.

mella NF **(a)** (*rotura*) nick, dent, notch; (*en dientes etc*) gap; **hacer ~** (*fig*) to make an impression, sink in, strike home; **hacer ~ en** (o **a**) to make an impression on, tell on.
(b) (*fig: daño*) harm, damage; **hacer ~ en** to do damage to, harm.

mellado ADJ *borde* jagged, nicked, ragged; *persona* gap-toothed; (*Cono Sur*) hare-lipped.

mellar [1a] VT **(a)** (*hacer muescas en*) to nick, dent, notch; to take a chip out of. **(b)** (*fig: dañar*) to damage, harm.

mellizo, -a ADJ, NM/F twin.

melo* NM = **melodrama.**

melocotón NM (*fruto*) peach; (*árbol*) peach-tree.

melocotonero NM peach-tree.

melodía NF **(a)** (*una ~*) melody; tune, air. **(b)** (*cualidad*) melodiousness.

melódico ADJ melodic.

melodiosamente ADV melodiously, tunefully.

melodiosidad NF melodiousness.

melodioso ADJ melodious, tuneful.

melodrama NM melodrama.

melodramáticamente ADV melodramatically.

melodramático ADJ melodramatic.

melómano, -a NM/F music-lover.

melón¹ NM **(a)** (*Bot*) melon; **los melones, a cata** the proof of the pudding is in the eating. **(b)** (**:** *cabeza*) head, nut**:**; **estrujarse el ~** to rack one's brains. **(c)** (**:** *idiota*) idiot, nutter**:**.

melón² NM (*Zool*) = **meloncillo.**

melonada NF silly thing, idiotic remark (*etc*).

melonar NM bed of melons, melon plot.

meloncillo NM (*Zool*) ichneumon, (kind of) mongoose.

melopea: NF spree, binge*; **coger** (*etc*) **una ~** to get canned**:**.

melosidad NF **(a)** (*lit*) sweetness; (*pey*) cloying sweetness. **(b)** (*fig*) sweetness; gentleness; (*pey*) smoothness.

meloso ADJ **(a)** (*dulce*) honeyed, sweet; (*pey*) cloying. **(b)** (*fig*) *voz etc* sweet, musical; gentle; (*pey*) smooth, soapy*.

membrana NF **(a)** (*piel*) membrane; (*Orn*) membrane, web; **~ mucosa** mucous membrane; **~ virginal** hymen. **(b)** (*Cono Sur Med*) diphtheria.

membranoso ADJ membranous.

membresía NF (*Méx*) membership.

membretado ADJ: **papel ~** headed notepaper.

membrete NM letterhead, heading.

membrillero NM quince tree.

membrillo NM **(a)** (*fruto*) quince; (*árbol*) quince tree; (**carne de**) **~** quince jelly. **(b)** (*: *cobarde*) softie*, coward. **(c)** (**:** *chivato*) nark**:**, informer.

membrudo ADJ burly, brawny, tough.

memela NF (*CAm*, *Méx*) (*tortilla*) maize tortilla; (*rellena*) fried tortilla filled with beans.

memez NF silly thing; farce, absurdity.

memo¹ **1** ADJ silly, stupid.
2 NM idiot.

memo²* NM memo*, memorandum.

memorabilia NF memorabilia.

memorable ADJ memorable.

memorablemente ADV memorably.

memorando NM, **memorándum** NM, PL **memorándums (a)** (*libreta*) notebook. **(b)** (*Pol etc*) memorandum.

memoria NF **(a)** (*gen*) memory; **de buena ~, de feliz ~** of happy memory; **digno de ~** memorable; **falta de ~** forgetfulness; **flaco de ~** forgetful; **aprender algo de ~** to learn sth by heart; to memorize sth, commit sth to memory; **hablar de ~** to speak from memory; **guardar la ~ de** to retain the memory of; **se le fue de la ~** he forgot it, it slipped his mind; **en ~ de** in memory of; **la peor tormenta de que hay ~** the worst storm in living memory; the worst storm on record; **hacer ~** to try to remember; **deben hacer ~** they should search their memories; **hacer ~ de algo** to recall sth, bring sth to mind; **no queda ~ de eso** there is no memory (o record) of that; **saber de ~** to know by heart; **tener mala ~** to have a bad memory; **si tengo buena ~** if my memory serves me; **traer algo a la ~** to recall sth; **no me viene a la ~** I can't remember.
(b) (*informe*) note, report, statement; (*relación*) record; (*memorándum*)

aide-mémoire, memorandum; (*petición*) petition; (*artículo*) (learned) paper; (*Univ*) thesis, dissertation; **~ anual** annual report; **~s** (*personales*) memoirs, (*de sociedad*) transactions.
(c) ~s (†: *saludo*) regards, remembrances.
(d) (*Inform*) memory; **~ de acceso aleatorio** random access memory, RAM; **~ auxiliar** backing storage; **~ burbuja** bubble memory; **~ caché** storage memory, cache memory; **~ central, ~ principal** main memory; **~ externa** external storage; **~ intermedia** buffer; **~ interna** internal storage, main memory; **~ muerta** read-only memory, ROM; **~ de núcleos** core memory; **~ programable** programmable read-only memory; **~ de sólo lectura = ~ muerta; ~ del teclado** keyboard memory; **~ virtual** virtual memory.

memorial NM memorial, petition; (*Jur*) brief.

memorialista NM amanuensis.

memorión **1** ADJ: **es muy ~** he has a wonderful memory.
2 NM good memory, amazing memory.

memorioso ADJ (*LAm*) having a retentive memory; that remembers everything.

memorista ADJ (*LAm*) having a retentive memory; **es ~** (*pey*) he just memorizes things.

memorístico ADJ memory (*atr*); **enseñanza memorística** learning by rote.

memorización NF memorizing.

memorizar [1f] VT to memorize.

mena NF ore.

menaje NM **(a)** (*familia*) family, household; **~ de tres** ménage à trois; **vida de ~** (*LAm*) family life, domestic life.
(b) (*economía doméstica*) housekeeping; (*quehaceres*) housework, upkeep of the house.
(c) (*Com etc*) household equipment, furnishings; (*de colegio*) school equipment; **sección de ~** (*en almacenes*) hardware and kitchen department.

menarquía NF menarche.

menchevique ADJ, NMF Menshevik.

Menchu NF *forma familiar de* **Carmen.**

mención NF mention; **~ honorífica** honourable mention; **hacer ~ de** to mention.

mencionado ADJ aforementioned.

▼ **mencionar** [1a] VT to mention, refer to; to name; **sin ~ ...** let alone ...; **dejar de ~** to fail to mention, leave unmentioned.

menda* PRON (*t ~s*) *p.ej.* **lo hizo este ~** (*lerenda*) yours truly did it*, I did it.

mendacidad NF **(a)** (*gen*) mendacity, untruthfulness. **(b)** (*una ~*) untruth, gross lie.

mendaz ADJ mendacious; lying, untruthful.

mendeliano ADJ Mendelian.

mendelismo NM Mendelism, Mendelianism.

mendicante ADJ, NMF mendicant.

mendicidad NF begging; mendicity.

mendigar [1h] **1** VT to beg (for).
2 VI to beg (for alms).

mendigo **1** NM, **mendiga** NF beggar.
2 ADJ (*Méx*: cobarde*) yellow, yellow-bellied**:**.

mendrugo NM **(a)** (hard) crust. **(b)** (*: *tonto*) dolt, blockhead.

meneado ADJ (*Carib*) drunk.

meneallo V **menear.**

menear [1a] **1** VT **(a)** (*gen*) to move, shift; *cabeza etc* to shake, toss; *cola* to wag; *caderas* to sway, swing, waggle; **sin ~ el dedo** without lifting a finger; **más vale no meneallo** it's best to leave that alone; don't go stirring all that up; **¡me la menean!:** they leave me cold!
(b) ~ cálamo to wield a pen.
(c) *asunto* to get on with, get moving; *negocio etc* to handle, conduct.
2 menearse VR **(a)** (*gen*) to move; (*agitarse*) to shake; (*cola*) to wag; (*caderas*) to sway, swing, waggle; **~:, meneársela** to wank**:**; **un vapuleo de no te menees** a terrific beating-up*.
(b) (*apurarse*) to hustle, bestir o.s., get a move on; **¡~!** get going!, jump to it!

Menelao NM Menelaus.

meneo NM **(a)** (*movimiento*) movement; shake, toss; wag; sway(ing), swing(ing); waggle; jerk, jolt; **dar un ~ a** to jerk, jolt, move suddenly. **(b)** (*) (*paliza*) hiding*; (*bronca*) dressing-down*. **(c)** (**:** *actividad etc*) = **movida.**

menequear [1a] VT, **menequetear** [1a] VT (*Cono Sur, Méx*) to shake, wag.

meneque(te)o NM (*Cono Sur, Méx*) shaking, wagging.

menester NM **(a)** **ser ~** to be necessary; **cuando sea ~** when it is necessary; **es ~ + infin** it is necessary to + *infin*, we (*etc*) must + *infin*; **todo es ~** everything is welcome.
(b) (*trabajo*) job, piece of business; (*recado*) errand; **~es** (*deberes*) duties, jobs, business; (*ocupación*) occupation; (*función*) function; **salir para un ~** to go out on an errand; **hacer sus ~es** (*euf*) to do one's

business (*euf*).
  (c) ~**es** (*Téc*) gear, tackle, tools.
menesteroso ADJ needy.
menestra NF **(a)** (*Culin: potaje*) vegetable soup, stew. **(b)** ~**s** dried vegetables.
menestral NMF (*t* **menestrala** NF) skilled worker, artisan.
menestrón NM (*And*) ≃ minestrone soup.
mengano, -a NM/F Mr (*o* Mrs *etc*) So-and-so; *V* **fulano.**
mengua NF **(a)** (*disminución*) decrease, diminishment; dwindling; (*decadencia*) decay, decline; **ir en ~ de** to contribute to the lessening of, assist the decrease (*o* restriction *etc*) of; **sin ~** complete, whole; untouched.
  (b) (*falta*) lack, want; (*pérdida*) loss.
  (c) (*pobreza*) poverty.
  (d) (*persona: debilidad*) spinelessness, weakness of character.
  (e) (*descrédito*) discredit; **ir en ~ de uno** to be to sb's discredit.
menguadamente ADV **(a)** (*fig*) wretchedly; weakly, spinelessly. **(b)** (*con tacañería*) meanly. **(c)** (*estúpidamente*) foolishly.
menguado [1] ADJ **(a)** (*disminuido*) decreased, diminished.
  (b) (*fig*) (*despreciable*) wretched, miserable; (*débil*) weak, spineless, weak in character; (*cobarde*) cowardly.
  (c) (*aciago*) unlucky; **en hora menguada** at an unlucky moment.
  (d) (*tacaño*) mean.
  (e) (*tonto*) foolish.
  (f) **medias menguadas** fully-fashioned stockings.
  [2] NM (*en punto*) decrease.
menguante [1] ADJ (*que disminuye*) decreasing, diminishing; dwindling; (*decadente*) decaying; *luna* waning; *marea* ebb (*atr*).
  [2] NF **(a)** (*Náut*) ebb tide, low water.
  (b) (*de luna*) waning; *V* **cuarto 2.**
  (c) (*fig*) decay, decline; **estar en ~** to be in decline.
menguar [1i] [1] VT **(a)** (*disminuir*) to lessen, diminish, reduce; (*labor de punto*) to decrease (by).
  (b) (*fig*) to discredit.
  [2] VI **(a)** (*disminuir*) to diminish, get less, dwindle, decrease; (*marea, número etc*) to go down; (*luna*) to wane.
  (b) (*fig*) to wane, decay, decline.
mengue* NM the devil; **¡malos ~s te lleven!** go to hell!
meninges: NFPL **estrujarse las ~** to rack one's brains.
meningitis NF meningitis.
menisco NM meniscus.
menjunje NM, **menjurje** NM = **mejunje.**
menopausia NF menopause.
menopáusico ADJ menopausal.
menor [1] ADJ (*Ecl*) *orden* minor; (*Mús*) minor.
  [2] ADJ COMP **(a)** (*en tamaño*) smaller (*que* than); less, lesser; **en ~ número** in smaller numbers; **celidonia ~** lesser celandine.
  (b) (*en edad*) younger (*que* than); junior (*que* to); **el hermano ~** the younger brother; **Juanito es ~ que Pepe** Johnnie is younger than Joe; *V* **edad.**
  [3] ADJ SUPERL **(a)** (*en tamaño*) smallest; least; **éste es el ~ de todos** this is the smallest of the lot; **no le doy la ~ importancia** I don't attach the least (*o* slightest) importance to it.
  (b) (*en edad*) youngest; most junior; **ella es la ~ de todas** she is the youngest of all.
  [4] NMF young person, juvenile; (*Jur*) minor; **un ~ de 14** an under-14; **los ~es de edad** those who are under age, the juveniles; **apto para ~es** (*Cine*) for all ages; **no apto para ~es** (*Cine*) not suitable for juveniles, 'Adults Only'.
  [5] NM **(a)** **al por ~** (*Com*) retail; **vender un género al por ~** to sell goods retail.
  (b) **contar algo por ~** to recount sth in detail.
Menorca NF Minorca.
menoría NF **(a)** (*Jur*) minority. **(b)** (*inferioridad*) inferiority; (*subordinación*) subordination.
menorista (*And, Cono Sur*) [1] ADJ retail (*atr*).
  [2] NMF retailer.
menorquín, -ina ADJ, NM/F Minorcan.
menos [1] ADJ **(a)** (*Mat*) *signo* minus.
  (b) (*comp*) less; fewer; **con ~ ruido** with less noise; **con ~ hombres** with fewer men; **A tiene ~ ventajas que B** A has fewer advantages than B; **A tiene ~ años que B** A is younger than B; **éste es ~ coche que el anterior*** this is not such a good car as the old one.
  (c) (*superl*) least; fewest; **es el que ~ culpa tiene** least blame attaches to him, he is least to blame.
  [2] ADV **(a)** (*comp*) less, (*superl*) least; **hoy se va ~** people don't go so much nowadays, nowadays people go less; **es el ~ inteligente de los 4** he is the least intelligent of the 4; **no quiero alquilarlo ni ~ comprarlo** I don't want to rent it and still less to buy it; **¿qué ~?*** what else did you expect?, it's the least one would expect; **~ de,** **~ de lo que,** **~ que** less than; **~ de lo que piensas** less than you think; **fue nada ~ que un rey** he was nothing less than a king, he

was a king no less; **hay 7 de ~** we're 7 short, there are 7 missing; **me dieron un paquete con medio kilo de ~** they gave me a packet which was half a kilo short (*o* under weight); **me han pagado 2 libras de ~** they have underpaid me by £2.
  (b) (*locuciones con lo*) **lo ~ 10** 10 at least; **lo ~ posible** as little as possible; **eso es lo de ~** that's the least of it; **es lo ~ que se puede esperar** it's the least one can expect; **al ~, a lo ~, por lo ~** at least.
  (c) (*modismos*) **a ~ de** without; **tener a ~ +** *infin* to consider it beneath o.s. to + *infin*; **ir a ~, venir a ~** to come down in the world; to decline, decay; to run to seed; **darse de ~** to underestimate o.s., hide one's light under a bushel; **echar a ~** to miss sb; **hacer de ~ a uno** to be unfaithful to sb; **hacer a uno de ~** to despise sb; to belittle sb; **no se quedó en ~** he was not to be outdone; **en ~ que se santigua un cura loco*** in no time at all; **no es para ~** it's worth all that and more; quite right too; *V* **cuando, mucho, poder.**
  [3] PREP **(a)** (*excepto*) except; **todos ~ él** everybody except him; **¡todo ~ eso!** anything but that!
  (b) (*Mat*) minus, less; **7 ~ 2 son 5** 2 from 7 leaves 5, 7 take away 2 leaves 5; **las 7 ~ 20** (*hora*) 20 to 7.
  [4] CONJ **a ~ que ...** unless ...
  [5] NM **(a)** (*Mat*) minus sign (-).
  (b) *V* **más.**
menoscabar [1a] VT **(a)** (*disminuir*) to lessen, reduce, diminish; (*dañar*) to damage, harm, impair. **(b)** (*desacreditar*) to discredit.
menoscabo NM lessening, reduction; damage, harm; loss; **con ~ de, en ~ de** to the detriment of; **sin ~** unimpaired; **sufrir ~** to suffer damage, suffer loss.
menospreciable ADJ contemptible.
menospreciador ADJ scornful.
menospreciar [1b] VT **(a)** (*despreciar*) to scorn, despise. **(b)** (*ofender*) to slight. **(c)** (*subestimar*) to underrate, undervalue.
menospreciativo ADJ scornful, contemptuous; slighting.
menosprecio NM **(a)** (*desdén*) scorn, contempt. **(b)** (*subestimación*) underrating, undervaluation. **(c)** (*falta de respeto*) disrespect; **con ~ del sexo de la víctima** without regard for the sex of the victim.
mensáfono NM bleeper, pager.
mensaje NM message; **~ de buenos augurios** goodwill message; **~ de la corona** (*Parl*) speech from the throne; **~ de error** (*Inform*) error message.
mensajería NF messaging; **~ electrónica** electronic messaging; **empresa de ~** courier company, messaging company; **servicio de ~** courier service, messaging service.
mensajero, -a NM/F messenger; courier.
menso* ADJ (*Méx*) stupid.
menstruación NF menstruation.
menstrual ADJ menstrual.
menstruar [1e] VI to menstruate.
menstruo NM **(a)** (*acción*) menstruation. **(b)** (*producto*) menses.
mensual ADJ monthly; **50 dólares ~es** 50 dollars a month.
mensualidad NF monthly payment (*o* salary, instalment *etc*).
mensualmente ADV monthly.
mensuario NM (*LAm*) monthly journal.
ménsula NF bracket; (*Arquit*) corbel.
mensura NF measurement.
mensurable ADJ measurable.
mensuración NF mensuration.
menta NF mint; **~ romana, ~ verde** spearmint.
mentada¹ NF: **hacer a uno una ~** (*LAm*) = **mentar la madre;** *V* **madre.**
mentada² NF (*Méx*) insult.
mentado ADJ **(a)** (*mencionado*) aforementioned. **(b)** (*famoso*) well-known, famous.
mental ADJ mental; *capacidad, trabajo etc* intellectual.
mentalidad NF mentality, mind.
mentalización NF (*mental*) preparation; conditioning; sensitization; persuasion; inspiration; (*pey*) brainwashing.
mentalizar [1f] [1] VT to prepare (mentally), condition; to sensitize, make aware; (*convencer*) to persuade, convince; (*inspirar*) to inspire; (*pey*) to brainwash.
  [2] **mentalizarse** VR to prepare o.s. (mentally); to make o.s. aware; to get used to an idea.
mentalmente ADV mentally.
mentar [1j] VT to mention, name.
mentas* NFPL (*And, Cono Sur*) **(a)** (*reputación*) good name, reputation; **una persona de buenas ~** a highly-regarded (*o* well-respected) person. **(b)** (*chismes*) rumours, gossip.
mente NF mind; intelligence, understanding; **~ consciente** conscious mind; **~ subconsciente** subconscious mind; **cambiar de ~** to change one's mind; **no está en mi ~ +** *infin*, **no tengo en ~ +** *infin* it is not in my mind to + *infin*, it is not my intention to + *infin*; **no lo tenía en ~** it slipped his mind; **se le fue completamente de la ~** it completely slipped his mind.

mentecatería NF, **mentecatez** NF stupidity, foolishness.

mentecato [1] ADJ silly, stupid.

[2] NM, **mentecata** NF idiot, fool.

mentidero NM place where people gossip, gossip shop*.

mentir [3i] [1] VT (*liter*) to feign, pretend; to suggest (falsely) to; **la sed me mintió un arroyo cercano** my thirst led me to suppose there was a stream nearby.

[2] VI (*gen*) to lie, tell a lie, tell lies; (*engañar*) to be deceptive; **¡miento!** sorry, I'm wrong!, my mistake!; **¡esta carta no me dejará ~!** this letter will bear me out!, this letter will confirm what I say!

mentira NF (a) (*una ~*) lie, falsehood; (*gen*) lying, untruthfulness, deceitfulness; (*Liter*) fiction, invention; **¡~!** it's a lie!; **una ~ como una casa*** (o **catedral**) a whopping great lie*; **~ caritativa, ~ oficiosa, ~ piadosa, ~ reverenda** (*Cono Sur*) white lie; **¡parece ~!** well (I never)!; you don't say so!; **aunque parezca ~** however incredible it seems, strange though it may seem; **parece ~ que ...** it seems impossible that ...; **parece ~ que no te acuerdas** I'm surprised you don't remember it; **no hay ~ que no salga** truth will out; **coger a uno en una ~** to catch sb in a lie.

(b) (*señal*) white mark (*on fingernail*).

(c) **sacar ~s** (*And, Cono Sur*) to crack one's knuckles.

(d) **de ~** (*LAm*: *artificial*) pretend, sham.

mentirijillas NFPL: **es de ~, va de ~** it's only a joke; (*a niño*) just pretend, it's just make-believe; **jugar de ~** to play for fun (*ie not for money*).

mentirilla NF fib; white lie.

mentirosillo, -a NM/F fibber.

mentiroso [1] ADJ (a) (*que miente*) lying, deceitful, untruthful; (*falso*) deceptive, false. (b) *texto* full of errors, full of misprints.

[2] NM, **mentirosa** NF liar; deceiver.

mentís NM INVAR denial; **dar el ~ a** to refute, deny, give the lie to.

mentol NM menthol.

mentolado ADJ mentholated.

mentolatum* NM: **ser un ~** (*Cono Sur*) to be a jack of all trades.

mentón NM chin.

mentor NM mentor.

menú NM (a) (*lista*) menu; (*menú del día*) table d'hôte, set meal. (b) (*Inform*) menu.

menudear [1a] [1] VT (a) (*repetir*) to repeat frequently, do repeatedly; *narración etc* to tell in great detail.

(b) (*LAm*: *vender*) to sell retail.

[2] VI (a) (*ser frecuente*) to be frequent, happen frequently; (*misiles etc*) to rain, come thick and fast; to come in abundance.

(b) (*al explicarse*) to go into great detail.

(c) (*Cono Sur, Méx*) (*abundar*) to abound; (*proliferar*) to increase, grow in number.

menudencia NF (a) (*bagatela*) trifle, small thing; **~s** little things, odds and ends. (b) (*minuciosidad*) minuteness; exactness; meticulousness. (c) **~s** (*Culin*) (*de cerdo*) pork products; (*menudillos*) offal.

menudeo NM (*Com*) retail trade; **vender al ~** to sell retail.

menudez NF smallness, minuteness.

menudillos NMPL giblets.

menudo [1] ADJ (a) (*pequeño*) small, tiny, minute; (*fig*) slight, petty, insignificant; **moneda menuda** small change, coins of low denomination.

(b) *persona* exact, meticulous.

(c) (*iró**) fine, some; **¡~ negocio!** some deal!; **¡menuda plancha!** what a bloomer!*; **¡menuda vidorra nos vamos a dar!** we won't half live it up!*; **¡menuda me la han hecho!** they've done it on me!*

(d) (*con prep*) **a ~** frequently, often; **a la menuda, por la menuda** (*Com*) retail; **contar algo por ~** to tell sth in detail.

[2] NM (a) (*Fin*) small change.

(b) **~s** (*Culin*) offal; giblets; (*Méx*: *guisado*) tripe stew.

meñique [1] ADJ tiny, very small; **dedo ~ = 2.**

[2] NM little finger.

meódromo: NM bog:, loo*.

meollo NM (a) (*Anat*) marrow, brains. (b) (*de pan*) soft part, inside, crumb. (c) (*fig: de persona*) brains. (d) (*fig: de asunto etc*) gist, essence, core; solid substance, solid part, meat.

meón* [1] ADJ *niño* that constantly wets itself.

[2] NM, **meona** NF baby (boy, girl).

meos: NMPL piss:.

meque* NM (*Carib*) rap.

mequetrefe NM (*vago*) good-for-nothing, whippersnapper; (*curiosón*) busybody.

meramente ADV merely, only, solely.

merca [1] NM food market; shopping centre.

[2] NF (*Méx*) shopping, purchases; (*Cono Sur*) contraband goods.

mercachifle NM (a) (*comerciante*) small-time trader, dealer; (*vendedor ambulante*) hawker, huckster. (b) (*fig*) moneygrubber.

mercadear [1a] [1] VT (*vender*) to market; (*regatear*) to haggle over.

[2] VI to deal, trade.

mercadeo NM marketing.

mercader NM (*esp Hist*) merchant.

mercadería NF commodity; **~s** goods, merchandise.

mercadillo NM street market; (*benéfico*) (charity) bazaar.

mercado NM market; **~ cambiario, ~ de divisas** foreign exchange market; **~ cautivo** captive market; **M~ Común** Common Market; **~ de demanda** seller's market; **~ de dinero** money market; **~ exterior** overseas market; **~ de futuros** futures market; **~ inmobiliario** property market; **~ interior, ~ nacional** home market; **~ libre** free market (*de* in); **~ mundial** world market; **~ negro** black market; **~ de oferta** buyer's market; **~ persa** (*Cono Sur*) cut-price store; **~ de trabajo** labour market; **~ único** single market; **~ de valores** stock market; **~ de viejo** flea-market; **~ de la vivienda** housing market; **~ de signo favorable al comprador, ~ de compradores** buyer's market; **~ de signo favorable al vendedor, ~ de vendedores** seller's market; **inundar el ~ de** to flood the market with; **salir al ~** to come on to the market.

mercadológico ADJ market (*atr*), marketing (*atr*).

mercadotecnia NF marketing; **estudios de ~** market research.

mercadotécnico ADJ marketing (*atr*).

mercancía [1] NF commodity; **~s** goods, merchandise; **~s de general** (*Náut*) general cargo; **~s perecederas** perishable goods.

[2] NM: **~s** goods train, freight train (*US*).

mercante [1] ADJ merchant (*atr*), trading, commercial; **buque ~ = 2.**

[2] NM merchantman, merchant ship.

mercantil ADJ mercantile, trading, commercial; *derecho* commercial.

mercantilismo NM mercantilism.

mercantilización NF commercialism; commercialization.

mercantilizar [1f] VT to commercialize.

mercar [1g] VT to buy.

merced NF (a) (†) (*favor*) favour; (*premio*) benefit, reward; (*placer*) pleasure, will; **hacer la ~ de + infin** to do sb the favour of + *ger*; **tenga la ~ de + infin** please be so good as to + *infin*.

(b) **~ a** thanks to.

(c) (††) **vuestra ~** your honour, your worship, sir.

(d) **estar a la ~ de** to be at the mercy of.

mercedario, -a ADJ, NM/F Mercedarian.

mercenario [1] ADJ mercenary.

[2] NM (*Mil*) mercenary; (*Agr*) day labourer; (*fig*) hack, hireling.

mercería NF (a) (*géneros*) haberdashery, notions (*US*). (b) (*tienda*) haberdasher's (shop), notions store (*US*); (*And, Carib, Méx*) draper's (shop), dry-goods store (*US*); (*Cono Sur*) ironmonger's, hardware store.

mercero, -a NM/F haberdasher; (*And, Carib, Méx*) draper.

Merche NF *forma familiar de* **Mercedes.**

merchero* NM petty criminal, delinquent.

Mercosur NM ABR *de* **Mercado Común del Cono Sur** *Common market between Argentina, Brazil, Paraguay and Uruguay.*

mercromina ® NF Mercurochrome ®.

mercurial ADJ mercurial.

Mercurio NM Mercury.

mercurio NM mercury.

mercurocromo NM Mercurochrome ®.

merdoso: ADJ filthy.

merecedor ADJ deserving, worthy (*de* of); **~ de crédito** solvent; **~ de confianza** trustworthy; **ser ~ de** to deserve, be deserving of.

merecer [2d] [1] VT (a) (*gen*) to deserve, be worthy of, merit; **~ + infin** to deserve to + *infin*; **merece que se le dé el premio** he deserves to receive the prize; **el trato que él nos merece** the treatment he deserves from us; **te lo tienes merecido** it serves you right. (b) (*And*) (*atrapar*) to catch; (*robar*) to snatch, pinch*; (*encontrar*) to find.

[2] VI to be deserving, be worthy; **~ mucho** to be very deserving; **bien de la patria** to deserve well of one's country, deserve one's country's gratitude.

merecidamente ADV deservedly.

merecido [1] ADJ well deserved, fully deserved; **bien ~ lo tiene** it serves him right.

[2] NM (just) deserts; **llevar su ~** to get one's deserts.

merecimiento NM (a) (*lo merecido*) deserts. (b) (*cualidad*) merit, worthiness.

merendar [1j] [1] VT (a) (*lit*) to have as an afternoon snack.

(b) **~ lo que escribe otro** to look at what sb else is writing; **~ las cartas de otro** to peep at sb else's cards, take a sly look at an opponent's cards.

[2] VI to have an afternoon snack, (*aprox*) to have tea; (*en el campo*) to picnic, take tea out.

[3] **merendarse*** VR (a) **~ algo** to wangle sth*, get sth by a fiddle*.

(b) **~ una fortuna** to squander a fortune.

(c) **~ a uno*** (*fig*) to gobble sb up, make short work of sb; (*And*) to beat sb; (*And, Cono Sur, Méx*: *matar*) to bump sb off:; (*Cono Sur*: *estafar*) to fleece sb.

merendero NM open-air café, snack bar; (*en el campo*) picnic spot; (*Méx: restaurán*) café, lunch counter.

merengar [1h] VT to upset, annoy.

merengue [1] ADJ (of) Real Madrid F.C.

[2] NM (a) (*Culin*) meringue. (b) (*And, Carib, Cono Sur*: *enclenque*) sickly person, invalid. (c) (*Cono Sur*: *alboroto*) row, fuss. (d) (*And, Carib*) a popular dance.

[3] NMPL Real Madrid F.C.

meretriz NF prostitute.

mergo NM cormorant.

meridiana NF (a) (*diván*) divan, couch; (†) chaise longue; (*cama*) day bed. (b) **a la ~** at noon.

meridianamente ADV (*fig*) clearly, with complete clarity; **eso queda ~ claro** that is crystal-clear.

meridiano [1] ADJ (a) (*calor, hora etc*) midday (*atr*). (b) (*fig*) *luz* very bright; *hecho etc* clear as day, crystal-clear.

[2] NM (*Astron, Geog*) meridian.

meridional [1] ADJ southern.

[2] NMF southerner.

merienda NF tea; afternoon snack; (*para viaje*) packed meal; (*en el campo*: *t* **~ campestre**) picnic; (*And*) supper; **~ de negros** (*confusión*) bedlam; (*trato sucio*) crooked deal*, dishonest share-out; **ir de ~** to go for a picnic; **juntar ~s** (*fig*) to join forces, pool one's resources.

merino [1] ADJ merino.

[2] NM merino (sheep); merino wool.

mérito NM (*valor*) merit; worth, value; (*excelencia*) excellence; (*ventaja*) advantage; **de ~** worthy, of merit; **~s de guerra** *corresponde a* mention in dispatches; **hacer ~ de** to mention; **hacer ~s** to strive to be deserving; to strive for recognition; **restar ~ de** to detract from; **alega los siguientes ~s** he quotes the following facts in support (*o* in his favour); **'serán ~s los idiomas'** (*anuncio*) 'languages an advantage'.

meritocracia NF meritocracy.

meritócrata NMF meritocrat.

meritoriaje NM actor's apprenticeship.

meritorio [1] ADJ meritorious, worthy, deserving; praiseworthy.

[2] NM unpaid employee, apprentice, unpaid trainee.

merla NF = **mirlo**.

merlan NM whiting.

merlango NM haddock.

Merlín NM Merlin; **saber más que ~** to know the lot.

merlo[1] NM (*Pez*) black wrasse.

merlo[2*] NM (*LAm*) idiot.

merlucera NF type of fishing boat, used especially for fishing hake.

merluza NF (a) (*Pez*) hake. (b) (*) **coger una ~** to get tight*; **estar ~***, **estar con la ~*** to get boozed up*.

merluzo ADJ silly, stupid.

merma NF (*disminución*) decrease; shrinkage; (*pérdida*) wastage, loss.

mermar [1a] [1] VT to reduce, lessen; to deplete; *pago, raciones etc* to cut down.

[2] VI *y* **mermarse** VR to decrease, dwindle; to be depleted; (*líquido*) to go down; (*fig*) to waste away.

mermelada NF jam; **~ de albaricoques** apricot jam; **~ de naranjas amargas** marmalade.

mero[1] [1] ADJ (a) mere, pure, simple; **el ~ hecho de ...** the mere (*o* simple) fact of ...

(b) (*Méx: preciso*) precise, exact; **a la mera hora** (*lit*) right on time; (*fig**) when it comes right down to it*.

(c) (*Méx: justo*) right; **en el momento ~** at the right moment (*o* time).

(d) (*Méx: mismo*) **el ~ centro** the very centre; **la mera verdad** the plain truth; **el ~ Pedro** Pedro himself; **en la mera calle** right there on the street; **tu ~ papá** your own father.

[2] NM: **el ~**, **el ~*** (*Méx*) the big boss, the top dog.

[3] ADV (a) (*And: sólo*) only.

(b) (*CAm, Méx: pronto*) soon; **ya ~ llega** he'll be here any minute now; **ahora ~** in a moment.

(c) (*CAm: de verdad*) really, truly.

(d) (*Méx: muy*) very.

(e) (*Méx*) (*hace poco*) just; (*precisamente*) exactly, precisely; **ahora ~** right now; **ahora ~ llegó** he's just got here; **aquí ~** right here; **¡ya ~!*** just coming!; **él va ~ adelante** he's just ahead; **¡eso ~!** right!, you've got it!

mero[2] NM (*Pez*) grouper.

merodeador [1] ADJ marauding; prowling.

[2] NM (*Mil etc*) marauder; raider; (*de noche*) prowler.

merodear [1a] VI (a) (*Mil etc*) to maraud; (*de noche*) to prowl (about), rove about. (b) (*Méx*) to make money by illicit means.

merodeo NM marauding; prowling, roving.

merolico NM (*Méx*) quack, medicine man.

merovingio, -a ADJ, NM/F Merovingian.

mersa*, **merza*** (*Cono Sur*) [1] ADJ (*de mal gusto*) naff*; (*ostentoso*) flashy.

[2] NMF parvenu.

[3] NF (*hampa*) mob, gang.

mes NM (a) (*lit*) month; **50 dólares al ~** 50 dollars a month; **~ lunar** lunar month; **el ~ corriente** the current month, this month; **el ~ que viene, el ~ próximo** next month.

(b) (*Fin*) (*sueldo*) month's pay; (*pago*) monthly payment; **el treceavo ~** the annual bonus.

(c) (*Med*) menses; **estar con el ~, tener el ~** to be having one's period.

mesa NF (a) (*gen*) table; (*t* **~ de trabajo**) desk; (*Com*) counter; **~ de alas abatibles** gate-leg(ged) table, table with flaps; **~ auxiliar** side-table; **~ de billar** billiard-table; **~ de café, ~ de centro** coffee-table; café table; **~ de comedor** dining-table; **~ de despacho** office desk; **~ digitalizadora** graph pad; **~ de negociación** negotiating table; **~ de noche** bedside table; **~ de operaciones, ~ operatoria** operating table; **~ ratona** (*Cono Sur*) coffee-table; **~ redonda** (*restaurante*) general table; (*Hist*) Round Table; (*Pol*) round table; (*conferencia*) round-table conference; **~ de tijera** folding table; **~ de trabajo** desk; **dinero sobre la ~** (offer of) money on the table; **alzar la ~, levantar la ~, quitar la ~** to clear away, clear the table; **bendecir la ~** to say grace; **poner la ~** to lay the table; **ponerlos sobre la ~:** to lay down the law; **sentarse a la ~** to sit down to table; **¡a la ~!** dinner's ready!; **servir a la ~** to wait at table; **vino de ~** table wine.

(b) (*pensión*) board; **~ y cama** bed and board; **tener a uno a ~ y mantel** to give sb free board.

(c) (*Geog*) meseta, tableland, plateau.

(d) (*Arqui*) landing.

(e) (*de herramienta*) side, flat.

(f) (*personas*) presiding committee, board; **~ electoral** officials in charge of a polling-station.

(g) (*negociación*) discussion, negotiating session.

mesada NF monthly payment.

mesana NF mizzen.

mesarse [1a] VR (a) (*2 personas*) to pull each other's hair. (b) **~ el pelo** (*o* **los cabellos**) to tear one's hair.

mescalina NF mescaline.

mescolanza NF = **mezcolanza**.

mesenterio NM mesentery.

mesera NF (*And, Méx*) waitress.

mesero NM (*And, Méx*) waiter.

meseta NF (a) (*Geog*) meseta, tableland, plateau. (b) (*Arqui*) landing.

mesetario ADJ of the Castilian meseta; (*fig*) Castilian.

mesiánico ADJ messianic.

Mesías NM Messiah.

mesilla NF (a) (*gen*) small table, side table, occasional table; **~ de chimenea** mantelpiece; **~ de noche** bedside table; **~ plegable** folding table; **~ de ruedas** trolley. (b) (*Carib*) market stall.

mesmeriano ADJ mesmeric.

mesmerismo NM mesmerism.

mesmerizante ADJ mesmerizing.

mesmerizar [1f] VT to mesmerize.

mesnada NF armed retinue; (*fig*) troop, band.

mesoamericano, -a ADJ, NM/F Indo-American.

mesolítico ADJ mesolithic; **el M~** the Mesolithic.

mesolito NM mesolith.

mesomorfo NM mesomorph.

mesón[1] NM (*Fís*) meson.

mesón[2] NM (a) (††: *hostería*) inn; (*moderno*) hotel with period décor, olde-worlde pub. (b) (*CAm*) lodging-house, rooming house (*US*). (c) (*Cono Sur*) large table; counter.

mesonera NF (††) innkeeper; (*dueña*) landlady; (*Carib*) waitress.

mesonero NM (††) innkeeper; (*dueño*) landlord; (*Carib*) waiter.

mesteño (*Méx*) [1] ADJ *caballo* wild, untamed.

[2] NM mustang.

mestizaje NM (a) (*acto*) crossbreeding; miscegenation. (b) (*personas*) half-castes (*collectively*).

mestizar [1f] VT to crossbreed; *raza* to adulterate by crossbreeding.

mestizo [1] ADJ *persona* half-caste, half-breed, mixed-race; (*Zool*) cross-bred; hybrid; mongrel.

[2] NM, **mestiza** NF mestizo, half-caste, half-breed; (*Zool*) crossbred animal; hybrid; mongrel.

mesura NF (a) (*gravedad*) gravity, dignity, calm. (b) (*moderación*) moderation, restraint. (c) (*cortesía*) courtesy.

mesurado ADJ (a) (*grave*) grave, dignified, calm. (b) (*moderado*) moderate, restrained. (c) (*cortés*) courteous.

mesurar [1a] [1] VT (a) (*contener*) to restrain, temper. (b) (*LAm*) to measure.

[2] **mesurarse** VR to restrain o.s., act with restraint.

meta [1] NF (a) (*Dep*) goal; (*de carrera*) winning post, finishing-line; **~ volante** (*ciclismo*) sprint; **entrar en ~** to finish, reach the finishing-line. (b) (*fig*) goal, aim, objective.

2 NM (*Dep*) goalkeeper.

meta... PREF meta...

metabólico ADJ metabolic.

metabolismo NM metabolism.

metabolizador ADJ metabolizing.

metabolizar [1f] VT to metabolize.

metacarpiano NM metacarpal.

metacrilato NM methacrylate.

metadona NF methadone.

metafísica[1] NF metaphysics.

metafísico **1** ADJ metaphysical.

2 NM, **metafísica**[2] NF metaphysician.

metáfora NF metaphor.

metafórico ADJ metaphoric(al).

metal NM (**a**) (*gen*) metal; (*Mús*) brass; (*Méx*) ore; **~ en láminas, ~ laminado** sheet metal; **~ pesado** heavy metal; **el vil ~** filthy lucre.
(**b**) (*de voz*) timbre; (*fig*) quality.

metalenguaje NM metalanguage.

metalero ADJ (*And, Cono Sur*) metal (*atr*).

metálico **1** ADJ metallic; metal (*atr*).

2 NM (*en barras*) specie, bullion; (*moneda*) coin; (*contante*) cash; **pagar en ~** to pay (in) cash; **premio en ~** cash prize.

metalista NMF metalworker.

metalistería NF metalwork.

metalizado ADJ (**a**) *pintura* metallic. (**b**) (*fig*) mercenary, dedicated to making money; who sees everything in terms of money.

metalizarse [1f] VR (*fig*) to become mercenary.

metalmecánico ADJ: **industria metalmecánica** (*Cono Sur*) metallurgical industry.

metalurgia NF metallurgy.

metalúrgico **1** ADJ metallurgic(al).

2 NM, **metalúrgica** NF metallurgist.

metamórfico ADJ metamorphic.

metamorfosear [1a] **1** VT to metamorphose, transform (*en* into).

2 **metamorfosearse** VR to be metamorphosed, be transformed, change.

metamorfosis NF INVAR metamorphosis, transformation, change.

metano NM methane.

metástasis NF INVAR metastasis.

metastatizar [1f] VI, **metastizar** [1f] VI to metastasize.

metatarsiano NM metatarsal.

metate NM (*CAm, Méx*) flat stone for grinding.

metátesis NF INVAR metathesis.

metedor(a) NM/F smuggler.

metedura NF (**a**) (*acto de meter*) putting, placing; insertion. (**b**) **~ de pata***** bloomer*, clanger*.

meteduría NF smuggling.

metejón* NM (**a**) (*Cono Sur*) violent love. (**b**) (*And: enredo*) mess.

metelón* ADJ (*Méx*) meddling.

metempsicosis NF INVAR metempsychosis.

meteórico ADJ meteoric (*t fig*).

meteorito NM meteor, meteorite.

meteoro NM (*esp fig*) meteor.

meteoroide NM meteoroid.

meteorología NF meteorology.

meteorológico ADJ meteorological, weather (*atr*).

meteorologista NMF, **meteorólogo, -a** NM/F meteorologist.

metepatas* NMF INVAR person who is always putting his (*o* her) foot in it.

meter [2a] **1** VT (**a**) (*gen*) to put, place; to insert, introduce (*en* in, into); to fit in; to squeeze in; (*Culin*) *ingrediente* to add (*en* to), put (*en* in); *herramienta* to use, ply; **a todo ~*** full-speed; **le están poniendo inyecciones a todo ~** they're pumping injections into him as fast as they can; **¡métetelo donde te quepa!**‡ you can stuff it!‡
(**b**) (*Dep*) *tanto* to score (*a* against).
(**c**) (*Com*: *t ~ de contrabando*) *géneros* to smuggle in.
(**d**) (*causar*) to make, cause; **~ ruido** to cause a stir (*y V* **ruido**); **~ un lío** to make a fuss, stir up trouble; **~ miedo a uno** to scare sb, frighten sb; **~ un susto a uno** to put the wind up sb; **~ prisa a uno** to make sb get a move on.
(**e**) (*apostar*) *dinero* to stake, wager (*en* on); (*Fin*) to invest (*en* in).
(**f**) **no hay quien le meta aquello** nobody seems able to make him understand that, nobody is able to get that idea into his head.
(**g**) *persona* to involve (*en* in); **tú me metiste en este lío** you got me into this mess; **A le metió a B en muchos disgustos** A let B in for a lot of trouble; **¿quién le mete en esto?** who told you to interfere?
(**h**) **~ a uno a trabajar** to put sb to work; **~ a uno a un oficio** to put sb to a trade; **~ a un chico de panadero** to apprentice a lad to a baker, put a lad to the baking trade.
(**i**) (*Cos*) *vestido* to take in, take up, gather.
(**j**) (*) *golpe* to give, deal.
(**k**) (*: encajar*) **~ algo a uno** to palm sth off on sb; to force sth on to ac-

cept sth; **nos metió un largo discurso** he gave us a terribly long speech; **le metieron 5 años de cárcel** they put him away for 5 years; **nos van a ~ más trabajo** they're going to lumber us with more work; **no me meta esas peras** don't try to foist those pears off on me.
(**l**) **~las** (*And*‡) to beat it*.

2 **meterse** VR (**a**) (*introducirse*) **~ en** to go into, get into, enter; **~ en un agujero** to get into a hole, squeeze into a hole; **se metió en la cama** she got into bed; **se metió en la tienda** he went into the shop; **~ en un negocio turbio** to take part in a shady deal, get involved in a shady deal; **~ en peligro** to get into danger; **~ en sí mismo** to withdraw into one's shell; **¿dónde se habrá metido el lápiz?** where can the pencil have got to?
(**b**) (*Geog*) to extend, project; **el cabo se mete en el mar** the cape extends (*o* goes out) into the sea; **el río se mete en el mar** the river flows into the sea.
(**c**) (*fig*) **~ en** to interfere in, meddle in; **¡no se meta en lo que no le importa!, ¡no se meta donde no le llaman!** mind your own business!
(**d**) **~ con uno** (*provocar*) to provoke sb, pick a quarrel with sb; (*abordar*) to accost sb, molest sb; (*mofarse*) to tease sb, have a go at sb.
(**e**) **se ha metido con las tijeras** she has taken the scissors to it.
(**f**) **~ monja** to become a nun; **~ a escritor** to become a writer, (*pey*) set o.s. up as a writer; **~ de aprendiz en un oficio** to go into a trade as an apprentice.
(**g**) **~ a** + *infin* to start (without due preparation) to + *infin*; to take it upon o.s. to + *infin*.

meterete* NM, **metereta*** NF (*Cono Sur*), **metete*** NM (*And, CAm, Cono Sur*) busybody, meddler.

metiche ADJ (*And, Méx**) meddling, meddlesome.

meticón* NM = metijón.

meticulosamente ADV meticulously, scrupulously, thoroughly.

meticulosidad NF meticulousness, scrupulousness, thoroughness.

meticuloso ADJ meticulous, scrupulous, thorough; (*esp LAm: pey*) fussy, petty, small-minded.

metida* NF = metedura.

metido **1** ADJ (**a**) **~ en sí, ~ para adentro** introspective.
(**b**) **estar muy ~ en un asunto** to be deeply involved in a matter.
(**c**) **~ en años** elderly, advanced in years; **está algo metidita en años** she must be getting on a bit now; **~ en carnes** (*Esp*) plump.
(**d**) **estar muy ~ con uno** to be well in with sb.
(**e**) (*LAm: entrometido*) meddling, meddlesome.
(**f**) (*Carib, Cono Sur**: *bebido*) half tight*.

2 NM (**a**) (*: reprimenda*) ticking-off*; **dar** (*o* **pegar**) **un ~ a uno** to give sb a dressing-down*.
(**b**) (‡: *sablazo*) touch*; **pegar un ~ a uno** to touch sb for money*.
(**c**) (*: golpe*) bash*; shove; **pegar un buen ~ a una tarta** to take a good chunk out of a cake.

metijón* NM busybody, meddler.

metilado ADJ: **alcohol ~** methylated spirit.

metílico ADJ: **alcohol ~** methylated spirit.

metilo NM methyl.

metimiento NM (**a**) (*inserción*) insertion. (**b**) (*) influence, pull.

metódicamente ADV methodically.

metódico ADJ methodical.

metodismo NM Methodism.

metodista ADJ, NMF Methodist.

método NM method.

metodología NF methodology.

metodológico ADJ methodological.

metomentodo **1** ADJ INVAR meddling, interfering.

2 NM meddler, busybody.

metonimia NF metonymy.

metraje NM length; (*Dep*) distance; (*Cine*) length; **cinta de largo ~** full-length film; **un discurso de largo ~** (*fig*) a long-winded speech; *V* **cortometraje, mediometraje**.

metralla NF (**a**) (*Mil*) shrapnel. (**b**) (*) coppers, small change.

metralleta NF submachine gun, tommy gun.

métrica NF metrics.

métrico ADJ metric(al).

metro[1] NM (**a**) (*Mat: medida*) metre, meter (*US*); **~ cuadrado** square metre; **~ cúbico** cubic metre; *ver también* | KILOS, METROS, AÑOS |. (**b**) (*Mat: instrumento*) rule, ruler (*t ~ plegable*); **~ de cinta** tape measure.

metro[2] NM (*Ferro: sistema*) underground, tube, subway (*US*); (*estación*) tube station.

metrobús NM combined bus and underground railway ticket.

metrónomo NM metronome.

metrópoli NF metropolis; (*de imperio*) mother country.

metropolitano **1** ADJ metropolitan.

2 NM (**a**) (*Ecl*) metropolitan. (**b**) (*Ferro*) = metro[2].

mexicano (*LAm*) = mejicano.

México NM (*LAm*) Mexico.
mezcal NM (*Méx*) mezcal.
mezcla NF (**a**) (*acto*) mixing.
(**b**) (*sustancia*) mixture; (*fig*) blend, combination; medley; (*Cos*) mixture; mixed cloth; **sin ~** pure, unadulterated; *bebida* neat; **~ explosiva** explosive mixture; (•) unholy mixture.
(**c**) (*Arquit*) mortar.
mezclado NM mixing.
mezclador ⓵ NM mixing bowl.
⓶ NM, **mezcladora¹** NF (**a**) (*TV*) **~ de imágenes** vision mixer; **~ de sonido** dubbing mixer. (**b**) (*Telec*) scrambler.
mezcladora² NF (*Culin*) mixer; **~ de hormigón** concrete mixer.
mezclar [1a] ⓵ VT (**a**) (*gen*) to mix, mix up (together); (*armonizar*) to blend; (*combinar*) to merge, combine; *cartas* to shuffle.
(**b**) (*fig*) **~ a A con B** to involve A with B, get A into trouble with B; **~ a la Iglesia en el debate** to drag the Church into the debate.
⓶ **mezclarse** VR (**a**) (*gen*) to mix, mingle (*con* with); to blend (*con* with).
(**b**) (*alternar*) **~ con cierta gente** to mix with certain people; **hizo mal en ~ con esa familia** she did wrong to marry (beneath herself) into that family.
(**c**) **~ en** (*entrometerse*) to get mixed up in, get involved in; to meddle in.
mezclillo NM (*Cono Sur*) denim.
mezcolanza NF hotchpotch, jumble.
mezquinamente ADV meanly.
mezquinar [1a] ⓵ VT (**a**) (*LAm*) to be stingy with, give sparingly.
(**b**) (*Cono Sur*) **~ el cuerpo** to dodge, swerve; **~ el saludo*** to ignore somebody.
(**c**) (*And*) **~ a uno** to defend sb; **~ a un niño** to let a child off a punishment.
⓶ VI (*LAm*) to be mean, be stingy.
mezquindad NF (**a**) (*cualidad*) meanness, stinginess; poor spirit; pettiness; ignoble nature; paltriness, wretchedness. (**b**) (*acto*) mean action, petty deed.
mezquino ⓵ ADJ (**a**) (*tacaño*) mean, stingy.
(**b**) (*de miras estrechas*) poor-spirited; small-minded, petty; (*vil*) ignoble; (*interesado*) materialistic, lacking the finer sentiments.
(**c**) *cualidad etc* miserable, paltry, tiny; *pago etc* wretched, wretchedly small.
⓶ NM (**a**) (*avaro*) mean person, miser; (*miserable*) petty individual, wretch.
(**b**) (*And, CAm, Méx: verruga*) wart.
mezquita NF mosque.
mezquite NM (*Méx*) mesquite (tree).
mezzanina NF (*LAm*), **mezzanine¹** NM (*LAm*) mezzanine.
mezzanine² [metsa'nine] NM (*And Teat*) circle.
mezzosoprano ['metso-] NF mezzo-soprano.
M.F. NF ABR *de* **modulación de frecuencia** frequency modulation, FM.
mg. ABR *de* **miligramo** milligram(me), mg.
MHz ABR *de* **megahercio** megahertz, MHz.
mi¹ ADJ POS my.
mi² NM (*Mús*) E; **~ mayor** E major.
mí PRON (*tras prep*) me; myself; **¡a ~!** (*Esp*) help!; **¡a ~ con ésas!** come off it!*, tell me another!; **¿y a ~ qué?** so what?, what has that got to do with me?; **para ~ no hay duda** so far as I'm concerned there's no doubt, I don't believe there can be any doubt; **por ~, puede ir** so far as I'm concerned she can go; **por ~ mismo** by myself; on my own account.
miaja NF (**a**) (*gen*) crumb. (**b**) (*fig*) bit, tiny portion; **ni (una) ~ de** not the least little bit of. (**c**) (*como adv*) a bit; **me quiere una ~** she likes me a bit.
mialgia NF myalgia.
miasma NM miasma.
miasmático ADJ miasmic.
miau NM mew, miaow.
Mibor NM ABR *de* **Madrid inter-bank offered rate**.
mica¹ NF (**a**) (*Min*) mica. (**b**) (*Carib Aut*) sidelight.
mica² NF (*And*) chamberpot.
mica³* NF (*CAm*) drunkenness; **ponerse una ~** to get drunk.
micada NF (*CAm, Méx*) flourish.
micción NF urination.
miccionar [1a] VI to urinate.
miche NM (**a**) (*Méx: gato*) cat. (**b**) (*Carib: licor*) liquor, spirits. (**c**) (*Cono Sur: juego*) game of marbles. (**d**) (*CAm: pelea*) fight, brawl.
michelín* NM spare tyre, roll of fat.
michi NM (*And*) noughts and crosses.
michino, -a NM/F, **micho, -a*** NM/F puss, pussy cat.
mico NM, **mica⁴** NF (**a**) (*Zool*) monkey, (*esp*) long-tailed monkey.
(**b**) (•) (*feo*) ugly devil; (*engreído*) conceited person, swank*; (*mariposón*) flirt; (*cachondo*) randy man*, old goat*; **¡~!** (*a niño*) you little monkey!

(**c**) **dar ~, hacer ~** to miss a date, stand sb up*; **dar el ~** (*estafar*) to cheat; (*decepcionar*) to disappoint, behave differently from what had been hoped; **volverse ~ para hacer algo** to be at one's wits' end to know how to do sth.
(**d**) (*CAm***) cunt**.
micoleón NM (*CAm*) kincajou.
micología NF mycology.
micra NF micron.
micrero NM (*Cono Sur*) minibus driver.
micro¹* NM (*Rad*) mike*, microphone.
micro² NM (*a veces* NF) (*And, Cono Sur: corta distancia*) minibus, bus; (*Cono Sur: larga distancia*) coach.
micro³ NM (*Inform*) micro, microcomputer.
micro... PREF micro...; mini...
microalgas NFPL micro-algae.
microbiano ADJ microbial.
microbio NM (**a**) microbe. (**b**) (‡) sprog‡, small child.
microbiología NF microbiology.
microbiológico ADJ microbiological.
microbiólogo, -a NM/F microbiologist.
microbús NM minibus.
microcasete NM o NF, **micro-cassette** NM o NF micro-cassette.
microchip NM, PL **microchips** microchip.
microcircuitería NF microcircuitry.
microcircuito NM microcircuit.
microcirugía NF microsurgery.
microclima NM microclimate.
microcomputador NM, **microcomputadora** NF micro(computer).
microcosmo(s) NM microcosm.
microeconomía NF microeconomy.
microeconómica NF microeconomics.
microeconómico ADJ microeconomic.
microelectrónica NF microelectronics.
microelectrónico ADJ microelectronic.
microespaciado NM microspacing.
microfalda NF micro-skirt.
microficha NF microfiche.
microfilm NM, PL **microfilms, microfilmes** microfilm.
microfilmar [1a] VT to microfilm.
micrófono NM microphone; (*Telec*) mouthpiece; **~ sin hilos, ~ inalámbrico** cordless microphone.
microforma NF microform.
microfotografiar [1c] VT to microphotograph .
microfundio NM smallholding, small farm.
microinformática NF microcomputing.
microinyectar [1a] VT to microinject.
microlentillas NFPL (*Esp*) contact lenses.
micrómetro NM micrometer.
microonda NF microwave; **~s** (*m*), **horno (de) ~s** microwave oven.
microordenador NM micro(computer).
microorganismo NM microorganism.
micropastilla NF (*Inform*) microchip.
microplaquita NF: **~ de silicio** silicon chip.
microprocesador NM microcomputer.
microprograma NM (*Inform*) microprogram.
micropunto NM microdot.
microscopía NF microscopy.
microscópico ADJ microscopic.
microscopio NM microscope; **~ electrónico** electron microscope.
microsegundo NM microsecond.
microsurco NM microgroove; **disco (de) ~** long-playing record (*LP*).
microtaxi NM minicab.
microtecnia NF, **microtecnología** NF microtechnology.
microtenis NM (*LAm*) table-tennis.
microtransmisor NM micro-transmitter.
Midas NM Midas.
midi NM, **midifalda** NF midiskirt.
MIE NM (*Esp*) ABR *de* **Ministerio de Industria y Energía**.
miéchica INTERJ (*LAm: euf*) damn!*, shoot!*.
miedica(s)* NMF coward.
mieditis* NF funk*; jitters*.
miedo NM (**a**) (*gen*) fear, dread (*a, de* of); apprehension, nervousness; **~ cerval, ~ espantoso** great fear; (*Teat etc*) **~ al público** stage fright; **por ~ a, por ~ de** for fear of; **por ~ de que ...** for fear that ...; **dar ~ a, infundir ~ a, meter ~ a** to scare, frighten, fill with fear; **me da ~** he scares me, he makes me nervous; **le daba ~ hacerlo** he was nervous about doing it; **en este punto siempre me entra un ~ terrible** I always get terribly nervous at this point; **tener ~** to be afraid (*a* of); **no tengas ~** don't worry; **tener ~ de** + *infin* to be afraid to + *infin*, be afraid (*o* nervous) of + *ger*.
(**b**) (*) **¡qué ~!** how awful!; **de ~** (ADJ) wonderful, smashing*, marvel-

lous; (*pey*) awful, ghastly*; (ADV) wonderfully, marvellously; (*pey*) awfully; **es un coche de ~** it's a smashing car*; **eso fue de ~** it was tremendous*, (*pey*) it was ghastly*; **hace un frío de ~** it's terribly cold.
miedoso ADJ fearful, fainthearted; timid, nervous, shy.
miel NF **(a)** (*lit*) honey.
  (b) (*melaza*: *t* ~ **de caña, ~ negra**) molasses.
  (c) (*locuciones*) **las ~es del triunfo** the sweets of success; **es ~ sobre hojuelas** it's marvellous, it's even better than I (*etc*) expected; **no hay ~ sin hiel** nothing is ever entirely perfect; **dejar a uno con la ~ en los labios** to snatch sth away from sb, spoil sb's fun; **quedarse con la ~ en los labios** to get a taste but no more, remain unsatisfied; to come close to success without attaining it; **hacerse de ~** to be excessively kind, be almost too sweet; **hazte de ~ y te comerán las moscas** if you are too nice people will take advantage of you.
mielero NM honeypot.
mielga NF lucerne, alfalfa.
miembro [1] NM **(a)** (*Anat*) limb, member; ~ **(viril)** (*male*) member, penis.
  (b) (*Ling, Mat etc*) member.
  [2] NMF (*persona*) member; fellow, associate; **no ~** non-member; **hacerse ~ de** to become a member of.
  [3] *como* ADJ member; **los países ~s** the member countries.
mientes NFPL: **¡ni por ~!** never!, not on your life!; **parar ~ en** to reflect on, consider carefully; **traer a las ~** to recall; **se le vino a las ~** it occurred to him, it came to his mind.
▼ **mientras** [1] CONJ **(a)** (*gen*) while; as long as; ~ **duraba la guerra** while the war lasted, as long as the war lasted; ~ **él estaba fuera** while he was abroad; ~ **no venga** until he comes.
  ▼ **(b)** ~ **(que)** whereas; ~ **más tienen más quieren** the more they have the more they want.
  (c) (*LAm*) ~ **más lo repetía, menos lo creía** the more he repeated it, the less I believed him.
  [2] ADV meanwhile, meantime (*t y ~, ~ tanto*); all the while.
miérc. ABR *de* **miércoles** Wednesday, Weds., Wed.
miércoles NM INVAR **(a)** Wednesday; ~ **de ceniza** Ash Wednesday. **(b)** (*: euf*) **¡~!** sugar!*
mierda⚹ NF **(a)** (*lit*) shit⚹; (*fig*) filth, dirt; **¡~!** shit!⚹
  (b) (*fig*) **es un(a)** ~ he's a shit⚹; **es un don M~** he's a nobody; **el libro es una ~** the book is crap⚹; **¡50 dólares, una ~!** 50 dollars, nearly nothing!; **es una ~ de coche** it's a bloody awful car⚹; **una película de ~** a crappy film⚹; **esos políticos de ~** those lousy politicians⚹; **marcó un gol de pura ~** he scored a goal by an almighty fluke*; **¿qué ~s ocurre?** what the hell is going on?; **coger** (*o* **pillar**) **una ~** (*Esp*) to get sozzled⚹; **¡vaya Vd a la ~!** go to hell!, piss off!⚹
  (c) (*droga*) hash*.
mierdear⚹ [1a] VT to upset, bother, mess around.
mierdoso⚹ ADJ filthy.
mies NF **(a)** (*granos*) (*ripe*) corn, wheat, grain. **(b)** (*temporada*) harvest time. **(c)** (*campos*) ~**es** cornfields.
miga NF **(a)** (*gen*) crumb; (*fig*) bit; ~**s** (*Culin*) fried breadcrumbs.
  (b) (*fig*) core, substance, essence; **esto tiene su ~** there's sth in this; there's more in this than meets the eye.
  (c) **hacer algo ~s** to break sth up, smash sth into little pieces; **hacer ~s a uno** to leave sb in a sorry state; **tener los pies hechos ~s** to be footsore; **hacer buenas ~s** to get on well, hit it off (*con* with).
migajas NFPL crumbs; bits; (*fig*) leavings, scraps.
migar [1h] VT to crumble, break up.
migra* NF (*LAm*) corps of immigration police, immigration authorities.
migración NF migration.
migraña NF migraine.
migrar [1a] VI to migrate.
migratorio ADJ migratory.
Miguel NM Michael; ~ **Ángel** Michelangelo.
mijo NM millet.
mil ADJ Y NM thousand; **tres ~ coches** three thousand cars; ~ **doscientos dólares** one thousand two hundred dollars; **lo ha hecho ~ veces** he's done it hundreds of times; ~**es y** ~**es** thousands and thousands; **a las ~*** at some ungodly hour*, terribly late.
miladi NF milady.
milagrero* [1] ADJ **(a)** (*que cree en milagros*) **personas milagreras** people who believe in miracles. **(b)** *curación, poder* miraculous; *persona* with miraculous powers.
  [2] NM, **milagrera** NF **(a)** (*que cree en milagros*) believer in miracles. **(b)** (*que hace milagros*) miracle-worker.
milagro [1] NM miracle; (*fig*) miracle, wonder, marvel; **económico** economic miracle; **¡ni de ~!** not a bit of it!; **es un ~ que ...** it is a miracle (*o* wonder) that ...; ~ **(sería) que ...** it would be a miracle if ...; **salvarse de ~** to escape miraculously, have a miraculous escape; **vivir de ~** to have a hard time of it, keep going somehow; to manage to stay alive; **hacer ~s** (*fig*) to work wonders.

  [2] ATR miracle (*atr*), miraculous, wonder-working; **cura ~** miracle cure; **entrenador ~** wonder-working coach.
milagrosa* NF police badge.
milagrosamente ADV miraculously.
milagroso ADJ miraculous.
Milán NM Milan.
milanesa NF (*Argentina*: *Culin*) schnitzel, escalope.
milano NM (*Orn*) kite.
mildeu (*t* **mildiu, mildiú**) NM mildew.
mildo ADJ (*Cono Sur*) timid, shy.
milenariamente ADV: **un pueblo ~ libre** a people which has been free for a thousand years.
milenario [1] ADJ millennial; (*fig*) very ancient, age-old.
  [2] NM millennium.
milenio NM millennium.
milenrama NF yarrow.
milésima NF thousandth.
milésimo ADJ, NM thousandth; **hasta el ~** to three places of decimals.
milhojas NM O NF INVAR (*pastel*) *cake made with puff pastry, filled with meringue*; (*Culin*) mille feuille.
mili* NF (*Esp*) military service; **estar en la ~, hacer la ~** to do one's military service.

    | MILI |

  La **mili** *is the colloquial term used in Spain to refer to the compulsory military service (***servicio militar***) which men are drafted into at 18. Exemption is possible on medical grounds and in certain family situations, while students and those living abroad can obtain a deferment (***prórroga***) which allows them to put off doing their military service until a more convenient time. Conscientious objectors (***objetores de conciencia***) can choose to do a longer period of community service, known as* **Prestación Social Sustitutoria (PSS)** *instead of military service. Over recent years, the length of* **la mili** *has been reduced to the current nine months, but there is still plenty of opposition to it and the number of those who refuse to do either military or community service, called* **insumisos**, *has increased. Plans have been drawn up to abolish military service and establish a professional army.*

⇨ *See also* | INSUMISO | , | PRESTACIÓN SOCIAL SUSTITORIA |

---

miliar ADJ: **piedra ~** milestone.
milibar NM millibar.
milicia NF **(a)** (*cuerpo, servicio*) militia; (*soldados*) military, soldiery. **(b)** (*arte*) art of war; science of warfare; (*profesión*) soldiering, military profession. **(c)** (*período*) (period of) military service.
miliciano NM (*And, Cono Sur*) (*soldado*) militiaman; (*conscripto*) conscript.
milico NM **(a)** (*And*) = **miliciano**. **(b)** (*And, Cono Sur**: *pey*) soldier; policeman; (*soldado raso*) squaddie*; **los ~s** the military.
miligramo NM milligram.
mililitro NM millilitre, milliliter (*US*).
milimetrado ADJ (*fig*) minutely calculated; **papel ~** graph paper.
milimétricamente ADV (*fig*) *calcular etc* precisely, minutely, down to the last detail.
milimétrico ADJ (*fig*) precise, minute; **con precisión milimétrica** with pinpoint accuracy.
milímetro NM millimetre, millimeter (*US*); **lo calculó hasta el ~** (*fig*) he calculated it very precisely; **nos siguió al ~** he stuck very close to us.
milisegundo NM millisecond.
militancia NF **(a)** (*cualidad*) militancy. **(b)** (*Pol*: *personas*) (active) membership; ~ **de base** rank-and-file members; ordinary supporters; **¿cuál es su ~ política?** what is his political affiliation?
militante [1] ADJ militant.
  [2] NMF militant; (*Pol*) (active) member; ~ **de base** rank-and-file member.
militantismo NM militancy.
militar [1] ADJ military; *espíritu etc* warlike; **ciencia ~** art of war.
  [2] NM (*soldado*) soldier, military man; serviceman; ~ **de carrera** professional soldier; career officer.
  [3] [1a] VI **(a)** (*Mil*) to serve (in the army); to soldier.
  (b) ~ **en un partido** (*fig*) to belong to a party, be an active member of a party.
  (c) (*fig*) ~ **contra** to militate against; ~ **en defensa de,** ~ **en favor de** to speak for, argue in favour of, lend weight to.
militarada NF military rising, putsch.
militarismo NM militarism.
militarista [1] ADJ militaristic.
  [2] NMF militarist.
militarización NF militarization.
militarizar [1f] VT to militarize; (*disciplinar*) to put under military discipline.
militarote NM (*LAm*: *pey*) rough soldier; blustering soldier.

milla NF mile; **~ marina** nautical mile; *ver también* ⏉KILOS, METROS, AÑOS⏉ .

millar NM thousand; **a ~es** in thousands, by the thousand; **los había a ~es** they were there in thousands.

millarada NF (about a) thousand.

millardo NM thousand million, billion.

millas-pasajero NFPL passenger miles.

millo NM, **millón**[1] NM (*CAm, Méx*) (*variety of*) millet.

millón[2] NM million; **un ~ de sellos** a million stamps; **3 millones de niños** 3 million children; **¡un ~ de gracias!** a thousand thanks!

millonada* NF million, vast number; **lo vendió por una ~** he sold it for a cool million.

millonario, -a NM/F millionaire.

millonésima NF millionth.

millonésimo ADJ, NM millionth.

milonga NF (**a**) (*: mentirilla*) fib, tale. (**b**) (*And, Cono Sur*) (*baile*) kind of dance rhythm; (*canción*) type of song; (*cabaret*) cabaret; (*: fiesta*) party. (**c**) (*And, Cono Sur: chismes*) gossip.

milonguero, -a NM/F (**a**) (*Mús*) singer of *milongas*. (**b**) (*And: fiestero*) partylover.

milor NM, **milord** [mi'lor] NM milord; **vive como un ~** he lives like a lord.

milpa NF (*CAm, Méx*) (*plantación*) maize field, cornfield (*US*); (*planta*) maize, Indian corn.

milpear [1a] [1] VT (*CAm, Méx*) to prepare for the sowing of maize. [2] VI (**a**) (*CAm, Méx*) to sow a field with maize. (**b**) (*Méx: maíz*) to sprout.

milpero NM (*CAm, Méx*) maize grower.

milpiés NM INVAR millipede.

milrayas ADJ INVAR *made of thinly striped fabric.*

miltomate NM (*CAm, Méx*) small green tomato.

mimado ADJ spoiled.

mimar [1a] VT *niño etc* to spoil, pamper, indulge.

mimbre NM O F (**a**) (*Bot*) osier, willow. (**b**) (*materia*) wicker; **de ~** wicker, wickerwork.

mimbrearse [1a] VR to sway.

mimbrera NF osier.

mimbreral NM osier bed.

mimeografiar [1c] VT to mimeograph.

mimeógrafo NM mimeograph.

miméticamente ADV mimetically, by way of imitation.

mimético ADJ mimetic, imitation (*atr*).

mimetismo NM mimetism; imitation; (*Zool etc*) mimicry.

mimetización NF copying, mimicry, imitation; camouflage.

mimetizarse [1f] VR to change colour, camouflage o.s.

mímica NF (**a**) (*señas*) sign language; (*ademanes*) gesticulation. (**b**) (*imitación*) mimicry; (*una ~*) mime.

mímico ADJ mimic; imitative; **lenguaje ~** sign language.

mimo NM (**a**) (*Teat: Hist*) mime; **hacer ~ de** to mime, mimic. (**b**) (*caricia*) affectionate caress; (*piropo*) nice remark (*etc*); (*gen*) pampering, indulgence; **dar ~s a un niño** to spoil a child; **hacer ~s a uno** to make a great fuss of sb, fuss over sb.

mimosa NF mimosa.

mimoso ADJ (**a**) (*mimado*) spoilt, pampered; (*blandengue*) soft; (*delicado*) fussy, finicky. (**b**) (*con relación al otro sexo*) arch, coy, provocative; kittenish.

min. (**a**) ABR *de* **minuto(s)** minute(s), min. (**b**) ABR *de* **minúscula** lower case, lc.

mina[1] NF (**a**) (*Min*) mine; **~ a cielo abierto** opencast mine; **~ de carbón, ~ hullera** coalmine. (**b**) (*galería*) underground passage; gallery; (*pozo*) shaft. (**c**) (*Mil, Náut*) mine. (**d**) (*de lapicero*) lead; refill. (**e**) (*fig*) mine, storehouse; gold-mine; **~ de información** mine of information.

mina[2]* NF (*Cono Sur*) bird*, girl.

minada NF (*Mil*) mining.

minador NM (**a**) (*Mil*) sapper; (*Min*) mining engineer. (**b**) (*Náut: t* **buque ~**) minelayer.

minar [1a] VT (**a**) (*Min*) to mine. (**b**) (*Mil, Náut*) to mine. (**c**) (*fig*) to undermine, sap, wear away.

minarete NM minaret.

mineral [1] ADJ mineral. [2] NM (*Geol*) mineral; (*Min*) ore; **~ de hierro** iron ore.

mineralero NM ore-carrier.

mineralizar [1f] VT to mineralize.

mineralogía NF mineralogy.

mineralogista NMF mineralogist.

minería NF mining.

minero [1] ADJ mining. [2] NM, **minera** NF miner; **~ de carbón** coalminer; **~ de interior** underground worker.

Minerva NF Minerva.

minestrone NF minestrone.

minga[1]* NF (*Esp*) prick*.

minga[2] NF (*LAm*) (**a**) (*trabajo*) voluntary communal labour, cooperative work. (**b**) (*equipo*) crew, team, gang (of cooperative workers).

mingaco NM (*And, Cono Sur*) = **minga**[2] (**a**).

mingar [1h] VT (**a**) (*And, Cono Sur*) *proyecto, tarea* to work communally on, contribute cooperatively to. (**b**) (*And, Cono Sur*) *obreros* to call together for a communal task. (**c**) (*And: atacar*) to set on, attack.

mingitorio* NM urinal.

Mingo NM *forma familiar de* **Domingo.**

mini [1] NF (*falda*) mini, miniskirt. [2] NM (*Aut*) Mini; (*Inform*) microcomputer.

mini... PREF mini...; (*como* PREF *hum*) **minibikini** microscopic bikini; **mininovillo** (*Taur*) baby bull, tiny bull.

miniacería NF small steelworks.

miniar [1b] VT *manuscrito* to illuminate.

miniatura [1] ADJ INVAR miniature; *perro etc* toy; **golf ~** miniature golf(course); **relojes ~** miniature watches. [2] NF miniature; **en ~** in miniature.

miniaturista NMF miniaturist.

miniaturización NF miniaturization.

miniaturizar [1f] VT to miniaturize.

minibar NM minibar.

minicadena NF mini hi-fi.

minicalculadora NF pocket calculator.

minicasino NM small gambling club.

minicines NMPL *cinema with several small screens.*

minicoche NM (*Esp*) minicar.

minicomputador NM minicomputer.

minidisco NM (*Inform*) diskette.

miniestadio NM small sports arena.

minifalda NF miniskirt.

minifaldero ADJ short-skirted, miniskirted.

minifundio NM smallholding, small farm.

minifundismo NM (*fig*) tendency to fragment, fragmentation.

minifundista NMF smallholder.

minigira NF short tour.

minigolf NM putting (green), miniature golf(-course).

minihorno NM small oven.

mínima NF (*Met*) low, lowest temperature.

minimalismo NM minimalism.

minimalista ADJ, NMF minimalist.

mínimamente ADV minimally.

minimizar [1f] VT to minimize.

mínimo [1] ADJ (*gen*) minimum; (*insignificante*) minimal; (*más pequeño*) smallest, slightest, least; **cifra mínima** minimum number, smallest figure; **sin el más ~ esfuerzo** without the slightest effort; **no contribuye en lo más ~** it doesn't help at all, it doesn't help in the least; **no me importa en lo más ~** it doesn't matter to me in the least. [2] NM (**a**) minimum; **como ~** as a minimum, at the very least; **~ de presión** (*Met*) low-pressure area, trough; **estar bajo ~s** to be at a low ebb. (**b**) (*Carib: Aut*) choke.

mínimum NM minimum.

minina[1]* NF (*Esp*) willie*.

minino, -a[2] NM/F puss, pussy-cat.

minio NM red lead, minium.

miniordenador NM microcomputer.

minipíldora NF minipill.

Minipimer ® NM electric mixer.

miniserie NF miniseries.

ministerial ADJ ministerial; governmental.

ministerio NM ministry; **M~ fiscal** Attorney General's Office; *V* **asunto, gobernación** *etc.*

ministrable NMF candidate for minister; possible minister, potential minister.

ministro, -a NM/F minister; **primer ~, primera ministra** prime minister; **~ portavoz** government spokesperson; **~ sin cartera** minister without portfolio; **~ en la sombra** shadow minister.

minivacaciones NFPL short break *sing.*

minivestido NM minidress.

minoración NF reduction, diminution.

minorar [1a] VT to reduce, diminish.

minoría NF minority; **~ de edad** minority.

minoridad NF minority (*of age*).

minorista NM (*Carib, Cono Sur*) retailer, retail trader.

minoritario ADJ minority (*atr*); **gobierno ~** minority government.

Minotauro NM Minotaur.

minucia NF (*detalle*) trifle, insignificant detail; (*bagatela*) mere nothing; (*pedazo*) morsel, tiny bit; **~s** petty details, minutiae.

minuciosamente ADV thoroughly, meticulously; in a very detailed way; minutely.

minuciosidad NF thoroughness, meticulousness; detailed nature; minuteness.

minucioso ADJ (*meticuloso*) thorough, meticulous; (*detallado*) very detailed; (*pequeño*) minute.

minué NM minuet.

minuetto NM (*Mús*) minuet, minuetto.

minúscula NF small letter; (*Tip*) lower case letter.

minúsculo ADJ tiny, minute, minuscule; (*Tip*) small.

minusvalía NF (a) (physical) handicap. (b) (*Com*) depreciation, capital loss.

minusvalidez NF state of being (physically) handicapped, disablement, disability.

minusválido ⊡ ADJ (physically) handicapped, disabled.
⊡ NM, **minusválida** NF handicapped person, disabled person; **los ~s** the handicapped; **~ físico** physically handicapped person; **~ psíquico** mentally handicapped person.

minusvalorar [1a] VT to undervalue; to underestimate.

minusvalorizar [1f] VT to undervalue.

minuta NF (a) (*borrador*) rough draft, first draft; (*copia*) carbon copy.
(b) (*apunte*) note, memorandum; (*Jur*) lawyer's bill.
(c) (*lista*) list, roll.
(d) (*Culin*) menu; **a la ~** (*Carib, Cono Sur*) rolled in breadcrumbs.
(e) (*Cono Sur*) (*basura*) junk, trash; (*tienda*) junk shop.
(f) (*CAm: bebida*) flavoured ice drink.

minutado NM, **minutaje** NM timing, running time; timing schedule.

minutar [1a] VT (a) *contrato* to draft. (b) *cliente* to bill.

minutario NM minute book.

minutero NM (*manecilla*) minute-hand; (*reloj*) timer.

minutisa NF sweet william.

minuto NM minute.

miñango* NM (*And, Cono Sur*) bit, small piece; **hecho ~s** smashed to pieces, in smithereens.

miñoco NM (*And*) grimace.

miñón ADJ (*LAm*) sweet, cute.

mío ADJ Y PRON mine, of mine; **es ~**, **es el ~** it is mine; **lo ~** (what is) mine, what belongs to me; **no es amigo ~** he's no friend of mine; **¡hijo ~!** my dear boy!; **los ~s** my people, my relations, my family.

miope ⊡ ADJ short-sighted, myopic.
⊡ NMF short-sighted person.

miopía NF short-sightedness, myopia.

miosis NF INVAR miosis, myosis.

miosotis NF INVAR myosotis, myosote, forget-me-not.

MIPS NMPL ABR *de* **millones de instrucciones por segundo** millions of instructions per second, MIPS.

MIR [mir] (a) NM (*Esp Med*) ABR *de* **Médico interno y residente**. (b) NM (*Bolivia*) ABR *de* **Movimiento de Izquierda Revolucionaria**.

mira NF (a) **estar a la ~** to be on the look-out, keep watch (*de* for).
(b) (*Mil, Téc etc*) sight(s); **~ de bombardeo** bombsight; **~ telescópica** telescopic sight; **con la ~ puesta en** (*fig*) with one's sights set on.
(c) (*Mil*) watchtower, look-out post.
(d) (*fig*) aim, intention; **con la ~ de** + *infin* with the aim of + *ger*; **con ~s a** with a view to; **llevar una ~ interesada** to have a selfish end in view; **poner la ~ en** to aim at, aspire to; **tener ~s sobre** to have designs on.
(e) (*fig*) **de amplias ~s** broad in outlook; tolerant, broad-minded; **de ~s estrechas** narrow-minded; insular, parochial.

mirada NF (a) (*gen*) look, glance; gaze; **~ fija** stare; hard look; **~ de soslayo** sidelong glance; **~ perdida**, **~ vaga** vague look, distant look; **aguantar la ~ de uno** to stare sb out; **apartar la ~** to look away (*de* from); **apuñalar** (*o* **fulminar**) **a uno con la ~** to look daggers at sb; **clavar la ~ en** to fix one's eyes on; **echar una ~ a** to glance at; to keep an eye on; **huir de las ~s de uno** to avoid looking sb in the eye; **lanzar una ~ a** to glance at, cast a glance at; **levantar la ~** to raise one's eyes; **no levanta la ~ del libro** he never takes his eyes off the book; **resistir la ~ de uno** to stare back at sb, stare sb out.
(b) (*expresión*) look, expression; **con una ~ triste** with a sad look.

miradero NM (a) (*atalaya*) look-out, vantage point. (b) (*atracción*) cynosure (of every eye), person (*etc*) that attracts every eye.

mirado ADJ (a) (*estimado*) well thought of, well liked, highly regarded; **no está bien ~ que ...** it is not thought proper that ...; **mal ~** disliked (*V t* **malmirado**).
(b) (*juicioso*) sensible; (*educado*) well-behaved; (*considerado*) considerate, thoughtful; (*cauto*) cautious; **ser ~ en los gastos** to be sensible about what one spends, be a careful spender.
(c) (*pey*) finicky, fussy.
(d) **bien ~** (*como ADV*) by rights, in justice, if everything is weighed up.

mirador NM (a) (*Arquit*) (*ventana*) bay window; (*balcón*) (enclosed) balcony; **~ de popa** (*Náut*) stern gallery. (b) (*atalaya*) viewpoint, vantage point.

miraguano NM (*material*) silk cotton, kapok; (*árbol*) silk cotton tree, kapok tree.

miramiento NM (a) (*consideración*) considerateness; (*cortesía*) courtesy; **sin ~** without consideration, discourteously.
(b) (*circunspección*) caution, circumspection, care; (*pey*) timidity, excessive caution.
(c) **~s** (*cortesías*) courtesies, attentions; **sin ~s** unceremoniously; high-handed(ly); **sin ~s de** regardless of; **andar con ~s** to tread carefully; **tratar sin ~s a uno** to treat sb without consideration, ride roughshod over sb.

miranda* NF: **estar de ~** (*gandulear*) to be idle, loaf around; (*mirar*) to look on, be an onlooker.

mirar [1a] ⊡ VT (a) (*gen*) to look at; to gaze at; (*observar*) to watch; **miraba la foto** she was looking at the photo; **miraba los barcos** she was watching the boats; **la miré subir la escalera** I watched her go (*o* going) upstairs; **le miraron la cartera** they looked at his wallet; **~ fijamente a uno** to stare at sb, look hard at sb; **~ algo por encima** to glance over sth, glance cursorily at sth.
(b) (*fig: pensar*) to consider, think over, think carefully about; **lo hago mirando el porvenir** I do it bearing the future in mind; **no mira las dificultades** he doesn't take account of the difficulties; **mirándolo bien** all in all; by rights; on second thoughts; **¡mira lo que haces!** just think what you're doing!; **¡mira con quien hablas!** just remember who you're talking to!
(c) **~ a uno como** (*fig: considerar*) to look on sb as, consider sb to be.
(d) (*fig: vigilar*) to watch, keep an eye on, be careful about; **conviene ~ el bolso** it's best to keep an eye on your handbag.
(e) (*fig: estimar*) to value, think highly of; **~ bien** to like; **~ mal** to dislike.
(f) (*LAm*) to see.
⊡ VI (a) (*gen*) to look; to glance; **no habla pero mira mucho** he never speaks but he keeps on looking; **¡mira!**, **¡mire!** look!; (*protesta*) look here!; **¡pero mire!** now look here!; **¡mira que no tenemos dinero!** remember that we haven't any money!; **¡mira lo que tenemos que aguantar!** look at what we have to put up with!; **¡mira que si es mentira!** just suppose it isn't true!, what if it's not true?; **mira si ha venido el taxi** look and see if the taxi has come; **¡(pues) mira por donde ...!** just imagine ...!; surprise, surprise!; **~ alrededor** to look around; **~ atrás** to look back (*fig*), think about the past; **~ hacia otro lado** to look the other way; **~ por la ventana** to look out of the window; **~ por un agujero** to look through a hole; **~ de través** to squint (*V t* **través 2**).
(b) (*Arquit*) to face; to look on to, open on to; **la casa mira al sur** the house faces south.
(c) **~ a** (*fig*) to aim at, have in mind.
(d) **por lo que mira a** as for, as regards.
(e) (*fig*) **~ por** to look after, take care of; **~ por sí** to look out for o.s., consider one's own safety.
⊡ **mirarse** VR (a) (*gen*) to look at o.s.; **~ al espejo** to look at o.s. in the mirror.
(b) (*2 personas*) to look at one another; **nos miramos asombrados** we looked at each other in amazement; **~ a los ojos** to look into each other's eyes.
(c) **se mire como se mire** whichever way one looks at it; **~ muy bien de hacer algo** to think twice about doing sth; to think carefully before doing sth; **~ en ello** to watch one's step.

mirasol NM sunflower.

miríada NF myriad; **~(s) de moscas** a myriad flies.

mirilla NF peephole, spyhole; (*Fot*) viewer.

miriñaque NM (a) (*Hist*) crinoline, hoop skirt. (b) (*Cono Sur Ferro*) cowcatcher. (c) (*Carib, Méx*) thin cotton cloth.

miriópodo NM millipede; myriapod.

miristiquívoro ADJ myristicivorous.

mirlarse [1a] VR to put on airs, act important.

mirlo NM (a) (*Orn*) blackbird.
(b) **~ blanco** (*fig*) exceptional thing, highly unusual thing; one in a million; impossible dream.
(c) (*fig*) self-important air, pompousness.
(d) (**‡**: *lengua*) tongue; **achantar el ~** to shut one's trap‡.

mirobrigense ⊡ ADJ of Ciudad Rodrigo.
⊡ NMF native (*o* inhabitant) of Ciudad Rodrigo; **los ~s** the people of Ciudad Rodrigo.

mirón ⊡ ADJ inquisitive, curious.
⊡ NM, **mirona** NF (*espectador*) onlooker, watcher, observer; (*pey*) nosey-parker*; (*voyer*) voyeur; (*Naipes*) kibitzer; **los mirones son de piedra** those watching the game are not allowed to speak; **estar de ~** to look on (without doing anything); to stand by (doing nothing); **ir de ~** to go along just to see.

mironismo NM voyeurism.

mirra NF (a) myrrh. (b) (*Carib: trocito*) small piece.

mirtilo NM bilberry, whortleberry.

mirto NM myrtle.

mis NF = **miss**.

misa NF mass; **~ del alba** early morning mass; **~ del gallo** midnight mass (on Christmas Eve); **~ mayor, ~ solemne** high mass; **~ negra** black mass; **~ rezada** low mass; **como en ~** in dead silence; **celebrar** (o **decir**) **~** to celebrate mass; **ir a ~** to go to mass, go to church; **oír ~** to go to mass, attend mass; **ser como ~ de pobre** to last all too short a time; **no saben de la ~ la media** they don't know the half of it; **eso va a ~** (fig) that's the honest truth; **estos datos van a ~** (fig) these facts are utterly trustworthy.

misacantano NM priest saying his first mass; ordained priest.

misal NM missal.

misantropía NF misanthropy.

misantrópico ADJ misanthropic.

misántropo, -a NM/F misanthrope, misanthropist.

misario NM acolyte, altar boy.

miscelánea NF (a) (lit) miscellany. (b) (Méx) corner shop.

misceláneo ADJ miscellaneous.

misera NF lobster.

miserable ⓵ ADJ (a) persona mean, stingy; miserly; suma etc miserable, paltry, pitifully small.
(b) (moralmente) rotten*, vile, contemptible, despicable; **¡~!** you rotter!*, you wretch!
(c) cuarto, lugar etc squalid, sordid.
⓶ NMF wretch; rotter*, cad; **¡eres un ~!** you're a rotter!*

miserando ADJ (esp LAm) pitiful.

miseria NF (a) (pobreza) poverty, destitution; (carencia) want; **caer en la ~** to fall into abject poverty; **vivir en la ~** to live in poverty.
(b) (condiciones) squalor, squalid conditions.
(c) (piojos) fleas, lice; **estar lleno de ~** to be covered with vermin.
(d) **una ~** (Fin) a tiny sum, a mere pittance; a tiny amount.
(e) (tacañería) meanness, stinginess.

misericordia NF (a) (compasión) pity, compassion. (b) (perdón) forgiveness; mercy.

misericordioso ADJ (V NF) (a) compassionate. (b) forgiving; merciful.

misero* ADJ churchy, fond of going to church.

mísero ADJ (a) (desgraciado) wretched. (b) = **miserable**.

misérrimo ADJ utterly wretched.

Misiá* NF, **Misia*** NF (esp Cono Sur: tratamiento) Missis*, Missus*; **~ Eugenia** Miss Eugenia.

misil NM missile; **~ de alcance medio** medium-range missile; **~ antimisil** antimissile missile; **~ autodirigido** guided missile; **~ balístico** ballistic missile; **~ buscador del calor** heat-seeking missile; **~ (de) crucero** cruise missile; **~ tierra-aire** ground-to-air missile.

misilístico ADJ missile (atr).

misión NF mission; job, task; **misiones** missions, missionary work (Ecl); **~ investigadora** fact-finding mission; **~ de buena voluntad** goodwill mission.

misional ADJ missionary.

misionero, -a NM/F missionary.

Misisipí NM Mississippi.

misiva NF missive.

miskito NM Miskito.

mismamente* ADV (sólo) only, just; (literalmente) literally; (hasta) even; (en realidad) really, actually; **ayer ~ vino** it was only yesterday he came.

mismísimo ADJ SUPERL selfsame, very same; **por mis ~s ojos** with my very own eyes; **es Vd el ~ diablo** you're the very devil in person; **estuvo el ~ obispo** the bishop himself was there; **es el ~ que yo perdí** it's the very (same) one I lost; **estoy hasta los ~s*** I'm utterly fed up*.

▼ **mismo** ⓵ ADJ (a) (lit) same (que as, that); **el ~ coche** the same car; **viven en la misma calle** they live in the same street; **es el ~ que vi ayer** it's the same (one) as I saw yesterday; **el policía y el ladrón son el ~** the policeman and the thief are one and the same; **quedar en las mismas** to be no further forward, show no progress.
▼(b) (con **lo**) **lo ~** the same, the same thing; **es lo ~** it's the same thing, it comes to the same thing; **no es lo ~** it's not the same (at all); **él diría lo ~** he would say the same; **por lo ~** for the same reason; **lo ~ A que B** both A and B; **o lo que es lo ~** or what amounts to the same thing; **lo ~ si viene que si no viene** whether he comes or not; **lo ~ no vienen** they may (equally well) not come; V **dar**.
(c) (con PRON PERS) -self; **yo ~** I myself; **yo ~ lo vi** I saw it myself; **lo hizo por sí ~** he did it by himself; **perjudicarse a sí ~** to harm one's own interests.
(d) (enfático) very; selfsame; **en ese ~ momento** at that very moment; **en Argentina misma, en la misma Argentina** in Argentina itself; **hoy ~** this very day; **ayer ~** only yesterday; **estuvo el ~ ministro** the (very) minister himself was there; **ella es la misma caridad** she is charity itself; **eso ~ digo yo** that's just what I say.
(e) (Méx: relativo) **~ que** who; which.

⓶ ADV right; **aquí ~** right here, on this very spot; **ayer ~** only yesterday; **delante ~ de la casa** right in front of the house.

⓷ como CONJ: **lo ~ que** just like, just as (if); **lo ~ que Vd es médico yo soy ingeniero** just as you are a doctor I am an engineer; **nos divertimos lo ~ que si hubiéramos ido al baile** we had just as good a time as if we had gone to the dance; **lo ~ que me levanto a las 6 me levantaría a las 5** just as I get up at 6 so I would gladly get up at 5.

misogamia NF misogamy.

misógamo, -a NM/F misogamist.

misoginia NF misogyny.

misógino NM misogynist.

miss [mis] NF beauty queen; **M~ España** Miss Spain.

míster NM (a) (hum) (any) Briton. (b) (Dep) trainer, coach.

misterio NM (a) (gen) mystery; **no hay ~** there's no mystery about it. (b) (lo secreto) secrecy; **obrar con ~** to go about sth secretly, go to work in secrecy. (c) (Teat: Hist) mystery play.

misteriosamente ADV mysteriously; puzzlingly.

misterioso ADJ mysterious; mystifying, puzzling.

mística¹ NF, **misticismo** NM mysticism.

místico ⓵ ADJ mystic(al).
⓶ NM, **mística²** NF mystic.

mistificación NF (a) (broma) hoax, practical joke; (jerga etc) hocus-pocus. (b) **sin mistificaciones** plain, without frills, with no nonsense about it; **una persona no dada a mistificaciones** a no-nonsense person.

mistificar [1g] VT (a) (embromar) to hoax, play a practical joke on; (engañar) to hoodwink, take in. (b) (confundir) to mix up, make a mess of. (c) (falsificar) to falsify.

mistongo* ADJ (Cono Sur) wretched, miserable.

Misurí NM Missouri.

mita (And, Cono Sur) NF (Hist: dinero) tax o tribute paid by Indians; (: trabajo) forced labour of Indians.

mitad NF (a) (gen) half; **~ y ~** half-and-half; (fig) so-so, yes and no; **es ~ blanco y ~ rojo** it's half white and half red; **mi otra ~, mi cara ~** my better half; **me queda la ~** I have half left; **a ~ de precio** half-price, at half the cost; **reducir en una ~** to cut by half, halve.
(b) (centro) middle; **a ~ de, en ~ de** halfway along (o through etc); **a ~ de la distancia entre A y Z** halfway between A and Z; **está a la ~** it's half empty, it's half gone (etc); **estar a ~ de camino** to be halfway there; **atravesar de ~ a ~** to pierce right through; **hacia la ~ de la película** halfway through the film; **cortar por la ~** to cut down the middle; **partir a uno por la ~** (fig) to upset sb's plans, queer sb's pitch; V **dividir**.
(c) (Dep) half; **la primera ~** the first half.

mítico ADJ mythical.

mitificar [1g] VT to mythologize, convert into a myth.

mitigación NF mitigation; relief; quenching; appeasement; tempering; reduction.

mitigar [1h] VT (gen) to mitigate, allay; dolor to relieve; sed to quench; ira to appease, mollify; dureza etc to temper, mitigate; inquietud to allay; calor to reduce; soledad to alleviate, relieve.

mitin NM (a) (esp Pol: reunión) meeting; **~ popular** mass meeting, rally. (b) (discurso) political speech; (pey) rabble-rousing speech; **dar un ~** to make a speech. (c) (*) rumpus*, riot, rough-house*; **dar el** (o **un**) **~*** to kick up a fuss.

mitinear [1a] VI to make a (political) speech; (pey) to make a rabble-rousing speech.

mitinero ⓵ ADJ demagogic, rabble-rousing.
⓶ NM, **mitinera** NF demagogue, rabble-rouser.

mitinesco ADJ rabble-rousing; (fig) rowdy, rough.

mito NM myth.

mitología NF mythology.

mitológico ADJ mythological.

mitómano, -a NM/F myth-maker, person who exaggerates; (pey) liar.

mitón NM mitten.

mitote NM (Méx) (Hist) Aztec ritual dance; (*: pelea) brawl; (*: jaleo) uproar; (*: charla) gossip, chat; **estar en el ~** to have a chat.

Mitra NM Mithras.

mitra NF mitre.

mitrado NM bishop, prelate.

mitraico ADJ Mithraic.

mitraísmo NM Mithraism.

mítulo NM mussel.

mixomatosis NF myxomatosis.

Mixteca NF (Méx) southern Mexico.

mixteco NM: **el ~** (Méx Hist) (pueblo) the Mixtecs; (civilización) Mixtec civilization.

mixtificar [1g] VT = **mistificar**.

mixtión NF mixture.

mixto ⓵ ADJ mixed.
⓶ NM (a) (fósforo) match; (Mil) explosive compound. (b) (Ferro) pas-

senger and goods train.

mixtolobo NM Alsatian (dog).

mixtura NF mixture (t *Farm*).

mixturar [1a] VT to mix.

ml. ABR *de* **mililitro** millilitre, ml.

MLN NM (*LAm*) ABR *de* **Movimiento de Liberación Nacional**.

mm. ABR *de* **milímetro** millimetre, mm.

M.N., m/n NF (*LAm*) ABR *de* **moneda nacional** national currency.

mnemónica NF, **mnemotécnica** NF mnemonics.

mnemotécnico ADJ mnemonic.

Mnez. ABR *de* **Martínez**.

MNR NM (*Bolivia*) ABR *de* **Movimiento Nacionalista Revolucionario**.

M.º (a) (*Pol*) ABR *de* **Ministerio** Ministry, Min. (b) (*Escol*) ABR *de* **Maestro** Master.

M.O. ABR *de* **mano de obra** manpower.

m/o (*Com*) ABR *de* **mi orden** my order.

moai NM, PL **moais** (*Chile*) *Easter Island statue*.

moaré NM moiré.

mobiliario NM (*muebles*) furniture; (*artículos domésticos*) household goods; (*juego*) suite (of furniture); **~ y enseres** furnishings and fittings; **~ sanitario** bathroom furnishings.

moblaje NM = **mobiliario**.

MOC NM ABR *de* **Movimiento de Objeción de Conciencia**.

moca[1] NM mocha.

moca[2] NF quagmire, muddy place.

moca[3] NF (*Méx*) coffee-flavoured cake (o biscuit).

mocarro NM mucus, snot*.

mocasín NM moccasin.

mocear [1a] VI to play around, live a bit wildly, sow one's wild oats.

mocedad NF (a) (*juventud*) youth; **en mis ~es** in my young days. (b) **~es** (*bromas*) youthful pranks; (*vida desordenada*) wild living; **pasar las ~es** to sow one's wild oats.

moceril ADJ youthful; typical of youth.

mocerío NM young people, lads and lasses (*collectively*).

mocero ADJ rakish, loose-living; fond of the girls.

mocetón NM strapping youth.

mocetona NF big girl, hefty wench.

mocha‡ NF (*Esp*) nut‡, head.

mochales‡ ADJ: **estar ~** (*Esp*) to be round the bend‡.

mochar [1a] VT (a) = **desmochar**. (b) (*And, Carib*) (*cortar*) to chop off, hack off (clumsily); (*Med*) to amputate. (c) (*Cono Sur*: *robar*) to pinch*. (d) (*And*: *despedir*) to fire*, sack*.

mochila NF rucksack, knapsack, back-pack (*US*); (*Mil*) pack; (*de bicicleta*) bag, basket; (*Cono Sur*) school satchel; **~ portabebés** baby-carrier; **tener algo casi en la ~*** to have sth almost in the bag*.

mochilear [1a] VI to go backpacking, backpack.

mochilero, -a NM/F back-packer.

mocho[1] ADJ (a) (*truncado*) cut off, short, truncated; *muñón* stubby; *herramienta etc* blunt, short; *árbol* lopped, pollarded; *vaca* hornless, polled; *torre* flat-topped; (*) *persona* shorn; (*LAm*) mutilated; (*Carib*) one-armed.
(b) (*And*: *grande*) big, huge.
(c) (*CAm, Méx*) (*reaccionario*) reactionary; (*beato*) sanctimonious.
[2] NM (a) (*de cigarrillo*) butt; (*de utensilio*) blunt end, thick end.
(b) (*) = **mochuelo** (b).
(c) (*And, Carib*: *caballo*) nag.
[3] NM, **mocha** NF (a) (*CAm*: *huérfano*) orphan.
(b) (*Méx*) (*reaccionario*) reactionary; (*beato*) bigot.

mochuelo NM (a) (*Orn*: *t* ~ **común**) little owl; **cada ~ a su sitio** everything in its place. (b) (*: *tarea*) burden, chore, bind*; **cargar con el ~** to get landed with it; to carry the can*; **colgar** (o **echar**) **el ~ a uno** to lumber sb with the job*, (*culpa*) to make sb carry the can*, (*crimen*) to frame sb. (c) (‡) cunt‡‡.

moción NF (a) (*movimiento*) motion, movement. (b) (*Parl etc*) motion; **~ de censura** motion of censure, censure motion; **~ de confianza** vote of confidence; **hacer** (o **presentar** o **plantar**) **una ~** to propose a motion.

mocionante NMF (*LAm*) proposer (of a motion).

mocionar [1a] VTI (*LAm*) to move, propose.

mocito[1] ADJ very young.
[2] NM, **mocita** NF youngster.

moco NM (a) (*gen*) mucus; snot*; **limpiarse los ~s** to blow one's nose; **llorar a ~ y baba**, **llorar a ~ tendido** to sob one's heart out, cry uncontrollably; **soltar el ~** to burst into tears; **tirarse el ~*** (*vacilar*) to hesitate; (*mentir*) to lie; (*exagerar*) to exaggerate, shoot a line*.
(b) (*Orn*) crest; **no es ~ de pavo** it's not just a small thing; you can't laugh this one off.
(c) (*mecha*) snuff, burnt wick; (*gotas*) candle grease, candle drippings; **a ~ de candil** by candlelight.
(d) (*Téc*) slag.
(e) (*: *farol*) brag, boast; tall story.

mocoso[1] ADJ (*lloroso*) snivelling; (*fig*) ill-bred, rude.

[2] NM, **mocosa*** NF brat; (*LAm*) child.

moda NF fashion; style; **a la ~** (ADJ) in fashion, fashionable; (ADV) fashionably; **un sombrero a la ~** a fashionable hat; **a la ~ de** after the fashion of; **estar a la ~** to be in fashion, be fashionable; **ponerse a la ~** to smarten up, get some new clothes; (*) to get with it*; **de ~** in fashion, fashionable; **fuera de ~** out of fashion; **pasado de ~** old-fashioned, out-dated; **pasarse de ~** to go out of fashion; **ponerse de ~** to become fashionable; **estar muy de ~** to be highly fashionable; **ha entrado la ~ de las medias amarillas** yellow stockings have come in, yellow stockings are in*.

modal[1] ADJ modal.
[2] **~es** NMPL manners.

modalidad NF (*clase*) form, kind, variety; (*moda*) fashion; (*manera*) way; **una nueva ~ teatral** a new dramatic form; a new fashion in the theatre; **~ de pago** (*Com*) method of payment; **~ de texto** (*Inform*) text mode; **hay varias ~es del juego** there are various forms of the game, there are several ways of playing the game.

modelado NM modelling.

modelador(a) NM/F modeller.

modelaje NM modelling.

modelar [1a] [1] VT (a) (*lit*) to model (*sobre, según* on). (b) (*formar*) to fashion, shape, form.
[2] **modelarse** VR: **~ sobre** to model o.s. on.

modélicamente ADV in a model way, in an exemplary fashion.

modélico ADJ model, ideal, exemplary.

modelismo NM modelling, model-making.

modelista NMF model-maker.

modelización NF modelling, creation of models; **~ cognoscitiva** cognitive modelling.

modelizar [1f] VT to model, create a model of.

modelo[1] NM (a) (*gen*) model; (*patrón*) pattern; (*norma*) standard; (*para hacer punto*) pattern; **~ a escala** scale model; **~ de maridos** model husband; **~ de vida** lifestyle, way of life; **presentar algo como un ~** to hold sth up as a model; **servir de ~** to serve as a model; **tomar por ~** to take as a model.
(b) (*Méx*: *forma*) blank form.
[2] NMF (*Alta Costura, Arte, Fot*) model; **~ de portada** cover-girl; **servir de ~ a un pintor** to sit for a painter, pose for a painter.
[3] ATR model; ideal, exemplary; **cárcel ~** model prison; **empresa ~** model company; pilot plant; **marido ~** model husband; **un coche último ~** a latest-model car.

módem NM modem.

moderación NF moderation; **~ salarial** wage restraint; **con ~** in moderation.

moderadamente ADV moderately.

moderado ADJ moderate.

moderador(a) NM/F (*TV etc*) presenter.

moderar [1a] [1] VT to moderate; *violencia* to restrain, control; *velocidad* to reduce.
[2] **moderarse** VR (*fig*) to restrain o.s., control o.s.; to calm down.

modernamente ADV nowadays, in modern times; (*recientemente*) recently.

modernez NF (a) (*calidad*) modernity. (b) (*truco*) gimmick.

modernidad NF modernity.

modernismo NM modernism.

modernista[1] ADJ modernist(ic).
[2] NMF modernist.

modernización NF modernization.

modernizador[1] ADJ modernizing.
[2] NM, **modernizadora** NF modernizer.

modernizar [1f] [1] VT to modernize.
[2] **modernizarse** VR to modernize (o.s.); to catch up, get up to date.

moderno[1] ADJ modern; present-day; up-to-date; **a la moderna** in the modern way; modern.
[2] NM, **moderna** NF trendy.

modestamente ADV modestly.

modestia NF modesty.

modesto ADJ modest.

modex NM (*Carib*) press-on sanitary towel.

modicidad NF reasonableness, moderateness.

módico ADJ reasonable, moderate; **la módica suma de ...** the modest sum of ...

modificable ADJ modifiable, that can be modified; **los precios son ~s** the prices are subject to change.

modificación NF modification; **~ de (la) conducta** change of behaviour.

modificar [1g] VT to modify.

modismo NM idiom.

modista NF dressmaker, modiste; **~ de sombreros** milliner.

modistilla NF seamstress.

modisto NM fashion designer, couturier.

▼ **modo** NM **(a)** (*manera*) way, manner; (*estilo*) fashion; (*método*) mode, method; '~ **de empleo'** (*en etiqueta*) 'instructions for use'; ~ **de gobierno** form of government; ~ **de pensar** way of thinking; **según mi** ~ **de pensar** according to my way of thinking; ~ **de ser = manera de ser; a mi** ~ **de ver** in my view; as I see it; **¡ni** ~**!** (*Méx*) but what can you do!; *ver también* MANERA, FORMA, MODO .
(b) (*locuciones con prep*) **a mi** ~ in my (own) way; **a** ~ **de** like; **uno a** ~ **de saco** a sort of bag, some kind of bag; **al** ~ **inglés** in the English way (*o* style); **de este** ~ (in) this way, like this; **de ese** ~ (*fig*) at that ▼ rate; **del mismo** ~ **(que), de igual** ~ **(que)** in the same way (as), just (as); **del mismo** ~ **otros dicen que no** similarly, others say no; **de igual** ~, ... in the same way, ...; **¡de** ~ **que sí fuiste tú!** so it was you after all!; **de diversos** ~s in various ways; **declaraba su edad de diversos** ~s she gave her several different versions of her age; **de un** ~ **o de otro** (in) one way or another; by some means or other; *para otras locuciones, V* **manera (a), (b).**
(c) (*modales*) ~s manners; **buenos** ~s good manners; **contestar con buenos** ~s to answer courteously; **contestar con malos** ~s to answer rudely.
(d) (*Inform, Mús*) mode.
(e) (*Ling*) mood; ~ **imperativo** imperative mood; ~ **indicativo** indicative mood; ~ **subjuntivo** subjunctive mood.
(f) (*fig*) moderation; **beber con** ~ to drink in moderation.
modorra NF **(a)** (*sueño*) drowsiness, heaviness. **(b)** (*Vet*) staggers.
modorro ADJ **(a)** (*soñoliento*) drowsy, heavy. **(b)** *fruta* soft, sleepy. **(c)** (*: tonto*) dull, stupid.
modosito ADJ = **modoso.**
modoso ADJ quiet, well-mannered, nicely-behaved; *muchacha* demure.
modulación NF modulation; ~ **de frecuencia** frequency modulation.
modulado ADJ modulated.
modulador NM modulator.
modulador-demodulador NM (*Inform*) modem.
modular [1a] **1** ADJ modular.
  2 VT to modulate.
  3 NM (*Cono Sur*) shelf unit.
modularidad NF modularity.
módulo NM module; (*And*) platform; ~ **lunar** lunar module; ~ **de mando** command module.
moer NM moiré.
mofa NF **(a)** (*gen*) mockery, ridicule, derision; **exponer a uno a la** ~ **pública** to hold sb up to public ridicule; **hacer** ~ **de** to scoff at, jeer at. **(b)** (*una* ~) jibe, taunt, sneer.
mofador **1** ADJ mocking, scoffing, sneering.
  2 NM, **mofadora** NF mocker, scoffer.
mofar [1a] **1** VI to mock, scoff, sneer.
  2 **mofarse** VR: ~ **de** to mock, scoff at, sneer at.
mofeta NF **(a)** (*Zool*) skunk. **(b)** (*Min*) firedamp, mephitis. **(c)** (**:**) fart**:**.
mofinco: NM (*Carib*) firewater*, gut-rot**:**.
mofle NM (*Méx Aut*) silencer.
moflete NM **(a)** (*mejilla*) fat cheek. **(b)** ~s (*fig*) chubbiness.
mofletudo ADJ fat-cheeked, chubby.
mogol: = **mongol; el Gran M~** the Great Mogul.
Mogolia NF = **Mongolia.**
mogolla NF (*And, Cono Sur*) bargain.
mogollón* **1** NM **(a)** (*t* **mogollona** NF) (*gorrón*) sponger*, hanger-on; spiv*; (*en fiesta etc*) gatecrasher; **colarse de** ~ **en un sitio** to get into a place without paying; **comer de** ~ to scrounge a meal*; **lograr un puesto de** ~ to wangle a job*.
(b) (*lío*) fuss, row.
(c) (*cantidad*) large amount, mass; **gente a** ~, **un** ~ **de gente** a mass of people, loads of people; **tengo un** ~ **de discos*** I've got loads of records.
  2 ADV *V* **cantidad 2.**
mogollónico: ADJ huge, colossal.
mogote NM (*otero*) flat-topped hillock; (*pila*) heap, pile; (*de gavillas etc*) stack, rick.
mohair [mo'xair, mo'air] NM mohair.
mohín NM (wry) face, grimace; pout; **hacer un** ~ to make a face; **con un leve** ~ **de chanza** with a faintly humorous expression.
mohína NF **(a)** (*enfado*) annoyance, displeasure; (*rencor*) resentment. **(b)** (*una* ~) grudge. **(c)** (*mal humor*) the sulks, sulkiness; **ser fácil a las** ~s to be easily depressed.
mohíno ADJ (*triste*) gloomy, depressed; (*malhumorado*) sulky, sullen; (*rencoroso*) resentful; (*displicente*) peevish.
moho NM **(a)** (*en metal*) rust.
(b) (*Bot*) mould, mildew; **cubierto de** ~ mouldy, mildewed.
(c) (*pereza*) lazy feeling; workshyness; **no cría** ~ he doesn't let the grass grow under his feet, he's always on the go; **no dejar criar** ~ **a uno** to keep sb on the go.
mohoso ADJ **(a)** (*metal*) rusty. **(b)** (*Bot*) mouldy, mildewed; musty. **(c)**

(*fig*) *chiste etc* stale.
Moisés NM Moses.
moisés NM Moses basket, cradle; carrycot.
moja: NF stab, thrust; stab wound.
mojada NF **(a)** (*al mojarse*) wetting, soaking. **(b)** (*herida*) stab (wound).
mojado **1** ADJ wet; damp, moist; drenched, soaked; **llover sobre** ~ to be quite unnecessary, be entirely superfluous; **luego llovió sobre** ~ then on top of all that sth else happened; **llueve sobre** ~ it never rains but it pours.
  2 NM (*Méx*) wetback (*US*), illegal immigrant.
mojadura NF wetting, soaking.
mojama NF salted tuna.
mojar [1a] **1** VT **(a)** (*gen*) to wet; (*humedecer*) to damp(en), moisten; (*empapar*) to drench, soak; ~**la:** to have a screw**:**; **la lluvia mojó a todos** the rain soaked everybody; **moje ligeramente el sello** moisten the stamp a little; ~ **la ropa en un líquido** to soak (*o* steep) clothes in a liquid.
(b) ~ **la pluma en la tinta** to dip one's pen into the ink; ~ **el pan en el café** to dip one's bread into one's coffee.
(c) (*Ling*) to palatalize.
(d) (*apuñalar*) to stab.
(e) (*) *triunfo etc* to celebrate (with a drink).
(f) (*Carib*) to tip; (*Carib*: *sobornar*) to bribe.
  2 VI **(a)** (**:**) to have a screw**:**. **(b)** ~ **en** (*fig*) to dabble in; to meddle in, get involved in.
  3 **mojarse** VR **(a)** to get wet; to get drenched, get soaked; ~ **las orejas** (*Cono Sur fig*) to give way, back down. **(b)** (*) **no se mojó** he kept out of it, he didn't get involved.
mojarra NF **(a)** (**:** *lengua*) tongue. **(b)** (*LAm*) short broad knife.
mojera NF whitebeam.
mojicón NM **(a)** (*Culin*) sponge cake; bun. **(b)** (**:** *bofetada*) punch in the face, biff*, slap.
mojiganga NF (*Hist*) masquerade, mummery; (*farsa*) farce, piece of clowning.
mojigatería NF hypocrisy; sanctimoniousness, affected piety; prudery, prudishness.
mojigato **1** ADJ (*hipócrita*) hypocritical; (*santurrón*) sanctimonious, affectedly pious; (*gazmoño*) prudish, strait-laced.
  2 NM, **mojigata** NF hypocrite; sanctimonious person; prude.
mojinete NM (*de techo*) ridge; (*de muro*) tiling, coping.
mojito NM (*Cuba*) long drink with a base of rum.
mojo NM (*Méx*) garlic sauce.
mojón **1** NM **(a)** (*hito*) landmark; (*piedra*) boundary stone; (*t* ~ **kilométrico**) milestone; (*señal*) signpost; (*montón*) heap, pile.
(b) (*And***:**) shit**:**; crap**:**.
  2 NM, **mojona** NF (*Carib***:**) (*bruto*) idiot, thickhead*; (*chaparro*) shortie*.
mol. (*Fís*) ABR *de* **molécula** molecule, mol.
mola NF rounded mountain.
molar¹ NM molar.
molar² [1a] **1** VT (*gustar*) to please; to suit; **lo que más me mola es ...** what I'm really into is ...*; **lo que mola mil** (*Esp*) what gets people really going; **tía, me molas mucho** (*Esp*) I'm crazy about you, baby*; **¿te mola un pitillo?** would you like a smoke?; **no me mola** I don't go for that*, I don't fancy that.
  2 VI **(a)** (*estar de moda*) to be in*, be fashionable; **eso mola mucho ahora** that's very in now*, it's all the rage now.
(b) (*dar tono*) to be classy*, be real posh*.
(c) (*darse tono*) to swank*.
(d) (*valer*) to be OK*; **por partes iguales, ¿mola?** equal shares then, OK?*
(e) **la cosa no mola** (*marchar*) it's not going well at all.
molcajete NM (*Méx*) mortar.
moldavo, -a ADJ, NM/F Moldavian, Moldovan.
molde NM **(a)** (*Téc*) mould; (*Culin*) mould, shape; (*vaciado etc*) cast; (*Tip*) forme; **romper** ~s (*fig*) to break the mould.
(b) (*Cos*) (*patrón*) pattern; (*aguja*) knitting needle.
(c) (*fig*) model.
(d) **de** ~ perfect, just right; **el vestido le está de** ~ the dress suits her perfectly, the dress is just right for (*o* on) her; **venir de** ~ to come just right; *V* **letra.**
moldeable ADJ *material* malleable; *carácter, persona* easily influenced, impressionable.
moldeado NM **(a)** moulding, molding (*US*), shaping; (*en yeso*) casting. **(b)** (*del pelo*) soft perm.
moldear [1a] VT **(a)** (*gen*) to mould, shape; (*en yeso etc*) to cast. **(b)** (*fig*) to mould, shape, form.
moldeo NM moulding.
moldura NF moulding; ~ **lateral** (*Aut*) side stripe.
mole¹ NF (*masa*) mass, bulk; (*de edificio*) pile; **se sentó con toda su** ~ he sat down with his full weight; **la enorme** ~ **del buque** the vast mass of the ship; **esa mujer es una** ~ that woman is massive.

mole² NM (*Méx*) black chili sauce; **~ de olla** meat stew; **ser el ~ de uno*** to be sb's favourite thing.

molécula NF molecule.

molecular ADJ molecular.

moledor [1] ADJ (a) (*que muele*) grinding, crushing. (b) (*) boring.
[2] NM (a) (*Téc*) grinder, crusher; roller. (b) (*) bore.

moledora NF (*Téc*) grinder, crusher; mill.

moledura NF (*de café etc*) grinding; (*de trigo*) milling.

moler [2h] VT (a) *café etc* to grind; (*machacar*) to crush; (*pulverizar*) to pound; *trigo* to mill; (*) to chew (up); **~ a uno a palos** to beat sb up*.
(b) (*fig*) (*cansar*) to tire out, weary, exhaust; **estoy molida de tanto trabajar** all that work has left me exhausted.
(c) (*fig*) (*fastidiar*) to annoy; (*aburrir*) to bore.

▼ **molestar** [1a] [1] VT (*fastidiar*) to annoy; (*incomodar*) to bother, inconvenience, put out; (*incordiar*) to upset; (*dolor*) to trouble, bother, hurt; **me molesta ese ruido** that noise upsets me, that noise gets on my nerves; **¿te molesta el ruido?** do you mind (o object to) the noise?, does the noise bother you?; **los críos me molestan para estudiar*** the kids disturb my work*, the kids stop me working*; **me molesta tener que repetirlo** I hate having to repeat it; **¿te molesta que abra la ventana?** do you mind if I open the window?; **¿te molesta que fume?** will it bother you if I smoke?
[2] VI (*fastidiar*) to be a nuisance; (*estorbar*) to get in the way, be awkward; **no quiero ~** I don't want to intrude, I don't want to be in the way, I don't wish to cause any trouble.
[3] **molestarse** VR (a) (*darse trabajo*) to bother (*con* about); (*incomodarse*) to go to trouble, put o.s. out; **~ en +** *infin* to bother to + *infin*; **¡no se moleste!** don't bother!, don't trouble yourself!
(b) (*enfadarse*) to get cross; (*ofenderse*) to take offence, get upset; **se molesta por nada** he gets annoyed at the slightest thing.

molestia NF bother, trouble, nuisance; inconvenience; (*Med*) discomfort; **es una ~** it's a nuisance; **no es ~** it's no trouble; **ahorrarse ~s** to save o.s. trouble, spare o.s. effort; **darse la ~ de +** *infin*, **tomarse la ~ de +** *infin* to take the trouble to + *infin*, go out of one's way to + *infin*.

molesto ADJ (a) (*que fastidia*) troublesome, annoying; (*pesado*) trying, tiresome; (*incómodo*) inconvenient; *tarea* irksome; *olor*, *sabor* nasty; **es muy ~ para mí** it's very inconvenient for me; **si no es ~ para Vd** if it's no trouble to you; **es una persona muy molesta** she's a very trying person.
(b) (*descontento*) discontented; (*inquieto*) restless; (*incómodo*) ill-at-ease; uncomfortable; (*ofendido*) upset, offended; (*azorado*) embarrassed; **estar ~** (*Med*) to be in some discomfort; **estar ~ con uno** to be cross with sb; **me sentí ~** I felt uncomfortable, I felt embarrassed.

molestoso ADJ (*And, Carib, Cono Sur*) annoying.

molibdeno NM molybdenum.

molicie NF (a) (*blandura*) softness. (b) (*fig*) soft living, luxurious living; effeminacy.

molido ADJ (a) (*machacado*) ground, crushed; (*pulverizado*) powdered. (b) **estar ~** (*fig*) to be exhausted, be dead beat; **estoy ~ de tanto viajar** I'm exhausted with all this travelling.

molienda NF (a) (*acto*) grinding; milling. (b) (*trigo*) quantity of corn (*etc*) to be ground. (c) (*molino*) mill. (d) (*: *cansancio*) weariness. (e) (*: *molestia*) nuisance.

moliente ADJ V **corriente**.

molinero NM miller.

molinete NM (toy) windmill.

molinillo NM (a) (*gen*) hand mill; **~ de aceite** olive press; **~ de café** coffee-mill, coffee grinder; **~ de carne** mincer. (b) (*juguete*) (toy) windmill.

molino NM (a) (*gen*) mill; (*trituradora*) grinder; **~ de agua** water mill; **~ de cubo** water-wheel; **~ de viento** windmill. (b) (*) (*inquieto*) restless person; (*pesado*) bore, tedious individual.

molla NF (*Anat*) fleshy part; (*de carne*) lean part; (*de fruta*) flesh; (*de pan*) breadcrumb, doughy part.

mollar ADJ (a) *fruta* soft, tender; easily shelled. (b) *carne* boned, boneless. (c) (*: *crédulo*) gullible. (d (*) *trabajo etc* cushy♯, easy. (e) (*: *bueno*) super*, brilliant*; *mujer* smashing*.

mollate NM plonk*.

molledo NM (a) (*Anat*) fleshy part (*of a limb*). (b) (*de pan*) crumb.

molleja NF gizzard; **~s** sweetbreads.

mollejón* NM softie*; (*pey*) fat slob*.

mollera NF (*Anat*) crown of the head; (*) brains, sense; **cerrado de ~**, **duro de ~** (*estúpido*) dense, dim; (*terco*) pigheaded; **no les cabe en la ~** they just can't believe it; **secar la ~ a uno** to drive sb crazy; **tener buena ~** to have brains, be brainy.

mollete NM (a) (*Culin*) muffin. (b) (*Anat*) (*brazo*) fleshy part of the arm; (*mejilla*) fat cheek.

molo NM (*Cono Sur*) breakwater, seawall.

molón* ADJ (a) (*bueno*) super*, smashing*. (b) (*Esp: elegante*) posh*, classy*. (c) (*Esp: engreído*) swanky*, stuck-up*. (d) (*CAm, Méx*) tire-

some.

molondra♯ NF bonce♯, head.

molote NM (a) (*Méx: ovillo*) ball of wool (*etc*). (b) (*Méx Culin*) fried maize pancake. (c) (*And, Méx*) dirty trick. (d) (*CAm, Carib, Méx*) riot, commotion.

molotov NM: **cóctel** (o **bomba**) **~** Molotov cocktail.

molturar [1a] VT to grind, mill.

Molucas NFPL: **las (Islas) ~** the Moluccas, the Molucca Islands.

molusco NM mollusc.

momentáneamente ADV momentarily.

momentáneo ADJ momentary.

momento NM (a) (*gen*) moment; (*instante*) instant; (*tiempo*) time; **¡momentito!** (*esp LAm*) just a moment!; **~s después** a few moments later; **al ~** at once; **a cada ~** every instant, all the time; **de ~** at the moment, for the moment; **continúa de ~ en el puesto** he stays in the job for the time being; **no los vi de ~** I didn't see them at first; **de un ~ a otro** at any moment; **en el ~ actual** at the present time; **en el ~ bueno** at the right moment, at the proper time; **en este ~** at this moment; right now; **en su ~** (*pasado*) in its time, (*futuro*) in due time, in due course, when the time is right; **hace un ~** not a moment ago; **por el ~** for the moment; **está cambiando por ~s** it is changing all the time; **atravesamos un ~ difícil** we are going through a difficult time; **ha llegado el ~ de +** *infin* the time has come to + *infin*.
(b) (*Mec*) momentum; moment.
(c) (*fig*) consequence, importance; **de poco ~** unimportant.

momería NF mummery, clowning.

momia NF mummy.

momificación NF mummification.

momificar [1g] [1] VT to mummify.
[2] **momificarse** VR to mummify, become mummified.

momio [1] ADJ *carne* lean.
[2] NM (a) (*ganga*) bargain; (*extra*) extra; (*prebenda*) cushy job♯; (*trato*) profitable deal; **de ~** free, gratis. (b) (*Cono Sur*) square*, fuddy-duddy*; (*Pol*) reactionary.

momo NM (a) (*cara*) funny face. (b) (*payasadas*) clowning, buffoonery.

mona NF (a) (*Zool*) female monkey; (*especie*) Barbary ape; **estar hecho una ~** to be embarrassed, be quite put out; **mandar a uno a freír ~s♯** to tell sb to go to blazes*.
(b) (*: *imitador*) ape, copycat*.
(c) (*) (*borrachera*) drunk*; (*resaca*) hangover*; **coger** (o **pillar**) **una ~** to get tight*; **dormir la ~** to sleep off a hangover*.
(d) (*And: rubio*) blonde.
(e) (*LAm**) Colombian golden marijuana.
(f) **andar** (o **estar**) **como la ~** (*Cono Sur*) to be broke; to feel wretched.

monacal ADJ monastic.

monacato NM monasticism; monastic life, monk's way of life.

monacillo NM acolyte, altar boy.

Mónaco NM Monaco.

monada NF (*esp Esp*) (a) (*acto*) (*mueca*) monkey face; *comportamiento* monkeyish way (o movement *etc*); *hábito* silly habit; *tontería* silly thing (to say *etc*).
(b) (*de niño*) charming habit, sweet little way.
(c) (*cualidad*) silliness, childishness.
(d) (*) (*objeto precioso*) lovely thing; beauty, cute little thing; (*chica*) pretty girl; **la casa es una ~** the house is lovely, the house is a gem; **¡qué ~!** isn't it cute?, isn't it lovely?; **¡hola, ~!** hullo, beautiful!*
(e) **~s** (*: *halagos*) flattery.

mónada NF monad.

monago NM, **monaguillo** NM acolyte, altar-boy.

monarca NMF monarch, ruler.

monarquía NF monarchy.

monárquico [1] ADJ monarchic(al); (*Pol*) royalist, monarchist.
[2] NM, **monárquica** NF royalist, monarchist.

monarquismo NM monarchism.

monasterio NM (*de hombres*) monastery; (*de mujeres*) convent.

monástico ADJ monastic.

Moncho NM *forma familiar de* **Ramón**.

Moncloa: la ~ NF *official residence of the Spanish prime minister* (*Madrid*).

monclovita ADJ of the Moncloa palace; (*frec*) of the prime minister, prime ministerial.

monda¹ NF (a) (*acto*) pruning, lopping, trimming; peeling. (b) (*temporada*) pruning season. (c) (*piel*) peel, peelings, skin. (d) (*And, Carib, Méx*) beating.

monda²* NF: **¡es la ~!** (a) (*fantástico*) it's great!*; (*pey: el colmo*) it's the limit, it's the end; it's sheer hell; **este nuevo baile es la ~** this new dance is the greatest*, (*pey*) this new dance is awful; **fue la ~** (*para reírse*) it was a scream*.
(b) (*persona*) he's great*, he's a knockout*; (*pey*) he's a shocker*, he's a terror.

mondadientes NM INVAR toothpick.
mondador NM (*Méx*) shredder.
mondadura NF (**a**) = **monda**[1] (a); (*limpieza*) cleaning, cleansing. (**b**) ~**s** = **monda**[1] (c).
mondar [1a] [1] VT (**a**) *árbol* to prune, lop, trim.
(**b**) *fruta* to peel, skin; *patata* to peel; *guisante, nuez* to shell; *palo* to peel, pare, remove the bark from; ~ **a uno** to cut sb's hair.
(**c**) (*limpiar*) to clean, cleanse; *canal etc* to clean out.
(**d**) (*: *pelar*) to fleece, strip bare, clean out*.
(**e**) **¡que te monden!*** get away!*, rubbish!
(**f**) (*And, Carib*: *dar una paliza a*) to beat, thrash; (*Carib Dep etc*) to wipe the floor with*.
[2] **mondarse** VR (**a**) ~ **los dientes** to pick one's teeth.
(**b**) ~ (**de risa**)* to die laughing*.
mondo ADJ (**a**) (*limpio*) clean; (*puro*) pure; (*sencillo*) plain; neat; *cabeza* completely shorn.
(**b**) (*fig*) bare, plain, without addition; **el asunto** ~ **es esto** the plain fact of the matter is; **tiene su sueldo** ~ **y nada más** he has his bare salary and nothing more; **me he quedado** ~* I'm cleaned out**;**, I haven't a cent; ~ **y lirondo*** plain, pure and simple.
mondongo NM (*: *entrañas*) guts, insides; (*Culin*) tripe.
mondongudo ADJ (*esp Cono Sur*) paunchy, potbellied.
monear [1a] VI (**a**) (*comportarse*) to act like a monkey; (*hacer muecas*) to make monkey faces. (**b**) (*Cono Sur, Méx**: *jactarse*) to boast, swank*.
moneda NF (**a**) (*gen*) currency, money, coinage; ~ **blanda**, ~ **débil** soft currency; ~ **convertible** convertible currency; ~ **de curso legal** legal tender; ~ **decimal** decimal currency; ~ **dura**, ~ **fuerte** hard currency; ~ **fraccionaria** money in small units; ~ **menuda**, ~ **suelta** small change, coins of low denomination; ~ **nacional** national currency; ~ **única** single currency; **en** ~ **española** in Spanish money; **pagar a uno con** (*o* **en**) **la misma** ~ to pay sb back in his own coin.
(**b**) (*una* ~) coin, piece; ~ **falsa** false coin, dud coin; **una** ~ **de 5 dólares** a 5-dollar piece; **es tan probable como que ahora lluevan** ~**s de 5 duros** it's about as likely as my becoming pope.
moned(e)ar [1a] VT to coin, mint.
monedero NM (**a**) ~ **falso** counterfeiter. (**b**) (*portamonedas*) purse.
monegasco [1] ADJ of Monaco.
[2] NM, **monegasca** NF native (*o* inhabitant) of Monaco; **los** ~**s** the people of Monaco.
monería NF (**a**) (*mueca*) funny face, monkey face; (*imitación*) mimicry. (**b**) (*payasada*) antic, prank, caper, playful trick. (**c**) (*pey*) trifle, triviality.
monetario ADJ monetary, financial.
monetarismo NM monetarism.
monetarista ADJ, NMF monetarist.
mongol, -ola [1] ADJ, NM/F Mongol, Mongolian.
[2] NM (*Ling*) Mongolian.
Mongolia NF Mongolia.
mongólico, -a ADJ, NM/F (*Med*) Mongol.
mongolismo NM mongolism, Down's syndrome.
moni* NF (*LAm*) money.
monicaco*, -a NM/F chump*, twit*.
monicongo NM (*LAm*) cartoon film.
monigote NM (**a**) (*muñeca*) rag doll; (*de papel*) paper doll; (*títere*) puppet; (*figura ridícula*) grotesque figure; ~ **de nieve** snowman; *see also* DÍA DE LOS (SANTOS) INOCENTES .
(**b**) (*fig*) colourless individual, weak character, little man; **¡~!** (*a niño*) you chump!*
(**c**) (*Arte*) humorous sketch, cartoon; (*pey*) bad painting (*o* statue), daub; doodle.
monises; NMPL brass*, dough**;**.
monitor [1] NM monitor (*t Inform, Téc*); ~ **en color** colour monitor; ~ **fósfor verde** green screen.
[2] NM, **monitora** NF (*persona*: *Escol*) monitor; (*Dep etc*) instructor, coach; (*de gira etc*) group leader; ~ **de campamento** camp leader; ~ **de esquí** ski instructor.
monitoreado NM monitoring.
monitorear [1a] VT to monitor.
monitorio ADJ admonitory.
monitorización NF monitoring.
monitorizar [1f] VT to monitor.
monja NF nun; sister.
monje NM (**a**) (*Rel*) monk. (**b**) (*Carib*) five-peso note.
monjil [1] ADJ nun's, of (*o* like) a nun; (*fig*) excessively demure.
[2] NM (*hábito*) nun's habit.
mono¹ NM (**a**) (*Zool*) monkey, ape; **¡~!** (*a niño*) you little monkey!
(**b**) (*fig*: *imitador*) ape, mimic; ~ **de imitación** (*niño etc*) copycat*; **ser un** ~ **de repetición** to repeat things like a parrot; to talk endlessly.
(**c**) (*: *engreído*) cocky youngster*, show-off*.
(**d**) (*Arte*) = **monigote** (c); ~**s** (*Cono Sur*) doodles, rough drawings; ~**s animados** (*Cono Sur*) cartoon(s).
(**e**) (*Naipes*) joker.

(**f**) (*: *feo*) ugly devil, ugly monkey.
(**g**) (**;**: *maricón*) pansy**;**, queer**;**.
(**h**) (**;**: *policía*) copper*.
(**i**) (*Med**) withdrawal symptoms (following deprivation of drugs), cold turkey; **estar con el** ~ to be suffering withdrawal symptoms.
(**j**) (*Carib**: *deuda*) debt.
(**k**) (*: *seña*) sign (*between lovers etc*); **hacerse** ~**s** to make eyes at each other, make little signs to each other.
(**l**) (*locuciones*) **no lo aguantaría ni que fuera yo un** ~ I wouldn't put up with it at any price; **no me mirarían más ni que tuviera** ~**s en la cara** they couldn't have stared at me more if I had come from the moon; **es el último** ~ he's a nobody; **estar de** ~**s** to be at daggers drawn; **meter los** ~**s a uno** (*And, Carib**) to put the wind up sb*.
mono² ADJ pretty, lovely, attractive; nice, charming, cute; **una chica muy mona** a very attractive girl, a very nice girl; **¡qué sombrero más** ~**!** what a cute little hat!
mono³ NM (*de obrero*) overalls; boilersuit; (*de niño*) rompers; (*de mujer*) jumpsuit; ~ **de esquí** ski suit.
mono⁴ [1] ADJ (*And*: *rubio*) blond, reddish blond.
[2] NM (*Cono Sur*) (*de fruta*: *montón*) pile; (*de sandía*) slice.
mono⁵* NM = **monofónico**.
mono... PREF mono...
monocarril NM monorail.
monocasco NM monohull.
monocigótico ADJ, **monocigoto** ADJ monozygotic.
monocolor ADJ one-colour, of a single colour; **gobierno** ~ one-party government.
monocorde ADJ (**a**) (*Mús*) single-stringed. (**b**) (*fig*) monotonous, unvaried.
monocromo [1] ADJ monochrome; (*TV*) black-and-white.
[2] NM monochrome.
monóculo NM monocle.
monocultivo NM monoculture, single crop; one-crop farming; **el** ~ **es un peligro para muchos países** in many countries dependence upon a single crop is dangerous.
monofónico ADJ monophonic.
monogamia NF monogamy.
monógamo ADJ monogamous.
monografía NF monograph; occasional paper.
monográfico ADJ: **estudio** ~ monograph; **número** ~ **de la revista** an issue of the journal devoted to a single subject; **programa** ~ programme devoted to a single subject.
monograma NM monogram.
monokini NM topless swimsuit, monokini.
monolingüe [1] ADJ monolingual, monoglot.
[2] NMF monoglot.
monolingüismo NM monolingualism.
monolítico ADJ monolithic.
monolitismo NM (*Pol etc*) monolithic nature; monolithic system.
monolito NM monolith.
monologar [1h] VI to soliloquize.
monólogo NM monologue; ~ **interior** stream of consciousness.
monomando NM mixer tap.
monomanía NF monomania; mania, obsession.
monomaniaco, -a ADJ, NM/F, **monomaníaco, -a** ADJ, NM/F monomaniac.
monomio NM monomial.
monomotor ADJ single-engined.
monono* ADJ (*Cono Sur*) pretty, attractive; dressed up.
mononucleado ADJ mononuclear.
mononucleosis NF: ~ **infecciosa** glandular fever.
monoparental ADJ: **familia** ~ single-parent family.
monoparentalidad NF single parenthood.
monopartidismo NM single-party system.
monopatín NM skateboard.
monopatinaje NM skateboarding.
monoplano NM monoplane.
monoplaza NM single-seater.
monopolio NM monopoly.
monopolista ADJ, NMF monopolist.
monopolístico ADJ monopolistic.
monopolización NF monopolization.
monopolizador ADJ (**a**) (*Econ*) monopolistic; **una empresa** ~**a del mercado** a company with a monopoly in the market. (**b**) **un niño** ~ **del cariño materno** a child who monopolizes the mother's attention.
monopolizar [1f] VT to monopolize.
monopsonio NM monopsony.
monoquini NM = **monokini**.
mono(r)rail NM monorail.
monorrimo ADJ *estrofa etc* having the same rhyme throughout.
monosabio NM (**a**) (*Zool*) trained monkey. (**b**) (*Taur*) picador's assis-

tant; employee who leads the horse team dragging the dead bull.

monosilábico ADJ monosyllabic.

monosílabo ☐1 ADJ monosyllabic. ☐2 NM monosyllable.

monoteísmo NM monotheism.

monoteísta ☐1 ADJ monotheistic. ☐2 NMF monotheist.

monotema NM: **ése fue el ~ de la entrevista** that was the main issue discussed in the interview; **su ~ de siempre** his old hobbyhorse.

monotemático ADJ having a single theme.

monoterapia NF monotherapy, single-drug therapy.

monotipia NF Monotype ®.

monotonía NF (_sonido_) monotone; (_fig_) monotony; sameness, dreariness.

monótono ADJ on one note; (_fig_) monotonous; humdrum, dreary.

monousuario ADJ single-user (_atr_).

mono-usuario ADJ INVAR (_Inform_) single-user.

monovalente ADJ monovalent, univalent.

monovía ADJ INVAR monorail (_atr_).

monovolumen ☐1 ADJ: **vehículo ~** people carrier. ☐2 NM people carrier.

monóxido NM monoxide; **~ de carbono** carbon monoxide; **~ de cloro** chlorine monoxide.

Mons. ABR _de_ Monseñor Monsignor, Mgr, Mons.

monseñor NM monsignor.

monserga NF (a) (_jerigonza_) gibberish, jargon. (b) (_disparates_) drivel, tedious talk; **dar la ~** to get on sb's nerves, be a bore; **¡no me vengas con ~s!** give my head peace!

monstruo ☐1 NM (a) (_gen: t fig_) monster; giant; (_del mundo pop_) idol, wonder boy; (_Mús, Teat etc_) great figure, all-time great*; (_Cine_) superstar, megastar; **ese niño es un monstruito** that child is the very devil; **~ sagrado** megastar; **Lope, ~ de la naturaleza** Lope, a marvel of nature.
(b) (_Bio_) freak, monster; **~ de circo** circus freak.
☐2 ATR* (a) (_grande_) huge, monster; **mitín ~** huge meeting. (b) (_maravilloso_) fantastic*, fabulous*; **idea ~** fantastic idea*; **es un plan ~** it's a fabulous scheme*.

monstruosidad NF monstrosity; (_Bio_) freak.

monstruoso ADJ monstrous, huge, monster (_atr_); (_Bio_) freakish, freak (_atr_); (_fig_) monstrous, hideous; **es ~ que ...** it is monstrous that ...

monta NF (a) (_acto_) mounting. (b) (_Mat_) total, sum. (c) (_fig_) value; **de poca ~** of small account, unimportant. (d) (_Agr_) (_caballeriza_) stud; (_temporada_) mating season (_of horses_); (_acto_) mating.

montacargas NM INVAR service lift, hoist, freight elevator (_US_).

montadito NM titbit, dainty item.

montado ☐1 ADJ (a) (_a caballo_) mounted; **artillería montada** horse artillery; **guardias montadas** horse guards; **estar ~⁝** (_con dinero_) to be flush⁝; (_boyante_) to be sitting pretty.
(b) (_Téc_) built-in.
☐2 **montada** NF: **la ~** (_CAm_) the mounted rural police.

montador NM (a) (_objeto_) mounting block. (b) (_persona_) fitter; **~ de escena** (_Cine_) (_diseñador_) set designer; (_que hace el montaje_) film editor.

montadura NF (a) (_acto_) mounting. (b) = **montura**.

montaje NM (a) (_Mec etc_) assembly; fitting-up; (_Arquit_) erection; (*: _arreglado de antemano_) set-up, put-up job*, frame-up*; (*: _estafa_) fiddle*, plot; (_apariencia_) (outward) show; **~ publicitario** advertising stunt, publicity stunt. (b) (_Rad_) hook-up. (c) (_Arte, Cine, Fot_) montage; (_Teat_) stage design, décor.

montante NM (a) (_Hist_) broadsword. (b) (_Téc_) (_poste_) upright, post; (_soporte_) stanchion; (_Arquit_) (_de puerta_) transom; (_de ventana_) mullion. (c) (_Arquit_) small window over a door. (d) (_suma_) total, amount; **~ compensatorio monetario** monetary compensation amount.

montaña ☐1 NF (a) (_gen_) mountain; mountains, mountainous area; **~ de mantequilla** butter mountain; **~ rusa** switchback, big dipper. (b) (_And, Carib_) forest; (_CAm_) virgin jungle.
☐2 NMF: **~ del Pirineo** Pyrenean mountain dog.

montañero ☐1 ADJ mountain (_atr_). ☐2 NM, **montañera** NF mountaineer, climber.

montañés ☐1 ADJ (a) (_gen_) mountain (_atr_); hill (_atr_); highland (_atr_). (b) (_de Santander_) of (o from) the Santander region.
☐2 NM, **montañesa** NF (a) (_gen_) highlander. (b) (_de Santander_) native (o inhabitant) of the Santander region.

montañismo NM mountaineering, climbing.

montañoso ADJ mountainous.

montaplatos NM INVAR service-lift, dumbwaiter (_US_).

montar [1a] ☐1 VT (a) _bicicleta, caballo etc_ to mount, get on; to ride; **hoy ella monta mi caballo** she's riding my horse today.
(b) **~ a uno sobre un tronco** to lift sb on to a log; **montó al niño en el burro** he lifted the child on to the donkey, he put the child up on the donkey, he sat the child on the donkey.
(c) (_Bio_) to cover, mate with; (⁝) _mujer_ to screw⁝.
(d) (_traslapar_) to overlap; **~ un color sobre otro** to overlap one col-

our with another, to cover one colour partially with another.
(e) (_Mec_) to assemble, fit (up), put together, set up; (_Arquit_) to erect, put up; _joya_ to set, mount; _pistola_ to cock; _reloj, resorte_ to wind (up); (_Cos_) _puntos_ to cast on; _guardia_ to mount; (_Cine_) _película_ to edit; (_Teat_) _obra_ to stage, put on; **~ una casa** to set up house, furnish a house; **~ una tienda** to open a shop; **~ un negocio** to start a business, found a business; **tiene una clínica ya montada** she has a fully-equipped clinic.
(f) (_Culin_) _huevo_ to beat, whip; _helado_ to whip.
(g) (*) **~la** to kick up a fuss.
☐2 VI (a) to mount (_a un caballo, en un caballo_ a horse), get up (_a, en_ on); to get on; to ride; **~ a caballo** to ride; **~ en bicicleta** to ride a bicycle, cycle; **me ayudó a ~** he helped me up; he helped me to mount; **montó en la bicicleta y desapareció** he got on his bicycle and disappeared; **mi hermana monta a diario** my sister rides every day; **~ para una cuadra de carreras** to ride for a racing stable.
(b) (_traslaparse_) to overlap; **el mapa monta sobre el texto** the map overlaps the text, the map covers part of the text.
(c) **~ en cólera, ~ en indignación** to get angry.
(d) **~ a** (_Fin_) to amount to, come to, add up to.
(e) **tanto monta** it makes no odds; it's all the same, it doesn't matter either way; **tanto monta que vengas o no** it's all the same whether you come or not.
☐3 **montarse** VR = 2 (a), (b) _y_ (c); (*) **montárselo** to set oneself up, get things going; to do one's thing*; **él se lo monta mejor** he does things better, he gets himself better organized; **él se lo ha montado realmente bien** he's got a nice little thing going for him*; **se lo monta muy mal** he's no idea how to manage things, he's just not with it*; **~ en el dólar*** to make a mint.

montaraz ☐1 ADJ (a) (_de montaña_) mountain (_atr_), highland (_atr_). (b) (_salvaje_) wild, untamed; (_pey_) rough, coarse, uncivilized; (_huraño_) unsociable.
☐2 NM (_guardabosque_) gamekeeper, game warden.

montarrón NM (_And_) forest.

monte NM (a) (_montaña_) mountain; **M~s Apalaches** Appalachians; **M~s Cárpatos** Carpathians; **M~ de la Mesa** Table Mountain; **los M~s Pirineos** the Pyrenees; **echarse al ~** to take to the hills.
(b) (_bosque_) woodland; (_despoblado_) wilds, wild country; **~ alto** forest; **~ bajo** scrub; **un conejo de ~** a wild rabbit; **batir el ~** to beat for game, go hunting; **creer que todo el ~ es orégano** to think everything in the garden is lovely; to think everything is plain sailing; **no todo el ~ es orégano** all that glitters is not gold.
(c) **~ de piedad** (state-owned) pawnshop.
(d) (_CAm, Carib: alrededores_) outskirts, surrounding country.
(e) (_Méx: pasto_) grass, fallow pasture.
(f) (_LAm*: droga_) hash*, pot⁝.
(g) (_Naipes: baraja_) pile; (_banca_) bank; (_juego_) a card game.
(h) (*: _obstáculo_) obstacle, snag; **todo se le hace un ~** he sees difficulties everywhere, he makes a mountain out of every molehill.

montear [1a] VT to hunt.

montecillo NM mound, hummock, hump.

montepío NM (a) (_sociedad_) charitable fund for dependants, friendly society. (b) (_LAm_) pawnshop. (c) (_And, Cono Sur_ = _viudedad_) widow's pension.

montera NF (a) (_sombrero_) cloth cap; (_Taur_) bullfighter's hat; **ponerse algo por ~** to laugh at sth; **ponerse el mundo por ~** not to care what anybody thinks. (b) (_Téc_) rise. (c) (_Arquit_) skylight.

montería NF (a) (_arte_) (art of) hunting; (_cacería_) hunt, chase.
(b) (_Arte_) hunting scene.
(c) (_personas_) hunting party.
(d) (_LAm_) (_animales_) animals, game; (_lugar_) hunting ground.
(e) (_And: canoa_) canoe.
(f) (_CAm: concesión_) concession.
(g) (_CAm, Méx: maderería_) timber camp.

montero NM huntsman, hunter; beater.

montés ADJ _gato etc_ wild.

montevideano, -a ADJ, NM/F Montevidean.

montículo NM = **montecillo**.

monto NM total, amount.

montón NM (a) (_gen_) heap, pile; (_de nieve_) drift.
(b) (_fig_) **del ~** ordinary, average, commonplace; **un hombre del ~** an ordinary chap; **salirse del ~** to be exceptional, stand out from the crowd.
(c) (*) stack*, heap*, lot; (_de gente_) crowd, mass; **un ~ de gente** a crowd, a mass of people, masses of people; **tengo un ~ de cosas que decirte** I have lots (o heaps*, stacks*) of things to tell you; **tenemos montones** we have heaps* (o tons*, loads); **a ~ together, all lumped together; **a montones** in great abundance, by the score (_etc_), galore.

montonera NF (a) (_LAm: guerrilla_) band of guerrilla fighters. (b) (_Carib: montón_) pile, heap; (_And: almiar_) haystack, strawstack.

montonero ☐1 ADJ (_Méx_) _persona_ overbearing.

2 NM (*LAm*) guerrilla fighter.

montuno ADJ (**a**) (*de montaña*) mountain (*atr*); forest (*atr*). (**b**) (*LAm*) (*salvaje*) wild, untamed; (*rústico*) rustic.

montuosidad NF hilliness, mountainous nature.

montuoso ADJ hilly, mountainous.

montura NF (**a**) (*cabalgadura*) mount. (**b**) (*silla*) saddle; (*arreos*) harness, trappings; **cabalgar sin ~** to ride bareback. (**c**) (*de joya etc*) mount, mounting, setting; (*de gafas etc*) frame.

monumental ADJ (**a**) (*enorme*) monumental. (**b**) (**: excelente*) tremendous*, terrific*.

monumentalidad NF monumental character.

monumentalismo NM tendency to construct vast buildings (*o* monuments).

monumento **1** NM (**a**) (*lit: t fig*) monument; memorial; **~ a los caídos** war memorial; **~ histórico-artístico** ≃ conservation area; listed building; **~ al soldado desconocido** tomb of the unknown soldier; **~s prehistóricos** prehistoric remains; **visitar los ~s de una ciudad** to see the sights of a town, visit the places of interest in a city.
(**b**) **~s** (*documentos*) documents, source material.
(**c**) (**: chica*) pretty girl.
2 ATR: **un éxito ~** a tremendous success*, a huge success.

monzón NM o F monsoon.

monzónico ADJ monsoon (*atr*); **lluvias monzónicas** monsoon rains.

moña NF (**a**) (*cinta*) hair ribbon, bow; (*Taur*) bullfighter's ribbon; (*de premio*) sash, prize ribbon. (**b**) (**: muñeca*) doll. (**c**) **estar con la ~** to be tight*. (**d**) (*Cono Sur*) bar. (**e**) (*‡: gay*) queer‡.

moño NM (**a**) (*de pelo*) bun, chignon; topknot; (*Cono Sur*) (*cabello*) man's hair; (*de caballo*) horse's forelock; **agarrarse del ~** to tear each other's hair; **estar con el ~ torcido** (*Carib, Méx*) to be in a bad mood; **estar hasta el ~*** to be fed up to the back teeth*; **ponerse ~s*** to give o.s. airs, put it on.
(**b**) (*Orn*) crest.
(**c**) = **moña** (**a**).
(**d**) **~s** (*fig*) frippery, buttons and bows.
(**e**) (*LAm: altivez*) pride, haughtiness; **agachar el ~** (*Cono Sur**) to give in; **bajar el ~ a uno** to take sb down a peg*.
(**f**) (*Cono Sur*) bar.

mopa NF mop.

MOPTMA NM (*Esp*) ABR *de* **Ministerio de Obras Públicas, Transportes y Medio Ambiente**.

MOPU ['mopu] NM (*Esp*) ABR *de* **Ministerio de Obras Públicas y Urbanismo**.

moquear [1a] VI to have a runny nose.

moqueo NM runny nose.

moquera NF: **tener ~** to have a runny nose.

moquero NM handkerchief.

moqueta NF moquette; (*fitted*) carpet.

moquete NM punch on the nose.

moquillo NM (*Vet*) distemper; pip.

mor: **por ~ de** PREP because of, on account of; for the sake of; **por ~ de la amistad** for friendship's sake.

mora¹ NF (**a**) (*Bot*) (*del moral*) mulberry; (*de zarzamora*) blackberry. (**b**) (*And*) bullet. (**c**) (*Méx**) pot‡, hash*.

mora² NF (*Jur*) delay; **ponerse en ~** to default, get into arrears.

mora³ NF (*Cono Sur*) blood sausage, black pudding.

morada NF (**a**) (*casa*) dwelling, abode, home; **la eterna ~** the great beyond; **última ~** (last) resting-place; **no tener ~ fija** to be of no fixed abode. (**b**) (*estancia*) stay, period of residence.

morado **1** ADJ purple, violet; **ojo ~** black eye; **pasarlas moradas** to have a tough time of it; **ponerse ~*** to do o.s. well, gorge o.s.
2 NM (**a**) bruise. (**b**) (*Cono Sur*) coward.

morador(a) NM/F inhabitant.

moradura NF bruise.

moral¹ NM (*Bot*) mulberry tree.

moral² **1** ADJ moral.
2 NF (**a**) (*moralidad*) morals, morality; (*como estudio*) ethics; **tiene más ~ que el alcoyano** he has the patience of Job, he keeps going against all the odds. (**b**) (*de ejército etc*) morale.

moraleja NF moral.

moralidad NF (**a**) (*moral*) morals, morality, ethics. (**b**) (*moraleja etc*) moral; **me tocó la ~*** it quite upset me; **sus críticas me tocan la ~** his criticisms get me down.

moralina NF moral.

moralista NMF moralist.

moralizador **1** ADJ moralizing; moralistic.
2 NM, **moralizadora** NF moralist.

moralizante ADJ moralizing; moralistic.

moralizar [1f] VT to moralize; to improve ethical standards in.

moralmente ADV morally.

morapio* NM (cheap) red wine, plonk*.

morar [1a] VI to live, dwell; to stay.

moratón NM bruise.

moratoria NF moratorium.

morbidez NF (*Arte etc*) softness, delicacy.

morbididad NF = **morbilidad**.

mórbido ADJ (**a**) (*enfermo*) morbid; diseased. (**b**) (*Arte etc*) soft, delicate.

morbilidad NF morbidity, sickness rate.

morbo NM (**a**) (*Med*) disease, illness. (**b**) (*fig*) unhealthy curiosity; ghoulish delight, morbid pleasure.

morbosidad NF (**a**) (*enfermedad*) morbidity, morbidness; unhealthiness. (**b**) (*estadística*) sick rate, morbidity.

morboso ADJ (**a**) (*enfermo*) morbid; (*malsano*) unhealthy, likely to cause disease(s). (**b**) (*fig*) diseased, morbid.

morcilla NF (**a**) (*Culin*) blood sausage, black pudding; (*Méx: callos*) tripe; **dar ~ a‡** (*matar*) to bump off‡, kill; (*dañar*) to hurt, harm; **¡vete a tomar ~!‡**, **¡que te den ~!‡** get stuffed!‡.
(**b**) (*Teat*) gag, unscripted lines, improvised part.
(**c**) (*‡*) prick‡.
(**d**) (*Carib: mentira*) lie.

morcillo ADJ *caballo* black with reddish hairs.

morcón NM (**a**) (*Culin*) big blood sausage. (**b**) (**: rechoncho*) stocky person. (**c**) (**: descuidado*) sloppy individual, shabby sort.

mordacidad NF sharpness, pungency; bite.

mordaga‡ NF, **mordaguera‡** NF drunkenness; **coger** (*o* **pillar**) **una ~** to get plastered‡.

mordaz ADJ *crítica etc* biting, scathing, pungent.

mordaza NF (**a**) (*de boca*) gag. (**b**) (*Téc*) clamp, jaw.

mordazmente ADV bitingly, scathingly.

mordedura NF bite.

mordelón **1** ADJ (**a**) (*CAm, Méx: sobornable*) given to taking bribes. (**b**) (*And, Carib*) *perro* snappy.
2 NM (*Méx‡*) traffic cop*.

morder [2h] **1** VT (**a**) (*gen*) to bite; (*pinchar*) to nip; (*mordisquear*) to nibble (at).
(**b**) (*Quím*) to corrode, eat away, eat into; *recursos etc* to eat into.
(**c**) (*Mec*) to catch; to clutch, seize.
(**d**) (**: denigrar*) to gossip about, run down.
(**e**) (*Méx: estafar*) to cheat; (*CAm, Méx: exigir soborno*) to exact a bribe from.
(**f**) (*‡: reconocer*) to recognize.
2 VI to bite (*t fig*); **estoy que muerdo** I'm simply furious; **está que muerde** he's hopping mad; **~ sobre** (*fig*) to bite into.

mordicar [1g] VI to smart, sting.

mordida NF (**a**) (*LAm*) bite. (**b**) (***) (*soborno*) bribe; (*tajada*) rake-off*, kickback*.

mordiscar [1g] **1** VT (*gen*) to nibble at; (*con fuerza*) to gnaw at; (*pinchar*) to nip; (*caballo*) to champ.
2 VI to nibble; to champ.

mordisco NM (**a**) (*acto*) bite, nip; nibble; (*fig*) attack, onslaught; **deshacer algo a ~s** to bite sth to pieces.
(**b**) (*trozo*) bite, piece bitten off.
(**c**) (*‡: beso*) love-bite.

mordisquear [1a] = **mordiscar**.

morena¹ NF (*Geol*) moraine.

morena² NF (*Pez*) moray.

morena³ NF dark girl, brunette.

morenal NM (*CAm*) shanty town.

morenear [1a] **1** VT to tan, brown.
2 **morenearse** VR to tan, brown.

morenez NF suntan, brownness.

moreno ADJ (dark) brown; *huevo* brown; *persona* dark; swarthy; dark-haired; (*bronceado*) brown, tanned; *pelo* dark, black; (*euf*) coloured (*euf*), Negro; (*And, Carib*) mulatto; **ponerse ~** to get brown, acquire a suntan.

morera NF mulberry tree.

morería NF (*Hist*) Moorish lands, Moorish territory; (*barrio*) Moorish quarter.

moretón NM (*esp LAm*) bruise.

morfa* NF = **morfina**.

morfar‡ [1a] (*Cono Sur*) **1** VT to eat; (*con gula*) to gobble up, put away*.
2 VI to nosh‡, scoff*.

morfema NM morpheme.

morfémico ADJ morphemic.

morfi‡ NM (*Cono Sur*) grub‡ nosh*, food.

morfina NF morphia, morphine.

morfinomanía NF morphine addiction, opium addiction.

morfinómano **1** ADJ addicted to morphine, addicted to opium.
2 NM, **morfinómana** NF morphine addict, opium addict.

morfofonología NF morphophonology.

morfología NF morphology.

morfológico ADJ morphological.

morfón: ADJ (*Cono Sur*) piggish, greedy.

morfosintaxis NF INVAR morphosyntax.

morganático ADJ morganatic.

morgue NF morgue.

moribundo [1] ADJ dying; (*esp fig*) moribund.

[2] NM, **moribunda** NF dying person.

moricho NM (*Carib*) hammock.

morigeración NF good behaviour.

morigerado ADJ well-behaved, law-abiding.

morigerar [1a] VT to restrain, moderate.

morillo NM firedog.

▼ **morir** [3j; PTP **muerto**] [1] VT (*sólo PTP y PERFECTO*) to kill; **le han muerto** they have killed him; **fue muerto en un accidente** he was killed in an accident; **fue muerto a tiros** he was shot (dead).

▼[2] VI (**a**) (*gen: t fig*) to die; **~ del corazón** to die of a heart-attack; **~ de difteria** to die of diphtheria; **~ joven** to die young; **~ de vejez** to die of old age; **~ ahogado** to drown; **~ ahorcado** to be hanged, die by hanging; **~ de frío** to die of cold, freeze to death; **~ fusilado** to be shot; **~ de hambre** to die of (o from) starvation, starve to death; **~ sin decir Jesús** to die very suddenly; **¡muera!** kill him!; **¡muera el tirano!** down with the tyrant!; **¡así se muera!** (*fig*) God rot him!; **y allí muere** (*LAm*) and that's all there is to it.

(**b**) (*irse apagando*) (*fuego*) to die down, burn low; to go out; (*luz*) to get dim, go out; **moría el día** the day was almost over, night was falling.

(**c**) (*Ferro etc: línea*) to end (*en* at); (*calle*) to come out (*en* at).

[3] **morirse** VR (**a**) (*gen*) to die; **se le murió el tío** an uncle of his died; **se nos va a ~ el burro** the donkey is going to die on us; **~ de hambre** = **muero de hambre!** (*fig*) I'm starving!; **no es cosa de ~** it's not as bad as all that.

(**b**) (*fig*) to be dying; **me moría de vergüenza** I nearly died of shame; **se moría de envidia** he was green with envy; **me moría de miedo** I was half-dead with fright; **se van a ~ de risa** they'll die of laughing.

(**c**) **~ por algo** to be dying for sth; **~ por uno** to be crazy about sb; **se muere por el fútbol** he's mad keen on football; **~ por + infin** to be dying to + infin.

(**d**) (*miembro*) to go to sleep, go numb.

morisco [1] ADJ Moorish; (*Arquit*) Mauresque, in the Moorish style.

[2] NM, **morisca** NF (**a**) (*Hist*) Moslem convert to Christianity, subject Moslem (*of 15th and 16th centuries*).

(**b**) (*Méx*: ††) quadroon.

morisma NF Moors (*collectively*).

morisqueta NF fraud, dirty trick.

mormón, -ona NM/F Mormon.

mormónico ADJ Mormon.

mormonismo NM Mormonism.

moro [1] ADJ (**a**) (*lit*) Moorish.

(**b**) *caballo* dappled, piebald.

[2] NM, **mora**[4] NF (**a**) (*lit*) Moor; **~ de paz** peaceful person; **¡hay ~s en la costa!** watch out!; **dar a ~ muerto gran lanzada** to kick a man when he's down.

(**b**) (*LAm: caballo*) piebald horse.

[3] NM (**a**) (*:*: *marido*) domineering husband.

(**b**) (*:*: *vendedor de droga*) drug pusher.

(**c**) **~s y cristianos** (*Carib*, *Culin*) rice with black beans.

(**d**) (*por extensión*) Morocco; **bajar al ~** to go to Morocco.

(**e**) (*Mús*) false note.

morocha NF (*Carib*) double-barrelled gun.

morocho [1] ADJ (**a**) (*LAm: moreno*) dark, swarthy; brunette.

(**b**) (*And, Carib, Cono Sur*) (*fuerte*) strong, tough; (*fornido*) well-built.

(**c**) (*Carib: gemelo*) twin.

[2] NM (**a**) (*LAm: maíz*) hard maize, corn (*US*).

(**b**) (*And, Carib, Cono Sur: duro*) persona tough person, hard guy*.

(**c**) (*Carib: gemelo*) twin.

morón NM hillock.

morondanga NF hotchpotch.

morondo ADJ (**a**) (*calvo*) bald; (*sin hojas*) leafless, bare. (**b**) (*fig*) bare, plain.

moronga NF (*CAm, Méx*) blood sausage, black pudding.

morosidad NF (**a**) (*lentitud*) slowness, sluggishness; dilatoriness; (*apatía*) apathy. (**b**) (*Fin*) slowness in paying up; (*atrasos*) arrears (of payment).

moroso [1] ADJ (**a**) (*lento*) slow, sluggish; dilatory; (*Com, Fin*) slow to pay up; **deudor ~** slow payer, defaulter; **una película de acción morosa** a film with slow action, a slow-moving film.

(**b**) **delectación morosa** lingering enjoyment, (*pey*) morbid enjoyment, unhealthy enjoyment.

[2] NM, **morosa** NF (*Com, Fin*) slow payer, bad debtor, defaulter.

morra NF top of the head; **andar a la ~** to exchange blows.

morrada NF (*cabezazo*) butt; bang on the head; (*golpe*) bash*, punch; **darse una ~** to fall flat on one's face.

morral NM (**a**) (*mochila*) haversack, knapsack; (*Caza*) pouch, gamebag; (*de caballo*) nosebag. (**b**) (*:*: *matón*) lout, rough type.

morralla NF (**a**) (*peces*) small fry, little fish. (**b**) (*basura*) rubbish. (**c**) (*personas*) rabble, common sort. (**d**) (*fig*) trinket. (**e**) (*Méx*) small change.

morrazo* NM (*golpe*) thump.

morrear: [1a] VTI to kiss.

morrena NF moraine.

morreo: NM kiss; kissing.

morrera: NF (*labios*) lips; (*boca*) kisser*.

morrillo NM (*Zool*) fleshy part of the neck; neck, back of the neck.

morriña NF (*Esp*) depression, depressed state, blues; **~ de la tierra** homesickness.

morriñoso ADJ homesick.

morrión NM (*Mil*) helmet, shako.

morrito* NM: **hacer ~s** to pout.

morro NM (**a**) (*Zool*) snout, nose; (*) lip, thick lip; **andar de ~ con uno** to be at odds with sb; **beber a ~** (*Esp*) to drink from the bottle; **dar a uno en los ~s*** to bash sb*; (*fig*) to get one's own back on sb; **estar de ~s** to be in a bad mood; **estar de ~(s) con uno** to be cross with sb; **¡cierra los ~s!:** shut your trap!:; **partir los ~s a uno*** to bash sb's face in*; **poner ~, torcer el ~** (*ofenderse*) to look cross, (*hacer una mueca*) to turn up one's nose; **poner morritos** to look sullen; **tiene un ~ que te lo pisas*** he's got a real brass neck*; **¡qué ~ tienes!*** you've got a nerve!*

(**b**) (*Aer, Aut etc*) nose; **caer de ~** to nose-dive (into the ground).

(**c**) (*Geog*) headland, promontory.

(**d**) (*guijarro*) pebble.

(**e**) (*cerro*) small rounded hill, rounded rock.

morrocotudo* ADJ (**a**) (*muy bueno*) smashing*, terrific*, splendid; *golpe, riña etc* tremendous*.

(**b**) (*fuerte*) strong; (*pesado*) heavy; (*Cono Sur*) clumsy, awkward.

(**c**) *asunto* (*difícil*) sticky, awkward; (*de peso*) important, weighty.

(**d**) (*Cono Sur, Méx: grande*) big.

(**e**) (*And: rico*) rich.

morrocoy NM (*CAm*) = **morrocoyo** (**a**).

morrocoyo NM (*Carib*) (**a**) (*Zool*) turtle. (**b**) (*:*) (*gordo*) fat person; (*tullido*) deformed person.

morrón NM (*LAm*) sweet pepper.

morrongo, -a NM/F cat.

morronguero* ADJ (*Carib*) (*tacaño*) stingy; (*cobarde*) yellow*.

morroña* NF (*CAm*) idleness, laziness.

morroñoso ADJ (**a**) (*CAm*) rough. (**b**) (*And*) (*pequeño*) small; (*endeble*) feeble; (*miserable*) wretched, poverty-stricken.

morrudo ADJ (**a**) thick-lipped, blubber-lipped. (**b**) (*Cono Sur*) tough, brawny.

morsa NF walrus.

morse NM morse.

mortadela NF bologna sausage.

mortaja NF (**a**) (*de muerto*) shroud. (**b**) (*Téc*) mortise. (**c**) (*LAm*) cigarette-paper.

mortal [1] ADJ (**a**) (*que muere*) mortal.

(**b**) *herida etc* mortal, fatal; *golpe* deadly.

(**c**) (*) *distancia, espera etc* deadly, unending.

(**d**) **quedarse*** **~** to be thunderstruck.

(**e**) **las señas son ~es** the signs are very clear.

[2] NMF mortal.

mortalidad NF (**a**) (*condición de mortal*) mortality. (**b**) (*cantidad de muertos*) mortality; loss of life, toll, number of victims; (*mortandad*) death rate; **~ infantil** (rate of) infant mortality.

mortalmente ADV (*V ADJ*) (**a**) mortally. (**b**) fatally.

mortandad NF toll, loss of life, number of victims; (*Mil*) slaughter, carnage.

mortecino ADJ (**a**) (*débil*) weak, failing; **hacer la mortecina** to pretend to be dead. (**b**) *luz* dim, fading, failing; *color* dull, faded.

morterada* NF: **gana una ~** he earns a small fortune, he earns a tidy bit*.

mortero NM mortar.

mortífero ADJ deadly, lethal.

mortificación NF mortification; humiliation.

mortificar [1g] [1] VT (**a**) (*Med*) to damage, affect seriously.

(**b**) *carne* to mortify; (*insecto, zapato etc*) to torment, plague; **me han mortificado toda la noche los mosquitos** the mosquitoes tormented me all night; **estos zapatos me mortifican** these shoes are killing me.

(**c**) (*fig*) to mortify, humiliate; to spite.

[2] **mortificarse** VR (*Méx*) (*avergonzarse*) to feel ashamed; (*ser tímido*) to be embarrassed, feel bashful.

mortuorio ADJ mortuary, death (*atr*); **casa mortuoria** house of mourning, home of the deceased.

morueco NM (*Zool*) ram.

moruno ADJ (*pey*) Moorish.

morza NF (*Cono Sur*) carpenter's vice.
Mosa NM Meuse.
mosaico[1] ADJ Mosaic, of Moses.
mosaico[2] NM mosaic; tessellated pavement; ~ **de madera** marquetry.
mosca [1] NF (**a**) (*Ent*) fly; ~ **blanca** whitefly; ~ **de burro** horsefly; ~ **de la carne** meatfly; ~ **doméstica** housefly; ~ **de España** Spanish fly, cantharides; ~ **de la fruta** fruitfly; ~ **muerta** (*fig*) hypocrite, slyboots; ~ **tsetsé** tsetse fly; **por si las ~s** just in case; **se asaban las ~s*** it was darned hot*; **mandar a uno a capar ~s‡** to tell sb to go to blazes*; **no se oía ni una ~** you could have heard a pin drop; **papar ~s*** to gape, gawp*; **pescar a ~** to fish with a fly; **le picó la ~** (*fig*) he suddenly got worried; **¿que ~ te picó?** what's eating you?; **tener la ~ en** (o **detrás de**) **la oreja** to be wary, be suspicious.
(**b**) (‡: *dinero*) dough‡; **aflojar la ~, soltar la ~** to fork out*, stump up. (**c**) (*: *persona*) pest, bore. (**d**) (*pelo*) tuft of hair, small growth of hair; (*barba*) small goatee beard. (**e**) ~**s** (*centellas*) sparks; ~**s volantes** spots before the eyes. (**f**) (*Méx**) sponger*.
[2] ADJ INVAR (*Esp**) **estar ~** (*recelar*) to smell a rat, be suspicious, be distrustful; (*harto*) to be utterly fed up*; **estar ~ con uno** to be cross with sb.
moscada ADJ: **nuez ~** nutmeg.
moscarda NF blowfly, bluebottle.
moscardón NM (**a**) (*Ent*) (*moscarda*) botfly, blowfly; (*abejón*) hornet. (**b**) (*) pest, bore, nuisance.
moscatel[1] ADJ, NM muscatel.
moscatel[2] NM (**a**) (*pesado*) bore, pest. (**b**) (*mocetón*) big lad, overgrown lad.
moscón NM (**a**) (*Ent*) = **moscarda**. (**b**) (*Bot*) maple. (**c**) (*: *pesado*) pest, nuisance.
moscoso* NM day off (*for personal matters, not deducted from annual leave*).
moscovita ADJ, NMF Muscovite.
Moscú NM Moscow.
Mosela NM Moselle.
mosqueado ADJ (**a**) (*moteado*) spotted. (**b**) (*enfadado*) angry, resentful.
mosqueador NM fly-whisk; (*: *cola*) tail.
mosqueante ADJ (**a**) (*molesto*) annoying, irritating. (**b**) (*sospechoso*) suspicious, fishy*.
mosquearse [1a] VR (*recelar*) to smell a rat, get suspicious; (*ofenderse*) to get cross, take offence; (*: *hartarse*) to get fed up (*de* with)*.
mosqueo NM (**a**) (*enfado*) annoyance, anger, resentment; **se llevó un ~** he got angry. (**b**) (*lío*) hassle, fuss.
mosquete NM musket.
mosquetero NM (*Hist*: *Mil*) musketeer; (*Teat*) groundling.
mosquita NF: ~ **muerta** (*fig*) hypocrite, slyboots; **hacerse la ~ muerta** to look as if butter would not melt in one's mouth.
mosquitero NM mosquito net.
mosquito NM mosquito; gnat.
mostacera NF, **mostacero** NM mustard pot.
mostacho NM moustache.
mostachón NM macaroon.
mostacilla NF (*And*) bead necklace.
mostaza NF (**a**) (*lit*) mustard; **un vestido ~** a mustard-yellow dress. (**b**) (*And*, *Méx‡*) pot‡, hash*.
mostela NF sheaf.
mosto NM must, unfermented grape juice.
mostrador NM (**a**) (*de tienda*) counter; (*de café etc*) bar; ~ **de caja** cashdesk; ~ **de facturación** check-in desk; ~ **de tránsito** transit desk. (**b**) (*de reloj*) face, dial. (**c**) (‡: *pecho*) bosom, tits‡.
mostrar [1l] [1] VT (*gen*) to show; (*exponer*) to display, exhibit; (*señalar*) to point out; (*explicar*) to explain; (*demostrar*) to demonstrate; ~ **en pantalla** (*Inform*) to display.
[2] **mostrarse** VR (**a**) (*gen*) to show o.s.; to appear.
(**b**) (*con adj*) to appear, show o.s. to be; **se mostró muy amable** he was very kind, he proved to be very kind; **se mostró ofendido** he appeared (to be) cross; **no se muestra muy imaginativa** she does not seem to be very imaginative.
mostrenco ADJ (**a**) (*sin dueño*) ownerless, unclaimed; *título* in abeyance; *animal* stray; *persona* homeless, rootless. (**b**) (*) (*lento*) dense, slow; (*gordo*) fat. (**c**) (*) *objeto* crude, roughly made.
mostro* ADJ (*And*) great*, superb.
mota[1] NF (**a**) (*partícula*) speck, tiny piece; (*pelusa*) piece of fluff; ~ **de carbonilla** smut, speck of coaldust; ~ **de polvo** speck of dust; **ver la ~ en el ojo ajeno** to see the mote in sb else's eye.
(**b**) (*dibujo*) dot; **diseño a ~s** design with (o of) dots.
(**c**) (*nudillo en paño*) burl, kink; (*fig*) fault, blemish, defect.
(**d**) **no ... ~** nothing, no, *p.ej.* **no hace ~ de aire** there isn't a breath of air.
(**e**) (*Geog*) hillock.
(**f**) (*Agr*: *mojón*) ridge, boundary mark.
(**g**) (*Agr*: *césped*) turf, clod (*used to block off irrigation channel*).
(**h**) (*LAm*: *pelo*) lock of wavy hair.
(**i**) (*And*, *Carib*, *Méx*: *borla*) powder puff.
(**j**) (*Méx*) (*Bot*) marijuana plant; (*: *droga*) grass‡, dope‡.
mote[1] NM (**a**) (*Hist*) motto, device. (**b**) (*apodo*) nickname, by-name.
mote[2] NM (**a**) (*LAm*) (*trigo*) boiled wheat; (*maíz*) boiled maize, boiled corn (*US*). (**b**) (*Cono Sur*) **pelar ~** to gossip; **como ~** in large numbers.
moteado ADJ *piel* speckled, mottled, dappled (*de* with); *tela etc* flecked, dotted, with a design of dots.
motear [1a] VT to speck (*de* with); to speckle, dapple.
motejar [1a] VT to nickname; ~ **a uno de** to brand sb as, accuse sb of being.
motel NM motel.
motero*, -a NM/F biker*, motorcyclist.
motete NM motet; anthem.
motín NM (*rebelión*) revolt, rising; (*disturbio*) riot, disturbance; ~ **carcelario** prison riot.
motivación NF motivation.
motivacional ADJ motivational.
motivar [1a] VT (**a**) (*causar*) to cause, motivate, give rise to. (**b**) (*explicar*) to explain, justify (*con*, *en* by, by reference to).
▼ **motivo** [1] ADJ motive.
▼ [2] NM (**a**) (*gen*) motive, reason (*de* for), cause (*de* of); ~**s de divorcio** grounds for divorce; ~ **oculto** ulterior motive; (*en formulario*) '**~ del viaje**' 'purpose of visit'; **con ~ de** because of, owing to; on the occasion of; in connection with; for the purpose of; **fue allí con ~ de la boda de su hija** he went there for his daughter's wedding; **con este ~** for this reason, because of this; **por cuyo ~** for which reason, on account of which; **por ~s de salud** for reasons of health; **sin ~** for no reason at all, without good reason; ~ **más que sobrado para ...** all the more reason to ...; **un crimen sin ~** a crime without a motive, a pointless crime; **tengo mis ~s** I have my reasons.
(**b**) (*Arte*, *Mús*) motif; ~ **principal** leitmotif; (*de musical etc*) theme song.
moto[1]* NF (*motocicleta*) motorbike*; (*escúter*) (motor) scooter.
moto[2] [1] ADJ (**a**) (*CAm*) orphaned, abandoned. (**b**) (*And*) tailless.
[2] NM, **mota**[2] NF (*CAm*) orphan.
motobomba NF fire engine.
motocarro NM three-wheeler, light delivery van.
motocicleta NF motorcycle; ~ **con sidecar** motorcycle combination.
motociclismo NM motorcycling.
motociclista NMF motorcyclist; ~ **de escolta** outrider.
moto-cross NM moto-cross.
motocultor NM cultivator.
motón NM (*Náut*) pulley.
motonauta NMF jet skier.
motonáutica NF speedboat racing.
motonave NF motor ship, motor vessel.
motoneta NF (*LAm*) motor scooter.
motoneurona NF motor neurone.
motonieve NF snowmobile.
motoniveladora NF bulldozer.
motor [1] ADJ (**a**) (*Téc*) motive; **potencia ~a** motive power.
(**b**) (*Anat*) motor.
[2] NM motor, engine; **con 6 ~es** 6-engined; **aviación con ~** powered flight; ~ **de arranque**, ~ **de puesta en marcha** starter, starting motor; ~ **de aviación** aircraft engine; ~ **de combustión interna**, ~ **de explosión** internal combustion engine; ~ **a chorro** jet engine; ~ **delantero** front-mounted engine; ~ **diesel** diesel engine; ~ **(de) fuera (de) borda** outboard motor; ~ **de (o a) inyección** fuel-injection engine; ~ **de pistón** piston engine; ~ **radial** radial engine; ~ **de (o a) reacción** jet engine; ~ **refrigerado por aire** air-cooled engine; ~ **trasero** rear-mounted engine; **calentar ~es** to warm up; **cargar ~es** (*fig*) to prepare oneself, get ready; to get charged up.
motora NF, **motorbote** NM motorboat, speedboat.
motorismo NM motorcycling.
motorista NMF (**a**) (*motociclista*) motorcyclist. (**b**) (*LAm*) driver.
motorístico ADJ motor-racing (*atr*).
motorización NF (**a**) (*acto*) motorization; mechanization. (**b**) (*capacidad*) engine size.
motorizado ADJ motorized; *tropas* mechanized; **patrulla motorizada** motorized patrol, mobile unit; **personas no motorizadas** people who do not own a car, people who do not have their own transport.
motorizar [1f] [1] VT to motorize; to mechanize.
[2] **motorizarse** VR (*hum*) to become mobile, get a car.
motorola* ® NF mobile phone.
motosegadora NF motor mower, motorized lawn mower.
motosierra NF mechanical saw, power saw.
motoso ADJ (*And*, *Cono Sur*) *pelo* kinky.
motricidad NF mobility.
motriz ADJ (*f irreg*: *de* **motor**) motive, driving; *V* **fuerza**.
motudo ADJ (*Cono Sur*) *pelo* kinky.

mousse [muːs] NF (*Culin*) mousse; (*de pelo*) hair-conditioner; (*de afeitar*) shaving foam.

movedizo ADJ (a) (*movible*) easily moved, movable; (*suelto*) loose; (*poco seguro*) unsteady, shaky; *arenas* shifting. (b) (*cambiadizo*) *persona* fickle; *situación etc* shifting, unsettled, changeable; troubled.

mover [2h] **1** VT (a) (*gen*) *objeto etc* to move; (*cambiar de sitio*) to shift; to move about, move along; *cabeza* (*negando*) to shake; (*asintiendo*) to nod; *cola* to wag; (*Ajedrez etc*) to move; (*LAm**) *droga* to push; '**no nos moverán**' (*eslogan*) 'we shall not be moved'.
(b) (*Mec*) to drive, power, work; to pull; **el agua mueve la rueda** the water turns (o drives) the wheel; **la máquina mueve 14 coches** the engine pulls 14 coaches; **el vapor mueve el émbolo** the steam drives (o works) the piston.
(c) (*fig*) to cause, provoke, induce; *descontento etc* to stir up; ~ **un jaleo** to cause a row, make a fuss; ~ **guerra a uno** to wage war on sb; ~ **pleito a uno** to take proceedings against sb; ~ **a uno a piedad** to move sb to pity, arouse compassion in sb; ~ **a uno a risa** to make sb laugh; ~ **a uno a hacer algo** to move (o prompt, lead) sb to do sth.
(d) **la empresa mueve X pesetas al año** the firm has an annual turnover of X pesetas.
2 VI (*Bot*) to bud, sprout.
3 moverse VR (a) (*gen*) to move; to stir (*de* from); (*hacer lugar*) to move over (o along, up *etc*); **no se ha movido de su asiento** he has not stirred from his place; **¡deja de moverte!** stop fidgeting!
(b) (*mar*) to get rough; (*viento*) to rise.
(c) (*fig*) (*apurarse*) to move o.s., get a move on; (*evolucionar*) to be on the move; **¡muévete!** hurry up!; **hay que** ~ (*darse prisa*) we must get a move on; (*estar alerta*) you have to keep on your toes; **si no te mueves lo perderás** if you don't hustle (o unless you do sth) it will be lost; **la moda masculina se mueve** men's fashions are changing, men's fashions are on the move.

movible ADJ (a) (*no fijo*) movable; (*móvil*) mobile. (b) (*fig*) changeable; fickle.

movida NF (a) (*Ajedrez etc*) move; ~ **clave** key-move.
(b) (*Pol etc*) movement.
(c) (*) (*asunto*) thing, affair, business; (*concentración*) gathering; (*acontecimiento*) happening; (*pelea*) scrap*, set-to*; **la** ~ **cultural** the cultural scene; **la** ~ **madrileña** the Madrid scene*, swinging Madrid*, where the action is in Madrid*.

┌─────────────────────┐
│ **MOVIDA MADRILEÑA** │
└─────────────────────┘

ⓘ *The **Movida Madrileña** was a cultural movement which sprang up in Madrid towards the end of the **Transición a la Democracia** (Transition to Democracy - 1975-82). In post-Franco Spain many were glad to shake off Catholic social and sexual mores and to experiment. This was the period that saw the emergence of exciting and innovative film directors like Pedro Almodóvar and bands like Radio Futura and Alaska y los Pegamoides. At the same time the media, music and fashion industries sought to distance themselves from the mass-produced popular culture of the US and UK and establish their own Spanish identity.*

movido ADJ (a) (*Fot*) blurred (*by camera shake etc*).
(b) *persona* (*activo*) active; (*inquieto*) restless, always on the go; *reunión etc* lively; turbulent; **unos días movidos** several furiously busy days; **la acción era muy movida** the action was pretty lively.
(c) (*And, CAm, Cono Sur*) *huevo* soft-shelled.
(d) (*And, CAm, Cono Sur: débil*) weak, feeble; (*CAm, Méx*) (*lento*) slow, sluggish; (*indeciso*) irresolute.

movidón* NM rave-up*, wild party.

móvil **1** ADJ = **movible** (a) *y* (b); *V* **material** *etc*.
2 NM (a) motive (*de* for); incentive. (b) (*Arte*) mobile.

movilidad NF mobility; ~ **ascendente** upward mobility; ~ **social** social mobility.

movilización NF mobilization; ~ **de capital** raising of capital; ~ **de los trabajadores** (call for) industrial action.

movilizar [1f] VT (a) (*organizar*) to mobilize. (b) (*Cono Sur*) to unblock, free.

movimiento NM (a) (*gen*) movement; (*Mec, Fís*) motion; (*estadística etc*) movement; (*de cabeza*) (*negando*) shake; (*asintiendo*) nod; ~ **ascensional de los precios** upward trend (o movement) of prices; ~ **ascendente de las líneas** upward sweep of the lines; ~ **continuo**, ~ **perpetuo** perpetual motion; ~ **de efectivo** cash flow; ~ **de mercancías** turnover, volume of business; ~ **de pinza** pincer movement; ~ **de los precios** changes in prices; ~ **sísmico** earth tremor; **estar en** ~ to be in motion, be moving; to be on the move; **mantener algo en** ~ to keep sth moving; **mantener en** ~ **la circulación** to keep the traffic on the move; **poner algo en** ~ to set sth in motion, start sth, get sth going.
(b) (*actividad etc*) movement; activity; (*bullicio*) bustle, stir; (*Aut*) traffic; **una tienda de mucho** ~ a busy shop, a much-frequented shop; ~ **máximo** (*Aut*) peak traffic; **había mucho** ~ **en el tribunal** there was great activity in the court.
(c) (*Liter, Teat etc*) action; **el libro no tiene bastante** ~ the book does not have enough action, not enough happens in the book.
(d) (*Mús*) (*compás*) tempo; (*tiempo*) movement.
(e) (*de emociones*) *cambio* change, alteration; (*arranque*) fit, outburst; ~ **de ánimo** perturbation; **en un** ~ **de celos** in a rush of jealousy; **obró en un** ~ **de pasión** he acted in a surge of passion.
(f) (*Arte, Liter, Pol etc*) movement; ~ **de liberación de la mujer** women's liberation movement; **el** ~ **revolucionario** the revolutionary movement; **el** ~ **iniciado por Picasso** the movement started by Picasso; **el M~** (*Esp, 1936 etc*) the Falangist Movement.
(g) ~ **de bloques** (*Inform*) block move.

moviolas NFPL magic-lantern (show); (*Cine*) hand viewer for film editing.

moza NF (*muchacha*) girl; (*criada*) servant; (*pey*) wench; **buena ~**, **real** ~ handsome girl, good-looking girl; ~ **de partido** prostitute; ~ **de servicio** (*Esp* †) domestic servant; ~ **de taberna** (*Esp* †) barmaid.

mozalbete NM lad.

Mozambique NM Mozambique.

mozambiqueño, -a ADJ, NM/F Mozambican.

mozárabe **1** ADJ Mozarabic. **2** NMF Mozarab; *see also* ⃞RECONQUISTA⃞ **3** NM (*Ling*) Mozarabic.

mozarrón NM big lad, strapping young fellow.

mozo **1** ADJ (a) (*joven*) young; **en sus años ~s** in his youth, in his young days.
(b) (*soltero*) single, unmarried.
2 NM youth, young fellow, lad; servant; (*en café*) waiter; (*Ferro etc*) porter; **buen** ~ handsome lad; well set-up young man; ~ **de caballos** groom; ~ **de café** waiter; ~ **de cámara** cabin boy; ~ **de cuadra** stableboy; ~ **de cuerda**, ~ **de estación**, ~ **de equipajes** porter; ~ **de hotel** page, buttons, bellhop (US); ~ **de laboratorio** laboratory assistant; ~ **de panadería** baker's boy.

mozuela NF girl; wench.

mozuelo NM (young) lad.

MPAIAC NM (*Esp*) ABR *de* **Movimiento para la Autodeterminación y la Independencia del Archipiélago Canario**.

MRTA NM (*Perú*) ABR *de* **Movimiento Revolucionario Túpac Amaru**.

MTC NM (*Esp*) ABR *de* **Ministerio de Transportes y Comunicaciones**.

mu‡: **¡achanta la ~!** (*Méx*) shut your face!‡; **no pasó ni** ~ nothing at all happened; **no dijo ni** ~ she didn't say a word.

muaré NM moiré.

mucama NF (*Cono Sur y LAm* ††) maid, servant.

mucamo NM (*Cono Sur*) servant.

muceta NF (*Univ*) cape.

muchá NMF (*LAm*) = **muchacho, muchacha**.

muchacha NF (a) (*chica*) girl. (b) (*criada: t* ~ **de servicio**) maid, servant.

muchachada NF (a) (*travesura*) childish prank. (b) (*esp LAm: grupo*) group of youths, bunch of youngsters.

muchacha-guía NF, PL **muchachas-guías** girl guide, girl scout (US).

muchachería NF = **muchachada** (a) *y* (b).

muchachil ADJ boyish, girlish.

muchacho NM (a) (*chico*) boy, lad; (*criado*) servant. (b) (*LAm: abrazadera*) clamp, holdfast; (*Cono Sur: de zapato*) shoehorn; (*And*) (*lámpara*) miner's lamp; (*sostén*) prop.

muchedumbre NF crowd, mass, throng; (*pey*) mob, herd; **una** ~ **de** a great crowd of, a great number of.

muchísimo ADJ, ADV SUPERL *de* **mucho**; very much, a very great deal (*etc*).

mucho **1** ADJ (a) (*sing*) a lot of; much, great; (*demasiado*) too much; ~ **tiempo** a long time (*y V* **tiempo**); ~ **dinero** a lot of money; **con** ~ **valor** with much courage, with great courage; **hace** ~ **calor** it's very hot; **es** ~ **dinero para un niño** it's too much money for a child; **con mucha menor frecuencia** much less often, with much less frequency.
(b) (*sing, colectivo*) **había** ~ **borracho** there were a lot of drunks*; **aquí hay** ~ **maricón‡** there are lots of queers here‡.
(c) (*sing**) **es** ~ **jugador** he's a great player; **es mucha mujer** what a woman she is!, there's a woman for you!; **ésta es mucha casa para nosotros** this house is far too big for us.
(d) (PL) ~**s** many, lots of; many a; (*demasiados*) too many; **hay ~s conejos** there are lots of rabbits; ~ **de los ausentes** many of those absent; **somos ~s** there are a lot of us; **se me hacen ~s** I think there are too many; **son ~s los que no quieren** there are many who don't want to.
2 PRON: **tengo** ~ **que hacer** I have a lot to do; ~**s dicen que** ... a lot of people say that ...; **el plan tiene** ~ **de positivo** there's a lot about the plan which is positive.
3 ADV (a) (*gen*) a lot, a great deal; much; ~ **más** much more, a lot more; ~ **menos** much less; **10 cuando** ~ 10 at the outside; ~ **peor** much worse; **toca** ~ she plays a lot, she plays a great deal; **me ale-**

gro ~ I'm very glad; **correr ~** to run fast; **trabajar ~** to work hard; **viene ~** he comes a lot, he comes often; **es ~** it's a lot, it's too much; **si no es ~ pedir** if that's not asking too much; **se guardará muy ~ de hacerlo*** he'll jolly well be careful not to do it*; *V* **antes** etc.

(b) (*tiempo*) long; **¿te vas a quedar ~?** are you staying long?

(c) (*como respuesta*) very; **¿estás cansado? - ¡~!** are you tired? - very (o I certainly am, yes indeed).

(d) (*locuciones*) **¡~ que sí!** I should jolly well think so!*, of course!; **¡~ lo sientes tú!** a fat lot you care!*; **con ~** by far, far and away, easily; **con ~ el mejor** far and away the best; **ni con ~** not nearly, nothing like; not by a long chalk; **ni ~ menos** far from it; **no es ~ que ...** it is no wonder that ...; **¿qué ~ si se odian?** is it any surprise if they loathe each other?; **no es para ~** it's not up to much; **tener a uno en ~** to think highly of sb, have a high opinion of sb.

(e) (*Méx*) **es ~ muy difícil** it's jolly difficult; **es ~ muy bueno** it's very good, it's excellent.

mucilaginoso ADJ mucilaginous.

mucílago NM mucilage.

mucosa NF mucous membrane; mucus.

mucosidad NF mucus.

mucoso ADJ mucous.

múcura NF (*And, Carib*) earthenware jug.

muda NF **(a)** (*ropa*) change of clothing. **(b)** (*Orn, Zool*) moult; (*de serpiente*) slough. **(c)** (*temporada*) moulting season. **(d) está de ~** (*chico*) his voice is breaking.

mudable ADJ, **mudadizo** ADJ changeable, variable; shifting; *carácter* etc fickle.

mudanza NF **(a)** (*gen*) change; **sufrir ~** to undergo a change. **(b)** (*de casa*) move, removal; **camión de ~s** removal van; **estar de ~** to be moving. **(c)** (*Baile*) figure. **(d) ~s** (*fig*) fickleness; moodiness, uncertainty of mood.

mudar [1a] **1** VT **(a)** (*cambiar*) to change, alter; **~ en** to change into, transform into; **me van a ~ la pluma** they're going to change the pen for me; **le han mudado a otra oficina** they've moved (o switched) him to another office; **esto mudó la tristeza en alegría** this changed (o turned, transformed) the sadness into joy; **le mudan las sábanas todos los días** they change his sheets every day.

(b) (*Orn, Zool*) to shed, moult; *piel* to slough.

2 VI to change; **~ de ropa** to change one's clothes; **~ de color** to change colour; **he mudado de parecer** I've changed my mind; **mandarse ~** (*esp LAm**) to clear off*, leave.

3 mudarse VR **(a)** = vi. **(b)** (*t ~ de casa*) to move, move house. **(c)** (*voz*) to break.

mudéjar **1** ADJ Mudejar. **2** NMF (*Hist*) Mudejar (*Moslem permitted to live under Christian rule*); see also RECONQUISTA .

mudejarismo NM (*Arte* etc) Mudejar character (o style etc).

mudenco ADJ (*CAm*) (*tartamudo*) stuttering; (*tonto*) stupid.

mudengo ADJ (*And*) silly.

mudez NF dumbness.

mudo ADJ **(a)** (*sin facultad de hablar*) dumb; (*callado*) silent, mute; **quedarse ~ de** (*fig*) to be dumb with; **quedarse ~ de asombro** to be dumbfounded, be speechless; **se quedó ~ durante 3 horas** he remained silent for 3 hours, he did not speak for 3 hours; **quedarse ~ de envidia** (*Esp*) to be green with envy.

(b) (*Ling*) *letra* mute, silent.

(c) *película* silent; *papel* ~ (*Teat*) walk-on part.

(d) (*And, CAm**) foolish, silly.

mueblaje NM = mobiliario.

mueble **1** ADJ movable.

2 NM **(a)** piece of furniture; **~s** furniture; (*de tienda* etc) fittings; **con ~s** furnished; **sin ~s** unfurnished; **~ combinado, ~ de elementos adicionables** piece of unit furniture; **~s y enseres** furniture and fittings; **~s de época** period furniture; **~ librería** bookcase unit; **~s de oficina** office furniture.

(b) (*Méx**: *coche*) car.

MUEBLE   **ver también la entrada**

- Para traducir la palabra *mueble* al inglés, hay que recordar que el sustantivo *furniture* es incontable y lleva el verbo en singular:
  Los muebles del comedor son muy antiguos
  The dining-room furniture is very old
- Si queremos traducir expresiones en las que se habla de un solo mueble, o en las que se precisa el número de muebles, utilizamos la construcción *piece/pieces of furniture*:
  Éste es un mueble muy valioso
  This is a very valuable piece of furniture
  He comprado un par de muebles antiguos
  I bought one or two pieces of antique furniture
  Para otros usos y ejemplos ver la entrada.

---

mueblé* NM brothel.

mueble-bar NM cocktail cabinet.

mueblería NF (*fábrica*) furniture factory; (*tienda*) furniture shop.

mueca NF (wry) face, grimace; **hacer ~s a** to make faces at.

muela NF **(a)** (*Anat*) tooth, (*estrictamente*) molar, back tooth; **~ del juicio** wisdom tooth; **dolor de ~s** toothache; **está que echa las ~s** he's hopping mad; **hacer la ~** (*Carib*) to skive*. **(b)** (*Téc*) (*de molino*) millstone; (*de afilar*) grindstone. **(c)** (*Geog*) mound, hillock. **(d)** (*And*) gluttony. **(e)** (*Carib*) trickery.

muellaje NM wharfage.

muelle[1] **1** ADJ **(a)** (*blando*) soft; (*delicado*) delicate; (*elástico*) springy, bouncy. **(b)** (*fig*) *vida* soft, easy, luxurious.

2 NM spring; **~ real** mainspring; **colchón de ~s** spring mattress, interior sprung mattress.

muelle[2] NM **(a)** (*Náut*) wharf, quay; pier; **~ de atraque** (*Náut*) mooring quay, (*Aer*) docking bay. **(b)** (*Ferro* etc: *t* **~ de carga**) loading bay.

muenda NF (*And*) thrashing.

muera etc V **morir.**

muérdago NM mistletoe.

muerdo: NM bite.

muérgano NM **(a)** (*And, Carib*: *cacharro*) useless object, piece of junk. **(b)** (*And*: *desharrapado*) shabby person; (*And*: *maleducado*) ill-bred person, lout. **(c)** (*And*: *caballo*) vicious horse.

muermo* **1** ADJ (*Esp*) (*pesado*) boring; (*débil*) wet*, indecisive; (*lento*) slow, slow-witted.

2 NM, **muerma** NF (*Esp*) (*pesado*) crashing bore; (*débil*) drip, wet fish*; (*tonto*) dolt, idiot; **¡no seas ~!** don't be an idiot!

3 NM **(a)** (*aburrimiento*) boredom; (*depresión*) blues. **(b)** (*asunto* etc) bore, pain*. **(c)** (*droga*) bad trip*.

muerte **1** NF **(a)** (*lit: t fig*) death; (*homicidio*) murder; **~ civil** loss of civil rights; **~ a mano airada, ~ violenta** violent death; **~ cerebral** brain death; **~ natural** natural death; **~ repentina** sudden death; **~ súbita** (*Dep*) sudden death (play-off); (*Tenis*) tiebreak; **causar la ~ a, producir la ~ a** to kill (*in an accident*), cause the death of, bring about the death of; **dar ~ a** to kill; **me da ~*** I can't be bothered; **encontrar la ~** to meet one's death; **estar a la ~** to be at death's door.

(b) (*locuciones fig*) **guerra a ~** war to the knife, war to the bitter end; **luchar a ~** to fight to the death; **un susto de ~** a terrible fright; **odiar a uno a ~** to loathe sb; **aburrirse de ~** to be bored to death; **un empleo de mala ~*** an awful job, a lousy job:; **un pueblo de mala ~*** an awful dump (of a town)*; **es la ~*** it's deadly (boring).

2 ADJ (*Cono Sur**) super*, brilliant*.

muerto **1** ADJ **(a)** (*gen, fig*) dead; lifeless; **~ en acción, ~ en campaña** killed in action; **nacido ~** stillborn; **más ~ que vivo** half-dead, more dead than alive; (*fig: aterrado*) frightened to death; **más ~ que mi abuela, más ~ que una piedra** as dead as a doornail, stone-dead; **dar por ~ a uno** to give sb up for dead; **no tener donde caerse ~** to be utterly destitute, not have a thing; **resultó ~ en el acto** he died instantly.

(b) (*fig*) **estar ~ de cansancio** to be dead tired, be dog-tired; **estar ~ de hambre** to be dying of hunger; **estar ~ de miedo** to be half-dead with fear, be panic-stricken; **estar ~ de risa** to be helpless with laughter.

(c) *color* dull.

(d) *lengua* dead; *V* **marea, naturaleza** etc.

(e) *cal* slaked.

2 NM, **muerta** NF **(a)** (*gen*) dead man, dead woman; (*difunto*) deceased; (*cadáver*) corpse; **los ~s** the dead; **Día de los M~s** (*LAm*) All Souls Day; **callarse como un ~** to keep absolutely quiet; **cargar con el ~*** to carry the can*; **doblar a ~, tocar a ~** to toll (for a death); **echar el ~ a uno** to put the blame on sb else; **no hablan los ~s** dead men tell no tales; **hacer el ~** (*nadador*) to float; **hacerse el ~** to pretend to be dead; **poner los ~s** to provide cannon-fodder.

(b) (*) (*lento*) slowcoach*; (*pesado*) bore, tedious sort.

3 NM **(a)** (*Naipes*) dummy. **(b)** (*: trabajo*) drag, slog.

DÍA DE LOS MUERTOS

ⓘ November 2, All Souls' Day, called the **Día de los Muertos** *elsewhere in the Spanish-speaking world and* **Día de los Difuntos** *in Spain, is the day when Christians throughout the Spanish-speaking world traditionally honour their dead. In Mexico the festivities are particularly spectacular with a week-long festival, starting on November 1, in which Christian and ancient pagan customs are married. November 1 itself is for children who have died, while November 2 is set aside for adults. Families meet to take food, flowers and sweets in the shape of skeletons, coffins and crosses to the graves of their loved ones. In Spain people celebrate the* **Día de los Difuntos** *by taking flowers to the cemetery.*

muesca NF (*corte*) notch, nick; (*ranura*) groove, slot.

muesli NM muesli.

muestra NF **(a)** (*señal*) indication, sign; (*ejemplo*) example; (*demostración*) demonstration; (*prueba*) proof; (*testimonio*) token; (*Com: exposición*) trade fair; **es ~ de cariño** it is a token of affection; **el no hacerlo es ~ de desprecio** not doing it is an indication of contempt; **quieren hacer una ~ de su poder** they want to give a demonstration of their power; **da ~s de deterioro** it's showing signs of wear.
(b) (*Com etc*) sample; specimen; **~ gratuita** free sample.
(c) (*estadística*) sample; **~ aleatoria, ~ al azar** random sample; **~ representativa** cross-section sample.
(d) (*pauta*) model, pattern, guide; (*Cos*) pattern; **es ~ de cómo debe hacerse** it is a model of how it should be done.
(e) (*de reloj*) face.
(f) (*de tienda etc*) sign, signboard.

muestral ADJ sample (*atr*).

muestrario NM collection of samples (*o* specimens); pattern book.

muestrear [1a] VT to sample.

muestreo NM sampling; survey.

mueva *etc* V **mover**.

mufa* NF (*Cono Sur*) (*mala suerte*) bad luck, misfortune; (*mal humor*) bad mood; (*aburrimiento*) boredom, tedium.

mufado* ADJ (*Cono Sur*): **estar ~** to be in a bad mood; to feel blue*.

mugido NM moo, lowing; bellow; roar, howl.

mugir [3c] VI (*vaca*) to moo, low; (*toro*) to bellow; (*con dolor*) to roar, howl; (*mar etc*) to roar.

mugre NF dirt, filth; grease, grime; **sacarse la ~*** (*Cono Sur: trabajar*) to work hard; (*sufrir un percance*) to have a nasty accident.

mugriento ADJ dirty, filthy; greasy, grimy.

mugrón NM (*de vid*) sucker, layer; (*vástago*) shoot, sprout.

mugroso ADJ = **mugriento**.

muguete NM lily of the valley.

mui: NF = **muy 2**.

muina* NF (*Méx*): **me da la ~** it gets on my nerves, it upsets me.

mujahedín, mujahidín, mujaidín NM mujaheddin.

mujer NF **(a)** (*gen*) woman; **~ alegre, ~ de vida alegre, ~ de la vida, ~ de mala vida, ~ pública** prostitute; **~ empresaria, ~ de negocios** businesswoman; **~ fatal** femme fatale; **~ de la limpieza** cleaning lady, cleaner; **~ piloto** (woman) pilot; **~ policía** policewoman; **~ sacerdote** woman priest; **ser muy ~** to be very feminine; **ser muy ~ de su casa** to be a good housewife; to be very houseproud.
(b) (*esposa*) wife; **mi ~** my wife; **~ golpeada, ~ maltratada** battered wife; **tomar ~** to take a wife, marry.
(c) **¡~!**: *en oración directa no se traduce*; **¡déjalo, ~!** leave it alone!

mujeraza NF shrew, bitch, horrid woman*.

mujercita NF little woman, little lady.

mujerengo ADJ (*CAm, Cono Sur*) **(a)** (*afeminado*) effeminate. **(b)** (*mujeriego*) fond of women.

mujerero ADJ (*LAm*) fond of women.

mujeriego **1** ADJ **(a)** fond of women, given to chasing the girls, wolfish. **(b)** **cabalgar a mujeriegas** to ride sidesaddle.
2 NM womanizer, wolf*.

mujeril ADJ womanly.

mujerío NM (*Esp*) **ir de ~** to go whoring; to go looking for a woman.

mujer-objeto NF, PL **mujeres-objeto** woman treated as an object, sex object.

mujerona NF big woman.

mujerzuela NF whore.

mújol NM grey mullet.

mula NF **(a)** (*Zool*) mule.
(b) (*Méx: trastos*) trash, junk, unsaleable goods.
(c) (*CAm: vergüenza*) shame.
(d) (*And: pipa*) pipe.
(e) (*And: idiota*) idiot.
(f) (*Méx: duro*) tough guy (*US**).
(g) (*Cono Sur**) (*mentira*) lie; (*engaño*) trick; **meter la ~** to tell lies; **meter la ~ a uno** to trick sb.

mulada NF drove of mules.

muladar NM dungheap, dunghill, midden.

mulato, -a ADJ, NM/F mulatto.

mulé: NM: **dar ~ a** to bump off:.

mulero **1** NM (*lit*) muleteer.
2 NM, **mulera** NF (*Cono Sur*: mentiroso*) liar.

muleta NF **(a)** (*para andar*) crutch. **(b)** (*Taur*) matador's stick with red cloth attached. **(c)** (*fig*) prop, support.

muletazo NM movement of the 'muleta' in bullfighting.

muletilla NF **(a)** (*bastón*) cross-handled cane; (*Téc: botón*) wooden toggle; large wooden button; (*Taur*) = **muleta (b)**. **(b)** (*fig*) (*palabra*) pet word, tag, cliché; (*de cómico etc*) catch-phrase.

muletón NM flanelette.

mullido **1** ADJ **(a)** *cama etc* soft, sprung; fluffy; *hierba etc* soft, springy.
(b) dejar a uno ~* to leave sb all in, wear sb out.
2 NM (*relleno*) stuffing, filling.

mullir [3a] VT **(a)** *almohada, lana etc* to make fluffy, fluff up; (*ablandar*) to soften; *cama* to shake up; *tierra* to hoe, loosen. **(b)** *plantas* to hoe round, loosen the earth round.

mullo NM (red) mullet.

mulo NM mule.

mulón ADJ (*And, Cono Sur*) (*tartamudo*) stammering; *niño* slow in learning to talk, backward.

multa NF fine; (*Dep etc*) penalty; **echar una ~ a, (im)poner una ~ a** to impose a fine (o penalty) on.

multar [1a] VT to fine; (*Dep etc*) to penalize; **~ a uno en 100 dólares** to fine sb 100 dollars.

multi... PREF multi...

multiacceso ADJ (*Inform*) multiaccess.

multicampeón, -ona NM/F (*perro*) champion.

multicanal ADJ (*TV*) multichannel.

multicapa ADJ INVAR multilayer(ed).

multicine NM multiscreen cinema, multiplex.

multicolor ADJ multicoloured, many-coloured; motley, variegated.

multiconfesional ADJ of (*o* for *etc*) several different faiths.

multicopiar [1b] VT to duplicate.

multicopista NF duplicator.

multicultural ADJ multicultural.

multiculturalidad NF multiculturalism.

multidimensional ADJ multidimensional.

multidireccional ADJ multidirectional.

multidisciplinar(io) ADJ: **estudio ~** cross-disciplinary study, study involving a variety of disciplines.

multifacético ADJ many-sided.

multifamiliar ADJ: **edificio ~** block of flats, block of tenements.

multifásico ADJ polyphase.

multiforme ADJ manifold, multifarious; multiform; having different forms.

multifuncional ADJ multifunctional.

multigrado ADJ *aceite etc* multigrade.

multilaminar NM (*t madera ~*) plywood.

multilateral ADJ, **multilátero** ADJ multilateral, many-sided.

multilingüe ADJ multilingual.

multimedia ADJ INVAR multimedia (*atr*).

multimillonario, -a NM/F multimillionaire.

multimotor **1** ADJ multi-engined.
2 NM multi-engined aircraft.

multinacional **1** ADJ multinational.
2 NF multinational (company).

multiorgánico ADJ: **donante ~** multiple organ donor.

multipartidismo NM multi-party system.

multipartidista ADJ multi-party (*atr*).

múltiple ADJ **(a)** (*Mat*) multiple; (*fig*) many-sided. **(b)** (*fig*) **~s** (*muchos*) many, numerous; (*variados*) manifold, multifarious; **tiene ~s actividades** he has multifarious activities, he has very numerous activities.

multiplexor NM multiplexor.

multiplicación NF multiplication.

multiplicado NM multiplicand.

multiplicador **1** ADJ: **efecto ~** multiplier effect.
2 NM (*Econ, Mat*) multiplier.

multiplicar [1g] **1** VT (*Mat y fig*) to multiply (*por* by); *posibilidades etc* to increase; (*Mec*) to gear up.
2 multiplicarse VR **(a)** (*Mat, Bio etc*) to multiply; to increase.
(b) (*fig*) to be everywhere at once; to attend to a lot of things all at once; **no puedo multiplicarme** I can't be in half-a-dozen places at once.

multiplicidad NF multiplicity.

múltiplo **1** ADJ multiple.
2 NM multiple; **mínimo común ~** lowest common multiple.

multiprocesador NM multiprocessor.

multiprocesamiento NM, **multiproceso** NM multiprocessing.

multipropiedad NF time-share.

multirracial ADJ multiracial.

multirregional ADJ multi-regional.

multirregulable ADJ adjustable (to a variety of positions).

multirreincidencia NF persistent offending.

multirreincidente NMF persistent offender.

multirriesgo *atr*: **póliza ~** fully comprehensive policy.

multisecular ADJ age-old, centuries-old, very ancient.

multitarea **1** ADJ INVAR multitasking.
2 NF multitask.

multitud NF multitude; (*de gente*) crowd; **la ~** (*pey*) the multitude, the masses; **~ de*** lots of, heaps of*; **tengo ~ de cosas que hacer** I have loads of things to do.

multitudinario ADJ massive, mass (*atr*); *reunión etc* big, attended by large numbers; *manifestación* mass *(atr)*; *recepción* tumultuous, exuberant.

multiuso ADJ INVAR for many uses, multipurpose.

multiusuario ADJ INVAR multiuser.

multiviaje ADJ INVAR: **billete ~** season ticket.

mun. ABR *de* **municipio** town.

mundanal ADJ *(liter)* worldly, of the world.

mundanalidad NF *(liter)* worldliness.

mundanería NF worldliness.

mundano [1] ADJ **(a)** *(del mundo)* worldly, of the world.
 (b) *(de alta sociedad)* society *(atr)*; fashionable; social; **son gente muy mundana** they're great society people; **una reunión mundana** a fashionable gathering, a gathering of society people.
 [2] NM, **mundana** NF society person, socialite.

mundial [1] ADJ world-wide, universal; *distribución, guerra, marca etc* world *(atr)*; **las comunicaciones ~es** world communications; **un invento de aplicación ~** an invention of world-wide application; **otra guerra ~** another world war.
 [2] NM world championship, *(esp)* **el M~** the World Cup *(soccer)*.

mundialización NF extension world-wide; internationalization.

mundialmente ADV throughout the world; universally; **~ famoso** world-famous; **hacer algo ~ popular** to make sth popular throughout the world.

mundillo NM **(a)** *(gen)* world, circle; **en el ~ teatral** in the theatre world, in theatrical circles. **(b)** *(Bot)* viburnum.

mundo NM world; *(fig)* world, people; society; *(Ecl)* world, secular life; **~ antiguo** ancient world; **~ feliz** brave new world; **Nuevo M~** New World; **Tercer M~** Third World; **Viejo M~** Old World; **el ~ hispánico** the Hispanic world; **el gran ~** high life, high society; **el ~ del espectáculo** show business; **este pícaro ~** this wicked world; **en el ~ de las ideas** in the world of ideas, in the realm of ideas; **medio ~** almost everybody, a huge number; **estaba medio ~** there were hordes of people; **el otro ~** the other world, the next world; **no es nada del otro ~** it's nothing extraordinary; **hacer algo del otro ~** to do sth quite extraordinary; **todo el ~** everybody; **en todo el ~** everywhere; throughout the world; **es lo que más desea en el ~** it's what she wants most in the world; **por esos ~s (de Dios)** there; all over, here there and everywhere; **el ~ es un pañuelo** it's a small world; **desde que el ~ es ~** since time began; **se le cae el ~ encima** he gets disheartened; **echar al ~** to bring into the world; **echarse al ~** to take to prostitution; **aunque se hunda el ~** come what may; **no por eso se hundirá el ~** it won't be the end of the world; **irse al otro ~** to pass away; **así va el ~** that's the way it is; **ponerse el ~ por montera** to care nothing for public opinion; **tener (mucho) ~** to be experienced, be sophisticated, know one's way around; **tener poco ~** to be inexperienced; **como Dios lo trajo al ~, tal como vino al ~** stark naked; **ver ~** to see life, see the world; **ha visto mucho ~** he's knocked around a lot.

mundología NF worldly-wisdom, experience of the world, savoir-faire.

mundonuevo NM peep show.

munición NF **(a)** *(t* **municiones)** *(balas etc)* ammunition; munitions; *(provisiones)* stores, supplies; **municiones de boca** provisions, rations. **(b) de ~** army *(atr)*, service *(atr)*; **botas de ~** army boots. **(c)** *(CAm)* uniform.

municionera NF *(Carib)* ammunition pouch.

municipal [1] ADJ municipal; *concejo etc* town *(atr)*; *piscina* public.
 [2] NM *(guardia)* (city) policeman.

municipalidad NF municipality.

municipio NM **(a)** *(distrito)* municipality; town, township. **(b)** *(ayuntamiento)* corporation; town council. **(c)** *(edificio)* town hall.

munificencia NF munificence.

munífico ADJ munificent.

muniqués [1] ADJ of Munich.
 [2] NM, **muniquesa** NF native (o inhabitant) of Munich; **los muniqueses** the people of Munich.

muñeca NF **(a)** *(Anat)* wrist. **(b)** *(de niño)* doll; *(de sastre)* dummy; *(‡: chica)* doll‡; **~ de trapo** rag doll. **(c)** *(trapos)* bunch of rags, cleaning (o polishing) pad. **(d)** *(Cono Sur*)* pull, influence.

muñeco NM **(a)** *(figura)* figure; *(juguete)* (boy) doll; *(espantapájaros)* guy, scarecrow; *(títere)* puppet, marionette; *(de sastre)* dummy; **~ de nieve** snowman.
 (b) *(fig: instrumento)* puppet, pawn.
 (c) *(*: niño)* pretty little boy, little angel; *(pey)* sissy*.
 (d) *(*: lío)* row, shindy*.
 (e) entrarle los ~s a uno *(And*)* to have butterflies in one's stomach.

muñeira NF *a popular Galician dance*.

muñequado* ADJ *(And)* jumpy, nervous.

muñequera[1] NF wristband.

muñequero, -a[2] NM/F puppeteer.

muñir [3h] VT **(a)** *(convocar)* to summon, convoke, call. **(b)** *(pey)* to rig,

fix, arrange in a fraudulent fashion.

muñón NM **(a)** *(Anat)* stump. **(b)** *(Mec)* trunnion; pivot, journal.

mural [1] ADJ mural, wall *(atr)*; **mapa ~** wall map.
 [2] NM mural.

muralista ADJ, NMF muralist.

muralla NF (city) wall, walls; rampart; *(LAm)* (any) wall; **la Gran M~ china** the Great Wall of China.

murar [1a] VT to wall.

Murcia NF Murcia.

murciano, -a ADJ, NM/F Murcian.

murciélago NM bat.

murga NF **(a)** *(banda)* street band. **(b)** *(*: lata)* bore, nuisance, bind*; **dar la ~** to be a pain*, be a pest.

murguista NM **(a)** *(músico)* street musician; *(hum*)* bad musician, poor player. **(b)** *(*: pesado)* bore.

múrido NM rodent.

murmullo NM **(a)** *(susurro)* murmur(ing); whisper(ing); mutter(ing). **(b)** *(de agua)* murmur, rippling; *(de hojas, viento)* rustle, rustling; *(ruido confuso)* hum(ming).

murmuración NF gossip; slanderous talk, backbiting; constant complaining.

murmurador [1] ADJ *(chismoso)* gossip; *(criticón)* backbiting; critical; complaining, grumbling.
 [2] NM, **murmuradora** NF *(chismoso)* gossip; *(criticón)* backbiter; critic; complainer, grumbler.

murmurar [1a] VI **(a)** *(persona)* *(susurrar)* to murmur, whisper; *(quejarse)* to mutter.
 (b) *(agua)* to murmur, ripple; *(hojas, viento etc)* to rustle; *(abejas, multitud etc)* to hum.
 (c) *(fig)* *(cotillear)* to gossip *(de* about); *(criticar)* to criticize *(de uno sb)*; *(quejarse)* to grumble *(de* about), mutter *(de* about); **siempre están murmurando del jefe** they're always grumbling about the boss, they're always criticizing the boss.

muro NM wall; **~ de Berlín** Berlin Wall; **~ de contención** containing wall; **M~ de las Lamentaciones** Wailing Wall.

murria NF *(Esp)* depression, blues; sulks; **tener ~** to feel blue, be down in the dumps*; to feel sulky.

murrio ADJ depressed, dejected; sulky, sullen.

murruco* ADJ *(CAm)* curly-haired.

mus[1] NM *a card game*.

mus[2] = **chus**; **sin decir ni ~** without saying a word.

musa NF muse; **las M~s** the Muses.

musaraña NF **(a)** *(Zool)* shrew; *(any)* small creature, bug, creepy-crawly*. **(b)** *(mota)* speck floating in the eye; **mirar a las ~s** to stare vacantly; **pensar en las ~s** to go woolgathering.

musculación NF muscle-building.

muscular ADJ muscular.

musculatura NF muscles, musculature; *(fig)* muscle; **doblar (o estirar) su ~** to flex one's muscles *(t fig)*.

músculo NM muscle.

musculoso ADJ muscular; tough, brawny.

museística NF museum studies.

museístico ADJ museum *(atr)*.

muselina NF muslin.

museo NM museum; gallery; **~ de arte, ~ de pintura** art gallery; **~ de cera** waxworks.

museografía NF museography.

musgaño NM shrew.

musgo NM moss.

musgoso ADJ mossy, moss-covered.

música NF **(a)** *(gen)* music; **~ ambiental** piped music; background music; **~ de cámara** chamber music; **~ celestial*** fine talk, empty promises, hot air*; **~ concreta** concrete music; **~ coreada** choral music; **~ enlatada*** canned music; **~ de fondo** background music; **~ ligera** light music; **~ mundana, ~ de las esferas, ~ de los planetas** music of the spheres; **~ sagrada** sacred music; **poner ~ a** to set to music; **irse con la ~ a otra parte** to take one's troubles elsewhere; to go away, go somewhere else; **me suena a ~ de caballitos** it sounds all too familiar; **¡con la ~ a otra parte!** off with you!, get out!
 (b) *(banda)* band.
 (c) *(*: tonterías)* **~s** drivel; **no estoy para ~s** I'm not in the mood to listen to such drivel.
 (d) *(Esp‡: cartera)* wallet.
 (e) *(‡: dinero)* bread‡, money.

musical ADJ, NM musical.

musicalidad NF musicality, musical quality.

musicalizar [1f] VT to set to music.

musicar [1g] VT to set to music.

músico [1] ADJ musical.
 [2] NMF **(a)** *(Mús)* musician, player; **~ callejero** street musician; **~ mayor** bandmaster. **(b)** *(*)* pickpocket.

musicología NF musicology.
musicólogo NM, **musicóloga** NF musicologist.
musiqueo NM monotonous sound.
musiquilla NF tune; piece of light music.
musitar [1a] VTI to mumble, mutter.
muslada: NF, **muslamen:** NM thighs.
muslera NF Tubigrip ®, thigh strap.
muslime ADJ, NMF Moslem.
muslímico ADJ Moslem.
muslo NM thigh.
mustango NM mustang.
mustela NF weasel.
mustiarse [1b] VR to wither, wilt.
mustio ADJ **(a)** (*Bot*) withered, faded. **(b)** (*poco tieso*) soft, slack. **(c)** (*triste*) depressed, gloomy. **(d)** (*Méx*) hypocritical.
musulmán, -ana ADJ, NM/F Moslem.
mutabilidad NF mutability; changeableness.
mutable ADJ mutable.
mutación NF **(a)** (*cambio*) (sudden) change. **(b)** (*Bio*) mutation. **(c)** (*Ling*) mutation. **(d)** (*Teat*) change of scene.
mutagene NM mutagen.
mutágeno ⟦1⟧ ADJ mutagenic.
⟦2⟧ NM mutagen.
mutante ADJ, NMF mutant.
mutar [1a] ⟦1⟧ VI (*Bio*) to mutate. **(b)** (*cambiar*) to mutate.
⟦2⟧ VT **(a)** (*Bio*) to mutate. **(b)** (*cambiar*) to transform, alter.
⟦3⟧ **mutarse** VR to mutate (*en* into).
mutil NM (*Hist*) Carlist soldier.
mutilación NF mutilation.
mutilado ⟦1⟧ ADJ crippled, disabled.

⟦2⟧ NM, **mutilada** NF cripple, disabled person; **~ de guerra** war cripple.
mutilar [1a] VT **(a)** (*gen*) to mutilate; (*lisiar*) to cripple, maim, disable. **(b)** (*fig*) *texto etc* to mutilate, hack about, spoil; *cuento* to garble; *objeto* to deface.
mutis NM INVAR (*Teat*) exit; ¡**~**! sh!; **hacer ~** (*Teat*) to exit, go off; (*fig*) to say nothing, keep quiet; **hacer ~ por el foro** (*fig*) to make oneself scarce.
mutismo NM dumbness; (*fig*) silence, uncommunicativeness.
mutua NF mutual (society).
mutual NF (*And, Cono Sur*) friendly society.
mutualidad NF **(a)** (*reciprocidad*) mutuality, mutual character. **(b)** (*ayuda*) mutual aid, reciprocal aid. **(c)** (*sociedad*) friendly society, mutual benefit society.
mutualista ⟦1⟧ ADJ mutual.
⟦2⟧ NMF *member or associate of a mutual (society)*.
mutuamente ADV mutually, reciprocally.
mutuo ADJ mutual, reciprocal; joint.
muy ⟦1⟧ ADV very; greatly, highly; (*demasiado*) too; **~ bueno** very good; **~ lentamente** very slowly; **~ buscado** very much sought-after, highly prized; **~ de noche** very late at night; **tener ~ en cuenta** to bear very much in mind; **venir ~ tarde** to come very late; **es ~ de sentir** it is much to be regretted; **eso es ~ español** that's very Spanish, that's typically Spanish; **eso es ~ de él** that's just like him; **es ~ hombre** he's a real man, he's pretty tough; **es ~ mujer** she's very feminine; as a woman she's terribly attractive; **el ~ bestia de Pedro** that great idiot Peter; ¡**el ~ bandido!** the rat!*
⟦2⟧ NF (‡) (*lengua*) tongue; (*boca*) trap‡, mouth; **achantar la ~** to shut one's trap‡; **irse de la ~** to spill the beans*; **largar por la ~** to speak, tell.

N

N (a) (*Geog*) ABR de **norte** ADJ Y NM north, N. **(b)** (*Aut*) ABR de **nacional** main road. **(c)** ABR de **noviembre** November, Nov.

> **20-N**
>
> *20-N is commonly used as shorthand to refer to the anniversary of General Franco's death on 20 November 1975. Every year supporters of the far right hold a commemorative rally in Madrid's Plaza de Oriente, the scene of many of Franco's speeches to the people.*

N, n ['ene] NF (*letra*) N, n.

n. (a) ABR de **nuestro** o **nuestra** our. **(b)** ABR de **nacido** born, b. **(c)** ABR de **número** number, No.

na*, ná* PRON *etc* = **nada**.

naba NF (*Bot*) swede.

nabab NM nabob.

nabina NF rapeseed.

nabiza NF (*Esp*) turnip greens.

nabo NM **(a)** (*Bot*) turnip; (*any*) root vegetable, thick root; **~ gallego, ~ sueco** swede.

(b) (*Anat*) root of the tail.

(c) (*Arquit*) newel, stair post.

(d) (*Náut*) mast.

(e) (ⁱⁱ) prickⁱⁱ.

Nabucodonosor NM Nebuchadnezzar.

nácar NM mother-of-pearl, nacre.

nacarado ADJ, **nacarino** ADJ mother-of-pearl (*atr*), pearly, nacreous.

nacatamal NM (*CAm, Méx*) *maíze, meat and rice wrapped in banana leaf.*

nacatete NM (*Méx*), **nacatón** NM, **nacatona** NF (*CAm, Méx*) unfledged chick.

nacedera NF (*CAm: t cerca ~*) hedge.

nacencia NF (*LAm*) = **nacimiento**.

nacer [2d] **1** VI **(a)** (*gen*) to be born; (*de huevo*) to hatch; **nací en Cuba** I was born in Cuba; **cuando nazca el niño** when the baby is born; **~ al amor** to awaken to love; **con esa exposición nació a la vida artística** that exhibition saw the beginning of his artistic career; **~ parado** (*And**) to be born with a silver spoon in one's mouth; **~ de pie** to be born lucky; **no nació para sufrir** she was not born to suffer; **nació para poeta** he was born to be a poet; **nadie nace enseñado** we all have to learn.

(b) (*Bot*) to sprout, bud; to come up; (*estrella etc*) to rise; (*río*) to rise; (*agua*) to spring up, appear, begin to flow; (*camino*) to begin, start (*de* from, *en* in); **le nacieron alas** it grew wings; **le nació mucho pelo** it sprouted a lot of hair.

(c) (*fig: idea etc*) to be born; to begin, originate, have its origin (*en* in); **nació una sospecha en su mente** a suspicion formed in her mind; **el error nace del hecho de que ...** the error springs (*o* stems) from the fact that ...; **entre ellos ha nacido una fuerte simpatía** a strong friendship has sprung up between them; **¿de dónde nace la idea?** where does the idea come from?

2 nacerse VR **(a)** (*Bot*) to bud, sprout.

(b) (*Cos*) to split.

Nacho NM *forma familiar de* Ignacio.

nacido **1** ADJ born; **~ a la libertad** born free; **~ para el amor** born to love; **~ de padres ricos** born of wealthy parents; **bien ~** of noble birth; well-bred; **mal ~** mean, base, wicked; ill-bred (*V t* malnacido); **recién ~** newborn.

2 NM **(a)** (*ser*) human being; **todos los ~s** everybody, all mankind; **ningún ~** nobody.

(b) (*Med*) tumour, growth; boil.

(c) (*Cos*) split.

naciente **1** ADJ (*que nace*) nascent; (*nuevo*) new, recent; (*creciente*) growing; *sol* rising; **el ~ interés por ...** the new-found interest in ..., the growing interest in ...

2 NM **(a)** (*este*) east.

(b) (*Cono Sur: t ~s*) spring, source.

▼ **nacimiento** NM **(a)** (*gen*) birth; (*Orn etc*) hatching; **~ sin violencia** natural childbirth; **ciego de ~** blind from birth; **un tonto de ~ a** born fool; **este defecto lo tiene de ~** he has had this defect since birth, he was born with this defect.

(b) (*fig: estirpe*) descent, family; **de ~ noble** of noble birth, of noble family.

(c) (*de agua, río*) source.

(d) (*fig*) birth; (*origen*) origin, beginning, start; **dar ~ a** to give rise to; **el partido tuvo su ~ en ...** the party had its origins in ...

(e) (*Arte, Ecl*) nativity (scene).

nación **1** NF nation; people; **Naciones Unidas** United Nations; **trato de ~ más favorecida** most favoured nation treatment; **ruritano de ~** Ruritanian by birth, of Ruritanian nationality.

2 NMF (*Cono Sur*) foreigner.

nacional **1** ADJ national; *industria, producto etc* home (*atr*), local; home-produced; indigenous; **páginas de ~** (*Prensa*) home news pages; (*anuncio*) **'vuelos ~es'** 'domestic flights'.

2 NMF national; **los ~es** (*España, 1936 etc*) the Franco forces.

nacionalcatolicismo NM Spanish Catholicism considered as an ally of Franco.

nacionalidad NF **(a)** nationality; **de ~ argentina** Argentine by birth, of Argentine nationality; **~ doble** dual nationality. **(b)** ((*Esp Pol*) autonomous region, regional government.

nacionalismo NM nationalism.

nacionalista **1** ADJ nationalist(ic).

2 NMF nationalist.

nacionalización NF **(a)** (*de inmigrante*) naturalization. **(b)** (*Econ*) nationalization.

nacionalizado **1** ADJ (*persona*) naturalized; (*industria*) nationalized.

2 NM, **nacionalizada** NF naturalized person.

nacionalizar [1f] **1** VT **(a)** *persona* to naturalize. **(b)** *industria* to nationalize.

2 nacionalizarse VR to become naturalized; to be nationalized.

nacionalsocialismo NM national socialism.

naco* **1** ADJ (*Méx*) (*bobo*) stupid; (*cobarde*) yellow.

2 NM **(a)** (*CAm: cobarde*) coward; (*endeble*) weakling, milksop.

(b) (*And, Cono Sur: tabaco*) plug of tobacco.

(c) (*And*) *maize kernels cooked with salt*; mashed potatoes.

(d) (*Cono Sur: susto*) fright, scare.

(e) **~s** (*Cono Sur*) roll of banknotes.

nada **1** PRON nothing; **no dijo ~** she said nothing, she didn't say anything; **¡~, ~!** not a bit of it!; **~ de ~** absolutely nothing, nothing at all; **~ de eso** nothing of the kind, far from it; **¡~ de eso!** not a bit of it!; **¡~ de excusas!** no excuses!; **¡~ de marcharse!** forget about leaving!; **¡de eso ~, monada!*** no way!*; **esto y ~, es lo mismo** it all boils down to nothing; **no tiene ~ de particular** there's nothing special about it; **no le conozco de ~** I don't know him from Adam; **~ entre dos platos** a lot of fuss, much ado about nothing; *V más*; **a cada (de) ~** (*LAm*) all the time, at every step; **antes de ~** very soon, right away; **antes de ~ tengo que ...** before I do anything else I must ...; **a cada ~*** (*LAm*) constantly; **casi ~** next to nothing; **¡casi ~!** a mere bagatelle!, just peanuts!*; **como si ~** as if it didn't matter, as if it were only a small thing; **¡de ~!** not at all!, don't mention it!; **estuvo en ~ que lo perdiesen** they very nearly lost it; **quedar(se) en ~** to come to nothing; **no reparar en ~** to stop at nothing; **en ~ de tiempo** in no time at all; **hace ~** just a moment ago; **no quiere comer ~** he won't eat or anything; **¡ni curas ni ~!*** blow the priests!*; I don't want to hear about the priests!; **no los mencionó para ~** he never mentioned them at all; **no servir para ~** to be no use at all, be utterly useless; **¡por ~!** (*Cono Sur*) not at all!, don't mention it! **llorar por ~** to cry for no reason at all; **por ~ del**

mundo not for anything in the world; **por menos de ~** for two pins; **no lo hago por ~ ni por nadie** I won't do it and that's that; **no por ~ le llaman 'tufos'** he's not called 'stinker' for nothing; **no por ~ decidimos comprar** we had good reason to buy; **¡pues ~!** not to worry!; **no ha sido ~** it's nothing; **y ~** and that was that, so there it was.

[2] ADV not at all, by no means; **no es ~ fácil** it's not at all easy, it's far from easy.

[3] NF nothingness; **la ~** the void; **el avión parecía salir de la ~** the aircraft seemed to come from nowhere.

nadaderas NFPL water wings.

nadador(a) NM/F swimmer.

nadar [1a] VI (a) (gen) to swim; (corcho etc) to float; (And) to take a bath; **querer ~ y guardar la ropa** to want to have it both ways, want to have one's cake and eat it.
(b) (Cos) **estos pantalones le quedan nadando** he's lost inside these trousers, these trousers are much too big for him.
(c) **~ en** (fig) dinero etc to wallow in, be rolling in.

nadería NF small thing, mere trifle.

nadie PRON (a) (gen) nobody, no-one; **~ lo tiene, no lo tiene ~** nobody has it; **no he visto a ~** I haven't seen anybody; **apenas ~** hardly anybody; **lo hace como ~** she does it jolly well.
(b) **no es ~** he's nobody (that matters); **es un don ~** he's a nobody.

nadir NM nadir.

nadita (LAm) = **nada**.

nado [1] ADV: **cruzar** (o **pasar**) **a ~** to swim, swim across.
[2] NM (*) swimming stroke, swimming style.

nafta NF naphtha; (Cono Sur) petrol, gasoline (US).

naftaleno NM, **naftalina** NF naphthalene.

nagual NM (a) (CAm, Méx: brujo) sorcerer, wizard. (b) (CAm: compañero) inseparable companion. (c) (Méx: mentira) lie.

nagualear: [1a] VI (Méx) (a) (mentir) to lie. (b) (robar) to nick things:. (c) (jaranear) to paint the town red.

naguas NFPL petticoat.

nagüeta NF (CAm) overskirt.

nahual NM (CAm, Méx) (Mit) spirit, phantom; (doble) double; (*: ladrón) cat burglar.

náhuatl NM (Ling) Nahuatl.

┌─ **NÁHUATL** ─┐

(i) *Náhuatl is the indigenous Mexican language that was once spoken by the Aztecs and which has given us such words as "tomato", "avocado" "chocolate" and "chilli". The first book to be printed on the American continent was a catechism in náhuatl, edited by a Franciscan monk in 1539. Today náhuatl is spoken in the central plateau of Mexico by a million bilingual and monolingual speakers.*

naide PRON (hum) = **nadie**.

naif ADJ, PL **naifs** o **naif** (Arte) naive, primitivist.

nailon NM nylon.

naipe NM playing card; **~ de figura** court card, picture; **~s** cards.

naipeador ADJ (Cono Sur) fond of cards.

naipear [1a] VI (Cono Sur) to play cards.

naja: **de ~(s)** at full speed, like the clappers*; **darse de ~, salir de ~** to get out, beat it*.

najarse: [1a] VR to beat it*.

najencia: INTERJ scram!:

nal. ABR de **nacional** national, nat.

nalga NF buttock; **~s** buttocks, backside, rump; **dar de ~s** to fall on one's bottom.

nalgada NF (a) (Culin) ham. (b) (azote) smack on the bottom; **~s** spanking.

nalguiento ADJ (And), **nalgón** ADJ (And), **nalgudo** ADJ big-bottomed, broad in the beam*.

Namibia NF Namibia.

namibio, -a ADJ, NM/F Namibian.

nana¹ NF (a) (abuela) grandma*, granny*; V **año**. (b) (Mús) lullaby, cradlesong. (c) (pelele) baby's sleeping bag. (d) (CAm, Méx) (nodriza) wet-nurse; (niñera) nursemaid. (e) (CAm: mamá) mum*, mummy*.

nana²: NF (Cono Sur: dolor) pain.

nanai*, nanay* INTERJ no way!*, not on your life!; **me hizo ver que ~ de la China** he made me see there was nothing doing, he showed me it just wasn't on*.

Nancy ® NF, PL **Nancys** ≃ Cindy doll ®.

nano, -a³: NM/F kid.

nao NF (Hist) ship.

napa NF imitation leather.

napalm NM napalm.

napia: NF (t **~s** PL) snout*, nose.

napo: NM 1000-peseta note.

Napoleón NM Napoleon.

napoleón NM (Cono Sur) pliers, wire-cutters.

napoleónico ADJ Napoleonic.

Nápoles NM Naples.

napolitano, -a ADJ, NM/F Neapolitan.

narajái: NM (Esp) priest.

naranja [1] NF (a) (gen) orange; **~ cajel, ~ zajarí** Seville orange; **~ sanguina** blood orange.
(b) (*) **¡~s!, ¡~s chinas!, ¡~s de la China!** nonsense!, rubbish!
(c) (Esp: pareja) **la media ~** one's better half; **esperar la media ~** to wait for Mr Right; **encontrar su media ~** to find one's life partner; **¡sí, naranjita!** yes darling!
(d) (Carib) bitter orange.
[2] ADJ INVAR orange.

naranjada NF orangeade.

naranjado ADJ orange, orange-coloured.

naranjal NM orange grove.

naranjero [1] ADJ orange-growing.
[2] NM, **naranjera** NF (agricultor) orange grower; (vendedor) orange seller.
[3] NM (árbol) orange tree.

naranjo NM orange tree.

Narbona NF Narbonne.

narcisismo NM narcissism.

narcisista ADJ narcissistic.

Narciso NM Narcissus.

narciso NM (a) (Bot) narcissus; **~ atrompetado, ~ trompón** daffodil.
(b) (fig) dandy, fop.

narco* NM = **narcotraficante**; = **narcotráfico**.

narco... PREF narco...; drug(s) ... (atr).

narcocorrupción NF drugs-related corruption.

narcodependencia NF drug dependency, drug dependence.

narcodólar NM narco-dollar, drug dollar.

narcosis NF narcosis.

narcoterrorismo NM drug-related terrorism.

narcótico [1] ADJ narcotic.
[2] NM narcotic; (somnífero) sleeping pill; **~s** (en sentido lato) drugs, dope.

narcotismo NM narcosis, narcotism.

narcotizante ADJ, NM narcotic.

narcotizar [1f] VT to narcotize; (en sentido lato) to drug, dope.

narcotraficante NMF drug dealer.

narcotráfico NM drugs traffic, traffic in drugs.

nardo NM nard; spikenard.

narguile NM hookah.

naricear* [1a] VT (And) to smell (out); (fig) to poke one's nose into.

narigada NF (LAm) snuff.

narigón [1] ADJ big-nosed.
[2] NM (Carib, Méx) nose ring.

narigudo ADJ big-nosed.

narigueta ADJ (Cono Sur) big-nosed.

nariz NF (a) (Anat) nose; nostril.
(b) (Anat) **narices** PL nostrils; (*) nose; **¡narices!*** rubbish!, nonsense!; **un rapapolvo de narices*** a real good telling-off*; **era guapa de narices*** she was pretty and then some*; **me encuentro de narices*** I'm on top of the world; **he dormido de narices*** I slept jolly well*; **cerrar la puerta en las narices de uno, dar con la puerta en las narices de uno** to shut the door in sb's face; **dar de narices** to fall flat on one's face; **dar de narices contra la puerta** to bang one's face on the door; **en mis propias narices** under my very nose; **estar hasta las narices*** to be completely fed up (de with)*; **hablar por las narices** to talk through one's nose, speak with a nasal twang; **lo hará por narices*** she'll do it because she wants to; **para el lunes por narices*** by Monday without fail; **se le hincharon las narices** he got very cross; **ese tío me hincha las narices*** that chap gets on my nerves; **meter las narices en algo** to poke one's nose into sth; **eso me lo paso por las narices*** I don't care tuppence about that*; **hazlo o te rompo las narices*** do it or I'll smash your face in*; **¡tiene narices la cosa!*** well I'm damned!; **tocarse las narices*** to slack, be idle; to stand idly by; to let one's attention wander.
(c) (olfato) sense of smell.
(d) (de vino) bouquet, nose.

narizota(s)* [1] NF(PL) big nose.
[2] NM (persona) big nose; **¡~s!*** (Esp) (canalla) you villain!; (idiota) you idiot!

narizudo ADJ (LAm) big-nosed.

narpias: NFPL = **napia**.

narración NF narration, account.

narrador(a) NM/F narrator.

narrar [1a] VT to tell, narrate, recount.

narrativa NF (a) (narración) narrative, story. (b) (arte) narrative skill, skill in storytelling. (c) (género) fiction.

narrativo ADJ narrative.

narval NM narwhal.

nasa NF (*de pan*) bread bin, flour bin; (*cesta*) basket, creel; (*trampa*) fish trap.

nasal ADJ, NF nasal.

nasalidad NF nasality.

nasalización NF nasalization.

nasalizar [1f] VT to nasalize.

nasalmente ADV nasally.

naso‡ NM (*Cono Sur*) nose, conk‡.

N.ª S.ʳª ABR de **Nuestra Señora** Our Lady, the Virgin.

nasti‡ ① INTERJ no way!*

　② ADV: **de eso ~, (monasti)**! no way!*, get away!*

nata NF (a) (*Esp*) (*gen*) cream; (*en leche hervida etc*) skin; **~ batida** whipped cream; **~ líquida** cream. (b) (*fig*) cream, choicest part, best part; *V flor.*

natación NF (a) (*gen*) swimming.

　(b) (*estilo*) style (of swimming), stroke; **~ a braza, ~ de pecho** breast-stroke; **~ de costado, ~ en cuchillo** sidestroke; **~ de espalda** backstroke; **~ sincronizada** synchronized swimming; **~ submarina** underwater swimming; skin diving.

natal ADJ natal; *suelo etc* native; *pueblo etc* home (*atr*).

natalicio ① ADJ birthday (*atr*).

　② NM birthday.

natalidad NF birth rate.

natalista ADJ *política* which supports a rising birth rate.

natatorio ① ADJ swimming; *vejiga* swim (*atr*).

　② NM (*Argentina*) swimming pool.

natillas NFPL (*Esp*) custard; **~ de huevo** egg custard.

natividad NF nativity.

nativo ① ADJ (a) (*gen*) native; *país etc* native, home (*atr*); **lengua nativa** native language, mother tongue.

　(b) (*natural*) natural, innate.

　(c) (*Min*) native.

　② NM, **nativa** NF native.

nato ADJ (a) (*gen*) born; **un actor ~** a born actor; **un criminal ~** a hardened criminal, an incorrigible criminal; **es un pintor ~** he's a natural painter.

　(b) (*por derecho*) ex officio; **el secretario es miembro ~ de ...** the secretary is ex officio a member of ...

natura NF (*Anat*) genitals.

naturaca‡ INTERJ naturally!, natch‡.

natural ① ADJ (a) (*gen*) natural; **es ~ que ...** it is natural that ...

　(b) *fruta* fresh, raw; *agua* plain; *flor* real.

　(c) (*Mús*) natural.

　② NMF native, inhabitant; **fue ~ de Sigüenza** he was a native of Sigüenza; **trató sin miramientos a los ~es** he treated the inhabitants unceremoniously; **¿de dónde es Vd ~?** where are you from?, where were you born?

　③ NM (a) (*temperamento*) nature, disposition, temperament; **buen ~** good nature.

　(b) **fruta al ~** fruit in its own juice; **se sirve al ~** it is served at room temperature; **una descripción al ~** a true-to-life description, a realistic description; **vivir al ~** to live according to nature; **está muy guapa al ~** she is very pretty just as she is (without make-up *etc*); **pintar del ~** to paint from life, paint from nature; **clase de dibujo del ~** life-class.

　(c) (*Taur*) natural, *a kind of pass with the cape.*

naturaleza NF (a) (*gen*) nature; **~ humana** human nature.

　(b) **~ muerta** (*Arte*) still life.

　(c) (*Pol*) nationality; **el joven es suizo de ~** the young man is Swiss by nationality.

　(d) (*Pol*) citizenship (*granted to a foreigner*); **carta de ~** naturalization papers.

　(e) **romper la ~** to reach puberty, start to menstruate.

naturalidad NF naturalness; **con la mayor ~ (del mundo)** as if nothing had happened; as if it were the most natural thing in the world; **lo dijo con la mayor ~** he said it in a perfectly ordinary tone; **allí le pegan un tiro con la mayor ~** they'll shoot you there and think nothing of it.

naturalismo NM (a) (*Arte etc*) naturalism; realism. (b) (*nudismo*) naturism.

naturalista ① ADJ naturalistic; realistic.

　② NMF (a) (*Arte etc*) naturalist. (b) (*nudista*) naturist.

naturalización NF naturalization.

naturalizar [1f] ① VT to naturalize.

　② **naturalizarse** VR to become naturalized.

naturalmente ADV (a) (*de modo natural*) naturally; in a natural way.

　(b) **¡~!** naturally!, of course!; you bet!

naturismo NM naturism; naturopathy.

naturista NMF naturist, naturopath.

naturópata NMF naturopath.

naturopatía NF naturopathy.

naufragar [1h] VI (a) (*barco*) to be wrecked, sink; (*persona*) to be shipwrecked. (b) (*fig*) to fail, miscarry, suffer a disaster.

naufragio NM (a) (*lit*) shipwreck. (b) (*fig*) failure, disaster, ruin.

náufrago ① ADJ shipwrecked.

　② NM, **náufraga** NF shipwrecked sailor, shipwrecked person; castaway.

náusea NF nausea, sick feeling; (*fig*) disgust, repulsion; **dar ~s a** to nauseate, sicken, disgust; **tener ~s** to feel nauseated, feel sick; (*fig*) to be nauseated, be sickened.

nauseabundo ADJ nauseating, sickening.

náutica NF navigation, seamanship.

náutico ADJ nautical.

nautilo NM nautilus.

navaja NF (a) (*cuchillo*) clasp knife, jack-knife; **~ (de afeitar)** razor; **~ automática, ~ de muelle, ~ de resorte** flick knife; **~ barbera** cut-throat razor; **~ multiuso(s)** Swiss army knife. (b) (*Zool*) (*colmillo*) tusk; (*molusco*) razor shell; (*Ent*) sting. (c) (*fig*) sharp tongue, evil tongue.

navajada NF, **navajazo** NM slash, gash, razor wound.

navajeo NM knifing, stabbing; (*fig*) infighting; back-stabbing, stabbing in the back.

navajero NM criminal who carries a knife.

naval ADJ naval; ship (*atr*), sea (*atr*).

Navarra NF Navarre.

navarrica* ADJ Y NMF = **navarro.**

navarro, -a ① ADJ, NM/F Navarrese.

　② NM (*Ling*) Navarrese.

nave NF (a) (*Náut*) ship, vessel; **quemar las ~s** to burn one's boats; **~ insignia** flagship; **la N~ de San Pedro** (*Ecl*) the Roman Catholic Church.

　(b) **~ espacial** spaceship, spacecraft.

　(c) (*Arqui*) (*de iglesia*) nave; (*de fábrica etc*) bay; **~ lateral** aisle.

　(d) (*Téc*) large building, large shed; factory, mill, plant; **~ industrial** factory premises; **~ de laminación** rolling mill.

　(e) (*Méx**: *coche*) car.

navegabilidad NF navigability; seaworthiness.

navegable ADJ *río etc* navigable; *barco* seaworthy.

navegación NF (a) (*gen: arte*) navigation; **~ a vela** sailing.

　(b) (*viaje*) sea voyage; **~ costanera** coasting, coastal traffic; **~ fluvial** river sailing, river navigation.

　(c) (*barcos*) ships, shipping; **cerrado a la ~** closed to shipping.

navegador NM, **navegante** NM navigator; **~ a vela** yachtsman.

navegar [1h] ① VT *barco* to sail; to navigate; *avión* to fly; **~ los mares** to sail the seas.

　② VI (a) (*Náut*) to sail; **~ a 15 nudos** to sail at 15 knots, go at 15 knots; **~ a (la) vela** to sail, go sailing. (b) (*Inform*) **~ por Internet** to surf the Net.

▼ **Navidad** NF Christmas; (**día de) ~** Christmas Day; **~es** Christmas time; **por ~es** at Christmas (time); **¡feliz ~!** happy Christmas!

navideño ADJ Christmas (*atr*).

naviera NF shipping company.

naviero ① ADJ shipping (*atr*).

　② NM shipowner.

navío NM ship; **~ de alto bordo, ~ de línea** (*Hist*) ship of the line.

náyade NF naiad.

naylón NM nylon.

nazarenas NFPL (*And, Cono Sur*) large *gaucho* spurs.

nazareno, -a ① ADJ Nazarene.

　② NM/F (a) (*Hist*) Nazarene. (b) (*Rel*) penitent in a Holy Week procession; *see also* SEMANA SANTA .

　③ NM (*) (a) (*fraude*) con trick*. (b) (*persona*) con man*.

Nazaret NM Nazareth.

nazi ADJ, NMF Nazi.

nazismo NM Nazism.

nazista ADJ Nazi.

NB ABR de **nota bene** NB.

N. de la R. ABR de **nota de la redacción** editor's note.

N. de la T, N. del T ABR de **Nota de la Traductora, Nota del Traductor** translator's note.

NE ABR de **nor(d)este** north-east, NE.

neblina NF mist; mistiness; (*fig*) fog.

neblinoso ADJ misty.

nebulizador NM atomizer, nebulizer.

nebulosa NF nebula.

nebulosidad NF (a) (*lit*) nebulosity; cloudiness; mistiness. (b) (*fig*) vagueness; obscurity.

nebuloso ADJ (a) (*Astron*) nebular, nebulous; *cielo* cloudy; *aire* misty, foggy; (*tétrico*) dark, gloomy. (b) (*fig*) nebulous, vague; obscure.

necedad NF (a) (*cualidad*) foolishness, silliness. (b) (*una ~*) silly thing; **~es** nonsense.

necesariamente ADV necessarily.

▼ **necesario** ADJ necessary; **es ~ que lo hagas** it is necessary that you should do it, it is necessary for you to do it; **todo es ~** it all helps, every little helps; **si es ~, de ser ~** if need(s) be.

neceser NM toilet case, dressing case; holdall; **~ de belleza** vanity case; **~ de costura** workbox; **~ de fin de semana** weekend bag, weekend case.

necesidad NF **(a)** (*gen*) necessity; need (*de* for); **~ imperiosa, ~ primordial** absolute necessity, pressing need; **de ~, por ~** of necessity; **esto es de primera ~** this is absolutely essential; **no hay ~ de + infin** there is no need to + infin; **satisfacer las ~es de uno** to satisfy sb's needs.

(b) (*apuro*) necessity; tight spot, awkward situation; **en caso de ~** in case of need; **encontrarse en una ~** to be in a difficult situation.

(c) (*miseria*) need, necessity, want; (*pobreza*) poverty; **están en la mayor ~** they are in great need.

(d) **~es** hardships; **pasar ~es** to suffer hardships.

(e) (*euf*) business; **hacer sus ~es** to do one's business, relieve o.s.; **sentir una gran ~** to be dying to relieve o.s.

necesitado ① ADJ **(a)** **~ de** in need of; **estamos ~s de mano de obra** we need workers, we are in need of labour. **(b)** (*pobre*) needy.
② NMPL: **los ~s** the needy, those in need.

▼**necesitar** [1a] ① VT to need, want; to necessitate, require; **necesitamos 2 más** we need 2 more; **necesita un poco de cuidado** it needs (*o* requires, takes) a little care; **~ + infin** to need to + infin, must + infin; **no necesitas hacerlo** you don't need to do it, you don't have to do it.
② VI: **~ de** to need.
▼③ **necesitarse** VR to be needed, be wanted; '**necesítase coche**' (*anuncio*) 'car wanted'.

neciamente ADV foolishly, stupidly.

necio ① ADJ **(a)** (*tonto*) silly, stupid.
(b) (*And etc*: *displicente*) peevish.
(c) (*And, Carib, Cono Sur*: *quisquilloso*) touchy, hypersensitive.
(d) (*CAm*) enfermedad stubborn, long-lasting.
(e) (*Méx*: *testarudo*) stubborn, pig-headed.
② NM, **necia** NF fool.

nécora NF small crab.

necrófago NM ghoul.

necrofilia NF necrophilia.

necrófilo, -a ADJ, NM/F necrophiliac.

necrología NF, **necrológica** NF obituary (notice), necrology.

necrológico ADJ necrological, obituary (*atr*).

necromancia NF, **necromancía** NF necromancy.

necrópolis NF INVAR necropolis.

necropsia NF autopsy.

necrosis NF INVAR necrosis.

néctar NM nectar (*t fig*); (*Culin*) fruit essence.

nectarina NF nectarine.

neerlandés ① ADJ Dutch, Netherlands (*atr*).
② NM, **neerlandesa** NF Dutchman, Dutchwoman, Netherlander.
③ NM (*Ling*) Dutch.

nefando ADJ unspeakable, abominable.

nefario ADJ nefarious.

nefasto ADJ influencia pernicious; harmful; viaje unlucky, ill-fated; (*LAm*: *atroz*) dreadful, terrible.

nefato* ADJ (*Carib*) stupid, dim*.

nefrítico ADJ nephritic.

nefritis NF nephritis.

negación NF **(a)** (*gen*) negation; (*negativa*) refusal, denial. **(b)** (*Ling*) negation; negative.

negado ① ADJ **(a)** (*tonto*) dull, stupid. **(b)** **~ para** inept at, unfitted for.
② NM, **negada** NF useless person.

▼**negar** [1h y 1j] ① VT **(a)** hecho, verdad etc to deny; acusación to deny, reject, refute; **~ que algo sea así** to deny that sth is so.
(b) permiso etc to deny, refuse (*a* to); to withhold (*a* from); **~ la mano a uno** to refuse to shake hands with sb; **~ el saludo a uno** to cut sb; **le negaron el paso por la frontera** they refused to let him cross the frontier; **pasé por la casa pero me la negaron** I called at the house but they refused to let me see her.
(c) relación, responsabilidad etc to disclaim, disown.
② VI: **~ con la cabeza** to shake one's head.
▼③ **negarse** VR **(a)** **~ a + infin** to refuse to + infin.
(b) **~ a una visita** to refuse to see a visitor, not be at home to a caller.

negativa NF negative; denial, refusal; **~ rotunda** flat refusal; **la ~ a comer es peligrosa** the refusal to eat is dangerous.

negativamente ADV negatively; **contestar ~** to answer in the negative; **valorar algo ~** to take a hostile (*o* critical) view of sth.

negatividad NF, **negativismo** NM negative attitude.

negativizar [1f] VT to neutralize.

negativo ① ADJ **(a)** (*gen*) negative; **voto ~** vote against, contrary vote, no vote. **(b)** (*Mat*) minus. **(c)** (*Fot*) negative.

② NM (*Fot*) negative.

negligencia NF negligence; neglect, slackness, carelessness; nonchalance.

negligente ADJ (*gen*) negligent; neglectful, slack, careless; postura etc careless, nonchalant.

negligentemente ADV negligently; slackly, carelessly; nonchalantly.

negociabilidad NF negotiability.

negociable ADJ negotiable.

negociación NF negotiation; deal, transaction; (*de cheque*) clearance; **~ colectiva (de salarios)** collective bargaining; **entrar en negociaciones con** to enter into negotiations with.

negociadamente ADV: **resolver un problema ~** to settle a problem by negotiation.

negociado NM **(a)** (*sección*) department, section. **(b)** (*Cono Sur*) shop, store. **(c)** (*And, Cono Sur*: *turbio*) illegal transaction, shady deal.

negociador ① ADJ negotiating; **comisión ~a** negotiating committee.
② NM, **negociadora** NF negotiator.

negociante NMF (*t* **negocianta** NF) businessman, businesswoman, merchant, dealer.

negociar [1b] ① VT to negotiate.
② VI **(a)** (*Pol etc*) to negotiate. **(b)** **~ en** (*Com*) to deal in, trade in.

negocio NM **(a)** (*asunto*) affair; **mal ~** bad business; **¡mal ~!** it looks bad!; **eso es ~ tuyo** that's your affair.
(b) (*Com, Fin: empresa*) business; **el ~ del libro** the book trade, the book business; **el ~ del espectáculo** show business; **montar un ~ de frutas** to start a fruit business; **traspasar un ~** to transfer a business, sell a business.
(c) (*Com, Fin: trato*) deal, transaction, piece of business; (*iró*) bargain; **buen ~** profitable deal, (good) bargain; **~ sucio, ~ turbio** shady deal; **el ~ es el ~** business is business; **hacer un buen ~** to pull off a profitable deal; **¡hiciste un buen ~!** (*iró*) that was a fine deal you did!; **hacer su propio ~** to look after one's own interests.
(d) (*Com, Fin: gen*) **~s** business; trade; **hombre de ~s** businessman, **el mundo de los ~s** the business world; **a malos ~s sombrero de copa** one must accept losses with dignity, one must make the best of a bad job; **estar de ~s** to be (away) on business; **retirarse de los ~s** to retire from business.
(e) (*And, Cono Sur*) (*firma*) firm, company; (*casa*) place of business.
(f) (*And, Carib**) **el ~** the fact, the truth; **pero el ~ es que ...** but the fact is that ...
(g) (*And*) tale, piece of gossip.

negocioso ADJ industrious; businesslike.

negra¹ NF **(a)** (*persona*) Negress*, black woman.
(b) (*Mús*) crotchet.
(c) (*Ajedrez*) black piece.
(d) (*CAm*: *fig*) black mark.
(e) (*mala suerte*) bad luck; **tener la ~** to be out of luck, have a run of bad luck; **le tocó la ~** he had bad luck; **ése me trae la ~** he brings me bad luck; **he mucks things up for me.

negrada NF (*LAm*) **(a)** (*grupo*) group of Negroes; Negroes (*collectively*).
(b) (*dicho etc*) remark (*o* act *etc*) typical of a Negro; (*fraude*) cheat, fraud.

negrear [1a] VI **(a)** (*volverse negro*) to go black, turn black. **(b)** (*tirar a negro*) to be blackish; (*mostrarse negro*) to show black, look black.

negrería NF (*LAm*), **negrerío** NM (*LAm*) = **negrada** (a).

negrero NM (*lit*) slave trader; (*fig*) slave driver.

negrilla NF **(a)** (*Tip*) = **negrita** (a). **(b)** (*Bot*) elm.

negrita NF **(a)** (*Tip*) bold face; **en ~** in bold type, in heavy type. **(b)** (*CAm*: *fig*) black mark.

negrito NM (*Carib*) black coffee.

negritud NF negritude.

negro ① ADJ **(a)** (*gen*) black; (*oscuro*) dark; persona black, Negro†; (*moreno*) dark, swarthy; **~ azabache** pitch-black; **~ como boca de lobo, ~ como un pozo** as black as pitch, pitch-dark; **más ~ que el azabache** (*etc*) as black as ink, coal-black.
(b) (*fig*) estado, humor etc sad; black, gloomy; suerte awful*, atrocious; **pasarlas negras** to have a tough time of it; **la cosa se pone negra** it's not going well, it looks bad; **ve muy ~ el porvenir** he's very gloomy about the future; **lo ve todo ~** he's terribly pessimistic about everything; **vérselas negras** to find o.s. in trouble; **verse ~ para + infin** to have one's work cut out to + infin; **nos veíamos ~s para salir del apuro** we had a tough time getting out of it.
(c) (*: *enfadado*) cross, peeved*; **estoy ~ con esto** I'm getting desperate about it; **poner ~ a uno** to make sb cross, upset sb; **ponerse ~** to get cross, cut up rough.
(d) (*ilegal*) black; **economía negra** black economy; **dinero ~** hot money, money not declared for tax.
(e) (*Pol*) fascist; **terrorismo ~** fascist terrorism.
② NM **(a)** (*color*) black; **en ~** (*Fot*) in black and white; **~ de humo** lampblack.
(b) (*persona*) Negro†, black, coloured person†; **¡no somos ~s!** we won't stand for it!, you can't do that to us!; **sacar lo que el ~ del**

► LENGUA Y USO: **necesitar: 3 → 37.1** **negar: 1a → 53.6 3a → 35.5, 39.3**

sermón to understand nothing of what has been said.
  (**c**) (*: *escritor*) ghost writer.
  (**d**) (*Carib*) black coffee.
  3 NM, **negra²** NF (*LAm: en oración directa*) dear, honey (*US*).
negroide ADJ negroid.
negrura NF blackness.
negruzco ADJ blackish.
nel: EXCL (*Méx*) yep*.
neli: ADV = **nada**.
nema NF (*Méx Admin*) seal.
neme NM (*And*) asphalt.
nemotécnica NF *etc* = **mnemoténica** *etc*.
nene, **nena** NF baby, small child; ¡sí, **nena!** (*a mujer*) yes dear!, yes darling!
nenúfar NM water lily.
neo NM neon.
neo... PREF neo...
neoaristotelismo NM neo-Aristotelianism.
neocapitalista ADJ, NMF neo-capitalist.
neocelandés ADJ New Zealand (*atr*), of (o from) New Zealand.
  2 NM, **neocelandesa** NF New Zealander.
neoclasicismo NM neoclassicism.
neoclásico ADJ neoclassical.
neocolonialismo NM neocolonialism.
neofascismo NM neofascism.
neofascista ADJ, NMF neofascist.
neófito, -a NM/F neophyte.
neogótico ADJ neogothic.
neoimpresionismo NM neo-impressionism.
neolatino ADJ: **lenguas neolatinas** Romance languages.
neolengua NF newspeak.
neolítico ADJ neolithic.
neologismo NM neologism.
neón NM neon; neon light.
neonatal ADJ *asistencia etc* postnatal, neonatal.
neonato, -a NM/F newborn child.
neonatólogo, -a NM/F neonatologist.
neonazi ADJ, NMF neonazi.
neonazista ADJ neonazi.
neoplatónico ADJ neoplatonic.
neoplatonismo NM neoplatonism.
neoplatonista NMF neoplatonist.
neoyorquino 1 ADJ New York (*atr*), of New York.
  2 NM, **neoyorquina** NF New Yorker.
neozelandés 1 ADJ New Zealand (*atr*), of (o from) New Zealand.
  2 NM, **neozelandesa** NF New Zealander.
Nepal NM Nepal.
nepalés, -esa ADJ, NM/F, **nepalí** ADJ, NMF Nepalese.
nepotismo NM nepotism.
Neptuno NM Neptune.
nereida NF nereid.
Nerón NM Nero.
nervadura NF (*Arquit*) ribs; (*Bot, Ent*) nervure, vein.
nervio NM (**a**) (*Anat: gen*) nerve; **crispar los ~s a uno, poner los ~s de punta a uno** to get on sb's nerves; to jar on sb, grate on sb; **estar de los ~s** to live on one's nerves; **perder los ~s** to lose one's temper; **poner a uno de los ~s** to get on one's nerves; **tener los ~s de punta** to be all keyed up, have one's nerves on edge; **tener los ~s a flor de piel** to be ready to explode; **tener los ~s como las cuerdas de un violín** to be as jumpy as a cat; **tener ~ de acero** to have nerves of steel.
  (**b**) (*Anat: tendón*) tendon, sinew; (*de carne*) sinew, tough part.
  (**c**) (*Arquit, Bot*) rib; (*Ent*) vein; (*de libro*) rib; (*Mús*) string.
  (**d**) (*fig*) (*vigor*) vigour, strength; fibre; (*resistencia*) stamina, toughness; (*moral*) moral fibre, moral strength; **un hombre sin ~** a weak man, a spineless man; **tener ~** to have character.
  (**e**) (*fig: persona*) soul, leading light, guiding spirit; **él es el ~ de la sociedad** he is the guiding spirit of the club.
  (**f**) (*fig: fondo*) core, crux.
nerviosamente ADV nervously.
nerviosera NF attack of nerves.
nerviosidad NF, **nerviosismo** NM nervousness; nervous anticipation, nerves; agitation, restlessness, impatience.
nervioso ADJ (**a**) (*Anat*) nerve (*atr*), nervous; **ataque ~** (attack of) hysterics; **centro ~** nerve centre; **crisis nerviosa, depresión nerviosa** nervous breakdown; **sistema ~** nervous system.
  (**b**) (*Anat*) *mano etc* sinewy, wiry.
  (**c**) *persona* (*de temperamento*) nervy, highly-strung, excitable; (*estado temporal*) nervous, nervy; (*impaciente*) restless, impatient; (*sobre-excitado*) overwrought; (*inquieto*) upset, agitated; **poner ~ a uno** to make sb nervous, get on sb's nerves; to get sb worked up; to make sb cross; **ponerse ~** to get nervous; to get worked up; to get upset,

get cross; to get rattled*; **¡no te pongas ~!** take it easy!, calm down!
  (**d**) *estilo etc* vigorous, forceful.
nervoso ADJ (**a**) *persona* = **nervioso** (**c**). (**b**) *carne* sinewy, tough.
nervudo ADJ (**a**) (*fuerte*) tough, strong. (**b**) *mano etc* sinewy, wiry.
nesga NF (*Cos*) flare, gore.
nesgado ADJ *falda etc* flared.
nesgar [1h] VT (*Cos*) to flare, gore.
netamente ADV clearly; purely; genuinely; **una construcción ~ española** a purely Spanish construction, a genuinely Spanish construction.
neto ADJ (**a**) (*gen*) clear; (*puro*) clean, pure; neat; *verdad etc* pure, simple; **tiene su sueldo ~** he has (just) his bare salary.
  (**b**) (*Com, Fin*) net; **peso ~** net weight; **sueldo ~** net salary, salary after deductions.
neumático 1 ADJ pneumatic; air (*atr*).
  2 NM (*Aut*) tyre; **~ balón** balloon tyre; **~ sin cámara** tubeless tyre; **~ radial** radial tyre; **~ de recambio, ~ de repuesto** spare tyre.
neumoconiosis NF pneumoconiosis.
neumonía NF pneumonia.
neura* NF (**a**) (*manía*) mania; obsession; crazy idea, strange notion. (**b**) (*depre*) depression; bad mood.
neural ADJ neural.
neuralgia NF neuralgia.
neurálgico ADJ neuralgic, nerve (*atr*); (*fig*) crucial, vital; most important.
neurastenia NF (**a**) (*Med*) neurasthenia; nervous exhaustion. (**b**) (*fig*) excitability, highly-strung nature, nerviness.
neurasténico ADJ (**a**) (*Med*) neurasthenic. (**b**) (*fig*) excitable, highly-strung, nervy, neurotic.
neuritis NF neuritis.
neuro... PREF neuro...
neuroanatomía NF neuroanatomy.
neurobiología NF neurobiology.
neurociencia NF neuroscience.
neurocirugía NF neurosurgery.
neurocirujano, -a NM/F neurosurgeon.
neurología NF neurology.
neurólogo, -a NM/F neurologist.
neurona NF neuron, nerve cell.
neurópata NMF neuropath.
neuropatológico ADJ neuropathological.
neuropsicología NF neuropsychology.
neuropsicólogo, -a NMF neuropsychologist.
neuropsiquiatra NMF neuropsychiatrist.
neuropsiquiatría NF neuropsychiatry.
neurosis NF INVAR neurosis; **~ de guerra** shellshock.
neurótico, -a ADJ, NM/F neurotic.
neurotizar [1f] 1 VT to make neurotic.
  2 **neurotizarse** VR to become neurotic.
neutral ADJ, NMF neutral.
neutralidad NF neutrality.
neutralismo NM neutralism.
neutralista ADJ, NMF neutralist.
neutralización NF neutralization.
neutralizar [1f] 1 VT to neutralize; *tendencia etc* to counteract.
  2 **neutralizarse** VR to neutralize each other; to cancel (each other) out.
neutro ADJ (**a**) (*gen*) neutral. (**b**) (*Bio*) neuter, sexless, without sex; **abeja neutra** worker bee. (**c**) (*Ling*) neuter; **género ~** neuter; **verbo ~** intransitive verb.
neutrón NM neutron.
nevada NF snowstorm; snowfall.
nevado 1 ADJ (**a**) (*cubierto de nieve*) snow-covered; *montaña* snow-capped. (**b**) (*fig*) snowy, snow-white.
  2 NM (*And, Cono Sur*) snow-capped mountain.
nevar [1j] 1 VT to cover with snow; (*fig*) to whiten.
  2 VI to snow.
nevasca NF snowstorm.
nevazón NF (*And, Cono Sur*) snowstorm.
nevera NF refrigerator, icebox; (*fig*) icebox.
nevera-congelador NF fridge-freezer.
nevero NM snowfield, icefield, place of perpetual snow.
nevisca NF light snowfall, flurry of snow.
neviscar [1g] VI to snow lightly.
nevoso ADJ snowy.
newtoniano ADJ Newtonian.
newtonio NM newton.
nexo NM link, connection; nexus.
n/f. ABR *de* **nuestro favor** our favour.
n/g. ABR *de* **nuestro giro** our money order.
ni CONJ (**a**) (*gen*) nor; neither; **no bebe ~ fuma** he doesn't smoke or drink, he neither smokes nor drinks; **~ el uno ~ el otro** neither one

nor the other; ~ **vino** ~ **llamó por teléfono** he neither came nor rang up; **no quiere** ~ **sal** ~ **mostaza** he doesn't want either salt or mustard; **sin temor** ~ **favor** without fear or favour; **sin padre** ~ **madre** without father or mother; ~ **yo** nor me; V **siquiera.**

(b) not ... even; ~ **uno** not even one; ~ **se sabe** even that is unknown; God knows!; **no lo sabrán** ~ **por fuerza** they won't find it out even by force; ~ **a ti te lo dirá** he won't tell even you.

(c) ~ **que** ... not even if ...; ~ **que fueses su mujer** not even if you were his wife; ~ **que fuera de plomo pesaría tanto** it wouldn't weigh so much even if it were lead; **¡~ que fueras su madre!** anyone would think you were his mother!

Niágara NM Niagara.

niara NF (*Agr*) stack, rick.

nica* ADJ, NMF (*CAm*) Nicaraguan.

nicabar‡ [1a] VT to rip off‡, nick‡.

Nicaragua NF Nicaragua.

nicaragüense ADJ, NMF Nicaraguan.

nicaragüismo NM word (o phrase *etc*) peculiar to Nicaragua.

nicho NM niche (*t fig*); recess; hollow; ~ **ecológico** ecological niche.

Nico NM *forma familiar de* **Nicolás.**

Nicolás NM Nicholas.

nicotiana NF nicotiana, tobacco plant.

nicotina NF nicotine.

nicotínico ADJ nicotinic, nicotine (*atr*).

nidada NF (*huevos*) sitting, clutch; (*pajarillos*) brood.

nidal NM (a) (*Orn*) nest; (*nido artificial*) nesting box. (b) (*dinero*) nest egg. (c) (*) (*guarida*) haunt, hang-out*; (*escondite*) hiding-place.

nidificación NF nesting; nest-building.

nidificante ADJ: **ave** ~ nesting bird.

nidificar [1g] VI to nest.

nido NM (a) (*lit, fig*) nest; ~ **de abeja** (*tela etc*) honeycomb pattern; ~ **de amor** love-nest; **caer del** ~ (*fig*) to come down to earth with a bump; **se ha caído de un** ~ he's dreadfully innocent, he's a bit wet behind the ears*; **manchar el propio** ~ to foul one's own nest.

(b) (*fig: guarida*) nest, haunt, abode, den; ~ **de ladrones** nest of thieves, den of thieves; ~ **de víboras** nest of vipers.

(c) (*fig*) (*escondite*) hiding-place; (*depósito*) secret store.

(d) (*fig: criadero*) centre, hotbed; **el reparto de premios fue un** ~ **de polémicas** the prize giving was a centre of controversy, the prize giving gave rise to heated arguments.

(e) (*Escol*) nursery-school.

(f) (*camita*) cot; (*corralito*) play-pen.

NIE NM ABR *de* **número de identificación de extranjero.**

niebla NF (a) (*lit*) fog, mist; ~ **artificial** smoke screen; ~ **de humo** smog; **un día de** ~ a foggy day; **hay** ~ it is foggy.

(b) (*fig*) fog, confusion.

(c) (*Bot*) mildew.

niego, niegue etc V **negar.**

nieta NF granddaughter.

nietísimo, -a NM/F (*hum*) extra-special grandchild (*esp with reference to Franco's grandchildren*).

nieto NM (a) (*lit*) grandson; ~**s** grandchildren. (b) (*fig*) descendant.

nieva etc V **nevar.**

nieve NF (a) snow; **las primeras** ~**s** the first snows, the first snowfall; ~ **abundante, copiosa** ~ heavy snow; ~ **artificial** artificial snow; ~**s perpetuas** permanent snow; ~ **(en) polvo** powdery snow. (b) (*LAm*) (*helado*) ice-cream; (*sorbete*) sorbet, water-ice. (c) (‡: *cocaína*) snow‡, cocaine. (d) (*TV*) snow.

NIF [nif] NM ABR *de* **número de identificación fiscal.**

nifear‡ [1a] VT: ~ **a uno** to muck sb about (bureaucratically), tie sb up in red tape.

Nigeria NF Nigeria.

nigeriano, -a ADJ, NM/F Nigerian.

night* [nait] NM nightclub.

nigromancia NF, **nigromancía** NF necromancy, black magic.

nigromante NM necromancer.

nigua NF (*And*) chigoe, jigger flea.

nihilismo NM nihilism.

nihilista ADJ, NMF nihilist.

niki NM (*Esp*) T-shirt.

Nilo NM Nile.

nilón [ni'lon, 'nailon] NM nylon.

nimbo NM (*Arte, Astron, Ecl*) halo; (*Met*) nimbus.

nimbostrato NM nimbostratus.

nimiamente ADV (*V ADJ*) (a) trivially; with a host of petty details. (b) fussily; small-mindedly; long-windedly. (c) excessively.

nimiedad NF (a) (*cualidad*) triviality; fussiness; small-mindedness; long-windedness; excess; **tratar un asunto con** ~ to discuss a subject in great detail, treat a theme exhaustively; (*pey*) to discuss a subject in excessive detail.

(b) (*una* ~) very small thing, tiny detail; **riñeron por una** ~ they quarrelled over some triviality.

nimiez NF bagatelle, trifle.

nimio ADJ (a) (*pequeño*) insignificant, trivial, tiny; **un sinfín de detalles** ~**s** a host of petty details.

(b) *persona* (*exigente*) fussy (about details), too meticulous; (*de miras estrechas*) small-minded; (*prolijo*) long-winded.

(c) (*excesivo*) excessive (*en* in).

ninchi‡ NM (a) (*imbécil*) berk‡, twit*. (b) (*niño*) kid*, child. (c) (*amigo*) pal*, buddy.

ninfa NF (a) (*lit*) nymph. (b) (*Esp*‡: *chica*) bird‡, girl.

ninfeta NF, **ninfilla** NF, **ninfita** NF nymphet.

ninfómana NF nymphomaniac.

ninfomanía NF nymphomania.

ninfómano ADJ nymphomaniac.

nínfula NF nymphet.

ningún ADJ V **ninguno.**

ningunear [1a] VT to scorn; ~ **a uno** (*despreciar*) to look down one's nose at sb; (*hacer el vacío a*) to cold-shoulder sb, pay no attention to sb; (*empequeñecer*) to make sb feel small; (*tratar mal*) to treat sb badly.

ninguno 1 ADJ (**ningún** *delante de* NM *sing*) no; **ningún hombre** no man; **ninguna belleza** no beauty; **no hay ningún libro que valga más** there is no book that is worth more; **no voy a ninguna parte** I'm not going anywhere; **sin ningún sentimiento** without any regret, without regret of any kind; **no es ningún tonto** he's no fool, he's no sort of fool.

2 PRON nobody, no-one; none; neither; **no lo sabe** ~ nobody knows; **lo hace como** ~ he does it like nobody else; ~ **de los dos** neither of them; **¿cuál prefieres?** — ~ which do you prefer? — neither (of them).

| NINGUNO | ver también la entrada |

Adjetivo

- Se traduce por *any* si el verbo va en forma negativa y por *no* si el verbo va en forma afirmativa. En general es más frecuente usar *not + any* (salvo como sujeto, posición en la que se debe emplear *no*), ya que *no* se utiliza normalmente con carácter más enfático:

  No tengo ninguna pregunta
  I haven't got any questions
  No se ha cometido ningún delito
  No crime has been committed
  No fui a ningún sitio
  I didn't go anywhere
  No hay ningún peligro
  There is no danger ◊ *There isn't any danger*
  NOTA: Hay que tener en cuenta que el sustantivo que sigue a *any* va en plural si es contable, como en el primer ejemplo.

- Con palabras que poseen un sentido negativo tales como *hardly*, *without* y *never* hay que utilizar *any*:
  Conseguí hacerlo sin ninguna ayuda
  I managed to do it without any help

Pronombre

- El uso de los pronombres *any* y *none* sigue las mismas pautas que los adjetivos *any* y *no*, ya que se emplea preferiblemente la forma *any* con verbos en forma negativa y *none* si la forma es negativa, e igualmente se prefiere la forma *none* para la posición de sujeto:

  No quiero ninguno de éstos
  I don't want any of these
  No me gusta ninguno de ellos
  I don't like any of them
  No queda ninguno
  There are none left
  No va a venir ninguno de sus amigos
  None of her friends is o are coming
  NOTA: Si el verbo va detrás de *none* puede ir tanto en singular como en plural.

- En lugar de *none* y *any*, si *ninguno* se refiere a dos personas o cosas se emplea *neither* y *either*, siguiendo las mismas reglas anotadas anteriormente:

  Ninguno de los dos equipos está jugando bien
  Neither of the teams o Neither team is playing well
  No conozco a ninguno de los dos
  I don't know either of them
  NOTA: El verbo va en singular si sigue a *neither*.
  Para otros usos y ejemplos ver la entrada.

---

niña NF (a) girl, little girl, child (*V t* **niño** 2 (a)); ~ **exploradora** girl guide, girl scout (*US*); ~ **bonita*** pride and joy, special treasure; (*15*) number fifteen.

(b) (*: *prostituta*) tart‡, whore.

(c) (*LAm: en oración directa*) miss, mistress; **la** ~ the mistress of the house.

(d) (*Anat*) pupil; **ser las ~s de los ojos de uno** to be the apple of sb's eye.

niñada NF = **niñería**.

niñato* NM (*pey*) kid*, youth; (*adulto*) playboy.

niñear [1a] VI to act childishly.

niñera NF nursemaid, nanny.

niñería NF **(a)** (*cualidad*) childishness. **(b)** (*acto*) childish thing; silly thing, triviality; **llora por cualquier ~** she cries about any triviality.

niñero ADJ fond of children.

niñez NF childhood; infancy (*t fig*).

niño [1] ADJ **(a)** (*gen*) young; (*sin experiencia*) immature, inexperienced; (*pey*) childish; **es muy ~ todavía** he's still very young (o small).
(b) (*And*) *fruta* green, unripe.
[2] NM **(a)** boy, little boy, child; (*gen*) child; (*no nacido, recién nacido*) baby; (*en oración directa*) my boy, my lad; **¡~!** look out!, be careful!; **los ~s** the children; **el N~ Jesús** the Christ-child, (*con menos formalidad*) Baby Jesus; **~ azul** blue baby; **~ bien, ~ bonito, ~ gótico** playboy; **el N~ de la bola** the infant Jesus; (*fig*) fortune's favourite; **el ~ bonito del toreo** the golden boy of bullfighting; **~ de coro** choirboy; **~ explorador** boy scout; **~ expósito** foundling; **~ maltratado** battered baby; **~ de pecho** small baby, babe-in-arms; **~ pera***, **~ pijo*** pampered child; daddy's boy; **~ probeta** test-tube baby; **~ prodigio** child prodigy; **~ terrible** enfant terrible; **de ~** as a child; when a child; **desde ~** since childhood, since I (*etc*) was a child; **¡no seas ~!** don't be such a baby!; **ser el ~ mimado de uno** to be sb's pet, be sb's white-haired boy; **¡qué coche ni qué ~ muerto!*** all this nonsense about a car!, car my foot!*; **hacer un ~ a una** to get a girl in the family way; **va a tener un ~** she's going to have a baby; **cuando nazca el ~** when the baby (o child) is born.
(b) (*LAm: en oración directa*) master, sir; **el ~** the (young) master.
(c) (*Cono Sur*) undesirable.

nipón, -ona ADJ, NM/F Japanese.

nipos⁣ NMPL dough⁣, money.

níquel NM **(a)** (*gen*) nickel; (*Téc*) nickel-plating. **(b)** (*LAm*) small coin, nickel (*US*); **~es** (*esp Cono Sur, Méx*) dough⁣.

niquelado ADJ nickel-plated.

niquelar [1a] [1] VT to nickel-plate.
[2] VI (*Esp*⁣) to shoot a line*.

niquelera NF (*And*) purse.

niqui NM T-shirt.

nirvana NM Nirvana.

níspero NM, **níspola** NF medlar.

nítidamente ADV brightly, cleanly; spotlessly; clearly, sharply.

nitidez NF **(a)** (*gen*) brightness; (*limpieza*) spotlessness; (*Fot etc*) clarity, sharpness. **(b)** (*fig*) unblemished nature.

nítido ADJ **(a)** (*gen*) bright, clean; (*limpio*) spotless; contorno (*t Fot*) clear, sharp. **(b)** (*fig*) pure, unblemished.

nitral NM nitrate deposit, saltpetre bed.

nitrato NM nitrate; **~ de cloro** chlorine nitrate; **~ potásico** potassium nitrate.

nitrera NF (*Cono Sur*) nitrate deposit.

nítrico ADJ nitric.

nitro NM nitre, saltpetre.

nitrobenceno NM nitrobenzene.

nitrogenado ADJ nitrogenous.

nitrógeno NM nitrogen.

nitroglicerina NF nitroglycerin(e).

nitroso ADJ nitrous.

nivel NM **(a)** (*Geog etc*) level, height; **~ de(l) aceite** (*Aut etc*) oil level; **~ del agua** water level; **~ freático** water-table; **~ del mar** sea level; **a los 900 m sobre el ~ del mar** at 900 m above sea level; **la nieve alcanzó un ~ de 1,5 m** the snow reached a depth of 1.5 m; **a ~** level; true; flush; horizontal; **al ~ de** on the same level as, on a level with, at the same height as.
(b) (*fig*) level, standard; **~es de audiencia** (*TV*) ratings; **el ~ cultural del país** the cultural standard of the country; **~ de vida** standard of living; **alto ~ de trabajo** high level of employment; **conferencia al más alto ~, conferencia de alto ~** high-level conference, top-level conference; **a ~ internacional** on the international level; **estar al ~ de** to be on a level with, be equal to; **no está al ~ de los demás** he is not up to the standard of the others; **estar al ~ de las circunstancias** to rise to the occasion; **de primer ~** top-level; **dar el ~** to come up to scratch.
(c) **a ~ de** PREP (*en cuanto a*) as for, as regards; (*como*) as; (*a tono con*) in keeping with; **a ~ de ministro es un desastre** as a minister he's a disaster; **a ~ de viajes** so far as travel is concerned, regarding travel.
(d) **~ de aire, ~ de burbuja** (*Téc*) spirit level.

nivelación NF levelling; levelling-up, levelling-out, equalization.

nivelado [1] ADJ level, flat; flush.
[2] NM levelling.

niveladora NF bulldozer.

nivelar [1a] VT **(a)** (*gen*) to level (out); (*Ferro etc*) to grade. **(b)** (*fig*) to

level (up), equalize, even (out, up), make even; (*Fin etc*) to balance (*con* against), adjust (*con* to); *déficit* to cover, deal with.

níveo ADJ (*liter*) snowy, snow-white.

nivosidad NF snowfall, (depth of) snow.

nixtamal NM (*CAm, Méx*) boiled maize, boiled corn (*US*) (*used for making tortillas*).

Niza NF Nice.

n/l. ABR de **nuestra letra** our letter.

NN ABR de **ningún nombre** no name (*mark on grave of unknown person*).

NNE ABR de **nornordeste** north-north-east, NNE.

NNO ABR de **nornoroeste** north-north-west, NNW.

NN.UU. ABR de **Naciones Unidas** United Nations, UN.

NO ABR de **noroeste** north-west, NW.

no ADV **(a)** (*en respuestas*) no; (*en frases sin verbo*) not; (*con verbo*) not; **un 'no' contundente** a resounding 'no', a firm 'no'; **¡no!** no!; **¡yo no!** not I!; **¡rey no!** we don't want a king!; **¡Paco no, Pepe sí!** Paco out, Pepe in!; **no sé** I do not know, I don't know; **me rogó no hacerlo** he asked me not to do it; **¿vives aquí, no?** *V* **¿no es verdad?** (*en verdad*); **decir que no** to say no; **creo que no** I don't think so; **¡que no!** I tell you it isn't! (*o doesn't etc*); **¡a que no!** I bet you can't!, I bet you it isn't! (*etc*); **¿oh no?, ¿a que no?** oh no?; do you dare me to?, do you think I can't?; **¡a que no lo sabes!** I bet you don't know!; **de no, ...** (*LAm*) if not, ...; **está de que no** he is in a mood to refuse, I guess he'll say no; **no sea que ...** lest ...; **si no** if not, otherwise; unless you (*etc*) do; **todavía no** not yet; *V* **más 1** (e), **sino** *etc*.
(b) (*en doble negación*) **no tengo nada** I have nothing, I don't have anything; *V* **nada, nunca** *etc*.
(c) (*palabras compuestas*) *p.ej.* **el no conformismo** non-conformism, non-conformity; **país no alineado** non-aligned country; **pacto de no agresión** non-aggression pact; **la política de no intervención** the policy of non-intervention, the non-intervention policy; **cosa no esencial** non-essential thing, inessential; **la no necesidad del latín en partes de la misa** the fact that Latin is not to be insisted upon in parts of the mass; *para otros casos, V el* N *o* ADJ.

n.º ABR de **número** number, No.

n/o. ABR de **nuestra orden** our order.

Nobel NM **(a)** (*t Premio ~*) Nobel Prize. **(b)** (*persona*) Nobel prizewinner.

nobiliario ADJ **(a)** *título etc* noble. **(b)** *libro etc* genealogical.

nobilizar [1f] VT to enhance, dignify, ennoble.

noble [1] ADJ **(a)** (*gen*) noble; (*honrado*) honest, upright. **(b)** *madera* fine.
[2] NM noble, nobleman; **los ~s** the nobles, the nobility.

noblemente ADV nobly; honestly, uprightly.

nobleza NF **(a)** (*cualidad*) nobility; honesty, uprightness; **~ obliga** noblesse oblige. **(b)** (*personas*) nobility, aristocracy.

nobuk NM nubuck.

nocaut NM, **nocáut** NM (*LAm*) knockout.

nocautear [1a] VT to knock out, K.O*.

nocdáun NM knockdown.

noche NF night; night-time; (*late*) evening; dark, darkness (*fig*); **ayer ~** last night; **esta ~** tonight; **¡buenas ~s!** good evening!, (*de despedida o al acostarse uno*) good night!; **Las mil y una ~s** The Arabian Nights; **~ de bodas** wedding-night; **~ de los cuchillos largos** night of the long knives; **~ de estreno** (*Teat*) first night; **~ toledana** sleepless night; **N~ vieja** New Year's Eve; **a primera ~** shortly after dark; **a la ~** at nightfall; **de ~** (ADV) at night, by night, in the night-time; **de ~** (ADJ) late-night (*atr*), evening (*atr*), *p.ej.* **función de ~** late-night show, evening performance, **traje de ~** evening dress; **de la ~ a la mañana** (*t fig*) overnight; **en la ~ de ayer** last night; **en la ~ de hoy** tonight; **hasta muy entrada la ~, hasta muy por la ~** until late at night; on into the small hours; **¡está para una ~!⁣, ¡qué ~ tiene!⁣** she's a bit of all right!⁣; **por la ~** at night, during the night; **ha cerrado la ~** the darkness has come down, night has closed in; **hacer ~ en un sitio** to spend the night in a place; **se hace de ~** it's getting dark, night is falling; **pasar la ~ en blanco, pasar la ~ de claro en claro** to have a sleepless night.

Nochebuena NF Christmas Eve.

⸢ **NOCHEBUENA** ⸣

ⓘ *Traditional Christmas celebrations in Spanish-speaking countries mainly take place on the night of* **Nochebuena**, *Christmas Eve. These include a large Christmas meal, going to Midnight Mass,* **Misa del Gallo**, *and, in Spain, watching the seasonal message from the King on TV. Presents are traditionally given at the Epiphany by* **los Reyes Magos**, *the Three Kings, but due to ever increasing Anglo-Saxon influence some people also give presents on Christmas Day.*
⇨ *See also* ⸢REYES, DÍA DE⸣

nochecita NF (*LAm*) dusk, nightfall.

nocherniego [1] ADJ nocturnal, that goes out (*etc*) at night, given to

wandering about at night.
[2] NM night-bird (fig).
nochero [1] ADJ (LAm) = **nocherniego**.
[2] NM (a) (And, Cono Sur: guardia) night watchman. (b) (CAm: mesilla) bedside table.
[3] NM, **nochera** NF (CAm) night worker.
Nochevieja NF, **nochevieja** NF New Year's Eve.

┌─ *NOCHEVIEJA* ─┐

ⓘ *Nochevieja, or New Year's Eve, is one of the most important seasonal celebrations in Spanish-speaking countries. Whereas* **Nochebuena** *is traditionally spent at home with the family,* **Nochevieja** *is an occasion for going out. In Spain, the highlight of the evening is* **las campanadas**, *the chimes of the* **Puerta del Sol** *clock in Madrid, which are broadcast live to usher in the New Year, like Big Ben in the UK. As the bells strike it is traditional to eat twelve grapes, one for each chime, a custom known as* **las uvas de la suerte** *or* **las doce uvas.**

nochote NM (Méx) cactus beer.
noción NF (a) (gen) notion, idea; **no tener la menor ~ de algo** to have not the faintest idea about sth. (b) **nociones** elements, rudiments; smattering; **tiene algunas nociones de árabe** he has a smattering of Arabic.
nocional ADJ notional.
nocividad NF harmfulness.
nocivo ADJ harmful, injurious (para to).
noctambulear [1a] VI to wander about at night.
noctambulismo NM sleepwalking.
noctámbulo [1] ADJ active at night.
[2] NM, **noctámbula** NF (sonámbulo) sleepwalker; (nocherniego) night-bird, person who goes around at night; (jaranero) roisterer.
noctiluca NF (Ent) glow-worm.
noctívago = **noctámbulo**.
nocturnidad NF evening hours, night hours; **obrar con ~** to operate under cover of darkness; **con la agravante de la ~** made more serious by the fact that it was done at night.
nocturno [1] ADJ night (atr); evening (atr); (Zool etc) nocturnal; **clase nocturna** evening class; **vida nocturna** night life.
[2] NM (a) (Mús) nocturne. (b) (Escol) evening class.
nodo[1] NM node.
nodo[2], **No-do** NM (Cine Hist) newsreel.
nodriza NF wet-nurse; **barco ~** supply ship.
nodular ADJ nodular.
nódulo NM nodule.
Noé NM Noah.
nogal NM (madera) walnut; (árbol) walnut tree.
noguera NF walnut tree.
noluntad NF unwillingness, reluctance, refusal.
nómada [1] ADJ nomadic.
[2] NMF nomad.
nomadear [1a] VI to wander.
nomadeo NM wanderings.
nomadismo NM nomadism.
nomás ADV (LAm) just; only; **y** V **más.**
nombradía NF fame, renown.
nombrado ADJ (a) (susodicho) aforementioned. (b) (fig) famous, renowned.
nombramiento NM (a) (denominación) naming; designation. (b) (mención) mention. (c) (para un puesto etc) nomination; appointment; (Mil) commission.
nombrar [1a] VT (a) (dar nombre a) to name; to designate.
(b) (mencionar) to mention.
(c) (para un puesto etc) to nominate; to appoint; (Mil) to commission; **~ a uno embajador** to nominate sb as ambassador, appoint sb ambassador.
nombre NM (a) name; **mal ~** nickname; **Bradomín, por mal ~ Tufo** Bradomín, nicknamed Stinker; **un sobre a mi ~** an envelope addressed to me; **~ y apellidos** name in full, full name; **~ artístico** (Liter) pen-name; (Teat) stage-name; **~ de bautismo** given name; **~ comercial** trade name; **~ de familia, ~ gentilicio** family name; V **hipocorístico; ~ de lugar** place-name; **~ de pila** first name, Christian name; **~ propietario** proprietary name; **~ propio** proper name; **~ de religión** name in religion; **~ social** corporate name; **no hay nadie a ~ de María** there's no one by the name of María; **bajo el ~ de** under the name of; **de ~** by name, p.ej. **de ~ García** García by name; **conocer a uno de ~** to know sb by name; **era rey tan sólo de ~, de rey no tenía más que el ~** he was king in name only; **no existe sino de ~** it exists in name only; **en ~ de** in the name of, on behalf of; **en ~ de la libertad** in the name of liberty; **¡abran en ~ de la ley!** open up, in the name of the law!; **por ~ de** by the name of, called; **sin ~** nameless; **poner ~ a** to call; name; **¿qué ~ le van a poner?** what are they going to call him?, what name are they giv-

ing him?; **le pusieron el ~ de su abuelo** they named him after his grandfather; **su conducta no tiene ~** his conduct is unspeakable.
(b) (Ling) noun; **~ abstracto** abstract noun; **~ colectivo** collective noun; **~ común** common noun; **~ concreto** concrete noun.
(c) (fig) name, reputation; **un médico de ~** a famous doctor; **tiene ~ en el mundo entero** it has a world-wide reputation.
nomenclador NM, **nomenclátor** NM catalogue of names.
nomenclatura NF nomenclature.
nomeolvides NF INVAR (a) (Bot) forget-me-not. (b) (pulsera) bracelet (with lover's name etc).
nómina NF list, roll; (Com, Fin) payroll; **tiene una ~ de 500 personas** he has 500 on his payroll.
nominación NF nomination.
nominal ADJ (a) jefe, rey etc nominal, titular, in name only. (b) valor face (atr), nominal; sueldo etc nominal. (c) (Ling) noun (atr), substantival.
nominalismo NM nominalism.
nominalización NF nominalization.
nominalizar [1f] VT to nominalize.
nominalmente ADV nominally, in name; **al menos ~** at least in name.
nominar [1a] VT to nominate.
nominativo [1] ADJ (a) (Ling) nominative. (b) (Com, Fin) bearing a person's name, made out to an individual; **el cheque será ~ a favor** (o **nombre**) **de X** the cheque should be made out to X.
[2] NM (Ling) nominative.
non [1] ADJ número odd, uneven.
[2] NM odd number; **pares y ~es** odds and evens; **los ~es** the odd ones; **un zapato de ~** an odd shoe; **queda uno de ~** there's an odd one, there's one left over; **estar de ~** (persona) to be odd man out, (fig) be useless; **andar de ~es** to have nothing to do.
nona* NF (Cono Sur) grandma*, granny*.
nonada NF trifle, mere nothing.
nonagenario [1] ADJ nonagenarian, ninety-year old.
[2] NM, **nonagenaria** NF nonagenarian, person in his (o her) nineties.
nonagésimo ADJ ninetieth.
nonato ADJ not born naturally; unborn.
noneco ADJ, **nonejo** ADJ (CAm) thick.
nones* ADV no; **¡~!** no way!*; **decir que ~** to say flatly no.
noningentésimo ADJ nine hundredth.
nono[1] ADJ ninth.
nono[2]* NM (Cono Sur) granddad*.
nopal NM prickly pear.
nopalera NF patch of prickly pears, area where prickly pears grow.
noqueada NF (esp LAm) (acto) knockout; (golpe) knockout blow.
noqueado* ADJ (LAm: cansado) shattered*, knackered*.
noquear [1a] VT to knock out, K.O.
noqueo NM (esp LAm) knockout, K.O.
noratlántico ADJ north-Atlantic.
noray NM bollard.
norcoreano, -a ADJ, NM/F North Korean.
nordeste [1] ADJ parte north-east, north-eastern; dirección north-easterly; viento north-east, north-easterly.
[2] NM (a) (región) north-east.
(b) (viento) north-east wind.
nordestino ADJ north-eastern.
nórdico [1] ADJ (a) (gen) northern, northerly; **es la ciudad más nórdica de Europa** it is the most northerly city in Europe.
(b) (Hist) Nordic, Norse.
[2] NM, **nórdica** NF (a) (gen) northerner.
(b) (Hist) Northman.
[3] NM (Ling) Norse.
noreste = **nordeste**.
noria NF (a) (Agr) waterwheel, chain pump. (b) (de feria) big wheel, Ferris wheel (US).
norirlandés [1] ADJ Northern Irish.
[2] NM, **norirlandesa** NF Northern Irishman, Northern Irishwoman.
norma NF (a) (gen) standard, norm, rule; (pauta) pattern; (método) method; **~ de comprobación** (Fís etc) control; **~s de conducta** (de periódico etc) policy; **~s de seguridad** safety regulations; **~ de vida** principle, guiding principle; **está sujeto a ciertas ~s** it is subject to certain rules.
(b) (Arquit, Téc) square.
normal [1] ADJ normal; regular, usual, natural; (Téc etc) standard; **es perfectamente ~** it's perfectly normal, it's completely usual.
[2] NF (a) (Aut) 3-star petrol. (b) (LAm Educ) teacher(s)' training college (primary).
normalidad NF normality, normalcy; (Pol) calm, normal conditions; **la situación ha vuelto a la ~** the situation has returned to normal; **la vuelta a la ~ es completa en la provincia** calm has been com-

pletely restored in the province.

normalillo, normalito ADJ quite ordinary; run-of-the-mill.

normalista NMF (*LAm*) student teacher; schoolteacher.

normalización NF normalization.

normalizado ADJ standard(ized).

normalizar [1f] ☐1 VT to normalize, restore to normal; (*Téc*) to standardize.

☐2 **normalizarse** VR to return to normal, settle down.

▼ **normalmente** ADV normally; usually.

Normandía NF Normandy.

normando ☐1 ADJ Norman; **Islas Normandas** Channel Isles.

☐2 NM, **normanda** NF Norman; Northman, Norseman.

normar [1a] VT (*LAm*) to lay down rules for, establish norms for.

normativa NF (set of) rules, regulations; guideline(s); **según la ~ vigente** according to current guidelines.

normativo ADJ (a) (*prescrito*) normative, preceptive.

(b) (*regular*) regular, standard; **español ~** standard Spanish, received Spanish; **es ~ en todos los coches nuevos** it is standard in all new cars, it is the norm in all new cars.

noroccidental ADJ north-western.

noroeste ☐1 ADJ *parte* north-west, north-western; *dirección* north-westerly; *viento* north-west, north-westerly.

☐2 NM (a) (*región*) north-west. (b) (*viento*) north-west wind.

nororiental ADJ north-eastern.

norsa NF (*LAm*) (*enfermera*) nurse; (*institutriz*) governess; (*niñera*) nursemaid.

nortada NF (steady) northerly wind.

norte ☐1 ADJ *parte* north, northern; *dirección* northerly; *viento* north, northerly.

☐2 NM (a) (*región*) north; **en la parte del ~** in the northern part; **al ~ de Segovia** to the north of Segovia, on the north side of Segovia; **eso cae más hacia el ~** that lies further (to the) north.

(b) (*viento*) north wind.

(c) (*fig*) (*guía*) guide; (*meta*) aim, objective; (*estrella*) lodestar; **pregunta sin ~** aimless question; **perder el ~** to lose one's way, go astray.

(d) (*Carib: se refiere vagamente a*) United States.

(e) (*Carib: llovizna*) drizzle.

norteafricano, -a ADJ, NM/F North African.

Norteamérica NF North America.

norteamericano, -a ADJ, NM/F North American, American.

nortear [1a] VI: **nortea** (*And, CAm, Carib*) the north wind is blowing.

norteño ☐1 ADJ northern.

☐2 NM, **norteña** NF northerner.

nortino = **norteño**.

Noruega NF Norway.

noruego, -a ☐1 ADJ, NM/F Norwegian.

☐2 NM (*Ling*) Norwegian.

norvietnamés, -esa ADJ, NM/F (*LAm*) North Vietnamese.

norvietnamita ADJ, NMF North Vietnamese.

nos PRON PERS PL (a) (*ac*) us.

(b) (*dativo*) (to) us; **~ lo dará** he will give it to us; **~ lo compró** he bought it from us; he bought it for us; **~ cortamos el pelo** we had our hair cut.

(c) (*reflexivo*) (to) ourselves; (*recíproco*) (to) each other; **~ lavamos** we washed; **no ~ hablamos** we don't speak to each other; **~ levantamos a las 7** we get up at 7.

nosocomio NM (*Méx*) hospital.

nosotros, nosotras PRON PERS PL (a) (*sujeto*) we. (b) (*tras prep*) us; ourselves; **entre ~** between you and me; between ourselves; **no irán sin ~** they won't go without us; **no pedimos nada para ~** we ask nothing for ourselves.

nostalgia NF nostalgia, homesickness; longing.

nostálgico ADJ nostalgic, homesick; longing.

nostalgioso ADJ (*Cono Sur*) = **nostálgico**.

nota ☐1 NF (a) (*gen*) note; memorandum; (*Liter*) footnote, marginal note; (*Com*) account; (*recibo*) receipt; (*en periódico*) note; (*LAm: pagaré*) IOU, promissory note; (*Méx: cuenta*) bill; **~ de cargo** debit note; **~ de entrega** delivery note; **~ de gastos** expense account; **~ informativa** press release; **~ de inhabilitación** (*Aut*) endorsement (*in licence*); **~ a pie de página** footnote; **~ de prensa** press release; **~ de la redacción** editor's note; **~ de sociedad** gossip column, column of society news; **texto con ~s de ...** text edited with notes by ..., text annotated by ...; **pagar la ~** (*fig*) to carry the can*; **tomar ~s** to take notes.

(b) (*Escol etc*) grade, mark, class; (*t* **~ escolar**) (*terminal*) report; **obtener buenas ~s** to get good marks; **ir para ~** to overdo it, put too much into it.

(c) (*Mús y fig*) note; **~ de adorno** grace note; **una ~ de buen gusto** a tasteful note; **como ~ de color** as a colourful note; as a bit of local colour; **~ dominante** dominant feature; **dar la ~** (*fig: dar el tono*) to set the tone; (*armar un lío*) to cause trouble; (*destacar*) to get one-

self noticed, act up; **entonar la ~** to pitch a note, give the note (*for singers to start*).

(d) (*fig: reputación*) reputation; **de ~** of note, famous; **de mala ~** notorious; of ill fame; **tiene ~ de tacaño** he has a reputation for meanness.

(e) **digno de ~** notable, worthy of note; **tomar ~** to take note.

(f) **quedarse ~** (INVAR) to be amazed.

(g) (*LAm*) effects of drugs.

☐2 NM (a) (*t*) bloke*. (b) **es un ~s*** he's an oddball*; his face doesn't fit.

notabilidad NF (a) (*cualidad*) noteworthiness, notability. (b) (*persona*) notable, worthy.

▼ **notable** ☐1 ADJ (a) (*gen*) noteworthy, notable; remarkable. (b) (*Escol*) outstanding. (c) (*Univ etc*) creditable, of the second class.

☐2 NMF (*gen*) notable, worthy.

☐3 NM (*Univ etc*) credit (mark), second class (mark).

notablemente ADV notably; remarkably, outstandingly.

notación NF notation; **~ binaria** binary notation; **~ hexadecimal** hexadecimal notation.

notar [1a] ☐1 VT (a) (*observar*) to note, notice; (*percibir*) to feel, perceive; (*ver*) to see; **no noto frío alguno** I don't feel cold at all; **no lo había notado** I hadn't noticed it; **te noto muy cambiado** I find you very changed; **hacer ~ que ...** to note that ..., observe that ...; **hacerse ~** to stand out, catch the eye, draw attention to o.s.

(b) (*apuntar*) to note down.

(c) (*marcar*) to mark, indicate.

(d) (*criticar*) to criticize; (*desacreditar*) to discredit; **~ a uno de oscuro** to brand sb as obscure, criticize sb for being obscure.

☐2 **notarse** VR to show, be apparent, be obvious; **se nota que ...** one observes that ..., one notes that ...; **la combinación no se le nota** your slip doesn't show; **no se nota en absoluto su origen extranjero** his foreign origin is not in the least obvious, you can't tell at all that he is foreign.

notaría NF (a) (*profesión*) profession of notary; **gastos de ~** legal fees, lawyer's fees. (b) (*despacho*) notary's office.

notariado NM (*profesión*) profession of notary; (*notarios*) notaries *pl*.

notarial ADJ notarial; *estilo etc* legal, lawyer's.

notarialmente ADV by legal process; **recurrir ~ a uno** to bring a legal action against sb; **tiene que certificarse ~** it must be legally certified, it must be certified before a commissioner for oaths.

notario, -a NM/F notary, notary public; (*en ciertos aspectos, equivale a*) solicitor.

▼ **noticia** NF (a) (*gen*) piece of news; (*en periódico, TV etc*) news item; **~s** news; **~ necrológica** notice of a death, obituary notice; **según nuestras ~s** according to our information; **eso no es ~** that's not news; **estar atrasado de ~s** to be behind the times, lack up-to-date information; **tener ~s de uno** to have news of sb, hear from sb; **hace tiempo que no tenemos ~s suyas** we haven't heard from her for a long time.

(b) (*conocimientos*) knowledge; notion; **no tener la menor ~ de algo** to know nothing at all about a matter, be completely ignorant of sth.

┌─ **NOTICIA** ──────────────── **ver también la entrada** ─┐

● Para traducir la palabra *noticia* al inglés, hay que tener en cuenta que el sustantivo *news* es incontable y lleva el verbo en singular:
    Las noticias de hoy no son nada buenas
    Today's news isn't very good
    Cuando recibió la noticia se puso a llorar
    When she received the news she burst into tears

● Cuando queremos precisar que se trata de una noticia en particular o de un número determinado de noticias utilizamos la expresión *piece/pieces of news*:
    Había dos noticias que nos parecieron preocupantes
    There were two pieces of news that we found worrying
    Para otros usos y ejemplos ver la entrada.

└──┘

noticiable ADJ newsworthy.

noticiar [1b] VT to notify.

noticiario NM (*Rad*) news bulletin; (*Cine*) newsreel.

noticiero ☐1 ADJ (a) (*relativo a noticias*) news (*atr*). (b) (*que da noticias*) news-bearing, news-giving. (c) (*ávido de noticias*) fond of receiving news.

☐2 NM (a) (*periódico*) newspaper, gazette. (b) (*Carib*) newsreel; (*LAm TV*) news bulletin, newscast.

notición NM bombshell.

noticioso ☐1 ADJ (a) *fuente etc* well-informed; *reportaje* news (*atr*); *suceso* newsworthy; **texto ~** news report. (b) **~ de que Vd quería verme ...** hearing that (o on being informed that) you wished to see me ...

☐2 NM (*LAm*) news bulletin, newscast.

notificación NF notification.

➤ LENGUA Y USO: **normalmente** → 53.1   **notable:** 1a → 53.1   **noticia: a** → 48.1, 48.2

notificar [1g] VT to notify, inform.

notoriamente ADV obviously; glaringly, blatantly, flagrantly; **una sentencia ~ injusta** a glaringly unjust sentence.

notoriedad NF fame, renown; wide knowledge; **hechos de amplia ~** widely-known facts.

notorio ADJ (a) (*conocido*) well-known, publicly known; (*famoso*) famous; **un hecho ~** a well-known fact; **es ~ que ...** it is well-known that ... (b) (*obvio*) obvious; *error etc* glaring, blatant, flagrant.

nov. ABR *de* **noviembre** November, Nov.

novador ① ADJ innovating, revolutionary.
② NM, **novadora** NF innovator.

noval ADJ *tierra* newly-broken.

novamás* NM INVAR: **es el ~** (*lo mejor*) it's the ultimate; (*lo último*) it's the latest thing.

novatada NF (a) (*broma*) rag, ragging, hazing (*US*) (*of new member etc*). (b) (*error*) beginner's mistake, elementary blunder; **pagar la ~** to learn the hard way.

novato ① ADJ (*inexperto*) raw, green, new.
② NM (*principiante*) beginner, tyro.

novecientos ADJ nine hundred; **en el ~** in the twentieth century.

novedad NF (a) (*cualidad*) newness, novelty; (*extrañeza*) strangeness. (b) (*objeto etc*) novelty; surprise; **~es** (*noticias*) latest news; **~es, últimas ~es** (*Com*) novelties, latest fashions, latest models. (c) (*innovación*) new feature, new development; (*cambio*) change; **sin ~ en el frente** all quiet on the front; **no hay ~es** there's nothing to report; **llegar sin ~** to arrive without mishap, arrive safely; **la jornada ha sido sin ~** it has been a quiet (o normal) day, it has been a day without incident; **el enfermo sigue sin ~** the patient's condition is unchanged.

novedoso ADJ (a) *idea, método etc* novel; new; full of novelties. (b) (*Cono Sur, Méx*) = **novelesco**.

novel ① ADJ (*nuevo*) new; inexperienced; **una escritora ~** a new writer.
② NM (*principiante*) beginner.

novela NF novel; **~ de amor** love story, romance; **~ de aprendizaje, ~ iniciática** Bildungsroman; **~s científicas** science fiction; **~ por entregas** serial; **~ epistolar** epistolary novel; **~ gótica** Gothic novel; **~ histórica** historical novel; **~ de misterio** mystery story; **~ negra** thriller; **~ policíaca** detective story, whodunit*; **~ radiofónica** radio serial; **~ río** saga; **~ rosa** romantic novel; **la ~ española en el siglo XX** the 20th century Spanish novel.

novelación NF fictionalization.

novelado ADJ fictionalized.

novelar [1a] ① VT to make a novel out of; to tell in novel form; to fictionalize.
② VI to write novels.

novelero ① ADJ (a) (*lleno de imaginación*) highly imaginative; (*romántico*) dreamy, romantic. (b) (*aficionado a novedades*) fond of novelty. (c) (*aficionado a novelas*) fond of novels. (d) *cuento etc* romantic, novelettish. (e) (*chismoso*) gossipy, fond of gossiping.
② NM, **novelera** NF novel reader.

novelesco ADJ (a) (*Liter*) fictional; **el género ~** fiction, the novel. (b) (*romántico*) romantic, fantastic, novelettish; *aventura etc* storybook (*atr*).

novelista NMF novelist.

novelística NF: **la ~** fiction, the novel.

novelón NM big novel, three-decker novel; (*pey*) pulp novel.

novelucha NF (*pey*) cheap novel, yellowback; pulp novel.

novena NF (*Ecl*) novena.

noveno ADJ, NM ninth.

noventa ADJ ninety; ninetieth; **los (años) ~** the nineties; **los escritores del ~ y ocho** the writers of the 1898 Generation.

noventayochista ADJ: *p.ej.* **un escritor ~** a writer of the 1898 Generation.

noventón ① ADJ ninety-year-old, ninetyish.
② NM, **noventona** NF person of about ninety.

novia NF (a) (*amiga*) sweetheart; (*prometida*) fiancée; (*en boda*) bride; (*recién casada*) newly-married girl; **echarse una ~** to get o.s. a girl; **Juan y su ~** John and his fiancée; **traje de ~** bridal gown, wedding dress. (b) (*Mil‡*) rifle, gun.

noviar [1b] VI: **~ con** (*Cono Sur*) to court, go out with, date.

noviazgo NM engagement.

noviciado NM apprenticeship, training; (*Ecl*) novitiate.

novicio, -a NM/F beginner, novice; apprentice; (*Ecl*) novice.

noviembre NM November.

noviero* ADJ: **es muy ~** he has had lots of girlfriends; he's always falling in love.

novilla NF heifer.

novillada NF (*Taur*) novillada, *bullfight with young bulls* (*and novice bull-*

fighters).

novillero NM (a) (*Taur*) novice, young bullfighter. (b) (*Escol**) truant.

novillo NM (a) (*Zool*) young bull, bullock, steer; **~s** = **novillada**. (b) (*) cuckold. (c) **hacer ~s** to stay away, not turn up; (*Escol*) to play truant.

novilunio NM (*Astron*) new moon.

novio NM (*amigo*) sweetheart; (*prometido*) fiancé; (*en boda*) bridegroom, (*recién casado*) newly-married man; **los ~s** (*prometidos*) the engaged couple; (*en boda*) the bride and groom; (*recién casados*) the newly-weds; **ser ~s formales** to be formally engaged; **Maruja y su ~** Mary and her young man, Mary and her fiancée; **viaje de ~s** honeymoon.

novísimo ADJ newest, latest, most recent; brand-new.

NPI‡ (*Esp*) ABR *de* **ni puta** (o **puñetera**) **idea** no bloody idea‡, not the faintest*.

nra., nro. ABR *de* **nuestra, nuestro** our.

N.S. ABR *de* **Nuestro Señor** Our Lord.

ns ABR *de* **no sabe(n)** don't know(s) (*in opinion poll*).

ns/nc ABR *de* **no sabe(n)/no contesta(n)** don't know(s)/non-respondents (*in opinion poll*).

N.T. (a) (*Rel*) ABR *de* **Nuevo Testamento** New Testament, NT. (b) (*Téc*) ABR *de* **nuevas tecnologías** new technology.

ntra. ABR *de* **nuestra.**

NU NFPL ABR *de* **Naciones Unidas** United Nations, UN.

nubada NF, **nubarrada** NF (a) (*chaparrón*) downpour, sudden shower. (b) (*fig*) shower; abundance; mass.

nubarrón NM storm cloud.

nube NF (a) (*gen*) cloud; **~ de lluvia** raincloud; **~ de tormenta** storm cloud. (b) (*fig: de humo, insectos etc*) cloud; crowd, mass, multitude; **una ~ de pordioseros** a swarm of beggars; **una ~ de críticas** a storm of criticism. (c) (*Med: en ojo*) cloud, film. (d) **los precios están por las ~s** prices are sky-high; **poner a uno en (o por, sobre) las ~s** to praise sb to the skies; **ponerse por las ~s*** (*persona*) to go up the wall*; (*precio*) to rocket, soar; **andar por las ~s, estar en las ~s** to have one's head in the clouds, be daydreaming, be remote from it all.

núbil ADJ marriageable, nubile.

nublado ① ADJ cloudy, overcast.
② NM (a) (*nube*) storm cloud, black cloud. (b) (*fig*) (*amenaza*) threat; (*peligro*) impending danger. (c) (*fig: multitud*) swarm, crowd, multitude; **un ~ de** a swarm of, a host of. (d) (*fig: enfado*) anger, black mood.

nublar [1a] ① VT (a) (*gen*) to darken, obscure. (b) (*fig*) *vista* to cloud, disturb; *razón* to affect; *felicidad etc* to cloud, destroy.
② **nublarse** VR to become cloudy, cloud over.

nublazón NM (*LAm*) = **nublado**.

nublo ADJ (*LAm*) cloudy.

nubloso ADJ (a) (*lit*) cloudy. (b) (*fig*) unlucky, unfortunate; gloomy.

nubosidad NF cloudiness, clouds; **~ de desarrollo, ~ de evolución** developing clouds.

nuboso ADJ cloudy.

nubuck NM nubuck.

nuca NF nape (of the neck), back of the neck.

nuclear ① ADJ nuclear.
② [1a] VT (a) (*reunir*) to bring together; (*combinar*) to combine; (*concentrar*) to concentrate; *miembros etc* to provide a focus for, act as a forum for. (b) (*liderar*) to lead.
③ NF nuclear power station.

nuclearización NF introduction of nuclear energy (*de* to); conversion to nuclear energy.

nuclearizarse [1f] VR (*Elec*) to build nuclear power stations, go nuclear; (*Mil*) to make (o acquire) nuclear weapons; **países nuclearizados** countries possessing nuclear weapons.

nucleizar [1f] VT = **nuclear 2**.

núcleo NM nucleus; (*Elec*) core; (*Bot*) kernel, stone; (*fig*) core, essence; **~ duro** hard core; **~ rural** (new) village, village settlement; **~ urbano** city centre.

nudillo NM knuckle.

nudismo NM nudism.

nudista NMF nudist.

nudo¹ ADJ: **nuda propiedad** bare ownership, bare title to property.

nudo² NM (a) (*gen*) knot; **~ corredizo** slipknot; **~ gordiano** Gordian knot; **~ llano, ~ de rizos** reef knot. (b) (*Náut*) knot. (c) (*Bot*) knot; node. (d) (*parte gruesa*) thick part, thickening, lump; **con un ~ en la garganta** with a lump in one's throat; **se me hizo un ~ en la garganta** I got a lump in my throat. (e) (*de comunicaciones etc*) centre; (*de carreteras*) cloverleaf, system of flyovers, motorway interchange; (*Ferro*) junction.

(f) *(fig: vínculo)* bond, tie, link.

(g) *(fig: de problema)* knotty point; core, crux; *(de drama etc)* crisis, point of greatest complexity.

nudoso ADJ *madera etc* knotty, full of knots; *tronco* gnarled; *bastón* knobbly.

nuégado NM nougat.

nuera NF daughter-in-law.

nuestro ① ADJ POS our; *(tras n)* of ours, *p.ej.* **un barco ~** a boat of ours, one of our boats; **no es amigo ~** he's not a friend of ours; **lo ~** (what is) ours, what belongs to us.

② PRON POS ours, of ours; **es el ~** it is ours; **los ~s** *(parientes)* our people, our relations, our family; *(Dep, Mil etc)* our men, our side.

nueva NF piece of news; **~s** news; **me cogió de ~s** it was news to me, it took me by surprise; **hacerse de ~s** to pretend not to have heard a piece of news before, pretend to be surprised.

Nueva Caledonia NF New Caledonia.

Nueva Delhi NF New Delhi.

Nueva Escocia NF Nova Scotia.

Nueva Gales NF **del Sur** New South Wales.

Nueva Guinea NF New Guinea.

Nueva Inglaterra NF New England.

nuevamente ADV again; anew.

nuevaolero ADJ new-wave *(atr)*.

Nueva Orleáns NF New Orleans.

Nueva York NF New York.

Nueva Zelanda NF, **Nueva Zelandia** NF *(LAm)* New Zealand.

nueve ① ADJ nine; *(fecha)* ninth; **las ~** nine o'clock.

② NM nine.

nuevecito ADJ brand-new.

nuevo ADJ *(gen)* new; fresh; novel; *(adicional)* further, additional; *sello* mint, unused; **de ~** again; **es ~ en la ciudad** he's new to the town; **es ~ en el oficio** he's new to the trade; **somos ~s aquí** we're new here; **no hay nada ~** there's nothing fresh; **no hay nada ~ bajo las estrellas** there's nothing new under the sun; **es más ~ que yo** he is junior to me; **con ~s argumentos** with new arguments, with further arguments; **la casa es nueva** the house is new; **la casa está nueva** the house is as good as new; **¿qué hay de ~?*** what's new?*, what's the news?

nuevomejicano, -a ADJ, NM/F New Mexican.

Nuevo Méjico NM New Mexico.

nuez NF **(a)** nut, *(esp)* walnut; *(Méx)* pecan nut; **~ del Brasil, ~ de Pará** Brazil nut; **~ moscada** nutmeg; **~ nogal** (o **de Castilla**) *(Méx)* walnut; **~ de la garganta** Adam's apple. **(b)** *(fig)* core, heart of the matter.

nulidad NF **(a)** *(Jur)* nullity. **(b)** *(incapacidad)* incompetence, incapacity. **(c)** *(persona)* nonentity; **es una ~** he's a dead loss, he's useless.

nulo ① ADJ **(a)** *(Jur)* void, null and void; invalid, without force; **~ y sin efecto** null and void.

(b) *persona* useless; **es ~ para la música** he's useless at music, he's no good at music, he's a dead loss as a musician.

(c) *partido* drawn, tied.

② NMPL: **~s** *(Naipes)* misère; **bridge con ~s** bridge with the misère variation.

núm. ABR *de* **número** number, No.

Numancia NF Numantia; *(fig)* symbol of heroic (o last-ditch) resistance.

numantino ① ADJ Numantine, of Numantia; *(fig)* *resistencia* heroic, last-ditch, *(pey)* diehard, stubborn.

② NMPL: **los ~s** the Numantines, the people of Numantia.

numen NM inspiration; talent, inventiveness; **~ poético** poetic inspiration; **de propio ~** out of one's head.

numeración NF **(a)** *(acto)* numeration, numbering. **(b)** *(números)* numbers, numerals; **~ arábiga** Arabic numerals; **~ romana** Roman numerals.

numerador NM numerator.

numeral ① ADJ numeral, number *(atr)*.

② NM numeral.

numerar [1a] ① VT to number; **páginas sin ~** unnumbered pages.

② **numerarse** VR *(Mil etc)* to number off.

numerario ① ADJ *claustral, miembro etc* full; *profesor* tenured, with tenure, permanent; **no ~** without tenure, not permanent.

② NM *(Fin)* cash, hard cash.

numererо* ADJ far-out*, over-the-top, outrageous.

numéricamente ADV numerically.

numérico ADJ numerical; *(Inform)* numeric.

numerito NM *(Teat)* short act; fill-in act.

número NM **(a)** *(gen)* number **~ arábigo** Arabic numeral; **~ binario**

binary number; **~ cardinal** cardinal number; **~ entero** whole number; **~ fraccionario** (o **quebrado**) fraction; **~ impar** odd number; **~ de identificación fiscal** ID number used for tax purposes; **~ de matrícula** *(Aut etc)* registration number; **~ ordinal** ordinal number; **~ par** even number; **~ primo** prime number; **~ redondo** round number; **en ~s redondos** in round numbers, in round figures; **~ de referencia** reference number; **~ romano** Roman numeral; **~ de serie** serial number; **N~ Uno** *(criminal)* Mr Big; **el jugador ~ uno de su país** the number one player of his country; **el ~ dos del grupo** second in command (o number two) of the group; **en ~ de** to the number of; **miembro de ~** full member; **sin ~** *(fig)* numberless, unnumbered; countless; **estar en** (o **tener**) **~s rojos** to be in the red; **tomar el ~~*, montar el ~*** *(engañar)* to try to put one over*; *(excederse)* to go too far; **volver a ~s negros** to get back into the black, return to profitability.

(b) *(de zapato etc)* size.

(c) *(de periódico etc)* number, issue; **~ atrasado** back number; **~ cero** *(Prensa)* dummy number, dummy run; **~ extraordinario** special edition, special issue; **~ suelto** single issue.

(d) *(de programa)* item, number; *(Teat etc)* turn, act, number; sketch; **hacer el ~*, montar el ~*** to do something pretty far-out*, go over the top; to make a scene; **¡ya empiezas con tus ~s!** there you go with your old tricks again!

(e) **de ~** *(Cono Sur)* first-class.

(f) **¡vaya ~!*** what a character!

(g) **profesor de ~** tenured teacher, teacher with tenure, teacher with a permanent post.

(h) *(Mil etc)* man; *(soldado raso)* private; *(policía)* policeman; **un sargento y 4 ~s** a sergeant and 4 men.

(i) *(*: billete de lotería)* ticket.

numerología NF numerology.

numeroso ADJ numerous; **familia numerosa** large family.

numerus clausus NM system of restricted (o selective) entry (to university etc), quota system.

numísmata NMF numismatist.

numismática¹ NF numismatics.

numismático ① ADJ numismatic.

② NM, **numismática²** NF numismatist.

núms ABR *de* **números** numbers, Nos.

nunca ADV never; ever; **no viene ~, ~ viene** he never comes, he doesn't ever come; **¡~!** never!; **casi ~** almost never, hardly ever; **¡hasta ~!** I don't care if I never see you again!; **más que ~** more than ever; **~ jamás, ~ más** never again, nevermore; **¿has visto ~ cosa igual?** have you ever seen anything like this?

nunciatura NF nunciature.

nuncio NM **(a)** *(Ecl)* nuncio; **~ apostólico, ~ pontificio** papal nuncio; **¡cuéntaselo al ~!** tell that to the marines!; **¡que lo haga el ~!** get sb else to do it! **(b)** *(mensajero)* messenger; *(fig)* herald, harbinger; **~ de la primavera** harbinger of spring.

nunquita ADV *(LAm)* = **nunca.**

nupcial ADJ wedding *(atr)*, nuptial.

nupcialidad NF rate of marriage, marriage statistics.

nupcias NFPL wedding, nuptials; **casarse en segundas ~, contraer nuevas ~** to marry again, get married a second time; **A, que se casó en segundas ~ con B** A, who made a second marriage to B.

nurse ['nurse] NF *(enfermera)* nurse; *(institutriz)* governess; *(niñera)* nursemaid.

nursería NF nursing mothers' room, mother-and-baby room.

nutria NF otter.

nutrición NF nutrition.

nutricional ADJ nutritional.

nutricionista NMF dietician, nutritionist.

nutrido ADJ **(a)** *(alimentado)* **bien ~** well-nourished; **mal ~** undernourished.

(b) *(fig)* *(grande)* large, considerable; *(numeroso)* numerous; *(abundante)* abundant; **~ de** full of, abounding in; **una nutrida concurrencia** a large attendance; **~s aplausos** loud applause; **fuego ~** *(Mil)* heavy fire.

nutriente NM nutrient.

nutrimento NM nutriment, nourishment.

nutrir [3a] VT **(a)** *(lit)* to feed, nourish. **(b)** *(fig)* to feed, strengthen; to support, foment, encourage.

nutritivo ADJ nourishing, nutritious; **valor ~** nutritional value, food value.

nylon [ni'lon, 'nailon] NM nylon.

Ñ, ñ ['eɲe] NF (*letra*) Ñ, ñ.
ña NF (*LAm*) = **doña, señora.**
ñaca-ñaca‡ NM rumpy-pumpy‡.
ñácara NF (*CAm*) ulcer, sore.
ñaco NM (*Méx*) popcorn.
ñafiar VT (*Carib*) to pilfer.
ñaka INTERJ quick as a flash.
ñam* INTERJ: ¡~, ~, ~! yum, yum!*
ñame NM yam.
ñandú NM (*Cono Sur*) rhea, South American ostrich.
ñandutí NM (*Cono Sur*) Paraguayan lace.
ñanga NF (a) (*CAm: pantano*) marsh, swampy ground. (b) (*And: trozo*) bit, small portion.
ñangada NF (*CAm*) (a) (*mordedura*) nip, bite. (b) ¡qué ~ hiciste!* that was a stupid thing to do!
ñangado ADJ (*Carib*) (*patizambo*) knock-kneed; (*estevado*) bow-legged.
ñangara NMF (*Carib Pol*) guerrilla.
ñango* ADJ (a) (*Cono Sur: patoso*) awkward, clumsy. (b) (*Cono Sur: de piernas cortas*) short-legged, waddling. (c) (*Méx: débil*) weak, feeble. (d) (*Carib*) = **ñangado.**
ñangotarse* [1a] VR (*And, Carib*) (a) (*agacharse*) to squat, crouch down. (b) (*desanimarse*) to lose heart.
ñangué: en los tiempos de ~ (*And**) way back, in the dim and distant past.
ñaña NF (a) (*Cono Sur*: hermana*) elder sister; (*Carib, Cono Sur*: nodriza*) nursemaid, wet-nurse. (b) (*CAm*‡) crap‡.
ñaño [1] ADJ (a) (*And, CAm, Cono Sur*) *amigo* close; (*And, CAm: mimado*) spoiled, pampered; **estar ~s** to be on very close terms. (b) (*Cono Sur: tonto*) silly. [2] NM (*And, CAm, Cono Sur: amigo*) close friend, chum; (*And, Cono Sur*: hermano*) elder brother; (*And: niño*) baby, child.
ñapa NF (*LAm*) extra, bonus; tip; **de ~** (*And, Carib*) as an extra, in addition.
ñapango NM (*And*) mulatto, mestizo, half-breed.
ñaque NM junk, worthless stuff; odds and ends.
ñata NF (a) (*LAm: nariz*) nose. (b) (*And: muerte*) death.
ñato [1] ADJ (a) (*LAm: de nariz*) flat-nosed, snub-nosed. (b) (*And: nasal*) nasal, twangy. (c) (*Cono Sur*) (*feo*) ugly; (*deforme*) bent, deformed. (d) (*CAm: afeminado*) effeminate. [2] NM (*Cono Sur**) chap*, guy*.
ñau EXCL (*LAm*) mew, miaow; **hacer ~ ~** (*lit*) to miaow; (*arañar*) to scratch.
ñauar [1a] VI (*LAm*) to miaow.
ñeque* [1] ADJ (*And, CAm, Cono Sur*) (*fuerte*) strong; (*vigoroso*) vigorous; (*listo*) clever, capable; (*CAm, Carib: valiente*) brave. [2] NM (a) (*LAm*) (*fuerza*) strength; (*vigor*) energy, vigour; (*valor*) courage. (b) (*CAm, Méx: golpe*) blow, punch.

(c) **~s** (*And*) fists.
ñique* NM (*CAm, Cono Sur: cabezazo*) butt with the head; (*CAm: puñetazo*) punch.
ñiquiñaque NM (a) (*trastos*) trash, junk, rubbish. (b) (*persona*) worthless individual.
ñisca NF (a) (*And, CAm, Cono Sur: pedazo*) bit, small piece. (b) (*And, CAm*‡: *excremento*) crap‡.
ñoca NF (*And*) crack, fissure.
ñoco [1] ADJ (*And, Carib*) (*sin dedo*) lacking a finger; (*sin mano*) one-handed. [2] NM (*Cono Sur: puñetazo*) straight punch.
ñola NF (a) (*And, CAm*‡: *excremento*) crap‡. (b) (*CAm*: úlcera*) ulcer, sore.
ñongarse [1h] VR (*And*) (a) (*agacharse*) to squat, crouch down. (b) **~ el pie** to twist one's foot.
ñongo ADJ (a) (*Carib, Cono Sur, Méx*: estúpido*) stupid; (*Cono Sur*) (*lento*) slow, lazy; (*perdido*) good-for-nothing; (*humilde*) creepy. (b) (*And, Carib: lisiado*) crippled. (c) (*Carib*) (*tramposo*) tricky, deceitful; (*feo*) unsightly; (*infausto*) of ill omen; (*quisquilloso*) touchy.
ñoñería NF, **ñoñez** NF (a) (*sosería*) insipidness; (*falta de carácter*) spinelessness; (*timidez*) shyness, bashfulness; (*melindrería*) fussiness. (b) (*Cono Sur: vejez*) senility; dotage. (c) (*Carib: estupidez*) inanity, stupid thing. (d) (*Carib*) (*nombre cariñoso*) endearment; (*halagos*) flattery.
ñoño [1] ADJ (a) (*soso*) characterless, insipid; (*insustancial*) insubstantial; *persona* spineless. (b) (*tímido*) shy, bashful. (c) (*quisquilloso*) fussy, finicky. (d) (*LAm*: viejo*) senile, decrepit. (e) (*And, Carib: vanidoso*) vain, that likes to be flattered. (f) (*Méx*: bruto*) thick*. [2] NM, **ñoña** NF spineless person, drip‡.
ñoqui NM (a) **~s** (*Culin*) gnocchi. (b) (*Cono Sur*: golpe*) thump.
ñoquis NMPL gnocchi.
ñorba NF (*And*), **ñorbo** NM (*And*) passionflower.
ñorda‡‡ NF turd‡‡, shit‡‡; ¡una ~! get away!*; **ser una ~** to be a shit‡‡.
ñu NM gnu, wildebeest.
ñuco ADJ (*And*) *animal* dehorned; (*) *persona* limbless.
ñudo: al ~ ADV (*LAm*) in vain; for nothing.
ñudoso ADJ = **nudoso.**
ñufla [1] NF (*Cono Sur*) piece of junk. [2] ADJ worthless.
ñuño* NF (*And*) wet-nurse.
ñusca‡‡ NF (*And*) crap‡‡.
ñusta NF (*And Hist*) princess of royal blood.
ñutir [3a] VI (*And*) to grunt.
ñuto* ADJ (*And*) crushed, ground.

O

O, o [o] NF (*letra*) O, o.

O (**a**) (*Geog*) ABR *de* **oeste** west, W. (**b**) ABR *de* **octubre** October, Oct.

o (*Com*) ABR *de* **orden** order, o.

o CONJ or; ~ ... ~ either ... or.

ó CONJ (*en números para evitar confusión*) or; **5 ó 6** 5 or 6.

OAA NF ABR *de* **Organización de las Naciones Unidas para la Alimentación y la Agricultura** Food and Agriculture Organization, FAO.

OACI NF ABR *de* **Organización de la Aviación Civil Internacional** International Civil Aviation Organization, ICAO.

oasis NM INVAR oasis.

obcecación NF blindness, blind obstinacy; mental blockage, disturbance; **en un momento de ~** when the balance of his (*etc*) mind was disturbed.

obcecadamente ADV blindly; stubbornly, obdurately; in a disturbed state.

obcecado ADJ (*ciego*) blind; mentally blinded; (*terco*) stubborn, obdurate; (*trastornado*) disturbed.

obcecamiento NM = **obcecación**.

obcecar [1g] VT to blind (mentally), disturb the mind of; **el amor le ha obcecado** love has blinded him (to all else).

obducción NF obduction.

obedecer [2d] VTI (**a**) (*gen*) to obey.
(**b**) **~ a** (*Med*) to yield to, respond to (treatment by).
(**c**) **~ a, ~ al hecho de que ...** to be due to ..., arise from ...; **su viaje obedece a dos motivos** his journey has two reasons.

obediencia NF obedience.

obediente ADJ obedient.

obelisco NM obelisk; (*Tip*) dagger.

obenques NMPL (*Náut*) shrouds.

oberol NM overalls.

obertura NF overture.

obesidad NF obesity.

obeso ADJ obese.

óbice NM obstacle, impediment; **eso no es ~ para que lo haga** that is not an obstacle to my doing it.

obispado NM bishopric.

obispo NM bishop.

óbito NM (*liter*) decease, demise.

obituario NM (*LAm*) (**a**) (*muerte*) decease, demise. (**b**) (*necrología*) obituary; (*sección de periódico*) obituary section.

objeción NF objection; **~ de conciencia** conscientious objection; **hacer objeciones** to raise objections; **no hacen ninguna ~** they make (o raise) no objection.

objetable ADJ objectionable, open to objection.

objetante NMF objector; (*en mitin*) heckler, protester.

objetar [1a] VTI (*gen*) to object; *objeción* to make, offer, raise; *argumento* to present, put forward; **le objeté que no había dinero para ello** I pointed out to him (o I protested to him) that there was no money for it.

objetivamente ADV objectively; clearly, obviously.

objetivar [1a] VT, **objetivizar** [1f] VT to objectify; to put in objective terms.

objetividad NF objectivity.

▼ **objetivo** 1 ADJ (**a**) (*no subjetivo*) objective. (**b**) (*claro*) clear, obvious.
▼ 2 NM (**a**) (*meta*) objective, aim, end. (**b**) (*Mil*) objective, target. (**c**) (*Fot*) lens; object lens; **~ zoom** zoom lens.

objeto NM (**a**) (*artículo*) object, thing; **~ de arte** objet d'art; **~ contundente** blunt instrument; **~s de escritorio** writing materials; **'~s perdidos'** (*letrero*) 'lost property'; **~ de recuerdo** souvenir; **~ sexual** sex object; **~s de tocador** toilet articles.
(**b**) (*meta*) object, aim, end, purpose; **al ~ de** + *infin*, **con ~ de** + *infin* with the object of + *ger*, with the aim of + *ger*; **esta carta tiene**

por **~** + *infin* this letter has the aim of + *ger*, this letter aims to + *infin*; **fue el ~ de un asalto** she was the target of an attack, she suffered an attack.
(**c**) (*tema etc*) theme, subject matter.
(**d**) (*Ling*) object.

objetor NM objector; **~ de conciencia** conscientious objector.

┌─ **OBJETOR DE CONCIENCIA** ─┐

i *The number of conscientious objectors to military service in Spain initially started to rise in the 1960's even though under the Francoist government of the time they could expect to be tried in a military court and to receive a long prison sentence. In the 1970's objectors tended to be assigned to non-fighting units like the medical corps and a law was finally passed in 1984 giving them legal status. In 1988 an alternative non-military programme (**Prestación Social Sustitutoria** or **PSS**) was developed allowing objectors to do social and community work. Events like Spain's membership of NATO in 1986 and the Gulf War in 1990 triggered a dramatic increase in the numbers of conscientious objectors.*

⇨ *See also* INSUMISO , PRESTACIÓN SOCIAL SUSTITUTORIA

oblación NF oblation, offering.

oblar [1a] VT (*Cono Sur*) *deuda* to pay in cash.

oblata NF oblation, offering.

oblea NF (**a**) (*Ecl y fig*) wafer; very thin slice; **quedar como una ~** to be as thin as a rake. (**b**) (*Cono Sur Correos*) stamp.

oblicuamente ADV obliquely.

oblicuar [1d] 1 VT to slant, place obliquely, cant, tilt.
2 VI to deviate from the perpendicular.

oblicuidad NF obliquity, oblique angle (o position *etc*).

oblicuo ADJ oblique; slanting; *mirada* sidelong.

obligación NF (**a**) (*gen*) obligation; duty; responsibility; **obligaciones** (*esp*) family responsibilities; **cumplir con una ~** to fulfil a duty; **faltar a sus obligaciones** to fail in one's duty, fail to carry out one's obligations; **tener ~ de** + *infin* to have a duty to + *infin*, be under an obligation to + *infin*; **primero es la ~ que la devoción** business before pleasure.
(**b**) (*Com, Fin*) bond; debenture; **obligaciones** bonds, securities; **~ de banco** bank bill; **~ convertible** convertible debenture; **~ tributaria** (*Méx*) tax liability.

obligacional ADJ compulsory; binding.

obligacionista NMF bondholder.

obligado ADJ obligatory, unavoidable.

▼ **obligar** [1h] 1 VT (**a**) (*gen*) to force, compel, oblige; **~ a uno a hacer algo** to force (o compel) sb to do sth; **verse obligado a** + *infin* to be obliged to + *infin*, find o.s. compelled to + *infin*; **estar** (o **quedar**) **obligado a uno** to be obliged to sb, be in sb's debt.
(**b**) *zapatos etc* to force, stretch; (*empujar*) to push; **el libro sólo entra allí obligándolo** the book goes in there but only with a hard push (o but only by forcing it).
2 **obligarse** VR to put o.s. under an obligation; **~ a** + *infin* to bind o.s. to + *infin*.

obligatoriamente ADV compulsorily; of necessity.

obligatoriedad NF obligatory nature; **de ~ jurídica** legally binding.

▼ **obligatorio** ADJ obligatory, compulsory; binding; **es ~** + *infin* it is obligatory to + *infin*; **escolaridad obligatoria** compulsory schooling, compulsory attendance at school.

obliteración NF (*Med*) obliteration.

obliterar [1a] VT (**a**) (*Med*) to obliterate. (**b**) (*LAm*) to obliterate, efface, destroy; (*Med*) *herida* to staunch.

oblongo ADJ oblong.

obnubilación NF = **ofuscación**.

obnubilado ADJ (*furioso*) furious, hopping mad; (*ofuscado*) flustered.

obnubilar [1a] VT = **ofuscar**.

➤ LENGUA Y USO: **objetivo: 2a** → 35.2 **obligar: 1a** → 37.1, 37.3 **obligatorio** → 37.1, 37.3

oboe [1] NM (*instrumento*) oboe.
[2] NMF (*persona*) oboist, oboe player.
oboísta NMF oboist.
óbolo NM (*fig*) mite, small contribution; ~ **de San Pedro** Peter's pence.
ob.ᵖᵒ. ABR *de* **obispo** Bishop, Bp.
obra NF (a) (*gen*) work; (*una* ~) piece of work; ~ **de arte** work of art; ~ **benéfica**, ~ **de misericordia**, ~ **piadosa** charity; **buenas ~s**, ~**s de caridad** good works; ~**s de carretera** roadworks; ~ **de construcción** building site; ~ **maestra** masterpiece; ~ **pía** religious foundation; ~**s públicas** public works; **Ministerio de O~s Públicas** Ministry of Works; **es ~ de benedictinos** it's a long job, it will take great patience; **es ~ de romanos** it's a huge task, it's a labour of Hercules; **¡manos a la ~!** to work!, let's get on with it!; **por ~ (y gracia) de** thanks to, thanks to the efforts of; **poner algo por ~** to put sth in hand; ~**s son amores que no buenas razones** actions speak louder than words.
(b) (*Arte*) work; (*Liter*) work, book; (*Teat*) play; ~ **de consulta** reference book, work of reference; ~ **de encargo** commission, commissioned work; ~ **literaria** literary work; ~ **de vulgarización** popular work; ~**s completas** complete works, collected works; **las ~s de Cervantes** the works of Cervantes.
(c) (*Teat*: ~ **dramática**, ~ **de teatro**) play.
(d) (*Mús*) work, opus, composition.
(e) (*Arquit*: *t* ~**s**) work; construction, building; (*LAm*: *solar, edificio en construcción*) building site; ~ **de hierro** ironwork; ~**s** (*frec*) repairs, alterations; '**cerrado por** ~**s**' 'closed for repairs (*o* alterations)'; **estamos en** ~**s** there are building repairs going on; we have the workmen in; **la autopista está en** ~**s entre A y B** there are roadworks on the motorway between A and B; **se han comenzado las** ~**s del nuevo embalse** work has been begun on the new dam.
(f) (*hechura*) workmanship, craftsmanship; handiwork; **la** ~ **es buena pero con malos materiales** the workmanship is good but the materials are bad.
(g) (*Cono Sur*) brickworks.
(h) ~ **de** about; **en** ~ **de 8 semanas** in about 8 weeks, in a matter of 8 weeks.
(i) (*Rel*) **la O~** (*Esp*) Opus Dei; *see also* OPUS DEI .
obradera* NF (*And, CAm euf*) diarrhoea.
obrador NM workroom, workshop.
obraje NM (a) (*And, Cono Sur*: *aserradero*) sawmill, timberyard. (b) (*Méx*: *carnicería*) butcher's (shop). (c) (*And*: *textil*) textile plant.
obrajero NM (a) (*capataz*) foreman, overseer. (b) (*Cono Sur*: *maderero*) lumberman. (c) (*And*: *artesano*) craftsman, skilled worker. (d) (*Méx*) pork butcher.
obrar [1a] [1] VT (a) *madera etc* to work.
(b) (*Med*) to work on, have an effect on.
(c) (*Cono Sur*: *construir*) to build.
(d) *milagro etc* to work, bring about.
[2] VI (a) (*actuar*) to act, behave; to proceed; ~ **de acuerdo con** to proceed in accordance with; ~ **con precaución** to act cautiously, proceed warily.
(b) (*medicina*) to work, have an effect.
(c) **su carta obra en mi poder** (*Com*) I have received your letter, your letter is to hand; **el expediente obra en manos del juez** (*Jur*) the file is in the judge's hands.
(d) (*) to relieve nature.
obr. cit. NF ABR *de* **obra citada** opere citato, op. cit.
obrerado NM work force.
obrerismo NM working-class movement.
obrero [1] ADJ *clase* working; *sindicato etc* labour (*atr*); **el movimiento** ~ the working-class movement.
[2] NM worker (*t Pol*), workman; man, hand; labourer; ~ **autónomo** self-employed worker; ~ **cualificado**, ~ **especializado** skilled worker; ~ **escenógrafo** stagehand; ~ **portuario** dock worker.
[3] **obrera** NF worker, woman worker.
obscenamente ADV obscenely.
obscenidad NF obscenity.
obsceno ADJ obscene.
obscu... *V* **oscu...**
obsecuente ADJ humble, obsequious.
obseder [2a] VT (*LAm*) to obsess.
obsequiar [1b] VT (a) (*gen*) to lavish attentions on, make a fuss of; **le obsequiaron con un reloj** they presented him with a clock, they gave him a clock; **le van a** ~ **con un banquete** (*Esp*) they are going to hold a dinner for him, they are going to honour him with a dinner.
(b) **le obsequiaron un reloj** (*LAm*) they presented him with a watch.
obsequio NM (a) (*regalo*) present, gift; (*de jubilación etc*) presentation; (*Com*) free gift; **ejemplar de** ~, ~ **del autor** complimentary copy, presentation copy.

(b) (*atenciones*) attention, kindness, courtesy; **en** ~ **de** in honour of; **hágame el** ~ **de** + *infin* please + *infin*.
obsequiosamente ADV obligingly, helpfully.
obsequioso ADJ (a) (*servicial*) obliging, helpful, attentive. (b) (*Méx*) fond of giving presents.
observable ADJ observable.
observación NF (a) (*acto*) observation; (*de ley etc*) observance; ~ **de aves** bird-watching; ~ **postal** interception of mail; ~ **telefónica** telephone tap; **estar en** ~ to be under observation.
(b) (*comentario*) observation, remark, comment; (*objeción*) objection; **hacer una** ~ to make a remark, comment, observe; **hacer una** ~ **a** (*objetar*) to raise an objection to.
observador [1] ADJ observant.
[2] NM, **observadora** NF observer; ~ **extranjero** foreign observer.
observancia NF observance.
observar [1a] VT (a) (*mirar*) to observe, watch; (*notar*) to see, notice, spot; (*Astron*) to observe; ~ **que ...** to observe that ..., notice that ...
(b) *ley etc* to observe, respect; to keep; *regla* to abide by, adhere to; ~ **buena conducta** (*And*) to behave o.s.
(c) ~ **algo a uno** (*LAm*) to point sth out to sb, draw sb's attention to sth.
(d) (*mostrar*) to show, give signs of; **el paciente observa una mejoría** the patient shows some improvement.
observatorio NM observatory.
obsesión NF obsession.
obsesionante ADJ haunting; obsessive.
obsesionar [1a] VT to obsess, haunt; **estar obsesionado con** (*o* **por**) **algo** to be obsessed by sth; to have sth on the brain.
obsesivo ADJ obsessive; obsessional.
obseso ADJ obsessed, haunted.
obsidiana NF obsidian.
obsolescencia NF obsolescence; ~ **incorporada** (*Com*) built-in obsolescence.
obsoleto ADJ obsolete.
obstaculización NF hindering, hampering.
obstaculizar [1f] VT to hinder, hamper, hold up; to prevent, stand in the way of.
obstáculo NM obstacle; hindrance; handicap, drawback; (*Mil, Dep etc*) obstacle; ~**s** (*carrera*) steeplechase; **no es** ~ **para que yo** + *subj* it is no obstacle to my + *ger*.
obstante: **no** ~ [1] ADV nevertheless, however; all the same.
[2] PREP in spite of.
obstar [1a] VI: ~ **a**, ~ **para** to hinder; to prevent; **eso no obsta para que lo haga** that is no obstacle to his doing it, that does not prevent him from doing it.
obstetra NMF obstetrician.
obstetricia NF obstetrics.
obstétrico [1] ADJ obstetric(al).
[2] NM, **obstétrica** NF obstetrician.
obstinación NF obstinacy, stubbornness.
obstinadamente ADV obstinately, stubbornly.
obstinado ADJ obstinate, stubborn.
obstinarse [1a] VR to be obstinate; to dig one's heels in; ~ **en** + *infin* to persist in + *ger*, continue obstinately to + *infin*.
obstrucción NF obstruction (*t Parl*).
obstruccionar [1a] VT (*LAm*) to obstruct.
obstruccionismo NM obstructionism.
obstruccionista [1] ADJ obstructionist, obstructive.
[2] NMF obstructionist.
obstructivismo NM obstructiveness.
obstructivo ADJ, **obstructor** ADJ obstructive.
obstruir [3g] VT (*gen*) to obstruct; (*bloquear*) to block; (*atascar*) to bung up, clog; (*estorbar*) to hinder, impede; (*dificultar*) to interfere with.
obtención NF obtaining, securing.
obtener [2k] VT to get, obtain, secure; *meta* to achieve.
obtenible ADJ obtainable, accessible; achievable.
obturación NF plugging, stopping; sealing off; filling; **velocidad de** ~ (*Fot*) shutter speed.
obturador NM plug, stopper; (*Mec*) choke; (*Fot*) shutter.
obturar [1a] VT to plug, stop (up); to seal off; *diente* to fill.
obtuso ADJ (a) *filo etc* blunt, dull. (b) (*Mat y fig*) obtuse.
obús NM (a) (*Mil*: *cañón*) howitzer; (*proyectil*) shell. (b) (*Aut*) core valve.
obvención NF bonus, perquisite.
obvencional ADJ bonus, extra; incidental.
obviamente ADV obviously.
obviar [1c] [1] VT (*evitar*) to obviate, remove.
[2] VI (*estorbar*) to stand in the way.
obviedad NF (a) (*gen*) obvious nature, obviousness. (b) (*una* ~) obvious remark (*etc*); **la respuesta parece ser una** ~ the reply seems to be an obvious one.
obvio ADJ obvious.

OC NF ABR *de* **onda corta** short wave, SW.

oca NF (a) goose; **¡es la ~!**: it's the tops!*. (b) (*And*) root vegetable.

ocasión NF (a) (*vez*) occasion, time; **con ~ de** on the occasion of; **en algunas ocasiones** sometimes; **en aquella ~** on that occasion, at that time, then; **venir en una mala ~** to come at a bad moment.
(b) (*oportunidad*) chance, opportunity, occasion; **aprovechar la ~** to take one's chance, seize one's opportunity; **dar a uno la ~ de** + *infin* to give sb a chance (*o* opportunity) to + *infin*; **a la ~ la pintan calva** it's an offer one can't refuse.
(c) (*motivo*) cause, motive; **no hay ~ para quejarse** there is no cause to complain.
(d) **de ~** (*Com*) secondhand; old, used; **librería de ~** secondhand bookshop.
(e) (*LAm: ganga*) bargain; **precio de ~** bargain price, reduced price.

ocasional ADJ (a) (*fortuito*) chance, accidental; incidental. (b) *composición etc* occasional. (c) *persona* part-time. (d) (*que ocurre a veces*) occasional.

ocasionalmente ADV by chance, accidentally; incidentally.

ocasionar [1a] VT to cause, produce, occasion.

ocaso NM (a) (*Astron*) sunset; (*de astro*) setting. (b) (*Geog*) west. (c) (*fig*) decline, end, fall.

occidental [1] ADJ western.
[2] NMF westerner.

occidentalidad NF (*Pol*) allegiance to the western bloc.

occidentalista ADJ (*Pol*) western; western bloc (*atr*).

occidentalizado ADJ westernized.

occidentalizar [1f] VT to westernize.

occidente NM west; **el O~** the West.

occipucio NM occiput.

occiso, -a NM/F murdered person, murder victim.

Occitania NF Occitania.

OCDE NF ABR *de* **Organización para la Cooperación y el Desarrollo Económico** Organization for Economic Cooperation and Development, OECD.

oceanario NM oceanarium.

Oceanía NF Oceania.

oceánico ADJ oceanic.

océano NM ocean; **O~ Atlántico** Atlantic Ocean; **O~ Glacial Ártico** Arctic Ocean; **O~ Índico** Indian Ocean; **O~ Pacífico** Pacific Ocean.

oceanografía NF oceanography.

oceanográfico ADJ oceanographic.

oceanógrafo, -a NM/F oceanographer.

ocelote NM ocelot.

ochar* [1a] (*Cono Sur*) [1] VT (a) *perro* to urge on, provoke to attack. (b) (*espiar*) to spy on.
[2] VI (*ladrar*) to bark.

ochavado ADJ eight-sided, octagonal.

ochavo NM († : *moneda*) ochavo; **no tener ni un ~*** to be broke*.

ochenta ADJ eighty; eightieth; **los (años) ~** the eighties.

ochentón [1] ADJ eighty-year-old, eightyish.
[2] NM, **ochentona** NF person of about eighty.

ocho [1] ADJ eight; (*fecha*) eighth; **las ~** eight o'clock. [2] NM (a) eight.
(b) (*Cos*) **~s** cable-stitch. (c) (*Dep*) eight.

ochocentista ADJ nineteenth-century (*atr*).

ochocientos ADJ eight hundred; **en el ~** in the eighteenth century.

ochote NM choir of eight voices.

OCI NF (*Venezuela, Perú: Pol*) ABR *de* **Oficina Central de Información.**

ocio NM (a) (*tiempo libre*) leisure, idleness; (*pey*) idleness; **~s, ratos de ~** leisure, spare time, free time; **entretener los ~s de uno** to occupy sb's spare time.
(b) **~s** (*pasatiempo*) pastime, diversion.

ociosamente ADV idly.

ociosear* [1a] VI (*Cono Sur*) to be at leisure; (*pey*) to idle, loaf about.

ociosidad NF idleness; **la ~ es madre de todos los vicios** the devil finds work for idle hands.

ocioso ADJ (a) (*inactivo*) idle; at leisure; inactive; **estar ~** to be idle.
(b) *acto, palabras etc* useless, pointless, idle; **dinero ~** money lying idle; **es ~ especular** it is idle to speculate.

oclusión NF (a) (*Ling etc*) occlusion; **~ glotal** glottal stop. (b) (*Met*) occluded front.

oclusiva NF (*Ling*) occlusive, plosive.

oclusivo ADJ (*Ling*) occlusive, plosive.

ocote NM (*CAm, Méx*) (*tea*) torch; (*Bot*) ocote pine; **echar ~** to make trouble.

ocozoal NM (*Méx*) rattlesnake.

-ocracia V Aspects of Word Formation in Spanish 2.

ocre NM ochre; **~ amarillo** yellow ochre; **~ rojo** red ochre.

OCSHA NF (*Rel*) ABR *de* **Obra de la Cooperación Sacerdotal Hispanoamericana.**

oct. NM ABR *de* **octubre** October, Oct.

octaedro NM octahedron.

octagonal ADJ octagonal.

octágono NM octagon.

octanaje NM octane number; **de alto ~** high-octane.

octano NM octane.

octava NF (*Mús, Poét*) octave.

octavilla NF pamphlet, leaflet.

octavín NM piccolo.

Octavio NM Octavian.

octavo [1] ADJ eighth.
[2] NM (a) eighth. (b) (*Tip*) **libro en ~** octavo. (c) **~s de final** (*Dep*) quarter-finals. (d) (‡: *droga*) small dose, small shot*.

octeto NM (*Mús*) octet(te); (*Inform*) byte.

octogenario [1] ADJ octogenarian, eighty-year-old.
[2] NM, **octogenaria** NF octogenarian, person in his (*o* her) eighties.

octogésimo ADJ eightieth.

octosílabo [1] ADJ octosyllabic.
[2] NM octosyllable.

octubre NM October.

OCU ['oku] NF (*Esp*) ABR *de* **Organización de Consumidores y Usuarios** ≃ Consumers' Association, CA.

ocular [1] ADJ ocular; eye (*atr*); **mediante examen ~** by visual inspection, with the eye; **testigo ~** eyewitness.
[2] NM eyepiece.

oculista NMF oculist.

ocultación NF, **ocultamiento** NM hiding, concealment.

ocultamente ADV secretly; mysteriously; stealthily.

ocultar [1a] [1] VT (*esconder*) to hide, conceal (*a, de* from); (*disfrazar*) to screen, mask.
[2] **ocultarse** VR to hide (o.s.); **~ a la vista** to keep out of sight; **~ con, ~ tras** to hide behind; **se me oculta la razón** I do not know the reason, the reason is a mystery to me; **no se me oculta que ...** I am fully aware that ...

ocultismo NM occultism.

ocultista NMF occultist.

oculto ADJ (a) (*escondido*) hidden, concealed; **permanecer ~** to stay hidden, remain in hiding.
(b) (*fig*) secret; mysterious; *ciencia* occult; *pensamiento* secret, inner; *motivo* ulterior.

ocupa* NMF squatter.

ocupable ADJ *persona* employable; **plaza ~** job/position available.

ocupación NF occupation; **fuerzas de ~** forces of occupation, occupying forces.

ocupacional ADJ occupational.

ocupado ADJ (a) *plaza etc* occupied, taken; **¿está ocupada la silla?** is that seat taken?
(b) **la línea está ocupada** (*Telec*) the line is engaged, the line is busy (*US*); **señal de ~** engaged tone, busy signal (*US*).
(c) *persona* (*atareado*) busy; **estoy muy ~** I'm very busy (*en* with).
(d) *persona* (*que tiene trabajo*) in work, working; **la población ocupada** the working population; **el porcentaje de ~s** the percentage of people in work.
(e) **estar ocupada** (*Esp: mujer*) to be pregnant.

ocupante NMF occupant; **~ de casa, ~ de vivienda** squatter.

▼ **ocupar** [1a] [1] VT (a) *espacio, silla etc* to occupy, fill, take up; *habitación* to occupy, live in, inhabit; *atmósfera* to fill, pervade; (*Mil*) *ciudad, país* to occupy; to take over, take control of.
(b) *puesto* to occupy, fill.
(c) *persona* to occupy, engage; to keep busy; *obreros* to employ, provide work for; **las obras ocupan más de 1000 hombres** the work keeps more than 1000 men busy, the work employs more than 1000 men.
(d) *tiempo* to occupy, fill up, take up; **ocupa sus ratos libres pintando** he uses his spare time to paint, he paints in his spare time.
(e) *confiscar* to seize, confiscate; **la policía le ocupó la navaja con que hirió a su mujer** the police impounded the razor with which he wounded his wife; **les ocuparon todo el contrabando** they seized all the contraband from them.
(f) (*Méx: emplear*) to use; **¿está ocupando la pluma?** are you using the pen?
▼[2] **ocuparse** VR: **~ con, ~ de, ~ en** to concern o.s. with; to pay attention to; to busy o.s. with; to take care of, look after; **los críticos no se ocuparon del libro** the critics paid no attention to the book, the critics did not take note of the book; **me ocuparé de ello mañana** I will deal with it tomorrow; I will look into it tomorrow; **en esta sección el autor se ocupa de los peces** in this section the author deals with fish; **conviene ~ de lo suyo** it's best to mind one's own business; **¡ocúpate de lo tuyo!*** mind your own business!

ocurrencia NF (a) (*suceso*) occurrence; incident, event.
(b) (*idea*) idea, bright idea; **me dio la ~ de** + *infin* it occurred to me to + *infin*, I had the idea of + *ger*; **¡qué ~!** (*iró*) what a bright idea.
(c) (*chiste*) witty remark, witticism.

ocurrente ADJ (*chistoso*) witty; (*listo*) bright, clever; (*gracioso*) entertaining, amusing.

ocurrido ADJ (a) lo ~ what has happened. (b) (*And: gracioso*) witty, funny.

▼ **ocurrir** [3a] **1** VI to happen, occur; **¿qué ocurre?** what's going on?; **por lo que pudiera ~** because of what might happen; **ocurre que ...** it (so) happens that ...; **lo que ocurre es que ...** the thing is ...

▼**2 ocurrirse** VR: **se le ocurre** + *infin* it occurs to him to + *infin*; **si se le ocurre huir** if he takes it into his head to escape; **se me ocurre que ...** it occurs to me that ...; **no se me ocurriría nunca** I wouldn't dream of it; **nunca se me había ocurrido** it had never crossed my mind.

oda NF ode.

odalisca NF odalisque.

ODECA [o'ðeka] NF ABR *de* **Organización de los Estados Centroamericanos**.

ODEPA [o'ðepa] NF ABR *de* **Organización Deportiva Panamericana**.

odiar [1b] VT (a) to hate. (b) (*Cono Sur*) (*fastidiar*) to irk, annoy; (*aburrir*) to bore.

odio NM (a) (*gen*) hatred; (*rencor*) ill will; (*antipatía*) dislike; ~ **de clases** class hatred; ~ **de sangre** feud, vendetta; **almacenar ~** to store up hatred; **tener ~ a** to hate.
(b) (*Cono Sur*) (*molestia*) annoyance, bother; (*tedio*) boredom, tedium.

odiosear* [1a] VT (*And, Cono Sur*) to pester, annoy.

odiosidad NF (*V adj*) (a) odiousness, hatefulness; nastiness. (b) (*And, Carib, Cono Sur*) irksomeness, annoyance.

odioso ADJ (a) (*gen*) odious, hateful, detestable; nasty, unpleasant; **hacerse ~ a uno** to incur sb's dislike.
(b) (*And, Cono Sur*) (*molesto*) irksome, annoying; (*presumido*) stuck-up*, snobbish.

Odisea NF Odyssey; **o~** odyssey.

odisea NF (*fig*) odyssey, epic journey.

Odiseo NM Odysseus.

odómetro NM milometer.

odontología NF dentistry, dental surgery, odontology.

odontólogo, -a NM/F dentist, dental surgeon, odontologist.

odorífero ADJ, **odorífico** ADJ sweet-smelling, odoriferous.

odre NM (a) (*liter*) wineskin. (b) (*: borracho*) toper, old soak*.

OEA NF ABR *de* **Organización de Estados Americanos** Organization of American States, OAS.

OECE NF ABR *de* **Organización Europea de Cooperación Económica** Organization for European Economic Cooperation, OEEC.

OELA NF ABR *de* **Organización de Estados Latinoamericanos**.

oeste **1** ADJ *parte* west, western; *dirección* westerly; *viento* west, westerly.
2 NM (a) (*región*) west; **en la parte del ~** in the western part; **al ~ de Bilbao** to the west of Bilbao, on the west side of Bilbao; **eso cae más hacia el ~** that lies further (to the) west; **una película del O~** a western, a film of the Wild West.
(b) (*viento*) west wind.

Ofelia NF Ophelia.

ofender [2a] **1** VT (a) (*gen*) to offend; (*insultar*) to slight, insult; (*hacer injusticia a*) to wrong; **por temor a ~le** for fear of offending him.
(b) *sentido* to offend, be offensive to; ~ **a la vista** to offend one's sight.
(c) (*Méx*) *mujer* to touch up*, feel*.
2 ofenderse VR to take offence (*de, por* at).

ofendido ADJ offended; **darse por ~** to take offence.

ofensa NF offence; slight; wrong.

ofensiva NF offensive; ~ **de paz** peace offensive; **tomar la ~** to take the offensive.

ofensivamente ADV (*Dep*) in attack.

ofensivo ADJ (a) (*Mil*) offensive. (b) (*gen*) offensive; (*grosero*) rude, insulting; (*asqueroso*) nasty, disgusting.

ofensor **1** ADJ offending.
2 NM, **ofensora** NF offender.

oferta NF (a) (*gen*) offer; (*propuesta*) proposal, proposition.
(b) (*Com*) offer; (*para contrato*) tender; (*en subasta*) bid; (*ganga*) special offer; ~ **cerrada** sealed bid; ~ **condicional** conditional offer; ~ **y demanda** supply and demand; ~ **monetaria** money supply; ~ **pública de adquisición (de acciones)** takeover bid; ~ **pública de venta (de acciones)** share offer; **la ~ es superior a la demanda** (the) supply exceeds (the) demand; **estar en** (o **de**) ~ to be on offer.
(c) (*regalo*) gift, present.

ofertante NMF (*Com*) bidder.

ofertar [1a] VT (a) *suma de dinero, producto* to offer. (b) (*Com*) to tender; to bid. (c) (*ofrecer barato*) to sell on special offer; to offer cheap, sell cheaply.

ofertorio NM offertory.

off [of] NM: **voz en ~** voice off; **ruido en ~** background noise; **pasa algo en ~** (*Cine*) something happens off-screen; **hay una discusión en ~** there is an argument offstage, there is an argument spoken by unseen actors; **poner un aparato en ~** to switch a machine off.

office ['ofis] NM (*Esp*) (*despensa*) pantry; (*trascocina*) scullery; utility room; (*cocina pequeña*) kitchenette; (*Aer*) galley.

offset ['ofset] NM (*Tip*) offset.

offside [of'sai] NM (*Dep*) offside; **¡~!** offside!; **estar en ~** to be offside; (*) to be out of touch, be out of date; to be daydreaming.

oficial **1** ADJ official.
2 NMF official, officer; (*Mil*) officer; (*Téc*) skilled workman; (*artesano*) craftsman; journeyman; (*de oficina*) clerk; **primer ~** (*Náut*) first officer, first mate; ~ **del día** orderly officer; ~ **ejecutivo** executive officer; ~ **de enlace** liaison officer; ~ **de guardia** (*Náut*) officer of the watch; ~ **mayor** chief clerk; ~ **médico** medical officer; ~ **pagador** paymaster.

oficiala NF skilled woman worker; clerk.

oficialada NF (*Cono Sur, Méx*) = **oficialidad**.

oficialidad NF (*Mil*) officers (*collectively*).

oficialismo NM government party; pro-government political forces; (*LAm*) government, authorities.

oficialista **1** ADJ governmental; of the party in power.
2 NMF member (o supporter) of the governing party; (*LAm*) governmental.

oficializar [1f] VT to make official, give official status to.

oficialmente ADV officially.

oficiante NM (*Ecl*) officiant, celebrant.

oficiar [1b] **1** VT (a) (*informar*) to inform officially. (b) *misa* to celebrate; *funeral etc* to conduct, officiate at.
2 VI (a) (*Ecl*) to officiate. (b) ~ **de** to officiate as, act as.

oficina NF office; (*Farm*) laboratory; (*Téc*) workshop; (*Cono Sur*) nitrate works; **horas de ~** business hours, office hours; ~ **de colocación,** ~ **de empleo** job centre, labour exchange, employment agency; ~ **de información** information bureau; ~ **meteorológica** weather bureau; ~ **paisaje** open-plan office; ~ **de objetos perdidos** lost property office, lost-and-found department (*US*); ~ **de prensa** press office.

oficinesco ADJ office (*atr*); clerical, white-collar (*atr*); (*pey*) bureaucratic.

oficinista NMF office worker, clerk; white-collar worker.

oficio NM (a) (*profesión*) job, profession, occupation; (*Téc*) craft, trade; **es del ~** (*experto*) he's an old hand; (*: prostituta*) she's on the game*; **un profesional con mucho ~** a seasoned professional; **sabe su ~** he knows his job; **aprender un ~** to learn a trade; **mi ~ es enseñar** my job is to teach; my profession is teaching; **tiene mucho ~** he is very experienced; **no tener ni ~ ni beneficio** to be out of work, be idle.
(b) (*puesto*) job, role, post; office; (*Mec etc*) function; **los deberes del ~** the duties of the post; **el ~ de esta pieza es de ...** the function (o job) of this part is to ...
(c) **buenos ~s** good offices; **ofrecer sus buenos ~s** to offer one's good offices.
(d) **Santo O~** (*Hist*) Holy Office, Inquisition.
(e) (*comunicado*) official letter.
(f) (*Ecl*) service; mass (*t* ~s PL); ~ **de difuntos** office for the dead, funeral service; ~ **divino** (divine) office.
(g) (*Arquit*) scullery.
(h) **de ~: 4 matones de ~** 4 professional thugs, 4 hired toughs*; **fue enterrado de ~** he was buried at the State's expense; **le informaremos de ~** we will inform you officially.

oficiosamente ADV (*V adj*) (a) semiofficially; informally. (b) helpfully. (c) (*pey*) officiously.

oficiosidad NF (a) (*amabilidad*) helpfulness. (b) (*pey*) officiousness, meddlesomeness.

oficioso ADJ (a) (*no oficial*) semiofficial; unofficial, informal; **de fuente oficiosa** from a semiofficial source.
(b) (*amable*) kind, helpful, obliging.
(c) (*pey*) officious, meddlesome, interfering.
(d) *V* **mentira**.

-ófilo SUFIJO: *V p.ej.* **anglófilo**.

ofimática NF office automation, office computerization (o computing).

ofimático ADJ: **sistema ~** office computer system; **gestión ofimática integrada** integrated computer system for office management.

Ofines [o'fines] NF ABR *de* **Oficina Internacional de Información y Observación del Español**.

-ófobo SUFIJO: *V p.ej.* **anglófobo**.

-ófono SUFIJO: *V p.ej.* **anglófono**.

▼ **ofrecer** [2d] **1** VT (*gen, t Com*) to offer; (*presentar*) to present; *gracias* to give, offer; *respetos* to pay; *bienvenida* to extend; **'ofrecen trabajo'** 'situations vacant'; ~ **a uno hacer algo** to offer to do sth for sb; **me ha ofrecido no fumar más** he has promised me that he won't smoke any more.
2 ofrecerse VR (a) (*persona*) to offer o.s., volunteer; ~ **a** + *infin* to offer to + *infin*, volunteer to + *infin*; **me ofrezco de guía** I offer myself as a guide.
(b) (*oportunidad, vista etc*) to offer itself, present itself.

➤ LENGUA Y USO: **ocurrir: 2 → 28.1, 28.2** | **ofrecer: 1 → 30**

(c) (*suceder*) to occur; **¿qué se ofrece?** what's going on?, what's happening?; **se me ofrece una duda** a doubt occurs to me.

(d) **¿se le ofrece algo?** do you want anything?; is there anything I can get you?; **no se me ofrece nada por ahora** I don't want anything for the moment.

ofrecimiento NM offer, offering; **~ de paz** peace offer.

ofrenda NF offering, gift; (*Ecl*) offering; (*fig*) tribute.

ofrendar [1a] VT to offer, give as an offering.

oftalmía NF ophthalmia.

oftálmico ADJ ophthalmic.

oftalmología NF ophthalmology.

oftalmólogo, -a NM/F ophthalmologist.

ofuscación NF, **ofuscamiento** NM (*fig*) dazzled state; blindness; bewilderment, confusion, mystification.

ofuscar [1g] VT **(a)** (*luz*) to dazzle.

(b) (*fig*) (*deslumbrar*) to dazzle; (*confundir*) to bewilder, confuse, mystify.

(c) (*fig: cegar*) to blind; **estar ofuscado por la cólera** to be blinded by anger.

Ogino, ogino NM: **método ~** rhythm method (of birth-control).

ogro NM ogre.

oh INTERJ oh!

ohmio NM ohm.

oíble ADJ audible.

OIC NF **(a)** (*Com*) ABR de **Organización Internacional del Comercio**. **(b)** (*Com*) ABR de **Organización Interamericana del Café**.

OICE [o'ise] NF ABR de **Organización Interamericana de Cooperación Económica**.

OICI [o'isi] NF ABR de **Organización Interamericana de Cooperación Intermunicipal** Inter-American Municipal Organization, IAMO.

OID NF ABR de **Oficina de Información Diplomática**.

oída NF hearing; **de ~s, por ~s** by hearsay.

-oide V Aspects of Word Formation in Spanish 2.

oído NM **(a)** (*sentido*) (sense of) hearing; **duro de ~, mal del ~** hard of hearing.

(b) (*Anat*) ear; **~ interno** inner ear; **¡~ a la caja!, ¡~ al parche!** pay attention!; **aguzar los ~s** to prick up one's ears; **aplicar el ~** to listen carefully; **dar ~s a** to listen to, give ear to; **apenas pude dar crédito a mis ~s** I could scarcely believe my ears; **decir algo al ~ de uno** to whisper sth to sb, whisper sth in sb's ear; **entra por un ~ y sale por otro** it goes in one ear and out (of) the other; **hacer ~s a** to pay attention to, take heed of; **hacer ~s sordos a** to turn a deaf ear to; **es una canción que se pega al ~** it's a catchy song; **prestar ~(s) a** to give ear to; **ser todo ~s** to be all ears; **le estarán zumbando los ~s** his ears must be burning.

(c) (*Mús*) ear; **~ by ear**; **tener (buen) ~** to have a good ear.

oidor NM (*Hist*) judge.

OIEA NF o NM ABR de **Organización** (u **Organismo**) **Internacional de Energía Atómica** International Atomic Energy Agency, IAEA.

oigo etc V **oír**.

OIN NF ABR de **Organización Internacional de Normalización** International Standards Organization, ISO.

OIP [o'ip] NF **(a)** ABR de **Organización Internacional de Periodistas. (b)** (*Aer*) ABR de **Organización Iberoamericana de Pilotos.**

OIR [o'ir] NF **(a)** ABR de **Organización Internacional para los Refugiados** International Refugee Organization, IRO. **(b)** ABR de **Organización Internacional de Radiodifusión.**

oír [3p] **1** VTI **(a)** (*gen*) to hear; to listen (to); *confesión* to hear; *misa* to go to, attend, hear; *consejo* to hear, pay attention to, heed; **~ decir que ...** to hear it said that ...; **~ hablar de to** hear about, hear of; **~ de** (*LAm*) to hear from; **le oí abrir la puerta** I heard him open (o opening) the door; **como lo oyes, lo que oyes** it really is so, just like I'm telling you; **lo oyó como quien oye llover** she paid no attention, she turned a deaf ear to it.

(b) (INTERJ *etc*) **¡oye!, ¡oiga!** listen!, listen to this!; (*llamando atención*) hi!, hey!; I say!; (*protesta*) now look here!; (*sorpresa*) I say!, say! (US); (*con permiso*) excuse me!; (*en tienda*) shop!; (*Telec*) **¡oiga!** hullo?

(c) *súplica* to hear, heed, answer; **Dios oyó mi ruego** God answered my prayer; **¡Dios te oiga!** I just hope you're right!

(d) (*Jur*) *causa* to hear.

2 **oírse** VR: **le gusta ~** he likes the sound of his own voice.

OIT NF ABR de **Oficina** (u **Organización**) **Internacional del Trabajo** International Labour Organization, ILO.

ojada NF (*And*) skylight.

ojal NM buttonhole.

▼ **ojalá** **1** INTERJ (*empleado sólo*) if only it were so!, if only it would! (*etc*); let's hope so!, I do hope you're right!; no such luck!, some hope!; '**mañana puede que haga sol**' ... '**¡~!**' 'it may be fine tomorrow' ... 'I hope it will be!', (*pesimista*) 'some hope!'.

▼ **2** CONJ (*t ~ que*) **(a)** (*gen*) I wish ...!, if only ...!, (*en tono retórico*) would that ...!; **¡~ venga pronto!** I hope he comes soon!, I wish he'd come!; **¡~ pudiera!** I wish I could!, if only I could!

(b) (*LAm*) even though; **no lo haré, ~ me maten** I won't do it even if they kill me.

ojazos NMPL big eyes, wide eyes; (*atractivos*) lovely big eyes; **echar los ~ a uno** to make eyes at sb.

OJD NF ABR de **Oficina de Justificación de la Difusión** office which keeps statistics of newspaper circulations.

OJE ['oxe] NF (†) ABR de **Organización Juvenil Española**.

ojeada NF glance; **echar una ~ a** to glance at, take a quick look at.

ojeador NM (*Caza*) beater; (*Dep etc*) talent scout, talent spotter.

ojear¹ [1a] VT (*mirar*) to eye; to stare at; **voy a ~ cómo va el trabajo** I'm going to see how the work is getting on.

ojear² [1a] VT **(a)** (*ahuyentar*) to drive away, drive off, shoo. **(b)** (*Caza*) to beat, put up, drive. **(c)** (*Cono Sur: hechizar*) to put the evil eye on.

ojén NM anisette.

ojeo NM (*Caza*) beating.

ojera NF **(a)** (*sombra*) ring under the eye; **tener ~s** to have rings (o circles) under the eyes. **(b)** (*Med*) eyebath.

ojeriza NF spite, ill will; **tener ~ a** to have a grudge against, have it in for∗.

ojeroso ADJ with rings under the eyes; tired, haggard.

ojete NM **(a)** (*Cos*) eyelet. **(b)** (*LAm∗∗*) arsehole∗∗.

ojiabierto ADJ wide-eyed.

ojillos NMPL bright eyes; lovely eyes; roguish eyes; **¡tiene unos ~!** you should see what eyes she's got!

ojímetro NM: **a ~** roughly, at a rough guess.

ojinegro ADJ black-eyed.

ojituerto ADJ cross-eyed.

ojiva NF (*Arquit*) ogive, pointed arch; (*Mil*) warhead.

ojival ADJ ogival, pointed.

ojo NM **(a)** (*Anat*) eye; **~s de almendra** almond eyes; **~ de cristal** glass eye; **~ a la funerala, ~ amoratado, ~ a la pava, ~ a la virulé, ~ morado** black eye; **~ del huracán** eye of the hurricane; **~ mágico** magic eye, photocell; **~ de pez** (*Fot*) wide-angle lens; **~s saltones** bulging eyes, goggle eyes; **~s que hablan** expressive eyes; **a los ~s de** in the eyes of; **a ~** (*de buen cubero*) by guesswork; roughly, at a rough guess; **a ~s cerrados** blindly; on trust; **dependiente a ~s cerrados en** blindly dependent on; **a ~ vistas** publicly, openly; *crecer etc* before one's (very) eyes; *suceder etc* right under one's nose; *disminuir* visibly; **con buenos ~s** kindly, favourably; **delante de mis propios ~s** before my very eyes; **estar hasta los ~s de trabajo** to be up to one's eyes in work; **~ por ~** an eye for an eye; tit for tat; **abrir el ~, abrir los ~s** to keep one's eyes open; to be careful; **abrir los ~s a uno** to open sb's eyes to sth; **en un abrir y cerrar de ~s** in the twinkling of an eye; **avivar el ~** to be on the alert; **cerrar los ~s a algo** to shut one's eyes to sth; **clavar los ~s en** to fix one's eyes on, stare at; **costar un ~ de la cara** to cost a small fortune; **dar en los ~s** to be conspicuous; to be self-evident; **dejar a uno con los ~s fuera de órbita** to make sb's eyes pop; **echar el ~ a** to have one's eye on, covet; **guiñar el ~** to wink (*a* at); to turn a blind eye (*a* on); **hacer del ~** to wink; **se le fueron los ~s tras la chica** he couldn't keep his eyes off the girl; **pasar los ~s por algo** to look sth over; **no pegué ~ en toda la noche** I didn't get a wink of sleep all night; **poner ~s** (u **ojitos**) **a una joven** to look longingly at a girl; **en mi vida le puse los ~s encima** I never set eyes on him in my life; **recrear los ~s en** to feast one's eyes on; **salir de ~** to be obvious, leap to the eye; **saltar a los ~s** to be blindingly obvious; **ser el ~ derecho de uno** to be the apple of sb's eye; **ser todo ~s** to be all eyes; **¡no es nada lo del ~!** there's a lot more to it than that!; there's more to it than meets the eye; **tener ~ clínico** to have good intuition; **tener a uno entre ~s** to loathe sb; **tener los ~s puestos en** (*fig*) to have set one's heart on; **torcer los ~s** to squint; **ver con malos ~s** to look unfavourably upon; **~s que no ven, corazón que no siente** out of sight, out of mind; V **alerta, avizor, besugo, blanco** etc.

(b) (*de aguja etc*) eye; (*en queso etc*) hole; **~ de la llave** keyhole.

(c) (*de puente*) span; space underneath the span; **un puente de 4 ~s** a bridge with 4 arches (o spans).

(d) **~ de agua** (*LAm*) spring.

(e) **~ del culo∗** arse∗∗.

(f) (*Arquit*) **~ de buey** bull's-eye window, (*Náut*) port-hole.

(g) **~ de gallo, ~ de pollo** (*LAm*) corn, callus; **~ de pescado** (*Carib*) callus (on the hand).

(h) (*fig*) (*perspicacia*) perspicacity; (*juicio*) judgement; (*agudeza*) sharpness; **tener ~ para conocer algo** to have the perspicacity to recognize sth.

(i) (*fig: cuidado*) care, caution; **¡~!** careful!, look out!; (*nota marginal*) N.B.; **hay que tener mucho ~ con los carteristas** one must be very careful of pickpockets, one must beware of pickpockets; **~ con creer que ...** let us beware of thinking that ...

ojón ADJ (*LAm*) big-eyed, having big eyes.

ojota NF **(a)** (*LAm: sandalia*) sandal. **(b)** (*And, Cono Sur: piel de llama*) tanned llama leather.

ojotes* NMPL (*And, CAm*) (*pey*) bulging eyes, goggle eyes; (*bellos*) lovely big eyes.

ojuelos NMPL = **ojillos**.

okapi NM okapi.

okupa* NMF squatter.

OL NF ABR *de* **onda larga** long wage, LW.

ola NF wave (*t fig*); **~ de calor** heat wave; **~ delictiva** crime wave; **~ de frío** cold wave; **~ de marea**, **~ sísmica** tidal wave; **la ~** (*Ftbl*) the Mexican wave; **la nueva ~** the latest fashion, the current trend, the most modern style; (*personas*) the new generation; (*Cine*) the new wave, the Nouvelle Vague; **batir las ~s** (*fig*) to ply the seas; **hacer ~s** to make waves; to rock the boat.

OLADE [o'laðe] NF ABR *de* **Organización Latinoamericana de Energía**.

OLAVU [o'laßu] NF ABR *de* **Organización Latinoamericana del Vino y de la Uva**.

olé INTERJ bravo!; well done!, jolly good!*; **¡y ~ morena!*** wow!*

oleada NF **(a)** (*Náut*) big wave; surge, swell.
(b) (*fig*) wave; surge; **una gran ~ de gente** a great surge of people; **la primera ~ del ataque** the first wave of the attack; **esta última ~ de huelgas** this latest wave of strikes.
(c) (*Méx*) run of luck.

oleaginosa NF oil product.

oleaginoso ADJ oily, oleaginous.

oleaje NM swell, surge; surf.

olear[1] [1a] VI to wave, flutter.

olear[2] [1a] VT to shout 'olé' to, cheer, encourage.

oleícola ADJ oil (*atr*); olive-oil (*atr*).

oleicultor(a) NM/F olive-grower.

oleicultura NF olive-growing.

oleo... PREF oleo...

óleo NM **(a)** (*Ecl*) oil; (*Arte*) oil; **santo(s) ~(s)** holy oil(s); **pintar al ~** to paint in oils. **(b)** (*Arte: cuadro*) oil painting. **(c)** (*LAm: fig*) baptism.

oleoducto NM (oil) pipeline.

oleoso ADJ oily.

oler [2i] [1] VT **(a)** (*gen*) to smell; (‡) **cocaína** to snort‡.
(b) (*fig: inquirir*) to pry into, poke one's nose into.
(c) (*fig: descubrir*) to smell out, sniff out, uncover.
[2] VI (*t fig*) to smell (*a of, like*); **huele mal** it smells bad.

oletear [1a] VT (*And*) to pry into.

oletón ADJ (*And*) prying.

olfa* NMF (*Cono Sur*) (*lameculos*) creep‡, bootlicker*; (*admirador*) admirer, follower.

olfacción NF smelling.

olfatear [1a] VT **(a)** (*gen*) to smell, sniff (*t fig*); (*perro*) to smell out, scent out, nose out (*t fig*).
(b) (*fig*) to pry into, poke one's nose into.

olfativo ADJ olfactory.

olfato NM **(a)** (sense of) smell. **(b)** (*fig*) good nose; instinct, intuition.

olfatorio ADJ olfactory.

oliente ADJ: **bien ~** sweet-smelling; **mal ~** foul-smelling.

oligarca NMF oligarch.

oligarquía NF oligarchy.

oligárquico ADJ oligarchic(al).

oligo... PREF oligo...

oligoelemento NM trace element.

oligofrénico [1] ADJ mentally retarded.
[2] NM, **oligofrénica** NF mentally retarded person.

oligopolio NM oligopoly.

oligopolístico ADJ oligopolistic.

oligopsonio NM oligopsony.

olimpiada NF, **olimpíada** NF Olympiad; **las O~s** the Olympics; **O~ de Invierno** Winter Olympics.

olímpicamente* ADV (*Esp*) totally, completely; **paso ~** I couldn't care less; **pasó de nosotros ~** he completely ignored us.

olímpico [1] ADJ Olympian; *juegos* Olympic.
[2] NM, **olímpica** NF Olympic athlete.

olimpismo NM Olympic movement; Olympic Games.

Olimpo NM Olympus.

oliscar [1g] [1] VT **(a)** (*gen*) to smell, sniff (gently). **(b)** (*fig*) to investigate, look into.
[2] VI to smell (bad).

olisco ADJ (*Cono Sur*), **oliscón** ADJ (*And*), **oliscoso** ADJ (*And, Carib*) smelly.

olisquear [1a] = **oliscar**.

oliva [1] NF **(a)** (*aceituna*) olive; (*árbol*) olive tree. **(b)** (*Orn*) = **lechuza**.
[2] ADJ INVAR olive.

oliváceo ADJ olive, olive-green.

olivar NM olive grove.

olivarero [1] ADJ olive (*atr*).
[2] NM, **olivarera** NF olive-producer, olive-oil producer.

Oliverio NM Oliver.

olivero ADJ olive (*atr*), olive-growing (*atr*); **región olivera** olive-growing region.

olivicultor(a) NM/F olive grower.

olivicultura NF olive growing.

olivo NM olive tree; **tomar el ~‡** to beat it*.

olla NF **(a)** (*recipiente*) pot, pan; (*para hervir agua*) kettle; **~ eléctrica** electric kettle; **~ exprés**, **~ de** (*o* **a**) **presión** pressure cooker; **se me va la ~*** I lose the thread.
(b) (*Culin*) stew; **~ podrida** Spanish stew; (*fig*) hotchpotch.
(c) (*de río*) pool; eddy, whirlpool.
(d) (*Alpinismo*) chimney.
(e) **~ común** soup-kitchen (*t* **~ popular**); (*Cono Sur*) canteen.

ollar NM (horse's) nose; **~es** (horse's) nostrils.

ollero, -a NM/F maker of (*o* dealer in) pots and pans.

olmeca [1] ADJ Olmec.
[2] NMF Olmec; **los ~s** the Olmecs.

olmeda NF, **olmedo** NM elm grove.

olmo NM elm, elm tree; **~ campestre** common elm; **~ de montaña** wych-elm.

ológrafo ADJ, NM holograph.

olor NM **(a)** (*gen*) smell; (*aroma*) odour, scent; **buen ~** nice smell, pleasant smell; **mal ~** bad smell, nasty smell, stink; **tiene mal ~** it smells bad; **~ corporal** body odour; **~ de santidad** odour of sanctity.
(b) (*fig*) smell; suspicion; **acudir al ~ del dinero** to come to where the money is, get wind of the money.
(c) **~es** (*Cono Sur, Méx Culin*) spices.

olorcillo NM faint smell; delicate aroma; (*fig, pey*) whiff (a *of*).

oloroso [1] ADJ sweet-smelling, scented, fragrant.
[2] NM oloroso (sherry).

olote NM (*CAm, Méx*) **(a)** (*Agr*) corncob; maize stalk. **(b)** **un ~** (*fig*) a nobody, a nonentity.

olotear [1a] VI (*CAm, Méx*) to gather (*o* harvest) maize (*o* corn: *US*).

olotera NF (*CAm, Méx*) **(a)** (*montón*) heap of corncobs. **(b)** (*máquina*) maize thresher.

OLP NF ABR *de* **Organización para la Liberación de Palestina** Palestine Liberation Organization, PLO.

olvidadizo ADJ forgetful; absent-minded.

olvidado ADJ **(a)** (*gen*) forgotten.
(b) *persona* forgetful; **~ de** forgetful of, oblivious to.
(c) (*fig: ingrato*) ungrateful.
(d) (*And, Cono Sur*) = **olvidadizo**.

olvidar [1a] [1] VT to forget; to leave behind; **¡olvídame!*** get lost!‡; **~ hacer algo** to forget to do sth.
[2] **olvidarse** VR **(a)** **se me olvidó** I forgot; **se me olvidó el paraguas** I forgot my umbrella; **se me olvida la fecha** I forget the date, the date escapes me, I can't think of the date; **~ de hacer algo** to forget to do sth, neglect to do sth.
(b) (*fig*) to be forgetful of self; (*pey*) to forget o.s.

OLVIDAR	**ver también la entrada**

Si se *nos olvida un objeto* en algún lugar, *olvidar* se puede traducir por *forget*, *leave* o *leave behind*:
- Por regla general, si no mencionamos el lugar donde se nos ha olvidado, *olvidar* se traduce por *forget* o *leave behind*:
  He olvidado la cartera
  I have forgotten my wallet ◊ *I have left my wallet behind*
  No olvides el pasaporte
  Don't forget your passport ◊ *Don't leave your passport behind*
- Si mencionamos el lugar donde se nos ha olvidado, *olvidar* se suele traducir por *leave*:
  He olvidado la cartera en el restaurante
  I have left my wallet in the restaurant
  Para otros usos y ejemplos ver la entrada.

---

olvido NM **(a)** (*estado*) oblivion; **caer en el ~** to fall into oblivion; **echar al ~** to forget; **enterrar** (*o* **hundir**) **en el ~** to forget (deliberately), cast into oblivion; **rescatar del ~** to save from oblivion.
(b) (*cualidad*) forgetfulness; (*acto*) omission, oversight; slip; **ha sido por ~** it was an oversight.

olvidón ADJ (*And*) forgetful.

OM (a) (*Pol*) NF ABR *de* **Orden Ministerial** ministerial decree. **(b)** (*Rad*) NF ABR *de* **onda media** medium wave, MW. **(c)** (*Geog*) NM ABR *de* **Oriente Medio** Middle East.

Omán NM Oman.

ombligo NM navel; **arrugársele el ~ a uno***, **encogérsele el ~ a uno*** to get the wind up*, get cold feet; **meter a uno el ~ para dentro*** to put the wind up sb*; **mirarse el ~** to contemplate one's navel.

ombliguera NF (*And*) striptease artiste.

ombú NM (*Argentina*) ombú (tree).

ombudsman NM ombudsman.

OMC NF ABR *de* **Organización Mundial del Comercio** World Trade Organization, WTO.

omega NF omega.
OMI NF ABR de **Organización Marítima Internacional** International Maritime Organization, IMO.
OMIC NF ABR de **Oficina Municipal de Información al Consumidor**.
ominoso ADJ **(a)** (*pasmoso*) awful, dreadful. **(b)** (*de mal agüero*) ominous.
omisión NF **(a)** (*gen*) omission; oversight; **~ de auxilio** (*Jur*) failure to give assistance, failure to go to somebody's aid; **su ~ de** + *infin* his failure to + *infin*, the fact that he omits to + *infin*. **(b)** (*cualidad*) neglect.
omiso ADJ V **caso**.
omitir [3a] VT **(a)** (*gen*) to leave out, miss out, omit. **(b)** **~ hacer algo** to omit to do sth, fail to do sth.
OMM NF ABR de **Organización Meteorológica Mundial** World Meteorological Organization, WMO.
omni... PREF omni...; all-...
omnibús NM (*Cono Sur*) bus.
ómnibus 1 ADJ V **tren**.
　　2 NM omnibus; (*And*) (*municipal*) bus.
omnicomprensivo ADJ all-inclusive.
omnidireccional ADJ omnidirectional.
omnímodo ADJ all-embracing; *poder* absolute.
omnipotencia NF omnipotence.
omnipotente ADV omnipotent, all-powerful.
omnipresencia NF omnipresence.
omnipresente ADJ omnipresent.
omnisapiente ADJ omniscient, all-knowing.
omnisciencia NF omniscience.
omnisciente ADJ, **omniscio** ADJ omniscient, all-knowing.
omnívoro ADJ omnivorous.
omoplato NM, **omóplato** NM shoulder-blade.
OMS NF ABR de **Organización Mundial de la Salud** World Health Organization, WHO.
OMT NF (*Esp*) ABR de **Oficina Municipal de Transportes**.
-ón, -ona V Aspects of Word Formation in Spanish 2.
onanismo NM onanism.
ONCE ['onθe] NF ABR de **Organización Nacional de Ciegos Españoles**.

┌─ ONCE ─────────────────────────────────

The **Organización Nacional de Ciegos Españoles** began life as a charity for the blind and is now one of the wealthiest and most successful organizations in Spain, with a wide-ranging sphere of activity, including assisting other groups for the disabled. The popular lottery which it set up to provide employment for its members is now its main source of income, generating plentiful capital for investment. One of **ONCE**'s main roles is to provide educational, occupational and rehabilitation centres for its members and to help them to achieve financial independence and social integration.

once 1 ADJ eleven; (*fecha*) eleventh; **las ~** eleven o'clock; **las ~*** elevenses*; (*de mañana*) mid-morning snack; (*And, Cono Sur*: **merienda**) tea, afternoon snack.
　　2 NM eleven.
oncear [1a] VI (*And*) to have an afternoon snack.
onceavo ADJ, NM eleventh.
onceno ADJ eleventh.
oncogén NM oncogene.
oncología NF oncology.
oncólogo, -a NM/F cancer specialist.
onda NF **(a)** (*gen*) wave; (*Cos*) scallop; **~ corta** short wave; **de ~ corta** shortwave (*atr*); **~ de choque, ~ expansiva, ~ sísmica** shock wave; **~ explosiva, ~ expansiva** blast, shock wave; **~ extracorta** ultra-short wave; **~ larga** long wave; **~ luminosa** light wave; **~ media** medium wave; **~ de radio** radio wave; **~ sonora** sound wave; **tratamiento de ~ ultravioleta** ultra-violet treatment.
(b) (*fig*) **buena ~*** good vibes*; **de ~*** in fashion, hip*, trendy; **coger** (*LAm*: **agarrar**) **la ~*** (*entender*) to get it*, get the point*; (*coger el tino*) to get the hang of it; **estar en ~⁑** (*drogado*) to be high⁑ (on drugs); **estar en la ~*** (*moda*) to be in*; *persona* (*a la moda*) to be hip*; (*al tanto*) to be on the ball, be up to date; **estar en ~ gay** to be of the gay persuasion, be into the gay thing*; **se merece un regalo en su ~*** he deserves a present suited to his needs; **perder la ~*** to lose one's touch; **¿qué ~?** (*LAm**) what gives?*
ondeante ADJ = **ondulante**.
ondear [1a] 1 VT *bandera* to wave; *pelo* to wave; (*Cos*) to pink, scallop.
　　2 VI to wave (up and down), undulate; to be wavy; to fluctuate; (*agua*) to ripple; (*bandera etc*) to fly, flutter, wave; (*pelo*) to flow, fall; (*flotar al viento*) to stream; **la bandera ondea en lo alto del edificio** the flag flies (*o* flutters) from the top of the building; **la bandera ondea a media asta** the flag is flying at half mast.
　　3 **ondearse** VR to swing, sway.
ondia* INTERJ (*euf*) = **hostia**.

ondímetro NM wavemeter.
ondina NF undine, water nymph.
ondulación NF undulation; wavy motion; (*en agua*) wave, ripple; (*en pelo*) wave; **ondulaciones** (*de superficie*) undulations, ups and downs; unevenness; **~ permanente** permanent wave.
ondulado 1 ADJ *pelo etc* wavy; *superficie* undulating, uneven; *camino* uneven, rough; *terreno* undulating, rolling; *hierro, papel etc* corrugated.
　　2 NM (*en pelo*) wave.
ondulante ADJ **(a)** *movimiento* undulating; from side to side, (gently) swaying; *sonido* rising and falling. **(b)** = **ondulado**.
ondular [1a] 1 VT *pelo* to wave; **hacerse ~ el pelo** to have one's hair waved.
　　2 VI y **ondularse** VR to undulate; to sway; to wriggle.
ondulatorio ADJ undulatory, wavy.
oneroso ADJ **(a)** (*pesado*) onerous, burdensome. **(b)** **comprar algo a título ~** to purchase sth compulsorily.
ONG NF ABR de **Organización No Gubernamental** Non-Governmental Organisation, NGO.
ónice NM, **ónix** NM onyx.
onírico ADJ oneiric, dream (*atr*).
ONO ABR de **oesnoroeste** west-north-west, WNW.
onomástica NF **(a)** personal names, proper names; onomastics, study of personal names. **(b)** (*t* **fiesta ~**) name day; *see also* SANTO .
onomástico 1 ADJ onomastic, name (*atr*), of names; **índice ~** index of names; **lista onomástica** list of names; **fiesta onomástica = 2**.
　　2 NM one's saint's day, one's name day (*celebrated in Spain and Latin America as equivalent to one's birthday*).
onomatopeya NF onomatopoeia.
onomatopéyico ADJ onomatopoeic.
ontología NF ontology.
ontológico ADJ ontological.
ONU NF ABR de **Organización de las Naciones Unidas** United Nations Organization, UNO.
onubense 1 ADJ of Huelva.
　　2 NMF native (*o* inhabitant) of Huelva; **los ~s** the people of Huelva.
ONUDI [o'nuði] NF ABR de **Organización de las Naciones Unidas para el Desarrollo Industrial** United Nations Industrial Development Organization, UNIDO.
onusiano ADJ United Nations (*atr*).
onza[1] NF ounce.
onza[2] NF (*LAm Zool*) snow leopard.
onzavo, -a ADJ, NM/F eleventh.
oolítico ADJ oolitic.
oolito NM oolite.
O.P. **(a)** ABR de **Obras Publicas** public works. **(b)** (*Ecl*) ABR de **Orden de Predicadores** Order of St Dominic, O.S.D.
OPA ['opa] NF ABR de **oferta pública de adquisición** takeover bid.
opa[1] ADJ (*And, Cono Sur*) **(a)** deaf and dumb; mentally retarded. **(b)** (*) stupid.
opa[2] INTERJ (*LAm*) = **hola**; (*Cono Sur*) stop it!
opacar [1g] 1 VT (*LAm*) **(a)** (*hacer opaco*) to make opaque; (*oscurecer*) to darken; (*empañar*) to mist up; (*deslustrar*) to dull, tarnish.
(b) (*persona*) to outshine, overshadow.
　　2 **opacarse** VR **(a)** (*LAm*: V VT **(a)**) to become opaque; to darken; to mist up; to lose its shine, become tarnished.
(b) (*And, CAm Met*) to cloud over.
opacidad NF **(a)** (*gen*) opacity, opaqueness. **(b)** (*fig*: *oscuridad*) dullness, lifelessness. **(c)** (*fig*: *melancolía*) gloominess.
opaco ADJ **(a)** (*gen*) opaque; dark; **una pantalla opaca a los rayos X** a screen which does not let X-rays through, a screen resistant to X-rays.
(b) (*fig*: *oscuro*) dull, lustreless, lifeless.
(c) (*fig*: *lúgubre*) gloomy, sad.
opado ADJ (*And, Carib*) pale.
OPAEP NF ABR de **Organización de Países Árabes Exportadores de Petróleo** Organization of Arab Petroleum Exporting Countries, OAPEC.
opalescencia NF opalescence.
opalescente ADJ opalescent.
ópalo NM opal.
opaparado ADJ (*And*) bewildered.
opar [1a] VTI to put in a takeover bid (for) (*V* **OPA**).
opción NF **(a)** (*elección*) option, choice; **opciones por defecto** default options; **no hay ~** there is no choice, you (*etc*) do not have the option.
(b) (*derecho*) right; **tiene ~ a viajar gratis** he has the right to travel free.
(c) (*Com*) option (*a* on); **~ de adquisición** option to purchase; **con ~ a 8 más, con ~ para 8 más** with an option on 8 more; **este dispositivo es de ~** this gadget is optional; **suscribir una ~ para la compra de** to take out an option on.

(d) (*posibilidad*) chance, likelihood; **no tiene ~ real al triunfo** she has no real chance of winning.

opcional ADJ optional.

opcionalmente ADV optionally.

op. cit. ABR *de opere citato* op. cit.

Op.D. NM (*Rel*) ABR *de* **Opus Dei.**

opear* [1a] VI (*And, Cono Sur*) to act the fool, fool about.

open NM INVAR (*Golf*) open.

OPEP ['opep] NF ABR *de* **Organización de Países Exportadores del Petróleo** Organization of Petroleum Exporting Countries, OPEC.

ópera NF opera; **~ bufa** comic opera; **gran ~** grand opera.

operable ADJ operable.

operación NF **(a)** (*Med*) operation; **~ cesárea** Caesarean operation; **~ a corazón abierto** open-heart surgery; **~ de estómago** stomach operation, operation on the stomach.

(b) (*Mil etc*) operation; **~ de ablandamiento** softening-up operation; **operaciones conjuntas** joint operations; **~ encubierta** under-cover operation; **~ de limpia, ~ de limpieza** mopping-up operation; **operaciones de rescate, operaciones de salvamento** rescue operations; **~ retorno** effort to control traffic returning to Madrid (*etc*) after a major holiday.

(c) (*Com*) transaction, deal; operation; **~ a plazo** forward transaction; **operaciones de bolsa, operaciones bursátiles** stock-exchange transactions; **~ 'llave en mano'** turnkey operation; **~ mercantil** business deal.

(d) (*Mat*) operation.

(e) (*LAm*) (*Min*) operation, working, exploitation; (*Com*) management.

(f) **operaciones accesorias** (*Inform*) housekeeping.

operacional ADJ operational.

operador(a) NM/F (*gen*) operator; (*Med*) operating surgeon; (*Cine: rodaje*) cameraman, film cameraman; (*t* **~ de cabina**) projectionist, operator; **~ del telégrafo** (*LAm*) telegraph operator; **~ de télex** telex operator; **~ turístico** tour operator.

operante ADJ **(a)** (*gen*) operating. **(b)** (*fig*) effective, active; **el motivo ~** the real reason, the actual motive.

operar [1a] **[1]** VT **(a)** *cambio, cura etc* to produce, bring about, effect; *milagro* to work.

(b) (*Med*) to operate on; **~ a uno de apendicitis** to operate on sb for appendicitis.

(c) (*LAm*) *máquina* to use, operate; *negocio* to manage, run; (*Min*) to work, exploit.

[2] VI **(a)** to operate (*t Mat*).

(b) (*Com*) to operate; to deal, do business; **hoy no se ha operado en la bolsa** there has been no dealing on the stock exchange today.

[3] **operarse** VR **(a)** (*ocurrir*) to occur, come about; **se han operado grandes cambios** great changes have come about, there have been great changes.

(b) (*Med*) to have an operation (*de* for).

operario, -a NM/F operative; (*unskilled*) worker, hand; **~ de máquina** machinist.

ópera-rock NF, PL **óperas-rock** rock opera.

operatividad NF **(a)** (*acto*) functioning, working; action. **(b)** (*eficacia*) effectiveness, efficiency.

operativizar [1f] VT to put into operation, make operative.

operativo **[1]** ADJ operative.

[2] NM (*LAm*) operation; **~ policial** police operation.

opereta NF operetta, light opera.

opería NF (*And, Cono Sur*) stupidity.

operista NMF opera singer.

operístico ADJ operatic, opera (*atr*).

operófilo, -a NM/F opera-lover.

operoso* ADJ (*Carib*) irritable.

opiáceo NM opiate.

opiarse* [1b] VR (*Cono Sur*) to get bored, get fed up*.

opiata NF opiate.

opimo ADJ plentiful, abundant, rich.

opinable ADJ debatable, open to a variety of opinions.

▼ **opinar** [1a] VI **(a)** (*pensar*) to think; **~ que ...** to think that ..., be of the opinion that ...

(b) **~ bien de** to think well of, have a good opinion of.

▼ **(c)** (*dar su opinión*) to give one's opinion; **fueron opinando uno tras otro** they gave their opinions in turn; **hubo un 7 por 100 que no quisieron ~, no opinaron el 7 por 100** (*sondeo*) there were 7% 'don't knows'.

▼ **opinión** NF opinion, view; **~ pública** public opinion; **en mi ~** in my opinion; **abundar en** (*o compartir*) **la ~ de uno** to share sb's opinion (*o* view); **cambiar** (*o mudar*) **de ~** to change one's mind; **formarse una ~** to form an opinion; **ser de ~ que ...** to be of the opinion that ..., take the view that ...

opio NM opium; **dar el ~ a uno*** to enchant sb, captivate sb; **ella le dio el ~*** she knocked him all of a heap; **la película es un ~** (*Cono*

Sur*) the film is a drag.

opiómano, -a NM/F opium addict.

opíparo ADJ *comida* sumptuous.

oponente **[1]** ADJ opposing, contrary.

[2] NMF opponent.

▼ **oponer** [2q] **[1]** VT **(a)** **~ A a B** to pit A against B, set up A in opposition to B; to play off A against B; **~ dos opiniones** to contrast two views.

(b) *objeción* to raise (*a* to); *resistencia* to put up, offer (*a* to); *arma* to use (*a* against); **~ la razón a la pasión** to use reason against passion, rely on reason and not passion; **~ un dique al mar** to set up defences against the sea.

▼ **[2]** **oponerse** VR to be opposed; (*2 personas*) to oppose each other, be in opposition; **yo no me opongo** I don't oppose it, I don't object; **~ a** to oppose, be opposed to, be against; to object to; to defy, resist; **se opone a hacerlo** he resists the idea of doing it, he is unwilling to do it, he objects to doing it; **se opone rotundamente a ello** he is flatly opposed to it.

Oporto NM Oporto.

oporto NM port.

oportunamente ADV opportunely, in a timely way; at the proper time; appropriately, suitably; conveniently; expediently.

oportunidad NF **(a)** (*cualidad*) opportuneness; timeliness; appropriateness; expediency.

(b) (*una ~*) opportunity, chance; **'~es'** (*en tienda*) 'bargains'; **igualdad de ~es** equality of opportunity; **en la primera ~** at the first opportunity; **tener la ~ de** + *infin* to have the chance of + *ger*, have a chance to + *infin*.

(c) (*vez*) time, occasion; **en dos ~es** on two occasions.

oportunismo NM opportunism.

oportunista **[1]** ADJ opportunist; opportunistic.

[2] NMF opportunist.

oportuno ADJ **(a)** (*en buena hora*) opportune, timely; (*apropiado*) appropriate, suitable; (*adecuado*) convenient; (*aconsejable*) expedient; **una respuesta oportuna** a suitable reply; **en el momento ~** at the right moment; at a convenient time; **las medidas que se estimen oportunas** the measures which may be considered appropriate; **sería ~ hacerlo en seguida** it would be best to do it at once.

(b) *persona* witty, quick.

oposición NF **(a)** (*gen*) opposition.

(b) (*Esp*) **oposiciones** public competition (for a post), public entrance (*o* promotion) examination; **hacer oposiciones a, presentarse a unas oposiciones a** to be a candidate for, go in for; **hacer oposiciones para una cátedra** (*etc*) to compete for a chair (*etc*); **ganar unas oposiciones** to be successful in a public competition.

OPOSICIONES

ⓘ *Oposiciones are exams that applicants for public-sector jobs, which are for life, must pass. The exams are held every year, every other year or every five years, depending on the speciality. The candidates (opositores) must sit a series of written exams and/or attend interviews. Some applicants can spend years studying for and resitting exams, so preparing candidates for oposiciones is a major source of students for many academias. All public-sector appointments that are open to competition are published in the BOE, an official government publication.*

⇨ *See also* ACADEMIA , BOE

---

oposicional ADJ (*Pol*) opposition (*atr*).

oposicionista **[1]** ADJ opposition (*atr*).

[2] NMF member of the opposition.

opositar [1a] VI (*Esp*) to go in for a public competition (for a post), sit for a public entrance (*o* promotion) examination.

opositor **[1]** ADJ (*contrario*) opposing; (*Pol*) opposition (*atr*), of the opposition; **el líder ~** the leader of the opposition, the opposing leader.

[2] NM, **opositora** NF **(a)** (*Univ etc*) competitor, candidate (*a* for). **(b)** (*Pol*) opponent.

opresión NF **(a)** (*gen*) oppression; oppressiveness. **(b)** (*Med*) difficulty in breathing, tightness of the chest; **sentir ~** to find it difficult to breathe.

opresivo ADJ oppressive.

opresor **[1]** ADJ oppressive, tyrannical.

[2] NM, **opresora** NF oppressor.

oprimente ADJ oppressive.

oprimir [3a] VT **(a)** (*presionar*) to squeeze, press, exert pressure on; *mango etc* to grasp, clutch; *botón etc* to press; *gas* to compress; (*ropa*) to be too tight for, constrict; to strangle.

(b) (*fig*) to oppress; to burden, weigh down, bear down on; to crush.

oprobio NM shame, ignominy, opprobrium.

oprobioso ADJ shameful, ignominious, opprobrious.

► LENGUA Y USO: **opinar: c → 33.1** **opinión → 29.2, 33.1, 33.2, 34.5, 38.1, 53.3, 53.5** **oponer: 2 → 41**

optar [1a] vi (**a**) (*gen*) to choose, decide; ~ **entre** to choose between; ~ **por** to choose, decide on, opt for; ~ **por** + *infin* to choose to + *infin*. (**b**) ~ **a** to compete for, challenge for, fight for; ~ **a un premio** to compete for a prize; **poder** ~ **a** to (have the right to) apply for, go in for; **ésos no pueden** ~ **a las becas** those do not have the right to apply for the scholarships.

optativa NF (*Educ*) option.

optativamente ADV optionally.

optativo ⊡ ADJ (**a**) (*opcional*) optional. (**b**) (*Ling*) optative. ⊡ NM (*Ling*) optative.

óptica¹ NF (**a**) (*ciencia*) optics. (**b**) (*tienda*) optician's (shop). (**c**) (*fig*) point of view, viewpoint; outlook; **bajo** (*o* **desde**) **esta** ~ from this point of view.

óptico ⊡ ADJ optic(al). ⊡ NM, **óptica²** NF optician.

óptico-cinético NM light show.

optimación NF optimization.

óptimamente ADV ideally; in ideal conditions.

optimar [1a] VT to optimize.

optimismo NM optimism; ~ **cauto**, ~ **matizado** cautious optimism.

optimista ⊡ ADJ optimistic, hopeful. ⊡ NMF optimist.

optimización NF optimization; improvement, perfection.

optimizar [1f] VT to optimize; to improve, perfect.

óptimo ADJ very good, very best; *condiciones etc* optimal, optimum.

optometrista NMF optometrist.

opuesto ADJ (**a**) *ángulo, lado etc* opposite; **en dirección opuesta** in the opposite direction. (**b**) *opinión etc* contrary, opposing, opposite.

opugnar [1a] VT to attack.

opulencia NF opulence; luxury; affluence; **sociedad de la** ~ affluent society; **vivir en la** ~ to live in luxury, live in affluence.

opulento ADJ opulent, rich; luxurious; affluent.

opuncia NF (*Méx*) prickly pear.

opúsculo NM booklet; short work, tract, brief treatise.

┌─ *OPUS DEI* ─────────────────────────┐

ⓘ *The* **Opus Dei**, *also referred to as* **la Obra**, *is an influential Catholic association formed in 1928 by the Spaniard José María Escrivá de Balaguer with the aim of spreading Christian principles in society. It has a direct link to the Vatican by virtue of a special "Personal Prelature" granted by John Paul II in 1982, which in practice means that it enjoys complete independence from local diocesan authorities. During the Franco era members of the* **Opus** *formed the intellectual backbone of the régime, and the technocrats who engineered the "economic miracle" of the 1950s and 60s were drawn largely from its number. Members of the* **Opus** *are particularly well-represented in educational circles: the universities of Pamplona in Spain and Piura in Peru are run by it.*

└──────────────────────────────────────┘

opusdeísta NMF member of Opus Dei.

OPV NF ABR *de* **Oferta Pública de Venta (de acciones)** share offer.

oquedad NF hollow, cavity; (*fig*) void; hollowness, emptiness.

oquedal NM wood of grown timber, plantation.

ORA ['ora] NF ABR *de* **Operación de Regulación de Aparcamientos**.

ora ADV (*liter*): ~ **A**, ~ **B** now A, now B; sometimes A, at other times B.

oración NF (**a**) (*discurso*) oration, speech; ~ **fúnebre** funeral oration; **pronunciar una** ~ to make a speech. (**b**) (*Ecl*) prayer; **oraciones por la paz** prayers for peace; **estar en** ~ to be at prayer. (**c**) (*LAm*) pagan invocation, magic charm. (**d**) (*Ling*) sentence; clause; ~ **compuesta** complex sentence; ~ **directa** direct speech; ~ **indirecta** to indirect speech, reported speech; ~ **subordinada** subordinate clause; **partes de la** ~ parts of speech.

oracional ADJ sentence (*atr*).

oráculo NM oracle.

orador(a) NM/F speaker, orator.

oral ADJ oral.

órale* INTERJ (*Méx*: *¡venga!*) come on!; (: *¡oiga!*) hey!

orangután NM orang-outang.

orante ⊡ ADJ: **actitud** ~ kneeling position, posture of prayer. ⊡ NMF (*persona*) worshipper, person at prayer.

orar [1a] vi (**a**) (*Ecl*) to pray (*a* to, *por* for). (**b**) (*disertar*) to speak, make a speech.

orate NMF lunatic.

orático ADJ (*CAm*) crazy, lunatic.

oratoria NF oratory.

oratorio ⊡ ADJ oratorical. ⊡ NM (**a**) (*Mús*) oratorio. (**b**) (*Ecl*) oratory, chapel.

orbe NM (**a**) (*gen*) orb, sphere. (**b**) (*fig*) world; **en todo el** ~ throughout the world.

órbita NF (**a**) (*gen*) orbit (*t fig*); **estar en** ~ to be in orbit; **entrar en** ~ **alrededor de la luna** to go into orbit round the moon; **poner en** ~

to place in orbit. (**b**) (*Méx*) socket (of the eye).

orbital ADJ orbital.

orbitar [1a] VTI to orbit.

orca NF grampus, killer whale.

Orcadas NFPL Orkneys, Orkney Islands.

órdago*: **de** ~ ADJ first-class, super*, swell* (*US*); (*pey*) awful, tremendous*.

ordalías NFPL (*Hist*) ordeal, trial by ordeal.

orden ⊡ NM (**a**) (*gen*) order; arrangement; ~ **del día** agenda; **de primer** ~ first-rate, of the first order; **en** ~ in order; **en** ~ **a** (*con miras a*) with a view to; (*en cuanto a*) with regard to; **en** ~ **a** + *infin* in order to + *infin*; **en** ~ **de batalla** in battle order; **en** ~ **de marchar** in marching order; **'en otro** ~ **de cosas ...'** (*en discurso*) 'passing now to other matters ...'; **hacemos progresos en todos los órdenes** we are making progress on all fronts; **fuera de** ~ out of order; out of turn; **por** (**su**) ~ in order; **por** ~ **de antigüedad** in order of seniority; **por** ~ **cronológico** in chronological order; **poner en** ~ to put in order, arrange (properly); to tidy up.
(**b**) (*Jur etc*) order; ~ **público** public order, law and order; **alterar el** ~ **público** to disturb the peace; **las fuerzas del** ~ the forces of law and order; **llamar al** ~ to take to task, reprimand; to call to order; **mantener el** ~ to keep order.
(**c**) **una cifra del** ~ **de 600** a figure of the order of 600.
(**d**) (*Arquit*) order; ~ **dórico** Doric order.
⊡ NF (**a**) (*mandamiento*) order; (*Jur*) order, warrant, writ; (*Méx: pedido*) order; ~ **de allanamiento** (*Méx*) search warrant; ~ **de búsqueda y captura**, ~ **de detención** arrest warrant; ~ **de citación** (*Méx*), ~ **de comparación** (*Méx*) summons, subpoena; ~ **del día** (*Mil*) order of the day; ~ **judicial** court order; **O~ Real** Order in Council; **a la** ~ (*Com*) to order; **¡a la** ~! (*LAm*) (*en tienda etc*) what can I get you?; (*no hay de qué*) you're welcome, don't mention it!; **a la** ~ **de Vd, a sus órdenes** at your service; **cheques a la** ~ **de Suárez** cheques to be made out to Suárez; **eso ahora está a la** ~ **del día** that is now the order of the day; **¡a las órdenes!** (*Mil*) yes sir?; **hasta nueva** ~ until further notice, till further orders; **por** ~ **de** on the orders of, by order of; **¡es una** ~! that's an order!; **dar una** ~ to give an order; **dar la** ~ **de** + *infin* to give the order to + *infin*.
(**b**) (*Ecl*) order; ~ **órdenes menores** minor orders; ~ **monástica** monastic order; ~ **religiosa** religious order; **órdenes sagradas** holy orders; **O~ de San Benito** Benedictine Order.
(**c**) (*Hist, Mil*) ~ **de caballería** order of knighthood; ~ **militar** military order; **O~ de Calatrava** Order of Caltrava.
(**d**) (*Com, Fin*) order; ~ **bancaria** banker's order; ~ **de compra** purchase order.
(**e**) (*Méx: porción*) portion, helping (of food).

ordenación NF (**a**) (*estado*) order; arrangement; (*acto*) ordering, arranging; (*Inform*) sorting; ~ **territorial** town and country planning. (**b**) (*Ecl*) ordination.

ordenada NF ordinate.

ordenadamente ADV in an orderly way; tidily; methodically.

ordenado ADJ (**a**) (*en orden*) (*estado*) orderly; tidy; well arranged. (**b**) *persona* methodical; tidy. (**c**) (*Ecl*) in holy orders.

ordenador NM computer; ~ **analógico** analog(ue) computer; ~ **central** mainframe computer; ~ **doméstico** home computer; ~ **de gestión** business computer; ~ **personal** personal computer; ~ **portátil**, ~ **transportable** portable computer; ~ **de (sobre)mesa** desktop computer.

ordenamiento NM (**a**) ordering, arranging. (**b**) (*Jur*) ~ **jurídico** (piece of) legislation; ~ **constitutional** statute.

ordenancista NMF disciplinarian, martinet.

ordenando NM (*Ecl*) ordinand.

ordenanza ⊡ NF (*decreto*) ordinance, decree; ~**s municipales** bylaws; **ser de** ~ to be the rule. ⊡ NM (*Com etc*) office boy, messenger; errand boy; (*Mil*) orderly, batman.

ordenar [1a] ⊡ VT (**a**) (*poner en orden*) to arrange, put in order; to marshal; to draw up; (*Inform*) to sort; ~ **sus asuntos** to put one's affairs in order; ~ **su vida** to arrange one's life.
(**b**) (*mandar*) to order; ~ **a uno hacer algo** to order sb to do sth; **tono de ordeno y mando** dictatorial tone.
(**c**) (*Ecl*) to ordain.
⊡ **ordenarse** VR (*Ecl*) to take holy orders, be ordained (*de* as).

ordeña NF (*Cono Sur, Méx*) milking.

ordeñadero NM milking pail.

ordeñadora NF milking machine.

ordeñar [1a] VT to milk.

ordeñe NM (*Carib*), **ordeño** NM milking.

órdiga: NF = **¡(anda) la** ~! (*Esp*) bloody hell!**:**

ordinal ADJ, NM ordinal.

ordinariamente ADV ordinarily, usually.

ordinariez NF (**a**) (*cualidad*) commonness, coarseness, vulgarity. (**b**) (*una* ~) coarse remark (*o* joke etc), piece of vulgarity.

ordinario [1] ADJ (a) (*normal*) ordinary; usual; (*corriente*) current; *gastos* daily; **de ~** usually, ordinarily.
(b) (*vulgar*) common, coarse, vulgar; (*grosero*) rude; *chiste* coarse, crude; **son gente muy ordinaria** they're very common people.
[2] NM (a) (*gastos*) daily household expenses.
(b) (*recadero*) carrier, delivery man.

ordinograma NM organization chart; flowchart.

orear [1a] [1] VT to air.
[2] **orearse** VR (a) (*ropa*) to air. (b) (*persona*) to get some fresh air, take a breather.

orégano NM marjoram; (*Méx‡*) grass‡.

oreja [1] NF (a) (*Anat*) ear; **con las ~s gachas** (*fig*) ashamed; embarrassed; **aguzar las ~s** to prick up one's ears; **asomar** (o **descubrir, enseñar**) **la ~** (*traicionarse*) to give o.s. away, reveal one's true nature; (*aparecer*) to show o.s., show up; **calentar las ~s a uno** (*golpear*) to box sb's ears; (*irritar*) to get on sb's nerves; (*despachar*) to send sb away with a flea in his ear; **chafar la ~‡** to kip‡, sleep; **estar hasta las ~s*** to be utterly fed up*; **hacer ~s de mercader** to turn a deaf ear; **planchar ~‡** to kip‡, sleep; **se la ve la ~*** you can see his little game; **verle las ~s al lobo** to escape from great danger.
(b) (*de zapato etc*) tab; tag; (*de jarra*) lug, handle; (*Mec*) lug, flange; (*de sillón*) wing; (*de libro*) flap; (‡) tit‡.
(c) (*LAm*) (*curiosidad*) curiosity; (*escucha*) eavesdropping; (*prudencia*) caution.
[2] NMF (‡: *soplón*) grass‡, informer.

orejano [1] ADJ (a) (*LAm*) *animal* unbranded, ownerless.
(b) (*LAm*) (*tímido*) shy, easily scared; (*huraño*) unsociable.
(c) (*Carib*: *cauteloso*) cautious.
[2] NM (*CAm, Carib*) peasant, countryman.

orejear* [1a] VI (a) (*LAm*: *escuchar*) to eavesdrop.
(b) (*And, Carib, Cono Sur*: *recelar*) to suspect, be distrustful.
(c) (*Cono Sur Naipes*) to uncover one's cards one by one.

orejera NF earflap.

orejero* [1] ADJ (a) (*LAm**) (*receloso*) suspicious; (*prudente*) cautious. (b) (*Cono Sur**: *chismoso*) telltale. (c) (*And**: *rencoroso*) malicious.
[2] NM (a) wing chair. (b) (*Cono Sur**) boss's right-hand man.

orejeta NF (*Téc*) lug.

orejón [1] ADJ (a) (*LAm*) = **orejudo**.
(b) (*And*: *distraído*) absent-minded.
(c) (*And, CAm, Méx*: *tosco*) rough, coarse.
[2] NM (a) (*tiró*) pull on the ear, tug at one's ear.
(b) (*fruta*) strip of dried peach (o apricot).
(c) (*And Med*) goitre.
(d) (*And*) (*vaquero*) herdsman; (*llanero*) plainsman.
(e) (*Méx‡*: *marido*) cuckold.
(f) (*And Hist*) Inca nobleman.

orejonas NFPL (*And, Carib*) big spurs.

orejudo ADJ big-eared, with big ears.

orensano [1] ADJ of Orense.
[2] NMF native (o inhabitant) of Orense; **los ~s** the people of Orense.

orfanato NM, **orfanatorio** NM (*LAm*) orphanage.

orfandad NF (a) (*lit*) orphanhood. (b) (*fig*: *abandono*) neglect, abandonment. (c) (*fig*: *escasez*) dearth, scarcity, paucity.

orfebre NM goldsmith, silversmith.

orfebrería NF gold work, silver work, craftsmanship in precious metals.

orfelinato NM orphanage.

Orfeo NM Orpheus.

orfeón NM glee club, choral society.

organdí NM organdie.

orgánicamente ADV organically.

orgánico ADJ organic; *V* **ley**.

organigrama NM flow chart; organization chart.

organillero NM organ-grinder.

organillo NM barrel organ, hurdy-gurdy.

organismo NM (a) (*Bio*) organism.
(b) (*Pol etc*) organization; body, institution; **~s de gobierno** organs of government, state bodies; **~ rector** governing body; **~ de sondaje** public-opinion poll, institute of public opinion.

organista NMF organist.

organito NM (*Cono Sur*) = **organillo**.

organización NF organization; **O~ de Estados Americanos** Organization of American States; **O~ de las Naciones Unidas** United Nations Organization.

organizadamente ADV in an organized way.

organizador(a) [1] NM/F organizer.
[2] NM: **~ personal** personal organizer

organizar [1f] [1] VT to organize.
[2] **organizarse** VR to manage one's affairs, organize one's life; to get one's priorities right.

organizativo ADJ organizational.

órgano NM (a) (*Anat, Mec etc*) organ; **~ del habla** speech organ. (b) (*Mús*) organ; **~ eléctrico** electric organ. (c) (*fig*) organ, means, medium; **~ de enlace** means of communication.

orgásmico ADJ orgasmic.

orgasmo NM orgasm.

orgía NF orgy.

orgiástico ADJ orgiastic.

orgullo NM pride; (*pey*) pride, haughtiness, arrogance.

orgullosamente ADV proudly; haughtily.

orgulloso ADJ proud; haughty; **estar ~ de algo** to be proud of sth; **estar ~ de** + *infin* to be proud to + *infin*.

oricio NM sea-urchin.

orientable ADJ adjustable.

orientación NF (a) (*gen*) orientation, position(ing); (*dirección*) direction, course; (*Arquit*) aspect, prospect; **~ sexual** sexual orientation; **la ~ actual del partido** the party's present course (o position); **una casa con ~ sur** a house with a southerly aspect, a house facing south.
(b) (*guía*) guidance; (*formación*) training; **~ profesional, ~ vocacional** vocational guidance; **me ayudó en la ~ bibliográfica** he helped me with bibliographical information; **importa mucho en la ~ de los maestros** it is very important in the training of teachers; **lo hizo para mi ~** he did it for my guidance.
(c) (*Dep*) orienteering.

orientador(a) NM/F careers adviser.

oriental [1] ADJ (a) oriental; eastern. (b) (*Cono Sur*) Uruguayan; (*Cuba*) of (o from) Oriente province.
[2] NMF (a) oriental. (b) (*Cono Sur*) Uruguayan; (*Cuba*) native (o inhabitant) of Oriente province.

orientalismo NM orientalism.

orientalista ADJ, NMF orientalist.

orientar [1a] [1] VT (a) (*gen*) to orientate, position; (*dirigir*) to point (*hacia* towards); to give a direction to, direct; (*Náut*) *vela* to trim; **la casa está orientada hacia el suroeste** the house faces (o looks) south-west; **hay que ~ las investigaciones en otro sentido** you will have to change the direction of your inquiries, you will have to pursue your researches in another direction.
(b) *persona* (*guiar*) to guide, direct; (*formar*) to train; **me ha orientado en la materia** he has guided me through the subject, he has given me guidance about the subject.
[2] **orientarse** VR (a) (*objeto etc*) to point, face (*hacia* towards).
(b) (*persona*) to get one's bearings, orient o.s., get orientated; (*fig*) to get one's bearings; to establish o.s.; to decide on a course of conduct (*etc*); **es difícil ~ en este terreno** it's hard to get one's bearings (o find one's way about) in this country.

orientativamente ADV by way of guidance.

orientativo ADJ guiding, illustrative; **los pesos reseñados son puramente ~s** the weights shown are for guidance only.

oriente NM (a) (*este*) east.
(b) **el O~** the Orient, the East; **Cercano O~, Próximo O~** Near East; **Extremo O~, Lejano O~** Far East; **O~ Medio** Middle East.
(c) (*viento*) east wind.
(d) (*de masones*) masonic lodge.

orificación NF gold filling.

orificar [1g] VT *muela* to fill with gold.

orificio NM orifice, hole; vent.

origen NM origin; source; **los orígenes de la guerra** the origins of the war, the causes of the war; **país de ~** country of origin; **de ~ argentino** of Argentinian origin; **dar ~ a** to cause, give rise to.

original [1] ADJ (a) (*gen*) original.
(b) (*fig*: *nuevo*) original; novel; (*raro*) odd, eccentric, strange.
(c) = **originario** (b).
[2] NM (a) (*gen*) original; **el ~ es mejor que la copia** the original is better than the copy.
(b) (*Tip*) manuscript, original; copy; **tenemos exceso de ~** we have too much copy.
(c) (*persona*) character, eccentric, original type.

originalidad NF (*V ADJ* a, b) (a) originality. (b) eccentricity, oddness.

originalmente ADV originally.

originar [1a] [1] VT to originate; to start, cause, give rise to.
[2] **originarse** VR to originate (*de* from, *en* in); to be started, be caused.

originariamente ADV originally.

originario ADJ (a) (*original*) original; **en su forma originaria** in its original form.
(b) **ser ~ de** to originate from, be a native of; **una familia originaria de Sicilia** a family originating from Sicily.
(c) **país ~** country of origin, native country.
(d) **una decisión originaria de disgustos** a decision which gave rise to trouble, a decision which was a source of trouble.

orilla NF (a) (*gen*) edge, border; (*de río*) bank; (*de lago*) side, shore; (*de mar*) shore; (*de mesa etc*) edge; (*de taza etc*) rim, lip; **~ del mar** seashore; **a ~s de** on the banks of; **vive ~ de mi casa*** he lives next

door to me.
(b) (*Cos*) edge, border, trimming; hem.
(c) **de ~** (*Carib*) trivial, of no account; worthless.
(d) (*LAm: acera*) pavement, sidewalk (*US*).
(e) **~s** (*LAm*) (*arrabales*) outlying districts; (*pey*) poor quarter; (*Méx*) shanty town.
orillar [1a] VT **(a)** (*Cos*) to edge, trim (*de* with).
(b) *bosque, lago etc* to skirt, go round; to pass along the edge of.
(c) *tema* to touch briefly on.
(d) *asuntos* to put in order, tidy up; (*concluir*) to wind up.
(e) *dificultad, obstáculo* to get round.
(f) **~ a uno a hacer algo** (*Méx*) to lead sb to do sth.
orillero ADJ (*LAm*) = **arrabalero**.
orillo NM selvage.
orín NM rust; **tomarse de ~** to get rusty.
orina NF urine.
orinal NM **(a)** (*gen*) chamberpot; **~ de cama** bedpan. **(b)** (*Mil**) tin hat*, helmet.
orinar [1a] **1** VTI to urinate.
2 **orinarse** VR to urinate (involuntarily); to wet o.s.; **~ en la cama** to wet one's bed.
orines NMPL urine.
Orinoco NM: **el río ~** the Orinoco (River).
orita* (*LAm*) ADV = **ahorita**.
oriundo **1** ADJ: **~ de** native to; **ser ~ de** to be a native of, come from, hail from.
2 NM, **oriunda** NF (*nativo*) native, inhabitant.
orla NF, **orladura** NF **(a)** border; fringe; trimming; **~ litoral** coastal strip. **(b)** (*Escol*) class graduation photograph.
orlar [1a] VT to border, edge, trim (*de* with).
ornamentación NF ornamentation, adornment.
ornamental ADJ ornamental.
ornamentar [1a] VT to adorn (*de* with).
ornamento NM **(a)** (*gen*) ornament, adornment; **~s** (*Ecl*) ornaments, vestments. **(b)** **~s** (*fig*) good qualities, moral qualities.
ornar [1a] VT to adorn (*de* with).
ornato NM adornment, decoration.
ornitofauna NF birds, bird population.
ornitología NF ornithology.
ornitológico ADJ ornithological.
ornitólogo, -a NM/F ornithologist.
ornitorrinco NM platypus.
oro NM **(a)** gold; **~ en barras** gold bars, bullion; **~ batido** gold leaf; **~ laminado** rolled gold; **~ molido** ormolu; **~ negro** black gold, oil; **~ en polvo** gold dust; **de ~** gold, golden; **como un ~** like new; spick and span; **no es ~ todo lo que reluce** all that glitters is not gold; **es de ~** (*fig*) he's a treasure; he's a marvel; **tiene una voz de ~** she has a marvellous voice; **apalear ~** to be rolling in money; **guardar algo como ~ en paño** to treasure sth; **hacerse de ~** to make a fortune; **poner a uno de ~ y azul** to lay into sb (verbally)*, heap insults on sb; **prometer el ~ y el moro** to promise the moon.
(b) **~s** (*Naipes*) diamonds.
orografía NF orography.
orográfico ADJ orographical.
orondo ADJ **(a)** *vasija etc* big, big-bellied, rounded; *persona* fat, pot-bellied.
(b) (*satisfecho*) smug, self-satisfied; (*pomposo*) pompous.
(c) (*LAm*) calm, serene.
oropel NM tinsel; **de ~** flashy, bright but tawdry; unsubstantial; **tener mucho ~** to be all show, (*esp*) make a pretence of being wealthy.
oropéndola NF golden oriole.
oroya NF (*And*) basket of a rope bridge; (*And Ferro*) funicular railway.
orozuz NM liquorice.
orquesta NF orchestra; **~ de baile** dance band; **~ de cámara** chamber orchestra; **~ de jazz** jazz band; **~ sinfónica** symphony orchestra.
orquestación NF orchestration (*t fig*).
orquestal ADJ orchestral.
orquestar [1a] VT to orchestrate (*t fig*).
orquestina NF band.
orquídea NF orchid, orchis.
orsay NM = **offside**.
ortiga NF nettle, stinging nettle.
orto¹ NM sunrise.
orto²* NM (*Cono Sur*) (*culo*) arse**; (*ano*) arsehole**.
orto... PREF ortho-.
ortodoncia NF orthodontics.
ortodoncista NMF orthodontist.
ortodoxia NF orthodoxy.
ortodoxo ADJ orthodox.
ortofonista NMF speech therapist.

ortografía NF spelling; orthography.
ortográfico ADJ spelling (*atr*); orthographic(al); **reforma ortográfica** spelling reform.
ortopeda NMF orthopaedist.
ortopedia NF orthopaedics.
ortopédico ADJ orthopaedic.
ortopedista NMF orthopaedist.
oruga NF **(a)** (*Ent*) caterpillar. **(b)** (*Bot*) rocket. **(c)** (*Téc*) caterpillar, caterpillar track; (*Mil*) tracked personnel carrier; **tractor de ~** caterpillar tractor.
orujo NM *refuse of grapes* (*u olives*) *after pressing*; (*bebida*) *liquor distilled from grape refuse*.
ovárico ADJ ovarian.
orza¹ NF (*jarra*) glazed earthenware jar.
orza² NF (*Náut*) luff, luffing; **ir de ~** (*fig*) to be on the wrong track.
orzar [1f] VI (*Náut*) to luff.
orzuelo NM (*Med*) stye.
os¹ PRON PERS PL **(a)** (*ac*) you.
(b) (*dativo*) (to) you; **~ lo di** I gave it to you; **~ lo compré** I bought it from you; I bought it for you; **~ quitáis el abrigo** you take off your coats.
(c) (*reflexivo*) (to) yourselves; (*recíproco*) (to) each other; **vosotros ~ laváis** you wash yourselves; **cuando ~ marchéis** when you leave.
os² INTERJ shoo!
osa NF she-bear; **O~ Mayor** Ursa Major, Great Bear; **O~ Menor** Ursa Minor, Little Bear; **¡la ~!*** gosh!*; **¡anda la ~!*** what a carry-on!*
osadamente ADV daringly, boldly.
osadía NF daring, boldness.
osado ADJ daring, bold.
osamenta NF bones; skeleton.
osar [1a] VI to dare; **~ hacer algo** to dare to do sth.
osario NM ossuary, charnel house.
Oscar, óscar NM Oscar.
oscarizado **1** ADJ *film* Oscar-winning.
2 NM, **oscarizada** NF Oscar winner.
oscense **1** ADJ of Huesca.
2 NMF native (*o inhabitant*) of Huesca; **los ~s** the people of Huesca.
oscilación NF **(a)** (*gen*) oscillation; (*vaivén*) swing, sway, to and fro movement; rocking; (*luz*) winking, blinking. **(b)** (*de precios*) fluctuation. **(c)** (*fig*) hesitation, wavering.
oscilador **1** ADJ oscillating.
2 NM oscillator.
oscilante ADJ oscillating; swinging.
oscilar [1a] VI **(a)** (*gen*) to oscillate; (*péndulo etc*) to swing, sway, move to and fro; (*mecerse*) to rock; (*luz*) to wink, blink.
(b) (*fig*) to fluctuate (*entre* between); to vary (*entre* between); to range (*entre* between); **la distancia oscila entre los 100 y 500 m** the distance ranges between 100 and 500 m; **los precios oscilan mucho** prices are fluctuating a lot.
(c) (*persona*) to hesitate; to waver (*entre* between); **oscila entre la alegría y el pesimismo** he passes from cheerfulness to pessimism.
oscilatorio ADJ oscillatory.
osciloscopio NM oscilloscope.
oscular [1a] VT (*liter*) to osculate, kiss.
ósculo NM (*liter*) osculation, kiss; **~ de paz** kiss of peace.
oscuramente ADV obscurely; in an obscure way.
oscurana NF (*CAm: de polvo*) cloud of volcanic dust; (*And**, *Méx*: *oscuridad*) darkness.
oscurantismo NM obscurantism.
oscurantista ADJ, NMF obscurantist.
oscurear [1a] (*Méx*) = **oscurecer**.
oscurecer [2d] **1** VT **(a)** (*gen*) to obscure, darken; to dim; to black out.
(b) (*fig*) *asunto* to confuse, cloud, fog; *rival* to overshadow, put in the shade; *fama* to dim, tarnish.
(c) (*Arte*) to shade.
2 VR, **oscurecerse** VR to grow dark, get dark.
oscuridad NF **(a)** (*gen*) darkness, obscurity; gloom, gloominess. **(b)** (*fig*) obscurity.
oscuro ADJ **(a)** (*gen*) dark; dim, gloomy, obscure; *contorno* confused, indistinct; **a oscuras** in the dark (*t fig*), in darkness; **quedarse a oscuras** to be left in the dark.
(b) *color* dark, deep; **un hermoso azul ~** a beautiful dark blue.
(c) (*Met*) overcast, cloudy.
(d) (*fig*) obscure; confused; *futuro etc* uncertain; *asunto* shady; **de origen ~** of obscure origin(s).
óseo ADJ bony, osseous.
osezno NM bear cub.
osificación NF ossification.
osificar [1g] **1** VT to ossify.
2 **osificarse** VR to ossify, become ossified.

-osis V Aspects of Word Formation in Spanish 2.

osito NM (*juguete*) toy bear; (*Cono Sur: de bebé*) all-in-one suit; **~ de felpa**, **~ de peluche** teddy bear; **~ panda** panda.

osmosis NF, **ósmosis** NF osmosis.

osmótico ADJ osmotic.

OSO ABR *de* **oessudoeste** west-south-west, WSW.

oso NM (a) bear; **~ blanco** polar bear; **~ colmenero** (*LAm*) anteater; **~ de las cavernas** cave bear; **~ gris** grizzly (bear); **~ hormiguero** anteater; **~ marsupial** koala bear; **~ pardo** brown bear; **~ de peluche** teddy bear; **ser un ~** to be a prickly sort; **hacer el ~** to play the fool; to play the sentimental lover.
(b) (*Carib*) braggart; bully.

Ostende NM Ostend.

ostensible ADJ obvious, evident; **hacer algo ~** to reveal sth, make sth clear; (*LAm*) to express sth, register sth; **procurar no hacerse ~** to keep out of the way, lie low.

ostensiblemente ADV obviously, evidently; openly; perceptibly, visibly; **se mostró ~ conmovido** he was visibly affected.

ostensorio NM monstrance.

ostenta NF (*And, Cono Sur*) = **ostentación**.

ostentación NF (a) (*gen*) ostentation, display; pomp. (b) (*acto*) show, display; **hacer ~ de** to show off, display, parade.

ostentar [1a] VT (a) (*mostrar*) to show; (*pey*) to show off, display, make a parade of, flaunt.
(b) (*tener*) to have, carry, show; **ostenta todavía las cicatrices** he still has (o carries) the scars.
(c) *poderes legales etc* to have, possess; *honor, título etc* to have, hold; **~ el título mundial en el deporte** to hold the world title in the sport, be the world record holder.

ostentativo ADJ ostentatious.

ostentosamente ADV ostentatiously.

ostentoso ADJ ostentatious.

osteo... PREF osteo...

osteoartritis NF osteoarthritis.

osteópata NMF osteopath.

osteopatía NF osteopathy.

osteoporosis NF INVAR osteoporosis.

osti INTERJ = **hostia**.

ostión NM large oyster.

ostionería NF (*LAm*) oyster bar.

ostra NF (a) (*Zool*) oyster.
(b) (*fig: pesado*) dull person; (*huraño*) retiring individual; (*permanente*) regular; **las ~s del café** the café regulars, the café habitués; **es una ~** he's a fixture here.
(c) **¡~s!** (*Esp**) hell!

ostracismo NM ostracism.

ostral NM oyster bed.

ostrería NF oyster bar.

ostrero NM (a) (*lugar*) oyster bed. (b) (*Orn*) oystercatcher.

osuno ADJ bear-like.

OTAN ['otan] NF ABR *de* **Organización del Tratado del Atlántico Norte** North Atlantic Treaty Organization, NATO.

otánico ADJ NATO (*atr*).

otanista NMF supporter of NATO.

otario* [1] ADJ (*Cono Sur*) simple, gullible.
[2] NM sucker.

OTASE [o'tase] NF ABR *de* **Organización del Tratado del Sudeste Asiático** South-East Asia Treaty Organization, SEATO.

otate NM (*Méx*) cane, stick; reed, rush.

-ote, -ota V Aspects of Word Formation in Spanish 2.

oteadero NM look-out post.

otear [1a] VT (a) (*alcanzar a ver*) to descry, make out, glimpse; (*mirar desde arriba*) to look down on, look over; (*espiar*) to watch (from above), spy on; *horizonte* to scan. (b) (*fig*) to examine, look into.

Otelo NM Othello.

otero NM low hill, hillock, knoll.

OTI ['oti] NF (*TV*) ABR *de* **Organización de la Televisión Iberoamericana**.

otitis NF earache.

otomana NF ottoman.

otomano, -a ADJ, NM/F Ottoman.

otomía NF (*Méx*) atrocity; **hacer ~s** to get up to no good, misbehave.

Otón NM Otto.

otoñada NF autumn, fall (*US*).

otoñal ADJ autumnal, autumn (*atr*), fall (*atr: US*).

otoño NM autumn, fall (*US*); (*fig: edad*) maturity.

otorgamiento NM (a) (*acto*) granting, conferring; consent; (*Jur*) execution. (b) (*documento*) legal document, deed.

otorgar [1h] VT (a) (*dar*) to grant, give (*a* to); *poderes etc* to confer (*a* on); *esfuerzo, tiempo* to devote (*a* to); *premio etc* to award (*a* to); *privilegio etc* to grant; (*Jur*) *instrumento etc* to execute; *testamento* to make.

(b) (*consentir en*) to consent, agree to.

otoronco NM (*And Zool*) mountain bear.

otorrino(laringólogo) NMF (*Med*) ear, nose and throat specialist.

otramente ADV in a different way.

otredad NF otherness.

otro [1] ADJ (*sing*) another, (*pl*) other; (*en serie: anterior*) last, previous; (*posterior*) next, following; **a la otra semana** the following week; **otra taza de café** another cup of coffee; **con ~s trajes** with other dresses; with different dresses; **con otras 8 personas** with another 8 people, with 8 other people; **¡otra!** (*Teat*) encore!; **otra cosa** sth else; **tropezamos con otra nueva dificultad** we run up against yet another (o a further) difficulty; **va a ser ~ Manolete** he's going to be another (o a second) Manolete; **~ que** other than; different from; **fue no ~ que el obispo** it was none other than the bishop, it was no lesser person than the bishop; **ser muy ~** to be very different; **los tiempos son ~s** times have changed.
[2] PRON (*sing*) another one, (*pl*) others; **el ~** the other one; **lo ~** the rest (of it); **los ~s** the others; the rest; **¿~?** another one?; **lo ~ es más triste** the rest of it is sadder; **lo ~ no importa** the rest isn't important; **tomar el sombrero de ~** to take somebody else's hat; **conformarse con las costumbres de los ~s** to adapt o.s. to other people's habits; **algún ~** somebody else; **que lo haga ~** let somebody else do it; **~ dijo que ...** somebody else said ...; **como dijo el ~** as the saying goes; **¡~ que tal!** here we go again!, we've heard all that before!; V **alguno, parte, tanto** etc.

otrora ADV (††, *liter*) (a) (*antiguamente*) formerly, in olden times. (b) (*como* ADJ INVAR) one-time, former; **el ~ señor del país** the one-time ruler of the country.

otrosí ADV furthermore.

OUA NF ABR *de* **Organización de la Unidad Africana** Organization of African Unity, OAU.

OUAA NF ABR *de* **Organización de la Unidad Afro-americana**.

ouija, oui-ja ® NM *o* NF Ouija ® board.

ourensano, -a ADJ, NM/F = **orensano**.

output ['autpu] NM, PL **outputs** ['autpu] (*Inform*) printout.

ovación NF ovation.

ovacionar [1a] VT to acclaim, cheer to the echo.

oval ADJ, **ovalado** ADJ oval.

óvalo NM oval; (*Méx Med*) pessary.

ovárico ADJ ovarian.

ovario NM ovary.

ovas NFPL fish eggs, roe.

oveja NF (a) sheep, ewe; **~ negra** (*fig*) black sheep (of the family); **cada ~ con su pareja** it's best to stick to people like o.s.; birds of a feather flock together; **apartar las ~s de los cabritos** (*fig*) to separate the sheep from the goats; **cargar con la ~ muerta** to be left holding the baby.
(b) (*Cono Sur*) whore.

ovejera NF (*Méx*) sheepfold.

ovejería NF (*Cono Sur*) sheep farm; sheep farming.

ovejero NM sheepdog; **~ alemán** German shepherd (dog), Alsatian.

ovejita* NF (*Argentina*) whore*.

ovejo NM, **ovejón** NM (*LAm*) ram.

ovejuno ADJ sheep (*atr*).

overbooking [oβer'βukin] NM overbooking.

overear [1a] VT (*And, Cono Sur Culin*) to cook to a golden colour, brown.

overol NM (*LAm*) overalls.

ovetense [1] ADJ of Oviedo.
[2] NMF native (o inhabitant) of Oviedo; **los ~s** the people of Oviedo.

Ovidio NM Ovid.

oviducto NM oviduct.

oviforme ADJ egg-shaped, oviform.

ovillar [1a] VT *lana etc* to wind, wind into a ball.
[2] **ovillarse** VR to curl up into a ball.

ovillo NM (*de lana etc*) ball; (*fig*) tangle; **hacerse un ~** (*descansando etc*) to curl up into a ball; (*con miedo*) to crouch, cower; (*en discurso etc*) to get tied up in knots.

ovino [1] ADJ ovine; sheep (*atr*); **ganado ~** sheep.
[2] NM (*animales*) sheep; **carne de ~** sheep meat; mutton, lamb.

ovíparo ADJ oviparous.

OVNI, ovni ['oβni] NM ABR *de* **objeto volante** (*o* **volador**) **no identificado** unidentified flying object, UFO.

ovoide [1] ADJ ovoid, egg-shaped.
[2] NM ovoid; (*LAm Dep*) rugby ball.

ovovegetariano, -a ADJ, NM/F ovo-vegetarian.

ovulación NF ovulation.

ovular [1a] VI to ovulate.

óvulo NM ovule, ovum.

ox [os] INTERJ shoo!

oxálico ADJ oxalic.

oxear [1a] VT to shoo (away).

oxiacanta NF hawthorn.
oxiacetilénico ADJ oxyacetylene *(atr)*.
oxidación NF rusting; *(Quím)* oxidation.
oxidado ADJ rusty; *(Quím)* oxidized.
oxidar [1a] **1** VT *(gen)* to rust; *(Quím)* to oxidize.
  2 oxidarse VR to rust, go rusty, get rusty; *(Quím)* to oxidize.
óxido NM rust; *(Quím)* oxide; **~ de hierro** iron oxide; **~ nitroso** nitrous oxide.
oxigenación NF oxygenation.
oxigenado **1** ADJ **(a)** *(Quím)* oxygenated.
  (b) *pelo* peroxided, bleached; **una rubia oxigenada** a peroxide blonde.
  2 NM peroxide *(for hair)*.

oxigenar [1a] **1** VT to oxygenate.
  2 oxigenarse VR **(a)** *(lit)* to become oxygenated. **(b)** *(fig)* to get some fresh air.
oxígeno NM oxygen.
oxímoron NM oxymoron.
oxte INTERJ shoo!; get out!, hop it!*; **sin decir ~ ni moxte** without a word.
oye, oyendo *etc* V oír.
oyente NMF **(a)** *(gen)* listener, hearer; *(Rad)* '**queridos ~s ...**' 'dear listeners ...'.
  (b) *(Univ)* unregistered student, occasional student, auditor *(US)*.
ozono NM ozone.
ozonosfera NF ozonosphere, ozone layer.

P

P, p [pe] NF (*letra*) P, p.
P **(a)** (*Ecl*) ABR de **Padre** Father, F., Fr. **(b)** ABR de **Papa** pope. **(c)** ABR de **pregunta** question, Q.
p. **(a)** (*Tip*) ABR de **página** page, p. **(b)** (*Cos*) ABR de **punto** stitch.
p.ª ABR de **para**.
PA NM (*Esp*) ABR de **Partido Andalucista**.
pa: PREP *pronunciación vulgar o jocosa de* **para**; *p.ej.* **es pal gato**; *V* **gato**.
p.a. **(a)** ABR de **por autorización**. **(b)** ABR de **por ausencia**.
PAAU NFPL ABR de **Pruebas para el Acceso a la Universidad**.
pabellón NM **(a)** (*tienda*) bell tent.
  (b) (*de cama*) canopy, hangings.
  (c) (*Arquit*) pavilion; (*en jardín*) summerhouse, hut; (*de hospital etc*) block, section; **~ de aduanas** customs house; **~ de caza** shooting box; **~ de conciertos**, **~ de música** bandstand; **~ (poli)deportivo** sports hall; **~ de hidroterapia** pumproom.
  (d) (*de trompeta etc*) mouth; **~ de la oreja** outer ear.
  (e) (*Mil*) stack.
  (f) (*bandera*) flag; **~ de conveniencia** flag of convenience; **~ nacional** national flag; **un buque de ~ panameño** a ship with Panamanian registration, a ship flying the Panamanian flag.
pabilo NM, **pábilo** NM wick; snuff (*of candle*).
Pablo NM Paul.
pábulo NM **(a)** (*gen*) food.
  (b) (*fig*) food, fuel, encouragement; **dar ~ a** to feed, encourage; **dar ~ a las llamas** to add fuel to the flames; **dar ~ a los rumores** to encourage rumours.
PAC NF ABR de **Política Agraria Común** Common Agricultural Policy, CAP.
Paca NF *forma familiar de* **Francisca**.
paca¹ NF bale.
paca² NF (*LAm: Zool*) paca, spotted cavy.
pacapaca NF (*And*) owl; **le vino la ~*** it all went wrong for him.
pacatería NF (*véase ADJ*) **(a)** timidity. **(b)** excessive modesty, prudishness.
pacato ADJ **(a)** (*tímido*) timid, quiet. **(b)** (*modesto*) excessively modest, prudish.
pacense [1] ADJ of Badajoz.
  [2] NMF native (*o* inhabitant) of Badajoz; **los ~s** the people of Badajoz.
paceño [1] ADJ of La Paz.
  [2] NM, **paceña** NF native (*o* inhabitant) of La Paz; **los ~s** the people of La Paz.
pacer [2d] [1] VT **(a)** *hierba etc* to eat, graze. **(b)** *ganado* to graze, pasture.
  [2] VI to graze.
pacha NF (*CAm*) baby's bottle.
pachá NM pasha; **vivir como un ~** to live like a prince.
pachacho ADJ (*Cono Sur*) (*rechoncho*) chubby; (*bajetón*) squat.
pachaco* ADJ (*CAm*) weak, feeble.
pachamama NF (*And, Cono Sur*) the good earth, Mother Earth.
pachamanca NF (*And*) barbecue; (*fig*) feast.
pachanga NF **(a)** (: *fiesta*) party; (*juerga*) binge*, booze-up:. **(b)** (*Carib*: lío*) mix-up. **(c)** (*Mús*) a Cuban dance.
pachanguear* [1a] VI to go on a spree.
pachanguero* ADJ **(a)** noisy, rowdy. **(b)** (*Méx*) (*alegre*) merry; (*chistoso*) witty; (*campechano*) expansive.
pacharán NM sloe brandy.
pacho* ADJ **(a)** (*CAm, Cono Sur**) *persona* (*rechoncho*) chubby; (*achaparrado*) squat; (*CAm*) *objeto* flat, flattened; *sombrero* flat-brimmed. **(b)** (*Carib*) slow, phlegmatic.
pachocha NF (*LAm*) = **pachorra**.
pachol NM (*Méx*) mat of hair.
pachón [1] ADJ **(a)** (*CAm, Cono Sur*: peludo*) shaggy, hairy; (*CAm, Méx**:

lanudo) woolly.
  (b) (*And: gordito*) plump.
  (c) (*And*: lerdo*) dim*, dense*.
  [2] NM **(a)** (*persona*) dull person, slow sort.
  (b) (*t* **perro ~**) beagle.
pachorra NF slowness, sluggishness; phlegm, phlegmatic nature; **Juan, con su santa ~** ... John, as slow as ever ...
pachorrada* NF (*Carib, Cono Sur*) blunder, gaffe.
pachorrear [1a] VI (*CAm*) to be slow, be sluggish.
pachorriento ADJ (*And, Cono Sur*), **pachorro** ADJ (*And, Carib*), **pachorrudo** ADJ slow, sluggish; phlegmatic.
pachotada NF (*And, Méx*) = **patochada**.
pachucho ADJ *fruta* overripe; *persona* (*enfermo*) off-colour, poorly.
pachuco* [1] ADJ (*Méx: majo*) flashy, flashily dressed.
  [2] NM (*bien vestido*) sharp dresser, snappy dresser; (*pey*) Chicano.
pachulí NM **(a)** (*Bot, perfume*) patchouli. **(b)** (*Esp:: tío*) bloke:, guy*.
paciencia NF patience; forbearance; **¡~!** be patient!; (*Cono Sur*) that's just too bad!; **¡~ y barajar!** keep trying!, don't give up! **se me acaba** (*o* **agota**) **la ~**, **no tengo más ~** my patience is running out, I'm at the end of my tether; **armarse** (*o* **cargarse**, **revestirse**) **de ~** to arm o.s. with patience, resolve to be patient; **perder la ~** to lose one's temper.
paciencioso ADJ (*And, Cono Sur*) long-suffering.
paciente ADJ, NMF patient.
pacientemente ADV patiently.
pacienzudo ADJ very patient, long-suffering.
pacificación NF pacification.
pacificador [1] ADJ pacifying, peace-making.
  [2] NM, **pacificadora** NF peace-maker.
pacíficamente ADV pacifically, peaceably.
pacificar [1g] [1] VT (*Mil*) to pacify; (*calmar*) to calm; (*apaciguar*) to appease.
  [2] **pacificarse** VR (*calmarse*) to calm down.
Pacífico NM (*t* **Océano ~**) Pacific (Ocean).
pacífico ADJ pacific, peaceable; peace-loving.
pacifismo NM pacifism.
pacifista ADJ, NMF pacifist.
Paco NM *forma familiar de* **Francisco**; **ya vendrá el tío ~ con la rebaja** it won't be as bad as you think.
paco¹ NM (*Mil*) sniper, sharpshooter.
paco²: NM (*LAm*) cop:, policeman.
paco³ [1] ADJ (*And, Cono Sur*) reddish.
  [2] NM (*And, Cono Sur*) alpaca.
pacota* NF (*Méx*) (*trasto*) piece of junk; (*persona*) layabout*.
pacotada* NF (*And*) blunder, gaffe.
pacotilla NF **(a)** (*gen*) trash, junk, inferior stuff; **de ~** trashy, shoddy; **hacer su ~** to be doing nicely, make a nice profit.
  (b) (*And, CAm, Cono Sur*) rabble, crowd, mob.
pacotillero [1] ADJ (*And*) rude, uncouth.
  [2] NM (*And, Carib, Cono Sur*) pedlar, peddler (*US*), hawker.
pactable ADJ negotiable.
pactar [1a] [1] VT to agree to, agree on; to stipulate, contract for.
  [2] VI to come to an agreement; to compromise.
pacto NM pact; agreement, covenant; **P~ Andino** Andean Pact; **~ de no agresión** non-aggression pact; **~ de** (*o* **entre**) **caballeros** gentlemen's agreement; **~ de recompra**, **~ de retro** (*Com*) repurchase agreement; **~ social** social contract; wages agreement; **P~ de Varsovia** Warsaw Pact.

┌─ *PACTOS DE LA MONCLOA* ─┐

ⓘ *In the unstable political environment that followed Franco's death and the narrow victory of Adolfo Suárez's* **UCD** *party in the 1977 general election, it became obvious that a great deal of cross-party cooperation* *would be needed if progress in Spain were to be made. The result was the* **Pactos de la Moncloa,** *named after the prime minister's official residence, where the pacts were signed in October 1977. They were designed to bring together all political groups in a spirit of consensus in order to push through vital legislation, specifically the Constitution, but also budgets and regional policies.*

⇨ *See also* LA CONSTITUCIÓN ESPAÑOLA , UCD

padecer [2d] ⬚1 VT (*gen*) to suffer (from); (*aguantar*) to endure, put up with; *error etc* to labour under, be a victim of.

⬚2 VI **~ de** to suffer from; **padece del corazón** he suffers with his heart, he has heart trouble; **padece en su amor propio** his self-respect suffers; **ella padece por todos** she suffers on everybody's account; **se embala bien para que no padezca en el viaje** it is well packed so that it will not get damaged on the journey.

padecimiento NM suffering; (*Med*) ailment.

padrastro NM (a) (*gen*) stepfather; (*fig*) harsh father, cruel parent. (b) (*fig: dificultad*) obstacle, difficulty. (c) (*Anat*) hangnail.

padrazo NM indulgent father.

padre ⬚1 NM (a) father; (*Zool*) father, sire; **~s** father and mother, parents; (*antepasados*) ancestors; **García ~** García senior, the elder García; (*en censo etc*) head of a household; **~ de familia** father of a family, man with family responsibilities; **~ de pila** godfather; **~ político** father-in-law; **~ soltero** single father; **su señor ~** your father; **es el ~ de estos estudios** he is the father of this discipline; **¡eres mi ~!*** you're a marvel!; **¡mi ~!*, ¡su ~!*** hell's bells!*; **¡tu ~!⁑** up yours!⁑

(b) (*Ecl*) father, priest; **el P~ Las Casas** Father Las Casas; **~ espiritual** confessor; **P~ Nuestro** Lord's Prayer, Our Father; **P~ Santo** Holy Father, Pope.

(c) **una paliza de ~ y muy señor mío*** a terrific bashing*, a beating and a half, the father and mother of a thrashing*.

⬚2 ADJ (*: enorme*) huge, tremendous*; **un éxito ~** a terrific success*; **un lío ~** an almighty row*; **un susto ~** an awful fright.

padrejón NM (*Cono Sur*) stallion.

padrenuestro NM Lord's Prayer, paternoster; **en menos que se reza un ~** in no time at all.

padrillo NM (*And, Cono Sur*) stallion.

padrinazgo NM being a godfather; (*fig*) sponsorship, patronage; protection.

padrino NM (a) (*Ecl*) godfather; (*t ~ de boda*) best man; (*en duelo*) second; (*de mafia*) godfather; (*fig*) sponsor, patron; **~s** godparents.

(b) (⁑: *víctima*) sucker⁑, victim.

padrísimo* ADJ (*Méx*) = **padre 2**.

padrón NM (a) (*lista de habitantes*) list of inhabitants, roll; (*censo*) census; (*de miembros etc*) register; (*Pol*) electoral register.

(b) (*Téc*) pattern.

(c) (*Arquit*) inscribed column, commemorative column.

(d) (*fig: t ~ de ignominia*) stain, blot; **el trabajo es un ~ para su autor** the work is a disgrace to its author; **será un ~ para todos nosotros** it will be a stain on all of us.

(e) (*: padrazo*) indulgent father.

(f) (*LAm: caballo*) stallion; (*And: toro*) breeding bull.

padrote NM (a) (*LAm*) (*caballo*) stallion; (*toro*) breeding bull. (b) (*Méx**: chulo*) pimp.

pae⁑, pai⁑: ¿qué ~? = ¿qué pasa? (V **pasar**).

paella NF paella.

paellada NF paella party.

paellera¹ NF (*Culin*) paella dish; (*hum*) dish aerial, TV satellite dish.

paellero ⬚1 ADJ paella (*atr*).

⬚2 NM, **paellera²** NF paella cook.

paf INTERJ bang!; plop!, splash!

pág. ABR *de* **página** page, p.

paga NF (a) (*acto*) payment; **entrega contra ~** cash on delivery. (b) (*sueldo*) pay, wages; (*pensión*) allowance; (*honorarios*) fee; **~ extra, ~ extraordinaria** salary bonus. (c) **mala ~*** bad payer.

PAGA EXTRAORDINARIA

ⓘ *Most long-term and permanent employment contracts in Spain stipulate that annual salary will be paid in 14 instalments. This means that most Spanish workers receive twice the normal monthly wage in June and December. These extra payments are generally known as* **paga extraordinaria** *or* **paga extra.**

pagadero ADJ payable, due; **~ a la entrega** payable on delivery; **~ a plazos** payable in instalments; **~ al portador** payable to bearer.

pagado ADJ (*fig*) pleased; **~ de sí mismo** self-satisfied, smug; **quedamos ~s** we're quits.

pagador(a) NM/F (a) (*que paga*) payer; **mal ~** bad payer. (b) (*de banco*) teller, cashier; (*Mil: t oficial ~*) paymaster.

pagaduría NF pay office, cashier's office; (*Mil*) paymaster's office.

paganini* NM: **ser el ~** to be the one who pays.

paganismo NM paganism, heathenism.

pagano¹, -a ADJ, NM/F pagan, heathen.

pagano², -a* NM/F person who pays for others; scapegoat, dupe, victim.

pagar [1h] ⬚1 VT (a) (*gen*) to pay; *deuda* to pay, pay off, repay; *compras* to pay for; *póliza* to pay out on; **su tío le paga los estudios** his uncle is paying for his education; **no lo podemos ~** we can't afford it; **paga 20 dólares de habitación** he pays 20 dollars for his room; **a ~** (*Correos*) postage due; **cuenta a ~, cuenta por ~** unpaid bill, outstanding account; **~ por adelantado** to pay in advance; **~ al contado** to pay cash.

(b) (*fig*) *favor* to repay; *amor* to return, requite; *visita* to return; *crimen, ofensa* to pay for, atone for; **lo pagó con la vida** he paid for it with his life; **¡me las pagarás!** I'll pay you out for this!, I'll get you for this!; **el que la hace la paga** one must face the consequences; **¡las vas a ~!** you'll catch it!*, you've got it coming to you!

⬚2 VI (a) (*LAm*) to pay; **el negocio no paga** the business doesn't pay. (b) (*Cono Sur: tomar apuestas*) to take bets, make a book.

⬚3 **pagarse** VR (a) **~ con algo** to be content with sth. (b) **~ de algo** to be pleased with sth; to take a liking to sth; (*pey*) to boast of sth; **~ de sí mismo** to be conceited, be smug; to be very full of o.s.; **se paga mucho de su pelo** she's terribly vain about her hair.

pagaré NM promissory note, IOU; **~ del Tesoro** Treasury bill, Treasury bond.

página NF page; **~s amarillas** yellow pages; **es primera ~** it's front-page news; **anuncio a toda ~, anuncio a ~ entera** full-page advertisement; **currarse la ~⁑** to pretend, try it on*.

paginación NF pagination.

paginar [1a] VT to paginate, number the pages of; **con 6 hojas sin ~** with 6 unnumbered pages.

▼**pago¹** ⬚1 NM (a) (*Fin*) payment; (*devolución*) repayment; **~ anticipado** advance payment; **~ al contado** cash payment; **~ a cuenta** payment on account; **~ a la entrega, ~ contra recepción** cash on delivery; **~ en especie** payment in kind; **~ fraccionado** instalment, part-payment; **~ inicial** first payment, down payment, deposit; **~ íntegro** gross payment; **~ a la orden** direct debit; **~ a plazos** payment by instalments, deferred payments; **~ a la presentación de factura** payment on invoice; **~ por resultados** payment by results; **~ simbólico** token payment; **'nada de ~'** (*en aduana*) 'nothing to declare'; **colegio de ~** fee-paying school; **huésped de ~** paying guest; **atrasarse en los ~s** to be in arrears; **efectuar un ~** to make a payment; **faltar en los ~s** to default on one's payments; **suspender los ~s** to stop payments.

(b) (*fig*) return, reward; **en ~ de** in return for; as a reward for.

⬚2 ADJ paid; **estar ~** to be paid; (*fig*) to be even, be quits.

pago² NM (*distrito*) district; (*finca*) estate, property (*esp planted with vines or olives*); (*Cono Sur*) region, area; home area, native part; **en estos ~s** hereabouts, round here, in this neck of the woods.

pagoda NF pagoda.

pagote* NM scapegoat.

págs ABR *de* **páginas** pages, pp.

pagua NF (a) (*Cono Sur*) (*hernia*) hernia; (*hinchazón*) large swelling. (b) (*Méx*) large avocado pear.

paguacha NF (*Cono Sur*) (a) = **pagua** (a). (b) (*melón*) large melon. (c) (⁑: *cabeza*) nut⁑, bonce⁑.

paguala NF (*Carib*) swordfish.

paguro NM edible crab.

pai NM (*LAm*) pie.

paiche NM (*And*) dried salted fish.

paila NF (a) large pan; (*sartén*) frying-pan. (b) (*Cono Sur*) meal of fried food.

pailero NM (a) (*And, Méx**: italiano*) immigrant Italian, Wop⁑. (b) (*CAm, Carib, Méx*) (*cobrero*) coppersmith; (*calderero*) tinker.

pailón NM (a) (*And, Carib*) pot, pan. (b) (*And, CAm Geog*) bowl. (c) (*Carib*) whirlpool.

paiño NM petrel.

paipai NM oriental-style fan.

pairo NM: **estar al ~** (*Náut*) to lie to; **quedarse al ~** (*fig*) to sit back and do nothing.

país NM (a) (*nación*) country; (*tierra*) land, region, area; (*paisaje*) landscape; **~ cliente** client state; **~ en (vías de) desarrollo** developing country; **~ deudor** debtor nation; **~ de las maravillas** wonderland; **~ natal** native land; **~ de nunca jamás** never-never land; **~ satélite** satellite country; **los ~es miembros, los ~es participantes** the member countries; **vino del ~** local wine; **así se cuece en mi ~** that's how it's cooked in my part of the country; **vivir sobre el ~** to live off the country.

(b) **P~es Bajos** Low Countries; **P~ Vasco** Basque Country.

paisa* NMF (*LAm*) = **paisano 2** (c).

paisaje NM landscape, countryside, scenery; **~ interior** state of mind.

paisajismo NM (*de jardines*) landscaping, landscape gardening; (*Arte*) landscape painting.

paisajista NMF landscape gardener; (*Arte*) landscape painter.

paisajístico ADJ landscape (*atr*), scenic.

paisanada NF (*Cono Sur*) group of peasants, peasants (*collectively*).

paisanaje NM (**a**) (*gen*) civil population. (**b**) (*Cono Sur*) = **paisanada**.

paisano ① ADJ of the same country.

② NM, **paisana** NF (**a**) (*Mil*) civilian; **vestir de ~** (*soldado*) to be in mufti, be in civvies*, (*policía*) be in plain clothes.

(**b**) (*compatriota*) compatriot, fellow countryman, fellow countrywoman; **es ~ mío** he's a fellow countryman (of mine).

(**c**) (*Cono Sur: extranjero*) foreigner; (*Cono Sur: árabe*) Arab; (*Méx*) Spaniard; (*And, Cono Sur*) Chinaman, Chinese woman.

paja NF (**a**) (*Agr*) straw; (*LAm: de beber*) straw; (*LAm: leña*) dried brushwood; **hombre de ~*** stooge*; **techo de ~** thatched roof.

(**b**) **hacerse una** (o **la**) **~*** to wank*, jerk off*; **riñeron por un quítame allá esas ~s** they fell out over some tiny thing, they quarrelled over some trifle; **lo hizo en un quitarme las ~s*** she did it in a jiffy*; **ver la ~ en el ojo ajeno y no la viga en el propio** to see the mote in sb else's eye and not the beam in one's own; **volarse la ~** (*CAm**) to wank*, jerk off*.

(**c**) (*fig*) trash, rubbish; (*lit*) padding, waffle*; **hinchar un libro con mucha ~** to pad a book out; **meter ~** to pad.

(**d**) (*And, CAm: t ~ de agua*) (*grifo*) tap, faucet (*US*); (*canal*) canal.

(**e**) (*Cono Sur: droga*) dope*.

(**f**) (*CAm*: mentira*) lie.

pajar NM straw loft; straw rick.

pájara NF (**a**) (*Orn*) hen, hen bird; (*esp*) hen partridge.

(**b**) (*cometa*) kite; (*pájaro de papel*) paper bird.

(**c**) (*putilla*) loose woman; (*ladrona*) thieving woman.

(**d**) **~ pinta** (game of) forfeits.

(**e**) (*Dep*) wall, collapse.

(**f**) **dar ~ a uno** (*And, CAm*) to swindle sb.

pajarada NF (*And*) flock of birds.

pajarear [1a] ① VT (**a**) (*LAm*) *pájaros* to scare, keep off.

(**b**) (*And: observar*) to watch intently.

(**c**) (*And: matar*) to murder.

② VI (**a**) (*holgazanear*) to loaf; to loiter.

(**b**) (*LAm: caballo*) to shy.

(**c**) (*Cono Sur*: estar distraído*) to have one's head in the clouds.

(**d**) (*Méx*: escuchar*) to keep an ear open.

pajarera NF aviary.

pajarería NF (**a**) (*tienda*) pet shop. (**b**) (*pájaros*) large flock of birds. (**c**) (*Carib**) vanity.

pajarero ① ADJ (**a**) (*Orn*) bird (*atr*).

(**b**) *persona* (*alegre*) fun-loving; (*chistoso*) facetious, waggish.

(**c**) *ropa etc* gaudy, flashy, loud.

(**d**) (*LAm*) *caballo* nervous; (*And, Carib, Méx*) *caballo* spirited.

(**e**) (*Carib*: entrometido*) meddlesome.

② NM (*cazador*) bird catcher; (*criador*) bird fancier, breeder of birds; (*Com*) bird dealer; (*And, CAm*) bird-scarer.

pajarilla NF paper kite; **se le alegraron las ~s*** he was tickled pink*.

pajarita NF (**a**) **~ de las nieves** white wagtail. (**b**) (*cometa*) paper kite; (*pájaro de papel*) paper bird. (**c**) (*corbata de*) **~** bow tie; V **cuello** (**b**).

pajarito NM (**a**) (*Orn*) baby bird, fledgling; (*hum*) birdie; (*fig*) very small person; **me lo dijo un ~** a little bird told me; **quedarse como un ~** to die peacefully, fade away.

(**b**) (*Carib: bichito*) bug, insect.

pájaro ① NM (**a**) (*Orn*) bird; **~ de mal agüero** bird of ill omen; **~ azul** bluebird; **~ bobo** penguin; **~ cantor**, **~ cantarín** songbird; **~ carpintero** woodpecker; **~ mosca** (*Esp*) hummingbird; **matar dos ~s de un tiro** to kill two birds with one stone; **quedarse como un ~** to die peacefully; **más vale ~ en mano que ciento volando** a bird in the hand is worth two in the bush; **tener ~s en la cabeza, tener la cabeza a ~s** (o **llena de ~s**) to be featherbrained.

(**b**) (*: *persona*; *t ~ de cuenta*) (*taimado*) wily bird, nasty type; (*de cuidado*) dangerous person; (*importante*) big noise*, big shot*; **~ bravo** (*Carib*) smart Alec*.

(**c**) (*) prick*.

(**d**) (*Carib**: *homosexual*) queer*, poof*.

② ADJ (**a**) (*Cono Sur*) (*atolondrado*) scatty, featherbrained; (*sospechoso*) shady, dubious; (*chillón*) loud, flashy.

(**b**) (*Carib*: afeminado*) poofy*, queer*.

(**c**) (*Cono Sur*) vague, distracted.

pajarón (*Cono Sur*) ① ADJ vague, ineffectual, stupid.

② NM, **pajarona** NF (**a**) (*poco fiable*) untrustworthy sort; (*ineficaz*) unbusinesslike person.

(**b**) (*charro*) flashily dressed person.

pajarota* NF (*Esp*) false rumour, canard.

pajarraca* NF to-do*, fuss.

pajarraco NM (**a**) (*Orn*) big ugly bird. (**b**) (*) slyboots*.

paje NM page; (*Náut*) cabin boy.

pajel NM sea-bream.

pajero ① ADJ (*CAm**) lying.

② NM, **pajera** NF (**a**) (*CAm**) liar. (**b**) (*CAm: fontanero*) plumber. (**c**) (*) tosser*, wanker*.

③ NF (*Agr*) straw loft.

pajilla NF (*CAm, Carib, Méx*) straw hat; (*LAm*) type of cigarette made from rolled maize.

pajillero* NM tosser*, wanker*.

pajita NF (drinking) straw; **quedarse mascando ~*** (*Carib*) to be left feeling foolish.

pajizo ADJ (**a**) (*de paja*) straw, made of straw; *techo* thatched. (**b**) (*color*) straw-coloured.

pajolero* ADJ (**a**) (*condenado*) blessed, wretched. (**b**) (*tonto*) stupid. (**c**) (*travieso*) naughty, mischievous; (*molesto*) irritating.

pajón ADJ (*Méx*) *pelo* (*lacio*) lank; (*crespo*) curly.

pajonal NM (*LAm*) scrubland.

pajoso ADJ (**a**) *grano* full of chaff. (**b**) (*color*) straw-coloured; (*como paja*) like straw.

pajuela NF spill; (*And*) match; (*And, Cono Sur, Méx*) toothpick; (*Carib Mús*) plectrum; **el tiempo de la ~** olden days, bygone times.

pajúo* ADJ (*Carib*) daft, stupid.

Pakistán NM Pakistan.

pakistaní ADJ, NMF Pakistani.

pala NF (**a**) (*gen*) shovel, spade; scoop; **~ cargadora** mechanical loader; **~ excavadora** digger; **~ mecánica** power shovel; **~ de patatas** potato fork; **~ quitanieves** snowplough; **~ topadora** (*Cono Sur*) power shovel.

(**b**) (*Culin*) slice; **~ para el pescado** fish slice.

(**c**) (*Dep*) bat; racquet; **jugar a ~** to play beach-tennis.

(**d**) (*de hélice, remo*) blade.

(**e**) **~ matamoscas** fly swat.

(**f**) (*de zapato*) vamp.

(**g**) (*: *mano*) mitt*, hand; **¡choca la ~!** shake on it!*

(**h**) (*fig*) cunning, wiliness.

palabra NF (**a**) (*vocablo*) word; **~ clave** keyword; **~s cruzadas** crossword (puzzle); **~s gruesas**, **~s mayores** strong words, abuse; **dos ~s, cuatro ~s** a couple of words; **medias ~s** hints, insinuations; **¡ni una ~ más!** not another word!; **de ~** by word of mouth; **en una ~** in a word; **~ por ~** word for word; verbatim; **a ~s necias, oídos sordos** it's best not to listen to such nonsense; **ser la última ~ en lujo** to be the last word in luxury; **cambiar unas ~s con uno** to have a few words with sb; **coger a uno la ~** to take sb at his word; to keep sb to his word; to call sb's bluff; **comerse las ~s** to mumble; **no cruzar** (una) **~ con uno** not to say a word to sb; **sin chistar ~** without a word; **dejar a uno con la ~ en la boca** to interrupt sb, leave sb in mid-sentence; **no encuentro ~s para expresarme** words fail me; **no entiendo ~** it's Greek to me; **gastar ~s** to waste words, waste one's breath; **medir las ~s** to choose one's words carefully; **negar la ~ de Dios a uno** to concede absolutely nothing to sb; **tuvo ~s de elogio para el ministro** he paid tribute to the minister; **trabarse de ~s** to get involved in an argument; to wrangle, squabble.

(**b**) (*facultad*) speech, power of speech, faculty of speech; **de ~ fácil** fluent; **perder la ~** to lose one's power of speech.

(**c**) (*Parl*) right to speak; **ceder la ~ a uno** to call on sb to speak; **dirigir la ~ a uno** to address sb; **hacer uso de la ~, tomar la ~** to speak; **pedir la ~** to ask to be allowed to speak; **tener la ~** to have the floor; **Vd tiene la ~** the floor is yours; **yo no tengo la ~** it's not for me to say; **tomar la ~** (*en un mitin*) to take the floor, begin one's speech.

(**d**) (*promesa*) word, promise; **¡~!** honest!, really!; **~ de casamiento**, **~ de matrimonio** promise to marry; **~ de honor** word of honour; **bajo ~** (*Mil*) on parole; **es hombre de ~** he is a man of his word; **cumplir la ~** to keep one's word; **dar su ~, empeñar su ~** to give one's word, give a pledge; **faltar a su ~** to go back on one's word.

palabrear [1a] VT (**a**) (*And, Cono Sur*) to agree verbally to; **~ a una** to promise to marry sb. (**b**) (*Cono Sur: insultar*) to abuse.

palabreja NF strange word; nasty-sounding word.

palabrería NF, **palabrerío** NM (*CAm, Cono Sur*) wordiness; verbiage, hot air.

palabrero ① ADJ wordy, windy.

② NM, **palabrera** NF windbag.

palabro* NM (*palabrota*) rude word; (*palabra rara*) odd word; pretentious term; (*barbarismo*) barbarism.

palabrota NF rude word, swearword.

palabrudo* ADJ (*Cono Sur*) foulmouthed.

palacete NM small palace.

palacial ADJ (*LAm*) palatial.

palaciego ① ADJ palace (*atr*), court (*atr*).

② NM (*persona*) courtier.

palacio NM (*de rey*) palace; (*casa grande*) mansion, large house; **~ de congresos** conference centre, conference hall; **P~ de las Comunicaciones** (*Madrid*) General Post Office; **~ de (los) deportes** sports centre; **~ episcopal** bishop's palace; **~ de justicia** courthouse; **~**

municipal city hall; **P~ Nacional** (*p.ej. Guatemala*) Parliament Building; **~ real** royal palace; **el ~ de los Marqueses de Tal** the house of the Marquis of Tal; **ir a ~** to go to court; **tener un puesto en ~** to have a post at court.

palada NF (**a**) (*gen*) shovelful, spadeful. (**b**) (*de remo*) stroke.

paladar NM (hard) palate, roof of the mouth; (*fig*) palate, taste; **tener un ~ delicado** to have a delicate palate.

paladear [1a] VT to taste; to relish, savour; **beber algo paladeándolo** to sip a drink (to see what it tastes like).

paladeo NM tasting; relishing, savouring; sipping.

paladín NM (*Hist*) paladin; (*fig*) champion.

paladinamente ADV openly, publicly; clearly.

paladino ADJ open, public; clear; **más ~ no puede ser** it couldn't be clearer.

palafrén NM palfrey.

palafrenero NM groom.

palana NF (*And*) (*pala*) shovel, spade; (*azadón*) hoe.

palanca NF (**a**) (*gen*) lever; crowbar; (*Mec*) lever; **~ de arranque** kick-starter; **~ de cambio(s)** gear-lever, gearshift (*US*); **~ de freno** brake lever; **~ de mando** control lever; (*Inform*) joystick.
(**b**) (*fig*) lever; pull, influence; **~s del poder** levers of power; **tener ~*** to have pull, to know people in the right places.
(**c**) (*And, Méx: de barca*) punting pole.

palangana [1] NF (**a**) (*gen*) washbasin.
(**b**) (*And, CAm*) platter, serving dish.
[2] NMF (**: t ~s*) (*Cono Sur: intruso*) intruder; (*LAm: frívolo*) shallow person; (*charlatán*) charlatan; (*jactancioso*) braggart.

palanganear* [1a] VI (*LAm*) to brag; to show off*.

palanganero NM washstand.

palangre NM fishing line (with multiple hooks).

palanquear [1a] [1] VT (**a**) (*And, CAm*) to lever (along), move with a lever; (*And, Carib, Méx*) *barca* to punt, pole along.
(**b**) (*fig*) **¿quién te palanqueó?** who got you fixed up?
[2] VI (*And, Carib, Cono Sur**) to pull strings.

palanquera NF stockade.

palanquero NM (*And, Cono Sur Ferro*) brakeman; (*And*) lumberman; (*Cono Sur*: ladrón*) burglar, housebreaker.

palanqueta NF small lever; (*de ladrón*) jemmy; (*Cono Sur, Méx: peso*) weight; (*Pesas*) bar.

palanquetazo* NM break-in, burglary.

palanquista* NM burglar.

p'alante: ADV = **para adelante**.

palatal ADJ, NF palatal.

palatalización NF palatalization.

palatalizar [1f] [1] VT to palatalize.
[2] **palatalizarse** VR to palatalize.

palatinado NM palatinate.

palatino ADJ (**a**) (*Pol*) palace (*atr*), court (*atr*), palatine. (**b**) (*Anat*) palatal.

palatosquisis NF cleft palate.

palca NF (*And*) crossroads.

palco NM (**a**) (*Teat etc*) box; (*Fút*) director's box; **~ de autoridades, ~ de honor** royal box; box for distinguished persons; **~ de la presidencia, ~ presidencial** (*Taur*) president's box; **~ de proscenio** stage box. (**b**) (***) balcony.

palde NM (*Cono Sur*) pointed digging tool; (*puñal*) dagger.

palé NM board game similar to Monopoly.

palear [1a] [1] VT (**a**) (*LAm*) *barca* to punt, pole. (**b**) (*LAm*) *tierra* to shovel; *zanja* to dig. (**c**) (*Cono Sur*) to thresh.
[2] VI (*piragüista*) to paddle.

palenque NM (**a**) (*estacada*) fence, stockade, palisade.
(**b**) (*recinto*) arena, ring, enclosure; (*de gallos*) pit.
(**c**) (*And, Cono Sur: de caballos*) tethering-post, rail.
(**d**) (*Cono Sur*: alboroto*) din, racket.

palenquear [1a] VT (*Cono Sur*) to hitch, tether.

palentino [1] ADJ of Palencia.
[2] NM, **palentina** NF native (*o* inhabitant) of Palencia; **los ~s** the people of Palencia.

paleo... PREF pal(a)eo...

paleografía NF paleography.

paleógrafo, -a NM/F paleographer.

paleolítico ADJ paleolithic.

paleontología NF paleontology.

paleontólogo, -a NM/F paleontologist.

palero* [1] ADJ (*And*) big-headed*.
[2] NM (*Méx*) front man*.

Palestina NF Palestine.

palestino, -a ADJ, NM/F Palestinian.

palestra NF arena; (*fig*) lists; **salir** (*o* **saltar**) **a la ~** (*fig*) to take the field, take the floor.

paleta [1] NF (**a**) (*pala*) small shovel, small spade; scoop (*t Culin*); fire shovel; (*Arquit*) trowel.

(**b**) (*Arte*) palette.
(**c**) (*Tec: de turbina etc*) blade; vane; (*de noria*) paddle; (*de rueda*) bucket; (*plataforma*) pallet, platform (*for lifting and stacking goods*).
(**d**) (*Anat*) shoulder-blade.
(**e**) (*LAm: pala*) wooden paddle for beating clothes.
(**f**) (*LAm: piruli*) lollipop.
(**g**) (*LAm Culin*) topside of beef.
[2] NM (*) building worker, brickie*.

paletada NF shovelful, spadeful.

paletear [1a] [1] VT (*Cono Sur*) *caballo* to pat; (*fig*) to flatter.
[2] VI (*Cono Sur*) to be out of work.

paletería¹ NF (*Culin*) palate, sense of taste.

paletería²* NF collection of yokels, shower:.

paletero NM (*And*) tuberculosis.

paletilla NF shoulder blade.

paletización NF (*Com*) palletization.

paleto [1] ADJ boorish, stupid.
[2] NM (**a**) (*Zool*) fallow deer. (**b**) (*) yokel, country bumpkin.

palia NF altar cloth, pall.

paliacate NM (*Méx*) scarf, kerchief.

paliar [1b] VT (**a**) (*gen*) to palliate, mitigate, alleviate; *dolor* to relieve; *efecto* to lessen, cushion; *importancia* to diminish.
(**b**) *defecto* to conceal, gloss over.
(**c**) *ofensa etc* to mitigate, excuse.

paliativo [1] ADJ palliative; mitigating; concealing.
[2] NM (**a**) palliative.
(**b**) **sin ~s** *desastre, fracaso* unmitigated; *rechazo* unreserved; *vulgaridad* utter; *condenar, rechazar* unreservedly.

palidecer [2d] VI to pale, turn pale.

palidez NF paleness, pallor; wanness; sickliness.

pálido ADJ pale, pallid (*t fig*); wan; (*enfermizo*) sickly.

palidoso ADJ (*And*) = **pálido**.

paliducho* ADJ pale.

palier NM (*Mec*) bearing; (*plataforma*) pallet.

palillero NM (*para palillos*) toothpick holder; (*para plumillas*) penholder.

palillo NM (**a**) (*gen*) small stick; (*mondadientes*) toothpick; (*Mús*) drumstick; (*Taur**) banderilla; (*Cono Sur*) knitting-needle; (*CAm, Méx*) penholder; **~s** (*Mús*) castanets; **~s chinos** chopsticks; **unas piernas como ~s de dientes** legs like matchsticks.
(**b**) (*hum*) very thin person; **estar hecho un ~** to be as thin as a rake.

palimpsesto NM palimpsest.

palindroma NM, **palindromo** NM palindrome.

palinodia NF recantation; **cantar la ~** to recant.

palio NM (*manto*) cloak; (*dosel*) canopy; (*Ecl*) pallium.

palique* NM chat; small talk, chitchat; **darle al ~, estar de ~** to be chatting, have a chat.

palista NMF (*Dep*) canoeist.

palitroque NM (**a**) (*Taur**) banderilla. (**b**) (*Cono Sur*) (*juego*) skittles, bowling (*US*); (*local*) skittle alley, bowling alley (*US*).

paliza [1] NF (**a**) (*golpes*) beating, thrashing; beating-up*; **dar una ~ a uno** to give sb a beating, beat sb up*; **dar la ~*** to be a pain*; **darse la ~** to flog o.s., slog; **el viaje fue una ~** the journey was ghastly*.
(**b**) (*Dep etc*) beating, drubbing; **¡qué ~ aquélla!** what a beating that was!; **los críticos le dieron una ~ a la novela** the critics panned the novel*, the novel took a beating from the critics.
[2] NMF INVAR (**: pesado*) bore, pain*.

palizada NF (**a**) (*valla*) fence, stockade, palisade. (**b**) (*recinto*) fenced enclosure.

palizas* NMF INVAR bore, pain*.

palizón NM = **paliza**.

palla NF (*And Hist*) Inca princess.

pallador NM (*LAm*) *etc* = **payador** *etc*.

pallar¹ [1a] VT (*Min*) to extract; (*Agr*) to glean.

pallar² NM (*And, Cono Sur*) Lima bean.

pallasca NF (*And, Cono Sur*), **pallaso** NM (*And, Cono Sur*) mattress.

Palma NF: **Isla de la ~** (*Canarias*) Island of Palma; **~ de Mallorca** Palma; **Las ~s** (*ciudad, provincia*) Las Palmas.

palma NF (**a**) (*Anat*) palm; **batir ~s, dar ~s** to clap hands, applaud; (*Mús*) to clap hands; **como la ~ de la mano** (*llano*) as flat as the palm of one's hand; (*fácil*) very easy, straightforward; **conocer como la ~ de la mano** to know like the back of one's hand.
(**b**) **~s** (*fig*) clapping, applause; **~s de tango** slow hand-clap.
(**c**) (*Bot*) (*árbol*) palm, palm tree; (*hoja*) palm leaf; **ganar la ~, llevarse la ~** to carry off the palm, triumph, win.

palmada NF (**a**) (*gen*) slap, pat (*on the shoulder etc*); **darse una ~ en la frente** to clap one's hand to one's brow.
(**b**) **~s** clapping, applause; **dar ~s** to clap, applaud.

palmadita NF pat, light tap.

palmado: ADJ (*CAm*) skint:, flat broke*.

palmar¹ NM (*Bot*) palm grove, cluster of palms.

palmar²: [1a] [1] VI (**a**) (*morir*) to peg out:, die. (**b**) (*en juego*) to lose.

2 VT: ~**la** = **1** (a).

palmar³ ADJ, **palmario** ADJ clear, obvious, self-evident.

palmarés NM (*Dep*) list of victories; list of winners; (*Mil etc*) service record.

palmariamente ADJ *demostrar* clearly; **estar ~ claro** to be abundantly clear.

palmario ADJ clear; *verdad* obvious.

palmarote: NM (*Carib*) yokel.

palmatoria NF (a) (*de vela*) candlestick. (b) (*de castigo*) cane.

palmazón: NM: **estar en el ~** (*CAm*) to be broke*.

palmeado ADJ *pata* webbed.

palmear [1a] VI to clap.

palmense **1** ADJ of Las Palmas.
2 NMF native (o inhabitant) of Las Palmas; **los ~s** the people of Las Palmas.

palmera¹ NF, **palmero¹** NM (*And, Cono Sur, Méx*) palm, palm tree; **~ datilera** date-palm; **estar en la ~** to be broke*.

palmero² **1** ADJ of the Island of Palma.
2 NM, **palmera²** NF native (o inhabitant) of the Island of Palma.

palmero, -a³ NM/F (*Mús*) *flamenco artiste who claps in time to the music*.

palmeta NF (*palo*) cane; (*acto*) caning, swish with a cane; **~ matamoscas** fly swat.

palmetazo NM caning, swish with a cane; (*fig*) blow, slap in the face; light slap (of admonition).

palmetón NM slap.

palmillas NFPL: **llevar a uno en ~** to treat sb with great consideration.

palmípedo ADJ web-footed.

palmista NMF (*LAm*) palmist.

palmiste NM palm kernel; palm oil.

palmita NF: **tener** (o **llevar, traer**) **a uno en ~s** (*mimar*) to spoil sb; (*tratar con cuidado*) to handle sb with kid gloves.

palmito NM (*LAm*) palm heart.

palmo NM (a) span; (*fig*) few inches, small amount; **~ a ~** inch by inch; **con un ~ de lengua fuera** with his tongue hanging out; **avanzar ~ a ~** to go forward inch by inch; **conocer el terreno ~ a ~** (o **a ~s**), **tener medido el terreno a ~s** to know every inch of the ground; **crecer a ~s** to shoot up; **dejar a uno un ~ de narices** to disappoint sb greatly, leave sb very crestfallen; **no hay un ~ de A a B** there's hardly any distance (o difference) between A and B, there's nothing to choose between A and B; **no levantaba un ~ del suelo cuando ...** he was knee-high to a grasshopper when ...
(b) (*CAm*:) cunt:.

palmotear [1a] VI to clap, applaud.

palmoteo NM clapping, applause.

palo NM (a) (*gen*) stick; (*Telec etc*) post, pole; (*porra*) club; (*de herramienta etc*) handle, haft, shaft; (*Taur*: *banderilla*) banderilla; (*: garrocha*) spear; (*Dep*: *de portería*) post; (*Dep Golf*) club; (:) prick:; **ensebado** greasy pole; **~ de escoba** broomstick; **~ de golf** golf club; **~ de tienda** tent pole; **de tal ~ tal astilla** like father like son; **¡~ y tentetieso!** be tough with him (*etc*)!; **la política del ~ y la zanahoria** the policy of the stick and the carrot; **estar hecho un ~** to be as thin as a rake; **meter ~s en las ruedas** (*fig*) to put a spanner in the works*.
(b) (*Náut*) mast; spar; **~ mayor** mainmast; **~ de mesana** mizzenmast; **~ de trinquete** foremast; **que cada ~ aguante su vela** everyone must take what's coming to him.
(c) (*Bot*) stalk (of grape etc).
(d) (*madera*) wood; **cuchara de ~** wooden spoon.
(e) (*árbol*: *esp LAm*) tree; **~ dulce** liquorice root; **~ de hule** (*CAm*) rubber tree; **~ de mango** mango tree; **~ rosa** (*CAm*) rosewood; **~ santo** lignum vitae.
(f) (*Tip*: *de letra*) ascender, descender.
(g) (*golpe*) blow, hit (with a stick); **andar a ~s** to be always squabbling; **dar un ~ a uno** (*fig*) to criticize sb severely, take sb to task; **los críticos le dieron un ~ a la obra** the critics panned (o slated) the play; **dar de ~s a uno, doblar** (o **matar**) (o **moler**) **a uno a ~s** to give sb a beating; **dar ~s de ciego** to lash out wildly; **es un ~** it's a blow, it's come as a shock.
(h) (*Naipes*) suit; **~ de(l) triunfo** trump suit, trumps; **asistir al ~, seguir el ~, servir del ~** to follow suit; **cambiar de ~** (*fig*) to change tack.
(i) (*LAm**) swig*, draught of liquor; **a medio ~** (*borracho*) half-drunk; **darse al ~** to take to drink; **pegarse unos ~s** to have a few drinks.
(j) **a ~ seco** bare; by itself, pure, with nothing else; **vermut a ~ seco** straight vermouth; **beber a ~ seco** to drink without having anything to eat; **tiene el sueldo a ~ seco** he has just his salary, he has his bare salary and nothing else.
(k) (:) **dar un ~, pegar un ~** (*robo*) to do a job*; (*mala pasada*) to play a dirty trick.
(l) **echar el** (o **un**) **~**:, **ir de ~**: to have a screw:.
(m) (*LAm*) **un ~ de casa** a splendid house, a marvellous house; **es un**

~ de hombre he's a great guy; **~ de agua** cloudburst, sudden downpour; **cayó un ~ de agua** there was a tremendous lot of rain*.
(n) **~ grueso** (*And**) big shot*; **tirar el ~** to brag.

paloma NF (a) (*Orn*) dove, pigeon; **~ buscadora de blancos** homing pigeon; **~ mensajera** carrier pigeon; **~ torcaz** wood-pigeon, ring-dove; **¡palomita!** darling!
(b) (*Pol*) dove; **~ sin hiel** pet, lamb.
(c) (*ejercicio*) handstand.
(d) (*CAm, Carib, Méx*: *cometa*) kite.
(e) **~s** (*Náut*) white caps (of waves), white horses.

palomar NM dovecot(e), pigeon loft.

palomear [1a] VT (a) (*Carib*) to swindle. (b) (*And*) *enemigos* to hunt down one by one; (*tirar a matar*) to shoot to kill, shoot dead; (*matar a traición*) to shoot down in cold blood.

palometa NF harvestfish, pompano, derbio.

palomilla NF (a) (*Ent*) moth; (*esp*) grain moth; (*crisálida*) nymph, chrysalis.
(b) (*Téc*: *tuerca*) wing nut.
(c) (*Téc*: *escuadra*) wall bracket, angle iron.
(d) (*de caballo*) back, backbone.
(e) (*And, Cono Sur*: *travieso*) urchin, ragamuffin; (*CAm, Cono Sur, Méx*: *de niños*) mob of kids*; (*: pandilla*) crowd of layabouts, band of hooligans.

palomino **1** ADJ (*And, Cono Sur, Méx*) *caballo* palomino; (*blanco*) white.
2 NM (a) (*Orn*) young pigeon. (b) (*And, Cono Sur, Méx*) palomino (horse); (*blanco*) white horse. (c) (*excremento*) pigeon droppings.

palomita NF (a) (*Dep*) full-length dive.
(b) (*Méx*) tick.

palomitas NFPL popcorn.

palomo **1** ADJ (*And, Cono Sur, Méx*) = **palomino.**
2 NM (cock) pigeon; **~ de arcilla** clay pigeon.

palotada NF: **no dar ~** (*no trabajar*) not to do a stroke of work; (*no hacer nada*) to do nothing; (*hacerlo mal*) to get nothing right.

palote NM (a) (*Mús*) drumstick. (b) (*en escritura*) downstroke; pothook.
(c) (*Carib, Cono Sur Culin*) rolling-pin; (*Cono Sur**: *persona*) beanpole*.

palotear [1a] VI to bicker, wrangle.

paloteo NM bickering, wrangling.

palpable ADJ palpable; (*fig*) tangible, palpable; concrete.

palpamiento NM (*LAm*) frisking, body-search.

palpar [1a] **1** VT (a) (*gen*) to touch, feel; (*amorosamente*) to feel, caress, fondle; (*esp LAm*) *sospechoso* to frisk, search for weapons; *muro etc* to feel one's way along, grope one's way past.
(b) (*fig*) to feel; to appreciate, understand; **ahora palpa las consecuencias** now he's really feeling the consequences; **ya palparás lo que es esto** one day you'll really understand all this.
2 palparse VR (*fig*) to be felt; **se palpaba el descontento** you could feel the restlessness; **hay una enemistad que se palpa** you can feel the hostility, there is a tangible hostility.

palpitación NF palpitation, throb(bing), beat(ing); quiver(ing); flutter(ing).

palpitante ADJ (a) (*gen*) palpitating, (*corazón*) throbbing. (b) (*fig*) *interés, cuestión* burning.

palpitar [1a] VI (a) (*gen*) to palpitate; (*corazón*) to throb, beat; (*nerviosamente*) to quiver; to flutter.
(b) (*fig*) to throb; **en la poesía palpita la emoción** the poem throbs with emotion.
(c) (*And, Cono Sur*) **me palpita** I have a hunch; **ya me palpitaba el fracaso** I had a hunch it would be a failure.

palpite NM, **pálpito** NM hunch, presentiment; (*Esp*) **me da el ~ de que ..., tengo el ~ de que ...** I have a hunch that ...

palquista: NM cat burglar.

palta NF (*Cono Sur*) avocado pear.

palto NM (*Cono Sur*) avocado tree.

paltó NM (*And, CAm, Carib*) jacket.

palúdico ADJ marshy; (*Med*) malarial.

paludismo NM malaria.

palurdo **1** ADJ rustic; coarse, uncouth.
2 NM rustic, yokel, hick (*US*); (*pey*) lout.

palustre¹ NM (*Téc*) trowel.

palustre² ADJ marsh (*atr*); marshy.

pamela NF picture hat, sun hat.

pamema NF (a) (*dicho etc*) silly thing, stupid remark (*etc*); **~s** nonsense, humbug; **¡déjate de ~s!** stop your nonsense.
(b) (*bagatela*) triviality, trifle.
(c) **~s** (*halagos*) flattery; coaxing, wheedling.
(d) **~s** (*quejas etc*) fuss; **¡déjate de ~s!** stop your fussing! that's enough of that!

pampa¹ NF (a) (*Geog*) pampa(s), prairie; **la P~** the Pampas; *see also* GAUCHO .
(b) (*Cono Sur*) (*Min*) region of nitrate deposits; (*descampado*) open area on the outskirts of a town.

(c) (*And: en la sierra*) high grassy plateau.

(d) **a** (*o* **en**) **la ~** (*LAm*: al aire libre*) in the open; **en ~** (*LAm*: desnudo*) in the nude, with nothing on; **estar en ~ y la vía** (*Cono Sur**) to be flat broke*; **quedarse en ~** (*Cono Sur**) to come to nothing, fall through.

pampa² [1] ADJ **(a)** (*And, Cono Sur**) *negocio* shady, dishonest.

(b) (*And: endeble*) weak, feeble.

[2] NMF (*Cono Sur*) pampean Indian.

[3] NM (*Ling*) language of the pampean Indians.

pámpana NF vine leaf; **zurrar la ~ a uno** (*Esp**) to give sb a hiding*.

pámpano NM vine shoot, vine tendril.

pampeano ADJ of (*o* from) the pampas.

pampear¹ [1a] VI (*Cono Sur*) to travel over the pampas.

pampear² [1a] VT (*And*) **(a)** (*tocar*) to tap, pat (on the shoulder). **(b)** *masa* to roll out.

pampero (*LAm*) [1] ADJ of (*o* from) the pampas.

[2] NM **(a)** (*persona*) inhabitant of the pampas, plainsman. **(b)** (*viento*) strong wind (*blowing over the pampas from the Andes*).

pampinflar‡ [1a] VT: **¡me la pampinflas!** you stupid git!‡

pampino [1] ADJ (*LAm*) of (*o* from) the pampas.

[2] NM, **pampina** NF (*Cono Sur*) inhabitant of the Chilean pampas.

pamplina NF **(a)** (*Bot*) chickweed.

(b) (*: *tontería*) silly remark; **~s** (*disparates*) nonsense; (*lío*) fuss; (*: *jabón*) soft soap*; **¡~s!** rubbish!; **sin más ~s** without any more beating about the bush; **esas son ~s** that's a load of rubbish*; **no me venga Vd con ~s** don't come to me with that soft soap*.

pamplinero ADJ **(a)** (*tonto*) silly, nonsensical. **(b)** (*aspaventero*) fussy, emotional, given to making a great fuss. **(c)** (*engreído*) vain.

pamplonada NF (*LAm*) triviality; silly thing, piece of nonsense.

pamplonés ADJ Y NM, **pamplonesa** NF = **pamplonica**.

pamplonica [1] ADJ of Pamplona. [2] NMF native (*o* inhabitant) of Pamplona; **los ~s** the people of Pamplona.

pampon NM (*And*) open space, open ground.

pamporcino NM cyclamen.

PAN NM (*Méx*) ABR de **Partido de Acción Nacional.**

pan NM **(a)** (*gen*) bread; (*un ~*) loaf; (*fig*) bread; **~ blanco, ~ candeal, ~ de flor** white bread; **~ casero** home-made bread; **~ cenceño** unleavened bread; **~ de centeno** rye bread; **~ integral** wholemeal bread; **~ de molde** standard loaf; **~ moreno** brown bread; **~ rallado** breadcrumbs *pl*; **el ~ nuestro de cada día** our daily bread; **es el ~ nuestro de cada día** (*fig*) it's a daily event, it happens every day; it's commonplace; **estar a ~ y agua** to be on (*o* condemned to a diet of) bread and water; **ganarse el ~** to earn one's living.

(b) (*Bot*) wheat; **~es** (*fig*) crops, harvest; **año de mucho ~** good year for wheat, year of a heavy wheat crop; **tierras de ~ llevar** arable land, wheat-growing land.

(c) **~ de azúcar** sugar loaf; **~ de hierba** turf, sod; **~ de higos** block of dried figs; **~ de jabón** bar of soap, cake of soap.

(d) (*Téc*) gold leaf, silver leaf.

(e) (*locuciones*) **eso es ~ comido** it's dead easy; **contigo ~ y cebolla** (with you I'd gladly have) love in a cottage; **con su ~ se lo coma** that's his look-out, it's his funeral*, let him get on with it; **echar ~es** (*And, Cono Sur*) to boast, brag; **llamar al ~ ~ y al vino vino** to call a spade a spade; **venderse como ~ bendito** to sell like hot cakes.

pan... PREF pan..., *p.ej.* **panasiático** pan-Asiatic.

pana¹ NF (*paño*) velveteen, corduroy.

pana² NF (*And Aut*) breakdown; **tener una ~** to break down.

pana³ NF (*Cono Sur*) liver; (*) guts, courage; **helársele a uno la ~** (*Cono Sur*) to lose one's nerve; **tirar ~s** (*And**) to put on airs.

pana⁴ NMF (*Carib*) pal*, buddy.

panacea NF panacea, cure-all.

panaché NM mixed salad.

panadería NF (*tahona*) bakery, bakehouse; (*tienda*) baker's (shop).

panadero NM baker.

panadizo NM (*Med*) whitlow.

panal NM honeycomb.

Panamá NM Panama.

panamá NM panama hat.

panameñismo NM word (*o* phrase *etc*) peculiar to Panama.

panameño, -a ADJ, NM/F Panamanian.

panamericanismo NM Pan-Americanism.

panamericano [1] ADJ Pan-American.

[2] NF: **la Panamericana** the Pan-American highway.

panamitos NMPL, **panamos** NMPL (*And*) beans; (*fig*) food, daily bread.

panca NF (*And*) dry leaf of maize.

pancarta NF placard, banner.

panceta NF streaky bacon.

pancha* NF = **panza.**

Pancho NM *forma familiar de* **Francisco.**

pancho¹ [1] ADJ **(a)** (*Cono Sur*) brown, tan. **(b)** (*And, Carib*) broad and

flat; squat; **ni tan ~ ni tan ancho** (*Carib‡*) neither one thing nor the other.

[2] NM (*Cono Sur Culin*) hot dog.

pancho² ADJ calm, unruffled; **estar tan ~** (*Cono Sur, Esp*) to remain perfectly calm, not turn a hair.

pancho³ NM (*pez*) young sea-bream.

pancista [1] ADJ unprincipled.

[2] NMF trimmer, opportunist.

pancita NF (*Méx Culin*) tripe.

pancito NM (*Méx*) lump of sugar.

páncreas NM pancreas.

pancreático ADJ pancreatic.

pancromático ADJ panchromatic.

panda¹ NMF (*Zool*) panda.

panda² NF (*Carib*) = **pandeo.**

panda³* NF = **pandilla.**

pandear [1a] VI y **pandearse** VR to bend, warp; to sag; to bulge.

pandemonio NM, **pandemónium** NM pandemonium; **fue el ~*** all hell broke loose, there was pandemonium.

pandeo NM bend; sag(ging); bulge, bulging.

pandereta NF tambourine; **zumbar la ~ a uno** (*Esp**) to tan sb's hide*.

panderetear [1a] VI to play the tambourine.

pandero NM **(a)** (*Mús*) tambourine. **(b)** (*cometa*) kite. **(c)** (*: *tonto*) idiot. **(d)** (*: *culo*) backside.

pandibó‡ NM slammer‡, prison.

pandilla NF set, group; (*pey*) clique, coterie, set; bunch, load; (*criminal etc*) gang.

pandillero NM member of a clique (*etc*); (*LAm*) gangster.

pando ADJ **(a)** *viga etc* sagging; *muro* bulging; *madera* warped. **(b)** *plato* shallow; flat. **(c)** *río, persona* slow. **(d)** (*CAm*) (*oprimido*) oppressed; (*: *saciado*) full (up). **(e)** (*CAm, Méx: de hombros*) round-shouldered.

Pandora NF: **la caja de ~** Pandora's box.

pandorga NF **(a)** (*gorda*) fat woman. **(b)** (*cometa*) kite. **(c)** (*And**) (*molestia*) bother, nuisance; (*mentira*) lie. **(d)** (*Méx**) (*broma*) practical joke; (*estudiantil*) student prank.

pandorgo ADJ **(a)** (*Méx*) dim, stupid. **(b)** (*Carib*) fat and slow-moving.

pane NM (*And Aut*) breakdown.

panear VI (*And, Cono Sur*) to boast, show off.

panecillo NM roll.

panegírico NM panegyric.

panel NM **(a)** (*madera etc*) panel; **~es** (*Arquit*) panelling; **~ explicativo** display panel; **~ de información de vuelos** flight information board; **~ solar** solar panel. **(b)** **~ de instrumentos** (*Aut etc*) dashboard; **~ de mandos** (*Aer etc*) controls. **(c)** (*jurado*) panel; **~ de audiencia** TV viewers' panel.

panela NF **(a)** (*LAm Culin*) brown sugar, coarse sugar; sugar loaf.

(b) (*Méx: sombrero*) straw hat.

(c) (*And, Méx**) (*pesado*) bore, drag; (*zalamero*) creep‡.

panelería NF panelling.

panelista NMF panellist, panelist (*US*).

panera NF bread basket.

panero ADJ **(a)** *industria, producción* bread (*atr*). **(b)** **ser muy ~*** to love bread.

pánfilo ADJ **(a)** (*tonto*) simple, gullible; stupid. **(b)** (*And*) pale, discoloured.

panfletario ADJ *estilo* violent, highly-coloured; *propaganda* cheap, demagogic.

panfletista NMF pamphleteer; satirist, lampoonist.

panfleto NM pamphlet; (*pey*) satire, lampoon, scandal sheet.

panga NF (*CAm, Méx: lancha*) barge, lighter; (*transbordador*) ferry(boat).

pangolín NM scaly anteater.

paniaguado NM (*Pol etc*) henchman; protégé.

paniaguarse [1i] VR (*Méx*) to become friends, pal up*.

pánico [1] ADJ panic.

[2] NM **(a)** panic, fear; **el ~ comprador** panic buying; **yo le tengo un ~ tremendo*** I'm scared stiff of him. **(b)** **de ~*** = **de miedo.**

paniego ADJ: **tierra paniega** cornland.

panificable ADJ: **granos ~s** bread grains.

panificación NF breadmaking.

panificadora NF bakery.

panil NM (*Cono Sur*) celery.

panizo NM **(a)** (*Bot*) millet; maize. **(b)** (*Cono Sur*) mineral deposit; (*fig*) treasure, gem, valuable object; (*Com*) profitable deal, gold mine.

panocha NF, **panoja** NF **(a)** (*Bot*) corncob, ear of maize; ear of wheat (*etc*).

(b) (*Méx: azúcar*) unrefined brown sugar; (*dulce*) brown sugar candy.

(c) (*And, CAm, Cono Sur*) large pancake of maize and cheese.

(d) (*: *dinero*) brass*, money.

(e) (*Méx‡‡*) cunt‡‡.

panocho [1] ADJ Murcian, of Murcia.

[2] NM, **panocha** NF Murcian.

3 NM (*Ling*) Murcian dialect.
panoli(s)* NMF, PL **panolis** (*Esp*) chump*, idiot.
panoplia NF panoply; collection of arms.
panorama NM panorama (*t fig*); vista, view, scene; (*perspectiva*) outlook, prospect; (*Arte, Fot*) view; **el ~ actual político** the present political scene.
panorámica NF general view, survey.
panorámico ADJ panoramic; **punto ~** viewpoint, vantage point.
panoramizar [1f] VTI (*Cine*) to pan.
panqué NM (*CAm, Carib*), **panqueque** NM (*LAm*) pancake.
panquequera NF pancake iron.
panquequería NF (*LAm*) pancake house.
pantagruélico ADJ lavish.
pantaleta NF (*LAm*) bloomers, drawers; panties.
pantalla NF **(a)** (*biombo*) screen; (*de lámpara*) shade, lampshade.
  (b) (*Cine etc*) screen; **~ acústica** loudspeaker; **~ grande** big screen; **~ plana** flat screen; **~ de radar** radar screen; **~ de rayos** (*en aeropuerto*) X-ray security apparatus; **~ de televisión** television screen; **~ de vídeo** video screen; **los personajes de la ~** screen personalities; **la pequeña ~** the small screen, the TV screen; **llevar una historia a la ~** to film a story.
  (c) (*Inform*) screen, display; **~ de ayuda** help screen; **~ de cristal líquido** liquid crystal display; **~ de plasma** plasma panel; **~ táctil** touch-sensitive screen.
  (d) (*Cono Sur: abanico*) fan.
  (e) (*fig*) blind, pretext; decoy; **hacer la ~** (*Dep*) to form the wall; **servir de ~ a** to be a blind for.
  (f) (*LAm: esbirro*) henchman, bodyguard.
  (g) (*CAm*) large mirror.
pantalón NM, **pantalones** NMPL **(a)** (*de hombre*) trousers, pants (*US*); (*de mujer: exterior*) slacks, trousers, (*interior*) knickers; **pantalones cortos** shorts; **pantalones de esquí** ski pants; **~ de montar** riding breeches; **~ pitillo** drainpipe trousers; **pantalones tejanos, pantalones vaqueros** jeans; **bajarse los pantalones** (*Esp*‡) to throw in the sponge; **no caber en los pantalones** to get too big for one's boots; **es ella la que lleva los pantalones*** she's the one who wears the trousers; **llevar los pantalones bien puestos** (*Carib**) to have guts.
  (b) (*And*) man, male.
  (c) (*Carib*) guts, courage.

┌─── *PANTALONES, ZAPATOS, GAFAS* ───┐

Uso de "pair"

• Para especificar el número de objetos que constan de dos piezas que forman parte de un juego de dos, se debe usar en inglés el partitivo *pair of* + SUSTANTIVO:
  Tengo dos pares de zapatos
  I've got two pairs of shoes

• La misma regla se aplica cuando se trata de objetos compuestos por dos piezas simétricas:
  ¿Cuántos pantalones meto en la maleta?
  How many pairs of trousers shall I pack?

! Si no queremos especificar el número de objetos, no es necesario utilizar *pair*:
  ¿Puede arreglarme las gafas?
  I wondered if you could mend my glasses?
  Para otros usos y ejemplos ver las entradas **gafa, pantalón** *y* **zapato.**

---

pantanal NM marshland.
pantano NM **(a)** (*natural*) marsh, swamp, bog; wetland; (*artificial*) reservoir, dam.
  (b) (*) jam*, fix*, difficulty; **salir de un ~** to get out of a jam*.
pantanoso ADJ **(a)** (*lit*) marshy, swampy, boggy. **(b)** (*fig*) difficult, problematic.
panteísmo NM pantheism.
panteísta **1** ADJ pantheistic.
  2 NMF pantheist.
panteón NM **(a)** (*gen*) pantheon; **~ familiar** family vault; **el ~ de los reyes** the burial place of the royal family, the pantheon of the kings.
  (b) (*Andalucía, LAm: cementerio*) cemetery.
  (c) (*Cono Sur*) ore, mineral.
panteonero NM (*LAm*) gravedigger.
pantera NF **(a)** (*Zool*) panther; (*Carib*) jaguar, ocelot. **(b)** (*Méx*) (*matón*) heavy*; (*atrevido*) risk taker.
pantimedias NFPL (*Méx*) panty-hose.
pantis NMPL tights, panty-hose.
pantógrafo NM pantograph.
pantomima NF pantomime, dumb show.
pantoque NM (*Náut*) bilge; **agua de ~** bilge water.
pantorra* NF (*Anat*) (fat) calf.
pantorrilla NF **(a)** (*Anat*) calf (of the leg). **(b)** (*And*) vanity.

pantorrilludo ADJ **(a)** (*de piernas gordas*) fat in the leg, thick-calved.
  (b) (*And**: *vanidoso*) vain.
pantufla NF, **pantuflo** NM slipper.
panty NM, PL **pantys, panties** (*Esp*: *medias*) tights, panty-hose; (*LAm*: *bragas*) panties.
panucho NM (*Méx*) stuffed tortilla.
panudo* (*And*) **1** ADJ boastful, bragging.
  2 NM, **panuda** NF loudmouth*.
panul NM (*Cono Sur*) celery.
panza NF belly; (*abultado*) belly, paunch; **~ de burro** (*Alpinismo*) overhang; **~ mojada** (*Méx*) wetback (*US*); **estrellarse de ~** to do a belly-flop, make a pancake landing.
panzada* NF **(a)** (*hartazgo*) bellyful; **una ~ de** (*fig*) a lot of, a bellyful of; **darse una ~‡, darse las grandes ~s‡** to have a blow-out‡.
  (b) (*golpe*) blow in the belly.
panzazo NM **(a)** (*And, Cono Sur*) blow in the belly.
  (b) (*Méx*) = **panzada (a)**.
  (c) **pasar de ~** (*LAm*‡) to get through by the skin of one's teeth.
panzón ADJ, **panzudo** ADJ paunchy, fat, potbellied.
pañal NM **(a)** (*de bebé*) nappy, diaper (*US*); (*de camisa*) shirttail; **~ desechable** disposable nappy.
  (b) **~es** baby clothes; (*fig*) early stages, infancy; **de humildes ~es** of humble origins; **criarse en buenos ~es** to be born with a silver spoon in one's mouth; **esto ha dejado en ~es a los rivales** this has left the competition way behind; **estar todavía en ~es** (*persona*) to be very innocent still; (*ciencia, técnica*) to be in its infancy; **yo de informática estoy en ~es** I'm completely in the dark about computing, I know nothing about computing.
pañería NF (*géneros*) drapery; (*tienda*) draper's (shop), dry-goods store (*US*), clothier's (shop).
pañero, -a NM/F draper, dry-goods dealer (*US*), clothier.
pañete NM **(a)** (*tela*) light cloth. **(b)** **~s** shorts, trunks. **(c)** (*And*) coat of fine plaster. **(d)** (*Cono Sur*) horse blanket.
pañí¹ NM (*Cono Sur*) sun trap.
pañí²‡ NF: **dar la ~** to give a tip-off, tip the wink*.
pañito NM (*Esp*) table runner; traycloth.
paño NM **(a)** (*gen*) cloth; stuff, material; **el buen ~ en el arca se vende** good wine needs no bush; **le conozco el ~** I know his sort, I know all about him, I recognize the type.
  (b) (*un ~*) (piece of) cloth; (*trapo*) duster, rag, cleaning cloth; **~ de altar** altar cloth; **~s calientes, ~s tibios** (*LAm fig*) half-measures, ineffective remedies; **no andarse con ~s calientes** to pull no punches, not go in for half-measures; **~ de cocina** dishcloth; **~ higiénico** (*Esp*) sanitary towel, sanitary napkin (*US*); **~ de lágrimas** (*fig*) standby, consolation; **~ de manos** towel; **~ mortuorio** pall; **~ de los platos, ~ de secar** tea towel; **jugar a dos ~s** to play a double game.
  (c) (*Cos*) piece of cloth, width; panel.
  (d) **~s** (*ropa*) clothes; (*Arte*) drapes; **~s menores** underclothes, undies*.
  (e) **al ~** (*Teat*) offstage.
  (f) (*Arquit*) stretch, length (*of wall*).
  (g) (*en cristal etc*) mist, cloud, cloudiness; (*en diamante*) flaw.
  (h) (*Carib*: *red*) fishing net.
  (i) (*And*: *tierra*) plot of land.
pañol NM (*Náut*) store, storeroom; **~ del agua** water store; **~ del carbón** coal bunker.
pañoleta NF fichu.
pañolón NM shawl.
pañuelo NM **(a)** (*gen*) handkerchief; (*de cabeza*) scarf, headscarf, shawl; **~ de cuello** cravate; **~ de papel** paper handkerchief. **(b)** (‡†: *billete*) 100-peseta note.
papa¹ NM (*Ecl*) pope; **~ negro** black pope (*General of the Jesuits*).
papa² NF **(a)** (*esp LAm*) potato; **~s colchas** (*CAm*) crisps; **echar las ~s** (*Esp**) to be sick; **cuando las ~s queman** (*Cono Sur*) when things hot up.
  (b) (*) **ni ~** not a blind thing*; **no entiendo ni ~** I don't understand a word; **no oyó ni ~** she didn't hear a thing.
  (c) (*Cono Sur**) bash*, blow.
  (d) (*Carib**) soft job*, plum.
  (e) (*Méx*: *sopa*) porridge, gruel; (*Cono Sur*) baby food.
  (f) (*Méx**: *mentira*) lie, fib; (*fraude*) hoax.
papa³ ADJ INVAR (*Cono Sur**) jolly good*, first-rate.
papá NM **(a)** (*) dad*, daddy*, papa, pop* (*US*); **P~ Noel** Father Christmas.
  (b) (*LAm*) father; **~s** mother and father, parents.
  (c) **~ grande** (*LAm**) grandfather, grandpa*.
papachar* [1a] VT (*Méx*) (*sobar*) to stroke; (*mimar*) to spoil.
papachos NMPL (*Méx*) cuddles, caresses.
papacote (*CAm*) **1** NM (*cometa*) kite.
  2 NMF (*fig*) bigwig, big shot*.
papada NF (*de persona*) double chin; (*de animal*) dewlap.
papadeno: NM (*Carib*) Jehovah's Witness.

papadilla NF dewlap.
papado NM papacy.
papagayo NM **(a)** (*Orn*) parrot.
(b) (*fig*) parrot; chatterbox; person who repeats parrot fashion.
(c) (*Carib, Méx*: *cometa*) large kite.
(d) (*And*: *bacinilla*) bedpan.
papaíto* NM daddy.
papal[1] ADJ (*Ecl*) papal.
papal[2] NM (*LAm*) potato field.
papalina NF **(a)** (*gorra*) cap with earflaps; bonnet; mobcap. **(b)** (*: *juerga*) binge*; **coger una ~** to get tight*. **(c)** (*CAm Culin*) crisps (*Brit*), potato chips (*US*).
papalón* NM (*Méx*) rat*, swine*.
papalote NM (*LAm*) (*cometa*) kite; (*molino: de niño*) windmill.
papalotear [1a] VI (*CAm, Méx**: *vagabundear*) to wander about; (*Méx**: *agonizar*) to give one's last gasp.
papamoscas NM INVAR **(a)** (*Orn*) flycatcher. **(b)** = **papanatas**.
papamóvil NM popemobile.
papanatas* NM INVAR simpleton, sucker‡.
papanatería NF, **papanatismo** NM gullibility, simple-mindedness.
papandujo ADJ (*Esp*) soft, overripe.
papapa NF (*CAm*) stupidity.
papar [1a] [1] VT (*tragar*) to swallow, gulp (down).
[2] **paparse*** VR **(a)** **~ algo** to eat sth up, scoff sth*; **se lo papó todo** he scoffed the lot*; **¡pápate ésa!** (*Esp*) put that in your pipe and smoke it!*
(b) (‡: *recibir un golpe*) to get a sudden knock, be hit real hard*.
paparazzo NM, PL **paparazzi** intrusive news photographer.
paparrucha NF **(a)** (*disparate*) piece of nonsense, silly thing. **(b)** (*chapuza*) botch, worthless object. **(c)** (*truco*) hoax.
paparruta NMF (*Cono Sur*) humbug.
paparulo* NM (*Cono Sur*) sucker‡.
papas NFPL pap, mushy food; (‡) grub‡.
papaya NF **(a)** (*LAm Bot*) papaya, pawpaw. **(b)** (*Carib*‡‡) cunt‡‡.
papayo NM (*LAm*) papaya (tree), pawpaw (tree).
papear‡ [1a] VI to eat, scoff*.
papel NM **(a)** (*gen*) paper; **~ (de) aluminio** tinfoil; (*Culin*) aluminium foil; **~ de arroz** rice paper; **~ atrapamoscas** flypaper; **~ biblia, ~ de China** India paper; **~ de calcar, ~ de calco** tracing-paper; **~ carbón** carbon paper, carbon; **~ de cartas** notepaper, stationery; **~ cel(l)o** adhesive tape; **~ craft** (*CAm, Méx*) waxed paper; **~ cuadriculado** squared paper; **~ charol** shiny wrapping paper; **~ de desecho** waste paper; **~ de embalar, ~ de envolver** brown paper, wrapping paper; **~ de empapelar** wallpaper; **~ encerado** wax(ed) paper; **~ engomado** gummed paper; **~ de estaño** tinfoil; **~ de estraza** brown paper, wrapping paper; **~ estucado** art paper; **~ de excusado** toilet-paper; **~ de filtro** filter paper; **~ de fumar** cigarette-paper; **entre A y B no cabía un ~ de fumar** (*Esp*) you couldn't have got a razor's edge between them; **yo no me lo cojo con ~ de fumar** (*Esp*) I wouldn't touch it with a bargepole; **~ de grasa** greaseproof paper; **~ higiénico** toilet-paper; **~ de lija** sandpaper; **~ madera** (*Cono Sur*) cardboard; **~ de mano** hand-made paper; **~ para máquinas de escribir** typing paper; **~ matamoscas** flypaper; **~ mojado** (*fig*) scrap of paper, worthless bit of paper; **~ de oficio** (*LAm*) official foolscap paper; **~ ondulado** corrugated paper; **~ de paja de arroz** rice paper; **~ de paredes, ~ pintado** wallpaper; **~ pautado** ruled paper; **~ de plata** silver paper; **~ prensa** newsprint; **~ reciclado** recycled paper; **~ de regalo** gift-wrap paper; **~ sanitario** (*CAm*) toilet-paper; **~ secante** blotting-paper; blotter; **~ de seda** tissue paper; **~ sellado** stamped paper; **~ timbrado** official form; **~ de tina** handmade paper; **~ (de) tornasol** litmus paper; **~ transparente** tracing-paper; **~ vitela** vellum paper; **sobre el ~** (*fig*) on paper, in theory.
(b) (*un ~*) piece of paper, sheet of paper; **~es** papers; **los ~es** (*prensa*) the papers, the newspapers; **~ usado, ~es usados, ~es viejos** waste paper.
(c) (*oficial*) **~es** papers, documents; identification papers; **los ~es, por favor** your papers, please; **tiene los ~es en regla** his papers are in order.
(d) (*Fin*: *billetes*) **~ moneda** paper money, banknotes; **mil dólares en ~** a thousand dollars in notes.
(e) (*Fin*: *valores*) stocks and shares; **~ del Estado** government bonds.
(f) (*Fin, Teat etc*: *recaudación*) takings, receipts.
(g) (*Fin*‡) 1000-peseta note; (*And*) one-peso note.
(h) (*LAm*) bag.
(i) (*Cine, Teat etc*) part, role; **~ estelar** star part; **desempeñar un ~** (*fig*), **hacer un ~** to play a part; **el ~ del gobierno en este asunto** the government's role in this matter; **hacer buen** (o **mal**) **~** to make a good (o bad) impression; **hizo el ~ de Cleopatra** she played the part of Cleopatra; **el equipo hizo un buen ~ en el torneo** the team did well in the tournament, the team put up a good show in the tournament; **hacer el ~ de** (*fig*) to act as, undertake the job of; **tuvo que desempeñar un ~ secundario** he had to play second fiddle, he

had to take a minor role.

┌─────────┐
│ **PAPEL** │   **ver también la entrada**
└─────────┘

El sustantivo *papel* se puede traducir en inglés por *paper* o por *piece of paper*.

• Lo traducimos por *paper* cuando nos referimos al *papel* como material:
    ¿Todo el mundo tiene lápiz y papel?
    Has everybody got a pencil and paper?

• Si *papel* se refiere a una hoja de papel no lo traducimos por *paper*, sino por *a piece of paper* si nos referimos a un trozo de papel pequeño y por *a sheet of paper* si nos referimos a una hoja de papel o a un folio:
    ¿Has visto el papel en el que estaba apuntando mis notas?
    Have you seen that sheet of paper I was making notes on?
    Apúntalo en ese papel
    Write it down on this piece of paper

• Si nos referimos a varias hojas o trozos de papel en blanco utilizamos *sheets* o *pieces*:
    Necesitamos varios papeles
    We need several pieces of paper

• Si nos referimos a *papeles* que ya están escritos, se pueden traducir por *papers*:
    Tengo que ordenar todos estos papeles
    I must put all these papers in order
    Para otros usos y ejemplos ver la entrada.

---

papela NF **(a)** (*Esp**) paper, document; identity card, ID. **(b)** (‡: *droga*) = **papelina**.
papelada NF (*CAm*) farce, pretence, charade.
papelamen* NM papers, masses of paper.
papelear [1a] VI **(a)** (*revolver papeles*) to rummage through papers. **(b)** (*atraer la atención*) to make a splash, draw attention to o.s.
papeleo NM (*trámites*) paperwork; (*pey*) red tape.
papelera NF **(a)** (*para basura*) litter bin; wastepaper basket. **(b)** (*mesa*) desk. **(c)** (*fábrica*) paper-mill.
papelería NF **(a)** (*papel etc para correspondencia*) stationery. **(b)** (*tienda*) stationer's (shop). **(c)** (*montón*) mass of papers, heap of papers; (*lío*) sheaf of papers.
papelerío NM (*LAm*) = **papelería** (c).
papelero [1] ADJ (*LAm*) paper (*atr*).
[2] NM **(a)** (*vendedor*) stationer; (*fabricante*) paper manufacturer. **(b)** (*Méx*) paper-boy. **(c)** (*Cono Sur*) ridiculous person.
papeleta NF **(a)** (*trozo de papel*) slip of paper, bit of paper; (*ficha*) card, index card, file card; (*Pol*) voting paper, ballot paper; (*CAm*) visiting card, calling card (*US*); **~ de empeño** pawn ticket; **~ de examen** (*Escol*) (examination) report; **¡vaya ~!** this is a tough one! **(b)** (*LAm*) bag. **(c)** (*And**: *multa*) fine.
papelillo NM cigarette; **~s** confetti.
papelina NF fold of paper (*containing drug*).
papelista NMF (*Carib, Cono Sur*) = **picapleitos**.
papelito NM **(a)** (*trozo de papel*) slip of paper, bit of paper. **(b)** (*Teat etc*) minor role, bit part.
papelón NM **(a)** (*papel usado*) (piece of) wastepaper; (*cartulina*) pasteboard.
(b) (*impostor*) impostor; (*engreído*) bluffer, show-off*.
(c) (*Teat etc*) leading role, big part; **hacer un ~** to do something ridiculous, make oneself a laughing-stock.
(d) (*And, Carib*) sugar loaf.
papelonero ADJ (*Cono Sur*) ridiculous.
papelote NM, **papelucho** NM useless bit of paper; worthless document; (*Liter*) trashy piece of writing.
papeo‡ NM (*comida*) grub‡, food; (*el comer*) eating.
papera NF goitre; (*t* **~s**) mumps.
papero [1] ADJ **(a)** (*LAm*) potato (*atr*). **(b)** (*Méx*) lying, deceitful.
[2] NM (*Agr*) potato grower; (*Com*) potato dealer.
papi* NM dad*, daddy*.
papiamento NM (*Ling*) Papiamento.
papila NF **(a)** (*de bebé*) baby food. **(b)** (*fig*) guile, deceit. **(c)** **estar hecho ~** (*roto*) to be smashed to pieces (o to pulp); (*cansado*) to be dog-tired.
papillote NM buttered paper, greased paper.
papiloma NF wart, papilloma (*Téc*); **~ genital** genital wart.
papilomavirus NM INVAR Papillomavirus
papira‡ NF letter.
papiro NM papyrus.
pápiro* NM (big) banknote; **~s** (*fig*) brass*, cash; **tener afán de ~s** to be greedy for money.
papiroflexia NF origami.
papirotazo NM, **papirote** NM flick.
papismo NM (*pey*) papism (*pey*), popery (*pey*).
papista [1] ADJ papist, popish (*pey*); **es más ~ que el papa** he's more

Catholic than the pope.

[2] NMF papist.

papo NM **(a)** (*Orn*) crop; (*Zool*) dewlap; (*de persona*) jowl, double chin; **estar de ~ de mona** (*Esp**) to be first-rate; **pasarlo de ~ de mona** (*Esp**) to have a super time*. **(b)** (*Med*) goitre. **(c)** (*Esp***) cunt**.

paprika NF paprika.

papudo ADJ *persona* with a heavy jowl, double-chinned; (*Zool*) dewlapped.

papujado ADJ swollen, puffed up.

papujo ADJ **(a)** (*Méx: hinchado*) swollen, puffed up; (*And*) fat-cheeked. **(b)** (*Méx: enfermizo*) wan, sickly, anaemic.

paquebote NM packet boat, packet.

paquero NM (*Méx*) swindler, crook.

paquete [1] NM **(a)** (*Correos*) packet, parcel, package; **~ de cigarrillos** (*Esp*) packet (*o* pack *US*) of cigarettes; **en un ~ discreto** under plain cover; **~ de flores** bunch of flowers; **~ de muestra** sample pack; **~s postales** (*como servicio*) parcel post; **dejar a una con el ~*** to put a girl in the family way; **ir** (*o* **viajar**) **de ~*** (*en moto*) to ride pillion; (*fig, con amantes*) to play gooseberry; **soltar el ~*** to give birth. **(b)** (*fig*) package; **~ de acciones, ~ accionarial** holding of shares; **~ de beneficios** benefits package; **~ de medidas económicas** package of financial measures. **(c)** (*: *majo*) dandy; **estar hecho un ~** to be all dressed up, be dressed in style. **(d)** **meter un ~ a uno** (*Mil**) to put sb on a charge. **(e)** (*Inform*) package; **~ de aplicaciones** application package; **~ estadístico** statistical package; **~ integrado** integrated package. **(f)** (*) equipment*, naughty bits*; **marcar ~** to wear very tight trousers. **(g)** (*Med**) dose (of VD)*. **(h)** (*LAm: cosa pesada*) nuisance, bore; **¡menudo ~!, ¡vaya ~!** what a bore! **(i)** **darse ~** (*CAm, Méx*) to give o.s. airs. **(j)** (*Méx: asunto*) tough job, hard one. **(k)** (*Cono Sur**) queer*, poof*. **(l)** (*LAm: vacaciones*) package holiday. **(m)** (*Náut*) packet boat, packet. [2] ADJ INVAR (*LAm*) chic, elegant, spruce; **estar de a ~** to look chic.

paquetear [1a] VI (*LAm*) to be very smart.

paquete-bomba NM, PL **paquetes-bomba** parcel-bomb.

paquetería NF **(a)** (*Cono Sur**) **¡qué ~!** how elegant!; **se puso toda su ~** she put on her Sunday best; **¡vaya ~ que lleva!*** she's wearing everything but the kitchen sink*! **(b)** (*LAm Com*) parcels; **servicio de ~** parcel service.

paquetero* NM card sharper.

paquetudo* ADJ (*LAm*) **(a)** = **paquete 2**. **(b)** (*orgulloso*) stuck-up*.

paquidermo NM pachyderm.

paquistaní = **pakistaní**.

Paquita NF *forma familiar de* **Francisca**.

Paquito NM *forma familiar de* **Francisco**.

PAR NM (*Esp*) ABR *de* **Partido Aragonés Regionalista**.

par [1] ADJ like, equal; *número* even. [2] NM **(a)** (*dos*) pair; couple; **un ~ de guantes** a pair of gloves; **por un ~ de dólares** for a couple of dollars; **solamente un ~ de veces** only a couple of times; **a ~es** in pairs, in twos; **un discurso a tres ~es*** a very lengthy speech. **(b)** (*igual*) equal; **al ~** equally; together, jointly; **es útil a ~ que** (*o y al ~*) **divertido** it is both useful and amusing, it is useful and amusing at the same time; **está al ~ de los mejores** it is on a level with the best, it's up to the standard of the best; **caminar al ~ de** to walk abreast of; **sin ~** matchless, peerless; unparalleled; **no tener ~** to have no parallel, be unique. **(c)** (*Mat*) even number; **~es o nones** odds or evens. **(d)** (*Golf*) par; **~ de(l) campo** par for the course; **lo hizo con 4 por debajo del ~** he did it in 4 under par. **(e)** (*Mec*) **~ de fuerzas** couple; **~ de torsión** torque. **(f)** **estar abierto de ~ en ~** to be wide open. **(g)** (*persona*) peer; **los doce ~es** the twelve peers. [3] NF **(a)** (*esp Com, Fin*) par; **a la ~** at par; (*fig*) = **al par**; **estar a la ~** to be at par; **estar por encima de la ~** to be above (*o* over) par; **estar por debajo de la ~** to be under (*o* below) par. **(b)** **a la ~ que** ... while ..., at the same time as ...

para¹ PREP **(a)** (*destino, finalidad, uso etc*) for; intended for; **un regalo ~ ti** a present for you; **lo traje ~ ti** I brought it for you; **~ mí que** ... in my opinion ..., if you ask me ...; **no tengo ~ el viaje** I haven't the money for the trip; **un hotel ~ turistas** a hotel (intended) for tourists, a tourist hotel; **una taza ~ café** a coffee cup, a cup for coffee; **no es ~ comer** it's not for eating, it's not to be eaten; **nació ~ poeta** he was born to be a poet; **ir ~ casa** to go home, head for home; **salir ~ Panamá** to leave for Panama; **decir ~ sí** to say to o.s.; **léelo ~ ti** read it to yourself; **~ esto, podíamos habernos quedado en casa** if this is all it is we might as well have stayed at home;

psicológicamente no estoy **~ ello** I'm not up to it psychologically.

┌───┐
│ **PAR** ver también la entrada │
└───┘

A la hora de traducir *par* (*de*) seguido de un sustantivo, hay que tener en cuenta la diferencia entre *pair* (*of*) y *couple* (*of*).

• Se traduce por *pair* (*of*) cuando nos referimos a objetos que normalmente se usan por *pares*:
   ...tres pares de guantes...
   ...three pairs of gloves...
   Voy a necesitar dos pares más de calcetines
   I'll need two more pairs of socks

• Lo traducimos por *couple* (*of*) en los demás casos, en los que *un par de* se puede emplear además en el sentido más vago de "dos o más de dos":
   Me he comprado un par de camisas
   I've bought a couple of shirts
   Regresaré en un par de minutos
   I'll be back in a couple of minutes
   ·> Ver también PANTALONES, ZAPATOS, GAFAS
   Para otros usos y ejemplos ver la entrada.

(b) **¿~ qué?** why?, for what purpose?, what's the use?; **¿~ qué lo quieres?** why do you want it?
(c) **~ + infin** (*finalidad*) to + *infin*, in order to + *infin*; **lo hizo ~ salvarse** he did it (in order) to save himself; **~ comprarlo necesitas 5 dólares más** to buy it you need another 5 dollars; **el rey visitará A ~ volar después a B** the king will visit A and then fly on to B.
(d) (*bastante, demasiado, muy:* **~ + infin**) **tengo bastante ~ vivir** I have enough to live on; **es demasiado cara ~ nuestros recursos** it's too dear for us, it's beyond our means; **tiene demasiada inteligencia ~ pensar así** he's too intelligent to think that.
(e) **~ que** CONJ in order that, so that; **lo traje ~ que lo veas** I brought it so that you could see it, I brought it for you to see; **~ que eso fuera posible habría que trabajar mucho** you would have to work hard for that to be possible (*o* to bring that about).
(f) **~ + infin** (*resultado*) only to + *infin*; **se casaron ~ separarse en seguida** they married only to separate at once.
(g) (*tiempo*) **~ mañana** for tomorrow; by tomorrow; **lo dejamos ~ mañana** we left it till tomorrow; **lo tendré listo ~ fin de mes** I'll have it ready by (*o* for) the end of the month; **~ las 2 estaba lloviendo** by 2 o'clock it was raining; **ahora ~ la feria de agosto hará un año** it'll be a year ago this (*o* come the) August holiday; **10 ~ las 8** (*LAm*) 10 to 8; V **ir** etc.
(h) (*relación, trato:* **t ~ con**) to, towards; **tan amable ~ todos** so kind to everybody; **no hay hombre grande ~ su ayuda de cámara** no man is a hero to (*o* in the eyes of) his valet.
(i) (*contrastes*) **~ profesor habla muy mal** he talks very badly for a professor; **~ niño lo hace muy bien** he does it very well for a child; **~ ruidosos, los españoles** for noisy people, there's nobody like the Spaniards; **~ locos, los nuestros** if it's madmen you want we've got plenty right here at home; **es mucho ~ lo que suele dar** this is a lot in comparison with what he usually gives; **¿quién es Vd ~ gritar así?** who are you to shout like that?
(j) V **estar 1** (r) y (s); V **ir 1** (b) etc.

para²* NM paratrooper, para*.

para... PREF para...

parabellum ® NF INVAR (*pistola*) (automatic) pistol; **balas del calibre 9 mm Parabellum** 9 mm Parabellum bullets.

parabién NM congratulations; **dar el ~ a uno** to congratulate sb (*por* on).

parábola NF **(a)** (*Mat*) parabola. **(b)** (*Liter*) parable.

parabólica NF satellite dish.

parabólico ADJ parabolic.

parabrisas NM INVAR windscreen, windshield (*US*).

paraca¹* NM paratrooper, para*.

paraca² NF (*And*) strong wind from the sea.

paracaídas NM INVAR parachute; **lanzar algo en ~** to send sth down by parachute; **lanzarse en ~** to parachute (down); (*en emergencia*) to bale out.

paracaidismo NM **(a)** parachuting; **~ acrobático** skydiving. **(b)** (*Méx*) squatting.

paracaidista NMF **(a)** parachutist; (*Mil*) paratrooper; **acrobático** skydiver. **(b)** (*Méx*) (*) (*colado*) gatecrasher; (*ocupante*) squatter.

paracetamol NM paracetamol.

parachispas NM fireguard, firescreen.

parachoques NM INVAR (*Aut*) bumper, fender (*US*); (*Ferro*) buffer(s).

parada NF **(a)** (*acto de parar*) stop; stopping; (*Dep*) save, stop; (*sitio*) stopping place; (*de industria etc*) shutdown, stoppage; standstill; (*de pagos*) suspension; **~ de autobús** bus-stop; **~ cardíaca** cardiac arrest; **~ discrecional** request stop; **~ en seco** sudden stop; **~ de taxis** taxi stand, cab-rank; **correr en ~** to run on the spot, run in place (*US*). **(b)** (*equipo de caballos*) relay, team.

(c) (*apuesta*) bet, stake.

(d) (*presa*) dam.

(e) (*Esgrima*) parry.

(f) (*caballeriza*) stud, breeding establishment.

(g) (*Mil etc*) parade; (*LAm*) civic procession; **~ nupcial** (*Orn*) courtship display; **formar en ~** to parade.

(h) (*CAm, Méx: cartuchos*) clip of cartridges.

(i) (*LAm*) (*vanidad*) vanity, pride, presumption; (*jactancia*) boastfulness; **meter ~** to boast, be proud.

(j) (*And*) crafty trick.

(k) (*And*) farmer's market (*US*), open market.

(l) **hacer ~ a uno** (*Cono Sur, Méx: desafiar*) to challenge sb.

paradear* [1a] VI (*Cono Sur*) to brag; to swank, show off; **~ con algo** to brag about sth, show sth off.

paradero NM **(a)** (*gen*) whereabouts; **no sabemos su ~** we do not know where it is; **averiguar el ~ de** to ascertain the whereabouts of, locate; **X, ahora en ~ desconocido** X, whose whereabouts are unknown.

(b) (*parada*) stopping place; (*alojamiento*) lodging; (*LAm Ferro*) wayside halt; (*And: de bus*)-bus stop.

(c) (*fin*) end; **seguramente tendrá mal ~** he's sure to come to a bad end.

paradigma NM paradigm.

paradigmático ADJ paradigmatic.

paradisiaco, paradisíaco ADJ heavenly.

parado 1 ADJ **(a)** **estar ~** *persona* to be motionless, be standing still; *fábrica* to be closed, be at a standstill; *coche etc* to be stopped, be standing; **salida parada** (*Dep*) standing start.

(b) **estar ~** (*Esp*) *obrero* to be unemployed, be idle; **los ~s** the unemployed.

(c) **estar ~** (*LAm*) to be standing (up); to be on one's feet; **estuve ~ durante 2 horas** I was standing for 2 hours, I stood for 2 hours.

(d) **dejar a uno ~** (*fig*) to amaze sb; to bewilder sb, leave sb confused; **to leave sb in doubt; ¡me deja Vd ~!** you amaze me!; **me quedé ~** I was completely confused, I was at a loss.

(e) **salir bien ~** to come off well, come out of it well; **salió mejor ~ de lo que cabía esperar** he came out of it better than could be expected; **estar bien ~** (*LAm*) (*estar bien colocado*) to be well placed; (*tener influencia*) to have influence; (*And, Carib: tener suerte*) to be lucky; **estar mal ~** (*And, Carib*) to be unlucky; **caer ~ (como los gatos)** (*LAm*) to land on one's feet, be lucky.

(f) **ser ~** (*Esp*) *persona* to be slow, be dull, be inactive; (*soso*) to lack character, be weak.

(g) (*LAm*) *pelo* stiff, straight; *poste etc* upright.

(h) (*Carib, Cono Sur*: vanidoso*) vain, cocky*.

2 NM **(a)** unemployed person; **los ~s** the unemployed; **los ~s de larga duración** the long-term unemployed. **(b)** (*Méx*) air, look, resemblance; **tener ~ de** to look like.

paradoja NF paradox.

paradójicamente ADV paradoxically.

▼ **paradójico** ADJ paradoxical.

paradón* NM (*Dep*) great save, fantastic stop*.

parador NM **(a)** (*Esp*) (*Hist*) inn; (*t ~ nacional de turismo*) parador, state-owned hotel. **(b)** (*jugador*) (heavy) gambler.

> ┌─ **PARADOR NACIONAL** ─────────────────
>
> *In the early days of the Spanish tourist industry in the 1950s, the government set up a network of high-class tourist hotels known as* **paradores**. *They are sited in rural beauty spots and places of historical interest, often in converted castles and monasteries. There are currently 57 paradors, all rated at 3 stars or above and aiming to provide a high standard of accommodation with the emphasis on local character and cuisine.*

paraestatal ADJ semi-official, public.

parafernalia NF paraphernalia.

parafina NF paraffin wax; (*Cono Sur*) paraffin; **~ líquida** liquid paraffin.

parafinado ADJ waxed, waterproofed.

parafrasear [1a] VT to paraphrase.

paráfrasis NF INVAR paraphrase.

paragolpes NM INVAR (*Cono Sur*) = **parachoques.**

parágrafo NM (*Carib*) paragraph.

paraguas NM INVAR **(a)** umbrella (*t fig*); **~ nuclear** nuclear umbrella; **~ protector** protective umbrella. **(b)** (*And, Carib, Méx*) (*seta comestible*) mushroom; (*no comestible*) toadstool; (*moho*) fungus. **(c)** (:) French letter.

Paraguay NM: **el ~** Paraguay.

paraguayismo NM word (*o phrase etc*) peculiar to Paraguay.

paraguayo 1 ADJ Paraguayan.

2 NM, **paraguaya** NF Paraguayan.

3 NM **(a)** (*And*) whip. **(b)** (*Carib*) long straight knife.

paragüero 1 NM umbrella stand.

2 NM, **paragüera** NF (*hum*) native (*o inhabitant*) of Orense; **los ~s** the people of Orense.

paraíso NM **(a)** (*Rel*) paradise, heaven; **~ fiscal** tax haven; **~ terrenal** earthly paradise. **(b)** (*Teat*) upper gallery, gods.

paraje NM place, spot.

paral NM (*Méx*) shore, prop; post.

paralela NF parallel (line); **~s** parallel bars.

paralelamente ADV parallel; (*fig*) in a parallel way, comparably.

paralelismo NM parallelism.

paralelo 1 ADJ **(a)** (*Mat etc*) parallel (*t fig: a* to). **(b)** (*fig*) unofficial, irregular; (*pey*) illegal; **medicina paralela** alternative medicine; **importaciones paralelas** unauthorized imports, illegal imports.

2 NM parallel; **en ~** (*Elec*) in parallel; **en ~ con** (*fig*) in parallel with; **circular en ~** to cycle (*etc*) two abreast.

paralelogramo NM parallelogram.

paralimpiada NF = **paraolimpiada.**

paralímpico ADJ = **paraolímpico.**

parálisis NF paralysis; **~ cerebral** cerebral palsy; **~ infantil** infantile paralysis; **~ progresiva** creeping paralysis.

paralítico, -a ADJ, NM/F paralytic.

paralización NF paralysis; (*Com*) stagnation.

paralizador ADJ, **paralizante** ADJ paralyzing.

paralizar [1f] 1 VT to paralyze (*t fig*); *tráfico etc* to stop, block; **estar paralizado de un brazo** to be paralyzed in one arm; **estar paralizado de miedo** to be paralyzed with fright.

2 **paralizarse** VR to become paralyzed; (*fig*) to be paralyzed, come to a standstill; (*Com etc*) to stagnate.

paramar (*And*) season of wind and snow.

param(e)ar [1a] VI (*And, Carib*) to drizzle.

paramédico ADJ paramedical.

paramento NM **(a)** (*adorno*) ornament, ornamental cover; (*colgadura*) hangings; (*de caballo*) trappings; **~s sacerdotales** liturgical vestments. **(b)** (*de pared, piedra*) face.

paramera[1] NF **(a)** (*Geog*) high moorland. **(b)** (*Carib*) mountain sickness.

paramero 1 ADJ (*And, Carib*) upland, highland.

2 NM, **paramera**[2] NF highlander.

parámetro NM parameter.

paramilitar ADJ paramilitary.

páramo NM **(a)** (*brezal*) bleak plateau, high moor. **(b)** (*descampado*) waste land. **(c)** (*And*) (*llovizna*) drizzle; (*tormenta*) storm of wind and snow. **(d)** (*Carib*) mountain heights.

paramoso ADJ (*And*) drizzly.

paramuno ADJ (*And*) upland, highland.

paranera NF (*LAm*) grassland.

parangón NM comparison; **sin ~** incomparable, matchless; **no tiene ~ en otro país** there is nothing comparable (*o equivalent*) in any other country.

parangonable ADJ comparable (*con* to).

parangonar [1a] VT to compare (*con* to).

paraninfo NM (*Univ*) central hall; auditorium.

paranoia NF paranoia.

paranoico NM paranoic.

paranoide ADJ paranoid.

paranormal ADJ paranormal.

paranza NF (*Caza*) hide.

paraolimpiada NF, **paraolimpiadas** NFPL Paralympics, Paralympic Games.

paraolímpico 1 ADJ Paralympic; **Juegos Paraolímpicos** Paralympics, Paralympic Games.

2 NM, **paraolímpica** NF Paralympic athlete.

parapente NM **(a)** (*deporte*) paragliding; **hacer ~** to go paragliding. **(b)** (*aparato*) paraglider.

parapetarse [1a] VR **(a)** (*gen*) to protect o.s., shelter (*tras* behind). **(b)** **~ tras media docena de excusas** (*fig*) to take refuge in half-a-dozen excuses.

parapeto NM parapet, breastwork; defence, barricade.

paraplejía NF paraplegia.

parapléjico, -a ADJ, NM/F paraplegic.

parapsicología NF parapsychology.

parar [1a] 1 VT **(a)** (*gen*) to stop; *coche, motor, respiración etc* to stop; *progresos* to stop, check, halt.

(b) *amenaza, golpe* to ward off; (*Esgrima*) to parry; (*Dep*) *pase* to intercept, cut off; *tiro* to stop, save.

(c) *atención* to fix (*en* on) V **mientes.**

(d) (*fig*) to lead; **ahí le paró esa manera de vida** that's where that way of life led him.

(e) (*Naipes etc*) to bet, lay, stake.

(f) (*arreglar*) to prepare, arrange.

(g) (*LAm*) to raise; to stand upright, cause to stand (up).

(h) **~la con uno** (*And**) to take it out on sb.

2 VI **(a)** (*gen*) to stop; to come to rest; to come to an end; (*en el trabajo*) to stop work, strike; **¡pare!** stop!; **el coche ha parado** the car has stopped; **el autobús para enfrente** the bus stops opposite; **sin ~** without stopping; without a break; **~ en seco** to stop dead, stop suddenly; **no parará hasta conseguirlo** he won't give up until he gets it; **¡y no para!** (*orador*) he just goes on and on!, there's no stopping him!; **vino a ~ a mis pies** it came to rest at my feet; **¿adónde vamos a ~ ?** (*fig*) where's it all going to end?

(b) **~ de** + *infin* to stop + *ger*; **ha parado de llover** it has stopped raining; **no para de quejarse** he never stops complaining, he complains all the time; ... **y pare Vd de contar** ... and that's the lot, ... and that's it.

(c) **~ con uno** (*And**) to hang about with sb.

(d) **~ en** (*proyecto etc*) to end up as, result in, come down to; (*persona*) to end up at; **no sabemos en qué va a ~ todo esto** we don't know where all this is going to end; **el edificio paró en hotel** the building ended up as a hotel; **fueron a ~ en la comisaría** they finished (o ended) up at the police station; **irá a ~ (en) mal** he'll come to a bad end.

(e) (*hospedarse*) to stay, put up, lodge (*en at*); **siempre paro en este hotel** I always stay at this hotel.

(f) (*Caza: perro*) to point.

3 **pararse** VR **(a)** (*persona etc*) to stop; (*coche etc*) to stop, pull up, draw up; (*proceso*) to come to a halt; (*trabajo etc*) to stop, come to a standstill, cease; **~ a** + *infin* to stop to + *infin*, pause to + *infin*; **~ en** (*Ferro*) to stop at, call at.

(b) **~ en algo** to pay attention to sth, notice sth.

(c) (*LAm*) (*levantarse*) to stand (up), get up; (*enderezarse*) to straighten up, sit (*etc*) erect; (*de la cama*) to get up; (*pelo*) to stand on end.

(d) (*Tip*) to set.

(e) (*LAm**) to make one's pile*, get rich.

pararrayos NM INVAR lightning conductor.
parasitar [1a] **1** VT to parasitize. **2** VI: **~ en** to parasitize.
parasitario ADJ, **parasítico** ADJ parasitic(al).
parasitismo NM parasitism.
parásito **1** ADJ parasitic (*de on*). **2** NM **(a)** (*gen*) parasite (*t fig*). **(b)** **~s** (*Rad*) atmospherics, statics, interference. **(c)** (*CAm*) squatter.
parasitología NF parasitology.
parasitólogo, -a NM/F parasitologist.
parasitosis NF parasitism.
parasol NM parasol, sunshade.
parateatral ADJ theatre-related; quasi-dramatic.
paratifoidea NF paratyphoid.
paratopes NM INVAR (*LAm: Ferro*) buffer.
parcamente ADV frugally, sparingly; parsimoniously; moderately.
Parcas NFPL: **las ~** the Parcae, the Fates.
parcela NF **(a)** (*solar*) plot, piece of ground; (*Agr*) smallholding. **(b)** (*fig*) part, portion; area; **~ de poder** power domain; sphere of influence.
parcelar [1a] VT to divide into plots; **finca** to break up, parcel out.
parcelario ADJ: **tierra parcelaria** land divided into plots.
parcelero, -a NM/F, **parcelista** NMF owner of a plot, smallholder.
parchar [1a] VT (*LAm*) to patch, put a patch on.
parche NM **(a)** (*Med*) sticking plaster; (*de ojo*) eye patch; (*en neumático*) patch; **~ de nicotina** nicotine patch.
(b) (*fig*) patch, mend, botch; temporary remedy, stopgap solution; **poner ~s a** to apply temporary remedies to.
(c) (*Mús*) drumhead; drum; (*fig*) busking; **dar el ~** to busk.
(d) **pegar un ~ a uno*** to put one over on sb*.
parchear¹ [1a] VT to patch (up).
parchear²* [1a] VT to feel*, touch up*.
parcheo NM (*fig*) temporary remedies, stopgap solutions.
parchís NM a board game.
parchita NF (*Carib*) passion fruit.
parcho NM (*Carib*) = **parche**.
parcial **1** ADJ **(a)** (*incompleto*) partial; part-; **examen ~** class examination. **(b)** (*opinión etc*) partial, prejudiced, biassed; (*partidista*) partisan. **2** **parciales** NFPL by-election.
parcialidad NF **(a)** (*cualidad*) partiality, prejudice, bias; partisanship. **(b)** (*grupo*) party, faction, group, (*esp*) rebel group.
parcidad NF = **parquedad**.
parco ADJ frugal, sparing; parsimonious; moderate, temperate; **muy ~ en comer** very frugal in one's eating habits; **~ en elogios** sparing in one's praises.
parcómetro NM parking meter.
pardal NM **(a)** (*Orn*) sparrow; linnet. **(b)** (*Bot*) aconite. **(c)** (*: *pillo*) sly fellow, rogue; **¡~!** (*a niño*) you rascal!
pardiez INTERJ (*Esp*††) by gad!
pardillo NM **(a)** (*paño*) brown cloth; **gente del ~** country folk. **(b)** (*persona: rústico*) yokel, rustic. **(c)** (*: *principiante*) beginner, novice. **(d)** (*Orn*: **t ~ común**) linnet.

pardo **1** ADJ **(a)** *color* dun; drab, dark grey; (*descolorado*) discoloured; **cerveza, nube** black, dark; **cielo** overcast. **(b)** *voz* flat, dull. **2** NM (*Carib, Cono Sur*) mulatto, half-breed; (*Méx*) poor devil.
pardusco ADJ = **pardo**.
pareado NM (*Liter*) couplet; (*slogan*) jingle.
parear [1a] **1** VT **(a)** (*formar pares de*) to match, put together; to form pairs of. **(b)** (*Bio*) to mate, pair. **2** VI (*Carib**) to skive*. **3** **parearse** VR to pair off.

PARECER   *ver también la entrada*

En español se utiliza *parecer* en relación a las impresiones que alguien o algo nos causa a los cinco sentidos. En cambio, en inglés se utilizan verbos diferentes dependiendo del sentido que se emplee.

Parecer en general
● Cuando *parecer* expresa una impresión general se traduce por *seem* (*to be*) o por *appear* (*to be*) (éste último en lenguaje más formal):
   Parece muy segura de sí misma
   She seems o appears (to be) very confident
   Parece que estás cansada
   You seem o appear (to be) very tired

Parecer a la vista
● Cuando *parecer* se refiere a la apariencia física de alguien o de algo, se traduce por *look* (con adjetivos) o *look like* (con sustantivos):
   Pareces cansado
   You look tired
   Ese cuadro parece una pintura del Renacimiento
   That picture looks like a Renaissance painting

Parecer al oído
● *Parecer* se traduce por *sound* (con adjetivos) o *sound like* (con sustantivos):
   No lo sé, la verdad es que eso parece un poco complicado
   I don't know. To be honest, that sounds a bit complicated
   Por el acento parecía extranjera
   She sounded foreign o She sounded like a foreigner

Parecer al gusto
● *Parecer* se traduce por *taste* (con adjetivos) o por *taste like* (con sustantivos):
   Parece más salado de lo normal
   It tastes saltier than usual
   Se parecen a las galletas que hacía mi abuela
   They taste like the biscuits my grandmother used to make

Parecer al tacto
● *Parecer* se traduce por *feel* (con adjetivos) o por *feel like* (con sustantivos):
   Al tocarlo, el paquete parecía sólido
   The package felt solid
   Esta tela parece algodón
   This material feels like cotton

Parecer por el olor
● *Parecer* se traduce por *smell* (con adjetivos) o por *smell like* (con sustantivos):
   Por como huele, esa sopa parece que va a estar picante
   This soup smells spicy
   Por el olor parece una mandarina
   It smells like a tangerine
   Para otros usos y ejemplos ver la entrada.

▼ **parecer** [2d] **1** NM **(a)** (*opinión*) opinion, view; **a mi ~** in my opinion; **al ~** apparently, seemingly; **por el bien** (o **buen**) **~** for form's sake, as a matter of courtesy; in order not to seem rude; **mudar de ~** to change one's mind.
(b) (*aspecto*) looks; **de buen ~** good-looking, nice-looking, handsome; **de mal ~** plain, ugly.
2 VI **(a)** (*gen*) to seem (to be), appear (to be); (*al tacto*) to feel; (*a la vista*) to look; (*al oído*) to sound; (*al gusto*) to taste; **parecía volar** it seemed to fly; **así parece** so it seems; **a lo que parece, según parece** to all appearances; seemingly, apparently; **aunque no lo parezca** surprising though it may seem, incredible though it is; **parece como si quisieras** ... it looks as if you wanted to ...; **parece que va a llover** it looks as though it's going to rain, it seems that it's going to rain.
(b) (*: *comparaciones: hum*) **parece un alfeñique** he's terribly thin; **parece una ballena** she's as fat as a cow*; **parece un juez** he looks terribly serious.
▼ **(c)** (*con pron pers*) **me parece que** ... I think (that) ..., it seems to me that ...; **como te parece, si a Vd le parece** as you wish; if you think

---

➤ LENGUA Y USO: **parecer: 1a** → 33.2, 53.5 **2c** → 28.1, 34.1, 36.1

so, if you want to; **¿te parece?** OK?*, all right?, does that suit you?; **¿qué te parece?** what do you think (of it)?; **vamos a la piscina, ¿te parece?** do you fancy the swimming pool?, what about going to the swimming pool?; **me parece bien que vayas** I think you should go, it seems to me proper you should go; **si a Vd le parece mal** if you don't like it; **le parece mal que no vayas** she takes a poor view of your not going, she doesn't like the idea of your not going; **¡me parece muy mal!** I think it's shocking!

(d) (*semejar*) to look like, seem like, resemble; **una casa que parece un palacio** a house that looks like a palace; **¡pareces una reina!** you look like a queen!

(e) (*aparecer*) to appear, show; (*persona*) to turn up, show up, appear; (*objeto perdido*) to turn up, reappear; **pareció el sol entre las nubes** the sun showed (*o* shone) through the clouds; **cuando la luna parezca** when the moon comes up; **ya parecieron los guantes** the gloves have turned up; **¡ya pareció aquello!** so that was it!

3 parecerse VR **(a)** (*2 cosas etc*) to look alike, resemble each other; **se parecen mucho** they look very much alike, they resemble each other closely; **ni cosa que se parezca** nor anything of the sort; far from it.

▼**(b)** **~ a** to look like, resemble; **se parece al abuelo** he takes after his grandfather, he has his grandfather's looks; **el retrato no se le parece (en nada)** the picture isn't a bit like him.

parecidamente ADV similarly, equally.

►**parecido** 1 ADJ **(a)** (*semejante*) similar (*de, en* in, in respect of); **~ a** like, similar to; **son muy ~s** they are very similar, they are very much alike.
(b) bien ~ good-looking, nice-looking, handsome; **no es mal parecido** he's not bad-looking.
▼2 NM (*semejanza*) similarity, likeness, resemblance (*a* to, *entre* between); **tienen mucho ~** they are very alike.
3 NM, **parecida** NF (*persona*) look-alike.

parecimiento NM **(a)** (*Cono Sur, Méx*) = **parecido 2. (b)** (*Cono Sur*) (*comparecencia*) appearance; (*aparición*) apparition.

pared NF **(a)** wall; (*Alpinismo*) face, wall; **~ arterial** wall of the artery; **~ celular** cell wall; **~ medianera** party wall; **~ por medio** next door; **estar cara a la ~** (*Escol*) to be stood in the corner; **ni que hablara uno a la ~** I might as well talk to a brick wall; **ponerse blanco como la ~** to go as white as a sheet; **subirse por las ~es*** to go up the wall*; **me hace subirme por las ~es*** it drives me up the wall*.

paredeño ADJ adjoining, next-door (*con* to).

paredón NM **(a)** (*muro*) thick wall; (*de ruina*) standing wall.
(b) (*de roca*) wall of rock, rock face.
(c) llevar a uno al ~ to put sb up against a wall, shoot sb; **¡al ~!** shoot him!

pareja NF **(a)** (*par*) couple; pair; (*policías*) pair of Civil Guards; (*esposos etc*) couple; (*Naipes*) pair; **~ abierta, ~ libre** open marriage; **~ de hecho** unmarried couple; **~ reproductora** (*Orn*) breeding pair.
(b) (*otro*) other one (of a pair); **~ de baile** dancing partner; **no encuentro la ~ de este guante** I can't find the glove that goes with this one, I can't find my other glove; **correr ~s** to be on a par, go together, keep pace (*con* with).
(c) (*amigo*) boyfriend, (*amiga*) girlfriend; (*amante*) lover; (*cónyuge*) other half, better half; **hogar sin ~** one-parent family; **madre sin ~, padre sin ~** single parent; **la vida en ~** living as a couple, life together; **nuestra vida como ~** our life together; **llevamos una relación de ~** we're an item*, we live together.
(d) (*LAm*) (*caballos*) pair of horses; (*de tiro*) team of draught animals; (*de bueyes*) yoke of oxen.

parejamente ADV equally.

parejería NF (*Carib*) vanity, conceit.

parejero 1 ADJ (*Carib**) (*demasiado confiado*) cheeky; (*presumido*) cocky, over-confident.
2 NM **(a)** (*LAm*) racehorse.
(b) (*Carib**) hanger-on.

parejita* NF pigeon pair (*son and daughter*).

parejo 1 ADJ **(a)** (*igual*) equal; (*semejante*) similar, alike; **6 todos ~s** 6 all the same; **por ~** on a par; **ir ~s** to be neck and neck; **ir ~ con** to be on a par with, be paralleled by.
(b) (*Téc*) smooth, even, flush; (*LAm*) flat, level.
2 ADV (*LAm*) at the same time, together.
3 NM (*CAm, Carib*) dancing partner, escort.

paremiología NF study of proverbs.

parentela NF relations.

parenteral ADJ parenteral; **inyección ~** intravenous injection.

parentesco NM relationship, kinship.

paréntesis NM INVAR **(a)** (*Ling*) parenthesis; digression; aside.
(b) (*Tip*) parenthesis, bracket; **~ cuadrados** square brackets; **entre ~** (ADJ) parenthetical, incidental; (ADV) parenthetically, incidentally; **y, entre ~ ...** and, by the way ..., and, I may add in passing ...
(c) (*fig*) interruption, interval, break; gap; lull; **el ~ vacacional** the

break for the holidays, the holiday interruption; **hacer ~** to digress.

pareo¹ NM pareo; (*de playa*) beach wrap; (*taparrabos*) loincloth; (*chal*) rectangular shawl.

┃ PAREJA ┃   **▌ ver también la entrada ▌**

Para traducir el sustantivo *pareja* referido a dos personas, hay que tener en cuenta la diferencia entre los sustantivos *pair* y *couple*:

● Se traduce por *couple* cuando se trata de un matrimonio o de dos personas que parecen tener una relación íntima, o cuando se refiere a una pareja de baile:
   En Salford conocí a una pareja de Ecuador
   In Salford I met a couple from Ecuador
   Algunas parejas prefieren no tener hijos
   Some couples prefer not to have children
   Había muchas parejas mayores bailando
   There were a lot of older couples dancing

● En un contexto de trabajo o de competiciones deportivas o cuando a la *pareja* no se le asocia ningún vínculo afectivo, se traduce por *pair*:
   Ahora vamos a trabajar por parejas
   Now we're going to work in pairs
   Detuvieron a la pareja al cruzar la frontera
   The pair were arrested when they were crossing the border

● La expresión *pareja de* se puede traducir tanto por *couple of* como por *pair of* cuando tiene el sentido de *par de*:
   Una pareja de pillos me robaron el reloj
   A couple o A pair of thugs stole my watch
   ⇨ Ver también ┃PAR┃
   Para otros usos y ejemplos ver la entrada.

---

pareo² NM (*unión*) pairing off; matching; (*Zool*) mating.

paria NMF pariah.

parián NM (*Méx*) market.

parida NF **(a)** (*mujer*) woman who has recently given birth. **(b)** (*: dicho etc*) silly thing, stupid remark (*etc*); **~s** nonsense; **salir con alguna ~** to come out with some silly remark.

paridad NF **(a)** (*igualdad*) parity, equality; (*semejanza*) similarity. **(b)** (*comparación*) comparison.

parido* ADJ successful.

paridora ADJ F fertile, productive.

parienta NF **(a)** (*gen*) relative, relation; **~ pobre** poor relation. **(b) la ~*** the wife*, the missus*.

pariente NM **(a)** (*gen*) relative, relation; **~ político** relative by marriage; **los ~s políticos** the in-laws; **medio ~** distant relative. **(b) el ~*** the old man*, my (*etc*) hubby*.

parietal ADJ parietal.

parihuela NF (*gen* **parihuelas** PL) stretcher; **~ de mariscos** (*LAm*) seafood platter.

paripé* NM: **hacer** (*o* **montar**) **el ~** to put on a show, keep up the show.

parir [3a] 1 VT **(a)** (*Bio*) to give birth to, bear. **(b) ~la‡** to drop a clanger‡.
2 VI (*mujer*) to give birth, have a baby; to be delivered; (*vaca*) to calve (*y hay verbos parecidos para otras especies*); **ha parido 4 veces** she has had 4 children, she has given birth 4 times; **poner a ~ a uno*** to run sb down*, criticize sb behind his back.

París NM Paris.

parisién ADJ, **parisino** ADJ Parisian.

parisiense ADJ, NMF Parisian.

paritario ADJ peer (*atr*); **grupo ~** peer group.

paritorio NM maternity ward.

parka NF parka.

parking ['parkin] NM car-park, parking lot; parking space.

parla NF chatter, gossip.

parlador ADJ talkative.

parlamentar [1a] VI to converse, talk; (*enemigos*) to parley.

parlamentario 1 ADJ parliamentary.
2 NM, **parlamentaria** NF parliamentarian; member of parliament; **~ autónomo** member of a regional parliament.

parlamento NM **(a)** (*Pol*) parliament; **~ autónomo** regional parliament; **P~ Europeo** European Parliament. **(b)** (*entre enemigos*) parley. **(c)** (*Jur, Teat*) speech.

parlana NF (*CAm Zool*) turtle.

parlanchín 1 ADJ loose-tongued, indiscreet.
2 NM, **parlanchina** NF **(a)** (*parlador*) chatterbox, great talker. **(b)** (*indiscreto*) indiscreet person.

parlante 1 ADJ *máquina etc* talking.
2 NM (*LAm*) loudspeaker.

-parlante SUF *en palabras compuestas, p.ej.* **castellanoparlante** (ADJ) Castilian-speaking, (NMF) Castilian speaker.

parlar [1a] VI to chatter (away), talk (a lot), gossip; (*loro*) to talk.

parlero ADJ **(a)** (*hablador*) talkative, garrulous; (*cotilla*) gossipy. **(b)**

parleta NF chat, small talk.

parlotear [1a] VI to chatter, prattle.

parloteo NM chatter, prattle.

PARM NM (Méx) ABR de **Partido Auténtico de la Revolución Mexicana**.

parmesano ADJ, NM Parmesan.

Parnaso NM Parnassus.

parné‡ NM dough‡, money.

paro[1] NM (Orn) tit.

paro[2] NM **(a)** (parada) stoppage (of work); standstill; (LAm: huelga) strike; **~ cardíaco** cardiac arrest; **hay ~ en la industria** work in the industry is at a standstill.
(b) (desempleo: t **~ forzoso, ~ obrero**) unemployment; **~ encubierto** hidden unemployment; **~ estacional** (Esp) seasonal unemployment; **enviar al ~** to put out of a job, make unemployed; **estar en ~** to be unemployed, be on the dole.
(c) (pago) unemployment benefit; **cobrar el ~** to receive unemployment benefit, (frec) be on the dole.
(d) (And, Carib: dados) throw.
(e) en ~ (And) all at once, in one go.

parodia NF parody, travesty, takeoff; (fig) travesty.

parodiar [1b] VT to parody, travesty, take off.

paródico ADJ parodic.

parodista NMF parodist, writer of parodies.

parola NF **(a)** (soltura) fluency; (verborrea) verbosity; (labia) gift of the gab*. **(b)** (charla) chitchat; wearisome talk; **son ~s** (Cono Sur*) it's all hot air*.

parolímpico, -a ADJ, NM/F = **paraolímpico**.

parón NM sudden halt, complete stop; general stoppage, shutdown.

paroxismo NM paroxysm; **~ histérico** hysterics; **~ de risa** convulsions of laughter; **en un ~ de celos** in a fit of jealousy, in a paroxysm of jealousy.

parpadear [1a] VI (ojo) to blink, wink; (luz) to blink, flicker; (estrella) to twinkle.

parpadeo NM blinking, winking; flickering; twinkling.

párpado NM eyelid; **restregarse los ~s** to rub one's eyes.

parpichuela‡ NF: **hacerse una ~** to wank‡.

parque NM **(a)** (gen) park; **~ acuático** waterpark; **~ de atracciones** funfair, fairground; **~ de automóviles, ~ de estacionamiento** car park, parking lot (US); **~ central** (Méx) town square; **~ cerrado** (Aut) pit, pits; **~ de chatarra** scrapyard; **~ eólico** windfarm; **~ infantil** playpark; **~ nacional** national park; **~ natural** nature reserve; **~ tecnológico** technology park; **~ zoológico** zoo.
(b) (Mil etc) depot; **~ de artillería** artillery depot, artillery stores; **~ de bomberos** fire-station.
(c) (Aut etc) fleet; **~ móvil** official cars; **el ~ nacional de automóviles** the total number of cars in the country; **el ~ provincial de tractores** the number of tractors in use in the province.
(d) ~ (de jugar) playpen.
(e) (LAm Mil) (equipo) equipment; (munición) ammunition; (depósito) ammunition dump.

parqué NM, **parquet** [par'ke] NM, PL **parquets** [par'ke] parquet; (Fin) **el ~** the Floor (of the stock exchange), (fig) the stock market.

parqueadero NM (LAm) (local) car park, parking lot (US); (espacio individual) parking-place.

parquear [1a] VTI (LAm) to park.

parquedad NF frugality, sparingness; parsimony; moderation.

parqueo NM (LAm) (acto) parking; (local) car-park, parking lot (US); (espacio individual) parking-place.

parquímetro NM parking meter.

parra NF grapevine; climbing vine, trained vine; **subirse a la ~*** to blow one's top*.

parrafada* NF (esp LAm) chat, talk; **echar la ~** to have a chat; **soltar la ~, tirarse la ~** to give a lengthy spiel*.

párrafo NM paragraph; **echar un ~*** to have a chat (con with); **hacer ~ aparte** to start a new paragraph; (fig) to change the subject.

parral NM vine arbour.

parranda NF **(a)** (*: juerga) spree, party; **andar** (o **ir** etc) **de ~** to go on a binge*. **(b)** (And, Cono Sur, Méx) lot, group, heap; **una ~ de** a lot of.

parrandear* [1a] VI to go on a binge*.

parricida NMF (persona) parricide.

parricidio NM (act) parricide.

parrilla NF **(a)** (objeto) grating, gridiron, grille; (de nevera) shelf; (Culin) grill; **carne a la ~** grilled meat.
(b) (restaurante) grillroom, steak restaurant.
(c) (Aut) (de radiador) radiator grille; (Cono Sur) roof-rack; **~ de salida** (Aut) starting grid; (de caballos) starting gate, starting stalls.
(d) (de bicicleta) carrier.

parrillada NF **(a)** grill; barbecue. **(b)** (restaurante) steak house.

párroco NM parish priest.

parroquia NF **(a)** (Ecl) (zona) parish; (iglesia) parish church.
(b) (Com) clientèle, customers; **hoy hay poca ~** there are few customers today; **una tienda con mucha ~** a shop with a large clientèle, a well-patronized shop.

parroquial ADJ parochial, parish (atr).

parroquiano, -a NM/F **(a)** (Ecl) parishioner.
(b) (Com) client, customer, patron; **ser ~ de** to be a regular client of, shop regularly at, patronize.

parsi NMF Parsee.

parsimonia NF **(a)** (prudencia) carefulness (about money etc); (frugalidad) sparingness.
(b) (calma) deliberateness, calmness; (flema) phlegmatic nature; **con ~** deliberately, calmly, unhurriedly.

parsimonioso ADJ **(a)** (prudente) sensible, careful (about money etc); economical; (frugal) sparing. **(b)** (tranquilo) slow, deliberate, calm, unhurried; phlegmatic.

parte[1] NM (Telec) message; (informe) report; (Mil) dispatch, communiqué; (Rad†) news bulletin; (Cono Sur: de boda) wedding invitation; (Cono Sur Aut) ticket for speeding; **~ de baja** sick note; **~ de clase** school report; **~ de defunción** death certificate; **~ facultativo** medical bulletin; **~ de guerra** military communiqué, war report; **~ matrimonial** wedding announcement; **~ médico** medical report, medical bulletin; **~ meteorológico** weather report, weather forecast; **~ de nacimiento** birth announcement; **dar ~ a uno** to report to sb, inform sb.

▼ **parte**[2] NF **(a)** (gen) part; (sección) portion, section; **cuarta ~** quarter, fourth part; **tercera ~** third; **reducir algo en una tercera ~** to reduce sth by a third; **primera ~** (Dep) first half; **la mayor ~ de** most of; the greater part of, the great majority of; **la mayor ~ de los argentinos** most of the Argentinians, most of the Argentinians; **~ del mundo** part of the world; **en las cinco ~s del mundo** (Esp) in the four corners of the earth; **~ de la oración** part of speech; **ser esencial** (o **integral, integrante**) **de** to be an essential part of; **de algún tiempo a esta ~** for some time past; **como ~ del pago** in part payment; in part exchange; **de una ~ a otra** back and forth, to and fro; **de ~ a ~** through and through, right through; **de ~ de** from, on behalf of; in the name of; **¿de ~ de quién?** (Telec) who's calling?, who is that talking?, who shall I say (is calling)?; **de ~ de todos nosotros** on behalf of us all; **salúdale de mi ~** give him regards from me, give him my regards; **en ~** in part, partly; **en gran ~** to a large extent, in large measure; **por ~ de** on the part of; **con concesiones por ambas ~s** with concessions on both sides; **por ~s** bit by bit; stage by stage, systematically; **por otra ~** (or) again, on the other hand; moreover; **por una ~ ... por otra (~)** on the one hand, ... on the other; **yo por mi ~** I for my part; **por la mayor ~** mostly, for the most part; **echar algo a mala ~** to look on sth with disapproval, be offended about sth; **echar una palabra a mala ~** to take offence at a remark; **(entrar a) formar ~ de** to form a part of, be a part of; (persona) to be a member of; **no formaba ~ del equipo** he was not in the team; **tomar algo en buena ~** to take sth in good part.
(b) (participación, porción) share; **la ~ del león** the lion's share; **a ~s iguales** in equal shares; **ir a la ~** to go shares; **llevar la mejor ~** to have the advantage, be on the way to winning; **llevarse la mejor ~** to come off best, get the best of it; **tener ~ en** to share in; **tomar ~** to take part (en in).
(c) (región, Geog etc) part; **en alguna ~** somewhere; **en alguna ~ de Europa** somewhere in Europe; **en cualquier ~** anywhere; **por ahí no se va a ninguna ~** that leads nowhere, (fig) this is getting us nowhere; **en ninguna ~ del país** in no part of the country, nowhere in the country; **no esperes ayuda de ninguna ~** don't expect help from any quarter; **ir a otra ~** to go somewhere else; **mirar a otra ~** to look the other way, look in another direction; **ha de estar en otra ~** it must be somewhere else; **¿en qué ~ del país?** in which part of the country? **¿en qué ~ lo dejaste?** whereabouts did you leave it?; **en todas ~s** everywhere; **en todas ~s de España** in all parts of Spain, everywhere in Spain, all over Spain; **por todas ~s se va a Roma** all roads lead to Rome.
(d) (lado) side; **por cualquier ~ que lo mires** from whichever side you look at it.
(e) (Mús, Teat) part.
(f) (de parentesco) side; **por ~ de madre** on the mother's side.
(g) (persona) contender; (Jur) party, side; **~ actora** prosecution; plaintiff; **las ~s contratantes** the contracting parties; **~ contraria** opposing party, other side; **tercera ~** third party; **ponerse de ~ de** to take the side of, side with.
(h) (cualidades) **~s** parts, qualities, talents; **buenas ~s** good parts.
(i) (Anat) **~s** parts; **~s íntimas** (o **~s pudendas**) pudenda, private parts; **la ~ donde la espalda pierde su honesto nombre** (hum) one's anatomy; **le dio en salva sea la ~** (Esp euf) it hit her on a part of her anatomy.
(j) (Méx Mec) spare part.

► LENGUA Y USO: **parte: a** → 48.2, 49, 50.6, 53.5

parteaguas NM INVAR divide, ridge; watershed; **~ continental** continental divide.

partear [1a] VT *mujer* to deliver.

parteluz NM mullion.

partenogénesis NF parthenogenesis.

Partenón NM Parthenon.

partenueces NM INVAR nutcracker.

partera NF midwife.

partero NM (*Méx*) gynaecologist.

parterre NF (**a**) (*de flores*) flower bed. (**b**) (*Teat etc*) stalls.

partición NF division, sharing-out; (*Pol etc*) partition.

participación NF (**a**) (*acto*) participation, taking part.
(**b**) (*interés, parte*) share; (*Fin*) share, stock (*US*), investment; interest, holding; **~ accionarial** holding, shareholding; **~ en los beneficios** profit-sharing; **~ electoral** turnout (of voters); **~ del mercado** market share, share in the market; **la ~ de la compañía A en la compañía B** company A's holding in company B; **su ~ en estos asuntos** his share (*o* part) in these matters.
(**c**) (*Dep*) entry; **hubo una nutrida ~** there was a big entry, there were numerous entrants.
(**d**) (*de lotería*) (part of a) lottery ticket; *see also* LOTERÍA PRIMITIVA, LOTERÍA NACIONAL .
(**e**) (*aviso*) notice, notification; **~ de boda** notice of a forthcoming wedding; **dar ~ a uno de algo** to inform sb of sth.

participante NMF participant; (*Dep*) entrant, entry; **los países ~s** the participating countries.

participar [1a] **①** VT (*informar*) to notify, inform; **~ algo a uno** to notify sb of sth; **le participo que ...** I have to tell you that ...; I warn you that ...
② VI (**a**) (*tomar parte*) to take part, participate (*en* in); **~ en una carrera** to enter for a race, run in a race, take part in a race.
(**b**) **~ de** (*o* en) **una herencia** to share in an estate; **~ en una empresa** (*Fin*) to invest in an enterprise.
(**c**) **~ de una cualidad** to share a quality, partake of a quality, have a quality in common.

participativo ADJ participatory, participating.

partícipe NMF participant; **hacer ~ a uno de algo** to share sth with sb, inform sb of sth.

participial ADJ participial.

participio NM participle; **~ de pasado, ~ pasivo, ~ de pretérito** past participle; **~ activo, ~ de presente** present participle.

partícula NF particle; **~ alfa** alpha particle; **~ atómica** atomic particle; **~ elemental** fundamental particle.

particular **①** ADJ (**a**) (*especial*) particular, special; (*propio*) peculiar (*a* to); **nada de ~** nothing special; **lo que tiene de ~ es que ...** what's remarkable about it is that ...; **en ~** in particular; **en este caso ~** in this particular case; **tiene un sabor ~** it has a special flavour, it has a flavour of its own.
(**b**) (*personal*) private, personal; **tiene coche ~** he has a car of his own, he has a car to himself; **clase ~** private lesson; **secretario ~** private secretary; **en ~** in private.
② NM (**a**) (*asunto*) particular, point, matter; **no dijo mucho sobre el ~** he didn't say much about the matter.
(**b**) (*persona*) individual, private individual; **iba vestido de ~** he was in civilian clothes; **no comerciamos con ~es** we don't do business with individuals.

particularidad NF (**a**) (*propiedad*) particularity, peculiarity; (*rasgo distintivo*) special feature, characteristic; **tiene la ~ de que ...** one of its special features is ..., it has the characteristic that ...
(**b**) (*amistad*) friendship, intimacy.

particularizar [1f] **①** VT (**a**) (*distinguir*) to distinguish, characterize, mark out.
(**b**) (*especificar*) to particularize, specify.
(**c**) (*distinguir con la amistad*) to show special friendship to.
(**d**) (*dar detalles*) to give details about.
② **particularizarse** VR (**a**) (*distinguirse*) to distinguish itself, stand out, mark itself out; (*persona*) to make one's mark, do sth outstanding.
(**b**) **~ con uno** to single sb out (for special treatment *etc*).

particularmente ADV (**a**) particularly, specially. (**b**) privately, personally.

partida NF (**a**) (*salida*) departure.
(**b**) (*registro*) register; (*documento*) certificate; (*entrada*) entry (in a register *etc*); **~ bautismal, ~ de bautismo** certificate of baptism; **~ de defunción** death certificate; **~ de matrimonio** marriage certificate; **~ de nacimiento** birth certificate.
(**c**) (*Com, Fin*) (*entrada*) entry, item; (*de presupuesto etc*) item, section, heading; **~ doble** double entry; **~ simple** single entry.
(**d**) (*Com: envío*) consignment, shipment; (*LAm*) consignment of drugs.
(**e**) (*Naipes*) game, hand; (*Ajedrez etc*) game; **~ de dobles** doubles match; **~ de individuales, ~ de simples** singles match; **echar una ~**

to have a game.
(**f**) (*apuesta*) stake, wager, bet.
(**g**) (*personas*) party; (*Mil etc*) band, group; faction; **~ de caza** hunting party; **~ de campo** picnic (party); **~ de excursión** group of trippers.
(**h**) (**mala**) **~, ~ serrana** dirty trick.

▼ **partidario** **①** ADJ partisan; **soy muy ~ de ...** I'm very fond of ..., I'm very partial to ...
▼ **②** NM, **partidaria** NF (**a**) (*gen*) supporter, follower (*de* of); partisan; **soy ~ de** + *infin* I'm in favour of + *ger*. (**b**) (*And, Carib*) sharecropper.

partidillo NM (*Dep*) practice game.

partidismo NM partisanship, bias; partisan spirit; (*Pol, pey*: *t ~*s) party feeling, party politics.

partidista **①** ADJ partisan; party (*atr*).
② NMF partisan.

partido NM (**a**) (*Pol etc*) party; **~ político** political party; **~ de la oposición** opposition party; **~ de la reforma** reforming party; **~ republicano** republican party; **sistema de ~ único** one-party system, single-party system; **P~ Verde** Green Party.
(**b**) (*Dep etc: encuentro*) game, match; fixture; **~ amistoso** friendly game; **~ de casa** home game; **~ de desempate** replay; **~ de exhibición** exhibition match; **~ de fútbol** football match; **~ (de) homenaje** benefit match; **~ de ida** away game; **~ internacional** international match; **~ de vuelta** return match.
(**c**) (*Dep etc: equipo*) team, side.
(**d**) (*distrito: t ~* **judicial**) district, administrative area.
(**e**) **darse a ~, venir(se) a ~** to give way; **tomar ~** to decide, make up one's mind; to take sides.
(**f**) (*provecho*) advantage, profit; **sacar ~ de** to profit from, benefit from; to put to use.
(**g**) (*apoyo*) support; **tiene ~ en todas las clases** he has support among all classes.
(**h**) **es un (buen) ~, es de ~** he's a good catch*, he's very eligible.
(**i**) (*Cono Sur Naipes*) hand.
(**j**) (*Méx: aparcía*) crop share.
(**k**) (*And, Carib:**) **a ~, al ~** share and share alike, in equal shares.

partija NF (**a**) (*partición*) partition, division. (**b**) (*pey*) = **parte²**.

partiota NF (*Carib*) dollar bill.

partir [3a] **①** VT (**a**) (*dividir*) to split (up, into two *etc*), divide (up); *nuez etc* to crack; (*abrir*) to break open; (*romper*) to split open; **~ la cabeza a uno** to split (*o* crack) sb's head open.
(**b**) (*repartir*) to share (out), distribute, divide (up); **~ algo con otros** to share sth with others.
(**c**) *cartas* to cut.
② VI (**a**) (*ponerse en camino*) to start, set off, set out, depart (*de* from, *para* for, *con rumbo a* for, in the direction of).
(**b**) (*comenzar*) to start (*de* from); **a ~ del lunes** from Monday, starting on (*o* from) Monday; **es el tercero a ~ de la esquina** it's the third one counting from the corner; **a ~ de estos datos** starting from these data; **hemos partido de un supuesto falso** we have started from a false assumption.
③ **partirse** VR to crack, split, break (in two *etc*); **~ de risa** to split one's sides laughing.

partisano, -a ADJ, NM/F partisan.

partitivo ADJ partitive.

partitura NF (*Mús*) score.

parto NM (**a**) (*Med*) birth, childbirth; delivery; labour; **~ sin dolor, ~ sin violencia** painless childbirth; **~ múltiple** multiple birth; **~ natural** natural childbirth; **~ de los montes** anticlimax, bathos; **estar de ~** to be in labour; **tener un ~ difícil** to have a difficult labour.
(**b**) (*fig*) product, creation; **~ del ingenio** brain child; **el ensayo ha sido un ~ difícil** I sweated blood over the essay.

parturición NF parturition.

parturienta NF woman in labour; woman who has just given birth.

party NM *o* F, PL **partys** party; (*cóctel*) cocktail party, reception.

parva NF (heap of) unthreshed corn; (*fig*) heap, pile.

parvada NF (*LAm*) flock.

parvedad NF littleness, smallness; fewness; **~ de recursos** limited resources, scant resources.

parvulario NM (*Esp*) nursery school, kindergarten, crèche.

parvulista NMF nursery teacher.

párvulo, -a NM/F child, infant; (*Escol*) infant.

pasa NF (**a**) raisin; **~ de Corinto** (*Esp*) currant; **~ de Esmirna** (*Esp*) sultana. (**b**) **está hecho una ~** (* *fig*) he's as shrivelled as a prune.

pasable ADJ (**a**) (*tolerable*) passable, tolerable. (**b**) (*LAm*) *arroyo etc* fordable, that can be forded. (**c**) (*Cono Sur*) saleable.

pasablemente ADV passably, tolerably (well).

pasabocas NM INVAR (*And*) snack, appetizer.

pasacalles NM INVAR street band; informal theatre troupe.

pasacintas NM INVAR suspender-belt.

pasada NF (**a**) (*acto*) passing, passage; (*con trapo etc*) rub, clean, polish; **~ de pintura** coat of paint; **dar dos ~s de jabón a la ropa** to soap

the clothes twice; **dar una ~ con la plancha a** to run the iron over.
(b) de ~ in passing, incidentally.
(c) (*Cos*) (*línea*) row of stitches; (*hilvanado*) tacking stitch; **~s** patch, mend.
(d) mala ~ dirty trick.
(e) una ~ de* a lot of, a whole heap of.
(f) (*ultraje*) outrage, excess; **esto fue una ~ suya** in this he went too far, with this he overstepped the bounds.
(g) (*CAm, Cono Sur**) telling-off*.
(h) (*And*) shame, embarrassment.

pasadera NF stepping stone.

pasadero ⓵ ADJ (*tolerable*) passable, tolerable.
⓶ NM (*piedra*) stepping stone.

pasadizo NM (*Arquit*) passage, corridor; (*callejón*) passageway, alley; (*con tiendas*) arcade; (*pasarela*) gangway; catwalk.

pasado ⓵ ADJ **(a)** (*gen*) past; **lo ~** the past; **lo ~, ~** let bygones be bygones; **el mes (próximo) ~** last month; **~ mañana** the day after tomorrow; **~s dos días** after two days.
(b) *comida* stale, bad; *fruta* overripe; *caza* (*en buen sentido*) high; (*muy hecho*) overdone; *cuento, noticia* stale; *idea* antiquated, out of date; *ropa etc* old, worn, threadbare; *belleza* faded; **la carne está pasada** the meat is off (o bad); **ella está un poco pasada** she's a little past her best.
⓶ NM **(a)** (*tiempo*) past.
(b) (*Ling*) past (tense).
(c) ~s ancestors.

pasador NM **(a)** (*pestillo etc*) bolt, fastener; (*de corbata*) (tie) pin; (*de pelo*) hairclip; (*Téc*) bolt; split pin.
(b) (*Culin*) colander; (*de té*) strainer; (*Téc*) filter.
(c) ~es (*gemelos*) cufflinks; (*And*) shoelaces.
(d) (*persona*) smuggler; (*LAm*) drug courier.

pasaje NM **(a)** (*acto*) passage, passing; (*Náut*) voyage, crossing.
(b) (*tarifa*) fare; **cobrar el ~** to collect fares.
(c) (*viajeros*) passengers (*collectively*).
(d) (*callejón*) passageway, alleyway; (*con tiendas*) arcade; (*Carib, Cono Sur, Méx*) cul-de-sac.
(e) (*Liter, Mús*) passage.
(f) (*And, Carib: cuento*) story, anecdote.
(g) (*And: pisos*) tenement building.

pasajeramente ADV fleetingly.

pasajero ⓵ ADJ **(a)** *momento etc* passing, fleeting, transient.
(b) pájaro ~ bird of passage, migratory bird.
(c) *calle etc* busy.
⓶ NM, **pasajera** NF passenger; traveller.
⓷ NM (*Méx*) ferryman.

pasamano(s) NM **(a)** (*barra*) rail, handrail; (*de escalera*) banisters. **(b)** (*Cos*) braid. **(c)** (*Cono Sur*) strap (*for standing passenger*). **(d)** (*Cono Sur: propina*) tip.

pasamontañas NM INVAR Balaclava (helmet), ski mask (*US*).

pasandito* ADV (*CAm, Méx*) on tiptoe.

pasante NM (*gen*) assistant; (*Escol*) assistant teacher; tutor; (*Jur*) articled clerk.

pasapalos NM INVAR (*Carib*) snack, appetizer.

pasapasa NM sleight of hand.

pasaporte NM passport; **dar el ~ a uno*** (*despedir*) to boot sb out; (*matar*) to bump sb off‡.

pasaport(e)ar‡ [1a] VT to bump off‡.

pasapuré(s) NM INVAR mixer, blender.

▼ **pasar** [1a] ⓵ VT **(a)** (*gen*) to pass; *objeto* to hand, give, pass (*a* to); *noticia, recado* to give, pass on; *cuenta* to send; *propiedad* to transfer; *persona* to take, lead, conduct (*a* to, into); *página* to turn; **¿me pasas la sal, por favor?** would you please pass the salt?; **nos hicieron pasar a otra habitación** they showed us into another room; **nos pasaron a ver al director** they took us to see the director; *V* **lista, revista** *etc*.
(b) *enfermedad* to give, infect with; **me has pasado tu tos** you've given me that cough.
(c) *visita etc* to make, carry out; **el médico pasará visita** the doctor will call.
(d) *calle, río* to cross, go over.
(e) *armadura etc* to pierce, penetrate, go through; *barrera* to pass through (o across, over), go through; *frontera, límite etc* to cross, go beyond; **el túnel pasa la montaña** the tunnel goes right through the mountain; **esto pasa los límites de lo razonable** this goes beyond anything that is reasonable.
(f) (*introducir*) to insert, put in; (*colar*) to put through; **~ el café por el colador** to put the coffee through a filter, strain the coffee.
(g) (*tragar*) to swallow; (*LAm*) to bear, stand, put up with; **no puedo ~ este vino** I can't get this wine down; **no puedo ~ a ese hombre** I can't bear that chap*.
(h) *examen etc* to pass.
(i) *falta etc* to overlook, tolerate; *persona* to forgive, indulge, be soft

on; **no te voy a ~ más** I'm not going to indulge you any more.
(j) *moneda falsa* to pass (off); *contrabanda* to smuggle (in, out); **a ése se le puede ~ cualquier cosa** you can get anything past him.
(k) (*superar*) to surpass, excel; *rival* to do better than, beat, outdistance; (*Aut*) to pass, overtake; **él me pasa ya 3 cms** he's already 3 cms taller than I am.
(l) *fecha, suceso etc* to pass, go past; *enfermedad* to get over; **hemos pasado el aniversario** we are past the anniversary, the anniversary is behind us.
(m) (*omitir*) to omit, leave out, pass over; to skip; to overlook; *V* **alto 3 (f).**
(n) *tiempo* to spend, pass; **~ las vacaciones** to spend one's holidays; **fuimos a ~ el día en la playa** we went to the seaside for a day; **~lo bien** to have a good time; **¡que lo pases bien!** have a good time!, enjoy yourself!; **lo pasaremos tan ricamente** we'll have such a good time; **~lo mal** to have a bad time (of it); **~las moradas o negras** (*etc*) to have a tough time of it.
(o) *penas* to suffer, endure, go through.
(p) ~ la mano por algo to pass (o run) one's hand over sth; to stroke sth; **~ el rosario** to tell one's beads; **~ el cepillo por el pelo** to run a brush through (o over) one's hair.
(q) *película, programa* to screen, show.
(r) (*Cono Sur**) to cheat, swindle.
⓶ VI **(a)** (*gen*) to pass, go; **pasó de mis manos a las suyas** it passed from my hands into his; **la cuerda pasa de un lado a otro de la calle** the rope goes from one side of the street to the other; **el hilo pasa por el agujero** the thread goes through the hole; **el río pasa por la ciudad** the river flows (o goes, runs) through the city; **el autobús pasa delante de nuestra casa** the bus goes past our house.
▼ **(b)** (*gen: persona*) to pass, to come in, go in; **¡pase Vd!** come in!; after you!; **~ a un cuarto contiguo** to go into an adjoining room, move into an adjoining room; **no se puede ~** you can't go in; you can't go through; **pasamos directamente a ver al jefe** we went straight in to see the boss; **nos hicieron ~** they showed us in (*a* to), they ushered us in; **~ a decir algo** to go on to say sth; **y luego pasaron a otra cosa** and then they went on to sth else; **los moros pasaron a España** the Moors crossed into (o over to) Spain; **~ adelante** to go on, continue, proceed; **~ de Inglaterra al Canadá** to move (o go, migrate) from England to Canada; **~ de teniente a general** to go from lieutenant to general; **~ por una crisis** to go through a crisis; **pasaré por tu casa** I'll call on you (at home), I'll drop in.
(c) (*ser aceptado*) (*propuesta*) to pass, get through, be approved; (*disculpa*) to be accepted; **puede ~** it's passable, it's O.K.*; **esta moneda no pasa** this coin is a dud*, this coin is no good; **que me llames carroza, pase, pero fascista, no** you can call me an old square if you like, but not a fascist.
(d) ~ de (*exceder*) to go beyond; to exceed; **~ de los límites** to exceed the limits; **pasa ya de los 70** he's over 70; **esto pasa de ser una broma** this goes beyond a joke; **no pasa de ser una mediocridad** he's no more than a mediocrity; **no pasan de 60 los que lo tienen** those who have it do not number more than 60; **de ésta no pasa** this is the very last time; **de hoy no pasa que le escriba** I'll write to him this very day; **yo de ahí no paso** that's as far as I can go; I draw the line at that; there I stick.
(e) (*Naipes*) to pass; **paso** I pass, no bid.
(f) Juan pasa por francés John could be taken for a Frenchman; **pasa por buen pintor** he is considered to be a good painter; **pasa por sabio** he has a reputation for learning; **se hace ~ por médico** he passes himself off as a doctor, he poses as a doctor.
(g) (*depender de*) **el futuro de la empresa pasa por este acuerdo** the company's future depends on this agreement (o requires this agreement as a condition).
(h) ir pasando (*fig*) to get by, manage (somehow); **~ con poco** to get along with very little; **tendrá que ~ sin coche** he'll have to get along without a car; **pasa por todo con tal que no le hagan trabajar** he'll put up with anything as long as they don't make him work.
(i) (*Esp*: como pasota*) to be indifferent, to stand back, stand aside, not take part; to drop out; **~ de** to do without, get by without; to have no interest in, have no concern for; (*desatender*) to ignore; **yo paso de política** I'm not into politics*, politics is not for me; **siguen pasando de este problema** they go on ignoring this problem.
(j) (*tiempo*) to pass, go by; **han pasado 4 años** 4 years have gone by, 4 years have elapsed; **¡cómo pasa el tiempo!** how time passes!
(k) (*condición*) to be over; to pass away; (*efecto*) to pass off, wear off; **ha pasado la crisis** the crisis is over; **ya pasó aquello** that's all over (and done with) now.
(l) (*suceder*) to happen; **aquí pasa algo misterioso** sth odd is going on here; **¿pasa algo?** is anything up?, is anything wrong?; **¿qué pasa?** what's happening?, what's going on?, what's up?; **¿qué le pasa a ése?** what's the matter with him?; **¿qué ha pasado con ella?**

what's become of her?; **¿qué pasa que no entra?** why on earth doesn't she come in?; **algo le pasa al motor** sth's the matter with the engine; lo que pasa es que ..., **pasa una cosa y es que ...** what's happening is that ..., what you find is that ..., it's like this ...; **como si no hubiese pasado nada** as if nothing (unusual) had happened; **pase lo que pase** whatever happens, come what may; **no me ha pasado otra (igual) en la vida** nothing like it has ever happened to me before; **siempre pasa igual** it's always the same; **siempre me pasa lo mismo** I'm always having the same trouble; **¿(qué) pas(s)a contigo?*** what gives?*, how are you?

3 **pasarse** VR (a) (*efecto etc*) to pass, pass off; **ya se te pasará** you'll get over it.

(b) (*perderse*) **se me pasó el turno** I missed my turn; **no se te pase la oportunidad** don't miss the chance this time.

(c) (*trasladarse etc*) = **1** (a); **~ al enemigo** to go over to the enemy.

(d) (*belleza, flor etc*) to fade; (*fruta*) to go soft, get overripe; (*comida*) to go bad, go off, get stale; (*té*) to stew; (*tela*) to wear, show signs of wear, get threadbare; (*mujer*) to lose her charms; **no se pasará si se tapa la botella** it will keep if you put the cap on the bottle.

(e) (*excederse*) to go too far, go over the line (*etc*); (*fig*) to overdo it; to say too much, go too far; **se pasa en mostrar agradecimiento** he overdoes the gratitude; **¡te has pasado, tío!*** bravo, friend!; well done, man!*

(f) (*tiempo*) = **1** (n); **se ha pasado todo el día leyendo** he has spent the whole day reading.

(g) **~ con, ~ sin;** *V* **2** (g).

(h) **no se le pasa nada** nothing escapes him, nothing gets past him, he misses nothing; **se me pasó** it slipped my mind, I forgot; **se me pasó llamarle** I forgot to ring him.

(i) **~ de** + ADJ to be too + ADJ, be excessively + ADJ; **se pasa de generoso** he's too generous; *V* **listo**.

4 NM: **un modesto ~** a modest competence; **tener un buen ~** to be well off.

| PASAR | ver también la entrada |

En expresiones temporales

• Se traduce por *spend* cuando *pasar* tiene un uso transitivo y queremos indicar un período de tiempo concreto, seguido de la actividad que en ese tiempo se desarrolla, o del lugar:

    Me pasé la tarde escribiendo cartas
    I spent the evening writing letters
    Ha pasado toda su vida en el campo
    He has spent his whole life in the country

• En cambio, cuando se describe la forma en que se pasa el tiempo mediante un adjetivo, se debe emplear en inglés la construcción *have* + (*a*) + ADJETIVO + SUSTANTIVO:

    Pasamos una tarde entretenida
    We had a lovely afternoon
    Pasamos un rato estupendo jugando al squash
    We had a fantastic time playing squash

    NOTA: La expresión *pasar el rato* se traduce por *pass the time*:
    No sé qué hacer para pasar el rato
    I don't know what to do to pass the time

• Cuando el uso es intransitivo, *pasar* se traduce por *pass* o *go by*.
    A medida que pasaba el tiempo se deprimía cada vez más
    As time passed o went by, he became more and more depressed
    Para otros usos y ejemplos ver la entrada.

---

pasarela NF (*puente*) footbridge; (*Teat etc*) walkway, catwalk; (*Náut*) gangway, gangplank; **~ telescópica** airport walkway.

pasarrato NM (*Carib, Méx*) = **pasatiempo.**

pasatiempo NM pastime, (leisure) pursuit; hobby; amusement.

pascana NF (a) (*And, Cono Sur: fonda*) wayside inn. (b) (*And, Cono Sur: etapa*) stage, part (of a journey). (c) (*And*) part of a journey done without stopping.

pascícola ADJ grazing, pasture (*atr*).

Pascua NF, **pascua** NF (a) **~ florida, ~ de Resurrección** Easter; **~ de Navidad** Christmas; **~ de Pentecostés** Whitsun, Whitsuntide; **~s** Christmas holiday, Christmas time (*strictly, Christmas Day to Twelfth Night*); **¡felices ~s!** merry Christmas!; **cumplir con P~** to do one's Easter duty.

(b) **~ de los hebreos, ~ de los judíos** Passover.

(c) (*locuciones*) **... y santas ~s ...** and that's that, ... and that's the lot; ... and there's nothing one can do about it; **de ~s a Ramos** once in a blue moon; **estar como unas ~s** to be as happy as a sandboy (*o* lark (*US*)); **hacer la ~ a uno*** to do the dirty on sb; to bug sb*; **¡que se hagan la ~!** (*Esp**) and they can lump it!

pascual ADJ paschal; **cordero ~** (older) lamb.

pase NM (a) (*documento*) pass; (*Com*) permit; **~ de embarque** (*Aer*) boarding-pass; **~ de favor** (*Pol etc*) safeconduct; (*Com*) complementary ticket; **~ de lista** (*Mil*) rollcall.

(b) (*Dep, Taur*) pass; **~ atrás** back pass.

(c) (*Cine*) showing; **~ de modas, ~ de modelos** fashion show.

(d) (⁑: *contrabando*) drug smuggling; (*LAm*⁑) dose (of a drug), fix⁑.

paseandero ADJ (*Cono Sur*) fond of strolling.

paseante NMF (a) (*que pasea*) walker, stroller; (*transeúnte*) passer-by; (*pey: t ~ en corte*) loafer, idler. (b) (*pretendiente*) suitor.

pasear [1a] **1** VT (a) *perro, niño etc* to take for a walk, walk.

(b) *pancarta etc* to parade, show off, exhibit; to walk about (the streets) with.

(c) **~ la calle a una muchacha** (*Esp*) to walk up and down the street where a girl lives.

(d) (*CAm*) *dinero* to squander.

(e) (*Esp* Hist*) = **dar el paseo a** (*V* **paseo** (e)).

2 VI *y* **pasearse** VR (a) (*gen*) to walk, go for a walk, stroll; to walk about, walk up and down; **~ en bicicleta** to go for a ride, go cycling; **~ en coche** to go for a drive, go driving, go for a run; **~ a caballo** to ride, go riding; **~ en bote** (*etc*) to go sailing, go on a trip.

(b) **~** (*Esp fig*) to idle, loaf about.

(c) **pasearse por un tema** (*Esp*) to deal superficially with a subject.

(d) **~** (*Méx*) to take a day off.

paseíllo NM (*Taur*) inaugural procession (*o* ceremonial entry) of bullfighters.

paseíto NM little walk, gentle stroll.

paseo NM (a) (*acto*) stroll, walk; (*excursión*) outing; **~ en bicicleta, ~ a caballo** ride; **~ en coche** drive, run, ride, outing; **~ espacial** walk in space; **~ por la naturaleza** nature trail; **~ de vigilancia** round, tour of inspection; **no va a ser un ~** (*Esp*) it's not going to be easy, it won't be a walkover; **dar un ~** to go for a walk, take a walk (*o* stroll); to go for a ride (*etc*); **estar de ~** to be out for a walk; **enviar** (*o* **mandar**) **a uno a ~**⁑ to tell sb to go to blazes*, to chuck sb out, send sb packing; **¡vete a ~!**⁑ get lost!⁑; **llevar** (*o* **sacar**) **a un niño de ~** to take a child out for a walk.

(b) (*avenida*) parade, avenue; **~ marítimo** promenade, esplanade.

(c) (*distancia*) short walk; **entre las dos casas no hay más que un ~** it's only a short walk between the two houses.

(d) **~ cívico** (*LAm*) civic procession.

(e) (*Esp* Hist*) (journey leading to the) summary execution of a political opponent; **dar el ~ a uno** to execute sb summarily; (*moderno*) to bump sb off⁑.

pasero NM (*And*) ferryman.

pashá NM = **pachá.**

pasible ADJ (*liter*) able to endure, long-suffering.

pasillear [1a] VI (*Parl*) to engage in lobby discussions, lobby.

pasilleo NM lobby discussions, lobbying.

pasillo NM (a) (*Arquit*) passage, corridor; (*Parl: fig*) lobby; (*Náut*) gangway; **~ aéreo** air corridor, airlane; **~ móvil, ~ rodante** travelator; **hacer ~s** to engage in lobby discussions, lobby. (b) (*Teat*) short piece, sketch.

pasión NF (a) passion; **la P~** (*Rel*) the Passion; **tener ~ por** to be passionately fond of, have a passion for. (b) (*pey*) bias, prejudice, partiality.

pasional ADJ (a) *persona etc* passionate; **crimen ~** crime of passion. (b) (*caprichoso*) temperamental.

pasionaria NF passionflower.

pasito ADV gently, softly.

pasivamente ADV passively.

pasividad NF passiveness, passivity.

pasivo **1** ADJ (a) (*gen*) passive; (*Econ*) inactive. (b) (*Ling*) passive.

2 NM (*Com, Fin*) liabilities, debts; (*de cuenta*) debit side; **~ circulante, ~ corriente** current liabilities; **~ diferido** deferred liabilities.

3 NF (*Ling*) passive (voice).

pasma⁑ **1** NM COP*.

2 NF (*Esp*) cops*, fuzz⁑.

pasmado ADJ (a) (*asombrado*) astonished, amazed; **dejar ~ a uno** to amaze sb; **estar** (*o* **quedar**) **~ de** to be amazed at, be astonished at; **mirar con cara de ~** to look in astonishment (at).

(b) (*atontado*) bewildered; **estar** (*o* **quedar**) **~** to stand gaping, be flabbergasted, be bewildered, look silly; **se quedó ahí ~** he just stood there gaping; **¡oye, ~!*** hey, you dope!*

(c) (*LAm*) *herida* infected, unhealthy; *persona* unhealthy-looking, ill-looking.

(d) (*CAm, Méx*) (*tonto*) thick; stupid; (*torpe*) clumsy.

(e) (*LAm*) *fruta* overripe.

pasmar [1a] **1** VT (a) (*asombrar*) to amaze, astonish, astound; to flabbergast; (*atontar*) to stun, dumbfound.

(b) (*enfriar*) to chill (to the bone); *planta* to nip, cut.

2 **pasmarse** VR (a) (*asombrarse*) to be amazed (*etc; de* at); to be dumbfounded; to marvel, wonder (*de* at).

(b) (*estar helado*) to be chilled to the bone; (*resfriarse*) to catch a chill.

(c) (*LAm*) (*infectarse*) to become infected; (*enfermar*) to fall ill; (*con fiebre*) to catch a fever; (*con trismo*) to get lockjaw.

(d) (*Carib, Méx: fruta*) to dry up, wither.

(e) (*color*) to fade.

---

pasmarota NF, **pasmarotada** NF display of shocked surprise, exaggerated reaction.

pasmarote* NMF halfwit; **¡no te quedes ahí como un ~!** don't just stand there like an idiot!

pasmazón NM (*CAm, Carib, Méx*) = **pasmo**.

pasmo NM (a) (*asombro*) amazement, astonishment; awe; (*fig*) wonder, marvel, prodigy; **es el ~ de cuantos lo ven** it is a marvel (o a source of wonder) to all who see it.
(b) (*Med: trismo*) lockjaw, tetanus.
(c) (*Med: enfriamiento*) chill.
(d) (*LAm: fiebre*) fever.

pasmosamente ADV amazingly; awesomely; wonderfully.

pasmoso ADJ amazing, astonishing; awesome, breathtaking; wonderful.

paso¹ ADJ *fruta* dried.

paso² [1] NM (a) (*acto*) passing, passage; crossing; (*Aut*) overtaking, passing; (*Orn, Zool*) migration, passage; (*fig*) transition; progress; **el ~ del tiempo** the passage of time; **lo recogeré al** (o **de**) **~** I'll pick it up when I'm passing; **salir al ~ a** (o **de**) to waylay; to confront; (*fig*) to nip in the bud; to strangle at birth; *rumor* to refute, deny, contradict; **de ~** (*al mismo tiempo*) in passing; (*a propósito*) by the way, incidentally; **estar de ~** to be passing through; **entrar de ~** to drop in, call in (for a moment).
(b) (*camino*) way through, passage; (*Arquit*) passage; **¡~!** make way!, gangway!; **~ de cebra** (*Esp*) zebra crossing; **~ elevado**, **~ a desnivel**, **~ a distinto nivel** (*Aut*) flyover; **~ franco**, **~ libre** free passage, free access; clear way through; **~ inferior** underpass; **~ a nivel** level-crossing, grade crossing (*US*); **~ a nivel sin barrera** unguarded level-crossing; **~ de** (o **para**) **peatones** pedestrian crossing; **~ salmonero** salmon ladder; **~ subterráneo** subway, underpass (*US*); **~ superior** (*Aut*) overpass, flyover; '**~ prohibido**', '**prohibido el ~**' 'no throughfare', 'no entry'; **abrir ~ para** to make way for; **abrirse ~** to make one's way (*entre, por* through), force a way through; **abrirse ~ luchando** to fight one's way through; **abrirse ~ a tiros** to shoot one's way through; **ceder el ~** to make way; (*Aut*) to give way, yield (*US*); '**ceda el ~**' (*Aut*) 'give way'; **ceder el ~ a** (*fig*), **dar ~ a** to give way to, give place to; **cerrar el ~**, **impedir el ~** to block the way; **dejar ~ a** to open the way for, leave the way clear for; **dejarle ~ a uno** to let sb by.
(c) (*Geog*) pass; (*Náut*) strait.
(d) (*de pie: acto*) step, pace; (*huella*) footprint; (*sonido*) footstep, footfall; (*distancia*) pace; **~ atrás** step backwards; **~ hacia atrás** (*fig*) backward step; **~ de baile** dance step; **~ a dos** pas de deux; **~ en falso** false step; **~ a ~** step by step; **a cada ~** at every step, at every turn; **a grandes ~s**, **a ~s agigantados** (*fig*) by leaps and bounds; **a dos ~s de aquí** two steps from here, very near here; **estar a un ~ mínimo de** to border on, verge closely on; **por sus ~s contados** step by step, systematically; **coger el ~** (*lit, fig*) to fall into step (*con* with); **dar un ~** to take a step; **dar un ~ en falso** to stumble; (*fig*) to take a false step; **no da un ~ sin hacer alguna barbaridad** he can't take a step without doing something awful; **llevar el ~** to keep in step, keep time; **marcar el ~** (*LAm*) (*lit*) to keep time, (*fig*) to mark time; **seguir los ~s a uno** to tail sb, shadow sb; **seguir los ~s de uno** to follow in sb's footsteps; **volver sobre los ~s** to retrace one's steps; (*fig*) to retract.
(e) (*modo de andar*) walk, gait; (*ritmo*) speed, pace, rate; (*de caballo*) gait; **~ de andadura** amble; **~ de ganso** (*LAm*), **~ de (la) oca** goose step; **buen ~** quick step, good pace; **a buen ~** quickly; (*fig*) at a good rate; **a ~ lento** at a slow pace, slowly; **a ~ ligero** (*Mil*), **a ~ redoblado** (*LAm*) at the double; **a ~ de tortuga** at a snail's pace; **a ese ~** (*fig*) at that rate; **al ~** slowly; **al ~ que vamos** at the rate we're going; **al ~ que ...** (*como* CONJ) at the same time as ...; while ..., whereas ...; **acelerar** (o **apretar, avivar** *etc*) **el ~** to go faster, quicken one's pace; **aflojar el ~** to slow down, slacken one's pace; **establecer el ~** to make the pace, set the pace; **romper el ~** to break step.
(f) (*de baile*) step; **~ a dos** pas de deux; **~ de vals** waltz step.
(g) (*fig*) step, move; measure; (*Inform*) step; **~ adelante** step forward, advance; **es un ~ hacia nuestro objetivo** it's a step towards our objective; **andar en malos ~s** to be mixed up in shady affairs; **dar un mal ~** to take a false step, make a false move; to get in the family way; **dar los primeros ~s** to make the first moves; *V t sentidos figurados en* (d).
(h) (*episodio*) episode, incident, event.
(i) (*Teat Hist*) sketch, interlude; (*Ecl*) float (o series of sculptures *etc*) *representing part of the Easter story, carried in procession; see also* SEMANA SANTA .
(j) (*Elec, Téc*) pitch.
(k) **~ de armas** (*Mil Hist*) passage of arms.
(l) (*apuro*) difficulty, awkward situation, crisis; **salir del ~** to get out of a jam*, get out of trouble.
(m) (*LAm: vado*) ford.
(n) (*Telec*) metered unit.
[2] ADV softly, gently; **¡~!** not so fast!, easy there!

pasodoble NM paso doble.

pasoso ADJ (a) (*LAm*) (*poroso*) porous, permeable; (*absorbente*) absorbent. (b) (*Cono Sur: sudoroso*) perspiring, sweaty. (c) (*And Med*) contagious.

pasota* [1] ADJ INVAR (a) (*Esp*) **filosofía ~** hippy (o drop-out) outlook (o mentality); **vida ~** hippy (o drop-out) life style.
(b) (*Méx: pasado de moda*) passé, out of fashion.
[2] NMF hippy, drop-out; non-conformist.

pasote* NM outrage; exaggeration.

pasotismo NM (*Esp*) hippy (o drop-out) mentality; hippy life-style.

paspa NF (*And*), **paspadura** NF (*Cono Sur*) chapped skin, cracked skin.

pasparse [1a] VR (*LAm: piel*) to chap, crack.

paspartú NM passe-partout.

pasquín NM (*Liter*) skit, satire, lampoon; (*Pol etc*) wall poster.

passar* [1a] VI (*hum*) *pronunciación de* **pasar** (*esp sentidos* 2 (i) *y* (l), 3 (e).

passim ADV passim.

pasta NF (a) (*gen*) paste; **~ de carne** meat paste; **~ de coca** cocaine paste; **~ de dientes**, **~ dentífrica** toothpaste; **~ de madera** wood pulp.
(b) (*de muelas*) filling; (*de lapicero*) lead.
(c) (*cartón*) cardboard; papier-mâché; (*Tip*) boards; **~ española** marbled leather binding; **media ~** half-binding; **libro en ~** book in boards.
(d) (*Culin: masa*) dough; (*para pastel*) pastry (mixture); **~s** (*pasteles*) pastries, cakes; (*fideos*) noodles, spaghetti.
(e) (*) dough*, money; **una ~** a lot of money; **~ gansa** big money; **soltar la ~** to cough up*.
(f) **de buena ~** (*Esp*) equable; kindly, good-natured.
(g) (*LAm*) drug tablet.

pastaje NM (*And, CAm, Cono Sur*), **pastal** NM (*LAm*) (*pastizal*) pasture, grazing land; (*pasto*) grass, pasture.

pastaplumón NM felt-tip pen.

pastar [1a] VTI to graze.

pastear [1a] VT to graze.

pastejón NM solid mass, lump.

pastel [1] NM (a) (*Culin*) (*de frutas etc*) cake; (*de carne etc*) pie; **~es** pastry, confectionery; **repartirse el ~** (*fig*) to divide up the cake (o pie (*US*)).
(b) (*Arte*) pastel; pastel drawing (*t* pintura al **~**).
(c) (*Naipes*) sharp practice; (*fig*) plot; undercover agreement, cynical compromise, deal; **descubrir el ~** to give the game away; **se le descubrió el ~** his little game was found out.
(d) (*: *chapuza*) botch, mess.
[2] ATR: **tono ~** pastel shade.

pastelado NM (*Carib*) choc-ice.

pastelear [1a] VI (a) (*trampear*) to go in for sharp practice; to plot; to make cynical compromises. (b) (*temporizar*) to stall, spin it out to gain time. (c) (*: *adular*) to creep*, be a bootlicker*.

pastelería NF (a) (*arte*) (art of) confectionery, pastry-making. (b) (*pasteles*) pastry, pastries (collectively). (c) (*tienda*) confectioner's, pastry shop, cake shop.

pastelero [1] ADJ (a) (*Culin*) **masa pastelera** dough; cake-mix; **rodillo ~** rolling-pin. (b) **no tengo ni pastelera idea*** (*euf*) I haven't a clue*.
(c) (*Cono Sur*) meddlesome, intriguing.
[2] NM, **pastelera** NF (a) (*Culin*) pastrycook; confectioner. (b) (*LAm Pol*) turncoat. (c) (*And*: traficante*) drug dealer, drug trafficker.

pastelillo NM small cake; **~ de mantequilla** (*Esp*) pat of butter; **~ de hígado de ganso** (*Esp*) pâté de foie gras.

pastelón NM (*Cono Sur*) large paving stone.

pasterizar [1f] VT *etc* = **pasteurizar** *etc*.

pasteurización NF pasteurization.

pasteurizado ADJ pasteurized.

pasteurizar [1f] VT to pasteurize.

pastiche NM pastiche.

pastilla [1] NF (*Med*) tablet, pastille; (*de jabón etc*) cake, bar; (*de chocolate*) bar, piece; (*Inform*) chip; **la ~** (*esp Med*) the pill; **~ de caldo** stock cube; **~ de freno(s)** (*Aut*) brake-lining; **~ de silicio** silicon chip; **~ para la tos** cough-drop, throat lozenge; **ir a toda ~** (*Esp**) to go full-belt*. [2] ADJ INVAR (*Esp**) boring.

pastillero NM pillbox.

pastinaca NF parsnip.

pastizal NM pasture.

pastizara* NF bread*, money; **una ~** a whole heap of money.

pasto NM (a) (*hierba*) grass, herbage, fodder; grazing; (*Méx**) grass*, pot*; **~ seco** fodder; **un sitio abundante en ~s** a place with rich grazing.
(b) (*comida*) (*any*) food, feed (*for cattle*).
(c) (*campo*) pasture, field; (*LAm*) grass, lawn; **echar el ganado al ~** to put animals out to pasture.
(d) (*fig*) food, nourishment; fuel; **fue ~ del fuego, fue ~ de las**

llamas it was fuel to the flames, the flames devoured it; **es ~ de la murmuración** it is a subject for gossip, gossip thrives on it; **fue ~ de los mirones** the onlookers lapped it up; **es ~ de la actualidad** it's headline material, it's highly newsworthy; **~ espiritual** spiritual nourishment.

(e) a ~ abundantly; **había fruta a ~** there was fruit in unlimited quantities; **beber a todo ~** to drink for all one is worth, drink to excess; **correr a todo ~** to run like hell*; **cita refranes a todo ~** he quotes vast quantities of proverbs, he greatly overdoes the proverbs.

(f) *vino de* **~** ordinary wine.

pastón NM: **un ~** a whole heap of money*.

pastor NM **(a)** (*Agr*) (*de ovejas*) shepherd; (*de ganado*) herdsman; (*de cabras*) goatherd; (*de vacas*) cowman (*etc*); **el Buen P~** the Good Shepherd.

(b) (*Ecl*) (Protestant) minister, clergyman, pastor.

(c) **~ alemán** Alsatian (dog); **viejo ~ inglés** old English sheepdog.

pastora NF **(a)** (*Agr*) shepherdess. **(b)** (*Ecl*) (woman) minister, (woman) pastor.

pastorada NF Nativity procession, moving tableau of the Nativity.

pastoral 1 ADJ pastoral.

2 NF **(a)** (*Liter etc*) pastoral, idyll. **(b)** (*Ecl*) pastoral letter.

pastorear [1a] VT **(a)** *rebaño* to pasture, graze, shepherd; to look after; (*Ecl*) to guide, lead.

(b) (*CAm, Cono Sur: acechar*) to lie in wait for.

(c) (*CAm: mimar*) to spoil, pamper.

pastorela NF (*Liter*) pastourelle.

pastoreo NM grazing.

pastoril ADJ (*Liter*) pastoral.

pastoso ADJ **(a)** *material* doughy; soft; pasty. **(b)** *voz* rich, mellow, pleasant; *vino* mellow, rich. **(c)** (*Cono Sur: con hierba*) grassy. **(d)** (*And*: *vago*) lazy.

pastura NF **(a)** (*campo*) pasture. **(b)** (*comida*) food, fodder, feed.

pasturaje NM common pasture.

pasudo ADJ (*Méx*) *pelo* kinky.

pat NM, PL **pats** [pat] putt.

pat. ABR *de* **patente** patent, pat.

pata 1 NF **(a)** (*Zool*) foot, leg; paw; (*Orn*) foot; (*de persona, hum*) foot; (*de mueble etc*) leg; (*Cono Sur: fig*) stage, leg; **~ de cabra** (*Téc*) crowbar; **~ de gallina** (*And, Carib*) crow's-feet (*wrinkles*); **~ de gallo** crow's-feet; (*: disparate*) silly remark, piece of nonsense; (*: plancha*) bloomer*; **~ hendida** cloven hoof; **andar a la ~ coja, andar a la ~ sola** (*And*) to play hopscotch; **eso lo sé hacer a la ~ coja** I can do that blindfold; **~s arriba** on one's back, upside down; (*fig*) upside down, topsy-turvy; **poner a uno ~s arriba*** to dumbfound sb; **a ~** on foot; **a cuatro ~s** on all fours; **a la ~ la llana** plainly, simply, directly; bluntly; **andar a ~s** (*niño*) to crawl, go on all fours; **andar a ~ renca** (*LAm*) to limp; **enseñar la ~, sacar la ~** to give oneself away; **estirar la ~** to peg out‡; **hacer la ~ a uno** (*Cono Sur*) to soft-soap sb*; **meter ~** (*Cono Sur: Aut*) to step on the gas*; **meter la ~*** to put one's foot in it, make a blunder; to blot one's copybook; to butt in; **ser ~(s)** to be even, tie; **es un diccionario con dos ~s** he's a walking dictionary; **es la virtud con dos ~s** she is virtue personified; **tener ~s*** (*Cono Sur*) to be brash; be cheeky*; **tener buena ~** to be lucky; **tener mala ~** (*suerte*) to be unlucky; (*torpe*) to be clumsy; **ser de mala ~** to be unlucky, bring bad luck; **ser ~ de perro** (*Cono Sur*) to be footloose, be fond of travelling.

(b) (*Zool*) (female) duck.

(c) **P~s*** Old Nick; **~s cortas*** shorty*, little man.

2 NMF (*And*) (*amigo*) pal*, mate*, buddy (*US*); (*tipo*) bloke‡, bird‡.

pataca NF Jerusalem artichoke.

patache NM **(a)** (*barca*) flat-bottomed boat. **(b)** (*And*) (*sopa*) soup; (‡: *comida*) food, grub‡.

patacho NM **(a)** (*Cono Sur: lancha*) flat-bottomed boat. **(b)** (*CAm, Méx: recua*) train of mules.

patacón NM **(a)** (*And Culin*) slice of fried banana. **(b)** (*Cono Sur: moretón*) bruise, welt.

patada NF **(a)** (*coz*) kick; (*en el suelo*) stamp; **~ hacia arriba*** kick upstairs; **a ~s** in abundance, galore; (*tratar etc*) roughly, inconsiderately; **en dos ~s*** (*sin esfuerzo*) with no trouble at all; (*en seguida*) in a jiffy*, right away; **esto lo termino en dos ~s** I'll finish (o be through with) this in no time at all, it won't take me any time to finish this; **dar ~s** to kick; to stamp; **dar ~s para conseguir algo** to take steps to obtain sth; **dar la ~ a uno*** to give sb the boot*; **dar a uno una ~ en el culo** (*Esp*) to kick sb up the backside; **me da cien ~s*** (*objeto*) it gets on my nerves; (*persona*) he gives me a pain in the neck*, I can't stand him; **echar a uno a ~s** to kick sb out; **me sentó como una ~ en el estómago*** (*o* **en los cojones‡**) it was like a kick in the teeth*; **tratar a uno a ~s** to kick sb around.

(b) *me etc* **fue de la ~** (*CAm, Méx**) it was a disaster, it all went wrong.

patadón NM big kick; (*Dep*) long kick, long ball; long clearance.

patagón, -ona ADJ, NM/F Patagonian.

patagónico ADJ Patagonian.

patalear [1a] VI **(a)** (*en el suelo*) to stamp (angrily).

(b) (*fig*) to protest; to make a fuss; **por mí, que patalee** so far as I'm concerned he can make all the fuss he likes.

(c) (*bebé etc*) to kick out, kick about.

pataleo NM **(a)** (*en el suelo*) stamping; (*en el aire*) kicking. **(b)** (*fig*) protest; (*lío*) scene, fuss; **derecho al ~** right to protest, right to make a fuss; **tener derecho al ~** (*fig*) to have the right to complain.

pataleta NF (*rabieta*) tantrum; (*Med*) fit, convulsion; **¡qué ~!** what a fuss!; **dar ~s** (*LAm: niño*) to stamp one's feet.

patán NM rustic, yokel; (*pey*) lout.

pataplaf, pataplás, pataplún (*LAm*) INTERJ bang!, crash!

patarata NF **(a)** (*afectación*) gush, affectation; (*aspaviento*) emotional fuss; excessive show of feeling. **(b)** (*disparate*) silly thing; (*bagatela*) triviality; **~s** nonsense, tomfoolery.

pataratero ADJ **(a)** (*afectado*) gushing, affected. **(b)** (*tonto*) silly.

pataruco ADJ (*Carib*) **(a)** (*tosco*) coarse, rough. **(b)** (*cobarde*) cowardly.

patasca NF (*And Culin*) pork stew with corn; **armar una ~*** to kick up a racket.

patata NF (*Esp*) **(a)** potato; **~s bravas** fried potatoes with spicy tomato sauce; **~ caliente** (*fig*) hot potato, hot issue; **~s deshechas** mashed potatoes; **~s enteras, ~s con su piel** jacket potatoes, potatoes in their jackets; **~s fritas** chips, French fries (*US*); **~ fritas (a la inglesa)** crisps, potato chips (*US*); **~s nuevas** new potatoes; **~ de siembra** seed potato; **~ temprana** early potato.

(b) (*: locuciones*) **ni ~** not a thing; **no se me da una ~, (no) me importa una ~** I don't care two hoots (*de* about); **no entendió una ~** he didn't understand a word of it; **pasar la ~ caliente*** to pass the buck*.

(c) (‡) cunt‡.

patatal NM, **patatar** NM potato field, potato patch.

patatera NF potato plant.

patatero* ADJ: **oficial ~** ranker.

patatín* **y ~ patatán** and so on; **que (si) ~, que (si) patatán** this, that and the other; **en el año ~** in such-and-such a year.

patato* ADJ (*Carib*), **patatuco*** ADJ (*Carib*) short.

patatús NM dizzy spell, queer turn.

paté NM pâté.

pateada NF **(a)** (*Cono Sur*) long tiring walk. **(b)** = **pateadura**.

pateador NM (*Dep*) kicker.

pateadura NF, **pateamiento** NM **(a)** (*acto*) stamping, kicking. **(b)** (*fig: en discusión*) flat denial; violent interjection; (*Teat*) noisy protest, catcalls.

patear[1] [1a] 1 VT **(a)** (*pisotear*) to stamp on, trample (on); (*dar patadas a*) to kick, boot; (*Dep*) *pelota* to kick.

(b) (*Esp*: *andar por*) to tramp round, cover, go over; **tuve que ~ toda la ciudad** I had to tramp round the whole town; **~ el mercado** to put in some legwork (and go looking for business).

(c) (*fig*) to trample on, treat roughly, treat inconsiderately.

(d) (*Carib*) to abuse.

(e) **la comida me ha pateado** (*Cono Sur**) the meal has upset my stomach.

2 VI **(a)** (*patalear*) to stamp (with rage), stamp one's foot; (*Teat etc*) to stamp.

(b) (*LAm: animal, arma*) to kick.

(c) (*: ir a pata*) to walk (it); (*Cono Sur*) to go long distances on foot.

(d) (*: ir y venir*) to be always on the go, bustle about.

3 **patearse*** VR **(a)** **nos hemos pateado Madrid** we explored (*o* did*) Madrid on foot. **(b)** **~ el dinero** to blow one's money*.

patear[2] [1a] VI to putt.

patena NF paten.

patentado ADJ patent; proprietary.

patentar [1a] VT to patent.

patente 1 ADJ **(a)** (*gen*) patent, obvious, evident; **hacer ~** to show clearly, establish.

(b) (*Com etc*) patent.

(c) (*Cono Sur*: *excelente*) superb, great.

2 NF **(a)** (*Jur etc*) grant; warrant; (*Com*) patent; **~ de corso** licence to do whatever one pleases; **~ de invención** patent; **~ de navegación** ship's certificate of registration; **~ de privilegio** letters patent; **~ de sanidad** bill of health; **de ~** patent; (*Cono Sur*) first-rate.

(b) (*LAm Aut*) (*placa*) number-plate; (*carnet*) driving licence.

3 NM (*Carib*) patent medicine.

patentizar [1f] 1 VT to show, reveal, make evident.

2 **patentizarse** VR to show plainly, become obvious.

pateo NM stamping; (*Teat*) stamping, noisy protest.

páter* NM (*Mil*) padre*.

patera NF (*Esp*) (small) boat.

paternal ADJ fatherly, paternal.

paternalismo NM paternalism; (*pey*) patronizing attitude.

paternalista 1 ADJ paternalistic; (*pey*) patronizing.

2 NM paternalist; (*pey*) patronizing person.

paternalmente ADV paternally, in a fatherly fashion.

paternidad NF (**a**) (*gen*) fatherhood, parenthood. (**b**) (*de hijo*) paternity; ~ **literaria** authorship.

paterno ADJ paternal; **abuelo** ~ paternal grandfather, grandfather on the father's side.

patero* ADJ (**a**) (*Cono Sur: adulador*) fawning. (**b**) (*And: embustero*) slippery, wily.

patéticamente ADV pathetically, movingly, poignantly.

patético ADJ (**a**) (*gen*) pathetic, moving, poignant. (**b**) (*Cono Sur*) clear, evident. (**c**) **es muy** ~ (*And: andador*) he loves walking.

patetismo NM pathos, poignancy.

patiabierto ADJ bow-legged.

patibulario ADJ (**a**) (*horroroso*) horrifying, harrowing. (**b**) *persona* sinister.

patíbulo NM scaffold; gallows, gibbet.

paticorto ADJ short-legged.

patidifuso* ADJ aghast, shattered; openmouthed; nonplussed; **dejar a uno** ~ to shatter sb; to nonplus sb.

patiestevado ADJ bandy-legged.

patihendido ADJ cloven-hoofed.

patilargo ADJ long-legged.

patilla [1] NF (**a**) (*Cono Sur*) bench.
  (**b**) (*And, Carib: sandía*) water-melon.
  (**c**) (*Cono Sur Bot*) layer.
  (**d**) (*de gafas*) sidepiece, temple (*US*); (*de vestido*) pocket flap.
  (**e**) (*Inform*) pin.
  (**f**) ~**s** (*esp Esp*) (*de hombre*) sideburns; (*de mujer*) kiss curl.
  [2] ~**s** NM: **P~s*** Old Nick; **ser un** ~**s** (*Esp**) to be a weak character, be a poor fish.

patimocho ADJ (*LAm: cojo*) lame.

patín NM (**a**) (*Dep*) skate; (*de trineo*) runner; (*Aer*) skid; **patines** (*Cono Sur*) soft over-slippers; ~ **de cola** (*Aer*) tailskid; ~ **de cuchilla**, ~ **de hielo** ice-skate; ~ **de ruedas** roller-skate. (**b**) (*Náut: t* ~ **a pedal**, ~ **playero**) pedalo, pedal-boat; (*de niño*) scooter; (*Aut**) banger‡, old car.

pátina NF patina.

patinadero NM skating rink.

patinado ADJ shiny, glossy.

patinador(a) NM/F skater.

patinadura NF (*Carib*) skid, skidding.

patinaje NM skating; ~ **artístico**, ~ **de figuras** figure-skating; ~ **sobre hielo** ice-skating; ~ **sobre ruedas** roller-skating; ~ **de velocidad** speed skating.

patinar [1a] VI (**a**) (*persona*) to skate. (**b**) (*Aut etc*) to skid, slip. (**c**) (*: *meter la pata*) to boob*, make a blunder. (**d**) (*Cono Sur*) to fail.

patinazo NM (**a**) (*Aut*) skid. (**b**) (*: *error*) boob*, blunder; **dar un** ~, **pegar un** ~ to make a boob*, blunder.

patinete NM, **patineta** NF scooter.

patio NM (*Arquit*) court, courtyard, patio; (*Teat*) pit; (*de garaje*) forecourt; (*Méx Ferro*) shunting yard; ~ **de armas** parade-ground; ~ **de luces** well (of a building); ~ **de operaciones** floor (of the stock exchange); ~ **de recreo** playground; **¡cómo está el** ~**!*** what a to-do!; **llevar el** ~ to rule the roost.

patiquín NM (*Carib*) fop, dandy.

patita NF: *V* **calle** (**a**).

patitieso ADJ (**a**) (*paralizado*) paralyzed with cold (*o* fright *etc*). (**b**) (*fig*) = **patidifuso**. (**c**) (*fig: engreído*) conceited, stuck-up*.

patito NM duckling; ~ **feo** ugly duckling (*also fig*); **los dos** ~**s*** number twenty-two.

patituerto ADJ bandy-legged.

patizambo ADJ knock-kneed.

pato NM (**a**) (*Orn*) duck; ~ (**macho**) drake; ~ **real**, ~ **silvestre** mallard, wild duck; ~ **de reclamo** decoy duck; **pagar el** ~***** to foot the bill; to take the blame, carry the can*; **ser el** ~ **de la boda** (*o* **fiesta**) (*LAm*) to be a laughing stock; **salga** ~ **o gallareta** (*LAm*) whatever the results.
  (**b**) (*Esp*: pesado*) bore, dull person; **estar hecho un** ~ to be terribly dull.
  (**c**) (*: *aburrimiento*) boredom; (*período aburrido*) boring time; (*fiesta etc sosa*) boring party (*etc*).
  (**d**) **ser un** ~ (*torpe*) to be clumsy.
  (**e**) (*And*: gorrón*) sponger*; **viajar de** ~ to stow away.
  (**f**) (*And*: inocentón*) sucker‡.
  (**g**) **hacerse el** ~, **hacerse** ~ (*Méx*) to act the fool.
  (**h**) (*Cono Sur**) **ser un** ~, **estar** ~ to be broke*; **pasarse de** ~ **a ganso** to go too far.
  (**i**) (*LAm Med*) bedpan.

patochada NF blunder, bloomer*.

patógeno NM pathogen.

patojo* [1] ADJ (*LAm*) lame.
  [2] NM, **patoja** NF (*And, CAm*) (*niño*) child; (*novio*) sweetheart, boyfriend/girlfriend; (*pey*) urchin, ragamuffin.
  [3] NM (*CAm*) (*niño*) kid*; (*muchacho*) lad, boy.

patología NF pathology.

patológico ADJ pathological.

patólogo, -a NM/F pathologist.

patomachera* NF (*Carib*) slanging match*.

patoso* [1] ADJ (**a**) (*aburrido*) boring, tedious.
  (**b**) (*sabihondo*) would-be clever.
  (**c**) (*molesto*) troublesome; **ponerse** ~ to get stroppy*, get awkward; to make trouble.
  (**d**) (*torpe*) clumsy, heavy-footed.
  [2] NM (**a**) (*pelmazo*) bore.
  (**b**) (*sabihondo*) clever Dick*, smart Aleck*.
  (**c**) (*agitador*) trouble-maker.

patota* NF (*Cono Sur: pandilla*) street gang, mob of young thugs, (*grupo*) large group; (*Carib, Cono Sur: amigos*) mob, crowd (of friends).

patotear* [1a] VT (*Cono Sur*) to beat up*.

patotero* NM (*Cono Sur*) rowdy, young thug.

patraña* NF (*cuento*) story, fib; (*mistificación*) hoax; (*narración confusa*) rigmarole, long involved story.

patraquear [1a] VT (*Cono Sur*) *objeto* to steal; *persona* to hold up, mug*.

patraquero NM (*Cono Sur*) thief; holdup man, mugger*.

patria NF native land, mother country; fatherland; ~ **adoptiva** country of adoption; ~ **chica** home town, home area; **madre** ~ mother country; **hacer** ~ to fly the flag*; **luchar por la** ~ to fight for one's country; *V* **merecer**.

patriada NF (*Cono Sur Hist*) rising, revolt.

patriarca NM patriarch.

patriarcado NM patriarchy.

patriarcal ADJ patriarchal.

Patricia NF Patricia.

Patricio NM Patrick.

patricio, -a ADJ, NM/F patrician.

patrilineal ADJ patrilineal.

patrimonial ADJ hereditary.

patrimonio NM (**a**) (*Jur*) inheritance.
  (**b**) (*fig*) heritage; birthright; **el** ~ **artístico de la nación** our national art heritage, the national art treasures; **nuestro** ~ **forestal** our national stock of trees, the forestry resources we have inherited; ~ **nacional** national wealth, national resources.
  (**c**) (*Com*) net worth, capital resources.

patrio ADJ (**a**) (*Pol*) native, home (*atr*); **amor** ~ love of one's country, patriotism; **el suelo** ~ one's native land, one's native soil. (**b**) (*Jur*) **poder** *etc* paternal.

patriota [1] NMF patriot.
  [2] NM (*CAm*) banana.

patriotería NF ostentatious patriotism, flag-waving; chauvinism; jingoism.

patrioterismo NM flag-waving, chauvinism, jingoism.

patriotero [1] ADJ ostentatiously patriotic; chauvinistic; jingoistic.
  [2] NM, **patriotera** NF flag-waver; chauvinist; jingoist.

patrióticamente ADV patriotically.

patriótico ADJ patriotic.

patriotismo NM patriotism.

patrocinado, -a NM/F (*Jur*) client.

patrocinador(a) [1] ADJ: **empresa patrocinadora** sponsoring company.
  [2] NM/F sponsor; patron(ess); promoter.

patrocinar [1a] VT to sponsor, act as patron to; to back, support; (*Dep*) to sponsor; **un movimiento patrocinado por** ... a movement under the auspices of (*o* under the patronage of) ...

patrocinazgo NM sponsorship; patronage.

patrocinio NM sponsorship, patronage; backing, support; (*Dep*) sponsorship.

patrón [1] NM (**a**) (*protector*) patron; (*Ecl: t* **santo** ~) patron saint; (*de esclavo*) master; (*fig: jefe*) master, boss, chief; (*Náut*) skipper; (*de pensión etc*) landlord.
  (**b**) (*Cos, Téc*) pattern; (*de medida etc*) standard; ~ **de distribución** distribution pattern; ~ **oro** gold standard; ~ **picado** stencilled pattern.
  (**c**) (*Agr: puntal*) prop, shore.
  (**d**) (*Agr: de árbol*) stock (*for* grafting).
  [2] ATR standard, regular; master (*atr*); sample (*atr*).

patrona NF patron(ess); (*Ecl*) patron saint; (*dueña*) employer, owner; (*de pensión etc*) landlady.

patronaje NM pattern-making; designing.

patronal [1] ADJ (**a**) **organización** ~ employers' organization, owners' organization; **la clase** ~ management, the managerial class; **cerrado por acto** ~ closed by the employers, closed by the owners (*o* management); **cierre** ~ lockout.
  (**b**) (*Ecl*) of a patron saint.
  [2] NF employers' organization; management.

patronato NM (**a**) (*acto*) patronage; sponsorship; **bajo el** ~ **de** under the auspices of, under the patronage of.

(b) (*Com, Fin*) employers' association, owners' organization; (*Pol*) the owners (*as a class*), management; **el ~ francés** French industrialists.
(c) (*junta*) board of trustees, board of management; **el ~ de turismo** the tourist board, the tourist organization.
(d) (*fundación*) trust, foundation.

patronear [1a] VT *barco* to skipper.

patronímico ADJ, NM patronymic.

patronista NMF pattern-maker; designer.

patronizar [1f] VT to patronize.

patrono NM patron; sponsor; protector, supporter; (*Ecl*) patron saint; (*Com, Fin*) owner, employer.

patrulla NF patrol.

patrullaje NM patrolling; **bajo un fuerte ~ policial** under heavy police patrol.

patrullar [1a] [1] VT to patrol, police.
[2] VI to patrol.

patrullera NF patrol-boat.

patrullero NM **(a)** (*Aut*) patrol-car. **(b)** (*Náut*) patrol-boat. **(c)** (*Méx*) patrolman, policeman.

patucho ADJ (*And*) short, squat.

patucos NMPL (*de bebé*) bootees; (*) shoes.

patudo [1] ADJ (*Cono Sur*) rough, brash.
[2] NM (*And*): **el ~** the devil.

patueco ADJ (*CAm*) = **patojo**.

patulea* NF mob, rabble.

patuleco ADJ (*LAm*), **patulejo** ADJ (*Cono Sur*), **patuleque** ADJ (*Carib*) = **patojo, patituerto**.

patulenco* ADJ (*CAm*) clumsy, awkward.

patullar [1a] VI **(a)** (*pisar*) to trample about, stamp around. **(b)** (*trajinar*) to bustle about. **(c)** (*charlar*) to chat; (*hacer ruido*) to talk noisily, make a lot of noise.

paturro ADJ (*And, Cono Sur*) chubby, plump; squat.

paúl NM marsh.

paular NM marshy ground.

paulatinamente ADV gradually, slowly.

paulatino ADJ gradual, slow.

paulina* NF **(a)** (*reprimenda*) telling-off*. **(b)** (*carta*) poison-pen letter.
Paulo NM Paul.

pauperismo NM pauperism.

pauperización NF impoverishment.

paupérrimo ADJ very poor, terribly poor.

pausa NF **(a)** (*gen*) pause; break, respite; interruption; (*Mús*) rest; **~ publicitaria** ad-break. **(b) con ~** slowly, deliberately.

pausadamente ADV slowly, deliberately.

pausado ADJ slow, deliberate.

pausar [1a] [1] VT to slow down; to interrupt.
[2] VI to go slow.

pauta NF **(a)** (*línea*) line, guideline.
(b) (*regla*) ruler.
(c) (*fig*) guide, guidelines, model; standard, norm; outline, plan, key; (*Med*) **~ del sueño** sleep pattern; **dar** (o **marcar**) **la ~** to set a standard, lay down a norm; **servir de ~** to act as a model for.

pautado [1] ADJ: **papel ~** ruled paper.
[2] NM (*Mús*) stave.

pautar [1a] VT **(a)** *papel* to rule. **(b)** (*fig: esp CAm*) to mark, characterize; to establish a norm for, lay down a pattern for, give directions for.

pava NF **(a)** (*Orn*) turkey (hen); **~ real** peahen; **pelar la ~** (*Esp**) to talk, court (*esp* at a balcony).
(b) (*LAm*) (*para hervir*) kettle; (*tetera*) teapot; (*para maté*) pot for making maté.
(c) (*And, Carib: sombrero*) broad-brimmed straw hat.
(d) (*And, CAm: fleco*) fringe.
(e) (*Cono Sur, Méx: orinal*) chamber-pot.
(f) (*And, Cono Sur*) (*guasa*) coarse banter; (*chiste*) tasteless joke; **hacer la ~ a uno*** to make sb look stupid.
(g) (*And, CAm**: *colilla*) cigarette-end, fag-end‡.
(h) (‡: *chica*) bird‡, girl.
(i) es una ~ (*Esp**) she's a dull person.
(j) (‡) **echar la ~** to be sick, throw up.

pavada NF **(a)** (*esp Cono Sur*) (*disparate*) silly thing; (*tontería*) silliness, stupidity; **no digas ~s** don't talk rubbish. **(b)** *Cono Sur*: *bagatela*) triviality; very small amount; **cuesta una ~** it costs next to nothing.
(c) (*Carib: mala suerte*) bit of bad luck.

pavear [1a] [1] VT **(a)** (*And*) to kill treacherously.
(b) (*And, Cono Sur*) to play a joke on.
[2] VI **(a)** (*Cono Sur**: *hacer el tonto*) to play the fool, mess about.
(b) (*Cono Sur**: *enamorados*) to whisper sweet nothings.
(c) (*And**: *hacer novillos*) to play truant.

pavería NF (*Cono Sur*) silliness, stupidity.

pavero, -a NM/F (*And, Cono Sur*) practical joker.

pavesas NFPL hot ash *sing.*

pavimentación NF paving.

pavimentar [1a] VT to pave; to floor.

pavimento NM (*de losas*) pavement, paving; (*de interior*) flooring; (*firme*) roadway, road surface.

pavipollo NM **(a)** (*Orn*) young turkey. **(b)** (*) twit*, idiot.

pavisoso* ADJ dull, graceless.

pavitonto* ADJ silly.

pavo [1] NM **(a)** (*Orn*) turkey (cock); **~ real** peacock; **estar en la edad del ~** to be going through the awkward stage (of adolescence).
(b) comer ~* to be a wallflower (*at a dance*); (*LAm*) to be disappointed.
(c) (*) (*necio*) idiot; (*víctima*) sucker‡; **¡no seas ~!** (*Esp*) don't be silly!
(d) (*Fin*‡) 5 pesetas, one *duro*.
(e) ponerse hecho un ~, subirse a uno el ~ to blush like a lobster; **tener mucho ~** to blush a lot.
(f) (*And: cometa*) large kite.
(g) (*And**) (*espadón*) big shot*; (*sospechoso*) evil-looking person.
(h) ir de ~ (*LAm**) to travel free, get a free ride.
(i) (*Carib**: *reprimenda*) telling-off*.
(j) (‡: *hombre*) bloke‡; (*Carib*‡: *joven*) youngster, kid*.
(k) (‡: *drogas*) cold turkey*.
[2] NM idiot, fool.
[3] ADJ (*LAm**) stupid, idiotic.

pavón NM **(a)** (*Orn*) peacock. **(b)** (*Téc*) bluing, bronzing.

pavonearse [1a] VR to swagger, strut (about); to swank*, show off.

pavoneo NM swagger(ing), strutting; swanking*, showing-off.

pavor NM dread, terror.

pavorosamente ADV frighteningly, terrifyingly.

pavoroso ADJ dreadful, frightening, terrifying.

pavoso ADJ (*Carib*) unlucky; that brings bad luck.

pay NM (*LAm*) pie.

paya NF (*Cono Sur*) improvised ballad.

payacate NM (*Méx*) (*de bolsillo*) handkerchief; (*prenda*) scarf, kerchief.

payada NF (*Cono Sur*) improvised gaucho folksong; **~ de contrapunto** contest between two *payadores*.

payador NM (*Cono Sur*) gaucho minstrel.

payar [1a] VI (*Cono Sur*) to improvise songs to a guitar accompaniment; (*fig**) to talk big*, shoot a line*.

payasada NF clownish trick, stunt; (*pey*) ridiculous thing (to do); **~s** clowning, tomfoolery; (*Teat etc*) slapstick, knockabout humour.

payasear [1a] VI (*LAm*) to clown around.

payaso, -a NM/F clown (*t fig*).

payés NM (*Cataluña, Islas Baleares*) peasant farmer.

payo [1] ADJ **(a)** (*Cono Sur*) albino. **(b)** (*Méx: simple*) rustic, simple. **(c)** (*Méx*) *ropa etc* loud, flashy, tasteless.
[2] NM (*entre gitanos*) non-gipsy.

payuelas NFPL chickenpox.

paz NF **(a)** (*gen*) peace; peacefulness, tranquility; **¡a la ~ de Dios!** God be with you!; **en ~ y en guerra** in peace and war, in peacetime and wartime; **no dar ~ a** to give no rest (o respite to); **no dar ~ a la lengua** to keep on and on; **dejar a uno en ~** to leave sb alone, leave sb in peace; **¡déjame en ~!** leave me alone!; **descansar en ~** to rest in peace; **su madre, que en ~ descanse, lo decía** her mother (God rest her soul) used to say so; **estar en ~** to be at peace; (*fig*) to be even, be quits, be all square (*con* with); (*Méx*‡) to be high‡ (on drugs); **¡haya ~!** stop it!, that's enough!; **mantener la ~** to keep the peace; **perturbar la ~** to disturb the peace; **¡... y en ~!, ¡aquí ~ y después gloria!** and that's that!, and Bob's your uncle!*
(b) (*tratado*) peace, peace treaty; **la ~ de los Pirineos** the Peace of the Pyrenees (*1659*); **hacer las paces** to make peace, (*fig*) to make it up.
(c) (*Ecl*) kiss of peace, sign of peace.

pazguato ADJ **(a)** (*necio*) simple, stupid. **(b)** (*remilgado*) prudish.

pazo NM (*Galicia*) country house.

PC NM ABR *de* **Partido Comunista** *p.ej.* **PCCH** ABR *de* **Partido Comunista Chileno; PCE** ABR *de* **Partido Comunista de España.**

p.c. NM ABR *de* **por cien(to)** per cent, %.

PCB NM ABR *de* **policlorobifenilo** polychlorinated biphenyl, PCB.

PCE NM ABR *de* **Partido Comunista Español.**

PCN NM (*El Salvador*) ABR *de* **Partido de Conciliación Nacional.**

PCUS NM ABR *de* **Partido Comunista de la Unión Soviética** former Soviet Communist Party.

PCV NM (*Venezuela*) ABR *de* **Partido Comunista Venezolano.**

P.D. ABR *de* **posdata** postscript, P.S.

PDC NM (*LAm*) ABR *de* **Partido Demócrata Cristiano.**

pdo. ABR *de* **pasado** ultimo, ult.

Pdte (*Chile: Prensa*) ABR *de* **presidente.**

pe NF the (name of the) letter *p*; **de ~ a pa** from A to Z, from beginning to end.

P.ᵉ ABR *de* **Padre** Father, F., Fr.

pea* NF: **coger una ~** to get smashed*, get legless*.

peaje NM toll.

peajista NMF collector of tolls.

peal NM (*LAm*) lasso.
pealar [1a] VT (*LAm*) to lasso.
peana NF stand, pedestal, base; (*Golf*) tee; (*) foot.
peatón NM pedestrian, person on foot; walker.
peatonal ADJ pedestrian (*atr*); **calle ~** pedestrian precinct.
peaton(al)ización NF pedestrianization.
peaton(al)izar [1f] VT to pedestrianize.
pebete ☐ NM (a) (*incienso*) joss stick. (b) (*de cohete*) fuse. (c) (*olor*) stink. (d) (*Cono Sur: panecillo*) roll.
　☐ NM, **pebeta** NF (*Cono Sur*) (*niño*) kid*, child; (*persona baja*) short person.
pebre NM (*esp Chile: Culin*) mild sauce made from vinegar, garlic, parsley and pepper.
peca NF freckle.
pecado NM sin; **~ capital** capital sin; **~ grave**, **~ mortal** mortal sin; **~ de comisión** sin of commission; **~ nefando** sodomy; **~ original** original sin; **~ venial** venial sin; **por mis ~s** for my sins; **sería un ~ no aprovecharlo** it would be a crime (*o* sin, pity) not to make use of it.
pecador ☐ ADJ sinful, sinning.
　☐ NM, **pecadora** NF sinner.
pecaminosidad NF sinfulness.
pecaminoso ADJ sinful.
pecar [1g] VI (a) (*Ecl*) to sin; (*fig*) to err, go astray; **si he pecado en esto, ha sido por ...** if I have been at fault in this, it is because ...; **si me lo pones delante, acabaré pecando** if you put temptation in front of me, I shall fall.
　(b) (*fig*) **~ de** + ADJ to be too + ADJ; **peca de generoso** he is too generous, he is generous to a fault; **nunca se peca por demasiado cuidado** one can't be too careful; **peca por exceso de confianza** he is too confident, he errs on the side of over-confidence.
pecari NM (*LAm*), **pécari** NM (*LAm*), **pecarí** NM (*LAm*) peccary.
peccata NF: **ser ~ minuta** to be no big deal, be unimportant.
pecé* ☐ NM (*Esp: partido*) Communist Party.
　☐ NMF (*persona*) Communist.
pececillos NMPL (*Pez*) fry.
pecera¹ NF fishbowl, fishtank.
pecero,* -a² NM/F (*Pol*) member of the Communist Party.
pecha NF (*Cono Sur*), push, shove.
pechada* NF (a) **una ~ de** a lot of, an excess of; **llevamos una ~ de andar** that's more than enough walking (for one day). (b) (*LAm*) push, shove; (*) scrounging*.
pechador* ADJ (*Cono Sur*) demanding.
pechar¹ [1a] VTI to pay (as a tax).
pechar² [1a] ☐ VT (a) (*LAm: empujar*) to push, shove. (b) **~ a uno** (*LAm**) to touch sb for a loan*. (c) (*Cono Sur**) to collar*, grab.
　☐ VI: **~ con*** (a) (*a desgana*) to get stuck with, get landed with; **siempre tengo que ~ con la más fea** I always get stuck with the plainest one. (b) *cometido etc* to shoulder, take on; *problema* to face up to.
pechazo NM (*LAm*) push, shove; (*) touch (for a loan)*.
pechblenda NF pitchblende.
peche: (*CAm*) ☐ ADJ skinny, weak.
　☐ NM child.
pechera NF (a) (*Cos: de camisa*) shirt front; (*de vestido*) front, bosom; (*Mil etc*) chest protector; **~ postiza** dicky. (b) (*Anat: hum*) (big) bosom. (c) (*Cono Sur Téc*) apron.
pechero¹ NM (*Hist*) commoner, plebeian.
pechero² NM (*Cos*) front (of dress); (*babero*) bib.
pechicato ADJ (*Carib*) = **pichicato**.
pechina NF scallop.
pecho¹ NM (a) (*Anat*) chest; **de ~ plano** flat-chested; **a ~ descubierto** unarmed, defenceless; (*fig*) openly, frankly; **dar el ~ a** to face things squarely; **estar de ~s sobre una barandilla** to be leaning on a railing; **gritar a todo ~** (*And, Carib*) to shout at the top of one's voice; **quedarse con algo entre ~ y espalda** to keep sth back; to have sth on one's mind; **sacar el ~** to thrust one's chest out, draw o.s. up.
　(b) (*de mujer*) breast; **los ~s** the breasts, the bosom, the bust; **dar el ~ a** to feed, suckle, nurse; **tener poco ~** to be small breasted.
　(c) (*fig*) heart, breast; **abrir** (*o* descubrir) **su ~ a uno** to unbosom o.s. to sb; **no le cabía en el ~ de alegría** he was bursting with happiness; **tomar algo a ~** to take sth to heart.
　(d) (*fig: valor*) courage, spirit; **¡~ al agua!** courage!; **a lo hecho ~;** *V* **hecho**.
　(e) (*Geog*) slope, gradient.
pecho² NM (*Hist*) tax, tribute.
pechoño ADJ (*And, Cono Sur*) sanctimonious.
pechuga NF (a) (*de pollo etc*) breast; (*hum: de mujer*) bosom; cleavage.
　(b) (*Geog*) slope, hill.
　(c) (*LAm: pey*) nerve*, gall, cheek.
　(d) (*And, CAm**: abuso de confianza*) abuse of trust.

(e) (*CAm: molestia*) trouble, annoyance.
pechugón* ☐ ADJ (a) (*de mucho pecho*) busty*, big-bosomed.
　(b) (*LAm*) (*descarado*) forward; (*franco*) outspoken; sponging, parasitical; (*egoísta*) egoistical, selfish.
　(c) (*Cono Sur: resuelto*) bold, single-minded.
　(d) (*: atractivo*) dishy*.
　☐ NM (*LAm*) (*descarado*) shameless individual, impudent person; (*gorrón*) sponger*, parasite.
pechuguera NF (*And, Méx*) (*ronquera*) hoarseness; (*resfriado*) chest cold.
pecio NM wrecked ship, shipwreck; **~s** flotsam, wreckage.
pecíolo NM, **peciolo** NM (leaf) stalk, petiole (*Téc*)
pécora NF (*esp* **mala ~**) (*lagarta*) bitch; (*arpía*) harpy; (*puta*) loose woman, whore.
pecoso ADJ freckled.
pecotra NF (*Cono Sur*) (*Anat*) bump, swelling; (*en madera*) knot.
pectina NF pectin.
pectoral ☐ ADJ pectoral.
　☐ NM (a) (*Ecl*) pectoral cross. (b) **~es** PL (*Anat*) pectorals.
pecuaca NF (*And, Carib*) = **pecueca**.
pecuario ADJ cattle (*atr*).
pecueca NF (*And, Carib*) (*pezuña*) hoof; (*hum*) smell of feet.
peculado NM peculation.
peculiar ADJ special, peculiar; typical, characteristic.
peculiaridad NF peculiarity; special feature, characteristic.
peculio NM one's own money; modest savings; **de su ~** out of one's own pocket.
pecunia* NF brass*; (*Carib: moneda*) coin.
pecuniario ADJ pecuniary, money (*atr*).
PED NM ABR *de* **Procesamiento Electrónico de Datos** Electronic Data Processing, EDP.
pedagogía NF pedagogy.
pedagógico ADJ pedagogic(al).
pedagogo, -a NM/F teacher; educator; (*pey*) pedagogue.
pedal NM (a) (*gen*) pedal; **~ de acelerador** accelerator (pedal); **~ de embrague** clutch (pedal); **~ de freno** footbrake, brake (pedal); **~ dulce**, **~ piano**, **~ suave** (*Mús*) soft pedal; **~ fuerte** (*Mús*) loud pedal.
　(b) **coger** (*o* tener) **un ~:** to get canned:.
pedalear [1a] VI to pedal; **~ en agua** to tread water.
pédalo NM pedal boat.
pedáneo ADJ: **alcalde ~** mayor of a small town; **juez ~** local magistrate.
pedanía NF district.
pedante ☐ ADJ pedantic; pompous, conceited.
　☐ NMF pedant.
pedantería NF pedantry; pompousness, conceit.
pedantescamente ADV pedantically.
pedantesco ADJ pedantic.
pedazo NM (a) (*fig*) piece, bit; scrap; morsel; **un ~ de papel** a piece of paper; **un ~ de pan** a bit of bread, a scrap of bread; **es un ~ de pan** (*Esp fig*) he's a terribly nice person; **trabaja por un ~ de pan** he works for a mere pittance; **hacer algo a ~s** to do sth in pieces, do sth piecemeal; **hacer ~s** to break to pieces, tear (*o* pull) to pieces; to shatter, smash; **se hizo ~s** it fell to pieces, it came apart; it broke up; it shattered, it smashed (itself); **estoy hecho ~s** I'm worn out.
　(b) (*fig*) **~ del alma**, **~ de las entrañas**, **~ del corazón** one's darling, the apple of one's eye; (*en oración directa*) my darling; **~ de animal***, **~ de atún*** blockhead; **¡~ de animal!***, **¡~ de bruto!*** you idiot!; you beast!
pederasta NM pederast.
pederastia NF pederasty.
pedernal NM flint; **como un ~** (*fig*) of flint, flinty.
pederse: [2a] VR to fart:.
pedestal NM pedestal, stand, base.
pedestre ADJ (a) *viajero etc* on foot; walking. (b) (*fig*) pedestrian.
pedestrismo NM race walking.
pediatra NMF, **pedíatra** NMF paediatrician.
pediatría NF paediatrics.
pediátrico ADJ paediatric.
pedicura NF chiropody.
pedicuro NMF chiropodist.
pedida NF: **~ de mano** engagement; *V* **pulsera**.
pedidera NF (*And, CAm, Carib*) = **petición**.
▼ **pedido** NM (*Com*) order; **~ al contado** cash order; **~ de ensayo** trial order; **~s pendientes** backlog; **~ de repetición** repeat order; **a ~** on request; **a ~ de** at the request of; **hacer algo bajo** (*o* sobre) **~** to make sth to order.
pedigree [pedi'gri] NM, **pedigrí** NM pedigree.
pedigüeño ADJ insistent, importunate; demanding.
pedilón ☐ ADJ (*LAm*) = **pedigüeño**.
　☐ NM (*LAm*) pest, nuisance.
pedimento NM petition; (*Jur*) claim, bill; (*Méx Com*) licence, permit.

► LENGUA Y USO: **pedido** → 47.2, 47.3, 47.4

pedir [3k] **1** VT **(a)** (*gen*) to ask for; to request; *comida etc* to order; (*Com*) to order (*a* from); ~ **algo a uno** to ask sb for sth; ~ **la paz** to sue for peace; ~ **que** ... to ask that ...; **me pidió que cerrara la puerta** he asked me to shut the door; **pidió que se volviera a estudiar la cuestión** he asked that the matter should be studied afresh; **el pescado es tal que no hay más que** ~ the fish is as good as it could possibly be.
(b) (*Com*) *precio* to ask; **¿cuánto piden por él?** how much are they asking for it?
(c) ~ **a una joven** to ask for a girl's hand in marriage; **fue anoche a ~la a su padre** he went last night to ask for permission to marry her.
(d) (*Jur*) to file a claim against; ~ **a uno en justicia** to sue sb.
(e) (*fig*) to need, demand, require; to cry out for; **la casa está pidiendo una mano de pintura** the house is crying out for a dab of paint; **ese color pide una cortina azul** that colour needs a blue curtain to go with it; **el triunfo pide que bebamos algo** the victory demands to be celebrated with a drink.
2 VI **(a)** to ask; **por ~ que no quede** it does no harm to ask, one might as well ask.
(b) (*t* ~ **por Dios**) to beg.
(c) *V* **boca** (a).

PEDIR ⬛ *ver también la entrada*

¿"Ask" o "Ask for"?
- La expresión española *pedir algo* se traduce por la inglesa *ask for sth*:
   Pidieron muchas cosas diferentes
   They asked for many different things
   NOTA: Si el verbo *pedir* lleva dos complementos, el complemento de persona siempre va delante:
   Pídele un lápiz a la profesora
   Ask the teacher for a pencil
- La estructura *pedir a alguien que haga algo*, se traduce al inglés por *ask* + OBJETO + CONSTRUCCIÓN DE INFINITIVO:
   Le pedí a mi hermana que me trajera una alfombra de Turquía
   I asked my sister to bring me a rug from Turkey
   Le pediremos que nos haga un descuento
   We'll ask him to give us a discount
   NOTA: Si el contexto es más formal *pedir* también se puede traducir por *request*:
   Ambas partes en conflicto están pidiendo ayuda al extranjero
   Both sides are requesting help from abroad
   Para otros usos y ejemplos ver la entrada.

---

pedo **1** NM **(a)** (⁑) fart⁑; **tirarse un** ~ to let off a fart⁑.
(b) ~ **de lobo** (*Bot*) puffball.
(c) ~ **de monja** (*Culin*) very light pastry.
(d) (‡) **agarrarse un** ~ to get sloshed‡; **estar en** ~ to be sloshed‡; **¡estás en** ~! (*al hablar*) you must be kidding!; **no me gusta trabajar al** ~ I don't like working for the sake of it.
(e) (‡: *drogas*) high‡.
2 ADJ INVAR (‡): **andar** ~, **estar** ~ (*borracho*) to be sloshed‡, (*drogado*) be high‡; **ponerse** ~ (*borracho*) to get sloshed‡; (*drogado*) to get high‡.
pedofilia NF paedophilia.
pedofílico NM paedophile, pedophile (*esp US*)
pedófilo NM paedophile.
pedología NF pedology, study of soils.
pedorrera⁑ NF string of farts⁑.
pedorrero⁑ ADJ given to farting⁑, windy.
pedorreta* NF raspberry*.
pedorro* **1** ADJ (*tonto*) daft; (*pelmazo*) annoying.
2 NM, **pedorra** NF (*tonto*) twit*; (*pelmazo*) pain*.
pedrada NF **(a)** (*acto*) throw of a stone; (*golpe*) hit (*o* blow) from a stone; **matar a uno a ~s** to stone sb to death; **pegar una ~ a uno** to throw a stone at sb.
(b) (*fig*) wounding remark, snide remark, dig.
(c) **la cosa le sentó como una** ~ he took it very ill, the affair went down very badly with him; **me sienta como una** ~ **tener que irme** I don't in the least want to go; **venir como** ~ **en ojo de boticario** to come just right, be just what the doctor ordered.
pedrea NF **(a)** (*combate*) stone-throwing, fight with stones. **(b)** (*Met*) hailstorm. **(c)** (*: premios*) small prizes in the lottery.
pedregal NM stony place, rocky ground; (*Méx*) lava field.
pedregón NM (*LAm*) rock, boulder.
pedregoso ADJ stony, rocky.
pedregullo NM (*Cono Sur*) crushed stone, grit.
pedrejón NM big stone, rock, boulder.
pedrera NF stone quarry.
pedrería NF precious stones, jewels.
pedrero NM **(a)** (*persona*) quarryman, stone cutter. **(b)** (*And, CAm,*

Cono Sur) = **pedregal**.
pedrisco NM **(a)** (*lluvia de piedras*) shower of stones; (*Met*) hailstorm. **(b)** (*montón*) heap of stones.
Pedro NM Peter; **entrar como** ~ **por su casa** to come in as if one owned the place.
pedrusco NM **(a)** rough stone; piece of stone, lump of stone. **(b)** (*LAm*) = **pedregal**.
peduncular ADJ stalk (*atr*), peduncular (*Téc*).
pedúnculo NM stem, stalk.
peerse⁑ [2a] VR = **pederse**⁑.
pega **1** NF **(a)** (*acto*) sticking.
(b) (*paliza*) beating; beating-up*.
(c) (*chasco*) practical joke; (*truco*) hoax, trick.
(d) (*dificultad*) snag, difficulty; **todo son ~s** there's nothing but problems; **poner ~s** to raise objections; to make trouble.
(e) (*pregunta*) searching question; catch question, trick question.
(f) **de ~*** false, dud*; fake, sham, bogus; **un billete (de banco) de** ~ a dud banknote*.
(g) (*Carib, Cono Sur, Méx: trabajo*) job, work.
(h) (*Carib: liga*) birdlime.
(i) (*Cono Sur: de enfermedad*) infectious period.
(j) **estar en la** ~ (*Cono Sur*) to be at one's best.
(k) **jugar a la** ~ (*And*) to play tag.
2 NM: **ser el ~*** to be the one who always sees problems.
pegachento ADJ sticky, (*esp*) that sticks to one's teeth.
pegada¹ NF (*Cono Sur*) **(a)** (*mentira*) fib, lie. **(b)** (*suerte*) piece of luck. **(c)** (‡: *atractivo*) charm, appeal; **tiene** ~ she's got plenty of it*.
pegada² NF (*Boxeo*) exchange of punches.
pegadillo NM (*And*) lace.
pegadizo **1** ADJ **(a)** (*pegajoso*) sticky.
(b) (*Med*) infectious, catching.
(c) (*Mús*) *melodía* catchy.
(d) (*postizo*) sham, imitation.
(e) *persona* parasitic, sponging*.
2 NM sponger*, hanger-on.
pegado **1** ADJ (*fig*): **dejar a uno** ~ to leave sb nonplussed; **estar** ~ to have no idea, be stuck; **quedarse** ~ to be bewildered, be nonplussed.
2 NM patch, sticking plaster.
pegadura NF (*And*) practical joke.
pegajoso ADJ **(a)** (*gen*) sticky, adhesive; viscous.
(b) (*Med*) infectious, catching; (*fig*) contagious; tempting.
(c) *persona* over-sweet; sloppy, cloying; clinging.
pegamento NM glue, adhesive; (*droga*) glue; ~ **de caucho** (*Aut etc*) rubber solution.
pegar [1h] **1** VT **(a)** (*gen*) to stick (on, together, up); (*con cola*) to glue, gum, paste; *cartel* to post, stick up; (*Cos*) to sew (on), fasten (on); *piezas* to join, fix together; ~ **un sello** to stick a stamp on; ~ **una estantería a una pared** to put a set of shelves against a wall; ~ **una silla a una pared** to move a chair up against a wall.
(b) (*Med*) *enfermedad* to give, infect with; *idea etc* to give, communicate (*a* to).
(c) *golpe* to give, hit, deal; *pelota* to hit; *persona* to hit, strike; to smack, slap; **dicen que pega a su mujer** they say he knocks his wife about; **es un crimen** ~ **a los niños** it's a crime to hit (*o* smack) children; **'pegad fuerte a Eslobodia'** (*eslogan*) 'hit Slobodia hard'; **hazlo o te pego** do it or I'll bash you*.
(d) (*) ~ **un grito** to let out a yell; ~ **un puntapié a uno** to give sb a kick; ~ **un salto** to jump (with fright *etc*); *V* **susto, fuego** *etc*.
(e) ~**la** (*LAm*) (*tener suerte*) to be lucky; (*lograrlo*) to manage it, get what one wants; (*caer en gracia*) to make a hit (*con* with).
(f) (*Méx*) to tie, fasten (down); *caballo etc* to hitch up.
(g) (*Carib*) *trabajo* to start.
2 VI **(a)** (*adherir*) to stick, adhere; *V* **cola**.
(b) ~ **en** to touch; **el piano pega en la pared** the piano is touching the wall.
(c) (*Bot*) to take root; (*remedio*) to take; (*fuego*) to catch.
(d) ~ **con uno** to run into sb.
(e) (*ser apropiado etc*) (*colores*) to match, go together; **no pega** (*fig*) it doesn't add up; **es una cosa que no pega** (*Culin*) it's a thing which does not go well with other dishes; **la cita no pega** the quotation is quite out of place, the quotation is most unsuitable; ~ **con** to match, go with; **ese sombrero no pega con el abrigo** that hat doesn't go with the coat.
(f) (*dar golpes*) to hit; to beat; ~ **en** to hit, strike (against); **la flecha pegó en el blanco** the arrow hit the target; **pegaba con un palo en la puerta** he was hitting (*o* pounding on) the door with a stick; **las ramas pegan en los cristales** the branches beat against the windows.
(g) (*sol*) to strike hot; **a estas horas el sol pega fuerte** the sun strikes very hot at this time; **esta canción está pegando muy fuerte** this song is rocketing up the charts; **este vino pega** this wine goes

to your head; **el sol pega en esta ventana** the sun comes (o shines) in through this window.

(h) (*Carib, Méx*: *trabajar duro*) to work hard.

3 pegarse VR **(a)** (*adherirse*) to stick.

(b) (*darse golpes*) to hit each other, fight.

(c) ~ **a uno** to stick to sb, attach o.s. to sb; ~ **a uno como una lapa** (*Esp*) to stick to sb like a limpet; ~ **a una reunión** to gatecrash a meeting.

(d) (*Med*) to be catching.

(e) (*Culin*) to burn, stick to the pot.

(f) (*) (*fracasar*) to fail, come a cropper*; **pegársela** (*con objeto*) to trick; to double-cross, do down*; *marido* to deceive, cuckold; **ella se la pega a su marido** she's deceiving her husband, she's unfaithful to her husband.

(g) ~ **un tiro** to shoot o.s.; **¡es para ~ un tiro!** it's enough to make you scream!; **se pega una vida de millonario*** he lives the life of Riley, he has a whale of a time* (*V t* **vida**).

Pegaso NM Pegasus.

pegata* NF, **pegatín** NM, **pegatina** NF sticker; badge.

pegativo ADJ (*CAm, Cono Sur*) sticky.

pego* NM (*Esp*) **(a) da el** ~ it looks great*, that looks just right. **(b) me ha dado el** ~ he's done me down.

pegón* ADJ **(a)** *persona* tough, hard, given to violence. **(b)** *vino* strong.

pegoste NM **(a)** (*LAm*) (*esparadrapo*) sticking plaster. **(b)** (*Carib**: *colado*) gatecrasher; (*CAm*‡: *parásito*) scrounger*.

pegote NM **(a)** (*Med*) sticking plaster; (*fig*) patch, ugly mend, botch.
(b) (*Culin**) sticky mess, sticky lump.
(c) (*: *chapuza*) botch, clumsy job.
(d) (*: *gorrón*) sponger*, hanger-on.
(e) echarse un ~*, **tirarse el** ~* to show off.

pegotear* [1a] VI to sponge*, cadge.

pegujal NM **(a)** (*Fin*) wealth, money; estate. **(b)** (*Agr*) small plot; small private plot, smallholding.

PEIN NM ABR *de* **Plan Electrónico e Informático Nacional**.

peina NF back comb, ornamental comb.

peinada NF combing; **darse una** ~ to comb one's hair.

peinado **1** ADJ **(a) bien** ~ *pelo* well-combed; *persona* neat, well-groomed.
(b) (*fig*) foppish, over elegant, overdressed; *estilo, ingenio* affected, overdone.
2 NM **(a)** (*de pelo*) hairdo; coiffure, hair style; ~ **de paje** pageboy hair style.
(b) (*: *investigación*) check, investigation; (*redada*) sweep, raid; house-to-house search.

peinador NM **(a)** (*persona*) hairdresser. **(b)** (*bata*) peignoir, dressing gown. **(c)** (*LAm*: *tocador*) dressing table.

peinadora NF hairdresser.

peinadura NF **(a)** combing. **(b)** ~s combings.

peinar [1a] **1** VT **(a)** *pelo* to comb; to do, arrange, style; *caballo* to comb, curry.
(b) *zona* to comb, search thoroughly.
(c) (*LAm*) *roca* to cut.
(d) (*Cono Sur*) to flatter.
(e) (*Dep**) *balón* to head.
2 peinarse VR to comb one's hair, do one's hair; ~ **a la griega** to do one's hair in the Greek style.

peine NM comb; **¡ya pareció el** ~**!** (*Esp*) so that was it!; **¡se va a enterar de lo que vale un** ~**!** (*Esp*) now he'll find out what's what!

peinecillo NM small back comb.

peineta NF back comb, ornamental comb.

peinilla NF (*And, Carib*) large machete.

p.ej. ABR *de* **por ejemplo** *exempli gratia*, for example, *e.g.*

peje **1** ADJ (*Méx*) stupid.
2 NM **(a)** (*Zool*) fish; ~ **araña** weever; ~ **sapo** monkfish. **(b)** (*: *listillo*) sly fellow, twister.

pejiguera* NF bother, nuisance.

Pekín NM Pekin(g).

pela NF **(a)** (*Culin*) peeling. **(b)** (‡) one peseta; (*gen*) money; **mucha ~**, ~ **larga** lots of dough‡; **cambiar** (o **echar**) **la ~** to throw up; **mirar la ~** to be concerned only about money. **(c)** (*LAm*: *zurra*) beating. **(d)** (*Méx*: *trabajo*) slog, hard work; (*CAm*: *fatiga*) exhaustion.

pelada NF **(a)** (*LAm*: *corte de pelo*) haircut.
(b) (*Cono Sur*) (*calva*) bald head; head of close-cropped hair.
(c) (*And, CAm, Carib*: *error*) blunder.
(d) la P~ (*And, Carib, Cono Sur*) death.

peladar NM (*Cono Sur*) arid plain.

peladera NF (*CAm, Méx*) **(a)** (*chismes*) gossip, backbiting. **(b)** = **peladar**.

peladero NM (*LAm*) = **pelador**.

peladez NF **(a)** (*And*: *pobreza*) poverty. **(b)** (*Méx*: *vulgaridad*) vulgarity; (*palabrota*) rude word, obscenity.

peladilla NF (*Esp*) sugared almond, coated almond.

pelado **1** ADJ **(a)** *cabeza etc* shorn; hairless; *tronco etc* bare, smooth; *hueso* clean; *manzana* peeled; *campo etc* treeless, bare; *paisaje* bare.
(b) (*fig*) bare; **cobra el sueldo** ~ he gets just the bare salary; **el cinco mil** ~ exactly five thousand; five thousand as a round number.
(c) (*LAm**: *sin dinero*) broke*, penniless, down and out.
(d) (*Méx**: *grosero*) coarse, crude.
(e) (*CAm, Carib*: *descarado*) impudent; barefaced.
2 NM **(a)** (*calva etc*) bare patch.
(b) (*pobre*) poor man, member of the lowest class; (*fig*) poor devil, wretch.
(c) (*: *joven* ~) skinhead.
(d) (*And, CAm**: *bebé*) baby.

┌─ **PELADO** ─┐

A stock figure in Mexican theatre and film, the **pelado** *is a kind of rural anti-hero cum lovable rogue who survives by his quick wits in the foreign environment of the city. The Mexican actor and comedian Mario Moreno (1911-94) based the character* **Cantinflas** *on the* **pelado**, *for which he is famous all over the Spanish-speaking world. The* **pelado** *is closely related to the literary figure of the* **pícaro** *and forms part of a long line of anti-heroic characters in Hispanic literature.*
⇨ *See also* PÍCARO , CARPA

pelador NM (*Culin*) peeler.

peladura NF **(a)** (*acción*) peeling. **(b)** (*calva etc*) bare patch. **(c)** ~s peel, peelings.

pelafustán NM, **pelafustana** NF layabout, good-for-nothing.

pelagallos NM INVAR = **pelagatos.**

pelagatos NM INVAR nobody; poor devil, wretch.

pelágico ADJ pelagic.

pelaje NM **(a)** (*Zool*) fur, coat. **(b)** = **pelambre (a).** **(c)** (*fig*) appearance; quality; **y otros de ese** ~ and others like him, and others of that ilk; **de todo** ~ of every kind.

pelambre NM **(a)** (*de persona*) thick hair, long hair, mop of hair; unkempt hair. **(b)** (*Zool*) fur, fleece (*cut from animal*). **(c)** (*calva*) bare patch. **(d)** (*Cono Sur*: *murmullos*) gossip, slander.

pelambrera NF = **pelambre (a).**

pelanas NM INVAR = **pelado 2 (b).**

pelandusca* NF (*Esp*) tart‡, slut.

pelapapas NM INVAR (*LAm*) potato peeler.

pelapatatas NM INVAR potato peeler.

pelar [1a] **1** VT **(a)** *animal* to cut the hair of, shear; *animal muerto* to flay, skin; *pollo* to pluck; *fruta* to peel, skin, take the skin off; *patatas etc* to peel; *guisantes etc* to shell.
(b) (*: *calumniar*) to blacken, slander, speak ill of; to criticize.
(c) (*: *Naipes etc*) to fleece, clean out*.
(d) (‡: *matar*) to do in‡, bump off‡.
(e) (*LAm*) to beat up*.
(f) ~**la** (*And**: *morir*) to die, kick the bucket‡.
2 VI **(a)** (*Cono Sur*) to gossip. **(b) hace un frío que pela** (*Esp*) it's bitterly cold.
3 pelarse VR **(a)** (*piel etc*) to peel off.
(b) (*persona*) to lose one's hair; **voy a pelarme** I'm going to get my hair cut.
(c) pelárselas por algo* to crave (for) sth; **pelárselas por** + *infin* to crave to + *infin*, long to + *infin*.
(d) corre que se las pela* he runs like nobody's business*.
(e) pelársela (‡) to toss off‡‡.
(f) (*Méx*‡) to peg out‡.

pelazón NF (*CAm, Méx*) **(a)** (*chismes*) gossip, backbiting. **(b)** (*pobreza*) chronic poverty.

peldaño NM step, stair; (*de escalera portátil*) rung.

pelea NF **(a)** (*gen*) fight, tussle, scuffle; (*riña*) quarrel, row; **armar una** ~ to kick up a row, start a fight. **(b)** ~ **de gallos** cockfight; **gallo de** ~ gamecock, fighting cock.

peleador ADJ brawling; combative, quarrelsome.

pelear [1a] **1** VI (*gen*) to fight; to scuffle, brawl; (*fig*) to fight, struggle (*por* for); (*reñir*) to quarrel; (*competir*) to vie.
2 pelearse VR **(a)** (*gen*) to fight; to scuffle, brawl; to come to blows; ~ **con uno** to fight sb (*por* for).
(b) (*fig*) to fall out, quarrel (*con* with; *por* about, over); **estamos peleados** we're not on speaking terms, we've fallen out.

pelechar [1a] VI **(a)** (*Zool*) to moult, shed its hair; to get new hair.
(b) (*persona: de salud*) to be on the mend; (*negocio*) to be turning the corner; (*Cono Sur: enriquecerse*) to improve one's position, prosper.

pelecho NM (*Cono Sur, Méx*) **(a)** (*pelo*) moulted fur; (*piel*) sloughed skin. **(b)** (*ropa*) old clothing.

pelele NM **(a)** (*figura*) guy, dummy, figure of straw; (*fig*) tool, cat's-paw, puppet. **(b)** (*de niño: traje*) rompers, creepers (*US*); (*de dormir*) baby's sleeping-bag.

pelendengue NM = **perendengue.**

peleón ADJ (a) *persona* pugnacious, aggressive; quarrelsome; argumentative. (b) *vino* cheap, ordinary; strong.

peleona* NF row, set-to*; brawl.

peleonero ADJ (*Lam*) = **peleón**.

pelero NM (a) (*CAm, Cono Sur*) horse blanket. (b) (*Carib*) = **pelambre**.

pelés‡‡ NMPL (*Esp*) balls‡‡; **estar en ~** to be stark naked.

pelete NM = **pelado 2** (b); **en ~** stark naked.

peletería NF furrier's, fur shop; (*Carib*) shoe shop.

peletero NM furrier.

peli* NF = **película** (b).

peliagudo ADJ *tema* tricky, ticklish.

pelicano¹ ADJ grey-haired.

pelicano² NM, **pelícano** NM pelican.

pelicorto ADJ short-haired.

película NF (a) (*Téc*) film; thin covering; **~ autoadherible** (*Méx*) Clingfilm ®.
(b) (*Cine*) film, movie (*US*), motion picture (*US*); **~ de animación** cartoon film; **~ en colores** colour film; **~ de dibujos (animados)** cartoon film; **~ estereofónica** stereophonic film; **~ muda** silent film; **~ del Oeste** western; **~ S** porn film; **~ de la serie B** B film; **~ sonora** talkie; **~ de terror** horror film; **~ vídeo** video film; **una cosa de ~** (*fig*) like something in the movies; an astonishing thing, something out of this world; **fue de ~** it was an incredible scene; **¡allí ~s!*** it's nothing to do with me!
(c) (*Fot*) film; roll of film, reel of film; **~ virgen** unexposed film.
(d) (*fig*) story, catalogue (of events); (*: *cuento*) tall story, tale; **¡cuánta ~!** what a load of rubbish!*
(e) (*Carib*: *disparate*) silly remark; (*lío*) row, rumpus.

peliculero [1] ADJ (a) film (*atr*), cine (*atr*), movie (*US atr*). (b) (*aficionado*) fond of films, fond of the cinema.
[2] NM film-maker; scenario writer; film-actor.

peligrar [1a] VI to be in danger; **~ de** + *infin* to be in danger of + *ger*.

peligro NM (*gen*) danger, peril; (*riesgo*) risk; (*amenaza*) menace, threat; **~ amarillo** yellow peril; **'~ (de muerte)'** (*aviso*) 'danger'; **con ~ de la vida** at the risk of one's life; **estar en ~** to be in danger; to be at stake; **estar fuera de ~** to be out of danger; **correr ~** to be in danger; to run a risk; **correr ~ de** + *infin* to run the risk of + *ger*; **poner algo en ~** to endanger sth; **estar enfermo de ~** to be seriously ill, be dangerously ill.

peligrosamente ADV dangerously; riskily.

peligrosidad NF danger; riskiness.

peligroso ADJ dangerous; risky; *herida etc* ugly, nasty.

pelilargo ADJ long-haired.

pelillo NM slight annoyance; triviality; **echar ~s a la mar** to make it up, bury the hatchet; **¡~s a la mar!** (*Esp*) let bygones be bygones!; **no se para en ~s** he doesn't stick at trifles, he won't let a little thing like that deter him.

pelín* [1] NM bit, small amount; **un ~ de música** a bit of music.
[2] ADV a bit, just a bit; **es un ~ tacaño** he's just a bit mean; **te pasaste un ~** you went a bit too far.

pelinegro ADJ black-haired.

pelirrojo ADJ red-haired, ginger; **la pequeña pelirroja** the little redhead.

pelirrubio ADJ fair-haired.

pella NF (a) (*gen*) ball, pellet, round mass; roll; dollop; (*Culin*) lump of lard. (b) (*Bot*: *de coliflor etc*) head. (c) (*) sum of money. (d) **hacer ~s*** to play truant.

pelleja NF (a) (*piel*) skin, hide. (b) (*: *puta*) whore. (c) (*: *persona delgada*) thin person. (d) (*Esp‡*: *cartera*) wallet.

pellejería NF (a) (*pieles*) skins, hides. (b) (*curtiduría*) tannery. (c) **~s** (*Cono Sur*) difficulty, jam.

pellejero‡ NM pickpocket.

pellejo NM (a) (*de animal*) skin, hide, pelt; (*de persona, esp LAm*) skin; (*Bot*) skin, peel, rind.
(b) (*odre*) wineskin; (*borracho*) drunk*, toper.
(c) (*) (*puta*) whore; (*mujeriego*) rake, womanizer.
(d) (*fig*) skin, hide; **arriesgarse el ~, jugarse el ~** to risk one's neck; **perder el ~** to lose one's life; **no quisiera estar en su ~** I wouldn't like to be in his shoes; **quitar el ~ a uno** to flay sb, criticize sb harshly; **salvar el ~** to save one's skin; **no tener más que el ~** to be all skin and bones.

pellet NM, PL **pellets** pellet.

pellingajo NM (*And, Cono Sur*) (a) (*trapo*) dishcloth. (b) (*objeto*) piece of junk.

pelliza NF fur jacket.

pellizcar [1g] VT (a) to pinch, nip; *comida etc* to take a small bit of. (b) (*fig**) to attract, tickle sb's fancy.

pellizco NM (a) (*gen*) pinch, nip. (b) (*Culin etc*) small bit; **un ~ de sal** a pinch of salt; **un buen ~*** a tidy sum*. (c) (*de sombrero*) pinch, dent.

pellón NM (*LAm*) sheepskin saddle blanket.

pelma [1] NMF (*) bore; **¡no seas ~!** don't be such a bore!, don't go on

about it!
[2] NM lump, solid mass.

pelmazamente* ADV boringly.

pelmazo* [1] ADJ boring, tedious.
[2] NM = **pelma**.

pelo NM (a) (*gen*) hair; (*de barba, bigote*) whisker; (*de animal*) hair, fur, coat; (*de cebada etc*) beard; (*de ave, de fruta*) down; (*de alfombra, tela*) nap, pile; (*Téc*) fibre, filament, strand; (*en joya*) flaw; (*de reloj*) hairspring; **un ~ rubio** a blonde hair; **tiene ~ rubio** she has blonde hair; **~ de camello** camel-hair, camel's hair (*US*); **dos caballos del mismo ~** two horses of the same colour; **cortarse el ~** to have one's hair cut; **hacer el ~ a una** to do sb's hair.
(b) (*locuciones*) **a ~** (*sin sombrero*) bareheaded, hatless; (*desnudo*) in the buff*; (*cabalgar*) bareback; **a medios ~s*** half-seas over; **al ~*** just right; **ha quedado al ~** it fits like a glove; **venir** (*o* **ir**) **al ~** to come just right, be exactly what one needs; **con es(t)os ~s*** unprepared, in a right state; **con** (**sus**) **~s y señales** with full details, with chapter and verse; **de medio ~** *persona* of no social standing, socially unimportant; *cosa* mediocre; **hombre de ~ en pecho** brave man; real man, he-man*, tough guy*; (*pey*) hard-hearted man; **en ~s*** naked; **por los ~s** by the skin of one's teeth; **escaparse por un ~** to have a narrow escape, have a close shave; **pasó el examen por los ~s** he scraped through the exam; **no afloja un ~** (*Cono Sur*) he won't give an inch; **agarrarse** (*o* **asirse**) **a un ~** to clutch at any opportunity; **¡se te va a caer el ~!** (*Esp**) you're for it now!, now you've really done it!; **no se cortó un ~** he didn't bat an eyelid; **cortar un ~ en el aire** (*fig*) to be pretty smart; **así nos crece** (*o* **luce**) **el ~*** and that's the awful state we're in, that's why we're so badly off; **dar a uno para el ~*** to knock sb silly*; (*en discusión*) to flatten sb; (*regañar*) to dress sb down*; **echar el ~** (*Cono Sur*) to waste time, idle; **estuvo en un ~ que lo perdiéramos** we came within an inch of losing it, we very nearly lost it; **no se mueve un ~ de aire** (*o* **viento**) there isn't a breath of air stirring; **se me pusieron los ~s de punta, se me paró el ~** (*LAm*) my hair stood on end; **ser de dos ~s** (*Cono Sur*) to be two-faced; **soltarse el ~*** to burst out, drop all restraint; to show one's true colours; **tener el ~ de la dehesa** to betray one's rustic (*o* humble) origins; **no tiene ~ de tonto** he's no fool; **no tener ~s en la lengua** to be outspoken, not mince words; **no tocar un ~ (de la ropa) a uno** not to lay a finger on sb; **tomar el ~ a uno*** to pull sb's leg*; to rag sb; **parece traído por los ~s** it seems far-fetched.
(c) (*Téc*: *grieta*) hairline, fine crack.
(d) (*Téc*: *sierra*) fine saw.

pelón [1] ADJ (a) (*calvo*) hairless, bald; (*rapado*) close-cropped, with a crew cut.
(b) (*) (*pobre*) poor; (*sin recursos*) broke*, penniless.
(c) (*And*) hairy, long-haired.
[2] NM (a) (*) = **pelado 2** (b).
(b) (*LAm*: *niño*) child, baby.
(c) (*Cono Sur*: *melocotón*) nectarine.
(d) (*Carib**: *error*) blunder, boob*.

pelona NF (a) (*calvicie*) baldness. (b) **la P~*** death.

peloso ADJ hairy.

pelota [1] NF (a) (*Dep etc*) ball; (‡) nut‡, head; **~ base** baseball; **~ de goma** (*Mil*) rubber bullet; **~ vasca** pelota; **devolver la ~ a uno** (*fig*) to turn the tables on sb; **echar ~s** (*fig*) to give it a go, let rip; **hacer la ~ a uno** (*Esp**) to suck up to sb*; **lanzar ~s fuera** (*fig*) to dodge the issue; **pasarse la ~** (*fig*) to pass the buck*; **la ~ sigue en el tejado** (*fig*) the situation is still unresolved.
(b) **~s** (‡‡) balls‡‡, bollocks‡‡; **¡las ~!** (*Cono Sur*) don't give me that!*
(c) **en ~*** stark naked; **coger** (*o* **pillar**) **a uno en ~s** to catch sb on the hop; **dejar a uno en ~** to strip sb of all that he has; (*en el juego*) to clean sb out*; **estar en ~s** (*sin dinero*) to be broke*.
(d) (*LAm‡*: *de amigos*) bunch, gang.
(e) (*CAm, Carib, Méx: pasión*) passion; **tener ~ por** to have a passion for; to be madly in love with.
(f) (*CAm, Carib, Méx: amante*) girlfriend, mistress.
(g) (‡: *en cárcel*) **estar en la ~** to be in solitary*.
[2] NMF (*) = **pelotillero**.

pelotari NM pelota player.

pelotazo NM (a) (*Dep*) (*fuerte*) fierce shot; (*largo*) long ball. (b) (*Esp‡*) drink; **pegarse un ~** to have a drink.

pelote‡ NM 5 pesetas.

pelotear [1a] [1] VT (a) *cuenta* to audit.
(b) **~ un asunto** (*And**) to turn sth over in one's mind.
(c) (*LAm**: *captar*) to catch, pick up.
[2] VI (a) (*Dep*) to knock (*o* kick) a ball about; (*Tenis*) to knock up (*before a game*).
(b) (*discutir*) to bicker, argue.

peloteo NM (*Tenis*) knock-up (*before a game*); rally, long exchange of shots; (*de notas etc*) exchange, sending back and forth; **hubo mucho ~ diplomático** there was a lot of diplomatic to-ing and fro-ing.

pelotera* NF row, scrap*, set-to*.

pelotero 1 ADJ (*) = **pelotillero**.
2 NM (a) (*LAm*) ball player, sportsman, (*esp*) footballer, baseball player. (b) (*: *lameculos*) creep‡, toady.
pelotilla* NF: **hacer la ~ a** to suck up to*, ingratiate o.s. with.
pelotilleo* NM boot-licking; favouritism.
pelotillero* 1 ADJ creeping, soapy*.
2 NM toady, creep‡, crawler; yes-man*, stooge*.
pelotón NM (a) (*pelota*) big ball.
(b) (*de hilos etc*) mass, tangle, mat.
(c) (*de personas*) knot, crowd; (*de atletas etc*) group, bunch; **~ de cabeza** leading group (of runners *etc*).
(d) (*Mil*) squad, party, detachment; **~ de abordaje** boarding party; **~ de demolición** demolition squad; **~ de ejecución**, **~ de fusilamiento** firing-squad.
pelotudo ADJ (a) (‡: *valiente*) tough, full of guts. (b) (*LAm*) *persona* (*inútil*) useless; (*tonto*) daft; (*descuidado*) slack, sloppy. (c) (*CAm**) *salsa* lumpy.
pelpa‡ NF (*LAm*) joint‡, reefer‡.
peltre NM pewter.
peluca NF (a) wig. (b) (*) dressing-down*.
peluche NM felt; plush; *V* **oso**.
peluchento ADJ silky, smooth.
peluco‡ NM clock, watch.
pelucón 1 ADJ (*And*) long-haired.
2 NM (*Cono Sur*: †) conservative; (*And*) bigwig, big shot*.
peludo 1 ADJ (a) (*gen*) hairy, shaggy; *animal* long-haired, shaggy; *furry*; *barba etc* bushy.
(b) (*CAm**: *difícil*) hard, sticky*.
2 NM (a) (*felpudo*) round mat.
(b) (*Cono Sur Zool*) (species of) armadillo.
(c) **agarrarse un ~** (*Cono Sur‡*) to get sloshed‡.
peluquearse [1a] VR (*LAm*) to have a haircut.
peluquería NF hairdresser's, barber's (shop), barber-shop (*US*).
peluquero NM (*de mujeres*) hairdresser; (*de hombres*) barber.
peluquín NM hairpiece, toupée; **ni hablar del ~** it's out of the question.
pelusa NF (a) (*Bot*) down; (*en cara*) down, fuzz; (*de paño*) fluff; (*bajo mueble etc*) fluff, dust. (b) (*: entre niños*) envy, jealousy.
pelusiento ADJ (*And, Carib*) hairy, shaggy.
peluso‡ NM (*Mil*) squaddie*, recruit.
pélvico ADJ pelvic.
pelvis NF pelvis.
peme* NM military policeman.
PEMEX ['pemeks] NM ABR *de* **Petróleos Mexicanos**.
PEN ['pen] NM (a) (*Esp*) ABR *de* **Plan Energético Nacional**. (b) (*Argentina*) ABR *de* **Poder Ejecutivo Nacional**.

▼ **pena** NF (a) (*tristeza*) grief, sadness, sorrow; (*congoja*) distress; (*malestar*) anxiety; (*sentimiento*) regret; **¡allá ~s!** I don't care!, that's not my worry!; **un partido sin ~ ni gloria** an ordinary sort of game; **pasó sin ~ ni gloria** it happened unnoticed, it happened but left no impression; **¡qué ~!** what a shame!; **es una ~** it's a shame, it's a pity (*que* that); **me dan ~** I'm sorry for them; **da ~ verlos así** it grieves me to see them like that; **da ~ que no vengan más** it's a pity they don't come more often; **me da (mucha) ~** (*Méx*) I'm (very) sorry; **merecer la ~**, **valer la ~** to be worth while; **no merece la ~** it's not worth the trouble; **merece la ~ (de) ir a verlo** it's worth taking the trouble to go and see it, it's worth seeing; **morir de ~** to die of a broken heart.
(b) (*: dolor*) pain; **tener una ~** to have a pain.
(c) (*dificultad*) trouble; **~s** hardships; toil; **alma en ~** soul in torment; **a duras ~s** (*con dificultad*) with great difficulty; (*apenas*) hardly, scarcely; **ahorrarse la ~** to save o.s. the trouble; **pasar las ~s del purgatorio** (*fig*) to go through hell; **con muchas ~s llegamos a la cumbre** after much toil we reached the top.
(d) (*Jur*) punishment, penalty; (*Com*) penalty; **~ capital** capital punishment; **~ de muerte** death penalty; **~ pecuniaria** fine; **bajo ~ de**, **so ~ de** on pain of, on penalty of.
(e) (*LAm*) (*timidez*) bashfulness, shyness, timidity; (*vergüenza*) embarrassment; **sentir (o tener) ~** (*tímido*) to be bashful, be shy; (*vergüenza*) to be ashamed; (*incómodo*) to be embarrassed, be ill at ease.
(f) (*And*) ghost.
penable ADJ punishable (by law).
penacho NM (a) (*Orn*) tuft, crest; (*en casco*) plume. (b) (*de humo etc*) plume; wreath. (c) (*fig*) pride, arrogance.
penado 1 ADJ = **penoso**.
2 NM convict.
penal 1 ADJ penal; criminal.
2 NM (a) (*prisión*) prison. (b) (*LAm Dep*) foul (in the penalty area); penalty (kick).
penales* NM INVAR police record.
penalidad NF (a) (*trabajos*) trouble, hardship. (b) (*Jur*) penalty, pun-

ishment.
penalista NMF penologist, expert in criminal law.
penalización NF (a) penalty; penalization; **recorrido sin penalizaciones** (*Dep*) clear round. (b) criminalization.
penalizar [1f] VT (a) (*penar*) to penalize. (b) (*hacer criminal*) to criminalize.
penalti NM, PL **~s**, **penálty** NM, PL **penálty(e)s**, **penalties** (*etc*) penalty (kick); **casarse de ~*** to have a shotgun wedding; **marcar de ~** to score from a penalty; **pitar ~**, **señalar ~** to award a penalty; **transformar un ~** to convert a penalty.
penar [1a] 1 VT to penalize; to punish.
2 VI (a) (*gen*) to suffer; (*alma*) to be in torment; **~ de amores** to be unhappy in love, go through the pains of love; **ella pena por todos** she takes everybody's sufferings upon herself.
(b) **~ por** to pine for, long for.
(c) (*And*: *ver fantasmas*) to see ghosts.
3 **penarse** VR to grieve, mourn.
penca NF (a) (*Bot*: *hoja*) fleshy leaf; main rib of a leaf; (*LAm*) palm leaf; (*chumbera*) prickly pear; (*Carib*) fan; (*Méx*: *de cuchillo*) blade.
(b) **hacerse de ~s** to have to be coaxed into doing something.
(c) (*And*) **~ de hombre/mujer** a fine-looking man/woman; **una ~ de casa** a great big house.
(d) **agarrar una ~** (*LAm**) to get drunk.
(e) (*LAm‡*) prick‡.
pencar‡ [1g] VI to slog away, work hard.
pencazo* NM (*CAm*) (*golpe*) smack; **cayó un ~ de agua** it pelted down, the skies opened.
penco 1 ADJ (*CAm**: *trabajador*) hard-working.
2 NM (a) (*CAm*, *Méx*: *caballo*) horse. (b) (*And*) **un ~ de hombre** a fine-looking man. (c) (*Carib‡*) poof‡, queer‡.
pendango ADJ (*Carib*) effeminate; cowardly.
pendejada NF (*LAm*) (a) (*acto*) (*disparate*) foolish act; (*cobardía*) cowardly act. (b) (*molestia*) curse, nuisance. (c) (*cualidad*) (*necedad*) foolishness, stupidity; (*cobardía*) cowardliness.
pendejear [1a] VI (*And, Méx*) to act the fool; to act irresponsibly.
pendejeta NMF (*And*) idiot.
pendejo 1 ADJ (a) (*LAm*) (*necio*) silly, stupid; (*irresponsable*) irresponsible; (*despreciable*) contemptible; (*cobarde*) cowardly, yellow.
(b) (*And**) (*listo*) smart; (*taimado*) cunning.
(c) (*Carib*, *Méx* ‡: *torpe*) ham-fisted.
2 NM (a) (*Cono Sur**) (*muchacho*) kid*, lad; (*sabelotodo*) know-all.
(b) (*LAm**: *del pubis*) pubic hair.
(c) (*LAm**) (*imbécil*) berk‡, idiot; (*cobarde*) wet*, coward.
pendencia NF quarrel; fight, brawl; **armar ~** to fight, brawl; to stir up trouble.
pendenciero 1 ADJ quarrelsome, argumentative; brawling, given to fighting.
2 NM rowdy, lout, tough*.
pender [2a] VI (a) (*gen*) to hang (*de, en* from; *sobre* over); to hang down, dangle; to droop.
(b) (*Jur*) to be pending.
(c) **~ sobre** (*fig*: *amenaza etc*) to hang over.
pendiente 1 ADJ (a) (*colgado*) hanging; **estar ~** to be hanging; to hang, dangle.
(b) (*fig*) *asunto* pending, unsettled; *cuenta* outstanding, unpaid; (*Univ*) *asignatura* to be retaken; **tener una asignatura ~** to have to resit a subject.
(c) (*fig*) **estar ~ de un cabello** to hang by a thread; **estar ~ de los labios de uno** to hang on sb's lips (*o* words); **estamos ~s de lo que él decida** we are dependent on what he may decide, everything hangs for us on his decision; **quedamos ~s de sus órdenes** we await your instructions.
(d) **estar ~ de un problema** (*LAm*) to be worried by a problem.
2 NM (*joya*) earring; pendant.
3 NF (*Geog*) slope, incline; (*Aut etc*) hill, slope; (*Arquit*) pitch; **estar en la ~ vital** to be over the hill.
pendil NM (woman's) cloak; **tomar el ~*** to pack up*, clear out*.
péndola NF (a) (*pluma*) pen, quill. (b) (*de puente etc*) suspension cable.
pendolear [1a] VI (a) (*LAm*: *escribir mucho*) to write a lot; (*Cono Sur*: *tener buena letra*) to write neatly. (b) (*Méx*) to be good in difficult situations, know how to manage people sensibly.
pendolista NMF penman, calligrapher.
pendón NM (a) (*estandarte*) banner, standard; pennant. (b) (*: persona*) tall shabby person. (c) (*) (*vaga*) lazy woman; (*marrana*) worthless woman, trollop, slut; (*puta*) whore. (d) **ser un ~*** to be an awkward customer*.
pendona* NF whore.
pendonear* [1a] VI to loaf around the streets.
péndulo NM pendulum.
pene NM penis.
Penélope NF Penelope.
penene NMF *V* **PNN**.

peneque [1] ADJ: **estar ~:** to be pickled**:**.
[2] NM (*Méx Culin*) stuffed tortilla.
penetrable ADJ penetrable.
penetración NF (a) (*acto*) penetration. (b) (*cualidad*) penetration, sharpness, acuteness; insight.
penetrador ADJ = **penetrante** (c).
penetrante ADJ (a) *herida* deep.
(b) *arma* sharp; *frío, viento* biting; *sonido* penetrating, piercing; *mirada* searching; sharp, penetrating; *vista* acute; *aroma* strong; *ironía etc* biting.
(c) *mente, persona* sharp, acute, keen.
penetrar [1a] [1] VT (a) *defensa, metal, roca etc* to penetrate, pierce; to permeate.
(b) *misterio etc* to fathom, grasp, see the explanation of; *secreto* to lay bare, understand; *intención* to see through, grasp; *significado* to grasp.
[2] VI (a) (*gen*) to penetrate; to go in; (*líquido etc*) to sink in, soak in; ~ **en**, ~ **entre**, ~ **por** to penetrate; **el cuchillo penetró en la carne** the knife went into (o entered, penetrated) the flesh; **penetramos poco en el mar** we did not go far out to sea; **el frío penetra en los huesos** the cold gets right into one's bones.
(b) (*persona*) to enter, go in; ~ **en** (*LAm*: a) **un cuarto** to go into a room.
(c) (*emoción etc*) to pierce; **la ingratitud penetró hondamente en su corazón** the ingratitude pierced him to the heart (o wounded him deeply).
[3] **penetrarse** VR: ~ **de** (a) (*absorber*) to become imbued with.
(b) (*Esp: comprender*) to understand fully, become fully aware of (the significance of).
peneuvista (*Esp*) [1] ADJ: **política** ~ policy of the PNV, PNV policy; *V* **PNV.**
[2] NMF member of the PNV.
penga NF (*And*) bunch of bananas.
penicilina NF penicillin.
penín* NF: **la** ~ Spain.
península NF peninsula; **P~ Ibérica** Iberian Peninsula.
peninsular [1] ADJ peninsular.
[2] NMF: **los ~es** the people(s) of the (Iberian) Peninsula.
penique NM penny.
penitencia NF (a) (*condición*) penitence.
(b) (*acto, castigo*) penance; **en** ~ as a penance; **imponer una** ~ **a uno** to give sb a penance; **hacer** ~ to do penance (*por* for); to do sth unpleasant; **ven a hacer** ~ **conmigo mañana*** come and eat with me tomorrow, but you'll have to take potluck.
penitenciado NM (*LAm*) convict.
penitencial ADJ penitential.
penitenciar [1b] VT to impose a penance on.
penitenciaría NF prison, penitentiary (*esp US*).
penitenciario [1] ADJ penitentiary, prison (*atr*).
[2] NM (*Ecl*) confessor.
penitente [1] ADJ (a) (*Ecl*) penitent. (b) (*And*) silly.
[2] NMF (*Ecl*) penitent; *see also* SEMANA SANTA .
[3] NM (*Cono Sur: pico*) rock pinnacle, isolated cone of rock; (*figura de nieve*) snowman.
penol NM yardarm.
penosamente ADV (a) (*dolorosamente*) painfully, distressingly. (b) (*con dificultad*) laboriously, with difficulty.
penoso ADJ (a) (*doloroso*) painful, distressing. (b) (*difícil*) arduous, laborious, difficult. (c) (*And, Carib, Méx: tímido*) bashful, timid, shy.
penquista (*Chile*) [1] ADJ of Concepción.
[2] NMF native (o inhabitant) of Concepción; **los ~s** the people of Concepción.
▼ **pensado** ADJ (a) **un proyecto poco** ~ a badly thought-out scheme; **lo tengo bien** ~ I have thought it over (o out) carefully; **tengo** ~ **hacerlo mañana** I have it in mind to do it tomorrow.
(b) **bien** ~ well-intentioned; **mal** ~ = **malpensado.**
(c) **en el momento menos** ~ when least expected; much sooner than one thinks.
pensador(a) NM/F thinker.
pensamiento NM (a) (*facultad*) thought; **como el** ~ (*fig*) in a flash.
(b) (*mente*) mind; **acudir** (o **venir**) **al** ~ to come to sb's mind; **envenenar el** ~ **de uno** to poison sb's mind (*contra* against); **ni por** ~ I wouldn't dream of it; **no le pasó por el** ~ it never occurred to him.
(c) (*un* ~) thought; ~ **desiderativo** wishful thinking; **mal** ~ nasty thought, wicked thought; **el** ~ **de Quevedo** Quevedo's thought; **nuestro** ~ **sobre este tema** our thinking on this subject; **adivinar los ~s de uno** to read sb's thoughts.
(d) (*propósito*) idea, intention; **mi** ~ **es** + *infin* my idea is to + *infin.*
(e) (*Bot*) pansy.
pensante ADJ thinking.
▼ **pensar** [1j] [1] VT (a) (*gen*) *etc* to think; ~ **que** ... to think that ...;

cuando menos lo pensamos when we least expect it; **¿qué piensas de ella?** what do you think of her?, what is your opinion of her?; **lo pensó mejor** she thought better of it; ~ **con los pies** to talk through one's hat; **dar que** ~ **a uno** to give sb food for thought; to give sb pause; **dar que** ~ **a la gente** to arouse suspicions, set people thinking; **¡ni ~lo!** not a bit of it!, forget it!
(b) *problema etc* to think over, think out; **lo pensaré** I'll think about it; **esto es para ~lo** this needs thinking about; **pensándolo bien** on reflection, after mature consideration.
▼ (c) ~ **que** ... (*concluir*) to decide that ..., come to the conclusion that ...
▼ (d) ~ + *infin* to intend to + *infin*, plan to + *infin*, propose to + *infin.*
(e) (*ideas*) *etc* to think up, invent; **¿quién pensó este plan?** who thought this one up?
▼ [2] VI (a) (*gen*) to think; ~ **en** to think of, think about; **¿en qué piensas?** what are you thinking about?; ~ **entre sí**, ~ **para sí** to think to o.s.; ~ **sobre** to think about, think over; **sin** ~ (*sin reflexionar*) without thinking; (*imprudentemente*) rashly; (*sin querer*) involuntarily; (*de repente*) unexpectedly.
(b) ~ **en** to aim at, aspire to; **piensa en una cátedra** he's aiming at a chair.
pensativamente ADV thoughtfully, pensively.
pensativo ADJ thoughtful, pensive.
penseque* NM careless mistake, thoughtless error.
Pensilvania NF Pennsylvania.
pensión NF (a) (*Fin*) pension; allowance; ~ **alimenticia** alimony, maintenance; ~ **asistencial** state pension; ~ **contributiva** contributory pension; ~ **de invalidez** disability allowance; ~ **de retiro** retirement pension; ~ **vitalicia** annuity; ~ **de viudedad** widow's pension.
(b) (*Univ etc*) scholarship, fellowship; travel grant.
(c) (*casa de huéspedes*) boarding house, guest house, lodging house; (*para estudiantes etc*) lodgings; (*And*) bar, café.
(d) (*precio*) board and lodging; ~ **completa** full board, room and all meals; **media** ~ half board.
(e) (*fig*) drawback, snag.
(f) (*And, Cono Sur*) (*preocupación*) worry, anxiety; (*remordimiento*) regret.
pensionado [1] NM boarding school.
[2] NM, **pensionada** NF pensioner.
pensionar [1a] VT (a) (*gen*) to pension, give a pension to; *estudiante* to give a grant to. (b) (*And, Cono Sur*) (*molestar*) to bother; (*preocupar*) to worry.
pensionista NMF (a) (*jubilado*) pensioner, old-age pensioner. (b) (*huésped*) lodger, paying guest. (c) (*interno*) boarder; boarding-school pupil. (d) (*LAm*) subscriber.
pentagonal ADJ pentagonal.
pentágono NM pentagon; **el P~** the Pentagon.
pentagrama NM (*Mús*) stave, staff.
pentámetro NM pentameter.
Pentateuco NM Pentateuch.
pentatlón NM pentathlon.
pentatónico ADJ pentatonic.
Pentecostés NM (*a veces* F) (a) (*cristiano*) Whitsun, Whitsuntide; **domingo de** ~ Whit Sunday. (b) (*judío*) Pentecost.
penúltima NF (a) (*Ling*) penult. (b) **la ~*** one for the road.
penúltimo ADJ penultimate, last but one, next to last.
penumbra NF penumbra; half-light, semi-darkness; shadows; **sentado en la** ~ seated in the shadows.
penuria NF (*escasez*) shortage, dearth; (*pobreza*) poverty, penury.
peña NF (a) (*Geog*) cliff, crag; ~ **viva** bare rock, living rock.
(b) (*grupo*) group, circle; (*pey*) coterie, clique; (*LAm*) (*club*) folk club; (*fiesta*) party; ~ **deportiva** supporters' club; ~ **taurina** club of bullfighting enthusiasts; **forma parte de la** ~ he's a member of the circle; **hay** ~ **en el café los domingos** the group meets in the café on Sundays.
(c) (*And, CAm, Carib*) *V* **sordo** 1 (a).
(d) (*Cono Sur: montepío*) pawnshop.
peñascal NM rocky place; rocky hill.
peñasco NM (a) (*piedra*) large rock, boulder. (b) (*risco*) rock, crag; (*pico*) pinnacle of rock; **no se me pasó por el ~*** it never occurred to me.
peñascoso ADJ rocky, craggy.
peñazo* [1] ADJ: **¡no seas tan ~!** don't be such a pain! (*).
[2] NM pain (in the neck)*; **dar el** ~ to be a pain*, be a bore*.
peñista NMF (*Dep*) member of a supporters' club, fan, supporter.
peñón NM mass of rock; wall of rock, crag; **el P~** the Rock (of Gibraltar).
peños: NMPL ivories*, teeth.
peñusco* NM (*Carib, Cono Sur*) crowd.
peo: NM: **¡vete al ~!** go to hell!
peón NM (a) (*Téc: persona*) unskilled workman; (*Taur*) assistant; (*Agr, esp LAm*) labourer, farmhand; (*Méx: aprendiz*) apprentice; (*ayudante*)

assistant; **~ de albañil** building labourer, bricklayer's mate; **~ caminero** navvy, roadman, roadmender.
(b) (*Mil Hist*) infantryman, foot-soldier.
(c) (*Ajedrez*) pawn.
(d) (*peonza*) spinning top.
(e) (*Mec*) spindle, shaft, axle.

peonada NF **(a)** (*Agr*) day's stint; period of time spent at work. **(b)** (*personas*) gang of workmen, gang of labourers.

peonaje NM labourers (*collectively*), group of labourers; (*Taur*) assistants.

peonar [1a] VI (*Cono Sur*) to work as a labourer.

peoneta NM (*Chile: Aut*) lorry driver's mate, truck driver's mate (*US*).

peonía NF peony.

peonza NF **(a)** spinning top, whipping top. **(b)** (*: persona*) busy little person; **ser un ~** (*fig*) to be always on the go. **(c) ir a ~:** to go on foot, hoof it*.

peor ADJ Y ADV (*comp*) worse; (*superl*) worst; **~ que ~** worse and worse; **A es ~ que B** A is worse than B; **Z es el ~ de todos** Z is the worst of all; **lo ~ es que ...** the worst of it is that ...; **tendencia a ~** tendency to worsen; **cambiar para ~** to change for the worse; **llevar lo ~** to get the worst of it; **o si no, será ~ para ti** or if you don't, it will be the worse for you; **~ es nada** (*LAm*) it's better than nothing; V **mal, tanto** *etc*.

peoría NF worsening, deterioration.

Pepa NF *forma familiar de* **Josefa**; **¡viva la ~!** as if he (*etc*) cared!, and to blazes with everybody else!*; jolly good!*

pepa NF **(a)** (*LAm Bot*) seed, pip, stone; **aflojar la ~*** to spill the beans*. **(b)** (*LAm: canica*) marble. **(c)** (*And*: *mentira*) lie. **(d)** (*And*: *pillo*) rogue.

pepazo NM **(a)** (*LAm*) shot, hit, throw; accurate shot. **(b)** (*And*) = **pepa** **(c)**.

Pepe NM *forma familiar de* **José**; **ponerse como un ~*** to have a great time*.

pepe NM **(a)** (*And, Carib* *: currutaco*) dandy. **(b)** (*CAm*) feeding-bottle.

pepena NF (*Méx*) rubbish collection.

pepenado, -a NM/F (*CAm, Méx*) orphan; foundling.

pepenador(a) NM/F (*Méx*) rubbish collector, dustman; scavenger (*on rubbish tip*).

pepenar [1a] **1** VT **(a)** (*And, CAm, Méx*) (*recoger*) to pick up; (*buscar*) to search out; *basura* to search through; (*escoger*) to choose; (*obtener*) to get, obtain.
(b) (*Méx*) (*agarrar*) to grab hold of; (*registrar*) to pick through, poke about in; (*robar*) to steal; *huérfano* to take in, bring up.
2 VI (*LAm*) to scour the rubbish.

pepián NM (*And, CAm, Méx*) = **pipián**.

pepinazo* NM **(a)** (*explosión*) bang. **(b)** (*Ftbl*) screamer*, scorcher*. **(c)** (*accidente*) smash.

pepinillo NM gherkin.

pepino NM **(a)** (*Bot*) cucumber; **no se me da un ~, (no) me importa un ~** I don't care two hoots (*de* about). **(b)** (*: cabeza*) bean:, head. **(c)** (*:*) prick:*.

Pepita NF *forma familiar de* **Josefa**.

pepita NF **(a)** (*Vet*) pip; **no tener ~ en la lengua** to be outspoken, not mince words; to talk nineteen to the dozen.
(b) (*Bot*) pip.
(c) (*Min*) nugget.

Pepito NM *forma familiar de* **José**.

pepito NM **(a)** (*Culin*) meat sandwich. **(b)** (*And, CAm, Carib*) dandy.

pepitoria NF **(a)** **pollo en ~** (*Esp Culin*) fricassée of chicken. **(b)** (*fig*) hotchpotch, mixture. **(c)** (*CAm: semillas*) dried pumpkin seeds.

pepón: ADJ (*And*) good-looking, dishy*.

pepona NF large cardboard doll.

pepsina NF pepsin.

péptico ADJ peptic.

peptona NF peptone.

peque* NMF kid*, child.

pequeñajo* **1** ADJ little, tiny.
2 NM, **pequeñaja** NF (*niño*) toddler, tot.

pequeñez NF **(a)** (*tamaño*) smallness, littleness, small size; shortness; (*infancia*) infancy.
(b) (*estrechez de miras*) pettiness, small-mindedness.
(c) (*bagatela*) trifle, triviality; **preocuparse por pequeñeces** to worry about trifles.

pequeño ADJ (*gen*) small, little; *cifra* small, low; *estatura* short; **los ~s** the children, the little ones; **un castillo en ~** a miniature castle; **un negocio en ~** a small-scale business.

pequeñoburgués **1** ADJ petit bourgeois.
2 NM, **pequeñoburguesa** NF petit(e) bourgeois(e).

pequero NM (*Cono Sur*) cardsharper.

pequinés¹, -esa ADJ, NM/F Pekinese.

pequinés² NM (*perro*) Pekinese.

pera¹ NF **(a)** (*Bot*) pear; (*:*) nut:, head; **esperar a ver de qué lado**

caen las **~s** to wait and see which way the cat will jump; **partir ~s con uno** to fall out with sb; **eso es pedir ~s al olmo** that's asking the impossible; **poner a uno las ~s a cuarto** to tell sb a few home truths.
(b) (*barba*) goatee; (*Cono Sur*: *barbilla*) chin.
(c) (*de atomizador, bocina etc*) bulb.
(d) (*Elec*) (*bombilla*) bulb; (*interruptor*) switch.
(e) hacerse una ~: to wank:*; **tocarse la ~:** to sit on one's backside (doing nothing).
(f) (*: empleo*) cushy job:.
(g) (*LAm Dep*) punchball.
(h) tirarse la ~ (*And*) to play truant.

pera²* **1** ADJ INVAR elegant; classy*, posh*; **niño ~** spoiled upper-class child; (*Com, Fin*) yuppie; **es un pollo ~** (*Esp*) he's a real toff*; **fuimos a un restaurante muy ~** (*Esp*) we went to a really swish restaurant*.
2 NF: **son la ~ de buenos** they're mighty good*, they're real good*; **esto nos viene de ~** this suits us fine.

pera³: NM fence*, receiver (of stolen goods).

peral NM pear-tree.

peraltado **1** ADJ canted, sloping; banked, cambered.
2 NM = **peralte**.

peralte NM (*Arquit*) cant, slope; (*de carretera*) banking, camber.

perca NF (*Pez*) perch.

percal NM, **percala** NF (*And, Méx*) **(a)** percale; **conocer el ~*** to know what the score is*. **(b)** (*: dinero*) bread:, money.

percán NM (*Cono Sur*) mould.

percance NM **(a)** (*gen*) misfortune, mishap; accident; (*de plan etc*) setback, hitch; **sufrir un ~, tener un ~** to have a mishap. **(b)** (*Fin*) perquisite.

percanque NM (*Cono Sur*) mould.

per cápita ADV per capita.

percatarse [1a] VR: **~ de** (*observar*) to notice, take note of; (*hacer caso de*) to heed; (*guardarse de*) to guard against; (*comprender*) to realize, come to understand.

percebe NM **(a)** (*Zool*) barnacle. **(b)** (*:*) idiot, twit*.

percentil NM percentile.

percepción NF **(a)** (*gen*) perception; **~ extrasensorial** extrasensory perception. **(b)** (*idea*) notion, idea. **(c)** (*Com, Fin*) collection; receipt.

perceptible ADJ **(a)** (*visible*) perceptible, noticeable, detectable. **(b)** (*Com, Fin*) payable, receivable.

perceptiblemente ADV perceptibly, noticeably.

perceptivo ADJ perceptive.

perceptor(a) NM/F recipient; (*de impuestos etc*) receiver; **~ de subsidio de desempleo** person who draws unemployment benefit.

percha NF **(a)** (*palo*) pole, support; (*perchero*) rack; coat-stand, hallstand; (*colgador*) coat-hanger; (*Orn*) perch; **vestido de ~** ready-made dress, dress off the peg; **~ de herramientas** toolrack.
(b) (*And*: *ostentación*) showiness; **tener ~** (*Cono Sur*) to be smart.
(c) (*fig*) clothes, wardrobe; (*And*: *ropa*) new clothes, smart clothing; (*Carib*) (*chaqueta*) jacket; (*traje*) suit.
(d) (*Cono Sur*: *montón*) pile.
(e) (*Méx**: *grupo*) gang.
(f) (*: tipo*) build, physique; (*de mujer*) figure.

perchero NM clothes rack, hallstand.

perchudo ADJ (*And*) smart, elegant.

percibir [3a] VT **(a)** (*notar*) to perceive, notice, detect; (*ver*) to see, observe; *peligro etc* to sense, scent; **~ que ...** to perceive that ..., observe that ...
(b) (*Com, Fin*) *sueldo* to earn, receive, get.

percollar [1a] VT (*And*) to monopolize.

percuchante NM (*And*) fool.

percudir [3a] VT (*deslustrar*) to tarnish, dull; *ropa etc* to dirty, mess up; *cutis* to spoil.

percusión NF percussion; **instrumento de ~** percussion instrument.

percusionar [1a] VT to hit, strike.

percusionista NMF percussionist, drummer.

percusor NM, **percutor** NM (*Téc*) striker, hammer.

percutir [3a] VT to strike, tap.

perdedor **1** ADJ **(a)** *baza, equipo etc* losing.
(b) (*olvidadizo*) forgetful, given to losing things.
2 NM, **perdedora** NF loser; **buen ~** good loser, good sport.

perder [2g] **1** VT **(a)** (*gen*) to lose; **¿dónde lo perdió?** where did you lose it?; **he perdido 5 kilos** I've lost 5 kilos; **he perdido la costumbre** I have got out of the habit (*y* V *costumbre*).
(b) *esfuerzo, tiempo etc* to waste; *oportunidad* to miss, lose, waste; *tren etc* to miss; (*Jur*) to lose, forfeit, give up; **no pierde nada** he doesn't miss a thing; **sin ~ un momento** without wasting a moment; **te he perdido*** I've lost you, I don't follow, I'm not with you*.
(c) (*arruinar*) to ruin, spoil; **ese vicio le perderá** that vice will be his ruin, that vice will destroy him; **ese error le perdió** that mistake was his undoing; **lo que le pierde es ...** where he comes unstuck is ...

(d) (*Univ*) *asignatura* to fail.

2 VI **(a)** (*gen*) to lose; **el equipo perdió por 2-5** the team lost 2-5; **salir perdiendo** to lose, be the loser; to lose on a deal; **saber ~, tener buen ~** to be a good loser; **tienen todas las de ~** they're on a hiding to nothing.

(b) (*decaer*) to decline, deteriorate, go down(hill); (*perder influencia*) to lose influence; **ha perdido mucho en mi estimación** he has gone down a lot in my estimation; **era guapísimo, pero ha perdido bastante** he used to be very good-looking, but he's deteriorated quite a bit.

(c) (*tela*) to fade, discolour.

(d) **echar a ~** *comida etc* to spoil, ruin; *oportunidad* to waste; **echarse a ~** to be spoiled, be ruined; to go downhill.

3 **perderse** VR **(a)** (*errar el camino*) to get lost (*t fig*), lose o.s.; to stray; to lose one's way; **¡piérdete!*** get lost!**;** **se perdieron en el bosque** they got lost in the wood; **se perdió en un mar de contradicciones** he got lost in a mass of contradictions; **¿qué se les ha perdido en Eslobodia?*** what business have they (to be) in Slobodia?

(b) (*desaparecer*) to disappear, be lost (to view); **el tren se perdió en la niebla** the train disappeared into the fog, the train was lost to sight in the fog; **el arroyo se pierde en la roca** the stream disappears into the rock.

(c) (*desperdiciarse*) to be wasted; to go (*o* run) to waste; **nada se pierde con intentar** there's no harm in trying.

(d) (*arruinarse*) to be ruined, get spoiled; **con la lluvia se ha perdido la mitad de la cosecha** with so much rain half the crop has been ruined (*o* lost).

(e) (*Náut*) to sink, be wrecked.

(f) (*persona*) to be ruined; **se perdió por el juego** he was ruined through gambling.

(g) **~ por** to be mad about, long for; **~ por** + *infin* to be mad keen to + *infin*, long to + *infin*.

(h) (*LAm**: *prostituirse*) to go on the streets.

(i) **¡no te lo pierdas!** don't miss it!; **no se pierde ni una** she doesn't miss out on anything.

perdición NF perdition (*t Rel*), undoing, ruin; **fue su ~** it was his undoing; **será mi ~** it will be the ruin of me.

perdida NF loose woman.

▼ **pérdida** NF (*gen*) loss; (*de tiempo etc*) waste; (*Jur*) forfeiture, loss; (*de líquido etc*) wastage; **~s** (*Fin, Mil etc*) losses; **~ de conocimiento** loss of consciousness; **~ contable** book loss; **~ efectiva** actual loss; **a ~ de vista** as far as the eye can see; **entrar en ~** (*Aer*) to stall; **¡no tiene ~!** you can't miss!, you can't go wrong!; **vender algo con ~** to sell sth at a loss.

perdidamente ADV: **~ enamorado** passionately in love, hopelessly in love.

perdidizo ADJ: **hacer algo ~** to hide sth away, deliberately lose sth; **hacerse el ~** (*en juego*) to lose deliberately; (*irse*) to make o.s. scarce, slip away.

perdido **1** ADJ **(a)** (*gen*) lost; *bala* stray; *momentos* idle; spare; **dar algo por ~** to give sth up for lost; **darse por ~** to give o.s. up for lost.

(b) (*vicioso*) vicious; incorrigible; *borracho etc* inveterate, hardened; (*Med*) terminally ill; **es un loco ~** he's a raving lunatic; **es un caso ~** he (*etc*) is a hopeless case; **de ~s, al río** in for a penny, in for a pound.

(c) **estar ~ por** to be mad about, be crazy about.

(d) **ponerse ~ de barro** to get covered in mud, be mud all over; **puso ~ su pantalón** he ruined his trousers.

(e) (*LAm*) (*vago*) idle; (*pobre*) down and out.

2 NM **(a)** **hacerse el ~** to make o.s. scarce, slip away.

(b) (*libertino*) rake, libertine, profligate.

perdidoso ADJ **(a)** (*que pierde etc*) losing. **(b)** (*que se pierde fácilmente*) easily lost, easily mislaid.

perdigar [1h] VT to half-cook, brown.

perdigón NM **(a)** (*Orn*) young partridge. **(b)** (*balita*) pellet; **~ zorrero** buckshot; **perdigones** shot, pellets.

perdigonada NF **(a)** (*disparo*) shot. **(b)** (*herida*) shotgun wound.

perdigonazo NM (*impacto*) blast of shot; (*herida*) shotgun wound.

perdiguero **1** ADJ: **perro ~** gundog.

2 NM gundog.

perdis* NM rake.

perdiz NF partridge; **~ blanca, ~ nival** ptarmigan.

perdón NM (*gen*) pardon (*t Jur*), forgiveness; (*indulto*) mercy; (*de pecado etc*) remission; **¡~!** sorry!, I beg your pardon!; **¡le pido ~!** I am so sorry!, do forgive me!; **pedir ~ a uno** to ask sb's forgiveness, apologize to sb; **con ~** if I may, if you don't mind, by your leave; excuse me; **con ~ de los presentes** present company excepted; **hablando con ~** if I may say so, if you'll pardon the expression; **no cabe ~** it's inexcusable.

perdonable ADJ pardonable, excusable.

perdonador ADJ forgiving.

▼ **perdonar** [1a] VTI **(a)** *ofensa etc, persona* to pardon (*t Jur*), forgive, excuse; **¡perdone (Vd)!** sorry!, I beg your pardon!!; **perdone, pero me parece que ...** excuse me, but I think ...; **perdónanos nuestras deudas** forgive us our trespasses; **Dios le haya perdonado** may God have mercy on him; **no perdona nada** he is wholly unforgiving; he doesn't miss a trick.

(b) **~ la vida a uno** to spare sb's life.

(c) (*de obligación etc*) to exempt, excuse; **les he perdonado las clases** I have excused them from classes.

(d) **no ~ esfuerzo** to spare no effort; **no ~ ocasión** to miss no chance (*de* + *infin* to + *infin*); **no ~ medio para** + *infin* to use all possible means to + *infin*; **sin ~ detalle** without omitting a single detail.

perdonavidas NM INVAR (*matón*) bully, tough, thug; (*suficiente*) superior person, condescending type.

perdulario **1** ADJ **(a)** (*olvidadizo*) forgetful, given to losing things. **(b)** (*descuidado*) careless, sloppy, inefficient. **(c)** (*vicioso*) vicious, dissolute.

2 NM rake.

perdurabilidad NF durability.

perdurable ADJ lasting, abiding; everlasting.

perdurar [1a] VI to last, endure, survive; to stand, still exist.

perecedero ADJ (*Com etc*) perishable; *vida etc* transitory, which must come to an end; *persona* mortal; **géneros no ~s** non-perishable goods.

perecer [2d] **1** VI to perish, die; (*objeto*) to shatter; **~ ahogado** to drown; to suffocate.

2 **perecerse** VR **(a)** **~ de risa** to die (of) laughing; **~ de envidia** to be dying of jealousy.

(b) **~ por algo** to long for, be dying for, crave; **~ por una mujer** to be crazy about a woman; **se perece por los calamares** he's passionately fond of squid; **~ por** + *infin* to long to + *infin*, be dying to + *infin*.

peregrinación NF **(a)** (*viajes*) long tour, travels; (*hum*) peregrination.

(b) (*Ecl*) pilgrimage; **ir en ~** to go on a pilgrimage, make a pilgrimage (*a* to).

peregrinar [1a] VI **(a)** (*ir*) to go to and fro; (*viajar*) to travel extensively (abroad). **(b)** (*Ecl*) to go on a pilgrimage (*a* to).

peregrino **1** ADJ **(a)** *persona* wandering; travelling; *ave* migratory.

(b) *costumbre, planta etc* alien, newly introduced; adventitious.

(c) (*fig: raro*) odd, strange, surprising.

(d) (*fig: excepcional*) fine, extraordinary, rare; (*exótico*) exotic.

2 NM, **peregrina** NF pilgrim.

perejil NM **(a)** (*Bot*) parsley.

(b) **~es** (*Cos** etc*) buttons and bows, trimmings, fripperies.

(c) **~es** (**: *títulos*) extra titles, handles (to one's name)*.

(d) **andar como ~** (*Cono Sur*) to be shabbily dressed.

perendengue NM **(a)** (*adorno*) trinket, cheap ornament; silly adornment.

(b) (**) **~s** (*pegas*) snags, problems; **el problema tiene sus ~s** the question has its tricky points; **un proyecto de muchos ~s** a plan with a lot of snags.

(c) **~s** (**: *categoría*) (high) standing, importance.

(d) **~s** (**: *valor*) bravery; spirit, guts.

perengano, -a NM/F somebody or other, someone or other.

perenne ADJ everlasting, constant, perennial; (*Bot*) perennial; **de hoja ~** evergreen.

perennemente ADV everlastingly, constantly, perennially.

perennidad NF perennial nature; perpetuity.

perentoriamente ADV urgently, peremptorily.

perentorio ADJ **(a)** *orden etc* urgent, peremptory. **(b)** *plazo* set, fixed.

pereque* NM (*LAm*) nuisance, bore.

perestroika NF perestroika.

pereza NF **(a)** (*gen*) sloth, laziness; slowness; idleness. **(b)** **¡qué ~!*** (*And*) what a drag!

perezosa NF (*And, Cono Sur*) deckchair.

perezosamente ADV lazily; slowly; sluggishly.

perezoso **1** ADJ slothful, lazy; slow, sluggish, idle.

2 NM **(a)** (*Zool*) sloth. **(b)** (*Carib, Méx*) safety-pin.

perfección NF **(a)** perfection; **a la ~** to perfection. **(b)** (*acto*) completion.

perfeccionamiento NM perfection; improvement.

perfeccionar [1a] VT **(a)** (*hacer perfecto*) to perfect; (*mejorar*) to improve. **(b)** *proceso etc* to complete, finish.

perfeccionismo NM perfectionism.

perfeccionista ADJ, NMF perfectionist.

perfectamente ADV perfectly; **¡~!** precisely!, just so!; of course!

perfectibilidad NF perfectibility.

perfectible ADJ perfectible, capable of being perfected; with scope for improvement.

▼ **perfecto** **1** ADJ **(a)** (*gen*) perfect; **¡~!** fine!; **me parece ~ que lo hagan** I think it right that they should. **(b)** (*completo*) complete, finished; perfected.

[2] NM (*Ling*) perfect (tense).

pérfidamente ADV perfidiously, treacherously.

perfidia NF perfidy, treachery.

pérfido ADJ perfidious, treacherous.

perfil NM (a) (*gen*) profile (*t fig*); (*contorno*) silhouette, outline; (*Arquit, Geol etc*) section, cross section, sectional view; (*Fot*) side view; ~ **aerodinámico** streamlining; **en** ~ in profile, from the side.

(b) ~**es** (*rasgos*) features, characteristics.

(c) ~**es** (*cortesías*) social courtesies; (*retoques*) finishing touches.

perfilado ADJ well-shaped, well-finished; *rostro* long and thin; *nariz* well-formed, shapely; (*Aer*) streamlined.

perfilador NM lip pencil.

perfilar [1a] [1] VT (a) (*gen*) to outline; (*fig*) to shape, give character to; **son los lectores los que perfilan los periódicos** it is the readers who shape their newspapers.

(b) (*Aer etc*) to streamline.

(c) (*fig: rematar*) to put the finishing touches to; to round off, perfect.

[2] **perfilarse** VR (a) (*persona*) to show one's profile, give a side view; (*Taur*) to draw o.s. up (and prepare for the kill); (*edificio etc*) to show in outline, appear in silhouette (*en* against).

(b) (*fig*) to take shape; to become more definite; **el proyecto se va perfilando** the plan is taking shape.

(c) (*LAm*) to slim, get slim.

(d) (*Cono Sur Dep*) to dribble and shoot.

perforación NF (a) (*gen*) perforation; (*proceso*) piercing; drilling, boring; punching. (b) (*Min*) drilling; drill, bore.

perforadora NF punch; drill; ~ **neumática** pneumatic drill; ~ **de tarjetas** card punch.

perforar [1a] [1] VT (*gen*) to perforate; to pierce; (*pinchar*) to puncture (*t Med*); *agujero* to make, drill, bore; *pozo* to sink; *tarjeta etc* to punch, punch a hole in; *ficha* to punch.

[2] VI (*Min*) to drill, bore.

perforista NMF (*Inform*) card puncher.

performance [per'formans] NF (*Aut, Mec*) performance.

perfumado ADJ scented; sweet-smelling.

perfumador NM perfume spray.

perfumar [1a] VT to scent, perfume.

perfume NM scent, perfume.

perfumería NF perfume shop; perfumery.

perfumista [1] ADJ *empresa* perfumery.

[2] NMF perfumer.

pergamino NM parchment; **una familia de muchos** ~**s** a very blue-blooded family, a very ancient family.

pergenio* NM (*Cono Sur: hum*) bright boy, clever kid*.

pergeñar [1a] VT (a) (*gen*) to sketch; to do roughly, do in rough; *texto etc* to do a draft of, prepare. (b) (*: *arreglar*) *cita etc* to fix up, arrange.

(c) (*Cono Sur**) *persona* to eye from head to toe.

pergeño NM aspect, appearance.

pérgola NF pergola.

peri... PREF peri...

perica NF (a) (*And, CAm*) (*navaja*) razor, knife; (*machete*) machete; (*espada*) short sword. (b) **agarrar una** ~ (*And, CAm**) to get sloshed*.

(c) (‡) (*chica*) bird‡; (*puta*) whore. (d) (‡: *droga*) cocaine, snow‡.

pericia NF skill, skilfulness; expertness, expertise.

pericial ADJ expert; **tasación** ~ expert valuation; **testigo** ~ expert witness.

periclitar [1a] VI (*liter*) (a) (*peligrar*) to be in danger. (b) (*declinar*) to decay, decline; (*quedar anticuado*) to become outmoded; **ésos quedan ya periclitados** those are out of date now.

Perico NM *forma familiar de* **Pedro**; ~ **el de los palotes** (*Esp*) anybody, somebody; so-and-so; any Tom, Dick or Harry; **ser p**~ **entre ellas** to be a ladies' man.

perico NM (a) (*Orn*) parakeet.

(b) (*peluca*) wig, toupé.

(c) (*: *orinal*) chamberpot.

(d) (‡: *puta*) whore, slut.

(e) (‡: *droga*) snow‡, cocaine.

(f) (*And*) coffee with a dash of milk.

(g) (*huevos*) ~**s** (*And, Carib*) scrambled eggs with fried onions.

pericote NM (a) (*And, Cono Sur: ratón*) large rat. (b) (*And, Cono Sur**: *niño*) kid*, nipper*.

periferia NF (a) (*gen*) periphery; (*de ciudad*) outskirts. (b) **los que viven en la** ~ **social** those who live on the fringes of society. (c) (*Inform*) peripherals.

periférico [1] ADJ peripheral; marginal; *barrio etc* outlying, on the outskirts; **carretera periférica** ring-road.

[2] NM (a) (*Méx Aut*) ring-road. (b) ~**s** (*Inform*) peripherals.

perifollo NM (a) (*Bot*) chervil. (b) ~**s** (*adornos*) buttons and bows, trimmings, fripperies.

perífrasis NF INVAR periphrasis.

perifrástico ADJ periphrastic.

perilla NF (*joya*) pear-shaped ornament, drop; (*Elec*) switch; (*Méx: manija*) handle; (*tirador*) doorknob; (*barba*) goatee; ~ **de la oreja** lobe of the ear; ~ **del timbre** bell-push; **venir de** ~(s) to come just right, be very welcome, be perfect.

perillán* NM rogue, rascal; **¡**~**!** (*a niño*) you rascal!

perimetral ADJ perimeter (*atr*); **vallado** ~ perimeter fence.

perímetro NM perimeter.

perinatal ADJ perinatal.

perinola [1] NF teetotum.

[2] ADV: **de** ~ (*Carib*) utterly, absolutely.

periódicamente ADV periodically.

periodicidad NF periodicity; regular recurrence, regular nature; (*Prensa*) frequency (of publication); **una revista de** ~ **mensual** a monthly review, a review which comes out monthly.

periódico [1] ADJ periodic(al); (*Mat*) recurrent.

[2] NM newspaper; periodical; ~ **del domingo** Sunday newspaper; ~ **mural** wall newspaper; ~ **de la tarde** evening newspaper.

periodicucho* NM rag*.

periodismo NM journalism; ~ **deportivo** sports journalism; ~ **gráfico** photoreportage; ~ **de investigación,** ~ **investigativo** investigative journalism.

periodista NMF journalist; (*m*) pressman, newsman, newspaperman; ~ **deportivo** sports writer; ~ **de televisión** television journalist.

periodístico ADJ journalistic; newspaper (*atr*); **estilo** ~ journalistic style, journalese; **de interés** ~ newsworthy.

periodización NF periodization.

periodo NM, **período** NM (a) (*gen*) period (*t Med*). (b) (*Ling*) sentence, period.

periodoncia NF periodontics, periodontology

peripatético ADJ peripatetic.

peripecia NF vicissitude; sudden change, unforeseen change; ~**s** vicissitudes, ups and downs; adventures, incidents.

periplo NM (long) journey, tour; (*Náut*) (long) voyage; (*errabundeo*) wanderings; (*hum*) peregrination; (*Hist*) periplus.

peripuesto* ADJ dressed up, smart; overdressed, dressy; **tan** ~ all dressed up (to the nines).

periquear* [1a] VI (*And*: *t* ~**se** VR) to get dressed up, get dolled up*.

periquete* NM: **en un** ~ in a tick.

periquito NM (a) (*Orn*) parakeet. (b) (‡: *droga*) snow‡, cocaine.

periscopio NM periscope.

perista* NM fence*, receiver (of stolen goods).

peristilo NM peristyle.

perita¹* ADJ = **pera**².

perita² N: ~ **en dulce** dainty.

peritaje NM (a) (*trabajo*) expert work; (*pericia*) expertise; (*informe*) report of an expert; specialist's report. (b) (*honorarios*) expert's fee. (c) (*formación*) professional training.

peritar [1a] VT to judge expertly, give an expert opinion on.

perito [1] ADJ skilled, skilful; expert; experienced, seasoned; ~ **en** skilled in, expert at.

[2] NM, **perita**³ NF expert; skilled person, qualified person; technician; ~ **agrónomo** agronomist; ~ **electricista** qualified electrician; ~ **forense** legal expert; ~ **en metales** metal expert, specialist in metals; ~ **testigo** (*Méx*) expert witness.

peritoneo NM peritoneum.

peritonitis NF peritonitis.

perjudicar [1g] VT (a) (*dañar*) to damage, harm, impair; *posibilidades etc* to damage, prejudice; **me perjudica que digan eso** for them to say that lowers me in the eyes of others.

(b) (*desfavorecer*) to be unbecoming to; **ese sombrero le perjudica** that hat does not become her, she doesn't look good in that hat.

(c) (*LAm*) to malign, slander.

perjudicial [1] ADJ harmful, injurious, damaging (*a, para* to); detrimental, prejudicial (*a, para* to).

[2] NM (*Méx*‡) secret policeman.

perjuicio NM damage, harm; (*Fin*) financial loss; **en** ~ **de** to the detriment of; **redundar en** ~ **de** to be detrimental to, harm; **sin** ~ **de** without prejudice to; without detriment to; **sin** ~ **de que pueda ocurrir** even though it might happen, in spite of the fact that it might happen; **sufrir grandes** ~**s** to suffer great damage.

perjurar [1a] [1] VI (a) (*Jur*) to perjure o.s., commit perjury. (b) (*jurar*) to swear a lot.

[2] **perjurarse** VR to perjure o.s.

perjurio NM perjury.

perjuro [1] ADJ perjured.

[2] NM, **perjura** NF perjurer.

perla NF (a) pearl; ~ **cultivada** cultivated pearl, cultured pearl; ~**s de imitación** imitation pearls.

(b) (*fig*) pearl (*de* of, among), gem; **me está de** ~**s, me viene de** ~**s** it comes just right; it suits me perfectly; **me parece de** ~**s** it all seems splendid to me; **ser una** ~ to be a treasure.

perlado ADJ pearly; **cebada perlada** pearl barley.
perlático ADJ paralytic, palsied.
perlesía NF paralysis, palsy.
perlífero ADJ pearl-bearing; **ostra perlífera** pearl oyster.
perlino ADJ pearly.
permagel NM permafrost.
permanecer [2d] VI (a) (gen) to stay, remain; **¿cuánto tiempo vas a ~?** how long are you staying?
(b) **~ + ADJ** to go on being + ADJ, remain + ADJ; **~ indeciso** to remain undecided, be still undecided; **~ dormido** to go on sleeping.
permanencia NF (a) (cualidad) permanence. (b) (estancia) stay; **~ en filas** (period of) military service. (c) **~s** (Escol: de profesores) obligatory administrative duties.
permanente ① ADJ permanent; constant; color fast; comisión, ejército etc standing.
② NF permanent wave, perm; **hacerse una ~** to have one's hair permed.
permanentemente ADV permanently; constantly.
permanganato NM permanganate.
permeabilidad NF permeability, pervious nature.
permeable ADJ permeable, pervious (a to).
permisible ADJ allowable, permissible.
permisionario, -a NM/F (LAm) official agent, official agency, concessionaire.
permisividad NF permissiveness; (Fin) liberal policies.
permisivo ADJ permissive.
▼ **permiso** NM (a) (gen) permission; **con (su) ~** (pidiendo ver algo etc) if I may; (queriendo entrar, pasar) excuse me; **con ~ de Vds me voy** excuse me but I must go, if you don't mind I must go; **¡permisito!** (LAm: para pasar) excuse me! **dar su ~** to give one's permission; **tener ~ para + infin** to have permission to + infin.
(b) (documento) permit, licence; **~ de armas** gun licence, firearms certificate; **~ de conducción, ~ de conducir, ~ de conductor, ~ de manejo** (LAm) driving licence; **~ de entrada** entry permit; **~ de exportación** export permit; **~ de importación** import permit; **~ de residencia** residence permit; **~ de salida** exit permit; **~ de trabajo** work permit.
(c) (Mil etc) leave; **~ de convalecencia** sick leave; **~ de (o por) maternidad, ~ por parto** maternity leave; **estar de ~** to be on leave.
permisología NF (LAm: hum) science of keeping on good terms with bureaucracy; craft of obtaining permits.
▼ **permitir** [3a] ① VT to permit, allow; to allow of; **~ a uno hacer algo** to allow sb to do sth; **¿me permite?** (¿le importa?) may I?, do you mind?; (al pasar) excuse me!; **¿me permite ver?** may I see (it)?, would you mind showing it to me? **permítame que le diga que ...** permit me to tell you that ...; **si el tiempo lo permite** weather permitting; **la fábrica permitirá una producción anual de ...** the factory will provide an annual production of ..., the factory will make possible an annual production of ...; **este método permite construir más casas** this method allows more houses to be built.
② **permitirse** VR (a) (gen) to be permitted, be allowed; **eso no se permite** that is not allowed; **si se me permite la expresión** if you'll pardon the expression; so to speak; **no se permite fumar** no smoking, you can't smoke here; **¿se permite fumar?** may I smoke?
(b) **~ algo** to permit o.s. sth; to (be able to) afford sth; **me permito 2 cigarrillos al día** I allow myself two cigarettes a day; **me permito recordarle que ...** may I remind you that ...
permuta NF barter, exchange; interchange.
permutación NF (a) (Mat etc) permutation. (b) = **permuta**.
permutar [1a] ① VT (a) (Mat etc) to permute.
(b) (cambiar) to exchange (con with, por for); to interchange (con with); **~ algo con uno** to exchange sth with sb; **~ destinos con uno** to exchange jobs with sb.
② VI: **~ con uno** to exchange (jobs) with sb, swap with sb.
pernada NF (a) (coz) kick; wild movement of the leg(s); **dar ~s** to kick out, lash out with the leg(s).
(b) (Hist) droit de seigneur.
pernear [1a] VI (a) (agitar las piernas) to shake one's legs; to kick one's legs. (b) (patear) to stamp one's foot (with rage). (c) (*: darse prisa) to hustle, get cracking*.
pernera NF trouser leg.
perneta NF: **en ~s** bare-legged, with bare legs.
perniabierto ADJ bow-legged.
perniche* NM blanket.
pernicioso ADJ pernicious (t Med); persona wicked, evil; insecto etc injurious (para to).
pernicorto ADJ short-legged.
pernigordo ADJ fat-legged.
pernil NM (a) (Zool) upper leg, haunch; (Culin) leg; (Carib) leg of pork, pork. (b) (Cos) trouser leg.
pernio NM hinge.

perno NM bolt; **estar hasta el ~** (And*) to be at the end of one's tether; to be at one's wits' end.
pernocta NF: **pase (de) ~** overnight pass.
pernoctación NF overnight stay; **con 3 pernoctaciones en hotel** with 3 nights in a hotel.
pernoctar [1a] VI to spend the night, stay for the night.
pero¹ ① CONJ (a) (gen) but; (sin embargo) yet.
(b) (*) **una chica guapa, ~ muy guapa** what you really call a pretty girl, a pretty girl and no mistake; **hizo muy mal, ~ muy mal** he was wrong, a thousand times wrong; I should jolly well say he was wrong*; **~ vamos a ver** well let's see; **¡~ que muy bien!** jolly good!*; **¡estoy ~ que muy harto!** I'm damn well fed up!*; **no había nadie, ~ que nadie** there was nobody, and I do mean nobody; **¡~ si no tiene coche!** I tell you he hasn't got a car!
② NM (a) (defecto) flaw, defect; snag; **el plan no tiene ~** there's nothing wrong with the plan, the plan hasn't any snags; **he encontrado un ~** I've found a snag.
(b) (objeción) objection; **poner ~s a** to raise objections to, find fault with; **el programa tiene dos ~s** the programme is open to two objections; **¡no hay ~ que valga!** there are no buts about it!
pero² NM (And, Cono Sur) pear tree.
perogrullada NF platitude, truism.
perogrullesco ADJ platitudinous.
Perogrullo NM, **Pero Grullo** NM: **verdad de ~** platitude, truism.
perol NM pan; (Carib: cacerola) saucepan; (Cono Sur, Méx: para poner al horno) metal casserole dish; (Carib: útil) kitchen utensil; (Carib: fig) piece of junk, worthless object.
perola NF saucepan.
perolero NM (a) (Carib: hojalatero) tinsmith. (b) (objetos) pile of junk; collection of odds and ends.
peronacho* NM (Cono Sur: pey) Peronist.
peroné NM fibula.
peronismo NM Peronism.

┌─── **PERONISMO** ───────────────────────────────
ⓘ *General Juan Domingo Perón (1895-1974) came to power in Argentina in 1946, on a social justice platform known as justicialismo. He aimed to break Argentina's dependence on exports by developing the domestic economy through state-led industrialization. Peronismo stood for nationalization of industry, trade unions, paid holidays, the welfare state, and the provision of affordable housing. Women were given the vote in 1947, a move championed by Perón's charismatic wife "Evita" (María Eva Duarte), who was extremely popular in certain circles and became a major public figure. Following her premature death from cancer in 1952, Perón's support began to crumble and he was driven into exile in 1955. His party was banned for almost a decade and did not regain power until 1973, when he was recalled from exile to become President. He died the following year and was succeeded by his second wife Isabel Martínez, who was ousted in a military coup in 1976. Peronismo as a movement has survived, and the Peronist party returned to power in 1989 under Carlos Menem.*
└──

peronista ADJ, NMF Peronist.
peroración NF (a) (discurso) peroration, speech; long speech. (b) (conclusión) conclusion of a speech.
perorar [1a] VI to make a speech; (hum) to orate, spout.
perorata NF long-winded speech; violent speech, harangue.
peróxido NM peroxide; **~ de hidrógeno** hydrogen peroxide.
perpendicular ① ADJ (a) perpendicular (a to).
(b) (en ángulo recto) at right angles (a to); **el camino es ~ al río** the road is at right angles to the river.
② NF perpendicular; vertical; **salir de la ~** to be out of the perpendicular (o vertical).
perpendicularmente ADV perpendicularly; vertically.
perpetración NF perpetration.
perpetrador(a) NM/F perpetrator.
perpetrar [1a] VT to perpetrate.
perpetuación NF perpetuation.
perpetuamente ADV perpetually; everlastingly, ceaselessly.
perpetuar [1e] VT to perpetuate.
perpetuidad NF perpetuity; **a ~** in perpetuity, for ever; **condena a ~** life sentence, sentence of life imprisonment; **le condenaron a prisión a ~** he was sentenced to life imprisonment.
perpetuo ADJ perpetual; everlasting; ceaseless; condena, exilio etc life (atr); (Bot) everlasting.
Perpiñán NM Perpignan.
perplejamente ADV perplexedly; in a puzzled way; in perplexity.
perplejidad NF (a) (gen) perplexity; bewilderment; puzzlement; hesitation. (b) (situación) perplexing situation; dilemma.
perplejo ADJ perplexed; bewildered; puzzled; **me miró ~** he looked at me in perplexity, he looked at me in a puzzled way; **dejar a uno ~** to perplex sb, puzzle sb; **se quedó ~ un momento** he looked perplexed for a moment, he hesitated a moment.

perra NF **(a)** (*Zool*) bitch; female dog, lady dog (*euf*); **~ salida** bitch on heat.
(b) (*Esp* Fin*) **~ chica** 5-céntimo coin; **~ gorda** 10-céntimo coin; **~s** small change; **costó unas ~s** it cost a few coppers; **no tener una ~** to be flat broke*.
(c) (*: *rabieta*) tantrum, pet; **el niño cogió una ~** the child had a tantrum, the child began to cry violently.
(d) (*: *manía*) mania, crazy idea; **está con la ~ de un abrigo de pieles** she's got the crazy idea that she must have a fur coat; **le cogió la ~ de ir a Eslobodia** he got an obsession (*o* thing*) about going to Slobodia.
(e) (*Cono Sur*) (*sombrero*) old hat; (*cantimplora*) leather water bottle.
perrada NF **(a)** (*perros*) pack of dogs. **(b)** (*: *acción*) dirty trick.
perraje NM (*And*) pack of dogs; (*) people of humble origins; lower orders, lower ranks.
perramus NM (*And, Cono Sur*) raincoat.
perrera[1] NF **(a)** (*para perros*) kennel; kennels; (*hum*) remand centre.
(b) (*carro*) cart in which stray dogs are picked up.
(c) (*trabajo*) badly-paid job; drudgery, grind.
(d) (*: *rabieta*) = **perra (c)**.
(e) (*Carib*) row, shindy.
perrería NF **(a)** (*perros*) pack of dogs; (*fig*) gang of villains.
(b) (*palabra*) harsh word, angry word; **decir ~s de uno** to say harsh things about sb.
(c) (*: *trampa*) dirty trick.
perrero, -a[2] NM/F dog catcher.
perrillo NM **(a)** (*perro joven*) puppy; (*raza pequeña*) small (breed of) dog; miniature dog; (*diminutivo sentimental*) doggie. **(b)** (*Mil*) trigger.
perrito, -a[1] NM/F puppy.
[2] NM: **~ caliente** hot dog.
perro[1] NM **(a)** (*Zool*) dog; **'~ peligroso'** 'beware of the dog'; **~ afgano** Afghan hound; **~ de agua** (*CAm*) coypu; **~ de aguas** spaniel; **~ antiexplosivos** sniffer dog; **~ buscadrogas** sniffer dog; **~ callejero** mongrel; **~ de caza** hunting dog; **~ de ciego**, **~ de guía**, **~ lazarillo** guide-dog; **~ cobrador** retriever; **~ dálmata** dalmatian; **~ danés** Great Dane; **~ dogo** bulldog; **~ esquimal** husky; **~ faldero** lapdog; **~ guardián** watchdog; **~ del hortelano** dog in the manger; **~ de lanas** poodle; **~ lebrel** whippet; **~ lobo** alsatian; wolfhound; **~ marino** dogfish; **~ de muestra** pointer, setter; **~ pastor** sheepdog; **~ pequinés** Pekinese; **~ policía** police dog; **~ de presa** bulldog; **~ raposero** foxhound; fox-terrier; **~ rastreador**, **~ rastrero** tracker dog; **~ salchicha*** sausage dog; **~ (de) San Bernardo** St Bernard; **~ tejonero** dachshund; **~ de Terranova** Newfoundland dog; **~ de trineo** husky; **~ vagabundo** stray (dog); **~ zorrero** foxhound; fox-terrier.
(b) (*locuciones*) **ser ~ viejo** to be an old hand; to be an old fox; **tiempo de ~s** dirty weather, awful weather; **¡a otro ~ con ese hueso!** tell that to the marines!; **atar ~s con longaniza** to court disaster; **darse a ~s** to get wild; **echar los ~s a uno*** to come down on sb like a ton of bricks; **echar a uno los ~s encima** to persecute sb, keep after sb; **echar una hora a ~s** to waste a whole hour, get absolutely nothing done in an hour; **hacer ~ muerto** (*And*) to avoid paying; **heder a ~ muerto** to stink to high heaven; **se llevan como ~s y gatos** they're always squabbling; **meter los ~s en danza** to set the cat among the pigeons; **¿qué ~ te mordió?** (*Carib**) what's up with you?*; what's got into you?; **~ que ladra no muerde**, **~ ladrador, poco mordedor** his bark is worse than his bite; **ser como ~ en misa** to be wholly out of place; **a ~ flaco no le faltan pulgas** it never rains but it pours; **tratar a alguien como a un perro** to treat sb like dirt.
(c) (*pey*) dog, swine, hound.
(d) (*And*) drowsiness.
(e) (*Cono Sur*) clothes-peg.
(f) (*Culin*) **~ caliente** hot dog.
[2] ADJ (*) awful, wretched; **esta perra vida** this wretched life; **he pasado una temporada perra** I've had a ghastly time*.
perro-guía NM, PL **perros-guía** guide-dog.
perrona NF (†: *moneda*) 10 céntimos; **de (a) ~*** cheapo*, cheap.
perronero* ADJ cheapo*, cheap.
perrucho NM (*pey*) hound, cur.
perruna NF dog biscuit.
perruno ADJ canine, dog (*atr*); **devoción** etc doglike.
persa[1] ADJ, NMF Persian.
[2] NM (*Ling*) Persian.
[3] NF (*Cono Sur*) cut-price store.
per saecula saeculorum ADV, **per secula seculorum** ADV for ever and ever.
persecución NF **(a)** (*acoso*) pursuit, hunt, chase; **~ individual** (*Ciclismo*) individual pursuit; **~ sexual** sexual harrassment; **estar en plena ~** to be in full cry. **(b)** (*Ecl, Pol etc*) persecution.
persecutorio ADJ: **manía persecutoria** persecution mania; **trato ~** cruel treatment.

perseguible ADJ **(a)** (*Jur*) *delito* indictable; *persona* liable to prosecution; **~ a instancia de parte** liable to private prosecution; **~ de oficio** liable to prosecution by the state.
perseguidor(a) NM/F **(a)** (*gen*) pursuer. **(b)** (*Ecl, Pol etc*) persecutor.
perseguimiento NM pursuit, hunt, chase; **en ~ de** in pursuit of.
perseguir [3d *y* 3k] VT **(a)** *caza, fugitivo* to pursue, hunt, chase; to hunt out, hunt down.
(b) (*fig*) *chica, empleo etc* to chase after, go after; *propósito* to pursue; **la persiguió durante 2 años** he was after her for 2 years, he pursued her for 2 years.
(c) (*Ecl, Pol etc*) to persecute; (*fig*) to persecute, harass; to pester, annoy; **me persiguieron hasta que dije que sí** they pestered me until I said yes; **le persiguen los remordimientos** he is gnawed by remorse, his conscience pricks him constantly; **le persigue la mala suerte** he is dogged by ill luck.
perseverancia NF perseverance, persistence.
perseverante ADJ persevering, persistent.
perseverantemente ADV perseveringly.
perseverar [1a] VI to persevere, keep on, persist; **~ en** to persevere in, persist with.
Persia NF Persia.
persiana NF (*Venetian*) blind; slatted shutter (*t* **~ enrollable**).
persignarse [1a] VR to cross o.s.
persistencia NF persistence.
persistente ADJ persistent.
persistentemente ADV persistently.
persistir [3a] VI to persist (*en* in; *en + infin* in + *ger*).
persoga NF (*CAm, Méx*) halter (of plaited vegetable fibre).
persona NF person; **20 ~s** 20 people; **aquellas ~s que lo deseen** those who wish; **es para animales y no para ~s** it's for animals not people; **es buena ~** he's a good sort, he's a decent chap*; **tercera ~** third party; (*Ling*) third person; **un pronombre de primera ~** a first person pronoun; **~ física** (*Jur*) natural person; **~ no grata** persona non grata; **~ de historia** person with a past, dubious individual; **~ jurídica** legal entity; **~s reales** royalty, king and queen; **en ~** in person; in the flesh; **en la ~ de** in the person of; **3 caramelos por ~** 3 sweets per person, 3 sweets each; **pagaron 2 dólares por ~** they paid 2 dollars a head (*o* each).

PERSONA	*ver también la entrada*

Mientras que *persona* en singular se traduce por *person*, el plural tiene dos traducciones: *people* y *persons*.
● *People* es la forma más utilizada, ya que *persons* se emplea solamente en el lenguaje formal o técnico. Las dos formas llevan el verbo en plural:
    Acaban de llegar tres personas preguntando por un tal Sr. Oliva
    Three people have just arrived asking for a Mr Oliva
    "Peso máximo: 8 personas"
    "Weight limit: 8 persons"
Para otros usos y ejemplos ver la entrada.

---

personaje NM **(a)** (*sujeto notable*) personage, important person; celebrity; **ser un ~** to be somebody, be important.
(b) (*Liter, Teat etc*) character.
personajillo NM insignificant person; minor character; (*hum*) minor celebrity.
personal[1] ADJ **(a)** (*gen*) personal.
(b) *habitación, asiento* etc single, for one person.
[2] NM **(a)** (*plantilla*) personnel, staff; (*total*) establishment; (*esp Mil*) force; (*Náut*) crew, complement; **~ de cabina** cabin staff; **~ de exterior** surface workers; **~ de interior** underground workers; **~ de servicios** maintenance staff; **~ de tierra** (*Aer*) ground-crew, groundstaff; **estar falto de ~** to be short-handed; **quedarse con el ~*** to make a hit with people.
(b) (*) **el ~** people; the public; **había exceso de ~ en el cine** there were too many people in the cinema.
[3] NF (*Dep*) foul.
personalidad NF **(a)** (*gen*) personality; **~ desdoblada** split personality. **(b)** (*Jur*) legal entity.
personalísimo ADJ intensely personal, highly individualistic.
personalismo NM **(a)** (*observación*) personal reference; **tenemos que proceder sin ~s** we must proceed without indulging in personalities (*o* personal attacks).
(b) (*egoísmo*) selfishness, egoism.
(c) (*parcialidad*) personal preference, partiality; **obrar sin ~s** to act with partiality towards none, act fairly with regard to the persons involved.
personalizar [1f] [1] VT to personalize; *virtud etc* to embody, personify.
[2] VI to make a personal reference.
[3] **personalizarse** VR to become personal.
▼ **personalmente** ADV personally.

► LENGUA Y USO: **personalmente** → 53.5

personarse [1a] VR to appear in person; **~ en** to present o.s. at; to report to; **~ en forma** (*Jur*) to be officially represented; **el juez se personó en el lugar del accidente** the judge made an official visit to the scene of the accident.

personería NF (a) (*Cono Sur*) (*personalidad*) personality; (*talento*) aptitude, talent. (b) (*LAm Jur*) proxy.

personero, -a NM/F (*LAm*) spokesperson; representative; (*Jur*) proxy.

personificación NF personification; embodiment.

personificar [1g] VT (a) (*encarnar*) to personify; to embody, be the embodiment of.

(b) **en esta mujer el autor personifica la maldad** the author makes this woman a symbol of wickedness.

(c) (*en discurso etc*) to single out for special mention.

perspectiva NF (a) (*Arte y fig*) perspective; **en ~** in perspective; **le falta ~** he lacks a sense of perspective.

(b) (*vista*) view, scene, panorama.

(c) (*porvenir etc*) outlook, prospect; future development; 'buenas **~s de mejora**' (*anuncio*) 'good prospects'; **las ~s de la cosecha son favorables** the harvest outlook is good; **es una ~ nada halagüeña** it's a most unwelcome prospect; **se alegró con la ~ de pasar un día en el campo** he cheered up with the prospect of spending a day in the country; **encontrarse ante la ~ de** + *infin* to be faced with the prospect of + *ger*; **tener algo en ~** to have sth in view, have a prospect of sth; **hay ocupaciones en ~** there's a busy time ahead.

perspicacia NF (a) (*agudeza de vista*) keen-sightedness. (b) (*fig*) perspicacity, shrewdness, discernment.

perspicaz ADJ (a) *vista* keen; *persona* keen-sighted. (b) (*fig*) perspicacious, shrewd, discerning.

perspicuidad NF perspicuity, clarity.

perspicuo ADJ clear, intelligible.

persuadir [3a] ① VT to persuade; to convince, prevail upon; **~ a uno a hacer algo** to persuade sb to do sth; **dejarse ~** to allow o.s. to be persuaded.

② **persuadirse** VR to be persuaded, become convinced.

persuasión NF (a) (*acto*) persuasion. (b) (*estado*) conviction; **tener la ~ de que ...** to have the conviction that ..., be convinced that ...

persuasiva NF persuasiveness, power of persuasion.

persuasivo ADJ persuasive; convincing.

pertenecer [2d] VI (a) (*gen*) to belong (*a* to). (b) (*fig*) **~ a** to concern; to apply to, pertain to; **le pertenece a él hacerlo** it's his job to do it.

perteneciente ADJ (a) **los países ~s** the member countries, the countries which belong; **las personas ~s al organismo** persons who are members of the organization. (b) (*relacionado*) **~ a** pertaining to, relevant to.

pertenencia NF (a) (*gen*) ownership; **las cosas de su ~** the things which belong to him, his possessions, his property.

(b) **~s** possessions, property; estate; (*de finca etc*) appurtenances, accessories.

pértica NF *land measure = 2.70 metres*.

pértiga NF pole; (*salto con ~*) pole-vault; **~ de trole** trolley pole.

pertiguero NM verger.

pertiguista NMF pole-vaulter.

pertinacia NF (a) (*persistencia*) persistence; prolonged nature. (b) (*obstinación*) pertinacity, obstinacy.

pertinaz ADJ (a) *tos etc* persistent; *sequía* persistent, long-lasting, prolonged. (b) *persona* pertinacious, obstinate.

pertinencia NF relevance, pertinence; appropriateness.

pertinente ADJ (a) (*gen*) relevant, pertinent; appropriate; **no es ~ hacerlo ahora** this is not the appropriate time to do it.

(b) **~ a** concerning, relevant to; **en lo ~ a libros** as regards books, as far as books are concerned.

pertinentemente ADV relevantly, pertinently; appropriately.

pertrechar [1a] ① VT to supply (*con, de* with); to equip (*con, de* with); (*Mil*) to supply with ammunition and stores, equip.

② **pertrecharse** VR: **~ de algo** to provide o.s. with sth.

pertrechos NMPL implements, equipment; gear; (*Mil*) supplies and stores, provisions; (*Mil*) munitions; **~ de pesca** fishing tackle.

perturbación NF (a) (*Met, Pol etc*) disturbance; **~ del orden público ▼** breach of the peace.

(b) (*Med*) upset, disturbance; (*mental*) perturbation, (*grave*) mental disorder, alienation.

perturbado ① ADJ mentally unbalanced.

② NM, **perturbada** NF mentally unbalanced person.

perturbador ① ADJ (a) *noticia etc* perturbing, disturbing.

(b) *conducta* unruly, disorderly; *movimiento* subversive.

② NM, **perturbadora** NF disturber (of the peace); (*Pol*) disorderly element, unruly person; subversive.

perturbadoramente ADV disturbingly.

perturbar [1a] VT (a) *orden etc* to disturb; *calma* to disturb, ruffle, upset.

(b) (*Med*) to upset, disturb; (*mentalmente*) to perturb; to cause mental disorder in.

Perú NM: **el ~** Peru.

peruanismo NM word (*o phrase etc*) peculiar to Peru.

peruano, -a ADJ, NM/F Peruvian.

Perucho* NM: **viven en plan de ~** (*Carib**) they get on like a house on fire.

peruétano* ① ADJ (*And, Carib, Méx*) boring, tedious; stupid.

② NM (*And, Carib, Méx*) (*pelma*) bore; (*necio*) dolt; **ese muchacho es un ~** (*Cono Sur: metido*) that lad is always sticking his nose where it doesn't belong.

perversamente ADV perversely; wickedly.

perversidad NF (a) (*cualidad*) perversity; depravity; wickedness. (b) (*una ~*) evil deed, wrongdoing.

perversión NF (a) (*gen*) perversion; deviance; **~ sexual** sexual perversion. (b) (*maldad*) wickedness; (*corrupción*) corruption.

perverso ADJ perverse; depraved; wicked.

pervertido ① ADJ perverted, deviant.

② NM, **pervertida** NF pervert; deviant.

pervertidor(a) NM/F corruptor; **~ de menores** corruptor of minors, child abuser.

pervertimiento NM perversion, corruption.

pervertir [3i] ① VT to pervert, corrupt; *texto etc* to distort, corrupt; *gusto* to corrupt.

② **pervertirse** VR to become perverted.

pervinca NF (*Bot*) periwinkle.

pervivencia NF survival.

pervivir [3a] VI to survive.

pesa NF (a) (*gen*) weight; (*Dep*) weight, shot; dumbbell; **~s y medidas** weights and measures; **hacer ~s** to do weight training. (b) **~s**:* balls:*. (c) (*And, CAm, Carib: carnicería*) butcher's shop.

pesabebés NM INVAR baby scales.

pesadamente ADV (a) (*gen*) heavily; **caer ~** to fall heavily. (b) (*lentamente*) slowly, ponderously; sluggishly; stiffly. (c) (*de manera aburrida*) boringly, tediously.

pesadez NF (a) (*peso*) heaviness; weight.

(b) (*lentitud*) slowness, ponderousness; sluggishness.

(c) (*Med*) drowsiness; dull feeling, heavy feeling.

(d) (*fatiga*) tediousness, boring nature; (*molestia*) annoyance; **es una ~ tener que ...** it's a bore having to ...; **¡qué ~!** what a bore!

pesadilla NF (a) (*gen*) nightmare, bad dream; **una experiencia de ~** a nightmarish experience.

(b) (*fig*) worry, obsession, nightmare; bogey; (*persona*) pet aversion; bogeyman; **ese equipo es nuestra ~** that is our bogey team; **ha sido la ~ de todos** it has been a nightmare for everybody.

pesado ① ADJ (a) (*gen*) heavy (*t fig*), weighty.

(b) (*tardo*) *persona etc* slow, slow-moving, ponderous; sluggish; *trabajo etc* slow; *mecanismo* stiff.

(c) (*Met*) heavy, sultry.

(d) *sueño* deep, heavy.

(e) **tengo la cabeza pesada** my head feels heavy, I can hardly keep my head up, my head feels like lead; **tener el estómago ~** to feel full up.

(f) *tarea etc* (*difícil*) tough, hard; (*aburrido*) tedious; boring; *lectura etc* boring, stodgy; *persona* tedious, boring; annoying; **esto se hace ~** this is becoming tedious; **la lectura del libro resultó pesada** the book was heavy going, I got bored with the book; **es una persona de lo más ~** he's a terribly dull sort, he's a person of the most boring kind; **ése me cae ~** (*Carib, Méx**) that chap gets on my nerves*; **es ~ tener que ...** it's such a bore having to ..., it's tough having to ...; **¡no seas ~!** come off it!; don't be so difficult!

(g) (*And*) very good, excellent.

② NM, **pesada** NF (a) (*aburrido*) boring person, bore; (*fanfarrón*) loudmouth*; **es un ~** he's such a bore.

(b) (*Carib**) big shot*.

③ NM (*acto*) weighing.

pesador NM (*And, CAm, Carib*) butcher.

pesadumbre NF grief, sorrow, affliction.

pesaje NM weighing; (*Dep*) weigh-in.

pésame NM expression of condolence, message of sympathy; **dar el ~** to express one's condolences, send one's sympathy (*por* for, on).

pesantez NF weight, heaviness; (*Fís*) gravity.

pesar [1a] ① VT (a) (*averiguar el peso de*) to weigh.

(b) (*resultar pesado para*) to weigh down, be heavy for; **me pesa el abrigo** the coat weighs me down.

(c) (*fig: resultar difícil para*) to weigh heavily on; **le pesa tanta responsabilidad** so much responsibility bears heavily on him (*o is a burden to him*).

(d) (*fig*) (*examinar*) to weigh; (*valorar*) to appraise, value; (*estimar*) to reckon up; **~ las posibilidades** to weigh up one's chances; **~ las palabras** to weigh one's words.

(e) (*fig: afligir*) to grieve, afflict, distress; **me pesa mucho** it grieves me, I am very sorry about it (*o to hear it etc*); **no me pesa haberlo** hecho I'm not sorry I did it; **le pesa que no le hayan nombrado** it grieves him that he has not been appointed; **¡ya le pesará!** you'll be sorry!; **pese a las dificultades** in spite of the difficulties; **pese a quien pese** regardless of the consequences; in spite of everything; come what may; *V* **mal.**

[2] VI (a) (*tener peso*) to weigh; (*Fís*) to have weight; **pesa 5 kilos** it weighs 5 kilos.

(b) (*pesar mucho*) to weigh a lot, be heavy; (*tiempo*) to drag, hang heavy; **ese paquete no pesa** that parcel isn't heavy, that parcel hardly weighs anything; **¿pesa mucho?** is it heavy?; **~ como una losa** to weigh like a millstone round one's neck.

(c) (*fig: resultar pesado*) to weigh heavily; **sobre ella pesan muchas obligaciones** many obligations bear heavily on her; **la hipoteca que pesa sobre la finca** the mortgage with which the estate is burdened.

(d) (*fig: opinión etc*) to carry weight, count for a lot; **esa consideración no ha pesado conmigo** that consideration has not weighed with me (o influenced me).

(e) (*And, CAm*) to sell meat.

[3] NM (a) (*arrepentimiento*) regret; (*tristeza*) grief, sorrow; **a mi ~** to my regret; **a ~ suyo** (*LAm*) in spite of himself; **con gran ~ mío** much to my sorrow; **causar ~ a uno** to grieve sb, cause grief to sb; **sentir** (*o* **tener**) **~ por no haber ...** to regret not having ...

(b) a ~ de in spite of, despite; **a ~ de eso** in spite of that, notwithstanding that; **a ~ de que no tiene dinero** in spite of the fact that he has no money; **a ~ de los ~es*** in spite of everything.

pesario NM pessary.

pesaroso ADJ sorrowful, regretful, sad.

pesca NF **(a)** (*acto*) fishing; **~ de altura** deep-sea fishing; **~ en bajura** shallow water fishing, coastal fishing; **~ de la ballena** whaling; **~ a caña** angling; **~ a mosca** fly-fishing; **~ de perlas** pearl fishing; **~ submarina** underwater fishing; skin diving; **allí la ~ es muy buena** the fishing is very good there; **ir de ~** to go fishing; **andar a la ~ de** (*fig*) to fish for, angle for.

(b) (*peces*) catch, quantity (of fish) caught; **la ~ ha sido mala** it's been a poor catch; **... y toda la ~*** and all the rest, and whatnot*.

pescada NF hake.

pescadería NF (*mercado*) fish-market; (*tienda*) fish-shop.

pescadero, -a NM/F fishmonger.

pescadilla NF whiting; small hake.

pescado NM **(a)** fish; **~ azul** blue fish. **(b)** (*And, Cono Sur**) secret police.

pescador(a) NM/F fisherman, fisherwoman; **~ de caña** angler, fisherman; **~ a mosca** fly-fisherman.

pescante NM **(a)** (*de carruaje*) coachman's seat, driver's seat. **(b)** (*Teat*) wire. **(c)** (*Téc*) jib; (*Náut*) davit.

pescar [1g] **[1] VT (a)** (*coger*) to catch; to land.

(b) (*intentar coger*) to fish for, try to catch; **¿qué pescáis aquí?** what are you fishing for here?, what fish are you after here?

(c) (*) (*lograr*) to catch, get hold of, land; *puesto etc* to land, manage to get; *enfermedad* to catch; *significación* to grasp; *hechos etc* to dredge up; (*detener*) to arrest; **viene a ~ un marido** she's come to get herself a husband; **logró ~ unos cuantos datos** he managed to bring up a few facts, he was able to find a few facts.

(d) (*) *persona* to catch (out), catch in a lie; to catch unawares; **¡ya te pesqué!** now I've found you out!

[2] VI (a) (*gen*) to fish; to go fishing; **~ a mosca** to fish with a fly; **~ al arrastre, ~ a la rastra** to trawl.

(b) (*) **la chica viene a ver si pesca** the girl is coming to see if she can get hitched‡.

(c) (*And, Cono Sur*) to nod, doze.

[3] pescarse* VR: **no sabe lo que se pesca** he hasn't a clue*, he has no idea.

pescata NF catch, haul.

pescocear [1a] VT (*LAm*) to grab by the scruff of the neck.

pescozón NM blow on the neck.

pescozudo ADJ thick-necked, fat in the neck.

pescuezo NM **(a)** (*Zool*) neck; (*: *de persona*) scruff of the neck; **retorcer a ~ a una gallina** to wring a chicken's neck; **¡calla, o te retuerzo el ~!** shut up, or I'll wring your neck!

(b) (*fig*) vanity; haughtiness, pride.

pescuezón ADJ (*LAm*) **(a)** = **pescozudo. (b)** (*de cuello largo*) long-necked.

pese: ~ a PREP despite, in spite of.

pesebre NM **(a)** (*Agr*) manger; stall. **(b)** (*esp LAm*) Nativity scene, crib.

pesebrera NF (*Cono Sur, Méx*) = **pesebre (b).**

pesera NF (*Méx*) = **pesero (b).**

pesero NM **(a)** (*And, CAm, Carib*) butcher; slaughterman. **(b)** (*Méx*) taxi bus.

peseta **[1]** NF peseta; **cambiar la ~*** to throw up.

[2] NM (‡) taxi driver.

pesetada NF (*LAm*) joke, trick.

pesetera NF (*CAm, Méx*) prostitute.

pesetero ADJ **(a)** (*avaro*) money-grubbing, mercenary. **(b)** (*Méx*) *comerciante* small-time. **(c)** (*Carib: tacaño*) mean. **(d)** (*And, CAm, Carib: gorrón*) sponging*, parasitic.

pésimamente ADV abominably, wretchedly.

pesimismo NM pessimism.

pesimista **[1]** ADJ pessimistic.

[2] NMF pessimist.

pésimo **[1]** ADJ abominable, wretched, vile.

[2] ADV: **lo hiciste ~** (*Méx**) you did it terribly.

peso NM **(a)** (*gen*) weight; weightiness, heaviness; (*Fís*) gravity; **~s y medidas** weights and measures; **~ atómico** atomic weight; **~ bruto** gross weight; **~ específico** specific gravity; (*fig*) influence; muscle, clout*; **~ muerto** dead weight; **~ neto** net weight; **~ en vivo** live weight; **comprar algo a ~ de oro** to buy sth at a very high price; **vender al ~** to sell by weight; **de poco ~** light, lightweight; **de mucho ~** (very) heavy; **eso cae de su ~** that goes without saying, that's obvious; **coger ~** to put on weight; **no da al ~** (*fig*) he doesn't make the grade; **echar a uno en ~ por una ventana** to throw sb bodily through a window; **sostener algo en ~** to support the full weight of sth; **lleva toda la dirección en ~** he carries all the burden of the management; **llevar el ~ de un ataque** to bear the brunt of an attack.

(b) (*objeto*) weight, weighty object; (*carga*) burden, load; (*Dep*) weight; shot; (*prueba*) shot-putting, putting the shot; **lanzar el ~** to put the shot; **levantamiento de ~s** weightlifting.

(c) (*Boxeo*) weight; **~ bantam** bantam-weight; **~ completo** (*CAm, Méx*), **~ fuerte** heavyweight (*t fig*); **~ gallo** bantam-weight; **~ ligero** lightweight; **~ medio** middle-weight; **~ medio fuerte** light heavyweight, cruiser-weight; **~ mosca** flyweight; **~ pesado** heavyweight; **~ pluma** featherweight; **~ welter** welterweight.

(d) (*modorra*) heavy feeling, dull feeling (*in head etc*).

(e) (*fig*) weight; **el ~ de los años** the weight of the years, the burden of age; **argumento de ~** weighty argument; **razones de ~** good reasons, sound reasons.

(f) (*balanza*) scales, balance, weighing machine; **~ de baño** bathroom scales; **~ de muelle** spring balance.

(g) (*Fin*) unit of currency of certain LAm countries.

pesor NM (*CAm, Carib*) weight, heaviness.

pespunte NM backstitch(ing).

pespunt(e)ar [1a] VTI to backstitch.

pesquera NF **(a)** (*zona*) fishing-ground, fishery. **(b)** (*presa*) weir.

pesquería NF fishing-ground, fishery.

pesquero **[1]** ADJ fishing (*atr*).

[2] NM fishing-boat.

pesquis* NM nous*; know-how; **tener el ~ para** + *infin* to have the nous to + *infin**.

pesquisa **[1]** NF (*indagación*) investigation, inquiry; (*registro*) search.

[2] NM (*And, Cono Sur**) (*policía*) secret police; (*detective*) detective.

pesquisador(a) NM/F investigator, inquirer; (*And, Cono Sur**) (*policía*) member of the secret police; (*detective*) detective.

pesquisar [1a] VT to investigate, inquire into.

pesquisidor NM investigator, inquirer.

pestaña **[1]** NF **(a)** (*Anat: de ojo*) eyelash; (*Anat, Bot etc: de pelo*) fringe; **no pegué ~*** I didn't get a wink of sleep; **quemarse las ~s** (*fig*) (*excederse*) to go too far, burn one's fingers; (*estudiar*) to burn the midnight oil; **tener ~** to be pretty smart. **(b)** (*Téc*) flange; (*de neumático*) rim.

[2] NM (*Esp‡*) (*policía*) cop*; (*policías*) cops*, fuzz‡.

pestañar [1a] VI (*LAm*), **pestañear** [1a] VI to blink, wink; **sin ~** without batting an eyelid.

pestañeo NM blink(ing), wink(ing).

pestazo* NM stink, stench.

peste NF **(a)** (*Med*) plague, epidemic; (*And, Carib*) bubonic plague; (*Cono Sur: viruela*) smallpox; (*And: resfrío*) cold; (*Cono Sur: enfermedad*) (*any*) infectious disease; **~ aviar** fowl pest; **~ bubónica** bubonic plague; **~ negra** Black Death; **~ porcina** swine fever.

(b) (*fig: plaga*) plague; evil menace; nuisance; **una ~ de ratones** a plague of mice; **los chiquillos son una ~** the kids are a pest, the kids are a nuisance.

(c) (*hedor*) stink, stench, foul smell; **¡qué ~ hay aquí!** what a stink!

(d) **echar ~s de** to swear about, fume at, utter bitter words about; **se hablan ~s de la cocina inglesa** awful things are said about English cooking.

pesticida NM pesticide.

pestífero ADJ (*dañino*) pestiferous; *olor* foul; *influencia etc* noxious, harmful.

pestilencia NF **(a)** (*plaga*) pestilence, plague. **(b)** (*hedor*) stink, stench.

pestilencial ADJ pestilential.

pestilente ADJ **(a)** (*dañino*) pestilent. **(b)** (*que huele*) smelly, foul.

pestillo NM bolt, latch; catch, fastener; (*Cono Sur: de puerta*) door handle.

pestiño* NM (*Esp*) (**a**) (*lata*) bore, drag; **fue un ~** it was a real drag. (**b**) (*chica*) plain girl.

pestozos: NMPL socks.

pesuña (*LAm*) NF = **pezuña**.

peta¹: NF (*Esp*) peseta.

peta²: NM (**a**) (*droga*) joint:, reefer:. (**b**) (*nombre*) name; **~ chungo** false name. (**c**) (*documentación*) papers.

petaca 1 NF (**a**) (*de cigarrillos*) cigarette-case; (*de puros*) cigar-case; (*de pipa*) tobacco pouch; **hacerle la ~ a uno** to make an apple-pie bed for sb. (**b**) (*cesto*) wicker basket; hamper; (*LAm*) leather-covered chest; (*Méx**) (*maleta*) suitcase; (*baúl*) trunk; (*equipaje*) luggage. (**c**) (*CAm, Méx**: *Anat*) hump; **~s** (*Carib, Méx*:) (*nalgas*) buttocks; (*pechos*) big breasts. 2 NMF (*LAm**: *rechoncho*) (**a**) short squat person. (**b**) (*vago*) lazy person. (**c**) **írsele las ~s a uno** to lose one's patience. 3 ADJ INVAR (**a**) (*LAm**: *vago*) lazy, idle; (*Cono Sur**: *torpe*) slow. (**b**) (*Carib**: *grosero*) coarse.

petacho NM patch, mend.

petacón* ADJ (*And, Cono Sur*: *gordito*) plump, chubby; (*And*: *barrigón*) potbellied, paunchy; **es petacona** (*CAm, Carib, Méx*) she's rather broad in the beam*.

petacudo* ADJ (**a**) (*And*) stout, fat; (*CAm*) hunchbacked; (*Méx*) broad in the beam*. (**b**) (*lento*) slow, ponderous, sluggish.

pétalo NM petal.

petanca NF pétanque.

petar* [1a] VI: **no me peta** (*gustar*) I don't like it, I'm not into it; (*apetecer*) I don't feel like it.

petardazo NM (**a**) (*fuegos artificiales*) firework display. (**b**) (*sonido*) crack, bang. (**c**) (*sorpresa*) shock result, upset.

petardear [1a] 1 VT (*) to cheat, swindle. 2 VI (*Aut*) to backfire.

petardista* NM cheat, swindler; (*Méx*) crooked politician*.

petardo NM (**a**) (*gen*) firework, firecracker; (small) explosive device, incendiary device; (*Mil*) petard. (**b**) (*estafa*) fraud, swindle; **pegar un ~** to practise a fraud, pull a fast one (*a* on); **ser un ~*** to be dead boring*. (**c**) (:: *droga*) joint:. (**d**) (:: *mujer*) old bag:.

petate NM (**a**) (*estera*) grass mat; (*LAm*) palm matting; (*de dormir*) sleeping mat. (**b**) (*lío de cama*) bedroll; (*equipaje*) baggage; **liar el ~*** to pack up; (*irse*) to pack up and go, clear out*; (*morir*) to peg out:. (**c**) (*: *estafador*) cheat, trickster. (**d**) (*: *pobre hombre*) poor devil. (**e**) **se descubrió el ~*** the fraud was discovered.

petatearse: [1a] VR (*Méx*) to peg out:, kick the bucket:.

peteneras NFPL: **salir por ~** (*Esp*) to butt in with some silly remark, say (*o* do) something quite inappropriate.

petición NF request, plea; petition; (*Jur*) plea; claim; **a ~** by request; **a ~ de** at the request of; **programa a ~ de radioyentes** listeners' request programme; **aborto a ~** abortion on demand; **~ de aumento de salarios** demand for higher wages, wage demand, wage claim; **~ de divorcio** petition for divorce; **~ de extradición** request for extradition; **cometer ~ de principio** to beg the question.

peticionar [1a] VT (*LAm*) to petition.

peticionario, -a NM/F petitioner, applicant.

petimetre 1 ADJ foppish. 2 NM fop, dandy.

petirrojo NM robin.

petiso (*And, Cono Sur*), **petizo** (*And, Cono Sur*) 1 ADJ (*bajo*) small, short; (*rechoncho*) stocky; chubby. 2 NM small horse. 3 NM, **petisa** NF, **petiza** NF short person.

petisú NM cream puff.

petitorio ADJ: **mesa petitoria** stall (*for charity collection*).

petizón ADJ (*And, Cono Sur*) = **petiso 1, petizo 1.**

peto NM (*corpiño*) bodice; (*babero*) bib; (*Mil*) breastplate; (*Taur*) protective covering of picador's horse.

petral NM breast-strap (*of harness*).

Petrarca NM Petrarch.

petrarquismo NM Petrarchism.

petrarquista ADJ Petrarchan.

petrel NM petrel.

pétreo ADJ stony; rocky.

petrificación NF petrifaction.

petrificado ADJ petrified.

petrificar [1g] 1 VT to petrify (*t fig*), turn to stone. 2 **petrificarse** VR to petrify, become petrified (*t fig*), turn to stone.

petrodólar NM petrodollar.

petroleado ADJ *animal, ave* oiled.

petróleo NM (*Min*) oil, petroleum; (*LAm*: *kerosene*) paraffin; **~ de alumbrado** paraffin (oil); **~ combustible** fuel oil; **~ crudo** crude oil.

petrolero 1 ADJ oil (*atr*), petroleum (*atr*); **flota petrolera** tanker fleet; **industria petrolera** oil industry; **sindicato ~** oil workers' union. 2 NM (**a**) (*Com*) oil man; (*obrero*) oil worker; (*criminal*) arsonist. (**b**) (*Náut*) tanker.

petrolífero ADJ (**a**) (*Min*) petroliferous, oil-bearing. (**b**) (*Com*) oil (*atr*); **compañía petrolífera** oil company.

petrología NF petrology.

petroquímica NF (*ciencia*) petrochemistry; (*Com*) petrochemical company; (*fábrica*) petrochemical factory.

petroquímico ADJ petrochemical.

petulancia NF vanity, self-satisfaction, opinionated nature.

petulante ADJ vain, self-satisfied, opinionated.

petunia NF petunia.

peuquino ADJ (*Cono Sur*) greyish.

peyorativo ADJ pejorative.

peyote NM (*LAm*) peyote cactus.

pez¹ 1 NM (**a**) fish; **~ de colores** goldfish; **~ espada** swordfish; **~ mujer** manatee; **~ sierra** sawfish; **~ volante** flying fish; **estar como el ~ en el agua** to feel completely at home, be in one's element; **¡me río de los peces de colores!*** I couldn't care less! (**b**) **~ gordo*** big shot*, fat cat*. (**c**) **buen ~*** rogue, rascal. 2 ADJ (*) **estar ~ de** (*o* en) **algo** to be completely ignorant of sth, know nothing at all about sth; **están algo peces en idiomas** they're rather backward at languages.

pez² NF pitch, tar.

pezón NM (**a**) (*Anat*) teat, nipple. (**b**) (*Bot*) stalk. (**c**) (*Mec*) **~ de engrase** nipple, lubrication point.

pezonera NF (*Cono Sur*) feeding bottle.

pezuña NF (**a**) (*Zool*) hoof; (*: *de persona*) hoof*, foot. (**b**) (*And, Méx*) dirt hardened on the feet.

PFCRN NM (*Méx*) ABR de **Partido del Frente Cardenista de Reconstrucción Nacional.**

PGB NM (*Chile*) ABR de **Producto Geográfico Bruto** gross domestic product, GDP.

pgdo. ABR de **pagado** paid, pd.

PGP NM (*Uruguay*) ABR de **Partido por el Gobierno del Pueblo.**

PGR NM (*Méx*) ABR de **Procuraduría General de la República.**

piada NF (**a**) (*Orn*) cheep, cheeping. (**b**) (*fig*) borrowed phrase.

piadosamente ADV (*V ADJ*) (**a**) piously, devoutly. (**b**) kindly, mercifully.

piadoso ADJ (**a**) (*Rel*) pious, devout. (**b**) (*amable*) kind, merciful (*para, con* to); *V* **mentira.**

piafar [1a] VI (*caballo*) to paw the ground, stamp.

pial NM lasso.

pialar [1a] VT to lasso.

Piamonte NM Piedmont.

piamontés, -esa ADJ, NM/F Piedmontese.

pianista NMF pianist.

pianístico ADJ piano (*atr*).

piano NM piano; **~ de cola** grand piano; **~ de media cola** baby grand; **~ mecánico** pianola; **~ recto, ~ vertical** upright piano; **como un ~** (*Esp**) real big*; **tocar el ~** to play the piano, (*: *lavar platos*) do the washing-up; (:: *huella dactilar*) to have one's fingerprints taken, be fingerprinted; **tocar ~** (*LAm**) to rob, steal.

piantado: (*Cono Sur*) 1 ADJ nuts:, crazy. 2 NM madman, nutcase:.

piantarse: [1a] VR (*Cono Sur*) to escape, get out.

piante* NMF: **es un ~** he's a pain*.

piar [1c] VI (**a**) (*Orn*) to cheep; (*: *hablar*) to talk, chatter. (**b**) **~ por*** to cry for, be dying for. (**c**) (*: *quejarse*) to whine, snivel, grouse*; **~las*** to be forever grousing*. (**d**) (*: *soplar*) to spill the beans*; **¡no la píes!** don't let on!*

piara NF herd; drove.

piastra NF piastre.

PIB NM ABR de **producto interior bruto** gross domestic product, GDP.

piba: NF whore.

pibe, -a* NM/F (*niño*) kid*, child; (*muchacho*) boy; (*muchacha*) girl; (*amiguito*) boyfriend; (*amiguita*) girlfriend.

pibil NM (*Méx*) chili sauce.

pica¹ NF (*Orn*) magpie.

pica² NF (*Mil*) pike; (*Taur*) goad; (:) prick::; **poner una ~ en Flandes** to bring off something difficult, achieve a signal success.

pica³ NF (*And Agr*) tapping (*of rubber trees*).

pica⁴ NF (*And*: *resentimiento*) pique, resentment; (*Cono Sur*: *mal humor*) annoyance, irritation; **sacar ~** to cause annoyance; to arouse envy.

pica⁵ NF (*And, CAm, Carib*: *camino*) forest trail, narrow path.

pica⁶ NF: **~s** (*Naipes*) spades.

pica⁷* NM (*de autobús etc*) inspector.

picacera* NF (*And, Cono Sur*) irritation.

picacho NM peak, summit.

picada¹ NF **(a)** (*gen*) prick; (*de insecto etc*) sting; bite; (*de ave*) peck. **(b)** (*Cono Sur: mal humor*) bad temper, anger. **(c)** ir en ~ (*LAm*) to nose-dive; (*fig*) to plummet, take a nose-dive. **(d)** (*Culin*) spicy sauce.

picada² NF (*LAm*) forest trail, narrow path; (*And*) ford.

picada³ NF (*Cono Sur*) small restaurant.

picadero NM **(a)** (*escuela*) riding-school. **(b)** (**⁑**: *habitación*) pad**⁑**, flat; (*pey*) apartment used for sexual encounters. **(c)** (*LAm*⁑) shooting gallery⁑ (*for drug taking*). **(d)** (*And: matadero*) slaughterhouse.

picadillo NM mince, minced meat; ser como el ~ (*Carib**) to be boring.

picado **1** ADJ **(a)** *material* pricked, perforated; with a row of holes; *superficie* pitted; ~ de viruelas pockmarked.
(b) *carne etc* minced; *tabaco* cut; *mar* choppy.
(c) *vino* pricked, slightly sour.
(d) estar ~ (*enojado*) to be offended, be cross; (*borracho*) to be tipsy; están picados desde hace muchos años they fell out years ago.
(e) estar ~ por algo to go for sth in a big way.*
(f) quedarse ~ to be frustrated.
2 NM **(a)** (*Aer, Orn*) dive; caer en ~ (*fig*) to take a dive, go downhill fast, slump.
(b) (*Mús*) pizzicato, staccato.
(c) (*de vino*) souring.

picador NM **(a)** (*gen*) horse-trainer, horse-breaker. **(b)** (*Taur*) picador, bullfighter's assistant (*mounted, with a lance*). **(c)** (*Min*) faceworker.

picadora NF: ~ de carne mincer, mincing machine.

picadura NF **(a)** (*gen*) prick; (*pinchazo*) puncture; (*de insecto etc*) sting, bite. **(b)** *tabaco* cut tobacco.

picaflor NM (*LAm*) **(a)** (*Orn*) humming-bird. **(b)** (*) (*tenorio*) ladykiller; (*mariposón*) flirt; (*amante*) lover, boyfriend.

picafuego NM poker.

picajón* ADJ, **picajoso*** ADJ touchy.

picamaderos NM INVAR woodpecker.

picana NF (*LAm*) cattle prod, goad; ~ eléctrica electric prod (*for torture*).

picanear [1a] VT (*LAm*) to spur on, goad on; *preso* to torture with electric shocks.

picante **1** ADJ **(a)** *comida, sabor* hot; peppery; spicy.
(b) (*fig*) *comentario* sharp, stinging, cutting; *chiste etc* racy, spicy; *situación, contraste* piquant.
2 NM **(a)** (*sabor*) hot taste.
(b) (*fig*) sharpness, pungency; raciness, spiciness; piquancy.
(c) (*And, Cono Sur: salsa*) chili sauce; (*And: guisado*) meat stew with chili sauce; (*LAm: chile*) chili.
(d) ~s⁑ socks.

picantería NF (*And, Cono Sur*) restaurant specializing in spicy dishes.

picantón NM spicy sauce.

picapedrero NM stonecutter, quarryman.

picapica NF **(a)** (*And: serpentina*) streamer. **(b)** V polvos.

picapleitos NM INVAR (*pey*) lawyer; litigious person.

picaporte NM (*tirador*) door-handle; (*pestillo*) latch; (*aldaba*) door-knocker; (*llave*) latchkey.

picar [1g] **1** VT **(a)** (*perforar*) to prick, puncture; *papel etc* to prick (a line of holes in, pierce with holes, perforate; *superficie* to pit, pock; (*Arte*) to stipple; (*Cos*) to pink; *ticket* to punch, clip.
(b) (*insecto*) to sting; to bite; (*culebra*) to bite; (*espina*) to prick.
(c) (*ave*) to peck; to peck at; (*persona*) *comida* to nibble (at), pick at; (*pez*) to bite.
(d) *caballo* to put spurs to, spur on; *toro* to stick, prick (with the goad); (*fig*) to incite, goad, stimulate; (*fig*) (*herir*) to wound; (*ofender*) to pique; (*molestar*) to annoy, bother; le pican los celos he is feeling pangs of jealousy.
(e) (*Mús*) to play staccato; (*: *escribir a máquina*) to type.
(f) *piedra* to chip, chip pieces off; *piedra de molino* to sharpen; *piedra* (*pulverizar*) to grind (up); (*Culin*) to mince, chop (up); *tabaco* to cut.
(g) *lengua* to burn, sting.
(h) (*Mil*) to harass.
(i) (**⁑**: *matar*) to bump off⁑.
(j) (**⁑**) to screw⁑.
2 VI **(a)** (*espina*) to prick; (*insecto*) to sting, bite; no es de los que pican it's not the kind that stings.
(b) (*ave*) ~ en to peck at; (*persona etc*) to nibble at, pick at; (*fig*) to dabble in, study superficially; ha picado en todos los géneros literarios he's dabbled in (o had a go at) all the literary genres; yo no pico en esas cosas I don't dabble in such things.
(c) (*pez*) to bite, take the bait; (*fig*) to rise to the bait; por fin picó he swallowed the bait eventually; ha picado mucha gente lots of people have fallen for it, it has caught on with lots of people.
(d) (*fig*) ~ en to border on, be akin to; eso pica en frescura that borders (o verges) on cheek*.
(e) (*Med*) to itch, sting; me pican los ojos my eyes hurt; me pica la

lengua my tongue is smarting (o stinging); me pica el brazo my arm itches.
(f) (*Esp: sol*) to burn, scorch; hoy sí pica el sol the sun is really burning today.
(g) (*Aer, Orn*) to dive.
(h) ~ muy alto to aim too high, be over-ambitious.
(i) (*Aut*) to pink.
3 **picarse** VR **(a)** (*ropa*) to get moth-eaten; (*sustancia*) to get holes in it; (*muela*) to decay.
(b) (*vino etc*) to turn sour, go off; (*fruta etc*) to spoil, go rotten.
(c) (*mar*) to get choppy.
(d) (*persona*) to take offence, get piqued; to get cross; to bridle (*por* at); (*emborracharse*) to get tipsy; el que se pica, ajos come if the cap fits, wear it.
(e) ~ con algo to get a longing for, get an obsession about; to take a strong liking to.
(f) ~ de puntual to take a pride in being punctual, make a strong point of punctuality; ~ de caballero to boast of being a gentleman.
(g) ~ de pecho (*Carib*) to become consumptive.
(h) (*: *inyectarse*) to give o.s. a shot (of drugs)*, shoot up⁑.

picarazado ADJ (*Carib*) pockmarked.

picardear [1a] **1** VT: ~ a uno to get sb into bad habits, lead sb into evil ways.
2 VI (*jugar*) to play about; (*dar guerra*) to play up, be mischievous.
3 **picardearse** VR to get into evil ways, go to the bad.

Picardía NF Picardy.

picardía NF **(a)** (*cualidad*) villainy, knavery; slyness, craftiness; naughtiness.
(b) (*una* ~) dirty trick; naughty thing (to do), mischievous act.
(c) (*grosería*) rude thing (to say), naughty word; (*insulto*) insult; le gusta decir ~s a la gente he likes saying naughty things to people.

picardías NM INVAR négligée.

picaresca NF **(a)** (*Liter*) (genre of the) picaresque novel. **(b)** (*astucia*) guile; chicanery, subterfuge; la ~ española Spanish guile, Spanish wiliness. **(c)** (*hampa*) (criminal) underworld.

picaresco ADJ **(a)** (*travieso*) roguish, rascally. **(b)** (*Liter*) *novela picaresque*, of roguery.

pícaro **1** ADJ **(a)** (*pillo*) villainous, knavish; (*taimado*) sly, crafty; (*travieso*) naughty, mischievous.
(b) (*precoz*) *etc* precocious, knowing, (*esp*) sexually aware before the proper age.
(c) (*hum*) naughty, wicked; ¡este ~ siglo! what naughty times we live in!; tiene inclinación a los ~s celos she gives way to that wicked jealousy.
2 NM **(a)** (*granuja*) villain, knave, scoundrel, rogue, rascal; (*ladino*) sly sort; (*niño*) rascal, scamp; ¡~! you rascal!
(b) (*Liter*) *pícaro* rogue.

┌──────────┐
│ **PÍCARO** │
└──────────┘

ⓘ *In Spanish literature, especially of the Golden Age, the* **pícaro** *is a roguish character whose travels and adventures are used as a vehicle for social satire. The anonymous* **Lazarillo de Tormes** *(1554), which relates the life and adventures of one such character, is thought to be the first of the genre known as the picaresque novel, or* **novela picaresca**. *Other well-known picaresque novels were written by Cervantes (* **Rinconete y Cortadillo** *) and Francisco de Quevedo (* **El Buscón** *).*

picarón NM **(a)** rogue. **(b)** (*And, Cono Sur, Méx Culin*) fritter.

picaruelo ADJ *mirada etc* roguish, naughty, sly; me dio una mirada picaruela she gave me a roguish look.

picatoste NM fried bread.

picaza NF magpie.

picazo NM peck; jab, poke.

picazón NF **(a)** (*comezón*) itch; (*ardor*) sting, stinging feeling; smart, smarting. **(b)** (*fig*) (*disgusto*) annoyance, pique; (*remordimiento*) uneasy feeling, pang of conscience.

píccolo NM piccolo.

pícea NF spruce.

picha¹ NF (*Méx*) blanket; (*hum*) mistress.

picha² NF (⁑) prick⁑.

pichado ADJ (*Cono Sur*) easily embarrassed.

pichana NF (*And, Cono Sur*) broom.

pichanga NF **(a)** (*And*) broom. **(b)** (*Cono Sur Dep*) friendly soccer match. **(c)** (*Cono Sur Culin*) tray of cocktail snacks.

pichango NM (*Cono Sur*) dog.

piche NM **(a)** (*CAm: avaro*) miser, skinflint.
(b) (*And, Cono Sur: Zool*) (*kind of*) armadillo.
(c) (*Carib, Cono Sur: miedo*) fright.
(d) (*And: empujón*) shove.
(e) (*And: suero*) whey.
(f) (*And: rojo*) red.

pichel NM tankard, mug; (*Méx*) water jug.

pichi¹: ① ADJ smart, elegant.
  ② NM (a) Madrid man in traditional dress. (b) (Cos) light knitted dress. (c) (en oración directa) mate*, man*.

pichi²: NM: **hacer ~** (And, Cono Sur) to have a pee:.

pichi³ NM (prenda) pinafore dress.

pichicata* NF (LAm) cocaine powder; (Cono Sur) (droga) hard drugs; (inyección) shot*; fix:.

pichicatero, -a* NM/F (And) drug addict.

pichicato ADJ (LAm) mean, miserly.

pichichi NM top goal-scorer.

pichicote ADJ (And) mean, miserly.

pichilingo NM (Méx) lad, kid*.

pichincha NF (And, Cono Sur) (ganga) bargain; (precio) bargain price; (trato) good deal; (suerte) lucky break.

pichingo NM (CAm) jar, vessel; (pey) piece of junk.

pichintún NM (Cono Sur) dash, smidgin*.

pichirre* ADJ (And, Carib) mean, stingy.

picholear* [1a] VI (a) (CAm, Cono Sur: jaranear) to have a good time. (b) (CAm, Méx: apostar) to have a flutter*.

pichón ① NM (a) (Orn) young pigeon; (Culin) pigeon; (LAm) chick, young bird; **~ de barro** clay pigeon; **sí, ~** yes, darling.
  (b) (LAm) (novato) novice, greenhorn; tyro; (Dep) young player, inexperienced player.
  (c) **un ~ de hombre** (Cono Sur) a well-bred man.
  ② **pichona** NF: **si, ~** yes, darling.

pichonear [1a] ① VT (a) (Cono Sur, Méx*: engañar) to swindle, con*.
  (b) (And, CAm: pillar) to catch out; (matar) to kill, murder.
  (c) (Cono Sur) = **pinchar**.
  (d) (And, CAm: tener prestado) to borrow, use temporarily; to occupy temporarily.
  ② VI (And, Cono Sur, Méx: triunfar) to win an easy victory.

pichoso ADJ (Carib) dirty.

pichula: NF (And) cock:, prick:.

pichuleador NM (Cono Sur) moneygrubber.

pichulear* [1a] VI (a) (Cono Sur) (negociar) to be a smalltime businessman; (ser mercenario) to be mercenary, be greedy for money. (b) (CAm, Méx: gastar poco) to be careful with one's money.

pichuleo* NM (a) (Cono Sur) meanness. (b) (CAm, Méx: negocio) small business, retail business.

pichulina: NF willie:.

picia* NF prank, escapade.

pick-up [pi'kap o pi'ku] NM pick-up.

picnic NM (a) (excursión) picnic.
  (b) (cesta) picnic basket, picnic set.

pico NM (a) (Orn) beak, bill; (Ent etc) beak; (hum: boca) mouth, lips; **callar** (o **cerrar**) **el ~:** to shut one's trap:, keep one's trap shut:; **darle al ~*** to talk a lot; **darse el ~*** (besar) to kiss; (fig) to hit it off; **hincar el ~*** (morir) to peg out:; (ceder) to give up, give in; **tener buen ~:** to like one's grub:.
  (b) (punta) corner, peak, sharp point; (de mesa, página) corner; **sombrero de tres ~s** cocked hat, three-cornered hat; **andar** (o **irse**) **de ~s pardos*** to go for a good time.
  (c) (de jarra etc) lip, spout.
  (d) (Téc) pick, pickaxe.
  (e) (Geog) peak, summit; pinnacle of rock.
  (f) **y ~** and a bit; **son las 3 y ~** it's just after 3; **tiene 50 libros y ~** he has 50-odd books; **quédese con el ~** keep what's left over; **me costó un ~** it cost me quite a bit.
  (g) (Orn: especie) woodpecker.
  (h) (*: labia) talkativeness; **ser un ~ de oro, tener buen** (o **mucho**) **~** to have the gift of the gab*, be a great talker; **irse del ~** to talk too much; **perderse por el ~** to harm o.s. by saying too much.
  (i) (Naipes) spade.
  (j) (And, CAm, Méx: beso) kiss.
  (k) (And, Cono Sur:) prick:.
  (l) (:: de droga) fix:, shot*; **darse el ~** to give o.s. a fix:.

picolargo* ADJ (Cono Sur) (respondón) pert, saucy; (murmurador) backbiting; (intrigante) intriguing, scheming.

picoleto: NM (Esp) Civil Guard.

picón* ① ADJ (a) (And, Carib: respondón) cheeky*. (b) (And, Carib: quisquilloso) touchy. (c) (Carib: burlón) mocking.
  ② NM, **picona** NF (And) gossip, telltale.

picor NM = **picazón (a)**.

picoreto ADJ (And, CAm, Carib) loose-tongued, indiscreet.

picoso ADJ (a) pockmarked. (b) (LAm: picante) hot, spicy.

picota NF (a) (gen) pillory; (fig) **poner a uno en la ~** to pillory sb.
  (b) (Arquit) point, top; (Geog) peak.
  (c) (Bot) bigarreau cherry.
  (d) (:: nariz) hooter:, nose.

picotada NF, **picotazo** NM peck; sting, bite; **tener mala picotada** (fig) to be bad-tempered.

picotear [1a] ① VT to peck.

② VI (a) (al comer) to nibble, pick. (b) (*: parlotear) to chatter, gas*, gab*.

③ **picotearse*** VR to squabble.

picotero ① ADJ chattering, gossipy, talkative.
  ② NM, **picotera** NF gossip, chatterer, gasbag*.

picotón NM (And, Cono Sur) peck.

picto ① ADJ Pictish.
  ② NM, **picta** NF Pict.
  ③ NM (Ling) Pictish.

pictograma NM pictogram.

pictóricamente ADV pictorially.

pictórico ADJ (a) (gen) pictorial.
  (b) escena etc worth painting; picturesque.
  (c) talento etc artistic; **tiene dotes pictóricas** she has artistic gifts, she has talent for painting.

picú NM record player.

picúa NF (Carib) (a) (cometa) small kite. (b) (comerciante) sharp businessman. (c) (puta) prostitute.

picuda NF (a) (Orn) woodcock. (b) (Carib: pez) barracuda.

picudo ADJ (a) (puntiagudo) pointed, with a point; jarra with a spout; persona long-nosed, sharp-nosed.
  (b) (*) = **picotero 1**.
  (c) (Carib) V **cursi**.
  (d) (Méx*: astuto) crafty, clever.

piculina NF (Esp) tart:, whore.

picure NM (And) (fugitivo) fugitive; (gandul) slacker. (b) (Carib) spicy sauce.

picurearse* [1a] VR (And, Carib) to scarper:.

PID NM ABR de **proceso integrado de datos** integrated data processing, IDP.

pida, pido etc V **pedir**.

pídola NF leapfrog.

pie NM (a) (Anat etc) foot; **~ de atleta** athlete's foot; **~ de cabra** crowbar; **~s de cerdo** (Culin) pig's trotters; **~s planos** flat feet; **ligero de ~s** light-footed, quick; **a ~** on foot; **ir a ~** to go on foot, walk; **a cuatro ~s** on all fours; **a ~ enjuto** dry-shod, (fig) without danger, without any risk; **a ~ firme** steadfastly; **a ~ juntillo, a ~s juntillos** with both feet together, (fig) creer firmly, absolutely; **con el ~ bien sentado** calmly, thoughtfully; with due care; **con ~s de plomo** warily, gingerly; **andar con ~s de plomo** to go very carefully; **con un ~ en el hoyo** with one foot in the grave; **entrar con buen ~** (o **con ~ derecho**) to get off to a good start; **hacer algo con los ~s** to bungle sth, make a mess of sth; **levantarse con el ~ izquierdo** (fig) to get up on the wrong side of the bed; **estar de ~** to be standing (up); **ponerse de** (o **en**) **~** to stand up, get up, rise; **caer de ~** (fig) to fall on one's feet, be lucky; **nacer de ~** to be born with a silver spoon in one's mouth, be born lucky; **cojear del mismo ~** to have the same faults; **saber de qué ~ cojea uno** to know sb's weak spots (o weaknesses); **de ~s a cabeza** from head to foot, from top to toe; **soldado de a ~** (Hist) foot-soldier; **de a ~** (fig) common, ordinary; **en ~** standing; upright; **ganado en ~** cattle on the hoof; **mantenerse en ~** to remain upright; **la duda sigue en ~** the doubt remains; **las víctimas salieron por su ~** those affected were able to leave unassisted (o without help); **irse** (o **salir**) **por ~s** to make off; **argumento sin ~s ni cabeza** pointless argument, absurd argument; unintelligible argument; **asentar el ~** to make a cautious start; **buscar tres ~s al gato** to split hairs, quibble; to look for trouble; **no dar ~ con bola** to do everything wrong, be no good at anything; **déle el ~ y se tomará la mano** give him an inch and he'll take a yard; **se le fueron los ~s** he slipped, he stumbled; **no hace ~** he's out of his depth; **parar los ~s a uno** to curb sb, clip sb's wings; to stop sb going too far; to take sb down a peg; **poner el ~** to tread, put one's foot; **poner el ~ en el acelerador** to step on the gas*; (fig) to speed things up, step up the pace; **poner los ~s en** (fig) to set foot in; **sacar los ~s del plato** to abandon all restraint; to kick over the traces; **volverse ~s atrás** to retrace one's steps.
  (b) (Mat) foot; **~ cuadrado** square foot; **~ cúbico** cubic foot; **tiene 6 ~s de largo** it is 6 feet long.
  (c) (Bot) trunk, stem; (de rosa etc) root, stock, stand; (de vaso) stem; (de estatua) foot, base; (de cama, colina, escalera, página etc) foot, bottom; (de carta, documento) ending; (de foto, grabado) colophon, caption; **~ de autor** byline; **~ de imprenta** imprint; **al ~ del monte** at the foot (o bottom) of the mountain; **a los ~s de la cama** at the foot of the bed; **al ~ de fábrica** cost price, ex-works; **al ~ de la letra** citar etc literally, verbatim; copiar exactly, word for word; cumplir impeccably, down to the last detail; **al ~ de la página** at the foot of the page; **al ~ de la obra** (Com) delivered, including delivery charges; **a ~ de obra** on the spot; **estar a ~ de obra** to be on site, be on the job; **a ~ de ese edificio** next to that building, right beside that building; **estar al ~ del cañón** to be ready to act; **morir al ~ del cañón** to die in harness.
  (d) (Teat) cue.

(e) (*de vino etc*) sediment.

(f) (*fig*) (*causa*) motive, basis; (*pretexto*) pretext; **dar ~ a** to give cause for; **dar ~ para que uno haga algo** to give sb a motive for doing sth; **tomar ~ para hacer algo** to use sth as a basis for action.

(g) (*fig: seguridad*) foothold; **no hacer ~** to be out of one's depth; **perder el ~** to lose one's foothold, slip.

(h) (*fig: posición*) standing, footing; **en ~ de guerra** on a war footing; **estar sobre un (mismo) ~ de igualdad** to be on an equal footing, be on equal terms (*con* with).

(i) (*Liter*) foot; measure, verse form.

(j) (*Cono Sur*: *enganche*) deposit, down payment.

(k) **~ de vía** (*CAm Aut*) indicator.

piecería NF, **piecerío** NM (*Mec*) parts.

piecero, -a NM/F tailor's cutter, garment worker.

piedad NF **(a)** (*Rel*) piety, devotion, devoutness; respect; **~ filial** filial respect.

(b) (*compasión*) pity; (*misericordia*) mercy; **¡por ~!** for pity's sake!; **mover a uno a ~** to move sb to pity, arouse compassion in sb; **tener ~ de** to take pity on; **¡ten un poco de ~!** show some sympathy!; **no tuvieron ~ de ellos** they showed no mercy.

piedra 1 NF **(a)** (*gen*) stone; (*roca*) rock; (*de encendedor etc*) flint; (*Med*) stone; (*Met*) hailstone; hail; **un puente de ~** a stone bridge; **tener el corazón de ~** to be hard-hearted; **primera ~** foundation stone; **~ de afilar** hone; **~ de amolar** grindstone; **~ angular** (*lit, fig*) cornerstone; **~ arenisca** sandstone; **~ de cal, ~ caliza** limestone; **~ de escándalo** source of scandal; bone of contention; **~ filosofal** philosopher's stone; **~ fundamental** (*fig*) basis, cornerstone; **~ imán** lodestone; **~ miliar** milestone; **~ de molino** millstone; **~ poma** (*Méx*), **~ pómez** pumice (stone); **~ preciosa** precious stone; **~ de toque** touchstone; **~ de tropiezo** stumbling block; **a tiro de ~** within a stone's throw; **no dejar ~ sobre ~** to raze to the ground; **no dejar ~ por mover** to leave no stone unturned; **¿quién se atreve a lanzar la primera ~?** which of you shall cast the first stone?; **colocar la primera ~** to lay the foundation stone; **hablar ~s** (*And*‡) to talk through the back of one's head*; **pasar a uno por la ~** to put sb through the mill; **pasar a una por la ~**‡ to screw sb‡; **quedarse de ~** to be thunderstruck, be rooted to the spot; **no soy de ~** I'm not made of stone, I do have feelings; **eso sería tirar ~s sobre su propio tejado** people who live in glass houses should not throw stones.

(b) (‡: *droga*) dope‡, pot‡.

(c) **en ~** (*Cono Sur Culin*) with hot sauce.

2 NMF (*Carib**: *pesado*) bore.

piel 1 NF **(a)** (*Anat*) skin; **estirarse la ~** to have a facelift, have cosmetic surgery.

(b) (*Zool*) skin, hide, pelt; fur; leather; **~ de ante** buckskin, buff, suède; **~ de becerro, ~ de ternera** calf, calfskin; **~ de cabra** goatskin; **~ de cerdo** pigskin; **~ de gallina** goosepimples; **~ de Suecia** suède; **~ de ternera** calfskin; **la ~ del toro** Spain; **abrigo de ~es** fur coat; **artículos de ~** leather goods; **una maleta de ~** a leather suitcase; **dejarse la ~** (*fig*) to give one's all.

(c) (*Bot*) skin, peel, rind.

2 NMF **~ roja** redskin; **los ~es rojas** the redskins.

piélago NM (*liter*) **(a)** (*océano*) ocean, deep. **(b)** **un ~ de dificultades** (*fig*) a sea of difficulties.

pienso¹ NM (*Agr*) feed, fodder; (‡) grub‡; **~s** feeding stuffs.

pienso²: **¡ni por ~!** (†) never!, the very idea!

pierna NF **(a)** (*Anat*) leg; **~ artificial** artificial leg; **en ~s** bare-legged; **estirar las ~s** (*fig*) to stretch one's legs; **salir por ~s*** to take to one's heels, leg it*; *V* **dormir.**

(b) (*de letra*) stroke; (*con pluma*) downstroke.

(c) (*Cono Sur*) player; partner.

piernas* NM INVAR twit*, idiot.

piernicorto ADJ short-legged.

pierrot [pie'ro] NM pierrot.

pietista ADJ pietistic.

pieza 1 NF **(a)** (*gen*) piece; (*de tela*) piece, roll; **~ de museo** museum piece; **~ arqueológica** object, find; **~ de ropa** piece of clothing, article of clothing; **de una ~** in one piece; solid; **prenda** one-piece; **taladro y destornillador en una sola ~** combined drill and screwdriver; **Juan es una ~** (*LAm**) Juan is as honest as the day is long; **formar ~ única con** to be all of a piece with, (*Mec*) be integral with; **dejar a uno de una ~** to strike sb all of a heap; **quedarse de una ~** to be dumbfounded; **vender algo por ~s** to sell sth by the piece.

(b) (*Mec*) part; **~ de recambio, ~ de repuesto** (*LAm*) spare, spare part, extra (*US*).

(c) (*Fin*) coin, piece; **~ de oro** gold coin, gold piece.

(d) (*Ajedrez etc*) piece, man.

(e) (*Caza*) example; **cobró dos bellas ~s** he obtained (*o* shot *etc*) two fine specimens.

(f) (*Arquit*) room; **~ amueblada** furnished room; **~ de recibo** reception room.

(g) (*Mús*) piece, composition; (*Teat*) piece, work, play; **~ corta**

sketch; **~ oratoria** speech.

(h) **~ de artillería** piece, gun.

(i) **~ de convicción** (*Jur*) exhibit, document, piece of evidence; (*fig*) convincing argument; **~ de examen** showpiece; point to bear in mind.

(j) **buena ~** rogue, villain.

2 NM **(a)** (‡: *camello*) drug pusher.

(b) **un dos ~s** a two-piece suit.

pífano NM fife.

pifia NF **(a)** (*Billar*) miscue, faulty shot, mis-hit.

(b) (*fig: error*) blunder, bloomer*.

(c) (*And, Cono Sur*) (*chiste*) joke; (*burla*) mockery; **hacer ~ de** (*bromear*) to make a joke of, joke about; (*burlarse*) to poke fun at.

(d) (*And: rechifla*) hissing, booing.

pifiador ADJ (*And, Cono Sur*) joking, mocking.

pifiar [1b] 1 VT **(a)** (*And, Cono Sur**: *arruinar*) to mess up, cock up‡, botch.

(b) (*And, Cono Sur, Ven: burlarse de*) to joke about, mock; (*engañar*) to play a trick on.

(c) (*And: rechifla*: *chiflar*) to boo, hiss at.

(d) (*Méx: robar*) to nick‡, lift*.

2 VI **(a)** (*Cono Sur*) (*fracasar*) to fail, come a cropper*; (*en el juego*) to mess up one's game.

(b) (*And, CAm*) to be disappointed, suffer a setback.

(c) (*: meter la pata: t ~la*) to blunder, make a bloomer*.

pigmentación NF pigmentation.

pigmentado 1 ADJ pigmented; (*euf*) *persona* coloured.

2 NM, **pigmentada** NF (*euf*) coloured person.

pigmento NM pigment.

pigmeo, -a ADJ, NM/F pigmy.

pignorable ADJ: **objeto fácilmente ~** a thing which it is easy to pawn.

pignorar [1a] VT to pawn.

pigricia NF **(a)** (*pereza*) laziness; sluggishness. **(b)** (*And, Cono Sur*) trifle, bagatelle; small bit, pinch.

pija¹‡ NF prick‡.

pija²* NF upper-crust girl; stuck-up female*.

pijada NF = **chorrada.**

pijama NM pyjamas; **~ de playa** beach pyjamas.

pijar‡ [1a] VT to fuck‡.

pije* NM (*Cono Sur*) toff*, fop.

pijo 1 ADJ (*) **(a)** (*engreído*) stuck-up*; posh*; yuppified*.

(b) (*quisquilloso*) fussy, demanding.

(c) (*tonto*) thick.

2 NM **(a)** (*: *mimado*) spoiled brat; posh youth; yuppy; upper-class twit*.

(b) (*: *tonto*) twit*, thickie*.

(c) (*Esp*‡) prick‡.

(d) (‡) **¡qué ~!** hell's bells!*; **¿qué ~s haces aquí?** what in hell's name are you doing here?; **no te oyen ni ~** they can't hear you at all.

pijolero‡ ADJ = **pijotero.**

pijotada* NF (*Méx*) **(a)** (*molestia*) nuisance, annoying thing. **(b)** (*dinero*) insignificant sum.

pijotear [1a] VI (*And, Cono Sur, Méx*) to haggle.

pijotería* NF **(a)** (*molestia*) nuisance, small annoyance; (*petición*) trifling request, silly demand.

(b) (*LAm*) (*pequeña cantidad*) insignificant sum, tiny amount; (*bagatela*) trifle, small thing.

(c) (*LAm: tacañería*) meanness.

pijotero 1 ADJ **(a)** (‡: *molesto*) tedious, annoying; wretched; (‡: *condenado*) bloody‡, bleeding‡.

(b) (*LAm**: *tacaño*) mean.

(c) (*Cono Sur: no fiable*) untrustworthy.

2 NM **(a)** (*: *persona molesta*) drag, pain*; **¡no seas ~!** don't be such a pain!*

(b) (*tonto*) berk‡, twit*.

pijudo‡ ADJ **(a)** = **pijotero. (b)** (*CAm: muy bueno*) great*, terrific*.

pila¹ NF **(a)** (*montón*) heap, pile, stack; (*Arquit*) pile.

(b) (*) heap*; (*LAm**) **una ~ de** a heap of*, a lot of; **una ~ de años** very many years; **una ~ de ladrones** a whole lot of thieves; **tengo una ~ de cosas que hacer** I have heaps of things to do*.

pila² NF **(a)** (*fregadero*) sink; (*artesa*) trough; (*abrevadero*) drinking trough; (*de fuente*) basin; (*LAm*) fountain; **~ de cocina** kitchen sink.

(b) (*Ecl*: *t ~ bautismal*) font; **~ de agua bendita** holy water stoup; **sacar de ~ a uno** to act as godparent to sb.

(c) (*Elec*) battery; cell; **~ atómica** atomic pile; **~ (de) botón** watch battery, calculator battery; **~ seca** dry cell; **~ solar** solar battery; **aparato a ~(s)** battery-run apparatus, battery-operated apparatus; **cargar las ~s** (*fig*) to recharge one's batteries; **ponerse las ~s*** to get one's act together.

(d) (*Carib*) tap, faucet (*US*).

pilado: ADJ: **está ~** (*And*) (*seguro*) it's a cert*; (*fácil*) it's a cinch:.

pilar¹ NM (**a**) (*poste*) post, pillar; (*mojón*) milestone.
(**b**) (*Arquit*) pillar; column, pier.
(**c**) (*fig*) prop, (chief) support, mainstay; **un ~ de la monarquía** a mainstay of the monarchy.

pilar² NM (*de fuente*) basin, bowl.

pilastra NF pilaster; (*Cono Sur: de puerta etc*) frame.

Pilatos NM Pilate.

pilatuna* NF (*LAm*) dirty trick.

pilatuno ADJ (*And*) manifestly unjust.

pilcha NF (**a**) (*Cono Sur*) garment, article of clothing; (*de caballo*) harness; **~s** old clothes; fine clothes. (**b**) (*Cono Sur**) mistress.

pilche NM (*And*) gourd, calabash.

píldora NF pill; **la ~** the pill; **~ abortiva** abortion pill; **~ antibaby**, **~ anticonceptiva** contraceptive pill; **~ antifatiga** anti-fatigue pill, pep pill*; **~ del día siguiente** morning-after pill; **dorar la ~** to sweeten the pill.

pildorazo* NM (*Mil*) burst of gunfire, salvo; (*Dep*) fierce shot.

pildorita NF (*Cono Sur*) small cocktail sausage.

pileta NF (**a**) (*gen*) basin, bowl; sink; trough; **~ de cocina** kitchen sink. (**b**) (*Cono Sur*) (*de baño*) wash-basin; **~ (de natación)** swimming-pool.

pilgua NF (*Cono Sur*) wicker basket.

pilier NM prop forward.

piligüe [1] ADJ (*CAm*) *fruta* shrivelled, empty.
[2] NMF (*CAm, Méx*) poor devil.

pilila: NF willie:.

pililo NM (*Cono Sur*) tramp; ragged person.

pilintruca NF (*Cono Sur*) slut.

pillada NF (**a**) (*trampa*) dirty trick. (**b**) (*Cono Sur*) surprise revelation; surprise encounter.

pillaje NM pillage, plunder.

pillar [1a] VT (**a**) (*Mil etc*) to pillage, plunder, sack.
(**b**) (*: atrapar*) to grasp, seize, lay hold of; (*suj: perro*) to catch, worry; **la puerta le pilló el dedo** the door trapped his finger, he got his finger caught in the door; **el perro le pilló el pantalón** the dog seized his trouser leg (in its teeth).
(**c**) (*: coger*) to catch; (*fig: sorprender*) to catch, catch out, catch in the act; **por fin le pilló la policía** the police nabbed him eventually*; **¡te he pillado!** got you!
(**d**) (*) *ganga, puesto etc* to get, land, lay hold of.
(**e**) (*) *significación* to grasp, catch on to.
(**f**) (*) (*caballo*) to knock down; (*coche*) to knock down, run over.
(**g**) (*) **~ una enfermedad** to catch a disease; **~ una borrachera** to get drunk.
(**h**) (*Esp**) **me pilla muy cerca** it's right here; **me pilla lejos** it's too far for me; **me pilla de camino** it's on my way.

pillastre* NM scoundrel.

pillería NF (**a**) (*trampa*) dirty trick. (**b**) (*banda*) gang of scoundrels.

pillete NM young rascal, scamp.

pillín, -ina NM/F little rascal.

pillo [1] ADJ villainous, blackguardly; sly, crafty; *niño* naughty.
[2] NM rascal, rogue, scoundrel; rotter*; (*niño*) rascal, scamp.

pilluelo NM = **pillo**; urchin.

pilmama NF (*Méx*) (*nodriza*) wet-nurse; (*niñera*) nursemaid.

pilme ADJ (*Cono Sur*) very thin.

pilón¹ NM (**a**) (*gen*) pillar, post; (*Elec etc*) pylon; **~ de azúcar** sugar loaf. (**b**) (*de romana*) weight. (**c**) (*Carib Agr*) dump, store.

pilón² NM (**a**) (*abrevadero*) drinking trough; (*de fuente*) basin; (*Méx*) drinking fountain. (**b**) (*mortero*) mortar. (**c**) (*Cono Sur*) pannier. (**d**) (*Méx*: *propina*) tip.

piloncillo NM (*Méx*) powdered brown sugar.

pilongo ADJ thin, emaciated.

pilosidad NF hairiness.

piloso ADJ hairy.

pilotaje NM piloting; navigation; **fallo de ~** navigational error.

pilotar [1a] VT *avión* to pilot; *coche* to drive; *barco* to steer, navigate; (*fig*) to guide, direct.

pilote NM (**a**) (*Arquit*) pile.
(**b**) (*CAm*: *fiesta*) party.

pilotear [1a] VT (**a**) = **pilotar**. (**b**) (*LAm*) *persona* to guide, direct; *negocio* to run, manage. (**c**) (*Cono Sur*) *persona* to exploit.

piloto [1] NMF (**a**) (*Aer*) pilot; **~ automático** automatic pilot; **~ de caza** fighter pilot; **~ de pruebas** test pilot; **segundo ~** co-pilot.
(**b**) (*Náut*) first mate; navigator, navigation officer; **~ de puerto** harbour pilot.
(**c**) (*Aut*) (*esp racing*) driver.
(**d**) (*fig*) guide; (*en exploración*) pathfinder.
(**e**) (*Elec*) pilot light; (*Aut*) rear light, tail light; **~ de alarma** flashing light.
(**f**) (*Cono Sur*) raincoat.
[2] ATR pilot (*atr*); trial (*atr*); experimental; **casa ~** model home, show

house; **estudio ~** pilot study; **planta ~** pilot plant; *V* **luz**.

pilpinto NM (*And, Cono Sur*) butterfly.

pilsen NF (*Cono Sur*) (*any*) beer.

piltra: NF kip:.

piltrafa NF (**a**) (*Culin*) useless bit of meat, skinny meat; **~s** offal, scraps.
(**b**) (*fig*) useless lump, worthless object; (*persona*) poor specimen, poor fish*, weakling.
(**c**) (*And, Cono Sur*) (*ganga*) bargain; (*suerte*) piece of luck; (*ganancia*) profit.
(**d**) **~s** (*LAm*) rags, old clothes.

piltrafiento ADJ (**a**) (*Cono Sur, Méx: harapiento*) ragged. (**b**) (*Cono Sur: marchito*) withered.

piltrafoso ADJ (*And*) ragged.

piltrafudo ADJ (*And*) weak, languid.

piltre [1] ADJ (**a**) (*And, Carib*) foppish. (**b**) (*Cono Sur*) *fruta* over-ripe; shrivelled, dried up; *persona* wizened.
[2] NMF (*And**) snappy dresser*.

pilucho (*Cono Sur*) [1] ADJ half-naked; half-dressed.
[2] NM (*de bebé*) cotton vest, dress.

PIM NMPL *abr de* **Programas Integrados Mediterráneos**.

pimentero NM (**a**) (*Culin*) pepperpot. (**b**) (*Bot*) pepper plant.

pimentón NM cayenne pepper, red pepper; paprika; **~ dulce** sweet pepper, capsicum; **~ picante** chili.

pimienta NF pepper; **~ inglesa** allspice; **~ negra** black pepper.

pimiento NM (**a**) (*Culin*) pepper, pimiento; **~ rojo** red pepper; **~ verde** green pepper; **no se me de un ~**, **(no) me importa un ~** I don't care two hoots (*de* about). (**b**) (*Bot*) pepper plant. (**c**) (**:**) cunt**:**.

pimpampúm* NM (**a**) (*de ferias*) shooting gallery. (**b**) (*ruido*) crash, bang, wallop.

pimpante* ADJ (**a**) (*encantador*) charming, attractive; chic. (**b**) (*pey: esp tan ~*) smug, self-satisfied.

Pimpinela NM: **el ~ escarlata** the Scarlet Pimpernel.

pimpinela NF pimpernel.

pimplar* [1a] [1] VI to booze*.
[2] **pimplarse** VR: **~ una botella** to down a bottle*, quaff a bottle*.

pimpollo NM (**a**) (*Bot*) (*serpollo*) sucker, shoot; (*arbolito*) sapling; (*capullo*) rosebud. (**b**) (*) (*niño*) bonny child; (*mujer*) attractive woman; **estar hecho un ~** (*elegante*) to look very smart; (*parecer joven*) to look very young for one's age.

pimpón NM ping-pong.

pimponista NMF ping-pong player.

PIN NM ABR *de* **producto interior neto** net domestic product, NDP.

pin NM, PL **pins** (**a**) (*chapa*) badge. (**b**) (*Elec*) pin.

pinabete NM fir, fir tree.

pinacate NM (*Méx*) black beetle.

pinacoteca NF art gallery.

pináculo NM pinnacle.

pinar NM pinewood, pine grove.

pinaza NF pinnace.

pincel NM (**a**) (*gen*) paintbrush, artist's brush; **estar hecho un ~** to be very smartly dressed. (**b**) (*fig*) painter.

pincelada NF brush-stroke; **última ~** (*fig*) finishing touch.

pincha¹* NF (*Carib*) job, spot of work.

pincha² NF (*Cono Sur*) hair-grip.

pincha³* NMF, **pinchadiscos*** NMF INVAR (*Esp*) disc-jockey, DJ.

pinchante ADJ *grito etc* piercing.

pinchar [1a] [1] VT (**a**) (*gen*) to prick, pierce, puncture; *neumático* to puncture; (*Esp* *Telec*) to tap, bug*; (*: con navaja*) to knife, stab; **ni ~ ni cortar*** to cut no ice; **tener un neumático pinchado** to have a puncture, have a flat tyre; **~ a uno** (*Med**) to give sb a jab* (*o* injection).
(**b**) (*fig: estimular*) to prod; **hay que ~le** he needs prodding; **le pinchan para que se case** they keep prodding him to get married.
(**c**) (*fig*) (*herir*) to wound, mortify; (*provocar*) to provoke, stir up.
(**d**) (*Rad**) *disco* to play, put on.
[2] VI (**a**) (*: perder*) to fail, suffer a defeat, get beaten.
(**b**) (**:**) to screw**:**.
[3] **pincharse** VR (**a**) (*gen*) to prick o.s.; (*: con droga*) to give o.s. a jab*, give o.s. a fix:.
(**b**) (*neumático*) to get punctured, go flat, burst.

pinchazo NM (**a**) (*gen*) prick; puncture (*t Aut*), flat (*US Aut*). (**b**) (*: de droga*) jab*, fix:. (**b**) (*fig*) prod. (**c**) (*Telec**) tap, bug*. (**d**) (*: derrota*) defeat; (*fracaso*) comedown*, débâcle.

pinche [1] NM (**a**) (*de cocina*) kitchen-boy, scullion. (**b**) (*Cono Sur*) (*oficinista*) minor office clerk; (*criminal*) small-time criminal. (**c**) (*Carib, Méx*) rascal. (**d**) (*And*) bad horse, nag. (**e**) (*Cono Sur*) hatpin.
[2] ADJ (**a**) (*Méx*: *maldito*) bloody:, lousy:. (**b**) (*CAm*: *tacaño*) stingy, tight-fisted; (*CAm, Méx*: *miserable*) wretched; **todo por unos ~s centavos** all for a few measly cents.

pinchito NM (*Esp: gen pl*) savoury, titbit (*served at bar with aperitif*).

pincho NM (a) (*gen*) point; (*Bot*) prickle, thorn; (*aguijón*) pointed stick, spike; (*Cono Sur*) spike, prickle; (**‡**: *navaja*) knife; (**••**) prick**‡‡**. (b) (*Culin*) = **pinchito**; **un ~ de tortilla** a portion of omelette (on a stick); **~ moruno** kebab.

pinchota‡ NMF user of drugs by injection.

pinciano (*Esp*) ① ADJ of (o from) Valladolid.
② NM, **pinciana** NF native (o inhabitant) of Valladolid; **los ~s** the people of Valladolid.

pindárico ADJ Pindaric.

Píndaro NM Pindar.

pindonga‡ NF gadabout.

pindonguear‡ [1a] VI to gad about.

pinga NF (*And, Carib, Méx‡‡*) prick**‡‡**; (*Carib*) **de ~‡** amazing, terrific‡.

pingajo NM rag, shred; tag.

pinganilla‡ NM (a) (*LAm*) poor man with pretensions to elegance.
(b) **en ~s** (*And, Méx: de puntillas*) on tiptoe; (*Méx*) (*en cuclillas*) squatting; (*poco firme*) wobbly.

pinganillo ADJ (*And*) chubby.

pinganitos NMPL: **estar en ~** to be well up, be well-placed socially; **poner a uno en ~s** to give sb a leg up (socially).

pingo NM (a) (*harapo*) rag, shred; (*cabo*) tag; (*prenda*) old garment, shabby dress; **~s** (‡: *ropa*) clothes; (‡: *trastos*) odds and ends; **no tengo ni un ~ que ponerme‡** I haven't a single thing I can wear; **andar** (o **ir**) **de ~** to gad about; **poner a uno como un ~** to abuse sb.
(b) (‡) (*marrana*) slut; (*puta*) prostitute.
(c) (*Cono Sur: caballo*) horse; good horse; (*Cono Sur, And: pey*) worthless horse, nag.
(d) (*Méx: niño*) scamp; **el ~** the devil.
(e) (*Cono Sur: niño*) lively child.

pingonear‡ [1a] VI to gad about.

pingorotear [1a] VI (*LAm*), **pingotear** [1a] VI (*LAm*) to skip about, jump.

ping-pong ['pimpon] NM ping-pong.

pinguchita‡ NF (*Cono Sur*) beanpole‡.

pingucho (*Cono Sur*) ① ADJ poor, wretched.
② NM urchin, ragamuffin.

pingüe ADJ (a) (*grasoso*) greasy, fat. (b) (*fig*) abundant, copious; *ganancia* rich, fat; *cosecha* heavy, bumper, rich; *negocio* lucrative.

pingui‡ NM swank.

pingüino NM penguin.

pininos NMPL (*esp LAm*), **pinitos** NMPL: **hacer ~** (*niño*) to toddle, take one's first steps; (*enfermo*) to start to get about again, to get back on one's feet again; (*novato*) to take one's first steps, try for the first time; **hago mis ~ como pintor** I play at painting, I dabble at painting.

pinja‡‡ NF (*And*) prick**‡‡**.

pino¹ NM (*Bot*) pine, pine-tree; **~ albar** Scots pine; **~ araucano** monkey-puzzle (tree); **~ bravo, ~ marítimo, ~ rodeno** cluster pine; **~ silvestre** Scots pine; **~ de tea** pitch-pine; **vivir en el quinto ~** to live at the back of beyond; **eso está en el quinto ~** that's terribly far away; **hacer el ~, ponerse de ~** to stand on one's head; **ponerle ~** (*Cono Sur‡*) to make a great effort.

pino² NM (a) **en ~** upright, vertical; standing. (b) **~s = pinitos**.

pinocha NF pine needle.

pinol(e) NM (*CAm, Méx*) roasted maize flour; *drink made of toasted maize*.

pinolero, -a‡ NM/F (*CAm*) Nicaraguan.

pinrel‡ NM hoof‡, foot.

pinsapo NM (*Esp*) Spanish fir.

pinta¹ NF (a) (*punto*) spot, dot; (*Zool etc*) spot, mark, marking; **una tela a ~s azules** a cloth with blue spots.
(b) (*Naipes*) spot (*indicating suit*); **¿a qué ~?** what's trumps?, what suit are we in?
(c) (*gota etc*) drop, spot; drop of rain; (‡) drink, drop to drink; **una ~ de grasa** a grease spot.
(d) (*fig: aspecto*) appearance, look(s); **¡a la ~!** (*Cono Sur*) perfect!, that's fine!; **estar a la ~** (*Cono Sur*) = **tener ~**; **por la ~** by the look of it; **tener ~** (*Cono Sur*) to be attractive; to be smart, be well-dressed; **tener buena ~** (*persona*) to look good, look well; (*comida*) to look good; **tener ~ de listo** to look clever, have a bright look about one; **tiene ~ de criminal** he has a criminal look; **tiene ~ de español** he looks Spanish, he looks like a Spaniard; **¿qué ~ tiene?** what does he look like?; **tirar ~‡** to impress, be impressive; **no se le vio ni ~** (*LAm‡*) there wasn't a sign (o trace) of him.
(e) (‡: *persona inútil*) worthless creature.
(f) (*And, Carib, Cono Sur: Zool etc: colorido etc*) colouring, coloration; (*LAm: señal*) birthmark; (*CAm: pintada*) graffito.
(g) (*And, Cono Sur*) (*juego*) draughts; (*dados*) dice.
(h) (*Cono Sur Min*) high-grade ore.
(i) **hacer ~** (*Méx*), **irse de ~** (*CAm*) to play truant.
(j) **ser de la ~** (*Carib: euf*) to be coloured.

pinta² NF (*medida inglesa*) pint.

pintada¹ NF (*Orn*) guinea-fowl.

pintada² NF graffiti, daub; slogan.

pintado ① ADJ (a) (*moteado*) spotted; (*pinto*) mottled, dappled; (*fig*) many-coloured, colourful; (*LAm*) black and white.
(b) (‡) **podría pasarle al más ~** it could happen to anybody; **lo hace como el más ~** he does it with (o as well as) the best.
(c) **me sienta que ni ~, viene que ni ~‡** it comes just right; it suits me a treat.
(d) (*LAm*) like, identical; **el niño salió** (o **está**) **~ al padre** the boy looks exactly like his father, the boy is the spitting image of his father; **ni ~ se le verá por aquí** (*Méx‡*) you won't catch sight of him round here.
② NM (a) (*con pintura*) painting; (*Téc*) coating; **~ de campo** marking-out of the pitch. (b) wine and vermouth cocktail.

pintalabios NM INVAR lipstick.

pintamonas‡ NMF INVAR (a) (*pintor*) dauber‡. (b) (*don nadie*): **un ~** a nobody.

pintar [1a] ① VT (a) (*gen*) to paint; *letra, letrero etc* to draw, make; **~ algo de azul** to paint sth blue.
(b) (*fig*) to paint, depict, describe; **lo pinta todo muy negro** (o **de negro**) he paints it all very black.
(c) **~la‡** to put it on, show off.
(d) (‡) **no pinta nada** he cuts no ice, he doesn't count; he has no say; **¿qué pinta?** (*de qué sirve*) what's it for?; (*qué hace*) what does he do?; **pero ¿qué pintamos aquí?** but what on earth are we doing here?
(e) (*LAm: zalamear*) to flatter.
② VI (a) (*gen*) to paint; **'ojo, (que) pinta'** (*aviso*) 'wet paint'; **~ como querer** to daydream, indulge in wishful thinking.
(b) (*Bot*) to ripen, turn red.
(c) **esto pinta mal‡** this looks bad, I don't like the look of this.
(d) **pintan corazones** hearts are trumps.
③ **pintarse** VR (a) (*maquillarse*) to use make-up; to put on make-up, (*pey*) paint o.s.
(b) **~las solo para algo** to be a dab hand at sth‡.
(c) (*LAm‡: escaparse*) to scarper**‡**.

pintarraj(e)ar [1a] VTI to daub.

pintarrajo‡ NM daub.

pintarroja NF dogfish.

pintas‡ NM INVAR ugly customer‡; scruffily dressed person.

pintear [1a] VI to drizzle, spot with rain.

pintiparado ADJ (a) (*idéntico*) identical (*a* to). (b) **me viene (que ni) ~** it comes just right, it's just what the doctor ordered.

pintiparar [1a] VT to compare.

Pinto NM: **estar entre ~ y Valdemoro** (*Esp‡*) (*dudoso*) to be in two minds; (*borracho*) to be tipsy.

pinto ADJ (a) (*LAm: moteado*) spotted; (*con manchas*) mottled, dappled; (*marcado*) marked (*esp* with black and white); (*abigarrado*) motley, colourful; *tez* blotchy.
(b) (*Carib: listo*) clever; (*pey*) sharp, shrewd.
(c) (*Carib: borracho*) drunk.

pintor, -a NM/F (a) painter; **~ de brocha gorda** house painter, (*fig*) bad painter, dauber; **~ decorador** house painter, interior decorator; **~ de suelo** pavement artist. (b) (*Cono Sur‡: fachendoso*) swank‡.

pintoresco ADJ picturesque.

pintoresquismo NM picturesqueness.

pintura NF (a) (*gen*) painting; (*fig*) painting, depiction, description; **no le podía ver ni en ~** she couldn't stand the sight of him.
(b) (*una ~*) painting; **~ a la acuarela, ~ a la aguada** watercolour; **~ al óleo** oil painting; **~ al pastel** pastel drawing; **~ rupestre** cave painting.
(c) (*material*) paint; **~ a la cola, ~ al temple** distemper, (*Arte*) tempera; **~ emulsionada** emulsion paint.

pinturero ① ADJ flashy, flashily dressed.
② NM, **pinturera** NF show-off‡, dandy.

pinza NF (*t ~s*) (*de ropa*) clothes-peg, clothespin (*US*); (*de depilar etc*) tweezers; (*Med*) forceps; (*Téc: tenazas*) pincers; (*Zool*) claw; **~s de azúcar** sugar tongs; **~ de pelo** (*Carib*) hair grip; **no se lo sacan ni con ~s** wild horses won't drag it out of him.

pinzón NM finch; **~ vulgar** chaffinch; **~ real** bullfinch.

piña ① NF (a) (*Bot*) pine-cone.
(b) (*t ~ de América, ~ de las Indias*) pineapple.
(c) (*fig*) group; cluster, knot; (*pey*) clique, closed circle.
(d) (*Carib, Méx*) hub.
(e) (‡: *golpe*) punch, bash‡; **darse ~s** to fight, exchange blows.
(f) (*Méx: de revólver*) chamber.
(g) (*And*) **¡qué ~!** bad luck!; **estar ~** to be unlucky.
② NMF (*CAm‡*) homosexual, poof**‡**.

piñal NM (*LAm*) pineapple plantation.

piñar‡ NM (*Méx*) lie.

piñata¹⁑ NF ivories*, teeth.

piñata² NF (*Cono Sur*) brawl, scrap*.

piñatería NF (*Cono Sur*) armed hold-up.

piño¹⁑ NM ivory*, tooth.

piño² NM (*Cono Sur*) lot, crowd.

piñón¹ NM (*Bot*) pine-nut, pine-seed; **estar a partir un ~** to be bosom pals (*con* with)*.

piñón² NM (*Orn, Téc*) pinion; **quedarse a ~ fijo** to have a mental block; **seguir a ~ fijo** to go on in the same old way, be stuck in one's old ways.

piñonate NM candied pine-nut.

piñonear [1a] VI to click.

piñoneo NM click.

piñoso* ADJ (*And*) unlucky.

PIO NM (*Esp*) ABR *de* **Patronato de Igualdad de Oportunidades** ≃ Equal Opportunities Commission.

Pío NM Pius.

pío¹ ADJ *caballo* piebald, dappled.

pío² ADJ (a) (*Rel*) pious, devout; (*pey*) sanctimonious; excessively pious. (b) (*compasivo*) merciful.

pío³ NM (a) (*Orn*) cheep, chirp; **no decir ni ~** not to breathe a word; **¡de esto no digas ni ~!** you keep your mouth shut about this!; **irse sin decir ni ~** to go off without a word. (b) **tener el ~ de algo*** to long for sth.

piocha ⬜1 NF (a) (*joya*) jewel (worn on the head). (b) (*LAm: piqueta*) pickaxe. (c) (*Méx*) goatee.
⬜2 ADJ (*Méx*) nice.

piojería NF (a) (*lugar*) lousy place, verminous place. (b) (*pobreza*) poverty. (c) (*: miseria*) tiny amount, very small portion.

piojo NM (a) (*Zool*) louse; **~ resucitado*** jumped-up fellow, vulgar parvenu; **dar el ~** (*Méx**) to show one's nasty side; **estar como ~s en costura** to be packed in like sardines. (b) (*And*) gambling den.

piojoso ADJ (a) (*gen*) lousy, verminous; (*fig*) dirty, ragged. (b) (*fig*) mean.

piojuelo NM louse.

piola ⬜1 NF (a) (*LAm*) (*soga*) rope, tether; (*And, Carib: cuerda*) cord, string, twine; (*maguey*) agave. (b) (*Cono Sur**) cock⁑.
⬜2 ADJ (*Cono Sur**) (*listo*) bright; (*taimado*) sly; (*servicial*) helpful; (*bueno*) great*, terrific*; (*elegante*) classy*, smart.

piolet [pio'le] NM, PL **piolets** [pio'les] ice-axe.

piolín NM (*LAm*) cord, twine.

pionco ADJ (a) (*Cono Sur*) naked from the waist down. (b) (*Méx: en cuclillas*) squatting. (c) (*Méx*) *caballo* short-tailed.

pionero ⬜1 ADJ pioneering.
⬜2 NM, **pionera** NF pioneer.

pioneta NM (*Chile: Aut*) lorry driver's mate, truck driver's mate (*US*).

piorrea NF pyorrhoea.

PIP NM (*Puerto Rico*) ABR *de* **Partido Independentista Puertorriqueño**.

pipa¹ NF (a) (*de fumar*) pipe; **fumar una ~, fumar en ~** to smoke a pipe. (b) (*de vino*) cask, barrel; (*medida*) pipe. (c) (*Bot*) pip, seed, edible sunflower seed. (d) (*Mús*) reed. (e) (*LAm*: *barriga*) belly. (f) (*And, CAm Bot*) green coconut. (g) (*: pistola*) rod⁑, pistol; (*ametralladora*) machine-gun. (h) **pasarlo ~*** to have a great time*.

pipa*² NM (*Mús*) assistant; (*mozo de carga*) porter; (*utillero*) boy, mate.

pipear⁑ [1a] ⬜1 VT to look at.
⬜2 VI to look.

pipero¹, -a NMF street vendor.

pipero² NM (a) (*estante*) pipe-rack. (b) (*fumador*) pipe-smoker.

pipeta NF pipette.

pipi⁑ NM (*Mil*) squaddie*, recruit; (*novato*) new boy.

pipí⁑ NM pee⁑, piss⁑, (*entre niños*) wee-wee⁑; **hacer ~** to have a pee⁑, go wee-wee⁑.

pipián NM (*CAm, Méx*) (*salsa*) thick chili sauce; (*guiso*) meat cooked in thick chili sauce.

pipiar [1c] VI to cheep, chirp.

pipiciego ADJ (*And*) short-sighted.

pipil* NM (*CAm: hum*) Mexican.

pipiolero* NM (*Méx*) crowd of kids*.

pipiolo, -a* NMF (*joven*) youngster; (*LAm: chico*) little boy, little girl; (*fig: novato*) novice, greenhorn, tyro. (b) (*Carib, Cono Sur: tonto*) fool. (c) **~s** (*CAm*) money.

pipirigallo NM sainfoin.

pipiripao NM (a) (*) slap-up do*, spread*. (b) **de ~** (*LAm*) worthless.

pipo ⬜1 ADJ (*And, Carib*) potbellied; **estar ~** (*Carib*) to be bloated.
⬜2 NM (a) (*Carib: niño*) child. (b) (*And, Carib: empleado*) crooked employee*. (c) (*And: golpe*) punch, bash*.

(d) (*And: licor*) contraband liquor.

pipón ADJ (*And, Carib, Cono Sur*) (*barrigón*) potbellied; (*después de comer*) bloated.

piporro NM (a) (*instrumento*) bassoon. (b) (*persona*) bassoonist.

pipote NM keg, cask; (*And*) dustbin.

pipudo⁑ ADJ great*, super*.

pique¹ NM (a) (*resentimiento*) pique, resentment; (*inquina*) ill will; (*rencor*) grudge; rivalry, competition; self-respect; **estar de ~** to have a grudge, be at loggerheads; **tener un ~ con uno** to have a grudge against sb. (b) **estar a ~ de** + *infin* to be on the point of + *ger*; to be in danger of + *ger*; **estuvo a ~ de hacerlo** he very nearly did it. (c) **echar a ~** *barco* to sink; (*fig*) to wreck, ruin; **irse a ~** to sink, founder; (*esperanza, familia etc*) to be ruined. (d) (*LAm: rebote*) bounce, rebound. (e) (*CAm, Cono Sur Min*) mineshaft; (*Méx*) drill, well. (f) (*Cam, Cono Sur: sendero*) trail, narrow path. (g) (*And: insecto*) jigger flea.

pique² NM (*Naipes*) spades.

pique³⁑ NM (*de droga*) fix⁑, shot*.

piquera NF (a) (*de tonel, colmena*) hole, vent. (b) (*CAm, Méx: taberna*) dive⁑. (c) (*Carib: de taxis*) taxi rank.

piquero NM (a) (*Hist*) pikeman. (b) (*And, Cono Sur*) miner. (c) (⁑) pick-pocket.

piqueta NF pick, pickaxe.

piquetazo NM (*LAm*) (*tijeretazo*) snip, small cut; (*mordida*) peck; (*de abeja etc*) sting, bite.

piquete NM (a) (*pinchazo*) prick, jab, slight wound. (b) (*agujero*) small hole (*in clothing*). (c) (*Mil*) squad, party; (*de huelguistas*) picket; picket line; **~ de ejecución** firing-squad; **~ informativo** picket; **~ móvil, ~ volante** flying picket. (d) (*Cono Sur*) yard, small corral. (e) (*And*) picnic. (f) (*Carib*) street band.

piquin NM (a) (*And: galán*) boyfriend. (b) (*Cono Sur**) (*pizca*) pinch, dash. (c) (*Cono Sur: persona*) irritable sort.

piquiña NF (a) (*And, Carib*) = **picazón**. (b) (*Carib: envidia*) envy.

pira¹ NF pyre.

pira²⁑ NF: **hacer ~, irse de ~** to clear off*; (*Escol*) to cut class*, go off and amuse o.s.

pirado⁑ ⬜1 ADJ (*tonto*) crazy; (*drogado*) high (on drugs)⁑.
⬜2 NM, **pirada** NF nutcase⁑; druggy⁑.

piragua NF canoe.

piragüismo NM canoeing.

piragüista NMF canoeist; oarsman.

piramidal ADJ (a) pyramidal. (b) (*And**) terrific*, tremendous*.

pirámide NF pyramid.

Píramo NM Pyramus.

piraña NF (*LAm*) piranha.

pirarse* [1a] VR (t **pirárselas**) (*largarse*) to beat it*, clear out*; (*Escol*) to cut class*; (*And*) to escape from prison; (*Méx*) to peg out⁑.

pirata ⬜1 NM/F (a) pirate; **~ aéreo** hijacker; **~ informático** hacker. (b) (*fig*) hard-hearted person. (c) (*: Liter etc*) plagiarist, borrower of other people's ideas (*etc*). (d) (*: granuja*) rogue, scoundrel; (*Com*) cowboy, shark, sharp operator; (*Inform*) hacker.
⬜2 ADJ pirate; illegal; unauthorized; **disco ~** bootleg record; **edición ~** pirated edition; **emisora ~** pirate radio station.

piratear [1a] ⬜1 VT (*Aer*) to hijack; (*esp Mús*) to pirate; *libro* to pirate; (*Inform*) to hack into.
⬜2 VI to buccaneer, practise piracy; (*fig*) to steal.

pirateo NM, **piratería** NF piracy; (*fig*) theft, stealing; (*de disco*) pirating; bootlegging; (*Inform*) hacking; **~ aérea** hijacking; **~s** depredations.

pirático ADJ piratical.

piraya NF (*LAm*) piranha.

pirca NF (*LAm*) dry-stone wall.

pire⁑ NM (*drogas*) trip⁑.

pirenaico ADJ Pyrenean.

pirético ADJ pyretic.

piretro NM pyrethrum.

pirgua NF (*And, Cono Sur*) shed, outhouse.

piri⁑ NM grub⁑, nosh⁑.

piridina NF pyridine.

pirineísta NMF mountaineer (who climbs in the Pyrenees).

Pirineo NM, **Pirineos** NMPL Pyrenees; **el ~ catalán** the Catalan (part of the) Pyrenees.

pirineo ADJ Pyrenean.

pirinola* NF (*Méx*) kid*, child.

piripez* NF: **coger una ~** to get merry.

piripi* ADJ: **estar ~** to be merry.

piritas NFPL pyrites.
pirlán NM (*And*) doorstep.
piro: NM: **darse el ~** to beat it*; **darse el ~ de** to escape from.
piro... PREF pyro...
pirófago, -a NM/F fire-eater.
piromanía NF pyromania.
pirómano, -a NM/F arsonist, fire-raiser, pyromaniac.
piropear [1a] VT to pay an amorous compliment to, make a flirtatious remark to.
piropo NM (a) (*cumplido*) amorous compliment, flirtatious remark; **echar ~s a** = piropear.
(b) (*piedra*) garnet; ruby.
(c) (*And**) ticking-off*.
piroso* ADJ lewd, dirty.
pirotecnia NF pyrotechnics; firework display (*t fig*).
pirotécnico ADJ pyrotechnic, firework (*atr*).
piroxidina NF pyridoxine.
pirquén NM: **mina al ~** (*Chile*) rented mine.
pirrar* [1a], **pirriar** [1b] [1] VT: **le pirraba el cine** the cinema really turned him on*.
[2] **pirr(i)arse** VR: **~ por** to rave about, be crazy about.
pírrico ADJ: **victoria pírrica** Pyrrhic victory.
Pirro NM Pyrrhus.
pirucho NM (a) (*CAm*) (ice-cream) cone (*o cornet*). (b) (*Cono Sur* *Pol*) Peronist.
pirueta NF (a) (*gen*) pirouette; (*cabriola*) caper. (b) (*fig*) remark which helps somebody out of an awkward situation; neat recovery. (c) **hacer ~s** (*fig*) to perform a balancing act (*between two policies etc*).
piruetear [1a] VI to pirouette; to caper.
pirula¹: NF (a) (*Anat*) willy:. (b) **hacer la ~ a** (*molestar*) to upset, annoy; (*jugarla*) to play a dirty trick on; (*embaucar*) to cheat, do down*.
piruleta NF lollipop.
pirulí NM (a) lollipop. (b) (:') prick:'. (c) **el P~*** Madrid television tower.
pirulo (*Cono Sur*) [1] NM: **tiene 40 ~s:** he's forty.
[2] NM, **pirula²** NF (*chico*) slim child.
pis: NM = pipí.
pisa NF (a) (*de uvas*) treading. (b) (*: zurra*) beating.
pisada NF footstep, footfall, tread; (*huella*) footprint.
pisadera NF (*And*) carpet.
pisadero NM (*Méx*) brothel.
pisado NM treading (of grapes).
pisapapeles NM INVAR paperweight.
pisar [1a] [1] VT (a) (*gen*) to tread (on), walk on; (*por casualidad*) to step on; (*dañando*) to flatten, crush, trample (on, underfoot); *uvas etc* to tread; *tierra* to tread down; **~ el acelerador** to step on the accelerator, press the accelerator; **~ (el coche) a fondo** to put one's foot down*; **'no ~ el césped'** 'keep off the grass'; **no volvimos a ~ ese sitio** we never set foot in that place again.
(b) (*Mús*) *tecla* to play, strike, press; *cuerda* to hold down.
(c) (*edificio etc*) to lie on, cover (part of).
(d) (*fig*) (*atropellar*) to trample on, walk all over; (*desatender*) to disregard; (*maltratar*) to abuse; **no se deja ~ por nadie** he doesn't let anybody trample over him.
(e) (*: robar*) to pinch*, steal; **A le pisó la novia a B** A pinched B's girl*; **~ una baza a uno** to trump sb's trick; **otro le pisó el puesto** sb got in first and collared the job*; **el periódico le pisó la noticia** the newspaper got in first with the news.
(f) (*And*) *hembra* to cover; (*CAm*:') to fuck:', screw:'.
[2] VI (a) (*andar*) to tread, step, walk; **hay que ~ con cuidado** you have to tread carefully.
(b) (*fig*) **~ fuerte** to act determinedly; to make a strong showing, make a real impression; **entró (o vino) pisando fuerte** she made a strong start; she made her position clear from the start, she showed she was not going to stand any nonsense; **ir pisando huevos** to tread carefully.
[3] **pisarse** VR (*Cono Sur*) to be mistaken.
pisaverde NM fop.
pisca NF (a) (*Méx*) maize harvest, corn harvest (*US*). (b) (*And: prostituta*) prostitute.
piscador NM (*Méx*) harvester.
piscar [1g] VI (*Méx*) to harvest maize (*o corn (US)*).
piscicultor(a) NM/F fish-farmer.
piscicultura NF fish-farming.
piscifactoría NF fish-farm.
piscigranja NF (*LAm*) fish-farm.
piscina NF (a) (*Dep*) swimming-pool; **~ climatizada** heated swimming-pool; **~ cubierta** indoor swimming-pool; **~ olímpica** Olympic-length pool. (b) (*tanque*) fishpond, fishtank.
Piscis NM (*Zodíaco*) Pisces.
pisco¹ NM (*And*) (a) (*Orn*) turkey. (b) (*fig*) fellow, guy* (*US*).
pisco² NM (*LAm*) strong liquor.

piscoiro* NM, **piscoira** NF (*Cono Sur**) bright child.
piscolabis NM INVAR (a) snack. (b) (*CAm, Méx*) money.
pisicorre NM (*Carib*) small bus.
piso NM (a) (*suelo*) floor; flooring.
(b) (*Arquit*) storey, floor; (*de autobús, barco*) deck; (*de cohete*) stage; (*de pastel*) layer; **~ alto** top floor; **~ bajo** ground floor, first floor (*US*); **primer ~** first floor, second floor (*US*); **un edificio de 8 ~s** an 8-storey building; **viven en el quinto ~** they live on the fifth floor; **autobús de dos ~s** double-decker bus; **ir en el ~ de arriba** to travel on the top deck, travel upstairs.
(c) (*apartamento*) flat, apartment (*US*); **~ franco** (*Esp*), **~ de seguridad** safe house, hide-out; **poner un ~ a una** (*Esp*) to set a woman up in a flat.
(d) (*Aut: de neumático*) tread.
(e) (*de zapato*) sole; **poner ~ a un zapato** to sole a shoe.
(f) (*Min*) set of workings; (*Geol*) layer, stratum.
(g) (*Cono Sur*) (*taburete*) stool; (*banco*) bench.
(h) (*estera*) mat; (*Cono Sur, Méx: tapete*) table runner; (*And, Cono Sur: alfombra*) long narrow rug; **~ de baño** bathmat.
pisón NM (a) (*herramienta*) ram, rammer. (b) (*LAm*) = pisotón (b). (c) (*Cono Sur: mortero*) mortar.
pisotear [1a] VT (a) (*gen*) to tread down, trample (on, underfoot); to stamp on. (b) (*fig*) to trample on; *ley etc* to abuse, disregard.
pisoteo NM treading, trampling; stamping.
pisotón NM (a) (*gen*) stamp on the foot. (b) (*: Periodismo*) newspaper scoop, reporting scoop.
pispar* [1a] [1] VT (*: robar*) to nick:, steal.
[2] VI (*Cono Sur*) to keep watch, spy.
pis-pas* NM: **en un ~** in a flash, in no time at all.
pisporra NF (*CAm*) wart.
pista NF (a) (*Zool y fig*) track, trail; (*fig: indicio*) clue; (*de cinta*) track; **~ falsa** false trail, false clue; (*en discusión etc*) red herring; **estar sobre la ~** to be on the scent; **estar sobre la ~ de uno** to be on sb's trail, be after sb; **seguir la ~ de uno** to be on sb's track, trail sb; to shadow sb; **la policía tiene una ~ ya** the police already have a lead (*o clue*).
(b) (*Dep etc*) track, course; (*cancha*) court; (*Aut*) carriageway; (*CAm: avenida*) avenue; (*de esquí*) run, slope; (*de circo etc*) floor, arena; (*Inform, Mús*) track; **~ de aprendizaje** nursery slope; **~ de aterrizaje** runway; landing-strip; **~ de atletismo** athletics track, running track; **~ de baile** dance-floor; **~ de bolos** bowling-alley; **~ de carreras** racetrack; **~ de ceniza** dirt track; **reunión de ~ cubierta** indoor athletics meeting; **~ de esquí** ski-run; **~ forestal** forest trail; **~ de hielo** ice-rink; **~ de hierba** grass court; **~ de patinaje** skating-rink; **~ de tenis** tennis-court; **~ de tierra batida** clay court; **atletismo en ~** track events.
pistacho NM pistachio.
pistero ADJ (*CAm*) mercenary, fond of money.
pistilo NM pistil.
pisto NM (a) (*Med*) chicken broth.
(b) (*Culin Esp*) fried vegetable hash.
(c) (*fig: revoltijo*) mixture, hotchpotch.
(d) **a ~s** little by little; sparingly.
(e) **darse ~*** to show off, swank*, shoot a line*.
(f) (*And, CAm*:) dough:, money.
(g) (*And: de revólver*) barrel.
(h) (*Méx*:) shot of liquor*.
pistola NF (a) (*Mil*) pistol; (*Téc*) spray gun; **~ de agua** water pistol; **~ ametralladora** submachine-gun, tommy-gun; **~ engrasadora**, **~ de engrase** grease-gun; **~ de juguete** toy pistol; **~ de pintar**, **~ rociadora de pintura** paint spray, spray gun. (b) (*Culin*) long loaf.
(c) (:') prick:'.
pistolera NF (a) holster; **salir de ~s** to get out of a tight spot. (b) (*Anat**) **~s** flabby thighs.
pistolerismo NM gun law, rule by terror.
pistolero NM gunman, gangster; **~ a sueldo** hired killer.
pistoleta NF (*And, Cono Sur*) small pistol.
pistoletazo NM pistol shot; (*Dep, fig*) starting signal.
pistolete NM pocket pistol.
pistolo: NM soldier.
pistón NM (a) (*Mec*) piston. (b) (*Mús*) key; (*LAm: corneta*) bugle, cornet. (c) (*CAm, Méx*) corn tortilla. (d) **de ~*** = pistonudo.
pistonudo* ADJ smashing*, terrific*.
pistudo ADJ (*CAm*) rich.
pita NF (a) (*Bot*) agave; (*fibra*) pita fibre, pita thread; (*esp Chile, Peru*) string; **enredar la ~** (*LAm**) to stir things up. (b) (*LAm*) **~s** lies.
pitada NF (a) (*silbido*) whistle; (*rechifla*) hiss. (b) (*LAm**: *de cigarrillo*) puff, drag*. (c) (*: salida inoportuna*) silly remark.
pitador, -a NM/F (*LAm*) smoker.
Pitágoras NM Pythagoras.
pitagorín* NM brainbox*.
pitandero, -a NM/F (*Cono Sur*) smoker.

pitanza NF (a) (*ración*) dole, daily ration; (‡) grub‡. (b) (*: precio*) price. (c) (*Cono Sur*) bargain; profit.

pitar [1a] **1** VT (a) *silbato* to blow; *partido* to referee; **el árbitro pitó falta** the referee whistled for a foul.
(b) *árbitro etc* to whistle at, boo; *actor, obra* to hiss, give the bird to*.
(c) (*LAm**) to smoke.
2 VI (a) (*silbar*) to whistle, blow a whistle; (*rechiflar*) to hiss, boo; (*Aut*) to sound one's horn; **pitó el árbitro** the referee blew (his whistle).
(b) (*LAm**) to smoke; to puff.
(c) (*) (*funcionar*) to work (well); (*dar resultados*) to give (good) results; **esto no pita** this is no good, this doesn't work; **la tele no pita** the telly is on the blink*; **~ bien** to give a good account of o.s.; **salir pitando** to beat it*; **salió pitando para X*** he went off at top speed to X.
3 **pitarse‡** VR to beat it*.

pitarra‡ NF grub‡, food.

pitay NM (*And, Cono Sur*) rash.

pitazo NM (*And, Méx*) whistle, hoot; **dar el ~ a uno** (*Carib**) to tip sb the wink*.

pítcher [pitʃer] NM (*CAm Béisbol*) pitcher.

pitear [1a] VI (*LAm*) = **pitar 2** (a).

pitido NM whistle.

pitilla NF (*Cono Sur*) string.

pitillera NF cigarette case.

pitillo NM (a) (*: cigarrillo*) cigarette; **echarse un ~** to have a smoke. (b) (*And, Carib*) pajita) drinking-straw.

pítima NF (a) (*Med*) poultice. (b) **coger una ~‡** to get plastered‡.

pitiminí NM: **de ~** (*fig*) trifling, trivial.

pitinsa* NF (*CAm*) overalls.

pitiusa **1** ADJ of (o from) Ibiza and Formentera (as opposed to the other Balearics islands).
2 NF: **las Pitiusas** Ibiza and Formentera.

pitiyanqui‡ NMF, **pitiyanki‡** NMF (*Carib*) Yankee-lover.

pito NM (a) (*silbato*) whistle; (*Aut*) horn, hooter; (*Ferro etc*) whistle, hooter; **tener voz de ~** to have a squeaky voice.
(b) **~ real** (*Orn*) green woodpecker.
(c) (*LAm Zool*) tick.
(d) (*: cigarrillo*) cigarette; (*LAm: pipa*) pipe.
(e) (*‡: pene*) prick‡.
(f) **~ de ternera** (*LAm*) steak sandwich.
(g) (*locuciones*) **~s flautos*** tomfoolery, absurdities; **cuando ~s, flautas** it's always the same, one way or another it always happens; **cuando no es por ~s es por flautas** if it isn't one thing it's another; **entre ~s y flautas** what with one thing and another; **~ ~ colorito ≃** eeny meeny miny mo; (*fig*) haphazard method of making decisions; **no se me da un ~**, (*no*) **me importa un ~*** I don't care two hoots (*de* about); **en este asunto no toca ~** he's got nothing to do with this matter; **tocarse el ~‡** to do damn-all‡, be bone-idle; **me tomaron por el ~ del sereno** (*Esp*) they thought I was something the cat had brought in; **no vale un ~** it's not worth tuppence.

pitón¹ NM (*Zool*) python.

pitón² NM (*bulto*) bump, lump, protuberance; (*Zool*) budding horn; (*Bot*) sprig, young shoot; (*de jarra etc*) spout; (*LAm: de manguera*) nozzle; **pitones** (*‡: senos*) tits‡; **~ de roca** sharp point of rock.

pitonisa NF (*adivinadora*) fortune-teller; (*bruja*) witch, sorceress.

pitopausia‡ NF male menopause.

pitorrearse* [1a] VR: **~ de** to tease, make fun of.

pitorreo* NM teasing, joking; **estar de ~** to be in a joking mood.

pitorro NM spout.

pitote* NM fuss, row.

pitra NF (*Cono Sur*) rash.

pituco* (*Cono Sur*) **1** ADJ stuck-up*, toffee-nosed*.
2 NM toff*.

pitufa‡ NF bird‡, chick*.

pitufo‡ NM (a) (*Pol*) career politician. (b) (*Méx*) cop*, policeman.

pituitario ADJ pituitary; **glándula pituitaria** pituitary (gland).

pituto* NM (a) (*Cono Sur*) (a) (*enchufe*) useful contact, connection. (b) (*chapuza*) odd job; moonlighting*.

piuco ADJ (*Cono Sur*) timid, scared.

piular [1a] VI to cheep, chirp.

pivotar [1a] VI (a) (*girar, Dep*) to pivot. (b) (*fig*): **~ alrededor de/sobre** to revolve around.

pivote NM pivot.

pixel NM, **píxel** NM (*Inform*) pixel.

píxide NF pyx.

pixtón NM (*CAm*) thick tortilla.

piyama NM (*t* F) (*LAm*) pyjamas.

pizarra NF (a) (*piedra*) slate; (*esquisto*) shale. (b) (*Escol etc*) blackboard; (*Cono Sur: tablero*) notice board.

pizarral NM slate quarry; shale bed.

pizarrín NM slate pencil.

pizarrón NM (*LAm Escol*) blackboard; (*Dep*) scoreboard.

pizarroso ADJ slaty.

pizca NF (a) (*partícula*) pinch, spot; (*migaja*) crumb; **una ~ de sal** a pinch of salt. (b) (*fig*) spot, speck, trace, jot; **ni ~** not a bit, not a scrap; **no tiene ni ~ de verdad** there's not a jot of truth in it. (c) (*Méx*) maize harvest.

pizcar [1g] VT to pinch, nip.

pizco NM pinch, nip.

pizcucha NF (*CAm*) kite (*toy*).

pizote NM (*CAm Zool*) coati(-mundi).

pizpireta* NF bright girl, lively (little) girl; smart little piece‡.

pizpireto* ADJ bright, lively, cheerful, saucy.

pizza NF (*Culin*) pizza.

pizzería [pitse'ria] NF pizzeria.

PJ NM (*Argentina*) ABR **de Partido Justicialista** Peronist party.

p.j. NM ABR **de partido judicial**.

PJF NF (*Méx*) ABR **de Policía Judicial Federal**.

PL NM ABR **de Parlamento Latinoamericano**.

placa NF (a) (*gen*) plate; (*lámina*) thin piece of material, (thin) sheet; tab; (*conmemorativa*) plaque, tablet; (*de horno*) plate; (*de dientes*) dental plate, denture; (*LAm Aut*) number-plate; (*Inform*) board; **~ conmemorativa** commemorative plaque; **~ giratoria** (*Ferro*) turntable; **~ de hielo** icy patch; **~ de matrícula** number-plate; **~ del nombre** nameplate; **~ de silicio** silicon chip; **~ solar** (*de techo*) solar panel; (*de pared*) radiator.
(b) (*Fot: t* **fotográfica**) plate; **~ esmerilada** focusing screen.
(c) (*esp LAm Mús*) gramophone record, phonograph record (*US*).
(d) (*distintivo*) badge, insignia.
(e) (*LAm*) (*erupción*) blotch, skin blemish; (*de dientes*) tartar.

placaje NM (*Rugby*) tackle.

placaminero NM persimmon.

placar [1g] VT (*Rugby*) to tackle.

placard [pla'kar] NM (*Cono Sur*) built-in cupboard.

placebo NM placebo; **efecto ~** placebo effect.

pláceme NM congratulations, message of congratulations; **dar el ~ a uno** to congratulate sb.

placenta NF placenta.

placentero ADJ pleasant, agreeable.

placentino (*Esp*) **1** ADJ of Plasencia.
2 NM, **placentina** NF native (o inhabitant) of Plasencia; **los ~s** the people of Plasencia.

▼ **placer¹** **1** NM (a) (*gen*) pleasure; (*contento*) enjoyment, delight; **a ~** at one's pleasure; as much as one wants; **es un ~ +** *infin* it is a pleasure to + *infin*; **con mucho ~, con sumo ~** with great pleasure; **tengo ~ en +** *infin* it is my pleasure to + *infin*, I have pleasure in + *ger*.
(b) (*deleite*) pleasure; **los ~es del ocio** the pleasures of idleness; **darse a los ~es** to give o.s. over to pleasures.
2 [2w] VT (*liter*) to please; **me place poder +** *infin* I am gratified to be able to + *infin*.

placer² NM (a) (*Geol, Min*) placer. (b) (*Náut*) sandbank. (c) (*And Agr*) ground prepared for sowing; plot, patch; (*Carib*) field.

placero, -a NM/F (a) (*Com*) stallholder, market trader. (b) (*fig*) loafer, gossip.

placeta NF (*Cono Sur*) plateau.

plácidamente ADV placidly.

placidez NF placidity.

plácido ADJ placid.

pladur ® NM plasterboard.

plaf INTERJ bang!; crash!; smack!

plafón NM (a) (*lámpara*) lamp with a lampshade stuck on the ceiling. (b) (*rosetón*) ceiling rosette. (c) (*panel*) soffit. (d) (*LAm*) ceiling.

plaga NF (a) (*Agr Zool*) pest, (*Bot*) blight; **~ del jardín** garden pest; **~ de la vid** pest of vines, pest on the vine; **~s forestales** pests on timber, forest pests.
(b) (*Med, de langostas etc*) plague; (*fig*) scourge; calamity, disaster; blight; **aquí la sequía es una ~** drought is a menace here; **una ~ de gitanos** a plague of gipsies.
(c) (*fig*) glut, abundance; **ha habido una ~ de lechugas** there has been a glut of lettuces.
(d) (*Med*) affliction, grave illness.

plagar [1h] **1** VT to infest, plague; to fill; **han plagado la ciudad de carteles** they have covered (o plastered) the town with posters; **un texto plagado de errores** a text full of errors, a text riddled with errors; **esta sección está plagada de minas** this part has mines everywhere.
2 **plagarse** VR: **~ de** to become infested with.

plagiar [1b] VT (a) *idea, libro etc* to plagiarize; *producto* to pirate, copy illegally. (b) (*LAm: secuestrar*) to kidnap.

plagiario, -a NM/F (V **plagio**) (a) plagiarist. (b) (*LAm*) kidnapper.

plagio NM (a) (*copia*) plagiarism; (*de producto*) piracy, illegal copying. (b) (*LAm: secuestro*) kidnap(ping).

plaguicida NM pest-control substance, insecticide.

plajo: NM fag:, gasper:.

plan NM **(a)** (*proyecto*) plan; scheme; (*intención*) idea, intention; **~ de desarrollo** development plan; **~ de jubilación** pension plan; **~ quinquenal** five-year plan; **~ de vuelo** flight plan; **mi ~ era comprar otro nuevo** my idea was to buy a new one; **realizar su ~** to put one's plan into effect.

(b) (*: idea*) (idea for an) activity, amusement; **ha sido un ~ muy pesado** it turned out to be a very tedious kind of amusement; **tengo un ~ estupendo para mañana** I've got a splendid idea about what to do tomorrow; **no es ~, tampoco es ~** that's not a good way to go about it, that's not a good idea, that's not on*.

(c) (*: aventura*) (*pey*) affair; (*persona*) date; boyfriend, girlfriend; **buscar ~** to try to pick somebody up*; **¿tienes ~ para esta noche?** are you booked for tonight?, have you a date for tonight?; **tiene un ~ con la mujer del alcalde** he's having an affair with the mayor's wife; **aquí hay ~** I'm in with a chance here; **estar en ~** to be in the mood; **ponerse en ~** to get in the mood.

(d) (*programa*) programme; **~ de estudios** curriculum, syllabus; **~ básico/de bachiller** (*CAm Escol*) basic secondary/advanced secondary curriculum.

(e) (*Med*) régime; course of treatment; **estar a ~** to be on a course of treatment.

(f) (*Agrimen*) level; height.

(g) a todo ~* with great ceremony; in a very posh way*, sparing no expense.

(h) no me hace ~* + *infin* it doesn't suit me to + *infin*.

(i) (*sistema*) set-up, system, arrangement; (*base*) basis, footing; (*actitud*) attitude; **chaparros en ~ disperso** scattered showers; **en ~ económico** in an economical way, on the cheap; **en ese ~** in that way; at that rate; **como sigas en ese ~** if you go on like that; **si te pones en ese ~** if that's your attitude; **no puedo con este ~ de esperar** I can't stand this business of waiting; **está en un ~ imposible** it's on an impossible basis, it's an impossible set-up; **en ~ de** as; on a basis of; **lo hicieron en ~ de broma** they did it for a laugh; **vamos en ~ de turismo** we're going as tourists; **no puedo porque estoy en ~ de viaje** I can't because I'm all set to go away; **unos jóvenes en ~ de divertirse** some youngsters out for a good time; **está en ~ de rehusar** he's in a mood to refuse, he's likely to refuse at the moment; **el negocio es en ~ timo** the deal is really a fraud; **lo hizo en ~ bruto** (*Esp*) he did it in a brutal way; **viven en ~ pasota** (*Esp*) they live like hippies.

(j) (*Cono Sur, Méx: de barco etc*) flat bottom.

(k) (*LAm: llano*) level ground; plain; (*Cono Sur: falda de cerro*) foothills.

(l) (*And, CAm, Carib: de espada etc*) flat.

plana NF **(a)** (*hoja*) sheet (of paper), page; (*Escol*) writing exercise, copywriting; (*Tip*) page; **~ de anuncios** advertisement page; **en primera ~** on the front page; **noticias de primera ~** front-page news; **corregir** (*o* **enmendar**) **la ~ a uno** to put sb right, (*pey*) find fault with sb; to improve upon sb's efforts; **escribir una ~ de castigo** to write 50 (*etc*) lines (as a punishment).

(b) ~ mayor (*Mil*) staff; (*fig*) persons in charge; (*) top brass*, big shots*.

(c) (*Téc*) trowel.

planazo NM **(a) se dio un ~** (*LAm*) he fell flat on his face.

(b) (*Carib: trago*) shot of liquor.

plancha NF **(a)** (*lámina*) plate, sheet; (*losa*) slab; (*Tip*) plate; (*Náut*) gangway; (*Med*) dental plate; **hacer la ~** (*bañista*) to float.

(b) (*utensilio*) iron; (*acto*) ironing; pressing; (*ropa planchada*) ironed clothes; (*ropa para planchar*) clothes to be ironed, ironing; **~ eléctrica** electric iron; **~ a** (*o* **de**) **vapor** steam iron.

(c) (*Culin*) grill; (*Cono Sur*) griddle pan; **a la ~** grilled.

(d) (*ejercicio*) press-up.

(e) (*: metedura de pata*) gaffe, blunder; **hacer una ~, tirarse una ~** to drop a clanger:, put one's foot in it; **pasar ~** (*Cono Sur*) to have an embarrassing time.

(f) (*Dep*) dive; **entrada en ~** sliding tackle; **cabecear en ~** to do a diving header; **lanzarse en ~** to dive (for the ball), dive headlong.

planchada NF (*LAm*) **(a)** (*desembarcadero*) landing stage. **(b)** = **plancha (e)**.

planchado 1 ADJ **(a)** *ropa* ironed; (*traje*) pressed.

(b) (*Culin*) pressed; **jamón ~** pressed ham.

(c) (*CAm, Cono Sur*: *elegante*) very smart, dolled up*.

(d) (*And, Carib, Cono Sur*: *sin dinero*) broke*.

(e) (*Méx*) (*listo*) clever; (*valiente*) brave.

2 NM ironing; pressing; (*Cono Sur*) panel-beating; **dar un ~ a** to iron; to press; **prenda que no necesita ~** non-iron garment.

planchar [1a] 1 VT **(a)** *ropa* to iron; *traje* to press; **prenda de no ~** non-iron garment.

(b) (*LAm*) to flatter, suck up to*.

(c) (*Méx*: *dejar plantado*) to stand up*.

2 VI **(a)** to iron, do the ironing.

(b) (*LAm*: *no bailar*) to sit out (a dance), be a wallflower.

(c) (*Cono Sur*) (*meter la pata*) to drop a clanger:; (*ponerse en ridículo*) to make oneself look ridiculous.

planchazo* NM = **plancha (e)**.

planchear [1a] VT to plate.

plancheta NF **(a)** (*Agrimen*) plane table. **(b) echárselas de ~*** to show off, swank*.

planchón NM (*Cono Sur*) snowcap; ice field.

plancton NM plankton.

planeador NM glider.

planeadora NF **(a)** (*niveladora*) leveller, bulldozer. **(b)** (*Náut*) speedboat, powerboat.

▼ **planear** [1a] 1 VT (*proyectar*) to plan; **~ hacer algo** to plan to do sth.
2 VI (*Aer*) to glide; (*fig*) to hover (**sobre** over), hang (**sobre** over).

planeo NM gliding; (*un ~*) glide.

planeta NM planet; **el ~ rojo** the red planet, Mars.

planetario 1 ADJ planetary.
2 NM planetarium.

planicie NF (*llanura*) plain; (*llano*) flat area, level ground; (*superficie plana*) flat surface.

planificación NF planning; (*Inform*) scheduling; **~ de familia, ~ familiar** family planning; **~ urbana** town planning.

planificador 1 ADJ planning (*atr*).
2 NM, **planificadora** NF planner.

planificar [1g] VT to plan.

planilla NF **(a)** (*esp LAm*) (*lista*) list; (*papelito*) slip of paper; (*tabla*) table, tabulation; (*nómina*) payroll; (*sujetapapeles*) clipboard.

(b) (*And, Cono Sur*) (*formulario*) form, application form; (*Fin*) (*cuenta*) account; (*cuenta de gastos*) expense account.

(c) (*And, CAm, Méx*) voting slip (*o* paper); (*nómina de electores*) electoral roll; (*candidatos*) ticket.

planimetría NF surveying, planimetry.

plan(n)ing ['planin] NM, PL **plan(n)ings** ['planin] agenda, schedule, plan.

plano 1 ADJ **(a)** (*gen*) flat, level, even; (*plano*) plane (*t Mat, Mec*); (*liso*) smooth; **caer de ~** to fall flat.

(b) (*fig*) **de ~**: **le daba el sol de ~** the sun shone directly on it; the sun was directly over it; **confesar de ~** to make a full confession; **rechazar algo de ~** to turn sth down flat, reject sth outright; *V* **cortar**.

2 NM **(a)** (*Mat, Mec*) plane; **~ focal** focal plane; **~ inclinado** inclined plane.

(b) (*fig*) plane; position, level; **de distinto ~ social** of a different social level; **están en un ~ distinto** they're on a different plane.

(c) (*Cine, Fot*) shot; **~ corto** close-up; **~ largo** long shot; **primer ~** foreground; close-up; **un primer ~ de la famosa actriz** a close-up of the famous actress.

(d) (*Aer*) plane; wing; **~ de cola** tailplane.

(e) (*Arquit, Mec etc*) plan; (*Geog*) map; (*de ciudad*) map, street plan; **~ acotado** contour map; **levantar el ~ de país** to survey, map, make a map of; *edificio etc* to draw up the designs for.

(f) (*de espada*) flat.

planta¹ NF **(a)** (*Anat*) sole of the foot; **asentar sus ~s en** to establish oneself in.

(b) (*Arquit*: *plano*) ground plan; **construir un edificio de (nueva) ~** to build a completely new building, rebuild from the foundations up.

(c) (*Arquit*: *piso*) floor, storey; **~ baja** ground floor, first floor (*US*); **una ventana de la ~ baja** a downstairs window, a ground-floor window; **~ noble** suite for functions.

(d) (*Baile, Esgrima*) position (of the feet).

(e) de buena ~ *hombre* well-built; *mujer* shapely; **tener buena ~** (*hombre*) to have a fine physique; (*mujer*) to be good-looking.

(f) (*Tec*) plant; **~ de ensamblaje** assembly plant; **~ piloto** pilot plant; **~ potabilizadora** waterworks, water treatment plant.

(g) (*proyecto*) plan, programme, scheme.

(h) echar ~s* to bluster; to threaten.

planta² NF (*Bot*) plant; **~ de interior** indoor plant, house plant; **~ de maceta** pot-plant; **~ trepadora** climbing plant.

plantación NF **(a)** (*acto*) planting. **(b)** (*plantas*) plantation; **~ de tabaco** tobacco plantation.

plantado* ADJ **(a) dejar a uno ~** to leave sb suddenly, leave sb in mid-sentence; to leave sb in the lurch, leave sb high and dry; **dejar ~ al novio** (*dar calabazas*) to jilt one's fiancé; (*en una cita*) to stand one's boyfriend up*; **ella dejó ~ a su marido** she left her husband.

(b) bien ~ *hombre* well-built; *mujer* shapely; good-looking.

plantador NM **(a)** (*Agr*) dibber. **(b)** (*persona*) planter.

plantaje* NM (*And, Carib*) looks.

plantar [1a] 1 VT **(a)** (*Bot*) to plant; (*: enterrar*) to bury.

(b) *poste etc* to put in; *monumento etc* to erect, set up; *tienda* to pitch; *creencia, reforma etc* to implant; *institución* to set up.

(c) *golpe* to plant (*en* on).

(d) *insulto* to offer, hurl.

(e) ~ **a uno en la calle** to pitch sb into the street, chuck sb out; ~ **a un obrero en la calle** to sack a workman*.
(f) (*) ~ **a uno** to curb sb, check sb; **le planté para que no dijera más** I stopped him before he could say any more.
(g) (*) = **dejar plantado** (*V* ADJ (a)).
[2] **plantarse** VR **(a)** (*resistir*) to stand firm, stay resolutely where one is; to plant o.s.; (*fig*) to stand firm, dig one's heels in, refuse to compromise; (*Naipes*) to stick; **35, y me planto** 35, and there I stop.
(b) (*caballo*) to balk, refuse.
(c) ~ **en** to reach, get to; **en 3 horas se plantó en Sevilla** he got to Seville in 3 hours.
(d) (*And, CAm, Méx*:*) to doll o.s. up*.

plante NM **(a)** (*huelga*) stoppage, protest strike. **(b)** (*postura*) stand, agreed basis for resistance; (*programa*) common programme of demands.

▼ **planteamiento** NM (*de problema*) posing, raising; (*aproximación*) approach.

▼ **plantear** [1a] [1] VT **(a)** *creencia, reforma etc* to implant; *cambio* to get under way; *institución* to set up, establish.
(b) (*proponer*) to plan.
▼ **(c)** *problema* to create, pose; *cuestión, dificultad* to raise; *debate, pleito etc* to start; **nos ha planteado muchos problemas** it has created a lot of problems for us; **se lo plantearé** I'll put it to him; I'll have it out with him; ~ **la cuestión de confianza** (*Parl*) to ask for a vote of confidence; **el estudio plantea que ...** the study proposes that ...
[2] **plantearse** VR (*pensar*) to think, reflect; **¡no me lo planteo!** I don't want to think about it!

plantel NM **(a)** (*Hort*) nursery.
(b) (*centro educativo*) training establishment.
(c) (*de profesionales, jugadores*) team; **un excelente** ~ **de actores** a pool of excellent actors.
(d) (*Cono Sur, Méx: personal*) staff, personnel.

plantificar [1g] [1] VT (*: colocar*) to plonk down, dump down*.
[2] **plantificarse** VR **(a)** (*Carib, Cono Sur, Méx**) (*plantarse*) to plant o.s.; (*no ceder*) to stand firm, stand one's ground; **se plantificó en la puerta** he planted himself in the doorway, he stood there in the doorway. **(b)** (*Méx: ataviarse*) to get dolled up*.

plantilla NF **(a)** (*de zapato*) inner sole, insole; (*de media etc*) sole.
(b) (*Téc*) pattern, template; stencil.
(c) (*personas*) establishment, personnel; list, roster; (*Dep*) team, squad; ~ **de personal** staff; **ser de** ~ to be established, be on the establishment.

plantillada* NF (*And*) bragging.

plantío NM **(a)** (*acto*) planting. **(b)** (*terreno*) plot, bed, patch.

plantista NM braggart.

plantón NM **(a)** (*Bot*) (*plántula*) seedling; (*esqueje*) cutting.
(b) (*: espera*) long wait, tedious wait; **dar (un)** ~ **a uno** to stand sb up (on a date*); **estar de** ~ (*Mil*) to be on sentry duty; (*fig*) to be stuck, have to wait around; **tener a uno de** ~ to keep sb waiting around.

plántula NF seedling.

plañidera NF (paid) mourner.

plañidero ADJ mournful, plaintive.

plañir [3h] VT to mourn, grieve over.

plaqueta NF (*Med*) platelet.

plas[1] INTERJ = **plaf**.

plas[2]; NM brother.

plasa; NF sister.

plasma NM plasma; ~ **sanguíneo** blood plasma.

plasmación NF shape, form.

plasmar [1a] [1] VT (*formar*) to mould, shape, form; (*crear*) to create; (*representar*) to represent, give visible (o concrete) form to.
[2] VI y **plasmarse** VR to take shape, appear in solid form, acquire a definite form; ~ **en** to take the form of, emerge as, turn into.

plasta [1] NF **(a)** (*masa*) soft mass, lump; (*cosa aplastada*) flattened mass.
(b) (*: desastre*) botch, mess; **es una** ~ **de edificio** it's a mess of a building; **el plan es una** ~ the plan is one big mess, the plan is a complete botch.
[2] NMF (*: pelmazo*) bore.
[3] ADJ INVAR (*) boring.

plástica NF (art of) sculpture, modelling.

plasticar [1g] VT (*LAm*) *documento* to cover with plastic, seal in plastic, laminate.

plasticidad NF **(a)** (*lit*) plasticity. **(b)** (*fig*) expressiveness, descriptiveness; richness, evocative character.

plasticina ® NF Plasticine ®.

plástico [1] ADJ **(a)** (*gen*) plastic; **artes plásticas** plastic arts.
(b) (*fig*) *imagen etc* expressive, descriptive; *descripción* rich, poetic, evocative.
(c) **chico** ~ (*CAm**) young trendy.

[2] NM **(a)** (*gen*) plastic; **es de** ~* it's fake, it's not for real*.
(b) (*Mús**) disc, record; **pinchar un** ~ to put a record on.
(c) (*Mil*) plastic explosive.

plasticoso ADJ plasticky*.

plastificación NF treatment with plastic, lamination.

plastificado ADJ treated with plastic, laminated.

plastificar [1g] VT **(a)** (*Téc*) = **plasticar**. **(b)** (*Mús*) to record, make a record of.

plastilina ® NF Plasticine ®.

plastrón NM (*LAm*) floppy tie, cravate.

plata NF **(a)** (*metal*) silver; (*vajilla*) silverware; (*Fin*) silver, silver coin(s); **como una** ~ shining bright, like a new pin.
(b) (*esp LAm*) (*dinero*) money; (*riqueza*) wealth; **apalear** ~, **pudrirse en** ~ to be rolling in money.
(c) **hablar en** ~ to speak bluntly, speak frankly.
(d) **La P~** (*río*) the (River) Plate.

platacho NM (*Cono Sur*) *dish of raw seafood*.

platada NF (*LAm*) dish, plateful.

plataforma NF **(a)** (*gen*) platform; stage; ~ **de carga** loading platform; ~ **continental** continental shelf; ~ **espacial** space-station; ~ **giratoria** turntable; ~ **de lanzamiento** launching-pad; ~ **de perforación**, ~ **petrolera**, ~ **petrolífera** drilling rig, oil-rig.
(b) (*Pol*: *t* ~ **electoral**) platform; (*programa*) programme; (*de negociación*) package, offer, set of proposals; ~ **reivindicativa** set of demands.

platal NM (*LAm*) fortune; wealth.

platanal NM, **platanar** NM, **platanera** NF (*LAm*) banana plantation.

platanero [1] ADJ banana (*atr*).
[2] NM (*CAm, Méx*) (*cultivador*) banana grower; (*comerciante*) dealer in bananas.

plátano NM **(a)** (*árbol*) plane, plane tree. **(b)** (*fruta*) banana; (*bananero*) banana tree. **(c)** (*llantén*) plantain. **(d)** (*:*) prick*:*.

platea NF (*Teat*) pit, orchestra (*US*).

plateado [1] ADJ **(a)** (*color*) silver; silvery; (*Téc*) silver-plated. **(b)** (*Méx*) wealthy.
[2] NM silver-plating.

platear [1a] [1] VT **(a)** (*gen*) to silver; (*Téc*) to silver-plate.
(b) (*CAm, Méx*) to sell, turn into money.
[2] VI to show silver; to turn silvery.

platense (*LAm*) [1] ADJ **(a)** = **rioplatense 1**. **(b)** (*de la ciudad*) of La Plata.
[2] NMF **(a)** = **rioplatense 2**. **(b)** native (*o* inhabitant) of La Plata; **los ~s** the people of La Plata.

plateresco ADJ plateresque.

platería NF **(a)** (*arte*) silversmith's craft. **(b)** (*tienda*) silversmith's; (*joyería*) jeweller's.

platero, -a NM/F silversmith; (*joyero*) jeweller.

plática NF (*esp CAm, Méx*) talk, chat; (*Ecl*) sermon; **estar de** ~ to be chatting, be having a talk.

platicador* ADJ (*Méx*) chatty, talkative.

platicar [1g] VI **(a)** (*charlar*) to talk, chat. **(b)** (*Méx*) to say, tell.

platija NF plaice, flounder.

platilla NF (*Carib*) water melon.

platillo NM **(a)** (*Culin*) saucer; small plate; (*de limosnas*) collecting bowl; ~ **de balance** scale, pan (*of scales*); ~ **volante**, ~ **volador** flying saucer; **pasar el** ~ to pass the hat round, make a collection.
(b) ~**s** (*Mús*) cymbals.
(c) (*CAm, Méx*) dish; **el tercer** ~ **de la comida** the third course of the meal.

platina NF (*de microscopio*) microscope slide; (*de tocadiscos*) deck; (*de casete*) tape deck; (*Tip*) platen.

platino [1] NM platinum; ~**s** (*Aut*) contact points.
[2] *como* ADJ: **rubia** ~ platinum blonde.

plato NM **(a)** (*Culin*) utensilio plate, dish; (*Téc*) plate; (*de balanza*) scale, pan; ~ **frutero** fruit-dish; ~ **giradiscos**, ~ **giratorio** turntable; ~ **hondo**, ~ **sopero** soup-dish; **del** ~ **a la boca se pierde la sopa** there's many a slip 'twixt cup and lip; **fregar** (*o* **lavar**) **los** ~**s** to wash the dishes, wash up; **pagar los** ~**s rotos** to pay for the damage, (*fig*) to carry the can*; *V* **nada**.
(b) (*contenido del* ~) plateful, dish; **un** ~ **de arroz** a dish of rice; **vender algo por un** ~ **de lentejas** to sell sth for a mess of pottage.
(c) (*Culin*) dish; course; ~ **combinado** set main course; ~ **dulce** sweet course; ~ **de fondo**, ~ **principal** main course; ~ **fuerte** (*principal*) main course; (*abundante*) heavy dish, meal in itself; (*fig: tema*) main topic, central theme; (*fig: punto fuerte*) strong point; ~ **precocinado** pre-cooked meal; ~ **preparado** ready-to-serve meal; **sopa y 4** ~**s** soup and 4 courses; **es mi** ~ **favorito** it's my favourite dish (*o* meal); **comen del mismo** ~ they're great pals; **ser** ~ **de segunda mesa*** to be second-best; to feel neglected, play second fiddle; **no es** ~ **de mi gusto** it's not my cup of tea.
(d) **es un** ~ (*Cono Sur**) he's very dishy*.
(e) (*Cono Sur**) **¡qué** ~**!** what a laugh!, that's a good one!

plató NM (*Cine*) set; (*TV*) floor.

Platón NM Plato.

platón NM (*LAm*) (a) (*Culin*) large dish; serving dish. (b) (*palangana*) washbasin.

platónicamente ADV platonically.

platónico ADJ platonic.

platonismo NM platonism.

platonista NMF platonist.

platudo* ADJ (*LAm*) rich, well-heeled*.

plausible ADJ (a) (*loable*) commendable, laudable, praiseworthy. (b) *razón etc* acceptable, admissible.

plausiblemente ADV commendably, laudably.

playa NF (a) (*orilla*) shore, beach; **P~ Girón** (*Carib*) Bay of Pigs; **una ~ de arenas doradas** a beach of golden sands; **pasar el día en la ~** to spend the day at (o on) the beach; **pescar desde la ~** to fish from the beach.
(b) (*fig*) seaside; seaside resort; **ir a veranear a una ~** to spend the summer at the seaside, go to the seaside for one's summer holidays.
(c) (*LAm*) (*llano*) flat open space; **~ de carga y descarga** (*Ferro*) goods-yard; **~ de estacionamiento** car-park, parking lot (*US*); **~ de juegos** playground.
(d) **una ~ de** (*Carib**) loads of.

playera NF sports shirt, T-shirt.

playeras NFPL sandals, sandshoes; tennis shoes.

playero ADJ beach (*atr*).

playo ADJ (*Cono Sur, Méx*) gently sloping.

play-off ['pleiof] NM, PL **play-offs** (*Dep*) play-off.

plaza NF (a) (*gen*) square; public square, open space; (*mercado*) market (place); **~ de armas** parade ground; **~ mayor** main square; **~ de toros** bullring; **abrir ~** to open a bullfight; **hacer la ~** (*Esp*) to do the daily shopping; **regar la ~** (*Esp**) to have a beer (as a starter).
(b) (*Com*) town, city, centre; **en esa ~** there, in your town.
(c) (*espacio*) room, space; (*lugar*) place; (*en vehículo etc*) seat, place; **¡~!** make way!; **~ de atraque** berth, mooring; **abrir ~** to make way; **el avión tiene 90 ~s** the plane has 90 seats, the plane carries 90 passengers; **de dos ~s** (*Aut etc*) two-seater; **'no hay ~s'** 'no vacancies'; **~s hoteleras** hotel beds; **reservar una ~** to reserve a seat.
(d) (*puesto*) post, job; (*vacante*) vacancy; **cubrir una ~** to fill a job, appoint to a post; **sentar ~** (*Mil*) to enlist, sign on (*de* as).
(e) (*Mil: t* **~ fuerte**) fortress, fortified town.

▼ **plazo** NM (a) (*tiempo*) time, period, term; (*término*) deadline, time limit; (*vencimiento*) date, expiry date; (*Com, Fin*) date; **~ de entrega** delivery time, delivery date; **~ previsto** specified period; **~ prudencial** reasonable time; **en un ~ de 6 meses** in the space of 6 months, in a period of 6 months; within a term of 6 months; before 6 months are up; **nos dan un ~ de 8 días** they allow us a week, they give us a week's grace; **¿cuándo vence el ~?** when is the payment due?, what is the time limit?; **se ha cumplido el ~** the time is up; **a ~** (*Com*) on credit; **a corto ~** (ADJ) *préstamo* short-dated, (*fig*) short-term; (ADV) in the short term; **a largo ~** (ADJ) *préstamo* long-dated, (*fig*) long-term; (ADV) in the long term; **a ~ medio** in the medium term; **es una tarea a largo ~** it's a long-term job.
(b) (*pago*) instalment, payment; **pagar el ~ de marzo** to pay the March instalment; **comprar a ~s** to buy on hire purchase, pay for in instalments.

plazoleta NF, **plazuela** NF small square.

pleamar NF high tide.

plebe NF: **la ~** the common people, the masses, the mass of the population; (*pey*) the plebs; the mob, the rabble.

plebeyez NF plebeian nature; (*fig*) coarseness, commonness.

plebeyo [1] ADJ plebeian; (*pey*) coarse, common.
[2] NM, **plebeya** NF plebeian, commoner; (*pey*) plebeian.

plebiscito NM plebiscite.

plectro NM plectrum.

plegable ADJ pliable, that bends; *silla etc* folding, that folds up, collapsible.

plegadera NF paperknife.

plegadizo ADJ = **plegable 1**.

plegado NM, **plegadura** NF (a) (*acto*) folding; bending; creasing. (b) (*pliegue*) fold; crease.

plegamiento NM (*de camión*) jack-knifing.

plegar [1h *y* `j] [1] VT to fold; to bend; to crease; (*Cos*) to pleat.
[2] VI (*fig*) to fold up.
[3] **plegarse** VR (a) (*gen*) to bend; to crease. (b) (*fig*) to yield, submit (*a* to).

plegaria NF prayer.

pleitear [1a] VI (a) (*Jur*) to plead, conduct a lawsuit; to go to law (*con, contra* with; *sobre* over), indulge in litigation. (b) (*esp LAm*) to argue.

pleitesía NF: **rendir ~ a** to show respect for, treat respectfully, show courtesy to; (*LAm*) to pay tribute to.

pleitista [1] ADJ (*lit*) litigious; (*fig: reñidor*) quarrelsome, argumentative.
[2] NMF (*lit*) litigious person; (*fig*) troublemaker; (*LAm: peleonero*)

brawler.

pleitisto ADJ (*LAm*) quarrelsome, argumentative.

pleito NM (a) (*Jur*) lawsuit, case; **~s** litigation; **~ de acreedores** bankruptcy proceedings; **~ civil** civil action; **andar a ~s** to be engaged in lawsuits; **entablar ~** to bring an action, bring a lawsuit; **ganar el ~** to win one's case; **poner ~** to sue, bring an action; **poner ~ a uno** to bring an action against sb, take sb to court.
(b) (*fig*) dispute, feud; controversy; (*LAm*) quarrel, argument; (*pelea*) fight, brawl; **estar a ~ con uno** to be at odds with sb.
(c) **~ homenaje** homage.

plenamente ADJ fully; completely.

plenaria NF plenary (session).

plenario ADJ plenary, full.

plenilunio NM full moon.

plenipotenciario, -a NM/F plenipotentiary.

plenitud NF plenitude, fullness; abundance; **en la ~ de sus poderes** at the height of his powers.

pleno [1] ADJ full; complete; *poderes* full; *sesión* plenary, full; **en ~ día** in broad daylight; **en ~ verano** at the height of summer; **tiene frío en ~ verano** he's cold even though it's summer; **en plena rebeldía** in open revolt; **en plena vista** in full view; **le dio en plena cara** it hit him full in the face.
[2] NM (a) (*Parl etc*) plenum, plenary session; **reunirse en ~** to hold a full meeting.
(b) (*quinielas*) maximum correct forecast.
(c) **en ~ decidir etc** unanimously.

pleonasmo NM pleonasm.

pleonástico ADJ pleonastic.

plepa NF (a) (*persona enfermiza*) sickly person. (b) (*: *antipático*) unpleasant sort. (c) (*molesto*) pain*, nuisance.

pletina NF = **platina**.

plétora NF (*abundancia*) plethora, abundance; flood; (*exceso*) excess, surplus.

pletórico ADJ abundant; **~ de** abounding in, full of, brimming with; **~ de salud** bursting with health.

pleuresía NF pleurisy.

plexiglás ® NM Perspex ®, Plexiglass ® (*US*).

plexo NM: **~ solar** solar plexus.

pléyade [1] NF (*liter*) group, gathering.
[2] NMPL **P~s** Pleiades.

plica NF sealed envelope, sealed document; (*en concurso*) sealed entry.

pliego NM (a) (*hoja*) sheet; (*carpeta*) folder; (*Tip*) section, signature.
(b) (*carta etc sellada*) sealed letter, sealed document; **~ cerrado** (*Náut*) sealed orders; **~ de condiciones** details, specifications (*of a tender etc*); **~ de cargos** list of accusations; *V* **descargo**.

pliegue NM (a) (*gen*) fold, crease; (*Cos*) pleat, crease; tuck. (b) (*Geol etc*) fold.

plima NF: **flor de la ~** (*Cono Sur*) wisteria.

plin*: **¡a mí ~!** EXCL I couldn't care less!

Plinio NM Pliny; **~ el Joven** Pliny the Younger; **~ el Viejo** Pliny the Elder.

plinto NM plinth.

plisado NM pleating; (*un ~*) pleat.

plisar [1a] VT to pleat.

PLN NM (*Costa Rica*) ABR *de* **Partido de Liberación Nacional**.

plomada NF (*Arquit etc*) plumb, plumb line; (*Náut*) lead; (*en red de pescar*) weights, sinkers.

plomar [1a] VT to seal with lead.

plomazo NM (a) (*CAm, Méx*) (*tiro*) shot; (*herida*) bullet wound. (b) (*) drag.

plombagina NF plumbago.

plomería NF (a) (*Arquit*) leading, lead roofing. (b) (*LAm*) (*sistema*) plumbing; (*taller*) plumber's workshop, plumber's shop.

plomero NM (*LAm*) plumber.

plomífero* ADJ boring.

plomizo ADJ (a) (*de plomo*) leaden, lead-coloured. (b) (*fig*) leaden.

plomo [1] NM (a) (*metal*) lead; **~ derretido** molten lead; **soldado de ~** tin soldier; **gasolina con ~** leaded petrol; **gasolina sin ~** unleaded petrol; **sacar ~ a** (*fig*) to make light of, play down.
(b) = **plomada**.
(c) (*de pesca*) weight, sinker; **a ~** plumb, true, vertical(ly); (*fig*) just right, exactly right; **caer a ~** to fall heavily, fall flat.
(d) (*Elec*) fuse; **se ha fundido el ~** it's fused; **se le fundieron los ~s** (*Esp**) he blew his top*.
(e) (*esp LAm: bala*) bullet, shot.
(f) (*) (*pesadez*) bore, dull affair; (*pelmazo*) drag.
(g) (*Méx: tiroteo*) gunfight.
[2] ADJ (a) (*LAm*) lead grey, lead-coloured.
(b) **ponerse ~*** to get cross.
(c) (*: *pesado*) boring, dull.

plomoso ADJ (*CAm*) boring.

plotter ['ploter] NM, PL **plotters** ['ploter] (*Inform*) plotter.

➤ LENGUA Y USO: **plazo: a** → 47.2, 47.3, 47.5

plugo, pluguiere *etc* V **placer**[1].

pluma [1] NF (**a**) (*Orn*) feather; quill; (*adorno*) plume, feather; (*volante*) shuttlecock; **colchón de ~s** feather-bed; **hacer a ~ y a pelo** to be versatile, be ready to undertake anything.
(**b**) (*de escribir, fig*) pen; **~ atómica** (*Méx*) ball-point pen; **~ electrónica** light pen; **~ esferográfica** (*LAm*) ball-point pen; **~ estilográfica**, **~ fuente** (*LAm*) fountain-pen; **y otras obras de su ~** and other works from his pen; **dejar correr la ~** to write spontaneously; **escribir a vuela ~** to write quickly, write without much thought.
(**c**) (*fig: caligrafía*) penmanship, writing.
(**d**) (*CAm: mentira*) fib, tale; hoax.
(**e**) (*Cono Sur*‡: *puta*) prostitute.
(**f**) (*And, Carib, Cono Sur: grifo*) tap, faucet (*US*).
(**g**) (*Cono Sur: grúa*) crane, derrick.
(**h**) (*Esp‡: peseta*) one peseta.
(**i**) (*Esp*‡‡: *pene*) prick‡‡.
(**j**) (*Esp‡: maricón*) queer‡, poofter‡.
(**k**) (*Esp*‡: *periodista*) hack (journalist).
[2] NM (*Dep*) featherweight.

plumada NF stroke of the pen; flourish.

plumado ADJ feathered, with feathers; *pollo* fledged.

plumafuente NF (*LAm*) fountain-pen.

plumaje NM (**a**) (*Orn*) plumage, feathers. (**b**) (*adorno*) plume, crest; bunch of feathers.

plumario, -a NM/F (*CAm, Méx*) (*periodista*) hack (journalist); (*: funcionario*) penpusher.

plumazo NM (**a**) (*trazo*) stroke of the pen (*t fig*); **de un ~** with one stroke of the pen; (*Carib*) in a jiffy*; **es un cuento que escribió de un ~** it's a story which she tossed off.
(**b**) (*colchón*) feather mattress; (*almohada*) feather pillow.

plumbemia NF lead poisoning.

plúmbeo ADJ leaden.

plúmbico ADJ plumbic.

plumear [1a] [1] VT (*CAm, Méx**) to write, scribble.
[2] VI (*Méx*‡) to be on the game*.

plumero [1] NM (**a**) (*para limpiar*) feather duster.
(**b**) (*adorno*) plume; bunch of feathers; **se le ve el ~** * you can see what he's really thinking, you can see what he's really like.
(**c**) (*portaplumas*) penholder.
(**d**) (*And*) plumber.
(**e**) (*Cono Sur*) powder-puff.
[2] ADJ (*) camp, exaggeratedly homosexual.

plumier(e) NM pencil-case.

plumífero, -a [1] NM/F (*hum*) poor writer, hack; hack journalist.
[2] NM quilted anorak.

plumilla [1] NF nib, pen-nib.
[2] NMF (*Prensa*) hack journalist.

plumín NM nib, pen-nib.

plumista NM/F clerk, scrivener.

plumón NM (**a**) (*Orn*) down. (**b**) (*cama*) feather bed. (**c**) (*LAm*) felt-tip pen.

plumoso ADJ feathery, downy.

plural [1] ADJ (**a**) plural. (**b**) (*fig: esp LAm*) many, manifold, numerous; diversified.
[2] NM plural; **en ~** in the plural.

pluralidad NF (**a**) (*gen*) plurality.
(**b**) **~ de votos** majority of votes.
(**c**) **una ~ de** a number of; numerous, diverse; **el asunto tiene ~ de aspectos** there are a number of sides to this question; **hay una alta ~ temática** there are many different themes; **existe una ~ de textos para esta asignatura** there is a duplication of textbooks for this course.

pluralismo NM pluralism.

pluralista [1] ADJ (**a**) (*gen*) pluralist; pluralistic. (**b**) (*polifacético*) many-sided, diverse.
[2] NMF pluralist.

pluralizar [1f] VT (*Ling*) to pluralize.

pluri... PREF pluri...; many ...; multi...

plurianual ADJ lasting for several years, covering a number of years; long-term.

pluricultural ADJ multicultural.

pluridimensional ADJ multifaceted, many-sided.

pluridisciplinar ADJ multidisciplinary.

pluriempleado [1] ADJ having more than one job.
[2] NM, **pluriempleada** NF person having more than one job, moonlighter*.

pluriempleo NM having more than one job, moonlighting*.

plurifamiliar ADJ: **vivienda ~** house (*etc*) for several families.

pluriforme ADJ very diverse, diversified, multifaceted.

plurilingüe ADJ multilingual.

plurilingüismo NM multilingualism.

plurinacional ADJ: **estado ~** state consisting of several nationalities.

pluripartidismo NM multi-party system.

pluripartidista ADJ: **sistema ~** multi-party system.

plurivalencia NF many-sided value; diversity of uses (*etc*); wide applicability.

plurivalente ADJ having numerous values; having diverse uses (*etc*); widely applicable.

plus NM extra pay, bonus; **~ de antigüedad** long-service bonus; **~ de carestía de vida** cost-of-living bonus; **~ de nocturnidad** extra pay for unsocial hours; **~ de peligrosidad** danger-money; **~ salarial** bonus; **con 5 dólares de ~** with a bonus of 5 dollars.

pluscafé NM (*LAm*) liqueur.

pluscuamperfecto NM pluperfect, past perfect.

plusmarca NF record; **batir la ~** to break the record.

plusmarquista NMF record-holder; record-breaker; top scorer.

plusvalía NF appreciation, added value; unearned increment; capital gain; **impuesto de ~** tax on rise in value (of land *etc*).

Plutarco NM Plutarch.

pluto‡ ADJ (*And*) drunk, sloshed‡.

plutocracia NF plutocracy.

plutócrata NMF plutocrat.

plutocrático ADJ plutocratic.

Plutón NM Pluto.

plutonio NM plutonium.

pluvial ADJ rain (*atr*).

pluviometría NF rainfall, precipitation.

pluviométrico ADJ rainfall (*atr*); **media pluviométrica** average rainfall.

pluviómetro NM rain-gauge, pluviometer.

pluviosidad NF rainfall.

pluvioso ADJ rainy.

pluviselva NF rain-forest.

PM NF ABR *de* **Policía Militar** Military Police, MP.

p.m. (**a**) ABR *de* **post meridiem** post meridiem, p.m. (**b**) ABR *de* **por minuto** per minute.

PMA NM ABR *de* **Programa Mundial de Alimentos** World Food Programme, WFP.

PMM NM ABR *de* **parque móvil de ministerios** official cars.

pmo ABR *de* **próximo**.

PN NMF (*Esp*) ABR *de* **profesor numerario, profesora numeraria**.

PNB NM ABR *de* **producto nacional bruto** gross national product, GNP.

P.N.D. NM (*Univ, Escol*) ABR *de* **personal no docente** non-teaching staff.

PNN [1] NMF (*Escol*) ABR *de* **profesor no numerario, profesora no numeraria**.
[2] NM (*Econ*) ABR *de* **producto nacional neto** net national product, NNP.

PNP NM (**a**) (*Puerto Rico*) ABR *de* **Partido Nuevo Progresista**. (**b**) (*Méx Hist*) ABR *de* **Partido Nacional Revolucionario**.

PNUD NM ABR *de* **Programa de las Naciones Unidas para el Desarrollo** United Nations Development Programme, UNDP.

PNV NM (*Esp*) ABR *de* **Partido Nacionalista Vasco**.

P.º ABR *de* **Paseo** Avenue, Ave, Av.

p.o. ABR *de* **por orden**.

poblacho NM, **poblachón** NM dump, one-horse town.

población NF (**a**) (*habitantes*) population; **~ activa**, **~ ocupada** working population; **~ flotante** floating population; **~ pasiva** non-working population, retired people. (**b**) (*ciudad*) town, city; (*pueblo*) village; (*Cono Sur*) small hamlet; main building and outbuildings. (**c**) (*Chile*) poor quarter, slum area, shanty-town.

poblacional ADJ population (*atr*); demographic; **estudio ~** population study.

poblada NF (**a**) (*And, Cono Sur* ††: *rebelión*) revolt, armed rising. (**b**) (*And, Cono Sur: multitud*) crowd.

poblado [1] ADJ (**a**) (*habitado*) inhabited.
(**b**) **poco ~** underpopulated, with a sparse population; **densamente ~** thickly populated; **la ciudad más poblada del país** the most populous city in the country.
(**c**) **~ de** peopled with, populated with; (*fig*) full of, filled with, covered with.
(**d**) *barba* big, thick; *cejas* bushy.
[2] NM (*pueblo*) village; (*población*) town; (*lugar habitado*) inhabited place; (*Aut etc*) built-up area; **~ de absorción**, **~ dirigido** new town, satellite town.

poblador(a) NM/F (**a**) (*colono*) settler, colonist; (*fundador*) founder; (*habitante*) inhabitant. (**b**) (*Chile*) slum-dweller.

poblano [1] ADJ (**a**) (*LAm*) village (*atr*), town (*atr*). (**b**) (*Méx*) of Puebla.
[2] NM, **poblana** NF (**a**) (*LAm*) villager. (**b**) (*Méx*) native (*o* inhabitant) of Puebla.

poblar [1l] [1] VT (**a**) *lugar* to settle, people, colonize; *colmena, río etc* to stock (*de* with); *tierra* to plant (*de* with).
(**b**) (*habitar*) to people, inhabit; **los peces que pueblan las profundidades** the fish that inhabit the depths; **las estrellas que**

pueblan el espacio the stars that fill space.

[2] **poblarse** VR (a) (*gen*) to fill (*de* with); (*ir aumentando*) to fill up, become stocked (*de* with); (*irse cubriendo*) to become covered (*de* with).

(b) (*Bot*) to come into leaf.

pobo NM white poplar.

pobre [1] ADJ (*gen*) poor (*de, en* in); **¡~ de mí!** poor old me!; **¡~ de él!** poor fellow!; **¡~ de ti si te pillo!** it'll be tough on you if I catch you!

[2] NMF (a) (*necesitado*) poor person; (*mendigo*) beggar, pauper; **un ~ a** poor man; **los ~s** the poor, poor people.

(b) (*fig*) wretch, poor devil; **la ~ estaba mojada** the poor girl was wet through; **el ~ está fatal de los ojos*** he's terribly short-sighted, poor chap*.

pobrecillo, -a NM/f poor thing.

pobremente ADV poorly.

pobrería NF, **pobrerío** NM (*Cono Sur*) poor people.

pobrete [1] ADJ poor, wretched.

[2] NM, **pobreta** NF poor thing, poor wretch.

pobretería NF (a) (*pobres*) poor people (*collectively*); (*reunión*) gathering of poor people. (b) (*pobreza*) poverty. (c) (*tacañería*) miserliness, meanness.

pobretón [1] ADJ terribly poor.

[2] NM poor man.

pobreza NF (*gen*) poverty; (*estrechez*) work, penury; **~ de espíritu** poorness of spirit, small-mindedness; **~ no es vileza** poverty is not a crime.

poca NM (*LAm*), **pócar** NM (*Méx*) poker.

pocero NM well-digger.

pocerón NM (*CAm, Méx*) pool.

pocha¹ NF (*Culin*) pinto bean.

pocha² NF (*Cono Sur*) (*mentira*) lie; (*trampa*) trick.

poch(e)ar [1a] VT (*Culin*) to poach.

pochismo NM (*Méx pey*) anglicism introduced into Spanish.

pocho [1] ADJ (a) color, flor faded, discoloured; *persona* pale; *fruta* soft, overripe; withered.

(b) (*fig*) depressed, gloomy.

(c) (*Cono Sur*) (*gordito*) chubby; (*rechoncho*) squat.

[2] NM, **pocha** NF (*Méx etc*) Mexican-American, Latino.

pochola* NF nice girl, attractive girl; (*en oración directa*) dear, darling.

pocholada* NF nice thing, pretty thing.

pocholez* NF gem, treasure; **el vestido es una ~** it's a dear little dress.

pocholo* [1] ADJ nice; pretty, attractive, cute.

[2] NM pretty boy.

pocilga NF piggery, pigsty; (*fig*) pigsty.

pocillo NM small cup; (*LAm esp: de café*) coffee cup; (*Méx*) mug.

pócima NF, **poción** NF (*Farm*) potion, draught; (*Vet*) drench; (*fig*) brew, concoction, nasty drink.

poco [1] ADJ (a) (*sing*) (*gen*) little; (*pequeño*) small; (*escaso*) slight, scanty; too little, *p.ej.* **era ~ para él** it was too little for him; **con ~ respeto** with little respect, with scant respect; **de ~ interés** of small interest; **de poca extensión** of small extent, not extensive; **hay ~ queso** there isn't much cheese; **nos queda ~ tiempo** we haven't much time; **el provecho es ~** the gain is small; **con lo ~ que me quedaba** with what little I had left; **ya sabes lo ~ que me interesa** you know how little it interests me; **todas las medidas son pocas** any measure will be inadequate; **por si fuera ~** if it were just a small thing; **y por si eso fuera ~** and as if that were not enough; and to add insult to injury.

(b) (PL) **~s** few; too few, *p.ej.* **eran ~s para ella** there were too few of them for her; **unos ~s** a few, some; **~s de entre ellos** few of them; **~s niños saben que ...** few (o not many) children know that ...; **~s son los que ...** there are few who ...; **me quedan pocas probabilidades** I don't have much chance; **un canalla como hay ~s** a real rotter*, an absolute rotter*.

[2] ADV (a) (*no mucho*) little, not much; (*ligeramente*) only slightly; **cuesta ~** it doesn't cost much; **ahora trabaja ~** he only works a little now; **¡~ (que) hemos trabajado!*** I should jolly well say we've been working!*; **los estiman ~** they hardly value them at all; **~ a ~** little by little; **¡~ a ~!** gently!, easy there!; **~ más o menos** more or less; **ser para ~** to be weak, be characterless, be very negative; **tener a uno en ~** to think little of sb, have no use for sb; **tiene la vida en ~** he holds his life cheap.

(b) (*con ADJ: se traduce a menudo con prefijo* dis-, un-*)* **~ dispuesto a ayudar** disinclined to help; **~ amable** unkind; **~ inteligente** unintelligent; **ser poca cosa** to be unimportant.

(c) **por ~** almost, nearly; **por ~ me ahogo** I very nearly drowned.

(d) (*locuciones de tiempo*) **a ~** shortly (after), presently; **a ~ de haberlo firmado** shortly after he had signed it; **a ~ que corras, lo alcanzas** if you run now you'll catch it; **cada ~** every so often; **dentro de ~** shortly; soon after; **hace ~** a short while back, a short time ago.

(e) (*LAm*) **¿a ~?** not really!, you don't say!; **¿a ~ no?** (well) isn't it?; **¿a ~ crees que ...?** do you really imagine that ...?; **a ~ vas a decir que ...** maybe you're going to say that ...; **a ~ que pueda** if at all possible.

[3] NM: **un ~** a little, a bit; **estoy un ~ triste** I am a little sad; **le conocía un ~** I knew him slightly; **un ~ de dinero** a little money, some money.

poda NF (a) (*acto*) pruning. (b) (*temporada*) pruning season.

podadera NF pruning knife, billhook; pruning shears, secateurs.

podadora NF (*Méx*) lawnmower.

podar [1a] VT (a) (*gen*) to prune; (*mondar*) to lop, trim (off).

(b) (*fig*) to prune, cut out.

podenco NM hound.

▼ **poder** [1] [2s] VI (a) (+ *infin: capacidad*) can, to be able to; **puede venir** he can come, he is able to come; **no puede venir** he cannot come; **puede ser** maybe, it may be so; **puede ser que ...** + *subj* it may be that ...; maybe ...; **pudiera ser que** + *subj* it might be that ...; **puede que esté en la biblioteca** he may be in the library, perhaps he's in the library; **este vino no se puede beber** this wine is not fit to drink.

▼ (b) (+ *infin: posibilidad*) may; **puede no venir** he may not come, it is possible that he won't come; **por lo que pudiera pasar** because of what might happen; **¡podías habérmelo dicho!** you might have told me!; **pudo hacerse daño** he might (o could) have hurt himself; **bien puedes pasar la noche aquí** you may perfectly well spend the night here.

▼ (c) (*absoluto*) can; **¿puedo?** may I (help you)? **lo haré si puedo** I'll do it if I can; **no puedo** I can't; **¡puede!** who knows!, maybe!; **¿se puede?** may I?, may I come in?; do you mind?; **los que pueden** those who can, those who are able (to); **el dinero puede mucho** money can do anything, money talks; **él puede mucho en el partido** he has great influence in the party; **causas respecto a las cuales nada puede el fabricante** causes over which the manufacturer has no control; **¿tú puedes con eso?** can you manage that?; **no puedo con él** I can't stand him; **no puedo con la maleta** I can't manage the case; **no puedo más** I've had enough; I can't go on any longer; I'm exhausted; **no puede ser** it's impossible; **a más no ~** to the utmost, as hard as possible, for all one is worth; **es terco a más no ~** he's utterly obstinate, he's as obstinate as they come; **comió a más no ~** he ate to excess; **me gusta el cine a más no ~** I'm passionately fond of the cinema; **no ~ menos de** + *infin* not to be able to help + *ger*, to have no alternative but to + *infin*.

(d) **puede que vaya** I may go, I might go; **puede que tenga uno ya** he may have one already; **puede que sí** it may be, maybe; **puede que no** maybe yes, maybe no.

(e) (*) **A le puede a B** A can beat B; A is tougher than B; A is more than a match for B.

(f) (*CAm, Méx**) to annoy, upset; **me pudo esa broma** that joke upset me; **su actitud me pudo** his attitude got on my nerves.

[2] NM (a) (*fuerza*) power; (*autoridad*) authority; (*posesión*) possession; **~ adquisitivo**, **~ de compra** purchasing power; **~ de convocatoria** drawing power; **~ de negociación** bargaining power; **~ de recuperación** resilience, recuperative power; **~ de** by dint of; **un partido jugado de ~ a ~** a hard-fought game; **bajo el ~ de** in the hands of; under the power of; **estar (u obrar) en ~ de** to be in the hands of, be in the possession of; **pasar a ~ de** to pass to, pass into the possession of; **el dinero es ~** money is power; **tiene ~ para arruinarnos** he has the power to ruin us; **esa droga no tiene ~ contra la enfermedad** that drug has no power (o is not effective) against the disease.

(b) (*Mec*) (*potencia*) power; strength; (*capacidad*) capacity; **el ~ del motor** the power of the engine; **tiene ~ para levantar X kilos** it has the power to lift X kilos.

(c) (*Pol etc*) power; authority; **~ absoluto** absolute power; **~ civil** civil power; **gobierno de ~ compartido** power-sharing government; **cuarto ~** fourth estate (*the Press*); **~ ejecutivo** executive power; **los ~es fácticos** the powers that be; **~ legislativo** legislative power; **~ negro** black power; **~es públicos** public authorities; **¡el pueblo al ~!** power to the people!; **¡Smith al ~!** Smith for leader!; **estar en el ~,** **ocupar el ~** to be in power.

(d) (*Jur*) power of attorney, proxy; **plenos ~es** full power, full authority (to act); **por ~(es)** by proxy.

(e) (*LAm*: persona*) drug pusher.

poderhabiente NMF (*Jur*) proxy; attorney (*US*).

poderío NM (a) (*gen*) power; (*fuerza*) might; (*señorío*) authority, jurisdiction. (b) (*Fin*) wealth.

poderosamente ADV powerfully.

poderoso ADJ powerful.

podiatría NF podiatry.

podio NM podium; (*Méx*) rostrum; **estar en el ~ de la actualidad** to be in the limelight, be the centre of current interest.

pódium NM, PL **pódiums** = **podio**.

podología NF chiropody.
podólogo, -a NM/F chiropodist.
podómetro NM pedometer.
podón NM billhook.
podre NF pus.
podredumbre NF (a) (*Med*) pus; rotten part, rot.
  (b) (*cualidad*) rottenness, putrefaction; (*fig: corrupción*) rottenness, decay, corruption; (*vino*) ~ **noble** noble rot.
  (c) (*fig: tristeza*) secret sorrow, secret sadness.
podrido [1] ADJ (a) (*gen*) rotten, bad; (*putrefacto*) putrid.
  (b) (*fig*) rotten, corrupt; **está ~ por dentro** he's rotten inside; **están ~s de dinero*** they're filthy rich*.
  (c) (*Cono Sur*: *harto*) fed-up*.
  [2] **podrida** NF: **armar la ~** (*Cono Sur*) to start a fight.
podrir [3a] = **pudrir**.
poema NM (a) (*gen*) poem, (*esp*) long poem. (b) (*fig*) **fue todo un ~** it was just like a fairy tale; it was all terribly romantic; (*hum*) it was a proper farce.
poemario NM book of poems.
poemático ADJ poetic.
poesía NF (a) (*gen*) poetry; **la ~ del Siglo de Oro** Golden Age poetry. (b) (*una ~*) poem, (*esp*) short poem, lyric.
poeta NMF (a) (*gen*) poet. (b) (*LAm*) writer, author, literary person.
poetastro NM poetaster.
poética NF poetics, art of poetry, theory of poetry.
poéticamente ADV poetically.
poético ADJ poetic(al).
poetisa NF poetess, (woman) poet.
poetizar [1f] [1] VT to poeticize; to idealize; to turn into poetry, make poetry out of.
  [2] VI to write poetry.
pogrom(o) NM pogrom.
póker NM (*Naipes*) poker.
polaco [1] ADJ Polish.
  [2] NM, **polaca** NF Pole.
  [3] NM (a) (*Ling*) Polish. (b) (*CAm*: *policía*) cop*.
  [4] NF (*And, Cono Sur: blusa*) smock.
polaina NF (a) (*sobrecalza*) gaiter, legging. (b) (*And, CAm, Cono Sur*) (*molestia*) annoyance; (*chasco*) setback.
polar ADJ polar.
polaridad NF polarity.
polarización NF polarization.
polarizado [1] ADJ polarized.
  [2] NM (*proceso*) polarizing
polarizar [1f] [1] VT to polarize.
  [2] **polarizarse** VR to polarize (*en torno a* around).
polca NF (a) (*Mús*) polka. (b) (*And*) blouse; (*And, Cono Sur*) long jacket.
  (c) (*: jaleo*) fuss, to-do*.
polcata* NF row, shindy*.
pólder NM, PL **pólders** polder.
polea NF pulley; (*Aut*) fan belt; (*Náut*) tackle, tackle block.
poleada NF (*CAm*) hot drink made of milk and flour.
polémica NF (a) (*gen*) polemics. (b) (*una ~*) polemic, controversy.
polémico ADJ polemic(al); controversial.
polemista NMF polemicist; debater, controversialist.
polemizar [1f] VI to indulge in a polemic, argue (*en torno a* about); **no quiero ~** I have no wish to get involved in an argument; **~ con uno en la prensa** to have a debate with sb in the press.
polemología NF war studies.
polen NM pollen.
polenta NF (a) (*And, Cono Sur*) (*maicena*) cornflour; (*sémola de maíz*) ground maize, polenta. (b) **tener ~** (*entusiasta*) to be enthusiastic; (*de calidad*) to be first-rate.
poleo NM (*Bot*) pennyroyal.
polera NF (*Cono Sur*) (*jersey*) polo neck jersey; (*camiseta*) T-shirt.
poli* [1] NM bobby*, copper*, cop*.
  [2] NF: **la ~** the cops*.
poli... PREF poly..., many ...
poliamida NM polyamide.
poliandria NF polyandry.
poliándrico ADJ polyandrous.
polibán NM hip-bath.
Polichinela NM Punch.
policía [1] NM policeman; **~ femenino** policewoman; **~ de paisano** plain-clothes policeman (*V t* **2(a)**).
  [2] NF (a) (*organización*) police; police force; **~ antidisturbios** riot police; **~ de barrio**, **~ de manzana** neighbourhood police; **~ fluvial** river police; **~ militar** military police; **~ montada** mounted police; **P~ Municipal** local police; **P~ Nacional** national police; **~ paralela** force of undercover police; **~ secreta** secret police; **~ de tráfico**, **~ de tránsito** (*LAm*) traffic police.
  (b) (*persona*) policewoman.

  (c) (*administración*) administration, (good) government; (*orden público*) public order.
  (d) (*cortesía*) courtesy, politeness.
  (e) (*limpieza*) cleanliness.

┌─── **POLICÍA** ───┐

*There are two types of **policía** in Spain, the **policía nacional**, in charge of national security and public order in general, and the **policía municipal**, with duties of regulating traffic and policing the local community. The Basque Country and Catalonia also have their own police forces, the **Ertzaintza** and the **Mossos d'Esquadra** respectively. In rural areas the **Guardia Civil** is responsible for policing duties.*
⇨ *See also* GUARDIA CIVIL , ERTZAINTZA

policiaco, policíaco ADJ police (*atr*); V **novela**.
policial [1] ADJ police (*atr*).
  [2] NM (*CAm*) policeman.
policlínico NM (*t* **hospital ~**) general hospital.
policromado [1] ADJ *escultura* polychrome-painted.
  [2] NM polychrome painting.
policromo ADJ, **polícromo** ADJ polychromatic; many-coloured, colourful.
polideportivo NM sports centre, sports complex; leisure centre.
poliedro NM polyhedron.
poliéster NM polyester.
poliestireno NM polystyrene.
polietileno NM polythene, polyethylene (*US*).
polifacético ADJ *persona, talento etc* many-sided, versatile.
polifacetismo NM many-sidedness, versatility.
Polifemo NM Polyphemus.
polifonía NF polyphony.
polifónico ADJ polyphonic.
polifuncional ADJ multifunctional, having many uses.
poligamia NF polygamy.
polígamo [1] ADJ polygamous.
  [2] NM polygamist.
poligénesis NF polygenesis.
poligloto, -a ADJ (*t* **polígloto** NM, **políglota** NMF) polyglot.
poligonal ADJ polygonal.
polígono NM (a) (*Mat*) polygon.
  (b) (*Esp*) (*solar*) site (for development), building lot; (*zona*) area; (*viviendas*) housing estate; **~ de descongestión** overspill area; **~ industrial** industrial estate; **~ residencial** housing estate; **~ de tiro** shooting-range; firing range, artillery range.
polígrafo, -a NM/F writer on a wide variety of subjects.
poliinsaturado ADJ polyunsaturated.
polilla NF (*lepidóptero*) moth, (*esp*) clothes moth; (*oruga*) grub, destructive larva; (*de los libros*) bookworm.
polímata NMF polymath.
polimerización NF polymerization.
polímero NM polymer.
poli-mili NMF member of the political-military wing of ETA.
polimorfismo NM polymorphism.
polimorfo ADJ polymorphic.
Polinesia NF Polynesia.
polinesio, -a ADJ, NM/F Polynesian.
polínico ADJ pollen (*atr*).
polinización NF pollination; **~ cruzada** cross-pollination.
polinizar [1f] VT to pollinate.
polinosis NF hay fever.
polio NF polio.
poliomielitis NF poliomyelitis.
polipiel ® NF synthetic leather.
pólipo NM polyp, polypus.
Polisario [poli'sarjo] NM (*t* **El Frente ~**) ABR *de* **Frente Popular de Liberación del Sáhara y Río de Oro**.
polisemia NF polysemy.
polisémico ADJ polysemic.
polisílabo [1] ADJ polysyllabic.
  [2] NM polysyllable.
polisón NM (a) bustle. (b) (*) bottom.
polista NMF polo player.
politécnica NF ≃ technical college.
politeísmo NM polytheism.
politeísta ADJ polytheistic.
politene NM, **politeno** NM polythene, polyethylene (*US*).
política¹ NF (a) (*Pol*) politics; **~ de pasillo(s)** lobbying; **la ~ ruritana en la posguerra** postwar Ruritanian politics; **meterse** (*o* **mezclarse**) **en la ~** to go in for politics, get mixed up in politics.
  (b) (*programa*) policy; **~ agraria** farming policy, agricultural policy; **~ de cañonera** gunboat diplomacy; **~ económica** economic policy; **~ exterior** foreign policy; **~ de ingresos y precios**, **~ de jornales y**

precios prices and incomes policy; **~ de mano dura** strong-arm policy, tough policy; **~ presupuestaria** budget policy; **~ de silla vacía** refusal to take one's seat (in parliament), **~ de tierra quemada** scorched earth policy.

(c) *(tacto)* tact, skill; *(cortesía)* politeness; *(educación)* good manners.

políticamente ADV politically.

politicastro NM *(pey)* politician, politico.

político ① ADJ (a) *(Pol)* political.

(b) *(diplomático)* politic; *(juicioso)* tactful, skilful; *(cortés)* polite, well-mannered, courteous.

(c) *(reservado)* stiff, reserved, stand-offish.

(d) *(pariente)* in-law, *p.ej.* **padre ~** father-in-law; **es tío ~ mío** he's an uncle of mine by marriage; *V* **familia** *etc.*

② NM, **política²** NF politician; **~ de café** armchair politician.

politicón* ADJ (a) *(Pol)* strongly political, keenly interested in politics.

(b) *(ceremonioso)* very ceremonious, obsequious.

politiquear [1a] VI to play at politics, dabble in politics; to talk politics.

politiqueo NM, **politiquería** NF *(pey)* party politics, the political game; political gossip.

politiquero, -a NM/F *(pey)* politician, party politician; political intriguer.

politiqués NM political jargon, special style of political journalese.

politiquillo, -a NM/F minor politician.

politización NF politicization.

politizar [1f] VT to politicize.

politología NF political science, study of politics.

politólogo, -a NM/F specialist in politics, political expert.

politoxicomanía NF multiple drug-addiction.

politraumatismo NM multiple injuries.

poliuretano NM polyurethane.

polivalente ADJ many-sided; multi-faceted; having diverse aspects, having diverse applications; *avión* multi-role; *edificio* multi-purpose.

polivinilo NM polyvinyl.

póliza NF (a) *(certificado)* certificate, voucher; *(Fin: giro)* draft; *(Fin: de seguro)* insurance certificate; insurance policy; **~ dotal** endowment policy; **~ de seguro(s)** insurance policy; **pagar una ~** to pay out on an insurance.

(b) *(impuesto)* tax stamp, fiscal stamp.

polizón NM (a) *(vago)* tramp, vagrant, bum *(US)*. (b) *(Aer, Náut, etc)* stowaway; **viajar de ~** to stow away *(en* on).

polizonte* NM bobby*, copper*.

polla NF (a) *(Orn)* pullet; chick; **~ de agua** moorhen.

(b) *(Naipes)* pool, kitty; *(And, CAm, Cono Sur)* stakes, pool; *(Cono Sur: lotería)* lottery.

(c) *(Esp‡: chica)* chick, bird‡.

(d) *(Esp‡‡)* prick‡‡; **¡una ~!** get away!*; **¡ni qué ~s!** no way!*; **¿qué ~s quiere?** what the hell does he want?

pollaboba‡ NM berk‡, wimp*.

pollada NF *(Orn)* brood.

pollastre* NM = **pollo** (b).

pollastro* NM, **pollastrón*** NM sly fellow.

pollera NF (a) *(criadero)* hencoop; *(gallinero)* chicken run; *(cesto)* basket for chickens. (b) *(And, Cono Sur)* skirt; *(Cono Sur Ecl)* soutane. (c) *(aparato)* walker.

pollería NF poulterer's (shop).

pollero NM (a) *(gen)* chicken farmer; poulterer. (b) *(LAm)* gambler. (c) *(Méx)* guide for illegal immigrants to USA).

pollerudo ADJ *(Cono Sur)* (a) *(cobarde)* cowardly; *(chismoso)* backbiting, gossipy. (b) *(santurrón)* self-righteous, sanctimonious.

pollino, -a NM/F (a) donkey. (b) (*) ass, idiot.

pollita NF (a) young pullet. (b) **echar ~s** to tell lies.

pollito NM (a) *(Orn)* chick; **~ de un día** day-old chick. (b) (*) = **pollo** (b).

pollo NM (a) *(Orn)* chicken; chick, young bird; *(Culin)* chicken; **~ asado** roast chicken; **echarse el ~** *(Cono Sur)* to pack up and go; **¡qué duquesa ni qué ~s en vinagre!*** duchess my foot!*; **¡ni eso ni ~s en vinagre!*** no way!*

(b) *(Esp*)* *(joven)* young man; *(señorito)* elegant youth, playboy; **~ pera*** dandy; *(chanchullero)* spiv*, flash Harry*; **¿quién es ese ~?** who is that chap?*; **es un ~ nada más** he's only a youngster.

(c) *(Esp‡: esputo)* spittle, spit; **soltar un ~** to spit.

(d) *(Méx)* (would-be) illegal immigrant (to USA).

polluelo NM chick.

polo¹ NM (a) *(Geog)* pole; **P~ Norte** North Pole; **P~ Sur** South Pole; **~ magnético** magnetic pole, magnetic north; **de ~ a ~** from pole to pole.

(b) *(Elec)* pole; *(borne)* terminal; *(de enchufe)* pin, point; **~ negativo** negative pole; **~ positivo** positive pole; **una clavija de 4 ~s** a 4-pin plug.

(c) *(fig: centro)* pole; focus, centre; **~ de atracción** focus of interest, centre of attraction; **los dos generales son ~s opuestos** the two generals are at opposite extremes; **esto es el ~ opuesto de lo que dijo antes** this is the exact opposite of what he said before.

(d) *(fig: Com etc)* **~ de desarrollo, ~ de promoción** growth point; development area.

(e) **~ helado** iced lolly*.

polo² NM *(Dep)* polo; **~ acuático** water polo.

polo³ NM *(suéter)* polo-necked sweater; *(niki)* T-shirt.

polola NF *(Cono Sur)* *(coqueta)* flirt, flirtatious girl; *(amiga)* girlfriend.

pololear [1a] *(And, Cono Sur)* ① VT *(pretender)* to court; *(coquetear con)* to flirt with.

② VI *(coquetear)* to flirt *(con* with); *(tener relación fija)* to be going steady* *(con* with); *(salir)* to go out together, date*.

pololeo NM *(And, Cono Sur)* (a) courting; flirting; dating*.

(b) *(chapuza)* small job, odd job.

pololito* NM *(Chile)* small job, odd job.

pololo NM *(Cono Sur)* (a) *(Ent)* buzzing insect. (b) *(soso)* bore, tedious person; *(coqueto)* flirt; *(amigo)* boyfriend; *(pretendiente)* (persistent) suitor. (c) *(chulo)* pimp.

polonesa NF polonaise.

Polonia NF Poland.

poltergeist NM INVAR poltergeist.

poltrón ADJ idle, lazy.

poltrona NF (a) easy chair; *(del presidente)* director's chair. (b) (‡) cushy number‡, soft job.

poltronear [1a] VI *(Cono Sur, Méx)* to loaf around.

polución NF (a) pollution; **~ de la atmósfera** air pollution. (b) **~ nocturna** *(Esp)* nocturnal emission, wet dream.

polucionante ADJ polluting.

polucionar [1a] VT to pollute.

polvareda NF (a) *(polvo)* dust cloud, cloud of dust. (b) *(fig)* storm, fuss, rumpus; **levantar una ~** to create a storm *(o* a stir).

polvata‡ NM = **polvo** (d).

polvera NF (a) *(gen)* powder compact, vanity case. (b) *(Méx)* = **polvareda**.

polvero NM (a) *(LAm)* = **polvareda**. (b) *(CAm)* handkerchief.

polvete‡ NM = **polvo** (d).

polvillo NM (a) *(And, Cono Sur Agr)* blight. (b) *(And, Cono Sur)* tobacco refuse. (c) *(CAm)* leather for shoemaking. (d) *(And)* rice bran.

polvo NM (a) *(gen)* dust; **lleno de ~** dusty; dust-covered; **limpiar un mueble de ~, quitar el ~ de** *(o* **a)** **un mueble** to dust a piece of furniture; **hacer algo ~** to smash sth, ruin sth; **hacer ~ a uno** to shatter sb; to wear sb out; to depress sb; *(en discusión)* to flatten sb, crush sb; **estoy hecho ~** I'm worn out; **hacer morder el ~ a** to humiliate, crush; **matar el ~** to lay the dust; **sacudir el ~ a uno** to thrash sb; to beat sb up*; **aquellos ~s traen estos lodos** such are the consequences.

(b) *(Quím, Culin, Med etc)* powder *(frec* **~s**); (*: *droga)* cocaine, heroin; **~s** *(esp)* face-powder; **~(s) de arroz** rice powder; **~s de blanqueo** bleaching-powder; **~s de chile** chili powder; **~(s) de hornear, ~(s) de levadura** baking-powder; **~ dentífrico, ~s para dientes** tooth powder; **~s de picapica** itching powder; **~s de talco** talcum powder; **en ~** powdered, in powdered form; **ponerse ~s** to powder one's face.

(c) *(porción)* pinch; **un ~ de rapé** a pinch of snuff.

(d) *(Esp‡‡)* screw‡‡; **echar un ~** to have a screw‡‡; **está para un ~, tiene mucho ~** she's hot stuff‡.

pólvora NF (a) *(Mil)* gunpowder; **~ de algodón** guncotton; **no ha descubierto** *(o* **inventado) la ~** he'll never set the Thames *(o* world) on fire; **gastar la ~ en salvas** to waste time and energy; to make empty gestures; to make a great song and dance; **levantar ~** to make a stir; **oler a ~** to smell fishy*; **propagarse como la ~** to spread like wildfire.

(b) *(fuegos artificiales)* fireworks.

(c) *(fig: mal genio)* bad temper, crossness.

(d) *(fig: viveza)* life, liveliness.

polvorear [1a] VT to powder, dust, sprinkle *(de* with).

polvoriento ADJ (a) *superficie etc* dusty. (b) *sustancia* powdery.

polvorilla* NMF touchy person, bad-tempered person, grouch*.

polvorín NM (a) *(pólvora)* fine gunpowder.

(b) *(Mil)* powder magazine; *(fig)* powder-keg.

(c) *(Cono Sur: insecto)* gnat.

(d) *(Cono Sur, Méx)* = **polvorilla**.

(e) *(And, Carib: polvareda)* cloud of dust.

polvorón NM shortbread; *(LAm)* cake.

polvorosa* NF road; **poner pies en ~** to beat it*.

polvoroso ADJ dusty.

polvoso ADJ *(CAm)* = **polvoriento**.

pom NM *(CAm)* incense.

poma NF (a) *(fig)* apple. (b) *(frasco)* scent bottle; *(Cono Sur)* small flask; *(And)* carafe. (c) *(Méx)* pumice (stone).

pomada NF (a) *(gen)* pomade, ointment; **estar en la ~*** *(metido)* to be mixed up in it, be involved; *(al tanto)* to be in the know.

(b) la ~: the cream, the top people, the nobs:.
(c) hacer algo ~ (*Cono Sur*) to break sth to bits.
pomar NM apple orchard.
pomelo NM **(a)** (*Esp*) grapefruit, pomelo. **(b)** (*Anat**) bottom, backside.
pómez NF: **piedra ~** pumice (stone).
pomo NM **(a)** (*Bot*) pome, fruit with pips. **(b)** (*frasco*) scent bottle. **(c)** (*de espada*) pommel; (*de puerta*) round knob, handle. **(d)** (*And*) powder-puff.
pompa NF **(a)** (*burbuja*) bubble; **~ de jabón** soap bubble. **(b)** (*Náut*) pump. **(c)** (*fausto*) pomp, splendour; (*ostentación*) show, display; procession; (*boato*) pageant, pageantry; **~s fúnebres** funeral ceremony; funeral procession; **'P~s fúnebres'** 'Undertaker', 'Funeral Parlour'.
Pompeya NF Pompeii.
Pompeyo NM Pompey.
pompis* NM INVAR bottom, behind*.
pompo ADJ (*And*) blunt.
pompón NM pompom.
pomposamente ADV splendidly, magnificently; majestically; (*pey*) pompously.
pomposidad NF splendour, magnificence; majesty; (*pey*) pomposity.
pomposo ADJ splendid, magnificent; majestic; (*pey*) pompous.
pómulo NM (*hueso*) cheekbone; (*mejilla*) cheek.
ponchada¹ NF bowlful of punch.
ponchada²* NF (*Cono Sur*) large quantity, large amount; **costó una ~** it cost a bomb*.
ponchadura NF (*Méx*) puncture.
ponchar [1a] **1** VT (*Carib, Méx*) **(a)** *billete** to punch. **(b)** *neumático* to puncture.
 2 VI (*LAm**: *resistir*) to chafe at the bit.
ponche NM punch.
ponchera NF **(a)** (*para ponche*) punch bowl. **(b)** (*And, Carib, Méx*: *palangana*) washbasin; (*And*: *bañera*) bath. **(c)** (*Cono Sur**: *barriga*) paunch, beer gut*.
poncho¹ ADJ **(a)** (*vago*) lazy, indolent; (*tranquilo*) quiet, peaceable. **(b)** (*And*: *gordito*) chubby.
poncho² NM **(a)** (*LAm*) (*prenda*) poncho; (*frazada*) blanket. **(b)** (*fig*) **los de a ~** (*And**) the poor; **arrastrar el ~** (*LAm**) to be looking (*o* spoiling) for a fight; **estar a ~** (*And**) to be in the dark; **pisarle el ~ a uno** (*And*) to humiliate sb; **pisarse el ~** (*Cono Sur**) to be mistaken.
ponchura NF (*Venezuela*) washbasin.
Poncio Pilato NM Pontius Pilate.
ponderación NF **(a)** (*contrapeso*) weighing, consideration; (*cuidado*) deliberation. **(b)** (*exageración*) high praise; **está sobre toda ~** it is too good for words. **(c)** (*Estadística*) weighting. **(d)** (*calma*) calmness, steadiness, balance.
ponderado ADJ **(a)** *carácter* calm, steady, balanced. **(b)** (*Estadística*) weighted; **media ponderada** weighted average.
ponderar [1a] VT **(a)** (*considerar*) to weigh up, consider. **(b)** (*elogiar*) to praise highly, speak in praise of; **~ algo a uno** to speak warmly of sth to sb, tell sb how good sth is; **le ponderan de inteligente** they speak highly of his intelligence. **(c)** (*Estadística*) to weight.
pondré *etc* V **poner**.
ponedero NM nest, nesting box.
ponedora ADJ: **gallina ~** laying hen, hen in lay; **ser buena ~** to be a good layer.
ponencia NF **(a)** (*comunicación*) (learned) paper, communication; report. **(b)** (*persona*) rapporteur.
ponente NMF speaker (*at a conference*), person giving a paper.
poner [2q] **1** VT **(a)** (*gen*) to put; (*colocar*) to place, set; *ropa, sombrero* to put on; *cuidado* to take, exercise (*en* in); *objeción* to raise; *mesa* to lay, set; (*Com*) *escaparate* to dress, arrange; *énfasis* to place (*en* on); **~ algo a secar al sol** to put sth (out) to dry in the sun; **~ la experiencia al servicio de** to put one's experience at the disposal of; **~ algo como ejemplo** to give (*o* quote) sth as an example, use sth as an illustration; **~ a uno por testigo** to cite sb as a witness; **~ algo en duda** to cast doubt on sth, call sth in question; **~ algo aparte** to put sth aside, put sth on one side.
(b) *huevo* to lay.
(c) *reloj etc* to adjust, set (right); **pone el reloj por esa campana** he sets his watch by that bell.
(d) *radio etc* to switch on, turn on, put on; **ponlo más fuerte** turn it up.
(e) *carta, telegrama* to send (*a* to).
(f) *problema* to set; *impuesto, multa* to impose (*a* on); *tarea* to give, assign (*a* to); **nos pone mucho trabajo** he gives us a lot of work.
(g) *tienda* to open, set up, establish; *casa* to fit up, equip; **han puesto la casa con todo lujo** they have fitted the house up most luxuriously.
(h) *dinero* to contribute, subscribe, give; (*en el juego*) to stake; (*Fin*) to put, invest; (*fig*) to contribute; *tiempo* to put, give; **yo pongo el dinero pero ella escoge** I put up the money but she chooses; **he**

puesto 5 minutos en firmarlo it took me 5 minutes to sign it; **esto no pone nada para la solución del problema** this does not contribute at all towards solving the problem.
(i) *nombre* to give; **al niño le pusieron Luis** they called the child Louis; **¿qué nombre le van a ~?** what are they going to call him?, what name are they giving him?
(j) **~ a uno de cochino** to call sb a swine*.
(k) (*añadir*) to add; **pongo 3 más para llegar a 100** I'll add 3 more to make it 100.
(l) (*Teat*) *obra* to put on, do, perform; *película* to show, put on; to screen; **¿qué ponen en el cine?** what's on at the cinema?
(m) *emoción, miedo etc* to cause; **me pone miedo** it frightens me, it scares me.
(n) *lengua, palabras etc* to translate, put (*en* into); **puso el discurso en alemán** he translated the speech into German.
(o) (*suponer*) to suppose; **pongamos 120** let's say 120, let's put it at 120; **pongamos que ...** let us suppose that ...; **poniendo que ...** supposing that ... assuming that ...
(p) (*Telec*) **~ a X con Y** to connect X to Y, give X a line to Y; **póngame con el conserje** get me the porter, put me through to the porter; **le pongo en seguida** I'm trying to connect you.
(q) (*conciliar*) **~ a P bien con Q** to reconcile P and Q, make things up between P and Q; **~ a Z mal con A** to cause a rift between Z and A, make Z fall out with A.
(r) (+ ADJ) to make, turn; **si añades eso lo pones azul** if you add that you turn it blue; **la medicina le puso bueno** the medicine made him better; **la has puesto colorada** now you've made her blush; **para no ~le de mal humor** so as not to make him cross.
(s) **~ a uno a** + *infin* to set sb to + *infin*; to start sb + *ger*.
(t) (*en colocación*) **puso a su hija de sirvienta** she got her daughter a job as a servant; **puso a sus hijos a trabajar** she sent her children out to work; V **aprendiz**; *para otros usos y muchas locuciones*, V **el** N.
(u) **¡no pongo ni una!** (*Carib**) I just can't get it right!
 2 VI **(a)** (*Orn*) to lay, lay eggs.
(b) **no pongo a la lotería** I don't go in for the lottery, I don't invest in the lottery.
 3 ponerse VR **(a)** (*gen*) to put o.s., place o.s.; **se ponía debajo de la ventana** he used to stand under the window; V **cómodo** *etc*.
(b) **~ un traje** to put a suit on.
(c) **~ de barro** to get covered in mud.
(d) **~ de conserje** to take a job as a porter.
(e) **~ a** (*lugar*), **~ en** to reach, get to, arrive at; **en 2 horas se puso a su lado** in 2 hours he reached her side, in 2 hours he was at her side.
(f) (*sol etc*) to set.
(g) **~ delante** (*estorbar*) to get in the way; (*intervenir*) to intercede, intervene; (*dificultad*) to arise, come up; **destruye al que se le pone delante** he destroys anyone who gets in his way.
(h) **~ a bien con uno** to get on good terms with sb, (*pey*) get in with sb; **~ a mal con uno** to get on the wrong side of sb.
(i) **~ con uno** (*reñir*) to quarrel with sb; (*oponerse*) to oppose sb; (*competir*) to compete with sb, play (against) sb.
(j) (+ ADJ) to turn, get, become; **se puso serio** he became serious; **en el agua se pone verde** it turns green in the water; **¡no te pongas así!** don't be like that!; V **furioso** *etc*.
(k) **~ a** + *infin* to begin to + *infin*, set about + *ger*; to proceed to + *infin*; **se pusieron a gritar** they started to shout.
(l) **ponérselos a*** to be unfaithful to.
(m) **~** (*Ⓕ*) to get high:.
(n) (*LAm*) **se me pone que ...** it seems to me that ...
(o) **~ al teléfono** to go on the phone, go to the phone.
poney ['poni] NM, PL **poneys** ['ponis] pony.
ponga, pongo¹ *etc* V **poner**.
pongaje NM (*And, Cono Sur*) *domestic service which Indian tenants are obliged to give free.*
pongo² NM orang-outang.
pongo³ NM (*And, Cono Sur*) **(a)** (*criado*) Indian servant, Indian tenant. **(b)** (*Geog*) ravine.
pongueaje NM = **pongaje**.
poni NM pony.
ponible ADJ *vestido* wearable.
poniente **1** ADJ west, western.
 2 NM **(a)** (*oeste*) west. **(b)** (*viento*) west wind.
ponja: (*And*) ADJ, NMF Jap*.
p.º n.º NM ABR *de* **peso neto** net weight, nt. wt.
pontaje NM, **pontazgo** NM toll.
pontevedrés (*Esp*) **1** ADJ of Pontevedra.
 2 NM, **pontevedresa** NF native (*o* inhabitant) of Pontevedra; **los pontevedreses** the people of Pontevedra.
pontificado NM papacy, pontificate.
pontifical ADJ papal, pontifical.
pontificar [1g] VI to pontificate (*t fig*).

pontífice NM pope, pontiff; **el Sumo P~** His Holiness the Pope.

pontificio ADJ papal, pontifical.

pontón NM **(a)** (*de puente etc*) pontoon; (*Aer: de hidroavión*) float. **(b)** (*puente:* t **~ flotante**) pontoon bridge; bridge of planks. **(c)** (*Náut*) converted ship.

pony ['poni] NM, PL **ponys** ['ponis] pony.

ponzoña NF poison, venom; (*fig*) poison.

ponzoñoso ADJ poisonous, venomous; (*fig*) *ataque etc* venomous; *propaganda* poisonous; *costumbre, idea etc* harmful.

pool [pul] NM, PL **pools** [pul] (*Fin*) consortium.

pop [1] ADJ pop.
[2] NM **(a)** (*Mús*) pop, pop music. **(b)** (*Arte*) pop artist.
[3] INTERJ bingo!*

popa NF **(a)** (*Náut*) stern; **a ~** astern, abaft; **de ~ a proa** fore and aft, from stem to stern. **(b)** (**‡**: *culo*) stern‡, bottom.

popar [1a] VT **(a)** *niño etc* to spoil; (*fig*) to make a fuss of, flatter. **(b)** (*mofarse de*) to scorn, jeer at.

pope NM **(a)** (*Ecl*) priest of the Orthodox Church. **(b)** (*: líder espiritual*) guru, spiritual leader; idol.

popelín NM, **popelina** NF, **poplín** NM (*LAm*) poplin.

popería* NF pop fans (*collectively*).

popero* [1] ADJ: **música popera** pop music.
[2] NM, **popera** NF pop fan.

popi* [1] ADJ pop.
[2] NMF pop fan.

popó‡ NM bottom, bum‡.

popof(f)* ADJ INVAR (*Méx*) posh*.

poporo NM **(a)** (*And, Carib:* *bulto*) bump, swelling. **(b)** (*Carib:* *porra*) truncheon, nightstick (*US*).

popote NM (*Méx*) (*tallo*) long thin stem; (*hierba*) tough grass used for making brooms; (*paja*) drinking-straw.

populachería NF cheap popularity, playing to the gallery.

populachero ADJ (*plebeyo*) common, vulgar; (*chabacano*) cheap; *discurso, política* rabble-rousing; *político* demagogic, who appeals to the lower orders, who plays to the gallery.

populacho NM populace, plebs, mob.

popular ADJ **(a)** (*ampliamente aceptado etc*) popular. **(b)** (*del pueblo*) *palabra etc* colloquial; *cultura etc* of the people; folk (*atr*).

popularidad NF popularity.

popularización NF popularization.

popularizar [1f] [1] VT to popularize.
[2] **popularizarse** VR to become popular.

populismo NM populism; populist policies.

populista ADJ, NMF populist.

populoso ADJ populous.

popurrí NM potpourri.

poquedad NF **(a)** (*escasez*) scantiness, paucity; (*pequeñez*) smallness; (*poca cantidad*) fewness. **(b)** (*una ~*) small thing, trifle; small quantity. **(c)** (*fig: timidez*) timidity.

póquer NM poker.

poquísimo ADJ **(a)** (*sing*) very little; hardly any, almost no. **(b)** (PL) **~s** very few, terribly few.

poquitín NM a little bit.

poquito NM **(a)** **un ~** a little bit (*de* of); (ADV) a little, a bit. **(b)** **a ~s** bit by bit; in dribs and drabs; **¡~ a poco!** gently!, easy there!

▼ **por** PREP **(a)** (+ *infin*) in order to; **~ no llegar tarde** in order not to be late, so as not to arrive late; **lo hizo ~ complacerle** he did it to please her; **hablar ~ hablar** to talk just for talking's sake; **moverse ~ no estar quieto** to move about simply so as to have a change from sitting still; *V* t **(c)**.
(b) (*objetivo*) for; **luchar ~ la patria** to fight for one's country; **trabajar ~ dinero** to work for money; **su amor ~ la pintura** his love for painting; **hazlo ~ mí** do it for me, do it for my sake; **(sí,) ¿~?** (*LAm*) (yes,) why?, why do you ask?
▼ **(c)** (*causa*) out of, because of, from; **fue ~ necesidad** it was from (*o* out of, because of) necessity; **~ temor** from fear; **~ temor a** for fear of; **lo hago ~ gusto** I do it because I like to; **no se realizó ~ escasez de fondos** it was not put into effect because of lack of money; **~ venir tarde perdió la mitad** through coming late he missed half of it; **se hundió ~ mal construido** it collapsed because it was badly built; **le expulsaron ~ revoltoso** they expelled him as a troublemaker; **lo dejó ~ imposible** he gave it up as (being) impossible.
(d) (*evidencia*) **~ lo que dicen** from what they say, judging by what they say; **~ las señas no piensa hacerlo** judging by the signs he's not intending to do it.
(e) (*en cuanto a*) **~ mí, que se vaya** so far as I'm concerned (*o* for myself, for my part) he can go.
(f) (*agente*) by; **~ su propia mano** by his own hand; **~ correo** by post, through the post; **~ mar** by sea, by boat; **~ sí mismo** by o.s.; **hablar ~ señas** to talk by signs, communicate by means of signs; **lo obtuve ~ medio de un amigo** I got it through a friend, I got it with the help of a friend.

(g) (*Mat*) **7 ~ 2 son 14** twice 7 is 14; **7 ~ 5 son 35** 5 times 7 is 35.
(h) (*modo*) in; by; (*según*) according to; **~ centenares** by the hundred, by hundreds; **~ orden** in order; **están dispuestos ~ tamaños** they are arranged according to size (*o* by sizes, in sizes); **punto ~ punto** point by point; **día ~ día** day by day.
(i) (*lugar*) by, by way of; (*a través de*) through; (*a lo largo de*) along; **ir a Bilbao ~ Santander** to go to Bilbao via Santander; **~ el lado izquierdo** on (*o* along) the left side; **cruzar la frontera ~ Canfranc** to cross the frontier at Canfranc; **~ la calle** along the street; **~ la caña** through the pipe, along the pipe; **~ todo el país** over the whole country, throughout the country; **llevar periódicos ~ las casas** to deliver papers round the houses; **pasar ~ Madrid** to pass through Madrid; to go via Madrid; **pasearse ~ el parque** to walk round the park, stroll through the park.
(j) (*tiempo*) **~ la mañana** in the morning; during the morning; **no sale ~ la noche** he doesn't go out at night.
(k) (*presente y futuro*) for; **se quedarán ~ 15 días** they will stay for a fortnight; **será ~ poco tiempo** it won't be for long.
(l) (*a cambio de*) for, in exchange for; **te doy éste ~ aquél** I'll swap you this one for that one; **le dieron uno nuevo ~ el viejo** they gave him a new one (in exchange) for the old one; **se vendió ~ 15 dólares** it was sold for 15 dollars; **me dieron 13 francos ~ una libra** they gave me 13 francs for a pound; **ha puesto B ~ V** he has put B instead of V.
(m) (*de parte de*) **vino ~ su jefe** he came instead of (*o* in place of) his boss; **interceder ~ uno** to intercede for sb, intercede on sb's behalf; **hablo ~ todos** I speak on behalf of (*o* in the name of) everybody.
(n) (*como*) **contar a uno ~ amigo** to count sb as a friend; **no se admite ~ válido** it is not accepted as valid; *V* **tener, tomar** etc.
(o) (*razón*) **10 dólares ~ hora** 10 dollars an hour; **revoluciones ~ minuto** revolutions per minute; *V* **persona** etc.
(p) (*indicación aproximativa*) **eso está allá ~ el norte** that's somewhere up in the north; **~ la feria** about carnival time, round about the carnival; *V* **fecha, Navidad** etc.
(q) **~ difícil que sea** however hard it is, however hard it may be; **~ mucho que lo quisieran** however much they would like to; *V* **más 1 (e)**.
(r) **ir a ~ uno** (*Esp*: *buscar*) to go for sb, go and fetch sb; (*atacar*) to attack sb, go for sb; **¡a ~ ellos!** after them!, get them!; *V* **venir ~** etc.
(s) **~ qué** why; **¿~ qué?** why?

porcachón* ADJ filthy, dirty.

porcada* NF = **porquería**.

porcallón* ADJ filthy, dirty.

porcelana NF (*sustancia*) porcelain; (*loza*) china, chinaware; **tienda de ~** china shop.

porcentaje NM percentage; proportion, ratio; rate; **un elevado ~ de** a high percentage of, a high proportion of; **~ de accesos** (*Inform*) hit rate; **el ~ de defunciones** the death-rate; **trabajar a ~** to work on a percentage basis.

porcentual ADJ percentage (*atr*).

porcentualmente ADV in percentage terms, percentage-wise; proportionally.

porche NM **(a)** (*tiendas etc*) arcade (*of shops, round square etc*). **(b)** (*de casa*) porch.

Porcia NF Portia.

porcino [1] ADJ porcine; pig (*atr*); **ganado ~** pigs.
[2] NM **(a)** (*animales*) pigs; (*lechón*) young pig; **carne de ~** pork; pig-meat. **(b)** (*Med*) bump, swelling.

porción NF **(a)** (*gen*) portion; (*parte*) part, share; (*en recetas etc*) quantity, amount, part; (*de chocolate etc*) piece, segment; **una ~ de patatas** a helping of potatoes.
(b) **una ~ de** (*fig*) a number of; **tengo una ~ de cosas que hacer** I have a number of things to do; **tuvimos una ~ de problemas** we had quite a few problems.

porcuno ADJ pig (*atr*).

pordiosear [1a] VI to beg (*t fig*).

pordiosero, -a NM/F beggar.

porende ADV (†† *o liter*) hence, therefore.

porfa* INTERJ please.

porfía NF **(a)** (*persistencia*) persistence; (*terquedad*) obstinacy, stubbornness. **(b)** (*disputa*) dispute; (*contienda*) continuous struggle, continuous competition. **(c)** **a ~** in competition.

porfiadamente ADV persistently; obstinately, stubbornly.

porfiado [1] ADJ (*insistente*) persistent; (*terco*) obstinate, stubborn.
[2] NM (*LAm*) doll; manikin, dummy.

porfiar [1c] VI (*persistir*) to persist, insist; (*disputar*) to argue stubbornly, doggedly maintain one's point of view; **~ con uno** to argue with sb; **~ en algo** to persist in sth; **porfía en que es así** he insists that it is so, he will have it that it is so; **~ por** + *infin* to struggle obstinately to + *infin*.

pórfido NM porphyry.

porfión ADJ dogged, stubborn.

porfirismo NM porphyria.
porfirista NMF (*Méx*) supporter of Porfirio Díaz.
pormenor NM detail, particular.
pormenorización NF: **sin entrar en la ~** without going into detail.
pormenorizadamente ADV in detail.
pormenorizado ADJ detailed.
pormenorizar [1f] ① VT (*detallar*) to detail, set out in detail; (*particularizar*) to particularize; to describe in detail.
② VI to go into detail, particularize.
porno* ① ADJ INVAR porno*, pornographic.
② NM porn*, pornography; **~ blando** soft porn; **~ duro** hard porn.
pornografía NF pornography.
pornográfico ADJ pornographic.
pornografista NMF pornographer.
poro¹ NM (*Anat*) pore.
poro² NM (*Méx*) leek.
poronga⚦ NF (*Cono Sur*) prick⚦, cock⚦.
porongo NM (*Cono Sur*) gourd, calabash; (*fig*) nobody.
pororó NM (*Cono Sur*) popcorn.
porosidad NF porousness, porosity.
poroso ADJ porous.
porotal NM (*LAm*) (a) (*gen*) beanfield, bean patch. (b) (*fig*) **un ~ de*** a lot of, a whole heap of.
poroto NM (a) (*And, Cono Sur*) kidney bean; **~ verde** green bean, runner bean; **~s*** food, grub⚦; **ganarse los ~** to earn one's daily bread; **no valer un ~** to be worthless. (b) (*Cono Sur: punto*) point; **anotarse un ~*** to make it. (c) (*Cono Sur**) (*niño*) kid*; (*débil*) weakling.
porpuesto NM (*Carib*) minibus, taxi.
porque CONJ (a) (+ *indic*) because; since, for. (b) (+ *subj*) so that, in order that.
porqué NM (a) (*motivo*) reason (*de* for), cause (*de* of); the whys and wherefores; **el ~ de la revolución** the factors that underlie the revolution; **'El ~ de los dichos'** 'Origins of our Sayings'; **no tengo ~ ir** there's no reason I should go.
(b) (*Fin*) amount, portion; **tiene mucho ~** he's got plenty of the ready*.
porquería NF (a) (*sustancia*) filth, muck, dirt; **me lo devolvieron cubierto de ~** they gave it back to me filthy all over; **estar hecho una ~** to be covered in muck, be dirty all over.
(b) (*cualidad*) nastiness; indecency.
(c) (*objeto*) small thing, trifle; **~s** old things, junk, lumber; **le regalaron alguna ~** they gave her some worthless present; **lo vendieron por una ~** they sold it for next to nothing.
(d) (*acto*) dirty trick, mean action; indecent act; **me han hecho una ~** they've played a dirty trick on me.
(e) (*Culin*) nasty food, awful meal; attractive but unwholesome dish.
(f) (*fig: basura*) rubbish; **una película de ~** (*LAm*) a rotten film*; **la novela es una ~** the novel is just rubbish; **escribió 3 ó 4 ~s** he wrote 3 or 4 rubbishy books.
porqueriza NF pigsty.
porquerizo NM, **porquero** NM pigman.
porra NF (a) (*palo*) stick, club, cudgel; (*de policía*) truncheon; (*Téc*) large hammer; (*Culin*) large club-shaped fritter; (⚦: *nariz*) conk⚦, nose; (⚦: *pene*) prick⚦.
(b) (*: *pesado*) bore.
(c) (*: *fachenda*) swank*, conceit; **gasta mucha ~** he's got loads of swank*.
(d) (*: *locuciones*) **¡~s!** bother!, dash it!*; (*a otro*) rubbish!; **¡una ~!** never!, no way!*; **¡a la ~!** (*fuera*) get out!, (*no hay tal*) no way!*, rubbish!; **¡a la ~ el ministro!** the minister can go to blazes!*; **mandar a uno a la ~** to chuck sb out, send sb packing; **¡vete a la ~!** go to blazes!*; **¡qué coche ni qué ~s!** car my foot!
(e) (*And, Cono Sur: mechón*) curl, forelock.
(f) (*CAm, Méx: Pol: pandilla*) political gang.
(g) (*Méx*) (*Dep*) fans; (*Teat*) claque.
(h) (*CAm: olla*) metal cooking-pot.
(i) (*juego*) sweep, sweepstake.
porracear* [1a] VT (*Carib, Méx*) to beat up.
porrada NF (a) (*porrazo*) thwack, thump, blow. (b) (*: *montón*) pile*, heap*; lot; **una ~ de** a whole heap of*, a lot of; **a ~s** in abundance, galore.
porrata⚦ NMF pot smoker.
porrazo NM (a) (*golpe*) thwack, thump, blow; (*al caer*) bump. (b) **de ~** (*LAm*) in one go, at one blow; **de golpe y ~** suddenly.
porrear [1a] VI (a) (*machacar*) to go on and on, harp on a theme. (b) (⚦: *droga*) to smoke pot⚦.
porrería* NF (a) (*petición*) annoying request, footling demand. (b) (*necedad*) stupidity.
porrero⚦, **-a** NM/F pot smoker⚦.
porreta NF (a) (*Bot*) green leaf. (b) **en ~(s)*** stark naked.
porretada NF = **porrada** (b).
porrillo: **a ~** ADV in abundance, by the ton.

porro* ① ADJ stupid, oafish.
② NM (a) idiot, oaf. (b) (*Esp⚦: canuto*) joint⚦; (*droga*) hash*. (c) (*And, Carib: baile*) a folk dance.
porrón¹ ADJ (*lerdo*) slow, stupid; (*soso*) dull; (*torpe*) sluggish.
porrón² NM *wine jar with a long spout*; **un ~ de*** a lot of; **me gusta un ~** I like it a lot.
porrón³ NM (*Orn*) pochard.
porrudo ADJ (a) (*abultado*) big, bulging. (b) (*Cono Sur: melenudo*) long-haired. (c) (*Cono Sur*) (*engreído*) big-headed.
porsiacaso NM (*Cono Sur*) knapsack.
port. ABR *de portugués* Portuguese, Port.
porta NF (*Náut*) port, porthole.
portaaeronaves NM INVAR aircraft-carrier.
porta(a)viones NM INVAR aircraft-carrier.
portabebés NM INVAR baby-carrier.
portabilidad NF portability.
portable ① ADJ portable.
② NM portable computer.
portabotellas NM INVAR (*para almacenar botellas*) wine rack; (*para llevar botellas*) bottle carrier.
portabultos NM INVAR carrier.
portabustos NM INVAR (*Méx*) brassière, bra*.
portacargas NM INVAR (*caja*) crate; (*de bicicleta etc*) carrier.
portacheques NM INVAR chequebook.
portación NF: **~ de armas** carrying (of) a weapon.
portacoches NM INVAR car transporter.
portacontenedores NM INVAR container ship.
portacubiertos NM INVAR knifebox, cutlery box.
portada NF (a) (*Arquit*) main front; (*fachada*) facade; (*pórtico*) porch, doorway; (*portal*) carriage door, gateway. (b) (*Tip*) title page; (*de revista*) cover; (*de disco*) sleeve.
portadiscos NM INVAR record rack.
portado ADJ: **bien ~** well-dressed; well-behaved; respectable.
portador(a) NM/F carrier, bearer; (*Com, Fin*) bearer; payee; **páguese al ~** pay the bearer; **~ de gérmenes** germ carrier; **el ~ de esta carta** the bearer of this letter.
portaequipajes NM INVAR (*Aut etc*) boot, trunk (*US*); (*de techo*) luggage-rack, roof-rack, grid; (*de bicicleta*) carrier.
portaesquíes NM INVAR (*Aut, Esquí*) ski rack.
portaestandarte NM standard-bearer.
portafolio(s) NM briefcase, attaché case.
portafotos NM INVAR locket.
portafusil NM rifle sling.
portahachón NM torchbearer.
portal NM (a) (*zaguán*) vestibule, hall.
(b) (*pórtico*) porch, doorway; (*puerta principal*) street door, main door; (*de ciudad*) gate; **~es** arcade (*of shops, around square, etc*).
(c) (*Dep*) goal.
(d) (*Ecl*): **~ de Belén** Nativity scene, crèche.
portalada NF large doorway; imposing entrance; gate.
portalámpara(s) NM INVAR lamp-holder, socket.
portalápices NM INVAR (*estuche*) pencil case; (*para escritorio*) penholder.
portaligas NM INVAR suspender-belt, garter belt (*US*).
portalón NM (a) (*Arquit*) = **portalada**. (b) (*Náut*) gangway.
portamaletas NM INVAR (*Aut*) luggage-rack, roof-rack, grid.
portamanteo NM (*Esp*) travelling bag.
portaminas NM INVAR propelling pencil.
portamisiles NM INVAR missile-carrier.
portamonedas NM INVAR purse.
portante NM: **tomar el ~*** to clear off*.
portañuela NF fly (*of trousers*).
portaobjeto(s) NM INVAR slide; stage.
portapapeles NM INVAR briefcase.
portaplacas NM INVAR (*Fot*) plateholder.
portaplatos NM INVAR plate rack.
portapliegos NM INVAR (*And*) office boy.
portaplumas NM INVAR penholder.
portar [1a] ① VT (*liter*) to carry, bear.
② **portarse** VR (a) (*conducirse*) to behave, conduct o.s.; **~ mal** to misbehave, behave badly; **se ha portado como un cochino** he has behaved like a swine; **se portó muy bien conmigo** he was very decent to me, he treated me very well.
(b) (*: *distinguirse*) to show up well, come through creditably.
(c) (*LAm*) to behave well.
portarretratos NM INVAR picture-frame, photograph frame.
portarrollos NM INVAR (*del baño*) toilet-roll holder; (*de la cocina*) kitchen-roll holder.
portasenos NM INVAR (*LAm*) bra*.
portátil ADJ portable.
portatostadas NM INVAR toast rack.
portatrajes NM INVAR suit bag.
portavelas NM INVAR candle-holder.

portaviandas NM INVAR lunch tin, dinner pail (US).

portavoz [1] NM (altoparlante) megaphone, loudhailer.

[2] NMF spokesperson, spokesman; (pey) mouthpiece.

portazgo NM toll.

portazo NM bang (of a door), slam; **dar un ~** to slam the door.

porte NM **(a)** (Com) (acto) carriage, transport; (gastos) (costs of) carriage, transport charges; (Correos) postage; **~ por cobrar** freight forward; **~ pagado** (Com) carriage paid, (Correos) post-paid; **franco de ~** (Com) carriage free, (Correos) post-free.
(b) (esp Náut) capacity.
(c) (conducta) conduct, behaviour.
(d) (comportamiento) bearing, demeanour; (presencia) air, appearance; **de ~ distinguido** with a distinguished air.

porteador NM carrier; (Alpinismo etc) porter; (Caza etc) bearer.

portear¹ [1a] VT (Com) to carry, convey, transport.

portear² [1a] VI **(a)** (puerta) to slam, bang. **(b)** (Cono Sur) to get out in a hurry.

portento NM marvel, wonder, prodigy; **es un ~ de belleza** she is extraordinarily beautiful.

portentosamente ADV marvellously, extraordinarily; extraordinarily well.

portentoso ADJ marvellous, extraordinary.

porteño [1] ADJ (Argentina) of Buenos Aires; (Chile) of Valparaíso.

[2] NM, **porteña** NF (Argentina) native (o inhabitant) of Buenos Aires o (Chile) Valparaíso; **los ~s** the people of Buenos Aires o (Chile) Valparaíso.

porteo NM carriage, transport, conveyance.

portera NF portress.

portería NF **(a)** (conserjería) porter's lodge, porter's office.
(b) (Dep) goal.

portero NM **(a)** (conserje) porter, janitor; doorman; (guardián) caretaker; **~ automático, ~ eléctrico, ~ electrónico** answering device.
(b) (Dep) goalkeeper.

portezuela NF **(a)** (gen) little door; (de vehículo) door; **~ de la gasolina** fuel-filler door. **(b)** (Cos) pocket flap.

portezuelo NM (Cono Sur Geog) pass.

pórtico NM **(a)** (portal) portico, porch; (fig) gateway (de to). **(b)** (de tiendas etc) arcade.

portilla NF porthole.

portillo NM **(a)** (abertura) gap, opening; (brecha) breach; (postigo) wicket, wicket gate; (puerta falsa) side entrance, private door.
(b) (Geog) narrow pass.
(c) (abolladura) dent; (saltadura) chip.
(d) (fig: punto débil) weak spot, vulnerable point; (para solución) opening (affording solution to a problem).

pórtland NM O F (esp LAm) cement.

portón NM (puerta grande) large door; (puerta principal) main door; (Aut: t ~ trasero) hatch, hatchback, tailgate (US); (LAm: de casa) main door, street door; (Cono Sur) back door.

portorriqueño, -a ADJ, NM/F Puerto Rican.

portuario ADJ port (atr), harbour (atr); dock (atr); **trabajador ~** docker.

Portugal NM Portugal.

portugués, -esa [1] ADJ, NM/F Portuguese.

[2] NM (Ling) Portuguese.

portuguesismo NM portuguesism, word (o phrase etc) borrowed from Portuguese.

porvenir NM future; **en el ~, en lo ~** in the future; **un hombre sin ~** a man with no future, a man with no prospects; **le espera un brillante ~** a brilliant future awaits him.

pos: en ~ de PREP after, in pursuit of; **ir en ~ de** to chase (after), pursue; **ella va en ~ de triunfo** she's after success.

posada NF **(a)** (hospedaje) shelter, lodging; **dar ~ a** to give shelter to, take in. **(b)** (mesón) inn; (pensión) lodging house. **(c)** (morada) house, dwelling, abode. **(d)** (CAm, Méx) Christmas party.

posaderas* NFPL backside, buttocks.

posadero NM innkeeper.

posar [1a] [1] VT carga to lay down, put down; mano etc to place, put gently; **~ los ojos en** to look vaguely at, glance idly at.

[2] VI (Arte, Cine, Fot) to sit, pose.

[3] **posarse** VR **(a)** (ave, insecto) to alight, settle, rest; (ave) to perch, sit; (avión) to land, come down; **el avión se encontraba posado** the aircraft was on the ground.
(b) (líquido) to settle, form sediment; (polvo) to settle.

posas* NFPL backside, buttocks.

posavasos NM INVAR dripmat, mat, coaster (US); (de taberna) beer-mat.

posbélico ADJ postwar.

poscolonial ADJ post-colonial.

poscombustión NF: **dispositivo de ~** afterburner.

posconciliar ADJ post-conciliar, after Vatican II.

posconcilio NM: **los 20 años de ~** the 20 years following Vatican II.

posdata NF postscript.

posdoctoral ADJ post-doctoral.

pose [pouz o 'pose] NF **(a)** (Arte, Cine, Fot) pose; (Fot) time exposure.
(b) (fig: actitud) attitude.
(c) (fig: aplomo) composure; poise.
(d) (fig) (afectación) pose; affectedness; (postura afectada) affected posture.

poseedor NM, **poseedora** NF owner, possessor; (de puesto, récord) holder.

poseer [2e] VT (gen) to have, possess, own; ventaja to have, enjoy; mujer to have; lengua, tema to know perfectly, have a complete mastery of; puesto, récord to hold.

poseído [1] ADJ **(a)** (lit) possessed (por by); (fig: enloquecido) maddened, crazed.
(b) **estar muy ~ de** to be very vain about, have an excessively high opinion of.

[2] NM, **poseída** NF: **gritar como un ~** to shout like one possessed.

poselectoral ADJ post-electoral.

posesión NF **(a)** (gen) possession; (de puesto) tenure, occupation; (de lengua, tema) complete knowledge, perfect mastery; **dar ~ a** to hand over to, make formal transfer to; **él está en ~ de las cartas** he is in possession of the letters; **las cartas están en ~ de su padre** the letters are in the possession of his father; **está en ~ del récord** he holds the record; **tomar ~** to take over, enter upon office (etc); **tomar ~ de** to take possession of, take over; **tomar ~ de un oficio** to take up a post.
(b) (una ~) possession (t Pol); (propiedad) property; (finca) piece of property, estate.
(c) (Cono Sur) country estate; (Carib) ranch, estate.

posesionar [1a] [1] VT: **~ a uno de algo** to hand sth over to sb.

[2] **posesionarse** VR: **~ de** to take possession of, take over.

posesividad NF possessiveness.

posesivo ADJ, NM possessive.

poseso = poseído.

posestructuralismo NM post-structuralism.

posfechar [1a] VT to postdate.

posfranquismo NM period after the death of Franco (1975).

posfranquista ADJ: **p.ej. cultura ~** post-Franco culture, culture since Franco.

posglacial ADJ postglacial.

posgrado NM: **curso de ~** postgraduate course.

posgraduado, -a ADJ, NM/F postgraduate.

posgradual ADJ postgraduate.

posguerra NF postwar period; **los años de la ~** the postwar years; **en la ~** in the postwar period, after the war.

▼ **posibilidad** NF possibility; chance; **no existe ~ alguna de que venga** there is no possibility of his coming; **tiene pocas ~es** he hasn't much chance; **si hay la ~ de verlo** if there's a chance to see it; **cabe la ~** there's always the chance; **estar en la ~ de +** infin to be in a position to + infin; **vivir por encima de sus ~es** to live above one's means.

posibilista [1] ADJ optimistic, positive.

[2] NMF optimist, positive thinker.

posibilitar [1a] VT to make possible, facilitate, permit; to make feasible; **~ que uno haga algo** to allow sb to do sth, make it possible for sb to do sth.

▼ **posible** [1] ADJ possible; feasible; **una ~ tragedia** a possible tragedy; **todas las concesiones ~s** all possible concessions; **a serme ~** if I possibly can; **de ser ~** if possible; **en lo ~ as** far as possible; **lo antes ~** as soon as possible; as quickly as possible; **lo más frecuentemente ~** as often as possible; **hacer ~ una cosa** to make sth possible; **hacer lo ~** to do all that one can (para o por + infin to + infin); **es ~ que +** subj it is possible that ...; perhaps ...; **¿es ~?** surely not?; can it really be true?; **¿será ~ que haya venido?** can he really have come (after all)?; **¿será ~ que no haya venido?** surely he has come, hasn't he?; **si es ~** if possible; **si me es ~** if I possibly can; V **dentro, pronto** etc.

[2] **~s** NMPL (medios) means; (fondos) funds, assets; **vivir dentro de sus ~s** to live within one's means.

▼ **posiblemente** ADV possibly.

posición NF **(a)** (gen) position; (status) status, standing, social position; **~ del misionero** missionary position; **estar en ~ de guardia** to be on guard (contra against); **perder posiciones** to fall away, lose strength.
(b) (Dep) position; (en liga etc) place, position; **posiciones de honor** first three places, medal positions; **terminar en primera ~** to finish first; **ganó A con B en segunda ~** A won with B in second place.
(c) (LAm: puesto) position, post, job.

posicionado NM positioning.

posicionamiento NM stance, attitude.

posicionar [1a] [1] VT to position.

[2] **posicionarse** VR (fig) to adopt an attitude, take up a stance; to define one's position, declare oneself.

posimperial ADJ post-imperial.

➤ LENGUA Y USO: **posibilidad** → 42.3, 43.3, 46.1   **posible: 1** → 31, 36.1, 42.3, 53.6   **posiblemente** → 53.6

posimpresionismo NM post-impressionism.
posimpresionista ADJ, NMF post-impressionist.
posindustrial ADJ post-industrial.
positiva NF (*Fot*) positive, print.
positivado NM (*Fot*) developing.
positivamente ADV positively.
positivar [1a] VT *foto* to develop.
positivismo NM positivism.
positivista ADJ, NMF positivist.
positivo ① ADJ (*gen*) positive; (*Mat*) positive, plus; *idea* useful, practical, constructive; **es ~ que** ... it is good that ..., it is encouraging that ...; **el atleta dio ~** the athlete failed a drugs test.
② NM (a) (*Ling*) positive. (b) (*Fot*) positive, print. (c) (*Dep*) point.
pósito NM (a) (*granero*) (public) granary. (b) (*cooperativa*) cooperative, association; **~ de pescadores** fishing cooperative.
positrón NM positron.
posma* NMF bore, dull person.
posmeridiano ADJ postmeridian, afternoon (*atr*).
posmodernidad NF post-modernity.
posmodernismo NM postmodernism.
posmoderno ADJ postmodern.
posnatal ADJ postnatal.
poso NM sediment, deposit; dregs; **~s de café** coffee grounds; **~s de té** tea-leaves.
posol NM (*CAm*) maize drink.
posología NF (*Med*) dosage.
posoperativo ADJ post-operative.
posoperatorio ① ADJ post-operative.
② NM post-operative period, period of recovery after an operation.
pososo ADJ (*CAm*) (*poroso*) porous, permeable; (*absorbente*) absorbent.
posparto ① ADJ postnatal.
② NM postnatal period.
posponer [2q] VT (a) (*subordinar*) **~ A a B** to put A behind (o below) B; **~ el amor propio al interés general** to subordinate one's self-respect to the general interest; **~ a uno** to downgrade sb.
(b) (*aplazar*) to postpone.
posposición NF (a) (*gen*) postposition; relegation; subordination. (b) (*aplazamiento*) postponement. (c) (*Ling*) post-position.
pospositivo ADJ postpositive.
posproducción NF post-production.
posquemador NM afterburner.
post... PREF post...
pos(t)... PREF post...; after...
posta ① NF (a) (*caballos*) relay, team; (*etapa*) stage; (*parada*) staging post; **a ~** on purpose, deliberately; **por la ~** post-haste, as quickly as possible.
(b) (*Naipes*) stake.
(c) (*Culin*) slice; **~ de pierna** (*CAm*) leg of pork.
(d) (*Caza*) slug, pellet.
(e) (*Cono Sur*) first-aid post.
② NM courier.
postal ① ADJ postal.
② NF postcard; **~ ilustrada** picture postcard.
postcolonial = **poscolonial**.
postdata NF postscript.
poste NM (*gen*) post, pole; (*columna*) pillar; (*estaca*) stake; (*Dep*) post, upright; (*de ejecución*) stake; **~s** (*Dep*) goalposts, goal; **~ de cerca** fencing post; **~ indicador** signpost; **~ de llegada** winning post; **~ de portería** goalpost; **~ de salida** starting post; **~ telegráfico** telegraph pole; **~ del tendido eléctrico** electricity pylon; **dar ~ a uno*** to keep sb hanging about; **mover los ~s** (*fig*) to move the goalposts; **oler el ~** to scent danger, see trouble ahead; to smell a rat.
postelectoral ADJ = **poselectoral**.
postema NF (a) (*Med*) abscess, tumour; (*Méx: pus*) pus; (*Méx: divieso*) boil. (b) (*: *pelmazo*) bore, dull person.
postemilla NF (*LAm*) gumboil.
póster NM, PL **pósteres** o **pósters** poster.
postergación NF (a) (*relegación*) passing over, ignoring. (b) (*retraso*) delaying; (*aplazamiento*) deferment, postponement.
postergar [1h] VT (a) *persona* to pass over, disregard; to ignore the seniority (o better claim) of. (b) (*esp LAm*) (*demorar*) to delay; (*aplazar*) to defer, postpone.
posteridad NF (a) posterity. (b) (*Esp*: culo*) bottom.
posterior ADJ (a) (*lugar*) back, rear; posterior; *motor* rear-mounted.
(b) (*en orden*) later, following.
(c) (*tiempo*) later, subsequent; **ser ~ a** to be later than.
posteriori V **a posteriori**.
posterioridad NF later nature; **con ~** later, subsequently; **con ~ a** subsequent to, later than.
posteriormente ADV later, subsequently, afterwards.
postgrado NM = **posgrado**.
postgraduado, -a ADJ, NM/F = **posgraduado**.

postguerra NF = **posguerra**.
postigo NM (a) (*puerta pequeña*) wicket, wicket gate; (*portillo*) postern; (*puerta falsa*) small door, side door. (b) (*contraventana*) shutter.
postillón NM postillion.
postín* NM (a) (*lujo*) elegance, luxury, poshness*; (*entono*) tone; **de ~** posh*, swanky*, smart.
(b) (*fachenda*) side*, swank*; **darse ~** to show off, swank*; **se da mucho ~ de que su padre es ministro** he swanks about his father being a minister*.
postinear* VI to show off, swank*.
postinero* ADJ (a) *persona* vain, conceited (*de* about); swanky*. (b) *traje etc* posh*, swish*.
postizas NFPL (*Esp*) (*small*) castanets.
postizo ① ADJ false, artificial; *dientes* false; *cuello* detachable; *exterior etc* dummy; *sonrisa etc* false, phoney*, sham.
② NM switch, false hair, hairpiece.
postnatal ADJ postnatal.
postoperatorio ADJ, NM = **posoperatorio**.
postor(a) NM/F bidder; **mayor** (o **mejor**) **~** highest bidder.
postparto ADJ, NM = **posparto**.
postproducción NF = **posproducción**.
postración NF prostration; **~ nerviosa** nervous exhaustion.
postrado ADJ (*t fig*) prostrate; **~ por el dolor** prostrate with grief.
postrar [1a] ① VT (a) (*derribar*) to cast down, overthrow; (*humillar*) to humble. (b) (*Med: debilitar*) to weaken, exhaust, prostrate.
② **postrarse** VR (*hincarse*) to prostrate o.s.
postre ① NM (*t ~s*) sweet, sweet course; dessert; **¿qué hay de ~?** what is there for dessert?; **para ~(s)*** to crown it all, on top of all that; **llegar a los ~s** (*fig*) to come too late, come after everything is over.
② NF: **a la ~** at last, in the end; when all is said and done.
postremo ADJ, **postrero** ADJ (**postrer** *delante de nm sing*) last; rear, hindermost; **palabras postremas** dying words.
postrimerías NFPL (a) (*gen*) dying moments; (*último período*) final stages, closing stages; **en las ~ del siglo** in the last few years of the century, right at the end of the century.
(b) (*Ecl*) four last things.
postulación NF (a) (*proposición*) postulation. (b) (*colecta*) collection.
postulado NM postulate, proposition; assumption, hypothesis.
postulador NM postulator.
postulante NMF petitioner; (*Ecl*) postulant; (*Pol*) candidate; (*LAm*) applicant.
postular [1a] ① VT (a) (*proponer*) to postulate.
(b) (*pedir*) to seek, demand; (*solicitar*) to petition for; (*pretender*) to claim; **en el artículo postula la reforma de** ... in the article he sets out demands for the reform of ...
(c) *dinero* to collect (for charity).
(d) (*CAm, Méx*) *candidato* to nominate.
② VI (*LAm*) to apply.
③ **postularse** VR (*LAm Pol*) to stand.
póstumo ADJ posthumous.
postura NF (a) (*del cuerpo*) posture, position; stance; pose; (*sexual*) position; **~ del loto** lotus position.
(b) (*fig*) attitude, position; stand; **adoptar una ~ poco razonable** to take an unreasonable attitude; **la ~ del gobierno en este asunto** the government's position in this matter; **tomar ~** to adopt a stance.
(c) (*en subasta*) bid; (*en el juego*) bet, stake; **hacer una ~** to lay a bet; to make a bid.
(d) (*Orn: acto*) egg-laying; (*huevos*) eggs (laid).
(e) (‡: *droga*) quantity of hash*; 1000-pesetas' worth of hash*.
postural ADJ postural.
posventa ADJ after-sales (*atr*); **servicio** (o **asistencia**) **de ~** after-sales service.
pota¹* NF wreck, clunker (*US*).
pota²‡ NF: **echar la ~** to puke‡, throw up.
potabilización NF purification.
potabilizadora NF water-treatment plant, waterworks.
potabilizar [1f] VT: **~ el agua** to make the water drinkable.
potable ADJ (a) drinkable; **agua ~** drinking water. (b) (*: *aceptable*) good enough, passable.
potaje NM (a) (*Culin*) broth; vegetable stew, stewed vegetables. (b) (*fig*) (*mezcla*) mixture; (*revoltijo*) jumble.
potar‡ [1a] VI to spew, throw up.
potasa NF potash.
potasio NM potassium.
pote NM (a) (*gen*) pot; (*tarro*) jar; (*jarra*) jug; (*Farm*) jar; (*Méx: lata*) tin, can; (*Méx: vasija*) mug; (*Hort*) flowerpot, pot; (*And, Carib*) flask; **a ~** in plenty; *V* **beber**.
(b) (*prov*) stew.
(c) (*: *puchero*) pout, sulky look.
(d) **darse ~*** to show off, swank*.

(e) (*: *trago*) drink; **tomar unos ~s** to have a few drinks.

potear* [1a] VI to have a few drinks.

potencia NF **(a)** (*gen*) power; potency; **~ electoral** voting power, power in terms of votes; **~ de fuego** firepower; **~ hidráulica** hydraulic power; **~ muscular** muscular power, muscular strength; **~ nuclear** nuclear power.
(b) (*Mec*) power; capacity; **~ (en caballos)** horsepower; **~ al freno** brake horsepower; **~ real** effective power.
(c) (*Pol*) power; **las ~s** the Powers; **las grandes ~s** the great powers; **~ colonial** colonial power; **~ mundial** world power; **éramos una ~ naval** we used to be a naval power.
(d) (*Mat*) power.
(e) (*Rel*: *t* **~ del alma**) faculty.
(f) **en ~** potential, in the making; **es una guerra civil en ~** it is a civil war in the making.

potenciación NF = **potenciamiento.**

potenciador ADJ: **~ de** favourable to, encouraging to.

potencial [1] ADJ potential.
[2] NM **(a)** (*gen*) potential; **~ comercial** market potential; **~ ganador** earning potential; **~ de ventas** sales potential. **(b)** (*Ling*) conditional.

potencialidad NF potentiality.

potencialización NF = **potenciamiento.**

potencializar [1f] VT = **potenciar.**

potencialmente ADV potentially.

potenciamiento NM favouring, fostering, promotion; development; strengthening, boosting, reinforcement.

potenciar [1b] VT (*promover*) to favour, foster, promote; (*desarrollar*) to develop; (*mejorar*) to improve, (*Inform*) to upgrade; (*fortalecer*) to strengthen, boost, reinforce.

potentado NM potentate; (*fig*) tycoon; baron, magnate; big shot*.

potente ADJ **(a)** (*poderoso*) powerful. **(b)** (*: *grande*) big, mighty, strong; **un grito ~** a great yell.

poteo* NM drinks, drinking; **ir de ~** to go round the bars.

potestad NF power, authority, jurisdiction; **~ marital** husband's authority; **patria ~** paternal authority.

potestativo ADJ optional, not mandatory; permissive.

potingue* NM concoction, brew.

potito NM **(a)** (*Esp*) small jar, (*esp*) (jar of) baby food. **(b)** (*LAm*) backside, bottom.

poto NM (*And, Cono Sur*) **(a)** (*) (*trasero*) backside, bottom; (*fondo*) lower end. **(b)** (*Bot*) calabash; (*vasija*) earthenware jug.

potoco* ADJ (*And, Cono Sur*) squat.

potón (*Cono Sur*) [1] ADJ coarse.
[2] NM rustic, peasant.

potosí NM fortune; **cuesta un ~** it costs the earth; **vale un ~** it's worth a fortune; **ella vale un ~** she's a treasure; **en ese negocio tienen un ~** they've got a gold mine in that business.

potra NF **(a)** (*Zool*) filly. **(b)** (*Med*) rupture, hernia. **(c)** (*: *suerte*) luck, jam*; **de ~** by luck, luckily; **tener ~** to be jammy*, be lucky.

potranca NF filly, young mare.

potranco NM (*LAm*) colt, young horse.

potrear [1a] [1] VT **(a)** (*And, CAm*) to beat. **(b)** (*Carib, Méx*) *caballo* to break, tame.
[2] VI (*CAm, Cono Sur*) to caper about, chase around.

potrero [1] NM **(a)** (*Agr*) pasture; paddock. **(b)** (*LAm*) (*de ganado*) cattle ranch; (*caballeriza*) stud farm, horse breeding establishment. **(c)** (*Cono Sur*: *parque*) playground; (*Méx*: *llanura*) open grassland.
[2] ADJ (*) jammy*, lucky.

potrillo NM **(a)** (*Cono Sur*: *caballo*) colt. **(b)** (*Cono Sur*: *vaso*) tall glass. **(c)** (*And*: *canoa*) small canoe.

potro NM **(a)** (*Zool*) colt; **~ de madera** vaulting-horse. **(b)** (*de tormento*) rack; (*cepo*) stocks; (*de herrar*) shoeing frame. **(c)** (*LAm Med*) hernia, tumour.

potroso* ADJ jammy*, lucky.

POUM NM (*Esp: Hist*) ABR de **Partido Obrero de Unificación Marxista.**

poyo NM stone bench.

poza NF puddle, pool; (*Méx*: *de río*) pool, backwater; (*LAm*: *escupitajo*) gob* of spit.

pozanco NM puddle, pool.

pozo NM **(a)** (*de agua*) well; **~ artesiano** artesian well; **~ ciego, ~ negro** cesspool; **~ de petróleo, ~ petrolífero** oil-well; **~ de riego** well used for irrigation; **~ séptico** septic tank; **caer en el ~** (*fig*) to fall into oblivion.
(b) (*Geog*) deep pool, deep part (of river).
(c) (*Min*) shaft; pit, mine; **~ de aire** air-shaft; **~ de registro, ~ de visita** manhole; inspection hatch; **~ de ventilación** ventilation shaft.
(d) (*Náut*) hold.
(e) (*fig*) **ser un ~ de ciencia** to be immensely learned; **es un ~ de maldad** he is utterly wicked.

pozol NM (*LAm*) = **posol.**

pozole NM (*Méx Culin*) maize stew.

PP (a) NMPL *abr de* **padres** Fathers, Frs. **(b)** NM (*Pol*) ABR *de* **Partido Popular.**

⌐ PP ⌐

i *The Spanish **Partido Popular** is a centre-right party, founded in 1976 under the name of **Alianza Popular** or **AP**, a confederation of various right-wing groups. It is now one of the three main political parties in Spain and the party which displaced the **PSOE** in the 1996 elections. Its first leader was Manuel Fraga, previously Franco's Minister of the Interior, who was succeeded by José María Aznar, the current Spanish prime minister.* ⇨ *See also* PSOE

P.P. (*Com*) ABR *de* **porte pagado** carriage paid, C/P.

p.p. (*Jur*) ABR *de* **por poder** per procurationem, by proxy, p.p.

PPM NM (*Esp*) ABR *de* **Patronato de Protección de la Mujer.**

ppm NFPL *abr de* **partes por millón** parts per million.

p.p.p. ABR *de* **puntos por pulgada** dots per inch, d.p.i.

PR NM ABR *de* **Puerto Rico.**

práctica NF (*gen*) practice; (*método*) method; (*destreza*) skill; **en la ~** in practice; **~ establecida** standard practice; **~s restrictivas (de la competencia)** restrictive practices; **~s profesionales** professional training, practical training for a profession; **~s de tiro** target practice; **la ~ hace maestro** practice makes perfect; **aprender con la ~** to learn by practice; **hacer ~ de clínica** to do one's hospital training, walk the wards; **poner algo en ~** to put sth into practice.

practicable ADJ **(a)** (*gen*) practicable; (*factible*) workable, feasible. **(b)** *camino etc* passable, usable. **(c)** (*Teat*) *puerta* that opens, that is meant to open.

prácticamente ADV practically; **está ~ terminado** it's practically finished, it's almost finished.

practicante [1] ADJ (*Ecl*) practising.
[2] NMF practitioner; (*Med*) medical assistant, doctor's assistant; (*Méx*) final year medical student; (*LAm*: *médico recién recibido*) houseman, intern (*US*).
[3] NM (*enfermero*) male nurse.

practicar [1g] [1] VT **(a)** *habilidad, virtud etc* to practise, exercise.
(b) *actividad etc* to practise; *deporte* to go in for, play; *profesión* to practise; **~ el francés con su profesor** to practise one's French with one's teacher.
(c) (*ejecutar*) to perform, carry out; *detención* to make.
(d) *agujero* to cut, make; to bore, drill.
[2] VI *y* **practicarse** VR: **~ en la enseñanza** to do teaching practice, do one's school practice.

practicidad NF practicality; effectiveness.

practicismo NM down-to-earth attitude, sense of realism.

práctico [1] ADJ **(a)** (*gen*) practical; *herramienta etc* handy; *casa etc* convenient; *ropa* sensible, practical; **no resultó ser muy ~** it turned out to be not very practical; **resulta ~ vivir tan cerca de la fábrica** it's convenient (*o* handy) to live so close to the factory.
(b) *estudio, formación etc* practical.
(c) *persona* skilled, expert (*en* at); **ser muy ~ en** to be very skilled at, be very adept at.
[2] NM (*Med*) practitioner; (*Náut*) pilot.

pradera NF (*prado*) meadow, meadowland; (*césped*) lawn; (*Canadá etc*) prairie; **unas extensas ~s** extensive grasslands.

pradería NF meadowlands, grasslands.

prado NM meadow, field; pasture; green grassy area; (*Cono Sur*) lawn.

Praga NF Prague.

pragmática NF (*Hist*) decree, proclamation.

pragmático ADJ pragmatic.

pragmatismo NM pragmatism.

pragmatista NMF pragmatist.

prángana* ADJ INVAR (*Méx*) poor.

PRD NM **(a)** (*Méx*) ABR *de* **Partido de la Revolución Democrática. (b)** (*República Dominicana*) ABR *de* **Partido Revolucionario Dominicano.**

pre... PREF pre...

preacordar [1l] VT to reach a preliminary agreement on, make a draft agreement about.

preacuerdo NM preliminary agreement; outline (*o* draft) agreement.

preadolescente [1] ADJ pre-adolescent; (*pey*) pre-pubescent.
[2] NMF pre-adolescent.

prealarma NF alert; early warning.

prealerta NF standby; **en estado de ~** on standby.

preámbulo NM **(a)** (*de libro, discurso*) preamble, introduction. **(b)** (*pey*) evasive talk, annoying digression; **gastar ~s** to talk evasively, beat about the bush; **sin más ~s** without more ado.

preautonómico ADJ (*Esp: Pol*) before the creation of the autonomous regional governments.

preaviso NM forewarning, early warning.

prebélico ADJ prewar.

prebenda NF **(a)** (*Ecl*) prebend. **(b)** (*: *oficio*) sinecure, soft job*; (*gaje*) perk*; **~s corporativas** business perks*.

prebendado NM prebendary.
preboste NM (a) (*Hist*) provost. (b) (*Pol*) chief, leader.
precalentamiento NM warm-up, warming-up.
precalentar [1j] [1] VT to preheat; to warm up.
  [2] **precalentarse** VR (*Dep etc*) to warm up.
precampaña NF (*t ~ electoral*) run-up to the election campaign.
precanceroso ADJ precancerous, pre-cancer.
precandidato, -a NM/F candidate not yet formally nominated.
precariamente ADV precariously.
precariedad NF precariousness.
precario [1] ADJ (*gen*) precarious; (*dudoso*) doubtful, uncertain; (*poco firme*) shaky; (*impredecible*) unpredictable.
  [2] NM precarious state; **dejar a uno en ~** to leave sb in a difficult situation; **estamos en ~** we are in difficult circumstances; **vivir en ~** to live from hand to mouth, scrape a living.
precaución NF (a) (*acto*) precaution; (*medida*) preventive measure; **extremar las precauciones** to be extra careful; **tomar precauciones** to take precautions.
  (b) (*cualidad*) foresight; caution, wariness; **ir con ~** to go cautiously, proceed warily; **lo hicimos por ~** we did it to be on the safe side, we did it as a safety measure.
precautorio ADJ precautionary.
precaver [2a] [1] VT (*prevenir*) to guard against, try to prevent; (*anticipar*) to forestall; (*evitar*) to stave off.
  [2] **precaverse** VR to be on one's guard, take precautions, be forewarned; **~ contra** to guard against; **~ de** to be on one's guard against, beware of.
precavidamente ADV cautiously, warily.
precavido ADJ cautious, wary.
precedencia NF (*gen*) precedence; (*prioridad*) priority; (*preeminencia*) greater importance, superiority.
precedente [1] ADJ (*anterior*) preceding, foregoing; (*primero*) former; **cada uno mejor que el ~** each one better than the one before.
  [2] NM precedent; **de acuerdo con el ~** according to precedent; **contra todos los ~s** against all the precedents; **sin ~(s)** unprecedented; unparalleled; **establecer un ~, sentar un ~** to establish (o set up) a precedent.
precedentemente ADV earlier, at an earlier stage, previously.
preceder [2a] [1] VT: **~ a** (a) (*anteceder*) to precede, go before; **le precedía un coche** he was preceded by a car; **el título precede al nombre** the title goes before the first name.
  (b) (*fig*) to have priority over; to take precedence over.
  [2] VI to precede; **todo lo que precede** all the preceding (part), all that which comes before.
preceptista NMF theorist.
preceptiva NF teaching, doctrine.
preceptivo ADJ compulsory, obligatory, mandatory; **es ~ utilizar el formulario** the application form must be used.
precepto NM precept; order, rule; **de ~** compulsory, obligatory.
preceptor(a) NM/F teacher; (*private*) tutor.
preceptorado NM tutorship.
preceptoral ADJ tutorial.
preceptuar [1e] VT to lay down, establish; to state as an essential requirement.
preces NFPL prayers, supplications.
preciado ADJ (a) (*estimado*) esteemed, valuable. (b) (*presuntuoso*) presumptuous.
preciarse [1b] VR to boast; **~ de algo** to pride o.s. on sth, boast of being sth; **~ de inteligente** to think o.s. clever, pride o.s. on one's intelligence; **~ de** + *infin* to boast of + *ger*.
precintado [1] ADJ sealed; (*Com*) prepackaged; **calle etc** sealed-off.
  [2] NM sealing; (*Com*) prepackaging.
precintar [1a] VT (*Com etc*) to seal; (*fig*) to seal off.
precinto NM seal; (*de aduana*) customs seal.
precio NM (a) (*gen*) price; (*costo*) cost; (*valor*) value, worth; (*de viaje*) fare; (*en hotel etc*) rate, charge; **~ de compra** purchase price; **~ al contado** cash price; **~ de coste** cost-price; **a ~ de coste, a ~ costo** at cost-price; **'a ~ de fábrica'** 'cost-price', 'at cost'; **~ en fábrica** price ex-factory; **~ de intervención** intervention price; **~ irrisorio, ~ de oportunidad, ~ de situación** (*LAm*) bargain price; **~ de lista** list price; **~ de mercado** market price; market value; **~ neto** net price; **~ obsequio** giveaway price; **~ de ocasión** bargain price; **~ orientativo** manufacturer's recommended price; **~ de pensión** school fees; **~ de referencia** suggested price; **a ~ de saldo** at a knockdown price; **~ de salida** starting price; **a (o por) un ~ simbólico** for a nominal (o token) sum; **~ tope** top price, ceiling price; **~ último** closing price; **~ de venta** sale price; **~ del viaje** price (for the journey); **al ~ de** (*fig*) at the cost of; **lo hará a cualquier ~** he'll do it whatever the cost; **evítelo a cualquier ~** avoid it at all costs; **'no importa ~'** 'cost no object'; **poner (o señalar) ~ a la cabeza de uno** to put a price on sb's head; **no tener ~** (*fig*) to be priceless.
  (b) (*fig*) value, worth; **hombre de gran ~** a man of great worth.

preciosamente ADV beautifully; charmingly.
preciosidad NF (a) (*excelencia*) preciousness; (*valor*) value, worth.
  (b) (*pey*) preciosity.
  (c) (*objeto*) beautiful thing; precious object; (*chica*) lovely girl; **es una ~** it's lovely, it's really beautiful; **¡oye, ~!** hey, beautiful!
preciosismo NM (*Liter etc*) preciosity.
preciosista (*Liter etc*) [1] ADJ precious, affected.
  [2] NMF precious writer, affected writer (*etc*).
precioso ADJ (a) (*excelente*) precious; (*valioso*) valuable.
  (b) (*exquisito*) pretty, lovely, beautiful; (*encantador*) charming; **una edición preciosa** a beautiful edition; **tienen un niño ~** they have a lovely child; **¿verdad que es ~?** isn't it lovely?
preciosura NF (*LAm*) = **preciosidad (c)**.
precipicio NM (a) (*gen*) cliff, precipice.
  (b) (*fig: abismo*) chasm, abyss; **tiene el ~ abierto a sus pies** the chasm yawns before him, he stands on the brink of disaster.
  (c) (*fig: ruina*) ruin.
precipitación NF (a) (*prisa*) haste; (*imprudencia*) rashness; **con ~** hastily; rashly, precipitately. (b) (*Met*) precipitation, rainfall. (c) (*Quím*) precipitation.
precipitadamente ADV headlong; hastily, suddenly; rashly, precipitately.
precipitado [1] ADJ *huida etc* headlong; *partida etc* hasty, sudden; *acto, conducta* hasty, rash, precipitate.
  [2] NM (*Quím*) precipitate.
precipitador NM precipitant.
precipitar [1a] [1] VT (a) (*arrojar*) to hurl down, cast down, throw (*desde* from).
  (b) (*apresurar*) to hasten; (*acelerar*) to speed up, accelerate; (*motivar*) to precipitate; **aquello precipitó su salida** that affair hastened his departure; **la dimisión precipitó la crisis** the resignation precipitated (o brought on, sparked off) the crisis.
  (c) (*Quím*) to precipitate.
  [2] **precipitarse** VR (a) (*arrojarse*) to throw o.s., hurl o.s. (*desde* from); (*lanzarse*) to launch o.s.
  (b) (*correr*) to rush, dash; to dart; **~ a hacer algo** to rush to do sth, hasten to do sth; **~ sobre** (*ave etc*) to swoop on, pounce on; **~ sobre uno** to rush at sb, hurl o.s. on sb; **~ hacia un sitio** to rush towards a place.
  (c) (*obrar impetuosamente*) to act rashly; **se ha precipitado rehusándolo** he acted rashly in rejecting it, it was rash of him to refuse it.
precipitoso ADJ (a) *lugar* precipitous, steep, sheer. (b) *acto etc* = **precipitado 1**.
precisa NF (a) (*CAm: urgencia*) urgency. (b) **tener la ~** (*Cono Sur**) to be on the ball.
precisado ADJ: **verse ~ a** + *infin* to be obliged (o forced) to + *infin*.
precisamente ADV (a) (*con precisión*) precisely, in a precise way.
  (b) (*justamente*) precisely, exactly, just; **¡~!** exactly!, precisely!; just so!; **~ por eso** for that very reason, precisely because of that; **~ fue él quien lo dijo** it so happens it was he who said it, as a matter of fact it was he who said it; **~ estábamos hablando de eso** we were just talking about that; **llegó ~ cuando nos íbamos** he arrived just as we were leaving; **yo no soy un experto ~** I'm not exactly an expert; **no es eso ~** it's not quite that, it's not really that.
precisar [1a] [1] VT (a) (*necesitar*) to need, require; **no precisa lavado** it needs no washing; **'vendedores precisa agencia internacional'** (*anuncio*) 'salesmen wanted by international agency'; **precisa que vengas** you must come; **no precisamos que el candidato tenga experiencia** we do not insist (o demand) that the candidate should be experienced.
  (b) (*determinar*) to determine exactly, fix; (*señalar*) to pinpoint, put one's finger on; *detalles etc* to specify, state precisely; **hay alguna rareza que no puedo ~** there is some oddity which I cannot pin down (o put my finger on).
  [2] VI (*ser necesario*) to be necessary; (*ser urgente*) to be urgent; **~ de algo** to need sth; **precisamos de más tiempo** we need more time.
precisión NF (a) (*exactitud*) precision; preciseness, accuracy, exactness; **instrumento de ~** precision instrument.
  (b) **hacer precisiones** to define matters more closely, make matters more precise, clarify matters.
  (c) (*necesidad*) need, necessity; **tener ~ de algo** to need sth, have need of sth; **verse en la ~ de** + *infin* to be obliged to + *infin*.
  (d) (*Méx*) urgency.
▼ **preciso** ADJ (a) (*exacto*) precise; exact, accurate; **una descripción precisa** a precise description.
  (b) **en aquel ~ momento** at that precise moment, at that very moment, just at that moment.
  (c) (*necesario*) necessary, essential; **las cualidades precisas** the essential qualities, the requisite qualities; **tener el tiempo ~ para** + *infin* to have (just) enough time to + *infin*; **cuando sea ~** when it becomes necessary; **es ~ que lo hagas** it is essential that you should

do it, you must do it; **es ~ tener coche** it is essential to have a car; **ser un Don P~** (*Cono Sur*) to believe o.s. to be indispensable. (**d**) (*Carib*) conceited.

precitado ADJ above-mentioned.

preclaro ADJ (*liter*) illustrious.

precocidad NF precociousness, precocity; (*Bot etc*) earliness.

precocinado ADJ precooked.

precocinar [1a] VT to precook.

precognición NF foreknowledge; precognition.

precolombino ADJ pre-Columbian; **la América precolombina** America before Columbus.

preconcebido ADJ preconceived; **idea preconcebida** preconception.

preconcepción NF preconception.

preconciliar ADJ preconciliar, before Vatican II.

precondición NF precondition.

preconizable ADJ foreseeable.

preconización NF (**a**) (*recomendación*) recommendation; favouring. (**b**) (*de algo futuro*) visualizing.

preconizar [1f] VT (**a**) (*elogiar*) to praise. (**b**) (*recomendar*) to recommend, advise. (**c**) (*proponer*) to suggest, propose; to advocate.

precontrato NM pre-contract.

precordillera NF (*LAm*) Andean foothills.

precoz ADJ precocious; forward; *calvicie etc* premature; (*Bot, Med etc*) early.

precozmente ADV precociously; prematurely; early.

precursor(a) NM/F predecessor, forerunner.

predación NF (*Bio*) predation; (*fig*) depredation, plundering.

predador NM, **predator** NM predator.

predecesor(a) NM/F predecessor.

predecir [3o] VT to predict, foretell, forecast.

predemocrático ADJ prior to the establishment of democracy (*esp* in Spain).

predestinación NF predestination.

predestinado ADJ predestined; **ser ~ a** + *infin* to be predestined to + *infin*.

predestinar [1a] VT to predestine.

predeterminación NF predetermination.

predeterminado ADJ predetermined.

predeterminar [1a] VT to predetermine.

prédica NF sermon; harangue; **~s** preaching (*t fig*).

predicación NF (**a**) (*gen*) preaching. (**b**) (*una ~*) = **prédica.**

predicado NM predicate.

predicador(a) NM/F preacher.

predicamento NM (**a**) (*dignidad*) standing, prestige; **no goza ahora de tanto ~** it has less prestige now, it is not so well thought of now. (**b**) (*LAm*) predicament.

predicar [1g] VTI to preach.

predicativo ADJ predicative.

predicción NF prediction; forecast; **~ del tiempo** weather forecast(ing).

predicho ADJ aforementioned.

predigerido ADJ predigested.

predilección NF predilection; **tener ~ por** to have a predilection for; **predilecciones y aversiones** likes and dislikes.

predilecto ADJ favourite.

predio NM property, estate; (*LAm*) premises; site; **~ rústico** country estate; **~ urbano** town property.

predisponente ADJ: **factor ~ de** factor which causes a tendency towards.

predisponer [2q] VT to predispose; (*pey*) to prejudice, bias (*contra* against).

predisposición NF predisposition, inclination; (*pey*) prejudice, bias (*contra* against); (*Med*) tendency, predisposition (*a* to).

predispuesto ADJ predisposed; **ser ~ a los catarros** to have a tendency to get colds; **ser ~ al abatimiento** to be inclined to depression; **estar ~ contra uno** to be prejudiced against sb.

predocumento NM draft, preliminary paper.

predominante ADJ predominant; major; prevailing; (*Com*) *interés* controlling.

predominantemente ADV predominantly.

predominar [1a] ① VT (*preponderar*) to dominate, predominate over. ② VI (**a**) (*dominar*) to predominate; (*prevalecer*) to prevail. (**b**) **esta casa predomina a aquélla** this house is higher than that one.

predominio NM (*dominio*) predominance; (*preponderancia*) prevalence; (*influencia*) sway, ascendancy, influence; (*superioridad*) superiority.

preelectoral ADJ: **sondeo ~** pre-election survey, survey taken before the election.

preeminencia NF pre-eminence, superiority.

preeminente ADJ pre-eminent; superior.

preeminentemente ADV pre-eminently.

preempción NF pre-emption.

preenfriar [1c] VT to precool.

pre(e)scoger [2c] VT *jugadores* to seed.

preescolar ① ADJ preschool; **educación ~** preschool education, nursery education. ② NM (*escuela*) nursery-school. ③ NMF child of nursery-school age.

preestablecido ADJ already-established.

preestrenar [1a] VT to preview, give a preview of.

preestreno NM preview, press view, private showing.

preexistencia NF pre-existence.

preexistente ADJ pre-existent, pre-existing.

preexistir [3a] VI to pre-exist, exist before.

prefabricado ① ADJ prefabricated. ② NM prefabricated building.

prefabricar [1g] VT to prefabricate.

prefacio NM preface, foreword.

prefecto NM prefect.

prefectura NF prefecture.

▼ **preferencia** NF preference; **de ~** for preference, preferably; **localidad de ~** seat in a reserved section; **tratamiento de ~** preferential treatment; **mostrar ~ por** to show preference to, be biassed in favour of.

preferencial ADJ preferential

preferente ADJ (**a**) (*preferido*) preferred; (*preferible*) preferable. (**b**) (*Fin*) *acción* preference (*atr*); *impuesto, trato etc* preferential; priority (*atr*); *derecho* prior. (**c**) **clase ~** (*Aer*) club class.

preferentemente ADV preferably.

preferible ADJ preferable (*a* to).

preferiblemente ADV preferably.

▼ **preferido** ADJ favourite; **es mi cantante ~** he's my favourite singer.

▼ **preferir** [3i] VT to prefer; **~ té a café** to prefer tea to coffee; **¿cuál prefieres?** which do you prefer?; (*en bar etc*) **¿qué prefieres?** what will you have?; **prefiero ir a pie** I prefer to walk, I'd rather go on foot.

┌─── PREFERIR ─────────────── ver también la entrada ─┐

Más verbo

• Cuando se habla de generalizaciones, *preferir* + INFINITIVO se traduce por *prefer* + -ING:

Prefiero nadar a correr

I prefer swimming to running

Juan siempre prefería leer a trabajar

Juan always preferred reading to working

• Cuando se habla de lo que se quiere hacer en una ocasión determinada, *prefiero/preferiría* se traducen por *would rather* + INFINITIVO *sin to* o en un contexto más formal, por *would prefer* + INFINITIVO *con to*:

"¿Vamos al cine?" - "Preferiría quedarme en casa"

"Shall we go to the cinema?" - "I'd rather stay o I'd prefer to stay at home"

Prefiero quedarme en un hotel a alquilar un apartamento.

I'd rather stay in a hotel than rent an apartment ◊ I'd prefer to stay in a hotel rather than rent an apartment

NOTA: Como se puede ver en el ejemplo anterior, *would prefer to* se usa en correlación con *rather than* + INFINITIVO *sin to* y nunca con *than* solo.

• Cuando se trata de traducir estructuras como *preferiría que* + ORACIÓN SUBORDINADA, en inglés se emplea la siguiente estructura: SUJETO DE LA ORACIÓN PRINCIPAL + *would rather* + SUJETO + VERBO EN PASADO:

Preferiría que él me llamara

I'd rather he phoned me

"¿Te importa que hable con ella?" - "Preferiría que no lo hicieras"

"Do you mind if I talk to her?" - "I'd rather you didn't"

NOTA: Otra posibilidad de expresar esta construcción en inglés sería: *would prefer it if* + RESTO DE LA ORACIÓN o *would prefer* + OBJETO + CONSTRUCCIÓN DE INFINITIVO:

Preferiría que él me llamara

I'd prefer it if he phoned me o *I'd prefer him to phone me*

Para otros usos y ejemplos ver la entrada.

└───┘

prefiguración NF foreshadowing, prefiguration.

prefigurar [1a] VT to foreshadow, prefigure.

prefijar [1a] VT (**a**) (*determinar*) to fix beforehand, arrange in advance, prearrange. (**b**) (*Ling*) to prefix (*a* to).

▼ **prefijo** NM prefix; (*Telec*) **~ local** area code; **~ telefónico** dialling code.

pregón NM proclamation, announcement (*by town crier*); (*Com*) street cry, vendor's cry; **~ literario de un acto** speech (*etc*) about a forthcoming public ceremony.

pregonar [1a] VT (*proclamar*) to proclaim, announce; *secreto* to disclose, reveal; *mercancía* to cry, hawk, advertise verbally; *méritos etc* to

praise publicly, proclaim (for all to hear).
pregonero NM (a) (*municipal*) town crier. (b) (*Méx: subastador*) auctioneer.
pregrabado ADJ prerecorded.
pregrabar [1a] VT to pre-record.
preguerra NF prewar period; **el nivel de la ~** the prewar level; **en la ~** in the prewar period, before the war.
pregunta NF question; **~ capciosa**, **~ indiscreta** catch question, loaded question; **~ retórica** rhetorical question; **~ sugestiva** (*Jur*) leading question; **andar** (o **estar**) **a la cuarta ~*** (*Esp**) to be broke*; **contestar a una ~** to answer a question; **hacer una ~** to ask (o put) a question; **estrechar a uno a ~s** to press sb closely with questions; **a ~s necias oídos sordos** ask a silly question (get a silly answer).
preguntar [1a] ☐1 VT to ask; to question, interrogate; **~ algo a uno** to ask sb sth; **~ si** to ask if, ask whether; **le fue preguntada su edad** he was asked his age; *V* **caber**.
☐2 VI to ask, inquire; **~ por uno** to ask for sb, inquire for sb; **~ por la salud de uno** to ask after sb's health, ask about sb's health.
☐3 **preguntarse** VR to wonder; **me pregunto si vale la pena** I wonder if it's worth while.
preguntón ADJ inquisitive.
prehispánico ADJ pre-Hispanic.
prehistoria NF prehistory.
prehistórico ADJ prehistoric.
preignición NF preignition.
preimpositivo ADJ: **beneficios ~s** pre-tax profits, profits before tax.
preinforme NM preliminary report.
preinscripción NF (*para congreso, cursillo*) provisional booking; (*Univ*) pre-enrolment, pre-enrollment (*US*).
preinstalación NF (*Aut*) factory-fitting; **~ de radio** radio (fitted) as standard.
preinstalado ADJ *software* preinstalled.
prejubilación NF early retirement.
prejubilado, -a NM/F person who takes early retirement.
prejuiciado ADJ (*LAm*) prejudiced (*contra* against).
prejuicio NM (a) (*acto*) prejudgement. (b) (*parcialidad*) prejudice, bias (*contra* against); (*idea preconcebida*) preconception.
prejuzgar [1h] VT to prejudge.
prelación NF preference, priority.
prelado NM prelate.
prelatura NF prelature; **~ personal** personal prelature.
prelavado NM prewash.
preliminar ADJ, NM preliminary.
preludiar [1b] ☐1 VT (*anunciar*) to announce, herald; (*introducir*) to introduce; (*iniciar*) to start off.
☐2 VI (*Mús*) to tune up, play a few scales.
preludio NM (a) (*Mús, fig*) prelude (*de* to). (b) (*Mús: ensayo*) tuning up, practice notes, scales.
premamá ATR: **vestido ~** maternity dress.
premarital ADJ premarital.
prematrimonial ADJ premarital; before marriage; *V* **relación** (c).
prematuramente ADV prematurely.
prematuro ADJ premature.
premedicación NF premedication.
premeditación NF premeditation; **con ~** with premeditation, deliberately.
premeditadamente ADV with premeditation, deliberately.
premeditado ADJ premeditated, deliberate; wilful; *insult etc* studied.
premeditar [1a] VT to premeditate; to plan, think out (in advance).
premenstrual ADJ premenstrual.
premiado ☐1 ADJ *novela etc* prize (*atr*), prize-winning.
☐2 NM, **premiada** NF prizewinner.
premiar [1b] VT (*recompensar*) to reward (*con* with); (*dar un premio a*) to give a prize to, make an award to; **salir premiado** to win a prize.
premier [pre'mjer] NMF prime minister, premier.
premio NM (a) (*recompensa*) reward, recompense; **como ~ a sus servicios** as a reward for his services.
(b) (*en concurso*) prize; award; (*persona*) prize-winner; **~ de consolación** consolation prize; **~ extraordinario** award (*of a degree etc*) with special distinction; **~ gordo** first prize, big prize; **Gran P~** Grand Prix; **~ en metálico** cash prize.
(c) (*Com, Fin*) premium; **a ~** at a premium.
premioso ADJ (a) *vestido etc* tight.
(b) *orden etc* strict.
(c) *persona* (*al hablar*) tongue-tied, slow of speech; (*al escribir*) slow in writing; (*al moverse*) slow in movement, heavy, awkward.
(d) (*fig*) *estilo* difficult.
premisa NF premise.
premonición NF premonition.
premonitoriamente ADV in a warning way, as a warning.
premonitorio ADJ indicative, warning, premonitory.
premunirse [3a] VR (*LAm*) = **precaverse**.

premura NF (a) (*presión*) pressure; **con ~ de tiempo** under (time) pressure, with very little time; **debido a ~ de espacio** because of pressure on space.
(b) (*prisa*) haste, urgency.
prenatal ADJ antenatal, prenatal.
prenavideño ADJ pre-Christmas, before Christmas.
prenda NF (a) (*garantía*) pledge; (*fig*) pledge, token; **dejar algo en ~** to pawn sth; to leave sth as security; **en ~ de** as a pledge of, as a token of; **al buen pagador no le duelen ~s** a good payer is not afraid of giving guarantees; **a mí no me duelen ~s** I don't mind saying nice things about others, it doesn't worry me that I'm not as good as others; **no soltar ~** to give nothing away, avoid committing o.s.; to give sb no chance (o opening).
(b) (*t* **~ de vestir**) garment, article of clothing; **~s deportivas** sports clothes, sportswear; **~ interior** undergarment, piece of underclothing; **~s de cama** bedclothes; **~s de mesa** table linen.
(c) **~s** (*fig: cualidades*) talents, gifts; (*t* **buenas ~s**) good qualities; **de todas ~s** first class, excellent.
(d) **~s** (*juego*) forfeits; **pagar ~** to pay a forfeit.
(e) (*joya: esp LAm*) jewel; **~s** jewellery.
(f) (***: en oración directa*) darling!, my treasure!; (*piropo: Esp**) **¡oye, ~!** hi, gorgeous!*
(g) **la ~** (*Cono Sur*) one's sweetheart, one's lover.
prendar [1a] ☐1 VT (a) (*encantar*) to captivate, enchant; (*ganar la voluntad*) to win over; **volvió prendado con** (o **de**) **la ciudad** he came back enchanted with the town.
(b) (*Méx: empeñar*) to pawn.
☐2 **prendarse** VR: **~ de** (*aficionarse*) to be captivated by, be enchanted with; to take a fancy to; **~ de uno** (*liter*) to fall in love with sb.
prendedera NF (*And*) waitress.
prendedero NM, **prendedor** NM clasp, brooch.
prender [2a] ☐1 VT (a) *persona* to catch, capture; (*detener*) to arrest.
(b) (*Cos etc*) (*sujetar*) to fasten; (*con alfiler*) to pin, attach (*en* to); (*atar*) to tie, do up; **~ el pelo con horquillas** to fix one's hair with hairpins, put clips in one's hair.
(c) (*esp LAm*) *fuego, horno etc* to light; *fósforo* to strike; *luz, TV etc* to switch on; *cigarrillo, vela* to light; *cuarto* to light up.
☐2 VI (a) (*engancharse*) to catch, stick; to grip; **el ancla prendió en el fondo** the anchor buried itself in the seabed, the anchor gripped firmly.
(b) (*fuego*) to catch; (*inyección*) to take; (*planta*) to take, take root; **el mal prendió más en la juventud** the evil spread most among young people, the evil infected youth most strongly.
☐3 **prenderse** VR (a) (*encenderse*) to catch fire (*en* on).
(b) (*mujer*) to dress up.
(c) (*Carib*) to get drunk.
prendería NF (*Esp: de cosas usadas*) secondhand (clothes) shop; (*de baratijas*) junkshop; (*de empeños*) pawnbroker's (shop).
prendero, -a NM/F secondhand (clothes) dealer, junk dealer; (*prestamista*) pawnbroker.
prendido ☐1 ADJ (a) **quedar ~** to be caught (fast), be stuck; (*fig*) to be captivated. (b) (*Cono Sur Med*) constipated. (c) (*Méx*) dressed up.
☐2 NM (*adorno*) clip, brooch.
prendimiento NM (a) (*captura*) capture, seizure; arrest. (b) (*Cono Sur Med*) constipation.
prensa NF (a) (*Mec*) press; (*Tip*) press, printing press; (*de raqueta*) press, frame; **~ de copiar** (*Fot*) printing frame; **~ hidráulica** hydraulic press; **~ rotativa** rotary press.
(b) (*fig*) **la P~** the press; **~ amarilla** gutter press; **~ del corazón**, **~ del hígado** (*hum*) periodicals specializing in real-life romance stories; women's magazines; **aprobar un libro para la ~** to pass a book for (the) press; **dar algo a la ~** to publish sth; **entrar en ~** to go to press; **estar en ~** to be in press; **tener mala ~** to have (o get) a bad press; **'libros en ~'** (*anuncio*) 'books in press', 'forthcoming publications'.

ⓘ ┌─ **PRENSA DEL CORAZÓN** ─────────────────────┐

*The **prensa del corazón** is the generic term given in Spain to weekly or fortnightly magazines specializing in society gossip and the social lives of the rich and famous. The pioneer was **Hola** which first appeared in 1944 (**Hello** magazine is the English-language version), while other popular titles include **Pronto, Lecturas, Semana** and **Diez Minutos**. They constitute a highly profitable sector of the market, occupying six of the top ten places in magazine sales.*

---

prensado NM (a) (*acto*) pressing. (b) (*lustre*) sheen, shine, gloss.
prensador NM press, pressing machine; **~ de paja** straw baler.
prensaestopas NM INVAR packing gland.
prensaje NM (*Mús*) recording.
prensalimones NM INVAR lemon-squeezer.
prensar [1a] VT to press.
prensil ADJ prehensile.

preñada ADJ pregnant; (*Zool*) pregnant, with young; ~ **de 6 meses** 6 months pregnant.

preñado [1] ADJ (*fig*) (a) *muro* bulging, sagging.

(b) ~ **de** pregnant with, full of; **una situación preñada de peligros** a situation full of danger, a situation fraught with dangers; **ojos ~s de lágrimas** eyes filled with tears, eyes brimming with tears.

[2] NM (*embarazo*) pregnancy.

preñar [1a] VT to get pregnant; (*Zool*) to impregnate, fertilize; (*fig*) to fill.

preñez NF pregnancy.

preocupación NF (a) (*cuidado*) worry, anxiety, concern, preoccupation.

(b) (*prejuicio*) prejudice.

(c) (*ofuscación*) preconception; (*inquietud*) unfounded fear, silly fear; (*noción*) notion, silly idea; **tiene la ~ de que su mujer le es infiel** he has an obsession that his wife is unfaithful to him.

(d) (*LAm*) special consideration, priority, preference.

preocupado ADJ worried, anxious, concerned, preoccupied.

preocupante ADJ worrying, disturbing.

preocupar [1a] [1] VT (a) (*inquietar*) to worry, preoccupy; to bother, exercise; **esto me preocupa muchísimo** this worries me greatly; **me preocupa cómo decírselo** I'm worried about how to tell him; **no le preocupa el qué dirán** public opinion doesn't bother him.

(b) (*influir*) to prejudice, influence.

[2] **preocuparse** VR (a) (*inquietarse*) to worry, care (*de, por* about); (*ocuparse*) to concern o.s. (*de* about); **¡no se preocupe!** don't worry!, don't bother!; **no te preocupes por eso** don't worry about that; **no se preocupa en lo más mínimo** he doesn't care in the least.

(b) **yo me preocuparé de que esté listo** I'll see to it that everything is ready; **tú preocúpate de que todo esté listo** you ensure that (*o* see to it that) everything is ready.

(c) ~ **de algo** (*LAm*) to give special attention to sth, give sth priority.

preolímpico [1] ADJ: **torneo ~** Olympic qualifying tournament.

[2] NM (*concurso*) Olympic qualifying tournament (*o* round *etc*).

[3] NM, **preolímpica** NF Olympic qualifier; athlete (*etc*) taking part in an Olympic qualifying tournament.

preoperatorio [1] ADJ pre-operative, pre-op*.

[2] NM pre-operative period.

prepago NM prepayment.

preparación NF (a) (*acto*) preparation; ~ **de datos** data preparation; **estar en** ~ to be in preparation.

(b) (*estado*) preparedness, readiness; ~ **militar** military preparedness.

(c) (*formación*) training (*t Dep*); **le falta** ~ **matemática** he lacks mathematical training, he is not trained in maths.

(d) (*competencia*) competence; ability.

(e) (*Bio, Farm*) preparation.

(f) (*Cono Sur: bocadito*) appetizer.

preparado [1] ADJ (a) (*dispuesto*) prepared (*para* for); (*Culin*) ready to serve, ready cooked; **¡~s, listos, ya!** ready, steady, go! (b) (*competente*) competent, able; (*con título*) qualified; (*informado*) well-informed.

[2] NM (*Farm*) preparation.

preparador(a) NM/F (a) (*Dep*) trainer, coach; (*de caballo*) trainer; ~ **físico** fitness trainer. (b) (*de laboratorio etc*) assistant.

preparar [1a] [1] VT (a) (*disponer*) to prepare, get ready; (*Téc*) to prepare, process, treat.

(b) (*enseñar*) to teach, train; (*Dep*) to train, coach; **X le prepara a Y de física** X is coaching Y in physics.

[2] **prepararse** VR (a) (*disponerse*) to prepare, prepare o.s., get ready; ~ **a** + *infin*, ~ **para** + *infin* to prepare to + *infin*, get ready to + *infin*.

(b) (*problema, tormenta etc*) to be brewing.

preparativo [1] ADJ preparatory, preliminary.

[2] **~s** NMPL (*aprestos*) preparations; (*disposiciones*) preliminaries; **hacer sus ~s** to make one's preparations (*para* + *infin* to + *infin*).

preparatorio [1] ADJ preparatory.

[2] **preparatoria** NF (*CAm, Méx Educ*) secondary school, high school (*US*).

pre-Pirineo NM Pyrenean foothills.

preponderancia NF preponderance; superiority.

preponderante ADJ preponderant; superior.

preponderar [1a] VI to preponderate; to dominate, prevail.

preponente ADJ (*And: jactancioso*) boastful, conceited.

preponer [2q] VT to place before.

preposición NF preposition.

preposicional ADJ prepositional.

prepósito NM (*Ecl*) prefect, superior.

prepotencia NF power, dominance, superiority; (*pey*) arrogance; abuse of power.

prepotente ADJ powerful, supreme; (*pey*) arrogant, overbearing, domineering; given to abusing power.

preproducción NF pre-production.

prepucio NM foreskin, prepuce.

prerrequisito NM prerequisite.

prerrogativa NF prerogative, right, privilege.

prerrománico ADJ pre-romanesque.

presa¹ NF (a) (*acto*) capture, seizure; **hacer ~** to seize.

(b) (*asimiento*) clutch, hold; ~ **de pie** foothold; **hacer ~ en** to clutch (on to), seize; to get a hold on; **el fuego hizo ~ en la cortina** the fire set light to (*o* caught, began to burn) the curtain.

(c) (*objeto*) capture, catch, prize; (*Mil*) spoils, booty; loot; (*Náut*) prize; (*Orn*) prey; (*Zool*) prey, catch; **ave de ~** bird of prey; **ser ~ de** (*fig*) to be a prey to, be a victim of.

(d) (*Orn*) claw; (*Zool*) tusk, fang.

(e) (*de río etc*) dam; (*represa*) weir, barrage.

(f) (*Agr*) ditch, channel.

(g) (*esp LAm*) (*de comida*) piece of food; (*de carne*) piece of meat.

presagiador ADJ ominous.

presagiar [1b] VT to betoken, forebode, presage.

presagio NM omen, portent.

presbicia NF (*Med*) long-sightedness.

presbiopía NF presbyopia.

présbita ADJ, **présbite** ADJ (*Med*) long-sighted.

presbítera NF (woman) priest; (woman) minister.

presbiteriano, -a ADJ, NM/F Presbyterian.

presbiterio NM presbytery, chancel.

presbítero NM priest.

presciencia NF prescience, foreknowledge.

presciente ADJ prescient.

prescindencia NF (*LAm*) doing without, going without; (*abstención*) non-participation, abstention.

prescindente ADJ (*LAm*) non-participating.

prescindible ADJ dispensable; **y cosas fácilmente ~s** and things we can easily do without.

prescindir [3a] VI: ~ **de** (*pasarse sin*) to do without, go without; (*deshacerse de*) to dispense with, get rid of; (*desatender*) to disregard; (*omitir*) to omit, (*pasar por alto*) overlook; **han prescindido del coche** they've given up their car, they've got rid of their car; **no podemos ~ de él** we can't manage without him; **prescindamos de todo aquello** let's forget about all that, let's leave all that aside.

prescribir [3a; PTP **prescrito**] [1] VT to prescribe.

[2] VI (*plazo*) to expire, run out.

prescripción NF (a) (*Med*) prescription; ~ **facultativa**, ~ **médica** medical prescription; **por ~ facultativa** on the doctor's orders. (b) (*Méx Jur*) legal principle.

prescriptivo ADJ prescriptive.

prescrito ADJ prescribed.

presea NF (a) (*liter*) jewel; treasure, precious thing. (b) (*LAm*) prize.

preselección NF (a) (*Dep*) seeding; (*de candidatos*) short-list(ing). (b) (*Dep: personas*) squad.

preseleccionado, -a NM/F short-listed candidate; (*Dep*) squad member, member of the squad.

preseleccionar [1a] VT (*Dep*) to seed; *candidatos* to short-list.

presencia NF presence; ~ **de ánimo**, ~ **de mente** presence of mind; **en ~ de** in the presence of; **tener (buena) ~** to have a good presence, be impressive, have an impressive bearing.

presencial ADJ: **testigo ~** eyewitness.

presenciar [1b] VT (*asistir a*) to be present at; to attend; (*ver*) to see, witness, watch.

presentable ADJ presentable.

presentación NF (a) (*gen*) presentation; (*de personas*) introduction; ~ **en directo**, ~ **en vivo** personal appearance; ~ **de modelos** fashion parade, fashion show; ~ **en (la) sociedad** coming-out, début. (b) (*LAm*) petition.

presentador(a) NM/F (*TV etc*) presenter; host, hostess.

presentar [1a] [1] VT (a) (*gen*) to present; to offer; to show, display; *armas, excusas, petición, prueba etc* to present; *dimisión* to tender; *moción* to propose, put forward; **presenta señales de deterioro** it shows signs of wear; **el coche presenta ciertas modificaciones** the car has certain modifications.

(b) (*Teat*) *obra* to perform, put on; *película* to show; *estrella* to present, feature; *espectáculo* (*TV etc*) to present, host, compère.

(c) *persona* to introduce; **le presento a Vd a mi hermana** may I introduce my sister to you?; **ser presentada en (la) sociedad** to come out, make one's début.

(d) **le presento mis consideraciones ...** (*en carta*) yours faithfully ...

(e) (*Com*) ~ **al cobro**, ~ **al pago** to present for payment.

[2] **presentarse** VR (a) (*comparecer*) to present o.s.; (*aparecer*) to appear (unexpectedly), turn up; ~ **a la policía** to report to the police, (*criminal*) give o.s. up to the police; **hay que ~ el lunes a las 9** you should report at 9 on Monday; **se presentó en un estado lamentable** he turned up in a dreadful state.

(b) (*hacerse conocer*) to introduce o.s. (*a* to); ~ **en (la) sociedad** to come out, make one's début.

(c) (*candidato*) to run, stand; **~ a** *puesto* to put in for, apply for; **~ a** (*o* **para**) *examen* to sit (for), enter for.

(d) (*ofrecerse*) to present itself; (*mostrarse*) to show, appear; **el día se presenta muy hermoso** it looks like being a lovely day, there are prospects of a fine day; **se presentó un caso singular** a strange case came up.

presente [1] ADJ **(a)** *persona* present; **¡~!** present!, here!; **los ~s** those present; **los señores aquí ~s** the gentlemen here present; **estar ~ en** to be present at; **mejorando lo ~, salvando a los ~s** present company excepted.

(b) la ~ carta, la ~ this letter; **le comunico por la ~** I hereby inform you.

(c) *tiempo* present; **hacer ~** to state, declare; **tener ~** to remember, bear in mind; **tennos ~** don't forget us; **ten muy ~ que ...** be sure to remember that ...; understand clearly that ...

(d) '**~**' (*LAm: en sobre*) 'by hand'.

[2] NM **(a)** present; **al ~** at present; **hasta el ~** up to the present.

(b) (*Ling*) present (tense).

(c) (*regalo*) present, gift.

presentimiento NM premonition, presentiment; foreboding.

▼ **presentir** [3i] VT to have a premonition of; **~ que ...** to have a premonition that ...

preservación NF protection, preservation.

preservante NM preservative.

preservar [1a] VT **(a)** (*proteger*) to protect, preserve (*contra* against, *de* from). **(b)** (*LAm*) to keep, preserve.

preservativo NM condom, sheath.

presi* NMF = **presidente**.

presidencia NF presidency; chairmanship; **P~** (*esp: oficina*) Prime Minister's office; **ocupar la ~** to preside, be in (*o* take) the chair.

presidenciable [1] ADJ: **ministro ~** minister who has the makings of a prime minister.

[2] NMF possible candidate (*o* contender) for the prime ministership (*o* presidency).

presidencial ADJ presidential.

presidencialismo NM autocratic leadership; abuse of presidential power.

presidente NMF (*t* **presidenta** NF) (*de asociación, país, Taur*) president; (*de comité, reunión*) chairman *m*, chairwoman *f*, chairperson *mf*; (*Pol Esp: t* **P~ del Gobierno**) prime minister; (*Pol: de la cámara*) speaker; (*Jur*) presiding judge, presiding magistrate; (*LAm*) mayor; **~ de honor** honorary president; **~ vitalicio** president for life; **candidato a ~** presidential candidate.

┌─────────────────────────┐
│ **PRESIDENTE DEL GOBIERNO** │
└─────────────────────────┘

ⓘ *The head of the Spanish government, or* **Presidente del Gobierno***, is elected not just by the winning party but by the entire* **Congreso de los Diputados** *following a general election. The* **Presidente** *is appointed for a four-year term and called upon by the King to form a cabinet. As in Britain, he has the power to call an early election, and can be forced to do so by a censure motion in the* **Congreso***.*

presidiario NM convict.

presidio NM **(a)** (*cárcel*) prison, penitentiary; **echar a uno a ~** to put sb in prison.

(b) (*trabajos forzados*) hard labour, penal servitude.

(c) (*Pol*) praesidium.

(d) (*Mil*) garrison; fortress.

presidir [3a] [1] VT **(a)** (*gobernar*) to preside at, preside over; (*dirigir*) to take the chair at.

(b) (*fig: dominar*) to dominate, rule, be the dominant element in.

[2] VI (*presidir*) to preside; (*dirigir*) to take the chair.

presilla NF **(a)** (*para cerrar*) fastener, clip. **(b)** (*lazo*) loop. **(c)** (*LAm*) shoulder badge, flash; (*Méx*) epaulette.

presintonía NF presetting, preprogram(m)ing.

presión NF **(a)** (*gen*) pressure; (*con mano etc*) press, squeeze; (*Fís, Met, Téc*) pressure; (*de explosión*) blast; **~ arterial, ~ sanguínea** blood pressure; **~ atmosférica** atmospheric pressure, air pressure; **a ~** under pressure; **de ~** (*Téc*) pressure (*atr*); **hacer ~** to press (*sobre* on).

(b) (*fig*) pressure; **~ fiscal, ~ impositiva** tax burden; **ejercer** (*o* **hacer**) **~ para que se haga algo** to press for sth to be done; **hay presiones dentro del partido** there are pressures within the party.

presionar [1a] [1] VT **(a)** (*pulsar*) to press.

(b) (*fig*) to press, put pressure on; **el ministro, presionado por los fabricantes, accedió** the minister, under pressure from the manufacturers, agreed.

[2] VI to press; **~ para, ~ por** to press for; **~ para que sea permitido algo** to press for sth to be allowed.

preso [1] PTP *de* **prender**; **llevar ~ a uno** to take sb away under arrest; **estar ~ de un terror pánico** to be panic-stricken; **~ por mil, ~ por mil quinientos** (*Esp*) in for a penny, in for a pound.

[2] NM, **presa²** NF convict, prisoner; **~ común** non-political prisoner;

~ de conciencia prisoner of conscience, political prisoner; **~ de confianza** trusty; **~ político** political prisoner; **~ preventivo** remand prisoner.

pressing ['presin] NM (*Dep*) pressure; = **presión** (b).

prestación NF **(a)** (*aportación*) lending, loan; (*subsidio*) benefit, payment; (*Méx*) fringe benefit, perk*; **~ de ayuda** giving of help; **~ de** (*o* **por**) **desempleo** unemployment benefit; **prestaciones económicas, prestaciones sociales** social security benefits; **~ por jubilación** retirement benefit; **~ personal** obligatory service (*of individual on communal work*); **~ social sustituoria** non-military alternative to national service.

(b) **~ de juramento** oath-taking, (ceremony of) swearing in.

(c) (*Aut, Mec*) feature, detail; **prestaciones** performance qualities.

(d) (*Inform*) capability.

┌─────────────────────────────────────┐
│ **PRESTACIÓN SOCIAL SUSTITUTORIA** │
└─────────────────────────────────────┘

ⓘ *The* **Prestación Social Sustitutoria** *(PSS) is the non-military alternative to* **la mili** *for Spanish conscientious objectors. It currently lasts 13 months, ie longer than normal military service, and involves a variety of largely unpaid community service ranging from social work to civil defence, to working on behalf of the local authority, the Red Cross or the Spanish equivalent of the Forestry Commission.*

⇨ *See also* MILI *,* INSUMISO

prestado ADJ: **dar algo ~** to lend sth; **eso está ~** that is on loan; **pedir ~ algo, tomar ~ algo** to borrow sth; **vivir de ~** to live at somebody else's expense, live on what one can borrow.

prestador(a) NM/F lender.

prestamista NMF moneylender; pawnbroker.

préstamo NM **(a)** (*acto*) loan, lending, borrowing. **(b)** (*empréstito*) loan; **~ bancario** bank loan; **~ cobrable a la vista** call loan; **~ colateral, ~ pignoraticio** collateral loan; **~ con garantía** secured loan; **~ hipotecario** mortgage (loan). **(c)** (*Ling*) loanword.

prestancia NF (*distinción*) distinction, excellence; (*elegancia*) elegance, dignity.

prestar [1a] [1] VT **(a)** *dinero etc* to lend, loan.

(b) (*fig*) to lend, give; *apoyo, ayuda* to give; *atención* to pay (*a* to); *servicio* to do, render; *encanto etc* to lend.

(c) *juramento* to take, swear.

(d) (*LAm: pedir prestado*) to borrow (*a* from).

(e) (*Carib, Cono Sur*) to do good to, be good for; to suit; **no le prestó el viaje** the trip was not good for him.

[2] VI **(a)** (*extenderse*) to give, stretch.

(b) **~ para** to be big enough for.

[3] **prestarse** VR **(a) no se presta a esas maniobras** he does not lend himself to manoeuvres of that kind; **la situación se presta a muchas interpretaciones** the situation lends itself to many interpretations.

(b) **~ a** + *infin* to offer to + *infin*, volunteer to + *infin*.

(c) **~ de algo** (*Carib*) to borrow sth.

prestatario, -a NM/F borrower.

preste NM (*hum*) priest.

presteza NF speed, promptness; alacrity; **con ~** promptly, with alacrity.

prestidigitación NF conjuring, juggling; sleight of hand.

prestidigitador(a) NM/F conjurer, juggler.

prestigiado ADJ (*LAm*) worthy, estimable, prestigious.

prestigiar [1b] VT to give prestige (*o* distinction, status) to; (*dar fama a*) to make famous; (*honrar*) to honour (*con* with); (*realzar*) to enhance.

prestigio NM **(a)** (*fama*) prestige; (*honra*) face; (*reputación*) good name; **de ~** prestigious. **(b)** (*ensalmo*) (magic) spell. **(c)** (*truco*) trick.

prestigioso ADJ worthy, estimable, prestigious; reputable; famous.

presto [1] ADJ **(a)** (*rápido*) quick, prompt. **(b)** (*listo*) ready (*para* for). **(c)** (*Mús*) presto.

[2] *adv* (*rápidamente*) quickly; (*en seguida*) at once, right away.

presumible ADJ presumable; probable; **es ~** it is to be presumed.

presumiblemente ADJ presumably.

presumido ADJ conceited.

presumir [3a] [1] VT **(a)** (*suponer*) to presume, conjecture, surmise; **~ que ...** to presume that ..., guess that ...

(b) (*And, Cono Sur: pretender*) to court; (*coquetear con*) to flirt with.

[2] VI **(a) según cabe ~** as may be presumed, presumably.

(b) (*engreírse*) to be conceited; (*fachendear*) to give o.s. airs, swank*, show off; **para ~ ante las amistades** in order to show off before one's friends; **no presumas tanto** don't be so conceited; **~ de listo** to think oneself very smart, boast of being clever; **~ de experto** to pride oneself on being an expert; **~ demasiado de sus fuerzas** to overestimate one's strength.

presunción NF **(a)** (*conjetura*) supposition, presumption; (*sospecha*) suspicion. **(b)** (*cualidad*) conceit, presumption; pretentiousness.

presuntamente ADV supposedly; **un hombre ~ rico** a supposedly rich man; **dos mujeres que ~ se dedican a esto** two women (who are) presumed to devote themselves to this, two women (who are) suspected of devoting themselves to this.

presunto ADJ (*supuesto*) supposed, presumed; (*llamado*) so-called; *heredero* presumptive; *criminal* suspected, alleged; **el ~ asesino** the alleged murderer; **X, ~ implicado en ...** X, alleged to be concerned in ...; **estos ~s expertos** these so-called experts.

presuntuosamente ADV conceitedly, presumptuously; pretentiously.

presuntuoso ADJ (*vanidoso*) conceited, presumptuous; (*pretencioso*) pretentious.

presuponer [2q] VT to presuppose.

presuposición NF presupposition.

presupuestal ADJ (*Méx etc*) budgetary, budget (*atr*).

presupuestar [1a] VT (*Fin*) to budget for; *gastos, ingresos* to reckon up, estimate for, estimate the cost of.

presupuestario ADJ budgetary, budget (*atr*).

presupuestívoro, -a NM/F (*LAm: hum*) public employee.

presupuesto NM (a) (*Fin*) budget; (*de obras, proyecto etc*) estimate; **~ operante** operating budget; **~ de ventas** sales budget.
(b) (*supuesto*) premise, assumption.

presurizado ADJ pressurized.

presurosamente ADV quickly, promptly; hastily.

presuroso ADJ (*rápido*) quick, prompt, speedy; (*apresurado*) hasty; *paso etc* light, quick.

pretal NM (*esp LAm*) strap, girth.

prêt-à-porter ADJ INVAR off-the-peg, ready-to-wear, off-the-rack (*US*).

pretecnología NF (*Escol*) practical subjects, technical courses.

pretemporada NF (*Dep*) pre-season (*t atr*).

pretenciosidad NF (a) pretentiousness; showiness. (b) (*LAm*) vanity, boastfulness.

pretencioso ADJ (a) (*vanidoso*) pretentious, presumptuous; showy. (b) (*LAm: presumido*) conceited, stuck-up*.

▼ **pretender** [2a] VT (a) (*intentar*) **~ + infin** to try to + infin, seek to + infin, endeavour to + infin; **pretendió convencerme** he sought to convince me; **han pretendido robarme** they have attempted to rob me; **¿qué pretende Vd decir con eso?** what do you mean by that?; **no pretendo ser feliz** it's not happiness I'm after.
(b) (*afirmar*) to claim; **~ ser rico** to claim to be rich, profess to be rich; **~ haber hecho algo** to claim to have done sth; **el libro pretende ser importante** the book tries to look (o make out that it is) important; **esto pretende poder curarlo todo** this purports to cure everything; **pretende que el coche le atropelló** he alleges that the car knocked him down.
▼(c) (*aspirar a*) to seek, try for; *puesto* to apply for; *honor* to aspire to; *objetivo* to aim at, try to achieve; **pretende llegar a ser médico** she hopes to become a doctor; **¿qué pretende Vd?** what are you after?; what do you hope to achieve.
(d) **~ que** + *subj* to expect that ..., suggest that ..., intend that ...; **él pretende que yo le escriba** he suggests that I should write to him, he wants me to write to him; **¿cómo pretende Vd que lo compre yo?** how do you expect me to buy it?
(e) *mujer* to woo, court; to seek the hand of.

pretendidamente ADV supposedly; allegedly.

pretendido ADJ supposed, pretended; alleged.

pretendiente [1] NM (*gen*) suitor.
[2] NM, **pretendienta** NF (*aspirante*) claimant; (*a puesto*) candidate, applicant (*a* for); (*a trono*) pretender (*a* to).

pretensado ADJ prestressed.

pretensión NF (a) (*reclamación, afirmación*) claim.
(b) (*objetivo*) aim, object; (*aspiración*) aspiration.
(c) (*pey*) pretension; exaggerated claim, false claim; **tener pretensiones de** to have pretensions to, lay claim to; **tener pocas pretensiones** to be undemanding, be content with very little; **tiene la ~ de que le acompañe yo** he expects me to go with him.
(d) (*LAm*) (*vanidad*) vanity; (*presunción*) presumption, arrogance.

pretensioso ADJ (*LAm*) = **pretencioso** (b).

pretensor NM: **cinturón con ~** inertia-reel seatbelt.

preterir [3a] VT to leave out, omit, pass over.

pretérito [1] ADJ (a) (*Ling*) past. (b) (*fig*) past, former; **las glorias pretéritas del país** the country's former glories.
[2] NM (*Ling*) preterite, past historic.

preternatural ADJ preternatural.

pretextar [1a] VT to plead, use as an excuse; **~ que ...** to plead that ..., allege that ..., claim that ...

pretexto NM (*gen*) pretext; (*disculpa*) excuse, plea; **a ~ de** on the pretext of; **bajo ningún ~** under no circumstances; **so ~ de** under pretext of; **tomar a ~** to use as an excuse.

pretil NM (a) (*parapeto*) parapet; (*baranda*) handrail, guardrail, railing.
(b) (*And*) forecourt; (*Carib, Méx: banco*) bench; (*Méx: encintado*) kerb.

pretina NF (a) girdle, belt, waistband; (*And, Cono Sur: correa*) leather strap; (*Carib: bragueta*) flies, fly. (b) (*Elec*) cassette-player.

pretor NM (*Méx*) lower-court judge, magistrate.

pretoriano ADJ: **guardia pretoriana** praetorian guard.

preu* NM one-year pre-university course.

preuniversitario [1] ADJ pre-university; **curso ~** one-year pre-university course.
[2] NM, **preuniversitaria** NF *student on a pre-university course.*

prevalecer [2d] VI (a) (*imponerse*) to prevail (*sobre* against, over); (*triunfar*) to triumph, win through; (*dominar*) to come to dominate. (b) (*prosperar*) to thrive; (*Bot*) to take root and grow.

prevaleciente ADJ prevailing, prevalent; dominant.

prevalerse [2p] VR: **~ de** to avail o.s. of; (*pey*) to take advantage of.

prevaricación NF, **prevaricato** NM (*Jur*) perversion of the course of justice.

prevaricar [1g] VI to pervert the course of justice.

preve* NF = **prevención** (f).

prevención NF (a) (*preparativo*) preparation; (*estado*) preparedness, readiness; **las prevenciones para la ceremonia** the preparations for the ceremony.
(b) (*acto de impedir*) prevention.
(c) (*cualidad*) foresight, forethought; **obrar con ~** to act with foresight.
(d) (*medida*) precaution; precautionary measure, safety measure; **de ~** precautionary; **medidas de ~** emergency measures, contingency plans; **hemos tomado ciertas prevenciones** we have taken certain precautions.
(e) (*prejuicio*) prejudice; **tener ~ contra uno** to have a prejudice against sb, be prejudiced against sb.
(f) (*comisaría*) police-station; (*Mil*) guardroom, guardhouse.

prevenido ADJ (a) **ser ~** to be cautious; to be far-sighted.
(b) **estar ~** to be prepared, be ready; to be forewarned, be on one's guard (*contra* against); **hombre ~ vale por dos** forewarned is forearmed.

prevenir [3r] [1] VT (a) (*disponer*) to prepare, get ready, make ready (*para* for).
(b) (*proveer*) **~ a uno de algo** to provide sb with sth.
(c) (*impedir*) to prevent; (*alertar*) to alert; (*anticipar*) to forestall; **hay accidentes que no se pueden ~** some accidents cannot be avoided.
(d) (*advertir*) **~ a uno** to warn sb, forewarn sb, put sb on his guard (*contra* against, *de* about); **pudieron ~le a tiempo** they were able to warn him in time.
(e) (*prever*) to foresee, anticipate; to provide for; **más vale ~ que curar** prevention is better than cure.
(f) (*predisponer*) to prejudice, bias (*a favor de* in favour of, *en contra de* against).
[2] **prevenirse** VR (a) (*disponerse*) to get ready, prepare; **~ para un viaje** to get ready for a trip; **~ de ropa adecuada** to provide o.s. with suitable clothing.
(b) **~ contra** to take precautions against, prepare for.
(c) **~ en contra de uno** to adopt a hostile attitude to sb.

preventivo ADJ preventive, precautionary; (*Med*) preventive.

▼ **prever** [2u] VT (a) (*antever*) to foresee.
▼(b) (*anticipar*) to anticipate, envisage, visualize; (*proyectar*) to plan; (*tener en cuenta*) to make allowances for; (*establecer*) to provide for, establish; **la elección es prevista para ...** the election is planned for ...; **no teníamos previsto nada para eso** we had not made any allowance for that; **~ que ...** to anticipate that ..., envisage that ..., expect that ...; **la ley prevé que ...** the law provides that ..., the law establishes that ...; **ya lo preveía** I expected as much.

previamente ADV previously.

previo [1] ADJ (a) (*gen*) previous, prior, earlier; *examen* preliminary; **autorización previa** prior authorization (*o* permission); **'previa cita'** 'by appointment only', 'appointment required'.
(b) *idea* preconceived, received, traditional.
[2] *como* PREP (a) (*tras*) after, following; **~ acuerdo de los otros** subject to the agreement of the others; **~ pago de los derechos** on payment of the fees.
(b) **~ a** before, prior to.
[3] NM (*Cine*) playback.

previsible ADJ foreseeable; predictable.

previsiblemente ADV predictably.

previsión NF (a) (*cualidad: clarividencia*) foresight, far-sightedness; (*prudencia*) caution.
(b) (*acto*) precaution, precautionary measure; **en ~ de** as a precaution against; in anticipation of.
(c) **caja de ~ social** social security.
(d) (*pronóstico*) forecast; **previsiones económicas** economic forecast; **~ meteorológica, ~ del tiempo** weather forecast(ing); **~ de ventas** sales forecast; **las previsiones del plan quinquenal** the forecasts of the five-year plan.

previsivo ADJ (*Méx*) = **previsor**.

previsor ADJ far-sighted; (*precavido*) prudent.

previsoramente ADV (a) far-sightedly; prudently. (b) (*por si acaso*) just in case.

previsto ADJ (*resultados*) predicted, anticipated; **empezó a la hora prevista** it started on time; **según lo ~** as planned; *V t* **prever**.

prez NM O F honour, glory.

PRI NM (*Méx*) ABR *de* **Partido Revolucionario Institucional**.

PRI - *Partido Revolucionario Institucional*
---

i The Mexican **Partido Revolucionario Institucional** *has been in power since 1929. Founded by General Plutarco E. Calles in 1928 as the* **Partido Nacional Revolucionario**, *it had its roots in the Revolution of 1910, and the subsequent need to "institutionalize" the revolution and achieve some continuity in a society long troubled by military coups and political assassinations. The present name was adopted in 1946.*

---

pribar [1a] VTI *etc* = **privar²**.

prieta NF (*Cono Sur Culin*) black pudding.

prieto 1 ADJ (a) (*oscuro*) blackish, dark; (*LAm*) dark, swarthy; *mujer* brunette.
(b) (*tacaño*) mean.
(c) (*apretado*) tight, compressed, tightly packed; **un siglo ~ de historia** a century packed full of history, a century rich in history.
2 NM (*LAm: dado*) loaded dice.

prietuzco ADJ (*CAm, Carib, Méx*) blackish.

priísta NMF (*Méx Pol*) member of the PRI; *V* **PRI**.

prima NF (a) (*pariente*) cousin.
(b) (*de sueldo etc*) bonus, extra payment; (*de exportación etc*) subsidy; **~ por coste de vida** cost of living bonus; **~ de incentivo, ~ a la** (o **de) producción** incentive bonus; **~ de seguro** insurance premium; **~ por trabajos peligrosos** danger money.
(c) (*Ecl*) prime.
(d) (*Cono Sur*) **bajar la ~** to moderate one's language; **subir la ~** to use strong language.

primacía NF (a) (*primer lugar*) primacy, first place; (*prioridad*) priority; (*supremacía*) supremacy; **~ de paso** (*Aut*) priority, right of way; **tener la ~ entre** to be supreme among.
(b) (*Ecl*) primacy.

primada NF piece of stupidity; silly mistake.

primado NM (*Ecl*) primate.

primadon(n)a NF prima donna (*t fig*).

primal 1 ADJ yearling.
2 NM, **primala** NF yearling.

primar [1a] 1 VT to give priority to; to place a high value on.
2 VI to occupy first place, be supreme; **~ sobre** to have priority over, take precedence over; to outweigh.

primaria NF (*t ~s* PL) primary election(s).

primariamente ADV primarily.

primariedad NF primacy.

primario ADJ primary; **escuela primaria** primary school.

primate 1 ADJ most important.
2 NM (a) (*Zool*) primate. (b) (*prócer*) important person, outstanding figure.

primavera 1 NF (a) (*estación*) spring; springtime (*t fig*). (b) (*Orn*) blue-tit. (c) (*Bot*) primrose.
2 NM: **ser un ~** (*Esp***) to be a simple soul.

primaveral ADJ spring (*atr*); spring-like.

prime* ADJ = **primero**.

primer ADJ *V* **primero**.

primera NF (a) (*Aut etc*) first gear, bottom gear.
(b) (*Ferro*) first class; **viajar en ~** to travel first.
(c) **de ~** first-class, first-rate; **comer de ~** to eat really well, have a first-class meal; **estar de ~** to feel fine.
(d) **~ de cambio** (*Com*) first of exchange; *V* **cambio** (c).
(e) **a las ~s de cambio** (*fig*) as soon as I turned my back; before you know where you are.

primeramente ADV first, firstly; chiefly.

primerear [1a] VI (*Cono Sur: fig*) to land the first blow, get in first.

primerizo 1 ADJ green, inexperienced.
2 NM, **primeriza** NF novice, beginner.

▼ **primero** 1 ADJ (**primer** *delante de* NM SING) (a) (*que precede*) first; (*anterior*) former; *página* first, front; **en los ~s años del siglo** in the early years of the century; **en los ~s años treinta** in the early thirties; **a ~s de siglo** at the start of the century, early in the century; **llegar el ~** to arrive first; **ser el ~ en** + *infin* to be the first to + *infin*; **venir a primera hora de la mañana** to come first thing in the morning.
▼(b) (*fig*) (*primordial*) first; (*principal*) prime; (*fundamental*) basic, fundamental; (*urgente*) urgent; *materia* raw; **lo ~ es que ...** the fundamental thing is that ...; **lo ~ es lo ~** first things first; **es nuestro primer deber** it is our first duty; **es el primer país en estos estudios** it is the foremost country in these studies.
2 ADV (a) (*primeramente*) first.
(b) (*antes*) rather, sooner; **~ se quedará en casa que pedir permiso para salir** she'd rather stay at home than have to ask for permission

to go out; **¡~ morir!** we'd rather die!

primicia NF (a) (*novedad*) novelty; (*estreno*) first appearance; **~ informativa** scoop. (b) **~s** first fruits (*t fig*).

primigenio ADJ primitive, original.

primitiva* NF: **la ~** = **lotería primitiva**.

primitivamente ADV (a) (*al principio*) at first; originally, in earlier times. (b) (*de un modo primitivo*) primitively, in a primitive way.

primitivo ADJ (a) (*temprano*) early; (*original*) first, original; (*Arte*) primitive; **el texto ~** the original text; **quedan 200 de los ~s 850** there remain 200 from the original 850; **es una obra primitiva** it is an early work; **devolver algo a su estado ~** to restore sth to its original state.
(b) *color* primary.
(c) (*Fin*) *acción* ordinary.
(d) (*Hist etc*) primitive; uncivilized; **en condiciones primitivas** in primitive conditions.

primo 1 ADJ (a) (*Mat*) prime.
(b) *materia* raw.
2 NM (a) (*pariente*) cousin; **~ carnal, ~ hermano** first cousin; **ser ~s hermanos** (*fig*) to be extraordinarily alike; **le vino el ~ de América*** she started her period.
(b) (*) (*cándido*) fool; (*incauto*) dupe, sucker‡; **hacer el ~** to be easily taken in, be taken for a ride*; to carry the can*; **tomar a uno por ~** to do sb down*, take sb in*.

primogénito ADJ first-born.

primogenitura NF (*Jur*) primogeniture; (*patrimonio*) birthright.

primor NM (a) (*belleza*) exquisiteness, beauty; (*elegancia*) elegance; (*delicadeza*) delicacy.
(b) (*maestría*) care, skill; **hecho con ~** done most skilfully, delicately made.
(c) (*objeto*) fine thing, lovely thing; **hace ~es con la aguja** she makes lovely things with her needlework; **cose que es un ~** she sews beautifully, she sews in a way that is a delight to see; **hijos que son un ~** delightful children, charming children.

▼ **primordial** ADJ basic, fundamental, essential; supreme; **esto es ~** this is top priority; **es de interés ~** it is of fundamental concern; **es ~ saberlo** it is essential to know it.

primordialidad NF overriding importance, essential nature; supremacy.

primordialmente ADV basically, fundamentally.

primorosamente ADV exquisitely, delicately, elegantly; neatly, skilfully.

primoroso ADJ exquisite, fine, delicate, elegant; neat, skilful.

prímula NF primrose.

princesa NF princess.

principado NM principality; **P~** (*Esp Pol*) Asturias.

▼ **principal** 1 ADJ (a) (*más importante*) principal, chief, main; (*más destacado*) foremost; *piso* first, second (*US*); **lo ~ es ...** the main thing is to ...
(b) *persona* illustrious.
2 NM (a) (*persona*) head, chief, principal.
(b) (*Fin*) principal, capital.
(c) (*Teat*) dress circle.

principalmente ADJ principally, chiefly, mainly.

príncipe NM (a) (*) prince; **~ azul** knight in shining armour, Prince Charming; **~ consorte** prince consort; **~ encantado** Prince Charming; **~ heredero** crown prince. (b) *V* **edición**.

principesco ADJ princely.

principiante 1 ADJ (*que comienza*) who is beginning; (*novato*) novice; (*inexperto*) inexperienced, green.
2 NM, **principianta** NF beginner; learner; novice.

principiar [1b] VTI to begin; **~ a** + *infin* to begin to + *infin*, begin + *ger*; **~ con** to begin with.

▼ **principio** NM (a) (*comienzo*) beginning, start; (*origen*) origin; (*primera etapa*) early stage; **al ~** at first, in the beginning; **a ~s de** at the beginning of; **a ~s del verano** at the beginning of the summer, early in the summer; **desde el ~** from the first, from the outset; **desde el ~ hasta el fin** from start to finish, from beginning to end; **en un ~** at first, to start with; **dar ~ a** to start off; **tener** (o **tomar) ~ en** to start from, be based on.
(b) **~s** (*nociones*) rudiments, first notions; '**P~s de física**' 'Introduction to Physics', 'Outline of Physics'.
▼(c) (*moral*) principle; **el ~ de la legalidad** the force of law, the rule of law; **persona de ~s** man of principles; **en ~** in principle; **por ~** on principle, as a matter of principle; **es inmoral por ~** it is immoral in principle; **sin ~s** unprincipled.
(d) (*Filos*) principle; (*Quím*) element, constituent.
(e) (*esp Esp Culin*) entrée.

principote* NM (*fachendoso*) swank*, show-off*; (*arribista*) parvenu, social climber.

pringada NF bread dipped in gravy (*etc*).

pringado*, -a NM/F (a) (*víctima*) (innocent) victim; (*sin suerte*) un-

lucky person; (*infeliz*) poor devil, wretch; down-and-out; **el ~ del grupo** the odd man out, the loser.
(**b**) (*gafe*) bringer of bad luck.
(**c**) (*tonto*) fool, idiot; **¡no seas ~!** don't be an idiot!
pringao* NM = **pringado**.
pringar [1h] **1** VT (**a**) (*Culin*) to dip in fat (*etc*); *asado* to baste; **~ el pan en la sopa** to dip one's bread in the soup.
(**b**) (*ensuciar*) to dirty, soil (with grease); (*rociar*) to splash grease (*o* fat) on; (*esp LAm*) to splash.
(**c**) (*: *herir*) **~ a uno** to wound sb, make sb bleed.
(**d**) (*: *denigrar*) to blacken, run down*.
(**e**) (*: *involucrar*) **~ a uno en un asunto** to involve sb in a matter; **están pringadas en esto unas altas personalidades** some top people are mixed up in this.
(**f**) (*Cono Sur*) *enfermedad* to give.
(**g**) (*Cono Sur**) *mujer* to put in the family way.
(**h**) **~la*** (*meter la pata*) to drop a brick*, make a boob*; **~la(s)** (*morir*) to peg out‡; **~la‡‡** (*Med*) to get a dose of clap‡.
(**i**) **estar pringado‡** to be hooked (on drugs)*.
2 VI (**a**) (*: *perder*) to take a beating, lose badly; to come a cropper*; **hemos pringado** we're done for.
(**b**) (*Mil etc**: *trabajar*) to sweat one's guts out‡, slog away.
(**c**) **~ en*** to dabble in; to take a hand in, get mixed up in.
(**d**) (*: *morir*) to peg out‡.
(**e**) (*CAm, Carib, Méx*: *lloviznar*) to drizzle.
3 **pringarse** VR (**a**) (*ensuciarse*) to get splashed, get soiled (*con, de* with).
(**b**) = **2** (**c**).
(**c**) (*) (*ganar por medios dudosos*) to make money on the side; (*sacar tajada*) to get a rake-off*; (*enriquecerse*) to make a packet*.
(**d**) **o nos pringamos todos, o ninguno*** either we all carry the can or none of us does*.
pringo NM (*LAm*) (*gota*) drop; (*pizca*) bit, pinch; **con un ~ de leche** with a drop of milk.
pringón **1** ADJ (*sucio*) dirty, greasy.
2 NM (**a**) grease stain, grease spot. (**b**) (‡) (*tajada*) rake-off*, (*ganancias*) packet*.
pringoso ADJ greasy; sticky.
pringue NM (*a veces* F) (**a**) (*Culin*) grease, fat, dripping.
(**b**) (*mancha*) grease stain, grease spot; (*suciedad*) (*any*) dirty object, sticky thing.
(**c**) (*: *molestia*) nuisance; cause of trouble; **es un ~ tener que ...** it's a bind having to ...*
(**d**) (*CAm, Méx*: *salpicadura*) splash (of mud *etc*); (*And*: *quemadura*) burn.
(**e**) (‡: *dinero*) dosh‡, money.
(**f**) (‡: *policía*) **P~** Crime Squad.
print-out NM (*Inform*) printout.
prior NM prior.
priora NF, **prioresa** NF †† prioress.
priorato NM priory.
priori V **a priori**.
prioridad NF (*precedencia*) priority; (*antigüedad*) seniority, greater age; **~ de paso** (*Aut*) right of way; **tener ~** to have priority (*sobre* over).
prioritariamente ADV (*primero*) as a priority, first; (*mayormente*) mainly, principally.
prioritario ADJ prior, priority (*atr*); main, principal; **un proyecto de carácter ~** a plan with top priority, a plan in the priority class; **lo ~es ...** the first thing (to do) is ...
priorizar [1f] **1** VT to give priority to, treat as a priority, prioritize.
2 VI to determine priorities.
prisa NF (*prontitud*) hurry, haste; (*rapidez*) speed; (*premura*) (sense of) urgency; **temporada de más ~(s)** rush period, busy period; **a ~, de ~** quickly, hurriedly; **a toda ~** as quickly as possible; **sin ~ pero sin pausa** in an unhurried way; **estar de ~** to be in a hurry; **voy con mucha ~** I'm in a great hurry; **correr ~** to be urgent; **¿te corre ~?** are you in a hurry?; **¿corren ~ estas cartas?** (*Esp*) are these letters urgent?, is there any hurry for these letters?; **dar ~ a uno, meter ~ a uno** to make sb get a move on; **darse ~** to hurry (up); **¡date ~!** hurry (up)!, come along!; **tener ~** to be in a hurry.
prisco **1** ADJ (*LAm**) simple.
2 NM (*esp Cono Sur*) apricot.
prisión NF (**a**) (*cárcel*) prison; **~ (de régimen) abierto** open prison; **~ de alta (o máxima) seguridad** top-security prison. (**b**) (*encierro*) imprisonment; **~ domiciliaria** house-arrest; **~ mayor** (*Esp*) sentence of more than six years and a day; **~ menor** (*Esp*) sentence of less than six years and a day; **~ perpetua** life imprisonment; **~ preventiva** preventive detention; **cinco años de ~** five years' imprisonment, prison sentence of five years. (**c**) *prisiones* (*grillos*) shackles, fetters.
prisionero, -a NM/F prisoner (of war); **hacer ~ a uno** to take sb prisoner.
prisma NM (**a**) prism. (**b**) (*fig*) point of view, angle; perspective; **bajo**

(*o* **desde**) **el ~ de** from the point of view of.
prismático **1** ADJ prismatic.
2 **~s** NMPL binoculars, field glasses.
pristinidad NF pristine nature, original quality.
prístino ADJ pristine, original.
priva‡ NF: **la ~** (*Esp*) the booze*, the drink.
privacidad NF privacy; secrecy.
privación NF (**a**) (*acto*) deprivation, deprival; **sufrir ~ de libertad** to suffer loss of liberty. (**b**) (*estado*) deprivation; want, privation; **privaciones** hardships, privations.
privadamente ADV privately.
privado **1** ADJ (**a**) (*particular*) private; personal; '**~ y confidencial**' 'private and confidential'.
(**b**) (*LAm*: *alocado*) mad, senseless; (*Carib*) weak, faint.
2 NM (**a**) (*Pol*) favourite, protégé; (*Hist*) royal favourite, chief minister.
(**b**) **en ~** privately, in private.
privanza NF favour; **durante la ~ de Lerma** when Lerma was royal favourite, when Lerma was chief minister.
privar¹ [1a] **1** VT (**a**) (*despojar*) **~ a uno de algo** to deprive sb of sth, take sth away from sb; **~ a uno del conocimiento** to render sb unconscious; **le privaron del carnet de conducir** they suspended his driving licence, they took away his driving licence; **nos vemos privados de ...** we find ourselves without ..., we find ourselves bereft of ...
(**b**) (*prohibir*) **~ a uno de** + *infin* to forbid sb to + *infin*, prevent sb from + *ger*; **lo cual me privó de verlos** which prevented me from seeing them; **no me prives de verte** don't forbid me to come to see you, don't tell me not to come again.
(**c**) (*extasiar*) to delight, overwhelm.
2 VI (**a**) (*Pol*) to be in favour (at court).
(**b**) (*existir*) to obtain, be present; (*predominar*) to prevail; (*: *estar de moda*) to be in fashion, be the thing; **la cualidad que más priva entre ellos** the quality which is most strongly present in them; **en ese período privaba la minifalda*** at that time miniskirts were in.
3 **privarse** VR: **~ de** (*abstenerse de*) to deprive o.s. of; (*renunciar*) to give up, go without, forgo; **no se privan de nada** they lack nothing, they have everything they want.
privar²‡ [1a] VTI to booze*, drink.
privata‡ NF = **priva**.
privativo ADJ exclusive; **~ de** exclusive to; **esa función es privativa del presidente** that function is the president's alone; **la planta es privativa del Brasil** the plant is peculiar to Brazil, the plant is restricted to Brazil.
privatización NF privatization.
privatizador ADJ *proceso, programa, política* privatisation (*atr*), of privatisation; *organismo* **~** privatisation body.
privatizar [1f] VT to privatize.
prive‡ NF = **priva**.
privilegiado **1** ADJ (*gen*) privileged; *memoria etc* exceptionally good.
2 NM, **privilegiada** NF privileged person; **los ~s** the privileged.
privilegiar [1b] VT to grant a privilege to; to favour.
privilegio NM (*gen*) privilege; concession; (*exención*) immunity, exemption; (*Jur*) sole right; (*Liter*) copyright; **~ fiscal** tax concession; **~ de invención** patent.
privota‡ NMF piss artist‡‡, boozer‡.
pro **1** NM Y NF (**a**) (*provecho*) profit, advantage; **los ~s y los contras** the pros and the cons, for and against; **buena ~ le haga** and much good may it do him; **en ~ de** for, on behalf of; for the benefit of.
(**b**) **de ~** (*bueno*) worthy; (*verdadero*) real, true; **hombre de ~** worthy man, honest man; **para los cinéfilos de ~** for real film buffs.
2 PREP for, on behalf of; **campaña ~ paz** peace campaign; **asociación ~ ciegos** association for (aid to) the blind.
pro... PREF pro-..., *p.ej.* prosoviético pro-Soviet.
proa NF (*Náut*) bow, bows; prow; (*Aer*) nose; **de ~** bow (*atr*), fore; **en la ~** in the bows; **poner la ~ a** (*Náut*) to head for, set a course for; (*fig*) to aim at; **poner la ~ a uno** to take a stand against sb, set o.s. against sb.
proamnistía ADJ INVAR pro-amnesty; **gestora ~** (*Esp*) *organization calling for an amnesty for ETA prisoners*.
▼ **probabilidad** NF (**a**) (*gen*) probability, likelihood; **según toda ~** in all probability.
▼(**b**) (*perspectiva*) chance, prospect; **~es** chances; **~es de vida** expectation of life; **hay pocas ~es de que venga** there is little prospect of his coming; **apenas tiene ~es** he hasn't much chance.
▼ **probable** ADJ probable, likely; **es ~ que** + *subj* it is probable (*o* likely) that ...; **es ~ que no venga** he probably won't come; **lo dio como ~** he said it was likely.
▼ **probablemente** ADV probably.
probadamente ADV provenly.
probado ADJ *remedio etc* proven.
probador NM (**a**) (*persona*) taster. (**b**) (*en tienda*) fitting room. (**c**)

(*LAm*) tailor's dummy.

probanza NF proof, evidence.

probar [1l] **1** VT (**a**) (*hecho, teoría etc* to prove; (*demostrar*) to show, demonstrate; (*asentar*) to establish; **~ que ...** to prove that ...
(**b**) *aparato, arma etc* to test, try (out); *ropa* to try on.
(**c**) *comida etc* to try, taste, sample; **prueba un poco de esto** try a bit of this; **no han probado nunca un buen jerez** they have never tasted a good sherry; **no lo pruebo nunca** I never touch it; **al ~ se ve el mosto** the proof of the pudding is in the eating.
2 VI (**a**) (*intentar*) to try; **¿probamos?** shall we try?, shall we have a go?; **~ no cuesta nada** there's no harm in trying; **~ a** + *infin* to try to + *infin*.
(**b**) **~ de = 1** (c).
(**c**) (*sentar*) to suit; **no me prueba** (**bien**) **el café** coffee doesn't agree with me; **le probó mal ese oficio** that trade did not suit him.
3 probarse VR: **~ un traje** to try a suit on.

probatorio ADJ (**a**) (*que testimonia*) evidential; **documentos ~s del crimen** documents in proof of the crime, documents which prove the crime. (**b**) (*convincente*) convincing.

probeta **1** NF test-tube; graduated cylinder.
2 ATR test-tube (*atr*); artificial; experimental; **niño ~** test-tube baby.

probidad NF integrity, honesty, rectitude.

▼ **problema** **1** NM (*gen*) problem; (*pega*) difficulty, snag; trouble; (*Méx*) accident, mishap; (*Mat*) problem; (*rompecabezas*) puzzle.
2 ATR problem (*atr*); **niño ~** problem child.

problemática NF problems, questions; issues; (*conjunto*) set of problems.

problemático ADJ problematic.

problematizar [1f] VT *asunto* to make problematic; *persona* to burden with problems.

probo ADJ honest, upright.

probóscide NF proboscis.

procacidad NF (**a**) (*desvergüenza*) insolence, impudence; (*descaro*) brazenness. (**b**) (*indecoro*) indecency, obscenity.

procaz ADJ (**a**) (*atrevido*) insolent, impudent; (*descarado*) brazen. (**b**) (*obsceno*) indecent, obscene.

procedencia NF (**a**) (*fuente*) source, origin; provenance (*punto de partida*) provenance; point of departure; (*Náut*) port of origin. (**b**) (*propiedad*) properness; (*justicia*) justification, soundness; (*Jur*) propriety.

procedente ADJ (**a**) **~ de** coming from, proceeding from, originating in. (**b**) (*razonable*) reasonable; (*apropiado*) proper, fitting; (*Jur*) proper; duly established.

procedentemente ADV properly, in a right and proper fashion.

proceder [2a] **1** VI (**a**) (*pasar*) to proceed; **~ a una elección** to proceed to an election; **~ contra uno** (*Jur*) to take proceedings against sb.
(**b**) **~ de** to come from, originate in; to flow from, spring from; **todo esto procede de su negativa** all this springs from his refusal; **estas patatas proceden de Israel** these potatoes come from Israel; **de donde procede que ...** (from) whence it happens that ...
(**c**) (*obrar*) to act; (*conducirse*) to proceed, behave; **ha procedido precipitadamente** he has acted hastily; **conviene ~ con cuidado** it is best to go carefully.
(**d**) (*ser apropiado*) to be right (and proper), be fitting; **si el caso procede** if the case warrants it; **no procede obrar así** it is not right to act like that; **táchese lo que no proceda** cross out what does not apply; **luego, si procede, ...** then, if appropriate, ...
(**e**) (*: estar de moda*) to be in*, be in fashion.
2 NM course of action; behaviour, conduct.

procedimental ADJ procedural; (*Jur*) legal.

procedimiento NM (*gen*) procedure; (*sistema*) process; (*medio*) means, method; (*Jur*) proceedings; **un ~ para abaratar el producto** a method of making the product cheaper; **por un ~ deductivo** by a deductive process.

proceloso ADJ (*liter*) stormy, tempestuous.

prócer NM (*persona eminente*) worthy, notable; (*magnate*) important person; (*Pol*) great man, leader; (*LAm*) leader of the independence movement.

procesado¹ **1** ADJ *alimento* processed.
2 NM (*Téc*) processing.

procesado², -a NM/F (*Jur*) accused (person).

procesador NM processor; **~ de datos** data processor; **~ de palabras**, **~ de textos** word processor.

procesadora NF (*LAm: t* **~ de alimentos**) food processor.

procesal ADJ (**a**) (*Parl etc*) procedural. (**b**) (*Jur*) *costas etc* legal; *derecho* procedural.

procesamiento NM (**a**) (*gen*) processing. (**b**) (*Inform*) processing; **~ concurrente** concurrent processing; **~ de datos** data processing; **~ interactivo** interactive processing; **~ por lotes** batch processing; **~ simultáneo** simultaneous processing; **~ de textos** word processing. (**c**) (*Jur*) prosecution; trial.

procesar [1a] VT (**a**) (*Jur: juzgar*) to try, put on trial; to prosecute; (*demandar*) to sue, bring an action against. (**b**) (*Téc*) to process.

procesión NF procession; **la ~ va por dentro** still waters run deep; there is more in this than meets the eye; **la ~ le va por dentro** he's a quiet one; he keeps his troubles to himself; **una ~ de quejas** a never-ending series of complaints.

procesional ADJ processional.

procesionaria NF processionary moth (o caterpillar).

proceso NM (**a**) (*gen*) process; **~ mental** mental process; **~ de una enfermedad** course (o progress) of a disease.
(**b**) (*transcurso*) lapse of time; **en el ~ de un mes** in the course of a month.
(**c**) (*Jur*) (*juicio*) trial; prosecution; (*pleito*) action, lawsuit, proceedings; **~ verbal** (*escrito*) record; (*audiencia*) hearing; **abrir** (o **entablar, formar**) **~** to bring a suit (a against).
(**d**) (*Inform*) processing; **~ de datos** data processing; **~ de imágenes** image processing; **~ por lotes** batch processing; **~ prioritario** foreground processing; **~ no prioritario** background processing; **~ de textos** word processing.

proclama NF (**a**) (*gen*) proclamation; (*discurso*) address; (*Pol*) manifesto. (**b**) **~s** (*Ecl*) banns.

proclamación NF proclamation.

proclamar [1a] **1** VT (*publicar*) to proclaim.
2 proclamarse VR: **~ rey** to proclaim o.s. king; **~ campeón** to become champion, win the championship.

proclive ADJ: **~ a** given to, inclined to.

proclividad NF proclivity, inclination.

procónsul NM proconsul.

procreación NF procreation, breeding.

procrear [1a] VTI to procreate, breed.

procura NF (*esp LAm*) obtaining, getting; **en ~ de** in search of; **andar en ~ de algo** to be trying to get sth.

procuración NF (*Jur*) power of attorney; proxy.

procurador(a) NM/F (**a**) (*Jur: abogado*) attorney, ≈ solicitor. (**b**) (*Jur: apoderado*) proxy. (**c**) **~ en Cortes**, **~ a Cortes** (*Pol Hist*) deputy, member of (the Spanish) parliament. (**d**) **~ general** attorney general.

procuraduría NF (**a**) lawyer's office; **~** (**general**) (*Méx*) attorney general's office. (**b**) (costs of) legal representation.

procurar [1a] **1** VT (**a**) (*intentar*) **~** + *infin* to try to + *infin*, endeavour to + *infin*; **procura conservar la calma** do try to keep calm; **procura que no te vean** take care not to let them see you, don't let them see you.
(**b**) (*conseguir*) to get, obtain; to secure; (*producir*) to yield, produce; **~ un puesto a uno** to get sb a job, find a job for sb; **esto nos procurará grandes beneficios** this will bring us great benefits, this will secure great benefits for us.
(**c**) (*lograr*) **~** + *infin* to manage to + *infin*, succeed in + *ger*; **por fin procuró dominarse** eventually he managed to control himself.
2 procurarse VR: **~ algo** to secure sth for o.s.

procurón* ADJ (*Méx*) interfering, nosey*.

Procustes NM, **Procusto** NM Procrustes; **lecho de ~** Procrustes' bed.

prodigalidad NF (**a**) (*abundancia*) bounty; richness. (**b**) (*liberalidad*) lavishness, generosity. (**c**) (*derroche*) prodigality; (*despilfarro*) extravagance, wastefulness.

pródigamente ADV (**a**) (*abundantemente*) bountifully; richly. (**b**) (*generosamente*) lavishly. (**c**) (*con prodigalidad*) prodigally; wastefully.

prodigar [1h] **1** VT (*disipar*) to lavish, give lavishly; (*despilfarrar*) (*pey*) to squander; **prodiga las alabanzas** he is lavish in his praise (a of); **nos prodigó sus atenciones** he was very generous in his kindnesses to us.
2 prodigarse VR to be generous with what one has, lay o.s. out to please; to be generous with one's time (o energies etc); (*dejarse ver*) to show o.s.; **no te prodigas que digamos** we don't see much of you to say the least.

prodigio **1** NM prodigy; wonder, marvel; **es un ~ de talento** he is wonderfully talented.
2 ATR: **niño ~** child prodigy.

prodigiosamente ADV prodigiously, marvellously.

prodigioso ADJ prodigious, marvellous.

pródigo **1** ADJ (**a**) (*exuberante*) bountiful; (*rico*) rich; (*fértil*) productive; **~ en** rich in, generous with; **la pródiga naturaleza** bountiful nature.
(**b**) (*liberal*) lavish, generous (*de* with); **ser ~ de sus talentos** to be generous in offering one's talents.
(**c**) (*derrochador*) prodigal; extravagant, wasteful; **hijo ~** prodigal son.
2 NM, **pródiga** (*manirroto*) spendthrift, prodigal.

producción NF (**a**) (*gen*) production; (*producto*) output; yield; **~ bruta** gross production; **~ en cadena** production-line assembly; **~ en serie** mass production. (**b**) (*objeto*) product; (*Cine*) production.

producir [3n] **1** VT (*gen*) to produce; (*hacer*) to make; (*dar, rendir*) to give, yield; (*motivar*) to cause, generate; *cambio etc* to bring about; *im-*

presión to give, cause; (*Fin*) *interés* to bear; **le produjo gran tristeza** it caused her much sadness; **¿qué impresión le produce?** how does it impress you?, what impression do you get from it?; **Ruritania no produce cohetes** Ruritania does not make rockets; **estos factores produjeron la revolución** these factors caused the revolution; **~ en serie** to mass-produce.

2 producirse VR (a) (*fabricarse*) to be produced, be made (*etc*).
(b) (*cambio etc*) to come about; (*dificultad, crisis*) to arise; (*accidente*) to happen, take place; (*disturbio etc*) to break out; **así se produjo la nueva creencia de que ...** in this way there arose the new belief that ...; **en ese momento se produjo una explosión** at that moment there was an explosion; **a no ser que se produzca un cambio** unless a change takes place, unless there is a change.

productividad NF productivity.
productivo ADJ productive; *negocio* profitable; **~ de interés** *bono etc* interest-bearing.
producto NM (*gen*) product (*t Mat*); production; (*Com, Fin: beneficio*) yield, profit; (*ingresos*) proceeds, revenue; **~s** products, (*Agr*) produce; **~ acabado, ~ terminado** finished product; **~s agrícolas** agricultural produce, farm produce; **~ alimenticio** foodstuff; **~s básicos** commodities; **~s de belleza** cosmetics; **~ bruto** gross (national) product; **~s de consumo** consumer goods; **~ derivado** by-product; **~ de desecho** waste product; **~s estancados** goods sold by state monopoly; **~ lácteo** dairy product; **~s de marca** branded goods; **~s perecederos** perishable goods; **~ secundario** by-product.
productor **1** ADJ productive, producing; **clase productora** those who produce; **nación productora** producer nation.
2 NM, **productora¹** NF (a) (*gen*) producer.
(b) (*obrero*) workman, labourer.
(c) (*Cine, TV*) producer; **~ asociado** associate producer; **~ ejecutivo** executive producer.
productora² NF (*Cine*) production company.
produje, produzco *etc* V **producir.**
proemio NM preface, introduction.
proeza NF (a) (*hazaña*) exploit, feat, heroic deed. (b) (*And, Méx*) boast.
Prof(a)., prof(a). ABR *de* **profesor(a).**
profa* NF = **profesora.**
profanación NF desecration.
profanar [1a] VT (*violar*) to desecrate, profane; (*deshonrar*) to defile; **~ la memoria de uno** to blacken the memory of sb.
profano **1** ADJ (a) (*laico*) profane, secular.
(b) (*irrespetuoso*) irreverent.
(c) (*no experto*) lay; (*ignorante*) ignorant.
(d) (*indecente*) indecent, immodest.
2 NM layman; outsider; **soy ~ en música** I'm ignorant of music, I'm a layman in matters of music.
profe* NM = **profesor.**
profecía NF prophecy.
proferir [3i] VT *palabra, sonido* to utter; *indirecta* to drop, throw out; *suspiro* to fetch; *insulto* to hurl, let fly (*contra* at); *maldición* to utter.
profesar [1a] **1** VT (a) *admiración, creencia etc* to profess; to declare.
(b) *materia* to teach; (*Univ*) to hold a chair in.
(c) *profesión* to practise.
2 VI (*Ecl*) to take vows.
profesión NF (a) (*de fe etc*) profession, declaration; avowal; (*Ecl*) taking of vows.
(b) (*carrera*) career; profession; (*vocación*) calling, vocation; '~' (*en formulario*) 'occupation'; **abogado de ~, de ~ abogado** a lawyer by profession; **~ liberal** liberal profession.
profesional **1** ADJ professional; **no ~** non-professional.
2 NMF professional; **~ del amor** prostitute.
profesionalidad NF (*de asunto*) professional nature; (*actitud*) professionalism, professional attitude.
profesionalismo NM professionalism.
profesionalización NF professionalization.
profesionalizar [1f] **1** VT to professionalize.
2 **profesionalizarse** VR to become (o turn) professional.
profesionalmente ADV professionally.
profesionista NMF (*LAm*) professional.
profeso ADJ (*Ecl*) professed.
profesor(a) NM/F (a) (*gen*) teacher; instructor; **~ de esgrima** fencing master; **~ de esquí** ski(ing) instructor; **~ de gimnasia** gym instructor; **~ de natación** swimming instructor; **~ de piano** piano teacher; **~ robot** teaching machine.
(b) (*Escol: gen*) teacher; **~ (de instituto)** schoolmaster, schoolmistress; **~ de biología** biology teacher (o master, mistress).
(c) (*Univ*) (*jefe*) professor; (*subordinado*) lecturer; **~ adjunto** (*kind of*) assistant lecturer, associate professor (*US*); **~ agregado** assistant professor (*US*); *V* **numerario, número; ~ titular** full professor; **es ~ de griego** he is professor of Greek, he is a lecturer in Greek; **nuestros ~es de universidad** our university teachers; **se reunieron los ~es** the staff met, the faculty met (*esp US*).

profesorado NM (a) (*profesión*) teaching profession; teaching, lecturing. (b) (*personas*) teaching staff, faculty (*esp US*). (c) (*cargo*) professorship.
profesoral ADJ professorial; teaching (*atr*).
profesoril ADJ donnish.
profeta NM prophet.
proféticamente ADV prophetically.
profético ADJ prophetic.
profetisa NF prophetess.
profetizar [1f] VTI to prophesy.
profiláctico **1** ADJ prophylactic.
2 NM prophylactic; (*condón*) condom.
profilaxis NF prophylaxis.
prófugo NM fugitive; (*Mil*) deserter; **~ de la justicia** fugitive from justice.
profundamente ADV deeply, profoundly; *dormir* deeply, soundly.
profundidad NF (a) (*hondura*) depth; (*Mat*) depth, height; **la poca ~ del río** the shallowness of the river; **tener una ~ de 30 cm** to be 30 cm deep (o in depth).
(b) **las ~es del océano** the depths of the ocean.
(c) (*fig*) depth, profundity; **investigación en ~** in-depth investigation.
profundímetro NM depth gauge.
profundización NF: **es necesaria una ~ de los conocimientos históricos** we need to deepen our awareness of historical knowledge; **eso significará la ~ de la crisis económica** that will mean a deepening of the economic crisis; **hemos de avanzar en la ~ de la democracia** we must make our country more democratic.
profundizar [1f] **1** VT (a) (*ahondar*) to deepen, make deeper.
(b) (*fig*) *tema* to study in depth, make a profound study of, go deeply into; *misterio* to fathom, get to the bottom of.
2 VI (a) **~ en** to penetrate into, enter.
(b) **~ en** (*fig*) = **1** (b).
profundo ADJ (a) (*hondo*) deep; **poco ~** shallow; **tener 20 cm de ~** to be 20 cm deep (o in depth); **¿cuánto tiene de ~?** how deep is it?
(b) (*fig*) *reverencia* low; *respiración, suspiro, voz* deep; *nota* low, deep; *sueño* deep, sound; *oscuridad* deep; *efecto, impresión etc* deep; *misterio, pensador* profound; **~ conocedor del arte** a very knowledgeable expert in the art; **en lo ~ del alma** in the depths of one's soul.
(c) **en la Francia profunda** in the French heartland; **en el Sussex ~** in deepest Sussex, deep in Sussex.
profusamente ADV profusely; lavishly, extravagantly.
profusión NF profusion; wealth, extravagance.
profuso ADJ (*abundante*) profuse; (*extravagante*) lavish, extravagant.
progenie NF (a) (*hijos*) progeny, offspring; (*pey*) brood. (b) (*familia*) family, lineage.
progenitor NM (*antepasado*) ancestor; (*padre*) father; **~es** (*hum*) parents.
progenitura NF offspring.
progesterona NF progesterone.
programa NM (a) (*gen*) programme; scheme, plan; **~ coloquio** chat-show; **~ concurso** game show; **~ continuo** (*Cine*) continuous showing; **~ doble** (*Cine*) double bill; **~ electoral** electoral manifesto; **~ de estudios** curriculum, syllabus; **~ de fomento de empleo** job creation scheme; **~ piloto** pilot scheme.
(b) (*Inform*) program; **~ de aplicación** application program; **~ fuente** source program; **~ objeto** object program; **~ verificador de ortografía** spell(ing) checker program.
(c) (*Cono Sur*: amorío*) love-affair.
programable ADJ that can be programmed.
programación NF (*Inform*) programming; (*Rad, TV*) programme planning; (*en periódico etc*) programme guide, viewing guide; (*Ferro etc*) scheduling, timetabling.
programado ADJ programmed; *visita etc* planned.
programador(a) NM/F programmer; (*Inform*) programmer; **~ de aplicaciones** applications programmer; **~ de sistemas** systems programmer.
programar [1a] VT (a) (*gen*) to plan; (*detalladamente*) to draw up a programme for; (*Inform*) to programme; (*Ferro etc*) to schedule, timetable; (*TV*) to put on, show.
(b) (*fig*) *futuro etc* to shape, mould, determine.
programático ADJ programmatical.
programería NF (*Inform*): **~ fija** firmware.
progre* **1** ADJ (*marchoso*) trendy; (*Pol*) leftish, liberal; (*en lo sexual etc*) liberal, permissive (in outlook); *mujer* liberated.
2 NMF trendy; lefty* (*pey*); liberal; sexual liberal.
3 NF liberated woman.
progresar [1a] VI to progress, make progress.
progresía NF (*V* **progre**) (a) (*actitud etc*) trendiness; leftish outlook (*pey*), liberal outlook; permissiveness; liberated outlook. (b) **la ~** (*personas*) the trendies; the lefties*, the liberals; the sexual liberals; liberated women.

progresión NF progression; ~ **aritmética** arithmetic progression; ~ **geométrica** geometric progression.

progresista ADJ, NMF progressive.

progresivamente ADV progressively; gradually, little by little.

progresividad NF progressiveness, progressive nature.

progresivo ADJ (*que avanza*) progressive; (*paulatino*) gradual; (*continuo*) continuous; (*Ling*) continuous.

progreso NM progress; advance; ~s progress; **hacer ~s** to progress, make progress, advance.

progubernamental ADJ pro-government.

prohibición NF prohibition (*de* of); ban (*de* on); embargo (*de* on); **levantar la ~ de** to remove the ban on, lift the embargo on.

prohibicionismo NM prohibitionism.

prohibicionista ADJ, NMF prohibitionist.

▼ **prohibir** [3a] [1] VT to prohibit, forbid, stop, ban; ~ **una droga** to prohibit a drug, ban a drug; ~ **algo a uno** to forbid sb sth; ~ **a uno** + *infin* to forbid sb to + *infin*; to stop sb + *ger*, ban sb from + *ger*; 'prohibido fumar' 'no smoking'; **está prohibido fumar aquí** smoking is not allowed here, you can't smoke in here; **queda terminantemente prohibido** + *infin* it is strictly forbidden to + *infin*; **el chico tiene prohibido salir de casa** the boy is not allowed out.

[2] **prohibirse** VR: 'se prohibe fumar' 'no smoking'.

prohibitivo ADJ prohibitive.

prohibitorio ADJ prohibitory.

prohijar [1a] VT to adopt (*t fig*).

prohombre NM outstanding man, great man; leader.

prójima NF (a) (*gen*) woman of dubious character, loose woman. (b) **la ~*** my old woman*, the wife*.

projimidad NF (*And, Carib, Cono Sur*) (*compasión*) fellow feeling, compassion (for one's fellows); (*solidaridad*) solidarity.

prójimo NM (a) (*semejante*) fellow man, fellow creature; (*vecino*) neighbour; **nuestros ~s los animales** our fellow animals. (b) (*: *tío*) so-and-so*, creature.

prolapso NM prolapse.

prole NF offspring; (*pey*) brood, spawn; **padre de numerosa ~** father of a large family.

prolegómeno NM preface, introduction (*t fig*); **los ~s del partido** the early stages of the match; the pre-match ceremonies.

proletariado NM proletariat.

proletario, -a ADJ, NM/F proletarian.

proletarismo NM proletarianism.

proletarizar [1f] VT to proletarianize.

proliferación NF proliferation; ~ **de armas nucleares** proliferation of atomic weapons, spread of nuclear arms; **tratado de no ~** non-proliferation treaty.

proliferar [1a] VI to proliferate.

prolífico ADJ prolific (*en* of).

prolijamente ADV long-windedly; tediously; with an excess of detail.

prolijidad NF prolixity, long-windedness; tediousness; excess of detail.

prolijo ADJ (a) (*extenso*) prolix, long-winded; (*pesado*) tedious; (*muy detallado*) excessively detailed; (*muy meticuloso*) excessively meticulous. (b) (*Cono Sur: incansable*) untiring. (c) (*LAm: pulcro*) smart, neat.

prologar [1h] VT to preface, write an introduction to; **un libro prologado por Ortega** a book with a preface by Ortega.

prólogo [1] NM (a) (*gen*) prologue (*de* to); (*preámbulo*) preface, introduction.

(b) (*fig*) prelude (*de* to).

[2] ATR: **etapa ~** preliminary stage, preparatory stage.

prologuista NMF author of the preface.

prolongación NF (a) (*acto*) prolongation, extension.

(b) (*de carretera etc*) extension; **por la ~ de la Castellana** along the new part of the Castellana, along the extension of the Castellana.

(c) (*Elec*) extension, flex.

prolongado ADJ *sobre, cuarto etc* long; *estancia, reunión etc* lengthy.

prolongar [1h] [1] VT (*alargar*) to prolong, extend; *línea* (*Mat*) to produce; *tubo etc* to make longer, extend; *reunión* to prolong.

[2] **prolongarse** VR to extend; to go on; **la carretera se prolonga más allá del bosque** the road goes on (*o* extends, stretches) beyond the wood; **el paisaje se prolonga hasta lo infinito** the countryside stretches away to infinity; **la sesión se prolongó bastante** the meeting went on long enough, it was a pretty long meeting.

prom. NM ABR *de* **promedio** average, av.

promedial ADJ average.

promedialmente ADV on the average, as an average.

promediar [1b] [1] VT (a) *objeto etc* to divide into two halves, divide equally.

(b) (*Mat etc*) to work out the average of, average (out).

(c) (*tener promedio de*) to average; **la producción promedia 100 barriles diarios** production averages 100 barrels a day.

[2] VI (a) (*mediar*) to mediate (*entre* between).

(b) **promediaba el mes** it was halfway through the month; **antes de ~ el mes** before the month is halfway through.

promedio NM (a) (*gen*) average; **el ~ de asistencia diaria** the average daily attendance; **el ~ es de 35 por 100** the average is 35%.

(b) (*de distancia etc*) middle, mid-point.

promesa NF [1] (*ofrecimiento*) promise; (*compromiso*) pledge; ~ **de matrimonio** promise of marriage; **absolver a uno de su ~** to release sb from his promise; **faltar a una ~** to break a promise, go back on one's word.

[2] ATR: **jugador ~** promising player, bright hope among players.

promesante NMF (*Cono Sur*), **promesero, -a** NM/F (*And, Cono Sur*) pilgrim.

prometedor ADJ, **prometente** ADJ promising.

prometedoramente ADV promisingly.

Prometeo NM Prometheus.

prometer [2a] [1] VT (*ofrecer*) to promise; (*comprometer*) to pledge; ~ **hacer algo** to promise to do sth, (*Ecl*) to take a vow to do sth; **esto promete ser interesante** this promises to be interesting; **esto no nos promete nada bueno** this does not look at all hopeful for us, this promises to be pretty bad for us.

[2] VI (*tener porvenir*) to have promise, show promise; **es un jugador que promete** he's a promising player, he's a player with promise.

[3] **prometerse** VR (a) (*esperar*) to expect, promise o.s.; ~ **algo bueno** to promise o.s. a treat; **prometérselas muy felices** to have high hopes; **nos habíamos prometido algo mejor** we had expected sth better; **se prometía que todo iba a ser fácil** he anticipated that everything was going to be easy.

(b) (*2 personas*) to get engaged; **se prometió con él en abril** she got engaged to him in April.

prometida NF fiancée.

▼ **prometido** [1] ADJ (a) (*ofrecido*) promised. (b) *persona* engaged; **estar ~ con** to be engaged to.

[2] NM (a) (*novio*) fiancé. (b) (*promesa*) promise.

prominencia NF (a) (*elevación*) protuberance; (*hinchazón*) swelling, bump; (*de terreno*) rise. (b) (*fig: esp LAm*) prominence.

prominente ADJ (a) prominent, protuberant; that sticks out. (b) (*fig*) prominent.

promiscuidad NF (a) (*mezcla*) mixture, jumble, confusion; (*confusión*) confused nature. (b) (*ambigüedad*) ambiguity.

promiscuo ADJ (a) (*revuelto*) mixed (up), in disorder; *multitud, reunión* motley. (b) *sentido* ambiguous.

promisión NF: **tierra de ~** land of promise, promised land.

promisorio ADJ (a) *futuro, artista* promising. (b) (*Jur*) promissory.

promoción NF (a) (*ascenso*) promotion, advancement, furtherance; (*Com, Dep etc*) promotion; ~ **inmobiliaria** property development; ~ **de ventas** sales promotion.

(b) (*profesional*) promotion; (*año*) class, year; **la ~ de 1995** the 1995 class; **fue de mi ~** he belonged to the same class as I did, he graduated (*o* got his commission *etc*) at the same time as I did.

(c) (*Com: ganga*) special offer.

promocional ADJ promotional.

promocionar [1a] [1] VT (*Com*) to promote; *persona* to give rapid promotion to, advance rapidly.

[2] **promocionarse** VR to improve o.s., better o.s.

promontorio NM promontory, headland.

promotor(a) [1] NM/F promoter (*t Com*); pioneer; instigator, prime mover; (*Parl: de ley*) sponsor; ~ **inmobiliario** property developer; ~ **de ventas** sales promoter; **el ~ de los disturbios** the instigator of the rioting.

[2] NF property development company.

promovedor(a) NM/F promoter; instigator.

promover [2h] VT (a) *proceso etc* to promote, advance, further; *intereses* to promote; *plan etc* to pioneer; (*Parl*) *ley* to sponsor; *acción* to begin, set on foot, get moving; *pleito* to bring.

(b) *escándalo etc* to cause; *disturbio* to instigate, stir up.

(c) (*ascender*) to promote (*a* to).

promulgación NF promulgation; (*fig*) announcement, publication.

promulgar [1h] VT to promulgate; (*fig*) to proclaim, announce publicly.

pronombre NM pronoun; ~ **personal** personal pronoun; ~ **posesivo** possessive pronoun; ~ **reflexivo** reflexive pronoun.

pronominal ADJ pronominal.

pronominalización NF pronominalization.

pronosticación NF prediction, prognostication, forecasting.

pronosticador(a) NM/F forecaster; (*en carreras*) tipster.

pronosticar [1g] VT to predict, foretell, forecast, prognosticate.

pronóstico NM (a) (*gen*) prediction, forecast; (*presagio*) omen; (*en carreras*) tip; ~ **del tiempo** weather forecast; ~s **para el año nuevo** predictions for the new year, prognostications for the new year.

(b) (*Med*) prognosis; **de ~ leve** slight, not serious; **de ~ reservado** of uncertain gravity, of unknown extent, possibly serious.

prontamente ADV quickly.

➤ LENGUA Y USO: **prohibir:** 1 → 36.3, 37.4 **prometido:** 1b → 51.2

prontito* ADV (a) double-quick; right away. (b) very early, nice and early.

prontitud NF (a) (*presteza*) speed, quickness, promptness. (b) (*viveza*) quickness, sharpness.

pronto ⃞1 ADJ (a) (*rápido*) *respuesta etc* prompt, quick, (*esp Com*) early; *cura* speedy; *servicio* quick, rapid, prompt.
(b) *persona* quick, sharp; **de inteligencia pronta** of keen (o sharp) intelligence; **es ~ en las decisiones** he is quick about taking decisions; **estuvo muy ~ para resolverse** he was quick to make up his mind, he decided on the spot.
(c) (*Cono Sur*) (*dispuesto*) ready; **la comida está pronta** lunch is ready; **estar ~ para** + *infin* to be ready to + *infin*.
(d) (*Cono Sur**: *borracho*) tight*.
⃞2 ADV (a) (*rápidamente*) quickly, promptly, speedily; (*en seguida*) at once, right away; (*dentro de poco*) soon; **cuanto más ~ mejor** the sooner the better; **lo más ~ posible** as soon as possible, as quickly as possible; **tan ~ como** as soon as; **tan ~ ríe como llora** he no sooner laughs than he cries; **tan ~ como me lo traigan** as soon as they bring it to me; **¡~!** hurry!, get on with it!; **al ~** at first; **de ~** suddenly; unexpectedly, without warning; **¡hasta ~!** see you soon!; **por de ~, por lo ~** (*entretanto*) meanwhile, for the present; (*al menos*) at least, anyway; (*al principio*) for a start, for one thing.
(b) (*temprano*) early; **levantarse ~** to get up early; **todavía es ~ para hacerlo** it's too early yet to do it, it's too soon to be doing it yet; **todavía es ~ para decidir si ...** it's early days to decide whether to ...; **iremos a comer un poco ~** we'll go and lunch a bit early.
⃞3 NM (*impulso*) urge, strong impulse; (*ocurrencia*) sudden feeling; **tener ~s de enojo** to be quick-tempered.

prontuario NM handbook, manual, compendium.

pronuncia NF (*Méx*) = **pronunciamiento**.

pronunciación NF pronunciation.

pronunciado ADJ (*marcado*) pronounced, strong; *curva etc* sharp; *rasgo etc* marked, noticeable.

pronunciamiento NM military revolt, military uprising.

▼ **pronunciar** [1b] ⃞1 VT (a) (*Ling*) to pronounce; (*articular*) to make, utter.
(b) (*fig*) *discurso* to make, deliver; *brindis* to propose; **~ palabras de elogio para ...** to say a few words of tribute to ...; **pronunció unas palabras en las que ...** she said that ...
(c) (*Jur*) *sentencia* to pass, pronounce.
▼⃞2 **pronunciarse** VR (a) (*declararse*) to declare o.s., state one's opinion; to make a pronouncement; **~ a favor de** to pronounce in favour of, declare o.s. in favour of; **~ sobre** to pronounce on, make a pronouncement about.
(b) (*Pol*) to revolt, rise, rebel.
(c) (*fig: hacerse más marcado*) to become (more) pronounced.
(d) (*: *soltar la pasta*) to cough up*, fork out*.

pronuncio NM (*And*) = **pronunciamiento**.

propagación NF propagation; (*fig*) propagation, spread(ing), dissemination.

propaganda NF (a) (*Pol etc*) propaganda. (b) (*Com*) advertising; **hacer ~ de un producto** to advertise a product.

propagandista NMF propagandist.

propagandístico ADJ propaganda (*atr*); (*Com*) advertising (*atr*).

propagar [1h] ⃞1 VT (*Bio*) to propagate; (*fig*) to propagate, spread, disseminate.
⃞2 **propagarse** VR (*Bio*) to propagate; (*fig*) to spread, be disseminated.

propalación NF disclosure; dissemination.

propalar [1a] VT (*divulgar*) to divulge, disclose; (*diseminar*) to disseminate; (*publicar*) to publish an account of.

propano NM propane.

propasarse [1a] VR to go too far, overstep the bounds; (*sexualmente*) to take liberties, overstep the bounds of propriety.

propela NF (*Carib, Méx*) (*hélice*) propeller; (*fueraborda*) outboard motor.

propelente NM propellent.

propender [2a] VI: **~ a** to tend towards, incline to; **~ a** + *infin* to tend to + *infin*, have a tendency to + *infin*.

propensión NF inclination, propensity, tendency (*a* to).

▼ **propenso** ADJ: **~ a** inclined to; prone to, subject to; **ser ~ a** + *infin* to be inclined to + *infin*, have a tendency to + *infin*.

propi* NF = **propina**.

propiamente ADV properly; really, exactly; *V* **dicho**.

propiciación NF propitiation.

propiciador(a) NM/F (*LAm*) sponsor.

propiciar [1b] VT (a) (*atraer*) to propitiate, to win over.
(b) (*favorecer*) to favour; to create a favourable atmosphere for; (*provocar*) to cause, give rise to; (*ayudar*) to aid; **tal secreto propicia muchas conjeturas** such secrecy causes a lot of speculation; **hecho que propició que el fuego llegara a ...** a fact which helped the fire to reach ...
(c) (*LAm*) to sponsor.

propiciatorio ADJ propitiatory.

propicio ADJ (*gen*) propitious, auspicious; *momento etc* favourable; *persona* kind, well-disposed, helpful.

propiedad NF (a) (*pertenencia*) possession, ownership; **~ colectiva** collective ownership; **ser de la ~ de** to be the property of, belong to; **una finca de la ~ del marqués** an estate belonging to the marquis; **ceder algo a uno en ~** to transfer sth completely to sb, transfer to sb the full rights over sth.
(b) (*objeto, tierras etc*) property; **~ particular** private property; **una ~** a property, a piece of property; **es ~ del municipio** it is the property of the town.
(c) (*Quím etc*) property; (*fig*) property, attribute.
(d) (*cualidad*: *lo apropiado*) propriety, properness; (*conveniencia*) suitability, appositeness; **discutir la ~ de una palabra** to discuss the appropriateness of a word.
(e) (*cualidad*: *exactitud*) accuracy, faithfulness; (*naturalidad*) naturalness; **lo reproduce con toda ~** he reproduces it faithfully.
(f) (*Com etc*) right(s); **~ industrial** patent rights; patents and trademarks; **~ intelectual**, **~ literaria** copyright; **'es ~'** 'copyright'; **tener una plaza en ~** to have tenure.
(g) **hablar español con ~** (*expresarse bien*) to have a good command of Spanish; (*hablar correctamente*) to speak Spanish correctly, speak correct Spanish.

propietaria NF owner, proprietress.

propietario ⃞1 ADJ proprietary.
⃞2 NM owner, proprietor; (*Agr etc*) landowner.

propina NF (a) tip, gratuity; **dar algo de ~** to give sth extra, give sth as a bonus; **con dos más de ~** (*fig*) with two more into the bargain.
(b) (*Mús*) encore.

propinar [1a] ⃞1 VT (a) **~ a uno** to treat sb to a drink, buy sb a drink.
(b) (*) *golpe* to deal, hit; *paliza* to give; **le propinó una serie de consejos** he gave him a lot of advice, he made him listen to several bits of advice.
⃞2 **propinarse** VR: **~ algo** to treat o.s. to sth.

propincuidad NF propinquity, nearness, proximity.

propincuo ADJ near.

propio ⃞1 ADJ (a) (*de uno*) own, of one's own; **con su propia mano** with his own hand; **lo vi con mis ~s ojos** I saw it with my own eyes; **los rizos son ~s** her curls are natural, her curls are her own; **lo hizo en beneficio ~** he did it for his own good; he did it in his own interest; **tienen casa propia** they have a house of their own; **ahora tiene una bicicleta suya propia** now she has a bicycle of her very own.
(b) (*particular*) peculiar (*de* to); (*especial*) special; (*típico*) characteristic, typical (*de* of); (*suyo ~*) of one's own; **una bebida propia del país** a typical drink of the country; **hace un sol ~ de país mediterráneo** this sunshine is more typical of a Mediterranean country; **fruta propia del tiempo** fruit in season; **eso es muy ~ de él** that's very characteristic of him; **tiene un olor muy ~** it has a very special smell, it has a smell of its own.
(c) (*apropiado*) proper; (*correcto*) correct, suitable, fitting (*para* for); **con los honores que le son ~s** with the honours which are proper (o due) to him; **ese bikini no es ~ para esta playa** that bikini is not suitable for this beach.
(d) (*mismísimo*) selfsame, very; **sus propias palabras** his very words; **me lo dijo el ~ ministro** the minister himself told me so; **yo haría lo ~ que tú** I'd do the same as you, I'd do exactly what you're doing.
(e) *sentido* proper, true; basic.
(f) **de ~** especially, deliberately, expressly; **al ~** (*CAm*) on purpose.
⃞2 NM (*mensajero*) messenger.

proponente NMF proposer.

▼ **proponer** [2q] ⃞1 VT *idea, proyecto etc* to propose, put forward; to suggest; *teoría* to propound; *problema* to pose; to outline, put up (for discussion); *moción* to propose; *candidato* to propose, nominate, put forward; **~ a uno para una beca** to propose sb for a scholarship; **le propuse que fuéramos juntos** I proposed to him that we should go together.
⃞2 **proponerse** VR (a) **~ hacer algo** to propose to do sth, plan to do sth, intend to do sth.
(b) (*pey*) **te has propuesto hacerme perder el tren** you set out deliberately to make me miss the train.

proporción NF (a) (*gen*) proportion; (*Mat etc*) ratio; (*relación*) relationship; (*porcentaje etc*) rate; **proporciones** proportions, (*fig*) dimensions; size, scope; **la ~ entre azules y verdes** the proportion of blues to greens; **en ~ con** in proportion to; **en una ~ de 5 a 1** in a ratio of 5 to 1; **a razón de 5 a 1** at a rate of 5 to 1; **estar fuera de ~** to be out of proportion; **guarda bien las proporciones** it remains in proportion; **esto no guarda ~ con lo otro** this is out of proportion to the rest; **una máquina de gigantescas proporciones** a machine of huge proportions (o size); **se desconocen las proporciones del desastre** the size (o extent, scope) of the disaster is unknown.

(b) (*oportunidad*) chance, opportunity, right moment.
(c) proporciones (*Méx*) wealth; **de proporciones** (*LAm: enorme*) huge, vast; (*Méx: rico*) wealthy.

proporcionadamente ADV proportionately, in proportion.

proporcionado ADJ **(a)** (*que guarda relación*) proportionate (*a* to).
(b) (*adecuado*) medium, middling, just right; **de tamaño ~** of the right size.
(c) *forma* well-proportioned; **bien ~** well proportioned; shapely, of pleasing shape.

proporcional ADJ proportional.

proporcionalmente ADV proportionally.

proporcionar [1a] VT **(a)** (*facilitar*) to give, supply, provide, furnish; to get, obtain (not without difficulty); (*fig*) to lend; **~ dinero a uno** to give sb money, supply sb with money; **esto le proporciona una renta anual de ...** this brings him in a yearly income of ...; **esto proporciona gran encanto a la narración** this lends (*o* gives) great charm to the story; **su tío le proporcionó el puesto** his uncle found him the job, his uncle helped him into the job.
(b) (*adaptar*) to adjust, adapt (*a* to).

proposición NF proposition; proposal; **~ de ley** proposed bill; **~ no de ley** motion.

▼ **propósito** NM purpose; aim, intention, objective; **buenos ~s** good intentions; good resolutions; **¿cuál es su ~?** what is his aim?; **nuestro ~ es de** + *infin* our aim is to + *infin*; **hacer(se) el ~ de** + *infin* to form an intention to + *infin*, set o.s. the aim of + *ger*; **a ~** (*como ADJ*) appropriate, suitable, fitting (*para* for); *observación etc* relevant, apt; **a ~** (*como ADV*) (*adrede*) intentionally, on purpose; (*de paso*) by the way, incidentally; **a ~ de** about, with regard to; **y a ~ de los toros ...** and talking of bulls ..., and while we're on the subject of bulls ...; **eso no viene a ~** that's not relevant, that's nothing to do with it; **de ~** on purpose, purposely, deliberately; **fuera de ~** irrelevant(ly), off the point, out of place; **mudar de ~** to change one's mind; **sin ~ fijo** aimless(ly), pointless(ly).

propuesta NF proposal; **~ salarial** pay offer; **a ~ de** at the proposal of, on the suggestion of.

propuesto PTP *de* **proponer**.

propugnación NF advocacy.

propugnar [1a] VT (*proponer*) to advocate, propose, suggest; (*apoyar*) to defend, support.

propulsado ADJ: **~ a cohete** rocket-driven; **~ a chorro** jet-propelled.

propulsante NM fuel, propellent.

propulsar [1a] VT **(a)** (*Mec*) to drive, propel. **(b)** (*fig*) to promote, encourage.

propulsión NF propulsion; **~ a cohete** rocket propulsion; **~ a chorro, ~ por reacción** jet propulsion; **con ~ a chorro** jet-propelled.

propulsor ① NM (*Téc: combustible*) propellent, fuel; (*motor*) motor, engine.
② NM, **propulsora** NF (*persona*) promoter.

propuse *etc* V **proponer**.

prorrata NF share, quota, prorate (*US*); **a ~** pro rata, proportionately.

prorratear [1a] VT to share out, apportion, distribute proportionately, prorate (*US*); **prorratearemos el dinero** we will share out the money pro rata.

prorrateo NM sharing (in proportion), apportionment; **a ~** pro rata, proportionately.

prórroga NF deferment; (*Com*) extension; (*Mil*) deferment; (*Jur*) stay (of execution), respite; (*Dep*) extra time.

prorrogable ADJ which can be extended.

prorrogación NF deferment, prorogation.

prorrogar [1h] VT *sesión etc* to prorogue, adjourn; *período etc* to extend; (*Mil*) to defer; (*Jur*) to grant a stay of execution to; *decisión etc* to defer, postpone; **prorrogamos una semana las vacaciones** we extended our holiday by a week.

prorrumpir [3a] VI to burst forth, break out; **~ en gritos** to start shouting; **~ en lágrimas** to burst into tears.

prosa NF **(a)** (*Liter*) prose.
(b) (*fig*) prosaic aspects, tedium; **la ~ de la vida** the humdrum aspects of life.
(c) (**: verborrea*) verbiage.
(d) (*Cono Sur: vanidad*) vanity, haughtiness.
(e) (*And, CAm: afectación*) pomposity, affectation.

prosador(a) NM/F **(a)** (*Liter*) prose writer. **(b)** (**: hablador*) chatterbox, great talker.

prosaicamente ADV **(a)** (*gen*) prosaically. **(b)** (*fig*) prosaically; tediously, monotonously.

prosaico ADJ **(a)** (*Liter*) prosaic, prose (*atr*). **(b)** (*fig*) prosaic, prosy; (*monótono*) tedious, monotonous; (*corriente*) ordinary.

prosaísmo NM (*fig*) prosaic nature; tediousness, monotony; ordinariness.

prosapia NF lineage, ancestry; **una familia de (mucha) ~** a (very) illustrious family.

proscenio NM proscenium.

proscribir [3a; PTP **proscrito**] VT to prohibit, ban; *partido etc* to proscribe; *criminal* to outlaw; to banish; *tema etc* to ban; **~ un tema de su conversación** to banish a topic from one's conversation.

proscripción NF prohibition (*de* of), ban (*de* on); proscription; outlawing; banishment.

proscrito ① PTP *de* **proscribir**.
② ADJ (*prohibido*) banned; (*desterrado*) outlawed; proscribed; **un libro ~** a banned book.
③ NM, **proscrita** NF (*exiliado*) exile; (*bandido*) outlaw.

prosecución NF (*continuación*) continuation; (*de demanda*) pressing; (*caza*) pursuit.

proseguir [3d y 3k] ① VT (*continuar*) to continue, carry on, go on with, proceed with; *demanda* to go on with, push, press; *investigación, estudio* to pursue.
② VI **(a) ~ en** (*o* **con**) **una actitud** to continue in one's attitude, maintain one's attitude.
(b) (*condición etc*) to continue, go on; **prosiguió con el cuento** he went on with the story; **¡prosigue!** continue!; **prosigue el mal tiempo** the bad weather continues.

proselitismo NM proselytism.

proselitista ADJ proselytizing.

proselito, -a NM/F proselyte.

prosificación NF (*texto*) prose version; (*acto*) rewriting as prose, turning into prose.

prosificar [1g] VT to rewrite as prose, write a prose version of.

prosista NMF prose writer.

prosodia NF prosody.

prosopopeya NF **(a)** (*Liter*) personification. **(b)** (*fig*) pomposity, affectation.

prospección NF exploration; (*Min*) prospecting (*de* for); **~ de mercados** market research; **~ del petróleo** prospecting for oil, drilling for oil.

prospeccionar [1a] VT *futuro* to look to, examine.

prospectar [1a] VT to survey.

prospectiva NF fortune-telling; futurology.

prospectivo ADJ prospective; future-orientated.

prospecto NM prospectus; (*Com etc*) leaflet, sheet of instructions.

prospector, -ora NM/F prospector; **~ de mercados** market researcher.

prósperamente ADV prosperously; successfully.

prosperar [1a] VI to prosper, thrive, flourish; to be successful; (*idea etc*) to prosper.

prosperidad NF prosperity; success; **en época de ~** in a period of prosperity, in good times; **desear a uno muchas ~s** to wish sb all success.

▼ **próspero** ADJ **(a)** (*rico*) prosperous, thriving, flourishing; (*venturoso*) successful; **¡~ año nuevo!** happy new year! **(b) con próspera fortuna** with good luck, favoured by fortune.

próstata NF prostate.

prosternarse [1a] VR (*postrarse*) to prostrate o.s.; (*humillarse*) to bow low, bow humbly.

prostético ADJ (*Ling, Med*) prosthetic.

prostibulario ADJ brothel (*atr*).

prostíbulo NM brothel.

prostitución NF (*t fig*) prostitution.

prostituir [3g] ① VT *mujer* to prostitute (*t fig*).
② **prostituirse** VR **(a)** to take up prostitution, become a prostitute.
(b) (*fig*) to prostitute o.s.

prostituta NF prostitute; **~ callejera** streetwalker.

prostituto NM male prostitute.

prosudo ADJ (*And, Cono Sur*) affected, pompous.

protagónico ADJ *papel* leading, major.

protagonismo NM **(a)** (*papel*) leading role; (*liderazgo*) leadership; **conceder el ~ al pueblo** to grant power to the people. **(b)** (*importancia*) prominence; (*iniciativa*) initiative; (*en sociedad*) taking an active part, being socially active; **afán de ~** urge to be in the limelight; **tuvo poco ~** he made little showing; he did not have much to do; **el tema adquiere gran ~ en este texto** the theme becomes a major one in this text. **(c)** (*defensa*) defence; (*apoyo*) support.

protagonista ① ADJ important, leading, influential.
② NMF protagonist; (*Liter etc, frec*) main character; hero, heroine.

protagonístico ADJ leading; **papel ~** leading role.

protagonizar [1f] VT **(a)** (*Teat etc*) to take the chief role in, play the lead in. **(b)** (*proceso, rebelión* to lead; *manifestación* to stage; *accidente* to figure in, be concerned in; **el mes ha estado protagonizado por ...** the month has been notable for ...; **una entrevista protagonizada por X** an interview whose subject was X.

proteaginosa NF protein product.

protección NF protection; **~ civil** civil defence; **~ de datos** data protection.

proteccionismo NM protectionism.

proteccionista ① ADJ (*Esp*) *política* protectionist; *impuesto etc* protec-

▶ LENGUA Y USO: **propósito → 35.2, 45.4   próspero: a → 50.2**

tive.

[2] NMF protectionist.

protector [1] ADJ protective, protecting.

[2] NM, **protectora** NF protector; (*Liter etc*) patron; (*de tradición etc*) guardian; **~ del pueblo** (*Esp*) ombudsman.

[3] NM: **~ solar** suntan oil.

protectorado NM protectorate.

proteger [2c] VT (*resguardar*) to protect (*contra* against, *de* from); (*escudar*) to shield; (*defender*) to defend; *artista, autor etc* to act as patron to; **~ contra grabación** (*Inform*) to write protect.

protegida NF protégée.

protegido [1] ADJ: **especie protegida** protected species.

[2] NM protégé.

proteico ADJ protean; many-sided, diverse.

proteína NF protein.

proteínico ADJ protein (*atr*); **contenido ~** protein content.

protervidad NF wickedness, perversity.

protervo ADJ wicked, perverse.

protésico [1] ADJ *aparato, miembro, técnica* prosthetic.

[2] NM, **protésica** NF prosthetist, limb-fitter; **~ dental** dental technician.

prótesis NF INVAR prosthesis (*Tec*); (*brazo, pierna*) artificial limb; **~ de cadera** artificial hip; **~ dental** false tooth; **~ de mama** breast implant; **~ de silicona** silicone implant.

protesta NF (a) (*queja*) protest; grumble; **bajo ~** under protest. (b) (*de inocencia etc*) protestation; **hacer ~s de lealtad** to protest one's loyalty.

protestación NF protestation; **~ de lealtad** protestation of loyalty, declaration of loyalty; **~ de fe** profession of faith.

protestante ADJ, NMF Protestant.

protestantismo NM Protestantism.

▼ **protestar** [1a] [1] VT (a) *inocencia etc* to protest, declare, avow; *fe* to profess.

(b) (*Fin*) **cheque protestado por falta de fondos** cheque referred to drawer (*R/D*).

▼[2] VI (a) (*quejarse*) to protest (*contra, de* about, against; *de que* that); (*objetar*) to object, remonstrate; **~ contra una demora** to protest about a delay; **¡protesto contra esa observación!** I resent that!, I object to that remark!

(b) **~ de** *inocencia etc* to protest.

protesto NM (*LAm*) protest.

protestón* (*pey*) [1] ADJ given to protesting, perpetually moaning.

[2] NM, **protestona** NF perpetual moaner, permanent protester.

proto... PREF proto...

protocolario ADJ (a) (*exigido por el protocolo*) established by protocol, required by protocol. (b) (*fig: ceremonial*) formal.

protocolo NM (a) (*Pol*) protocol (*t Inform*). (b) (*fig*) protocol, social etiquette, convention. (c) (*fig*) **sin ~s** informal(ly); without formalities, without a lot of fuss. (d) (*Med*) medical record.

protón NM proton.

protoplasma NM protoplasm.

prototipo NM prototype.

protuberancia NF protuberance; (*fig: en estadística etc*) bulge.

protuberante ADJ protuberant.

prov. NF ABR *de* **provincia** province, prov.

provecho NM advantage, benefit, profit; (*Fin*) profit; **de ~** *negocio* profitable; *actividad* useful; *persona* worthy, honest; **¡buen ~!** *phrase used to those at table, hoping they will enjoy their meal*; **¡buen ~ le haga!** and much good may it do him!; **en ~ de** to the benefit of; **en ~ propio** to one's own advantage, for one's own profit; **ese alimento no le hace ~ a uno** that food(stuff) doesn't do one any good; **sacar ~ de algo** to benefit from sth, profit by (*o* from) sth.

provechosamente ADV advantageously, beneficially, profitably.

provechoso ADJ advantageous, beneficial, profitable; useful; (*Fin*) profitable.

provecto ADJ aged; **de edad provecta** elderly.

proveedor(a) NM/F supplier, purveyor; dealer; **'P~es de la Real Casa'** 'By appointment to His (*o* Her) Majesty'; **consulte a su ~ habitual** consult your usual dealer.

proveeduría NF (*Cono Sur*) grocer's, grocery.

proveer [2e; PTP **provisto** y **proveído**] [1] VT (a) (*suministrar*) to provide, supply, furnish (*de* with).

(b) (*disponer*) to provide, get ready; **~ todo lo necesario** to provide all that is necessary (*para* for).

(c) *vacante* to fill.

(d) *negocio* to transact, dispatch.

(e) (*Jur*) to decree.

[2] VI: **~ a** to provide for; **~ a las necesidades de uno** to provide for sb's wants; **~ a un vicio de uno** to pander to sb's vice.

[3] **proveerse** VR: **~ de** to provide o.s. with.

proveniente ADJ: **~ de** coming from.

provenir [3r] VI: **~ de** to come from, arise from, stem from; **esto**

proviene de no haberlo curado antes this comes from (*o* is due to) not having treated it earlier.

Provenza NF Provence.

provenzal [1] ADJ, NMF Provençal.

[2] NM (*Ling*) Provençal.

proverbial ADJ (*lit, fig*) proverbial.

proverbialmente ADV proverbially.

proverbio NM proverb.

próvidamente ADV providently.

provida, pro-vida ADJ INVAR pro-life.

providencia NF (a) (*cualidad*) foresight; (*prevención*) forethought, providence; (**Divina**) **P~** (Divine) Providence.

(b) (*precauciones*) **~s** measures, steps; **dictar** (*o* **tomar**) **~s para +** *infin* to take steps to + *infin*.

(c) (*Jur*) ruling, decision.

providencial ADJ providential.

providencialmente ADV providentially.

providente ADJ, **próvido** ADJ provident.

provincia NF province; **las P~s Vascongadas** the Basque Provinces, the Basque Country; **un pueblo de ~(s)** a provincial town, a country town.

ⓘ │ PROVINCIA │

Spain is divided into 55 administrative **provincias**, *including the islands and territories in North Africa. Each one has a* **capital de provincia** *which generally has the same name as the province itself.* **Provincias** *are grouped by geography, history and culture into* **comunidades autónomas**. *Most* **comunidades autónomas** *are made up of two or more provinces (for example the* **comunidad autónoma** *of* **Aragón** *includes the provinces of* **Huesca, Zaragoza** *and* **Teruel**), *though some consist of just one province of the same name (e.g.* **Asturias** *and* **Navarra**).

⇨ *See also* │ COMUNIDAD AUTÓNOMA │

---

provincial [1] ADJ provincial.

[2] NM, **provinciala** NF (*Ecl*) provincial.

provincialismo NM (*Ling*) provincialism, dialect(al) word (*o* phrase etc).

provincianismo NM provincialism; **~ de cortas luces, ~ de vía estrecha** narrow provincialism, deadening provincialism.

provinciano [1] ADJ (a) (*gen, t pey*) provincial; (*rural*) country (*atr*).

(b) (*vasco*) Basque, of the Basque Provinces.

[2] NM, **provinciana** NF (*V ADJ* (a)) (a) provincial; country dweller.

(b) (*vasco*) Basque.

proviniente ADJ: **~ de** coming from, arising out of.

provisión NF (a) (*acto*) provision.

(b) (*suministro*) provision, supply; **provisiones** provisions, supplies, stores.

(c) (*Fin*) **~ de fondos** financial cover; **cheque sin ~** bad cheque.

(d) (*medida*) (precautionary) measure, step.

provisional ADJ provisional.

provisionalidad NF provisional nature, temporary character.

provisionalmente ADV provisionally.

provisionar [1a] VT *deuda* to cover, to make bad-debt provision for.

provisorio ADJ (*LAm*) provisional.

provista NF (*Cono Sur*) provisions, supplies.

provisto [1] PTP *de* **proveer**. [2] ADV: **~ de** provided with, supplied with; having, possessing.

provocación NF provocation.

provocador [1] ADJ (*hostil*) provocative; (*irritante*) provoking.

[2] NM, **provocadora** NF trouble-maker.

▼ **provocar** [1g] [1] VT (a) *persona* to provoke; (*enojar*) to rouse, stir up (to anger etc); (*tentar*) to tempt, invite; **~ a uno a cólera** (*o* **indignación**) to rouse sb to fury; **~ a uno a lástima** to move sb to pity; **~ a uno a risa** to make sb laugh; **el mar provoca a bañarse** the sea tempts one to bathe, the sea invites one to go for a swim.

▼(b) *cambio etc* to bring about, lead to; *proceso* to promote; *explosión, protesta, guerra etc* to cause, spark off; *fuego* to cause, start (deliberately); *parto* to induce, bring on.

(c) (*mujer*) to rouse, stir, stimulate (sexually).

(d) (*LAm: gustar, apetecer*) **¿te provoca un café?** would you like some coffee?, do you fancy a coffee?; **¿qué le provoca?** what would you like?, what do you fancy?; **no me provoca la idea** the idea doesn't appeal to me, I don't fancy the idea; **¿por qué no vas? — no me provoca** why aren't you going? — I don't feel like it; **no me provoca estudiar hoy** I'm not in the mood for (*o* I don't feel like) studying today.

[2] VI (*: *vomitar*) to be sick.

provocativo ADJ (a) (*gen*) provocative, provoking.

(b) *mujer* provocative, sexually stimulating; *vestido* daring, immodest; *ademán, risa etc* inviting.

proxeneta NMF pimp, procurer, (*f*) procuress.

proxenetismo NM procuring.

---

próximamente ADV shortly, soon.
proximidad NF nearness, closeness, proximity.
próximo ADJ (a) (*cercano*) near, close; neighbouring; *pariente* close; **en fecha próxima** soon, at an early date; **estar ~ a** to be close to, be near; **estar ~ a** + *infin* to be on the point of + *ger*, be about to + *infin*.
(b) (*anterior, siguiente*) next; **el mes ~** next month; **el mes ~ pasado** last month; **el ~ 5 de junio** on 5th June next; **bajarán en la próxima** they will get off at the next stop.
proyección NF (a) (*acto, parte*) projection.
(b) (*Cine etc: acto*) showing; **el tiempo de ~ es de 35 minutos** the showing lasts 35 minutes, the film runs for 35 minutes.
(c) (*Cine, Fot: diapositiva*) slide, transparency.
(d) (*fig*) hold, sway, influence; **la ~ de los periódicos sobre la sociedad** the hold of newspapers over society, the influence which newspapers have on society.
proyeccionista NMF projectionist.
proyectable ADJ: **asiento ~** (*Aer*) ejector seat.
proyectar [1a] VT (a) *objeto* to hurl, throw; *luz* to cast, shed, project; *chorro, líquido etc* to send out, give out; to direct (*hacia* at); *sombra* to cast.
(b) (*Cine, Fot*) to project; to screen, show.
(c) (*Mat etc*) to project.
(d) (*Arquit etc*) to plan; (*Mec*) to design; **está proyectado para** + *infin* it is designed to + *infin*.
(e) **~** + *infin* to plan to + *infin*.
proyectil NM projectile, missile; (*Mil: de cañón*) shell, (*con cohete*) missile; **~ de aire a aire** air-to-air missile; **~ balístico intercontinental** intercontinental ballistic missile; **~ (tele)dirigido** guided missile; **~ de iluminación** flare, rocket.
proyectista NMF planner; (*Aer, Aut, Téc etc*) designer; (*delineante*) draughtsman; (*Cine*) projectionist.
proyecto NM (a) (*Téc*) plan, design; project; (*Fin*) detailed estimate.
(b) (*fig*) plan; scheme, project; **~ piloto** pilot scheme; **cambiar de ~** to change one's plans; **tener ~s para** to have plans for; **tener algo en ~** to be planning sth; **tener sus ~s sobre algo** to have designs on sth.
(c) (*Parl*) **~ de declaración** draft declaration; **~ de ley** bill.
proyector NM (a) (*Cine*) projector; **~ de diapositivas** slide projector.
(b) (*Mil etc*) searchlight; (*Teat*) spotlight; **~ antiniebla** foglamp.
prudencia NF wisdom, prudence; care; soundness, sound judgement.
prudencial ADJ (a) (*adecuado*) prudential; (*razonable*) sensible; **tras un intervalo ~** after a decent interval, after a reasonable time.
(b) *cantidad, distancia etc* roughly correct, more or less correctly guessed.
prudenciarse [1b] VR (*And, CAm, Méx*) (*ser cauteloso*) to be cautious; (*contenerse*) to hold back, control o.s.
▼ **prudente** ADJ sensible, wise, prudent; *conductor etc* careful; *decisión etc* sensible, judicious, sound.
prudentemente ADV sensibly, wisely, prudently; carefully; judiciously, soundly.
prueba NF (a) (*gen, t Mat*) proof; (*Jur*) proof, evidence; exhibit; **~s** (*Jur*) documents; **~ documental** documentary evidence; **~ indiciaria** circumstantial proof; **~ palpable** clear proof; **a la ~ me remito** the proof of the pudding is in the eating, the event will show; **en ~ de** in proof of; **en ~ de lo cual** in proof whereof; **en ~ de que no es así te lo ofrezco gratis** to prove that it isn't so I offer it to you free; **¿tiene Vd ~ de ello?** can you prove it?; do you have proof?
(b) (*fig: indicio*) proof, sign, token; **es buena ~** it's a good sign; **sin dar la menor ~ de ello** without giving the faintest sign of it.
(c) (*Téc etc*) test, trial; (*Quím etc*) experiment; **~s** (*Aer, Aut, Náut*) trials; **~ de acceso** entrance test; **~ de aptitud** aptitude test; **~ de campo** field trial; **~ por carretera** road trials; **~ clínica** clinical test; **~ de embarazo** pregnancy test; **~ de fuego** (*fig*) acid test; **~ de imagen, ~ de luces, ~ de pantalla** screen test; **~ de inteligencia** intelligence test; **~ nuclear** nuclear test; **~ de selectividad** entrance examination; **~ de tornasol** litmus test; **a ~** (*Téc*) on trial; (*Com*) on approval, on trial; **libertad a ~** (release on) probation; **ingresar con un nombramiento a ~** to take up a post for a probationary period; to come in with a probationary appointment; **a ~ de** proof against; **a ~ de agua** waterproof; **a ~ de bala** bulletproof; **a ~ de bombas** bombproof, shellproof; **a ~ de choques** shockproof; **a ~ de fallo** with a failsafe device; **a ~ de grasa** greaseproof; **a ~ de impericia, a toda ~** foolproof; **a ~ de ladrones** burglar-proof; **a ~ de lluvia** rainproof; **a ~ de ruidos** soundproof; **a ~ de viento** windproof; **poner a ~, someter a ~** to test, put to the test, try out; **poner a ~ los nervios de uno** to test sb's nerves; **poner a ~ la paciencia de uno** to try sb's patience; **hacer ~ de** to test, put to the test.
(d) (*de comida etc: acto*) testing, sampling; (*cantidad*) taste, sample.
(e) (*Cos*) fitting, trying on; **sala de ~s** fitting room.
(f) (*Tip*) **~s** proofs; **primeras ~s** first proofs, galleys; **~s de planas** page-proofs.

(g) (*Fot*) proof, print; **~ negativa** negative; **~ positiva** positive, print.
(h) (*Dep*) event; race; **~s** trials; **~ clasificatoria, ~ eliminatoria** heat; **~ de descenso** downhill run; **~ de obstáculos** obstacle race; **~ de relevos** relay race; **~ contra reloj** time trial; **~ de resistencia** endurance test; **~ de vallas** hurdles, hurdles race.
(i) (*LAm*) circus act; (*And: función*) circus show, performance.
(j) (*Méx*) examination.
pruebista NMF (a) (*LAm*) (*acróbata*) acrobat; (*funámbulo*) tightrope walker; (*prestidigitador*) conjurer; (*malabarista*) juggler; (*contorsionista*) contortionist. (b) (*Cono Sur: de libros*) proofreader.
prurito NM (a) (*Med*) itch, pruritis.
(b) (*fig*) itch, urge; **tener el ~ de** + *infin* to have the urge to + *infin*; **por un ~ de exactitud** out of an excessive desire for accuracy, because of his urge (*o* eagerness) to get everything just right.
Prusia NF Prussia.
prusiano, -a ADJ, NM/F Prussian.
PS NM (*Pol gen*) ABR *de* **Partido Socialista**; *p.ej.* **PSA** ABR *de* **Partido Socialista Argentino**; **PST** ABR *de* **Partido Socialista de los Trabajadores** *etc.*
pse..., psi...: *the Academy recommends the spellings* **se..., si...**; *all forms are pronounced* [se-, si-].
PSE-EE NM (*Esp*) ABR **Partido Socialista de Euskadi-Euskadiko Eskerra**.
psefología NF psephology.
psefólogo, -a NM psephologist.
pseudocientífico ADJ pseudo-scientific.
psic... PREF, **psiqu...** PREF psych...
psicoactivo ADJ psychoactive.
psicoafectivo ADJ mental, psychological.
psicoanálisis NM psychoanalysis.
psicoanalista NMF psychoanalyst.
psicoanalítico ADJ psychoanalytic(al); **diván ~** psychiatrist's couch.
psicoanalizar [1f] VT to psychoanalyse.
psicocirugía NF psychosurgery.
psicodélico [1] ADJ psychedelic.
[2] NM light show.
psicodepresor NM depressant
psicodinámica NF psychodynamics.
psicodrama NM psychodrama.
psicoestimulante NM (mental) stimulant.
psicofármaco NM psychotropic drug, mood-altering drug.
psicolingüística NF psycholinguistics.
psicolingüístico ADJ psycholinguistic.
psicología NF psychology.
psicológicamente ADV psychologically.
psicológico ADJ psychological.
psicólogo, -a NM/F psychologist.
psicomotricidad NF psychomotor skills *pl*.
psiconeurosis NF INVAR psychoneurosis.
psicópata NMF psychopath.
psicopático ADJ psychopathic.
psicopatología NF psychopathology.
psicopedagogo, -a NM/F educational psychologist.
psicoquinesis NF psychokinesis.
psicoquinético ADJ psychokinetic.
psicosis NF INVAR psychosis; **~ puerperal** puerperal psychosis.
psicosomático ADJ psychosomatic.
psicotécnico ADJ: **test ~, prueba psicotécnica** response test.
psicoterapeuta NMF psychotherapist.
psicoterapia NF psychotherapy.
psicótico, -a ADJ, NM/F psychotic.
psicotrópico ADJ psychotropic, psychoactive.
Psique NF Psyche.
psique NF psyche.
psiquiatra, psiquíatra NMF psychiatrist.
psiquiatría NF psychiatry.
psiquiátrico [1] ADJ psychiatric.
[2] NM mental hospital; psychiatric ward.
psíquico ADJ psychic(al); **enfermedades psíquicas** mental illnesses, psychological illnesses.
psitacosis NF psittacosis.
PSOE [pe'soe] NM (*Esp Pol*) ABR *de* **Partido Socialista Obrero Español**.

┌─ *PSOE* ─────────────────────────────┐

i The *Partido Socialista Obrero Español* is Spain's oldest political party, dating from 1879. It was the largest element of the **Frente Popular** (FP), the left-wing coalition that won the 1936 elections. Like all political parties, it was banned under Franco and its leadership had to remain in hiding until going into exile in France in 1952. After the restoration of democracy and the legalization of political parties in 1977, the PSOE went on to become the prime political mover in the transition to democracy,

► LENGUA Y USO: **prudente** → 29.2

winning the elections of 1982, 1986, 1989 and 1993 under the leadership of Felipe González. However, in the 1990s its image became seriously tarnished by various scandals involving corruption, nepotism and civil rights abuses in the fight against **ETA** *and it lost to the* **PP** *in the 1996 elections.*

psoriasis NF INVAR psoriasis.

PSS NF ABR *de* **prestación social sustitutoria** *non-military alternative to national service; see also* INSUMISO, MILI

PSUM NM (*Méx*) ABR *de* **Partido Socialista Unificado de México.**

Pta. ABR *de* **Punta** Point, Pt.

pta. (a) (*Fin*) ABR *de* **peseta.** (b) ABR *de* **presidenta.**

ptas. ABR *de* **pesetas.**

PTB NM (*And*) ABR *de* **Producto Territorial Bruto** gross domestic product, GDP.

pte ABR *de* **presidente.**

pterodáctilo [te-] NM pterodactyl.

ptmo. (*Com*) ABR *de* **préstamo.**

ptomaína [to-] NF ptomaine.

ptomaínico [to-] ADJ: **envenenamiento ~** ptomaine poisoning.

pts. ABR *de* **pesetas.**

púa NF (a) (*punta*) sharp point; (*Bot, Zool*) prickle, spike, spine; (*de erizo*) quill; (*de peine*) tooth; (*de tenedor*) prong, tine; (*de gancho, alambre*) barb; (*Carib, Cono Sur: de gallo*) spur; (*Mús*) plectrum; (*Mús*) gramophone needle, phonograph needle (*US*). (b) (*Bot*) graft, cutting. (c) (‡) one peseta.

puaf* INTERJ yuck!*

puazo NM (*Argentina*) stab.

pub [pub, paß] NM, PL **pubs** [pub, paß] bar *m.*

púber ① ADJ adolescent.
② NMF adolescent child, child approaching puberty.

pubertad NF puberty.

pubescencia NF pubescence.

pubescente ADJ pubescent.

púbico ADJ pubic.

pubis NM pubis.

publicación NF publication.

públicamente ADV publicly.

publicar [1g] VT (*gen*) to publish; (*difundir*) to publicize; *secreto etc* to make public, disclose, divulge.

publicidad NF (a) (*gen*) publicity; **dar ~ a** to publicize, give publicity to.
(b) (*Com*) advertising; **~ directa** direct advertising; **~ estática** (advertising on) hoardings; **~ de lanzamiento** advance publicity, advertising campaign to launch a product; **hacer ~ por** to advertise; **se ha prohibido la ~ de cigarrillos** cigarette advertising has been banned.

publicista NMF publicist.

publicitar [1a] VT to publicize; (*Com*) to advertise.

publicitario ① ADJ advertising (*atr*); publicity (*atr*).
② NM advertising man, advertising agent.

público ① ADJ public; **hacer ~** to publish, make public; to publicize; to disclose.
② NM (*concurrencia*) public; (*Mús, Teat etc*) audience; (*Dep*) spectators, crowd; (*de café etc*) clients, clientèle, patrons; (*de periódico*) readers, readership; **hay poco ~** there aren't many people; **el ~ que se paseaba por la calle** the people who were strolling in the street; **hubo un ~ de 800** there was a crowd (*o* gathering, audience *etc*) of 800; **el gran ~** the general public; **en ~** in public.

public relations [pußlıkre'laʃonz] NMF INVAR public relations man/woman.

publirreportaje NM feature, special report.

pucará NF (*LAm Arqueol*) pre-Columbian fort.

pucelano* ① ADJ of (*o* from) Valladolid.
② NM, **pucelana** NF native (*o* inhabitant) of Valladolid.

pucha¹ NF (a) (*Carib*) bouquet. (b) (*Méx*) ring-shaped loaf.

pucha²* NF (*LAm: euf = puta*); **¡(la) ~!** (*sorpresa*) well I'm damned (*o* blowed*)!; (*irritación*) drat!

puchana NF (*Cono Sur*) broom.

puchar‡ [1a] VT to speak, say.

puchera NF stew.

pucherazo* NM (*Esp*) electoral fiddle*; **dar ~** to rig an election, fiddle the votes*.

puchero NM (a) (*Culin: olla*) cooking-pot. (b) (*Culin: guiso*) stew; (*fig*) food, daily bread; **apenas gana para el ~** he hardly earns enough to eat. (c) (*: *mueca*) pout; **hacer ~s** to pout, make a face, screw up one's face.

puches NMPL (*Esp*) porridge, gruel.

puchica‡ INTERJ (*And*) blast!*, damn!

puchito, -a* NM/F (*Cono Sur*) youngest child.

pucho* NM (a) (*colilla*) (*de cigarrillo*) fag-end‡; (*de puro*) cigar stub; (*cigarrillo*) fag‡.
(b) (*LAm*) (*resto*) scrap, left-over(s); dregs; (*Cos*) remnant; (*Fin*) coppers, small change; (*fig: nimiedad*) trifle, mere nothing; **a ~s** in dribs and drabs.
(c) (*And, Cono Sur*) youngest child.

puco NM (*And, Cono Sur*) earthenware bowl.

pude *etc* V **poder.**

pudendo ① ADJ: **partes pudendas** pudenda, private parts.
② NM (*pene*) penis.

pudibundez NF false modesty, affected modesty; excess of modesty.

pudibundo ADJ affectedly modest; over-shy (*about sexual matters*), excessively modest; prudish.

pudicicia NF modesty; chastity.

púdico ADJ modest; chaste.

pudiendo V **poder.**

pudiente ADJ (*rico*) wealthy, well-to-do; (*poderoso*) powerful, influential; **las gentes menos ~s** the less well-off.

pudín NM pudding.

pudinga NF puddingstone.

pudo *etc* V **poder.**

pudor NM (a) (*recato*) modesty; (*timidez*) shyness; (*vergüenza*) (sense of) shame, (sense of) decency; **con ~** modestly; discreetly; **tenía ~ de confesarlo** he was ashamed to confess it. (b) (*castidad*) chastity, virtue; **atentado al ~** indecent assault.

pudorosamente ADV (a) (*recatadamente*) modestly; shyly. (b) (*virtuosamente*) chastely, virtuously.

pudoroso ADJ (a) (*recatado*) modest; shy. (b) (*casto*) chaste, virtuous.

pudrición NF (a) (*proceso*) rotting. (b) (*lo podrido*) rot, rottenness; **~ seca** dry rot.

pudridero NM rubbish heap, midden.

pudrimiento NM (a) (*proceso*) rotting. (b) (*lo podrido*) rot, rottenness.

pudrir [3a] ① VT (a) (*descomponer*) to rot.
(b) (*: *molestar*) to upset, vex, annoy, exasperate.
② VI (*fig: haber muerto*) to rot, be dead and buried.
③ **pudrirse** VR (a) (*corromperse*) to rot, decay; (*descomponerse*) to rot away.
(b) (*fig*) to rot, languish; **mientras se pudría en la cárcel** while he was languishing in jail; **te vas a ~ de aburrimiento** you'll die of boredom; **¡que se pudra!** let him rot!; **¡ahí (o así) te pudras!** (*Esp‡*) get away!*, not on your nelly!‡.

pueblada NF (*LAm*) (*motín*) riot; (*sublevación*) revolt, uprising; (*Cono Sur: multitud*) (*gen*) mob; (*de obreros*) gathering of workers.

pueblerino ① ADJ countrified, small-town (*atr*); *persona* rustic, provincial.
② NM, **pueblerina** NF rustic, country person, provincial.

pueblero (*LAm*) ① ADJ town (*atr*), city (*atr*).
② NM townsman, city dweller; (*pey*) city slicker.

pueblo NM (a) (*Pol etc*) people, nation; **~ elegido** chosen people; **el ~ español** the Spanish people; **hombre del ~** man of the people; **la voluntad del ~** the nation's will; **hacer un llamamiento al ~** to call on the people, call on the nation.
(b) (*plebe*) common people, lower orders; **~ de mala muerte** (*gente*) dregs of society.
(c) (*aldea*) village; (*población*) small town, country town; **~ fantasma** ghost town; **~ joven** (*LAm: euf*) shanty-town.

puedo *etc* V **poder.**

puente ① NM (a) (*lit, fig*) bridge; **~ aéreo** (*en crisis*) airlift; (*servicio*) airbus service, shuttle (service); **~ atirantado** suspension bridge; **~ de barcas**, **~ de pontones** pontoon bridge; **~ colgante** suspension bridge; **~ giratorio** swing bridge; **~ grúa** bridge crane; **~ levadizo** drawbridge; **~ de peaje** tollbridge; **~ para peatones** footbridge; **tender un ~** (*fig*) to offer a compromise, go part-way to meet somebody's wishes; **tender ~s de plata a uno** to make it as easy as possible for sb.
(b) (*fig: de gafas, Mús etc*) bridge.
(c) (*Náut: t ~ de mando*) bridge; (*cubierta*) deck; **~ del timón** wheelhouse.
(d) (*fig*) gap; hiatus; **habrá que salvar el ~ de una cosecha a otra** something will have to be done to fill the gap between one harvest and the next.
(e) **hacer ~*** to take a long weekend, take extra days off work between two public holidays.
(f) (*And*) collarbone.
② ATR temporary; provisional, transitional; that bridges the gap; **crédito ~**, **préstamo ~** bridging loan; **gabinete ~** caretaker government; **hombre ~** linkman; intermediary; **solución ~** temporary solution.

 HACER PUENTE

ⓘ *When a public holiday in Spain falls on a Tuesday or Thursday it is common practice for employers to make the Monday or Friday a holiday as well and to give everyone a four-day weekend. This is known as* **hacer puente.** *When a named public holiday such as the* **Día de la**

Constitución falls on a Tuesday or a Thursday, people refer to the whole holiday period as e.g. the puente de la Constitución.

puentear* [1a] ① VT (a) (*autoridad etc*) to bypass, pass over; **le puentearon con el ascenso** they passed him over for the promotion. (b) (*Fin*) to take out a bridging loan on.
② VI to jump a grade (in the hierarchy), go up to the grade next but one.

puenting ['pwentin] NM bungee jumping (*from a bridge*).

puerca NF (a) (*cerda*) sow. (b) (*****: *puta*) slut. (c) (*cochinilla*) woodlouse.

puercada NF (*And, CAm, Carib*) (*acto*) dirty trick; (*dicho*) obscene remark.

puerco ① NM (a) (*cerdo*) pig, hog (*US*); (*jabalí*) wild boar; **~ espín** porcupine; **~ jabalí, ~ montés, ~ salvaje** wild boar, wild pig; **~ de mar** porpoise; **~ marino** dolphin; *V* **Martín**.
(b) (*****) (*sinvergüenza*) pig; (*canalla*) swine*, rotter*.
② ADJ (a) (*sucio*) dirty, filthy.
(b) (*asqueroso*) nasty, disgusting; (*grosero*) coarse.
(c) (*canallesco*) vile, rotten*, mean.

puericia NF boyhood.

puericultor(a) NM/F (*t médico* **~**) paediatrician.

puericultura NF paediatrics.

pueril ADJ (a) (*gen*) childish, child (*atr*); **edad ~** childhood. (b) (*pey*) puerile, childish.

puerilidad NF puerility, childishness.

puerperal ADJ puerperal.

puerqueza NF (*Cono Sur*) (a) (*objeto*) dirty thing, filthy object. (b) (*trampa*) dirty trick. (c) (*Zool*) bug, creepy-crawly*.

puerro NM leek.

puerta NF door; gate; doorway; (*esp fig*) gateway (*de* to); (*Aer*) gate; (*Inform*) port, gate; (*Dep*) goal; **~ accesoria** side door; **~ de artistas** stage door; **~ (de) corredera, ~ deslizante** sliding door; **~ cortafuegos** fire-door; **~ de cristales** glass door; **~ chica** side door, private door; **entrar por la ~ chica*** to get in by the back door; **~ de embarque** boarding gate; **~ excusada** private door, side door; **~ giratoria** revolving door; **~ oscilante** swing door; **~ (de transmisión en) paralelo** (*Inform*) parallel port; **~ principal** front door; main entrance; **~ (de transmisión en) serie** (*Inform*) serial port; **~ de servicio** tradesmen's entrance; **~ trasera** back door; **~ ventana** French window; **~ vidriera** glass door, French window; **a ~ cerrada** behind closed doors; **a las ~s de la muerte** at death's door; **tenemos la guerra a las ~s** war is upon us, the threat of war is imminent; **coche de 2 ~s** (*t un dos ~s*) 2-door car; **coche de 4 ~s** 4-door car; **~s adentro** (ADV) behind closed doors; (ADJ: *sirviente*) live-in; **política de ~s adentro** home policy, domestic policy; **lo que pasa de ~s afuera** (*fuera de casa*) what happens on the other side of one's door; (*en el extranjero*) what happens abroad, foreign affairs; **de ~s afuera se dice que ...** for public consumption it is being said that ...; **de ~ en ~** from door to door; **abrir la ~ a** (*fig*) to open the door to; **cerrarle todas las ~s a uno** to close off all avenues to sb; **coger la ~*** to leave in a huff; **dar con la ~ en las narices a uno** to slam the door in sb's face; **dar ~ a uno*** to chuck sb out; **dejar la ~ abierta a** (*fig*) to leave the door open for; **enseñar la ~ a uno** to show sb the door; **entrar por la ~ grande** to take a big step up; to find promotion (*etc*) easy; **estar en ~s** to be imminent; **estar hasta la ~** to be chock-a-block; **franquear las ~s a uno** (*Esp*) to welcome sb in; **pegarse una ~*** to storm out, leave in a huff; **quedarse a la ~** to almost get a job; **querer poner ~s al campo** to try to stem the tide; **sacar de ~** to take a goal-kick; **salir por la ~ de los carros** (*apurado*) to leave in a hurry; (*destituido etc*) to leave in disgrace; **tomar la ~*** to leave, get out.

puertaventana NF shutter; French window.

puertear [1a] VI (*Cono Sur*) to make a dash for the exit.

puerto NM (a) (*gen*) port, harbour; (*de mar*) seaport; **~ comercial** trading port; **~ de contenedores** container port; **~ deportivo** yachting harbour, marina; **~ de escala** port of call; **~ de entrada** port of entry; **~ franco, ~ libre** free port; **~ de gran calado** deep-water port; **~ de origen** home port; **~ naval** naval port, naval harbour; **~ pesquero** fishing port; **entrar a ~, tomar ~** to enter port, come into port.
(b) (*fig: refugio*) haven, refuge; **llegar a ~** to solve a problem, get over a difficulty, come through safely.
(c) (*Geog*) pass.
(d) (*Inform*) gate, port; **~ (de transmisión en) paralelo** parallel port; **~ (de transmisión en) serie** serial port.

Puerto Rico NM Puerto Rico.

puertorriqueñismo NM word (*o phrase etc*) peculiar to Puerto Rico.

puertorriqueño, -a ADJ, NM/F Puerto Rican.

▼ **pues** ① ADV (a) (*entonces*) then; (*bueno*) well, well then; (*así que*) so; **~ no voy** well I'm not going, in that case I'm not going; **¿no vas con ella, ~?** aren't you going with her after all?; so you're not going with her?; **llegó, ~, con 2 horas de retraso** so he arrived 2 hours late; **~ sí** well yes, why yes; certainly; **~ no** well no; not at all; **¡~ qué!** come now!; what else did you expect!; **¿~?** so?, well?; what next?
(b) (*vacilando*) **~ ... no sé** well ... I don't know.
(c) (*afirmación*) **¡~!** yes!, certainly!; *V* **ahora, bien** *etc.*
▼ ② CONJ since, for; **cómpralo, ~ lo necesitas** buy it, since you need it; **nos marchamos, ~ no había más remedio** we left, since there was no alternative.

puesta NF (a) (*acto*) putting, placing; **~ en antena** (*TV*) showing; **~ al día** revision, updating; **~ en escena** staging; **~ de largo** coming-out (in society); **~ en libertad** freeing, release; **~ en marcha** (*acto*) starting; launch; (*dispositivo*) self-starter; **~ en práctica** putting into effect, implementation; **~ a punto** final preparation; perfection, fine-tuning.
(b) (*Astron*) setting; **~ del sol** sunset.
(c) (*Orn*) egg-laying; **una ~ anual de 300 huevos** an annual lay (*o* output) of 300 eggs.
(d) (*Naipes etc*) stake, bet.
(e) (*Cono Sur*) **¡~!** it's a tie!, it's a draw!; (*Carreras*) it's a dead heat!

puestero NM (a) (*LAm Com*) stallholder, market vendor. (b) (*Cono Sur*) (*mayoral*) farm overseer; (*agricultor*) small farmer, tenant farmer; (*trabajador*) ranch hand.

▼ **puesto** ① PTP *de* poner.
② ADJ (a) **con el sombrero ~** with one's hat on, wearing a hat; **una mesa puesta para 9** a table laid for 9.
(b) (**bien**) well dressed, smartly turned out.
(c) **tenerlos bien ~s** (*Esp**) to be a real man.
(d) **no está muy ~ en este tema** he's not very well up in these matters.
③ NM (a) (*lugar*) place; position; **~ de amarre** berth, mooring; **~ de honor** leading position; **~ de trabajo** (*Inform*) work-station; **el ~ de la especie en la clasificación** the place of the species in the classification; **ocupa el tercer ~ en la liga** it is in third place in the league; **ceder el ~ a uno** to give up one's place to sb; **guardar** (*o* **mantener**) **su ~** to know one's place; to keep the proper distance.
▼ (b) (*cargo*) **~ (de trabajo)** post, position, job; **tiene un ~ de conserje** he has a post as a porter; **se crearán 200 ~s de trabajo** 200 new jobs will be created.
(c) (*Mil etc*) post; **~ de control** checkpoint; **~ de escucha** listening-post; **~ fronterizo** border post; **~ de observación** observation post; **~ de policía** police post, police station; **~ de socorro** first-aid post.
(d) (*Caza*) stand, place.
(e) (*Com*) stall; stand, booth; kiosk; pitch; **~ callejero** street stall; **~ de mercado** market-stall; **~ de periódicos** newspaper stand.
(f) (*Cono Sur*) small farm.
④ **~ que** CONJ since, as.

puf INTERJ ugh!

puff [puf] NM, PL **puffs** [puf] pouffe.

pufo* NM (a) (*trampa*) trick, swindle; **dar el ~ a uno** to swindle sb.
(b) (*deuda*) debt.
(c) (*persona*) con man*.

púgil NM boxer.

pugilato NM boxing.

pugilismo NM boxing.

pugilista NM (*LAm*) boxer.

pugilístico ADJ boxing (*atr*).

pugío NM (*And, Cono Sur*) spring.

pugna NF battle, struggle, conflict; **entrar en ~ con** to clash with, come into conflict with; **estar en ~ con** to clash with, conflict with.

pugnacidad NF pugnacity, aggressiveness.

pugnar [1a] VI (a) (*luchar*) to fight; **~ en defensa de** to fight in defence of; **~ por** to fight for.
(b) (*esforzarse*) to struggle, fight, strive (*por + infin* to + *infin*); **~ por no reírse** to struggle not to laugh.
(c) **~ con** (*opinión etc*) to clash with, conflict with.

pugnaz ADJ pugnacious, aggressive.

puja NF (a) (*esfuerzo*) attempt, effort. (b) (*en subasta*) bid; **~ de salida** opening bid. (c) **sacar de la ~ a uno** (*adelantarse*) to get ahead of sb; (*sacar de apuro*) to get sb out of a jam*. (d) (*And**) ticking-off*.

pujante ADJ (*fuerte*) strong, vigorous; (*potente*) powerful; (*enérgico*) pushful, forceful.

pujanza NF strength, vigour; power; pushfulness, forcefulness, drive.

pujar [1a] VI (a) (*en subasta*) to bid, bid up; (*Naipes*) to bid; **~ en** (*o* **sobre**) **el precio** to bid the price up.
(b) (*esforzarse*) to struggle, strain; **~ para hacer algo** to struggle to do sth; **~ para adentro** (*CAm, Carib*) to grin and bear it.
(c) (*vacilar*) to falter, dither, hesitate.
(d) (*no encontrar palabras*) to struggle for words, be at a loss for words.
(e) (*hacer pucheros*) to be on the verge of tears.
(f) (*CAm**: *quejarse*) to moan, whinge*.

puje* NM (*And*) ticking-off*.

➤ LENGUA Y USO: **pues: 2** → 44.1 **puesto: 3b** → 46.1, 46.5

pujo NM **(a)** (Med) difficulty in relieving o.s., tenesmus.
  (b) (fig; ansia) longing, strong urge; **sentir ~ de llorar** to be on the verge of tears; **sentir ~ de reírse** to have an uncontrollable urge to laugh.
  (c) (fig: intento) attempt, try, shot; **~s** pretensions; **tiene ~s de caballero** he has pretensions to being a gentleman.

pulcramente ADV neatly, tidily, smartly; exquisitely; delicately.

pulcritud NF neatness, tidiness, smartness; exquisiteness, delicacy.

pulcro ADJ (aseado) neat, tidy, smart; (elegante) smartly dressed, smartly turned out; (exquisito) exquisite; (delicado) dainty, delicate.

pulga NF **(a)** (Zool) flea.
  (b) (de juego) tiddlywink; **juego de ~s** tiddlywinks.
  (c) (locuciones) **un tío de malas ~s** a bad-tempered chap, a peppery individual; **tener malas ~s** to be bad-tempered, be violent, be unpredictable; **no aguantar ~s*** to stand no nonsense; **buscar las ~s a uno*** to tease sb, needle sb*; **hacer de una ~ un elefante** (o **camello**) to make a mountain out of a molehill; to exaggerate sb's defects.
  (d) (Inform) bug.

pulgada NF inch.

pulgar NM thumb.

pulgarada NF **(a)** (capirotazo) flick, flip. **(b)** (de rapé etc) pinch.

Pulgarcito NM Tom Thumb.

pulgón NM plant louse; bug.

pulgoso ADJ, **pulguiento** ADJ (LAm) full of fleas, verminous.

pulguero NM (Esp) kip*, bed; (CAm, Carib) gaol.

pulidamente ADV **(a)** (con pulcritud) neatly, tidily; (con esmero) carefully; (refinadamente) in a polished way; (pey) affectedly. **(b)** (con cortesía) courteously.

pulido ① ADJ (pulcro) neat, tidy; (limpio) clean; (esmerado) careful; (refinado) polished, refined; (pey) over-nice, affected, finicky.
  ② NM polish, polishing.

pulidor(a) NM/F polisher.

pulimentado NM polishing.

pulimentar [1a] VT (pulir) to polish; (dar lustre a) to put a gloss on, put a shine on; (alisar) to smooth.

pulimento NM **(a)** (acto) polishing; polish, shine; (brillo) gloss. **(b)** (sustancia) polish.

pulique NM (CAm) dish of chilis and maize.

pulir [3a] ① VT **(a)** (gen) to polish; (dar lustre a) to put a gloss on, put a shine on.
  (b) (alisar) to smooth; (acabar) to finish (off).
  (c) (fig) to polish up, touch up, rub up; persona to polish up.
  (d) (‡) (robar) to pinch*; (vender) to sell, flog‡; to sell off (cheap); (gastar) to blow*, spend.
  ② **pulirse** VR (fig: refinarse) to acquire polish; (acicalarse) to spruce o.s. up.

pull [pul] NM pullover.

pulla NF **(a)** (injuria) cutting remark, wounding remark; (mofa) taunt; (indirecta) dig. **(b)** (obscenidad) obscene remark, rude word.

pullman NM **(a)** (And, Cono Sur: Ferro) sleeping car, Pullman car. **(b)** (Chile: autobús) long-distance coach.

pulmón NM **(a)** (gen) lung; **~ de acero** iron lung; **a pleno ~** respirar deeply; gritar at the top of one's voice; funcionar full-blast, at full throttle. **(b)** **pulmones‡** tits‡.

pulmonar ADJ pulmonary, lung (atr).

pulmonía NF pneumonia; **~ doble** double pneumonia.

pulmotor NM iron lung.

pulóver NM, **pull-over** NM pullover.

pulpa NF pulp; soft mass; (de fruta, planta) flesh, soft part; (Anat) soft flesh; (Cono Sur) boneless meat, fillet; **~ de madera** wood pulp; **~ de papel** paper pulp.

pulpejo NM fleshy part, soft part.

pulpería NF (And, CAm, Cono Sur) (tienda) general store, food store; (bar) bar, tavern.

pulpero, -a NM/F (And, CAm, Cono Sur) (comerciante) storekeeper, grocer; (tabernero) tavernkeeper.

púlpito NM pulpit.

pulpo NM **(a)** (Zool) octopus. **(b)** (Aut etc) elastic strap.

pulposo ADJ pulpy; soft, fleshy.

pulque NM (And, Méx) fermented drink made from maguey sap.

| PULQUE |

ⓘ *Pulque is a traditional alcoholic drink from Mexico. Thick, slightly sweet and milky, it is brewed from the juice of the agave plant, or maguey, and roughly equivalent in strength to beer. It was the sacred drink of the Aztecs, who used it in offerings to the gods and also for medicinal purposes. In modern-day Mexico it is often given to children since it is rich in vitamins, and in the cities it sold in special bars called **pulquerías**.*

---

pulquear [1a] (Méx) ① VI to drink pulque.
  ② **pulquearse** VR to get drunk on pulque.

pulquería NF (Méx) bar, tavern, pulque shop.

pulquérrimo ADJ SUPERL de pulcro.

pulsación NF **(a)** (latido) beat, pulsation; (Anat) throb(bing), beat(ing).
  (b) (en máquina de escribir etc) tap; (de mecanógrafo, pianista) touch. **(c)** (Inform) **~ doble** strikeover.

pulsador NM button, push-button; (Elec) switch.

pulsar¹ [1a] ① VT tecla etc to strike, touch, tap; botón, interruptor to press; (Mús) to play.
  (b) **~ a uno** (Med) to take sb's pulse, feel sb's pulse.
  (c) (fig) opinión etc to sound out, take, explore.
  ② VI to pulsate; to throb, beat.

pulsar² NM pulsar; (fig) black hole.

pulsear [1a] VI **(a)** (entre dos personas) to arm-wrestle. **(b)** (Cono Sur) to aim at a target.

pulsera NF wristlet, bracelet; **~ de pedida** (Esp) engagement bracelet; **~ para reloj** watch strap; **reloj de ~** wristwatch.

pulsión NF urge, drive, impulse.

pulso NM **(a)** (Anat) pulse; **tomar el ~ a uno** to take sb's pulse, feel sb's pulse; **tomar el ~ a la opinión** to sound out opinion.
  (b) (Anat: muñeca) wrist; (fig: fuerza) strength of wrist; (fig: contienda) trial of strength; battle of wills; showdown; **echar un ~** to arm-wrestle; **echar un ~ a** (fig: contender con) to have a trial of strength with; (desafiar) to challenge; **a ~** by sheer strength; with the strength of one's arm; (fig) by sheer hard work; unaided, all alone; the hard way; **a ~ sudando** by the sweat of one's brow; **dibujo (hecho) a ~** freehand drawing; **orquesta de ~ y púa** string orchestra; **ganar algo a ~** to get sth the hard way; **levantar una silla a ~** to lift a chair with one hand; **tomar un mueble a ~** to lift a piece of furniture clean off the ground; **con ~ firme** with a firm hand.
  (c) (fig: firmeza) steadiness, steady hand, firmness of touch; **tener ~** (Cono Sur) to have a good aim.
  (d) (fig: tacto) tact, good sense; **con mucho ~** very sensibly; with great tact.
  (e) (And) = **pulsera**.

pulular [1a] ① VT (LAm) to infest, swarm in, overrun.
  ② VI (estar plagado) to swarm (de with); (fig) to abound.

pululo* ADJ (CAm) short and fat.

pulverización NF **(a)** (de sólidos) pulverization. **(b)** (de perfume, insecticida) spray; spraying.

pulverizador NM spray, sprayer, spray-gun; **~ nasal** inhaler.

pulverizar [1f] VT **(a)** sustancia to pulverize; (reducir a polvo) to powder, convert into powder. **(b)** líquido, plantas etc to spray. **(c)** (fig) ciudad, enemigo to pound, pulverize, smash.

pulverulento ADJ **(a)** sustancia powdered, powdery. **(b)** superficie dusty.

pum INTERJ bang!; thud!; pop!

puma NM puma.

pumba INTERJ (indicando un golpe) bang!, crash!; (indicando una explosión) boom!, bang!

puna NF (LAm) **(a)** (Geog) high Andean plateau, puna. **(b)** (Med) mountain sickness. **(c)** (viento) cold mountain wind.

punch NM **(a)** (puñetazo) punch. **(b)** (fig) (empuje) vigour, strength, punch; (agilidad) agility. **(c)** **~es** (CAm) popcorn.

punchar [1a] VT (LAm) to punch.

punching ['punʃin] NM punchball.

punching-ball ['punʃinbal] NM punchball; (fig) whipping-boy.

punción NF (Med) puncture.

pundonor NM (dignidad) self-respect, pride; (honra) honour; face.

pundonoroso ADJ (honrado) honourable; (escrupuloso) punctilious, scrupulous.

punga‡ ① NF (Cono Sur) thieving, nicking‡.
  ② NMF (Cono Sur) pickpocket, thief.

pungir [3c] VT **(a)** (punzar) to prick, puncture; (picar) to sting. **(b)** (hacer sufrir) to cause suffering to.

punguista‡ NM (And, Cono Sur) (carterista) pickpocket; (ladrón) thief.

punible ADJ punishable.

punición NF punishment.

púnico ADJ, NM (Ling) Punic.

punitivo ADJ, **punitorio** ADJ punitive.

punki(e) ADJ, NMF punk.

punta ① NF **(a)** (extremo) end; (extremo puntiagudo) tip, point, sharp end; (de madera etc) thin end; (Geog) point; headland; (Cos) dentelle; **~s de espárrago** asparagus tips; **~ de lanza** spearhead (t fig); **con la ~ de la lengua** with the tip of one's tongue; **la ~ del iceberg** the tip of the iceberg; **la ~ de la lengua** the tip of one's tongue; **~ del pie** toe; **a ~ de cuchillo** at knife-point; **a ~ de pistola** at gunpoint; **línea ~ a ~** (Telec) direct line; **de ~** on end; endways; **de ~ a ~** from one end to the other; **ir de ~ en blanco** to be dressed up to the nines; **se la pusieron los pelos de ~** her hair stood on end; **energía de ~** peak power demand; **estoy hasta la ~ de los pelos de él*** I'm utterly fed up with him*; **ponerse de ~ en blanco** to get all dressed up; **sacar ~ a** to sharpen, point, put a point on; **sacar ~ a una**

observación to read too much into a remark; **sacar ~ a una máquina** to get the most out of a machine; to use a machine in ways which were never intended.

(b) (*fig: elemento*) touch, trace; tinge; **tiene una ~ de loco** he has a streak of madness, he's a bit mad; **tiene sus ~s de filósofo** there's a little of the philosopher about him.

(c) (*fig: locuciones*) **a ~ pala*** by the ton; by the score; **lo tenemos a ~ pala*** we have loads of it; **andar** (o **estar**) **de ~** to be at odds (*con* with); **estar de ~** to be edgy; to be in a bad mood; **ponerse de ~ con uno** to fall out with sb; to adopt a hostile attitude to sb; **tener de ~ a uno** to be at daggers drawn with sb.

(d) (*Téc: clavo*) small nail.

(e) (*colilla*) stub, butt.

(f) (*Zool: de toro*) horn; (*de ciervo*) point, tine.

(g) (*Agr: vacas*) group of cows.

(h) (*Carib: tabaco*) best quality tobacco (leaf).

(i) (*Méx: arma*)) sharp weapon.

(j) (*Carib: mofa*) taunt, snide remark.

(k) (*LAm: grupo*) group, gathering; lot; **una ~ de** a lot of, a bunch of.

(l) **en ~** (*CAm*) wholesale.

(m) (*Dep*) striker, forward; **media ~** midfield player.

(n) **~s** (*Ballet*) points; ballet-shoes.

2 ATR (*máximo*) top, maximum; (*más moderno*) latest; (*primero*) leading; (*de mayor carga*) peak; **horas ~** peak hours, rush hours; **industrias ~** sunrise industries; **tecnología ~** latest technology, leading edge technology; **velocidad ~** maximum speed, top speed.

3 NM (*Dep*) striker, forward.

puntada NF **(a)** (*Cos*) stitch; **~ cruzada** cross-stitch; **~ invisible** invisible mending; **dar unas ~s en** to put a few stitches in, stitch up; **no ha dado ~** (*fig*) he hasn't done a stroke; he's done nothing at all about it.

(b) (*: *indirecta*) hint; **pegar** (o **soltar**) **una ~** to drop a hint.

(c) (*LAm Med*) stitch; (*dolor agudo*) sharp pain.

(d) (*Méx*) witty remark, witticism.

puntaje NM (*LAm*) score.

puntal NM **(a)** (*Arquit*) prop, shore, support; (*Agr*) prop; (*Téc*) strut, crosspiece; stanchion. **(b)** (*fig*) prop, support; chief supporter. **(c)** (*LAm*) snack.

puntapié NM kick; (*Rugby*) **~ de bote pronto** drop kick; **~ colocado** place kick; **~ de saque** drop-out; **echar a uno a ~s** to kick sb out; **pegar un ~ a uno** to give sb a kick.

puntazo NM (*Taur*) jab (*with a horn*); (*LAm*) (*pinchazo*) jab, poke; (*puñalada*) stab; (*herida*) stab wound, knife wound.

punteado **1** ADJ (*moteado*) dotted, covered with dots; (*grabado con puntos*) stippled; *plumaje etc* flecked (*de* with); *diseño* of dots. **2** NM **(a)** (*V ADJ*) series of dots; stippling; flecking. **(b)** (*Mús*) punteado, pizzicato.

puntear [1a] **1** VT **(a)** (*marcar con puntos*) to dot, cover (o mark) with dots; to stipple; to fleck. **(b)** *artículos* to tick, put a mark against; (*LAm*) *lista* to check off. **(c)** (*Cos*) to stitch (up). **(d)** (*Mús*) to play pizzicato, pluck. **(e)** (*Cono Sur*) *tierra* to fork over. **(f)** (*Cono Sur*) *marcha etc* to head, lead. **2** VI (*Náut*) to luff.

punteo NM plucking.

puntera NF **(a)** (*de zapato*) toecap. **(b)** (*de lapicero*) pencil top. **(c)** (*: *puntapié*) kick.

punterazo NM (*Dep*) powerful shot, drive.

puntería NF **(a)** (*el apuntar*) aim, aiming; **enmendar** (o **rectificar**) **la ~** to correct one's aim; **hacer la ~ de un cañón** to aim a gun, sight a gun. **(b)** (*fig: destreza*) marksmanship; **tener buena ~** to be a good shot; **tener mala ~** to be a bad shot.

puntero **1** ADJ (*primero*) top, leading; (*moderno*) up-to-date; **más ~** (*sobresaliente*) outstanding, furthest ahead; (*último*) latest; **equipo ~** top club. **2** NM **(a)** (*palo*) pointer; **~ luminoso** light pen. **(b)** (*Téc*) stonecutter's chisel. **(c)** (*persona*) outstanding individual; leader, top man. **(d)** (*LAm*) (*Dep*) leading team, team which is ahead; (*de rebaño*) leading animal; (*de desfile*) leader. **(e)** (*LAm: de reloj*) hand.

puntiagudo ADJ sharp, sharp-pointed.

puntilla NF **(a)** (*Téc*) tack, brad. **(b)** (*de pluma*) point, nib. **(c)** (*Cos*) lace edging. **(d)** (*Taur*) short dagger for giving the coup de grâce; **dar la ~** to give the coup de grâce, finish off the bull. **(e)** **de ~s** on tiptoe; **andar de ~s** to walk on tiptoe.

puntillazo NM **(a)** (*Taur*) the decisive, mortal blow in a bullfight. **(b)** **dar el ~ a algo** to put an end to sth.

puntillismo NM pointillism.

puntillo NM **(a)** punctilio; (*pey*) exaggerated sense of honour, excessive amour propre. **(b)** (‡) **ligar un ~** (*drogas*) to get high‡; (*bebida*) to get plastered‡.

puntilloso ADJ punctilious; (*pey*) touchy, sensitive.

▼ **punto** NM **(a)** (*en diseño etc*) dot, spot; fleck; (*en plumaje etc*) spot, speckle; (*en carta, dominó*) spot, pip; **diseño a ~s** design of dots, pattern of dots.

(b) (*Tip*) full stop, period (*US*); **~ acápite** (*LAm*) full stop, new paragraph; **~ de admiración**, **~ de exclamación** exclamation mark; **'~ y aparte'** (*al dictar*) 'new paragraph'; **~ y coma** semicolon; **~ final** full stop; **~ de interrogación** question mark, query; **'~ y seguido'** 'full stop, new sentence'; **~s suspensivos** dots, suspension points (...); **dos ~s** colon; **¡y ~ (final)!** and that's that!; **sin faltar ~ ni coma** accurately, faithfully; minutely; **hacer algo con ~s y comas** to get sth right down to the last detail; **poner los ~s sobre las íes** to dot the i's and cross the t's; **le puso los ~s sobre las íes** she corrected him, she drew attention to his inaccuracies.

(c) (*tanto: Dep*) point; (*en examen*) mark; (*en bolsa*) point; **con 8 ~s a favor y 3 en contra** with 8 points for and 3 against; **los dos están empatados a ~s** the two are level on points; **ganar a los ~s, vencer por ~s** to win on points.

▼ **(d)** (*en discusión*) point; item, matter, question; **contestar ~ por ~** to answer point by point; **~ capital** crucial point, basic point; crux; **~s de consulta** terms of reference; points referred for decision (o report); **~s a tratar** matters to be discussed, agenda.

(e) **~ de taxis** taxi stand, cab rank.

(f) (*Mús*) pitch.

(g) (*Cos*) stitch; (*de tela*) mesh; (*en media*) ladder, run; (*Med*) stitch; **una herida que necesitó 10 ~s** a wound which needed 10 stitches; **~ del derecho** plain knitting; **~ de media** plain knitting; **~ del revés** purl; **hacer ~** to knit; **¡~ en boca!** mum's the word!, keep it under your hat!; **chaqueta de ~** knitted jacket.

(h) **~ de costado** (*Med*) stitch, pain in the side.

(i) (*agujero etc*) hole; **darse dos ~s en el cinturón** to let out one's belt, (*fig*) overeat; **calzar muchos ~s** to know a lot; **calzar pocos ~s** to know very little, be pretty dim.

(j) (*Com*) **~ de equilibrio** break-even point.

(k) (*Inform*) pixel; **~ de parada** break-point; **~ de referencia** benchmark.

▼ **(l)** (*lugar etc*) spot, place, point; (*Geog*) point; (*Mat*) point; (*de proceso*) point, stage; (*de tiempo*) point, moment; **~ de apoyo** fulcrum; **~ de arranque** starting point; **~ de atraque** berth, mooring; **~ cardinal** cardinal point; **~ céntrico** central point; **~ ciego** (*Anat*) blind spot; **~ clave** (**de las defensas**) key point (in the defences); **~ de congelación** freezing-point; **~ de contacto** point of contact; **~ de control** checkpoint; **~ crítico** critical point, critical moment; **~ culminante** culminating moment; topmost point, limit; **~ débil**, **~ flaco** weak spot, weak point; **~ de ebullición** boiling-point; **~ de fuga** vanishing point; **~ de fusión** melting-point; **~ de inflamación** flashpoint; **estar en el ~ de mira de uno** to be in sb's sights; **~ muerto** (*Mec*) dead centre; (*Aut etc*) neutral (gear); (*fig*) deadlock, stalemate; **las negociaciones están en un ~ muerto** the negotiations are deadlocked, there is stalemate in the talks; **hemos llegado a un ~ muerto** we have reached deadlock; **~ negro** (*Aut*) blackspot; (*Anat*) blackhead; (*fig*) blemish, defect; **~ neurálgico** (*Anat*) nerve centre; (*fig*) key point; **~ neutro** (*Mec*) dead centre; (*Aut etc*) neutral (gear); **~ de no** (o **sin**) **retorno** point of no return; **~ panorámico** viewpoint, vantage point; **~ de partida** starting point; **~ de penalti** penalty spot; **~ de referencia** point of reference; **~ de venta** point of sale; **~ de veraneo** summer resort, holiday resort; **~ de vista** point of view, viewpoint; criterion; **él lo mira desde otro ~ de vista** he looks at it from another point of view.

(m) (*locuciones etc + prep*) **a ~** ready; **con sus máquinas a ~ para disparar** with their cameras ready to shoot; **llegar a ~** to come just at the right moment; **al llegar a este ~** at this moment, at this stage; **saber algo a ~ fijo** to know sth for sure; **al ~** at once, instantly; **está a ~** it's ready; **estar a ~ de** + *infin* to be on the point of + *ger*, be about to + *infin*; **estar a ~ de caramelo** to be at the point of realization; **estar al ~*** (*LAm*) to be high (on drugs)‡; **poner a ~** (*fig*) to fine-tune; **poner un motor a ~** to tune an engine; **de todo ~** completely, absolutely; **bajar de ~** to decline, fall off, fall away; **subir de ~** to grow, increase; to get worse; **a las 7 en ~** at 7 sharp, at 7 on the dot, punctually at 7; **en ~ a** with regard to; **estar en su ~** (*Culin*) to be done to a turn; **una medida muy puesta en su ~** a very timely (o proper) measure; **para dejar las cosas en su ~** to be absolutely precise; **llegar a su ~** to reach its peak; **pongamos las cosas en su ~** let's be absolutely clear about this; **poner algo en su ~** to bring sth to perfection; **hasta el ~ de** + *infin* to the extent of + *ger*; **hasta cierto ~** up to a point, to some extent; in a way; **hasta tal ~ que ...** to such an extent that ...

(n) (*Esp*) (*hombre*) bloke‡, guy*; (*pey*) rogue; **¡vaya (un) ~!, ¡está he-**

cho un ~ filipino! he's a right rogue!*

(o) (‡) **ligar un ~** V **puntillo** (b).

puntuable ADJ ranking; championship *(atr)*; **una prueba ~ para el campeonato** a race counting towards the championship.

puntuación NF (a) *(Ling, Tip)* punctuation.

(b) *(acto: Escuela etc)* marking; *(Dep)* scoring; **sistema de ~** system of scoring.

(c) *(Escuela: puntos)* mark(s); *(grado)* class, grade; *(Dep)* score.

puntual ADJ (a) *persona (fiable)* reliable, conscientious; *(rápido)* prompt; *(al acudir etc)* punctual.

(b) *llegada etc* punctual.

(c) *informe etc* reliable; precise; *cálculo* exact, accurate.

(d) *(concreto)* specific, concrete, precise.

puntualidad NF (a) *(seguridad)* reliability, conscientiousness; *(diligencia)* promptness; *(exactitud)* punctuality. (b) *(precisión)* precision; exactness, accuracy.

puntualización NF specification, detailed statement (o explanation etc).

puntualizador ADJ specific, detailed.

puntualizar [1f] VT (a) *(precisar)* to fix, specify, state in detail; *(determinar)* to settle, determine. (b) *(recordar)* to fix in one's mind (o memory).

puntualmente ADV *(V N)* (a) reliably, conscientiously; promptly; punctually. (b) precisely, exactly, accurately.

puntuar [1c] [1] VT (a) *(Ling, Tip)* to punctuate. (b) *(valorar)* to evaluate, assess; *examen* to mark.

[2] VI (a) *(Dep: valer)* to score, count; **eso no puntúa** that doesn't count. (b) *(marcar)* to score.

puntudo ADJ *(LAm)* sharp.

puntura NF puncture, prick.

punzada NF (a) *(puntura)* puncture, prick; jab.

(b) *(Med)* stitch; *(dolor)* twinge (of pain), shooting pain; *(espasmo)* spasm.

(c) *(fig)* pang, twinge (of regret etc).

(d) *(Carib*: insolencia)* cheek*.

punzante ADJ (a) *dolor* shooting, sharp. (b) *herramienta etc* sharp. (c) *(fig) comentario etc* biting, caustic.

punzar [1f] [1] VT (a) *(pinchar)* to puncture, prick, pierce; *(Téc)* to punch; to perforate.

(b) *(fig)* to hurt, grieve; **le punzan remordimientos** he feels pangs of regret, his conscience pricks him.

[2] VI *(dolor)* to shoot, stab; to sting.

punzó ADJ *(Carib, Cono Sur)* bright red.

punzón NM *(Téc)* punch; graver, burin; bodkin.

puñada NF punch, clout; **dar de ~s en** to punch, pound, beat on.

puñado NM handful *(lit, fig)*; **a ~s** by handfuls; in plenty, galore; **me mola un ~‡** I like it a lot.

puñal NM dagger; **poner el ~ al pecho a uno** *(fig)* to hold a pistol to sb's head.

puñalada NF (a) *(golpe)* stab, thrust; *(herida)* stab wound; **~ de misericordia** coup de grâce; **~ trapera** stab in the back; dirty trick; V **coser**. (b) *(fig)* stab, grievous blow; **~ encubierta** stab in the back, treacherous thrust.

puñeta [1] NF (a) (‡) *(bobada)* silly thing; *(queja)* silly complaint; *(dicho)* stupid remark; *(bagatela)* silly trifle; **¡no me vengas con ~s!** don't come whining to me!; **perder el tiempo en ~s** to waste time on piddling trifles.

(b) (‡) **hacer la ~ a uno** to muck sb around, screw sb up‡; **me han hecho la ~** they've screwed it up for me‡.

(c) (፡‡) **hacer ~s** to wank‡፡; **¡(vete) a hacer ~s!** get stuffed!‡፡; **mandar a uno a hacer ~s** to tell sb to get stuffed‡፡.

(d) (‡: otras locuciones) **tengo un catarro de la ~** I've got a bloody awful cold‡; **ese conserje de la ~** that swine of a porter*; **fue un lío de ~s** it was one hell of a mess; **es un problema de ~** it's a devil of a problem; **no entiende ni ~** he doesn't understand a blind thing; **¡qué coche ni qué ~s!** what car?, car my foot!; **¿qué ~s le habrá pasado?** what in hell's name can have happened to her?; **viven en la quinta ~** they live in the middle of nowhere.

[2] INTERJ (‡) **¡~s!, ¡qué ~s!** *(enojo)* hell!; *(asombro)* bugger me!‡፡, well I'm damned!; **¡una ~!** get away!*; **¡es enorme, ~!** it's bloody huge!‡; **¡escucha, ~!** you bloody well listen!‡

puñetazo NM punch; **a ~s** with (blows of) one's fists; **dar a uno de ~s** to punch sb; **andaba a ~s con las lágrimas** he was struggling to keep back his tears.

puñetería‡ NF bore, drag; = **puñeta** (a).

puñetero ADJ (a) (‡: condenado) bloody‡፡; lousy‡. (b) *(malévolo)* bloody-minded‡; *(nimio)* niggling, hair-splitting.

puño NM (a) *(Anat)* fist; **~ de hierro** knuckleduster; **a ~ cerrado** with one's clenched fist; **apretar los ~s** *(fig)* to struggle hard; **comerse los ~s** to be starving; **como un ~** *(pequeño)* tiny, very small; *(grande)* huge, enormous; *verdad etc* obvious *(V t* **verdad***)*; *(tangible)* tangible, visible; **mentiras como ~s** whopping great lies*; **de propio ~** in

one's own handwriting; **de ~ y letra del poeta** in the poet's own handwriting; **meter a uno en un ~** to intimidate sb, cow sb; to bring sb under control; **su mujer le tiene en un ~** his wife's got him completely under her thumb.

(b) *(cantidad)* handful, fistful.

(c) *(Cos)* cuff.

(d) *(de espada)* hilt; *(de herramienta)* handle, haft, grip; *(de vasija)* handle; *(de puerta)* handle.

(e) *(fig)* **~s** strength; brute force; **es hombre de ~s** he's strong, he's tough; **ganar algo con los ~s** to get sth by sheer hard work; **hacer algo a ~s** to do sth by hand.

(f) *(fig)* **un ~ de casa** a tiny house, a very small house.

pupa NF (a) *(Med) (ampolla)* blister, pimple; *(úlcera)* lip sore, ulcer; *(palabra de niños)* sore, pain; **hacer ~ a uno** to hurt sb. (b) (*: error) gaffe, blunder. (c) *(Ent)* pupa.

pupas* NMF unpredictable person; *(gruñón)* moaner*.

pupila NF (a) *(Anat)* pupil. (b) *(en orfelinato)* inmate; *(pensionista)* boarder. (c) *(Jur)* ward. (d) (*: puta) prostitute. (e) *(perspicacia)* sharpness, intelligence; good sense.

pupilo NM (a) *(en orfelinato)* inmate; *(interno)* boarder. (b) *(Jur)* ward. (c) *(Dep*)* player.

pupitre NM *(Escol etc)* desk; *(Inform)* console.

pupo NM *(And, Cono Sur)* navel.

pupón ADJ (a) *(Cono Sur, Méx*: lleno de comida)* stuffed, full (up). (b) *(Cono Sur‡: barrigón)* pot-bellied, paunchy.

pupurri NM pot-pourri.

pupusa NF *(CAm)* (a) *(Culin)* stuffed tortilla. (b) (፡‡) cunt፡፡.

puque NM *(Méx)* *(podrido)* rotten, bad; *(débil)* weak, sickly; *(estéril)* sterile.

puquío NM *(And, Cono Sur)* spring, fountain.

Pura NF ABR de **Purificación**.

puramente ADV purely, simply.

pura-sangre NMF, PL **pura-sangres** thoroughbred.

puré NM purée, (thick) soup; **~ de guisantes** pea soup; *(fig)* peasouper*, thick fog; **~ de patata(s)** mashed potatoes, creamed potatoes; **~ de tomate** tomato paste; **estoy hecho ~*** I'm knackered*.

purear [1a] VI *(And)* to drink one's liquor neat.

pureta‡ [1] ADJ old, elderly.

[2] NMF (a) *(viejo)* old crock, old geezer‡. (b) *(carca)* old square*.

pureza NF purity.

purga NF (a) *(Med)* purge, cathartic, purgative. (b) *(Pol)* purge. (c) *(Mec)* venting, draining, airing; **válvula de ~** vent.

purgación NF (a) *(Med)* purging, purgative. (b) *(de mujer)* menstruation.

purgante NM purgative.

purgar [1h] [1] VT (a) *(gen)* to purge, cleanse *(de of)*; *(Mec)* to vent, drain, air; *(Pol)* to purge, liquidate.

(b) *(purificar)* to purify, refine.

(c) *(Med)* to purge, administer a purgative to.

(d) *(fig) pecado* to purge, expiate; *pasiones* to purge.

[2] **purgarse** VR (a) *(Med)* to take a purge.

(b) *(fig)* **~ de** to purge o.s. of.

purgativo ADJ purgative.

purgatorio NM purgatory *(lit, fig)*; **¡fue un ~!** it was purgatory!

puridad NF *(lit)* secrecy; **en ~** *(llanamente)* plainly, directly; *(secretamente)* in secret; *(estrictamente)* strictly, in the strict sense.

purificación NF purification.

purificador NM: **~ de agua** water filter; **~ de aire** air purifier, air filter.

purificante ADJ cleansing.

purificar [1g] VT to purify; to cleanse; *(Téc)* to purify, refine.

purili‡ NMF old geezer‡.

Purísima ADJ superl: **la ~** the Virgin.

purismo NM purism.

purista NMF purist.

puritanismo NM puritanism.

puritano [1] ADJ *actitud etc* puritanical; *iglesia, tradición etc* puritan.

[2] NM, **puritana** NF puritan.

puro [1] ADJ (a) *color, lengua, sustancia etc* pure; *(sin mezcla)* unadulterated; *oro* solid; *cielo* clear.

(b) *(fig)* pure, simple; sheer; *verdad* plain, simple; **de ~ aburrimiento** out of sheer boredom; **de ~ tonto** out of sheer stupidity; **por pura casualidad** by sheer chance; **por las puras*** *(Cono Sur)* just for the hell of it.

(c) *(moralmente)* pure, virtuous, chaste.

(d) *(Méx: solo)* only, just; **me queda una pura porción** I have just one ration left, I have only one ration left.

(e) *(And, Carib Méx: idéntico)* identical; **el hijo es ~ el padre** the son is exactly like his father.

[2] COMO ADV: **de ~ bobo** out of sheer stupidity; **de ~ cansado** out of sheer tiredness; **no se le ve el color de ~ sucio** it's so dirty you can't tell what colour it is; **cosas que se olvidan de ~ sabidas**

things which are so well known that they get overlooked. **3** NM (**a**) (*cigarro*) cigar; **~ habano** Havana cigar.
(**b**) **a ~ de** by dint of, thanks only to.
(**c**) **meter un ~ a uno** (*Mil‡*) to put sb on a charge.
púrpura ADJ INVAR, NF purple.
purpurado NM (*Ecl*) cardinal.
purpurar [1a] VT to dye purple.
purpúreo ADJ, **purpurino** ADJ purple.
purpurina NF metallic paint (*gold, silver etc*).
purrela NF (**a**) (*vino malo*) bad wine, cheap wine, plonk*. (**b**) **una ~** (*fig*) a mere trifle, chicken feed.
purrete* NM (*Cono Sur*) kid*, child.
purulento ADJ purulent.
pus NM pus, matter.
puse *etc V* **poner.**
pusilánime ADJ fainthearted, pusillanimous.
pusilanimidad NF faintheartedness, pusillanimity.
pústula NF pustule, sore, pimple.
put [put] NM, PL **puts** [put] (*Golf*) putt.
puta NF (**a**) (*gen*) whore, prostitute; **¡la muy ~!** the slut!, the bitch!‡; **~ callejera** streetwalker; **casa de ~s** brothel; **ir de ~s** to go whoring. (**b**) (‡) **¡~!** bloody hell!‡, Jesus!‡; **¡la ~!** (*sorpresa*) well I'm damned!
(**c**) (*LAm Naipes*) jack.
2 ADJ INVAR (‡) bloody‡; bloody awful‡; **¡ni ~ idea!** I've no bloody idea!‡; **de ~ madre** (ADJ) (*bueno*) terrific*, smashing*; (*malo*) bloody awful‡; (ADV) marvellously; **ella cocina de ~ madre** she's a bloody marvellous cook‡; **por toda la ~ calle** all along the bloody street‡; **¡qué ~ suerte!** (*mala*) what bloody awful luck!‡, (*buena*) what incredible luck!; **pasarlas ~s** to have a terrible time.
putada NF dirty trick; **¡qué ~!** what a bloody shame‡!; **es una ~** it's a bloody nuisance‡.
putañear [1a] VI to go whoring, consort with prostitutes.
putañero **1** ADJ (**a**) (*que va de putas*) whoring.
(**b**) (*cachondo*) randy, oversexed.
2 NM whoremonger.
putativo ADJ putative, supposed.
puteada NF (*Cono Sur, Méx*) insult; (*palabrota*) swearword.
puteado ADJ (**a**) (*maleado*) corrupted, perverted. (**b**) (*harto*) fed up*, browned off‡.
putear‡ [1a] **1** VT (**a**) (*malear*) to corrupt, pervert. (**b**) (*fastidiar*) to bugger about‡, muck around. (**c**) (*maltratar*) to kick around, abuse, misuse; **uno está puteado** you get fed up (to the teeth)*. (**d**) (*enfadar*) to upset, send up the wall*. (**e**) (*LAm: insultar*) to swear at, curse. (**f**)

(‡) to screw.
2 VI (**a**) (*ir de putas*) to go whoring; (*ser puta*) to be on the game*. (**b**) (*padecer*) to have a rough time of it.
3 **putearse** VR to go down the drain*.
puteo‡ NM : **ir de ~** (*Esp*) to go whoring.
putería NF (**a**) (*gen*) prostitution; life (*etc*) of the prostitute. (**b**) (*prostíbulo*) brothel. (**c**) (‡: *zalamería*) soft soap*.
puterío NM whoring, prostitution.
puticlub* [putɪ'klu] NM (*hum*) singles club, singles bar.
putilla‡ NF scrubber‡.
putiza‡ NF (*Méx*) brawl, set-to*.
puto‡ **1** ADJ bloody‡; bloody awful‡; (**no me hizo**) **ni ~ caso** she completely bloody ignored me‡; *V t* **puta 2.**
2 NM (**a**) (*prostituto*) male prostitute; (*homosexual*) queer‡, fairy‡. (**b**) (*insulto*) sod‡‡.
putrefacción NF (**a**) (*acto*) rotting, putrefaction; decay. (**b**) (*materia*) rot, rottenness; **~ fungoide** dry rot; **sujeto a ~** *comestible etc* perishable.
putrefacto ADJ rotten, putrid; decayed.
putrescente ADJ rotting, putrefying, putrescent.
pútrido ADJ putrid, rotten.
putt [put] NM, PL **puts** [put] putt.
putter ['puter] NM, PL **putters** ['puter] putter.
puya NF (**a**) (*punta acerada*) goad, pointed stick; point; (*Taur*) point of the picador's lance. (**b**) (*Carib*) one cent.
puyar [1a] **1** VT (**a**) (*LAm*) to jab, wound, prick. (**b**) (*CAm, Carib**: *molestar*) to upset, needle*.
2 VI (*Carib: planta*) to shoot, sprout.
puyazo NM (*Taur*) jab with the lance.
puyero NM (*Carib*) pile of money; **divertirse un ~*** to have a great time*, have a whale of a time*.
puyo NM (*Cono Sur*) coarse woollen poncho.
puyón NM (**a**) (*And, Cono Sur: de gallo*) cock's spur; (*Méx: punta*) sharp point; (*Méx: espina*) prickle, spine, thorn; (*And, CAm, Méx: renuevo*) shoot, bud. (**b**) (*And, CAm, Carib: pinchazo*) jab, prick.
puzcua NF (*Méx*) puffed maize.
puz(z)le ['puθle] NM puzzle (*t fig*).
PVC NM ABR *de* **polyvinyl-chloride** PVC.
PVP NM ABR *de* **precio de venta al público.**
PYME NF ABR *de* **Pequeña y Mediana Empresa** small and middle-sized businesses.
PYRESA [pi'resa] NF ABR *de* **Prensa y Radio Española, Sociedad Anónima.**

Q, q [ku] NF (*letra*) Q, q.

Qatar NM Qatar.

q.b.s.m. ABR *de* **que besa sus manos** *courtesy formula.*

q.b.s.p. ABR *de* **que besa sus pies** *courtesy formula.*

q.D.g. ABR *de* **que Dios guarde** *courtesy formula.*

QED ABR *de* **quod erat demonstrandum** QED.

q.e.g.e. ABR *de* **que en gloria esté** ≃ R.I.P.

q.e.p.d. ABR *de* **que en paz descanse** R.I.P.

q.e.s.m. ABR *de* **que estrecha su mano** *courtesy formula in letters.*

QH NF ABR *de* **quiniela hípica** *horse-racing totalizator.*

qm ABR *de* **quintal(es) métrico(s).**

qts ABR *de* **quilates** carats, c.

quáker NM (*And*) porridge.

quantum ['kwantum] NM, PL **quanta** ['kwanta] (*Fís*) quantum.

quark NM, PL **quarks** quark.

quásar NM quasar.

quattrocentista ADJ quattrocento (*atr*).

que¹ ⬚1 REL PRON (a) (*persona: sujeto*) who, that; (*acusativo*) whom, that; (*pero a menudo se omite el relativo, p.ej.*) **la joven ~ invité** the girl I invited.

(b) (*cosa*) that, which; (*pero a menudo se omite el relativo, p.ej.*) **el coche ~ compré** the car I bought; **la cama en ~ pasé la noche** the bed in which I spent the night, the bed I spent the night in; **el día ~ ella nació** the day (that) she was born, the day when she was born; **la reunión a ~ yo asistí** the meeting I attended, the meeting I was at; **los disgustos ~ tiene que aguantar** the unpleasantness he has to put up with.

⬚2 PRON REL (*con artículo*) V **el³, lo⁴.**

que² CONJ (a) (*tras verbo*) that; (*pero a menudo se omite, p.ej.*) **creo ~ va a venir** I think (that) he will come; **no sabía ~ tuviera coche** I didn't know he had a car; **decir ~ sí** to say yes; **la idea de ~ haya oro en Ruritania** the idea that there is gold in Ruritania; **estoy seguro de ~ lloverá** I am sure (that) it will rain; **¡~ si lo tengo!** of course I've got it!; **¡~ tenga que escuchar tales cosas!** why do I have to listen to such things?; **vergonzoso, ~ dice tu padre** shameful, as your father says; **¿~ no estabas allí?** (are you telling me) you weren't there?; *V* **claro, decir** *etc.*

(b) (*con verbo en subj*) **esperar ~ uno haga algo** to hope that sb will do sth; **querer ~ uno haga algo** to want sb to do sth; **alegrarse de ~ uno haya llegado** to be glad (that) sb has arrived; **no digo ~ sea traidor** I'm not saying (that) he's a traitor; **¡~ lo haga él!** let him do it!, get him to do it!; **¡~ entre!** let him come in!, send him in!; **¡~ venga pronto!** let's hope he comes soon.

(c) (*elíptico*) **¡a ~ no!** *etc: V* **no** (a); **tengo una sed ~ me muero** I'm dying of thirst.

(d) **el que** + *subj* the fact that ...; **el ~ tenga dos hermanas guapas no me interesa** the fact that he has two pretty sisters doesn't concern me; **el ~ quiera estar con su madre es natural** it is natural (that) he should want to be with his mother.

(e) (*resultado*) that; **soplaba tan fuerte ~ no podíamos salir** it was blowing so hard (that) we couldn't go out; **huele ~ es un asco** it smells disgusting; *V* **bendición, primor** *etc.*

(f) (*locuciones*) **siguió toca ~ toca** he just kept on playing, he played and played; **estuvieron habla ~ habla toda la noche** they talked and talked all night.

(g) (*ya que, porque*) for, since, because; **vine un poco pronto ~ está lloviendo** I came a bit early because it's raining; **¡vamos, ~ cierro!** off with you, (because) I'm closing!; **¡cuidado, ~ nos vamos!** hold tight, we're off!; **¡suéltame, ~ voy a gritar!** let go or I'll scream.

(h) (*comparación*) than; **yo ~ tú** if I were you, if I were in your place; *V* **más** *etc.*

qué ⬚1 PRON INTERROG: **¿~?** what?; **¿~ dijiste?** what did you say?; **no sé ~ quiere decir** I don't know what it means; **¿a ~?** why?; **¿a ~ has**

venido? why have you come?, what have you come for?; **¿y a mí ~?** so what?, what has that got to do with me?; **¿y ~?** so what?, well?; **¿con ~ lo vas a pagar?** what are you going to pay with?; how are you going to pay it?; **¿de ~ le conoces?** how do you recognize him?; **¿en ~ lo notas?** in what way do you see that?; **ahí estaba el ~** that was the reason; **sin ~ ni para ~** without rhyme or reason; *V* **más, para** *etc.*

⬚2 ADJ (a) (*interrog*); **¿~ libro?** what book?; which book?; **¿~ edad tiene?** what age is he?, how old is he?; **¿~ traje te vas a poner?** which suit are you wearing (o going to wear)?; **¿a ~ velocidad?** at what speed?, how fast?; **¿de ~ tamaño es?** what size is it?, how big is it?; **dime ~ libro buscas** tell me which book you are looking for.

(b) (EXCL) **¡~ día más espléndido!** what a glorious day!; **¡~ bonito!** (*lit*) isn't it pretty!, how pretty it is!; (*lit, iró*) very nice too! **¡~ asco!** how awful!, how revolting!; **¡~ susto!** what a scare!; **¡~ de cosas te diría!** what a lot I'd have to say to you!; **¡~ de gente había!** what a lot of people there were!

quebracho NM (*LAm*) (a) (*Bot*) quebracho; (*madera*) break-ax (*US*). (b) (*Téc*) extract used in leather-tanning.

quebrada NF (a) (*hondonada*) gorge, ravine; (*puerto*) gap, pass. (b) (*LAm: arroyo*) mountain stream.

quebradero NM: **~ de cabeza** headache, worry.

quebradizo ADJ (a) (*gen*) fragile, brittle, delicate; *hojaldre* short; *galleta etc* crumbly; *voz* weak.

(b) (*Med*) sickly, frail.

(c) (*muy sensible*) emotionally fragile, sensitive, readily upset.

(d) (*moralmente*) frail, easily tempted.

quebrado ⬚1 ADJ (a) *terreno* broken, rough, uneven; *línea* irregular, zigzag.

(b) (*t ~ de color*) *rostro* pale; *tez* pallid.

(c) (*Med*) ruptured.

(d) (*Fin*) bankrupt.

⬚2 NM (a) (*Mat*) fraction.

(b) (*Fin*) bankrupt.

quebradora NF (*CAm Med*) dengue fever.

quebradura NF (a) (*grieta*) fissure, slit, crack. (b) (*Geog*) = **quebrada** (a). (c) (*Med*) rupture.

quebraja NF fissure, slit, crack.

quebrantadura NF, **quebrantamiento** NM (a) (*V* **quebrantar 1** (a), (b), (c)) (*acto*) breaking; cracking; weakening; forcing; violation; **~ de forma** (*Jur*) breach of normal procedure.

(b) (*estado*) exhaustion, exhausted state; broken health.

quebrantahuesos NM INVAR bearded vulture.

quebrantar [1a] ⬚1 VT (a) (*romper*) to break; to crack; to shatter.

(b) *cimientos, furia, moral etc* to weaken; *resistencia* to break, weaken; *salud, posición* to undermine, shatter, destroy; *persona* to shatter, break.

(c) *cerradura* to force; *caja fuerte, sello* to break open; *cárcel* to break out of; *sagrado* to break into, violate; *terreno vedado etc* to trespass on.

(d) *ley, promesa* to break.

(e) *color* to tone down.

(f) (*LAm*) *caballo* to break in.

⬚2 **quebrantarse** VR (*persona*) to be shattered, be broken (in health *etc*).

quebranto NM (a) (*daño*) damage, harm; (*pérdida*) severe loss. (b) (*agotamiento*) exhaustion, weakness; (*mala salud*) broken health; (*depresión*) depression. (c) (*aflicción*) sorrow, affliction.

quebrar [1j] ⬚1 VT (a) (*romper*) to break, smash.

(b) *cuerpo* to bend (at the waist); (*torcer*) to twist.

(c) *carrera, formación, proceso etc* to interrupt; to alter the course of, interfere seriously with.

(d) *color* to tone down.

(e) *para diversos significados* V **quebrantar.**
[2] VI **(a)** *(Fin)* to fail, go bankrupt.
(b) *(debilitarse)* to weaken.
(c) ~ **con uno** to break with sb.
[3] **quebrarse** VR **(a)** to break, smash, get broken.
(b) *(Med)* to be ruptured; to have a rupture.

quebraza NF crack; *(Med)* crack (on the skin), chap.

quebrazón NF **(a)** *(LAm: de vidrio etc)* smashing, shattering. **(b)** *(Cono Sur: contienda)* quarrel.

quebroso ADJ *(And)* brittle, fragile.

queche NM smack, ketch.

quechua [1] ADJ, NMF Quechua.
[2] NM *(Ling)* Quechua.

┌─── **QUECHUA** ───────────────────────────────┐

i *Quechua, the language spoken by the Incas, is the most widely spoken indigenous language in South America, with some 13 million speakers in the Andean region. The first Quechua grammar was compiled by a Spanish missionary in 1560, as part of a linguistic policy intended to aid the process of evangelization. In 1975 Peru made Quechua an official state language. From Quechua come words such as "llama", "condor" and "puma".*

└──┘

queda NF (*t* **toque de** ~) curfew.

quedada¹ †† NF *(CAm, Carib, Méx)* spinster, old maid.

quedada²* NF joke, tease; hoax.

quedado ADJ *(Cono Sur, Méx)* lazy.

quedar [1a] [1] VI **(a)** *(gen)* to stay, remain; **quedamos una semana** we stayed a week; ~ **atrás** to remain behind; to fall behind.
(b) *(en un estado:* + PREP, + ADJ*)* to remain, be; ~ **asombrado** to be amazed; ~ **inmóvil** to remain *(o be, stand etc)* motionless; *(vehículo etc)* to remain stationary; ~ **de pie** to remain standing; ~ **ciego** to go blind; ~ **cojo** to go lame; **después de eso ha quedado en ridículo** as a result of that he made a fool of himself; **A pretendía que B quedara en ridículo** A was trying to make B look ridiculous; **ha quedado sin hacer** it remained undone, nothing was done about it; **el proyecto quedó sin realizar** the plan was never carried out; **ir quedando atrás** to fall behind; **con las reformas el edificio queda mejor** as a result of the alterations the building looks better; **la cosa queda así** there the matter rests, that's how the affair stands; **¿cuánto te quedo a deber?** how much do I owe you?; **quedó heredero del título** he became heir to the title, that made him heir to the title.
(c) *(~ bien etc)* ~ **bien** to come off well; to do o.s. justice; to make a good impression; ~ **bien con uno** to be on good terms with sb, stand well with sb; **por** ~ **bien** (so as) to make a good impression; ~ **mal** to do badly, come off badly; ~ **mal con uno** to be at odds with sb; **por no** ~ **mal** in order to do the right thing, so as not to cause any offence; **ha quedado como un canalla** he showed himself to be a rotter*, he was shown up as the rotter he is*.
(d) *(lugar)* to be; **eso queda muy lejos** that's a long way (away); **queda un poco más al oeste** it is *(o lies)* a little further west; **esa cuestión queda fuera de nuestros límites** that matter lies *(o falls)* is) outside the bounds of our inquiry.
(e) *(sobrar)* to remain, be left; **quedan 6** there are 6 left; **me quedan 6** I have 6 left; **nos queda poco dinero** we haven't much money left; **no quedan más que escombros** there is nothing left but rubble; **ya no queda motivo para ello** there is no longer any reason for it; **no me queda otro remedio** I have no alternative (left).
(f) *(faltar)* to be ... still; **quedan pocos días para la fiesta** only a few days remain till the party, there are only a few days to go to *(o* left till) the party; **nos quedan 12 kms para llegar al pueblo** there are still 12 kms to go to the village.
(g) **¿cómo quedamos entonces?** what's the arrangement then?
(h) ~ **con uno** *(citarse)* to arrange to meet sb, make a date with sb; *(flirtear)* to give sb the eye* *(o* the come-on*)*; *(burlarse de)* to poke fun at sb; ~ **de verse con uno** *(LAm)* to arrange to meet sb.
(i) ~ **en** to turn out to be, result in, end up as; **todo ese trabajo quedó en nada** all that work came to nothing; **las discusiones quedaron en un informe más** the discussions merely resulted in one more report.
(j) ~ **en** + *infin* (*t* ~ **de**, *Méx*) to agree to + *infin*, arrange to + *infin*; ~ **en que ...** to agree that ...; **¿en qué quedamos?** what do we decide to do then?
(k) ~ **por** + *infin* to be still to be + PTP, remain to be + PTP; **las cartas quedan aún por escribir** the letters are still to be written; **eso queda todavía por estudiar** that remains to be studied, that still has to be studied.
(l) ~ + *ger* to be + *ger*, go on + *ger*; **él quedaba trabajando en casa** he went on working at home.
[2] **quedarse** VR **(a)** *en sentidos básicos,* = 1 **(a)** *y* **(b)**, *p.ej.* ~ **atrás** to remain behind; to fall behind; *(sentidos adicionales)* to stay on, stay

behind, linger (on); ~ **en una pensión** to stay at a boarding-house, put up at a boarding-house; ~ **con unos amigos** to stay with some friends; **se me queda pequeña esta camisa** this shirt has got too small for me, I've outgrown this shirt; ~ **sin** to find o.s. out of, run out of; **nos hemos quedado sin café** we've run out of coffee; ~ **sin empleo** to lose one's job; ~ **helado** *(fig)* to be scared stiff.
(b) *(mar, viento)* to fall calm.
(c) ~ **con** *(retener)* to keep, hold on to, retain; to acquire, get hold of; *(fig)* to take, prefer; **se quedó con mi pluma** he kept my pen, he walked off with my pen; **quédese con la vuelta** keep the change; **el vencedor se queda con todo** winner takes all; **entre A y B, me quedo con B** if I have to choose between A and B, I'll take B; **así que me quedé con el más tonto de los tres** so I got left with the stupidest of the three.
(d) ~ **con uno** (*: *estafar)* to swindle sb, cheat sb; *(tratar de engañar)* to try to fool sb; *(convencer)* to win sb round, talk sb round; **¿quieres quedarte conmigo?** are you trying to kid me?*
(e) ~ **con uno** *(Esp*: *tomar el pelo)* to take the mickey out of sb*, pull sb's leg*.
(f) ~ **con uno** *(Esp*: *mirar)* to give sb the come-hither look, look invitingly at sb.
(g) ~ **con uno** *(Esp*: *aburrir)* to bore the pants off sb*.
(h) *(locuciones)* **no se queda con la cólera dentro** he can't control his anger, he can't keep his anger bottled up; ~ **en nada** to come to nothing; **no se quedó en menos** he was not to be outdone.
(i) *(Cono Sur)* *(miembro)* to become paralysed; *(persona)* to die, pass away *(euf)*.
(j) ~ + *ger* to be + *ger*, go on + *ger*; **se nos quedó mirando asombrado** he stood *(etc)* looking at us in amazement.
[3] VT (*): **me quedo este paraguas** I'll take this umbrella; **así que me lo quedé** so I took it; **me la quedo** *(acepto)* I'll buy it*, I'll stay with it*.

quedito ADV very softly, very gently.

quedo [1] ADJ **(a)** *(inmóvil)* still. **(b)** *voz* quiet, soft, gentle; *paso etc* soft.
[2] ADV softly, gently; **¡~!** gently now!

quedón: ADJ *(Esp)* **(a)** *(guasón)* jokey, waggish. **(b)** *(ligón)* flirtatious, fond of the opposite sex.

quehacer NM job, task; **~es (domésticos)** household jobs, chores; **agobiado de** ~ overburdened with work; **atender a sus ~es** to go about one's business; **tener mucho** ~ to have a lot to do.

queimada NF *traditional Galician hot drink made with flamed 'orujo', sugar and lemon.*

queja NF **(a)** *(gen)* complaint; *(protesta)* protest; grumble, grouse*; *(rencor)* grudge, resentment; *(Jur)* protest; **una** ~ **infundada** an unjustified complaint; **presentar** ~ **de uno** to make a complaint about sb; **tener** ~ **de uno** to have a complaint to make about sb; **tengo** ~ **de ti** I've a bone to pick with you.
(b) *(quejido)* moan, groan; ~ **de dolor** groan of pain.

quejadera NF *(And, Méx)*, **quejambre** NF *(And, Méx)* moaning.

quejarse [1a] VR **(a)** *(gen)* to complain *(de* about, of); *(refunfuñar)* grumble *(de* about, at); *(protestar)* to protest *(de* about, at); ~ **de que ...** to complain (about the fact) that ...; ~ **a un oficial** to complain to an official.
(b) *(gemir)* to moan, groan; to whine.

quejica* NMF, **quejicas*** NMF INVAR, **quejicoso, -a*** NM/F = **quejón.**

quejido NM moan, groan; whine; **dar ~s** to moan, groan; to whine.

quejigal NM, **quejigar** NM gall-oak grove.

quejigo NM gall-oak.

quejón* [1] ADJ grumbling, complaining.
[2] NM, **quejona** NF grumbler, constant complainer, misery*.

quejoso ADJ *persona* complaining; *tone* querulous, whining; plaintive.

quejumbre NF moan, groan.

quejumbroso ADJ = **quejoso.**

quela: NF, **quel(i)**¹: NM house; **ir a** ~ to go home.

queli²: NM mate, pal*.

quelite NM *(CAm, Méx)* *(verduras)* greens, vegetables; *(renuevo)* shoot, tip, green part; **poner a uno como un** ~ *(Méx*)* to make mincemeat of sb.

quelonia NF *(Carib)* turtle.

quelonio NM chelonian.

quelpo NM kelp.

quema NF **(a)** *(acto)* fire; burning, combustion; *(Méx)* burning-off (of scrub). **(b)** *(Cono Sur: vertedero)* rubbish-dump. **(c)** *(Méx: fig)* danger. **(d)** **hacer** ~ to hit the target.

quemable ADJ inflammable.

quemado [1] ADJ **(a)** *(gen)* burned, burnt; **aquí huele a** ~ I smell something burning in here; **esto sabe a** ~ this has a burnt taste. **(b)** *persona (agotado)* burned out, finished; *(resentido)* bitter; **espía** ~ spy who has had his cover blown. **(c)** *(moralmente, políticamente)* discredited. **(d)** *(Cono Sur: muy oscuro)* very dark.
[2] NM **(a)** *(acto)* burning; *(Med)* cauterization; *(nuclear)* burn-out. **(b)** *(LAm)* burnt field.

quemador NM burner; hob; (*LAm: mechero*) lighter; **~ de gas** gas burner.

quemadura NF (**a**) (*gen*) burn; (*con líquido*) scald; (*por el sol*) sunburn; (*de fusible*) blowing, blow-out; **~ de primer grado** first-degree burns. (**b**) (*Bot: por helada*) cutting; withering. (**c**) (*Bot: tizón*) smut.

quemar [1a] **1** VT (**a**) to burn (*t Culin; por ácido, sol*); to burn up; to set on fire, kindle; to scorch; (*con líquido*) to scald; *fusible* to blow, burn out.
(**b**) *plantas* (*helada*) to cut, wither, burn.
(**c**) (*fig*) *fortuna etc* to burn up, squander; *persona* to burn out; *organismo, gobierno* to damage, affect seriously; *suma* to spend quickly, get through in no time; *recursos* to use up, exhaust; *precios* to slash, cut; *géneros* to sell off cheap.
(**d**) (*fig: molestar*) to annoy, upset; **estar muy quemado** to be very hurt; **estar quemado con** (*o* **por**) **algo** to be sick and tired of sth.
(**e**) (*CAm, Méx: denunciar*) to denounce, inform on.
(**f**) (*Carib, Méx: estafar*) to swindle.
(**g**) (*Carib: con arma de fuego*) to shoot.
2 VI (**a**) to be burning hot; **esto está que quema, está quemando** it's burning hot; **es una especia que quema en la lengua** it's a spice that tastes really hot, it's a spice that burns the tongue.
(**b**) (*piel*) to get tanned.
3 quemarse VR (**a**) (*hacerse daño*) to burn o.s.; (*consumirse*) to burn up, burn away; (*edificio etc*) to burn down; (*ropa etc*) to scorch, get scorched; (*con el sol*) to get sunburnt; **~ con la sopa** to burn one's mouth on the soup; **¡que me quemo!*** I'm scorching!, I'm terribly hot.
(**b**) (*en juego*) to get warm; **¡que te quemas!** you're getting warm!
(**c**) (*fig: agotarse*) to burn o.s. out, exhaust o.s.
(**d**) (*fig: inquietarse*) to fret.
(**e**) (*Carib, Cono Sur: deprimirse*) to get depressed.
(**f**) (*moralmente, políticamente*) to be discredited, lose credibility.

quemarropa: a ~ ADV (*lit, fig*) point-blank.

quemazón NF (**a**) (*gen*) burn; burning, combustion; (*CAm, Carib, Méx*) fire.
(**b**) (*calor*) intense heat.
(**c**) (*Med*) burning sensation; (*fig*) itch; smarting, sting.
(**d**) (*fig: dicho*) cutting remark, wounding thing (to say).
(**e**) (*fig: rencor*) pique, resentment, annoyance.
(**f**) (*Com*) bargain sale, cut-price sale.
(**g**) (*And, Cono Sur: espejismo*) mirage (*on the pampas*).

quemón, -ona: NM/F (*Méx*) dope smoker‡.

quena NF (*And, Cono Sur*) Indian flute.

queo¹‡ NM (*Esp*) house.

queo²* NM: **dar el ~** to shout a warning.

quepis NM INVAR kepi.

quepo *etc* V **caber**.

queque NM (*And*) various types of cake; (*CAm, Méx*) bun, cake.

queratina NF keratin.

queratinizarse [1f] VR to keratinize

querella NF (**a**) (*queja*) complaint. (**b**) (*Jur: acusación*) charge, accusation; (*proceso*) suit, case. (**c**) (*controversia*) dispute, controversy.

querellado, -a NM/F defendant.

querellante **1** ADJ: **parte ~ = 2**.
2 NMF (*Jur*) plaintiff.

querellarse [1a] VR (**a**) (*quejarse*) to complain. (**b**) (*Jur*) to file a complaint, bring an action (*ante* before, *contra, de* against).

querencia NF (**a**) (*Zool*) lair, haunt; (*Taur*) (bull's) favourite spot; (*fig*) favourite spot, home ground, haunt; **buscar la ~** to home, head for home.
(**b**) (*Zool: instinto*) homing instinct; (*fig: nostalgia*) longing for home, homesickness.

querendón (*LAm*) **1** ADJ affectionate, loving, of an affectionate nature.
2 NM, **querendona** NF (*favorito*) favourite, pet; (*amante*) lover.

▼ **querer** [2t] **1** VTI (**a**) (*desear*) to want, wish (for); **¿cuál quieres?** which one do you want?; **no quiero más** I don't want any more; **hablaremos otro día, ¿quieres?** we'll talk another day, shall we?; **pero ¡que quieres!** but what do you expect?; **¿qué más quieres?** what more do you want?; **¡qué mas quisiera yo!** would that I could!, my wishes entirely!; **¿quiere un café?** would you like some coffee?; **¿cuánto quieren por el coche?** how much do they want for the car?, what are they asking for the car?; **como Vd quiera** as you wish, as you please; **ven cuando quieras** come when you like; **quiera o no, quiera que no** willy-nilly, whether he (*etc*) likes it or not; **hace lo que quiere** she does what she wants; **¡lo que quieras!** anything you say!; have it your own way!; **lo hizo queriendo*** he did it deliberately; **lo hizo sin ~** he didn't mean to do it, he did it inadvertently, he did it by mistake; **~ es poder** where there's a will there's a way; **¡está como quiere!** (*Esp*) she's a bit of all right!‡
▼ (**b**) (+ *verbo*) **~ hacer algo** to want to do sth; **~ que uno haga algo** to want sb to do sth; **no quiso pagar** he didn't want to pay; he re-

fused to pay; **no queremos vender** we're not about to sell; **ha querido quedarse en casa** he preferred to stay at home, he decided to stay at home; **quiso hacerlo pero no pudo** he tried to do it but couldn't; **¿quiere abrir la ventana?** would you mind opening the window?, please open the window; **¿qué quieres que te diga?** how should I put it?, what can I say?; **más quiero** + *infin* I would rather + *infin*, I would prefer to + *infin*; **mejor quisiera** + *infin* I would rather + *infin*; **la ley quiere que seamos buenos** the law requires us to be good; **este crítico quiere que Góngora haya sido loco** this critic tries to make out that Góngora was mad, this critic would have us believe that Góngora was mad; **la tradición quiere que ...** tradition has it that ...; **éste quiere que le rompan la cabeza*** this fellow is asking for a crack on the head*.
(**c**) (*absoluto*) **¡no quiero!** I won't!, I refuse!; **sí quiero** (*matrimonio*) I will; **'él no quiere venir' ... '¡sí (que) quiero!'** 'he doesn't want to come' ... 'but I do!'; **lo hago porque quiero** I do it because I want to; **pero no quiso** but he refused; but he was unwilling; **¿quiere?** do you want some?, would you like some?
(**d**) (*requerir*) to need, demand; **tal traje quiere un sombrero ancho** that dress needs a big hat to go with it; **¡esto quiere unas copas!** we must have a drink on that!, that deserves a drink to celebrate it!
(**e**) (*impersonal*) **quería amanecer** dawn was about to break; **parece que quiere llover** it looks like rain, it seems that it's trying to rain.
(**f**) (*amar*) to love; to like; **~ bien a uno** to be fond of sb; **¡te quiero, bobo!** I love you, you idiot!; **en la oficina le quieren mucho** he is well liked at the office; **¿no me quieres siquiera un poquito?** don't you like me just a little bit?; **hace tiempo que te quiero** I've been in love with you for a long time; **hacerse ~ por uno** to endear o.s. to sb; **¡por lo que más quieras!** by all that's sacred!; (*arrancando pétalos etc*) **me quiere ... no me quiere** she loves me ... she loves me not.
(**g**) **como quiera** *etc*: V **comoquiera, dondequiera.**
2 NM love, affection; **tener ~ a** to be fond of.

QUERER   *ver también la entrada*

● La estructura española *querer que alguien haga algo* no se traduce literalmente al inglés, sino que debe emplearse la construcción *want* + *somebody* + INFINITIVO *con to*:
   Quiero que me ayude con esto
   I want him to help me with this
   Quería que la conocieras
   I wanted you to meet her
● Si se trata de una petición directa a alguien, hecha de forma más cortés, es preferible el uso de *I'd like you* + INFINITIVO *con to*:
   Quisiera que limpiara primero la cocina
   I'd like you to clean the kitchen first
   Para otros usos y ejemplos ver la entrada.

---

querida NF (**a**) (*persona amada*) darling, beloved; **¡sí, ~!** yes, darling!
(**b**) (*amante*) mistress, lover.

querido **1** ADJ (*amado*) dear, darling, beloved; (*en carta*) dear; **nuestra querida patria** our beloved country.
(**b**) (*And*) nice.
2 NM (**a**) (*persona amada*) darling, beloved; **¡sí, ~!** yes, darling!; **el ~ de las musas** the darling of the muses.
(**b**) (*amante*) lover.

querindongo, -a NM/F lover.

quermes, quermés NF kermes.

querosén NM, **queroseno** NM, **querosín** NM (*LAm*) kerosene, paraffin.

querúbico ADJ cherubic.

querubín NM cherub.

quesadilla NF (*torta*) cheesecake; (*Méx*) folded tortilla.

quesera NF (**a**) (*persona*) dairymaid; cheesemaker. (**b**) (*plato*) cheesedish.

quesería NF (**a**) (*tienda*) dairy; (*fábrica*) cheese factory. (**b**) (*quesos*) cheeses; dairy products.

quesero **1** ADJ cheese (*atr*); **la industria quesera** the cheese industry.
2 NM dairyman; cheesemaker.

quesillo NM (*CAm*) tortilla with cream cheese filling.

queso NM (**a**) cheese; **~ azul** blue cheese; **~ de bola** Dutch cheese; **~ crema, ~ de nata** cream cheese; **~ helado** ice-cream brick; **~ de puerco** (*Méx*) jellied pork; **~ rallado** grated cheese; **darla a uno con ~*** to swindle sb, pull a fast one on sb. (**b**) **~s** (‡: *pies*) plates‡, feet.

quetzal NM (**a**) quetzal (*Guatemalan unit of currency*). (**b**) (*ave*) quetzal.

quevedos NMPL pince-nez.

quey NM (*And*) cake.

quiá INTERJ (*Esp* †) surely not!

quíbole* INTERJ (*Méx*) **¿~?** how's things?

quiche NM quiche.

quichua **1** ADJ, NMF Quechua.
2 NM (*Ling*) Quechua.

---

quichuismo NM Quechuan word (o expression).

quichuista NM (a) (*LAm: especialista*) Quechua specialist. (b) (*And, Cono Sur: hablante*) Quechua speaker.

quicio NM upright, jamb; **estar fuera de ~** (*fig*) to be out of joint; **sacar a uno de ~** (*fig*) to irritate sb, get on sb's nerves; to get sb worked up; **estas cosas me sacan de ~** these things make me see red.

quico* NM: **ponerse como el ~** (*Esp*) (*comer mucho*) to stuff o.s.; (*engordar*) to get as fat as a pig.

quid NM core, crux; **dar en el ~** to hit the nail on the head; **he aquí el ~ del asunto** here we have the nub of the matter.

quídam NM (a) (*alguien*) somebody, somebody or other. (b) (*pey*) nobody, nonentity.

quiebra NF (a) (*grieta*) crack, fissure; slit.
(b) (*Fin*) bankruptcy; failure; (*Econ*) slump, crash, collapse; (*fig*) failure; risk of failure; **dar en ~, ir a la ~** to go bankrupt; **es una cosa que no tiene ~** it just can't go wrong, it's a venture that carries no risk.

quiebre NM breaking, rupture.

quiebro NM (a) (*Taur etc*) dodge, swerve; avoiding action; **dar el ~ a uno** (*fig*) to dodge sb. (b) (*Mús*) grace note(s), trill.

quien PRON REL (a) (*sujeto*) who, (*ac*) whom; **la señorita con ~ hablaba** the young lady to whom I was talking, the young lady I was talking to; **las personas con ~es estabas** the people you were with; **esta señora es a ~ tienes que dar el recado** this is the lady to whom you are to give the message.
(b) (*indefinido*) **~ dice eso es tonto** whoever says that is a fool; **~ lo sepa, que lo diga** o **que lo diga ~ lo sepa** let whoever knows it speak up about it; **~ habla más trabaja menos** he who talks most works least; **contestó como ~ no quería** he answered as if he was reluctant to; **hay ~ no lo acepta** there are some who do not accept it; **no hay ~ lo aguante** nobody can stand him.
(c) **~ más, ~ menos tiene sus problemas** everybody has problems; **cada ~** each one, every one.

quién PRON INTERROG (*sujeto*) who, (*ac*) whom; **¿~ es?** who is it?; who's there?; (*Telec*) who's calling?; **'¿Q~ es ~?'** 'Who's Who?'; **¿a ~ lo diste?** to whom did you give it?, who did you give it to?; **¿a ~ le toca jugar?** whose turn is it to play?, whose go is it?; **¿con ~ estabas anoche?** who were you with last night?; **¿de ~ es la bufanda esa?** whose scarf is that?, who does that scarf belong to?; **¡~ pudiese!** if only I could!; **¿~ de ustedes lo reconoce?** which of you recognizes it?; **no sé ~ lo dijo primero** I don't know who said it first.

quienquiera PRON INDEF, PL **quienesquiera** whoever; **le cazaremos ~ que sea** we'll catch him whoever he is.

quiera *etc* V **querer**.

quietismo NM quietism.

quietista NMF quietist.

quieto ADJ (a) (*inmóvil*) still; motionless; **¡~!** (*a perro*) down boy!; **¡~!**, **¡estáte ~!** (*a niño*) keep still!, stop fidgeting!; behave yourself!; **dejar ~ a uno** to leave sb alone; **estar ~ como un poste** (o **una estatua**) to stand stock-still.
(b) *carácter* calm, staid, placid.

quietud NF stillness; quietude; calm.

quif NM hashish.

quihubo EXCL (*Méx*) how's it going?

quijada NF jaw, jawbone.

quijotada NF quixotic act.

quijote NM quixotic person; dreamer, hopelessly unrealistic person, do-gooder*; well-meaning busybody; **Don Q~** Don Quixote.

quijotería NF (a) = **quijotismo**. (b) = **quijotada**.

quijotescamente ADV quixotically.

quijotesco ADJ quixotic.

quijotismo NM quixotism.

quil. ABR **de quilates** carats, c.

quilar* [1a] VT (*Esp*) to screw*.

quilatar [1a] VT = **aquilatar**.

quilate NM carat.

quilco NM (*Cono Sur*) large basket.

quiligua NF (*Méx*) large basket.

quilla¹ NF (*Náut*) keel; **colocar la ~ de un buque** to lay down a ship; **dar de ~** to keel over.

quilla² NF (*LAm*) cushion.

quillango NM (*And, Cono Sur*) fur blanket.

quilo¹ NM (*Anat*) chyle; **sudar el ~*** to have a tough time; to slave, slog.

quilo² NM kilo, kilogramme.

quilo... = **kilo...**

quilombear [1a] VI (*Cono Sur*) to go whoring.

quilombera NF (*Cono Sur*) whore.

quilombero ADJ (*Cono Sur*) rowdy.

quilombo NM (a) (*And, Cono Sur: burdel*) brothel. (b) (*And, Cono Sur: lío*) row, set-to*. (c) (*And, Carib*) (*lugar apartado*) out-of-the-way spot;

(*choza*) rustic hut, shack.

quiltrear* [1a] VT (*Cono Sur*) to annoy.

quiltro NM (*Cono Sur*) (a) (*perrito*) lapdog; (*callejero*) stray dog, mongrel. (b) (*: *tipo pesado*) pest, nuisance.

quimba NF (a) (*And, Carib: zapato*) sandal. (b) (*And: mueca*) grimace. (c) **~s** (*And*) (*dificultades*) difficulties; (*deudas*) debts.

quimbo NM (*Carib*) knife, machete.

quimera NF (a) (*Mit*) chimera.
(b) (*alucinación*) hallucination; (*noción*) fancy, fantastic idea; (*sueño*) impossible notion, pipe dream.
(c) (*sospecha*) unfounded suspicion; **tener la ~ de que ...** to suspect quite wrongly that ...
(d) (*riña*) quarrel.

quimérico ADJ fantastic, fanciful; *esperanza, proyecto etc* impossible.

quimerista ① ADJ (a) (*pendenciero*) quarrelsome; (*ruidoso*) rowdy. (b) (*soñador*) dreamy.
② NMF (*V ADJ*) (a) quarrelsome person; rowdy, brawler. (b) dreamer, visionary.

quimerizar [1f] VI to indulge in fantasy, indulge in pipe dreams.

química¹ NF chemistry; **~ inorgánica** inorganic chemistry; **~ orgánica** organic chemistry.

químico ① ADJ chemical.
② NM, **química²** NF chemist.

quimioterapia NF chemotherapy.

quimono NM kimono.

quimoterapia NF chemotherapy.

quina NF quinine, Peruvian bark; **tragar ~*** to have to put up with it.

quincalla NF (a) (*gen*) hardware, ironmongery. (b) (*una* ~) trinket.

quincallería NF ironmonger's (shop), hardware store (*US*).

quincallero, -a NM ironmonger, hardware dealer (*US*).

quince ① ADJ fifteen; (*fecha*) fifteenth; **~ días** (*frec*) fortnight; **dar ~ y raya a uno** to be able to beat sb hollow (*en* at), be more than a match for sb (*en* at).
② NM fifteen.

quinceañera¹ NF (*Méx*) coming-out balls for girls who have reached their 15th birthday.

quinceañero ① ADJ fifteen-year old, (*frec*) teenage.
② NM, **quinceañera²** NF fifteen-year old, (*frec*) teenager.

quinceavo, -a ADJ, NM fifteenth.

quincena NF (a) (*quince días*) fortnight. (b) (*condena*) fortnight's imprisonment. (c) (*pago*) fortnightly pay.

quincenal ADJ fortnightly.

quincenalmente ADV fortnightly, once a fortnight.

quinceno ADJ fifteenth.

quincha NF (*LAm*) wall (o roof *etc*) made of rushes and mud.

quinchar [1a] VI (*LAm*) to build walls (*etc*) of **quincha**.

quincho NM (*Cono Sur: choza*) mud hut; (*And, Cono Sur: cerco*) mud fence; (*Cono Sur: restaurán*) steak restaurant.

quincuagenario, -a ADJ, NMF fifty-year old.

Quincuagésima NF Quinquagesima Sunday.

quincuagésimo ADJ fiftieth.

quindécimo ADJ fifteenth.

quinfa NF (*And*) sandal.

quingentésimo ADJ five-hundredth.

quingo NM (*And*) twist, turn; **~s** zigzag.

quinguear [1a] VI (*And*) to twist, turn; to zigzag.

quiniela NF pools coupon; **~s** football pool(s); **~ hípica** horse-racing totalizator; **hacer ~s** to do the pools.

QUINIELA

ⓘ The **quiniela** is the Spanish equivalent of the football pools and coupons are available from **estancos**. Players can predict a home win (1), a draw (X) or an away win (2) for most premier and first division matches. 12 or more correct forecasts wins a prize, the size of which varies from week to week depending on the takings or **recaudación**. There is also a a version for horse-racing, the **quiniela hípica**, although most betting on horses is done at the racecourse.

⟶ See also ENCANCO
---

quinielista NMF punter, participant in a football pool.

quinielístico ADJ pools (*attr*); **boleto ~** pools coupon; **peña quinielística** pools syndicate.

quinientos ADJ five hundred; **en el ~** in the sixteenth century; **volvió a las quinientas*** she got back at some unearthly hour.

quinina NF quinine.

quino NM (*LAm*) cinchona (tree).

quinqué NM (a) (*lámpara*) oil lamp. (b) (*: *astucia*) know-how, shrewdness; **tener mucho ~** to know what's going on, know what the score is*.

quinquenal ADJ quinquennial; **plan ~** five-year plan.

quinquenalmente ADV every five years.

quinquenio NM quinquennium, five-year period.

quinqui* NM (*bandido*) bandit, gangster; (*delincuente*) delinquent, criminal; (*vendedor*) small-time dealer, tinker.

quinta NF (**a**) (*casa*) villa, country house; (*LAm*) small estate on the outskirts of a town.
(**b**) (*Mil*) draft, call-up; **la ~ de 1998** the 1998 call-up, the class called up in 1998; **ser de la ~ de uno** to be the same age as sb; **entrar en ~s** to reach the call-up age; to be called up.
(**c**) (*Mús*) fifth.

quintacolumnista NMF fifth columnist.

quintada* NF rag, trick.

quintaesencia NF quintessence.

quintaesencial ADJ quintessential.

quintal NM (*Castilla*) measure of weight, = 46 kg; **~ métrico** = 100 kg.

quintar [1a] VT (*Mil*) to call up, conscript, draft (*US*).

quintería NF farmhouse.

quintero NM (*dueño*) farmer; (*bracero*) farmhand, labourer.

quinteto NM quintet(te).

quintilla NF (*Liter: Hist*) a five-line stanza.

quintillizo NM, **quintilliza** NF quintuplet.

Quintín NM: **se armó la de San ~*** all hell broke loose; **se va a armar la de San ~** there will be an almighty row*; **costó la de San ~*** it cost a bomb*.

quinto [1] ADJ fifth.
[2] NM (**a**) (*Mat*) fifth. (**b**) (*Mil*) conscript, national serviceman. (**c**) (*: juego*) bingo. (**d**) (*Méx Fin*) nickel. (**e**) (*botellín*) small bottle of beer.

quíntral (*And, Cono Sur*) NM (**a**) (*Zool*) armadillo. (**b**) (*Mús*) ten-stringed guitar.

quintuplicar [1g] [1] VT to quintuple.
[2] **quintuplicarse** VR to quintuple.

quíntuplo [1] ADJ quintuple, fivefold.
[2] NM quintuple; **X es el ~ de Y** X is five times the size of Y.

quinzavo = quinceavo.

quiña NF (*And*), **quiñadura** NF (*And*) scratch.

quiñar* [1a] VT (*And*) to scratch.

quiñazo NM (*LAm*) smash, collision.

quiño NM (*LAm: puñetazo*) punch.

quiñón NM piece of land, plot of land.

quiñonero NM part-owner (of a piece of land).

quiosco NM (*Com*) kiosk, stand, stall; (*de jardín*) summerhouse, pavilion; (*de parque*: **t ~ de música**) bandstand; **~ de necesidad** public lavatory; **~ de periódicos** news-stand.

quiosquero, -a NM/F proprietor of a news-stand, newspaper seller.

quipe NM (*And*) knapsack, rucksack, backpack (*US*).

quipu NM (*And Hist*) quipu (*system used by the Incas to record information using knotted strings*).

quiqui* NM screw**.

quiquiriquí NM cock-a-doodle-doo.

quirico NM (*Carib*) (*criado*) servant; (*mensajero*) messenger; (*ladrón*) petty thief.

quirófano NM operating theatre.

quirógrafo NM (*Méx*) IOU.

quirología NF palmistry.

quiromancia NF palmistry.

quiromántico, -a NM/F palmist.

quiromasaje NM massage.

quiropodia NF chiropody.

quiropráctica[1] NF chiropractic.

quiropráctico, -a[2] NM/F chiropractor.

quiroterapeuta NMF chiropractor

quirúrgicamente ADV surgically; **intervenir ~ a uno** to operate on sb.

quirúrgico ADJ surgical.

quise *etc* V querer.

quisicosa* NF puzzle, conundrum.

quisling ['kizlin] NM, PL **quislings** ['kizlin] quisling.

quisque* NM: **cada ~, todo ~** every man-Jack; **como cada ~** like everyone else; **ni ~** not a living soul.

quisqui* NM: **ser un ~** to be a fusspot*; to have a mania for details.

quisquilla NF (**a**) (*bagatela*) trifle, triviality.
(**b**) (*pega*) slight snag, minor difficulty.
(**c**) (*sofisterías*) **~s** quibbles, quibbling, hair-splitting; **¡déjate de ~s!** stop fussing!; don't quibble!; **pararse en ~s** to bicker; to quibble.
(**d**) (*Zool*) shrimp.
(**e**) (*:*) cunt**.

quisquilloso ADJ (**a**) (*sensible*) touchy, oversensitive; (*irritable*) irritable; (*delicado*) pernickety*, choosy*, fussy. (**b**) (*sofístico*) quibbling, hair-

splitting.

quiste NM cyst.

quisto ADJ: **bien ~, mal ~** V bienquisto, malquisto.

quita NF (**a**) *de deuda* release (from a debt); (*LAm: descuento*) rebate. (**b**) **de ~ y pon** V quitapón.

quitacutículas NM INVAR cuticle remover.

quitaesmalte NM nail-polish remover.

quitagusto NM (*And*) intruder, gatecrasher.

quitaipón NM: **de ~** removable; *capucha* detachable.

quitalodos NM INVAR boot-scraper.

quitamanchas NM INVAR (**a**) (*líquido etc*) cleaning material, stain remover. (**b**) (*Esp: persona*) dry cleaner; (*tienda*) dry-cleaner's (shop).

quitamiedos NM INVAR (*Esp*) handrail.

quitamotas* NM INVAR creep**, toady.

quitanieves NM INVAR snowplough.

quitapelillos* NM INVAR creep**, toady.

quitapenas: NM INVAR (*pistola*) pistol, rod**; (*US*); (*navaja*) knife, chiv**.

quitapesares NM INVAR comfort; distraction.

quitapiedras NM INVAR (*Ferro*) cowcatcher.

quitapintura NF paint-remover, paint-stripper.

quitapón: **de ~** detachable, removable.

quitar [1a] [1] VT (**a**) (*gen*) to take away, remove; *ropa etc* to take off; *mancha* to remove, get rid of, get out; *dolor etc* to relieve, stop, kill; *felicidad* to destroy; *vida* to take; (*Mec*) *pieza* to remove, take out, take off; *mesa* to clear; *abuso, dificultad, obstáculo* to remove, do away with, put an end to; *tiempo* to take (up); *molestia, inquietud* to save, prevent; (*Mat*) to take away, subtract; *valor etc* to reduce; (*robar*) to remove, steal; **quitando el postre comimos bien** apart (*o* aside) from the dessert we had a good meal; **~ extensión a un campo** to reduce the size of a field; **~ importancia a un acontecimiento** to diminish the importance of an event; **no quita nada de su valor** it does not detract at all from its value; **me quita mucho tiempo** it takes up a lot of my time; **le van a ~ ese privilegio** they are going to take that privilege away from him; **le quitaron la cartera en el tren** he had his wallet stolen on the train; **me quitó las ganas de comer** it took away my appetite; **el café me quita el sueño** coffee stops me sleeping; **quitando 3 ó 4, van a ir todos** except for 3 or 4 everybody is going; V medio, mesa.
(**b**) *golpe* to avert, ward off; (*Esgrima*) to parry.
(**c**) (*impedir*) **~ a uno de hacer algo** to stop sb doing sth, prevent sb (from) doing sth; **esto no quita que tú tenías la culpa** this doesn't mean it wasn't your fault; **eso no quita para que me ayudes** that doesn't stop you helping me, that is no bar to your helping me.
(**d**) (*:*) *dinero* to make.
[2] VI (**a**) **¡quita!, ¡quita de ahí!** get away!, not a bit of it!
(**b**) **ni quito ni pongo** I'm not saying one thing or the other; I'm strictly neutral; **ni me quita ni me pone** it doesn't bother me.
[3] **quitarse** VR (**a**) (*retirarse*) to remove o.s.; to withdraw (*de* from); **~ de la vista de uno** to remove o.s. from sb's sight; **esa mancha de vino no se quita** that wine stain won't come off (*o* come out); **¡quítate de ahí!** come (*o* get) out of there!, off with you!; **me quito** (*And**) I'm off, I must be going; V medio *etc*.
(**b**) **~ algo de encima** to get rid of sth; to cast sth off, shake sth off; **~ la ropa** to take off one's clothing; **~ una jaqueca andando** to walk off a headache.
(**c**) **~ de un vicio** to give up a vice, wean o.s. away from a bad habit; **~ del tabaco** to give up smoking; **se me ha quitado el gusto de fumar** I've lost my taste for smoking; **~ la preocupación** to stop worrying; **quitémonos de tonterías** let's stop being silly.

quitasol NM sunshade, parasol.

quitasueño NM worry, problem.

quite NM (**a**) (*acto*) removal.
(**b**) (*Esgrima*) parry.
(**c**) (*movimiento*) dodge, sidestep, swerve; (*Taur*) manoeuvre whereby bullfighters draw the bull away from an injured colleague, horse etc. **estar al ~** to be ready to go to somebody's aid; **hacer el ~ a uno** (*Cono Sur*) to avoid somebody; **esto no tiene ~** there's no help for it.
(**d**) (*LAm Dep*) tackle.

quiteño [1] ADJ of (*o* from) Quito.
[2] NM, **quiteña** NF native (*o* inhabitant) of Quito; **los ~s** the people of Quito.

quitrín NM (*CAm, Carib, Cono Sur*) trap (*vehicle*).

▼ **quizá(s)** [ki'θa(s)] ADV perhaps, maybe.

quórum ['kworum] NM, PL **quórums** ['kworum] quorum; **constituir ~** to constitute (*o* make up) a quorum.

R

R, r ['ere] NF (*letra*) R, r.
R. (**a**) (*Rel*) ABR *de* **Reverendo** Reverend, Rev. (**b**) ABR *de* **Real** royal. (**c**) ABR *de* **remite, remitente** sender.
rabada NF hindquarter, rump.
rabadán NM head shepherd.
rabadilla NF (*Anat*) coccyx; (*Culin*: *de pollo*) parson's nose; (*) rear*, tail*.
rabanillo NM wild radish.
rábano NM radish; **~ picante** horseradish; **¡un ~!*** get away!; **no se me da un ~, (no) me importa un ~** I don't care two hoots (*de* about); **tomar el ~ por las hojas** to get hold of the wrong end of the stick, bark up the wrong tree.
rabear [1a] VI (*perro*) to wag its tail.
rabelasiano ADJ Rabelaisian.
rabí NM (*delante de nombre*) rabbi.
rabia NF (**a**) (*Med*) rabies.
  (**b**) (*fig*: *ira*) fury, rage, anger; bad feeling; **¡qué ~!** isn't it infuriating!; **me da ~** it maddens me, it infuriates me, it makes my blood boil; **tener ~ a uno** to have a grudge against sb, have it in for sb; **el maestro le tiene ~** the teacher has it in for him, the teacher doesn't like him; **tomar ~ a** to take a dislike to.
  (**c**) (*LAm*) **con ~** extremely, terribly; **llueve con ~** it's raining with a vengeance; **es fea con ~** she's terribly ugly.
rabiadero NM (*And*) fit of temper.
rabiar [1b] VI (**a**) (*Med*) to have rabies.
  (**b**) (*fig*: *sufrir*) to suffer terribly, be in great pain; **estaba rabiando de dolor de muelas** she had raging toothache.
  (**c**) (*fig*) **esto quema (o pica) que rabia** this is hot enough to burn your mouth; **este cóctel está que rabia*** this cocktail has got a real kick to it*.
  (**d**) (*fig*: *enfadarse*) to rage, rave, be furious; **~ contra** to storm at, rave about; **hacer ~ a uno** to rouse sb to a fury; **las cosas así le hacen ~** things like that make him see red; **está que rabia** he's hopping mad, he's furious; **¡para que rabies!** so there!; just to turn you green with envy.
  (**e**) (*fig*: *anhelar*) **~ por algo** to long for sth, be dying for sth; **~ por + infin** to be dying to + *infin*.
  (**f**) **me gusta a ~*** I'm terribly fond of it.
rabiasca NF (*Carib*) fit of temper.
rabieta* NF fit of temper; paddy*, pet, tantrum*; **tomarse una ~** to get cross, fly into a rage.
rabietas* NMF INVAR touchy sort, bad-tempered person.
rabillo NM (**a**) (*Anat*) small tail.
  (**b**) (*Bot*) leaf stalk.
  (**c**) (*punta*) tip; (*ángulo*) corner; (*parte delgada*) thin part; (*tira*) thin strip of material; **mirar con el ~ del ojo** to look out of the corner of one's eye.
rabimocho ADJ (*And, Carib, Méx*) short-tailed.
rabínico ADJ rabbinical.
rabino NM rabbi; **gran ~** chief rabbi.
rabión NM (t **rabiones**) rapids.
rabiosamente ADV (*fig*) furiously; terribly, violently; rabidly.
rabioso ADJ (**a**) (*Med*) rabid, suffering from rabies; **perro ~** (*fig*) mad dog.
  (**b**) (*fig*: *furioso*) *enfado* furious; *dolor* terrible, raging, violent; *aficionado etc* rabid; *sabor* hot; **poner ~ a uno** to enrage sb.
  (**c**) (*fig*: *enorme*) huge, vast; **de rabiosa actualidad** highly topical.
rabo NM (**a**) (*Anat*) tail; **~ de toro** (*Culin*) oxtail; **con el ~ entre las piernas** crestfallen, dejected; **queda el ~ por desollar** we've still got the most difficult part to do.
  (**b**) (*fig*) tail, train, hanging part; = **rabillo** (**b**) *y* (**c**).
  (**c**) **~ verde** (*CAm*) dirty old man.
rabón ADJ (**a**) *animal* short-tailed; bobtailed; tailless.

  (**b**) (*LAm*: *pequeño*) short, small.
  (**c**) (*Cono Sur*: *desnudo*) stark naked.
  (**d**) (*Carib, Cono Sur*) *cuchillo* damaged.
  (**e**) (*Méx*: *desgraciado*) down on one's luck.
rabona NF (**a**) **hacer ~** (*ausentarse*) to play truant. (**b**) (*LAm*) campfollower.
rabonear [1a] VI (*LAm*) to play truant.
rabosear [1a] VT to mess up, rumple, crumple.
rabotada NF rude remark; coarse expression.
rabudo ADJ long-tailed.
raca*¹ NF (*CAm*) mummy*.
raca:² NM (*Aut*) crate*, old car.
racanear* [1a] VI (*trabajo*) to slack; to swing the lead; (*jugar mal*) to have a bad spell; (*con dinero*) to be stingy.
racaneo* NM, **racanismo*** NM slackness, idleness; stinginess.
rácano* ① ADJ (**a**) (*vago*) bone-idle. (**b**) (*tacaño*) stingy, mean. (**c**) (*artero*) sly, artful.
  ② NM (**a**) (*vago*) slacker, idler; **hacer el ~** to slack; to swing the lead*. (**b**) (*tacaño*) mean devil. (**c**) (*Aut*) crate*, old car.
RACE ['raθe] NM ABR *de* **Real Automóvil Club de España** ≃ Royal Automobile Club, RAC.
racha NF (**a**) (*Met*) gust of wind; squall.
  (**b**) (*fig*: *serie*) string, series; run; **buena ~** piece of luck, stroke of luck, lucky break; **mala ~** piece of bad luck; unlucky spell, spell when everything goes wrong; **a ~s** by fits and starts; **estar de ~** to be in luck; (*Dep*) to be in form.
rache NM (*Carib*) zip.
racheado ADJ *viento* gusty, squally.
rachi: NM night.
rachir [3h] VT (*Cono Sur*) to scratch.
rachoso ADJ (*Cono Sur*) ragged.
racial ADJ racial, race (*atr*); **odio ~** race hatred.
racimo NM bunch, cluster; (*Bot*) raceme.
raciocinación NF ratiocination.
raciocinar [1a] VI to reason.
raciocinio NM (**a**) (*facultad*) reason. (**b**) (*acto*) reasoning.
ración NF (**a**) (*Mat*) ratio. (**b**) (*porción*) portion, helping; **raciones** (*Mil*) rations; **~ de hambre** starvation wage; **~ de reserva** emergency ration; iron ration; **darse una ~ de vista** to have a good look. (**c**) (*Ecl*) prebend.
racional ADJ (**a**) (*Mat, Filos etc*) rational. (**b**) rational, reasonable, sensible.
racionalidad NF rationality.
racionalismo NM rationalism.
racionalista ADJ, NMF rationalist.
racionalización NF rationalization.
racionalizador ADJ rationalizing; streamlining.
racionalizar [1f] VT to rationalize; (*Com*) to streamline.
racionalmente ADV rationally, reasonably, sensibly.
racionamiento NM rationing.
racionar [1a] VT (**a**) (*limitar*) to ration; **estar racionado** to be rationed, be on the ration. (**b**) (*repartir*) to ration out, share out.
racionero NM (*Ecl*) prebendary.
racionista NMF (**a**) (*gen*) person living on an allowance. (**b**) (*actor*) (*Teat*) player of bit parts; ham*, third-rate actor (o actress).
racismo NM racialism, racism.
racista ① ADJ racial, racialist.
  ② NMF racist.
raco* NM (*CAm*) daddy*.
rada NF (*Náut*) roads, roadstead; natural bay.
radar NM (*sistema*) radar; (*estación*) radar station.
radárico ADJ radar (*atr*).
radiación NF (**a**) (*Fís*) radiation; **~ solar** solar radiation; sun's rays; **~**

ultravioleta ultraviolet radiation. **(b)** (*Rad*) broadcasting.
radiactividad NF radioactivity.
radiactivo ADJ radioactive.
radiado ADJ **(a)** (*Bot etc*) radiate. **(b)** (*Rad*) radio (*atr*), broadcast; **en una interviú radiada** in a radio interview.
radiador NM radiator.
radial ADJ **(a)** (*Mec etc*) radial. **(b)** (*Aut*) road (*atr*). **(c)** (*LAm: Rad*) radio (*atr*), broadcasting (*atr*); **comedia ~** radio play.
radiante ADJ (*Fís y fig*) radiant; **estaba ~** she was radiant (*de* with).
radiar[1] [1b] VT **(a)** (*Fís etc*) to radiate; to irradiate. **(b)** (*Rad*) to broadcast. **(c)** (*Med*) to treat with X-rays.
radiar[2] [1b] VT (*LAm*) (*borrar*) to delete, cross off (a list); (*expulsar*) to expel; (*suprimir*) to remove.
radicado ADJ: **~ en** based in.
radical [1] ADJ radical.
　[2] NM **(a)** (*Ling, Mat*) root; square-root sign. **(b)** (*Quím*) radical.
　[3] NMF (*Pol*) radical.
radicalidad NF radical nature; (*Pol*) radicalism.
radicalismo NM radicalism.
radicalización NF radicalization.
radicalizar [1f] [1] VT to radicalize.
　[2] **radicalizarse** VR **(a)** (*Pol*) to be radicalized, become more radical. **(b)** (*situación etc*) to worsen, deteriorate.
radicalmente ADV radically.
radicar [1g] [1] VI **(a)** (*Bot y fig*) to take root.
　(b) (*estar*) to be, be situated, lie.
　(c) (*dificultad etc*) **~ en** to lie in.
　[2] **radicarse** VR to establish o.s., put down one's roots (*en* in).
radicha NMF (*Cono Sur*) radical.
radicheta* NF (*Cono Sur: hum*) radical.
radícula NF (*Bot*) radicle.
radiestesia NF water divining, dowsing.
radio[1] NM **(a)** (*Mat*) radius; **~ de acción** sphere of jurisdiction, extent of one's authority; (*Aer*) range; **un avión de largo ~ de acción** a long-range aircraft; **~ de giro** turning circle; **en un ~ de 10 km alrededor de la ciudad** within a radius of 10 km round the city.
　(b) (*de rueda*) spoke.
　(c) (*Anat*) radius.
　(d) (*Quím*) radium.
　(e) (*Rad*: mensaje*) wireless message.
　(f) (*LAm*) = **radio**[2].
radio[2] NF **(a)** (*gen*) radio, wireless; broadcasting; **R~ Eslobodia** Radio Slobodia; **~ libre** pirate radio; **~ macuto*** the grapevine; **~ pirata** pirate radio (station); **por ~** by radio, on the radio, over the radio; **hablar por ~** to talk on the radio.
　(b) (*aparato*) radio (set), wireless (set).
radio... PREF radio...
radioactividad NF radioactivity; **detector de ~** Geiger counter.
radioactivo ADJ = **radiactivo**.
radioaficionado, -a NM/F radio ham*, amateur radio enthusiast.
radioantena NF antenna; (*Astron*) radio telescope.
radioastronomía NF radio astronomy.
radiobaliza NF radio beacon.
radiobiología NF radiobiology.
radiobúsqueda NF radiopaging.
radiocaptar [1a] VT *emisora* to listen in to, pick up.
radiocarbono NM radiocarbon.
radiocasete NM o F radiocassette (player).
radiocomunicación NF radio contact, contact by radio.
radiodespertador NM radio clock radio.
radiodiagnóstico NM X-ray diagnosis.
radiodifundir [3a] VT to broadcast.
radiodifusión NF broadcasting.
radiodifusora NF (*LAm*) radio station, transmitter.
radioemisora NF radio station, transmitter.
radioenlace NM radio link.
radioescucha NMF listener.
radioestesia NF water divining, dowsing.
radiofaro NM radio beacon.
radiofonía NF radio, wireless.
radiofónico ADJ radio (*atr*).
radiogoniómetro NM direction finder.
radiografía NF **(a)** (*gen*) radiography, X-ray photography. **(b)** (*una ~*) radiograph, X-ray photograph (o picture).
radiografiar [1c] VT **(a)** (*Med*) to X-ray. **(b)** (*Rad*) to radio, send by radio.
radiográfico ADJ X-ray (*atr*).
radiógrafo, -a NM/F radiographer.
radiograma NM wireless message.
radiogramola NF (*Esp*) radiogram; **~ tragamonedas, ~ tragaperras** jukebox.
radioisótopo NM radioisotope.

radiola NF (*And*) radiogram.
radiólisis NF INVAR radiolysis.
radiolocación NF radiolocation.
radiología NF radiology.
radiólogo, -a NM/F radiologist.
radiomensajería NF radiopaging.
radionavegación NF radio navigation.
radionovela NF radio series.
radiooperador(a) NM/F (*LAm*) radio operator, wireless operator.
radiopatrulla NM patrol-car.
radiorreceptor NM radio (set), wireless (set), receiver; **~ de contrastación** monitor set.
radioscopia NF radioscopy.
radioso ADJ (*LAm*) radiant.
radiotaxi NM radio cab, radio taxi.
radiotécnica[1] NF radio engineering.
radiotécnico, -a[2] NM/F radio engineer.
radiotelefonía NF radiotelephony.
radiotelefonista NMF radiotelephonist.
radioteléfono NM radiotelephone.
radiotelegrafía NF radiotelegraphy, wireless (telegraphy).
radiotelegrafiar [1c] VT to radiotelegraph.
radiotelegrafista NMF radio operator, wireless operator.
radiotelescopio NM radiotelescope.
radioterapeuta NMF radiotherapist.
radioterapia NF radiotherapy.
radiotransmisión NF radio transmission.
radiotransmisor NM radio transmitter.
radioyente NMF listener.
radón NM radon.
RAE NF (*Esp*) ABR de **Real Academia Española**.

> ┌─ *RAE* ─┐
>
> ⓘ *The Real Academia Española de la Lengua was created in 1713 and given royal approval by Philip V in 1714 with the motto "limpia, fija y da esplendor" to protect the purity of the Spanish language. There are 46 members appointed for life from among Spain's most prestigious writers and linguists. Its first dictionary, the six-volume **Diccionario de Autoridades**, was published between 1726 and 1739. A condensed single-volume version was published in 1780, since when more than 20 new editions have appeared.*

raedera NF scraper; spokeshave.
raedura NF **(a)** (*acto*) scrape, scraping; (*Med*) abrasion, graze. **(b)** **~s** scrapings, filings.
raer [2y] [1] VT **(a)** (*gen*) to scrape; (*quitar*) to scrape off; (*borrar*) to erase; (*Med*) to abrade, graze; to chafe; *paño etc* to fray.
　(b) *contenido* to level off, level with the brim.
　[2] **raerse** VR to chafe; (*paño*) to fray.
raf NM (*Golf*) rough.
Rafael NM Raphael.
ráfaga NF **(a)** (*Met*) gust, squall; sudden blast.
　(b) (*de tiros*) burst.
　(c) (*de intuición, luz*) flash; **dar ~s de luces a** to flash one's headlights at.
　(d) (*And, Cono Sur: racha*) run of luck; **estar de** (*o* en) (mala) **~** to have a spell of bad luck.
rafaguear [1a] [1] VT to direct a burst of machine-gun fire at.
　[2] VI to fire a burst with a machine-gun.
rafañoso* ADJ (*Cono Sur*) (*sucio*) dirty; (*ordinario*) coarse, common.
rafia NF raffia.
rafting ['raftin] NM white-water rafting.
raglán ADJ INVAR: **manga ~** raglan sleeve.
RAH NF (*Esp*) ABR de **Real Academia de la Historia**.
rai ADJ, NM (*Mús*) rai.
raicear [1a] VI (*CAm, Carib*) to take root.
raicero NM (*LAm*) mass of roots, root system.
raid [raid] NM, PL **raids** [raid] **(a)** (*Mil*) raid, attack; expedition; (*plaga*) attack, infestation.
　(b) (*de policía*) police raid; (*de criminales*) criminal raid.
　(c) (*esfuerzo*) attempt, endeavour; (*empresa*) enterprise; (*hazaña*) heroic undertaking.
　(d) (*Dep*) endurance test; (*Aer*) long-distance flight; (*Aut*) rally drive; transcontinental expedition by car.
　(e) (*Méx Aut*) lift; **pedir ~** to hitch a lift.
raído ADJ **(a)** *paño* frayed, threadbare; *persona, prenda* shabby. **(b)** (*fig*) shameless.
raigambre NF (*a veces* M) **(a)** (*Bot*) mass of roots; root system.
　(b) (*fig*) (*tradición*) tradition; (*antecedentes*) antecedents, history; **una familia de fuerte ~ local** a family with deep roots in the area; **tienen ~ liberal** they have a liberal tradition.
raigón NM (*Bot*) thick root, stump; (*Anat*) root, stump.

rail, raíl NM rail; ~ **electrizado** electrified rail, live rail.
Raimundo NM Raymond.
▼ **raíz** ⒈ NF (a) (*Bot etc*) root; **arrancar algo de** ~ to root sth out completely, destroy sth root and branch; **cortar un peligro de** ~ to nip a danger in the bud; **echar raíces** to take root (*t fig*).
(b) (*Mat*) root; ~ **cuadrada** square root; ~ **cúbica** cube root.
(c) (*Ling*) root.
▼ (d) (*fig*) root, origin; **a** ~ **de** immediately after, immediately following; as a result of.
⒉ ATR root (*atr*); **causa** ~ root cause; **fuente** ~ principal source.
raja NF (a) (*hendedura*) slit, split; (*grieta*) crack; (*abertura*) gash, chink.
(b) (*pedacito*) sliver, splinter, thin piece; (*de limón etc*) slice.
(c) (⁑) cunt⁑.
(d) **sacar** ~* to get a rake-off*, get a share.
(e) **tener** ~ (*Carib*) to have Negro blood.
(f) **estar en la** ~ (*And**) to be broke*.
(g) ~**s** (*Méx Culin*) pickled green pepper.
rajá NM rajah.
rajada NF (a) (*Cono Sur: huida*) flight, hasty exit. (b) (*Méx*) (*cobardía*) cowardly act; (*el retroceder*) backing down, going back on one's word.
rajado* NM (a) (*canalla*) swine*. (b) (*cobarde*) coward.
rajador ADJ (*Cono Sur*) fast.
rajadura NF = **raja** (a) y (b).
rajamacana* NM (*Carib*) (a) (*trabajo duro*) tough job. (b) (*persona*) (*dura*) tough character; (*terca*) stubborn person. (c) (*experto*) expert. (d) **a** ~ = **a rajatabla**.
rajante* ADJ (*Cono Sur*) (*perentorio*) peremptory, sharp; (*inmediato*) immediate.
rajar [1a] ⒈ VT (a) (*hender*) to split, crack; to cleave; to slit; *fruta etc* to slice; *tronco etc* to chop (up), split; *neumático etc* to slash; *persona* to stab.
(b) (*LAm: difamar*) to slander, run down.
(c) (*LAm⁑ Univ*) to flunk*.
(d) (*And, Carib*) (*aplastar*) to crush, defeat; (*arruinar*) to ruin; (*fastidiar*) to annoy.
(e) (*Cono Sur**) *obrero* to fire*.
(f) (*Carib*: *fastidiar*) to pester, bug*.
⒉ VI (a) (*hablar*) to chatter, talk a lot; (*jactarse*) to brag; (*And*: *chismear*) to gossip.
(b) (*LAm: salir*) to rush off, rush out.
⒊ **rajarse** VR (a) (*henderse*) to split, crack.
(b) (*) (*desistir*) to back out (de *of*); (*acobardarse*) to get cold feet; (*desdecirse*) to go back on one's word; **¡me rajé!** that's enough for me!, I'm quitting!
(c) (*And, Carib, Cono Sur*) (*huir*) to run away; to bolt; (*irse*) to rush off; **salir rajando** to go off at top speed.
(d) (*And, Cono Sur: equivocarse*) to be mistaken.
(e) (*Carib: emborracharse*) to get drunk.
(f) (*And, CAm, Carib, Cono Sur: ser pródigo*) to splash out*.
rajatabla: a ~ ADV (*estrictamente*) strictly, rigorously; (*exactamente*) exactly; (*imparcialmente*) without fear or favour, (*a toda costa*) at all costs; (*pase lo que pase*) regardless (of the consequences), by hook or by crook; **cumplir las órdenes a** ~ to carry out one's orders to the letter; **pagar** (*etc*) **a** ~ (*LAm*) to pay (*etc*) on the dot, pay (*etc*) promptly.
rajatablas* NM INVAR (*And, Carib*) ticking-off*.
raje* NM (*Cono Sur*) firing*, sacking*; **al** ~ in a hurry; **dar el** ~ **a uno** to fire sb*; **tomar(se) el** ~ to beat it*; to rush off.
rajita NF (*Culin*) (thin) slice.
rajo NM (*LAm*) tear, rip.
rajón ⒈ ADJ (a) (*Andalucía, LAm: liberal*) generous, lavish, free-spending.
(b) (*Andalucía, CAm, Méx*) (*cobarde*), cowardly; (*pesimista*) readily disheartened; (*Méx: de poca confianza*) unreliable.
⒉ NM (a) (*LAm: rajo*) tear, rip.
(b) (*Andalucía, CAm, Méx: remolón*) quitter.
(c) (*CAm, Méx*) (*matón*) bully; (*jactancioso*) braggart.
(d) (*And, Méx: chismoso*) gossip, telltale.
rajonada NF (*CAm*) (a) (*baladronada*) boast, brag; (*jactancia*) bragging. (b) (*ostentación*) ostentation.
rajuñar [1a] VT (*Cono Sur*) = **rasguñar**.
RAL NF ABR *de* **red de área local** local area network, LAN.
rala NF (*And*) birdlime.
rale NM (*Cono Sur*) wooden bowl, wooden dish.
ralea NF (*pey*) kind, sort, breed; **de esa** ~ of that ilk; **de baja** ~ evil, wicked; wretched.
ralear [1a] VI to become thin, become sparse; to thin out; to become less dense.
ralentí NM (a) (*Cine*) slow motion; **al** ~ in slow motion. (b) (*Aut*) neutral; **estar al** ~, **funcionar al** ~ to be ticking over.
ralentización NF slowing down, deceleration; (*Econ etc*) slowing

down.
ralentizar [1f] VTI to slow down.
rallado ADJ *queso etc* grated.
rallador NM grater.
ralladura NF: ~ **de limón** grated lemon rind; ~**s de patata** potato peelings.
rallar [1a] VT (a) (*Culin*) to grate. (b) (*: dar dentera a*) to grate on; to annoy, needle*. (c) (*Carib: provocar*) to goad.
rallo NM (*Culin*) grater; (*Téc*) file, rasp.
rallón ADJ (*And*) bothersome, irritating.
rally(e) ['rali] NM (a) (*Aut*) rally; (*concurso*) contest, competition; (*reunión*) gathering. (b) (*Fin*) rally.
rallye-paper NM paper chase.
ralo ⒈ ADJ *pelo etc* thin, sparse; *tela* loosely woven; *bosque* open; *aire* rare, rarified; (*Cono Sur*) insubstantial, lacking body.
⒉ ADV: ~-~ (*Cono Sur*) sometimes.
rama NF (a) (*Bot etc*) branch; **en** ~ *algodón, seda* raw; *libro* unbound; ~ **de olivo** olive branch; **andarse por las** ~**s** to beat about the bush; to get bogged down in details; **poner algo en la última** ~ to leave sth till last; to consider sth unimportant.
(b) (*LAm⁑*) pot⁑, hash*.
(c) **mi** ~ (*Esp**) the wife*, my better half.
ramada NF (a) (*de árbol*) branches, foliage. (b) (*LAm: cobertizo*) shed, hut; shelter (o covering *etc*) made of branches; (*Cono Sur*) festival stall.
ramadán NM Ramadan.
ramaje NM branches, foliage.
ramal NM (a) (*de soga*) strand (of a rope); (*de caballo etc*) halter. (b) (*fig*) off-shoot; (*Aut*) branch, branch road; (*Ferro*) branch line.
ramalazo NM (a) (*azote*) lash; (*verdugón*) weal, bruise, mark left by a lash; (*cicatriz*) scar.
(b) (*fig*) (*dolor*) stab of pain, sharp pain; (*depresión*) fit of depression, (*pesar*) sudden grief; (*golpe*) blow; (*locura*) fit of madness.
(c) (*fig: Met*) gust of wind; lash of rain.
ramazón NF (*CAm, Cono Sur, Méx*) antler, horns.
rambla NF (a) (*arroyo*) watercourse; stream, torrent. (b) (*Esp: avenida*) avenue. (c) (*LAm*) (*paseo marítimo*) promenade; (*muelle*) quayside.
ramera NF whore.
ramificación NF ramification.
ramificarse [1g] VR to ramify, divide, branch (out).
ramillete NM (a) (*de flores*) bouquet, bunch of flowers, posy; (*llevado en el vestido*) corsage; (*Bot*) cluster. (b) (*fig: selección*) collection; choice bunch, select group.
ramita NF twig, sprig; (*flores*) spray.
ramo NM (a) (*de árbol*) (*t fig*) branch; (*ramillete*) bunch of flowers, bouquet.
(b) (*fig*) branch; (*Com*) section, department; (*de géneros*) line; **el ministro del** ~ the appropriate minister, the minister concerned with this; **es del** ~ **de la alimentación** he's in the food business; **es del** ~ (*: homosexual*) he's one of them*.
(c) (*Med; t* ~**s**) touch; **tiene** ~**s de loco** he has a streak of madness.
ramojo NM brushwood.
Ramón NM Raymond.
ramonear [1a] VT (a) *árboles* to lop, lop the twigs of. (b) (*ovejas*) to browse on.
rampa NF ramp, incline; ~ **de la basura**, ~ **de desperdicios** refuse chute; ~ **de lanzamiento** launching-ramp; (*fig*) springboard; ~ **móvil** mobile launching-pad.
rampante ADJ rampant.
rampla NF (*Cono Sur*) trailer.
ramplón ADJ common, coarse, uncouth.
ramplonería NF commonness, coarseness, uncouthness.
rana NF (a) (*Zool*) frog; ~ **toro** bullfrog; **no es** ~ (*fig*) he's no fool, he knows his stuff*; **pero salió** ~* but he turned out badly, but he was a big disappointment; **cuando las** ~**s críen pelo** when pigs learn to fly; **¡hasta que las** ~**s críen pelo!** if I never see you again it'll be too soon! (b) (*LAm*) *game of throwing coins into the mouth of an iron frog*.
ranchada NF (a) (*CAm: canoa*) canoe. (b) (*Cono Sur: cobertizo*) shed, hut.
ranchar [1a] VI (a) (*Cono Sur, Méx: vagar*) to wander from farm to farm. (b) (*And, Carib, Méx*) (*pasar la noche*) to spend the night; (*establecerse*) to settle. (c) (*Carib: obstinarse*) to persist.
ranchear [1a] ⒈ VT (*Carib, Méx*) (*saquear*) to loot, pillage; (*robar*) to rob.
⒉ VI (a) (*LAm: formar rancho*) to build a camp, make a settlement. (b) (*And, Cono Sur: comer*) to have a meal.
ranchera NF (a) (*Méx*) typical Mexican song. (b) (*Carib*) station wagon.
ranchería NF (a) (*Cono Sur*) = **rancherío**. (b) (*And: de rancho*) labourers' quarters, bunkhouse (*US*). (c) (*Carib: taberna*) poor country inn. (d) (*Carib: chabolas*) shantytown.
rancherío NM (*LAm*) settlement.
ranchero ⒈ ADJ (*Méx*) (a) (*rudo*) uncouth; (*ridículo*) ridiculous, silly.

(b) es muy ~ (*conocedor del campo*) he's a real countryman. **(c)** huevos ~s fried eggs in a hot chili and tomato sauce; **música ranchera** ≃ country and western music.

2 NM **(a)** (*LAm: jefe de rancho*) rancher, farmer; (*Méx*) peasant. **(b)** (*cocinero*) mess cook.

ranchitos NMPL (*Carib*) shanty town.

rancho NM **(a)** (*choza*) hut, thatched hut; (*And: cobertizo*) shed; (*And: casa de campo*) country house, villa; (*Carib: chabola*) shanty, shack; ~s (*And, Carib*) shanty town.
(b) (*Náut*) crew's quarters.
(c) (*LAm: granja*) ranch, large farm; (*Méx*) small farm.
(d) (*de gitanos etc*) camp, settlement; (*Méx*) village.
(e) (*Mil etc*) mess, communal meal; (*pey*) bad food, grub*; **asentar el ~** to prepare a meal; (*fig*) to get things organized, settle in; **hacer ~** to make room; **hacer el ~** to have a meal; **hacer ~ aparte** to set up on one's own, go one's own way, keep to oneself.
(f) (*Cono Sur: sombrero*) straw hat.

rancidez NF, **ranciedad** NF **(a)** (*madurez*) age, mellowness; (*pey*) rankness, rancidness; mustiness. **(b)** (*fig*) great age, antiquity; (*pey*) antiquatedness.

rancio 1 ADJ **(a)** *vino* old, mellow; *comestible* (*pey*) rank, rancid, stale; musty.
(b) (*fig*) *linaje* ancient; *tradición etc* very ancient, time-honoured; (*pey*) antiquated, old-fashioned; **esas dos rancias** those two old girls.
2 NM = **rancidez**.

rancontán ADV (*And, CAm, Carib*) in cash.
rand [ran] NM, PL **rands** [ran] rand.
randa[1] NF (*Cos*) lace, lace trimming.
randa[2]* NM (*ladrón*) pickpocket, petty thief; (*sospechoso*) suspicious character, prowler.
randar: [1a] VT to nick*, rip off*.
randevú NM (*Cono Sur*) rendez-vous.
randevuses NMPL (*Cono Sur*) courtesies.
ranfaña* NM (*And, Cono Sur*) scruff*.
ranfañoso* (*And, Cono Sur*) 1 ADJ shabby, scruffy.
2 NM scruff.
ranfla NF (*And, Méx*) ramp, incline.
ranga NF (*And*) nag, old horse.
ranglán ADJ INVAR = **raglán**.
rango[1] NM **(a)** (*categoría*) rank; (*status*) standing, status, class; **de ~** of high standing, of some status; **de alto ~** high-ranking. **(b)** (*LAm*) (*lujo*) luxury; (*pompa*) pomp, splendour.
rango[2] NM (*And*) = **ranga**.
rangosidad* NF (*Cono Sur*) generosity.
rangoso* ADJ (*CAm, Carib, Cono Sur*) generous.
Rangún NM Rangoon.
ránking ['raŋkin] NM, PL **ránkings** ['raŋkin] ranking, ranking list, ranking order; classification; (*And Mús*) hit parade.
rantifuso ADJ (*Cono Sur*) **(a)** (*sucio*) dirty, grubby; (*ordinario*) common.
(b) (*sospechoso*) suspicious.
ranúnculo NM ranunculus; (*esp Esp*) buttercup.
ranura NF groove; slot; **~ de expansión** (*Inform*) expansion slot.
rap NM rap (music); **hacer ~** to rap; **música ~** rap (music).
rapacidad NF rapacity, greed.
rapado 1 ADJ *pelo* close-cropped.
2 NMF (*persona*) skinhead.
3 NM (*corte de pelo*) crew-cut.
rapadura NF **(a)** (*afeitado*) shave, shaving; (*corte de pelo*) close haircut.
(b) (*LAm*) (*azúcar*) brown sugar; (*caramelo*) sweet made of milk and syrup.
rapapolvo* NM ticking-off*; **echar un ~ a uno** to give sb a ticking-off*, tick sb off*.
rapar [1a] VT **(a)** *barba* to shave; *pelo* to crop, cut very close. **(b)** (*arrebatar*) to snatch; (*) to pinch*.
rapaz[1] 1 ADJ (*ávido*) rapacious, greedy; (*ladrón*) thieving; (*Zool*) predatory; (*Orn*) raptorial, of prey.
2 NF (*Zool*) predatory animal; (*Orn*) bird of prey.
rapaz[2] NM lad, youngster; kid*; **sí, ~** yes, my lad.
rapaza NF lass, girl.
rape[1] NM **(a)** (*afeitado*) quick shave; (*corte de pelo*) close haircut; **al ~** cut close. **(b)** (*: bronca*) ticking-off*.
rape[2] NM (*Zool*) anglerfish.
rapé NM snuff.
rapero* 1 ADJ rap *atr*.
2 NM, **rapera** NF rapper.
rápida NF (*Méx*) chute.
rápidamente ADV rapidly, fast, quickly, swiftly.
rapidez NF rapidity, speed; speediness, swiftness.
rápido 1 ADJ **(a)** (*gen*) rapid, fast, quick, swift; *tren* fast, express.
(b) (*And, Carib, Cono Sur*) *campo* fallow; *paisaje* fallow; flat, open.
(c) (*Carib*) *tiempo* clear.
2 ADV (*) quickly; **¡y ~, eh!** and make it snappy!*
3 NM **(a)** (*Ferro*) express.

(b) (*And, Carib, Cono Sur: campo*) open country.
(c) ~s rapids.
rapiña NF robbery (with violence); V **ave**.
rapiñar [1a] VT to steal.
raposa NF **(a)** fox (*t fig*), vixen. **(b)** (*Carib*) carrier bag.
raposera NF foxhole.
raposero ADJ: **perro ~** foxhound.
raposo NM **(a)** (*zorro*) fox, dog fox. **(b)** (*And, Carib: mocoso*) kid*.
rap(p)el NM abseiling; **a ~** by abseiling; **hacer ~** to abseil (down *etc*).
rap(p)elar [1a] VI to abseil (down *etc*).
rapsodia NF rhapsody.
rapsódico ADJ rhapsodic.
raptar [1a] VT to kidnap, abduct; to carry off.
rapto NM **(a)** (*secuestro*) kidnapping, abduction; carrying-off. **(b)** (*fig: impulso*) sudden impulse; **en un ~ de celos** in a sudden fit of jealousy. **(c)** (*fig: éxtasis*) ecstasy, rapture.
raptor(a) NM/F kidnapper.
raque[1] NM beachcombing; **andar al ~** to beachcomb, go beach-combing.
raque[2] NM (*Carib*) bargain.
raquear[1] [1a] VI to go beachcombing.
raquear[2] [1a] VT (*Carib*) to rob, hold up.
Raquel NF Rachel.
raquero, -a NM/F beachcomber.
raqueta NF racquet; **~ de nieve** snowshoe.
raquetazo NM shot, hit, stroke.
raquítico ADJ **(a)** (*Med*) rachitic; *árbol etc* weak, stunted. **(b)** (*fig*) small, inadequate, miserly.
raquitis NF, **raquitismo** NM rickets.
raramente ADV rarely, seldom.
rarefacción NF rarefaction.
rareza NF **(a)** (*cualidad*) rarity, rareness, scarcity.
(b) (*objeto*) rarity.
(c) (*fig*) oddity, peculiarity; eccentricity; **tiene alguna ~** there's something odd about him; **tiene sus ~s** he has his peculiarities, he has his little ways.
raridad NF rarity.
rarificar [1g] VT to rarefy.
rarífico ADJ (*Cono Sur*) = **raro** (b).
raro ADJ **(a)** (*poco frecuente*) rare, scarce, uncommon; **son ~s los que saben hacerlo** very few people know how to do it; **con alguna rara excepción** with rare exceptions.
(b) (*extraño*) odd, peculiar, strange; (*excéntrico*) eccentric; (*notable*) notable, remarkable; **de rara perfección** of rare perfection, of remarkable perfection; **es ~ que ...** it is odd that ..., it is strange that ...; **¡qué ~!** how (very) odd!; **¡qué cosa más rara!** how strange!, most odd!; **es un hombre muy ~** he's a very odd man.
(c) (*Fís*) rare, rarefied.
ras NM levelness, evenness; **~ con ~** level, on a level; flush; **a ~ de** level with; flush with; **volar a ~ de tierra** to fly (almost) at ground level.
rasado ADJ level; **cucharada rasada** level teaspoonful.
rasante 1 ADJ low; **tiro ~** low shot; **vuelo ~** low-level flight.
2 NM slope; **cambio de ~** (*Aut*) brow of a hill.
rasar [1a] 1 VT **(a)** *contenido* to level (with the rim).
(b) (*casi tocar*) to skim, graze; **la bala pasó rasando su sombrero** the bullet grazed his hat.
(c) = **arrasar**.
2 **rasarse** VR (*cielo*) to clear.
rasca[1]: NF (*And, CAm, Carib*) drunkenness.
rasca[2]* ADJ (*Cono Sur*) tacky*, inferior.
rascacielos NM INVAR skyscraper.
rascacio NM scorpion fish.
rascadera NF scraper; (*de caballo*) currycomb.
rascado ADJ **(a)** (*LAm: borracho*) drunk. **(b)** (*CAm: casquivano*) feather-brained.
rascador NM **(a)** (*Téc*) scraper; file, rasp. **(b)** (*de pelo*) ornamental hairclasp.
rascaespalda NF backscratcher.
rascamoño NM **(a)** = **rascador** (b). **(b)** (*Bot*) zinnia.
rascapies NM INVAR (*And*) firecracker.
rascar [1g] 1 VT **(a)** (*raer*) to scrape, rasp; (*quitar*) to scrape off; *cabeza etc* to scratch.
(b) (*Mús: hum*) to scrape, scratch away.
(c) (*: descubrir*) to sniff out, smell out, find out about.
2 VI (*Cono Sur: picar*) to itch.
3 **rascarse** VR **(a)** to scratch, scratch o.s.
(b) (*LAm*: *emborracharse*) to get drunk.
(c) **~ juntos** (*CAm, Cono Sur*) to band together (for a criminal purpose); **~ la barriga, ~ la panza** (*Méx, Cono Sur*) to take it easy; **no ~ con uno** (*And*) not to hit it off with sb.
rascatripas NMF INVAR fiddler, third-rate violinist.

rasco ADJ (*Cono Sur*) common, low; low-class.
rascón¹ ADJ (a) (*amargo*) sharp, sour (to taste). (b) (*Méx: pendenciero*) quarrelsome.
rascón² NM (*Orn*) water rail.
rascuache ADJ (*CAm, Méx*) (*pobre*) poor, penniless; (*desgraciado*) wretched; (*ridículo*) ridiculous, in bad taste; (*grosero*) coarse, vulgar; (*tacaño*) mean, tightfisted.
rascucho ADJ (*Cono Sur*) drunk.
RASD NF ABR *de* **República Árabe Saharaui Democrática** Democratic Saharan Arab Republic.
raseado ADJ level; **cucharada raseada** level teaspoonful.
rasear [1a] VT (a) (*casi tocar*) to skim, graze. (b) (*nivelar*) to level (off). (c) *balón* to play low, play along the ground.
rasera NF (*Culin*) fish slice.
rasero [1] ADJ low, level.
　[2] NM strickle; **doble ~** double standards *pl*; **medir dos cosas con el mismo ~** to treat two things alike.
rasete NM satinet(te).
rasgado ADJ (a) *ventana* wide; deep, which reaches to the floor; *ojos* wide; almond-shaped; *boca* wide, big. (b) (*LAm: franco*) outspoken. (c) (*And: generoso*) generous.
rasgadura NF tear, rip, slash.
rasgar [1h] VT (a) (*gen*) to tear, rip, slash; *papel* to tear up, tear to pieces. (b) = **rasguear**.
rasgo NM (a) (*de pluma*) stroke, flourish; (*adorno*) adornment; (*raya*) dash; **~s** characteristics (*of one's handwriting*); **a grandes ~s** (*fig*) with broad strokes, in outline; briefly; broadly speaking.
　(b) **~s** (*Anat*) features; **de ~s enérgicos** of energetic appearance, with an energetic look.
　(c) (*fig: característica*) characteristic, feature, trait; **~s característicos** typical features; **~s distintivos** distinctive features.
　(d) (*acto*) generous deed; noble gesture; **~ de ingenio** flash of wit; stroke of genius.
　(e) (*Cono Sur: acequia*) irrigation channel.
　(f) (*Cono Sur: terreno*) plot (of land); (*trozo*) piece, portion.
rasgón NM tear, rent.
rasguear [1a] VT (a) (*Mús*) to strum. (b) (*escribir*) to write with a flourish; (*fig*) to write.
rasguñadura NF (*LAm*) scratch.
rasguñar [1a] VT (a) (*gen*) to scratch. (b) (*Arte*) to sketch, draw in outline.
rasguño NM (a) (*gen*) scratch; **salir sin un ~** to come out of it without a scratch. (b) (*Arte*) sketch, outline drawing.
rasmillón NM (*Cono Sur*) scratch.
raso [1] ADJ (a) (*llano*) flat, level; (*despejado*) clear, bare, open; (*liso*) smooth; *silla* backless; **aprobado ~** bare pass (mark).
　(b) *cielo* clear; **está ~** the sky is clear, the weather is clear.
　(c) *contenido* level (with the brim); **una cucharada rasa** a level teaspoonful.
　(d) *pelota, vuelo etc* very low, almost at ground level; **fusila el gol por ~** he scores with a low shot.
　(e) **soldado ~** private.
　[2] ADV: **tirar ~** (*Dep*) to shoot low.
　[3] NM (a) (*Cos*) satin.
　(b) (*campo llano*) flat country; (*abierto*) open country; **al ~** in the open.
raspa NF (a) (*Bot: de cebada*) beard; (*de uva*) stalk.
　(b) (*de pez*) fishbone, (*esp*) backbone.
　(c) (*) sharp-tongued woman; (*criada*) servant.
　(d) (*LAm*: reprimenda*) scolding; dressing-down*.
　(e) (*Carib, Méx: azúcar*) brown sugar.
　(f) (*Cono Sur: herramienta*) rasp.
　(g) **ni de ~** (*And*) under no circumstances, no way.
　(h) (*CAm, Méx: burla*) joke.
　(i) (*LAm: chusma*) riffraff.
raspada* NF (*Carib, Méx*) scolding; dressing-down*.
raspado [1] ADJ (a) (*CAm, Carib*) shameless. (b) **un aprobado ~** a bare pass; **lo pasé ~** I just scraped through.
　[2] NM (a) (*Med*) D and C, (*dilation and curettage*); (b) (*LAm: bebida*) water ice.
raspador NM scraper, rasp; (*Méx Culin*) grater.
raspadura NF (a) (*acto*) scrape, scraping, rasping. (b) **~s** scrapings; filings. (c) (*raya*) scratch, mark; (*borradura*) erasure. (d) (*LAm: azúcar*) brown sugar.
raspante ADJ *vino* sharp, rough.
raspar [1a] [1] VT (a) (*gen*) to scrape; (*limar*) to rasp, file; (*alisar*) to smooth (down); (*quitar*) *etc* to scrape off, remove by scraping; *superficie* to scratch; *piel* to chafe; to graze; *palabra* to erase, scratch out.
　(b) (*fig: casi tocar*) to skim, graze; to scrape past.
　(c) **este vino raspa la boca** this wine tastes sharp.
　(d) (*) to pinch*.
　(e) (*Carib*: matar*) to kill.

(f) (*Carib, Méx: regañar*) to scold, tell off*.
(g) (*Méx: maltratar*) to say unkind things to, make wounding remarks to.
　[2] VI (a) (*manos*) to be rough.
　(b) (*vino*) to be sharp, have a rough taste.
　(c) (*Carib*) (*irse*) to leave, go off; (*morir*) to die.
raspear [1a] [1] VT (*And, Cono Sur*) to tick off*.
　[2] VI (*pluma*) to scratch.
raspón NM (a) (*rasguño*) scratch, graze; (*LAm*) (*abrasión*) abrasion; (*cardenal*) bruise.
　(b) (*LAm*: regaño*) scolding; ticking-off*.
　(c) (*Méx*: dicho*) cutting remark.
　(d) (*And: sombrero*) straw hat.
rasponear* [1a] VT (*And*) to scold; to tick off*.
rasposo ADJ (a) sharp-tasting, rough. (b) (*Méx*) joking, teasing. (c) (*Cono Sur*) (*raído*) scruffy, threadbare; (*miserable*) wretched.
rasqueta NF (*LAm*) scraper, rasp; (*de caballo*) currycomb.
rasquetear [1a] VT (*LAm*) *caballo* to brush down; (*Cono Sur*) to scrape.
rasquiña NF (*LAm*) itch.
rasta ADJ, NMF Rasta.
rastacuerismo NM (*LAm*) (*ambición social*) social climbing; (*tren de vida*) rich living; (*ostentación*) ostentation, display.
rastacuero† NM (*LAm*) upstart, parvenu.
rastafario, -a ADJ, NM/F Rastafarian.
rastra NF (a) (*Agr*) (*rastrillo*) rake; (*grada*) harrow.
　(b) = **rastro**; = **ristra**.
　(c) (*de transporte*) sledge (*for moving heavy objects*); (*carga pesada*) weighty object, thing being pulled along.
　(d) (*de pesca*) trawl; dredge; **pescar a la ~** to trawl.
　(e) (*Cono Sur: cinturón*) gaucho's thick leather belt.
　(f) (*Méx: puta*) prostitute.
　(g) (*fig*) (*consecuencia*) unpleasant consequence, disagreeable result; (*castigo*) punishment; (*merecido*) deserts.
　(h) **a ~s** by dragging, by pulling; (*fig*) unwillingly; **avanzar a ~s** to crawl (along), drag oneself along; **llevar un piano a ~s** to pull a piano along; **andar a ~s** (*fig*) to have a difficult time of it, suffer hardships.
rastreable ADJ traceable.
rastreador NM (a) (*persona*) tracker. (b) (*Náut: t* **barco ~**) trawler; **~ de minas** minesweeper.
rastrear [1a] [1] VT (a) (*seguir*) to track, trail, follow the trail of; *satélite* to track; (*localizar*) to track down, trace, run to ground; **~ el monte** to comb the woods; **~ los archivos** to trawl through the files.
　(b) (*sacar a la superficie*) to dredge (up), drag (up); *pesca* to trawl; *minas* to sweep.
　[2] VI (a) (*Agr*) to rake, harrow.
　(b) (*Pesca*) to trawl.
　(c) (*Aer*) to skim the ground; to fly low, hedgehop.
rastreo NM (a) (*gen*) dredging, dragging; (*pesca*) trawling. (b) (*de satélite*) tracking.
rastrerismo; NM (*LAm*) toadying, bootlicking*.
rastrero ADJ (a) (*Zool*) creeping, crawling; (*Bot*) creeping.
　(b) *vestido etc* trailing, hanging close to the ground; (*Aer*) *vuelo* very low.
　(c) (*fig*) *conducta* mean, despicable; *método* low; *disculpa* abject, humble; *persona* cringing; soapy*, bootlicking*, fawning.
rastrillada NF (*Cono Sur*) track, trail.
rastrillar [1a] [1] VT (a) (*Agr*) (*gen*) to rake; (*recoger*) to rake up, rake together; (*alisar*) to rake smooth.
　(b) *lino etc* to dress.
　(c) (*LAm*) *fusil* to fire; *fósforo* to strike.
　(d) (*CAm, Méx*) *pies* to drag.
　[2] VI (a) (*And, Carib, Cono Sur: errar el tiro*) to miss; (*Carib, Cono Sur: disparar*) to fire, shoot.
　(b) (*Cono Sur*: robar*) to shoplift.
rastrillazo NM (*CAm*) (*sueñecito*) light sleep; (*piscolabis*) light meal, snack.
rastrillero*, -a NM/F (*Cono Sur*) shoplifter.
rastrillo NM (a) (*Agr etc*) rake.
　(b) (*Téc*) hackle, flax comb.
　(c) (*de cerradura, llave*) ward.
　(d) (*Mil*) portcullis; (*Arquit etc*) spiked gate.
　(e) (*Ferro*) **~ delantero** cowcatcher.
　(f) (*Com*) jumble sale; charity fête; (*And*) barter; deal.
rastro NM (a) (*Agr etc*) (*rastrillo*) rake; (*grada*) harrow.
　(b) (*huella*) track, trail; mark on the ground; (*pista*) scent; (*de cohete etc*) track, course; (*de tormenta*) path; **perder el ~** to lose the scent; **seguir el ~ de uno** to follow sb's trail.
　(c) (*fig*) trace, sign; **desaparecer sin dejar ~** to vanish without trace; **no quedaba ni ~ de ello** not a trace of it was to be seen.
　(d) (*mercado*) fleamarket; **el R~** secondhand market in Madrid.

(e) (†: *matadero*) slaughterhouse.

rastrojear [1a] VI (*LAm*) to glean; (*animales*) to feed in the stubble.

rastrojera NF stubble field.

rastrojero NM **(a)** (*Cono Sur: campo*) stubble field. **(b)** (*Cono Sur Aut*) jeep. **(c)** (*Méx: maíz*) maize (o corn *US*) stalks (*used as fodder*).

rastrojo NM **(a)** (*de campo*) stubble; (*Cono Sur: terreno cultivado*) ploughed field. **(b)** ~s waste, remains, left-overs.

rasura NF **(a)** (*llanura*) flatness, levelness; (*lisura*) smoothness. **(b)** (*afeitado*) shave, shaving; (*Téc*) scrape, scraping. **(c)** ~s scrapings; filings.

rasurado NM shave.

rasurador NM, **rasuradora** NF (electric) shaver, electric razor.

rasurar [1a] □ VT **(a)** (*afeitar*) to shave. **(b)** (*Téc*) to scrape.
□ **rasurarse** VR to shave.

rata □ NF rat; ~ **de biblioteca** bookworm.
□ NM (*) **(a)** (*ladrón*) sneak thief. **(b)** (*tacaño*) mean devil.

rataplán NM drumbeat, rub-a-dub.

ratear¹ [1a] □ VT to steal, pilfer; to filch.
□ VI to crawl, creep (along).

ratear² [1a] VT **(a)** (*repartir*) to share out. **(b)** (*reducir*) to reduce proportionately.

ratera NF (*Méx*) rat-trap.

ratería NF **(a)** (*gen*) petty larceny, small-time thieving, pilfering. **(b)** (*una* ~) theft. **(c)** (*cualidad*) crookedness, dishonesty.

raterismo NM (*LAm*) thieving.

ratero □ ADJ thievish, light-fingered.
□ NM (*carterista*) pickpocket; (*ladrón*) sneak thief, small-time thief; (*Méx: de casas*) burglar.

raticida NM rat poison.

ratificación NF ratification; confirmation; support.

ratificar [1g] VT *tratado etc* to ratify; *noticia etc* to confirm; *opinión* to support; ~ **que ...** to confirm that ...

rating ['ratin] NM, PL **ratings** ['ratin] rating; (*Náut*) class; (*TV etc*) popularity rating.

ratio NM (*a veces* F) ratio.

Ratisbona NF Regensburg, Ratisbon.

rato NM **(a)** (short) time, while; spell, period; **un** ~ (*como adv*) a while, a time; **un buen** ~, **largo** ~ a long time, a good while; ~**s libres**, ~**s de ocio** leisure, spare time, free time; **a** ~**s** at times, from time to time; **a** ~**s perdidos** at (o in) odd moments; **al** ~ **viene** (*LAm**) he'll be here in a moment; **al poco** ~ shortly after; **de a** ~**s** (*Cono Sur*) from time to time; **dentro de un** ~ in a little while; **hace** ~ **que se fue** (*LAm**) he's been gone a while, he left a while ago; **¡hasta cada** (o **el**) ~! (*LAm**), **¡hasta otro** ~!* so long!; **matar el** ~, **pasar el** ~ to kill time, pass the time, while away the time; **pasar un buen** ~ to have a good time; **pasar** (o **llevarse**) **un mal** ~ to have a bad time of it, have a rough time; **dar malos** ~**s a uno** to give sb a hard time of it; to cause sb a lot of worry; **hay para** ~ there's still a long way to go; **tener sus** ~**s** (*persona*) to have one's moments; **tenemos para** ~ we've still a lot to do, we're still far from finished; **¿vas a tardar mucho** ~? will you be long?

(b) (*) **es un** ~ **difícil** it's a bit tricky; **pesan un** ~ they weigh a bit; **sabe un** ~ **de matemáticas** she knows a heck of a lot of maths*.

ratón NM **(a)** (*Zool*) mouse; ~ **de archivo**, ~ **de biblioteca** bookworm; ~ **almizclero** muskrat; **mandar a uno a capar ratones** to tell sb to go to blazes*.
(b) (*Carib: petardo*) squib, cracker.
(c) (*Carib*: resaca*) hangover*.
(d) (*: *pelusa*) ball of fluff.
(e) (*Inform*) mouse.

ratonar [1a] VT to gnaw, nibble.

ratonera NF **(a)** (*trampa*) mousetrap. **(b)** (*agujero*) mousehole. **(c)** (*And, Cono Sur: barrio bajo*) hovel, slum; (*Carib: tienda*) ranch store. **(d)** (*fig*) trap; **caer en la** ~ to fall into a trap.

ratonero NM: ~ **común** buzzard.

RAU NF ABR *de* **República Árabe Unida** United Arab Republic, UAR.

raudal NM **(a)** (*torrente*) torrent, flood. **(b)** (*fig*) plenty, abundance; great quantity; **a** ~**es** in abundance, in great numbers; **entrar a** ~**es** to pour in, come flooding in.

raudo ADJ swift; rushing, impetuous.

ravioles NMPL ravioli.

raya¹ NF **(a)** (*gen*) line; streak; (*en piedra etc*) scratch, mark; (*en mano*) line; (*en diseño, tela*) stripe, pinstripe; ~ **magnética** magnetic stripe; ~ **de puntos** dotted line; ~ **en negro** black line; **a** ~**s** striped.
(b) (*del pelo*) parting; (*del pantalón*) crease; **hacerse la** ~ to part one's hair.
(c) (*límite*) line, boundary, limit; (*Dep*) line, mark; **hacer** ~ (*fig*) to be outstanding (*en* in); **mantener a** ~ **a uno** to keep sb at bay; to keep sb in line; **pasar de la** ~ to overstep the mark, go too far; **poner a** ~ to check, hold back; **tener a** ~ to keep off, keep at bay, keep in check, control.
(d) (*Tip*) line, dash; (*Telec*) dash.

(e) (*Méx* ††: *sueldo*) pay, wages.
(f) (*: *droga*) fix*, dose.

raya² NF (*pez*) ray, skate.

rayadillo NM (*Cos*) striped material, (*esp*) blue-and-white striped material.

rayado □ ADJ **(a)** *papel* ruled; *cheque* crossed; *diseño, tela* striped; (*Téc*) *fusil etc* rifled. **(b)** (*And, Cono Sur**: *loco*) cracked, crazy. **(c)** (*Cono Sur**: *fanático*) extreme, fanatical.
□ NM **(a)** *ruling*, ruled lines; crossing; stripes, striped pattern; (*Téc*) rifling. **(b)** (*Carib Aut*) no parking area.

rayador NM **(a)** (*Méx* ††: *contador*) paymaster, accountant. **(b)** (*Cono Sur: árbitro*) umpire. **(c)** (*Cono Sur*) = **rallador**.

rayadura NF scratch.

rayajo NM scrawl.

rayano ADJ **(a)** (*lindante*) adjacent, contiguous; (*fronterizo*) border *atr*. **(b)** ~ **en** bordering on.

rayar [1a] □ VT **(a)** *papel* to line, rule lines on; *cheque* to cross; *piedra etc* to scratch, score, mark; *texto* to underline, underscore; *error* to cross out; (*como diseño*) to stripe, streak; (*Téc*) to rifle.
(b) (*Méx: pagar*) to pay (his wages to).
(c) (*Cono Sur*) = **rallar**.
(d) (*LAm*) *caballo* to spur on.
□ VI **(a)** ~ **con** to border on, be next to, be adjacent to.
(b) ~ **en** (*fig*) to border on, verge on; **esto raya en lo increíble** this verges on the incredible, this is well-nigh incredible; ~ **en los sesenta** to be nearly sixty, be pushing sixty.
(c) (*arañar*) to scratch, make scratches; **este producto no raya al fregar** this product scrubs without scratching.
(d) **al** ~ **el alba** at break of day, at first light.
(e) (*Méx: cobrar*) to draw one's wages.
□ **rayarse** VR **(a)** (*objeto*) to get scratched.
(b) (*And: ver realizados sus deseos*) to see one's wishes fulfilled; (*Méx: enriquecerse*) to get rich.
(c) (*And, Cono Sur**: *enojarse*) to get angry.
(d) (*Cono Sur**: *enloquecer*) to go crazy.

rayero NM (*Cono Sur*) linesman, line judge.

rayo¹ NM **(a)** (*de luz*) ray, beam; shaft (of light); ~ **láser** laser beam; ~ **de luna** moonbeam; ~ **de la muerte** death ray; ~ **de partículas** stream of particles; ~ **de sol**, ~ **solar** sunbeam, ray of sunlight; ~**s catódicos** cathode rays; ~**s cósmicos** cosmic rays; ~**s gamma** gamma rays; ~**s infrarrojos** infrared rays; ~**s luminosos** light rays; ~**s ultravioleta** ultraviolet rays; ~**s X** X-rays.
(b) (*Téc*) spoke.
(c) (*Met*) lightning, flash of lightning; thunderbolt; **¡~s!*** dammit!*; **¿qué** ~**s es eso?*** what in hell's name is that?*; **cayó un** ~ **en la torre** the tower was struck by lightning; **huele/sabe a** ~**s*** it smells/tastes awful; **como un** ~ like lightning, like a shot; **la noticia cayó como un** ~ the news was a bombshell; **entrar como un** ~ to dash in; **salir como un** ~ to dash out; **pasar como un** ~ to rush past, flash past; **echar** ~**s y centellas** to rage, fume; **¡que le parta un** ~!*, **¡mal** ~ **le parta!*** damn him!; **¡que me parta un** ~ **(si lo sé)!** I'm damned if I know; **¡a los demás que les parta un** ~! and the rest of them can go to hell!
(d) (*fig: desgracia*) blow, misfortune.
(e) (*fig: persona*) fast worker; **es un** ~ he's like lightning.

rayo² *etc* V **raer**.

rayón NM rayon.

rayuela NF pitch-and-toss; (*LAm*) hopscotch.

raza¹ NF **(a)** (*gen*) race; (*de animal*) breed, strain; (*estirpe*) stock; (*Bio*) race; ~ **blanca** white race; ~ **humana** human race; ~ **negra** black race; **de** ~, **de pura** ~ *caballo* thoroughbred; *perro etc* pedigree. **(b)** (*And**) cheek*, impudence; **¡qué tal** ~! some cheek!*, what a cheek!*

raza² NF **(a)** (*grieta*) crack, slit, fissure; (*en tela*) run. **(b)** (*rayo*) ray of light.

razano ADJ (*And*) thoroughbred.

▼ **razón** NF **(a)** (*facultad*) reason; **hacer que uno entre en** ~, **meter** (o **poner**) **a uno en** ~ to make sb see sense; **avenirse a razones**, **meterse en** ~ to see sense, listen to reason; **perder la** ~ to lose one's reason, go out of one's mind; **muy puesto en** ~ very reasonable; **¡eso es ponerse en** ~! that's better!, now you're talking!

▼ **(b)** (*lo correcto*) right, rightness; (*justicia*) justice; **con** ~ **o sin ella** rightly or wrongly; **le asiste la** ~ he has right on his side; **cargarse de** ~ to have right fully on one's side; **quiero cargarme de** ~ **antes de ...** I want to be sure of my case before ...; **dar la** ~ **a uno** to agree that sb is right, prove sb right; to side with sb; **tener** ~ to be right; **no tener** ~ to be wrong; **tener plenamente** ~ **en** + *infin* to be fully justified in + *ger*; **tratar de quitar a uno la** ~ to try to put sb in the wrong.

▼ **(c)** (*motivo*) reason, motive, cause; '~: **Princesa 4**' 'inquiries to 4 Princesa Street'; 'for further details, apply to 4 Princesa Street'; ~ **que le sobra** she's only too right, she can say that again; **¿cuál es la** ~? what is the reason?; **la** ~ **por qué** the reason why; **la** ~ **por la**

► LENGUA Y USO: **razón: b** → 38.1, 40.3 **c** → 44.1, 44.2, 53.2, 53.6

que lo hizo the reason why he did it, the reason for his doing it; **~ de estado** reasons of state; **~ de más** all the more reason (*para* + *infin* to + *infin*); **~ de ser** raison d'être; **con ~** with good reason; **¡con ~!** naturally!; **con ~ o sin ella** rightly or wrongly; **en ~ de** with regard to; **no atiende a razones** he'll not listen to reason, he's not open to argument; **dar ~ de** to give an account of, report on; to give information about; to deal with; to give some idea of, convey; **nadie me daba ~ de ella** nobody could tell me anything about her; **dar ~ de sí** to give an account of o.s.; **tener ~ para** + *infin* to have cause to + *infin*.

(d) (*Com*) **~ social** trade name, firm's name.

(e) (**: recado*) message; **mandar a uno ~ de que haga algo** to send sb a message telling him to do sth.

(f) (*Mat*) ratio, proportion; rate; **a ~ de 5 a 7** in the ratio of 5 to 7; **a ~ de 8 por persona** at the rate of 8 per head; **abandonan el país a ~ de 800 cada año** they are leaving the country at the rate of 800 a year; **en ~ directa con** in direct ratio to.

razonabilidad NF reasonableness.

▼ **razonable** ADJ reasonable.

razonablemente ADV reasonably.

razonado ADJ reasoned; *cuenta etc* itemized, detailed.

razonamiento NM reasoning.

razonar [1a] ① VT **(a)** (*gen*) to reason, argue. **(b)** *problema etc* to reason out. **(c)** *cuenta* to itemize.

② VI **(a)** (*argüir*) to reason, argue. **(b)** (*hablar*) to talk (together).

raz(z)ia [ˈraθia] NF raid.

raz(z)iar [raθiˈar] VI to raid.

rbdo. (*Com*) ABR *de* **recibido** received, recd.

RCE NF (*Rad*) ABR *de* **Radio Cadena Española**.

RCN NF (*Méjico, Colombia*) ABR *de* **Radio Cadena Nacional**.

RD NM ABR *de* **Real Decreto**.

RDA NF (*Hist*) ABR *de* **República Democrática Alemana** German Democratic Republic, GDR.

Rdo. ABR *de* **Reverendo**.

RDSI NF ABR *de* **Red Digital de Servicios Integrados** Integrated Services Digital Network, ISDN.

re NM (*Mús*) D; **~ mayor** D major.

re... PREF **(a)** re...

(b) (*intensivo*) very, awfully, terribly, *p.ej.* **rebueno** very good, jolly good*; **reguapa** awfully pretty; **resalada** (*Esp*) terribly attractive; **¡rebomba!** (*Esp*) how utterly amazing!; **¡rediez!** (*Esp*) well I'm damned!

reabastecer [2d] ① VT (*t* **~ de combustible, ~ de gasolina**) to refuel.

② **reabastecerse** VR to refuel.

reabastecimiento NM refuelling.

reabrir [3a; PTP **reabierto**] ① VT to reopen; **~ las heridas** to open old wounds.

② **reabrirse** VR to reopen.

reacción NF **(a)** (*gen*) reaction (*a, ante* to; *t Med*); response (*a* to); **~ en cadena** chain reaction; **~ nuclear** nuclear reaction; **la ~ blanca** the white backlash.

(b) (*Pol*) reaction.

(c) (*Téc*) **avión a** (*o* **de**) **~** jet plane; **propulsión por ~** jet propulsion.

reaccionar [1a] VI **(a)** (*gen*) to react (*a, ante* to; *contra* against; *sobre* on); to respond (*a* to); **¿cómo reaccionó?** how did she take it? **(b)** (*sobreponerse*) to pull oneself together.

reaccionario, -a ADJ, NM/F reactionary.

reacio ADJ stubborn; reluctant; **ser ~ a, estar ~ a** to be opposed to, resist (the idea of), be unwilling to accept (the need for); **estar ~ a** + *infin* to be unwilling to + *infin*.

reacondicionamiento NM reconditioning; reorganization, restructuring.

reacondicionar [1a] VT to recondition; *organismo* to reorganize, restructure.

reactivación NF reactivating; (*Econ*) recovery, upturn.

reactivar [1a] VT to reactivate.

reactividad NF reactivity.

reactivo NM reagent.

reactor NM **(a)** (*Fís*) reactor; **~ de agua a presión** pressurized-water reactor; **~ enfriado por gas** gas-cooled reactor; **~ generador, ~ reproductor** breeder reactor; **~ nuclear** nuclear reactor. **(b)** (*Aer*) (*motor*) jet engine; (*avión*) jet plane; **~ ejecutivo** executive jet.

readaptación NF readaptation; readjustment; **~ profesional** industrial retraining; **~ social** social rehabilitation; assimilation into society.

readmisión NF readmission.

readmitir [3a] VT to readmit.

readquirir [3a] VT *poder etc* to recover, regain.

reafirmación NF reaffirmation; reassertion.

reafirmar [1a] VT to reaffirm; to reassert.

reagrupación NF regrouping.

reagrupar [1a] ① VT to regroup.

② **reagruparse** VR to regroup.

reagudizarse [1f] VR (*Med*) to become acute again, recrudesce.

reaje: NM (*Cono Sur*) mob, rabble.

reajustar [1a] ① VT to readjust; (*Pol*) to reshuffle; *precios etc* (*euf*) to increase, put up.

② **reajustarse** VR to readjust.

reajuste NM readjustment; (*fig*) readjustment, reappraisal; **~ agonizante, ~ doloroso** agonizing reappraisal; **~ ministerial** cabinet reshuffle; **~ de precios** (*euf*) rise in prices, price increase; **~ salarial** wage increase.

real¹ ADJ (*verdadero*) real.

real² ① ADJ **(a)** (*del rey*) royal.

(b) (*fig*) royal; grand, splendid; *V* **moza** etc.

② NM **(a)** (*Hist*) (*Mil*) army camp; (*de feria*) fairground; **(a)sentar sus ~es** to settle down; to establish o.s.

(b) (*Fin Hist*) coin of 25 céntimos, one quarter of a peseta; **costó 6 ~es** it cost 1½ pesetas; **está sin un ~*, no tiene un ~*** he hasn't a bean*.

③ **~es** NMPL (*Méx**) cash, dough:.

reala NF (*CAm, Méx*) rope.

realada NF (*Méx*) roundup, rodeo.

realar [1a] VT (*Méx*) *ganado* to round up.

realce NM **(a)** (*Téc*) raised work, embossing.

(b) (*Arte*) highlight.

(c) (*fig*) (*esplendor*) lustre, splendour; (*importancia*) importance, significance; (*aumento*) enhancement; **dar ~ a** to add lustre to, enhance the splendour of; to highlight; **un asunto sin ~** a matter of no importance.

realengo ADJ **(a)** (*LAm*) *animal* stray, lost, ownerless. **(b)** (*Méx, Carib*) (*ocioso*) idle; (*libre*) free, unattached.

realeza NF royalty.

▼ **realidad** NF (*gen*) reality; (*verdad*) truth; **~ virtual** virtual reality; **la ~ de la política** the realities of politics; **atengámonos a la ~** let's face the facts; **en ~** in fact, really, actually; **la ~ es que ...** the fact of the matter is that ...

realimentación NF (*Rad, Inform etc*) feedback; (*Aer etc*) refuelling.

realineamiento NM realignment.

realinear [1a] VT to realign.

realísima NF *V* **gana**.

realismo NM realism; **~ mágico** magic(al) realism.

ⓘ **REALISMO MÁGICO**

Realismo mágico, which derives from a term coined by the Cuban writer Alejo Carpentier in 1949, lo real maravilloso, refers to a primarily Latin American literary genre in which the writer combines elements of the fantastic and realistic in a conscious effort to reconcile tradition with modernity and American-Indian and Black oral culture with European literary writing. Such writers felt that post-Enlightenment European culture had sacrificed imaginative experimentation and themes of instinct and desire to an intellectual rationalism which restricted their capacity to explore. The most celebrated magical realist writer is Colombian Nobel Prize winner Gabriel García Márquez.

---

realista ① ADJ realistic.

② NMF realist.

reality show [reˈalitiʃow] NM, PL **reality shows** real-life drama show, reality show (*US*).

realizable ADJ **(a)** *bienes etc* realizable. **(b)** *objetivo* attainable; *plan* practical, feasible.

realización NF **(a)** (*Fin*) realization; (*venta*) sale, selling-up; (*liquidación*) clearance sale; **~ de beneficios** profit-taking. **(b)** (*acto*: *V* VT **(b)**) realization; fulfilment, carrying out; achievement. **(c)** (*Cine, TV*) production; (*Rad*) broadcast. **(d)** (*Ling*) performance.

realizado ADJ (*V* VT, VR); **sentirse ~** to feel fulfilled.

realizador(a) NM/F (*TV etc*) director.

realizar [1f] ① VT **(a)** (*Fin*) *bienes* to realize; *existencias* to sell off, sell up; *beneficios* to take.

(b) *objetivo etc* to attain, achieve, realize; *promesa* to fulfil, carry out; *plan* to carry out, put into effect.

(c) *viaje etc* to make; *visita* to carry out; *expedición, vuelo etc* to undertake, make; *compra* to make.

(d) **~ que ...** (*LAm*) to realize that ...

② **realizarse** VR **(a)** (*sueño etc*) to come true; (*esperanza*) to materialize; (*plan*) to be carried out.

(b) (*persona*) to fulfil o.s.; **~ como persona** to fulfil one's aims in life.

realmente¹ ADV (*en efecto*) really; (*de hecho*) in fact, actually.

realmente² ADV (*fig*) royally.

realojar [1a] VT to rehouse.

realojo NM rehousing.

realquilado ① ADJ sublet.

② NM, **realquilada** NF sublessee.

realquilar [1a] VT to sublet, sublease; to relet.

realzar [1f] VT (**a**) (*Téc*) to emboss, raise. (**b**) (*Arte*) to highlight. (**c**) (*fig*) to enhance, heighten, add to.

reanimación NF revival (*t fig*); resuscitation.

reanimar [1a] ⊞ VT (**a**) (*lit*) to revive; to resuscitate. (**b**) (*fig*) to revive, encourage, stimulate; to give new life to.

⊡ **reanimarse** VR to revive; to acquire new life.

reanudación NF renewal; resumption.

reanudar [1a] VT to renew; *cuento, viaje etc* to resume.

reaparecer [2d] VI to reappear; to return; to recur.

reaparición NF reappearance; return; recurrence.

reapertura NF reopening.

reaplicar [1g] VT to reapply.

reaprovisionamiento NM replenishment, restocking.

reaprovisionar [1a] VT to replenish, restock.

rearmar [1a] ⊞ VT to rearm.

⊡ **rearmarse** VR to rearm.

rearme NM rearmament.

reasegurar [1a] VT to reinsure; to underwrite.

reaseguro NM reinsurance; underwriting.

reasentar [1j] VT to resettle.

reasfaltado NM resurfacing.

reasfaltar [1a] VT to resurface.

reasumir [3a] VT to resume, reassume.

reata NF (**a**) (*cuerda*) rope (*joining string of pack animals*); (*LAm: lazo*) rope, lasso; (*LAm: correa*) strap; (*And: tira de algodón*) strip of cotton cloth.
(**b**) (*caballos*) string (of horses *etc*), pack train; **de ~** in single file, one after the other; (*fig*) submissively.
(**c**) (*And, Carib, Méx: de flores*) flowerbed, border.
(**d**) (*Méx: enrejado*) bamboo screen.
(**e**) (*Méx*⁚) prick⁚; cock⁚; **echar ~** to fuck⁚.

reavivar [1a] VT to revive.

rebaja NF lowering, lessening, reduction; (*Com*) discount, rebate; (*en saldo*) reduction; '**~s**' 'sale'; **las ~s** the sales; **~s de marzo** spring sales; '**grandes ~s**' 'big reductions'.

rebajamiento NM (**a**) = **rebaja**. (**b**) **~ de sí mismo** self-abasement.

rebajar [1a] ⊞ VT (**a**) *tierra etc* to lower, lower the level of.
(**b**) *precio* to reduce, lower, cut (down); *valor* to detract from, reduce; **~ el precio a uno en un 5 por 100** to give sb a discount of 5%, knock 5% off the price for sb.
(**c**) *intensidad etc* to lessen, diminish; *color* to tone down; *sonido* to turn down, reduce; *calor* to lessen; (*LAm*) *droga* to cut.
(**d**) *persona etc* to humble; to bring down a peg or two, deflate; *ventajas etc* to decry, disparage; **llamarlo así es ~lo de categoría** calling it by that name reduces its (real) importance, calling it that makes it less important than it is.

⊡ **rebajarse** VR: **~ ante uno** to bow before sb; **~ a** + *infin* to humble o.s. sufficiently to + *infin*; to stoop to + *ger*, descend to + *ger*, condescend to + *infin*.

rebaje NM (**a**) (*Téc*) recess; groove. (**b**) (*acto*) lowering; (*Econ, Fin*) cut.

rebajo NM recess; (*Téc*) rabbet.

rebalsa NF pool, puddle.

rebalsar [1a] ⊞ VT (**a**) *agua* to dam (up), block. (**b**) (*LAm*) *orillas etc* to burst, overflow.

⊡ **rebalsarse** VR to form a pool (*o* lake); to become dammed up.

rebanada NF (**a**) (*Culin*) slice. (**b**) (*Méx: pestillo*) latch.

rebanar [1a] VT (*Culin*) to slice, cut in slices; *árbol etc* to slice through, slice down; *miembro etc* to slice off.

rebañar [1a] VT (**a**) *restos* to scrape up, scrape together; to sweep up, sweep into a pile; **logró ~ ciertos fondos** he managed to scrape some money together; **~ el plato del arroz** to scrape a dish clean of rice.
(**b**) **~ una tienda de joyas** (*fig*) to clear a shop of jewellery, clean out all the jewellery from a shop.

rebaño NM flock, herd; (*fig*) flock.

rebasar [1a] VT (*t* VI: **~ de**) (*en calidad, número*) to exceed, surpass; (*en carrera, progreso*) to overtake, leave behind; (*Aut*) to overtake, pass; *punto* to pass, go beyond; (*Náut*) to sail past; *límite de tiempo* to exceed; (*agua*) to overflow, rise higher than; **han rebasado ya los límites razonables** they have already gone beyond all reasonable limits; **la cifra no rebasa de mil** the number does not exceed a thousand.

rebatible ADJ (**a**) *argumento* easily refuted. (**b**) *silla* tip-up.

rebatinga NF (*CAm, Méx*) = **rebatiña**.

rebatiña NF (*LAm*) scramble, rush; **les echó caramelos a la ~** he threw sweets so that they could scramble for them; **andar a la ~ de algo** to scramble for sth, fight over sth; (*fig*) to argue fiercely over sth.

rebatir [3a] VT (**a**) *ataque* to repel; *golpe* to parry, ward off.
(**b**) *argumento etc* to reject, rebut, refute; *tentación* to resist; *sugerencia* to reject.

(**c**) *suma* to reduce; *descuento* to deduct, knock off.

rebato NM (*Mil: alarma*) alarm, warning of attack, call to arms; (*ataque*) surprise attack; **llamar** (*o* **tocar**) **a ~** (*t fig*) to sound the alarm.

rebautizar [1f] VT to rechristen.

Rebeca NF Rebecca.

rebeca NF cardigan.

rebeco NM chamois, ibex.

rebelarse [1a] VR to revolt, rebel, rise; **~ contra** (*fig*) to rebel against.

rebelde ⊞ ADJ (**a**) (*gen*) rebellious; mutinous; **el gobierno ~** the rebel government; **ser ~ a** (*fig*) to be in revolt against, rebel against; to resist.
(**b**) *niño etc* unruly; unmanageable, uncontrollable; stubborn; *problema etc* difficult; *tos etc* persistent, hard to cure; *sustancia* difficult to work, awkward to treat.
(**c**) (*Jur*) defaulting; in contempt of court.
⊡ NMF (**a**) (*Mil, Pol*) rebel.
(**b**) (*Jur*) defaulter; person in contempt of court.

rebeldía NF (**a**) rebelliousness; defiance, disobedience; **estar en plena ~** to be in open revolt.
(**b**) (*Jur*) default; contempt of court; **caer en ~** to be in default; to be in contempt of court; **fue juzgado en ~** he was sentenced by default.

rebelión NF revolt, rebellion, rising.

rebelón ADJ *caballo* hard-mouthed.

rebencudo ADJ (*Carib*) stubborn.

rebenque NM (*LAm*) riding-crop, whip.

rebenqueada NF (*LAm*) whipping.

rebenquear⁎ [1a] VT (*LAm*) to whip.

reblandecer [2d] VT to soften.

reblandecido⁎ ADJ (*And*) (*loco*) soft in the head; (*senil*) senile.

reblandecimiento NM softening; **~ cerebral** softening of the brain.

reble⁚ NM bum⁚, bottom.

rebobinado NM rewind(ing).

rebobinar [1a] VT to rewind.

rebojo NM crust, piece (of bread).

rebolichada NF (*Méx*) opportunity.

rebolludo ADJ thickset, chunky⁎.

reborde NM ledge; (*Téc*) flange, rim; border.

rebosadero NM overflow.

rebosante ADJ: **~ de** (*t fig*) brimming with, overflowing with.

rebosar [1a] VI (**a**) (*líquido, recipiente*) to overflow, run over; **el café rebosa de la taza** the coffee cup is running over, the coffee is running over the cup; **llenar una sala a ~** to fill a room to overflowing.
(**b**) (*abundar*) to abound, be plentiful; **allí rebosa el mineral** the mineral abounds there, a lot of the mineral is found there; **le rebosa la alegría** merriment bubbles out of him.
(**c**) **~ de, ~ en** to overflow with, be brimming with; **~ de salud** to be bursting with health, be brimming with health; **ellos rebosan en dinero** they have pots of money.

reboso NM (*Carib, Cono Sur*) driftwood.

rebotado⁎ NM (*sacerdote*) ex-priest; (*monje*) former monk.

rebotar [1a] ⊞ VT (**a**) *pelota* to bounce; *ataque* to repel; *rayos etc* to send back, turn back, cause to bounce off.
(**b**) *clavo* to clinch.
(**c**) *persona* to annoy; to put out, upset.
(**d**) (*And, Méx*) *agua* to muddy, stir up.
⊡ VI (**a**) (*pelota etc*) to bounce; to rebound (*de* off); (*bala*) to ricochet (*de* off), glance (*de* off). (**b**) (*fig*) to bounce back, recover.

rebote NM bounce, rebound; **de ~** on the rebound; (*fig*) indirectly, as an indirect consequence.

reboteador, -a NM/F (*Baloncesto*) rebounder.

rebotear [1a] VI (*Baloncesto*) to get rebounds.

rebotica NF back room.

rebozado ⊞ ADJ (*Culin*) fried in batter (*o* breadcrumbs *etc*).
⊡ NM batter.

rebozar [1f] ⊞ VT (**a**) *cabeza, cara* to muffle up, wrap up. (**b**) (*Culin*) to roll in batter (*o* breadcrumbs *etc*), fry in batter.
⊡ **rebozarse** VR to muffle (o.s.) up.

rebozo NM (**a**) (*mantilla etc*) muffler, wrap; (*LAm: chal*) shawl. (**b**) (*fig: disfraz*) disguise; dissimulation; **de ~** secretly; **sin ~** (ADV) openly, frankly, (ADJ) plain, straight; aboveboard.

rebrotar [1a] VI to break out again, reappear.

rebrote NM new outbreak, reappearance; (*Econ*) upsurge, (sudden) rise.

rebufar [1a] VI to snort loudly.

rebufo NM loud snort.

rebujo NM (*maraña*) mass, knot, tangle, ball; (*paquete*) badly-wrapped parcel.

rebullicio NM hubbub, uproar; agitation.

rebullir [3a] ⊞ VT (*Méx*) to stir up.
⊡ VI y **rebullirse** VR to stir, begin to move; to show signs of life.

rebultado ADJ bulky.
rebumbio* NM (*Méx*) racket, din, hubbub.
rebusca NF **(a)** (*busca*) search.
  (b) (*Agr*) gleaning.
  (c) (*restos*) leavings, left-overs, remains.
  (d) (*And, Cono Sur*) (*negocio*) small business; (*: *negocio ilegal*) shady dealing, illicit trading; (*ganancia*) profit on the side.
rebuscado ADJ *palabra* recherché; out-of-the-way; *estilo* studied, elaborate; (*LAm: afectado*) affected, stuck-up*.
rebuscar [1g] ① VT **(a)** *objeto etc* to search carefully for, search out; (*Agr*) to glean.
  (b) *lugar* to search carefully; *montón etc* to search through, rummage in.
  ② VI to search carefully; (*Agr*) to glean.
  ③ **rebuscarse*** VR **(a)** (*And, Cono Sur*) to look for work.
  (b) (*And**) to live on one's wits.
rebuznar [1a] VI to bray.
rebuzno NM bray; braying.
recabar [1a] VT **(a)** (*obtener*) to obtain by entreaty, manage to get (*de* from); *fondos* to collect.
  (b) (*reclamar*) to claim as of right, assert one's claim to.
  (c) (*solicitar*) to ask for, apply for; (*exigir*) to demand, insist on.
recadero NM (*mensajero*) messenger; (*repartidor*) errand boy, deliveryman; (*trajinante*) carrier.
recado NM **(a)** (*mensaje*) message; errand; (*regalo*) gift, small present; **coger** (o **tomar**) **un ~** (*Telec etc*) to take a message; **dejar ~** to leave a message; **enviar a uno a un ~** to send sb on an errand; **mandar ~** to send word; **salir a hacer un ~, salir a un ~** (*Méx*) to go out on an errand.
  (b) (*compras*) provisions, daily shopping.
  (c) (*equipo*) equipment, materials; **~ de escribir** writing case, set of writing materials.
  (d) (*LAm: montura*) saddle and trappings, riding gear.
  (e) (*Carib: saludos*) greetings; **déle ~s a su familia** give my regards to his family.
recaer [2n] VI **(a)** (*Med*) to suffer a relapse.
  (b) (*criminal etc*) to fall back, relapse (*en* into); to backslide.
  (c) **~ en** (*elección etc*) to fall on, fall to; (*legado*) to pass to; (*deber*) to devolve upon; (*premio*) to go to; **las sospechas recayeron sobre el conserje** suspicion fell on the porter; **este peso recaerá más sobre los pobres** this burden will bear most heavily on the poor; **la acusación recayó sobre él mismo** the charge recoiled upon him.
  (d) (*Arquit*) **~ a** to look out on, look over.
recaída NF relapse (*en* into); backsliding.
recalar [1a] ① VT to saturate, soak.
  ② VI **(a)** (*Náut*) to sight land, reach port. **(b)** (*) to end up (*en* at). **(c)** **~ a uno** (*LAm*) to go to sb for help.
▼ **recalcar** [1g] ① VT **(a)** *contenido* to press down, press in, squeeze in; *recipiente* to cram, stuff (*de* with).
  ▼ **(b)** (*fig*) to stress, emphasize; to make great play with; **~ algo a uno** to insist on sth to sb; **~ a uno que ...** to tell sb emphatically that ...
  ② VI (*Náut*) to list, heel.
  ③ **recalcarse** VR: **~ un hueso** (*LAm*) to dislocate a bone.
recalcitrante ADJ recalcitrant.
recalcitrar [1a] VI **(a)** (*echarse atrás*) to take a step back (the better to resist). **(b)** (*resistir*) to resist, be stubborn, refuse to take heed.
recalentado ADJ warmed-up (*t fig*).
recalentamiento NM **(a)** overheating; **~ global** global warming. **(b)** (*Culin etc*) warming-up, reheating.
recalentar [1j] ① VT **(a)** (*gen*) to overheat. **(b)** *comida etc* to warm up, reheat.
  ② **recalentarse** VR to become overheated, get too hot.
recalificación NF (*de terrenos*) reassessment, reclaim.
recalificar [1g] VT *terrenos* to reassess.
recalmón NM lull.
recamado NM embroidery.
recamar [1a] VT to embroider.
recámara NF **(a)** (*cuarto*) side room; (*vestidor*) dressing room; (*And, CAm, Méx*) bedroom.
  (b) (*de cañón*) breech, chamber.
  (c) (*fig: cautela*) caution, wariness; reserve; **tener mucha ~** to be on the careful side, be wary by nature.
recamarera NF (*Méx*) chambermaid.
recambiar [1b] VT *pieza* to change over.
recambio NM (*Mec*) spare; (*de pluma*) refill; **~s** spares, spare parts, extras (*US*); **neumático de ~** spare tyre.
recañí NF window.
recapacitar [1a] ① VT to think over, reflect on.
  ② VI to think things over, reflect.
recapitulación NF recapitulation, summing-up, summary.
recapitular [1a] VTI to recapitulate, sum up, summarize.
recargable ADJ rechargeable.

recargado ADJ **(a)** (*sobrecargado*) overloaded. **(b)** *adorno, estilo etc* over-elaborate.
recargar [1h] VT **(a)** (*cargar demasiado*) to overload; to overload on one side, unbalance.
  (b) (*Fin*) to put an additional charge on, increase (the price of, the tax on *etc*).
  (c) (*Jur*) *sentencia* to increase.
  (d) (*Téc*) to reload, recharge; *pila* to recharge.
  (e) (*fig*) to overload (*de* with); **~ a uno de deberes** to overload sb with duties; **~ el café de azúcar** to put too much sugar in the coffee, make the coffee too sweet; **~ un diseño de adornos** to overload a pattern with decoration.
recargo NM **(a)** (*nueva carga*) new burden; (*aumento de carga*) extra load, additional load.
  (b) (*Fin*) extra charge, surcharge; increase.
  (c) (*Jur*) new charge, further charge; increase of sentence.
  (d) (*Med*) rise in temperature.
recatado ADJ **(a)** *mujer* modest, shy, demure. **(b)** (*prudente*) cautious, circumspect.
recatar [1a] ① VT to hide.
  ② **recatarse** VR **(a)** (*ocultarse*) to hide o.s. away (*de* from).
  (b) (*ser discreto*) to act discreetly; **sin ~** openly.
  (c) (*ser prudente*) to be cautious; (*vacilar*) to hesitate; **~ de algo** to fight shy of sth; **no se recata ante nada** nothing daunts her.
recato NM **(a)** (*modestia*) modesty, shyness, demureness. **(b)** (*cautela*) caution, circumspection; reserve, restraint; **sin ~** openly, unreservedly.
recatón NM (*And*) miner's pick.
recauchutado NM **(a)** (*neumático*) retread. **(b)** (*proceso*) retreading, re-moulding.
recauchutar [1a] VT *neumático* to retread, remould.
recaudación NF **(a)** (*acto*) collection; recovery. **(b)** (*cantidad*) takings, sum taken, income; (*Dep*) gate, gate money; *ver también* QUINIELA . **(c)** (*oficina*) tax office.
recaudador(a)¹ NM/F: **~ de contribuciones** tax collector.
recaudadora² NF (*And*) tax office.
recaudar [1a] VT *impuestos* to collect; *dinero* to collect, take (in), receive; *deuda* to recover.
recaudería NF (*Méx*) greengrocer's shop.
recaudo NM **(a)** (*Fin*) collection.
  (b) (*Jur*) surety, security.
  (c) (*cuidado*) care, protection; (*precaución*) precaution; **estar a buen ~** to be in safekeeping; **poner algo a buen ~** to put sth in a safe place.
  (d) (*CAm, Cono Sur, Méx: especias*) spices, condiments.
  (e) (*CAm, Cono Sur, Méx: legumbres*) daily supply of fresh vegetables.
recebo NM gravel.
recechar [1a] VT *caza* to stalk.
rececho NM stalking; **cazar a** (o **en**) **~** to stalk.
recechor(a) NM/F stalker.
recelar [1a] ① VT: **~ que ...** to suspect that ..., fear that ...
  ② VI *y* **recelarse** VR: **~ de** to suspect, fear, distrust; **~ + infin** to be afraid of + *ger*.
recelo NM (*suspicacia*) suspicion; (*temor*) fear, apprehension; (*desconfianza*) distrust, mistrust.
receloso ADJ suspicious, distrustful; apprehensive.
recensión NF recension; review.
recepción NF **(a)** (*acto*) reception, receiving; (*Rad*) reception; (*en academia etc*) admission.
  (b) (*ceremonia*) reception.
  (c) (*cuarto*) drawing room; (*de hotel*) reception, reception desk.
recepcionar [1a] VT (*esp LAm*) to receive, accept.
recepcionista NMF (hotel) receptionist, desk clerk (*US*).
receptación NF (crime of) receiving.
receptáculo NM receptacle; holder.
receptar [1a] VT (*Jur*) to receive.
receptividad NF receptivity.
receptivo ADJ receptive.
receptor ① NM **(a)** (*Téc*) receiver; **~ de control** (*TV*) monitor; **~ de televisión** television receiver, television set; **descolgar el ~** (*Telec*) to pick up the receiver. **(b)** (*Dep*) catcher.
  ② NM, **receptora** NF person who receives a transplant.
recesar [1a] VI (*LAm, Pol*) to recess, go into recess.
recesión NF (*Com, Fin*) recession; slump; (*de precios*) slide, fall.
recesivo ADJ (*Bio*) recessive; (*Econ*) recession (*atr*), recessionary.
receso NM **(a)** (*LAm Parl*) recess. **(b)** (*descanso*) coffee break; **hacer un ~** to pause, stop. **(c)** **~ económico** downturn in the economy.
receta NF (*Culin*) recipe (*de* for); (*Med*) prescription.
recetar [1a] VT **(a)** (*Med*) to prescribe. **(b)** (*CAm, Méx*) *golpe* to deal out, hit.
recetario NM collection of recipes, recipe book.
rechace NM **(a)** rejection. **(b)** (*Dep*) rebound.

➤ LENGUA Y USO: recalcar: 1b → 53.6

rechazamiento NM (a) repelling, beating off; driving back; reflection. (b) rejection; refusal; resistance.

▼ **rechazar** [1f] VT (a) *persona* to push back, push away; *ataque* to repel, beat off; *enemigo* to throw back, drive back; *luz etc* to reflect, turn back; *agua etc* to throw off.

▼ (b) *acusación, idea, moción* to reject; *oferta* to reject, refuse, turn down; *tentación* to resist; (*Med*) *corazón etc* to reject.

rechazo NM (*rebote*) bounce, rebound; (*de cañón*) recoil; (*Med*) rejection; (*fig*) repulse, rebuff; **de ~** on the rebound; (*bala*) as it glanced off, as it ricocheted; (*fig*) in consequence, as a result.

rechifla NF (a) (*silbido*) whistling; (*siseo*) hissing; (*abucheo*) booing; (*Teat*) catcall. (b) (*fig*) mockery, derision.

rechiflar [1a] [1] VT to whistle at, hiss, boo.
[2] VI to whistle, hiss.
[3] **rechiflarse** VR (a) (*de broma*) to take things as a huge joke; **~ de** to make a fool of. (b) (*Cono Sur: enojarse*) to get cross, lose one's temper.

rechín NM (*And*) piece of burnt food; **huele a ~** I can smell food burning.

rechinamiento NM creaking, grating; squeaking; clanking, clattering; humming, whirring; grinding, gnashing.

rechinar [1a] [1] VI (a) (*gen*) to creak, grate; to squeak; (*madera, puerta etc*) to creak; (*máquina*) to clank, clatter; (*piezas sin lubricar*) to grate; (*motor*) to hum, whirr; (*dientes*) to grate, grind, gnash; **hacer ~ los dientes** to grind one's teeth, gnash one's teeth.
(b) (*fig*) to do (o accept *etc*) something with an ill grace.
(c) (*) (*And, Cono Sur, Méx: rabiar*) to rage, fume; (*Carib: quejarse*) to grumble; (*Carib: contestar*) to answer back.
[2] VT (*CAm Culin*) to burn, overcook.
[3] **rechinarse** VR (a) (*CAm, Méx*) to burn, overcook.
(b) (*Cono Sur**) to get furious, lose one's temper.

rechinido NM, **rechino** NM = **rechinamiento**.

rechistar [1a] VI to complain; **se fue a la cama sin ~** he went to bed without (a word of) complaint; **nadie se atrevió a ~** nobody dared complain.

rechonchez NF stockiness; plumpness.

rechoncho ADJ thickset, stocky, squat; plump.

rechupete*: **de ~** [1] ADJ splendid, jolly good*; *comida* delicious, scrumptious*.
[2] ADV splendidly, jolly well*; **me ha salido de ~** it turned out marvellously for me; **pasarlo de ~** to have a fine time.

recial NM rapids.

reciamente ADV strongly; severely; intensely; loudly.

recibí NM 'received with thanks', receipt; **poner el ~ en** to sign one's receipt on.

recibidero ADJ receivable.

recibido ADJ (*LAm*) *persona* qualified.

recibidor¹ NM (*de casa*) entrance hall.

recibidor² NM, **recibidora** NF (*persona*) receiver, recipient.

recibimiento NM (a) (*acto*) reception, welcome; **dispensar a uno un ~ apoteósico** to give sb an enthusiastic welcome.
(b) (*antecámara*) anteroom. vestibule, lobby; (*hall*) hall; (*sala*) reception room.

▼ **recibir** [3a] [1] VT (a) (*gen*) to receive; **'recibido'** (*Rad*) 'message received'.
(b) (*acoger*) *persona* to welcome, receive, greet; to go and meet; *propuesta etc* to receive; to welcome, greet; **~ a uno con los brazos abiertos** to welcome sb with open arms; **el torero recibe al toro** the bullfighter awaits the bull's charge; **le recibió el ministro** the minister received him, the minister granted him an interview; **la oferta fue mal recibida** the offer was badly received; **reciba un saludo de ...** (*en carta*) Yours sincerely ...
(c) (*Univ*) *título etc* to receive, take.
[2] VI to receive; to entertain; **reciben mucho en casa** they entertain at home a good deal; **la baronesa recibe los lunes** the baroness receives visitors on Mondays, the baroness's 'at home' day is Monday.
[3] **recibirse** VR (*LAm*) to qualify; (*Univ*) to graduate; **~ de** to qualify as; to graduate in; *V* **abogado**; **~ de doctor** to take one's doctorate, receive one's doctor's degree; **~ de médico** to graduate in medicine (o as a doctor).

recibo NM (a) = **recibimiento** (a) *y* (b); **estar de ~** (*vestido etc*) to be ready for collection; (*persona*) to be dressed, be ready to receive (visitors); **no es de ~** it is not acceptable, it is intolerable (*que* that).
(b) (*Com*) receipt; (*factura*) bill, account; **de la luz** electricity bill; **acusar ~** to acknowledge receipt (*de* of).

reciclado [1] ADJ recycled.
[2] NM recycling; retraining.

reciclador ADJ recycling.

recicladora NF (*planta*) recycling plant; (*empresa*) recycling firm.

reciclaje NM, **reciclamiento** NM (*V* VT) recycling; retraining; modification, adjustment.

reciclar [1a] [1] VT (*Téc*) to recycle; *persona* to retrain; *plan* to modify,

adjust.
[2] **reciclarse** VR (*fig*) to retrain; to go on a refresher course; (*rejuvenecerse*) to rejuvenate oneself.

recidiva NF (*Med*) relapse.

reciedumbre NF strength, toughness; solidity; severity, harshness; loudness.

recién ADV (a) newly, recently (+ PTP).
(b) (*LAm*) just, only just; **~ se acordó** (*apenas*) she only just remembered; **~ me lo acaban de decir** they've only just told me; **~ ahora** right now, this very moment; **~ aquí** right here, just here; **~ llego** I've (only) just arrived; **~ llegó** he has (only) just arrived, he arrived not long ago.

recién casado ADJ newly-wed; **los ~s** the newly-weds.

recién hecho ADJ newly-made.

recién llegado [1] ADJ newly arrived.
[2] NM, **recién llegada** NF newcomer, new person; (*en fiesta etc*) latecomer.

recién nacido [1] ADJ newborn.
[2] NM, **recién nacida** NF newborn child.

recién puesto ADJ *huevo* new-laid.

reciente ADJ recent; *pan etc* new, fresh, newly-made.

recientemente ADV recently.

Recife NM Recife; (††) Pernambuco.

recinto NM (*cercado*) enclosure; (*zona*) precincts; (*lugar*) area, spot, place; **~ amurallado** walled enclosure; **~ ferial** trades fair pavilion; **~ fortificado** fortified place; strongpoint; **dentro del ~ universitario** on the university campus.

recio [1] ADJ (a) (*fuerte*) *cuerda etc* thick, strong; *persona* strong, tough, robust; *tierra* solid; *prueba etc* tough, demanding, severe.
(b) *voz* loud.
(c) *tiempo* harsh, severe.
(d) (*veloz*) swift, fast, quick.
(e) **en lo más ~ del combate** in the thick of the fight; **en lo más ~ del invierno** in the depths of winter.
[2] ADV *golpear* hard; *soplar* hard, strongly; *pasar etc* swiftly; *cantar, gritar* loud, loudly.

recipiendario, -a NM/F newly-elected member.

recipiente NM (a) (*persona*) recipient. (b) (*vaso etc*) recipient, container, vessel.

recíproca NF (*Mat*) reciprocal.

reciprocación NF reciprocation.

recíprocamente ADV reciprocally, mutually.

reciprocar [1g] VT to reciprocate.

reciprocidad NF reciprocity; mutual character; **usar de ~** to reciprocate.

recíproco ADJ (a) (*mutuo*) reciprocal, mutual. (b) (*inverso*) inverse. (c) **a la recíproca** vice versa; **estar a la recíproca** to be ready to respond.

recitación NF recitation.

recitado NM recitation; (*Mús*) recitative.

recital NM (*Mús*) recital; (*Liter*) reading; **~ de poesías** poetry reading.

recitar [1a] VT to recite.

recitativo NM recitative.

reclamable ADJ reclaimable.

reclamación NF (a) (*gen*) reclamation. (b) (*reivindicación*) claim, demand; **~ salarial** wage claim. (c) (*objeción*) objection; (*queja*) complaint, protest; **formular una ~** to make (o lodge) a complaint.

reclamar [1a] [1] VT (a) (*exigir*) to claim, demand (*de* from); **~ algo para sí** to claim sth for o.s.; **~ su porción de la herencia** to claim one's share of the estate; **esto reclama toda nuestra atención** this demands our full attention.
(b) **~ a uno ante los tribunales** (*Jur*) to take sb to court, file a suit against sb.
[2] VI to protest (*contra* against), complain (*contra* about); **~ contra una sentencia** (*Jur*) to appeal against a sentence.
[3] **reclamarse** VR to proclaim o.s., declare o.s.; **~ de** to claim to be, describe o.s. as.

reclame NM Y F (*LAm*) advertisement; **mercadería de ~** loss leader.

reclamo NM (a) (*Orn*) call, bird call; (*Caza*) decoy, lure.
(b) (*a persona*) call; **acudir al ~** to answer the call.
(c) (*Tip*) catchword.
(d) (*fig: aliciente*) inducement, lure, attraction; (*Com*) (*anuncio*) advertisement; (*slogan*) advertising slogan; (*editorial*) publisher's blurb.
(e) (*Jur*) claim.
(f) (*afirmación*) claim, statement.
(g) (*LAm: protesta*) complaint, protest.

reclinable ADJ: *asiento* **~** reclining seat.

reclinar [1a] [1] VT to lean, recline (*contra* against, *sobre* on).
[2] **reclinarse** VR to lean; to recline, lean back.

reclinatorio NM (*Ecl*) prie-dieu.

recluir [3g] [1] VT to shut away; to confine; (*Jur*) to imprison.
[2] **recluirse** VR to shut o.s. away.

➤ LENGUA Y USO: **rechazar: b → 39.1   recibir: 1a → 47.4**

reclusión NF **(a)** (*acto*) seclusion; (*Jur*) imprisonment, confinement; **~ mayor** imprisonment in conditions of maximum security; **~ perpetua** life imprisonment. **(b)** (*cárcel*) place of imprisonment, prison.

recluso ⊞ ADJ imprisoned; **población reclusa** prison population. ⊡ NM, **reclusa** NF **(a)** *solitario* recluse. **(b)** (*Jur*) prisoner; **~ de confianza** trusty; **~ preventivo** prisoner on remand.

reclusorio NM (*esp Méx*) prison.

recluta ⊞ NF (*acto*) recruitment. ⊡ NMF (*persona*) recruit.

reclutamiento NM recruitment; conscription.

reclutar [1a] VT **(a)** (*Mil*) to recruit (*t fig*). **(b)** (*Cono Sur*) *ganado* to round up; *obrero* to contract, hire.

recobrar [1a] ⊞ VT to recover, get back, retrieve; *ciudad, fugitivo etc* to recapture; *amistad etc* to win back; *tiempo* to make up (for). ⊡ **recobrarse** VR **(a)** (*Med*) to recover, convalesce, get better; (*volver en sí*) to come to, regain consciousness. **(b)** (*fig*) to collect o.s.

recobro NM recovery, retrieval; recapture.

recocer [2b y 2h] ⊞ VT **(a)** (*Culin*: *calentar*) to cook again, warm up; (*cocer demasiado*) to overcook. **(b)** (*Metal*) to anneal. **(c)** (*Cono Sur*: *cocer*) to cook. ⊡ **recocerse** VR (*) to be eaten up inside, suffer a lot.

recochinearse: [1a] VR: **~ de uno** (*Esp*) to take the mickey out of sb:.

recochineo: NM mickey-taking*.

recocina NF scullery.

recodar [1a] VI to twist, turn; to form a bend.

recodo NM turn, bend; elbow; loop.

recogecables NM INVAR automatic cable retractor.

recogedor NM **(a)** (*Agr*: *persona*) picker, harvester; gleaner; **~ de basura** dustman. **(b)** (*herramienta*) rake, scraper; (*recipiente*) pan.

recogepelotas NMF INVAR ballboy, ballgirl.

recoger [2c] ⊞ VT **(a)** *objeto caído* to pick up; *objetos dispersos* to gather (up), gather together; (*Dep*) *pelota* to gather, stop, field; *detalle, información etc* to pick up, come across; *cuentos, romances etc* to collect; *basura etc* to collect, pick up, take; **el informe recoge que ...** the report says that ... **(b)** *dinero etc* to collect, get together; *sellos etc* to collect. **(c)** *periódico etc* to take up, call in, seize; **las autoridades recogieron todos los ejemplares** the authorities took up all the copies; **van a ~ las monedas antiguas** they are going to call in the old coins. **(d)** (*Agr*) *cosecha* to harvest, get in; *fruta* to pick; (*fig*) to harvest, reap; to get as one's reward; **no recogió más que censuras** all he got was criticisms; **de todo esto van a ~ muy poco** they won't get much back out of all this. **(e)** *agua etc* to absorb, take up; *polvo* to gather; (*en recipiente*) to collect. **(f)** *cuerda, velas* to take in; *alas* to fold; *cuernos etc* to draw in; *falda* to roll up, lift, gather up; *mangas* to roll up; (*Cos*) to take in, reduce, shorten. **(g)** *ropa lavada* to take in, get in; *aparato, platos etc* to put away. **(h)** (*ir a buscar*) *persona* to get, fetch, come for; (*en coche*) to pick up; **te vendremos a ~ a las 8** we'll come for you at 8 o'clock; **me recogieron en la estación** they picked me up at the station. **(i)** *necesitado* to take in, shelter. ⊡ **recogerse** VR (*retirarse*) to withdraw, retire; (*ir a casa*) to go home; (*acostarse*) to go to bed; (*refugiarse*) to take shelter; (*ir aparte*) to go off alone (to meditate *etc*).

recogida NF **(a)** (*retiro*) withdrawal, retirement. **(b)** (*Agr*) harvest; (*de basura, correo etc*) collection; **~ de basuras** rubbish collection; **~ de datos** (*Inform*) data collection; **~ de equipajes** (*Aer*) baggage reclaim; **hay 6 ~s diarias** there are 6 collections daily. **(c)** (*Méx Agr*) round-up; (*Cono Sur*: *de policía*) sweep, raid.

recogido ⊞ ADJ **(a)** *vida* quiet; *escenario, lugar* secluded; *carácter* modest, retiring, (*pey*) shy, inhibited; **ella vive muy recogida** she lives very quietly. **(b)** (*pequeño*) small; (*apretado*) bunched up, tight. ⊡ NM tuck, gathering.

recogimiento NM **(a)** (*Agr etc*: *acto*) harvesting, picking; collection; gathering. **(b)** (*acto*: *retiro*) withdrawal, retirement; (*Fin*) retrenchment. **(c)** (*estado*) absorption, concentration; seclusion; quietness. **(d)** (*Ecl*) recollection. **(e)** (*Ecl*: *cualidad*) devotion, devoutness.

recolección NF **(a)** (*Agr etc*) harvesting, picking; collection; gathering. **(b)** (*época*) harvest time, picking season. **(c)** (*Liter*) compilation; summary. **(d)** (*Ecl*) retreat. **(e)** **~ de basura** (*esp LAm*) rubbish collection.

recolectar [1a] VT = **recoger** (d).

recolector(a) NM/F (*Agr*) picker; (*liter etc*) collector.

recoleto ADJ *persona* quiet, retiring; *calle* peaceful, quiet; (*aislado*) isolated.

recolocación NF relocation.

recolocar [1g] VT to relocate.

recomendable ADJ recommendable; laudable; advisable; **poco ~** inadvisable.

▼ **recomendación** NF **(a)** (*indicación*) recommendation; (*sugerencia*) suggestion. **(b)** (*elogio*) praise. ▼ **(c)** (*escrito*) reference, testimonial; **carta de ~** letter of introduction (*para* to); **tiene muchas recomendaciones** he is strongly recommended to us, (*fig*) there's a lot to be said for him. **(d)** (*Ecl*) **~ del alma** prayers for the dying.

recomendado ADJ (*LAm Correos*) registered.

▼ **recomendar** [1j] VT **(a)** (*indicar*) to recommend; (*sugerir*) to suggest; (*aconsejar*) to advise; **~ a uno que haga algo** to recommend sb to do sth, advise sb to do sth; **se lo recomiendo** I recommend it to you. **(b)** (*confiar*) to entrust, confide (*a* to). **(c)** (*elogiar*) to praise, commend. **(d)** (*LAm Correos*) to register.

recomendatorio ADJ recommendatory; **carta recomendatoria** letter of introduction (*para* to).

recomenzar [1f y 1j] VTI to begin again, recommence.

recomerse [2a] VR to bear a secret grudge, harbour resentment.

recompensa NF recompense, reward; compensation (*de una pérdida* for a loss); **en ~ de** in return for, as a reward for.

recompensar [1a] VT to reward, recompense (*por* for); to compensate (*algo* for sth).

recomponer [2q] ⊞ VT **(a)** (*Téc*) to mend, repair; (*Tip*) to reset. **(b)** *persona* to dress up, doll up*. ⊡ **recomponerse*** VR to dress up, doll o.s. up*.

recompra NF repurchase, buying back.

recomprar [1a] VT to repurchase, buy back.

reconcentrar [1a] ⊞ VT **(a)** *atención etc* to concentrate (*en* on), devote (*en* to). **(b)** *personas etc* to bring together. **(c)** *solución* to make more concentrated; to reduce the volume of, compress, increase the density of. **(d)** *emoción* to hide. ⊡ **reconcentrarse** VR **(a)** to concentrate hard, become totally absorbed. **(b)** *emoción* to harbour, conceal in one's heart.

reconciliable ADJ reconcilable.

reconciliación NF reconciliation.

reconciliar [1b] ⊞ VT to reconcile. ⊡ **reconciliarse** VR to become (o be) reconciled.

reconcomerse [2a] VR to bear a secret grudge, harbour resentment.

reconcomio NM **(a)** (*rencor*) grudge, resentment. **(b)** (*deseo*) urge, longing, itch. **(c)** (*sospecha*) suspicion.

recóndito ADJ recondite; **en lo más ~ de** in the depths of; **en lo más ~ del corazón** in one's heart of hearts; **en lo más ~ de mi ser** deep inside me.

reconducir [3n] VT **(a)** *persona* to take back, bring back (*a* to). **(b)** (*Jur*) to renew, extend.

reconfortante ⊞ ADJ comforting; cheering; heart-warming. ⊡ NM (*LAm*) tonic; pick-me-up.

reconfortar [1a] ⊞ VT (*confortar*) to comfort; (*animar*) to cheer, encourage; (*Med*) to strengthen. ⊡ **reconfortarse** VR: **~ con** to fortify o.s. with.

▼ **reconocer** [2d] VT **(a)** (*gen*) to recognize (*por* by); (*distinguir*) to identify, know, tell, distinguish (*por* by); **se le reconoce por el pelo** you can recognize him by his hair. **(b)** (*aceptar*) to recognize (*por* as); *firma, gobierno, hijo etc* to recognize; **no le reconocieron por jefe** they did not recognize (o accept) him as their leader; **le reconocen por inteligente** they agree that he is intelligent; **reconoció al niño por suyo** he recognized that the child was his, he recognized the child as his. ▼ **(c)** (*admitir*) *cualidad, deber, derecho etc* to recognize, admit, acknowledge; **~ los hechos** to face the facts; **~ que ...** to admit that ...; to realize that ...; **reconozco que no existen pruebas de ello** I realize that there is no proof of it; **hay que ~ que no es normal** one must admit that it isn't normal; **por fin reconocieron abiertamente que era falso** eventually they openly admitted that it was untrue. **(d)** *regalo, servicio etc* to be grateful for. **(e)** (*registrar*) *persona* to search; *equipaje etc* to search, inspect, examine; *terreno* to survey; (*Mil*) to reconnoitre, spy out; (*Med*) to examine.

reconocible ADJ recognizable.

▼ **reconocido** ADJ **(a)** *jefe etc* recognized, accepted. **(b)** **quedar ~** to be grateful.

▼ **reconocimiento** NM **(a)** recognition; identification; **~ de firma** (*Méx*) authentication of a signature; **~ óptico de caracteres** optical

➤ LENGUA Y USO: **recomendación**: c → 46.5   **recomendar**: a → 28.1, 29.1, 40.4, 46.5   **reconocer**: c → 38.1, 40.2, 53.4, 53.6   **reconocido**: b → 49

character recognition; **~ de la voz** speech recognition. **(b)** recognition, admission, acknowledgement. ▼**(c)** gratitude; **en ~ de** in gratitude for. **(d)** search(ing); inspection, examination; survey; (*Mil*) reconnaissance; (*Med*) examination, check-up; **~ físico** physical examination; **~ médico** medical examination; **vuelo de ~** reconnaissance flight.

reconquista NF reconquest; recapture; **la R~** the Reconquest (of Spain).

┌─ RECONQUISTA ─┐

ⓘ The term **Reconquista** *refers to the eight centuries during which the Christian kings of the Spanish kingdoms gradually reclaimed their country from the Moors, who had invaded the Iberian Peninsular in 711. It is generally accepted that the reconquest began in 718 with the Christian victory at Covadonga in Asturias, and ended in 1492, when Ferdinand and Isabella, the* **Reyes Católicos**, *Catholic Monarchs, retook Granada, the last Muslim stronghold. In the intervening centuries there had been a great deal of contact and overlap between the two cultures. Christians living under Arab rule were called* **mozárabes**, *while* **mudéjares** *were practising Muslims living under Christian rule. In contrast with the pluralistic society that had existed under the Arabs, the final years of the* **Reconquista** *were a time of great intolerance with Arabs and Jews being forcibly converted to Christianity, after which they were known as* **conversos**. *Those refusing to be converted were expelled in 1492.*
---

reconquistar [1a] VT **(a)** (*Mil*) *territorio* to reconquer; *ciudad, posición* to recapture (*a* from). **(b)** (*fig*) *estima etc* to recover, win back.

reconsideración NF reconsideration.

reconsiderar [1a] VT to reconsider.

reconstitución NF reconstitution, reforming; reconstruction.

reconstituir [3g] VT to reconstitute, reform; *crimen, escena* to reconstruct.

reconstituyente NM tonic, restorative, pick-me-up.

reconstrucción NF reconstruction; reshuffle.

reconstruir [3g] VT (*gen*) to reconstruct; *gobierno* to reshuffle.

recontar [1l] VT **(a)** *cantidad* to recount, count again; to count up carefully. **(b)** *cuento* to retell, tell again.

recontra* **1** PREF (*LAm: intensivo*) extremely, terribly; *p.ej.* **recontracaro** terribly dear, **recontrabueno** really good; **estoy ~cansado** I'm terribly tired. **2** INTERJ **¡~!** (*euf*) well I'm ...!*

reconvención NF **(a)** *reproches* reprimand; expostulation, remonstrance. **(b)** (*Jur*) counterclaim.

reconvenir [3r] VT **(a)** (*reprender*) to reprimand; (*tratar de convencer a*) to expostulate with, remonstrate with. **(b)** (*Jur*) to counterclaim.

reconversión NF reconversion; restructuring, reorganization; streamlining; **~ industrial** (*euf*) industrial rationalization; **~ profesional** industrial retraining.

reconvertir [3i] VT to reconvert (*en* to); to restructure, reorganize; to streamline; (*euf*) *industria* to rationalize; **~ profesionalmente** to retrain for industry, give industrial retraining to.

recopa NF cup-winners' cup.

recopilación NF summary; compilation; (*Jur*) code; **la R~** *Spanish law code of 1567*; **la Nueva R~** *Spanish law code of 1775*; **~ de datos** (*Inform*) data collection.

recopilador(a) NM/F compiler.

recopilar [1a] VT **(a)** (*reunir*) to compile, gather, collect (together); (*resumir*) to summarize. **(b)** *leyes* to codify.

recopilatorio **1** ADJ compilation (*atr*). **2** NM compilation.

record, récord [re'kor, 'rekor] **1** ADJ INVAR record; **cifras ~** record quantities; **en un tiempo ~** in a record time. **2** NM, PL **records, récords** [re'kor, 'rekor] record; **batir** (*o* **establecer**) **el ~** to break the record.

recordable ADJ memorable.

recordación NF recollection; remembrance; **de feliz ~** of happy memory; **de infeliz** (*o* **triste**) **~** of unhappy memory; **digno de ~** memorable.

recordar¹ [1l] **1** VT **(a)** (*acordarse de*) to remember; to recollect, recall; **no lo recuerdo** I don't remember it; **recuerda haberlo dicho** he remembers saying it.
(b) (*traer a la memoria*) to recall; to call up, evoke (memories of), bring to mind; **esto recuerda aquella escena de la película** this recalls that scene in the film; **la frase recuerda a Garcilaso** the phrase is reminiscent of Garcilaso, the phrase has echoes of Garcilaso.
(c) (*acordar a otro*) to remind; **~ algo a uno** to remind sb of sth; **~ a uno que haga algo** to remind sb to do sth; **recuérdale que me debe 5 dólares** remind him that he owes me 5 dollars.
(d) (*Cono Sur, Méx*: despertar*) to awaken, wake up.
2 VI to remember; **no recuerdo** I don't remember; **que yo recuerde** as far as I can remember; **creo ~, si mal no recuerdo** if my memory serves me right; *V* **desde**.
3 **recordarse** VR **(a)** **~ que ...** to remind o.s. that ...
(b) (*Cono Sur, Méx*: despertar*) to wake up.

(c) (*And, Carib, Cono Sur: volver en sí*) to come to, come round.

recordar² [1l] VT (*CAm, Carib, Méx*) *voz etc* to record.

recordativo ADJ reminiscent; **carta recordativa** reminder.

recordatorio NM **(a)** (*gen*) reminder; *recuerdo* memento. **(b)** (*tarjeta*) in memoriam card. **(c)** **esto te servirá de ~** let this be a lesson to you.

recordman NM, PL **recordmans** (*titular*) record-holder; (*campeón*) champion; (*jugador destacado*) outstanding player (*etc*).

recorrer [2a] VT **(a)** (*pasar por*) *lugar, zona* to go over, go across, go through, traverse; *país* to cross, tour, travel; (*buscadores*) to cover, range, scour; *distancia* to travel, cover, do; (*Mec*) to travel (along); **~ una provincia a pie** to go over a province on foot, have a walking tour through a province; **~ un escrito** to run one's eye over a document, look through a document; **en 14 días los Jones han recorrido media Europa** the Jones have done half Europe in a fortnight.
(b) (*registrar*) to look over, go over, survey; to check; to search.
(c) (*Mec etc*) to repair, mend; to overhaul.
(d) *sillas etc* to move along, put closer together; (*Tip*) *letras* to take over.

recorrido NM **(a)** (*viaje*) run, journey; (*ruta*) route, course, path; (*distancia*) distance covered, distance travelled; (*de golf, saltos; de repartidor etc*) round; (*de émbolo etc*) stroke; **el ~ del primer día fue de 450 km** the first day's run was 450 kms; **un ~ en 5 bajo par** a round in 5 under par; **tren de largo ~** long-distance train; **~ de aterrizaje** (*Aer*) landing run; **~ electoral** (*Pol*) campaign trail.
(b) (*Mec etc*) repair; overhaul.
(c) (*) detailed reprimand.

recortable NM cut-out.

recortada NF sawn-off shotgun.

recortado **1** ADJ **(a)** *borde* jagged; uneven, irregular. **(b)** (*CAm, Carib: chaparro*) short and stocky. **(c)** (*CAm, Carib*: necesitado*) broke*.
2 NM (*And, Carib, Cono Sur*) sawn-off rifle, pistol.

recortar [1a] **1** VT **(a)** *exceso* to cut away, cut off, cut back, trim; *pelo* to trim; *grabado, recorte etc* to cut out; *escopeta* to saw off.
(b) (*Arte*) to draw in outline.
(c) (*fig*) to cut out, remove, suppress; *plantilla* to cut, cut back; *víveres etc* to cut down.
2 **recortarse** VR to stand out, be outlined, be silhouetted (*en, sobre* against).

recorte NM **(a)** (*acto*) cutting, trimming; (*de pelo*) trim; (*para economizar*) cutback (*de* in); **~ presupuestario** budget cut, spending cut.
(b) (*de juguete*) cut-out.
(c) **~s** trimmings, clippings; **~s de periódico, ~s de prensa** newspaper cuttings, press clippings; **álbum de ~s** scrapbook; **el libro está hecho de ~s** the book is a scissors-and-paste job.
(d) (*CAm*: comentario*) nasty remark.

recoser [2a] VT to patch up, darn.

recosido NM patch, darn.

recostable ADJ: **asiento ~** reclining seat.

recostado ADJ reclining, recumbent; **estar ~** to be lying down.

recostar [1l] **1** VT to lean (*en* on).
2 **recostarse** VR **(a)** (*reclinar*) to recline, lie back; to lie down. **(b)** (*fig*) to have a short rest.

recotín* ADJ (*Cono Sur*) restless.

recova NF **(a)** (*negocio*) poultry business, dealing in poultry; (*mercado*) poultry market.
(b) (*And, Cono Sur: mercado*) food market; (*And: carnicería*) butcher's (shop).
(c) (*Cono Sur Arquit*) arcade, covered corridor (*along the front of a house*); porch.

recoveco NM **(a)** (*de calle etc*) turn, bend.
(b) (*en casa*) nook, odd corner; cubbyhole.
(c) (*fig: complejidades*) **~s** ins and outs; **el asunto tiene muchos ~s** it's a very complicated matter, the affair has lots of pitfalls.
(d) (*fig: subterfugios*) **~s** subterfuges, devious ways; **sin ~s** plainly, frankly.

recovero, -a NM/F poultry dealer.

recreación NF **(a)** recreation. **(b)** = **recreo**.

recrear [1a] **1** VT **(a)** (*crear de nuevo*) to recreate.
(b) (*divertir*) to amuse, divert, entertain.
2 **recrearse** VR to enjoy o.s.; to amuse o.s., entertain o.s. (*con* with); **~ viendo los infortunios de otros** to take pleasure in (*o* gloat over) others' misfortunes.

recreativo **1** ADJ recreative; recreational; **instalaciones recreativas** recreational facilities.
2 NM games arcade.

recrecer [2d] **1** VT to increase.
2 VI **(a)** (*crecer*) to increase, grow. **(b)** (*volver a ocurrir*) to happen again.
3 **recrecerse** VR to cheer up, recover one's spirits.

recreo NM **(a)** (*gen*) recreation, relaxation; (*diversión*) amusement. **(b)**

(*Escuela*) break, playtime, recreation.

recriminación NF (a) (*gen*) recrimination; ~ **mutua** mutual recrimination. (b) (*Jur*) countercharge.

recriminar [1a] ① VT (a) (*reprochar*) to reproach. (b) (*Jur*) to countercharge.
② VI to recriminate.
③ **recriminarse** VR to reproach each other, indulge in mutual recrimination.

recrudecer [2d] VI *y* **recrudecerse** VR to recrudesce, break out again; to worsen.

recrudecimiento NM, **recrudescencia** NF recrudescence, new outbreak, upsurge.

recrudescente ADJ recrudescent.

recta NF straight line; **la ~** (*Dep*) the straight; **~ final, ~ de llegada** home straight; (*fig*) closing stages, final stage; final dash.

rectal ADJ rectal.

rectamente ADV (a) (*correctamente*) *comportarse, entender* properly, correctly. (b) (*directamente*) straight; **mirar a uno ~ a los ojos** to look sb straight in the eyes.

rectangular ADJ = **rectángulo 1.**

rectángulo ① ADJ rectangular, oblong; *triángulo etc* right-angled.
② NM rectangle, oblong.

rectificable ADJ rectifiable; **fácilmente ~** easily rectified, easy to put right.

rectificación NF rectification; correction.

rectificador(a) NM/F (*Mec*) rectifier.

rectificar [1g] ① VT (a) *carretera etc* to straighten (out).
(b) (*Mec etc*) to rectify; to balance; *cilindro* to rectify, rebore.
(c) *cálculo etc* to rectify, correct; *conducta* to change, reform.
② VI to correct oneself; **'No, eran 4', rectificó** 'No', he said, correcting himself, 'there were 4'; **rectifique, por favor** please see that this is put right.

rectilíneo ADJ rectilinear.

rectitud NF (a) (*gen*) straightness. (b) (*fig*) rectitude, honesty, uprightness.

recto ① ADJ (a) *línea etc* straight; *ángulo* right; *componente etc* upright; *curso* straight, direct, unswerving; **la flecha fue recta al blanco** the arrow went straight to the target; **siga todo ~** go straight on.
(b) (*fig*) *persona* honest, upright; *juez etc* fair, just, impartial; *juicio* sound; *intención* lawful, proper.
(c) (*fig*) *sentido* literal, proper, basic; **en el sentido ~ de la palabra** in the proper sense of the word.
(d) (*Ling*) *caso* nominative.
② NM (*Anat*) rectum.

rector ① ADJ *persona* leading; governing; managing; *idea, principio* guiding, governing; **los deberes ~es del régimen** the régime's guiding principles; **una figura ~a** an outstanding figure, a leading figure.
② NM, **rectora** NF (a) head, chief, leader; principal.
(b) (*Univ*: *t* ~ **magnífico**) rector, president (*US*), (*aprox*) vice-chancellor.

rectorado NM (*Univ*) (a) (*oficio*) rectorship, presidency (*US*), (*aprox*) vice-chancellorship. (b) (*oficina*) rector's office.

rectorar [1a] VT (*CAm*) to rule, govern, direct.

rectoría NF = **rectorado** (a) *y* (b).

recua NF mule train, train of pack animals; **una ~ de chiquillos** a bunch of kids*.

recuadro NM (*Tip*) inset; (*Esp: de formulario*) box.

recubrir [3a; PTP **recubierto**] VT to cover (*con, de* with); to coat (*con, de* with).

recuento NM (*acto*) count, recount; (*inventario*) inventory, survey; **~ de espermas** sperm count; **~ polínico** pollen count; **hacer el ~ de** to make a survey of, draw up an inventory of; to count up, reckon up.

▼ **recuerdo** ① ADJ (*And**) awake.
② NM (a) (*memoria*) memory; recollection; reminiscence; **'R~s de la vida de hace 80 años'** 'Reminiscences of life 80 years ago'; **contar los ~s** to reminisce; **entrar en el ~, pasar al ~** (*euf*) to pass away; **guardar un feliz ~ de uno** to have happy memories of sb.
(b) (*regalo*) souvenir, memento, keepsake; **'R~ de Mallorca'** 'A souvenir from Majorca'; **toma esto como ~** take this as a keepsake.
(c) (*: joya*) jewel, piece of jewellery.
▼ (d) (*saludo*) ~**s** regards, best wishes; **¡dale ~s míos!** give him my regards!, remember me to him!; **os manda muchos ~s para todos** he sends you all his warmest regards.

recuero NM muleteer.

recuesto NM slope.

reculada NF (a) (*lit*) backward movement; (*de fusil*) recoil. (b) (*Méx*) retreat; (*fig*) backing down, weakening.

recular [1a] VI (a) (*animal, vehículo*) to go back, back; (*cañón*) to recoil; (*ejército etc*) to fall back, retreat.
(b) (*fig*) to back down, weaken (in one's resolve).

reculativa NF (*Méx*) = **reculada** (b).

reculón NM (a) (*LAm*) = **reculada**. (b) **andar a reculones** to go backwards.

recuperable ADJ recoverable, retrievable.

▼ **recuperación** NF recovery, recuperation, retrieval; **~ de datos** data retrieval; **~ de informaciones** information retrieval; **~ de tierras** land reclamation.

recuperar [1a] ① VT (a) (*recobrar*) to recover, recuperate, retrieve; (*Inform*) to retrieve; *pérdida* to recoup; *tiempo* to make up; *tierras* to reclaim; *fuerzas* to restore, repair.
(b) (*Téc*) *residuos etc* to reclaim, process for re-use.
② **recuperarse** VR (*Med etc*) to recover, recuperate.

recuperativo ADJ recuperative.

recurrencia NF (a) (*Med*) recurrence. (b) (*apelación*) recourse, appeal.

recurrente ① ADJ recurrent.
② NMF (*Jur*) appellant.

recurrir [3a] ① VT (*Jur*) to appeal against.
② VI (a) **~ a medio etc** to resort to, have recourse to; to fall back on; *persona* to turn to, appeal to. (b) (*Jur*) to appeal (*a* to; *contra, de* against).

recurso NM (a) (*gen*) recourse, resort; (*medio*) means; (*expediente*) expedient; **como último ~** as a last resort.
(b) ~**s** (*Fin etc*) resources; means; ~**s ajenos** (*Fin*) borrowed capital; ~**s económicos** economic resources; ~**s humanos** human resources ~**s naturales** natural resources; ~**s no renovables** non-renewable resources; **la familia está sin ~s** the family has nothing to fall back on.
(c) (*Jur*) appeal; **interponer ~ contra** to lodge an appeal against.

recusación NF (a) (*rechazo*) rejection. (b) (*Jur*) challenge.

recusante ADJ, NMF recusant.

recusar [1a] VT (a) (*rechazar*) to reject, refuse. (b) (*Jur*) to challenge.

red NF (a) (*Pesca etc*) net; (*Dep*) net; (*del pelo*) hairnet; (*malla*) mesh, meshes; (*Ferro*) rack; (*cerca*) fence; (*reja*) grille; **~ de alambre** wire mesh, wire-netting; **~ barredera** trawl; **~ metálica** metal screen; **~ de seguridad** safety net.
(b) (*fig*) network, system; (*Elec, cañerías etc*) mains, supply system; grid; (*de almacenes etc*) chain; **~ de área extendida** extended area network; **~ de área local** local area network; **~ de comunicaciones** communications network; **~ de conmutación de circuito** circuit switching network; **~ de distribución** distribution network; **~ de emisoras** radio network; **~ de espionaje** spy network, spy ring; **~ ferroviaria** railway network, railway system; **~ informática, ~ informativa** information network; **~ local** local network; **~ rastreadora, ~ de rastreo** tracking network; **~ de transmisión de datos** data network; **~ vascular** vascular system; **~ vial** road network; **funciona a (la) ~** it works from the mains; **con agua de la ~** with mains water, with water from the mains; **estar conectado con la ~** to be connected to the mains.
(c) (*fig: trampa*) snare, trap; **aprisionar a uno en sus ~es** to have sb firmly caught in one's toils, have sb well and truly snared; **caer en la ~** to fall into the trap; **tender una ~ para uno** to set a trap for sb.

redacción NF (a) (*acto*) writing, redaction; editing. (b) (*fraseología*) wording. (c) (*oficina*) newspaper office. (d) (*personas*) editorial staff. (e) (*Escuela*) composition; (*Univ*) essay.

redactar [1a] VT (a) (*escribir*) to write; to draft, draw up; (*expresar*) to word, express; **una carta mal redactada** a badly-worded letter. (b) *periódico etc* to edit.

redactor, -a NM/F (a) (*escritor*) writer, drafter. (b) (*director*) editor; sub-editor.

redada NF (a) (*acto*) cast, casting, throw. (b) (*de policía*) sweep, raid. (c) (*cantidad*) catch, haul (*t fig*).

redaje NM (*And*) (*red*) net; (*maraña*) mess, tangle.

redaño NM (a) (*Anat*) mesentery; caul. (b) ~**s** guts, pluck.

redargüir [3g] ① VT (a) (*Jur*) to impugn, hold to be invalid. (b) **~ que ...** to argue on the other hand that ...
② VI to turn an argument against its proposer.

redecilla NF hairnet.

rededor: al ~ V **alrededor.**

redefinición NF redefinition.

redefinir [3a] VT to redefine.

redemocratización NF return to democracy, reestablishment of democracy.

redención NF redemption.

redentor ① ADJ redeeming.
② NM redeemer; **R~** Redeemer, Saviour; **meterse a ~** to intervene (with the best intentions).

redescubrir [3a; PTP **redescubierto**] VT to rediscover.

redesignar [1a] VT (*Inform*) to rename.

redespachar [1a] VT (*Cono Sur Com*) to send on, forward (directly).

redicho ADJ affected, overrefined, stilted.

redil NM sheepfold.

redimensionamiento NM remodelling; rationalization; streamlining, cutting back.

▶ LENGUA Y USO: **recuerdo: 2d** → 48.2   **recuperación** → 50.4

redimensionar [1a] VT (a) (*Econ etc*) to remodel; (*euf*) to rationalize, streamline, cut back.
(b) (*disminuir*) to play down.
redimible ADJ redeemable.
redimir [3a] VT to redeem (*t Fin, fig*); *cautivo* to ransom; *esclavo* to purchase the freedom of.
rediós* INTERJ good God!
redistribución NF redistribution.
redistribuir [3g] VT to redistribute.
redistributivo ADJ redistributive; **programa ~** programme for the redistribution of wealth (*etc*).
rédito NM interest, yield, return.
redituable ADJ (*Cono Sur*) profitable.
redituar [1e] VT to yield, produce, bear.
redivivo ADJ new; revived, resuscitated.
redoba NF (*Méx Mús*) *wooden board hung round neck and used as a percussion instrument.*
redoblado ADJ (a) (*Mec*) *pieza* reinforced, extra strong; *persona* stocky, thickset. (b) *celo etc* redoubled. (c) *paso* double-quick.
redoblante NM (long-framed) side drum.
redoblar [1a] ① VT (a) *papel etc* to bend back, bend over, bend down; *clavo* to clinch.
(b) *celo, esfuerzo etc* to redouble.
(c) (*Bridge*) to redouble.
② (*Mús*) to play a roll on the drum; (*trueno*) to roll, rumble.
redoble NM (*Mús*) drumroll, drumbeat; (*de trueno*) roll, rumble.
redoma NF (a) (*frasco*) flask, phial. (b) (*Cono Sur: de pez*) fishbowl. (c) (*Carib Aut*) roundabout, traffic circle (*US*).
redomado ADJ (a) (*taimado*) sly, artful. (b) *pícaro etc* complete, utter, out-and-out.
redomón ADJ (a) (*Méx*) *caballo* wild, unbroken; *persona* (*inexperto*) untrained, unskilled; (*torpe*) slow, dense; (*ordinario*) crude, rough. (b) (*LAm*) *caballo* half-trained.
redonda NF (a) (*Mús*) semibreve.
(b) (*Tip*) roman, rounded characters, ordinary letters.
(c) **en muchas millas a la ~** for many miles round about; **se olía a un kilómetro a la ~** you could smell it a mile off.
(d) (‡: *droga*) pill.
redondear [1a] ① VT (a) (*lit*) to round, round off. (b) (*fig: completar*) to round off. (c) *cifra* to round up (*t ~ por arriba, ~ por defecto*), round down (*t ~ por abajo, ~ por exceso*). (d) (*complementar*) to top up.
② **redondearse** VR (a) (*enriquecerse*) to acquire money, become wealthy. (b) (*librarse de deudas*) to get clear of debts.
redondel NM (a) (*Taur*) bullring, arena. (b) (‡: *círculo*) ring, circle; **~ de humo** smoke-ring. (c) (*Aut*) roundabout, traffic circle (*US*).
redondez NF roundness; **en toda la ~ de la tierra** in the whole wide world.
redondilla NF (*Liter Hist*) quatrain.
redondo ① ADJ (a) *forma* round; rounded; **3 m en ~** 3 metres round; **¿cuánto tiene de ~?** how far is it round?; **caer ~** to fall in a heap; (*dormido*) to fall asleep; (*borracho*) to pass out; **girar en ~** to turn right round; **rehusar en ~** to give a flat refusal, refuse flatly.
(b) *cantidad, cifra* round; **en números ~s** in round numbers, in round figures.
(c) *viaje* round.
(d) *negativa etc* straight, flat, square; *afirmación etc* blunt.
(e) *negocio etc* complete, finished; successful; **todo le ha salido ~** it all went well for him; **el negocio era ~** the business was really profitable; **será un negocio ~** it will be a really good deal; **triunfo ~** complete success.
(f) *vino* full, rounded.
(g) (‡) AC/DC‡, bisexual.
(h) (*Méx**) (*lerdo*) dense*, thick*; (*débil*) weak.
② NM (a) (*Mús**) disc, record.
(b) (*Culin*) rumpsteak.
(c) (‡) bisexual.
redopelo NM (a) (*) scrap*, rough-and-tumble. (b) **a ~ = a contrapelo**; **una lógica a ~** logic stood on its head, logic in reverse; **traer al ~ a uno** to treat sb very badly, ride roughshod over sb.
redor: **en ~** V **alrededor**.
redro ADV behind; backwards.
redrojo NM (a) (*Bot*) late fruit, withered fruit.
(b) (*Cono Sur: exceso*) rest, remainder.
(c) (*Méx**: *harapos*) rags.
redropelo = redopelo.
reducción NF (a) (*gen*) reduction; (*disminución*) diminution, lessening (*de* of); cut, cutback (*de* in); **~ del activo** divestment. (b) (*Med*) setting. (c) (*LAm Hist*) settlement of Christianized Indians.
reduccionismo NM reductionism.
reducible ADJ reducible.
reducido ADJ (a) (*gen*) reduced; (*limitado*) limited; *número etc* small; *in-*

gresos, recursos limited, small; *espacio* confined, limited; *precio* reduced. (b) **quedar ~ a** to be reduced to.
reducir [3n] ① VT (a) *cantidad, número etc* to reduce; to diminish, lessen, cut (down); *discurso etc* to cut down, abridge; *tamaño* to reduce, cut down; *actividad, intervención etc* to limit (*a* to); (*Aut*) to change down; **~ algo al absurdo** to make sth seem ridiculous.
(b) (*Mat etc*) to reduce (*a* to), convert (*a* into); **~ las millas a kilómetros** to convert miles into kilometres; **~ los dólares en pesetas** to change dollars into pesetas; to express dollars as pesetas; **~ una casa a escombros** to reduce a house to rubble; **todo lo reduce a cosas materiales** he reduces everything to material terms.
(c) *país etc* to subdue; *persona peligrosa* to overpower; *rebeldes* to overcome, bring under control; *fortaleza* to reduce; **~ a uno al silencio** to silence sb, reduce sb to silence; **~ a uno a la obediencia** to bring sb to heel.
(d) (*Med*) *hueso* to set.
② **reducirse** VR (a) to diminish, lessen, fall, be reduced (*a* to).
(b) (*Fin*) to economize.
(c) **~ a** to come down to, amount to no more than; **el escándalo se redujo a un simple chisme** the scandal amounted to nothing more than a piece of gossip; **~ a + infin** to come down to + *ger*, find o.s. reduced to + *ger*.
reductible ADJ (*Cono Sur, Méx*) reducible.
reductivo ADJ *régimen etc* slimming.
reducto NM (*Mil y fig*) redoubt; **el último ~ de** the last redoubt of.
reduje *etc* V **reducir**.
redundancia NF redundancy, superfluity; **valga la ~** forgive the repetition.
redundante ADJ redundant, superfluous.
redundar [1a] VI: **~ en** to redound to; **~ en beneficio de** to be to the advantage of.
reduplicación NF reduplication; redoubling.
reduplicar [1g] VT to reduplicate; *esfuerzo etc* to redouble.
reedición NF reissue, reprint(ing).
reedificación NF rebuilding.
reedificar [1g] VT to rebuild.
reeditar [1a] VT to reissue, republish, reprint.
reeducación NF re-education; **~ profesional** industrial retraining.
reeducar [1g] VT to re-educate; **~ profesionalmente** to give industrial retraining to.
reelección NF re-election.
reelegible ADJ eligible for re-election.
reelegir [3c y ₃k] VT to re-elect.
reembalar [1a] VT to repack.
reembolsable ADJ repayable; refundable, returnable; (*Fin*) **no ~ valores** irredeemable; *depósito* non-returnable, not refundable.
reembolsar [1a] ① VT *persona* to reimburse; to repay; *dinero* to repay, pay back; *depósito* to refund, return.
② **reembolsarse** VR to reimburse o.s.; **~ una cantidad** to recover a sum.
reembolso NM reimbursement; repayment, refund; **enviar algo contra ~** to send sth cash on delivery (ABR: *COD*).
reemisor NM booster station.
reemplazable ADJ replaceable.
reemplazante NMF (*Méx*) replacement, substitute.
reemplazar [1f] VT to replace (*con* with, *por* by).
reemplazo NM (a) replacement. (b) (*Mil*) reserve; annual draft of recruits; **de ~** reserve (*atr*), from the reserve.
reemprender [2a] VT to resume.
reencarnación NF reincarnation.
reencarnar [1a] ① VT to reincarnate.
② VI to be reincarnated.
reencauchado NM (*LAm Aut*) retread, remould.
reencauchar [1a] VT (*LAm Aut*) to retread, remould.
reencender [1j] VT to light again, rekindle.
reencontrarse [1l] VR to meet again.
reencuadernar [1a] VT to rebind.
reencuentro NM reunion.
reengancharse [1a] VR to re-enlist, sign on again.
reenganche NM (*Mil*) reenlistment.
reentrada NF re-entry.
reenvasar [1a] VT to repack, rewrap.
reenviar [1c] VT (*hacer seguir*) to forward, send on; (*devolver*) to send back.
reenvío NM cross-reference.
reescribir [3a] VT to rewrite.
reestatificación NF renationalization.
reestatificar [1g] VT to renationalize.
reestrenar [1a] VT (*Teat*) to revive, put on again; (*Cine*) to reissue.
reestreno NM (*Teat*) revival; (*Cine*) reissue.
reestructuración NF restructuring, reorganizing.
reestructurar [1a] VT to restructure, reorganize.

reevaluación NF reappraisal.
reevaluar [1e] VT to reappraise.
reexaminación NF re-examination.
reexaminar [1a] VT to re-examine.
reexpedir [3k] VT to forward; to redirect.
reexportación NF (*Com*) re-export.
reexportar [1a] VT to re-export.
REF NM (*Esp Econ*) ABR de **Régimen económico fiscal**.
Ref.ª ABR de **referencia** reference, ref.
refacción NF (**a**) (*comida*) light refreshment, refection.
(**b**) (*LAm Arquit, Mec*) repair(s).
(**c**) (*LAm Agr: gastos*) running costs.
(**d**) (*Carib, Méx*) (*préstamo*) short-term loan, (*subvención*) financial assistance.
(**e**) (*Méx Mec*) **refacciones** spares, spare parts.
refaccionar [1a] VT (**a**) (*LAm Arquit, Mec*) to repair. (**b**) (*LAm: subvencionar*) to finance, subsidize.
refaccionaria NF (*LAm*) repair shop.
refajo NM (*enagua*) flannel underskirt; (*falda*) short extra skirt; (*combinación*) slip.
refalar* [1a] (*Cono Sur*) ① VT (**a**) **~ algo a uno** to take sth from (*u* off) sb.
(**b**) (*hurtar*) to steal.
② **refalarse*** VR (**a**) **~ los zapatos** to kick off one's shoes.
(**b**) (*huir*) to make off, beat it*; (*resbalar*) to slip.
refalón* NM (*Cono Sur*) slip, fall.
refaloso* ADJ (*Cono Sur*) (**a**) (*resbaladizo*) slippery. (**b**) (*tímido*) shy, timid.
refanfinflar* [1a] VT: **me la refanfinfla** I couldn't give a damn*.
refectorio NM refectory.
referencia NF (**a**) (*gen*) reference; **con ~ a** with reference to; **hacer ~ a** to refer to, allude to; **~ cruzada** cross-reference; **~ multiple** general cross-reference.
(**b**) (*informe*) account, report; **~ bancaria** banker's reference; **una ~ completa del suceso** a complete account of what took place.
referenciar [1b] VT to index.
referendo NM referendum.
referéndum NM, PL **referéndums** referendum.
referente ADJ: **~ a** relating to, about, concerning.
referí NMF (*LAm*) referee, umpire.
referible ADJ: **~ a** referable to.
referido ADJ (**a**) above-mentioned. (**b**) **discurso ~** reported speech.
referir [3i] ① VT (**a**) (*contar*) to recount, report; to tell; **~ que ...** to say that ..., tell how ..., relate how ...
(**b**) **~ al lector a un apéndice** to refer the reader to an appendix.
(**c**) (*relacionar*) to refer, apply, relate; **todo lo refiere a su teoría favorita** he refers (*o* relates) everything to his favourite theory; **han referido el cuadro al siglo XVII** they have referred the picture to the 17th century.
(**d**) **~ a** (*Fin*) to convert into, express in terms of.
(**e**) (*CAm: insultar*) to abuse, insult.
(**f**) **~ algo a uno en cara** (*Méx*) to throw sth in sb's face.
② **referirse** VR: **~ a** to refer to; **me refiero a lo de anoche** I refer to what happened last night; **por lo que se refiere a eso** as for that, as regards that.
refilón: de ~ ADV obliquely, slantingly, aslant; **el sol da de ~** the sun strikes obliquely, the sun comes slanting in; **mirar a uno de ~** to take a sideways glance at; to take a quick look at.
refinación NF refining.
refinado ADJ refined, distinguished.
refinador NM refiner.
refinadura NF refining.
refinamiento NM refinement; **con todos los ~s modernos** with all the modern refinements; **~ por pasos** (*Inform*) stepwise refinement.
refinanciación NF refinancing, refunding.
refinanciar [1b] VT to refinance.
refinar [1a] VT (**a**) (*Téc*) to refine. (**b**) (*fig*) *sistema etc* to refine, perfect; *estilo etc* to polish.
refinería NF refinery.
refino ① ADJ extra fine, pure, refined.
② NM refining.
refirmar [1a] VT (*LAm*) to reaffirm.
refistolería NF (*V ADJ*) (**a**) (*CAm*) scheming nature; scheming, troublemaking.
(**b**) (*Méx: presunción*) vanity.
(**c**) (*Carib**) boot-licking*; oiliness.
refistolero ADJ (**a**) (*CAm*) (*mañoso*) intriguing, scheming; (*dañoso*) mischievous. (**b**) (*Carib: pedante*) pedantic. (**c**) (*Carib*: zalamero*) greasy, oily.
reflación NF reflation.
reflacionar [1a] VT to reflate.
reflectante ADJ reflective.

reflector NM (**a**) (*gen*) reflector. (**b**) (*Elec*) spotlight; (*Aer, Mil*) searchlight.
reflejar [1a] ① VT (**a**) (*lit*) to reflect. (**b**) (*fig*) to reflect, mirror, show, reveal.
② **reflejarse** VR to be reflected (*t fig*).
reflejo ① ADJ (**a**) *luz* reflected.
(**b**) *movimiento* reflex.
(**c**) (*Ling*) *verbo* reflexive.
② NM (**a**) (*imagen*) reflection; **mirar su ~ en el agua** to look at one's reflection in the water.
(**b**) (*fig*) reflection.
(**c**) (*Anat etc*) reflex; (*condicionado*) reflex action; **perder ~s** (*fig*) to lose one's touch.
(**d**) **~s** gleam, glint; (*en el pelo*) highlight; streaks; **tiene ~s metálicos** it has a metallic glint.
(**e**) (*tratamiento del pelo*) rinse; streak; **darse un ~ azul** to give one's hair a blue rinse.
reflejoterapia NF reflex therapy.
reflex, réflex (*Fot*) ① ADJ INVAR SLR, reflex.
② NF SLR camera.
reflexión NF (**a**) (*Fís*) reflection. (**b**) (*fig*) reflection; thought; meditation; **con ~** on reflection; **sin ~** without thinking; **mis reflexiones sobre el problema** my reflections on the problem; **hacer reflexiones** to meditate, philosophize.
reflexionar [1a] ① VT to reflect on, think about, think over.
② VI to reflect (*en, sobre* on); (*antes de obrar*) to think, pause, reflect; **¡reflexione!** you think it over!, think for a moment!
reflexivamente ADV (**a**) (*Ling*) reflexively. (**b**) *obrar* thoughtfully, reflectively.
reflexividad NF (*Ling*) reflexiveness.
reflexivo ADJ (**a**) (*Ling*) reflexive. (**b**) *persona etc* thoughtful, reflective. (**c**) *acto* considered.
reflexología NF reflexology.
reflexoterapia NF reflex therapy.
reflotar [1a] VT to refloat; (*fig*) to relaunch, re-establish.
refluir [3g] VI to flow back.
reflujo NM ebb, ebb tide.
refocilación NF, **refocilamiento** NM huge enjoyment, great pleasure; (*pey*) unhealthy pleasure, cruel pleasure; coarse merriment.
refocilar [1a] ① VT (*encantar*) to give great pleasure to; (*divertir*) to amuse hugely, amuse in a coarse way; (*alegrar*) to cheer up.
② VI (*Cono Sur*: relámpago*) to flash.
③ **refocilarse** VR (**a**) (*divertirse*) to enjoy o.s. hugely; (*pey*) to enjoy o.s. in a coarse way; **~ con algo** to enjoy sth hugely, have a fine time with sth; **~ viendo lo que sufre otro** to gloat over sb else's sufferings.
(**b**) (*alegrarse*) to cheer up no end.
refocilo NM (**a**) = **refocilación**. (**b**) (*Cono Sur*: rayo*) lightning, flash of lightning.
reforestación NF reforestation, reafforestation.
reforestar [1a] VT to reforest, reafforest.
reforma NF (**a**) reform; reformation; improvement; **R~** (*Ecl*) Reformation; **la R~** (*Méx Pol*) *19th century reform movement*; **~ agraria** land reform.
(**b**) (*Arquit etc*) **~s** alterations, repairs, improvements; **'cerrado por ~s'** 'closed for repairs'.
reformación NF reform, reformation.
reformado ADJ reformed.
reformador(a) NM/F reformer.
reformar [1a] ① VT (**a**) (*gen*) to reform; (*modificar*) to change, alter; (*mejorar*) to improve; (*reorganizar*) to reorganize; *abuso etc* to correct, put right; *texto* to revise.
(**b**) (*formar de otro modo*) to re-form.
(**c**) (*Arquit etc*) to alter, repair; to improve; to redecorate; (*Mec*) to mend, repair; (*Cos*) to alter.
② **reformarse** VR to reform, mend one's ways.
reformatear [1a] VT (*Inform*) to reformat.
reformatorio NM reformatory; **~ de menores** remand home.
reformismo NM reforming policy, reforming attitude.
reformista ① ADJ reforming.
② NMF reformist, reformer.
reforzado ADJ reinforced.
reforzador NM (*Elec*) booster; (*Fot*) intensifier.
reforzamiento NM reinforcement, strengthening.
reforzar [1f y 1l] VT (**a**) (*Arquit etc*) to reinforce, strengthen; (*Mil*) to reinforce; (*Elec etc*) to boost, raise, step up; *dosis* to increase; (*Fot*) to bring up, intensify.
(**b**) (*fig*) *resistencia etc* to strengthen, buttress, bolster up; *persona* to encourage.
refracción NF refraction.
refractante ADJ refractive.
refractar [1a] VT to refract.

refractario ADJ (a) (*Téc*) fireproof, heat-resistant; (*Culin*) ovenproof. (b) (*fig*) refractory, recalcitrant; stubborn; **ser ~ a una reforma** to resist a reform, be opposed to a reform; **ser ~ a las lenguas** to be hopeless where languages are concerned.

refractivo ADJ refractive.

refractor NM refractor.

refrán NM proverb, saying; **como dice el ~** as the saying goes.

refranero NM collection of proverbs.

refraniento ADJ (*Cono Sur*) much given to quoting proverbs.

refregar [1h y 1j] VT (a) (*frotar*) to rub (hard), brush (repeatedly); to scrub. (b) (*fig*) **~ algo a uno** to rub sth in; to harp on about sth to sb.

refregón NM (a) (*acto*) rub(bing), brush(ing); scrub(bing). (b) (*señal*) mark left by rubbing (*etc*).

refrenar [1a] VT (a) *caballo* to rein back, rein in; to hold back. (b) (*fig*) to curb, restrain, hold in check.

refrendar [1a] VT (a) (*firmar*) to endorse, countersign; (*autenticar*) to authenticate; (*aprobar*) to give one's approval to; *pasaporte* to stamp. (b) (*: repetir*) to do again, repeat; *comida* to order more of, have a second helping of. (c) (*Méx*) to redeem (from pawn).

refrendo NM endorsement; counter-signature; authentication; approval.

refrescante ADJ refreshing, cooling.

refrescar [1g] ① VT (a) (*gen*) to refresh; (*enfriar*) to cool (down). (b) *memoria* to refresh; *conocimientos* to brush up, polish up. (c) *acto* to repeat; *enemistad etc* to renew. ② VI (a) (*Met*) to get cooler, cool down. (b) (*persona*) to refresh o.s.; (*salir*) to take the air, go out for a walk. (c) (*beber*) to take some refreshment, have a drink. (d) (*Méx Med*) to get better. ③ **refrescarse** VR (a) = VI (*esp* b). (b) (*And, esp Colombia*) to have tea.

refresco NM cool drink, soft drink, non-alcoholic drink; **~s** refreshments; **'R~s'** 'Refreshments'.

refresquería NF (*LAm*) refreshment stall.

refri* NM (*Méx*) fridge*, refrigerator.

refriega NF scuffle, set-to*; affray, brawl.

refrigeración NF refrigeration; (*Mec*) cooling; air conditioning; **~ por agua** water-cooling; **~ por aire** air-cooling.

refrigerado ADJ cooled; *cinema, room etc* air-conditioned; **~ por agua** water-cooled; **~ por aire** air-cooled.

refrigerador NM refrigerator; cooling unit, cooling system.

refrigeradora NF (*LAm*) refrigerator.

refrigerante ① ADJ cooling, refrigerating. ② NM (*Quím*) refrigerant, coolant.

refrigerar [1a] VT to cool, refresh; (*Téc*) to refrigerate; (*Mec*) to cool; *sala* to air-condition.

refrigerio NM (a) (*piscolabis*) snack; (*bebida*) cooling drink. (b) (*fig*) relief.

refrior NM chill (in the air).

refrito ① ADJ (a) (*Culin*) refried; over-fried. (b) (*fig*) revised, rehashed. ② NM rehash, revised version.

refucilar [1a] VI (*And, Cono Sur*) = **refocilar 2**.

refucilo NM (*Cono Sur*) = **refocilo** (b).

refuerzo NM (a) (*acto*) strengthening; reinforcement. (b) (*Téc*) brace, support. (c) **~s** (*Mil*) reinforcements. (d) (*fig: ayuda*) aid.

refugiado, -a ADJ, NM/F refugee.

refugiarse [1b] VR to take refuge; to shelter (*en* in); to go into hiding; **~ en un país vecino** to flee to a neighbouring country, seek asylum in a neighbouring country.

refugio NM (a) (*gen*) refuge, shelter; asylum; (*Ecl*) sanctuary; (*fig*) refuge, haven; **acogerse a un ~** to take refuge, shelter (*en* in); to seek sanctuary. (b) (*edificio*) refuge, shelter; (*Esp Aut*) street island; **~ alpino**, **~ de montaña** mountain hut; **~ antiaéreo** air-raid shelter; **~ antiatómico**, **~ antinuclear** fallout shelter; **~ de caza** hunting lodge; **~ subterráneo** underground shelter; dugout.

refulgencia NF brilliance, refulgence.

refulgente ADJ brilliant, refulgent.

refulgir [3c] VI to shine (brightly).

refundar [1a] VT to relaunch.

refundición NF (a) (*acto*) revision, recasting. (b) (*texto etc*) new version, adaptation; revision.

refundidor(a) NM/F reviser, adapter.

refundir [3a] ① VT (a) (*Téc*) to recast. (b) (*Liter etc*) to adapt; to revise, rewrite; to remodel. (c) (*And, CAm, Méx: perder*) to lose, mislay. (d) (*Cono Sur: arruinar*) to ruin, crush; (‡) *candidato* to plough‡. (e) (*CAm: guardar*) to keep carefully. ② **refundirse** VR (*And, CAm, Méx*) to get lost, be mislaid.

refunfuñar [1a] VI (*gruñir*) to growl, grunt; (*quejarse*) to grumble.

refunfuño NM growl, grunt; grumble.

refunfuñón* ① ADJ growling, grunting; grumbling, grouchy*. ② NM, **refunfuñona** NF grumbler, groucher*.

refusilo NM (*And, Chile*) flash of lightning.

refutable ADJ refutable; **fácilmente ~** easily refuted.

refutación NF refutation.

refutar [1a] VT to refute.

regada NF watering.

regadera NF (a) (*gen*) sprinkler; (*Hort*) watering-can. (b) (*Méx*) shower. (c) (*Esp*) **estar como una ~, ser una ~*** to be crazy, be as mad as a hatter.

regadío NM (*t* **tierra de ~**) irrigated land, irrigation land; **cultivo de ~** crop that grows on irrigated land, crop that needs irrigation.

regadizo ADJ irrigable.

regador NM (*Cono Sur*) watering can.

regadura NF sprinkling, watering; (*Agr*) irrigation.

regala NF gunwale.

regaladamente ADV **vivir** in luxury; **comer ~** to eat extremely well.

regalado ADJ (a) *vida etc* of luxury; (*cómodo*) comfortable, pleasant; (*pey*) soft. (b) (*delicado*) dainty, delicate. (c) (*Com, Fin*) free, given away; **me lo dio medio ~** he gave it to me for a song; **no lo quiero ni ~** I won't have it at any price, I don't want it even as a present. (d) **hace su regalada gana** (*LAm*) she does exactly what she likes.

regalar [1a] ① VT (a) (*dar*) to give, present; to give away; **~ algo a uno** to give sb sth, make sb a present of sth; **en su jubilación le regalaron este reloj** they gave him this clock on his retirement, they presented him with this clock on his retirement; **están regalando plumas** they're giving pens away, they're issuing pens free; **regaló el balón** (*Dep*) he gave the ball away. (b) *persona* to treat royally, make a great fuss of; (*pey*) to indulge, pamper; **~ a uno con un banquete** to entertain sb to a dinner, (*menos formal*) treat sb to a dinner; **le regalaron con toda clase de atenciones** they regaled him with all manner of hospitality, they lavished attentions on him. ② **regalarse** VR (a) (*darse gusto*) to indulge o.s., pamper o.s.; to do o.s. well. (b) **~ con** to regale o.s. with.

regalía NF (a) **~s** (*del rey*) royal prerogatives. (b) (*fig: privilegio*) privilege, prerogative; (*Fin*) perquisite, bonus. (c) (*And, CAm, Carib: regalo*) gift, present. (d) (*Liter, Mús*) **~s** (*derechos*) royalty; (*avance*) advance payment. (e) (*Carib: excelencia*) excellence, goodness.

regaliz NM, **regaliza** NF liquorice, licorice; **~ de palo** stick of liquorice.

regalo NM (a) (*gen*) gift, present; **~ de boda** wedding present; **~ de Navidad, ~ de Reyes** Christmas present; **entrada de ~** complimentary ticket; **un libro de ~** a free book. (b) (*fig: placer*) pleasure; (*comestible*) treat, delicacy, dainty; **es un ~ para el oído** it's a treat to listen to. (c) (*fig: comodidad*) luxury, comfort.

regalón ADJ (a) *niño* spoiled, pampered; *persona* comfort-loving, (*pey*) soft, lapped in luxury. (b) *vida* of luxury, comfortable; (*pey*) soft. (c) (*LAm*) **es el ~ de su padre** he's the apple of his father's eye, he's his daddy's pet. (d) (*And: obsequioso*) fond of giving presents.

regalonear [1a] ① VT (*Cono Sur: mimar*) to spoil, pamper. ② VI (*Cono Sur: dejarse mimar*) to allow o.s. to be pampered.

regañada* NF (*CAm, Méx*) = **regaño**.

regañadientes: a ~ ADV unwillingly, reluctantly.

regañado ADJ: **estar ~ con uno** to be at odds with sb.

regañar [1a] ① VT to scold; to tell off*, reprimand; to nag (at). ② VI (a) (*perro*) to snarl, growl. (b) (*persona*) to grumble, grouse*; to nag. (c) (*2 personas*) to fall out, quarrel.

regañina NF = **regaño** (b).

regaño NM (a) (*gruñido*) snarl, growl; (*mueca*) scowl; (*queja*) grumble, grouse*. (b) (*reprimenda*) scolding; telling-off*; **merecerse un ~** to get a telling off*.

regañón ADJ grumbling, grouchy*; irritable; *mujer* nagging, shrewish.

regar [1h y 1j] ① VT (a) *planta* to water; *tierra* to water, irrigate; *calle* to water, hose (down); *herida etc* to wash, bathe (*con, de* with); (*con insecticida etc*) to spray (*con, de* with); **~ la garganta** to spray one's throat; **~ un plato con vino** to have wine with a dish, accompany a dish with wine; **regó la carta con lágrimas** she bathed the letter in tears. (b) (*Geog: río*) to water; (*mar*) to wash, lap against; **una costa regada por un mar tranquilo** a coast washed by a calm sea. (c) (*fig: esparcir*) to sprinkle, strew (in all directions), scatter; **iba regando monedas** he was dropping money all over the place. (d) (*And, CAm*) (*derramar*) to spill; (*derribar*) to knock over, knock down.

(**e**) (*Carib*: *pegar*) to hit.

2 VI (**a**) (*Carib**: *bromear*) to joke; **está regando** she's having us on.

(**b**) (*Carib*: *actuar sin pensar*) to act rashly.

(**c**) **~la** (*Méx*: *fracasar*) to screw it up*, make a mess of it.

3 **regarse** VR (**a**) (*CAm, Méx*: *dispersarse*) to scatter (in all directions).

(**b**) (*Carib**: *enfadarse*) to get cross.

(**c**) (*LAm*: *ducharse*) to shower, take a shower.

regata¹ NF (*Agr*) irrigation channel.

regata² NF (*Náut*) race, boat-race; regatta.

regate NM (**a**) (*desvío*) swerve, dodge; (*Dep*) dribble. (**b**) (*fig*) dodge, ruse.

regatear¹ [1a] VI (*Náut*) to race.

regatear² [1a] **1** VT (**a**) (*Com*) *objeto, trato* to haggle over, bargain over; *precio* to try to beat down.

(**b**) *provisión etc* to be mean with, economize on; to give (*o issue etc*) sparingly; **su padre no le regatea dinero** her father does not keep her short of money; **aquí regatean el vino** they are mean with their wine here; **no hemos regateado esfuerzo para** + *infin* we have spared no effort to + *infin*.

(**c**) (*fig*: *negar*) to deny, refuse to allow; **no le regateo buenas cualidades** I don't deny his good qualities.

2 VI (**a**) (*Com*) to haggle, bargain; (*fig*) to bicker.

(**b**) (*desviarse*) to swerve, dodge; to duck; (*Dep*) to dribble.

3 **regatearse** VR: **~ algo** (*LAm*) to haggle over sth.

regateo NM (**a**) (*Com*) haggling, bargaining. (**b**) (*Dep*) dribbling.

regatista NMF (*sailing*) competitor; yachtsman, yachtswoman.

regato NM pool.

regatón¹ NM (*de bastón*) tip, ferrule.

regatón² **1** ADJ (*Com*) haggling; (*fig*) bickering, niggling, argumentative.

2 NM (*Carib**: *restos*) dregs.

3 NMF (*Méx**: *comerciante*) small-time dealer.

regazo NM (*t fig*) lap.

regencia NF regency.

regeneración NF (**a**) (*gen*) regeneration. (**b**) (*Téc*) reclaiming, reclamation.

regenerado ADJ regenerate.

regenerador ADJ regenerative.

regeneramiento NM regeneration.

regenerar [1a] VT (**a**) (*gen*) to regenerate. (**b**) (*Téc*) to reclaim, process for re-use.

regentar [1a] VT (**a**) *cátedra etc* to occupy, hold; *puesto* to hold temporarily; *hotel etc* to run, manage, administer; (*fig*) *destinos etc* to guide, preside over. (**b**) (*: *dominar*) to domineer, boss.

regente **1** ADJ (**a**) *príncipe etc* regent.

(**b**) *director etc* managing.

2 NMF (*t* **regenta** F) (**a**) (*Pol*) regent.

(**b**) (*de fábrica, finca*) manager; (*Esp Farm*) chief pharmacist; (*Tip*) foreman.

(**c**) (*Méx*: *alcalde*) mayor of Mexico City.

reggae ['reɣe] NM reggae.

regiamente ADV regally.

regicida NMF regicide (*person*).

regicidio NM regicide (*act*).

regidor **1** ADJ *principio* governing, ruling.

2 NM (**a**) (*Teat*) stage manager. (**b**) (*Hist*) alderman.

regiego = **rejego**.

régimen NM, PL **regímenes** (**a**) (*Pol*) régime; rule; **el ~ anterior** (*esp*) Franco's rule, the Franco period; **antiguo ~** ancien régime; **~ marioneta** puppet régime; **~ del terror** reign of terror; **bajo el ~ del dictador** under the dictator's régime (*o rule*).

(**b**) (*Med esp Esp*) diet (*t* **~ alimenticio**); **~ lácteo** milk diet; **estar a ~** to be on a diet; **poner a uno a ~** to put sb on a diet; **ponerse a ~** to go on a diet.

(**c**) (*reglas*) rules, set of rules, régime, system; (*manera de vivir*) way of life; **prisión de ~ abierto** open prison; **he cambiado de ~** I have changed my whole way of life, I have made myself a new set of rules; **alojamiento en ~ de pensión completa** full board; **viviendas en ~ de alquiler** homes for rent.

(**d**) (*Ling*) government.

regimentación NF regimentation.

regimiento NM (**a**) (*Pol etc*) administration, government, organization. (**b**) (*Mil*) regiment. (**c**) (*LAm**: *gentío*) mass, crowd.

Reginaldo NM Reginald.

regio **1** ADJ (**a**) royal, regal; kingly. (**b**) (*fig*) royal; splendid, majestic. (**c**) (*Cono Sur*) super*, brilliant*.

2 INTERJ (*LAm**) great!*, terrific!*

regiomontano (*Méx*) **1** ADJ of (*o from*) Monterrey.

2 NM, **regiomontana** NF native (*o inhabitant*) of Monterrey.

región NF (**a**) (*Geog etc*) region; district, area, part; (*Pol*) region. (**b**) (*Anat*) region, tract.

regional ADJ regional.

regionalismo NM regionalism.

regionalista ADJ, NMF regionalist.

regionalización NF regionalization.

regir [3c *y* 3k] **1** VT (**a**) *país etc* to rule, govern; *colegio etc* to run, be in charge of, be at the head of; *empresa* to manage, run, control.

(**b**) (*Jur, Ling etc*) to govern; **según el reglamento que rige estos casos** according to the statute which governs these cases; **ese verbo rige el dativo** that verb takes the dative; **los factores que rigen los cambios del mercado** the factors which govern (*o determine, control*) changes in the market.

2 VI (**a**) (*Jur*) to be in operation, be in force, apply; (*precio*) to be in force; (*condición etc*) to prevail, obtain; **esa ley ya no rige** that law no longer applies; **el mes que rige** the present month, the current month; **cuando estas condiciones ya no rijan** when these conditions no longer obtain.

(**b**) (*Mec*) to work, go; **el timbre no rige** the bell doesn't work.

(**c**) **no ~*** to have a screw loose*, be not all there*.

3 **regirse** VR: **~ por** to be ruled by, be guided by, go by; to follow.

regista NMF (*Cine*) producer.

registrado ADJ registered.

registrador(a)¹ **1** NM/F (**a**) (*persona*) recorder, registrar. (**b**) **~ de sonido** (*TV*) sound recordist.

2 NM: **~ de vuelo** flight recorder.

registradora² NF (*Com*) cash register.

registrar [1a] **1** VT (**a**) (*anotar etc*) to register, record; to enter; to file; **~ un libro** to mark one's place in a book.

(**b**) (*Esp Mús etc*) to record; **~ la voz en una cinta** to record one's voice on tape.

(**c**) *equipaje, lugar, persona* to search; *archivo, documento* to survey, inspect; *cajón* to look through; **lo hemos registrado todo de arriba abajo** we have searched the whole place from top to bottom; **¡a mí que me registren!*** search me!*

(**d**) (*Méx*) *correo* to register.

2 **registrarse** VR (**a**) (*persona*) to register; (*en hotel*) to check in, sign in.

(**b**) (*hecho etc*) to be recorded; (*ocurrir*) to happen; **se han registrado algunos casos de tifus** a few cases of typhus have been reported; **no se ha registrado nunca nada parecido** nothing of the kind has ever been recorded before; **el cambio que se ha registrado en su actitud** the change which has occurred in his attitude.

registro NM (**a**) (*acto*) registration, recording.

(**b**) (*libro*) register; visitor's book; (*Inform*) record; **~ catastral**, **~ de la propiedad inmobiliaria** land registry; **~ de defunciones** register of deaths; **~ electoral** voting register, electoral roll; **~ de hotel** hotel register; **~ lógico** logical record; **~ de matrimonios** register of marriages; **~ mercantil** business register; **~ de nacimientos** register of births; **~ parroquial** parish register; **capacidad de ~** storage facility, recording capacity; **firmar el ~** to sign the register.

(**c**) (*lista*) list, roll, record; (*apunte*) note; **~ de erratas** list of errata.

(**d**) (*entrada*) entry (in a register).

(**e**) (*oficina*) registry, record office; **~ civil** registry office; **~ de patentes y marcas** patents office; **~ de la propiedad** land registry (office).

(**f**) (*búsqueda*) search; (*inspección*) survey, inspection; **~ domiciliario** search of a house; **~ policíaco** police search; **orden de ~** search warrant; **practicar un ~** to make a search (*en* of).

(**g**) (*Mús etc*: *grabación*) recording; **es un buen ~ de la sinfonía** it is a good recording of the symphony.

(**h**) (*Mús*) (*timbre*) register; (*del órgano*) stop; (*del piano*) pedal; **salir por** (*o* **adoptar**) **un ~ muy raro** (*fig*) to adopt a very odd tone, adopt a most inappropriate attitude; **mira por qué ~ nos sale ahora** look what he's coming out with now; **tocar todos los ~s** (*fig*) to pull out all the stops.

(**i**) (*Téc*) manhole, manhole cover; (*de fuego*) damper; inspection plate, inspection hatch.

(**j**) (*de libro*) bookmark.

(**k**) (*de reloj*) regulator.

(**l**) (*Tip*) register; **estar en ~** to be in register.

(**m**) (*And, Cono Sur*: *tienda*) wholesale textiles store.

regla NF (**a**) (*instrumento*) ruler, rule; **~ de cálculo** slide rule; **~ de un pie** foot-rule; **~ T**, **~ en T** T-square.

(**b**) (*ley etc*) rule; regulation; (*Dep etc*) rule; (*científico*) law, principle; norm; **~s del juego** rules of the game (*t fig*), laws of the game; **~s de la circulación** traffic regulations; **~s para el uso de una máquina** instructions for the use of a machine; **no hay ~ sin excepción** every rule has its exception; **ser de ~** to be the rule, be usual, be the norm; **salir de ~** to overstep the mark; to be abnormal, have abnormal features; **en ~** in order; **es un español en toda ~** he's a real Spaniard, he's a Spaniard through and through; **todo está en ~** everything is in order; all is as it should be; **hacer algo en toda ~** to do sth properly, do sth by the book; **poner algo en ~** to put sth

straight; **no tenía los papeles en ~** his papers were not in order; **por ~ general** generally, usually, as a rule; on the average; **hacerse una ~ de** + *infin* to make it a rule to + *infin*.
(c) (*Mat*) rule; law; **~ de 3** rule of 3; **¿por qué ~ de tres ...?** (*Esp**) why on earth ...?
(d) (*Ecl*) rule, order; **viven según la ~ benedictina** they live according to the Benedictine rule.
(e) (*Med*) period.
(f) (*fig: moderación*) moderation, restraint; **comer con ~** to eat in moderation.
reglable ADJ adjustable.
reglaje NM (a) (*Mec*) checking, overhaul; adjustment; **~ en altura** (*en anuncios de coches*) height adjustment; **~ de neumáticos** wheel alignment. (b) (*Mil*) correction (of aim).
reglamentación NF (a) (*acto*) regulation. (b) (*reglas*) rules, regulations (*collectively*).
reglamentar [1a] VT to regulate; to make rules for, establish regulations for.
reglamentariamente ADV in due form, according to the rules; properly.
reglamentario ADJ regulation (*atr*), obligatory, set; (*estatuario*) statutory; (*apropiado*) proper, due; **pistola reglamentaria** standard issue pistol; **en el traje ~** in the regulation dress; **en la forma reglamentaria** in due form, in the properly established way; **es ~** + *infin* the law requires that ..., the regulation makes it obligatory to + *infin*.
reglamento NM (*reglas*) rules, regulations (*collectively*); (*de reunión, sociedad*) standing order(s); (*municipal etc*) by-law; (*de profesión*) code of conduct; **~ de aduana** customs regulations; **~ del tráfico** rule of the road; **pistola de ~** standard issue pistol.
reglar [1a] ① VT (a) *línea, papel etc* to rule.
(b) (*Mec*) to check, overhaul; to adjust; (*Mil*) *puntería* to correct.
(c) (*fig*) to regulate, make regulations for.
② **reglarse** VR: **~ a** to abide by, conform to; **~ por** to be guided by; to follow.
regleta NF (*Tip*) space.
regletear [1a] VT (*Tip*) to space out.
regocijadamente ADV merrily; joyously, joyfully; exultantly.
regocijado ADJ (a) *carácter* jolly, cheerful, merry. (b) *estado, humor* merry; joyous, joyful; exultant.
regocijar [1a] ① VT to gladden, delight, cheer (up); **un cuento que regocijó a todos** a story which made everyone laugh; **crear un personaje para ~ a los niños** to create a character to amuse children; **la noticia regocijó a la familia** the news delighted the family, the news filled the family with joy.
② **regocijarse** VR (a) (*alegrarse*) to rejoice, be glad, express one's happiness (*de, por* about, at).
(b) (*reírse*) to laugh; **~ con un cuento** to laugh at a story.
(c) (*pasarlo bien*) to make merry, have a merry time, celebrate.
(d) (*pey*) to exult; **~ por un desastre ajeno** to exult in sb else's misfortune.
regocijo NM (a) (*alegría*) joy, happiness; rejoicing; delight, elation; gaiety, merriment.
(b) (*pey*) exultation; unhealthy pleasure, cruel delight (*por* in).
(c) **~s** festivities, rejoicings, celebrations; **~s navideños** Christmas festivities; **~s públicos** public rejoicings.
regodearse [1a] VR (a) (*: bromear*) to crack jokes*; to indulge in coarse humour.
(b) (*deleitarse*) to be glad, be delighted; **~ haciendo algo** to enjoy o.s. hugely doing sth; (*pey*) **~ con, ~ en** to gloat over, take a cruel delight in; **~ porque otro está sufriendo** to be perversely glad that sb else is suffering.
(c) (*LAm**: *ser exigente*) to be fussy, be hard to please.
regodeo NM (a) joking; coarse humour. (b) delight; huge enjoyment; (*pey*) cruel delight, perverse pleasure.
regodeón (*LAm*) ① ADJ (a) (*exigente*) fussy, hard to please. (b) (*egoísta*) self-indulgent.
② NM pet.
regodiente ADJ (*And*) fussy, hard to please.
regojo NM (a) (*pan*) piece of left-over bread. (b) (*: persona*) ti(t)ch*.
regoldar [1l] VI to belch.
regordete ADJ *persona* chubby, plump; *manos etc* fat.
regosto NM longing, craving (*de* for).
regresar [1a] ① VT (*LAm*) to give back, send back, return.
② VI to come back, go back, return.
③ **regresarse** VR (*LAm*) = **2**.
regresión NF regression; (*fig*) retreat; backward step.
regresivo ADJ *movimiento* backward; (*fig*) regressive, retrogressive, backward; downward.
regreso NM return; **viaje de ~** return trip, homeward journey; **emprender el ~ a** to return to, come back to; **estar de ~** to be back, be home.

regro ADJ (*Carib*) great*, fabulous*.
regto. ABR *de* **regimiento** Regiment, Regt., Rgt.
regüeldo NM belch, belching.
reguera NF (a) (*Agr*) irrigation channel. (b) (*Náut*) cable, mooring rope, anchor chain.
reguero NM (a) (*Agr*) irrigation ditch; (*LAm: surco*) furrow.
(b) (*pista*) track; (*señal*) streak, line, mark; (*de sangre etc*) trickle; (*de pólvora etc*) train; (*de humo, vapor*) trail; **propagarse como un ~ de pólvora** to spread like wildfire.
reguío NM (*And*) = **riego**.
regulable ADJ adjustable.
regulación NF (a) (*gen*) regulation; adjustment; control; **~ de la natalidad** birth-control; **~ del tráfico** traffic control; **~ del volumen sonoro** (*Rad*) volume control. (b) (*euf: reducción*) reduction; **~ de empleo** dismissal, redundancy; reduction of the workforce; **~ de jornada** cut in working hours; **~ de plantilla** staff cut; reduction of the workforce.
regulador ① ADJ regulating, regulatory.
② NM (*Mec*) regulator, throttle, governor; (*Rad etc*) control, knob, button; **~ de intensidad** dimmer, dimmer switch; **~ de volumen** volume control.
regular ① ADJ (a) (*gen, t Ecl, Mat, Mil*) regular; (*normal*) normal, usual, customary; (*corriente*) ordinary; *vida etc* regular, orderly, well-organized; **a intervalos ~es** at regular intervals; **tiene un latido ~** it has a regular beat.
(b) (*fig: mediano*) regular; middling, medium, average; fair; (*pey*) fair, so-so, not too bad; **es una novela ~** it's an average sort of novel, it's a fair novel; **de tamaño ~** medium-sized, fair-sized; **'¿cómo es el profesor?'** ... **'~'** 'what's the teacher like?' ... 'not too bad', 'nothing special'.
(c) **por lo ~** as a rule, generally.
② ADV (*) **estar ~** to be all right, be so-so; **'¿qué tal estás?'** ... **'~'** 'how are you?' ... 'so-so' (o 'all right', 'can't complain').
③ [1a] VT (a) (*gen*) to regulate, control; (*ley etc*) to govern; *tráfico* to control, direct; *precio etc* to control.
(b) (*Mec etc*) to adjust, regulate; *reloj* to put right; *despertador* to set.
(c) (*Méx*) to calculate.
regularcillo ADJ = **regular 1 (b)**.
regularidad NF regularity; **con ~** regularly.
regularización NF regularization; standardization.
regularizar [1f] VT to regularize; to standardize, bring into line.
regularmente ADV regularly.
régulo NM kinglet, petty king.
regurgitación NF regurgitation.
regurgitar [1a] VT to regurgitate.
regustado ADJ (*Carib*) well-satisfied.
regustar [1a] VT (*Carib, Méx*) to taste, relish, savour.
regusto NM (*t fig*) aftertaste; **queda siempre el ~** it leaves a bad taste in the mouth.
rehabilitación NF (a) (*de persona*) rehabilitation; (*en puesto*) reinstatement; (*de quebrado*) discharge. (b) (*Arquit etc*) restoration; (*Mec*) overhaul.
rehabilitar [1a] VT (a) to rehabilitate; to reinstate; *quebrado* to discharge. (b) to restore, renovate; to overhaul.
rehacer [2r] ① VT (a) (*volver a hacer*) to redo, do again; (*repetir*) to repeat.
(b) (*recrear*) to remake; (*reparar*) to mend, repair; (*renovar*) to refurbish, renew, do up.
② **rehacerse** VR (a) (*Med*) to recover; to regain one's strength; (*fig: reponerse*) to recover one's calm (o self esteem *etc*); **~ de** to get over, recover from.
(b) (*Mil*) to re-form; to rally.
rehecho ADJ thickset, chunky; (*fig: descansado*) rested.
rehén NM hostage.
rehenchir [3l] VT to fill, stuff, pack (*de* with).
rehilar [1a] VI (a) (*temblar*) to quiver, shake. (b) (*flecha etc*) to hum.
rehilete NM (a) (*flecha*) dart; (*Taur*) banderilla. (b) (*volante*) shuttlecock. (c) (*fig: comentario*) dig, cutting remark, taunt, barb.
rehogar [1h] VT (*Culin*) to sauté, toss in oil.
rehostia: ① INTERJ damn it!
② NF: **es la ~** it's altogether too much; it's the bloody end:; **él se cree que es la ~** he thinks he's the best thing since sliced bread*.
rehuir [3g] VT to shun, avoid; to shrink from; **~** + *infin* to avoid + *ger*, shrink from + *ger*.
rehusar [1a] ① VT to refuse, decline; **~ hacer algo** to refuse to do sth.
② VI to refuse (*t caballo*).
reidero ADJ amusing, funny.
reidor ADJ merry, laughing.
reilón ADJ (*Carib*) (*que se ríe*) given to laughing a lot, giggly; (*alegre*) merry.
reimplantar [1a] VT to re-establish, reintroduce.

reimponer [2q] VT to reimpose.

reimpresión NF reprint(ing).

reimprimir [3a] VT to reprint.

reina ☐1 NF (a) queen (*t Ajedrez, Ent etc*); ~ **de belleza** beauty-queen; ~ **claudia** (*Bot*) greengage; ~ **de la fiesta** carnival queen; ~ **madre** queen mother; ~ **mora** (*juego*) hopscotch; ~ **viuda** dowager queen.
(b) (*****: *droga*) pure heroin.
☐2 ATR top, ultimate; **prueba** ~ ultimate test.

reinado NM reign; **bajo el** ~ **de** in the reign of.

Reinaldos NM Reginald.

reinante ADJ (a) (*lit*) reigning. (b) (*fig*) prevailing.

reinar [1a] VI (a) (*Pol*) to reign, rule.
(b) (*fig: prevalecer*) to reign; to prevail, be general; **reinan las bajas temperaturas** there are low temperatures everywhere; **reina una confusión total** total confusion reigns; **entre la población reinaba el descontento** unrest was rife in the population, there was widespread discontent in the population.

reinauguración NF reinauguration.

reinaugurar [1a] VT to reinaugurate.

reincidencia NF (*acto*) relapse (*en* into); (*tendencia*) recidivism.

reincidente NMF recidivist; hardened offender; backslider.

reincidir [3a] VI to relapse (*en* into); (*criminal*) to repeat an offence; (*pecador etc*) to backslide.

reincorporación NF (*al trabajo*) return; (: *tras despido*) reinstatement.

reincorporar [1a] ☐1 VT to reincorporate (*a* in), reunite (*a* to).
☐2 **reincorporarse** VR: ~ **a** to rejoin; ~ **al trabajo** to return to work.

reindustrialización NF restructuring of industry.

reineta ☐1 ADJ: **manzana** ~ pippin.
☐2 NF pippin.

reingresar [1a] VI: ~ **en** to re-enter.

reingreso NM re-entry (*en* into).

reinicializar [1f] VT (*Inform*) to reset.

reiniciar [1b] VT to rehabilitate; to resume.

reinicio NM new beginning; resumption.

reino NM kingdom; **el R~ Unido** the United Kingdom.

reinona* NF fairy*.

reinoso, -a NM/F (a) (*And*: *del interior*) inlander, inhabitant of the interior (*esp of the cold eastern upland*). (b) (*Carib*) Colombian.

reinserción NF: ~ **social**, ~ **en la sociedad** social rehabilitation, assimilation into society.

reinsertado, -a NM/F former terrorist now socially rehabilitated.

reinsertar [1a] ☐1 VT to rehabilitate, assimilate into society.
☐2 **reinsertarse** VR: ~ **en la sociedad** to resume an ordinary social life.

reinstalar [1a] VT to reinstall; *persona* to reinstate.

reinstauración NF restoration.

reinstaurar [1a] VT to restore.

reintegrable ADJ *depósito* returnable, refundable.

reintegración NF (a) *rehabilitación* reinstatement (*a* in). (b) (*Fin*) refund, repayment, reimbursement. (c) (*vuelta*) return (*a* to).

reintegrar [1a] ☐1 VT (a) (*completar*) to make whole again, reintegrate.
(b) *persona* to reinstate (*a* in).
(c) (*Fin*) ~ **a uno una cantidad** to refund (*o* repay, pay back) a sum to sb, reimburse sb for a sum; **ha sido reintegrado de todos sus gastos** he has been reimbursed in full for all his expenses.
(d) *suma* to pay back.
(e) *documento* to attach a fiscal stamp to.
☐2 **reintegrarse** VR (a) ~ **a** to return to.
(b) ~ **de una cantidad** to recover a sum, recoup a sum, secure repayment of a sum; ~ **de los gastos** to reimburse o.s. for one's expenses.

reintegro NM (a) (*Fin*) refund, repayment, reimbursement; (*de cuenta bancaria*) withdrawal. (b) (*lotería*) return of one's stake. (c) (*sello*) (cost of a) fiscal stamp.

reintroducción NF reintroduction.

reintroducir [3n] VT to reintroduce.

reinventar [1a] VT to reinvent.

reinversión NF reinvestment.

reinvertir [3i] VT to reinvest.

reír [3l] ☐1 VT to laugh at; **todos le ríen los chistes** everybody laughs at his jokes.
☐2 VI (a) (*lit*) to laugh; **sólo para hacer** ~ just to make people laugh, just for a laugh; **¡no me hagas** ~! don't make me laugh!; ~ **como un loco** to laugh like a hyena; **el que ríe al último ríe mejor** he who laughs last laughs longest.
(b) (*fig*: *ojos etc*) to laugh, sparkle, be merry; (*campo, mañana, naturaleza*) to smile, be bright.
☐3 **reírse** VR (a) (*lit*) to laugh (*con, de* about, at, over); ~ **con uno** to laugh at sb's jokes; ~ **de uno** to laugh at sb, make fun of sb; **¿se ríe Vd de mí?** are you laughing at me?; **¡déjeme que me ría!** that's a

good one!; ~ **el último** to have the last laugh; **fue para** ~ it was utterly absurd; *V* **echar** *etc*.
(b) (*) to split, come apart; **la chaqueta se me ríe por los codos** my jacket is out at the elbows; **estos zapatos se ríen** these shoes are coming apart.

reiteración NF reiteration, reaffirmation; repetition; (*Com*) **llamada de** ~ follow-up call; **visita de** ~ follow-up visit.

reiteradamente ADV repeatedly.

reiterado ADJ repeated.

reiterar [1a] VT to reiterate, reaffirm; to repeat.

reiterativo ADJ reiterative; (*pey*) repetitive, repetitious.

reivindicable ADJ recoverable (at law).

reivindicación NF (a) (*reclamación*) claim (*de* to); (*queja*) grievance; ~ **salarial** wage claim. (b) (*justificación*) vindication; *restauración* restoration of rights. (c) (*Jur*) recovery.

reivindicar [1g] ☐1 VT (a) (*reclamar*) to claim (the right to), claim as of right; to assert one's claim to; (*intentar cobrar*) to make a bid to recover; ~ **un atentado** to claim responsibility for an outrage.
(b) *reputación etc* to vindicate; (*restaurar*) to restore; (*cobrar*) to win back; to restore one's rights.
(c) (*Jur*) *derecho* to recover.
(d) (*LAm**: *exigir*) to demand.
☐2 **reivindicarse** VR (*LAm*) to vindicate o.s.; to restore one's reputation.

reivindicativo ADJ *movimiento, acto, plataforma* protest (*atr*); **adoptar una postura más reivindicativa** to be more aggressive in one's demands.

reja NF (a) grating, grid, gridiron; (*de ventana*) bars, grille; (*Ecl*) screen; **estar entre ~s** to be behind bars; **meter a uno entre ~s** to put sb behind bars.
(b) (*Agr*) ~ **del arado** ploughshare.
(c) (*LAm**: *cárcel*) prison, nick*****.
(d) (*Méx Cos*) darn, darning.
(e) (*Cono Sur Agr*) cattle truck.

rejado NM grille, grating.

rejeada NF (*And, CAm*) thrashing.

rejear [1a] VT (*CAm*) to jail, put in jail.

rejego ☐1 ADJ (a) (*Méx*) (*salvaje*) wild, untamed; (*fig: revoltoso*) troublesome, unruly; obstinate. (b) (*Méx*: *lento*) slow, sluggish.
☐2 NM (*CAm*) stud bull.

rejiego ADJ (*Carib, Méx*) = **rejego**.

rejilla NF (a) (*reja*) grating, grille; lattice; screen; (*Rad*) grille; (*Ferro*) luggage-rack; (*Méx Aut*) luggage-rack, roof-rack; (*de mueble*) wickerwork; **silla de** ~ wicker chair.
(b) (*brasero*) small stove, footwarmer.
(c) (*Cono Sur*: *fresquera*) meat safe.

rejo NM (a) (*punta*) spike, sharp point.
(b) (*Ent*) sting.
(c) (*Bot*) radicle.
(d) (*fig*) strength, vigour, toughness.
(e) (*LAm*: *látigo*) whip; (*Carib*: *tira*) strip of raw leather.
(f) (*Carib*: *porra*) stick, club; ~ **tieso** brave person.
(g) (*And*) (*ordeño*) milking; (*vacas*) herd of cows.

rejón NM pointed iron bar; spike; (*Taur*) lance.

rejoneador NM (*Taur*) *mounted bullfighter who uses the lance*.

rejonear [1a] (*Taur*) ☐1 VT to wound the bull with the lance.
☐2 VI to fight the bull on horseback with the lance.

rejoya NF (*Geog CAm*) deep valley.

rejudo ADJ (*And, Carib*: *pegajoso*) sticky, viscous; (*Carib*: *líquido*) runny.

rejugado ADJ (a) (*And, Carib*: *astuto*) cunning, sharp. (b) (*CAm*: *tímido*) shy.

rejunta NF (*Cono Sur, Méx*) round-up, rodeo.

rejuntar [1a] VT (a) (*Cono Sur*: *recoger*) to collect, gather in. (b) (*Méx*) *ganado* to round up. (c) (*Cono Sur*) *suma* to add up.

rejuvenecedor ADJ rejuvenating; (*fig*) refreshing, stimulating.

rejuvenecer [2d] ☐1 VT to rejuvenate.
☐2 **rejuvenecerse** VR to be rejuvenated, become young again.

rejuvenecimiento NM rejuvenation.

relación NF (a) (*gen*) relation, relationship (*con* to, with); **relaciones** relations, relationship; **la** ~ **entre X y Z** the relationship between X and Z; **sus relaciones con el jefe** his relations with the boss; **buenas relaciones** good relations; **relaciones amistosas** friendly relations; **relaciones carnales** (*o* **sexuales**) sexual relations; **relaciones comerciales** business connections, trade relations; **relaciones empresariales, relaciones laborales** industrial relations; **Ministerio de Relaciones Exteriores** Foreign Ministry; **relaciones humanas** human relations, (*como sección, profesión*) personnel management; **estar en buenas relaciones con** to be on good terms with; **mantener relaciones con** to keep in touch with; **romper las relaciones con** to break off relations with; **con** ~ **a**, **en** ~ **a** in relation to; **un aumento de 3 por cien con** ~ **al año anterior** an increase of 3% over the previous year; *V t* **relaciones públicas**.

(b) (*Mat*) ratio; proportion; **~ de compresión** compression ratio; **en una ~ de 7 a 2** in a ratio of 7 to 2; **guardar cierta ~ con** to bear a certain relation to; **no guardar ~ alguna con** to be out of all proportion to, bear no relation whatsoever to.

(c) relaciones (*amorosas*) courting, courtship; affair; **relaciones formales** engagement; **relaciones ilícitas** illicit sexual relations; **relaciones prematrimoniales** premarital sex, sex before marriage; **llevan varios meses de relaciones** they've been going out (*o* courting) for some months; their affair has been going on for some months; **A está en** (*o* **tiene**) **relaciones con B** A and B are going out together, A and B are courting; A and B are having an affair.

(d) relaciones (*personas*) acquaintances; (*esp*) influential friends, contacts, connections; **para eso conviene tener relaciones** for that it helps to have contacts; **tener** (**buenas**) **relaciones** to be well connected, have powerful friends.

(e) (*narración*) account, report; story; (*de dificultades etc*) tale, recital; **hizo una larga ~ de su viaje** he gave a lengthy account of his trip.

(f) (*lista*) list; (*informe*) record, (official) return.

(g) (*Teat*) long speech.

relacionado ADJ **(a)** related; **un tema ~ con Lorca** a subject that has to do with Lorca, a subject that concerns Lorca; **A está íntimamente ~ con B** A is closely connected with B; A is much bound up with B.

(b) una persona relacionada (*LAm*), **una persona bien relacionada** a well-connected person.

relacional ADJ: **estudio ~** study of (human) relationships.

relacionar [1a] ① VT **(a)** (*asociar*) to relate (*con* to), connect (*con* with).

(b) (*hacer constar*) to list.

② **relacionarse** VR **(a) es hombre que se relaciona** he's a man with (powerful) connections.

(b) (*dos cosas etc*) to be connected, be related.

(c) (*formar amistades*) to make contacts, get to know people; to get in the swim; **~ con uno** to get to know sb; to get into touch with sb.

(d) en lo que se relaciona con as for, with regard to.

relaciones públicas ① NMF INVAR (*persona*) public relations officer, publicity agent.

② NFPL (*acto etc*) public relations.

relai(s) [re'le] NM (*Elec*) relay.

relajación NF **(a)** (*sosiego*) relaxation. **(b)** (*acto*) relaxation; slackening, loosening; weakening. **(c)** (*fig: diversión*) relaxation, amusement. **(d)** (*fig: moral*) laxity, looseness. **(e)** (*Med*) hernia, rupture.

relajado ADJ **(a)** (*sosegado*) relaxed. **(b)** (*inmoral*) dissolute, loose. **(c)** (*Med*) ruptured.

relajadura NF (*Méx Med*) hernia, rupture.

relajante ① ADJ **(a)** *ejercicio etc* relaxing. **(b)** (*Med*) laxative. **(c)** (*Cono Sur*) *comida* sickly, sweet and sticky. **(d)** (*repugnante*) revolting, disgusting.

② NM laxative.

relajar [1a] ① VT **(a)** (*sosegar*) to relax.

(b) (*aflojar*) to relax; to slacken, loosen; (*debilitar*) to weaken.

(c) (*fig: moralmente*) to weaken, corrupt, make lax.

(d) (*LAm: comida*) to cloy, sicken, disgust.

(e) (*Carib*) (*hacer mofa*) to mock, deride; (*escarnecer*) to poke fun at.

② **relajarse** VR **(a)** (*sosegarse*) to relax; **conviene relajarte más** you should relax more, you should take more time for relaxation.

(b) (*aflojarse*) to relax; to slacken, loosen; (*debilitarse*) to weaken.

(c) (*fig: moralmente*) to become dissolute, go to the bad; (*moralidad etc*) to become lax.

(d) (*Med*) **~ un tobillo** to sprain one's ankle, lose the feeling in an ankle; **~ un órgano** to rupture an organ.

relajo NM (*esp LAm*) **(a)** (*libertinaje*) laxity, dissipation, depravity; (*indecencia*) lewdness.

(b) (*acto inmoral*) immoral act; (*acto indecente*) indecent act.

(c) (*bullicio*) boisterous gathering; (*fiesta*) lewd party; (*desorden*) commotion, disorder; (*lío*) fuss, row.

(d) (*chiste*) rude joke; (*trastada*) practical joke; (*mofas*) derision; **cuento de ~** blue joke; **echar algo a ~** to make fun of sth.

(e) (*Méx: opción fácil*) easy ride, soft option.

(f) (**: descanso*) rest, break.

relajón ADJ **(a)** (*Carib*) (*mofador*) mocking; (**: obsceno*) dirty. **(b)** (*Méx: depravado*) depraved, perverse.

relamer [2a] ① VT to lick repeatedly.

② **relamerse** VR **(a)** (*animal*) to lick its chops; (*persona*) to lick one's lips (*t* **~ los labios**).

(b) ~ con algo (*fig*) to relish sth, smack one's lips over sth; (*pey*) to gloat over sth.

(c) (*fig: jactarse*) to brag.

(d) (*fig: maquillarse*) to paint one's face.

relamido ADJ **(a)** (*remilgado*) prim and proper; (*afectado*) affected; (*muy elegante*) overdressed, dolled-up*. **(b)** (*CAm, Carib**) shameless,

cheeky*.

relámpago ① NM lightning, flash of lightning; (*fig*) flash; **~ difuso** sheet lightning; **como un ~** as quick as lightning, in a flash.

② ATR lightning; **guerra ~** blitzkrieg; **viaje ~** lightning trip; **visita ~** rushed visit, rapid visit, flying visit.

relampaguear [1a] VI (*Carib, Méx*) to twinkle; to flicker; to gleam.

relampagueo NM (*Carib, Méx*) twinkle; flicker, gleam.

relampagueante ADJ flashing.

relampaguear [1a] VI **(a)** (*gen*) to lighten; to flash; **relampagueó toda la noche** the lightning was flashing all night, there was lightning all night.

(b) (*Carib*) (*parpadear*) to twinkle, flicker; (*brillar*) to gleam, shine.

relampagueo NM **(a)** (*gen*) flashing. **(b)** (*Carib*) (*parpadeo*) twinkle, flicker; (*brillo*) gleam, shine.

relampuso ADJ (*Carib*) shameless, brazen.

relance NM (*Cono Sur*) **(a) = piropo** (a). **(b) de ~** (*al contado*) in cash.

relanzamiento NM relaunch(ing).

relanzar [1f] VT **(a)** *plan etc* to relaunch. **(b)** (*rechazar*) to repel, repulse.

relatar [1a] VT to relate, tell; to report.

relativamente ADV relatively.

relatividad NF relativity.

relativismo NM relativism.

relativista ① ADJ relativistic.

② NMF relativist.

relativizar [1f] VT to play down, (seek to) diminish the importance of.

relativo ① ADJ relative (*t Ling*); **~ a** relative to; regarding, relating to.

② NM (*Ling*) relative.

relato NM story, tale; account, report.

relator(a) NM/F teller, narrator; (*Jur*) court reporter.

relatoría NF post of court reporter.

relauchar* [1a] VI (*Cono Sur*) to skive off‡.

relax [re'las] NM (*Esp*) **(a)** (*sosiego*) (state of) relaxation; (*descanso*) rest, break; **hacer ~** to relax; **vamos a hacer un poco de ~** let's take a break.

(b) (*euf*) sexual services; (*anuncio*) '**R~**' 'Massage'.

relé NM (*Elec*) relay.

releer [2e] VT to reread.

relegación NF **(a)** (*gen*) relegation. **(b)** (*Hist*) exile, banishment.

relegar [1h] VT **(a)** (*gen*) to relegate; **~ algo al olvido** to banish sth from one's mind; to consign sth to oblivion. **(b)** (*desterrar*) to exile, banish.

relente NM night dew.

releso ADJ (*Cono Sur*) stupid, thick*.

relevación NF **(a)** (*gen*) relief (*t Mil*); replacement. **(b)** (*Jur*) exoneration; release (*de* from).

relevante ADJ **(a)** (*destacado*) outstanding. **(b)** (*pertinente*) relevant.

relevar [1a] VT **(a)** (*Téc*) to emboss; to carve (*o* paint *etc*) in relief.

(b) (*Mil*) *guardia* to relieve; *colega* to replace, substitute for.

(c) ~ a uno de una obligación to relieve sb of a duty, free sb from an obligation; **~ a uno de la culpa** to exonerate sb, free sb from blame; **~ a uno de** + *infin* to free sb from the obligation to + *infin*.

(d) ~ a uno de un cargo to relieve sb of his post, replace sb in his post; **ser relevado de su mando** to be relieved of one's command.

relevista NMF relay runner; relay swimmer.

relevo NM **(a)** (*Mil: acto*) relief, change; (*personas*) relief; **~ de la guardia** changing of the guard; **~ de los tiros** change of horses; **tomar el ~** to take over. **(b)** (*Dep*) **~s** relay (race); **400 metros ~s** 400 metres relay.

reliar [1c] VT *cigarrillo* to roll.

relicario NM **(a)** (*Ecl*) shrine; reliquary. **(b)** (*medallón*) locket.

relieve NM **(a)** (*Arte, Téc*) relief; raised work, embossing; raised part; **alto ~** high relief; **bajo ~** bas-relief; **en ~** raised pattern, embossed pattern, pattern in relief; **película en ~** stereoscopic film, three-dimensional (ABR: *3-D*) film; **estampar en ~, grabar en ~** to emboss.

(b) (*importancia*) importance, prominence; (*status*) social standing; **un personaje de ~** an important man, a man of some importance; **dar ~ a** to enhance; to give prominence to, bring out; **poner algo de ~** to emphasize (the importance of), point out the interest of, stress the qualities of.

(c) ~s (*restos*) left-overs.

religión NF **(a)** (*Rel*) religion.

(b) (*fig*) religion, cult; **tiene la ~ de la promesa** he believes utterly in keeping his word.

(c) (*religiosidad*) religiousness; (*piedad*) religious sense, piety.

(d) (*Ecl*) the religious life, religion; **entrar en ~** to take vows, enter a religious order.

religiosa NF nun.

religiosamente ADV religiously.

religiosidad NF religiosity, religiousness; (*fig*) religiousness.

religioso ① ADJ religious (*t fig*).

2 NM religious, member of a religious order, monk.
relimpio ADJ absolutely clean; spick and span.
relinchada NF (*Méx*) = **relincho**.
relinchar [1a] VI to neigh, whinny, snort.
relincho NM neigh(ing), whinny(ing), snort(ing).
reliquia NF **(a)** (*Ecl*) relic; (*Méx*) (votive) offering.
  (b) (*tesoro etc*) relic; **~s** relics, remains; (*vestigios*) traces, vestiges; **~ de familia** heirloom, family treasure.
  (c) (*Med*) **~s** after-effects, lingering effects, resultant weakness.
rellano NM (*Arquit*) landing.
rellena NF (*LAm*) black pudding; (*CAm*) *type of turnover*.
rellenable ADJ refillable; reusable.
rellenado NM refill; replenishment; (*Aer etc*) refuelling.
rellenar [1a] **1** VT **(a)** (*volver a llenar*) to refill, replenish; (*Aer etc*) to refuel.
  (b) (*llenar completamente*) to fill up; to pack, stuff, cram (*de* with); (*Culin*) to stuff; (*Cos etc*) to pad; *espacios etc* to fill in; *formulario* to fill in, fill up.
  2 rellenarse VR to stuff o.s. (*de* with).
rellenito ADJ *persona* plump.
relleno **1** ADJ **(a)** (*lleno*) packed, stuffed, crammed (*de* with); very full, full right up (*de* of); (*Culin*) stuffed (*de* with).
  (b) *persona* plump; *cara* full.
  (c) (*rellenado*) **envíe el cupón debidamente ~ a ...** send the completed coupon to ...
  2 NM **(a)** (*gen*) filling; (*Arquit*) plaster filling; (*Culin*) stuffing; (*Cos*) padding; wadding; (*Mec*) packing; (*de caramelo*) **~ blando** soft centre; **~ duro** hard centre; **frases** (*etc*) **de ~** padding, stuffing.
  (b) (*And*: *vertedero*) tip, dump.
reloj [re'lo] NM (*grande*) clock; (*de bolsillo, de pulsera*) watch; (*Téc*) clock, meter; **~ de arena** sandglass, hourglass; **~ automático** timer, timing mechanism; **~ biológico** biological clock; **~ de bolsillo** pocket watch; **~ de caja** grandfather clock; **~ de carillón** chiming clock; **~ de cuco** cuckoo-clock; **~ despertador** alarm-clock; **~ digital** digital watch; **~ eléctrico** electric clock; **~ de estacionamiento** parking meter; **~ de fichar** time-clock; **~ de la muerte** (*Ent*) deathwatch beetle; **~ de pie** grandfather clock; **~ parlante** talking clock; **~ de pulsera** wristwatch; **~ registrador** time-clock; **~ de sol** sundial; **como un ~** like clockwork; **estar como un ~** to be regular; to be as fit as a fiddle; **marchar como un ~** to go like clockwork; **contra** (**el**) **~** against the clock.
relojear [1a] VT (*Cono Sur*) **(a)** *carrera* to time. **(b)** (*: vigilar*) to spy on, keep tabs on; (*controlar*) to check, keep a check on.
relojería NF **(a)** (*arte*) watchmaking, clockmaking. **(b)** (*tienda*) watchmaker's (shop). **(c)** (*t aparato de ~*) clockwork; **bomba de ~** time-bomb; **mecanismo de ~** timing device.
relojero NM watchmaker, clockmaker.
reluciente ADJ **(a)** (*brillante*) shining, brilliant; glittering, gleaming, sparkling; bright. **(b)** *persona* (*pulcro*) sleek; (*gordo*) well-fed; (*de buen aspecto*) healthy-looking.
relucir [3f] VI **(a)** (*brillar*) to shine; to glitter, gleam, sparkle; to be bright. **(b) siempre saca a ~ sus éxitos** he's always bringing up (*o* harping on) his triumphs.
relujar [1a] VT (*CAm, Méx*) *zapatos* to shine.
relumbrante ADJ brilliant, dazzling; glaring.
relumbrar [1a] VI to shine brilliantly, be bright; to dazzle; to glare.
relumbrón NM **(a)** flash; sudden glare. **(b)** (*fig*) flashiness, ostentation; **joyas de ~** flashy jewellery; **vestirse de ~** to dress flashily, dress to kill.
remachado ADJ (*And*) quiet, reserved.
remachador NM riveter.
remachar [1a] **1** VT **(a)** (*Téc*) *clavo etc* to clinch; *metales* to rivet.
  (b) (*fig*) *aspecto* to hammer home, drive home; to stress; *caso* to tie up, finish; **para ~lo todavía** to clinch matters; to make it entirely certain.
  2 remacharse * VR (*And*) to remain stubbornly silent.
remache NM **(a)** (*Téc*) rivet. **(b)** (*acto*) clinching; riveting. **(c)** (*And*: *terquedad*) stubbornness, obstinacy.
remada NF stroke.
remador(a) NM/F rower.
remaduro ADJ (*LAm*) overripe.
remake [ri'meik] NM (*Cine*) remake.
remalladora NF mender, darner.
remallar [1a] VT to mend, darn.
remalo ADJ (*LAm*) really bad.
remandingo NM (*Carib*) row, uproar; scandal.
remanente **1** ADJ remaining; (*Fís*) remanent; (*Com etc*) surplus.
  2 NM remainder; (*Com, Fin*) retained earnings; balance; (*de producción*) surplus.
remangar = **arremangar**.
remango * ADJ lively, energetic, vigorous.
remangue * NM liveliness, energy, vigour; go; **hacer algo con ~** to

do sth energetically, tackle sth vigorously.
remansarse [1a] VR to form a pool; to become stagnant.
remanso NM **(a)** (*de río*) pool; backwater. **(b)** (*fig*) quiet place, peaceful area; **un ~ de paz** an oasis of peace, a haven of peace.
remaque NM (*Cine*) remake.
remar [1a] VI **(a)** (*Náut*) to row. **(b)** (*fig*) to toil, struggle; to suffer hardships.
remarcable ADJ remarkable.
remarcación NF (*Com*) mark-up.
remarcar [1g] VT **(a)** (*observar*) to notice, observe, remark on. **(b)** (*distinguir*) to distinguish. **(c)** (*subrayar*) to emphasize, underline. **(d)** *precio* to mark up.
rematadamente ADV terribly, hopelessly; **~ mal** terribly bad; **es ~ tonto** he's utterly stupid.
rematado ADJ **(a)** (*inútil*) hopeless; (*total*) complete, out-and-out; **es un loco ~** he's a raving lunatic; **es un tonto ~** he's an utter fool. **(b)** (*Esp*) *niño* very naughty.
rematador NM **(a)** (*Dep*) goal-scorer. **(b)** (*And, Cono Sur*) auctioneer.
rematadora NF auction house, auctioneer's.
rematante NM highest bidder.
rematar [1a] **1** VT **(a)** (*matar*) *persona* to finish off; to kill off; *animal* to shoot dead, kill instantly; *animal herido* to put out of its misery.
  (b) (*fig*) *trabajo etc* to finish off, bring to a conclusion; *proceso* to finish, round off; *abuso* to put an end to; *bebida etc* to finish up, drink (*etc*) the last of; (*Cos*) to cast off.
  (c) (*Arquit etc*) to top, be at the very top of, crown.
  (d) (*Com*: *vender*) to sell off cheaply, sell at a bargain price.
  (e) ~ algo a uno (*Com*: *en subasta*) to knock sth down to sb (*en* for).
  (f) (*LAm*) (*en subasta, comprar*) to buy at an auction, (*vender*) to sell at auction; (*CAm, Méx*: *vender*) to sell.
  (g) (*Cono Sur*) *caballo* to pull up.
  2 VI **(a)** (*terminar*) to end, finish off; **remató con un par de chistes** he finished with a couple of jokes.
  (b) ~ en to end in, come to; **es del tipo que remata en punta** it's the sort which comes to a point; **fue una situación que remató en tragedia** it was a situation which ended in tragedy.
  (c) (*Dep*) to shoot, score; **~ de cabeza** to head a goal.
remate NM **(a)** (*acto*) finishing (off); killing off; (*Dep*) shot; **equipo sin ~** a team with no finishing power.
  (b) (*cabo*) end; (*punta*) tip, point; (*Arquit*) top, crest; (*de mueble etc*) ornamental top.
  (c) (*fig*) conclusion; finishing touch; **de ~ = rematado (a)**; **para ~** to crown it all, on top of all that; **por ~** finally, as a finishing touch; **poner ~ a** to cap; to put the finishing touch to, round off.
  (d) (*Com*: *postura*) highest bid.
  (e) (*Com*: *venta*) sale (by auction); (*Bridge*) bidding, auction.
rematista NM (*And, Carib*) auctioneer.
rembolsar *etc* = **reembolsar**.
remecer [2d] **1** VT to rock, swing (to and fro); (*Méx*) to shake; to wave.
  2 remecerse VR to rock, swing (to and fro).
remedar [1a] VT to imitate, copy; (*pey*) to ape; (*burlándose*) to ape, mimic.
remediable ADJ remediable, that can be remedied; **fácilmente ~** easy to remedy, easily remedied.
remediar [1b] VT **(a)** (*poner remedio a*) to remedy; *daño, pérdida* to make good, repair; (*compensar*) to make up for; *abuso* to correct, put right, put a stop to; **llorando no remedias nada** you won't do any good by crying.
  (b) *necesidades etc* to meet, help with; *necesitado* to help (out); *persona en peligro* to help, save.
  (c) (*evitar*) to avoid, prevent; **sin poder ~lo** without being able to prevent it; **a ver si lo remediamos** let's see if we can do anything about it; **no poder ~ el echarse a reír** not to be able to help laughing.
▼ **remedio** NM **(a)** (*gen*) remedy (*t Med*; *contra* against); (*Med*) cure; (*ayuda*) help; **~ casero** ordinary remedy, simple domestic remedy; **~ heroico** extreme remedy; (*fig*) extreme measure; **como último ~** as a last resort; **sin ~** inevitable; irremediable; **es un tonto sin ~** he's a hopeless idiot, he's so stupid he's past redemption; **no se podía encontrar ni para un ~** it couldn't be had for love nor money; **¡ni por un ~!*** not on your life!; **no hay más ~** there's no help for it, there's nothing one can do, there's no other way; **no hay más ~ que +** *infin* the only thing is to + *infin*; **no hay ~ para él** it's all up with him, he's had it; **esto no tiene ~** it is unavoidable; there's nothing one can do about it; it's beyond repair; **él no tiene ~** he's hopeless, he's past redemption; **¿qué ~ tengo?** what else can I do?; **no tener más ~ que +** *infin* to have no alternative but to + *infin*; **poner ~ a un abuso** to correct an abuse, put a stop to an abuse; **ruego que se ponga ~** I hope something can be done about it.
  (b) (*alivio*) relief, help; **buscar ~ en su aflicción** to look for some relief in one's distress.

➤   LENGUA Y USO: **remedio: a → 37.1, 45.4**

(c) (*Jur*) remedy, recourse.

(d) (*CAm, Méx Med*) medicine.

remedo NM imitation, copy; (*pey*) poor imitation, travesty, parody.

rememorar [1a] VT (*liter*) to remember, recall.

remendar [1j] VT **(a)** (*Cos*) to mend, repair; to patch, darn. **(b)** (*fig*) correct.

remendón NM cobbler.

remera NF (*Cono Sur*) T-shirt.

remero NM **(a)** (*persona*) oarsman. **(b)** (*máquina*) rowing machine.

remesa NF remittance; shipment, consignment; **~ de fondos** (*Méx Com*) (financial) settlement.

remesar [1a] VT *dinero* to remit, send; *mercancías* to send, ship, consign.

remeter [2a] VR to put back; *camisa, ropa de cama etc* to tuck in.

remezón NM (*LAm*) earth tremor, slight earthquake.

remiendo NM **(a)** (*acto*) mending; patching.

(b) (*parche etc*) mend; patch, darn; **a ~s** piecemeal; **echar un ~ a** to patch, put a patch on.

(c) (*fig*) correction; (*Med*) improvement.

(d) (*Zool*) spot, patch.

remilgado ADJ prudish, prim; affected; finicky, fussy, particular, overnice; squeamish, oversensitive; **don R~*** (*Esp hum*) Lord Muck*.

remilgarse [1h] VR to react prudishly; to show one's affectation; to be fussy; to be squeamish.

remilgo NM **(a)** (*gazmoñería*) prudery, primness; (*afectación*) affectation; (*melindre*) fussiness; (*sensibilidad*) squeamishness, excess of sensitivity.

(b) (*mueca*) prim look; simper; smirk; **hacer ~s a** to react in a prudish (*etc*) way to; **él no hace ~s a ninguna clase de trabajo** he won't turn up his nose at any kind of work.

(c) **don R~s** (*: *hum*) Lord Muck*.

remilgoso ADJ (*LAm*) = **remilgado**.

reminiscencia NF reminiscence.

remirado ADJ **(a)** (*prudente*) cautious, circumspect, careful; (*pey*) overcautious. **(b)** (*pey*) (*gazmoño*) prudish; (*afectado*) affected, over-nice; (*melindroso*) fussy, pernickety*.

remirar [1a] **1** VT to look at again; to look hard at.

2 remirarse VR to be extra careful (*en* about), take great pains (*en* over).

remise NM O F (*Cono Sur*) hired car, taxi.

remisión NF **(a)** (*envío*) sending; (*LAm*) shipment, consignment.

(b) (*referencia*) reference (*a* to).

(c) (*aplazamiento*) postponement; adjournment.

(d) (*disminución*) remission (*t Med*); slackening.

(e) (*Ecl*) forgiveness, remission.

remiso ADJ **(a)** *persona* slack, slow (to obey), remiss; **mostrarse ~** to be reluctant; **estar ~ a** + *infin* to be reluctant to + *infin*, be unwilling to + *infin*. **(b)** *movimiento* slow, sluggish.

remisor(a) NM/F (*LAm Com*) sender.

remite NM sender's name and address (*written on back of envelope*).

remitente NMF sender.

remitido NM **(a)** (*en periódico*) paid insert. **(b)** (*Méx: consignación*) shipment, consignment.

remitir [3a] **1** VT **(a)** (*Correos: enviar*) to send; *dinero* to remit; (*Com*) to send, ship, consign.

(b) *lector, usuario* to refer (*a* to).

(c) (*aplazar*) to postpone; *sesión* to adjourn.

(d) **~ una decisión a uno** to leave a decision to sb, refer a matter to sb for a decision.

(e) (*Ecl*) *pecados* to forgive, pardon.

2 VI **(a)** (*disminuir*) to slacken, diminish, let up.

(b) **'remite: X ...'** (*en sobre*) 'sender: X ...'

3 remitirse VR: **a las pruebas me remito** the proof of the pudding is in the eating.

remo NM **(a)** (*Náut*) oar; **a ~ y vela** (*fig*) speedily; **cruzar un río a ~** to row across a river; **pasaron los cañones a ~** they rowed the guns across.

(b) (*Dep*) rowing; **practicar el ~** to row, go in for rowing.

(c) (*Anat*) arm, leg; (*Orn*) wing.

(d) (*fig*) toils, hardships; **andar al ~** to work like a (galley) slave.

remoción NF **(a)** (*gen*) removal. **(b)** (*de persona: esp LAm*) sacking*, dismissal.

remodelación NF remodelling; (*renovación*) refurbishment; (*Aut*) restyling; (*Pol*) reshuffle, restructuring; **~ ministerial** cabinet reshuffle.

remodelar [1a] VT to remodel; (*Aut*) to restyle; (*Pol*) to reshuffle, restructure.

remojar [1a] VT **(a)** (*gen*) to steep, soak (*en* in); (*bañar*) to dip (*en* in, into); (*sin querer*) to soak, drench (*con* with); *galleta etc* to dip, dunk (*en* in).

(b) (*) *suceso* to celebrate with a drink.

(c) (*Méx**: *sobornar*) to bribe.

remojo NM **(a)** (*gen*) steeping, soaking; drenching; (*galleta*) dip, dip-

ping; **dejar la ropa en ~** to leave clothes to soak; **poner los garbanzos a ~** to put chickpeas in to soak.

(b) (*Carib, Méx*) (*regalo*) gift, present; (*propina*) tip.

remojón NM **(a)** (*gen*) soaking, drenching; **darse un ~*** to go in for a dip. **(b)** (*Culin*) piece of bread soaked in milk (*etc*).

remolacha NF (*t ~ de mesa, ~ roja*) beet, beetroot; **~ azucarera** sugar beet.

remolachero **1** ADJ beet (*atr*).

2 NM, **remolachera** NF beet farmer.

remolcable ADJ that can be towed.

remolcador NM (*Náut*) tug; (*Aut*) tow car, breakdown lorry.

remolcar [1g] VT to tow, tow along; to take in tow; (*Ferro*) to pull.

remoledor* ADJ (*And, Cono Sur*) roistering, party-going.

remoler [2h] **1** VT **(a)** (*moler*) to grind up small. **(b)** (*And, CAm: fastidiar*) to annoy, pester.

2 VI (*Cono Sur, And**) to live it up*.

remolienda* NF (*And, Cono Sur*) party, wild time*.

remolinar(se) [1a], **remolinear(se)** [1a] = **arremolinarse**.

remolino NM **(a)** (*agua*) swirl, eddy; (*en río*) whirlpool; (*de aire*) whirl; disturbance; (*viento*) whirlwind; (*de humo, polvo*) whirl, cloud.

(b) (*de pelo*) tuft.

(c) (*de gente*) crowd, throng, crush, moving mass.

(d) (*fig*) commotion.

remolón **1** ADJ **(a)** (*terco*) stubborn; (*difícil*) awkward, cantankerous.

(b) (*vago*) slack, lazy.

2 NM, **remolona** NF stubborn individual; slacker, shirker; **hacerse el ~** = **remolonear**.

remolonear [1a] VI **(a)** (*estar resuelto*) to be stubborn, refuse to budge; to hold out on sb. **(b)** (*no trabajar*) to slack, shirk.

remolque NM **(a)** (*acto*) towing; **a ~** on tow, being towed; **ir a ~** to be on tow; **llevar un coche a ~** to tow a car; **lo hizo a ~** (*fig*) he did it reluctantly; they had to push him to do it, he did it because somebody made him; **dar ~ a** to tow, take in tow.

(b) (*Náut: cable*) towrope; cable, hawser; (*Aut etc*) towrope.

(c) (*vehículo etc: Aut*) tow; (*caravana*) trailer, caravan; (*Náut*) ship on tow.

remonda: NF: **¡es la ~!** this is the end!; it's sheer hell!

remonta NF **(a)** (*Cos etc*) mending, repair. **(b)** (*Mil*) remount, supply of cavalry horses; cavalry horses; cavalry depot.

remontada NF (*fig*) recovery.

▼ **remontar** [1a] **1** VT **(a)** *media* to mend (a ladder in); *zapato* to mend, repair, resole.

(b) **~ el vuelo** to soar (up).

(c) *río etc* to go up.

(d) *obstáculo* to negotiate, get over, surmount.

(e) (*Mil*) *caballería* to remount.

(f) *reloj* to wind.

(g) (*Caza*) *animales* to frighten away.

(h) **~ un gol** (*Dep*) to pull a goal back.

2 remontarse VR **(a)** (*Aer, Orn etc*) to rise, soar; (*edificio*) to soar, tower; (*fig*) to soar; **~ en alas de la imaginación** to take flight on the wings of fantasy.

(b) **~ a** (*Fin*) to amount to.

▼**(c)** (*en el tiempo*) **~ a** to go back to; **sus recuerdos se remontan al siglo pasado** her memories go back to the last century; **este texto se remonta al siglo XI** this text dates from (*o* back to) the 11th century; **tenemos que remontarnos a los mismos orígenes** we must get back to the very origins.

remonte NM ski-lift.

remoquete NM **(a)** (*puñetazo*) punch. **(b)** (*fig: comentario*) cutting remark, dig. **(c)** (*apodo*) nickname; **poner ~ a uno** to give sb a nickname. **(d)** (*) (*coqueteo*) flirting, spooning*; (*pretendiente*) suitor.

rémora NF **(a)** (*Zool*) remora. **(b)** (*fig*) drawback; hindrance.

remorder [2h] **1** VT *persona* to grieve, distress; to cause remorse to; *conciencia* to prick; *mente* to afflict, prey upon.

2 remorderse VR to suffer (*o* show) remorse; to suffer inwardly, harbour a grudge (*o* jealousy *etc*).

remordimiento NM remorse, regret (*t ~s*); **tener ~s** to feel remorse, suffer pangs of conscience.

remotamente ADV **(a)** *parecerse, recordar* vaguely, slightly; **no se le parece ni ~** he doesn't look even remotely like him. **(b)** *pensar etc* vaguely, tentatively.

remotidad* NF (*CAm*) remote spot, distant place.

▼ **remoto** ADJ remote; **¡ni por lo más ~!*** not on your life!; **no tengo lo más ~*** I haven't the faintest.

remover [2h] VT **(a)** *tierra etc* to turn over, dig up; *objetos* to move round, change over, shift about; *cóctel etc* to shake; *sopa etc* to stir (round); *sentimientos* to disturb, upset; **~ un asunto** to turn a matter over, go into a matter again; **~ el pasado** to stir up the past; to rake up the past; **~ un proyecto** to revive a scheme; **~ cielo y tierra, ~ Roma con Santiago** to move heaven and earth.

(b) (*quitar*) *obstáculo etc* to remove; (*Med*) to excise, cut out; *persona*

➤ LENGUA Y USO: **remontar:** 2c → 44.2 **remoto** → 42.3

to discharge, remove (from office); (*esp LAm*) to sack*, fire*.

removimiento NM removal.

remozado NM rejuvenation; renovation.

remozamiento NM rejuvenation; renovation.

remozar [1f] ☐1 VT *persona etc* to rejuvenate; *aspecto etc* to brighten up, polish up; *organización etc* to give a new look to, give a face-lift to; *edificio, fachada* to renovate.

☐2 **remozarse** VR to be rejuvenated; to look much younger; **la encuentro muy remozada** I find her looking much younger.

remplazar *etc* = **reemplazar** *etc*.

rempujar* [1a] VT to keep at it, persist.

rempujón* NM shove, push.

remuda NF change, alteration; replacement; ~ **de caballos** change of horses; ~ **(de ropa)** change of clothes, spare clothes.

remudar [1a] VT to remove; to change, alter; to replace.

remuneración NF remuneration.

remunerado ADJ: **trabajo mal** ~ badly-paid job.

remunerador ADJ remunerative; rewarding, worthwhile; **poco** ~ unremunerative.

remunerar [1a] VT to remunerate; to pay; to reward.

remunerativo ADJ remunerative.

renacentista ADJ Renaissance (*atr*).

renacer [2d] VI (a) (*gen*) to be reborn; (*Bot*) to appear again, come up again.
(b) (*fig*) to revive; to acquire new vigour (*o* life); **hacer** ~ to revive; **hoy me siento** ~ today I feel renewed, I feel I am coming to life again today; **sentían** ~ **la esperanza** they felt new hope.

renaciente ADJ renascent.

renacimiento NM rebirth, revival; **R**~ Renaissance.

renacuajo NM (a) (*Zool*) tadpole. (b) (*) shrimp; (*pey*) runt, little squirt*.

renal ADJ renal, kidney (*atr*).

Renania NF Rhineland.

renano ADJ Rhenish, Rhine (*atr*).

rencilla NF (a) (*riña*) quarrel; (*enemistad*) feud; ~s dissension; arguments, bickering. (b) (*rencor*) bad blood; ill will; grudge; **me tiene** ~ he's got it in for me, he bears me a grudge.

rencilloso ADJ quarrelsome.

renco ADJ lame.

rencor NM rancour, bitterness; ill feeling, resentment; spitefulness; **guardar** ~ to bear malice, have a grudge (*a* against); **no le guardo** ~ I bear him no malice.

rencorosamente ADV (*V* ADJ) (a) spitefully, maliciously. (b) resentfully; bitterly.

rencoroso ADJ (a) (*malicioso*) (*ser*) spiteful, nasty, malicious. (b) (*resentido*) (*estar*) resentful; (*amargado*) bitter, embittered.

rendición NF (a) (*Mil etc*) surrender; ~ **incondicional** unconditional surrender. (b) (*Fin*) yield, profit(s), return. (c) (*Cono Sur*) (*Com*) trading balance; (*Fin*: *t* ~ **de cuentas**) balance.

rendidamente ADV submissively; obsequiously; humbly, devotedly.

rendido ADJ (a) (*sumiso*) submissive; (*servil*) obsequious; *admirador* humble, devoted. (b) **estar** ~ (**de cansancio**) to be exhausted, be all in.

rendidor ADJ (*LAm*) highly productive; (*Fin*) highly profitable.

rendija NF (a) crack, cleft, crevice; chink; aperture. (b) (*fig*) rift, split. (c) (*Jur*) loophole.

rendimiento NM (a) (*parte útil*) usable part, proportion of usable material.
(b) (*Mec*) efficiency, performance; (*capacidad*) capacity; (*producción*) output; **el** ~ **del motor** the performance of the engine; **aumentar el** ~ **de una máquina** to increase the output of a machine; **funcionar a pleno** ~ to work all-out, work at full throttle.
(c) (*Fin*) yield, profit(s), return; ~ **del capital** return on capital; **ley del** ~ **decreciente** law of diminishing returns.
(d) (*cualidad*) (*sumisión*) submissiveness; (*servilismo*) obsequiousness; (*devoción*) devotion; **su** ~ **total a la voluntad de ella** his complete submissiveness to her will.
(e) (*agotamiento*) exhaustion.

rendir [3k] ☐1 VT (a) (*producir*) to produce, yield, bear; *producto, total etc* to produce; *beneficios etc* to yield; *interés* to bear.
(b) (*vencer*) *enemigo* to defeat, conquer, overcome; *país* to conquer, subdue; *fortaleza* to take, capture, reduce.
(c) *persona* to exhaust, tire out; **le rindió el sueño** sleep overcame him.
(d) *voluntad* to subject to one's own will, dominate, assume control of; **logró** ~ **el albedrío de la joven** he came to dominate the young woman's will completely; **había que** ~ **su entereza** he had to overcome his honest doubts, he had to fight down his moral objections.
(e) (*devolver*) to give back, return; (*entregar*) to hand over; (*Mil*) to surrender; (*Mil*) *guardia* to hand over; (*Esp**) to vomit, bring up.
(f) (*Com*) *factura* to send.
(g) (*Mil*) *bandera* to dip; *armas* to lower, reverse.

(h) *tributo* to pay; *homenaje* to do, pay; *gracias* to give; ~ **culto a** to worship; (*fig*) to pay homage to, pay tribute to.
(i) ~ **examen** (*Cono Sur*) to sit (*o* take) an exam.
☐2 VI (a) (*producir*) to yield, produce; to be profitable, give good results; **el negocio no rinde** the business doesn't pay; **este año ha rendido poco** it has done poorly this year; **la finca rinde para mantener a 8 familias** the estate produces enough to keep 8 families; **trabajo, pero no rindo** I work hard, but without much to show for it.
(b) (*LAm*: *durar*) to last longer, keep going.
(c) (*LAm*: *henchirse*) to swell up (in the cooking *etc*).
☐3 **rendirse** VR (a) (*ceder*) to yield (*a* to); (*Mil*) to surrender; (*entregarse*) to give o.s. up; ~ **a la evidencia** to bow before the evidence; ~ **a la fuerza** to yield to violence; ~ **a la razón** to yield to reason.
(b) (*cansarse*) to wear o.s. out, exhaust o.s.

renditivo ADJ (*Cono Sur*) productive; profitable.

renegado ☐1 ADJ (a) (*traidor*) renegade; (*Ecl*) apostate.
(b) (*) (*brusco*) gruff; (*malhumorado*) cantankerous, bad-tempered.
☐2 NM, **renegada** NF (a) renegade; (*Ecl*) apostate; (*Pol*) turncoat.
(b) (*) bad lot, nasty piece of work.

renegar [1h y 1j] ☐1 VT (a) (*negar*) to deny vigorously, deny repeatedly.
(b) (*odiar*) to abhor, detest.
☐2 VI (a) (*apostatar*) to turn renegade, go over to the other side, be a traitor; (*Ecl*) to apostatize.
(b) ~ **de** (*abandonar*) to forsake, disown; (*renunciar*) to renounce, give up; ~ **de su familia** to disown one's family; ~ **de la amistad de uno** to break completely with sb; **reniego de ti** I want nothing more to do with you.
(c) ~ **de** (*odiar*) to abhor, detest.
(d) (*jurar*) to curse, swear; (*Rel*) to blaspheme.
(e) (*quejarse*) to grumble; to protest, complain.
(f) (*And, Méx*: *enojarse*) to get angry, get upset; (*gritar*) to shout, rage.
(g) (*And, Cono Sur, Méx*: *protestar*) to protest.

renegociación NF renegotiation.

renegociar [1b] VT to renegotiate.

renegón* ADJ grumbling, cantankerous, grouchy*.

renegrido ADJ (*LAm*) very black, very dark.

RENFE, Renfe ['renfe] NF (*Ferro*) ABR *de* **Red Nacional de los Ferrocarriles Españolas.**

renglón NM (a) (*línea*) line (of writing); **a** ~ **seguido** in the very next line, (*fig*) straight after, without a break; **escribir un** ~ **a, poner unos renglones a** to drop a line to; **leer entre renglones** to read between the lines; **estos pobres renglones** these humble jottings.
(b) (*Com etc*) item (of expenditure).
(c) (*LAm Com*) (*género*) line of goods; (*departamento*) department, area.

rengo ADJ (*LAm*) lame, crippled.

rengue NM train.

renguear [1a] VI (a) (*LAm*: *cojear*) to limp, hobble. (b) (*Cono Sur*: *perseguir*) to pursue a woman.

renguera NF (*LAm*) limp, limping; lameness.

reniego NM (a) (*juramento*) curse, oath; (*Rel*) blasphemy, blasphemous remark.
(b) (*queja*) grumble; complaint.

reno NM reindeer.

renombrado ADJ renowned, famous.

renombre NM (a) (*fama*) renown, fame; **de** ~ renowned, famous. (b) (*apellido*) surname.

renovable ADJ renewable.

renovación NF (a) (*gen*) renewal; renovation; ~ **espiritual** spiritual renewal; ~ **de la suscripción** renewal of one's subscription; ~ **urbana** urban renewal.
(b) (*Arquit etc*) renovation; restoration; redecoration.
(c) (*Pol etc*) reorganization, remodelling, transformation.

renovado ADJ renewed, redoubled; **con renovada energía** with renewed energy.

renovador (*Pol*) ☐1 ADJ reformist.
☐2 NM, **renovadora** NF reformer.

renoval NM (*Cono Sur, Méx*) area of young trees.

renovar [1l] VT (a) (*gen*) to renew; *aviso etc* to renew, repeat; *abono* to renew.
(b) (*Arquit etc*) to renovate; to restore; *cuarto* to redecorate.
(c) (*Pol etc*) to reorganize, remodel, transform.

renquear [1a] VI (a) (*cojear*) to limp, hobble. (b) (*: *ir tirando*) to get along, manage with difficulty. (c) (*motor*) to splutter. (d) (*: *vacilar*) to dither.

renqueo NM limp.

renta NF (a) (*ingresos*) income; (*interés etc*) interest, return, yield; **política de** ~s incomes policy; ~ **devengada** earned income; ~ **dis-**

ponible disposable income; ~ **gravable,** ~ **imponible** taxable income; ~ **nacional** national income; ~ **bruta nacional** gross national income; ~**s públicas** revenue; ~ **del trabajo** earned income; ~ **vitalicia** annuity; **título de** ~ **fija** fixed-interest income; **valores de** ~ **fija** fixed-yield securities; **tiene** ~**s particulares** she has a private income; **vivir de sus** ~**s** to live on one's private income.
(b) (*deuda*) public debt, national debt.
(c) (*alquiler, esp LAm*) rent; **'casa de** ~' 'house to let'.
(d) (*Dep*) lead, advantage.
rentabilidad NF (*V* ADJ) profitability; cost-effectiveness.
rentabilizar [1f] VT to make (more) profitable; to promote; to exploit to the full, (*pey*) cash in on.
rentable ADJ profitable; (*de coste-beneficio favorable*) cost-effective, economic; **no** ~ unprofitable; uneconomical; **el avión no es** ~ the aircraft is not an economic proposition; **la línea ya no es** ~ the line is no longer economic (to run).
rentado ADJ (*Cono Sur*) *trabajo* paid.
rentar [1a] ① VT **(a)** (*rendir*) to produce, yield. **(b)** (*LAm*) *casa* to let, rent out, rent.
② **rentarse** VR: **'se renta'** (*Méx*) 'to let'.
rentero, -a NM/F tenant farmer.
rentista NMF **(a)** (*accionista*) stockholder, person who lives on income from shares, (*como miembro de clase*) rentier; (*que vive de sus rentas*) person of independent means. **(b)** (*experto*) financial expert.
rentístico ADJ financial.
renuencia NF **(a)** *persona* unwillingness, reluctance. **(b)** *objeto etc* awkwardness.
renuente ADJ **(a)** *persona* unwilling, reluctant. **(b)** *sustancia* awkward, difficult.
renuevo NM **(a)** (*acto*) renewal. **(b)** (*Bot*) shoot, sprout.
renuncia NF renunciation; resignation; relinquishment; abdication.
renunciar [1b] ① VT (*t vi:* ~ **a**) *derecho etc* to renounce (*en* in favour of), surrender, relinquish; *hábito, proyecto etc* to give up; *demanda* to drop, waive; *puesto, responsabilidad* to resign; *trono* to abdicate (*en* in favour of); ~ **a hacer algo** to give up doing sth, stop doing sth.
② VI (*Naipes*) to revoke.
renuncio NM **(a)** (*Naipes*) revoke. **(b)** **coger a uno en un** ~ to catch sb in a fib, catch sb out.
reñidamente ADV *luchar etc* bitterly, hard, stubbornly.
reñidero NM: ~ **de gallos** cockpit.
reñido ADJ **(a)** *batalla, concurso* bitter; **un partido** ~ a hard-fought game; a bitter struggle; **en lo más** ~ **de la batalla** in the thick of the fight.
(b) **estar** ~ **con uno** to be at odds with sb, be on bad terms with sb; **está** ~ **con su familia** he has fallen out with his family.
(c) **estar** ~ **con** (*principio etc*) to be at variance with, be divorced from, be in opposition to.
reñidor ADJ quarrelsome.
reñir [3h y 3k] ① VT **(a)** (*regañar*) to scold; (*reprender*) to tell off, reprimand (*por* for).
(b) *batalla* to fight, wage.
② VI (*disputar*) to quarrel, fall out (*con* with); (*pelear*) to fight, scrap, come to blows; **ha reñido con su novio** she's fallen out with her boyfriend; she's broken it off with her fiancé; **se pasan la vida riñendo** they spend their whole time quarrelling; **riñeron por cuestión de dinero** they quarrelled about (*o* over) money.
reo¹ NMF **(a)** (*delincuente*) culprit, offender; criminal; (*Jur*) accused, defendant; ~ **de Estado** person accused of a crime against the state; ~ **de muerte** person under sentence of death.
(b) (*Cono Sur: vagabundo*) tramp, bum (*US*).
reo² NM (*pez*) sea-trout.
reoca: NF: **es la** ~ (*Esp*) (*bueno*) it's the tops*; (*malo*) it's the pits*.
reojo: **mirar a uno de** ~ to look at sb out of the corner of one's eye; (*fig*) to look askance at sb, look dubiously at sb.
reordenación NF realignment.
reordenar [1a] VT to realign.
reorganización NF reorganization.
reorganizar [1f] ① VT to reorganize; to reshuffle.
② **reorganizarse** VR to reorganize.
reorientación NF reorientation; new direction; readjustment.
reorientar [1a] VT to reorientate; to give a new direction to; to readjust.
reóstato NM rheostat.
Rep ABR *de* **República** Republic, Rep.
repaminonda: NF: **es la** ~ (*Esp*) it's the tops*.
repanchigarse [1h] VR, **repantigarse** [1h] VR to lounge, sprawl, loll (back); **estar repanchigado en un sillón** to loll back in a chair.
repanocha* NF: **¡eres la** ~**!** you're unbelievable!; **¡aquello fue la** ~**!** it was unbelievable!
reparable ADJ repairable.
reparación NF **(a)** (*acto*) repairing, mending.
(b) (*Téc*) repair; **'reparaciones en el acto', 'reparaciones**

instantáneas' 'repairs while you wait'; **efectuar reparaciones en** to carry out repairs to.
(c) (*fig*) amends, reparation, redress.
reparador ① ADJ **(a)** *persona* critical, faultfinding.
(b) *comida* fortifying, strengthening, restorative; *sueño* refreshing.
② NM (*Téc*) repairer.
③ NM, **reparadora¹** NF (*criticón*) carping critic, faultfinder.
reparadora² NF: ~ **de calzados** (*Méx*) shoe repairer's.
reparar [1a] ① VT **(a)** (*Téc*) to repair, mend.
(b) *energías etc* to repair, restore; *fortunas* to retrieve.
(c) *ofensa etc* to make amends for; *daño, pérdida* to make good; *consecuencia* to undo.
(d) *golpe* to parry.
(e) *observar* to observe, notice.
(f) (*Cono Sur: imitar*) to mimic, imitate.
② VI **(a)** (*notar*) ~ **en** to observe, notice, note, see; **no reparó en la diferencia** he didn't notice the difference; **sin** ~ **en que ya no funcionaba** without noticing that it was no longer working.
(b) ~ **en** (*hacer caso de*) to pay attention to, take heed of; (*considerar*) to consider; **no** ~ **en las dificultades** to take no heed of the difficulties, refuse to consider the difficulties; **repara en lo que vas a hacer** reflect on what you are going to do; **sin** ~ **en los gastos** heedless of expense, regardless of the cost; **no** ~ **en nada** to stop at nothing.
(c) (*CAm, Méx: caballo*) to rear, buck.
③ **repararse** VR **(a)** to check o.s., restrain o.s.
(b) (*CAm, Méx: caballo*) to rear, buck.
reparista ADJ (*And, CAm, Carib*), **reparisto** ADJ (*CAm, Carib*) = **reparón** 1.

▼ **reparo** NM **(a)** (*Téc*) repair; (*Arquit etc*) restoration.
(b) (*Esgrima*) parry; (*fig: protección*) defence, protection.
(c) (*Med*) remedy; restorative.
▼**(d)** (*objeción*) objection; (*crítica*) criticism; (*duda*) doubt; **poner** ~**s** to raise objections (*a* to); to criticize, express one's doubts; (*pey*) to find fault (*a* with).
(e) (*escrúpulo*) hesitation; scruple, doubt; **no tuvo** ~ **en** + *infin* he did not hesitate to + *infin*; he did not scruple to + *infin*.
(f) (*CAm, Méx: caballo*) bucking, rearing; **tirar un** ~ to rear, buck.
reparón ① ADJ carping, critical, faultfinding.
② NM, **reparona** NF critic, faultfinder.
repartición NF **(a)** (*distribución*) distribution; sharing out, division. **(b)** (*Cono Sur Admin*) government department, administrative section. **(c)** (*LAm Pol: de tierras*) redistribution.
repartida NF (*CAm, Cono Sur*) = **repartición** (a).
repartido NM (*Correos*) delivery; (*de lechero etc*) round.
repartidor NM distributor; (*Com*) roundsman, deliveryman; ~ **de leche** milkman; ~ **de periódicos** paperboy.
repartija* NF share-out, carve-up*.
repartimiento NM distribution; division; (*de impuestos*) assessment.
repartir [3a] ① VT (*distribuir*) to distribute; (*dividir entre varios*) to divide (up), share (out); to parcel out; *trabajos* to allot, assign; *tierras* to parcel up, divide, split up; *país* to partition; *folletos, premios etc* to give out, hand out; *comida* to serve out; *bebidas, vasos* to hand round; *dividendo* to declare, pay out; *cartas, leche, pan, periódicos etc* to deliver; *cartas* to deal; (*Teat*) *papeles* to cast; *castigos* to issue, impose, mete out; **el premio está muy repartido** the prize is shared among many; **las cartas están repartidas en 4 palos** the cards are distributed among 4 suits; **los diamantes están repartidos 4-3** the diamonds are split 4-3; **las guarniciones están repartidas por toda la costa** the garrisons are distributed all round the coast, there are garrisons dotted about all along the coast.
② **repartirse** VR to be distributed, be shared out (*etc*); **'se reparte a domicilio'** 'home delivery service'.
reparto NM **(a)** (*acto*) = **repartición** (a).
(b) (*distribución*) distribution (*t Bridge*); **un** ~ **poco uniforme** a very uneven distribution.
(c) (*Com, Correos*) delivery.
(d) (*Teat: acto*) casting; (*lista*) cast, cast list.
(e) (*CAm, Carib, Méx: solar*) building site, building lot (*US*); (*LAm: urbanización*) housing estate, real estate development (*US*).
(f) ~ **de utilidades** (*Fin*) profit sharing.
repasador NM (*Cono Sur*) dishcloth.
repasar [1a] VT **(a)** *lugar* to pass (by) again; *calle* to go along again; **pasar y** ~ **una calle** to go up and down a street repeatedly.
(b) ~ **la plancha por una prenda** to give a garment another iron.
(c) (*Cos*) to sew, sew up, darn; to mend.
(d) (*Mec*) to check, overhaul.
(e) *cuenta etc* to check; *texto* to revise, re-examine; *notas* to go over again; to read through rapidly, flick through; *lección* to revise; *publicación etc* to put the finishing touches to, polish up.
(f) (*Cono Sur*) *platos etc* to dust, polish; *mueble* to polish; *ropa* to brush (down).
repasata* NF ticking-off*.

▶ LENGUA Y USO: **reparo: d** → 38.3

repaso NM (*gen*) review, revision; check; (*Cos*) mending; (*Mec*) check-up, overhaul; (*lectura*) rapid reading, quick re-reading; **~ general** general overhaul; **curso de ~** revision course, refresher course; **ropa de ~** mending, darning; **dar un ~ a una lección** to revise a lesson; **los técnicos daban el último ~ al cohete** the technicians were giving the rocket a final check; **pegar un buen ~ a uno*** to give sb a proper ticking-off*.

repatear: [1a] VT: **ese tío me repatea** (*Esp*) that chap gets on my wick‡, that chap turns me right off*.

repatriación NF repatriation.

repatriado [1] ADJ repatriated.

[2] NM, **repatriada** NF repatriate, repatriated person.

repatriar [1b] [1] VT to repatriate; *criminal etc* to deport; to send home, send back to one's country of origin; **van a ~ el famoso mármol** they are going to send the famous marble back to its original country.

[2] **repatriarse** VR to return home, go back to one's own country.

repe*¹ [1] ADJ repeated, duplicated; **un sello que tengo ~** a duplicate stamp I have, a stamp I have twice over; **los tengo ~s** I've got stacks*.

[2] NMF (*Univ*) student who is repeating a course.

[3] NF (*TV etc*) repeat (of a programme).

repe² NM (*And*) mashed bananas with milk.

repechar [1a] VI: **~ contra** (*Méx*) to lean (one's chest) against.

repecho NM (a) (*vertiente*) sharp gradient, steep slope; **a ~** uphill. (b) (*Carib, Méx: parapeto*) parapet. (c) (*Méx: refugio*) shelter, refuge, hut.

repela NF (*And, CAm*) gleaning (of coffee crop).

repelar [1a] [1] VT (a) (*pelar completamente*) to leave completely bare, shear; *hierba* to nibble, crop; *uñas* to clip.

(b) **~ a uno** to pull sb's hair.

(c) (*Méx: criticar*) to raise objections to, call into question.

(d) (*Méx*: reprender*) to scold, tell off*.

[2] **repelarse** VR (*Cono Sur*) to feel remorse.

repelencia NF revulsion, disgust.

repelente [1] ADJ (a) (*asqueroso*) repellent, repulsive, disgusting. (b) (*LAm*: impertinente*) cheeky*, insolent; (*Méx*: fastidioso*) annoying, irritating.

[2] NM (insect) repellent.

repeler [2a] [1] VT (a) *enemigo etc* to repel, repulse, drive back; *persona* to push away.

(b) **este material repele el agua** this material is water-repellent; **la pared repele la pelota** the wall sends the ball back, the ball bounces off the wall.

(c) *idea, oferta* to reject.

(d) (*fig*) to repel, disgust, fill with repulsion.

[2] **repelerse** VR: **los dos se repelen** the two are (mutually) incompatible.

repellar [1a] VT (a) (*Arquit*) to plaster, stucco; (*LAm: enjalbegar*) to whitewash. (b) (*Carib: menear*) to wriggle, wiggle.

repello NM (a) (*LAm: jalbegue*) whitewash(ing). (b) (*Carib etc: en baile*) wiggle, grind.

repelo NM (a) (*pelo*) hair out of place, hair (*etc*) that sticks up; (*en madera*) snag, knot; (*Anat*) hangnail.

(b) (*: *riña*) tiff, slight argument.

(c) (*fig*) aversion.

(d) (*And, Méx*) (*baratijas*) junk, bric-a-brac; (*trapo*) rag, tatter.

repelón [1] ADJ (*Méx*) grumbling, grumpy.

[2] NM (a) (*tirón*) tug (at one's hair).

(b) (*Cos*) ruck, snag.

(c) (*pedacito*) small bit, tag, pinch.

(d) (*de caballo*) dash, short run.

(e) (*Méx: reprimenda*) telling-off*, scolding.

repelús* NM inexplicable fear; **me da ~** it gives me the willies‡, it gives me the shivers.

repeluz: en un ~ ADV (*Cono Sur*) in a flash, in an instant.

repeluzno* NM nervous shiver, slight start of fear.

repensar [1j] VT to rethink, reconsider, think out again.

repente NM (a) (*movimiento*) sudden movement, start, jerk; (*fig*) sudden impulse; **~ de ira** fit of anger.

(b) **de ~** (*de pronto*) suddenly; (*sin avisar*) unexpectedly; (*de golpe*) all at once.

(c) (*Méx Med*) (*acceso*) fit; (*desmayo*) fainting fit.

repentinamente ADV suddenly; unexpectedly; **torcer ~** to turn sharply, make a sharp turn.

repentino ADJ (a) (*súbito*) sudden; (*imprevisto*) unexpected; *cambio* sudden, swift; *curva, vuelta* sharp. (b) **tener repentina compasión** to be quick to pity.

repentización NF sight-reading; ad-lib*, improvisation.

repentizar [1f] VI (*Mús*) to sight-read; (*en discurso etc*) to ad-lib, improvise.

repentón* NM violent start.

repera* NF: **es la ~** it's the tops*.

repercusión NF (a) (*sonido*) (*gen*) repercussion; (*reverberación*) reverberation; echo.

(b) (*fig: consecuencia*) repercussion; **repercusiones** repercussions, after-effects; **las repercusiones de esta decisión** the repercussions of this decision; **de amplia ~, de ancha ~** far-reaching; **tener ~(es) en** to have repercussions on.

repercutir [3a] [1] VT (*And*) to contradict.

[2] VI (a) (*objeto*) to rebound, bounce off; (*sonido*) to re-echo; to reverberate, go on sounding (*o beating etc*).

(b) (*fig*) **~ en** to have repercussions on, have effects on, have an effect on.

(c) (*Méx: oler mal*) to smell bad, stink.

[3] **repercutirse** VR to reverberate.

reperiquete NM (*Méx*) (a) (*baratija*) cheap jewellery. (b) (*baladronada*) brag, boast.

repertoriar [1b] VT to catalogue, list.

repertorio NM (a) (*lista*) list, index, compendium; (*catálogo*) catalogue. (b) (*Teat*) repertoire; repertory. (c) (*Inform*) repertoire.

repesca NF (a) (*Univ*) repeat exam. (b) (*Dep**) play-off (for third place); second chance to qualify.

repescar [1g] VT to give a second chance to.

repeso NM (*And*) bonus, extra.

repetición NF (a) (*gen*) repetition; recurrence. (b) (*Teat etc*) encore; **pedir la ~ de una canción** to encore a song. (c) **fusil de ~** repeater rifle.

repetidamente ADV repeatedly.

repetido ADJ repeated; (*numeroso*) numerous; *sello etc* duplicate; **el tan ~ aviso** the oft-repeated warning; **repetidas veces** repeatedly, over and over again, many times.

repetidor NM (*Rad, TV*) booster, booster station.

repetidora NF repeater rifle.

repetir [31] [1] VT (*gen*) to repeat; (*volver a decir*) to say again; (*volver a hacer*) to do again; (*Teat*) to repeat as an encore, sing (*etc*) again; *lección* to recite, rehearse, go over; *sonido o echo*; *grabación* to repeat, play back; **le repito que es imposible** I repeat that it is impossible, I tell you again it is impossible; **los niños repiten lo que hacen las personas mayores** children imitate adults, children ape their seniors.

[2] VI (a) (*gen*) to repeat; **el pepino repite mucho** cucumber keeps coming back, cucumber gives one bad hiccups.

(b) **~ de un plato** to have a second helping of a dish.

[3] **repetirse** VR (a) (*persona*) to repeat o.s.

(b) (*suceso*) to recur; **¡ojalá no se repita esto!** I hope this won't happen again!

repetitivo ADJ repetitive.

repicado NM copying of (video) tapes, video piracy.

repicar [1g] [1] VT (a) *carne etc* to chop up small.

(b) (*picar*) to prick (again).

(c) *campanas* to ring, peal (merrily).

(d) **~ gordo un acontecimiento*** to celebrate an event in style.

(e) *cinta* to copy, pirate.

[2] **repicarse** VR to boast (*de* about, of).

repintar [1a] [1] VT (*volver a pintar*) to repaint; (*pintar de prisa*) to paint hastily, paint roughly.

[2] **repintarse** VR to pile the make-up on.

repipi* ADJ (*esnob*) posh*; (*afectado*) la-di-da*, affected; arty*; (*precoz*) precocious, knowing for one's years; (*engreído*) stuck-up*; **es una niña ~** she's a little madam, she's an insufferably affected child.

repipiez* NF poshness*; affectation; artiness*; precociousness; stuck-up ways*.

repique NM (a) (*Mús*) peal(ing), ringing; chime. (b) (*: *riña*) tiff, squabble.

repiquete NM (a) (*Mús*) merry peal(ing). (b) (*Mil*) clash. (c) (*Cono Sur Orn*) trill, song. (d) (*And: resentimiento*) pique, resentment.

repiquetear [1a] [1] VT (a) *campanas* to peal joyfully, ring merrily.

(b) *mesa, tambor etc* to tap, beat rapidly, drum lightly on.

[2] VI (a) (*Mús*) to peal out, ring.

(b) (*máquina*) to clatter.

[3] **repiquetearse:** VR to exchange insults, slag one another off‡.

repiqueteo NM (a) (*Mús*) joyful peal(ing), merry ringing. (b) (*en mesa etc*) tapping, drumming; (*de máquina*) clatter.

repisa NF ledge, shelf; (wall) bracket; **~ de chimenea** mantelpiece; **~ de ventana** windowsill.

replana NF (*And*) underworld slang.

replantar [1a] VT to replant.

replanteamiento NM rethink, reconsideration.

replantear [1a] [1] VT *cuestión* to raise again, reopen.

[2] **replantearse** VR: **~ algo** to rethink sth, think again about sth.

replantigarse [1h] VR (*LAm*) = **repanchigarse**.

repleción NF repletion.

replegable ADJ folding, that folds (up); (*Aer*) *tren de aterrizaje* retractable.

replegar [1h y 1j] **1** VT (*doblar*) to fold over; (*de nuevo*) to fold again, refold; *tren de aterrizaje* to retract, draw up.
2 replegarse VR (*Mil*) to withdraw, fall back (in good order; *sobre* on).
repletar [1a] **1** VT to fill completely, stuff full, pack tight.
2 repletarse VR to eat to repletion.
repleto ADJ (a) (*lleno*) replete, full up; ~ **de** filled with, absolutely full of, crammed with; **la plaza estaba repleta de gente** the square was solid with people; **una colección repleta de rarezas** a collection containing innumerable rarities.
(b) **estar** ~ (*persona*) to be full up (*with food*), be replete.
(c) *aspecto* sleek, well-fed.
réplica NF (a) (*respuesta*) answer; retort, rejoinder; (*refutación*) rebuttal; (*Jur*) answer to a charge; ~**s** backchat; **dejar a uno sin ~s** to leave sb speechless. (b) (*Arte*) replica, copy.
replicar [1g] VI to answer, retort, rejoin; (*pey*) to argue, answer back; **¡no repliques!** don't answer back!, I don't want any backchat!
replicón* ADJ argumentative; cheeky, saucy.
repliegue NM (a) (*pliegue*) fold, crease. (b) (*Mil*) withdrawal, retirement.
repoblación NF (*gente*) repopulation, repeopling; (*objetos*) restocking; ~ **forestal** (re)afforestation.
repoblar [1l] VT *país, zona* to repopulate, repeople; *río etc* to restock; (*Bot*) to (re)afforest, plant trees on.
repollo NM cabbage.
repollonco* ADJ (*Cono Sur*), **repolludo*** ADJ tubby*, chunky*.
reponer [2q] **1** VT (a) (*devolver a su lugar*) to replace, put back; *persona* to reinstate; *combustible, surtido etc* to replenish; (*Fin*) to plough back, reinvest; *objeto dañado etc* to replace, pay for (the replacement of).
(b) (*Teat*) to revive, put on again; (*TV*) to repeat.
(c) (*contestar*) to reply (*que that*).
2 reponerse VR (*Med etc*) to recover; ~ **de** to recover from, get over.
repóquer NM (*t* ~ **de ases**) four aces *pl*.
reportaje NM report, article, news item; ~ **gráfico** illustrated report, story in pictures.
reportar [1a] **1** VT (a) (*traer*) to bring, fetch, carry.
(b) *beneficio etc* to obtain.
(c) (*producir*) to give, bring; **esto le habrá reportado algún beneficio** this will have brought him some benefit; **esto le habrá reportado 2 millones** it must have landed him 2 million; **la cosa no le reportó sino disgustos** the affair brought him nothing but trouble.
(d) (*fig: moderar*) to check, restrain.
(e) (*LAm*) (*informar*) to report; (*denunciar*) to denounce, accuse; (*notificar*) to notify, inform.
2 VI (*LAm: a cita*) to turn up (for an appointment).
3 reportarse VR (a) (*controlarse*) to control o.s.; to calm down; **¡repórtate!** control yourself!
(b) (*CAm, Méx: presentarse*) to present o.s., be present.
reporte NM (*CAm, Méx*) report, piece of news.
reportear [1a] **1** VT (a) *suceso* to report (on). (b) (*LAm*) to interview (for the purpose of writing an article); to photograph (for the press).
2 VI to report; to work as a journalist.
reportero, -a NM/F reporter; ~ **gráfico** news photographer, press photographer.
reposabrazos NM INVAR armrest.
reposacabeza(s) NM INVAR headrest.
reposacodos NM INVAR elbow-rest.
reposadamente ADV quietly; gently, restfully; unhurriedly, calmly.
reposadera NF (*CAm*) drain, sewer.
reposado ADJ (*tranquilo*) quiet; (*descansado*) gentle, restful; (*sin prisa*) unhurried, calm.
reposapiés NM INVAR footrest.
reposaplatos NM INVAR tablemat.
reposar [1a] **1** VT: ~ **la comida** to let one's meal go down, settle one's stomach.
2 VI (*descansar*) to rest, repose; (*dormir*) to sleep; (*muerto*) to lie, rest.
3 reposarse VR (*líquido*) to settle.
reposera NF (*LAm*) deckchair, garden chair.
reposición NF (a) (*gen*) replacement. (b) (*Fin*) ploughing-back, reinvestment. (c) (*Teat*) revival; (*TV*) repeat. (d) (*Med y fig*) recovery.
reposicionar [1a] VT to reposition.
repositorio NM repository.
reposo NM rest, repose; ~ **absoluto** (*Med*) complete rest; **guardar** ~ (*Med*) to rest, stay in bed.
repostada NF (*CAm*) rude reply, sharp answer.
repostadero NM refuelling stop.
repostaje NM refuelling, filling up.
repostar [1a] **1** VT *surtido etc* to replenish, renew; ~ **combustible**, ~ **gasolina** (*Aer*) to refuel, (*Aut*) to fill up (with petrol).

2 VI to refuel.
3 repostarse VR to replenish stocks, take on supplies; ~ **de combustible** to refuel.
repostería NF (a) (*tienda*) confectioner's (shop), cake shop. (b) (*arte*) confectionery; (art of) pastrymaking. (c) (*despensa*) larder, pantry.
repostero, -a NM/F (a) (*cocinero*) confectioner, pastrycook. (b) (*And: estantería*) kitchen shelf unit; (*cuarto*) pantry.
repostón* ADJ (*CAm, Méx*) rude, surly.
repregunta NF (*Jur*) cross-examination, cross-questioning.
repreguntar [1a] VT (*Jur*) to cross-examine, cross-question.
reprender [2a] VT to reprimand, tell off*, take to task; *niño* to scold; ~ **algo a uno** to reprimand sb for sth; to criticize sb about sth, reproach sb for sth.
reprensible ADJ reprehensible.
reprensión NF reprimand, rebuke; scolding; criticism, reproach.
represa NF (a) (*captura*) recapture. (b) (*represión*) repression; (*parada*) check, stoppage. (c) (*presa*) dam; (*vertedero*) weir; (*estanque*) pool, lake; (*Carib, Cono Sur*) reservoir; ~ **de molino** millpond.
represalia NF reprisal; **como** ~ **por** as a reprisal for; **tomar** ~**s** to take reprisals, retaliate (*contra* against).
represaliado, -a NM/F victim of a reprisal; person victimized.
represaliar [1b] VT to take reprisals against; to victimize.
represar [1a] VT (a) (*Náut*) to recapture. (b) (*reprimir*) to repress; (*parar*) to check, put a stop to; (*refrenar*) to restrain. (c) *agua* to dam (up); (*fig*) to stem.
representable ADJ (*Teat*): **la obra no es** ~ the play cannot actually be staged, it is not a play for the stage.
representación NF (a) (*gen*) representation; ~ **diplomática** diplomatic representation; embassy; ~ **proporcional** proportional representation; **en** ~ **de** representing, as a representative of; **por** ~ by proxy; **hacer representaciones a** to make representations to; **tener la** ~ **exclusiva de** (*Com*) to be sole agent for.
(b) (*Teat*) (*función*) performance; production; (*de un actor*) playing, acting; **una serie de 350 representaciones** a run of 350 performances.
(c) (*fig: status*) importance, standing; **hombre de** ~ man of some standing.
(d) ~ **visual** (*Inform*) visual display.
representado, -a NM/F (*Jur*) client.
representante NMF (a) (*Com, Pol etc*) representative; (*Teat*) agent. (b) (*Teat: actor*) performer, actor, actress.
representar [1a] **1** VT (a) (*gen*) to represent; to act for; (*simbolizar*) to stand for, symbolize; (*expresar*) to express, depict.
(b) (*Teat*) *obra* to perform, put on, do; to produce; *papel* to act, play, take.
(c) *edad etc* to look; **representa unos 55 años** he looks about 55, from his appearance he's about 55; **ella no representa los años que tiene** she doesn't look her age; **el conserje no representaba ser muy listo** the porter didn't seem to be any too intelligent; **ese traje no representa lo que has gastado en él** that suit does not look as though it's worth what you paid for it.
(d) *detalles, hechos etc* to state, explain; to enumerate; to express; ~ **una dificultad a uno** to represent a difficulty to sb, explain a snag to sb; **representa que lo vendió por ...** he claims that he sold it for ...
(e) (*significar*) to mean; *amenaza* to pose, constitute; **tal acto representaría la guerra** such an act would mean war.
2 representarse VR: ~ **una escena** to imagine a scene, picture a scene to o.s.; ~ **una solución** to envisage a solution; **se me representa la cara que pondrá** I can just imagine his face.
representatividad NF representativeness; representative nature.
representativo ADJ representative.
represión NF repression; suppression.
represivo ADJ, **represor** ADJ repressive.
reprimenda NF reprimand, rebuke.
reprimido **1** ADJ repressed.
2 NM, **reprimida** NF repressed person.
reprimir [3a] **1** VT to repress, suppress; (*refrenar*) to curb, check; *bostezo, risa etc* to suppress, hold in, smother; *rebelión etc* to suppress.
2 reprimirse VR: ~ **de** + *infin* to stop o.s. from + *ger*.
reprisar [1a] VT (*CAm, Cono Sur, Méx*) *obra* to revive, put on again.
reprise[1] NF (*Teat*) revival.
reprise[2] [re'pris] NM (*a veces* F) (*Aut*) acceleration.
repristinación NF restoration to its original state.
repristinar [1a] VT to restore to its original state.
reprivatización NF (re)privatization.
reprivatizar [1f] VT to (re)privatize.
reprobable ADJ blameworthy, to be condemned, reprehensible.
reprobación NF reproval, reprobation; blame; condemnation; **escrito en** ~ **de ...** written in condemnation of ...
reprobador ADJ *mirada etc* reproving, disapproving.
reprobar [1l] VT (a) (*censurar*) to reprove, condemn; (*culpar*) to blame;

(*condenar*) to damn. (**b**) *candidato* to fail.

reprobatorio ADJ = **reprobador.**

réprobo ADJ (*Ecl*) damned.

reprocesado NM, **reprocesamiento** NM reprocessing.

reprocesar [1a] VT to reprocess.

reprochabilidad NF blameworthiness, culpability.

reprochable ADJ blameworthy, culpable.

reprochar [1a] ① VT to reproach; to condemn, censure; **~ algo a uno** to reproach sb for sth; **le reprochan (por) su descuido** they reproach him for his negligence.

② **reprocharse** VR to reproach o.s.; **no tienes nada que reprocharte** you have nothing to reproach yourself for (*o* about).

reproche NM reproach (*a* for); reflection (*a* on); **es un ~ a su honradez** it is a reflection on his honesty; **nos miró con ~** he looked at us reproachfully.

reproducción NF reproduction.

reproducir [3c] ① VT to reproduce; (*Bio*) to reproduce, breed.

② **reproducirse** VR (**a**) to reproduce; to breed.

(**b**) (*condiciones etc*) to be reproduced; (*suceso*) to happen again, recur; **se le han reproducido los síntomas** the symptoms have recurred; **si se reproducen los desórdenes** if the disorders happen again.

reproductor ① ADJ reproductive.

② **~ de compact disc, ~ de discos compactos** CD player, compact disc player.

reprografía NF reprography.

reprogramar [1a] VT to reprogram(me); *deuda etc* to reschedule.

reps NM (*tela*) rep.

reptar [1a] VI to creep, crawl; to snake along.

reptil ① ADJ reptilian.

② NM reptile.

república NF republic; **~ bananera** banana republic; **R~ Dominicana** Dominican Republic; **R~ Árabe Unida** United Arab Republic; **Segunda R~** Second Spanish Republic.

republicanismo NM republicanism.

republicano, -a ADJ, NM/F republican.

repudiación NF repudiation.

repudiar [1b] VT *mujer, violencia etc* to repudiate; (*desconocer*) to disown, disavow; *herencia* to renounce.

repudio NM repudiation.

repudrir [3a] ① VT (**a**) (*pudrir*) to rot.

(**b**) (*fig*) to gnaw at, eat up, devour.

② **repudrirse** VR to suffer inwardly, suffer gnawing doubts (*etc*); to eat one's heart out, pine away.

repuesto ① PTP *de* **reponer.**

② NM (**a**) (*provisión*) stock, store; (*abastecimiento*) supply.

(**b**) (*reemplazo*) replacement; (*de pluma*) refill.

(**c**) (*Aut, Mec*) spare, spare part, extra (*US*); **rueda de ~** spare wheel; **y llevamos otro de ~** and we have another as a spare (*o* in reserve).

(**d**) (*Esp: mueble*) sideboard, buffet.

repugnancia NF (**a**) (*asco*) disgust, loathing, repugnance; (*aversión*) aversion (*hacia, por* to).

(**b**) (*moral*) repugnance.

(**c**) (*desgana*) reluctance; **lo hizo con ~** he did it reluctantly.

(**d**) (*Filos*) opposition, incompatibility.

repugnante ADJ disgusting, loathsome, revolting.

repugnar [1a] ① VT (**a**) (*dar asco a*) to disgust, revolt, nauseate; to fill with loathing; **ese olor me repugna** that smell revolts me, I loathe that smell; **me repugna tener que mirarlo** I hate having to watch it, I loathe having to watch it.

(**b**) (*odiar*) to hate, loathe; **siempre repugnaba el engaño** he always hated deceit.

(**c**) (*contradecir*) to contradict.

② VI (**a**) (*ser asqueroso*) to be disgusting, be revolting.

(**b**) = **3.**

③ **repugnarse** VR to conflict, be in opposition; to contradict each other; **las dos teorías se repugnan** the two theories are not compatible, the two theories contradict each other.

repujado ADJ embossed.

repujar [1a] VT to emboss, work in relief.

repulgado ADJ affected.

repulgar [1h] VT (**a**) (*Cos*) to hem, edge. (**b**) (*Culin*) to crimp.

repulgo NM (**a**) (*Cos*) hem; hemstitch. (**b**) (*Culin*) crimping, fancy edging, decorated border; **~s de empanada** silly scruples.

repulido ADJ (**a**) *objeto* polished, repolished. (**b**) (*fig*) *persona* dressed up, dolled up*; spick and span, very smart.

repulir [3a] ① VT (**a**) *objeto* to polish up; to repolish (*t fig*).

(**b**) (*fig*) *persona* to dress up; to spruce up.

② **repulirse** VR (*fig*) to dress up, doll o.s. up*; to smarten up.

repulsa NF (**a**) (*Mil*) check. (**b**) (*fig: rechazo*) rejection, refusal; rebuff; **sufrir una ~** to meet with a rebuff. (**c**) (*fig*) (*censura*) strong condemnation; (*reprimenda*) severe reprimand.

repulsar [1a] VT (**a**) (*Mil*) to repulse; to check. (**b**) (*fig*) *solicitud* to reject, refuse; *oferta, persona* to rebuff. (**c**) (*fig: condenar*) to condemn in strong terms.

repulsión NF (**a**) = **repulsa.** (**b**) (*emoción*) repulsion, disgust, aversion. (**c**) (*Fís*) repulsion.

repulsivo ADJ disgusting, revolting, loathsome.

repunta NF (**a**) (*Geog*) point, headland. (**b**) (*indicio*) sign, indication, hint. (**c**) (*resentimiento*) pique. (**d**) (*disgusto*) slight upset, tiff. (**e**) (*LAm Agr*) round-up. (**f**) (*And: riada*) sudden rise (*of a river*), flash flood.

repuntar [1a] ① VT (*Cono Sur, Méx*) *ganado* to round up.

② VI (**a**) (*marea*) to turn.

(**b**) (*LAm*) (*manifestarse*) to (begin to) make itself felt, give the first signs; (*persona*) to turn up unexpectedly.

(**c**) (*LAm: río*) to rise suddenly; (*Cono Sur*) to rise to its previous level.

③ **repuntarse** VR (**a**) (*vino*) to begin to sour, turn.

(**b**) (*persona*) to get cross.

(**c**) (*2 personas*) to fall out, have a tiff.

repunte NM (**a**) (*Náut*) turn of the tide; (*de río*) level; rise. (**b**) (*LAm Agr*) round-up. (**c**) (*Fin*) rise in share prices; (*Econ*) upturn, recovery.

reputación NF reputation; standing.

reputado ADJ (*t bien ~*) highly reputed, reputable.

reputar [1a] VT (*gen*) to repute; (*estimar*) to esteem; (*considerar*) to deem, consider; **~ a uno de** (*o por*) **inteligente** to consider sb intelligent; **le reputan no apto para el cargo** they think him unsuitable for the post; **una colección reputada en mucho** a highly esteemed collection.

requebrar [1j] VT to say nice things to, flatter, compliment; **~ a una de amores** to court sb.

requemado ADJ scorched; parched; *piel* tanned, bronzed; *comida* overdone.

requemar [1a] ① VT (**a**) (*fuego etc*) to scorch; *planta* to parch, scorch, dry up; *piel* to tan; *comida* to overdo, burn; *lengua* to burn, sting.

(**b**) (*fig*) *sangre* to inflame, set afire.

② **requemarse** VR (*V* VT) (**a**) to scorch; to parch, get parched, dry up; to tan; to burn.

(**b**) (*fig*) to harbour resentment, smoulder with indignation (*etc*).

requenete ADJ (*Carib*), **requeneto** ADJ (*And, Carib*) = **rechoncho.**

requerimiento NM (**a**) (*petición*) request; (*demanda*) demand; (*llamada*) summons (*t Jur*); **a ~ de** at the request of. (**b**) (*notificación*) notification.

requerir [3i] ① VT (**a**) (*necesitar*) to need, require; **esto requiere cierto cuidado** this requires some care.

(**b**) (*pedir*) to request, ask, invite; **~ a uno para que haga algo** to ask sb to do sth.

(**c**) (*mandar traer*) to send for, call for; (*buscar*) to hunt around for; (*con dedos*) to feel for; *persona* to send for, summon; **el ministro requirió sus gafas** the minister sent for his spectacles; **el ministro le requirió para que lo explicara** the minister summoned him to explain it.

(**d**) (*t ~ de amores a*) *mujer* = **requebrar.**

② VI: **~ de** (*LAm*) to need, require.

requesón NM cottage cheese; curd(s).

requete...* PREFIJO INTENSIVO, *p.ej.* **requeteguapa** quite extraordinarily pretty; **me parece requetebién** it seems absolutely splendid to me; **lo tendré muy requetepensado** I'll think it over very thoroughly; **una joven requetemonísima** a fabulously attractive girl*; **una requetesuperminifalda** an ultrashort miniskirt.

requeté NM (**a**) (*Hist*) Carlist militiaman. (**b**) (*) he-man*, tough guy*.

requiebro NM amorous compliment, flirtatious remark.

réquiem NM, PL **réquiems** requiem.

requilorios NMPL (**a**) (*trámites*) tedious formalities, red tape; petty conditions.

(**b**) (*adornos*) silly adornments, unnecessary frills.

(**c**) (*preliminares*) time-wasting preliminaries; (*rodeos*) roundabout way of saying something.

(**d**) (*elementos dispersos*) bits and pieces.

requintar [1a] ① VT (**a**) (*LAm*) *cuerda* to tighten, make taut.

(**b**) **~ a uno** (*And, Méx*) to impose one's will on sb, push sb around.

(**c**) (*And: insultar*) to abuse, swear at.

② VI (*Carib: parecerse*) to resemble each other.

requisa NF (**a**) (*inspección*) survey, inspection. (**b**) (*Mil*) requisition. (**c**) (*LAm: confiscación*) seizure, confiscation.

requisar [1a] VT (**a**) (*Mil*) to requisition. (**b**) (*LAm: confiscar*) to seize, confiscate. (**c**) (*Cono Sur: registrar*) to search.

requisición NF (**a**) (*Mil*) requisition. (**b**) (*Cono Sur, Méx: embargo*) seizure, requisition. (**c**) (*Cono Sur, Méx: registro*) search.

▼ **requisito** NM requirement, requisite; qualification; **~ previo** prerequisite; **llenar los ~s** to fulfil the requirements; **tener los ~s para un cargo** to have the essential qualifications for a post.

requisitoria NF demand; (*LAm Jur*) examination, interrogation; (*orden*) writ.

res NF (**a**) (*animal*) beast, animal; **~ lanar** sheep; **~ vacuna** cow, bull, ox; **100 ~es** 100 animals, 100 head of cattle. **(b)** (*Méx: carne*) steak; beef. **(c)** (*Cono Sur*) body.

resabiado ADJ cunning, crafty; that has learned his lesson; *caballo* vicious.

resabiarse [1b] VR to acquire a bad habit, get into evil ways.

resabido ADJ **(a)** *dato* thoroughly well known; **lo tengo sabido y ~** of course I know all that perfectly well. **(b)** *persona* pretentious, pedantic, know-all.

resabio NM **(a)** (*dejo*) nasty taste (in the mouth), unpleasant aftertaste; **tener ~s de** (*fig*) to smack of. **(b)** (*vicio*) bad habit, unpleasant way; (*de caballo*) vicious nature.

resabioso ADJ (*And, Carib*) = **resabiado.**

resaca NF **(a)** (*Náut*) undertow, undercurrent; backward movement (of the waves).
(b) (*: después de beber*) hangover*.
(c) (*fig*) reaction, backlash; **la ~ blanca** the white backlash.
(d) (*And, CAm, Méx*: *aguardiente*) strong liquor; bad liquor.
(e) (*Cono Sur: en playa*) line of driftwood and rubbish (*left by the tide*).
(f) (*Cono Sur*: *personas*) dregs of society.
(g) (*Carib: paliza*) beating.
(h) la ~ (*Méx*) the very essence; (*iró*) the hardened criminal.

resacado [1] ADJ (*Méx*) (*tacaño*) mean, stingy; (*débil*) weak; (*estúpido*) stupid; **es lo ~** (*Méx*) it's the worst of its kind.
[2] NM (*And*) (contraband) liquor.

resacar [1g] VT (*And, Méx*) to distil (a second time).

resacoso [1] ADJ hung-over*.
[2] NM, **resacosa** NF person with a hangover*.

resalado ADJ lively, vivacious, attractive; *V* **re...**

resaltable ADJ notable, noteworthy.

resaltante ADJ (*LAm*) outstanding.

resaltar [1a] VI **(a)** (*salir*) to jut out, stick out, stick up, project.
(b) (*rebotar*) to bounce, rebound.
(c) (*fig*) to stand out; to be outstanding; **hacer ~ algo** to throw sth into relief, set sth off (*contra* against a background of); (*fig*) to emphasize sth; **~ como una mosca en la leche** to stick out like a sore thumb.

resalte NM projection.

resalto NM **(a)** (*saliente*) projection. **(b)** (*rebote*) bounce, rebound.

resanar [1a] VT to restore, repair, make good.

resaquero ADJ (*LAm*) = **remolón 1.**

resarcimiento NM repayment; indemnification, compensation.

resarcir [3b] [1] VT (*pagar*) to repay; (*compensar*) to indemnify, compensate; **~ a uno de una cantidad** to repay sb a sum; **~ a uno de una pérdida** to compensate sb for a loss.
[2] **resarcirse** VR: **~ de** to make up for, compensate o.s. for; to retrieve.

resbalada NF (*LAm*) slip.

resbaladero NM slippery place; (*de parque etc*) slide, chute.

resbaladilla NF (*LAm*) slide, chute.

resbaladizo ADJ slippery.

resbalar [1a] [1] VT **(a)** (*sin querer*) to slip, slip up (*en, sobre* on); (*deslizarse*) to slide, slither (*por* along, down); (*Aut etc*) to skid; **el embrague resbala** the clutch is slipping; **le resbalaban las lágrimas por las mejillas** tears were trickling down her cheeks.
(b) (*fig: fallar*) to slip up, make a slip.
(c) (*) **me resbala** its leaves me cold; **las críticas le resbalan** criticism runs off him like water off a duck's back.
[2] **resbalarse** VR **(a)** = **1. (b)** (*: rajarse*) to cop out*.

resbalón NM **(a)** slip; slide, slither; skid. **(b)** (*fig*) slip, error; **dar un ~** to slip up.

resbalosa NF a Peruvian dance.

resbaloso ADJ **(a)** (*LAm: resbaladizo*) slippery. **(b)** (*Méx*: *coqueta*) flirtatious, coquettish.

rescatar [1a] [1] VT **(a)** *cautivo* to ransom; *ciudad etc* to recapture, recover; *prenda* to redeem; *póliza* to surrender.
(b) (*salvar*) to save, rescue.
(c) *dinero, posesión etc* to get back, recover, regain possession of.
(d) *tiempo perdido* to make up; *delitos* to atone for, redeem, expiate.
(e) *tierras* to reclaim.
(f) (*Méx*: *revender*) to resell.
[2] VI (*And*) to peddle goods from village to village.

rescate NM (*V* VT) **(a)** ransom; recapture, recovery; redemption.
(b) rescue; **operaciones de ~** rescue operations; **acudir** (*o* **venir**) **al ~ de** to go (*o* come) to the rescue of.
(c) recovery.
(d) atonement, expiation.
(e) reclamation; **~ de terrenos** land reclamation.

rescindible ADJ: **contrato ~ por ambas partes** a contract that can be cancelled by either side.

rescindir [3a] VT *contrato etc* to rescind, cancel; *privilegio* to withdraw; *puestos de trabajo* to cut back.

rescisión NF cancellation; withdrawal; cutback.

rescoldo NM **(a)** (*lit*) embers, hot ashes. **(b)** (*fig*) lingering doubt, scruple; **avivar el ~** (*fig*) to stir up the dying embers.

rescontrar [1l] VT (*Com, Fin*) to offset, balance.

resecamiento NM drying.

resecar¹ [1g] [1] VT (*secar*) to dry off, dry thoroughly; (*quemar*) to parch, scorch, burn.
[2] **resecarse** VR to dry up, get too dry.

resecar² [1g] VT (*Med*) to cut out, remove; to resect.

resección NF resection.

reseco ADJ **(a)** (*lit*) very dry, too dry; parched. **(b)** (*fig*) skinny, lean.

reseda NF, **resedá** NF (*LAm*) mignonette.

resellarse* [1a] VR to switch parties, change one's views.

resembrado NM re-sowing, re-seeding.

resembrar [1j] VT to re-sow, re-seed.

resentido ADJ resentful; bitter; sullen; **es un ~** he's bitter, he's got a chip on his shoulder, he feels hard done by.

resentimiento NM resentment; bitterness.

resentirse [3i] VR **(a)** **~ con algo, ~ por algo** (*t* **estar resentido por algo**) to resent sth, be offended about sth, feel bitter about sth.
(b) (*debilitarse*) to remain weak, be weakened, suffer; **con los años se resintió su salud** his health suffered (*o* was affected) over the years; **los cimientos se resintieron con el terremoto** the foundations were weakened by the earthquake; **sin que se resienta el dólar** without the dollar being affected.
(c) **~ de** *defecto* to suffer from, labour under; *consecuencias etc* to feel the effects of; **me resiento todavía del golpe** I can still feel the effects of the injury.

reseña NF **(a)** (*resumen*) outline, account, summary; (*Liter*) review; (*Dep etc*) report (*de* on), account (*de* of).
(b) (*descripción*) brief description (*for identification purposes*).
(c) (*Mil*) review.
(d) (*Cono Sur: esp Chile*) procession held on Passion Sunday.

reseñable ADJ **(a)** *ofensa* for which one can be booked. **(b)** (*destacado*) noteworthy, notable; worth mentioning.

reseñante NMF (*Liter*) reviewer.

reseñar [1a] VT **(a)** (*describir*) to describe (*for identification purposes*); (*narrar*) to write up, write a brief account of; (*Liter*) to review; *partido* to report on.
(b) *delincuente* to book.

reseñista NMF (*Liter*) reviewer.

resero NM (*And, CAm, Cono Sur*) cowboy, herdsman; (*comerciante*) cattle dealer.

▼ **reserva** [1] NF **(a)** (*acto*) reservation; **la ~ de asientos no se paga** there is no charge for seat reservation (*o* for reserving seats).
(b) (*provisión, surtido*) reserve (*t Com*); stock, holding; **~ para amortización, ~ para depreciaciones** depreciation allowance; **~ en metálico** cash reserves; **~s monetarias** financial reserves; **~s ocultas** hidden reserves; **~ de oro** gold reserve; **las ~s mundiales de petróleo** world reserves of oil, world stocks of oil; **de ~** spare, reserve (*atr*), emergency *atr*); **tener algo de ~** to have sth in reserve, keep sth for an emergency.
(c) (*Geog etc*) reserve, reservation; **~ de caza** game reserve; **~ de indios** Indian reservation; **~ natural** nature reserve.
(d) (*Mil*) reserve.
(e) (*cualidad*) reserve; discretion, reticence; (*pey*) coldness, distance.
▼ **(f)** (*secreto*) privacy; **con ~ in** confidence; **escribir con la mayor ~** to write in the strictest confidence; **'absoluta ~'** (*anuncio*) 'strictest confidence'.
▼ **(g)** (*salvedad*) reserve, reservation; **~ mental** mental reservation; **con ciertas ~s** with certain reservations; **hay que tomar esa noticia con ~** that news should be taken with reservations; **sin ~(s)** unreservedly, without qualification.
(h) a ~ de except for; **a ~ de que ...** unless ..., unless it should turn out that ...
[2] NM (*vino*) wine which is at least 3 years old.

RESERVA

🛈 *Quality Spanish wine is often graded* **Crianza,** **Reserva** *or* **Gran Reserva** *according to the length of bottle-ageing and barrel-ageing it has undergone. Red* **Reserva** *wines are at least three years old, having spent a minimum of one year in cask, and white* **Reserva** *wines are at least two years old with at least six months spent in cask. A* **Gran Reserva** *wine is a top-quality wine. A red must be aged for at least 2 years in an oak cask and 3 years in the bottle. White wine must be aged for 48 months, with at least 6 months in cask.*
⇨ *See also* CRIANZA

---

reservación NF reservation.

reservadamente ADV confidentially, privately.

reservado [1] ADJ **(a)** *asiento etc* reserved; **'~s todos los derechos'** 'all rights reserved'.
(b) *actitud, persona* reserved; discreet, reticent; (*pey*) cold, distant.

(c) *asunto etc* confidential, private.
　2 NM (*en restaurante etc*) private room; (*Ferro*) reserved compartment.
▼ **reservar** [1a] 1 VT **(a)** (*gen*) to reserve; (*guardar*) to keep, keep in reserve, set aside; *asientos etc* to reserve, book; **lo reserva para el final** he's keeping it till last; **ha reservado lo mejor para sí** he has kept the best part for himself.
(b) (*ocultar*) to conceal; (*callar*) to keep to oneself, refuse to tell; *opinión etc* to reserve; **prefiero ~ los detalles** I prefer to keep the details to myself.
　2 **reservarse** VR to save o.s. (*para* for); to keep up one's strength; to bide one's time; **no bebo porque me reservo para más tarde** I'm not drinking because I have to be fit for later on.
reservista NMF reservist.
reservón* ADJ excessively reserved; cagey*, close; very quiet.
resfriado 1 ADJ **(a)** **estar ~** to have a cold. **(b)** (*Cono Sur**) indiscreet, loud-mouthed.
　2 NM cold; chill; **coger un ~** to catch a cold.
resfriar [1c] 1 VT **(a)** (*gen*) to cool, chill.
(b) (*fig*) *ardor* to cool.
(c) **~ a uno** (*Med*) to give sb a cold.
　2 VI (*Met*) to turn cold.
　3 **resfriarse** VR **(a)** (*Med*) to catch (a) cold.
(b) (*fig: relaciones*) to cool off.
resfrío NM (*LAm*) cold.
resguardar [1a] 1 VT to protect, shield (*de* from); to safeguard.
　2 **resguardarse** VR **(a)** (*protegerse*) to defend o.s., protect o.s.; to safeguard o.s.
(b) (*obrar con cautela*) to go warily, proceed with caution.
resguardo NM **(a)** (*protección*) defence, protection; safeguard; **servir de ~ a uno** to be a protection to sb; **~ de consigna** cloakroom check.
(b) (*Com etc*) (*vale*) voucher, certificate; (*garantía*) guarantee; (*recibo etc*) slip, check, cover note, receipt; (*de cheque*) stub; (*de consigna etc*) ticket.
(c) (*Náut*) sea room; safe distance.
residencia NF **(a)** (*gen*) residence; (*Univ*) hall of residence, hostel; **~ para ancianos, ~ para jubilados** rest home, old people's home; **~ canina** dogs' home, kennels; **~ sanitaria** hospital; **~ secundaria, segunda ~** second home. **(b)** (*Jur*) investigation, inquiry. **(c)** **~ vigilada** (*And*) house arrest.
residencial 1 ADJ residential.
　2 NM (*And*) small hotel, boarding-house.
　3 NF estate, housing development; (*CAm*) residential area.
residenciar [1b] 1 VT (*Jur*) to conduct a judicial inquiry into, investigate.
　2 **residenciarse** VR to take up residence, establish o.s., settle.
residente 1 ADJ resident; **no ~** non-resident.
　2 NMF resident; **no ~** non-resident.
residir [3a] VI **(a)** (*gen*) to reside, live, dwell.
(b) (*fig*) **~ en** to reside in, lie in; to consist in; **la autoridad reside en el gobernador** authority rests with the governor; **la dificultad reside en que ...** the difficulty lies in the fact that ...
residual ADJ residual, residuary; **aguas ~es** sewage.
residuo NM residue; (*Mat*) remainder; (*Quím etc*) residuum; **~s** (*restos*) remains; (*basura*) refuse, waste; rubbish; (*sobras*) left-overs; (*Téc*) waste products; **~s nucleares** nuclear waste; **~s radiactivos** radioactive waste; **~s sólidos** solid waste; **~s tóxicos** toxic waste.
resignación NF resignation.
resignadamente ADV resignedly, with resignation.
resignado ADJ resigned.
resignar [1a] 1 VT to resign, give up, renounce; *mando* to hand over (*en* to); *puesto* to resign.
　2 **resignarse** VR to resign o.s. (*a, con* to); **~ a + infin** to resign o.s. to + *ger*.
resina NF **(a)** resin. **(b)** (*Méx*) torch (of resinous wood).
resinoso ADJ resinous.
resistencia NF **(a)** (*gen*) resistance; stand; **la R~** (*Pol*) the Resistance; **~ a la enfermedad** resistance to disease; **~ pasiva** passive resistance; **oponer ~ a** to resist, oppose, stand out against.
(b) (*del cuerpo etc*) endurance, stamina; (*fuerza*) strength; staying power; (*dureza*) toughness; (*de tela etc*) strength, toughness; **el maratón es una prueba de ~** the marathon is a test of endurance; **la ~ que necesitan tener los montañistas** the toughness (o stamina) which mountaineers need.
(c) (*oposición*) opposition; (*renuencia*) unwillingness (*para* + *infin* to + *infin*); **luchar con la ~ de sus colegas** to fight against the opposition of one's colleagues, try to overcome the hostility of one's colleagues.
resistente 1 ADJ resistant (*a* to); *tela etc* strong, tough; hard-wearing; (*Bot*) hardy; **~ al calor** resistant to heat, heat-resistant; **~ al fuego** fireproof; **hacerse ~** (*Med*) to build up a resistance (*a* to).
　2 NMF resistance fighter.

resistible ADJ resistible.
resistir [3a] 1 VT **(a)** *peso* to bear, support; *presión etc* to bear, withstand.
(b) *enemigo* to resist; *ataque* to resist, withstand; to stand up to; *propuesta* to resist, oppose, make a stand against; *tentación* to resist.
(c) *agotamiento, decepción etc* to put up with, endure, withstand; **no puedo ~ este frío** I can't bear (o stand) this cold; **no lo resisto un momento más** I'm not putting up with this a moment longer.
(d) **~ la mirada de uno** to stare back at sb; to stare sb out.
　2 VI **(a)** (*gen*) to resist; (*luchar*) to struggle; (*combatir*) to put up a fight, fight back; (*seguir resistiendo*) to hold out.
(b) (*durar*) to last, still go on, endure; **el coche resiste todavía** the car is still going; **el equipo no puede ~ mucho tiempo más** the team can't last out much longer; **no podíamos ~ del cansancio** we were so tired we couldn't go on any longer.
　3 **resistirse** VR **(a)** = 2 **(a)**.
(b) **~ a + infin** to refuse to + *infin*, find it hard to + *infin*, resist + *ger*; to be unwilling to + *infin*, be reluctant to + *infin*; **no me resisto a citar algunos versos** I can't resist quoting a few lines; **me resisto a creerlo** I refuse to believe it, I find it hard to believe; **se me resiste pasar sin saludarle** I cannot possibly pass by without calling on him.
(c) **se le resiste la química** he can't get on with chemistry, chemistry comes very hard to him.
resituar [1e] VT *país* to put back on track; *debate, concepto* to redefine.
resma NF ream.
resobado ADJ (*fig*) hackneyed, trite, well-worn.
resobar [1a] VT **(a)** (*manosear*) to finger, paw; to muck about*. **(b)** (*fig*) *tema* to work to death.
resobrino, -a NM/F first cousin once removed.
resol NM glare of the sun; reflected sunlight.
resolana NF (*LAm*) **(a)** (*luz del sol*) sunlight. **(b)** = **resol**. **(c)** = **resolano**.
resolano NM suntrap, sunny place.
resollar [1l] VI **(a)** (*respirar*) to breathe heavily, breathe noisily; (*jadear*) to puff and blow; to wheeze.
(b) (*fig*) **escuchar sin ~** to listen without saying a word in reply, listen scarcely daring to breathe; **hace tiempo que no resuella** he has given no sign of life for some time, it's a long time since we heard from him.
resoltarse [1l] VR (*And*) to overstep the mark.
resolución NF **(a)** (*decisión*) decision; **~ fatal** decision to take one's own life; **tomar una ~** to take a decision.
(b) (*de problema: acto*) solving; (*respuesta*) solution; **un problema de ~ nada fácil** a problem which it is not easy to (re)solve.
(c) (*Parl etc*) resolution; motion; **~ judicial** legal ruling.
(d) (*cualidad*) resolution, resolve, determination; decisiveness; **obrar con ~** to act with determination, act boldly.
(e) **en ~** in a word, in short, to sum up.
(f) (*Inform*) **alta ~** high resolution; **baja ~** low resolution.
(g) (*Cono Sur: terminación*) finishing, completion.
resolutivo ADJ decisive.
resoluto ADJ = **resuelto 2.**
resolver [2h; PTP **resuelto**] 1 VT **(a)** *problema* to solve, resolve; *crimen* to solve; *duda* to settle; *asunto* to decide, settle; *modo de obrar* to decide on; **crimen sin ~** unsolved crime.
(b) (*Quím*) to dissolve.
(c) *cuerpo de materiales etc* to analyse, divide up, resolve (*en* into).
　2 VI **(a)** to resolve, decide; **~ a favor de uno** to resolve in sb's favour.
(b) **~ hacer algo** to resolve to do sth.
　3 **resolverse** VR **(a)** (*problema etc*) to resolve itself, work out.
(b) **~ en** to resolve itself into; to be transformed into; **todo se resolvió en una riña más** in the end it came down to one more quarrel.
(c) (*decidir*) to decide, make up one's mind; **~ a + infin** to resolve to + *infin*; **~ por algo** to decide on sth; **hay que ~ por el uno o el otro** you'll have to make up your mind one way or the other.
resonador NM resonator.
resonancia NF **(a)** (*repercusión*) resonance; (*eco*) echo. **(b)** (*fig: consecuencia*) wide importance, widespread effect; **tener ~** to have repercussions, cause a stir, have a considerable effect.
resonante ADJ **(a)** (*lit*) resonant; ringing, echoing, resounding. **(b)** (*fig*) *éxito etc* tremendous, resounding.
resonar [1l] VI to resound, ring, echo (*de* with).
resondrar* [1a] VI (*And*) to tell off*, tick off*.
resongar [1a] VT (*LAm*) = **rezongar.**
resoplar [1a] VI = **resollar**; (*de ira etc*) to snort; to pant.
resoplido NM **(a)** (*respiración*) heavy breathing, noisy breathing; (*jadeo*) puff, puffing; (*resuello*) wheeze; (*bufido*) snort; **dar ~s to** breathe heavily, puff; (*de motor*) to chug, puff; to labour.
(b) (*fig*) sharp answer.

---

resorber [2a] VT to reabsorb.

resorción NF resorption, reabsorption.

resorte NM (**a**) (*muelle*) spring.
(**b**) (*cualidad*) elasticity; springiness, resilience.
(**c**) (*fig*) (*medio*) means, expedient; (*enchufe*) contact; (*influencia*) influence; **tocar ~s** to pull strings; **tocar todos los ~s** to mobilize all one's influential friends, bring influence to bear from all sides.
(**d**) (*LAm*: *gomita*) elastic band.
(**e**) (*LAm*) (*responsabilidad*) responsibility; (*incumbencia*) concern; (*Jur*) authority; jurisdiction; **no es de mi ~** it's not my concern.

respaldar [1a] ☐1 VT (**a**) *documento* to endorse.
(**b**) (*fig*) to back, support.
(**c**) (*LAm*) (*asegurar*) to ensure; (*garantizar*) to guarantee, safeguard.
(**d**) (*Inform*) to back up.
☐2 **respaldarse** VR (**a**) to lean back, sprawl, loll (*contra* against, *en* on).
(**b**) **~ con, ~ en** (*fig*) to take one's stand on, base o.s. on.

respaldo NM (**a**) (*de silla etc*) back.
(**b**) (*Hort*) wall.
(**c**) (*de documento*) back; (*firma etc*) endorsement; **firmar al ~, firmar en el ~** to sign on the back.
(**d**) (*fig*) support, backing; (*esp LAm*) (*ayuda*) help; (*garantía*) guarantee; **operación de ~** back-up operation, support operation.

respectar [1a] VT to concern, relate to; **por lo que respecta a** as for, with regard to.

respectivamente ADV respectively.

respective NMF: **mi ~** (*Esp*) my other half (*spouse*).

respectivo ☐1 ADJ respective.
☐2 **en lo ~ a** *como* PREP as regards, with regard to.

respecto NM: **al ~** in the matter, with regard to the subject under discussion; **a ese ~** on that score; **no sé nada al ~** I know nothing about it; **bajo ese ~** in that respect; (**con**) **~ a, ~ de** with regard to, in relation to; (**con**) **~ a mí** as for me.

respetabilidad NF respectability.

respetable ☐1 ADJ respectable.
☐2 NM: **el ~** (*Teat*) the audience; (*hum*) the public, ≃ the great British sporting public.

respetablemente ADV respectably.

▼ **respetar** [1a] VT to respect; **hacerse ~** to win respect; (*establecerse*) to establish o.s., win a proper position; (*imponerse*) to impose one's will.

respeto NM (**a**) (*consideración*) respect, regard, consideration; **~ a la opinión ajena** respect for other people's opinions; **~ de sí mismo** self-respect; **~ a la conveniencia, ~s humanos** respect for the conventions, consideration for the susceptibilities of others; **por ~ a** out of consideration for; **¡un ~!** show some respect!; watch what you're saying!; **campar por sus ~s** to act independently, strike out on one's own; (*pey*) to show no consideration for others, be entirely self-centred; **faltar al ~, perder el ~** to be disrespectful (*a* to).
(**b**) **~s** respects; **presentar sus ~s a** to pay one's respects to.
(**c**) **de ~** best, reserve (*atr*); special; **cuarto de ~** best room; **estar de ~** to be all dressed up.

respetuosamente ADV respectfully.

respetuosidad NF respectfulness.

respetuoso ADJ respectful.

réspice NM (**a**) (*respuesta*) sharp answer, curt reply. (**b**) (*reprimenda*) severe reprimand.

respingado ADJ *nose* snub, turned-up.

respingar [1h] ☐1 VI (**a**) (*caballo*) to shy, balk; to start.
(**b**) (*fig*) to kick, show oneself unwilling, dig one's heels in.
(**c**) = **2**.
☐2 **respingarse** VR (*vestido*) to ride up, curl up.

respingo NM (**a**) (*sobresalto*) shy; start; (*de dolor*) wince; **dar un ~ to** start, jump.
(**b**) (*fig*) gesture of disgust; flounce.
(**c**) (*Cos*) **la chaqueta me hace un ~ aquí** the jacket rides up here.
(**d**) (*fig*) = **réspice** (**a**) y (**b**).

respingón ADJ *nariz* snub, turned-up.

respingona NF *traditional Castilian dance*.

respirable ADJ breathable.

respiración NF (**a**) (*gen*) breathing, respiration; (*una ~*) breath; **~ artificial, ~ mecánica** artificial respiration; **~ boca a boca** kiss of life, mouth-to-mouth resuscitation; (*fig*) revitalization; **contener la ~ to** hold one's breath; **quedarse sin ~** (*lit*) to be out of breath; (*fig*) to be knocked all of a heap; **llegar sin ~** to arrive exhausted.
(**b**) (*ventilación etc*) ventilation.

respiradero NM (**a**) (*Téc*) vent, valve. (**b**) (*fig*) respite, breathing space.

respirador NM breathing tube, snorkel.

respirar [1a] ☐1 VT (**a**) to breathe; *gas etc* to breathe in, inhale.
(**b**) **respira confianza** she exudes (*o* oozes) confidence.
☐2 VI (**a**) (*gen*) to breathe; to draw breath; **~ con dificultad** to

breathe with difficulty, gasp for breath; **sin ~** without a break, without respite; **paramos durante 5 minutos para ~** we stopped for 5 minutes to get our breath back.
(**b**) (*fig*: *después de esfuerzo, choque etc*) to breathe again; **¡respiro!** that's a relief! **no dejar ~ a uno** to keep on at sb, badger sb, make sb's life a misery; **no poder ~** to be all in; to be up to one's eyes (with work *etc*).
(**c**) **no ~** (*fig*) to say absolutely nothing; **estuvo escuchándole sin ~** he listened to him in complete silence; **los niños le miraban sin ~** the children watched him with bated breath.
(**d**) (*ventilarse*) to be ventilated.

respiratorio ADJ respiratory; breathing (*atr*).

respiro NM (**a**) (*gen*) breathing. (**b**) (*fig*) respite, breathing space; (*descanso*) rest; (*Com etc*) extension of time, period of grace; (*Jur*) suspension; reprieve.

respis NM = **réspice**.

resplandecer [2d] VI (**a**) (*relucir*) to shine; to gleam, glitter, glow; to blaze. (**b**) (*fig*) to shine; **~ de felicidad** to shine with happiness, be radiant with happiness.

resplandeciente ADJ (**a**) (*brillante*) shining; gleaming, glittering, glowing; blazing. (**b**) (*fig*) radiant (*de* with).

resplandor NM (**a**) (*brillantez*) brilliance, brightness, radiance; gleam, glitter, glow; blaze. (**b**) (*Cono Sur, Méx*) = **resolana**. (**c**) (*Méx*) (*luz del sol*) sunlight; (*resol*) warmth of the sun; (*brillo*) glare.

responder [2a] ☐1 VT to answer; to reply to; **pero él me responde con injurias** but he answers me with insults.
☐2 VI (**a**) (*gen*) to answer, reply; (*eco*) to answer; **~ a una pregunta** answer a question.
(**b**) (*fig*) to reply, respond; **~ con grosería a una cortesía** to return rudeness for courtesy, answer a courteous request rudely.
(**c**) (*replicar*) to answer back.
(**d**) **~ a** *necesidad* to answer, obey; *mandos etc* to obey; *situación, tratamiento etc* to respond to; **la cápsula no responde a los mandos** the capsule is not obeying the controls; **pero no respondió a tal tratamiento** but he did not respond to such treatment.
(**e**) (*sustancia*) to be workable, be easily worked.
(**f**) (*corresponder etc*) to correspond (*a* to); **~ a una descripción** to fit a description, agree with a description; **la obra no responde al título** the book is not what the title implies.
(**g**) **~ de** to be responsible for; to answer for; **yo no respondo de lo que hagan mis colegas** I am not responsible for what my colleagues may do; **yo no respondo de lo que pueda pasar** I cannot answer for the consequences; **en estas circunstancias, ¿quién responde?** who is responsible in these circumstances?
(**h**) **~ por uno** to vouch for sb, guarantee sb.
(**i**) **~ al nombre de** to be called, go by the name of.

respondida NF (*LAm*) reply.

respondón ADJ cheeky, insolent.

responsabilidad NF responsibility; liability; **~ civil** public liability (insurance); **~ contractual** contractual liability; **~ objetiva** (*Jur*) strict liability; **~ solidaria** joint responsibility; **de ~ limitada** limited liability (*atr*); **bajo mi ~** on my responsibility; **cargo de ~** position of responsibility; **hay que exigir ~es al Gobierno por los hechos** the government must be held accountable (*o* responsible) for what happened.

responsabilizar [1f] ☐1 VT: **~ a uno** to make sb responsible; (*encargar*) to put sb in charge; **~ a uno de un desastre** to hold sb responsible for a disaster, place the blame for a disaster on sb.
☐2 **responsabilizarse** VR to make o.s. responsible (*de* for); to acknowledge one's responsibility; to take charge; **~ de un atentado** to claim responsibility for an outrage.

responsable ☐1 ADJ (**a**) (*gen*) responsible (*de* for); **la persona ~** the person in charge; **la policía busca a los ~s** the police are hunting for those responsible; **hacer a uno ~** to hold sb responsible (*de* for); **hacerse ~ de algo** to assume responsibility for sth; to acknowledge one's responsibility for sth; **no me hago ~ de lo que pueda pasar** I take no responsibility for what may happen.
(**b**) (*ante otro*) accountable, answerable; **ser ~ ante uno de algo** to be answerable to sb for sth.
☐2 NMF: *p.ej.* **~ de prensa** press secretary.

responso NM (*Rel*) prayer for the dead.

responsorio NM (*Ecl*) response.

▼ **respuesta** NF answer, reply; response; **~ inmune, ~ inmunitaria** immune response.

resquebra(ja)dura NF crack, split, cleft.

resquebrajar [1a] ☐1 VT to crack, split.
☐2 **resquebrajarse** VR to crack, split.

resquebrar [1j] VI to begin to crack.

resquemar [1a] VT (**a**) (*lit*) to burn slightly; (*Culin*) to scorch; burn; *lengua* to burn, sting; *planta* to parch, dry up. (**b**) (*fig*) to cause bitterness to, upset.

resquemor NM (**a**) (*sensación*) burn, sting, stinging feeling; (*Culin*)

► LENGUA Y USO: **respetar** → 38.3   **respuesta** → 46.1, 46.5, 47.1, 48.2

scorching, burnt taste. **(b)** (*fig: resentimiento*) resentment, bitterness; (*enojo*) concealed anger; (*sospecha*) secret suspicion.

resquicio NM **(a)** (*abertura*) chink, crack.
(b) (*fig*) (*posibilidad*) chance, possibility; (*oportunidad*) opening, opportunity; ~ **legal** loophole.
(c) (*And, Carib: vestigio*) vestige, trace.
(d) (*Carib: pedacito*) little bit, small piece.

resta NF (*Mat*) **(a)** (*acto*) subtraction. **(b)** (*residuo*) remainder.
restablecer [2d] ⃞1 VT to re-establish; to restore.
⃞2 **restablecerse** VR (*Med*) to recover.
restablecimiento NM re-establishment; restoration; (*Med*) recovery.
restallar [1a] VI to crack; to click one's tongue; to crackle.
restallido NM (*de látigo*) crack; (*de lengua*) click; (*de papel etc*) crackle.
restante ADJ remaining; **lo** ~ the rest, the remainder; **los** ~**s** the remaining ones, the rest, those that are left (over).
restañar [1a] VT to stanch, stop (the flow of).
restañasangre NM bloodstone.
restar [1a] ⃞1 VT **(a)** (*quitar*) to take away, reduce; (*descontar*) to deduct; (*Mat*) to take away, subtract (*de* from); ~ **autoridad a uno** to take away authority from sb, reduce sb's authority; **le restó importancia** he did not give it much importance.
(b) (*Dep*) *pelota, saque* to return.
⃞2 VI to remain, be left; **restan 3 días para terminarse el plazo** there are 3 days left before the period expires; **ahora sólo me resta** + *infin* it only remains for me now to + *infin*.
restauración NF **(a)** restoration; **la R~** (*Esp*) *the restoration of the Spanish monarchy (1873).* **(b)** (*Com*) **la** ~ the restaurant industry; **la** ~ **rápida** the fast-food industry.
restaurador(a) ⃞1 NM/F **(a)** (*Arte etc*) restorer. **(b)** (*Com*) restauranteur, restaurant owner.
⃞2 NM: ~ **del cabello** hair-restorer.
restaurán NM, **restaurante** [resto'ran] NM restaurant.
restaurar [1a] VT to restore.
restinga NF sandbar, shoal, mudbank.
restitución NF return; restoration.
restituir [3g] ⃞1 VT **(a)** (*devolver*) to return, give back, restore (*a* to).
(b) (*Arquit etc*) to restore.
⃞2 **restituirse** VR: ~ **a** to return to, go back to, rejoin.
resto NM **(a)** (*lo que queda*) rest, remainder; (*Mat*) remainder; ~**s** remains; (*Culin*) left-overs, scraps; (*Náut etc*) wreckage; (*escombros*) debris, rubble; ~**s de edición** remainders; ~**s humanos** human remains; ~**s mortales** mortal remains; ~ **de serie** remainder, remaindered item; ~**s de serie** (*fig*) left-overs.
(b) (*Dep*) return (of a ball *o* of service); (*persona*) receiver; **estar al** ~ to be ready to return service.
(c) (*apuesta*) stake; **a** ~ **abierto** with no limit on stakes; (*fig*) without limit; **echar el** ~* to stake all one's money; (*fig*) to go all out, go the whole hog; **echar el** ~ **por** + *infin* to do one's utmost to + *infin*.
restorán NM restaurant.
restregar [1h *y* 1j] VT **(a)** (*fregar*) to scrub; to rub (hard). **(b)** (*mueble etc*) to rub on, rub against.
restricción NF restriction; limitation; restraint; **restricciones eléctricas** electricity cuts; ~ **mental** mental reservations; **restricciones presupuestarias** budgetary constraints; ~ **salarial** wage-restraint; **sin** ~ **de** without restrictions as to, with no limitation upon; **hablar sin restricciones** to talk freely.
restrictivo ADJ restrictive, limiting.
restrillar [1a] ⃞1 VT (*And, Carib*) *látigo* to crack.
⃞2 VI (*Carib: madera*) to crack, creak.
restringido ADJ restricted, limited.
restringir [3c] VT to restrict, limit (*a* to).
resucitación NF resuscitation.
resucitador NM (*Med*) respirator.
resucitar [1a] ⃞1 VT **(a)** (*lit*) to resuscitate, revive.
(b) (*fig*) to revive; to resurrect, give a new existence to.
⃞2 VI **(a)** (*lit*) to revive, return to life.
(b) (*fig*) to be resuscitated, be resurrected; to revive.
resudar [1a] VTI to sweat a little; (*recipiente etc*) to leak slightly.
resuello NM **(a)** (*aliento*) breath; (*respiración*) breathing; **corto de** ~ short of breath, short-winded; **sumir el** ~ **a uno** (*LAm*⁑) to bump sb off⁑.
(b) (*jadeo*) puff; (*respiración difícil*) heavy breathing; (*ruidoso*) wheeze.
(c) **meter a uno el** ~ **en el cuerpo** (*dar un susto a*) to put the wind up sb*, give sb a nasty fright; (*quitar los humos a*) to puncture sb's vanity.
(d) (*LAm*) breathing space; (*descanso*) rest; **tomar un** ~ to take a breather.
(e) (⁑: *dinero*) bread⁑, money.
resueltamente ADV resolutely, with determination; boldly; steadfastly.
▼ **resuelto** ⃞1 PTP *de* **resolver.**
▼⃞2 ADJ (*decidido*) resolute, resolved, determined; (*audaz*) bold; (*firme*) steadfast, firm; **estar** ~ **a algo** to be set on sth; **estar** ~ **a** + *infin* to be determined to + *infin*.

resulta NF result; **de** ~**s de** as a result of; **estar a** ~**s de** (*esp Esp*) to keep track of, keep up-to-date with.
resultado NM (*gen*) result; (*conclusión*) outcome, sequel; (*efecto*) effect; ~**s** (*Com, Fin*) results; **dar** ~ to produce results.
resultante ADJ resultant, consequential.
▼ **resultar** [1a] VI **(a)** (*ser*) to be; (*llegar a ser*) to prove (to be), turn out (to be); **me resulta simpático** I like him, he's nice; **si resulta** (*ser*) **verdadero** if it proves (to be) true; **el conductor resultó muerto** the driver was killed; **resultó** (*ser*) **el padre de mi cocinera** he turned out to be my cook's father, it emerged that he was my cook's father; **la casa nos resulta muy pequeña** we find the house very small; **resulta difícil decidir si** ... it is difficult to decide whether ...; **este trabajo está resultando un poco aburrido** this job is turning out to be a bit boring; **resulta que** ... it follows that ...; it seems that ..., it emerges that ...; **ahora resulta que no vamos** now it turns out that we're not going; **resulta que no me gusta** the thing is that I don't like it; **resulta de todo esto que no lo podemos pagar** it follows from all this that we can't afford it.
(b) ~ **de** to result from; (*derivarse de*) to stem from; (*verse en*) to be evident from; **de ese negocio resultaron 4 más** from that deal there resulted 4 others, that deal produced 4 more; **me resultan 8 menos que a ti** that leaves me with 8 less than you.
(c) (*seguir*) to ensue; **con lo que después resultó** with what ensued, with what happened in consequence.
(d) (*salir bien*) to turn out well; **resultó de lo mejor** it worked out very well; **no resultó** it didn't work; **no me resultó muy bien aquello** that didn't work out very well for me; **este tema no me resulta** I can't get along with this subject.
(e) (*Fin*) to cost, work out at, amount to; **la serie completa nos resultó en 50 dólares** the complete set cost us 50 dollars; **entre unos y otros resultan 800 pesetas** all together they amount to 800 pesetas.
(f) (*: ser prudente*) ~ + *infin* to be best to + *infin*, be wise to + *infin*; **no resulta dejar el coche fuera** it's best not to leave the car outside, it's not a good idea to leave the car outside.
(g) (*parecer bien*) to look well, have a pleasing effect; **esa corbata no resulta con ese traje** that tie doesn't go with the suit.
resultón* ADJ **(a)** (*agradable*) pleasing; (*impresionante*) impressive, that makes a good impression. **(b)** *hombre, mujer* attractive (to the opposite sex).
▼ **resumen** ⃞1 NM summary, résumé; abstract; **en** ~ (*en conclusión*) to sum up; (*brevemente*) in short.
⃞2 ATR: **comparecencia** ~ brief concluding appearance; **exposición** ~ summary; **programa** ~ programme in summary form.
resumidero NM (*LAm*) = **sumidero.**
▼ **resumir** [3a] ⃞1 VT **(a)** (*recapitular*) to sum up; (*condensar*) summarize; (*reducir*) to abridge, shorten, cut down.
⃞2 **resumirse** VR **(a)** **la situación puede resumirse en pocas palabras** the situation can be summed up in a few words.
(b) ~ **en** to be reduced to; come down to; boil down to; **todo se resumió en algunos porrazos** the affair amounted to no more than a few punches.
resunta NF (*And: resumen*) summary.
resurgimiento NM resurgence; revival.
resurgir [3c] VI **(a)** (*reaparecer*) to reappear, revive; (*resucitar*) to be resurrected. **(b)** (*fig*) to acquire a new spirit, pick up again; (*Med*) to recover.
resurrección NF resurrection.
retablo NM (*Ecl*) **(a)** reredos, altarpiece. **(b)** (*Méx*) exvoto, votive offering.
retacada NF (*Billar*) foul stroke.
retacado ADJ (*Méx*) full.
retacarse* [1g] VR (*Cono Sur*) to dig one's heels in; to go back on a promise (*etc*).
retacear [1a] VT (*Cono Sur*) *dinero etc* to give grudgingly, give bit by bit.
retachar [1a] VTI (*LAm*) to bounce (back).
retacitos NMPL (*CAm*) confetti.
retaco* NM **(a)** (*persona*) midget. **(b)** (*en billar*) short cue.
retacón ADJ (*And, Cono Sur*) short and fat, squat.
retador ⃞1 ADJ challenging; defiant.
⃞2 NM, **retadora** NF (*LAm Dep*) challenger.
retaguardia NF **(a)** (*Mil etc*) rearguard; **a** ~ in the rear; **3 millas a** ~ 3 miles to the rear, 3 miles further back. **(b)** (*Anat**) rear*, bottom.
retahíla NF string, series; (*de insultos etc*) volley, stream.
retajado (*Cono Sur*) ⃞1 ADJ (*Zool*) castrated, gelded.
⃞2 NM, **retajada** NF (⁑) wanker⁑⁂.
retajar [1a] VT **(a)** to cut out, cut round. **(b)** (*LAm*) to castrate, geld.
retal NM remnant, piece left over.
retaliación NF (*LAm*) retaliation.

retallones NMPL (*Carib*) left-overs.

retama NF (*Bot*), **retamo** NM (*LAm Bot*) broom.

retar [1a] VT (**a**) (*desafiar*) to challenge; to defy. (**b**) (*reprender*) to reprimand, tell off; (*regañar*) to scold. (**c**) (*Cono Sur*: *insultar*) to insult, abuse; **~le a uno algo** to throw sth in sb's face.

retardación NF retardation, slowing down; delaying; (*Mec*) deceleration.

retardado [1] ADJ (**a**) *espoleta* time delay (*atr*); **caja de apertura retardada** time delay safe; **bomba de efecto ~** time bomb. (**b**) *persona* retarded, mentally handicapped.
[2] NM, **retardada** NF (*t* **~ mental**) retarded person, mentally handicapped person.

retardar [1a] VT to slow down, slow up, retard; *marcha, progresos etc* to hold up, retard; *tren etc* to delay, make late; *reloj* to put back.

retardatriz ADJ (F) *acción etc* delaying.

retardo NM delay; time lag.

retazar [1f] VT (*cortar*) to cut up, snip into pieces; (*dividir*) to divide up; *leña* to chop.

retazo NM (**a**) (*Cos etc*) remnant; (*recorte*) snippet; (*trocito*) bit, piece, fragment; **~s** (*Liter etc*) snippets, bits and pieces; (*fragmentos*) disjointed fragments. (**b**) (*Carib*) bargain.

RETD NF (*Esp Telec*) ABR de **Red Especial de Transmisión de Datos.**

rete... PREFIJO INTENSIVO very ..., *p.ej.* **retebién** very well, terribly well; **una persona retefina** a terribly refined person.

retemblar [1j] VI to shudder, shake (*de* at, with).

retemplar [1a] VT (*And, CAm, Cono Sur*) to cheer up, revive.

retén NM (**a**) (*Téc*) stop, catch; lock; (*Aut*) oil-seal. (**b**) (*reserva*) reserve, store. (**c**) (*puesto de policía*) police post; (*control*) checkpoint, roadblock; (*pelotón*) post of armed men kept in reserve for an emergency; (*Mil*) reserves, reinforcements; **hombre de ~** reserve; **estar de ~** to be on call. (**d**) (*Carib*) remand home; detention centre.

retención NF (**a**) (*gen*) retention (*t Med*). (**b**) (*Fin*) deduction, stoppage (of pay *etc*); **~ a cuenta** deduction at source; **~ fiscal** retention for tax purposes. (**c**) (*Aut*) stoppage, hold-up, back-up. (**d**) (*Telec*) hold facility.

retener [2k] VT (*gen*) to retain; to keep (back), hold back; (*Fin*) to deduct; to withhold (part of); *atención* to hold; *memoria* to retain; *artículo prestado* to keep, hold on to; *tesoros, víveres* to hoard; **~ a uno preso** to keep sb in detention.

retenida NF guy-rope.

retentiva NF memory, capacity for remembering.

retentivo ADJ retentive.

reteñir [3h y 3k] VT to redye.

reticencia NF (**a**) (*sugerencia*) insinuation, (malevolent) suggestion; (*trascendencia*) implication; (*ironía*) irony, sarcasm. (**b**) (*engaño*) half-truth, misleading statement. (**c**) (*reserva*) reticence, reserve. (**d**) (*renuencia*) unwillingness, reluctance.

reticente ADJ (**a**) (*insinuador*) insinuating; (*irónico*) ironical, sarcastic; full of (unpleasant) implications. (**b**) (*reservado*) deceptive, misleading. (**c**) reticent, reserved. (**d**) (*desinclinado*) unwilling, reluctant; **estar o ser ~ a** to be unwilling for, be resistent to; **se mostró ~ a aceptar** she was unwilling to accept, she was reluctant to accept; **se declara ~ a la política** he says he doesn't like the idea of politics.

rético, -a [1] ADJ, NM/F Romansch.
[2] NM (*Ling*) Romansch.

retícula NF (*Ópt*) reticle; (*Fot*) screen.

reticular ADJ reticulated.

retículo NM reticle; net, network; (*de medir etc*) grid.

retina NF retina.

retinol NM retinol.

retintín NM (**a**) (*tilín*) tinkle, tinkling; (*tintineo*) jingle, jangle; (*del oído*) ringing. (**b**) (*fig*) sarcastic tone; **decir algo con ~** to say sth sarcastically.

retinto ADJ (*LAm*) *tez* very dark.

retiñir [3a] VI to tinkle; to jingle, jangle; (*en el oído*) to go on ringing (in one's ears).

retirada NF (**a**) (*Mil*) retreat, withdrawal; **batirse en ~, emprender la ~** to begin to) retreat.
(**b**) (*de dinero, embajador etc*) withdrawal; **~ de tierras de la producción** taking of land out of cultivation.
(**c**) (*refugio*) retreat, safe place, place of refuge.

retiradamente ADV *vivir* quietly, in seclusion.

retirado ADJ (**a**) *vida* quiet; *lugar* remote, secluded, quiet. (**b**) *oficial etc* retired. (**c**) **la tiene retirada** (*Esp*) he keeps her as his mistress.

retirar [1a] [1] VT (**a**) (*mover*) *silla etc* to move away, move back; (*quitar*) to put away, take away, remove; *tentáculo etc* to draw in; *cortina, mano etc* to draw back; *tapa* to take off; (*Mec*) *pieza* to take out, remove; (*Mil*) *fuerzas* to withdraw; **~ tierras de la producción** to take land out of cultivation, set land aside.
(**b**) (*Fin*) to withdraw (*de* from), take out; *embajador* to recall, withdraw; *atleta, caballo* to scratch.
(**c**) *moneda, sello etc* to withdraw (from circulation); *permiso* to with-

draw, cancel; (*Aut*) *carnet* to suspend, confiscate, take away.
(**d**) (*jubilar*) to retire, pension off.
(**e**) *acusación, palabras* to withdraw.
[2] **retirarse** VR (**a**) (*apartarse*) to move back, move away (*de* from); (*Mil*) to retreat, withdraw; **~ ante un peligro** to shrink back from a danger; **no se retire** (*Telec*) don't hang up.
(**b**) (*Dep*) to retire; to scratch.
(**c**) (*recluirse*) to go into seclusion, go off into retreat, withdraw from active life; (*jubilarse*) to retire (*de* from); **se retiró a vivir a Mallorca** he went off to live in Majorca, he retired to Majorca; **cuando me retire de los negocios** when I retire from business.
(**d**) (*después de cenar etc*) to retire (to one's room *o* to bed), go off to bed.

retiro NM (**a**) (*acto*) retirement; withdrawal; (*Dep*) retirement; scratching; (*de dinero etc*) withdrawal; **~ prematuro** early retirement.
(**b**) (*estado*) retirement; **un oficial en ~** an officer in retirement, a retired officer.
(**c**) (*Fin*) retirement pay, pension.
(**d**) (*lugar*) quiet place, secluded spot; (*apartamiento*) seclusion; retreat; **vivir en el ~** to live in seclusion; live quietly.
(**e**) (*Ecl*) (*t* **~s**) retreat.

reto NM (**a**) (*desafío*) challenge; (*amenaza*) threat, defiant statement (*etc*). (**b**) (*Cono Sur*: *reprimenda*) telling off, scolding. (**c**) (*Cono Sur*: *insulto*) insult.

retobado ADJ (**a**) (*LAm*: *salvaje*) *animal* wild, untamed; *persona* wild, unruly; (*rebelde*) rebellious; (*terco*) obstinate; (*hosco*) sullen; (*caprichoso*) unpredictable, capricious.
(**b**) (*And, CAm, Méx**) (*gruñón*) grumbling; (*descarado*) saucy, cheeky*.
(**c**) (*And, Cono Sur*: *taimado*) cunning, crafty.
(**d**) (*And*: *ofendido*) cheesed-off*, offended.

retobar [1a] [1] VT (**a**) (*LAm*) (*forrar o cubrir*) to line (*o* cover) with leather; (*And, Cono Sur*) *etc* to line (*o* cover) with leather (*o* sacking *o* oilcloth).
(**b**) (*And*) *pieles* to tan.
[2] VI y **retobarse** VR (*LAm*) (*obstinarse*) to be stubborn, dig one's heels in; (*quejarse*) to grumble, protest.

retobo NM (**a**) (*LAm*) (*forro*) lining; (*cubierta*) covering; (*Cono Sur*: *hule etc*) sacking, oilcloth, wrapping material.
(**b**) (*LAm*) (*terquedad*) stubbornness; (*protesta*) grumble, moan; (*capricho*) whim.
(**c**) (*And, CAm Agr*) old stock, useless animals; (*fig*) (*persona*) useless person; (*objeto*) worthless object; (*trastos*) junk, rubbish.
(**d**) (*LAm*: *resabio*) aftertaste.

retobón ADJ (*Cono Sur*) = **retobado** (**a**).

retocar [1g] [1] VT (**a**) *foto etc* to retouch, touch up. (**b**) *grabación* to play back.
[2] **retocarse** VR (*Esp*) to redo one's make-up.

retomar [1a] VT to take up again.

retoñar [1a] VI (**a**) (*Bot*) to sprout, shoot. (**b**) (*fig*) to reappear, recur.

retoño NM (**a**) (*Bot*) sprout, shoot, new growth. (**b**) (*: niño*) kid*.

retoque NM (**a**) (*acto*) retouching, touching-up; (*último trazo*) finishing touch. (**b**) (*Med*) symptom, sign, indication.

retorcer [2b y 2h] [1] VT (**a**) *brazo etc* to twist; *cuello, manos, ropa lavada* to wring; *hebras* to twine (together).
(**b**) (*fig*) *argumento* to turn, twist; *sentido* to twist, force.
[2] **retorcerse** VR (**a**) (*cuerda etc*) to get into knots, twist up, curl up.
(**b**) **~ el bigote** to twirl one's moustache.
(**c**) (*persona*) to writhe; to squirm; **~ de dolor** to writhe in pain, squirm with pain; **~ de risa** to double up with laughter.

retorcido ADJ (**a**) *estilo* involved. (**b**) *método, persona* crafty, devious.

retorcijón NM (*LAm*) = **retortijón.**

retorcimiento NM (**a**) twisting; wringing; entwining; writhing.
(**b**) (*fig*: *complejidad*) involved nature.
(**c**) (*fig*: *astucia*) craftiness, deviousness.

retórica NF (**a**) (*lit*) rhetoric; (*pey*) affectedness, windiness, grandiloquence. (**b**) (*) **~s** (*palabrería*) hot air, mere words; (*sofisterías*) quibbles.

retóricamente ADV rhetorically.

retórico [1] ADJ rhetorical; (*pey*) affected, windy; grandiloquent.
[2] NM rhetorician.

retornable ADJ returnable; **envase no ~** non-returnable empty.

retornar [1a] [1] VT (**a**) (*devolver*) to return, give back. (**b**) (*devolver a su lugar*) to replace, return to its place. (**c**) (*mover*) to move back.
[2] VI to return, come back, go back.

retorno NM (**a**) (*vuelta*) return; **'R~ a Brideshead'** 'Brideshead Revisited'; **~ hacia atrás** flashback. (**b**) (*recompensa*) reward; (*pago*) repayment; (*cambio*) exchange, barter; (*de regalo, servicio etc*) return. (**c**) (*Elec*) **~ terrestre** earth wire, ground wire (US). (**d**) (*Méx Aut*) turning place; **'~ prohibido'** 'No U turns'. (**e**) (*Inform*) **~ del carro** carriage return; **~ (del carro) automático** wordwrap, word wraparound.

retorsión NF = **retorcimiento** (**a**).

retorta NF (*Quím*) retort.

retortero NM: **andar al ~** to bustle about, have heaps of things to do; **andar al ~ por algo** to crave for sth; **andar al ~ por uno** to be madly in love with sb; **llevar** (o **traer**) **a uno al ~** to have sb under one's thumb; to keep sb constantly on the go; (*fig*) to push sb around.

retortijón NM rapid twist; **~ de estómago** gripe, stomach cramp.

retostar [1l] VT to burn, overcook.

retozar [1f] VI to romp, frolic, frisk about; to gambol.

retozo NM **(a)** (*holgorio*) romp, frolic, (*jugueteo*) gambol; **~s** romping, frolics; gambolling. **(b)** **~ de la risa** giggle, titter, suppressed laugh.

retozón ADJ **(a)** (*juguetón*) playful, frolicsome, frisky. **(b)** *risa* bubbling.

retracción NF retraction, retractation.

retractable ADJ retractable.

retractación NF retraction, recantation.

retractar [1a] ① VT to retract, withdraw.
② **retractarse** VR to retract, recant; **me retracto** I take that back; **me retracto de la acusación hecha** I withdraw the accusation.

retráctil ADJ (*Aer etc*) retractable; (*Bio*) retractile.

retraer [2o] ① VT **(a)** *garras etc* to draw in, retract.
(b) (*volver a traer*) to bring back, bring again.
(c) (*fig*) to dissuade; to keep away.
② **retraerse** VR to withdraw, retire, retreat (*de* from); to stay away; **~ a** to take refuge in; **~ de** (*fig*) (*retirarse de*) to withdraw from; (*renunciar a*) to give up; (*evitar*) to avoid, shun, stay away from.

retraído ADJ retiring, shy, reserved; (*pey*) aloof, unsociable.

retraimiento NM **(a)** (*acto*) withdrawal, retirement; (*estado*) seclusion. **(b)** (*cualidad*) retiring nature, shyness, reserve; (*pey*) aloofness. **(c)** (*lugar*) refuge, retreat.

retranca NF (*LAm*) brake.

retrancar [1g] ① VT (*LAm*) to brake.
② **retrancarse** VR **(a)** (*LAm: frenar*) to brake, apply the brakes. **(b)** (*Méx: fig*) to come to a halt, seize up.

retransmisión NF repeat (broadcast), rebroadcast.

retransmitir [3a] VT *mensaje* to relay, pass on; (*Rad, TV*) to repeat, rebroadcast, retransmit; (*en vivo*) to broadcast live, do an outside broadcast of.

retrasado ADJ **(a)** **estar ~** (*industria, persona etc*) to be behind, be behindhand, lag behind; **está ~ en química** he is behind in chemistry, he has a lot to make up in chemistry; **vamos ~s en la producción** we lag behind in production, our production is lagging; **estar ~ en los pagos** to be behind in one's payments, be in arrears.
(b) **estar ~** (*reloj*) to be slow; **tengo el reloj 8 minutos ~** my watch is 8 minutes slow.
(c) *país* backward, underdeveloped; *actitud etc* antiquated, old-fashioned.
(d) *comida etc* unused, left over; **tengo trabajo ~** I have work piling up, I am behindhand in my work.
(e) (*Med*) subnormal, mentally retarded.

retrasar [1a] ① VT **(a)** (*demorar*) to delay, put off, postpone; (*retardar*) to retard, slow down; to hold up.
(b) *reloj* to put back.
② VI y **retrasarse** VR (*reloj*) to be slow; (*persona, tren etc*) to be late, be behind time; (*en estudios, producción etc*) to lag behind; (*producción etc*) to decline, fall away.

retraso NM **(a)** (*demora*) delay; (*intervalo*) time lag; (*tardanza*) slowness, lateness; **llegar con ~** to be late, arrive late; **llegar con 25 minutos de ~** to be 25 minutes late; **llevo un ~ de 6 semanas** I'm 6 weeks behind (with my work *etc*).
(b) (*de país*) backwardness, backward state, underdevelopment.
(c) **~ mental** (*Med*) subnormality, mental deficiency.
(d) **~s** (*Com, Fin*) (*de pagos*) arrears; (*deudas*) deficit, debts.

retratar [1a] ① VT **(a)** to portray; (*Arte*) to paint a picture of, paint the portrait of; (*Fot*) to photograph, take a picture of; **hacerse ~** (*Arte*) to have one's portrait painted; (*Fot*) to have one's photograph taken (as a portrait).
(b) (*fig: representar*) to portray, depict, describe.
② **retratarse** VR **(a)** (*Arte*) to have one's picture painted; (*Fot*) to have one's photograph taken.
(b) (***) *dinero* to pay (up), fork out*; to let people see the colour of one's money.

retratería NF (*LAm*) photographer's (studio).

retratista NMF (*Arte*) portrait painter; (*Fot*) photographer.

retrato NM **(a)** (*Arte*) portrait; (*Fot*) photograph, portrait.
(b) (*fig: descripción*) portrayal, depiction, description.
(c) (*fig: semejanza*) likeness; **ser el vivo ~ de** to be the very image of.

retrato-robot NM, PL **retratos-robot** identikit picture, photofit picture.

retrechería NF **(a)** (**: truco*) dodge*, wheeze*, crafty trick; (*hum*) rascally trick.
(b) (**: encantos*) **~s** winning ways, charming ways.
(c) (**: atractivo*) charm, attractiveness.

(d) (*V* ADJ (c)) meanness; deceitfulness; suspicious nature.

retrechero ADJ **(a)** (***) (*dado a trucos*) full of dodges*; (*astuto*) wily, crafty; (*hum*) rascally.
(b) (**: encantador*) winning, charming, attractive.
(c) (*LAm*) (*tacaño*) mean; (*tramposo*) unreliable, deceitful; (*sospechoso*) suspicious.

retreparse [1a] VR to lean back; to sprawl, loll, lounge.

retreta NF **(a)** (*Mil*) retreat; (*exhibición*) tattoo, display. **(b)** (*LAm Mús*) open-air band concert. **(c)** (*LAm: serie*) series, string.

retrete NM lavatory.

retribución NF **(a)** (*pago*) pay, payment; (*recompensa*) reward; compensation. **(b)** (*Téc*) compensation.

retribuido ADJ *trabajo* paid; *puesto* salaried, that carries a salary; **un puesto mal ~** a badly paid post.

retribuir [3g] VT **(a)** (*pagar*) to pay; (*compensar*) to reward, compensate. **(b)** (*LAm*) *favor etc* to repay, return.

retro* ① ADJ INVAR *moda etc* backward-looking; revivalist; (*Pol*) reactionary.
② NM (*Pol*) reactionary.

retro... PREF retro...

retroacción NF feedback.

retroactivamente ADV retroactively, retrospectively.

retroactividad NF (*de ley*) retroactivity; (*de pago*) backdating.

retroactivo ADJ retroactive, retrospective; **ley de efecto ~** retrospective law; **un aumento ~ desde abril** a rise backdated to April; **dar efecto ~ a un pago** to backdate a payment.

retroalimentación NF feedback.

retroalimentador ADJ feedback (*atr*).

retroalimentar [1a] VT to feed back.

retrocarga: de ~ breechloading; **arma de ~** breechloader.

retroceder [2a] VI **(a)** (*moverse atrás*) to move back; (*retirarse*) to draw back, stand back; (*ir atrás*) to go backwards; (*volver atrás*) to turn back; (*Mil*) to fall back, retreat; (*cañón*) to recoil; (*agua, nivel, precio etc*) to fall, go down, (*Tip*) to backspace; **retrocedió unos pasos** he went back a few steps; **la policía hizo ~ a la multitud** the police forced the crowd back, the police pushed the crowd back.
(b) (*fig*) to back down; to give up; to flinch (*ante un peligro* from a danger); **no ~** to stand firm.

retroceso NM **(a)** (*movimiento hacia atrás*) backward movement; drawing back; (*Mil*) withdrawal, retreat; (*de cañón*) recoil; **cañón sin ~** recoil-less gun.
(b) (*fig*) backing down.
(c) (*Com, Fin*) recession (of trade), slump, depression; (*de apoyo, precio etc*) fall, decline.
(d) (*Med*) renewed attack, new outbreak.
(e) (*Tip*) backspace.

retrocohete NM retrorocket.

retrocuenta NF count-down.

retrogradación NF retrogression.

retrógrado ADJ retrograde, retrogressive; (*Pol etc*) reactionary.

retrogresión NF retrogression.

retronar [1l] VI = **retumbar**.

retropropulsión NF retropropulsion; (*Aer*) jet propulsion.

retroproyector NM overhead projector.

retrospección NF retrospection.

retrospectiva NF **(a)** (*Arte*) retrospective (exhibition). **(b)** **en ~** with hindsight.

retrospectivamente ADV retrospectively; in retrospect.

retrospectivo ADJ retrospective; **escena retrospectiva** flashback; **mirada retrospectiva** backward glance, look back (*a* at).

retrotraer [2o] VT to carry back (in time), take back; **retrotrajo su relato a los tiempos del abuelo** he carried his tale back into his grandfather's day; **ahora podemos ~ su origen al siglo XI** now we can take its origin further back to the 11th century; **piensa ~ el problema a su origen** he hopes to trace the problem back to its origin.

retroventa NF resale; **precio de ~** resale price.

Retrovir ® NM Retrovir ®.

retrovírico ADJ retroviral.

retrovirus NM INVAR retrovirus.

retrovisión NF **(a)** hindsight. **(b)** (*Cine*) flashback (technique).

retrovisor ① ADJ: **espejo ~ = 2**.
② NM driving mirror, rear-view mirror; wing mirror.

retrucar [1g] VT **(a)** *argumento* to turn against its user. **(b)** (*prov, LAm*) to retort; **le retruqué diciendo que ...** I retorted to him that ... **(c)** (*Billar*) to kiss.

retruécano NM pun, play on words.

retruque NM **(a)** (*And, Cono Sur*) sharp retort, brusque reply. **(b)** **de ~** (*Cono Sur, Méx*) on the rebound; as a consequence, as a result.

retumbante ADJ **(a)** booming, rumbling; resounding. **(b)** (*fig*) bombastic.

retumbar [1a] VI (*artillería, trueno etc*) to boom, roll, thunder, rumble;

(*pasos, voz*) to echo, resound; to reverberate; **la cascada retumbaba a lo lejos** the waterfall boomed (*o* roared) in the distance; **la caverna retumbaba con nuestros pasos** the cave echoed with our steps; **sus palabras retumban en mi cabeza** his words still echo in my mind.

retumbo NM boom, roll, thunder, rumble; echo; reverberation.

reubicación NF (*de trabajadores, empresas*) relocation; (*de comunidad, pueblo*) resettlement.

reubicar [1g] VT *trabajador, empresa* to relocate; *comunidad, pueblo* to resettle.

reuma NM, **reúma** NM rheumatism.

reumático ADJ rheumatic.

reumatismo NM rheumatism.

reumatoide(o) ADJ rheumatoid.

reunificación NF reunification.

reunificar [1g] VT to reunify.

reunión NF (a) (*asamblea*) meeting, gathering; (*fiesta*) social gathering, party; (*Pol*) meeting; rally; (*Dep*) meeting; **~ (en la) cumbre** summit meeting; **~ ilícita** unlawful assembly; **~ informativa** press conference; **~ plenaria** plenary session.
(b) (*encuentro*) reunion.

reunir [3a] **1** VT (a) (*juntar*) *partes etc* to reunite, join (together); **~ dos cuartos** to knock two rooms together, make one room out of two.
(b) (*recoger*) *cosas dispersas etc* to gather (together), get together, put together; *datos etc* to assemble, collect, gather; *recursos* to pool; *colección* to make; *dinero* to collect; *fondos* to raise; (*ahorrar*) to save (up); **los 4 reunidos no valen lo que él** the 4 of them together are not as good as he is; **la producción de los demás países reunidos no alcanzará al nuestro** the production of the other countries put together will not come up to ours.
(c) *personas* to assemble, bring together, invite together; **reunió a sus amigos para discutirlo** he assembled his friends to talk it over; **está** (*o* **se encuentra**) **reunida** (*Esp*) she's in a meeting.
(d) *cualidades* to combine; *condiciones* to have, possess; **~ esfuerzos** to join forces; **la casa reúne la comodidad con la economía** the house combines comfort with economy.

2 reunirse VR (a) (*unirse*) to unite, join together; (*de nuevo*) to re-unite.
(b) (*personas*) to meet, gather, assemble; to get together; **~ para** + *infin* to get together to + *infin*; **~ con uno para una excursión** to join sb for an outing.
(c) (*circunstancias*) to conspire (*para* + *infin* to + *infin*).

reutilizable ADJ reusable.

reutilización NF reuse; recycling.

reutilizar [1f] VT to reuse.

revalida NF (*Escol etc*) resit.

revalidar [1a] VT (a) (*confirmar*) to confirm, ratify. (b) (*Escol etc*) to re-sit.

revalor(iz)ación NF revaluation; reassessment.

revalorar [1a] VT, **revalorizar** [1f] VT to revalue; to reassess.

revaluación NF (*Fin*) revaluation.

revaluar [1e] VT (*Fin*) to revalue.

revancha NF (a) revenge; **en ~** in retaliation; **tomar su ~** to get one's revenge, get one's own back. (b) (*Dep*) return match; (*Boxeo*) return fight. (c) (*fig*) revision, reassessment.

revanchismo NM revanchism.

revanchista ADJ, NMF revanchist.

revejido ADJ (*And*) weak, feeble.

revelación **1** NF revelation (*t fig*); disclosure; **fue una ~ para mí** it was a revelation to me.
2 ATR surprise (*atr*); **el coche ~ de 1998** the surprise car of 1998; **el diputado ~ del año** the surprise of the year among members.

revelado NM (*Fot*) developing.

▼ **revelador** **1** ADJ revealing; telltale.
2 NM (*Fot*) developer.

revelar [1a] VT (a) (*gen*) to reveal; *secreto* to disclose; (*mostrar*) to betray, show; (*delatar*) to give away. (b) (*Fot*) to develop.

revendedor(a) NM/F (*al por menor*) retailer; (*pey*) speculator; (*de calle etc*) vendor, hawker, seller; (*Dep, Teat etc*) ticket tout.

revender [2a] VT (*volver a vender*) to resell; (*al por menor*) to retail; (*pey*) to speculate in; (*por la calle etc*) to hawk; *entradas* to tout.

revendón NM (*And*) middleman.

revenirse [3r] VR (a) (*encogerse*) to shrink.
(b) (*comida*) to go bad, go off; (*vino etc*) to sour, turn.
(c) (*enlucido etc*) to dry out; to give off moisture.
(d) (*Culin*) to get tough; get leathery.
(e) (*fig: ceder*) to give way (at last).

reventa **1** NF resale; speculation; hawking; touting; **precio de ~** resale price.
2 NMF (*persona*) ticket tout.

reventadero NM (a) (*terreno áspero*) rough ground; (*escarpado*) steep

terrain. (b) (*fig: trabajo*) tough job, heavy work, grind. (c) (*And, Cono Sur, Méx: hervidero*) bubbling spring. (d) (*Cono Sur*) = **rompiente.**

reventado* ADJ exhausted.

reventador(a) NM/F (a) (*en mitín etc*) troublemaker, heckler. (b) (*ladrón*) safebreaker.

reventar [1j] **1** VT (a) *globo etc* to burst, explode, pop; *neumático, tubo etc* to burst; *barrera etc* to break, smash; **tengo una cubierta reventada** I have a puncture, I have a flat tyre, I have a flat (*US*).
(b) *caballo* to flog, ride hard, ride to death; *persona* to work to death, overwork, exhaust.
(c) (*) *proyecto etc* to sink, ruin; (*Teat etc*) *obra* to hiss off the stage; *orador* to heckle, barrack; *asamblea* to disturb, disrupt, break up.
(d) (*: *perjudicar*) to do down, do serious harm to.
(e) (*: *fastidiar*) to annoy, rile*; **me revienta tener que ponérmelo** it riles me to have to wear it.
2 VI (a) (*globo etc*) to burst, pop, go off pop; to explode; (*granada, neumático, tubo etc*) to burst; (*contenido*) to burst forth, burst out.
(b) (*ola*) to break.
(c) (*: *morir*) to peg out‡.
(d) **~ de** (*fig*) to be bursting with; **me revienta de aburrimiento** it bores me to tears; **~ de gordo** to be as fat as a pig; **~ de indignación** to be bursting with indignation; **casi reventaba de ira** he almost exploded with anger; **~ de risa** to burst out laughing, split one's sides; **~ de ganas de decirlo todo** to be bursting to tell all about it; **~ por algo** to crave sth; **~ por** + *infin* to be bursting to + *infin*, be dying to + *infin*.
3 reventarse VR (a) = **2** (a).
(b) (*caballo*) to die of overwork, die of exhaustion; (*en carrera*) to blow up; (*: *persona*) to slog away, sweat one's guts out‡.
(c) (*: *morir*) to peg out‡; **se revienta trabajando** he's killing himself with work.

reventazón NF (a) (*Cono Sur: colina*) low ridge. (b) (*Méx: de estómago*) flatulence. (c) (*Méx: fuente*) bubbling spring.

reventón NM (a) (*estallido*) burst, bursting; explosion; (*Aut*) puncture, blow-out, flat (*US*); **dar un ~** to burst, explode.
(b) (*: *muerte*) death (from overeating); **dar un ~** to peg out‡.
(c) (*pendiente*) steep slope; (*subida*) tough climb.
(d) (*) (*esfuerzo*) killing effort; (*trabajo*) toil, slog; **le dio un ~ al caballo** he flogged his horse, he half-killed his horse; **darse un ~, pegarse un ~** to slog, flog o.s., sweat one's guts out‡ (*para* + *infin* to + *infin*).
(e) (*apuro*) jam, difficulty.
(f) (*Cono Sur Min*) outcrop of ore.
(g) (*Cono Sur: estallido*) explosion, outburst; (*Med*) relapse.
(h) (*CAm: empujón*) shove, push.
(i) (*Méx**) party, binge*.

rever [2u] VT (a) to see again, look again at. (b) (*Jur*) *sentencia* to review; *pleito* to retry.

reverberación NF reverberation.

reverberador NM reverberator.

reverberar [1a] VI (a) (*luz*) to play, be reflected; (*superficie*) to shimmer, shine; (*nieve etc*) to glare; **la luz reverberaba en el agua** the light played (*o* danced) on the water; **la luz del farol reverberaba en la calle** the lamplight lay in a pool on the street, the lamplight was reflected on the street.
(b) (*sonido*) to reverberate.

reverbero NM (a) (*de luz*) play, reflection; shimmer, shine; glare; **el ~ de la nieve** the glare of the snow, the dazzle of the snow.
(b) (*de sonido*) reverberation.
(c) (*reflector*) reflector (*t Aut*).
(d) (*LAm: cocinilla*) small spirit stove.
(e) (*Carib*: licor*) cheap liquor.

reverdecer [2d] **1** VT (*fig*) to renew, reawaken.
2 VI (a) (*Bot*) to grow green again. (b) (*fig*) to come to life again, revive, acquire new vigour.

reverencia NF (a) (*gen*) reverence. (b) (*inclinación*) bow, curtsy; **hacer una ~** to bow, curtsy. (c) (*título*) **R~** (*t* **Su R~, Vuestra R~**) Your Reverence.

reverencial ADJ reverential.

reverenciar [1b] VT to revere, venerate.

reverencioso ADJ reverent, respectful.

reverendísimo ADJ Most Reverend.

reverendo ADJ (a) (*estimado*) respected, revered.
(b) (*Ecl*) reverend; **el ~ padre X** Reverend Father X.
(c) (*: *solemne*) solemn.
(d) (*LAm*: inmenso*) big, tremendous*, awful; **un ~ imbécil** an awful idiot.

reverente ADJ reverent.

reverentemente ADV reverently.

reversa NF (*LAm Aut*) reverse.

reversible ADJ reversible.

reversión NF reversion.

reversionario ADJ reversionary.

reverso NM back, other side; wrong side; (*de moneda*) reverse; **el ~ de la medalla** (*fig*) the other side of the coin; the exact opposite.

revertir [3i] VI (a) (*posesión*) to revert (*a* to).
(b) **~ a su estado primitivo** to revert to its original state.
(c) **~ en** to end up as, come to be.
(d) **~ en beneficio de** to be to the advantage of; **~ en perjuicio de** to be to the detriment of.

revés NM (a) (*dorso*) back; (*contrahaz*) other side, wrong side; (*lado inferior*) underside; **el ~ de la medalla** (*fig*) the other side of the coin.
(b) (*golpe*) backhand (blow *o* shot *etc*); slap, swipe; (*Dep*) backhand; **~ cruzado** cross-court backhand.
(c) (*fig*) reverse (*t fig*), setback; **sufrir un ~** to suffer a setback; **los reveses de la fortuna** the blows of fate.
(d) **al ~** the wrong (*o* other) way round; upside down; *vestido etc* inside out; **y al ~** and vice versa; **entender algo al ~** to get hold of the wrong end of the stick; to have quite a different idea; **todo nos salió al ~** it all turned out wrong for us; **al ~ de lo que se cree** contrary to what is believed; **al ~ de lo corriente** against the usual practice, contrary to what normally happens; **llevar algo del ~** to wear sth the wrong way round (*o* inside out); **volver algo del ~** to turn sth round (the other way); to turn sth inside out.

revesado ADJ (a) *asunto* complicated, involved. (b) *niño etc* unruly, uncontrollable.

revesero ADJ (*And*) treacherous.

revestimiento NM (*Téc*) coating, facing, covering; lining; (*de carretera*) surface; (*Mil*) revetment; **~ antiadherente** non-stick coating.

revestir [3k] **1** VT (a) *ropa* to put on, don; to wear.
(b) (*Téc*) (*cubrir*) to coat, face, cover (*de* with); (*forrar*) to line (*de* with); *tubo etc* to sheathe (*de* in); (*fig*) *suelo etc* to carpet (*de* with).
(c) (*fig*) (*encubrir*) to cloak, disguise (*de* in); *persona* to invest (*con, de* with); *cuento etc* to adorn (*de* with); **revistió su acto de generosidad** he gave his action an appearance of generosity.
(d) *cualidad, importancia* to have, possess; **el acto revestía gran solemnidad** the ceremony had great dignity, the ceremony was a very solemn one.
2 revestirse VR (a) (*Ecl*) to put on one's vestments.
(b) (*fig: ponerse*) to deck o.s. in, put on; **los árboles se revisten de hojas** the trees put on their leaves again.
(c) **~ con, ~ de** (*fig*) *autoridad etc* to be invested with, have; *cualidad etc* to arm o.s. with; **se revistió de valor y fue a hablarle** he screwed up his courage and went to speak to her; **V t paciencia.**
(d) (*fig*) (*apasionarse*) to get carried away; (*engreírse*) to be vain, be haughty.

reviejo ADJ very old; *niño* wise beyond his years; old before his time.

revientapisos NM INVAR burglar, housebreaker.

revirado* ADJ (*Cono Sur*) (a) (*de mal genio*) bad-tempered, irritable; (*revoltoso*) unruly, wild. (b) (*loco*) crazy.

revirar [1a] **1** VT to turn (round), twist (round).
2 revirarse VR (a) (*Carib, Cono Sur*) (*rebelarse*) to rebel. (b) (*Cono Sur: enloquecer*) to go crazy. (c) **~ contra uno** (*Carib, Cono Sur*) to turn on sb.

revirón 1 ADJ (*CAm, Carib*) disobedient, rebellious, unruly.
2 NM (*CAm, Carib, Méx*) rebellion, revolt.

revisación NF (*Cono Sur*), **revisada** NF (*LAm*) = **revisión.**

revisar [1a] VT (a) *apuntes, texto etc* to revise, look over, go through; *edición* to revise; *cuenta* to check; to audit; (*Jur*) to review; *teoría etc* to re-examine, review.
(b) (*Mil*) *tropas* to review.
(c) (*Mec*) to check, overhaul; (*Aut*) to service.

revisión NF (a) (*repaso*) revision; check, checking; (*revista*) re-examination, review; **~ aduanera** customs inspection; **~ de cuentas** audit; **~ de sueldos** salary review. (b) (*Mec*) check, overhaul; (*Aut*) service.

revisionismo NM revisionism.

revisionista ADJ, NMF revisionist.

revisor(a) 1 NM/F reviser; inspector; (*Ferro*) ticket collector, inspector, conductor (*US*); **~ de cuentas** auditor; **~ de guión** (*Cine, TV*) script editor.
2 NM: **~ ortográfico** spellchecker.

revista NF (a) (*acto: examen*) review, revision; (*inspección*) inspection; (*Jur*) retrial; **pasar ~ a** to review, revise, re-examine.
(b) (*Mil*) review, inspection; (*Náut*) review; **pasar ~ a** to review, inspect.
(c) (*periódico*) review, journal, magazine; **~ comercial** trade paper; **~ cómica** comic; **~ del corazón** magazine of real-life romance stories; women's magazine; **~ de destape** girlie magazine; **~ gráfica** illustrated paper; **~ juvenil** teenage magazine; **~ literaria** literary review; **~ de modas** fashion paper; **~ para mujeres** women's magazine; **~ semanal** weekly review.
(d) (*Liter: sección*) section, page; **~ de libros** book review section, literary page; **~ de toros** bullfighting page, section of bullfight reports.
(e) (*Teat*) revue; variety show, vaudeville show (*US*).
(f) (*And: del pelo*) trim.

revistar [1a] VT (*Mil*) to review, inspect; (*Náut*) to review.

revistero, -a 1 NM/F reviewer, critic; contributor; **~ deportivo** sporting journalist; **~ literario** literary critic, book reviewer.
2 NM (*mueble*) magazine rack.

revisto PTP *de* **rever.**

revitalización NF revitalization.

revitalizador 1 ADJ revitalizing.
2 NM stimulant.

revitalizante ADJ revitalizing, invigorating.

revitalizar [1f] VT to revitalize.

revival 1 NM (*Mús etc*) revival; (*de persona*) comeback.
2 ATR: **canción ~** revived hit song, hit song from the past; **prenda ~** garment enjoying a new popularity.

revivificar [1g] VT to revivify.

revivir [3a] **1** VT *suceso etc* to revive memories of; (*vivir de nuevo*) to relive, live again; *sospecha* to revive.
2 VI to revive, be revived; to come to life again; **hacer ~ = 1.**

revocación NF revocation, repeal; reversal.

revocar [1g] VT (a) *decisión* to revoke, repeal; to cancel; to reverse; *persona* to remove from his post, axe.
(b) *humo etc* to send in a different direction, blow back, blow the wrong way.
(c) (*disuadir*) to dissuade (*de* from).
(d) (*Arquit*) (*enlucir*) to plaster, stucco; (*encalar*) to whitewash.

revocatoria NF (*LAm*) revocation, repeal.

revoco NM (a) = **revocación.** (b) = **revoque.**

revolar [1l] VI (*alzar el vuelo*) to take to flight again; (*revolotear*) to flutter about, fly around.

revolcadero NM (*Zool*) mudhole, mudbath.

revolcar [1g y 1l] **1** VT (a) (*derribar*) *persona* to knock down, knock over, send flying; (*Taur*) to knock down and trample on.
(b) (*) *adversario* to floor, crush; to wipe the floor with*.
(c) *orgulloso* to deflate, puncture.
(d) (*Esp: Univ*) to plough*.
2 revolcarse VR (a) (*persona*) to roll about, flounder about; to turn over and over; (*animal*) to wallow; (*: *amantes*) to have a romp in the hay; **~ en la tumba** to turn over in one's grave; **~ en los vicios** to wallow in vice.
(b) (*fig*) to dig one's heels in.

revolcón* NM fall, tumble; (*Fin*) slump; **dar un ~ a uno** (*fig*) to floor sb, crush sb; to wipe the floor with sb*; to deflate sb.

revolear [1a] **1** VT (*Cono Sur, Méx*) *lazo* to whirl, twirl.
2 VI to fly round.

revolera NF whirl, twirl.

revolica NF (*CAm*) confusion.

revolotear [1a] VI to flutter, fly about; to flit; to wheel, circle; to hover.

revoloteo NM fluttering; flitting; wheeling, circling; hovering.

revolqué V **revolcar.**

revoltijo NM, **revoltillo** NM (a) (*confusión*) jumble, confusion; (*desorden*) mess, litter; (*fig*) mess; **~ de huevos** scrambled eggs. (b) (*CAm, Cono Sur, Méx*) bundle.

revoltoso 1 ADJ rebellious, unruly, turbulent; *niño* naughty, uncontrollable.
2 NM, **revoltosa** NF (*rebelde*) rebel; (*Pol*) troublemaker, agitator; (*manifestante*) rioter.

revoltura NF (a) (*LAm: confusión*) confusion, jumble. (b) (*Méx: mezcla*) mixture; (*Culin*) scrambled eggs with vegetables; (*Arquit*) mortar, cement.

revolución NF (a) (*Téc*) revolution; **revoluciones por minuto** revolutions per minute. (b) (*Pol etc*) revolution; **R~ Cultural** Cultural Revolution; **R~ Industrial** Industrial Revolution; **~ islámica** Islamic revolution; **R~ de Octubre** October Revolution; **~ de palacio** palace revolution; **R~ Verde** Green Revolution.

revolucionar [1a] VT (a) *industria, moda etc* to revolutionize, cause a revolution in.
(b) *persona* to arouse intense excitement in, rouse to a pitch of excitement.
(c) (*Pol*) to stir up, sow discontent among; to rouse to revolt.

revolucionario, -a ADJ, NM/F revolutionary.

revoluta NF (*CAm*) revolution.

revolvedora NF (*Cono Sur, Méx*) concrete mixer.

revolver [2h; PTP **revuelto**] **1** VT (a) (*mover*) *objetos* to move about; (*poner al revés*) to turn round, turn over, turn upside-down; (*Culin*) to turn over; *tierra* to turn over, turn up, dig over; *recipiente* to shake; *líquido etc* to stir; *papeles etc* to look through; to rummage through, rummage among; (*Méx*) to revolve, turn around; **~la** (*fig*) to mess everything up; **¡deja de ~!, ¡no revuelvas!** (*a niño*) stop messing about with things!, stop fidgeting!

(b) (*desordenar*) to disturb, disarrange, mix up, mess up; **han revuelto toda la casa** they've messed up the whole house, they've turned the whole house upside-down.

(c) (*indagar*) to go into, inquire into, investigate; **~ algo en la cabeza** to turn sth over in one's mind.

(d) (*Pol etc*) to stir up, rouse, cause unrest among; *persona* to provoke, rouse to anger; **~ Eslobodia con Ruritania** to stir up trouble between Slobodia and Ruritania; **~ al secretario con el jefe** to get the secretary into trouble with his boss.

(e) (*volver*) *ojos, caballo etc* to turn.

(f) (*envolver*) to wrap up.

(g) (*And*) to weed.

2 VI: **~ en una maleta** to rummage (about) in a case, hunt through the contents of a case; **~ en los bolsillos** to feel in one's pockets, fumble in one's pockets.

3 revolverse VR **(a)** (*volverse*) to turn (right) round; to turn over; (*en cama*) to toss and turn; (*con dolor*) to writhe, squirm; (*Astron*) to revolve; **~ al enemigo** to turn to face the enemy; **se revolvía en su silla** he was fidgeting about on his chair; he was squirming uncomfortably on his chair.

(b) (*fig*) **~ contra uno** to turn on sb, turn against sb, attack sb.

(c) (*sedimento*) to be stirred up, be disturbed; (*líquido*) to become cloudy.

(d) (*Met*) to break, turn stormy.

(e) (*And*: prosperar*) to get a lucky break, have a change of fortunes; (*pey*) to look after Number One.

revólver NM revolver.

revoque NM **(a)** (*acto*) plastering; whitewashing. **(b)** (*materia*) (*enlucido*) plaster, stucco; (*cal*) whitewash.

revuelco NM fall, tumble; wallow(ing).

revuelo NM **(a)** flutter(ing).

(b) (*fig*) (*conmoción*) stir, commotion, disturbance; (*jaleo*) row, rumpus; **de ~** incidentally, in passing; **armar** (*o* **levantar** *etc*) **un gran ~** to cause a great stir.

revuelta NF **(a)** (*vuelta*) turn; **dar vueltas y ~s a algo** to go on turning sth over and over.

(b) (*de carretera etc*) bend, turn.

(c) (*fig*) (*conmoción*) commotion, disturbance; (*jaleo*) fuss; (*riña*) quarrel, row; (*Pol*) disturbance, riot; (*motín*) revolt.

(d) (*And*) weeding.

revuelto **1** PTP *de* **revolver**.

2 ADJ **(a)** *objetos* mixed up, in disorder, confused; *huevos* scrambled; *agua* cloudy, muddy; *mar* rough; *tiempo* unsettled, changeable; stormy; **todo estaba ~** everything was in disorder, everything was upside-down; **los tiempos están ~s** the times are out of joint, these are disturbed times; **viven ~s los animales y las personas** people and animals live on top of each other.

(b) *carácter* (*revoltoso*) unruly; (*inquieto*) restless, discontented; *niño etc* mischievous, naughty; *población* rebellious, mutinous; **la gente está revuelta por tales abusos** people feel mutinous about such scandals, people are properly on the boil about such abuses.

(c) *asunto* complicated, involved.

3 NM **(a)** **~ de huevos** mixed eggs and vegetables; **~ de morcilla** dish of mixed blood-sausage and vegetables.

(b) (*And*) must, grape juice.

revulsar [1a] VT (*Méx**) to vomit, throw up.

revulsionar [1a] VT: **~ a uno** to turn sb's stomach.

revulsivo NM **(a)** (*Med*) enema, revulsive. **(b)** (*fig*) nasty but salutary shock.

rey NM **(a)** king (*t Ajedrez, Naipes y fig*); **los ~es** (*frec*) the king and queen; royalty; **los R~es Católicos** the Catholic Monarchs (*Ferdinand and Isabella of Aragon and Castile*); **~ de armas** king of arms; **a ~ muerto ~ puesto** off with the old, on with the new; **ni ~ ni roque** no-one at all, not a single living soul; **lo mismo me da ~ que roque** it's all the same to me.

(b) (*Rel*) **los R~es** (**Magos**) the Magi, the Three Wise Men; (*fecha*) Twelfth Night, Epiphany; **nos veremos por R~es** we'll meet after Christmas; **¿qué te han traído los R~es?** ≃ what did Father Christmas bring you?

┌─ **DÍA DE REYES** ─┐

El Día de Reyes or Día de los Reyes Magos, often shortened to Reyes, which is on 6 January (Epiphany), is the day when children and adults in Spain traditionally receive presents for the Christmas season. When children go to bed on the night of 5 January, they leave their shoes outside their bedroom doors or by their windows for the Reyes Magos to leave presents beside. They may already have written letters to SS.MM. los Reyes Magos de Oriente with a list of what they would like. For Reyes it is traditional to eat Roscón de Reyes, a ring-shaped cake studded with frosted fruits and containing a little trinket or coin.

---

reyerta NF quarrel; fight, brawl, affray.

reyezuelo NM **(a)** petty king, kinglet. **(b)** (*Orn*) **~ sencillo** goldcrest.

rezaga NF (*LAm*) = **zaga**.

rezagado **1** ADJ **(a) quedar ~** (*quedar atrás*) to be left behind; (*llevar retraso*) to be late, be behindhand; (*en pagos, progresos etc*) to fall behind, be backward.

(b) carta rezagada (*And, Méx*) unclaimed letter.

2 NM, **rezagada** NF latecomer; loiterer, dawdler; (*Mil*) straggler.

rezagamiento NM falling behind, lagging behind; (*fig*) backwardness.

rezagar [1h] **1** VT **(a)** (*dejar atrás*) to leave behind; to outpace, outdistance.

(b) (*aplazar etc*) to postpone.

2 rezagarse VR (*quedar atrás*) to stay behind, fall behind, get left behind; to lag (behind); (*ir despacio*) to loiter, dawdle; to straggle; **nos rezagamos en la producción** we are falling behind in production.

rezago NM **(a)** (*géneros*) left-over goods (*etc*); (*sobra*) unused material, material which is left over; (*Cono Sur*) (*mercancías*) unsold (*o* remaindered) goods; (*ganado*) cattle rejected at the abattoir.

(b) (*vacas dispersas*) group of straggling cattle.

(c) (*And, Méx Correos*) unclaimed letters.

rezar [1f] **1** VT **(a)** *oración* to say.

(b) (*pedir*) to call for, plead for; **el periódico reza agua** the paper says we need rain.

2 VI **(a)** (*Rel*) to pray (*a* to); to say one's prayers; to be at prayer.

(b) (*texto*) to read, say, run, go; **el anuncio reza así** the notice reads as follows.

(c) (**: quejarse*) to grumble.

(d) **~ con*** to concern, have to do with; **eso no reza conmigo** that has nothing to do with me; that doesn't apply to me.

rezo NM **(a)** (*un ~*) prayer(s); devotions; (*oficio*) daily service; **estar en el ~** to be at prayer. **(b)** (*acto, gen*) praying.

rezondrada* NF (*And*) telling off*, scolding.

rezondrar [1a] VT (*And*) = **rezongar**.

rezongador ADJ = **rezongón**.

rezongar [1h] **1** VT (*CAm, Cono Sur*) to tell off, scold.

2 VI to grumble; to mutter; to growl.

rezongo NM **(a)** (*quejido*) grumble, moan. **(b)** (*CAm*) (*reprimenda*) reprimand; (*regaño*) scolding.

rezongón ADJ grumbling, grouchy*, cantankerous.

rezumar [1a] **1** VT to ooze, exude; to leak.

2 VI **(a)** (*contenido*) to ooze (out), seep, leak out; (*recipiente*) to ooze, leak.

(b) (*fig*) to ooze; **le rezuma el orgullo** he oozes pride; **le rezuma el entusiasmo** he is bursting with enthusiasm, he overflows with enthusiasm.

3 rezumarse VR **(a)** = **2 (a)**.

(b) (*fig*) to leak out, become known.

RFA NF (*Hist*) ABR *de* **República Federal Alemana** West Germany, FRG.

RFE NF ABR *de* **Revista de Filología Española**.

Rh NM ABR *de* **Rhesus** Rh; **ser Rh positivo** to be rhesus positive.

ría¹ *etc* V **reír**.

ría² NF estuary; **R~s Altas** northern coast of Galicia; **R~s Bajas** southern coast of Galicia.

riachuelo NM brook, stream; **~s de gente** crowds of people.

Riad NM Riyadh.

riada NF flood (*t fig*); **hasta aquí llegó la ~** that's how bad things were.

ribazo NM steep slope, steep bank.

ribeiro NM young white wine from Galicia.

ribera NF **(a)** (*de lago, río*) bank; (*de mar*) beach, shore; (*zona*) riverside.

(b) (*Agr*) irrigated plain.

(c) (*Cono Sur, Méx*) (*de campo*) riverside community; (*chabolas*) shanty town, slum quarter.

riberano ADJ (*LAm*) = **ribereño**.

ribereño **1** ADJ riverside (*atr*); coastal; (*Jur*) riparian.

2 NM, **ribereña** NF person who lives near a river; riverside dweller.

ribete NM **(a)** (*Cos*) edging, border, trimming.

(b) (*fig: adorno*) addition, adornment; **~s** (*de cuento*) embellishments, trimmings, personal touches.

(c) **~s** (*fig: elementos*) touch, quality; **tiene sus ~s de pintor** he has some pretensions to being a painter, he is not without some of the painter's talents.

ribetear [1a] VT to edge, border, trim (*de* with).

ribo NM (*And*) (*de río*) bank; (*de mar*) shore.

riboflavina NF riboflavin.

ricacho*, **ricachón*** NM fabulously rich man; nouveau riche (*Pol: pey*) well-heeled bourgeois*, dirty capitalist.

ricamente ADV **(a)** (*lit*) richly.

(b) (*fig*) **muy ~, tan ~** very well, jolly well*; **comeremos tan ~** we'll have a really good meal; **he dormido tan ~** I've slept splendidly; **viven muy ~ sin él** they manage perfectly well without him.

Ricardo NM Richard.

ricino NM castor-oil plant; **aceite de ~** castor oil.

ricito NM ringlet, kiss-curl.

rico ① ADJ (a) (*Fin*) rich, wealthy; **llueva sobre el más ~** to him that hath shall be given.
(b) (*fig*) *suelo, vena etc* rich; **~ de, ~ en** rich in.
(c) *joya etc* valuable, precious; *muebles etc* luxurious, sumptuous, valuable; *tela* fine-quality, rich.
(d) (*sabroso*) delicious, tasty; *fruta* luscious; **estos pasteles son riquísimos** these cakes are exceptionally tasty, these cakes are really lovely.
(e) (*) *niño* bonny; cute, lovely; (*en oración directa: a marido etc*) **¡~!** darling!; **¡oye, ~!** hey, man!*; **¡que no, ~!** (*Esp*) no way, mate!* **¡oye, rica!** (*Esp*) hey, beautiful!; hullo, gorgeous!*; **¡qué ~ está el pequeño!** isn't he a lovely baby!; **¡qué ~!** (*iró*) isn't that just splendid?; **está muy rica la tía** she's a bit of all right‡.
② NM, **rica** NF rich person; wealthy man, wealthy woman; **nuevo ~** nouveau riche.

rictus NM (involuntary) curl of the lip, rictus; (*de desprecio*) sneer; (*de burla*) grin; **~ de dolor** wince of pain; **~ de amargura** bitter smile.

ricura* NF (a) (*lo sabroso*) tastiness, delicious quality,
(b) (*chica*) smashing girl*; **¡oye, ~!** hey, beautiful!; hullo, gorgeous*.
(c) **¡qué ~ de pastel!** isn't this a lovely cake?; what a smashing cake!*; **¡qué ~ de criatura!** what a lovely baby!

ridi* ① ADJ ridiculous; **¡no seas ~!** don't be ridiculous!
② NM: **hacer el ~** to make a fool of oneself.

ridículamente ADV ridiculously, absurdly.

ridiculez NF absurdity.

ridiculización NF mockery; parody.

ridiculizador ADJ, **ridiculizante** ADJ mocking, derisive.

ridiculizar [1f] VT to ridicule, deride; to mock, guy, parody.

ridículo ① ADJ ridiculous, absurd, ludicrous.
② NM (a) **hacer el ~** to make o.s. ridiculous, make a fool of o.s.
(b) ridicule; **exponerse al ~** to lay o.s. open to ridicule; **poner a uno en ~** to ridicule sb, make a fool of sb; **ponerse en ~** to make o.s. ridiculous, make a fool of o.s.

riego NM (*aspersión*) watering; (*Agr*) irrigation; (*fig*) sprinkling; **~ por aspersión, ~ por goteo** watering by spray, watering by sprinklers; **la política del ~ en esta provincia** irrigation policy in this province.

riel NM (a) (*Ferro*) rail; **~es** rails, track, permanent way. (b) (*Téc*) ingot.

rielar [1a] VI (*poét*) to shimmer; to glitter, gleam.

rielazo* NM (*CAm*) blow, smack.

rielero NM (*Méx*) railwayman.

ríen *etc* V **reír**.

rienda NF rein; (*fig*) restraint, moderating influence; **a ~ suelta** at top speed; (*fig*) without the least restraint; violently; **aflojar las ~s** to let up; **dar ~ suelta a** to give free rein to; **dar ~ suelta al llanto** to weep uncontrollably; **dar ~ suelta a los deseos** to indulge one's desires freely; **dar ~ suelta a uno** to give sb a free hand; **empuñar las ~s** to take charge; **llevar las ~s** to be in charge, be in control; **soltar las ~s** to relinquish control; to take off the brakes; to kick over the traces; **tener a uno a ~ corta** to keep a tight rein on sb.

riendo V **reír**.

riente ADJ (a) (*risueño*) laughing, merry. (b) (*fig*) *paisaje etc* bright, pleasant.

riesgo NM risk, danger; **con ~ de** at the risk of; **seguro a** (o **contra**) **todo ~** comprehensive insurance; **grupos de ~** groups at risk; **correr ~ de** + *infin* to run the risk of + *ger*, be in danger of + *ger*.

riesgoso ADJ risky, dangerous.

Rif NM: **el ~** the Rif(f).

rifa NF (a) (*lotería*) raffle. (b) (*riña*) quarrel, dispute, fight.

rifar [1a] ① VT to raffle; **~ algo para fines benéficos** to raffle sth for charity.
② VI to quarrel, fight.
③ **rifarse*** VR (a) **~ algo** to quarrel over sth, fight for sth; **~ el amor de una** to vie for sb's love.
(b) (*CAm: arriesgarse*) to take a risk.

rifeño ① ADJ Riffian, of the Riff.
② NM, **rifeña** NF Riffian.

rififí* NM (a) (*acto*) burglary, robbery, (*esp*) bank robbery. (b) burglar, robber, bank-robber.

rifir(i)rafe* NM* shindy*, row.

rifle NM rifle; (*Dep*) sporting rifle; (*Caza*) hunting gun; **~ de repetición** repeater rifle.

riflero ① ADJ (*Cono Sur, Méx*) *tirador* ace, crack.
② NM (a) (*Mil*) rifleman. (b) (*Cono Sur, Méx: tirador*) marksman, crack shot.

rígidamente ADV (V ADJ) (a) rigidly, stiffly. (b) (*fig*) rigidly. (c) (*fig*) strictly, sternly, harshly. (d) woodenly.

rigidez NF (V ADJ) (a) rigidity, stiffness; **~ cadavérica** rigor mortis. (b) (*fig*) rigidity; inflexibility. (c) (*fig*) strictness, sternness, harshness. (d) woodenness.

rígido ADJ (a) (*tieso*) rigid, stiff; **quedarse ~** to go rigid; (*aterirse*) to get stiff (with cold).
(b) (*fig: actitud*) rigid, inflexible, unadaptable.
(c) (*fig: moralmente*) strict, stern (*con, para* towards), harsh, unbending.
(d) *mirada, cara* wooden, expressionless.

rigor NM (a) severity, harshness; strictness; toughness, stringency.
(b) (*Met*) harshness, severity; **el ~ del verano** the worst of the summer, the hottest part of the summer; **los ~es del clima** the rigours of the climate.
(c) (*severidad*) rigour; (*exigencia*) exacting nature; (*precisión*) accuracy, meticulousness; **con todo ~ científico** with complete scientific rigour; **una edición hecha con el mayor ~ crítico** an edition produced with absolute meticulousness.
(d) **ser de ~** (*esencial*) to be de rigueur, be absolutely essential; **después de los saludos de ~** after the customary greetings; **me dio los consejos de ~** he gave the expected advice, he gave me the advice which he felt he had to; **en ~** strictly speaking.
(e) **un ~ de cosas** (*And*) a whole lot of things.
(f) **dar un ~ a uno** (*Cono Sur*: *paliza*) to give sb a hiding*.

rigorismo NM strictness, severity; austerity.

rigorista ① ADJ strict.
② NMF strict disciplinarian; strict observer (*de* of), stickler (*de* for).

rigue NM (*CAm Culin*) tortilla.

rigurosamente ADV (a) (*severamente*) severely, harshly; (*estrictamente*) strictly; stringently.
(b) (*con precisión*) rigorously; accurately, meticulously.
(c) **un estudio ~ científico** an absolutely scientific study; **eso no es ~ exacto** that is not strictly accurate, that is not wholly true.

rigurosidad NF rigour, harshness, severity.

riguroso ADJ (a) *actitud, disciplina etc* severe, harsh; *aplicación etc* strict; *medida* severe, tough, stringent; **su tratamiento ~ de los empleados** his harsh treatment of the employees.
(b) (*Met*) harsh, severe, hard; extreme.
(c) *estudio, método etc* rigorous; exacting; accurate; meticulous.
(d) (*liter*) cruel; **los hados ~s** the cruel fates.

rija NF quarrel, dispute, fight.

rijio NM (a) (*CAm*) = **rijo**. (b) (*CAm, Méx*) spirit, spirited temperament (*of a horse*).

rijioso ADJ (*CAm, Méx*) = **rijoso**.

rijo NM lustfulness, sensuality; randiness*.

rijosidad NF (a) (*sensibilidad*) touchiness, susceptible nature; quarrelsomeness. (b) (*deseo sexual*) lustfulness, sensuality; randiness*.

rijoso ADJ (a) (*sensible*) touchy, susceptible; (*peleador*) quarrelsome. (b) (*cachondo*) lustful, sensual, randy*. (c) (*caballo*) in rut.

rila NF (a) (*And, Méx: de carne*) gristle. (b) (*And: excremento*) bird droppings.

rilado‡ ① ADJ knackered*, shagged out‡.
② NM coward.

rilarse‡ [1a] VI (a) (*agotarse*) to knacker o.s.*, get shagged out‡. (b) (*rajarse*) to back out, fall down on the job; to get cold feet. (c) (*asustarse*) to be dead scared. (d) (*temblar*) to shiver. (e) (*peerse*) to fart‡.

rima NF (a) (*gen*) rhyme; **~ imperfecta** assonance, half-rhyme; **~ interna** internal rhyme; **~ perfecta** full rhyme; **octava ~** ottava rima; **tercia ~** terza rima. (b) **~s** poems, verse, poetry.

rimado ADJ rhymed, rhyming.

rimador(a) NM/F rhymester.

rimar [1a] VTI to rhyme (*con* with).

rimbombancia NF (a) resonance, echo. (b) (*fig*) pomposity, bombast. (c) (*fig*) showiness, flashiness.

rimbombante ADJ (a) (*resonante*) resounding, echoing. (b) (*fig: pomposo*) pompous, bombastic. (c) (*fig: ostentoso*) showy, flashy.

rimbombar [1a] VI to resound, echo, boom.

rimel NM, **rímel** NM, **rimmel** NM mascara, eye-shadow.

rimero NM stack, pile, heap.

Rin NM Rhine.

rin NM (*And*) (*teléfono*) public telephone (using tokens); (*ficha*) token (for telephone).

rinche ADJ (*And, Cono Sur*) full to the brim, brimming over.

rincón NM (a) (*gen*) (inside) corner. (b) (*fig*) corner, nook; (*retiro*) retreat; niche. (c) (*Agr: esp LAm*) patch of ground.

rinconada NF corner.

rinconera NF (a) (*mueble*) corner-piece (of furniture); (*armario*) corner-cupboard, dresser. (b) (*Arquit*) wall between corner and window.

ring ['riŋ] NM, PL **rings** (boxing) ring.

ringla NF, **ringle** NM, **ringlera** NF row, line; (*Agr*) swath.

ringlete (*And, Cono Sur*) ① ADJ fidgety*, restless.
② NMF fidget*, restless person.

ringletear [1a] VI (*Cono Sur*) to fidget.

ringorrango NM (a) (*en escritura*) flourish. (b) **~s** (*adornos*) frills, buttons and bows, useless adornments.

ringuelete NMF (a) (*Cono Sur, And: inquieto*) rolling stone (*fig*). (b) (*And*) (*rehilete*) dart; (*molinillo*) toy windmill.

ringueletear [1a] VI (*And, Cono Sur*) = **callejear**.

rinitis NF: ~ **alérgica** hay fever.

rinoceronte NM rhinoceros.

rintoso: NM (*Carib*) skiver:, shirker.

riña NF (*disputa*) quarrel, argument; (*pelea*) fight, brawl, scuffle; ~ **de gallos** cockfight; ~ **de perros** dogfight(ing).

riñendo etc V **reñir**.

riñón NM (a) (*Anat*) kidney; (*más general*) lower part of the back; ~ **artificial** artificial kidney; **me costó un ~*** it cost me a bomb*; **tener riñones*** to have guts, be tough; **tener el ~ bien cubierto*** to be well-heeled*.

(b) (*fig*) heart, core; innermost part; **aquí en el ~ de Castilla** here in the very heart of Castile.

riñonada* NF: **me costó una ~** it cost the earth.

riñonera NF money belt, money pouch.

riñonudo* ADJ full of guts, tough.

río¹ [1] NM (*gen*) river; (*fig*) stream, torrent; ~ **abajo** downstream; ~ **arriba** upstream; **un ~ de gente** a stream of people, a flood of people; **es un ~ de oro** it's a gold mine; **a ~ revuelto, ganancia de pescadores** there are bound to be pickings for some, it's an ill wind that blows nobody any good; **cuando el ~ suena, agua lleva, cuando el ~ suena, piedras trae** there's no smoke without fire.

[2] ATR lengthy, long-lasting; epic; (*pey*) interminable; **novela ~ saga; programa ~** blockbuster of a programme; **serie ~** long-running series.

río², rió etc V **reír**.

Río de la Plata NM River Plate.

Rioja NF: **La ~** La Rioja.

rioja NM Rioja, Riojan wine.

riojano [1] ADJ Riojan, of La Rioja.

[2] NM, **riojana** NF Riojan.

[3] NM (a) (*vino*) Rioja. (b) (*Ling*) Riojan dialect.

riolada* NF flood, stream.

rioplatense [1] ADJ of the River Plate region.

[2] NMF native (*o* inhabitant) of the River Plate region; **los ~s** the people of the River Plate region.

riostra NF brace, strut.

Ripalda NM catechism of Jerónimo Ripalda; (*fig*) bible, handbook.

ripiado ADJ (a) (*And: harapiento*) ragged. (b) (*Carib: pobre*) wretched, down-at-heel.

ripiar [1b] VT (a) (*Arquit*) to fill with rubble. (b) (*And, Carib*) (*cortar*) to shred, cut into shreds; (*desmenuzar*) to crumble. (c) (*And, Carib: despilfarrar*) to squander. (d) (*And*) persona to leave badly off; **dos personas** to mix up. (e) (*Méx: espigar*) to glean. (f) (*Carib: pegar*) to hit.

ripiería NF (*And*) mob, populace.

ripio NM (a) (*basura*) refuse, waste; (*Arquit*) rubble; debris; (*Cono Sur*) roadstone.

(b) (*Liter*) padding, word (*o* phrase) put in to fill up the line; (*fig*) padding, verbiage, empty words; **no perder ~** not to miss a trick, to miss nothing of what is going on.

ripioso ADJ (*And, Carib*) ragged.

riquerío NM: **el ~** (*Cono Sur**) rich people (*collectively*).

riqueza NF (a) (*bienes*) wealth, riches; ~ **imponible** taxable wealth; **vivir en la ~** to live in luxury. (b) (*fig: cualidad*) richness.

riquiña NF (*Carib*) sewing basket.

riquiñeque NM (*And*) quarrel.

risa NF (*una ~*) laugh; (*gen, t ~s*) laughter; **hubo ~s** there was laughter; **no es cosa de ~** it's no laughing matter; **¡qué ~!** how very funny!, what a joke!; **el libro es una verdadera ~** the book is a laugh from start to finish; **~s enlatadas** canned laughter; **~ retozona** suppressed giggle, titter; **ahogarse** (*o* **caerse, descoserse, desternillarse, mondarse, morirse**) **de ~** to split one's sides laughing, die laughing*; **causar ~ a uno, mover** (*o* **provocar**) **a uno a ~** to make sb laugh; **entrar ganas de ~** to feel like laughing; **la ~ va por barrios** you'll all get your turn, every dog has his day; **soltar la ~** to burst out laughing; **tomar algo a ~** to take sth as a joke, laugh sth off.

risco NM (a) (*inclinado*) cliff, crag; steep rock. (b) **~s** (*terreno áspero*) rough parts, difficult pieces.

riscoso ADJ steep, craggy.

risible ADJ ludicrous, laughable.

risión NF derision, mockery; **ser un objeto de ~** to be a laughing-stock.

risotada NF guffaw, loud laugh.

rispiar [1b] VI (*CAm*) to rush off.

rispidez NF (a) coarseness, uncouthness. (b) roughness, sharpness.

ríspido ADJ (*esp LAm*) (a) (*maleducado*) coarse, uncouth. (b) (*áspero*) rough, sharp.

risquería NF (*Cono Sur*) craggy place.

ristra NF string (*t fig*); **una ~ de ajos** a string of garlic.

ristre NM: **en ~** at the ready, all set; V **lanza**.

risueñamente ADV smilingly; cheerfully.

risueño ADJ (a) cara smiling; **muy ~** smiling all over, with a big smile, wreathed in smiles.

(b) temperamento etc cheerful, sunny, gay; paisaje etc smiling, pleasant.

(c) perspectiva bright, favourable.

RITD NF (*Telec*) ABR de **Red Iberoamericana de Transmisión de Datos**.

rítmico ADJ rhythmic(al).

ritmo NM (a) (*Mús etc*) rhythm.

(b) (*fig*) rhythm; rate, pace; speed; ~ **cardíaco** pulse-rate; ~ **de crecimiento**, ~ **de expansión** rate of growth; ~ **de publicación** rate of publication; ~ **de vida** pace of life; lifestyle, way of life; **el trabajo se mantiene a un ~ intenso** the work is going on at a rapid rate (*o* pace); **trabajar a ~ lento** to go slow; **de acuerdo con el ~ de las estaciones** in keeping with the rhythm of the seasons.

rito NM rite, ceremony; ~ **iniciático** initiation rite; **~s de paso** rites of passage.

ritual ADJ, NM ritual; **de ~** ritual, customary.

ritualismo NM ritualism.

ritualista [1] ADJ ritualistic, ritual.

[2] NMF ritualist.

ritualizado ADJ ritualized; (*fig*) familiar; stereotyped, fixed.

rival [1] ADJ rival, competing.

[2] NMF rival, competitor; contender; **el eterno ~** (*fig*) the old enemy.

rivalidad NF rivalry, competition.

rivalizar [1f] VI to vie, compete, contend; ~ **con** to rival, compete with; **los dos rivalizan en habilidad** they rival each other in skill.

rizado ADJ pelo curly; superficie ridged, crinkly; terreno undulating; mar choppy.

rizador NM curling iron, hair-curler.

rizadura NF ripple.

rizapestañas NM INVAR eyelash curlers pl.

rizar [1f] [1] VT pelo to curl; to ruffle; superficie to ridge, crinkle; agua to ripple, ruffle; V **rizo¹** 2 (b).

[2] **rizarse** VR (*agua*) to ripple; ~ **el pelo** to perm one's hair.

rizo¹ [1] ADJ curly.

[2] NM (a) (*de pelo*) curl, ringlet; (*en superficie*) ridge; (*en agua*) ripple. (b) (*Aer*) loop; **hacer el ~, rizar el ~** to loop the loop; (*fig*) to split hairs.

rizo² NM (*Náut*) reef; **tomar ~s** to reef in (the sails).

rizoma NM rhizome.

R.M. ABR de **Reverenda Madre** Reverend Mother.

Rma. ABR de **Reverendísima** courtesy title.

Rmo. ABR de **Reverendísimo** Right Reverend, Rt. Rev.

RNE NF (*Rad*) ABR de **Radio Nacional de España**.

R.O. ABR de **Real Orden** royal order.

roano [1] ADJ roan.

[2] NM roan (horse).

robacarros NMF INVAR (*LAm*) car thief.

robacarteras NMF INVAR pickpocket.

robagallinas* NMF INVAR (*fig*) petty thief.

robalo NM, **róbalo** NM sea-bass.

robaperas* NMF INVAR (*fig*) petty thief.

robar [1a] VT (a) dueño to rob; objeto to steal (*a* from); casa etc to break into, burgle; cajafuerte to break open, break into, rifle (the contents of); ~ **algo a uno** to steal sth from sb, rob sb of sth; **en ese negocio me han robado** I was cheated in that deal; **X robó el balón a Y** X stole the ball from Y.

(b) persona to kidnap, abduct.

(c) (*fig*) atención etc to steal, capture; interés to command; paciencia to exhaust; tranquilidad to destroy; vida to take; ~ **el corazón a uno** to steal sb's heart; **tuve que ~ 3 horas al sueño** I had to use up 3 hours when I should have been sleeping.

(d) (*río*) to carry away.

(e) (*Naipes*) to draw, take (from the pile).

Roberto NM Robert.

robinsón NM castaway.

roblar [1a] VT to rivet, clinch.

roble NM oak, oak tree; **de ~** oak (*atr*), oaken; **de ~ macizo** of solid oak.

robledal NM, **robledo** NM oakwood.

roblón NM rivet.

roblonar [1a] VT to rivet.

robo NM (a) (*un ~*) theft; (*gen*) robbery, theft, thieving; ~ **a mano armada** armed robbery; ~ **con allanamiento**, ~ **con escalamiento**, ~ **con escalo**, ~ **en vivienda** housebreaking, burglary; ~ **relámpago** smash-and-grab raid; ~ **en la vía pública** highway robbery; **¡esto es un ~!** this is sheer robbery!

(b) (*cosa robada*) stolen article, stolen goods.

robot [ro'ßo] [1] NM, PL **robots** [ro'ßo] (a) robot. (b) (*fig*) puppet, tool.

[2] ATR stereotyped; identikit (*atr*).

robótica NF robotics.
robotización NF robotization; automation.
robotizar [1f] VT to automate; (*fig*) to turn into a robot.
robustecer [2d] **1** VT to strengthen.
　2 robustecerse VR to grow stronger.
robustecimiento NM strengthening.
robustez NF strength, toughness, robustness.
robusto ADJ strong, tough, robust.
ROC ABR *de* **Reconocimiento Óptico de Caracteres** Optical Character Recognition, OCR.
roca NF (**a**) rock; **en ~ viva** in(to) the living rock; **la R~** the Rock (of Gibraltar). (**b**) **ser firme como una ~** (*fig*) to be as solid as a rock. (**c**) (‡: *droga*) crack.
rocalla NF small stones, pebbles; stone chippings.
rocalloso ADJ pebbly, stony.
rocambolescamente ADV bizarrely, in a bizarre fashion; ornately, over-elaborately.
rocambolesco ADJ (*raro*) odd, bizarre; *estilo* ornate, baroque, over-elaborate.
rocanola NF jukebox.
rocanrol NM rock-'n'-roll.
rocanrolear* [1a] VI to rock and roll.
roce NM (**a**) (*acto*) rub, rubbing; (*Téc*) friction; (*fig: Pol etc*) friction. (**b**) (*señal*) rub, mark of rubbing; (*en la piel*) graze, chafing mark. (**c**) (*) (*contacto*) close contact; (*familiaridad*) familiarity; (*disgusto*) brush; **tener ~ con** to be in close contact with, have a lot to do with; **tuvo algún ~ con la autoridad** he had a few brushes with the law.
rochabús* NM (*Perú*) (police) water cannon truck.
Rochela NF: **La ~** La Rochelle.
rochela* NF (*And, Carib*) rowdy party; (*alboroto*) din, racket.
rochelear* [1a] VI (*And, Carib*) (*juguetear*) to play about; (*ir de juerga*) to go out on the town.
rochelero* ADJ (*And, Carib: ruidoso*) unruly, rowdy; (*Carib: travieso*) mischievous, naughty.
rociada NF (**a**) (*aspersión*) shower, spray, sprinkling; (*en bebida etc*) dash, splash; (*Agr*) spray. (**b**) (*fig: de piedras*) shower; (*de balas*) hail; (*de perdigones*) scatter; (*de insultos*) hail, stream, torrent.
rociadera NF watering can.
rociado NM sprinkling; (*Agr*) spraying.
rociador NM spray; sprinkler; **~ de moscas** fly spray.
rociar [1c] **1** VT to sprinkle, spray (*de* with); (*de lodo etc*) to spatter, bespatter (*de* with); (*de balas*) to spray (*de* with).
　2 VI: **empieza a ~** the dew is beginning to fall; **rocía esta mañana** there is a dew this morning.
rocín NM (**a**) (*caballo*) hack, nag, poor horse; (*Cono Sur*) riding horse; (*And*) draught ox. (**b**) (*: persona*) lout, ignorant fellow.
rocinante NM broken-down old horse.
rocío NM (**a**) (*Met*) (*de noche*) dew; (*llovizna*) light drizzle. (**b**) (*fig*) sprinkling; dew; drops of condensation (*etc*).
rock ADJ, NM (*Mús*) rock.
rockero **1** ADJ rock (*atr*); **música rockera** rock music; **es muy ~** he's a real rock fan.
　2 NM, **rockera** NF (*cantante*) rock singer; (*músico*) rock musician; (*aficionado*) rock fan.
rococó ADJ, NM rococo.
rocola NF (*LAm*) jukebox.
rocosidades NFPL rocky places.
rocoso ADJ rocky.
rocote NM, **rocoto** NM (*LAm*) large pepper, large chili.
roda¹ NF (*Náut*) stem.
roda² NM (*Aut*) crate*, car.
rodaballo NM turbot; **~ menor** brill.
rodada NF (**a**) (*de rueda*) rut, wheel track. (**b**) (*Cono Sur, Méx: caída*) fall (from a horse).
rodadero NM (*And*) cliff, precipice.
rodado **1** ADJ (**a**) *tráfico* wheeled, on wheels. (**b**) *piedra etc* rounded; **esto vino ~** this just happened (without my having to do anything); by luck the chance came up; **salir** (*o* **venir**) **~** to go smoothly. (**c**) *caballo* dappled. (**d**) *estilo* well-rounded, fluent. (**e**) (*fig: experimentado*) experienced.
　2 NM (*Cono Sur*) (wheeled) vehicle.
rodadura NF (**a**) (*acto*) roll, rolling. (**b**) (*rodada*) rut. (**c**) (*de neumático: t* **banda de ~**) tread.
rodaja NF (**a**) (*ruedecilla*) small wheel; (*disco*) small disc; (*de mueble*) castor. (**b**) (*de pan, fruta etc*) slice; **limón en ~s** sliced lemon.
rodaje NM (**a**) (*Téc*) wheels, set of wheels. (**b**) (*Cine*) shooting, filming. (**c**) (*Aut*) running-in; **'en ~'** 'running in'. (**d**) (*And: impuesto*) vehicle tax, road tax (*Brit*). (**e**) (*fig*) **período de ~** initial phase; **poner en ~**

to launch. (**f**) (*experiencia*) experience; know-how.
rodamiento NM (**a**) **~ a bolas**, **~ de bolas** ball-bearing. (**b**) (*Aut: de neumático, t* **banda de ~**) tread.
Ródano NM Rhône.
rodante **1** ADJ rolling; **material ~** rolling stock.
　2 NM (‡: *coche*) crate*, car; (*carro*) cart.
rodapié NM skirting board, baseboard (*US*); (*estera*) doormat.
rodar [1l] **1** VT (**a**) *vehículo* to wheel (along); *objeto* to roll, drag (along).
　(**b**) (*viajar por*) to travel, go over; **ha rodado medio mundo** he's been round half the world.
　(**c**) *coche* (*en carreras*) to race, drive; *coche nuevo* to run in.
　(**d**) (*Cine*) to shoot, film.
　(**e**) (*Inform*) *programa* to run.
　(**f**) (*Carib*) (*agarrar*) to seize; (*encarcelar*) to imprison.
　(**g**) **~** (**a patadas**) (*LAm*) to knock over, kick over.
　(**h**) (*LAm*) *ganado etc* to round up.
　2 VI (**a**) (*ir rodando*) to roll (*por* along, down, over *etc*); (*sobre ruedas*) to go, run, travel; (*Aut*) to go, drive; **~ de suelo** (*Aer*) to taxi; **se oía el ~ de los carros** one could hear the rumbling of the tanks; **~ por la escalera** to fall downstairs, go tumbling down the stairs; **echarlo todo a ~** (*fig*) to mess it all up, spoil everything; to throw one's hand in.
　(**b**) (*girar etc*) to go round, turn, rotate.
　(**c**) (*persona*) **andar** (*o* **ir**) **rodando** to move about (from place to place); (*gandulear*) to roll around, drift; **no hace más que ir rodando** he just drifts about; **me han hecho ir rodando de acá para allá** they kept shunting me about from place to place.
　(**d**) (*fig: existir todavía*) to be still going, exist still; **no sabía que ese modelo rodaba todavía por esos mundos** I didn't know that model was still about.
　(**e**) **~ por uno** to be at sb's beck and call, dance attendance on sb.
　(**f**) (*Cine*) to shoot, film; **llevamos 2 meses de ~ en Méjico** we've spent 2 months filming in Mexico.
　(**g**) (*Cono Sur: caballo*) to stumble, fall.
Rodas NF Rhodes.
rodear [1a] **1** VT (**a**) (*gen*) to surround (*de* by, with); (*encerrar*) to ring, encircle, enclose, shut in; (*brazos, ropa etc*) to encircle, enclose; **los soldados rodearon el edificio** the soldiers surrounded the building; **le rodeó el cuello con los brazos** she threw her arms round his neck.
　(**b**) (*LAm*) *ganado* to round up.
　2 VI (**a**) *ruta* to go round, go by an indirect route; to make a detour.
　(**b**) (*fig*) to beat about the bush.
　3 rodearse VR (**a**) **~ de** to surround o.s. with.
　(**b**) (*volverse*) to turn round; (*en la cama*) to turn over (and over), toss and turn.
rodela NF (**a**) (*Hist: escudo*) buckler, round shield. (**b**) (*Cono Sur: rosca*) padded ring (*for carrying loads on one's head*).
rodenticida NM rat-poison.
rodeo NM (**a**) (*ruta indirecta*) long way round, roundabout way; (*desvío*) detour; **dar un ~** to make a detour.
　(**b**) (*escape*) dodge; (*fig*) dodge, stratagem, subterfuge.
　(**c**) (*en discurso*) circumlocution; (*evasión*) evasion; **andarse con ~s, ir por ~s** to beat about the bush; **no andarse con ~s, dejarse de ~s** to talk straight, stop beating about the bush; **hablar sin ~s** to speak out plainly.
　(**d**) (*LAm*) round-up, rodeo (*US*).
rodera NF rut, wheel track.
Rodesia NF (*Hist*) Rhodesia.
rodesiano, -a ADJ, NM/F (*Hist*) Rhodesian.
rodete NM (**a**) (*de pelo*) coil, bun; (*de grasa*) roll; (*para llevar carga*) pad. (**b**) (*de cerradura*) ward.
rodilla NF (**a**) (*Anat*) knee; **de ~s** kneeling; **caer de ~s** to fall on one's knees; **doblar** (*o* **hincar**) **la ~** to kneel down; (*fig*) to bow, humble oneself, bend the knee (*ante* to); **estar de ~s** to kneel, be kneeling (down); **hincarse de ~s, ponerse de ~s** to kneel (down); **pedir algo de ~s** to ask for sth on bended knee; **poner de ~s a un país** to bring a country to its knees.
　(**b**) (*para llevar carga*) pad.
　(**c**) (*paño*) floorcloth, mop.
rodillazo NM push with the knee; **dar un ~ a** to knee.
rodillera NF (**a**) (*protección*) knee guard; (*remiendo*) kneepad, patch on the knee. (**b**) (*bolsa*) baggy part (*in knee of trousers*). (**c**) (*para llevar carga*) pad.
rodillo NM (*gen*) roller; (*Culin*) rolling pin; (*Tip*) ink roller; (*de máquina de escribir*) cylinder, roller; (*exprimidor*) mangle; (*Agr*) roller; **~ pastelero** rolling-pin; **~ pintor** paint roller; **~ de vapor** steamroller.
rodillón NM (*And*‡) old geezer*.
rodillona NF (*Carib*‡: *solterona*) old maid; (*And*‡: *bruja*) old bag*.
rodio NM rhodium.
rododendro NM rhododendron.

Rodrigo NM Roderick; **~ el último godo** Roderick, the last of the Goths.

rodrigón NM (*Agr*) stake, prop, support.

Rodríguez NM: **estar de ~** (*Esp*) to be a grass widower, be bacheloring it (*US*), be left on one's own.

roedor [1] ADJ **(a)** (*Zool*) gnawing. **(b)** (*fig*) *remordimiento etc* gnawing, ever-present, nagging.

[2] NM rodent.

roer [2z] VT **(a)** *comida* to gnaw; (*mordiscar*) to nibble at; *hueso* to gnaw, pick.

(b) *metal* to corrode, eat away, eat into.

(c) (*fig*) *capital etc* to eat into bit by bit.

(d) (*fig: remordimiento etc*) to gnaw, nag, torment.

rogación NF **(a)** petition. **(b)** **rogaciones** (*Ecl*) rogations.

▼ **rogar** [1h y 1l] [1] VT **(a)** *persona* to beg; to plead with; *cosa* to ask for, beg for, plead for; **~ a uno** + *infin* to ask sb to + *infin*, beg sb to + *infin*; **~ que** + *subj* to ask that ...; **ruegue a este señor que nos deje en paz** please ask this gentleman to leave us alone.

(b) (*Rel*) to pray.

[2] VI **(a)** (*pedir*) to beg, plead; **hacerse ~** to have to be coaxed, be unwilling to agree; to play hard to get; **no se hace de ~** he doesn't have to be asked twice.

(b) (*Rel*) to pray.

▼ [3] **rogarse** VR: '**se ruega la mayor puntualidad**' 'please be punctual'; '**se ruega no fumar**' 'please do not smoke'.

rogativas NFPL (*Ecl*) rogations.

rogatoria NF (*LAm*) request, plea.

rogatorio ADJ: **comisión rogatoria** investigative commission, committee of inquiry.

roja: NF 2000-peseta note.

rojamen* NM: **el ~** the reds, the commies*.

rojear [1a] VI **(a)** (*volverse rojo*) to redden, turn red.

(b) (*tirar a rojo*) to be reddish; (*mostrarse rojo*) to show red, look red.

rojeras* NMF INVAR red, commie*.

rojerío* NM: **el ~** the reds, the commies*.

rojete NM rouge.

rojez NF redness; (*en la piel*) blotch.

rojigualdo ADJ red-and-yellow (*colours of the Spanish flag*).

rojillo [1] ADJ (*Pol*) pink; (*fig*) suspicious, subversive.

[2] NM, **rojilla** NF pinko*, leftie*.

rojizo ADJ reddish; ruddy.

rojo [1] ADJ **(a)** (*gen*) red; ruddy; **~ burdeos** maroon, dark red; **~ cereza** cherry-red; **~ sangre** blood-red; **~ teja** brick-red; **poner ~ a uno** to make sb blush; **ponerse ~** to turn red, blush; **ponerse ~ de la ira** to be fighting mad.

(b) *pelo* red; sandy.

(c) (*Pol*) red; (*entre nacionalistas en España, 1936 y después*) Republican.

[2] NM **(a)** (*gen*) red, red colour; **calentar al ~** to make red-hot; **la atmósfera está al ~ vivo** the atmosphere is electric; **la emoción está al ~ vivo** excitement is at fever pitch; **un semáforo en ~** a red light.

(b) **~ de labios** rouge, lipstick.

(c) (*Pol*) red; Republican (*V* **1 c**).

rojura NF redness.

rol NM **(a)** (*lista*) list, roll; (*catálogo*) catalogue; (*Náut*) muster. **(b)** (*Teat y fig*) role, part. **(c)** (*Méx*) **dar un ~** to take a walk.

rola* [1] NF (*Carib: comisaría*) police-station.

[2] NMF (*Cono Sur: matón*) lout; (*zonzo*) thickhead*, dope*.

Rolando NM Roland.

rolar [1a] [1] VT **(a)** (*And, Cono Sur*) to touch on, mention (in conversation); **la conversación roló la religión** the conversation touched on religion.

(b) (*And, Cono Sur*) to associate with, be in contact with.

(c) (*Méx: pasar*) to pass from hand to hand.

[2] VI **(a)** (*Náut: viento*) to veer round.

(b) (*Cono Sur: ser arribista*) to be a social climber.

(c) (*And, Cono Sur: hablar*) to talk, converse (*con* with); (*And, Cono Sur: alternar con*) to associate, be in contact (*con* with).

Roldán NM Roland.

roldana NF pulley wheel.

rollazo* [1] ADJ dead boring*.

[2] NM deadly bore.

rollista* NMF (*pesado*) bore; (*mentiroso*) liar; (*chismoso*) gossip.

rollístico* ADJ dead boring*.

rollito NM roll; **~ de primavera** spring roll.

rollizo ADJ **(a)** *objeto* round, cylindrical. **(b)** *persona* plump; stocky; *niño* chubby; *mujer* plump, buxom.

rollo [1] ADJ INVAR boring, tedious.

[2] NM **(a)** (*gen: de paño, papel, película*) roll; (*de cuerda*) coil; (*Hist*) scroll; **en ~** rolled, rolled up; *madera* whole, uncut.

(b) (*Culin: rodillo*) rolling-pin.

(c) (*madera*) round log, uncut log.

(d) (*Culin: empanada etc*) roll.

(e) (*Anat**) roll of fat.

(f) (*Esp**) (*cosa pesada*) bore; (*discurso*) boring speech; (*explicación*) tedious explanation, lengthy justification; (*sermón: fig*) sermon; (*conferencia*) lecture; (*cuento*) tale, story; **~ macabeo, ~ patatero** deadly bore, awful drag; **la conferencia fue un ~** the lecture was an awful bore; **¡menudo ~ nos colocó!** some sermon he gave us!; **¡qué ~ más pobre!** what awful rubbish!; **nos soltó el ~ de siempre** he gave us the usual stuff*; **cortar el ~** to stop the flow (of talk *etc*), break in, interrupt; **estar de ~** to be doing something dead boring*.

(g) (*Esp**) (*asunto*) thing, affair; (*actividad*) activity; (*negocio*) business; **está metido en muchos ~s** he's stuck into so many things*; **no sabemos de qué va el ~** we're not in the picture*, we don't know what the score is*; **tirarse el ~** to shoot a line*.

(h) (*Esp**) (*contracultura*) alternative culture, alternative life-style, life-style of young people; **darle al ~** to go in for an alternative life-style; **montarse el ~** to organize one's life-style; **traerse un mal ~** to adopt a false life-style; **tener un ~ muy bueno** to have style.

(i) (*Esp**) (*ambiente*) ambience, atmosphere; **el ~ madrileño** the Madrid scene*; **me va el ~** I like this scene*, I'm having a great time*; **se estableció un buen ~ entre los dos** they really hit it off, they got a good scene going between them*.

(j) **largar el ~** (*And, Cono Sur*: vomitar*) to be sick, throw up.

(k) **~ de pelo** (*Carib*) (hair) curler, roller.

rolo NM (*LAm*) stick, truncheon.

Roma NF Rome; **~ no se construyó en un día** Rome was not built in a day; **por todas partes se va a ~** all roads lead to Rome; *V* **remover (a)**.

romadizo NM (*resfriado*) head cold; (*permanente*) catarrh; (*Carib: reuma*) rheumatism.

romana NF steelyard; **cargar la ~** (*Cono Sur**) to heap the blame on somebody else.

romance [1] ADJ *lengua* Romance.

[2] NM **(a)** (*Ling*) Romance language; (*castellano*) Spanish, Spanish language; **hablar en ~** (*fig*) to speak plainly.

(b) (*Liter*) ballad.

(c) (*: *amorío*) romance, love-affair.

(d) (*: *amante*) lover; (*de antes*) old flame*.

romancear [1a] [1] VT to translate into Spanish.

[2] VI (*Cono Sur*) **(a)** (*charlar*) to waste time chatting. **(b)** (*galantear*) to flirt.

romancero NM collection of ballads; **el R~** the Spanish ballads (*collectively*).

romancístico ADJ ballad (*atr*).

romaní ADJ, NM/F Romany, gipsy.

Romania NF Romance countries, Romance-speaking regions.

románico ADJ **(a)** (*Ling*) Romance. **(b)** (*Arquit*) Romanesque, Romanic; (*en Inglaterra*) Norman.

romanizar [1f] [1] VT to romanize.

[2] **romanizarse** VR to become romanized.

romano, -a [1] ADJ, NM/F Roman.

[2] NM (*Esp:*) cop*.

romanó NM (*Ling*) Romany.

románticamente ADV romantically.

romanticismo NM romanticism.

romántico, -a ADJ, NM/F romantic.

romanticón* ADJ *persona* sentimental, soppy*; *película, novela* slushy*, soppy*.

romaza NF dock, sorrel.

rombal ADJ rhombic.

rombo NM rhomb, rhombus; (*TV*) diamond (*warning of sexually explicit scene*); (*en diseño etc*) diamond, diamond shape.

romboidal ADJ rhomboid.

romboide NM rhomboid.

Romeo NM Romeo.

romereante NMF (*And, Carib*) pilgrim.

romería NF **(a)** (*Ecl*) pilgrimage; gathering at a local shrine; **ir en ~** to go on a pilgrimage; (*fig*) to go in throngs, go thronging. **(b)** (*fig: excursión*) trip, excursion; (*feria*) fair, (*baile*) open-air dance; (*fiestas*) festivities. **(e)** (*Aut*) queue (of cars); slow procession.

┌─ **ROMERÍA** ─┐

(i) *In Spain* **romerías** *are annual religious pilgrimages to chapels and shrines associated with particular saints or miracles of the Virgin. The pilgrims, called* **romeros**, *make their way on foot to the particular holy site, often covering long distances, and make offerings before gathering at* **el prado de la romería** *for a picnic. The day's festivities often include sports fixtures, fireworks and traditional music and dancing. Some* **romerías** *are large-scale events, one of the best known being the* **Romería de la Virgen del Rocío** *at Huelva in Andalusia, which involves spectacular processions of pilgrims in traditional Andalusian dress, some on horseback and some in brilliantly-decorated waggons.*

▶ LENGUA Y USO: **rogar: 1a** → 45.1, 46.1, 46.4, 48.1 **3** → 31

romero[1] NM, **romera** NF pilgrim.
romero[2] NM (*Bot*) rosemary.
romo ADJ **(a)** (*gen*) blunt; *persona* snub-nosed. **(b)** (*fig*) dull, lifeless.
rompebolas NMF INVAR (*Argentina*) pain in the arse.
rompecabezas NM INVAR **(a)** (*gen*) puzzle; (*acertijo*) riddle; (*juego*) jigsaw (puzzle). **(b)** (*fig*) puzzle; problem, teaser, headache.
rompecojones NMF INVAR pain in the arse.
rompecorazones NMF INVAR breaker of hearts.
rompedero 1 ADJ breakable, delicate, fragile.
   2 NM: ~ **de cabeza** (*Cono Sur*) puzzle, brain teaser.
rompedora-cargadora NF (*Min*) power-loader.
rompehielos NM INVAR icebreaker.
rompehuelgas NM INVAR strikebreaker, blackleg.
rompenueces NM INVAR nutcrackers.
rompeolas NM INVAR breakwater.
rompepelotas NM INVAR ball-breaker.
romper [2a; PTP **roto**] 1 VT **(a)** *juguete, plato etc* to break, smash, shatter; *barrera, cerca etc* to break down, break through; to breach; *cuerda etc* to snap, break; *paño, papel* to tear (up), rip (up); *niebla, nubes* to break through; **está a punto de ~ aguas** her water is about to break.
   (b) (*gastar*) to wear out, wear a hole in.
   (c) *olas* (*rompeolas*) to break the force of; (*barco*) to cleave.
   (d) (*roturar*) to break (up), plough.
   (e) (*Mil*) *línea etc* to break (through); V **fila**.
   (f) *ayuno, continuidad, silencio, sucesión etc* to break.
   (g) *contrato, pacto* to break; *amistad, relaciones* to break off.
   (h) (*Mil*) ~ **el fuego** to open fire; ~ **las hostilidades** to start hostilities.
   2 VI **(a)** (*olas*) to break.
   (b) (*capullo*) to open, burst.
   (c) (*guerra*) to break out.
   (d) (*diente*) to break through; (*sol*) to break through, appear, begin to shine; (*alba, día*) to break; ~ **entre** to burst one's way through; ~ **por** to break through.
   (e) ~ **a** + *infin* to start (suddenly) to + *infin*; ~ **a proferir insultos** to begin to pour forth abuse; ~ **a llorar** to burst into tears; **luego rompió a hacer calor** then it suddenly began to get hot.
   (f) ~ **en llanto** to burst into tears.
   (g) ~ **con uno** to fall out with sb, break with sb; **ha roto con su novio** she has broken it off with her fiancé.
   (h) de rompe y rasga brash, tearaway, impetuous; full of self-confidence; utterly inconsiderate; **rompe por todo** he presses on regardless; **quien rompe paga** one must pay the consequences.
   3 **romperse** VR to break, smash; to snap; to tear, rip; to wear out; **no te vayas a ~** don't be so fussy; you're not that delicate.
rompestómagos NM INVAR vile concoction.
rompiente NM reef, shoal.
rompimiento NM **(a)** (*acto*) breaking, smashing; (*de cristal, porcelana*) shattering; (*de muro etc*) breaching; (*de madera*) snapping; (*de tela, papel*) tearing; ~ **de aguas** downpour.
   (b) (*abertura*) opening, breach; (*grieta*) crack.
   (c) (*acto: fig*) break (*con* with); ~ **de contacto** (*Mil*) disengagement; ~ **de relaciones** breaking-off of relations.
   (d) ~ **de hostilidades** outbreak of hostilities.
romplón: de ~ ADV (*CAm, Méx*) off the cuff, on the spur of the moment.
rompope NM (*CAm, Méx*) eggnog.
Rómulo NM Romulus.
ron NM rum.
ronca NF **(a)** (*Zool*) (*sonido*) roar (*of rutting stag*); (*época*) rutting season.
   (b) (*fig*) threat; **echar ~s** to bully, threaten.
roncadoras NFPL (*LAm*) large spurs.
roncar [1g] VI **(a)** (*estando dormido*) to snore. **(b)** (*ciervo, mar, viento*) to roar. **(c)** (*amenazar*) to threaten, bully; (*And, Cono Sur*) to be bossy, domineer; to be jealous of one's authority.
roncear [1a] 1 VT **(a)** (*pedir repetidas veces*) to cajole, pester, keep on at. **(b)** (*LAm*) = **ronzar**[1]. **(c)** (*LAm: espiar*) to keep watch on, spy on.
   2 VI **(a)** (*Náut*) to move slowly. **(b)** (*trabajar a desgana*) to work (*etc*) unwillingly; (*gandulear*) to slack, kill time.
roncería NF **(a)** (*desgana*) unwillingness. **(b)** (*lisonja*) cajolery.
roncero ADJ **(a)** (*Náut*) slow, slow-moving, sluggish.
   (b) (*desganado*) unwilling; (*gandul*) slack, slow; **estar ~** to find reasons for shirking work (*etc*).
   (c) (*gruñón*) grumpy, grouchy.
   (d) (*cobista*) smooth, smarmy.
   (e) (*And, CAm, Cono Sur*) (*taimado*) sly, sharp; (*entrometido*) nosey, meddling.
roncha NF **(a)** (*cardenal*) bruise, weal, welt; (*hinchazón*) swelling; **hacer ~** (*Cono Sur*) to create an impression; **levantar ~** (*Carib*) to pass a dud cheque; **sacar ~** to cause an upset. **(b)** (*rodaja*) slice.
ronco ADJ *persona* hoarse; *voz* throaty, husky; *sonido* harsh, raucous.

roncón ADJ (*And, Carib*) boastful, bragging.
ronda NF **(a)** (*esp Hist*) night patrol, night watch; (*de policía*) beat; (*personas*) watch, patrol, guard; **ir de ~** to go the rounds, do one's round.
   (b) (*Mús*) group of serenaders.
   (c) (*de bebidas, negociaciones etc*) round; **pagar una ~** to pay for a round.
   (d) (*Naipes*) hand, round, game; (*en concurso*) round; (*Golf*) round.
   (e) (*Mil*) sentry walk.
   (f) (*Aut*: *t* ~ **de circunvalación**) outer road, ringroad.
   (g) (*Cono Sur*: *juego*) ring-a-ring-a-roses.
   (h) en ~ (*Cono Sur*) in a ring, in a circle.
rondalla NF **(a)** (*Mús*) band of street musicians. **(b)** (*ficción*) fiction, invention.
rondana NF (*LAm*) pulley; winch.
rondar [1a] 1 VT **(a)** (*Mil etc*) to patrol; (*inspeccionar*) to inspect, go the rounds of; (*fig*) to haunt, frequent, hang about; ~ **la calle a una joven** to hang about the street where a girl lives.
   (b) *persona* to hang round; (*acosar*) to harass, pester; *chica* to court.
   (c) *luz* (*mariposa*) to flutter round, fly about.
   (d) me está rondando un catarro (*fig*) I've got a cold hanging about.
   (e) el precio ronda los mil dólares the price is nearly a thousand dollars; **rondaba los 30 años** he was about 30.
   2 VI (*policía*) to patrol, go on patrol, go the rounds; (*fig*) to prowl round, go up and down, hang about; to roam the streets after dark; (*Mús*) to go serenading.
rondín[1] NM (*And, Cono Sur*) night watchman.
rondín[2] NM (*And Mús*) harmonica, mouth organ.
rondó NM (*Liter*) rondeau; (*Mús*) rondo.
rondón: de ~ ADV unexpectedly; unannounced, without warning; **entrar de ~** to rush in; (*en fiesta*) to crash a party.
ronquear [1a] VI to be hoarse, talk hoarsely.
ronquedad NF, **ronquera** NF hoarseness; huskiness.
ronquido NM snore; snoring; (*fig*) roar(ing); snort.
ronronear [1a] VI to purr.
ronroneo NM purr.
ronzal NM halter.
ronzar[1] [1f] VT (*Náut*) to move with levers, lever along.
ronzar[2] [1f] 1 VT to munch, crunch, eat noisily.
   2 VI to crunch.
roña 1 NF **(a)** (*Vet: de oveja*) scab, (*de perro*) mange; (*Bot*) rust.
   (b) (*mugre*) crust of dirt, filth, grime; (*en metal*) rust.
   (c) (*Bot*) pine bark.
   (d) (*fig: peligro moral*) moral danger, contagion.
   (e) (*fig: tacañería*) meanness, stinginess.
   (f) (*estratagema*) stratagem.
   (g) (*Carib, Méx*) (*envidia*) envy; (*inquina*) grudge, ill will.
   (h) (*And: Med*) feigned illness.
   (i) jugar a la ~ to play for fun, play without money stakes.
   2 NMF (*) skinflint.
   3 ADJ INVAR (*CAm, Cono Sur*) mean, stingy.
roñería NF meanness, stinginess.
roñica NMF skinflint.
roñoso ADJ **(a)** (*Vet*) scabby, mangy.
   (b) (*sucio*) dirty, filthy, grimy; rusty; (*fig: inútil*) broken down, useless.
   (c) (*fig: tacaño*) mean, tight.
   (d) (*And: tosco*) unpolished, coarse.
   (e) (*And: tramposo*) tricky, slippery.
   (f) (*Carib, Méx*) (*rencoroso*) bitter, resentful; (*hostil*) hostile.
ropa NF (*gen*) clothes, clothing; (*vestido*) dress; ~ **amplia** loose-fitting clothes; ~ **blanca** linen; ~ **blanca de mujer** lingerie; ~ **de cama** bed linen, bed-clothes; ~ **hecha** ready-made clothes; ~ **interior**, ~ **íntima** (*LAm*) underwear, underclothes; ~ **interior térmica** thermal underwear; ~ **lavada**, ~ **por lavar** washing; ~ **de mesa** table linen; ~ **planchada** ironing; ~ **sucia** dirty clothes, washing; ~ **usada** used clothing, secondhand clothes; ~ **vieja** (*Méx Culin*) meat stew; **a quema** ~ point-blank; **hay** ~ **tendida** be careful what you say, walls have ears; **guardar la** ~ to speak cautiously; **la** ~ **sucia se lava en casa** (*fig*) dirty linen should not be washed in public; **tentarse la** ~ to think long and hard (before doing anything); **no tocar la** ~ **a uno** not to touch a hair of sb's head, keep one's hands off sb; V **ligero, nadar**, *etc*.
ropaje NM **(a)** (*vestiduras*) gown, robes, ceremonial garb; ~**s** (*Ecl*) vestments.
   (b) (*fig*) drapes, drapery.
   (c) (*pey*) (*raro*) odd garb; (*excesivo*) heavy clothing, excessive amount of clothes.
   (d) (*Liter*) trappings, rhetorical adornments.
ropalócero NM butterfly.
ropavejería NF old-clothes shop.

ropavejero, -a NM/F old-clothes dealer.

ropería NF (**a**) (*tienda*) clothier's, clothes shop. (**b**) (*negocio*) clothing trade.

ropero [1] ADJ for clothes, clothes (*atr*); **armario ~ = 2** (**b**).
[2] NM (**a**) (*persona*) clothier.
(**b**) (*mueble*) wardrobe, clothes cupboard.

ropita NF baby clothes.

ropón NM (*de ceremonia*) long robe; (*bata*) loose coat, housecoat.

roque[1] NM (*Ajedrez*) rook, castle.

roque²• ADJ: **estar ~** to be asleep; **quedarse ~** to fall asleep.

roquedal NM, **roquedo** NM rocky place.

roqueño ADJ (**a**) (*rocoso*) rocky. (**b**) (*duro*) hard as rock, rock-like, flinty; (*fig*) rock-solid.

roquero = **rockero**.

rorcual NM rorqual, finback (whale).

ro-ro NM car ferry, roll-on/roll-off ferry.

rorro NM (**a**) (*: niño*) baby, kid•. (**b**) (*Méx*) fair blue-eyed person; (*muñeca*) doll.

Rosa NF Rose.

rosa [1] NF (**a**) (*Bot*) rose; **~ almizcleña** musk-rose; **~ laurel** rosebay, oleander; **~ palo** rosewood; **no hay ~ sin espinas** there's no rose without a thorn; **un cutis como una ~** a skin as soft as silk; **estar como una ~** to be fresh and clean; to feel as fresh as a daisy; **estar como las propias ~s** to feel entirely at ease; **florecer como ~ en mayo** to blossom, flourish.
(**b**) **de ~, color de ~** pink, rose, rose-coloured; **vestidos color de ~** pink dresses; *V t* **color.**
(**c**) (*Anat*) red spot, red mark, birthmark.
(**d**) (*Arquit*) rose window.
(**e**) **~ náutica, ~ de los vientos** compass (card), compass rose.
(**f**) **~s** (*Culin*) popcorn.
[2] ADJ INVAR pink, rose, rose-coloured; **revista ~** magazine of sentimental stories.

rosáceo ADJ = **rosado 1.**

rosacruciano ADJ Rosicrucian.

rosado [1] ADJ pink, rosy, roseate; (*fig*) *panorama* favourable, rosy.
[2] NM (*vino*) rosé.

rosal NM (**a**) (*planta*) rosebush, rosetree; **~ silvestre** wild rose, dog rose; **~ de China, ~ japonés** japonica. (**b**) (*Carib, Cono Sur: rosaleda*) rosebed, rosegarden.

rosaleda NF rosebed, rosegarden.

rosario NM (**a**) (*Rel*) rosary; chaplet, beads; **acabar como el ~ de la aurora** (o **del alba**) to end up in confusion, end with everybody falling out; **rezar el ~** to say one's rosary, tell one's beads.
(**b**) (*Agr*) chain of buckets (*of a waterwheel*).
(**c**) (*Anat•*) backbone.
(**d**) (*fig*) string, series; **un ~ de maldiciones** a string of curses.
(**e**) (*Arquit*) beading.

rosbif NM roast beef.

rosca NF (**a**) (*de humo etc*) coil, spiral, ring; (*Culin*) ring, ring-shaped roll; **estaba hecho una ~** he was all curled up in a ball; **comerse una ~:** to make it (with a woman):; **no comerse una ~:** to get absolutely nowhere (*con* with); **no me como** (o **jalo**) **una ~:** I don't understand a word of it.
(**b**) (*de tornillo*) thread; (*de espiral*) turn; **hacer la ~ a uno•** to suck up to sb•; **pasarse de ~** (*tornillo*) to have a crossed thread; (*fig*) to go too far, overdo it.
(**c**) (*Anat*) (*hinchazón*) swelling; (*de grasa*) roll of fat.
(**d**) (*Cono Sur: para llevar carga*) pad.
(**e**) (*Cono Sur: Naipes*) (circle of) card players.
(**f**) (*Cono Sur: discusión*) noisy argument; (*jaleo*) uproar, commotion; **se armó una ~** there was uproar.
(**g**) **tirarse una ~** (*Esp• Univ*) to plough•.
(**h**) (*And Pol*) ruling clique.

rosco[1] NM (*LAm Com*) middleman.

rosco² NM (**a**) (*Culin*) doughnut. (**b**) (*: Univ*) zero, nought.

roscón NM ring-shaped cake.

rosedal NM (*Cono Sur*) = **rosaleda.**

Rosellón NM Roussillon.

róseo ADJ rosy, roseate.

roseta NF (**a**) (*Bot*) small rose.
(**b**) (*Dep etc*) rosette.
(**c**) (*de regadera*) rose, nozzle.
(**d**) (*Anat*) red spot (on the cheek).
(**e**) (*Cono Sur*) prickly fruit, burr.
(**f**) (*And, Cono Sur: de espuela*) rowel.
(**g**) **~s (de maíz)** (*Culin*) popcorn.

rosetón NM (**a**) (*Arquit*) rose; rose window. (**b**) (*Dep etc*) rosette.

rosicler NM dawn pink, rosy tint of dawn.

rosita NF (**a**) (*Bot*) small rose. (**b**) (*Cono Sur: pendiente*) earring. (**c**) **de ~** (*And, Méx*) free, gratis; **andar de ~** (*Cono Sur, Méx*) to be out of work.
(**d**) **~s** (*Culin*) popcorn.

rosquero• ADJ (*Cono Sur*) quarrelsome.

rosquete NM (**a**) (*And, CAm: bollo*) bun. (**b**) (*And:*) queer:.

rosquetón• ADJ, NM (*Perú*) queer:.

rosquilla NF (**a**) (*de humo*) ring. (**b**) (*Ent*) grub, small caterpillar. (**c**) (*Culin*) ring-shaped pastry, doughnut; **venderse como ~s** to sell like hot cakes.

rosticería NF = **rotisería.**

rostizado ADJ roast.

rostizar [1a] VT to spit-roast.

rostro NM (**a**) (*Anat*) face (*para locuciones, compárese* **cara**); **retrato de ~ entero** full-face portrait. (**b**) (*Náut: Hist*) beak. (**c**) (*Zool, Hist etc*) rostrum.

rostropálido, -a NM/F paleface.

rotación NF (*gen*) rotation; (*una ~*) turn, revolution; (*Téc: de producción etc*) turnover; **~ de cultivos** rotation of crops; **~ de existencias** (*Com*) turnover of stock; **~ de la tierra** rotation of the earth.

rotacional ADJ rotational.

rotaje• NM (*Chile*) plebs• *pl*.

rotar [1a] VT (*Inform*) to rotate.

rotarianismo NM (*esp LAm*) Rotarianism.

rotariano ADJ, NM (*LAm*) = **rotario.**

rotario, -a ADJ, NM/F Rotarian.

rotativamente ADV by turns.

rotativo [1] ADJ rotary, revolving; *prensa* rotary.
[2] NM (**a**) (*Tip*) rotary press. (**b**) (*periódico*) newspaper. (**c**) (*luz*) revolving light. (**d**) (*Cono Sur Cine*) continuous performance.

rotatorio ADJ *puesto* rotating; **la secretaría será rotatoria** the secretaryship will rotate.

rotería NF (*Cono Sur*) (**a**) (*plebe*) common people, plebs. (**b**) (*truco*) dirty trick; (*dicho*) coarse remark.

rotisería NF (*Cono Sur, Méx*) grillroom, steak restaurant; eating-house.

roto [1] PTP *de* **romper.**
[2] ADJ (**a**) (*gen*) broken, smashed; *vestido etc* torn; ragged; *vida* shattered, destroyed; wasted; **estar ~ de cansancio** to be exhausted.
(**b**) (*fig*) debauched, dissipated.
(**c**) (*Cono Sur*) bad-mannered.
[3] NM (**a**) (*en vestido*) hole, torn piece, worn part; **nunca falta un ~ para un descosido** you can always find a companion in misfortune; birds of a feather flock together.
(**b**) (*Cono Sur: pobre*) poor wretch, down-and-out; (*iró*) fop, toff•.
(**c**) (*And, Cono Sur:: chileno*) *nickname given to a Chilean;* **el ~ chileno** the Chilean man in the street.
(**d**) (*And: mestizo*) half-breed.

rotograbado NM rotogravure.

rotonda NF (*Arquit*) rotunda; circular gallery; (*Ferro*) engine shed, roundhouse; (*Cono Sur Aut*) roundabout, traffic circle (*US*).

rotor NM rotor.

rotoso ADJ (**a**) (*LAm: harapiento*) ragged, shabby. (**b**) (*And, Cono Sur•: ordinario*) low-life, common.

rótula NF (**a**) (*Anat*) kneecap. (**b**) (*Mec*) ball-and-socket joint.

rotulación NF (**a**) (*escritura*) labelling; lettering. (**b**) (*profesión*) sign painting.

rotulador NM felt-tip pen, marking pen.

rotular [1a] VT *objeto* to label, put a label (o ticket *etc*) on; *mapa etc* to letter, inscribe; *carta, documento* to head, entitle.

rotulata NF (**a**) (*etiquetas*) labels, inscriptions *etc* (*collectively*). (**b**) (•) = **rótulo.**

rotulista NMF sign painter.

rótulo NM (*etiqueta*) label, ticket, tag; (*en museo etc*) label; (*título*) heading, title; (*en mapa etc*) lettering; inscription; (*letrero*) sign, notice; (*Com*) sign; (*cartel*) placard, poster; **~ luminoso** illuminated sign; **~ de salida** (*TV*) credits.

▼ **rotundamente** ADV *negar* flatly, roundly; *afirmar, expresar acuerdo etc* emphatically.

rotundidad NF (*V ADJ*) (**a**) rotundity. (**b**) forthrightness; clearness, convincing nature. (**c**) well-rounded character, expressiveness.

rotundo ADJ (**a**) (*redondo*) round. (**b**) *negativa etc* flat, round, forthright; *victoria* clear, convincing; **me dio un 'sí' ~** he gave me an emphatic 'yes'. (**c**) *estilo* well-rounded, expressive.

rotura NF (**a**) (*acto*) breaking *etc* (*V* **rompimiento** (**a**)); **~ de servicio** break of service.
(**b**) (*abertura*) opening, breach; (*grieta*) crack; (*en tela*) tear, rip, hole.
(**c**) (*acto: fig*) break (*con* with); **~ de relaciones** breaking-off of relations.

roturación NF breaking-up, ploughing.

roturar [1a] VT to break up, plough.

rough [ruf] NM: **el ~** (*Golf*) the rough.

roulotte [ru'lo] NF caravan, trailer (*US*).

round ['raun] NM, PL **rounds** (*Boxeo*) round.

roya NF (*Bot*) rust, blight.

royalty NM, PL **royalties** royalty.

➤ LENGUA Y USO: **rotundamente → 39.3**

roza NF **(a)** (*Arquit*) groove, hollow (*in a wall*). **(b)** (*prov, Cono Sur*) weeds. **(c)** (*Méx: matas*) brush, stubble. **(d)** (*And*) planting in newly-broken ground. **(e)** (*CAm: tierra limpia*) cleared ground.

rozado ADJ worn, grazed.

rozador NM (*Carib*) machete.

rozadura NF mark of rubbing, chafing mark; (*Med*) abrasion, graze, sore place.

rozagante ADJ **(a)** *vestido etc* showy, gorgeous; striking. **(b)** (*fig*) proud.

rozamiento NM **(a)** (*gen*) rubbing, chafing; (*Mec*) friction; wear. **(b) tener un ~ con uno*** to have a slight disagreement with sb.

rozar [1f] **①** VT **(a)** (*frotar*) to rub (on), rub against; (*raer*) to scrape (on); to chafe; (*Mec*) to grate on, cause friction with; (*Med*) to chafe, graze; (*tocar ligeramente etc*) to graze, shave, touch lightly; (*ave*) *superficie* to skim; **~ a uno al pasar** to brush past sb.
(b) (*arrugar*) to rumple, crumple; (*ensuciar*) to dirty.
(c) (*fig*) to touch on, border on; **es cuestión que roza la política** it's partly a political question.
(d) (*Arquit*) to make a groove (o hollow) in.
(e) (*Agr*) *hierba* to graze, crop, nibble.
(f) (*Agr*) *tierra* to clear.
② VI **(a) ~ en = 1 (a)**.
(b) ~ con (*fig*) = **1 (c)**.
③ rozarse VR **(a) ~ el cuello** to rub (o wear, chafe) one's collar; **~ los puños** to graze one's knuckles.
(b) (*ajarse*) to get worn, get rubbed (*etc*).
(c) (*: *tropezar*) to trip over one's own feet.
(d) ~ con* to hobnob with, rub shoulders with, mix with.
(e) ~ en un sonido to stutter over a sound, have trouble pronouncing a sound.

roznar¹ [1a] VTI = **ronzar.**

roznar² [1a] VI (*burro*) to bray.

roznido NM bray(ing).

R.P. ABR *de* **Reverendo Padre** Reverend Father.

r.p.m. NFPL *abr de* **revoluciones por minuto** revolutions per minute, rpm.

rrollo* NM = **rollo (g)**, **(h)**, **(i)**.

RRPP NFPL *abr de* **relaciones públicas** public relations, PR.

Rte. (*Correos*) *abr de* **remite, remitente** sender.

RTVE NF (*TV*) ABR *de* **Radiotelevisión Española.**

rúa NF (*prov*) street.

Ruán NM Rouen.

ruana NF (*And, Carib*) ruana, poncho, wool cape.

ruanetas NMF INVAR (*And*) peasant.

ruano ADJ, NM = **roano.**

rubeola NF, **rubéola** NF German measles, rubella.

rubí NM ruby; (*de reloj*) jewel.

rubia NF **(a)** (*gen*) blonde; **~ de bote, ~ de frasco, ~ oxigenada** peroxide blonde; **~ ceniza** ash blonde; **~ miel** honey blonde; **~ platino** platinum blonde. **(b)** (*Aut*) estate car, station wagon (*US*). **(c)** (*Fin**) one peseta.

rubiales NMF INVAR blond(e), fair-headed person; **R~** Goldilocks.

rubiato **①** ADJ fair, blond(e).
② NM, **rubiata** NF fair-haired person, blond(e).

Rubicón NM Rubicon; **pasar el ~ to** cross the Rubicon.

rubicundo ADJ **(a)** *cara, persona* ruddy, rubicund. **(b)** (*rojizo*) reddish.

rubiez NF blondness.

rubio **①** ADJ **(a)** *pelo, persona* fair, fair-haired, blond(e); *animal, pelo de animal etc* light-coloured, golden. **(b) tabaco ~ = 2.**
② NM Virginian tobacco.

rublo NM rouble.

rubor NM **(a)** (*color*) bright red. **(b)** (*en la cara*) blush, flush; **causar ~ a una** to make sb blush (*t fig*). **(c)** (*fig*) bashfulness; shame.

ruborizado ADJ blushing; flushed; (*avergonzado*) ashamed.

ruborizante ADJ blush-making.

ruborizar [1f] **①** VT (*t fig*) to cause to blush, make blush.
② **ruborizarse** VR to blush, flush, redden (*de* at).

ruboroso ADJ **(a) ser ~** to have a tendency to blush, blush easily. **(b) estar ~** to blush, be blushing, have a flush; (*fig*) to feel bashful.

rúbrica NF **(a)** (*señal*) red mark. **(b)** (*de la firma*) paraph, flourish. **(c)** (*título*) title, heading, rubric; **bajo la ~** under the heading of. **(d) de ~ = de rigor;** *V* **rigor.**

rubricar [1g] VT to sign with a flourish, sign with one's paraph; *documento* to initial; (*en sentido lato*) to sign and seal.

rubro NM **(a)** (*LAm: título*) heading, title; (*Tip*) headline; section heading.
(b) (*LAm: de cuenta*) book-keeping (entry).
(c) (*LAm: sección*) section, department (*of a business*).
(d) ~ social (*Cono Sur*) trading name, company name.

ruca NF **(a)** (*Cono Sur: cabina*) hut, cabin. **(b)** (*Méx: soltera*) old maid.

rucho ADJ (*And*) **(a)** rough. **(b)** *fruta* overripe.

rucio **①** ADJ *caballo* grey, silver-grey; *persona* grey-haired; (*Cono Sur*) fair, blond(e).
② NM grey (horse).

ruco ADJ **(a)** (*CAm, Méx*) (*usado*) worn-out; (*agotado*) exhausted. **(b)** (*And, Méx: viejo*) old.

ruda NF rue.

rudamente ADV simply, plainly; (*pey*) roughly, coarsely.

rudeza NF **(a)** (*simplicidad*) simplicity; plainness; (*pey*) roughness, coarseness, commonness. **(b)** (*estupidez*): **t ~ de entendimiento** stupidity.

rudimental ADJ, **rudimentario** ADJ rudimentary.

rudimento NM **(a)** (*Anat etc*) rudiment. **(b) ~s** rudiments.

rudo ADJ **(a)** *madera etc* rough; (*sin labrar*) unpolished, unworked.
(b) (*Mec*) *pieza* stiff.
(c) *persona* (*sencillo*) simple, uncultured; (*llano*) plain; (*pey*) rough, coarse, common.
(d) *golpe* hard.
(e) (*estúpido*) simple, stupid.

rueca NF distaff.

rueda NF **(a)** (*Mec etc*) wheel; (*neumático*) tyre; (*de mueble*) roller, castor; **~ de agua, ~ hidráulica** waterwheel; **~ de alfarero** potter's wheel; **~s de aterrizaje** (*Aer*) landing wheels; **~ de atrás** rear wheel, back wheel; **~ de cadena** sprocket wheel; **~ dentada** cog, cogwheel; gearwheel; **~ de la fortuna** wheel of fortune; **~ impresora** daisy-wheel; **~ libre** freewheel; **~ de molino** millwheel; **~ motriz** driving-wheel; **~ de paletas** paddle wheel; **~ de recambio** spare wheel; **~ de trinquete** ratchet wheel; **comulga con ~s de molino** he'd swallow anything; he's pretty thick*; **chupar ~** to bide one's time; **ir sobre ~s*** to go for a spin*; (*fig*) to go smoothly; to go with a swing. **(b)** (*círculo*) circle, ring; **en ~** in a ring; **~ de identificación, ~ de presos** identity parade; **~ informativa, ~ de prensa** press-conference. **(c)** (*Culin*) slice, round. **(d)** (*de torneo*) round. **(e)** (*Hist*) rack. **(f)** (*pez*) sunfish. **(g)** (*Orn: de pavón*) spread tail; **hacer la ~** to spread its tail; **hacer la ~ a una** (*fig*) to court sb; **hacer la ~ a uno** (*fig*) to play up to sb, ingratiate o.s. with sb. **(h) dar ~ (en)** (*Carib Aut*) to drive (around).

ruedecilla NF small wheel; roller, castor.

ruedero NM wheelwright.

ruedo NM **(a)** (*revolución*) turn, rotation. **(b)** (*contorno*) edge, circumference; (*borde*) border; (*de falda*) hem, bottom. **(c)** (*Taur*) bullring, arena; (*Pol etc*) ring. **(d)** (*esterilla*) (round) mat. **(e)** (*Cono Sur: suerte*) luck, gambler's luck.

ruega *etc* V **rogar.**

ruego NM request, entreaty; **a ~ de** at the request of; **accediendo a los ~s de ...** in response to the requests of ...; (*en orden del día*) **'~s y preguntas** 'any other business'.

rufián NM **(a)** (*coime*) pimp, pander. **(b)** (*gamberro*) lout, hooligan; (*canalla*) scoundrel.

rufiancete NM villain, rogue.

rufianería NF, **rufianismo** NM pimping, procuring; (*Jur*) living off immoral earnings.

rufianesca NF criminal underworld.

rufianesco ADJ **(a)** pimping, pandering. **(b)** loutish; villainous.

rufo ADJ **(a)** (*pelirrojo*) sandy-haired, red-haired; (*rizado*) curly-haired. **(b)** (*) (*satisfecho*) smug, self-satisfied; (*engreído*) cocky*, boastful.

rugbista NM rugby player.

rugby ['rugbi] NM rugby.

rugido NM roar; bellow; howl; **~ de dolor** howl of pain; **~ de tripas** intestinal rumblings, collywobbles*.

rugir [3c] VI **(a)** (*león etc*) to roar; (*toro*) to bellow; (*mar*) to roar; (*tormenta, viento*) to roar, howl, rage; (*persona*) to roar; (*tripas*) to rumble; **~ de dolor** to roar with pain, howl with pain. **(b)** (‡: *oler mal*) to pong‡, stink.

rugosidad NF roughness.

rugoso ADJ (*arrugado*) wrinkled, creased; (*desigual*) ridged; (*áspero*) rough.

ruibarbo NM rhubarb.

ruido NM **(a)** (*gen*) noise, sound; (*alboroto*) din, row; (*lo ruidoso*) noisiness; **~ blanco** white noise; **~ de fondo** background noise; **~ de sables** (*fig*) sharpening of knives; **sin ~** quietly, soundlessly, without making a noise; **no hagas ~** don't make a sound; **no hagas tanto ~** don't make such a noise; **mucho ~ y pocas nueces** much ado about nothing; **es más el ~ que las nueces** there's a lot of talk but nothing much gets done.
(b) (*fig*) (*escándalo*) commotion, stir; (*jaleo*) fuss; row, rumpus; (*grito*) outcry; **hacer ~, meter ~** to cause a stir, be a sensation; to have repercussions; to cause an outcry; **quitarse de ~s** to keep out of trouble.

ruidosamente ADV (*V* ADJ) **(a)** noisily, loudly. **(b)** (*fig*) sensationally.

ruidoso ADJ (a) (*estrepitoso*) noisy, loud. (b) (*fig*) *noticia* sensational; much talked-of.

ruin [1] ADJ (a) (*vil*) *persona* mean, despicable, low, contemptible; *trato* (*injusto*) mean, shabby; (*cruel*) heartless, callous.
(b) (*tacaño*) mean, stingy.
(c) (*pequeño*) small, weak.
(d) *animal* vicious.
[2] NM mean person (*etc*); **en nombrando al ~ de Roma, luego asoma** talk of the devil!; well, look who's here!

ruina NF (a) (*Arquit etc*) ruin; **~s** ruins, remains; **estar hecho una ~** to be a wreck; to be a shadow of one's former self.
(b) (*colapso*) collapse; **amenazar ~** to threaten to collapse, be about to fall down.
(c) (*fig*) ruin, destruction; (*de imperio*) fall, decline; (*de persona*) ruin, downfall; (*de esperanzas*) destruction; **será mi ~** it will be the ruin of me; **la empresa le llevó a la ~** the venture ruined him (financially).
(d) (*Jur*) bird‡, prison sentence.

ruindad NF (a) (*cualidad*) meanness, lowness; shabbiness; callousness.
(b) (*acto*) mean act, low trick, piece of villainy.

ruinoso ADJ (a) (*Arquit*) ruinous; tumbledown. (b) (*Fin etc*) ruinous, disastrous.

ruiseñor NM nightingale.

rula NF (*And, CAm*) hunting knife.

rular‡ [1a] VT *droga* to pass round.

rulemán NM (*Cono Sur*) ball-bearing, roller bearing.

rulenco, rulengo ADJ (*Cono Sur*) weak, underdeveloped.

rulero NM (*And*) hair curler, roller.

ruleta NF roulette; **~ rusa** Russian roulette.

ruletear [1a] VI (*CAm, Méx*) to drive a taxi, drive a cab.

ruleteo NM (*CAm, Méx*) taxi driving, cab driving.

ruletero NM (*CAm, Méx*) (*taxista*) taxi driver, cab driver; (*camionero*) lorry driver.

rulo¹ NM (a) (*pelota*) ball, round mass. (b) (*rodillo*) roller; (*Culin*) rolling pin. (c) (*del pelo*) hair-curler. (d) (*Cono Sur*) (*natural*) curl.

rulo² NM (*Cono Sur*) well-watered ground.

rulota NF caravan, trailer (*US*).

ruma* NF (*LAm*) heap, pile.

Rumania NF, **Rumanía** NF Romania.

rumano, -a [1] ADJ, NM/F Romanian.
[2] NM (a) (*lengua nacional*) Romanian. (b) (*: lenguaje*) special language, jargon; (*argot*) slang.

rumba¹ NF (a) (*Mús*) rumba. (b) (*Carib: fiesta*) party, celebration.

rumba² NF (*Cono Sur*) = **ruma**.

rumbar [1a] [1] VT (*LAm*) to throw.
[2] VI (a) (*And: zumbar*) to buzz. (b) (*And, Cono Sur: orientarse*) to get one's bearings.
[3] **rumbarse** VR (*And*) to make off, go away.

rumbeador NM (*And, Cono Sur*) pathfinder, tracker.

rumbear [1a] VI (a) (*LAm Mús*) to dance the rumba.
(b) (*LAm*) (*seguir un rumbo*) to follow a direction; (*orientarse*) to find one's way, get one's bearings.
(c) (*LAm*) to go out on the town, go on a binge*.
(d) (*Méx: en bosque*) to clear a path (through undergrowth).

rumbero [1] ADJ (a) (*And, Cono Sur*) tracking, pathfinding.
(b) (*Carib: juerguista*) party-going, fond of a good time.
[2] NM (*And*) (*en bosque etc*) pathfinder, guide; (*de río*) river pilot.

rumbo¹ NM (a) (*camino*) route, direction; (*Náut*) course; bearing; **con ~ a** in the direction of; **ir con ~ a** to be heading for, be going in the direction of, be bound for; (*Náut*) to be bound for; **corregir el ~** to correct one's course; **hacer ~ a** (o **hacia**) to head for; **poner ~ a** (*Náut*) to set a course for.
(b) (*fig*) (*tendencia*) course of events; (*conducta*) line of conduct; **~ nuevo** new departure; **los nuevos ~s de la estrategia occidental** the new lines of western strategy; **tomar ~ nuevo** to set off on a different tack, change one's approach; **los acontecimientos vienen tomando un ~ sensacional** events are taking a sensational turn.
(c) (*fig*) (*liberalidad*) generosity, lavishness; (*boato*) lavish display; (*ostentación*) showiness, pomp; **de mucho ~** = **rumboso**; **viajar con ~** to travel in style, travel in state.
(d) (*CAm*: *fiesta*) party, binge*.
(e) (*Cono Sur: herida*) cut (on the head).

rumbo² NM (*And Orn*) hummingbird.

rumbón* ADJ = **rumboso**.

rumbosidad NF lavishness.

rumboso ADJ (a) *persona* generous, lavish; free-spending. (b) *regalo* lavish; *boda etc* big, splendid, slap-up*.

rumia NF, **rumiación** NF rumination.

rumiante ADJ, NM ruminant.

rumiar [1b] [1] VT (a) (*masticar*) to chew. (b) (*fig*) *asunto* to chew over; to brood over, ponder (over).
[2] VI (a) (*pensar*) to chew the cud. (b) (*fig*) to ruminate, brood, ponder; (*pey*) to take too long to make up one's mind.

rumor NM (a) (*murmullo*) murmur, mutter; (*ruido sordo*) confused noise, low sound; (*de voces*) buzz; (*de agua*) murmur. (b) (*fig*) rumour.

rumoreado ADJ rumoured.

rumorearse [1a] VR: **se rumorea que ...** it is rumoured that ...

rumoreo NM murmur(ing).

rumorología NF rumours; gossip.

rumorólogo, -a NM/F scandal-monger.

rumorosidad NF noise level.

rumoroso ADJ full of sounds; *arroyo etc* murmuring, musical.

runa¹ NF rune.

runa² NM (*LAm*) Indian.

runcho ADJ (a) (*And*) (*ignorante*) ignorant; (*obstinado*) stubborn. (b) (*CAm*) mean.

rundir [3a] (*Méx*) [1] VT (*guardar*) to keep; (*ocultar*) to hide, put away.
[2] VI to become drowsy.
[3] **rundirse** VR to fall fast asleep.

rundún NM (*Cono Sur*) hummingbird.

runfla* NF, **runflada*** NF (*LAm*) (*masa*) mass, (*montón*) lot, heap; (*multitud*) crowd; (*pandilla*) gang (of kids*).

rúnico ADJ runic.

runrún NM (a) *de voces* sound of voices, buzz of conversation, murmur. (b) (*fig: rumor*) rumour, buzz. (c) (*de máquina etc*) whirr.

runrunearse [1a] VR: **se runrunea que ...** it is rumoured that ...

runruneo NM = **runrún** (a).

ruñir [3h] VTI (*And, Méx*) = **roer**; (*Carib*) = **roer** (a), (b).

rupestre ADJ rock (*atr*); **pintura ~** cave painting; **planta ~** rock plant.

rupia NF rupee; (‡) one peseta.

ruptor NM contact-breaker.

ruptura NF (*fig*) rupture; (*escisión*) split; (*de contrato etc*) breaking; (*de relaciones*) breaking-off; **~ matrimonial** breakdown of a marriage.

rural [1] ADJ rural, country (*atr*).
[2] NM (a) (*Cono Sur*) estate car, station wagon (*US*). (b) **los ~es** (*Méx Hist*) the rural police.

Rusia NF Russia; **~ Soviética** Soviet Russia.

ruso, -a [1] ADJ, NM/F Russian.
[2] NM (*Ling*) Russian.

rústica NF: **en ~** unbound, in paper covers; **libro en ~** paperback (book).

rusticidad NF (a) (*gen*) rusticity, rural character. (b) (*ordinariez*) coarseness, uncouthness; (*grosería*) crudity; (*descortesía*) unmannerliness.

rústico [1] ADJ (a) (*del campo*) rustic, rural, country (*atr*). (b) (*pey: tosco*) coarse, uncouth; (*grosero*) crude; (*sin educación*) unmannerly.
[2] NM rustic, peasant, yokel.

rustidera NF roasting tin.

ruta NF route; (*Cono Sur*) road; (*fig*) course, course of action; **~ aérea** air route, airway; **R~ Jacobea** Way of St James (*pilgrim road to Santiago de Compostela*).

rutero ADJ road (*atr*).

rutilancia NF sparkle.

rutilante ADJ (*liter*) shining, sparkling, glowing.

rutilar [1a] VI (*liter*) to shine, sparkle, glow.

rutina NF routine; **~ diaria** daily routine, daily round; **por** (o **de**) **~** as a matter of course, as a matter of routine; (*fig*) from force of habit.

rutinariamente ADV in a routine way; unimaginatively.

rutinario ADJ (a) (*ordinario*) *procedimiento* routine; ordinary, everyday. (b) *persona* ordinary; unimaginative; *creencia etc* unthinking, automatic.

rutinero [1] ADJ who sticks to routine; ordinary; unimaginative.
[2] NM, **rutinera** NF person who sticks to routine; ordinary sort, unimaginative person.

rutinizarse [1f] VR to become routine, become normal.

Rvdo. ABR de **Reverendo** Reverend, Rev(d).

S

S, s ['ese] NF (*letra*) S, s.
S (**a**) ABR *de* **sur** South, S. (**b**) (*Rel*) ABR *de* **San, Santa, Santo** Saint, St. (**c**) ABR *de* **septiembre** September, Sept. (**d**) (*Cine*) **película S** ABR *de* **película porno** pornographic film.
s. (**a**) ABR *de* **siglo** century, c. (**b**) ABR *de* **siguiente** following, foll.
s/ (*Com*) ABR *de* **su, sus.**
S.ª ABR *de* **Sierra** Mountains, Mts.
S.A. (**a**) (*Com*) ABR *de* **Sociedad Anónima** Limited, Ltd; public limited company, plc; (*US*) Corporation, Corp., Incorporated, Inc. (**b**) ABR *de* **Su Alteza** His Highness, Her Highness, H.H.
sáb. ABR *de* **sábado** Saturday, Sat.
sábado NM Saturday; (*judío*) Sabbath; **S~ de Gloria, S~ Santo** Easter Saturday; **hacer ~** to have a good clean-up, do the weekly clean.
sábalo NM (*pez*) shad.
sabana NF (*LAm*) savannah.
sábana NF (**a**) (*de cama*) sheet; (*Ecl*) altar cloth; **~ de agua** sheet of rain; **la S~ Santa de Turín** the Holy Shroud of Turin; **encontrar las ~s*** to hit the hay*; **estirarse más de lo que dan de sí las ~s** to bite off more than one can chew, over-reach oneself; **se le pegan las ~s** he loves his sleep; he's bad about getting up; **ponerse uno en la ~** to strike it lucky.
(**b**) (*Fin‡*) 1000-peseta note; **media ~** 500-peseta note; **~ verde** 10000-peseta note.
sabandija NF (**a**) (*insecto*) bug, insect, creepy-crawly*, creature; **~s** bugs, vermin. (**b**) (*fig*) wretch, louse‡.
sabanear [1a] **1** VT (**a**) (*CAm: agarrar*) to catch.
(**b**) (*CAm: halagar*) to flatter.
(**c**) (*CAm, Carib: perseguir*) to pursue, chase.
2 VI (*LAm*) to travel across a plain; to round up cattle on the savannah, scour the plain for cattle.
sabanero (*LAm*) **1** ADJ plain (*atr*), savannah (*atr*); of (*o* from) the plains (*o* savannah).
2 NM, **sabanera** NF plainsman, plainswoman.
3 NM (*CAm*: matón*) bully, thug.
sabanilla NF small sheet, piece of cloth; (*Ecl*) altar cloth; (*Cono Sur*) bedspread.
sabañón NM chilblain.
sabara NF (*Carib*) light mist, haze.
sabatario, -a ADJ, NM/F sabbatarian.
sabateño NM (*Carib*) boundary stone.
sabático ADJ sabbatical; (*del sábado*) Saturday (*atr*).
sabatino ADJ Saturday (*atr*).
sabedor ADJ: **ser ~ de** to know about; to be aware of.
sabelotodo* NM INVAR know-all.
▼ **saber** [2m] **1** VTI (**a**) (*gen*) to know; **~ de** to know about, be aware of; to know of; **desde hace 6 meses no sabemos nada de él** we haven't heard from him for 6 months, it's 6 months since we had news of him; **un 5 por ciento 'no sabe, no contesta'** there were 5% 'don't knows'; **lo sé** I know; **sin ~lo yo** without my knowledge; **hacer ~ algo a uno** to inform sb of sth, let sb know about sth.
(**b**) (*en pretérito, frec*) to find out, learn; to hear, get to know; (*darse cuenta*) to realize; **cuando lo supe** when I heard about it; **lograron ~ el secreto** they managed to learn the secret.
(**c**) (*locuciones*) **a ~** namely; **a ~ dónde lo tiene guardado** I wonder where he has it hidden away; **a ~ si realmente lo compró** I wonder whether he really did buy it; **es a ~** namely, that is to say; **¡haberlo sabido!** if only I'd known!; **¡yo qué sé!; ¡qué sé yo!** how should I know!, search me!*; **demasiado sé que ...** I know only too well that ...; **tú sabrás (lo que haces)** I suppose you know (what you're doing); **¡no lo sabes bien!*** not half!*; **que yo sepa** as far as I know; **que sepamos** as far as we know; **ya lo sabía yo** I thought as much; **un no sé qué** a certain something; **un no sé qué de afectado** a certain (element of) affectation; **nos sirvió no sé qué vino** he gave us

some wine or other; **A y B y no sé qué** (*o* **cuántos**) A and B and so forth; **¿tú qué sabes?** what do you know about it?; **vete a ~** your guess is as good as mine; **¡vete a ~!** God knows!; **¡vete a ~ de dónde ha venido!** goodness only knows where he came from!; **cualquiera sabe si ...** it's anybody's guess whether ...; **¿sabe?*** you know?*, you know what I mean?*; **costó muy caro, ¿sabe Vd?** it was very dear, you know; **¿quién sabe?** who knows?, who can tell?, who's to say?; **sepa Vd, para que lo sepa** let me tell you, just for your information; **cada uno sabe dónde le aprieta el zapato** everyone knows his own weaknesses; **no sabía dónde meterse** he didn't know what to do with himself; **no ~ ni papa** not to know the first thing about something; **no ~ a qué quedarse** to be in a dilemma; *V* **cuánto, más, convenir, Briján** *etc*.
▼ (**d**) **~ +** *infin* to know how to + *infin*, can + *infin*; **sé conducir** I can drive, I know how to drive; **¿sabes nadar?** can you swim?; **tiene que ~ contenerse** he must know how to control himself, he must be able to control himself.
(**e**) **~ +** *infin* (*movimiento*): **~ ir a un sitio** to know one's way to a place; **no sabe todavía andar por la ciudad** he still doesn't know his way about the town.
(**f**) **~ +** *infin* (*LAm: tener costumbre*) to be in the habit of + *ger*; **no sabe venir por aquí** he doesn't usually come this way, he's not in the habit of coming along here.
2 VI: **~ a** to taste of, taste like; (*fig*) to smack of; **esto sabe a queso** this tastes of cheese; **esto sabe mal, sabe a demonio(s)** this tastes awful; **le sabe mal que otro la saque a bailar** it upsets him that anybody else should ask her to dance, he doesn't like other people dancing with her.
3 saberse VR (**a**) **se sabe que ...** it is known that ..., we know that ...; **no se sabe** it's not known, nobody knows; **¿se puede ~ si ...?** may one inquire whether ...?; **¿quién es Vd, si puede ~?** who are you, may I ask?; **tiene que perder sépase cuánto tiempo para recuperarlo** he has to waste goodness knows how much time getting it back; **sépase que ...** let it be known that ...
(**b**) **se supo que ...** it was learnt that ..., it was discovered that ...; **por fin se supo el secreto** finally the secret was revealed.
4 NM (**a**) knowledge, learning; **~ popular** folk wisdom; **según mi leal ~ y entender** to the best of my knowledge, as far as I can honestly tell.
(**b**) **~ hacer** know-how.

┌─ **SABER** ─────────────────── **ver también la entrada** ─┐

Por regla general, si *saber* va seguido de un infinitivo, se traduce por *can* cuando indica una habilidad permanente y por **know how** cuando se trata de la capacidad de resolver un problema concreto. La construcción correspondiente habrá de ser *can* + INFINITIVO *sin to* o *know how* + INFINITIVO con to:

> Jaime sabe tocar el piano
> *Jaime can play the piano*
> ¿Sabes cambiar una rueda?
> *Do you know how to change a wheel?*

NOTA: Hay que tener en cuenta que *know* (sin *how*) nunca puede ir seguido directamente de un infinitivo en inglés.
Para otros usos y ejemplos ver la entrada.

└──┘

sabiamente ADV (**a**) (*eruditamente*) learnedly; expertly. (**b**) (*prudentemente*) wisely, sensibly.
sabichoso* ADJ (*Carib*) = **sabihondo.**
sabidillo, -a* NM/F know-all.
sabido **1** PTP *de* **saber**: **es ~ que ...** it is well known that ...; **como es ~** as we know, as is well known.
2 ADJ (**a**) = **consabido.**
(**b**) (*iró*) highly knowledgeable, learned.

(c) **de ~** (*por supuesto*) for sure, certainly.

(d) (*And*) lively, mischievous, saucy.

sabiduría NF wisdom; learning, knowledge; **~ popular** popular knowledge; folklore.

sabiendas: a ~ ADV (*sabiendo*) knowingly; (*con intención*) consciously, deliberately; **a ~ de que ...** knowing full well that ..., in the full knowledge that ...

sabihondo* [1] ADJ know-all, pedantic.

[2] NM, **sabihonda** NF know-all, self-proclaimed expert; smart Aleck*; pedant.

sabio [1] ADJ (a) (*docto*) learned; expert; (*iró*) know-all.

(b) (*juicioso*) wise, sensible, judicious; **más ~ que Salomón** wiser than Solomon.

(c) *acto, decisión etc* wise, sensible.

(d) *animal* trained.

[2] NM, **sabia** NF learned man, learned woman; wise person; scholar, expert, savant; (*Hist*) sage; **de ~s es rectificar** it takes a wise man to recognize that he was wrong; **¡hay que escuchar al ~!** (*iró*) just listen to the professor!

sabiondo, -a ADJ, NM/F = **sabihondo**.

sablazo NM (a) (*herida*) sword wound; (*golpe*) slash with a sword.

(b) (*: *gorronería*) sponging*; **dar un ~, pegar un ~** to make a touch* (*de for*); **dar un ~ a uno** to touch sb for a loan*, to scrounge money off sb*; **vivir de ~s** to live by sponging*.

(c) **la cuenta fue un ~** the bill was astronomical.

sable¹ NM sabre, cutlass.

sable² NM (*Her*) sable.

sablear* [1a] [1] VT: **~ algo a uno** to scrounge sth from sb*.

[2] VI (*por costumbre*) to live by sponging*; (*dar un sablazo*) to ask for a loan.

sablista* NMF sponger*, cadger.

sabor NM taste, flavour; savour, savouriness; (*fig*) flavour; **con ~ a** (*o* **de**) **queso** with a cheese flavour(ing), cheese-flavoured; **con ligero ~ arcaico** with a slightly archaic flavour (to it); **sin ~** tasteless; **le deja a uno mal ~ de boca** (*fig*) it leaves a nasty taste in the mouth.

saborcillo NM slight taste.

saborear [1a] [1] VT (a) *comida* to savour, relish (the savour of); (*probar*) to taste; (*deleitarse con*) to enjoy.

(b) (*dar sabor a*) to flavour, add a flavour to.

(c) (*fig*) to relish, enjoy; **~ el triunfo** to enjoy one's triumph, relish one's victory (to the full).

[2] **saborearse** VR (a) to smack one's lips (in anticipation).

(b) **~ algo** (*fig*) to relish the thought of sth.

saborete NM slight taste.

saborizante NM flavouring.

sabotaje NM sabotage.

saboteador NM saboteur.

sabotear [1a] VT to sabotage (*t fig*).

Saboya NF Savoy.

saboyano [1] ADJ of Savoy.

[2] NM, **saboyana** NF native (*o* inhabitant) of Savoy; **los ~s** the people of Savoy.

sabré *etc V* **saber**.

sabrosera NF (*LAm*) tasty thing, titbit.

sabroso ADJ (a) *comida* (*rico*) tasty, delicious; (*agradable*) nice, pleasant, agreeable.

(b) (*Esp Culin*) slightly salty.

(c) (*fig*) *libro etc* solid, meaty.

(d) (*fig*) *cuento, chiste etc* salty, racy, daring.

(e) (*And, Carib*: *agradable*) lovely, nice, pleasant.

(f) (*And, Carib, Méx: parlanchín*) talkative.

(g) (*Méx: fanfarrón*) bigheaded, stuck-up.

sabrosón* ADJ (a) (*LAm*) = **sabroso** (a). (b) (*And: parlanchín*) talkative, chatty.

sabrosura NF (*LAm*) (a) (*de comida*) tastiness. (b) (*fig*) pleasantness, delightfulness, sweetness; delight, enjoyment.

sabueso NM (a) (*Zool*) bloodhound. (b) (*fig*) sleuth.

saburra NF coat, fur (*on tongue etc*).

saburroso ADJ *lengua* coated, furred.

saca¹ NF (a) big sack; **~ de correo(s)** mailbag. (b) (*LAm*) (moving) herd of cattle.

saca² NF (*acto*) taking out; withdrawal; (*Com*) export; **~ carcelaria** illegal removal of a prisoner from prison (for execution); **estar de ~** (*Com*) to be on sale; (*fig*) to be at the right age to marry.

sacabocados NM INVAR (*Téc*) punch.

sacabotas NM INVAR bootjack.

sacabuche NM sackbut.

sacabullas* NM (*Méx*) bouncer*.

sacaclavos NM INVAR nail-puller, pincers.

sacacorchos NM INVAR corkscrew.

sacacuartos NM INVAR = **sacadineros**.

sacada NF (*And, Cono Sur*) = **sacadura**.

sacadera NF (*Pesca*) landing-net.

sacadineros NM INVAR (a) (*baratija*) cheap trinket. (b) (*diversión*) money-wasting spectacle, worthless sideshow (*etc*); (*truco criminal*) small-time racket. (c) (*persona*) cheat.

sacador(a) NM/F (*Tenis*) server.

sacadura NF (*And, Cono Sur*) extraction.

sacafaltas NMF INVAR faultfinder.

sacamanchas NM INVAR cleaning material, stain remover.

sacamuelas NMF INVAR (a) (*hum: dentista*) tooth-puller; (*Med*) charlatan, quack. (b) (*parlanchín*) chatterer.

sacaniguas NM INVAR (*And*) squib, Chinese cracker.

sacaperras* NMF INVAR con artist*.

sacapuntas NM INVAR pencil sharpener.

sacar [1g] VT (a) (*gen*) to take out, get out; to pull out, draw out, extract; (*Quím*) to extract; *carbón etc* to mine, bring up; (*del bolsillo etc*) to get out; *arma* to draw; *dinero* (*de banco*) to draw out, withdraw; (*borrar etc*) to remove, exclude; **~ fuera a uno** to chuck sb out, get rid of sb.

(b) (*fig: extraer*) to get (out); **~ una información a uno** to get information out of sb; **los datos están sacados de 2 libros** the data is taken from 2 books; **~ un secreto a uno** to get (*o* worm) a secret out of sb; **¿de dónde has sacado esa idea?** where did you get that idea?; **no conseguirán ~le nada** they'll get nothing out of him; **lo que se saca de todo esto es que ...** what I gather from all this is that ..., the result of this is that ...

(c) *mancha etc* to remove, get out, get off.

(d) (*Tenis*) to serve; (*Fútbol*) to throw in.

(e) *parte del cuerpo* to stick out, put out, thrust out; **~ la barbilla** to stick one's chin out; **~ la lengua** to put (*o* stick) one's tongue out; **~ la mano** (*Aut etc*) to put one's hand out.

(f) *prenda de vestir* (*Cos*) to let out.

(g) *ropa etc* (*esp LAm*) to take off; **~ la funda a un fusil** to take the cover off a rifle.

(h) *entradas etc* to get; *reservas* to make, book.

(i) *solución* to reach, obtain, get; *conclusión* to draw.

(j) (*producir*) *obra* to produce, make; *producto* to make; *novela etc* to bring out, publish; *modelo nuevo* to bring out; *moda* to create; *canción etc* to compose, make up; **aquí sacan 200 coches diarios** they make 200 cars a day here; **he sacado 20 páginas de notas** I've made 20 pages of notes; **para** (*o* **con**) **este propósito han sacado unos versos** they've made up some verses about this.

(k) (*Fot*) to take; *copia* to make, have made; **saca buen retrato** he takes well; **nos quiso ~ una foto** he wanted to take a photo of us; **no tenía la intención de ~ ese coche** I didn't mean to include that car in the photograph.

(l) (*obtener*) *beneficio, legado, premio etc* to get; to receive; *ganancia* to make; (*fig*) to derive (*de* from); **sacó el premio gordo** he got (*o* won) the big prize; **así no vas a ~ nada** you won't get anything that way; **sacó un buen número para la lotería** he drew a good number for the lottery; **la sociedad saca una ganancia de ...** the company makes a profit of ...

(m) (*Parl etc*) to elect; **han sacado 35 diputados** they have got 35 members elected; **por fin sacaron presidente a X** they finally elected X (as) president.

(n) *cualidad etc* to show; **por fin en esto sacó su habilidad** in this he finally showed (*o* demonstrated *o* proved) his skill; **~ faltas a uno** to point out sb's defects.

(o) *lustre etc* to put on, bring up, bring out; **~ los colores a la cara de uno** to bring the colour to sb's cheeks, put some colour into sb's cheeks.

(p) (*en periódico etc*) to mention, put; **no me vayas a ~ en tu discurso** don't mention me in your speech; **le han sacado en el periódico** they've put him in the paper.

(q) (*) **le saca 10 cm a su hermano** he is 10 cm taller than his brother, he has an advantage in height of 10 cm over his brother; **al terminar la carrera le sacaba 10 metros al adversario** at the end of the race he was 10 metres ahead of his rival.

(r) **~ adelante** *niño* to bring up; *licenciado etc* to produce, turn out; *negocio* to carry on, go on with; **~ a una adelante*** to get a girl in the family way.

(s) **~ a uno de sí** to infuriate sb.

(t) (*And, CAm: lisonjear*) to flatter, fawn on.

(u) (*And, Méx*) **~ algo a uno** to reproach sb for sth, throw sth back in sb's face.

[2] **sacarse*** VR (a) (*Méx*) to leave, go away; **¡sáquese de aquí!** get out of here!

(b) (*LAm*) **~ la ropa** to take off one's clothes.

sacarina NF saccharin(e).

sacarino ADJ saccharine.

sacatín NM (*And*) still.

sacerdocio NM priesthood.

sacerdotal ADJ priestly.

sacerdote NM priest; **~ obrero** worker priest; **sumo ~** high priest.
sacerdotisa NF priestess.
sacha ADJ INVAR (*LAm*) **(a)** (*fingido*) false, sham; **~ médico** quack. **(b)** (*desmañado*) bungling, unskilled; **~ carpintero** clumsy carpenter.
sachadura NF weeding.
sachar [1a] VT to weed.
sacho NM weeding hoe.
saciado ADJ: **~ de** sated with; (*fig*) steeped in, saturated in, full of.
saciar [1b] **⒈** VT **(a)** *hambre etc* to satisfy, satiate, sate; (*sed*) to quench. **(b)** (*fig*) *deseos etc* to appease; *curiosidad, anhelo etc* to satisfy; *ambición* to fulfil, more than satisfy.
⒉ saciarse VR to satiate o.s.; to be satiated (*con, de* with).
saciedad NF satiation, satiety; **demostrar algo hasta la ~** to prove sth up to the hilt; **repetir algo hasta la ~** to repeat sth over and over again.
saco[1] NM **(a)** (*bolso*) bag; (*costal*) sack; (*Mil*) kitbag; (*medida*) bagful; sackful; **~ de arena** (*Mil*) sandbag, (*Dep*) punchball; **~ de dormir, ~ manta** sleeping-bag; **~ de mano, ~ de noche, ~ de viaje** travelling bag; **~ postal** mailbag, postbag; **~ terrero** sandbag; **a ~s** (*fig*) by the ton; **la petición cayó en ~ roto** the appeal fell on deaf ears; **eso es echarlo en ~ roto** that's like throwing it down the drain; **no echar algo en ~ roto** to be careful not to forget sth; **no es** (*o* **no parece**) **~ de paja** he can't be written off as unimportant; **lo tenemos en el ~*** we've got it in the bag*; **tomar a una por el ~⁑** to screw sb⁑; **mandar a uno tomar por el ~⁑** to tell sb to get stuffed⁑.
(b) (*Anat*) sac.
(c) (*) **ser un ~ de gracia** to be very witty; **es un ~ de picardías** he's full of tricks; **ser un ~ de huesos** (*LAm*) to be a bag of bones.
(d) (*prenda*) long coat, loose-fitting jacket; (*LAm*) coat, jacket; (*And*) jumper; (*Cono Sur*) woman's overcoat.
(e) (⁑) 1000-peseta note; **medio ~** 500-peseta note.
(f) (⁑: *cárcel*) nick⁑, prison.
saco[2] NM (*Mil*) sack; **entrar a ~ en** to sack, loot, plunder.
sacón **⒈** ADJ **(a)** (*CAm*⁑) (*soplón*) sneaky; (*cobista*) flattering, soapy*. **(b)** (*LAm: entrometido*) nosey*, prying.
⒉ NM, **sacona** NF (⁑) **(a)** (*CAm: zalamero*) flatterer, creep⁑. **(b)** (*LAm: entrometido*) nosey-parker*.
⒊ NM (*Cono Sur*) woman's outdoor coat.
saconear* [1a] VT (*CAm*) to flatter, soap up*.
saconería* NF **(a)** (*CAm: zalamería*) flattery, soft soap*. **(b)** (*LAm: curiosidad*) prying.
SACRA NM (*Argentina*) ABR *de* **Sindicato de Amas de Casa de la República Argentina**.

┌─── ⓘ **SACRA** ───────────────────────────┐

ⓘ *Founded in 1984, SACRA, or the* **Sindicato de Amas de Casa de la República Argentina** *was the world's first trade union for housewives. One of its main aims has been to redefine housework as employment and to obtain for its members the salaries, pensions and health benefits traditionally associated with union membership. It has developed an educational programme designed to improve women's job opportunities, organized cheap holidays for housewives and obtained free medical treatment for its members. While union membership has allowed thousands of women to take part in public affairs, critics believe that the idea that housewives should have salaries simply reaffirms the stereotypical view that women function best in the home and, in the long run, may encourage non-participation outside.*

└──┘

sacral ADJ religious, sacral; totemic.
sacralización NF (*hum*) consecration, canonization.
sacralizar [1f] VT (*hum*) to consecrate, canonize; to give official approval to.
sacramental ADJ **(a)** (*Ecl*) sacramental. **(b)** (*fig*) ritual, ritualistic; time-honoured; **pronunció las palabras ~es** he spoke the time-honoured words.
sacramentar [1a] VT to administer the last sacraments to.
sacramento NM sacrament; **el Santísimo S~** the Blessed Sacrament; **recibir los ~s** to receive the last sacraments.
sacrificado ADJ *profesión, vida* demanding; *persona* self-sacrificing.
sacrificar [1g] **⒈** VT **(a)** (*gen*) to sacrifice (*t fig; a* to). **(b)** *animal* (*para carne*) to slaughter; *animal doméstico* to put down, destroy, put to sleep.
⒉ sacrificarse VR to sacrifice o.s.; to make a sacrifice.
sacrificio NM **(a)** (*gen, t fig*) sacrifice; **el ~ de la misa** the sacrifice of the mass. **(b)** (*de animal*) slaughter(ing); putting down, painless destruction.
sacrilegio NM sacrilege.
sacrílego ADJ sacrilegious.
sacristán NM verger, sacristan; sexton.
sacristía NF **(a)** (*Ecl*) vestry, sacristy. **(b)** (⁑) (*bragueta*) flies; (*horcajadura*) crotch.
sacro[1] ADJ sacred, holy.

sacro[2] NM (*Anat*) sacrum.
sacrosanto ADJ most holy; (*fig*) sacrosanct.
sacuara NF (*And Bot*) bamboo plant.
sacudida NF **(a)** (*gen*) shake, shaking; (*tirón*) jerk; (*choque*) jolt, jar, bump; (*de terremoto*) shock; (*de explosión*) blast; (*de la cabeza*) jerk, toss; **~ eléctrica** electric shock; **dar una ~ a una alfombra** to beat a carpet; **el coche avanzaba dando ~s** the car moved forward in a series of jolts, the car went jerkily forwards; **la ~ de la bomba llegó hasta aquí** the blast of the bomb was felt as far away as this.
(b) (*fig*) violent change; sudden jolt; (*Pol etc*) upheaval; **hay que darle una ~** he needs a jolt.
sacudido ADJ **(a)** (*brusco*) ill-disposed, unpleasant; (*difícil*) intractable. **(b)** (*resuelto*) determined.
sacudidura NF, **sacudimiento** NM = **sacudida**.
sacudir [3a] **⒈** VT **(a)** *árbol, edificio, miembro, persona, tierra etc* to shake; *persona* (*como castigo*) to beat, thrash; *ala etc* to flap, move up and down; *alfombra* to beat; *colchón* to shake (the dust out of); *cuerda etc* to jerk, tug; *pasajero, vehículo etc* to shake, jolt, jar, bump; to rock (to and fro); *cabeza* to jerk, toss.
(b) (*quitar*) *moscas etc* to chase away, brush off; *carga* to shake off.
(c) (*conmover*) to shake; **una tremenda emoción sacudió a la multitud** a great wave of excitement ran through the crowd; **~ a uno de su depresión** to shake sb out of his depression; **~ los nervios a uno** to shatter sb's nerves.
(d) **~ a uno** (*: *pegar*) to belt sb*, to beat sb up*.
(e) **~ dinero a uno*** to screw money out of sb.
⒉ sacudirse VR: **~ (de) un peso** to shake off a burden, get rid of a burden; **por fin se le han sacudido** they've finally got rid of him; **el caballo se sacudía las moscas con la cola** the horse brushed off the flies with its tail.
sacudón NM (*LAm*) violent shake, severe jolt; (*fig*) shake-up, upheaval.
sádico **⒈** ADJ sadistic.
⒉ NM, **sádica** NF sadist.
sadismo NM sadism.
sadista NMF sadist.
sado* ADJ = **sadomasoquista**.
sadoca⁑ NMF = **sadomasoquista**.
sado-maso* NM S & M, sado-masochism.
sadomasoquismo NM sadomasochism.
sadomasoquista **⒈** ADJ sadomasochistic.
⒉ NMF sadomasochist.
saeta NF **(a)** (*Mil*) arrow, dart. **(b)** (*de reloj*) hand; (*de brújula*) magnetic needle. **(c)** (*Mús*) *sacred song in flamenco style sung during Holy Week processions*. **(d)** (*Rel*) ejaculatory prayer.
saetera NF (*Mil*) loophole.
saetín NM **(a)** (*de molino*) millrace. **(b)** (*Téc*) tack, brad.
safado ADJ (*LAm*) = **zafado**.
safagina NF, **safajina** NF (*And*) uproar, commotion.
safari NM safari; **estar de ~** to be on safari; **contar ~s*** to shoot a line*.
safo⁑ NM hankie*, handkerchief.
saga NF **(a)** (*Liter*) saga. **(b)** (*fig*) clan, dynasty; family.
sagacidad NF shrewdness, cleverness, sagacity; astuteness.
sagaz ADJ **(a)** (*listo*) shrewd, clever, sagacious; (*astuto*) astute. **(b)** *perro* keen-scented.
sagazmente ADV shrewdly, cleverly, sagaciously; astutely.
Sagitario NM (*Zodíaco*) Sagittarius.
sagrado **⒈** ADJ sacred, holy (*t fig*); *escritura, órdenes etc* holy.
⒉ NM sanctuary, asylum; **acogerse a ~** to seek sanctuary.
sagrario NM shrine; tabernacle, sacrarium.
sagú NM sago.
Sahara NM, **Sáhara** NM ['saxara] Sahara.
saharaui **⒈** ADJ Saharan.
⒉ NM/F Saharan, native (*o* inhabitant) of the Sahara; **los ~s** the people of the Sahara.
sahariana[1] NF safari jacket.
sahariano, -a[2] ADJ, NM/F = **saharaui**.
Sahel NM Sahel.
sahumadura NF = **sahumerio**.
sahumar [1a] VT (*incensar*) to perfume (with incense); (*fumigar*) to smoke, fumigate.
sahumerio NM **(a)** (*acto*) perfuming with incense. **(b)** (*humo*) aromatic smoke; (*sustancia*) aromatic substance.
S.A.I. ABR *de* **Su Alteza Imperial** His (*o* Her) Imperial Highness, H.I.H.
saibó NM (*LAm*), **saibor** NM (*And, Carib*) sideboard.
saín NM **(a)** (*grasa*) animal fat, grease; *de pescado* fish oil (*used for lighting*). **(b)** (*en la ropa*) dirt, grease.
sainete NM **(a)** (*Culin*) seasoning, sauce; (*fig*) titbit, delicacy, pleasant adornment, nice extra. **(b)** (*fig*) spice, relish, tastiness. **(c)** (*Teat*) one-act farce (*o* comedy); comic sketch, skit.

> **SAINETE**
>
> ℹ️ A **sainete** is a humorous short, generally one-act, verse play sometimes performed as an interlude between the acts of a major play. **Sainetes** were developed in the 18th century by playwrights such as Ramón de la Cruz, and were largely based on satirical observations of ordinary people's lives and reflected this in the language they were written in. They were still being written by authors such as Carlos Arniches well into the 20th century.
>
> ⇨ See also **ENTREMÉS**

sainetero, -a NM/F, **sainetista** NMF writer of farces (*etc*).

sajar [1a] VT (*Med*) to cut open, lance.

sajín* NM (*CAm*), **sajino*** NM (*CAm*) underarm odour, smelly armpits.

sajón, -ona ADJ NM/F Saxon.

Sajonia NF Saxony.

sajornar [1a] VT (*Carib*) to pester, harrass.

sal¹ NF **(a)** (*gen*) salt; **~ amoníaca** sal ammoniac; **~es (aromáticas)** smelling-salts; **~es de baño** bath-salts; **~ de cocina, ~ común, ~ gorda** kitchen salt, cooking salt; **~ de eno** (*CAm*) fruit-salts, liver-salts; **~ de fruta(s)** fruit-salts; **~ gema** rock salt; **~ de la Higuera** Epsom salts; **~ de mesa** table salt; **~es minerales** mineral salts; **~ volátil** sal volatile.
(b) (*Esp: fig*) salt; (*gracia*) wit, wittiness; (*encanto*) charm, liveliness; **~ de la tierra** salt of the earth; **esto es la ~ de la vida** this is the spice of life; **tiene mucha ~** he's a great wit, he's very amusing, he's good company; **ella tiene mucha ~** she's delightful, she's absolutely charming.
(c) (*fig: LAm*) misfortune, piece of bad luck.

sal² V **salir**.

sala NF **(a)** (*de casa: t ~ de estar*) drawing-room; (*cuarto grande*) (large) room; (*edificio público*) hall; (*Teat*) house, auditorium; (*Jur*) court; (*Med*) (hospital) ward, section; **~ de alumbramiento** labour ward; **~ de autoridades** (*Aer*) VIP lounge; **~ de banderas** guardroom; **~ capitular** chapterhouse, meeting room; **~ de cine**, **~ cinematográfica** cinema; **~ de lo civil** civil court; **~ de conciertos** concert-hall; **~ de conferencias** lecture-room, lecture-hall; **~ de lo criminal** criminal court; **~ de embarque** (*Aer*) departure lounge; **~ de espectáculos** concert-room, hall; (*teatro*) theatre; (*cine*) cinema; **~ de espera** waiting-room; **~ de fiestas** dance-hall; nightclub; **~ de juntas** (*Com*) boardroom; **~ de justicia** lawcourt; **~ de lectura** reading room; **~ de máquinas** (*Náut*) engine-room; **~ de muestras** showroom; **~ de operaciones** operating theatre; **~ de partos** labour ward; **~ de prensa** press room; **~ de profesores** staffroom; **~ de pruebas** fitting room; **~ de recibo** parlour; **~ de salidas** (*Aer*) departure lounge; **~ de subastas** saleroom, auction-room; **~ del trono** throneroom; **~ de urgencias** casualty department; **~ X** cinema showing 'adult' films; **deporte en ~** indoor sport, indoor game.
(b) (*muebles*) suite of drawing-room (*etc*) furniture.

salacidad NF salaciousness, prurience.

sala-cuna NF, PL **salas-cuna** (*Cono Sur*) day-nursery.

saladar NM salt marsh, saltings.

saladería NF (*Cono Sur*) meat-salting plant.

saladito NM (*Cono Sur*) nibble, (bar) snack.

salado ADJ **(a)** (*Culin*) salty; savoury; *agua* salt; **muy ~** very salty, over-salted.
(b) (*Esp: fig*) (*gracioso*) witty, amusing; (*vivo*) lively; (*encantador*) charming, attractive, cute; *lenguaje* rich, racy; **es un tipo muy ~** he's a very amusing chap, he's a very lively sort; **¡qué ~!** how amusing!, (*iró*) very droll!, wasn't that clever of you?
(c) (*LAm: desgraciado*) unlucky, unfortunate.
(d) (*Cono Sur*) *artículo* dear, expensive; *precio* very high.

salamanca NF (*Cono Sur*) **(a)** (*cueva*) cave, grotto; (*lugar oscuro*) dark place. **(b)** (*brujería*) witchcraft, sorcery.

salamandra NF salamander.

salamanqués = **salmantino**.

salamanquesa NF lizard, gecko.

salame* NM (*Cono Sur*) idiot, thickhead*.

salami NM salami.

salar ① NM (*And, Cono Sur*) (*mina*) salt mine; (*yacimiento*) salt pan.
② [1a] VT **(a)** (*Culin*) *plato* to put salt in, add salt to.
(b) (*Culin: para conservar*) to salt, cure.
(c) (*And*) *ganado* to feed salt to.
(d) (*LAm*) (*arruinar*) to ruin, spoil; (*gafar*) to bring bad luck to, jinx*; (*maldecir*) to curse, wish bad luck on.
(e) (*CAm, Carib: deshonrar*) to dishonour.

salarial ADJ wage (*atr*); **reclamación ~** wage-claim.

salario NM wages, pay; (*LAm*) salary; **~ base** basic wage; **~ de hambre**, **~ de miseria** starvation wage; pittance; **~ inicial** starting salary; **~ mínimo interprofesional** guaranteed minimum wage.

salaz ADJ salacious, prurient.

salazón NF **(a)** (*acto*) salting. **(b)** (*carne*) salted meat; (*pescado*) salted fish. **(c)** (*CAm, Carib, Méx*) bad luck.

salazonera NF salting plant (*for salting fish*).

> **SALADO** | *ver también la entrada*
>
> • **Salado** se traduce por **salt** al referirse al agua de mar (por oposición a agua dulce) o a un producto que ha sido curado con sal:
>   El Caspio es un lago de agua salada
>   *The Caspian Sea is a salt lake*
>   El bacalao salado se emplea mucho en la cocina española
>   *Salt cod is used a great deal in Spanish cooking*
> • **Salado**, por oposición a dulce, se traduce por **savoury**:
>   ...platos dulces y salados...
>   *...sweet and savoury dishes...*
> • Si algo está **salado** porque sabe a sal o porque contiene demasiada sal, se debe traducir por **salty**:
>   Estas albóndigas están muy saladas
>   *These meatballs are very salty*
>   NOTA: **Salty** es la única de estas tres traducciones que se puede usar en grado superlativo o comparativo:
>   Esta carne está mucho más salada que la de ayer
>   *This is much saltier than the meat we had yesterday*
>   NOTA: Si nos referimos a almendras o cacahuetes salados se debe emplear **salted**.
>   *Para otros usos y ejemplos ver la entrada.*

salbeque NM (*CAm*) knapsack, backpack (*esp US*).

salbute NM (*Méx*) stuffed tortilla.

salceda NF, **salcedo** NM willow plantation.

salchicha NF sausage.

salchichería NF pork butcher's (shop).

salchichón NM (salami-type) sausage.

salchipapa NF (*And*) (kind of) kebab.

salcochar [1a] VT to boil in salt water.

saldar [1a] VT **(a)** *cuenta* to pay; *deuda* to pay off. **(b)** (*fig*) *diferencias* to settle, resolve; *V* **cuenta**. **(c)** *existencias* to sell off, sell up; *libros* to remainder.

saldo NM **(a)** (*acto*) settlement; payment.
(b) (*balance*) balance (*t fig*); **~ acreedor, ~ a favor, ~ positivo** credit balance; **~ activo** active balance; **~ del banco, ~ de cuentas** bank statement; **~ deudor, ~ en contra, ~ negativo** debit balance, adverse balance; **~ final** final balance; **~ vencido** balance due; **el ~ es a su favor** (*fig*) the balance is in his favour, on balance he comes off best.
(c) (*Com: liquidación*) clearance sale; **precio de ~** bargain price.
(d) (*restos*) remnant(s), remainder, left-over(s).

saledizo ① ADJ projecting.
② NM projection; overhang; **en ~** projecting, overhanging.

salera NF (*Cono Sur*) = **salina**.

salero NM **(a)** (*Culin: de mesa*) salt cellar. **(b)** (*reserva*) salt store. **(c)** (*Agr*) salt lick. **(d)** (*Esp: fig*) (*gracia*) wit, wittiness; (*encanto*) charm; (*sesapil*) sex appeal, allure, glamour. **(e)** (*Cono Sur*) = **salina**.

saleroso* ADJ = **salado (b)**.

saleta NF small room; vestibule.

salga *etc* V **salir**.

salida NF **(a)** (*acto*) leaving, going out, exit; emergence; (*viaje*) outing; (*Aer, Ferro etc*) departure; (*Astron*) rising; (*de gas etc*) leak, escape; (*Dep*) start; (*Golf*) drive; (*Teat: a escena*) appearance, entry, coming-on; (*Teat: para recibir aplausos*) curtain-call; **'S~s'** (*Ferro etc*) 'Departures'; **~ al campo**, (*Aer, Ferro etc*) field trip; **~ lanzada** running start, flying start; **~ parada** standing start; **~ del sol** sunrise; **oferta de ~** opening bid; **precio de ~** starting price; **la ~ fue triste** leaving was sad, our departure was sad; **a la ~ del trabajo** on leaving work; **a la ~ del teatro** as we (*etc*) came out of the theatre; **para García, dos orejas y ~ en hombros** (*Taur*) García won two ears and was carried out shoulder-high; **dar la ~** (*Dep*) to give the signal to start; **tomar la ~** (*Dep*) to line up (for the start); to start (*t fig*).
(b) (*Mil*) sally, sortie; (*Aer*) sortie.
(c) (*Naipes*) lead; **si la ~ es a trébol** if the lead is in clubs.
(d) (*Téc: producción*) output, production; (*Fin: inversion*) outlay; (*Inform*) output; **~ impresa** (*Inform*) hard copy.
(e) (*lugar etc*) exit, way out; (*Mec*) outlet, vent, valve; (*Geog*) outlet; **'S~'** 'Exit', 'Way Out'; **~ de artistas** (*Teat*) stage door; **~ de emergencia**, **~ de urgencia** emergency exit; **~ de incendios** fire-exit; **dar ~ a su indignación** to vent one's anger; **tener ~ a** (*Arquit*) to lead to, open on to, (*Geog*) have an outlet to.
(f) (*fig: solución*) way out; (*escapatoria*) pretext, loophole; (*truco*) dodge; **es una ~ cómoda** it's a simple solution; **no hay ~** there's no way out of it; **no tenemos otra ~ que firmarlo** there's nothing we can do but sign it, we have no option but to sign it; **dio con una ~ ingeniosa** he hit upon a clever way out; **es sólo una ~** it's only a pretext.

(g) (*fig: resultado*) issue, result, outcome.

(h) **~s** (*profesionales*) job opportunities.

(i) (*Com*) (*venta*) sale; (*posibilidad de venta*) sales outlet, opening; **dar ~ a** to sell, place, find an outlet for; **tener ~** to sell well; **el bikini no tiene ~ en Groenlandia** bikinis don't sell in Greenland; **tener una ~ difícil** to be a hard sell; **tener una ~ fácil** to have a ready market, be a soft sell.

(j) (*saliente*) projection, protuberance.

(k) (*prenda*) **~ de baño** bathing robe; beach robe; **~ de cama** dressing gown; **~ de teatro** evening wrap.

(l) (*Com*) (*de cuenta: gen*) item; (*cargo*) debit entry.

(m) (*chiste*) crack*, joke, witty remark; piece of repartee; **tener ~s** to be amusing, be full of wisecracks; to have amusing ideas.

(n) (*fig: comentario*) **~ de pie de banco, ~ de tono, ~ de bombero, ~ de torero** inept remark, ill-judged remark.

salido ADJ **(a)** (*gen*) projecting, sticking out; *ojos* bulging. **(b)** (*Esp*: *cachondo*) randy*, lustful; **estar ~** to be in the mood, feel randy*; (*Zool*) **estar salida** to be on heat. **(c)** (*) (*osado*) daring; (*pey*) foolishly confident, reckless.

salidor ADJ (*Carib, Cono Sur*) (*andariego*) restless, roving; (*fiestero*) partygoing; (*entusiasta*) lively, enthusiastic; (*Carib: buscapleitos*) argumentative.

saliente ① ADJ **(a)** (*Arquit etc*) projecting, protuberant; raised, overhanging; *rasgo* prominent.
(b) (*fig*) salient; outstanding.
(c) *sol* rising.
(d) *miembro etc* outgoing, retiring.
② NM projection; (*de carretera etc*) shoulder; (*Mil*) salient.

salina NF (*mina*) salt mine; (*depresión*) salt pan; **~s** (*fábrica*) saltworks; (*saladar*) salt flats.

salinera NF (*And, Carib*) = **salina**.

salinidad NF salinity; saltness, saltiness.

salinización NF (*acto*) salinization; (*estado*) salinity.

salinizar [1f] ① VT to salinify, make salty.
② **salinizarse** VR to become salty.

salino ADJ saline; salty.

salir [3q] ① VI **(a)** (*gen: persona*) to come out, go out (*de* of); to leave; to appear, emerge (*de* from); to get out (*de* of), escape (*de* from); **salimos a la calle** we went out into the street, we went out; **~ a ver algo** to go out to see sth; **~ de** to leave; **al ~ del cine** on leaving the cinema, when we (*etc*) came out of the cinema; **lo buscaremos al ~ de aquí** we'll look for it on the way out of here; **¿de dónde has salido?** where did you spring from?; **~ del coma** to emerge from a coma; **~ del enojo** to get over one's anger; **~ de un apuro** to get out of a jam; **~ de un puesto** to leave one's post, give up one's post; **este año sale de presidente** this year he ceases to be chairman, he gives up the chairmanship this year; **por fin salió de pobre** he finally left poverty behind him; **~ para** to leave for.

(b) (*gen: objetos etc*) to come out; to emerge, appear; (*Astron*) to rise, come up; (*Bot*) to appear, come up, show; (*revista etc*) to come out, appear, be published; (*moda etc*) to come in; (*mancha, suciedad*) to come off, come out; **el agua sale aquí** the water comes out here; **le salió un diente** he cut a tooth; **esta calle sale a la plaza** this street comes out in the square, this street leads to the square; **el vino sale de la uva** wine comes from grapes; **el anillo no le sale del dedo** the ring won't come off her finger, she can't get the ring off her finger; **le salió la satisfacción a la cara** satisfaction showed in his face; **la noticia salió en el periódico de ayer** the news came out in yesterday's paper; **por fin salió la causa de todo ello** eventually the reason for the whole thing came to light; **¡ya salió aquello!** so that was it!, so now we know!; **cuando salga la ocasión** when the opportunity comes up (*o* arises, presents itself); **si sale un puesto apropiado** if the right job comes up; **no le sale novio** she doesn't seem to be able to get a young man; **~ por la tele*** to appear on the telly*; **no sale ningún hombre en la peli*** there's not a man to be seen in the movie; **~ adelante** to do well, make progress, get on.

(c) (*resultar etc*) to turn out; to prove, be, turn out to be; **salga lo que salga** (*o* saliere) come what may; regardless of the consequences; whatever turns up; **si sale cierto** if it proves (to be) true; **la prueba salió positiva** the test proved positive; **la criada nos salió muy trabajadora** the girl turned out to be very hard-working; **el conserje salió un sinvergüenza** the porter turned out to be a rogue; **si sale cara** (*al echar moneda*) if it comes down heads; **este crucigrama no me sale** this crossword won't work out, I can't do this crossword; **le salen los problemas sin dificultad** he works problems out with no trouble at all; **~ a** (*precio*) to come to, amount to, work out at; **el traje le salió muy caro** the suit worked out very expensive for him; **esto nos va a ~ carísimo** this is going to cost us a fortune; **me sale a menor precio que a ti** it's working out cheaper for me than it is for you; **~ ganando** to gain, be the gainer; to come out on top; to emerge as the winner; to gain on a deal; **~ perdiendo** to lose, be the loser; to lose on a deal; **~ bien** (*persona*) to succeed,

make good; to do well; (*en examen*) to pass; (*fiesta etc*) to go off well; **~ mal** (*persona*) to fail, do badly, come unstuck; (*en examen*) to fail; (*fiesta etc*) to be a failure; **les salió mal el proyecto** the scheme miscarried, the plan went badly for them; **~ con la suya*** to get one's own way.

(d) (*Teat*: *t* **~ a escena**) to enter, come on; **sale vestido de policía** he comes on dressed as a policeman; **'sale el rey'** (*acotación*) 'enter the king'.

(e) (*autobús, tren etc*) to leave, depart; (*Náut*) to sail; **sale a las 8** it leaves at 8; **~ para** to leave for.

(f) **~ con** (*novios*) to go out with, date (*US*); **salen juntos desde hace 2 años** they've been going out (*o* around) together for two years.

(g) (*huevo, pollito*) to hatch.

(h) (*Arquit etc*) to project, jut out; to stick out; to overhang; **sale un poco más cada día** it comes out a little further each day; **el balcón sale unos 2 metros** the balcony projects about 2 metres.

(i) (*número de lotería etc*) to come up, win (a prize); (*Pol*: *t* **~ elegido**) to be elected, win; **salió alcalde por 3 votos** he was elected mayor by 3 votes.

(j) (*Naipes*) to lead; (*Ajedrez*) to have first move; (*Dep*) to start; **~ con un as** to lead an ace; **~ de triunfo** to lead a trump, play a trump.

(k) **y ahora sale con esto** (*decir*) and now he comes out with this.

(l) **~ por uno** to come out in defence of sb, stick up for sb.

(m) **~ con un propósito** to carry out a plan; **~ con una pretensión** to succeed in a claim; **ella sale con todo el trabajo** she manages to keep up with all the work; she is fully up to all the work.

(n) (*parecerse*) **~ a** to take after; **salió a su padre** he took after his father, he was exactly like his father.

(o) (*Fin*) **~ a los gastos de uno** to meet (*o* pay, defray) sb's expenses; **~ por uno** to back sb financially; to stand security for sb.

(p) (*Inform*) to quit, exit.

② **salirse** VR **(a)** (*gen*) = 1; **el camión se salió de la carretera** the lorry left (*o* ran off) the road; **~ del tema** to wander from the point; to make a digression, go outside one's subject; **se salió del partido** he left the party; **~ con la suya** to have it one's own way.

(b) (*animal, ave etc*) to escape (*de* from), get out (*de* of); (*aire, líquido etc*) to leak out; to overflow; (*al hervir*) to boil over; (*recipiente, río*) to leak; to overflow; **el barril se sale** (*Esp*) the barrel is leaking.

(c) (*Mec*) to become disconnected; **~ de la vía** (*Ferro*) to leave the rails, jump the track.

(d) **~ de costumbre** to break with custom, depart from tradition; **~ de lo normal** to go beyond what is normal; **~ de los límites** to go beyond the limits.

(e) **~ de un compromiso** to get out of an obligation.

SALIR	ver también la entrada

Para precisar la forma de salir

Aunque *salir* (*de*) se suele traducir por *come out* (*of*) o por *go out* (*of*) según la dirección del movimiento, cuando se quiere especificar la forma en que se realiza ese movimiento, estos verbos se pueden reemplazar por otros como *run out*, *rush out*, *jump out*, *tiptoe out*, *climb out*, etc.

Se vio a tres hombres enmascarados salir del banco corriendo
Three masked men were seen running out of the bank
Salió del coche con un salto
He jumped out of the car
Salió de puntillas de la habitación
He tiptoed out of the room
Para otros usos y ejemplos ver la entrada.

---

salita NF small room; (*Teat*) small auditorium.

salitre NM saltpetre, nitre.

salitrera NF (*fábrica*) nitre works; (*mina*) nitrate fields.

saliva NF saliva, spit; **gastar ~** (*fig*) to waste one's breath (*en* on); **tragar ~** to swallow one's feelings; to swallow hard.

salivación NF salivation.

salivadera NF (*Andalucía, Cono Sur*) spittoon, cuspidor (*US*).

salival ADJ salivary.

salivar [1a] VI to salivate; (*LAm*) to spit.

salivazo NM gobbet of spit; **arrojar un ~** to spit.

salivera NF (*Cono Sur*) spittoon, cuspidor (*US*).

salmantino ① ADJ of (*o* from) Salamanca.
② NM, **salmantina** NF native (*o* inhabitant) of Salamanca; **los ~s** the people of Salamanca.

salmear [1a] VI to sing psalms.

salmo NM psalm.

salmodia NF **(a)** (*Ecl*) psalmody. **(b)** (*: canturreo*) monotonous singing; drone, singsong.

salmodiar [1b] VI **(a)** (*Ecl*) to sing psalms. **(b)** (*) to drone, sing monotonously; to chant.

salmón NM salmon.

salmonela NF salmonella.

salmonelosis NF salmonellosis, salmonella food-poisoning.

salmonero ADJ: **río ~** salmon river.

salmonete NM red mullet.

salmuera NF pickle, brine.

salobre ADJ salt, salty; *agua* salt, brackish.

saloma NF (*Náut*) sea shanty, sea song; (*de trabajo*) working song.

Salomé NF Salome.

Salomón NM Solomon.

salomónicamente ADV with the wisdom of Solomon.

salomónico ADJ: **juicio ~** judgement of Solomon.

salón NM **(a)** (*de casa*) drawing-room, lounge; (*Arte e Hist*) salon; (*sala pública*) hall, assembly-room; (*Náut*) saloon; (*de colegio etc*) common-room; (*Com*) show, trade fair, exhibition; **~ de actos** assembly-room, hall; **~ del automóvil** motor show; **~ de baile** ballroom, dance-hall; **~ de belleza** beauty-parlour; **~ de demostraciones** showroom; **~ de fiestas** dance-hall; **~ de fumar** smoking room; **~ de masaje** massage parlour; **~ náutico** boat show; **~ de los pasos perdidos*** waiting-room; **~ de pintura** art exhibition, art gallery; **~ de reuniones** conference room; **~ de sesiones** assembly hall; (*Pol*) chamber; **~ de té** tearoom; **juego de ~** parlour game. **(b)** (*muebles*) suite of drawing-room furniture.

saloncillo NM (*Teat etc*) private room; restroom.

salonero NM (*And*) waiter.

salpicadera NF (*Méx*) mudguard.

salpicadero NM (*Aut*) dashboard.

salpicado [1] ADJ **(a)** **~ de** splashed with, spattered with; sprinkled with; **un diseño ~ de puntos rojos** a pattern with red dotted about in it; **una llanura salpicada de granjas** a plain with farms dotted about on it, a plain dotted with farms. **(b)** **un discurso ~ de citas latinas** a speech sprinkled with Latin quotations, a speech full of Latin quotations. **(c)** (*Cono Sur, Méx*) *animal* spotted, dappled, mottled.

[2] NM **(a)** (*acto*) splashing, spattering. **(b)** (*diseño*) sprinkle.

salpicadura NF **(a)** (*acto*) splashing, spattering; sprinkling; flecking. **(b)** (*mancha etc*) splash, spatter; sprinkle; dot, fleck. **(c)** (*fig*) spatter, peppering; sprinkling.

salpicar [1g] VT **(a)** (*de lodo, pintura etc*) to splash, spatter (*de* with); (*de agua etc*) to sprinkle (*de* with); *flores etc* to scatter, strew (about); *diseño, tela* to dot, fleck (*de* with); **~ un coche de barro** to splash a car with mud, splash mud over a car; **~ agua sobre el suelo** to sprinkle water on the floor; **la multitud de islas que salpican el océano** the host of islands dotted about the ocean; **este asunto salpica al gobierno** the government has got egg on its face over this affair. **(b)** (*fig*) *conversación, oración etc* to sprinkle, interlard (*de* with); to pepper (*de* with).

salpicón NM **(a)** = **salpicadura. (b)** (*Culin*) salmagundi. **(c)** (*And*: *jugos mixtos*) cold mixed fruit juice. **(d)** (*And, Cono Sur*) raw vegetable salad. **(e)** **~ de mariscos** seafood cocktail.

salpimentar [1a] VT **(a)** (*Culin*) to season, add salt and pepper to. **(b)** (*fig*) to season, improve, sweeten (*de* with).

salpiquear [1a] VT (*And, Carib*) = **salpicar.**

salpresar [1a] VT to salt (down).

salpreso ADJ (*Culin*) salted, salt.

salpullido NM **(a)** (*Med*) rash, skin disease. **(b)** (*picadura*) fleabite; (*hinchazón*) swelling (from a bite). **(c)** (*fig*) problem, tricky situation.

salsa NF **(a)** (*gen*) sauce; (*para asado*) gravy; (*para postre*) sauce; (*para ensalada*) dressing; **~ de ají** chili sauce; **~ holandesa** hollandaise sauce; **~ mahonesa, ~ mayonnaise; **~ de soja** soy sauce; **~ de tomate** tomato sauce, ketchup; **~ tártara** tartar sauce; **cocerse en su propia ~** to stew in one's own juice; **estar en su ~** to be in one's element, be absolutely at home. **(b)** (*fig*) seasoning, spice; appetizer; **es la ~ de la vida** it's the spice of life. **(c)** (**:** *ambiente*) scene*; **la ~ madrileña** the Madrid scene*. **(d)** **música ~** salsa music.

salsera[1] NF sauce boat; gravy boat.

salsero [1] ADJ (*Mús*) salsa-loving; **ritmo ~** salsa rhythm. [2] NM, **salsera²** NF salsa music player.

salsifí NM salsify.

saltabanco NM **(a)** (*Hist*) quack, mountebank. **(b)** = **saltimbanqui.**

saltado ADJ **(a)** (*loza etc*) **estar ~** to be chipped, be damaged; **la corona tiene varias piedras saltadas** the crown has several stones missing. **(b)** *ojos* bulging.

saltador [1] NM (*comba*) skipping rope. [2] NM, **saltadora** NF (*atleta*) jumper; (*en agua*) diver; **~ de altura** high-jumper; **~ de longitud** long-jumper; **~ de pértiga** polevaulter.

saltadura NF chip.

saltamontes NM INVAR grasshopper.

saltante ADJ (*And, Cono Sur*) outstanding, noteworthy.

saltaperico NM (*Carib*) squib, firecracker.

saltar [1a] [1] VT **(a)** *muro, obstáculo etc* to jump (over), leap (over), vault. **(b)** (*quitar*) to remove; **le saltó 3 dientes** he knocked out 3 of his teeth; **me has saltado un botón** you've torn off one of my buttons. **(c)** (*fig: omitir*) to skip, miss out, leave out; **saltó un párrafo entero** he skipped a whole paragraph.

[2] VI **(a)** (*persona etc*) to jump, leap, spring (*a* on to, into; *por, por encima de* over); to vault; to bound; (*niño*) to hop, skip; to gambol; **~ a la silla** to leap into the saddle; **~ al agua** to jump (o dive, plunge) into the water; **~ de la cama** to leap out of bed; **~ de alegría** to jump with joy, jump for joy; **~ en tierra** to leap ashore; **~ en paracaídas** to jump, come down by parachute; **~ por una ventana** to jump out of a window, leap from a window; **~ sobre uno** to pounce on sb; **hacer ~ un caballo** to jump a horse, make a horse jump. **(b)** (*Inform*) to jump; (*fig: en discurso etc*) to skip about, skip from one subject to another. **(c)** (*pelota*) to bounce, fly up; (*resorte*) to unroll suddenly; (*líquido*) to spurt up, shoot up; (*lágrimas*) to well up; (*cantidad, cifra*) to leap (up); **~ a la mente** to leap to one's mind; **estar a la que salta** to watch out for an opportunity, look for an opening; to live for the day; **la mayoría ha saltado a 900 votos** the majority has shot up (o leaped up) to 900 votes. **(d)** (*desprenderse*) (*pieza*) to come off, fly off; (*corcho*) to blow out, pop out; (*astilla etc*) to fly off; (*botón*) to come off; (*madera etc*) to crack, snap, break; (*resorte*) to break; (*recipiente*) to crack; (*explosivo*) to explode, burst; **hacer ~ un edificio** to blow a building up; **hacer ~ una trampa** to spring a trap; **hacer ~ la banca** to break the bank. **(e)** (*fig: de ira*) to explode, blow up. **(f)** **~ con una patochada** (*fig*) to come out with a ridiculous (o foolish) remark. **(g)** (*fig*) **~ de un puesto** to surrender a post, give up a job; **hacer ~ a uno de un puesto** to boot sb out of a job. **(h)** **~ atrás** (*Bio*) to revert (to type).

[3] **saltarse** VR **(a)** **~ un párrafo** to skip a paragraph; **me he saltado dos renglones** I've left out a couple of lines; **~ un semáforo en rojo*** to jump (o shoot) the lights*; *V* 1 (c). **(b)** **~ todas las reglas** to break all the rules. **(c)** (*pieza, botón etc*) to come off, fly off; *V* 2 (d).

saltarín [1] ADJ restless; full of movement, always on the go; (*pey*) unstable, volatile. [2] NM, **saltarina** NF dancer.

salteado ADJ (*Culin*) sauté.

salteador NM (**t ~ de caminos**) holdup man; (*Hist*) highwayman, footpad.

salteamiento NM highway robbery, holdup.

saltear [1a] [1] VT **(a)** (*atracar*) to hold up; (*robar*) to rob, assault, attack; (*sorprender*) to take by surprise. **(b)** (*fig: duda etc*) to assail. **(c)** (*Culin*) to sauté. [2] VI to work (*etc*) fitfully, do sth by fits and starts; **lo leyó salteando** he read bits of it here and there.

salteña NF (*And*) meat pie.

salterio NM **(a)** (*Ecl*) psalter; (*Bib*) Book of Psalms. **(b)** (*Mús*) psaltery.

saltimbanqui NM (*malabarista*) juggler; (*acróbata*) acrobat; (*volatinero*) tightrope walker, mountebank; (*fig*) playboy.

salto NM **(a)** (*gen*) jump, leap; bound, spring; vault; hop, skip; (*al agua*) jump, dive, plunge; (*sobre víctima*) pounce; **~ a ciegas, ~ en el vacío** leap in the dark; **el gran ~ (hacia) adelante** the great leap forward; **un vuelo de tres ~s** a flight in three hops; **a ~s** by jumping, in a series of jumps; (*fig*) by fits and starts; **avanzar a ~s** to jump along, go hopping along; **de un ~** at one bound, with one jump; **subió de un ~** he jumped up; **bajó de un ~** he jumped down; **en un ~** (*fig*) in a jiffy*; **en dos ~s estoy de vuelta*** I'll be back in a moment; **dar un ~, pegar un ~** to jump (with fright *etc*); **dar un ~ por la casa de alguien** to drop by sb's house; **me daba ~s el corazón** my heart was pounding; **hacer el ~*** to be unfaithful; **pegar el ~ a*** to be unfaithful to, cuckold; **vivir a ~ de mata** (*pobre*) to live from hand to mouth, keep one's head just above water; (*fugitivo*) to keep one jump ahead of justice; **escapar a ~ de mata** to flee headlong; **hacer algo a ~ de mata** to do sth thoughtlessly, do sth unmethodically; **el libro fue su ~ a la fama** the book marked his leap to fame. **(b)** (*Dep: acto*) jump; (*al agua*) dive; **~ de altura** high jump; high dive; **~ de ángel** swallow-dive; **~ de cabeza** header; **~ de carpa** jack-knife dive; **~s de esquí** ski-jumping; **~ a la (o con) garrocha, ~ con (o de) pértiga** polevault; **~ de longitud** long-jump; **~ mortal** somersault; **~ ornamental** fancy dive; **~ de palanca** high dive; **~ de trampolín** springboard dive; **triple ~** triple jump; hop, step and jump. **(c)** **~ atrás** (*Bio*) throwback, reversion to type. **(d)** (*Geol*) fault; chasm, rift.

(e) (*fig*) (*diferencia, vacío*) gap; jump; (*sección etc omitida*) passage skipped, part missed; **aquí hay un ~ de 50 versos** there is a gap here of 50 lines; **de él al otro hermano hay un ~ de 9 años** there is a gap of 9 years between him and the other brother, there are 9 years between him and the other brother.

(f) (*barricada*) barricade; (*barrera*) human barrier, line; (*Dep: barra etc*) jump; (*cerca*) fence; (*valla*) hurdle, obstacle; **~ de agua** water-jump.

(g) **~ de agua** (*Geog*) waterfall, cascade; (*Tec*) chute.

(h) **~ de cama** négligé, peignoir.

(i) **a** (*o* **al**) **~** (*Carib*) in cash.

(j) (*Inform*) jump; **~ de línea** line feed; **~ de línea automática** wordwrap; **~ de página** form feed.

saltón [1] ADJ **(a)** *ojos* bulging, popping; *dientes* prominent, protruding.

(b) (*LAm*) undercooked, half-cooked.

[2] NM grasshopper; (*Méx*) young locust.

saltona NF (*Cono Sur*) young locust.

salubre ADJ healthy, salubrious.

salubridad NF **(a)** (*sanidad*) healthiness, salubrity, salubriousness. **(b)** (*estadística*) health statistics.

salud NF **(a)** (*Med*) health; state of health; **~ ambiental** environmental health; **~ mental** mental health; **~ ocupacional** health at work; **estar bien de ~** to be in good health; **estar mal de ~** to be in bad health; **¿cómo vamos de ~?** how are we today?; **mejorar de ~** to improve in health, get better; **devolver la ~ a uno** to give sb back his health, restore sb to health.

(b) (*fig*) health; welfare, wellbeing; **la ~ moral de la nación** the country's moral welfare; **curarse en ~** to see one's own defects, put one's own house in order; (*precaverse*) to be prepared, take precautions.

(c) (*brindis*) **¡~!**, **¡a su ~!**, **¡~ y pesetas!** good health!, here's to you!, here's luck!; **beber a la ~ de** to drink to the health of.

(d) (*LAm: al estornudar*) **¡~!** bless you!

(e) (*Rel*) salvation; state of grace.

saludable ADJ **(a)** (*Med*) healthy. **(b)** (*fig*) salutary, good, beneficial; **un aviso ~** a salutary warning.

saludador(a) NM/F quack doctor.

▼ **saludar** [1a] VT **(a)** (*gen*) to greet; (*hacer reverencia a*) to bow to; (*quitarse el sombrero a*) take off one's hat to; **ir a ~ a uno** to go and say hullo to sb, drop in to see sb; **salude de mi parte a X** give my regards to X; **no ~ a uno** to cut sb, refuse to acknowledge sb.

(b) (*en carta*) **le saluda atentamente** yours faithfully.

(c) (*Mil*) to salute.

(d) (*fig*) to salute, hail, welcome.

saludo NM **(a)** (*gen*) greeting; bow; **negar el ~ a uno** to cut sb, ignore sb.

(b) (*en carta*) **~s** best wishes, greetings, regards; **un ~ afectuoso**, **un ~ cordial** yours sincerely; **os envía muchos ~s** he sends you warmest regards; **atentos ~s** best wishes; **un ~ cariñoso a Jane** warm regards to Jane; **~s respetuosos** respectfully yours.

(c) (*Mil*) salute.

Salustio NM Sallust.

salutación NF greeting, salutation.

salva[1] NF **(a)** (*Mil etc*) salute, salvo; (*fig: de aplausos*) storm, volley; **~ de advertencia** warning shots. **(b)** (*saludo*) greeting. **(c)** (*promesa*) oath, solemn promise.

salva[2] NF (*bandeja*) salver, tray.

salvabarros NM INVAR mudguard.

salvación NF **(a)** (*gen*) rescue, delivery (*de* from), salvation. **(b)** (*Rel*) salvation; **~ eterna** eternal salvation.

salvada NF (*LAm*) = **salvación** (a).

salvado NM bran.

Salvador NM **(a)** **el ~** (*Rel*) the Saviour. **(b)** **El ~** (*Geog*) El Salvador.

salvador(a) NM/F rescuer, saviour; (*de playa*) life-saver.

salvadoreñismo NM word (*o* phrase *etc*) peculiar to El Salvador.

salvadoreño, -a ADJ, NM/F Salvadorian.

salvaguarda NF = **salvaguardia**.

salvaguardar [1a] VT to safeguard; (*Inform*) to backup, make a backup copy of.

salvaguardia NF safe-conduct; (*fig*) safeguard.

salvajada NF savage deed, piece of savagery; barbarity, atrocity; brutal act.

salvaje [1] ADJ **(a)** (*Bot, Zool etc*) wild; *huelga* wildcat; *construcción etc* unauthorized, uncontrolled; *tierra* wild, uncultivated. **(b)** *pueblo, tribu etc* savage. **(c)** (*LAm**) terrific*, smashing*.

[2] NMF savage (*t fig*).

salvajería NF = **salvajada**.

salvajez NF = **salvajismo**.

salvajino ADJ **(a)** (*gen*) wild, savage. **(b)** **carne salvajina** meat from a wild animal.

salvajismo NM savagery.

salvamanteles NM INVAR tablemat.

salvamento NM **(a)** (*acto*) rescue; delivery; salvage; (*fig*) salvation; **de ~** life-saving (*atr*); rescue (*atr*); **bote de ~** lifeboat; **operaciones de ~** rescue operations; **~ y socorrismo** life-saving.

(b) (*refugio*) place of safety, refuge; haven.

salvaplatos NM INVAR tablemat.

salvar [1a] [1] VT **(a)** *persona etc* to save, rescue (*de* from); *barco* to salvage; *apariencias* to save, keep up; **me salvó la vida** he saved my life; **apenas salvaron nada del incendio** they hardly rescued anything from the fire; **~ a uno de tener que** + *infin* to save sb from having to + *infin*.

(b) (*Rel*) to save.

(c) *barrera, línea, montañas, río etc* to cross; *rápidos* to shoot; *arroyo* to jump across, jump over, clear; *dificultad* to overcome, resolve; *obstáculo* to get round, negotiate.

(d) *distancia* to cover, do, travel; **el tren salva la distancia en 2 horas** the train covers the distance in 2 hours.

(e) (*excluir*) to except, exclude.

(f) (*árbol, edificio etc*) to rise above.

(g) (*nivel del agua etc*) to reach, rise as high as; **el agua salvaba el peldaño más alto** the water came up to the topmost step.

(h) (*Cono Sur*) *examen* to pass.

[2] **salvarse** VR **(a)** to save o.s., escape (*de* from); **¡sálvese el que** (*o* **quien**) **pueda!** every man for himself!

(b) (*Rel*) to save one's soul, be saved.

salvavidas [1] NM INVAR lifebelt.

[2] ADJ life-saving (*atr*); **bote ~** lifeboat; **cinturón ~** lifebelt; **chaleco ~** life-jacket.

salvedad NF reservation, qualification, proviso; **con la ~ de que ...** with the proviso that ...; **hacer una ~** to make a qualification.

Salvi NM *forma familiar de* **Salvador**.

salvia NF (*Bot*) sage.

salvilla NF salver, tray; (*Cono Sur*) cruet.

salvo [1] ADJ safe; *V* **sano**.

[2] ADV Y PREP **(a)** except (for), save; barring; **~ aquellos que ya contamos** except for those we have already counted; **de todos los países ~ de Ruritania** from all countries except Ruritania.

(b) **a ~** safely; out of danger; **a ~ de** safe from; **en ~** out of danger, in a safe place; **dejar algo a ~** to make an exception of sth, leave sth out of it; **para dejar a ~ su reputación** in order to keep his reputation safe; **poner algo a ~** to put sth in a safe place, put sth out of harm's way; **ponerse a ~** to escape, reach safety; **nada ha quedado a ~ de sus ataques** nothing has been safe from his attacks.

[3] **~ que**, **~ si** CONJ unless ...; except that ...; **iré ~ que me avises al contrario** I'll go unless you tell me not to.

salvoconducto NM safe-conduct.

salvohonor NM (*hum*) backside.

samaritano, -a ADJ, NM/F Samaritan; **buen ~** good Samaritan.

samaruco NM (*Cono Sur*) hunter's pouch, gamebag.

samba NF samba.

sambenito NM (*Hist*) sanbenito; (*fig*) dishonour, disgrace, infamy; **le colgaron el ~ de fascista** they branded him a fascist; **le colgaron el ~ de haberlo hecho** they attached to him the stigma of having done it; **echar el ~ a otro** to pin the blame on somebody else; **quedó con el ~ toda la vida** he was disgraced for life.

sambo, -a NM/F offspring of black person and (American) Indian.

sambumbia NF **(a)** (*And, Carib, Méx: bebida*) watery drink (*: mazamorra*) mush, hash.

(b) (*Carib*) drink of sugar-cane syrup, water and peppers; (*Méx: de ananás*) pineapple drink; (*Méx: hordiate*) barleywater drink.

(c) (*And: trasto*) old thing, battered object; **volver algo ~** to smash sth to pieces.

sambutir [3a] VT (*Méx*) (*: meter a fuerza*) to stick in, stuff in; (*: hundir*) to sink in, shove in.

samotana NF (*CAm*) row, uproar, racket.

samovar NM samovar.

sampablera NF (*Carib: jaleo*) racket, row.

sampán NM sampan.

Samuel NM Samuel.

samurear [1a] VI (*Carib*) to walk with bowed head.

San NM (*apocopated form of* **santo**) saint; **San Juan** Saint John, (*escrito en general*) St John; **cerca de San Martín** near St Martin's (church); **se casarán por San Juan** they'll get married sometime in midsummer (*estrictamente*, round about St John's Day); *V t* **santo, Juan**, etc.

sanable ADJ curable, susceptible to treatment.

sanaco ADJ (*Carib*) silly.

sanalotodo NM cure-all, universal remedy.

sanamente ADV healthily; wholesomely.

sananería NF (*Carib*) stupid remark, silly comment.

sanar [1a] [1] VT to heal; to cure (*de* of).

[2] VI (*persona*) to recover, get well; (*herida*) to heal.

sanativo ADJ healing, curative.
sanatorio NM sanatorium; (private) nursing-home.
San Bernardo NM St Bernard.
sancho NM (a) (prov) pig. (b) (Méx: carnero) ram, (cordero) lamb; (macho cabrío) billygoat; (animal abandonado) orphan animal, suckling.
sanción NF sanction; punishment, penalty; **sanciones comerciales** trade sanctions; **~ disciplinaria** punishment, disciplinary measure; **sanciones económicas** economic sanctions; **imponer sanciones** to impose sanctions; **levantar sanciones a uno** to lift sanctions against sb.
sancionable ADJ punishable.
sancionado, -a NM/F guilty person; **los ~s** (Pol) those who have been punished for a political offence, those guilty of political crimes.
sancionar [1a] VT (a) (castigar) to sanction; (Jur) to penalize. (b) (permitir) to sanction.
sancionatorio ADJ (Jur) penal, penalty (atr).
sancochado NM (And) = sancocho.
sancochar [1a] VT to parboil; (CAm, Méx) to throw together, rustle up*.
sancocho NM (a) (comida malguisada) undercooked food; (carne) parboiled meat. (b) (LAm: guisado) stew (of meat, yucca etc). (c) (CAm, Carib, Andes) fuss; confusion; row (d) (Carib: bazofia) pigswill.
San Cristóbal NM (a) (Ecl) St Christopher. (b) (Geog) St Kitts.
sandalia NF sandal.
sándalo NM sandal, sandalwood.
sandez NF (a) (cualidad) foolishness. (b) (acto, dicho) stupid thing, piece of stupidity; **decir sandeces** to talk nonsense; **fue una ~ obrar así** it was silly to do that.
sandía NF watermelon.
sandinismo NM Sandinista movement.
sandinista ADJ, NMF Sandinista.
sandío ADJ foolish, silly, stupid.
sanduche NM (And) sandwich.
sandunga NF (a) (*) (atractivo) charm; (gracia) wit. (b) (And, Carib, Cono Sur, Méx: juerga) party, binge*.
sandunguero* ADJ charming, witty, amusing.
sandwich [san'gwitʃ, sam'bitʃ] NM, PL **sandwichs** o **sandwiches** sandwich.
sandwichera NF toasted sandwich maker.
sandwichería NF (esp LAm) sandwich bar.
saneamiento NM (a) (alcantarillado) draining; drainage (system), sanitation; sewerage. (b) (fig) remedy; ending; cleaning-up. (c) (garantía) guarantee; insurance. (d) (compensación) compensation, indemnification. (e) (Com, Fin) restructuring, reorganization, streamlining.
sanear [1a] VT (a) tierra to drain; casa to remove the dampness from; (Téc) to instal drainage (o sewerage) in, lay sewers in. (b) (fig) daño to remedy, repair; abuso to end; centro de vicio to clean up, purge. (c) (garantizar) to guarantee; (asegurar) to insure. (d) (Jur) comprador to compensate, indemnify. (e) (Com, Fin) capital, compañía to restructure, reorganize, streamline.
sanfasón: a la ~ ADV (LAm) unceremoniously, informally; (pey) carelessly.
sanfermines NMPL festivities in celebration of San Fermín (Pamplona).

SANFERMINES

ⓘ The **Sanfermines** are a week-long festival starting on July 7 in Pamplona (Navarre) to honour **San Fermín**, the town's patron saint. As with many other local Spanish festivities, one of the main events is bullfighting. In Pamplona, however, the bulls have to be led from their enclosure to the bullring early in the morning through the city's main streets. Young men, dressed in the traditional Navarrese attire of red berets, white shirts and trousers and red sashes round their waist, run through the streets leading the fast-moving bulls. This activity, known as the **encierro**, in which people risk serious injury and even death, was popularized by writers such as Ernest Hemingway and now attracts visitors from all over the world. The festivities start with the **txupinazo**, a large rocket fired from Pamplona's main square, and for a full week Pamplona becomes one large street party punctuated by the daily **encierro**.

---

sanforizar [1f] ® VT to Sanforize ®.
sango NM (And Culin) yucca and maize pudding.
sangradera NF (a) (Med) lancet. (b) (Agr: acequia) irrigation channel; (desagüe) sluice, outflow.
sangradura NF (a) (Anat) inner angle of the elbow. (b) (Med) (incisión) cut made into a vein; (sangría) bleeding, blood-letting. (c) (Cono Sur) outlet, drainage channel.
sangrante ADJ (a) herida, persona bleeding. (b) (fig) injusticia etc crying, flagrant.

sangrar [1a] ① VT (a) (Med) to bleed.
(b) (Agr etc) tierra to drain, drain the water from; agua to drain off, let out, allow to drain away; árbol to tap; horno to tap.
(c) (Tip) to indent.
(d) (*) to filch, filch from.
② VI (a) (t fig) to bleed.
(b) (fig) **estar sangrando** (ser actual) to be still fresh, be very new still; (ser obvio) to be obvious; **aún sangra la humillación** the humiliation still rankles.
sangre NF blood (t fig); **~ azul** blue blood; **~ fría** sangfroid, coolness; (pey) callousness; **a ~ fría** in cold blood, callously; **mala ~** bad blood; **pura ~** (NMF) thoroughbred; **~ vital** lifeblood; **a ~** by animal power, by horsepower; **a ~ caliente** in the heat of the moment; **a ~ y fuego** by fire and sword; **es de ~ de reyes** he has royal blood, he is of the blood royal; **fue de ~ de conquistadores** he was descended from conquistadors; **le bulle la ~ (en las venas)** he is full of youthful vigour, he is bursting with energy; **esto chorrea ~** this cries out to heaven; **chupar la ~ a uno** (fig) to exploit sb, suck out sb's lifeblood; to bleed sb white; **dar su ~** to give one's blood; **echar ~** to bleed (de from); **echar ~ por los ojos** to be furious; **encender** (o **quemar, revolver**) **la ~ a uno** to infuriate sb, make sb's blood boil; **freír la ~ a uno*** to rile sb*, needle sb*; **me he hecho ~** I'm bleeding; **hacerse mala ~** to get upset; to fret; **se me heló la ~** my blood froze, my blood ran cold; **llegar a la ~** to come to blows; **la ~ no llegará al río** it's not as bad as all that; **sin que la ~ llegue al río** without disastrous results, without going to extremes; **no creo que llegue la ~ al río** I don't think it will be too disastrous; **lo lleva en la sangre** it runs in her blood; **sudar ~** to undergo hardships; to slog, toil; **tener la ~ gorda** (o **de horchata**), **no tener ~ en las venas** (ser frío) to be excessively phlegmatic, be unemotional, be stone cold; (ser pesado) to be dull, be boring.
sangregorda* NMF bore.
sangría NF (a) (Med) bleeding, bloodletting; **~ suelta** excessive flow of blood; (fig) outflow, drain, continuous loss.
(b) (Anat) inner angle of the elbow.
(c) (Agr) (acequia) irrigation channel; (desagüe) outlet, outflow; (zanja) ditch; (drenaje) drainage.
(d) (Téc) (acto) tapping (of a furnace); (metal fundido) stream of molten metal.
(e) (Culin) sangría, (aprox) fruit cup.
(f) (Tip) indentation.
sangrientamente ADV bloodily.
sangriento ADJ (a) herida bleeding.
(b) arma, ropa etc bloody, bloodstained, gory.
(c) batalla bloody.
(d) (liter) blood-red.
(e) (fig) injusticia etc crying, flagrant; insulto deadly; chiste cruel.
sangrigordo ADJ (Carib) (aburrido) tedious, boring; (insolente) rude, insolent.
sangriligero ADJ (LAm), **sangriliviano** ADJ (LAm) pleasant, nice, congenial.
sangripesado ADJ (LAm), **sangrón** ADJ (Carib, Méx‡), **sangruno** ADJ (Carib) (grosero) rude; (desagradable) unpleasant, nasty; (aburrido) boring, tiresome; (obstinado) obstinate, pig-headed; (triste) miserable.
sanguarañas NFPL (And*) circumlocutions, evasions.
sánguche NM, **sanguchito** NM (LAm) sandwich.
sangüich NM (Esp) sandwich.
sanguijuela NF leech (t fig).
sanguinario ADJ bloodthirsty, cruel, callous.
sanguíneo ADJ (a) (Anat) blood (atr); **vaso ~** blood vessel. (b) (fig: color) blood-red.
sanguinolento ADJ (a) herida bleeding; ropa etc bloody, bloodstained; streaked (o tinged) with blood; ojos bloodshot.
(b) (Culin) underdone, rare.
(c) (fig: color) blood-red.
sanidad NF (a) (gen) health, healthiness; (fig) salubrity.
(b) (asunto público) public health; (aguas residuales etc) sanitation; (**Ministerio de**) **S~** Ministry of Health; **~ pública** public health (department); **inspector de ~, oficial de ~** sanitary inspector.
San Isidro NM Saint Isidore.

SAN ISIDRO

ⓘ **San Isidro** is the patron saint of Madrid, and gives his name to the week-long festivities which take place round May 15. Originally an 18th-century trade fair, the **San Isidro** celebrations now include music, dance, a famous **romería**, theatre and bullfighting. The **isidrada** is in fact one of the most important dates in the bullfighting calendar.
⇨ See also ROMERÍA

---

sanitaría NF (Cono Sur) plumber's (shop).
sanitario ① ADJ condiciones sanitary; centro etc health (atr); sanitation (atr).

2 NM (a) (*Med*) stretcher bearer. (b) ~s PL bathroom fittings. (c) ~s PL (*wáter*) toilets; (*Méx*) toilet.

sanjacobo NM escalope with cheese filling.

San Juan NM Saint John.

SAN JUAN

ⓘ The *Día de San Juan* on June 24 fuses Christian tradition with ancient summer solstice celebrations. In many areas, particularly near the sea, it is customary to light large bonfires on open ground on the night of June 23 and to burn an effigy, normally a large rag doll, at the stake. These *hogueras de San Juan*, which are accompanied by fireworks and music, draw crowds of people wanting to dance or simply to enjoy the summer evening until the fire dies out in the small hours. Some legends credit this night with magical qualities and talk of ghostly apparitions.

San Lorenzo NM: **el** (*Río*) ~ the St Lawrence.

sano ADJ (a) (*Med etc*) healthy; fit; *madera, órgano etc* sound; *fruta* good; **cortar por lo** ~ to take extreme measures, go right to the root of the trouble; to cut one's losses.
(b) *clima etc* healthy; *comida* good, wholesome.
(c) *objeto* whole, intact, undamaged; ~ **y salvo** safe and sound; **esa silla no es muy sana** that chair is not too strong; **no ha quedado plato** ~ **en toda la casa** there wasn't a plate left whole (o unbroken) in the house.
(d) (*fig*) (*sin vicios*) (morally) healthy, wholesome; *doctrina, enseñanza* sound; *deseo* earnest, sincere; *objetivo etc* worthy.

sansalvadoreño 1 ADJ of San Salvador.
2 NM, **sansalvadoreña** NF native (o inhabitant) of San Salvador; **los ~s** the people of San Salvador.

sánscrito ADJ, NM Sanskrit.

sanseacabó*: **y** ~ and that's the end of it, and there's no more to be said.

Sansón NM Samson; **es un** ~ he's tremendously strong.

santa NF saint; *V* **santo**.

Santa Bárbara NF Santa Barbara.

santabárbara NF (*Náut*) magazine.

santamente ADV: **vivir** ~ to live a saintly (o holy) life.

santanderino (*Esp*) 1 ADJ of Santander.
2 NM, **santanderina** NF native (o inhabitant) of Santander; **los ~s** the people of Santander.

santateresa NF (*Ent*) praying mantis.

santería NF (a) (*LAm: tienda*) shop selling religious images, prints etc. (b) (*) = **santidad**. (c) (*Carib Rel*) religion of African origin.

santero 1 NM (*LAm*) maker (o seller) of religious images, prints etc.
2 NM, **santera** NF person excessively devoted to the saints.

Santiago NM St James.

santiaguero, -a* NM/F (*Cono Sur*) faith-healer.

santiagués = **santiaguino**.

santiaguino 1 ADJ of Santiago de Chile.
2 NM, **santiaguina** NF native (o inhabitant) of Santiago de Chile; **los ~s** the people of Santiago de Chile.

santiamén* NM: **en un** ~ in a jiffy*, in no time at all.

santidad NF holiness, sanctity; saintliness; **su S~** His Holiness.

santificación NF sanctification.

santificar [1g] VT (a) (*gen*) to sanctify, make holy, hallow; *lugar* to consecrate; *fiesta* to keep; **santificado sea Tu Nombre** hallowed be Thy Name. (b) (*: *perdonar*) to forgive.

santiguada NF sign of the Cross; act of crossing oneself.

santiguar [1i] 1 VT (a) (*persignar*) to make the sign of the Cross over; to bless.
(b) (*LAm: sanear*) to heal (by blessing).
(c) (*: *pegar*) to slap, hit.
2 **santiguarse** VR (a) to cross o.s., make the sign of the Cross.
(b) (*: *exagerar*) to make a great fuss, react in an exaggerated way, overdo the emotion.

santísimo ADJ SUPERL (most) holy; **hacer la santísima a uno*** (*jorobar*) to drive sb up the wall*; (*perjudicar*) to do sb down*.

santo 1 ADJ (a) (*gen*) holy; sacred; *tierra* holy, consecrated; *persona* saintly; *mártir* blessed.
(b) (*fig*) *remedio etc* wonderful, miraculous.
(c) (*: *total*) utter, complete; blessed; ~ **y bueno** well and good; **todo el** ~ **día** the whole livelong day; the whole blessed day; **y él con su santa calma** and he utterly unmoved, and he so completely calm; *V* **voluntad** etc.
2 NM (a) (*Ecl*) saint; ~ **patrón**, ~ **titular** patron saint; **S~ Domingo** (*Ecl*) St Dominic; (*Geog*) Santo Domingo, Dominican Republic; **S~ Tomás** St Thomas; *V t* **San**.
(b) (*locuciones*) **¿a qué** ~? what on earth for?; **¿a** ~ **de qué** ...? why on earth ...?; **¡por todos los ~s!** for pity's sake!; **no es** ~ **de mi devoción** I'm not very keen on him; **alzarse con el** ~ **y la limosna*** to clear off with the whole lot*; **comerse los ~s*** to be terribly devout; **desnudar a un** ~ **para vestir otro** to rob Peter to pay Paul; **se**

le fue el ~ **al cielo** he forgot what he was about to say (o do *etc*), he clean forgot; he was day-dreaming; **¡que se te va el** ~ **al cielo!** you're miles away!; **llegar y besar el** ~ to pull it off at the first attempt; **nacer con el** ~ **de espaldas** to be born unlucky; **poner a uno como un** ~* to give sb a telling-off*; **quedarse para vestir ~s** to be left on the shelf; **tener el** ~ **de cara*** to have tremendous luck*; **tener el** ~ **de espaldas*** to have bad luck.
(c) (*fig: persona*) saint; **es un** ~ he's a saint; **estaba hecho un** ~ he was terribly sweet.
(d) (*día*) saint's day; ~ **y seña** (*Mil*) password; (*fig*) watchword, slogan; **mañana es mi** ~ tomorrow is my saint's day, tomorrow is my name day (*celebrated in Spain etc as equivalent to a birthday*).
(e) (*Cono Sur Cos*) patch, darn.

SANTO

ⓘ As well as celebrating their birthday, many Spaniards celebrate their *santo* or *onomástica*. This is the day when the saint whose name they have is honoured in the Christian calendar. It used to be relatively common for newborn children to be called after the saint whose day they were born on. So a boy born on July 25 (Saint James's day) stood a good chance of being christened "Santiago". The tradition may be dying out now that parents are no longer restricted to names from the Christian calendar, as was the case in the past. As with birthdays, the person whose *santo* it is normally buys the drinks.

---

santón* NM (*hum*) big shot*, big wheel*.

santoral NM calendar of saints' days.

santuario NM (a) (*Rel*) sanctuary, shrine; (*lugar seguro*) sanctuary. (b) (*And, Carib*) (*ídolo*) native idol; (*tesoro*) buried treasure.

santulario ADJ (*Cono Sur*) = **santurrón**.

santurrón 1 ADJ sanctimonious; hypocritical.
2 NM, **santurrona** NF sanctimonious person; hypocrite.

saña NF (a) (*furor*) anger, rage, fury; (*crueldad*) cruelty; (*fig*) fury, viciousness. (b) (⁑: *cartera*) wallet.

sañero⁑ NM (*Esp*) pickpocket.

sañoso ADJ = **sañudo**.

sañudamente ADV angrily, furiously; cruelly; viciously.

sañudo ADJ furious, enraged; cruel; *golpe etc* vicious, cruel.

sapaneco ADJ (*CAm*) plump, chubby.

sáparo NM (*And*) wicker basket.

sapiencia NF knowledge, wisdom.

sapo[1] NM (a) (*Zool*) toad; (*fig: Zool*) small animal, bug, creature; (*persona*) ugly creature; thick-set individual; **echar ~s y culebras** to produce a stream of abuse, curse and swear.
(b) (*prov, LAm*) game of throwing coins into the mouth of an iron toad.
(c) (*CAm, Carib*⁑: *soplón*) informer, grass⁑; (*Cono Sur*⁑) soldier.

sapo[2] ADJ (*And, CAm, Cono Sur: astuto*) cunning, sly; (*Cono Sur: hipócrita*) hypocritical, two-faced; (*CAm, Carib*) telltale, gossipy.

saporro ADJ (*And, CAm*) chubby, plump.

sapotear [1a] VT (*And*) to finger, handle.

saprófago ADJ saprophagous.

saprófito 1 ADJ saprophytic.
2 NM saprophyte.

saque NM (a) (*acto: Tenis*) service, serve; ~ **de banda** (*Fútbol*) throw-in, (*Rugby*) line-out; ~ **de castigo** penalty kick; ~ **de esquina** corner-kick; ~ **de falta** free kick; ~ **de honor** guest appearance; ~ **inicial** kick-off; ~ **libre** free kick; ~ **de mano** (*LAm Dep*) throw-in; ~ **de portería**, ~ **de puerta** goal-kick.
(b) (*Tenis: persona*) server.
(c) **tener buen** ~ to eat heartily, be a good trencherman.

saqué etc V **sacar**.

saqueador NM looter.

saquear [1a] VT (*Mil*) to sack; (*robar*) to loot, plunder, pillage; (*fig*) to rifle, ransack; to turn upside down.

saqueo NM sacking; looting, plundering; (*fig*) rifling, ransacking.

saquito NM small bag; sachet; ~ **de papel** paper bag.

S.A.R. ABR de **Su Alteza Real** His (o Her) Royal Highness, H.R.H.

sarampión NM measles.

sarao NM (a) (*fiesta*) soirée, evening party. (b) (*: *lío*) fuss, to-do*.

sarape NM (*Méx*) blanket.

sarasa⁑ NM pansy⁑, fairy⁑.

saraviado ADJ (*And*) spotted, mottled; *persona* freckled.

sarazo (*LAm*) = **zarazo**.

sarazón ADJ (*Méx*) = **zarazo**.

sarcasmo NM sarcasm; **es un** ~ **que** ... it is ludicrous that ...

sarcásticamente ADV sarcastically.

sarcástico ADJ sarcastic.

sarcófago NM sarcophagus.

sarcoma NM sarcoma.

sardana NF Catalan dance and music.

sardina NF sardine; pilchard; ~ **arenque** herring; ~ **noruega** brisling; **como ~s en lata** (packed) like sardines.

sardinero ADJ sardine (atr).
sardo, -a ADJ, NM/F Sardinian.
sardónico ADJ (esp LAm) sardonic; ironical, sarcastic.
sargazo NM (Carib) seaweed.
sargentear [1a] ① VT (Mil) to command; (*) to boss about.
　② VI (*) to be bossy, boss people about.
sargento NM sergeant; (pey*) bossy female.
sargentona* NF tough mannish woman.
sargo NM bream.
sari NM sari.
sarita NF (And) straw hat.
sarmentoso ADJ (a) planta twining, climbing. (b) dedos etc long and thin; gnarled.
sarmiento NM vine shoot.
sarna NF (Med) itch, scabies; (Vet) mange.
sarniento ADJ (CAm, Méx), **sarnoso** ADJ (a) (Med) itchy, infected with the itch; (Vet) mangy. (b) (fig) weak, feeble. (c) (And, Cono Sur*: despreciable) contemptible, lousy‡, wretched.
sarpullido NM = **salpullido**.
sarraceno, -a ADJ, NM/F Saracen.
sarracina NF (a) (disputa) quarrel; (pelea) brawl, free fight.
　(b) (matanza) mass slaughter; (fig) wholesale destruction; **han hecho una ~** (Univ*) they've ploughed almost everybody*.
Sarre NM Saar.
sarrio NM Pyrenean mountain goat.
sarro NM (a) (gen) incrustation, deposit; (en dientes) tartar, scale, plaque; (en caldera, lengua) fur. (b) (Bot) rust.
sarroso ADJ incrusted; covered with tartar; furred, furry.
sarta NF, **sartal** NM, **sartalada** NF (Cono Sur) (serie) string, series; (fila) line, row; (fig) string; **una ~ de mentiras** a pack of lies.
sartén NF (M en LAm) frying-pan; **coger la ~ por donde quema** to act rashly; **saltar de la ~ y dar en la brasa** to jump out of the frying pan into the fire; **tener la ~ por el mango** to be the master, rule the roost; to hold all the cards.
sarteneja NF (And, Méx) dried-out pool; (Méx) (bache) pothole; (tierra seca) cracked soil, parched soil.
sasafrás NM sassafras.
sastra NF seamstress.
sastre NM (a) tailor; **~ de teatro** costumier; **hecho por ~** tailor-made. (b) (prenda) tailor-made costume.
sastrería NF (a) (oficio) tailoring, tailor's trade. (b) (tienda) tailor's (shop).
Satán NM, **Satanás** NM Satan.
satánico ADJ satanic; devilish, fiendish.
satanismo NM Satanism, devil-worship.
satanización NF demonizing.
satanizar [1f] VT to demonize.
satelitario ADJ satellite (atr).
satélite ① NM (a) (Astron) satellite; **~ artificial** artificial satellite; **~ de comunicaciones** communications satellite; **~ espía** spy satellite; **~ meteorológico** weather satellite.
　(b) (satélite; minion; (esbirro) henchman; (compañero) crony.
　② ATR satellite; **ciudad ~** satellite town; **país ~** satellite country.
satén NM sateen.
satín NM (LAm) sateen, satin.
satinado ① ADJ glossy, shiny.
　② NM gloss, shine.
satinar [1a] VT to gloss, make glossy.
sátira NF satire.
satíricamente ADV satirically.
satírico ADJ satiric(al).
satirizar [1f] VT to satirize.
sátiro NM satyr.
satisfacción NF (a) (gen) satisfaction; **~ laboral, ~ profesional** job satisfaction; **a ~ de** to the satisfaction of; **a su entera ~** to his complete satisfaction; **con ~ de todos** to the general satisfaction.
　(b) (de ofensa) satisfaction, redress; (disculpa) apology; **pedir ~ a uno** to demand an apology from sb, demand satisfaction from sb.
　(c) (de sí mismo) self-satisfaction, smugness.
satisfacer [2s] ① VT (a) (gen) to satisfy; (éxito etc) to gratify, please; necesidad, solicitud to meet, satisfy; deuda, sueldo etc to pay; (Com) letra de cambio to honour; gastos to meet.
　(b) culpa to expiate; pérdida to make good.
　(c) **~ a uno de** (o por) **una ofensa** to give sb satisfaction for an offence.
　② **satisfacerse** VR (a) (gen) to satisfy o.s., be satisfied; **~ con muy poco** to be content with very little.
　(b) (resarcirse) to obtain redress, obtain satisfaction; (vengarse) to take revenge.
satisfactoriamente ADV satisfactorily.
satisfactorio ADJ satisfactory.
satisfecho ADJ (a) (gen) satisfied; content(ed); **darse por ~ con algo**

to declare o.s. satisfied (o content) with sth; **dejar ~s a todos** to satisfy everybody; **quedarse ~** (comida) to be full.
　(b) (t ~ **consigo mismo, ~ de sí mismo**) self-satisfied, smug; conceited; **nos miró ~** he looked at us smugly.
sativa NF (Cono Sur) marijuana.
satrústegui* INTERJ well!, well I'm blowed!*
satsuma NF satsuma.
saturación NF saturation; permeation.
saturado ADJ saturated.
saturar [1a] VT to saturate; to permeate; **~ el mercado** to flood the market; **estos aeropuertos son los más saturados** these airports are the most crowded (o overused).
saturnales NFPL Saturnalia.
saturnino ADJ saturnine.
Saturno NM Saturn.
sauce NM willow (tree); **~ de Babilonia, ~ llorón** weeping willow.
saucedal NM willow plantation.
saúco NM (Bot) elder.
saudí, saudita ADJ, NMF Saudi.
Saúl NM Saul.
sauna NF (M en LAm) sauna.
saurio NM saurian.
savia NF sap.
saxífraga NF saxifrage.
saxo* NM (Mús) sax*; (persona) saxist.
saxofón, saxófono ① NM (instrumento) saxophone.
　② NMF (persona) saxophonist.
saxofonista NMF saxophonist.
saya NF (a) (falda) skirt; (enaguas) petticoat; (vestido) dress. (b) (And: mujer) woman.
sayal NM coarse woollen cloth.
sayo NM (a) smock, tunic; loose garment, long loose gown. (b) (Esp) **cortar un ~ a uno** to gossip about sb, talk behind sb's back; **¿qué ~ se me corta?** what are they saying about me?
sayón NM (a) (Jur) executioner. (b) (fig) cruel henchman; (*) ugly customer*.
sayuela NF (Carib) long shirt, smock.
sazo* NM hankie*.
sazón ① NF (a) (Agr) good heart; proper condition (of land) for planting, tilth.
　(b) (de fruta) ripeness, maturity; **en ~** ripe, ready (to eat); (fig) opportunely; **fuera de ~** at the wrong moment, inopportunely.
　(c) (liter) time, moment, season; **a la ~** then, at that time.
　(d) (Culin) flavour.
　② ADJ (And, CAm, Méx) ripe.
sazonado ADJ (a) fruta etc ripe; mellow; plato tasty. (b) **~ de** (Culin) seasoned with, flavoured with. (c) (fig) witty.
sazonar [1a] ① VT (a) fruta to ripen, bring to maturity. (b) (Culin) to season, flavour (de with). (c) (Carib) to sweeten.
　② VI to ripen.
s/c (Com) (a) ABR de **su casa** your firm. (b) ABR de **su cuenta** your account.
scalextric NM complicated traffic interchange, spaghetti junction*.
schop [tʃop] NM (Cono Sur) (vaso) mug, tankard; (cerveza) keg beer.
schopería NF (Cono Sur) bar.
scooter [es'kuter] NM motor scooter.
scotch [es'kotʃ] NM adhesive tape.
script [es'kri] NF, PL **scripts** [es'kri] script-girl.
scruchante* NM (Argentina) burglar.
SD NF (Pol) (a) ABR de **Social Democracia.** (b) ABR de **Solidaridad Democrática.**
Sdo. (Com) ABR de **Saldo** balance, bal.
SE ABR de **sudeste** south-east, SE.
S.E. ABR de **Su Excelencia** His (o Her) Excellency, H.E.
se[1] PRON REFLEXIVO (sing: M) himself, (F) herself, (de cosa) itself, (de Vd) yourself; (PL) themselves, (de Vds) yourselves; **se está lavando, está lavándose** he's washing, he's washing himself; **se retira** he withdraws; **se tiró al suelo** she threw herself to the ground; **¡siéntese!** sit down.
　(b) (recíproco) each other, one another; **se ayudan** they help each other; **se miraron el uno al otro** they looked at one another; **no se hablan** they are not on speaking terms, they don't speak; **procuran no verse** they try not to meet each other.
　(c) (gen) oneself; **conviene lavarse después del uso** it is advisable to wash after use.
　(d) (dativo) **se ha comprado un sombrero** he has bought himself a hat, he has bought a hat for himself; **se rompió la pierna** he broke his leg; **han jurado no cortarse la barba** they have sworn not to cut their beards.
　(e) (uso impersonal: se traduce frec por la voz pasiva, por one, some o people) **se compró hace 3 años** it was bought 3 years ago; **se comprende que ...** it can be understood that ..., it is understandable

that ...; **no se sabe por qué** it is not known why; **en esa parte se habla galés** in that area Welsh is spoken, in that area people speak Welsh; **en ese hotel se come realmente bien** the food is really good in that hotel, you eat (*o* one eats) really well in that hotel; **se hace cuando se puede** one does it when one can; **se avisa a los interesados que** ... those concerned are informed that ...; '**véndese: solar** ...' (*anuncio*) 'for sale: plot ...'; '**véndese coche**' (*anuncio*) 'car for sale'.

se² PRON PERSONAL (*que corresponde a* **le, les**) **se lo arrancó** he snatched it from her; **voy a dárselo** I'll give it to him; **se lo buscaré** I'll look for it for you; **no se lo agradecerán** they won't thank you for it.

sé *V* **saber, ser**.

SEA ['sea] NM (*Esp Agr*) ABR *de* **Servicio de Extensión Agraria**.

sea *etc V* **ser**.

SEAT, Seat ['seat] NF (*Esp Com*) ABR *de* **Sociedad Española de Automóviles de Turismo**.

sebáceo ADJ sebaceous.

sebear [1a] VT (*Carib*) to inspire love in; to court.

sebo NM (a) (*grasa*) grease, fat; (*para velas*) tallow; (*Culin*) suet.
(b) (*) (*gordura*) fat; (*mugre*) grease, filth, grime.
(c) **hacer ~** (*Cono Sur*) to idle, loaf; **dar ~ a** (*And*) to pester; **hacer** (*o* **volver**) **~ a** (*Carib*) to crush, ruin; **helarse a uno el ~*** (*fracasar*) to come a cropper*; (*morir*) to peg out‡.

sebón ADJ (*And, CAm, Cono Sur*) idle, lazy.

seboso ADJ (a) (*gen*) greasy, fatty; (*de vela*) tallowy; (*de comida*) suety.
(b) (*: *mugriento*) greasy, filthy, grimy.

Sec. ABR *de* **Secretario** secretary, sec.

seca NF (a) (*Agr*) drought; (*Met*) dry season. (b) (*Náut*) sandbank.

secadero NM (a) (*lugar*) drying place; drying shed. (b) (*And*: *terreno*) dry plain, scrubland.

secado NM drying.

secador NM (a) (*lugar*) place where clothes are hung to dry. (b) **~ de cabello**, **~ para el pelo** hair-drier; **~ centrífugo** spin-drier.

secadora NF drier, clothes drier; **~ centrífuga** spin-drier; (*CAm, Méx*) **~ de cabello** hair-drier.

secamanos NM INVAR hand dryer, hand drier.

secamente ADV (*V ADJ* (c)) brusquely, sharply, curtly; drily.

secano NM (a) (*Agr*: *t* **tierra ~**) dry land, dry region; unirrigated land; **cultivo de ~** crop for dry farming.
(b) (*Náut*) (*banco de arena*) sandbank; (*islote*) small sandy island.

secante¹ 1 ADJ (a) (*viento etc*) drying; **papel ~ = 2**. (b) (*Cono Sur*: *latoso*) tedious, irritating.
2 NM blotting paper, blotter.

secante² NF (*Mat*) secant.

secapelos NM INVAR hair drier.

secar [1g] 1 VT (a) (*gen*) to dry, dry up, dry off; *plato, superficie* to wipe dry; *lágrimas* to dry; *frente* to wipe, mop; *líquido derramado* to mop up; *tinta* to blot; *planta* to dry up, wither.
(b) (*fig*) (*fastidiar*) to annoy, vex; (*aburrir*) to bore.
2 **secarse** VR (a) (*ropa lavada etc*) to dry, dry off; (*río*) to dry up, run dry; (*planta*) to dry up, wither, wilt; (*persona*) to dry o.s., get dry (*con una toalla* on a towel, with a towel).
(b) (*herida*) to close up, heal up.
(c) (*: *adelgazar*) to get thin.
(d) (*: *t* **~ de sed**) to have a raging thirst.

secarral NM dry plain, arid area.

secarropa NM clothes-horse.

sección NF (a) (*Arquit, Mat etc*) section; (*t* **~ transversal**) cross-section; **~ cónica** conic section; **~ longitudinal** longitudinal section; **~ vertical** vertical section.
(b) (*fig*) section; (*de almacén, compañía*) division, department, branch; **~ de contactos** personal column (containing offers of marriage *etc*); **~ de cuerdas** string section; **~ deportiva** sports section, sports page; **~ económica** financial pages.
(c) (*Mil*) section, platoon.

seccional ADJ sectional.

seccionar [1a] VT (*dividir*) to divide up, divide into sections; (*cortar*) to cut (off); (*disecar*) to dissect; **~ la garganta a uno** to cut sb's throat.

secesión NF secession.

secesionista ADJ, NMF secessionist.

seco ADJ (a) (*gen*) dry; *fruta etc* dried; *planta* dried up, withered, dead; *batería, clima, época, lago, vino* dry; **estar en ~** (*Náut y fig*) to be high and dry.
(b) (*flaco*) thin, skinny.
(c) *carácter* (*frío*) cold; (*antipático*) disagreeable; (*brusco*) blunt; *actitud, respuesta etc* brusque, sharp, curt; *estilo* plain, bare, flat, inexpressive; *explicación* plain, unvarnished; *estudio, tema* dry.
(d) *golpe, ruido etc* dull; *tos* dry.
(e) (*puro*) bare; *coñac* neat; **vivir a pan ~** to live on bread alone, eat only bread; **tiene el sueldo ~** he has just his salary; **estar ~*** to be broke*.
(f) **dejar a uno ~** (*matar*) to kill sb stone-dead; (*atolondrar*) to dumb-

found sb; **quedarse ~** to be dumbfounded.
(g) **a secas: habrá pan a secas** there will be just bread; **decir algo a secas** to say sth curtly, say sth abruptly; **se llama Rodríguez a secas** he is called plain Rodríguez, he is just called Rodríguez.
(h) **en ~: callarse en ~** to stop talking suddenly; to stop talking at once; **frenar en ~** to brake sharply. pull up sharply; **parar en ~** to stop dead, stop suddenly.
(i) (*LAm*: *golpe*) slap, smack.

secoya NF redwood, sequoia.

secre* NMF = **secretario**.

secreción NF secretion.

secreta 1 NF secret police; plain-clothes police.
2 NM secret policeman; plain-clothes policeman.

secretamente ADV secretly.

secretar [1a] VT to secrete.

secretaría NF (a) (*plantilla*) secretariat. (b) (*oficina*) secretary's office. (c) (*cargo*) secretaryship. (d) (*Méx Pol*) Ministry, Department of State (*US*).

secretariado NM (a) (*plantilla*) secretariat. (b) (*cargo*) secretaryship. (c) (*LAm*: *curso*) secretarial course. (d) (*LAm*: *profesión*) career as a secretary, profession of secretary.

secretario, -a NM/F (a) secretary; **~ adjunto** assistant secretary; **~ de dirección** executive secretary; **~ general** general secretary, (*Pol*) secretary general; **~ de imagen** public relations officer; **~ municipal** town clerk; **~ particular** personal secretary, private secretary; **~ de prensa** press secretary; **~ de rodaje** script clerk. (b) (*Méx Pol*) Minister (of State), Secretary of State (*US*).

secretear [1a] VI (a) (*conversar*) to talk confidentially, exchange secrets. (b) (*cuchichear*) to whisper unnecessarily; to whisper ostentatiously.

secreter NM writing-desk.

secretismo NM (excessive) secrecy.

secreto 1 ADJ (a) (*gen*) secret; (*escondido*) hidden; *información* secret, confidential, (*Mil*) classified; **alto ~** top secret; **todo es de lo más ~** it's all highly secret.
(b) *persona* secretive.
2 NM (a) (*un ~*) secret; **~ de confesión** confessional secret; **~ de estado** state secret; **~ de fabricación** industrial secret; **~ de Polichinela**, **~ a voces** open secret; **debido al ~ sumarial** (*o* **del sumario**) because the matter is sub judice; **la juez ha levantado el ~ sumarial sobre el caso** the judge has lifted the ban on reporting the case; **estar en el ~** to be in on the secret; **guardar un ~** to keep a secret; **hacer ~ de algo** to be secretive about sth.
(b) (*cualidad*) secrecy; **~ de correspondencia** sanctity of the mails; **de** (*o* **en**) **~** in secret, secretly, in secrecy; **lo han hecho con mucho ~** they have done it in great secrecy.
(c) (*cajón*) secret drawer.
(d) (*de cerradura*) combination.

secta NF sect; denomination.

sectario 1 ADJ sectarian; denominational; **no ~** non-sectarian, non-denominational.
2 NM, **sectaria** NF follower, devotee; member; (*Ecl*) sectarian, member of a sect (*o* denomination).

sectarismo NM sectarianism.

sector NM sector; (*de opinión etc*) section; **~ privado** private sector; **~ público** public sector; **~ terciario** tertiary sector, service industries, service sector.

sectorial ADJ local, regional; relating to a particular sector (*o* industry *etc*).

sectorialmente ADV locally, regionally; in a way which relates to a particular sector (*o* industry *etc*).

secuaz NM follower, supporter; (*pey*) underling, hireling.

secuela NF (a) (*consecuencia*) consequence; sequel. (b) (*Méx Jur*) proceedings, prosecution.

secuencia NF (*Cine, Ling etc*) sequence.

secuenciación NF (*Bio*) sequencing.

secuencial ADJ sequential.

secuencialmente ADV sequentially, in sequence.

secuenciar [1b] VT to arrange in sequence.

secuestración NF (a) (*Jur*) sequestration. (b) = **secuestro**.

secuestrador(a) NM/F kidnapper; **~ aéreo** hijacker.

secuestrar [1a] VT (a) *niño* to kidnap; *persona* to kidnap, abduct; (*Aer*) to hijack. (b) (*Jur*) *artículos* to seize, confiscate.

secuestro NM (a) (*rapto*) kidnapping, abduction; (*Aer*) hijack(ing). (b) (*Jur*) seizure, confiscation.

secular ADJ (a) (*Ecl*) secular; lay. (b) (*que dura 100 años*) century-old; (*fig*: *antiguo*) centuries-old, age-old, ancient; **según una tradición ~** according to an age-old tradition.

secularización NF secularization.

secularizar [1f] VT to secularize.

secundar [1a] VT to second, help, support; *huelga* to take part in, join.

secundario ADJ secondary; minor, of lesser importance; **actor ~** supporting actor.

secundinas NFPL afterbirth.

secuoia, secuoya NF (*LAm*) = **secoya.**

sed NF thirst; thirstiness; (*Agr*) thirst, drought, dryness; (*fig*) thirst, lust, longing (*de* for); **~ inextinguible, ~ insaciable** unquenchable thirst; **apagar la ~** to quench one's thirst; **tener ~** to be thirsty; **tener mucha ~** to be very thirsty; **tener ~ de** (*fig*) to thirst for, long for.

seda NF (a) (*gen*) silk; **~ artificial** artificial silk; **~ de coser** sewing silk; **~ dental** dental floss; **~ floja** floss silk; **~ hilada** spun silk; **~ en rama** raw silk; **como una ~** (*ADJ*) as smooth as silk, beautifully smooth; *persona* very meek, very sweet-tempered; (*ADV*) smoothly; **de ~** silk (*atr*); silken, silky; **hacer ~:** to sleep, kip:. (b) (*Zool*) bristle.

sedación NF sedation.

sedal NM fishing-line.

sedán NM (*Aut*) saloon, sedan (*US*).

sedante 1 ADJ (*Med*) sedative; (*fig*) soothing, calming. 2 NM sedative.

sedar [1a] VT to sedate.

sedativo ADJ sedative.

sede NF (a) (*de gobierno*) seat; (*de sociedad*) headquarters, central office; (*Dep*) venue; **~ diplomática** diplomatic quarter (of a city); **~ social** head office, central office; headquarters. (b) (*Ecl*) see; **Santa S~** Holy See.

sedentario ADJ sedentary.

sedentarismo NM (a) sedentary nature. (b) (*Med*) sedentary lifestyle; lack of exercise.

sedente ADJ *estatua* seated.

sedeño ADJ (a) (*sedoso*) silken, silky. (b) (*Zool*) bristly.

sedería NF (a) (*cría*) silk raising; (*manufactura*) silk manufacture, sericulture; (*comercio*) silk trade. (b) (*géneros*) silks, silk goods.

sedero 1 ADJ silk (*atr*); **industria sedera** silk industry. 2 NM, **sedera** NF silk dealer; draper, haberdasher.

SEDIC [se'ðik] NF ABR *de* **Sociedad Española de Documentación e Información Científica.**

sedicente ADJ, **sediciente** ADJ self-styled; so-called, would-be.

sedición NF sedition.

sedicioso 1 ADJ seditious; mutinous, rebellious. 2 NM, **sediciosa** NF subversive element, disloyal individual; rebel; troublemaker.

sediente ADJ: **bienes ~s** (*Jur*) real estate.

sediento ADJ (a) (*lit, t Agr*) thirsty. (b) (*fig*) thirsty, eager (*de* for).

sedimentación NF sedimentation.

sedimentar [1a] 1 VT (a) (*depositar*) to deposit. (b) (*fig*) to calm, quieten. 2 **sedimentarse** VR (a) (*depositarse*) to settle. (b) (*fig*) to calm down, quieten down.

sedimentario ADJ sedimentary.

sedimento NM sediment, deposit.

sedosidad NF silkiness.

sedoso ADJ silky, silken.

seducción NF (a) (*acto*) seduction. (b) (*cualidad*) seductiveness; charm, allure; lure, fascination.

seducir [3o] 1 VT (a) *mujer* to seduce. (b) (*fig*) (*moralmente*) to lead on, seduce from one's duty; (*sobornar*) to bribe. (c) (*fig: cautivar*) to charm, attract, captivate, fascinate; **seduce a todos con su simpatía** she captivates everyone with her charm; **la teoría ha seducido a muchos** the theory has attracted many people; **no me seduce la idea** I don't like the idea, I'm not taken with the idea. 2 VI to be charming, be fascinating; **es una película que seduce** it's a captivating film.

seductivo ADJ = **seductor 1.**

seductor 1 ADJ (a) seductive. (b) (*fig*) (*encantador*) charming, captivating, fascinating; *idea etc* tempting. 2 NM seducer.

Sefarad NF (*historia de los judíos*) Spain; (*fig*) homeland.

sefardí 1 ADJ Sephardic. 2 NMF Sephardi, Sephardic Jew(ess); **sefardíes** Sephardim.

sefardita = **sefardí.**

segable ADJ *cosecha* ready to cut.

segadera NF sickle.

segador NM harvester, reaper.

segadora NF (a) (*persona*) harvester, reaper. (b) (*Mec*) mower, reaper, mowing machine; **~ de césped** lawnmower.

segadora-atadora NF binder.

segadora-trilladora NF combine harvester.

segar [1h y 1k] VT (a) (*Agr*) *trigo etc* to reap, cut, harvest; *heno, hierba* to mow, cut; *otro objeto* to cut off. (b) (*fig*) to mow down. (c) (*fig*) *esperanzas etc* to ruin, destroy; **~ la juventud de uno** to cut sb off in his prime.

seglar 1 ADJ secular, lay. 2 NMF layman, laywoman.

segmentación NF segmentation.

segmentar [1a] 1 VT to segment. 2 **segmentarse** VR to segment.

segmento NM segment; (*Com, Fin*) sector, group; **~ de émbolo** piston ring.

segoviano 1 ADJ of (o from) Segovia. 2 NM, **segoviana** NF native (o inhabitant) of Segovia; **los ~s** the people of Segovia.

segregación NF (a) (*gen*) segregation; **~ racial** racial segregation. (b) (*Anat*) secretion.

segregacionista NMF segregationist, supporter of racial segregation.

segregar [1h] VT (a) (*gen*) to segregate, separate. (b) (*Anat*) to secrete.

seguida NF (a) (*método normal*) normal way (of doing sth); (*ritmo*) proper rhythm, habitual speed; **coger la ~** to get into the swing of it, get into the proper way (of doing sth). (b) **a ~ = seguidamente; de ~** uninterruptedly, straight off; at once; **en ~** at once, right away; **en ~ termino** I've very nearly finished, I shan't be long now; **en ~ tomó el avión para Madrid** he immediately caught the plane to Madrid.

seguidamente ADV (a) (*sin parar*) uninterruptedly, straight off, without a break; continuously. (b) (*inmediatamente después*) immediately after, next; **dijo ~ que ...** he went on at once to say that ...

seguidilla NF (a) (*Mús*) seguidilla (*dance (and piece of music) in a fast triple rhythm*). (b) (*Liter*) seguidilla (*poem with four to seven lines used in popular songs*). (c) **una ~ de protestas** a series of complaints.

seguidista ADJ copycat (*atr*).

seguido 1 ADJ (a) *línea etc* continuous, unbroken. (b) *camino, ruta etc* straight. (c) **~s** consecutive, successive; **5 días ~s** 5 days running; **5 blancos ~s** 5 bull's-eyes in a row, 5 consecutive bull's-eyes. (d) (*largo*) long-lasting; **una enfermedad muy seguida** a very lengthy illness, a long drawn-out illness. (e) **todos sus hijos son muy ~s** she had all her children one after the other. 2 ADV (a) (*directo*) straight; **vaya Vd todo ~** just keep straight on; **por aquí ~** straight on past here. (b) (*detrás*) after; **ese coche iba primero y ~ el mío** that car was in front and mine was immediately behind it. (c) (*LAm*) often; **le gusta visitarnos ~** she likes to visit us often. 3 NM: **a ~** then, next, right away.

seguidor(a) NM/F follower; (*Dep*) fan, follower, supporter.

seguimiento NM (a) (*caza*) chase, pursuit; (*continuación*) continuation; (*Med*) follow-up; monitoring; (*TV*) report, follow-up; **estación de ~** tracking-station; **ir en ~ de** to go in pursuit of, chase (after). (b) **el ~ de la huelga** the support for the strike.

seguir [3d y 3l] 1 VT (a) (*gen*) to follow; to follow on, come next to, come after. (b) *caza* to chase, pursue; to hound; *pista* to follow; *satélite* to track; *pasos* to dog; *pista (de crimen)* to follow up; *mujer* to court. (c) *autoridad, inclinación, jefe, orden, texto etc* to follow; *consejo* to follow, adopt, take; (*Med*) to follow up, monitor; **~ los acontecimientos de cerca** to monitor events closely. (d) *carrera, rumbo* to follow, pursue. (e) **~ su camino** to continue on one's way. 2 VI (a) (*venir después*) to follow; to follow on, come next, come after; **y los que siguen** and the next ones, and those that come next; **como sigue** as follows. (b) (*continuar*) to continue, to carry on, go on; to proceed; **sigue** (*en carta*) PTO, (*en libro, TV*) continued; **¡siga!** go on!; (*And*) come in!; **¡síguele!** (*Méx*) go on!; **siga a la derecha** keep to the right; **~ con una idea** to go on with an idea; **sigue en su sitio** it is still in its place; **sigue en Caracas** he is still in Caracas; **seguía en su error** he continued in his error; **~ adelante** to go on, carry on; to go straight on; (*Aut*) to drive on, go straight ahead; **siga Vd adelante hasta Toboso** go straight ahead as far as Toboso; **~ por un camino** to carry on along a path; **hacer ~ una carta** to forward a letter; **¿cómo sigue?** how is he?; **sigue bien, que siga Vd bien** I hope you keep well, look after yourself. (c) (*con adj o n etc*) to be still, go on being; **sigue enfermo** he's still ill; **si el tiempo sigue bueno** if the weather continues (o stays) fine; **sigue tan misterioso como antes** it's still as mysterious as ever; **sigue soltera** she's still single; **sigue sin poderlo comprar** he is still unable to buy it; **sigo sin comprender** I still don't understand. (d) **~ + *ger*** to go on + *ger*, keep (on) + *ger*; **sigue lloviendo** it's still raining; **sigue siendo lo mismo** it's still the same, it remains unchanged; **siguió mirándola** he went on looking at her; **siguió sentado** he stayed sitting down, he remained seated.

3 **seguirse** VR (a) (*venir después*) to follow; **una cosa se sigue a otra** one thing follows another.
(b) (*deducirse etc*) to follow, ensue, happen in consequence; **de esto se sigue que ...**, **síguese que ...** it follows that ...

▼ **según** 1 ADV (*) according to circumstances; ~ (**y**) **como**, ~ **y conforme** it all depends; '**¿lo vas a comprar?**' — '**~**' 'are you going to buy it?' — 'it all depends'.

▼ 2 PREP (a) (*gen*) according to; (*de acuerdo con*) in accordance with, in line with; ~ **el jefe** according to the boss; ~ **este mapa** according to this map; **obrar ~ las instrucciones** to act in accordance with one's instructions; ~ **lo que dice** from what he says, according to what he says; ~ **lo que se decida** according to what is decided; **iremos o no, ~ el tiempo** we'll go or not, depending on the weather; **eso es ~ el dinero de que se disponga** that depends on what money is available; ~ **parece** it would seem so.
(b) **está ~ lo dejaste** it is just as you left it.
3 CONJ as; ~ **me consta** as I know for a fact; ~ **esté el tiempo** depending on the weather; ~ **que vengan 3 ó 4** depending on whether 3 or 4 come.

segunda NF (a) (*Mús*) second. (b) (*intención*) second meaning, veiled meaning; **decir algo con ~(s)** to say sth with an implied second meaning. (c) (*Aut*) second gear. (d) **viajar en ~** (*Ferro*) to travel second class.

segundar [1a] 1 VT (a) (*repetir*) to do again. (b) (*Cono Sur*) **golpe** to return. (c) (*Méx*) to earth up.
2 VI to come second, be in second place.

segundero NM second hand (*of a watch*).

segundo 1 ADJ second; **educación** secondary; **intención** double.
2 NM (a) (*gen*) second; second one; (*Mil etc*) second in command, second in authority; (*Náut*) first mate; (*Boxeo*) second; ~ **de a bordo** (*fig*) second in command; right-hand man; **sin ~** unrivalled.
(b) (*tiempo*) second.
(c) (*Méx Teat etc*) ~**s** upstairs seats.

segundón 1 NM second son, younger son.
2 NM, **segundona** NF (*fig*) second-class citizen.

segur NF (*hoz*) sickle; (*hacha*) axe.

▼ **seguramente** ADV (a) *con certeza etc* for sure, with certainty.
(b) (*muy probablemente*) surely; ~ **tendrán otro** surely they'll have another, they must have another; ~ **van a estar contentos** no doubt they'll be pleased; '**¿lo va a comprar?**' — '**~**' 'is he going to buy it?' — 'I should think so'.
▼ (c) (*probablemente*) probably, possibly; ~ **llegarán mañana** they'll probably arrive tomorrow.

▼ **seguridad** NF (a) (*lo salvo*) safety; security; safeness; (*Mil, Pol*) security; ~ **en la carretera**, ~ **vial** road safety; ~ **ciudadana** law and order; ~ **colectiva** collective security; ~ **contra incendios** fire precautions; ~ **industrial** industrial safety, safety at work; ~ **social** social security; (*contribución*) national insurance (contribution); **de ~** safety (*atr*), *p.ej.* **cinturón de ~** safety belt; **con la mayor ~** with (*o* in) complete safety; **para mayor ~** to be on the safe side, for safety's sake; **estar en ~** to be in a safe place.
▼ (b) (*certeza*) certainty; **en la ~ de su victoria** in the certainty of winning, being sure of winning; **con toda ~** with complete certainty, for sure; **no lo sabemos con ~** we don't know for sure; **tener la ~ de que ...** to have the certainty that ..., be sure that ...; **tengan Vds la ~ de que ...** rest assured that ...
(c) (*t ~ en sí mismo*) confidence, self-confidence.
(d) (*fiabilidad*) trustworthiness; reliability.
(e) (*firmeza*) firmness; stability, steadiness.
(f) (*Jur*) security, surety.

▼ **seguro** 1 ADJ (a) (*a salvo*) safe; secure; **un puerto ~** a safe harbour; **está más ~ en el banco** it's safer in the bank; **lo más ~ es + infin** the safest thing is to + infin, the best thing is to + infin; **lo más ~ es que no quieren** it's highly likely they don't want to, most probably they don't want to; **conviene atenerse a lo ~** it's best to be on the safe side.
(b) *método, resultado etc* sure, certain; (*inevitable*) bound to come, certain to happen; **ir a una muerte segura** to go to certain death; **es ~ que ...** it is certain that ...; **en estas investigaciones no hay nada ~** nothing is certain in these researches.
▼ (c) (*cierto*) sure, certain; **¿estás ~?** are you sure?; **estar ~ de** to be sure of; **estar ~ de que ...** to be sure that ...
(d) **estar ~ de sí mismo** to be self-confident, be sure of o.s.
(e) (*de fiar*) amigo etc firm, sure, trustworthy; fuente etc reliable, dependable, trustworthy.
(f) (*firme*) objeto firm; firmly fastened, securely tied (*etc*); stable, steady; fecha etc firm, definite.
(g) (*LAm: honesto*) honest, straight.
(h) (*probable*) probable, possible.
2 ADV (a) for sure; **todavía no lo ha dicho ~** he still hasn't said for sure.

(b) **¡~!** sure!, I'm sure it is! (*etc*).
3 NM (a) (*dispositivo*) safety device; (*de cerradura*) tumbler; (*Mil*) safety catch; (*Téc*) catch, pawl, lock, stop.
(b) (*fig*) safety, certainty, assurance; **a buen ~**, **de ~** surely; truly; **en ~** in a safe place; **sobre ~** safely, without risk; **ir sobre ~** to be on safe ground.
(c) (*Com, Fin*) insurance; ~ **de desempleo**, ~ **de paro** unemployment benefit; ~ **de enfermedad** medical insurance; ~ **de incendios** fire insurance; ~ **multiriesgo** multirisk insurance; ~ **mutuo** mutual insurance; ~ **social** social insurance, social security; ~ **contra terceros** third-party insurance; ~ **a** (*o* **contra**) **todo riesgo** comprehensive insurance; ~ **de vida**, ~ **sobre la vida** life insurance.
(d) (*Méx: alfiler*) safety pin.

seibó NM (*And, Carib*) sideboard.

seis 1 ADJ six; (*fecha*) sixth; **las ~** six o'clock.
2 NM six.

seiscientos 1 ADJ six hundred; **en el ~** in the seventeenth century.
2 NM (*Aut*) small car.

seísmo NM tremor, shock, earthquake.

seisporocho NM (*Carib*) a Venezuelan folk dance.

SEL NF ABR *de* **Sociedad Española de Lingüística.**

selección NF (a) (*gen*) selection; ~ **biológica**, ~ **natural** natural selection; ~ **múltiple** multiple choice. (b) (*Dep*) team, side. (c) (*Liter, Mús*) **selecciones** selections.

seleccionable ADJ eligible.

seleccionado NM team.

seleccionador(a) NM/F (*Dep*) selector; team manager.

seleccionar [1a] VT to pick, choose, select.

selectividad NF (a) selectivity. (b) (*Univ*) entrance examination.

selectivo ADJ selective.

selecto ADJ (a) (*en calidad*) select, choice, fine; *club etc* select, exclusive. (b) (*Liter*) obras selected.

selector NM (*Téc*) selector.

selenizaje NM moon-landing.

selenizar [1f] VI to land on the moon.

self* NM, **self-service** NM self-service restaurant.

sellado 1 ADJ sealed; stamped, franked.
2 NM (a) (*acto*) sealing; stamping. (b) (*Cono Sur*) stamps, stamp duty.

selladora NF primer, sealant.

selladura NF (a) (*sello*) seal. (b) (*acto*) sealing; stamping.

sellar [1a] VT (a) documento, carta to seal. (b) pasaporte etc to stamp. (c) (*marcar*) to brand. (d) (*cerrar*) labios, pacto to seal; calle to seal off.

sello NM (a) (*personal, de rey etc*) seal; (*administrativo*) (official etc) stamp; signet; (*LAm: en reverso de moneda*) tails; ~ **real** royal seal; ~ **de caucho**, ~ **de goma** rubber stamp.
(b) (*señal*) impression, mark; stamp; (*Com*) brand, seal; (*Mús: t ~ discográfico*) record label; recording company; (*Liter*) publishing house; ~ **fiscal** revenue stamp; **lleva el ~ de esta oficina** it carries the stamp of this office.
(c) (*Esp Correos*) stamp; ~ **aéreo** airmail stamp; ~ **conmemorativo** commemorative stamp; ~ **de correo** postage stamp; ~ **de urgencia** express-delivery stamp; **no pega ni un ~*** he's useless, he's a waste of space.
(d) (*Med*) cachet, wafer.
(e) (*fig: t ~ distintivo*) hallmark, stamp; **lleva el ~ de su genialidad** it carries the hallmark of his genius.

seltz [selθ, sels]: **agua (de) ~** seltzer (water).

selva NF (*bosque*) forest, woods; (*jungla*) jungle; **S~ Negra** Black Forest.

selvático ADJ (a) (*de la selva*) woodland (atr), sylvan; (*de la jungla*) jungle (atr); (*fig: rústico*) rustic. (b) (*Bot etc*) wild.

selvoso ADJ wooded, well-wooded.

sem ABR *de* **semana** week, wk.

S.Em.ª ABR *de* **Su Eminencia** His Eminence, H.E.

semaforazo* NM robbery (of occupants of a car) at traffic lights.

semáforo NM (*Náut etc*) semaphore; (*Ferro*) signal; (*Aut*) traffic-lights; ~ **sonoro** pelican crossing.

semana NF week; ~ **inglesa** working week of 5½ days; ~ **laboral** working week; **S~ Santa** Holy Week; **entre ~** during the week; **vuelo de entre ~** midweek flight.

┌─── **SEMANA SANTA** ───┐

ⓘ In Spain celebrations for Semana Santa (Holy Week) are often spectacular. Viernes Santo, Sábado Santo and Domingo de Resurrección (Good Friday, Holy Saturday, Easter Sunday) are all national public holidays, with additional days being given as local holidays. There are long processions through the streets with pasos - religious floats and sculptures. Religious statues are carried along on the shoulders of the cofrades, members of the cofradías or lay brotherhoods that organize the processions. These are accompanied by penitentes and nazarenos generally wearing long hooded robes. Seville and Málaga are particularly well-known for their spectacular Holy Week processions.

► LENGUA Y USO: **según:** 2a → 53.5   **seguramente:** c → 43.2   **seguridad:** b → 42.1, 43.1, 53.6   **seguro:** 1c → 42.1, 43.1, 52.6

semanal ADJ weekly.

semanalmente ADV weekly, each week.

semanario [1] ADJ weekly.
[2] NM (*revista*) weekly (magazine).

semanero, -a NM/F (*LAm*) weekly-paid worker; worker specially engaged for a week's work.

semántica NF semantics.

semántico ADJ semantic.

semblante NM (*Liter Anat*) face, visage; (*exterior*) face, appearance; (*perspectiva*) outlook; (*aspecto*) aspect; **alterar** (*o* **demudar**) **el ~ a uno** to make sb look alarmed, upset sb; **componer el ~** to regain one's composure; **mudar de ~** to change colour; **el caso lleva otro ~ ahora** the matter looks different now; **tener buen ~** (*salud*) to look well; (*humor*) to be in a good mood.

semblantear [1a] VT (a) (*CAm, Cono Sur, Méx*) *persona* to look straight in the face, look deeply into the eyes of.
(b) (*CAm Méx: examinar*) to study, examine, look at.

semblanza NF biographical sketch.

sembradera NF seed drill.

sembradío NM = **sembrío**.

sembrado NM sown field.

sembrador(a) [1] NM/F (*persona*) sower.
[2] NF (*Agr*) seed drill.

sembradura NF sowing.

sembrar [1k] VT (a) (*Agr*) *campo, semilla* to sow; **~ de** to sow with.
(b) **~ minas en un estrecho**, **~ un estrecho de minas** (*Náut*) to mine a strait, lay mines in a strait.
(c) (*fig*) *objetos* to sprinkle, scatter about, spread around; *superficie* to sprinkle, strew (*de* with); *discordia* to sow; *noticia* to spread; **el que siembra recoge** one reaps what one has sown.
(d) (*Méx*) *jinete* to throw; (*derribar*) to knock down.

sembrío NM (*LAm*) land prepared for sowing.

semejante [1] ADJ (a) (*parecido*) similar; **~s** alike, similar, the same; **~ a** like; **es ~ a ella en el carácter** she is like her in character; **son muy ~s** they are very much alike.
(b) (*Mat*) similar.
(c) (*tal*) such; **nunca hizo cosa ~** he never did such a thing, he never did anything of the kind; **¿se ha visto frescura ~?** did you ever see such cheek?*.
(d) (*Cono Sur, Méx*) huge, enormous.
[2] NM (a) (*ser humano*) fellow man, fellow creature; **nuestros ~s** our fellow men.
(b) **no tiene ~** (*equivalente*) it has no equal, there is nothing to equal it.

▼ **semejanza** NF similarity, resemblance; **a ~ de** like, as; **~ de familia** family likeness; **tener ~ con** to look like, resemble, bear a resemblance to.

semejar [1a] [1] VI to seem like, resemble, seem to be.
[2] **semejarse** VR to look alike, be similar, resemble each other; **~ a** to look alike, resemble.

semen NM semen.

semental [1] ADJ stud, breeding (*atr*).
[2] NM (*Zool*) sire, stud animal; (‡: *hombre*) stud‡.

sementera NF (a) (*acto*) sowing. (b) (*época*) seedtime, sowing season. (c) (*tierra*) sown land, sown field. (d) (*fig*) hotbed (*de* of), breeding ground (*de* for).

semestral ADJ half-yearly, biannual.

semestralmente ADV half-yearly, biannually.

semestre NM (a) (*seis meses*) period of six months; (*US: Univ etc*) semester. (b) (*Fin*) half-yearly payment.

semi... PREF semi..., half-...

semiacabado ADJ (*Com*) half-finished.

semialfabetizado ADJ semiliterate.

semiamueblado ADJ semi-furnished.

semiautomático ADJ semiautomatic.

semibola NF (*Bridge*) small slam.

semibreve NF semibreve.

semicircular ADJ semicircular.

semicírculo NM semicircle.

semiconductor NM semiconductor.

semiconsciente ADJ semiconscious, half-conscious.

semiconsonante NF semiconsonant.

semicorchea NF semiquaver.

semicualificado ADJ semiskilled.

semiculto ADJ half-learned.

semicultismo NM half-learned word.

semicupio NM (*CAm, Carib*) hip-bath.

semiderruido ADJ half-ruined, half-collapsed.

semidesconocido ADJ virtually unknown.

semidescremado ADJ semi-skimmed.

semidesértico ADJ semidesert (*atr*).

semidesierto ADJ half-empty.

semidesnatado ADJ semi-skimmed.

semidesnudo ADJ half-naked.

semidiós NM demigod.

semidormido ADJ half-asleep.

semidúplex ADJ (*Inform*) half duplex.

semielaborado ADJ half-finished.

semienterrado ADJ half-buried.

semiexperto ADJ semiskilled.

semifallo NM (*Bridge*) singleton (*a* in).

semifinal NF semifinal.

semifinalista NMF semifinalist.

semifondo NM (*Dep*) middle-distance running; **carrera de ~** middle-distance race.

semifracaso NM partial failure, near failure.

semiinconsciente ADJ semiconscious.

semilla NF (a) (*Bot, t fig*) seed; **~ de césped** grass seed. (b) (*Cono Sur*) brad, tack. (c) (*Cono Sur: niño*) baby, small child; **la ~*** the kids (*collectively*).

semillero NM (a) (*terreno*) seedbed; nursery; (*caja*) seedbox.
(b) (*fig*) hotbed (*de* of), breeding ground (*de* for); **un ~ de delincuencia** a hotbed of crime; **la decisión fue un ~ de disgustos** the decision caused a host of troubles, the decision became a battleground of controversy.

semimedio NM (*Boxeo*) welterweight.

seminal ADJ seminal.

seminario NM (a) (*Agr*) seedbed; nursery. (b) (*Ecl*) seminary. (c) (*Univ etc*) seminar.

seminarista NM seminarist.

seminuevo ADJ (*Com*) nearly new; pre-owned (*US*).

semioficial ADJ semi-official.

semiología NF semiology.

semiolvidado ADJ half-forgotten.

semioruga NF (*t* **camión ~**) half-track.

semioscuridad NF half-darkness; gloom.

semiótica NF semiotics.

semiótico ADJ semiotic.

semipesado ADJ (*Boxeo*) light-heavyweight.

semiprecioso ADJ semiprecious.

semiprofesional ADJ, NMF semi-professional.

semisalado ADJ *agua* brackish.

semiseco ADJ *vino* medium-dry.

semiseparado ADJ semidetached.

semisótano NM semibasement.

semita [1] ADJ Semitic.
[2] NMF Semite.

semítico ADJ Semitic.

semitono NM semitone.

semivacío ADJ half-empty.

semivocal NF semivowel.

semivolea NF half-volley.

sémola NF semolina.

semoviente ADJ: **bienes ~s** livestock.

sempiterno ADJ everlasting.

sen NM, **sena** NF (*Bot, Med*) senna.

Sena NM Seine.

senado NM senate; (*fig*) assembly, gathering.

SENADO

The **Senado** *is the Upper Chamber of the Spanish Parliament. Approximately 80% of its 256 members acquire their seats in the general elections while the remaining 20% are nominated by each of the Autonomous Regions (*Comunidades Autónomas*). Like the* **Congreso de los Diputados***, the term of office for the* **Senado** *is no longer than four years.*
⇨ *See also* CONGRESO DE LOS DIPUTADOS

---

senador(a) NM/F senator; *ver también* SENADO .

senatorial ADJ senatorial.

sencillamente ADV simply; **es ~ imposible** it's simply impossible.

sencillez (*V* ADJ) NF (a) simplicity, plainness. (b) simplicity, straightforwardness. (c) naturalness, unaffectedness, lack of sophistication; (*pey*) simplicity; (*LAm*) foolishness.

sencillo [1] ADJ (a) (*gen*) simple, plain, unadorned; *costumbres, estilo, ropa etc* simple.
(b) *asunto, problema* simple, easy, straightforward; **es muy ~** it's very simple.
(c) *persona* natural, unaffected, unsophisticated; (*pey*) simple, (*LAm*) foolish.
(d) *billete, flor, hilo etc* single.
[2] NM (a) (*disco*) single. (b) (*LAm: moneda*) small change, loose change.

senda NF path, track; (*fig*) path; (*Aut*) lane.

senderismo NM hill walking.

senderista [1] ADJ (*Perú: Pol*) of (*o* pertaining) to the Shining Path guerrilla movement.
[2] NMF (a) (*Perú: Pol*) member (*o* supporter) of Shining Path. (b) (*Dep*) hill walker.
sendero NM path, track; **S~ Luminoso** (*Perú*) Shining Path.

SENDERO LUMINOSO

(*i*) **Sendero Luminoso** (*Shining Path*) is a Maoist terrorist group operating in Peru and founded by a former philosophy lecturer, Abimael Guzmán. Its aims are to bring about a Communist revolution. Since 1980 it has been conducting a guerrilla war against the Peruvian government and its institutions.

---

sendos ADJ PL one each; each; **les dio ~ libros** she gave them each a book; **los criados recibieron ~ regalos** each servant received a present; **con sendas peculiaridades** each with its own peculiarity.
Séneca NM Seneca.
senectud NF old age.
Senegal NM: **El ~** Senegal.
senegalés, -esa ADJ, NM/F Senegalese.
senescencia NF ageing.
senil ADJ senile.
senilidad NF senility.
seno NM (a) (*Anat*) bosom, bust; **~s** breasts; **~ (frontal)** frontal sinus; **~ materno** womb; (*fig*) bosom; **en el ~ de Abrahán** on Abraham's bosom; **morir en el ~ de la familia** to die in the bosom of one's family; **lo escondió en su ~** she hid it in her bosom, she put it down the front of her dress.
(b) (*hueco*) hollow, cavity; (*Náut*) trough (*between waves*); (*Met*) trough.
(c) (*Geog: ensenada*) small bay, inlet; (*golfo*) gulf.
(d) (*fig*) refuge, haven.
(e) (*de club etc*) headquarters; (*fig*) heart, core; **el ~ del movimiento** the heart of the movement.
(f) (*Mat*) sine.
SENPA ['senpa] NM (*Esp*) ABR de **Servicio Nacional de Productos Agrarios**.
sensación NF (a) (*gen*) sensation, feeling; (*impresión*) sense; feel; **una ~ de placer** a feeling of pleasure; **tengo una ~ de inutilidad** I have a feeling of being useless.
(b) (*fig*) sensation; **causar ~, hacer ~** to cause a sensation.
sensacional ADJ sensational.
sensacionalismo NM sensationalism.
sensacionalista ADJ sensationalist.
sensacionalizar [1f] VT to sensationalize.
sensatamente ADV sensibly.
sensatez NF good sense, sensibleness.
sensato ADJ sensible.
sensibilidad NF sensitivity (*a* to), sensitiveness; sensibility; **~ artística** artistic feeling, sensitivity to art.
sensibilización NF sensitizing.
sensibilizado ADJ sensitized.
sensibilizar [1f] VT to sensitize; (*fig*) to alert (*a* about, to), make aware (*a* of).
sensible [1] ADJ (a) (*que siente*) feeling, sentient; (*que reacciona*) sensitive (*a* to); (*Med*) *lugar* sensitive, tender, sore; (*Fot*) sensitive; **un aparato muy ~** a very sensitive (*o* delicate) piece of apparatus; **una placa ~ a la luz** a plate sensitive to light; **es muy ~ a los cambios de temperatura** it is very sensitive to changes in temperature.
(b) *carácter* sensitive (*a* to); responsive (*a* to); impressionable, emotional, easily hurt.
(c) *cambio etc* perceptible, appreciable, noticeable; *diferencia etc* tangible, palpable; *golpe* heavy; *pérdida* heavy, considerable; **una ~ mejoría** a noticeable improvement, a marked improvement.
(d) (*capaz*) **~ de** capable of; **~ de mejora** capable of improvement, having a capacity for improvement.
(e) **soy ~ del honor que se me hace** I am conscious of the honour being done me.
(f) (*lamentable*) regrettable, lamentable; **es muy ~** it is highly regrettable; **es ~ que ...** it is regrettable that ...
[2] NF (*Mús*) leading note.
sensiblemente ADV perceptibly, appreciably, noticeably; markedly; **~ más** substantially more.
sensiblería NF sentimentality; mushiness, sloppiness; squeamishness.
sensiblero ADJ sentimental; mushy, sloppy; squeamish.
sensitiva NF (a) (*Bot*) mimosa. (b) (*: persona*) highly sensitive person, delicate flower.
sensitivo ADJ (a) *órgano etc* sense (*atr*). (b) *ser etc* sentient; sensitive.
sensomotor ADJ sensorimotor.
sensor NM sensor; **~ de calor** heat sensor; **~ de fin de papel** paper-out sensor.
sensorial ADJ sensorial, sensory.

sensorio ADJ sensory.
sensual ADJ (a) (*sexual*) sensual; (*sensorio*) sensuous. (b) (*esp LAm*) alluring, sexy.
sensualidad NF (a) sensuality, sensuousness. (b) (*esp LAm*) attractiveness, allure, sexiness.
sensualismo NM sensualism.
sensualista NMF sensualist.
sentada NF (a) (*gen*) sitting; **de una ~, en una ~** at one sitting. (b) (*Pol etc*) sit-down (protest); sit-in.
sentadera NF (a) (*LAm*) seat (*of a chair etc*). (b) (*Méx*) **~s** backside.
sentadero NM seat.
sentado ADJ (a) (*gen*) **estar ~** to sit, be sitting (down), be seated; **permanecer ~** to remain seated.
(b) (*fig*) settled, established; firm; **dar algo por ~** to take sth for granted, assume sth; **dejar algo ~** to establish sth firmly; **dejar ~ que ...** to lay down that ..., have it clearly understood that ...
(c) (*fig*) *carácter* solid, sensible, steady; sedate.
sentador ADJ (*Cono Sur*) *vestido* smart, elegant.
sentadura NF (*en piel*) sore; (*en fruta*) mark.
sentar [1k] [1] VT (a) *persona* to sit, seat.
(b) *objeto* to place (firmly), settle (in its place); **~ el último ladrillo** to tap the last brick into place; **~ las costuras** to press the seams; **~ las bases** to lay the foundations.
(c) **~ una suma en la cuenta de uno** (*Com*) to put a sum down to sb's account.
(d) (*fig*) *base, cimientos* to lay, establish, create; *principio* to set up, establish; *precedente* to lay down, set up.
(e) (*And, Carib*) *persona* to crush, squash.
(f) (*And*) *caballo* to rein in (*o* pull up) sharply.
[2] VTI (a) (*ropa etc*) to suit; to fit; to look well on, be becoming to; **ese peinado le sienta horriblemente*** that hair style doesn't suit her one little bit*, she looks awful with that hairdo*.
(b) (*comida*) **bien a** to agree with; **~ mal a** to disagree with; **no me sientan las gambas** prawns disagree with me.
(c) (*fig*) **~ bien** to go down well; **~ mal** to go down badly, produce a bad impression; **le ha sentado mal que lo hayas hecho tú** he took it badly that you should do it, he didn't like your doing it; **a mí me sienta como un tiro*** it suits me like a hole in the head.
[3] **sentarse** VR (a) (*persona*) to sit, sit down; to seat o.s.; to settle o.s.; **siéntese (do)** sit down, take a seat; **sentémonos aquí** let's sit (down) here; **se sentó a comer** she sat down to eat.
(b) (*sedimento etc*) to settle.
(c) (*tiempo etc*) to settle (down); to become steady, stabilize.
(d) (*Arquit*) to settle.
(e) (*zapato etc*) to leave a mark, rub.
sentencia NF (a) (*Jur*) sentence; (*fig*) decision, ruling; opinion; **~ de muerte** death sentence; **dictar ~, pronunciar ~** to pronounce sentence.
(b) (*Liter*) maxim, saying; dictum.
(c) (*Inform*) statement.
sentenciar [1b] [1] VT (a) (*Jur*) to sentence (*a* to). (b) (*LAm*) **~ a uno** to swear revenge on sb.
[2] VI to pronounce, give one's opinion.
sentenciosamente ADV (*V ADJ*) (a) pithily. (b) sententiously.
sentenciosidad NF (a) pithiness; oracular nature. (b) sententiousness.
sentencioso ADJ (a) *dicho* pithy; oracular. (b) *persona* sententious.
sentidamente ADV (*V ADJ*) (a) regretfully. (b) sincerely, with great feeling.
sentido [1] ADJ (a) (*lamentable*) regrettable; deeply felt; **una pérdida muy sentida** a deeply felt loss, a most regrettable loss.
(b) *compasión etc* sincere, deeply felt, keen; **le doy mi más ~ pésame** I offer my deepest sympathy.
(c) *carácter* sensitive, tender, easily wounded.
(d) (*Méx*) (*de buen oído*) having good hearing, sharp-eared.
(e) (*Méx: resentido*) bitter.
[2] NM (a) (*del cuerpo*) sense; **los cinco ~s** the five senses; **~ del olfato** sense of smell; **~ del color** sense of colour; **~ del humor** sense of humour; **~ de la medida, ~ de las proporciones** sense of proportion; **~ de los negocios** business sense; **~ de orientación** sense of direction; **sexto ~** sixth sense; **tener ~ del ridículo** to be too self-conscious; **no tiene ~ del ritmo** he has no sense of rhythm; **sin ~** senseless, unconscious; **aguzar el ~** to prick up one's ears; **costar un ~*** to cost the earth; **embargar los ~s a uno** to enrapture sb; **perder el ~** to lose consciousness; **poner los cinco ~s en algo** to give one's whole attention to sth; **quitar el ~ a uno** to take one's breath away; **recobrar el ~** to regain consciousness.
(b) (*juicio*) sense; discernment, judgement; **buen ~** good sense; **~ común** common sense; **tener ~ para distinguir algo** to have enough sense to distinguish sth.
(c) (*Ling*) sense, meaning; **doble ~** double meaning; **~ figurado** figurative sense; **en el buen ~ de la palabra** in the best sense of the

word; **en el ~ amplio, en ~ lato** in the broad sense; **en el ~ estricto** in the strict sense; **en cierto ~** in a sense; **en todos los ~s** in every sense; **en este ~** in this respect; **en tal ~** to this effect; **en el ~ de que ...** to the effect that ...; **sin ~** meaningless; **cobrar ~** to begin to make sense; **no le encuentro ningún ~** I can't make any sense of it; **tener ~** to make sense; **no tiene ~ que lo haga él** it doesn't make any sense for him to do it; **la vida no tiene ~ para él** life has no meaning for him; **tomar algo en buen** (o **mal**) **~** to take sth the right (o wrong) way.

(d) (*sensibilidad etc*) feeling; **leer con ~** to read with feeling; **tener ~ de la música** to have a feeling for music.

(e) (*Geog*) direction; way; '**~ único**' 'one way (street)'; **en ~ contrario, en ~ opuesto** in the opposite direction, the other way; **en el ~ de las agujas del reloj** clockwise; **en ~ contrario al de las agujas del reloj** anticlockwise; **algo en este ~** (*fig*) something along these lines; **iban en ~ inverso al nuestro** they were travelling in the opposite direction to us.

(f) (*Méx: oreja*) ear.

sentimental ADJ (a) (*gen*) sentimental; emotional; *mirada* soulful. (b) *asunto, vida etc* love (*atr*); V **aventura**.

sentimentalismo NM sentimentality.

sentimentalmente ADV: **estar unido ~ a uno** to be (romantically) involved with sb.

sentimentaloide* ADJ sugary, over-sentimental; mushy, soppy*.

sentimentero ADJ (*Carib, Méx*) = **sensiblero**.

sentimiento NM (a) (*emoción*) feeling, emotion, sentiment; **un ~ de insatisfacción** a feeling of dissatisfaction; **buenos ~s** fellow feeling, sympathy; **herir los ~s de uno** to hurt (o wound) sb's feelings.

(b) (*sentido*) sense; **~ del deber** sense of duty; **~ de la responsabilidad** sense of responsibility.

(c) (*pesar*) regret, grief, sorrow; **con profundo ~** with profound regret; V **acompañar**.

sentina NF (a) (*Náut*) bilge; (*en ciudad*) sewer, drain. (b) (*fig*) sink, sewer.

▼ **sentir** [3i] **1** VT (a) (*gen*) to feel; (*percibir*) to perceive, sense; (*esp LAm: oír*) to hear; (*oler*) to smell; *emoción* to feel; *dignidad, responsabilidad etc* to feel, be aware of, realize; *música, pintura etc* to feel, have a feeling for; **~ un dolor** to feel a pain; **~ el ruido de un coche** to hear the noise of a car; **sin ~ el frío** without feeling the cold; **~ ganas de +** *infin* to feel an urge to + *infin*; **lo siento ajeno a mí** I feel it is foreign to me, I feel detached from it; **siente la profesión como un sacerdocio** he feels the profession like a sacred calling; **dejarse ~, hacerse ~** to let itself be felt; **se deja ~ el frío** it's beginning to feel cold.

(b) *enfermedad etc* to feel the effects of, suffer from the aftermath of.

▼ (c) (*lamentar*) to regret, be sorry for; **lo siento** I'm sorry; **¡lo siento muchísimo!, ¡cuánto lo siento!** I'm very sorry!, I'm so sorry!; **sintió profundamente esa pérdida** he felt (o regretted, mourned *etc*) that loss deeply; **~ que ...** to regret that ..., be sorry that ...; **sentiré que me obligue Vd a venderlo** I shall be sorry if you force me to sell it; **siento no haberlo hecho antes** I am sorry not to have done it before; **siento molestarle** I'm sorry to bother you.

2 VI (a) (*gen*) to feel; **estaba que ni oía ni sentía** he was in such a state that he could neither hear nor feel anything; **sin ~** without noticing, quite inadvertently; imperceptibly, so quickly (o smoothly *etc*) that one does not notice.

(b) (*lamentar*) to feel sorry; **dar que ~** to give cause for regret.

3 **sentirse** VR (a) (*gen*) to feel; **~ pesimista** to feel pessimistic; **~ herido** (*fig*) to feel hurt; **~ mal(o)** to feel ill, feel bad; **~ como en su casa** to feel at home; **~ en ridículo** to feel ridiculous; **~ actor** to feel o.s. to be an actor.

(b) (*Med*) **~ del costado** to have a pain in one's side; **~ del paludismo** to suffer from malaria.

(c) (*ofenderse*) to be offended, feel resentful (*de* about, at); **~ de una observación** to take offence at a remark.

(d) (*LAm: enfadarse*) to get cross, get angry; **~ con uno** to fall out with sb.

(e) (*recipiente*) to crack.

4 NM opinion, judgement; **a mi ~, en mi ~** in my opinion; **compartir el ~ de** to share the view of, echo the opinion of.

sentón NM (a) (*CAm, Méx: caída*) heavy fall. (b) **dar un ~ a** (*And*) *caballo* to rein in suddenly; **dar un ~** (*Méx: caerse*) to fall on one's backside.

▼ **seña** NF (a) (*del cuerpo etc*) mark, distinguishing mark; **~s** description; **~s de identidad, ~s particulares** identifying marks, distinguishing marks; **~s personales** personal description; **~s mortales** sure signs; **las ~s son mortales** the signs are unmistakable; **dar las ~s de uno** to give a personal description of sb.

(b) (*indicio etc*) sign; (*fig*) sign, token, secret sign; (*Mil*) password; **por las ~s** so it seems; **por más ~s** just to prove it, to clinch matters; into the bargain, moreover; **dar ~s de** to show signs of; **hablar por ~s** to talk by signs, communicate by means of signs; **hacer una ~ a**

uno to make a sign to sb; **hacer una ~ a uno para que +** *subj* to signal to sb to + *infin*.

▼ (c) **~s** (*Correos*) address.

señá NF = **señora**.

señal NF (a) (*gen*) sign; (*síntoma*) symptom; (*indicio*) token, indication; **en ~ de** as a token of, as a sign of, in sign of; **es buena ~** it's a good sign; **dar ~es de** to show signs of; **hacer la ~ de la cruz** to make the sign of the Cross; **hacer ~es de humo** to send up smoke-signals; (*) to talk on the phone.

(b) (*Com, Fin*) token payment; deposit; pledge; **dejar una suma en ~** to leave a sum as a deposit.

(c) (*con la mano*) sign, signal; **~ de la victoria** victory sign, V-sign; **dar la ~ de** (o **para**) to give the signal for; **hacer una ~ a uno** to make a sign to sb; **hacer una ~ grosera** to make a rude sign; **al hacerse una ~ predeterminada** at a prearranged signal.

(d) (*seña*) mark; (*vestigio*) trace, vestige, sign; (*Med*) scar, mark; (*en animal*) mark, marking; brand; (*Geog*) landmark; (*Liter*) bookmark; **sin la menor ~ de** without the least trace of, without the slightest sign of; **no quedaba ni ~** there wasn't the slightest trace of it; **lo hicieron sin dejar ~** they did it without leaving a trace.

(e) (*Aut, Ferro etc*) signal; **~ de alto, ~ de stop** stop sign; **~ de auxilio, ~ de socorro** distress-signal; **~ de carretera, ~ de tránsito, ~ vertical** roadsign; **~ horizontal** road marking; **~es luminosas, ~es de tráfico** traffic-lights, traffic-signals; **~ de peligro** danger-signal.

(f) (*Rad*) signal; **~ horaria** time signal.

(g) (*Telec*) signal, tone; buzz; **~ de llamada** calling signal; **~ para marcar** dialling tone; **~ de ocupado** (o **comunicando**) engaged tone, busy signal (*US*).

(h) (*LAm*) earmark.

señala NF (*Cono Sur*) earmark.

señaladamente ADV (a) (*especialmente*) especially. (b) (*claramente*) clearly, plainly.

señalado ADJ (a) **estar ~ como** to be marked down as, be known to be.

(b) **dejar ~ a uno** to scar sb permanently.

(c) (*claro*) distinct, clear, plain.

(d) *día, favor etc* special; *persona* distinguished, notable, (*pey*) notorious.

señalador NM bookmark.

señalar [1a] **1** VT (a) (*significar*) to mark; to denote, betoken; **señalan la llegada de la primavera** they announce the arrival of spring; **eso señaló el principio del descenso** that marked the start of the decline.

(b) *papel etc* to mark; to stamp; *persona* to mark (for life), scar (permanently); (*Med*) to leave a scar on; (*LAm*) *ganado* to brand.

(c) *carretera etc* to put up signs on; *ruta* to signpost.

(d) (*con el dedo*) to point to, point out, indicate; (*fig*) to show, indicate; (*aguja de reloj etc*) to show, point to, say; **iba señalando los edificios importantes** he went round pointing out the interesting buildings; **tuve que ~le varios errores** I had to point out several mistakes to him.

(e) (*en conversación*) to allude to; (*pey*) to criticize.

(f) *fecha, precio etc* to fix, settle; *tarea* to set; *persona* to appoint; **¿qué precio ha señalado al cuadro?** what price has he put on the picture?; **se negó a ~me hora** he refused to offer me an appointment, he refused to arrange a time to meet.

2 **señalarse** VR to make one's mark (*como* as); to distinguish o.s. (*por* by, by reason of), achieve distinction.

señalero NM (*Cono Sur*) signalman.

señalización NF (*acto*) signposting; (*sistema*) system of signs (o signals), signal code; **~ horizontal** markings on the road; **~ vertical** (system of) roadsigns.

señalizador NM roadsign, signpost.

señalizar [1f] VT *carretera etc* to put up signs on; *ruta* to signpost.

señero ADJ (a) (*solo*) alone, solitary. (b) (*sin par*) unequalled, outstanding.

seño* NF (*Esp: en la escuela*) Miss.

señor **1** NM (a) man; (*caballero*) gentleman; **le espera un ~** there's a gentleman waiting to see you; **es todo un ~** he's a real gentleman; **dárselas de ~** to put on airs; **hacer el ~** to lord it; **quiere parecer un ~** he tries to look like a gentleman.

(b) (*de bienes*) owner, master; (*de criados*) master; (*fig*) master; **el ~ de la casa** the master of the household; **¿está el ~?** is the master in?; **no es ~ de sus pasiones** he cannot control his passions.

(c) (*delante de apellido*) Mister (*se escribe siempre* Mr); **es para el Sr Meléndez** it's for Mr Meléndez; **los ~es Poblet** the Poblets, Mr and Mrs Poblet; **Señor Don Jacinto Benavente** (*en sobre*) Mr J. Benavente, J. Benavente Esq.

(d) (*delante de cargo profesional: no se traduce*) **el ~ alcalde** the mayor; **el ~ cura** the priest; **el ~ presidente** the president (*pero V* (e)).

(e) (*en oración directa*) sir (*pero frec no se traduce*); (*a noble*) my lord; **~es** (*en discurso*) gentlemen; **¡mire Vd, ~!** look here!; **¡oiga Vd, ~!** I

say!; ~ **alcalde** Mr Mayor; ~ **director** ... (*de periódico*) Dear Sir ...; **sí,
~ guardia** (*Esp*) yes, officer; ~ **juez** my Lord; ~ **presidente** Mr Chairman, Mr President; **¡no ~!** (*fig*) not a bit of it!, never!, absolutely
not!; **¡sí ~!** (*fig*) yes indeed!, I should jolly well think it is!*, it certainly does! (*etc*); **pues sí ~** well that's how it is.

(**f**) (*Com etc*) **muy ~ mío** Dear Sir; **muy ~es nuestros** Gentlemen.

(**g**) (*Hist*) noble, lord; ~ **feudal** feudal lord; lord of the manor; ~ **de
la guerra** warlord; ~ **de horca y cuchillo** (*fig*) despot.

(**h**) (*Rel*) **El S~** The Lord; **Nuestro S~** Our Lord; **S~ de los Ejércitos**
Lord of Hosts; **recibir al S~** to take communion.

(**i**) **los ~es*** the fuzz*, the police.

2 ADJ (*) (**a**) (*señoril*) posh*; **un coche muy ~** a really posh car*.

(**b**) (*verdadero, grande*) real, really big; **una casa para un ~ ~** a house
for a gentleman who really is a gentleman; **eso es un ~ melón** now
that really is a melon, that's some melon; **fue una ~a herida** it was
a real big wound*.

señora NF (**a**) (*gen*) lady; ~ **de compañía** chaperon; companion; **le
espera una ~** there's a lady waiting to see you.

(**b**) (*de bienes*) owner, mistress; **¿está la ~?** is the lady of the house
at home?

(**c**) (*esposa*) wife; **mi ~** my wife; **el jefe y su ~** the boss and his wife;
la ~ de Smith Mrs Smith.

(**d**) (*en oración directa: pero frec no se traduce*) madam, (*a noble*) my
lady; **¡~s y señores!** ladies and gentlemen!; **sí, ~** yes, madam; **¡oiga
Vd, ~!** I say!

(**e**) **muy ~ mía** (*Com etc*) Dear Madam.

(**f**) **Nuestra S~** (*Rel*) (*para católicos*) Our Lady, (*para protestantes*) the
Virgin (Mary).

(**g**) (*Esp*) fuzz*, police; secret police.

señorear [1a] **1** VT (**a**) (*gobernar*) to rule, control; (*pey*) to domineer,
lord it over.

(**b**) (*edificio*) to dominate, soar above, tower over.

(**c**) *pasiones* to master, control.

2 **señorearse** VR (**a**) (*dominarse*) to control o.s.

(**b**) (*darse humos*) to adopt a lordly manner.

(**c**) ~ **de** to seize, seize control of.

señoría NF (**a**) (*dominio*) rule, sway. (**b**) (*títulos*) **su S~** (*t* **vuestra S~**)
your lordship, his lordship, your ladyship, her ladyship; my lord,
my lady.

señorial ADJ, **señoril** ADJ lordly; aristocratic; noble, majestic, stately.

señorío NM (**a**) (*Hist*) manor, feudal estate; domain.

(**b**) (*fig: dominio*) rule, sway, dominion (*sobre* over).

(**c**) (*cualidad*) lordliness; majesty, stateliness.

(**d**) (*) (*personas*) distinguished people; (*pey*) toffs*, nobs*.

señorita NF (**a**) (*gen*) young lady.

(**b**) (*delante de nombre o apellido*) Miss.

(**c**) (*en oración directa, no se traduce*) **¿qué busca Vd, ~?** what are you
looking for?

(**d**) (*LAm: profesora*) schoolteacher.

señoritingo*, **-a** NM/F rich kid.

señorito **1** NM (**a**) (*gen*) young gentleman; (*en lenguaje de criados*)
master, young master. (**b**) (*pey*) rich kid*.

2 ADJ (*hum**) lordly; high-class, classy*; (*excessively*) genteel.

señorón* NM big shot*.

señuelo NM (**a**) (*lit*) decoy. (**b**) (*fig*) bait, lure. (**c**) (*And, Cono Sur: buey*)
leading ox.

seo NF (*Aragón*) cathedral.

sep. NM ABR *de* **septiembre** September, Sept.

sepa *etc* V **saber**.

separable **1** ADJ separable; (*Mec etc*) detachable, removable.

2 NM pull-out feature, supplement.

separación NF (**a**) (*acto etc*) separation; division; (*Mec*) removal; (*de
puesto*) removal, dismissal (*de* from); ~ (**del matrimonio**), ~ **judicial**
legal separation; ~ **racial** racial segregation; ~ **del servicio** (*Mil*) discharge.

(**b**) (*distancia*) gap, distance.

separadamente ADV separately.

separado ADJ separated; separate; (*Mec*) detached; **vive ~ de su mujer**
he is separated from his wife, he doesn't live with his wife; **por ~**
(*aparte*) separately; (*uno por uno*) individually, one by one; (*Correos*)
under separate cover; **firmar una paz por ~** to sign a separate peace.

separador NM (**a**) separator. (**b**) (*Inform*) delimiter.

separadora NF (*Inform*) burster.

separar [1a] **1** VT (**a**) *objeto* to separate (*de* from); *silla etc* to move
away (*de* from), take away, remove; ~ **un trozo de pan** to put aside
a piece of bread.

(**b**) *peleadores etc* to separate, pull apart, keep apart; *palabras, sílabas*
to divide; *conexión etc* to sever, cut; *cartas etc* to sort (out); **saber ~ las
buenas de las malas** to know how to separate (*o* tell, distinguish)
the good ones from the bad; **los negocios le separan de su familia**
business keeps him away from his family.

(**c**) (*Mec*) *pieza* to detach, remove (*de* from).

(**d**) (*destituir*) to remove, dismiss (*de* from); **ser separado del servicio**
(*Mil*) to be discharged.

2 **separarse** VR (**a**) (*fragmento*) to come away, detach itself (*de*
from); (*componentes*) to come apart; (*Pol*) to secede.

(**b**) (*persona*) to leave, go away, withdraw; ~ **de un grupo** to leave a
group; to part company with a group; **no quiere ~ de sus libros** she
and her books are inseparable; **se ha separado de todos sus amigos**
he has cut himself off from all his friends; **me separé de ella a las
11** I left her at 11; **se ha separado de su mujer** he has left his wife.

(**c**) (*Jur*) to withdraw (*de* from).

separata NF offprint.

separatismo NM separatism, separatist tendency.

separatista ADJ, NMF separatist.

separo NM (*Méx*) cell.

sepelio NM burial.

sepia NF (**a**) (*Zool*) cuttlefish. (**b**) (*Arte etc*) sepia.

SEPLA NM ABR *de* **Sindicato Español de Pilotos de Líneas Aéreas**.

sepsis NF sepsis.

sept. ABR *de* **septiembre** September, Sept.

septentrión NM north.

septentrional ADJ north, northern.

septeto NM septet.

septicemia NF septicaemia.

séptico ADJ septic.

se(p)tiembre NM September.

septillizo, -a NM/F septuplet.

séptimo ADJ, NM seventh.

septuagenario **1** ADJ septuagenarian, seventy-year-old.

2 NM, **septuagenaria** NF septuagenarian, person in his (*o* her)
seventies.

septuagésimo ADJ seventieth.

séptuplo ADJ sevenfold.

sepulcral ADJ sepulchral; (*fig*) sepulchral, gloomy, dismal.

sepulcro NM tomb, grave; (*esp Bib*) sepulchre; ~ **blanqueado** whited
sepulchre.

sepultación NF (*Cono Sur*) burial.

sepultar [1a] VT (**a**) (*enterrar*) to bury; (*fig: en mina etc*) to bury, entomb; **quedaban sepultados en la caverna** they were trapped in
the cave, they were cut off in the cave.

(**b**) (*fig: esconder*) to hide away, bury, conceal.

sepultura NF (**a**) (*acto*) burial; **dar ~ a** to bury; **dar cristiana ~ a uno**
to give sb a Christian burial; **recibir ~** to be buried.

(**b**) (*tumba*) grave, tomb.

sepulturero NM gravedigger, sexton.

seque *etc* V **secar**.

sequedad NF (**a**) (*gen*) dryness. (**b**) (*fig*) bluntness; brusqueness, curtness; plainness, bareness (*V* **seco**).

sequerío NM (*prov*) dry place, dry field.

sequía NF (**a**) (*falta de lluvias*) drought; (*época*) dry season. (**b**) (*prov,
And*) thirst.

sequiar [1c] VI (*Cono Sur*) to inhale.

séquito NM (**a**) (*comitiva*) retinue, suite, entourage.

(**b**) (*Pol etc*) group of supporters, adherents, devotees.

(**c**) (*de sucesos*) train; aftermath; **con todo un ~ de calamidades**
with a whole train of disasters.

SER [ser] NF (*Rad*) ABR *de* **Sociedad Española de Radiodifusión**.

ser [2v] **1** VI (**a**) (*gen: absoluto, de carácter, identidad, etc*) to be; ~ **o no
~** to be or not to be; **es difícil** it's difficult; **él es pesimista** he's a
pessimist, he's a pessimistic sort; **soy ingeniero** I'm an engineer; **soy
yo** it's me, it is I (*liter*); (*Telec*) **¡soy Pedro!** this is Peter, Peter here,
Peter speaking; **somos seis** there are six of us; **el gran pintor que
fue Goya** the great painter (known to us as) Goya; **¿quién es?** who
is it?; who's there?; (*Telec*) who's calling?; **es él quien debiera
hacerlo** it is he who should do it, he's the one who ought to do it;
¿qué ha sido? what happened?, what is going on?; **libros, como ~
diccionarios** (*LAm*) books, for example (*o* such as) dictionaries.

(**b**) (*origen*) ~ **de** to be from, come from; **ella es de Calatayud** she's
from Calatayud; **estas naranjas son de España** these oranges come
from Spain; **¿de dónde es Vd?** where are you from?

(**c**) (*sustancia*) ~ **de** to be (made) of; **es de piedra** it is of stone, it is
made of stone, it's a stone one.

(**d**) (*possesión*) ~ **de** to belong to; **éste es suyo** this is his; **el parque
es del municipio** the park belongs to the town; **esta tapa es de
otra caja** this top belongs to another box; **¿de quién es este lápiz?**
whose is this pencil?, who does this pencil belong to?

(**e**) (*destino*) **¿qué será de mí?** what will become of me?; **¿qué ha
sido de él?** what has become of him?, what happened to him?; **el
trofeo fue para Rodríguez** the trophy went to Rodríguez; **el sexto
hoyo fue para García** the sixth hole went to García; **después ella
fue su mujer** later she became his wife.

(**f**) (*lo adecuado*) **esas finuras no son para mí** those niceties are not
for me; **ese coche no es para correr mucho** that car isn't made to

go very fast; **esa manera de hablar no es de una dama** that talk does not come well from a lady, one does not expect to hear a lady say such things.

(g) (*hora*) **es la una** it is one o'clock; **son las 7** it is 7 o'clock; **serán las 8** it must be about 8 o'clock; **serían las 9 cuando llegó** it must have been about 9 when he arrived; V *hora etc.*

(h) (*uso especial del imperfecto, en juegos*) **yo era la reina** pretend I was the queen, let's pretend I'm the queen.

(i) (*uso especial del pretérito: cargos*) **presidente que fue de Ruritania** ex-president of Ruritania, former(ly) president of Ruritania.

(j) (*uso especial del futuro: hipótesis*) **¿será posible?** is it possible?, can it really be so? (*y V posible*); **¡serás burro!** can you really be so stupid?; **serán delincuentes** they must be criminals.

(k) (*corresponde a* estar) **soy en todo con Vd** I entirely agree with you, I'm with you all the way; **en un momento soy con Vd** I'll be with you in a moment.

(l) (**~ de** + *infin*) **es de creer que ...** it may be assumed that ...; and yet ...; in spite of the fact that ..., even though the truth of the matter is that ...; **es de desear que ...** it is to be wished that ...; **es de esperar que ...** it is to be hoped that ...; **era de ver** it was worth seeing, you ought to have seen it.

(m) (*locuciones con indic*) **siendo así que ...** since ...; **¡o somos o no somos!*** let's get on with it!, make your minds up!; **érase que se era, érase una vez** once upon a time (there was); **a no ~ por** but for; were it not for, had it not been for; **a no ~ que ... unless ...; ¡ahí fue ella!** what a row there was!, you should have heard the fuss!; **es que no pude** but I couldn't; **es que no quiero** but I don't want to; **¿cómo es que ...?** how is it that ...?, how does it happen that ...?; **¡cómo ha de ~!** what else do you expect!; **hizo como quien es** he acted as one might expect, he did what one could expect of him; **con ~ ella su madre** even though she is his mother, despite the fact that she's his mother; **de no ~ esto así** if it were not so, were it not so; **no vaya a ~ que ...** unless.

(n) (*locuciones con subj*) **¡sea!** agreed!, all right!; **o sea ...** that is to say ..., or rather ..., in other words; **sea ... sea ...** either ... or, whether ... or whether; **sea lo que sea** (o **fuere**) be that as it may; **no sea que ... lest ...**, in case ..., for fear that ...; **hable con algún abogado que no sea Pérez** speak to some lawyer other than Pérez, consult any lawyer you like except Pérez.

2 *forma la voz pasiva:* **fue construido** it was built; **ha sido asaltada una joyería** there has been a raid on a jeweller's; **será fusilado** he will be shot; **está siendo estudiado** it is being examined.

3 NM (*ente*) being; (*existencia*) life; (*esencia*) essence; **~ humano** human being; **~ imaginario** imaginary being; **S~ Supremo** Supreme Being; **~ vivo** living creature, living organism; **la que le dio su ~** she who gave him life, she who brought him into the world; **en lo más íntimo de su ~** in his inmost being, deep within himself.

SER	ver también la entrada

En español decimos *somos 15, son 28, etc.* Esta estructura se traduce al inglés por *there are/were/etc* + NÚMERO + of *us/you/them*:
Somos 50.
There are 50 of us
Eran 38 en total
There were 38 of them altogether
Para otros usos y ejemplos ver la entrada.

---

sera NF pannier, basket.

seráficamente ADV angelically, like an angel.

seráfico ADJ **(a)** (*angélico*) angelic, seraphic. **(b)** (*: *humilde*) poor and humble.

serafín NM **(a)** (*gen*) seraph; (*fig*) angel; cherub. **(b)** (*Carib: broche*) clip, fastener.

serape NM (*Méx*) = **sarape**.

serbal NM, **serbo** NM service tree, sorb; rowan, mountain ash.

Serbia NF Serbia.

serbio **1** ADJ Serbian.
2 NM, **serbia** NF Serb.
3 NM (*Ling*) Serbo-Croat.

serbobosnio, -a ADJ, NM/F Bosnian Serb.

serbocroata **1** ADJ, NMF Serbo-Croatian.
2 NM (*Ling*) Serbo-Croat.

serenamente ADV **(a)** *con calma* calmly, serenely. **(b)** *tranquilamente* peacefully, quietly.

serenar [1a] **1** VT **(a)** (*calmar*) to calm; (*tranquilizar*) to quieten, pacify.
(b) *líquido* to clarify.
2 VI (*And**) to drizzle.
3 **serenarse** VR **(a)** (*persona etc*) to calm down, grow calm; to compose o.s.
(b) (*mar*) to grow calm; (*tiempo*) to clear up.
(c) (*líquido*) to clear, settle.

serenata NF serenade.

serendipia NF serendipity.

serenera NF (*And, CAm, Carib*) cape, wrap.

serenero NM (*Cono Sur*) (*pañuelo*) headscarf; (*chal*) wrap, cape.

serenidad NF **(a)** (*calma*) calmness, serenity. **(b)** (*tranquilidad*) peacefulness, quietness.

serenísimo ADJ: **su Alteza Serenísima** his (o Her) Serene Highness.

sereno **1** ADJ **(a)** *persona* calm, serene, unruffled.
(b) *tiempo* settled, fine; *cielo* cloudless, clear.
(c) *ambiente* calm, peaceful, quiet.
(d) **estar ~*** to be sober.
2 NM **(a)** (*rocío*) night dew, night dampness; **dormir al ~** to sleep out in the open; **le perjudica el ~** the night air is bad for her.
(b) (*Esp: persona*) night watchman.

sereta NF builder's bucket, basket.

seriado ADJ mass-produced.

serial NM serial; **~ radiofónico** radio serial; **~ televisivo** television serial.

serialización NF serialization.

serializar [1f] VT to serialize.

seriamente ADV seriously.

seriar [1b] VT **(a)** (*poner en serie*) to arrange in series, arrange serially.
(b) (*producir*) to mass-produce. **(c)** (*TV etc*) to make a serial of, serialize.

sericultura NF silk raising, sericulture.

serie NF series (*t Bio, Elec, Mat*); set, sequence, succession; (*Liter, Rad etc*) series, serial; (*de sellos*) set; (*de inyecciones*) course; **~ eliminatoria** heats; **una ~ inacabable de** an endless series of; **arrollado en ~** (*Elec*) series-wound; **fabricación en ~** mass production; **fabricar** (o **producir**) **en ~** to mass-produce; **casas construidas en ~** mass-produced houses; **matanzas en ~** mass murders; **fuera de ~** out of order, not in the proper sequence; (*fig*) special; **un fuera de ~** a person out of the ordinary, an extraordinary person; **artículos fuera de ~** (*Com*) goods left over, remainders, remnants; **tamaño de ~** (*Com*) stock size, regular size; **equipamiento de ~** standard equipment; **modelo de ~** (*Aut etc*) standard model; **esta adición es de ~ en el coche** this addition is now standard on the car; **artículo de ~** mass-produced article; **ser de la ~ B*** to be one of them* (*homosexual*); **película de la ~ B*** gay film.

SERIE	ver también la entrada

Serie en relación con la literatura, la televisión o la radio se puede traducir al inglés por *serial* o *series*.

- Si se refiere a una historia de ficción cuyo argumento continúa a lo largo de varios días se debe emplear *serial*:
  Muchas novelas solían publicarse en forma de serie
  Novels used often to be published in serial form
  La novela se va a emitir próximamente como serie televisiva
  The novel is going to be broadcast soon as a television serial
- En cambio, si se trata de una historia de ficción dividida en partes, en la que cada una de estas partes forma una historia por sí misma, se traduce por *series*:
  Hay una nueva serie de humor en la tele
  There is a new comedy series on T.V.
- Si se trata de documentales también se traduce por *series*:
  Me encantan las series sobre la naturaleza
  I love wildlife series
  Para otros usos y ejemplos ver la entrada.

---

seriedad NF **(a)** (*gen*) seriousness; (*gravedad*) gravity, solemnity; (*formalidad*) staidness; **hablar con ~** to speak seriously, speak in earnest.
(b) (*dignidad*) dignity; properness; (*sensatez*) seriousness, (sense of) responsibility; **falta de ~** frivolity; irresponsibility.
(c) (*en negocio etc*) reliability, dependability, trustworthiness; straightness, honesty; fair-mindedness.
(d) (*en crisis etc*) gravity, seriousness.

serigrafía NF silkscreen printing; **una ~** a silkscreen print.

serigrafista NMF silkscreen printer.

serimiri NM (*prov*) drizzle.

serio ADJ **(a)** *actitud, expresión, persona etc* serious; grave, solemn; staid; **ponerse ~** to look serious, adopt a solemn expression (*etc*); **se quedó mirándome muy ~** he looked at me very seriously, he stared gravely at me; **pareces muy ~** you're looking very serious.
(b) (*formal*) *actitud, persona etc* dignified; (*decente*) proper; (*responsable*) serious, responsible; **el negro es el único color ~ para esto** black is the only proper colour for this; **un traje ~** a formal suit; **poco ~** undignified; frivolous, not to be taken seriously; **es una persona poco seria** he's an irresponsible sort, he's rather a silly individual.
(c) (*de fiar etc*) *persona* reliable, dependable, trustworthy; responsible; fair-minded; *negocio, trato* straight, honest; **poco ~** unreliable; irresponsible; **es una casa seria** it's a reliable firm.

(d) *estudio, libro etc* serious.
(e) *(grave)* etc grave, serious; **esto se pone ~** this is getting serious.
(f) **en ~** seriously; **hablo perfectamente en ~** I'm perfectly serious, I'm in dead earnest; **¿lo dices en ~?** do you really mean it?; **tomar un asunto en ~** to take a matter seriously.

sermón NM sermon (*t* *); **el S~ de la Montaña** the Sermon on the Mount.

sermonear* [1a] **1** VT to lecture, read a lecture to.
　2 VI to sermonize.

sermoneo* NM lecture, sermon.

sermonero* ADJ given to sermonizing.

sernambí (*And, Carib*) inferior rubber.

serología NF serology.

serón NM pannier, large basket; *(de bebé)* cot.

seronegativo ADJ seronegative.

seropositivo ADJ seropositive.

seroso ADJ serous.

serpa NF *(Bot)* runner.

serpear [1a] VI, **serpentear** [1a] VI **(a)** *(Zool)* to wriggle; to creep. **(b)** *(fig) (camino)* to wind, snake, twist and turn; *(río)* to wind, meander.

serpenteante ADJ *(fig)* winding, twisting; meandering.

serpenteo NM **(a)** *(Zool)* wriggling; creeping. **(b)** *(fig)* winding, twisting; meandering.

serpentín NM coil.

serpentina NF **(a)** *(Min)* serpentine. **(b)** *(de papel)* streamer.

serpentino ADJ snaky, sinuous; winding, meandering; serpentine.

serpiente NF *(culebra)* snake; *(Mit etc)* serpent; **la S~** the (European monetary) Snake; **~ de anteojos** cobra; **~ boa** boa constrictor; **~ de cascabel** rattlesnake; **~ de mar** sea-serpent; **~ pitón** python; **~ de verano** silly story, non-story *(used to fill papers in the slack season)*; **~ de vidrio** slow-worm.

serpol NM wild thyme.

serpollo NM sucker, shoot.

serrado ADJ serrated; toothed; jagged, uneven, rough.

serraduras NFPL sawdust.

serrallo NM seraglio, harem.

serrana¹ NF = **serranilla**.

serranía NF **(a)** mountainous area, hilly country; range of mountains. **(b)** *(Méx)* wood, forest.

serraniego ADJ = **serrano**.

serranilla NF *15th-century verse-form*.

serrano 1 ADJ **(a)** *(Geog)* highland *(atr)*, hill *(atr)*, mountain *(atr)*.
　(b) *(fig)* coarse, rustic.
　(c) **partida serrana** *(Esp)* dirty trick.
　2 NM, **serrana²** NF highlander.

serrar [1j] VT to saw (off, up).

serrería NF sawmill.

serrín NM sawdust.

serrote NM *(Méx)* = **serrucho**.

serruchar [1a] VT *(LAm)* to saw (off, up).

serrucho NM **(a)** saw, handsaw.
　(b) *(Carib: puta)* whore.
　(c) **hacer un ~** *(And, Carib)* to split the cost.

Servia NF *etc* = **Serbia** *etc*.

servible ADJ serviceable, usable.

servicial 1 ADJ helpful, obliging.
　2 NM *(And: t* **serviciala** NF*)* servant.

servicialidad NF helpfulness, obliging nature.

servicio NM **(a)** *(gen)* service; **¿su ~, señor?** your order, sir?; **a su ~** at your service; **al ~ de** in the service of; **estar al ~ de** to be in the service of; **estar al ~ del gobierno** to be on government service; **estar de ~** to be serviceable, be in service; **entrar en ~** to come into service; **tiene 8 camiones en ~** he has 8 lorries in service; **hacer un ~ para uno** to do sb a service; **te ha hecho un flaco ~** he's done you a poor service.
　(b) *(Mil etc)* service; **~ activo** active service; **~ militar** military service; **apto para el ~** fit for military service; **en condiciones de ~** operational; **entrar de ~** to go on duty; **estar de ~** to be on duty; **estar fuera de ~, estar libre de ~** to be off duty; **prestar ~** to serve, see service *(de as)*.
　(c) **~s de administración** management services; *(~ individual)* **~ aduanero, ~ de aduana** customs service; **~ de asistencia, ~ de atención** after-sales service; **~s en autopista** motorway services; **~ comunitario** community service; **~ consultivo** advisory service; **~ de contraespionaje** secret service; **~ doméstico** domestic service; domestic help; *(personas)* servants; **'~ a domicilio'** 'we deliver'; **~ de entrega** delivery service; **~ de guardia** *(Aut)* breakdown service, emergency service; **~ de incendios** fireservice; **~ de información** *(Mil)*, **~ de inteligencia** intelligence service; **~ médico** medical service; **~ de megafonía** public address system; **~s mínimos** essential services *(maintained during strike)*; **~ de orden** *(Pol)* marshals, stewards; **~ permanente** round-the-clock service; **~s postales** postal services; **~ posventa** after-sales service; **~s públicos** public services; **~ secreto** secret service; **~s sociales** social services; welfare work; **~ sustitutorio** community service in place of military service; **~ de transportes** transport service.
　(d) *(Culin etc)* service, set; **~ de café** coffee-set; **~ de mesa** set of dishes, *(esp)* dinner-service; **~ de tocador** toilet set.
　(e) *(euf: wáter)* toilet; *(Esp: orinal)* chamberpot; **~s** *(de casa)* services, *(euf)* sanitation; **'S~s'** *(letrero)* 'Toilets'; **'Todos ~s'** *(anuncio)* 'all main services'.
　(f) *(Ecl)* service; **~ divino** divine service.
　(g) *(en hotel etc)* service, service charge; **~ incluido** service charge included.
　(h) *(Tenis)* serve, service; **romper el ~ de uno** to break sb's service.
　(i) *(de policía)* job, case, inquiry.
　(j) *(Fin)* servicing (of a debt).

servidor(a) 1 NM/F **(a)** *(criado)* servant; **un ~** *(yo mismo)* yours truly*, my humble self; **aquí me tiene al ~ para lo que se le ofrezca** I am always at your service, please count on me for whatever it may be; **¡~ de Vd!** at your service!
　(b) **¡~!** *(Esp: en clase etc)* present!
　(c) *(en cartas)* **su seguro ~, atento y s.s.** (= *seguro servidor*) yours faithfully.
　(d) **'~'** *(LAm: formal)* 'your servant', 'at your service'.
　2 NM *(Inform)* server.

servidumbre NF **(a)** *(estado)* servitude; **~ de la gleba** serfdom.
　(b) *(fig)* compulsion.
　(c) *(Jur)* obligation; **~ de paso** right of way.
　(d) *(personas)* servants, staff.

servil ADJ **(a)** *(gen)* slave *(atr)*, serf's; *trabajo etc* menial. **(b)** *actitud etc* servile; obsequious, grovelling; *imitación etc* slavish.

servilismo NM servility; obsequiousness; slavishness.

servilla NF slipper, pump.

servilleta NF serviette, napkin.

servilletero NM serviette ring, napkin holder.

▼ **servir** [3l] 1 VT **(a)** *(gen)* to serve; to do a favour to, oblige; **~ a Dios** to serve God; **~ a la patria** to serve one's country; **dígame en qué puedo ~le** tell me in what way I can be of service, tell me how I can help you; **para ~le** at your service; **para lo que me va a ~** for all the good it will do me; **ser servido de** + *infin* to be pleased to + *infin*.
　(b) *(en restaurante)* to wait on, serve.
　(c) *(Com)* *cliente* to serve; *pedido* to attend to, fill; *libro (en biblioteca)* to issue; *programa (TV)* to show, put on, present; **¿ya le sirven, señora?** are you being attended to, madam?; **el libro está servido** the book is out, the book is in use.
　(d) *(Culin)* *comida* to serve (out o up); **~ patatas a uno** to serve sb with potatoes, help sb to potatoes; **la cena está servida** dinner is served; **~ vino a uno** to pour out wine for sb.
　(e) *cargo* to hold, fill; *responsabilidad* to carry out.
　(f) *cañón* to man; *máquina* to tend, mind, man.
　(g) *(Tenis etc)* to serve; *cartas* to deal.
　(h) *(‡: detener)* to nick‡, arrest.
　2 VI **(a)** *(gen)* to serve; *(criado)* to be in service; **sirvió 10 años** he served 10 years, he did 10 years; **está sirviendo** *(Mil)* he's doing his military service; **para ~ a Vd** at your service.
　(b) *(camarero)* to serve, wait *(a* at, on*)*.
▼　**(c)** *(ser útil)* to serve *(de* as, for*)*; to be of use, be useful; **eso no sirve** that's no good, that won't do; **~ en lugar de** to do duty for; **~ de guía** to act as guide, serve as a guide; **no sirve de nada que vaya él** it's no use his going; **~ para** to be good for, be used for; **no sirve para nada** it's no use at all, it's utterly useless; **él no sirve para nada** he's a dead loss; **yo no serviría para futbolista** I shouldn't be any good as a footballer.
　(d) **~ del palo** *(Naipes)* to follow suit.
　3 **servirse** VR **(a)** *(en la mesa)* to serve o.s., help o.s.; **se sirvió patatas** he helped himself to potatoes; **se sirvió café** he poured himself some coffee; **¡sírvete más!** have some more!; **¿no te sirves más ensalada?** wouldn't you like more salad?; **¿qué se sirven?** *(LAm)* what are you going to have?
　(b) **~ de algo** to make use of sth, use sth; to put sth to use.
▼　**(c)** **~** + *infin* to be kind enough to + *infin*; to deign to + *infin*, condescend to + *infin*; **sírvase sentarse** please sit down, would you like to sit down?; **sírvase darme su dirección** could you give me your address, please?; **si la señora se sirve pasar por aquí** if madam would care to come this way.

servo NM servo.

servo... PREF servo...

servoasistido ADJ servoassisted.

servodirección NF power steering.

servofrenos NMPL power-assisted brakes.

servomecanismo NM servo(mechanism).

▶ LENGUA Y USO: **servir:** 2c → 43.4 **3c** → 47.5, 48.3, 48.4

sésamo NM sesame; **¡~ ábrete!** open sesame!

sesapil NM sex-appeal.

sesear [1a] VI *to pronounce c* (*before* e, i) *and* z [θ] *as* [s] (*a feature of Andalusian and much LAm pronunciation*).

sesenta ADJ sixty; sixtieth; **los (años) ~** the sixties.

sesentañera NF woman of about sixty.

sesentañero NM man of about sixty.

sesentón [1] ADJ sixty-year old, sixtyish.
[2] NM, **sesentona** NF person of about sixty.

seseo NM *pronunciation of* c (*before* e, i) *and* z [θ] *as* [s].

sesera NF (*Anat*) brainpan; (*) brains, intelligence.

sesgado ADJ (a) slanted, slanting, oblique; leaning; awry, askew; *pelota* swerving, sliced. (b) (*fig*) biased, slanted.

sesgar [1h] VT (a) (*inclinar*) to slant, slope, place obliquely; (*ladear*) to put askew, twist to one side; *pelota* to swerve, cut, slice.
(b) (*Cos*) to cut on the slant, cut on the bias.
(c) (*Aut*) to cut across, cut in on.
(d) (*fig*) *reportaje etc* to bias, slant.

sesgo NM (a) (*inclinación*) slant, slope; (*torcimiento*) warp, twist, twisted position; (*Cos*) bias; (*de pelota*) swerve, slice; **estar al ~** to be aslant, be awry; **cortar algo al ~** to cut sth on the bias.
(b) (*fig*) direction; twist, turn; **ha tomado otro ~** it has taken a new turn.
(c) (*: truco*) dodge*.

sésil ADJ sessile.

sesión NF (a) (*Parl etc*) session, sitting, meeting; (*Inform*) session; **~ de preguntas al gobierno** question-time; **~ de trabajo** (*acto*) working period; (*grupo*) working party; (*de gimnasio*) work-out; **~ secreta** secret session; **abrir la ~** to open the meeting; **celebrar una ~** to hold a meeting; **levantar la ~** to close the meeting, adjourn.
(b) (*Teat*) show, performance; **~ de espiritismo** séance; **~ de prestidigitación** conjuring show, exhibition of conjuring; **~ de lectura de poesías** poetry reading.
(c) (*Cine*) showing; **~ continua** continuous showing; **iremos a la segunda ~** we'll go to the second house; **hay 3 sesiones diarias** there are 3 showings a day.

sesionar [1a] VI to sit; to be in session; to hold a meeting.

seso NM (a) (*Anat*) brain; **~s** (*Culin*) brains.
(b) (*fig*) brains, sense, intelligence; **calentarse los ~s, devanarse los ~s, estrujarse los ~s** to rack one's brains; **perder el ~** to go off one's head (*por* over); **eso le tiene sorbido el ~** he's crazy about it.

sesquicentenario NM 150th anniversary, sesquicentenary.

sesquipedal ADJ sesquipedalian.

sestear [1a] VI to take a siesta, have a nap.

sesteo NM (*LAm*) siesta, nap.

sesudamente ADV sensibly, wisely.

sesudo ADJ (a) (*juicioso*) sensible, wise. (b) (*inteligente*) brainy. (c) (*Cono Sur: terco*) stubborn, pig-headed.

set NM, PL **set** o **sets** (*Tenis*) set.

set. ABR *de* setiembre September, Sept.

seta NF (a) mushroom; **~ venenosa** toadstool. (b) (*) cunt*.

setecientos ADJ seven hundred; **en el ~** in the eighteenth century.

setenta ADJ seventy; seventieth; **los (años) ~** the seventies.

setentañera NF woman of about seventy.

setentañero NM man of about seventy.

setentón [1] ADJ seventy-year old, seventyish.
[2] NM, **setentona** NF person of about seventy.

setero [1] ADJ mushroom (*atr*).
[2] NM, **setera** NF mushroom gatherer.

setiembre NM September.

seto NM (a) (*cercado*) fence; **~ vivo** hedge. (b) (*Carib: pared*) dividing wall, partition.

setter NM, PL **setters** [se'ter] setter.

SEU ['seu] NM (*Hist*) ABR *de* **Sindicato Español Universitario**.

seudo... PREF pseudo...

seudohistoria NF pseudohistory.

seudónimo [1] ADJ pseudonymous.
[2] NM pseudonym; pen name, nom de plume.

Seúl NM Seoul.

s.e.u.o. ABR *de* **salvo error u omisión** errors and omissions excepted, E.&O.E.

severamente ADV (*V* ADJ (a), (c)) (a) severely, harshly; strictly.
(b) severely; grimly, sternly.

severidad NF (*V* ADJ (a), (c)) (a) severity, harshness; strictness; stringency. (b) severity; grimness, sternness.

severo ADJ (a) *carácter etc* severe, harsh; *disciplina* strict; *crítica, castigo* harsh; *padre etc* strict, harsh; *condiciones* harsh, stringent; **ser ~ con uno** to be hard on sb, treat sb harshly.
(b) *invierno etc* severe, harsh, hard; *frío* bitter.
(c) *cara, expresión* severe; grim, stern; *estilo, vestido etc* severe.

seviche NM = cebiche.

Sevilla NF Seville.

sevillanas NFPL (a) (*melodía*) popular Sevillian tune. (b) (*baile*) typical Sevillian dance.

sevillano [1] ADJ Sevillian, of Seville.
[2] NM, **sevillana** NF Sevillian, native (o inhabitant) of Seville.

sexagenario [1] ADJ sexagenarian, sixty-year old.
[2] NM, **sexagenaria** NF sexagenarian, person in his (o her) sixties.

sexagésimo ADJ sixtieth.

sexar [1a] VT *pollitos* to sex.

sexenio NM (*Méx Pol*) (six-year) presidential term.

sexería NF sex shop.

sexi = **sexy**.

sexismo NM sexism.

sexista ADJ, NMF sexist.

sexo NM sex; **el bello ~** the fair sex; **el ~ débil** the gentle sex; **el ~ femenino** the female sex; **el ~ fuerte** the stronger sex; **el ~ masculino** the male sex; **~ en grupo** group sex; **~ oral** oral sex; **de ambos ~s** of both sexes; **sin ~** sexless; **hablar del ~ de los ángeles** to talk in a pointless way, indulge in pointless discussion.

sexofobia NF aversion to sex.

sexología NF sexology.

sexólogo, -a NM/F sexologist.

sex shop [sek'ʃop] NF, PL **sex shops** sex shop.

sex symbol [sek'simβol] NMF, PL **sex symbols** sex symbol.

sextante NM sextant.

sexteto NM sextet(te).

sextillizo, -a NM/F sextuplet.

sexto ADJ, NM sixth.

séxtuplo ADJ sixfold.

sexual ADJ sexual; sex (*atr*); **vida ~** sex life.

sexualidad NF (a) (*gen*) sexuality. (b) (*sexo*) sex; **determinar la ~ de** to determine the sex of.

sexualmente ADV sexually.

sexy [sesi] [1] ADJ INVAR (*a veces* PL **sexys**) *mujer* sexy, full of sex-appeal; *libro, escena etc* warm, hot; *película ~* pornographic film; **~ show** adult show, nude show.
[2] NM sexiness, sex-appeal.
[3] NF nude artiste; stripper.

s.f. ABR *de* **sin fecha** no date, n.d.

s/f (*Com*) ABR *de* **su favor** your favour.

SGAE NF ABR *de* **Sociedad General de Autores de España**.

SGEL [se'xel] NF ABR *de* **Sociedad Española General de Librería**.

SGR NF ABR *de* **sociedad de garantía recíproca**.

sgte(s). ABR *de* **siguiente(s)** following, foll.

share [ʃear] NM (*TV*) audience share.

shiatsu ['sjatsu] NM shiatsu.

shock [ʃok] NM, PL **shock** o **shocks** [ʃok] (*Med*) shock.

short [ʃor] NM, PL **shorts** [ʃor] shorts.

show [tʃo, ʃou] NM (a) (*Teat etc*) show; spectacle. (b) (*farsa*) farce, masquerade. (c) (*: jaleo*) fuss, bother; display of bad temper; **menudo ~ hizo** (*Esp*) he made a great song-and-dance about it.

si¹ CONJ (a) if; **~ lo quieres te lo doy** if you want it I'll give it to you; **~ me lo pedía se lo daba** if he asked me for it I gave it to him; **~ me lo hubiese pedido se lo hubiera dado** if he had asked me for it I would have given it to him; **~ lo sé te lo digo*** if I had known about it I would have told you.
(b) (*en pregunta indirecta*) if, whether; **me pregunto ~ vale la pena** I wonder whether (o if) it's worth the trouble; **no sé ~ hacerlo o no** I don't know whether to do it or not; **hablaban de ~ hacerlo o no** they were talking about whether to do it or not; **que ~ lavar los platos, que ~ limpiar el suelo, que ~ ...** what with washing up and sweeping the floor and ...
(c) (*locuciones etc*) **~ no** if not; unless; otherwise, or else; **~ no estudias no aprobara's** you won't pass if you don't study, you won't pass unless you study; **¿~ vendrá?** I wonder if he'll come?; **¿~ será verdad?** what if it's true?; **¿~ nos lo roban?** what if somebody steals it?, suppose it gets stolen?; **lleva un revólver por ~** (*acaso*) **resulta útil** he carries a gun in case it should come in handy; **¡por ~ eso fuera poco!** as if that wasn't enough!; **¡~ fuera verdad!** if only it were true!; **¡~ viniese pronto!** I wish he'd come!; **¡~ (es que) acabo de llamar!** but I've only just phoned you!; **¡~ no está!** but it isn't there!; **¡~ no sabía que estabas allí!** but I didn't know you were there!; **¡~ es el cartero!** why, it's the postman!

si² NM (*Mús*) B; **~ mayor** B major.

sí¹ [1] ADV (a) (*afirmativo*) yes; indeed, certainly; **él no quiere pero yo ~** he doesn't want to but I do; **ellos no van pero nosotros ~** they aren't going but we are; **~, pero menos** (*iró*) that's a bit much, that's pushing things a bit; **~ pues** (*LAm*) of course; **creo que ~** I think so; **¡que ~, hombre!** I tell you it is! (*etc*); **está de que ~*** he seems likely to agree; **¡(pues) ~ que estoy yo para bromas!** (*iró*) I should say I'm in the mood for jokes!; **por ~ o por no** in any case, just in case; **porque ~** because that's the way it is; because I say so; **lo hizo porque ~** he did it because he just felt like doing it; he did it because he thought it had to be done; (*pey*) he did it out of sheer cussedness; **una semana ~ y otra no** in alternate weeks, every other week.

(b) (*énfasis*) **¿sí?** oh?, really?, is that so?; **ella ~ vendrá** she will certainly come, she is sure to come; **ellos ~ tienen uno** they certainly have one; **¡~ que lo es!** I'll say it is!, you're dead right there!; **¡eso ~ que no!** never!, not on your life!

[2] NM consent, agreement; **dar el ~** to agree, consent; (*mujer*) to accept a proposal; **todavía no tengo el ~** I have not yet received his consent, he still hasn't said yes.

| **SI** | **ver también la entrada** |

La conjunción *si* se puede traducir al inglés por *if* o *whether*; *si no* se traduce por *if not* o *unless*.

Si

● Por regla general, *si* se traduce al inglés por *if* en las oraciones condicionales y por *whether* o *if* en las dubitativas:
  Si me has mentido te arrepentirás
  If you have lied to me you'll regret it
  Si tuviera mucho dinero me compraría un caballo
  If I had lots of money, I would buy myself a horse
  No sé si me dejará quedarme
  I don't know whether o if she'll let me stay

● *Si* se puede traducir sólo por *whether*, y nunca por *if*, cuando se presentan dos opciones a elegir, cuando va detrás de una preposición, delante de un infinitivo o de una oración interrogativa indirecta:
  No sé si ir a Canadá o a Estados Unidos
  I can't decide whether to go to Canada or the United States
  Quiero que hablemos de si deberíamos mandar a los niños a un colegio interno
  I want to talk to you about whether we should send the children to boarding school
  Todavía no tenemos muy claro si vamos a mudarnos o no
  We still haven't made up our minds about whether to move or not

Si no

● *Si no* generalmente se traduce al inglés por *if not* aunque, cuando en español se puede reemplazar por *a no ser que*, se puede utilizar también *unless* y cuando equivale a *de lo contrario* se emplea preferentemente *otherwise* o *else*:
  Iría al cine más a menudo si no fuera tan caro
  I would go to the cinema more often if it weren't so expensive
  No te puedes quedar aquí si no pagas el alquiler
  You cannot stay here unless you pay your rent o You cannot stay here if you don't pay your rent
  Tenemos que estar allí antes de las diez; si no, vamos a tener problemas
  We must be there by ten, otherwise o or else we'll be in trouble
  NOTA: Las oraciones del tipo *si/si no hubiera(s)/hubiera(n) hecho algo...* se pueden traducir, en un registro más culto, omitiendo la partícula *if* e invirtiendo el orden del sujeto y el verbo auxiliar:
  Si hubieras estado aquí esto no habría ocurrido
  Had you been here this would not have happened
  Si no hubiese robado el dinero, ahora no estaría en la cárcel
  Had he not stolen the money, he wouldn't be in prison now
  Para otros usos y ejemplos ver la entrada.

---

sí² PRON REFLEXIVO **(a)** (*sing*) (M) himself, (F) herself, (*de objeto*) itself, (*de Vd*) yourself, (*gen*) o.s.; (PL) themselves, (*de Vds*) yourselves; **~ mismo** himself *etc*; **lo quieren todo para ~** they want the whole lot for themselves; **no lo podrá hacer por ~ solo** he won't be able to do it by himself; **conviene guardarlo para ~** it's best to keep it to o.s.; **se ríe de ~ misma** she laughs at herself; **no lo tiene en ~ misma** she doesn't have it in her.

(b) (*recíproco*) each other; **cambiaron una mirada entre ~** they exchanged a look, they gave each other a look.

(c) (*locuciones*) **de ~** in itself; spontaneously; **el problema es bastante difícil de ~** the problem is difficult enough in itself; **de por ~** in itself; per se; separately, individually; **estar en ~** to be in one's right mind; **pensar entre ~, pensar para ~** to think to o.s.; **estar fuera de ~** to be beside o.s.; **estar sobre ~** (*alerta*) to be on one's guard; (*engreído*) to be puffed up with conceit; *V* **decir, volver** *etc*.

Siam NM Siam.
siamés, -esa ADJ, NM/F Siamese.
sibarita [1] ADJ sybaritic, luxury-loving; epicurean.
  [2] NMF sybarite, lover of luxury; epicure, bon vivant.
sibarítico ADJ sybaritic, luxury-loving; epicurean.
sibaritismo NM sybaritism, love of luxury; epicureanism.
Siberia NF Siberia.
siberiano, -a ADJ, NM/F Siberian.

sibil NM (*cueva*) cave; (*sótano*) vault, underground store; (*de trigo*) corn-storage pit.
Sibila NF Sibyl.
sibila NF sibyl.
sibilante ADJ, NF sibilant.
sibilino ADJ sibylline.
sic... PREF = **psic...**, *p.ej., para* **sicología** *V* **psicología.**
sicalipsis NF eroticism, suggestiveness; pornography.
sicalíptico ADJ erotic, suggestive; pornographic.
sicario NM hired assassin.
Sicilia NF Sicily.
siciliano, -a [1] ADJ, NM/F Sicilian.
  [2] NM (*Ling*) Sicilian.
sicofanta NM, **sicofante** NM sycophant.
sicomoro NM, **sicómoro** NM sycamore, sycamore tree.
sicote* NM (*LAm*) foot odour.
sida, SIDA ['siða] NM ABR *de* **síndrome de inmuno-deficiencia adquirida** acquired immuno-deficiency syndrome, AIDS; **~ declarado** full-blown AIDS.
sidatorio NM AIDS clinic.
SIDE NF (*Argentina*) ABR *de* **Secretaría de Inteligencia del Estado** *Peronist secret service.*
sidecar ['saikar] NM sidecar.
sideral ADJ, **sidéreo** ADJ **(a)** astral, sidereal; space (*atr*). **(b)** (*fig*) *coste etc* astronomic.
siderometalurgia NF (*industria*) iron and steel industry.
siderometalúrgico ADJ iron and steel (*atr*).
siderurgia NF iron and steel industry.
siderúrgico [1] ADJ iron and steel (*atr*).
  [2] **siderúrgica** NF iron and steel works.
sídico ADJ AIDS (*atr*).
sidoso [1] ADJ relating to AIDS, AIDS (*atr*).
  [2] NM, **sidosa** NF AIDS sufferer.
sidra NF cider.
sidrería NF cider bar.
sidrero [1] ADJ cider (*atr*).
  [2] NM, **sidrera** NF cider-maker.
sidrina NF cider.
siega NF **(a)** (*acto*) reaping, harvesting; mowing. **(b)** (*época*) harvest (time).
siembra NF **(a)** (*acto*) sowing; **patata de ~** seed potato. **(b)** (*época*) sowing time.
siembre NM (*Carib*) sowing.
siempre [1] ADV **(a)** (*gen*) always; all the time; ever; (*LAm*) still; (*Méx*) in the end, eventually; **como ~** as usual, as always; **la hora de ~** the usual time; **somos amigos de ~** we're old friends; **es la historia de ~, es lo de ~** it's the same thing as it always is, it's the same old story; **desde ~** always; **lo vienen haciendo así desde ~** they've always done it this way; **¡hasta ~!*** see you!*; **para ~, por ~** for ever; for good (and all); **por ~ jamás** for ever and ever.
  (b) (*LAm*) (*seguramente*) certainly, definitely; (*sin embargo*) still, in any case; **~ sí me voy** I'm going anyway; **~ no** (*Méx*) certainly not; **~ sí** certainly, of course.
  [2] CONJ: **~ que ... (a)** (+ *indic*) whenever; each time that ..., as often as ...
  (b) (+ *subj*; *t* **~ y cuando ...**) provided that ...
siempreverde ADJ evergreen.
siempreviva NF houseleek.
sien NF (*Anat*) temple.
siena¹ NF sienna.
siena²* NF (*Esp*) mug*, face.
siento *etc V* **sentar; sentir.**
sierpe NF snake, serpent.
sierra NF **(a)** (*Téc*) saw; **~ de arco, ~ para metales** hacksaw; **~ de cadena** chainsaw; **~ de calados, ~ de calar** fretsaw; **~ circular** circular saw; **~ de espigar** tenon saw; **~ mecánica** power saw; **~ de vaivén** jigsaw.
  (b) (*Geog*) mountain range, sierra; **la ~ madrileña** the hills close to Madrid; **van a la ~ a pasar el fin de semana** they're off to the mountains for the weekend.
  (c) (*Méx: pez*) swordfish.
Sierra Leona NF Sierra Leone.
siervo, -a NM/F slave; **~ de la gleba** serf.
siesta NF **(a)** (*parte del día*) hottest part of the day, afternoon heat.
  (b) (*sueñecito*) siesta, nap; **dormir la ~, echarse una ~, tomar una ~** to have one's afternoon nap, have a doze.
siestecita NF nap, doze.
siete¹ [1] ADJ seven; (*fecha*) seventh; **las ~** seven o'clock; **hablar más que ~** to talk nineteen to the dozen.
  [2] NM **(a)** (*número*) seven. **(b)** (*roto*) **hacerse un ~ en el pantalón** to tear one's trousers (*making an L-shaped tear*).
siete²* NM (*LAm: euf*) bum*, backside.

sietecueros NM INVAR (*LAm*) gumboil, whitlow.

sietemesino ADJ *niño* premature; (*fig*) half-witted.

sífilis NF syphilis.

sifilítico, -a ADJ, NM/F syphilitic.

sifón NM (a) (*Téc*) trap, U-bend; siphon. (b) (*de agua*) siphon (of soda water); **whisky con ~** whisky and soda. (c) (*And: cerveza*) (bottled) beer. (d) (*Geol*) flooded underground chamber; underground stream.

sifrino ADJ (*Carib*) stuck-up*, full of airs and graces.

sig. ABR *de* **siguiente** following, f.

siga NF (*Cono Sur*) pursuit; **ir a la ~ de algo** to chase after sth.

sigilo NM (*secreto*) secrecy; (*discreción*) discretion; (*pey*) stealth; slyness; **~ sacramental** secrecy of the confessional; **con mucho ~** with great secrecy.

sigilosamente ADV secretly; discreetly; (*pey*) stealthily, slyly.

sigiloso ADJ secret; discreet; (*pey*) stealthy, sly.

sigla NF (*símbolo*) symbol; (*abreviatura*) abbreviation; acronym (*p.ej.* NATO, CAMPSA).

siglo NM (a) century; **S~ de las Luces** Age of Enlightenment (*18th century*); **~ de oro, ~ dorado** (*Mit*) golden age; **S~ de Oro** (*de España*) Golden Age (*Spain: about 1492-1650*); **los ~s medios** the Middle Ages; **el jugador del ~** the player of the century. (b) (*fig: época*) age, time, times. (c) (*fig: largo tiempo*) age(s); **hace un ~ que no le veo** I haven't seen him for ages. (d) **por los ~s de los ~s** (*Rel*) world without end. (e) (*Ecl*) **el ~** the world; worldly affairs; **retirarse del ~** to withdraw from the world, become a monk.

signar [1a] ① VT (a) (*sellar*) to seal; (*marcar*) to put one's mark on. (b) (*firmar*) to sign. (c) (*Rel*) to make the sign of the Cross over. ② **signarse** VR to cross o.s.

signatario, -a ADJ, NM/F signatory.

signatura NF (a) (*Mús, Tip*) signature. (b) (*de biblioteca*) catalogue number, press mark.

significación NF significance, importance; (*sentido*) meaning.

significado ① ADJ well-known; outstanding. ② NM (*importancia*) significance; (*de palabra etc*) meaning; **su ~ principal es ...** its chief meaning is ...; **una palabra de ~ dudoso** a word of uncertain meaning.

significante ADJ (*esp LAm*) significant.

▼ **significar** [1g] ① VT (a) (*palabra etc*) to mean; to signify (*t fig*); **¿qué significa 'nabo'?** what does 'nabo' mean?; **50 dólares significan muy poco para él** 50 dollars doesn't mean much to him; **significará la ruina de la sociedad** it will mean the ruin of the company; **él no significa gran cosa en estos asuntos** he doesn't count for much in these matters. (b) (*expresar*) to make known, express (*a* to); **le significó la condolencia de la familia real** he expressed (*o* conveyed) the royal family's sympathy to him. ② **significarse** VR (a) (*distinguirse*) to become known, make a name, become famous (*o* notorious); **~ como** to become known as, be recognized as. (b) to declare o.s., take sides; **no ~** to refuse to take sides.

significativamente ADV significantly; meaningfully.

significativo ADJ (a) (*gen*) significant; *mirada etc* meaning, expressive; **es ~ que ...** it is significant that ...; **calcularlo a 3 cifras significativas** to work it out to 3 significant figures. (b) (*influyente*) important, influential.

signo NM (a) (*gen*) sign; (*Mat*) sign, symbol; (*de analfabeto*) mark; **~ de admiración** exclamation mark; **~ de la cruz** sign of the Cross; **~ igual** equals sign; **~ de interrogación** question-mark; **~ (de) más, ~ de sumar** plus sign; **~ (de) menos** minus sign; **~ positivo** positive sign; **~ postal** postage-stamp; **~s de puntuación** punctuation marks; **~ de los tiempos** sign of the times; **~ de la victoria** victory sign, V-sign; **~ del zodíaco** sign of the zodiac; **bajo el ~ de** (*fig*) marked by, in the spirit of. (b) (*fig: tendencia*) tendency; **una situación de ~ alentador** an encouraging situation; *V* **mercado.**

sigo *etc V* **seguir.**

sigs. ABR *de* **siguientes** following, ff.

siguiente ADJ following; next; **dijo lo ~** he said the following; **¡que pase el ~!** next please!; **el día ~, al día ~** the following day, next day.

sij NMF, PL **sijs** Sikh.

sijolaj NM (*CAm Mús*) clay whistle, type of ocarina.

sílaba NF syllable.

silabario NM spelling book.

silabear [1a] VT to syllabify, syllabicate, divide into syllables; to pronounce syllable by syllable.

silabeo NM syllabification, syllabication, division into syllables.

silábico ADJ syllabic.

silba NF hissing, catcalls; **armar una ~, dar una ~ (a)** to hiss.

silbar [1a] ① VT (a) *melodía* to whistle; *silbato etc* to blow. (b) *comedia, orador etc* to hiss. ② VI (a) (*Mús*) to whistle; (*Anat*) to wheeze; (*viento*) to whistle; (*bala*) to whistle, whine; (*flecha etc*) to whizz, swish, hum. (b) (*Teat etc*) to hiss, catcall, boo.

silbatina NF (*And, Cono Sur*) hissing, booing.

silbato NM whistle.

silbido NM, **silbo** NM whistle, whistling; hiss; wheeze; whine, whizz, swish, hum; **~ de oídos** ringing in the ears.

silenciador NM silencer.

silenciamiento NM (*de oposición etc*) silencing; (*de suceso etc*) hushing up.

silenciar [1b] ① VT (a) *suceso etc* to hush up; *hecho etc* to keep silent about, pass over in silence. (b) *persona etc* to silence. (c) (*Téc*) to silence. ② **silenciarse** VR: **se silenció el asunto** the matter was hushed up; **se silenció su labor** a veil of silence was drawn over his work.

silencio ① NM (a) (*gen*) silence; (*calma*) quiet, hush; **¡~!** silence!, quiet!; **~ administrativo** policy of doing nothing about a matter; **en ~** in silence; **en el ~ más absoluto** in dead silence; **entregar algo al ~** to cast sth into oblivion; **guardar ~** to keep silent, say nothing (*sobre* about); **había un ~ sepulcral** it was as quiet as the grave, there was a deathly silence; **imponer ~ a uno** to make sb be quiet; to force sb to remain silent; **mantener el ~ radiofónico** to keep radio silence; **pasar algo en ~** to pass over sth in silence; **reducir al ~** *persona* to silence, reduce to silence; *artillería* to silence. (b) (*Mús*) rest. ② ADJ (*And, CAm, Méx*) (*silencioso*) silent, quiet; (*tranquilo*) still.

silenciosamente ADV silently, quietly; soundlessly; noiselessly.

silencioso ① ADJ silent, quiet; soundless; *máquina* silent, noiseless. ② NM silencer, muffler.

silense ADJ (*Esp*) of Silos, of Santo Domingo de Silos.

silente ADJ silent, noiseless.

sílex NM silex, flint.

sílfide NF (*t fig*) sylph.

silfo NM sylph.

silicato NM silicate.

sílice NF silica.

silíceo ADJ siliceous.

silicio NM silicon.

silicona NF silicone.

silicosis NF silicosis.

silla NF (a) (*asiento*) seat; chair; **~ alta** high chair; **~ de balanza, ~ de hamaca** (*LAm*) rocking-chair; **~ eléctrica** electric chair; **~ giratoria** swivel chair; **~ de manos** sedan chair; **~ plegable, ~ plegadiza, ~ de tijera** folding chair, folding stool, camp-stool; **~ de ruedas** wheelchair; **política de la ~ vacía** policy of not taking one's seat (*in parliament etc*); **calentar la ~** to stay too long, overstay one's welcome; **movieron la ~ para que cayese** (*fig*) they pulled the rug out from under him. (b) (*t ~ de montar*) saddle.

sillar NM block of stone, ashlar.

sillería NF (a) (*sillas*) chairs, set of chairs; (*Teat etc*) seating; (*Ecl*) choir-stalls. (b) (*taller*) chairmaker's workshop. (c) (*Arquit*) masonry, ashlar work.

sillero NM (a) (*artesano*) chairmaker. (b) (*Cono Sur: caballo*) horse, mule.

silleta NF (a) (*silla pequeña*) small chair; (*LAm: silla*) seat, chair; (*LAm: taburete*) low stool. (b) (*Med*) bedpan.

sillico NM chamberpot; commode.

sillín NM saddle, seat.

sillita NF small chair; **~ de ruedas** pushchair.

sillón NM (a) (*butaca*) armchair; easy chair; (*LAm*) rocking-chair; **~ de lona** deckchair; **~ de orejas, ~ orejero** wingchair; **~ de ruedas** wheelchair. (b) (*de montar*) woman's saddle, sidesaddle.

silo NM (*Agr*) silo; (*sótano*) underground store; (*depósito*) storage pit; (*Mil*) silo, bunker.

silogismo NM syllogism.

silogístico ADJ syllogistic.

silueta NF silhouette; (*de edificio*) outline; (*de ciudad*) skyline; (*de persona*) figure; (*Arte*) silhouette, outline drawing; **en ~** in silhouette.

siluetear [1a] VT to outline; (*fig*) to shape, mould.

silvático ADJ = **selvático.**

silvestre ADJ (*Bot*) wild; (*fig*) rustic, rural.

silvicultor(a) NM/F forestry expert.

silvicultura NF forestry.

SIM [sim] NM (*Esp*) ABR *de* **Servicio de Investigación Militar.**

sima NF abyss, chasm; pit; deep fissure, pothole.

Simbad NM Sinbad; **~ el marino** Sinbad the sailor.

simbiosis NF symbiosis.

simbiótico ADJ symbiotic.

simbólicamente ADV symbolically.
simbólico ADJ symbolic(al); token *(atr)*.
simbolismo NM symbolism.
simbolista ADJ, NMF symbolist.
simbolizar [1f] VT *(gen)* to symbolize; *(representar)* to represent, stand for, be a token of; *(ser ejemplo de)* to typify.
símbolo NM symbol; **~ de los apóstoles**, **~ de la fe** Creed.
simbología NF **(a)** *(símbolos)* symbols *(collectively)*; system of symbols. **(b)** *(estudio)* study of symbols.
simbombo ADJ *(Carib)* cowardly.
simetría NF symmetry; *(fig)* harmony.
simétricamente ADV symmetrically; *(fig)* harmoniously.
simétrico ADJ symmetrical; *(fig)* harmonious.
simetrizar [1f] VT to make symmetrical; *(fig)* to bring into line, harmonize.
símico ADJ = **simiesco**.
simiente NF seed.
simiesco ADJ simian, apish.
símil ☐1 ADJ similar. ☐2 NM comparison; *(Liter)* simile.
similar ADJ similar.
similaridad NF = **similitud**.
similitud NF similarity, resemblance, similitude.
similor NM pinchbeck; **de ~** *(fig)* pinchbeck, showy but valueless; fake, sham.
similñaca NF *(Carib)* tangle, mess.
simio NM ape, simian.
Simón NM Simon.
simonía NF simony.
simpatía NF **(a)** *(gen)* liking; *(afecto)* affection; **~ hacia**, **~ por** liking for; **~s y antipatías** likes and dislikes; **coger ~ a uno** to take to sb, take a liking to sb; **ganarse la ~ de todos** to win everybody's affection, come to be well liked by everybody; **tener ~ a** to like; **tener mucha ~** to be likeable, nice; **no le tenemos ~ en absoluto** we don't like him at all; **no tiene ~s en el colegio** nobody at school likes him, he has no friends at school.
(b) *(de ambiente etc)* friendliness, warmth, congeniality; *(de lugar, persona etc)* charm, attractiveness, likeableness; **la famosa ~ andaluza** that well-known Andalusian charm.
(c) *(solidaridad)* fellow feeling; mutual support, solidarity, sympathy; *(comprensión)* understanding; **explosión por ~** secondary explosion; **mostrar su ~ por** to show one's support for, show one's solidarity with.
(d) *(compasión)* sympathy, compassion.
simpático ADJ *persona* nice, likeable, genial, pleasant; *(bondadoso)* kind; *(encantador)* charming, attractive; *ambiente etc* congenial, agreeable; **¡qué policía más ~!** what a nice policeman!; **no le hemos caído muy ~s** she didn't much take to us; **siempre procura hacerse ~** he's always trying to ingratiate himself; **me es ~ ese muchacho** I like that lad.
simpatiquísimo ADJ *(superl)* de **simpático**.
simpatizante NMF sympathizer *(de* with).
simpatizar [1f] VI **(a)** *(2 personas)* to get on (well together); **pronto simpatizaron** they hit it off at once, they soon became friends.
(b) **~ con** to get on well with, take to, hit it off with; to be congenial to.
simplada NF *(And, CAm)* *(cualidad)* simplicity, stupidity; *(acto etc)* stupid thing (to do o to say).
simple ☐1 ADJ **(a)** *(gen)* simple; *(sin adornos)* uncomplicated, unadorned, bare; *(Ling, Quím etc)* simple; *(Bot)* single; *método etc* simple, easy, straightforward.
(b) *(delante de N: puro)* mere; pure, sheer; alone; **por ~ descuido** through sheer (o pure) carelessness; **es cosa de una ~ plumada** it's a matter of a mere stroke of the pen; **me basta con tu ~ palabra** your word alone is good enough for me; **somos ~s aficionados** we're just amateurs.
(c) *(delante de N: corriente)* ordinary; **un ~ soldado** an ordinary soldier; **un ~ abogado** a solicitor of little importance.
(d) *persona* simple, simple-minded, innocent; *(crédulo)* gullible; *(pey)* foolish, silly.
☐2 NM **(a)** *(persona)* simpleton.
(b) *(And: licor)* liquor.
(c) **~s** *(Bot)* simples.
(d) **~s** *(Tenis)* singles.
simplemente ADV *(V* ADJ **(a)**, **(b))** **(a)** simply. **(b)** simply, merely; purely.
simpleza NF **(a)** *(cualidad)* simpleness, simple-mindedness; gullibility; *(pey)* foolishness.
(b) *(una ~)* silly thing (to do *etc)*; **~s** nonsense.
(c) *(fig)* trifle, small thing; **se contenta con cualquier ~** she's happy with any little thing; **se enojó por una ~** he got annoyed over nothing.

simplicidad NF simplicity, simpleness.
simplificable ADJ simplifiable.
simplificación NF simplification.
simplificar [1g] VT to simplify.
simplista ADJ simplistic.
simplón ☐1 ADJ simple, gullible.
☐2 NM, **simplona** NF simple soul, gullible person.
simplote = **simplón**.
simposio NM symposium.
simulación NF simulation; make-believe; *(pey)* pretence; **~ por ordenador** computer simulation.
simulacro NM **(a)** *(ídolo)* simulacrum; image, idol. **(b)** *(apariencia)* semblance; *(fingimiento)* sham, pretence; **un ~ de ataque** a mock attack; **un ~ de combate** a sham fight; **~ de incendio** fire-practice, fire-drill; **~ de salvamento** *(Náut)* boat-drill.
simulado ADJ simulated; *(fingido)* feigned; mock, sham.
simulador NM simulator; **~ de vuelo** flight simulator.
simular [1a] VT to simulate; *(fingir)* to feign, sham.
simultáneamente ADV simultaneously.
simultanear [1a] VT: **~ dos cosas** to do two things simultaneously; **~ A con B** to contrive to do A at the same time as B, fit in A and B at the same time, synchronize A and B; **jugar con 16 tableros simultaneados** to play 16 boards simultaneously.
simultaneidad NF simultaneousness.
simultáneo ADJ simultaneous.
simún NM *(viento)* simoom; *(tempestad de arena)* sandstorm.
sin ☐1 PREP **(a)** *(gen)* without; with no ...; apart from, not counting, not including; **~ nosotros** without us; **costó 5 dólares ~ los gastos de envío** it cost 5 dollars not counting postage and packing; **salió ~ sombrero** he went out without a hat (o hatless); **me he quedado ~ cerillas** I've run out of matches; **~ compromiso** without obligation; **~ protección contra el sol** with no protection against the sun.
(b) **~ + infin** without + *ger, p.ej.* **~ verlo** without seeing it; **~ verlo yo** without my seeing it; **¡~ empujar!** don't push!, stop pushing!; **las 2 y el padre ~ venir** 2 o'clock and father hasn't come home yet; *(frec se traduce por 'un' + ptp, p.ej.)* **~ lavar** unwashed, **~ pagar** unpaid.
☐2 **~ que** CONJ without + *ger;* **~ que lo sepa él** without his knowing; **entraron ~ que nadie les observara** they came in without anyone seeing them.
sinagoga NF synagogue.
Sinaí NM Sinai.
sinalefa NF elision.
sinalefar [1a] VT to elide.
sinapismo NM **(a)** *(Med)* mustard plaster; **hay que ponerle un ~*** he needs gingering up.
(b) *(fig)* bore; nuisance, pest.
sinarquismo NM *(Méx Pol)* Sinarquism *(Mexican fascist movement of the 1930s)*.
sinarquista NM *(Méx Pol)* Sinarquist.
sinceramente ADV sincerely.
sincerarse [1a] VR *(justificarse)* to vindicate o.s.; *(decir la verdad)* to tell the truth, be honest; **~ a**, **~ con** to open one's heart to; to square o.s. with, give a full explanation to; **~ ante el juez** to justify one's conduct to the judge; **~ de su conducta** to explain one's conduct, justify one's conduct.
sinceridad NF sincerity; **con toda ~** in all sincerity.
▼ **sincero** ADJ sincere.
síncopa NF **(a)** *(Ling)* syncope. **(b)** *(Mús)* syncope, syncopation.
sincopar [1a] ☐1 VT to syncopate.
☐2 **sincoparse** VR *(corazón)* to miss a beat.
síncope NM **(a)** *(Ling)* syncope. **(b)** *(Med)* syncope; *(desmayo)* fainting fit, queer turn, blackout.
sincopizarse [1f] VR to have a fainting fit, have a blackout.
sincorbatismo NM habit of going without a tie.
sincretismo NM syncretism.
sincronía NF synchronous character; simultaneity.
sincrónico ADJ synchronous; *(Téc)* synchronized; *sucesos etc* simultaneous, coincidental; *(Ling)* synchronic.
sincronismo NM synchronism; simultaneity; *(de fechas etc)* coincidence.
sincronización NF synchronization.
sincronizadamente ADV simultaneously.
sincronizador NM timer.
sincronizar [1f] VT to synchronize *(con* with).
síncrono ADJ synchronous.
sincrotrón NM synchrotron.
sindicación NF **(a)** *(de obreros)* unionization. **(b)** *(Prensa)* syndication. **(c)** *(LAm Jur)* charge, accusation.
sindical ADJ union *(atr)*, trade-union *(atr)*; *(Pol)* syndical.
sindicalismo NM trade(s) unionism; *(Pol)* syndicalism.
sindicalista ☐1 ADJ union *(atr)*, trade-union *(atr)*; *(Pol)* syndicalist.

2 NMF trade(s) unionist; (*Pol*) syndicalist.
sindicalizar [1f] **1** VT to unionize.
2 sindicalizarse VR to form a union.
sindicar [1g] **1** VT (a) *obreros* to unionize, form into a trade(s) union. (b) (*LAm*) to charge, accuse.
2 sindicarse VR (*obrero*) to join a union; (*obreros*) to form themselves into a union.
sindicato NM (a) (*gen*) syndicate; **casarse por el ~** to have a shotgun wedding. (b) (*de obreros*) trade(s) union, labor union (*US*).
sindicatura NF (*Fin*) syndicate.
síndico, -a NM/F trustee; (*Jur*) official receiver.
síndrome NM syndrome; **~ de abstinencia** withdrawal symptoms; **~ de Down** Down's syndrome; **~ premenstrual** premenstrual tension; **~ tóxico** poisoning.
sinécdoque NF synecdoche.
sinecura NF sinecure.
sine die ADV sine die.
sine qua non ADJ: **condición ~** sine qua non.
sinergía NF synergy.
sinfín NM (a) = **sinnúmero**. (b) (*Téc*) conveyor-belt; spiral conveyor.
sinfonía NF (a) symphony. (b) (*Carib Mús*) harmonica, mouth-organ.
sinfónico ADJ symphonic; **orquesta sinfónica** symphony orchestra.
sinfonieta NF sinfonietta.
sinfonola NF (*LAm*) jukebox.
Singapur NM Singapore.
singar [1h] **1** VT (*Carib‡*) to pester, annoy.
2 VI (*CAm, Carib‡‡*) to fuck‡‡, screw‡‡.
singladura NF (*Náut*) (*recorrido*) day's run; (*día*) nautical day (*from noon to noon*).
single NM (*Mús*) single.
singlista NMF (*LAm Dep*) singles player.
singón NM (*Carib, Méx*) womanizer, philanderer.
singuisarra‡ NF (*And, Carib*) row, racket.
singular **1** ADJ (a) (*Ling*) singular.
(b) combate ~ single combat.
(c) (*fig*) outstanding, exceptional; (*pey*) singular, peculiar, odd.
2 NM (*Ling*) singular; **en ~** in the singular; (*fig*) **en ~** in particular; **se refiere a él en ~** it refers to him in particular; **que hable él en ~** let him speak solely for himself.
singularidad NF singularity, peculiarity, oddity.
singularizar [1f] **1** VT to single out; to refer specifically to.
2 singularizarse VR (*distinguirse*) to distinguish o.s., stand out, excel; (*llamar la atención*) to be conspicuous; (*ser el solo*) to be the odd one out; **~ con uno** to single sb out for special treatment.
singularmente ADV (a) (*extrañamente*) singularly, peculiarly, oddly. (b) (*especialmente*) especially.
sinhueso‡ NF tongue; **soltar la ~** to shoot one's mouth off‡.
siniestra NF (*liter*) left hand; **a mi ~** on my left.
siniestrado, -a **1** ADJ involved in an accident; damaged, wrecked, crashed; **la zona siniestrada** the affected area, the disaster zone.
2 NM/F victim (of an accident *etc*), person who has suffered a loss (*o* damage).
siniestralidad NF accident rate.
siniestro **1** ADJ (a) (*liter*) left.
(b) (*fig*) (*funesto*) sinister; (*de mal agüero*) ominous; (*maligno*) evil, malign.
(c) (*fig*: *nefasto*) fateful, disastrous.
2 NM (a) natural disaster, catastrophe, calamity; accident; **~ marítimo** shipwreck, disaster at sea. (b) (*Fin*) insurance claim, claim on an accident (*etc*) insurance policy; **~ total** total loss, total write-off.
sinnúmero NM: **un ~ de** a great many, no end of, a huge number of.
sino¹ NM fate, destiny.
sino² CONJ (a) but; **no son 8 ~ 9** there are not 8 but 9; **no cabe otra solución ~ que vaya él** there is no other solution but that he should go; **no lo hace sólo para sí ~ para todos** he's not doing it only for himself but for everybody.
(b) (*salvo*) except, save, only; **todos aplaudieron ~ él** everybody except him applauded; **no te pido ~ una cosa** I ask only (*o* but) one thing of you; **no deseo ~ verte** my sole wish is to see you; **no lo habría dicho ~ en broma** he could only have said it jokingly, he wouldn't have said it except as a joke.
sino... PREF Chinese ..., Sino...
sínodo NM synod.
sinología NF Sinology.
sinólogo, -a NM/F Sinologist.
sinonimia NF synonymy.
sinónimo **1** ADJ synonymous (*con* with).
2 NM synonym.
sinopsis NF INVAR synopsis.
sinóptico ADJ synoptic(al); **cuadro ~**, diagram, chart.

sinovitis NF: **~ del codo** tennis elbow.
sinrazón NF wrong, injustice, outrage.
sinsabor NM (a) (*disgusto*) trouble, unpleasantness. (b) (*dolor*) sorrow; (*inquietud*) uneasiness, worry.
sinsentido NM absurdity, the absurd.
sinsilico‡ ADJ (*Méx*) stupid, thick‡.
sinsombrerismo NM hatlessness, custom of going hatless.
sinsonte NM mockingbird.
sinsostenismo NM bralessness, habit of going without a bra.
sinsustancia‡ NMF idiot.
sintáctico ADJ syntactic(al).
sintagma NM syntagma, syntagm.
Sintasol ® NM (*a kind of*) lino.
sintaxis NF syntax.
▼ **síntesis** NF INVAR synthesis; **~ de la voz humana** voice (*o* speech) synthesis.
sintéticamente ADV synthetically.
sintético ADJ synthetic(al).
sintetizador NM synthesizer; **~ de la voz humana** voice (*o* speech) synthesizer.
sintetizar [1f] VT to synthesize; (*resumir*) to summarize, sum up.
sintiendo *etc* V **sentir**.
sintoísmo NM Shintoism.
síntoma NM symptom; sign, indication.
sintomático ADJ symptomatic.
sintomatizar [1f] VT to typify, characterize, be symptomatic of.
sintomatología NF symptomatology.
sintonía NF (a) (*acto*: *Elec*) syntony; (*Rad*) tuning. (b) (*Mús, Rad*) signature tune.
sintonización NF (*Rad*) tuning.
sintonizado NM tuning.
sintonizador NM (*Rad*) tuner.
sintonizar [1f] VT (*Elec*) to syntonize; (*Cine*) to synchronize; (*Rad*) *emisora* to tune (in to; to pick up, receive.
sinuosidad NF (a) (*gen*) sinuosity; waviness. (b) (*curva*) bend, curve, wave; **las ~es del camino** the windings of the road, the bends in the road. (c) (*fig*) deviousness.
sinuoso ADJ (a) *camino etc* winding, sinuous; *línea* wavy; *rumbo* devious. (b) (*fig*) *medio, persona etc* devious.
sinusitis NF sinusitis.
sinvergonzón‡ NM rotter‡, swine‡.
sinvergüencería NF (a) (*cualidad*) villainy; rottenness; shamelessness. (b) (*acto*) = **sinvergüenzada**.
sinvergüenza NMF (a) (*pillo*) scoundrel, villain, rascal; (*canalla*) rotter‡; **¡~!** (*hum*) you villain! (b) (*descarado*) shameless person.
sinvergüenzada NF (*LAm*) villainous trick, rotten thing (to do)‡.
sinvergüenzura NF (*LAm*) shamelessness.
Sión NM Zion.
sionismo NM Zionism.
sionista ADJ, NMF Zionist.
sipo ADJ (*And*) pockmarked.
sipotazo NM (*CAm*) slap (in the face), punch.
siqu... PREF = **psiqu...**, *p.ej. para* **siquiatría** V **psiquiatría**.
siquiera **1** ADV (a) (*por lo menos*) at least; **una vez ~** once at least, just once; **dame un abrazo ~** at least give me a hug; **deja ~ trabajar a los demás** at least let the others work; **~ come un poquito** (*LAm*) at least eat a bit.
(b) ni ~, ni ... ~ not even, not so much as; **ni él ~ vino** not even he came; **ella ni me miró ~** she didn't even look at me; **ni ~ probó la sopa** he hardly touched the soup.
2 CONJ (a) (*aunque*) even if, even though; **ven ~ sea por pocos días** do come even if only for a few days.
(b) ~ venga, ~ no venga whether he comes or not.
Siracusa NF Syracuse.
sirena NF (a) (*Mit*) siren; mermaid; **~ de la playa** bathing beauty. (b) (*Téc*) siren, hooter; **~ de buque** ship's siren; **~ de niebla** foghorn.
sirga NF (*Náut*) towrope.
sirgar [1h] VT to tow.
sirgo NM (piece of) twisted silk.
Siria NF Syria.
sirimba NF (*Carib*) faint, fainting fit.
sirimbo ADJ (*Carib*) silly.
sirimbombo ADJ (*Carib*) (*débil*) weak; (*tímido*) timid.
sirimiri NM (*prov*) drizzle.
siringa NF (*LAm*) rubber tree.
siringal NM (*LAm*) rubber plantation.
Sirio NM Sirius.
sirio, -a ADJ, NM/F Syrian.
sirla‡ NF (a) (*arma*) chiv‡, knife. (b) (*atraco*) hold-up, armed robbery, stick-up‡.
sirlero‡ NM armed robber, hold-up man.
siró NM (*Carib*) syrup.

siroco NM sirocco.
sirope NM (*LAm*) syrup.
sirsaca NF seersucker.
sirte NF shoal, sandbank.
sirviendo *etc* V **servir**.
sirvienta NF servant, maid.
sirviente NM servant; waiter.
sisa NF **(a)** (*robo*) petty theft; (*ganancia*) dishonest profit (*made by a servant*); (*tajada*) cut, percentage*; **~s** pilfering, petty thieving. **(b)** (*Cos*) dart; armhole.
sisal NM sisal; sisal plant.
sisar [1a] VT **(a)** *artículos* to thieve, pilfer, filch; *persona* to cheat; *cuenta* to cheat on. **(b)** (*Cos*) to put darts in, take in.
sisear [1a] VTI to hiss.
siseo NM hiss(ing).
Sísifo NM Sisyphus.
sísmico ADJ seismic.
sismo NM = **seísmo**.
sismografía NF seismography.
sismógrafo NM seismograph.
sismología NF seismology.
sismólogo, -a NM/F seismologist.
sisón[1] 1 ADJ thieving, light-fingered.
  2 NM, **sisona** NF petty thief.
sisón[2] NM (*Orn*) little bustard.
sistema NM system; method; **~ de alarma** alarm system; **~ binario** binary system; **~ de calefacción** heating (system); **~ de diagnosis** diagnostic system; **~ educativo** education system; **~ experto** expert system; **~ de facturación** invoicing system; **~ de gestión de base de datos** database management system; **~ impositivo, ~ tributario** taxation, tax system; **~ inmunitario, ~ inmunológico** immune system; **~ de lógica compartida** shared logic system; **S~ Monetario Europeo** European Monetary System; **~ montañoso** mountain range; **~ nervioso (central)** (central) nervous system; **~ operativo** operating system; **~ operativo de disco** disk operating system; **~ pedagógico** teaching method; **~ rastreador** tracking system; **~ de seguridad** security system; **trabajar con ~** to work systematically, work methodically; **yo por ~ lo hago así** I make it a rule to do it this way.
sistemática NF systematics.
sistemáticamente ADV systematically.
sistematicidad NF systematic nature.
sistemático ADJ systematic.
sistematización NF systematization.
sistematizar [1f] VT to systematize.
sitiador NM besieger.
sitial NM seat of honour; ceremonial chair.
sitiar [1b] VT to besiege, lay siege to; (*fig*) to surround, hem in.
sitio NM **(a)** (*lugar*) place; spot; part; site, location; **real ~** royal country house; **en cualquier ~** anywhere; **en todos los ~s** everywhere, all over; **en el mejor ~ de la ciudad** in the best part of the city; **cambiar de ~** to shift, move; **cambiar de ~ con uno** to change places with sb; **dejar a uno en el ~** to kill sb (on the spot); **así no vas a ningún ~** you'll get nowhere doing that; **poner a uno en su ~** (*fig*) to put sb firmly in his place; **quedarse en el ~** to die instantly, die on the spot.
  (b) (*espacio*) room, space; **¿hay ~?** is there any room?; **hay ~ de sobra** there's plenty of room; **hacer ~** to make room (*a uno* for sb); **te haremos ~** we'll make room for you.
  (c) (*empleo*) job, post.
  (d) (*Mil*) siege; **en estado de ~** in a state of siege; **levantar el ~** to raise the siege; **poner ~ a** to besiege.
  (e) (*CAm, Cono Sur: solar*) building site, vacant lot (*US*).
  (f) (*Carib, Méx Agr*) small farm, smallholding.
  (g) (*LAm*) (*parada*) taxi rank, cab rank (*US*); **carro de ~** taxi, cab (*US*).
sito ADJ situated, located (*en* at, in).
situ V **in situ**.
situación NF **(a)** (*gen*) situation, position; (*status*) position, standing; **~ B** (*Mil y fig*) retirement; **~ económica** financial position; **~ límite** extreme situation; **crearse una ~** to attain a position of financial security, make good; **estar en ~ de** + *infin* to be in a position to + *infin*.
  (b) **precio de ~** (*LAm*) bargain price.
situacional ADJ situational.
situado ADJ **(a)** (*gen*) situated, placed. **(b) estar ~** (*Fin*) to be financially secure, be well placed.
situar [1e] 1 VT **(a)** (*gen*) to place, put, set; *edificio etc* to locate, situate, site; (*Mil*) to post, station; **sitúan esta etapa en el siglo XIII** they place this stage in the 13th century; **esto le sitúa entre los mejores** this places him among the best.
  (b) (*Fin*) (*invertir*) to place, invest; (*depositar en banco*) to bank; (*destinar*) to set aside; to assign, earmark; **~ una pensión para uno**

to settle an income on sb; **ha venido situando fondos en el extranjero** he has been placing money in accounts abroad.
  2 **situarse** VR to get a position; to establish o.s., do well for o.s.
siútico ADJ (*Cono Sur*) = **cursi**.
siutiquería NF (*Cono Sur*) = **cursilería**.
skay [es'kai] NM imitation leather.
sketch [es'ketʃ] NM, PL **sketches** [es'ketʃ] (*Teat*) sketch.
skin [es'kin] ADJ, NMF, PL **skins, skinhead** [es'kinxeð] ADJ, NMF, PL **skinheads** skinhead.
S.L. **(a)** (*Com*) ABR *de* **Sociedad Limitada** Limited Company, Ltd. **(b)** ABR *de* **Sus Labores** self-employed (*V t* **labor** (a)).
slalom [ez'lalom] NM slalom; **~ gigante** giant slalom.
slam [ez'lam] NM (*Bridge*) slam; **gran ~** grand slam; **pequeño ~** little slam.
slip [ez'lip] NM, PL **slips** [ez'lip] (*Esp*) briefs, pants; (*LAm*) bathing-trunks.
s.l. ni f. (*Tip*) ABR *de* **sin lugar ni fecha** no place or date, n.p. or d.
slogan [ez'loɣan] NM, PL **slogans** [ez'loɣan] slogan.
slot [es'lot] NM: **~ de expansión** (*Inform*) expansion slot.
S.M. **(a)** NF (*Esp Rel*) ABR *de* **Sociedad Marianista**. **(b)** ABR *de* **Su Majestad** His (*o Her*) Majesty, HM.
smash [ez'mas] NM (*Tenis*) smash.
SME NM ABR *de* **Sistema Monetario Europeo** European Monetary System, EMS.
SMI NM ABR *de* **salario mínimo interprofesional**.
smog [ez'smo] NM smog.
smoking [ez'mokin] NM, PL **smokings** [ez'mokin] dinner-jacket, tuxedo (*US*).
s/n ABR *de* **sin número** no number.
snack [ez'nak] NM, PL **snacks** [ez'nak] (*merienda etc*) snack; (*cafetería*) snackbar.
s.n.m. ABR *de* **sobre el nivel del mar** (*height*) above sea-level.
snob [ez'noß] *etc* = **esnob** *etc*.
SO ABR *de* **suroeste** south-west, SW.
so[1] PREP under; *V* **capa** *etc*.
so[2] INTERJ **(a)** (*para parar*) whoa! **(b)** (*LAm: ¡silencio!*) quiet!, shut up!* **(c)** (*Carib*) (*a animal*) shoo!
so[3] *como* INTERJ (*contraction of* señor): **¡~ indecente!** you swine!; **¡~ burro!** you idiot!, you great oaf!
s/o (*Com*) ABR *de* **su orden** your order.
soasar [1a] VT to roast lightly.
soba NF **(a)** (*amasar*) kneading. **(b)** (*) (*bofetada*) slap, punch; (*paliza*) hiding*; **dar ~ a uno** to wallop sb*. **(c)** (*: reprimenda*) telling-off*.
sobacal ADJ underarm (*atr*).
sobaco NM (*Anat*) armpit; (*Cos*) armhole; **lo pasó por el ~*** he dismissed it, he totally disregarded it.
sobado ADJ **(a)** *ropa* worn, shabby; (*ajado*) rumpled, crumpled, messed up; *libro* well-thumbed, dog-eared.
  (b) (*fig*) *tema* well-worn; *chiste* hoary, corny*.
  (c) (*Culin*) hojaldre short.
  (d) (*Cono Sur*: *enorme*) big, huge.
sobador NM **(a)** (*And, Méx*: *Med*) bonesetter; quack. **(b)** (*And, Carib, Méx*: *lisonjero*) flatterer.
sobajar [1a] VT **(a)** (*gen*) to crush, rumple, mess up. **(b)** (*And, Méx*: *humillar*) to humiliate, demean.
sobajear [1a] VT (*LAm*) (*apretar*) to squeeze, press; (*desordenar*) to mess up.
sobandero NM (*And, Carib*) bonesetter; (*And*) quack.
sobao 1 ADJ (*) **quedarse ~** to fall asleep; *V t* **sobado**.
  2 NM *sponge cake made with cream or lard*.
sobaquera NF **(a)** (*Cos*) armhole. **(b)** (*pistolera*) shoulder holster. **(c)** (*CAm, Carib*: *olor*) underarm odour.
sobaquero ADJ: **funda sobaquera** shoulder holster.
sobaquina NF underarm odour.
sobar [1a] 1 VT **(a)** *tela etc* to handle, finger, dirty (with one's fingers); *ropa etc* to crush, rumple, crumple, mess up; *masa* to knead; *masilla etc* to squeeze (in the hands), soften; *músculo* to massage, rub.
  (b) *persona* to fondle, feel (amorously); (*pey*) to finger, paw*, lay hands on.
  (c) (*LAm*) *hueso* to set.
  (d) (*And*: *despellejar*) to skin, flay.
  (e) (*: pegar*) to wallop*.
  (f) (*: molestar*) to pester; to annoy.
  (g) (*And, Carib, Méx*: *lisonjear*) to flatter.
  (h) (*CAm, Méx*: *reprender*) to tell off*.
  2 VI (‡) to kip‡, sleep.
  3 **sobarse** VR (*amantes*) to pet*, fondle, cuddle.
sobasquera NF (*CAm, Carib, Méx*) = **sobaquina**.
sobeo NM fondling, caresses, love-play.
soberanamente ADV (*fig*) supremely.
soberanía NF sovereignty.
soberano 1 ADJ **(a)** (*Pol etc*) sovereign.
  (b) (*fig*) supreme.

(c) (*) real, really big; **una soberana paliza** a real walloping*.
2 NM, **soberana** NF sovereign; **los ~s** the king and queen, the royal couple.

soberbia NF **(a)** (*orgullo*) pride; (*altanería*) haughtiness, arrogance.
(b) (*fig*) magnificence, grandeur, pomp.
(c) (*ira*) anger; (*malhumor*) irritable nature.

soberbio ADJ **(a)** (*orgulloso*) proud; haughty, arrogant. **(b)** (*fig*) magnificent, grand, superb; **¡~!** splendid! **(c)** (*enojado*) angry; irritable. **(d)** (*) = soberano (c).

sobeta ADJ INVAR: **estar ~, quedarse ~** to be kipping.

sobijo NM **(a)** (*And, CAm*) = soba. **(b)** (*And*) (*desolladura*) skinning, flaying.

sobijón NM (*CAm*) = sobijo.

sobón ADJ **(a)** (*que soba*) too free with one's hands, given to pawing*; (*fig*) fresh*, too familiar by half; *amantes* mushy, wet*; **¡no seas ~!** get your hands off me!, stop pawing me!*
(b) (*gandul*) lazy, workshy.
(c) (*And*: *adulón*) soapy*, greasy.

sobornable ADJ bribable, venal.

sobornar [1a] VT to bribe, suborn; to buy off; (*hum*) to get round.

soborno NM **(a)** (*un ~*) bribe; (*el ~*) bribery, graft. **(b)** (*And, Cono Sur*) (*sobrecarga*) extra load; (*prima*) extra, bonus; extra charge; **de ~** extra, in addition.

▼ **sobra** NF **(a)** (*excedente*) excess, surplus; **~s** leavings, left-overs, scraps; (*Cos*) remnants.
▼ **(b)** **de ~** spare, surplus, extra; **aquí tengo de ~** I've more than enough here, I've got plenty (and to spare) here; **tengo tiempo de ~** I've got plenty of time; **tuvo motivos de ~** he had plenty of justification, he was more than justified; **lo sé de ~** I know it only too well; **aquí estoy de ~** I'm not needed here; I'm in the way here.

sobradamente ADV too; amply; over...; **saber** only too well; **con eso queda ~ satisfecho** he is only too happy with that, with that he is more than fully satisfied.

sobradero NM overflow pipe.

sobradillo NM penthouse.

sobrado **1** ADJ **(a)** (*más que suficiente*) more than enough; (*excesivo*) superfluous, excessive; (*muy abundante*) superabundant; **hay tiempo ~** there's plenty of time; **motivo más que ~ para + infin** all the more reason to + *infin*; **tuvo razón sobrada** he was amply justified; **sobradas veces** repeatedly.
(b) **estar ~ de algo** to have more than enough of sth, be well provided with sth.
(c) (*rico*) wealthy; **no anda muy ~** he's not very well off.
(d) (*atrevido*) bold, forward.
(e) (*Cono Sur: enorme*) colossal.
(f) **darse de ~** (*And*) to be full of oneself.
2 ADV too, exceedingly.
3 NM **(a)** attic, garret.
(b) **~s** (*Andalucía, Cono Sur: restos*) left-overs.

sobrador ADJ (*Cono Sur*) stuck-up*, conceited.

sobrancero ADJ unemployed.

sobrante **1** ADJ (*que sobra*) spare, remaining, extra, surplus; *obrero* redundant.
2 NM **(a)** (*lo que sobra*) surplus, remainder; (*Com, Fin*) surplus; (*saldo*) balance in hand.
(b) **~s** odds and ends.
3 NMF redundant worker, person made redundant.

sobrar [1a] **1** VT to exceed, surpass.
2 VI (*quedar de más*) to remain, be left (over), be (to) spare; (*ser más que suficiente*) to be more than enough; (*ser superfluo*) to be superfluous; **por este lado sobra** there's too much on this side; **no es que sobre talento** it's not that there's a surplus of talent; **todo lo que has dicho sobra** all that you've said is quite unnecessary; **nos sobra tiempo** we have plenty (o lots o heaps) of time; **al terminar me sobraba medio metro** I had half a metre left over when I finished; **veo que aquí sobro** I see that I'm not needed here; I see that I'm in the way; **más vale que sobre que no que falte** better too much than too little.

sobrasada NF Majorcan sausage.

sobre¹ NM **(a)** (*gen*) envelope; **~ de primer día** (*de circulación*) first-day cover; **~ de paga, ~ de pago** pay-packet; **~ de sellos** packet of stamps. **(b)** (*: cama*) kip, bed; **meterse en el ~** to hit the hay*.

sobre² PREP **(a)** (*lugar*) on, upon; (*encima de*) on top of; over, above; **está ~ la mesa** it's on the table; **volamos ~ Cádiz** we're flying over Cádiz; **prestar juramento ~ la Biblia** to swear on the Bible.
(b) (*cantidad etc*) over, over and above; more than; (*además de*) in addition to, on top of, besides; **un aumento ~ el año anterior** an increase over last year; **10 dólares ~ lo estipulado** 10 dollars over and above what was agreed; **~ todas mis obligaciones hay una nueva** on top of all my duties here comes another; **crimen ~ crimen** crime upon crime; **~ ser traidor es asesino** in addition to being a traitor he is a murderer.

(c) **estar ~ uno** (*fig*) (*acosar*) to keep on at sb; (*vigilar*) to keep constant watch over sb; **quiere estar ~ todos** he wants to control everyone.
(d) (*Fin etc*) on; **un préstamo ~ una propiedad** a loan on a property; **un tributo ~ las medias** a tax on stockings.
(e) (*cifras*) about; **~ las 6** at about 6 o'clock; **ocupa ~ 20 páginas** it fills about 20 pages, it occupies roughly 20 pages.
(f) (*porcentaje*) in, out of; **3 ~ 100** 3 in a 100, 3 out of every 100.
(g) (*tema*) about, on; **un libro ~ Tirso** a book about Tirso.
(h) (*comparaciones*) **si medimos julio ~ julio** if we measure this July against last July, if we compare this July with last July.

sobre... PREF super..., over...

sobreabundancia NF superabundance, overabundance.

sobreabundante ADJ superabundant, overabundant.

sobreabundar [1a] VI to superabound (*en* in, with), be very abundant.

sobreactuación NF overacting.

sobreactuar [1e] VI to overact.

sobrealimentación NF overfeeding.

sobrealimentado ADJ (*Mec*) supercharged.

sobrealimentador NM supercharger.

sobrealimentar [1a] VT **(a)** *persona etc* to overfeed. **(b)** (*Mec*) to supercharge.

sobreañadido ADJ additional; (*pey*) superfluous.

sobreañadir [3a] VT to give in addition, add (as a bonus); to superinduce.

sobrecalentamiento NM overheating (*t fig*).

sobrecalentar [1j] VT to overheat (*t fig*).

sobrecama NM bedspread.

sobrecaña NF (*Vet*) splint.

sobrecapacidad NF overcapacity, excess capacity.

sobrecapitalización NF overcapitalization.

sobrecapitalizar [1f] VT to overcapitalize.

sobrecarga NF **(a)** (*carga*) extra load; (*peso*) excess weight; (*fig*) new burden.
(b) (*Com*) surcharge; (*Correos*) surcharge, overprint(ing); **~ de importación** import surcharge.
(c) (*cuerda*) rope.

sobrecargar [1h] VT **(a)** *camión etc* to overload; (*Elec*) to overcharge; *persona* to weigh down, overburden (*de* with); **~ el mercado** (*Cono Sur*) to glut the market.
(b) (*Com*) to surcharge; (*Correos*) to surcharge, overprint (*de* with).

sobrecargo NM (*Náut*) supercargo, purser.

sobrecejo NM **(a)** (*ceño*) frown. **(b)** (*Arquit*) lintel.

sobreceño NM frown.

sobrecito NM (*LAm*) sachet.

sobrecogedor ADJ (*imponente*) *paisaje, silencio* imposing, impressive; (*horrible*) horrific; **~as escenas de guerra** horrific scenes of war.

sobrecoger [2c] **1** VT (*sobresaltar*) to startle, take by surprise; (*asustar*) to scare, frighten.
2 **sobrecogerse** VR **(a)** (*asustarse*) to be startled, start (*a* at, *de* with); to get scared, be frightened.
(b) (*quedar impresionado*) to be overawed (*de* by); **~ de emoción** to be overcome with emotion.

sobrecontrata NF overbooking.

sobrecontratar VTI to overbook.

sobrecoste NM extra charges; extra costs.

sobrecubierta NF outer cover; (*de libro*) jacket.

sobredicho ADJ aforementioned.

sobredimensionado ADJ **(a)** extra large; (*pey*) excessively large, oversized. **(b)** **estar ~ de** to have a surplus (o excess) of, have too much of.

sobredimensionamiento NM (*tamaño*) excessive size; (*de personal etc*) excessive number; overmanning; (*aumento*) increase in size, expansion.

sobredorar [1a] VT to gild; (*fig*) to gloss over.

sobredosis NF INVAR overdose.

sobre(e)ntender [2g] **1** VT to understand; (*adivinar*) to guess, deduce, infer.
2 **sobre(e)ntenderse** VR: **aquí se sobre(e)ntienden dos palabras** here two words are understood; **se sobre(e)ntiende que ...** it is implied that ..., one infers that ...

sobre(e)scribir [3a] VT (*Inform*) to overwrite.

sobre(e)sfuerzo NM superhuman effort; (*Med*) overstrain.

sobre(e)stimación NF overestimate.

sobre(e)stimar [1a] VT to overestimate.

sobre(e)xcitación NF overexcitement.

sobre(e)xcitado ADJ overexcited.

sobre(e)xcitar [1a] **1** VT to overexcite.
2 **sobre(e)xcitarse** VR to get overexcited.

sobreexplotación NF (*de recursos*) over-exploitation, draining; (*de trabajadores*) exploitation.

sobreexplotar [1a] VT *recursos* to over-exploit, drain; *trabajadores* to exploit.

sobre(e)xponer [2q] VT to overexpose.

sobre(e)xposición NF (*Fot*) overexposure.

sobrefunda NF (*CAm*) pillowslip, pillowcase.

sobregirar [1a] VTI to overdraw.

sobregiro NM overdraft.

sobrehilar [1a] VT to whipstitch, overcast.

sobrehumano ADJ superhuman.

sobreimpresión NF (*Correos*) overprint(ing).

sobreimpresionar [1a] VT to overprint.

sobreimprimir [1a] VT (*Correos*) to overprint.

sobrellevar [1a] VT *peso* to carry, help to carry, help with; *carga de otro* to ease; *desastre, enfermedad, problemas etc* to bear, endure; *faltas ajenas* to be tolerant towards.

sobremanera ADV exceedingly; **me interesa ~** I'm most interested in it.

sobremarca NF (*Bridge*) overbid; raise (in a suit).

sobremarcha NF (*Aut*) overdrive.

sobremesa NF (a) (*mantel*) table cover.
(b) (*postre*) dessert.
(c) (*período etc del postre*) sitting on after a meal; **conversación de ~** table talk; **lámpara de ~** table lamp; **orador de ~** after-lunch speaker; **ordenador de ~** desktop computer; **programa de ~** (*TV*) afternoon programme; **un cigarro de ~** an after-lunch cigar, a postprandial cigar; **estar de ~** to sit round the table after lunch; **hablaremos de eso de ~** we'll talk about that after lunch.
(d) (*de mueble*) desktop.

┌─ **SOBREMESA** ─┐

i After the main meal of the day, which usually takes place at around 2 or 3 p.m., the Spanish often linger on at table drinking coffee and/or liqueurs and chatting, playing cards or watching TV before returning to work later in the afternoon. While **estar de sobremesa** is also occasionally applied to the period after the evening meal, it is more usually taken to mean after lunch, and the **sobremesa** time band used in TV programme listings applies only to between 2.00 and 5.00 p.m.

---

sobremodo ADV = **sobremanera**.

sobrenadar [1a] VI to float.

sobrenatural ADJ supernatural; (*misterioso*) weird, unearthly; **lo ~** the supernatural; **ciencias ~es** occult sciences; **vida ~** life after death.

sobrenombre NM by-name, extra name; nickname.

sobrentender *etc* = **sobre(e)ntender** *etc*.

sobrepaga NF extra pay, bonus.

sobreparto NM confinement after childbirth; **dolores de ~** afterpains; **morir de ~** to die in childbirth.

sobrepasar [1a] ① VT (*gen*) to exceed, surpass, outdo; *límite* to exceed; *esperanzas etc* to surpass; *rival, récord* to beat; *pista* (*Aer*) to overshoot.
② **sobrepasarse** VR = **propasarse**.

sobrepelliz NF surplice.

sobrepelo NM (*Cono Sur*) saddlecloth.

sobrepesca NF over-fishing.

sobrepeso NM (*carga*) extra load; (*de paquete, persona*) excess weight, overweight.

sobrepoblación NF overcrowding.

sobreponer [2r] ① VT (a) (*objeto*) to put on top (*en* of), superimpose (*en* on), add (*en* to).
(b) **~ A a B** (*persona*) to give A preference over B, give more weight to A than to B.
② **sobreponerse** VR (a) (*recobrar la calma*) to master o.s., pull o.s. together; (*triunfar*) to win through, pull through, overcome adversity (*etc*); to pull o.s. together.
(b) **~ a una enfermedad** to pull through an illness; **~ a un rival** to triumph over a rival; **~ a un enemigo** to overcome an enemy; **~ a un susto** to get over a fright, recover from a fright.

sobreprecio NM surcharge; increase in price.

sobreprima NF (*en seguros*) extra premium.

sobreproducción NF overproduction.

sobreproducir [3n] VT to overproduce.

sobreprotección NF over-protection.

sobreprotector ADJ over-protective.

sobreproteger [2c] VT to overprotect.

sobrepuerta NF lintel.

sobrepuesto ADJ added, superimposed.

sobrepujar [1a] VT to outdo, excel, surpass; **sobrepuja a todos en talento** he excels all the rest in talent.

sobrereacción NF over-reaction.

sobrereserva NF overbooking.

sobrereservar [1a] VTI to overbook.

sobrero ① ADJ extra, spare.

---

② NM (*Taur*) spare bull, reserve bull.

sobresaliente ① ADJ (a) (*Arquit etc*) projecting; overhanging.
(b) (*fig*) outstanding, excellent; (*Univ etc*) *calificación* first class.
② NMF substitute; (*Teat*) understudy.
③ NM (*Univ etc*) first class (mark), distinction.

sobresalir [3r] VI (a) (*Arquit etc*) to project, jut out; to overhang; to stick out, protrude; to stick up, stand up; to be conspicuous.
(b) (*fig*) to stand out, be outstanding, excel.

sobresaltar [1a] ① VT to startle, scare, frighten.
② **sobresaltarse** VR to start, be startled (*con, de* at).

sobresalto NM (*sorpresa*) start; (*susto*) scare; (*conmoción*) sudden shock; **de ~** suddenly.

sobresanar [1a] VI (*Med*) to heal superficially; (*fig*) to conceal itself, hide its true nature.

sobrescrito NM (*señas*) address; (*inscripción*) superscription.

sobreseer [2e] ① VT: **~ una causa** (*Jur*) to stop a case, stay a case.
② VI: **~ de** to desist from, give up.

sobreseído ADJ: **causa sobreseída** (*Jur*) case dismissed.

sobreseimiento NM (*Jur*) stay, dismissal.

sobresello NM double seal.

sobrestadía NF (*Com*) demurrage.

sobrestante NM (*capataz*) foreman, overseer; (*gerente*) site manager.

sobresueldo NM bonus.

sobretasa NF surcharge.

sobretensión NF (*Elec: transitoria*) surge.

sobretiempo NM (*LAm*) overtime.

sobretiro NM (*Méx*) offprint.

sobretítulo NM (*Prensa*) general title, general heading.

sobretodo NM overcoat.

sobrevaloración NF overvaluation; (*fig*) overrating.

sobrevalorado ADJ *persona* overrated; *dinero, moneda* overvalued.

sobrevalorar [1a] VT to overvalue; (*fig*) to overrate, put too high a value on.

sobrevender [2a] VT to overbook.

sobrevenir [3s] VI (*ocurrir*) to happen (unexpectedly), come up, supervene; (*resultar*) to follow, ensue.

sobrevirar [1a] VI to oversteer.

sobrevivencia NF survival.

sobreviviente = **superviviente**.

sobrevivir [3a] VI to survive; **~ a** *accidente, desastre etc* to survive; *persona* to survive, outlive; (*durar más tiempo que*) to outlast.

sobrevolar [1m] VT to fly over, overfly.

sobrevuelo NM overflying; **permiso de ~** permission to overfly.

sobriedad NF soberness; moderation, restraint; quietness; plainness.

sobrina NF niece.

sobrinanieta NF great-niece.

sobrino NM nephew.

sobrinonieto NM great-nephew.

sobrio ADJ (*templado*) sober; (*moderado*) moderate, temperate, restrained; *color* quiet; *estilo, moda etc* plain, sober; **ser ~ en la bebida** to be temperate in one's drinking habits; **ser ~ de palabras** to speak with restraint.

sobros NMPL (*CAm*) left-overs, scraps.

soca[1] NF (a) (*And*) (*de arroz*) young shoots of rice; (*de tabaco*) top leaf of tobacco plant, high quality tobacco leaf. (b) (*CAm*: embriaguez*) drunkenness.

soca[2]* NM: **hacerse el ~** to act dumb*.

socaire NM (*Náut*) lee; **al ~** to leeward; **al ~ de** (*fig*) enjoying the protection of; **using ... as an excuse**; **estar** (*o* **ponerse**) **al ~** (*fig*) to shirk, dodge the column*.

socaliña ① NF (*astucia*) craft, cunning; (*porfía*) clever persistence.
② NMF (*) twister, swindler.

socaliñar [1a] VT to get by a swindle.

socaliñero ADJ crafty, cunning; cleverly persistent.

socapa* NF dodge, subterfuge; **a ~** surreptitiously.

socapar [1a] VT: **~ uno** (*And, Méx**) to cover up for sb.

socar [1g] ① VT (*CAm*) (a) (*comprimir*) to press down, squeeze, compress.
(b) (*: *enojar*) to annoy, upset.
② VI (*CAm*) to make an effort.
③ **socarse** VR (*CAm*) (a) (*emborracharse*) to get drunk.
(b) **~ con uno** to fall out (*o* squabble) with sb.

socarrar [1a] VT to scorch, singe.

socarrón ADJ (a) (*sarcástico*) sarcastic, ironical; *humor* sly. (b) (*taimado*) crafty, cunning.

socarronería NF (a) (*sarcasmo*) sarcasm, irony; sly humour. (b) (*astucia*) craftiness, cunning.

socava NF, **socavación** NF undermining.

socavar [1a] VT (a) (*excavar*) to undermine; to dig under, dig away; (*agua*) to hollow out. (b) (*fig*) to sap, undermine.

socavón NM (a) (*Min*) gallery, tunnel; (*hueco*) hollow; (*cueva*) cavern; (*en la calle*) hole. (b) (*Arquit etc*) subsidence, sudden collapse.

soche NM (*And*) tanned sheepskin (o goatskin).

socia* NF (*Esp*) whore.

sociabilidad NF sociability, friendliness; gregariousness; conviviality.

sociable ADJ *persona* sociable, friendly; *animal* social, gregarious; *reunión etc* convivial.

sociablemente ADV sociably; gregariously; convivially.

social ⅠADJ (a) (*gen*) social. (b) **acuerdo ~, pacto ~** wages agreement; **paz ~** industrial harmony, agreement between employers and unions. (c) (*Com, Fin*) company (*atr*), company's; V **capital, razón.**

② **~es*** NMPL (*Escol*) social studies.

socialdemocracia NF social democracy.

socialdemocracia NF social democracy.

socialdemócrata NMF social democrat.

socialdemocrático ADJ social democratic.

socialismo NM socialism.

socialista Ⅰ ADJ socialist(ic).

② NMF socialist.

socialización NF socialization; nationalization.

socializar [1f] VT to socialize; to nationalize.

socialmente ADV socially.

sociata: ADJ, NMF socialist.

sociedad NF (a) (*gen*) society; **los males de la ~ actual** the ills of contemporary society; **~ benéfica** welfare state; **~ de consumo** consumer society; **~ del ocio** leisure society; **~ opulenta** affluent society; **~ permisiva** permissive society; **hacer ~** to join forces.

(b) (*asociación*) society, association; (*cuerpo*) body; **~ científica, ~ docta** learned society; **~ gastronómica** dining club; **~ inmobiliaria** building society; **S~ de Jesús** Society of Jesus; **S~ de las Naciones** League of Nations; **~ secreta** secret society; **~ de socorro mutuo** friendly society, provident society.

(c) (*Com, Fin*) company; partnership; **~ anónima** limited liability company, corporation; **~ anónima laboral** workers' cooperative; **Góngora y Quevedo S~ Anónima** (ABR SA) Góngora and Quevedo Limited (Incorporated *US*); **~ de cartera, ~ de control** holding company; **~ en comandita** limited partnership; **~ mercantil** company, trading company.

(d) (*mundo elegante*) society; **alta ~, buena ~** (high) society; **notas de ~** gossip column, column of society news; **entrar en ~, presentarse en (la) ~** to come out, make one's début.

(e) **~ conyugal** marriage partnership.

societal ADJ societal.

socio NMF (*t* **socia**) (a) (*gen*) associate; (*de club*) member; (*de sociedad docta etc*) fellow; **se ruega a los señores ~s ...** members are asked to ...; **~ honorario, ~ de honor** honorary member; **~ numerario, ~ de número** full member; **~ vitalicio** life member.

(b) (*Com, Fin*) partner; **~ activo** active partner; **~ capitalista, ~ comanditario, ~ pasivo** sleeping partner, silent partner (*US*).

(c) (*: *amigo*) buddy, mate*; (*coime*) pimp.

socio... PREF socio...

sociobiología NF sociobiology.

sociocultural ADJ sociocultural.

socioeconómico ADJ socioeconomic.

sociolingüística NF sociolinguistics.

sociolingüístico ADJ sociolinguistic.

sociología NF sociology.

sociológico ADJ sociological.

sociólogo, -a NM/F sociologist.

sociopolítico ADJ sociopolitical.

sociosanitario ADJ public health (*atr*).

soco Ⅰ ADJ (a) (*CAm: borracho*) drunk, tight*.

(b) = **zoco** 1.

② NM (a) (*And Anat, Bot*) stump.

(b) (*And: cuchillo*) short blunt machete.

(c) = **zoco** 2.

socola NF (*And, CAm*) clearing of land.

socolar [1a] VT (a) (*And, CAm*) *tierra* to clear, clear of scrub.

(b) (*And*) *trabajo etc* to bungle, do clumsily.

socollón NM (*CAm, Carib*) violent shaking.

socollonear [1a] VT (*CAm*) to shake violently.

socón: ADJ (*CAm*) studious, swotty*.

soconusco NM (a) (*chocolate*) (*Carib*) chocolate; (*CAm, Méx*) high quality chocolate. (b) (*Carib*: trato*) shady deal, dirty business.

socorrer [2a] VT *persona* to help; *necesidad* to relieve, meet, help with; *ciudad* to relieve; *expedición etc* to bring aid to.

socorrido ADJ (a) *tienda etc* well-stocked. (b) *objeto etc* handy; useful. (c) *persona* helpful, obliging, cooperative. (d) (*fig: probado*) well-tried; (*corriente*) ordinary, usual, common; *frase* well-worn.

socorrismo NM life-saving.

socorrista NMF lifeguard, life-saver.

socorro NM (a) (*ayuda*) help, aid, assistance; relief (*t Mil*); **¡~!** help!; **~s mutuos** mutual aid; **trabajos de ~** relief work, rescue work.

(b) (*Cono Sur: pago adelantado*) advance payment, sub*.

socoyote NM (*Méx*) smallest child.

Sócrates NM Socrates.

socrático ADJ Socratic.

socrocio NM (*Med*) plaster.

socucha NF, **socucho** NM (*Cono Sur, Méx*) (*cuartito*) poky little room, den; (*casucha*) hovel, slum.

soda NF (a) (*Quím*) soda. (b) (*bebida*) soda water.

sódico ADJ sodium (*atr*).

sodio NM sodium.

Sodoma NF Sodom.

sodomía NF sodomy.

sodomita NM sodomite.

sodomizar [1f] VT to sodomize.

SOE NM (*Esp*) ABR de **Seguro Obligatorio de Enfermedad.**

soez ADJ dirty, rude, obscene.

sofá NM sofa, settee.

sofá-cama NM, **sofá-nido** NM studio couch, sofa-bed.

sofero ADJ (*And*) huge, enormous.

Sofia NF, **Sofía¹** NF Sophia.

Sofía² NF (*Geog*) Sofia.

sofión NM (*bufido*) angry snort; (*reprimenda*) sharp rebuke; (*réplica*) sharp retort.

sofisma NM sophism.

sofista NM sophist; (*fig*) quibbler.

sofistería NF sophistry.

sofisticación NF sophistication; (*pey*) affectation, over-refinement.

sofisticado ADJ sophisticated; (*pey*) affected, over-refined.

sofístico ADJ sophistic(al); false, fallacious.

soflama NF (a) (*fuego*) dull glow, flicker. (b) (*sonrojo*) blush. (c) (*fig: arenga*) fiery speech, harangue. (d) (*fig**) (*engaño*) deceit; (*halagos*) cajolery, blarney. (e) (*Méx: chisme*) piece of trivia, bit of gossip.

soflamar [1a] VT (a) (*quemar*) to scorch; (*Culin*) to singe. (b) *persona* to shame, make blush. (c) (*: *engañar*) to deceive, swindle; (*halagar*) to cajole, blarney.

sofocación NF (a) (*gen*) suffocation. (b) (*fig*) = **sofoco** (b).

sofocado ADJ: **estar ~** (*fig*) to be out of breath; to feel stifled; to be hot and bothered; to be upset.

sofocante ADJ stifling, suffocating.

sofocar [1g] Ⅰ VT (a) *persona* to suffocate, stifle.

(b) *incendio* to smother, put out; *rebelión etc* to crush, put down; *epidemia* to stop.

(c) (*fig*) **~ a uno** (*hacer sonrojar*) to make sb blush; (*avergonzar*) to put sb to shame; (*azorar*) to embarrass sb; (*enojar*) to anger sb, get sb worked up, provoke sb, upset sb.

② **sofocarse** VR (a) (*ahogarse*) to suffocate, stifle; (*jadear*) to get out of breath, (begin to) pant; (*no poder respirar*) to choke.

(b) (*fig*) to blush; to feel embarrassed; to get angry, get worked up, get upset, upset o.s.; **no vale la pena de que te sofoques** it's not worth upsetting yourself about it.

(c) (*CAm, Méx: preocuparse*) to worry, be anxious.

Sófocles NM Sophocles.

sofoco NM (a) (*gen*) suffocation; stifling sensation; **~ de calor** hot flush.

(b) (*fig*) (*azoro*) embarrassment; (*ira*) anger, rage, feeling of indignation.

(c) **pasar un ~** to have an embarrassing time.

sofocón* NM shock, nasty blow; **se le dio un ~** he really blew up*, he got really worked up; **llevarse un ~** to have a sudden shock.

sofoquina* NF (a) (*calor*) stifling heat; **hace una ~** it's stifling hot. (b) = **sofocón.**

sofreír [3l; PTP **sofrito**] VT to fry lightly.

sofrenada NF (a) sudden check, sudden jerk on the reins. (b) (*) ticking-off*.

sofrenar [1a] VT (a) *caballo* to rein back sharply. (b) (*fig*) to restrain, control. (c) (*: *echar una bronca*) to tick off*.

sofrito ADJ lightly fried.

sofrología NF sleep therapy.

software ['sofwer] NM software; **~ de aplicación** application software; **~ del sistema** system software; **~ del usuario** user software.

soga NF (*gen*) rope, cord; (*de animal*) halter; (*del verdugo*) hangman's rope; **dar ~ a uno** to make fun of sb; **echar la ~ tras el caldero** to chuck it all up*, throw in one's hand; **estar con la ~ al cuello** to be in imminent danger, be in a real fix*; **hablar de (o mentar) la ~ en casa del ahorcado** to say something singularly inappropriate; **no hay que hablar de (o mentar) la ~ en casa del ahorcado** there's a time and a place for everything; **hacer ~** to lag behind.

sogatira NM tug of war.

soguear [1a] VT (a) (*And, CAm, Cono Sur: atar*) to tie with a rope; (*Carib: lazar*) to lasso. (b) (*Carib: domesticar*) to tame. (c) (*And*: burlarse*) to make fun of.

soguero ADJ (*Carib*) tame.

sois V **ser.**

soja NF soya; **semilla de ~** soya bean.

sojuzgar [1h] VT (*vencer*) to conquer; to subdue; (*tiranizar*) to rule despotically.

sol¹ NM (**a**) (*gen*) sun; (*luz solar*) sunshine, sunlight; **~ artificial** sunlamp; **~ naciente** rising sun; **~ poniente** setting sun; **como un ~** as bright as a new pin; **día de ~** sunny day; **de ~ a ~** from sunrise to sunset; **dejar algo al ~** to leave sth in the sun; **tostarse al ~** to sit in the sun, acquire a sun tan; **arrimarse al ~ que más calienta** to know which side one's bread is buttered; to climb on the bandwagon; **no dejar a uno ni a ~ ni a sombra** to chase sb all over, pester sb continually; **mirar algo a contra ~** to look at sth against the light; **hay ~, hace ~** it is sunny, the sun is shining; **salga el ~ por donde quiera** come what may; press on regardless; **tomar el ~, tumbarse al ~** to sun o.s., sunbathe, bask.
(**b**) (*Fin*) sol (*Peruvian unit of currency*).
(**c**) (*Carib**) **~ y luna** machete, cane knife.
(**d**) (*) **¡es un ~!** he's great!*, he's the greatest!*; **el niño es un ~** he's a lovely child.
(**e**) (*: *bebida*) glass of brandy and anisette.

sol² NM (*Mús*) G; **~ mayor** G major.

solada NF sediment.

solado NM tiling, tiled floor.

solamente ADV only; solely; just.

solana NF (*sitio*) sunny spot, suntrap; (*en casa*) sun-lounge, sun gallery.

solanas* ADJ INVAR alone, all on one's own.

solanera NF scorching sunshine; (*Med*) (*quemadura*) sunburn; (*insolación*) sunstroke.

solano NM east wind.

solapa NF (**a**) (*de chaqueta*) lapel; (*de bolsillo, libro, sobre*) flap. (**b**) (*fig*) pretext.

solapadamente ADV slyly, in an underhand way, by underhand means.

solapado ADJ (*furtivo*) sly, underhand, sneaky; (*evasivo*) evasive; (*secreto*) undercover.

solapamiento NM overlapping.

solapante ADJ overlapping.

solapar [1a] **1** VT (**a**) (*lit*) to overlap.
(**b**) (*fig*) to cover up, cloak, keep dark.
2 VI to overlap (**con** with).
3 solaparse VR to overlap; **se ha solapado** it has got covered up, it has got hidden underneath.

solapo NM (**a**) (*Cos*) lapel; overlap. (**b**) **a ~* = solapadamente.**

solar¹ NM (**a**) (*Arquit*) lot, piece of ground, site; **~ para edificaciones** building site.
(**b**) (*casa*) ancestral home, family seat; (*fig: familia*) family, lineage, line.
(**c**) (*CAm, Carib: corral*) patio, yard.
(**d**) (*And, Carib: tugurio*) tenement house.

solar² [1m] VT *suelo* to floor, tile; *zapato* to sole.

solar³ ADJ solar, sun (*atr*).

solariego ADJ (**a**) **casa solariega** family seat, ancestral home. (**b**) (*Hist*) *familia* ancient and noble; *derechos etc* manorial; **tierras solariegas** demesne.

solario NM sunbed; solarium.

solárium NM solarium.

solateras* ADJ INVAR alone, all on one's own.

solaz NM (*descanso*) recreation, relaxation; (*consuelo*) solace, spiritual relief.

solazar [1f] **1** VT (*divertir*) to provide relaxation for; (*consolar*) to console; (*alegrar*) to comfort, cheer.
2 solazarse VR to enjoy o.s., relax.

solazo* NM = **solanera.**

solazoso ADJ restful; recreative, relaxing; leisure (*atr*).

soldada NF pay; salary; (*Mil*) service pay.

soldadera NF (*Méx Hist*) camp-follower.

soldadesca NF (**a**) (*profesión*) military profession, military. (**b**) (*pey*) (brutal and licentious) soldiery.

soldadesco ADJ soldierly.

soldadito NM: **~ de plomo** tin soldier.

soldado¹ NMF soldier; **~ de infantería** infantryman; **~ de marina** marine; **~ de plomo** tin soldier; **~ de primera** lance-corporal; **~ raso** private; **una joven ~** a young woman soldier.

soldado² ADJ *juntura etc* welded; **totalmente ~** welded throughout.

soldador NM (**a**) (*Téc*) soldering iron. (**b**) (*persona*) welder.

soldadura NF (**a**) (*sustancia*) solder. (**b**) (*acto*) soldering, welding; **~ autógena** welding. (**c**) (*juntura*) soldered joint, welded seam.

soldar [1m] **1** VT (**a**) (*Téc*) to solder, weld.
(**b**) (*unir*) to join, unite; (*cementar*) to cement; *partes diversas* to weld together; *disputa* to patch up.
2 soldarse VR (*huesos*) to knit (together).

soleado ADJ sunny.

solear [1a] VT (*dejar al sol*) to put in the sun; (*blanquear*) to bleach.

solecismo NM solecism.

soledad NF (**a**) (*estado*) solitude; (*aislamiento*) loneliness. (**b**) (*duelo*) grieving, mourning. (**c**) (*lugar*) lonely place; **~es** wilderness.

solejar NM = **solana.**

solemne ADJ (**a**) (*serio*) solemn; (*ceremonioso*) dignified, impressive. (**b**) (*) *mentira* downright; *disparate* utter; *error* complete, terrible.

solemnemente ADV solemnly; impressively.

solemnidad NF (**a**) (*cualidad*) solemnity; impressiveness; formality, gravity, dignity.
(**b**) (*acto*) solemnity, solemn ceremony; **~es** solemnities.
(**c**) **~es** (*hum*) (bureaucratic) formalities.
(**d**) **pobre de ~*** miserably poor, penniless.

solemnización NF solemnization, celebration.

solemnizar [1f] VT to solemnize, celebrate.

solenoide NM solenoid.

▼ soler [2h; *defectivo*] VI (**a**) **~ + infin** to be in the habit of + *ger*, be accustomed to + *infin*, be wont to + *infin*; **suele pasar por aquí** he usually comes this way; **solíamos ir todos los años** we used to go every year; **como se suele** as is normal, as is customary; **¿beber? pues no suele** drink? well he doesn't usually.
(**b**) (*Cono Sur: ocurrir*) to occur rarely, happen only occasionally; *ver también* |ACOSTUMBRAR|.

solera NF (**a**) (*puntal*) prop, support; (*plinto*) plinth.
(**b**) (*de cuneta etc*) bottom.
(**c**) (*piedra de molino*) lower millstone.
(**d**) (*Méx: baldosa*) flagstone.
(**e**) (*Cono Sur: de acera*) kerb.
(**f**) (*carácter*) inherited character, collective character; traditional nature; **éste es país de ~ celta** this is a country of basically Celtic character; **es de ~ de médicos** he comes from a line of doctors; **vino de ~** sherry; older wine (for blending); **es un barrio con ~** it is a typically Spanish (*etc*) quarter, it is a quarter with lots of character.

SOLERA

*ⓘ Sherry does not have a specific vintage since it is a mixture of the vintages from different years; the solera method is used to ensure uniformity of quality. In the **bodega** (cellar) the casks are arranged in horizontal rows, with the bottom row, known as the **solera**, containing the oldest wine. When part of this is bottled, the casks are replenished with wine from the row immediately above, which in turn is refilled with wine from the next row, and so on.*

⇨ *See also* |JEREZ|

---

solería NF flooring.

soleta NF (**a**) (*Cos*) patch, darn.
(**b**) (*: *mujer*) shameless woman.
(**c**) (*) **dar ~ a uno** to chuck sb out; **tomar ~** to beat it*; **dejar a uno en ~s** (*And*) to leave sb penniless.
(**d**) (*Méx Culin*) wafer, ladyfinger.

solevantamiento NM (**a**) pushing up, raising. (**b**) (*Pol*) rising; upheaval.

solevantar [1a] VT (**a**) *objeto* to push up, raise, heave up. (**b**) (*Pol etc*) to rouse, stir up.

solfa NF (**a**) (*Mús*) solfa; (*signos*) musical notation; (*fig*) music. (**b**) (*: *paliza*) tanning*. (**c**) **poner a uno en ~*** to make sb look ridiculous, hold sb up to mockery.

solfear [1a] VT (**a**) (*Mús*) to solfa. (**b**) (*: *zurrar*) to tan*. (**c**) (*: *reprender*) to tick off*. (**d**) (*Cono Sur*: hurtar*) to nick‡, swipe‡.

solfeo NM (*Mús*) solfa, singing of scales, voice practice; **clase de ~** singing lesson. (**b**) (*: *paliza*) tanning*; ticking-off*.

solicitación NF request; solicitation; canvassing.

solicitado ADJ: **estar muy ~** to be in great demand, be much sought after.

solicitante NMF applicant; petitioner.

solicitar [1a] VT (**a**) *permiso etc* to ask for, request, seek; *aprobación* to seek; *puesto* to apply for; *apoyo* to solicit, canvass for; *votos* to canvass; **~ algo a uno** to ask sb for sth, request sth of sb.
(**b**) *atención, interés* to attract (*t Fís*).
(**c**) *persona* to pursue, chase after, try to attract; *mujer* to court; **le solicitan en todas partes** he is in great demand all over, he is much sought after, he's very popular.

solícito ADJ (*diligente*) diligent, careful; (*preocupado*) solicitous, concerned (*por* about, for); (*afectuoso*) affectionate.

solicitud NF (**a**) (*cualidad*) diligence, care; solicitude, concern; affection.
(**b**) (*acto*) request (*de* for); petition; application (*de un puesto* for a post); **a ~** on request; **~ de extradición** request for extradition; **~ de pago** (*Com*) demand note; **presentar una ~** to put in an application, make an application; **denegar** (*o* **desestimar** *etc*) **una ~** to re-

fuse a request, reject an application.

sólidamente ADV solidly.

solidariamente ADV jointly, mutually.

solidaridad NF solidarity; **por ~ con** (*Pol etc*) out of sympathy with, out of solidarity with.

solidario ADJ (a) *obligación etc* mutually binding, jointly shared, shared in common; *participación etc* joint, common; *persona* jointly liable; **responsabilidad solidaria** joint liability.

(b) **hacerse ~ de** to sympathize with, declare one's solidarity with; **hacerse ~ de una opinión** to echo an opinion.

solidarizarse [1f] VR: **~ con** to declare one's solidarity with, affirm one's support for, line up with; **me solidarizo con esa opinión** I share that view.

solideo NM (*Ecl*) calotte, skullcap.

solidez NF solidity; hardness.

solidificación NF solidification; hardening.

solidificar [1g] 1 VT to solidify, harden.

2 **solidificarse** VR to solidify, harden.

sólido 1 ADJ (a) (*gen*) solid (*t Mat, Fís*); (*duro*) hard.

(b) (*Téc etc*) solidly made; well built; *zapatos etc* stout, strong; *color* fast.

(c) (*fig*) solid, sound; firm, stable, secure; *base, moralidad, principio etc* sound.

2 NM solid.

soliloquiar [1b] VI to soliloquize, talk to oneself; to meditate aloud.

soliloquio NM soliloquy, monologue.

solimán NM corrosive sublimate; (*fig*) poison.

solio NM throne.

solipsismo NM solipsism.

solista NMF soloist.

solitaria[1] NF (*Zool*) tapeworm.

solitario 1 ADJ (a) *persona, vida* lonely, solitary; **vivir ~** to live alone.

(b) *lugar* lonely, desolate; bleak; **a tal hora la calle está solitaria** at such a time the street is deserted (*o* empty).

2 NM, **solitaria**[2] NF recluse; hermit; solitary person.

3 NM (a) (*Naipes*) patience, solitaire.

(b) (*diamante*) solitaire.

(c) **en ~** alone, on one's own; single-handed; **ir en ~** to go it alone, do something unaided; **vuelta al mundo en ~** solo (sailing) trip round the world; **tocar en ~** to play solo.

solito* ADJ: **estar ~** to be all alone, be on one's own.

sólito ADJ usual, customary.

soliviantar [1a] VT (a) (*amotinar*) to stir up, rouse (to revolt).

(b) (*enojar*) to anger; (*irritar*) to irritate, exasperate.

(c) (*inquietar*) to worry, cause anxiety to; **le tienen soliviantado los celos** he is eaten up with jealousy.

(d) (*causar anhelos a*) to fill with longing; (*dar esperanzas a*) to buoy up with false hopes; (*engreír*) to make vain, fill with conceit; **anda soliviantado con el proyecto** he has tremendous hopes for the scheme.

soliviar [1b] 1 VT to lift, push up.

2 **soliviarse** VR to half rise, partly get up; to get up on one elbow.

solla NF plaice.

sollamar [1a] VT to scorch, singe.

sollastre NM rogue, villain.

sollo NM sturgeon.

sollozar [1f] VI to sob.

sollozo NM sob; **decir algo entre ~s** to sob sth.

solo 1 ADJ (a) (*uno*) single, sole; (*único*) one; unique; **hay una sola dificultad** there is just one difficulty; **con esta sola condición** with this single condition; **su sola preocupación es ganar dinero** his one concern is to make money; **no hubo ni una sola objeción** there was not a single objection; **es ~ en su género** it is unique of its kind.

(b) (*solitario*) alone; lonely; by o.s.; **venir ~** to come alone; **pasa los días ~ en su cuarto** he spends the days alone in his room; **iré ~** I'll go alone; **estos días me siento muy ~** I feel very lonely nowadays; **dejar ~ a uno** to leave sb all alone; **tendremos que comer pan ~** we shall have to eat plain bread, we shall have to eat bread and nothing with it; **se quedó ~ a los 7 años** he was left an orphan (*o* alone in the world) at 7; **se queda ~ en contar mentiras** there's nobody to touch him when it comes to telling lies; **lo hace como él ~** he does it as no-one else can.

(c) **a solas** alone, by oneself; **lo hizo a solas** he did it (all) by himself; **volar a solas** to fly solo; **vuelo a solas** solo flight.

(d) (*Mús*) solo; **cantar ~** to sing solo.

2 NM (a) (*Mús*) solo; **un ~ para tenor** a tenor solo.

(b) (*Naipes*) patience, solitaire.

(c) (*Cono Sur: lata*) tedious conversation.

sólo ADV only, solely, merely, just; **~ quería verlo** I only (*o* just) wanted to see it; **es ~ un teniente** he's only a lieutenant, he's merely a lieutenant; **no ~ A sino también B** not only A but also B; **~**

que ... except that ...; but for the fact that ...; **ven aunque ~ sea para media hora** come even if it's just for half an hour; **con ~ que sepas tocar algunas notas** even if you only know how to play a few notes; **con ~ que estudies dos horas diarias** by studying for as little as two hours a day; **tan ~** only, just.

solomillo NM sirloin.

solomo NM sirloin; loin of pork.

solón NM (*Carib*) scorching heat, very strong sunlight.

solsticio NM solstice; **~ de estío** summer solstice; **~ de invierno** winter solstice.

soltar [1m] 1 VT (a) (*dejar ir*) to let go of; (*dejar caer*) to drop; to release; *nudo* to undo, untie; *amarra* to cast off; *hebilla etc* to undo, unfasten, loosen; *embrague* (*Aut*) to release, disengage; *freno* to release, take off; *cuerda etc* to loosen, slacken; to pay out; *cuerda trabada etc* to free; *agua* to let out, run off; *cautivo* to release, let go, set free; *animales* to let out, turn out, turn loose; to set free; *presa* to let go of; (*) *dinero* to cough up*; *puesto, privilegio etc* to give up; **¡suéltame, querido!** let go of me, dear!; **¡suélteme, señor!** unhand me, sir! (*liter*); **no quiere ~ el puesto por nada del mundo** he won't give up the job for anything.

(b) *estornudo, risa, exclamación etc* to let out; *suspiro* to fetch, heave; *blasfemia etc* to utter, come out with, let fly; *indirecta* to drop; *verdad* to let out, let slip; **¡suelta!** out with it!, spit it out!; **soltó un par de palabrotas** he came out with a couple of rude words, he let fly a couple of obscenities; **les volvió a ~ el mismo sermón** he read them the same lecture all over again.

(c) *golpe* to deal, strike, let fly.

(d) (*culebra*) *piel* to cast, slough.

(e) *dificultad* to solve; *duda* to resolve; *objeción etc* to satisfy, deal with.

(f) (*And: ceder*) to cede, give, hand over.

2 **soltarse** VR (a) (*cordón, nudo etc*) to come undone, come untied; (*costura etc*) to come unstitched; (*animal etc*) to get loose, break loose, free itself; to escape; (*Mec: pieza*) to work loose; to come off, fly off, fall off; **~ de las manos de uno** to escape from sb's clutches; **se le soltó un grito** a cry escaped him, he let out a yell; **no se vaya a ~ el perro** don't let the dog get out (*o* get loose *etc*); **~ del estómago** to have diarrhoea.

(b) (*fig: independizarse*) to achieve one's independence, win freedom.

(c) (*fig: perder el control*) to lose control (of o.s.); **~ a su gusto** to let fly, let o.s. go.

(d) (*fig: adquirir pericia etc*) to become expert, acquire real proficiency; (*en un idioma*) to become fluent.

(e) **~ a** + *infin* to begin to + *infin*.

(f) **~ con una idea absurda** to come up with a silly idea; **~ con una contribución de 50 dólares** to come up with a 50-dollar contribution; **por fin se soltó con algunos peniques** he eventually parted with a few coppers.

soltera NF single woman, unmarried woman, spinster; **apellido de ~** maiden name; **la señora de X, de ~ Z** Mrs X, née Z; Mrs X, whose maiden name was Z.

solterear [1a] VI (*Cono Sur*) to stay single.

soltería NF (*gen*) single state, unmarried state; (*de hombre*) bachelorhood, (*de mujer*) spinsterhood.

soltero 1 ADJ single, unmarried; **madre soltera** unmarried mother.

2 NM bachelor, unmarried man.

solterón NM confirmed bachelor, old bachelor.

solterona NF spinster, maiden lady; (*pey*) old maid; **tía ~** maiden aunt.

soltura NF (a) (*de cuerda etc*) looseness, slackness; (*Mec*) looseness; (*de miembros*) agility, nimbleness, ease of movement, freedom of action.

(b) (*Med: t ~ de vientre*) looseness of the bowels, diarrhoea.

(c) (*en hablar etc*) fluency, ease; **habla árabe con ~** he speaks Arabic fluently.

(d) (*pey*) shamelessness; licentiousness; dissipation.

solubilidad NF solubility.

soluble ADJ (a) (*Quím*) soluble; **~ en agua** soluble in water. (b) *problema* solvable, that can be solved.

solución NF (a) (*Quím*) solution.

(b) (*de problema etc*) solution; answer (*de* to); **~ final** final solution; **~ salomónica** compromise solution; **esto no tiene ~** there's no answer to this, there's no solution to this one.

(c) (*Teat*) dénouement.

(d) **~ de continuidad** break in continuity, interruption.

solucionar [1a] VT to solve; to resolve, settle.

solucionista NMF solver.

solvencia NF (a) (*Fin: estado*) solvency.

(b) (*Fin: acto*) settlement, payment.

(c) (*fig*) reliability; trustworthiness; (*Fin*) financial standing; **~ moral** character; **de toda ~ moral** of excellent character, completely trustworthy; **fuentes de toda ~** completely reliable sources.

(d) (*reputación*) solid reputation; (*valor*) recognized worth.

(e) (*Cono Sur: aptitud*) ability, competence; (*brillantez*) brilliance.

solventar [1a] VT **(a)** *cuenta, deuda* to settle, pay. **(b)** *dificultad* to resolve; *asunto* to settle.

solvente [1] ADJ **(a)** (*Fin*) solvent, free of debt. **(b)** (*fig*) reliable, trustworthy; *fuente etc* reliable. **(c)** (*fig*) respectable, worthy. **(d)** (*Cono Sur: hábil*) able, gifted, talented; brilliant. [2] NM (*Quím*) solvent.

solysombra* NF = **sol¹** (e).

somalí ADJ, NMF Somali.

Somalia NF Somalia; (*Hist*) Somaliland.

somanta NF beating, thrashing.

somantar [1a] VT to beat, thrash.

somatada NF (*CAm*) blow, punch.

somatar [1a] (*CAm*) [1] VT **(a)** (*zurrar*) to beat, thrash; (*pegar*) to punch. **(b)** to sell off cheap. [2] **somatarse** VR to fall and hurt o.s., knock o.s. about badly.

somatén NM **(a)** (*alarma*) alarm; **tocar a ~** to sound the alarm. **(b)** (*: *jaleo*) uproar, confusion.

somático ADJ somatic; physical.

somatizar [1f] VT **(a)** to externalize, express externally. **(b)** (*fig*) to characterize.

somatón NM (*CAm*) = **somatada**.

sombra NF **(a)** (*proyectada por objeto*) shadow; (*protección etc*) shade; (*Arte*) shaded part, shaded area, dark part; **~ de ojos** eyeshadow; **~s** shadows, darkness; **~s chinescas** shadow play, shadow pantomime; **luz y ~** light and shade; **lugar de ~** shady spot; **a la ~ de** in the shade of; (*fig*) under the protection of; thanks to the support of; (*pey*) under the cloak of; **estar a la ~** to be in the shade; (*) to be inside*; **dar ~, hacer ~** to give shade; to cast a shadow; **dar ~ a** to shade; **hacer ~ a uno** (*fig*) to put sb in the shade; **hacer ~** (*Boxeo*) to shadow box; **no quiere que otros le hagan ~** he doesn't want to be overshadowed by anybody else, he refuses to tolerate any rivals; **se ha constituido en ~ de sí mismo** he is a shadow of his former self; **quedar en la ~** (*fig*) to stay in the background, remain on the sidelines; **dirigente en la ~** shadow leader; **gobierno en la ~** shadow cabinet.

(b) **~s** (*fig*) (*oscuridad*) darkness, obscurity; (*ignorancia*) ignorance; (*pesimismo*) sombreness, pessimism.

(c) (*fantasma*) shade, ghost.

(d) (*mancha etc*) dark patch, stain; (*fig*) stain, blot; **es una ~ en su carácter** it is a stain on his character.

(e) (*fig: vestigio*) shadow; sign, trace, bit; **sin ~ de avaricia** without a trace of greed; **sin ~ de duda** without a shadow of doubt; **no se fía ni de su ~** he doesn't even trust his own shadow; **no tiene ni ~ de talento** he hasn't the least bit of talent; **tiene una ~ de parecido con su tío** he has a faint resemblance to his uncle; **ni por ~** by no means; not in the least bit.

(f) (*suerte*) luck; **tener buena ~** to be lucky; **ser de mala ~** to be unlucky.

(g) (*atractivo*) charm; (*gracia*) wit; (*talento*) talent, aptitude; **tiene mucha ~ para contar chistes** she's got a great talent for telling jokes; **tener buena ~** to be likeable, have lots of charm; **tener mala ~** to be a nasty piece of work; to have an unfortunate effect (on people *etc*); **el cuento tiene (buena) ~** it's a good story.

(h) (*CAm, Cono Sur: quitasol*) parasol, sunshade; (*CAm, Méx*) (*toldo*) awning; (*pórtico*) porch.

(i) (*CAm, Cono Sur: para escribir*) guidelines.

(j) (*Dep*) shadow-boxing.

(k) (*: *persona*) shadow, tail*.

sombraje NM, **sombrajo** NM shelter from the sun; **hacer ~s** to get in the light.

sombreado [1] ADJ shady. [2] NM (*Arte etc*) shading; hatching.

sombreador NM: **~ de ojos** eyeshadow.

sombrear [1a] VT to shade; (*Arte etc*) to shade; to hatch; (*maquillar*) to put eyeshadow on.

sombrerera NF **(a)** (*persona*) milliner. **(b)** (*caja*) hatbox. **(c)** (*And, Carib*) hatstand.

sombrerería NF **(a)** (*sombreros*) hats, millinery. **(b)** (*tienda*) hat shop; (*fábrica*) hat factory.

sombrerero NM **(a)** (*fabricante*) hatter, hatmaker. **(b)** (*And, Cono Sur*) hatstand.

sombrerete NM **(a)** (*sombrero*) little hat. **(b)** (*de hongo*) cap. **(c)** (*Téc*) bonnet; (*de cubo etc*) cap; (*de chimenea*) cowl.

sombrero NM **(a)** hat; headgear; **~ ancho, ~ jarano** (*Méx*) broad-brimmed Mexican hat; **~ apuntado** cocked hat; **~ de bola** (*Méx*), **~ hongo** bowler (hat); **~ de candil, ~ de tres picos** cocked hat, three-cornered hat; **~ de copa, ~ de pelo** (*LAm*) top hat; **~ flexible** soft hat, trilby; **~ gacho** slouch hat; **~ de jipijapa** Panama hat; **~ de paja** straw hat; **~ safari** safari hat; **~ tejano** stetson, ten-gallon hat*; **quitarse el ~ a** (*fig*) to take off one's hat to.

(b) (*Bot*) cap.

sombríamente ADV sombrely; dismally; gloomily.

sombrilla NF parasol, sunshade.

sombrío [1] ADJ **(a)** *lugar* shaded, (too much) in the shade, dark. **(b)** (*fig*) *lugar* sombre, sad, dismal; *persona* gloomy; *perspectiva etc* sombre. [2] NM (*Méx*) shady place.

someramente ADV superficially.

somero ADJ superficial; shallow.

someter [2a] [1] VT **(a)** *país* to conquer; *persona* to subject to one's will, force to yield.

(b) **~ una decisión a lo que se resuelva en una reunión** to make one's decision depend on what is resolved in a meeting; **~ su opinión a la de otros** to subordinate one's opinion to that of others.

(c) *informe etc* to present, submit (*a* to); to send in; **~ algo a la aprobación de uno** to submit sth for sb's approval; **~ un trabajo a la censura** to send a work to the censor.

(d) **~ un asunto a una autoridad** to refer a matter to an authority for decision.

(e) **~ a** *prueba etc* to put to, subject to; **~ una sustancia a la acción de un ácido** to subject a substance to the action of an acid; *V* **prueba** *etc*.

[2] **someterse** VR **(a)** (*rendirse*) to give in, yield, submit; **~ a la mayoría** to give way to the majority.

(b) **~ a una operación** to undergo an operation; **~ a un tratamiento con drogas** to have treatment with drugs.

sometico ADJ (*And*), **sometido** ADJ (*And, CAm*) = **entrometido**.

sometimiento NM **(a)** (*estado*) submission, subjection. **(b)** (*acto*) presentation, submission; reference.

somier [so'mjer] NM, PL **somiers** spring mattress.

somnambulismo NM sleepwalking, somnambulism.

somnámbulo, -a NM/F sleepwalker, somnambulist.

somnífero [1] ADJ sleep-inducing. [2] NM sleeping pill.

somnílocuo [1] ADJ given to talking in one's sleep. [2] NM, **somnílocua** NF person who talks in his (*o* her) sleep.

somnolencia NF sleepiness, drowsiness, somnolence.

somnolento, somnoliento ADJ sleepy, drowsy.

somorgujar [1a] [1] VT to duck; to plunge, dip, submerge. [2] **somorgujarse** VR to dive, plunge (*en* into).

somormujo NM grebe; **~ menor** dabchick.

somos *V* **ser**.

sompopo NM (*El Salvador*) yellow ant.

son¹ NM **(a)** (*gen*) sound; (*sonido agradable*) pleasant sound, sweet sound; **a ~ de** to the sound of; **a los ~es de la marcha nupcial** to the sounds (*o* strains) of the wedding march.

(b) (*fig: rumor*) rumour; **corre el ~ de que ...** there is a rumour going round that ...

(c) (*fig: estilo etc*) manner, style; **¿a qué ~ ...?, ¿a ~ de qué ...?** why ...?; **en ~ de** as, like, in the manner of; by the way of; **en ~ de broma** as a joke; **en ~ de guerra** in a warlike fashion; **lo dijo en ~ de riña** he said it as though he was trying to pick a quarrel; **no vienen en ~ de protesta** they're not coming in a protesting mood; **por este ~** in this way; **sin ~** for no reason at all; *V* **bailar**.

(d) (*Carib*) Cuban folk song and dance.

(e) **~ huasteca** (*Méx*) folk song from Veracruz.

son² *V* **ser**.

sonado ADJ **(a)** (*comentado*) talked-of; (*famoso*) famous; (*sensacional*) sensational; (*escandaloso*) scandalous; **un crimen muy ~** a particularly ghastly crime, a most notorious crime; **un suceso muy ~** a much talked-of event, an event which made a great stir.

(b) **hacer una (que sea) sonada** to do something really frightful; to cause a major scandal.

(c) **estar ~*** to be crazy; (*Boxeo*) to be punch-drunk.

sonaja NF little bell; (*Cono Sur*) (*Mús*) rattle, maracas; (*juguete*) rattle.

sonajera NF (*Cono Sur*), **sonajero** NM rattle.

sonambulismo NM sleepwalking.

sonámbulo, -a NM/F sleepwalker.

sonanta* NF guitar.

sonante ADJ audible; resounding; tinkling, jingling; *V* **contante**.

sonar¹ [1m] [1] VT **(a)** *moneda, timbre* to ring; *trompeta etc* to play, blow; *sirena* to blow.

(b) **~ (las narices) a un niño** to blow a child's nose.

[2] VI **(a)** (*gen*) to sound, make a noise; (*hacerse oír*) to sound out, make itself heard, be heard; (*Mús*) to play; (*timbre*) to ring; (*reloj*) to chime, strike; **han sonado las 10** it has struck 10; **le estaban sonando las tripas** his stomach was rumbling; **~ a cascado** to sound cracked; **~ a hueco** to sound hollow.

(b) (*Ling*) to be sounded, be pronounced; **la h de 'hombre' no suena** the h in 'hombre' is not pronounced (*o* is silent); **en esa región 'fue' suena casi como 'juez'** in that area 'fue' sounds (*o* is pronounced) almost like 'juez'.

(c) (*fig: parecer etc*) to sound; **esas palabras suenan extrañas** those words sound strange; **no me suena bien** it sounds all wrong to me; **no le ha sonado muy bien aquello** that did not make a good impression on him, he wasn't very well impressed with that; **me suena a camelo** (*Esp*) it sounds like a hoax to me; **se llama Anastasio, así como suena** he's called Anastasius, just like I'm telling you; **ni ~ ni tronar** not to count.

(d) (*fig: ser mencionado*) to be talked of; **es un nombre que suena** it's a name that's in the news, it's a name that people are talking about; **no quiere que suene su nombre** he doesn't want his name mentioned; **el asunto no ha sonado para nada en la reunión** the matter did not come up at all at the meeting.

(e) (*fig: ser conocido*) to sound familiar, seem familiar; **no me suena el nombre** the name doesn't ring a bell with me; **me suena ese coche** that car looks familiar.

(f) (*Cono Sur*) (*fracasar*) to come a cropper*, blow it‡; (*resentirse*) to suffer consequences, begin to feel it; (*perder*) to lose (in a game); (*ser despedido*) to lose one's job; (*morir*) to peg out‡; (*enfermar*) to suffer a mental illness.

(g) hacer ~ a uno (*Cono Sur*) to thrash sb within an inch of his life; (*derrotar*) to defeat sb.

3 sonarse VR **(a)** (*t ~ las narices*) to blow one's nose.

(b) se suena que ... it is rumoured that ...

sonar² NM sonar.

sonata NF sonata.

sonda NF **(a)** (*acto*) sounding. **(b)** (*Náut*) lead; (*Téc*) bore, drill; (*Med*) probe; **~ acústica** echo-sounder; **~ espacial** space probe.

sondaje NM (*Náut*) sounding; (*Téc*) boring, drilling; **conversaciones de ~** exploratory talks; **organismo de ~** public opinion poll, institute of public opinion.

sond(e)ar [1a] VT (*Náut*) to sound, take soundings of; (*Med*) to probe, sound; (*Téc*) to bore, bore into, drill; (*fig*) *terreno etc* to explore; *misterio* to plumb, delve into, inquire into; *intenciones, persona etc* to sound out.

sondeo NM sounding; (*Téc*) boring, drilling; (*fig*) poll, inquiry, investigation; (*Pol etc*) feeler, overture, approach; **~ de audiencia** audience research; **~ de opinión** opinion poll.

sonería NF (*de reloj*) chimes.

soneto NM sonnet.

songa NF **(a)** (*Carib: sarcasmo*) sarcasm, irony. **(b)** (*Méx: grosería*) dirty joke, vulgar remark. **(c) a la ~(~)** (*And, CAm, Cono Sur*) slyly, underhandedly.

songo [1] ADJ **(a)** (*And, Méx*: *estúpido*) stupid, thick*. **(b)** (*And, Méx*: *taimado*) sly, crafty.

[2] NM (*And*) buzz, hum.

sónico ADJ sonic, sound (*atr*).

sonidista NMF sound engineer.

sonido NM sound.

soniquete NM = **sonsonete (b)**.

sonista NMF (*Cine, TV*) sound engineer, sound recordist.

sonoboya NF sonar buoy.

sonoridad NF sonority, sonorousness.

sonorización NF **(a)** (*de local*) installation of a sound system; (*Cine*) soundtracking. **(b)** (*Ling*) voicing.

sonorizar [1f] [1] VT **(a)** *local* to fit with a sound system, install a sound system in. **(b)** (*Ling*) to voice.

[2] **sonorizarse** VR (*Ling*) to voice, become voiced.

sonoro ADJ **(a)** (*gen*) sonorous; (*ruidoso*) loud, resonant, resounding; *versos etc* sonorous; *cueva etc* echoing; *voz* rich.

(b) (*Ling*) voiced.

(c) banda sonora sound-track; **efectos ~s** sound effects.

sonotone NM hearing-aid.

sonreír [3m] [1] VI **(a)** to smile; **~ a uno** to smile at sb, beam at sb; **~ de un chiste** to smile at a joke; **~ forzadamente** to force a smile.

(b) (*fig*) **le sonríe la fortuna** fortune smiles upon him; **el porvenir le sonríe** he has a bright future.

[2] **sonreírse** VR to smile.

sonría etc V **sonreír.**

sonriente ADJ smiling.

sonrisa NF smile; **~ amarga** bitter smile, wry smile; **~ forzada** forced smile.

sonrojante ADJ embarrassing.

sonrojar [1a] [1] VT: **~ a uno** to make sb blush.

[2] **sonrojarse** VR to blush, flush (*de* at).

sonrojo NM **(a)** (*rubor*) blush. **(b)** (*dicho etc*) offensive word, naughty remark (that brings a blush).

sonrosado ADJ rosy, pink.

sonrosarse VR to turn pink.

sonsacar [1g] VT (*obtener*) to get by cunning; (*quitar*) to remove surreptitiously; *criado etc* to entice away; (*engatusar*) to wheedle, cajole; **~ a uno** to pump sb for information; **~ un secreto a uno** to worm a secret out of sb.

sonsear [1a] VI (*Cono Sur*) = **zoncear.**

sonsera NF, **sonsería** NF (*LAm*) = **zoncera** etc.

sonso ADJ (*LAm*) = **zonzo.**

sonsonete NM **(a)** (*golpecitos*) tap, tapping; (*traqueteo*) rattle; (*cencerreo*) jangling; (*ruido monótono*) monotonous din.

(b) (*voz*) monotonous delivery, singsong (voice), chant.

(c) (*copla etc*) jingle, rhyming phrase.

(d) (*tono mofador*) mocking undertone.

sonsoniche NM (*Carib*) = **sonsonete.**

sonza NF **(a)** (*Carib: astucia*) cunning, deceit. **(b)** (*Méx: sarcasmo*) sarcasm, mockery.

soñación* NF: **¡ni por ~!** not on your life!

soñado ADJ **(a)** (*gen*) dreamed-of, that one has dreamed of; **el hombre ~** one's ideal man, one's dream man; Mr Right.

(b) (*) **hemos encontrado un sitio que ni ~** we've found an absolutely perfect spot; **me va que ni ~** it suits me a treat*.

soñador [1] ADJ dreamy.

[2] NM, **soñadora** NF dreamer.

soñar [1l] VTI (*t fig*) to dream; **~ con algo** to dream of sth; **soñé contigo anoche** I dreamed about you last night; **soñaba con una lavadora** she dreamed of (one day) having a washing machine; **~ con + infin, ~ en + infin** to dream of + *ger*; **~ que ...** to dream that ...; **~ despierto** to daydream; **~ en voz alta** to talk in one's sleep; **¡ni ~lo!** not on your life!; **nunca me lo hubiera soñado** I'd never have believed it.

soñarra NF, **soñarrera** NF, **soñera** NF **(a)** (*modorra*) drowsiness, deep desire to sleep. **(b)** (*sueño*) deep sleep.

soñolencia NF = **somnolencia.**

soñolientamente ADV sleepily, drowsily.

soñoliento ADJ sleepy, drowsy, somnolent.

sopa NF **(a)** (*caldo*) soup; **~ de cebolla** onion soup; **~ de cola** (*CAm*) oxtail soup; **~ chilena** (*And*) corn and potato soup; **~ de fideos, ~ de pastas** noodle soup; **~ de letras** morass of political parties (*known by initials*); **~ de sobre** packet soup; **~ de verduras** vegetable soup; **comer o andar a, vivir a) la ~ boba** to scrounge one's meals*, live on other people; **poner a uno como ~ de Pascua*** to give sb a ticking-off*; **los encontramos hasta en la ~** they're everywhere, they're ten a penny.

(b) (*pan mojado etc*) sop; **~s de leche** bread and milk; **dar ~s con honda a uno** to be streets ahead of sb; **estar como una ~*** to be tight*; **estar hecho una ~** to be sopping wet.

(c) (*Méx: t ~ seca*) second course.

(d) (*: resaca*) hangover*; **quitar la ~ a uno** to sober sb up; **quitarse la ~** to sober up.

sopaipilla NF (*And, Cono Sur Culin*) fritter.

sopapear [1a] VT **(a)** (*golpear*) to punch, bash*; to slap; (*sacudir*) to shake violently. **(b)** (*maltratar*) to maltreat; (*insultar*) to insult.

sopapié NM (*And*) kick.

sopapina NF series of punches, bashing*.

sopapo NM punch, thump.

sopar* [1a] (*Cono Sur*) [1] VT *pan etc* to dip, dunk.

[2] VI to meddle.

sopear [1a] VT (*Cono Sur*) to dunk, dip, moisten.

sopenta: cenar a la ~ to sup very late.

sopera NF soup tureen.

sopero [1] ADJ **(a) plato ~** = **2.**

(b) (*And: curioso*) nosey*, gossipy.

[2] NM soup plate.

▼ **sopesar** [1a] VT **(a)** (*levantar*) to try the weight of, try to lift. **(b)** (*fig*) *palabras* to weigh, consider; *situación* to weigh up.

sopetón NM **(a)** (*golpe*) punch.

(b) de ~ suddenly, unexpectedly; **entrar de ~** to pop in, drop in; **entrar de ~ en un cuarto** to burst into a room, appear unexpectedly in a room.

sopimpa NF (*Carib*) series of punches; beating, bashing*.

soplacausas* NMF INVAR incompetent lawyer.

soplado [1] ADJ **(a)** (*limpio*) clean; (*pulcro*) extra smart, overdressed; (*afectado*) affected; (*engreído*) stuck-up*. **(b) estar ~*** to be tight*. **(c)** (*Cono Sur*) **ir ~** to drive very fast.

[2] NM (*Téc*) air-cooling; **~ de vidrio** glass-blowing.

soplador NM **(a)** (*t ~ de vidrio*) glass blower. **(b)** (*ventilador*) fan, ventilator. **(c)** (*fig*) troublemaker. **(d)** (*And, CAm Teat*) prompter.

soplagaitas* NMF INVAR idiot, twit*.

soplamocos NM INVAR **(a)** (*puñetazo*) punch, bash*. **(b)** (*Méx: comentario*) put-down.

soplapollas‡ NMF INVAR berk‡, prick‡.

soplar [1a] [1] VT **(a)** *polvo etc* to blow away, blow off; *superficie* to blow on; *vela* to blow out; *globo* to blow up, inflate; *vidrio* to blow; *cenizas, fuego* to blow on.

(b) (*fig: musa etc*) to inspire.

(c) ~ a uno (*respuesta*) to whisper to sb; (*ayudar a recordar*) to prompt sb, help sb along; (*CAm Teat*) to prompt; **~ a X algo**

---

referente a **Y** to tell X sth to Y's discredit.
(d) (*: *delatar*) to split on*.
(e) (‡: *birlar*) to pinch*, nick‡.
(f) (‡: *cobrar*) to charge, rush‡, sting*; **¿cuánto te soplaron?** what did they rush you?‡; **me han soplado 8 dólares** they stung me for 8 dollars*.
(g) (*) *golpe* to deal, fetch.
[2] VI **(a)** (*persona, viento*) to blow; to puff; **¡sopla!*** well I'm blowed!*
(b) (*: *delatar*) to split*, squeal‡.
(c) (‡: *beber*) to drink, booze*.
(d) (‡*: *copularse*) to screw‡*.
[3] **soplarse** VR **(a)** (*) ~ **una docena de pasteles** to wolf a dozen cakes; **se sopla un litro entero** he knocks back a whole litre*.
(b) (*: *engreírse*) to get conceited.
(c) ~ **de uno*** to split on sb*, sneak on sb*.
soplete NM **(a)** (*lit*) blowlamp, torch; ~ **oxiacetilénico** oxyacetylene burner; ~ **soldador** welding torch. **(b)** (*Cono Sur*) = **soplo** (c).
soplido NM strong puff, blast.
soplo NM **(a)** (*con la boca*) blow, puff; (*de viento*) puff, gust; (*Téc*) blast; **la semana pasó como** (o **en**) **un** ~ the week sped by, the week seemed no more than an instant.
(b) (‡) (*aviso*) tip, tip-off, secret warning; (*pronóstico*) tip; (*denuncia*) denunciation, informing; **dar el** ~ to tell tales; to split*, squeal‡; to inform; **ir con el** ~ **al director** to take one's tales to the headmaster, go and split to the head*.
(c) (*) (*chismoso*) telltale, talebearer, sneak; (*de policía etc*) informer, grass‡.
(d) ~ **cardíaco**, ~ **al corazón** heart murmur.
soplón, -ona NM/F **(a)** (*) = **soplo** (c). **(b)** (*: *policía*) (*Méx*) cop*; (*And*) member of the secret police. **(c)** (*CAm Teat*) prompter.
sopón ADJ (*Carib*) interfering.
soponcio NM queer turn, dizzy spell; (*fig*) upset.
sopor NM (*Med*) drowsiness; (*fig*) torpor, lethargy.
soporífero, soporífico [1] ADJ sleep-inducing; (*fig*) soporific. [2] NM nightcap; (*Med*) sleeping-pill, sleeping-draught.
soportable ADJ bearable.
soportal NM **(a)** (*pórtico*) porch; portico. **(b)** ~**es** arcade; colonnade.
soportante ADJ supportive.
▼ **soportar** [1a] VT **(a)** (*Arquit etc*) to bear, carry, support, hold up; *pre-*
▼ *sión etc* to resist, withstand. **(b)** (*fig: aguantar*) to stand, bear, endure, put up with.
soporte NM **(a)** (*gen*) support; (*pedestal*) base, stand, mounting; (*de repisa*) holder, bracket. **(b)** (*Her*) supporter. **(c)** (*fig*) pillar, support. **(d)** (*Inform*) medium; ~ **de entrada** input medium; ~ **físico** hardware; ~ **lógico** software; ~ **de salida** output medium.
soprano NF soprano.
soquete NM (*LAm*) sock, ankle sock.
sor NF **(a)** (*delante de nombre*) Sister; **S~ María** Sister Mary. **(b)** **una ~*** a nun.
sorber [2a] VT **(a)** (*con los labios*) to sip; to suck up; ~ **por una paja** to drink through a straw; ~ **por las narices** to sniff (in, up); (*Med*) to inhale.
(b) (*esponja*) to soak up, absorb, suck up; (*papel secante*) to dry up; (*con trapo*) to mop up.
(c) (*fig: mar*) to suck down, swallow up.
(d) (*fig*) *palabras* to drink in.
sorbete NM **(a)** sherbet; iced fruit drink, water-ice; (*CAm*) ice-cream. **(b)** (*Carib, Cono Sur: pajita*) drinking-straw. **(c)** (*Méx: sombrero*) top hat.
sorbetera NF ice-cream freezer.
sorbetería NF (*CAm*) ice-cream parlour (o shop).
sorbetón NM gulp, mouthful.
sorbito NM sip.
sorbo NM (*gen*) sip; (*trago*) gulp, swallow; (*por las narices*) sniff; **un** ~ **de té** a sip of tea; **beber a** ~**s** to sip; **tomar de un** ~ to down in one, to drink in one gulp.
sorche‡ NM, **sorchi‡** NM soldier.
sordamente ADV dully, in a muffled way.
sordera NF deafness.
sordidez NF **(a)** (*suciedad*) dirt, dirtiness, squalor. **(b)** (*tacañería*) meanness.
sórdido ADJ **(a)** (*sucio*) dirty, squalid. **(b)** *palabra etc* nasty, dirty. **(c)** (*tacaño*) mean.
sordina NF (*Mús*) mute, muffle, damper. **(b)** **a la** ~ on the quiet, surreptitiously, by stealth.
sordo [1] ADJ **(a)** *persona* deaf; ~ **como una tapia** as deaf as a post, stone deaf; **quedarse** ~ to go deaf; **a la sorda, a sordas** on the quiet, surreptitiously, by stealth; **mostrarse** ~ **a**, **permanecer** ~ **a** (*fig*) to remain deaf to; **se quedó** ~ **a sus súplicas** he was unmoved by her entreaties.
(b) *máquina etc* quiet, noiseless; *ruido* dull, muffled; *dolor* dull; (*Ling*) voiceless; *emoción, ira* suppressed, inward.
[2] NM, **sorda** NF deaf person; **hacerse el** ~ to pretend not to hear,

turn a deaf ear.
sordociego [1] ADJ blind and deaf.
[2] NM, **sordociega** NF blind and deaf person.
sordomudez NF deaf-muteness.
sordomudo [1] ADJ deaf and dumb.
[2] NM, **sordomuda** NF deaf-mute.
sorgo NM sorghum.
soriano [1] ADJ (*Esp*) of Soria.
[2] NM, **soriana** NF native (o inhabitant) of Soria; **los ~s** the people of Soria.
soriasis NF psoriasis.
Sorlinga, Sorlingen: Islas NFPL ~ Scilly Isles.
sorna NF **(a)** (*malicia*) slyness; (*sarcasmo*) sarcasm, sarcastic tone; **con** ~ slyly, mockingly, sarcastically. **(b)** (*lentitud*) slowness; (*deliberación*) (humorous) deliberation.
sornar‡ [1a] VI to kip‡, sleep.
sorocharse [1a] VR **(a)** (*And, Cono Sur*) = **asorocharse**. **(b)** (*Cono Sur: ponerse colorado*) to blush.
soroche NM **(a)** (*LAm Med*) mountain sickness, altitude sickness. **(b)** (*Cono Sur: rubor*) blush(ing). **(c)** (*And, Cono Sur Min*) galena, natural lead sulphide.
sorprendente ADJ surprising; amazing; startling; **no es** ~ **que ...** it is hardly surprising that ..., it is small wonder that ...
▼ **sorprender** [2a] [1] VT **(a)** (*gen*) to surprise; (*asombrar*) to amaze; (*sobresaltar*) to startle.
(b) (*Mil etc*) to surprise; (*coger desprevenido*) to catch unawares, take by surprise; *conversación* to overhear; *secreto* to find out, discover; *escondrijo* to come across; ~ **a uno en el hecho** to catch sb in the act.
[2] VI: **sorprende observar cómo lo hace** it's surprising to see how he does it; **sorprende la delicadeza de su verso** the delicacy of her poetry is surprising.
[3] **sorprenderse** VR to be surprised (*de* at), be amazed (*de* at); **no me sorprendería de que fuera así** I shouldn't be surprised if it were like that; **se sorprendió mucho** he was very surprised.
sorprendido ADJ surprised.
sorpresa [1] NF **(a)** (*emoción*) surprise; amazement; **causar** ~ **a**, **producir** ~ **a** to surprise; **con gran** ~ **mía, para mi** ~ much to my surprise, to my great surprise.
(b) (*acto*) surprise; **¡qué** ~**!, ¡vaya** ~**!** what a surprise!; **coger a uno de** ~ to take sb by surprise, come as a surprise to sb.
(c) (*regalo*) surprise.
(d) (*Mil*) surprise attack; **coger por** ~ to surprise.
[2] ATR surprise (*atr*); **ataque** ~ surprise attack; **inspección** ~ spot check; **regalo** ~ mystery present; **resultado** ~ surprise result, unexpected result; **sobre** ~ mystery envelope; **visita** ~ unannounced visit.
sorpresivamente ADV surprisingly; suddenly, unexpectedly, without warning.
sorpresivo ADJ (*sorprendente*) surprising; (*repentino*) sudden, (*imprevisto*) unexpected.
sorrajar [1a] VT (*Méx*) (*golpear*) to hit; (*herir*) to wound.
sorrasear [1a] VT (*Méx*) to part-roast (o grill).
sorrongar [1h] VI (*And*) to grumble.
sorrostrigar [1h] VT (*And*) to pester, annoy.
sortario ADJ (*Carib*) lucky, fortunate.
sortear [1a] [1] VT **(a)** (*gen*) to draw lots for, decide by lot; to draw out of a hat; (*rifar*) to raffle (for charity); (*Dep etc*) *lados* to toss up for.
(b) *obstáculo* to dodge, avoid; to get round; to manage to miss, swerve past; **el torero sorteó al toro** the bullfighter eluded the bull; **el esquiador sorteó muy bien las banderas** the skier swerved round the flags skilfully; **aquí hay que** ~ **el tráfico** one has to dodge the traffic here.
(c) (*fig*) *dificultad* to avoid; to get round, overcome; *pregunta* to handle, deal with (skilfully).
[2] VI to draw lots; (*con moneda*) to toss, toss up.
sorteo NM **(a)** (*lotería etc*) draw, drawing lots; (*rifa*) raffle; (*Dep*) toss; **ganar el** ~ to win the toss; **esto se realizará mediante** ~ this shall be determined by lot; **ver también** LOTERÍA PRIMITIVA, LOTERÍA NACIONAL
(b) (*el evitar*) dodging, avoidance; swerving.
sortija NF **(a)** (*anillo*) ring; ~ **de compromiso**, ~ **de pedida** engagement ring; ~ **de sello** signet ring. **(b)** (*bucle*) curl, ringlet.
sortilegio NM **(a)** (*brujería*) sorcery; (*adivinación*) fortunetelling; (*vaticinio*) magical prediction. **(b)** (*un* ~) spell, charm (*t fig*).
sos (*Argentina*) = **sois**; *V* **ser**.
sosa NF soda; ~ **cáustica** caustic soda.
sosaina* [1] ADJ dull. [2] NMF dull person.
sosco NM (*And*) bit, piece.
sosegadamente ADV quietly, calmly, peacefully; gently.
sosegado ADJ **(a)** (*tranquilo*) quiet, calm, peaceful; (*apacible*) gentle. **(b)** *persona* calm, sedate, steady.

sosegar [1h y 1k] **1** VT (*calmar*) to calm, quieten; (*arrullar*) to lull; *ánimos etc* to reassure; *dudas, temores* to allay.
2 VI to rest.
3 **sosegarse** VR to calm down, become calm; to quieten down.
soseras* ADJ = **soso** (b).
sosería NF (a) (*insipidez*) insipidity. (b) (*fig*) dullness; flatness, colourlessness. (c) **es una ~** it's boring, it's terribly dull*.
sosia NMF double, lookalike.
sosiego NM (a) (*de lugar, ambiente etc*) calm(ness), quiet(ness); peacefulness. (b) (*de persona*) calmness, sedateness, steadiness, composure; **hacer algo con ~** to do sth calmly.
soslayar [1a] VT (a) (*ladear*) to put across, put sideways, place obliquely. (b) (*fig*) *dificultad* to get round; *pregunta* to dodge, sidestep; *encuentro* to avoid.
soslayo: al ~, de ~ ADV obliquely, sideways, aslant; **mirada de ~** sidelong glance; **mirar de ~** to look out of the corner of one's eye (at); (*fig*) to look askance (at), look down one's nose (at).
soso ADJ (a) (*Culin*) (*insípido*) tasteless, insipid; (*sin sal*) unsalted; (*sin azúcar*) unsweetened. (b) (*fig*) dull, uninteresting, flat, colourless.
sospecha NF suspicion.
sospechar [1a] **1** VT to suspect.
2 VI: **~ de** to suspect, be suspicious of, have one's suspicions about.
sospechosamente ADV suspiciously.
sospechoso **1** ADJ suspicious; suspect; suspected; **todos son ~s** everybody is under suspicion; **es ~ de desafecto al régimen** he is suspected of being hostile to the régime, it is suspected that he is hostile to the régime; **tiene amistades sospechosas** some of his acquaintances are suspect.
2 NM, **sospechosa** NF suspect.
sosquín NM (*Carib*) (a) (*ángulo*) wide corner, obtuse angle. (b) (*golpe*) backhander, unexpected blow.
sosquinar [1a] VT (*Carib*) to hit (*o wound etc*) unexpectedly.
sostén NM (a) (*Arquit etc*) support, prop; stand; pillar, post.
(b) (*prenda*) brassière, bra.
(c) (*alimento*) sustenance, food, nourishment.
(d) (*fig*) support, pillar, mainstay; **el principal ~ del gobierno** the mainstay of the government; **el único ~ de su familia** the sole support of his family.
sostener [2l] **1** VT (a) (*Arquit etc*) to hold up, support; to prop up; *carga* to carry; *peso* to bear; (*persona*) to hold up, hold on to; **¡sostén!** hold this!; **los dos sosteníamos la cuerda** we were both holding the rope; **la cinta le sostiene el pelo** the ribbon keeps her hair in place.
(b) (*fig*) *persona* to support, back; (*ayudar*) to help; (*defender*) to defend; **su partido le sostiene en el poder** his party keeps him in power; **esta manifestación de apoyo sirve para ~me** this demonstration of support strengthens my resolve; **le sostienen los nervios** his nerves keep him going.
(c) (*con alimentos*) to sustain, keep going.
(d) (*Mús*) *nota* to hold.
(e) (*fig*) *acusación etc* to maintain; *opinión* to stand by, stick to, uphold; *promesa* to stand by; *proposición, teoría* to maintain; *presión* to keep up, sustain; *resistencia* to strengthen, boost, bolster up; **sostenella y no emendalla** firm defence of a decision (*etc*).
(f) (*fig*) *lucha, posición, velocidad etc* to keep up, maintain.
(g) (*Fin*) to maintain, pay for; *gastos* to meet, defray.
(h) **~ la mirada de uno** to stare sb out; to look sb in the eye without flinching.
2 **sostenerse** VR (a) (*lit*) to hold o.s. up, support o.s.; (*mantenerse en pie*) to stand up; **apenas podía ~ de puro cansado** he was so utterly tired he could hardly stand.
(b) (*fig*) (*ganarse la vida*) to support o.s.; (*continuar*) to keep (o.s.) going; (*resistir*) to last out; **~ en el poder** to stay in power; **~ vendiendo corbatas** to support o.s. by selling ties.
(c) (*fig: continuar*) to continue, remain; **el mercado se sostiene firme** the market remains firm, the market continues steady; **se sostiene el régimen lluvioso** rainy conditions prevail.
sostenible ADJ sustainable.
sostenidamente ADV steadily, continuously.
sostenido **1** ADJ (a) (*continuo*) steady, continuous; *esfuerzo* sustained; (*prolongado*) prolonged. (b) (*Mús*) sharp.
2 NM (*Mús*) sharp.
sostenimiento NM (a) (*mantenimiento*) support; holding up; maintenance; upholding; strengthening; bolstering. (b) (*Fin*) maintenance; (*alimentos*) sustenance.
sota¹ NF (a) (*Naipes*) jack, knave; **de ~, caballo y rey** first-rate, top-class. (b) (*) (*descarada*) hussy, brazen woman; (*puta*) whore.
sota² NM (*Cono Sur**) overseer, foreman.
sotabanco NM (a) (*desván*) attic, garret. (b) (*Cono Sur: cuartucho*) poky little room.
sotabarba NF double chin, jowl.
sotacura NM (*And, Cono Sur*) curate.
sotana NF (a) (*Ecl*) cassock, soutane. (b) (*: *paliza*) hiding*.

sotanear* [1a] VT to tick off*.
sótano NM (*de casa*) basement; (*bodega*) cellar; (*de banco etc*) vault.
Sotavento: Islas NFPL **de ~** Leeward Isles.
sotavento NM lee, leeward; **a ~** to leeward; **de ~** leeward (*atr*).
sotechado NM shed.
soterradamente ADV in an underhand way.
soterrado ADJ (*fig*) buried, hidden.
soterramiento NM excavation; **obras de ~** excavations, underground works.
soterrar [1j] VT to bury; (*fig*) to bury, hide away.
soto NM (a) (*matorral*) thicket; (*arboleda*) grove, copse. (b) (*And*) (*en la piel*) rough lump, bump; (*nudo*) knot.
sotobosque NM undergrowth.
sotreta NF (*And, Cono Sur*) (a) (*caballo*) horse; (*brioso*) frisky horse; (*viejo*) useless old nag. (b) (*persona*) loafer, idler; bum (*US*).
soturno ADJ taciturn, silent; unsociable.
soufflé [su'fle] NM (*Culin*) soufflé.
soul ADJ INVAR, NM (*Mús*) soul.
souvenir [suße'nir] NM, PL **souvenirs** souvenir.
soviet [so'ßie] NM, PL **soviets** [so'ßie] soviet.
soviético **1** ADJ Soviet (*atr*).
2 NM: **los ~s** the Soviets, the Russians.
soy V ser.
soya NF (*LAm*) soya bean.
S.P. NM (a) (*Rel*) ABR de **Santo Padre** Holy Father. (b) (*Esp Aut*) ABR de **Servicio Público**. (c) (*Admin*) ABR de **Servicio Postal**.
spaghetti(s) NMPL, **spaguetti(s)** NMPL [espa'ɤeti] spaghetti.
spárring [es'parin] NM sparring partner.
speed [es'pið] NM (*droga*) speed.
spi* [es'pi] NM spinnaker.
spleen [es'plin] NM = **esplín**.
SPM NM ABR de **síndrome premenstrual** premenstrual tension, PMT.
sponsor [espon'sor] NM, PL **sponsors** [espon'sor] sponsor.
sport [es'por] **1** NM sport; **camiseta ~** sleeveless vest; **chaqueta (de) ~** sports coat; **vestido de ~** wearing sports clothes; (*fig*) casually dressed; **hacer algo por ~** to do sth (just) for fun.
2 **de ~** ADV (*con aplomo*) casually, nonchalantly; (*alegremente*) merrily; (*en broma*) for fun, as a joke; just for laughs.
spot [es'pot] NM, PL **spots** [es'pot] (a) (*TV*) slot, space; **~ electoral** party political broadcast; **~ publicitario** commercial, ad*. (b) (*Cono Sur Elec*) spotlight.
spray [es'prai] NM, PL **sprays** [es'prai] spray, aerosol.
sprint [es'prin] NM, PL **sprints** [es'prin] (a) (*Dep*) sprint; (*fig*) sprint, sudden dash; burst of speed; **tengo que hacer un ~** I must dash, I must get a move on. (b) (*fig: t ~ final*) final dash, last-minute rush.
sprintar [esprin'tar] [1a] VI to sprint.
sprínter [es'printer] NMF sprinter.
squash [es'kwas] NM squash.
Sr. ABR de **Señor** Mister, Mr; ver también DON, DOÑA.
Sra. ABR de **Señora** Mistress, Mrs; ver también DON, DOÑA.
S.R.C. ABR de **se ruega contestación** please reply, RSVP.
Sres., Srs. ABR de **Señores** Messieurs, Messrs.
Sria., Srio. ABR de **Secretaria, Secretario** secretary, sec.
Sri Lanka NM Sri Lanka.
Srta. ABR de **Señorita** Miss; ver también DON, DOÑA.
SS ABR de **Santos, Santas** Saints, SS.
S.S. (a) (*Rel*) ABR de **Su Santidad** His Holiness, H.H. (b) NF ABR de **Seguridad Social** ≃ Social Security. (c) ABR de **Su Señoría** His Lordship, Her Ladyship.
ss. ABR de **siguientes** following, foll.
s.s. ABR de **seguro servidor** courtesy formula.
SSE ABR de **sudsudeste** south-south-east, SSE.
SSI NM ABR de **Servicio Social Internacional** International Social Service, ISS.
SS.MM. ABR de **Sus Majestades** their Royal Highnesses.
SSO ABR de **sudsudoeste** south-south-west, SSW.
s.s.s. ABR de **su seguro servidor** courtesy formula.
SSS NM ABR de **servicio social sustitutorio**.
Sta. ABR de **Santa** Saint, St.
staccato [esta'kato] ADV, ADJ INVAR staccato.
staff [es'taf] NM, PL **staffs** [es'taf] (a) (*equipo*) (*Mil*) staff, command; (*Pol*) ministerial team. (b) (*individuo*) top executive. (c) (*Cine, Mús*) credits, credit titles.
stage [es'teiʒ] NM period, phase.
stagflación [estagfla'θjon] NF stagflation.
Stalin [es'talin] NM Stalin.
stand [es'tan] NM, PL **stands** [es'tan] stand.
standar(d) [es'tandar] ADJ y NM etc V **estándar** etc.
standing [es'tandin] NM standing; rank, category; **de alto ~** high-class, high-ranking; *piso etc* luxury, top quality.
stárter [es'tarter] NM (a) (*Aut: aire*) choke; (*LAm: arranque*) starting-motor; ignition. (b) (*LAm Dep*) starter; (*puerta*) starting-gate.

statu quo [es'tatu kwo] NM status quo.
status [es'tatus] NM INVAR status.
Sto. ABR de **Santo** Saint, St.
stock [es'tok] NM, PL **stocks** [es'tok] (Com) stock, supply.
stop [es'top] NM (Aut) stop sign, halt sign.
store [es'tor] NM sunblind, awning.
stress [es'tres] NM stress.
strip-tease [es'triptis] NM striptease.
su ADJ POS (a) (sing) (de él) his; (de ella) her; (de objeto) its; (impersonal) one's; (de Vd) your. (b) (PL) (de ellos, de ellas) their; (de Vds) your.
suampo NM (CAm) swamp.
suato* ADJ (Méx) silly.
suave [1] ADJ (a) superficie smooth, even; piel, pasta etc smooth.
(b) color, curva, movimiento, reprimenda, viento etc gentle; aire soft, mild, sweet; clima mild; trabajo easy; operación mecánica smooth, easy; música, voz soft, sweet, mellow; ruido soft, gentle, quiet; olor sweet; sabor smooth, mild; droga soft; **~ como el terciopelo** (fig) smooth as silk.
(c) persona, carácter gentle; meek, docile; **estuvo muy ~ conmigo** he was very sweet to me, he was very helpful to me, he behaved very nicely to me.
(d) (Cono Sur, Méx) (enorme) vast, huge; (destacado) outstanding.
(e) (Méx) (atractivo) good-looking, fanciable*; (estupendo) great*, fabulous*; **¡~! great idea*!, right on*!** (US*), you bet!
(f) **dar la ~** (LAm) to flatter.
[2] ADV (a) (LAm) sonar etc softly, quietly.
(b) (Méx) **toca ~** she plays beautifully.
suavemente ADV smoothly; gently; softly, sweetly.
suavidad NF smoothness, evenness; gentleness; softness, mildness; sweetness.
suavización NF (a) smoothing; softening. (b) softening, tempering; relaxation.
suavizador NM razor strop.
suavizante NM (para ropa) (fabric) softener; (para el pelo) conditioner.
suavizar [1f] VT (a) (alisar) to smooth (out, down); (ablandar) to soften; pasta etc to make smoother; navaja to strop; cuesta etc to ease, make more gentle; color to tone down; tono to soften.
(b) persona to mollify, soften, make gentler; carácter to mellow; severidad to soften, temper; medida to relax.
sub... PREF sub..., under...; **subprivilegiado** underprivileged, **subvalorar** to undervalue; **la selección española ~-21** the Spanish under-21 team.
suba NF (CAm, Cono Sur) rise (in prices).
subacuático ADJ underwater.
subalimentación NF underfeeding, undernourishment.
subalimentado ADJ underfed, undernourished.
subalpino ADJ subalpine.
subalquilar [1a] VT to sublet.
subalterno [1] ADJ importancia etc secondary; personal etc minor, auxiliary.
[2] NM, **subalterna** NF (a) subordinate. (b) (Taur) assistant bull-fighter.
subarbustivo ADJ shrubby.
subarrendador(a) NM/F subtenant.
subarrendar [1k] VT to sublet, sublease.
subarrendatario, -a NM/F subtenant.
subarriendo NM subtenancy, sublease.
subártico ADJ subarctic.
subasta NF (a) (venta) auction, sale by auction; **~ a la baja** Dutch auction; **poner en** (o **sacar a**) **pública ~** to put up for auction, sell at auction.
(b) (Com: oferta de obras) tender.
(c) (Naipes) auction.
subastador(a)¹ NM/F auctioneer.
subastadora² NF (casa) auction-house.
subastar [1a] VT to auction, auction off, sell at auction.
subatómico ADJ subatomic.
subcampeón, -ona NM/F runner-up.
subcampeonato NM runner-up position, second place.
subcomisario, -a NM/F deputy superintendent.
subcomisión NF subcommittee.
subcomité NM subcommittee.
subconjunto NM (Inform) subset; (Pol) subcommittee; (Zool) subspecies.
subconsciencia NF subconscious.
subconsciente [1] ADJ subconscious.
[2] NM: **el ~** the subconscious; **~ colectivo** collective subconscious; **en el ~** in the subconscious.
subconscientemente ADV subconsciously.
subcontinente NM subcontinent.
subcontrata NF subcontract.
subcontratación NF subcontracting.

subcontratar [1a] VT (Com) to subcontract.
subcontratista NMF subcontractor.
subcontrato NM subcontract.
subcultura NF subculture.
subcutáneo ADJ subcutaneous.
subdesarrollado ADJ underdeveloped.
subdesarrollo NM underdevelopment.
subdirección NF section, subdepartment.
subdirector(a) NM/F subdirector, assistant manager, deputy manager; **~ de biblioteca** sub-librarian, under-librarian.
subdirectorio NM subdirectory.
súbdito, -a ADJ, NM/F (Pol) subject.
subdividir [3a] [1] VT to subdivide.
[2] **subdividirse** VR to subdivide.
subdivisión NF subdivision.
sube NM (LAm): **~ y baja** see-saw; **dar un ~ a uno** to give sb a hard time.
subempleado ADJ underemployed.
subempleo NM underemployment.
subespecie NF subspecies.
subestación NF substation.
subestimación NF underestimation; undervaluation; understatement.
subestimar [1a] VT capacidad, enemigo etc to underestimate, underrate; objeto, propiedad to undervalue; argumento to understate.
subexponer [2q] VT (Foto) to underexpose.
subexposición NF under-exposure.
subexpuesto ADJ under-exposed.
subfusil NM automatic rifle.
subgénero NM (Liter) minor genre; (Zool) subspecies.
subgerente NMF assistant director.
subgrupo NM subgroup; (Pol) splinter group.
subibaja NM seesaw.
subida NF (a) (de montaña etc) climb, climbing; ascent; **una ~ en globo** a balloon ascent; **en la ~ había muchas flores** there were a lot of flowers on the way up; **es una ~ difícil** it's a tough climb.
(b) (de cantidad, precio etc) rise, increase (de in); raising; (en escalafón) promotion (a to); **~ salarial** wage increase; **esto va de ~** this is increasing, this is on the increase; **el calor va de ~** it's getting hotter.
(c) (cuesta) slope, hill; (en nombres de calles) rise, hill.
subido ADJ (a) precio etc high. (b) color bright, strong, intense; high; olor strong; V **color**. (c) persona vain, proud.
subienda NF (And) shoal.
subilla NF awl.
subíndice NM (Inform) subscript.
subinquilino, -a NM/F subtenant.
subir [3a] [1] VT (a) objeto to raise, lift up; to put up; to take up, get up; cabeza etc to raise; **que me suban los equipajes** please see that my luggage is brought up (o taken up); **lo subieron a la repisa** they put it up on the rack.
(b) calle, cuesta etc to go up; escalera to climb, mount, ascend.
(c) persona to promote (a to).
(d) (Arquit) to build, raise, put up; **~ una pared** to build a wall.
(e) precio, sueldo etc to raise, put up, increase; artículo en venta to put up the price of.
(f) (Mús) to raise the pitch of.
[2] VI (a) (gen) to go up, come up; to move up; to climb; (a caballo etc) to get on, mount; (a vehículo) to get in, get on; **le subieron los colores a la cara** she blushed; **el vino me sube a la cabeza** wine goes to my head; **~ a caballo** to mount, get on one's horse; **~ al tren** get on to the train; **seguíamos subiendo** we went on climbing; **bajar es peor que ~** coming down is worse than going up; **¡sube pronto!** come up quickly!
(b) (marea, mercurio, muro, río etc) to rise.
(c) **~ a** (Fin) to amount to.
(d) (persona: fig) to be promoted (a to), rise, move up.
(e) (precio, valor etc) to rise, increase, go up; (epidemia etc) to spread; (fiebre etc) to get worse; **sigue subiendo la bolsa** the market is still rising.
[3] **subirse** VR (a) (a un árbol etc) to get up, climb (a on to); to go up, rise; **~ al tren** to get on the train; **el niño se le subió a las rodillas** the child climbed on to her knees; **se me sube el vino a la cabeza** wine goes to my head; V **tono** etc.
(b) (fig) (engreírse) to get conceited; (descararse) to become bolder; (portarse mal) to forget one's manners.
(c) (Bot) to run to seed.
súbitamente ADV suddenly; unexpectedly.
súbito [1] ADJ (a) (repentino) sudden; (imprevisto) unexpected. (b) (*: precipitado) hasty, rash. (c) (*: irritable) irritable.
[2] ADV (t **de ~**) suddenly; unexpectedly.
subjefatura NF local (police) headquarters.
subjetivamente ADV subjectively.

subjetivar [1a] VT, **subjetivizar** [1f] VT to subjectivize, perceive in subjective terms.
subjetividad NF subjectivity.
subjetivismo NM subjectivism.

┌─── *SUBIR* ─────────────────── *ver también la entrada* ───┐

De vehículos

• *Subir(se) a* un vehículo privado o a un taxi se traduce por *get in(to)*, mientras que *subir a* un vehículo público (tren, autobús, avión, *etc*), se traduce por *get on(to)*:
   Fui la primera en subir al coche
   I was the first to get in(to) the car
   Se despidió de nosotros y subió al autobús
   She said goodbye to us and got on(to) the bus
• Debe emplearse *get on* cuando nos referimos a bicicletas, motos y animales de montura:
   Se subió a la moto
   She got on the motorbike

Otros verbos de movimiento

• *Subir la cuesta/la escalera etc*, por regla general, se suele traducir por *to come up* o por *to go up*, según la dirección del movimiento (hacia o en sentido contrario al hablante), pero *come* y *go* se pueden reemplazar por otros verbos de movimiento si la oración española especifica la forma en que se sube mediante el uso de adverbios o construcciones adverbiales:
   Tim subió las escaleras a gatas
   Tim crept up the stairs
   El mes pasado los precios subieron vertiginosamente
   Prices shot up last month
   Para otros usos y ejemplos ver la entrada.

└───┘

subjetivo ADJ subjective.
subjuntivo ⊡ ADJ subjunctive.
⊡ NM subjunctive (mood).
sublevación NF revolt, rising; (*Mil*) mutiny; (*de cárcel*) riot.
sublevar [1a] ⊡ VT (a) (*amotinar*) to rouse to revolt, stir up a revolt among.
(b) (*fig*) to upset, put out, irritate; to rouse to fury.
⊡ **sublevarse** VR to revolt, rise, rebel.
sublimación NF sublimation.
sublimado NM (*Quím*) sublimate.
sublimar [1a] VT (a) *persona* to exalt, praise. (b) *deseos etc* to sublimate. (c) (*Quím*) to sublimate.
sublime ADJ (a) sublime; (*elevado*) noble, lofty, grand; **lo ~** the sublime. (b) (*liter*) high, tall, lofty.
sublimemente ADV sublimely.
sublimidad NF sublimity.
subliminal ADJ, **subliminar** ADJ subliminal.
subliteratura NF third-rate literature, pulp writing.
submarinismo NM underwater exploration, diving; (*pesca*) underwater fishing.
submarinista ⊡ ADJ: **exploración ~** underwater exploration.
⊡ NMF underwater fisherman, underwater diver (*o explorer etc*); frogman.
submarino ⊡ ADJ underwater, submarine; **pesca submarina** underwater fishing.
⊡ NM (a) (*Náut*) submarine. (b) (*Pol etc*) infiltrator; undercover man.
submundo NM underworld.
subnormal ⊡ ADJ subnormal.
⊡ NMF subnormal person.
subnormalidad NF subnormality, mental handicap.
suboficial NMF non-commissioned officer.
subordinación NF subordination.
subordinado ⊡ ADJ subordinate; **X queda ~ a Y** X is subordinate to Y.
⊡ NM, **subordinada** NF subordinate.
subordinar [1a] ⊡ VT to subordinate.
⊡ **subordinarse** VR: **~se a** to subordinate o.s. to.
subpárrafo NM subparagraph.
subproducto NM by-product; spin-off.
subprograma NM subprogramme.
subrayable ADJ worth emphasizing; **el punto más ~** the point which should particularly be noted, the most important point.
subrayado ⊡ ADJ underlined; (*en bastardilla*) italicized, in italics.
⊡ NM underlining; italics; **el ~ es mío** my italics, the italics are mine.
subrayar [1a] VT (a) to underline; (*poner en bastardilla*) to italicize, put in italics. (b) (*fig*) to underline, emphasize.
subrepticiamente ADV surreptitiously.
subrepticio ADJ surreptitious.
subrogación NF substitution, replacement.

subrogante (*Cono Sur*) ADJ, NMF substitute.
subrogar [1h] VT to substitute (for), replace (with).
subrutina NF subroutine.
subsahariano ADJ sub-Saharan.
subsanable ADJ (*perdonable*) excusable; (*reparable*) repairable; **un error fácilmente ~** an error which is easily rectified; **un obstáculo difícilmente ~** an obstacle which is hard to overcome.
subsanar [1a] VT *falta* to overlook, excuse; *daño, defecto* to repair, make good; *error* to rectify, put right; *deficiencia* to make up for; *dificultad, obstáculo* to get round, overcome.
subscr... PREF = **suscr...**
subsecretaría NF undersecretaryship.
subsecretario, -a NM/F undersecretary.
subsector NM subsection, subsector.
subsecuente ADJ subsequent.
subsede NF (*Dep*) secondary venue.
subsidiar [1b] VT to subsidize.
subsidiariedad NF subordination, subsidiary nature; complementary nature.
subsidiario ADJ subsidiary; complementary.
subsidio NM (a) (*subvención*) subsidy, grant; (*ayuda*) aid, financial help; benefit; **~ de desempleo**, **~ de paro** unemployment benefit; **~ de enfermedad** sick benefit, sick-pay; **~ de exportación** export subsidy; **~ familiar** family allowance; **~ de huelga** strike pay; **~ de natalidad** maternity benefit; **~ de vejez** old-age pension.
(b) (*And: inquietud*) anxiety, worry.
subsiguiente ADJ subsequent.
subsistema NM subsystem.
subsistencia NF subsistence; sustenance; **salario de ~** subsistence wage.
subsistente ADJ lasting, enduring; surviving; **una costumbre aún ~** a still surviving custom.
subsistir [3a] VI (a) (*malvivir*) to subsist, live (*con, de* on); (*perdurar*) to survive, last out, endure; **todavía subsiste el edificio** the building still stands; **es una creencia que subsiste** it is a belief which still exists; **sin ayuda económica no podrá ~ el colegio** the college will not be able to survive without financial aid.
(b) (*And: vivir juntos*) to live together.
subsónico ADJ subsonic.
subsótano NM basement.
subst... PREF = **sust...**
subsuelo NM subsoil.
subsumir [3a] VT to subsume.
subte* NM (*Cono Sur*) tube, underground.
subteniente, -enta NM/F sub-lieutenant, second lieutenant.
subterfugio NM subterfuge.
subterráneo ⊡ ADJ underground, subterranean.
⊡ NM (a) (*túnel*) underground passage; (*almacén*) underground store (*o cellar etc*).
(b) (*LAm Ferro*) underground, subway (*US*).
subtexto NM subtext.
subtitulado NM subtitling.
subtitular [1a] VT to subtitle.
subtítulo NM subtitle (*t Cine*), subheading.
subtotal NM subtotal.
subtropical ADJ subtropical.
suburbano ⊡ ADJ suburban.
⊡ NM suburban train.
suburbial ADJ suburban; (*pey*) slum (*atr*).
suburbio NM (a) (*afueras*) suburb, outlying area. (b) (*barrio bajo*) slum quarter; (*chabolas*) shantytown.
subutilizado ADJ under-used, under-utilized.
subvaloración NF undervaluing.
subvalorar [1a] VT to undervalue, to underrate; (*por anticipado*) to underestimate.
subvención NF subsidy, subvention, grant; **~ estatal** state subsidy; **subvenciones agrícolas** agricultural subsidies.
subvencionar [1a] VT to subsidize, aid.
subvenir [3s] VI: **~ a** *gastos* to meet, defray; *necesidades etc* to provide for; **con eso subviene a sus vicios** with that he pays for his vices; **así subviene a la escasez de su sueldo** in that way he makes up for his low salary.
subversión NF (a) (*gen*) subversion.
(b) (*una ~*) revolution; **la ~ del orden establecido** the overthrow of the established order.
subversivo ADJ subversive.
subvertir [3i] VT (*minar*) to subvert; (*derrocar*) to overthrow, undermine; (*perturbar*) to disturb.
subyacente ADJ underlying.
subyacer [2x] VI: **~ a o en** to underlie.
subyugación NF subjugation.
subyugador ADJ, **subyugante** ADJ dominating; (*fig*) captivating, en-

chanting.

subyugar [1h] VT **(a)** *país etc* to subjugate, subdue; *enemigo* to overpower; *voluntad etc* to dominate, gain control over. **(b)** *(fig)* to captivate, charm.

succión NF suction.

succionar [1a] VT *(sorber)* to suck; to apply suction to; *(Téc)* to absorb, soak up, suck up.

sucedáneo ☐1 ADJ substitute, ersatz.
☐2 NM substitute (food).

suceder [2a] ☐1 VTI **(a)** *(pasar)* to happen; **pues sucede que no vamos** well it happens we're not going; **no le había sucedido eso nunca** that had never happened to him before; **suceda lo que suceda** come what may, whatever happens; **¿qué sucede?** what's going on?, whatever's all this?; **lo que sucede es que ...** the fact is that ..., the trouble is that ...; **lo más que puede ~ es que ...** the worst that can happen is that ...; **llevar algo por lo que pueda ~** to take sth just in case; **lo mismo sucede con éste que con el otro** it's the same with this one as it is with the other.
(b) *(seguir)* to succeed, follow; *(heredar)* to inherit; **~ a uno en un puesto** to succeed sb in a post; **~ al trono** to succeed to the throne; **~ a una fortuna** to inherit a fortune; **al otoño sucede el invierno** winter follows autumn; **a este cuarto sucede otro mayor** a larger room leads off this one, a large room lies beyond this one.
☐2 **sucederse** VR to follow one another.

sucesión NF **(a)** *(gen)* succession (*a* to); *(secuencia)* sequence, series; **~ apostólica** apostolic succession; **una ~ de acontecimientos** a succession of events, a series of happenings; **en rápida ~** in quick succession; **la princesa ocupa el quinto puesto en la línea de ~ al trono** the princess is fifth in the line of succession to the throne.
(b) *(herencia)* inheritance; *(bienes)* estate; **derechos de ~** death duty.
(c) *(hijos)* issue, offspring; **morir sin ~** to die without issue.

sucesivamente ADV successively, in succession; **y así ~** and so on.

sucesivo ADJ *(subsiguiente)* successive, following; *(consecutivo)* consecutive; **3 días ~s** 3 days running, 3 successive days; **en lo ~** henceforth, in future; *(desde entonces)* thereafter, thenceforth.

suceso NM **(a)** *(acontecimiento)* event, happening; *(incidente)* incident; *(en periódico)* **capítulo de ~s** section of accident and crime reports.
(b) *(resultado)* issue, outcome; **buen ~** happy outcome.

sucesor(a) NM/F successor; heir.

sucesorio ADJ *lucha, derechos, crisis* succession *(atr)*; *impuesto* inheritance *(atr)*; **tercero en la línea sucesoria** third in (the) line of succession.

suche ☐1 ADJ *(Carib*)* sharp, bitter.
☐2 NM **(a)** *(Cono Sur*: grano)* pimple. **(b)** *(Cono Sur*: funcionario)* penpusher. **(c)** *(Cono Sur*: coime)* pimp.

súchil NM *(LAm)* an aromatic flowering tree.

sucho ADJ *(And)* maimed, paralytic, crippled.

suciamente ADV **(a)** *(gen)* dirtily, filthily. **(b)** *(fig)* vilely, meanly; obscenely, unfairly.

suciedad NF **(a)** *(sustancia)* dirt, filth, grime; *(cualidad)* dirtiness; filthiness. **(b)** *(fig)* vileness, meanness; obscenity; unfairness. **(c)** *(una ~)* dirty act; filthy remark; obscenity.

sucintamente ADV succinctly, concisely, briefly.

sucinto ADJ **(a)** *declaración etc* succinct, concise, brief. **(b)** *prenda* short, brief, scanty.

sucio ☐1 ADJ **(a)** *(gen)* dirty; *(mugriento)* filthy, grimy; *(manchado)* grubby, soiled; *color* dirty; *blurred*, smudged; *bosquejo etc* rough, messy; *lengua* coated, furred.
(b) *(fig) conducta* vile, mean, despicable; *acto, palabra etc* dirty, filthy, obscene; *jugada* foul, dirty; *táctica* unfair.
(c) *conciencia* bad.
(d) *precio, sueldo* gross.
☐2 ADV: **jugar ~*** to play unfairly, indulge in dirty play.
☐3 NM *(And)* smut, bit of dirt.

suco¹ ADJ *(And)* muddy, swampy.

suco² ADJ *(And)* *(rojizo)* bright red; *(rubio)* blond, fair; *(anaranjado)* orange.

sucre NM sucre *(Ecuadorian unit of currency)*.

sucrosa NF sucrose.

sucucho NM *(Carib)* = **socucho**.

suculencia NF tastiness, richness; succulence, lusciousness, juiciness.

suculento ADJ *(sabroso)* tasty, rich; *(jugoso)* succulent, luscious, juicy.

sucumbir [3a] VI to succumb *(a* to).

sucursal NF *(oficina)* branch, branch office; *(filial)* subsidiary.

sucusumuco: a lo ~ ADV *(And, Carib)* pretending to be stupid, feigning stupidity.

sud NM *(esp LAm)* south.

sudaca* ADJ, NMF *(pey)* South American.

sudadera NF *(CAm, Méx)* sweatshirt.

sudado ☐1 ADJ sweaty.
☐2 NM *(And)* stew.

Sudáfrica NF South Africa.

sudafricano, -a ADJ, NM/F South African.

Sudamérica NF South America.

sudamericano, -a ADJ, NM/F South American.

Sudán NM Sudan.

sudanés, -esa ADJ, NM/F Sudanese.

sudar [1a] ☐1 VT **(a)** *(gen)* to sweat; **~ a chorros*** to drip with sweat; V **sangre** *etc.*
(b) *(Bot etc)* to ooze, give out, give off; *(recipiente)* to ooze; *(pared etc)* to sweat, give off.
(c) *ropa etc* to make sweaty, make damp with sweat.
(d) (*) **~lo** to sweat it out; **~ un aumento de sueldo** to sweat for a rise in pay, work hard for some extra money; **ha sudado el premio** he really sweated to get the prize; **~ la gota gorda** to sweat blood.
(e) (*) *dinero* to cough up*, part with.
(f) **es un asunto que me la suda*** it's a matter which bores the pants off me*.
☐2 VI to sweat; **hacer ~ a uno** *(fig)* to make sb sweat.

sudario NM shroud.

sudestada NF *(Cono Sur)* = **surestada**.

sudeste ☐1 ADJ *parte* south-east, south-eastern; *dirección* south-easterly; *viento* south-east, south-easterly.
☐2 NM **(a)** *(Geog)* south-east. **(b)** *(viento)* south-east wind.

sudista ☐1 ADJ southern.
☐2 NMF Southerner.

sudoeste ☐1 ADJ *parte* south-west, south-western; *dirección* south-westerly; *viento* south-west, south-westerly.
☐2 NM **(a)** *(Geog)* south-west. **(b)** *(viento)* south-west wind.

sudón ADJ *(LAm)* sweaty.

sudor NM sweat; *(fig: t ~es)* sweat, toil, labour; **con el ~ de su frente** by the sweat of one's brow; **estar bañado en ~** to be dripping with sweat.

sudoración NF *(Med)* sweating.

sudoriento ADJ, **sudoroso** ADJ, **sudoso** ADJ sweaty, sweating; covered with sweat; **trabajo sudoroso** thirsty work, work that makes one sweat a lot.

Suecia NF Sweden.

suecia NF suède.

sueco¹ ☐1 ADJ Swedish.
☐2 NM, **sueca** NF Swede.
☐3 NM *(Ling)* Swedish.

sueco²* NM: **hacerse el ~** to pretend not to hear (*o* understand); to act dumb, not let on*.

suegra NF mother-in-law.

suegro NM father-in-law; **~s** parents-in-law, in-laws.

suela NF **(a)** *(de zapato)* sole; *(trozo de cuero)* piece of strong leather; **media ~** half sole; *(fig)* patch, botch; *(fig)* temporary remedy; temporary relief; **A no le llega a la ~ del zapato a B** A can't hold a candle to B; **un pícaro de siete ~s** a proper rogue; **duro como la ~ de un zapato** tough as leather, tough as old boots.
(b) **~s** *(Ecl)* sandals; **de siete ~s** utter, downright.
(c) *(Pez)* sole.
(d) *(LAm Téc)* washer.

suelazo* NM *(LAm)* *(caída)* heavy fall, nasty bump; *(golpe)* blow, punch.

▼ **sueldo** NM *(gen)* pay; *(mensual)* salary; *(semanal)* wage; **~ atrasado** back pay; **~ base** basic salary; **~ de hambre** starvation wage; **asesino a ~** hired assassin, contract killer; **estar a ~** to be on a salary, earn a salary; **estar a ~ de una potencia extranjera** to be in the pay of a foreign power.

suelear* [1a] VT *(Cono Sur)* to throw, chuck.

suelo NM **(a)** *(tierra)* ground; *(superficie)* surface; **~ natal**, **~ patrio** native land, native soil; **arrastrar (o poner o tirar) por los ~s** to blacken, run down, speak ill of; **caer al ~** to fall to the ground; **caerse al ~** (o fig) to fail, collapse; **echar al ~** *edificio* to demolish; *esperanzas* to dash; *plan* to ruin; **echarse al ~** to hurl o.s. to the ground; to fall on one's knees; **echarse por los ~s** *(fig)* to grovel; **estar por el ~*** to feel very low; **los precios están por el ~** prices are at rock bottom; **esos géneros están por los ~s** those goods are dirt cheap; **irse al ~** to fall through; **medir el ~** to fall full-length; **tirarse por los ~s*** to roll in the aisles (with laughter)*; **venirse al ~** *(fig)* to fail, collapse, be ruined.
(b) *(de cuarto etc)* floor; flooring.
(c) *(Cono Sur: tierra)* ground, soil, earth; **~ vegetal** topsoil.
(d) *(de pan, vasija etc)* bottom.

suelta NF: **habrá una ~ de globos** balloons will be released.

suelte *etc* V **soltar**.

sueltista NMF *(LAm)* freelance journalist.

suelto ☐1 ADJ **(a)** *(libre)* free; *(no atado)* untied, undone; *pieza etc* detached, unattached, separate; *cabo, hoja, tornillo* loose; *(sin trabas)* unhampered; *prenda etc* loose, loose-fitting; **~ de lengua** *(hablador)* talkative; *(respondón)* cheeky, given to answering back; *(soplón)* not to be trusted with secrets; *(obsceno)* foulmouthed; **~ de vientre**

loose; **el libro tiene dos hojas sueltas** the book has two pages loose; **llevas ~s los cordones** your shoelaces are undone; **el perro anda ~** the dog is loose; **su marido anda ~** her husband is on the loose; **lo ató con el cabo ~** he tied it up with the free (o loose) end; **lo dejamos ~** we leave it untied, we leave it free; **iba con el pelo ~** she had her hair down.

(b) *fragmento, pasaje etc* detached, isolated; individual; (*Com: no envasado*) loose, in bulk; (*desparejado*) odd; *número, volumen* odd, single; **es un trozo ~ de la novela** it's a separate piece from the novel, it's an isolated passage from the novel; **son 3 poesías sueltas** these are 3 separate poems; **los tomos no se venden ~s** the volumes are not sold singly (o separately); **hay un calcetín ~** there is one odd sock; **una mesa con números ~s de revistas** a table with odd copies of magazines.

(c) (*en movimiento*) free, easy; (*ágil*) light; quick, agile, unhampered; *estilo* fluent, free, flowing; **está muy ~ en inglés** his English is fluent.

(d) (*moralmente*) free and easy; (*atrevido*) daring; (*licencioso*) licentious, lax.

(e) (*Liter*) *verso* blank.

2 NM **(a)** (*Fin*) change, loose change, small change.

(b) (*Tip*) paragraph; (*en periódico*) item, note, short article.

suene *etc* V **sonar**.

sueña *etc* V **soñar**.

sueñera* NF (*LAm*) drowsiness, sleepiness.

sueño NM **(a)** (*el dormir*) sleep; **~ eterno** eternal rest; **~ invernal** (*Zool*) winter sleep; **~ pesado**, **~ profundo** deep sleep, heavy sleep; **coger el ~**, **conciliar el ~** to get to sleep; **descabezar un ~**, **echarse un ~** to have a nap; **dormir el ~ de los justos** to sleep the sleep of the just; **pasar una noche sin ~** to have a sleepless night; **perder el ~ por algo** to lose sleep over sth; **tengo ~ atrasado** I haven't had much sleep lately; **tener el ~ ligero** to be a light sleeper; **tener el ~ pesado** (o **profundo**) to be a heavy sleeper.

(b) (*somnolencia*) sleepiness, drowsiness; **caerse de ~** to be so sleepy one can hardly stand; **espantar el ~** to struggle to keep awake; **tener ~** to be sleepy; **sentirse con ~** to feel sleepy; **se me ha quitado el ~** I'm not sleepy any more.

(c) (*lo soñado*) dream (*t fig*); **¡ni en ~s!**, **¡ni por ~!** not on your life!; **es su ~ dorado** it's the dream of his life, it's his great dream; **es un ~ hecho realidad** it's a dream come true; **estar entre ~s** to be half asleep; **ver algo en** (o **entre**) **~s** to see sth in a dream; **vive en un mundo de ~s** she lives in a dream world; **tiene una casa que es un ~** she has a real dream of a house, she has a real dream-house.

suero NM **(a)** (*Med*) serum. **(b)** whey; **~ de la leche** buttermilk.

suertaza* NF great stroke of luck.

▼ **suerte** NF **(a)** (*destino*) fate, destiny; (*azar*) chance, fortune; **por ~** by chance, as it happened; **abandonado a su ~** left to one's own devices; **confiar algo a la ~** to leave sth to chance; **dejar a uno a su ~** to abandon sb to his fate; **la ~ que les espera** the fate which awaits them; **quiso la ~ que ...** as fate would have it ..., as luck would have it ...; **seguir la ~ a uno** to keep track of sb; **tentar a la ~** to tempt fate; **unirse a la ~ de uno** to throw in one's lot with sb, make common cause with sb.

(b) (*elección*) lot; **caber en ~ a uno**, **caer en ~ a uno** to fall to sb, fall to sb's lot; **no me cupo tal ~** I had no such luck; **echaron ~s entre los 4** the 4 of them drew lots, the 4 of them tossed up; **lo echaron a ~s** they drew lots for it, they tossed up for it; **la ~ está echada** the die is cast.

▼**(c)** (*fortuna*) luck; **buena ~** luck, good luck; **¡buena ~!** good luck!; **¡~, y al toro!*** the best of luck to you!; **mala ~** bad luck, hard luck; **~ perra*** bad luck, rotten luck; **hombre de ~** lucky man; **un número de mala ~** an unlucky number; **por ~** luckily, fortunately; **dar ~**, **traer ~** to bring luck; **trae mala ~ escupir allí** it's unlucky to spit there; **estar de ~** to be in luck; **probar ~** to try one's luck; **tener ~** to be lucky; to have a piece of luck; **¡que tengas ~!** good luck!, I wish you luck!, and the best of luck!; **tuvo una ~ loca*** he was fantastically lucky; **tuvo la ~ de que hacía buen tiempo** he was lucky that it was fine.

(d) (*condición*) lot; state, condition; **mejorar de ~** to improve one's lot.

(e) (*billete de lotería*) lottery ticket.

(f) (*especie*) sort, kind; **es una ~ de** it is a kind of; **no podemos seguir de esta ~** we cannot go on in this way; **de otra ~** otherwise, if not; **de ~ que ...** in such a way that ..., so that ...; **¿de ~ que no hay más dragones?** so there are no more dragons?

(g) (*Taur*) stage, part (of the bullfight); **~ de varas** *opening section (of play with the capes).*

suertero 1 ADJ (*LAm*) lucky.

2 NM, **suertera** NF (*And, CAm*) seller of lottery tickets.

suertoso ADJ (*And*) lucky.

suertudo ADJ lucky.

suestada NF (*Argentina*) southeast wind.

sueste NM **(a)** (*Náut: sombrero*) sou'wester. **(b)** (*LAm: viento*) south-east wind.

suéter NM sweater.

Suetonio NM Suetonius.

Suez NM Suez; **Canal de ~** Suez Canal.

suficiencia NF (*V* ADJ) **(a)** sufficiency; adequacy; **una ~ de ...** enough ...; **a ~** sufficiently, adequately.

(b) competence; suitability, fitness; adequacy; capacity; (*Escol*) proficiency; **demostrar su ~** to prove one's competence, show one's capabilities.

(c) (*pey*) self-importance; superiority; condescension; smugness, self-satisfaction, complacency; *V* **aire**.

suficiente ADJ **(a)** (*bastante*) enough, sufficient (*para* for); (*adecuado*) adequate.

(b) *persona* competent; (*idóneo*) suitable, fit; (*adecuado*) adequate; (*capaz*) capable; (*Escol*) proficient.

(c) (*pey*) (*engreído*) self-important; superior; (*desdeñoso*) condescending; (*satisfecho de sí*) smug, self-satisfied, complacent.

suficientemente ADV sufficiently, adequately.

sufijo NM suffix.

suflé NM soufflé.

sufragáneo ADJ suffragan.

sufragar [1h] **1** VT **(a)** (*ayudar*) to aid, help, support.

(b) *gastos* to meet, defray, cover; *proyecto etc* to pay for, defray the costs of.

2 VI (*LAm*) to vote (*por* for).

sufragio NM **(a)** (*voto*) vote; **los ~s emitidos a favor de X** the votes cast for X.

(b) (*derecho de votar*) suffrage; franchise; **~ universal** universal suffrage.

(c) (*apoyo*) help, aid.

(d) (*Ecl*) suffrage.

sufragista NF suffragette.

sufrible ADJ bearable.

sufrido 1 ADJ **(a)** *persona* (*duro*) tough; (*paciente*) long-suffering, patient.

(b) *tela etc* hard-wearing, long-lasting, tough; *color* that does not show the dirt, that wears well.

(c) *marido* complaisant.

2 NM complaisant husband.

sufridor 1 ADJ suffering.

2 NM **(a)** (*persona*) sufferer. **(b)** (*And*) saddlecloth.

sufrimiento NM **(a)** (*estado*) suffering; misery, wretchedness.

(b) (*cualidad*) toughness; patience; tolerance; **tener ~ en las dificultades** to be patient in hard times, bear troubles patiently.

sufrir [3a] **1** VT **(a)** (*gen*) to suffer; *accidente, ataque* to have, suffer; *consecuencias, desastre, revés etc* to suffer; *cambio* to undergo, experience; *pérdida* to suffer, sustain; *operación* to have, undergo.

(b) (*soportar*) to bear, stand, put up with; **no sufre la menor descortesía** he won't tolerate the slightest rudeness; **A no le sufre a B** A can't stand B.

(c) (*sostener*) to hold up, support.

(d) *examen, prueba* to take, undergo.

2 VI to suffer; **~ de** to suffer from, suffer with; **sufre de reumatismo** she suffers from (o with) rheumatism; **sufre mucho de los pies** she suffers a lot with her feet; **aprender a ~ silenciosamente** to learn to suffer in silence.

▼ **sugerencia** NF suggestion.

sugerente ADJ full of suggestions, rich in ideas, thought-provoking; *escena etc* evocative.

sugerible ADJ = **sugestionable**.

sugerimiento NM suggestion.

▼ **sugerir** [3i] VT (*gen*) to suggest; (*insinuar*) to hint, hint at; *pensamiento etc* to prompt; **~ que ...** to suggest that ...

sugestión NF **(a)** (*sugerencia*) suggestion; (*insinuación*) hint; (*estímulo*) prompting, stimulus; **las sugestiones del corazón** the promptings of the heart; **un sitio de muchas sugestiones** a place rich in associations.

(b) (*autosugestión*) autosuggestion, self-hypnotism.

(c) (*poder*) fascination (for others); hypnotic power, power to influence others; **emanaba de él una fuerte ~** a strong hypnotic power flowed from him.

sugestionable ADJ impressionable, suggestible; open to influence, readily influenced.

sugestionar [1a] **1** VT to influence, dominate the will of, hypnotize; to exercise a powerful fascination over; **~ a uno para que haga algo** to influence sb to do sth.

2 **sugestionarse** VR to indulge in autosuggestion; **es probable que se haya dejado ~ por ...** he may have allowed himself to be influenced by ...; **te lo has sugestionado** you've talked yourself into it.

sugestivo ADJ **(a)** (*estimulante*) stimulating, thought-provoking; (*evoca-*

---

dor) evocative. (**b**) (*atractivo*) attractive; (*fascinante*) fascinating.

sugiera *etc V* **sugerir**.

suiche NM (**a**) (*LAm, Elec*) switch. (**b**) (*Carib Aut*) ignition key.

suicida [1] ADJ, ATR suicidal; **comando ~** suicide squad; **conductor ~** suicidal driver; **piloto ~** suicide pilot, kamikaze pilot.
[2] NMF suicidal case, person with a tendency to suicide; (*muerto*) person who has committed suicide; **es un ~ conduciendo** he's a maniac behind the wheel.

suicidado, -a NM/F person who commits suicide.

suicidar [1a] [1] VT (*iró*) to murder, assassinate (so as to convey an impression of suicide), fake the suicide of.
[2] **suicidarse** VR to commit suicide, kill oneself.

suicid(i)ario ADJ suicidal.

suicidio NM suicide.

sui géneris ADJ INVAR individual, idiosyncratic.

suite [swit] NF, PL **suites** (*t Mús*) suite; **la ~ nupcial** the bridal suite.

Suiza NF Switzerland.

suiza¹ NF (**a**) (*CAm, Carib: juego*) skipping, skipping game.
(**b**) (*And, CAm: paliza*) beating.

suizo¹, -a² ADJ, NM/F Swiss.

suizo² NM (*Culin*) bun.

suje* NM bra*.

sujeción NF (**a**) (*estado*) subjection. (**b**) (*acto*) fastening; seizure; (*fig*) subjection (*a* to); **con ~ a** subject to.

sujetacorbata NM tiepin.

sujetador NM fastener; (*para pelo*) clip, pin, grip; (*para papeles*) clip; (*de pluma*) clip; (*prenda*) brassiere, bra; **~ de libros** book-end.

sujetalibros NM INVAR book-ends.

sujetapapeles NM INVAR paperclip.

sujetar [1a] [1] VT (**a**) (*dominar*) *nación* to subdue, conquer; to hold down; keep down, keep under; to exercise control over; *precio etc* to keep down, hold down; **~ A a B** to put A under B's authority, subordinate A to B.
(**b**) (*agarrar*) to seize, clutch, lay hold of; (*sostener*) to hold, (*fuertemente*) to hold tight; *persona* to hold down, keep hold of; (*Téc*) to fasten; (*con clavo*) to nail down; (*con cola*) to stick down; (*con tornillo*) to screw down (*etc*); *pelo etc* to keep in place, hold in place; *papeles etc* to fasten together.
[2] **sujetarse** VR: **~ a** (*someterse a*) to subject o.s. to; *regla* to abide by; *circunstancias etc* to act in accordance with, recognize the limitations of; *autoridad* to submit to; **~ a + infin** to agree to + infin, give way before the necessity of + ger.

sujeto [1] ADJ (**a**) (*fijo*) fastened, secure; (*firme*) firm; (*ajustado*) tight; **la cuerda está bien sujeta** the rope is securely fastened.
(**b**) **~ a** subject to; (*propenso a*) liable to; **~ a la aprobación de** subject to the approval of; **~ a derechos** subject to duty, dutiable; **estar ~ a cambios inesperados** to be liable to sudden changes.
(**c**) **tener a alguien ~** to keep sb under supervision.
[2] NM (**a**) (*Ling*) subject.
(**b**) (*persona*) individual; (*Med etc*) subject, case; (*) fellow, character*, chap*; **un ~ sospechoso** a suspicious character*; **buen ~** good chap*.

sulfamida NF sulphonamide.

sulfatar [1a] VT to fertilize (with sulphate).

sulfato NM sulphate; **~ amónico** ammonium sulphate; **~ de cobre** copper sulphate; **~ de hierro** iron sulphate; **~ magnésico** magnesium sulphate; **~ potásico** potassium sulphate.

sulfurado* ADJ cross, angry.

sulfurar [1a] [1] VT (**a**) (*Quím*) to sulphurate.
(**b**) (*) to annoy, rile*.
[2] **sulfurarse** VR (*) to get mad*, see red, blow up*.

sulfúreo ADJ sulphurous.

sulfúrico ADJ sulphuric.

sulfuro NM sulphide.

sulfuroso ADJ sulphurous.

sultán NM sultan.

sultana NF sultana.

sultanato NM sultanate.

▼ **suma** [1] NF (**a**) (*Mat: acto*) adding (up), addition; (*cantidad*) total, sum; (*de dinero*) sum; '**~ y sigue**' (*en cuenta*) 'carried forward'; (*) and it's still going on; **~ global** lump sum; **en ~** in short; **hacer ~s** to add up, do addition.
(**b**) (*fig: resumen*) summary; essence; **una ~ de perfecciones** perfection itself; **es la ~ y compendio de todas las virtudes** she is the personification of all the virtues.
[2] NM: **un ~ y sigue de grandes aportaciones al mundo del automóvil** a whole host of great contributions to the world of cars.

sumador NM (*Inform*) adder circuit.

sumadora NF adding machine.

sumamente ADV extremely, exceedingly, highly.

sumando NM (*Mat*) addend.

sumar [1a] [1] VT (**a**) (*Mat*) to add (up), total; (*fig: resumir*) to summa-

rize, sum up.
(**b**) (*recoger*) to collect, gather.
(**c**) **la cuenta suma 6 dólares** the bill adds up to (*o* comes to, amounts to, works out at) 6 dollars.
[2] VI to add up.
[3] **sumarse** VR: **~ a un partido** to join a party; **~ a una protesta** to associate o.s. with a protest, join in a protest.

sumarial ADJ *V* **secreto**.

sumariamente ADV summarily.

sumario [1] ADJ brief, concise; (*Jur*) summary; **información sumaria** summary proceedings.
[2] NM (**a**) (*resumen*) summary. (**b**) (*Jur*) indictment.

sumarísimo ADJ (*Jur*) summary.

Sumatra NF Sumatra.

sumergible [1] ADJ submersible; that can go under water.
[2] NM submarine.

sumergido ADJ (**a**) submerged, sunken. (**b**) (*ilegal*) illegal, unauthorized; **economía sumergida** black economy; **tratos ~s** black-market deals.

sumergimiento NM submersion, submergence.

sumergir [3c] [1] VT (**a**) (*gen*) to submerge; (*hundir*) to sink; (*bañar*) to immerse, dip, plunge (*en* in).
(**b**) (*fig*) to plunge (*en* into).
[2] **sumergirse** VR (**a**) (*gen*) to submerge, sink beneath the surface; (*submarino etc*) to dive.
(**b**) **~ en** (*fig*) to immerse o.s. in, become absorbed in.

sumersión NF (**a**) (*gen*) submersion, submergence; immersion. (**b**) (*fig*) absorption (*en* in).

sumidero NM (**a**) (*cloaca*) drain, sewer; (*fregadero*) sink; (*Téc*) sump; (*And, Carib*) cesspool, cesspit.
(**b**) (*Carib: tremedal*) quagmire.
(**c**) (*fig*) drain; **es el gran ~ de las reservas** it is the chief drain on our reserves.

sumiller NM wine-waiter.

suministrador(a) NM/F supplier.

suministrar [1a] VT *artículos, información etc* to supply, furnish, provide; *persona* to supply; **me ha suministrado muchos datos** he has given me a lot of data, he has supplied me with a lot of information.

suministro NM (*provisión*) supply; (*acto*) supplying, furnishing, provision; **~s** (*Mil*) supplies; **~s de combustible** fuel supply.

sumir [3a] [1] VT (**a**) (*hundir*) to sink, plunge, submerge; (*mar, olas*) to swallow up, suck down.
(**b**) (*fig*) to plunge (*en* into); **el desastre le sumió en la tristeza** the disaster plunged him into sadness.
(**c**) (*And, Cono Sur, Méx: abollar*) to dent.
[2] **sumirse** VR (**a**) (*objeto*) to sink; (*agua etc*) to run away, disappear.
(**b**) (*boca, pecho etc*) to sink, be sunken, become hollow.
(**c**) **~ en el estudio** to become absorbed in one's work; **~ en la tristeza** to plunge into grief, give o.s. over entirely to one's grief.
(**d**) (*LAm*) (*encogerse*) to cower, cringe; (*desanimarse*) to lose heart; (*callar*) to fall silent from fear, clam up.
(**e**) **~ el sombrero** (*LAm*) to pull one's hat down over one's eyes.

sumisamente ADV submissively, obediently; unresistingly; uncomplainingly.

sumisión NF (**a**) (*acto*) submission. (**b**) (*cualidad*) submissiveness, docility.

sumiso ADJ (*dócil*) submissive, docile, obedient; (*que no resiste*) unresisting; (*que no se queja*) uncomplaining.

súmmum NM: **el ~ de la elegancia** the height of elegance; *persona* the epitome of elegance.

sumo¹ ADJ (**a**) (*supremo*) great, extreme, supreme; **con suma dificultad** with the greatest (*o* utmost) difficulty; **con suma indiferencia** with supreme indifference; **con suma destreza** with consummate skill.
(**b**) (*en rango*) high, highest; **~ sacerdote** high priest; *V* **pontífice**; **la suma autoridad** the highest authority, the supreme authority.
(**c**) **a lo ~** at most.

sumo² NM sumo (wrestling).

sunco ADJ (*And*) = **manco**.

sungo ADJ (*And*) Negro; (*de piel liso*) with a shiny skin; (*tostado*) tanned.

suní, sunita ADJ, NMF Sunni.

suntuario ADJ sumptuary.

suntuosamente ADJ sumptuously, magnificently; lavishly, richly.

suntuosidad NF sumptuousness, magnificence; lavishness.

suntuoso ADJ sumptuous, magnificent; lavish, rich.

sup. ABR de **superior** superior, sup.

supe *etc V* **saber**.

supeditar [1a] [1] VT (**a**) (*subordinar*) to subordinate (*a* to); **tendrá que ser supeditado a lo que decidan ellos** it will have to depend on what they decide.
(**b**) (*sojuzgar*) to subdue; (*oprimir*) to oppress, crush.

2 supeditarse VR: ~ **a** (*subordinarse*) to make o.s. subordinate to, come to depend on; (*ceder*) to give way to, allow o.s. to be overridden by; **no voy a supeditarme a su capricho** I am not going to depend on her whims.

super... PREF super..., over... (**a**) **superambicioso** overambitious; **superatraco** major hold-up; **superdesarrollo** overdevelopment.
(**b**) *prefijo de adj: equivale frec a superlativo*: **supercaro** impossibly expensive; **superfamoso** extremely famous; **superreservado** excessively shy; **un texto supercomentado** a text which has so often been commented on.

súper 1 ADJ (*) super*.
2 ADV (*) really well, real good*.
3 NM (**a**) (*Aut*) four-star petrol. (**b**) (*Com*) supermarket.

superable ADJ *dificultad* surmountable, that can be overcome; *tarea etc* that can be performed; **un obstáculo difícilmente ~** an obstacle not easily surmounted.

superabundancia NF superabundance.

superabundante ADJ superabundant.

superación NF (**a**) (*acto*) overcoming, surmounting; transcending; excelling. (**b**) (*mejora*) improvement, doing better; *V* **afán**.

superagente* NMF supercop*, super-sleuth*.

superar [1a] 1 VT (**a**) *rival* to surpass, excel (*in* en), beat, do better than; *adversario* to overcome; *esperanzas* to exceed; *límite, punto* to go beyond, transcend; *récord* to break; **las escenas superan a toda imaginación** the scenes are more extraordinary than anyone could imagine, the scenes defeat one's imagination; **~ a uno en brillantez** to outshine sb; **superó 2 veces la marca de los 200 metros** she twice broke the 200-metre record.
(**b**) *dificultad* to overcome, surmount; *prueba* to pass.
(**c**) *etapa, período* to get past, leave behind, emerge from; **ya hemos superado lo peor** we're over the worst now.
2 **superarse** VR to do extremely well, excel o.s.

superávit NM INVAR surplus.

superavitario ADJ surplus (*atr*).

superbombardero NM superbomber.

supercarburante NM high-grade fuel.

supercarretera NF superhighway.

superchería NF fraud, trick, swindle.

superchero ADJ fraudulent; sham, bogus.

supercola NF superglue.

superconductividad NF superconductivity.

superconductor 1 ADJ superconductive.
2 NM superconductor.

superconsumo NM overconsumption.

supercopa NF cup-winners' cup.

supercotizado ADJ much sought-after, in very great demand.

supercuenta NF high interest account.

superdirecta NF (*Aut*) overdrive.

superdotado 1 ADJ extremely gifted.
2 NM, **superdotada** NF extremely gifted person.

superego NM superego.

superempleo NM overemployment,

superentender [2g] VT to supervise, superintend.

supererogación NF supererogation.

superestrella NF superstar.

superestructura NF superstructure.

superferolítico* ADJ (**a**) (*afectado*) affected; (*muy refinado*) excessively refined. (**b**) (*delicado*) overnice, finicky, choosy*.

superficial ADJ (**a**) *medida etc* surface (*atr*), of the surface; *herida etc* superficial, flesh (*atr*). (**b**) (*fig*) *interés, mirada etc* superficial; (*breve*) brief, perfunctory; *carácter* superficial, shallow; (*frívolo*) facile.

superficialidad NF superficiality; shallowness.

superficialmente ADV superficially.

superficie NF (**a**) (*gen*) surface; (*cara*) face; (*exterior*) outside; (*del mar etc*) surface; **~ inferior** lower surface, underside; **~ de rodadura** (*Aut*) tread; **el ave rozó la ~** the bird skimmed the surface; **el submarino salió a la ~** the submarine surfaced, the submarine came to the surface; **ruta de ~** surface route, land (*o* sea) route.
(**b**) (*medidas etc*) area; **~ útil** useful area, usable space; **se regará una ~ de 200 hectáreas** an area of 200 hectares will be irrigated; **todo quedó destruido en una extensa ~** everything was destroyed over a wide area.
(**c**) (*fig*) surface, outward appearance.
(**d**) (*Com*) **gran ~** superstore.

superfino ADJ superfine.

superfluamente ADV superfluously.

superfluidad NF superfluity.

superfluo ADJ superfluous.

superfosfato NM superphosphate.

superhéroe NM superhero.

superhombre NM superman.

superíndice NM (*Inform*) superscript.

superintendencia NF supervision, superintendence.

superintendente NMF supervisor, superintendent; overseer; (*Com*) shop walker, floorwalker (*US*); **~ de división** sectional head.

▼ **superior** 1 ADJ (**a**) (*posición: más alto*) upper; (*el más alto*) uppermost, top; (*más elevado*) higher; *clase* upper; *estudio* advanced, higher; **labio ~** upper lip; **vive en el piso ~** he lives on the upper (*o* top) floor; **viven en el piso ~ al mío** they live on the floor above mine; **un estudio de nivel ~ a los existentes** a study on a higher plane than the present ones.
▼ (**b**) (*en calidad etc*) superior, better; **ser ~ a** to be superior to, be better than; **de calidad ~** of superior quality.
(**c**) (*en número*) higher, greater, larger; **cualquier número ~ a 12** any number above (*o* higher than) 12.
(**d**) (*en actitud*) superior; condescending, patronizing.
2 NM superior; **mis ~es** my superiors, those above me (*in* rank); (*fig*) my betters.

superiora NF mother superior.

superioridad NF superiority.

superitar [1a] VT (*And, Cono Sur*) (**a**) (*superar*) to overcome. (**b**) (*aventajar*) to improve.

superlativo ADJ, NM superlative.

superlujo NM: **hotel de ~** super-luxury hotel; **tiene categoría de ~** it is in the super-luxury class.

supermercado NM supermarket.

superministro, -a NM/F minister with an overall responsibility, senior minister, overlord.

supermoda NF: **vestido de ~** high-fashion dress.

supermujer NF superwoman.

supernova NF supernova.

supernumerario, -a ADJ, NM/F supernumerary.

superordenador NM supercomputer.

superpetrolero NM supertanker.

superpoblación NF overpopulation, excess of population; overcrowding, congestion.

superpoblado ADJ *país, región* overpopulated; *barrio etc* overcrowded, congested.

superponer [2q] VT to superimpose, superpose, put on top.

superposición NF superposition.

superpotencia NF superpower, great power.

superpredador NM top predator, superpredator.

superproducción NF overproducton.

superprotector ADJ over-protective.

supersecreto ADJ top secret.

supersensible ADJ ultra-sensitive.

supersimplificación NF oversimplification.

supersónico ADJ supersonic.

supersoplón, -ona‡ NM/F supergrass‡.

superstición NF superstition.

supersticiosamente ADV superstitiously.

supersticioso ADJ superstitious.

supertalla NF (*Cos*) outsize.

supervalorar [1a] VT to overvalue, overstate; (*Com, Fin*) to overvalue.

superventa 1 ADJ best-selling.
2 NF best-seller, best-selling article.
3 NMF (*persona*) top salesperson.

superventas* NM INVAR best seller; **lista de ~** (*Mús*) charts.

supervigilancia NF (*LAm*) supervision.

supervisar [1a] VT to supervise.

supervisión NF supervision.

supervisor(a) NM/F supervisor; (F: *de hospital*) matron.

supervivencia NF survival; **~ de los más aptos, ~ de los mejor dotados** survival of the fittest.

superviviente 1 ADJ surviving.
2 NMF survivor.

supervivir [3a] VI to survive.

superyo NM superego.

supino ADJ, NM supine.

súpito ADJ (**a**) = **súbito**. (**b**) (*And*: *atónito*) dumbfounded.

suplantación NF (**a**) (*gen*) supplanting; (*de persona*) impersonation. (**b**) (*And*: *falsificación*) forgery.

suplantar [1a] VT (**a**) (*gen*) to supplant; (*hacerse pasar por otro*) to take the place of (fraudulently), impersonate. (**b**) (*And*: *falsificar*) to falsify, forge.

suplefaltas NMF INVAR (**a**) (*chivo expiatorio*) scapegoat. (**b**) (*suplente*) substitute, stopgap, fill-in.

suplemental ADJ supplementary.

suplementario ADJ supplementary; extra, additional; **empleo ~, negocio ~** sideline; **tren ~** extra train, relief train; **tiempo ~** overtime.

suplementero NM (*Cono Sur*) newsboy, news vendor.

suplemento NM (**a**) (*gen*) supplement; (*Ferro etc*) excess fare, supplement. (**b**) (*revista etc*) **~ a** (*o* en) **color** colour supplement; **~**

dominical Sunday supplement; **~ separable** pull-out supplement.

suplencia NF (*LAm*) substitution, replacement.

suplente ⊡ ADJ substitute, deputy; reserve; **maestro ~** supply teacher.
⊡ NMF substitute, deputy; replacement; (*Dep*) substitute, reserve.

supletorio ⊡ ADJ supplementary; extra, reserve, additional; stopgap *(atr)*; **con la ventaja supletoria de que ...** with the additional advantage that ...; **llevar una lámpara supletoria** to take a spare bulb.
⊡ NM (*Telec*) extension.

súplica NF request; entreaty, supplication; (*Jur*) petition; **~s** entreaties, pleading; **acceder a las ~s de uno** to grant sb's request; **se publica a ~(s) de ...** it is published at the request of ...

suplicante ⊡ ADJ *tono etc* imploring, pleading.
⊡ NMF applicant; (*Jur*) petitioner, supplicant.

suplicar [1g] ⊡ VT **(a)** *cosa* to beg (for), plead for, implore.
(b) *persona* to beg, plead with, implore; **~ a uno no hacer algo** to implore sb not to do sth.
(c) (*Jur*) to appeal to, petition (*de* against).
⊡ **suplicarse** VR: **'se suplica cerrar la puerta'** 'please shut the door'.

suplicatorio NM **(a)** (*Pol*) Supreme Court petition asking Parliament to ovelook an MP's parliamentary immunity so that (s)he can be prosecuted.
(b) (*Jur*) letter supplicatory.

suplicio NM (*tortura*) torture; (*Hist*) (*castigo*) punishment; (*ejecución*), execution; (*fig*) torment, torture; (*mental*) anguish; (*sufrimiento*) ordeal; **~ de Tántalo** torments of Tantalus; **es un ~ tener que escucharle** it's torture having to listen to him.

suplir [3a] ⊡ VT **(a)** *necesidad, omisión* to supply; *falta* to make good, make up for; *palabra etc que falta* to supply; to understand.
(b) (*sustituir*) **~ A con B** to replace A by B, substitute B for A; **suplen el aceite con grasa animal** they replace olive oil by animal fat.
⊡ VI: **~ a, ~ por** to replace, take the place of, substitute for, do duty for; **suple en el equipo al portero lesionado** he's replacing the injured goalkeeper in the team.

supo *etc V* **saber**.

supondré *etc V* **suponer**.

▼ **suponer** [2r] ⊡ VT **(a)** (*dar por sentado*) to suppose, assume; **supongamos que ...** let us suppose (o assume) that ...; **supongo que sí** I suppose so; **era de ~ que ...** it was to be expected that ...; **con las dificultades que son de ~** with all the difficulties that one might expect.
▼ **(b)** (*imaginarse*) to think, imagine; (*adivinar*) to guess; **ya puedes ~ lo que ella sufría** you can just imagine how she was suffering; **Vd puede ~ lo que pasó** you can guess what happened; **no puedes ~ lo bruto que es** you can't begin to imagine what a lout he is; **es un ~** I was only thinking aloud, of course that's just guesswork.
(c) (*atribuir*) to attribute; to credit (with); **le supongo unos 60 años** I give him (an age of) about 60; **se le supone una gran antigüedad** it is thought to be very ancient, it is credited with great antiquity; **hubo poco público y se ve que el equipo no tenía tanta 'fuerza' como se le suponía** there were few spectators and it is clear that the team did not have the 'pull' it was credited with.
(d) (*significar*) to mean, imply; (*acarrear*) to involve, entail; **el traslado le supone grandes gastos** the move involves a lot of expense for him; **tal distancia no supone nada yendo en coche** that distance doesn't amount to anything in a car; **esa cantidad supone mucho para ellos** that amount means a lot to them.
⊡ VI to have authority, count (for a lot); **casi no supone en la organización** he hardly counts for anything in the organization.

suponga *etc V* **suponer**.

suposición NF **(a)** (*supuesto*) supposition, assumption, surmise. **(b)** (*autoridad*) authority; (*distinción*) distinction. **(c)** (*calumnia*) slander; (*engaño*) imposture.

supositorio NM suppository.

supra... PREF supra...

supradicho ADJ aforementioned.

supranacional ADJ supranational.

supremacía NF supremacy.

supremo ADJ supreme.

supresión NF (*V* VT) suppression; abolition; removal, elimination; cancellation, lifting; deletion, omission; banning.

supresivo ADJ suppressive.

supresor NM (*Elec*) suppressor.

suprimido ADJ *libro etc* suppressed, banned.

suprimir [3a] VT *crítica, rebelión etc* to suppress; *costumbre, derecho, institución etc* to abolish; *dificultad, obstáculo, residuos* to remove, eliminate; *restricciones* to cancel, lift; *detalle, pasaje etc* to delete, cut out, omit; *libro etc* to suppress, ban.

supuestamente ADV supposedly; allegedly.

▼ **supuesto** ⊡ PTP *de* **suponer**.
⊡ ADJ **(a)** (*aparente*) supposed, ostensible; (*pretendido*) self-styled; (*según se afirma*) alleged; **el ~ jefe del movimiento** the self-styled

leader of the movement; **bajo un nombre ~** under an assumed name, under a false name.
(b) **dar por ~ algo** to take sth for granted; **demos por ~ que ...** let us take it for granted that ...
⊡ **~ que** CONJ (*ya que*) since; (*dado que*) granted that; (*pues*) inasmuch as.
⊡ NM **(a)** (*hipótesis*) assumption, hypothesis; **~ previo** prior assumption; **en el ~ de que** (+ *subj*) on the assumption that ...
▼ **(b)** **¡por ~!** of course!, naturally! **pero ¡por ~!** (*LAm*) please do!, you're welcome!

supuración NF suppuration.

supurar [1a] VI to suppurate, discharge, fester.

supuse *etc V* **suponer**.

sur ⊡ ADJ *parte* south, southern; *dirección* southerly; *viento south, southerly*.
⊡ NM **(a)** south; **en la parte del ~** in the southern part; **al ~ de León** to the south of Leon, on the south side of Leon; **eso cae más hacia el ~** that lies further (to the) south.
(b) (*viento*) south wind.

sura NM sura.

Suráfrica NF = **Sudáfrica**.

surafricano ADJ, NM/F = **sudafricano**.

Suramérica NF = **Sudamérica**.

suramericano = **sudamericano**.

surazo NM (*And, Cono Sur*) strong southerly wind.

surcar [1g] VT **(a)** *tierra* to plough (through), furrow; *superficie* (*cortar*) to cut, score, groove; (*rayar*) to make lines across; **una superficie surcada de ...** a surface lined with ..., a surface criss-crossed with ...
(b) (*fig*) *agua, olas* to cut through, cleave; **los barcos que surcan los mares** (*liter*) the ships which ply the seas; **las aves que surcan los aires** (*liter*) the birds which ride the winds.

surco NM (*Agr etc*) furrow; (*de rueda*) rut, track; (*en metal etc*) groove, score, line; (*de disco*) groove; (*Anat*) wrinkle; (*en agua*) track, wake; **echarse al ~** *persona perezosa* to sit down on the job; (*terminar*) to knock off*, think one has done enough.

surcoreano, -a ADJ, NM/F South Korean.

sureño ⊡ ADJ southern.
⊡ NM, **sureña** NF Southerner.

surero NM (*And*) cold southerly wind.

surestada NF (*Cono Sur*) wet south-easterly wind.

sureste = **sudeste**.

surf NM surfboarding; **~ a vela** windsurfing.

surfero ⊡ ADJ surfing.
⊡ NM, **surfera** NF surfer.

surfista NMF surfboarder.

surgencia NF, **surgimiento** NM rise; emergence.

surgir [3c] VI **(a)** (*aparecer*) to arise, emerge, spring up, appear; (*líquido*) to spout (out), spurt (up), gush (forth); (*en niebla etc*) to loom up; (*persona*) to appear unexpectedly; (*dificultad*) to arise, come up, crop up; **la torre surge en medio del bosque** the tower rises (o soars) up in the middle of the woods; **han surgido varios problemas** several problems have arisen.
(b) (*Náut*) to anchor.

suriano ADJ (*Méx*) southern.

surja *etc V* **surgir**.

surmenage, surmenaje NM (*trabajo excesivo*) overwork; (*estrés*) stress, mental fatigue; (*crisis*) nervous breakdown.

suroeste = **sudoeste**.

surrealismo NM surrealism.

surrealista ⊡ ADJ surrealist(ic).
⊡ NMF surrealist.

surtido ⊡ ADJ **(a)** (*variado*) mixed, assorted, varied.
(b) **estar bien ~ de** to be well supplied with, have good stocks of; **estar mal ~ de** to be badly off for.
⊡ NM (*selección*) selection, assortment, range; (*existencias*) supply, stock; **gran ~** large assortment, wide range; **artículo de ~** article from stock.

surtidor NM **(a)** (*chorro*) jet, spout; (*fuente*) fountain. **(b)** **~ de gasolina** petrol pump. **(c)** (*LAm: de droga*) drug pusher.

surtir [3a] ⊡ VT **(a)** (*suministrar*) to supply, furnish, provide; **~ a uno de combustible** to supply sb with fuel; **~ el mercado** to supply the market; **~ un pedido** to fill an order.
(b) *efecto* to have, produce; *V* **efecto (a)**.
⊡ VI to spout, spurt (up), rise.
⊡ **surtirse** VR: **~ de** to provide o.s. with.

surto ADJ anchored.

suruca NF (*Carib*) **(a)** (*algazara*) din, uproar. **(b)** (*borrachera*) drunkenness.

suruco⁑ NM (*Cono Sur*) crap⁑, shit⁑.

surumbático ADJ (*LAm*) = **zurumbático**.

surumbo ADJ (*CAm*) = **zurumbo**.

surumpe NM (*And*) inflammation of the eyes (*caused by snow glare*),

➤ LENGUA Y USO: **suponer:** 1a → 53.1, 53.2   1b → 53.6   **supuesto:** 4b → 36.2, 40.2

snow blindness.

surupa NF (*Carib*) cockroach, roach (*US*).

suruví NM (*Cono Sur*) catfish.

survietnamita ADJ, NMF South Vietnamese.

susceptibilidad NF **(a)** (*V* ADJ **(b)**) susceptibility (*a* to); sensitivity; touchiness; impressionable nature.
(b) ~**es** susceptibilities; **ofender las ~es de uno** to offend sb's susceptibilities.

susceptible ADJ **(a)** ~ **de** capable of; ~ **de mejora(r** capable of improvement, open to improvement; ~ **de sufrir daño** liable to suffer damage.
(b) *persona* susceptible; (*sensible*) sensitive; (*quisquilloso*) touchy; (*impresionable*) impressionable.

suscitar [1a] VT *rebelión etc* to stir up; *conflicto, escándalo, revuelo etc* to make, cause, provoke; *debate* to start; *duda, problema* to raise; *interés, sospechas* to arouse; *consecuencia* to cause, give rise to, bring with it.

▼ <u>**suscribir**</u> [3a; PTP **suscrito**] ☐1 VT **(a)** *contrato, petición etc* to sign; *promesa* to make, agree to, ratify.
▼ **(b)** *opinión* to subscribe to, endorse.
(c) (*Fin*) *acciones etc* to take out an option on; *seguro* to underwrite.
(d) ~ **a uno a una revista** to enter sb as a subscriber to a journal, put sb on the subscription list of a journal; **A le suscribió a B por 100 dólares** A put B down for a 100-dollar contribution.
☐2 **suscribirse** VR to subscribe (*a* to, for); **¿te vas a suscribir?** are you going to subscribe?; ~ **a una revista** to take out a subscription for a magazine (*o* journal).

suscripción NF subscription; **por ~ popular** by public subscription; **abrir una ~** to take out a subscription; **cerrar su ~** to cancel one's subscription.

suscriptor(a) NM/F subscriber.

suscrito PTP *de* **suscribir**.

Suso NM *familiar form of* **Jesús**.

susodicho ADJ above-mentioned.

suspender [2a] VT **(a)** *objeto* to hang, hang up, suspend (*de* from, on).
(b) (*fig*) *pago, trabajo etc* to stop, suspend; *reunión, sesión* to adjourn; *proceso etc* to interrupt; ~ **hasta más tarde** to put off till later, postpone for a time.
(c) (*Univ etc*) *candidato, asignatura* to fail.
(d) (*fig: pasmar*) to astound, astonish; to fill with wonder, cause to marvel.

suspense NM suspense.

suspensión NF **(a)** (*acto*) hanging (up), suspension.
(b) (*Aut, Mec*) suspension; ~ **hidráulica** hydraulic suspension; **con ~ independiente** with independent suspension.
(c) (*fig*) stoppage, suspension; adjournment; interruption; postponement; (*Jur*) stay; ~ **de empleo** suspension (from work) on full pay; ~ **de empleo y sueldo** suspension without pay; ~ **de fuego, ~ de hostilidades** ceasefire, cessation of hostilities; ~ **de pagos** suspension of payments.
(d) (*pasmo*) astonishment; wonderment; (*Liter, Teat etc*) suspense.

suspensivo ADJ: **puntos ~s** dots, suspension points.

suspenso ☐1 ADJ **(a)** (*colgado*) hanging, suspended; hung (*de* from).
(b) (*Univ etc*) *candidato* failed.
(c) (*fig*) **estar ~, quedarse ~** (*pasmarse*) to be astonished, be amazed; (*maravillarse*) to be filled with wonder; (*aturdirse*) to be bewildered, be baffled.
☐2 NM **(a)** (*Univ etc*) fail, failure.
(b) (*esp LAm*) suspense; **estar en ~, quedar en ~** to be in suspense, be pending; (*Jur: ley*) to be suspended, be in abeyance; (*pleito*) to stand over, be postponed.

suspensores NMPL (*LAm*) braces, suspenders (*US*).

suspensorio ☐1 ADJ suspensory.
☐2 NM jockstrap; (*Med*) suspensory (bandage).

suspicacia NF suspicion, mistrust.

suspicaz ADJ suspicious, distrustful.

suspirado ADJ longed-for, yearned for.

suspirar [1a] VI (*t fig*) to sigh (*por* for).

suspiro NM **(a)** (*gen*) sigh; (*fig*) sigh, breath, rustle, whisper; ~ **de alivio** sigh of relief; **deshacerse en ~s** to sigh deeply, heave a great sigh; **exhalar el último ~** to breathe one's last. **(b)** (*LAm Culin*) meringue.

sustancia NF (*gen*) substance; (*esencia*) essence; (*materia*) matter; ~ **(de carne)** (*Culin*) stock; ~ **gris** (*Anat*) grey matter; **en ~** in substance, in essence; **sin ~** lacking in substance; (*poco profundo*) shallow, superficial.

sustancial ADJ **(a)** (*lit*) substantial; (*fundamental*) essential, vital, fundamental. **(b)** = **sustancioso**.

sustancialmente ADV (*V* ADJ) substantially; essentially, vitally, fundamentally.

sustancioso ADJ *discurso etc* solid; meaty; *comida* solid, substantial; (*nutritivo*) nourishing.

sustantivación NF nominalization.

sustantivar [1a] VT to use as a noun.

sustantivo ☐1 ADJ substantive; (*Ling*) substantival, noun (*atr*).
☐2 NM noun, substantive; ~ **contable** count-noun; ~ **no contable** mass noun.

sustentabilidad NF viability.

sustentable ADJ viable, sustainable.

sustentación NF sustenance; support; (*Aer*) lift.

sustentar [1a] ☐1 VT **(a)** *objeto* to hold up, support, (bear the weight of).
(b) (*alimento*) to sustain, nourish, feed, keep going.
(c) (*fig*) *esperanza etc* to sustain, keep going, buoy up.
(d) *idea, teoría* to maintain, uphold, defend.
☐2 **sustentarse** VR: ~ **con** to sustain o.s. with, subsist on; ~ **de esperanzas** to sustain o.s. with hopes, live on hopes; ~ **del aire** to live on air.

sustento NM (*apoyo*) support; (*alimento*) sustenance, food; (*mantenimiento*) maintenance; (*fig*) livelihood; **ganarse el ~** to earn one's living, earn a livelihood; **es el ~ principal de la institución** it is the lifeblood of the institution.

sustitución NF substitution (*por* for), replacement (*por* by).

sustituible ADJ replaceable; expendable.

sustituir [3g] ☐1 VT to substitute, replace; ~ **A por B** to substitute B for A, replace A by B, replace A with B, put A in place of B; **tendremos que ~ el neumático pinchado** we shall have to change (*o* replace) the flat tyre; **le quieren ~** they want to remove him, they want him replaced.
☐2 VI to substitute; to deputize; ~ **a** to replace; to substitute for, deputize for; **los sellos azules sustituyen a los verdes** the blue stamps are replacing the green ones.

sustitutivo ☐1 ADJ substitute; **géneros propios ~s de los importados** home-produced goods in substitution of (*o* to replace) imported ones.
☐2 NM substitute (*de* for); **es un ~ del café** it is a coffee substitute.

sustituto, -a NM/F substitute, replacement; deputy.

sustitutorio ADJ substitute, replacement (*atr*); equivalent; *V* **servicio (c)**.

susto NM **(a)** (*gen*) fright, scare; **¡qué ~!** what a scare!; **caerse del ~** to be frightened to death; **dar un ~ a uno** to give sb a fright (*o* scare); **darse un ~, pegarse un ~** to have a fright, give o.s. a fright; **no gana para ~s** she never gets a moment's peace; **este año no ganamos para ~s** it's been one blow after another this year; **meter un ~ a uno** to put the wind up sb.
(b) (*And: crisis nerviosa*) nervous breakdown.
(c) **el ~** (*hum: en restaurante*) the bill.

sustracción NF **(a)** (*acto*) removal; (*Mat*) subtraction, taking away; deduction; extraction. **(b)** (*robo*) theft; ~ **de menores** child abduction.

sustraer [2p] ☐1 VT **(a)** (*llevarse*) to remove, take away; (*Mat*) to subtract, take away; (*descontar*) to deduct; *agua etc* to extract.
(b) (*robar*) to steal; *persona* to abduct.
☐2 **sustraerse** VR: ~ **a** (*evitar*) to avoid; (*apartarse de*) to withdraw from, contract out of; ~ **a** + *infin* to avoid + *ger*, get out of + *ger*; **no pude sustraerme a la tentación** I could not resist the temptation.

sustrato NM substratum.

susurrante ADJ (*fig*) (*viento*) whispering; (*arroyo*) murmuring; (*follaje*) rustling.

susurrar [1a] VI **(a)** (*persona*) to whisper; ~ **al oído de uno** to whisper to sb, whisper in sb's ear.
(b) (*fig*) (*viento*) to whisper; (*insecto*) to hum; (*arroyo*) to murmur; (*hojas*) to rustle.
☐2 **susurrarse** VR: **se susurra que ...** it is being whispered that ..., it is rumoured that ...

susurro NM **(a)** (*cuchicheo*) whisper. **(b)** (*V* VI **(b)**) whisper; hum, humming; murmur; rustle.

sutil ADJ **(a)** *hebra, hilo etc* fine, delicate, tenuous; *rodaja* thin; *tela* (*fino*) thin, light; (*suave*) very soft; *aire* thin; *olor* delicate; subtle; *brisa etc* gentle. **(b)** *diferencia* fine, subtle, nice. **(c)** *mente, persona* sharp, keen, observant; subtle; *observación* subtle.

sutileza NF **(a)** (*cualidad*) fineness, delicacy; thinness; subtlety, subtleness; sharpness, keenness. **(b)** (*una ~*) subtlety; (*pey*) artifice, artful deceit.

sutilizar [1f] ☐1 VT **(a)** *objeto* (*reducir*) *etc* to thin down, fine down; (*fig: pulir*) to polish, perfect; (*fig: perfeccionar*) to refine (upon).
(b) *concepto etc* (*pey*) to quibble about, split hairs about.
☐2 VI (*pey*) to quibble, split hairs.

sutura NF suture.

suturar [1a] VT to suture; to stitch.

suyo ADJ Y PRON POS ☐1 (*tras verbo* **ser** *o con artículo*) **(a)** (*de él*) his, (*de ella*) hers, (*de cosa*) its, (*de uno mismo*) one's; (*de Vd*) yours; **es ~, es el ~** it is his (*etc*); **¿es ~ esto?** is this yours?; **lo ~** (what is) his, what belongs to him; **los ~s** (*parientes*) his people, his relations, his family; (*partidarios*) his people, his supporters.

(b) (*de ellos, de ellas*) theirs; (*de Vds*) yours.

2 (*tras* N) **(a)** (*de él*) of his, (*de ella*) of hers; (*de la cosa misma*) of its own, (*de uno mismo*) of one's own; (*de Vd*) of yours; **no es amigo ~** he is no friend of hers.

(b) (*de ellos, de ellas*) of theirs; (*de Vds*) of yours.

3 ADJ Y PRON (*locuciones*): **de ~** in itself, per se; intrinsically; on its own; **eso es muy ~** that's just like him, that's typical of him; **él es un hombre muy ~** (*reservado*) he's a man who keeps very much to himself; (*quisquilloso*) he's a very fussy sort; **él pesa lo ~*** he's really heavy, he weighs a bit; **aguantar lo ~** to shoulder one's burden; to put up with a lot; **eso cae de ~** that's obvious, that goes without saying; **estar en lo mejor ~*** to be on top form, be in one's best form; **hizo suyas mis palabras** he echoed my words, he supported what I had said; **hacer de las suyas** to get up to one's old tricks; **ir a la suya, ir a lo ~** to go one's own way; (*pey*) to act selfishly, think only of o.s.; **salirse con la suya** to get one's way; (*en discusión*) to carry one's point; **valorar lo ~** to be worth one's keep; **cada cual a lo ~** it's best to mind one's own business.

svástica NF swastika.

swing [es'win] NM **(a)** (*Mús*) swing. **(b)** (*Golf*) swing.

switch [switʃ] NM (*esp Méx*) switch; (: *Aut*) ignition.

T

T, t [te] NF (*letra*) T, t.

t. NM(PL) ABR *de* **tomo(s)** volume(s), vol(s).

TA NF ABR *de* **traducción automática** automatic translation, A.T.

taba NF (*Anat*) anklebone; (*juego*) knucklebones, jackstones (*US*); **menear las ~s*** to bustle about; to get cracking*, get moving.

tabacal NM (*LAm*) (*sembrío*) tobacco field; (*plantación*) tobacco plantation.

Tabacalera NF *Spanish state tobacco monopoly; ver también* ESTANCO .

tabacalera NF (*Méx*) cigarette factory.

tabacalero ① ADJ tobacco (*atr*).

② NM (*en tienda*) tobacconist; (*cultivador*) tobacco grower; (*comerciante*) tobacco merchant.

tabaco ① NM (**a**) (*gen*) tobacco; (*cigarrillos*) cigarettes, (*puro*) cigar (*esp LAm*); (*Bot*) tobacco plant; **~ amarillo, ~ americano** Virginian tobacco; **~ de hebra** loose tobacco; **~ de mascar** chewing tobacco; **~ negro** dark tobacco; **~ de pipa** pipe-tobacco; **~ en polvo** snuff; **~ en rama** leaf tobacco; **~ rubio** Virginian tobacco; **~ turco** Turkish tobacco; **¿tienes ~?** have you any cigarettes?; **se me acabó el ~** I've run out of cigarettes, I had nothing left to smoke; **se le acabó el ~** (*Cono Sur**) he ran out of dough‡; **estar de mal ~** (*CAm**) to be in a bad mood; **estaba hecho ~** (*: *persona*) he was all in; (*objeto*) it was all torn to pieces; **quitar el ~ a uno‡** to do sb in‡.

(**b**) (*LAm*: *droga*) reefer‡, joint‡.

(**c**) (*Carib**: *golpe*) slap, smack.

② ADJ (*LAm*) dusty brown.

tabacón‡ NM (*Méx*) marijuana, grass‡.

tabalada NF bump, heavy fall.

tabalear [1a] ① VT to rock; to swing.

② VI to drum (with one's fingers), tap.

tabaleo NM rocking; swinging; drumming, tapping.

tabanco NM (**a**) (*CAm*: *desván*) attic. (**b**) (*Méx*: *puesto*) stall.

tábano NM horsefly, gadfly.

tabaqueada* NF (*Méx*) (*paliza*) beating-up*; (*pelea*) fist-fight.

tabaquear [1a] VI (*And*) to smoke.

tabaquera NF (*para tabaco*) tobacco-jar; (*para rapé*) snuffbox; (*de pipa*) bowl; (*LAm*) (*bolsa para tabaco*) tobacco-pouch; (*para puros*) cigar-case; (*para cigarrillos*) cigarette-case.

tabaquería NF (**a**) (*tienda*) tobacconist's (shop), cigar store (*US*) (**b**) (*Carib*: *fábrica*) cigar factory.

tabaquero ① ADJ (*LAm*) tobacco (*atr*).

② NM (*en tienda*) tobacconist; (*cultivador*) tobacco grower; (*comerciante*) tobacco merchant.

tabaquismo NM addiction to tobacco, tobacco habit.

tabaquito NM (*LAm*) small cigar.

tabarra* NF nuisance, bore; **dar la ~** to be a nuisance, be a bore; **dar la ~ a uno** to get on sb's nerves, annoy sb.

tabasco NM Tabasco ®.

tabear [1a] VI (*Cono Sur*) to chat, gossip; to gossip about a person not present.

taberna NF bar, pub; (*Hist*) tavern; (*Cono Sur*) gambling-den; (*Carib*) small grocery shop.

tabernáculo NM tabernacle.

tabernario ADJ *lenguaje etc* rude, dirty, coarse, tavern (*atr*).

tabernero NM (*dueño*) publican, landlord; (*mozo*) barman, bartender.

tabicar [1g] ① VT *puerta* to wall up; *cuarto* to partition off; *nariz* to stop up.

② **tabicarse** VR to get stopped up.

tabicón NM (*Méx*) breeze block.

tabique NM (*pared*) thin wall, partition (wall); (*Méx*: *ladrillo*) brick.

tabla ① NF (**a**) (*de madera*) plank, board; (*estante*) shelf; (*de piedra etc*) slab; (*Arte*) panel; (*Carib*) shop counter; **~ deslizadora, ~ de surf, ~ a vela, ~ de windsurf** surfboard, windsurfing board; **~ de dibujo** drawing-board; **~ de esmeril** emery board; **~ de lavar** washboard; **~**

de picar chopping board; **~ de planchar** ironing-board; **~ de quesos** cheeseboard; **~ de salvación** (*fig*) last resort, sole hope; thing that saves one's life; **~ del suelo** floorboard; **es lo que canta** (*o* **marca**) **la ~** it's the rule, it's what the book says; **escaparse** (*o* **salvarse**) **en una ~** to have a narrow escape, have a close shave; **estar en las ~s** (*Carib*) to be destitute; **hacer ~ rasa de** to disregard utterly, sweep aside, ride roughshod over; **lo hizo por ~s*** she (only) just managed it, she very nearly didn't manage it.

(**b**) **~s** (*Taur*) boards, fence.

(**c**) **~s** (*Teat*) boards, stage; **coger ~s** to gain acting experience; (*fig*) to get the hang of it; **pisar las ~s** to walk the stage; **salir a las ~s** to have a good stage presence; **tener muchas ~s** (*fig*) to be an old hand, be an expert.

(**d**) **~s** (*Ajedrez*) draw; tie; (*fig*) stalemate, deadlock; **~s por ahogado** stalemate; **hacer ~s, quedar** (**en**) **~s** to draw, reach a drawn position; (*fig*) to reach stalemate, be deadlocked; **el partido quedó ~s** the game was a draw, the game was drawn.

(**e**) (*Anat*) flat area, wide part.

(**f**) (*Agr*) plot, patch, bed.

(**g**) (*Cos*) broad pleat.

(**h**) (*Com*) meat stall.

(**i**) (*fig*) table, list, chart; (*Dep*: *t ~ clasificatoria*) table, league table; (*Mat*) table; (*Tip*) table, index; (*Inform*) array; **~s actuariales** actuarial tables; **~ de decisiones** decision table; **~ de ejercicios, ~ de gimnasia** exercise routine, set of exercises; **~ de logaritmos** table of logarithms; **~ de materias** table of contents; **~ de multiplicar** multiplication table; **~ salarial** wage scale; **~ trazadora** plotter; **~ de valores** set of values.

(**j**) (*And*) **cantarle las ~s a uno** to tell it to sb straight; **salir con las ~s** to fail.

② NM (‡) queer‡, fairy‡.

tablada NF (*Cono Sur*) slaughterhouse.

tablado NM (*suelo*) plank floor, boards; (*plataforma*) stand, stage, platform; (*de baile*) dance-floor; (*Hist*) scaffold; (*Teat*) stage.

tablaje NM, **tablazón** NF planks, planking, boards.

tablao NM (= **tablado**) (*espectáculo*) flamenco show; (*escenario*) dance-floor (for flamenco dancing); (*local*) venue for flamenco.

tablear [1a] VT (**a**) *madera* to cut into boards (*o* planks).

(**b**) (*Agr*) *tierra* to divide up into plots.

(**c**) *terreno* to level off; (*Cono Sur*) *masa* to roll out.

(**d**) (*Cos*) to pleat.

tablero NM (**a**) (*de madera*) board(s), plank(s); panel; (*de mármol etc*) slab; (*Escol etc*) blackboard; (*Com*) counter; (*de juegos*) board; (*Cono Sur*: *de anuncios*) notice-board, bulletin board (*US*); (*Elec*) switchboard; **~ de ajedrez** chessboard; **~ de dibujo** drawing-board; **~ de gráficos** (*Inform*) graph pad; **~ de instrumentos, ~ de mandos** instrument panel, (*Aut*) dashboard; **~ posterior** tailboard.

(**b**) (*Agr*) bed(s), plot(s).

(**c**) (*garito*) gambling-den.

tableta NF (**a**) (*de madera*) small board; block; (**b**) (*de escribir*) writing-pad. (**c**) (*Med*) tablet; (*de chocolate*) bar, stick.

tabletear [1a] VI to rattle, clatter; (*ametralladora*) to rattle.

tableteo NM rattle, clatter.

tablilla NF (**a**) small board; (*Med*) splint. (**b**) (*Méx*) bar (of chocolate).

tablista NMF windsurfer.

tabloide NM tabloid.

tablón NM (**a**) plank, beam; **~ de anuncios** notice board, bulletin board (*US*).

(**b**) (*) **coger un ~, pillar un ~** to get tight*.

(**c**) (*LAm Agr*) plot, bed.

tablonazo NM (*Carib*) trick, swindle.

tabú ① ADJ INVAR taboo; **varias palabras ~** several taboo words.

② NM, PL **~s** (*o* **~es**) taboo.

tabuco NM (*chabola*) slum, shack; (*cuarto*) tiny room, poky little room.

tabulación NF (*Inform*) tabbing.

tabulador NM (*Inform*) tab.

tabular [1a] [1] VT to tabulate; (*Inform*) to tab; to tabulate.
[2] ADJ tabular.

taburete NM stool.

tacada NF (*Billar*) stroke; (*serie de puntos*) break; **de una ~** (*fig*) all at once; all in one go.

tacana NF (a) (*And, Cono Sur Agr*) cultivated hillside terrace. (b) (*Cono Sur, Méx: de mortero*) pestle. (c) (*Cono Sur*: *policía*) fuzz*, police.

tacanear [1a] VT (*Cono Sur*) to tread down; to pound, crush.

tacañería NF (V ADJ) (a) meanness, stinginess. (b) craftiness.

tacaño ADJ (a) (*avaro*) mean, stingy. (b) (*astuto*) crafty.

tacar [1g] VT (*And*) (a) (*disparar*) to shoot at. (b) (*llenar*) to fill, pack tightly (*de* with).

tacataca• NM baby-walker.

tacha¹ NF (a) (*Téc*) large tack, brad, stud. (b) (*LAm*) = **tacho**.

tacha² NF flaw, blemish, defect; **sin ~** perfect, flawless; **poner ~ a** to find fault with.

tachadura NF erasure, correction.

tachar [1a] VT (a) (*borrar*) to cross out, erase; (*corregir*) to correct. (b) (*criticar*) to criticize, attack, find fault with; (*Jur*) *testigo* to challenge; **~ a uno de incapaz** to accuse sb of being incompetent.

tachero NM (*Cono Sur*) tinsmith.

tachines: NMPL (*Esp*) (*pies*) plates:, feet; (*zapatos*) shoes.

tacho NM (*LAm*) (*caldero*) boiler, large boiling pan; (*para azúcar*) sugar pan, sugar evaporator; (*balde*) bucket, pail; (*arcón*) bin, container; (*Cono Sur*) washbasin; **~ de basura**, **~ para la basura** dustbin, garbage can (*US*); **~ para lavar la ropa** clothes boiler; **irse al ~** (*Cono Sur•*) to be ruined, fail.

tachón¹ NM (a) (*Téc*) large stud, ornamental stud, boss. (b) (*Cos*) trimming.

tachón² NM erasure, stroke, crossing-out.

tachonado ADJ: **~ de estrellas** star-studded, star-spangled.

tachonar [1a] VT to stud, adorn with studs; (*Cos*) to trim; (*fig*) to stud (*de* with).

tachoso ADJ defective, faulty.

tachuela NF (a) (*clavito*) tack, tintack; (*en vestido*) stud; (*LAm: chincheta*) drawing-pin; (*Carib*) long pin; **me hace ~s** it gives me goosepimples. (b) (*Aut*) speed ramp, sleeping policeman. (c) (*And, Carib: recipiente*) metal pan; (*Carib, Méx: taza*) metal cup, dipper. (d) (*CAm, Cono Sur, Méx*) (*persona*) short stocky person; (*pey*) runt.

tacita NF small cup; **la T~ de Plata** (*affectionate name for*) Cadiz; **como una ~ de plata** as bright as a new pin.

tácitamente ADV tacitly.

Tácito NM Tacitus.

tácito ADJ tacit; *comentario etc* unspoken; *ley* unwritten; (*Ling*) unexpressed, understood.

taciturnidad NF taciturnity, silent nature; moodiness, sullenness; glumness.

taciturno ADJ taciturn, silent; moody, sullen, sulky; glum.

tacizo NM (a) (*And, Carib: hacha*) narrow-bladed axe. (b) (*And: celda*) small prison cell.

taco¹ NM (a) (*de fusil etc*) wad, wadding; (*tarugo*) wooden peg; (*tapón*) stopper, plug, bung; **~ de salida** (*Dep*) starting block. (b) (*de bota*) stud; (*LAm: de zapatos*) heel; (*CAm Dep*) football boot. (c) (*para escribir*) pad; (*calendario*) calendar; (*de billetes etc*) book of travel tickets (*o coupons etc*); (*de cheque etc*) stub; (*Cono Sur*) desk calendar; **~ de papel** writing-pad, pad of notepaper. (d) (*Billar*) cue. (e) (*Mil Hist*) ramrod. (f) (*fusil de juguete*) popgun. (g) (•) (*bocado*) snack, bite; (*trago*) swig of wine•. (h) (*Esp•: palabrota*) rude word, swearword; **dice muchos ~s** he swears a lot; **soltar un ~** to swear. (i) (•: *lío*) tangle, mess; **armarse un ~**, **hacerse un ~** to get into a mess, get all tied up; **dejar a uno hecho un ~** to flatten sb (in an argument). (j) (:: *año*) **tener 16 ~s** to be 16 (years old); **cumple 5 ~s** he's doing 5 years' bird:. (k) (*Cono Sur, Méx: obstáculo*) obstruction, blockage; (*Aut*) traffic jam. (l) (*Méx Culin*) rolled tortilla, taco. (m) (*Cono Sur: chaparro*) short stocky person. (n) (*CAm, Carib: preocupación*) worry, anxiety; fear. (o) **darse ~s** (*CAm, Méx•*) to give o.s. airs.

taco² [1] ADJ (*Carib*) (a) (*currutaco*) foppish. (b) (*emprendedor*) bold, enterprising. [2] NM (a) (*CAm, Carib, Méx*) fop, dandy; **darse ~** to put on airs. (b) (*And•*) big shot•.

tacógrafo NM tacograph.

tacómetro NM tachometer.

tacón NM (a) heel; **~** (**de**) **aguja** stiletto heel; **tacones altos** high heels; **de ~ alto** high-heeled. (b) (:) purse.

taconazo NM (*golpecito*) heel tap; (*patada*) kick with one's heel, blow with the heel; **~s** (*Mil*) heel-clicking; **entró y dio un ~** he came in and clicked his heels.

taconear [1a] [1] VT (*Cono Sur*) to pack tight, fill right up. [2] VI (a) (*dar golpecitos*) to tap (*o stamp*) with one's heels; (*Mil etc*) to click one's heels; (*caminar ruidosamente*) to walk noisily on one's heels; (*con arrogancia*) to strut. (b) (•: *apresurarse*) to bustle about.

taconeo NM tapping (*o stamping*) with one's heels; heel-clicking; noisy walking on one's heels; strutting.

tacote: NM (*Méx*) marijuana, grass:.

táctica NF tactics; (*una ~*) tactic, move; (*gámbito*) gambit; **~ de cerrojo** stonewalling, negative play.

tácticamente ADV tactically.

táctico [1] ADJ tactical. [2] NM tactician; (*Dep*) coach.

táctil ADJ tactile.

tacto NM (a) (*sentido*) touch, sense of touch; (*de mecanógrafa etc*) touch. (b) (*acto*) touch, touching; feel; **ser áspero al ~** to feel rough, be rough to the touch. (c) (*cualidad*) feel; **tiene un ~ viscoso** it has a sticky feel (to it). (d) (*fig*) tact; **tener ~** to be tactful.

tacuache NM (*Carib*) fib, lie.

tacuacín NM (*Méx*) sloth.

tacuaco ADJ (*Cono Sur*) chubby.

tacuche [1] NM (*Méx*) bundle of rags. [2] ADJ worthless.

TAE NF ABR *de* **tasa anual efectiva** (*o* **equivalente**) annual percentage rate, APR.

taekwondista NMF taekwondist.

taekwondo, tae-kwon-do NM taekwondo, tae-kwon-do.

tafetán NM (a) taffeta; **~ adhesivo**, **~ inglés** sticking plaster. (b) **tafetanes** (*fig*) flags; (•) frills, buttons and bows.

tafia NF (*LAm*) rum.

tafilete NM morocco leather.

tagalo, -a [1] ADJ, NM/F Tagalog. [2] NM (*Ling*) Tagalog.

tagarnia• NF: **comer hasta la ~** (*And, CAm*) to stuff o.s.•.

tagarnina NF (a) (*puro*) (cheap) cigar. (b) (*Méx*) leather tobacco pouch. (c) (*And, CAm, Méx•*) drunkenness; **agarrar una ~•** to get tight•.

tagarote NM (a) (*Zool*) sparrowhawk. (b) (•: *persona*) tall shabby person. (c) (•: *empleadillo*) lawyer's clerk, penpusher. (d) (*CAm•*) big shot•.

tagua NF (*And*) ivory palm.

tahalí NM swordbelt.

Tahití NM Tahiti.

tahona NF (*panadería*) bakery, bakehouse; (*molino*) flourmill.

tahonero NM baker; miller.

tahur NM gambler; (*pey*) cardsharper, cheat.

taifa• NF gang, crew; gang of thieves.

taiga NF taiga.

tailandés, -esa [1] ADJ, NM/F Thai. [2] NM (*Ling*) Thai.

Tailandia NF Thailand.

taima NF (a) (*astucia*) slyness, craftiness, slickness. (b) (*Cono Sur•: terquedad*) obstinacy, pigheadedness.

taimadamente ADV craftily, cunningly.

taimado ADJ (a) (*astuto*) sly, crafty, slick. (b) (*hosco*) sullen. (c) (*And: perezoso*) lazy.

taimarse [1a] VR (a) (*volverse taimado*) to get sly, adopt crafty tactics. (b) (*amostazarse*) to go into a huff, sulk; (*obstinarse*) to be obstinate, dig one's heels in.

taita NM (a) (•) (*padre*) dad, daddy; (*tío*) uncle. (b) (*Cono Sur etc*) in direct address, term of respect used before a name. (c) (*Cono Sur*) (*matón*) tough, bully; (*pendenciero*) quarrelsome person. (d) (*coime*) pimp.

Taiwán NM Taiwan.

taiwanés, -esa ADJ, NM/F Taiwanese.

taja NF cut.

tajada NF (a) (*Culin*) slice; slab, chunk. (b) (*Fin•*) rake-off•; **sacar ~** to get one's share, get something out of it; to get a rake-off•, take one's cut; (*fig*) to look after Number One. (c) (*Med*) hoarseness. (d) (:) **coger una ~, pillar una ~** to get tight•. (e) (*tajo*) cut, slash; **¡te haré ~s!•** I'll cut you up!

tajadera NF (a) (*hacha*) chopper; (*cincel*) cold chisel. (b) (*tajadero*) chopping block.

tajadero NM chopping block.

tajado ADJ *peña* sheer.

tajador NM (*And*) pencil sharpener.

tajalán ⟨1⟩ ADJ (*Carib*) lazy.

⟨2⟩ NM, **tajalana** NF idler, layabout.

tajaleo* NM (*Carib*) (a) (*comida*) food, grub‡. (b) (*pelea*) row, brawl.

tajaloseo* NM (*Carib*) row.

tajamar NM (a) (*Náut*) stem; (*de puente*) cutwater. (b) (*CAm, Cono Sur: muelle*) mole; (*And, Cono Sur: presa*) dam, dike.

tajante ADJ (a) sharp, cutting.

(b) (*fig*) incisive, sharp, emphatic; *distinción etc* sharp; **contestó con un 'no' ~** he answered with an emphatic 'no'; **una crítica ~ del gobierno** some sharp criticism of the government; **es una persona ~** he's an incisive person.

tajantemente ADV (*fig*) incisively, sharply, emphatically.

tajar [1a] VT to cut, slice, chop.

tajarrazo NM (*CAm, Méx*) slash, wound; (*fig*) damage, harm.

tajeadura NF (*Cono Sur*) long scar.

tajear* [1a] VT (*LAm*) to cut up, chop; to slash.

Tajo NM Tagus.

tajo NM (a) (*acto, herida*) cut, slash; **darse un ~ en el brazo** to cut one's arm; **tirar ~s a uno** to slash at sb.

(b) (*Geog*) cut, cleft; (*precipicio*) steep cliff, sheer drop.

(c) (*zona*) working area; (*: *empleo*) work, job; (*: *oficina, fábrica etc*) workplace; **largarse al ~*** to get off to work, go back on the job; **¡vamos al ~!*** let's get on with it!

(d) (*filo*) cutting edge.

(e) (*Culin*) chopping block; (*Hist*) block (*for executions*).

(f) (*taburete*) small three-legged stool.

tajón NM (*Méx*) slaughterhouse.

tal ⟨1⟩ ADJ such; **~ cosa** such a thing; **~es cosas** such things; **no hay ~ cosa** there's no such thing; **con ~ atrevimiento** with such boldness; **con un resultado ~** with such a result; **el ~ país no existió nunca** such a country never existed; **necesitas tanto dinero para ~ cosa** you need so much money for such-and-such a thing; **~ día hace 10 años** on the corresponding day 10 years ago; **un ~ García** a man called García, one García; **el ~ cura** this priest, this priest we were talking about; (*pey*) this priest person.

⟨2⟩ PRON (*persona*) such a one, sb; (*cosa*) such a thing, sth; **el ~** this man (*etc*) I mentioned, this man we're talking about; such a person; **una ~** (*euf*) a prostitute; **no haré ~** I won't do anything of the sort; **¡no hay ~!** nothing of the sort!; **en la calle de ~** in such-and-such a street; **es jefe de ~ y ~** he's the boss of this and that; **~ como** such as; **~ como es, todavía vale algo** such as it is, it is still worth sth; **y como ~, tiene que pagar los derechos** and as such, he has to pay the fees; **se para aquí ~ cual autocar** an odd coach stops here, a coach stops here occasionally; **vive en ~ o cual hotel** he lives in such-and-such a hotel; **son ~ para cual** they're two of a kind; **sí ~** yes indeed, yes of course; **~ hay que lo piensa** there are some who think so; **hablábamos de que si ~ que si cual** we were talking about this that and the other; **había ruritanos y eslobodos y ~** there were Ruritanians and Slobodians and such (o such like, others of that kind); **fuimos al cine y ~** we went to the pictures and that kind of thing.

⟨3⟩ ADV so; in such a way; **~ como** just as; **estaba ~ como lo dejé** it was just as I had left it; **~ cual** just as it is; **es ~ cual siempre deseaba** it is just what he had always wanted; **ella sigue ~ cual** (*regular*) she's so-so, she's middling fair; (*sin cambio*) she hasn't changed; **~ la madre, cual la hija** like mother, like daughter; **tomaremos algo ligero ~ que una tortilla*** we'll have sth light such as an omelette; **¿qué ~?** how goes it?, how's things?; **¿qué ~ es?** what's she like?; **¿qué ~ estás?** how are you?; **¿qué ~ estoy?** how do I look?; **¿qué ~ el partido?** what was the game like?, how did the game go?; **¿qué ~ tu tío?** how's your uncle?; **¿qué ~ del profesor?** what's the news of the professor?; **¿qué ~ te gusta?** what do you think of it?, how do you like it? **¿qué ~ si lo compramos?** how about buying it?, suppose we buy it?; *V t* **cual** *para otras comparaciones*.

⟨4⟩ CONJ: **con ~ (de) que** ... provided (that) ..., on condition that ...; **con ~ de no volver nunca** on condition that he (*etc*) never comes back; **no importa el frío con ~ de ir bien abrigado** the cold doesn't matter if you're well wrapped up.

tala NF (a) *acto*) tree felling, wood cutting; (*fig*) havoc, destruction. (b) (*Carib: hacha*) axe. (c) (*Carib: huerto*) vegetable garden. (d) (*Cono Sur: pasto*) grazing.

talabarte NM sword belt.

talabartería NF (a) (*taller*) saddlery, harness-maker's shop. (b) (*LAm: tienda*) leather-goods shop.

talabartero NM saddler, harness maker.

talacha NF, **talache** NM (*Méx*) mattock.

talado NM felling.

taladradora NF drill; **~ de fuerza** power drill; **~ neumática** pneumatic drill.

taladrante ADJ piercing.

taladrar [1a] VT (a) (*gen*) to bore, drill, punch, pierce; *billete* to punch; *lóbulo* to pierce.

(b) (*fig: dolor, ruido*) to pierce; **un ruido que taladra los oídos** an ear-splitting noise; **es un ruido que taladra** it's a shattering noise.

taladro NM (a) (*herramienta*) drill; auger, gimlet; borer; **~ de billetes** ticket punch; **~ mecánico** power drill; **~ neumático** pneumatic drill.

(b) (*agujero*) drill hole.

talaje NM (a) (*Cono Sur: pasto*) pasture. (b) (*Cono Sur, Méx: pastoreo*) grazing.

tálamo NM marriage bed.

talamoco ADJ (*And*) albino.

talante NM (a) (*voluntad*) mood, disposition, frame of mind; (*humor*) will, willingness; (*tendencia*) tendency; **estar de buen ~** to be in a good mood, be in the right frame of mind; **hacer algo de buen ~** to do sth willingly; **recibir a uno de buen ~** to give sb a warm welcome; **estar de mal ~** to be in a bad mood; **responder de mal ~** to answer with an ill grace, answer bad-temperedly.

(b) (*aspecto*) mien, look, appearance.

talar [1a] VT (a) *árbol* to fell, cut down. (b) (*fig*) to lay waste, devastate. (c) (*Prov, LAm: podar*) to prune.

talco NM talcum powder; (*Min*) talc.

talcualillo* ADJ so-so, middling, fair.

talega NF (a) (*bolsa*) sack, bag. (b) (*pañal*) baby's nappy, diaper (*US*).

(c) **~s** (‡) money. (d) **~s** (⁂) balls⁂.

talegada NF, **talegazo** NM heavy fall, severe bump.

talego NM (a) (*bolsa grande*) big sack, long sack, poke. (b) (*: *persona*) fat person, lump. (c) **tener ~*** to have money stashed away*; **no tengo ~** I'm broke*. (d) (‡: *droga*) small bar of hash*. (e) (‡: *cárcel*) nick‡, jail. (f) (*Fin*‡) 1000 pesetas; **medio ~** 500 pesetas.

taleguilla NF bullfighter's breeches.

talejo NM (*And*) paper bag.

talento NM (a) (*gen*) talent; ability, gift; **~s** talents; accomplishments. (b) (*Bib*) talent.

talentoso ADJ talented, gifted.

talero NM (*Cono Sur*) whip.

Talgo ['talɣo] NM (*Ferro*) ABR de **tren articulado ligero Goicoechea-Oriol** *Inter-city high-speed train.*

talidomida NM thalidomide.

talión NM: **la ley del ~** an eye for an eye.

talismán NM talisman.

talla¹ NF (a) (*t obra de ~*) (*Arte: esp de madera*) carving; (*escultura*) sculpture; (*grabado*) engraving.

(b) (*altura: de persona*) height, stature; (*fig*) stature; (*de prenda*) size, fitting; **camisas de todas las ~s** shirts in all sizes; **tener poca ~** to be short, be on the short side; **ha crecido de ~** (*fig*) he has grown in stature; (*fig*) **dar la ~** to set the standard; **no dio la ~** he didn't measure up (to the task), he wasn't up to it.

(c) (*vara*) measuring rod.

(d) (*Med*) gallstones operation.

(e) (*Naipes*) hand.

(f) (*Jur*) reward (*for capture of a criminal*); **poner a uno a ~** to offer a reward for the capture of sb.

talla² NF (a) (*CAm: mentira*) fib, lie. (b) (*Cono Sur*) (*chismes*) gossip, chit-chat; (*piropo*) compliment; **echar ~s** to put on airs; **echar ~(s) a uno** to tease somebody; **echar ~s a una** to pay a compliment to a woman. (c) (*And: paliza*) beating. (d) (*Méx*: pelea*) set-to*, squabble.

tallado ⟨1⟩ ADJ (a) carved; sculpted; engraved.

(b) **bien ~** shapely, well-formed; **mal ~** misshapen.

⟨2⟩ NM carving; sculpting; engraving; **~ en madera** woodcarving.

tallador NM (a) carver; sculptor; engraver. (b) (*LAm*) dealer, banker.

tallar¹ [1a] ⟨1⟩ VT (a) *madera etc* to carve, shape, work; *piedra* to sculpt; *metal* to engrave; *joya* to cut.

(b) *persona* to measure (the height of).

(c) (*Naipes*) to deal.

⟨2⟩ VI (*Naipes*) to deal, be banker.

tallar² [1a] ⟨1⟩ VT (a) (*And: fastidiar*) to bother, annoy.

(b) (*And: azotar*) to beat.

⟨2⟩ VI (*Cono Sur*) (*chismear*) to chat, gossip; to gossip maliciously; (*amantes*) to whisper sweet nothings.

tallarín NM (a) (*Culin*) noodle.

(b) (*And*: galón*) stripe.

talle NM (a) (*Anat, Cos*) waist; **~ de avispa** wasp waist.

(b) (*Cos etc: medidas*) waist and chest measurements; (*número*) size, fitting.

(c) (*tipo: de mujer*) figure; (*de hombre*) build, physique; **de ~ esbelto** with a slim figure; **tiene buen ~** she has a good figure.

(d) (*fig*) (*aspecto*) look, appearance; (*contorno*) outline.

(e) (*CAm, Cono Sur: corpiño*) bodice.

taller NM (*Téc*) workshop; (*fábrica*) mill, factory; (*Arte*) studio; (*Cos*) workroom; (*en lenguaje sindical*) shop; **~ agremiado** union shop, closed shop; **~ de coches** car repair shop, garage (for repairs); **~es gráficos** printing works; **~ de máquinas** machine-shop; **~ mecánico** garage (for repairs); **~ de montaje** assembly-shop; **~ de reparaciones** repair shop; **~ de trabajo** (*en congreso etc*) workshop.

tallero NM (*LAm*) **(a)** (*verdulero*) vegetable merchant, greengrocer. **(b)** (*embustero*) liar.

tallista NM = **tallador (a)**, (*esp*) wood carver.

tallo NM **(a)** (*Bot*) stem, stalk; (*de hierba*) blade, sprig; shoot.
(b) (*And: repollo*) cabbage.
(c) **~s** (*LAm*) vegetables, greens.
(d) (*Culin*) crystallized fruit.

talludito* ADJ grown-up; quite old; **el actor es ~ ya para este papel** the actor is getting on a bit now for this rôle; **la talludita actriz X** actress X, no longer as young as she was.

talludo ADJ **(a)** (*Bot*) tall; *persona* big, tall, lanky; (*fig*) grown-up; **ya eres una talluda** you're a big girl now, you're too big for that at your age; **es una talluda ya** (*pey*) she's not exactly a youngster, she's no spring chicken.
(b) (*CAm, Méx*) *fruta etc* tough, (*duro*) leathery; (*difícil de pelar*) hard to peel.
(c) (*CAm, Méx*) **es un viejo ~*** he's old but there's life in him yet; **es una máquina talluda*** it's an old machine but it still serves its purpose.

talmente* ADV (*tal*) so, in such a way; (*tan*) to such an extent; (*exactamente*) exactly, literally; **la casa es ~ una pocilga** the house is such a pigsty, the house is literally a pigsty.

Talmud NM Talmud.

talmúdico ADJ Talmudic.

talón NM **(a)** (*Anat*) heel; (*de zapato etc*) heel; **~ de Aquiles** Achilles' heel; **pisar los talones a uno** to be on sb's heels, follow close behind sb; (*fig*) to run sb very close.
(b) (*Aut*) flange, rim.
(c) (*Com etc*) stub, counterfoil; (*Ferro*) luggage receipt; (*cheque*) cheque; **~ en blanco** blank cheque; **~ sin fondos** bad cheque; **~ al portador** bearer cheque, cheque payable to bearer.

talonador NM (*Rugby*) hooker.

talonar [1a] VT **(a)** (*Rugby*) to heel. **(b)** (*en carrera*) to be hard on the heels of.

talonario ① ADJ: **libro ~ = 2.**
② NM receipt book; book of tickets, book of counterfoils; **~ (de cheques)** cheque book.

talonear [1a] ① VT **(a)** (*Dep*) to heel. **(b)** (*LAm*) *caballo* to dig one's heels into, spur along.
② VI **(a)** (*precipitarse*) to walk briskly, hurry along. **(b)** (*Méx: prostituta*) to walk the streets, ply her trade.

talonera NF heel-pad; (*And*) heel.

talquera NF talcum powder container; (*con borla*) compact.

talquina* NF (*Cono Sur*) deceit, treachery.

taltuza NF (*CAm*) raccoon.

talud NM slope, bank; (*Geol*) talus.

tamal NM **(a)** (*LAm Culin*) tamale.
(b) (*Cono Sur*) bundle of clothing; (*Méx*) pile, bundle.
(c) (*LAm*) (*trampa*) fraud, trick, hoax; (*intriga*) intrigue; **hacer un ~** to prepare a trick, set a trap.

tamalero (*LAm*) ① ADJ **(a)** fond of tamales. **(b)** (*intrigante*) intriguing, fond of intrigue.
② NM, **tamalera** NF tamale maker, tamale seller.

tamango NM (*Cono Sur*) **(a)** (*zapato*) sandal. **(b)** (*vendas*) bandages.

tamañito ADJ: **dejar a uno ~** to make sb feel very small; to crush sb, flatten sb (in an argument); **me quedé ~** I felt about so high; I felt utterly bewildered.

tamaño ① ADJ **(a)** (*tan grande*) so big, such a big; (*tan pequeño*) so small, such a small; **parece absurdo que cometiera ~ error** it seems absurd that he should make so grave an error (*o* such a great error); **una piedra tamaña como una naranja** a stone as big as an orange.
(b) (*LAm*) huge, colossal.
② NM size; **~ de bolsillo** pocket-size; **una foto ~ carnet** a passport-size photo; **de ~ extra, de ~ extraordinario** outsize, extra large; **~ familiar** family-size; **~ gigante** king-size, vast; **de ~ natural** full-size, life-size; **ser del mismo ~, tener el mismo ~** to be the same size; **¿de qué ~ es?** what size is it?, how big is it?

támara NF date-palm; **~s** dates, cluster of dates.

tamarindo NM **(a)** (*Bot*) tamarind. **(b)** (*Méx‡*) traffic policeman, traffic cop (*).

tamarisco NM, **tamariz** NM tamarisk.

tambache NM (*Méx*) (*de ropa*) bundle of clothes; (*bulto*) big package.

tambaleante ADJ staggering, tottering; unsteady; swaying.

tambalearse [1a] VR (*LAm: t* **tambalear**) (*persona*) to stagger, totter, reel; to zigzag; to wobble (from side to side); (*vehículo*) to lurch, sway; (*mueble*) to wobble; **ir tambaleándose** to stagger along; to lurch along, sway about (as one walks *etc*).

tambaleo NM (*de persona*) staggering; (*de vehículo*) swaying; (*de mueble*) wobble.

tambar [1a] VT (*And*) to swallow.

tambarria* NF (*And, CAm*) binge*, booze-up*.

tambero NM (*Cono Sur*) (*fondista*) innkeeper; (*granjero*) dairy farmer.

▼ **también** ADV also, as well, too; besides; **¿Vd ~?** you too?; **y bebe ~** and he drinks as well, he also drinks; **no sólo A sino ~ B** not only A but also B; **'¿y es guapa?'** ... **'~'** 'and is she pretty?' ... 'she's that as well'; **los ~ parados X y Z** X and Z, who are also out of work.

tambo NM **(a)** (*And†† : taberna*) country inn, roadside inn. **(b)** (*Cono Sur: corral*) milking yard. **(c)** (*Cono Sur: burdel*) brothel.

tambocha NF (*LAm*) red ant.

tambor NM **(a)** (*Mús, Téc*) drum; (*botella*) bottle; (*Arquit, Cos*) tambour; (*Anat*) eardrum; **~ de tostar café** coffee roaster; **~ del freno** brake-drum; **~ magnético** (*Inform*) magnetic drum; **venir** (*o* **salir**) **a ~ batiente** to come out with flying colours, emerge in triumph.
(b) (*Mús: persona*) drummer; **~ mayor** drum-major.
(c) (*Carib, Méx: tela*) burlap, sackcloth.

tambora NF **(a)** (*Mús*) (*tambor*) bass drum; (*Méx*) brass band. **(b)** (*Carib*: mentira*) lie, fib.

tamboril NM small drum.

tamborilada NF, **tamborilazo** NM (*batacazo*) bump on one's bottom; (*sacudida*) severe jolt; (*espaldarazo*) slap on the shoulder.

tamborilear [1a] ① VT (*) to praise up, boost.
② VI (*Mús*) to drum, play the drum; (*con dedos*) to drum with one's fingers; (*lluvia*) to patter, drum.

tamborileo NM drumming; patter(ing).

tamborilero, -a NM/F drummer.

tambre NM (*And*) dam.

tamegua NF (*CAm, Méx*) weeding, cleaning.

tameguar [1d] VT (*CAm, Méx*) to weed, clean.

Tamerlán NM Tamburlaine.

Támesis NM Thames.

tamil ADJ, NMF Tamil.

tamiz NM sieve.

tamizado ① ADJ sifted; *luz* filtered.
② NM sifting.

tamizar [1f] VT to sieve, sift.

tamo NM fluff, down, dust; (*Agr*) dust; chaff.

tampa NF (*Cono Sur*) matted hair.

támpax ['tampaks] NM, PL **támpax** ['tampaks] ® (*LAm*) Tampax ®, tampon.

tampiqueño ① ADJ of (*o* from) Tampico.
② NM, **tampiqueña** NF native (*o* inhabitant) of Tampico.

tampoco ADV neither, not ... either; nor; **ni A ni B ~** neither A nor B, not A nor B either; **yo ~ lo compré, yo no lo compré ~** I didn't buy one either; **ni yo ~ nor I;** **'¿lo sabes tú?'** ... **'~'** 'do you know?' ... 'No, I don't either'; **'pero ¿vendrás a la fiesta?'** ... **'~'** 'but you'll be coming to the party?' ... 'No, I shan't come to that either'.

tampón ① NM (*Med*) tampon; (*Téc*) plug; (*Elec, Inform etc*) buffer; **~ de entintar** inking-pad.
② ATR: **parlamento ~** rubber-stamp parliament. **(b)** **sistema ~** buffer system; **zona ~** buffer zone.

tamuga NF **(a)** (*CAm*) (*lío*) bundle, pack; (*mochila*) knapsack. **(b)** (*LAm‡*) joint‡, reefer‡.

▼ **tan** ADV **(a)** so; **~ rápido** so fast; **~ rápidamente** so fast; **no es buena idea comprar un coche ~ grande** it's not a good idea to buy such a big car; **¡qué idea ~ rara!** what an odd notion!; **A es ~ feo como B** A is as ugly as B; **es ~ caro que nadie puede comprarlo** it's so expensive that nobody can afford it; **no te esperaba ~ pronto** I wasn't expecting you so soon; **de ~ rico resulta incomible** it's so rich that one can't eat it; **~ es así que ...** so much so that ...; **~ sólo** just.
(b) (*Méx*) **¿qué ~ grande es?** how big is it?; **¿qué ~ grave está el enfermo?** how ill is the patient?; **¿qué ~ lejos?** how far?

tanaca NF (*And*) slut.

tanaceto NM tansy.

tanaco ADJ (*Cono Sur*) foolish, silly.

tanate NM (*CAm, Méx*) **(a)** (*cesta*) basket, pannier. **(b)** **~s** (*fig*) odds and ends, bits and pieces, gear.

tanatorio NM morgue.

tanda NF **(a)** (*serie etc*) series, set; batch; (*de huevos etc*) layer; (*de inyecciones*) course, series; (*de ladrillos*) course; (*de golpes*) series; **~ de penaltis** series of penalties, penalty shoot-out.
(b) (*turno de trabajo*) shift, turn, spell; (*tarea*) job; task, piece of work; (*de riego*) turn (to use water); (*personas*) shift, relay; gang; **~ de noche** nightshift, spell of night work; **ahora estás de ~** now it's your turn.
(c) (*Billar etc*) game; (*Béisbol*) innings.
(d) (*LAm Teat*) show, performance; (*Cono Sur: farsa*) farce; (*Cono Sur: comedia musical*) musical; **primera ~** first show, early performance.

tándem NM tandem; duo, pair, partnership; **en ~** (*Elec*) in tandem;

➤ LENGUA Y USO: **también** → 53.5   **tan: a** → 32.3

(*fig*) jointly, in association, together.

tanga[1] NF (*a veces* M) tanga, G-string.

tanga[2]: NM (*chulo*) pimp.

tangada: NF trick, swindle.

tangana NF (*Perú*) large oar.

tanganear [1a] VT (*And, Carib*) to beat.

tanganillas: en ~ ADV unsteadily; (*fig*) uncertainly, dubiously; unsafely.

tanganillo NM prop, wedge, temporary support.

tangar: [1h] VT to swindle; **~ algo a uno** to do sb out of sth.

tangencial ADJ tangential; (*fig*) oblique.

tangencialmente ADV tangentially; (*fig*) obliquely.

tangente NF tangent; **salirse por la ~** (*fig: hacer una digresión*) to go off at a tangent; (*esquivar una pregunta*) to dodge the issue, give an evasive answer.

Tánger NM Tangier(s).

tangerino [1] ADJ of Tangier(s).
[2] NM, **tangerina** NF native (o inhabitant) of Tangier(s); **los ~s** the people of Tangier(s).

tangibilidad NF tangibility.

tangible ADJ tangible; (*fig*) tangible, concrete.

tango NM tango.

tanguear [1a] VI (a) (*LAm: bailar*) to tango. (b) (*And: borracho*) to reel drunkenly.

tanguero, -a NM/F, **tanguista** NMF tango dancer.

tánico ADJ tannic; **ácido ~** tannic acid.

tanino NM tannin.

tano* NM (*Cono Sur: pey*) Italian.

tanque NM (a) (*gen*) tank; water store, reservoir; (*Mil*) tank; (*Aut*) tanker, tanker lorry; **~ de cerebros, ~ de ideas** think-tank. (b) (*Esp*) handbag.

tanquero NM (*Carib*) (*Náut*) tanker; (*Aut*) tanker, tank wagon.

tanqueta NF small tank, armoured car.

tanquista NM (*Mil*) member of a tank-crew.

tanta NF (*And*) maize bread.

tantán NM gong; tomtom.

tantarán NM, **tantarantán** NM (a) (*de tambor*) drumbeat, rub-a-dub. (b) (*) (*golpe*) hefty punch; (*sacudida*) violent shaking.

tanteada NF (a) (*LAm*) = **tanteo**. (b) (*Méx*) (*mala pasada*) dirty trick; (*estafa*) hoax, swindle.

tanteador [1] NM scoreboard.
[2] NM, **tanteadora** NF (*persona*) scorer.

tantear [1a] [1] VT (a) *número, total, valor etc* to reckon (up), work out roughly, try to calculate, guess; *tela, cantidad etc* to size up, take the measure of; *peso* to feel, get the feel of, try the weight of; (*fig*) to weigh up, consider carefully.
(b) (*poner a prueba*) to test, try out; (*sondear*) to probe; *intenciones, persona* to sound out; **~ si la superficie está bien segura** to test the surface to see if it is safe, see if the surface is safe.
(c) (*Arte*) to sketch in, draw the outline of.
(d) (*Dep*) to keep the score of.
(e) (*CAm, Méx: acechar*) to lie in wait for.
(f) (*Méx*) (*estafar*) to swindle; (*burlarse*) to make a fool of, take for a ride*.
[2] VI (a) (*Dep*) to score, keep (the) score.
(b) (*LAm: ir a tientas*) to grope, feel one's way; **¿tantee Vd?** what do you think?

tanteo NM (a) reckoning, rough calculation, guesswork; weighing up, careful consideration; **a ~, por ~** by guesswork.
(b) test(ing), trial; trial and error; **al ~** by trial and error; **conversaciones de ~** exploratory talks.
(c) (*Dep*) scoring.

tantico*: **un ~** ADV a bit, quite a bit; **es un ~ difícil** it's a wee bit awkward*.

tantísimo ADJ SUPERL so much; **~s** so many; **había tantísima gente** there was such a crowd, there were so many people; **te lo he dicho tantísimas veces** I've told you lots of times.

tantito* [1] ADJ (*Méx*) a little; **~ pulque** a little pulque.
[2] NM = **tantico**.
[3] ADV (*Méx*) a little; **~ antes** a little earlier.

▼ **tanto** [1] ADJ so much, as much; so many, as many; **tiene ~ dinero como yo** he has as much money as I have; **tiene ~ dinero que no sabe qué hacer con él** he has so much money he doesn't know what to do with it; **hay ~s sellos verdes como azules** there are as many green stamps as (there are) blue ones; **hubo tanta manzana** there were so many apples; **es uno de ~s** it's one of many, it's one of a number; **quedan por ver otros ~s candidatos** there are as many candidates again still to be seen; **se dividen el trabajo en otras tantas porciones** they divide up the work into a like number of parts; **20 y ~s** 20-odd; **treinta y ~s** thirty-something; **tiene 40 y ~s años** he's over 40; **hay ciento y ~s concursantes** there are 100-odd competitors; **a ~s de marzo** on such-and-such a day in March;

a ~s de ~s on such-and-such a day in this or that month; **a las tantas de la madrugada** at some time in the small hours; **volver a casa a las tantas** to come home terribly late; **estar fuera hasta las tantas** to stay out until all hours; **yo no sé qué ~s de libros hay** I don't know how many books there are.
[2] ADV so much, as much; **permanecer ~** to stay so long; **trabajar ~** to work so hard; **venir ~** to come so often; **él gasta ~ como yo** he spends as much as I do; **gastó ~ que se quedó sin dinero** he spent so much that he ran out of money; (*para for*); **~ A como B** both A and B; **~ como eso** ... I don't think it's as bad as all that, I think you're exaggerating; **~ como estafador, no** well, not really a swindler; I wouldn't go so far as to call him a swindler; **~ como corre va a perder la carrera** with all his carry-on he'll end up with no qualifications; **~ como habla no dice más que tonterías** all his talk is just hot air; **es ~ más difícil** it is all the more difficult; **es ~ más loable cuanto que** ... it is all the more praiseworthy because ...; **~ mejor** all the better, so much the better (*para for*); **~ peor** so much the worse; **¡y ~!** and how!, I'll say it is! (*etc*); **~ es así que** ... so much so that ..., so much is this the case that ...; **~ si viene como si no viene** whether he comes or whether he doesn't; **en ~, entre ~** meanwhile, meantime; **no es para ~** it's not as bad as all that;
▼ there's no need to make such a fuss; **por ~, por lo ~** so, therefore; **¡ni ~ así!** not a scrap!; **¡ni ~ ni tan calvo!, ¡ni ~ ni tan poco!** don't exaggerate!, it's not that bad!; **no le tengo ni ~ así de lástima** I haven't a scrap of pity for him; **¿qué ~ será?** (*LAm*) how much (is it)?
[3] CONJ: **con ~ que** ... provided (that) ...; **en ~ (que)** ... while ...; until ...; **hasta ~ que** ... until (such time as) ...
[4] NM (a) (*Com, Fin etc*) certain amount, so much; **~ alzado** agreed price; overall estimate; **por un ~ alzado** for a lump sum; at a flat rate; **~ por palabra** rate per word, so much a word; **~ por ciento** percentage; rate; **un ~ por cada semana de trabajo** so much for each week's work; **al ~** at the same price; **las máquinas costaron otro ~** the machines cost as much again (o the same again).
(b) (*Dep: punto*) point; (*gol*) goal; (*ficha*) counter, chip; **~ en contra** point against; **~ a favor** point for; **~ del honor** consolation goal; **apuntar los ~s** to keep score; **apuntarse un ~** to score a point; (*fig*) to stay one up.
(c) **estar al ~** to be fully informed; to know the score (*fig*); **estar al ~ de los acontecimientos** to be fully abreast of events, be in touch with events; **poner a uno al ~** to give sb the news (*de about*), put sb in the picture (*de about*).
(d) **al ~ de** because of; **al ~ de que** ... because of the fact that ...; with the excuse that ..., on the pretext that ...
(e) **algún ~, un ~** (*como adv*) rather, somewhat; **estoy un ~ cansado** I'm rather tired; **es un ~ difícil** it's a bit awkward.

Tanzania NF Tanzania.

tanzano, -a ADJ, NM/F Tanzanian.

tañar: [1a] VT to grasp, understand; **~ a uno** to twig what sb is saying.*

tañer [2f] [1] VT (*Mús*) to play; *campana* to ring;
[2] VI to drum with one's fingers.

tañido NM (*Mús*) sound; strains, notes; (*de campana*) ringing, pealing.

T/año ABR *de* **toneladas por año**.

TAO NF ABR *de* **traducción asistida por ordenador** computer-assisted translation, CAT.

tapa NF (a) (*de caja, olla*) lid; cover, top; (*de botella*) cap; (*de libro*) cover; (*de cilindro*) head; **~ de registro** manhole cover, inspection cover; **~ de los sesos** brainbox, skull; (*libro de*) **~ dura** hardback (book); **levantarse la ~ de los sesos** to blow one's brains out.
(b) (*de zapato*) heelplate.
(c) (*de canal*) sluicegate.
(d) (*Esp Culin*) dish of hors d'oeuvres; snack, delicacy (*taken at the bar counter with drinks*); **ir de ~s** (*V* **tapeo**).
(e) (*And Culin*) rumpsteak.
(f) (*Méx Aut*) hubcap.
(g) (*Carib*: *comisión*) commission.

tapa(a)gujeros* NM INVAR (a) (*Arquit*) jerry-builder. (b) (*fig*) stand-in, substitute.

tapabarro NM (*And, Cono Sur*) mudguard.

tapaboca NF, **tapabocas** NM INVAR (a) (*manotada*) slap. (b) (*prenda*) muffler.

tapaboquetes NM INVAR stopgap.

tapacubos NM INVAR hubcap.

tapada NF (a) **un gay de ~*** a closet gay*.
(b) (*mentira*) lie.

tapadera NF (a) (*tapa*) lid, cover; cap. (b) (*fig: de organización*) cover, front (organization) (*de for*); (*de espía*) cover.

tapadero NM stopper.

tapadillo: de ~ ADV secretly, stealthily.

tapado [1] ADJ (a) (*Cono Sur*) *animal* all one colour.
(b) (*And*) (*vago*) lazy, slack; (*ignorante*) ignorant.

➤ LENGUA Y USO: **tanto: 2 → 44.1**

2 NM (**a**) (*And, Cono Sur: tesoro*) buried treasure.
(**b**) (*CAm, Cono Sur*) (*abrigo de mujer*), woman's coat; (*de niño*) child's coat; (*Méx: chal*) headscarf, shawl.
(**c**) (*And, CAm Culin*) dish of plantain and barbecued meat.
(**d**) (*Pol*) officially-backed candidate.

tapagrietas NM INVAR filler.

tapalcate NM (*CAm, Méx*) (*objeto*) piece of junk, useless object; (*persona*) useless person.

tapalodo NM (*And, Carib*) mudguard.

tapanca NF (**a**) (*And, Cono Sur*) (*de caballo*) horse trappings; (*LAm: gualdrapa*) saddle blanket. (**b**) (*Cono Sur**: *culo*) backside.

tapaojo NM (*LAm: venda*) blindfold, bandage (over the eyes); (*parche*) patch.

tapaporos NM INVAR primer.

tapar [1a] **1** VT (**a**) (*gen*) to cover, cover up (*de* with); *olla, recipiente* to put the lid on; *botella* to put the cap on, put the stopper in, stopper, cork; *cara* to cover up, hide; (*en cama*) to wrap up; *tubo etc* to stop (up), block (up), obstruct; *agujero* to plug; (*Arquit*) to fill up, wall up, wall in; (*LAm*) *diente* to fill; *objeto* to hide; *vista* to obstruct, block; **el árbol tapa el sol a la ventana** the tree keeps the sunlight off the window, the tree prevents the sun from reaching the window; **el muro nos tapaba el viento** the wall protected us from the wind; **el atleta se encontraba tapado** the athlete was shut in (*o* boxed in).
(**b**) (*fig*) *derrota etc* to cover up, conceal; *fugitivo* to hide, conceal; *criminal* to cover up for.
(**c**) (*And: aplastar*) to crush, flatten; (*chafar*) to rumple.
(**d**) (*And: insultar*) to abuse, insult.
2 taparse VR (**a**) to wrap (o.s.) up, (*esp*) to wrap up warmly (in bed). (**b**) (*: *con sombrero*) to put one's hat on.

tapara NF (*Carib*) calabash, gourd.

táparo NM (*And*) (**a**) (*yescas*) tinderbox. (**b**) (*tuerto*) one-eyed person; (*fig*) dolt.

taparrabo NM, **taparrabos** NM INVAR (swimming) trunks; (*oriental etc*) loincloth.

tapatío **1** ADJ of Guadalajara.
2 NM, **tapatía** NF native (*o* inhabitant) of Guadalajara; **los ~s** the people of Guadalajara.

tapayagua NF (*CAm, Méx*), **tapayagüe** NM (*Méx*) (*nubarrón*) stormcloud; (*llovizna*) drizzle.

tape* NM (*Carib*) cover.

tapear [1a] VI V **tapeo**.

tapeo* NM: **ir de ~** (*Esp*) to go round the bars (eating snacks).

tapeque NM (*And*) equipment for a journey.

tapera NF (*LAm*) (*casa*) ruined house; (*pueblo*) abandoned village.

taperujarse* [1a] VR to cover up one's face.

tapesco NM (*CAm, Méx*) (*armazón*) bedframe; (*cama*) camp bed.

tapete NM (*alfombrita*) rug; (*de mesa*) table runner, table cover; **~ verde** card table; **estar sobre el ~** (*fig*) to be under discussion; **poner un asunto sobre el ~** to put a matter up for discussion.

tapetusa NF (*And*) contraband goods, contraband liquor.

tapia NF (**a**) garden wall; mud wall, adobe wall. (**b**) (‡) partner.

tapial NM = **tapia**.

tapialera NF (*And*) = **tapia**.

tapiar [1b] VT to wall in; *ventana* to block up; (*fig*) to block, stop up.

tapicería NF (**a**) (*arte*) tapestry making; upholstery. (**b**) (*tapiz*) tapestry; (*tapices*) tapestries, hangings; (*de coche, mueble etc*) upholstery.

tapicero, -a NM/F upholsterer.

tapiñar‡ [1a] VT to scoff*, eat.

tapioca NF tapioca.

tapir NM tapir.

tapisca NF (*CAm, Méx*) maize harvest, corn harvest (*US*).

tapiscar [1g] VT (*CAm*) *maíz* to harvest.

tapita* *como* ADJ: **estar ~** (*Carib*) to be as deaf as a post.

tapiz NM (*de pared*) tapestry; (*de suelo*) carpet; **~ volador** magic carpet.

tapizado NM tapestries; carpeting; upholstery.

tapizar [1f] VT (**a**) *pared* to hang with tapestries; *mueble* to upholster, cover; *coche* to upholster; *suelo* to carpet, cover.
(**b**) (*fig*) to carpet (*con, de* with).

tapón **1** ADJ (*CAm, Cono Sur*) tailless.
2 NM (**a**) (*de botella*) stopper, cap, top; (*corcho*) cork; (*Téc*) plug, bung, wad; (*para el oído*) ear-plug; (*Aut*) filler-cap; (*Med*) tampon; (*Méx Elec*) fuse; **~ de corona, ~ de rosca** screw top; **al primer ~, zurrapa*** well, the first shot was a failure.
(**b**) (*: *persona*) chubby person.
(**c**) (*estorbo*) obstacle, hindrance; (*Aut* *) slowcoach*.
(**d**) (*Aut: t ~ circulatorio*) traffic-jam.

taponar [1a] VT *botella* to stopper, cork, put the cap on; *tubo* to plug, stop up, block; (*Dep*) to block, stop; (*Med*) to tampon; **~ los oídos** to stop up one's ears.

taponazo NM (*de corcho*) pop.

tapujar* [1a] **1** VT to cheat, con*.

2 tapujarse VR to muffle o.s. up.

tapujo* NM (**a**) (*embozo*) muffler.
(**b**) (*engaño*) deceit, humbug; (*subterfugio*) subterfuge, dodge*; (*secreto*) secrecy; **sin ~s** honestly, openly, aboveboard; without beating about the bush; **andar con ~s** to behave deceitfully, be involved in some shady business; **llevan no sé qué ~ entre manos** they're up to some dodge or other*.

taquear [1a] **1** VT (*LAm: llenar*) to fill right up, pack tight (*de* with); *arma* to fire.
2 VI (**a**) (*And, Cono Sur, Méx: jugar al billar*)) to play billiards.
(**b**) (*Carib: vestirse*) to dress in style.
(**c**) (*Méx: comer tacos*) to have a snack.
3 taquearse VR (*And*) to get rich.

taquería NF (**a**) (*Carib*) cheek. (**b**) (*Méx*) taco restaurant, taco stall.

taquete NM (*Méx*) plug, bung.

taquicardia NF abnormally rapid heartbeat, tachycardia.

taquigrafía NF shorthand, stenography.

taquigráficamente ADV: **tomar un discurso ~** to take a speech down in shorthand.

taquigráfico ADJ shorthand (*atr*).

taquígrafo, -a NM/F shorthand writer, stenographer.

taquilla NF (**a**) (*Ferro*) booking-office, ticket-office; ticket-window; (*Teat*) box-office.
(**b**) (*Teat: recaudación*) takings; (*Dep etc*) gate-money, proceeds.
(**c**) (*carpeta*) file; (*archivador*) filing-cabinet; (*armario*) locker.
(**d**) (*CAm*) (*bar*) bar; (*tienda*) liquor store.
(**e**) (*And, CAm, Cono Sur. clavo*) tack.

taquillaje NM (*Teat etc*) takings, box-office receipts; (*Dep*) gate-money, gate.

taquillero **1** ADJ popular, successful (at the box-office); **ser ~** to be good (for the) box-office, be a draw, be popular; **función taquillera** box-office success, big draw; **el actor más ~ del año** the actor who has been the biggest box-office draw of the year.
2 NM, **taquillera** NF clerk, ticket clerk.

taquimeca NF, **taquimecanógrafa** NF shorthand typist.

taquimecanografía NF shorthand typing.

taquímetro NM (*Aut*) speedometer; (*Agrimensura*) tachymeter.

taquito NM (*Culin*) small slice.

tara¹ NF (**a**) (*Com*) tare.
(**b**) (*fig*) defect, blemish.

tara² NF tally stick.

tarabilla **1** NF (**a**) latch, catch. (**b**) (*: *charla*) chatter.
2 NMF (*) (*hablador*) chatterbox; (*casquivano*) featherbrained person; (*inútil*) useless individual, dead loss.

tarabita NF (**a**) (*de cinturón, hebilla*) tongue. (**b**) (*And*) cable of a rope bridge (*with hanging basket for carrying passengers across ravines*).

taracea NF inlay, marquetry.

taracear [1a] VT to inlay.

tarado **1** ADJ (**a**) (*Com etc*) damaged, defective, imperfect; *animal etc* maimed, weak. (**b**) (*Cono Sur*) *persona* (*mutilado*) physically impaired, crippled; (*raro*) odd, eccentric. (**c**) (*LAm**) (*idiota*) stupid; (*loco*) crazy.
2 NM, **tarada*** NF idiot, cretin.

tarambana(s) NMF (**a**) (*casquivano*) harum-scarum, fly-by-night; (*estrafalario*) crackpot; (*no fiable*) unreliable person. (**b**) (*parlanchín*) chatterbox.

taranta NF (**a**) (*And, Cono Sur Zool*) tarantula. (**b**) (*And, CAm: locura*) mental disturbance, madness; (*CAm*) bewilderment. (**c**) (*Méx: embriaguez*) drunkenness.

tarantear [1a] VI (*Cono Sur: hacer algo imprevisto*) to do something unexpected; (*cambiar*) to chop and change a lot; (*hacer cosas raras*) to behave strangely, be eccentric.

tarantela NF tarantella.

tarantín NM (**a**) (*CAm, Carib Culin*) kitchen utensil. (**b**) (*Carib: patíbulo*) scaffold. (**c**) (*Carib: puesto*) stall. (**d**) **tarantines** (*Carib**), odds and ends.

taranto ADJ (*And*) dazed, bewildered.

tarántula NF tarantula.

tarar [1a] VT (*Com*) to tare.

tarareable ADJ: **melodía ~** catchy tune, tune that you can hum.

tararear [1a] VTI to hum.

tararí* **1** ADJ (*Esp*) crazy.
2 INTERJ no way!*, you must be joking!

tarasca NF (**a**) (*monstruo*) carnival dragon, monster.
(**b**) (*fig*) (*comilón*) glutton; (*sumidero de recursos*) person who is a drain on one's resources.
(**c**) (*: *mujer*) old hag, old bag*; termagant.
(**d**) (*And, CAm, Cono Sur. boca*) big mouth.

tarascada NF (**a**) (*mordisco*) bite; snap. (**b**) (*: *réplica*) tart reply, snappy answer.

tarascar [1g] VT to bite, snap at.

tarasco NM (*And*) bite, nip.

tarascón NM (*LAm*) bite, nip.

tarasquear [1a] VT (*CAm, Cono Sur, Méx*) to bite, snap at; to bite off.

tardanza NF (**a**) (*lentitud*) slowness. (**b**) (*demora*) delay.

tardar [1a] VI (**a**) (*tomar mucho tiempo*) to take a long time, be long; (*llegar tarde*) to be late; (*retardarse*) to delay, linger (on); **a más ~, a todo ~** at the latest; **aquí tardan mucho** they are very slow here, they take a long time here; **he tardado un poco debido a la lluvia** I'm a bit late because of the rain, I took longer (to get here) because of the rain; **tardamos 3 horas de A a B** we took 3 hours (to get) from A to B; **escribiré sin ~** I'll write without delay.

(**b**) **~ a** + *infin* to delay + *ger*, be slow to + *infin*; **no tardes a hacerlo** don't put off doing it.

(**c**) **~ en** + *infin* to be slow to + *infin*, take a long time to + *infin*, be long in + *ger*; to be late in + *ger*; **tardó mucho en repararlo** he took a long time to repair it; **tardó 3 horas en encontrarlo** it took him 3 hours to find it, he spent 3 hours looking for it; **no tardes en informarme** tell me at once, inform me without delay; **¿cuánto tardaremos en terminarlo?** how long shall we take to finish it?; **el público no tardó en reaccionar** the spectators were not slow to react.

tarde [1] ADV late; (*demasiado ~*) too late; **un poco más ~** a little later; **de ~ en ~** from time to time; **~ o temprano** sooner or later; **se hace ~** it's getting late; **es ~ para eso** it's too late for that.

[2] NF (*primeras horas*) afternoon; (*últimas horas*) evening, early evening; **¡buenas ~s!** good afternoon!; good evening!; **a la ~** in the evening; by evening; **en la ~ de hoy** this afternoon, this evening; **por la ~** in the afternoon, in the evening; **función de la ~** matinée; **de la ~ a la mañana** overnight, during the night; (*fig*) in no time at all.

tardecer [2d] VI = **atardecer**.

tardecica NF, **tardecita** NF evening, approach of night, dusk.

tardecito ADV (*LAm*) rather late.

tardíamente ADV late, belatedly; too late.

tardío ADJ (*gen*) late; (*atrasado*) overdue, belated, slow to arrive (*etc*); *fruta, patata etc* late.

tardo ADJ (**a**) (*lento*) slow, sluggish; dilatory. (**b**) (*lerdo*) slow (of understanding), dull, dense; **~ de oído** hard of hearing.

tardo... PREF late, *p.ej.* **tardorromano** late Roman; **el tardofranquismo** the last years of the Franco régime.

tardón* ADJ (**a**) (*lento*) slow; dilatory. (**b**) (*lerdo*) dim.

tarea NF (**a**) (*gen*) job, task; (*faena*) chore; (*trabajo asignado*) set piece of work, stint, amount of work set; (*de colegial*) homework; (*Inform*) task; **~ de ocasión** chore; **~ suelta** odd job; **todavía me queda mucha ~** I've still got a lot left to do; **es una ~ poco grata** it's not a very satisfying job; **¡~ te mando!*** you've got a job on there!; you'll have your work cut out!

tareco NM (*And*) old thing, piece of junk; **~s** (*fig*) things, gear, odds and ends.

tarifa NF (*precio*) tariff; (*tasa*) rate; (*lista de precios*) price list, list of charges; (*en vehículo*) fare; **~ de agua** water rate, water charges; **~ de anuncios** advertisement rates; **~ nocturna** (*Telec*) cheap rate; **~ de suscripción** subscription rate; **~ turística** tourist class, tourist rates.

tarifar [1a] [1] VT to price.

[2] VI to fall out, quarrel.

tarifario ADJ price (*atr*); rate (*atr*); tariff (*atr*).

tarificación NF metering.

tarificar [1g] VT (*Telec*) to meter.

tarima NF (*plataforma*) platform; (*estrado*) low dais; (*soporte*) stand; (*banquillo*) low bench.

tarimaco NM (*Carib*) = **tareco**.

tarja¹ NF tally, tally stick.

tarja² NF (*: *golpe*) swipe, bash*.

tarjar [1a] VT (**a**) to keep a tally of, notch up. (**b**) (*And, Cono Sur*: *tachar*) to cross out.

tarjeta NF card; **~ amarilla** (*Dep*) yellow card; **~ bancaria** bank-card; **~ de circuitos impresos** printed circuit board; **~ comercial** business card; **~ de crédito** credit-card; **~ de embarque** boarding-pass; **~ de expansión** expansion board; **~ de felicitaciones, ~ de saludo** greetings card; **~ de gráficos** graphics card; **~ de identidad** identity card; **~ inteligente** smart card; **~ de lector** reader's ticket; **~ de multifunción** multifunction card; **~ de Navidad, ~ navideña** Christmas card; **~ perforador** punched card; **~ de periodista** press card; **~ postal** postcard; **~ de presentación** business card; **~ de respuesta** reply card; **~ de respuesta pagada** reply-paid postcard; **~ roja** (*Dep*) red card; **~ de sonido** sound card; **~ telefónica** phonecard; **~ verde** green card; **~ de visita** visiting card, calling card (*US*); **dejar ~** to leave one's card; **pasar ~** to send in one's card.

tarjetear [1a] VT: **~ a un jugador** to show a card to a player.

tarjetero [1] ADJ: **el árbitro se mostró muy ~** (*Ftbl*) the referee was constantly reaching for his pocket, the referee booked a lot of players.

[2] NM (*cartera*) credit card holder, credit card wallet.

tarot NM tarot.

tarpón NM tarpon.

tarquín NM mud, slime, ooze.

tarra* NMF old geezer*.

tarraconense [1] ADJ of Tarragona.

[2] NMF native (*o* inhabitant) of Tarragona; **los ~s** the people of Tarragona.

tarrajazo NM (**a**) (*And, Carib*: *suceso*) unpleasant event. (**b**) (*CAm*) (*golpe*) blow; (*herida*) wound.

tarramenta NF (*Carib, Méx*) horns.

tarrayazo NM (**a**) (*And, Carib, Méx*) (*de red*) cast (of a net). (**b**) (*Carib*: *golpe*) violent blow.

tarrear [1a] VT (*Carib*) to cuckold.

tarrina NF small container; pot, jar; (*de helado*) tub.

tarro NM (**a**) (*pote*) pot, jar.

(**b**) (*) **comer el ~ a uno** (*engañar*) to put one over on sb*; (*lavar el cerebro*) to brainwash sb; **comerse el ~** (*Esp*) to think hard, rack one's brains.

(**c**) (*And, Cono Sur*) (*lata*) tin, can; (*bidón*) drum; **arrancarse con los ~s*** to run off with the loot*.

(**d**) (*Carib, Cono Sur, Méx*: *cuerno*) horn.

(**e**) (*And††*: *chistera*) top hat.

(**f**) (*Cono Sur*: *chiripa*) stroke of luck, fluke.

(**g**) (*Carib*: *del marido*) cuckolding.

(**h**) (*Carib*: *asunto*) difficult matter, complicated affair.

tarsana NF (*LAm*) soapbark.

tarso NM tarsus.

tarta NF (**a**) (*pastel*) cake; (*torta*) tart; flan, sponge; **~ de bodas, ~ nupcial** wedding cake; **~ de cumpleaños** birthday-cake; **~ de frutas** fruit-cake; **~ de queso** cheesecake; **~ de Reyes** Christmas cake; **repartir la ~ nacional** to divide up the national cake. (**b**) (*Inform*) pie-chart.

tártago NM (**a**) (*Bot*) spurge.

(**b**) (*: *desgracia*) mishap, misfortune.

(**c**) (*: *trastada*) practical joke.

tartaja [1] ADJ stammering, tongue-tied.

[2] NMF stammerer.

tartajear [1a] VI to stammer.

tartajeo NM stammer(ing).

tartajoso, -a ADJ, NM/F = **tartaja**.

tartalear [1a] VI (**a**) (*al andar*) to walk in a daze; to stagger, reel. (**b**) (*al hablar*) to stammer, be stuck for words.

tartamudeante ADJ stuttering, stammering.

tartamudear [1a] VI to stutter, stammer.

tartamudeo NM stutter(ing), stammer(ing).

tartamudez NF stutter, stammer, speech defect.

tartamudo [1] ADJ stuttering, stammering.

[2] NM, **tartamuda** NF stutterer, stammerer.

tartán NM tartan.

tartana NF trap, light carriage.

tartancho ADJ (*And, Cono Sur*) = **tartamudo**.

Tartaria NF Tartary.

tartárico ADJ tartaric; **ácido ~** tartaric acid.

tártaro¹ NM (*Quím etc*) tartar.

tártaro², -a ADJ, NM/F Tartar.

tartera NF cake-tin.

Tarteso NM Tartessus; (*Biblia*) Tarshish.

tarugo [1] ADJ (**a**) (*esp LAm*) stupid.

(**b**) (*Carib*) fawning.

[2] NM (**a**) (*pedazo de madera*) lump, chunk (of wood *etc*); (*clavija*) wooden peg; (*tapón*) plug, stopper; (*pan*) chunk of stale bread; (*adoquín*) wooden paving block.

(**b**) (*Carib**: *susto*) fright, scare.

(**c**) (*esp LAm*: *imbécil*) chump*, blockhead.

(**d**) (*Méx*: *miedo*) fear, anxiety.

(**e**) (:) backhander*.

tarumba* ADJ INVAR: **volver ~ a uno** to get sb all mixed up; to daze sb, fog sb; **volverse ~** to get all mixed up, get completely bewildered; **esa chica me tiene ~** I'm crazy about that girl.

tasa NF (**a**) (*acto*) valuation; estimate, appraisal.

(**b**) (*medida, norma*) measure, standard, norm.

(**c**) (*precio, tipo*) fixed price, official price, standard rate; **~ de aeropuerto** airport tax; **~ de basuras** rubbish-collection charge; **~ de cambio** exchange rate; **~ de crecimiento, ~ de desarrollo** growth rate; **~ de descuento bancario** bank rate; **~ de desempleo** level of unemployment; **~ de instrucción** tuition fee; **~ de interés** rate of interest; **~ de nacimiento, ~ de natalidad** birthrate; **~ de paro** level of unemployment; **~ de rendimiento** rate of return; **sin ~** boundless, limitless; unstinted; **gastar sin ~** to spend like there's no tomorrow.

tasable ADJ ratable.

tasación NF valuation, assessment; (*fig*) appraisal; **~ pericial** expert valuation; **~ de un artículo** fixing of a price for an article.

tasadamente ADV sparingly.

tasador(a) NM/F valuer; **~ de averías** average adjuster; **~ de impuestos** tax appraiser.

tasajear [1a] VT (*LAm*) **(a)** (*cortar*) to cut, slash. **(b)** *carne* to jerk.

tasajo NM **(a)** (*carne de vaca*) dried beef, jerked beef; (*carne*) (*any*) piece of meat. **(b)** (*And: persona*) tall thin person.

tasajudo ADJ (*LAm*) tall and thin.

tasar [1a] VT **(a)** *artículo* to fix a price for, price (*en* at); (*regular*) to regulate; *trabajo etc* to rate (*en* at).
(b) (*fig*) to value, appraise, assess (*en* at).
(c) (*restringir*) to limit, put a limit on, restrict; ration; (*escatimar*) to be sparing with, (*pey*) be mean with, stint; **les tasa a los niños hasta la leche** she even rations her children's milk.

tasca* NF (*Esp*) bar; **ir de ~s** to go on a crawl round the bars*.

tascar [1g] VT **(a)** *lino etc* to swingle, beat. **(b)** *hierba* to munch, champ; *freno* to champ at; (*And: masticar*) to chew, crunch.

Tasmania NF Tasmania.

tasquear* [1a] VI (*Esp*) to go drinking, go round the bars.

tasqueo* NM: **ir de ~** (*Esp*) = **tasquear**.

tata [1] NM **(a)** (*Murcia, LAm*: padre*) dad, daddy. **(b)** (*LAm*) = **taita** (b).
[2] NF **(a)** (*: *niñera*) nanny, nursemaid; (*chacha*) maid. **(b)** (*LAm: hermana menor*) younger sister.

tatarabuelo NM great-great-grandfather; **los ~s** one's great-great-grandparents.

tataranieto NM great-great-grandson.

tatas: **andar a ~** (*hacer pinitos*) to toddle; (*ir a gatas*) to crawl, get down on all fours.

tate¹ INTERJ (*sorpresa*) good heavens!; well well!; (*admiración*) bravo!; (*ira*) come now!; watch your step!; (*dándose cuenta*) so that's it!; oh I see!; (*aviso*) look out!

tate²: NM hash*, pot:.

tato* NM (*Cono Sur*) younger brother.

tatole* NM (*Méx*) plot.

tatuaje NM **(a)** (*dibujo*) tattoo. **(b)** (*acto*) tattooing.

tatuar [1d] VT to tattoo.

tauca NF (*And*) **(a)** (*objetos*) heap of things. **(b)** (*bolsa*) large bag.

taumaturgia NF miracle working, thaumaturgy.

taumaturgo NM miracle-worker; (*fig*) wonder-worker.

taurinamente ADV in bullfighting terms.

taurino ADJ bullfighting (*atr*); **el negocio ~** the bullfighting business; **leía una revista taurina** he was reading a bullfighting magazine.

Tauro NM (*Zodíaco*) Taurus.

taurofobia NF dislike of bullfighting.

taurófobo, -a NM/F opponent of bullfighting.

taurómaco [1] ADJ bullfighting (*atr*).
[2] NM bullfighting expert.

tauromaquia NF (art of) bullfighting, tauromachy.

tauromáquico ADJ bullfighting (*atr*).

tautología NF tautology.

tautológico ADJ tautological.

TAV NM ABR *de* **tren de alta velocidad** high-velocity train, HVT.

taxativamente ADV in a restricted sense, specifically.

taxativo ADJ (*restringido*) limited, restricted; *sentido* particular, concrete; specific.

taxi NM taxi, cab, taxicab.

taxidermia NF taxidermy.

taxidermista NMF taxidermist.

taximetrero, -a NM/F, **taximetrista** NMF (*Argentina*) cab driver, taxi driver.

taxímetro NM taximeter, clock.

taxista NMF **(a)** taxidriver, cabby. **(b)** (*: *chulo*) pimp.

taxonomía NF taxonomy.

taxonomista NMF taxonomist.

Tayikistán NM Tadzhikistan.

taza NF **(a)** cup; (*contenido*) cupful; **~ de café** cup of coffee; **~ para café** coffee cup, cup for coffee.
(b) (*de fuente*) basin, bowl; (*de lavabo*) bowl; (*Cono Sur: palangana*) washbasin; **~ de noche** (*Cono Sur: euf*) chamberpot; **~ del wáter** lavatory pan.

tazado ADJ *ropa* frayed, worn; *persona* shabby.

tazar [1f] [1] VT **(a)** (*cortar*) to cut; to cut up, divide. **(b)** (*desgastar*) to fray.
[2] **tazarse** VR to fray.

tazón NM (*taza*) large cup; (*cuenco*) bowl, basin; (*prov*) washbasin.

TBC NM ABR *de* **tren de bandas en caliente** hot-strip mill.

TC NM ABR *de* **Tribunal Constitucional** Constitutional Court.

TCI NM ABR *de* **Tablero de Circuito Impreso** Printed Circuit Board, PCB.

TDV NF ABR *de* **tabla deslizadora a vela** windsurfing board.

te PRON PERS **(a)** (*ac*) you; (*††, a Dios*) thee.
(b) (*dativo*) (to) you; (*††, a Dios*) (to) thee; **te he traído esto** I've brought you this, I've brought this for you; **¿te duele mucho el brazo?** does your arm hurt much?

(c) (*reflexivo*) (to) yourself; (*††, a Dios*) (to) thyself; **te vas a caer** you'll fall; **te equivocas** you're wrong; **¡cálmate!** calm yourself!

té NM **(a)** (*planta, bebida*) tea; (*reunión*) tea party; **dar un ~** to give a tea party. **(b) dar el ~ a uno*** to bore sb to tears.

tea NF **(a)** (*antorcha*) torch; (*astillas*) firelighter. **(b)** (:: *cuchillo*) chiv:, knife.

teatral ADJ **(a)** theatre (*atr*); dramatic; **obra ~** dramatic work; **temporada ~** theatre season.
(b) (*fig*) theatrical, dramatic; (*pey*) histrionic, stagey.

teatralidad NF theatricality; drama; sense of the theatre, stage sense; (*pey*) showmanship; histrionics, staginess.

teatralizar [1f] VT to stage; to dramatize.

teatralmente ADV theatrically.

teatrero* [1] ADJ **(a)** (*exagerado*) theatrical. **(b)** (*aficionado*) **ser muy ~** to be a great theatre-goer.
[2] NM, **teatrera** NF **(a)** (*aficionado*) theatre-goer. **(b)** (*artista*) theatre-worker.

teatro NM **(a)** (*gen*) theatre; **el ~** (*como profesión*) the theatre, the stage, acting; **~ del absurdo, ~ de lo absurdo** theatre of the absurd; **~ de aficionados** amateur theatre, amateur theatricals; **~ de calle** street theatre; **~ de la ópera** opera-house; **~ de repertorio** repertory theatre; **~ de títeres** puppet theatre; **~ de variedades** variety theatre, music-hall, vaudeville theater (*US*); **escribir para el ~** to write for the stage; **en el ~ es una persona muy distinta** she's a very different person on the stage; **hacer que se venga abajo el ~** to bring the house down.
(b) (*Liter*) drama, plays; **el ~ de Cervantes** Cervantes' plays, Cervantes' dramatic works; **selecciones del ~ del siglo XVIII** selections from 18th century drama.
(c) (*de suceso*) scene; (*Mil*) theatre; **~ de guerra, ~ de operaciones** theatre of war, front.
(d) (*fig*) **hacer ~** to exaggerate, act affectedly; **ella tiene mucho ~** she's terribly dramatic, she's given to histrionics.
(e) (*LAm: cine*) cinema, movies.

Tebas NF Thebes.

tebeo NM (children's) comic; **eso está más visto que el ~** that's old hat; **~ de terror** horror comic.

tebeoteca NF collection of comics.

TEC NFPL abr de **toneladas equivalentes de carbón** equivalent tons of coal.

teca¹ NF teak.

teca²* NF (*Esp*) disco.

techado NM roof, covering; **bajo ~** under cover, indoors.

techar [1a] VT to roof (in, over).

techo NM **(a)** (*exterior*) roof; (*interior*) ceiling; (:) lid:, hat; **~ corredizo, ~ solar** (*Aut*) sunroof; **bajo ~** under cover, indoors; **tenis bajo ~** indoor tennis; **sin ~** *casa* roofless; *persona* homeless. **(b)** (*Aer*) ceiling.
(c) (*fig*) limit, ceiling, upper limit; peak; (*Fin*) ceiling; **ha tocado ~** it has reached its ceiling (*o* limit).

techumbre NF roof.

tecito NM (*esp LAm*) cup of tea.

tecla¹ NF (*Mús, de máquina de escribir etc*) key; **dar en la ~*** to get it right; to get the hang of sth; **dar en la ~ de** + *infin** to fall into the habit of + *ger*; **hay que tocar muchas ~s a la vez*** there are too many things to think about all together; **no le queda ninguna ~ por tocar** there's nothing else left for him to try; **~ de anulación** cancel key; **~ de borrado** delete key; **~ de cambio** shift-key; **~ de control** control key; **~s de control direccional del cursor** cursor control keys; **~ del cursor** cursor key; **~ de desplazamiento** scroll key; **~ de edición** edit key; **~ con flecha** arrow key; **~ de función** function key; **~ de iniciación** booting-up switch; **~ programable** user-defined key; **~ de retorno** return key; **~ de tabulación** tab key.

teclado NM (*Mús, de máquina de escribir etc*) keyboard, keys; (*de órgano*) manual; **~ numérico** numeric keypad; **marcación por ~** push-button dialling.

tecle ADJ (*Cono Sur*) weak, sickly.

teclear [1a] [1] VT **(a)** (*LAm*) *instrumento* to play clumsily, mess about on; *máquina de escribir* to use clumsily.
(b) (*) *problema* to approach from various angles.
[2] VI **(a)** (*Mús*) to strum, thrum, play a few chords.
(b) (*: *con dedos*) to drum, tap (with one's fingers).
(c) (*Cono Sur: estar enfermo*) to be weak, be ill.
(d) (*Cono Sur: ser pobre*) to be very poor.
(e) (*And, Cono Sur: negocio*) to be going very badly.

tecleo NM **(a)** (*Mús*) fingering, playing; touch; strumming, thrumming. **(b)** (*: *con dedos*) drumming, tapping.

tecleteo NM = **tecleo**.

teclista NMF (*Inform*) keyboard operator, key-puncher; (*Mús*) keyboard player.

teclo (*And*) [1] ADJ old.
[2] NM, **tecla²** NF old man/woman.

técnica¹ NF (*gen*) technique; technology; (*método*) method; (*destreza*) craft, skill.

técnicamente ADV technically.

tecnicidad NF technicality, technical nature.

tecnicismo NM (a) technical nature. (b) (*Ling*) technical term, technicality.

técnico [1] ADJ technical.

[2] NM, **técnica²** NF technician; expert, specialist; (*Dep*) trainer, coach; ~ **informático** computer programmer; ~ **de mantenimiento** maintenance engineer; ~ **de sonido** sound engineer; ~ **de televisión** television engineer, television repairman; **es un ~ en la materia** he's an expert on the subject.

tecnicolor ® NM Technicolor ®; **en** ~ in Technicolor.

tecnificar [1g] [1] VT to make more technical.

[2] **tecnificarse** VR to become more technical.

tecno... PREF techno....

tecnocracia NF technocracy.

tecnócrata NMF technocrat.

tecnocrático ADJ technocratic.

tecnología NF technology; ~ **de alimentos** food technology; **alta** ~, ~ **(de) punta** high technology, advanced technology; ~ **de estado sólido** solid-state technology; ~ **de la información** Information Technology, IT.

tecnológico ADJ technological.

tecnólogo, -a NM/F technologist.

teco* ADJ (*CAm, Méx*) drunk.

tecolote [1] ADJ (a) (*CAm*) *color* reddish-brown. (b) (*CAm, Méx: borracho*) drunk.

[2] NM (a) (*CAm, Méx Orn*) eagle owl. (b) (*Méx*: *policía*) policeman, cop*.

tecomate NM (*Méx*) (a) (*Bot*) gourd, calabash. (b) (*recipiente*) earthenware cup.

tecorral NM (*Méx*) dry-stone wall.

tectónica NF tectonics.

tecuán [1] ADJ (*CAm, Méx*) greedy, voracious.

[2] NM monster.

tedio NM (a) (*aburrimiento*) boredom, tedium. (b) (*falta de interés*) lack of interest; (*depresión*) depression; (*vaciedad*) sense of emptiness; **a mí no me produce sino** ~ it just depresses me.

tedioso ADJ boring, tedious; wearisome; depressing.

tefe NM (a) (*And*) (*cuero*) strip of leather, (*tela*) strip of cloth. (b) (*And*: *cicatriz*) scar on the face.

tegumento NM tegument.

Teherán NM Teheran.

tehuacán NM (*Méx*) mineral water.

Teide NM: **el** (**Pico de**) ~ Teide, Teyde.

teína NF theine.

teísmo NM theism.

teísta [1] ADJ theistic.

[2] NMF theist.

teja¹ NF tile; **por fin le cayó la** ~ (*Cono Sur*) finally the penny dropped; **pagar a toca** ~ to pay cash; to pay on the nail; **de** ~**s a-bajo** in this world, in the natural way of things; **de** ~**s arriba** in the next world; up aloft; with God's help.

teja² NF (*Bot*) lime (tree).

tejadillo NM top, cover.

tejado NM roof, tiled roof; (*fig*) housetop; **tiene el** ~ **de vidrio** he himself is open to the same charge, he lives in a glass house and should not throw stones.

tejamaní NM, **tejamanil** NM (*LAm*) roofing board, shingle.

tejano, -a [1] ADJ, NM/F Texan.

[2] **tejanos** NMPL (*vaqueros*) jeans.

tejar [1a] VT to tile, roof with tiles.

Tejas NM Texas.

tejaván NM (*LAm*) shed; (*cobertizo*) corridor; (*galería*) gallery; (*choza*) rustic dwelling.

tejavana NF (*cobertizo*) shed; (*tejado*) shed roof, plain tile roof.

tejedor(a) NM/F (a) (*artesano*) weaver. (b) (*And, Cono Sur*: *intrigante*) intriguer, meddler.

tejedura NF (a) (*acto*) weaving. (b) (*textura*) weave, texture.

tejeduría NF (a) (*arte*) (art of) weaving. (b) (*fábrica*) textile mill.

tejemaneje* NM (a) (*actividad*) bustle; (*jaleo*) fuss, to-do*; **se trae un tremendo** ~ **con sus papeles** he's making a tremendous to-do with his papers*, he's getting all worked up with his papers.

(b) (*intriga*) intrigue, shady business.

tejer [2a] [1] VT (a) (*Cos*) to weave; to make; *telaraña* to make, spin; *capullo* to spin; (*esp LAm*: *tricotar*) to knit; (*coser*) to sew; (*hacer de ganchillo*) to crochet.

(b) (*fig*) *complot* to weave; *cambio etc* to bring about little by little; *escándalo, mentira etc* to fabricate.

[2] VI: ~ **y destejer** to chop and change, blow hot and cold.

tejerazo NM: **el** ~ *the coup attempted by Col. Tejero on 23 February 1981.*

tejeringo NM (*prov*) fritter.

tejido NM (a) (*tela*) weave, woven material; web; fabric; ~**s** textiles; ~ **de punto** knitting; knitted fabric; **un** ~ **de intrigas** a web of intrigue. (b) (*textura*) weave, texture. (c) (*Anat*) tissue; ~ **conjuntivo** connective tissue.

tejo¹ NM (a) (*aro*) ring, quoit; **echar los** ~**s** (*fig*) to set one's cap at somebody, make a play for somebody. (b) (*juego*) hopscotch. (c) (*Esp**) 5 peseta piece.

tejo² NM (*Bot*) yew (tree).

tejoleta NF bit of tile, shard; brickbat.

tejón NM badger.

tejudo NM label (*on spine of book*).

tel. ABR *de* **teléfono** telephone, Tel.

tela NF (a) (*gen*) cloth, fabric, material; ~ **de cebolla** onion skin; ~**s del corazón** (*fig*) heartstrings; ~ **cruzada** twill; ~ **metálica** wire netting; ~ **mosquitera** mosquito net(ting); ~ **de saco** sackcloth; **en** ~ (*Tip*) clothbound.

(b) (*LAm Arte*) painting.

(c) (*Ent etc*) web; ~ **de araña** spider's web, cobweb.

(d) (*en liquido*) skin, film.

(e) (*Bot*) skin.

(f) (*Fin**) dough*, money; **sacudir** (o **soltar**) **la** ~ to cough up*.

(g) (*fig: materia*) subject, matter; **hay** ~ **que cortar**, **hay** ~ **para rato** there's plenty of material, there's lots to talk about; it's a long job; it's a tricky business; **el asunto trae mucha** ~ it's a complicated matter; **hay** ~ **de eso*** there's lots of that; **tiene** ~***** there's a lot to it. (h) **poner algo en** ~ **de juicio** to question, call in question, cast doubt on.

(i) (*And*: *tortilla*) thin maize pancake.

telabrejos NMPL (*LAm*) things, gear, odds and ends.

telanda* NF brass*, money.

telar NM (a) loom; ~**es** (*fig*) textile mill. (b) (*Teat*) gridiron.

telaraña NF spider's web, cobweb.

tele* NF telly*; **salir en** (o **por**) **la** ~ to be on telly*, be on the box*.

tele... PREF tele...

teleadicto, -a* NM/F telly-addict*.

telealarma NF alarm (system).

telebaby NM, PL **telebabys** cable-car.

telebanco NM cash-dispenser.

telebasura* NF junk TV.

telebrejos NMPL (*Méx*) = **telabrejos**.

telecabina NF cable-car.

telecámara NF television camera.

telecargar [1h] VT (*Inform*) to download.

telecomando NM remote control.

telecomedia NF television comedy show.

telecompra NF home shopping.

telecomunicación NF telecommunication.

teleconferencia NF teleconference; teleconferencing.

telecontrol NM remote control.

telecopia NF fax system; fax message.

telecopiadora NF fax copier.

telediario NM television news-bulletin.

teledifusión NF telecast.

teledirigido ADJ remote-controlled, radio-controlled.

telef. ABR *de* **teléfono** telephone, Tel.

telefacsímil NM, **telefax** NM fax system; fax message.

teleférico NM ski lift; cable railway, cableway.

telefilm NM, PL **telefilms, telefilme** NM telefilm.

telefonazo NM telephone call; **te daré un** ~ I'll give you a ring, I'll call you up.

telefonear [1a] VTI to telephone.

telefonema NM telephone message.

telefonía NF telephony; **red de** ~ **móvil** mobile phone network; **servicios de** ~ **móvil** mobile phone services.

Telefónica NF: **la** ~ *Spanish national telephone company.*

telefónicamente ADV by telephone; **fue amenazado** ~ he received threats by telephone.

telefónico ADJ telephonic; telephone (*atr*).

telefonillo NM portable telephone.

telefonista NMF (telephone) operator, telephonist.

▼ **teléfono** NM telephone, phone; (*número*) telephone number; ~ **árabe*** bush telegraph*, grapevine*; ~ **erótico** sex line; ~ **de la esperanza** helpline; ~ **gratuito** free phone; ~ **sin hilos**, ~ **inalámbrico**, cordless telephone; ~ **interior** house phone, interphone; ~ **móvil** mobile phone; ~ **móvil de coche** car-phone; ~ **rojo** hot line; ~ **de socorro** (*Aut*) emergency telephone; **está hablando por** ~ he's on the phone; **llamar a uno al** (o **por**) ~ to telephone sb, phone sb, ring sb up, call sb (up); **te llaman al** ~ you're wanted on the phone.

telefoto(grafía) NF telephoto.

telefotográfico ADJ telephoto (*atr*).

telegenia NF telegenic quality.

➤ LENGUA Y USO: **teléfono** → 27.2, 27.7

telegénico ADJ telegenic.
telegrafía NF telegraphy.
telegrafiar [1c] VTI to telegraph.
telegráfico ADJ telegraphic; telegraph (atr).
telegrafista NMF telegraphist.
telégrafo NM telegraph; **~ óptico** semaphore.
telegrama NM telegram; **poner un ~ a uno** to send sb a telegram.
teleimpresor NM, **teleimpresora** NF teleprinter.
teleindicador NM TV monitor.
teleinformático ADJ telematic.
telele NM fainting fit, queer turn; **le dio un ~** he came over queer.
telemandado ADJ remote-controlled.
telemando NM remote control.
telemanía NF TV addiction.
telemarketing NM, **telemárketing** NM telesales pl.
telemática NF data transmission, telematics.
telemático ADJ telematic.
telemedida NF telemetry.
telemedir [3k] VT (Inform) to telemeter.
telémetro NM rangefinder.
telengues NMPL (CAm) things, gear, odds and ends.
telenoticias NFPL television news sing, TV news sing.
telenovela NF television serial, soap-opera.
telenque ADJ (Cono Sur) weak, feeble.
teleobjetivo NM telephoto lens, zoom-lens.
teleología NF teleology.
teleoperador(a) NM/F telemarketing phone operator.
telépata NMF telepathist.
telepate NM (CAm) bedbug.
telepatía NF telepathy.
telepáticamente ADV telepathically.
telepático ADJ telepathic.
teleproceso NM teleprocessing.
telequinesia NF telekinesis.
telerregulación NF adjustment by remote control.
telescopar [1a] **1** VT to telescope.
2 telescoparse VR to telescope.
telescópico ADJ telescopic.
telescopio NM telescope.
teleserie NF television serial, soap-opera.
telesilla NM ski lift, chair lift.
telespectador(a) NM/F viewer.
telesquí NM ski lift.
teletaxi NM radio cab, radio taxi.
teletex NM, **teletexto** NM teletext.
teletienda NF home shopping.
teletipista NMF teletypist, teleprinter operator.
teletipo NM teletype, teleprinter.
teletratamiento NM teleprocessing.
teletubo NM cathode-ray tube, television tube.
televendedor(a) NM/F telesales person.
televenta NF telesales pl.
televidente NMF viewer, televiewer.
televisar [1a] VT to televise.
televisión NF television; **~ por cable** cable television; **~ en color(es)** colour television; **~ comercial** commercial television; **~ matinal** breakfast television; **~ pagada** pay-television, pay-TV; **~ por satélite** satellite television; **hacer ~** to be doing television, be working in television, be engaged in television work; **mirar la ~** to watch television; **salir en** (o **por**) **la ~** to be on television.
televisivo **1** (a) ADJ television (atr); **serie televisiva** television serial (o series). (b) (de interés ~) televisual; **persona** telegenic.
2 NM, **televisiva** NF television personality.
televisor NM television set.
televisual ADJ television (atr).
télex NM INVAR telex.
telón NM (Teat) curtain; **~ de acero** (Pol) iron curtain; **~ de boca** front curtain; **~ de fondo**, **~ de foro** backcloth, backdrop; **~ metálico** fire-curtain; **~ de seguridad** safety curtain.
telonero NM (Teat) first turn, curtain-raiser; (Mús) support band, support act.
telúrico ADJ of the earth, telluric; (fig) earthy; **tendencias telúricas** back-to-nature tendencies.
▼ **tema** **1** NM (a) theme; subject, topic; (Mús) theme, motif; (Arte) subject; **~ de actualidad** current issue; **~s de actualidad** current affairs; **~s verdes** green issues; **el ~ de su discurso** the theme (o subject) of his speech; **es un tema muy manoseado** it's a subject which has often been discussed; **pasar del ~*** to dodge the issue; **las autoridades tienen ~ de meditación** the authorities have food for thought, the authorities have sth to think about; **tienen tema para un rato** they have plenty to talk about.

(b) (Ling) stem.
2 NM o NF (a) (idea fija) fixed idea, mania, obsession; **tener ~** to be stubborn. (b) (inquina) ill will, unreasoning hostility; **tener ~ a uno** to have a grudge against sb.
temar [1a] VI (Cono Sur) (a) (tener idea fija) to have a mania, be obsessed. (b) (tener inquina) to bear ill will; **~ con uno** to have a grudge against sb.
temario NM (temas) set of themes, collection of subjects; (programa) programme; (oposiciones) topics to be examined; (asignaturas, etc) curriculum; (de junta) agenda, subjects for discussion.
temascal NM (CAm, Méx) bathroom; (fig) hot place, oven.
temática NF (collection of) themes, subjects; range of topics.
temático ADJ (a) (gen) thematic. (b) (Ling) stem (atr). (c) (And: poco prudente) injudicious, tasteless.
tembladera NF (a) (*) violent shaking; trembling fit. (b) (LAm) = **tembladeral**.
tembladeral NM (Cono Sur, Méx) quagmire.
temblar [1j] VI (a) (persona: de miedo) to tremble, shake; (de frío) to shiver; (edificio etc) to shake, quiver, shudder; **~ de frío** to shiver with cold; **~ de miedo** to tremble with fright; **~ ante una escena** to shudder at a sight; **~ como un azogado** to shake like a leaf, tremble all over; **dejar una botella temblando*** to use most of a bottle, make a bottle look pretty silly.
(b) (fig) to tremble; **tiemblo de pensar en lo que pueda ocurrir** I tremble (o shudder) to think what may happen; **~ por su vida** to fear for one's life.
tembleque* NM (a) violent shaking, shaking fit; **le entró un ~** he began to shake violently, he got the shakes. (b) (LAm: persona) weakling.
temblequeante ADJ andar doddery, wobbly, tottering; voz quivering, tremulous.
temblequear* [1a] VI to shake violently, be all of a quiver; to wobble.
temblequera NF (a) shaking; wobbling. (b) (And, Carib) (miedo) fear; (temblor) trembling.
temblón **1** ADJ trembling, shaking; tremulous; **álamo ~** = **2**.
2 NM aspen.
temblor NM (a) trembling, shaking; shiver, shivering, shudder, shuddering; **le entró un ~ violento** he began to shake violently. (b) (LAm: t ~ de tierra) earthquake.
tembloroso ADJ trembling, tremulous; quivering; shivering; **con voz temblorosa** in a shaky voice, in a tremulous tone; **~ de sugerencias** alive with suggestions, bursting with suggestions.
tembo ADJ (And) featherbrained, stupid.
temer [2a] **1** VT (a) to fear, be afraid of; to dread; to go in awe of; **~ + infin** to fear to + infin; **~ a Dios** to fear God.
(b) (fig) **temo que lo ha perdido** I'm afraid he has lost it, I fear he has lost it; **teme que no vaya a volver** she's afraid he won't come back.
2 VI to be afraid; **no temas** don't be afraid, (fig) don't worry; **~ por la seguridad de uno** to fear for sb's safety.
3 temerse VR = **1** (b).
temerariamente ADV rashly, recklessly; hastily.
temerario ADJ acto, persona rash, reckless; juicio etc hasty, rash.
temeridad NF (a) (cualidad) rashness, recklessness; hastiness. (b) (acto) rash act, folly.
temerón **1** ADJ bullying, ranting, loud-mouthed.
2 NM bully, ranter.
temerosamente ADV timidly, fearfully.
temeroso ADJ (a) (tímido) timid; (miedoso) fearful, frightened. (b) **~ de Dios** God-fearing, full of the fear of God. (c) (espantoso) dread, frightful.
temible ADJ fearsome, dread, frightful; adversario etc redoubtable.
temor NM (miedo) fear, dread; (recelo) suspicion, mistrust; **~** a fear of; **~ de Dios** fear of God; **por ~** from fear; **por ~ a** for fear of; **sin ~ a** fearless of; regardless of.
témpano NM (a) (t ~ de hielo) ice floe; **quedarse como un ~ *** to be chilled to the marrow.
(b) (Mús: tamboril) small drum, kettledrum.
(c) (Mús: parche) drumhead.
(d) (Arquit) tympan.
(e) **~ de tocino** (Culin) flitch of bacon.
témpera NM tempera.
temperadero NM (LAm) summer resort.
temperado ADJ (And) = **templado**.
temperamental ADJ (a) temperamental. (b) (*: fuerte) vigorous, forceful, strong.
temperamento NM (a) (naturaleza) temperament, nature, disposition.
(b) (constitución) constitution.
(c) (genio) temperament; **tener ~** to have a temperament, be temperamental.

(d) (*Pol etc*) compromise.

(e) (*LAm*) (*clima*) climate, weather; (*verano*) summer; **ir de ~** to spend a (summer) holiday .

temperancia NF temperance, moderation.

temperante (*LAm*) ⬚1 ADJ teetotal.

⬚2 NMF teetotaller, abstainer.

temperar [1a] ⬚1 VT (*moderar*) to temper, moderate; (*calmar*) to calm; (*aliviar*) to relieve.

⬚2 VI (*And, Carib: veranear*) to spend the summer, summer; (*cambiar de aires*) to have a change of air.

temperatura NF temperature; **a ~** (**de**) **ambiente** at room temperature.

temperie NF (state of the) weather.

tempestad NF storm (*t fig*); **~ de arena** sandstorm; **~ de nieve** snowstorm; **~ de polvo** dust-storm; **~ en un vaso de agua** storm in a teacup; **levantar una ~ de protestas** to cause a storm of protests.

tempestivo ADJ timely.

tempestuoso ADJ stormy (*t fig*).

templado ⬚1 ADJ (a) (*moderado*) moderate, restrained; (*en comer*) frugal; (*en beber*) of sober habits, abstemious.

(b) (*algo caliente*) (pleasantly) warm; *agua* lukewarm; *clima* mild, temperate; (*Geog*) *zona* temperate.

(c) (*Mús*) in tune, well-tuned.

(d) (*) (*franco*) bold, forthright; (*valiente*) courageous.

(e) (*: listo*) *niño* bright, lively; (*CAm, Méx: hábil*) able, competent.

(f) (*And: severo*) severe.

(g) (*And, Carib*: *borracho*) tipsy.

(h) **estar ~** (*And, Cono Sur*) to be in love.

⬚2 NM (*Téc*) tempering, hardening.

templanza NF (a) *cualidad* moderation, restraint; frugality; abstemiousness. (b) (*Met*) mildness.

templar [1a] ⬚1 VT (a) (*gen*) to temper; to moderate, soften; *ira* to restrain, control; *clima* to make mild; *calor* to reduce; *solución* to dilute.

(b) *agua, cuarto* to warm up (slightly).

(c) (*Mús*) to tune (up).

(d) (*Mec*) to adjust; *tornillo etc* to tighten up; *resorte etc* to set properly.

(e) *acero* to temper, harden.

(f) (*Arte*) *colores* to blend.

(g) (*And: derribar*) to knock down; (*CAm*) (*golpear*) to hit; (*pegar*) to beat; (*And*⚇: *matar*) to kill, bump off⚇.

(h) (*Carib*⚇) to screw⚇⚇, fuck⚇⚇.

⬚2 VI (a) (*frío etc*) to moderate.

(b) (*Carib: huir*) to flee.

⬚3 **templarse** VR (a) (*persona*) to be moderate, be restrained, act with restraint; **~ en la comida** to eat frugally.

(b) (*agua*) to warm up, get warm.

(c) (*And, CAm*⚇: *morir*) to die, kick the bucket⚇.

(d) (*Carib: huir*) to flee; **templárselas** (*Carib, Méx: huir*) to flee.

(e) (*And, Carib: emborracharse*) to get drunk.

(f) (*Cono Sur: enamorarse*) to fall in love.

(g) (*Cono Sur: excederse*) to go too far, overstep the mark.

(h) **templárselas** (*And*) to stand firm.

templario NM Templar.

temple NM (a) (*Téc*) temper; tempering.

(b) (*Mús*) tuning.

(c) (*Met*) state of the weather, temperature.

(d) (*humor*) mood; **estar de mal ~** to be in a bad mood.

(e) (*espíritu*) spirit, temper, mettle; (*LAm: valentía*) courage, boldness.

(f) (*pintura*) distemper; (*Arte*) tempera; **pintar al ~** to distemper; (*Arte*) to paint in tempera.

(g) (*LAm*⚇: *enamoramiento*) infatuation.

templete NM (a) (*quiosco*) pavilion; kiosk; **~ de música** bandstand.

(b) (*Rel: templo*) small temple; (*santuario*) shrine; (*nicho*) niche.

templo NM (*masónico, pagano, fig*) temple; (*Ecl*) church, chapel; **~ metodista** Methodist chapel; **~ protestante** Protestant church; **como un ~** (*esp LAm*) (*grande*) huge, tremendous; (*excelente*) first-rate, excellent.

tempo NM tempo (*t fig*).

temporada NF time, period, spell; (*Met*) spell; (*del año, social, Dep etc*) season; **~ alta** high season; **~ baja** low season; **~ de fútbol** football season; **~ de ópera** opera season; **~ de exámenes** examination period; **~ de lluvias** rainy spell; rainy season; **en plena ~** at the height of the season; **por ~s** on and off; **estar fuera de ~** to be out of season.

temporadista NMF (*Carib*) holiday-maker.

temporal ⬚1 ADJ (a) temporary; *trabajador* temporary, casual; seasonal.

(b) (*Ecl etc*) temporal; **poder ~** temporal power.

⬚2 NM (a) (*tormenta*) storm; (*período de lluvia*) rainy weather, spell of rough weather; **capear el ~** (*t fig*) to weather the storm, ride out the storm.

(b) (*Carib: persona*) shady character.

temporalidad NF temporariness, temporary nature.

temporalmente ADV temporarily.

temporáneo ADJ temporary.

temporario ADJ (*LAm*) temporary.

témporas NFPL ember days.

temporero ⬚1 ADJ *obrero* temporary, casual.

⬚2 NM, **temporera** NF casual worker.

temporizador ⬚1 ADJ: **mecanismo ~ = 2**.

⬚2 NM timing device, timer.

temporizar [1f] VI to temporize.

tempozonte ADJ (*Méx*) hunchbacked.

tempranal ADJ *planta, tierra etc* early.

tempranear [1a] VI (a) (*LAm: madrugar*) to get up early. (b) (*Cono Sur Agr*) to sow early.

tempranero ADJ (a) (*Bot*) early. (b) *persona* early, early-rising.

temprano ⬚1 ADJ (a) *fruta etc* early.

(b) *años* youthful; *obra, período etc* early.

⬚2 ADV (*gen*) early; (*demasiado ~*) too early, too soon; **lo más ~ posible** as soon as possible.

ten V **tener**.

tenacidad NF (*V ADJ*) (a) toughness. (b) tenacity. (c) ingrained nature; persistence; stubbornness.

tenacillas NFPL (*para azúcar*) sugar tongs; (*para pelo*) curling tongs; (*Med etc*) tweezers, forceps; (*para velas*) snuffers.

tenamaste ⬚1 ADJ (*CAm, Méx*) stubborn.

⬚2 NM (a) (*CAm, Méx: piedra*) cooking stone. (b) (*CAm*) = **cachivache**.

tenaz ADJ (a) *materia* tough, durable, resistant.

(b) *persona* tenacious.

(c) *mancha etc* hard to remove, that sticks fast; *suciedad* ingrained; *dolor* persistent; *creencia, resistencia etc* stubborn.

tenaza NF (a) (*Bridge*) squeeze (*a in*). (b) **~s** (*Téc*) pliers, pincers; tongs; (*Med*) forceps; **unas ~s** a pair of pliers (*etc*); **avance en ~** pincer movement.

tenazmente ADV tenaciously; stubbornly.

tenazón: a ~, de ~ ADV suddenly; *disparar* without taking aim.

tenca[1] NF (*pez*) tench.

tenca[2] NF (*Cono Sur*) lie, swindle.

tencal NM (*Méx*) wicker box, wicker poultry cage.

tencha⚇ NF (*CAm*) prison.

tendajo NM = **tendejón**.

tendal NM (a) (*toldo*) awning.

(b) (*Agr*) sheet spread to catch olives (*when shaken from the tree*).

(c) (*LAm*) (*montón*) heap, lot, abundance; (*objetos etc desparramados*) lot of scattered objects (*o bodies etc*); (*desorden*) confusion, disorder; **un ~ de** a lot of, a whole heap of.

(d) (*Cono Sur Agr*) shearing shed; (*And, Carib: fábrica*) brickworks, tileworks; (*And, CAm*) sunny place for drying coffee.

(e) (*And: campo*) flat open field.

tendalada NF (*LAm*) = **tendal**.

tendalera NF mess, litter (of scattered objects).

tendear [1a] VI (*Méx*) to go window-shopping.

tendedera NF (a) (*CAm, Carib, Méx: cuerda*) clothes-line. (b) (*And*) = **tendal**.

tendedero NM (*lugar*) drying place; (*cuerda*) clothes-line, frame for drying clothes.

tendejón NM small shop; stall, booth.

▼ **tendencia** NF tendency; trend; inclination; **~ imperante** dominant trend, prevailing tendency; **~ del mercado** (*Fin*) run of the market, price movement; **la ~ hacia el socialismo** the tendency (*o trend*) towards socialism; **una palabra con ~ a quedarse arcaica** a word tending to become archaic; **tener ~ a** + *infin* to have a tendency to + *infin*, tend to + *infin*, be inclined to + *infin*; **tener ~s de zurdo** to have a tendency towards left-handedness.

tendenciosidad NF tendentiousness.

tendencioso ADJ tendentious.

tendente ADJ: **una medida ~ a** + *infin* a measure tending to + *infin*; a measure designed to + *infin*.

▼ **tender** [2g] ⬚1 VT (a) (*estirar*) to stretch; (*extender, desplegar*) to spread, spread out, extend, lay out; *pintura etc* to put on, apply; *mantel* to lay, spread; **tendieron el cadáver sobre el suelo** they stretched the corpse out on the floor.

(b) *ropa lavada* to hang out; *cuerda etc* to stretch (*a to, de from*), hang (*de from*); *mano* to stretch out, reach out; *ferrocarril, puente* to build; *cable, vía* to lay.

(c) *arco* to draw; *trampa* to set (*a for*).

(d) (*LAm*) *cama* to make the bed; **~ la mesa** to lay the table.

▼⬚2 VI: **~ a** to tend to, tend towards, have a tendency towards; **~ a** + *infin* to tend to + *infin*; **las plantas tienden a la luz** plants grow (*o turn*) towards the light; **el color tiende a verde** the colour tends towards green; **ella tiende al pesimismo** she has a tendency to be pessimistic.

➤ LENGUA Y USO: **tendencia** → 53.1   **tender: 2** → 53.1

3 **tenderse** VR (a) (*echarse*) to lie down, stretch (o.s.) out.
(b) (*fig*) to let o.s. go; to give up, let things go, stop bothering.
(c) (*caballo*) to run at full gallop.
(d) (*Naipes*) to lay down.

ténder NM (*Ferro*) tender.

tenderete NM (a) (*para ropa lavada*) = **tendedero**. (b) (*puesto de mercado*) stall, market booth; (*carretón*) barrow. (c) (*Com: géneros*) display of goods for sale (*etc*); (*fig*) litter (of objects), mess.

tendero, -a NM/F shopkeeper, (*esp*) grocer.

tendida NF (*Cono Sur: de caballo*) shy, start.

tendido **1** ADJ (a) (*tumbado*) lying down; (*llano*) flat.
(b) *galope* fast, flat out.
2 NM (a) (*Arquit*) coat of plaster.
(b) (*ropa lavada: t ~s*) washing, clothes (hung out to dry).
(c) (*Taur*) front rows of seats.
(d) (*de cable, vía*) laying; (*cables*) wires; **~ de alta tensión** high voltage power line; **~ eléctrico** power line.
(e) (*Culin*) batch of loaves.
(f) (*And, Méx: ropa de cama*) bedclothes.
(g) (*CAm, Carib: cuerda*) long tether, rope.
(h) (*And, Méx: puesto de mercado*) stall, booth.

tendinitis NF INVAR tendinitis, tendonitis.

tendinoso ADJ sinewy.

tendón NM tendon, sinew; **~ de Aquiles** Achilles' tendon.

tendonitis NF INVAR tendinitis, tendonitis.

tendré *etc* V **tener.**

tenducho NM poky little shop.

tenebrosidad NF (V ADJ) (a) darkness; gloom(iness). (b) (*fig*) gloominess, dimness, blackness. (c) (*fig*) sinister nature, shadiness. (d) (*fig*) obscurity.

tenebroso ADJ (a) (*oscuro*) dark; (*sombrío*) gloomy, dismal. (b) (*fig*) *perspectiva etc* gloomy, dim, black. (c) (*pey*) *complot etc* sinister, dark; *pasado etc* shady. (d) (*fig*) *estilo etc* obscure.

tenedor **1** NM (a) (*Culin*) fork. (b) **restaurante de 5 ~es** ≃ five-star restaurant, top-class restaurant.
2 NM, **tenedora** NF (*Com, Fin etc*) holder, bearer; **~ de acciones** shareholder; **~ de libros** book-keeper; **~ de obligaciones** bondholder; **~ de póliza** policyholder.

teneduría NF: **~ de libros** book-keeping.

tenencia NF (a) (*de casa, apartamento etc*) tenancy, occupancy; (*de puesto*) tenure; (*de propiedad*) possession; **~ ilícita de armas** illegal possession of weapons.
(b) (*oficio*) deputyship; **~ de alcaldía** post of deputy mayor.
(c) (*Mil*) lieutenancy.

▼ **tener** [2k] **1** VT (a) (*gen*) to have; to have got; to possess; **~ ojos azules** to have blue eyes; **hemos tenido muchas dificultades** we have had a lot of difficulties; **hoy no tenemos clase** we have no class today, we are not having a class today; **¿tienes una pluma?** have you got a pen?; **¿tiene Vd permiso para esto?** do you have permission for this?, have you (got) permission for this?; **va a ~ un niño** she's going to have a baby; **tiene un tío en Venezuela** he has an uncle in Venezuela; **tiene muchas preocupaciones encima** he has a lot of worries, he is burdened with anxieties; **el cargo tiene una buena retribución** the post carries a good salary; **de bueno no tiene nada** there's nothing good about it; **ya saben dónde me tienen** you always know where you can find me; *V* **particular, suerte** *etc.*
(b) (*locuciones con ciertos n*) **~ 7 años** to be 7, be 7 years old; **~ hambre** to be hungry; **~ mucha sed** to be very thirsty; **~ calor** to be hot; **~ mucho frío** to be very cold; *para más detalles, V* **celos, cuidado, ganas, miedo** *etc.*
(c) (*medidas*) **~ 5 cm de ancho** to be 5 cm wide; *V* **ancho, largo** *etc.*
(d) *objeto* to hold; (*agarrar*) to hold on to, hold up, grasp; (*llevar*) to carry, bear; **ten esto** take this, hold on to this; **¡ten!, ¡tenga!** here you are!; catch!; **lo tenía en la mano** he was holding it in his hand; he was carrying it in his hand; **los dos que tenían la bandera** the two who were carrying the flag.
(e) (*recipiente*) to hold, contain; **una caja para ~ el dinero** a box to hold the money, a box to keep (*o* put) the money in.
(f) *promesa* to keep.
(g) (*sentimiento*) to have, profess (*a* for); **~ gran admiración a uno** to have (a) great admiration for sb; **le tengo mucho cariño** I'm very fond of him; *V* **cariño** *etc.*
(h) (*pensar, considerar*) to think, consider, deem; **~ a bien** + *infin* to see fit to + *infin*, deign to + *infin*; to think it proper to + *infin*; **~ a menos** + *infin* to consider it beneath o.s. to + *infin*; **~ a uno en más** to think all the more of sb; **te tendrán en más estima** they will hold you in higher esteem; **~ para sí que ...** to think that ...; **~ a uno por** + ADJ to think sb + ADJ, consider sb to be + ADJ, deem sb to be + ADJ; **no quiero que me tengan por informal** I don't want them to think me unreliable; **le tengo por poco honrado** I consider

er him to be rather dishonest; **lo tienen por cosa cierta** they believe it to be true; **ten por seguro que ...** rest assured that ...; *V* **más, mucho** *etc*; *V* **gala, honra** *etc.*
(i) (+ ADJ) **procura ~ contentos a todos** he tries to keep everybody happy; **me tiene perplejo la falta de noticias** the lack of news perplexes me, I am bewildered by the absence of news; *V* **cuidado, frito** *etc.*
(j) (+ *infin*) **no tengo nada que deciros** I have nothing to tell you; **tengo trabajo que hacer** I have work to do.
▼ (k) **~ que** + *infin* to have to + *infin*, must + *infin*; **tengo que comprarlo** I have to buy it; **tenemos que marcharnos** we have to leave, we must go; **así tiene que ser** it has to be this way; **¡tú tenías que ser!** it would be you!, it had to be you!
(l) (+ PTP) **tenemos alquilado un piso** we have rented a flat; **tenía el sombrero puesto** he had his hat on; **te lo tengo dicho muchas veces** I've told you hundreds of times; **yo no le tengo visto** I've never set eyes on him; **nos tenían preparada una sorpresa** they had prepared a surprise for us; **teníamos andados unos 10 kilómetros** we had walked (*o* covered) some 10 kilometres.
(m) (*locuciones*) **¿qué tienes?** what's the matter with you?; **¿(conque) ésas tenemos?** so that's it!; so that's the game, is it?; here we go again!; **no ~las todas consigo** to be worried, feel uneasy; **no las tengo todas conmigo de que lo haga** I'm none too sure that he'll do it; **quien tuvo retuvo** it's gone for good, I've said goodbye to that; **ten con ten** (*como n*) good sense, tact; ability to find a middle way; **~ todas las de ganar** to hold all the winning cards, look like a winner; **~ todas las de perder** to be fighting a losing battle, look like losing.
(n) (*LAm*) **tengo 4 años aquí** I've been here for 4 years; **tenía 5 años sin verlo** I hadn't seen him for 5 years; **tienen 3 meses de no cobrar** they haven't been paid for 3 months, it's 3 months since they've been paid; **este cadáver tiene un mes de muerto** this corpse has been dead for a month; **¿cuánto tiempo tiene manejando este coche?** (*Méx*) how long have you been driving this car?
(o) **~lo** (⁑: *eyacular*) to come ⁑.
2 **tenerse** VR (a) (*estar de pie*) to stand, stand up; **la muñeca se tiene de pie** the doll stands up; **~ firme** to stand upright; (*fig*) to stand firm; **no poder ~** (*cansado*) to be all in, be tired out; (*borracho*) to be incapable (with drink).
(b) **~ sobre algo** to lean on sth, support o.s. on sth.
(c) (*fig: dominarse*) to control o.s.; to stop in time.
(d) **~ por** to consider o.s. to be, think o.s.; **se tiene por muy listo** he thinks himself very clever; **~ en mucho** to have a high opinion of o.s.; (*fig*) to be dignified; to be incapable of a mean action.

teneraje NM (*LAm*) calves.

tenería NF tannery.

Tenerife NM Tenerife.

tenga, tengo *etc* V **tener.**

tenguerengue⁑ NM (*Carib*) hovel.

tenia NF tapeworm.

tenida NF (a) (*LAm*) (*reunión*) meeting, session; (*de masones*) meeting of a masonic lodge. (b) (*Cono Sur: vestido*) suit, dress; (*Mil*) uniform; **~ de gala, ~ de noche** evening dress; **~ de luto** mourning.

tenienta NF (woman) lieutenant; (*Hist*) lieutenant's wife.

teniente **1** NM lieutenant; (*ayudante*) deputy; **~ de alcalde** deputy mayor; **~ coronel** lieutenant-colonel; **~ fiscal** assistant prosecutor; **~ general** lieutenant-general; **~ de navío** lieutenant.
2 ADJ: **estar ~⁑** to be deaf.

tenis NM (a) (*juego*) tennis; **~ de mesa** table-tennis. (b) (PL: *zapatos*) tennis-shoes; **colgar los ~⁑** to peg out⁑. (c) (*construcción*) set of tennis-courts.

tenista NMF tennis-player.

tenístico ADJ tennis (*atr*).

tenor¹ NM (*Mús*) tenor.

tenor² NM tenor; meaning, sense, purport; **el ~ de esta declaración** the sense of this statement, the tenor of this declaration; **a este ~** like this, in this fashion; **a ~ de** on the lines of, like; (*Com*) in accordance with.

tenorio NM ladykiller, Don Juan.

tensado NM tensioning; tension.

tensamente ADV tensely.

tensar [1a] VT to tauten; *arco* to draw.

tensión NF (a) (*física*) tension, tautness; (*Mec*) stress, strain; rigidity; **~ superficial** surface tension.
(b) (*Fís: de gas etc*) pressure.
(c) (*Elec*) voltage; tension; **alta ~** high tension; **cable de alta ~** high-tension cable.
(d) (*Anat*) **~ arterial** blood-pressure; **tener ~⁑, tener la ~ alta** to have high blood-pressure; **tomarse la ~** to have one's blood-pressure taken.
(e) (*Med*) tension; (*estrés*) strain, stress; **~ excesiva** (over)strain; **~**

nerviosa nervous strain; **~ premenstrual** premenstrual tension, PMT.

(f) *(fig)* tension, tenseness; **~ racial** racial tension; **la ~ de la situación política** the tenseness of the political situation.

tensionado ADJ tense, in a state of tension.

tensional ADJ tense, full of tension.

tensionar [1a] VT **(a)** to tense, tauten. **(b)** *(fig) adversario* to put pressure on; *relaciones* to put a strain on.

tenso ADJ **(a)** *(estirado)* tense, taut.

(b) *(fig)* tense; strained; **es una situación muy tensa** it is a very tense situation; **las relaciones entre los dos están muy tensas** relations between the two are very strained.

tensor [1] ADJ tensile.

[2] NM *(Téc)* guy, strut; *(Anat)* tensor; *(de cuello)* stiffener; *(Med)* chestexpander.

tentación NF **(a)** *(gen)* temptation; **resistir (a) la ~** to resist temptation; **no puedo resistir (a) la ~ de** + *infin* I can't resist the temptation of + *ger*; **vencer la ~** to overcome temptation.

(b) (*: *objeto*) tempting thing; **las gambas son mi ~** I can't resist prawns; **¡eres mi ~!** you'll be the ruin of me!

tentacular ADJ tentacular.

tentáculo NM tentacle; feeler.

tentador [1] ADJ tempting.

[2] NM tempter.

tentadora NF temptress.

tentar [1j] VT **(a)** *(tocar)* to touch, feel; *(Med)* to probe; **ir tentando el camino** to feel one's way, grope one's way along.

(b) *(probar)* to try, test, try out; *(emprender)* to undertake, venture on; **~ (a) hacer algo** to try to do sth, attempt to do sth.

(c) *(atraer: t Rel)* to tempt; *(seducir)* to attract, lure, entice; **me tentó con una copita de anís** she tempted me with a glass of anise; **no me tienta nada la idea** the idea doesn't attract me at all; **~ a uno a hacer algo** to tempt sb to do sth; **ella podría estar tentada también a probarlo** she might be tempted to try it too.

tentativa NF *(intento)* attempt; *(esfuerzo)* effort; *(Jur)* criminal attempt; **~ de asesinato** attempted murder; **~ de robo** attempted robbery; **~ de suicidio** suicide attempt.

tentativo ADJ tentative.

tentebonete* NM *(puesto)* cushy job*, plum; *(gaje)* perk*.

tentempié* NM snack, bite.

tenue ADJ **(a)** *palo etc* thin, slim, slender; *alambre* fine.

(b) *(fig)* tenuous; insubstantial, slight; *aire, olor* thin; *neblina* light; *línea* faint; *sonido* faint, weak; *relación etc* slight, tenuous; *estilo* simple.

tenuidad NF *(V ADJ)* **(a)** thinness, slimness, slenderness; fineness.

(b) tenuousness; slightness; thinness; lightness; faintness; simplicity.

(c) *(una ~)* triviality.

teñide NM dyeing.

teñir [3h y 3k] VT **(a)** *(con tinte)* to dye; *(colorar)* to tinge, colour; to stain; **~ una prenda de azul** to dye a garment blue; **el jersé ha teñido los pañuelos** the jersey has come out on the handkerchiefs.

(b) *(Arte)* color to darken.

(c) *(fig)* to tinge *(de* with); **una poesía teñida de añoranza** a poem tinged with longing.

teocali NM *(Méx)* teocalli, Aztec temple.

teocracia NF theocracy.

teocrático ADJ theocratic.

teodolito NM theodolite.

teogonía NF theogony.

teologal ADJ: **las virtudes ~es** the three Christian virtues *(faith, hope and charity)*.

teología NF theology; **~ de la liberación** liberation theology.

teológico ADJ theological.

teólogo NM theologian.

teorema NM theorem.

teorético ADJ *(LAm)* theoretic(al).

▼ **teoría** NF theory; **~ atómica** atomic theory; **~ cuántica, ~ de los cuanta** quantum theory; **~ de la información** information theory; **~ de la relatividad** theory of relativity; **en ~** in theory, theoretically.

teóricamente ADV theoretically, in theory.

teoricidad NF theoretical nature.

teórico [1] ADJ theoretic(al).

[2] NM, **teórica** NF theorist.

teorización NF theorizing.

teorizante NMF theoretician, theorist; *(pey)* theorizer.

teorizar [1f] VI to theorize.

teosofía NF theosophy.

teosófico ADJ theosophical.

teósofo, -a NM/F theosophist.

tepalcate NM *(CAm, Méx)* **(a)** *(vasija)* earthenware jar; *(fragmento)* fragment of pottery, shard. **(b)** *(cachorro)* piece of junk.

tepalcatero, -a NM/F *(Méx)* potter.

tepe NM sod, turf, clod.

tepetate NM *(CAm, Méx)* **(a)** *(residuo)* slag. **(b)** *(caliza)* limestone.

tepocate NM *(CAm, Méx)* **(a)** *(guijarro)* stone, pebble. **(b)** (*: *niño*) kid*.

teporocho* ADJ *(Méx)* tight*, drunk.

tequi: NM car.

tequila NF *(Méx)* tequila.

tequilero* ADJ *(Méx)* tight*, drunk.

tequío NM *(CAm, Méx)* *(molestia)* trouble; *(fardo)* burden; *(daño)* harm, damage.

tequioso ADJ *(CAm, Méx: V n)* burdensome; harmful; annoying, bothersome.

TER [ter] NM ABR *de* **Tren Español Rápido** ≈ *inter-city high-speed train*.

terapeuta NMF therapist.

terapéutica NF therapeutics; therapy.

terapéutico ADJ therapeutic(al).

terapia NF therapy; **~ aversiva, ~ por aversión** aversion therapy; **~ de choque** *(fig)* shock treatment; **~ electroconvulsiva** electroconvulsive therapy; **~ de electrochoque** electroshock therapy; **~ de grupo** group therapy; **~ laboral, ~ ocupacional** occupational therapy, work therapy; **~ lingüística** speech therapy; **~ táctil** touch therapy.

teratogénico ADJ teratogenic.

tercamente ADV obstinately, stubbornly.

tercena NF **(a)** *(Méx:††)* government warehouse. **(b)** *(And: carnicería)* butcher's (shop).

tercenista NM *(And)* butcher.

tercer ADJ V **tercero**.

tercera NF **(a)** *(Mús)* third. **(b)** *(pey)* go-between, procuress.

tercería NF *(arbitración)* mediation, arbitration; *(buenos oficios)* good offices; *(pey)* pimping, procuring.

tercermundismo NM attitudes *(o policies etc)* akin to those of a third-world country; backwardness, under-development.

tercermundista [1] ADJ third-world *(atr)*; under-developed.

[2] NM third-world country.

tercero [1] ADJ *(tercer delante de NM SING)* third; **~ grado** *(penitenciario) lowest category within the prison system which allows day release privileges*; **Tercer Mundo** Third World; **a la tercera va la vencida** third time lucky; **un hotel de ~** a third-class hotel.

[2] NM **(a)** *(árbitro)* mediator, arbitrator; *(Jur)* third person, third party; **~ en discordia** three's a crowd.

(b) *(pey)* pimp, pander, procurer.

tercerola NF *(Carib)* shotgun.

terceto NM **(a)** *(Mús)* trio. **(b)** *(Liter)* tercet, triplet.

terciada NF *(LAm)* plywood.

terciado ADJ **(a)** **azúcar terciada** brown sugar.

(b) **llevar algo ~** to wear sth diagonally *(o across one's chest etc)*; **con el sombrero ~** with his hat on the slant, with his hat at a rakish angle.

(c) **está ~ ya** a third of it has gone *(o been used etc)* already.

terciana NF tertian (fever).

terciar [1b] [1] VT **(a)** *(Mat)* to divide into three.

(b) *(Agr)* to plough a third time.

(c) *(inclinar)* to slant, slope; *faja etc* to wear (diagonally) across one's chest; *sombrero etc* to tilt, wear on the slant, put on at a rakish angle.

(d) *(And, Cono Sur, Méx)* to hoist on to *(o carry on)* one's shoulder.

(e) *(LAm)* vino etc to water down; *(Méx: mezclar)* to mix, blend.

[2] VI **(a)** *(completar el número)* to fill in, stand in, make up the number.

(b) **~ en** to take part in, join in; **yo terciaré con el jefe** I'll have a word with the boss; **~ entre dos rivales** to mediate between two rivals.

[3] **terciarse** VR **(a)** **si se tercia una buena oportunidad** if a good chance presents itself *(o comes up)*; **si se tercia, él también sabe hacerlo** on occasion he knows how to do it too, in the right circumstances he can manage it too.

(b) **si se tercia alguna vez que yo pase por allí** if I should happen sometime to go that way.

terciario ADJ tertiary.

tercio NM **(a)** *(tercera parte)* third; **dos ~s** two thirds.

(b) *(Mil Hist)* regiment, corps; **~ extranjero** foreign legion; **~ de la guardia civil** division of the civil guard.

(c) *(Taur)* stage, part (of the bullfight).

(d) **hacer buen ~ a uno** to do a service for sb; to serve sb well, be useful to sb; **hacer mal ~ a uno** to do sb a bad turn; **estar mejorado en ~ y quinto** to come out of it very well.

(e) *(LAm)* pack, package, bale.

(f) *(Carib*: *hombre)* fellow, guy*.

terciopelo NM velvet.

terco ADJ **(a)** *(obstinado)* obstinate, stubborn; **~ como una mula** as stubborn as a mule. **(b)** *material* hard, tough, hard to work. **(c)** *(And: duro)* harsh, unfeeling; indifferent.

Tere NF *forma familiar de* **Teresa**.

▶ LENGUA Y USO: **teoría** → 53.2

tere ADJ (*And*) niño weepy, tearful.
terebrante ADJ *dolor* sharp, piercing.
tereco NM (*And*) = **tereque**.
Terencio NM Terence.
tereque NM (*And, Carib*) **(a)** = **cachivache**. **(b)** ~s things, gear*, odds and ends.
Teresa NF T(h)eresa.
teresiano ADJ: **las obras teresianas** the works of Saint Teresa (of Ávila).
tergal ® NM Tergal ®.
tergiversación NF **(a)** (*falseamiento*) distortion, misrepresentation. **(b)** (*vacilación*) prevarication.
tergiversar [1a] **①** VT (*torcer*) to distort, twist (the sense of), misrepresent.
② VI (*no resolverse*) to prevaricate; (*vacilar*) to chop and change, blow hot and cold.
terliz NM ticking.
termal ADJ thermal.
termalismo NM hydrotherapy, bathing at a spa.
termalista **①** ADJ spa (*atr*).
② NMF person who visits a spa.
termas NFPL hot springs, hot baths.
termes NM INVAR termite.
termia NF (*gas*) therm.
térmica NF thermal, hot-air current.
térmico ADJ thermic, heat (*atr*); *cristal etc* heated; *ropa* thermal.
terminacho NM (*de palabra*) (*fea*) ugly word; (*incorrecta*) incorrect word, malapropism, linguistic monstrosity; (*malsonante*) nasty word, rude word.
terminación NF **(a)** (*acto*) ending, termination. **(b)** (*conclusión*) ending, conclusion. **(c)** (*Ling*) ending, termination. **(d)** (*Téc*) finish, finishing.
terminado NM (*Téc*) finish, finishing.
terminajo NM = **terminacho**.
terminal **①** ADJ terminal; **los enfermos ~es** the terminally ill.
② NM (*Elec, Inform*) terminal; **~ de computadora**, **~ informático** computer terminal; **~ interactivo** interactive unit; **~ de vídeo** video terminal.
③ NF (*Aer, Ferro etc*) terminal; (*LAm Ferro etc*) terminus; **~ de carga** freight terminal; **~ de contenedores** container terminal; **~ de pasajeros**, **~ de viajeros** passenger terminal.
terminante ADJ (*definitivo*) final, decisive, definitive; *decisión* final; *contestación* categorical, conclusive; *negativa* flat, forthright; *prohibición* strict.
▼ **terminantemente** ADV finally, decisively, definitively; categorically, conclusively; flatly; strictly; **queda ~ prohibido** + *infin* it is strictly forbidden to + *infin*.
▼ **terminar** [1a] **①** VT to end; to conclude; to finish, complete.
② VI **(a)** (*forma, objeto etc*) to end, finish; **termina en punta** it ends in a point, it comes to a point; **esto va a ~ en tragedia** this will end in tragedy.
(b) (*acabar*) to end (up), finish; to stop; (*Inform*) to quit; **al ~ el acto se fueron todos** at the end of the ceremony everyone went off; **¡hemos terminado!** that's an end of the matter!; **~ de hacer algo** to finish doing sth; to stop doing sth; **cuando termine de hablar** when he finishes speaking; **terminaba de salir del baño** she had just got out of the bath; **terminó de llenar el vaso con helado** he topped (o filled) the glass up with ice-cream; **~ por hacer algo** to end (up) by doing sth; **terminó marchándose enfadado** he ended up by going off in a huff, he finally went off very cross; **terminó diciendo que ...** he ended by saying that ..., he said in conclusion that ...
③ **terminarse** VR to end, come to an end, draw to a close, stop.
terminista NMF (*Cono Sur*) pedant.
término NM **(a)** (*fin*) end, finish, conclusion; **dar ~ a** to finish off, conclude; **llevar a ~** to carry out; **llevar a feliz ~** to carry through to a happy conclusion; **poner ~ a** to put an end to, put a stop to.
(b) (*de tierra etc*) boundary, limit; (*mojón*) boundary-stone.
(c) (*Ferro etc*) terminus.
(d) (*Pol*) area, district; (*Jur*) jurisdiction; **~ municipal** township; **tiene mucho ~** he has a big patch (to look after).
(e) (*Teat*) **primer ~** downstage; **segundo ~** middle distance; **último ~** upstage.
(f) (*Mat, Filos*) term; **~ medio** middle term; average; (*fig*) compromise, middle way; happy medium; **de ~ medio** average; **por ~ medio** on the average; **tendrán que buscar un ~ medio** they will have to look for a compromise (o middle way); **en primer ~** firstly; primarily; **en último ~** in the last analysis; as a last resort, if there is no other way out.
(g) (*plazo etc*) term, time, period; **en el ~ de 10 días** within a period of 10 days.
(h) (*de argumento etc*) point; **invertir los ~s** to stand an argument on

its head; (*fig*) to switch things round completely, turn a situation upside down.
(i) (*Ling*) term; **~s de intercambio** terms of trade; **según los ~s del contrato** according to the terms of the contract; **en ~s generales** generally speaking; **en ~s reales** in real terms; **en ~s sencillos** in simple terms; **en otros ~s** in other words; **en ~s de la productividad** in terms of productivity; **se expresó en ~s conciliatorios** he expressed himself in conciliatory terms.
(j) **estar en buenos ~s con uno** to be on good terms with sb.
terminología NF terminology.
terminológico ADJ terminological.
terminólogo, -a NM/F specialist in technical terminology.
termita NF, **termite** NM termite.
termitero NM (*montículo*) termite mound; (*nido*) termite nest, termitarium (*Téc*).
termo NM (*botella*) thermos (bottle, flask); (*calentador*) water-heater.
termo... PREF thermo...
termoaislante ADJ heat-insulating.
termodinámica NF thermodynamics.
termodinámico ADJ thermodynamic.
termoeléctrico ADJ thermoelectric.
termoimpresora NF thermal printer.
termoiónico ADJ thermionic.
termómetro NM thermometer.
termonuclear ADJ thermonuclear.
termopar NM thermocouple.
termopila NF thermopile.
Termópilas NFPL: **Las ~** Thermopylae.
termos NM INVAR = **termo**.
termostático ADJ thermostatic.
termostato NM thermostat.
termotanque NM (*Cono Sur*) immersion heater.
terna NF list of three candidates (*among whom a final choice is made*), shortlist.
ternario ADJ ternary.
terne **①** ADJ **(a)** (*fuerte*) tough, strong, husky; (*pey*) bullying. **(b)** (*terco*) stubborn; **~ que ~** out of sheer stubbornness.
② NM **(a)** bully, tough*. **(b)** (*Cono Sur*) rogue.
ternejo ADJ (*And*) spirited, vigorous.
ternera NF **(a)** (*Agr*) calf, heifer calf. **(b)** (*Culin*) veal.
ternero NM calf, bull calf.
ternerón ADJ **(a)** (*: compasivo*) soft-hearted. **(b)** (*Cono Sur, Méx*) mozo overgrown, big.
terneza NF **(a)** (*cualidad*) tenderness. **(b)** ~s (*palabras*) nice things, endearments, tender words.
ternilla NF gristle, cartilage; (*CAm, Carib, Méx*) cartilage of the nose.
ternilloso ADJ gristly, cartilaginous.
terno NM **(a)** (*grupo de tres*) set of three, group of three; trio; (*traje*) three-piece suit; (*Carib: joyas*) necklace set.
(b) (*: palabrota*) curse, swearword; **echar** (*o* **soltar**) **~s** to curse, swear.
ternura NF **(a)** (*cualidad*) tenderness; fondness; affection. **(b)** (*palabra*) endearment, tender word.
ternurismo NM sentimentality.
ternurista ADJ sentimental.
Terpsícore NF Terpsichore.
terquedad NF **(a)** (*obstinación*) obstinacy, stubbornness. **(b)** (*dureza*) hardness, toughness. **(c)** (*And: severidad*) harshness, lack of feeling; indifference.
terracota NF terracotta.
terrado NM **(a)** terrace; flat roof. **(b)** (*: cabeza*) bonce*, head.
terraja NF diestock.
terral **①** NM (*LAm*) cloud of dust.
② ADJ: **viento ~** wind from the land.
Terranova NF Newfoundland.
terranova NM Newfoundland dog.
terraplén NM **(a)** (*Ferro etc*) embankment; (*Agr*) terrace; (*Mil*) rampart, bank, earthwork; mound. **(b)** (*cuesta*) slope, gradient.
terraplenar [1a] VT *terreno* to (fill and) level (off); (*Agr*) to terrace; *hoyo* to fill in; (*elevar*) to bank up, raise.
terráqueo **①** ADJ earth (*atr*); **globo ~** (*bola del mundo*) globe; **el globo ~** (*la tierra*) the Earth.
② NM, **terráquea** NF earthling.
terrario NM terrarium.
terrateniente NMF landowner.
terraza NF **(a)** (*Arquit*) (*techo*) flat roof; (*balcón*) balcony; (*terraza*) terrace. **(b)** (*Agr*) terrace. **(c)** (*Hort*) flowerbed, border, plot. **(d)** (*Culin*) two-handled glazed jar. **(e)** (*café*) pavement café. **(f)** (*: cabeza*) nut*, head.
terrazo NM terrazzo.
terregal NM (*LAm*: *terrón*) clod, hard lump of earth; (*Méx*: *tierra*) loose earth, dusty soil; (*polvareda*) cloud of dust.

terremoto NM earthquake.

terrenal ADJ earthly, worldly.

terreno 1 ADJ terrestrial; earthly, worldly.
2 NM (a) (*gen, Geol etc*) terrain; (*tierra, suelo*) soil, earth, ground, land; (*Agr*) soil, land; **los accidentes del ~** the characteristics of the terrain, the features of the landscape; **~ abonado para el vicio** hotbed of vice, breeding-ground of vice; **en todos los ~s** in any place you care to name; **un coche para todo ~** a car for every type of surface, a car for all conditions; **sobre el ~** on the spot; **hay que fiarse del hombre sobre el ~** you have to trust the man on the spot; **resolveremos el problema sobre el ~** we will solve the problem as we go along; **ceder ~, perder ~** to give ground, lose ground (*a, ante* to); **ganar ~** to gain ground; **llegar al ~** to arrive on the scene, get to the spot; **medir el ~** (*fig*) to see how the land lies; **minar** (*o* **socavar**) **el ~ a uno** to undermine sb's position; **preparar el ~** (*fig*) to pave the way (*a* for); **vencer a uno en su propio ~** to defeat sb on his home ground.
(b) (*un ~*) piece of land, piece of ground; (*para construcción*) plot, lot, site; (*Agr*) plot, field, patch; (*Dep*) field, pitch, ground; **~ beneficial** (*Ecl*) glebe, glebe land; **~ de camping** campsite; **~ de fútbol** football ground, football pitch; **~ de juego** field of play, pitch; **~ de pasto** pasture; **~ de pruebas** testing-ground; **un ~ plantado de patatas** a field planted with potatoes; **vender unos ~s** to sell some land; **repartir ~ a los campesinos** to distribute land to the peasants.
(c) (*fig*) field, sphere; **en el ~ de la química** in the field of chemistry; **eso no es mi ~** that's not (in) my field.

térreo ADJ earthen; earthy.

terrero 1 ADJ (a) (*de la tierra*) earthy; (*de tierra*) of earth. (b) *vuelo* low, skimming. (c) (*fig*) humble.
2 NM pile, heap; (*Min*) dump.

terrestre ADJ (*gen*) terrestrial; (*de la tierra*) earthly; ground (*atr*), land (*atr*); *ruta* land (*atr*), overland (*atr*); *fuerzas* (*Mil*) ground (*atr*).

terrible ADJ terrible, dreadful, awful.

terriblemente ADV terribly, dreadfully, awfully.

terrícola ADJ, NMF earthling.

terrier NM terrier.

terrífico ADJ terrifying.

terrina NF terrine.

territorial ADJ territorial.

territorialidad NF territoriality.

territorio NM territory; **~ bajo mandato** mandated territory.

terrón NM (a) (*Geol*) clod, lump, sod. (b) (*de azúcar, harina etc*) lump; **azúcar en ~** lump sugar. (c) (*Agr*) field, patch; **terrones** (*fig*) land.

terronera NF (*And*) terror, fright.

terror NM terror; **~ pánico** panic.

terrorífico ADJ terrifying, frightening.

terrorismo NM terrorism; **~ de Estado** state terrorism.

terrorista ADJ, NMF terrorist.

terroso ADJ earthy.

terruño NM (a) (*tepe*) lump, clod. (b) (*parcela*) plot, piece of ground; (*fig*) native soil, home (ground); **apego al ~** attachment to one's native soil.

terso ADJ (a) (*liso*) smooth; (*y brillante*) glossy, polished, shining; **piel tersa** smooth skin, soft skin. (b) *estilo* smooth, polished, flowing.

tersura NF (*V* ADJ) (a) smoothness; glossiness, polish, shine. (b) smoothness, flow.

tertulia NF (a) (*reunión informal*) social gathering, regular informal gathering; (*en café etc*) group, circle, set; **~ literaria** literary circle, literary gathering; **~ radiofónica** (radio) talk show; **estar de ~** to talk, sit around talking; **hacer ~** to get together, meet informally and talk; **hoy no hay ~** there's no meeting today, the group is not meeting today.
(b) (*sala*) clubroom, games room.
(c) (*Cono Sur: galería*) gallery; (*Carib: palcos*) boxes.

TERTULIA

i *The term **tertulia** is used for groups of people who meet informally on a regular basis to chat about current affairs, the Arts, etc and is also used to refer to the gathering itself. In early 20th Century Spain, **tertulias literarias** were much in vogue, and critics and writers would meet to discuss the literary issues of the day in places such as the famous Café Gijón. In more recent times, the term has been used to refer to the highly organized PR platforms in which writers of the moment engage in round-table discussions to promote their latest work.*

Tertuliano NM Tertullian.

tertuliano, -a NM/F member of a social gathering (*etc*); (*Rad*) talk show guest.

tertuliar [1b] VI (*LAm*) to attend a social gathering; to get together, meet informally and talk.

terylene ® NM Terylene ®.

Tesalia NF Thessaly.

tesar [1j] VT to tauten, tighten up.

tesauro NM thesaurus.

tescal NM (*Méx*) stony ground.

tesela NF tessera.

Teseo NM Theseus.

tesina NF minor thesis, dissertation (*for first degree*).

▼ **tesis** NF INVAR thesis.

tesitura NF attitude, frame of mind.

teso ADJ taut, tight; tense.

tesón NM insistence; tenacity, persistence; firmness; **resistir con ~** to resist firmly, resist staunchly.

tesonero ADJ (*LAm*) tenacious, persistent.

tesorería NF treasurership, office of treasurer.

tesorero, -a NM/F treasurer.

tesoro NM (a) (*dineral*) treasure; hoard; **~ escondido** buried treasure; secret hoard; **valer un ~** to be worth a fortune; (*persona*) to be a real treasure.
(b) (*Fin, Pol etc*) treasury; **T~ público** Exchequer, Treasury.
(c) (*Fin: pagaré*) treasury bond.
(d) (*Liter*) thesaurus.
(e) (*fig*) treasure; **¡sí, ~!** yes, darling!, **el libro es un ~ de datos** the book is a mine of information; **es un ~ de recuerdos** it is a treasure-house of memories; **tenemos una cocinera que es todo un ~** we have a real gem of a cook, we have a cook who is a real treasure.

Tespis NM Thespis.

test [tes] NM, PL **tests** [tes] test; **~ de comprensión** comprehension test; **~ de embarazo** pregnancy test; **examen tipo ~** multiple-choice exam.

testa NF (a) (*cabeza*) head; **~ coronada** crowned head. (b) (**: inteligencia*) brains; (*sentido común*) gumption*.

testador NM testator.

testadora NF testatrix.

testaduro ADJ (*Carib*) = **testarudo**.

testaferro NM (a) (*persona*) figurehead; front man. (b) (*Com*) dummy.

testamentaria NF executrix.

testamentaría NF (a) (*acto*) execution of a will. (b) (*bienes*) estate.

testamentario 1 ADJ testamentary.
2 NM executor.

testamento NM (a) (*gen*) will, testament; **hacer ~, otorgar ~** to make one's will.
(b) **Antiguo T~** Old Testament; **Nuevo T~** New Testament.
(c) (***) screed.

testar[1] [1a] VI to make a will.

testar[2] [1a] VT (*And*) to underline.

testar[3] [1a] VT *coche, producto* to test.

testarada* NF, **testarazo*** NM bump on the head; bang, bash*; **darse una testarada** to bump one's head, give o.s. a bang on the head.

testarudez NF stubbornness, pigheadedness.

testarudo ADJ stubborn, pigheaded.

testear [1a] (*LAm*) 1 VT to test.
2 VI to do a test, undergo a test.

testera NF front, face; (*Zool*) forehead.

testero NM (a) = **testera**. (b) (*de cama*) bedhead. (c) (*Arquit*) wall.

testes NMPL testes.

testiculamen*: NM balls*:, equipment*.

testículo NM testicle.

testificación NF (a) testification. (b) = **testimonio**.

testificar [1g] 1 VT (a) (*atestiguar*) to attest; (*dar testimonio de*) to testify to, give evidence of. (b) (*fig*) to attest, testify to.
2 VI to testify, give evidence; **~ de** = 1 (a).

testigo 1 NMF (a) (*Jur etc*) witness; **~ de cargo** witness for the prosecution; **~ de descargo** witness for the defence; **~ de Jehová** Jehovah's witness; **~ del novio** ≃ best man; **~ ocular, ~ presencial, ~ de vista** eyewitness; **~ pericial** expert witness; **poner a uno por ~** to cite sb as a witness.
(b) (*en experimento*) control; (*Geol*) sample core.
(c) (*en carrera de relevos*) baton.
(d) (*Aut*) **~ luminoso** warning light.
2 ATR: **grupo ~** control group; **sujeto ~** particular case, case used as an example.

testimonial ADJ token, nominal.

testimonialmente ADV as a token gesture; nominally; (*fig*) half-heartedly.

testimoniar [1b] VT to testify to, bear witness to; (*fig*) to show, demonstrate.

testimonio NM testimony, evidence; affidavit; **~ de oídas** hearsay evidence; **falso ~** perjured evidence; **dar ~** to testify (*de* to), give evidence (*de* of); **en ~ de mi afecto** as a token (*o* mark) of my affection.

testosterona NF testosterone.

testuz NM (*frente*) forehead; (*nuca*) nape (of the neck).

teta [1] NF (*de biberón*) teat; (*pezón*) nipple; (*) breast; **dar (la) ~ a** to suckle, breast-feed; **quitar la ~ a** to wean; **niño de ~** baby still at the breast; **mejor que ~ de monja:** really great*.

[2] ADJ INVAR: **estar ~** (*Esp*:) to be really great*.

tetamen: NM big bust, lots of bosom.

tétanos NM tetanus.

tete* NM (*Cono Sur*) mess, trouble.

tetelque ADJ (*CAm, Méx*) sharp, bitter.

tetera¹ NF teapot; tea urn; **~ eléctrica** electric kettle.

tetera² NF (*Méx*) (*biberón*) feeding bottle; (*vasija*) vessel with a spout.

tetero NM (*And, Carib*) feeding bottle.

tetilla NF (a) (*Anat: de hombre*) nipple. (b) (*de biberón*) rubber teat.

tetina NF teat.

Tetis NF Thetis.

tetón¹ NM (*en neumático etc*) bubble, swelling.

tetón²: ADJ (*Cono Sur*) stupid, thick*.

tetona* ADJ busty*.

tetra brik ® NM INVAR, **tetrabrik** ® NM INVAR Tetra-Pak ®, carton.

tetracilíndrico ADJ: **motor ~** four-cylinder engine.

tetracloruro NM tetrachloride; **~ de carbono** carbon tetrachloride.

tetraedro NM tetrahedron.

tetrágono NM tetragon.

tetrámetro NM tetrameter.

tetramotor ADJ four-engined.

tetra pak ® NM INVAR, **tetrapak** ® NM INVAR Tetra-Pak ®.

tetrarreactor NM four-engined jet plane.

tetratlón NM tetrathlon.

tétrico ADJ *pensamiento* gloomy, dismal; *humor* gloomy, pessimistic; sullen; *luz* dim, wan.

tetuda* ADJ busty*.

tetunte NM (*CAm*) bundle.

teutón, -ona NM/F Teuton.

teutónico ADJ Teutonic.

teveo NM = **tebeo**.

textil [1] ADJ textile.

[2] (a) **~es** NMPL textiles. (b) (*hum**) non-naturist, person who wears a swimsuit.

texto NM text; **grabado fuera de ~** full-page illustration.

textual ADJ (a) (*de texto*) textual. (b) (*fig*) exact; literal; **son sus palabras ~es** those are his exact words.

textualmente ADV (a) (*de texto*) textually. (b) (*fig*) exactly; literally; **dice ~ que ...** he says (and I quote his own words) that ...

textura NF texture (*t fig*).

tez NF complexion, skin; colouring.

tezontle NM (*Méx*) volcanic rock.

Tfno., tfno. ABR *de* **teléfono** telephone, Tel.

TGV NM ABR *de* **tren de gran velocidad** ≃ Advanced Passenger Train, APT.

ti PRON (*tras PREP*) you; yourself; (††, *a Dios*) thee, thyself; **es para ~** it's for you; **¿lo has comprado para ~?** did you buy it for yourself?; **esto no se refiere a ~** this doesn't refer to you.

tía NF (a) (*pariente*) aunt; **~ abuela** great-aunt; **¡no hay tu ~!** nothing doing!; **¡cuéntaselo a tu ~!** pull the other one!*

(b) *delante de nombre en tono respetuoso, no se traduce*: **unos dulces para la ~ Dulcinea** some sweets for Dulcinea.

(c) (*) (*mujer*) woman; (*chica*) bird:, chick*; **~ buena** smashing girl*; **¡oye, ~ buena!** hi, gorgeous!*; **las ~s piensan así** that's the way women think.

(d) (*: *puta*) whore.

(e) (:: *bruja*) old bat*, old bag*.

(f) **la ~:** (*María etc*) the curse (of Eve).

tiamina NF thiamine.

tiangue NM (*CAm*) small market; booth, stall.

tianguis NM (*CAm, Méx*) market.

TIAR [ti'ar] NM ABR *de* **Tratado Interamericano de Asistencia Recíproca**.

tiara NF tiara.

tiarrón* NM big chap*, huge fellow.

tiarrona* NF big girl, hefty wench*.

tibante ADJ (*And*) haughty.

tibe NM (*And, Carib*) whetstone.

Tíber NM Tiber.

Tiberio NM Tiberius.

tiberio* [1] ADJ (*CAm, Méx*) sloshed*.

[2] NM (a) (*jaleo*) uproar, row; (*pelea*) set-to*. (b) (*CAm, Méx*) binge*.

Tibet NM: **El ~** Tibet.

tibetano, -a [1] ADJ, NM/F Tibetan.

[2] NM (*Ling*) Tibetan.

tibia NF tibia.

tibiarse [1b] VR (*CAm, Carib*) to get cross.

tibieza NF (a) (*de sustancia*) lukewarmness, tepidness. (b) (*fig*) luke-

warmness; coolness, lack of enthusiasm.

tibio ADJ (a) *agua etc* lukewarm, tepid.

(b) (*fig*) *fe, persona etc* lukewarm; cool, unenthusiastic; **estar ~ con uno** to be cool to sb, behave distantly towards sb.

(c) **poner ~ a uno** to hurl abuse at sb, give sb a verbal battering; to say dreadful things about sb.

(d) (*CAm, Carib*) cross, angry.

tibor NM large earthenware jar; (*Carib*) chamber pot; (*Méx*) gourd.

tiburón NM (a) shark; **~ de río** pike. (b) (*) go-getter*, unscrupulous person; (*en bolsa*) secret purchaser of shares; (*Cono Sur*) wolf*, Don Juan.

tiburoneo NM (*Com*) share raiding.

tic NM, PL **tics** [tik] (a) tap; click; tick, tick-tock. (b) (*Med: t* **~ nervioso**) tic.

Ticiano NM Titian.

tícket ['tike] NM, PL **tíckets** ticket; (*de una compra*) receipt.

tico*, -a ADJ, NM/F (*CAm*) Costa Rican.

tictac NM (*de reloj*) tick, tick-tock; (*de corazón*) beat; (*de máquina de escribir*) tapping, tip-tap; **hacer ~** to tick; to beat, go pit-a-pat; to tip-tap.

tiempecito NM (*LAm*) (spell of) very bad weather.

tiemple NM (a) (*Cono Sur: galanteo*) love-making, courting. (b) (*Cono Sur: amante*) lover. (c) (*LAm: enamoramiento*) infatuation.

tiempo NM (a) (*gen*) time; **breve ~** short while; **~ del bocadillo** teabreak; **~ compartido** timeshare; time-sharing; **~ libre** spare time, free time, leisure; **~ máquina** machine time; **~ muerto** (*Dep*) time out; (*fig*) breather, breathing-space; **~ real** real time; **~ de respuesta** response time; **a ~** in time, in good time, early; at the right time; **a un ~, al mismo ~** at the same time; **a su debido ~** in due course; **al poco ~** very soon, soon after; **a ~ que ..., al ~ que ...** at the same time that ..., while ...; **al mismo ~ que ...** at the same time as ...; **trabajo a ~ parcial** part-time work; **trabajar a ~ completo** to work fulltime; **cada cierto ~** every so often; **con ~** in time, in good time, early; **con el ~** eventually, in time; **cuánto ~, ¿eh?*** long time no see!; **¿cuánto ~ se va a quedar?** how long is he staying?; **de ~ en ~** from time to time; **de algún ~ a esta parte** for some time past; **una costumbre de mucho ~** a long-standing custom; **fuera de ~** at the wrong time; **necesito más ~** I need longer, I need more time; **no puede quedarse más ~** he can't stay any longer; **mucho ~** a long time, a long while; **todo el ~** all the time; **el ~ es de oro** time is money; time is precious; **el ~ lo es todo** time is everything, time is of the essence; **es ~ perdido hablar con él** it's a waste of time talking to him; **andando el ~** in due course, in time; in the fullness of time; **el ~ apremia** time presses; **dar ~ al ~** to consider all the possibilities; to let matters take their course; **darse buen ~** to have a good time; **el ~ dirá** time will tell; **apenas dispongo de mi ~** I can scarcely call my time my own; **engañar el ~, matar el ~** to kill time; **ganar ~** to save time; **hacer ~** to while away the time, kill time; to mark time; **hace mucho ~** a long time ago; **hace bastante ~ que lo compré** I bought it a good while ago; **desde hace mucho ~** for a long time; **hace mucho ~ que no voy** I haven't been for a long time; **perder el ~** to waste time; to fool around; **sería simplemente perder el ~** it would be just a waste of time; **sin perder ~** without delay; **sacar ~ para hacer algo** to take time out to do sth; **tener ~ para** to have time for.

(b) (*específico, limitado*) time, period, age; **~s modernos** modern times; **a través de los ~s** through the ages; **en ~ de los griegos** in the time of the Greeks; **en estos ~s nuestros** in this day and age; **en los ~s que corremos** in these dreadful times; **en mis ~s** in my day; **en los buenos ~s** in the good old days; **en mis buenos ~s** when I was in my prime; **en otro ~** formerly; once upon a time; **en los últimos ~s** recently, lately, in recent times; **en ~ de Maricastaña, en ~ del rey que rabió** way back, long ago; in the good old days; **estar en el ~ de las vacas flacas** to have fallen on hard times; **los ~s están revueltos** the times are out of joint, these are disturbed times; **hay que ir con los ~s** one must keep abreast of the times.

(c) (*de niño*) age; **A y B son del mismo ~** A and B are the same age; **¿cuánto o qué** (*LAm*) **~ tiene el pequeño?** how old is the child?

(d) (*Dep*) half; **primer ~** first half.

(e) (*Mús: compás*) tempo, time.

(f) (*Mús: de sinfonía etc*) movement.

(g) (*Ling*) tense; **~ compuesto** compound tense; **en ~ presente** in the present tense.

(h) (*Met: t* **~ atmosférico**) weather; **si dura el mal ~** if the bad weather continues; **hace buen ~** it's fine, the weather is good, the weather is fine; **¿qué ~ hará mañana?** what will the weather be like tomorrow?; **a mal ~, buena cara** one must make the best of a bad job.

(i) (*Náut*) stormy weather, rough weather.

(j) (*Mec*) cycle; **motor de 2 ~s** two-stroke engine.

tienda NF (a) (*Com*) shop, store; (*esp*) grocer's; (*Carib, Cono Sur*:

mercería) draper's, clothier's; **~ de coloniales, ~ de comestibles, ~ de ultramarinos** (*Esp*) grocer's (shop), grocery (*US*); **~ por departamento** (*Carib*) department store; **~ de deportes** sports shop; **~ libre de impuestos** duty-free shop; **~ de regalos** gift-shop; **ir de ~s** to go shopping; **poner ~** to set up shop.

(b) (*Náut etc*) awning; **~ de campaña** tent; **~ de oxígeno** oxygen tent.

tienta NF (a) (*Med*) probe.

(b) (*habilidad*) cleverness; (*astucia*) astuteness.

(c) **a ~s** (*a ciegas*) gropingly, blindly; **andar a ~s** to grope one's way along, feel one's way; (*fig*) to feel one's way; **decir algo a ~s** to throw out a remark at random, say sth to see what effect it has.

(d) (*Taur*) trial, test.

tiento NM (a) (*sensación física*) feel, feeling, touch; (*Fin**) touch*, tickle*; (*: *amoroso*) pass*; **a ~** by touch; gropingly; (*fig*) uncertainly; **echar un ~ a una chica*** to make a pass at a girl*, try it on with a girl*; **a 40 dólares nadie le echó un ~** at 40 dollars nobody was biting, at 40 dollars he didn't get a tickle*; **perder el ~** to lose one's touch.

(b) (*fig*) (*tacto*) tact; (*prudencia*) care; (*cautela*) wariness, circumspection; **ir con ~** to go carefully, go cautiously.

(c) (*Arte etc*) steadiness of hand, steady hand.

(d) (*Zool*) feeler, tentacle; (*Circo*) balancing pole; (*de ciego*) blind man's stick.

(e) (*Mús*) preliminary flourish, scale, notes played in tuning up.

(f) (*: *puñetazo*) blow, punch; **dar ~s a uno** to hit sb.

(g) (*: *trago*) swig*; **dar un ~** to take a swig* (*a* from).

(h) (*Cono Sur*: *tira*) thong of raw leather, rawhide strap.

tiernamente ADV tenderly.

tierno ADJ (*gen*) tender; soft; *pan etc* new, fresh.

tierra NF (a) (*Astron*: *el mundo*) earth, world.

(b) (*superficie*) land; **~ firme** mainland; terra firma, dry land; **~ de nadie** no-man's land; **~ quemada** scorched earth; **~ adentro** inland; (*LAm*) interior, remote area; **por ~** by land, overland; **¡~ a la vista!** land!; **besar la ~** to fall flat; **caer a ~** to fall down; **caer por ~** (*t fig*) to fall to the ground; **dar con algo en ~** to drop sth; to knock sth over; (*fig*) to overthrow sth; **echar a ~** to demolish, pull down; to raze to the ground; **echar** (*o* **tirar**) **algo por ~** to ruin sth, upset sth; **perder ~** (*perder el pie*) to lose one's footing; (*en agua*) to get out of one's depth; **poner un avión en ~** to land a plane; **poner ~ por medio** to get out quick, get as far away as possible; **saltar en** (*o* **a**) **~** (*desde barco*) to leap ashore; **tocar ~** (*Aer*) to touch down; **tomar ~** (*Aer*) to land, come down; (*Náut*) to reach harbour; **venirse a** (*o* **por**) **~** to collapse.

(c) (*Geol etc*) land, soil, earth, ground; **~ de batán** fuller's earth; **~ batida** (*Dep*) clay (court); **~ de brezo** peat; **~ vegetal** topsoil; **echar ~ a un asunto** to hush an affair up; to forget about a matter; **echar ~ a uno** (*Cono Sur, Méx*) to speak damagingly of sb.

(d) (*Agr*) land; **~s** lands, estate(s); **~ baldía** wasteland; **~ de labor** agricultural land; **~ de pan llevar** arable land, corn-growing land; **en cualquier ~ de garbanzos** all over; **heredó unas ~s en la provincia** he inherited some land in the province.

(e) (*Pol etc*) country; **su ~** one's own country, one's native land; one's own region, one's home area; **~ natal** native land; **~ prometida, ~ de promisión** land of promise, promised land; **ver ~** to see the world; **vamos a nuestra ~ a pasar las Navidades** we go home for Christmas; **no es de estas ~s** he's not from these parts; **¿tienen tractores en tu ~?** do they have tractors where you come from?, do they have tractors in your part of the world?

(f) (*Elec*) earth, ground (*US*); **conectar un aparato a ~** to earth a piece of apparatus, ground a piece of apparatus (*US*).

(g) (*LAm*: *polvo*) dust.

tierra-aire ATR: **misil ~** surface-to-air missile.

tierrafría NMF (*And*) highlander.

tierral NM (*LAm*), **tierrazo** NM (*LAm*) cloud of dust.

Tierra Santa NF Holy Land.

tierra-tierra ATR: **misil ~** surface-to-surface missile.

tierrero NM (*LAm*) cloud of dust.

tierruca NF native land, native heath.

tieso ① ADJ (a) (*rígido*) stiff, rigid; (*erecto*) erect; (*tenso*) taut; **con las orejas tiesas** with its ears pricked; **quedarse ~** (*fig*) (*de frío*) to be frozen stiff; (‡: *muerto*) to peg out‡.

(b) (*fig*) (*sano*) fit; (*vivo*) sprightly; (*alegre*) chirpy*; **le encontré muy ~ a pesar de su enfermedad** I found him very cheerful in spite of his illness.

(c) (*fig*) (*estirado*) stiff (in manner); (*rígido*) rigid (in attitude); **como un ajo** as stiff as a poker; **me recibió muy ~** he received me very stiffly.

(d) (*) (*orgulloso*) proud; (*presumido*) conceited, stuck-up*; (*satisfecho*) smug; **~ de cogote** haughty; **iba tan ~ con la novia al brazo** he was walking so proudly with his girl on his arm.

(e) (*terco*) stubborn; (*firme*) firm, confident; **~ que ~** as stubborn as

they come; **ponerse ~ con uno** to stand one's ground, insist on one's rights; (*pey*) to be stubborn with sb; **tenerlas tiesas con uno** to put up a firm resistance to sb, stand one's ground for o.s.

(f) **estar ~** (*Fin**) to be broke*.

(g) **estar ~** (*: *parado*) to be out of work.

② ADV strongly, energetically, hard.

tiesto NM (a) (*Hort*) flowerpot. (b) (*casco*) shard, piece of pottery. (c) (*Cono Sur*) (*vasija*) pot, vessel; (*orinal*) chamberpot.

tiesura NF (a) (*rigidez*) stiffness, rigidity; erectness; tautness. (b) (*fig*) stiffness; rigidity. (c) (*) conceit. (d) (*terquedad*) stubbornness; (*confianza*) firmness, confidence.

tifiar‡ [1b] VT (*Carib*) to nick‡, lift*.

tifitifi* NM (*Carib*) theft.

tifo NM typhus; **~ de América** yellow fever; **~ asiático** cholera; **~ de Oriente** bubonic plague.

tifoidea NF (*t* **fiebre ~**) typhoid.

tifón NM (a) (*huracán*) typhoon. (b) (*tromba*) waterspout. (c) (*Méx Min*) outcrop of ore.

tifus NM (a) (*Med*) typhus; **~ exantemático** spotted fever; **~ icteroides** yellow fever.

(b) (*Teat**) persons having complimentary tickets (*o* free seats); claque; **entrar de ~** to get in free.

tigra NF (*LAm Zool*) female tiger; (*jaguar*) female jaguar; **ponerse como una ~ parida** (*And, Cono Sur**) to fly off the handle*.

tigre NM (a) (*Zool*) tiger; (*LAm*) jaguar; **~ de Bengala** Bengal tiger; **~ de colmillo de sable** sabre-toothed tiger; **~ de papel** paper tiger. (b) (*And*: *café*) black coffee with a dash of milk; (*And*: *combinado*) cocktail. (c) (‡: *wáter*) bog‡, loo*; **esto huele a ~** this pongs‡, this smells awful.

tigrero ① ADJ (*Cono Sur*) brave.
② NM (*LAm*) jaguar hunter.

tigresa NF tigress.

tigridia NF tiger lily.

tigrillo NM (*LAm*) member of the cat tribe, *eg* ocelot, lynx.

Tigris NM Tigris.

tigrón* NM (*Carib*) bully, braggart.

tigüila NF (*Méx*) trick, swindle.

tija NF (*Aut*) shank.

tijera NF (a) (*de bicicleta*) fork; (*LAm*) scissors; **meter la ~ en** to cut into.

(b) (*LAm Zool*) claw, pincer.

(c) (*: *persona*) gossip; **ser una buena ~, tener buena ~** to be a great gossip; to have a sharp tongue; to indulge constantly in backbiting, be a scandalmonger.

(d) **de ~** folding; **escalera de ~** steps, step-ladder; **silla de ~** folding chair, folding stool, camp stool.

(e) **es un trabajo de ~** it's a scissors-and-paste job.

tijeral NM (*Cono Sur Orn*) stork.

tijeras NFPL scissors; (*Hort etc*) shears, clippers; **~ de coser** sewing scissors; **~ podadoras, ~ de podar** secateurs; **~ para las uñas** nail-scissors; **unas ~** a pair of scissors (*etc*), some scissors (*etc*).

tijereta NF (a) (*Ent*) earwig. (b) (*Bot*) vine tendril. (c) (*Dep*) scissors kick, overhead kick.

tijeretada NF, **tijeretazo** NM snip, snick, small cut.

tijeretear [1a] ① VT to snip, snick, cut.
② VI (a) (*entrometerse*) to meddle. (b) (*CAm, Cono Sur, Méx*: *chismear*) to gossip, backbite.

tijereteo NM (a) (*lit*) snipping, snicking, cutting. (b) (*fig*) meddling. (c) (*CAm, Cono Sur, Méx*: *chismes*) gossiping, backbiting.

tila NF (a) (*Bot*) lime tree. (b) (*Culin*) lime(-blossom) tea. (c) (‡: *droga*) hash*, pot‡.

tildar [1a] VT (a) (*Tip*) to put an accent on; to put a tilde over. (b) (*fig*) **~ a uno de** + ADJ to brand sb as (being) + ADJ, stigmatize sb as (being) + ADJ.

tilde *gen* NF (a) (*Tip*) accent (´), tilde (˜). (b) (*fig*: *defecto*) blemish, defect, flaw. (c) (*fig*) (*bagatela*) triviality; (*pizca*) jot, bit; **en una ~*** in a jiffy*.

tilichera NF (*CAm, Méx*) hawker's box, glass-covered box.

tilichero NM (*CAm, Méx*) hawker, pedlar, peddler (*US*).

tiliches NMPL (*CAm, Méx*) trinkets; belongings; (*pey*) junk.

tilín NM (a) tinkle, ting-a-ling.

(b) (*) **hacer ~** to be well liked; **me hace ~** I like it, I go for it*; **no me hace ~** it doesn't appeal to me; **tener ~** to be nice, be attractive, have a way with people; **tener algo al ~** (*Carib*) to have sth at one's fingertips.

(c) **en un ~** (*And, Carib, Cono Sur*: *) in a flash.

tilinches* NMPL (*Méx*) rags.

tilingada* NF (*Cono Sur, Méx*) silly thing (to do *etc*).

tilingo* (*And, Cono Sur, Méx*) ① ADJ silly, stupid.
② NM fool.

tilinguear* [1a] VI (*And, Cono Sur, Méx*) to act the fool, do (*etc*) silly things.

tilinguería* NF (*And, Cono Sur, Méx*) (a) (*estupidez*) silliness, stupidity. (b) **~s** nonsense.

tilintar [1a] VT (*CAm*) to stretch, tauten.

tilinte ADJ (*CAm*) (a) (*tenso*) tight, taut. (b) (*elegante*) elegant. (c) (*repleto*) replete.

tilma NF (*Méx*) blanket, cape.

tilo NM (a) (*Bot*) lime, lime tree. (b) (*Cono Sur*) = **tila** (b).

tiloso* ADJ (*CAm*) dirty, filthy.

timador(a) NM/F swindler, trickster.

timar [1a] ① VT (a) *propiedad* to steal.
(b) *persona* to swindle, play a confidence trick on, con*; **le timaron la herencia** they swindled him out of the inheritance.
② **timarse*** VR to make eyes at each other; **~ con uno** (*amorosamente*) to make eyes at sb, ogle sb; (*engatusar*) to play sb along, lead sb on.

timba NF (a) (*en juego de azar*) hand. (b) (*garita*) gambling den. (c) (*CAm, Carib, Méx*) pot-belly. (d) (*Carib*) **esto tiene ~** it's a sticky business.

timbal NM (a) (*Mús*) small drum, kettledrum. (b) (*Culin*) meat pie. (c) **~es** (ⁱⁱ) balls ⁱⁱ.

timbembe* ADJ (*Cono Sur*) weak, trembling.

timbero* (*Cono Sur*) ① ADJ given to gambling.
② NM, **timbera** NF gambler.

timbiriche NM (*Carib, Méx*) small shop.

timbrado ADJ: **voz bien timbrada** well-toned voiced.

timbrar [1a] VT (a) (*estampillar*) to stamp; (*sellar*) to seal. (b) (*Correos*) to postmark.

timbrazo NM ring; **dar un ~** to ring the bell.

timbre NM (a) (*Com, Fin*) fiscal stamp, revenue stamp; *sello* seal; (*Fin*) stamp duty.
(b) (*Méx Correos*) postage stamp.
(c) (*LAm: descripción*) personal description; description of goods (*etc*).
(d) (*fig*) **~ de gloria** mark of honour; action (*etc*) which is to one's credit.
(e) (*Elec etc*) bell; **~ de alarma** alarm bell; **tocar el ~** to ring the bell.
(f) (*Mús etc*) timbre; **~ nasal** (*Ling*) nasal timbre, twang.

timbrear [1a] VI to ring (the bell).

timbusca NF (*And: sopa*) thick soup; (*plato rústico*) spicy local dish.

tímidamente ADV timidly, shyly, nervously; bashfully.

timidez NF timidity, shyness, nervousness; bashfulness.

tímido ADJ timid, shy, nervous; bashful.

timo NM (*estafa*) swindle, confidence trick, confidence game (*US*); (*broma*) gag, hoax; **dar un ~ a uno** to swindle sb; to hoax sb.

timón NM (a) (*Aer, Náut*) rudder; helm; **~ de deriva, ~ de dirección** (*Aer*) rudder; **~ de profundidad** (*Aer*) elevator; **poner el ~ a babor** to turn to port, port the helm.
(b) (*de carruaje*) pole; (*de arado*) beam.
(c) (*fig*) helm; **coger el ~, empuñar el ~** to take the helm, take charge.
(d) (*And Aut*) steering-wheel.

timonear [1a] ① VT (*LAm*) (*dirigir*) to direct, manage; (*guiar*) to guide.
② VI to steer; (*And Aut*) to drive.

timonel NM (*Náut*) steersman, helmsman; (*de bote de carreras*) cox.

timonera NF wheelhouse.

timonería NF (*Náut*) rudders, steering mechanisms; (*Ferro*) linkage.

timonero NM = **timonel**.

timorato ADJ (a) (*tímido*) timorous, feeble-spirited, small-minded. (b) (*mojigato*) prudish. (c) (*Rel*) God-fearing; (*pey*) excessively pious; sanctimonious.

Timoteo NM Timothy.

tímpano NM (a) (*Anat*) tympanum, eardrum. (b) (*Arquit*) tympanum. (c) (*Mús*) small drum, kettledrum. **~s** (*de orquesta*) tympani.

tina NF (*recipiente*) vat, tub; (*bañera*) bathtub; **~ de lavar** washtub.

tinaco NM (*And, Méx: vasija*) tall earthenware jar; (*Méx: cisterna*) water tank.

tinaja NF large earthen jar.

tinajero NM stone water filter.

tinca NF (a) (*Cono Sur: capirotazo*) flip, flick. (b) (*And*) bowls. (c) (*Cono Sur*: pálpito*) hunch.

tincada NF (*Cono Sur*) hunch.

tincanque NM (*Cono Sur*) = **tinca** (a).

tincar* [1g] VT (*Cono Sur*) (a) (*dar un capirotazo a*) to flip, flick. (b) (*presentir*) to have a hunch about. (c) (*apetecer*) to like, fancy; **me tinca** I like him (*etc*); **no me tinca** I don't like the idea, I don't fancy it.

tincazo NM (*Cono Sur*) = **tinca** (a).

tinctura NF tincture.

tinerfeño ① ADJ of Tenerife.
② NM, **tinerfeña** NF native (*o* inhabitant) of Tenerife; **los ~s** the people of Tenerife.

tinga* NF (*Méx*) row, uproar.

tingar [1h] VT (*And*) to flip, flick.

tinglado NM (a) (*tablado*) platform; (*cobertizo*) shed, covering.
(b) (*fig*) set-up, system; (*pey*) trick; plot, intrigue; **armar un ~** to lay a plot; **conocer el ~** to see through it, see sb's little game; **está metida en el ~ del espiritismo*** she's into the spiritualism thing; **montar el ~** to get going, set up in business; **montar su ~*** to do one's own thing*.

tingo NM, **tingue** NM (*And*) = **tinca** (a).

tinieblas NFPL (a) (*oscuridad*) darkness, dark; (*sombras*) shadows; (*tenebrosidad*) gloom.
(b) (*fig*) confusion, fog; black ignorance; **estamos en ~ sobre sus proyectos** we are in the dark about his plans, we are entirely ignorant of what he plans to do.

tino¹ NM (a) (*habilidad*) skill, knack; feel; (*seguridad*) (sureness of) touch; (*conjeturas*) (good) guesswork, (good) reckoning; (*Mil*) (accurate) aim, (good) marksmanship; **a ~** gropingly; **a buen ~** by guesswork; **coger el ~** to get the feel of it, get the hang of it.
(b) (*fig*) (*tacto*) tact; (*juicio*) good judgement; (*perspicacia*) insight, acumen; **sin ~** foolishly; aimlessly; **obrar con mucho ~** to act wisely, act with great good sense; **perder el ~** to act foolishly, go off the rails; **sacar de ~ a uno** to bewilder sb; to exasperate sb, infuriate sb.
(c) (*fig: moderación*) moderation; **sin ~** immoderately; **comer sin ~** to eat to excess; **gastar sin ~** to spend recklessly.

tino² NM (a) (*tina*) vat; (*de piedra*) stone tank. (b) (*lagar*) winepress; (*de aceite*) olive press.

tinoso ADJ (*And*) (*hábil*) skilful, clever; (*juicioso*) sensible; (*moderado*) moderate; (*diplomático*) tactful.

tinque NM (*Cono Sur*) = **tinca** (a).

tinta NF (a) (*Tip etc*) ink; **~ china** Indian ink; **~ de imprenta** printer's ink, printing ink; **~ indeleble, ~ de marcar** marking ink; **~ invisible, ~ simpática** invisible ink; **con ~** in ink; **sudar ~*** to slog, slave; **saber algo de buena ~** to know sth on good authority.
(b) (*Tec*) dye.
(c) (*de pulpo*) dye, ink.
(d) (*Arte*) colour; **~s** (*fig*) tints, shades, hues; **media ~** half-tone, tint; **medias ~s** (*fig*) (*medidas*) half measures; (*ideas*) half-baked ideas; (*respuestas*) inadequate answers; **presentar una situación bajo ~s muy negras** to paint a situation very black; **cargar las ~s** to exaggerate.

tintado ① ADJ *vidrio* tinted.
② NM tinting.

tintar [1a] VT to dye.

tinte NM (a) (*acto*) dyeing.
(b) (*Quím*) dye, dyestuff; stain.
(c) (*Com*) dyer's (shop); dry-cleaning establishment, dry cleaner's.
(d) (*fig: matiz*) tinge, colouring; **sin el menor ~ político** without the slightest political colouring, devoid of all political character.
(e) (*fig: barniz*) veneer, gloss, light covering; **tiene cierto ~ de hombre de mundo** he has a slight touch of the man of the world about him.

tinterillo NM (a) (*empleado*) penpusher, small-time clerk. (b) (*LAm: abogado*) shyster lawyer*.

tintero NM (a) (*lit*) inkpot, inkwell, inkstand; **lo dejó en el ~, se le quedó en el ~** (*fig*) he clean forgot about it; **no deja nada en el ~** she leaves nothing unsaid. (b) (*LAm: plumas etc*) writing materials, desk set.

tintillo NM (*Cono Sur*) red wine.

tintín NM tinkle, tinkling; ting-a-ling; jingle; clink, chink.

tintinear [1a] VI (*campanilla*) to tinkle; (*timbre*) to go ting-a-ling; (*cadena etc*) to jingle; (*tazas etc*) to clink, chink.

tintineo NM = **tintín**.

tinto ① ADJ (a) (*teñido*) dyed; (*manchado*) stained; tinged; **~ en sangre** stained with blood, bloodstained. (b) *vino* red.
② NM (*vino*) red wine. (b) (*And*) black coffee.

tintorera NF shark; (*And, CAm, Méx*) female shark.

tintorería NF (a) (*arte*) dyeing. (b) (*Téc: fábrica*) dyeworks; (*tienda*) dyer's (shop). (c) (*de lavar en seco*) dry cleaner's.

tintorero NM (a) (*que tiñe*) dyer. (b) (*que lava en seco*) dry cleaner.

tintorro* NM plonk*, cheap red wine.

tintura NF (a) (*acto*) dyeing.
(b) (*Quím*) dye, dyestuff; (*Téc*) stain; (*Farm*) tincture; **~ de tornasol** litmus; **~ de yodo** iodine.
(c) (*fig*) smattering; thin veneer.

tinturar [1a] VT (a) (*teñir*) to dye; to tinge. (b) **~ a uno** (*fig*) to give sb a rudimentary knowledge, teach sb superficially.

tiña NF (a) (*Med*) ringworm. (b) (*fig: pobreza*) poverty. (c) (*fig: tacañería*) meanness.

tiñoso ADJ (a) (*Med*) scabby, mangy. (b) (*fig: miserable*) poor, wretched. (c) (*fig: tacaño*) mean.

tío NM (a) uncle; **~ abuelo** great-uncle; **~ carnal** real uncle; **mi ~ Eduardo** my uncle Edward; **T~ Sam** Uncle Sam; **mis ~s** (*frec*) my uncle and aunt.
(b) *delante de nombre en tono respetuoso, no se traduce*: **ha muerto el ~**

Francisco Francis has died.

(c) (*Esp**) (*viejo*) old fellow; (*sujeto*) fellow, chap*, guy*; **los ~s** guys*, men; **¿quién es ese ~?** who's that chap?*; **ese ~ del sombrero alto** that chap with the tall hat*; **¡qué ~!** what a fellow!; (*pey*) isn't he a so-and-so?*; **~ legal** good sort*; **es un ~ grande, es un ~ con toda la barba** he's a great guy*.

tiovivo NM roundabout, merry-go-round.

tipa¹ NF (*And, Cono Sur*) large wicker basket.

tipa²* NF dame*, chick*; (*pey*) bitch‡, cow‡.

tipaza* NF: **es una ~** she's got a smashing figure*.

tipazo* NM (*grande*) tall chap*, big guy*; (*arrogante*) arrogant fellow; (*And*: *persona importante*) bigwig.

tipear [1a] VTI (*LAm*) to type.

tipejo*, **-a** NM/F queer fish*, odd sort; bad lot*.

tiperrita NF (*Carib*) typist.

tipiadora NF (a) (*máquina*) typewriter. (b) (*persona*) typist.

típicamente ADV typically; characteristically.

tipicidad NF genuineness, authenticity.

típico ADJ (a) (*característico*) typical; characteristic.

(b) (*pintoresco*) quaint, picturesque; (*lleno de color local*) full of local colour; (*folklórico*) rich in folklore, full of folkloric interest; (*tradicional*) traditional; (*regional*) regional; (*de interés turístico*) of interest to tourists; **baile ~** regional dance, national dance; **es la taberna más típica de la ciudad** it's the most picturesque pub in town; **unas jóvenes con su ~ peinado** some girls with their hair done in the traditional (and local) fashion; **no hay que perderse tan típica fiesta** you shouldn't miss a festivity so rich in local colour and tradition.

tipificación NF classification.

tipificar [1g] VT (a) (*ser típico de*) to typify; to characterize. (b) (*clasificar*) to class, consider (*como* as).

tipismo NM quaintness, picturesqueness; local colour; folkloric interest; traditionalism; regional character; **estoy harto de tanto ~ bobo** I'm fed up with all this nonsensical local colour and traditionalism.

tiple ① NM (a) (*persona*) treble, boy soprano. (b) (*voz*) soprano (voice).

② NF soprano.

tipo ① NM (a) (*gen*) type; (*norma*) norm, standard; (*pauta*) pattern, model; **un sombrero ~ Bogart** a Bogart-style hat, a hat like Bogart's; **una joven ~ Marilyn** a girl in the Marilyn mould; **un vehículo ~ jeep** a jeep-type vehicle.

(b) (*clase*) type, sort, kind; **un nuevo ~ de bicicleta** a new kind of bicycle; **de otro ~ pero del mismo precio** of a different type but at the same price.

(c) (*Liter etc*) type, character.

(d) (*: *hombre*) fellow, chap*, guy*; **dos ~s sospechosos** two suspicious characters*; **un ~ que yo conozco** a fellow I know; **¿quién es ese ~?** who's that chap*?

(e) (*Com, Fin*) rate; **~ bancario, ~ de descuento** bank rate; **~ de cambio** exchange rate, rate of exchange; **~ impositivo** tax coding, tax bracket; tax rate; **~ de interés** interest rate; **~ (de) oro** gold standard; **~ de seguro** insurance rates.

(f) (*Anat*: *de hombre*) build, physique; (*de mujer*) figure; **él tiene buen ~** he's well built; **ella tiene buen ~** she has a good figure; **tener mal ~** to be misshapen.

(g) (*Tip*: *t ~s*) type; **~ de datos** data type; **~ gótico** Gothic type, black letter; **~ de letra** typeface, font; **~ menudo** small print.

(h) (*) **aguantar el ~, mantener el ~** to hold out; to put up with a lot; **jugarse el ~** to risk one's neck.

② ATR standard; ordinary, average, typical; representative; **dos conductores ~** two average drivers; **lengua ~** standard language.

tipografía NF (a) (*arte*) typography; printing. (b) (*taller*) printing works; (*imprenta*) printing press.

tipográfico ADJ typographical; printing (*atr*).

tipógrafo, -a NM/F typographer; printer.

tipología NF typology.

tiposo ADJ (*And*) ridiculous, eccentric.

típula NF cranefly, daddy-long-legs.

tique NM = **tíquet**.

tiquear [1a] VT (*Cono Sur*) to punch.

tíquet ['tike] NM, PL **tíquets** ['tike], **tiquete** NM (*LAm*) ticket; (*en tienda*) cash slip; (*And*: *etiqueta*) label.

tiquismiquis NMPL (a) (*escrúpulos*) silly scruples; (*detalles*) fussy details; (*quejas*) silly objections.

(b) (*cortesías*) affected courtesies, bowing and scraping.

(c) (*riñas*) bickering, squabbles.

(d) (*molestias*) minor irritations, pinpricks.

tiquitique* NM: **estar en el ~** to be gossiping.

tira¹ ① NF (a) strip; long strip, narrow strip; band; (*de papel*) slip of paper; **~ (cómica)** comic strip; **~ de películas** film strip; **~ publicitaria** flysheet, leaflet. (b) **la ~ de*** lots of, masses of; **estoy desde hace la ~ de tiempo** I've been here for absolute ages; **eso fue**

hace la ~ that was ages ago.

② NM: **~ y afloja** (a) (*cautela*) prudence, caution; (*tacto*) tact.

(b) (*lucha*) tug-of-war (*fig*); (*concesiones*) give and take, mutual concessions; **3 horas de ~** 3 hours of touch and go.

tira²‡ ① NM (*And, Cono Sur*) cop*.

② NF: **la ~** the cops*, the fuzz‡; (*Uruguay*) the secret police.

tirabuzón NM (a) (*sacacorchos*) corkscrew; **sacar algo a uno con ~** (*fig*) to drag sth out of sb. (b) (*rizo*) curl, ringlet. (c) (*Natación*) twist, corkscrew.

tirachinas NM INVAR catapult.

tirada NF (a) (*acto*) cast, throw; (*Caza*) shoot; **~ de patos** duck shoot.

(b) (*distancia*) distance; (*tramo*) stretch; (*Cos*) length; (*fig*) series, number; time; (*Liter*) stanza; sequence; epic laisse; **de una ~** at one go, in a stretch; **lo recitó todo de una ~** he recited the whole lot straight off, he reeled the lot off; **estuvo con nosotros una ~ de días** he spent a number of days with us; **de B a C hay una ~ de 18 kms** from B to C there is a stretch of 18 kms.

(c) (*Tip*: *acto*) printing, edition; (*cantidad*) print-run; **~ aparte** offprint, reprint.

(d) (*LAm*: *discurso*) boring speech, tedious discourse.

(e) (*Cono Sur*: *indirecta*) hint.

(f) (*Carib*: *mala pasada*) dirty trick.

(g) (‡: *puta*) whore, slut.

tiradera NF (a) (*CAm, Carib, Cono Sur*) (*faja*) sash; (*correa*) belt, strap; (*Carib*: *de caballo*) harness strap, trace. (b) (*And, CAm**: *mofa*) taunt.

tiradero NM (*Méx*) tip, rubbish-dump; (*fig*) mess; **esta casa es un ~** this house is a tip*.

tirado ADJ (a) (*Náut*) rakish; *escritura* cursive.

(b) estar ~* (*Com*) to be dirt-cheap; to be a glut on the market; (*tarea etc*) to be very simple; **esa asignatura está tirada** that subject is dead easy*. **(c) quedarse ~** to be left in the lurch.

tirador NM (a) (*persona*) marksman, shot; shooter; (*CAm, Méx*) hunter; **~ apostado** sniper; **~ certero** sharpshooter; **~ de élite** marksman.

(b) (*puño*) handle, knob, button; (*de puerta*) doorknob; (*Elec*) cord; **~ de campanilla** bellrope, bellpull.

(c) (*tirachinas*) catapult.

(d) (*Arte, Téc*: *pluma*) drawing-pen.

(e) (*And, Cono Sur*: *cinturón*) wide gaucho belt.

(f) **~es** (*And, Cono Sur*) braces, suspenders (*US*).

tiragomas NM INVAR catapult.

tiraje NM (a) (*Tip*) (*impresión*) printing; (*cantidad*) print run. (b) (*CAm, Cono Sur, Méx*: *de chimenea*) chimney flue.

tiralevitas NM INVAR bootlicker*; creep‡.

tiralíneas NM INVAR drawing-pen, ruling pen.

tiranía NF tyranny.

tiránicamente ADV tyrannically.

tiranicida NM tyrannicide (*person*).

tiranicidio NM tyrannicide (*act*).

tiránico ADJ tyrannical; despotic; *amor* possessive, domineering; *atracción* irresistible, all-powerful.

tiranizar [1f] VT to tyrannize, rule despotically; to domineer.

tirano ① ADJ tyrannical, despotic; domineering.

② NM, **tirana** NF tyrant, despot.

③ NM (*Méx**) cop*.

tirantas NFPL (*And, Méx*) braces, suspenders (*US*).

tirante ① ADJ (a) *cuerda etc* tight, taut; tensed; drawn tight.

(b) *relaciones, situación etc* tense, strained; **las cosas andan algo ~s** things are rather strained.

(c) (*Fin*) tight.

② NM (a) (*Arquit*) tie, brace, crosspiece; (*Mec*) brace, stay, strut.

(b) (*de arreos*) trace; (*de vestido*) shoulder strap; **~s** braces, suspenders (*US*); **vestido sin ~s** strapless dress.

tirantear [1a] VT (*CAm, Cono Sur*) to stretch.

tirantez NF (a) (*tensión*) tightness, tautness; tension.

(b) (*fig*) tension, strain; **la ~ de las relaciones con Eslobodia** the strained relations with Slobodia, the tense state of relations with Slobodia; **ha disminuido la ~** the tension has lessened.

(c) (*Fin*) tightness; stringency.

tirar [1a] ① VT (a) (*lanzar*) to throw; to hurl, fling, cast, sling; (*sin querer*) to drop; (*volcar*) to knock over, knock down; *edificio* to pull down; *tiro* to fire, shoot; *cohete* to fire, launch; *bomba* to drop; **el aparato tira el proyectil a 2000 metros** the machine throws the projectile 2000 metres; **estaban tirando la fruta con palos largos** they were knocking the fruit down with long poles; **el viento ha tirado la valla** the wind has knocked the fence down; **me tiró un beso** she blew me a kiss.

(b) *basura etc* to throw away; to chuck out; *fortuna* to waste, squander; **estos calcetines están para ~los** these socks are ready to be thrown away; **hay que ~ los podridos** the rotten ones ought to be thrown out; **has tirado el dinero comprando eso** you've thrown your money away buying that.

(c) *alambre* to draw out.

(d) *línea* to draw, trace, rule.

(e) *(Tip)* to print, run off.

(f) *golpe etc* to give, deal, fetch; **~ una coz a uno** to give sb a kick; **~ un mordisco a uno** to give sb a bite; **~ tajos a uno** to slash at sb.

(g) *(And: usar)* to use; to work with; **~ brazo** to swim.

(h) *(And, Carib, Cono Sur: acarrear)* to cart, haul, transport.

(i) **~la de** to fancy oneself, pose as.

2 VI **(a)** *(Mil etc)* to shoot *(a at)*, fire *(a at, on)*; **~ a matar** to shoot to kill; **~ con bala** to use live ammunition; **¡no tires!** don't shoot.

(b) **~ de** *objeto* to pull, tug; *carro etc* to draw (along), haul; *cuerda etc* to pull (on), tug (at); *cartera, pañuelo etc* to pull out, take out (suddenly), yank out; *espada* to draw; **~ de la manga de uno** to tug at sb's sleeve; **tire de ese cabo** pull that end; **este vestido tira un poco de aquí** this dress is a bit tight here; **tiraron de cuchillos** they drew their knives; **'~', 'tirad'** *(Esp)*, **'tire'** *(LAm)* *(en puerta etc)* 'pull'; **el motor no tira** the engine is sluggish.

(c) *(imán etc)* to draw, attract; *(fig)* to draw, pull, have a pull; to appeal; **no le tira el estudio** study does not attract him; **la patria tira siempre** one's native land always exerts a powerful pull.

(d) *(chimenea etc)* to draw.

(e) *(Esp•)* **ir tirando** to get along, manage; **vamos tirando** we manage, we keep going; **esos zapatos tirarán todavía otro invierno** those shoes will last out another winter.

(f) *(•: ir)* to go; **tire Vd adelante** go straight on; **¡tira (adelante)!** get on with it!; **~ a la derecha** to turn right; to keep right; **~ por una calle** to turn down a street, go off along a street.

(g) **~ a** *(tender)* to tend to, tend towards; **~ a rojo** to have some red in it, have a touch of red about it; **~ a viejo** to be getting old, be elderly; **~ a su padre** to take after one's father, resemble one's father; **él tira más bien a cuidadoso** he's on the careful side; **tira a hacerse servir** he tends to make others wait on him; **~ para médico** to have inclinations towards a medical career, feel like becoming a doctor, be attracted towards a career in medicine.

(h) **~ a** *(proponerse)* to aim at being, work to become; *(pey)* to intrigue to become; **~ a +** *infin* to aim to + *infin*; *(pey)* to intrigue in order to + *infin*, go surreptitiously to work to + *infin*.

(i) *(Dep: a portería etc)* to shoot; *(jugar)* to go, play, have one's turn; **tira tú ahora** it's your go now; **tiró fuera de la portería** he shot wide of the goal; **¡tira!** shoot!

(j) **a todo ~** at the most; **nos queda gasolina para 20 kms a todo ~** we have only enough petrol for 20 kms at the outside (*o* at the most); **llegará el martes a todo ~** he'll arrive on Tuesday at the latest.

(k) *(••)* to screw••.

3 tirarse VR **(a)** *(lanzarse)* to throw o.s., hurl o.s.; **~ al agua** to dive (*o* plunge) into the water; **~ al suelo** to throw o.s. to the ground; **~ por una ventana** to throw o.s. out of a window; to jump from a window; **~ por un risco** to throw o.s. over a cliff; **~ en paracaídas** to parachute (down), *(en emergencia)* bale out; **~ en la cama** to lie down on one's bed; **~ sobre uno** to rush at sb, spring on sb.

(b) *(fig)* to cheapen o.s., demean o.s.; to waste o.s. in an unworthy job.

(c) **~ a una••** *(t* **tirársela)** to screw sb••.

(d) **me tiré mucho tiempo haciéndolo** I spent a lot of time doing it, it took me a lot of time to do it.

(e) *(•: irse)* **~ a otra parte** to clear off somewhere else•.

tirilla NF **(a)** band, strip; *(Cos)* neckband. **(b)** *(Cono Sur)* shabby dress, ragged garment.

tirillas• NMF **(a)** *(sin importancia)* unimportant person, nobody; **¡vete, ~!** get along, little man! **(b)** *(pequeño)* undersized individual, runt.

tirillento ADJ *(LAm)* ragged, shabby.

tirita NF *(Cos)* tag, tape *(for name, on clothing)*; *(Med)* (sticking) plaster, bandaid *(US)*.

tiritaña• NF mere trifle.

tiritar [1a] VI **(a)** to shiver *(de* with).

(b) *(•)* **dejaron el pastel tiritando** they almost finished the cake off; **este plato ha quedado tiritando** there isn't much left of this dish.

tiritón NM shiver.

tiritona NF shivering (fit).

Tiro NM Tyre.

tiro NM **(a)** *(lanzamiento)* throw.

(b) *(Mil etc)* shot; *(ruido)* sound of a shot, report; *(impacto)* impact of a shot, hit; *(señal)* bullet mark; *(gen)* shooting, firing; **~ con arco** archery; **~ al blanco** target practice, shooting practice; **~ de escopeta**, **~ de fusil** gunshot; **~ al** (*o* **de**) **pichón** clay-pigeon shooting; **~ al plato** trap-shooting; **cañón de ~ rápido** quick-firing gun; **descargar un ~** to fire a shot; **errar el ~** to miss, miss with one's shot; **se oyó un ~** a shot was heard; **se pegó un ~** he shot himself; **le pegó un ~ a su novio** she shot her lover; **¡que le peguen cuatro ~s!** he ought to be shot!; **le salió el ~ por la culata** the scheme (*etc*) backfired; **hacer ~ a** *(fig)* to have designs on, aim at; **no lo haría ni a ~s** I wouldn't do it for love nor money; **esperar a ver por dónde van**

los ~s to wait and see which way the wind is blowing; **liarse a ~s con** *(fig)* to get involved in a violent argument with; **matar a uno a ~s** to shoot sb (dead); **tendrán que decidirlo a ~s** they'll have to shoot it out; **me cae** (*o* **sienta**) **como un ~** I need it like I need a hole in the head.

(c) *(Dep)* shot; drive; **~ de aproximación** *(Golf)* approach shot; **~ libre** *(fútbol)* free kick; *(básquet)* free throw; **~ a gol** shot at goal; **~ de revés** backhand drive; **parar un ~** to stop a shot.

(d) *(Mil etc: alcance)* range; **a ~ de fusil** within gunshot; **a ~ de piedra** within a stone's throw; **estar a ~** to be within range; *(fig)* to be accessible; **si se pone a ~ se lo diré** if he comes my way I'll tell him; **ponerse a ~•** *(mujer)* to offer herself.

(e) *(campo de tiro)* rifle-range; *(galería de tiro)* shooting-gallery.

(f) *(caballos etc)* team of horses (*etc*); **caballo de ~** cart-horse, draught horse.

(g) *(Cos)* length (of cloth *etc*); **andar de ~s largos** to be all dressed up, be very smartly turned out.

(h) *(cuerda)* rope, cord; *(cadena)* chain; *(de timbre)* bellpull; *(de arreos)* trace, strap; **~s** *(Mil)* swordbelt; **~s** *(Cono Sur)* braces, suspenders *(US)*.

(i) *(Arquit)* flight of stairs.

(j) *(de chimenea etc)* draught; *(Min)* shaft; **~ de mina** mineshaft.

(k) *(fig: revés)* blow; setback.

(l) *(fig)* *(ataque)* veiled attack; *(alusión)* damaging allusion.

(m) *(fig: broma)* trick, hoax; practical joke.

(n) *(fig: robo)* petty theft; *(engaño)* petty deceit.

(o) *(And, Cono Sur, Méx: canica)* marble.

(p) *(Cono Sur Carreras)* distance, course.

(q) *(Méx)* *(número)* issue; *(edición)* edition.

(r) *(Cono Sur: indirecta)* hint.

(s) *(Carib: astucia)* craftiness, cunning.

(t) *(CAm, Cono Sur: locuciones)* **al ~** at once, right away; **a ~ de +** *infin* about to + *infin*, on the point of + *ger*; **de a ~** completely; **del ~** consequently; **hacer algo de un ~** to do sth in one go.

(u) **~ de cuerda**, **~ de soga** tug-of-war.

tiroideo ADJ thyroid.

tiroides **1** ADJ INVAR thyroid.

2 NM *(a veces* NF*)* INVAR thyroid.

Tirol NM: **El ~** the Tyrol.

tirolés, -esa ADJ, NM/F Tyrolese.

tirón¹ NM **(a)** *(acción brusca)* pull, tug, sudden jerk; hitch; *(Pol etc)* shake-up; **~ (de bolsos)** bag-snatching; **~ de orejas** *(fig)* reminder; rebuke, reprimand; **dar un ~ a** to pull at, tug at; to jerk suddenly; **le dieron un ~ al bolso** they snatched her bag; **me lo arrancó de un ~** she suddenly jerked it away from me; **el coche se movía a tirones** the car moved along in a series of jerks, the car went jerkily forward; **pegar un ~ a•** to shoot up.

(b) *(fig)* **de un ~** all at once; in one go, straight off, without a break; **leyó la novela de un ~** she read the novel straight through; **se lo bebió de un ~** he drank it down in one go; **trabajan 10 horas de un ~** they work 10 hours at a stretch.

(c) **ganar el ~ a uno** *(Cono Sur•)* to steal a march on sb, beat sb to it.

(d) *(fuerza de atracción)* pull, power, attraction.

tirón² NM *(persona)* tyro, novice.

tirona• NF whore.

tironear [1a] VT *(LAm)* = **tirar 2 (b)**.

tironero NM, **tironista** NM bag-snatcher.

tirotear [1a] **1** VT to shoot at, fire on; to blaze away at; to snipe at; *(y matar etc)* to shoot, shoot down.

2 tirotearse VR to exchange shots; to blaze away at each other.

tiroteo NM *(tiros)* firing, shooting, exchange of shots; *(escaramuza)* skirmish; *(batalla)* gunfight; *(con policía)* shoot-out; **~ cruzado** crossfire.

Tirreno ADJ: **Mar ~** Tyrrhenian Sea.

tirria NF dislike; ill will; **tener ~ a** to dislike, have a grudge against.

tisaje NM weaving.

tisana NF tisane, infusion.

tísico **1** ADJ consumptive, tubercular.

2 NM, **tísica** NF consumptive.

tisiqu(i)ento ADJ *(Cono Sur)* *(Med)* consumptive; *(fig)* pale and thin.

tisis NF consumption, tuberculosis.

tisú NM, PL **tisus** lamé, tissue.

tisular ADJ tissue *(atr)*.

tít. ABR *de* **título** title.

tita• NF auntie•, aunty•.

titán NM Titan.

titánico ADJ titanic.

titanio NM titanium.

titeador• ADJ *(And, Cono Sur)* mocking, derisive.

titear• [1a] VT *(And, Cono Sur)* to mock, scoff at; to make fun of.

titeo• NM *(And, Cono Sur)* mockery, scoffing; **tomar a uno para el ~** to scoff at sb; to make fun of sb.

títere [1] NM (a) puppet, marionette; **~s** puppets; (*espectáculo*) puppet show; (*arte*) puppetry; **~ de guante** glove puppet; **no dejar ~ con cabeza** to turn everything upside down; to break up everything in sight; to spare no-one.

(b) (*fig*) puppet; (*instrumento*) cat's-paw; (*débil, soso*) weak person, colourless individual; (*poco fiable*) untrustworthy person; (*de aspecto raro*) odd-looking person.

[2] ATR: **gobierno ~** puppet government.

titi: [1] NM bloke‡, chap*; (*en oración directa*) man.

[2] NF bird‡, chick* (*US*).

tití NM (*LAm*) capuchin (monkey).

titilante ADJ twinkling.

titilar [1a] VI (*párpado etc*) to flutter, tremble; (*estrella, luz*) to twinkle.

titipuchal NM (*Méx*) (noisy) crowd.

titiritaña NF (*Méx*) (a) (*espectáculo*) puppet show. (b) (*fig*) piece of trivia; **de ~** sickly.

titiritero, -a NM/F (*que maneja títeres*) puppeteer; (*acróbata*) acrobat; (*malabarista*) juggler; (*artista de circo*) circus artist.

tito NM uncle.

Tito Livio NM Livy.

titubeante ADJ (a) tottery; *mueble etc* shaky, unsteady. (b) stammering; halting. (c) hesitant.

titubear [1a] VI (a) (*al andar*) to totter; to stagger; (*mueble etc*) to be unstable, be shaky, be unsteady; (*borracho*) to reel.

(b) (*Ling*) to stammer; to falter.

(c) (*vacilar*) to hesitate, vacillate; **no ~ en** + *infin* not to hesitate to + *infin*.

titubeo NM (*V VI*) (a) tottering; staggering; instability, shakiness, unsteadiness.

(b) (*Ling*) stammering; faltering.

(c) hesitation, vacillation; **proceder sin ~s** to act resolutely, act without hesitation.

▼ **titulación** NF (*Univ*) (system of) degrees and diplomas.

titulado [1] ADJ (a) *libro etc* entitled.

(b) *persona* titled.

(c) *persona* (*Univ etc*) with a degree, having a degree; qualified; (*Téc etc*) trained, skilled.

[2] NM, **titulada** NF (*Univ*) graduate.

titular [1] ADJ titular, official; *campeón* reigning; defending.

[2] NM (*Tip*: *t ~es*) headline.

[3] NMF (*de puesto*) holder, occupant; (*jefe*) head; (*Dep*) regular player, first-team player; (*LAm Dep*) captain; (*Ecl*) incumbent; (*de pasaporte, récord etc*) holder; (*de coche etc*) owner.

[4] VT [1a] to title, entitle, call.

[5] **titularse** VR (a) (*llamarse*) to be entitled, be called; to call o.s., style o.s. (b) (*Univ*) to graduate.

titularidad NF (a) (*propiedad*) ownership; **empresa de ~ pública** publicly-owned company. (b) (*Fin*) bond. (c) (*Dep*) first(-team) place, top spot. (d) (*Pol*: *puesto*) ministerial post; (*período*) term of office, tenure; **durante la ~ de Bush** during Bush's period of office.

titulillo NM (*Tip*) running title, page heading; (*Prensa*) subhead, section heading; **andar en ~s** to watch out for every little thing.

titulitis NF (*hum*) mania for employing graduate personnel; obsession with acquiring an academic degree.

título NM (a) (*gen*) title; (*Jur etc*) section heading; (*artículo*) article; (*de presupuesto*) item; (*Tip*) title; (*de periódico*) headline; **~s de crédito** credits, credit titles; **a ~ de** by way of; in the capacity of; **a ~ de curiosidad** as a matter of interest; **el dinero fue a ~ de préstamo** the money was given as a loan, the money was by way of being a loan; **nos lo dijo a ~ de noticia alentadora** he told us it as being a cheering piece of news; **a ~ no exclusivo detallamos ...** for purposes of illustration we specify the following ...; **a ~ personal** for one's own part, personally, in a personal way; **a ~ póstumo** posthumously.

(b) (*de persona*) title; **~ de nobleza, ~ nobiliario** title of nobility.

(c) (*fig: noble*) titled person; **casarse con un ~** to marry a titled person, marry into the nobility.

(d) (*calificación profesional*) professional qualification; (*diploma*) diploma, certificate; (*Univ*) degree; (*fig*) qualification; (*Carib Aut*) driving licence; **~s** qualifications, credentials; **con ~ superior** with higher education; **~ universitario** university degree; **maestro sin ~** unqualified teacher; **obtener un ~** to obtain a qualification; to take a degree; **tener los ~s para un puesto** to have the qualifications for a job.

(e) (*de carácter etc*) quality; **no es precisamente un ~ de gloria para él** it is not exactly a quality on which he can pride himself; **tiene varios ~s honrosos** he has several noble qualities, he has a number of worthy attributes.

(f) (*Jur*) title; **~ de propiedad** title deed.

(g) (*Fin*) bond; **~ al portador** bearer bond; **~ de renta fija** fixed-interest security; **~ de renta variable** variable-yield security.

(h) (*fig: derecho*) right; **con justo ~** rightly; **¿con qué ~?** by what

right?; **tener ~ de** + *infin* to be entitled to + *infin*, have the right to + *infin*; **le sobran ~s para hacerlo** he has every right to do it.

tiza NF (a) (*para escribir*: *t Billar*) chalk; (*de zapatos*) whitening; **una ~ a** piece of chalk. (b) (*And*) exaggeration.

tizar [1f] VT (*Cono Sur*) to plan; to design, model; (*And*) *traje* to mark out for cutting.

tizate NM (*CAm, Méx*) chalk.

Tiziano NM Titian.

tizna NF black, grime.

tiznado: NM (*pey*) darkie‡.

tiznajo NM black mark, dirty smear.

tiznar [1a] [1] VT (a) (*ennegrecer*) to blacken, black; (*manchar*) to smudge, soil, stain, spot; (*untar*) to smear (*de* with).

(b) (*fig*) to stain, tarnish; to defame, blacken.

[2] **tiznarse** VR (a) **~ la cara con un corcho quemado** to blacken one's face with burnt cork.

(b) (*mancharse*) to get smudged, get soiled (*etc*).

(c) (*CAm, Cono Sur, Méx*: *emborracharse*) to get drunk.

tizne NM (a) (*hollín*) soot; (*mancha negra*) black smear, blackening; (*mugre*) grime; smut. (b) (*fig*) stain.

tiznón NM smut, speck of soot; smudge.

tizo NM burning piece of wood, brand.

tizón NM (a) (*tea*) burning piece of wood, brand; half-burned piece of wood. (b) (*Bot*) smut. (c) (*fig: mancha*) stain.

tizonazos NMPL (*fig*) pains of hell.

tizonear [1a] VT *fuego* to poke, stir.

tizos: NMPL dabs‡, fingers.

tlacanear [1a] VT (*Méx*) to feel up‡.

tlachique NM (*Méx*) unfermented *pulque*.

tlacote NM (*Méx*) growth, tumour.

tlacual: NM (*Méx*) (a) (*comida*) food; meal. (b) (*olla*) cooking pot.

tlapalería NF (*Méx*) (*ferretería*) ironmonger's, hardware store; (*papelería*) stationer's.

tlapiloya: NF (*Méx*) clink‡, jail.

tlapisquera NF (*Méx*) shed, barn, granary.

tlascal NM (*Méx*) tortilla.

TLC NM ABR *de* **Tratado de Libre Comercio** North American Free Trade Agreement, NAFTA.

tlecuil NM (*Méx*) brazier.

T.m., Tm, tm ABR *de* **tonelada(s) métrica(s)** metric ton(s).

TNT NM ABR *de* **trinitrotolueno** trinitrotoluene, TNT.

toa NF (*LAm*) hawser, rope, towrope.

toalla NF towel; **~ de baño** bath-towel; **~ de playa, ~ playera** beach-towel; **~ de rodillo** roller towel; **arrojar** (*o* **tirar**) **la ~** to throw in the towel.

toallero NM towel-rail.

toba: NF (a) (*colilla*) dog-end‡. (b) (*puñetazo*) punch, bash*.

tobar [1a] VT (*And*) to tow.

tobera NF nozzle.

tobillera NF (a) ankle-sock. (b)(*) teenager, bobbysoxer* (*US*).

tobillero [1] ADJ ankle-length.

[2] NM ankle-sock; (*Dep*) ankle-guard.

tobillo NM ankle.

tobo NM (*Carib*) bucket.

tobogán NM (a) (*trineo*) toboggan. (b) (*de feria*) switchback; **~ gigante** roller-coaster. (c) (*para niños*) children's slide; (*en piscina*) chute, slide; **~ acuático** water-slide.

toc ADV: **¡~ ~!** (*en puerta*) rat-a-tat!; knock, knock!

toca[1] NF (*sombrero*) headdress; (*de mujer*) bonnet; toque; **~s de viuda** widow's weeds.

toca[2] NMF (*LAm*) = **tocayo**.

tocacasete NM cassette recorder.

tocadiscos NM INVAR record player, phonograph (*US*); **~ automático** auto-change record player; **~ tragamonedas, ~ tragaperras** juke-box.

tocado[1] ADJ (a) *fruta* bad, rotten; *carne etc* tainted, bad; **estar ~** (*Dep*) to be injured; **estar ~ de la cabeza** to be weak in the head.

(b) **una creencia tocada de heterodoxia** a belief tainted with heterodoxy.

(c) **estar ~ de piedad** to be all piety, have got religion.

tocado[2] [1] ADJ: **~ con un sombrero de paja** wearing a straw hat, with a straw hat on his head.

[2] NM (a) (*sombrero*) headdress, headgear, hat.

(b) (*peinado*) coiffure, hair-do.

(c) (*atavío*) toilet.

tocador[1] NM (a) (*mueble*) dressing table; **jabón de ~** toilet soap; **juego de ~** toilet set.

(b) (*neceser*) toilet case.

(c) (*cuarto*) boudoir, dressing room; **~ de señoras** ladies' room.

tocador[2](a) NM/F (*Mús*) player.

tocadorista NMF (*Cine, TV*) dresser.

tocamientos NMPL (sexual) molestation.

tocante [1]: ~ **a** PREP with regard to, about; **en lo** ~ **a** so far as concerns, as for.
[2] ADJ (*Cono Sur*) moving, touching.

tocar¹ [1g] [1] VT (**a**) (*gen*) to touch; to feel; to handle; *timbre* to touch, press; ~ **las cosas de cerca** to experience things for oneself, learn about things at first hand; **sin ~ un pelo de su ropa** without laying a finger on her; **¡no me toques!** don't touch me!; **que nadie toque mis papeles** don't let anyone touch my papers, don't interfere with my papers.
(**b**) (*2 objetos*) to touch, be touching; **la mesa toca la pared** the table touches the wall, the table is up against the wall.
(**c**) (*Mús*) to play; *campana* to ring; to toll, peal; *tambor* to play, beat; *trompeta* to play, blow, sound; *sirena etc* to sound; *disco, cinta* to play; *hora* to chime, strike; ~ **la generala** (*Mil*) to sound the call to arms; ~ **la retirada** to sound the retreat.
(**d**) (*Arte*) to touch up.
(**e**) (*fig: conmover*) to touch; ~ **el corazón de uno** to touch sb's heart.
(**f**) *obstáculo etc* to hit, strike, collide with, run into; (*Náut*) to go aground on, run on to; (*Caza*) to hit, wing; *blanco etc* to hit.
(**g**) *tema* to touch on, refer to, allude to; **no tocó para nada esa cuestión** he didn't refer to that matter at all.
(**h**) *consecuencias* to suffer, undergo, come in for; **él tocará las consecuencias de todo esto** he will suffer the consequences of all this.
(**i**) (*afectar*) to concern, affect; **esto no te toca a ti** this doesn't concern you; **ello me toca de cerca** it concerns me closely; **por lo que a mí me toca** as far as I'm concerned.
(**j**) (*) to be related to; **X no le toca para nada a Y** X is not related at all to Y, X is no relation to Y.
[2] VI (**a**) ~ **a una puerta** to knock on (*o* at) a door.
(**b**) **tocan a misa** they are ringing the bell for mass; **ese timbre toca a fuego** that bell sounds the fire alarm; **¡a pagar tocan!** it's time to pay up!
(**c**) ~**le a uno** to fall to sb, fall to sb's lot; to fall to sb's share; **les tocó un dólar a cada uno** each one got a dollar as his share; **¿les tocará algo de herencia?** will they get anything under the will?; **le ha tocado otro premio** he has won another prize; **te toca jugar** it's your turn (to play), it's your go; **¿a quién le toca?** whose turn is it?; **¿a quién le toca pagar esta vez?** whose turn is it to pay this time?; **le toca a Vd reprenderle** it is up to you to reprimand him.
(**d**) (*impersonal*) **no toca hacerlo hasta el mes que viene** it's not due to be done until next month; **ahora toca torcer a la derecha** now you have to turn right, now there's a right turn coming up.
(**e**) (*Náut*) ~ **en** to call at, touch at; **el barco no toca en Barcelona** the ship does not call at Barcelona.
(**f**) (*fig*) ~ **en** to border on, verge on; **esto toca en locura** this verges on madness.
[3] **tocarse** VR (**a**) to touch each other, be in contact.
(**b**) **tocárselas*** to beat it*.
(**c**) **tocársela** (*Esp⁑: masturbarse*) to wank⁑; (*fig*) not to do a stroke (of work).
(**d**) (*LAm⁑: drogarse*) to be on drugs.

tocar² [1g] [1] VT *pelo* to do, arrange, set.
[2] **tocarse** VR to cover one's head, put on one's hat.

tocata* NM record-player.

tocateja: a ~ ADV on the nail.

tocayo, -a NM/F (**a**) (*gen*) namesake. (**b**) (*And: amigo*) friend.

toche NM (*Méx*) hare.

tochimbo NM (*And*) smelting furnace.

tocho* NM big fat book, tome; mass of reading matter.

tocineta NF (*And, Carib*) bacon.

tocinillo NM: ~ **de cielo** pudding made with egg yolk and syrup.

tocino NM (*t* ~ **de panceta**) bacon; salt pork; ~ **veteado** streaky bacon.

toco¹, -a NM/F (*CAm*) = **tocayo**.

toco² NM (*Carib*) = **tocón**.

toco³⁑ NM: **costó un** ~ (*Cono Sur*) it cost a hell of a lot.

tocoginecología NF obstetrics.

tocoginecólogo, -a NM/F obstetrician.

tocología NF obstetrics.

tocólogo, -a NM/F obstetrician.

tocolotear [1a] VI (*Carib Naipes*) to shuffle (the cards).

tocomocho* NM con*, swindle.

tocón¹ [1] ADJ (**a**) (*And: sin rabo*) tailless; (*Carib: sin cuernos*) hornless.
(**b**) = **sobón**.
[2] NM (*Anat, Bot*) stump.

tocón²* NM person given to excessive touching; (*fig*) dirty old man.

tocuyo NM (*And, Cono Sur*) coarse cotton cloth.

todavía ADV still, yet; ~ **no** not yet; ~ **en 1980** as late as 1980, right up to 1980; ~ **no lo ha encontrado** he still has not found it, he has not found it yet; **está nevando** ~ it is still snowing; **es** ~ **más**

inteligente que su hermano he is still (*o* even) more intelligent than his brother.
(**b**) (*LAm: no obstante*) nonetheless, nevertheless.

TODAVÍA	ver también la entrada

En oraciones afirmativas e interrogativas, *todavía* se traduce principalmente al inglés por *still* o *yet*.

• Se traduce por *still* cuando nos referimos a una situación o acción que comenzó en el pasado y que todavía continúa. Generalmente *still* se coloca detrás de los verbos auxiliares o modales y delante de los demás verbos:
  Todavía tienen hambre
  They are still hungry
  Todavía toco el piano
  I still play the piano
  ¿Puedes verlos todavía?
  Can you still see them?

• También se puede traducir *todavía* por *still* para expresar insatisfacción o sorpresa en oraciones negativas. En este caso, *still* se coloca detrás del sujeto:
  Todavía no sé cómo ayudarle
  I still don't know how to help him
  Después de veinte años todavía no puede olvidarlo
  After twenty years she still can't forget him

• Se traduce generalmente por *yet* en frases negativas e interrogativas cuando nos referimos a una situación o acción que no ha tenido lugar todavía y que esperamos que ocurra. *Yet* va al final de la frase, aunque a veces puede ponerse delante del verbo principal en frases negativas:
  El doctor no ha llegado todavía
  The doctor hasn't arrived yet o *hasn't yet arrived*
  ¿Todavía no han llamado?
  Haven't they phoned yet?
  NOTA: En lenguaje formal, se puede traducir *todavía* por *yet* en frases afirmativas para expresar que algo no se ha realizado. Para ello utilizamos la estructura *to have yet* + INFINITIVO *con to*:
  Todavía tienen que comunicarnos los resultados
  They have yet to tell us the results

• En oraciones comparativas *todavía* se traduce por *even*:
  Su prima es todavía más alta que ella
  Her cousin is even taller than she is
  NOTA: El adverbio *aún* sigue las mismas pautas que *todavía*:
  Aún no sé cómo decírselo
  I still don't know how to tell him
  ¿Aún no has hablado con ella?
  Haven't you talked to her yet?
  Aún está trabajando para esa compañía de seguros
  She's still working for that insurance company
  Este pastel está aún mejor que el de la semana pasada
  This cake is even better than last week's
Para otros usos y ejemplos ver la entrada.

---

toditito* ADJ, **todito** ADJ (absolutely) all.

todo [1] ADJ (**a**) (*gen*) all; (*entero*) whole, entire; (*cada*) every; ~ **el bosque** all the wood, the whole wood, the entire wood; **el universo** ~ the whole universe; **lo sabe** ~ **Madrid** all Madrid knows it, the whole of Madrid knows it; **lo golpeó con toda su fuerza** he hit him with his full strength, he hit him with all his might; **a toda velocidad** at full speed, at top speed; **con toda prisa** in all haste, with all speed; **en toda España** all over Spain, throughout Spain; **en toda España no hay más que 5** there are only 5 in the whole of Spain; ~ **lo demás** all the rest, all else; ~**s vosotros** all of you; ~**s los libros** all the books; **todas las semanas** every week; **viene** ~**s los martes** he comes every Tuesday; ~ **el que quiera ...** everyone who wants to ...; whoever wants to ...; ~**s los que quieran ...** all those who want to ...; ~ **lo que ves aquí** all that you see here; ~ **lo que necesites** whatever you need; **con toda su inteligencia** with all his intelligence; in spite of all his intelligence; **de todas todas*** the whole lot, all of them without exception; **¡te digo que sí de todas todas!** (*Esp*) I tell you it jolly well is!*; **es verdad de todas todas** it's absolutely true; V **cuanto** etc.
(**b**) (*negativo*) **en** ~ **el día** not once all day; **en toda la noche he dormido** I haven't slept all night; **en toda España lo encuentras** you won't find it anywhere in Spain; **dio un portazo por toda respuesta** his only response was to slam the door.
(**c**) (*locuciones*) **es** ~ **un hombre** he's every inch a man; **es** ~ **un palacio** it's a real palace; **es** ~ **un héroe** he's a real hero; **la hija es toda su madre** the daughter is exactly like her mother; **tiene toda la nariz de su abuela** her nose is exactly like her grandmother's; **el niño estaba** ~ **ojos** the child was all eyes; **ese hombre es** ~ **ambición** that man is all ambition (and nothing else); **a** ~ **esto** (*entretanto*) meanwhile; (*de pasada*) by the way.

2 ADV (a) all, entirely, completely; **estaba ~ rendido** he was completely worn out; **para las 8 estará ~ hecho** it will be completely finished by 8 o'clock; **lleva un vestido ~ roto** she's wearing a dress that's all torn.

(b) **puede ser ~ lo sencillo que Vd quiera** it can be as simple as you wish; V **más** etc.

3 CONJ **con ~ y** (LAm) in spite of; **el equipo, con ~ y estar integrado por buenos jugadores** ... the team, in spite of being (o for all that it is) made up of good players ...

4 NM Y PRON (a) all, everything; **~s** everybody; every one of them; **el ~** the whole; **en un ~** together, as a whole; **~s y cada uno** all and sundry; **lo comió ~** he ate it all; **lo han vendido ~** they've sold it all, they've sold the lot; **~ lo sabemos** we know everything; **~ o nada** all or nothing; **~ es** (o **son**) **reveses** it's all setbacks, there's nothing but troubles; **y luego ~ son sonrisas** and then it's all smiles; **~ cabe en él** he is capable of anything; **ser el ~** to be the most important thing; (*: persona) to be the mainstay; to run the show, dominate everything; **y ~ y** and so on, and what not; **tienen un coche nuevo y ~** they have a new car and everything; **los zapatos, viejos y ~, durarán otro año** these shoes, old though they are, will last another year; **andando rápidamente y ~, no llegaron a tiempo** even though they walked quickly they still didn't get there in time; V **jugarse** etc.

(b) (locuciones con prep) **ir a ~** to go forward resolutely, be prepared to do or die; **ante ~** first of all, in the first place; primarily; **a pesar de ~** even so, in spite of everything; all the same; **con ~** still, however; in spite of everything; **de ~ como en botica** everything under the sun; **de ~ hay en este mundo de Dios, de ~ hay en la viña del Señor** it takes all sorts to make a world; **le llamaron de ~** they called him every name under the sun; **del ~** wholly, completely; **no es del ~ verdad** it is not entirely true, it is not quite true; **no es del ~ malo** it is not wholly bad; **después de ~** after all; **está en ~** * he's on the ball, he doesn't miss a trick; **para ~** all-purpose; **por ~** all in all; **sobre ~** especially; above all, most of all.

┌─ **TODO** ─────────── ver también la entrada ─┐

● Para traducir **todo** con el sentido de **en su totalidad** se usa **all**, seguido del sustantivo en singular y sin determinante:
  Se pasó toda la tarde viendo la tele
  He spent all afternoon watching T.V.

● Con el mismo sentido anterior, también se puede traducir por **whole** o **entire** - éste último es más enfático. En este caso, el indefinido tiene que ir acompañado de un sustantivo contable en singular y precedido por un determinante:
  Se pasó toda la tarde viendo la tele
  He spent the whole o the entire afternoon watching TV

● **Todos** se traduce por **every** cuando se hace hincapié en todos y cada uno de los individuos de un grupo de personas o cosas y también cuando se habla de acciones repetidas:
  Todos los niños deben llevar el uniforme del colegio
  Every child must wear school uniform
  Salimos a cenar todos los viernes
  We go out for dinner every Friday

NOTA: El sustantivo que sigue a **every** va en singular y nunca lleva determinante. El verbo va también en singular.

● Cuando **todos** se emplea para generalizar, se traduce por **all**. En este caso el sustantivo que sigue a **all** no lleva determinante:
  Todos los alemanes saben hablar inglés
  All Germans can speak English

● **Todos** también se traduce por **all** para referirse al conjunto de individuos de un grupo pero, a diferencia de **every**, sin dar importancia a los elementos. En este caso el sustantivo lleva determinante y va en plural, como el verbo:
  Todos los libros de la biblioteca eran antiguos
  All the books in the library were old
  Para otros usos y ejemplos ver la entrada.

└──┘

todopoderoso ADJ almighty, all-powerful; **el T~** the Almighty.

todoterreno **1** NM INVAR jeep, (type of) Land Rover ®, all-purpose vehicle.
2 atr multi-purpose; adaptable; persona for all seasons.

tofo NM (Cono Sur) white clay; fireclay.

toga NF (Hist) toga; (Jur etc) gown, robe; (Univ) gown; **tomar la ~** to qualify as a lawyer.

togado, -a NM/F lawyer.

Togo NM Togo.

Togolandia NF Togoland.

togolés, -esa ADJ, NM/F Togolese.

toilette [tua'le] NF (Cono Sur) toilet, lavatory.

toisón NM: **~ (de oro)** Golden Fleece.

tojo[1] NM (Bot) gorse, furze.

tojo[2] ADJ (And) twin.

Tokio, Tokío NM Tokyo.

tol NM (CAm) gourd.

tolda NF (a) (And, Carib: tela) canvas.
(b) (And) (tienda) tent, improvised hut; (refugio) shelter; (de barco) awning.
(c) (Carib: bolsa grande) large sack.
(d) (Carib: cielo nublado) overcast sky.
(e) **él es de la ~ Acción Democrática** (Carib Pol) he belongs to Acción Democrática.

toldería NF (And, Cono Sur) Indian village, camp of Indian huts.

toldillo NM (And, Carib) mosquito net.

toldo NM (a) (de playa etc) sunshade, awning; (de tienda) sunblind; (entoldado) marquee; (encerado etc) cover, cloth, tarpaulin.
(b) (And, Cono Sur: choza) Indian hut; (Méx: tienda) tent.
(c) (And, Carib) mosquito net.
(d) (Méx Aut) hood, top (US).
(e) (fig) pride, haughtiness.

tole[1]* NM (a) (t **toletole**: disturbio) hubbub, commotion, uproar; (protesta) outcry; **levantar el ~** to kick up a fuss; **venir a uno con el ~** to badger sb about something, complain perpetually about something.
(b) (t **toletole**: chismes) gossip, rumour; (campaña difamatoria) slander campaign.
(c) **coger el ~, tomar el ~** to get out, pack up and go.

tole[2] NM (And) track, trail.

toledano **1** ADJ Toledan, of Toledo; V t **noche**.
2 NM, **toledana** NF Toledan, inhabitant (o native) of Toledo; **los ~s** the people of Toledo.

tolempo NM (And) = **lempo**.

tolerable ADJ tolerable.

tolerado ADJ: **película tolerada** ≃ PG.

tolerancia NF (a) tolerance; toleration. (b) (Mec) tolerance.

tolerante ADJ tolerant.

tolerantismo NM religious toleration.

tolerar [1a] VT (gen) to tolerate; (aguantar) to bear, endure, put up with; (permitir) to allow; **no se puede ~ esto** this cannot be tolerated; **no tolera que digan eso** he won't allow them to say that, he won't put up with their saying that; **su madre le tolera demasiado** his mother spoils him, his mother lets him get away with too much; **su estómago no tolera los huevos** eggs don't agree with him; **el cosmonauta toleró muy bien esta situación difícil** the cosmonaut stood up very well to this awkward situation; **el puente no tolera el peso de los tanques** the bridge will not support the weight of the tanks.

tolete NM (a) (Náut) tholepin. (b) (LAm: palo) short club, stick, cudgel. (c) (And, Carib: pedazo) piece, bit. (d) (And: balsa) raft.

toletole NM (a) (Cono Sur*: jaleo) row. (b) (And: terquedad) obstinacy, persistence. (c) (Carib*) (vida alegre) high life; (vagabundeo) roving life; V t **tole**[1] (b).

tolla NF (a) (pantano) marsh, quagmire. (b) (Carib, Méx: abrevadero) drinking trough.

tollina* NF hiding*; bashing*.

Tolomeo NM Ptolemy.

Tolón NM Toulon.

toloncho NM (And) piece of wood.

tolondro **1** ADJ scatterbrained.
2 NM (Med) bump, lump, swelling.

tolondrón ADJ, NM = **tolondro**.

Tolosa (de Francia) NF Toulouse.

tolosarra **1** ADJ of Tolosa (Navarre).
2 NMF native (o inhabitant) of Tolosa (Navarre); **los ~s** the people of Tolosa.

tolteca **1** ADJ Toltec.
2 NMF Toltec.

tolva NF (a) (recipiente) hopper; chute. (b) (Cono Sur, Méx: Ferro) hopper wagon, hopper car (US). (c) (Méx Min) shed for storing ore.

tolvanera NF dustcloud.

toma NF (a) (gen) taking; **~ de beneficios** profit-taking; **~ de conciencia** (conocimiento) awareness; increasing awareness; (el darse cuenta) realization; **~ de contacto** initial contact; first approach; **~ de decisiones** decision-making, decision-taking; **~ de declaración** taking of evidence; **~ de hábito** (Ecl) taking of vows; **~ de posesión** taking over; (de presidente) taking up of office, inauguration; **~ de tierra** (Aer) landing, touchdown; (Elec) earth (wire).
(b) (Mil) capture, taking; seizure.
(c) (cantidad) amount, portion; (Med) dose; (de bebé) feed; **~ de rapé** pinch of snuff.
(d) (Mec etc) (entrada) inlet, intake; (salida) outlet; (de agua etc) tap, outlet; (Elec) (enchufe) plug, socket; (cable) lead; (borne) terminal; **~ de agua** source of water supply; **~ de aire** air-inlet, air-intake; **~ de antena** (Rad) aerial socket; **~ de corriente, ~ de fuerza** power point, plug; **~ directa** (Aut) top gear; **~ de tierra** earth wire, ground wire

(*US*).
(e) (*Cine, TV*) take, shot; **~ directa** live shot; live broadcast.
(f) (*LAm: acequia*) irrigation channel; (*CAm: arroyo*) brook.
tomacorriente NM (*Elec*) plug.
tomada NF (*LAm Elec*) plug.
tomadero NM **(a)** (*asidero*) handle. **(b)** (*entrada*) inlet, intake; (*grifo*) tap.
tomado ADJ **(a)** (*t* **~ de orín**) rusty. **(b)** *voz* (*LAm*) hoarse. **(c) estar ~** to be drunk.
tomador 1 ADJ (*LAm**) drunken, boozy‡.
2 NM **(a)** (*Com*) drawee. **(b)** (*: *ladrón*) thief; **~ del dos, ~ del pico** pickpocket. **(c)** (*LAm: bebedor*) drunkard, boozer‡.
tomadura NF = **toma** (a) *y* (b); **~ de pelo*** (*burla*) hoax; deception, rip-off‡; (*guasa*) leg-pull*; (*mofa*) mockery; (*insulto*) abuse.
tomaína NF ptomaine.
tomante‡ NM queer‡.
tomar [1a] 1 VT **(a)** (*gen*) to take; to accept; to get, acquire; *aire, baño, curva, decisión, medida, oportunidad, paso, ruta, sol, temperatura etc* to take; *armas, pluma etc* to take up; *actitud* to adopt, take up; to strike; *aspecto, forma etc* to take on; *pelota* to catch, stop; *catarro* to take, get, catch; *hábito* to get into, fall into, acquire; *negocio* to take over; *lección* to have; *nombre* to take, adopt; *criado* to take on, engage; *fuerza* to get, gain, acquire; *billete* to take, get, buy; **¡toma!** here you are!, here!, catch!; **¡tómate ésa!** take that!; **es a ~ o a dejar** it's take it or leave it; **~ y dejar pasajeros** to take up and set down passengers; **~ a uno por policía** to take sb for a policeman, think that sb is a policeman; **~ a uno por loco** to think sb mad; **¿por quién me toma Vd?** what do you take me for?, who do you think I am?; **~ algo sobre sí** to take sth upon o.s.; *V* **mal, serio** *etc*.
(b) (*Mil*) to take, capture; to seize; (*ocupar*) to occupy, take over.
(c) (*Culin*) to eat, drink, have; **~ el pecho** to suck, feed at the breast; **tomamos unas cervezas** we had a few beers; **¿qué quieres ~?** what will you have?, what would you like?
(d) *autobús, tren etc* to take.
(e) (*Cine, Fot, TV*) to take; (*Cine*) to shoot; **~ una foto de** to take a photo of.
(f) *apuntes* to take; *discurso etc* to take down; **~ por escrito** to write down; **~ en taquigrafía** to take down in shorthand; **~ en cinta** to record on tape.
(g) *afecto, asco etc* to acquire, take (*a* to); *V* **cariño** *etc*.
(h) (*dominar*) to overcome; **le tomaron ganas de reír** she was overcome by an urge to laugh.
(i) **~la con uno** to pick a quarrel with sb; **tenerla tomada con uno** to have a down on sb*, adopt a consistently hostile attitude to sb.
(j) (*And: molestar*) to upset, annoy.
(k) (‡) *mujer* to have.
2 VI **(a)** (*Bot*) to take, take root; (*injerto*) to take.
(b) ~ a la derecha to go off to the right, turn right; **~ por una calle** to go off along a street, turn down a street.
(c) (*LAm: beber*) to drink; **estaba tomando en varios bares** he was drinking in a number of bars.
(d) (*) **tomó y lo rompió** he went and broke it; **tomó y se fue** off he went, he upped and went *.
(e) toma y daca (*como* N) give and take; (*pey*) mutual concessions (for selfish reasons), horse-trading, log-rolling; **más vale un ~ que dos te daré** a bird in the hand is worth two in the bush.
(f) ¡toma! well!; there!, fancy that!; I told you so!; (*a perro*) here boy!; **¡toma ya!** believe it or not!
3 **tomarse** VR **(a)** to take; **~ la venganza por su mano** to take vengeance with one's own hands; **no te lo tomes así** don't take it that way; **se lo sabe tomar bien** he knows how to take it, he can take it in his stride; **se tomó unas vacaciones larguísimas** he took tremendously long holidays; **se tomó un tremendo disgusto** he received a very severe blow; **se tomó 13 cervezas seguidas** he drank down 13 beers one after the other.
(b) ~ por to think o.s., consider o.s. to be; **¿por quién se toma aquel ministro?** who does that minister think he is?
(c) **~ de orín**) to get rusty.
Tomás NM Thomas; **~ Moro** Thomas More.
tomatal NM **(a)** (*sembrío*) tomato bed, tomato field. **(b)** (*LAm: planta*) tomato plant.
tomatazo NM: **recibió una lluvia de ~s** he was pelted with tomatoes.
tomate NM **(a)** tomato; **ponerse como un ~** to turn as red as a beetroot. **(b)** (‡: *jaleo*) fuss, row, to-do*; (*pelea*) set-to*; (*pega*) snag, difficulty; **¡qué ~!** what a mess!; **esto tiene ~** this is tough, this is a tough one.
tomatera¹ NF **(a)** (*planta*) tomato plant. **(b)** (*Cono Sur*: juerga*) drunken spree; rowdy party.
tomatero, -a² NM/F (*cultivador*) tomato grower; (*comerciante*) tomato dealer.
tomavistas NM INVAR film camera, cine-camera.

tombo‡ NM (*And*) fuzz‡, police.
tómbola NF tombola.
tomillo NM thyme; **~ salsero** garden thyme.
tominero ADJ (*Méx*) mean.
tomismo NM Thomism.
tomista ADJ, NMF Thomist.
tomiza NF esparto rope.
tomo¹ NM (*libro*) volume; **en 3 ~s** in 3 volumes.
tomo² NM (*bulto*) bulk, size; (*fig*) importance; **de ~ y lomo** utter, out-and-out; **un canalla de ~ y lomo** a real swine*.
tomografía NF scanner.
tomo-homenaje NM, PL **tomos-homenaje** homage volume, Festschrift.
tomón ADJ (*And*) teasing, jokey.
tompiate NM (*Méx*) (*canasta*) basket (*of woven palm leaves*); (*bolsa*) pouch (*of woven palm leaves*).
ton: sin ~ ni son 1 ADV for no particular reason; without rhyme or reason.
2 ADJ *argumento etc* hopelessly confused.
tonada NF **(a)** (*Mús*) tune, song, air. **(b)** (*LAm: acento*) accent, local peculiarity, typical intonation. **(c)** (*Carib*) (*embuste*) fib; (*juego de palabras*) pun.
tonadilla NF little tune; merry tune, light-hearted song.
tonal ADJ tonal.
tonalidad NF **(a)** (*Mús*) key; tonality; (*Rad*) tone; **~ mayor** major key; **~ menor** minor key; **control de ~** tone control.
(b) (*Arte*) shade; colour scheme; **una bella ~ de verde** a beautiful shade of green; **cambiar la ~ de un cuarto** to change the colour scheme of a room.
tonel NM **(a)** barrel, cask, vat, keg; **(b)** (*: *persona*) fat lump.
tonelada NF ton; **~ americana, ~ corta** short ton; **~ inglesa, ~ larga** long ton, gross ton; **~ métrica** metric ton; **~ de registro** register ton; **un buque de 30.000 ~s de registro bruto** a ship of 30,000 gross register tons.
tonelaje NM tonnage.
tonelería NF cooperage, barrel-making.
tonelero NM cooper.
tonelete NM **(a)** (*tonel*) cask, keg. **(b)** (*falda*) short skirt.
Tonete NM *forma familiar de* **Antonio.**
tonga NF **(a)** layer, stratum; (*de ladrillos*) course. **(b)** (*Carib, Méx: montón*) pile. **(c)** (*And, Aragón, Cono Sur*) (*tarea*) job, task; (*tanda*) spell of work. **(d)** (*And: siesta*) nap.
tongada NF layer; coat, covering.
tongo¹ NM (*Dep etc*) fixing, throwing of a game (*o* fight *etc*); **¡hay ~!** it's been fixed!, it's been rigged!; **hubo ~ en las elecciones** the elections were rigged.
tongo² NM (*Cono Sur*) **(a)** (*sombrero*) bowler hat. **(b)** (*bebida*) rum punch.
tongonearse [1a] VR (*LAm*) = **contonearse.**
tongoneo NM (*LAm*) = **contoneo.**
tongorí NM (*And, Cono Sur*) (*hígado*) liver (*of cow etc*); (*menudencias*) offal; (*bofe*) lights.
tongoy NM (*LAm*) bowler hat.
Toni NM *forma familiar de* Antonio.
tónica NF **(a)** (*Mús: t fig*) tonic; keynote; **es una de las ~s del estilo moderno** it is one of the keynotes of the modern style. **(b)** (*fig: tendencia*) tone, trend, tendency. **(c)** (*bebida*) tonic, tonic water.
tonicidad NF tonicity.
tónico 1 ADJ **(a)** (*Mús*) tonic; (*Ling*) *sílaba* tonic, stressed, accented. **(b)** (*Med: t fig*) tonic, invigorating, stimulating.
2 NM tonic (*t fig*).
tonificador ADJ, **tonificante** ADJ invigorating, stimulating.
tonificar [1g] VT to tone up; to invigorate, fortify.
tonillo NM **(a)** (*monótono*) singsong, monotone, monotonous voice. **(b)** (*mofador*) sarcastic tone, mocking undertone. **(c)** (*peculiar*) (local) accent.
tono NM **(a)** (*Mús*) tone; (*altura*) pitch; (*tonalidad*) key; **~ mayor** major key; **~ menor** minor key; **estar a ~** to be in key; **estar a ~ con** (*fig*) to be in tune with.
(b) (*de voz etc, t fig*) tone; **~ de marcar** (*Telec*) dialling tone; **~ de voz** tone of voice; **a este ~** in the same fashion, in the same vein; **en ~ bajo** in low tones; **en ~ de enojo** in an angry tone; **bajar el ~** to lower one's voice; (*fig*) to change one's tune, quieten down; **cambiar el** (*o* de) **~** to change one's tune; **subir de ~** to get louder, increase in volume; **la expresión tiene un ~ despectivo** the expression has a pejorative tone; **la discusión tomó un ~ áspero** the discussion took on a harsh tone.
(c) (*social etc*) tone; **buen ~** tone, good tone; **una familia de ~** a good family, a family of some social standing; **de buen ~** elegant, fashionable; (*hum*) genteel, refined; **de mal ~** common, coarse; **eso no es de ~** that's not done, that's not nice; **fuera de ~** inappropriate; **dar el ~** to set the tone; **darse ~** to put on airs; **ponerse a ~**

(*portarse bien*) to behave o.s.; (*conformarse*) to toe the line; (*: *en la onda*) to get with it*; **subirse de** ~ to get more haughty (*o* angry), take a more arrogant (*o* indignant) line; **no venir a** ~ to be inappropriate, be out of place.
(**d**) (*Mús: diapasón*) tuning fork.
(**e**) (*Mús: corredera*) slide.
(**f**) (*Anat, Med*) tone.
(**g**) (*de color*) shade, hue; ~ **pastel** pastel shade.
tonsura NF tonsure.
tonsurado ADJ tonsured.
tonsurar [1a] VT to clip, shear; (*Ecl*) to tonsure.
tontada NF = **tontería**.
tontaina* NMF idiot, dimwit*.
tontamente ADV foolishly, stupidly.
tontear* [1a] VI (**a**) (*hacer el tonto*) to fool about, act the fool; to talk nonsense. (**b**) (*amorosamente*) to flirt.
tontera NF (*LAm*) = **tontería**.
tontería NF (**a**) (*cualidad*) silliness, foolishness, stupidity.
(**b**) (*una* ~) (*cosa*) silly thing; (*acto*) foolish act; (*dicho*) stupid remark; ~**s** nonsense, rubbish; **¡déjate de** ~**s!** stop that nonsense!, quit fooling!; **dejémonos de** ~**s** let's be serious; **hacer una** ~ to do a silly thing, do sth silly; **no es ninguna** ~ it's not such a bad idea; it's not just a small thing, it's more serious than you think.
(**c**) (*fig: bagatela*) triviality; **lo vendió por una** ~ he sold it for a song; **estima cualquier** ~ **de ese autor** he values any little thing by that writer.
(**d**) (*fig: escrúpulo*) silly scruple; ~**s** display of delicacy (*o* squeamishness *etc*).
tonto [1] ADJ (**a**) (*necio*) silly, foolish, stupid; (*Med*) imbecile; (***) **chica** stuck-up*; **¡qué** ~ **soy!** how silly of me!; **¡no seas** ~**!** don't be silly!; **es lo bastante** ~ **como para** + *infin* he's fool enough to + *infin*; **es más** ~ **que Abundio*** he's as thick as two short planks*; **dejar a uno** ~ to dumbfound sb; **tener el día** ~ to have an off-day.
(**b**) *amante* silly, soft, mushy.
(**c**) **a tontas y a locas** anyhow, unsystematically, haphazardly; **hablar a tontas y a locas** to talk without rhyme or reason; **lo hace a tontas y a locas** he does it just anyhow, he does it any old how; **repartir golpes a tontas y a locas** to hit out wildly, hit out blindly.
[2] NM, **tonta** NF fool, idiot; (*Med*) imbecile; **¡**~**!** you idiot!; **soy un** ~ I'm an idiot, I must be crazy; ~ **del bote**, ~ **de capirote**, ~ **de remate** prize idiot, utter fool; ~ **del lugar** village idiot; ~ **útil*** stooge; **hacer(se) el** ~ to act the fool, play the fool.
[3] NM (**a**) (*Circo, Teat*) clown, funny man.
(**b**) (*And, CAm, Cono Sur: palanca*) jemmy.
(**c**) (***) cunt*.
tontón[1], -ona* NM/F = **tonto 2**.
tontón[2]* NM (*vestido premamá*) smock, maternity dress.
tontorrón*, -ona* NM/F dimwit*.
tontura NF = **tontería** (**a**).
tontureco ADJ (*CAm*) = **tonto 1**.
tonudo* ADJ (*Cono Sur*) classy*.
tony ['toni] NM (*LAm**) clown.
toña: NF (**a**) (*puñetazo*) bash*, punch; (*patada*) kick. (**b**) **pillarse una** ~ (*Esp*) to get plastered:.
top* [1] ADJ top, best; leading; (*Com*) best-selling, leading.
[2] NM INVAR (**a**) (*vestido*) top.
(**b**) top person; leading personality; **el** ~ **del** ~ la crème de la crème; **el** ~ **de la gama** the best in its range.
topacio NM topaz.
topadora NF (*LAm*) bulldozer.
topar [1a] [1] VT (**a**) (*Zool*) to butt, horn.
(**b**) *persona* to run into, come across, bump into; *objeto* to find, come across; **le topé por casualidad en el museo** I happened to bump into him in the museum.
(**c**) (*And, Cono Sur, Méx: apostar*) to bet, stake.
[2] VI (**a**) ~ **contra**, ~ **en** to run into, hit, bump into, knock against.
(**b**) ~ **con** = 1 (**b**); ~ **con un obstáculo** to run up against an obstacle, encounter an obstacle.
(**c**) **la dificultad topa en eso** that's where the trouble lies, there's the rub.
(**d**) (*Méx: reñir*) to quarrel.
[3] NM = 2 (**b**).
toparse VR = 2 (**b**).
tope[1] [1] (**a**) *como* ADJ INVAR top, maximum; **edad** ~ **para un puesto** maximum (*o* minimum) age for a job; **fecha** ~ closing date, last date; **precio** ~ top price, ceiling price; **sueldo** ~ top salary, maximum salary.
(**b**) ADJ (*) great*, super*; ~ **guay** clean over the top*.
[2] NM (**a**) (*cabo*) end; (*límite*) top, maximum, limit; (*techo*) ceiling; (*Náut*) top, masthead; ~ **salarial** wage ceiling; **al** ~ end to end; **hasta el** ~ to the brim, to the limit; **estar hasta los** ~**s** (*Náut*) to be overloaded, be loaded to the gunwales; (*fig: t* **estar a** ~) to be full to bursting; **voy a estar a** ~ I'm going to be up to the eyes (with work

etc); **estoy hasta los** ~**s*** I'm utterly fed up*; **ir a** ~ to go flat out; **trabajar a** ~ to work flat out, work to the limit; **vivir a** ~ to live life to the full.
(**b**) (*Náut: persona*) lookout.
(**c**) (*And, Cono Sur: cumbre*) peak, summit.
(**d**) (*LAm*) (*saliente*) protuberance; (*obstáculo*) impediment; (*Méx Aut*) speed ramp, sleeping policeman.
tope[2] NM (**a**) (*golpe*) bump, knock, bang; (*con cabeza*) butt; (*Aut*) collision.
(**b**) (*fig*) (*riña*) quarrel; (*pelea*) scuffle.
(**c**) (*Mec etc*) catch, stop, check; (*Ferro*) buffer; (*Aut*) bumper; (*de revólver*) catch; ~ **de tabulación** tab stop.
(**d**) (*fig: pega*) snag, difficulty; **ahí está el** ~ that's just the trouble.
(**e**) (:) burglary, breaking and entering.
topera NF (**a**) molehill. (**b**) (:) tube, metro.
topero: NM burglar.
toperol NM (*Cono Sur, Méx*) brass tack.
topetada NF butt, bump, bang, collision.
topetar [1a] VT (**a**) (*golpear*) to butt, bump. (**b**) (*fig*) to bump into.
topetazo NM = **topetada**.
topetear [1a] VT (*And*) = **topetar**.
topetón NM = **topetada**.
▼ **tópico** [1] ADJ (*Med*) for external application.
▼[2] NM (**a**) (*lugar común*) commonplace, platitude; cliché; catchphrase.
(**b**) (*LAm*) topic, subject.
topillo[1] NM (*Méx*) trick, swindle.
topillo[2] NM (*Zool*) vole.
topista: NM burglar.
top-less NM habit of going topless; topless bathing; topless entertainment; **ir en** ~, **practicar el** ~ to go topless.
top-model NMF, PL **top-models** supermodel.
topo[1] NM (**a**) (*Zool*) mole. (**b**) (*fig: torpe*) clumsy person, blunderer. (**c**) (*espía*) mole, spy, inside informer. (**d**) (*Mec*) mole, tunnelling machine.
topo[2] NM (*LAm*) large pin.
topo[3] NM (*And*) measurement of distance of 1.5 leagues.
topocho[1] ADJ (*Carib*) plump, chubby.
topocho[2] NM (*Carib Bot*) plantain.
topografía NF topography.
topográfico ADJ topographic(al).
topógrafo, -a NM/F topographer; surveyor.
topolino [1] NF (**a**) teenager, bobbysoxer (*US*). (**b**) (*Aut*) small car (*Fiat 500 cc*).
[2] NMPL: ~**s** wedge-heeled shoes.
topón NM (*LAm*) = **topetada**.
toponimia NF (**a**) (*nombres*) toponymy, place-names. (**b**) (*estudio*) study of place-names.
toponímico ADJ toponymic; *índice* of place names; *referencia* place names (*atr*).
topónimo NM place-name.
toposo ADJ (*Carib*) meddlesome.
toque NM (**a**) (*acto*) touch; **dar los primeros** ~**s a** to make a start on; **dar el último** ~ **a** to put the finishing touch to; **dar un** (*o* **el**) ~ **a uno** (*estimular*) to give sb a prod; (*avisar*) to pass the message to sb, tip the wink to sb*; **faltan algunos** ~**s para completarlo** it needs a few touches to finish it off.
(**b**) (*Arte*) touch; dab (of colour); ~ **de luz** light, highlight.
(**c**) (*Quím*) test; assay; **dar un** ~ **a** to test; *persona* to sound out.
(**d**) (*Mús*) (*de campana*) peal, chime; (*de reloj*) stroke; (*de timbre*) ring; (*de tambor*) beat; (*de sirena*) hoot, blast; (*Mil*) bugle call; ~ **de atención** (*fig*) warning note; ~ **de diana** reveille; ~ **de difuntos** passing bell, knell; ~ **de oración** call to prayer; ~ **de queda** curfew; ~ **de retreta** tattoo; ~ **de silencio** ≃ lights out; **al** ~ **de las doce** on the stroke of twelve; **dar el** ~ **a uno** (*visitar*) to drop in on sb; (*Telec*) to give sb a ring.
(**e**) (*fig: quid*) crux; essence, heart of the matter; **ahí está el** ~ that's the crux of the matter.
(**f**) (*And: vuelta*) turn.
toquetear [1a] VT (**a**) (*manosear*) to touch repeatedly, handle, keep fingering. (**b**) (*Mús*) to mess about on, play idly. (**c**) (:: *amorosamente*) to fondle, feel up:, touch up:.
toqueteo: NM fondling, feeling up:.
toquido NM (*CAm, Méx*) = **toque**.
toquilla NF headscarf; knitted shawl, woollen bonnet; (*And*) straw hat.
torácico ADJ thoracic.
torada NF herd of bulls.
tórax NM thorax.
torbellino NM (**a**) (*viento*) whirlwind; (*polvareda*) dust cloud. (**b**) (*fig*) whirl. (**c**) (*fig: persona*) whirlwind.
torcaz ADJ: **paloma** ~ wood pigeon, ring dove.

---

torcecuello NM (*Orn*) wryneck.

torcedor NM (**a**) (*Téc*) spindle. (**b**) (*fig*) torture, torment.

torcedura NF (**a**) (*gen*) twist(ing); (*Med*) sprain, strain, wrench. (**b**) (*vino*) weak wine.

torcer [2b y 2h] ① VT (**a**) (*gen*) to twist; (*doblar*) to bend; *madera etc* to warp; *miembro* to twist, wrench, put out; *músculo* to strain; *tobillo* to sprain, twist; *ojos* to turn, squint; *pelota* to spin, cut.
(**b**) *cuello, manos, ropa* to wring; *hebras, cuerda* to plait.
(**c**) (*fig*) *decisión, sucesos, tendencia* to influence, affect; *voluntad* to bend; *pensamientos* to turn (*de* from); *persona* to dissuade, turn (*de* from).
(**d**) (*fig*) *justicia* to pervert; *persona* to corrupt, bribe.
(**e**) (*fig*) *sentido* to twist, pervert, distort.
② VI (**a**) (*camino, vehículo, viajero*) to turn; **el coche torció a la izquierda** the car turned left; **al llegar allí tuerza Vd a la derecha** when you reach there turn right.
(**b**) (*pelota*) to spin; to swerve.
③ **torcerse** VR (**a**) to twist; to bend; to warp.
(**b**) ~ **un pie** to twist one's foot, sprain one's foot.
(**c**) (*fig: perverterse*) to go astray, be perverted; (*Med etc*) to suffer in one's development; (*suceso*) to take a strange turn; (*esperanzas, proyecto etc*) to go all wrong, go awry; **si no se tuerce** as long as nothing turns up to prevent it.
(**d**) (*leche, vino*) to turn sour.

torcida NF wick.

torcidamente ADV (**a**) (*gen*) in a twisted way, crookedly. (**b**) (*fig*) deviously, in a crooked way.

torcido ① (*gen*) ADJ (**a**) twisted; bent; *camino etc* crooked, twisty, full of turns; **el cuadro está** ~ the picture is askew, the picture is not straight; **llevaba el sombrero algo** ~ he had his hat on not quite straight.
(**b**) (*fig*) devious, crooked.
(**c**) (*And, CAm, Carib*: *desgraciado*) unlucky.
② NM (*de seda etc*) twist.

torcijón NM (**a**) sudden twist. (**b**) = **retortijón**.

torcimiento NM = **torcedura**.

tordillo ① ADJ dappled, dapple-grey.
② NM dapple.

tordo ① ADJ dappled, dapple-grey.
② NM (*Orn*) thrush.

torear [1a] ① VT (**a**) *toro* to fight, play.
(**b**) (*fig: esquivar*) to dodge, avoid.
(**c**) (*fig*) (*mantener a raya*) to keep at bay; (*embromar*) to tease, draw on; (*dar largas a*) to put off, keep guessing.
(**d**) (*fig*) (*acosar*) to plague; (*confundir*) to confuse.
(**e**) (*CAm, Cono Sur*) *animal* to provoke, enrage; (*Cono Sur, Méx*) *persona* to infuriate.
(**f**) (*And, Cono Sur: perro*) to bark furiously at.
② VI (**a**) (*Taur*) to fight, fight bulls; to be a bullfighter; **toreó bien Suárez** Suárez fought well; **no volverá a** ~ he will never fight again; **el muchacho quiere** ~ the boy wants to be a bullfighter.
(**b**) (*) to spin it out, procrastinate.
(**c**) (*And, Cono Sur: ladrar*) to bark furiously.

toreo NM (**a**) (*Taur*) (art of) bullfighting. (**b**) (*Méx: alambique*) illicit still.

torera[1] NF (**a**) (*chaqueta*) short tight jacket. (**b**) **saltarse un deber a la** ~ to disregard a duty; **saltarse una ley a la** ~ to flout a law.

torería NF (**a**) (*toreros*) (class of) bullfighters; (*mundo del toreo*) bullfighting world. (**b**) (*Carib, CAm: broma*) prank.

torero, -a[2] NM/F bullfighter; **decir una de** ~* to say sth wholly off the point; **un problema que no se lo salta un** ~ a huge problem.

torete NM (**a**) (*animal*) small bull, young bull. (**b**) (*fig: niño*) strong boy, robust child; (*pey*) rough child; bad-tempered boy.

toril NM bullpen.

torio NM thorium.

torito NM (*And Ent*) bluebottle.

tormenta NF (**a**) storm; ~ **de arena** sandstorm; ~ **de cerebros** brainstorm(ing); ~ **de polvo** dust-storm.
(**b**) (*fig: tempestad*) storm; turmoil, upheaval; ~ **en un vaso de agua** storm in a teacup; **sufrió una** ~ **de celos** she suffered a great pang of jealousy; **desencadenó una** ~ **de pasiones** it unleashed a storm of passions.
(**c**) (*fig*) (*desgracia*) misfortune; (*revés*) reverse, setback.

tormento NM torture; (*fig*) torture, torment; anguish, agony; **dar** ~ **a** to torture; (*fig*) to torment, plague; **darse** ~ to torment o.s.; **estos zapatos son un** ~ these shoes are agony; **sus dos hijos son un** ~ **perpetuo** her two sons are a perpetual torment to her.

tormentoso ADJ stormy (*t fig*).

tormo NM lump, mass.

torna NF (**a**) (*vuelta*) return.
(**b**) **volver las** ~**s a uno** to turn the tables on sb; **se han vuelto las** ~**s** now it's all changed, now the boot's on the other foot.

tornada NF return.

tornadera NF pitchfork, winnowing fork.

tornadizo ① ADJ changeable; fickle.
② NM, **tornadiza** NF (*Hist*) renegade.

tornado NM tornado.

tornar [1a] ① VT (**a**) (*devolver*) to give back, return.
(**b**) (*transformar*) to change, alter, transform (*en* into).
② VI (**a**) (*volver*) to go back, come back, return.
(**b**) ~ **a hacer algo** to do sth again; **tornó a llover** it began to rain again; **tornó a estudiar el problema** he returned to the study of the problem.
(**c**) ~ **en sí** to regain consciousness, come to.
③ **tornarse** VR (**a**) (*volver*) to return.
(**b**) (*volverse*) to turn, become.

tornasol NM (**a**) (*Bot*) sunflower. (**b**) (*Quím*) litmus; **papel de** ~ litmus paper. (**c**) (*fig*) sheen, iridescence.

tornasolado ADJ iridescent, sheeny; full of different lights; *tela* shot.

tornasolar [1a] ① VT to make iridescent, put a sheen on.
② **tornasolarse** VR to be (*o* become) iridescent, show different lights.

tornavía NF (*Ferro*) turntable.

tornavoz NF baffle; sounding board; (*de púlpito*) sounding board, canopy; **hacer** ~ to cup one's hands to one's mouth.

torneado ① ADJ (**a**) (*Téc*) turned (on a lathe). (**b**) *brazo etc* shapely, delicately curved; pleasingly rounded.
② NM turning.

tornear [1a] VT to turn (on a lathe).

torneo NM tournament, competition; (*Hist*) tourney, joust; ~ **de tenis** tennis tournament; ~ **por equipos** team tournament.

tornero, -a NM/F machinist, turner, lathe operator.

tornillería NF bolts; nuts and bolts.

tornillo NM (**a**) (*gen*) screw; bolt; ~ **de banco** vice, vise (*US*), clamp; ~ **sin fin** worm gear; **apretar los** ~**s a uno** to apply pressure on sb, put the screws on sb*; **le falta un** ~* he has a screw loose*.
(**b**) **hacer** ~ (*Mil*) to desert.
(**c**) (*Cono Sur*: *frío*) bitter cold.

torniquete NM (**a**) (*gen*) turnstile. (**b**) (*Med*) tourniquet.

torniscón NM (**a**) (*apretón*) pinch, squeeze. (**b**) (*manotada*) slap on the face; smack on the head, cuff.

torno NM (**a**) (*Téc: cabrestante*) winch, windlass; drum; winding machine.
(**b**) (*Téc: de tornear*) lathe; ~ **de banco** vice, vise (*US*), clamp; ~ **de tornero** turning lathe; **labrar a** ~ to turn on the lathe.
(**c**) (*Téc*) ~ **de alfarero** potter's wheel; ~ **de asador** spit; ~ **de hilar** spinning wheel.
(**d**) (*freno etc*) brake.
(**e**) (*de rió*) (*curva*) bend; (*rabiones*) race, rapids.
(**f**) **en** ~ **a** round, about; **se reunieron en** ~ **suyo** they gathered round her; **todo estaba inundado en muchos kilómetros en** ~ for many miles all round everything was flooded; **en** ~ **a este tema** on this theme, about this subject; **polemizar en** ~ **a un texto** to argue about a text.

toro NM (**a**) (*Zool*) bull; ~ **bravo**, ~ **de lidia** fighting bull; **a** ~ **pasado** with hindsight, in retrospect; **coger el** ~ **por los cuernos, irse a la cabeza del** ~ to take the bull by the horns; **echar** (*o* **soltar**) **el** ~ **a uno*** to give sb a severe dressing-down*; **hacer un** ~* (*Teat*) to stand in for somebody; **esto está hecho para que nos coja el** ~ the dice are loaded against us; **pillar el** ~ **a uno*** to get sb into a corner (*in an argument*).
(**b**) (*fig*) strong man, he-man*; solidly-built man; tough guy*; **ser** ~ **corrido** to be an old hand at it, be an old fox.
(**c**) **los** ~**s** (*función*) bullfight; (*arte*) (art of) bullfighting; **este año no habrá** ~**s** there will be no bullfight this year; **ir a los** ~**s, ir de** ~**s** to go to the bullfight; **no me gustan los** ~**s** I don't like bullfighting; **ciertos son los** ~**s** it turns out that it's true; **ver los** ~**s desde la barrera** to be able to take an independent view, remain uncommitted; to sit on the fence.
(**d**) **hacer** ~**s*** to play truant, cut class.
(**e**) **T~** (*Zodíaco*) Taurus.

torombolo ADJ (*Carib*) (*gordito*) plump; (*barrigón*) pot-bellied.

toronja NF grapefruit.

toronjil NM balm, (*Esp*) lemon balm.

toronjo NM grapefruit tree.

torpe ADJ (**a**) *persona* (*desmañado*) clumsy, awkward; (*poco ágil*) slow, ungainly; *movimiento* slow, sluggish, heavy.
(**b**) *llave etc* stiff.
(**c**) *persona* (*lerdo*) dense, dim, slow-witted.
(**d**) (*fig*) (*vil*) morally vile; (*nada honrado*) dishonest, dishonourable.
(**e**) (*fig: obsceno*) crude, obscene.

torpear [1a] VI (*Cono Sur*) to be dishonest, behave dishonourably.

torpedear [1a] VT to torpedo; (*fig*) *proyecto* to torpedo; ~ **a uno con preguntas** to bombard sb with questions.

torpedeo NM (*fig*) bombardment.
torpedero NM torpedo boat.
torpedo NM torpedo.
torpemente ADV (*V* ADJ) (a) clumsily, awkwardly; slowly, sluggishly, heavily.
　(b) stiffly.
　(c) slow-wittedly.
　(d) (*fig*) vilely, dishonestly.
　(e) (*fig*) crudely, obscenely.
torpeza NF (*V* ADJ) (a) clumsiness, awkwardness; slowness, ungainliness; sluggishness, heaviness.
　(b) stiffness.
　(c) denseness, dimness, slowness of wit.
　(d) (*fig*) moral vileness; dishonesty.
　(e) (*fig*) crudeness, obscenity.
　(f) (*una ~*) mistake, error of taste, lack of tact; **fue una ~ mía** it was tactless of me; **fue una ~ más** it was yet another instance of tastelessness.
torpón ADJ (*Cono Sur*) = **torpe**.
torpor NM torpor.
torrado NM (a) (*Anat*:) bonce:, head. (b) **~s** (*Culin*) toasted chickpeas.
torrar [1a] ① VT (a) (*Culin*) to toast, roast. (b) (:: *robar*) to pinch*, nick:.
　② **torrarse** VR to go off to sleep.
torre NF (a) (*Arquit etc*) tower; (*Rad, TV etc*) mast, tower; (*de pozo de petróleo*) derrick; (*de oficinas, viviendas*) tower block; **T~ de Babel** Tower of Babel; **~ de alta tensión, ~ de conducción eléctrica** electricity pylon; **~ de control** (*Aer*) control tower; **~ del homenaje** keep; **~ de marfil** ivory tower; **~ de observación** observation tower, watchtower; **~ de perforación** drilling rig; **~ de refrigeración** cooling-tower; **~ (de) vigía** (*Náut*) crow's-nest, (*de submarino*) conning-tower; **~ de vigilancia** watchtower.
　(b) (*Ajedrez*) rook, castle.
　(c) (*Aer, Mil, Náut*) turret; (*Mil*) watchtower; **~ de mando** (*de submarino*) conning-tower.
　(d) (*Carib, Méx: chimenea*) factory chimney.
　(e) **dar en la ~** (*Méx*) to hit where it hurts most.
torrefacción NF toasting, roasting.
torrefacto ADJ high roast.
torreja NF (*LAm*) (fried) slices of fruit and vegetables; (*Cono Sur*) slice of fruit.
torrencial ADJ torrential.
torrencialidad NF torrential nature.
torrencialmente ADV torrentially, in a torrent; in great quantities.
torrente NM (a) (*río etc*) rushing stream, mountain stream, torrent; **llover a ~s** to rain cats and dogs, rain in torrents.
　(b) (*Anat*: *t* **~ circulatorio, ~ sanguíneo**) bloodstream.
　(c) (*fig*) stream, torrent, rush, flood; onrush; **~ de palabras** torrent of words, rush of words; **~ de voz** loud strong voice.
torrentera NF gully, watercourse.
torrentoso ADJ (*LAm*) *río* torrential, rushing; *lluvia* torrential.
torreón NM tower; (*Arquit*) turret.
torrero NM lighthouse keeper.
torreta NF (a) (*Aer, Mil, Náut*) turret; (*de submarino*) conning-tower; **~ de observación, ~ de vigilancia** watchtower. (b) (*Elec*) pylon, mast.
torrezno NM rasher, slice of bacon.
tórrido ADJ torrid.
torrificar [1g] VT (*Méx*) *café* to toast, roast.
torrija NF French toast.
torsión NF (*torcedura*) twist(ing); warp(ing); (*Mec*) torsion, torque.
torsional ADJ torsional.
torso NM (*Anat*) torso; (*Arte*) head and shoulder; (*Escultura*) bust.
torta NF (a) (*pastel*) cake; tart, flan; (*hojuela*) pancake; (*Méx*) sandwich; (*fig*) cake, flat mass, round lump; **la ~ costó un pan** it worked out dearer than expected, (*fig*) it was more trouble than it was worth; **eso es ~s y pan pintado** it's child's play, it's a cinch; **no entendió ni ~*** he didn't understand a word of it; **¡ni ~!*** I haven't a clue!*, not the foggiest!*; **nos queda la ~** (*fig*) there's a lot left over.
　(b) (*Esp*) **agarrar una ~** to get plastered:; **estar con la ~** to be all at sea, be totally bemused.
　(c) (*CAm, Méx*: *t* **~ de huevos**) omelet(te).
　(d) (*Tip*) fount.
　(e) (*: puñetazo*) punch, sock*; (*caída*) crash, fall; **liarse a ~s** to get involved in a punch-up*.
　(f) (*CAm, Méx*:*) cunt::.
tortazo* NM slap, punch, sock*; **pegarse el ~** to get hurt, have a bad accident.
tortear [1a] ① VT (*Cono Sur*) *masa* to flatten, roll; (*CAm, Méx*) *tortilla* to shape (with the palms of one's hands).
　② VI (*Méx*) to clap, applaud.
tortero ADJ (*And*) round and flat, disc-shaped.
tortícolis NF INVAR crick in the neck, stiff neck.

tortilla NF (a) (*de huevo*) omelet(te); **~ española, ~ de patatas** Spanish potato omelette; (*fig*) **cambiar** (*o* **volver**) **la ~ a uno** to turn the tables on sb; **se le volvió la ~** it came out all wrong for him, his luck let him down; **se ha vuelto la ~** now the boot is on the other foot; **hacer algo una ~** to smash sth up; **hacer a uno una ~*** to beat sb up*; **van a hacer el negocio una ~** they're sure to mess the deal up.
　(b) (*CAm, Méx: de maíz*) flat maize pancake, tortilla.
　(c) (::) lesbian intercourse, lesbian practices.
tortillera NF (a) (*CAm, Méx*) tortilla seller. (b) (::) dyke:, lesbian.
tortita NF pancake.
tórtola NF turtledove.
tortoleo NM (*Méx*) billing and cooing.
tórtolo NM (a) (*Orn*) (male) turtledove. (b) (*amante*) lovebird, loverboy; **~s*** pair of lovers, lovebirds.
tortuga NF tortoise; **~** (*marina*) turtle.
tortuguismo NM (*Méx Ind*) go-slow.
tortuoso ADJ (a) (*camino etc*) winding, tortuous, full of bends. (b) (*fig*) devious.
tortura NF torture (*t fig*).
torturado, -a NM/F torture victim.
torturar [1a] VT to torture.
toruno NM (a) (*CAm: semental*) stud bull; (*Cono Sur: toro viejo*) old bull; (*Cono Sur: buey*) ox. (b) (*Cono Sur: hombre*) fit old man.
torvisca NF, **torvisco** NM spurge flax.
torvo ADJ grim, stern, fierce.
torzal NM cord, twist (of silk); (*Cono Sur*) plaited rope.
tos NF cough; coughing; **acceso de ~** coughing fit; **~ ferina** whooping cough.
toscamente ADV coarsely, roughly, crudely.
Toscana NF: **La ~** Tuscany.
toscano, -a ① ADJ, NM/F Tuscan.
　② NM (a) (*Ling*) Tuscan; (*Hist*) Italian. (b) (*puro*) (a kind of) cigar.
tosco ADJ coarse, rough, crude (*t fig*).
tosedera NF (*LAm*) nagging cough.
toser [2a] ① VT (*fig*) (a) **no le tose nadie, no hay quien le tosa** nobody can compete with him, he's in a class by himself.
　(b) **a mí no me tose nadie** I'll not stand for that, I'm not taking that from anybody.
　② VI to cough.
tosido NM (*CAm, Cono Sur, Méx*) cough.
tósigo NM poison.
tosquedad NF coarseness, roughness, crudeness (*t fig*).
tostada NF (a) toast, piece of toast; (*Méx: tortilla*) fried tortilla; (*CAm: plátano*) toasted slice of banana; **una ~ de*** a lot of, masses of; **hace una ~ de años*** ages ago; **se olía la ~*** you could tell there was trouble coming.
　(b) (*) **dar una ~ a uno, pegar una ~ a uno** to put one over on sb*, cheat sb.
　(c) (*Cono Sur: conversación*) long boring conversation.
tostado ① ADJ (a) (*Culin*) toasted. (b) *color* dark brown, ochre, burnt; *persona, piel* (*t* **~ por el sol**) brown, tanned, sunburnt.
　② NM tan.
tostador NM toaster; roaster; **~ eléctrico, ~ de pan** electric toaster.
tostadora NF toaster.
tostadura NF (*de café*) roasting.
tostar [1l] ① VT (a) *pan etc* to toast; *café* to roast; (*Culin*) to brown.
　(b) *persona, piel* to tan.
　(c) **~ a uno** (*Carib, Cono Sur*:*) to tan sb's hide*.
　(d) (*Carib, Cono Sur: proseguir*) to continue vigorously, push on with.
　(e) (*Méx*) (*ofender*) to offend; (*perjudicar*) to harm, hurt; (*matar*) to kill.
　② **tostarse** VR (*t* **~ al sol**) to tan, brown, get brown.
tostelería NF (*CAm*) cake shop.
tostón NM (a) (*Culin: cubito*) small cube of toast, crouton; (*tostada*) toast dipped in oil; (*garbanzo*) toasted chickpea.
　(b) (*Culin: lechón*) roast sucking-pig.
　(c) (*Culin: tostada quemada*) piece of bread (*etc*) toasted too much.
　(d) (*) (*lata*) bore, boring thing; (*discurso*) long boring speech; (*cuento*) tedious tale; **dar el ~** to be a bore, get on everybody's nerves; to be a nuisance.
　(e) (*: comedia etc*) bad play (*o* film *etc*), dreadful piece of work.
　(f) (*Carib: banana*) slice of fried green banana.
　(g) (*Méx*) 50-cent piece.
tostonear* [1a] VTI (*Méx*) to sell at bargain prices.
total ① ADJ (a) total; whole, complete; utter, sheer; *anestésico* general; **una revisión ~ de su teoría** a complete revision of his theory; **ha sido una calamidad ~** it was an utter disaster. (b) (*: excelente*) smashing*, brilliant*; **es un libro ~** it's a super book*.
　② ADV (*en resumen*) in short, all in all; (*así que*) and so; (*al fin*) when all is said and done; **~ que ...** to cut a long story short ..., the upshot of it all was that ...; **~, usted manda** well, you're the boss,

after all; **~ que no fuimos** so we didn't go after all.
[3] NM (a) (*Mat*) (*suma*) total, sum; (*totalidad*) whole; **~ de comprobación** hash total; **el ~ de la población** the whole (of the) population; **en ~** in all.
(b) **en ~** (*fig*) = 2.
(c) (*Com*) total; **~ debe** debit total; **~ haber** assets total.

totalidad NF whole; totality; **en su ~** as a whole, in its entirety; **la ~ de los obreros** all the workers; **la casi ~ de ellos, la práctica ~ de ellos** nearly all of them; **la ~ de la población** the whole (of the) population; **pero el hombre en su ~ se nos escapa** but the whole man eludes us.

totalitario ADJ totalitarian.

totalitarismo NM totalitarianism.

totalizador [1] ADJ all-embracing, all-encompassing.
[2] NM totalizator.

totalizar [1f] [1] VT to totalize, add up.
[2] VI to total, add up to; to come to, amount to.

▼ **totalmente** ADV totally, wholly, completely.

totazo NM (a) (*And: explosión*) bursting, explosion. (b) (*And, Carib: golpe*) bang on the head.

totear [1a] (*And, Carib*) [1] VI to burst, explode.
[2] **totearse** VR (*reventar*) to burst; (*agrietarse*) to crack, split.

tótem NM, PL **tótems** o **tótemes** totem.

totémico ADJ totemic.

totemismo NM totemism.

totopo NM, **totoposte** NM (*CAm, Méx*) fried tortilla.

totora NF (*LAm*) reed.

totoral NM (*LAm*) reedbed.

totoreco* ADJ (*CAm*) thick*, stupid.

totovía NF woodlark.

totuma NF (a) (*And, Carib Bot*) gourd, calabash. (b) (*Cono Sur*) (*cardenal*) bruise; (*chichón*) bump, lump. (c) (*And, Carib, Cono Sur:* *cabeza*) nut*, head; **cortarse ~** (*Carib*) to get one's hair cut.

totumo NM (a) (*And, Carib: árbol*) calabash tree. (b) (*Cono Sur: chichón*) bump on the head.

touroperador(a) NM/F tour-operator.

toxicidad NF toxicity, poisonous nature; poisonous properties.

tóxico [1] ADJ toxic, poisonous.
[2] NM poison, toxic.

toxicodependencia NF drug-addiction.

toxicodependiente NMF drug-addict.

toxicología NF toxicology.

toxicológico ADJ toxicological.

toxicólogo, -a NM/F toxicologist.

toxicomanía NF drug-addiction.

toxicómano [1] ADJ addicted to drugs.
[2] NM, **toxicómana** NF drug addict.

toximia NF toxaemia.

toxina NF toxin.

toxinfección NF poisoning; **~ alimentaria** food poisoning.

tozudez NF obstinacy.

tozudo ADJ obstinate.

traba NF (a) (*gen*) bond, tie; (*de mesa etc*) crosspiece; (*Mec*) clasp, clamp; (*de caballo*) hobble; (*de prisionero*) fetter, shackle; (*Cono Sur*) hair slide.
(b) (*fig: vínculo*) bond, link, tie; (*pey*) hindrance, obstacle; **~s** trammels, shackles; **desembarazado de ~s** free, unrestrained; **poner ~s a** to shackle; to restrain, check; **ponerse ~s** to place restrictions on o.s., limit one's own freedom to act.
(c) (*Carib, Méx: de gallos*) cockfight; cockpit.

trabacuenta NM mistake, miscalculation; **andar con ~s** to be engaged in endless controversies.

trabado ADJ (a) (*unido*) joined; (*vinculado*) linked; *discurso etc* coherent, well constructed. (b) (*fig*) strong, tough. (c) (*And: bizco*) cross-eyed. (d) (*Méx: tartamudo*) stammering.

trabajado ADJ (a) *persona* worn out, weary from overwork. (b) (*Arte etc*) carefully worked, elaborately fashioned; (*pey*) forced, strained, artificial.

trabajador [1] ADJ hard-working, industrious.
[2] NM, **trabajadora** NF worker; labourer; (*Pol*) worker; **~ autónomo** self-employed person; freelance; **~ por cuenta ajena** employee, employed person; **~ por cuenta propia** self-employed person; freelance; **~ eventual** casual worker; **~ portuario** docker; **~ social** social worker.

trabajar [1a] [1] VT (a) *tierra* to work, till; *madera etc* to work; *masa* to knead; *ingredientes* to mix, stir, work in.
(b) *estudio, tema* to work at, work on; *aspecto, detalle* to give special attention to, to work to bring out; *negocio, proyecto etc* to work at, carry forward, pursue, follow up; (*Com*) *géneros* to run a line in, deal particularly with, handle; **estoy trabajando el latín** I am working away at Latin; **es mi colega quien trabaja esos géneros** it is my colleague who handles that line; **el pintor ha trabajado muy bien los**

árboles the painter has taken special care over the trees.
(c) *caballo* to train.
(d) *persona* to work, drive, push.
(e) *persona* (*fig*) to work on, get to work on, persuade; **trabaja a su tía para sacarle los ahorros** he's working on his aunt in order to get hold of her savings.
(f) *mente etc* to trouble, bother.
[2] VI (a) (*gen*) to work (*de* as; *en* in, at); (*Teat etc*) to act, perform; **~ mucho** to work hard; **~ más** to work harder; **~ como un buey** (*etc*) to work like a Trojan; **~ como un condenado** to work like a slave; **~ por horas** to be paid by the hour; to work part-time; **~ al mínimo legal** to work to rule; **~ a ritmo lento** to go slow; **~ a tiempo parcial** to work part-time; **~ por** + *infin* to strive to + *infin*; **hacer ~ dinero etc** to put to good use, make work; *agua, recursos etc* to harness.
(b) (*fig*) **~ con uno para que** + *subj* to work on sb to + *infin*, persuade sb to + *infin*.
(c) (*fig: proceso, tiempo etc*) to work, operate; **el tiempo trabaja a nuestro favor** time is working for us.
(d) (*fig: árbol, suelo etc*) to bear, produce, yield.

trabajo NM (a) (*gen*) work; (*Mec*) work; (*un ~*) job, task; (*Arte, Liter etc*) work, piece of work; (*Inform*) job; **~ autónomo** self-employment; **~ de campo, ~ en el terreno** fieldwork; **~ de clase** schoolwork; **~ de chinos** hard slog; **~ a destajo** piecework; **~ a domicilio** work at home, outwork; **~ en equipo** teamwork; **~ eventual** casual work, temporary work; **~ fijo** permanent job; **~ excesivo, ~ intenso** overwork; **~s forzados** hard labour; **~ intelectual** brainwork; **~ manual** manual labour; **~s manuales** (*Escol etc*) handicraft; **~ nocturno** night work; **~ social** social work; **~ sucio** dirty work; **~ a turnos, ~ por turno** shift work; **ropa de ~** working clothes; **los sin ~** the unemployed; **estar sin ~** to be out of a job, be unemployed; **hacer ~ lento** to go slow; **ir al ~** to go to work.
(b) (*Pol*) labour; the workers, the working class.
(c) **Ministerio de T~** Ministry of Labour; **en T~ dicen que ...** at the Ministry of Labour they say that ...
(d) (*fig*) (*esfuerzo*) effort, labour; (*dificultad*) trouble; **~s** troubles, difficulties, hardships; **ahorrarse el ~** to save o.s. the trouble; **tomarse el ~ de** + *infin* to take the trouble to + *infin*; **lo hizo con mucho ~** he did it after a lot of trouble, it took him a lot of effort to do it; **le cuesta ~** + *infin* he finds it hard to + *infin*, it is difficult for him to + *infin*; **dar ~** to cause trouble; **~ te doy, ~ te mando** it's no easy task, it's a tough job; **tener ~ de sobra para poder** + *infin* to have one's work cut out to + *infin*.

trabajosamente ADV laboriously; painfully.

trabajoso ADJ (a) (*difícil*) hard, laborious; (*doloroso*) painful.
(b) (*Med*) pale, sickly.
(c) (*Cono Sur*) (*exigente*) exacting, demanding; (*astuto*) wily.
(d) (*And*) (*poco amable*) unhelpful; (*malhumorado*) bad-tempered, tetchy.
(e) (*Cono Sur: molesto*) annoying.

trabalenguas NM INVAR tongue-twister.

trabar [1a] [1] VT (a) (*unir*) to join, unite, link.
(b) (*agarrar*) to seize; to lay hold of, catch, grasp; (*sujetar*) to tie down; (*encadenar*) to shackle, fetter; (*Mec*) to clamp, fasten; to jam; *caballo* to hobble.
(c) (*Culin etc*) to thicken.
(d) *sierra* to set.
(e) (*fig*) *conversación, debate etc* to start (up); *batalla* to join, engage in; *amistad* to strike up.
(f) (*fig: impedir*) to impede, hinder, obstruct.
(g) (*CAm, Carib: engañar*) to deceive.
[2] VI (*planta*) to take, strike; (*ancla etc*) to grip, hold.
[3] **trabarse** VR (a) (*con cuerda etc*) to get entangled, get tangled up; (*mecanismo*) to lock, jam; to seize up; **se le traba la lengua** he gets tongue-tied, he stammers.
(b) (*LAm: ~ la lengua*) to get tongue-tied, stammer; (*Carib: perder el hilo*) to lose the thread (of what one is saying).
(c) (*t ~ de palabras*) to get involved in an argument; to wrangle, squabble.

trabazón NF (a) (*Téc*) joining, assembly; (*fig*) link, bond, (close) connection. (b) (*de líquido*) consistency; (*fig*) coherence.

trabilla NF (*tira*) small strap; (*broche*) clasp; (*de cinturón*) belt loop; (*puntada*) dropped stitch.

trabucar [1g] [1] VT to confuse, to jumble up, mix up, mess up; *palabras, sonidos* to switch over, misplace, interchange.
[2] **trabucarse** VR to get all mixed up.

trabuco NM (a) (*Hist*) catapult; (*t ~ naranjero*) blunderbuss; (*prov*) pop-gun.
(b) (*:*) prick*:*.

traca NF string of fireworks; (*fig*) series of noises; row, racket; **es de ~*** it's killingly funny.

trácala NF (a) (*And: gentío*) crowd, mob. (b) (*Carib, Méx: trampa*) trick, ruse. **(c)** (*Méx: tramposo*) trickster.

tracalada NF **(a)** (*LAm: gentío*) crowd; lot, mass; **una ~ de** a lot of, a huge amount of; **a ~s*** by the hundred. **(b)** (*Méx: trampa*) trick, ruse.

tracalero (*Carib, Méx*) ① ADJ (*astuto*) crafty; (*tramposo*) sly, deceitful. ② NM cheat, trickster.

tracamundana* NF **(a)** (*jaleo*) row, rumpus. **(b)** (*cambio*) swap, exchange.

tracatrá* INTERJ no way!*, get away!*

tracción NF traction; haulage; (*Mec*) drive, traction; **~ delantera** front-wheel drive; **~ trasera** rear-wheel drive; **~ integral, ~ total, ~ a las cuatro ruedas** four-wheel drive.

tracería NF tracery.

tracoma NM trachoma.

tractivo ADJ tractive.

tractor ① ADJ: **rueda ~a** drive wheel. ② NM tractor; **~ agrícola** agricultural tractor, farm tractor; **~ (de) oruga** caterpillar tractor.

tractorada NF *demonstration where farmers block the streets with their tractors.*

tractorista NMF tractor-driver.

trad. ABR *de* **traducido** translated, trans.

tradición NF tradition.

tradicional ADJ traditional.

tradicionalidad NF traditionality, traditional character.

tradicionalismo NM traditionalism.

tradicionalista ADJ, NMF traditionalist.

tradicionalmente ADV traditionally.

tráding ['tradin] ① ADJ: **empresa ~ = 2.** ② NF trading company.

traducción NF translation (*a* into, *de* from); (*fig*) rendering, interpretation; **~ asistida por ordenador** computer-assisted translation; **~ automática, ~ automatizada** automatic translation, machine translation; **~ simultánea** simultaneous translation.

traducible ADJ translatable.

traducir [3n] ① VT to translate (*a* into, *de* from); (*fig*) to render, interpret; to express. ② **traducirse** VR: **~ en** (*fig*) to mean in practice; to entail, result in.

traductor(a) NM/F translator; **~ jurado** official translator.

traer [2o] ① VT **(a)** (*gen*) to bring, get, fetch; to carry; to take; **¡trae!, ¡traiga!** hand it over!, give it here!; **el muchacho que trae los periódicos** the lad who brings the papers; **¿has traído el dinero?** have you brought the money? **(b)** (*llevar encima*) to wear; *objeto* to wear, carry, have about one. **(c)** (*imán etc*) to draw, attract, pull. **(d)** (*fig: causar*) to bring (about), cause; to involve; *consecuencias* to bring, have; **~ consigo** to involve, entail; **nos trajo grandes perjuicios** it did us great harm, it caused a lot of trouble for us. **(e)** (*periódico etc*) to carry, have, print; **este periódico no trae nada sobre el particular** this newspaper doesn't carry anything about the affair. **(f)** *autoridad, razón etc* to adduce, bring forward; V **colación, cuento**. **(g)** **~ + ADJ** *etc* to have + ADJ, keep + ADJ; **~ de cabeza a uno** to upset sb, bother sb; **el juego le trae perdido** gambling is his ruin; **la ausencia de noticias me trae muy inquieto** the lack of news is making me very anxious; V **frito, loco** *etc*. **(h)** (*locuciones*) **~ a mal a uno** (*maltratar*) to abuse sb, maltreat sb; (*irritar*) to upset sb; (*exasperar*) to exasperate sb; (*mandar de acá para allá*) to keep sb chasing about all over the place; **~ y llevar a uno** to gossip about sb.

② **traerse** VR **(a)** **~ algo** to have sth (improper) on hand; to be planning sth (disreputable); **los dos se traen algún manejo sucio** the two of them are up to something shady. **(b)** **~ bien** to dress well; to behave properly; **~ mal** to dress shabbily; to behave badly. **(c)** **~las** (*molestar*) to be annoying; (*ser difícil*) to be difficult, be awkward; (*ser excesivo*) to be excessive; **es un problema que se las trae** it's a difficult problem; **ese punto realmente se las trae** that point really is a sticky one; **hace un calor que se las trae** this heat is too much of a good thing; **tiene un padre que se las trae** she has an excessively severe father.

trafagar [1h] VI to bustle about; to be on the move, keep on the go.

tráfago NM **(a)** (*Com*) traffic, trade. **(b)** (*trabajo*) drudgery, toil; routine job. **(c)** (*ajetreo*) bustle, hustle, intense activity.

trafaguear [1a] VI (*Méx*) to bustle about, keep on the go.

traficante NMF trader, dealer (*en* in); **~ de armas** arms dealer; **~ de drogas** (drug) pusher.

traficar [1g] VI **(a)** (*Com*) to trade, deal (*con* with, *en* in); to buy and sell; (*pey*) to traffic (*en* in). **(b)** **~ con** (*pey*) to deal illegally in, do illegal business in. **(c)** (*moverse mucho*) to be on the move, keep on the go; (*viajar*) to travel a lot.

tráfico NM **(a)** (*Com*) trade, business; (*esp pey*) traffic (*en* in); **~ de estupefacientes, ~ en narcóticos** drug-traffic; **~ de influencias** peddling of political favours. **(b)** (*Aut, Ferro etc*) traffic; **~ de carga** (*LAm*), **~ de mercancías** goods traffic; **~ por ferrocarril** rail traffic; **~ rodado** road traffic, vehicular traffic; **T~ pide que ...** the Dirección General de Tráfico asks that ... **(c)** (*LAm: tránsito*) transit, passage.

tragabalas NM INVAR (*Méx*) bully, braggart.

tragaderas NF (*LAm*) slap-up do*, blow-out:.

tragaderas NFPL **(a)** (*garganta*) throat, gullet. **(b)** (*fig*) (*credulidad*) gullibility; (*tolerancia*) tolerance, broad-mindedness; **tener buenas ~** (*crédulo*) to be gullible, be prepared to swallow anything; (*permisivo*) to be very easy-going, be prepared to put up with a lot, be excessively tolerant.

tragadero NM throat, gullet; **la comida fue un ~** (*Méx**) we stuffed ourselves*.

tragador(a) NM/F glutton; **~ de leguas*** great walker.

tragafuegos NMF INVAR fire-eater.

trágala* NMF **(a)** (*glotón*) glutton, greedy sort. **(b)** **cantar el ~ a uno** to mock sb's authority by doing precisely what he has forbidden. **(c)** **es el país del ~** it's the country where you accept something whether you like it or not.

tragaldabas* NMF INVAR glutton, greedy sort.

tragaleguas* NMF INVAR quick walker, great walker.

tragalibros NMF INVAR (*lector*) bookworm; (*empollón*) swot*.

tragallón ADJ (*Cono Sur*) greedy.

tragaluz NM skylight.

tragamonedas NM INVAR = **tragaperras**.

traganíqueles* NM INVAR (*CAm*) = **tragaperras**.

tragantada* NF swig*, mouthful.

tragantón* ADJ greedy, gluttonous.

tragantona* NF **(a)** (*comida*) blow-out:, slap-up meal*. **(b)** (*acto*) (act of) swallowing hard.

tragaperras NM (*a veces* F) INVAR slot-machine; (*en bar etc*) fruit-machine; V t **máquina, tocadiscos** *etc*.

tragar [1h] ① VT **(a)** (*gen*) to swallow; to swallow down, drink up; (*pey: rápidamente etc*) to bolt, devour, swallow whole (*o* quickly); to gulp down, get down. **(b)** (*absorber etc*) to absorb, soak up, drink in; V t **3**. **(c)** *insultos, reprimenda* to have to listen to; *trampa etc* to swallow, fall for, be taken in by; *injusticia etc* to put up with; **hacer ~ algo a uno** to force sb to listen to sth; to force sb to swallow sth, make sb believe sth; **no le puedo ~** I can't stand him, I can't stomach him. ② VI (:) to sleep around*, be free and easy. ③ **tragarse** VR **(a)** (*comer etc*) to swallow; to eat, get down; **se lo tragó entero** he swallowed it whole; **el perro se ha tragado un hueso** the dog has swallowed a bone; **eso me lo trago en dos minutos** I could eat that up in a couple of minutes. **(b)** (*tierra etc*) to absorb, soak up; (*abismo, mar*) to swallow up, engulf; to suck down; *ahorros etc* to swallow up, use up, absorb. **(c)** (*fig*) *hecho desagradable, cuento etc* to swallow; **se tragará todo lo que se le diga** he'll swallow whatever he's told; **ya se lo tenía tragado** he had already learned to live with the idea, he had already prepared himself for that happening; **se las tragó como ruedas de molino** he swallowed it hook, line and sinker; **el árbitro se tragó dos penaltis** the referee did not award two penalties, the referee overlooked two penalties.

tragasables NMF INVAR sword-swallower.

tragasantos NMF INVAR excessively pious person.

tragavenado NM (*And, Carib*) boa constrictor.

tragedia NF tragedy.

trágicamente ADV tragically.

trágico ① ADJ tragic(al); **lo ~ es que ...** the tragedy of it is that ..., the tragic thing about it is that ... ② NM tragedian.

tragicomedia NF tragicomedy.

tragicómico ADJ tragicomic.

trago NM **(a)** (*cantidad etc*) drink, draught; (*bocado*) swallow, mouthful, swig*; sip; **~ largo** long drink; **el ~ del estribo** one for the road; **beber algo de un ~** to drink sth at a gulp; **brindar el ~ a uno** (*LAm*) to stand sb a drink; **echarse un ~** to have a drink, have a swig*; **no vendría mal un ~ de vino** a drop of wine would not come amiss. **(b)** (*bebida en general*) drink, drinking; (*LAm*) hard liquor; **ser demasiado aficionado al ~** to be too fond of the drink. **(c)** (*fig*) **mal ~, ~ amargo** (*rato difícil*) hard time, rough time; (*golpe*) nasty blow; (*desgracia*) misfortune, calamity; **fue un ~ amargo** it was a cruel blow; **nos quedaba todavía el ~ más amargo** the worst of it was still to come. **(d)** **hacer algo a ~s** to do sth bit by bit.

tragón ADJ greedy, gluttonous.

tragona: ADJ (*Esp*) easy, promiscuous.

traguear* [1a] ① VTI (*CAm, Méx: beber*) to drink; (*Carib*) to get sloshed*.

2 traguearse VR (*And, CAm, Méx*) to get sloshed*.
trai NM (*Cono Sur: rugby*) try.
traición NF (*gen*) treachery; (*Jur etc*) treason; (*una ~*) betrayal, act of treason, treacherous act; **alta ~** high treason; **matar a uno a ~** to kill sb treacherously; **hacer ~ a uno** to betray sb.
traicionar [1a] VT to betray (*t fig*).
traicionero ADJ treacherous.
traída NF carrying, bringing; **~ de aguas** water supply.
traído 1 ADJ (a) (*usado*) worn, old, threadbare. (b) **~ y llevado** (*fig*) well-worn, trite, hackneyed.
2 NMPL: **~s** (*And*) presents.
traidor 1 ADJ *persona* treacherous; *acto* treasonable.
2 NM traitor; betrayer; (*Teat*) villain, bad character.
traidora NF traitress; betrayer.
traidoramente ADV treacherously, traitorously.
traiga *etc* V **traer.**
trailer, tráiler NM, PL **~s** (a) (*Cine*) trailer. (b) (*Aut: caravana*) caravan, trailer (*US*); (*de camión*) trailer, trailer unit.
traílla NF (a) (*Téc*) scraper, leveller; (*Agr*) harrow. (b) (*de perro*) lead, leash; (*azote*) lash. (c) (*equipo de perros*) team of dogs.
traillar [1a] VT to scrape; to level; (*Agr*) to harrow.
traína NF, **traiña** NF sardine-fishing net, dragnet.
trainera NF small fishing-boat.
Trajano NM Trajan.
traje¹ *etc* V **traer.**
traje² NM (*gen*) dress, costume; (*de hombre*) suit; (*esp And, Cono Sur: de mujer*) woman's dress; (*fig*) garb, guise; **~ de agua** wetsuit; **~ de baño** bathing-costume, swimming-costume, swimsuit; **~ de calle** lounge suit; **un policía en ~ de calle** a policeman in plain clothes; **~ de campaña** battledress; **~ de casa** casual dress; **~ de ceremonia, ~ de etiqueta** full dress; dress suit, evening dress; **~ (de) chaqueta** suit, skirt and jacket; **~ de cóctel** cocktail dress; **~ de cuartel** (*Mil*) undress; **~ de época** period costume; **~ espacial** spacesuit; **en ~ de Eva** in her birthday suit; **~ de faena** fatigues; **~ hecho** ready-made suit; **~ (hecho) a la medida** made-to-measure suit; **~ isotérmico** wetsuit; **~ largo** evening gown; **~ de luces** bullfighter's costume; **~ de madera*** coffin, box*; **~ de malla** tights; **~ de montar** riding-habit; **~ de noche** evening dress; **~ de novia** wedding-dress, bridal gown; **~ de oficina** business suit; **~ de paisano** (*Esp*) civilian clothes; **~ pantalón** trouser suit; **~ de playa** sunsuit; **~ regional** regional costume, regional dress; **~ serio** business suit; **cortar un ~ a uno** to gossip about sb.
trajeado ADJ: **ir bien ~** to be well dressed, be well turned out; **estar ~ de** to be dressed in; (*hum*) to be got up in, be rigged out in; **estar bien ~ para la temporada** to be well equipped with clothes for the season.
trajear [1a] 1 VT to clothe, dress (*de* in); (*hum*) to get up, rig out (*de* in).
2 trajearse VR to dress up; to provide o.s. with clothes.
trajelarse‡ [1a] VR: **~ una botella*** to knock a bottle back*.
traje-pantalón NM, PL **trajes-pantalón** trouser suit.
trajera *etc* V **traer.**
traje-sastre NM, PL **trajes-sastre** tailor-made suit.
trajín NM (a) (*acarreo*) haulage, carriage, transport.
(b) (*) (*ir y venir*) coming and going, movement; (*ajetreo*) hustle, bustle, commotion; (*jaleo*) fuss.
(c) **trajines** (*: *actividades*) affairs, (suspicious) doings, goings-on; **trajines de la casa** household chores.
trajinado ADJ *tema etc* well-worked, overworked, trite.
trajinante NM (a) carrier, carter; haulage contractor. (b) (*pey**) person who indulges in a lot of useless activity.
trajinar [1a] 1 VT (a) (*acarrear*) to carry, cart; to transport.
(b) (*Cono Sur: estafar*) to swindle, deceive.
(c) (*Cono Sur: registrar*) to search.
(d) (‡) to fuck‡.
2 VI (*ajetrearse*) to bustle about; (*viajar*) to travel around a lot; (*moverse mucho*) to be on the go, keep on the move.
trajinería NF carriage; haulage.
trajinista NMF (*Carib, Cono Sur*) busybody, snooper.
tralla NF whipcord, whiplash; lash.
trallazo NM (a) (*de látigo*) crack of a whip; lash. (b) (*: *bronca*) telling-off*. (c) (*Dep*) fierce shot, hard shot.
trama NF (a) (*Téc*) weft, woof. (b) (*fig: vínculo*) connection, link; (*correlación*) correlation. (c) (*fig: complot*) plot, scheme, intrigue; (*Liter*) plot. (d) (*Tip*) shading; area.
tramar [1a] 1 VT (a) (*Téc*) to weave.
(b) (*fig*) to plan, plot; to scheme for, intrigue for; *complot* to lay, hatch; **están tramando algo** they're up to sth; **¿qué estarán tramando?** I wonder what they're up to?
2 tramarse VR: **algo se está tramando** (*fig*) there's sth afoot, there's sth going on.
trambucar [1g] VI (a) (*And, Carib: naufragar*) to be shipwrecked. (b)

(*Carib*: enloquecer*) to go out of one's mind, lose one's marbles‡.
trambuque NM (*And*) shipwreck.
trámil ADJ (*Cono Sur*) awkward, clumsy.
tramitación (*V* VT) NF transaction; negotiation; steps, procedure; handling.
tramitar [1a] VT (*despachar*) to transact; (*negociar*) to negotiate; (*proseguir*) to proceed with, carry forward; (*manejar*) to handle.
trámite NM (*etapa*) step, stage; (*negocio*) transaction; **~s** (*procedimientos*) procedure; (*formalidades*) formalities; (*pey*) red tape; (*Jur*) proceedings; **~s de costumbre** usual channels; **~s oficiales** official channels; **~ de quejas** grievance procedure; **los ~s para la obtención de un visado** the procedure for obtaining a visa; **para acortar los ~s de costumbre lo hacemos así** in order to get it quickly through the usual procedure we do it this way; **hacer los ~s para un viaje** to make the arrangements for a journey; **el gobierno se limita a resolver asuntos de ~** the government is dealing only with ordinary ongoing business; **en ~** in hand; **lo tenemos en ~** we have the matter in hand, we are pursuing the matter; **el proyecto de ley está en ~ parlamentario** the bill is going through parliament; **'patente en ~'** 'patent applied for'.
tramo NM (a) (*sección*) section, stretch; (*de carretera etc*) section, length; (*de puente*) span; (*de escalera*) flight; **~ cronometrado** time trial. (b) (*Agr*) plot. (c) (*Fin*) share issue.
tramontana NF (a) (*viento*) north wind; (*dirección*) north. (b) (*fig: vanidad*) conceit, pride; (*lujo*) luxury. (c) **perder la ~*** to lose one's head.
tramontar [1a] 1 VI (*sol*) to sink behind the mountains.
2 tramontarse VR to escape over the mountains.
tramoya NF (a) (*Teat*) piece of stage machinery. (b) (*estafa*) trick, scheme, swindle; (*parte oculta*) concealed part, secret part (of a deal). (c) **armar una ~*** to kick up a fuss.
tramoyar [1a] VT (*And, Carib*) to swindle.
tramoyero ADJ (*CAm, Carib*) tricky, sharp.
tramoyista NM (a) (*Teat*) scene shifter, stagehand. (b) (*estafador*) swindler, trickster; (*farsante*) humbug; (*impostor*) impostor; (*intrigante*) schemer.
trampa NF (a) (*escotilla*) trapdoor; hatch; (*bragueta*) fly.
(b) (*Caza etc*) trap; snare; (*Golf*) bunker; (*fig*) snare; catch, pitfall; **~ cazabobos, ~ explosiva** booby-trap; **~ de fuera de juego** offside trap; **~ mortal** deathtrap; **~ para ratas** rat-trap; **caer en la ~** to fall for it, fall into the trap; **coger a alguien en la ~** to catch sb red-handed; **hay ~** there's a catch in it; there's something fishy here*; **esto es sin ~ ni cartón** this is the real thing; **este juego no tiene ~ ni cartón** there are no catches in this game.
(c) (*juego de manos*) conjuring trick; **hacer ~s** to juggle, conjure.
(d) (*fig*) (*estafa*) trick, swindle, fraud; (*chanchullo*) wangle*, fiddle*; (*broma*) hoax; (*Fin etc*) racket; **hacer ~s** to cheat; to be on the fiddle*; **hicieron (una) ~ con los votos** they fiddled the voting*, they juggled with the votes; V **ley** (a).
(e) (*Com*) bad debt.
trampantojo* NM (*juego de manos*) sleight of hand, trick; (*fig: chanchullo*) fiddle*, cheat; (*método poco limpio*) underhand method.
trampear [1a] 1 VT to cheat, swindle.
2 VI (a) to cheat; to get money by false pretences. (b) (*ir tirando*) to manage, get by; (*vestido, zapatos etc*) to last out.
trampería NF = **tramposería.**
trampero 1 ADJ (*CAm, Cono Sur, Méx*) = **tramposo.**
2 NM (a) (*persona*) trapper. (b) (*Cono Sur: trampa*) trap for birds.
trampilla NF (a) (*mirilla*) peephole. (b) (*escotilla*) trap-door, hatchway; (*bragueta*) fly; **~ de carburante** filler-cap, fuel-cap.
trampista NM = **tramposo 2.**
trampolín NM (*de piscina*) springboard, diving-board; (*Dep*) trampoline; (*de esquí*) ski-jump.
trampón* ADJ crooked*.
tramposería NF crookedness*; guile, deceit.
tramposo 1 ADJ crooked*, tricky, swindling; **pregunta tramposa** catch question.
2 NM, **tramposa** NF crook*, twister, swindler; (*tahur*) cardsharper; (*Fin*) bad payer.
tranca NF (a) (*porra*) stick, cudgel, club; (*Méx**) **~s** legs. (b) (*viga*) beam, pole; (*de puerta, ventana*) bar. (c) = **tranquera** (b). (d) (*: *borrachera*) drunken spree, binge*; **tener una ~** (*LAm*) to be drunk. (e) (*Cono Sur: de escopeta etc*) safety-catch. (f) (*Carib*) dollar, peso. (g) (*Carib Aut*) traffic-jam. (h) (‡: *pene*) prick‡. (i) **a ~s y barrancas** with great difficulty, against many obstacles; through fire and water. (j) **saltar las ~s** (*Méx*) to rebel; to lose one's patience. (k) (*Cono Sur**) complex, neurosis.
trancada NF stride; **en dos ~s** in a couple of strides; (*fig*) in a couple of ticks.
trancantrulla NF (*Cono Sur*) trick, fraud.
trancaperros NM INVAR (*Carib*) row, scrap.
trancar [1g] 1 VT (a) *puerta, ventana* to bar. (b) (*Carib Aut etc*) to box

in, block, shut in. [2] VI to stride along.

[3] **trancarse** VR (a) (*Carib*) to get drunk. (b) (*Cono Sur, Méx Med*) to be constipated.

trancazo NM (a) (*golpe*) blow, bang (with a stick). (b) (*Med**) flu.

trance NM (a) (*momento difícil*) (difficult) moment, (awkward) juncture, (tough) situation; critical juncture, moment of peril; ~ **mortal, último** ~, **postrer** ~ last moments, dying moments; **a todo** ~ at all costs; **estar en** ~ **de muerte** to be at the point of death, be at death's door; **estar en** ~ **de** + *infin* to be on the point of + *ger*, be in process of + *ger*; **puesto en tal** ~ placed in such a situation. (b) (*estado hipnótico*) hypnotic state; (*estado drogado*) drugged condition; (*de médium*) (spiritualistic) trance; (*Rel*) trance, ecstasy.

tranco NM (a) (*paso*) stride, big step; **a** ~**s*** pell-mell, hastily, in a rush; **andar a** ~s to walk with long strides, take big steps; **en dos** ~s in a couple of strides; (*fig*) in a couple of ticks. (b) (*Arquit*) threshold.

trancón NM (*Colombia: Aut*) traffic jam.

tranque NM (*Cono Sur*) dam; reservoir.

tranquera NF (a) (*cercado*) palisade, fence. (b) (*LAm: para ganado*) cattle-gate.

tranquero NM (*And, Carib, Cono Sur*) = **tranquera** (b).

tranqui* [1] EXCL cool it!*, calm down!
[2] ADJ = **tranquilo**.

tranquilamente ADV calmly; peacefully; quietly.

tranquilidad (*V ADJ*) NF stillness, calmness, tranquillity; peacefulness; quietness; freedom from anxiety; unruffled state; **dijo con toda** ~ he said calmly; **perder la** ~ to lose patience; to get worked up.

tranquilino NM (*LAm*) drunkard.

tranquilizador ADJ *música etc* soothing; lulling; *hecho etc* reassuring.

tranquilizadoramente ADV soothingly; reassuringly.

tranquilizante [1] ADJ = **tranquilizador**.
[2] NM (*Med*) tranquillizer.

tranquilizar [1f] [1] VT to calm, quieten, still; *mente* to reassure, relieve, set at ease; *persona* to calm down; to reassure.
[2] **tranquilizarse** VR to calm down; to stop worrying; **¡tranquilícese!** calm yourself!; don't worry!, never fear!

tranquilla NF (a) (*pasador*) latch; pin. (b) (*en conversación*) trap, catch. (c) (*And*) hindrance, obstacle.

tranquillo* NM knack; **coger el** ~ **a un problema** to get the hang of a problem, find the knack of solving a problem.

tranquilo ADJ (a) (*gen*) still, calm, tranquil; peaceful; quiet; *mar etc* calm; *mente* calm, free of worry, untroubled; *carácter, estado* calm, unruffled; **dejar a uno** ~ to leave sb alone; **ir con la conciencia tranquila** to go with a clear conscience; **¡estad** ~**s!** don't worry!; keep calm!; **tú estáte** ~ **hasta que yo vuelva** you stay put till I come back, you just sit tight till I get back; **¡tú,** ~**!*** calm down!, take it easy!; **mientras no lo hagan, todos** ~s provided they don't do it, everyone's happy; **se quedó tan** ~ he didn't bat an eyelid. (b) (*pey*) thoughtless, unreliable, inconsiderate; **es un tío de lo más** ~ he's an utterly inconsiderate chap.

tranquis* ADJ: **hacer algo en plan** ~ to do sth on the quiet.

tranquiza NF (*And, Méx*) beating.

Trans. (*Com*) ABR *de* **transferencia** transfer.

trans... PREF trans...; *V t* **tras...**

transacción NF (a) (*Com etc*) transaction; deal, bargain; ~ **comercial** business deal. (b) (*componenda*) compromise, compromise settlement; **llegar a una** ~ to reach a compromise.

transandino ADJ trans-Andean.

transar¹ [1a] [1] VT (*Cono Sur*) to trade.
[2] VI (*LAm*) = **transigir**.

transar² [1a] VT (*Méx*) to cheat, swindle, defraud.

transatlántico [1] ADJ *cable etc* transatlantic; *travesía* Atlantic; **los países** ~s the countries on the other side of the Atlantic.
[2] NM (*Náut*) liner.

transbordador NM (a) (*Náut*) ferry; (*Aer*) shuttle; ~ **para coches** car ferry; ~ **espacial** space shuttle. (b) **puente** ~ transporter bridge. (c) ~ **funicular** cable railway.

transbordar [1a] [1] VT to transfer, move across, switch; (*Náut*) to tranship; (*a través de río etc*) to ferry across.
[2] VI *y* **transbordarse** VR (*Ferro etc*) to change.

transbordo NM (a) (*traslado*) transfer; move, switch; (*Náut*) transhipment; ferrying. (b) (*Ferro etc*) change; **hacer** ~, **realizar** ~ to change (*en* at).

transcender [2g] VT = **trascender**.

transceptor NM transceiver.

transcribir [3a; PTP **transcrito**] VT (*copiar*) to transcribe; (*de alfabeto distinto*) to transliterate.

transcripción NF transcription; transliteration.

transcultural ADJ cross-cultural.

transculturización NF cross-cultural influence(s); transculturation.

transcurrir [3a] VI (a) (*tiempo*) to pass, go by, elapse; **han transcu-**

rrido **7 años** 7 years have passed. (b) (*suceso etc*) to be, turn out; **la tarde transcurrió aburrida** the evening was boring; **las fiestas transcurren con gran alegría** the festivities are being held in a very happy atmosphere, the celebrations are turning out to be very merry.

transcurso NM: ~ **del tiempo** course of time, passing of time, lapse of time; **en el** ~ **de 8 días** in the course of a week, in the space of a week; **en el** ~ **de los años** in the course of the years.

transecto NM transect.

transepto NM transept.

transeúnte [1] ADJ transient, transitory; *miembro etc* temporary.
[2] NMF (*en la calle etc*) passer-by; (*no permanente*) temporary member (*o inhabitant etc*), non-resident.

transexual ADJ, NMF transsexual.

transexualidad NF transsexuality.

transexualismo NM transsexualism.

transferencia NF transference; (*Dep, Jur*) transfer; ~ **bancaria** banker's order; bank transfer; ~ **por cable,** ~ **cablegráfica** cable transfer; ~ **de crédito** credit transfer; ~ **electrónica de fondos** electronic funds transfer.

transferible ADJ transferable.

transferir [3i] VT (a) (*trasladar*) to transfer. (b) (*aplazar*) to postpone.

transfiguración NF transfiguration.

transfigurar [1a] VT to transfigure (*en* into).

transformable ADJ transformable; (*Aut*) convertible.

transformación NF transformation (*en* into); change, conversion (*en* into); change-over; (*Rugby*) conversion.

transformacional ADJ transformational.

transformador NM (*Elec*) transformer.

transformar [1a] VT to transform (*en* into); to change, convert (*en* into); (*Dep*) *penalti* to convert.

transformismo NM (a) (*Bio*) evolution, transmutation. (b) (*sexual*) transvestism.

transformista NMF (a) (*Teat*) quick-change artist(e). (b) (*sexual*) transvestite.

transfronterizo ADJ cross-border *atr*; **seguridad transfronteriza** cross-border security.

tránsfuga NMF (*Mil*) deserter; (*Pol*) (*de partido*) turncoat; (*de nación*) defector.

transfuguismo NM tendency to desert (*o* defect).

transfundir [3a] VT (a) *sangre etc* to transfuse. (b) *noticia* to tell, spread, disseminate.

transfusión NF transfusion; ~ **de sangre** blood transfusion; **hacer una** ~ **de sangre a uno** to give sb a blood transfusion.

transgénico ADJ transgenic.

transgredir [3a: *defectivo*] VTI to transgress.

transgresión NF transgression.

transgresor(a) NM/F transgressor.

transiberiano ADJ trans-Siberian.

transición NF transition (*a* to, *de* from); **período de** ~ transitional period; **la** ~ (*Esp Pol*) the transition to democracy in Spain after Franco's death (1975).

TRANSICIÓN A LA DEMOCRACIA

*The death of General Franco on 20 November 1975 ushered in a period of transition to democracy in Spain which was to end with the democratic transfer of power to the **PSOE** (Spanish Socialist Party) on November 28, 1982. On 22 November 1975 Juan Carlos I was proclaimed king. Though initially handicapped by a constitutional system devised by Franco, the King was able to appoint the **aperturista** Adolfo Suárez as Prime Minister in July 1976. Within three months Suárez rushed through a political reform bill introducing universal suffrage and a two-chamber parliament which was put to a referendum and endorsed by 94.2% of the electorate. Political parties were legalized and elections were held on 15 June 1977. Suárez and his party, the newly-formed **UCD** (**Unión de Centro Democrático**) won without gaining an overall majority. Through accords with the other parties - the **Pactos de la Moncloa** - they were able to manage the transitional process, which included the drafting and endorsement of the 1978 Constitution. The **UCD** went on to win the next general election in 1979 by an even tighter margin. Splits within the party finally led to Suárez's resignation in 1981, which was seized upon by sections of the military as the opportunity for a coup. Early general elections in November 1982 led to a landslide victory for the Socialists.*
⏵ *See also* APERTURISMO , 23-F

transicional ADJ transitional.

transido ADJ: ~ **de angustia** beset with anxiety; ~ **de dolor** racked with pain; ~ **de frío** frozen to the marrow; ~ **de hambre** overcome with hunger.

transigencia NF (a) (*acto*) compromise; yielding. (b) (*actitud etc*) accommodating attitude, spirit of compromise.

transigente ADJ accommodating, compromising; tolerant.

transigir [3c] **1** VT: ~ **un pleito** (*Jur*) to settle (a suit) out of court. **2** VI (*llegar a un acuerdo*) to compromise (*con* with; *en cuanto a* on, about); (*ceder*) to give way, yield, make concessions; ~ **en** + *infin* to agree to + *infin*; **yo no transijo con tales abusos** I cannot tolerate such abuses, I cannot compromise with such abuses; **hemos transigido con la demanda popular** we have bowed to the people's demand.

Transilvania NF Transylvania.

transistor NM transistor.

transistorizado ADJ transistorized.

transitable ADJ *camino etc* passable.

transitar [1a] VI to go, go from place to place, travel; ~ **por** to go along, pass along.

transitivamente ADV transitively.

transitivo ADJ transitive.

tránsito NM **(a)** (*acto*) transit, passage, movement; **'se prohíbe el ~'** 'no thoroughfare'; **estar de ~** to be in transit, be passing through; **el ~ de este camino presenta dificultades** this road has its problems, the going on this road is not easy. **(b)** (*Aut etc*) movement, traffic; ~ **rodado** wheeled traffic, vehicular traffic; **calle de mucho ~** busy street; **horas de máximo ~** rush hours, peak traffic hours. **(c)** (*traslado*) move, transfer. **(d)** (*Rel*) passing, death. **(e)** (*parada*) stop; stopping place; **hacer ~** to make a stop. **(f)** (*pasillo*) passageway.

transitoriedad NF transience.

transitorio ADJ (*pasajero*) transitory; fleeting; (*provisional*) temporary; *período etc* transitional, of transition.

transliteración NF transliteration.

transliterar [1a] VT to transliterate.

translucidez NF translucence.

translúcido ADJ translucent.

transmarino ADJ overseas.

transmigración NF migration, transmigration.

transmigrar [1a] VI to migrate, transmigrate.

transmisibilidad NF (*Med*) contagiousness, ability to be transmitted.

transmisible ADJ transmissible; (*Med*) contagious.

transmisión NF **(a)** (*acto*) transmission; (*Jur etc*) transfer; ~ **de dominio** (*Jur*) transfer of ownership. **(b)** (*Mec*) transmission. **(c)** (*Elec*) transmission; (*Rad, TV*) transmission, broadcast(ing); ~ **en circuito** hookup; ~ **en diferido** recorded programme, repeat broadcast; ~ **exterior** outside broadcast; ~ **por satélite** satellite broadcasting. **(d)** **transmisiones** (*Mil*) signals (corps). **(e)** (*Inform*) ~ **de datos** data transmission; ~ **de datos en paralelo** parallel data transmission; ~ **de datos en serie** serial data transmission; **media ~ bidireccional** half duplex; **plena ~ bidireccional** full duplex.

transmisor **1** ADJ transmitting; **aparato ~** transmitter; **estación ~a** transmitter. **2** NM transmitter.

transmisora NF transmitter; radio relay station.

transmisor-receptor NM transceiver; (*portátil*) walkie-talkie.

▼ **transmitir** [3a] VTI to transmit (*a* to); (*Rad, TV*) to transmit, broadcast; *posesiones* to pass on, hand down; (*Jur*) to transfer (*a* to); (*Med*) *enfermedad* to give, infect with; *gérmenes* to carry.

transmutable ADJ transmutable.

transmutación NF transmutation.

transmutar [1a] VT to transmute (*en* into).

transnacional **1** ADJ international, transnational; that crosses national borders. **2** NF multinational (company).

transoceánico ADJ transoceanic.

transparencia NF **(a)** transparency; clarity, clearness; ~ **informativa** willingness to disclose information. **(b)** (*Fot*) slide, transparency. **(c)** (*fig*) (*franqueza*) openness; (*como sistema*) open government.

transparentar [1a] **1** VT to reveal, allow to be seen; *emoción etc* to show, reveal, betray. **2** VI to be transparent; to allow the contents (*etc*) to show through. **3** **transparentarse** VR **(a)** (*vidrio etc*) to be transparent, be clear; (*objeto etc*) to show through, be able to be seen. **(b)** (*fig*) to show clearly, become perceptible; **se transparentaba su verdadera intención** his real intention became plain, his true intention was betrayed. **(c)** (*: ropa*) to become threadbare, show what is underneath. **(d)** (*: persona*) to be dreadfully thin.

transparente **1** ADJ transparent; *aire* clear; *vestido* diaphanous, filmy; (*fig*) transparent, clear, plain. **2** NM curtain, blind, shade.

transpiración NF perspiration; (*Bot*) transpiration.

transpirar [1a] VI **(a)** (*sudar*) to perspire; (*Bot*) to transpire; (*líquido*) to seep through, ooze out. **(b)** (*fig*) to transpire, become known.

transpirenaico ADJ, **transpireneo** ADJ *ruta etc* trans-Pyrenean; *tráfico* passing through (o over) the Pyrenees; **la nación transpirenaica** the country on the other side of the Pyrenees.

transplantar *etc* V **trasplantar** *etc*.

transpondedor NM transponder.

transponer [2q] **1** VT **(a)** (*gen*) to transpose; (*cambiar de sitio*) to switch over, move about, change the places of. **(b)** (*trasplantar*) to transplant. **(c)** ~ **la esquina** to disappear round the corner. **2** VI (*desaparecer*) to disappear from view; (*ir más allá*) to go beyond, get past; (*sol*) to go down, go behind the mountain (*etc*). **3** **transponerse** VR **(a)** (*cambiar de sitio*) to change places. **(b)** (*esconderse*) to hide, hide behind sth; (*sol*) to go down, go behind the mountain (*etc*). **(c)** (*dormirse*) to doze (off).

transportable ADJ transportable; **fácilmente ~** easily carried, easily transported.

transportación NF transportation.

transportador NM **(a)** (*Mec*) conveyor, transporter; ~ **de banda**, ~ **de correa** conveyor belt. **(b)** (*Mat*) protractor.

transportar [1a] **1** VT **(a)** (*acarrear*) to transport; to haul, carry, take; (*Náut*) to ship; (*cable etc*) to carry, transmit; **el avión podrá ~ 400 pasajeros** the plane will be able to carry 400 passengers. **(b)** *diseño etc* to transfer (*a* to). **(c)** (*Mús*) to transpose. **2** **transportarse** VR (*fig*) to get carried away, be enraptured.

transporte NM **(a)** (*acto*) transport; haulage, carriage; ~**s** transport, transportation; (*empresa*) haulage business, transport company; removals company; ~ **por carretera** road transport; ~ **colectivo**, ~ **público** public transport; ~ **escolar** school buses; **Ministerio de T~s** Ministry of Transport. **(b)** (*de diseño etc*) transfer. **(c)** (*Náut*) transport, troopship. **(d)** (*Méx*) vehicle. **(e)** (*fig*) transport, rapture, ecstasy.

transportista NM (*Aer etc*) carrier; (*Aut*) haulier, haulage contractor; freight transporter.

transposición NF transposition (*t Mús*).

transpuesto PTP *de* **transponer**.

transustanciación NF transubstantiation.

transustanciar [1b] VT to transubstantiate.

transvasar [1a] VT = **trasvasar**.

transversal **1** ADJ transverse, cross; oblique; **calle ~** cross street; **otra calle ~ de la calle mayor** another street which crosses the high street. **2** NF cross street.

transversalmente ADV transversely, across; obliquely.

transverso ADJ = **transversal 1**.

transvestido, -a ADJ, NM/F transvestite.

transvestismo NM transvestism.

tranvía NM (*vehículo*) tram, tramcar, streetcar (*US*); (*ferro*) local train; (*sistema*) tramway.

trapacear [1a] VI to cheat, be on the fiddle*; to run a racket; to make mischief.

trapacería NF **(a)** (*trampa*) racket*, fiddle*, swindle; **(b)** (*chisme*) piece of gossip, malicious tale.

trapacero **1** ADJ dishonest, swindling. **2** NM, **trapacera** NF **(a)** (*tramposo*) cheat, swindler; racketeer. **(b)** (*chismoso*) gossip, mischief-maker.

trapacista NM = **trapacero 2**.

trapajoso ADJ **(a)** *ropa* shabby, ragged. **(b)** *pronunciación* defective; incorrect; *persona* who talks incorrectly; who has a speech defect.

trápala **1** NF **(a)** (*de caballo*) clatter, noise of hooves, clip-clop, hoofbeat. **(b)** (*: jaleo*) row, uproar, shindy*. **(c)** (*: trampa*) swindle. **2** NM (*garrulidad*) talkativeness, garrulity. **3** NMF (*) **(a)** (*parlanchín*) chatterbox. **(b)** (*tramposo*) cheat, trickster, swindler.

trapalear [1a] VI **(a)** (*caballo*) to clatter, beat its hooves, clip-clop; (*persona*) to clatter, go clattering along. **(b)** (*: parlotear*) to chatter, jabber. **(c)** (*mentir*) to fib, lie; (*trampear*) to be on the fiddle*.

trapalero ADJ (*Carib*) = **trapalón**.

trapalón ADJ (*mentiroso*) lying; (*tramposo*) dishonest, swindling.

trapalonear [1a] VI (*Cono Sur*) = **trapalear** (c).

trapatiesta NF (*jaleo*) commotion, shindy*; (*pelea*) roughhouse*.

trapaza NF = **trapacería**.

trapeador NM (*CAm, Cono Sur, Méx*) floor mop.

trapear [1a] VT **(a)** (*LAm*) *suelo* to mop. **(b)** (*CAm**) (*pegar*) to beat, tan*; (*fig: insultar*) to insult; (*fig: regañar*) to tick off*.

trapecio NM trapeze; (*Mat*) trapezium.

trapecista NMF trapeze artist(e).

trapería NF (a) (*trapos*) rags; (*ropa vieja*) old clothes. (b) (*tienda*) old-clothes shop; junk shop.

trapero NM ragman.

trapezoide NM trapezoid.

trapicar [1g] VI (*Cono Sur*) (*comida*) to taste very hot; (*herida etc*) to sting, smart.

trapichar [1a] VT (*And, Méx*) to smuggle (in); (*Carib*) to deal in.

trapiche NM (*de aceite*) olive-oil press; (*de azúcar*) sugar mill; (*And, Cono Sur: Min*) ore-crusher.

trapichear [1a] ① VT to deal in, trade in.
② VI (a) (*trampear*) to be on the fiddle*; (*andar en malos pasos*) to be mixed up in something shady; (*intrigar*) to plot, scheme. (b) (*Cono Sur: comerciar*) to scrape a living by buying and selling.

trapicheo ① NM fiddle*, shady deal.
② NMPL: ~s (a) (*Com*) dealing, trading; (*pey: trampas*) fiddles*, shady dealing; (*intrigas*) plots, schemes, tricks. (b) (*Cono Sur: comercio*) small-time business. (c) (*Méx*) clandestine affair.

trapichero NM (a) (*LAm: obrero*) sugar-mill worker. (b) (*And, Carib*: *entrometido*) busybody. (c) (*Cono Sur*:* Com*) small-time dealer.

trapiento ADJ ragged, tattered.

trapillo NM: **estar de ~, ir de ~** to be dressed in ordinary clothes, be informally dressed.

trapío NM (a) (*atractivo*) charm; (*garbo*) elegant carriage, attractive way of moving; **tener buen ~** to have a fine presence, carry o.s. elegantly, move beautifully; (*fig*) to have real class. (b) (*de toro*) fine appearance.

trapisonda NF (a) (*jaleo*) row, commotion; shindy*; (*pelea*) brawl, scuffle. (b) (*estafa*) swindle; (*asunto sucio*) monkey business*, shady affair, fiddle*; (*intriga*) intrigue.

trapisondear [1a] VI (*intrigar*) to scheme, plot, intrigue; (*trampear*) to be on the fiddle*.

trapisondeo NM, **trapisondería** NF scheming, plotting, intrigues; fiddling*, wangling*.

trapisondista NMF schemer, intriguer; fiddler*, wangler*.

trapito NM (*trapo*) rag; ~s (*: ropa*) clothes; ~s **de cristianar** Sunday best, glad rags; **él y sus ~s** he and all his troubles.

trapo NM (a) (*paño*) rag; **dejar a uno hecho un ~, poner a uno como un ~** (*: reprender*) to give sb a dressing-down*; to haul sb over the coals; (*en debate*) to flatten sb, give sb a battering; to shower abuse on sb.
(b) (*t ~ del polvo*) duster; (*de limpiar*) rag, cleaning cloth; **~ de fregar** dishcloth; **pasar un ~ por algo** to give sth a wipe over (*o* down).
(c) (*Taur*) cape.
(d) (*: vestidos*) ~s (woman's) clothes, dresses; **gasta una barbaridad en ~s** she spends an awful lot on clothes; **lavar los ~s sucios ante el mundo entero** to wash one's dirty linen in public; **trataron de ocultar los ~s sucios** (*fig*) they tried to sweep it under the carpet; **sacar los ~s** (**a relucir**) to let fly, tell a lot of home truths; to bring out all the skeletons in the cupboard.
(e) (*Náut*) canvas, sails; **a todo ~** with all sails set, under full sail; (*fig*) quickly; **llorar** (*etc*) **a todo ~** to cry (*etc*) uncontrollably.
(f) **soltar el ~** (**a llorar**) to burst into tears; **soltar el ~** (**a reír**) to burst out laughing, collapse in helpless laughter.
(g) (*: velocidad*) speed; **a todo ~** at full speed, flat-out; **¡qué ~ llevaba!** what a lick he was going at!

traposiento ADJ (*And*) ragged.

traposo ADJ (a) (*And, Carib, Cono Sur: harapiento*) ragged. (b) (*Cono Sur*) = **trapajoso** (b). (c) (*Cono Sur*) *carne* tough, stringy.

trapujear [1a] VI (*CAm*) to smuggle.

trapujero NM (*CAm*) smuggler.

traque NM (a) crack, bang. (b) (*:*) noisy fart**:**.

tráquea NF trachea, windpipe.

traquear [1a] ① VTI = **traquetear**.
② VT (a) (*CAm, Cono Sur, Méx: dejar huella*) to make deep tracks on.
(b) (*Carib*) *persona* to take about from place to place; (*Cono Sur*) *ganado* to switch from place to place.
(c) (*Carib*) (*probar*) to test, try out; (*entrenar*) to train.
③ VI (a) (*Cono Sur: frecuentar*) to frequent a place.
(b) (*Carib: beber*) to drink.
④ **traquearse** VR (*Carib*) to go out of one's mind.

traqueo NM = **traqueteo**.

traqueotomía NF tracheotomy, tracheostomy.

traquetear [1a] ① VT (a) *recipiente* to shake; *sillas etc* to rattle, bang about, make a lot of noise with.
(b) (*: estropear*) to mess up, muck about with.
② VI (a) (*cohete etc*) to crackle, bang; (*vehículo etc*) to rattle, jolt; (*ametrallador*) to rattle, clatter.
(b) (*Cono Sur, Méx: apresurarse*) to bustle, go to and fro a lot; (*Cono Sur: cansarse*) to tire o.s. out at work.

traqueteo NM (a) (*V VT*) crackle, bang; rattle, rattling, jolting; clatter; **se le da el ~*** she likes to live it up*. (b) (*And, Carib, Méx*) (*ruido*) row,

din; (*movimiento*) hustle and bustle, coming and going.

traquidazo NM (*Méx*) = **traquido**.

traquido NM (*de látigo*) crack; (*de disparo*) crack, bang, report.

traquinar [1a] VI (*Carib*) = **trajinar**.

tras¹ ① PREP (a) (*lugar*) behind; after; **día ~ día** day after day; **uno ~ otro** one after the other; **andar ~ algo, estar ~ algo** to be looking for sth, be on the track of sth; **andamos ~ un coche que han anunciado** we're after a car which has been advertised; **correr ~ uno, ir ~ uno** to chase (after) sb.
(b) (*al otro lado de*) across, beyond; **~ los Pirineos** beyond the Pyrenees; **~ el río** on the other side of the river.
(c) (*tiempo*) after.
(d) **~ de** + *infin* besides + *ger*, in addition to + *ger*.
(e) (*And, Méx*) **~ de** + *infin* after + *ger*; **~ de que** ... after ...
② NM (*) bottom, backside.

tras² INTERJ: **¡~, ~!** tap, tap!; knock, knock!

tras... PREF trans...; *V t* **trans...**

trasalcoba NF dressing-room.

trasaltar NM retrochoir.

trasbocar [1g] VTI (*And, Cono Sur*) to throw up.

trasbucar [1g] VT (*Carib, Cono Sur*) to upset, overturn.

trasbuscar [1g] VT (*Cono Sur*) to search carefully.

trascendencia NF (a) (*importancia*) importance, significance, momentousness; far-reaching nature; implications, consequences; **encuentro sin ~** casual meeting; **discusión sin ~** discussion of no particular significance.
(b) (*Filos*) transcendence.

trascendental ADJ (a) (*importante*) important, significant, momentous; (*esencial*) vital; *consecuencias* far-reaching. (b) (*Filos*) transcendental.

trascendente ADJ = **trascendental**.

trascender [2g] VI (a) (*oler*) to smell (*a* of); **el olor de la cocina trascendía hasta nosotros** the smell of the kitchen floated across to us, the kitchen smell reached as far as us; **la carne trasciende a pasada** the meat smells bad.
(b) **~ a** (*fig*) to smack of, be suggestive of; to evoke, suggest; **en esta novela todo trasciende a romanticismo** everything in this novel smacks of romanticism; **de su gesto trasciende cierta serenidad** his expression suggests a certain calmness, a certain serenity shines through his expression.
(c) (*saberse*) to come out, leak out; **~ a** to become known to, spread to; **por fin ha trascendido la triste noticia** the sad news has come out at last; **no queremos que ello trascienda a los demás** we do not want this to be known to the others.
(d) (*propagarse*) to spread, have a wide effect; **~ a** to reach, get across to, have an effect on; **su influencia trasciende a los países más remotos** his influence extends to the most remote countries; **~ de** to go beyond, go outside of, go beyond the limits of.

trascocina NF scullery.

trascolar [1l] VT to strain.

trasconejarse [1a] VR to get lost, be misplaced.

trascordarse [1l] VR: **~ algo** to forget sth, lose all memory of sth; **estar trascordado** to be completely forgotten.

trascoro NM retrochoir.

trascorral NM (a) inner yard. (b) (*: culo*) bottom.

trascuarto NM back room.

trasegar [1h *y* 1j] ① VT (a) (*cambiar de sitio*) to move about, switch round; *puestos* to reshuffle; *vino* (*para la mesa*) to decant; (*en bodega*) to rack, pour into another container (*o* bottle).
(b) (*trastornar*) to mix up; to upset, turn upside down.
(c) (*) *bebida* to knock back*, put down*.
② VI (*) to drink, booze*.

trasera NF back, rear.

trasero ① ADJ back, rear; hind; **motor ~** rear-mounted engine; **rueda trasera** back wheel, rear wheel.
② NM (a) (*Anat*) bottom, buttocks; (*Zool*) hindquarters, rump. (b) ~s (*antepasados*) ancestors.

trasfondo NM background; (*de crítica etc*) undertone, undercurrent.

trasgo NM (a) (*duende*) goblin, imp. (b) (*niño*) imp.

trasgredir [3a] VT = **transgredir**.

trashojar [1a] VT *libro* to leaf through, glance through.

trashumación NF transhumance, seasonal migration, move to new pastures.

trashumante ADJ *animales* migrating, on the move to new pastures; *persona, tribu* nomadic.

trashumar [1a] VI to make the seasonal migration, move to new pastures.

trasiego NM (*V VT*) (a) move, switch; reshuffle; decanting; racking.
(b) mixing; upset.

trasigar [1h] VT (*And*) to upset, turn upside down.

trasijado ADJ skinny.

traslación NF (a) (*Astron*) movement, passage; removal. (b) (*copia*) copy; copying. **(c)** (*Liter*) metaphor; figurative use.

trasladar [1a] ☐ VT **(a)** (*mudar*) to move; (*quitar*) to remove; *persona* to move, change, transfer (*a* to).
(b) (*aplazar*) to postpone (*a* until), move (*a* to); *reunión* to adjourn (*a* to).
(c) (*copiar*) to copy, transcribe.
(d) *pensamiento, sentimiento etc* to translate; to express, interpret; to convey in a different form; **~ su pensamiento al papel** to put one's thoughts on paper; **~ una novela a la pantalla** to transfer a novel to the screen, interpret a novel as a film.
(e) (*Ling*) to translate (*a* into).
☐ **trasladarse** VR to go, move (*a* to); to betake o.s. (*a* to); (*LAm*) to move (house); **~ a otro puesto** to move to a new job, change to a new post; **los que se trasladan a la oficina en coche** those who go to their offices by car; **después nos trasladamos al bar** later we moved to the bar.

traslado NM **(a)** (*mudanza*) move; removal; (*cambio*) change, transfer. **(b)** (*copia*) copy; (*Jur*) notification; **dar ~ a uno de una orden** to give sb a copy of an order.

traslapar [1a] ☐ VT to overlap.
☐ **traslaparse** VR to overlap.

traslapo NM overlap, overlay.

traslaticiamente ADV figuratively.

traslaticio ADJ figurative.

traslucir [3f] ☐ VT to show, reveal, betray; **dejar ~ algo** to hint at sth, suggest sth.
☐ **traslucirse** VR **(a)** (*ser transparente*) to be translucent, be transparent.
(b) (*ser visible*) to show through, be perceptible.
(c) (*fig*) (*revelarse*) to reveal itself, be revealed; (*ser obvio*) to be plain to see; **en su cara se traslucía cierto pesimismo** a certain pessimism was revealed in his expression, a certain pessimism was written on his face.
(d) (*fig: saberse*) to leak out, come to light.
(e) (*fig: persona*) to reveal one's inmost thoughts, betray one's hidden feelings.

traslumbrar [1a] ☐ VT to dazzle.
☐ **traslumbrarse** VR **(a)** (*ser deslumbrado*) to be dazzled.
(b) (*ir y venir*) to appear and disappear suddenly, come and go unexpectedly; (*pasar rápidamente*) to flash across.

trasluz NM **(a)** (*luz difusa*) diffused light; (*luz reflejada*) reflected light, glint, gleam.
(b) **mirar algo al ~** to look at sth against the light.
(c) (*Carib: semblanza*) resemblance.

trasmano **(a)** **a ~** ADV out of reach; (*fig*) out of the way, remote.
(b) **por ~** (*LAm*) ADV secretly, in an underhand way.

trasminante ADJ (*Cono Sur*) *frío* bitter, piercing.

trasminarse [1a] VR to filter through, pass through.

trasmundo NM hidden world, secret world.

trasnochada NF **(a)** (*vigilia*) vigil, watch; (*noche sin dormir*) sleepless night.
(b) (*Mil*) night attack.
(c) (*noche anterior*) last night, previous night, night before.

trasnochado ADJ **(a)** *comida etc* stale, old; (*fig*) stale, obsolete, ancient; *proyecto etc* that has been too long in the preparation, that has been overtaken by events.
(b) *persona* wan, haggard, hollow-eyed.

trasnochador ☐ ADJ given to staying up late; **son muy ~es** they turn in very late, they keep very late hours.
☐ NM, **trasnochadora** NF night-bird (*fig*).

trasnochar [1a] ☐ VT *problema* to sleep on.
☐ VI **(a)** (*acostarse tarde*) to stay up late, go to bed late; (*no acostarse*) to stay up all night; (*no dormir*) to have a sleepless night; (*ir de juerga*) to have a night out, have a night on the tiles.
(b) **~ en un sitio** to spend the night in a place.
☐ **trasnocharse** VR (*LAm*) = 2.

trasoír [3p] VTI to mishear.

trasojado ADJ haggard, hollow-eyed.

traspaís NM interior, hinterland.

traspalar [1a] VT to shovel about, move with a shovel.

traspapelar [1a] ☐ VT to lose, mislay, misplace.
☐ **traspapelarse** VR to get mislaid.

traspapeleo NM misplacement.

traspar [1a] VI (*Méx*) to move house.

traspasar [1a] ☐ VT **(a)** (*penetrar*) to pierce, penetrate, go through; to transfix; (*líquido*) to go through, come through, soak through; **la bala le traspasó el pulmón** the bullet pierced his lung; **~ a uno con una espada** to run sb through with a sword.
(b) (*fig: dolor, grito etc*) to pierce; to pain, grieve mortally; **un ruido que traspasa el oído** a noise which pierces your ear, a noise which drills into your ear; **ese grito me traspasó** that yell transfixed me; **la escena me traspasó el corazón** the scene pierced me to the core.

(c) *calle, río etc* to cross over.
(d) *límite* to go beyond, overstep; to transcend; **esto traspasa los límites de lo tolerable** this goes beyond the limits of what is tolerable.
(e) *ley* to break, infringe, transgress.
(f) *jugador, propiedad etc* to transfer; to sell, make over; (*Jur*) to convey; **'traspaso negocio'** (*anuncio*) 'business for sale'.
☐ **traspasarse** VR to go too far, overstep the mark.

traspaso NM **(a)** (*venta*) transfer, sale; (*Jur*) conveyance.
(b) (*propiedad, bienes*) property transferred, goods (*etc*) sold; (*Jur*) property being conveyed; (*Esp Pol*) **~s** fields of competence and powers transferred to an autonomous region.
(c) (*Com, Dep*) transfer fee; (*de piso etc*) key money.
(d) (*fig: pena*) anguish, pain; grief.
(e) (*de ley*) infringement, transgression.

traspatio NM (*LAm*) backyard.

traspié NM **(a)** (*tropiezo*) slip, stumble, trip; **dar un ~** to slip, trip, stumble. **(b)** (*fig*) slip, blunder.

traspintarse [1a] VR **(a)** (*en papel*) to come through, show through.
(b) (*: *acabar mal*) to backfire, turn out all wrong.

trasplantado, -a NM/F transplant patient.

trasplantar [1a] ☐ VT to transplant.
☐ **trasplantarse** VR to emigrate, uproot o.s.

trasplante NM **(a)** (*Bot*) transplanting. **(b)** (*Med*) transplant, transplantation; **~ de corazón** heart transplant; **~ hepático** liver transplant.

trasponer [2q] VT = **transponer**.

traspontín NM = **traspuntín**.

traspuesta NF **(a)** (*transposición*) transposition; (*cambio*) switching, changing over; removal.
(b) (*Geog*) rise.
(c) (*huida*) flight, escape; (*acto de esconderse*) hiding.
(d) (*patio*) backyard; (*dependencias*) outbuildings.

traspuesto ADJ, PTP de **trasponer**; **quedarse ~** to doze off.

traspunte NM (*Teat: botones*) callboy; (*apuntador*) prompt, prompter.

traspuntín NM **(a)** (*asiento*) tip-up seat, folding seat. **(b)** (*: *culo*) backside, bottom.

trasque CONJ (*LAm*) in addition to the fact that ..., besides being ...

trasquiladura NF shearing, clipping.

trasquilar [1a] VT **(a)** *oveja* to shear, clip; *pelo, persona* to crop. **(b)** (*: *cortar*) to cut down, curtail, chop off.

trasquilón NM: **¡menudo ~ que le han dado!** what a mess they've made of his hair!

trastabillar [1a] VI = **trastrabillar**.

trastabillón NM (*LAm*) stumble, trip.

trastada* NF **(a)** (*acto insensato*) stupid act, senseless act; (*travesura*) mischief, prank; (*broma pesada*) practical joke; (*grosería*) piece of bad behaviour.
(b) (*mala pasada*) dirty trick; **hacer una ~ a uno** to play a dirty trick on sb.

trastajo NM piece of junk.

trastazo NM bump, bang, thump.

traste[1] NM **(a)** (*Mús*) fret.
(b) **dar al ~ con algo** to ruin sth, spoil sth, mess sth up; **dar al ~ con una fortuna** to squander a fortune; **dar al ~ con los planes** to ruin one's plans; **esto ha dado al ~ con mi paciencia** this has exhausted my patience; **ir al ~** to fail, fall through, be ruined.

traste[2] NM **(a)** (*LAm*) = **trasto**. **(b)** (*Cono Sur**) bottom, backside.

trastear [1a] ☐ VT **(a)** (*Mús*) to play.
(b) *objetos* (*mover*) to move around; (*desordenar*) to mess up, disarrange.
(c) (*Taur*) to play with the cape.
(d) *persona* (*manipular*) to lead by the nose, twist round one's little finger.
(e) *persona* (*entretener*) to keep waiting, keep at bay, keep dangling.
(f) (*Méx*: *acariciar*) to feel up*, touch up*.
☐ VI **(a)** (*mover objetos*) to move things around; **~ con, ~ en** (*buscando*) to rummage among; (*manosear*) to fiddle with; (*desordenar*) to mess up, disarrange.
(b) (*And, CAm: mudar de casa*) to move house.
(c) (*conversar*) to make bright conversation.
☐ **trastearse** VR (*And, Cono Sur*) to move house.

trastera NF **(a)** (*cuarto*) lumber room. **(b)** (*Méx: armario*) cupboard. **(c)** (*Carib*) heap of junk.

trastería NF **(a)** (*trastos*) lumber, junk. **(b)** (*tienda*) junkshop. **(c)** = **trastada**.

trastero NM **(a)** (*cuarto*) lumber room; storage room. **(b)** (*Méx*) cupboard, closet (*US*). **(c)** (*Méx**: *culo*) backside. **(d)** (*CAm, Méx: para platos*) dishrack.

trastienda NF **(a)** back room (of a shop), room behind a shop; **obtener algo por la ~** to get sth under the counter; (*fig*) to get sth by underhand means.

(b) tiene mucha ~ (*: *astucia*) he's a sharp one; he's a deep one, he hides a lot inside himself.
(c) (*Cono Sur, Méx*) backside.

trasto NM **(a)** (*mueble*) piece of furniture; (*utensilio*) household utensil; (*cosa inútil*) piece of lumber, piece of junk; (*olla etc*) old crock, old pot; **~s viejos** lumber, junk, rubbish; **tirarse los ~s a la cabeza** to have a blazing row.
(b) ~s (*Teat*) (*decorado*) scenery; (*accesorios*) stage furniture, properties.
(c) (*: *avíos*) **~s** gear, tackle; **~s de matar** weapons; **~s de pescar** fishing tackle; **coger los ~s, liar los ~s** to pack up and go.
(d) (*: *persona*) useless individual, good-for-nothing; dead loss; nuisance; unreliable person; odd type*.

trastocar [1g y 1l] VT = **trastrocar**.

trastornado ADJ *persona* mad, crazy; *mente* unhinged.

trastornar [1a] **1** VT **(a)** (*volcar*) to overturn, upset; to turn upside down; *objetos* to mix up, jumble up, turn upside down; *orden* to confuse, disturb.
(b) (*fig*) *ideas etc* to upset, confuse; *proyecto* to upset; *vida* to disturb, disorganize; *sentidos* to daze, confuse; *nervios* to shatter; *orden público etc* to disturb; *persona (molestar)* to upset, trouble, disturb; (*marear*) to make dizzy.
(c) (*volver loco*) *mente* to unhinge; *persona* to drive crazy, disturb mentally; **esa chica le ha trastornado** that girl has bowled him over, that girl is driving him crazy.
(d) (*: *encantar*) to delight; **la trastornan las joyas** she's crazy about jewels, she just lives for jewels.
2 trastornarse VR **(a)** (*proyecto etc*) to fall through, be ruined.
(b) (*persona*) to go crazy, go out of one's mind.

trastorno NM **(a)** (*acto*) overturning, upsetting; mixing up, jumbling up.
(b) (*fig: perturbación*) confusion, disturbance; (*molestia*) trouble, inconvenience; (*Pol*) disturbance, upheaval; **los ~s políticos de Eslobodia** the Slobodian political disturbances.
(c) (*Med*) upset, disorder; **~ digestivo, ~ estomacal** stomach upset.
(d) ~ mental mental disorder, breakdown.

trastrabillar [1a] VI **(a)** (*tropezar*) to trip, stumble. **(b)** (*tambalearse*) to totter, reel, stagger. **(c)** (*trabarse la lengua*) to stammer, stutter.

trastrocar [1g y 1l] VT **(a)** *objetos* to switch over, change round; *orden* to reverse, invert. **(b)** (*transformar*) to change, transform.

trastrueco NM, **trastrueque** NM (*V* VT) **(a)** switch, changeover; reversal. **(b)** change, transformation.

trastumbar [1a] VT: **~ la esquina** (*Méx*) to disappear round (o turn) the corner.

trasudar [1a] VI to sweat a little.

trasudor NM slight sweat.

trasuntar [1a] VT **(a)** (*copiar*) to copy, transcribe. **(b)** (*resumir*) to summarize. **(c)** (*fig: mostrar*) to show, exude; **su cara trasuntaba serenidad** his face exuded calm.

trasunto NM **(a)** (*copia*) copy, transcription.
(b) (*fig: semejanza*) image, likeness; carbon copy; **fiel ~** exact likeness; faithful representation; **esto es un ~ en menor escala de lo que ocurrió ayer** this is a repetition on a smaller scale of what happened yesterday.

trasvasable ADJ transferable.

trasvasar [1a] VT *vino etc* to pour into another container, decant, transfer; *río* to divert; (*fig*) to move, shift, transfer.

trasvase NM pouring, decanting; diversion; (*fig*) movement, shift, transfer; (*fuga*) drain.

trasvasijar [1a] VT (*Cono Sur*) = **trasvasar**.

trasvolar [1l] VT to fly over, cross in an aeroplane.

trata NF (*t* **~ de esclavos, ~ de negros**) slave trade; **~ de blancas** white slave trade.

tratable ADJ **(a)** (*amable*) friendly, sociable, easy to get on with. **(b)** (*Cono Sur*) passable.

tratadista NMF writer (of a treatise); essayist.

tratado NM **(a)** (*Com etc*) agreement; (*Pol*) treaty, pact; **T~ de Adhesión** Treaty of Accession (to EC); **T~ de paz** peace treaty; **T~ de Roma** Treaty of Rome; **T~ de Utrecht** Treaty of Utrecht.
(b) (*Liter*) treatise, tract; essay; **un ~ de física** a treatise on physics.

tratamiento NM **(a)** (*Med, Quím, Téc etc*) treatment; (*Téc*) processing; (*de persona, problema*) treatment, handling; management; **~ de choque** shock treatment; **~ de gráficos** graphics processing; **~ de la información** information processing; **~ de márgenes** margin settings; **~ médico** medical treatment; **~ con rayos X** X-ray treatment; **~ de textos** word-processing.
(b) (*título*) title, style (of address); **~ de tú** familiar address (*in 2nd person singular of verb*); **apear el ~ a uno** to drop sb's title, address sb without formality; **dar ~ a uno** to give sb his full title.

tratante NMF dealer, trader (*en* in).

tratar [1a] **1** VT **(a)** (*gen*) to treat, handle; **la tratan muy bien en esa pensión** they treat her well in that boarding house; **~ a alguien a**

patadas (*o* con la punta del pie) to kick sb around (*t fig*); **hay que ~ los libros con cuidado** books should be handled carefully; **trata a todos con poca ceremonia** he treats everyone very unceremoniously.
(b) (*Med, Quím, Téc*) to treat (*con, por* with); (*Inform*) to process; **~ a uno con un nuevo fármaco** to treat sb with a new drug.
(c) ~ a uno (*tener relaciones*) to have dealings with sb, have to do with sb, know sb; **le trato desde hace 6 meses** I have known him for 6 months.
(d) ~ a uno de tú to address sb as 'tú' (*familiar 2nd person sing*); **¿cómo le hemos de ~?** how should we address him?, what ought we to call him?; **~ a uno de vago** to call sb idle.
2 VI **(a) ~ de** (*libro etc*) to deal with, be about, discuss; (*personas, reunión*) to talk about, discuss; **este libro trata de las leyendas épicas** this book is about the epic legends; **ahora van a ~ del programa** they're going to talk about the programme now.
(b) ~ con (*Com*) to deal in, trade in, handle.
(c) ~ con *tema etc* to have to do with, deal with; *persona* to know, have dealings with, have contacts with; *enemigo* to negotiate with, treat with; **el geólogo trata con rocas** the geologist deals with rocks; **no tratamos con traidores** we do not treat with traitors, there can be no negotiations with traitors; **no había tratado con personas de esa clase** I had not had dealings with people of that class.
(d) ~ de + *infin* to try to + *infin*, endeavour to + *infin*.
3 tratarse VR **(a)** (*1 persona*) **~ bien** to do o.s. well, live well; **ahora se trata con mucho cuidado** he looks after himself very carefully now.
(b) (*2 personas*) to treat each other, behave towards each other.
(c) (*2 personas*) **se tratan de usted** they address each other as 'usted' (*polite form of verb*); **¿aquí nos tratamos de tú o de usted?** are we on 'tú' or 'usted' terms here?; **¿cómo nos hemos de ~?** how should we address each other?
(d) ~ con uno to have to do with sb, have dealings with sb.
(e) (*ser cuestión de*) **se trata de la nueva piscina** it's about the new pool, it's a question of the new pool; **se trata de aplazarlo un mes** it's a question of putting it off for a month; **¿de qué se trata?** what's it about?; what's up?, what's the trouble?; **ahora, tratándose de Vd ...** now, in your case ...; **si no se trata más que de eso** if there's no more to it than that, if that's all it is.

tratativas NFPL (*Cono Sur*) negotiations; steps, measures.

trato NM **(a)** (*entre personas*) intercourse, dealings; (*relación*) relationship; (*conocimiento*) acquaintance; **~ carnal, ~ sexual** sexual intercourse; **~ doble** double-dealing, dishonesty; **entrar en ~s con uno** to enter into relations (o negotiations) with sb; **no querer ~s con uno** to want no dealings with sb; **romper el ~ con uno** to break off relations with sb.
(b) (*de persona: t ~s*) treatment; **~ preferente** priority treatment; **malos ~s** ill-treatment, rough treatment, ill-usage.
(c) (*manera de ser*) manner; (*conducta*) behaviour; **de fácil ~** easy to get on with; **de ~ agradable** pleasant, affable; **~ de gentes = don de gentes; tener buen ~** to be easy to get on with, have a pleasant manner, be affable.
(d) (*Com, Jur*) agreement, contract; deal, bargain; (*fig*) deal; **~s dealings;** **~ colectivo** collective bargaining; (*fig*) deal; **~ comercial** business deal; **~ equitativo** fair deal, square deal; **~ preferente** preferential treatment; **¡~ hecho!** it's a deal!; **cerrar un ~** to do a deal, strike a bargain; **hacer buenos ~s a uno** to offer sb advantageous terms.
(e) (*Ling*) title, style of address; **dar a uno el ~ debido** to give sb his proper title.
(f) (*Méx: puesto*) market stall.
(g) (*Méx: negocio*) small business.

trauma NM **(a)** (*mental*) trauma. **(b)** (*lesión*) injury.

traumar [1a] VT to traumatize.

traumático ADJ traumatic.

traumatismo NM traumatism.

traumatizante ADJ traumatic.

traumatizar [1f] VT (*Med, Psic*) to traumatize; (*fig*) to shock, affect profoundly, shake to the core.

traumatología NF orthopedic surgery.

traumatólogo, -a NM/F orthopedic surgeon.

trauque NM (*Cono Sur*) friend.

travelín, travel(l)ing NM, PL **travel(l)ing(s)** (*Cine: aparato*) dolly, travelling platform; (*: movimiento*) tracking shot.

través **1** NM **(a)** (*Arquit*) crossbeam.
(b) (*Mil*) traverse; protective wall.
(c) (*curva*) bend, turn; (*inclinación*) slant; (*sesgo*) bias; (*deformación*) warp.
(d) (*fig*) reverse, misfortune; upset.
2 al ~ ADV across, crossways; **de ~** across, crossways; obliquely; sideways; **con el sombrero puesto de ~** with his hat on askew;

hubo que introducirlo de ~ it had to be squeezed in sideways; **ir de ~** (*Náut*) to drift off course, be blown (*etc*) to the side; **mirar de ~** to squint; **mirar a uno de ~** to look at sb out of the corner of one's eye, (*fig*) look askance at sb.

3 a ~ de, al ~ de PREP across; over; (*por medio de*) through; **un árbol caído a ~ de los carriles** a tree fallen across the lines; **lo sé a ~ de un amigo** I know about it through a friend.

travesaño NM (a) (*Arquit*) crosspiece, crossbeam; (*Dep*) crossbar.
(b) (*de cama*) bolster.
(c) (*CAm, Carib, Méx Ferro*) sleeper.

travesear [1a] VI (a) (*jugar*) to play around; (*ser travieso*) to play up, be mischievous, be naughty; (*pey*) to live a dissipated life.
(b) (*fig: hablar*) to talk wittily, sparkle.
(c) (*Méx: de jinete*) to show off one's horsemanship.

traveseo NM (*Méx*) display of horsemanship.

travesero 1 ADJ cross (*atr*); slanting, oblique; *V* **flauta.**
2 NM bolster.

travesía NF (a) (*calle*) cross-street, short street which joins two others; (*de pueblo*) road that passes through a village.
(b) (*Náut*) crossing, voyage; (*Aer*) crossing; distance travelled, distance to be crossed; **~ del desierto** (*fig*) period in the wilderness.
(c) (*viento: Náut*) crosswind; (*Cono Sur*) west wind.
(d) (*en el juego*) amount won, amount lost.
(e) (*And, Cono Sur: desierto*) arid plain, desert region.

travesti, travestí 1 NM (*Teat*) (a) (*persona*) drag artist. (b) (*arte*) art of drag.
2 NMF transvestite.

travestido ADJ disguised, in disguise; *V t* **travestí.**

travestirse [3k] VR to cross-dress.

travestismo NM transvestism.

travesura NF (a) (*broma etc*) prank, lark, piece of mischief; escapade; **son ~s de niños** they're just childish pranks; **las ~s de su juventud** the wild doings of his youth, the waywardness of his young days.
(b) (*mala pasada*) sly trick.
(c) (*gracia*) wit, sparkle.

traviesa NF (a) (*Arquit*) tie, crossbeam, rafter.
(b) (*Ferro*) sleeper.
(c) (*Min*) cross-gallery.
(d) = **travesía** (b); *V* **campo.**

travieso ADJ (a) *niño* naughty, mischievous; *adulto* (*inquieto*) restless; (*vivo*) lively, (*voluble*) unpredictable; (*pey*) dissolute.
(b) (*listo*) bright, clever, shrewd; (*gracioso*) witty.

trayecto NM (a) (*camino*) road, route, way; (*tramo*) stretch, section; **destrozó un ~ de varios kilómetros** it destroyed a stretch several kilometres long; **final del ~** end of the line, terminus; **recorrer un ~** to cover a distance.
(b) (*viaje: de persona*) journey; (*de vehículo*) run, journey; (*de bala etc*) flight, trajectory; **comeremos durante el ~** we'll eat on the journey, we'll lunch on the way.

trayectoria NF (a) (*camino*) trajectory, path; **~ de vuelo** flightpath.
(b) (*fig*) course of development, evolution, path; **~ profesional** career; **la ~ poética de Garcilaso** Garcilaso's poetic development; **la actual del partido** the party's present line (o course, path).

trayendo *etc V* **traer.**

traza NF (a) (*Arquit, Téc*) plan, design; (*disposición*) layout.
(b) (*aspecto etc*) looks, general appearance, air; **por las ~s, según las ~s** from all the signs, to judge by appearances; **llevar buena ~** to look well, seem impressive; (*proyecto etc*) to seem promising; **llevar** (*o* **tener**) **~s de** + *infin* to look like + *ger*; **esto tiene ~s de nunca acabar** this looks as though it will never end.
(c) (*medio*) means; (*pey*) trick, device, expedient; **darse ~** to find a way, get along, manage; **darse ~ para hacer algo, discurrir ~s para hacer algo** to contrive (schemes) to do sth, look for a way of achieving sth.
(d) (*habilidad*) skill, ability; **tener** (**buena**) **~ para hacer algo** to be skilful at doing sth; **para pianista tiene poca ~** she's not much of a pianist.
(e) (*Cono Sur: huella*) track, trail.
(f) (*Inform*) trace.

trazable ADJ traceable.

trazada NF line, course, direction; **cortar la ~ a uno** (*Aut*) to cut in on sb.

trazado 1 ADJ: **bien ~** shapely, well-formed; good-looking; **mal ~** ill-favoured, unattractive.
2 NM (a) (*Arquit, Téc*) plan, design; (*disposición*) layout; (*esbozo etc*) outline, sketch; (*de carretera*) line, route.
(b) (*fig*) lines, outline.
(c) (*And: cuchillo*) machete.

trazador 1 ADJ (*Mil, Fís*) tracer (*atr*); **bala ~a** tracer bullet; **elemento ~** tracer element.
2 NM (a) (*persona*) planner, designer.
(b) (*Fís*) tracer.

(c) (*Inform*) **~ gráfico, ~ de gráficos** plotter; **~ plano** flatbed plotter.

trazadora NF tracer, tracer bullet.

trazar [1f] VT (a) (*Arquit, Téc*) (*planificar*) to plan, design; (*disponer*) to lay out; *línea etc* to draw, trace; (*Arte*) to sketch, outline; *límites* to mark out; *curso, huella* to trace, plot, follow.
(b) (*fig*) *desarrollo, política etc* to lay down, mark out.
(c) (*fig: en discurso etc*) to trace, describe, explain, outline.
(d) *medios etc* to contrive, devise.

trazo NM (a) (*línea*) line, stroke; **~ discontinuo** broken line; **~ de lápiz** pencil stroke, pencil mark.
(b) (*esbozo*) sketch, outline; **~s** (*de rostro*) lines, features, cast; **de ~s enérgicos** vigorous-looking; **de ~s indecisos** with an indecisive look about him (*etc*).
(c) (*Arte: de ropaje*) fold.

TRB NFPL ABR *de* **toneladas de registro bruto** gross register tons, GRT.

TRC NM ABR *de* **tubo de rayos catódicos** cathode ray tube, CRT.

trébede(s) NF, PL **trébedes** trivet.

trebejos NMPL (a) (*avíos*) equipment, gear, things; **~ de cocina** kitchen utensils, kitchen things.
(b) (*Ajedrez*) chessmen.
(c) (*fig*) old-fashioned things.

trébol NM (a) (*Bot*) clover, trefoil. (b) (*Arquit*) trefoil. (c) **~es** (*Naipes*) clubs.

trebolar NM (*Cono Sur*) clover field, field covered in clover.

trece ADJ thirteen; (*fecha*) thirteenth; **estar** (*o* **mantenerse, seguir** *etc*) **en sus ~** to stand firm, stick to one's guns.

treceavo ADJ, NM thirteenth.

trecho NM (a) (*tramo*) stretch; (*distancia*) length, distance; (*de tiempo*) while; **andar un buen ~** to walk a good way, go on a good distance; **a ~s** in parts, here and there; intermittently; by fits and starts; **de ~ en ~** at intervals, every so often; **muy de ~ en ~** very occasionally, only once in a while.
(b) (*Agr*) plot, patch.
(c) (*: pedazo*) bit, piece, part; **he terminado ese ~ de punto** I've finished that bit of knitting; **queda un buen ~ que hacer** there's still quite a bit to do.

trefilar [1a] VT *alambre* to draw (out).

tregua NF (a) (*Mil*) truce. (b) (*fig*) lull, respite, let-up; **sin ~** without respite; **dar ~s** (*dolor etc*) to come and go, let up from time to time; (*asunto*) not to be urgent; **no dar ~** to give no respite.

treinta ADJ thirty; (*fecha*) thirtieth; **los** (**años**) **~** the thirties.

treintañero 1 ADJ thirtyish, about thirty.
2 NM, **treintañera** NF person of about thirty, person in his (*o* her) thirties.

treintena NF thirty; about thirty.

treintón 1 ADJ thirty-year old, thirtyish.
2 NM, **treintona** NF person of about thirty.

trekking NM pony-trekking.

trematodo NM (*Zool*) fluke.

tremebundo ADJ terrible, frightening; *palabras etc* fierce, threatening, savage.

tremedal NM quaking bog.

tremendamente* ADV tremendously*; awfully, terrifically*.

tremendismo NM crudeness, coarse realism; use of realism to shock.

tremendista 1 ADJ crude, coarsely realistic.
2 NMF coarsely realistic writer, writer who shocks by his realism.

tremendo ADJ (a) (*terrible*) terrible, dreadful, frightful.
(b) (*imponente*) imposing, awesome.
(c) (*: asombroso*) tremendous*; awful, terrific*; **una roca tremenda de alta** a terrifically high rock*; **le dio una tremenda paliza** he gave him a tremendous beating*; **un error ~** a terrible mistake.
(d) (*) *persona* inventive, witty, entertaining; **es ~, ¿eh?** isn't he a scream?*, isn't he great?*
(e) **echar la tremenda** to speak angrily; **dar** (*o* **tomar**) **algo por la tremenda** to make a great fuss about sth.

trementina NF turpentine.

tremolar [1a] 1 VT (a) *bandera* to wave. (b) (*fig*) to show off, flaunt.
2 VI to wave, flutter.

tremolina* NF row, fuss, commotion; shindy*; **armar una ~** to start a row, make a fuss.

tremotiles NMPL (*And, Carib*) tools, tackle.

trémulamente ADV tremulously; quaveringly; timidly.

trémulo ADJ quivering, tremulous; *voz* quavering; timid, small; *luz etc* flickering.

tren NM (a) (*Ferro*) train; **~ de alta velocidad** high-speed train; **~ ascendente** up train; **~ botijo*, ~ de excursión, ~ de recreo** excursion train; **~ de carga** goods train, freight train (*US*); **~ de cercanías** suburban train; **~ de contenedores** container train; **~ correo** slow train; (*Correos*) mailtrain; **~ de cremallera** funicular (railway); **~ descendente** down train; **~ directo** through train; **~ expreso** fast train; **~ de largo recorrido** long-distance train; **~ (de) mercancías** goods train, freight train (*US*); **~ mixto** passenger and goods train; **~**

ómnibus stopping train, local train, accommodation train (US); **~ de pasajeros** passenger train; **~ postal** mailtrain; **~ rápido** express (train); **~ suplementario** extra train, relief train; **cambiar de ~** to change trains; **coger un ~, tomar un ~** to catch a train; **coger el ~ (en marcha)** (fig), **subirse al ~** (fig) to climb (o jump) on the bandwagon; **tenemos libros para parar un ~*** we have loads of books; **está como (para parar) un ~** (Esp*) she's hot stuff*, she looks terrific*; **ir en ~** to go by train; **perder el ~** (fig) to miss the boat.

(b) (equipaje) baggage; (equipo) outfit, equipment; **~ de viaje** equipment for a journey.

(c) (Mec) set; set of gears (o wheels etc); **~ de aterrizaje** (Aer) undercarriage, landing gear; **~ de bandas en caliente** hot-strip mill; **~ de laminación** rolling-mill; **~ de lavado** (Aut) carwash.

(d) (Mil) convoy.

(e) **~ de vida** life style; (Fin) rate of spending; **vivir a todo ~** to live in style, live expensively; **no pudo sostener ese ~ de vida** he could not keep up that style of living.

(f) (velocidad) speed; **a fuerte ~** at a rapid pace, fast; **forzar el ~** to force the pace; **ir a buen ~** to go at a good speed.

(g) (LAm) **en ~ de** in the process of, in the course of; **estamos en ~ de realizarlo** we are carrying it out; **estar en ~ de recuperación** to be on one's way to recovery.

(h) (Carib) (taller) workshop; (empresa) firm, company; **~ de mudadas** removal company; **~ de lavado** laundry.

(i) (CAm, Méx: trajín) coming and going; **~es** shady dealings.

(j) (Cono Sur, Méx: tranvía) tram, streetcar (US).

(k) (Carib: majadería) cheeky remark.

trena: NF clink:, prison.

trenca NF duffle-coat.

trencilla 1 NF braid.

2 NM (Dep) referee.

trencillo NM braid.

tren-cremallera NM, PL **trenes-cremallera** funicular (railway).

trenista NM **(a)** (Carib) (patrón) owner of a workshop; (gerente) company manager. **(b)** (Méx Ferro) railwayman.

Trento NM Trent; **Concilio de ~** Council of Trent.

trenza NF **(a)** (de pelo) plait; pigtail, ponytail; tress; (Cos) braid; (de pajas etc) plait; (de hilos) twist; **~ postiza** switch, hairpiece; **encontrar a una en ~** to find a woman with her hair down.

(b) (LAm: de cebollas etc) string.

(c) **~s** (Carib) shoelaces.

(d) (Culin) plaited pastry.

(e) (Cono Sur: recomendación) recommendation, suggestion.

(f) (Cono Sur: pelea) hand-to-hand fight.

trenzado 1 ADJ plaited; braided; twisted together, intertwined.

2 NM **(a)** (de pelo) plaits. **(b)** (Ballet) entrechat.

trenzar [1f] 1 VT pelo to plait, braid; pajas etc to plait; hilos etc to twist (together), intertwine, weave.

2 VI (bailadores) to weave in and out; (caballo) to caper.

3 **trenzarse** VR **(a)** **~ en una discusión** (LAm) to get involved in an argument.

(b) (And, Cono Sur*: pelear) to come to blows.

trepa¹ 1 NF **(a)** (subida) climb, climbing.

(b) (voltereta) somersault.

(c) (Caza) hide.

(d) (ardid) trick, ruse, deception.

(e) (*: paliza) tanning*.

2 NMF (:) (cobista) creep:; (arribista) social climber; **ser un ~*** to be on the make*.

trepa² NF **(a)** (Téc) drilling, boring. **(b)** (Cos) trimming. **(c)** (de madera) grain.

trepada NF climb; (fig) rise, ascent.

trepaderas NFPL (Carib, Méx) climbing-irons.

trepado NM **(a)** (Téc) drilling, boring. **(b)** (de sello etc) perforation.

trepador 1 ADJ **(a)** planta climbing, rambling.

(b) **este vino es bien ~** (And*) this wine goes right to your head.

2 NM **(a)** (Bot) climber, rambler.

(b) (*: persona) social climber.

(c) (Orn) nuthatch.

(d) **~es** climbing-irons.

trepadora NF (Bot) climber, rambler.

trepanar [1a] VT to trepan.

trepar¹ [1a] VTI to climb (a up), clamber up; to scale; (Bot) to climb (por up); **~ a un avión** to climb into an aircraft; **~ a un árbol** to climb (up) a tree.

trepar² [1a] VT **(a)** (Téc) to drill, bore. **(b)** (Cos) to trim.

trepe* NM telling-off*; **echar un ~ a uno** to tell sb off*.

trepetera* NF (Carib) hubbub, din.

trepidación NF shaking, vibration.

trepidante ADJ shaking, vibrating; (fig) shattering; frío extreme; ruido etc intolerable, shattering.

trepidar [1a] VI **(a)** (temblar) to shake, vibrate. **(b)** (And, Cono Sur:

vacilar) to hesitate, waver; **~ en** + infin to hesitate to + infin.

treque ADJ (Carib) witty, funny.

tres 1 ADJ three; (fecha) third; **las ~** three o'clock; **como ~ y 2 son 5** as sure as sure can be, as sure as eggs is eggs; **de ~ al cuarto** cheap, poor quality; **ni a la de ~** on no account, not by a long shot; not by any manner of means; **no ve ~ en un burro** he's as blind as a bat.

2 NM three; **~ en raya** (juego) noughts and crosses.

trescientos ADJ three hundred.

tresillo NM **(a)** (muebles) three-piece suite. **(b)** (Mús) triplet.

tresnal NM (Agr) shock, stook.

treso ADJ (Méx) dirty.

treta NF **(a)** (Esgrima) feint. **(b)** (fig) (truco) trick; (ardid) ruse, stratagem; (Com etc) stunt, gimmick; **~ publicitaria** advertising gimmick.

tri... PREF tri...; three-...

tríada NF triad.

trial 1 NM (Dep) trial.

2 NF trial motorcycle.

triangulación NF triangulation.

triangular 1 ADJ triangular; three-cornered.

2 [1a] VT to triangulate.

triángulo NM triangle (t Mús); **~ de aviso** warning triangle; **~ de las Bermudas** Bermuda Triangle.

triates NMPL (Méx) triplets.

triatlón NM triathlon.

tribal ADJ tribal.

tribalismo NM tribalism.

tribu NF tribe; **~ urbana** youth subculture.

tribulación NF tribulation.

tribulete* NM trainee journalist.

tribuna NF **(a)** (de orador) platform, rostrum, dais; (en mitin) platform.

(b) (Dep etc) stand, grandstand; **~ cubierta** covered stand; **~ libre, ~ pública** (Parl) public gallery, (Prensa) open forum, forum for debate; **~ de la prensa** (Parl) press-gallery, (Dep) press-box.

(c) (Ecl) gallery; **~ del órgano** organ loft.

(d) (Jur) **~ del acusado** dock; **~ del jurado** jury-box.

(e) (fig) political oratory, public speechmaking.

tribunal NM **(a)** (Jur) court; (personas) court, bench; **~ constitucional** constitutional court; **~ de familia** family court; **T~ de la Haya, T~ Internacional de Justicia** International Court of Justice; **~ juvenil, ~ (tutelar) de menores** juvenile court; **T~ Supremo** High Court, Supreme Court (US); **en pleno ~** in open court; **llevar a uno ante los ~es** to take sb to court.

(b) (Pol, comisión investigadora etc) tribunal.

(c) (Univ) (examinadores) board of examiners; (de selección) appointments committee.

(d) (fig) tribunal; forum; **~ de la conciencia** one's own conscience; **el ~ de la opinión pública** the forum of public opinion.

(e) (Cono Sur Mil) court-martial.

TRIBUNAL CONSTITUCIONAL

The role of the Spanish **Tribunal Constitucional** is to see that the 1978 Constitution is adhered to by the organs of government. It has jurisdiction in conflicts of power between the Spanish State and the **Comunidades Autónomas** and between the Autonomous Communities themselves, and it also has powers to safeguard the basic rights of citizens. It consists of 12 members, 4 nominated by Congress and 4 by Senate, 2 by the Government and 2 by the governing body of the Spanish judiciary, the **Consejo General del Poder Judicial.**

⇨ See also LA CONSTITUCIÓN ESPAÑOLA
---

tribuno NM tribune.

tributación NF **(a)** (pago) payment. **(b)** (impuestos) taxation; **~ directa** direct taxation.

tributar [1a] 1 VT **(a)** (Fin) to pay. **(b)** (fig) homenaje, respeto etc to pay; gracias to give; afecto etc to have, show (a for).

2 VI (pagar impuestos) to pay taxes.

tributario 1 ADJ **(a)** (Geog, Pol) tributary.

(b) (Fin) tax (atr), taxation (atr); **privilegio ~** tax concession; **sistema ~** taxation, tax system.

2 NM tributary.

tributo NM **(a)** (Hist: t fig) tribute. **(b)** (Fin) tax.

tricampeón, -ona NM/F triple champion, three-times champion.

tricentenario NM tercentenary.

tricentésimo ADJ three hundredth.

trichina NF (LAm) trichina.

triciclo NM tricycle.

tricófero NM (And, Cono Sur, Méx) hair restorer.

tricola NF (Cono Sur) knitted waistcoat.

tricolor 1 ADJ tricolour, three-coloured; **bandera ~ = 2.**

2 NF tricolour.

tricornio NM three-cornered hat.

tricota NF (LAm) sweater.

tricotar [1a] VTI to knit; **tricotado a mano** hand-knitted.
tricotosa NF knitting-machine.
tridente NM trident.
tridentino ADJ Tridentine, of Trent; **Concilio T~** Council of Trent; **misa tridentina** Tridentine Mass.
tridimensional ADJ three-dimensional.
trienal ADJ triennial.
trienalmente ADV triennially.
trienio NM (**a**) period of three years. (**b**) (*pago*) monthly bonus for each three-year period worked with the same employer.
trifásico [1] ADJ (*Elec*) three-phase, triphase.
　[2] NM: **tener ~** to have pull, have influence.
triforio NM (*Ecl*) triforium, clerestory.
trifulca* NF row, shindy*.
trifulquero* ADJ rowdy, trouble-making.
trifurcación NF trifurcation.
trifurcarse [1g] VR to divide into three.
trigal NM wheat field.
trigésimo ADJ thirtieth.
trigo NM (**a**) (*Bot*) wheat; **~ candeal** bread wheat; **~ sarraceno** buckwheat; **de ~ entero** wholemeal; **no es ~ limpio** (*fig*) he's (o it's) dishonest; **no todo era ~ limpio** it wasn't completely aboveboard; it was a bit fishy*.
　(**b**) **~s** wheat, wheat field(s); **meterse en ~s ajenos** to meddle in sb else's affairs; to trespass on sb else's subject (*etc*).
　(**c**) (‡: *dinero*) dough‡, money.
trigonometría NF trigonometry.
trigonométrico ADJ trigonometric(al).
trigueño [1] ADJ (**a**) *pelo* corn-coloured, dark blonde. (**b**) *piel* light brown, golden-brown; (*LAm euf*) coloured.
　[2] NM, **trigueña** NF (*LAm euf*) coloured man, coloured woman.
triguero [1] ADJ wheat (*atr*).
　[2] NM (**a**) (*comerciante*) corn merchant. (**b**) (*tamiz*) corn sieve.
trila NF, **triles** NMPL (game of) 'find the lady'.
trilateral, trilátero ADJ trilateral, three-sided.
trilero NM card-sharp.
trilingüe ADJ trilingual.
trilita NF trinitrotoluene.
trilla NF (**a**) (*Agr*) threshing. (**b**) (*Carib, Cono Sur**: *paliza*) thrashing, beating. (**c**) (*Méx: senda*) track. (**d**) (*Carib: atajo*) short cut.
trillado [1] ADJ (**a**) (*Agr*) threshed.
　(**b**) (*fig*) *camino* beaten, well-trodden.
　(**c**) (*fig*) *tema* (*gastado*) trite, hackneyed, well-worn; (*conocido*) well-known; (*sencillo*) straightforward.
　[2] NM (**a**) (*fig*) thorough investigation. (**b**) (*Carib*) path, track.
trillador NM thresher.
trilladora NF threshing machine.
trilladura NF threshing.
trillar [1a] VT (**a**) (*Agr*) to thresh. (**b**) (*fig*) to use a lot, wear out by frequent use.
trillizo NM, **trilliza** NF triplet.
trillo NM (**a**) (*máquina*) threshing machine. (**b**) (*CAm, Carib: sendero*) path, track.
trillón NM trillion (*Brit*), quintillion (*US*).
trilogía NF trilogy.
trimarán NM trimaran.
trimestral ADJ quarterly, three-monthly; (*Univ*) termly.
trimestralmente ADV quarterly, every three months.
trimestre NM (**a**) (*período de tiempo*) quarter, period of three months; (*Univ*) term. (**b**) (*Fin*) (*pago*) quarterly payment; (*alquiler*) quarter's rent (*etc*).
trinado NM (*Orn*) song, warble; (*Mús*) trill.
trinar [1a] VI (**a**) (*Mús*) to trill; (*Orn*) to sing, warble. (**b**) (*: *enfadarse*) to fume, be angry; (*Cono Sur*) to shout; **está que trina** he's hopping mad*.
trinca NF (**a**) (*tres*) group of three, set of three, threesome.
　(**b**) (*And, Cono Sur*) (*pandilla*) band, gang; (*facción*) faction; (*complot*) plot, conspiracy.
　(**c**) (*Carib, Méx: embriaguez*) drunkenness.
　(**d**) (*Cono Sur: canicas*) marbles.
trincar¹ [1g] [1] VT (**a**) (*atar*) to tie up, tie firmly; (*Náut*) to lash.
　(**b**) (*inmovilizar*) to pinion, hold by the arms; (‡: *detener*) to nick*, arrest, lift*.
　(**c**) (*agarrar*) to pick up, grab, lay hold of; (‡: *robar*) to nick‡.
　(**d**) (*‡: *copularse*) to screw‡.
　(**e**) (‡: *matar*) to do in‡.
　(**f**) (*CAm, Cono Sur, Méx*) to squeeze, press.
　(**g**) (*Cono Sur**) **me trinca que ...** I have a hunch that ...
　[2] **trincarse** VR: **~ a** + *infin* (*CAm, Méx*) to start to + *infin*, set about + *ger*.
trincar² [1g] VT (*romper*) to break up; (*tajar*) to chop up; *papel etc* to tear up.

trincar³ [1g] [1] VTI (*beber*) to drink.
　[2] **trincarse** VR (*Carib, Méx**) to get drunk.
trinchador NM carving-knife, carver.
trinchante NM (**a**) (*cuchillo*) carving-knife, carver; (*tenedor*) carving-fork. (**b**) (*mueble*) sidetable; (*Cono Sur*) sideboard.
trinchar [1a] VT (**a**) (*cortar*) to carve, slice, cut up. (**b**)(‡: *matar*) to do in‡.
trinche [1] NM (**a**) (*LAm: tenedor*) fork. (**b**) (*And, Cono Sur, Méx: mueble*) sidetable. (**c**) (*Méx Agr*) pitchfork.
　[2] ADJ: **pelo ~** (*And*) frizzy hair.
trinchera NF (**a**) (*zanja*) trench, entrenchment; (*Mil*) trench; (*Ferro*) cutting; **guerra de ~s** trench warfare.
　(**b**) (*prenda*) trenchcoat.
　(**c**) (*LAm: cercado*) fence, stockade.
　(**d**) (*Méx: cuchillo*) curved knife.
trinchete NM shoemaker's knife; (*And*) table knife.
trincho NM (*And*) (*parapeto*) parapet; (*zanja*) trench, ditch.
trinco NM (*Carib, Méx*) drunkard.
trincón‡ ADJ murderous.
trineo NM sledge, sleigh; **~ de balancín** bobsleigh; **~ de perros** dog sleigh.
Trini NF *forma familiar de* **Trinidad.**
Trinidad NF (**a**) (*Rel*) Trinity. (**b**) (*Geog*) Trinidad.
trinidad NF (*fig*) trio, set of three.
trinitaria NF (*de jardín*) pansy; (*silvestre*) heart's-ease.
trinitrotolueno NM trinitrotoluene.
trino NM (*Orn*) warble; trill; (*Mús*) trill.
trinomio ADJ, NM trinomial.
trinque* NM liquor, booze*.
trinquetada NF (*Carib*) period of danger; (*And, Méx*) hard times.
trinquete¹ NM (*Mec*) pawl, trip, catch; ratchet.
trinquete² NM (**a**) (*Náut*) (*mástil*) foremast; (*vela*) foresail. (**b**) (*Dep*) pelota court.
trinquete³ NM (*Méx*) (**a**) (*soborno*) bribe; (*asunto turbio*) shady deal, corrupt affair. (**b**) **es un ~ de hombre*** he really is a tough customer. (**c**) (*And*) small room.
trinquis* INVAR [1] NM drink, swig*.
　[2] ADJ (*Méx**) drunk, sloshed*.
trío NM trio.
tripa NF (**a**) (*Anat*) intestine, gut; **~s** (*Anat*) guts, insides*, innards*; (*Culin*) tripe; **me duelen las ~s** I have a stomach ache; **echar las ~s** to retch, vomit violently; **le gruñían las ~s** his tummy was rumbling*; **hacer de ~s corazón** to pluck up courage, screw up one's courage; **llenar la ~*** to eat well at somebody else's expense; **quitar las ~s a un pez** to gut a fish; **revolver las ~s a uno** (*fig*) to turn sb's stomach; **¡te sacaré las ~s!*** I'll tear your guts out!‡; **tener malas ~s** to be cruel.
　(**b**) (*fig**: *vientre*) belly, tummy*; (*de mujer encinta*) bulge; **echar ~** to put on weight, start to get a paunch; **dejar a una con ~** (*Esp*) to get a girl in the family way; **estar con ~** (*Esp*) to be in the family way; **tener mucha ~** to be fat, be paunchy.
　(**c**) (*de fruta*) core, seeds.
　(**d**) (*Mec*) **~s*** innards*, works; parts; **sacar las ~s de un reloj** to take out the works of a watch.
　(**e**) (*de vasija*) belly, bulge.
　(**f**) (*Com, Jur etc*) file, dossier.
　(**g**) (*Carib: de neumático*) inner tube.
tripartito ADJ tripartite.
tripe NM shag.
tripear* [1a] VI to stuff o.s.*, scoff*.
triperío NM (*And, Méx*) guts, entrails.
tripero* ADJ greedy.
tripi‡ NM LSD; dose of LSD.
tripicallos NMPL (*Culin Esp*) tripe.
tripitir [3a] VT to repeat again, do a third time.
triple [1] ADJ triple; threefold; (*de 3 capas*) of three layers (o thicknesses *etc*); **~ salto** triple jump.
　[2] NM (**a**) triple; **es el ~ de lo que era** it is three times what (o as big as) it was; **su casa es el ~ de grande que la nuestra** their house is three times bigger than ours. (**b**) (*Dep*) triple jump.
　[3] ADV: **esta cuerda es ~ gruesa que ésa*** this string is three times thicker than that bit.
tripleta NF trio, threesome.
triplicado ADJ triplicate; **por ~** in triplicate.
triplicar [1g] [1] VT to treble, triple; **las pérdidas triplican las ganancias** losses are three times the profits.
　[2] **triplicarse** VR to treble, triple.
triplo NM = **triple 2 (a).**
trípode NM tripod.
Trípoli NM Tripoli.
tripón* [1] ADJ fat, potbellied.
　[2] NM, **tripona** NF (*Méx*) little boy, little girl; **los tripones** the kids*.

tríptico NM (a) (*Arte*) triptych. (b) (*formulario*) form in three parts, three-part document (c) (*Com*) folder, brochure, leaflet.

triptongo NM triphthong.

tripudo ADJ fat, potbellied.

tripulación NF crew.

tripulado ADJ: **vuelo ~** manned flight; **vuelo no ~** unmanned flight; **~ por** manned by.

tripulante NM crew member, crewman; **~s** crew, men.

tripular [1a] VT (a) *barco etc* to man. (b) (*Aut etc*) to drive. (c) (*Cono Sur*) to mix (up).

tripulina* NF (*Cono Sur*) row, brawl.

trique NM (a) (*ruido*) crack, sharp noise, swish.
(b) **a cada ~** at every moment; repeatedly.
(c) (*And, Méx*) trick, dodge.
(d) **~s** (*Méx**) things, gear, odds and ends.
(e) (*And, CAm: juego*) noughts and crosses.

triquina NF trichina.

triquinosis NF trichinosis.

triquiñuela NF trick, dodge; **~s** dodges, funny business; **es un tío ~s*** he's an artful old cuss*; **saber las ~s del oficio** to know the tricks of the trade, know all the dodges.

triquis NMPL (*Méx*) = **trique** (d).

triquitraque NM string of fire-crackers.

trirreactor NM tri-jet.

trirreme NM trireme.

tris NM (a) (*estallido*) crack; (*al rasgarse*) tearing noise.
(b) **está en un ~** it's touch and go; **estaba en un ~ que lo perdiera** he very nearly lost it, he was within an inch of losing it; **los dos coches evitaron el choque por un ~** the two cars avoided a collision by a hair's breadth.
(c) (*LAm: juego*) noughts and crosses.

trisar [1a] VT (*And, Cono Sur*) to crack; to chip.

trisca NF (a) (*crujido*) crunch, crushing noise. (b) (*jaleo*) uproar, rumpus, row. (c) (*Carib*) mockery; (*chiste*) private joke.

triscar [1g] ① VT (a) (*mezclar*) to mix, mingle; (*confundir*) to mix up.
(b) *sierra* to set.
(c) (*And, Carib: mofar*) to mock, joke about; to tease.
② VI (a) (*patalear*) to stamp one's feet about.
(b) (*corderos etc*) to gambol, frisk about; (*personas*) to romp, play about.

triscón ADJ (*And*) hypercritical, overcritical.

trisecar [1g] VT to trisect.

trisemanal ADJ triweekly.

trisemanalmente ADV triweekly, thrice weekly.

trisilábico ADJ trisyllabic, three-syllabled.

trisílabo ① ADJ trisyllabic, three-syllabled.
② NM trisyllable.

trisito NM (*And*) (*pizca*) pinch; (*pedacito*) scrap, piece.

trismo NM lockjaw.

Tristán NM Tristram, Tristan.

triste ① ADJ (a) (*estado*) *persona* sad; (*desgraciado*) miserable; gloomy; sorrowful; *carácter* gloomy, melancholy; *aspecto, cara* sad-looking; **poner ~ a uno** to make sb sad, make sb unhappy, make sb miserable; **ponerse ~** to become sad; to look sad.
(b) *cuento, noticia etc* sad; *canción* sad, mournful; *paisaje* dismal, desolate, dreary; *cuarto etc* gloomy, dismal.
(c) (*fig*) sorry, sad; **hizo un ~ papel** he cut a sorry figure; **la ~ verdad es que ...** the sorry truth is that ...; **es ~ verle así** it is sad to see him like that, it grieves one to see him like that; **es ~ no poder ir, es ~ que no podamos ir** it's a pity we can't go.
(d) (*) *flor etc* old, withered.
(e) (*: *desgraciado*) miserable, wretched; single; **no queda sino una ~ peseta** there's just one miserable peseta left, there's just one poor little peseta left; **su padre es un ~ vigilante** his father is just a poor old watchman; **le mató algún ~ campesino** some wretched peasant killed him.
(f) (*LAm: pobre*) poor, valueless, wretched.
(g) (*And: tímido*) shy, timid.
② NM (*And, Cono Sur: canción*) sad love song.

tristemente ADV sadly; miserably; gloomily; sorrowfully; mournfully; **el ~ famoso lugar** the place which is well known for such unhappy reasons, the place which enjoys a sorry fame.

tristeza NF (V ADJ (a), (b)) (a) sadness; misery; gloom; sorrow; gloominess, melancholy. (b) dismalness, desolation, dreariness. (c) **~s*** (*noticias*) sad news; (*sucesos*) unhappy events. (d) (*Bot*) (type of) tree virus.

tristón ADJ rather sad; given to melancholy; pessimistic, gloomy.

tristura NF (*LAm*) = **tristeza.**

Tritón NM Triton.

tritón NM (*Zool*) newt.

trituración NF trituration; grinding, crushing.

triturador NM, **trituradora** NF (*Téc*) grinder, crushing machine;

(*Culin*) mincer, mincing machine; **~ de basuras** waste-disposal unit; **~ (de papel)** shredder.

triturar [1a] VT to triturate; to grind, crush, pulverize.

triunfador ① ADJ triumphant; (*ganador*) winning.
② NM, **triunfadora** NF victor, winner.

triunfal ADJ (a) *arco etc* triumphal. (b) *grito, sonrisa etc* triumphant.

triunfalismo NM euphoria, excessive optimism; over-confidence; self-congratulation; smugness; **lo digo sin ~s** I say it without wishing to exult.

triunfalista ADJ euphoric, excessively optimistic; over-confident; self-congratulatory; smug.

triunfalmente ADV triumphantly.

triunfante ADJ (a) triumphant; (*ganador*) winning; **salir ~** to come out the winner, emerge victorious. (b) (*jubiloso*) jubilant, exultant.

triunfar [1a] VI (a) (*gen*) to triumph (*de, sobre* over); (*ganar*) to win; (*salir victorioso*) to emerge victorious; (*tener éxito*) to be a success, be successful; **~ de los enemigos** to triumph over one's enemies; **~ en la vida** to succeed in life, make a success of one's life; **~ en un concurso** to win a competition.
(b) (*pey*) to exult (*de, sobre* over).
(c) (*Naipes: jugador*) to trump (in), play a trump.
(d) (*Naipes: ser triunfos*) to be trumps; **triunfan corazones** hearts are trumps.

triunfo NM (a) (*gen*) triumph; (*victoria*) win, victory; (*éxito*) success; **adjudicarse el ~** to win; **ha sido un verdadero ~** it has been a real triumph; **fue el sexto ~ consecutivo del equipo** it was the team's sixth consecutive win.
(b) (*Mús etc*) hit, success; **lista de ~s, lista del ~** hit parade, top ten (o twenty *etc*).
(c) (*Naipes*) trump; **6 sin ~s** 6 no-trumps; **palo del ~** trump suit, trumps; **tener todos los ~s en la mano** (*fig*) to hold all the trumps.

triunvirato NM triumvirate.

trivial ADJ trivial, trite, commonplace.

trivialidad NF (a) (*cualidad*) triviality, triteness.
(b) (*una ~*) trivial matter; trite remark (*etc*); **~es** trivia, trivialities; **decir ~es** to talk trivially, talk in platitudes.

trivialización NF trivializing; minimizing (the importance of), playing-down.

trivializar [1f] VT to trivalize; to minimize (the importance of), play down.

trivialmente ADV trivially, tritely.

triza NF bit, fragment; shred; **hacer algo ~s** to smash sth to bits; to tear sth to shreds; **hacer ~s a uno** to wear sb out; to flatten sb, crush sb; **los críticos dejaron la obra hecha ~s** the critics pulled the play to pieces, the critics tore the play to shreds.

trizar [1f] VT to smash to bits; to tear to shreds.

troca NF (*Méx*) lorry, truck.

trocaico ADJ trochaic.

trocar [1g y 1l] ① VT (a) (*Com*) to exchange, barter (*por* for).
(b) *dinero* to change (*en* into).
(c) (*cambiar*) to change (*con, por* for); (*intercambiar*) to interchange, switch round, move about; *palabras* to exchange (*con* with); **~ la alegría en tristeza** to change gaiety into sadness.
(d) (*confundir*) to mix up, confuse.
(e) *comida* to vomit.
(f) (*Cono Sur: vender*) to sell; (*And: comprar*) to buy.
② **trocarse** VR to change (*en* into); to get switched round; to get mixed up.

trocear [1a] VT to cut up, cut into pieces.

trocha NF (a) (*senda*) by-path, narrow path; (*atajo*) short cut. (b) (*LAm Ferro*) gauge; **~ normal** standard gauge. (c) (*Cono Sur Aut*) lane (of a motorway). (d) (*And: trote*) trot. (e) (*And: porción*) portion, helping (of meat).

trochar [1a] VI (*And*) to trot.

troche: a ~ y moche, a trochemoche ADV *correr etc* helter-skelter, pell-mell; *desparramarse etc* all over the place; *repartir, usar etc* haphazardly, unsystematically, regardless of distinctions.

trofeo NM (a) (*objeto*) trophy. (b) (*fig*) victory, success, triumph.

troglodita NMF (a) (*Hist*) cave dweller, troglodyte. (b) (*fig*) (*grosero*) brute, coarse person; (*huraño*) unsociable individual, recluse. (c) (*: *glotón*) glutton.

troica NF troika.

troja NF (*LAm*) = **troj(e).**

troj(e) NF granary, barn.

trola¹* NF fib, lie.

trola² NF (*And*) (*jamón*) slice of ham; (*cuero*) piece of raw hide; (*corteza*) piece of loose bark.

trole NM (a) (*Elec*) trolley, trolley pole. (b) (*Cono Sur Hist: autobús*) trolley bus.

trolebús NM trolley bus.

trolero* NM fibber, liar.

tromba NF whirlwind; **~ marina** waterspout; **~ terrestre** whirlwind, tornado; **~ de agua** violent downpour; **~ de polvo** column of dust; **entrar en ~** to come in in a torrent, come rushing in; **pasar como una ~** to go by like a whirlwind.

trombo NM thrombus (*Téc*), clot.

trombón [1] NM (*instrumento*) trombone.
   [2] NMF (*persona*) trombonist.

trombonista NMF trombonist.

trombosis NF thrombosis; (*t ~ cerebral*) cerebral haemorrhage.

trome* ADJ (*And*) bright, smart.

trompa [1] NF (a) (*Mús*) horn; **~ de caza** hunting horn; **sonar la ~ marcial** to sound a warlike note, blow a martial trumpet.
   (b) (*peonza*) humming-top; whipping-top.
   (c) (*Ent*) proboscis; (*Zool*) trunk; (*: nariz*) snout‡, hooter‡; (*LAm: labios*) thick lips, blubber lips; **¡cierra la ~!** (*CAm, Méx*‡) shut your trap‡!
   (d) (*Anat*) tube, duct; **~ de Eustaquio** Eustachian tube; **~ de Falopio** Fallopian tube.
   (e) (*Met*) = **tromba**.
   (f) (*: borrachera*) drunkenness; **cogerse** (*LAm*: **agarrarse**) **una ~** to get tight*.
   (g) (*Méx Ferro*) cowcatcher.
   [2] NM (a) (*Mús*) horn player. (b) (*Cono Sur*: *patrón*) boss, chief.

trompada NF, **trompazo** NM (a) (*choque*) bump, bang; head-on collision. (b) (*puñetazo*) punch, swipe. (c) (*Méx: zurra*) thrashing, beating-up*.

trompeadura NF (*LAm*) (a) (*choques*) bumping, banging. (b) (*puñetazos*) series of punches; (*paliza*) beating-up*.

trompear [1a] (*LAm*) [1] VT (a) (*chocar con*) to bump, bang into; to collide head-on with. (b) (*pegar*) to punch, thump.
   [2] VI (a) to spin a top. (b) = **3**.
   [3] **trompearse** VR to exchange blows, fight.

trompeta [1] NF (a) (*instrumento*) trumpet; (*corneta*) bugle; (*fig*) clarion. (b) (*: droga*) reefer‡, joint‡. (c) (*Cono Sur Bot*) daffodil.
   [2] NMF (*Mús*) trumpeter; bugler.
   [3] NM (*) (*imbécil*) twit*; (*borracho*) drunk*, old soak*.
   [4] ADJ (*Méx*) sloshed*, tight*.

trompetazo NM (*Mús*) trumpet blast; (*fig*) blast, blare.

trompetear [1a] VI to play the trumpet.

trompeteo NM sound of trumpets, (*esp*) fanfare.

trompetero NM (*de orquesta*) trumpet player; (*Mil etc*) trumpeter; bugler.

trompetilla NF (a) (*t ~ acústica*) ear trumpet. (b) (*Carib*) raspberry*.

trompetista NMF trumpet player, (*jazz*) trumpeter.

trompeto* ADJ (*Méx*) drunk.

trompezar [1f] VI (*LAm*) = **tropezar**.

trompezón NM (*LAm*) = **tropezón**.

trompicar [1g] [1] VT (*tropezar*) to trip up.
   (b) **~ a uno*** to fiddle sb's promotion*, promote sb improperly.
   [2] VI to trip up a lot, stumble repeatedly.

trompicón NM (a) (*tropiezo*) stumble, trip; **a trompicones** in fits and starts; with difficulty. (b) (*Carib: puñetazo*) blow, punch.

trompis* NM INVAR punch, bash*.

trompiza* NF (*And, Méx*) punch-up‡.

trompo NM (a) (*juguete*) spinning top; **~ de música** humming-top; **ponerse como un ~** to eat to bursting point.
   (b) (*LAm*) (*desmañado*) clumsy person; (*bailador*) rotten dancer*.
   (c) (*Fin*‡) 1000-peseta note; **medio ~** 500-peseta note.
   (d) (*Dep*) spin.

trompón NM (a) (*) (*choque*) bump, bang; (*puñetazo*) hefty punch, vicious swipe. (b) = **trompo** (b). (c) (*Bot: t narciso ~*) daffodil.

trompudo ADJ (*LAm*) thick-lipped, blubber-lipped.

tron‡ NM = **tronco** (d).

tronada NF, **tronadera** NF (*Méx*) thunderstorm.

tronado ADJ (a) (*viejo*) old, broken-down, useless. (b) **estar ~*** (*loco*) to be potty*; (*arruinado*) to be ruined. (c) **estar ~** (*CAm*‡) to be broke*. (d) **estar ~** (*LAm*‡) to be high (on drugs)‡.

tronadura NF (*Chile: Min*) blasting.

tronamenta NF (*And, Méx*) thunderstorm.

tronar [1l] [1] VT (a) (*CAm, Méx*‡: *fusilar*) to shoot, execute; (*pegar un tiro a*) to shoot.
   (b) **la tronó** (*Méx*‡) he blew it‡, he messed it up.
   [2] VI (a) to thunder; (*cañones etc*) to thunder, rumble, boom; **por lo que pueda ~** just in case, to be on the safe side.
   (b) (*Fin*‡) to go broke*; (*fracasar*) to fail, be ruined.
   (c) **~ con uno*** to fall out with sb.
   (d) (*fig: enfurecerse*) to rave, rage; **~ contra** to fulminate against, thunder against; to storm at.
   [3] **tronarse*** VR (a) (*CAm, Méx*) to shoot o.s., blow one's brains out.
   (b) (*LAm*) to take drugs.

tronazón NF (*CAm, Méx*) thunderstorm.

tronca‡ NF bird‡.

troncal ADJ: **línea ~** main line, trunk line; **materia ~** core subject.

troncar [1g] VT = **truncar**.

troncha NF (a) (*LAm*) (*tajada*) slice; (*trozo*) chunk, piece. (b) (*LAm*‡: *prebenda*) sinecure, soft job. (c) (*Méx: comida*) soldier's rations; meagre meal.

tronchacadenas NM INVAR chain cutters *pl*.

tronchado* [1] NM (*Méx: buen negocio*) gold mine (*fig*), prosperous business.
   [2] ADJ (*And: lisiado*) maimed, crippled.

tronchante* ADJ killingly funny.

tronchar [1a] [1] VT (a) (*talar*) to bring down; to chop down, lop off; (*cortar*) to cut up, cut off; (*hender*) to split, rend, smash.
   (b) (*fig*) vida to cut off, cut short; *esperanzas etc* to shatter.
   (c) (*: cansar*) to tire out.
   [2] **troncharse** VR (a) (*árbol*) to fall down, split.
   (b) (*: cansarse*) to tire o.s. out.
   (c) (*) **~ de risa** to split one's sides laughing.

troncho [1] ADJ (*Cono Sur*) maimed, crippled.
   [2] NM (a) (*Bot*) stem, stalk (of cabbage *etc*). (b) (*Cono Sur: trozo*) piece, chunk. (c) (*And: enredo*) knot, tangle. (d) (*‡*) prick‡‡.

tronco NM (a) (*Bot*) (*de árbol*) trunk; (*de flor etc*) stem, stalk; (*leño*) log; (*LAm*) tree stump; **~ de Navidad** (*Culin*) yule log; **dormir como un ~** to sleep like a log; **estar hecho un ~** (*dormido*) to be sound asleep; (*inmóvil*) to be completely deprived of movement.
   (b) (*Anat*) trunk.
   (c) (*‡: pene*) prick‡‡.
   (d) (*‡*) (*hombre*) bloke‡, chap*; (*amigo: en oración directa*) mate, chum*; **oye, ~** hey, friend; hey, brother*; **María y su ~** María and her bloke‡.
   (e) (*Ferro*) main line, trunk line.
   (f) (*de familia*) stock.

tronera [1] NF (a) (*Mil*) loophole, embrasure; (*Arquit*) small window.
   (b) (*Billar*) pocket.
   (c) (*Méx: chimenea*) chimney, flue.
   [2] NMF (*: tarambana*) crazy person, harum-scarum.
   [3] NM (*: libertino*) rake, libertine.

tronido NM (*Met*) thunderclap; (*explosión*) loud report, bang, detonation; boom; **~s** thunder, booming.

tronío NM lavish expenditure, extravagance.

trono NM throne; (*fig: frec*) crown; **heredar el ~** to inherit the crown; **subir al ~** to ascend the throne, come to the throne; **nuestra lealtad al ~** our loyalty to the crown.

tronquista NMF (*LAm*) lorry driver, truck driver (*US*).

tronzar [1f] VT (a) (*cortar*) to cut up; (*romper*) to split, rend, smash. (b) (*Cos*) to pleat. (c) (*) persona to tire out.

tropa NF (a) (*multitud*) troop, body, crowd; (*pey*) troop, mob.
   (b) (*Mil*) army, military; **~s** troops; **~s de asalto, ~ de choque** storm-troops; **ser de ~*** to be in the army, be a soldier.
   (c) (*Mil: soldados rasos*) men, rank and file, ordinary soldiers.
   (d) (*LAm Agr*) flock, herd.
   (e) (*Cono Sur: vehículos*) line of carts; stream of vehicles; line of cars.
   (f) (*Méx*: *maleducado*) rude person; (*Carib*: *tonto*) dope*.

tropear [1a] VT (*Cono Sur*) to herd.

tropecientos* ADJ PL umpteen*.

tropel NM (a) (*multitud*) mob, crowd, throng. (b) (*revoltijo*) jumble, mess, litter. (c) (*prisa*) rush, haste; **acudir** (*etc*) **en ~** to come in a mad rush, all rush together, come thronging in confusion.

tropelía NF (a) = **tropel** (c). (b) (*atropello*) outrage, abuse of authority, violent act; **cometer una ~** to commit an outrage.

tropero NM (a) (*Cono Sur*) cowboy. (b) (*Méx*) boor.

tropezar [1f y 1j] [1] VT = VI (b).
   [2] VI (a) (*dar con los pies*) to trip, stumble (*con, contra, en* on, over); **~ con** to run into, run up against.
   (b) (*fig: topar*) **~ con uno** to run into sb, bump into sb; **~ con algo** to run across sth.
   (c) **~ con una dificultad** (*fig*) to run into a difficulty, run up against a difficulty.
   (d) **~ con uno** (*fig: reñir*) to have an argument with sb; to fall out with sb.
   (e) (*fig: cometer un error*) to slip up, blunder; (*moralmente*) to slip, fall.
   [3] **tropezarse** VR to run into each other.

tropezón NM (a) (*traspié*) trip, stumble; **dar un ~** to trip, stumble; **proceder a tropezones** to proceed by fits and starts; **hablar a tropezones** to talk jerkily, talk falteringly.
   (b) (*fig: error*) slip, blunder; (*moral*) slip, lapse.
   (c) (*Culin*) small piece of meat (*added to soup etc*).

tropical ADJ (a) tropical. (b) (*Cono Sur: melodramático*) rhetorical, melodramatic, highly-coloured.

tropicalismo NM (*Cono Sur*) rhetoric, melodramatic style, excessive colourfulness.

trópico NM (a) (*Geog*) tropic; **~s** tropics; **~ de Cáncer** Tropic of Cancer; **~ de Capricornio** Tropic of Capricorn.
   (b) (*Carib*) **~s** hardships, difficulties; **pasar los ~s** to suffer hard-

ships, have a hard time.

tropiezo NM (a) (*error*) slip, blunder; (*desliz moral*) moral lapse. (b)(*desgracia*) misfortune, mishap; (*revés*) setback; (*en el amor*) disappointment in love. (c) (*obstáculo*) obstacle, snag; stumbling block. (d) (*riña*) quarrel; tiff, argument.

tropilla NF (*Cono Sur*) drove, team.

tropo NM trope, figure of speech.

troquel NM (*Téc*) die.

troquelado NM (*Téc*) hot-die forging, punching; (*fig*) moulding, shaping.

troqueo NM trochee.

trosco, -a* NM/F Trot*, Trotskyist.

trotacalles* NMF INVAR bum*.

trotaconventos NF INVAR go-between, procuress.

trotamundos NM INVAR globetrotter.

trotar [1a] VI (a) (*caballo etc*) to trot. (b) (*: *persona*) to travel about, chase around here and there; to hustle.

trote NM (a) (*de caballo etc*) trot; ~ **cochinero**, ~ **de perro** jogtrot; **ir al ~** to trot, go at a trot; **irse al ~** to go off in a great rush. (b) (*) (*viajes*) travelling, chasing around; (*ajetreo*) bustle; **yo ya no estoy para esos ~s** I can't go chasing around like that any more; **tomar el ~** to dash off. (c) **de mucho ~** *ropa* tough, hard-wearing; **chaqueta para todo ~** a jacket for everyday use, a jacket for ordinary wear. (d) (*: *asunto turbio*) ~**s** shady affair, dark doings; **meterse en malos ~s** to get mixed up in something improper. (e) (*: *apuros*) ~**s** hardships; **andar en malos ~s** to have a rough time of it, suffer hardships.

trotskismo NM Trotskyism.

trotskista ADJ, NMF Trotskyist.

trova NF ballad.

trovador NM troubadour.

Troya NF Troy; **aquí fue ~** and now this is all you see, now there's nothing but ruins; **¡aquí fue ~!** * you should have heard the fuss!; **¡arda ~!** press on regardless!, never mind the consequences!

troyano, -a ADJ, NM/F Trojan.

troza NF log.

trozo NM (a) (*pedazo*) bit, piece; chunk; fragment; **a ~s** in bits, piecemeal; **es un ~ de pan*** he's a dear, he's a sweetie*. (b) (*Liter, Mús*) passage; section; ~**s escogidos** selections, selected passages.

trucaje NM (*Cine*) trick photography; special effects; (*fig*) rigging, fixing, fiddling*.

trucar [1g] **1** VT (*) (a) *resultado* to fix, rig; *baraja* to arrange (fraudulently); **las cartas estaban trucadas** (*fig*) the dice were loaded against us. (b) (*Aut*) *motor* to soup up*.
2 VI (*Billar*) to pocket the ball, pot.

trucha¹ NF (a) (*pez*) trout; ~ **arco iris** rainbow trout; ~ **marina** sea trout. (b) (*Téc*) crane, derrick.

trucha² NF (*CAm Com*) stall, booth.

trucha³* NMF tricky individual, wily bird; cheat.

truche: NM (*And*) snappy dresser*, dude* (*US*).

truchero¹ NM (*CAm*) hawker, vendor.

truchero² ADJ trout (*atr*); **río ~** trout river.

truchimán NM (a) (*Hist*) interpreter. (b) (*) rogue, villain.

trucho ADJ (*And*) sharp, rascally.

truco NM (a) (*ardid*) trick, device, dodge; (*destreza*) knack; (*Cine*) trick effect, piece of trick photography; **arte de los ~s** conjuring; ~ **de naipes** card trick; ~ **publicitario** advertising stunt, publicity gimmick; **el tío tiene muchos ~s** the fellow is up to all the dodges; **coger el ~** to get the knack, get the hang of it, catch on; **coger el ~ a uno** to see how sb works a trick; (*fig*) to catch on to sb's little game. (b) ~**s** (*Billar*) billiards, pool. (c) (*And, Cono Sur**: *puñetazo*) punch, bash*. (d) (*Cono Sur Naipes*) popular card game.

truculencia NF gruesomeness.

truculento ADJ gruesome; (*horroroso*) horrifying; (*extravagante*) full of extravagant effects.

trueco NM = **trueque**.

trueno NM (a) (*gen*) thunder; (*un ~*) clap of thunder, thunderclap; (*de cañón etc*) bang, boom, report. (b) (*) (*tarambana*) wild youth, madcap; (*libertino*) rake. (c) ~ **gordo*** finale (*of firework display*); (*fig*) big row, major scandal. (d) (*Carib**: *juerga*) binge*, noisy party. (e) (*And:*) rod:, gun. (f) ~**s** (*And Fin*) stout shoes.

trueque NM (a) (*cambio*) exchange; switch; (*Com*) barter; **a ~ de** in exchange for; in place of; **aun a ~ de perderlo** even at the cost of losing it. (b) ~**s** (*And Fin*) change.

trufa NF (a) (*Bot*) truffle. (b) (*: *cuento*) fib, story.

trufado ADJ stuffed with truffles.

trufar [1a] **1** VT (a) (*Culin*) to stuff with truffles. (b) (*: *estafar*) to take in*, swindle.
2 VI (*) to fib, tell stories.

trufi* NM (*And*) taxi.

truhán NM (a) (*Hist*) jester, buffoon, funny man. (b) (*estafador*) rogue, crook*, swindler; (*charlatán*) mountebank.

truhanería NF (a) (*Hist*) buffoonery. (b) (*picardía*) roguery, crookedness, swindling.

truhanesco ADJ (a) buffoonish. (b) (*tramposo*) crooked*, dishonest.

truísmo NM truism.

truja: NM fag:, gasper:.

trujal NM (*de vino*) winepress; (*de aceite*) olive-oil press.

trujimán NM = **truchimán**.

trujis: NM INVAR fag:, gasper:.

trulla NF (a) (*bullicio*) bustle, commotion, noise. (b) (*multitud*) crowd, throng. (c) (*And: broma*) practical joke.

trullada NF (*Carib*) crowd, throng.

trullo: NM nick:, jail.

truncado ADJ (*reducido*) truncated, shortened; (*incompleto*) incomplete.

truncamiento NM truncation, shortening; curtailing; cutting; mutilation.

truncar [1g] VT (a) (*acortar*) to truncate, shorten; *texto etc* to cut off; to cut short, curtail; *discurso* to cut, slash; *cita* to mutilate; *sentido* to affect, upset, destroy. (b) (*fig*) *carrera, vida* to cut short; *esperanzas, proyecto* to ruin; *desarrollo* to stunt, check, seriously affect.

trunco ADJ (*reducido*) truncated, shortened; (*incompleto*) incomplete.

truquero (*LAm*) **1** ADJ tricky; gimmicky.
2 NM, **truquera** NF trickster.

truqui* NM = **truco** (a).

trusa NF (a) (*Carib*: *bañador*) bathing trunks. (b) (*And, Méx*) (*de hombre*) underpants; (*de mujer*) panties, knickers; (*de bebé*) pants.

trust [trʌst] NM, PL **trusts** [trʌsts] (*Fin*) trust, cartel.

truzas* NFPL knickers.

Tte. ABR *de* **teniente** Lieutenant, Lt.

TU NM ABR *de* **tiempo universal** universal time, U.T.

tu ADJ POS your; (††, *a Dios*) thy.

tú PRON PERS (a) you; (††, *a Dios*) thou; **tratar a uno de ~ a ~** to treat sb on equal terms; **en el partido se mantuvo el ~ a ~** the game was between equals, the game was an equal struggle. (b) (:) (*usado solo, en oración directa*) (*enfático*) you know, you see; (*rechazo*) no way!*, get away!*; (*insulto*) get lost!:

tualé (*LAm*) **1** NM toilet, lavatory.
2 NF (*feminine*) toilet.

tuareg ADJ, NMF, PL **tuareg(s)** Tuareg.

tubercular ADJ tubercular.

tubérculo NM (a) (*Bot*) tuber. (b) (*Anat, Med etc*) tubercle.

tuberculosis NF tuberculosis.

tuberculoso ADJ tuberculous, tubercular.

tubería NF (*tubos*) pipes, piping; tubes, tubing; (*oleoducto etc*) pipeline.

tubero NM plumber, pipe-fitter.

Tubinga NF Tübingen.

tubo NM (a) tube (*t Anat, TV etc*); pipe; (*LAm Telec*) handset, earpiece; ~ **acústico** speaking-tube; ~ **capilar** capillary; ~ **de chimenea** chimneypot; ~ **de desagüe** drainpipe, waste-pipe; ~ **digestivo** alimentary canal; ~ **de ensayo** test-tube; ~ **de escape** exhaust (pipe); ~ **fluorescente** fluorescent tube; ~ **de humo** chimney, flue; ~ **de imagen** television tube; ~ **intestinal** intestine; ~ **de lámpara** lamp glass; ~ **lanzatorpedos** torpedo-tube; ~ **de órgano** organ pipe; ~ **de radio** wireless valve, tube (*US*); ~ **de rayos catódicos** cathode-ray tube; ~ **de respiración** breathing-tube; ~ **de vacío** valve, vacuum tube (*US*); **pasar por el ~*** to knuckle under; **lo vendió por un ~*** he sold it for a packet*. (b) (:) (*Ferro*) tube, underground; (*Telec*) phone, blower:; (*cárcel*) nick:.

tubular 1 ADJ tubular.
2 NM (*prenda*) roll-on.

tucán NM, **tucano** NM (*Carib, Cono Sur*) toucan.

Tucídedes NM Thucydides.

tuco¹ 1 ADJ (a) (*LAm*) (*mutilado*) maimed, limbless; (*manco*) lacking a finger (o hand). (b) (*CAm**: *achaparrado*) squat.
2 NM (*LAm Anat*) stump.
3 NM, **tuca** NF (*persona*) cripple.

tuco² NM (*And, Cono Sur: Ent*) glow-worm.

tuco³, -a NM/F (*CAm: tocayo*) namesake.

tuco⁴ NM (*And, Cono Sur Culin*) tomato sauce.

tucura NF (a) (*Cono Sur: langosta*) locust. (b) (*And*) (*libélula*) dragonfly; (*mantis*) praying mantis; (*saltamontes*) grasshopper. (c) (*fig: cura*) corrupt priest.

tucuso NM (*Carib*) hummingbird.

tudesco, -a ADJ, NM/F German.

tuerca NF nut; ~ **mariposa** wingnut; **apretar las ~s a uno** to tighten the screws on sb.

tuerce: NM (*CAm*) misfortune, setback.
tuerto [1] ADJ (**a**) (*torcido*) twisted, bent, crooked.
(**b**) (*mutilado*) one-eyed, blind in one eye.
(**c**) **a tuertas** upside-down; back to front; **a tuertas o a derechas** (*con razón o sin ella*) rightly or wrongly; (*por fas o por nefas*) by hook or by crook; (*sin pensar*) thoughtlessly, hastily.
[2] NM, **tuerta** NF one-eyed person, person blind in one eye.
[3] NM (*injusticia*) wrong, injustice.
tuesta• NF (*Carib*) binge•.
tueste NM (*de café*) roasting.
tuétano NM (**a**) (*Anat*) marrow; (*Bot*) pith; **hasta los ~s** through and through, utterly, to the core; **enamorado hasta los ~s** head over heels in love.
(**b**) (*fig*) core, essence.
tufarada NF (*olor*) bad smell; (*racha de olor*) gust of foul smell, cloud of evil-smelling gas (*etc*).
tufillas• NMF INVAR bad-tempered person.
tufillo NM (*fig*) slight smell (*a of*).
tufo[1] NM (**a**) (*vapor*) vapour, gas, exhalation.
(**b**) (*olor*) bad smell, stink; (*de cuerpos*) body odour; (*halitosis*) bad breath; (*de cuarto etc*) fug; **se le subió el ~ a las narices** (*fig*) he got very cross.
(**c**) **~s**• swank•, conceit; **tener ~s** to be swanky•, be conceited.
tufo[2] NM (*de pelo*) curl, sidelock.
tugurio NM (*Agr*) shepherd's hut; (*chabola*) hovel, slum, shack; (*cuartucho*) poky little room; (*cafetucho*) den, joint:; **~s** (*And*) slum quarter, shanty town.
tuja NF (*And*) hide-and-seek.
tul NM tulle, net.
tulenco ADJ (*CAm*) splay-footed.
tulipa NF lampshade.
tulipán NM tulip; (*And, Carib, Méx*) hibiscus.
tulipanero NM, **tulipero** NM tulip-tree.
tulis NM INVAR (*Méx*) highway robber, brigand.
tullida[1] NF (*Carib*) dirty trick.
tullido [1] ADJ crippled; paralysed, paralytic.
[2] NM, **tullida**[2] NF cripple.
tullir [3h] VT (**a**) (*lisiar*) to cripple, maim; (*paralizar*) to paralyze. (**b**) (*fig: agotar*) to wear out, exhaust. (**c**) (*fig: maltratar*) to abuse, maltreat.
tumba[1] NF (*sepultura*) tomb, grave; **ser (como) una ~** to keep one's mouth shut; **llevar a uno a la ~** (*euf*) to carry sb off; **hablar a ~ abierta** to speak openly.
tumba[2] NF (**a**) (*sacudida*) shake, jolt; lurch.
(**b**) (*voltereta*) somersault.
(**c**) (*LAm*) (*tala*) felling of timber, clearing of ground; (*tierra*) ground cleared for sowing; (*claro*) forest clearing.
(**d**) (*Cono Sur: carne*) boiled meat of poor quality.
tumba[3] NF (*Carib, Cono Sur*) African drum.
tumbacuartillos• NM INVAR old soak:.
tumbacuatro NM (*Carib*) braggart.
tumbadero NM (*Carib, Méx*) (**a**) (*Agr*) ground cleared for sowing. (**b**) (•: *burdel*) brothel.
tumbadora NF (*Carib*) large conga drum.
tumbar [1a] [1] VT (**a**) (*derribar*) to knock down, knock over, knock to the ground; (•: *vino*) to lay out; (:: *matar*) to do in:.
(**b**) (::: *copularse*) to lay::, screw::.
(**c**) (*Univ*•) to plough•.
(**d**) (•: *olor etc*) to lay out•, knock back•; (*impresionar etc*) to amaze, stun; **su presunción tumbó a todos** his conceit amazed everybody, his conceit knocked everybody sideways.
(**e**) (*LAm*) árboles to fell; *tierra* to clear.
[2] VI (**a**) (*caerse*) to fall down.
(**b**) (*Náut*) to capsize.
(**c**) (•) **un olor que tumba** a smell which knocks you back•; **tiene una desfachatez que tumba de espaldas** his brazenness is enough to stun you.
[3] **tumbarse** VR (**a**) (*acostarse*) to lie down; (*estirarse*) to stretch out; (*repantigarse*) to sprawl, loll; **estar tumbado, quedar tumbado** to lie, be lying down.
(**b**) (*trigo etc*) to go flat.
(**c**) (*fig*) to give up, decide to take it easy; to let o.s. go (*after achieving a success etc*).
tumbilla NF (*CAm*) wicker suitcase.
tumbo[1] NM (**a**) (*caída*) fall, tumble; (*sacudida*) shake, jolt; lurch; **dar un ~** to tumble; to jolt; to lurch; **dando ~s** (*fig*) with all sorts of difficulties, despite the upsets, after a lot of setbacks.
(**b**) (*momento crítico*) critical moment.
tumbo[2] NM (*Hist*) monastic cartulary.
tumbón• ADJ slack, lazy, bone-idle.
tumbona NF (*butaca*) easy chair; (*de playa*) deckchair, beach chair (*US*).
tumefacción NF swelling, tumefaction.

tumefacto ADJ swollen.
tumescente ADJ tumescent.
túmido ADJ swollen, tumid.
tumor NM tumour, growth; **~ cerebral** brain tumour; **~ maligno** malignant growth.
túmulo NM tumulus, barrow, burial mound; (*Geog*) mound.
tumulto NM turmoil, commotion, uproar, tumult; (*Pol etc*) riot, disturbance; **~ popular** popular rising.
tumultuario ADJ = tumultuoso.
tumultuosamente ADV tumultuously; (*pey*) riotously; rebelliously.
tumultuoso ADJ tumultuous; (*pey*) riotous, disorderly; rebellious.
tuna[1] NF (*Bot*) prickly pear.
tuna[2] NF (**a**) (*Esp Mús*) student music group.
(**b**) (*vida picaresca*) rogue's life, vagabond life; (*fig*) merry life; **correr la ~** to have a good time, live it up•.
(**c**) (*CAm: embriaguez*) drunkenness.

┌─────────┐
│ **TUNA** │
└─────────┘

🛈 *Tunas, also known as **estudiantinas** are groups of students dressed in 17th century costumes who play guitars, lutes and tambourines and go serenading through the streets. They also make impromptu appearances at weddings and parties singing traditional Spanish songs, often of a bawdy nature, in exchange for drinks or a few pesetas.*

tunantada NF dirty trick, villainous act.
tunante NM rogue, villain, crook; **¡~!** you villain!, (*a niño*) you young scamp!
tunantear [1a] VI to live a rogue's life, be a crook•.
tunantería NF (**a**) (*cualidad*) villainy, crookedness. (**b**) (*una ~*) villainy, dirty trick.
tunar [1a] VI to loaf, idle, bum around (*US*).
tunco (*CAm, Méx*) [1] ADJ (*lisiado*) maimed, crippled; (*manco*) one-armed.
[2] NM (**a**) (*persona*) cripple. (**b**) (*Zool*) pig.
tunda[1] NF (*esquileo*) shearing.
tunda[2] NF (**a**) (*paliza*) beating, thrashing. (**b**) **darse una ~** to wear o.s. out.
tundir[1] [3a] VT *paño* to shear; *hierba etc* to mow, cut.
tundir[2] [3a] VT (**a**) (*pegar*) to beat, thrash. (**b**) (*fig*) to exhaust, tire out.
tundra NF tundra.
tunear [1a] VI (**a**) (*vivir como pícaro*) to live a rogue's life. (**b**) (*gandulear*) to loaf, idle; (*divertirse*) to have a good time.
tunecino, -a ADJ, NM/F Tunisian.
túnel NM (**a**) tunnel; **~ aerodinámico, ~ de pruebas aerodinámicas, ~ de viento** wind-tunnel; **~ del Canal de la Mancha** Channel Tunnel; **~ de lavado** car-wash; **~ del tiempo** timewarp; **~ de vestuarios** tunnel leading to the changing-rooms.
(**b**) (*fig*) dark passage; dark period. (**c**) (*Dep*) nutmeg kick (*o pass etc*).
tuneladora NF tunnelling machine.
tunelar [1a] VI to tunnel.
tunes NMPL (*And, CAm*) first steps (*of a child*); **hacer ~** to toddle, start to walk, take one's first steps.
Túnez NM (*ciudad*) Tunis; (*Hist: país*) Tunisia.
tungo [1] ADJ (*And*) short, shortened; blunt.
[2] NM (**a**) (*And: trozo*) bit, chunk. (**b**) (*Cono Sur Anat*) neck; jowl.
tungsteno NM tungsten.
túnica NF (**a**) (*gen*) tunic; (*vestido largo*) robe, gown, long dress; **~ de gimnasia** gymslip. (**b**) (*Anat, Bot*) tunic.
Tunicia NF Tunisia.
túnico NM (*LAm*) shift, long undergarment.
túnido NM tuna (fish).
tuno NM (**a**) (*hum*) rogue, villain; scamp; **el muy ~** the old rogue. (**b**) (*Mús*) member of a student *tuna* (V **tuna**[2] (**a**)).
tunoso ADJ (*And*) prickly.
tuntún: **al (buen) ~** ADV thoughtlessly, without due calculation; trusting to luck; haphazardly; **juzgar al buen ~** to judge hastily, jump to conclusions.
tuntuneco• ADJ (*CAm, Carib*) stupid, dense•.
tuñeco ADJ (*Carib*) maimed, crippled.
tupamaro, -a NM/F (*Uruguay Pol*) Tupamaro.
tupé NM (**a**) (*peluca*) toupée, hairpiece. (**b**) (•: *caradura*) nerve•, cheek•.
tupí [1] NMF Tupi (Indian).
[2] NM (*Ling*) Tupi.
tupia NF (*And*) dam.
tupiar [1b] VT (*And*) to dam up.
tupición NF (**a**) (*LAm*) (*obstrucción*) blockage, stoppage, obstruction; (*Med*) catarrh.
(**b**) (*LAm: multitud*) dense crowd, throng.
(**c**) (*And, Méx: vegetación*) dense vegetation.
(**d**) **una ~ de cosas** (*Cono Sur*•) a lot of things.
(**e**) (*LAm: fig*) bewilderment, confusion.
tupido [1] ADJ (**a**) (*denso*) thick, dense; impenetrable; *tela* close-woven.

(b) (*LAm: obstruido*) blocked, stopped up, obstructed.
(c) (*: *estúpido*) dense*, dim*.
(d) (*Méx: frecuente*) common, frequent.
[2] ADV (*Méx*) (*con tesón*) persistently, steadily; (*a menudo*) often, frequently.

tupí-guaraní [1] ADJ Tupi-Guarani.
[2] NMF Tupi-Guarani (Indian).
[3] NM (*Ling*) Tupi-Guarani.

tupinambo NM Jerusalem artichoke.

tupir [3a] [1] VT **(a)** (*apretar*) to pack tight, press down, compact.
(b) (*LAm: obstruir*) to block, stop up, obstruct.
[2] **tupirse** VR **(a)** (*: *comer mucho*) to stuff oneself*.
(b) (*LAm: desconcertarse*) to feel silly, get embarrassed.

turba¹ NF peat, turf.

turba² NF crowd, throng; swarm; (*pey*) mob; rabble.

turbación NF **(a)** (*disturbio*) disturbance. **(b)** (*alarma*) perturbation, worry, alarm; (*vergüenza*) embarrassment; (*confusión*) bewilderment, confusion; (*agitación*) trepidation.

turbado ADJ disturbed, worried, upset; embarrassed; bewildered.

turbador ADJ disturbing, alarming; embarrassing.

turbal NM peat bog.

turbamulta NF mob, rabble.

turbante NM **(a)** (*sombrero*) turban. **(b)** (*Méx Bot*) gourd, calabash.

turbar [1a] [1] VT **(a)** *orden, paz, razón etc* to disturb.
(b) *persona* (*inquietar*) to disturb, worry, alarm; (*desconcertar*) to disconcert; (*alterar*) to upset; (*azorar*) to embarrass; (*aturdir*) to bewilder.
(c) *agua etc* to stir up.
[2] **turbarse** VR to be disturbed, get worried, become alarmed; to be embarrassed; to be bewildered, get confused, get all mixed up.

turbera NF peat bog.

turbiedad NF (*V ADJ*) **(a)** cloudiness, thickness.
(b) dimness, mistiness; disturbance; lack of clarity, confusion.
(c) turbulence.
(d) (*pey*) shadiness; dubious character.

turbina NF turbine; **~ eólica** wind turbine; **~ de gas** gas turbine; **~ a** (*o* **de**) **vapor** steam-engine.

turbio [1] ADJ **(a)** *agua etc* cloudy, thick, turbid, muddy.
(b) *vista* dim, misty, blurred; disturbed; *asunto, lenguaje* unclear, confused.
(c) (*fig*) *período etc* restless, unsettled, turbulent.
(d) (*pey*) *negocio* shady; *método* dubious.
[2] ADV: **ver ~** to have disturbed vision, not see clearly.
[3] NMPL: **~s** sediment; sludge.

turbión NM **(a)** (*Met*) heavy shower, downpour; squall. **(b)** (*fig*) shower, torrent; swarm; (*de balas*) hail.

turbo [1] NM INVAR (*Mec*) turbo, turbocharger; (*coche*) turbocharged car.
[2] ATR turbo (*atr*).

turbo... PREF turbo...

turboalimentado ADJ turbocharged.

turbocompresor NM turbo-compressor, (*diesel*) turbo-supercharger.

turbodiesel ADJ INVAR, NM turbo diesel.

turbohélice [1] NM turboprop (aeroplane).
[2] ATR turboprop (*atr*).

turbonada NF (*Cono Sur*) sudden storm, squall.

turbopropulsado ADJ turboprop (*atr*).

turbopropulsor, turborreactor [1] NM turbojet (aeroplane).
[2] ATR turbojet (*atr*).

turbulencia NF (*V ADJ*) **(a)** turbulence; troubled nature, unsettled character; storminess.
(b) restlessness; unruliness, rebelliousness; disorderly state, mutinous state.

turbulento ADJ **(a)** *elementos, río etc* turbulent; *período* troubled, unsettled, turbulent; *reunión* stormy.
(b) *carácter* restless; unruly, rebellious; *niño* noisy, troublesome, unruly; *ejército etc* disorderly, mutinous.

turca:¹ NF booze-up:, binge*; **coger** (*o* **pillar** *etc*) **una ~** to get sozzled:; **estar con la ~** to be under the weather.

turco [1] ADJ Turkish.
[2] NM, **turca²** NF **(a)** (*de Turquía*) Turk; **joven ~** (*Pol*) young Turk. **(b)** (*LAm*) (*árabe*) Arab, (*sirio*) Syrian, (*de Medio Oriente*) Middle Easterner; (*buhonero*) pedlar, peddler (*US*), hawker.
[3] NM (*Ling*) Turkish.

turcochipriota ADJ, NMF Turkish-Cypriot.

túrdiga NF thong, strip of leather.

Turena NF Touraine.

turf NM **(a)** **el ~** the turf, horse-racing. **(b)** (*LAm†: pista*) racetrack.

turfista [1] ADJ fond of horse-racing.
[2] NM racing man.

turgencia NF turgidity.

turgente ADJ, **túrgido** ADJ turgid, swollen.

Turín NM Turin.

Turingia NF Thuringia.

turismo NM **(a)** (*gen*) tourism; (*excursionismo*) touring, sightseeing; (*industria*) tourist trade; **~ blanco** winter holidays, skiing holidays; **~ rural** rural tourism; **casas de ~ rural** ≃ holiday cottages; **hacer ~** to go touring (abroad), go travelling as tourists; **ahora se hace más ~ que nunca** numbers of tourists are greater now than ever; **se desarrolla mucho el ~ en Eslobodia** facilities for tourists are being much developed in Slobodia; **el ~ constituye su mayor industria** the tourist trade is their biggest industry. **(b)** (*Aut*) (private) car.

turista NMF tourist; sightseer, visitor, holidaymaker, vacationist (*US*).

turístico ADJ tourist (*atr*).

turistizado ADJ touristy.

Turkmenistán NM Turkmenistan.

turma NF **(a)** (*Anat*) testicle. **(b)** (*Bot*) truffle; (*And*) potato.

túrmix NF (*a veces* M) mixer, blender.

turnar [1a] VI *y* **turnarse** VR to take (it in) turns; **ellos se turnan para usarlo** they take it in turns to use it.

turné NM tour, trip.

turno NM **(a)** (*lista*) rota; (*orden*) order (of priority).
(b) (*vez, oportunidad*) turn; (*tanda*) spell, period of duty; (*de día etc*) shift; (*en juegos*) turn, go; (*en reunión etc*) opportunity to speak; **~ de día** day shift; **~ de noche** nightshift; **~ de oficio** spell of court duty; **~ de preguntas** question-and-answer session; **~ rotativo** rotating shift; **por ~** in rotation, in turn; **por ~s** by turns; **trabajar por ~s** to work shifts; **trabajo de ~s** shift work(ing); **es su ~, es el primero en ~, le toca el ~** it's his turn (next); **esperar su ~** to wait one's turn, take one's turn; **cuando le llegue el ~** when her turn comes; **estar de ~** to be on duty; **estuvo con la querida de ~** he was with his girlfriend of the moment.

turolense [1] ADJ of Teruel.
[2] NMF native (*o* inhabitant) of Teruel; **los ~s** people of Teruel.

turón NM polecat.

turqueo* NM (*CAm*) fight.

turquesa NF turquoise.

turquesco ADJ Turkish.

turquí ADJ: **color ~** indigo, deep blue.

Turquía NF Turkey.

turra: NF (*Cono Sur*) whore, prostitute.

turrón NM **(a)** nougat. **(b)** (*) cushy government job:; sinecure, political plum.

┌─ **TURRÓN** ─┐

ⓘ *Turrón is a type of Spanish sweet rather like nougat which is eaten particularly around Christmas. It has Arabic origins and is made of honey, egg whites, almonds and hazelnuts. There are two traditional varieties:* **alicante**, *which is hard and contains whole almonds, and* **jijona**, *which is soft and made from crushed almonds.*

turulato* ADJ dazed, stunned, flabbergasted; **quedó ~ con la noticia** he was stunned by the news.

tururú* [1] ADJ: **estar ~** to be crazy.
[2] INTERJ no way!*, you're joking!

tus¹ INTERJ (*a perro*) good dog!, here boy!

tus²: **sin decir ~ ni mus** without saying a word; **no decir ~ ni mus** to remain silent, say nothing.

tusa NF **(a)** (*And, CAm, Carib*) (*mazorca*) cob of maize, corncob; (*cascabillo*) maize husk; (*Carib: cigarro*) cigar rolled in a maize leaf; (*Cono Sur: seda*) cornsilk.
(b) (*Cono Sur: crin*) horse's mane.
(c) (*Cono Sur: esquileo*) clipping, shearing.
(d) (*And: hoyo*) pockmark.
(e) (*And††*) (*susto*) fright; (*inquietud*) anxiety.
(f) (*CAm, Carib: puta*) whore.
(g) **no vale ni una ~** (*CAm, Carib*) it's worthless.

tusar [1a] VT (*LAm*) (*esquilar*) to cut, clip, shear; (*cortar*) to cut roughly, cut badly.

tuse NM (*Cono Sur*) = **tusa**.

tuso ADJ **(a)** (*And, Carib: esquilado*) cropped, shorn. **(b)** (*Carib: rabón*) docked, tailless. **(c)** (*And, Carib: picado de viruelas*) pockmarked.

tútano NM (*LAm*) = **tuétano**.

tute NM *a card game similar to bezique*; **darse un ~** to work extra hard, make a special effort.

tutear [1a] [1] VT **(a)** **~ a uno** to address sb as 'tú' (*familiar 2nd person sing*). **(b)** (*fig*) **~ a** to be on equal terms with.
[2] **tutearse** VR: **se tutean desde siempre** they have always addressed each other as 'tú', they have always been on familiar terms.

tutela NF (*Jur*) guardianship; (*fig: protección*) protection, tutelage; (*fig: guía*) guidance; **bajo ~** in ward; **estar bajo ~ jurídica** (*niño*) to be a ward of court; **estar bajo la ~ de** (*amparo*) to be under the protection of; (*auspicios*) to be under the auspices of.

tutelado, -a NM/F (*Univ etc*) pupil; (*Jur*) ward.

tutelaje NM (*LAm*) = **tutela**.

tutelar [1] ADJ tutelary; **genio ~** tutelary genius.

2 [1a] VT (*proteger*) to protect, guard; (*guiar*) to advise, guide; (*vigilar*) to supervise, oversee.

tuteo NM addressing a person as 'tú', familiar usage; **se ha extendido mucho el ~** the use of 'tú' has greatly increased.

tutilimundi NM (*LAm*) everybody.

tutiplé(n): a ~ ADV *dar etc* freely; *repartir* haphazardly, without discernment; *comer etc* hugely, to excess.

tutor NM (**a**) (*Jur*) guardian; (*Univ*) tutor; **~ de curso** form master. (**b**) (*Agr*) prop, stake.

tutora NF (*Jur*) guardian; (*Univ*) tutor; **~ de curso** form mistress.

tutoría NF (**a**) (*Jur*) guardianship. (**b**) (*Univ*) tutorial, class.

tutorial ADJ tutorial.

tutorizar [1f] VT = **tutelar 2**.

tutú NM tutu.

tutuma NF (*And, Cono Sur*) (**a**) (‡: *cabeza*) nut‡, head; (*bollo*) bump; (*joroba*) hump; (*moretón*) bruise. (**b**) (*fruta*) *type of cucumber*.

tutumito NM (*And, CAm*) idiot.

tuturuto **1** ADJ (**a**) (*CAm, Carib, Méx: borracho*) drunk. (**b**) (*And, CAm, Carib*) (*tonto*) stupid; (*aturdido*) dumbfounded, stunned. **2** NM (*Cono Sur: chulo*) pimp.

tuve *etc* V **tener.**

tuyo ADJ Y PRON yours, of yours; (††, *a Dios*) thy, of thine; **es ~, es el ~** it is yours; **lo ~** (what is) yours, what belongs to you; **cualquier amigo ~** any friend of yours; **los ~s** (*frec*) your people, your relations, your family.

tuza NF (*LAm Zool*) mole.

TV NF ABR *de* **televisión** television, TV.

TVE NF ABR *de* **Televisión Española.**

tweed [twi] NM tweed.

txistu ['tʃistu] NM (Basque) flute.

txistulari [tʃistu'lari] NMF (Basque) flute player.

U

U, u [u] NF (*letra*) U, u; **~ doble** (*Méx*) w; **curva en ~** hairpin bend.
U ABR *de* **Universidad** university, univ., U.
u CONJ (*delante de* **o~, ho~**) or; **siete ~ ocho** seven or eight.
ualabi NM wallaby.
UAM NF **(a)** (*Esp*) ABR *de* **Universidad Autónoma de Madrid. (b)** (*Méx*) ABR *de* **Universidad Autónoma Metropolitana.**
ubérrimo ADJ exceptionally fertile, marvellously productive, very rich; (*LAm*) abundant.
ubicación NF **(a)** (*acto*) placing; siting. **(b)** (*lugar*) whereabouts; place, position, location, situation.
ubicado ADJ **(a) una tienda ubicada en la calle X** a shop situated in X street. **(b) bien ubicada, ubicadísima** (*Méx*) well located, in a desirable location.
ubicar [1g] **1** VT (*esp LAm*) **(a)** (*colocar*) to place, put, locate, situate; *edificio* to site.
(b) (*encontrar*) to find, locate; **no hemos podido ~ al jefe** we haven't been able to get hold of the boss; **a ver si logras ~lo** let's see if you can track it down.
(c) (*fig: instalar*) to instal in a place (*o post etc*), fix up with a job.
(d) (*fig: clasificar*) to classify, place, judge.
2 VI to be, be situated, be located; to lie, stand.
3 **ubicarse** VR **(a)** = **2**.
(b) (*orientarse*) to find one's way about; (*Cono Sur: fig*) to appreciate one's situation.
(c) (*LAm: en un puesto*) to get a job, fix o.s. up with a job; (*establecerse*) to settle in, establish o.s.
ubicuidad NF ubiquity; **el don de la ~** the gift for being everywhere at once.
ubicuo ADJ ubiquitous.
ubre NF udder; teat.
ubrera NF (*Med*) thrush.
UBS NFPL (*Esp*) ABR *de* **Unidades Básicas de Salud.**
UCD NF (*Esp: Pol*) ABR *de* **Unión de Centro Democrático**; *see also* TRANSICIÓN A LA DEMOCRACIA .

i *The* **Unión de Centro Democrático** *was the Spanish political party which, under the leadership of Adolfo Suárez, held office for two successive terms between 1977 and 1982 and guided Spain's transition from dictatorship to parliamentary democracy. When the relatively unknown Suárez was appointed Prime Minister by King Juan Carlos in July 1976 he did not belong to a political party. When the date for the general elections was set for 15 June 1977, Suárez approached the* **Centro Democrático** *with a deal: he would lead them to success in the elections if they accepted his leadership and took his team of collaborators and supporters on board. The party was renamed the* **Unión de Centro Democrático** *and they won the next two general elections. It now no longer exists.*

UCE NF **(a)** (*Fin*) ABR *de* **Unidad de Cuenta Europea** European Currency Unit, ECU. **(b)** ABR *de* **Unión de Consumidores de España.**
ucedista **1** ADJ: **política ~** policy of UCD, UCD policy.
2 NMF member of UCD.
-ucho, -ucha V Aspects of Word Formation in Spanish 2.
uchuvito* ADJ (*And*) drunk, tight*.
UCI NF ABR *de* **unidad de cuidados intensivos** intensive care unit, ICU.
UCM NF (*Esp*) ABR *de* **Universidad Complutense de Madrid.**
-uco, -uca V Aspects of Word Formation in Spanish 2.
UCP NF ABR *de* **unidad central de proceso** central processing unit, CPU.
UCR NF (*Argentina*) ABR *de* **Unión Cívica Radical.**
Ucrania NF Ukraine.

ucranio, -a, ucraniano, -a ADJ, NM/F Ukrainian.
ucronía NF uchronia, imaginary time.
ucrónico ADJ uchronic, imaginary.
Ud. PRON ABR *de* **usted** you.
-udo V Aspects of Word Formation in Spanish 2.
Uds. PRON ABR *de* **ustedes** you.
UDV NF ABR *de* **unidad de despliegue visual** visual display unit, VDU.
UE NF ABR *de* **Unión Europea** European Union, EU.
UEFA NF ABR *de* **Union of European Football Associations** UEFA.
UEI NF ABR *de* **Unidad Especial de Intervención** *special force of the Guardia Civil.*
-uelo, -uela V Aspects of Word Formation in Spanish 2.
UEM NF ABR *de* **unión económica y monetaria** economic and monetary union, EMU.
UEO NF ABR *de* **Unión Europea Occidental** Western European Union, WEU.
UEP NF ABR *de* **Unión Europea de Pagos** European Payments Union, EPU.
UEPS ABR *de* **último en entrar, primero en salir** last in, first out, LIFO.
UER NF ABR *de* **Unión Europea de Radiodifusión** European Broadcasting Union, EBU.
uf INTERJ (*calor, cansancio*) phew!; (*repugnancia*) ugh!
ufanamente ADV proudly; cheerfully; exultantly; (*pey*) conceitedly; boastfully; smugly.
ufanarse [1a] VR to boast; to be vain, be conceited; **~ con, ~ de** to boast of, pride o.s. on, be vain about; to glory in.
ufanía NF **(a)** (*orgullo*) pride; (*pey*) vanity, conceit; boastfulness. **(b)** (*Bot*) = **lozanía.**
ufano ADJ **(a)** (*orgulloso*) proud; (*alegre*) gay, cheerful; exultant; (*pey: vanidoso*) vain, conceited; (*jactancioso*) boastful; (*altivo*) overweening; (*satisfecho*) smug; **iba muy ~ en el nuevo coche** he was going along so proudly in his new car; **está muy ~ porque le han dado el premio** he is very proud that they have awarded him the prize.
(b) (*Bot*) = **lozano.**
ufología NF study of unidentified flying objects, ufology.
ufólogo, -a NM/F student of unidentified flying objects, ufologist.
Uganda NF Uganda.
ugandés, -esa ADJ, NM/F Ugandan.
ugetista **1** ADJ: **política ~** policy of the UGT, UGT policy.
2 NMF member of the UGT.
UGT NF (*Esp*) ABR *de* **Unión General de Trabajadores.**

i *The* **Unión General de Trabajadores** *is a socialist trade union which was founded by the* **Partido Socialista Obrero Español** *in 1888. Relegalized in 1977 after the dictatorship of General Franco, it is nowadays one of the two major unions in Spain, together with CCOO.*

UIT NF ABR *de* **Unión Internacional para las Telecomunicaciones** International Telecommunications Union, ITU.
ujier NM usher; doorkeeper, attendant.
-ujo, -uja V Aspects of Word Formation in Spanish 2.
újule INTERJ (*Méx*) (*para indicar desprecio*) huh!; (*para indicar sorpresa*) wow!
úlcera NF ulcer, sore; **~ de decúbito** bedsore; **~ duodenal** duodenal ulcer; **~ gástrica** gastric ulcer.
ulceración NF ulceration.
ulcerar [1a] **1** VT to make sore, make a sore on, ulcerate.
2 **ulcerarse** VR to ulcerate; to fester.
ulceroso ADJ ulcerous; full of sores, covered with sores.
ule NM (*CAm, Méx*) = **hule 1 (a).**
ulerear [1a] VT (*Cono Sur*) *masa* to roll out.
ulero NM (*Cono Sur*) rolling pin.

Ulises NM Ulysses.

ulluco NM (*And, Cono Sur*) manioc.

ulpo NM (*And, Cono Sur*) maize gruel.

ulterior ADJ (a) *lugar* farther, further. (b) *tiempo etc* later, subsequent; eventual.

ulteriormente ADV later, subsequently.

ultimación NF completion, conclusion.

ultimador(a) NM/F (*LAm*) killer, murderer.

últimamente ADV (a) (*por último*) lastly, finally. (b) (*en último caso*) as a last resort. (c) (*recientemente*) recently, lately. (d) ¡~! (*LAm*) well I'm damned!, that's the absolute end!

ultimar [1a] VT (a) (*terminar*) to finish, complete, conclude; *detalles, preparativos* to finalize; *acuerdo* to conclude; **lo tengo ultimado** I have it in the final stages.
(b) (*LAm*) *persona* (*rematar*) to finish off, give the coup de grâce to; (*matar*) to kill, murder.

ultimato NM, **ultimátum** NM, PL **ultimátums** ultimatum.

ultimizar [1f] VT = **ultimar**.

▼ **último** ① ADJ (a) (*en orden, tiempo*) (*final*) last; (*más reciente*) latest, most recent; (*de dos*) latter; **éste ~, éstos ~s** the latter; **el ~ día del mes** the last day of the month; **a ~s del mes** in the latter part of the month, towards the end of the month; **las últimas noticias** the latest news; **en estos ~s años** in recent years, in the last few years; **llegó el ~** he arrived last, he came last, he was last; (*en carrera*) he came (in) last; **hablar el ~** to speak last, (*fig*) have the last word, have the final say; **reírse el ~** to have the last laugh; **ser el ~ en +** *infin* to be the last to + *infin*; **estar a lo ~ de** to be nearly at the end of, have nearly finished; **estar en las últimas** (*: moribundo*) to be about to peg out ⁑; (*pobrísimo*) to be down and out, be on one's last legs; (*casi falto de*) to be down to one's last little bit (of a stock *etc*); **está dando las últimas** it's on its last legs; **por ~** lastly, finally; **por última vez** for the last time.
(b) (*lugar*) furthest, most remote; (*más al fondo*) back; (*más alto*) top, topmost; (*más bajo*) lowest, bottom; **en el ~ rincón del país** in the furthest corner of the country; **un asiento de última fila** a seat in the back row; **el equipo en última posición** the team in the lowest position, the bottom team; **viven en el ~ piso** they live on the top floor.
(c) (*fig: extremo*) final, extreme, last; utmost; **la última solución** the final solution; **el ~ remedio** the ultimate remedy; **en ~ caso** as a last resort, in the last resort; **decir la última palabra** to have the final say.
(d) (*Com*) *precio* lowest, bottom; **dígame lo ~, dígame el ~ precio** tell me what your lowest price is.
(e) (*fig*) *calidad* finest, best, superior.
(f) (*) **estar ~** (*o vivir*) **a la última** to be thoroughly with it*, be utterly up-to-date; **vestido a la última** dressed in the latest style; **tienen un coche que es lo ~** they have the very latest thing in cars; **¡es lo ~!** it's the greatest!*, it's tremendous!*; (*pey*) this is the end!; **viven en un puebiucho que es lo ~** they live in a dump which is unbelievably awful*; **pedirme eso encima ya es lo ~** for him to ask that of me as well really is the limit.
② ADV (*LAm*): **ahora ~** lately, recently.

ultra (*Pol*) ① ADJ extreme, extremist; ultra-conservative.
② NMF (*esp right-wing*) extremist; ultra-conservative.

ultra... PREF ultra..., extra...

ultracongelación NF (*Esp*) (deep-)freezing.

ultracongelado ADJ (*Esp*) (deep-)frozen.

ultracongelador NM (*Esp*) deep-freeze, freezer.

ultracongelar [1a] VT to deep-freeze.

ultraconservador(a) ADJ, NM/F ultra-conservative.

ultracorrección NF hypercorrection.

ultracorto ADJ ultra-short.

ultraderecha NF (*Pol*) extreme right(-wing).

ultraderechista ① ADJ extreme right(-wing).
② NMF extreme right-winger.

ultrafino ADJ ultrafine.

ultraísmo NM revolutionary poetic movement of the 1920s (*imagist, surrealist etc*).

ultraizquierda NF extreme left(-wing).

ultraizquierdista ① ADJ extreme left(-wing).
② NMF extreme left-winger.

ultrajador ADJ, **ultrajante** ADJ outrageous; offensive; insulting.

ultrajar [1a] VT (a) (*gen*) to outrage; (*ofender*) to offend; (*insultar*) to insult, revile, abuse. (b) (*liter*) to spoil, to crumple, disarrange.

ultraje NM outrage; insult.

ultrajoso ADJ outrageous; offensive; insulting.

ultraligero NM microlight (aircraft).

ultramar NM countries beyond the seas, foreign parts; **de ~, en ~** overseas; **los países de ~** the overseas countries; **productos venidos de ~** products from overseas, goods from abroad; **pasó 8 años en ~** he spent 8 years overseas.

ultramarino ① ADJ overseas; foreign; (*Com*) imported.
② **~s** NMPL (*Esp*) (a) (*género*) (imported) groceries, foodstuffs; **tienda de ~s** = (b). (b) **un ~s** (*tienda*) a grocer's (shop), a grocery (*US*).

ultramoderno ADJ ultramodern.

ultramontanismo NM ultramontanism.

ultramontano ADJ, NM ultramontane.

ultranza ① **: a ~** ADV: **luchar a ~** to fight to the death; **lo quiere hacer a ~** he wants to do it at all costs (*o* come what may, regardless of the difficulties); **paz a ~** peace at any price.
② **: a ~** ADJ all-out, extreme; **revolucionario a ~** out-and-out revolutionary, utterly uncompromising revolutionary.

ultrapotente ADJ extra powerful.

ultrarrápido ADJ extra fast.

ultrarrojo ADJ = **infrarrojo**.

ultrasecreto ADJ top secret.

ultrasensitivo ADJ ultrasensitive.

ultrasofisticado ADJ *arma* highly sophisticated.

ultrasónico ADJ ultrasonic.

ultrasonido NM (*Fís*) ultrasound.

ultrasur NMF INVAR extremist fan of Real Madrid FC.

ultratumba NF what lies beyond the grave; **la vida de ~** life beyond the grave, life in the next world; **una voz de ~** a voice from beyond the grave.

ultravioleta ADJ INVAR ultraviolet; **rayos ~** ultraviolet rays.

ulular [1a] VI (*animal, viento*) to howl, shriek; (*búho*) to hoot, screech.

ululato NM howl, shriek; hoot, screech.

UM NF (*Esp*) ABR *de* **Unión Mallorquina**.

umbilical ADJ umbilical.

umbral ① NM (a) (*de entrada*) threshold; **pasar** (*o* **traspasar**) **el ~ de uno** to set foot in sb's house.
(b) (*fig: comienzo*) threshold; first step, beginning; **~ de la pobreza** poverty line; **estar en los ~es de** to be on the threshold of, be on the verge of, be on the point of; **eso está en los ~es de lo imposible** that borders (*o* verges) on the impossible.
② ATR: **libro de nivel ~** basic level textbook, book for the beginner's stage.

umbralada NF (*And, Cono Sur*), **umbralado** NM (*And, Cono Sur*), **umbraladura** NF (*And*) threshold.

umbrío ADJ, **umbroso** ADJ shady.

UME NF ABR *de* **Unión Monetaria Europea** European Monetary Union, EMU.

UMI NF ABR *de* **unidad de medicina intensiva** intensive care unit, ICU.

un, una ① ART INDEF a, (*delante de vocal y h muda*) an.
② ADJ one; **la una** one o'clock; **¡a la una, a las dos, a las tres!** (*en subasta*) going, going, gone!; (*Dep*) ready, steady, go!
③ NM one.

U.N.A.M. NF ABR *de* **Universidad Nacional Autónoma de México**.

unánime ADJ unanimous.

unánimemente ADV unanimously.

unanimidad NF unanimity; **por ~** unanimously.

uncial ADJ, NF uncial.

unción NF (a) (*Med*) anointing. (b) (*Ecl y fig*) unction.

uncir [3b] VT to yoke.

undécimo ADJ eleventh.

UNED [u'neð] NF (*Esp Escol*) ABR *de* **Universidad Nacional de Educación a Distancia** ≃ Open University.

ungido ADJ anointed; **el U~ del Señor** the Lord's Anointed.

ungir [3c] VT (a) (*Med*) to anoint, put ointment on, rub with ointment. (b) (*Ecl*) to anoint.

ungüento NM ointment, unguent; (*fig*) salve, balm.

ungulado ① ADJ ungulate, hoofed.
② NM ungulate, hoofed animal.

uni... PREF uni..., one-..., single-...

únicamente ADV only; solely.

unicameral ADJ (*Pol*) single-chamber.

unicameralismo NM system of single-chamber government.

unicelular ADJ unicellular, single-cell.

unicidad NF uniqueness; oneness.

único ADJ (a) (*solo*) only; sole, single, solitary; unique; **hijo ~** only child; **sistema de partido ~** one-party system, single-party system; **la única dificultad es que ...** the only difficulty is that ...; **fue el ~ sobreviviente** he was the sole survivor; **es el ~ ejemplar que existe** it is the only copy (*o* specimen) in existence; **es lo ~ que nos hacía falta** (*iró*) that's all we needed; **este ejemplar es ~** this specimen is unique.
(b) (*fig*) unique; unusual, extraordinary.

unicolor ADJ one-colour, all one colour.

unicornio NM unicorn.

unidad NF (a) (*cualidad*) unity; oneness; togetherness; **~ de acción** (*Liter*) unity of action; **~ de lugar** (*Liter*) unity of place.
(b) (*Mat, Mil, Téc etc*) unit; (*Ferro*) coach, wagon; **~ de cola** (*Aer*) tail unit; **~ de cuenta europea** European currency unit; **~ de cuidados**

intensivos intensive care unit; ~ **monetaria** monetary unit; ~ **móvil** (*TV*) mobile unit; ~ **vecinal de absorción de Toboso** overspill town for Toboso; ~ **de quemados** burns unit; ~ **de vigilancia intensiva** intensive care unit; ~ **de visualización** visual display unit.
(c) **nueve dólares (la)** ~ (*Com*) nine dollars each.
(d) (*Inform*) ~ **central de proceso** central processing unit; ~ **de cinta** tape unit; ~ **de control** control unit; ~ **de disco** disk drive, disk unit; ~ **de discos flexibles** floppy disk drive; ~ **de entrada** input device; ~ **de información** bit (of information); ~ **periférica** peripheral device; ~ **central de procesamiento** central processing unit; ~ **de salida** output device.
unidimensional ADJ one-dimensional; (*fig*) flat; restricted, limited.
unidireccional ADJ: **calle** ~ one-way street.
unido ADJ (a) (*juntado*) joined (*por* by), linked (*por* by).
(b) (*fig*) united; **una familia muy unida** a very united family; **mantenerse** ~s to remain united, maintain their (*etc*) unity, keep together.
unifamiliar ADJ single-family (*atr*).
unificación NF unification.
unificador ADJ unifying.
unificar [1g] VT to unite, unify.
uniformado 1 ADJ uniformed.
2 NM man in uniform, (*esp*) policeman.
uniformar [1a] VT (a) (*igualar*) to make uniform; to level up; to standardize, make the same. (b) *persona* to put into uniform, provide a uniform for.
uniforme 1 ADJ (*gen*) uniform; *superficie etc* level, even, smooth; *velocidad etc* uniform, steady; regular.
2 NM uniform; ~ **de campaña**, ~ **de combate** battledress; ~ **de gala** full-dress uniform.
uniformemente ADV uniformly.
uniformidad NF (*V* **uniforme** 1) uniformity; levelness, evenness, smoothness; steadiness; regularity.
uniformización NF standardization.
uniformizar [1f] VT = **uniformar**.
unigénito ADJ (*Rel*) only begotten; **el U~** the Only Begotten Son.
unilateral ADJ unilateral, one-sided.
unilateralismo NM unilateralism.
unilateralmente ADV unilaterally.
unión NF (a) (*acto*) union, uniting, joining; **en** ~ **de** with, together with; **la** ~ **hace la fuerza** united we stand.
(b) (*cualidad*) unity; closeness, togetherness.
(c) (*Com, Pol etc*) union; (*Jur*) union, marriage; **en** ~ **con** with, together with, accompanied by; ~ **aduanera** customs union; ~ **consensual** common-law marriage; ~ **monetaria** monetary union; **U~ Panamericana** Pan-American Union; **U~ Soviética** Soviet Union; **U~ Sudafricana** Union of South Africa; **vivir en** ~ **libre con** to live with.
(d) (*Mec*) joint, union; (*t* **punto de** ~) junction (*entre* between).
unipartidario ADJ one-party (*atr*).
unipartidismo NM one-party system, one-party state.
unipersonal ADJ for one (person); single, individual.
unir [3a] 1 VT (a) *objetos, piezas* to join, unite; (*atar*) to tie (*o* fasten, bolt *etc*) together; *persona* to unite; *familias* to unite (by marriage); *compañías, intereses etc* to merge, join; to pool; *cualidades* to combine (*a* with); **les une una fuerte simpatía** they are bound by a strong affection, there are bonds of affection between them.
(b) *líquidos etc* to mix; *masa, salsa etc* to mix thoroughly, make smooth; to beat (up).
2 VI (*ingredientes*) to mix well, make a smooth mixture.
3 **unirse** VR (a) (*2 personas etc*) to join together, unite; (*compañías*) to merge, combine; ~ **en matrimonio** to marry, be united in marriage.
(b) ~ **a** to join; ~ **con** to unite with, merge with; **se unen las ramas por encima** the branches meet overhead.
(c) (*ingredientes*) to mix well, cohere.
unisex(o) ADJ unisex.
unísono ADJ unisonous, on the same tone; *voces etc* in unison; **al** ~ on the same tone; (*fig*) in unison, with one voice, in harmony, harmoniously; **al** ~ **con** (*fig*) in tune with, in harmony with.
unitario 1 ADJ unitary; (*Ecl*) Unitarian.
2 NM, **unitaria** NF Unitarian.
unitarismo NM Unitarianism.
univalente ADJ univalent.
univalvo ADJ univalve.
universal ADJ (*gen*) universal; (*mundial*) world (*atr*), world-wide; **historia** ~ world history; **de fama** ~ known all over the world, internationally famous; **una especie de distribución** ~ a species with a world-wide distribution.
universalidad NF universality.
universalizar [1f] VT to universalize, make universal; to extend widely, bring into general use.

universalmente ADV universally; all over the world.
universiada NF university games, student games.
universidad NF university; **U~ Nacional de Educación a Distancia** ≃ Open University (*Brit*); ~ **laboral** technical college, college of advanced technology; ~ **popular** extramural classes, extension courses.
universitario 1 ADJ university (*atr*); academic.
2 NM, **universitaria** NF (*profesor*) university teacher; (*estudiante*) university student; (*graduado*) university graduate.
universo NM universe; world.
unívoco ADJ unanimous, single-minded.
UNO NF (*Nicaragua*) ABR *de* **Unión Nacional Opositora**.
uno 1 ADJ (a) (*gen*) one; (*idéntico*) one and the same, identical; **es todo** ~, **es** ~ **y lo mismo** it's all one, it's all the same; **Dios es** ~ God is one; **la verdad es una** truth is one and indivisible.
(b) ~s (*t* ~s **cuantos**) some, a few; about, *p.ej.* ~s **80 dólares** about 80 dollars.
(c) **¡hubo una** (*enfático*) **gente!** there were so many people!, you should have seen the people!; **se dio una** (*enfático*) **hostia en la pierna** he banged his leg terribly.
2 PRON (a) (*gen*) one; *persona* somebody; ~ **mismo** oneself; **ha venido** ~ **que dice que te conoce** sb who says he knows you came; ~s **que estaban allí protestaron** some (people) who were there protested; **los** ~s **dicen que sí y los otros que no** some say yes and some say no; **es mejor hacerlo** ~ **mismo** it's better to do it o.s.
(b) **cada** ~ each one, every one; **cada** ~ **a lo suyo** everyone should mind his own business; **había 3 manzanas para cada** ~ there were 3 apples each.
(c) (*sujeto indef*) one, you; ~ **nunca sabe qué hacer** one never knows what to do; ~ **necesita descansar** a man has to rest, you have to rest.
(d) **uno(s) a otro(s)** each other, one another; **se detestan** ~s **a otros** they hate each other; **se miraban fijamente el** ~ **al otro** they stared at each other; ~ **tras otro** one after the other.
(e) (*locuciones*) ~ **a** ~, ~ **por** ~, **de** ~ **en** ~, **de** ~ **en fondo** in single file, one by one; **a una** all together; **juntarlo todo en** ~ to put it all together; **estar en** ~ to be at one; **no gustará a más de** ~ there are quite a few who will not like this; **una de dos** either one thing or the other; the choice is simple, it's a straight choice; ~ **con otro salen a 3 dólares** on an average they work out at 3 dollars each; **el** ~ **y el otro están locos** they're both mad; **ser** ~ **de tantos** to be run of the mill; **para mí es** ~ **de tantos** so far as I'm concerned he's just one of many; in my view he's a very ordinary sort; **salen una que otra vez** they go out from time to time; **lo** ~ **por lo otro** it comes to the same thing, what you lose on the swings you gain on the roundabouts.
uno-equis-dos NM (*1-X-2*) (*fig*) football pool(s).
untadura NF (a) (*acto*) smearing, dabbing, rubbing; greasing; spreading. (b) (*Med*) ointment; (*Mec etc*) grease, oil. (c) (*mancha*) mark, smear, dab.
untar [1a] 1 VT (a) to smear, dab, rub (*con, de* with); (*Med*) to anoint, rub (*con, de* with); (*Mec etc*) to grease, oil; ~ **su pan en la salsa** to dip one's bread in the gravy, soak one's bread in the gravy; ~ **los dedos de tinta** to smear one's fingers with ink; ~ **el pan con mantequilla** to spread butter on one's bread, put butter on one's bread.
(b) (*: sobornar*) to bribe, grease the palm of.
2 **untarse** VR (a) ~ **con**, ~ **de** to smear o.s. with.
(b) (*Fin**) to take a rake-off*, get a cut in the profits; to line one's pockets.
unto NM (a) (*materia blanda*) soft substance; (*Med*) ointment, unguent; (*Zool*) grease, (animal) fat. (b) (*Cono Sur: betún*) shoe-polish.
untuosidad NF greasiness, oiliness; stickiness.
untuoso ADJ greasy, oily, sticky.
untura NF = **untadura**.
uña NF (a) (*Anat*) (*de la mano*) nail, fingernail; (*del pie*) toenail; (*Zool etc*) claw; ~ **encarnada** ingrowing nail; **ser** ~ **y carne** to be inseparable, be as thick as thieves; **largo de** ~s light-fingered, thieving; **estar de** ~s **con uno** to be at daggers drawn with sb; **caer en las** ~s **de uno** to fall into sb's clutches; **comerse las** ~s to bite one's nails; (*fig*) to get very impatient, get furious; (*LAm: pobre*) to be terribly poor; **se dejó las uñas en ese trabajo** he wore his fingers to the bone at that job; **enseñar** (*o* **mostrar, sacar**) **las** ~s (*t fig*) to show one's claws; **tener las** ~s **afiladas** to be light-fingered.
(b) (*pezuña*) hoof; ~ **de caballo** (*Bot*) coltsfoot; **escapar a** ~ **de caballo** to ride off at full speed; ~ **de vaca** (*Culin*) cow heel.
(c) (*de alacrán*) sting.
(d) (*Téc*) claw; nailpuller.
(e) (*de ancla*) fluke.
uñada NF nail mark; scratch.
uñalarga NMF (*LAm*) thief.
uñarada NF = **uñada**.

uñero NM (**a**) (*panadizo*) whitlow. (**b**) (*uña encarnada*) ingrowing nail. (**c**) (*Tip*) thumb-notch; **2 tomos con ~** 2 volumes with thumb index.

uñeta NF (*Cono Sur Mús*) plectrum.

uñetas NMF INVAR (*And, CAm*) thief.

uñetear [1a] VT (*Cono Sur*) to steal.

uñilargo NM (*And*), **uñón** NM (*And*) thief.

UOE NF (*Esp Mil*) ABR de **Unidad de Operaciones Especiales.**

UP NF (**a**) (*Chile*) ABR de **Unidad Popular.** (**b**) (*Colombia*) ABR de **Unión Patriótica.** (**c**) (*Perú*) ABR de **Unión Popular.**

UPA NF ABR de **Unión Panamericana** Pan-American Union, PAU.

upa¹ NM (*And*) idiot.

upa² INTERJ up, up!

UPAE NF ABR de **Unión Postal de las Américas y España.**

upar* [1a] VT (**a**) to lift up, lift in one's arms. (**b**) (*LAm*) = **aupar.**

uperización NF UHT treatment.

uperizado ADJ: **leche uperizada** UHT milk.

UPN NF (*Esp*) ABR de **Unión del Pueblo Navarro** *Navarrese nationalist party.*

UPU NF ABR de **Unión Postal Universal** Universal Postal Union, UPU.

Urales NMPL (*t* Montes **~**) Urals.

uralita ® NF *corrugated asbestos and cement roofing material.*

uranio NM uranium; **~ enriquecido** enriched uranium.

Urano NM Uranus.

urbanícola NMF city-dweller.

urbanidad NF courtesy, politeness, urbanity.

urbanificar [1g] VT = **urbanizar.**

urbanismo NM (**a**) (*planificación*) town planning; (*desarrollo*) urban development. (**b**) (*Carib*) real-estate development.

urbanista NMF town planner.

urbanístico ADJ town-planning (*atr*); urban, city (*atr*).

urbanita NMF city dweller.

urbanizable ADJ: **tierras ~s** building land; **zona no ~** green belt, land designated as not for building.

urbanización NF (**a**) (*acto*) urbanization; urban development. (**b**) (*colonia etc*) housing estate, residential development.

urbanizado ADJ built-up.

urbanizadora NF property development company.

urbanizar [1f] VT (**a**) *tierra* to develop, build on, urbanize; to lay out and prepare for city development. (**b**) *persona* to civilize.

urbano ADJ (**a**) (*de la ciudad*) urban, town (*atr*), city (*atr*). (**b**) (*cortés*) courteous, polite, urbane.

urbe NF large city, metropolis; (*capital*) capital city; (*Esp*) **La U~** Madrid, the Capital.

urbícola NMF city dweller.

urco NM (*And, Cono Sur*) ram; (*) alpaca.

urdimbre NF (**a**) (*en tela*) warp. (**b**) (*fig*) scheme, intrigue.

urdir [3a] VT (**a**) *tela* to warp. (**b**) (*fig*) to plot, scheme for, contrive.

urdu NM Urdu.

urea NF urea.

urente ADJ (*Med etc*) burning, stinging.

uréter NM ureter.

uretra NF urethra.

urgencia NF (**a**) (*gen*) urgency; (*presión*) pressure; (*prisa*) haste, rush; **con toda ~** with the utmost urgency, posthaste; **de ~** urgent, pressing; (*Correos*) express; **pedir algo con ~** to press for sth. (**b**) (*emergencia*) emergency; **medida de ~** emergency measure; **salida de ~** emergency exit. (**c**) (*necesidad*) pressing need; **en caso de ~** in case of necessity, if the need arises; **acudió a mí en una ~ de dinero** he came to me with a pressing need for money. (**d**) **urgencias** PL (*Med*) casualty department.

urgente ADJ urgent; pressing; *exigencia etc* pressing, imperative, insistent; **carta ~** express letter; **pedido ~** rush order.

urgentemente ADV urgently; imperatively, insistently.

urgir [3c] VI to be urgent, be pressing; **urge el dinero** the money is urgently needed; **me urge la respuesta** the reply is required with the utmost urgency; **el tiempo urge** time presses, time is short; **me urge terminarlo** I must finish it as soon as I can, I must finish it with the utmost speed; **me urge partir** I have to leave at once; '**Úrgeme vender: dos gatos ...**' (*anuncio*) 'Must be sold: two cats.'

úrico ADJ uric.

urinario ⓵ ADJ urinary. ⓶ NM urinal, public lavatory, comfort station (*US*).

urna NF (*gen*) urn; (*de cristal*) glass case; (*Pol etc*: *t* **~ electoral**) ballot-box; **al cierre de las ~s** when voting closed; **acudir a las ~s** to vote, go and vote, go to the polls.

URNG NF (*Guatemala*) ABR de **Unidad Revolucionaria Nacional Guatemalteca.**

uro NM aurochs.

urogallo NM capercaillie.

urogenital ADJ urogenital.

urología NF urology.

urólogo, -a NM/F urologist.

urpo NM (*Cono Sur*) = **ulpo.**

urraca NF (**a**) (*Orn*) magpie. (**b**) (*) (*habladora*) chatterbox; (*chismosa*) gossip.

URSS [urs] NF ABR de **Unión de Repúblicas Socialistas Soviéticas** Union of Soviet Socialist Republics, USSR.

ursulina NF (**a**) (*Rel*) Ursuline nun. (**b**) (*Esp**) goody-goody*.

urticaria NF urticaria, nettlerash.

urubú NM (*Cono Sur*) black vulture.

Uruguay NM: **El ~** Uruguay.

uruguayismo NM word (o phrase *etc*) peculiar to Uruguay.

uruguayo, -a ADJ, NM/F Uruguayan.

USA ATR United States, American; **dos aviones ~** two American planes.

usado ADJ *sello etc* used; *ropa* worn; secondhand; **muy ~** worn out, old, shabby.

usagre NM (*Med*) impetigo; (*Vet*) mange.

usanza NF usage, custom; **a ~ india, a ~ de los indios** according to the custom of the Indians, in the Indian fashion.

usar [1a] ⓵ VT (**a**) (*utilizar*) to use, make use of; *ropa* to wear; **sin ~** unused; **botella de ~ y tirar** disposable bottle. (**b**) **~ + infin** (*soler*) to be accustomed to + infin, to be in the habit of + ger. ⓶ VI: **~ de** to use, make use of. ⓷ **usarse** VR (*gen*) to be used, be in use; (*ropa*) to be worn; to be in fashion; (*práctica*) to be the custom; **la chistera ya no se usa** top hats are not worn nowadays, top hats are no longer in fashion.

usía PRON PERS (††) Your Lordship, Your Ladyship.

usina NF (**a**) (*LAm*) factory, plant. (**b**) (*Cono Sur*: *de electricidad*) power-plant; (*de gas*) gasworks; (*de tranvías*) tram depot.

uslero NM (*Cono Sur*) rolling-pin.

USO ['uso] NF (*Esp*) ABR de **Unión Sindical Obrera.**

uso NM (**a**) (*empleo*) use; **de ~ corriente** in everyday use; **objeto de ~ personal** article for personal use; **de ~ externo** (*Med*) for external application; **de un solo ~** disposable, to be used once only; **estar fuera de ~** to be out of use, be obsolete; **estar en ~** to be in use; **estar en buen ~** to be in good condition; **estar en el ~ de la palabra** to be speaking, have the floor; **hacer ~ de** to make use of; **hacer ~ de la palabra** to speak; **retirar algo del ~** to withdraw sth from service. (**b**) (*Mec etc*) wear, wear and tear; **~ y desgaste** wear and tear; **deteriorado por el ~** worn. (**c**) (*costumbre*) custom, usage; (*estilo, moda*) fashion, style; **es un ~ muy antiguo** it is a very ancient custom; **al ~** as is customary, in keeping with custom; **con bigotes al ~** with the usual sort of moustache, with the sort of moustache which was then fashionable; **un hombre al ~** an ordinary man; **al ~ de** in the style of, in the fashion of; **un libro hecho al ~ de los principiantes** a book written for beginners.

usted, PL **ustedes** PRON PERS (*gen abr* **Vd., Vds.**) you (*polite or formal address*); **el coche de ~** your car; **mi coche y el de ~** my car and yours; **para ~** for you; **sin ~** without you; **¡a ~!** (*dando gracias*) thank you!

usual ADJ usual, customary; ordinary; regular.

usualmente ADV usually; ordinarily, regularly.

usuario, -a NM/F user; (*de biblioteca*) reader; **~ de la vía pública** road user; **~ final** end-user.

usufructo NM usufruct, use; **~ vitalicio** life interest (*de* in).

usufructuario, -a NM/F usufructuary.

usura NF usury; (*fig*) profiteering, racketeering.

usurario ADJ usurious.

usurear [1a] VI to lend money at an exorbitant rate of interest; (*fig*) to profiteer, run a racket.

usurero, -a NM/F usurer; (*fig*) profiteer, racketeer.

usurpación NF usurpation; seizure, illegal taking; (*fig*) encroachment (*de* upon), inroads (*de* into).

usurpador, -a NM/F usurper.

usurpar [1a] VT *corona, derechos etc* to usurp; *tierra etc* to seize, take illegally; (*fig*) to encroach upon, make inroads into.

usuta NF (*And*) = **ojota.**

utensilio NM tool, implement; (*Culin*) utensil; **~s de cirujano** surgeon's instruments; **~s para escribir** writing materials; **~s para pescar** fishing tackle; **~s de pintor** painter's materials; **con los ~s de su oficio** with the tools of his craft, with the equipment of his trade.

uterino ADJ uterine; **hermanos ~s** children born of the same mother; *V* furor.

útero NM womb, uterus; **~ alquilado, ~ de alquiler** surrogate motherhood.

útil ⓵ ADJ (**a**) (*gen*) useful; (*servible*) usable, serviceable; handy; **las plantas ~es para el hombre** the plants which are useful to man; **el coche es viejo pero todavía está ~** the car is old but it is still serviceable; **es muy ~ tenerlo aquí cerca** it's very handy having it here

close by; **¿en qué puedo serle ~?** can I do anything for you?, can I be of any help?
(b) día ~ working day, weekday.
(c) ~ para el servicio (*Mil*) *persona* fit for military service, *vehículo etc* operational.
[2] **~es** NMPL tools, implements; tackle, equipment; **~es de chimenea** fire irons; **~es de labranza** agricultural implements.
utilería NF (*Cono Sur, Méx Teat*) properties, props*.
utilero, -a NM/F (*Cono Sur, Méx: Teat*) property manager, *person in charge of stage props.*
utilidad NF **(a)** (*cualidad de útil*) usefulness, utility; (*provecho*) benefit.
(b) (*Com, Fin etc*) profit, benefit; **~es ocasionales** windfall profits; **~es líquidas** net profits. **(c)** (*Inform*) utility.
utilitario [1] ADJ **(a)** (*gen*) utilitarian. **(b)** *coche, ropa etc* utility (*atr*).
[2] NM **(a)** (*Inform*) utility. **(b)** (*Aut*) small car, compact car (*US*).
utilitarismo NM utilitarianism.
utilitarista NMF utilitarian.
utilizable ADJ (*gen*) usable; serviceable; (*disponible*) fit for use, ready to use; (*Téc*) *residuos* reclaimable, useful.
utilización NF use, utilization; (*Tec*) reclamation.
utilizar [1f] VT to use, make use of, utilize; *fuerzas, recursos etc* to harness; (*Tec*) *residuos* to reclaim.
utillaje NM (set of) tools; tackle, equipment.
utillero NM (plumber's *etc*) mate.
útilmente ADV usefully.
utopía NF, **utopia** NF Utopia.

utópico ADJ Utopian.
utopista ADJ, NMF Utopian.
utrículo NM utricle.
UV [1] ADJ ABR *de* **ultravioleta** ultraviolet, UV.
[2] NF (*Esp*) ABR *de* **Unión Valenciana**.
UVA NF ABR *de* **unidad vecinal de absorción**.
uva NF **(a)** grape; **~ blanca** white grape; **~ de Corinto** currant; **~ crespa, ~ espina** gooseberry; **~s del diablo** (*Bot*) nightshade; **~ de gato** (*Bot*) stonecrop; **~s de mesa** dessert grapes; **~ moscatel** muscatel grape; **~ pasa** raisin; **~s verdes** (*fig*) sour grapes; **de ~s a peras** very occasionally, once in a blue moon; **ir de ~s a peras** to switch the subject for no reason; **entrar a por ~s** (*fig*) to take the plunge; **estar de mala ~** (*Esp**) to be in a bad mood; **estar de mala ~ con uno** (*Esp**) to have it in for sb; **estar hecho una ~** to be drunk as a lord. **(b)** (*) (*vino*) wine; (*bebida*) drink (*in general*). **(c)** (*Cono Sur: beso*) kiss. **(d) las doce ~s, las ~s de la suerte** twelve grapes eaten at midnight on New-Year's Eve; (*fig*) New-Year's Eve, New Year.
uve NF the (name of the) letter *v*; **~ doble** the (name of the) letter *w*; **de forma de ~** V-shaped; **escote en ~** V-neck.
UVI ['uβi] NF ABR *de* **unidad de vigilancia intensiva** intensive care unit, ICU.
úvula NF uvula.
uvular ADJ uvular.
uxoricida NM uxoricide.
uxoricidio NM wife-murder.
-uzo, -uza V Aspects of Word Formation in Spanish 2.

V, v ['uβe, (*LAm*) be'korta] NF (*letra*) V,v; **~ doble** (*Esp*), **doble ~** (*LAm*) W; **~ de la victoria** V for victory; victory sign, V-sign; **escote en ~** V-neck.

V. (**a**) ABR *de* **Usted** you. (**b**) ABR *de* **Visto** approved, passed, OK.

v. (**a**) (*Elec*) ABR *de* **voltio(s)** volt(s), V. (**b**) ABR *de* **ver, véase** vide, see, v. (**c**) (*Liter*) ABR *de* **verso** line, l.

V.A. ABR *de* **Vuestra Alteza** Your Highness.

va *etc V* **ir.**

vaca NF (**a**) (*Zool*) cow; **~ de leche, ~ lechera** dairy cow, milking cow; (*LAm: fig*) good business, profitable deal; **~ marina** manatee, sea cow; **~ sagrada** (*t fig*) sacred cow; **~ de San Antón** ladybird, ladybug (*US*); **(los años de) las ~s flacas** the lean years; **(los años de) las ~s gordas** the fat years, the boom years; **pasar las ~s gordas** (*fig*) to have a grand time of it.
(**b**) (*Culin: carne de vaca*) beef; (*cuero*) cowhide.
(**c**) (*LAm*) enterprise with profits on a pro rata basis.
(**d**) **hacer(se) la ~** (*And*) to play truant, play hooky (*US*).

vacaburra* NF boor; **¡~! animal!***.

vacación NF **vacation;** **vacaciones** holiday(s), vacation (*esp US*); **vacaciones escolares** school holidays; **vacaciones pagadas, vacaciones retribuidas** holidays with pay; **estar de vacaciones** to be (away) on holiday; **hacer vacaciones** to take a day off; **marcharse de vacaciones** to go off on holiday.

VACACIONES	ver también la entrada

¿"Holiday" o "holidays"?

- En inglés británico, *vacaciones* se puede traducir tanto por *holiday* como por *holidays* cuando hablamos de un período de tiempo sin colegio o trabajo:

  ¿Dónde pasaste las vacaciones?
  Where did you spend your holiday(s)?
  Larry fue a Londres un par de días durante las vacaciones
  Larry went to London for a couple of days during the holiday(s)

- *Vacaciones* se traduce por *holiday* cuando se habla de un viaje en particular:

  El año pasado pasamos unas vacaciones maravillosas en Mallorca
  We had a lovely holiday in Majorca last year
  ¿Te lo has pasado bien en las vacaciones?
  Did you have a good holiday?

  NOTA: Aquí *holiday* funciona como un sustantivo contable normal; se añade una "s" cuando se trata de más de un viaje.

- *Estar de vacaciones* se traduce por *to be on holiday*. En este caso *holiday* no acepta el plural:

  Estaré de vacaciones dos semanas
  I'll be on holiday for a fortnight
  Para otros usos y ejemplos ver la entrada.

---

vacacional ADJ vacation (*atr*), holiday (*atr*); **período ~** holiday period.

vacacionista NMF holidaymaker, vacationer (*US*).

vacada NF herd of cows.

vacaje NM (*Cono Sur*) cows, cattle; herd of cows; (*Méx*) herd of beef cows.

vacante [1] ADJ vacant, empty, unoccupied; *puesto* vacant.
[2] NF (**a**) vacancy, place, (unfilled) post; **proveer una ~** to fill a post.
(**b**) (*LAm: asiento*) empty seat.

vacar [1g] VI (**a**) (*puesto*) to fall vacant, become vacant; to remain unfilled.
(**b**) (*persona*) to cease work; to be idle.
(**c**) **~ a, ~ en** to attend to, engage in, devote o.s. to.
(**d**) **~ de** to lack, be without.

vacarí ADJ cowhide (*atr*).

vaccinio NM (*Esp*) bilberry; blueberry (*US*).

vaciadero NM (**a**) (*desaguadero*) sink, drain; sump. (**b**) (*vertedero*) rubbish tip, dumping ground.

vaciado [1] ADJ (**a**) *estatua etc* cast in a mould; *herramienta* hollow-ground; **~ a troquel** die-cast. (**b**) (*Méx*: estupendo*) great*, terrific*.
[2] NM (**a**) (*objeto*) cast, mould(ing); **~ de yeso** plaster cast. (**b**) (*acto*) hollowing out; excavation. (**c**) (*rápido*) (*Aer*) jettisoning.

vaciar [1c] [1] VT (**a**) *recipiente* to empty (out); *vaso etc* to drain; *contenido* to empty out; *líquido* (*verter*) to pour, pour away; to run off; (*beber*) to drink up; (*Aer etc*) to jettison; **vació los bolsillos en la mesa** he emptied out his pockets on the table; **vació la leche en un vaso** he poured (*o* emptied) the milk into a glass; **lo vació todo sobre su cabeza** he poured the lot over his head.
(**b**) *madera, piedra etc* to hollow out; *estatua etc* to cast.
(**c**) *cuchillo etc* to grind, sharpen.
(**d**) *tema, teoría* to expound at length.
(**e**) *texto* to copy out.
[2] VI (*río*) to flow, empty, run (*en* into).
[3] **vaciarse** VR (**a**) to empty.
(**b**) (**: t ~ por la lengua*) to blab, spill the beans*.

vaciedad NF (**a**) (*estado*) emptiness. (**b**) (*fig*) silliness; piece of nonsense; **~es** nonsense, rubbish.

vacila* NM tease, joker.

vacilación NF hesitancy, hesitation, vacillation; **sin vacilaciones** unhesitatingly.

vacilada* NF (*Méx*) (**a**) (*borrachera*) spree, binge*. (**b**) (*chiste*) joke; (*chiste verde*) dirty joke; **de ~** as a joke, (just) for a laugh. (**c**) (*truco*) trick.

vacilante ADJ (**a**) *mano, paso* unsteady; *mueble* wobbly, tottery; *habla* faltering, halting; *memoria* uncertain. (**b**) *luz* flickering. (**c**) (*fig*) hesitant, uncertain, vacillating; indecisive, dithery.

vacilar [1a] [1] VT (**a**) (*Carib, Méx*: burlarse*) to make fun of, tease.
(**b**) (*CAm*: engañar*) to trick.
(**c**) (***) to mess about, make difficulties for; **¡no me vaciles!** stop messing me about!
[2] VI (**a**) (*mueble etc*) to be unsteady; to wobble, rock, move, shake; (*persona*) to totter; to reel, stagger; to stumble; (*fig: moralidad etc*) to be indecisive, be collapsing; (*habla*) to falter; (*memoria*) to fail.
(**b**) (*luz*) to flicker.
(**c**) (*fig*) to hesitate, waver, vacillate; to hang back; **sin ~** unhesitatingly; **~ en** + *infin* to hesitate to + *infin*; **~ entre dos posibilidades** to hesitate between two possibilities; **es un hombre que vacila mucho** he is a very indecisive man, he is a man who dithers a lot; **no vaciles en decírmelo** don't hesitate to tell me about it.
(**d**) (*fig: variar*) **~ entre** to vary between; **un sabor que vacila entre agradable y desagradable** a taste which varies between nice and nasty, a taste which ranges from nice to nasty.
(**e**) **~ con uno** (**: guasearse*) to tease sb, take the mickey out of sb‡.
(**f**) **~ con uno** (**: hablar*) to talk pointlessly to sb, bore sb with one's talk.
(**g**) (**: fachendear*) to talk big*, show off, swank*.
(**h**) (*CAm, Carib, Méx‡*) (*emborracharse*) to get plastered‡; (*ir de juerga*) to go on a spree; (*bromear*) to lark about*, have fun.

vacile* NM (**a**) (*duda*) hesitation. (**b**) (*guasa*) teasing, amusing talk; **estar de ~** to chat, indulge in teasing talk. (**c**) (*guasón*) tease, joker.

vacilón* [1] ADJ (**a**) (*guasón*) teasing, jokey; (*CAm, Méx*) fun-loving; **estar ~** to be in a jokey mood. (**b**) (**: fachendón*) swanky*, stuck-up*.
[2] NM (**a**) tease, joker. (**b**) poser*, show-off*. (**c**) (*Méx*) reveller, merry-maker; **andar de ~** to be out on the town. (**d**) (*CAm, Méx: juerga*) party, revels; fun.

vacío [1] ADJ (**a**) (*gen*) empty; *puesto etc* vacant, unoccupied; unfilled; *piso* unfurnished; *papel* blank; **~ de todo contenido serio** empty of any serious contents, devoid of any serious purpose; **el teatro estaba medio ~** the theatre was half empty; **irse con las manos**

vacías to leave empty-handed. **(b)** (*fig*) (*insustancial*) insubstantial; (*superficial*) superficial; *charla etc* light, idle, frivolous; *esfuerzo* vain, useless. **(c)** (*fig*) (*vanidoso*) vain; (*orgulloso*) proud. **(d)** (*fig: ocioso*) idle, unemployed. **(e) pan ~** (*And, CAm, Carib*) bread alone, just bread, bread by itself. ⟨2⟩ NM (*gen*) emptiness; void; (*Fís*) vacuum; (*un ~*) empty space, gap; vacant place; (*hueco*) hollow; (*Anat*) side, flank, ribs; **~ legislativo** gap in legislation; **~ político** political vacuum; **han dejado un ~ para el nombre** they have left a space for the name; **se nota ahora un gran ~ en la familia** one is conscious now of a big gap in the family; **el libro llenará un ~** the book will fill a gap; **empaquetado al ~, envasado al ~** vacuum-packed; **el camión volvió de ~** the lorry came back empty; **lo pedí pero tuve que marcharme de ~** I asked for it but had to go away empty-handed; **caer en el ~** to fail, be ineffective, produce no result; **dar un golpe en ~** to miss, fail to connect; **esta viga parece que está en el ~** this beam seems to be unsupported, this beam seems to rest on nothing at all; **marchar en ~** (*Mec*) to tick over; **tener un ~ en el estómago** to feel hungry; **hacer el ~ a uno** to send sb to Coventry, pretend that sb does not exist; to ignore sb.

vacuidad NF **(a)** emptiness. **(b)** (*fig*) vacuity; superficiality, frivolity; empty-headedness.

vacuna NF **(a)** (*sustancia*) vaccine; **~ antigripal** flu vaccine. **(b)** (*LAm: acto*) vaccination.

vacunación NF **(a)** vaccination. **(b)** (*fig*) preparation; inuring; forearming.

vacunar [1a] ⟨1⟩ VT **(a)** (*Med*) to vaccinate (*contra* against). **(b)** (*fig: preparar*) to prepare; (*habituar*) to inure; (*prevenir*) to forearm. ⟨2⟩ **vacunarse** VR to get (oneself) vaccinated.

vacuno ⟨1⟩ ADJ bovine; cow (*atr*); **ganado ~** cattle. ⟨2⟩ NM (*ganado*) cattle; **carne de ~** beef.

vacuo ADJ **(a)** (*vacío*) empty; vacant. **(b)** (*fig*) vacuous; superficial, frivolous, empty-headed.

vade NM (*Esp Escuela etc*) satchel, case.

vadeable ADJ **(a)** (*lit*) fordable, which can be forded. **(b)** (*fig*) not impossible, not insuperable.

vadear [1a] ⟨1⟩ VT **(a)** *río* to ford; *agua* to wade through, wade across. **(b)** *dificultad* to surmount, get round, overcome. **(c)** (*fig*) *persona* to sound out. ⟨2⟩ VI to wade; **cruzar un río vadeando** to wade across a river; **llegar a tierra vadeando** to wade ashore.

vademécum NM, PL **vademécums (a)** (*libro*) vademecum. **(b)** (*Escuela etc*) satchel, schoolbag.

vadera NF wide ford.

vade retro INTERJ go away!, get thee behind me (Satan)! *hum.*

vado NM **(a)** (*de río*) ford. **(b)** (*Esp Aut*) garage entrance; (*letrero*) **'~ permanente'** 'Garage Entrance', 'Keep Clear'. **(c)** (*fig: salida*) way out, solution, expedient; **no hallar ~** to see no way out, find no solution; **tentar el ~** to look into possible solutions. **(d)** (*fig: respiro*) respite.

vagabundaje NM vagrancy.

vagabundear [1a] VI (*errar*) to wander, roam, rove; (*haraganear*) to loaf, idle, bum (*US*).

vagabundeo NM wandering, roving; tramp's life; loafing, idling, bumming (*US*).

vagabundo ⟨1⟩ ADJ (*errante*) wandering, roving; (*pey*) vagrant; vagabond; *perro* stray. ⟨2⟩ NM, **vagabunda** NF wanderer, rover; (*pey*) vagrant; vagabond, tramp, bum (*US*).

vagación NF (*Mec*) free play.

vagamente ADV vaguely.

vagamundería NF (*LAm*) idleness, laziness.

vagamundero ADJ (*LAm*) idle, lazy.

vagancia NF **(a)** (*vagabundaje*) vagrancy. **(b)** (*gandulería*) idleness, laziness.

vagante ADJ **(a)** wandering, vagrant. **(b)** (*Mec*) free, loose.

vagar ⟨1⟩ [1h] VI **(a)** (*errar*) to wander (about), roam, rove; (*rondar*) to prowl about; (*pasearse*) to saunter up and down, wander about the streets; (*entretenerse*) to loiter; (*gandulear*) to idle, loaf, laze about; **como alma en pena** to wander about like a lost soul. **(b)** (*Mec*) to be free, be loose, move about. ⟨2⟩ NM (*tiempo libre*) leisure, free time; (*pereza*) idleness; (*calma*) lack of anxiety, freedom from worry; **andar de ~** to be at leisure; to feel at ease.

vagido NM baby's first cry, cry of new-born baby.

vagina NF vagina.

vaginal ADJ vaginal.

vaginalmente ADV vaginally.

vaginitis NF INVAR vaginitis.

vago ⟨1⟩ ADJ **(a)** (*gen*) vague; (*indistinto*) ill-defined, indistinct; indeterminate; (*Arte, Fot*) blurred.

(b) (*errabundo*) roving, wandering. **(c)** (*gandul*) lazy, slack; (*poco fiable*) unreliable; (*ocioso*) idle, unemployed; *objeto* idle, unused; *espacio etc* empty. **(d) en ~ mantenerse en pie etc** unsteadily; (*sin apoyo*) unsupported; *esforzarse* in vain; aimlessly, pointlessly; **dar golpes en ~** to flail about, beat the air. ⟨2⟩ NM **(a)** (*vagabundo*) tramp, vagrant; (*pobre*) down-and-out. **(b)** (*gandul*) idler, slacker; (*unreliable person*); (*inútil*) useless individual, dead loss; **hacer el ~** to loaf around.

vagón NM (*de pasajeros*) coach, carriage, car; (*de mercancías*) truck, wagon; car, van; **~ cisterna, ~ tanque** tanker, tank wagon; **~ de cola** guard's-van; (*fig*) rear, tail-end; **~ directo** through carriage; **~ de equipajes** luggage-van; **~ de ganado, ~ de hacienda** (*Cono Sur*), **~ de reja** (*Cono Sur*) cattle-truck; **~ de mercancías** goods van, freight-car (*US*); **~ mirador** observation car; **~ postal** mailcoach, mailcar (*US*); **~ de primera** first-class carriage; **~ de segunda** second-class carriage; **~ restaurante** dining-car; **~ tolva** hopper.

vagonada NF truckload, wagonload.

vagoneta NF light truck.

vaguada NF watercourse, stream bed.

vaguear [1a] VI = **vagar 1.**

vaguedad NF **(a)** (*cualidad*) vagueness; indistinctness; indeterminacy. **(b)** (*una ~*) vague remark; woolly idea; **hablar sin ~es** to get straight to the point, speak with precision.

vaguería NF laziness, slackness; unreliability.

vaguitis* NF (*Esp*) congenital idleness.

vaharada NF (*soplo*) puff, gust of breath; (*olor*) whiff, reek; smell.

vahear [1a] VI (*echar vapor*) to steam; (*humear*) to fume, give off fumes, smoke; (*oler*) to whiff, reek, smell.

vahído NM dizzy spell, blackout.

vaho NM **(a)** (*vapor*) vapour, steam; (*en cristal etc*) mist, condensation; (*Quím etc*) fumes; (*aliento*) breath; (*olor*) whiff, reek, smell. **(b) ~s** (*Med*) inhalation.

vaina ⟨1⟩ NF **(a)** (*de espada etc*) sheath, scabbard; (*de herramienta*) sheath, case; (*de cartucho*) case. **(b)** (*Bot*) (*de guisante etc*) pod; (*de nuez etc*) husk, shell; **~s** (*judías*) green beans. **(c)** (*pega*) problem, snag; (*LAm*: molestia*) nuisance, bother; **¡qué ~!** what a nuisance! **(d)** (*And: chiripa*) fluke, piece of luck. **(e)** (*Cono Sur: estafa*) swindle. **(f) echar ~** (*Carib*‡*) to screw‡‡, fuck‡‡. ⟨2⟩ NM (*) twit*, nitwit*. ⟨3⟩ ADJ (*LAm*) annoying.

vainica NF (*Cos*) hemstitch.

vainilla NF vanilla.

vainillina NF vanillin.

vainita NF (*LAm*) green bean.

vais V **ir**.

vaivén NM **(a)** (*ir y venir*) to-and-fro movement, oscillation; (*mecerse*) rocking, backward and forward movement; (*balanceo*) swing(ing), sway(ing); (*sacudidas*) lurch(ing). **(b)** (*de tráfico etc*) coming and going, constant movement. **(c)** (*fig: de la suerte*) change of fortune; **vaivenes** ups and downs, vicissitudes. **(d)** (*fig: Pol etc*) swing, seesaw, violent change of opinion.

vaivenear [1a] VT to oscillate; to rock, move backwards and forwards; to swing, sway.

vajear [1a] VT (*CAm, Carib, Méx*) (*culebra*) to fascinate, hypnotize; (*hechizar*) to bewitch; (*seducir*) to win over by flattery, seduce.

vajilla NF (*gen*) crockery, china; dishes; (*una ~*) service, set of dishes; **~ de oro** gold plate; **~ de porcelana** chinaware; **lavar la ~** to wash up.

valdiviano ⟨1⟩ ADJ of Valdivia. ⟨2⟩ NM, **valdiviana** NF native (*o* inhabitant) of Valdivia; **los ~s** the people of Valdivia. ⟨3⟩ NM *typical Chilean dish of dried meat and vegetables.*

valdré *etc* V **valer.**

vale¹ NM (*Fin*) promissory note, IOU; (*recibo*) receipt; (*cupón*) voucher, coupon, warrant; (*LAm: cuenta*) bill, check (*US*); **~ de comida, ~ (de) restaurante** luncheon voucher; **~ de correo, ~ postal** money order; **dar el ~** (*fig*) to O.K., pass as suitable; to give the go-ahead.

vale²* NM (*LAm*: ABR *de* **valedor**) pal*, chum*, buddy (*US*); **~ corrido** (*Carib*) old crony; **ser ~ con** (*And*) to be pals with*.

valedero ADJ valid; (*Jur*) binding; **~ para 6 meses** valid for 6 months; **~ hasta el día 16** valid until the 16th.

valedor NM **(a)** (*protector*) protector, guardian. **(b)** (*LAm*) = **vale².**

valedura NF **(a)** (*Méx*) (*ayuda*) help; (*protección*) protection; (*favor*) favour. **(b)** (*And, Carib: propina*) gift made by a gambler out of his winnings.

valemadrista* ADJ (*Méx*) indifferent, laid-back*; cynical.

valencia NF (*Quím*) valency.

valencianismo NM (a) (*Ling*) word (*o phrase etc*) peculiar to Valencia. (b) sense of the differentness of Valencia; (*Pol*) doctrine of (*o belief in*) Valencian autonomy.

valenciano, -a ADJ, NM/F ⚀ Valencian.
⚁ NM (*Ling*) Valencian.

valentía NF (a) (*valor*) bravery, courage; boldness; (*resolución*) resoluteness.
(b) (*pey*) boastfulness.
(c) (*acto*) brave deed, heroic exploit; bold act.
(d) (*pey: dicho*) brag, boast.

valentón ⚀ ADJ boastful; blustering, bullying; arrogant.
⚁ NM braggart; bluster, bully.

valentonada NF (*dicho*) boast, brag; piece of bluster; (*acto*) arrogant act.

▼ **valer** [2p] ⚀ VT (a) (*proteger*) to aid, protect; (*servir*) to serve; (*ayudar*) to help, avail; **¡válgame (Dios)!** *V* **Dios**; **no le vale ser hijo del ministro** it's of no help to him being the minister's son, it doesn't help his case that he's the minister's son; **su situación privilegiada no le valió** his privileged position did not save him; **no le valdrán excusas** excuses won't help him, excuses will avail him nothing.
(b) (*Mat: ser igual a*) to equal, be equal to; (*sumar*) to amount to, come to; **la suma vale 99** the total comes to 99; **el ángulo B vale 38°** angle B is 38°; **en ese caso X vale 9** in that case X equals 9.
(c) (*causar*) to cause; (*ganar*) to earn; to win; (*costar*) to lose, cost; **el asunto le valió muchos disgustos** the affair caused him lots of trouble; **esa tontería le valió un rapapolvo** that piece of stupidity got (*o earned*) him a dressing-down; **son las cualidades que le valieron el premio** these are the qualities which won him the prize; **su ausencia le valió la pérdida del contrato** his absence lost (*o cost*) him the contract.
⚁ VTI (a) (*Com, Fin*) to be worth; (*costar*) to cost, be priced at, be valued at; (*ser valioso*) to be valuable; (*fig: representar*) to be equivalent to, represent; **este libro vale 5 dólares** this book costs (*o is worth*) 5 dollars; **ésas valen 20 pesetas el kilo** those are 20 pesetas a kilo; **esta tela vale a 60 pesetas** this cloth costs 60 pesetas; **¿cuánto vale?** how much is it?; **¿vale mucho?** is it valuable?; **4 fichas azules valen por una negra** 4 blue counters are worth one black one; **cada cupón vale por un paquete** each coupon represents (*o counts for*) a packet.
▼ (b) (*fig: tener valor*) to be worth; **no vale nada** it's worthless, it's rubbish; **no vale un higo** (*Esp*) it's not worth a brass farthing; **vale lo que pesa** it's worth its weight in gold; **esa mirada suya me valió un sinfín de palabras** that look of hers told me more (*o was worth more to me*) than a hundred words; **más vale así** it's better this way; **A vale más que B** A is better than B; **más vale tarde que nunca** better late than never; **más vale no hacerlo** it's better not to do it; **más vale que vayas tú** it would be better for you to go; **más vale que me vaya** I had better go; *V* **pena**.
(c) (*fig: persona*) to be worthy; to have one's merits (*o qualities*); **es un hombre que vale** he's a worthy man, he's a man of some quality, he has his points; **no vale para este trabajo** he's no good for this job; **no vale para nada** he's useless, he's a dead loss.
(d) **¡me vale (madre)!** (*Méx**) I don't give a damn!
⚂ VI (a) (*servir*) to be of use, be useful; (*bastar*) to do, be enough; **es viejo pero todavía vale** it's old but it still serves; **este sombrero me vale aún** this hat is still useful to me; **hay que tirar todo lo que no vale** we must throw out everything that is no use; **este trozo no me vale para hacer la cortina** this piece won't do to make the curtain.
(b) (*ser valedero*) to be valid; (*ser aplicable*) to be applicable, apply; (*en juegos*) to count, score; to be permitted; **¿vale?** is that all right?, will that do?; how about that?; **¡vale!** (*Esp*) that's right!, O.K.!*; that'll do!, that's enough!; **es una teoría que no vale ya** it is a theory which no longer holds; **esa sección no vale ahora** that section is not now applicable; **¡eso no vale!** that doesn't count!; that's not allowed!, you can't do that!; **ese tanto no vale** that point doesn't count; **no vale golpearlo segunda vez** you aren't allowed to have a second shot at it; **¡no hay 'querido' que valga!** it's no good saying 'darling' to me!, you can cut out the 'darling'!
(c) **hacer ~ su derecho** to assert one's right; **hacer ~ sus argumentos** to make one's arguments felt, establish the validity of one's arguments.
(d) **está un poco chiflado, valga la expresión** he's a bit cracked, so to speak; he's a bit cracked, for want of a better way of putting it.
⚃ **valerse** VR (a) **~ de** to make use of, avail o.s. of; to take advantage of; *derecho* to exercise.
(b) **~ por sí mismo** to help o.s., shift for o.s., manage by o.s.; **poder ~** to be able to manage; **no poder ~** to be helpless.
⚄ NM worth, value.

valeriana NF valerian.
valerosamente ADV bravely, valiantly.
valeroso ADJ brave, valiant.

valet [ba'le] NM, PL **valets** [ba'le] (*Naipes*) jack, knave.
valetudinario, -a ADJ, NM/F valetudinarian.
valga *etc V* **valer**.
Valhala NM Valhalla.
valía NF (a) (*valor*) worth, value; **de gran ~** of great worth, very valuable; *persona* worthy, estimable. (b) (*fig: influencia*) influence.
validación NF validation; ratification.
validar [1a] VT to validate, give effect to; (*Pol etc*) to ratify.
validez NF validity; **dar ~ a** to validate, give effect to; (*Pol etc*) to ratify.
valido NM (*Hist*) (royal) favourite.
válido ADJ (a) valid (*hasta until, para for*). (b) (*Med*) strong, robust; fit.
valiente ⚀ ADJ (a) (*valeroso*) brave, valiant; (*audaz*) bold.
(b) (*pey*) boastful, blustering.
(c) (*fig*) fine, excellent; noble; strong; (*iró*) fine, wonderful; **¡~ amigo!** a fine friend you are!; **¡~ gobierno!** some government!, do you call this a government?
⚁ NMF (a) (*héroe*) brave man, brave woman; hero, heroine.
(b) (*pey*) braggart.
valientemente ADV (*V* ADJ) (a) bravely, valiantly; boldly. (b) (*pey*) boastfully. (c) (*fig*) excellently; nobly; (*iró*) wonderfully.
valija NF (a) (*maleta*) case; (*LAm*) suitcase. (b) (*portamantas*) valise; (*cartera*) satchel; (*Correos*) mailbag; (*fig*) mail, post; **~ diplomática** diplomatic bag.
valijería NF (*Cono Sur*) travel-goods shop.
valimiento NM (a) (*valor*) value; benefit.
(b) (*Pol etc*) favour, protection; (*Hist*) position of royal favourite, status of the royal favourite; **~ con uno, ~ cerca de uno** influence with sb.
valioso ADJ (a) (*de valor*) valuable; (*útil*) useful, beneficial; (*estimable*) estimable. (b) (*rico*) wealthy; (*poderoso*) powerful.
valisoletano = **vallisoletano**.
valla NF (a) (*cercado*) fence; (*Mil*) barricade; palisade, stockade; (*Dep*) hurdle; **~ de protección, ~ de seguridad** barrier; **~ publicitaria** hoarding, billboard (*US*); **400 metros ~s** 400 metres hurdles.
(b) (*fig*) (*barrera*) barrier; (*límite*) limit; (*obstáculo*) obstacle, hindrance; **romper las ~s, saltar(se) la ~** to disregard the social conventions, do away with social niceties; to burst through the barriers of convention.
(c) (*And, Carib, Méx: de gallos*) cockpit.
(d) (*And: zanja*) ditch.
valladar NM (a) = **valla** (a). (b) (*fig*) defence, barrier.
vallado ⚀ ADJ fenced.
⚁ NM (a) = **valla** (a). (b) (*Mil*) defensive wall, rampart. (c) (*Méx: zanja*) deep ditch.
vallar [1a] VT to fence in, put up a fence round, enclose.
valle NM (a) valley; vale, dale; **~ de lágrimas** vale of tears. (b) **energía de ~** off-peak power demand (*o supply*); **horas de ~** off-peak hours.
vallero (*Méx*) ⚀ ADJ valley (*atr*).
⚁ NM, **vallera** NF valley dweller.
vallino ADJ (*And*) valley (*atr*).
vallisoletano ⚀ ADJ of Valladolid.
⚁ NM, **vallisoletana** NF native (*o inhabitant*) of Valladolid; **los ~s** the people of Valladolid.
vallista NMF hurdler.
vallisto ADJ (*Cono Sur, Méx*) valley (*atr*).
vallunco ADJ (*CAm*) rustic, peasant (*atr*).
valón, -ona ADJ, NM/F ⚀ Walloon.
⚁ NM (*Ling*) Walloon.
valona NF (a) (*And, Carib*) artistically trimmed mane; **hacer la ~** (*Carib*) to shave. (b) (*Méx*) = **valedura** (a).
valonar [1a] VT (*And*) to trim, cut; to shear.
valonearse [1a] VR (*CAm*) to lean from the saddle.
valor NM (a) (*gen*) value, worth; (*precio*) price; (*de moneda, sello*) value, denomination; (*Mat, Mús etc*) value; (*de palabras etc*) value, importance; meaning; (*tasa*) rate; **objetos de ~** valuables; **sin ~** worthless, valueless; **~ adquisitivo** purchasing power; **~ alimenticio** food value, nutritional value; **~ añadido** added value; (*Econ*) surplus value; profit; (*Com*) mark-up; **~ según balance, ~ en libros** book value; **~ calorífico** calorific value; **~ catastral** official valuation of property (for tax purposes); **~ comercial** commercial value; **'sin ~ comercial'** 'no commercial value'; **~ contable** asset value; **~ por defecto** default value; **~ de desecho** salvage value; **~ facial, ~ nominal** face-value, nominal value; **~ a la par** par value; **~ sentimental** sentimental value; **por ~ de** to the value of, for; **conceder ~ a, dar ~ a** to attach importance to; to value, esteem; **quitar ~ a** to minimize the importance of; **esas cosas ya no tienen ~ para mí** such things no longer have any importance for me, I no longer value such things; **se han medido ~es de 80 al m³** rates of 80 to the cubic metre have been recorded.
(b) (*fig*) great name, great figure; **Cervantes, máximo ~ nacional**

Cervantes, one of our country's greatest figures; Cervantes, part of our great national heritage.

(c) **~es** (*Com, Fin*) securities, bonds; stock; (*And, Cono Sur*) assets; **~es en cartera**, **~es habidos** investments, holdings, share portfolio; **~es fiduciarios** fiduciary issue, banknotes; **~es inmuebles** real estate; **~es de renta fija** fixed-interest securities; **~es de renta variable** variable-yield securities.

(d) (*valentía*) bravery, courage, valour; **~ cívico** (sense of) civic duty; **armarse de ~** to gather up one's courage.

(e) (*: caradura*) nerve*, cheek*; **¡qué ~!** of all the cheek!*; **tuvo el ~ de pedírmelo** he had the nerve to ask me for it*.

valoración NF **(a)** (*valuación*) valuation; (*fig*) assessment, appraisal. **(b)** (*Quím*) titration.

valorar [1a] VT **(a)** to value (*en* at); (*tasar*) to price; (*esp fig*) to assess, appraise; to rate; **~ mucho** to value highly, esteem; **~ poco** to attach little value to; (*anuncio*) **'se valorarán conocimientos de eslóbodo'** 'Knowledge of Slobodian an advantage'. **(b)** (*Quím*) to titrate.

valorización NF valuation; (*fig*) appraisal, assessment.

valorizar [1f] VT **(a)** = **valorar. (b)** (*And, Cono Sur: subir el precio de*) to put up the price of. **(c)** (*And: vender barato*) to sell cheaply.

Valquiria NF Valkyrie.

vals NM waltz.

valsar [1a] VI to waltz.

valse NM **(a)** (*LAm*) waltz. **(b)** (*Carib*) Venezuelan folk dance.

valsear [1a] VI (*LAm*) to waltz.

valuable ADJ (*LAm*) **(a)** (*valioso*) valuable. **(b)** (*calculable*) calculable.

valuación NF = **valoración (a)**.

valuador(a) NM/F (*LAm*) valuer.

valuar [1e] VT = **valorar (a)**.

valumen NM **(a)** (*Cono Sur Bot*) luxuriance, rankness. **(b)** (*Méx*) (*lío*) bundle; (*masa*) mass, bulk.

valumoso ADJ **(a)** (*CAm, Cono Sur*) luxuriant, rank. **(b)** (*And, CAm, Méx: voluminoso*) bulky. **(c)** (*Carib: vanidoso*) vain, conceited.

valva NF (*Bot, Zool*) valve.

válvula NF (*Mec etc*) valve; **~ de admisión** inlet valve; **~ de escape** exhaust valve; (*fig*) relief, escape; **~ de purga** vent; **~ de seguridad** safety valve.

vamos *etc* V **ir**.

vampi* NF = **vampiresa**.

vampiresa NF vamp.

vampirizar [1f] VT to sap, milk, bleed dry.

vampiro NM **(a)** (*Zool*) vampire. **(b)** (*fig*) vampire; exploiter, bloodsucker.

van V **ir**.

vanagloria NF vainglory.

vanagloriarse [1b] VR **~ de** to boast; to be vain, be arrogant; **~ de** to boast of; **~ de** + *infin* to boast of + *ger*, boast of being able to + *infin*.

vanaglorioso ADJ vainglorious; vain, boastful, arrogant.

vanamente ADV uselessly, vainly.

vanarse [1a] VR (*And, Carib, Cono Sur*) to shrivel up; (*fig*) to fall through, come to nothing, produce no results.

vandálico ADJ Vandal(ic); (*fig*) loutish, destructive.

vandalismo NM vandalism.

vándalo [1] ADJ Vandal(ic).

[2] NM, **vándala** NF (*Hist*) Vandal; (*fig*) vandal.

vanguardia NF vanguard, van (*t fig*); **estar en la ~ del progreso** to be in the van of progress; **ir a la ~**, **ir en ~** to be in the vanguard; to be foremost, be ahead, be in front; **un pintor de ~** an ultramodern painter, a painter with a revolutionary style.

vanguardismo NM (*Arte, Liter etc*) avant-garde movement; ultramodern manner, revolutionary style; new tendency.

vanguardista [1] ADJ avant-garde; ultramodern, revolutionary; **coche de tecnología ~** technically advanced car.

[2] NMF avant-garde artist (*etc*).

vanidad NF **(a)** (*irrealidad*) unreality; (*sospecha*) groundlessness; (*inutilidad*) uselessness, futility; (*superficialidad*) shallowness; (*necedad*) inanity; (*falta de sentido*) pointlessness.

(b) (*presunción*) vanity; **por pura ~** out of sheer vanity; **halagar la ~ de uno** to play up to sb's vanity.

(c) **~es** vanities.

vanidoso ADJ vain, conceited; smug.

vano [1] ADJ **(a)** (*irreal*) unreal, imaginary, vain; *temor etc* idle; *sospecha* groundless; *superstición* foolish, unreasonable.

(b) (*inútil*) vain, useless; *pasatiempo* idle; **en ~** in vain; **no en ~** not in vain.

(c) *persona* (*frívolo*) shallow, superficial; frivolous; *placer etc* empty, inane, pointless; *adorno* silly.

(d) *cáscara* empty, hollow.

[2] NM (*Arquit*) space, gap.

vapor NM **(a)** (*gen*) vapour; (*Tec*) steam; (*Quím*) fumes; (*Met*) mist, haze; **~ de agua** water vapour; **al ~** by steam, (*fig*) very fast; **cocer**

---

un plato al ~ to steam a dish; **a todo ~** at full steam, (*t fig*) full-steam; **de ~** steam (*atr*); **acumular ~** to get steam up; **echar ~** to give off steam, steam.

(b) (*Náut*) steamer, steamship; **~ correo** mailboat; **~ de paletas**, **~ de ruedas** paddle-steamer; **~ volandero** tramp steamer.

(c) (*Med*) giddiness, faintness; dizzy spell; **~es** vapours, hysteria.

vapora NF **(a)** (*barco*) steam launch. **(b)** (*Carib Ferro*) steam engine.

vapor(e)ar [1a] [1] VT to evaporate.

[2] VI to give off vapour.

[3] **vapor(e)arse** VR to evaporate.

vaporización NF vaporization.

vaporizador NM vaporizer; spray.

vaporizar [1f] [1] VT to vaporize, convert into vapour; *perfume etc* to spray.

[2] **vaporizarse** VR to vaporize, turn into vapour.

vaporizo NM (*Carib, Méx*) **(a)** (*calor*) strong heat, steamy heat. **(b)** (*Med*) inhalation.

vaporoso ADJ **(a)** (*de vapor*) vaporous; steamy, misty; steaming. **(b)** *tela* light, airy, diaphanous.

vapulear [1a] VT **(a)** *alfombra etc* to beat; *persona* (*pegar*) to beat; (*azotar*) to thrash; flog; (*dar paliza a*) to beat up*. **(b)** (*fig*) to give a tongue-lashing to.

vapuleo NM **(a)** (*paliza*) beating; thrashing, flogging; beating-up. **(b)** (*fig*) tongue-lashing.

vaquerear [1a] VI (*And*) to play truant.

vaquería NF **(a)** (*lechería*) dairy. **(b)** (*LAm*) (*cuidado de ganado*) cattle farming, cattle tending; (*arte del vaquero*) craft of the cowboy. **(c)** (*And, Carib*) (*cubo*) milking pail; (*lechería*) milking shed. **(d)** (*Carib: ganado*) herd of dairy cows. **(e)** (*Carib: caza*) hunting with a lasso. **(f)** (*Méx: baile*) barn dance, country dance.

vaqueriza NF (*establo*) cowshed; (*corral*) cattle yard.

vaquerizo [1] ADJ cattle (*atr*).

[2] NM cowman; herdsman.

vaquero [1] ADJ cattle (*atr*).

[2] NM **(a)** (*que cuida ganado*) cowman; herdsman, cattle tender; (*en US, LAm*) cowboy. **(b)** (*LAm: lechero*) milkman. **(c)** (*And: ausente*) truant. **(d)** (*Carib: látigo*) rawhide whip. **(e)** **~s** (*pantalones*) jeans.

vaqueta [1] NF **(a)** (*cuero*) cowhide, leather. **(b)** (*Carib: de afeitarse*) razor strop.

[2] NM (*Carib*) shifty sort.

vaquetón ADJ **(a)** (*Carib: poco fiable*) unreliable, shifty. **(b)** (*Méx*) (*lerdo*) dim-witted; (*flemático*) phlegmatic, slow. **(c)** (*Méx: descarado*) bare-faced, brazen.

vaquetudo ADJ (*Carib, Méx*) = **vaquetón, baquetudo**.

vaquilla NF (*LAm*) **(a)** (*Agr*) heifer. **(b)** **~s** (*Taur*) amateur bullfight with young bulls.

vaquillona NF (*LAm*) heifer.

vara NF **(a)** (*palo*) stick, pole; (*barra*) rod, bar; (*Mec*) rod; (*de carro*) shaft; (*Bot*) branch, twig (stripped of its leaves), wand, switch; (*Bot*) central stem, main stalk; **~ mágica**, **~ de las virtudes** magic wand; **~ de medir** yardstick, measuring rod; **~ de oro**, **~ de San José** goldenrod; **~ de pescar** fishing rod.

(b) (*Pol etc*) wand (of office); sign of authority; **~ alta** (*autoridad*) authority, power; (*influencia*) influence; (*dominio*) dominance; **doblar la ~ de la justicia** to pervert justice; **empuñar la ~** to take over, take up office (*as mayor etc*); **tener (mucha) ~ alta**, **tener ~** (*And*) to have great influence, be influential.

(c) (*Mat: prov, LAm*) ≈ yard (= .836 m, = 2.8 feet).

(d) (*Taur: lanza*) lance, pike; (*herida*) wound with the lance; **poner ~s al toro** to wound the bull with the lance.

(e) (*: revés*) blow; upset, setback.

(f) **dar la ~*** to annoy, pester.

varada NF **(a)** (*lanzamiento*) launching. **(b)** (*encalladura*) stranding, running aground.

varadero NM dry dock.

varado [1] ADJ **(a)** (*Náut*) stranded; **estar ~** to be aground; to be beached.

(b) **estar ~*** (*Cono Sur: sin trabajo*) to be without regular work; (*CAm, Cono Sur, Méx: sin dinero*) to be broke*.

[2] NM (*Cono Sur*) drifter, man without a regular job.

varadura NF stranding, running aground.

varajillo NM (*Carib*) liqueur coffee.

varal NM **(a)** (*palo*) long pole, stout stick; (*armazón*) framework of poles; (*puntal*) strut, support; (*de carro*) shaft; (*Teat*) batten. **(b)** (*: persona*) thin person, lamppost.

varapalear [1a] VT (*fig*) to slate, tear to pieces.

varapalo NM **(a)** (*palo*) long pole. **(b)** (*golpe*) blow with a stick; (*paliza*) beating. **(c)** (*fig: regañada*) dressing-down*. **(d)** (*fig: revés*) setback, disappointment, blow.

varar [1a] [1] VT **(a)** (*botar*) to launch.

(b) (*llevar a la playa*) to beach, run up on the beach.

[2] VI y **vararse** VR **(a)** (*Náut*) to be stranded, run aground.

(b) *(fig)* to get stuck, get bogged down; to come to a standstill; *(And, Cono Sur)* to stop; to stay.

varayoc NM *(And)* Indian Chief.

varazo NM blow with a stick.

varazón NF *(And, Carib, Méx)* sticks, bunch of sticks.

vardasca NF green twig; switch.

varé: NM *(Esp)* 100 pesetas.

vareador(a) NM/F olive picker, olive harvester.

varear [1a] VT **(a)** *persona* to beat, hit; *fruta* to knock down (with poles); *alfombra etc* to beat; *toro* to prick with the lance, goad, stir up. **(b)***(Com)* *paño* to sell by the yard. **(c)** *(Cono Sur: hacer ejercicio)* to exercise, train.

varec NM kelp, wrack.

varejón NM *(Cono Sur)* **(a)** = **vardasca**. **(b)** *(palo)* stick, straight branch (stripped of leaves).

vareta NF **(a)** *(ramita)* twig, small stick; *(con liga)* lime twig for catching birds.
(b) *(Cos)* stripe.
(c) *(indirecta)* insinuation; *(pulla)* taunt; **echar ~s** to make insinuations.
(d) estar de ~, irse de ~ *(Med)* to have diarrhoea.

varetazo NM *(Taur)* sideways thrust with the horn.

varga NF steepest part of a slope.

variabilidad NF variability.

variable [1] ADJ variable, changeable; *(Mat)* variable.
[2] NF *(Mat)* variable.

variación NF variation *(t Mús)*; **sin ~** without varying, unchanged.

variado ADJ varied; mixed; assorted; *colores, superficie* variegated.

variante [1] ADJ variant.
[2] NM **(a) ~s** *(Esp Culin)* pickled vegetables *(as hors d'oeuvres)*. **(b)** *(And)* *(senda)* path; *(atajo)* short cut.
[3] NF **(a)** variant. **(b)** *(Aut)* by-pass.

variar [1c] [1] VT *(cambiar)* to vary, change, alter; *(modificar)* to modify; *menu etc* to vary, introduce some variety into; *posiciones* to change round, switch about.
[2] VI to vary; to change; **~ de opinión** to change one's mind; **varía de 3 a 8** it ranges from 3 to 8, it goes from 3 to 8; **este producto varía mucho de precio** this article varies a lot in price; **esto varía de lo que dijo antes** this differs from what he said earlier; **para ~** for a change; **para no ~** as usual, the same as always.

varicela NF chickenpox.

várices, varices NFPL varicose veins.

varicoso ADJ **(a)** *pierna etc* varicose. **(b)** *persona* suffering from varicose veins.

variedad NF **(a)** *(diversidad)* variety; variation; *(Bio)* variety. **(b)** *(Teat)* **~es** variety show; **teatro de ~es** variety theatre, music hall, vaudeville theater *(US)*.

variétés NMPL *(Teat)* = **variedades**.

varilla NF **(a)** *(palito)* (thin) stick; *(Bot)* twig, wand, switch; *(Mec)* rod, bar; *(Aut)* dipstick; *(eslabón)* link; *(de rueda)* spoke; *(de corsé)* rib, stay; *(de abanico, paraguas)* rib; *(de gafas)* sidepiece, earpiece; *(Anat)* jawbone; **~ mágica, ~ de virtudes** magic wand; **~ de zahorí** divining rod.
(b) *(Méx)* cheap wares, trinkets.
(c) *(Carib: vaina)* nuisance, bother.

varillaje NM *(Mec)* rods, links, linkage; *(de abanico, paraguas)* ribs, ribbing.

varillar [1a] VT *(Carib)* *caballo* to try out, train.

vario ADJ **(a)** *(variado)* varied; *(de color)* variegated, motley.
(b) *(cambiable)* varying, variable, changeable; *persona* fickle.
(c) ~s several, some; a number of; **hay varias posibilidades** there are several (o various) possibilities; **en ~s libros que he visto** in a number of books which I have seen; **los inconvenientes son ~s** there are several drawbacks.

varioloso ADJ pockmarked.

variopinto ADJ many-coloured, colourful; of diverse colours; **~s** *(fig)* diverse, miscellaneous; very mixed.

varita NF wand; **~ mágica, ~ de las virtudes** magic wand.

varón [1] ADJ male; **hijo ~** male child, boy, son.
[2] NM **(a)** *(hombre)* man, male; adult male; *(fig)* worthy man, great man; **~ de Dios** saintly man; **santo ~** simple old man; **tuvo 4 hijos, todos varones** she had 4 children, all boys.
(b) *(And: marido)* husband.
(c) *(Cono, Sur, Méx: vigas)* beams, timber.

varona NF, **varonesa** NF mannish woman.

varonil ADJ **(a)** *(viril)* manly, virile; *(enérgico)* vigorous. **(b)** *(Bio)* male.
(c) una mujer de aspecto ~ a woman of mannish appearance.

Varsovia NF Warsaw.

vas V *ir*.

vasallaje NM *(Hist)* vassalage; *(fig)* subjection, serfdom.

vasallo NM vassal.

vasar NM kitchen dresser.

vasco, -a ADJ, NM/F [1] Basque.
[2] *(Ling)* Basque.

vascófilo, -a NM/F expert in Basque studies.

vascófono [1] ADJ Basque-speaking.
[2] NM, **vascófona** NF Basque speaker.

vascofrancés [1] ADJ: **País V~** French Basque Country.
[2] NM, **vascofrancesa** NF French Basque.

vascohablante [1] ADJ Basque-speaking.
[2] NMF Basque speaker.

Vascongadas NFPL: **las ~** the Basque Provinces.

vascongado = **vasco**.

vascuence NM *(Ling)* Basque.

vascular ADJ vascular.

vase (= **se va**) V *ir*.

vasectomía NF vasectomy.

vaselina NF ® Vaseline ®, petroleum jelly; **poner ~*** to calm things down; to make things go smoothly.

vasera NF kitchen shelf, rack.

vasija NF vessel; container, receptacle.

vaso NM **(a)** *(Culin)* glass, tumbler; vessel; container; *(liter)* vase, urn; *(de pila)* cell; *(And)* small cup; *(And Aut)* hub-cap; **~ de agua** glass of water; **~ para vino** wineglass; **~ de engrase** *(Mec)* grease cup; **~ de noche** chamberpot; **~ litúrgico, ~ sagrado** liturgical vessel; **ahogarse en un ~ de agua** to get worked up about nothing at all.
(b) *(cantidad)* glassful, glass.
(c) *(Anat)* vessel; tube, duct; **~ capilar** capillary; **~ sanguíneo** blood vessel.
(d) *(Zool)* hoof.
(e) *(Náut)* *(casco)* hull; *(barco)* boat, ship, vessel.

vasoconstrictor [1] ADJ vasoconstrictive, vasoconstrictor.
[2] NM vasoconstrictive substance, vasoconstrictor.

vasodilatador [1] ADJ vasodilating.
[2] NM vasodilator.

vasquismo NM sense of the differentness of the Basque Country; *(Pol)* doctrine of (o belief in) Basque autonomy.

vasquista [1] ADJ that supports *(etc)* Basque autonomy; **el movimiento ~** the movement for Basque autonomy; **la familia es muy ~** the family strongly supports Basque autonomy.
[2] NMF supporter *(etc)* of Basque autonomy.

vástago NM **(a)** *(Bot)* shoot, sprout, bud.
(b) *(Mec)* rod; stem; **~ de émbolo** piston rod.
(c) *(hijo, descendiente)* scion, offspring.
(d) *(And, CAm, Carib: tronco)* trunk of the banana tree.

vastedad NF vastness, immensity.

vasto ADJ vast, huge, immense.

vataje NM wattage.

vate NM **(a)** *(Hist)* seer, prophet. **(b)** *(Liter)* poet, bard.

váter NM = **wáter**.

Vaticano NM Vatican; **la Ciudad del ~** Vatican City.

vaticano ADJ Vatican; papal.

vaticinador NM seer, prophet; forecaster.

vaticinar [1a] VT to prophesy, predict; to forecast.

vaticinio NM prophecy, prediction; forecast.

vatio NM watt.

vaya *etc* V *ir*.

VCL NM ABR *de* **visualizador cristal líquido** liquid crystal display, LCD.

Vd. PRON ABR *de* **usted** you.

Vda. de ABR *de* **viuda de** widow of.

Vds. PRON ABR *de* **ustedes** you.

V.E. ABR *de* **Vuestra Excelencia** Your Excellency.

ve NF *(LAm)*: **~ corta** (o **chica**) *name of the letter v*; **~ doble** *name of the letter w*.

vea *etc* V **ver**.

vecinal ADJ **(a)** *camino etc* local; *impuesto* local, municipal; **padrón ~** list of residents. **(b)** *(LAm: vecino)* neighbouring, adjacent.

vecindad NF **(a)** *(barrio)* neighbourhood, vicinity; *(LAm: barrio pobre)* inner-city slum.
(b) *(vecinos)* neighbours, neighbourhood; local community; *(habitantes)* residents (of a block of flats).
(c) *(proximidad)* nearness, proximity.
(d) *(Jur etc)* residence, abode; **declarar su ~** to state where one lives, give one's place of abode.

vecindario NM neighbourhood; local community; residents; *(estadística etc)* population, inhabitants.

vecino [1] ADJ **(a)** *(contiguo)* neighbouring, adjacent, adjoining; *(cercano)* near, nearby, close; *casa etc* next; **el garaje ~ del mío** the garage next to mine; **no aquí sino en el pueblo ~** not here but in the next village; **las dos fincas son vecinas** the two estates adjoin.
(b) *(fig)* alike, similar; **~ a** like, similar to.
[2] NM, **vecina** NF **(a)** *(de al lado)* neighbour; **~ de rellano** ≃ next-door neighbour.
(b) *(habitante)* resident, inhabitant, citizen; **un pueblo de 800 ~s** a

village of 800 inhabitants; **asociación de ~s** residents' association; **una vecina de la calle X** a resident in X street.

vector NM vector.

Veda NM Veda.

veda NF **(a)** (*acto*) prohibition; imposition of a close season. **(b)** (*temporada*) close season.

vedado NM preserve; **~ de caza** game preserve; **cazar** (o **pescar**) **en ~** to poach, hunt (o fish) illegally.

vedar [1a] VT (*prohibir*) to prohibit, forbid, ban; (*impedir*) to stop, prevent; *idea, plan etc* to veto; **~ a uno hacer algo** to forbid sb to do sth; to stop sb doing sth, prevent sb from doing sth.

vedeta NF, **vedette** [be'ðet] NF **(a)** (*Cine*) star; starlet; (*fig: número*) star turn, main attraction. **(b)** (*Méx: corista*) chorus-girl.

vedetismo NM insistence on being in the forefront, insistence on playing the star role; star quality; stardom.

védico ADJ Vedic.

vedija NF **(a)** (*lana*) tuft of wool. **(b)** (*greña*) mat of hair, matted hair.

vega NF **(a)** (*terreno*) fertile plain, rich lowland area; water meadow(s); (*And*) stretch of alluvial soil. **(b)** (*Carib: tabacal*) tobacco plantation.

vegetación NF **(a)** (*plantas*) vegetation. **(b)** (*acto*) growth, growing. **(c)** (*Med*) **vegetaciones adenoideas** adenoids.

vegetal [1] ADJ vegetable, plant (*atr*); **patología ~** plant pathology. [2] NM **(a)** (*planta*) plant, vegetable; **~es** (*CAm, Méx*) vegetables. **(b)** (*persona*) vegetable.

vegetar [1a] VI **(a)** (*Bot*) to grow. **(b)** (*fig: persona*) to vegetate, live like a vegetable; (*negocio*) to stagnate.

vegetarianismo NM vegetarianism.

vegetariano, -a ADJ, NM/F vegetarian.

vegetativo ADJ vegetative.

vegoso ADJ (*Cono Sur*) *tierra* soggy, damp.

veguero [1] ADJ lowland (*atr*), of the plain. [2] NM **(a)** (*agricultor*) lowland farmer. **(b)** (*Carib*) tobacco planter. **(c)** (*cigarro*) coarse cigar; (*Cono Sur*) good-quality Cuban tobacco, good cigar.

vehemencia NF vehemence; passion, impetuosity; fervour; eagerness, violence.

vehemente ADJ **(a)** (*insistente*) vehement; (*apasionado*) passionate, impetuous; *partidario etc* fervent, passionate; *deseo* strong, eager, violent; *orador* passionate, forceful. **(b)** *señal, sospecha etc* strong.

vehicular [1a] VT to transport; to transmit, convey.

vehiculizar [1f] VT = **vehicular**.

vehículo NM **(a)** (*Aut etc*) vehicle; **~ astral**, **~ cósmico** spacecraft; **~ de carga**, **~ de transporte** goods vehicle; **~ carretero** road vehicle. **(b)** (*fig*) vehicle (*de* for); (*Med*) carrier, transmitter (*de* of).

veinte ADJ twenty; (*fecha*) twentieth; **los** (**años**) **~** the twenties.

veintena NF twenty, a score; about twenty, about a score.

veintiañero [1] ADJ twentyish, about twenty. [2] NM, **veintiañera** NF person of about 20, person in his (o her) twenties.

veintipocos ADJ PL twenty-odd.

veintiuna NF (*Naipes*) pontoon.

vejación NF vexation, annoyance; **sufrir vejaciones** to suffer vexations.

vejamen NM **(a)** = **vejación**. **(b)** (*pasquín*) satire, lampoon; (*pulla*) shaft, taunt.

vejaminoso ADJ (*And, Carib*) irritating, annoying.

vejancón*, **vejarrón*** [1] ADJ ancient, doddery. [2] NM old chap*, old dodderer.

vejancona* NF, **vejarrona*** NF (decrepit) old woman.

vejar [1a] VT (*molestar*) to vex, annoy; (*mofarse de*) to scoff at; (*acosar*) to harass.

vejarano ADJ (*LAm* ††) ancient, doddery, decrepit.

vejatorio ADJ (*molesto*) vexatious, annoying; (*humillante*) humiliating, degrading; **es ~ para él tener que pedirlo** it is humiliating for him to have to beg for it.

vejestorio NM, **vejete** NM dodderer, gaffer, old crock.

vejez NF **(a)** old age; **¡a la ~, viruelas!** fancy that happening at his (*etc*) age! **(b)** (*fig: displicencia*) peevishness; grouchiness*, grumpiness. **(c)** (*fig*) (*cuento*) old story; (*noticia*) piece of stale news.

vejiga NF **(a)** (*Anat*) bladder; **~ de la bilis** gall-bladder; **~ natatoria** air bladder. **(b)** (*Med, en pintura etc*) blister.

vela¹ NF **(a)** (*despierto*) wakefulness, state of being awake; sleeplessness; **estar en ~** to be unable to get to sleep, be still awake; **pasar la noche en ~** to have a sleepless night, not sleep all night. **(b)** (*vigilia*) vigil; (*trabajo nocturno*) evening work, night work; (*Mil*) (period of) sentry duty. **(c)** (*candela*) candle; **~ de sebo** tallow candle; **no se le dará ~ en este entierro** he will not be given any say in this matter; **¿quién te ha dado ~ en este entierro?** who asked you to poke your nose in?; **encender una ~ a San Miguel y otra al diablo** to want to have it

both ways; **quedarse a dos ~s** (*fig*) to be in the dark. **(d)** (*Taur**) horn. **(e)** **~s** * mucus, snot*. **(f)** (*CAm, Carib, Méx: velorio*) wake. **(g)** (*Cono Sur: molestia*) nuisance, bother; **¡qué ~!** what a nuisance!; **aguantar la ~** to put up with it for sb else's sake. **(h)** (*Carib, Méx*: *bronca*) telling-off*; **aguantar la ~** to face the music.

vela² NF (*Náut*) sail; (*deporte*) sailing; **~ balón** spinnaker; **~ mayor** mainsail; **a toda ~, a ~s desplegadas** under full sail, (*fig*) vigorously, energetically, straining every nerve; **barco de ~** sailing ship; **estar a dos ~ s*** to be broke*; **estar entre dos ~s*, ir a la ~*** to be half-seas over; **arriar ~s, recoger ~s** (*fig*) to back down; to give up, chuck it up*; **darse a la ~, hacerse a la ~, largar las ~s** to set sail, get under way; **hacer ~** to go sailing; **ir como las ~s** (*Cono Sur*) to drive very fast; **plegar ~s** (*fig*) to slow down.

velación NF wake, vigil.

velada NF (evening) party, social gathering, soirée; **~ de boxeo** fight night, boxing evening; **~ musical** musical evening.

veladamente ADV in a veiled way.

velado ADJ veiled (*t fig*); (*Fot*) fogged, blurred; *sonido* muffled.

velador NM **(a)** (*vigilante*) watchman, caretaker; (*Hist*) sentinel. **(b)** (*candelero*) candlestick. **(c)** (*mesa*) pedestal table; (*LAm: mesita*) night table. **(d)** (*Cono Sur: lámpara*) night light. **(e)** (*Méx: pantalla*) lampshade.

veladora NF (*LAm: vela*) candle; (*Méx*) table-lamp, bedside lamp; (*Ecl*) paraffin lamp.

velamen NM sails, canvas.

velar¹ [1a] [1] VT **(a)** (*vigilar*) to watch, keep watch over; *enfermo* to sit up with, stay by the bedside of. **(b)** (*LAm: codiciar*) to look covetously at. [2] VI **(a)** (*no dormir*) to stay awake; to go without sleep; (*seguir sin acostarse*) to stay up, sit up at night; (*trabajar de noche*) to work late, do night duty; (*vigilar*) to keep watch, (*Ecl*) keep vigil. **(b)** (*ser solícito*) to be solicitous; **~ por** (*cuidar*) to watch over, look after; (*proteger*) to guard, protect; **~ por que se haga algo** to see to it (o ensure) that sth is done; **no hay quien vele por sus intereses** there is nobody to watch over his interests. **(c)** (*Náut: arrecife*) to appear.

velar² [1a] [1] VT **(a)** (*lit*) to veil. **(b)** (*fig*) to shroud, hide, veil. **(c)** (*Fot*) to fog, blur. [2] **velarse** VR **(a)** (*esconderse*) to hide itself. **(b)** (*ojos*) to glaze over; (*Fot*) to fog, blur.

velar³ ADJ (*Ling*) velar.

velarizar [1f] VT to velarize.

velarte NM (*Hist*) broadcloth.

velatorio NM funeral wake.

Velázquez NM Velázquez, Velasquez.

veleidad NF **(a)** (*cualidad*) fickleness, capriciousness, flightiness. **(b)** (*una ~*) whim, caprice; unpredictable mood; strange fancy.

veleidoso ADJ fickle, capricious, flighty.

velero [1] ADJ *barco* fast. [2] NM **(a)** (*Náut: barco*) sailing ship. **(b)** (*Aer*) glider. **(c)** (*Náut: persona*) sailmaker.

veleta [1] NF **(a)** weather-vane, weathercock. **(b)** (*Pesca*) float. [2] NMF (*persona*) weathercock, fickle person.

veletería NF (*Cono Sur*) chopping and changing, fickleness.

velís NM, **veliz** NM (*Méx*) (*pequeño*) overnight bag, valise; (*maleta*) suitcase; **velises, velices** cases, luggage, bags.

vello NM (*Anat*) down, fuzz, hair; (*Bot*) down; (*en fruta*) bloom; (*en cuerna*) velvet; **~ púbico** pubic hair.

vellocino NM fleece; **V~ de Oro** Golden Fleece.

vellón¹ NM **(a)** (*lana*) fleece; (*piel*) sheepskin. **(b)** (*mechón*) tuft of wool.

vellón² NM **(a)** (*Téc*) copper and silver alloy. **(b)** (*CAm, Carib: moneda*) five-cent coin.

vellonera NF (*Carib*) jukebox.

vellosidad NF downiness, fuzziness, hairiness; fluffiness.

velloso ADJ downy, fuzzy, hairy; fluffy.

velludo [1] ADJ hairy, shaggy. [2] NM plush, velvet.

velo NM **(a)** (*gen*) veil; **tomar el ~** to take the veil, become a nun; **corramos un tupido ~ sobre esto** let us draw a discreet veil over this. **(b)** (*fig: cobertura*) veil, light covering; shroud; film; (*en cristal*) mist; (*Fot*) fog, veiling. **(c)** (*fig: pretexto*) pretext, cloak. **(d)** (*fig: falta de claridad*) mental fog, confusion, lack of clarity. **(e)** **~ del paladar** (*Anat*) soft palate, velum.

velocidad NF **(a)** (*gen*) speed, rate, pace, velocity; (*lo veloz*) speediness, swiftness; **~ adquirida** momentum; **de alta ~** high-speed; **~ de crucero, ~ económica** cruising speed; **~ máxima, ~ punta** maximum speed, top speed; **~ máxima de impresión** maximum print speed; **~ máxima permitida** speed-limit; **~ de**

obturación, ~ de obturador shutter speed; **~ de transferencia** transfer rate; **a gran ~** at high speed; **a máxima ~, a toda ~** at full speed, at top speed; **¿a qué ~?** at what speed?, how fast?; **¿a qué ~ ibas?** what speed were you doing?; **cobrar ~** to pick up speed, gather speed; **disminuir ~, moderar la ~, perder ~** to slow down; **exceder la ~ permitida** to speed, exceed the speed-limit.

(b) (*Mec*) gear, speed; **primera ~, ~ corta** low gear, bottom gear, first gear; **segunda ~** second gear; **~es de avance** forward gears; **4 ~es hacia adelante** 4 forward gears.

velocímetro NM speedometer.

velocípedo NM velocipede.

velocista NMF sprinter.

velódromo NM cycle track.

velomotor NM (*Hist*) autocycle.

velón NM **(a)** (*lámpara*) oil lamp. **(b)** (*And, Cono Sur, Méx: vela*) thick tallow candle. **(c)** (*CAm*: *parásito*) sponger*, parasite. **(d)** (*And, Carib*) person who casts covetous glances.

velorio¹ NM **(a)** (*fiesta*) party, celebration; (*And, Carib, Cono Sur*) dull party, flat affair.

(b) (*esp LAm: de entierro*) wake, vigil for the dead; **~ del angelito** wake for a dead child.

velorio² NM (*Ecl*) (ceremony of) taking the veil.

veloz ADJ fast, quick, swift; **~ como un relámpago** as quick as lightning.

velozmente ADV fast, quickly, swiftly.

ven V **venir**.

vena NF **(a)** (*Anat*) vein; **~ yugular** jugular vein.

(b) (*Min*) vein, seam, lode.

(c) (*en madera, piedra*) grain.

(d) (*Bot*) vein, rib.

(e) (*Geog*) underground stream.

(f) (*fig: disposición*) vein; mood, disposition; **~ de loco** streak of madness; oddity, mania; **coger a uno de** (*o* **en**) **~** to catch sb in the right mood; **le daba la ~ por ello** he took a fancy to it, the mood took him that way; **estar de** (*o* **en**) **~** to be in the vein, be in the mood (*para* for); to be in good form.

(g) (*fig: talento*) talent, promise; **tiene ~ de pintor** he has the makings of a talent, he shows a talent for painting.

venablo NM javelin, dart; **echar ~s** (*fig*) to burst out angrily.

venado NM **(a)** (*Zool*) deer, stag.

(b) (*Culin*) venison.

(c) (*Carib: piel*) deerskin.

(d) (*Carib: puta*) whore.

(e) (*And: contrabanda*) contraband.

(f) **correr el ~, pintar el ~** (*CAm, Méx*) to play truant.

venal¹ ADJ (*Anat*) venous.

venal² ADJ **(a)** (*Com*) commercial, that can be bought (*o* sold). **(b)** (*pey*) venal, corrupt.

venalidad NF venality, corruptness.

venático ADJ rather crazy, a bit mad.

venatorio ADJ hunting (*atr*).

vencedor ① ADJ *equipo, jugador* winning, victorious; *general etc* victorious, successful; *nación* conquering, victorious.

② NM, **vencedora** NF winner, victor; conqueror.

vencejo¹ NM (*Orn*) swift.

vencejo² NM (*Agr*) straw plait, string (*used in binding sheaves*).

vencer [2b] ① VT **(a)** (*derrotar*) *enemigo* to defeat, beat; to conquer, vanquish, overcome; (*Dep*) to beat; *rival* to outdo, surpass; *pasión etc* to master, control, fight down; *tentación* to overcome; (*sueño etc*) to overcome; **vence a todos en elegancia** he outdoes them all in elegance, he beats them all for elegance; **por fin le venció el sueño** finally sleep overcame him; **dejarse ~** to yield, give in; **no te dejes ~** don't give in, don't let yourself be beaten (by it).

(b) *dificultad, obstáculo* to overcome, surmount, get round.

(c) *soporte, rama etc* to break down, snap, prove too heavy for; **el peso de los libros ha vencido el anaquel** the weight of the books has broken the shelf.

(d) *cuesta, montaña* to get to the top of, reach the summit of.

② VI **(a)** (*ganar*) to win; to win through, succeed, triumph; **¡venceremos!** we shall win!; we shall overcome!

(b) (*Com etc: plazo*) to expire, end; (*pago etc*) to fall due; (*bono*) to mature, become due for redemption; (*póliza etc*) to become invalid, cease to apply, expire.

③ **vencerse** VR **(a)** (*persona*) to control o.s.

(b) (*soporte etc*) to break, snap, collapse (under the weight); (*Cono Sur*) (*gastarse*) to wear out, get worn out; (*deshacerse*) to come apart.

(c) se venció el plazo (*LAm*) the time's up.

vencido ① ADJ **(a)** (*gen*) beaten, defeated; *equipo etc* losing; **¡ay de los ~s!** woe to the conquered!; **darse por ~** to give up, acknowledge defeat; **ir de ~** to be all in, be on one's last legs; **la enfermedad va de vencida** the illness is past its worst; **la tormenta va de vencida** the worst of the storm is over.

(b) (*Com etc*) mature; due, payable; **con los intereses ~s** with the interest which is due; **pagar por meses ~s** to pay at the end of the month.

(c) (*LAm*) *billete, permiso etc* out of date.

② ADV: **pagar ~** to pay in arrears, pay for the month (*etc*) which is past.

vencimiento NM **(a)** (*bajo peso*) breaking, snapping; collapse. **(b)** (*Com etc*) expiration; maturity; **al ~, a su ~** when it matures, when it falls due.

venda NF bandage.

vendaje¹ NM (*Med*) dressing, bandaging.

vendaje² NM **(a)** (*Com*) commission. **(b)** (*LAm: plus*) bonus, perk*.

vendar [1a] VT **(a)** *herida* to bandage, dress; *ojos etc* to cover, put a bandage over, tie a cloth (*etc*) round. **(b)** (*fig*) (*cegar*) to blind; (*engañar*) to hoodwink.

vendaval NM gale, strong wind, hurricane; (*fig*) storm.

vendedor ① ADJ selling; (*Fin*) **corriente vendedora** selling tendency, tendency to sell.

② NM seller, vendor; retailer; (*en tienda*) salesman; **~ ambulante** street seller; hawker, pedlar, peddler (*US*); **~ a domicilio** door-to-door salesman; **~ por teléfono** telephone salesperson.

vendedora NF seller; (*dependienta*) salesgirl, saleswoman.

vendeja NF **(a)** (*venta*) public sale. **(b)** (*géneros*) collection of goods offered for sale.

vendepatrias NMF INVAR traitor.

vender [2a] ① VT **(a)** (*gen*) to sell; to market; **~ por las casas** to peddle round the houses; **~ al contado** to sell for cash; **~ al descubierto** to sell short; **~ al por mayor** to sell wholesale; **~ al por menor** to sell retail; **estar sin ~** to remain unsold; **¡a mí que las vendo!** you can't catch an old bird with chaff!, I'm not falling for that one!

(b) (*fig*) to sell, betray.

② **venderse** VR **(a)** (*Com*) to sell; to be sold; **~ a, ~ por** to sell at, sell for; to fetch, bring in; **este artículo se vende muy bien** this article is selling very well; **'se vende'** (*anuncio*) 'for sale'; **'véndese coche'** (*anuncio*) 'car for sale'; **no se vende** not for sale.

(b) ~ caro (*fig*) to play hard to get, be terribly choosy about one's friends*.

(c) (*fig: traicionarse*) to betray o.s., give o.s. away.

vendetta [ben'ðeta] NF vendetta.

vendí NM certificate of sale.

vendibilidad NF saleability; marketability.

vendible ADJ saleable; marketable.

vendido ADJ: **estar ~ a algo/uno** to be at the mercy of sth/sb.

vendimia NF **(a)** (*de uvas*) grape harvest, wine harvest; (*relativo a calidad, año*) year; **la ~ de 1999** the 1999 vintage. **(b)** (*fig*) big profit, killing.

vendimiador(a) NM/F vintager.

vendimiar [1b] VT **(a)** *uvas* to harvest, pick, gather. **(b)** (*fig*) to take a profit from, squeeze a profit out of, make a killing with. **(c)** (‡: *matar*) to bump off‡.

vendré *etc* V **venir**.

venduta NF **(a)** (*LAm: subasta*) auction, public sale.

(b) (*Carib: frutería*) greengrocer's (shop), fruiterer's (shop); (*abacería*) small grocery store.

(c) (*Carib: estafa*) swindle.

vendutero NM **(a)** (*LAm: en subasta*) auctioneer. **(b)** (*Carib: comerciante*) greengrocer, fruiterer.

Venecia NF Venice.

veneciano, -a ADJ, NM/F Venetian.

veneno NM poison, venom.

venenoso ADJ poisonous, venomous.

venera NF scallop; scallop shell; *see also* CAMINO DE SANTIAGO .

venerable ADJ venerable.

veneración NF veneration; worship.

venerando ADJ venerable.

venerar [1a] VT to venerate, revere; to worship.

venéreo ADJ venereal; **enfermedad venérea** venereal disease.

venero NM **(a)** (*Min*) lode, seam. **(b)** (*fuente*) spring. **(c)** (*fig*) source, origin; **~ de datos** mine of information.

venezolanismo NM word (*o* phrase *etc*) peculiar to Venezuela.

venezolano, -a ADJ, NM/F Venezuelan.

Venezuela NF Venezuela.

venga *etc* V **venir**.

vengador ① ADJ avenging.

② NM, **vengadora** NF avenger.

venganza NF vengeance, revenge; retaliation; **tomar ~ de uno** to take vengeance on sb.

vengar [1h] ① VT to avenge.

② **vengarse** VR to take revenge (*de una ofensa* for an offence; *de uno, en uno* on sb), avenge o.s.; to retaliate (*en* against, on).

vengativo ADJ *espíritu, persona* vindictive; *acto* retaliatory.

vengo *etc* V **venir**.

venia NF **(a)** *(perdón)* pardon, forgiveness.

(b) *(permiso)* permission, consent; **con su ~** by your leave, with your permission; **casarse sin la ~ de sus padres** to marry without the consent of one's parents.

(c) *(LAm Mil)* salute.

venial ADJ venial.

venialidad NF veniality.

venida NF **(a)** *(llegada)* coming; arrival; *(vuelta)* return. **(b)** *(fig)* impetuosity, rashness.

venidero ADJ coming, future; **los ~s** future generations, posterity, our *(etc)* descendants; **en lo ~** in (the) future.

▼ **venir** [3r] **1** VI **(a)** *(gen)* to come *(a* to, *de* from); to arrive; **¡ven!**, **¡venga!** come along!; come on (now)!; **¡ven acá!** come (over) here!; **¡ahora vengo!** I'm coming!, I'll be right there!; **vino a vernos** she came to see us; **~ por** to come for; **no me vengas con historias** don't come telling tales to me; **hacer ~ a uno** to summon sb; to call sb, have sb fetched; **le hicieron ~ desde Londres** they fetched him (all the way) from London; **en el periódico viene una nota** there's a note about it in the press.

(b) *(suceder)* to come, happen; **le vino una desgracia** she had a mishap, sth untoward happened to her; **venga lo que venga** *(o* **viniere)** come what may; **con todo lo que vino después** with everything that happened afterwards, with all that ensued; **(estar a) ver ~** to wait and see what happens; to sit on the fence; **se puede ver ~ la noche** one can face the evening ahead; **le vinieron muchos problemas** he was beset by problems.

(c) *(tiempo)* ... **que viene** next ..., *p.ej.* **el mes que viene** next month.

(d) *(provenir)* to come; **~ de** to come from, proceed from, stem from; to originate in; **la finca le viene de su hermano** the estate comes to him from his brother; **de ahí vienen muchos males** many evils spring from that; **de ahí viene que** ... hence it is that ..., and so it is that ...; thus it follows that ...; **la relación de X con Y viene desde lejos** the association of X and Y goes back a long way.

(e) *(fig: ocurrir etc)* to come; **le vino la idea de** + *infin* he got the idea of + *ger*, the idea of + *ger* came to him; **sentía ~me sueño** I felt sleep coming over me; **me vinieron ganas de llorar** I felt like crying, I had an urge to cry; **le vino un gran dolor de cabeza** he got a terrible headache.

(f) **~ a** + *infin* to come to + *infin*, serve to + *infin*; **el desastre vino a turbar nuestra tranquilidad** the disaster served to destroy our peace; **viene a llenar un gran vacío** it serves to fill a large gap; **viene a cumplir lo que habíamos empezado** it helps to finish off what we had begun; **venimos a conocerle en Bolivia** we got to know him in Bolivia; **vino a dar en la cárcel** he ended up in jail; V **caso, menos** *etc*.

(g) **~ a ser: viene a ser lo mismo** it comes to (about) the same thing; **viene a ser 84 en total** it amounts to 84 in all, it comes to 84 all together; **viene a ser más difícil que nunca** it's turning out to be more difficult than ever.

▼ **(h)** **~ bien** to come just right; to be suitable, be convenient; to fit; *(Bot)* to do well, grow nicely; **eso vendrá bien para el invierno** that will come in handy for the winter; **me vendría bien una copita** I could do with a drink; **no me viene muy bien aquello** that doesn't suit me all that well; **~ bien a** *(ropa)* to suit, look well on, fit, be right for; **el tapón viene justo a la botella** the stopper fits the bottle exactly; **el abrigo te viene algo pequeño** the coat is rather small on you; **te viene estrecho por las espaldas** it's too tight round your shoulders; **~ mal** to come awkwardly, be inconvenient *(a* for); **~ mal a** *(ropa)* to look wrong on, not fit.

(i) *(locuciones)* **¿a qué viene esto?** what's behind all this?; **¿a qué vienes?*** what do you want?, what are you doing here?; **¿a qué viene afligirte?** why get so worked up?, what's the point of distressing yourself?; **¡venga!*** *(dámelo)* let's have it!, hand it over!; *(vamos)* let's go!; *(hagámoslo)* let's do it!; **¡venga ya!*** *(déjalo)* come off it!*; **¡venga la pluma esa!** let's have (a look at) that pen!; **¡venga una canción!** let's have a song!; **venga a** *(o* **de) pedir** she keeps on asking; **venga de preguntas** with endless questions, asking questions all the time.

(j) *(en tiempos continuos)* **venían andando desde mediodía** they had been walking since midday; **viene gastando mucho** she has been spending a lot; **eso vengo diciendo** that's what I've been saying all along.

(k) *(+ PTP)* **vengo cansado** I'm tired; **venía hecho polvo** he was worn out.

2 **venirse** VR **(a)** *(vino)* to ferment; *(masa)* to work.

(b) **~ abajo**, **~ al suelo**, **~ a** *(la)* **tierra** to fall down, collapse, tumble down; *(fig)* to fail, collapse, be ruined.

(c) **se nos vino encima la guerra** the war came upon us; **parece que todo se nos viene encima a la vez** everything seems to be happening to us all at once; **cualquier cosita se le viene encima** any

little thing gets him down.

(d) **lo que se ha venido en llamar ...** what we have come to call ...

(e) *V* **mano.**

(f) *(CAm* ‡‡*)* to come‡‡.

VENIR | *ver también la entrada*

Aunque *venir* y *come* generalmente dan una idea de movimiento en dirección al hablante, e *ir* y *go* implican que hay un movimiento en dirección opuesta al hablante, tenemos que distinguir algunos casos en los que hay diferencias entre los dos idiomas.

● En español no solemos describir el movimiento de una acción desde el punto de vista de la otra persona, mientras que en inglés sí. Por ejemplo, si alguien nos llama, respondemos:
   Ya voy
   I'm coming
● Si estamos organizando algo por teléfono, por carta, o en una conversación:
   Iré a recogerte a las cuatro
   I'll come and pick you up at four
   ¿Voy contigo?
   Shall I come with you?
● Por lo tanto, tenemos que traducir *ir* por *come* cuando, si vamos a algún sitio, nos unimos a alguien o a un grupo que va o ya está en ese sitio.
   Para otros usos y ejemplos ver la entrada.

---

venoso ADJ **(a)** *sangre* venous. **(b)** *hoja etc* veined, ribbed.

venta NF **(a)** *(Com)* sale; selling; marketing; **~ por balance**, **~ postbalance** stocktaking sale; **~s brutas** gross sales; **~ al contado** cash sale; **~ por correo** mail-order selling; **~s al detalle** retail sales; **~s directas** direct selling; **~ a domicilio** door-to-door selling; **~s de exportación** export sales; **~ por inercia** inertia selling; **~ de liquidación** sale, clearance sale, closing-down sale; **~ a plazos**, **~ por cuotas** hire purchase; **~ al (por) mayor** wholesale; **~ al (por) menor**, **~ piramidal** pyramid selling; **~ pública** public sale, auction; **~s por teléfono** telephone sales; **precio de ~** sale price; **servicio de ~** sales department; **poner algo a la ~** to put sth on sale, put sth up for sale; to market a product; **estar de** *(o* **en) ~** to be (up) for sale, be on the market.

(b) *(posada)* country inn.

(c) *(Carib, Méx)* small shop, stall; *(Cono Sur: de feria etc)* stall, booth.

ventada NF gust of wind.

ventaja NF **(a)** *(gen)* advantage; *(en carrera)* start, advantage; *(Tenis)* advantage; *(en apuestas)* odds; **es un plan que tiene muchas ~s** it is a plan that has many advantages; **me dio una ~ de 4 metros, me dio 4 metros de ~** he gave me 4 metres start; **me dio una ~ de 20 puntos** he gave me an advantage of 20 points, he handicapped himself by 20 points; **llevar (la) ~ a** to have the advantage over; to be ahead of; to be one up on; **la ~ que A le lleva a B es grande** A has a big advantage over B; **sacar ~ de** to derive profit from, *(pey)* use to one's own advantage.

(b) *(Fin: esp LAm)* profit, gain; **dejar buena ~** to bring in a good profit.

(c) **~s** *(en empleo)* extras, perks*; **~s supletorias** fringe benefits.

ventajear [1a] VT *(And, CAm)* **(a)** *(rebasar)* to outstrip, surpass; *(llevar ventaja a)* to get the advantage of. **(b)** *(mejorar)* to better, improve on. **(c)** *(preferir)* to prefer, give preference to. **(d)** **~ a uno** *(pey)* to beat sb to it, get the jump on sb*.

ventajero ADJ *(LAm)* = **ventajista**.

ventajismo NM **(a)** opportunism. **(b)** *(LAm)* cheek*, nerve*.

ventajista ADJ *(poco escrupuloso)* unscrupulous; *(egoísta)* self-seeking, grasping; *(taimado)* sly, treacherous.

ventajosamente ADV advantageously; *(Fin)* profitably; **estar ~ colocado** to be well placed.

ventajoso ADJ **(a)** *(gen)* advantageous; *(Fin)* profitable. **(b)** *(LAm)* = **ventajista**.

ventana NF **(a)** *(gen)* window; **~s dobles** double glazing; **~ de guillotina** sash-window; **~ de la nariz** nostril; **~ salediza** bay window; **tirar algo por la ~** to throw sth out of the window; *(fig)* to throw sth away, fail to make any use of sth.

(b) *(And: claro de bosque)* forest clearing, glade.

ventanaje NM windows.

ventanal NM large window.

ventanear [1a] VI to be always at the window, be forever peeping out.

ventanilla NF **(a)** *(gen)* small window; *(de sobre, taquilla, Aut, Ferro etc)* window; *(Fin)* bank counter; *(fig)* administrative office, public office; **programa de ~ única** programme to simplify bureaucratic procedures; **pasar por ~** *(fig)* to seek *(o* obtain) official approval. **(b)** *(Anat: t ~ de la nariz)* nostril.

ventanillero, -a NM/F counter-clerk.

ventanillo NM (*ventana*) small window; (*mirilla*) peephole.

ventarrón* NM gale, violent wind, blast.

ventear [1a] **1** VT (**a**) (*perro etc*) *aire* to sniff.
(**b**) *ropa etc* to air, put out to dry, expose to the wind.
(**c**) (*CAm, Méx*) *animal* to brand.
(**d**) (*Cono Sur*) *adversario* to get far ahead of, leave far behind.
(**e**) (*And, Carib*) (*abanicar*) to fan; (*Agr*) to winnow.
2 VI (*curiosear*) to snoop, pry, come poking about; (*investigar*) to inquire, investigate.
3 **ventearse** VR (**a**) (*henderse*) to split, crack; (*ampollarse*) to blister; (*secarse*) to get too dry, spoil.
(**b**) (*Anat*) to break wind.
(**c**) (*And, Carib, Cono Sur: estar mucho fuera*) to be outdoors a great deal.
(**d**) (*And, Carib: engreírse*) to get conceited.

ventero, -a NM/F innkeeper.

ventilación NF (**a**) (*gen*) ventilation; **sin ~** unventilated. (**b**) (*corriente*) draught, air. (**c**) (*ventilador*) ventilator, opening for ventilation. (**d**) (*fig*) airing, discussion.

ventilado ADJ draughty, breezy.

ventilador NM ventilator; fan; **~ eléctrico** electric fan.

ventilar [1a] **1** VT (**a**) *cuarto etc* to ventilate.
(**b**) *ropa etc* to air, put out to air, dry in the air.
(**c**) (*fig*) *asunto* to air, discuss, talk over.
(**d**) (*fig*) *asunto privado* to make public, reveal.
2 **ventilarse** VR (**a**) (*cuarto etc*) to ventilate, air.
(**b**) (*persona*) to get some air, take a breather.
(**c**) (*Esp***) **~ a una** to screw sb**.
(**d**) (**: *matar*) **~ a uno** to do sb in**.

ventisca NF blizzard, snowstorm.

ventiscar [1g] VI, **ventisquear** [1a] VI (*nevar*) to blow a blizzard, snow with a strong wind; (*nieve*) to drift.

ventisquero NM (**a**) (*tormenta*) blizzard, snowstorm. (**b**) (*montón*) snowdrift; (*barranco*) gully (o slope *etc*) where the snow lies.

vento* NM (*Cono Sur*) dough*.

ventolada NF (*LAm*) strong wind, gale.

ventolera NF (**a**) (*ráfaga*) gust of wind, blast.
(**b**) (*juguete*) windmill.
(**c**) (*fig*) (*vanidad*) vanity, conceit; (*satisfacción*) smugness; (*arrogancia*) arrogance; (*jactancia*) boastfulness; **tiene mucha ~*** she's terribly big-headed*.
(**d**) (*fig: capricho*) whim, wild idea; **le dio la ~ de** + *infin* he suddenly took it into his head to + *infin*.
(**e**) (*Méx***) fart**.

ventolina NF (**a**) (*Náut*) light wind. (**b**) (*Cono Sur, Méx*) sudden gust of wind. (**c**) (*Cono Sur Med*) wind, flatulence.

ventorrillo NM (**a**) (*taberna*) small inn, roadhouse. (**b**) (*Carib, Méx: tienda*) small shop.

ventosa NF (**a**) (*agujero*) vent, airhole. (**b**) (*Zool*) sucker; (*Téc*) peg (*etc*) that adheres by suction, suction pad. (**c**) (*Med*) cupping glass.

ventosear [1a] VI to break wind.

ventosidad NF wind; flatulence, windiness.

ventoso **1** ADJ (**a**) (*Met*) windy. (**b**) (*Anat*) windy, flatulent.
2 NM (**a**) (*Esp**) burglar. (**b**) (*CAm***) fart**.

ventral ADJ ventral.

ventregada NF brood, litter.

ventrículo NM ventricle.

ventrílocuo, -a NM/F ventriloquist.

ventriloquia NF ventriloquism.

ventrudo ADJ fat, potbellied.

ventura NF (**a**) (*dicha*) happiness.
(**b**) (*suerte*) luck, (good) fortune; chance; **mala ~** ill luck; **por su mala ~** as ill luck would have it; **a la ~** at random; **ir a la ~** to go haphazardly, go without a fixed plan; **vivir a la ~** to live in a disorganized way; **todo lo hace a la ~** he does it all in a hit-or-miss fashion; **por ~** fortunately; perhaps, by chance, *p.ej.* **¿piensas ir, por ~?** are you by any chance thinking of going?; **echar la buena ~ a uno** to tell sb's fortune; **probar la ~** to try one's luck; **~ te dé Dios** I wish you luck; **viene la ~ a quien la procura** God helps them that help themselves.

venturero ADJ (**a**) (*Méx*) **cosecha venturera** second crop. (**b**) (*fig*) temporary; casual; irregular.

venturoso ADJ (*dichoso*) happy; (*afortunado*) lucky, fortunate.

Venus **1** NF Venus.
2 NM (*Astron*) Venus.

venus NF (*fig*) venery, love-making, sexual delights.

venusiano, -a ADJ, NM/F Venusian.

veo-veo NM (*juego*) I spy (with my little eye).

ver [2u] **1** VTI (**a**) (*gen*) to see; (*esp LAm*) to look at, watch; **la vi bajar la escalera** I saw her come downstairs; **lo he visto hacer muchas veces** I have often seen it done; **no lo veo** I can't see it; **desde aquí lo verás** you can see it from here; **¡lo que ves!** can't you see?, it's

there for you to see!; **no veo nada en contra de eso** I see nothing against it; **te veo muy triste** you look really sad; **~ y creer** seeing is believing; **~ y callar** it's best to keep one's mouth shut about this; **un coche que no veas*** a car like you never saw before; **ir a ~ a uno** to go to see sb, go and see sb; **voy a ~** I'll go and see; **¡a ~!** let's see!, let's have a look!, show me!; (*fig*) I say!, hey!; (*And Telec*) hullo?; **¿a ~?** what's all this?; **a ~ qué nos dices** let's see what you've got to say; **¡a ~ qué pasa!*** just you dare!; **a ~ si ...** I wonder if ...; **a ~ si acabas pronto** I hope you can finish this off quickly; **es de ~ it's** worth seeing, you really should see it; **eso está por ~** that remains to be seen.
(**b**) (*fig: entender*) to see, understand; **¿ves?** do you see?, (do you) get it?; **¿viste?** (*Cono Sur*) right?, are you with me?; **lo veo** I see; **¡verás!** you'll see!; **veremos** we'll see (about that); **¿no ves que ...?** don't you see that ...?; **como vimos ayer en la conferencia** as we saw in the lecture yesterday; **como veremos más adelante** as we shall see later; **según voy viendo** as I am now beginning to see; **no veo claro por qué lo quiere** I don't really see why he wants it; **a mi modo de ver** in my view; as I see it.
(**c**) (*fig: indagar*) to look into, examine, inquire into; **lo veremos** we'll look into it.
(**d**) (*Jur*) *pleito* to try, hear.
(**e**) **~ de** + *infin* to see about + *ger*; to try to + *infin*.
(**f**) (*locuciones*) **¡para que veas!** so there!; **si te vi no me acuerdo** they (*etc*) just don't want to know; there was no recognition, there was not a hint of gratitude; **me lo estoy viendo de almirante** I can just imagine him as an admiral; **lo estaba viendo** it's just what I expected, one could see this coming; **parece que lo estoy viendo** I can picture it quite clearly; **dejarse ~** (*etc*) to show, become apparent; to begin to tell; (*persona*) to show up, show one's face; **no dejarse ~** to keep away; to lie low, stay hidden; **la preocupación se dejaba ~ en su cara** the worry showed in his face; **las vi y las deseé** I just managed it by a great effort, it was a sweat but I did it; **echar de ~ algo** to notice sth; **¡hay que ~!** it just goes to show!; **hacer ~ que ...** to point out that ..., prove that ...; **no le puedo ~** I hate the sight of him, I can't stand him; **tener que ~ con** to concern, have to do with; **A no tiene nada que ~ con B** A has nothing to do with B; A is irrelevant to B; **vamos a ~** let's see ..., let me see ...; **y Vd que lo vea** and the same to you; **¿por qué no lo compraste, vamos a ~?** why didn't you buy it, I'd like to know?; V t **visto**.
(**g**) (*LAm: locuciones*) **¡vieras aquello!, ¡hubieras visto aquello!** you should have seen that!, if only you'd seen that!; **¡nos estamos viendo!** (*Méx*) (I'll) be seeing you!; **eso está en veremos** that's still a long way off, that's very much in the future; **lo dijo por ~** (*Carib*), **lo dijo de por ~** (*Cono Sur*) he said it just as a joke; **todo quedó en veremos** it was all left in the air.
2 **verse** VR (**a**) (*2 personas*) to see each other; to meet; **~ con uno** to see sb, have a talk (o interview) with sb; **vérselas con uno** to confront sb, have it out with sb; **ahora apenas nos vemos** we hardly see (anything of) each other nowadays.
(**b**) (*1 persona etc*) to see o.s., imagine o.s.; (*ser visto*) to be seen; **véase la página 9** see page 9; **se le veía mucho en el parque** he used to be seen a lot in the park; **desde aquí no se ve** you can't see it from here; **se ve que sí** so it seems, apparently; **ya se ve** naturally, plainly; **ya se ve que ...** it is obvious that ...; apparently, it's turned out that ...; **¿cuándo se vio nada igual?** did you ever see the like?; **no se ha visto un lío parecido** you never saw such a mess, it was the biggest mess ever; **eso ya se verá** that remains to be seen; **¡habráse visto!*** did you ever!*, of all the cheek!*, well I like that!; **¡que se vean los forzudos!** let's see how tough you are!; come on, you tough guys*!
(**c**) (*encontrarse*) to find o.s., be; **~ en un apuro** to be in a jam; **se veía en la cumbre de la fama** he was at the height of his fame.
(**d**) (*Jur*) **el proceso se verá en mayo** the case will be heard in May.
(**e**) (*LAm: parecer*) to seem; **te ves cansado** you look tired; **te vas a ver precioso así** you'll look lovely like that.
3 NM (**a**) (*aspecto*) looks, appearance; **de buen ~** good-looking, of agreeable appearance; **tener buen ~** to be good-looking; **no tiene mal ~** she's not bad-looking.
(**b**) **a mi ~** in my view, as I see it.
(**c**) **a más ~, hasta más ~** au revoir.

vera NF edge, verge, border; (*del río*) bank; **a la ~ de** near, beside, next to; **a la ~ del camino** beside the road, at the roadside; **se sentó a mi ~** he sat down beside me.

veracidad NF truthfulness, veracity.

veracruzano **1** ADJ of Veracruz.
2 NM, **veracruzana** NF native (o inhabitant) of Veracruz; **los ~s** the people of Veracruz.

veragua NF (*CAm*) mildew (*on cloth*).

veranda NF veranda(h).

veraneante NMF holidaymaker, (summer) vacationer (*US*).

veranear [1a] VI to spend the summer (holiday); **veranean en Jaca**

they go to Jaca for the summer, they holiday in Jaca; **es un buen sitio para ~** it's a nice place for a summer holiday.

veraneo NM summer holiday; **lugar de ~, punto de ~** summer resort, holiday resort; **estar de ~** to be away on one's summer holiday; **ir de ~ a la montaña** to go off to spend one's summer holidays in the mountains.

veraniego ADJ **(a)** (*del verano*) summer (*atr*). **(b)** (*fig*) slight, trivial.

veranillo NM **(a)** **~ de San Martín** Indian summer. **(b)** (*CAm*) dry spell in the rainy season; **~ de San Juan** (*Cono Sur*) = Indian summer.

verano NM **(a)** summer. **(b)** (*And, Méx*) dry season.

veranoso ADJ (*LAm*) dry.

veras NFPL **(a)** (*verdad*) truth, reality; (*cosas serias*) serious things; (*hechos*) hard facts; V **burla**.
(b) **de ~** really, truly; sincerely; in earnest; **¿de ~?** really?, indeed?, is that so?; **lo siento de ~** I am truly sorry; **ahora me duele de ~** now it really does hurt me; **esto va de ~** this is serious; I'm in earnest; **ahora va de ~ que lo hago** now I really am going to do it; **esta vez va de ~** this time it's the real thing.

veraz ADJ truthful, veracious.

verbal ADJ verbal; oral.

verbalizar [1f] VT to verbalize, express.

verbalmente ADV verbally; orally.

verbena NF **(a)** (*Bot*) verbena. **(b)** (*fiesta*) fair; (*de santo*) open-air celebration on the eve of a saint's day; (*baile*) open-air dance.

verbenero ADJ of (o relating to) a *verbena* (V **verbena (b)**); **alegría verbenera** fun of the fair; **música verbenera** fairground music.

verbigracia ADV for example, eg.

verbo NM **(a)** (*Ling*) verb; **~ activo** transitive verb; **~ auxiliar** auxiliary verb; **~ defectivo** defective verb; **~ deponente** deponent verb; **~ finito** finite verb; **~ intransitivo** intransitive verb; **~ neutro** intransitive verb; **~ reflexivo** reflexive verb; **~ transitivo** transitive verb.
(b) (*juramento*) curse, oath; **echar ~s** to swear, curse.
(c) (*Liter*) language, diction, style; **de ~ elegante** elegant in style.
(d) **el V~** (*Rel*) the Word.

verborragia NF, **verborrea** NF logorrhoea, verbal diarrhoea; torrent of words.

verborreico ADJ verbose; prone to fits of verbal diarrhoea.

verbosidad NF verbosity, wordiness; verbiage.

verboso ADJ verbose, wordy.

▼ **verdad** NF **(a)** (*gen*) truth; (*veracidad*) truthfulness; (*fiabilidad*) reliability, trustworthiness; **la ~ de su relato** the truthfulness of his tale, the reliability of his account; **la ~ amarga** the bitter truth; **la ~ lisa y llana** the plain truth; **la pura ~ es que ...** the plain truth is that ...; **a la ~** really, in truth; **de ~** (ADJ) real, proper, *p.ej.* **un héroe de ~** a real hero; (ADV) really, properly, *p.ej.* **entonces la pegó de ~** then he really did hit her; **¿de ~?** really?; **en ~** really, truly; **pues, la ~ no sé** well, the truth is I don't know; well, truth to tell, I don't know; **decir la ~** to tell the truth; **la ~ sea dicha** truth to tell, in all truth; **a decir ~ ...** to tell the truth ...; **faltar a la ~** to lie, be untruthful; **hablar con ~** to speak truthfully; **hay una parte de ~ en esto** there is some truth in this.
▼ **(b)** **es ~** it is true, it is so; (*confesión*) yes; I'm afraid so; **eso no es ~** that is not true; **es ~ que ...** it is true that ...; **bien es ~ que ...** it is of course true that ..., it is certainly true that ...; **si bien es ~ que ...** even though ..., despite the fact that ...; **¿~?**, **¿no es ~?** isn't it?, aren't you?, don't you? (*etc*), isn't that so?
(c) **media ~, ~ a medias** half-truth; **~ de Pero Grullo** (*Esp*), **~ de Perogrullo** (*Esp*) platitude, truism; **sigo la ~ de Pero Grullo** I follow accepted truth; **~es del barquero** plain truths; **es una ~ como un puño** it's as plain as a pikestaff; **decir cuatro ~es a uno** to tell sb a few home truths, give sb a piece of one's mind.

verdaderamente ADV really, indeed; truly; **~, no sé** I really don't know; **un hombre ~ bueno** a truly good man; **es ~ triste** it's really sad.

verdadero ADJ **(a)** (*gen*) true, truthful; (*de fiar*) reliable, trustworthy.
(b) *persona* truthful.
(c) (*fig*) true, real, veritable; **es un ~ héroe** he's a real hero; **fue un ~ desastre** it was a real disaster, it was a veritable disaster; **es un ~ amigo** he's a true friend.

verde ① ADJ **(a)** green; **~ botella** bottle-green; **~ lima** lime-green; **~ manzana** apple-green; **~ oliva** olive-green.
(b) *fruta etc* green, unripe; *planta* green, fresh; *madera* unseasoned; (*fig*) *proyecto etc* premature; **¡están ~s!** sour grapes!; **segar la hierba en ~** to cut the grass while it is still green.
(c) (*fig*) *persona* unduly amorous, randy* (despite one's advanced years); **viejo ~** randy old man*, dirty old man*; **viuda ~** merry widow.
(d) (*fig*) *canción, chiste etc* blue, smutty, scabrous, dirty.
(e) (*Pol*) green.
(f) (*locuciones*) **está ~*** (*inocente*) he's very green; (*ignorante*) he doesn't know a thing; **estar ~ de envidia** to be green with envy; **¡si**

piensan eso, están ~s! if that's what they think, they've got another think coming!; **pasar las ~s y las maduras** to have a rough time of it; **poner ~ a uno** (*: *regañar*) to give sb a dressing-down*; (*insultar*) to abuse sb violently; (*denigrar*) to run sb down.
② NM **(a)** (*color*) green, green colour.
(b) (*Bot*) (*hierba*) green, green grass; (*de árboles*) foliage; (*Agr*) green fodder; **sentarse en el ~** to sit on the grass.
(c) **darse un ~** to eat a lot, eat one's fill (*de* of); **darse un ~ de conciertos** to have a surfeit of concerts, have one's fill of concerts.
(d) (:) 1000-peseta note.
(e) (*Cono Sur*) (*pasto*) grass, pasture; (*mate*) maté; (*ensalada*) salad.
(f) (*And*) plantain.
(g) (*Carib, Méx: campo*) country, countryside.
(h) (*Carib**: *policía*) policeman.
③ NMF (*Pol*) Green; **los V~s** the Greens, the Green Party.

verdear [1a] VI **(a)** (*volverse verde*) to go green, turn green.
(b) (*tirar a verde*) to be greenish; (*mostrarse verde*) to show green, look green.
(c) (*Cono Sur*) to drink maté.
(d) (*Cono Sur Agr*) to graze.

verdecer [2d] VI to turn green, grow green; (*persona*) to go green.

verdegay ADJ, NM light green.

verdemar ADJ, NM sea-green.

verderón NM **(a)** (*Orn*) greenfinch. **(b)** (*Esp*:) 1000-peseta note.

verdete NM verdigris.

verdiazul ADJ greenish-blue.

verdiblanco ADJ light green.

verdín NM **(a)** (*color*) bright green, fresh green. **(b)** (*Bot*) (*capa*) scum; (*musgo*) moss; (*verdete*) verdigris. **(c)** (*en la ropa etc*) green stain.

verdinegro ADJ dark green.

verdino ADJ bright green.

verdirrojo ADJ green and red.

verdolaga NF: **crecer como la ~** (*CAm*) to spread like wildfire.

verdón ① ADJ (*Cono Sur*) **(a)** (*gen*) bright green. **(b)** *fruta* slow to ripen.
② NM **(a)** (*Orn*) = **verderón**. **(b)** (*Cono Sur: cardenal*) bruise, welt.

verdor NM **(a)** (*color*) greenness; (*Bot*) verdure, lushness. **(b)** (*fig: t ~es*) youthful vigour, lustiness.

verdoso ADJ greenish.

verdugo NM **(a)** (*Hist*) executioner; hangman.
(b) (*fig*) (*amo*) cruel master, slave-driver; (*tirano*) tyrant; (*atormentador*) tormentor.
(c) (*fig: tormento*) torment.
(d) (*látigo*) lash.
(e) (*cardenal*) weal, welt.
(f) (*Bot*) twig, shoot, sprout.
(g) (*arma*) slender rapier.
(h) (*de lana*) balaclava, woollen hood.

verdugón NM **(a)** (*cardenal*) weal, welt. **(b)** (*Bot*) twig, shoot, sprout.
(c) (*And: rasgón*) rent, rip.

verdulera NF **(a)** (*comerciante*) greengrocer. **(b)** (*pey*) coarse woman, fishwife.

verdulería NF greengrocer's (shop).

verdulero NM greengrocer.

verdura NF **(a)** (*gen*) greenness; (*Bot*) greenery, verdure. **(b)** **~s** (*Culin*) greens, green vegetables, (*esp*) cabbage. **(c)** (*fig*) smuttiness, scabrous nature.

verdusco ADJ dark green, dirty green.

vereco* ADJ (*CAm*) cross-eyed.

verecundia NF bashfulness, sensitivity, shyness.

verecundo ADJ bashful, sensitive, shy.

vereda NF **(a)** path, lane; **entrar en ~** (*persona*) to toe the line; (*elemento*) to fall into place, fit into the normal pattern; **hacer entrar en ~ a uno, meter en ~ a uno** to make sb toe the line; **ir por la ~** (*fig*) to do the right thing; to keep to the straight and narrow.
(b) (*LAm: acera*) pavement, sidewalk (*US*).
(c) (*And*) (*pueblo*) village, settlement; (*zona*) section of a village.
(d) (*Méx: raya*) parting.

veredicto NM verdict; **~ de culpabilidad** verdict of guilty; **~ de inculpabilidad** verdict of not guilty.

veredón NM (*Cono Sur*) broad pavement, broad sidewalk (*US*).

verga NF **(a)** (*vara*) rod, stick; (*Náut*) yard, spar. **(b)** (*CAm**) **a ~** by hook or by crook; **por la ~ grande** miles away, at the back of beyond*. **(c)** (*Zool*) penis; (*:*) prick*:, cock*:; **me vale ~*:** I don't give a toss*:; **¡ni ~!** no way !*, you must be joking!

vergajo NM **(a)** (*Anat: de toro*) pizzle; (*:*) prick*:; **dar un ~*:** to have a screw*:. **(b)** (*látigo*) lash, whip. **(c)** (*And**) swine*, rat*.

vergazo NM: **un ~ de** (*CAm**) lots of, loads of.

vergel NM (*liter*) (*jardín*) garden; (*huerto*) orchard.

vergonzante ADJ **(a)** (*avergonzado*) shamefaced; (*tímido*) bashful; **pobre ~** poor but too ashamed to beg openly. **(b)** (*vergonzoso*) shameful, shaming.

➤ LENGUA Y USO: **verdad: a** → 45.1 **b** → 38.1

vergonzosamente ADV (*V* ADJ) (**a**) bashfully, shyly; modestly. (**b**) shamefully, disgracefully.

vergonzoso ADJ (**a**) *persona* bashful, shy, timid; modest. (**b**) *acto, asunto etc* shameful, disgraceful, shocking; **es ~ que** ... it is disgraceful that ... (**c**) **partes vergonzosas** (*Anat*) private parts.

vergüenza NF (**a**) (*sentimiento*) shame; sense of shame, feelings of shame; **perder la ~** to lose all sense of shame, cast aside all restraints; **sacar a uno a la ~** to hold sb up to shame; **tener ~** to be ashamed; **tener ~ de** + infin to be ashamed to + infin; **si tuviera ~ no lo haría** if he had any shame he wouldn't do it.

(**b**) (*timidez*) bashfulness, shyness, timidity; (*azoramiento*) embarrassment; (*modestia*) (sexual) shame, modesty; **me da ~ decírselo** I feel too shy to say it to him, it embarrasses me to say it to him, it upsets me to say it to him; **sentir ~ ajena** to feel embarrassed on somebody else's account.

(**c**) (*escándalo*) disgrace; **¡qué ~!** what a disgrace!, what a scandal!; shame (on you)!; **el hijo es la ~ de su familia** the son is a disgrace to his family; **es una ~ que esté tan sucio** it's a disgrace that it should be so dirty.

(**d**) **~s** (*Anat*) private parts.

vericueto NM rough part, rough track, piece of difficult terrain.

verídico ADJ true, truthful.

verificabilidad NF verifiability.

verificable ADJ verifiable.

verificación NF (**a**) (*inspección*) check, checkup, inspection; (*prueba*) testing; verification; proving. (**b**) (*cumplimiento*) carrying out; performance; holding. (**c**) (*de profecía etc*) realization.

verificar [1a] ⬚**1** VT (**a**) (*Mec etc*) to check, inspect; to test; *resultados* to check (up on); *hechos* to verify, establish, substantiate; *testamento* to prove.

(**b**) *inspección etc* to carry out; *ceremonia* to perform; *elecciones* to hold.

⬚**2** **verificarse** VR (**a**) (*suceso etc*) to occur, happen; (*reunión etc*) to be held, take place.

(**b**) (*profecía etc*) to come true, prove true, be realized.

verija NF (**a**) (*Anat*) groin, genital region. (**b**) (*LAm: de caballo*) flank.

verijón* ADJ (*Méx*) idle, lazy.

veringo ADJ (*And*) nude, naked.

veringuearse [1a] VR (*And*) to undress.

verismo NM realism, truthfulness; factual nature.

verista ADJ realistic, true to life; factual.

verja NF (*reja*) grating, grille; (*cerca*) railing(s); (*puerta*) iron gate.

vermicida NM vermicide.

vermicular ADJ vermicular.

vermífugo NM vermifuge.

verminoso ADJ infected, wormy.

vermú NM, PL **vermús, vermut** [ber'mʊ] NM, PL **vermuts** [ber'mʊ] ⬚**1** NM vermouth.

⬚**2** NF (*And, Cono Sur Teat*) early performance.

vernáculo ADJ vernacular.

vernal ADJ spring (*atr*), vernal.

Verónica NF Veronica.

verónica NF (**a**) (*Bot*) veronica, speedwell. (**b**) (*Taur*) *a kind of pass with the cape*.

verosímil ADJ (*probable*) likely, probable; (*creíble*) credible.

verosimilitud NF likeliness, probability; credibility; (*Liter*) verisimilitude.

verosímilmente ADV in a likely way; credibly.

verraco NM boar, male pig; (*And*) ram; (*Carib*) wild boar.

verraquear [1a] VI (**a**) (*gruñir*) to grunt. (**b**) (*niño*) to wail, howl with rage.

verraquera NF (**a**) (*enfado*) crying spell, fit of rage, tantrum. (**b**) (*Carib: borrachera*) drunken spell.

verruga NF (**a**) (*Anat, Bot*) wart. (**b**) (*latoso*) bore, pest, nuisance. (**c**) (*: *defecto*) fault, bad habit.

verrugoso ADJ warty, covered in warts.

versación NF (*Cono Sur, Méx*) expertise, skill.

versada NF (*LAm*) long tedious poem.

versado ADJ: **~ en** versed in, conversant with; expert in, skilled in.

versal (*Tip*) ⬚**1** ADJ capital.

⬚**2** NF capital (letter).

versalitas NFPL (*Tip*) small capitals.

Versalles NM Versailles.

versallesco ADJ (**a**) (*Arte, Hist*) Versailles (*atr*). (**b**) (*fig*) *lenguaje, modales* extremely refined.

versar [1a] VI (**a**) (*girar*) to go round, turn.

(**b**) **~ sobre** to deal with, discuss, be about; to turn on.

(**c**) (*Carib: versificar*) to versify, improvise verses.

(**d**) (*Carib: charlar*) to chat, talk.

(**e**) (*Méx*: guasearse*) to tease, crack jokes.

versátil ADJ (**a**) (*Anat etc*) versatile, mobile, loose, easily turned. (**b**) (*fig*) versatile. (**c**) (*fig: pey*) fickle, changeable.

versatilidad NF (**a**) versatility, mobility, looseness, ease of movement. (**b**) (*fig*) versatility. (**c**) (*fig: pey*) fickleness, changeableness.

versículo NM (*Biblia*) verse.

versificación NF versification.

versificador(a) NM/F versifier.

versificar [1g] ⬚**1** VT to versify, put into verse.

⬚**2** VI to write verses, versify.

versión NF version; translation; adaptation; **~ (de) concierto** concert performance.

versionar [1a] VT (*traducir*) to translate; (*adaptar*) to adapt, make a new version of; (*Mús*) to adapt; to record a version of.

vers.º NM (*Rel*) ABR **de versículo** verse, v.

verso NM (**a**) (*gen*) verse; **~ libre** free verse; **~ suelto** blank verse; **teatro en ~** verse drama.

(**b**) (*un ~*) line; **en el segundo ~ del poema** in the second line of the poem.

(**c**) **echar ~** (*Carib, Méx**) to rabbit on*.

versolari NM (*País Vasco, Aragón*) improviser of verse.

versus PREP versus, against.

vértebra NF vertebra.

vertebración NF (*V* VT) (**a**) support. (**b**) structuring, essential structure.

vertebrado ADJ, NM vertebrate.

vertebrador ADJ: **fuerza ~a** unifying force, force making for cohesion; **columna ~a** central column; **soporte ~** principal support.

vertebral ADJ vetebral.

vertebrar [1a] VT (**a**) (*apoyar*) to hold up, support. (**b**) (*estructurar*) to provide the backbone of, be the essential structure of.

vertedero NM (**a**) (*de basura*) rubbish dump, tip. (**b**) = **vertedor** (**a**). (**c**) (*Cono Sur: pendiente*) slope, hillside.

vertedor NM (**a**) (*salida*) runway, overflow; (*desagüe*) drain, outlet; spillway. (**b**) (*Náut*) scoop, bailer. (**c**) (*cuchara etc*) scoop, small shovel.

verter [2g] ⬚**1** VT (**a**) *contenido, líquido etc* to pour (out); to empty (out); (*sin querer*) to pour, spill; *luz, sangre* to shed; *basura* to dump, tip, shoot; **~ los granos del saco en el camión** to pour grain from a sack into a lorry; **~ el café sobre el mantel** to spill (o upset) one's coffee on the tablecloth.

(**b**) *recipiente* to empty (out); to tip up; (*sin querer*) to upset.

(**c**) (*Ling*) to translate (*a* into).

⬚**2** VI (*río*) to flow, run (*a* into); (*pendiente etc*) to fall (*a* towards).

vertical ⬚**1** ADJ vertical; upright.

⬚**2** NF vertical; **en ~** straight (up).

verticalidad NF (*posición*) vertical position; (*dirección*) vertical direction.

verticalmente ADV vertically.

vértice NM (**a**) (*cúspide*) vertex, apex; top; **~ geodésico** bench mark, survey point. (**b**) (*Anat*) crown of the head.

verticilo NM whorl.

vertido NM (**a**) (*acto*) spillage; dumping; pouring. (**b**) **~s** (*residuo*) waste; residue; effluent; **el ~ de residuos nucleares** the disposal of nuclear waste.

vertiente NF (**a**) (*declive*) slope. (**b**) (*fig*) (*lado*) side, aspect; (*punto de vista*) point of view, viewpoint. (**c**) (*And, Cono Sur, Méx*) spring, fountain.

vertiginosamente ADV (*V* ADJ) (**a**) giddily, dizzily. (**b**) (*fig*) excessively; very rapidly; **los precios suben ~** prices are rising rapidly, prices are spiralling up.

vertiginoso ADJ (**a**) (*Med*) giddy, dizzy, vertiginous. (**b**) (*fig*) *velocidad* dizzy, excessive; *subida etc* very rapid.

vértigo NM (**a**) (*Med*) giddiness, dizziness, vertigo; dizzy spell; **puede provocar ~s** it may cause giddiness; **bajar así me produce ~** going down like that makes me dizzy.

(**b**) (*fig*) (*frenesí*) sudden frenzy; (*locura*) fit of madness, aberration; (*actividad*) intense activity; (*remolino*) whirl, maelstrom; **el ~ de los negocios** the frenzied rush of business; **el ~ de los placeres** the whirl of pleasures; **¡es el ~, tío!*** it's great, man!*

(**c**) (*Esp**) **de ~: con una velocidad de ~** at a giddy speed; **fue un jaleo de ~** it was an almighty row*; **tiene un talento de ~** he has a fantastic talent*; **es de ~ cómo crece la ciudad** the city grows at a frenzied speed, the town spreads at a tremendous rate*.

vesania NF rage, fury; (*Med*) insanity.

vesánico ADJ raging, furious; (*Med*) insane.

vesícula NF vesicle; blister; **~ biliar** gall-bladder.

vespa NF Vespa, motor scooter.

vespertino ⬚**1** ADJ evening (*atr*).

⬚**2** NM (*diario*) evening paper.

vespino NM small motorcycle.

vesr(r)e* NM (*Cono Sur*) backslang.

vestal ADJ, NF vestal.

veste NF (*liter*) garb.

vestíbulo NM vestibule, lobby, hall; (*Teat*) foyer.

vestiditos NMPL (*frec*) baby clothes.
vestido NM (a) (*gen*) dress, costume, clothing; **historia del ~** history of costume.
(b) (*un ~: de mujer*) dress, frock; costume, suit; (*And, CAm, Cono Sur: de hombre*) suit; **~ de debajo** undergarment; **~ de encima** outer garment; **~ isotérmico** wetsuit.
vestidor NM dressing-room.
vestidura NF (a) (*liter*) clothing, apparel.
(b) (*Ecl*) **~s** vestments; **~s sacerdotales** priestly vestments; **rasgarse las ~s** to tear one's hair.
vestigial ADJ vestigial.
vestigio NM vestige, trace; sign; **~s** remains, relics; **no quedaba el menor ~ de ello** there was not the slightest trace of it.
vestimenta NF (a) (*ropa*) clothing; (*pey*) gear, stuff*, things. (b) **~s** (*Ecl*) vestments.
vestir [3k] **1** VT (a) *cuerpo, persona* to dress (*de* in), clothe (*de* in, with); *estatua, superficie etc* to clothe, cover, drape (*de* in, with); *pared* to hang (*de* with); (*adornar*) to dress up, adorn, deck, embellish (*de* with); **estar vestido de** to be dressed in, be clad in; (*como disfraz*) to be dressed as; **vístame lentamente, que tengo prisa** more haste less speed.
(b) *ropa* (*ponerse*) to don, put on; (*llevar*) to wear; **vestía traje azul con sombrero** he was wearing a blue suit and a hat; **lo viste siempre** she always wears it.
(c) (*pagar la ropa de etc*) to clothe, pay for the clothing of.
(d) (*sastre*) to dress, make clothes for; **le viste un buen sastre** he has his clothes made at a good tailor's.
(e) *idea etc* to express (*de* in); *defecto etc* to conceal, cover up, disguise; **~ el rostro de gravedad** to put on a serious expression.
2 VI (a) (*persona*) to dress; **~ bien** to dress well; **~ con elegancia** to dress smartly; **~ de negro** to dress in black, wear black; **~ de sport** to dress casually; **~ de uniforme** to wear a uniform; **el mismo que viste y calza** the selfsame, the very same.
(b) (*ropa*) to look well, be right (for an occasion); **traje de (mucho) ~** formal suit, (*pey*) suit that is too dressy; **el vestido negro viste más que el azul** the black dress is more formal (*o* suitable) than the blue one.
3 vestirse VR (a) (*persona*) to dress o.s., get dressed, put on one's clothes; (*fig*) to cover itself, become covered (*de* in); **~ de azul** to wear blue, dress in blue; **el árbol se está vistiendo de verde** the tree is coming out in leaf, the tree is turning green; **le gusta vestirse en París** he likes to buy his clothes in Paris; **apenas gana para ~** she hardly earns enough to keep her in clothes.
(b) (*fig: Med*) to get up again (after an illness).
(c) (*fig*) **~ de cierta actitud** to adopt a certain attitude; **~ de severidad** to adopt a severe tone (*etc*).
vestón NM (*Cono Sur*) jacket.
vestuario NM (a) (*ropa*) clothes, wardrobe; (*Teat*) wardrobe, costumes; (*Mil*) uniform.
(b) (*cuarto: Teat*) dressing-room, (*gen*) backstage area; (*en edificio público etc*) cloakroom; (*Dep*) changing-room; pavilion.
Vesubio NM Vesuvius.
veta NF (*Min*) seam, vein, lode; (*en madera*) grain; (*en carne, piedra etc*) streak, stripe.
vetar [1a] VT to veto; *socio* to blackball.
vetazo NM (*And*) lash.
veteada NF (*And*) flogging, beating.
veteado **1** ADJ veined; grained; streaked, striped (*de* with); *tocino* streaky.
2 NM veining; graining; streaks, markings.
vetear [1a] VT (a) (*gen*) to grain; to streak. (b) (*And: azotar*) to flog, beat.
veteranía NF (*status*) status (*o* dignity *etc*) of being a veteran; (*servicio*) long service; (*antigüedad*) seniority.
veterano **1** ADJ veteran.
2 NM, **veterana** NF veteran; (*fig*) old hand, old stager.
veterinaria¹ NF veterinary science, veterinary medicine.
veterinario, -a² NM/F veterinary surgeon, vet, veterinarian (*US*).
vetevé NM (*And*) sofa.
veto NM veto; **poner (su) ~ a** to veto; **tener ~** to have a veto.
vetulio NM (*And*) old man.
vetustez NF (*liter*) great age, antiquity; (*iró*) venerable nature; hoariness.
vetusto ADJ (*liter*) very old, ancient, venerable; (*iró*) venerable, ancient; hoary.
▼ **vez** NF (a) (*gen*) time, occasion; instance; **aquella ~ en Tánger** that time in Tangiers; **a veces** at times; **a la ~** at a time, at the same time; **a la ~ que ...** at the same time as ...; **alguna ~, algunas veces** sometimes; **¿lo viste alguna ~?** did you ever see it?; **alguna que otra ~** occasionally, now and again; **cada ~** every time; **cada ~ que ..., ~ que ...** (*And*) (*como* CONJ) each time that ..., whenever ...; **cada ~ más** increasingly, more and more; **iba cada ~ más lento** it went

slower and slower; **le encuentro cada ~ más inaguantable** he gets more and more unbearable; **contadas veces** seldom, rarely; **¿cuántas veces?** how often?, how many times?; **de ~ en cuando** now and again, from time to time, occasionally; **en veces** by fits and starts; with interruptions; **las más de las veces** most of the times, mostly, in most cases; **muchas veces** often; **otra ~** again; **pocas veces** seldom, rarely; **por esta ~** this time, this once; **rara ~** seldom, rarely; **repetidas veces** repeatedly, over and over again; **tal ~** perhaps; **toda ~ que ...** (*como* CONJ) since ...; although ...; in view of the fact that ...; **varias veces** several times; repeatedly.
(b) (*con número*) **una ~** once; **una ~ que** (*como* CONJ) once ...; as soon as ..., when ...; **una ~ dice que sí y otra que no** first he says yes and then he says no; **érase una ~** once upon a time (there was); **había una ~ una princesa** there was once a princess; **de una ~** in one go, all at once; outright; without a break, straight off; **¡acabemos de una ~!** let's get it over!, let's have done with it!; **una y otra ~** time and (time) again; **de una ~ para siempre** (*o* **por todas**) once and for all, for good; **dos veces** twice; **dos veces tanto** twice as much; **con una velocidad dos veces superior a la del sonido** at a speed twice that of sound; **tres veces** three times; **cien veces** hundreds of times, lots of times; **la primera ~ que le vi** first time I saw him; **por primera ~** for the first time; **por última ~** for the last time; **por enésima ~** for the umpteenth time*; **no se permite golpearlo segunda ~** you can't hit it again, you aren't allowed a second shot at it.
(c) (*Mat*) **7 veces 9** 7 times 9.
(d) (*turno*) turn; **a su ~** in his turn; **en ~ de** instead of, in place of; **ceder la ~** to give up one's turn, (*en cola etc*) give up one's place; **cuando le llegue la ~** when his turn comes; **hacer las veces de** to take the place of, act for, stand in for; to serve as, do duty as; **pedir la ~** to speak out, establish one's rights.
veza NF vetch.
v.g. = v.gr.
v.gr. ABR *de* **verbigracia** videlicet, namely, *viz.*
vía **1** NF (a) (*calle etc*) road; (*ruta*) route; track; (*And Aut*) lane (*of a motorway*); (*fig*) way; (*Rel etc*) way; **~ de acceso** access road; service road; **~ aérea** airway; lane; (*Correos*) airmail; **por ~ aérea** by air, (*Correos*) (by) airmail; **~ de agua** leak; **abrirse una ~ de agua** to spring a leak; **~ de circunvalación** bypass, ringroad; **~ de comunicación** communication route; **V~ Crucis** Way of the Cross; **~ de escape** escape route, way out; **~ férrea** railway; **~ fluvial** waterway; **V~ Láctea** Milky Way; **¡~ libre!** make way!, clear the way!; **dar ~ libre a** to give the go-ahead to; **~ marítima** sea route, seaway; **por ~ marítima** by sea; **~ pública** public thoroughfare; **~ romana** Roman road; **~ terrestre** overland route, (*Correos*) surface route; **por ~ terrestre** overland, by land, (*Correos*) by surface mail; **por ~ de** via, by way of; through; (*fig*) by way of, as, as a kind of; **dejar la ~ libre al desafuero** to leave the way open for abuse.
(b) (*Ferro*) track; line; (*ancho*) gauge; **~ ancha** broad gauge; **~ doble** double track; **de ~ estrecha** narrow-gauge (*atr*); **~ muerta** siding, (*fig*) dead end; **~ normal** standard gauge; **~ única** single track; **de ~ única** single-track (*atr*); **el tren está en la ~ 8** the train is at platform 8; **la estación tiene 18 ~s** the station has 18 platforms.
(c) (*Anat*) passage, tube; tract; **~s digestivas** digestive tract; **~s respiratorias** respiratory tract; **~s urinarias** urinary tract; **por ~ bucal** through the mouth, by mouth; **por ~ interna** (*Med*) internally.
(d) (*fig*) system; way, means; channel; **~s de hecho** physical violence, assault and battery; **~ judicial** process of law, legal means; **recurrir a la ~ judicial** to go to law, have recourse to the law; **por ~ oficial** through official channels; by official means; **tercera ~** middle way, compromise.
(e) (*fig*) **en ~s de** in process of; **un país en ~s de desarrollo** a developing country; **una especie en ~s de extinción** an endangered species, a species on the verge of extinction; **el asunto está en ~s de una solución** the matter is on its way to a solution, the question is in process of being solved.
2 PREP (*Ferro etc*) via, by way of; through.
viabilidad NF (a) viability; feasibility. (b) (*Aut*) road conditions.
viabilizar [1f] VT to make viable.
viable ADJ viable; *plan etc* feasible.
viacrucis NM Way of the Cross; (*fig*) load of disasters, heap of troubles; **hacer el ~** ≈ to go on a pub-crawl*.
viada NF (*And*) speed.
viaducto NM viaduct.
viajado ADJ: **ser muy ~** to be well-travelled.
viajante **1** ADJ travelling.
2 NM (*t ~ de comercio*) commercial traveller, salesman; **~ en jabones** traveller in soap.
viajar [1a] VI (a) to travel (*t Com*); to journey; **ha viajado mucho** he has travelled a lot; **~ en coche** to go in a car, ride (in a car); **~ por Ruritania** to travel through (*o* across) Ruritania; to tour Ruritania.

(b) (‡) to trip‡.

viajazo NM **(a)** (*Méx: empujón*) push, shove. **(b)** (*Carib: azote*) lash. **(c)** (*CAm*: bronca*) telling-off*.

viaje[1] NM **(a)** (*gen*) journey; trip; (*Náut*) voyage; **los ~s** (*actividad*) travelling; **~ en barco** boat trip, sail; **~ de buena voluntad** goodwill trip, goodwill mission; **~ en coche** ride, trip by car; **~ de compras** shopping trip; **~ de ensayo** trial run; **~ de Estado** state visit; **~ de fin de curso** end-of-year trip; **~ de ida** outward journey, trip out; **~ de ida y vuelta** (*o* **ida y retorno**), **~ redondo** (*LAm*) round trip, journey there and back; **~ de negocios**, **~ de trabajo** business trip; **~ de novios** honeymoon; **~ organizado** package tour; **~ de recreo** pleasure trip; **¡buen ~!**, **¡feliz ~!** bon voyage!, have a good trip!; **estar de ~** to be travelling, be on a trip.
(b) (*Com etc: carga*) load; cartload, cartful (*etc*); **un ~ de leña** a load of wood.
(c) (*Carib: vez*) time; **lo repitió varios ~s** he repeated it several times; **de un ~** (*Carib*) all in one go, at one blow; all at once.
(d) **echar un ~ a uno** (*CAm*) to give sb a telling-off*.
(e) (‡: *droga*) trip‡; **estar de ~** to be high‡, be on a trip‡; **ir de ~** to trip‡.

VIAJE	ver también la entrada

¿"Journey", "voyage", "trip" o "travel"?
- *Viaje* se traduce por *journey* cuando se refiere a un *viaje* en particular, tanto por aire como por tierra:
  El viaje de Londres a Madrid dura unas dos horas
  The journey from London to Madrid takes about two hours
- Un largo *viaje* por mar se traduce por *voyage*:
  Muchos marineros murieron en el primer viaje de Colón a América
  Many sailors died on Columbus's first voyage to America
- Cuando *viaje* hace referencia no sólo al trayecto de ida y vuelta, sino también a la estancia en un lugar, se suele traducir por *trip*. Normalmente se trata de un viaje con un fin concreto o de un viaje corto:
  Fui a Alemania en viaje de negocios
  I went to Germany on a business trip
- Como sustantivo incontable, *travel* se utiliza sólo en lugar de *travelling* para traducir la actividad de viajar; también, en muy contadas ocasiones, puede usarse en plural referido a viajes concretos:
  No le gusta nada viajar en barco
  He hates travelling by sea o *He hates sea travel*
  Colecciona recuerdos en sus viajes al extranjero
  He collects souvenirs on his travels abroad
  Para otros usos y ejemplos ver la entrada.

---

viaje[2]* NM (*tajada*) slash (with a razor); (*golpe*) bash*; (*puñalada*) stab; **tirar un ~ a uno** to take a slash at sb.

viajero [1] ADJ travelling; (*Zool*) migratory.
[2] NM, **viajera** NF traveller; (*en vehículo, Ferro etc*) passenger; **¡señores ~s, al tren!** will passengers kindly board the train?

vial [1] ADJ road (*atr*); traffic (*atr*); **circulación ~** road traffic; **fluidez ~** free movement of traffic; **reglamento ~** (*control*) traffic control; (*código*) rules of the road, highway code; **seguridad ~** road safety, safety on the road(s).
[2] NM road.

vialidad NF highway administration.

vianda NF **(a)** (*t ~s*) food. **(b)** (*Carib: verduras*) vegetables. **(c)** (*And, Cono Sur*) lunch tin, dinner pail (*US*).

viandante NMF (*viajero*) traveller, wayfarer; (*en ciudad*) passer-by; pedestrian.

viaraza NF (*And, CAm, Cono Sur*) **(a)** (*enojo*) fit of anger (*o* temper); **estar con la ~** to be in a bad mood. **(b)** (*idea*) bright idea.

viario ADJ road (*atr*); **red viaria** road network; **sistema ~** transport system, system of communications.

viático NM **(a)** (*Hist*) food for a journey. **(b)** (*Fin*) travel allowance; **~s** travelling expenses. **(c)** (*Ecl*) viaticum.

víbora NF **(a)** viper (*t fig*). **(b)** (*Méx: cartera*) money belt.

viborear [1a] VI **(a)** (*Cono Sur: serpentear*) to twist and turn, snake along. **(b)** (*Carib Naipes*) to mark the cards.

vibración NF **(a)** (*temblor*) vibration; shaking; (*pulsación*) throbbing, pulsating. **(b)** (*Ling*) roll, trill. **(c)** (*Psic*) **vibraciones** vibrations, vibes*; **vibraciones negativas** bad vibes*.

vibracional ADJ vibratory.

vibrador NM vibrator.

vibráfono NM vibraphone.

vibrante [1] ADJ **(a)** (*gen*) vibrant, vibrating.
(b) (*Ling*) rolled, trilled.
(c) (*fig*) *voz, slogan etc* ringing; *reunión etc* exciting, lively; **~ de** ringing with, vibrant with.
[2] NF (*Ling*) vibrant.

vibrar [1a] [1] VT **(a)** (*gen*) to vibrate; (*agitar*) to shake, rattle. **(b)** (*Ling*) to roll, trill.
[2] VI to vibrate; to shake, rattle; (*pulsar*) to throb, beat, pulsate.

vibratorio ADJ vibratory.

viburno NM viburnum.

vicaria NF woman priest.

vicaría NF vicarage; **pasar por la ~** to tie the knot*.

vicario NM (*Ecl*) curate; deputy; **~ general** vicar-general; **V~ de Cristo** Vicar of Christ (*the Pope*).

vice* NMF deputy; second in command; vice-president.

vice... PREF vice...

vicealcalde, -esa NM/F deputy mayor.

vicealmirante NM vice-admiral.

vicecampeón, -ona NM/F runner-up.

viceconsejero, -a NM/F deputy minister in a regional government.

vicecónsul NMF vice-consul.

vicedecanato NM vice-deanship.

vicedecano, -a NM/F subdean.

vicedirector(a) NM/F (*Com etc*) deputy director; (*Escol*) deputy headmaster, deputy headmistress; (*Prensa*) deputy editor.

vicegerente NMF assistant manager.

vicelendakari NM, **vicelehendakari** NM *vice-president of the Basque autonomous government*.

vicelíder NMF deputy leader.

viceministro, -a NM/F deputy minister.

Vicente NM Vincent.

vicepresidencia NF vice-presidency; vice-chairmanship.

vicepresidente NMF (*Pol*) vice-president; (*de comité etc*) vice-chairman.

vicetiple NF chorus-girl.

viceversa ADV vice versa.

vichadero NM (*Cono Sur*) = **bichadero**.

vich(e)ar [1a] VT (*Cono Sur*) = **bichear**.

viciado ADJ **(a)** *aire* foul, thick, stale. **(b)** *texto* corrupt.

viciar [1b] [1] VT **(a)** *costumbres etc* to corrupt, pervert, subvert.
(b) (*Jur*) to nullify, invalidate.
(c) *texto* to corrupt, vitiate, falsify; to interpret erroneously.
(d) *sustancia* to adulterate; *aire* to make foul; *comida etc* to spoil, taint, contaminate.
(e) *objeto* to bend, twist, put out of shape; to warp.
[2] **viciarse** VR **(a)** (*persona*) to take to vice, get depraved, become corrupted; *V t* **enviciarse**.
(b) (*objeto*) to warp, lose its shape.

vicio NM **(a)** *gen* vice; (*carácter vicioso*) viciousness, depravity.
(b) (*mala costumbre*) bad habit, vice; **el ~** (*droga*) the drug habit, drug addiction; **~ inveterado**, **~ de origen** ingrained bad habit; **tiene el ~ de no contestar las cartas** he has the bad habit of not answering letters; **no le podemos quitar el ~** we can't get him out of the habit; **darse al ~** (*droga*) to take to drugs; **de ~**, **por ~** out of sheer habit; for no reason at all; **hablar de ~** to chatter away; **quejarse de ~** to complain for no reason at all; **eso tiene mucho ~*** that's very addictive.
(c) (*defecto*) defect, blemish; (*Jur etc*) error; (*Ling*) mistake, incorrect form; solecism; **adolece de ciertos ~s** it has a number of defects, there are certain things wrong with it.
(d) (*de superficie etc*) warp; (*de línea*) twist, bend.
(e) (*con niño*) excessive indulgence.
(f) (*Bot*) rankness, luxuriance, lushness.
(g) **estar de ~** (*LAm*) to be idle.
(h) **de ~*** very tasty; great*, super*.

viciosamente ADV **(a)** viciously; dissolutely. **(b)** (*Bot*) rankly, luxuriantly.

viciosidad NF viciousness.

vicioso [1] ADJ **(a)** vicious; depraved, dissolute; *niño* spoiled.
(b) (*Mec etc*) faulty, defective.
(c) (*Bot*) rank, luxuriant, lush.
[2] NM, **viciosa** NF **(a)** vicious person, depraved person.
(b) (*adicto*) addict, fiend.

vicisitud NF (*desgracia*) accident, upset, mishap; (*cambio*) sudden change; **~es** vicissitudes.

víctima NF **(a)** (*gen*) victim; (*fig, t de ave etc*) prey; **fue ~ de una estafa** she was the victim of a swindle; **es ~ de alguna neurosis** he is a prey to some neurosis; **hay pocas ~s mortales** there are not many dead; **no hay que lamentar ~s del accidente** there were no casualties in the accident.
(b) (*Hist*) sacrifice.

victimar [1a] VT (*herir*) to wound; (*matar*) to kill.

victimario, -a NM/F **(a)** (*gen*) person responsible for somebody's suffering (*o* accident *etc*).
(b) (*LAm*) person responsible for wounding (*o* killing), killer.

victimismo NM victimization; persecution.

victimizar [1f] VT to victimize.

Victoria NF Victoria.

victoria NF victory; triumph; **~ moral** moral victory; **~ pírrica** Pyrrhic victory.

victoriano ADJ Victorian.

victoriosamente ADV victoriously.

victorioso ADJ victorious.

victrola NF (*LAm†*) gramophone, phonograph (*US*).

vicuña NF vicuna.

vid NF vine.

vid. ABR *de* **vide** see.

vida NF (**a**) (*gen*) life; (*modo de vivir*) way of life; (*años de ~*) lifetime, life span; (*profesión etc*) livelihood; **tuvo una ~ ejemplar** he lived an exemplary life; **la ~ de estos edificios es breve** the life of these buildings is short; **así es la ~** such is life, that's life; **¿qué es de tu ~?** what's the news?; **este sol es la ~** this sunshine is a real tonic; **¡esto es ~!** this is living!; **¡es la ~!, ¡qué ~ ésta!** well, that's life!; **está escribiendo la ~ de Quevedo** he is writing the life (*o* a biography) of Quevedo.

(**b**) (*locuciones con PREP*) **¡hermana de mi ~!** my dear sister!; **de por ~** for life, for the rest of one's life; **un amigo de toda la ~** a lifelong friend; **en ~** during his (*etc*) lifetime, while still alive; **en la ~, en mi ~** (*negativo*) never, never in my life; **entre ~ y muerte** at death's door; **¡por ~ de ... !** upon my soul!; **¡por ~ del chápiro verde!** I'll be darned!

(**c**) (*locuciones con ADJ etc*) **~ airada** criminal life; underworld; **de ~ airada** loose-living, immoral; **~ arrastrada** wretched life; **la ~ cotidiana** everyday life; **doble ~** double life; **~ eterna** everlasting life; **~ íntima** private life; **de ~ libre** loose-living, immoral; **mala ~** dissolute life; prostitution; **mujer de ~ alegre, mujer de mala ~** prostitute; **~ y milagros de uno*** full details about sb; **cuéntame tu ~ y milagros** tell me all about yourself; **la otra ~** the next life; the life to come; **~ perra, ~ de perros** dog's life, wretched life; **~ privada** private life; **~ sentimental** love-life; **~ útil** (*Com*) life span; (*Téc*) useful life.

(**d**) (*locuciones con VERBO*) **estar con ~** to be still alive; **amargar la ~ a uno** to make sb's life a misery; **complicarse la ~** to make life difficult for o.s.; **cortar la ~ de uno** to cut sb off (in his prime); **darse buena ~, darse ~ de canónigo, darse la ~ padre*** to live well, live in style, do o.s. proud*; **dar la ~ ~** to sacrifice one's life; **dar mala ~ a uno** to ill-treat sb, give sb a wretched time of it; **enterrarse en ~** to go into seclusion; **escapar con ~** to escape alive; **ganarse la ~** to make a living; **desde hace 5 años goza de mejor ~** she passed away 5 years ago; **hacer ~ marital** to live together (as man and wife); **hacer por la ~*** to eat; **no le va la ~ en esto** it's not as though his life depends on it; **meterse en ~s ajenas** to pry, snoop; to meddle; **pasar a mejor ~** (*euf*) to pass away; **pasar la ~ a tragos*** to have a miserable life; **pegarse la gran ~*, pegarse la ~ padre*** to live it up*, live the life of Riley; **perder la ~** to lose one's life; **quitar la ~ a uno** to take sb's life; **quitarse la ~** to kill o.s., do away with o.s.; **rehacer la ~** to start a new life; **tener siete ~s como los gatos** (*hum*) to have nine lives; **vender cara la ~** to sell one's life dearly.

(**e**) (*de ojos, mirada etc*) liveliness, brightness.

(**f**) (*en oración directa*) **¡~!, ¡~ mía!, ¡mi ~!** my darling!, my love!

(**g**) (*euf) prostitution; **una mujer de la ~** a prostitute, a woman on the game*; **echarse a la ~** to take up prostitution; **hacer la ~** to be on the game*.

(**h**) (**‡**: *hachís*) pot‡, hash*.

videncia NF clairvoyance; fortune-telling.

vidente ①️ ADJ sighted, able to see.

②️ NMF (**a**) (*no ciego*) sighted person, person who can see. (**b**) (*profeta*) seer, prophet; clairvoyant(e). (**c**) (*TV*) viewer.

vídeo NM (*gen*) video; (*aparato*) video, video recorder; (*cinta*) video; **~ comunitario** community video; **~ doméstico** home video; **~ musical** music video; **~ promocional** promotional video; **cinta de ~** videotape; **película de ~** videofilm; **grabar en ~** to videotape, record.

vídeo... PREF video ...

videoadicción NF video addiction.

videoadicto, -a NM/F video addict.

videoaficionado, -a NM/F video fan.

videocámara NF video camera.

videocasete NM video cassette.

videocasetera NF video cassette recorder.

videocassette NM *o* NF video cassette.

videocine NM video films.

videocinta NF videotape.

videoclip NM, PL **videoclips** videoclip, video.

videoclub NM, PL **videoclubs** *o* **videoclubes** videoclub.

videoconferencia NF videoconference, teleconference.

videoconsola NF (video) games console.

videocopia NF pirate video.

videodisco NM video disc.

videoedición NF video editing.

videofilm(e) NM videofilm.

videófono NM videophone.

videofrecuencia NF video frequency.

videograbación NF (*acto*) videotaping, video recording; (*cinta*) recording.

videograbadora NF video recorder.

videograbar [1a] VT to video(tape).

videográfico ADJ video (*atr*).

videograma NM video recording, videogram, video.

videojuego NM video game.

videolibro NM video book.

videomarcador NM electronic scoreboard.

videopiratería NF video piracy.

videopresentación NF video-presentation.

videoproyección NF video-screening; **pantalla de ~** video-screen.

videoproyector NM video projector.

videorregistrador NM video (tape-)recorder.

videorrevista NF video magazine.

videoteca NF video (film) library; videotape library.

videotelefonía NF videotelephony.

videoteléfono NM videophone.

videoterminal NM video terminal; video display unit.

videotex NM Videotex ®.

videotexto NM videotext.

vidilla* NF: **dar ~ a algo** to spice sth up, liven sth up; **dar ~ a uno** to liven sb up.

vidorra* NF good life, easy life; **pegarse la ~** to live it up*.

vidorria NF (**a**) (*Cono Sur*: *vida alegre*) gay life, easy life. (**b**) (*And, Carib*: *vida triste*) miserable life.

vidriado ①️ ADJ glazed.

②️ NM (**a**) (*barniz*) glaze, glazing. (**b**) (*loza*) glazed earthenware.

vidriar [1b] ①️ VT to glaze.

②️ **vidriarse** VR to become glazed.

vidriera NF (**a**) (*Ecl*: *t ~ de colores*) stained glass window; (*t* **puerta ~**) glass door; glass partition.

(**b**) (*LAm*) (*escaparate*) shop window; (*vitrina*) showcase.

(**c**) (*Carib*) tobacco stall, tobacco kiosk.

vidriería NF (**a**) (*fábrica*) glassworks. (**b**) (*objetos*) glassware.

vidriero NM glazier.

vidrio NM (**a**) (*gen*) glass; **~ cilindrado** plate glass; **~ de color(es), ~ coloreado, ~ pintado** stained glass; **~ deslustrado** (*o* **esmerilado**) frosted glass, ground glass; **~ inastillable** laminated glass, splinterproof glass; **~ plano** sheet glass; **~ tallado** cut glass; **bajo ~** under glass; **pagar los ~s rotos*** to carry the can*; **soplar ~*** to booze*.

(**b**) (*: *vaso*) glass; **tomar unos ~s** to have a few drinks.

(**c**) (*Cono Sur*: *botella*) bottle of liquor.

(**d**) (*LAm*: *ventanilla*) window.

vidrioso ADJ (**a**) (*gen*) glassy; (*como vidrio*) glass-like; (*frágil*) brittle, fragile, delicate.

(**b**) *ojo* glassy; fishy; *expresión, mirada* glazed; *superficie* slippery as glass, glassy.

(**c**) *persona* touchy, sensitive.

(**d**) *asunto* delicate.

vidurria NF (*And, Carib, Cono Sur*) = **vidorria**.

vieira NF scallop.

vieja NF (**a**) (*gen*) old woman.

(**b**) (*) **la ~** (*madre*) my mum*; **la ~** (*esposa*) my old woman*.

(**c**) (*Cono Sur*: *petardo*) cracker, squib.

(**d**) (*Méx*: *de cigarro*) cigar stub.

viejada NF (*Cono Sur*) group of old people.

viejales* NM INVAR old chap*.

viejera NF (**a**) (*Carib*: *vejez*) old age. (**b**) (*Carib*: *trasto*) bit of old junk.

viejito*, -a NM/F (**a**) (*anciano*) old man, old woman. (**b**) (*LAm*: *amigo*) friend.

viejo ①️ ADJ (**a**) (*gen*) old; **~ como el mundo, más ~ que el cagar‡** as old as the hills; **se cae de ~** (*persona*) he's so old he can hardly walk; (*objeto*) it's falling to bits (*o* pieces); **hacerse ~** to grow old, get old; **no parece más ~ de un día** he doesn't look a day older.

(**b**) **zapatero de ~** cobbler.

(**c**) **Plinio el V~** Pliny the Elder.

②️ NM (**a**) (*persona*) old man; **el V~ de Pascua** (*LAm*) Father Christmas; **V verde**.

(**b**) (*) **el ~** (*padre*) my dad*; **mi ~** (*esposo*) my old man*; **los ~s** the old folks, my (*etc*) mum and dad*.

(**c**) (*LAm**: *amigo*) mate, pal*; (*en oración directa*) old chap*.

viejón ADJ (*And, Cono Sur, Méx*) elderly.

Viena NF Vienna.

viene *etc* V **venir**.

vienés, -esa ADJ, NM/F Viennese.

viento NM (**a**) (*corriente de aire*) wind, breeze; **corre ~, hay ~, hace ~** it is windy, there is a wind; **hace mucho ~** it is very windy; **cuando**

sopla el ~ when the wind blows; **~s alisios** trade winds; **~ ascendente** up-current; **~ de cara** headwind; **~ de cola, ~ de espalda, ~ a favor, ~ trasero** tailwind; **~ colado** draught; **~ contrario, ~ de proa** headwind; **~ de costado** crosswind, sidewind; **~ de la hélice** slipstream; **~ huracanado** hurricane wind, violent wind; **~ lateral** sidewind; **~s nuevos** (*fig*) winds of change; **~ en popa** following wind; **ir ~ en popa** to go splendidly; to do extremely well; (*de negocio*) to prosper, boom; **~ portante** prevailing wind; **~ racheado** gusty wind, squally wind; **~ terral** land breeze; **estar lleno de ~** to be empty, have nothing inside; **beber los ~s por uno** to be crazy about sb; **echar a uno con ~ fresco*** to chuck sb out; **¡vete con ~ fresco!*** go to blazes!*, and good riddance!; **le mandé a tomar ~** I sent him packing; **publicar algo a los cuatro ~s** to tell all and sundry about sth, shout sth from the rooftops; **soplan ~s de fronda** there's trouble brewing; **sorber los ~s por uno** to be crazy about sb; **como el ~** like the wind; **contra ~ y marea** come hell or high water, come what may.

(b) (*Anat*) wind, flatulence.

(c) (*Mús*) wind; wind instruments, wind section.

(d) (*Caza*) scent.

(e) (*de perro*) keen scent, sense of smell.

(f) (*fig: vanidad*) conceit, vanity; **estar lleno de ~** to be puffed up (with conceit).

(g) (*de poste, tienda*) guy, guy-rope.

(h) (*And: de cometa*) strings of a kite.

(i) (*CAm, Carib Med*) rheumatism.

vientre NM (a) (*Anat*) (*estómago etc*) belly; (*matriz*) womb; **bajo ~** lower abdomen; **llevar un hijo en su ~** to carry a child in one's womb.

(b) (*intestino*) bowels; **~ flojo** looseness of the bowels; **descargar el ~, exonerar el ~, hacer de ~** to have a bowel movement.

(c) (*de animal muerto*) guts, entrails, offal.

(d) (*Zool*) foetus, unborn young.

(e) (*de vasija*) belly, wide part.

vier. ABR *de* **viernes** *m* Friday, Fri.

viernes NM INVAR Friday; **V~ Santo** Good Friday.

Vietnam NM Vietnam; **~ del Norte** North Vietnam; **~ del Sur** South Vietnam.

vietnamita¹ [1] ADJ, NMF Vietnamese.

[2] NM (*Ling*) Vietnamese.

vietnamita² NF (*máquina*) duplicator.

viga NF (*de madera*) balk, timber; (*Arquit*) beam, rafter; (*metal*) girder; **~ maestra** main beam; **~ transversal** crossbeam; **estar contando las ~s** (*fig*) to be gazing vacantly at the ceiling.

vigencia NF (a) (*ley etc*) operation; (*validez*) validity, applicability; (*de contrato etc*) term, life; **estar en ~** to be in force; to be valid, apply; **entrar en ~** to take effect, come into operation; **perder ~** to go out of use, be no longer applicable; **tener ~** to be valid, apply; to prevail.

(b) (*norma social*) social convention, norm of society.

vigente ADJ valid, applicable, in force; prevailing.

vigésimo ADJ, NM twentieth.

vigía [1] NM look-out, watchman; **los ~s** (*Náut*) the watch.

[2] NF (a) (*Mil etc*) watchtower. (b) (*Geog*) reef, rock.

vigilancia NF vigilance, watchfulness; **burlar la ~ de uno** to escape sb's vigilance; **tener a uno bajo ~** to keep watch on sb, keep sb under observation.

vigilante [1] ADJ vigilant, watchful; alert.

[2] NM (a) (*guardián*) watchman, caretaker; (*de cárcel*) warder; (*de trabajo*) supervisor; (*en tienda*) shopwalker, store detective; (*de museo*) keeper; **~ jurado** security guard; **~ de noche, ~ nocturno** night watchman.

(b) (*Cono Sur: policía*) policeman.

vigilantemente ADV vigilantly, watchfully.

vigilar [1a] [1] VT (*velar por*) to watch, watch over; (*cuidar*) to look after, keep on eye on; (*instalación, prisionero etc*) to guard; (*máquina*) to tend; (*frontera etc*) to guard, police, patrol; (*trabajo etc*) to supervise, superintend; **~ a los niños para que no se hagan daño** to see that the children come to no harm; **~ la leche para que no se salga** to keep an eye on the milk so that it does not boil over.

[2] VI to be vigilant, be watchful, stay alert; to keep watch; **~ por, ~ sobre** to watch over.

vigilia NF (a) (*estar sin dormir*) wakefulness, being awake; (*vigilancia*) watchfulness; **pasar la noche de ~** to spend a night without sleep, stay awake all night.

(b) (*trabajo*) night work, late work; time spent working late; (*estudio*) night-time study, lucubrations.

(c) (*Ecl*) vigil; abstinence; **día de ~** day of abstinence; **comer de ~** to fast, abstain from meat.

vigor NM (a) (*fuerza*) vigour; (*vitalidad*) vitality; (*resistencia*) toughness, stamina, hardiness; (*empuje*) drive; **con ~** vigorously.

(b) = **vigencia**; **en ~** in force; valid, applicable, operative; **entrar en ~** to take effect, come into force; **poner en ~** to put into effect, put

into operation, enforce; *V* **mantenerse**.

vigorización NF strengthening; encouragement, stimulation; revitalization.

vigorizador ADJ, **vigorizante** ADJ invigorating; bracing; revitalizing; *medicina* tonic.

vigorizar [1f] VT to invigorate; to strengthen, encourage, stimulate; to revitalize.

vigorosamente ADV vigorously; strongly, forcefully; strenuously.

vigoroso ADJ vigorous; strong, tough, forceful; *esfuerzo* strenuous; *protesta etc* vigorous, forceful; *niño* sturdy, strong.

viguería NF beams, rafters; girders, metal framework.

vigués [1] ADJ of Vigo.

[2] NM, **viguesa** NF native (*o* inhabitant) of Vigo; **los vigueses** the people of Vigo.

vigueta NF joint, small beam.

VIH NM ABR *de* **virus de la inmunodeficiencia humana** human immunodeficiency virus, HIV; **~ positivo** HIV positive.

vihuela NF (*Hist*) *an early form of the guitar.*

vihuelista NMF (*Hist*) *vihuela* player.

vijúa NF (*And*) rock salt.

vikingo, -a NM/F Viking.

vil ADJ *persona* low, villainous, blackguardly; *acto* vile, foul, rotten; *conducta* despicable; *trato* unjust, shabby, mean.

vileza NF (a) (*cualidad*) low character, villainy; vileness, foulness; despicable nature; injustice, shabbiness, meanness.

(b) (*una ~*) vile act, base deed, villainy.

vilipendiar [1b] VT (*V N*) (a) to vilify, revile, abuse. (b) to despise, scorn.

vilipendio NM (a) (*denuncia*) vilification, abuse. (b) (*desprecio*) contempt, scorn; humiliation.

vilipendioso ADJ contemptible; humiliating.

villa NF (a) (*romana etc*) villa. (b) (*pueblo*) small town; (*Pol*) borough, municipality; **la V~ (y Corte)** Madrid; **~ miseria** slum quarter, shanty-town; **~ olímpica** Olympic village.

Villadiego: tomar las de ~* to beat it quick*.

villanaje NM (a) (*status*) humble status, peasant condition. (b) (*personas*) peasantry, villagers.

villancico NM (Christmas) carol.

villanesco ADJ peasant (*atr*); village (*atr*), rustic.

villanía NF (a) (*Hist*) humble birth, lowly status.

(b) (*cualidad*) villainy, baseness.

(c) (*una ~*) = **vileza** (b).

(d) (*dicho*) obscene expression, filthy remark.

villano [1] ADJ (a) (*Hist*) peasant (*atr*); rustic.

(b) (*fig: grosero*) coarse.

(c) (*fig: vil*) villainous, base.

[2] NM, **villana** NF (a) (*Hist*) villein, serf; (*esp fig*) peasant, rustic.

(b) (*fig*) rotter*, rat*, swine*.

(c) (*LAm*) villain.

villista NMF (*Méx Pol*) supporter of Pancho Villa.

villorrio NM one-horse town, dump*; (*LAm*) shantytown.

vilmente ADV villainously; vilely, foully; despicably; unjustly, shabbily, meanly.

vilo: en ~ ADV (a) **en ~** (up) in the air; suspended, unsupported; **sostener algo en ~** to hold sth up.

(b) (*fig*) **estar en ~, quedar en ~** to be left in the air, be left in suspense.

vilote NM (*LAm*) coward.

vinagre NM vinegar; **~ de sidra** cider vinegar; **~ de vino** wine vinegar.

vinagrera NF (a) (*recipiente*) vinegar bottle; **~s** cruet stand. (b) (*LAm Med*) heartburn, acidity.

vinagreta NF (*Culin: t* **salsa ~**) vinaigrette (sauce).

vinagroso ADJ (a) (*amargo*) vinegary, tart. (b) (*fig*) *persona* bad-tempered, sour.

vinatería NF (a) (*tienda*) wine shop. (b) (*comercio*) wine trade.

vinatero, -a NM/F wine-merchant, vintner.

vinaza NF nasty wine, wine from the dregs.

vinazo NM strong wine.

vincha NF (*And, Cono Sur*) hairband.

vinculación NF (a) (*gen*) linking, binding; (*fig*) bond, link, connexion. (b) (*Jur*) entail.

vinculante ADJ *fallo* binding (*para* on).

vincular [1a] [1] VT (a) (*liar*) to link, bind, tie (*a* to); *esperanzas etc* to base, found (*en* on); **~ su suerte a la de otro** to make one's fate depend on sb else's; **están estrechamente vinculados entre sí** they are closely bound together.

(b) (*Jur*) to entail.

[2] **vincularse** VR to link o.s. (*a* to).

vínculo NM (a) (*gen*) link, bond, tie; **~ de parentesco** family ties, ties of blood; **los ~s de la amistad** the bonds of friendship; **hay un fuerte ~ histórico** there is a strong historical link.

(b) *(Jur)* entail.

vindicación NF **(a)** *(gen)* vindication. **(b)** *(venganza)* vengeance, revenge.

vindicar [1g] ① VT **(a)** *(vengar)* to avenge.
(b) *(justificar)* to vindicate.
(c) *(Jur)* = **reivindicar**.
② **vindicarse** VR **(a)** *(vengarse)* to avenge o.s.
(b) *(justificarse)* to vindicate o.s.

vine *etc* V **venir**.

vineo* NM: **ir de ~** to go boozing*.

vinería NF *(And, Cono Sur)* wine-shop.

vínico ADJ *(Quím)* wine *(atr)*.

vinícola ADJ *industria etc* wine *(atr)*; *región* wine-growing *(atr)*; wine-making *(atr)*.

vinicultor(a) NM/F wine-grower.

vinicultura NF wine-growing, wine production.

vinificable ADJ that can be made into wine, suitable for wine-making.

vinificación NF fermentation.

vinílico ADJ vinyl *(atr)*.

vinillo NM thin wine, weak wine.

vinilo NM vinyl.

vino NM **(a)** wine; **~ añejo** mellow wine, mature wine; **~ del año** new wine, wine for early drinking; **~ base** base; **~ blanco** white wine; **~ de la casa** house wine; **~ corriente** ordinary wine, plonk*; **~ espumoso** sparkling wine; **~ generoso** strong wine, full-bodied wine; **~ de Jerez** sherry; **~ litúrgico**, **~ de misa**, **~ para consagrar** communion wine; **~ de Málaga** Malaga (wine); **~ de mesa** table wine; **~ de Oporto** port (wine); **~ de pasto** ordinary wine; **~ peleón** coarse wine, plonk*; **~ de postre** dessert wine; **~ seco** dry wine; **~ de solera** vintage wine; **~ tinto** red wine; **~ tranquilo** still wine; **aguar** (o **bautizar, cristianar**) **el ~** to water the wine; **dormir el ~** to sleep off a hangover*; **echar agua al ~** *(fig)* to water down a statement; **tener buen ~** to know how to carry one's liquor; **tener mal ~** to get wild after a few drinks.
(b) *(recepción)* drinks, reception, party; **~ de honor** official reception; *(Cono Sur)* special wine; **después de la conferencia hubo un ~** there were drinks after the lecture.

vinolento ADJ boozy‡, fond of the bottle.

vinoso ADJ *sabor* like wine, vinous; *color* wine-coloured.

vinoteca NF collection of wines.

vinotería NF *(Méx)* wine-shop.

viña NF **(a)** *(viñedo)* vineyard. **(b)** *(Méx)* rubbish-dump.

viñador(a) NM/F vine grower; wine grower.

viñal NM *(Cono Sur)* vineyard.

viñatero, -a NM/F *(And, Cono Sur)* vine-grower; wine-grower.

viñedo NM vineyard.

viñeta NF *(Arte y fig)* vignette; *(Prensa)* cartoon, sketch, drawing; *(emblema)* emblem, badge, device.

viola NF **(a)** *(Bot)* viola. **(b)** *(Mús)* viola; *(Hist)* viol; **~ de gamba** viola da gamba.

violáceo ADJ violet.

violación NF *(V* VT*)* **(a)** violation. **(b)** rape. **(c)** offence, infringement.
(d) **~ de contrato** *(Com)* breach of contract.

violado ① ADJ violet.
② NM violet (colour).

violador ① NM rapist.
② NM, **violadora** NF violator; offender *(de* against*)*.

violar [1a] VT **(a)** *sagrado, territorio etc* to violate.
(b) *mujer* to rape.
(c) *ley etc* to break, offend against, infringe; *acuerdo, principio etc* to violate, break.

violatorio ADJ: **ser ~ de** to be in breach (o violation) of.

violencia NF **(a)** *(gen)* violence; *(fuerza)* force; *(Jur)* violence, assault; *(Pol)* rule by force; **no ~** non-violence; **usar ~ para abrir una caja** to use force to open a box; **no se consigue nada con él usando la ~** you will not achieve anything with him by using force; **amenazar ~** to threaten violence, *(turba etc)* to turn ugly; **apelar a la ~** to resort to violence, use force; **hacer ~ a = violentar (b)**, **(c)**.
(b) *(una ~)* unjust act, damaging act; outrage.
(c) *(azoramiento)* embarrassment; *(situación)* embarrassing situation; **si eso te cuesta ~** if that embarrasses you; **estar con ~** to be (o feel) embarrassed.

violentamente ADV *(V* ADJ*)* **(a)** violently; furiously, wildly.
(b) awkwardly, unnaturally.
(c) embarrassingly, awkwardly.
(d) *(interpretación)* distortedly.
(e) *(LAm)* quickly.

violentar [1a] ① VT **(a)** *puerta etc* to force; *rama etc* to bend, twist (out of shape); *casa* to break into, enter forcibly.
(b) *persona* to force, use force on, persuade forcibly; to subject to violence; *(Jur)* to assault.

(c) *(fig)* *principio* to violate, outrage.
(d) *(fig)* *sentido* to distort, twist, force.
② **violentarse** VR to force o.s.

violentismo NM *(Cono Sur)* agitation; social unrest; political violence.

violentista ADJ, NMF *(Cono Sur: Pol)* subversive.

violento ADJ **(a)** *(gen)* violent; *esfuerzo etc* furious, wild; *discurso, medio, persona, temperamento etc* violent; *deporte* tough, physically demanding, *(pey)* rough; **mostrarse ~** to turn violent, offer violence.
(b) *postura etc* awkward, unnatural; cramped; *acto* unnatural, forced; **me es muy ~ consentir en ello** it goes against the grain with me to agree with it.
(c) *situación etc* embarrassing, awkward; **para mí todo esto es un poco ~** this is all a bit awkward for me.
(d) *estado de persona* embarrassed, awkward; **estar** (o **sentirse**) **~** to be (o feel) embarrassed; **me encuentro ~ estando con ellos** I feel awkward when I'm with them; **la discusión entre los dos me hacía estar ~** the argument between them made me feel embarrassed.
(e) *(fig)* *interpretación* forced, distorted.
(f) *(LAm)* quick, sudden; **tuvo que hacer un viaje ~** she had to make a sudden trip.

violeta ① NF **~** violet; **~ africana** African violet; **~ de genciana** gentian violet; **conservador a la ~** dyed-in-the-wool conservative.
② ADJ INVAR violet.

violín ① NM **(a)** *(instrumento)* violin.
(b) **~ de Ingres** spare-time occupation (o art, hobby *etc)* at which one shines.
(c) *(Carib)* bad breath.
(d) **de ~** *(Méx)* gratis, free.
(e) **embolsar el ~** *(Carib*)* to get egg on one's face*; **meter ~ en bolsa** *(Cono Sur*)* to be embarrassed; **pintar un ~*** *(Méx)* to make a rude sign; **tocar ~*** *(And)* to play gooseberry.
② NMF *(persona)* violinist; **primer ~** first violin.

violinista NMF violinist.

violón ① NM *(instrumento)* double bass; **tocar el ~*** to talk rot*.
② NMF *(persona)* double bass player.

violonc(h)elista NMF cellist.

violonc(h)elo NM cello.

vip* NM, PL **vips** VIP.

viperino ADJ viperish.

vira[1] NF *(Mil etc)* dart.

vira[2] NF *(de zapato)* welt.

viracho ADJ *(Cono Sur)* cross-eyed.

Viracocha NM **(a)** *(And, Cono Sur: Hist)* name of an Inca god. **(b)** *(And*, Hist: título)* name given by Incas to the Spanish Conquistadors.

virada NF *(Náut)* tack, tacking.

virador NM *(Fot)* toner.

virago NF mannish woman.

viraje NM **(a)** *(Náut)* tack; turn, going about; *(de vehículo)* turn; swerve; *(de carretera etc)* bend, curve; **~ en horquilla** hairpin bend.
(b) *(fig)* change of direction; *(de política)* abrupt switch, volte-face; *(de votos)* swing.
(c) *(Fot)* toning.

virar [1a] ① VT **(a)** *(Náut)* to put about, turn.
(b) *(Fot)* to tone.
(c) *(And, Cono Sur)* *(volver)* to turn round; *(invertir)* to turn over, turn upside down.
(d) *(Carib)* *azotar)* to whip.
② VI **(a)** *(cambiar de dirección)* to change direction; *(Náut)* to tack; to turn, go about, put about; *(conductor, vehículo)* to turn; to swerve; **~ a estribor** to turn to starboard; **~ hacia el sur** to turn towards the south; **~ en redondo** to turn completely round; **tuve que ~ a la izquierda para no atropellarle** I had to swerve left to avoid hitting him.
(b) *(fig)* to change one's views, switch round; to veer *(a, hacia* to, towards); *(Pol: votos)* to swing; **~ en redondo** to switch round completely, veer round, make a complete volte-face; **el país ha virado a la derecha** the country has swung (to the) right.
(c) *(And, Cono Sur)* to turn.
③ **virarse** VR *(Carib‡)* to kick the bucket‡.

virgen ① ADJ virgin; *cinta* blank; *película* unexposed.
② NF virgin; **la V~** the Virgin; **la V~ de las Angustias** Our Lady of Sorrows; **la Santísima V~** the Blessed Virgin; **¡Santísima V~!** by all that's holy!; **es un viva la V~*** he doesn't give a damn, he doesn't care one little bit; **ser (devoto) de la V~ del Puño*** to be very tight-fisted; **se le apareció la V~*** he got his big chance, he struck lucky*.

virgencita NF *(frec)* small picture of the Virgin.

Vírgenes: Islas NFPL **~** Virgin Isles.

virgiliano ADJ Virgilian.

Virgilio NM Virgil.

virginal ADJ **(a)** *(gen)* maidenly, virginal. **(b)** *(Ecl)* of (o relating to) the Virgin.

virginidad NF virginity.

Virgo NF (*Zodíaco*) Virgo.

virgo NM virginity.

virguería NF (*adorno*) silly adornment, frill; (*objeto delicado*) pretty thing, delicately made object; (*fig*) **hacer ~s** to do clever things; **hacer ~s con algo** to be clever enough to handle sth well.

virguero• ADJ (a) (*bueno*) super•, smashing•. (b) (*elegante*) smart, nattily dressed•; (*exquisito*) pretty, delicately made. (c) (*hábil*) clever.

viricida ① ADJ viricidal.
② NM viricide.

vírico ADJ viral, virus (*atr*); **enfermedad vírica** virus disease.

viril ADJ virile; manly; *V* **edad** etc.

virilidad NF (a) (*cualidad*) virility; manliness. (b) (*estado*) manhood.

virilizar [1f] ① VT to make like a man, induce male characteristics in.
② **virilizarse** VR to become like a man, acquire male characteristics.

viringo ADJ (*And*) (a) (*desnudo*) bare, naked. (b) (*despellejado*) skinned. skinless.

viroca NF (*Cono Sur*) serious mistake.

virola NF (a) (*gen*) metal tip, ferrule; (*de lanza, herramienta etc*) collar. (b) (*Cono Sur, Méx*) (*argolla*) silver ring; (*disco*) metal disc (*fixed to harness etc as an adornment*).

virolento ADJ pockmarked.

virolo ADJ (*And*) cross-eyed.

virología NF virology.

virólogo, -a NM/F virologist.

virote NM (a) (*flecha*) arrow. (b) (*Méx: pan*) bread roll. (c) (•) (*señorito*) playboy; (*estirado*) stuffed shirt. (d) (*And, Méx: tonto*) simpleton.

virreinato NM viceroyalty.

virrey NM viceroy.

virriondo• ADJ (*Méx*) (a) *animal* (*hembra*) on heat; (*macho*) in rut. (b) *persona* randy•, horny•.

virtual ADJ (a) (*real*) virtual. (b) (*potencial etc*) potential; future, possible. (c) (*Fís*) apparent.

virtualidad NF potentiality; **tiene ciertas ~es** it has certain potentialities.

virtualmente ADJ virtually.

▼ **virtud** NF (a) (*cualidad*) virtue; **~ cardinal** cardinal virtue.
▼(b) (*capacidad*) virtue, power; (*eficacia*) efficacy; **en ~ de** by virtue of, by reason of; **tener la ~ de** + *infin* to have the virtue of + *ger*, have the power to + *infin*; **una planta que tiene ~ contra varias enfermedades** a plant which is effective against certain diseases. (c) (*Carib•*) (*pene*) prick•; (*vagina*) cunt•.

virtuosamente ADV virtuously.

virtuosismo NM virtuosity.

virtuosista ADJ virtuoso.

virtuoso ① ADJ virtuous.
② NM virtuoso.

viruela NF (a) (*Med*) smallpox. (b) **~s** pockmarks; **picado de ~s** pockmarked.

virulé: a la ~ ADJ (a) (*viejo*) old; (*estropeado*) damaged; (*torcido*) bent, twisted; (*raído*) shabby. (b) (•) *persona* cracked, potty•.

virulencia NF virulence.

virulento ADJ virulent.

virus NM INVAR virus (*t Inform*); **~ gripal** flu virus; **~ de inmunodeficiencia humana** human immunodeficiency virus.

viruta NF ① (a) (*Téc*) shaving; **~s de acero** steel wool. (b) (•: *dinero*) bread•, money.
② NM (*t ~s*) carpenter.

vis NF: **~ cómica** comic sense, sense of comedy; **tener ~ cómica** to be witty, sparkle.

visa NM (F *en LAm*) visa.

visado NM visa; permit; **~ de permanencia** residence permit; **~ de salida** exit visa; **~ de tránsito** transit visa; **~ turístico** tourist visa.

visaje NM (wry) face, grimace; **hacer ~s** to pull faces, grimace, smirk.

visar [1a] VT (a) *pasaporte* to visa. (b) *documento* to pass, approve, endorse.

vis a vis ① ADV face to face.
② NM face to face (meeting); (*en la cárcel*) private visit.

visceral ADJ (*fig*) innate, fundamental; intense, profound, deep-rooted; **aversión ~** gut aversion; **sentimientos ~es** gut feelings.

visceralidad NF gut feelings, gut reaction; strong feelings.

visceralmente ADV innately, fundamentally; intensely, profoundly.

vísceras NFPL viscera, entrails; (*fig*) guts, bowels.

visco NM birdlime.

viscosa NF viscose.

viscosidad NF (a) (*cualidad*) viscosity, stickiness; thickness. (b) (*Bot, Zool*) slime; sticky secretion.

viscoso ADJ viscous, sticky; *líquido* thick, stiff; *secreción* slimy.

visera NF (*Mil*) visor; (*de gorra*) peak; (*de jugador etc*) eyeshade; (*Carib: de caballo*) (horse's) blinkers; (*de estadio*) canopy; **~ de béisbol** baseball cap.

visibilidad NF visibility; **la ~ es de 200 m** there is a visibility of 200 m; **la ~ queda reducida a cero** visibility is down to nil; **una curva de escasa ~** (*Aut*) a bend that leaves a driver with a poor view.

visible ADJ (a) (*gen*) visible. (b) (*fig*) (*claro*) clear, plain; (*obvio*) evident, obvious. (c) *persona* (*libre*) free (to receive a visit); **¿está ~ el profesor?** is the professor free? (d) *persona* (*vestida*) decent, presentable; **¿estás ~?** are you decent?

visiblemente ADV (a) (*lit*) visibly. (b) (*fig*) clearly; evidently; **parecía crecer ~** it seemed to grow as one watched it, it seemed to get bigger before one's eyes.

visigodo ① ADJ Visigothic.
② NM, **visigoda** NF Visigoth.

visigótico ADJ Visigothic.

visillo NM (a) (*cortina*) lace curtain, net curtain. (b) (*antimacasar*) antimacassar.

visión NF (a) (*Anat*) vision, (eye)sight; **~ de túnel** tunnel vision; **perder la ~ de un ojo** to lose the sight in one eye. (b) (*Rel etc*) vision; (*fantasía*) fantasy; (*ilusión*) illusion; **se le apareció en ~** it came to him in a vision; **ver ~es** to be seeing things, suffer delusions. (c) (*vista*) view; **~ de conjunto** complete picture, overview, overall view; **su ~ del problema** his view of the problem. (d) (*pey*) scarecrow, fright•; **ella iba hecha una ~** she looked a real fright•; **han comprado una ~ de cuadro** they've bought a frightful picture, they've bought an absolutely ghastly picture•.

visionado NM (a) viewing, inspection. (b) (*TV*) viewing-room.

visionador(a) NM/F (*Fot*) viewer.

visionar [1a] VT (a) (*Fot etc*) to view, have a viewing (*o showing*) of; (*TV*) to view, see; to preview. (b) (*entrever*) to glimpse; (*prever*) to foresee. (c) (*presenciar*) to witness.

visionario ① ADJ (a) (*gen*) visionary. (b) (*pey*) deluded, subject to hallucinations.
② NM, **visionaria** NF (a) (*gen*) visionary. (b) (*pey*) deluded person, crazy individual.

visir NM vizier; **gran ~** grand vizier.

visita NF (a) (*gen*) visit; (*breve*) call; **derecho de ~** right of search; **~ conyugal**, **~ íntima** conjugal visit; **~ de cortesía**, **~ de cumplido** formal visit, courtesy call; **~ de despedida** farewell visit; **~ de Estado** state visit; **~ de intercambio** exchange visit; **~ de médico•** very short call; **~ de pésame** call to express one's condolences; **~ relámpago** lightning visit, flying visit; **estar de ~ en** to be on a visit to; **hacer una ~, rendir una ~** to visit, pay a visit; **devolver una ~, pagar una ~** to return a visit; **tener ~** (*Med*) to have an appointment at the surgery. (b) (*persona*) visitor, caller; **'no se admiten ~s'** 'no visitors allowed'; **hoy tenemos ~** we have visitors today. (c) (*Carib Med*) enema. (d) **tener la ~, tener ~s•** to have the curse (of Eve).

visitación NF (*Ecl*) visitation.

visitador(a) ① NM/F (a) (*visitante*) frequent visitor, person much given to calling. (b) (*inspector*) inspector; (*Com, Med*) drug-company salesman.
② **visitadora** NF (*LAm*) (*jeringa*) syringe; (*enema*) enema.

visitante ① ADJ visiting
② NMF visitor.

visitar [1a] ① VT to visit; to call on, go and see; *ciudad, museo etc* to visit; (*oficialmente*) to visit; to inspect.
② VI: **el médico está visitando** the doctor is holding his surgery.
③ **visitarse** VR (a) (2 *personas*) to visit each other. (b) (*Med*) to attend the doctor's surgery.

visiteo NM frequent visiting, constant calling.

visitero ① ADJ fond of visiting, much given to calling.
② NM, **visitera** NF frequent visitor, constant caller.

visitón• NM long and boring visit; visitation.

vislumbrar [1a] VT (a) (*entrever*) to glimpse, catch a glimpse of, see briefly. (b) (*fig*) to glimpse, see some slight possibility of; *solución etc* to begin to see; *futuro* to get a slight idea of, make a conjecture about; *hecho desconocido etc* to surmise.

vislumbre NF (a) (*vista*) glimpse, brief view. (b) (*brillo*) gleam, glimmer. (c) (*fig*) (*posibilidad*) glimmer; slight possibility; (*noción*) vague idea; (*conjetura*) conjecture; **tener ~s de** to get an inkling of, get a vague idea of.

viso NM (a) (*de metal*) gleam, glint. (b) (*de tela*) **~s** sheen, gloss; shot-silk appearance; **negro con ~s azules** black with a bluish sheen, black with bluish lights in it; **hacer ~s** to shimmer. (c) (*fig: aspecto*) appearance; **a dos ~s, de dos ~s** (*fig*) with a double purpose, two-edged; **hay un ~ de verdad en esto** this has the ap-

pearance of truth, there is an element of truth in this; **tiene ~s de ser puro cuento** it looks like being just a tale; **tenía ~ de nunca acabar** it seemed that it was never going to finish.
(d) (*Cos*) coloured undergarment (*worn under a filmy outer garment*).
(e) (*Geog*) viewpoint, vantage point.
(f) ser persona de ~ to be somebody, have some standing.
visón NM mink.
visor NM **(a)** (*Mil*) sight; (*Aer*) bombsight; **~ nocturno** nightsight; **~ telescópico** telescopic sight. **(b)** (*Fot*: *t ~* **de imagen**) viewfinder.
víspera NF eve, day before, evening before; **~ de Navidad** Christmas Eve; **la ~ de, en ~ s de** on the eve of (*t fig*); **estar en ~s de** + *infin* to be on the point of + *ger*, be on the verge of + *ger*.
▼ **vista** ① NF **(a)** (*Anat*) sight, eyesight, vision; (*acto*) look, gaze, glance; **~ de águila, ~ de lince** very keen sight, eagle eye; **~ corta** short sight; **~ doble** double vision; second sight; **¡~ a la derecha!** (*Mil*) eyes right!
(b) (*gen*: *locuciones con* PREP) **a primera ~** at first sight; on the face of it; **traducción hecha a primera ~** unseen translation; **a simple ~** with the naked eye; at a glance; **lo teníamos a la ~** we could see it, we had it before our eyes; **la parte que quedaba a la ~** the part that was visible (or uncovered); **no tenemos ningún cambio a la ~** we do not have any change in view; **a la ~ está** it's obvious, you can see for yourself; **está a la ~ que ...** . it is obvious that ...; **estar a la ~ de** to be within sight of; **a la ~ de muchas personas** in the presence of many people; **a la ~ de todo el mundo** openly, publicly, for all to see; **a la ~ de tal espectáculo** at the sight of such a scene, on beholding such a scene; **a la ~ de sus informes** in the light of his reports; **estaré a la ~ de lo que pase** I will keep an eye on developments; **yo me quedo a la ~ del fuego** I'll keep an eye on the fire; **con la ~ puesta en** with one's eyes (*fig*: thoughts) fixed on; **conocer a uno de ~** to know sb by sight; **en plena ~** in full view; **en ~ de** (*fig*) in view of; **en ~ de que ...** in view of the fact that ...; **¡hasta la ~!** au revoir!; so long!; **hasta donde alcanza la ~** as far as the eye can see; **no muy agradable para la ~** not a pretty sight, not nice to look at.
(c) (*gen*: *locuciones con* VERBO) **aguzar la ~** to look sharp, look more carefully; **alzar la ~** to look up; (*fig*) to raise one's eyes to; **alzar la ~ a uno** (*fig*) to turn to sb for help; **apartar la ~** to look away, glance away; (*fig*) to turn a blind eye (*de* to); **no apartar la ~ de** to keep one's eyes glued to; **bajar la ~** to look down; to cast one's eyes down; **clavar la ~ en** to stare at, fix one's eyes on; to clap eyes on; **comer** (*o* **devorar**) **con la ~** to look angrily at; to look curiously at; to look lovingly at (*pey*: lustfully) at; **dirigir la ~ a** to look at, look towards; to turn one's gaze on; **echar una ~ a** to take a look at: **fijar la ~ en** to stare at, fix one's eyes on; **hacer la ~ gorda** to pretend not to notice, turn a blind eye; **hacer la ~ gorda a** to wink at, close one's eyes to; **luz que hiere la ~** light that dazzles, light that hurts one's eyes; **leer con la ~** to read to o.s.; **medir a uno con la ~** to size sb up; **se me nubló la ~** my eyes clouded over; **pasar la ~ por** to look over, glance quickly at; **perder algo de ~** to lose sight of sth (*t fig*); **se pierde de ~** (*fig*) he's very sharp, he's terribly clever; **no perder a uno de ~** to keep sb in sight; **poner algo a la ~** to put sth on view; **recorrer algo con la ~** to run one's eye over sth; **salta a la ~** it hits you in the eye; **torcer la ~** to squint; **volver la ~** to look back (*t fig*); to look away; **nunca volvió la ~ atrás** he never looked back, he never had regrets about the past.
(d) **a la ~** (*esp Com*) at sight, on sight; **a 30 días ~** (*Com*) thirty days after sight; **a 5 años ~** 5 years from then; **dinero a la ~** (*Com*) money on call; **año ~ de las elecciones** a year before the elections.
(e) (*aspecto*) appearance, looks; **un coche con una ~ estupenda** a splendid-looking car; **de ~ poco agradable** of unattractive appearance, unprepossessing; **a la ~, no son pobres** from what one can see, they're not poor.
(f) (*fig*: *perspicacia*) foresight, perception; **ha tenido mucha ~** he was very far-sighted.
▼ **(g)** (*fig*: *intención*) intention; **con ~s a una solución del problema** with a view to solving the problem.
(h) (*panorama etc*) view, scene, vista, panorama; **~s** (*de casa etc*) outlook; (*fig*) outlook, prospect; **la ~ desde el castillo** the view from the castle; **~ anterior, ~ frontal** front view; **con ~s a la montaña** with views across to the mountains; **con ~s al mar** overlooking the sea; **con ~s al oeste** facing west, with westerly aspect.
(i) (*Arte, Fot etc*) view; **~ fija** still; **frontal** front view; **~ de pájaro** bird's-eye view; **una tarjeta con una ~ de Venecia** a card with a view of Venice.
(j) (*Jur*) hearing; trial; **~ de una causa** hearing of a case; **~ oral** first hearing.
(k) **~s** (*Hist*) meeting, conference.
② NM customs inspector.
vistar* [1a] VT (*LAm*) to have a look at, look over, look round.
vistazo NM look, glance; **de un ~** at a glance; **dar un ~*** to pop in, drop in; **dar un ~ a, echar un ~ a** to glance at, take a look at, have

a quick look at.
vistillas NFPL viewpoint, height, high place.
visto ① PTP *de* **ver**.
② PTP Y ADJ **(a)** **~ todo esto** in view of all this; **por lo ~** evidently, apparently; by the look of it; **ni ~ ni oído** like lightning; **cosa no vista, cosa nunca vista** an unheard-of thing; **lo fusilaron, ~ y no ~** they shot him just like that.
(b) **~ bueno** approved, passed, O.K.*.
(c) **está muy ~** it is very commonly worn (*o* used), one sees it about a lot; everyone's wearing it.
(d) **está ~ que ...** it is clear that ...; **estaba ~** it had to be, it was expected all along.
(e) **lo que está bien ~** what is socially acceptable, what is done; **eso está muy mal ~** that's not done, that is thought highly improper; **está muy mal ~ que una joven vaya sola** it is thought most improper for a girl to go alone.
③ **: ~ que ...** CONJ seeing that ...; since ..., inasmuch as ...
④ **: ~ bueno** NM approval, O.K.*, authorization; **dar su ~ bueno** to give one's approval.
vistosamente ADV showily, colourfully; attractively; (*pey*) gaudily.
vistosidad NF showiness, colourfulness; attractiveness; (*pey*) gaudiness; spectacular nature, liveliness.
vistoso ADJ *ropa etc* showy, colourful; gay, attractive; (*pey*) gaudy; *partido etc* spectacular, lively.
Vístula NM Vistula.
visual ① ADJ visual; **campo ~** field of vision.
② NF **(a)** (*gen*) line of sight. **(b)** (*: *vistazo*) look, glance; **echar una ~** to take a look (*a* at).
visualización NF **(a)** (*Inform*) display(ing); **pantalla de ~** display screen. **(b)** **~ radiográfica** (*Med*) scan(ning).
visualizador NM (*Inform*) display.
visualizar [1f] VT **(a)** (*LAm*: *divisar*) to see, make out, descry. **(b)** (*fig*: *imaginarse*) to visualize. **(c)** (*Inform*) to display. **(d)** **~ radiográficamente** (*Med*) to scan.
visualmente ADV visually.
vital ADJ **(a)** life (*atr*), living (*atr*); **espacio ~** living space, (*Pol*) lebensraum; **fuerza ~** life force.
(b) (*fig*) vital, essential, fundamental; **de importancia ~** of vital importance.
(c) (*fig*) *persona* vital, full of vitality.
vitaliciamente ADV for life.
vitalicio ① ADJ life (*atr*); for life; **cargo ~** post held for life; **interés ~** life interest.
② NM life annuity.
vitalidad NF vitality.
vitalismo NM **(a)** (*Fil*) vitalism. **(b)** (*de persona*) vitality.
vitalista ① ADJ **(a)** (*Fil*) vitalist. **(b)** *persona* vital, full of life.
② NMF (*Fil*) vitalist.
vitalizador ADJ: **acción ~a, efecto ~** revitalizing effect.
vitalizante ADJ revitalizing.
vitalizar [1f] VT (*esp LAm*) to vitalize; to revitalize.
vitamina NF vitamin.
vitaminado ADJ vitaminized, with added vitamins.
vitaminar [1a] VT to vitaminize, add vitamins to.
vitamínico ADJ vitamin (*atr*).
vitaminizado ADJ vitaminized, with added vitamins.
vitando ADJ to be avoided; to be condemned.
vitela NF vellum.
vitícola ADJ vine (*atr*), vine-growing (*atr*).
viticultor(a) NM/F (*cultivador*) vine grower; (*dueño*) proprietor of a vineyard
viticultura NF vine growing, viticulture.
vitíligo NM vitiligo.
vitivinicultura NF grape and wine-growing.
vitoco* ADJ (*Carib*) vain, stuck-up*.
vitola NF **(a)** (*de cigarro*) cigar band. **(b)** (*aire, aspecto*) looks, appearance, general air.
vitoquear* [1a] VI (*Carib*) to be conceited, swank*.
vítor ① INTERJ hurrah!
② NM cheer; **entre los ~es de la multitud** among the cheers of the crowd; **dar ~es a** to cheer on.
vitorear [1a] VT to cheer, acclaim.
vitoriano ① ADJ of (*o* from) Vitoria.
② NM, **vitoriana** NF native (*o* inhabitant) of Vitoria.
vitral NM stained-glass window.
vítreo ADJ glassy, vitreous; glass-like.
vitrificación NF vitrification.
vitrificar [1g] ① VT to vitrify.
② **vitrificarse** VR to vitrify.
vitrina NF **(a)** (*aparador*) glass case, showcase; (*en casa*) display cabinet. **(b)** (*LAm*: *escaparate*) shop window.
vitriolo NM vitriol.

➤ LENGUA Y USO: **vista: 1b** → 44.1 **1g** → 35.2

vitro ADJ, ADV *V* **in vitro**.
vitrocerámica NF: **placa de ~** glass-ceramic hob.
vitrocerámico ADJ glass-ceramic; **placa vitrocerámica** glass-ceramic hob.
vitrola NF (*LAm*†) gramophone, phonograph (*US*).
vitualla NF, **vituallas** NFPL provisions, victuals.
vituperable ADJ reprehensible.
vituperación NF condemnation, censure.
vituperar [1a] VT to condemn, censure, inveigh against.
vituperio NM (a) (*condena*) condemnation; (*reproche*) reproach, censure; (*injuria*) insult; **~s** abuse, insults; vituperation. (b) (*deshonra*) stigma, dishonour.
vituperioso ADJ abusive; vituperative.
viuda NF (a) (*persona*) widow; **~ verde** merry widow. (b) (*And, Cono Sur: fantasma*) ghost. (c) (*And Culin*) fish stew. (d) (*Carib: cometa*) large kite.
viudedad NF (a) (*esp LAm*) widowhood. (b) (*Fin*) widow's pension.
viudez NF widowhood.
viudo [1] ADJ (a) widowed; **estar ~*** to be a grass widow(er). (b) **garbanzos ~s** (*Culin**) chick peas by themselves.
[2] NM widower.
viva NM cheer; **dar un ~** to give a cheer; **prorrumpir en ~s** to start to cheer, burst out cheering.
vivac NM, PL **vivacs** bivouac.
vivacidad NF (a) (*vigor*) vigour. (b) (*personalidad*) liveliness, vivacity; keenness, sharpness; (*inteligencia*) brightness.
vivalavirgen* [1] ADJ INVAR happy-go-lucky*.
[2] NMF happy-go-lucky person*.
vivales* NM INVAR wide boy*, smooth operator.
vivamente ADV in lively fashion; *describir, recordar etc* vividly; *protestar* sharply, strongly; *sentir* acutely, intensely; **lo siento ~** I am deeply sorry, I sincerely regret it; **se lo deseo ~** I sincerely hope he gets (*etc*) it.
vivaque NM bivouac.
vivaquear [1a] VI to bivouac.
vivar[1] NM (a) (*Zool*) warren. (b) (*estanque*) fishpond; (*criadero*) fish nursery.
vivar[2] [1a] VT (*LAm*) to cheer.
vivaracho ADJ (a) *persona* jaunty, lively, sprightly; vivacious; bouncy; (*atractivo*) superficially attractive; *ojos* bright, lively, twinkling. (b) (*Méx*) sharp, sly.
vivaz ADJ (a) (*de larga vida*) long-lived; (*duradero*) enduring, lasting; (*Bot*) perennial. (b) (*vigoroso*) vigorous. (c) (*vivo*) lively; (*listo*) keen, sharp, quick-witted.
vivencia NF (*t* **~s**) experience, knowledge gained from experience.
vivencial ADJ existential.
vivenciar [1b] VT to experience.
víveres NMPL provisions; (*esp Mil*) stores, supplies.
vivero NM (a) (*Hort etc*) nursery; (*semillero*) seedbed; (*de árboles*) tree nursery.
(b) (*de peces: estanque*) fishpond; (*criadero*) hatchery, fish nursery; (*Zool*) vivarium; **~ de ostras** oyster bed.
(c) (*fig*) breeding ground; (*pey*) hotbed; **es un ~ de discordias** it's a hotbed of discord.
viveza NF liveliness, vividness; brightness; sharpness; strength, depth, intensity; acuteness; **la ~ de su inteligencia** the sharpness of his mind; **la ~ de sus sentimientos** the strength of his feelings; the sincerity of his regret; **contestar con ~** to answer sharply, answer with spirit.
vividero ADJ habitable, inhabitable, that can be lived in.
vivido ADJ personally experienced; **un episodio ~ por el autor** an episode which the author himself lived (through).
vívido ADJ vivid, graphic.
vividor [1] ADJ (*pey*) sharp, clever; opportunistic; unscrupulous.
[2] NM wide boy*.
vivienda NF (a) (*gen*) housing, accommodation; **escasez de ~s** housing shortage; **el problema de la ~** the housing problem.
(b) (*una ~*) dwelling, accommodation unit; (*piso*) flat, apartment (*US*), tenement; **~ campestre** small house in the country, cottage; **bloque de ~s** block of flats, block of tenements; **~ libre** (house *etc* with) freehold; **~s para obreros** workers' housing; **~ de protección oficial** ≃ council house, council flat; **~s protegidas, ~s de renta limitada, ~s sociales** ≃ council houses, public housing (*US*); **segunda ~** second home, holiday home.
viviente ADJ living; **los ~s** the living.
vivificador ADJ, **vivificante** ADJ life-giving; (*fig*) revitalizing.
vivificar [1g] VT (a) (*lit*) to give life to, vivify. (b) (*fig*) to revitalize, bring to life, bring new life to; to enliven.
vivillo ADJ Y NM (*Cono Sur*) = **vividor**.
vivíparo ADJ viviparous.
vivir [3a] [1] VT to live through; to experience, go through; **los que hemos vivido la guerra** those of us who lived through the war; **ha**

vivido momentos de verdadera angustia she went through moments of real agony.
[2] VI (a) (*gen*) to live (*en* at, in); (*ser vivo*) to be alive; **~ bien** to live well, be prosperous; to live an honest life; (*2 personas*) to live happily together, live in harmony; **~ para ver** you live and learn; would you believe it?; that'll be the day!; **¡viva!** hurray!; **¡viva el rey!** long live the king!; hurray for the king!; **¿quién vive?** (*Mil*) who goes there?; **dar el quién vive a uno** to challenge sb; **~ como un pachá** to live like a prince; **saber ~** to know how to get the best out of life; **no dejar ~ a uno** to give sb no peace, harass sb; **no le dejan ~ los celos** she is eaten up with jealousy; **no vivo de intranquilidad** I'm worried to death; **ya no vivo de vergüenza** the shame of it is killing me; **y a pesar de todo eso vive todavía** and in spite of all that she's still alive today.
(b) (*Fin*) to live (*de* by, off, on); **~ muy justo** to be hard up*, have only just enough to live on; **~ dentro de los medios** to live within one's means; **~ por encima de sus posibilidades** to live beyond one's means; **~ de la pluma** to live by one's pen; **~ de las rentas** to live on one's private income; **no tienen con qué ~** they haven't enough to live on; **ganar lo justo para ~** to earn a bare living.
(c) (*fig: durar*) to last (out); **el abrigo no vivirá mucho** the coat won't last much longer.
(d) (*fig: memoria*) to live, remain.
[3] NM life, way of life; living; **de mal ~** (*inmoral*) dissolute, loose-living; (*criminal*) criminal, delinquent.
vivisección NF vivisection.
vivisector(a) NM/F vivisectionist.
vivito ADJ: **estar ~ y coleando** to be alive and kicking.
vivo [1] ADJ (a) (*gen*) living; live, alive; *carne* living, raw; *lengua* living; **los ~s y los muertos** the living and the dead; **los venden en ~** they sell them alive; **actuación en ~** live show, live performance; **transmitir algo en ~** to broadcast sth live; **le ha llegado al ~** it touched him on the raw, it really came home to him; **me dio** (*o* **hirió**) **en lo más ~** it got me on the raw, it cut me to the quick.
(b) (*fig*) *descripción* lively, vivid, graphic; *escena, memoria* vivid; *brillo etc* bright, sudden; *mirada, ojos, ritmo* lively; *movimiento, paso* quick, lively; *color* bright, rich, vivid; *filo* sharp; *protesta etc* sharp, strong; *emoción* strong, deep, intense; *dolor* sharp, acute; *genio* sharp, quick; *inteligencia* sharp, keen, acute; *ingenio* ready; *imaginación* lively; **¡~!** hurry up!; **describir algo al ~** (*o* **a lo ~**) to describe sth to the life, describe sth very realistically; **lo explica al ~** (*o* **a lo ~**) he explains it very expressively.
(c) *persona* (*listo*) sharp, clever; (*animado*) lively; (*pey*) sharp; (*esp LAm*) sly, crafty; unscrupulous; **pasarse de ~** to be too clever by half.
(d) (*Cono Sur: travieso*) naughty.
[2] NM (*Cos*) trimming, edging, border.
vizacha NF (*LAm: Zool*) viscacha.
vizcaíno, -a ADJ, NM/F Biscayan.
Vizcaya NF Biscay (*Spanish province*); **el Golfo de ~** the Bay of Biscay.
vizcondado NM viscounty.
vizconde NM viscount.
vizcondesa NF viscountess.
V.M. ABR *de* **Vuestra Majestad** Your Majesty.
V.° B.° ABR *de* **visto bueno** approval, O.K.
V.O. NF ABR *de* **versión original** original version, undubbed version (of a film).
vocablo NM word; term; **jugar del ~** to make a pun, play on words.
vocabulario NM vocabulary.
vocación NF vocation, calling; **errar la ~** to miss one's vocation; **tener ~ por** to have a vocation for.
vocacional [1] ADJ vocational.
[2] NF (*Méx Educ*) ≃ technical college.
vocal [1] ADJ vocal.
[2] NMF member (of a committee *etc*); (*portavoz*) chairperson; (*director*) director, member of the board of directors.
[3] NF (*Ling*) vowel.
vocalía NF committee; **lleva la ~ de la mujer** she is the person responsible for women's affairs.
vocálico ADJ vocalic, vowel (*atr*).
vocalismo NM vowel system.
vocalista NMF vocalist, singer.
vocalizar [1f] [1] VT to vocalize.
[2] VT (*Mús*) (*canturrear*) to hum; (*hacer prácticas*) to sing scales, practise.
[3] **vocalizarse** VR to vocalize.
vocalmente ADV vocally.
vocativo NM vocative.
voceado ADJ vaunted, much-trumpeted.
voceador [1] ADJ loud, loud-mouthed, vociferous.
[2] NM (a) (*pregonero*) town crier. (b) (*And, Méx*) newsboy, paperboy.
vocear [1a] [1] VT (a) *mercancías* to cry.

(b) (*llamar a*) to call loudly to, shout to, shout the name of.
(c) (*dar vivas a*) to cheer, acclaim.
(d) *secreto etc* to shout to all and sundry, shout from the rooftops; (*fig*) to proclaim; **su cara voceaba su culpabilidad** his face proclaimed his guilt.
(e) (**: reivindicar*) to boast publicly about, lay public claim to.
[2] VI to shout, yell, bawl.
vocejón NM loud voice, big voice.
voceo NM shouting, yelling, bawling.
voceras NM INVAR loudmouth*.
vocería NF, **vocerío** NM (*griterío*) shouting, yelling; (*jaleo*) clamour, uproar, hullabaloo.
vocero, -a NM/F (*esp LAm*) spokesperson.
vociferación NF vociferation.
vociferador ADJ loud, loud-mouthed.
vociferar [1a] [1] VT (**a**) (*gritar*) to shout, scream, vociferate.
(b) (*proclamar*) to proclaim boastfully.
[2] VI to shout, yell, clamour.
vocinglería NF (**a**) (*griterío*) clamour, uproar. (**b**) (*cualidad*) loudness, noisiness; garrulity.
vocinglero ADJ (**a**) (*vociferador*) vociferous, loud, loud-mouthed. (**b**) (*hablador*) loquacious, garrulous. (**c**) (*fig*) blatant.
vodevil NM vaudeville (*US*), music-hall, variety show (*o theatre*).
vodevilesco ADJ music-hall (*atr*).
vodka NM vodka.
vodú NM (*LAm*) voodoo.
voduísmo NM (*LAm*) voodooism.
vol ABR *de* **volumen** volume, vol.
volada NF (**a**) (*vuelo*) short flight, single flight. (**b**) (*LAm: diversos sentidos*) = **bolada**.
voladizo ADJ (*Arquit*) projecting.
volado [1] ADJ (**a**) (*Tip*) superior, superscript.
(b) estar ~ (*preocupado*) to be worried, feel anxious (*con* about); to be ill-at-ease; (**: loco*)) to be crazy; (*LAm: despistado*) to be absent-minded; (*LAm: enamorado*) to be in love; (*LAm: soñador*) to be in a dreamy state.
(c) (*Cono Sur*) (*saledizo*) projecting; (*abultado*) protuberant, big.
(d) ~ de genio (*Cono Sur, Méx*) quick-tempered.
[2] NM (**a**) (*CAm: mentira*) fib, lie.
(b) (*Carib, Cono Sur Cos*) flounce, ruffle.
(c) (*Méx: juego*) game of heads or tails; **echar ~** to toss a coin.
(d) (*Méx*) (*aventura*) adventure; (*incidente*) incident, happening.
[3] ADV (*And, CAm, Méx*) in a rush, hastily.
volador [1] ADJ (**a**) flying.
(b) (*fig*) swift; fleeting.
[2] NM (**a**) (*pez*) flying fish; (*calamar*) (*a species of*) squid.
(b) (*cohete*) rocket.
(c) (*And, CAm: molinillo*) toy windmill; (*Carib: cometa*) kite.
voladura NF (**a**) blowing up, demolition; blast; **~ controlada** controlled explosion. (**b**) (*Cos*) flounce, ruffle.
volandas: en ~ ADV (**a**) in the air, off the ground (**b**) (*fig*) swiftly, as if on wings; **¡voy en ~!** (*hum*) I fly!
volandera NF (**a**) (*piedra*) millstone, grindstone. (**b**) (*Mec*) washer. (**c**) (**: mentirilla*) fib.
volandero ADJ (**a**) *pieza* loose, movable, not fixed; *cuerda, hoja etc* loose; *dolor* that moves about.
(b) (*fortuito*) random, casual; (*imprevisto*) unexpected.
(c) (*Orn*) fledged, ready to fly; (*fig*) *persona* restless.
volanta NF (**a**) (*And, Carib: rueda*) flywheel; large wheel. (**b**) (*Carib, Méx: carro*) break.
volantazo NM (*Aut*) sharp turn; (*fig*) sudden switch, sudden change of direction.
volante [1] ADJ (**a**) (*que vuela*) flying; *V* **escuadrón** *etc*.
(b) (*fig*) unsettled.
[2] NM (**a**) (*Téc*) flywheel; (*de reloj*) balance.
(b) (*Aut*) steering wheel; **ir al ~** to be at the wheel, be driving.
(c) (*nota*) note; (*folleto*) pamphlet; **un ~ para el especialista** (*Med*) a referral to a specialist.
(d) (*Dep: objeto*) shuttlecock; (**juego del**) **~** badminton.
(e) (*Dep: jugador*) winger.
(f) (*Cos*) flounce, ruffle.
(g) (*LAm*) (*Aut*) driver; (*de carreras*) racing driver.
volantín [1] ADJ loose, unattached.
[2] NM (**a**) (*sedal*) fishing line. (**b**) (*LAm: cometa*) kite. (**c**) (*And: cohete*) rocket. (**d**) (*LAm: voltereta*) somersault.
volantista NMF (*Aut*) driver; (*de carreras*) racing driver; (*pey*) roadhog, speed merchant*.
volantón [1] ADJ fledged, ready to fly.
[2] NM fledgling.
volantusa NF (*LAm*) prostitute.
volantuzo NM (*And*) snappy dresser*.
volapié NM (*Taur*) wounding thrust; **a ~** (*ave*) half walking and half

flying; **de ~** in a split second.
volar [1l] [1] VT (**a**) *edificio, puente etc* to blow up, demolish (with explosive); *mina* to explode; *roca* to blast.
(b) (*Caza*) to put up, put to flight, rouse; (*LAm*) to put to flight, chase off, repel.
(c) (**: irritar*) to irritate, upset, exasperate.
(d) (*CAm*) **~ lengua** to talk, speak; **~ diente** to eat; **~ pata** to walk; **~ máquina** to type.
(e) (*Méx*: robar*) to pinch*.
(f) (*Méx*: estafar*) to swindle.
(g) (*Méx*: coquetear con*) to flirt with.
[2] VI (**a**) (*gen*) to fly; (*irse*) to fly away, fly off; to get blown away; **una alfombra que vuela** a carpet that flies, a flying carpet; **~ a solas** to fly solo; **echar a ~ una noticia** to spread a piece of news; **echarse a ~** (*fig*) to leave the parental nest.
(b) (*fig: tiempo*) to fly, pass swiftly; (*noticia*) to spread rapidly.
(c) (*fig*) (*correr*) to fly; to rush, hurry; (*coche etc*) to scorch, hurtle (along, past *etc*), go like the wind; **¡volando!** get a move on!; **voy volando** I'll go as quickly as I can; I must dash; **prepárame volando la cena** get my supper double-quick, please; **~ a** + *infin* to fly to + *infin*, rush to + *infin*.
(d) (**: desaparecer*) to disappear, vanish, walk*; **han volado mis pitillos** my fags have walked*.
(e) (*LAm Naipes*) to bluff.
(f) (**: droga*) to trip**.
[3] **volarse** VR (**a**) to fly away.
(b) (*LAm: enfadarse*) to get angry, lose one's temper.
(c) **~ algo** (*Méx*) to spirit sth away.
volate NM (**a**) (*And: confusión*) confusion, mess. (**b**) (*And: objetos*) lot of odd things. (**c**) **echar ~** (*Carib*: desesperarse*) to throw up one's hands in despair.
volatería NF (**a**) (*Caza*) hawking, falconry; fowling.
(b) (*Orn*) birds; fowls; flock of birds.
(c) (*fig: pensamientos*) random thoughts, formless collection of ideas.
(d) (*And: fuegos artificiales*) fireworks.
volatero NM (*And*) rocket.
volátil ADJ (**a**) (*Quím*) volatile. (**b**) (*fig*) changeable, inconstant.
volatilidad NF (**a**) (*Quím*) volatility, volatile nature. (**b**) (*fig*) changeableness, inconstancy.
volatilizar [1f] [1] VT (**a**) (*Quím*) to volatilize, vaporize.
(b) (*fig*) to spirit away, cause to vanish.
[2] **volatilizarse** VR (**a**) (*Quím*) to volatilize, vaporize.
(b) (*fig*) to vanish into thin air; **¡volatilízate!** get lost!**
volatín NM (**a**) (*acrobacia*) acrobatics, tightrope walking. (**b**) = **volatinero**.
volatinero, -a NM/F acrobat, tightrope walker.
volcado NM: **~ de memoria** (*Inform*) dump.
volcán NM (**a**) volcano.
(b) (*And, Cono Sur*) (*torrente*) summer torrent; (*avalancha*) avalanche.
(c) (*CAm, Carib: montón*) pile, heap; **un ~ de cosas** a lot of things, a whole heap of things.
(d) (*Carib: estrépito*) deafening noise; confusion, hubbub.
(e) (*And*) breakdown; collapse, fall.
volcanada NF (*Cono Sur*) whiff.
volcanarse [1a] VR (*And*) to break down; to collapse, fall down.
volcánico ADJ volcanic.
volcar [1g y 1l] [1] VT (**a**) *recipiente* to upset, overturn, tip over, knock over; (*adrede*) to empty out; *contenido* to upset; to empty out; *camión etc* to tip; *carga* to dump, shoot; *coche etc* to overturn; *barco* to overturn, capsize, upset.
(b) ~ a uno (*fig: marear*) to make sb dizzy, make sb's head swim.
(c) ~ a uno (*fig: convencer*) to force sb to change his mind.
(d) (*fig*) (*irritar*) to irritate, exasperate; (*desconcertar*) to upset; (*embromar*) to tease.
(e) estar volcado a un cometido to be dedicated to a task.
(f) estar volcado* to be broke*.
[2] VI (*coche etc*) to overturn.
[3] **volcarse** VR (**a**) (*recipiente*) to be upset, get overturned; to tip over; (*coche etc*) to overturn; (*barco*) to capsize.
(b) (*fig*) to go out of one's way, be excessively kind; to be welcoming; **~ para** (*o* **por**) **conseguir algo** to do one's utmost to get sth; **~ por complacer a uno** to lean over backwards to satisfy sb.
(c) ~ en una actividad to throw o.s. into an activity.
volea NF volley; **media ~** half-volley.
volear [1a] VTI to volley; **~ por alto** to lob.
voleibol NM volleyball.
voleiplaya NM beachball, beach volleyball.
voleo NM (**a**) (*gen*) volley; **de un ~, del primer ~** (*rápidamente*) quickly; (*bruscamente*) brusquely, suddenly; (*de un golpe*) at one blow; **sembrar a** (*o* **al**) **~** to broadcast the seed, scatter the seed; **repartir algo a** (*o* **al**) **~** to distribute sth haphazardly.
(b) (**: puñetazo*) punch, bash*.

volframio NM wolfram.
volibol NM volleyball.
volición NF volition.
volido NM (*LAm*) flight; **de un ~** quickly, at once.
volitivo ADJ volitional, volitive.
volován NM vol-au-vent.
volquete NM (*carro*) tipcart; (*Aut*) dumping lorry, dumper, dump truck (*US*).
voltaico ADJ voltaic.
voltaje NM voltage.
voltario ADJ (*Cono Sur*) **(a)** (*cambiable*) fickle, changeable. **(b)** (*voluntarioso*) wilful, headstrong. **(c)** (*pulcro*) spruce, dapper.
volteada NF **(a)** (*Cono Sur Agr*) round-up. **(b)** (*CAm, Cono Sur, Méx Pol*) defection.
volteado NM (*And Mil*) deserter; (*Pol*) turncoat.
volteador(a) NM/F acrobat.
voltear [1a] **1** VT **(a)** (*volver al revés*) to turn over, roll over; (*invertir*) to turn upside down; (*dar vuelta a*) to turn round; *recipiente* to upset, overturn; (*LAm*) *espalda etc* to turn; (*Cono Sur, Méx: volcar*) to knock down; to knock over, spill.
(b) *campanas* to peal.
(c) (*lanzar al aire*) to throw into the air; (*toro*) to toss.
(d) (*esp LAm*) *lazo etc* to whirl, twirl.
(e) **~ a uno** (*And, Carib, Cono Sur*) to force sb to change his mind.
(f) (*Carib: buscar*) to search all over for.
2 VI **(a)** (*dar vueltas*) to roll over, go rolling over and over; (*Teat etc*) to somersault.
(b) (*LAm: torcer*) to turn (*a la derecha* to the right); (*volverse*) to turn round.
(c) (*LAm*) **~ a hacer algo** to do sth again.
(d) **volteó con mi amiga** (*Carib*) he went off with my girlfriend.
3 **voltearse** VR (*LAm*) **(a)** (*dar la vuelta*) to turn round; (*volcarse*) to overturn, turn over.
(b) (*Pol*) to change one's allegiance, go over to the other side; to change one's ideas.
voltereta NF somersault; roll, tumble; **~ lateral** cartwheel; **dar ~s** to turn somersaults, do cartwheels.
voltímetro NM voltmeter.
voltio NM **(a)** (*gen*) volt. **(b) darse un ~*** to take a stroll.
volubilidad NF fickleness, changeableness; unpredictability; instability.
voluble ADJ **(a)** (*Bot*) twining, clinging; climbing. **(b)** *persona* (*inconstante*) fickle, changeable; (*imprevisible*) erratic, unpredictable; (*inestable*) unstable.
volumen NM **(a)** (*gen*) volume; (*lo abultado*) bulk, bulkiness; (*masa*) mass; **~ sonoro** volume (of sound); **~ de negocios, ~ de ventas** amount of business done, volume of business, turnover; **~ de capital invertido** amount of capital invested; **una operación de mucho ~** a very substantial operation; **poner la radio a todo ~** to turn the radio up full (*o* as loud as possible).
(b) (*tomo*) volume.
volumétrico ADJ volumetric.
voluminoso ADJ voluminous; sizeable, bulky, massive.
voluntad NF **(a)** (*gen*) will; (*resolución: t* **fuerza de ~**) willpower; (*volición*) volition; (*deseo*) wish, desire; (*intención*) intention; **buena ~** goodwill; good intention, honest intention; **mala ~** ill will, malice; evil intent; **última ~** last wish, (*Jur*) last will and testament; **~ débil** weak will, lack of willpower; **~ divina** divine will; **~ férrea, ~ de hierro** will of iron; **~ popular** will of the people; **a ~** at will; at one's discretion; *cantidad* as much as one likes; whatever you (*etc*) can afford, 'all donations gratefully received'; **se abre a ~** it opens at will; **a ~ de uno** as one wishes; **por causas ajenas a mi ~** for reasons beyond my control; **por ~ propia** of one's own volition, of one's own free will; **su ~ es +** *infin* his wish is to + *infin*; **no lo dije con ~ de +** *infin* I did not say so with any wish to + *infin*, I did not say it with any intention of + *ger*; **hacer su santa ~** to do exactly as one pleases, have one's own way at all costs; **hace falta ~ para escucharlo hasta el final** you need a strong will to sit right through it; **ganar(se) la ~ de uno** to win sb over; to dominate sb's will; **tener ~ de ganar** to have the will to win; **no tener ~ propia** to have no will of one's own; **no tiene ~ para dejar de beber** he hasn't the willpower to give up drinking; **reiterar su ~ de +** *infin* to reaffirm one's intention to + *infin*; **le viene ~ de +** *infin* he feels a need to + *infin*, he feels like + *ger*.
(b) (*****: *afecto*) fondness, affection; **tener ~ a** to be fond of, feel affection for.
voluntariado NM (*trabajo*) voluntary work; (*trabajadores*) voluntary workers *pl*.
voluntariamente ADV voluntarily.
voluntariedad NF wilfulness, unreasonableness.
voluntario **1** ADJ **(a)** (*gen*) voluntary. **(b)** (*Mil*) voluntary; *fuerza etc* volunteer.

2 NM, **voluntaria** NF volunteer; **alistarse** (*u* **ofrecerse**) to volunteer (*para* for).
voluntariosamente ADV **(a)** (*pey*) wilfully, unreasonably. **(b)** (*con buenas intenciones*) dedicatedly, in a well-intentioned way.
voluntarioso ADJ **(a)** (*pey*) headstrong, wilful, unreasonable. **(b)** (*bienintencionado*) dedicated, willing, well-intentioned.
voluntarismo NM headstrong nature, wilfulness; arbitrariness.
voluntarista ADJ headstrong, wilful; *decisión etc* arbitrary.
voluptuosamente ADV voluptuously; sensually.
voluptuosidad NF voluptuousness; sensuality.
voluptuoso **1** ADJ voluptuous; sensual.
2 NM, **voluptuosa** NF voluptuary; sensualist.
voluta NF **(a)** (*Arquit*) scroll, volute. **(b)** (*de humo*) spiral, column.
volvedor **1** ADJ: **este caballo es ~** (*And, Carib*) this horse always finds its way home.
2 NM **(a)** (*llave inglesa*) wrench; (*destornillador*) screwdriver.
(b) (*And: plus*) bonus, extra.
volver [2h; PTP **vuelto**] **1** VT **(a)** *objeto* (*gen*) to turn, turn round; (*poner boca abajo*) to turn over, turn upside down; (*poner al revés*) to turn back to front; *cabeza, espalda* to turn; (*Culin*) to turn (over); (*Cos*) to turn; *tierra* to turn over; *ojos* to turn (*a* on, towards), cast (*a* on); *arma* to aim (*a* at), turn (*a* on); **~ un calcetín** to turn a sock inside out; **tener a uno vuelto como un calcetín** (*o* **media**) to have got sb where one wants him; **~ el pensamiento a Dios** to turn one's thoughts to God; **me volvió la espalda** he turned his back on me (*V t* **espalda**); **~ la proa al viento** to turn the bow into the wind; **~ la vista atrás** to look back.
(b) *página* to turn (over); *puerta, ventana* (*abrir*) to push open, swing open; (*cerrar*) to close, pull to, swing to.
(c) *manga etc* to roll up.
(d) *objeto lanzado etc* to turn back, send back; *comida* to bring up; *imagen* to reflect.
(e) (*****: *devolver*) to return, give back, send back; *vuelta* to give; *visita* to repay, return; **~ algo a su lugar** to return sth to it place, put sth back (in its place); **~ bien por mal** to return good for evil.
(f) (*transformar*) to change, turn, transform; (+ ADJ) to turn, make, render; **~ la casa a su estado original** to restore a house to its original state; **vuelve fieras a los hombres** it turns men into wild beasts; **esto le vuelve furioso** this makes him mad; **todo lo volvió muy triste** it made it all very sad; **el ácido lo vuelve azul** the acid turns it blue; *V* **loco**.
(g) (*Ling*) to translate (*a* into).
2 VI **(a)** (*camino, viajero etc*) to turn (*a* to).
(b) (*regresar*) to return (*a* to, *de* from), come back, go back, get back; **~ atrás** to go back, turn back; **~ victorioso** to come back victorious, return in triumph; **volvió muy cansado** he got back tired out; **~ a una costumbre** to revert to a habit; **volviendo ahora a mi tema ...** returning (*o* reverting) now to my theme ...
(c) **~ a hacer algo** to do sth again; **han vuelto a pintar la casa** they have painted the house again; **he vuelto a salir con ella** I've started going out with her again.
(d) **~ en sí** to come to, come round; regain consciousness; **~ sobre sí** to give up an idea, change one's mind; **~ por** to come out in defence (*o* support) of, stand up for.
3 **volverse** VR **(a)** (*persona*) to turn round, (*objeto*) to turn over, turn upside down, turn inside out; **se le volvió el paraguas** his umbrella turned inside out; **se volvió riendo a mí** she turned laughingly to me; **se volvió para mirarlo** he turned (round) to look at it; **~ atrás** (*recordando*) to look back; (*desdecirse*) to back down, go back on one's word; **~ contra uno** to turn against (*o* on) sb.
(b) = **2 (b)**; **vuélvete a buscarlo** go back and look for it.
(c) (+ ADJ) to turn, become, go, get; **se ha vuelto imposible** he has become quite impossible; **en el ácido se vuelve más oscuro** it turns darker in the acid; **todo se le vuelve dificultades** troubles come thick and fast for him; *V* **loco** etc.
(d) (*vino etc*) to go off, turn sour.
vomitado ADJ *persona* sickly; seedy.
vomitar [1a] **1** VT **(a)** (*devolver*) to vomit, bring up, throw up; **~ sangre** to spit blood.
(b) (*fig*) *humo, llamas etc* to belch, belch forth; *lava* to spew, throw up, hurl out; *injurias* to hurl (*contra* at).
(c) (*fig*) *secreto* to tell reluctantly, finally come out with; *ganancias etc* to disgorge, shed.
2 VI (*devolver*) to vomit, be sick; **eso me da ganas de ~** (*fig*) that makes me sick, that turns my stomach.
vomitera NF (*Carib*), **vomitina** NF vomiting, retching.
vomitivo **1** ADJ **(a)** (*Med*) emetic. **(b)** (*fig*) disgusting; *chiste etc* sick-making, repulsive.
2 NM **(a)** (*Med*) emetic. **(b)** (*Cono Sur: fastidio*) nuisance, bore.
vómito NM **(a)** (*acto*) vomiting, being sick; **~ de sangre** spitting of blood. **(b)** (*materia*) vomit.
vomitona* NF bad sick turn.

vomitorio NM vomitorium, vomitory.

voquible NM (*hum*) word.

VOR NM ABR *de* valor objetivo de referencia.

voracear [1a] VT (*Cono Sur*) to challenge in a loud voice.

voracidad NF voracity, voraciousness.

vorágine NF whirlpool, vortex, maelstrom; (*fig*) maelstrom; whirl.

voraz ADJ (**a**) (*devorador*) voracious, ravenous; (*pey*) greedy. (**b**) (*fig*) *fuego* all-devouring, fierce. (**c**) (*Méx: audaz*) bold.

vorazmente ADV voraciously, ravenously; greedily.

vórtice NM (**a**) (*agua*) whirlpool, vortex; (*viento*) whirlwind. (**b**) (*Met*) cyclone, hurricane.

vos PRON PERS (**a**) (††) you, ye††. (**b**) (*Cono Sur*) you (*sing*).

vosear [1a] VT (*Cono Sur*) to address as 'vos'.

voseo NM (*Cono Sur*) addressing a person as 'vos' (*familiar usage*).

Vosgos NMPL Vosges.

vosotros, vosotras PRON PERS (**a**) (*sujeto*) you.
(**b**) (*tras PREP*) you; (*reflexivo*) yourselves; **entre ~** among yourselves; **irán sin ~** they'll go without you; **¿no pedís nada para ~?** are you not asking anything for yourselves?; **¿es de ~?** is it yours?

votación NF voting; vote; **~ a mano alzada** show of hands; **por ~** popular by popular vote; **por ~ secreta** by secret vote, by secret ballot; **~ táctica** tactical voting; **~ unánime** unanimous vote; **la ~ ha sido nutrida** voting has been heavy; **someter algo a ~** to put sth to the vote, take a vote on sth.

votante ① ADJ voting.
② NMF voter.

votar [1a] ① VT (**a**) (*Pol*) *candidato, partido* to vote for; *moción, proyecto de ley* to pass, approve (by vote); **Pérez fue el más votado** Pérez received the highest number of votes, Pérez got most votes.
(**b**) (*Ecl*) to vow, promise (a to).
② VI (**a**) (*Pol etc*) to vote (*por* for).
(**b**) (*Ecl*) to vow, take a vow.
(**c**) (*echar pestes*) to curse, swear.

votivo ADJ votive.

voto NM (**a**) (*Pol etc*) vote; **~ afirmativo** vote in favour, **~ en blanco**, **~ nulo** blank vote, spoiled ballot-paper; **~ de calidad** casting vote; **~ de castigo** protest vote; **~ cautivo** captive vote; **~ de censura** vote of censure, vote of no confidence; **~ de conciencia** free vote; **~ de confianza** vote of confidence; **~ por correo** postal vote; **~ de desconfianza** vote of no confidence; **~ fluctuante**, **~ de los indicisos** floating vote; **~ secreto** secret vote, secret ballot; **dar su ~** to cast one's vote (*a* for), give one's vote (*a* to); **emitir su ~** to cast one's vote, (*fig*) give one's opinion; **ganar por 7 ~s** to win by 7 votes; **hubo 13 ~s a favor y 11 en contra** there were 13 votes for and 11 against; **tener ~** to have a vote.
(**b**) (*Ecl: promesa*) vow; **~ de castidad** vow of chastity; **~ de pobreza** vow of poverty; **~s monásticos** monastic vows; **hacer ~ de** + *infin* to take a vow to + *infin*.
(**c**) (*Ecl: ofrenda*) ex voto.
(**d**) (*juramento*) oath, curse; (*palabrota*) swearword.
(**e**) (*deseos*) **~s** wishes; good wishes; **mis mejores ~s por su éxito** my best wishes for its success; **hacer ~s por el restablecimiento de uno** to wish sb a quick recovery, hope that sb will get well; **hago ~s para que se remedie pronto** I pray that it may be speedily put right, I earnestly hope that something will soon be done about it.

vox populi ADJ: **ser ~** to be common knowledge.

voy etc V **ir**.

voye(u)r NM voyeur.

voye(u)rismo NM voyeurism.

vóytelas INTERJ (*Méx*) wow!*

voz NF (**a**) (*gen*) voice; **~ argentina** silvery voice; **~ empañada**, **~ opaca** thin voice, voice weak with emotion; **~ en off** voice-over; **la ~ de la conciencia** the voice of conscience, the promptings of conscience; **la ~ del pueblo** the voice of the people; **a una ~** with one voice, unanimously; **a media ~** in a low voice; **a ~ en cuello, a ~ en grito** at the top of one's voice; **de viva ~** personally, in person; orally; **en alta ~** loud(ly), in a loud voice; V **bajo**; **estar en ~** to be in good voice; (*) to be fit, be ready for anything; **aclarar la ~** to clear one's throat; **alzar la ~, levantar la ~** to raise one's voice; **ahuecar la ~** to adopt a serious tone, try to make o.s. sound impressive; **se me anudó la ~ (en la garganta)** I got a lump in my throat; **desanudar la ~** to manage to speak again, find one's voice; **tener la ~ tomada** to be hoarse.
(**b**) (*Mús etc: sonido*) sound, note; (*de trueno etc*) noise; **la ~ del órgano** the sound of the organ, the strains of the organ.
(**c**) (*Mús: de cantante*) voice, part; **canción a cuatro voces** song for four voices, four-part song; **cantar a dos voces** to sing a duet; **~ cantante** leading part; **llevar la ~ cantante** (*fig*) to be the boss, have the chief say.
(**d**) (*grito*) shout; yell; **voces** shouts, shouting, yelling; **~ de mando** (*Mil*) command; **dar** (*o* **pegar**) **voces** to shout, call out, yell; **dale una ~** give him a shout; **dar la ~ de alarma** to sound the alarm;

dar cuatro voces to make a great fuss; **discutir a voces** to argue noisily; **llamar a uno a voces** to shout to sb; **está pidiendo a voces que se remedie** it's crying out (to heaven) to be put right.
(**e**) (*Naipes*) call.
(**f**) (*fig: rumor*) rumour; **común** hearsay, gossip, rumour; **corre la ~ de que ...** there is a rumour going round that ...
(**g**) (*fig: en junta etc*) voice, say; vote, support; **asistir con ~ y voto** to be present as a full member; **tener ~ y voto** to be a full member, (*fig*) have a say; **no tener ~ en capítulo** to have no say in a matter; to have no influence, not count.
(**h**) (*Ling: vocablo*) word; **una ~ de origen árabe** a word of Arabic origin.
(**i**) (*Ling: forma*) voice; **~ activa** active voice; **~ pasiva** passive voice.

vozarrón NM loud voice, big voice.

VPO NFPL ABR *de* viviendas de protección oficial.

vra., vro. PRON POS ABR *de* vuestra, vuestro your.

vto. (*Com*) ABR *de* vencimiento due date, maturity.

vudú NM voodoo.

vuduísmo NM voodooism.

vuela etc V **volar**.

vuelapluma: a ~ ADV quickly, without much thought.

vuelco NM (**a**) (*gen*) upset, overturning, spill; **dar un ~** (*coche etc*) to overturn; (*barco*) to capsize.
(**b**) **mi corazón dio un ~** my heart missed a beat; I had a presentiment.
(**c**) (*fig*) collapse; catastrophe, ruin; **este negocio va a dar un ~** this business is heading for a catastrophe.

vuelillo NM lace, frill.

vuelo NM (**a**) (*gen*) flight; **~ con alas delta, ~ libre** hang-gliding; **~ a baja cota** low flying; **~ a ciegas** blind flying, flying on instruments; **~ charter** charter flight; **~ de ensayo** test-flight; **~ sin escalas, ~ sin etapas** non-stop flight; **~ espacial** space-flight; **~ con motor** powered flight; **~ sin motor, ~ a vela** gliding; **~ nacional** domestic flight; **~ de órbita** orbital flight; **~ en picado** dive; **~ de prueba(s)** test-flight; **~ rasante** ground flying; hedge-hopping; **~ regular** scheduled flight; **~ a solas** solo flight; **alzar el ~, levantar el ~** to take flight, take off; (*fig: partir*) to dash off; (*fig*: largarse) to clear off*; (*fig: joven*) to leave the parental nest, spread one's wings; **se oía el ~ de una mosca** you could hear a pin drop; **remontar el ~** to soar (up); **tocar las campanas a ~** to peal the bells; **tomar ~** to grow, develop; to assume great importance; **de un ~, en un ~** rapidly.
(**b**) **al ~: cazar** (*o* **coger**) **algo al ~** to catch sth in flight; (*fig*) to overhear sth in passing; **tirar al ~** to shoot at a bird on the wing; **cogerlas** (*o* **pescarlas, pillarlas** etc) **al ~** (*fig*) (*comprender*) to catch on immediately, get it at once*; (*ser listo*) to be pretty smart.
(**c**) (*Orn: t* **~s**) (*plumas*) flight feathers; (*ala*) wing, wings; **de altos ~s** (*fig*) grandiose, ambitious, far-reaching; **cortar los ~s a uno** to clip sb's wings.
(**d**) (*Cos: de bocamangas*) lace, frill.
(**e**) (*Cos: de falda etc*) loose part; **el ~ de la falda** the spread of the skirt, the swirl of the skirt; **falda de mucho ~** full skirt, wide skirt.
(**f**) (*Arquit*) projection, projecting part.

▼ **vuelta** NF (**a**) (*gen*) turn; (*Astron, Mec etc*) revolution; **una ~ de la tierra** one revolution of the earth; **~ al mundo** trip round the world; **~ atrás** backward step (*t fig*); (*Cine etc*) flashback; **¡media ~!** (*Mil*) about turn!; **~ en redondo** complete turn; **a ~ de** by dint of; **andar a ~s con** to be engaged in, be immersed in; **dar la ~ a una página** to turn a page; **dar la ~ al mundo** to go round the world; **el coche dio la ~** the car turned over; **dar una ~ de campana** to overturn, turn completely over, somersault; **dar media ~** (*Mil*) to face about; to turn half round; (*) to about-turn, walk out; **al llegar allí hay que dar media ~** when you get there make a half turn; **dar ~ a una llave** to turn a key; **dar ~ a un coche** (*Esp*) to reverse a car, turn a car round; **el libro dio la ~ por muchas oficinas** the book went round a lot of offices; **dar la ~ a la tortilla** to change things completely; **dar la ~ a uno** (*CAm*) to con sb*; **dar ~s** to turn, revolve, go round; (*cabeza*) to spin, swim, be in a whirl; **dar ~s alrededor de un eje** to spin round an axle; **dar ~s alrededor de un planeta** to revolve round a planet, go round a planet; **dar ~s al calcetín** (*fig*) to try sth different ways; **dar ~s a una manivela** to turn (*o* wind, crank) a handle; **dar ~s a un botón** to turn a knob; **dar ~s a un asunto** to think a matter over, turn a matter over in one's mind; **le estás dando demasiadas ~s** you're worrying too much about it; **dar ~s a un palo entre los dedos** to twirl a stick in one's fingers; **no hay que darle ~s** that's the way it is, there's no mistake about it; **poner a uno de ~ y media*** (*insultar*) to heap abuse on sb; (*reprender*) to give sb a good telling-off*; **sacar a ~ a uno** (*And*) to cuckold sb.
(**b**) (*cambio*) turn, change; (*pey*) volte-face, reversal; **~ de calcetín** complete turnaround; **~ de la marea** turn of the tide; **~ de tuerca** (*fig*) turn of the screw; twist; **las ~s de la vida** the ups and downs of life; **dar la ~, dar una ~** to change right round, alter radically.

➤ LENGUA Y USO: **vuelta: a → 35.2**

(c) (*de camino, río*) bend, curve, turn; ~ **cerrada** sharp turn, tight bend; **a la ~ de la esquina** round the corner; **en una ~ del río** at a bend in the river; **dar ~s** to twist and turn.

(d) (*de cuerda*) loop; coil; ~ **de cabo** (*Náut*) hitch.

(e) (*de elecciones, negociaciones, torneo etc*) round; (*en carrera*) lap, circuit; (*Golf*) round; ~ **ciclista** long-distance cycle race; **V~ de Francia** Tour de France; ~ **de honor** lap of honour; ~ **al ruedo** (*Taur*) *circuit of the ring made by a triumphant bullfighter*; **dio 3 ~s al ruedo** he went round the ring 3 times; **segunda ~** (*Univ*) repeat examinations, resits; **la segunda ~ de la Liga** the second half of the League programme.

(f) (*rodaja etc*) round, slice.

(g) (*Cos*) (*de puntos*) row of stitches; (*al hacer calceta*) row.

(h) (*Cos*) (*tira*) strip; (*guarnición*) facing; (*puño*) cuff; (*del pantalón*) turn-up, cuff (*US*).

(i) (*de papel, tela etc*) back, reverse, other side; (*de disco*) flip side; **a la ~** on the next page, overleaf; **a la ~ de la esquina** round the corner; **a la ~ de varios años** after some years; **lo escribió a la ~ del sobre** he wrote it on the back of the envelope; **buscar las ~s a uno** to try to catch sb out; **no tiene ~ de hoja** there's no alternative; there are no two ways about it; there's no gainsaying it, it's unanswerable.

(j) (*acto*) return; (*Ferro etc*) return journey, homeward journey; **a ~ de correo** by return (of post); **a la ~** on one's return; **lo haré a la ~** I'll do it when I get back; **partido de ~** return match; **de ~, iremos a verlos** we'll go and see them on the way back; **estar de ~** to be back, be home (again); (*fig*) to have no illusions, know from experience; **el público está de ~ de todo** the public has seen it all before, the public knows all about it; **¡hasta la ~!** au revoir!, good-bye for now!; **envase sin ~** non-returnable bottle (*etc*).

(k) (*acto*) = **devolución**.

(l) (*Fin: t ~s*) change; **quédese con la ~** keep the change.

(m) (*paseo*) stroll, walk; **dar una ~** to take a stroll, go for a walk.

(n) (*: paliza*) beating, tanning*.

vueltero ADJ (*Cono Sur*) *persona* difficult.

vuelto ① PTP *de* **volver**.
② NM (*LAm*) change.

vuelva *etc* V **volver**.

vuestro ① ADJ POS your; (*tras* N) of yours, *p.ej.* **una idea vuestra** an idea of yours, one of your ideas; **lo ~** (what is) yours, what belongs to you.

② PRON POS yours, of yours; **es el ~** it is yours; **los ~s** (*frec*) your people, your relations, your family; your men, your side.

vulcanita NF vulcanite.

vulcanización NF vulcanization.

vulcanizar [1f] VT to vulcanize.

Vulcano NM Vulcan.

vulcanología NF vulcanology.

vulcanólogo, -a NM/F vulcanologist.

vulgar ADJ **(a)** *lengua* vulgar; *término* common, ordinary; *canción, cuento* popular; (*pey*) vulgar.

(b) *persona* ordinary, common; *modales, rasgos etc* coarse; **el hombre ~** the ordinary man, the common man.

(c) *suceso, vida etc* ordinary, everyday; (*rutinario*) humdrum; *observación etc* banal, trivial, commonplace; inane.

vulgaridad NF **(a)** (*cualidad*) (*ordinariez*) ordinariness, commonness; (*lo grosero*) coarseness; (*banalidad*) banality; (*trivialidad*) triviality; (*necedad*) inanity. **(b)** (*acto*) vulgarity, coarse thing; (*locución*) coarse expression. **(c)** **~es** banalities, trivialities, platitudes; inanities.

vulgarismo NM popular form (of a word); (*pey*) slang word, vulgarism, popular expression.

vulgarización NF **(a)** (*gen*) popularization; **obra de ~** popular work. **(b)** (*Ling*) translation into the vernacular.

vulgarizar [1f] VT **(a)** (*gen*) to popularize; to spread a knowledge of. **(b)** (*Ling*) to translate into the vernacular.

vulgarmente ADV commonly, ordinarily; vulgarly; **A, llamado ~ B** A, popularly (*o* commonly) known as B.

Vulgata NF Vulgate.

vulgo ① NM common people; (*pey*) lower orders, common herd; mob.
② ADV: **el mingitorio, ~ 'meadero'** the urinal, commonly (*o* popularly) known as the 'bog'.

vulnerabilidad NF vulnerability.

vulnerable ADJ vulnerable (*de* to).

vulneración NF infringement, contravention.

vulnerar [1a] VT **(a)** (*perjudicar*) to damage, harm; *costumbre, derecho etc* to interfere with, affect seriously. **(b)** *ley* to break, infringe, contravene.

vulpeja NF fox; vixen.

vulpino ADJ vulpine; (*fig*) foxy.

vulva NF vulva.

W, w [ˈuβe ˈdoβle, (*LAm*) ˈdoβle be] NF (*letra*) W, w.
wachimán NM (*LAm*) watchman.
walki-talki NM walkie-talkie.
Walkman ® NM Walkman ®.
walquiria [balˈkirja] NF Valkyrie.
wambas NFPL sandshoes.
wat, watt NM [bat, wat] watt.
wáter [ˈbater] NM lavatory, water closet.
waterpolista NMF water polo player.

waterpolo NM water polo.
wedge [weʒ] NM (*Golf*) wedge.
wélter [ˈbelter] NM welterweight.
whiskería NF, **wisquería** NF bar (*specializing in whisky*).
whisky [ˈwiski, ˈgwiski] NM whisk(e)y; **~ de malta** malt whisky.
windsurf [ˈwinsurf] NM windsurfing.
windsurfista [winsurˈfista] NMF windsurfer.
wolfram [ˈbolfram] NM, **wolframio** [bolˈframjo] NM wolfram.
wonderbra ® NM, **wonderbrá** NM Wonderbra ®.

X, x ['ekis] NF (*letra*) X, x.
xantofila NF xanthophyll.
XDG NF (*Esp Pol*) ABR *de* **Xunta Democrática de Galicia.**
xeno NM xenon.
xenofilia NF xenophilia.
xenófilo [1] ADJ xenophilic.
　　[2] NM, **xenófila** NF xenophile.
xenofobia NF xenophobia.
xenófobo [1] ADJ xenophobic.
　　[2] NM, **xenófoba** NF xenophobe.
xenón NM xenon.

xerocopia NF photocopy.
xerocopiar [1b] VT to photocopy.
xerófito ADJ xerophytic.
xerografía NF (*proceso*) photocopying; (*resultado*) photocopy, Xerox ®.
xerografiar [1b] VT to photocopy, xerox ®.
xilófono NM xylophone.
xilografía NF (**a**) (*arte*) xylography. (**b**) (*una* ~) xylograph, wood engraving.
xilográfico ADJ xylographic.
Xunta NF *Galician autonomous government.*

Y

Y, y [i'ɣrjeɣa] NF (*letra*) Y, y.

y ...: *para algunas palabras escritas con* **y**... *en LAm, V t* **ll**...

y CONJ and; ¿**~**? so?, well?; ¿**~ eso**? why?, how so?*; ¿**~ los demás**? what about the rest?

▼ **ya** 1 ADV (a) (*pasado*) already, yet; **lo hemos visto ~** we've seen it already; **han dado las 8 ~** it's past 8 already; ¿**ha venido ~**? has he come yet?; **~ en el siglo X** as long ago as the 10th century, as early as the 10th century; **~ no viene** he no longer comes, he doesn't come any more.
(b) (*presente: ahora*) now; (*en seguida*) at once, right away; (*pronto*) soon, presently; (*más adelante*) in due course; **~ veremos** (*eso*) we'll see (about) that; **~ es hora de irnos** it's time for us to go now; **~ viene el autobús** the bus is coming now, here's the bus; **~ se lo traerán** they'll bring it for you right away; **~ no lo volverás a ver** you won't see it any more; **~ arreglarán todo eso** they'll soon put all that right.
(c) (*como* INTERJ) ¡**~**! (*sí recuerdo*) of course!, that's it!, now I remember!; (*bien*) sure!; (*comprendo*) I understand!; (*por fin*) at last!, so you've managed it at last!; ¡**~**, **~**! yes, yes!; all right!; O.K.!*; **~, pero ...** yes, but ...
(d) (*enfático: no se suele traducir*) ¡**~ voy**! coming!; **~ lo sé** I know; **~ se acabó** it's all over; ¿**~ estás aquí otra vez**? are you here again?; **~ te llegará el turno a ti** your turn will come (don't you worry); **esto ~ es un robo** this really is robbery, you can't call this anything other than robbery; **~ gasta, ~** he really does spend a lot.
(e) (*LAm*) now; **~ mismo** right now; **desde ~** (*Esp*) (*a partir de ahora*) from now, (*fig*) of course.
2 CONJ (a) **~ por una cosa, ~ por otra** now for one thing, now for another; **~ dice que sí, ~ dice que no** first he says yes, then he says no; **~ te vas, ~ te quedas, me es igual** whether you go or stay is all the same to me.
(b) **no ~** not only; **no ~ aquí, sino en todas partes** not only here, but everywhere.
▼(c) **~ que ...** as ...; since ...; now that ...; seeing that ...; **~ que no ...** but not ...

yac NM, PL **yacs** [jak] yak.

yacaré NM (*LAm*) alligator.

yacente ADJ *estatua* reclining, recumbent.

yacer [2x] VI (*gen* ††) to lie; **aquí yace X** here lies X; **~ con** to sleep with.

yacija NF (a) (*cama*) bed; rough bed; **ser de mala ~** to sleep badly, be a restless sleeper; (*fig*) to be a vagrant, be a ne'er-do-well. (b) (*sepultura*) grave, tomb.

yacimiento NM (*Geol*) bed, deposit; (*arqueológico*) site; **~ petrolífero** oilfield.

yacuzzi ® NM, PL **yacuzzis** Jacuzzi ®.

yagua NF (*LAm*) royal palm; fibrous tissue from the wood of the royal palm.

yagual NM(*CAm, Méx*) padded ring (*for carrying loads on the head*).

yaguareté NM(*And, Cono Sur*) jaguar.

yaguré NM (*LAm*) skunk.

yaíta ADJ (*LAm*) = **ya**.

yak NM, PL **yaks** [jak] yak.

Yakarta NF Jakarta.

yámbico ADJ iambic.

yana ADJ (*And*) black.

yanacón, -ona NM/F (*And, Cono Sur*) (*aparcero*) Indian tenant farmer, Indian sharecropper; (*criado*) unpaid Indian servant.

yancófilo ADJ (*LAm*) pro-American, pro-United States.

yanomami ADJ, NMF Yanomami.

yanqui 1 ADJ Yankee.
2 NMF Yank, Yankee.

yanquilandia* NF (*pey*) Yankeedom, the States *pl*.

yantar (†† *o hum*) 1 NM food.
2 [1a] VT to eat.
3 VI to have lunch.

yapa NF (a) (*LAm*) (*plus*) extra, extra bit, bonus; (*trago*) one for the road, last drink; **dar algo de ~** to add a bit, give sth as a bonus; (*fig*) to add sth for good measure.
(b) (*Carib, Méx: propina*) tip.
(c) (*Cono Sur Mec*) attachment, end piece.

yapada NF (*LAm*) extra, extra bit, bonus.

yapar [1a] (*LAm*) 1 VT (a) (*dar de más*) to give as a bonus, add as an extra. (b) (*extender*) to stretch; (*alargar*) to add a bit to, lengthen.
2 VI to add an extra, give an extra bit.

yarará NF (*And, Cono Sur*) rattlesnake.

yaraví NM (*And, Argentina*) plaintive Indian song.

yarda NF yard.

yate NM (*de vela*) yacht; (*de motor*) pleasure cruiser, motor cruiser.

yatista NMF yachtsman, yachtswoman.

yaya¹ NM (a) (*And, Carib, Cono Sur*) (*herida*) slight wound; (*cicatriz*) scar; (*dolor*) slight pain. (b) (*Carib: bastón*) stick, walking stick.

yaya²* NF nan, nana.

yaz NM jazz.

yazca *etc* V **yacer**.

ye...: *para ciertas palabras, V* **hie**..., *p.ej. para* **yerra** *V* **hierra**.

yedra NF ivy.

yegua 1 NF (a) (*Zool*) mare; **~ de cría** breeding mare.
(b) (*And, Cono Sur*) (*: pey*) old bag*; (*puta*) whore, slag*.
(c) (*And, CAm: de cigarro*) cigar stub.
2 ADJ (a) (*CAm, Carib*) (*tonto*) stupid; (*ordinario*) rough, coarse.
(b) (*Cono Sur: grande*) big, huge.

yeguada NF (a) (*caballeriza*) stud; (*Cono Sur: yeguas*) group of breeding mares. (b) (*CAm, Carib: estupidez*) piece of stupidity, foolish act (*etc*).

yeguarizo NM (*Cono Sur*) (a) (*de cría*) stud, group of breeding mares.
(b) (*caballos gen*) horses.

yegüerío NM (*CAm, Carib*) = **yeguarizo** (a).

yeísmo NM *pronunciation of Spanish 'll' as 'y'.*

yelmo NM helmet.

yema NF (a) (*de huevo*) yolk; (*LAm: huevo*) egg; **~ mejida** egg flip.
(b) (*Bot*) leaf bud, eye; young shoot.
(c) **~ del dedo** (*Anat*) fingertip.
(d) (*fig: lo mejor*) best part.
(e) (*fig: pega*) snag; **dar en la ~** to put one's finger on the spot, hit the nail on the head.
(f) **en la ~ del invierno** (*fig*) in the dead of winter.

Yemen NM: **el ~** the Yemen.

yemenita ADJ, NMF Yemeni.

yen NM, PL **yens** *o* **yenes** yen.

yendo V **ir**.

yerba NF (a)=**hierba**.
(b) (*LAm*) green.
(c) (*And, Cono Sur: t* **~ mate**, **~ de mate**) maté.
(d) (*: marijuana*) marijuana, grass*.

yerbabuena NF (*LAm*) mint.

yerbal NM (*Cono Sur*), **yerbatal** NM (*And*) maté plantation.

yerbatero 1 ADJ pertaining to maté.
2 NM (a) (*LAm*) (*herbolario*) herbalist; (*curandero*) quack doctor. (b) (*Cono Sur*) (*comerciante*) dealer in maté; (*cultivador*) grower of maté.

yerbear [1a] VI (*Cono Sur*) to drink maté.

yerbera NF (*Cono Sur*) maté container.

yerbero NM (*LAm*) = **yerbatero**.

yerga *etc* V **erguir**.

yermar [1a] VT to lay waste.

yermo 1 ADJ uninhabited; waste, uncultivated.
2 NM waste land; waste, wilderness.

➤ LENGUA Y USO: **ya: 2c → 44.1**

yerna NF (*And, Carib*) daughter-in-law.
yerno NM son-in-law.
yernocracia* NF nepotism.
yeros NMPL lentils.
yerre *etc* V **errar**.
yerro NM error, mistake.
yersey NM, **yersi** NM jersey.
yerto ADJ stiff, rigid; ~ **de frío** stiff with cold.
yesca NF **(a)** (*materia inflamable*) tinder; (*Cono Sur: piedra*) flint; **~s** tinderbox; **arder como si fuera** ~ to burn like tinder.
   (b) (*fig*) (*pábulo*) fuel; (*situación*) inflammable situation; (*grupo*) group (*etc*) which is easily inflamed.
   (c) (*fig: Culin*) thirst-making food.
   (d) (*And Fin*) debt.
yesería NF plastering, plasterwork.
yesero NM plasterer.
yeso NM **(a)** (*Geol*) gypsum.
   (b) (*Arquit etc*) plaster; ~ **mate** plaster of Paris; **dar de** ~ **a una pared** to plaster a wall.
   (c) (*Arte etc*) plaster cast.
   (d) (*Escuela*) chalk.
yesquero NM (*And, Carib*) cigarette lighter.
yeta* NF (*Méx, Cono Sur*) bad luck, misfortune.
yetar* [1a] VT (*Cono Sur*) to put a jinx on*, jinx*.
yeti NM yeti.
ye-yé: ① ADJ groovy:, trendy.
   ② NMF groover:, trendy.
yíd(d)ish NM Yiddish.
yihad NM jehad.
yip NM jeep.
yirante* NF (*Cono Sur*) streetwalker.
yo PRON PERS **(a)** (*gen*) I; **soy** ~ it's me, (*liter*) it is I. **(b) el** ~ the self, the ego.
yod NF yod.
yodado ADJ iodized, with added iodine; **sal yodada** iodized salt.
yodo NM iodine.
yodoformo NM iodoform.
yoga[1] NM yoga.
yoga[2] NF (*Méx*) dagger.
yogui NM yogi.
yogur NM **(a)** yoghurt; **mal** ~ (*euf*) = **mala leche**. **(b)** (:: *coche de policía*) police-car, squad-car.
yogurtera NF **(a)** yoghurt-maker. **(b)** (:) (*Esp*) police-car, squad-car.
yol NM yawl.
yola NF gig, yawl; sailing boat; (*de carreras*) (racing) shell.
yonqui* NMF junkie*.
yoquei NM = **yóquey**.

yoquepierdismo* NM (*CAm*) self-interest, I'm-all-right-Jack attitude*.
yóquey NMF, PL **yóqueis** jockey.
YPFB NMPL (*Bolivia*) ABR *de* **Yacimientos Petrolíferos Fiscales Bolivianos**.
yuca ① NF **(a)** (*Bot*) yucca; (*LAm*) manioc root, cassava. **(b)** (*Carib*) poverty; **pasar** ~ (*LAm*) to be poor. **(c)** (*And: comida*) food. **(d)** (*And: pierna*) leg. **(e)** (*And, CAm: mentira*) lie.
   ② ADJ (*CAm: difícil*) tough, hard.
yucateco ① ADJ of Yucatan.
   ② NM, **yucateca** NF native (*o* inhabitant) of Yucatan; **los ~s** the people of Yucatan.
yudo NM judo.
yugar [1a] VI (*CAm**) to slog away.
yugo NM yoke (*t fig*); ~ **del matrimonio** marriage tie; **sacudir el** ~ (*fig*) to throw off the yoke.
Yugo(e)slavia NF Yugoslavia, Jugoslavia.
yugo(e)slavo ① ADJ Yugoslavian, Jugoslavian.
   ② NM, **yugo(e)slava** NF Yugoslav, Jugoslav.
yuguero NM ploughman.
yugular ① ADJ jugular.
   ② [1a] VT to slaughter.
yuju INTERJ yipee!
yungas NFPL (*And, Cono Sur*) hot valleys.
yungla NF jungle.
yunque NM **(a)** (*herramienta*) anvil. **(b)** (*fig*) (*estoico*) stoical person; (*trabajador*) tireless worker; **hacer de** ~, **servir de** ~ to have to put up with hardships (*o* abuse *etc*).
yunta NF **(a)** (*bueyes*) yoke, team (of oxen). **(b) ~s** (*esp LAm*) (*pareja*) couple, pair; (*gemelos*) cufflinks.
yuntero NM ploughman.
yuppie ['jupi] ADJ, NMF yuppie.
yuta NF **(a)** (*Cono Sur Bio*) slug. **(b) hacer la** ~ (*And, Cono Sur*) to play truant.
yute NM jute.
yuxtaponer [2q] VT to juxtapose.
yuxtaposición NF juxtaposition.
yuxtapuesto PTP *de* **yuxtaponer**.
yuyal NM (*Cono Sur*) scrub(land).
yuyería NM (*And, Cono Sur*) (*malas hierbas*) weeds; (*plantas silvestres*) wild plants.
yuyero, -a NM/F (*Cono Sur*) herbalist.
yuyo NM **(a)** (*And, Cono Sur*) (*mala hierba*) weed; (*planta silvestre*) wild plant, useless plant; (*Cono Sur Med*) medicinal plant, herb; (*And*) herb flavouring; (*And*) cooking herb; **estar como un** ~ (*Cono Sur*) to be wet*.
   (b) (*And: emplasto*) herbal poultice.
   (c) ~s (*CAm: ampollas*) blisters on the feet.

Z

Z, z [θeta, (*esp LAm*) seta] NF (*letra*) Z, z.
zabordar [1a] VI to run aground.
zabullir [3h] VI *etc* = **zambullir** *etc*.
ZAC NF ABR *de* **zona de atmósfera contaminada**.
zacapel(l)a NF rumpus*, row.
zacatal NM (*CAm, Méx*) pasture.
zacate NM (**a**) (*CAm, Méx*) (*hierba*) grass; (*heno*) hay, fodder. (**b**) (*Méx: trapo*) dishcloth.
zacatear [1a] (*CAm, Méx*) ☐1 VT to beat.
  ☐2 VI to graze.
zacatera NF (*CAm, Méx*) (*pasto*) pasture; (*almiar*) haystack.
zafacoca NF (**a**) (*LAm*) (*riña*) row, quarrel; (*pelea*) brawl. (**b**) (*Méx: paliza*) beating. (**c**) (*Carib: disturbio*) riot.
zafacón NM (*Carib*) rubbish bin, trash can (*US*).
zafado ADJ (**a**) (*prov, LAm: descarado*) brazen, shameless; insolent. (**b**) (*Cono Sur: despierto*) alert, sharp, wide awake. (**c**) (*And, Méx‡: loco*) crazy, nuts‡.
zafadura NF (*LAm*) dislocation, sprain.
zafaduría* NF (*LAm*) (**a**) (*descaro*) cheek*, nerve*. (**b**) (*una ~*) bit of cheek*.
zafante PREP (*Carib*) except (for).
zafar [1a] ☐1 VT (**a**) (*soltar*) to loosen, untie.
  (**b**) *barco* to lighten; *superficie etc* to clear, free.
  (**c**) (*LAm: excluir*) to exclude.
  ☐2 **zafarse** VR (**a**) (*huir*) to escape, run away; (*irse*) to slip away; (*soltarse*) to break loose; (*ocultarse*) to hide o.s. away.
  (**b**) (*Mec: correa*) to slip off, come off.
  (**c**) ~ *de persona* to get away from; to dodge, shake off; *deber, trabajo* to get out of, dodge; *acuerdo* to get out of, wriggle out of; *dificultad* to get round.
  (**d**) (*) ~ **con algo** (*robar*) to pinch sth*; (*quedar sin castigo*) to get away with sth.
  (**e**) ~ **un brazo** (*LAm*) to dislocate one's arm.
  (**f**) (*CAm, Cono Sur: esquivar*) to dodge (a blow).
  (**g**) (*And‡: volverse loco*) to go a bit crazy, to lose one's marbles‡.
zafarrancho NM (**a**) (*Náut*) clearing for action; ~ **de combate** call to action stations.
  (**b**) (*fig*) havoc, destruction; mess; **hacer un ~** to cause havoc; to break everything up; to make a dreadful mess.
  (**c**) (*: *riña*) quarrel, row.
zafio ADJ coarse, uncouth.
zafiro NM sapphire.
zafo ☐1 ADJ (**a**) (*Náut*) clear; unobstructed. (**b**) (*ileso*) unharmed; (*intacto*) undamaged, intact; **salir ~ de** to come unscathed out of. (**c**) (*LAm: libre*) free.
  ☐2 PREP (*CAm: excepto*) except (for).
zafón NM (*And*) slip, error.
zafra[1] NF oil jar, oil container.
zafra[2] NF (*esp LAm*) (*cosecha*) sugar harvest; (*fabricación*) sugar making.
zaga NF (**a**) rear; **a la ~, en ~** behind, in the rear; **dejar en ~** to leave behind, outstrip; **A ha quedado muy a la ~ de B** A is well behind B; **A no le va a la** (*o en*) **~ a B** A is every bit as good as B, A is in no way inferior to B; **no le va a la ~ a nadie** he is second to none. (**b**) (*Dep*) defence.
zagal NM boy, lad, youth; (*Agr*) shepherd boy.
zagala NF girl, lass; (*Agr*) shepherdess.
zagalejo NM lad; (*Agr*) shepherd boy.
zagalón NM big boy, strapping lad.
zagalona NF big girl, hefty wench*.
zagual NM paddle.
zaguán NM (**a**) (*entrada*) vestibule, hallway, entry. (**b**) (*CAm: garaje*) garage.
zaguero ☐1 ADJ (**a**) (*trasero*) rear, back; *carro* too heavily laden at the back; **equipo ~** bottom team, team that is trailing. (**b**) (*fig*) slow, laggard.
  ☐2 NM, **zaguera** NF (*Dep*) back.
zahareño ADJ wild; shy, unsociable.
zaherimiento NM criticism; mortification; reprimand; reproach.
zaherir [3i] VT (*criticar*) to criticize sharply (*o sarcastically*), attack, lash; (*herir*) to wound, mortify; (*reprender*) to upbraid; ~ **a uno con algo** to reproach sb for sth, cast sth in sb's teeth.
zahiriente ADJ wounding, mortifying.
zahones NMPL chaps.
zahorí NM (*vidente*) seer, clairvoyant; (*que busca agua*) water diviner; (*fig*) highly perceptive person.
zahurda NF (**a**) (*Agr*) pigsty. (**b**) (*: *chabola*) hovel, shack.
zahurra NF (*And*) din, hullabaloo*.
zaino[1] ADJ *caballo* chestnut; *vaca* black.
zaino[2] ADJ (*pérfido*) treacherous; *animal* unreliable, vicious; **mirar a lo** (*o de*) **~** to look sideways, look shiftily.
zainoso ADJ (*Cono Sur*) treacherous.
Zaire NM Zaire.
zaireño, -a ADJ, NM/F Zairean.
zalagarda NF (**a**) (*Mil*) (*emboscada*) ambush, trap; (*ardid*) ruse; (*escaramuza*) skirmish; (*Caza*) trap. (**b**) (*ruido*) row, din; (*riña*) noisy quarrel; (*jaleo*) shindy*, hullabaloo*.
zalamerear [1a] VI (*And, Méx*) to flatter, cajole, wheedle.
zalamería NF (*t ~s*) flattery; cajolery, wheedling. (**b**) (*cualidad*) suaveness; oiliness, soapiness*.
zalamero ☐1 ADJ (*lisonjero*) flattering; (*mimoso*) cajoling, wheedling; (*fino*) suave; (*cobista*) oily, soapy‡.
  ☐2 NM flatterer; wheedler; suave person; oily sort, soapy individual*.
zalea NF sheepskin.
zalema NF salaam, deep bow; **~s** bowing and scraping, flattering courtesies.
zalenco ADJ (*Carib*) crippled, lame.
zalenquear [1a] VI (*And*) to limp.
zamacuco, -a NM/F crafty person.
zamarra NF (*piel*) sheepskin; (*chaqueta*) sheepskin jacket, fur jacket.
zamarrazo NM (*fig*) blow; setback; nasty jolt.
zamarrear [1a] VT (**a**) (*perro*) to shake, worry.
  (**b**) (*) (*sacudir*) to shake up, knock around; (*empujar*) to shove around.
  (**c**) (*: *en discusión*) to corner, beat, squash.
  (**d**) (‡) to rob, pick the pocket of.
zamarro NM (**a**) (*piel*) sheepskin; (*chaqueta*) sheepskin jacket. (**b**) **~s** (*And, Carib*) chaps. (**c**) (*) (*rústico*) boor, yokel; (*taimado*) sly person.
zamba[1] NF (*esp LAm*) zamba (*a dance*).
zambada NF (*And*) group of half-breeds.
zambardo NM (**a**) (*Cono Sur: desmañado*) clumsy person. (**b**) (*Cono Sur*) (*desmaña*) clumsiness; (*daño*) damage, breakage. (**c**) (*Cono Sur**: *chiripa*) fluke.
zambeque (*Carib*) ☐1 ADJ silly.
  ☐2 NM (**a**) (*idiota*) idiot. (**b**) (*: *jaleo*) uproar, hullabaloo*.
zambequería NF (*Carib*) silliness.
zamberío NM (*And*) half-breeds* (*collectively*).
Zambeze NM Zambesi.
Zambia NF Zambia.
zambiano, -a ADJ, NM/F Zambian.
zambo ☐1 ADJ knock-kneed.
  ☐2 NM, **zamba**[2] NF (**a**) (*LAm*) half-breed (*of Negro and Indian parentage*). (**b**) (*And, Cono Sur: mulato*) mulatto.
zambomba NF (**a**) (*tambor*) a kind of rustic drum. (**b**) (*) **¡~!** phew!
zambombazo NM (**a**) (*estallido*) bang, explosion. (**b**) (*golpe*) blow, punch.
zambombo NM boor, yokel.

zambra NF (**a**) (*de gitanos*) gipsy festivity. (**b**) (*: *jaleo*) uproar, shindy*; commotion.

zambrate NM (*CAm*), **zambrera** NF (*Carib*) row, commotion.

zambucar [1g] VT to hide, tuck away, cover up.

zambuir [3g] VI (*And, Carib*) = **zambullir**.

zambullida NF dive, plunge; dip; ducking.

zambullir [3h] ⓵ VT (*en el agua*) to dip, plunge (*en* into); (*debajo del agua*) to duck (*en* under).

⓶ **zambullirse** VR (**a**) (*debajo del agua*) to dive, plunge (*en* into); to duck (*en* under).

(**b**) (*ocultarse*) to hide, cover o.s. up.

zambullón NM (*And, Cono Sur*) = **zambullida**.

zamorano ⓵ ADJ of Zamora.

⓶ NM, **zamorana** NF native (*o* inhabitant) of Zamora; **los ~s** the people of Zamora.

zampa NF (*Arquit*) pile.

zampabollos NMF INVAR (**a**) (*glotón*) greedy pig, glutton. (**b**) (*grosero*) coarse individual.

zampar [1a] ⓵ VT (**a**) (*ocultar*) to put away hurriedly (*en* in), whip smartly (*en* into); (*sumergir*) to dip, plunge (*en* into).

(**b**) (*arrojar*) to hurl, dash (*en* against, to); **lo zampó en el suelo** he dashed it to the floor.

(**c**) *comida* to gobble, wolf.

(**d**) (*LAm*) *golpe* to fetch, deal.

⓶ VI to gobble, eat voraciously.

⓷ **zamparse** VR (**a**) (*lanzarse*) to bump, crash, hurtle; **se zampó en medio del corro** he thrust himself roughly into the circle.

(**b**) (*fig: en fiesta etc*) to gatecrash, go along uninvited.

(**c**) **~ en** to dart into, whip into, shoot into; **pero se zampó en el cine** but he shot into the cinema.

(**d**) **~ algo** to wolf sth, tuck sth away*; **se zampó 4 porciones enteras** he wolfed 4 whole helpings.

zampatortas* NMF INVAR = **zampabollos**.

zampón* ADJ greedy.

zampoña NF panpipes.

zampuzar [1f] VT = **zambullir**; = **zampar**.

zamuro NM (*Venezuela*) turkey vulture, turkey buzzard (*US*).

zanahoria ⓵ NF carrot (*t fig*).

⓶ NM (*Cono Sur**) (*imbécil*) idiot, nitwit*; (*desmañado*) clumsy oaf; (*pobre*) poor wretch.

zanate NM (*CAm, Méx Orn*) rook.

zanca NF (**a**) (*Orn*) shank. (**b**) (*Anat hum*) shank.

zancada NF stride; **alejarse a grandes ~s** to go off with big strides, stride away; **en dos ~s** (*fig*) (*rápidamente*) in a couple of ticks; (*fácilmente*) very easily.

zancadilla NF trip; (*fig*) stratagem, trick (*to get sb out of a job*); **echar la ~ a uno** to trip sb up; (*fig*) to put the skids under sb*, scheme to get sb out.

zancadillear [1a] VT to trip (up); (*fig*) to undermine, put the skids under.

zancajear [1a] VI to rush around.

zancajo NM (**a**) (*Anat, Cos*) heel; **A no le llega a los ~s a B** A can't hold a candle to B, A is much inferior to B. (**b**) (*: *enano*) dwarf, runt.

zancajón ADJ (*Méx*) (**a**) (*alto*) tall, lanky. (**b**) (*torpe*) clumsy, misshapen.

zancarrón NM (**a**) (*Anat*) leg bone; big bone. (**b**) (*: *viejo*) old bag of bones. (**c**) (*: *maestro*) ignorant teacher.

zanco NM stilt; **estar en ~s** (*fig*) to be well up, be in a good position.

zancón ADJ (**a**) (*de piernas largas*) long-legged. (**b**) (*CAm: alto*) lanky; clumsy-looking. (**c**) (*LAm*) *vestido* too short.

zancudero NM (*CAm, Carib, Méx*) swarm of mosquitoes.

zancudo ⓵ ADJ long-legged; **ave zancuda** wader, wading bird.

⓶ NM (*LAm*) mosquito.

zanfona NF hurdy-gurdy.

zangamanga* NF trick; funny business.

zanganada NF stupid remark, silly thing (to say).

zanganear [1a] VI (**a**) (*gandulear*) to idle, loaf; (*hacer el tonto*) to fool around, waste one's time. (**b**) (*decir disparates*) to make stupid remarks.

zángano NM (**a**) (*Ent*) drone. (**b**) (*fig: gandul*) drone; idler, slacker. (**c**) (*imbécil*) idiot, fool. (**d**) (*pesado*) bore. (**e**) (*CAm, Méx*: malvado*) rogue.

zangarriana NF (**a**) (*Med*) headache, migraine; minor upset. (**b**) (*fig*) blues, depression.

zangolotear [1a] ⓵ VT (*manosear*) to keep playing with, fiddle with; (*agitar*) to shake, jiggle.

⓶ VI y **zangolotearse** VR (**a**) (*ventana etc*) to rattle, shake.

(**b**) (*persona*) to fidget; to jiggle; to fiddle about, fuss around.

zangoloteo NM fiddling; shaking, jiggling; fidgeting; rattling.

zangolotino ⓵ ADJ: **niño ~** older boy with childish habits (*o* clothes *etc*); silly child.

⓶ NM youth, lad.

zangón NM big lazy lad, lazy lump*.

zanguanga* NF fictitious illness; **hacer la ~** to swing the lead*, malinger.

zanguango* ⓵ ADJ idle, slack.

⓶ NM, **zanguanga** NF slacker, shirker; malingerer.

zanja NF (**a**) (*fosa*) ditch; (*de drenaje*) drainage channel; (*foso*) trench; (*hoyo*) pit; (*tumba*) grave; **abrir las ~s** (*Arquit*) to lay the foundations (*de* for).

(**b**) (*LAm: barranco*) gully, watercourse.

(**c**) (*And: límite*) fence, low wall.

zanjar [1a] VT (**a**) (*gen*) to ditch, trench; to dig trenches in. (**b**) (*fig*) *dificultad, problema* to get around, surmount; *desacuerdo* to resolve, clear up.

zanjón NM (**a**) (*zanja profunda*) deep ditch. (**b**) (*Carib, Cono Sur*) (*risco*) cliff; (*barranco*) gully, ravine.

zanquear [1a] ⓵ VT (*CAm, Carib, Méx*) to hunt for.

⓶ VI (**a**) (*andar mal*) to waddle; to walk awkwardly. (**b**) (*ir rápidamente*) to stride along. (**c**) (*fig*) to rush about, bustle about.

zanquilargo ADJ long-legged, leggy.

zanquivano ADJ spindly-legged.

Zanzíbar NM Zanzibar.

zapa¹ NF sharkskin; shagreen.

zapa² NF (**a**) (*pala*) spade.

(**b**) (*Mil*) sap, trench.

zapador NM sapper.

zapallada NF (**a**) (*Cono Sur*) (*chiripa*) fluke; (*suerte*) lucky break; (*conjetura*) lucky guess (*etc*). (**b**) (*And: comentario*) silly remark.

zapallo NM (**a**) (*LAm Bot*) gourd, pumpkin. (**b**) (*Cono Sur*) = **zapallada** (**a**). (**c**) (*And: gordo*) fat person. (**d**) (*And, CAm*: tonto*) dope*, fool. (**e**) (*Cono Sur‡: cabeza*) nut‡.

zapallón* ADJ (*And, Cono Sur*) chubby, fat.

zapapico NM pick, pickaxe; mattock.

zapar [1a] VTI to sap, mine.

zaparrazo NM claw, scratch.

zapata NF (**a**) boot. (**b**) (*Mec, Náut*) shoe; **~ de freno** brake shoe.

zapatazo NM (**a**) (*golpe dado con zapato*) blow with a shoe; (*caída, ruido*) thud; bump; bang; (*de pies*) stamping; pounding; (*Dep*) fierce kick, hard shot; **tratar a uno a ~s*** to treat sb very rudely. (**b**) (*Náut*) violent flapping of a sail.

zapateado NM (*gen*) tap dance; (*baile típico español*) zapateado.

zapatear [1a] ⓵ VT (**a**) (*dar golpecitos en*) to tap with one's foot.

(**b**) (*patear*) to kick, prod with one's foot.

(**c**) (*: *maltratar*) to ill-treat, treat roughly.

⓶ VI (**a**) (*dar golpecitos*) to tap with one's feet; (*bailar*) to tap-dance; (*conejo*) to thump.

(**b**) (*Náut: vela*) to flap violently.

zapatería NF (**a**) (*fabricación*) shoemaking. (**b**) (*tienda*) shoeshop; (*fábrica*) shoe factory, footwear factory.

zapatero ⓵ ADJ (**a**) shoemaking (*atr*). (**b**) *patatas etc* hard, undercooked; poor-quality.

⓶ NM shoemaker; **~ remendón**, **~ de viejo** cobbler; **~, a tus zapatos** let the cobbler stick to his last.

zapatiesta* NF set-to*, shindy*.

zapatilla NF (**a**) (*para casa*) slipper; (*de baile*) pump; (*Dep*) trainer, training shoe, running shoe; **~s de clavos** spiked shoes; **~s de deporte** sports shoes; **~s de tenis** tennis-shoes. (**b**) (*Mec*) washer, gasket.

zapato NM shoe; **~s de color** brown shoes; **~s de cordones** lace-up shoes; **~s de golf** golf shoes; **~s de goma** (*LAm*), **~s de hule** (*Méx*) tennis-shoes, gymshoes, plimsolls; **~s de plataforma** platform shoes; **~s de salón** pumps; **~s de tacones altos** high-heeled shoes; **~s de tenis** tennis-shoes; **estaban como tres en un ~** they were packed in like sardines; **meter a uno en un ~** to bring sb to heel; **saber dónde aprieta el ~** to be alive to all the difficulties, have the right feeling about a situation; to know which side one's bread is buttered; to know where somebody's weakness lies; *ver también* PANTALONES, ZAPATOS, GAFAS .

zapatón NM big shoe; (*LAm*) overshoe, galosh.

zape ⓵ INTERJ (**a**) (*a animal*) shoo! (**b**) (*sorpresa*) good gracious!

⓶ NM (‡) queer‡.

zapear [1a] ⓵ VI (*TV*) to channel-hop.

⓶ VT (**a**) *gato etc* to shoo, scare away; *persona* to shoo away, get rid of. (**b**) (*And, CAm: espiar*) to spy on, watch.

zapeo NM channel-hopping.

zaperoco* NM (*Carib*) muddle, mess.

zapote NM (*LAm Bot*) sapodilla (plum), sapota.

zapoteca NM, NMF Zapotec.

zapping ['θapin] NM INVAR channel-hopping; **hacer ~** to channel-hop.

zaque NM (**a**) (*de vino*) wineskin. (**b**) (‡: *borracho*) boozer‡, old soak‡.

zaquizamí NM (**a**) (*buhardilla*) attic, garret. (**b**) (*fig: cuartucho*) poky little room, hole; hovel.

zar NM tzar, czar.

zarabanda NF (a) (*Hist*) sarabande. (b) (*fig*) confused movement, rush, whirl. (c) (*Méx**: *paliza*) beating.

zaragata NF (a) (*: *ajetreo*) bustle, turmoil; (*jaleo*) hullabaloo*; (*riña*) row, set-to*. (b) **~s** (*Carib*) cajolery, wheedling.

zaragate NM (a) (*Cono Sur*: *malvado*) rogue, rascal; (*entrometido*) busybody. (b) (*Carib**: *zalamero*) flatterer, creep‡.

zaragatero [1] ADJ (*ruidoso*) rowdy, noisy; (*pendenciero*) quarrelsome. [2] NM rowdy, hooligan.

Zaragoza NF Saragossa.

zaragozano [1] ADJ of Saragossa. [2] NM, **zaragozana** NF native (o inhabitant) of Saragossa; **los ~s** the people of Saragossa.

zaragüelles NMPL *baggy trousers that form part of the traditional dress of Valencia and Murcia.*

zaramullo [1] ADJ (a) (*And, CAm, Carib*) (*afectado*) affected; (*engreído*) conceited; (*delicado*) finicky.
(b) (*And, Carib*: *divertido*) amusing, witty.
[2] NM (a) (*And*: *tontería*) silly thing.
(b) (*And**) (*entrometido*) busybody; (*tonto*) fool.

zaranda NF (a) (*tamiz*) sieve. (b) (*Méx*: *carrito*) wheel-barrow. (c) (*Carib*: *juguete*) spinning top; (*Mús*) horn.

zarandajas* NFPL trifles, odds and ends, little things.

zarandear [1a] [1] VT (a) (*cribar*) to sieve, sift.
(b) (*: *sacudir*) to shake vigorously to and fro, shake up, toss about; (*empujar*) to shove, jostle, push around.
(c) (*: *dar prisa a*) *persona* to keep on the go, keep hustling about.
(d) (*LAm*: *balancear*) to swing, push to and fro; (*fig*) to abuse publicly.
[2] **zarandearse** VR (a) (*prov, LAm*: *pavonearse*) to strut about.
(b) (*ir y venir*) to keep on the go, hustle about.

zarandillo NM active person, bustler; (*pey*) restless individual; (*niño*) fidget; **llevar a uno como un ~** to keep sb on the go.

zarapito NM (*t* ~ **real**) curlew.

zaraza NF printed cotton cloth, chintz.

zarazas NFPL rat poison.

zarazo ADJ (*LAm*) (a) *fruta* underripe. (b) (*: *bebido*) rather drunk, tight*.

zarcillo NM (a) (*pendiente*) earring. (b) (*Bot*) tendril. (c) (*Cono Sur, Méx Agr*) earmark.

zarco ADJ light blue.

zarigüeya NF opossum.

zarina NF tsarina.

zarista ADJ, NMF Tsarist, Czarist.

zaroche NM (*LAm*) = **soroche.**

zarpa NF (a) (*Zool*) claw, paw; **echar la ~ a** to claw at, paw; (*: *agarrar*) to grab, lay hold of. (b) (*salpicadura*) splash of mud, smear of mud.

zarpada NF clawing; blow with the paw; **dar una ~ a** to claw, scratch; to hit with its paw.

zarpar [1a] VI to weigh anchor, set sail, get under way.

zarpazo NM (a) = **zarpada.** (b) (*fig*) thud; bang, bump. (c) **dar un ~*** to beat it quick*.

zarpear [1a] VT (*CAm, Méx*) to splash with mud.

zarrapastrón* ADJ, **zarrapastroso*** ADJ shabby, dirty, rough-looking.

zarria NF (a) (*salpicadura*) splash of mud, spattering of mud, smear of mud. (b) (*harapo*) rag, tatter.

zarza NF bramble, blackberry (bush).

zarzal NM bramble patch, clump of brambles.

zarzamora NF blackberry.

zarzaparrilla NF sarsaparilla.

zarzo NM (a) (*Agr etc*) hurdle; (*para construir*) wattle. (b) (*And*: *buhardilla*) attic.

zarzuela NF (a) (*Mús*) operetta, light opera, (Spanish-style) musical comedy. (b) **~ de mariscos** (*Culin Esp*) seafood casserole. (c) (**Palacio de**) **la Z~** *royal palace in Madrid.*

┌─ ⓘ ZARZUELA ─┐

ⓘ **Zarzuelas**, named after the Zarzuela Palace where they were first performed in the 17th century for the entertainment of Philip IV, are a kind of Spanish comic folk opera. They are usually in three acts, and their chief ingredients include stock characters, traditional scenes and a mixture of dialogue, music and traditional song. After a decline in popularity in the 18th century, interest in this very Spanish genre was rekindled as part of the 19th century revival of Spanish nationalism.

---

zarzuelista NMF composer of light opera, musical-comedy writer.

zas INTERJ bang!, slap!; crash!; **le pegó un porrazo** ..., **¡~!** ... **que** ... he gave him a swipe ... bang! ... which ...; **apenas habíamos puesto la radio y** ... **¡~!** ... **se cortó la corriente** we had only just switched on the radio when ... click! ... and off went the current; **cayó ¡~! al agua** she fell right into the water.

zasca EXCL (a) bang!, crash! (b) (*como* ADV) all of a sudden.

zascandil NM (a) (*casquivano*) featherbrained person; (*poco fiable*) unreliable person; (*frívolo*) frivolous individual.
(b) (*entrometido*) busybody.

zascandilear [1a] VI (a) (*obrar sin dar resultado*) to buzz about uselessly, fuss a lot; to behave frivolously, do featherbrained things.
(b) (*entrometerse*) to pry, meddle.

zaya NF (*Carib*) whip.

zeda NF the (name of the) letter z.

zen ADJ INVAR, NM Zen.

Zenón NM Zeno.

zenzontle NM (*Cam, Méx*) mockingbird.

zepelín NM zeppelin.

zeta [1] NF the (name of the) letter z. [2] NM (*Aut*) police-car, Z-car.

Zetlandia: Islas NFPL **de ~** Shetland Isles.

ZID NF ABR *de* **zona industrializada en declive.**

zigoto NM zygote.

zigzag [1] ADJ zigzag. [2] NM, PL **zigzagues** zigzag (line *etc*); **relámpago en ~** forked lightning, chain lightning (*US*).

zigzagueante ADJ (*LAm*) zigzag (*atr*).

zigzaguear [1a] VI to zigzag.

zigzagueo NM zigzag, zigzagging movement.

Zimbabue NM, **Zimbabwe** NM Zimbabwe.

zimbabuo, -a ADJ, NM/F Zimbabwean.

zinc NM zinc.

zíngaro = **cíngaro.**

zíper NM (*Méx*) zip, zipper (*esp US*).

zipizape* NM set-to *, rumpus*; **armar un ~** to cause a rumpus; **los dos están de ~** the two of them are always squabbling.

zócalo NM (a) (*Arquit*: *pedestal*) plinth, base.
(b) (*de pared*) skirting board, baseboard (*US*); (*paneles*) panelling.
(c) (*Méx*) (*Mil*) parade ground; (*plaza*) town square; (*bulevar*) walk, boulevard; (*parque*) park.

zocato [1] ADJ (a) *fruta, legumbre* hard, rubbery; damaged. (b) *persona* left-handed.
[2] NM (*And*: *pan*) stale bread.

zoclo NM = **zueco.**

zoco[1] [1] ADJ (a) (*zurdo*) left-handed. (b) (*And*: *manco*) one-armed; (*And, Carib, Cono Sur*: *tullido*) maimed, limbless.
[2] NM (a) (*zurdo*) left-handed person. (b) (*Carib*: *tonto*) fool. (c) (*Cono Sur*: *puñetazo*) hefty punch.

zoco[2] NM (*Com*) (*Arab*) market, soq, souk.

zocotroco NM (*And, Cono Sur*) chunk, big lump; **~ de hombre*** hefty man*.

zodiaco NM, **zodíaco** NM zodiac.

zollenco ADJ (*Méx*) big and tough.

zollipar* [1a] VI to sob.

zombi NM zombie.

zona NF zone; belt, area; (*Inform*) area; **~ acuosa, ~ húmeda** wetland; **~ ancha** (*Dep*) midfield; **~ de batalla** battle zone; **~ catastrófica, ~ de desastre** disaster area; **~ común** communal area; **~ construida, ~ edificada** built-up area; **~ desnuclearizada** nuclear-free zone; **~ de ensanche** development area; **~ erógena** erogenous zone; **~ fronteriza** border area, border land; **~ de guerra** war-zone; **~ lumbar** lumbar region; **~ marginada** (*CAm*) slum area; **~ peatonal** pedestrian precinct; **~ de peligro** danger-area, danger-zone; **~ en penumbra, ~ de sombra** (*fig*) grey area; **~ de pruebas** testing-ground; **~ de tiendas** shopping centre; **~ tórrida** torrid zone; **~ verde** (*cinturón*) green belt; (*parque*) park, green area.

zonación NF zoning.

zonal ADJ zonal.

zoncear [1a] VI (*CAm, Cono Sur*) to behave stupidly.

zoncera NF (a) (*LAm*) = **zoncería.** (b) (*Cono Sur*) mere trifle; small amount; **costar una ~** to cost next to nothing; **comer una ~** to have a bite to eat.

zoncería NF silliness, stupidity; dullness; boredom, boring nature.

zonchiche NM (*CAm, Méx*) buzzard.

zonda NF (*And, Cono Sur*) hot northerly wind.

zonificar [1g] VT to divide into zones.

zonzo [1] ADJ (*esp LAm*) (*tonto*) silly, stupid; (*pesado*) boring, inane; (*Méx*) dazed, weary. [2] NM (*LAm*) idiot; bore, drag.

zonzoneco ADJ (*CAm*), **zonzoreco** ADJ (*CAm*), **zonzoreno** ADJ (*CAm*) stupid.

zoo NM zoo.

zoo... PREF zoo...

zoología NF zoology.

zoológico [1] ADJ zoological. [2] NM zoo.

zoólogo, -a NM/F zoologist.

zoom [θum] NM (*objetivo*) zoom-lens; (*toma*) zoom shot.

zoomórfico ADJ zoomorphic.
zoomorfo NM zoomorph.
zooplancton NM zooplankton.
zoo-safari NM safari park.
zope NM (*CAm*) vulture.
zopenco* [1] ADJ dull, stupid.
  [2] NM clot‡, nitwit*.
zopilote NM (*LAm*) buzzard; (*) thief.
zopilotear [1a] VT (*Méx*) to eat greedily, wolf; (*fig*) to steal.
zopo ADJ crippled, maimed.
ZOPRE NF ABR *de* **zona de promoción económica**.
zoquetada NF (*LAm*) stupidity.
zoquetazo NM (*Cono Sur, Méx*) swipe, punch.
zoquete NM (a) (*de madera*) block, piece, chunk (of wood).
  (b) (*de pan*) crust of old bread.
  (c) (*: *rechoncho*) squat person.
  (d) (*) (*zopenco*) duffer, blockhead; (*patán*) lout, oaf.
  (e) (*LAm: suciedad*) body dirt, human dirt.
  (f) (*Carib, Méx*) (*puñetazo*) punch; (*trompada*) smack in the face.
zoquetillo NM shuttlecock.
zorenco ADJ (*CAm*) stupid.
Zoroastro NM Zoroaster.
zorongo NM (*Mús*) popular song and dance of Andalusia.
zorra NF (a) (*animal*) fox; vixen. (b) (‡: *mujer*) whore, tart‡; ¡~! you slut! (c) **pillar una ~*** to get tight*.
zorral ADJ (a) (*And, CAm: molesto*) annoying. (b) (*And: obstinado*) obstinate.
zorrear* [1a] VI to be up to one's tricks again, be up to no good.
zorrera NF (a) (*madriguera*) foxhole; (*fig: cuarto*) smoky room, room with a fug. (b) (*consternación*) dismay; (*inquietud*) worry, anxiety. (c) (*modorra*) drowsiness, lethargy.
zorrería NF (a) (*cualidad*) foxiness, craftiness. (b) (*una ~*) sly trick.
zorrero ADJ foxy, crafty.
zorrillo NM (*Cono Sur*), **zorrino** NM (*Cono Sur*) skunk.
zorro [1] ADJ (a) foxy, crafty.
  (b) (‡) bloody‡; **toda la zorra noche** the whole bloody night‡; **no tengo ni zorra** (*idea*) I haven't a clue*.
  [2] NM (a) (*Zool*) fox, dog fox.
  (b) (*piel*) fox-fur, foxskin; **~ plateado** silver fox (fur).
  (c) (*fig*) (*taimado*) old fox, crafty person, rascal; (*gandul*) slacker, shirker; **hacerse el ~** to act dumb; **estar hecho un ~** to be very drowsy; **estar hecho unos ~s*** to be all in, be done up; to be in an awful state.
  (d) **~s** (*trapo*) duster.
zorrón ADJ sluttish.
zorruno ADJ foxy, fox-like.
zorrupia‡ NF tart‡, whore.
zorzal NM (a) (*Orn*) thrush. (b) (*fig*) (*listo*) shrewd person; (*taimado*) sly fellow. (c) (*Cono Sur*) (*tonto*) simpleton; (*inocente*) dupe, innocent person.
zorzalear* [1a] VI (*Cono Sur*) to sponge*.
zorzalero* ADJ (*Cono Sur*) sponging*, parasitical.
zorzalino* ADJ: **la vida zorzalina** the easy life.
zosco NM (*Carib*) idiot.
zotal NM ® disinfectant.
zote* [1] ADJ dense, dim, stupid.
  [2] NM dimwit*.
zozobra NF (a) (*Náut*) capsizing, overturning; sinking. (b) (*fig*) (*inquietud*) worry, anxiety; (*nerviosismo*) jumpiness, nervous state.
zozobrar [1a] VI (a) (*Náut*) (*peligrar*) to be in danger (of foundering); (*volcar*) to capsize, overturn; (*hundirse*) to founder, sink.
  (b) (*fig: intención, proyecto*) to fail, come to naught, collapse; (*negocio*) to be ruined.
  (c) (*fig: persona*) to be anxious, worry, fret.
zueco NM clog, wooden shoe.
zulla NF (human) excrement.
zullarse [1a] VR (*ensuciarse*) to dirty o.s.; (*ventosear*) to break wind.
zullón NM breaking wind.
zulo NM (*de armas*) cache; (*de documentos etc*) hiding-place.
zulú [1] ADJ (a) Zulu. (b) (*) thick*, stupid.
  [2] NMF (a) Zulu. (b) (*) idiot, dimwit*.
Zululandia NF Zululand.
zumaque NM sumac(h).
zumba NF (a) (*charla*) banter, chaff, teasing; humour; **dar ~ a**, **hacer ~ a** to rag, tease. (b) (*LAm: paliza*) beating. (c) (*Méx*) drunkenness.
zumbado* ADJ (a) **estar ~** to be crazy, be off one's head. **andar ~, ir ~** to be in a rush.
zumbador NM (a) (*Elec*) buzzer. (b) (*Carib, Méx Orn*) hummingbird.
zumbar [1a] [1] VT (a) *persona* to rag, tease.
  (b) (*Univ**) to plough*.
  (c) *golpe* to fetch, hit.

  (d) (*LAm*) (*lanzar*) to throw, chuck*, toss; (*expulsar*) to chuck out.
  (e) (‡: *robar*) to nick‡.
  (f) (‡̣) to fuck‡̣.
  [2] VI (a) (*insecto*) to buzz, hum, drone; (*máquina*) to hum, whirr; (*zumbador*) to buzz; (*oídos*) to hum, sing, buzz; **me zumban los oídos** I have a buzzing in my ears (*V t* **oído**).
  (b) (*: *quedar cerca*) to be very close; **no está en peligro ahora, pero le zumba** he's not actually in danger now, but it's not far away.
  [3] **zumbarse** VR (a) **~ de** to rag, tease; to poke fun at.
  (b) (*And, Carib*: marcharse*) to clear off*.
  (c) (*Carib: pasarse*) to overstep the mark.
  (d) **~ a una‡̣** to screw sb‡̣.
  (e) **~la‡̣** to wank‡̣.
zumbido NM (a) *insecto* buzz(ing), hum(ming), drone; *máquina etc* whirr(ing); **~ de oídos** buzzing in the ears, ringing in the ears. (b) (*: *puñetazo*) punch, biff*.
zumbo¹ NM (*And, CAm*) gourd, calabash.
zumbo² NM = **zumbido** (a).
zumbón [1] ADJ *persona* waggish, funny; *tono etc* teasing, bantering; (*pey*) sarcastic.
  [2] NM wag, joker, funny man; tease.
zumiento ADJ juicy.
zumo NM (a) juice; (*bebida*) juice, squash; **~ de naranja** orange squash. (b) (*fig*) (solid) profit, (real) gain.
zumoso ADJ juicy.
zuncho NM metal band, hoop.
zupia NF (a) (*heces*) dregs; (*vino*) muddy wine; (*bebistrajo*) nasty drink, evil-tasting liquid. (b) (*fig: gente*) dregs; human trash. (c) (*And*: aguardiente*) rough liquor.
ZUR NF ABR *de* **zona de urgente reindustrialización**.
zurcido NM (a) (*acto*) darning, mending. (b) (*remiendo*) darn, mend, patch.
zurcidura NF = **zurcido**.
zurcir [3b] VT (a) (*Cos*) to darn, mend, sew up. (b) (*fig*) to join, combine, put together; *mentira* to concoct, think up. (c) (‡) **¡que las zurzan!** to blazes with them!; **¡que te zurzan!** get lost!‡
zurdazo NM (*golpe*) left-handed punch; (*tiro*) left-footed shot.
zurdear [1a] VT (*LAm*) to do with the left hand.
zurdo [1] ADJ *mano* left; *persona* left-handed; **a zurdas** with the left hand, (*fig*) the wrong way, clumsily; **no es ~** (*fig*) he's no fool; **ser ~ a algo** (*Carib**) to be bad at sth.
  [2] NM, **zurda** NF (a) (*gen*) left-handed person.
  (b) (*Cono Sur Pol: pey*) lefty*, left-winger.
zurear [1a] VI (*paloma*) to coo.
zureo NM coo, cooing.
zuri‡ NM: **darse el ~** to clear out*.
zurito NM small glass (of beer).
zuro NM beard (on corn).
zurra NF (a) (*Téc*) dressing, tanning.
  (b) (*: *paliza*) tanning*, hiding*.
  (c) (*: *trabajo*) hard grind*, drudgery.
  (d) (*: *pelea*) roughhouse*.
zurrador NM tanner.
zurrapa NF (a) (*masa*) soft lump, dollop; (*mancha*) smudge, smear; (*hilo*) thread, stream (of dirt *etc*); **~s** dregs. (b) (*fig*) trash, muck, rubbish.
zurraposo ADJ full of dregs, thick, muddy.
zurrar [1a] VT (a) (*Téc*) to dress, tan.
  (b) (*: *pegar*) to tan*, wallop*, lay into*.
  (c) (*: *en discusión*) to sit heavily on*, flatten.
  (d) (*: *criticar*) to lash into, criticize ferociously.
zurria* NF (a) (*And, CAm: paliza*) tanning*, hiding*. (b) (*And: multitud*) lot, crowd, mass.
zurriaga NF whip, lash.
zurriagar [1h] VT to whip, lash.
zurriagazo NM (a) (*azote*) lash, stroke, cut.
  (b) (*fig*) (*revés*) severe blow, bad knock; (*mala suerte*) stroke of bad luck.
  (c) (*fig: trato injusto*) piece of unjust (*o* harsh) treatment.
zurriago NM whip, lash.
zurribanda* NF = **zurra** (b) *y* (d).
zurriburri* NM (a) (*confusión*) turmoil, bustle, confusion; (*lío*) mess, mix-up; (*ruido*) hubbub. (b) (*persona*) worthless individual. (c) (*pandilla*) gang; (*turba*) rabble.
zurrón NM pouch, bag.
zurullo NM, **zurullón** NM (a) (*en líquido*) lump, hard bit.
  (b) (‡̣) turd‡̣.
  (c) (*persona*) lout, hooligan.
zurumato ADJ (*Méx*) (*turulato*) light-headed, woozy*; (*estúpido*) stupid.
zurumbanco ADJ (*CAm, Méx*) (a) = **zurumato**.
  (b) (*: *medio borracho*) half-drunk, half cut*.
zurumbático ADJ: **estar ~** to be stunned, be dazed.

zurumbo ADJ (*CAm*) (**a**) = **zurumato**. (**b**) (*: *medio borracho*) fuddled, stupid with drink.

zutano, -a NM/F (Mr, Mrs *etc*) So-and-so; **si se casa fulano con zutana** if Mr X marries Miss Y; *V* **fulano**.

LANGUAGE IN USE

LENGUA Y USO

First Edition
by
Beryl T. Atkins and Hélène M. A. Lewis

New Edition
by
Teresa Álvarez García   Diana Feri   José Miguel Galván Déniz   Cordelia Lilly

Language in Use

Contents

Spanish-English

Lengua y Uso

Índice de materias

Inglés-Español

Corpus Acknowledgements

We would like to acknowledge the assistance of the many hundreds of individuals and companies who have kindly given permission for copyright material to be used in The Bank of English. The written sources include many national and regional newspapers in Britain and overseas; magazine and periodical publishers in Britain, the United States and Australia. Extensive spoken data has been provided by radio and television broadcasting companies; research workers at many universities and other institutions; and individual numerous contributors. We are grateful to them all.

Agradecimientos

Agradecemos especialmente la valiosa colaboración de los periódicos EL MUNDO y ABC, así como del Laboratorio de Lingüística Informática de la Universidad Autónoma de Madrid, en el que se realizó el 'Corpus de Referencia de la Lengua Española Contemporánea: corpus oral centro-peninsular' dirigido por el Prof. Dr. Francisco A. Marcos-Marín.

Introduction to Language in Use - New Edition

Our aim in writing Language in Use has been to help non-native speakers find fluent, natural ways of expressing themselves in the foreign language, without risk of the native-language distortion that sometimes results from literal translation.

To achieve this, we have identified a number of essential language functions, such as *agreement, suggestions* and *apologies,* and provided a wealth of examples to show typical ways of expressing them. Users can select phrases to meet their needs using either their knowledge of the foreign language alone or by looking at the translations of the key elements.

In this completely revised and updated edition of Language in Use, the authentic examples are taken from Collins vast computerized databases of modern English and Spanish. These databases consist of around 230 million English and Spanish words from a variety of modern written and spoken sources: literature, magazines, newspapers, letters, radio and television.

The fresh new layout is designed to make consultation even easier. Clear headings and subdivisions enable you to find the topic of your choice at a glance. We have given style guidance, where appropriate, so that you can be confident that the phrase you have chosen is as assertive, tentative, direct or indirect as you want it to be.

Also new, is the linking of the main dictionary text to the Language in Use section. Certain words, *suggestion,* for example, have been marked in the main dictionary to show that additional material is given in Language in Use. In these cases, the headword is underlined, an arrow symbol appears in the margin beside it and beside any relevant categories, and a footnote (**suggestion (a)** 1.1, 1.2) tells you which Language in Use section(s) to go to - in this case, sections 1.1 and 1.2 for examples relating to category (a). For added clarity, where a particular phrase within the entry is cross-referred, it is underlined. As all cross-referred words are underlined in the relevant Language in Use section, you will quickly be able to locate them there.

Since Spanish forms of address corresponding to the English *you* vary according to the formality of the relationship, we have tried to reflect this in a consistent manner. As a general rule, *tú/te* has been shown in everyday one-to-one situations where there is no evidence of formality. Where the situation or language suggests a more formal relationship, *usted/le* has been used. Where more than one person is addressed, *vosotros/as* and *ustedes/les* have been used in a similar way. Nevertheless, as usage of *tú/usted* and *vosotros/ustedes* varies depending on which variety of Spanish is being spoken and the age of the speakers, you should be prepared to make adjustments accordingly.

Lengua y Uso - Introducción a la nueva edición

Nuestro objetivo al escribir este suplemento de Lengua y Uso ha sido ayudar a los estudiantes de ambas lenguas a encontrar formas de expresarse con naturalidad en el idioma extranjero y evitar así las distorsiones que a veces resultan de una traducción literal.

Para ello, se ha analizado el acto de la comunicación partiendo de ciertas funciones del tipo *consejos, permiso* o *posibilidad,* para agrupar toda una serie de frases y expresiones bajo las secciones correspondientes. De esta manera el lector puede seleccionar la frase que le hace falta gracias tanto a sus conocimientos pasivos del idioma extranjero como a la traducción dada a su propia lengua de dichas frases.

En esta nueva edición, totalmente revisada y actualizada, hemos hecho uso de ejemplos de la lengua hablada y escrita tomados de la base de datos electrónica de la que dispone Collins para su labor lexicográfica: más de 230 millones de palabras en inglés y español, recogidas de libros, revistas, periódicos, cartas, programas de radio y televisión.

La presentación gráfica se ha renovado también para facilitar aún más la labor de consulta, mediante unos encabezamientos y subdivisiones más claros que permiten encontrar en un momento el tema buscado. Además, se da una orientación de estilo en los casos apropiados para que pueda saberse con seguridad si la frase se usa de forma más o menos directa, o en un contexto más o menos familiar etc.

Otra novedad más es la conexión del texto central del diccionario con este suplemento. En algunas entradas (como *recomendar,* por ejemplo), hay una llamada que indica que podrán verse más ejemplos relacionados con ellas en la sección correspondiente de Lengua y Uso. En estos casos, la palabra cabeza de artículo viene subrayada y a su lado y junto a la categoría gramatical o acepción correspondiente aparece una flecha, además de una nota a pie de página (**recomendar (a)** 28.1, 29.1, 40.4. 46.5) que indica en qué sección pueden encontrarse dichos ejemplos. En el caso de *recomendar,* se verán ejemplos relacionados con la acepción (a) en las secciones 28.1, 29.1, 40.4, 46.5. Algunas frases concretas que se han remitido a Lengua y Uso se verán tambien subrayadas para mayor claridad. Como además todas las palabras remitidas a este suplemento vienen subrayadas en el mismo, se las puede localizar rápidamente.

En cuanto al tratamiento de *tú* o *usted* en las frases en español y en las traducciones de este suplemento, se ha decidido usar como norma general el *tuteo,* excepto en los ejemplos de situaciones que requieren un trato más formal y por lo tanto el uso de *usted.*

1 Suggestions

1.1 Making suggestions

Using direct questions

¿**Quieres que** ponga la maceta en la ventana?	*would you like me to*
¿**Te apetece que** vayamos a verle esta tarde?	*do you <u>fancy</u> going*
¿**Por qué no** lo dejas hasta que volvamos a casa?	*<u>why</u> don't you*
¿**Y si** organizáramos una fiesta para darle una sorpresa?	*what if we*
¿**Te parece bien** que la invitemos a la fiesta?	*do you think we <u>should</u>*
¿**Qué te parece** decírselo por carta?	*what do you think about*
¿**No se te ha ocurrido que** el mejor regalo no es siempre el más caro?	*hasn't it ever occurred to you that*
¿**No cree que sería mejor** hacerlo ahora?	*mightn't it be better to*
¿**Puedo hacerle una propuesta** que quizá le parezca interesante?	*may I make a <u>suggestion</u>*

Assertively

Yo que tú no haría nada por ahora	*if I were you*
Lo que sugiero es lo siguiente: por ahora no cambiemos los planes	*what I <u>suggest</u> is that*
Lo que deberíamos hacer es no preocuparnos demasiado de los demás	*what we <u>should</u> not do is*
Propongo que busquemos ayuda profesional	*I <u>suggest</u> that*
Lo mejor sería no involucrarse en un conflicto en el que no tenemos ni arte ni parte	*it would be best not to*
No se olvide de avisarme en cuanto llegue	*don't forget to*
Yo propondría que la actual reforma de la ley se negocie buscando el consenso de todos	*I would <u>suggest</u> that*
Les sugeriría que llamaran antes por teléfono	*I would <u>advise</u> you to*
Quisiera hacer una propuesta para mejorar el servicio	*I should like to make a <u>suggestion</u> to*
Si se me permite una sugerencia, yo creo que debemos trazar un plan de actuación detallado	*if I may make a <u>suggestion</u>*

Tentatively

Sería cuestión de hacer una prueba para ver si funciona	*we/you would have to*
Si le parece bien, podemos enviárselo por correo urgente	*if you agree, we <u>could</u>*
Lo que podríamos hacer es hablar con él antes de que se marche a Italia	*what we <u>could</u> do is*
Sería mejor que el ganador del premio fuera un escritor novel	*it would be best if*
Sería buena idea aprovechar la atención que va a atraer el acontecimiento	*it would be a good idea to*
No sería mala idea levantarse un poco más temprano	*it mightn't be a bad idea to*
Quizás habría que ser un poco más firmes con ellos	*perhaps you/we <u>should</u>*
En estas circunstancias **sería muy poco aconsejable** enviar más tropas a la zona	*it would be very inadvisable to*
Sería preferible tener mejor calidad de vida para nuestra población	*it would be preferable to*
Convendría encontrar una alternativa más sencilla	*it would be <u>advisable</u> to*
Convendría que recurriera a los servicios de un especialista	*you would do well to*
Sería conveniente que acudieran a un abogado con la documentación	*it would be <u>advisable</u> for ... to*

1.2 Asking for suggestions

¿**Alguna idea**?	*any <u>ideas</u>?*
¿**Tú qué dices**?	*what do you <u>think</u>?*
¿**Cómo lo ves**?	*what do you <u>think</u>?*
¿**Tú qué harías**?	*what would you do?*
¿**Qué hacemos ahora**?	*what shall we do now?*
¿**A tí qué te parece que podemos** hacer ahora?	*what do you <u>think</u> we can*
Si se le ocurre algo ...	*if you have any <u>ideas</u>*
¿**Qué haría usted en mi lugar**?	*what would you do if you were me?*
¿**Tiene usted alguna sugerencia** al respecto?	*have you any <u>suggestions</u>?*

2 Advice

2.1 Asking for advice

¿Tú qué me aconsejas?	*what would you <u>advise</u> me to do?*
¿Tú qué harías (si estuvieras) en mi lugar?	*what would you do if you were me?*
¿Te puedo pedir un consejo?	*can I ask your <u>advice</u> about something?*
¿Tú crees que a estas alturas sirve de algo que desconvoquen la huelga?	*do you think there is any point in ... at this late stage?*
Necesito que alguien me aconseje	*I need some <u>advice</u>*
¿Qué es lo más recomendable en esta situación?	*what would be <u>advisable</u>*
Quería pedirle un consejo	*I'd like to ask your <u>advice</u> about something*
¿Usted qué me aconsejaría que hiciera?	*what would you <u>advise</u> me to*
Le agradecería que me asesorase sobre ese asunto	*I would be grateful for your <u>advice</u> on*

2.2 Giving advice

Yo que tú no haría nada por ahora	*if I were you*
Yo en tu lugar no lo dudaría	*if I were you*
Hay que tomarse las cosas con más calma	*you <u>must</u>*
Te interesa más comprar acciones de la otra empresa	*you would be better to*
Deberías mostrarte más abierto y sincero en tu relación	*you <u>should</u>*
Lo que ella debería hacer es cambiar su imagen ligeramente	*what she <u>should</u> do is*
Harías bien en visitar a un especialista	*you would do well to*
Más vale no decir nada por el momento	*it would be better or best not to*
Mi consejo es que te sinceres con ellos y les digas la verdad	*my <u>advice</u> would be to*
Habría que sopesar los pros y los contras antes de tomar una decisión definitiva	*we/you <u>ought</u> to*
Lo que habría que hacer es consultarlo con quien sepa sobre el tema	*what we/you <u>ought</u> to do is*
Lo que haría falta es que instalaran un nuevo sistema de refrigeración	*what they <u>should</u> do is*
Lo mejor que puede hacer es dirigirse a la oficina central	*the best thing you can do is*
Le recomiendo que abandone el hábito del cigarrillo si quiere mejorar su estado de salud	*I would <u>advise</u> you to*
Sería totalmente desaconsejable intervenir ahora	*it would be extremely <u>inadvisable</u> to*
Permítanme ustedes que insista en la necesidad de presionar a la compañía	*I'd like to emphasize the <u>need</u> to*
Me permito sugerirle que corrija dichos errores, para mejorar aún más si cabe la calidad de su periódico	*I should like to <u>suggest</u> that you*

More tentatively

¿Y si fueras a verle y le pidieras perdón?	*what if you*
Yo te aconsejaría un cambio de aires	*I'd <u>recommend</u>*
Quizás habría que preparar unos planes más detallados	*perhaps we <u>should</u>*
Yo le diría que fuera prudente a la hora de tomar una decisión	*I would <u>advise</u> you to*
No sería mala idea enviarlo todo exprés	*it wouldn't be a bad idea to*
Sería prudente llamar antes por teléfono, por si acaso está fuera	*it would be <u>wise</u> to*

2.3 Warnings

Os advierto que no vamos a dar ninguna información	*I should <u>warn</u> you that*
Debo advertirle que esa agencia no es de fiar	*I must <u>warn</u> you that*
Si no pides disculpas ahora, **deberás atenerte a las consecuencias**	*if you don't ... you must accept the consequences*
Corremos el riesgo de perder toda credibilidad	*we run the <u>risk</u> of*
Que sirva de advertencia: si continuáis con esa actitud, las consecuencias pueden ser nefastas	*be <u>warned</u>:*
Sería cosa de locos *or* **una locura** proseguir en estas pésimas condiciones	*it would be <u>madness</u> to*
Es necesario cambiar de rumbo **antes de que sea demasiado tarde**	*we <u>need</u> to ... before it is too late*
Es absolutamente indispensable que modifiquemos nuestra política de ventas	*it is absolutely <u>vital</u> that*

3 Offers

Using direct questions

¿Te ayudo?	can I <u>help</u> (you)?
¿Cierro la ventana?	<u>shall</u> I close
¿Quieres que vaya a recoger al niño al colegio?	would you like me to
¿Necesitas ayuda?	do you need any <u>help</u>?
¿Me dejas que te eche una mano con los preparativos?	can I lend (you) a hand with
¿Puedo ayudarle en algo?	can I do anything to <u>help</u>?
¿Me permite que le ofrezca mi colaboración de cara al proyecto?	perhaps you will allow me to <u>offer</u> some <u>help</u>

Direct offers

No te preocupes, **ya lo hacemos nosotros**	we'll do it
Si quieres te acompaño	... if you like
Puedo ir yo si no hay nadie disponible	I could go if
Déjeme que le ayude	<u>let</u> me <u>help</u> you
Estoy para lo que haga falta	I'm ready and <u>willing</u> to do whatever's needed
Estoy dispuesto a hacer todo lo que sea necesario	I'm <u>prepared</u> to
No dude en venir a mí si le surge algún problema	don't <u>hesitate</u> to come back to me if
Permítame usted por lo menos que le lleve a la estación	at least <u>let</u> me
Me tiene a su entera disposición para todo lo que necesite	I'm entirely at your <u>disposal</u>
Sería un placer poder servirle en todo lo que haga falta	it would be a <u>pleasure</u> to

4 Requests

Using direct questions

¿Me traes un vaso de agua?	<u>would</u> you fetch me
¿Me dejas tu chaqueta?	<u>can</u> I borrow
¿Quieres cambiarme el turno?	<u>would</u> you <u>mind</u>
¿Te importa echar esta carta al correo?	<u>would</u> you <u>mind</u>
¿Te puedo pedir un favor?	<u>would</u> you do me a <u>favour</u>?
¿Podría decirme qué pone en ese cartel, **por favor?**	<u>could</u> you tell me ..., please?
¿Le importaría cerrar un poco la ventana?	<u>would</u> you <u>mind</u>
¿Sería tan amable de enseñármelo usted mismo?	<u>would</u> you be so <u>kind</u> as to
¿Podría aclararme unas dudas sobre su patrimonio, **si tiene la bondad?**	<u>would</u> you <u>mind</u>

Assertively

Déjame el coche, anda, sólo por una noche	lend me the car, <u>won't</u> you
Por favor, házmelo cuanto antes	please <u>can</u> you do it for me
Sólo te pido que bajes un poco la voz	I'm only asking you to
Alcánzame las gafas, **si me haces el favor**	pass me ..., <u>will</u> you?
Haga el favor de no poner los pies en el asiento	<u>please</u> don't
Vuelva a llamar en cinco minutos, **si es tan amable**	if you don't <u>mind</u>
Le ruego que se apresure en responder	<u>please</u>

More tentatively

Si no es mucho pedir, mándame un listado de direcciones	<u>please</u> ..., if it isn't too much <u>trouble</u>
Nos vendría bien saberlo mañana, antes de la reunión	it would be good if we could
Preferiría que no lo utilizara a partir de las ocho	I would <u>rather</u> you didn't
Si no es demasiada molestia, ¿podrías comentarnos cómo es el panorama musical en tu ciudad?	if it isn't too much <u>trouble</u>, <u>could</u> you
Le agradecería que me ayudara a resolver el problema	I'd be <u>grateful</u> if you <u>would</u>

In writing

Tenga la amabilidad de presentarse en nuestras oficinas en horario laboral	<u>please</u>
Agradeceríamos su colaboración en cualquier aspecto de nuestra investigación	we should be <u>grateful</u> if you <u>would</u> help us in
Les quedaríamos muy agradecidos si se pudieran poner en contacto con nuestros representantes	we should be very <u>grateful</u> if
Tengan a bien comunicarnos la respuesta por télex	<u>please</u>

5 Comparisons

5.1 Contrasting facts

Las carreteras están **relativamente** tranquilas para esta época del año	*comparatively*
Las nuestras son producciones modestas, **comparadas con** las más "aparatosas" de otros teatros	*compared* with
En comparación con el interior del país, el clima en la costa **no es tan** extremo	in *comparison* with ... is not *so*
Si comparamos el actual estado del río **y** or **con** el anterior, podemos observar un aumento en el grado de contaminación	if we *compare* ... and or with
Los países desarrollados consumen en exceso, **mientras que** los del Tercer Mundo no llegan a cubrir las necesidades básicas	*while*

5.2 Comparing similar things

Estos dos cuadros **son igualitos**	are just the *same*
Su programa político **es igual que** el de la oposición	is the *same* *as*
En nuestras carreteras se producen **casi tantos** accidentes **como** en las de Grecia y Portugal	almost *as* many ... *as*
El paisaje es **tan** bello **como** lo describió el poeta	*as* ... *as*
García Márquez se limita a transcribir la realidad **tal como es**	just *as* or *like* it is
Ambos coches valen **exactamente lo mismo**	exactly the *same*
Ha vuelto a suceder **lo mismo que** hace unos años	the *same* thing as
Al igual que sucede en el reino animal, las plantas también luchan por su supervivencia	just *as* happens
Los dos hermanos **se parecen mucho** físicamente	are very *alike*
Las temperaturas aquí **son muy parecidas** or **similares a** las de mi tierra	are very *similar* to
Esto **equivale a** veinte horas de trabajo	is *equivalent* to

5.3 Comparing dissimilar things

Los pros **son (muchos) más que** los contras	there are (far) *more* ... *than*
En su tierra se le aprecia **(muchísimo) menos que** en el extranjero	far *less* *than*
Es aún **(mucho) más** nacionalista **que** su hermano	far *more* ... *than*
Un coche nuevo contamina **bastante menos que** uno viejo	considerably *less* *than*
Al contribuyente se le cobra **mucho menos de lo que** cuestan los servicios	much *less* *than*
Lo que diga una revista del corazón **no es lo mismo que** las manifestaciones públicas de un presidente	is not the *same* *as*
Esa canción ya **no** suena **tanto como** el año pasado	not ... *as* much *as*
No se parece en nada a su padre	he is not at all *like*
¡Hay diferencia entre este vino y el otro ...!	there's quite some *difference* between
Un modelo **se diferencia** or **distingue del** otro en el número de extras que lleva incorporados	the *difference* between ... and ... lies in
La realidad **es muy diferente** or **distinta de** lo que teníamos creído	is very *different* from

5.4 Comparing favourably

Me encuentro **muchísimo mejor** ahora que me han operado	much *better*
Este vino **es muy superior** al otro	is vastly *superior* to

5.5 Comparing unfavourably

Para muchos perder su cargo público resulta **mucho peor que** perder la dignidad	much *worse* *than*
Las posibilidades que ofrece una máquina de escribir **no tienen (ni punto de) comparación con** las prestaciones de un procesador de textos	there's (absolutely) no *comparison* between ... and
Este premio **no es tan** importante **como** el que consiguió hace unos años	is not *as* ... *as*
Como deportista, Juan **no le llega ni a la suela de los zapatos**	isn't a patch on him

5.6 Increasing and decreasing

Estos juegos **tienen cada vez más aceptación entre** los estudiantes	are becoming *more* and *more* popular with
Las desigualdades **son cada vez mayores**	are becoming greater and greater
A decir verdad, yo escribo **cada vez menos**, y acabaré sin duda por dejar de escribir	*less* and *less*
Son cada vez menos los que se casan antes de los 29 años	fewer and fewer people
Cuanto más madura un vino, **más** añejo es su sabor	the *more* ..., the *more*

6 Opinions

6.1 Asking for someone's opinion

¿Qué piensas de su actitud?	*what do you <u>think</u> of*
¿Qué te parece mi trabajo?	*what do you <u>think</u> of*
¿Crees que le gustará el regalo?	*do you <u>think</u> that*
¿Piensas que se puede estudiar en estas condiciones?	*do you <u>think</u> that*
¿Qué opina usted de la exportación de animales vivos?	*what do you <u>think</u> of or about*
¿Qué opinión tiene usted de sus compatriotas?	*what is your <u>opinion</u> of*
¿Qué opinión le merece la subida del precio de los carburantes?	*what is your <u>opinion</u> of*
¿Nos puede ofrecer su opinión sobre la liberalización del mercado?	*could you give us your <u>opinion</u> on*
Quisiera saber lo que opina sobre el informe publicado en la prensa	*I should like to know what you <u>think</u> about*
Me interesaría conocer su opinión en torno a la nueva política exterior del gobierno	*I should be interested to know your <u>opinion</u> of*

6.2 Expressing your opinion

Creo que le va a encantar tu visita	*I <u>think</u> that*
Me parece que le has caído muy bien a todos	*I <u>think</u> that*
Para ser sincero, su obra no me apasiona	*to be <u>honest</u>*
En mi opinión, fue un error no haberle contratado antes	*in my <u>opinion</u>*
A mi parecer *or* **A mi manera de ver**, las cosas se deberían hacer de otro modo	*in my <u>view</u>*
Mi opinión personal es que se debería nombrar un comité al respecto	*my personal <u>opinion</u> is that*
Yo considero que eso no es perjudicial para el sistema democrático	*it is my <u>belief</u> that*
Personalmente, creo que es un gasto innecesario	*personally, I <u>think</u> that*
Debo reconocer *or* **admitir que** nuestra posición se ha visto debilitada	*I must <u>admit</u> that*
Mi posición al respecto difiere de la suya	*my <u>position</u> on the matter*
En mi calidad de *or* **Como** Premio Nobel de la Paz, **quiero reafirmar** mi apoyo inequívoco a una solución pacífica y negociada	*as ..., I should like to reaffirm*
Si me permite que le dé mi opinión, me parece que esa oferta es un engaño	*if I may be allowed to offer my <u>opinion</u>, I <u>think</u> that*

With more conviction

Lo que es yo, no lo veo necesario	*<u>personally</u>*
Si quieres mi opinión, déjame que te diga que no tienes de qué quejarte	*if you want my <u>opinion</u>*
Si quieren que les dé mi opinión, hay necesidades más importantes en las que gastar el dinero	*if you want my <u>opinion</u>*
Tengo que decir que no me gusta nada	*I must say that*
Estoy totalmente seguro de que nos lo van a devolver	*I'm quite <u>sure</u> that*
Estoy convencida de que no cuentan con fondos suficientes	*I'm <u>convinced</u> that*
No puedo menos que pensar que es un acto deliberado	*I can't help <u>thinking</u> that*

More tentatively

Me da que no va a venir	*I <u>suspect</u> that*
Me da la sensación de que no va a dar resultado	*I have a (funny) <u>feeling</u> that*
Tengo la impresión de que algo marcha mal	*I have the <u>impression</u> that*
Supongo que es una posibilidad tan buena como cualquier otra	*I <u>suppose</u> that*
Los padres, **imagino que** también tendrán que contribuir a ello	*I <u>suppose</u> that*
Con el debido respeto, debo decirle que eso no es así	*with all due respect, I have to tell you that*

6.3 Replying without giving an opinion

No sabría decir	*I couldn't say*
Preferiría reservarme la opinión	*I would rather reserve judgement*
Es difícil dar una opinión sin conocer las circunstancias	*it's difficult to give an <u>opinion</u>*
No puedo opinar sobre un tema del que no tengo conocimiento	*I can't express an <u>opinion</u> on*
No deseamos ofrecer ninguna opinión hasta que la situación se haya aclarado	*we would rather not express an <u>opinion</u> until*
No estoy en posición de hacer declaraciones al respecto	*I'm not in a position to make a statement*
No puedo pronunciarme a favor de ninguna de las opciones	*I cannot say I am in <u>favour</u> of*
No me es posible emitir una opinión objetiva sobre este asunto	*I cannot give an objective <u>opinion</u> on*

7 Likes, dislikes and preferences

7.1 Asking people what they like

¿**Te gusta** el yogur de fresa?	do you <u>like</u>
¿**Cuál de** las tres camisas **te gusta más**?	which of ... do you <u>like</u> best?
¿**Le gustaría** viajar a otra época?	would you <u>like</u> to
De las dos posibilidades, ¿**cuál prefiere**?	which do you <u>prefer</u>?
Quería saber si prefieren salir ahora **o** después de comer	I wanted to know if you would <u>prefer</u> to ... or
¿**Podrían darme su parecer sobre** el nuevo programa?	could you give me your opinion on

7.2 Saying what you like

Me agrada que hayan venido a verme desde tan lejos	it was good of them to
A todos nos gusta que nos reconozcan un trabajo bien hecho	we all <u>like</u> it when
Me ha gustado mucho el regalo que me has enviado	I was <u>delighted</u> with the present
A mí los turistas que vienen por aquí **me caen (muy) bien**	I (really) <u>like</u> ...
Lo que más me gusta es observar a la gente	what I <u>like</u> (doing) best is
Disfruto charlando con los niños	I <u>enjoy</u>
Disfruto con sus atrevidos comentarios en televisión	I <u>enjoy</u>
Me seduce la idea de viajar a Finlandia, no sé por qué	the idea of ... really <u>appeals</u> to me
Para muchos ver la televisión **es su pasatiempo favorito**	is their <u>favourite</u> pastime
Soy muy aficionado a la danza contemporánea	I'm very <u>keen</u> on
Me encanta el mar y navegar a vela	I <u>love</u>
Me fascina observar el firmamento en una noche clara	I <u>love</u> watching
Me apasiona la luminosidad del paisaje mediterráneo	I <u>love</u>
Siento verdadera debilidad por los postres cremosos	I have a weakness for

7.3 Saying what you dislike

No me gusta comer fuera de casa	I don't <u>like</u>
Sus canciones **no son nada del otro mundo**	aren't anything to write home about
Me cuesta tener que criticarle en público	I find it hard to have to
No me gusta nada que me mientan	I don't <u>like</u> ... at all
No me resulta nada agradable ir a trabajar a estas horas de la noche	I'm not at all <u>keen</u> on
Me molesta el olor de las sardinas asadas	I find ... very <u>unpleasant</u>
Mis nuevos vecinos **me caen muy mal** or **no me caen nada bien**	I don't <u>like</u> ... at all
Le he cogido manía a ese chico	I've really taken a <u>dislike</u> to
No soporto que me hagan esperar	I can't <u>stand</u>
Lo que más me fastidia es que suban tanto el volumen	what really <u>annoys</u> me is when
Si hay algo que no aguanto es que cambien la programación sin avisar	if there's one thing I can't <u>bear</u>, it's when
Detesto cualquier tipo de violencia	I <u>hate</u>
Me horrorizan las corridas de toros	I really <u>hate</u>

7.4 Saying what you prefer

Prefiero la lectura **a** la televisión	I <u>prefer</u> ... to
Prefiero que llegues tarde **a que** no vengas	I'd <u>rather</u> you ... than
Es mejor or **preferible** hablar en el idioma del cliente	it's better to
Preferiría que nadie me acompañara	I would <u>rather</u>
Nos vendría mejor or **Nos convendría más** salir antes para evitar la hora de más tráfico	we would do better to
Tengo especial predilección por la música de Falla	I am particularly <u>fond</u> of

7.5 Expressing indifference

Vamos a esperar hasta encontrar la persona idónea, **no pasa nada porque** no haya titular durante un tiempo	it doesn't <u>matter</u> if
Me da igual or **Me da lo mismo** vivir aquí **que** allí	it's all the same to me whether ... or
Me es (completamente) indiferente que salga de presidente uno **u** otro	it makes (absolutely) no difference to me whether ... or
Si no le veo hoy **no importa**	it doesn't <u>matter</u> if
No tiene (la mayor) importancia que se demoren unos minutos	it doesn't <u>matter</u> (in the slightest) if

8 Intentions and desires

8.1 Asking what someone intends or plans to do

¿**Qué piensas hacer**? — *what do you <u>intend</u> to do?*

¿**Qué vas a hacer** con las plantas estas vacaciones? — *what are you going to do*

¿**Qué planes tienes** para la familia? — *what <u>plans</u> have you got*

¿**Qué intentas hacer**? — *what are you trying to do?*

¿**Qué esperan ustedes conseguir con** esta propuesta? — *what do you hope to <u>achieve</u> with*

Quisiera saber cómo piensa actuar en lo referente al tema que nos ocupa — *I'd like to know how you <u>intend</u> to*

8.2 Talking about intentions

Voy a tomar el tren de las siete — *I'm going to*

Pienso marcharme cuando me haya recuperado por completo — *I <u>intend</u> to*

Haremos los preparativos para la fiesta la noche antes — *we shall*

Tengo la intención de empezar una serie de conciertos para niños — *I <u>plan</u> or <u>intend</u> to*

Mi intención no es otra que explicar que la promoción de la salud es el objetivo principal de la salud pública — *my sole <u>aim</u> is to*

Me propongo alcanzar la cima en un tiempo récord — *my <u>aim</u> is to*

Tienen previsto casarse coincidiendo con las vacaciones — *they are <u>planning</u> to*

Los vecinos **tienen pensado** denunciar la situación a las autoridades — *are <u>planning</u> to*

El objetivo de la directiva **es** remodelar los estatutos del partido — *the <u>aim</u> of … is to*

El médico **está decidido a** salvar la vida del niño como sea — *is <u>determined</u> to*

Está resuelta a no dejarlo hasta que acabe — *she is <u>determined</u> not to*

La presidencia alemana **se ha planteado unos objetivos muy ambiciosos** — *has set itself some very ambitious <u>goals</u>*

Desconozco sus intenciones — *I don't know what he is <u>intending</u> to do*

8.3 Saying what you would like

Me gustaría saber qué se propone hacer como nuevo director — *I'd <u>like</u> to*

Me gustaría que el partido tuviera una actitud más realista — *I'd <u>like</u> … to*

Mi único deseo es volver a mi hogar — *all I <u>want</u> is to*

Nuestro deseo es que, de una vez por todas, se nos tome en serio — *what we <u>want</u> is for … to*

Como actriz, **me encantaría poder** trabajar con un director como él — *I'd <u>love</u> to be able to*

Ojalá no lloviera tanto para poder salir más a menudo — *if only it didn't rain*

Esperemos que todo salga bien — *let's <u>hope</u> that*

Es de esperar que las negociaciones lleguen a buen puerto — *it's to be <u>hoped</u> that*

Quisiera dedicar una canción a mi hija Gemma, que cumple mañana 12 años — *I should <u>like</u> to*

Querría que mis cuadros estuviesen colgados junto a los de los grandes maestros — *I'd <u>like</u> … to*

Desearía que se le prestara mayor atención a los desamparados — *I should <u>like</u> … to*

Sueña con llegar a ser modelo — *her <u>dream</u> is to*

8.4 Saying what you don't intend or don't want to do

No quiero que vayan a pensar otra cosa — *I don't <u>want</u> you to*

Por ahora **no me planteo** hacer una película sobre temas tan delicados — *I'm not <u>considering</u>*

Convocar elecciones anticipadas **no entraba en nuestros planes** — *was not on our agenda*

No se trata de hablar otra vez con ellos, sino de que acepten lo que hemos propuesto ya varias veces — *it's not a question of*

No desearíamos causarles molestias — *we would not <u>wish</u> to*

With more determination

No pienso hacerle caso — *I do not <u>intend</u> to*

No tenía la más mínima intención de dimitir — *he didn't have the slightest <u>intention</u> of*

Jamás haría una cosa así — *I would <u>never</u> do*

Me niego (rotundamente) a entrar en la polémica — *I (categorically) <u>refuse</u> to*

9 Permission

9.1 Asking for permission

¿Puedo pasar?	<u>may</u> I
¿Me dejas que lo use yo antes?	will you <u>let</u> me ... please?
¿Se puede aparcar aquí?	<u>can</u> I
¿Te importa si subo la tele un poco?	do you <u>mind</u> if I
¿Podría hacerle unas preguntas?	<u>could</u> I
¿Le importaría que me sentara?	would you <u>mind</u> if I
¿Les molesta que abra la ventana?	do you <u>mind</u> if I
Con su permiso vamos a cerrar el tema de una vez	... if you don't <u>mind</u>
¿Sería mucha molestia dejarlo para más tarde?	would it be an awful <u>nuisance</u> if
¿Me permite usar su teléfono?	<u>may</u> I
¿Tendrían inconveniente en que tomáramos unas fotografías?	would you <u>mind</u> if
Espero que no les importe que hagamos uso de esta información	I hope you don't <u>mind</u> if

9.2 Giving permission

¡Naturalmente que puedes ir!	of <u>course</u>
Puede escoger otro modelo, si le conviene más	you <u>can</u> (always)
Les autorizamos a que actúen como estimen más conveniente	you have our <u>permission</u> to
Tiene mi autorización para llevar a cabo el proyecto	you have my <u>authorization</u> to
No tengo ningún inconveniente en responder a sus preguntas	I don't have any <u>objection</u> to

9.3 Refusing permission

¿Es que piensas que te voy a dejar el coche? **¡Ni pensarlo**!	no way!
No puedo dejarte ir de excursión con el tiempo tan malo que hace	I <u>can't</u> <u>let</u> you
¡No consiento ese tipo de lenguage en esta casa!	I will not <u>tolerate</u>
No se puede fumar aquí	you <u>can't</u>
Me opongo a que se les permita acudir a la reunión	I am opposed to their being <u>allowed</u> to
Eso es imposible, porque no lo permite el decreto de 1983	that's impossible because ... doesn't <u>allow</u> it
Lo siento, pero no está permitido entrar si no se pertenece a la organización	I'm sorry, but you aren't <u>allowed</u> to
Le prohíbo (terminantemente) que se dirija a mí de esa manera	I absolutely <u>forbid</u> you to

9.4 Saying that permission is granted

Le dejan acostarse a la hora que quiera	he's <u>allowed</u> to
Me dijo que podía venir cuando quisiera	she said I <u>could</u>
Nuestros padres **nos dieron permiso para** organizar una fiesta	gave us <u>permission</u> to
Nos han concedido la licencia de importación	we have been <u>granted</u>
El alcohol es la única droga cuyo consumo público **está permitido**	is <u>allowed</u>
Tengo autorización para firmar en nombre del Consejo de Administración	I am <u>authorized</u> to

9.5 Saying that permission is refused

No me dejan participar en la carrera por problemas de salud	I'm not <u>allowed</u> to
Me han denegado la beca de estudios que necesitaba	I've been <u>refused</u>
No nos han otorgado la autorización necesaria	we haven't been given the necessary <u>authorization</u>
No nos está permitido hablar del tema con la prensa	we aren't <u>allowed</u> to
No estoy autorizado para hacer declaraciones de ningún tipo	I'm not <u>authorized</u> to
No tengo autorización para darles acceso a las instalaciones	I'm not <u>authorized</u> to
El médico **me ha prohibido** fumar	has <u>forbidden</u> me to
Tengo totalmente prohibido el alcohol, a causa de problemas hepáticos	I'm not <u>allowed</u>

10 Obligation

10.1   Saying what someone must do

Tenemos que levantarnos a primera hora de la mañana	*we have to*
Hagas lo que hagas, **no te olvides de** avisarme si tienes problemas	*don't forget to*
No le queda más remedio que *or* **No tiene más remedio que** soportar la afrenta con dignidad	*he has no option but to*
Me han encargado que realice esta inspección	*I've been given the job of*
En nombre del gobierno **debo** hacer la siguiente declaración: ...	*I must*
Las circunstancias políticas **me obligaron a** salir de mi país	*forced me to*
Todos **estamos obligados a** *or* **tenemos la obligación de** actuar con un gran sentido de la responsabilidad	*have a duty to*
Por razones de seguridad a bordo **nos vemos obligados a** limitar el equipaje de mano de nuestros pasajeros	*we are obliged to*
Tengo el deber de informarles de que su petición ha sido rechazada	*it is my duty to inform you that*
Aquí **hace falta que alguien** ponga un poco de orden	*what we need is someone to*
En verano **hay que** proteger la piel contra las radiaciones solares	*you must*
Para viajar a Copiapó **es preciso** atravesar desiertos de arena y riscos áridos	*you have to*
Es obligatorio que figure en el envase la fecha de elaboración	*it is compulsory for ... to*
Es esencial *or* **imprescindible** *or* **indispensable** devolver el agua al medio natural sin contaminaciones	*it is essential to*
Para que sea válida la renuncia al puesto **se requiere que** esté hecha libremente	*in order to be ... must*
La ley **estipula que hay que** superar los dieciséis años para solicitar una licencia	*stipulates that you have to*
Es un país donde **se exige que** los automóviles lleven un nivel de equipamiento y automatización muy alto	*are required to*
Se exige experiencia en ventas	*... required*
Es requisito indispensable tener cumplido el servicio militar	*it is essential to have*

10.2   Enquiring if someone is obliged to do something

¿De verdad tengo que pagar para entrar?	*do I really have to*
¿Qué debo hacer para empezar a escribir novelas?	*what must I do in order to*
¿Se necesita carnet de conducir?	*do I need*
¿Estoy obligada a atenerme a estas normas?	*do I have to*
¿Tiene un ciudadano **la obligación de** demostrar su identidad si así lo requiere la policía?	*is ... obliged to*

10.3   Saying what someone is not obliged to do

No vale *or* **merece la pena que** te molestes en acompañarme	*there's no need for ... to*
Los ciudadanos europeos **no necesitan** pedir un permiso de trabajo	*do not need to*
No hace falta que tomen las comidas en el hotel **si no quieren**	*you needn't ... if you don't want to*
No está obligada a contestar si no quiere	*you're not obliged to*
No tiene por qué aceptar una oferta que no le interesa	*there is no reason why you should*
No es obligatorio llevar el pasaporte	*it is not compulsory to*
No es necesario hacer trasbordo para ir a Barcelona	*you don't need to*
Los militares de reemplazo **no tendrán obligación de** obedecer órdenes si no están de servicio	*will not be under any obligation to*
No es indispensable que lleguemos antes de las ocho	*we don't absolutely have to*
No se sientan obligados a aceptar la propuesta de la Delegación del Gobierno	*don't feel obliged to*

10.4   Saying what someone must not do

No puedes presentarte a votar en nombre de otra persona	*you cannot*
No se puede solicitar permiso de residencia **hasta que** no se tenga un contrato de trabajo	*you cannot ... until you have*
No me hable más del tema	*would you mind not saying*
No le permito que hable a los clientes de ese modo	*I won't have you*
No tiene usted derecho a tratarme como si fuera un esclavo	*you have no right to*
Le prohíbo nombrar al director para nada	*I forbid you to*
Está prohibido pisar el césped en los parques	*you are not allowed to*
El régimen ha advertido que **no tolerará que critiquen** abiertamente al Gobierno	*it will not tolerate any ... criticism*

11.1   Agreeing with a statement

Claro que la colección más importante de bonsais es la del Palacio Imperial Japonés — *of <u>course</u>*

¡Exacto! Ahí está la raíz del problema — *<u>exactly</u>*

Naturalmente. Esa es la única forma de acabar con la corrupción política — *of <u>course</u>*

Yo también pienso lo mismo. Nuestro equipo no tiene posibilidades en el campeonato — *I <u>agree</u>*

Estoy de acuerdo contigo en lo que dices del machismo — *I <u>agree</u> with what you say about*

Por supuesto que no hay derecho a que nos traten así — *of <u>course</u>*

Todo el pueblo cree todavía hoy que está vivo. **Y puede que tengan razón** — *they may be <u>right</u>*

En eso tienes *or* **te doy toda la razón**, el emigrante trabaja mucho y nunca se queja — *you are quite <u>right</u> there*

Te entiendo perfectamente: yo he pasado por lo mismo hace años — *I know exactly what you mean*

Mi maestra **tenía razón** al decir que para ser bailarín profesional hay que ser bueno — *was <u>right</u>*

Es cierto que es un tema que nunca se ha tratado en serio — *it is <u>true</u> that*

Comprendo muy bien que es un asunto muy delicado — *I quite understand that*

Admito que estaba equivocado — *I <u>admit</u> that*

Los dos **somos del mismo parecer** *or* **de la misma opinión** — *are of the same <u>opinion</u>*

Compartimos la misma opinión *or* **el mismo punto de vista** — *we share the same <u>view</u>*

En eso coincido totalmente con usted — *I entirely <u>agree</u> with ... on that*

Estamos en completo acuerdo — *we are in complete <u>agreement</u>*

Ningún experto podrá refutar dicho principio — *no one could <u>argue</u> with*

11.2   Agreeing to a proposal

¡Me apunto! — *count me in!*

¡Claro! Podéis venir cuando queráis — *of <u>course</u>*

¡Vale! Nos vemos a las cuatro — *<u>fine</u>*

De acuerdo: publicaremos el artículo en el próximo número de la revista — *<u>agreed</u>*

Perfecto. Allí estaremos — *<u>fine</u>*

Me parece bien que le invites a cenar — *I think it's a good idea (for you) to*

Me parece una idea estupenda — *I think it's a great idea*

Tengo que reconocer *or* **admitir que la idea me gusta** — *I must <u>admit</u> that I like the idea*

Estamos conformes con el precio que piden — *we <u>agree</u> to*

Apoyaremos su propuesta ante el consejo ejecutivo — *we will <u>back</u> your proposal*

Acepto con mucho gusto su invitación a visitarle en México — *I am very pleased to <u>accept</u>*

El parlamento **está dispuesto a aceptar** la nueva ley reguladora — *is <u>willing</u> to <u>accept</u>*

La asamblea de accionistas **aprobó el plan** presentado por la junta directiva — *<u>approved</u> the plan*

Tendré en cuenta sus consejos a la hora de firmar el acuerdo — *I'll bear your advice in mind*

Quiero expresarle mi total conformidad con su plan de actuación para los próximas meses — *I should like to say that I wholeheartedly endorse*

11.3   Agreeing to a request

¡Claro, hombre! ¡Para eso están los amigos! — *of <u>course</u>! That's what friends are for!*

¿Que si puedo echar una mano mañana? **¡Por supuesto que sí!** — *of <u>course</u> I will*

Sí, mujer, **faltaría más**, úsalo cuando quieras — *but of <u>course</u>*

Bueno. Mañana estaré libre si me necesitas — *<u>fine</u>*

Las fechas que propones **me vienen bien** — *are <u>fine</u> for me*

Si me necesitas, no tienes más que avisarme — *if you need me, just let me know*

Puedes contar con nuestro apoyo — *you can <u>count on</u>*

Estaré encantado de participar en ese intercambio — *I'll be <u>delighted</u> to*

El famoso cantante **accedió a que** la prensa estuviera presente — *<u>agreed</u> to*

No tengo ningún inconveniente en que se haga público el informe judicial — *I have no <u>objection</u> to*

12 Disagreement

12.1 Disagreeing with what someone has said

¿5.000? No, **¡qué va!**, 10.000 por lo menos	*no way!*
¿Madridista yo? **¡Pero que dices, hombre!** Yo del Real Betis y nadie más	*you must be <u>joking</u>!*
Yo no lo veo así	*that's not how I see it*
¿No lo dirás en serio?	*you can't be <u>serious</u>*
En eso te equivocas *or* **estás equivocado**	*you're <u>wrong</u> there*
No estoy de acuerdo contigo en ese punto	*I <u>disagree</u> with you on*
Estamos en contra de toda clase de extremismos	*we are <u>against</u>*
No entiendo tu actitud ante el problema	*I can't <u>understand</u> your attitude*
No se trata de *or* **No es cuestión de** hacer nuevas leyes, **sino de** poner en práctica las que ya existen	*it's not a question of ... but of*
Yo personalmente me inclino por la segunda opción	*<u>personally</u>, I favour*
Sus críticas **no tienen justificación alguna**	*there is absolutely no <u>justification</u> for*
Deseo expresar mi total disconformidad con esta medida	*I should like to express my total <u>disagreement</u> with*

More tentatively

Yo opino de manera distinta	*I see it differently*
En lo que se refiere al tema de la seguridad social tengo **una opinión muy distinta** a la suya	*I take a very different view*
Siento (tener que) contradecirte *or* **llevarte la contraria, pero** las cosas son como son	*I'm sorry to (have to) <u>contradict</u> you, but*
No comparto tu opinión al respecto	*I do not <u>share</u> your view*
No coincidimos con su planteamiento	*we do not <u>agree</u> with*

12.2 Disagreeing with what someone proposes

¡Vaya ocurrencia!	*what a <u>ridiculous</u> idea!*
Me parece una idea descabellada el cambiar ahora de táctica	*I think it would be <u>madness</u> to*
No estamos dispuestos a aceptar sus planteamientos	*we are not <u>prepared</u> to accept*
Resulta (más que) discutible que sea la única solución	*it's (highly) <u>debatable</u> whether*
Me niego a votar sin estar debidamente informado	*I <u>refuse</u> to*
No podemos adherirnos a la propuesta del portavoz de la oposición	*we cannot <u>agree</u> to the proposal made by*
No podemos suscribir el ultimátum dado por la OTAN	*we cannot support*

More tentatively

No lo veo muy claro	*I'm not <u>sure</u>*
No me hace mucha gracia levantarme tan temprano	*I'm not <u>keen</u> on (the idea of)*
Lo de introducirnos en el mercado extranjero **no nos convence**	*we're not <u>keen</u> on the idea of*
Me es imposible apoyar su solicitud	*I cannot give you my <u>support</u> for*
Su plan **no nos parece factible**	*does not seem <u>feasible</u> to us*
Me temo que no me será posible aceptar su proyecto	*I'm afraid I shall not be able to*

12.3 Refusing a request

¡Ni pensarlo!	*it's out of the <u>question</u>*
No puede ser. Ya no hay tiempo para cambiar el procedimiento	*it's <u>impossible</u>*
Lo siento, pero no estamos en condiciones de aceptar su propuesta en este momento	*I'm sorry, but we are not in a position to*
Es totalmente imposible reducir el personal de la empresa	*... is out of the <u>question</u>*
No accederemos jamás a introducir la semana de 32 horas	*we shall never <u>agree</u> to*

More tentatively

Me gustaría, pero no voy a poder	*I'd like to, but I <u>can't</u>*
Lo sentimos, pero no podemos atender su petición	*we regret that we cannot <u>grant</u> your <u>request</u>*
Por desgracia *or* **Desgraciadamente, su demanda no puede ser atendida**	*unfortunately, your <u>request</u> cannot be <u>granted</u>*
Aun sintiéndolo mucho, he de negarme a hacer lo que nos piden	*I'm very sorry, but I must <u>refuse</u> to*
Lamentamos comunicarle que su petición ha sido denegada	*we are sorry to have to inform you that*

13   Approval

Y si se quieren casar, **pues muy bien**, que se casen	_fine_
¡**Así se hace**!	_well done!_
¡**Estupendo**!, por mi ahora mismo	_great!_
Me parece perfecto. Podemos empezar cuando queráis	_that seems _fine_ to me_
¡**Buena idea**! Yo también me voy a bañar	_good idea!_
No hay problema. Dame tu dirección y te lo mando por correo urgente	_no _problem__
Conforme: No tomaremos ninguna medida hasta previo aviso	_agreed_
Trato hecho	_it's a _deal__
Sigue así _or_ **por ese camino**	_carry on just as you are doing_
Has hecho bien en decírmelo	_you were right to_
Me parece muy bien que te estés tomando las cosas con tranquilidad	_I think it's _great_ that_
Me alegro mucho de que tomes un paso tan importante	_I'm so _pleased_ that_
Estoy muy contento con el rendimiento de los jugadores	_I'm very _pleased_ with_
Todos **han dado por bueno** el resultado del referéndum que se convocó el pasado mes de diciembre	_has _welcomed__

More formally

Estoy satisfecho con la decisión del organismo mundial	_I am _satisfied_ with_
Nos parece una idea excelente que haya decidido usted encargarse del asunto	_we think it is _excellent_ that_
Cualquier propuesta **será bien recibida**	_will be _welcomed__
Celebro que se hayan desmentido los rumores	_I am _delighted_ that_
Será un placer colaborar con ustedes	_I shall be _delighted_ to_

14   Disapproval

Pero ¿**qué dices**, Pedro Morán el mejor corredor del mundo?	_what are you on about?_
Sólo a tí se te ocurre una cosa así	_trust you to come up with something like that!_
¡**Menuda ocurrencia**!	_what a _ridiculous_ idea!_
¿**Cómo voy a aprobar su conducta si** va en contra de mis principios?	_how could I possibly _approve of_ such behaviour when_
Me parece fatal que la gente fume en los vagones de no fumadores	_I think it's _awful_ that_
Lo que me parece mal es que se hagan inversiones desmesuradas a costa de otras zonas mucho más necesitadas	_what I think is _wrong_ is that_
De ninguna manera deben paralizarse las obras	_under no _circumstances__
Hay capítulos que **no deberían haber sido** publicados	_should not have been_
Muchos de los encuestados **no están nada contentos con** el rumbo actual de la economía	_are _unhappy_ with_
¿**Con qué derecho se atreven a** prohibirme que hable?	_who do they think they are to_
¡**Eso no se puede tolerar**!	_this cannot be _tolerated__
No estoy dispuesto a tolerar tales afirmaciones	_I am not prepared to _put up_ with_
Es intolerable que no se haya llegado a un acuerdo definitivo todavía	_it is _intolerable_ that_
Es inconcebible que en los albores del siglo XXI se sigan produciendo este tipo de intoxicaciones	_it is _unbelievable_ that_
Todas las instituciones democráticas **condenan** la violencia	_condemn_
Deseamos protestar contra la severidad de la pena impuesta por el juez	_we should like to _protest_ against_
El gobierno **expresó su más enérgica repulsa por** el atentado cometido ayer	_expressed its strongest _condemnation_ of_

More tentatively

No estamos conformes con el tono en que se expuso el informe	_we are not _happy_ about_
Los profesores universitarios **están poco satisfechos con** las instituciones para las que trabajan	_are _unhappy_ with_
Me decepciona que no haya conseguido su objetivo todavía	_I am _disappointed_ that_
Nos disgusta el tratamiento que algunas tertulias radiofónicas dan a Cataluña y el catalán	_we are _unhappy_ about_
Es deplorable que ocurran cosas de esta naturaleza	_it is _deplorable_ that_

15 Certainty, probability, possibility and capability

15.1 Expressing certainty

Seguro que no está en casa	I'm <u>sure</u>
Está claro que lo que pretende la publicidad de estos productos es satisfacer el deseo de muchos de perder unos kilos	it is <u>obvious</u> that
Salta a la vista que no son del lugar ... por la vestimenta, digo	it's patently <u>obvious</u> that
Estoy segura de que ésa es la fecha exacta de su nacimiento	I'm <u>sure</u> that
Estamos convencidos de que los coches se roban para venderlos	we are <u>convinced</u> that
Es obvio que or **Es evidente que** se va a convertir en el principal tema de conversación en los próximos días	it is <u>clear</u> that
Por supuesto que siempre va a haber alguien que se crea eso	of <u>course</u>
La fecha de inicio **será, casi con toda** or **total seguridad**, el primer domingo de septiembre	will almost <u>certainly</u> be
Se tiene la certeza de que los secuestradores fueron como máximo tres	we know for <u>certain</u> that
Sin lugar a dudas or **Sin duda alguna**, esta nueva victoria es un gran aliciente para el equipo	without a <u>doubt</u>
No cabe la menor duda de que sus condiciones de vida eran infrahumanas	there can't be the slightest <u>doubt</u> that
Es innegable que determinadas melodías perdurarán siempre	it is <u>undeniable</u> that

15.2 Expressing probability

Aquí en este barrio **es fácil que** te atraquen	you are quite <u>likely</u> to be
Ya verás como todo sale bien	you'll see how
Seguramente se ha retrasado por el camino	... <u>probably</u> ...
Debe (de) haberse olvidado de su compromiso	he <u>must</u> have
Lo más seguro or **probable es que** esa no fuera su verdadera intención	... <u>probably</u> ...
Es muy posible or **probable que** lleguemos a nuestro destino dentro del horario previsto	it seems very <u>likely</u> that
(Muy) posiblemente or **probablemente** se trate de una falsa alarma	... (very) <u>probably</u> ...
Parece ser que la autoridad monetaria podría tomar la decisión de subir los tipos de interés el próximo día 23	it <u>seems</u> that
No sería de extrañar que or **No sería extraño que** los animales fueran al final los más perjudicados	it wouldn't be <u>surprising</u> if
No me sorprendería que el ciclista francés ganara la etapa de hoy	I shouldn't be <u>surprised</u> if
Según la agencia meteorológica, **hay muchas** or **grandes posibilidades de que** se produzcan nuevas erupciones	it is very <u>likely</u> that
Todavía tiene mucha or **una buena chance de** ganar la carrera (LAm)	he still has a good <u>chance</u> of
Todo lleva a suponer or **Todo parece indicar que** las rupturas matrimoniales seguirán en aumento	all the <u>indications</u> are that

15.3 Expressing possibility

Igual no tengo suerte y suspendo	I <u>may</u>
A lo mejor hago escala en Tenerife de camino a Montevideo	<u>maybe</u>
Quizá(s) tengamos que volver antes de lo previsto	<u>perhaps</u>
Tal vez nuestras sospechas son infundadas	<u>perhaps</u>
Puede que la situación se convierta en irreversible	... <u>may</u>
Dicho comando **podría ser** el autor de diversos atentados terroristas cometidos en la región desde octubre	<u>could</u> be
Siempre existe la posibilidad de que el nivel de precios aumente	there's always the <u>possibility</u> that
Cabe la posibilidad de que los afectados hayan bebido agua contaminada	it is <u>possible</u> that
Cabe pensar que el error haya sido a propósito	it is <u>possible</u> that

15.4 Expressing capability

¿**Sabes** escribir a máquina?	<u>can</u> you
¿**Sabes** usar el nuevo procesador de textos?	do you <u>know</u> how to
Hablo francés y **entiendo** el italiano	I <u>can</u> speak ... I <u>can</u> understand
Puedo invertir hasta trece millones en las obras	I <u>can</u>
Se exigen **conocimientos básicos de** mecánica	a basic <u>knowledge</u> of
El niño **tiene aptitudes para** la física y las matemáticas	has an <u>aptitude</u> for
El ser humano **tiene la capacidad del** raciocinio	has the <u>capacity</u> for

16 Doubt, improbability, impossibility and incapability

16.1 Expressing doubt

No sé si debemos discutir ese tema ahora	I don't _know_ whether
No estoy seguro de cuáles son sus condiciones	I'm not _sure_ what ... are
No es seguro que el viaje de vuelta sea en el mismo tren	it isn't _certain_ that
No está claro quién va a salir más perjudicado de la situación	it isn't _clear_ who
No tengo muy claro que sirva de algo el que vayamos a la huelga	I'm not very _sure_ that
Me pregunto si realmente merece la pena trabajar fuera	I _wonder_ whether
No estoy (plenamente) convencido de que su propuesta sea la solución más acertada	I'm not (entirely) _convinced_ that
Dudo que vuelva a haber otra oferta similar	I _doubt_ whether
Todavía quedan dudas sobre las circunstancias en que acontecieron los hechos	_doubts_ still remain about
No hay ninguna seguridad de que el proyecto esté finalizado el mes que viene	we cannot be _certain_ that
Ya veremos si conviene o no meterse en ese tipo de aventuras	we shall see in due course whether
No se sabe con certeza si es una enfermedad hereditaria	no one knows for _certain_ whether

16.2 Expressing improbability

Es difícil que el número uno español participe en el campeonato el próximo año	... is _unlikely_ to
Dudo mucho que el cambio se traduzca en una mejora de la calidad	I very much _doubt_ whether
Es bastante dudoso que se convoque el referéndum	it is rather _doubtful_ whether
No parece que vaya a hacer buen tiempo	it doesn't _look_ as if
Me extrañaría _or_ **Me sorprendería (mucho) que** la fruta madurara en esas condiciones	I should be (very) _surprised_ if
Es (muy) poco probable que una subida de las multas se traduzca en un descenso del número de infracciones	... is (very) _unlikely_ to
No parece muy probable que se logre desarrollar una vacuna eficaz	it doesn't seem very _likely_ that
Es (muy/bastante) improbable que ocurra un accidente en una central nuclear moderna	... is (very/pretty) _unlikely_ to
Quien pierde su empleo **cada vez tiene menos probabilidades de** encontrar uno nuevo a corto plazo	has less and less _chance_ of

16.3 Expressing impossibility

No, no estuve en París. **¡Qué más quisiera yo!**	_chance_ would be a fine thing!
A estas horas **no puede ser** el cartero	it _can't_ be
No es posible que se trate de la misma persona	it _can't_ be
Es totalmente _or_ **completamente imposible que** la vegetación crezca en unas condiciones tan adversas	... _can't_ _possibly_
Me resulta (materialmente) imposible despedirme de todos en persona	it would be (physically) _impossible_ for me to
El camino de la negociación **tiene escasas posibilidades de** éxito	has very little _chance_ of
No hay _or_ **No existe ninguna posibilidad de que** los sindicatos lleguen a un acuerdo con el gobierno en tan poco tiempo	there isn't the slightest _chance_ of
Me es imposible llamarle hasta mañana	I _can't_
No parece factible que el delantero uruguayo vaya a fichar por el Barcelona	it doesn't _seem_ feasible that
Se ha demostrado que el plan de regulación del tráfico **es poco viable**	is not very _practicable_

16.4 Expressing incapability

No veo nada desde aquí	I _can't_ see anything
No sé cómo explicar lo que vi	I _can't_ explain
Apenas se podía uno mover de la cantidad de gente que había	one _could_ hardly
Muchos industriales de nuestro país **no se sienten capaces de** competir de igual a igual con los extranjeros	feel _incapable_ of
Yo soy (totalmente) incapaz de montar escenas en público porque soy muy pudorosa	I am (quite) _incapable_ of
Este chico **no sirve para** este trabajo	is no _good_ at
Carece de las aptitudes necesarias para una misión de tal envergadura	he hasn't the necessary _aptitude_ for
Muy a menudo la policía **se ve imposibilitada para** actuar con una mayor efectividad	find themselves _unable_ to

17 Explanations

17.1 Emphasizing the reason for something

Tuvimos que marcharnos **porque** se puso a llover	*because*
Como tardabas en llegar, decidimos irnos	*as*
Las plantas se han marchitado **por** exceso de riego	*due to*
Tiene 10.000 acciones **gracias a** los ahorros de toda la vida	*thanks to*
Con la nevada que ha caído no hay correo	*what with*
Es que llevamos tanto tiempo agarrados al kalashnikov que no podemos soltarlo fácilmente	*it's just that*
Ha tenido muy mala suerte. **Por eso** le tengo tanta lástima	*that's <u>why</u>*
Habla tan bajo que a menudo parece que susurrara. **Por eso mismo** le aconsejaron que interviniera lo menos posible en mítines populares	*that's <u>why</u>*
El fenómeno **tiene muchísimo que ver con** las nuevas formas de vida que aíslan cada vez más al hombre de la ciudad	*has a great deal to do with*
No toleraba flores junto a ella **por miedo a que** la intoxicaran	*for <u>fear</u> that*
No es la religión **la causa de** tanta guerra	*it is not ... that <u>causes</u>*
En vista de que el fuego había provocado una densa humareda, se decidió la evacuación del recinto	*seeing that*

More formally

El problema es grave, **ya que** el consumo anual es mayor que la producción	*for*
Se recomienda ir pronto, **puesto que** se forman colas importantes	*since*
La cuantía de las donaciones no era demasiado elevada, **pues** únicamente había monedas de bajo valor	*as*
La evacuación del edificio se vio dificultada **a causa del** bloqueo de una de las salidas de emergencia	*because of*
En todo el mundo se ha desencadenado una gran competencia por las áreas de pesca. **Por este motivo** han surgido grandes problemas	*for this <u>reason</u>*
El absentismo entre los eurodiputados es muy preocupante, **dado que** el Parlamento europeo toma cada vez más decisiones	*given that*
Por razones de seguridad, aparcamos el automóvil lejos de la casa	*for ... <u>reasons</u>*
Sus motivos para abrir una nueva oficina **son** de orden económico	*his reasons for ... are*
La capital se hallaba ayer prácticamente paralizada **a consecuencia de** la huelga general	*as a <u>result</u> of*
Como consecuencia de la crisis económica, las ventas se redujeron en un porcentaje considerable	*as a <u>result</u> of*
Como resultado de las acciones emprendidas, los trabajadores lograron parte de sus reivindicaciones	*as a <u>result</u> of*
Debido a condiciones meteorológicas adversas, nos vemos obligados a suspender la celebración anunciada	*owing to*
Los problemas de suciedad en la zona **se deben a** una mala gestión municipal	*are <u>due</u> to*
La falta de lluvias **ha ocasionado** una grave sequía al sur del país	*has <u>caused</u>*
Su especial percepción de la atmósfera parisina **arranca de** una infancia llena de vivencias	*dates back to*
Dicha teoría sostiene que la evolución **resulta de** una interacción entre la variación y la selección	*is a <u>result</u> of*
El descenso de la competitividad **procede principalmente de** los elevados costes y del declive de la productividad	*is mainly <u>due</u> to*
La fuerza de esta poesía **radica en** su brillante capacidad verbal	*lies in*
Ocurre que a veces a algunos les da por hablar en un tono ofensivo	*what happens is that*
La explosión, **provocada por** una bomba, ha causado un alto número de heridos	*which was <u>caused</u> by*
Yo personalmente **lo atribuyo a** un error del conductor	*I <u>attribute</u> it to*

17.2 Emphasizing the result of something

No quería ir con el estómago vacío, **así que** me preparé un sandwich previo	*<u>so</u>*
Me atrae **tanto** lo que hago **que** no me merece la pena restarle tiempo para dedicarlo a otras cosas	*<u>so</u> much that*
Salieron temprano, **de modo que** cuando él llegó se encontró la casa vacía	*<u>so</u> that*
El recuerdo del hambre infantil le marcó **de tal manera que** siempre devoraba grandes cantidades de pan	*in such a way that*
No fabrican anticuerpos **y por lo tanto** no pueden inmunizarse contra los parásitos y los virus	*and <u>therefore</u>*

18 Apologies

18.1   Apologizing

Perdona, me había olvidado de tí — *I'm _sorry_*
Perdona que no avisara con tiempo suficiente — *I'm _sorry_*
No consigo acordarme del autor. **Lo siento** — *I'm _sorry_*
Siento mucho no haber podido conseguir la información — *I'm so _sorry_ that I wasn't able to*
Pido perdón a la familia **por** lo que hicimos — *I ask ... to _forgive_*
Cualquiera que se atreva a hacer una cosa así es, **con perdón**, un perfecto imbécil — *if you'll _forgive_ me for saying so*
Lo lamento. A veces me cuesta reprimirme — *I am very _sorry_*

More formally

El escritor **pidió disculpas por** su ausencia en el acto inaugural — *_apologized_ for*
En cualquier caso **acepte mis disculpas, por favor** — *please accept my _apologies_*
Disculpen si les he causado alguna molestia — *I _apologize_ if*
Rogamos disculpen las molestias que esta deficiencia pueda causarles — *we _apologize_ for any _inconvenience_ that*

Espero que el avisado lector **excuse** estas generalidades que seguramente conoce — *I hope that ... will _excuse_*
Espero dispensen lo ocurrido — *I hope you'll _forgive_ us/me for this _unfortunate_ incident*

Lamentamos profundamente que haya ocurrido este incidente — *we are very _sorry_ that*

18.2   Apologizing for being unable to do something

Por desgracia la empresa **no puede** atender su petición en estos instantes — *_unfortunately_ or I'm _afraid_ ... is unable to*
Sentimos comunicarle que a partir de la fecha dejaremos de abonar el importe correspondiente al seguro de las pólizas — *we _regret_ to inform you that*
Desgraciadamente or **Lamentablemente, nos es imposible** aceptar su propuesta — *_unfortunately_, we are unable to*
Muy a nuestro pesar nos vemos obligados a prescindir de sus servicios a partir de hoy — *we very much _regret_ that we are obliged to*

18.3   Admitting responsibility

Es culpa mía. Me lo he buscado — *it's my _fault_*
Reconozco que estaba equivocado — *I _admit_ I was _wrong_*
Sé que mis palabras de anoche **no tienen perdón** — *I know that ... was _unforgivable_*
Debo confesar que el error **fue culpa mía** — *I must _confess_ that ... was my _fault_*
Me responsabilizo plenamente de lo ocurrido — *I take full _responsibility_ for*
Admitimos que existen defectos en la organización — *we _admit_ that*
Asumimos plenamente nuestra responsabilidad — *we fully accept our _responsibility_*

18.4   Disclaiming responsibility

De verdad que **no lo hice a posta** — *I didn't do it on _purpose_*
Ha sido sin querer — *it was an _accident_*
Lo dijeron sin mala intención — *they didn't _mean_ any _harm_*
No era mi intención ofenderle: hablaba en broma — *I didn't _mean_ to _offend_ you*
Pensé que hacía bien en dirigirme a ellos directamente — *I thought I was doing the right thing in*
Teníamos entendido que ellos estaban de acuerdo — *we thought that*
Habría querido actuar de otro modo, **pero no tenía otra salida** — *but I had no _alternative_*
Espero que comprenda usted lo difícil de nuestra situación — *I hope you will understand*

18.5   Replying to an apology

No pasa nada, hombre: si se ha roto me compro otro y ya está — *don't _worry_ about it*
No te preocupes. ¿Qué culpa tienes tú? — *don't _worry_*
Fue un lapsus: **no se hable más** — *we won't say any more about it*
No importa, ya lo sabíamos — *it doesn't _matter_*
No te guardo (ningún) rencor — *I don't bear you any grudge*
No es ninguna molestia — *it's no _trouble_*
El retraso **no tiene (ninguna) importancia** — *is of no _importance_*
Aceptamos de buen grado sus disculpas — *we are happy to accept your _apologies_*

Julia Guedes Tola
Paseo Buenos Aires 141, 5° A
07052 Alicante   12 de julio, 1996

Sr. Director Gerente
INFOCOMP, Sistemas informáticos
C/ Primero de Mayo 73, 1°
46002 VALENCIA

Muy Señor mío:

Me dirijo a usted para solicitar el puesto de Director de ventas
anunciado en EL PAÍS el día 9 de este mes.

Como podrá ver en la copia del currículum vitae que adjunto, tengo
considerable experiencia en el sector comercial, además de numerosas
relaciones con empresas de la zona, sin duda de gran utilidad para un
puesto como el que solicito.

Adjunto también toda la documentación justificativa que se exige.

Quedo a su disposición para cualquier aclaración que necesite y le
agradezco la atención prestada.

Atentamente,

Julia Guedes

CURRICULUM VITAE

NOMBRE Y APELLIDOS	**Julia Guedes Tola**
DOMICILIO	Paseo Buenos Aires 141, 5° A
	07052 Alicante
TELÉFONO	(965) 93 15 58
FECHA DE NACIMIENTO	5 de septiembre de 1966
ESTADO CIVIL	soltera

ESTUDIOS [1]

1984-89 :	Licenciatura en Ciencias Empresariales, Universidad de Valencia
1988 marzo-junio :	Universidad de Dublín, intercambio Erasmus
1983-84 :	COU, Instituto Salzillo, Murcia

EXPERIENCIA PROFESIONAL

Desde mayo 1994 :	Directora de Ventas, ELECTRÓNICA COSTA BLANCA, Alicante
Febrero 1990 - marzo 1994 :	Encargada de Administración, Agencia de Publicidad PLENA PLANA, Castellón
Veranos 1988 y 1989 :	Profesora de matemáticas, Academia ESTUDIOS, Alcoy
Enero - marzo 1989 :	Prácticas laborales en INTER-CHIP, Valencia

INFORMACIÓN COMPLEMENTARIA

Idiomas: inglés, uso habitual en el entorno laboral. Numerosos contactos
empresariales en toda la Costa Blanca. Asesoramiento empresarial ofrecido con
regularidad a pequeñas y medianas empresas de la industria turística. Destreza
en el uso y aprovechamiento de recursos informáticos en la empresa.

[1] People with British, American or other qualifications applying for jobs in Spanish-speaking countries might use some form of wording to explain their qualifications such as *"equivalente al bachillerato superior español/mejicano"* etc. (3 A-levels), *"equivalente a una licenciatura en Letras/Ciencias"* etc. (B.A. B.Sc. etc) etc. Alternatively, *"Licenciado en Lenguas Clásicas"* etc. might be used.

19.1 Starting your letter

En referencia al anuncio publicado en la edición de hoy de La Gaceta,
le agradecería que me enviara los datos y la documentación pertinente
al puesto anunciado
with reference to your advertisement in ..., I should be grateful if you would send me details of

En respuesta a su anuncio de hoy en Noticias, **les agradecería que me considerasen para el puesto de** jefe de ventas
in response to your advertisement in today's ..., I should be grateful if you would consider me for the position of

Me permito enviarles mis detalles para que los tomen en consideración
en el caso de que necesiten los servicios de alguien con mis cualificaciones/mi experiencia
I am writing to you with my particulars in the hope that you may consider them

19.2 Detailing your experience and giving your reasons for applying

Soy licenciado en Ciencias de la Información y llevo seis meses trabajando en la redacción de un periódico local, **donde estoy al cargo de** la sección de sucesos
I have a degree in Media Studies and for the last six months have been working on ... where I am in charge of

Tengo dos años de experiencia como auxiliar administrativo **en** una empresa de importación-exportación
I have two years' experience as ... in

Además del inglés, mi lengua materna, **hablo español con fluidez** or **soltura, tengo conocimientos de francés y entiendo el italiano escrito**
I speak Spanish fluently, have a working knowledge of French, and can understand written Italian

Aunque no tengo experiencia previa en este tipo de trabajo, **he desempeñado otros trabajos eventuales durante las vacaciones de verano.** Si lo desean, puedo darles los nombres de las entidades en las que he estado empleado
although I have no previous experience of ..., I have had other holiday jobs

Mi sueldo actual es de ... ptas **al año, e incluye cuatro semanas de vacaciones remuneradas**
my current salary is ... a year, with four weeks paid holiday

Desearía trabajar en su país durante algún tiempo **con objeto de perfeccionar mis conocimientos de español y adquirir experiencia en** el sector hotelero
I should like to work in your country ... so as to improve my Spanish and gain experience in

He terminado recientemente mis estudios de Filología Hispánica y **estoy muy interesado en usar mis conocimientos de español dentro de un entorno laboral**
I am very keen to use my Spanish in a work environment

Tengo extremo interés en trabajar con una empresa de su prestigio
I should very much like to work for

19.3 Closing the letter

Estoy a su entera disposición para ofrecerles cualquier información complementaria que necesiten
I should be happy to supply any further information that you may need

Podría incorporarme a su empresa a partir de primeros de junio
I would be available for work from

Tendré mucho gusto en entrevistarme con ustedes cuando lo consideren conveniente
I should be delighted to attend for interview

Le agradezco la atención prestada y quedo a la espera de su respuesta
thanking you for your kind attention, I look forward to hearing from you

19.4 Asking for and giving references

Le ruego se sirva comunicarnos cuánto tiempo lleva trabajando la Sra. Fernández en su empresa, cuáles eran sus responsabilidades **y qué opinión le merece su capacidad profesional para el puesto que solicita. Trataremos su respuesta con la mayor reserva y confidencialidad**
please would you let us know ... what you think of her suitability for the post that she has applied for. We shall treat your reply in the strictest confidence

Durante los cinco años que la Sra. Díaz **ha trabajado en nuestra empresa, siempre ha demostrado** gran constancia, sentido de la responsabilidad y capacidad de organización. **No dudo en recomendarla para el puesto mencionado**
in the five years ... has worked for us, she has shown ... I have no hesitation in recommending her for the post in question

19.5 Accepting and refusing

Acudiré con mucho gusto a sus oficinas de la calle Rato **para una entrevista** el próximo día 15 de octubre a las 10 de la mañana
I shall be delighted to attend for interview at your offices

Deseo confirmar mi aceptación del puesto que me han ofrecido y la fecha de mi incorporación al mismo
I am writing to confirm my acceptance of the post

Antes de tomar una decisión, les agradecería que discutiéramos algunos puntos de su oferta
before coming to a decision, I should be grateful if we could discuss a few points

Tras considerarla detenidamente, lamento tener que rechazar su oferta de trabajo
after much consideration, I am sorry to have to decline

TODOLIBRO S.A.
EDITORES – DISTRIBUIDORES
Av. del Guadalquivir, 144 - 41005 Sevilla
Tel (954) 34 34 90 - Fax (954) 34 00 39

West Distribution Services Ltd   Sevilla, 12 de octubre de 1995
14 St David's Place
Birmingham B12 5TS

Estimados señores:

Acusamos recibo de su carta del 20 de septiembre, en la que nos sugieren la posibilidad de que su representante el Sr. John Kirk nos visite en Sevilla aprovechando su próximo viaje por España, al objeto de establecer una relación más estrecha entre nuestras respectivas casas.

Tendremos, naturalmente, mucho gusto en recibirle y en principio sugerimos la fecha del lunes 23 de octubre para nuestro primer contacto, que podría tener lugar en nuestras oficinas a las 10 de la mañana.

Sin otro particular, quedamos a la espera de sus noticias.

Atentamente,

J. J. Rodríguez

Juan José Rodriguez
Director Comercial

Calzados la Mallorquina
Casa fundada en 1928

Carretera de la Finca, s/n - 07034 Palma de Mallorca - Teléfono (971) 100303

Palma, 2 de marzo de 1996

Dña Ana Hernández
Import-Export. S.A.
Mellado 38
28034 Madrid

Estimada Sra. Hernández,

Con referencia a su carta del 20-2-96, sobre la liquidación de nuestra factura núm 86-109876, le informo que aún existe un saldo pendiente de 120.000 ptas., debido al parecer a que han deducido una nota de crédito por dicha cantidad de la que no tenemos conocimiento.

Sin duda se trata de un error fácilmente subsanable, por lo que le rogamos que revisen sus cálculos con el fin de aclarar su cuenta y podamos continuar nuestras transacciones como de costumbre.

Reciba un atento saludo,

Andrés Carbonell

Andrés Carbonell
Jefe de Ventas

20.1 Enquiries

Hemos visto en el último número de nuestro boletín industrial **su oferta especial en** artículos de oficina

having seen your special offer on ... in the last issue of

Les agradeceríamos que nos enviaran información más detallada sobre los productos que anuncian, **incluyendo descuentos por pedidos al por mayor, forma de pago y fechas de entrega**

we should be grateful if you would send us details of ..., including wholesale discounts, payment terms and delivery times

20.2 ... and replies

Acusamos recibo de su carta con fecha de 10 de febrero, **interesándose por** nuestros equipos. **Adjunto encontrará** nuestro catálogo general y lista de precios en vigor

thank you for your letter of ..., inquiring about .... Please find enclosed

En respuesta a su consulta del 20 del corriente, **nos complace enviarle los detalles que nos solicitaba**

in reply to your inquiry of ..., we are pleased to send you the information you requested

20.3 Orders

Les rogamos nos envíen por avión los siguientes artículos a la mayor brevedad

please send us the following items by airmail as soon as possible

Les agradeceríamos que tomaran nota de nuestro pedido núm. 1.443 **y nos confirmen su aceptación a vuelta de correo**

we should be grateful if you would note our order ... and confirm acceptance by return of post

Adjunta le remitimos nota de pedido núm. 8.493, **que esperamos se sirva cumplimentar con la mayor urgencia**

please find enclosed order no ..., which we hope can be executed with all possible speed

Tengan la amabilidad de efectuar la entrega dentro del plazo especificado. De no ser así nos reservamos el derecho a rechazar la mercancía

please ensure that delivery is within the specified time. Otherwise, we must reserve the right to refuse the merchandise

20.4 ... and replies

Acusamos recibo de su pedido núm. 7721

we acknowledge receipt of your order no.

Le agradecemos su pedido con fecha del 3 de septiembre, **al que daremos salida** tan pronto como nos sea posible

thank you for your order of ..., which we will dispatch

La entrega se efectuará en un plazo no superior a veinte días

you should allow 20 days for delivery

20.5 Deliveries

Efectuaremos entrega de los productos en cuanto recibamos sus instrucciones

orders will be dispatched as soon as

No nos responsabilizamos de los daños que la mercancía pueda sufrir en tránsito

we cannot accept responsibility for goods damaged in transit

Sírvanse enviar acuse de recibo

please confirm receipt

Le informamos que **la mercancía ha sido despachada según lo acordado**

the goods were dispatched as agreed

20.6 Payments

Cumpliendo su encargo, **le remitimos adjunta factura por valor de** 35.000 ptas, **con vencimiento a** diez días **vista**

please find enclosed our invoice for the sum of .... Payment is due within ... of receipt

El importe total se eleva a 320.700 ptas

the final total amounts to

Sírvase remitirnos el pago a vuelta de correo

please send payment by return

Adjuntamos cheque por valor de 356.000 ptas **en liquidación de su factura**

please find enclosed our cheque for the sum of ... in settlement of your invoice

20.7 Complaints

Les comunicamos que no hemos recibido nuestro pedido del 4 de julio dentro del plazo acordado. Les rogamos que hagan las indagaciones pertinentes

please note that we have not received our order of ... within the agreed time

Nos permitimos recordarle que estamos a la espera del pago de nuestra factura núm. 43.809, **cuyo plazo venció** el 2 del corriente. Le rogamos se ponga en contacto con nosotros a la mayor brevedad

we should like to remind you that we are awaiting payment for invoice no. ... which fell due on

Hemos apreciado un error de suma en su factura núm. 7.787, por lo que les rogamos se sirvan remitirnos rectificación

we have found an addition error in invoice

Santander, 10 de marzo de 1996

Querido César:

Recibí la carta que nos escribiste hace unos meses. Siento no haberte contestado hasta ahora, aunque ya te imaginarás que no se debe a que no nos hayamos acordado de tí, simplemente hemos estado demasiado ocupados con el traslado.

Tanto Rosa como yo tenemos recuerdos muy agradables de la temporada que pasamos en tu casa de Puebla. En realidad, el objeto principal de esta carta es invitarte a pasar unas semanas con nosotros este verano. Sabemos lo mucho que te gustaría visitar nuestra tierra y en estas fechas nosotros vamos a poder respirar por fin tras unos meses de intensa actividad.

Espero que te encuentres bien y que podamos verte pronto.

Un saludo muy afectuoso de Rosa y un abrazo de

José

Liverpool, 5 de noviembre de 1996

Sra. Dña. Agustina Martos
Dpto de Historia Moderna
Facultad de Filosofía y Letras
Universidad de Salamanca
C/ Fray Luís de León
37002 SALAMANCA
Spain

Estimada señora,

Me dirijo a usted para solicitarle su inestimable colaboración sobre un tema del que tengo entendido que es una gran experta.

Estoy realizando una investigación sobre el comercio durante el reinado de los Reyes Católicos para una futura tesis doctoral y tenía pensado pasar unos meses en España para estudiar el asunto con detenimiento a partir de las fuentes. Un amigo me recomendó que me pusiera en contacto con usted, de ahí esta carta.

En principio mi idea era visitar el Archivo de Simancas, pero antes quisiera saber su opinión; si me aconseja que empiece mis investigaciones en otros archivos o bibliotecas y si debería realizar algún trámite previo para acceder a los mismos.

A pesar de llevar poco tiempo estudiando este periodo de la historia, ha llegado ya a apasionarme y, si no es inconveniente, le estaría inmensamente agradecido si me permitiera visitarla en algún momento de mi viaje a España.

Una vez más, le agradezco de antemano cualquier ayuda que pueda prestarme.

Atentamente,

J. Hamilton

When the recipient is not personally known to you

Muy señor mío: (*esp Sp*)	Reciba un respetuoso saludo de	More formal
Distinguido señor: Distinguida señora:		
Estimado señor: Estimada señora:	Atentamente Le saluda(n)[1] atentamente	[1] *if the signatory is more than one person*

When the person is known to you (fairly formal)

Estimado señor (García): [1]	Reciba un cordial saludo de	[1] *the forms Sr., Sra., Srta. can be used before the surname*
Estimada señorita (González): [1]		
Estimado colega:	Un cordial saludo	
Estimada Carmen:		

(fairly informal)

Mi apreciado amigo:	Afectuosamente
Mi apreciada amiga:	
Mi querido amigo:	Un afectuoso saludo de
Mi querida amiga:	

To close friends and family

Querido Juan:	Recibe un fuerte abrazo de
Querida Elvira:	Muchos besos y abrazos de
Mi querido Pepe:	Tu amigo que no te olvida
Mis queridos primos:	
Queridísima Julia:	Con mucho cariño

Writing to a firm or an institution (see also page 786)

Muy señor mío:[1] (*esp Sp*)	Le saluda atentamente	[1] *if the addressee's job title etc is given*
Muy señores míos:[2]	Les saluda atentamente	
Estimados señores:[2]	Atentamente	[2] *if not naming individual addressee*
De nuestra consideración: (*LAm*)		

To a person in an important position

Señor Director: Señor Secretario General:	Respetuosamente le saluda

21.1 Starting a letter

To a friend or acquaintance

Como hace tanto tiempo que no sé de tí me he decidido a mandarte unas líneas ...
as it's been so long since I had news of you, I decided to

Me alegró mucho recibir noticias tuyas, después de tanto tiempo
it was lovely to hear from you

Gracias por la amable carta que me enviaste
thank you for the very nice <u>letter</u>

Perdona que no te haya escrito antes pero mis ocupaciones profesionales me dejan poco tiempo para más
please forgive me for not having <u>written</u> before but

In formal correspondence

Me dirijo a ustedes para solicitar mayor información sobre los cursos de verano organizados por su entidad
I am <u>writing</u> to ask for further <u>information</u> on

Les ruego que me envíen los números de abril y mayo pasados de su revista. Adjunto el cupón con detalles de mi tarjeta de crédito
please <u>send</u> me

Le agradecería que me informara si han encontrado una chaqueta negra que creo haber olvidado en la habitación que ocupamos en su hotel
I should be grateful if you would let me know if

... and replies

En contestación a su carta del 19 de noviembre, **he de informarle que** no hemos encontrado los documentos por los que se interesa
in <u>answer</u> to your <u>letter</u> of ..., I regret to <u>inform</u> you that

Acusamos recibo de su carta, en la que pregunta por nuestros cursos de verano
thank you for your <u>letter</u> <u>inquiring</u> about

He recibido su carta en la que solicita autorización para reproducir uno de mis cuadros en la portada de su revista
I have received your <u>letter</u> asking for

Gracias por su carta del 29 de enero y disculpe la tardanza en responder
thank you for your <u>letter</u> of

En referencia a su petición para que se reforme el reglamento del club, **tengo el gusto de comunicarle que** ya ha sido remitida a órgano de dirección
with <u>reference</u> to your request for ..., I am pleased to <u>advise</u> you that

21.2 Ending a letter

Espero que tardes menos en escribirme esta vez
I hope that this time you won't take so long to <u>write</u> to me

No te olvides de darle mis recuerdos a todos por ahí
do give my best <u>wishes</u> to

A ver si podemos vernos pronto
let's see if we can get together

Recuerdos de parte de mi madre
... sends her best <u>wishes</u>

In formal correspondence

Quedo a la espera de sus noticias
I <u>look</u> <u>forward</u> to hearing from you

No dude en ponerse en contacto con nosotros si requiere más información
don't hesitate to <u>contact</u> us if you need further <u>information</u>

Muchas gracias de antemano por su colaboración
thanking you in advance for your help

21.3 Travel plans

¿Disponen ustedes de un listado de cámpings de la región?
do you have a list of campsites for

Sírvanse enviarme su guía de actividades deportivas y lista de precios
please would you <u>send</u> me your guide to sports activities

¿Podría decirme si quedan plazas para el viaje por el Marruecos interior que anuncian en el número de este mes de su revista?
please could you tell me if there are any places left for

21.4 Bookings

Me han recomendado encarecidamente su hotel, por lo que **les agradeceré que me reserven** dos **habitaciones individuales con cuarto de baño** para la primera semana de junio
I should be grateful if you would <u>reserve</u> me ... single <u>rooms</u> with en suite bathroom ...

Deseo confirmar mi reserva. Tenga la amabilidad de decirme si requiere el pago por adelantado
I should like to <u>confirm</u> my <u>booking</u>. Please would you let me know if you require <u>payment</u> in <u>advance</u>

Por circunstancias ajenas a mi voluntad, **me veo obligado a cancelar la reserva hecha** la semana pasada
I am obliged to <u>cancel</u> the <u>booking</u> I made

22 Thanks

Gracias por todo	<u>thank</u> you for everything
Te escribo esta nota para darte las gracias por haber ayudado tanto a mi hija a superar sus problemas	I am writing to <u>thank</u> you for
Te agradezco mucho las molestias que te has tomado	I am very <u>grateful</u> to you for
Te estoy muy agradecido por el interés que has demostrado	I am very <u>grateful</u> to you for
Ha sido muy amable de su parte acompañarme durante tan grata visita	it was very <u>kind</u> of you to
Le estamos profundamente agradecidos por las atenciones que ha mostrado con nosotros	we are very <u>grateful</u> to you for
Quisiera expresarles mi más sincero agradecimiento por la inestimable ayuda que nos han prestado	I should like to express my heartfelt <u>gratitude</u> for
Le ruego que transmita a sus colegas **nuestro reconocimiento por** el interés que mostraron en nuestras propuestas	please would you convey our <u>thanks</u> to ... for

23 Best wishes

23.1 For any occasion

Les deseamos un feliz fin de semana	have a good
Le deseo una feliz estancia en nuestra compañía	I <u>wish</u> you a <u>happy</u>
Le deseamos lo mejor en estas fechas tan señaladas	all best <u>wishes</u> on
Un cariñoso saludo de todos nosotros	very best <u>wishes</u> from
Espero que se encuentren todos bien y que podamos tener el placer de volver a verlos pronto	I <u>hope</u> you are all well and that we shall have the pleasure of seeing you again soon
Transmita mis mejores deseos al Sr. Giménez **por** su candidatura	please convey my best <u>wishes</u> to ... for

23.2 Season's greetings

Feliz Navidad y Próspero Año Nuevo	<u>Merry</u> <u>Christmas</u> and a <u>Happy</u> <u>New</u> <u>Year</u>
Felices Pascuas	<u>Happy</u> <u>Christmas</u>
Les deseamos unas Felices Navidades y lo mejor para el año entrante	best <u>wishes</u> for a <u>Merry</u> <u>Christmas</u> and a <u>Happy</u>, <u>Prosperous</u> <u>New</u> <u>Year</u>
Felices Fiestas a todos	<u>Happy</u> <u>Christmas</u> to you all

23.3 Birthdays and saint's day

¡Felicidades!	<u>Happy</u> <u>Birthday</u>!
¡Feliz cumpleaños!/**¡Feliz aniversario!** (*CAm*)	<u>Happy</u> <u>Birthday</u>!
Te deseamos muchas felicidades y que cumplas muchos más	<u>Happy</u> <u>Birthday</u> and Many <u>Happy</u> Returns of the Day
Muchísimas felicidades en el día de tu santo	With All Best <u>Wishes</u> on your <u>Saint's</u> Day
¡Feliz onomástico! (*LAm*)	<u>Happy</u> <u>Saint's</u> Day!

23.4 Get well wishes

Que te mejores pronto	get well soon
Espero que te pongas bien cuanto antes	I <u>hope</u> that you'll be better soon
Le deseamos una pronta recuperación	we <u>hope</u> that you'll soon be better

23.5 Wishing someone luck

¡Suerte!	good <u>luck</u>!
¡Buena suerte con tu nuevo trabajo!	good <u>luck</u> with
Adiós y **muchísima suerte**	the best of <u>luck</u>
Te deseo toda la suerte del mundo en el examen	the very best of <u>luck</u>
Espero que te salga todo bien	I <u>hope</u> that everything goes well for you
Os deseamos mucho éxito para el estreno de la obra	we <u>wish</u> you every possible success for

23.6 Congratulations

Felicidades por tu reciente paternidad, Antonio	<u>congratulations</u> on becoming a father
¡Enhorabuena (*Sp*) por la noticia!	<u>congratulations</u>!
Mi más cordial *or* **calurosa enhorabuena** (*Sp*)	many <u>congratulations</u>
Ha estado usted inmejorable. **¡Le felicito!**	<u>congratulations</u>!
Reciba mis más sinceras felicitaciones por el premio	warmest <u>congratulations</u> on

24 Announcements

NB: In Spain and South America, births, engagements and marriages are not usually announced in the formal way that they are in English-speaking countries

24.1 Announcing a birth and responding

El matrimonio Rodríguez García **se complace en anunciar el nacimiento de su hijo** Guillermo el 10 de julio de 1996 en Edimburgo
are pleased to announce the birth of their son

Me alegra comunicarte que Lola y Fernán **han sido padres de una niña**, que nació el 25 de septiembre y que recibirá el nombre de Emma. Tanto la madre como la niña se encuentran en perfecto estado de salud
I am very glad to tell you that ... have had a daughter

Nuestra más cordial felicitación por el nacimiento de su hijo, con nuestro deseo de una vida llena de salud y prosperidad
warmest congratulations on the birth of your son

Nos ha dado una gran alegría recibir las noticias del nacimiento de Ana y les felicitamos de todo corazón
we were delighted to learn of the birth of ...

24.2 Announcing an engagement and responding

Los señores de Ramírez López y Ortega de los Ríos **se complacen en anunciar el compromiso matrimonial de** sus hijos Roberto y María José
are happy to announce the engagement of

Deseamos participarte que Ana y Manolo **se han prometido**. Como es natural, **nos alegramos mucho de que** hayan tomado esta decisión
we wanted to let you know that ... have got engaged .... We are delighted that

Hemos sabido que se ha anunciado su compromiso matrimonial con la Srta Gil de la Casa y **aprovechamos esta oportunidad para darle la enhorabuena** (*Sp*) *or* **felicitarle** en tan dichosa ocasión
we should like to take this opportunity to offer you our very best wishes and congratulations

Me he enterado de que se ha formalizado el compromiso de boda. **Me alegro enormemente y les deseo lo mejor** a los novios
it is splendid news and I should like to send ... my very best wishes

24.3 Announcing a change of address

Deseamos comunicarles nuestra nueva dirección a partir del 1 de marzo: Fernández de la Hoz, 25, 2° derecha, 28010 Madrid. Teléfono 543 43 43
please be advised that from ... our address will be

24.4 Announcing a wedding

See page 805 for **invitations to a wedding**

Helena Pérez Cantillosa y Antonio Fayos de la Cuadra **tienen el placer de anunciar el próximo enlace matrimonial de su hija** María de los Angeles **con** Pedro Carbonell i Trueta, **que se celebrará** en la parroquia de Santa María la Grande el próximo día 3 de mayo a las doce del mediodía
are pleased to announce the forthcoming marriage of their daughter ... and ... which will take place

Me alegra comunicarles que la boda de mi hijo Juan y Carmen **se celebró** el pasado día 4 en el Juzgado Municipal (*Sp*) *or* Registro Civil (*LAm*)
I am pleased to be able to tell you that ... were married on

24.5 Announcing a death and responding

Dña Juana Gómez Rivero, viuda de Tomás Alvarez Ramajo, **falleció en el día de ayer a la edad de 72 años después de recibir los Santos Sacramentos** y la bendición apostólica. **D.E.P.** Sus hijos, hermanos, y demás familia **ruegan a** sus amistades y personas piadosas **una oración por su alma. El funeral por su eterno descanso tendrá lugar mañana** a las diez de la mañana en la Iglesia de Nuestra Señora de los Remedios
... passed away yesterday aged 72, having received the Holy Sacrament. R.I.P. ... would ask ... to pray for her .... The funeral will take place tomorrow

Con gran dolor anunciamos que nuestro querido padre, D. Carlos Delgado, ha fallecido en la madrugada del día 10. Rogamos una oración por su alma
it is with deepest sorrow that we have to announce that

Deseamos expresarle nuestro más sentido pésame por tan dolorosa pérdida, y hacemos votos para que logren hacer frente a estos difíciles momentos con la mayor entereza
we should like to extend our deepest sympathy to you on your sad loss and to say that we very much hope you will be able to find the strength to bear up in this sad time

Me he enterado con gran tristeza de la muerte de tu hermano Carlos. De verdad **lo siento en el alma. Comprendo que estas palabras no te servirán de consuelo, pero ya sabes que puedes contar conmigo para lo que necesites**....
I was very sad to learn of the death of I am so very sorry. Words are of little comfort, but you know you can count on me if there is anything you need

25.1   Marriages

Las familias Herrera Martínez y Gil Pérez **tienen el placer de comunicarles el próximo enlace matrimonial de** sus hijos Cristina y Andrés. **La ceremonia religiosa tendrá lugar el** 5 de junio en la Iglesia de San Francisco de Villalta, a la una de la tarde **y a continuación se dará un almuerzo en** el hotel Las Encinas

... are pleased to announce the <u>marriage</u> of .... The <u>ceremony</u> will take place on ... and there will be a <u>reception</u> afterwards at

... and replies

Tenemos sumo gusto en aceptar su amable invitación a la boda de su hija. **Aprovechamos la ocasión para felicitar sinceramente a los novios**

we are delighted to accept your kind <u>invitation</u> to ..., and we should like to offer our warmest congratulations to the happy couple

25.2   Other formal receptions

María Luisa Gómez y Roberto Espinedo **tienen el gusto de invitarles al bautizo de su hija** Leticia, **que se celebrará** el domingo día 3 a las once de la mañana en la Iglesia parroquial de S. Marcos. **La recepción tendrá lugar en** el restaurante "Los Molinos", Calle de S. Juan 27

request the pleasure of your company at the <u>christening</u> of their daughter ..., which will take place .... A <u>reception</u> will be held afterwards at

A la atención de la Srta. Marta Goikoetxea: El Decano de la Facultad de Estudios Empresariales de la Universidad de Donosti **se complace en invitarla a la cena que tendrá lugar el** 3 de julio **con motivo del** décimo aniversario de su incorporación a nuestra facultad. **S.R.C.**

requests the pleasure of your company at a <u>dinner</u> on ... to <u>celebrate</u> the ... <u>R.S.V.P.</u>

En Ediciones Frontera **celebramos** el lanzamiento de nuestra nueva colección "Letras históricas" **con un cóctel en** la Galería de Arte de Carmen Villarroel el martes a las ocho de la tarde. **Esperamos que le sea posible acudir** al mismo

we are having a cocktail <u>party</u> to <u>celebrate</u> .... We hope you will be able to attend

... and replies

Agradecemos su amable invitación, que aceptamos con mucho gusto

thank you very much for your kind <u>invitation</u>, which we are delighted to <u>accept</u>

Gracias por su invitación a la cena de homenaje del Presidente de la Asociación, **a la que acudiré encantada**

thank you for your <u>invitation</u> to .... I shall be delighted to attend

He recibido su invitación, pero lamento no poder asistir, como hubiera sido mi deseo, por tener un compromiso previo

thank you for your <u>invitation</u>. I greatly regret that, owing to a <u>prior engagement</u>, I shall not be able to attend

25.3   Less formal invitations

Quisiéramos corresponder de alguna forma a su amabilidad al tener en su casa a nuestra hija el verano pasado, **por lo que hemos pensado que podrían pasar con nosotros** las vacaciones de Semana Santa, si les viene bien

we should like to do something to show our appreciation for your kindness in ... and we wondered if you would be able to spend ... with us

Nos gustaría mucho que María Teresa y tú **vinierais a cenar con nosotros** el viernes por la noche

we should be so glad if ... would come to <u>dinner</u>

Quedas invitado a una fiesta que damos el sábado a las nueve de la noche **y a la que esperamos que puedas venir**

you are <u>invited</u> to a <u>party</u> ... and we very much hope you can come

Vamos a reunirnos unos cuantos amigos en casa el sábado por la tarde para tomar unas copas y picar algo **y nos encantaría que pudieras venir tú también**, sola o acompañada, como prefieras

we are having a little gathering with some friends ... and we should be delighted if you could come too

Pascual y yo normalmente pasamos todo el mes de agosto en el apartamento de Gandía, pero en julio **lo tienes a tu disposición. No tienes más que avisar si quieres** pasar allí una temporada

you would be very welcome to use it. Just let us know if you would like to

... and replies

Le agradezco enormemente su amabilidad al invitarme a pasar unos días con ustedes. **Estoy deseando que lleguen** las vacaciones para ponerme en marcha

it was extremely kind of you to <u>invite</u> me to .... I'm so much <u>looking forward</u> to

Muchas gracias por tu invitación para el viernes. María Teresa y yo **acudiremos con mucho gusto**

thank you very much for your <u>invitation</u> .... would be delighted to come

Lo siento en el alma pero no me es posible cenar contigo el domingo

I am extremely sorry but I am <u>unable</u> to

26 Essay writing

26.1 The broad outline of the essay

Introductory remarks

Hoy es un hecho bien sabido que ciertas corrientes vanguardistas de la Europa de entreguerras tuvieron especial eco en Canarias
nowadays, it is a well-known fact that

La historia ha sido testigo en repetidas ocasiones de la ambición de las naciones dominantes
throughout history there have been repeated examples of

Una actitud muy extendida hoy día es la de considerar que nada tiene valor permanente
the attitude that ... is very widespread these days

Hoy en día todo el mundo está de acuerdo en que el progreso significa un aumento del nivel de vida. **Sin embargo, cabe preguntarse si** esta mejora repercute por igual en todos los sectores de la población
nowadays, everyone agrees that .... However, we should perhaps ask ourselves whether

Normalmente, al hablar de "cultura", **nos referimos al** sentido antropológico de la palabra
when we talk about ..., we usually mean

Se suele afirmar que la televisión tiene una influencia excesiva en el comportamiento de los más jóvenes. **Convendría analizar esta afirmación a la luz de** nuevas investigaciones psicológicas
it is often said that .... This statement needs to be examined in the light of

Uno de los temas que más preocupa a la opinión pública es el de la seguridad ciudadana
one of the issues which the public is particularly concerned about is

Existe una gran divergencia de opiniones sobre la dirección que ha de tomar la reforma educativa
there are many different opinions about

Un tema que se ha planteado reiteradamente es el de la presencia de la mujer en el mundo empresarial
one issue which has often been raised is

Se debate con frecuencia en nuestros días el problema de los cambios estructurales en la familia
a problem which is often discussed these days is

Explaining the aim of the essay

En el presente informe vamos a abordar la influencia que el turismo puede haber ejercido en el desarrollo de la España contemporánea
in this paper we shall examine

En este trabajo trataremos de averiguar si las bacterias deberían incluirse en el reino animal o vegetal
in this essay we shall try to establish whether

Este ensayo es un intento de dar respuesta a una pregunta de crucial importancia: ¿a qué se debe que la industria de la defensa sea la única que no esté recorrida por los aires desreguladores del liberalismo?
this essay is an attempt to answer a fundamental question

Nuestro propósito es hacer justicia a la obra de España en América, tantas veces criticada entre nosotros
our aim is to

Este trabajo tiene como objetivo aclarar las circunstancias que llevaron a este pueblo a ser una fuerza invasora
the aim of this essay is to

Con objeto de profundizar el papel que ciertos productos tienen en el desarrollo de las alergias, se ha llevado a cabo un estudio en dos escuelas de la ciudad
with the aim of

Developing the argument

Empecemos diciendo que ninguna filosofía se puede considerar la panacea de todos los problemas
let us begin by saying that

Para comenzar, debemos hacer hincapié en la diferencia entre adictos y consumidores ocasionales de drogas
first of all, ... must be emphasized

Damos por sentado que la situación económica del país en el siglo pasado dificultaba la adopción de las nuevas tendencias artísticas
we are assuming that

Centrémonos primero en el problema de la congestión en el centro de las grandes ciudades
first, let us concentrate on the problem of

En primer lugar conviene examinar si existe algún uso o costumbre que no permita la agrupación de accionistas
first, we need to consider whether

Como punto de partida hemos tomado la situación inmediatamente anterior al estallido del conflicto
we have taken as a starting-point

Si partimos del principio del equilibrio del ecosistema, **podremos comprender cómo** muchas de nuestras actividades lo rompen constantemente
if we start from the principle of ..., we shall be able to see how

Los que abogan por una disminución de la actividad pesquera esgrimen varios argumentos de peso. **El primero que vamos a analizar es** la reducción acelerada de los bancos de pesca
the first ... that we shall examine is

Connecting elements

Pero debemos concentrar la atención en el aspecto realmente importante del problema	*however, we should now focus our attention on*
Pasemos ahora a considerar otro aspecto del tema que nos ocupa	*let us move on to another aspect of*
Dirijamos la atención al segundo aspecto que apuntábamos	*let us turn our attention to the second point that*
A continuación trataremos un punto estrechamente relacionado	*next, we shall look at another closely related issue*
Nos ocupamos seguidamente de los detalles que muchos críticos han ignorado	*next, we shall consider*
Continuemos con una mención detallada de los distintos apartados de la declaración	*let us now move on to*
Pero volvamos de nuevo al asunto que nos ocupa	*but, to return to the issue*
Examinemos con más detalle los orígenes de la situación	*let us look in greater detail at*

The other side of the argument

Pero pasemos al segundo argumento planteado, según el cual tener el dinero inutilizado en una cuenta corriente perjudica al Tesoro, pero beneficia al banco emisor	*now let us move on to the second argument, according to which*
Consideremos ahora lo que ocurriría si contáramos con un aparato que pudiese grabar cada acto de nuestra existencia de manera que tuviéramos un rápido acceso a todo lo que nos ha sucedido	*now let us consider what would happen if*
Pero existe otro factor sin el cual no se puede comprender la importancia de la ingeniería genética para la naciente bioindustria	*but there is another factor that should be taken into account if we are to understand the importance of*
Un segundo enfoque consiste en decidir si las limitaciones impuestas a los extranjeros que quieran participar en las empresas privatizadas se adapta a la normativa comunitaria	*a second approach would be to decide whether*
Sin embargo, también merece atención el planteamiento de quienes aseguran que el transporte es un servicio social subvencionado	*however, it is also worthwhile considering the view of those who maintain that*
Es preciso advertir, no obstante, que esta biografía es muy elemental y está orientada a lectores con mínimos conocimientos sobre el asunto	*it should be pointed out, however, that*
Lo que digo sobre la poesía oriental **puede ser aplicado igualmente a** la poesía occidental, tanto la europea como la americana	*my comments on ... can equally well be applied to*
En contrapartida, la creencia de que es bueno romper estereotipos hace que nuestro estilo de diálogo aparente ser más violento que en otras culturas	*on the other hand, the belief that*
Ante tal afirmación se puede objetar que uno debe votar a aquéllos ante los cuales se siente más representado	*such an assertion can be countered with the argument that*

In conclusion

En resumen, los servicios ferroviarios del país necesitan una planificación seria y a largo plazo	*in short*
En definitiva, la búsqueda de lo absoluto es esencial en su obra	*in the final analysis*
Se trata, en suma, de desarrollar un método de diseño que permita que la arquitectura aproveche las posibilidades tecnológicas en beneficio de todos	*in short, it is a question of*
Todos los argumentos vistos aquí llevan a la misma conclusión: se tardarán tantos años en recuperar la biodiversidad perdida que es importante que empecemos a conservarla ya	*all the arguments set out here lead to the same conclusion*
De todo lo que antecede se deduce que durante algunos años al menos, no se puede esperar llegar a un acuerdo sobre este tema a nivel universal	*from what has been said, it can be seen that*
Todo ello demuestra la inviabilidad de los sistemas de reparto del trabajo como método de reducir el paro	*all of this demonstrates*
Llegamos así a la conclusión de que la responsabilidad recae en los países desarrollados	*we are therefore drawn to the conclusion that*
En conclusión, existe un grave problema de vivienda en la ciudad, que debemos intentar resolver cuanto antes	*in conclusion*
Para concluir, diremos que los argumentos con los que nos hallamos más de acuerdo son aquellos refrendados por la investigación científica	*let us conclude by saying that*
Como colofón, hagamos mención de lo que decía el dramaturgo: "Y los sueños, sueños son"	*finally, let us remember*

26.2 Constructing a paragraph

Ordering elements

Ante todo, entendemos por escalada libre la progresión por una pared sin emplear más que la roca, los pies y las manos	*first* and *foremost*
En esta discusión median poderosas razones políticas; **primero**, porque el tradicional apoyo a la iniciativa privada del Gobierno de Estados Unidos influye también en las actividades culturales; **en segundo lugar**, porque la cultura europea ha estado siempre sujeta al Estado y no es fácil separarlas de repente	*firstly* ...; *secondly*
Pero antes de examinar esta cuestión, veamos primeramente cuáles son las enfermedades hereditarias que podrían beneficiarse de esta terapia y cuáles son los equipos que trabajan en este campo	*before examining this question in detail, let us look at*
Finalmente, habría que pedir con urgencia a todos los responsables públicos que se comiencen a discutir los temas de bioética con la mayor transparencia	*finally*
Por último, hay que resaltar que la obra hace gala de un estilo que rebasa la simple eficacia	*lastly*

Connecting elements

La tendencia de las sociedades humanas es a endiosar mitos y anatemizar diablos. De **los primeros** se esperan milagrosas salvaciones; contra **los segundos** se descargan las miserias	*the former* ... *the latter*
No sólo *or* **solamente** se ha creado la esperanza de una paz duradera **sino que también** *or* **además** se han sentado las bases para que así ocurra	*not only* ... *but also*
En relación con *or* **En conexión con** lo expuesto anteriormente, hemos de añadir la falta de previsión	*in connection with*
A este respecto hay que destacar que las enfermedades de transmisión sexual están más extendidas entre los hombres que entre las mujeres	*in this regard we should point out that*
Tanto la forma **como** el contenido muestran una estructura simétrica	*both* ... *and*
El estudio determina, **por otra parte**, la relación de causa-efecto que se da en la construcción española entre la crisis que padece y su efecto multiplicador	*moreover*
El libro tiene dos virtudes. **Por una parte**, reúne toda la información sobre los maltratos a menores **y por otra**, pone sobre la mesa lo que está pasando	*on the one hand* ... *and on the other*
Si por un lado en sus mejores obras consigue una trascendentalización del arte, **por otro**, en las más repetitivas, se reduce a una mera manifestación convencional	*while on the one hand* ..., *on the other*
Las operaciones se llevaron a cabo, **bien** por negligencia de los supervisores, **bien** por astucia del perpetrante	*either* ... *or*
Ni sus colegas **ni** sus ayudantes, **ni siquiera** los más allegados, tenían idea de lo que el artista se proponía lograr	*neither* ... *nor* ... *nor even*

Adding elements

Un ajuste de tal magnitud afectaría, **además**, a otras empresas estatales	*moreover*
Además de los instrumentos señalados para el fomento de la investigación científica por parte de la Administración, **existen** otras medidas indirectas que pueden tomar diferentes Ministerios	*in addition to* ..., *there are*
Otro dato a tener en cuenta es la aprobación de un comunicado conjunto	*another factor to take into account is*
Otro acontecimiento que tuvo también gran importancia fue la firma de un acuerdo de cooperación entre ambos países	*another very important event was*
Y no sólo eso *or* **eso no es todo**: tales medidas no compensan a los afectados de ninguna manera	*and that is not all*
Todo ejercicio aeróbico estresa el sistema central. **Es más**, el corazón no puede saber qué ejercicio está realizando	*moreover*
Cabe destacar igualmente que la transferencia genética se ha empleado con éxito en células de mamífero	*it should also be noted that*
Por lo que respecta a las novedades de producto, la gama todo terreno se ha ampliado con la llegada de tres nuevas versiones	*as far as* ... *are concerned*
En cuanto a las tendencias para los 12 meses siguientes, el gasto en software se incrementará en el 59,9% de las empresas	*as for*

Introducing one's own point of view

Soy de la opinión de que es mejor que los medios de comunicación estén en manos de los propietarios de la edición y de la comunicación que controlados por los propietarios de entes financieros	*I am of the opinion that*

La exposición más destacada del pintor aragonés fue, **a mi criterio**, la exhibida en el Casón del Buen Retiro a principios de los sesenta — *to my <u>mind</u>*

Para muchos la diferencia es simplemente administrativa, **y yo lo suscribo totalmente** — *and I would <u>agree</u> wholeheartedly*

Hasta cierto punto **comparto esta opinión** — *I share that <u>view</u>*

Nuestra hipótesis es que el pintor busca plasmar la fugacidad, aunque tal vez nos equivoquemos — *our <u>hypothesis</u> is that*

Podemos afirmar que las raíces del levantamiento armado hay que buscarlas en las condiciones de vida de la población indígena — *it is true to say that*

Vaya por delante mi firme convicción de que, en un tiempo razonable, vamos a ser capaces de relanzar el arte de nuestra tierra hasta volverle a situar en lugar destacado dentro de Europa — *<u>first</u> and <u>foremost</u> I am <u>convinced</u> that*

El problema, **desde mi punto de vista**, reside en que aún no se ha conseguido sintetizar culturalmente una nueva idea de España, como comunidad de pueblos o nación de naciones — *as I <u>see</u> it*

Basta comenzar a leer la obra **para sentirse** transportado a la época — *you only need to ... to feel*

Introducing someone else's point of view

Tras ellos el arte posmodernista - **según concluye el autor** - ha terminado por ser un barrio de Disneylandia, un paraíso de masas — *as the author <u>concludes</u>*

Esta y otras consideraciones, **como señala el autor**, deben estimular a nuevas y específicas investigaciones y debates — *as the author <u>points out</u>*

Como afirmó Platón, ningún hombre puede aspirar al conocimiento total de la verdad absoluta — *as Plato stated*

Parece que fue una clara agresión, **a juzgar por los comentarios de** la prensa y de algunas personas — *<u>judging</u> by the <u>comments</u> of*

La comisión que investiga el caso **mantiene la teoría de** la existencia de "un poder político paralelo sin cuyo concurso no hubiera sido posible el fraude masivo detectado" — *the <u>theory</u> supported by ... is that*

El proponente **reiteró su tesis sobre** la inadmisibilidad de la tortura en ningún supuesto — *repeated his <u>argument</u> about*

El museo **asegura que** la retirada del logotipo había sido decidida en la etapa del ministro anterior — *<u>maintains</u> that*

Introducing an example

Sirva de ejemplo la situación descrita por uno de los viajeros — *as an <u>example</u>, let us take*

Y mencionaré como ejemplo de ello el episodio independiente compuesto por unas jornadas de cacería en las que el protagonista participa — *and I shall take as an <u>example</u>*

Podemos hacer uso de un ejemplo gráfico — *to give a graphic <u>example</u>:*

Pongamos por caso or **Supongamos que** uno de los rivales decide retirarse — *let us <u>suppose</u> that*

Procederé a ilustrar con algunos ejemplos la idea de que se ha producido un desfase entre la ciencia económica y la sociedad — *with the help of some <u>examples</u>, I shall move on to*

Las autoridades arguyen que la medida supone un importante ahorro de energía, pero yo disiento. **Veamos un ejemplo** — *let us look at an <u>example</u>*

Introducing a quotation or source

Ya lo dice el refrán, "Dime con quién andas y te diré quién eres" — *as the <u>saying</u> goes*

Tal convicción animó al Realismo decimonónico, **que, en palabras de** Clarín, exigía del novelista la facultad de "saber ver y copiar" — *which, in the words of*

Según la frase atribuida al famoso pintor, "Yo no busco, encuentro" — *as ... is supposed to have said*

Ya dice d'Ors **que** el dandismo de Valle-Inclán "no es sino el uniforme de los estudiantes de Coimbra y Santiago, perpetuado toda una vida" — *as ... says*

Podemos citar un pasaje que ilustra esta posibilidad — *let us take a passage which <u>illustrates</u>*

Tomemos como referencia el momento en que todo se descubre — *let us take as our <u>point</u> of reference the moment when*

26.3   The mechanics of the argument

Stating facts

La característica más destacada del problema es su universalidad — *the most notable <u>aspect</u> of the <u>problem</u> is*

A medida que se avanza en la lectura de la obra, **se abren nuevas perspectivas**

as one progresses ..., new perspectives open up

Podemos observar que, en estos momentos, **existe** una clara tendencia común en los ejecutivos europeos

it can be seen that ... there is

Se puede constatar que hay un gran índice del alcoholismo en la isla

it can be seen that

Es un hecho que la industria está demostrando interés por este tipo de buques ya que se han hecho varios pedidos de barcos porta-barcazas

it is a <u>fact</u> that

Si partimos de la base de que las corrientes que se engloban bajo el título de "Nuevas tecnologías" nunca han tenido un especial prestigio en este país ...

if we <u>start</u> from the <u>premise</u> that

Making a supposition

Por los documentos que existen **podemos suponer que** Ferri sea valenciano, descendiente tal vez de Féliz Ferri, pintor levantino del siglo XVIII

it can be <u>assumed</u> that

Esta novedad **permite pensar que** será posible un tratamiento de afecciones neuromusculares humanas en un futuro próximo

leads us to <u>believe</u> that

La ruptura entre ambos **podría interpretarse como** una celosa competencia de naturaleza literaria

could be <u>interpreted</u> as

Me atrevo a pensar que aquellos años fueron los más felices en su matrimonio, como así lo pude constatar en dos ocasiones en que fui a visitarle

I would <u>venture</u> to <u>suggest</u> that

Podría quizá pensarse que la física da una respuesta clara al problema de la naturaleza del tiempo, pero nada más alejado de la verdad, como observan los dos libros objeto del presente comentario

one might (be tempted to) <u>think</u> that

La simplicidad del método **hace suponer que** se continuará empleando en el futuro

<u>suggests</u> that

Especulemos con la hipótesis de un descenso acelerado de la temperatura del planeta

let us take the <u>hypothetical</u> situation in which there is

Expressing a certainty

Lo cierto es que los mecanismos de lucha contra el terrorismo no sólo no han mejorado, sino que se encuentran en uno de sus peores momentos

one thing is <u>certain</u>:

La salida de presos preventivos produce una sensación de inseguridad en los ciudadanos, pero **está claro que** la justicia debe predominar sobre todo

it is <u>clear</u> that

Es indudable que Chigorin fue un precursor del nuevo ajedrez, que sería creado en el primer cuarto de este siglo por la llamada escuela hipermoderna

without a <u>doubt</u>

No hay duda de que esta nueva medida del gobierno supone un peligro para la libertad de expresión

there can be no <u>doubt</u> that

No se puede negar que el yogur es el derivado lácteo preferido por los españoles

it cannot be <u>denied</u> that

Todos coinciden en que hay argumentos de peso para defender la filosofía como pilar básico de la formación académica

everyone <u>agrees</u> that

Es evidente que si la informática y las telecomunicaciones no pudiesen ser utilizadas para reforzar el poder existente, habrían sido dejadas totalmente de lado

it is <u>clear</u> that

Más allá de la guerra de cifras, **es incontestable que** la convocatoria de huelga tuvo un seguimiento mayoritario en el sector industrial

<u>unquestionably</u>

Un político dimite - **como es obvio en cualquier democracia** - por sentido de la responsabilidad y no por disciplina de partido

as is the case in any normal democracy

Expressing doubt

Es improbable que un académico empleara la forma "andase"

it is <u>unlikely</u> that

Resulta difícil creer que una obra de tal celebridad pueda ser vendida en el mercado secreto del arte robado

it is hard to <u>believe</u> that

Y aún **cabría preguntarse si** la auténtica literatura no ha sido siempre la manifestación de lo individual e incluso de lo íntimo

the question arises as to whether

Todavía está por ver, sin embargo, cuáles van a ser las tendencias en las subastas de arte cuando cese la actual recesión

it still remains to be seen

Su parecido físico con el autor del crimen, **introduce un elemento de duda** en la identificación

introduces an element of <u>doubt</u>

Un nuevo atraco **pone en cuestión** la seguridad de los furgones blindados

raises <u>doubts</u> about

Conceding a point

España, que debe considerarse un país desarrollado en el conjunto occidental, no tiene, **sin embargo**, una política medioambiental integral

<u>nevertheless</u>

Todavía no estamos en situación de valorar su trabajo, **aunque** sí creemos que es un autor con mucho que decir

<u>although</u>

Asegura que lo que le interesa es la felicidad. Habría que saber, **no obstante**, en qué consiste para ella ese concepto tan abstracto — *however*

Aunque hayan surgido escépticos por todas partes, el acuerdo de paz entre ambos países se irá construyendo poco a poco — *even if*

Es la operación más importante que haya pactado nunca una empresa española en el exterior. **Pero** amenaza también con convertirse en la más controvertida — *however*

A pesar de que la obre carece de la unidad que poseen otras "semióperas" de Purcell, el conjunto es de una frescura, una variedad y un encanto admirables — *in spite of the fact that*

Por mucho que se complique el lenguaje de la clase política, existe una gran masa de población capaz de descifrarlo — *however complicated ... becomes*

El hombre es capaz de mantener su temperatura corporal en unos límites muy estrechos, **sea cual sea** la temperatura ambiental — *whatever ... is*

Estos viajes cuasidiplomáticos al extranjero por parte de un candidato de la oposición durante el año electoral son, **como mínimo**, insólitos — *to say the least*

No se puede caer en la tentación, comprensible **hasta cierto punto**, de disminuir los precios de los productos petrolíferos a los usuarios — *up to a point*

En el plano social, **hay que reconocer que** los resultados obtenidos a lo largo de más de una década de aplicación de esta ley son, en términos generales, muy satisfactorios — *it must be recognized that*

Hemos de admitir que el turismo también ha afectado negativamente a la zona — *it must be admitted that*

Emphasizing particular points

Ante todo debemos subrayar que esta obra es muy superior a las anteriores — *first and foremost, it should be stressed that*

Conviene también precisar que el hecho de pasar unas vacaciones en la nieve no tiene por qué suponer obligatoriamente pasarse el día exclusivamente esquiando — *it should also be pointed out that*

De todos modos, es evidente que fue un pionero, **no sólo** en lo ideológico, **sino también** en lo que se refiere a la acción social — *not only ... but also*

La gente no le ha apoyado en parte por las sospechas que levanta su personalidad. **Pero un factor aún más importante es** que su discurso democrático hace temblar a una región poco democrática — *but an even more important factor is*

En cuanto al tema de la corrupción, **sería preciso matizar que** no son sólo los cargos públicos los culpables, ya que también se han beneficiado individuos de la sociedad civil — *it should be pointed out that*

La cuestión fundamental es que la lucha de los ecologistas no está únicamente encaminada a salvar a tal o cual animal, sino a recuperar el equilibrio entre el hombre y la Tierra — *the fact is that*

La poesía explica el tiempo, y **yo diría incluso que** la poesía no tiene tiempo, que la poesía "es" el tiempo — *I would go as far as to say that*

Es precisamente la teoría cuántica, aun con sus paradojas, la que hace posible la creación de una máquina del tiempo — *it is precisely ...*

Moderating a statement

Sería deseable la implantación de un impuesto verde que gravase las energías contaminantes — *... would be desirable*

Quizás muchos tan sólo relacionen al director con aquellos años de apertura erótica, **pero sería injusto** condicionar toda su obra a esa etapa transitoria — *but it would be unfair to*

Probablemente por ello se han vertido inexactitudes que, **sin ánimo polémico**, quisiera aclarar — *without wishing to be controversial*

La cuestión no tendría más importancia si no fuera porque ese dinero procede de los fondos de ayuda al desarrollo teóricamente destinados a financiar proyectos en países del Tercer Mundo — *this would not be particularly important were it not for the fact that*

A pesar de ser una tesis bien construida, **se hace necesario en cierta medida cuestionarse** su validez en el mundo de hoy — *although it is ..., should perhaps be questioned*

Indicating agreement

Por lo que conocemos del autor, bastantes de los episodios aquí narrados son, **efectivamente**, autobiográficos — *in fact*

Nada más cierto que la afirmación que la autora hace al final del libro: "Saber dialogar es una asignatura pendiente en la sociedad democrática" — *... is absolutely right*

Debido a la actual necesidad de prudencia, **sí parece justificada** la lentitud del Consejo en la toma de decisiones — *does indeed seem justified*

Es cierto que el poder consultar los microfilmes indexados por temas y fechas ayuda considerablemente al historiador	it is <u>true</u> that
Soy partidario del acuerdo, porque el diálogo y la concordia son siempre armas justas	I am in <u>favour</u> of
Como reacción contra ese concepto de realismo, que el autor da **justamente** como extinguido, se alzó el contrario	<u>rightly</u>
La exposición del problema que realizó el nuevo presidente de la organización parece **razonable y convincente**	<u>reasonable</u> and convincing

Indicating disagreement

En cambio, lo que sí **resulta altamente discutible** es la atención morbosa con que los medios de comunicación han seguido el caso	is highly <u>questionable</u>
El resultado de sus obras **es poco convincente**	is not very impressive
Pero el trabajo tiene inconvenientes metodológicos que **lo ponen en tela de juicio**	raise <u>doubts</u> about it
Con la debida humildad, **expreso mis reservas sobre** lo radical de dicha revisión	I should like to express my <u>doubts</u> about
Esas interpretaciones **carecen de base sólida**	there are no real <u>grounds</u> for ...
Las soluciones por ellos aportadas **distan mucho de ser indiscutibles**	are <u>questionable</u>, to say the least
Pecaríamos de ingenuos si creyéramos que ése es el único argumento válido	it would be extremely <u>naïve</u> to <u>believe</u> that
El punto de vista antropocentrista que pretende que somos los únicos hombres del universo **es** hoy día **totalmente inaceptable**	is totally <u>unacceptable</u>
Sería un grave error acabar con el cinturón de dunas en el que se ubicaría la urbanización	it would be a serious <u>mistake</u> to
Es de todo punto absurdo mantener que los acontecimientos del este de Europa no han repercutido sobre los nacionalismos de los países occidentales	it is completely <u>absurd</u> to <u>suggest</u> that

Making a correction

El segundo lienzo de la subasta estaba valorado en 4-6 millones y fue vendido por 3.500.000; **en realidad**, 3.920.000	or, to be <u>precise</u>
La idea de este proyecto es difundir el conocimiento de las Reales Academias. **No se trata propiamente de** una historia de las Academias, **sino de** una presentación de las mismas	it is not really ..., but <u>rather</u>
Si rechazan escribir sobre literatura **no es porque** tengan mucho que ocultar sobre el proceso de la escritura. **Me parece más bien que** carecen de una sólida cultura literaria	it is not <u>because</u> ..., but <u>rather</u>, it seems to me, <u>because</u>
Tal vez sería más adecuado hablar de problemas por resolver **que de** inconvenientes, dado que con el ritmo de desarrollo actual los problemas analizados a continuación tendrán solución a corto o medio plazo	perhaps it would be better to talk about ... <u>rather</u> than
La transexualidad **tiene más de** conflicto **que de** la perversión sexual que muchos le atribuyen	is more a <u>question</u> of ... than of

Indicating the reason for something

La tierra está agotada **debido a** la agricultura y a la ganadería intensiva que practicó la cooperativa durante años	<u>owing</u> to
En estas tierras habría habido una ruptura total con el pasado anterior, **lo cual explica** la inexistencia de siervos y libertos y el clima de libertad personal de la época medieval	which <u>explains</u>
El descubrimiento fue posible **gracias a** los grandes progresos técnicos que pusieron el radiotelescopio a disposición de los astrónomos	<u>thanks</u> to
Y si quienes conocían el manuscrito no concedieron importancia a esas disquisiciones, **es, sin duda, porque** nada en ellas les resultaba digno de especial mención	it is <u>doubtless</u> <u>because</u>
Ambas pinturas necesitan ser restauradas, **dado que** su estado de conservación no es bueno	<u>since</u>
En la semiótica de entrada cabe todo, **puesto que** todo es signo, o signo de un signo	<u>since</u>
El estudio ha demostrado que esta enfermedad **es el motivo de** baja laboral de un 8%	is <u>responsible</u> for
Si no se observan distorsiones, **es porque** los rayos viajan una distancia corta y bajo un ángulo demasiado empinado para que se curven apreciablemente	if ..., it is <u>because</u>

Indicating the consequences of something

El informe prevé una reactivación en la demanda de pisos, **lo que llevará a** un ligero aumento de los precios	which will lead to
La enmienda fue aprobada por unanimidad, **lo que significa** que irá directamente al Congreso Federal del partido sin que sea debatida por el pleno	which <u>means</u> that

Las galas televisivas recaudan centenares de millones, **por lo que** la ayuda final superará fácilmente los mil millones de pesetas — *for which <u>reason</u>*

La industria auxiliar de la automoción atraviesa una fuerte crisis **como consecuencia de** la recesión en las ventas de automóviles — *as a <u>result</u> of*

El carácter documental de sus libros, unido a la técnica literaria de los mismos, **daba como resultado** una fórmula muy bien acogida por la industria editorial y su público — *<u>resulted</u> in*

El uso de la mitad del arsenal atómico mundial existente **provocaría** en el hemisferio Norte un largo invierno nuclear y la desaparición de la vida humana — *would <u>cause</u>*

Este insecto-palo, carece de alas y es idéntico a una ramita seca. **De ahí que** resulte tan difícil distinguirlo entre la maleza — *that is <u>why</u>*

Tendrán que perfeccionar su producto y seguir las tendencias del mercado, **lo que implica** producir coches para todos los niveles adquisitivos — *which <u>involves</u>*

Contrasting or comparing

Las ciencias sociales se verán severamente afectadas con la reforma universitaria, **por el contrario** las ciencias aplicadas y las carreras técnicas serán muy favorecidas — *<u>whereas</u>*

Las causas clásicas de mortalidad tienden a disminuir en los países desarrollados, **en cambio**, las enfermedades hereditarias toman cada vez mayor relieve — *<u>whereas</u>*

El olfato humano está muy poco desarrollado **en comparación con** el de algunos animales — *in <u>comparison</u> with*

La exportación mantuvo ritmos positivos de crecimiento, **en contraste con** el comportamiento medio de los países de la OCDE — *in <u>contrast</u> with*

En contraposición al descenso que se observa en la venta de libros a Europa, las exportaciones a otros países han experimentado un aumento respecto al año anterior — *<u>unlike</u>*

En *La Riqueza de las Naciones*, de Adam Smith, se puede ver **la diferencia entre** la tradición liberal **y** el neoliberalismo actual — *the <u>difference</u> between ... and*

Esta zona posee la mayoría de los yacimientos de crudo **mientras que** en Esmeralda está la principal refinería y puerto de exportación del crudo — *<u>while</u>*

La organización se ha gastado una suma **muy superior a** la prevista — *far higher ... than*

Este material se compone de microfibras con un diámetro **diez veces inferior al de** las fibras de poliéster corriente — *ten times smaller than*

27 El teléfono

The telephone

27.1 Para obtener un número

Getting a number

Could you get me Newhaven 465786, please?
(four-six-five-seven-eight-six)

Por favor, ¿me puede poner con el 043 65 27 82?
(cero cuarenta y tres, sesenta y cinco, veintisiete, ochenta y dos)

Could you give me <u>directory</u> enquiries *(Brit)* o <u>directory</u> assistance *(US)*, please?
Can you give me the number of Europost, of 54 Broad Street, Newham?
It's not in the book
They're ex-directory *(Brit)* o They're unlisted *(US)*
What is the code for Exeter?
Can I <u>dial</u> direct to Peru?
How do I make an outside <u>call</u>? o What do I <u>dial</u> for an outside line?
What do I <u>dial</u> to get the speaking clock?
You'll have to look up the number in the <u>directory</u>
You should get the number from International <u>Directory</u> Enquiries
You omit the '0' when <u>dialling</u> England from Spain

¿Me pone con Información (Urbana/Interurbana), por favor?

¿Me puede decir el número de Europost? La dirección es Plaza Mayor, 34. Carmona, provincia de Sevilla.
No está en la guía
No figura en la guía *or* Es un número privado *(Mex)*
¿Cuál es el <u>prefijo</u> de León?
¿Puedo <u>llamar</u> a Perú <u>marcando</u> directamente?
¿Qué hay que hacer para obtener línea?

¿Cuál es el número de Información Horaria?
Tendrá usted que consultar la guía telefónica
Le podrán dar el número si <u>llama</u> a Información Internacional

No <u>marque</u> el cero del <u>prefijo</u> cuando <u>llame</u> a Londres desde España

27.2 Diferentes tipos de llamadas

Different types of call

It's a local <u>call</u>
It's a long-distance <u>call</u> from Worthing
I want to make an international <u>call</u>
I want to make a reverse charge <u>call</u> to a London number *(Brit)* o I want to call a London number collect *(US)*
I'd like to make a personal <u>call</u> *(Brit)* o a person-to-person call *(US)* to Joseph Broadway on Jamestown 123456
I want to make an ADC <u>call</u> to Bournemouth

I'd like to make a credit card <u>call</u> to Berlin

I'd like an alarm <u>call</u> for 7.30 tomorrow morning

Es una <u>llamada</u> local or urbana
Es una <u>llamada</u> interurbana desde Barcelona
Deseo <u>llamar</u> al extranjero
Quisiera hacer una <u>llamada</u> a cobro revertido a Londres

Quería hacer una <u>llamada</u> personal a don Juan Crespo; el número es el 25 46 79 de Córdoba
Deseo <u>llamar</u> a Valencia y que me digan lo que ha costado la llamada
Quería hacer una <u>llamada</u> a Berlín pagando con tarjeta de crédito
Por favor, ¿me podrían avisar por <u>teléfono</u> mañana por la mañana a las siete y media?

27.3 Habla el telefonista

The operator speaks

Number, please
What number do you want? o What number are you <u>calling</u>?
Where are you <u>calling</u> from?
Would you repeat the number, please?
You can <u>dial</u> the number direct
Replace the receiver and <u>dial</u> again
There's a Mr Campbell calling you from Canberra and wishes you to pay for the <u>call</u>. Will you accept it?

Go ahead, caller
(Información) There's no listing under that name
There's no reply from 45 77 57 84
I'll try to reconnect you
Hold the line, caller
All lines to Bristol are engaged - please try later
I'm trying it for you now
It's <u>ringing</u> o <u>Ringing</u> for you now
The line is engaged *(Brit)* o busy *(US)*

¿Dígame? ¿Qué número desea?
¿Con qué número desea comunicar?
¿Desde dónde <u>llama</u> usted?
¿Podría repetir el número, por favor?
Puede <u>marcar</u> el número directamente
Cuelgue y vuelva a <u>marcar</u>
Hay una <u>llamada</u> para usted del Sr. López, que telefonea desde Bilbao y desea hacerlo a cobro revertido. ¿Acepta usted la <u>llamada</u>?
Ya puede hablar, señor/señora/señorita
(Directory Enquiries) Ese nombre no viene en la guía
El 945 77 57 84 no contesta
Voy a intentar otra vez comunicar con este número
No se retire, señor/señora/señorita
Las líneas están saturadas; <u>llame</u> más tarde, por favor
Le voy a poner ahora *(Sp)* or Le estoy conectando *(LAm)*
Está sonando or <u>llamando</u>
Está comunicando

27.4 Cuando contestan

Could I have extension 516? *o* Can you give me extension 516?
Is that Mr Lambert's phone?
Could I speak to Mr Swinton, please? *o* I'd like to speak to
  Mr Swinton, please *o* Is Mr Swinton there?
Could you put me through to Dr Henderson, please?

Who's speaking?
I'll try again later
I'll call back in half an hour
Could I leave my number for her to call me back?

I'm ringing from a callbox *(Brit)* *o* I'm calling from a pay station
  (US)
I'm phoning from England
Would you ask him to ring me when he gets back?

27.5 Contesta la centralita/el conmutador

Queen's Hotel, can I help you?
Who is calling, please?
Who shall I say is calling?
Do you know his extension number?

I am connecting you now *o* I'm putting you through now
I have a call from Tokyo for Mrs Thomas
I've got Miss Trotter on the line for you
Miss Paxton is calling you from Paris
Dr Craig is talking on the other line
Sorry to keep you waiting
There's no reply
You're through to our Sales Department

27.6 Para contestar

Hello, this is Anne speaking
(Is that Anne?) Speaking
Would you like to leave a message?
Can I take a message for him?
Don't hang up yet
Put the phone down and I'll call you back
This is a recorded message
Please speak after the tone

27.7 En caso de dificultad

I can't get through
The number is not ringing
I'm getting 'number unobtainable' *o* I'm getting the 'number
  unobtainable' signal
Their phone is out of order
We were cut off
I must have dialled the wrong number
We've got a crossed line
I've called them several times with no reply
You gave me a wrong number
I got the wrong extension
This is a very bad line

When your number answers

¿Me da la extensión *or* interno *(SC)* 615?
¿Es éste el número del señor Lambert?
Por favor, ¿podría hablar con Carlos García? *or* Quisiera hablar
  con Carlos García, por favor *or* ¿Está Carlos García?
¿Me pone *(Sp)* *or* conecta *(LAm)* con el doctor Rodriguez,
  por favor?
¿De parte de quien? *or* ¿Me puede decir quien habla?
Volveré a llamar más tarde
Llamaré otra vez dentro de media hora
¿Podría darle mi número y decirle que haga el favor de
  llamarme?
Llamo desde una cabina (telefónica)

Llamo desde Inglaterra
¿Puede decirle que me llame cuando vuelva?

The switchboard operator speaks

Hotel Castellana. ¿dígame?
¿Me puede decir quién llama?
¿De parte de quién?
¿Sabe usted qué extensión *or* interno *(SC)* es?

Le pongo *(Sp)* *or* Le conecto *(LAm)*
Hay una llamada de Tokio para la Sra. Martínez
Pilar Martín quiere hablar con usted
Carmen Pérez le llama desde París
El doctor Rodríguez está hablando por el otro teléfono
Perdone la demora, pero no se retire
No contesta
Ya tiene línea con el departamento de ventas

Answering the telephone

Sí, soy Ana, dígame
(¿Es Ana?) Si, soy yo *or* Sí, aquí Ana *or* Al aparato
¿Quiere dejar (algún) recado?
¿Quiere que le pase un recado?
No cuelgue *or* No se retire
Cuelgue y espere que le llame
Este es el contestador automático de ...
Deje su mensaje después de la señal

In case of difficulty

No consigo comunicar
El teléfono no suena
Me sale la señal de línea desconectada

Ese teléfono está estropeado
Nos han cortado (la comunicación)
Debo de haberme equivocado de número
Hay un cruce de líneas
He llamado varias veces y no contestan
No me han dado el número que pedí
Me han dado una extensión que no era la que yo quería
Se oye muy mal *or* La línea está muy mal

28 Sugerencias

28.1   Para hacer sugerencias

You might like to think it over before giving me your decision | *tal vez quiera*
If you were to give me the negative, **I could** get copies made | *si me diera ... yo podría*
You could help me clear out my office, **if you don't mind** | *podría ... si no le importa*
We could stop off in Venice for a day or two, **if you like** | *podríamos ... si te apetece*
I've got an idea - **let's organize** a surprise birthday party for Megan! | *vamos a organizar*
If you've no objection(s), I'll speak to them personally | *si no tienes <u>inconveniente</u>, hablaré*
If I were you, I'd go | *yo que tú, iría*
If you ask me, you'd better take some extra cash | *en mi opinión, más <u>vale</u> que*
I'd be very careful not to commit myself at this stage | *tendría cuidado de no*
I would recommend (that) you discuss it with him before making a decision | *te <u>recomendaría</u> que*
It could be in your interest to have a word with the owner first | *te <u>convendría</u>*
There's a lot to be said for living alone | *... tiene muchas ventajas*
Go and see Pompeii - **it's a must**! | *no dejes de ir a ver*

Más directamente

I suggest that you go to bed and try to sleep | *te <u>sugiero</u> que*
I'd like to suggest that you seriously consider taking a long holiday | *te <u>sugeriría</u>*
We propose that half the fee be paid in advance, and half on completion | *<u>proponemos</u> que*
It is very important that you take an interest in what he is trying to do | *es muy importante que*
I am convinced that this would be a dangerous step to take | *estoy convencido de que*
I cannot put it too strongly: **you really must** see a doctor | *de verdad, tienes que*

Menos directamente

Say you were to approach the problem from a different angle | *y si*
In these circumstances, **it might be better to** wait | *quizás sería <u>mejor</u>*
It might be a good thing o **a good idea to** warn her about this | *estaría bien*
Perhaps it would be as well to change the locks | *quizás <u>convendría</u>*
Perhaps you should take up a sport | *tal vez <u>deberías</u>*
If I may make a suggestion, a longer hemline might suit you better | *si me permite una <u>sugerencia</u>*
Might I be allowed to offer a little advice? - talk it over with a solicitor before you go any further | *¿me permite que le dé un pequeño consejo?*
If I might be permitted to suggest something, installing bigger windows would make the office much brighter | *si se me permite hacer una <u>sugerencia</u>*

Haciendo una pregunta

How do you fancy a holiday in Australia? | *¿te <u>apetece</u> ...?*
I was thinking of going for a drink later. **How about it?** | *¿qué te <u>parece</u>?*
What would you say to a trip up to town next week? | *¿qué te <u>parecería</u> ...?*
Would you like to stay in Paris for a couple of nights? | *¿te <u>gustaría</u> ...?*
What if you try ignoring her and see if that stops her complaining? | *¿y si ...?*
What you need is a change of scene. **Why not** go on a cruise? | *¿por qué no ...?*
Suppose o **Supposing** you left the kids with your mother for a few days? | *¿y si ...?*
How would you feel about taking calcium supplements? | *¿qué te <u>parecería</u> ...?*
Have you ever thought of starting up a magazine of your own? | *¿no se te ha <u>ocurrido</u> ...?*
Would you care to have lunch with me? | *¿querría ...?*

28.2   Para pedir sugerencias

What would you do if you were me? | *¿qué harías tú en mi lugar?*
Have you any idea how I should go about it to get the best results? | *¿tienes idea cómo debería ...?*
I've no idea what to call our new puppy: **have you any suggestions?** | *¿se te <u>ocurre</u> algo?*
I can only afford to buy one of them: **which do you suggest?** | *¿cuál me <u>aconsejas</u>?*
I wonder if you could suggest where we might go for a few days? | *¿podría <u>sugerirnos</u> ...?*
I'm a bit doubtful about where to start | *no estoy muy seguro de*

29 Consejos

29.1   Para pedir consejo

What would you do **if you were me?**	*en mi lugar*
Would a pear tree grow in this spot? If not, **what would you recommend?**	*qué <u>recomendaría</u> usted*
Do you think I ought to tell the truth if he asks me where I've been?	*crees que <u>debería</u>*
What would you advise me to do in the circumstances?	*¿qué me <u>aconsejaría</u> que hiciera?*
Would you advise me to seek promotion within this firm or apply for another job?	*¿me <u>aconsejaría</u> usted que ...?*
I'd like o **I'd appreciate your advice on** personal pensions	*me gustaría que me <u>aconsejara</u> sobre*
I'd be grateful if you could advise me on how to treat this problem	*le agradecería que me <u>aconsejara</u> sobre*

29.2   Para aconsejar

De manera impersonal

It might be wise o **sensible to** consult a specialist	*quizás sería <u>prudente</u>*
It might be a good idea to seek professional advice	*quizás sería buena idea*
It might be better to think the whole thing over before taking any decisions	*sería <u>mejor</u>*
You'd be as well to state your position at the outset, so there is no mistake	*más te <u>valdría</u>*
You would be well-advised to invest in a pair of sunglasses if you're going to Spain	*haría bien en*
You'd be ill-advised to have any dealings with this firm	*sería poco <u>aconsejable</u> que*
It would certainly be advisable to book a table	*se <u>aconseja</u>*
It is in your interest o **your best interests to** keep your dog under control if you don't want it to be reported	*le <u>conviene</u>*
Do be sure to read the small print before you sign anything	*<u>asegúrate</u> de*
Try to avoid upsetting her; she'll only make your life a misery	*intenta evitar*
Whatever you do, don't drink the local schnapps	*no se te ocurra*

De manera más personal

If you ask me, you'd better take some extra cash	*para mí que es <u>mejor</u> que lleves*
If you want my advice, you should steer well clear of them	*si quieres un <u>consejo</u>, aléjate*
If you want my opinion, I'd go by air to save time	*si quieres mi <u>opinión</u>, yo iría*
In your shoes o **If i were you, I'd** be thinking about moving on	*yo que tú, me pondría a pensar*
Take my advice and don't rush into anything	*hazme <u>caso</u>*
I'd be very careful not to commit myself at this stage	*yo tendría mucho <u>cuidado</u> de no*
I think you ought to o **should** seek professional advice	*creo que <u>deberías</u>*
My advice would be to have nothing to do with them	*yo te <u>aconsejaría</u> que*
I would advise you to pay up promptly before they take you to court	*yo te <u>aconsejaría</u> que*
I would advise against call**ing** in the police unless he threatens you	*yo <u>aconsejaría</u> no*
I would strongly advise you to reconsider this decision	*yo le <u>aconsejo</u> que*
I would urge you to reconsider selling the property	*le ruego encarecidamente que*
Might I be allowed to offer a little advice? - talk it over with a solicitor before going any further	*¿me permite que le dé un <u>consejo</u>?*

29.3   Para hacer una advertencia

It's really none of my business but **I don't think you should** get involved	*creo que no <u>deberías</u>*
A word of caution: watch what you say to him if you want it to remain a secret	*una <u>advertencia</u>:*
I should warn you that he's not an easy customer to deal with	*te <u>advierto</u> que*
Take care not to lose the vaccination certificate	*ten <u>cuidado</u> de no*
Watch you don't trip over your shoelaces	*<u>cuidado</u> no*
Make sure that o **Mind that** o **See that you don't** say anything they might find offensive	*ten <u>cuidado</u> de no*
I'd think twice about shar**ing** a flat with him	*me lo pensaría dos veces antes de*
It would be sheer madness to attempt to drive without your glasses	*sería una auténtica <u>locura</u>*
You risk a long delay in Amsterdam **if** you come back by that route	*corre el riesgo de ... si*

30 Propuestas

De manera directa

I would be delighted to help out, if I may — *me encantaría*
It would give me great pleasure to show you round the city — *sería un placer*
We would like to offer you the post of Sales Director — *quisiéramos <u>ofrecerle</u>*
I hope you will not be offended if I offer a contribution towards your expenses — *espero que no se ofenda si le <u>ofrezco</u>*
Do let me know if I can help in any way — *avísame si puedo*
If we can be of any further assistance, **please do not hesitate to** contact us — *si podemos ... no dude en*

Haciendo una pregunta

Say we were to offer you a 5% rise, **how would that sound?** — *¿qué le parecería si le <u>ofreciéramos</u> ...?*
What if I were to call for you in the car? — *¿y si yo ...?*
Could I give you a hand with your luggage? — *¿puedo ...?*
Shall I do the photocopies for you? — *¿te hago ...?*
Is there anything I can do to help you find suitable accommodation? — *¿puedo hacer algo para ...?*
May o **Can I offer you** a drink? — *¿le pongo ...?*
Would you like me to find out more about it for you? — *¿quieres que ...?*
Would you allow me to pay for dinner, at least? — *¿me deja que ...?*
You will let me show you around Glasgow, **won't you?** — *¿me dejarás que ... ¿no?*

31 Peticiones

Please would you drop by on your way home and pick up the papers you left here? — *¿<u>puedes</u> ...?*
Could you please try to keep the noise down while I'm studying? — *haced el <u>favor</u> de*
Would you mind look**ing** after Hannah for a couple of hours tomorrow? — *¿te <u>importaría</u> ...?*
Could I ask you to watch out for anything suspicious in my absence? — *¿podrías ...?*

Por escrito

I should be grateful if you could confirm whether it would be possible to increase my credit limit to £5000 — *le <u>agradecería</u> que confirmara*

We would ask you not to use the telephone for long-distance calls — *le pedimos que no*
You are requested to park at the rear of the building — *se <u>ruega</u>*
We look forward to receiv**ing** confirmation of your order within 14 days — *quedamos a la <u>espera</u> de*
Kindly inform us if you require alternative arrangements to be made — *tenga la <u>amabilidad</u> de comunicarnos si*

De manera más indirecta

I would rather you didn't breathe a word to anyone about this — *preferiría que no*
I would appreciate it if you could let me have copies of the best photos — *te <u>agradecería</u> que*
I was hoping that you might have time to visit your grandmother — *esperaba que tendrías*
I wonder whether you could spare a few pounds till I get to the bank? — *¿te sería <u>posible</u> ...?*
I hope you don't mind if I borrow your exercise bike for half an hour — *espero que no te <u>importe</u> que ...*
It would be very helpful o **useful if you could** have everything ready beforehand — *nos <u>vendría</u> muy bien si*
If it's not too much trouble, would you pop my suit into the dry cleaners on your way past? — *si no es mucha molestia, podrías*
You won't forget to lock up before you leave, **will you?** — *no te olvidarás de ..., ¿no?*

32 Comparaciones

32.1   Objetivas

The streets, though wide for China, are narrow **compared with** English ones — *comparadas con*

The bomb used to blow the car up was small **in** o **by comparison with** those often used nowadays — *en comparación con*

If you compare the facilities we have here **with** those in other towns, you soon realize how lucky we are — *si se comparan ... con*

It is interesting to note **the similarities and the differences between** the two approaches — *las semejanzas y las diferencias entre*

In contrast to the opulence of the Kirov, the Northern Ballet Theatre is a modest company — *en contraste con*

Only 30% of the females died **as opposed to** 57% of the males — *frente a*

Unlike other loan repayments, those to the IMF cannot simply be rescheduled — *a diferencia de*

The quality of the paintings is disappointing **beside** that of the sculpture section — *al lado de*

Whereas burglars often used to make off only with video recorders, they now also tend to empty the fridge — *mientras que*

What differentiates these wines from a good champagne is their price — *lo que diferencia ... de*

32.2   Comparaciones favorables

Orwell was, indeed, **far superior to** him intellectually — *muy superior a*

Personally I think high-speed trains **have the edge over** both cars and aircraft for sheer convenience — *aventajan a*

Michaela was astute beyond her years and altogether **in a class of her own** — *única en su género*

32.3   Comparaciones desfavorables

Matthew's piano playing **is not a patch on** his sister's — *no le llega a la suela del zapato a*

My old chair **was nowhere near as** comfortable **as** my new one — *no era ni mucho menos tan ... como*

The parliamentary opposition **is no match for** the government, which has a massive majority — *no puede con*

Commercially-made ice-cream **is far inferior to** the home-made variety — *es muy inferior a*

The sad truth was that **he was never in the same class as** his friend — *no estaba a la misma altura que*

Ella doesn't rate anything **that doesn't measure up to** Shakespeare — *que no esté al nivel de*

Her brash charms **don't bear comparison with** Marlene's sultry sex appeal — *no tienen comparación con*

The Australians are far bigger and stronger than us - **we can't compete with** their robot-like style of play — *no podemos competir con*

32.4   Para destacar el parecido

The new computerized system costs **much the same as** a more conventional one — *prácticamente lo mismo que*

When it comes to performance, **there's not much to choose between** them — *no hay mucha diferencia entre*

The impact was **equivalent to** 250 hydrogen bombs exploding — *equivalente a*

English literature written by people of the ex-colonies **is** clearly **on a par with** the writings of native-born British people — *está al mismo nivel que*

In Kleinian analysis, the psychoanalyst's role **corresponds to** that of mother — *corresponde a*

The immune system **can be likened to** o **compared to** a complicated electronic network — *se le puede comparar con*

There was a close resemblance between her **and** her son — *había un gran parecido entre ... y*

It's swings and roundabouts - what you win in one round, you lose in another — *al final viene a ser lo mismo*

32.5   Para destacar el contraste

You cannot compare a small local library **with** a large city one — *no se puede comparar con*

Homemade clothes **just cannot compare with** bought ones — *no se pueden comparar con*

There's no comparison between the sort of photos I take **and** those a professional could give you — *no hay comparación entre ... y*

His books **have little in common with** those approved by the Party — *tienen poco en común con*

We might be twins, but **we have nothing in common** — *no tenemos nada en común*

The modern army **bears little resemblance to** the army of 1940 — *se parece poco a*

33 Opiniones

33.1 Para pedir la opinión de alguien

What do you think of the new Managing Director?	¿qué _piensas_ de ...?
What is your opinion on women's rights?	¿qué _opinas_ sobre ...?
What are your thoughts on the way forward?	¿cuál es su _opinión_ sobre ...?
What is your attitude to people who say there is no such thing as sexual inequality?	¿cuál es su _actitud_ hacia ...?
What are your own feelings about the way the case was handled?	¿qué _opina_ usted acerca de ...?
How do you see the next stage **developing**?	¿cómo ve el desarrollo de ...?
How do you view an event like the Birmingham show in terms of the cultural life of the city?	¿cóme ve ...?
I would value your opinion on how best to set this all up	apreciaría su _opinión_ sobre
I'd be interested to know what your reaction is to the latest report on food additives	me interesaría conocer su reacción ante

33.2 Para expresar la opinión propia

In my opinion, eight years as President is quite enough for anyone	en mi _opinión_
As I see it, everything depended on Karlov being permitted to go to Finland	según lo veo yo
I feel that there is an epidemic of fear about cancer which is not helped by all the publicity about the people who die of it	_pienso_ que
Personally, I believe the best way to change a government is through the electoral process	personalmente, _creo_ que
It seems to me that the successful designer leads the public	a mi _parecer_
I am under the impression that he is essentially a man of peace	mi _impresión_ es que
I have an idea that you are going to be very successful	_presiento_ que
I am of the opinion that the rules should be looked at and refined	soy de la _opinión_ de que
I'm convinced that we all need a new vision of the future	estoy convencido de que
I daresay there are so many names that you get them mixed up once in a while	me _figuro_ que
We're prepared to prosecute the company, which **to my mind** has committed a criminal offence	a mi _parecer_
From my point of view activities like these should not be illegal	desde mi _punto de vista_
As far as I'm concerned, Barnes had it coming to him	en lo que a mí respecta
It's a matter of common sense, nothing more. **That's my view of the matter**	Esa es mi _opinión_ sobre el tema
It is our belief that to be proactive is more positive than being reactive	nosotros _creemos_ que
If you ask me, there's something a bit strange going on	para mí que
If you want my opinion, if you don't do it soon you'll lose the opportunity altogether	si quiere mi _opinión_

33.3 Para responder sin expresar una opinión

Would I say she had been a help? **It depends what you mean by** help	depende de lo que quiera decir con
It could be seen as a triumph for capitalism but **it depends on your point of view**	depende de su punto de vista
It's hard o **difficult to say whether** she has benefited from the treatment or not	resulta difícil decir si
I'm not in a position to comment on whether the director's accusations are well-founded	no estoy en situación de comentar si
I'd prefer not to comment on operational decisions taken by the service in the past	preferiría no _pronunciarme_ sobre
I'd rather not commit myself at this stage	preferiría no comprometerme
I don't have any strong feelings about which of the two companies we decide to use for the job	no tengo una _opinión_ firme sobre cuál de las dos compañías
This isn't something I've given much thought to	es algo en lo que no me he parado a pensar
I know nothing about fine wine	no sé nada sobre

34 Gustos y preferencias

34.1 Para preguntarle a alguien sus preferencias

Would you like to visit the castle, while you are here?   ¿te _gustaría_ ...?
How would you feel about Simon join**ing** us?   ¿qué te _parecería_ si ...?
What do you like do**ing best** when you're on holiday?   ¿qué es lo que más te _gusta_ hacer ...?
What's your favourite film?   ¿cuál es tu ... _preferida_?
Which of the two proposed options **do you prefer?**   ¿cuál de las dos ... _prefiere_?
We could either go to Rome or stay in Florence - **which would you rather** do?   ¿qué _preferirías_ ...?

34.2 Para expresar gustos

I'm very keen on garden**ing**   me _gusta_ mucho
I'm very fond of white geraniums and blue petunias   me _gustan_ mucho
I really enjoy a good game of squash after work   _disfruto_ con
There's nothing I like more than a quiet night in with a good book   no hay nada que me _guste_ más que
I have a weakness for rich chocolate gateaux   siento _debilidad_ por
I've always had a soft spot for the Dutch   siempre he sentido _debilidad_ por

34.3 Para decir lo que a uno no le gusta

Acting **isn't really my thing** - I'm better at singing   no es lo mío
Watching football on television **isn't my favourite** pastime   no es mi ... _preferido_
Some people might find it funny but **it's not my kind of** humour   no es mi tipo de
I enjoy playing golf, although this type of course **is not my cup of tea**   no es plato de mi gusto
Sitting for hours on motorways **is not my idea of fun**   no es lo que yo llamo divertirse
The idea of walking home at 10 or 11 o'clock at night **doesn't appeal to me**   no me resulta nada atractiva
I've gone off the idea of cycling round Holland   se me han quitado las ganas de
I can't stand o **can't bear** the thought of seeing him   no _soporto_
I am not enthusiastic about shopp**ing** in large supermarkets   no me _entusiasma_
I'm not keen on seafood   no me _entusiasma_
I don't like the fact that he always gets away with not helping out in the kitchen   no me _gusta_ que
What I hate most is waiting in queues for buses   lo que más _detesto_ es
I dislike laziness since I'm such an energetic person myself   me _desagrada_
There's nothing I dislike more than having to go to work in the dark   no hay nada que me _guste_ menos que
I have a particular aversion to the religious indoctrination of schoolchildren   siento una _aversión_ especial por
I find it intolerable that people like him should have so much power   me resulta _intolerable_ que

34.4 Para decir lo que uno prefiere

I'd prefer to o **I'd rather** wait until I have enough money to go by air   _preferiría_
I'd prefer not to o **I'd rather not** talk about it just now   prefiero no
I'd prefer you to give o **I'd rather you** gave me your comments in writing   prefiero que
I'd prefer you not to o **I'd rather you didn't** invite him   prefiero que no lo invites
I like the blue curtains **better than** the red ones   ... me gustan más que ...
I prefer red wine **to** white wine   prefiero ... a

34.5 Para expresar indiferencia

It makes no odds whether you have a million pounds or nothing, we won't judge you on your wealth   _da_ lo mismo que tengas
I really don't care what you tell her as long as you tell her something   me trae sin _cuidado_ lo que
It's all the same to me whether he comes **or** not   me _da_ igual que ... o que
I don't mind at all - let's do whatever is easiest   me da exactamente lo _mismo_
It doesn't matter which method you choose to use   no _importa_ qué
I don't feel strongly about the issue of privatization   no tengo una _opinión_ definida sobre
I have no particular preference   no tengo _preferencias_

35 Intenciones y deseos

35.1 Para preguntar a alguien lo que piensa hacer

Will you take the job?   ¿vas a ...?
What do you intend to do?   ¿qué _piensas_ hacer?
Did you mean to _o_ **intend to** tell him about it, or did it just slip out?   ¿tenías _intención_ de ...?
What do you propose to do with the money?   ¿qué _piensas_ hacer ...?
What did you have in mind for the rest of the programme?   ¿qué tenías _pensado_ ...?
Have you anyone in mind for the job?   ¿tienes a alguien _pensado_ para ...?

35.2 Para expresar las proprias intenciones

We're toying with the idea of releasing a compilation album   le estamos dando _vueltas_ a la posibilidad de

I'm thinking of retiring next year   estoy _pensando_ en
I'm hoping to go and see her when I'm in Paris   _espero_
I studied history, **with a view to** becoming a politician   con _vistas_ a
We bought the land **in order to** farm it   para
We do not penetrate foreign companies **for the purpose of** collecting business information   con el _fin_ de
We plan to move _o_ **We are planning on** moving next year   estamos _planeando_
Our aim _o_ **Our object in** buying the company **is to** provide work for the villagers   nuestro _propósito_ al ... es
I aim to reach Africa in three months   _pretendo_

Con mayor convicción

I am going to sell the car as soon as possible   voy a
I intend to put the house on the market   tengo la _intención_ de
I have made up my mind to _o_ **I have decided to** go to Japan   he _decidido_
I went to Rome **with the intention of** visiting her, but she had gone away   con _intención_ de
We have every intention of winning a sixth successive championship   estamos _decididos_ a
I have set my sights on recapturing the title   mi _objetivo_ es volver a ganar
My overriding ambition is to get into politics   mi gran _ambición_ es
I resolve to do everything in my power to help you   estoy _resuelto_ a

35.3 Para expresar lo que no se piensa hacer

I don't mean to offend you, but I think you're wrong   no es mi _intención_
I don't intend to pay unless he completes the job   no es mi _intención_
I have no intention of accepting the post   no tengo _intención_ de
We are not thinking of taking on more staff   no tenemos _previsto_
We do not envisage making changes at this late stage   no _contemplamos_

35.4 Para expresar lo que se desea hacer

I'd like to see the Sistine Chapel some day   me _gustaría_
I want to work abroad when I leave college   _quiero_
We want her to be an architect when she grows up   _queremos_ que sea
I'm keen to develop the business   tengo mucho _interés_ en

Con gran entusiasmo

I'm dying to leave home   me muero de _ganas_ de
My ambition is to become an opera singer   lo que _ambiciono_ es
I long to go to Australia but I can't afford it   tengo el _anhelo_ de
I insist on speaking to the manager   _insisto_ en

35.5 Para expresar lo que no se quiere hacer

I would prefer not to _o_ **I would rather not** have to speak to her about this   _preferiría_ no
I wouldn't want to have to change my plans just because of her   no _quisiera_
I don't want to take the credit for something I didn't do   no _quiero_
I have no wish _o_ **desire to** become rich and famous   no tengo ningún _deseo_ de
I refuse to be patronized by the likes of her   me _niego_ a

36.1 Para pedir permiso

Can I o **Could I borrow** your car this afternoon?	¿me _dejas_ ...?
Can I use the telephone, please?	¿_puedo_ ...?
Can I have the go-ahead to order the supplies?	¿me das luz verde para ...?
Are we allowed to say what we're up to or is it top secret at the moment?	¿_podemos_ ...?
Would it be all right if I arrived on Monday instead of Tuesday?	¿te _importaría_ que ...?
Would it be possible for us to leave the car in your garage for a week?	¿nos sería _posible_ dejar ...?
We leave tomorrow. **Is that all right by you**?	¿te _parece_ bien?
Do you mind if I come to the meeting next week?	¿te _importa_ que ...?
Would it bother you if I invited him?	¿te _molestaría_ que lo invitara ...?
Would you let me come into partnership with you?	¿me _dejaría_ ...?
Would you have any objection to sail**ing** at once?	¿tiene algún _inconveniente_ en ...?
With your permission, I'd like to ask some questions	con su _permiso_, quisiera

Con más cautela

Is there any chance of borrow**ing** your boat while we're at the lake?	¿nos sería _posible_ ...?
I wonder if I could possibly use your telephone?	¿_podría_ ...?
Might I be permitted to suggest the following ideas?	¿me _permitirían_ que ...?
May I be allowed to set the record straight?	¿me _dejan_ que ...?

36.2 Para dar permiso

You can have anything you want	_puedes_
You are allowed to visit the museum, as long as you apply in writing to the Curator first	_puedes_
It's all right by me if you want to skip the Cathedral visit	por mí _puedes_ ... si
You have my permission to be absent for that week	te doy _permiso_ para
I've nothing against her go**ing** there with us	no me opongo a que
The Crown **was agreeable to** hav**ing** the case called on March 23	dio su _consentimiento_ para que
I do not mind if my letter is forwarded to the lady concerned	no veo _inconveniente_ en que
You have been authorized to use all necessary force to protect relief supply routes	está _autorizado_ a
We should be happy to allow you to inspect the papers here	no tenemos _inconveniente_ en que

Con más insistencia

If you need to keep your secret, **of course you must keep it**	guárdalo, claro
By all means charge a reasonable consultation fee	por _supuesto_
I have no objection at all to your quot**ing** me in your article	no tengo ningún _inconveniente_ en que
We would be delighted to have you	sería un _placer_

36.3 Para denegar permiso

You can't o **you mustn't** go anywhere near the research lab	no _puedes_
I don't want you to see that man again	no _quiero_ que
I'd rather you didn't give them my name	_preferiría_ que no
You're not allowed to leave the ship until relieved	no tienes _permiso_ para
I've been forbidden to swim for the moment	me han _prohibido_ que
I've been forbidden alcohol **by** my doctor	... me ha _prohibido_
I couldn't possibly allow you to pay for all this	¿cómo te voy a _dejar_ ...?
You must not enter the premises without the owners' authority	no se le _autoriza_ a
We cannot allow the marriage **to** take place	no podemos _permitir_ que

Con más insistencia

I absolutely forbid you to take part in any further search	te _prohíbo terminantemente_
You are forbidden to contact my children	tienes _prohibido_
Smoking **is strictly forbidden** at all times	está _terminantemente prohibido_
It is strictly forbidden to carry weapons in this country	está _terminantemente prohibido_
We regret that it is not possible for you to visit the castle at the moment, owing to the building works (_por escrito_)	_lamentamos_ informarle que no se _puede_

37 Obligación

37.1 Para explicar lo que se está obligado a hacer

You've got to o **You have to** be back before midnight	*tienes* que
You must have an address in Prague before you can apply for the job	*tienes* que
You need to have a valid passport if you want to leave the country	*hay* que
I have no choice: this is how **I must** live and I cannot do otherwise	*debo*
He was forced to ask his family for a loan	*se vio obligado a*
Jews **are obliged to** accept the divine origin of the Law	*están obligados a*
A degree **is indispensable** for future entrants to the profession	*es indispensable*
Party membership **is an essential prerequisite of** a successful career	*es un requisito indispensable para*
It is essential to know what the career options are before choosing a course of study	*es esencial*
Wearing the kilt **is compulsory for** all those taking part	*es obligatorio para*
One cannot admit defeat, **one is driven to** keep on trying	*algo te empuja a*
We have no alternative but to fight	*no nos queda otro remedio más que*
Three passport photos **are required**	*se necesitan*
Club members **must not fail to** observe the regulations about proper behaviour	*han de*
You will go directly to the headmaster's office and wait for me there	*vete*

37.2 Para saber si se está obligado a hacer algo

Do I have to o **Have I got to** be home by midnight?	*¿tengo que ...?*
Does one have to o **need to** book in advance?	*¿hay que ...?*
Is it necessary to go into so much detail?	*¿es necesario ...?*
Ought I to tell my colleagues?	*¿debería ...?*
Should I call the police?	*¿debería ...?*
Am I meant to o **Am I expected to** o **Am I supposed to** fill in this bit of the form?	*¿tengo que ...?*

37.3 Para explicar lo que no se está obligado a hacer

I don't have to o **I haven't got to** be home so early now the nights are lighter	*no tengo que*
You don't have to o **You needn't** go there if you don't want to	*no hace falta que*
You are not obliged to o **You are under no obligation to** invite him	*no estás obligado*
It is not compulsory o **obligatory to** have a letter of acceptance but it does help	*no es obligatorio*
The Council **does not expect you to** pay all of your bill at once	*no espera que*

37.4 Para explicar lo que no se debe hacer

On no account must you be persuaded to give up the cause	*no debes de ninguna manera*
You are not allowed to sit the exam more than three times	*no puedes*
Smoking **is not allowed** in the dining room	*no se puede*
You mustn't show this document to any unauthorized person	*no debe*
These are tasks **you cannot** ignore, delegate or bungle	*no puedes*
You're not supposed to o **meant to** use this room unless you are a club member	*no puede*
I forbid you to return there	*te prohíbo que*

De forma menos directa

It is forbidden to bring cameras into the gallery	*está prohibido*
You are forbidden to talk to anyone while the case is being heard	*le está prohibido*
Smoking **is prohibited** o **is not permitted** in the dining room	*está prohibido*

38 Acuerdo

38.1 Para expresar acuerdo con lo que se dice

I **fully agree with you** o I **totally agree with you** on this point	estoy <u>totalmente</u> de <u>acuerdo</u> contigo
We are in complete agreement on this	estamos <u>totalmente</u> de <u>acuerdo</u>
I entirely take your point about the extra vehicles needed	tienes toda la <u>razón</u> en que
I think **we see completely eye to eye** on this issue	pensamos <u>exactamente</u> lo mismo
I talked it over with the chairman and **we are both of the same mind**	ambos somos de la misma <u>opinión</u>
You're quite right in pointing at distribution as the main problem	tienes <u>razón</u> en
We share your views on the proposed expansion of the site	<u>compartimos</u> su opinión
My own experience certainly **bears out** o **confirms** what you say	mi experiencia personal confirma
It's true that you had the original idea but many other people worked on it	es <u>verdad</u> que
As you have quite rightly pointed out, this will not be easy	como bien dijo usted
I have to concede that the results are quite eye-catching	he de <u>reconocer</u> que
I have no objection to this being done	no tengo <u>inconveniente</u> en que
I agree in theory, but in practice it's never quite that simple	en principio estoy de <u>acuerdo</u>
I agree up to a point	estoy de <u>acuerdo</u> hasta cierto punto

De forma más familiar

Go for a drink instead of working late? **Sounds good to me!**	me parece <u>estupendo</u>
That's a lovely idea	¡qué buena idea!
I'm all for encouraging a youth section in video clubs such as ours	soy <u>partidario</u> de
I couldn't agree with you more	estoy <u>totalmente</u> de <u>acuerdo</u> contigo

De forma menos directa

I am delighted to wholeheartedly endorse your campaign	me complace dar mi <u>incondicional</u> <u>apoyo</u> a
Our conclusions are entirely consistent with your findings	nuestras conclusiones <u>confirman</u> ... <u>totalmente</u>
Independent statistics **corroborate** those of your researcher	<u>corroboran</u>
We applaud the group's decision to stand firm on this point	<u>celebramos</u>

38.2 Para expresar acuerdo con lo propuesto

This certainly **seems the right way to go about it**	parece ser la forma <u>correcta</u> de proceder
I will certainly give my backing to such a scheme	cuenta con todo mi <u>apoyo</u>
It makes sense to enlist helping hands for the final stages	tiene sentido
We certainly welcome this development	nos alegra

De forma más familiar

It's a great idea	es una idea <u>estupenda</u>
Cruise control? **I like the sound of that**	suena bien
I'll go along with Ted's proposal that we open the club up to women	<u>apoyo</u>

De forma menos directa

This solution **is most acceptable** to us	nos parece muy <u>aceptable</u>
The proposed scheme **meets with our approval**	<u>aprobamos</u>
This is a proposal which **deserves our wholehearted support**	merece nuestro <u>apoyo</u> incondicional
I shall do my best to **fall in with** her wishes	<u>acceder</u> a

38.3 Para expresar acuerdo con lo que pide alguien

Of course **I'll be happy to** organize it for you	estaré <u>encantado</u> de
I'll do as you suggest and send him the documents	seguiré tu consejo
There's no problem about getting tickets for him	podemos/puedo ... sin problema

De forma menos directa

Reputable builders **will not object to** this reasonable request	no podrán <u>reparos</u> a
We should be delighted to cooperate with you in this enterprise	con mucho <u>gusto</u>
An army statement said it **would comply with** the ceasefire	<u>respetaría</u>
I consent to the performance of such procedures as are considered necessary	<u>accedo</u> a

39 Desacuerdo

39.1   Para mostrarse en desacuerdo con lo que se ha dicho

There must be some mistake - **it can't possibly** cost as much as that	*no es posible que*
I'm afraid he **is quite wrong** if he has told you that	*se _equivoca_*
You're wrong in thinking that I haven't understood	*te _equivocas_ al pensar que*
The article **is mistaken in** claim**ing** that debating the subject is a waste of public money	*comete un _error_ al*
Surveys **do not bear out** Mrs Fraser's assumption that these people will return to church at a later date	*no confirman*
I cannot agree with you on this point	*no estoy de _acuerdo_ contigo*
We cannot accept the view that the lack of research and development explains the decline of Britain	*no _aceptamos_ la opinión de que*
To say we should forget about it, no **I cannot go along with that**	*no puedo _aceptar_ eso*
We must agree to differ on this one	*habrá que _aceptar_ que nunca nos pondremos de _acuerdo_ en este punto*

Con más insistencia

This is most emphatically not the case	*insisto en que no es así*
I entirely reject his contentions	*_rechazo_ totalmente*
I totally disagree with the previous two callers	*no estoy en absoluto de _acuerdo_ con*
This is your view of the events: **it is certainly not mine**	*yo _desde luego_ no lo veo así*
I cannot support you on this matter	*no puedo _apoyarte_*
Surely you can't believe that he'd do such a thing?	*¿no creerás que ...?*

39.2   Para mostrarse en desacuerdo con lo que se ha propuesto

Con decisión

I'm dead against this idea	*estoy _totalmente_ en _contra_ de*
Right idea, wrong approach	*es una buena idea, pero mal enfocado*
I will not hear of such a thing	*no quiero ni oír hablar de*
It is not feasible to change the schedule at this late stage	*no es viable*
This **is not a viable alternative**	*no es una alternativa viable*
Trade sanctions will have an immediate effect but it **is the wrong approach**	*no es forma de hacer las cosas*

Con menos insistencia

I'm not too keen on this idea	*no me _convence_ mucho*
I don't think much of this idea	*no me _convence_ mucho*
This doesn't seem to be the right way of deal**ing** with the problem	*esta no parece la mejor forma de*
While we are grateful for the suggestion, **we are unfortunately unable to** implement this change	*por desgracia nos es _imposible_*
I regret that I am not in a position to accept your kind offer	*_lamento_ no hallarme en condiciones de*

39.3   Para mostrarse en desacuerdo con lo que se ha pedido

I wouldn't dream of do**ing** a thing like that	*no se me ocurriría*
I'm sorry but **I just can't** do it	*es que no _puedo_*
I cannot in all conscience leave those kids in that atmosphere	*en conciencia no _puedo_*

Con más decisión

This is quite out of the question for the time being	*no _puede_ ser*
I won't agree to any plan that involves your brother	*no voy a _apoyar_*
I refuse point blank to have anything to do with this affair	*me _niego_ _rotundamente_*

De forma menos directa

I am afraid I must refuse	*lo _siento_ pero he de _negarme_*
I cannot possibly comply with this request	*me es _imposible_ _acceder_ a*
It is unfortunately impracticable for us to commit ourselves at this stage	*nos es, _por desgracia_, _imposible_*
In view of the proposed timescale, **I must reluctantly decline to** take part	*aun _sintiéndolo_, me veo obligado a _declinar_*

40 Aprobación

40.1 Para aprobar lo que se ha dicho

I couldn't agree (with you) **more** — *Estoy <u>totalmente</u> de <u>acuerdo</u> (contigo)*
I couldn't have put it better myself — *tal y como lo hubiera dicho yo mismo*
We must oppose terrorism, whatever its source. - **Hear, hear!** — *¡sí, señor!*
I endorse his feelings regarding the condition of the Simpson memorial — *<u>suscribo</u>*

40.2 Para aprobar una propuesta

It's just the job! — *¡<u>perfecto</u>!*
This is just the sort of thing I wanted — *es <u>justo</u> lo que quería*
This is exactly what I had in mind — *es <u>justo</u> lo que yo tenía pensado*
Thank you for sending the draft agenda: **I like the look of it very much** — *me ha causado muy buena impresión*
We are all very enthusiastic about *o* **very keen on** his latest set of proposals — *estamos todos <u>entusiasmados</u> con*
I shall certainly give it my backing — *<u>por supuesto</u> que lo voy a <u>apoyar</u>*
Any game which is as clearly enjoyable as this **meets with my approval** — *tiene mi <u>aprobación</u>*
Skinner's plan **deserves our total support** *o* **our wholehearted approval** — *merece todo nuestro <u>apoyo</u>*
There are considerable advantages in the alternative method you propose — *... comporta numerosas ventajas*
We recognize the merits of this scheme — *<u>reconocemos</u> los méritos de*
We view your proposal to extend the site **favourably** — *... nos merece una opinión <u>favorable</u>*
This project **is worthy of our attention** — *merece de nuestra atención*

40.3 Para aprobar una idea

You're quite right to wait before making such an important decision — *tienes toda la <u>razón</u> al*
I entirely approve of the idea — *<u>apruebo</u> totalmente*
I'd certainly go along with that! — *estoy totalmente de <u>acuerdo</u>*
I'm very much in favour of that sort of thing — *soy muy <u>partidario</u> de*
What an excellent idea! — *¡Qué idea tan <u>estupenda</u>!*

40.4 Para aprobar una acción

I applaud Noble's perceptive analysis of the problems — *... merece un <u>aplauso</u>*
I have a very high opinion of their new teaching methods — *tengo muy buena opinión de*
I have a very high regard for the work of the Crown Prosecution Service — *tengo muy buen <u>concepto</u> de*
I think very highly of the people who have been leading thus far — *... me merecen muy buena opinión*
I certainly admire his courage in telling her what he thought of her — *siento gran <u>admiración</u> por*
I must congratulate you on the professional way you handled the situation — *debo <u>felicitarle</u> por*
I greatly appreciated the enormous risk that they had all taken — *les <u>agradecí</u> mucho*
I can thoroughly recommend the event to field sports enthusiasts — *<u>recomiendo</u> plenamente*

41 Desaprobación

This doesn't seem to be the right way of going about it — *no parece ésta la mejor manera de*
I don't think much of what this government has done so far — *no tengo muy buena opinión de*
I can't say I'm pleased about what has happened — *no es que esté muy <u>contento</u> con*
The police **took a dim view of** her attempt to help her son break out of jail — *veía ... con malos ojos*
We have a low *o* **poor opinion of** opportunists like him — *sentimos poca estima por*
They **should not have refused to** give her the money — *no deberían haberse negado a*

Más directamente

I'm fed up with having to wait so long for payments to be made — *estoy hasta la <u>coronilla</u> de*
I've had (just) about enough of this whole supermodel thing — *... (ya) me tiene <u>harto</u>*
I can't bear *o* **stand** people who smoke in restaurants — *no <u>soporto</u>*
How dare he say that! — *¡cómo se atreve a ...!*
He was quite wrong to repeat what I said about her — *hizo muy mal en*
I cannot approve of *o* **support** any sort of testing on live animals — *me <u>resulta</u> <u>inaceptable</u>*
We are opposed to all forms of professional malpractice — *nos <u>oponemos</u> a*
We condemn any intervention which could damage race relations — *<u>condenamos</u>*
I must object to the tag "soft porn actress" — *tengo que <u>protestar</u> contra*
I'm very unhappy about your (idea of) going off to Turkey on your own — *me hace muy poca gracia*
I strongly disapprove of such behaviour — *<u>desapruebo</u> totalmente*

42 Certeza, probabilidad, posibilidad y capacidad

42.1   Certeza

She was bound to discover that you and I had talked — *era de esperar que*
It is inevitable that they will get to know of our meeting — *es inevitable que se enteren*
I'm sure o **certain (that)** he'll keep his word — *estoy seguro de que*
I'm positive o **convinced (that)** it was your mother I saw — *estoy convencido de que*
We now know for certain o **for sure that** the exam papers were seen by several students before the day of the exam — *sabemos ya con seguridad*
I made sure o **certain that** no one was listening to our conversation — *me aseguré de que*
From all the evidence **it is clear that** they were planning to sell up — *está claro que*
What is indisputable is that a diet of fruit and vegetables is healthier — *lo que es indiscutible es que*
It is undeniable that racial tensions in Britain have been increasing — *no se puede negar que*
There is no doubt that the talks will be long and difficult — *no hay ninguna duda de que*
There can be no doubt about the objective of the animal liberationists — *no cabe ninguna duda acerca de*
This crisis has demonstrated **beyond all (possible) doubt** that effective political control must be in place before the creation of such structures — *sin lugar a dudas*
Her pedigree **is beyond dispute** o **question** — *está fuera de dudas*
You have my absolute assurance that this is the case — *tiene mi garantía absoluta de que*
I can assure you that I have had nothing to do with any dishonest trading — *puedo asegurarle que*
Make no mistake about it - I will return when I have proof of your involvement — *que quede bien claro*

42.2   Probabilidad

There is a good o **strong chance that** they will agree to the deal — *hay bastantes probabilidades de que*
It seems highly likely that it was Bert who told Peter what had happened — *parece muy probable que*
The chances o **the odds are that** he will play safe in the short term — *lo más probable es que*
The probability is that your investment will be worth more in two years time — *lo más probable es que*
The child's hearing will, **in all probability,** be severely affected — *con toda probabilidad*
You will **very probably** be met at the airport by one of our men — *es muy probable que*
It is highly probable that American companies will face retaliation abroad — *es muy probable que*
It is quite likely that you will get withdrawal symptoms at first — *es bastante probable que*
The likelihood is that the mood of mistrust and recrimination will intensify — *lo más probable es que*
The person indicted is, **in all likelihood**, going to be guilty as charged — *con toda probabilidad*
There is reason to believe that the books were stolen from the library — *hay motivo para creer que*
He must know of the paintings' existence — *debe de*
The talks **could very well** spill over into tomorrow — *podrían muy bien*
The cheque **should** reach you by Saturday — *debería*
It wouldn't surprise me o **I wouldn't be surprised if** he was working for the Americans — *no me sorprendería que*

42.3   Posibilidad

The situation **could** change from day to day — *podría*
Britain **could perhaps** play a more positive role in developing policy — *podría quizá*
I venture to suggest (that) a lot of it is to do with his political ambitions — *me atrevería a sugerir que*
It is possible that psychological factors play some unknown role in the healing process — *es posible que*
It is conceivable that the economy is already in recession — *cabe la posibilidad de que*
It is well within the bounds of possibility that England could be beaten — *no se puede descartar la posibilidad de que*
It may be that the whole battle will have to be fought over again — *puede ser que*
It may be (the case) that they got your name from the voters' roll — *puede ser que*
There is an outside chance that the locomotive may appear in the Gala — *hay una remota posibilidad de que*
There is a small chance that your body could reject the implants — *existe una pequeña posibilidad de que*

42.4   Para expresar lo que alguien es capaz de hacer

Our Design and Print Service **can** supply envelopes and package your existing literature — *pueden*
Applicants must **be able to** use a word processor — *saber*
He is qualified to teach physics — *tiene titulación para*

43 Incertidumbre, improbabilidad, imposibilidad e incapacidad

43.1 Incertidumbre

I doubt if o **It is doubtful whether** he knows where it came from	_dudo_ que
There is still some doubt surrounding his exact whereabouts	sigue habiendo _dudas_ acerca de
I have my doubts about replac**ing** private donations with taxpayers' cash	tengo mis _dudas_ sobre la sustitución de
It isn't known for sure o **It isn't certain** where she is	no se sabe con _certeza_
No one can say for sure how any child will develop	no se puede decir con _seguridad_
It's all still up in the air - **we won't know for certain** until next week	no lo sabremos con _seguridad_
You're asking why I should do such an extraordinary thing and **I'm not sure** o **certain that** I really know the answer	no estoy _seguro_ de
I'm not convinced that you can really teach people who don't want to learn	no estoy _convencido_ de que
We are still in the dark about where the letter came from	seguimos sin saber
How long this muddle can last **is anyone's guess**	cualquiera sabe
Sterling is going to come under further pressure. **It is touch and go whether** base rates will have to go up	está por ver si
I'm wondering if I should offer to help?	no sé

43.2 Improbabilidad

You have **probably not** yet seen the document I am referring to	_seguramente_ no
It is highly improbable that there will be a challenge for the party leadership in the near future	hay poquísimas _probabilidades_ de que
It is very doubtful whether the expedition will reach the summit	es muy _dudoso_ que
In the unlikely event that the room was bugged, the music would drown out their conversation	si se diera el caso poco _probable_ de que
It was hardly to be expected that democratization would be easy	_apenas_ cabía esperar que

43.3 Imposibilidad

There can be no changes in the schedule	no puede haber
Nowadays Carnival **cannot** happen **without** the police tell**ing** us where to walk and what direction to walk in	no _puede_ ... sin que
People said prices would inevitably rise; **this cannot be the case**	esto es _imposible_
I couldn't possibly invite George and not his wife	¿cómo voy a ...?
The report **rules out any possibility of** exceptions, and amounts to little more than a statement of the obvious	descarta cualquier _posibilidad_ de
There is no question of us gett**ing** this finished on time	es _imposible_ que
A West German spokesman said **it was out of the question that** these weapons would be based in Germany	que ... de ninguna manera
There is not (even) the remotest chance that o **There is absolutely no chance that** he will succeed	no existe la más remota _posibilidad_ de que
The idea of trying to govern twelve nations from one centre **is unthinkable**	es _impensable_
Since we had over 500 applicants, **it would be quite impossible to** interview them all	sería del todo _imposible_

43.4 Para expresar lo que uno es incapaz de hacer

I can't drive, I'm afraid	no _sé_
I don't know how to use a word processor	no _sé_
The army **has been unable to** suppress the political violence in the area	no ha _podido_
The congress had shown itself **incapable of** real reform	_incapaz_ de
His fellow-directors **were not up** to runn**ing** the business without him	no eran _capaces_ de
We hoped the sales team would be able to think up new marketing strategies, but they **were** unfortunately **not equal to the task**	no fueron _capaces_ de hacerlo
I'm afraid the task **proved** (to be) **beyond his capabilities**	resultó demasiado para él
I'd like to leave him but sometimes I feel that such a step **is beyond me**	es superior a mis fuerzas
He simply couldn't cope with the stresses of family life	es que no _podía_ con
Far too many women accept that they're **hopeless at** o **no good at** manag**ing** money	no _sirven_ para controlar
I'm not in a position to say now how much substance there is in the reports	no estoy en situación de
It is quite impossible for me to describe the confusion and horror of the scene	me _resulta_ casi _imposible_

44 Explicaciones

44.1 Para dar las razones de algo

He was sacked **for the simple reason that** he just wasn't up to it any more	por la sencilla <u>razón</u> de que
The reason that we admire him is that he knows what he is doing	la <u>razón</u> de que
He said he could not be more specific **for** security **reasons**	por <u>razones</u> de
The students were arrested **because of** suspected dissident activities	<u>por</u>
Parliament has prevaricated, **largely because of** the unwillingness of the main opposition party to support the changes	sobre todo a <u>causa</u> de
Teachers in the eastern part of Germany are assailed by fears of mass unemployment **on account of** their communist past	a <u>causa</u> de
Morocco has announced details of the austerity package it is adopting **as a result of** pressure from the International Monetary Fund	como <u>consecuencia</u> de
They are facing higher costs **owing to** rising inflation	<u>debido</u> a
The full effects will be delayed **due to** factors beyond our control	<u>debido</u> a
Thanks to their generosity, the charity can afford to buy new equipment	gracias a
What also had to go was the notion that some people were born superior to others **by virtue of** their skin colour	en <u>virtud</u> de
Both companies became profitable again **by means of** severe cost-cutting	<u>mediante</u>
He shot to fame **on the strength of** a letter he had written to the papers	a <u>raíz</u> de
The King and Queen's defence of old-fashioned family values has acquired a poignancy **in view of** their inability to have children	en <u>vista</u> de
The police have put considerable pressure on the Government to toughen its stance **in the light of** recent events	a la <u>luz</u> de
In the face of this continued disagreement, the parties have asked for the polling to be postponed	ante
His soldiers had been restraining themselves **for fear of** harming civilians	por temor a herir
A survey by the World Health Organization says that two out of every five people are dying prematurely **for lack of** food or health care	por <u>falta</u> de
Babies have died **for want of** o **for lack of** proper medical attention	por <u>falta</u> de
I refused her a divorce, **out of** spite I suppose	<u>por</u>
The warder was freed unharmed **in exchange for** the release of a colleague	a <u>cambio</u> de
The court had ordered his release, **on the grounds that** he had already been acquitted of most of the charges against him	<u>basándose</u> en que
I am absolutely in favour of civil disobedience **on** moral **grounds**	por <u>motivos</u>
It is unclear why they initiated this week's attack, **given that** negotiations were underway	<u>dado</u> que
Seeing that he had a police escort, the only time he could have switched containers was on the way to the airport	<u>dado</u> que
As he had been up since 4 a.m., he was doubtless very tired	como
International intervention was appropriate **since** tensions had reached the point where there was talk of war	ya que
She could not have been deaf, **for** she started at the sound of a bell (*literario*)	<u>pues</u>
I cannot accept this decision. **So** I confirm it is my intention to appeal to a higher authority	<u>así que</u>
What the Party said was taken to be right, **therefore** anyone who disagreed must be wrong	<u>por lo tanto</u>
Following last weekend's rioting in central London, Conservatives say some left-wing Labour MPs were partly to blame	tras
The thing is that once you've retired there's no going back	lo que <u>pasa</u> es que

44.2 Para explicar la causa o el origen de algo

The serious dangers to your health **caused by** o **brought about by** cigarettes are now better understood	<u>provocados</u> por
When the picture was published recently, **it gave rise to** o **led to** speculation that the three were still alive and being held captive	dio lugar a
The army argues that security concerns **necessitated** the demolitions	hacían necesarias
This lack of recognition **was at the root of** the dispute	fue la <u>razón</u> fundamental de
I attribute all this mismanagement **to** the fact that the General Staff in London is practically non-existent	<u>atribuyo</u> ... a
This unrest **dates from** colonial times	data de
The custom **goes back to** pre-Christian days	se <u>remonta</u> a

45.1   Para disculparse

I'm really sorry, Steve, **but** we won't be able to come on Saturday — de _verdad_ lo _siento_ ... pero

I'm sorry that your time has been wasted — _siento_ que

I am sorry to have to say this to you but you're no good — _siento_ tener que

Apologies if I wasn't very good company last night — _disculpa_ si

I must apologize for what happened. Quite unforgivable, and the man responsible has been disciplined — le _ruego disculpe_

I owe you an apology. I didn't think you knew what you were talking about — te debo una _disculpa_

The general back-pedalled, saying that **he had not meant to** offend the German government — no había sido su intención ofender

Do forgive me for be**ing** a little abrupt — le _ruego_ me _perdone_ que haya sido

Please forgive me for behav**ing** so badly — _perdóname_ por haberme comportado

Please accept our apologies if this has caused you any inconvenience — les _rogamos_ acepten nuestras _disculpas_

45.2   Para aceptar responsabilidad de algo

I admit I overreacted, but someone needed to speak out against her — _admito_ que

I have no excuse for what happened — no tengo _excusa_ para explicar

It is my fault that our marriage is on the rocks — es _culpa_ mía que

The Government **is not entirely to blame for** the crisis — no tiene toda la _culpa_ de

I should never have let him rush out of the house in anger — no _tenía que_ haber

Oh, but **if only I hadn't** lost the keys — _ojalá_ no hubiera

I hate to admit that the old man was right, but **I made a stupid mistake** — fue un _fallo_ tonto

My mistake was in fail**ing** to push my concerns and convictions as hard as I could have done — mi _error_ fue no conseguir

My mistake was to arrive wearing a jacket and polo-neck jumper — cometí el _error_ de

In December and January the markets raced ahead, and I missed out on that. **That was my mistake** — ese fue mi _error_

45.3   Para expresar lo que se lamenta

I'm very upset about her decision but I accept she needs to move on to new challenges — estoy muy disgustado por

It's a shame that the press gives so little coverage to these events — es una _pena_ que

I feel awful about saying this but you really ought to spend more time with your children — me sabe mal

I'm afraid I can't help you very much — (me temo que) no puedo

It is a pity that my profession can make a lot of money out of the misfortunes of others — es una _lástima_ que

It is unfortunate that the matter should have come to a head just now — es de _lamentar_ que

David and I **very much regret that** we have been unable to reach an agreement — _lamentamos_ mucho

The accused **bitterly regrets** this incident and it won't happen again — _lamenta_ de corazón

We regret to inform you that the post of Editor has now been filled — _lamentamos_ tener que informarle que

45.4   Para rechazar toda responsabilidad

I didn't do it on purpose, it just happened — no lo hice a _propósito_

Sorry, Nanna. **I didn't mean to** upset you — no era mi _intención_

Sorry about not coming to the meeting **I was under the impression that** it was just for managers — tenía idea de que

We are simply trying to protect the interests of local householders — intentamos sencillamente

I know how this hurt you but **I had no choice**. I had to put David's life above all else — no me quedaba otro _remedio_

We were obliged to accept their conditions — nos vimos obligados a

We are unhappy with 1.5%, but under the circumstances **we have no alternative but to** accept — no nos queda otra _alternativa_ que

I had nothing to do with the placing of any advertisement — no tuve nada que ver con

A spokesman for the club assured supporters that **it was a genuine error** and **there was no intention to** mislead them — se trataba de un error auténtico y que no hubo _intención_ de

89 Short Street
Glossop
Derby SK13 4AP

The Personnel Director
Norton Manufacturing Ltd
Sandy Lodge Industrial Estate
Northants NN10 8QT

3 February 1995

Dear Sir or Madam[1]

With reference to your advertisement in the <u>Guardian</u> of 2 February 1995, I wish to apply for the post of Export Manager in your company.

I am currently employed as Export Sales Executive for United Engineering Ltd. My main role is to develop our European business by establishing contact with potential new distributors and conducting market research both at home and abroad.

I believe I could successfully apply my sales and marketing skills to this post and therefore enclose my curriculum vitae for your consideration. Please do not hesitate to contact me if you require further details. I am available for interview at any time.

I look forward to hearing from you.

Yours faithfully

Janet Lilly

---

[1] Cuando no se sabe si el destinatario es hombre o mujer, se debe usar esta fórmula. Por otra parte, si se conoce la identidad del destinatario se puede utilizar una de estas formas al escribir el nombre y dirección:

Mr Derek Balder
Mrs Una Claridge
Ms Nicola Stokes
o
Personnel Director
Messrs. J.M. Kenyon Ltd. *etc.*

En el encabezamiento de la carta, las fórmulas correspondientes serían: "Dear Mr Balder", "Dear Mrs Claridge" etc, "Dear Sir/Madam" (según corresponda, si se sabe si es hombre o mujer), "Dear Sir or Madam" (si no se sabe).

Las cartas que comienzan con el nombre de la persona en el encabezamiento (e.g. "Dear Mr Balder") pueden terminar con la fórmula de despedida "Yours sincerely"; las que empiezan con "Dear Sir/Madam" normalmente acaban con "Yours faithfully", seguido de la firma. Véanse más detalles en las páginas 822-825.

[2] Si se solicita un puesto en el extranjero se puede emplear una frase que explique el título académico que se posee, p.ej. "Spanish/Mexican etc. equivalent of A-Levels (bachillerato superior)", "equivalent to a degree in English Studies etc. (licenciatura en Filología Inglesa etc)".

CURRICULUM VITAE

Name: Margaret Sinclair

Address: 12 Poplar Avenue, Leeds LS12 9DT, England

Telephone: 0113 246 6648

Date of Birth: 2.2.70

Marital Status: Single

Nationality: British

Qualifications[2]: Diploma in Business Management, Liverpool College of Business Studies (1994)
B.A. Honours in French with Hispanic Studies (Upper 2nd class), University of York (1993)
A-Levels: English (B), French (A), Spanish (A), Geography (C) (1988)
O-Levels: in 8 subjects (1986)

Employment History: Assistant Manager, Biblio Bookshop, York (October 1994 to present)
Sales Assistant, Langs Bookshop, York (summer 1994)
English Assistant, Lycée Victor Hugo, Nîmes, France (1991-92)
Campsite courier, Peñíscola, Spain (summer 1989)

Other Information: I enjoy reading, the cinema, skiing and amateur dramatics. I hold a clean driving licence and am a non-smoker.

References: Mr John Jeffries   Ms Teresa González
Manager   Department of Spanish
Biblio Bookshop   University of York
York   York
YT5 2PS   YT4 3DE

46.1 Para empezar la carta

In reply to your advertisement for a Trainee Manager in today's *Guardian*, I would be grateful if you would send me further details of the post

en *respuesta* a su *anuncio*

I wish to apply for the post of bilingual correspondent, as advertised in this week's *Euronews*

desearía que se me considerara para el *puesto* de

I am writing to ask if there is any possibility of work in your company

le *ruego* me informe si existe alguna *posibilidad* de *empleo* dentro de su empresa

I am writing to enquire about the possibility of joining your company on work placement for a period of 3 months

le *agradecería* me informara sobre la *posibilidad* de efectuar *prácticas* de trabajo en su empresa

46.2 Para hablar de la experiencia profesional propia

I have three **years' experience of** office work
tengo ... años de *experiencia* en

I am familiar with word processors
tengo *experiencia* en proceso de textos

As well as speaking fluent English, **I have a working knowledge of** German
además de hablar ... con fluidez, tengo buenos *conocimientos* de

As you will see from my CV, I have worked in Belgium before
como verá en mi *currículum*

Although I have no experience of this type of work, I have had other holiday jobs and can supply references from my employers, if you wish
a pesar de carecer de *experiencia* en

My current salary is ... per annum and I have four weeks' paid leave
mi *sueldo* actual es de

46.3 Para exponer las motivaciones propias

I would like to make better use of my languages
quisiera hacer más uso de los *idiomas* que conozco

I am keen to work in public relations
tengo mucho interés en trabajar en

46.4 Para terminar la carta

I will be available from the end of April
estaré libre a partir de

I am available for interview at any time
me tendrá a su disposición para una *entrevista* personal

Please do not hesitate to contact me for further information
no dude en ponerse en contacto conmigo

Please do not contact my current employers
le *rogaría* que no se comunicara con mi empresa

I enclose a stamped addressed envelope for your reply
adjunto

46.5 Como pedir y redactar referencias

In my application for the position of lecturer, I have been asked to provide the names of two referees and **I wondered whether you would mind if I gave your name** as one of them
le *agradecería* me permitiera dar su nombre

Ms Lee has applied for the post of Marketing Executive with our company and has given us your name as a reference. **We would be grateful if you would let us know whether you would recommend her for this position**
le *agradeceríamos* nos informase si merece su *recomendación* para tal *puesto*

Your reply will be treated in the strictest confidence
su *respuesta* será tratada con absoluta *reserva*

I have known Mr Chambers for four years in his capacity as Sales Manager and **can warmly recommend him for the position**
me *complace recomendarlo* para el *puesto*

46.6 Para aceptar o rechazar una propuesta de empleo

Thank you for your letter of 20 March. **I will be pleased to attend for interview** at your Manchester offices on Thursday 7 April at 10am
con mucho gusto me presentaré a la entrevista personal que me solicitan

I would like to confirm my acceptance of the post of Marketing Executive
deseo confirmar que *acepto*

I would be delighted to accept this post. However, would it be possible to postpone my starting date until 8 May?
aceptaría encantado el puesto. *Sin embargo,*

I would be glad to accept your offer; however, the salary stated is somewhat lower than what I had hoped for
aceptaría con mucho gusto su oferta; *sin embargo*

Having given your offer careful thought, **I regret that I am unable to accept**
lamento no poder *aceptarla*

47 Correspondencia comercial

Ms Sharon McNeillie
41 Courthill Street
Beccles NR14 8TR

18 January 1995

Dear Ms McNeillie

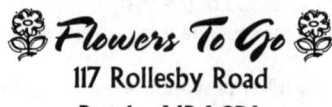

Flowers To Go
117 Rollesby Road
Beccles NR6 9DL
☎ 61 654 31 71

Special Offer! 5% discount on orders received in January!

Thank you for your recent enquiry. We can deliver fresh flowers anywhere in the country at very reasonable prices. Our bouquets come beautifully wrapped, with satin ribbons, attractive foil backing, a sachet of plant food and, of course, your own personalized message. For that special occasion, we can even deliver arrangements with a musical greeting, the ideal surprise gift for birthdays, weddings or Christmas!

Whatever the occasion, you will find just what you need to make it special in our latest brochure, which I have pleasure in enclosing, along with our current price list. All prices include delivery within the UK.

During the promotion, a discount of 5% will apply on all orders received before the end of January, so hurry!

We look forward to hearing from you.

Yours sincerely

Daisy Duckworth

Daisy Duckworth
Promotions Assistant

Carrick Foods Ltd

Springwood Industrial Estate
Alexandra Road
Sheffield S11 5GF

Ms J Birkett
Department of English
Holyrood High School
Mirlees Road
Sheffield S19 7KL

14 April 1995

Dear Ms Birkett

Thank you for your letter of 7 April enquiring if it would be possible to arrange a group visit to our factory. We would of course be delighted to invite you and your pupils to take part in a guided factory tour. You will be able to observe the process from preparation through to canning, labelling and packaging of the final product ready for dispatch. Our factory manager will be available to answer pupils' questions at the end of the tour.

I would be grateful if you could confirm the date of your proposed visit, as well as the number of pupils and teachers in the party, at your earliest convenience.

Thank you once again for your interest in our company. I look forward to meeting you.

Yours sincerely

George Whyte

George Whyte

47.1 Peticiones de información

We see from your advertisement in the Healthy Holiday Guide that you are offering cut-price holidays in Scotland, and **would be grateful if you would send us** details

hemos visto ... Les agradeceríamos que nos enviaran

I read about the Happy Pet Society in the NCT newsletter and would be very interested to learn more about it. **Please send me details of** membership — les _agradecería_ que me _enviaran_ información detallada sobre

... y cómo responder

In response to your enquiry of 8 March, **we have pleasure in enclosing** full details on our activity holidays in Cumbria, **together with** our price list, valid until May 1997 — en _respuesta_ a su consulta del ... _adjuntamos_ ... acompañados de

Thank you for your enquiry about the Society for Wildlife Protection. **I enclose** a leaflet explaining our beliefs and the issues we campaign on. **Should you wish** to join, a membership application form is also enclosed — le _agradecemos_ el interés mostrado por .... Le _envío_ .... Si se decidiera a

47.2 Pedidos y cómo responder

We would like to place an order for the following items, in the sizes and quantities specified below — desearíamos hacer un _pedido_ de

Please find enclosed our order no. 3011 for ... — _adjunto_ encontrará nuestro _pedido_ n°

The enclosed order is based on your current price list, assuming our usual discount — el _pedido adjunto_

I wish to order a can of "Buzz off!" wasp repellent, as advertised in the July issue of Gardeners' Monthly, **and enclose a cheque for** £2.50 — desearía _encargar_ ... para lo que _adjunto_ un cheque por valor de

Thank you for your order of 3 May, which will be dispatched within 30 days — le _agradecemos_ su _pedido_ de fecha

We acknowledge receipt of your order no. 3570 and advise that the goods will be dispatched within 7 working days — acusamos recibo de su _pedido_ n°

We regret that the goods you ordered are temporarily out of stock — _lamentamos_ tener que informarle que los artículos solicitados se hallan agotados temporalmente

Please allow 28 days **for delivery** — la _entrega_ se efectuará en un _plazo_ de

47.3 Entregas

Our delivery time is 60 days from receipt of order — nuestro _plazo_ de _entrega_ es de

We await confirmation of your order — quedamos a la espera de _confirmación_ de su _pedido_

We confirm that the goods were dispatched on 4 September — _confirmamos_ que el _envío_ de la mercancía tuvo lugar el

We cannot accept responsibility for goods damaged in transit — _lamentamos_ no poder responsabilizarnos de

47.4 Para hacer una reclamación

We have not yet received the items ordered on 6 May (ref. order no. 541) — no hemos _recibido_ aún

Unfortunately, the goods were damaged in transit — _desgraciadamente_

The goods received differ significantly from the description in your catalogue — los artículos recibidos difieren sustancialmente de los descritos

If the goods are not received by 20 October, **we shall have to cancel our order** — nos veremos obligados a _anular_ nuestro _pedido_

47.5 Pagos

The total amount outstanding is ... — el _importe_ pendiente se eleva a

We would be grateful if you would attend to this account immediately — les _agradeceríamos_ que nos enviaran _liquidación_ de esta _cuenta_

Please remit payment by return — _sírvase_ remitirnos el _pago_ a vuelta de correo

Full payment **is due within** 14 working days from receipt of goods — vence en un _plazo_ de

We enclose a cheque for ... **in settlement of your invoice no.** 2003L/58 — _adjuntamos_ ... como _liquidación_ de su _factura_ n°

We must point out an error in your account and **would be grateful if you would adjust your invoice** accordingly — les _agradeceríamos_ que rectificaran su _factura_

This mistake was due to an accounting error, and **we enclose a credit note for** the sum involved — _abonamos_

Thank you for your cheque for ... in settlement of our invoice — le _agradecemos_ su _cheque_ por valor de

We look forward to doing further business with you in the near future — Esperamos poder volver a servirles

48 Correspondencia de carácter general

226 Wilton Street
Leicester LE8 7SP

20th November 1994

Dear Hannah,

Sorry I haven't been in touch for a while. It's been hectic since we moved house and we're still unpacking! Anyway, it's Leah's first birthday on the 30th and I wondered if you and the kids would like to come to her party that afternoon. We were planning to start around 4 o'clock and finish around 5.30 or so. I've invited a clown and a children's conjurer, mainly for the entertainment of the older ones. With a bit of luck, you and I might get a chance to catch up on all our news!

Drop me a line or give me a ring if you think you'll be able to make it over on the 30th. It would be lovely if you could all come!

Hoping to hear from you soon. Say hello to Danny, Paul and Jonathan for me.

Love,

Jackie

---

14 Apsley Grove
Aberdeen AB4 7LP
Scotland

14th April 1995

Dear Paloma and Paco,

How are you? I hope you and the children enjoyed Montse's birthday party yesterday. I wish I could have been there too.

My flight from Madrid was delayed, so we didn't reach Gatwick till after midnight last night. I am a bit tired, but at least I have the weekend ahead to recover before going back to work on Monday!

You were so kind to me and I can't thank you enough for all your warmth and hospitality. It was a truly unforgettable stay. I took lots of photographs, as you know, and I intend to have them developed as soon as possible so I can look at them and think of you all. I shall, of course, send you copies of the best ones.

Remember that you are only too welcome to come and stay with me any time. It would be lovely to see you both and to have the opportunity to do something for you at last.

Keep in touch and take care!

With love from

Sandra

El esquema siguiente proporciona ejemplos de fórmulas de saludo y de despedida que se usan a menudo en la correspondencia. Dentro de cada sección son posibles las permutaciones:

A alguien conocido personalmente

Dear Mr Brown		
Dear Mrs Drake		
Dear Mr & Mrs Charlton	Yours sincerely	
Dear Miss Baker		
Dear Ms Black		
Dear Dr Armstrong	With all good wishes, Yours sincerely	
Dear Professor Lyons		*tratamiento más cordial*
Dear Sir Gerald	With kindest regards, Yours sincerely	
Dear Lady Mcleod		
Dear Andrew		
Dear Margaret		

A un(a) amigo(a), a un pariente

Dear Victoria	With love from	
Dear Aunt Eleanor	Love from	
Dear Granny and Grandad	Love to all	
Dear Mum and Dad	Love from us all	
My dear Elizabeth	Yours	*tratamiento familiar*
My dear Albert		
Dearest Norman	All the best	
My dearest Mother		
My dearest Lucy	With much love from	
My darling Peter	Lots of love from	*tratamiento afectuoso*
	Much love, as always	
	All my love	

Cartas comerciales (véase también pág. 822)

Dear Sirs[1]		[1] *para dirigirse a una empresa*
Dear Sir[2]		[2] *para dirigirse a un hombre*
Dear Madam[3]	Yours faithfully	[3] *para dirigirse a una mujer*
Dear Sir or Madam[4]		[4] *cuando no se sabe si se dirige uno a un hombre o una mujer*

A un conocido o un(a) amigo(a)

Dear Alison	Yours sincerely	
Dear Annie and George		
Dear Uncle Eric	With best wishes, Yours sincerely	
Dear Mrs Newman	With kindest regards, Yours sincerely	*tratamiento más cordial*
Dear Mr and Mrs Jones	All good wishes, Yours sincerely	
My dear Miss Armitage		
	With best wishes, *(etc)* Yours ever	
	Kindest regards,	*tratamiento familiar*
	Best wishes	
	With best wishes, As always	

48.1 Para comenzar una carta

Para escribir a alguien que se conoce

Thank you o **Thanks for your letter** which arrived yesterday	*gracias* por tu *carta*
It was good o **nice** o **lovely to hear from you**	me *alegró* recibir *noticias* tuyas
It's such a long time since we were last in touch that **I felt I must write a few lines** just to say hello	*pensé* que tenía que *escribirte* unas líneas
I'm sorry I haven't written for so long, and hope you'll forgive me; I've had a lot of work recently and ...	*perdona* que no te haya *escrito* desde hace tanto tiempo

Para escribir a una organización

I am writing to ask whether you have in stock a book entitled ...	*el motivo de mi carta* es preguntarles si
Please send me ... I enclose a cheque for ...	les *ruego* me *envíen*
When I left your hotel last week, I think I may have left a red coat in my room. **Would you be so kind as to** let me know whether it has been found?	si fueran tan *amables*, ¿podrían ...?
I have seen the details of your summer courses, and **wish to know whether** you still have any vacancies on the Beginners' Swedish course	*desearía* saber si

48.2 Para terminar el cuerpo de la carta (antes de la despedida)

A un conocido

Gerald joins me in sending very best wishes to you all	Gerald y yo os *deseamos* lo mejor a todos
Please remember me to your wife - I hope she is well	dele mis *recuerdos* a
I look forward to hearing from you	quedo a la *espera* de tu *respuesta*

A un amigo

Say hello to Martin for me	*saluda* a Martin de mi *parte*
Give my warmest regards to Vincent	un *abrazo* para Vincent
Do write when you have a minute	*escríbeme*
Hoping to hear from you before too long	*esperando* recibir *noticias* tuyas pronto

A amigos íntimos

Rhona **sends her love**/Ray **sends his love**	*abrazos/besos* de *parte* de
Give my love to Daniel and Laura, and tell them how much I miss them	*abrazos/besos* a
Jodie and Carla **send you a big hug**	te mandan un muy fuerte *abrazo*

48.3 Preparativos de viaje

Para reservar una habitación

Please send me details of your prices	*sírvanse* enviarme *información* detallada sobre
Please let me know by return of post if you have one single room with bath, half board, for the week commencing 3 October	*sírvanse informarme* a vuelta de correo si
I would like to book bed-and-breakfast accommodation with you	*desearía reservar*

48.4 Para confirmar o anular una reserva

Please consider this a firm booking and hold the room until I arrive, however late in the evening	le ruego considere esta como una *reserva* en firme
Please confirm the following by fax: one single room with shower for the nights of 20-23 April 1996	*sírvanse* confirmarme por fax los siguientes datos
We expect to arrive in the early evening, unless something unforeseen happens	*esperamos* llegar
I am afraid I must ask you to alter my booking from 25 August **to** 3 September. I hope this will not cause too much inconvenience	me veo obligado a solicitarle que cambie mi *reserva* del ... al
Owing to unforseen circumstances, **I am afraid (that) I must cancel the booking** made with you for the week beginning 5 September	*lamento* tener que *anular* la *reserva*

49 Agradecimientos

Just a line to say thanks for the lovely book which arrived today — *sólo unas letras para darle las <u>gracias</u> por*

I can't thank you enough for find**ing** my watch — *no se cómo darle las <u>gracias</u> por*
(Would you) please thank him from me — *dele las <u>gracias</u> de mi <u>parte</u>*
We greatly appreciated your support during our recent difficulties — *<u>agradecemos</u> enormemente*
Your advice and understanding **were much appreciated** — *le quedamos muy <u>reconocidos</u> por*
I am writing to thank you *o* **to say thank you for** allow**ing** me to quote your experience in my article on multiple births — *me dirijo a usted para darle las <u>gracias</u> por permitirme*
Please accept our sincere thanks for all your help and support — *le damos nuestro más sincero <u>agradecimiento</u> por*

A big thank you to everyone involved in the show this year — *muchísimas <u>gracias</u> a todos*
We would like to express our appreciation to the University of Durham Research Committee for providing a grant — *queremos expresar nuestro <u>reconocimiento</u> a*

De parte de un grupo

Thank you on behalf of the Manx Operatic Society **for** all your support — *<u>gracias</u> en nombre de ... por*
I am instructed by our committee **to convey our sincere thanks for** your assistance at our recent Valentine Social — *... me ha encomendado que les <u>transmitiera</u> nuestro <u>sincero</u> <u>agradecimiento</u> por*

50 Saludos de cortesía y felicitaciones

50.1 Expresiones para cualquier ocasión

I hope you have a lovely holiday — *<u>espero</u> que tengas*
With love and best wishes for your wedding anniversary — *os <u>deseo</u> un <u>feliz</u>*
(Do) give my best wishes to your mother **for** a happy and healthy retirement — *dile a ... que le <u>deseo</u> lo mejor en*
Len **joins me in sending you our very best wishes for** your future career — *... y yo te <u>deseamos</u> lo mejor en*

50.2 En Navidad y Año Nuevo

Merry Christmas and a happy New Year — *<u>Feliz</u> <u>Navidad</u> y <u>Próspero</u> Año Nuevo*
With season's greetings and very best wishes from (*+ firma*) — *les <u>deseamos</u> unas <u>felicés</u> <u>fiestas</u>*
May I send you all our very best wishes for 1997 — *quisiera <u>desearles</u> a todos un <u>feliz</u>*

50.3 Para un cumpleaños

All our love and best wishes on your 21st **birthday**, from Simon, Liz, Kerry and the cats — *te <u>deseamos</u> muchísimas <u>felicidades</u> en tu 21 <u>cumpleaños</u>. Con todo nuestro <u>cariño</u>*

I am writing to wish you **many happy returns (of the day)**. Hope your birthday brings you everything you wished for — *muchas <u>felicidades</u> (en el día de tu <u>cumpleaños</u>)*

50.4 Para desear una pronta recuperación

Sorry (to hear) you're ill - **get well soon!** — *que te <u>mejores</u> pronto*
I was very sorry to learn that you were ill, and **send you my best wishes for a speedy recovery** — *le <u>deseo</u> una pronta <u>recuperación</u>*

50.5 Para desear buena suerte

Good luck in your driving test. I hope things go well for you on Friday — *buena <u>suerte</u> en el*
Sorry to hear you didn't get the job - **better luck next time!** — *¡que haya más <u>suerte</u> la próxima vez!*
We all wish you the best of luck in your new job — *te <u>deseamos</u> mucha <u>suerte</u> con*

50.6 Para felicitar a alguien

You're expecting a baby? **Congratulations!** When is the baby due? (*hablado*) — *¡<u>enhorabuena</u>! (esp Sp), ¡<u>felicitaciones</u>! (esp LAm)*

You've finished the job already? **Well done!** (*hablado*) — *¡muy bien!*
We all send you our love and congratulations on such an excellent result (*escrito*) — *<u>enhorabuena</u> de <u>parte</u> de todos por*
This is to send you our warmest congratulations and best wishes on your engagement (*escrito*) — *recibe nuestra más cordial <u>enhorabuena</u> por*

51 Notas y avisos de sociedad

51.1 Para anunciar un nacimiento

Julia Archer **gave birth to** a 6lb 5oz **baby son**, Andrew, last Monday. **Mother and baby are doing well**

... *dio a luz un niño. Tanto la madre como el niño se encuentran en perfecto estado*

Ian and Zoë Pitt **are delighted to announce the birth of a daughter**, Laura, on 1st May, 1994, at Minehead Hospital (*en una carta o periódico*)

se <u>complacen</u> en <u>anunciar</u> el <u>nacimiento</u> de su hija

At the Southern General Hospital, on 1st December, 1994, **to Paul and Diane Kelly (née Smith) a son, John Alexander,** a brother for Helen (*en un periódico*)

Paul y Diane Kelly tienen el <u>placer</u> de <u>anunciar</u> el <u>nacimiento</u> de su hijo, John Alexander

... y para responder

Congratulations on the birth of your son

<u>enhorabuena</u> por el <u>nacimiento</u> de

We were delighted to hear about the birth of Stephanie, and send our very best wishes to all of you

nos <u>alegró</u> mucho saber del <u>nacimiento</u> de

51.2 Para anunciar un compromiso matrimonial

I'm sure you'll be pleased to hear that Jim and I **got engaged** yesterday

estamos <u>prometidos</u> desde

It is with much pleasure that the engagement is announced between Michael, younger son of Professor and Mrs Perkins, York, **and** Jennifer, only daughter of Dr and Mrs Campbell, Hucknall (*en un periódico*)

nos <u>complace</u> anunciar el <u>compromiso</u> matrimonial entre ... y

... y para responder

Congratulations to you both on your engagement, and very best wishes for a long and happy life together

<u>enhorabuena</u> a los dos por vuestro <u>compromiso</u>

I was delighted to hear of your engagement, and wish you both all the best for your future together

me ha <u>alegrado</u> mucho saber de su <u>compromiso</u>

51.3 Para anunciar una boda

I'm getting married in June, to a wonderful man named Lester Thompson

me <u>caso</u> el 1 de junio de 1996 tuvo lugar el

At Jurby Church, on 1st June, 1996, Eve, daughter of Ian and Mary Jones, Jurby, to John, son of Ray and Myra Watt, Ayr (*en un periódico*)

<u>enlace</u> matrimonial de Eve Jones, hija de Ian y Mary Jones, vecinos de Jurby, con John Watt, hijo de Ray y Myra Watt de Ayr. La ceremonia fue celebrada en la Iglesia de Jurby

... y para responder

Congratulations on your marriage, and best wishes to you both for your future happiness

<u>enhorabuena</u> por vuestra <u>boda</u>. Os <u>deseamos</u> lo mejor para el futuro

We were delighted to hear about your daughter's marriage to Iain, and wish them both all the best for their future life together

nos hemos <u>alegrado</u> mucho de saber de la <u>boda</u> de su hija con

51.4 Para anunciar un fallecimiento

My husband **died suddenly** in March

<u>murió</u> de repente

It is with great sadness that I have to tell you that Joe's father **passed away** three weeks ago

con gran <u>dolor</u> tengo que <u>comunicarte</u> el <u>fallecimiento</u>

Suddenly, at home, in Newcastle-upon-Tyne, on Saturday 2nd July, 1994, Alan, aged 77 years, **the beloved husband of** Helen and **loving father of** Matthew (*en un periódico*)

... <u>falleció</u> repentinamente ... dejando a su desconsolada esposa ... e hijo

... y para responder

My husband and I **were greatly saddened to learn of the passing of** Dr Smith, and send (*o* offer) you and your family our most sincere condolences

nos <u>entristeció</u> enormemente enterarnos del <u>fallecimiento</u> de

We wish to extend our deepest sympathy for your sad loss to you and your wife

queremos expresarle nuestro más sentido <u>pésame</u> a su mujer y a usted por su dolorosa <u>pérdida</u>

51.5 Para anunciar el cambio de dirección

We are moving house next week. **Our new address** as of 4 May 1996 **will be ...**

las nuevas <u>señas</u> ... son

52.1 Invitaciones oficiales

Mr and Mrs James Waller **request the pleasure of your company at the marriage of** their daughter Mary Elizabeth to Mr Richard Hanbury at St Mary's Church, Frampton on Saturday, 21st August, 1997 at 2 o'clock and afterwards at Moor House, Frampton

tienen el <u>placer</u> de <u>invitarles</u> al <u>enlace</u> de

The Chairman and Governors of Hertford College, Oxford **request the pleasure of the company of** Miss Charlotte Young and partner **at a dinner** to mark the anniversary of the founding of the College

tienen el <u>placer</u> de <u>invitar</u> a ... a la cena

... y para responder

We thank you for your kind invitation to the marriage of your daughter Annabel on 20th November, **and have much pleasure in accepting**

<u>gracias</u> por su amable <u>invitación</u> a ..., que <u>aceptamos</u> con mucho <u>gusto</u>

Mr and Mrs Ian Low **thank** Dr and Mrs Green for **their kind invitation to** the marriage of their daughter Ann on 21st July **and are delighted to accept**

<u>agradecen</u> su amable <u>invitación</u> a ... y aceptan <u>encantados</u>

We regret that we are unable to accept your invitation to the marriage of your daughter on 6th May

<u>sentimos</u> no poder <u>aceptar</u> su <u>invitación</u> a

52.2 Invitaciones a fiestas

We are celebrating Rosemary's engagement to David by holding a dinner dance at the Central Hotel on Friday 11th February, 1997, **and very much hope that you will be able to join us**

celebramos el <u>compromiso matrimonial</u> de Rosemary y David ... y esperamos que podáis acompañarnos

We are giving a dinner party next Saturday, **and would be delighted if you and your wife could come**

damos una cena ... y nos <u>encantaría</u> que vinierais tu mujer y tú

I'm having a party next week for my 18th - **come along, and bring a friend**

voy a hacer una <u>fiesta</u> ... te espero. Y puedes traer a un amigo

52.3 Para quedar con alguien

Would you and Gordon like to come to dinner next Saturday?

¿os <u>gustaría</u> venir a tí y a Gordon ...?

Would you be free for lunch next Tuesday?

¿tienes tiempo para ...?

Perhaps we could meet for coffee some time next week?

podíamos

52.4 Para aceptar una invitación

Yes, I'd love to meet up with you tomorrow

sí, me <u>encantaría</u> verte

It was good of you to invite me, I've been longing to do something like this for ages

me <u>alegro</u> de que me hayas <u>invitado</u>

Thank you for your invitation to dinner - **I look forward to it very much**

<u>gracias</u> por su <u>invitación</u> a ... iré con mucho <u>gusto</u>

52.5 Para declinar una invitación

I'd love to come, but I'm afraid I'm already going out that night

me <u>encantaría</u> ir, pero

I wish I could come, but unfortunately I have something else on

<u>ojalá</u> pudiera ir, pero por <u>desgracia</u>

It was very kind of you to invite me to your dinner party next Saturday. **Unfortunately I will not be able to accept**

<u>desgraciadamente</u> no voy a poder aceptar

Much to our regret, we are unable to accept

<u>sentimos</u> tener que decirle que nos es imposible <u>aceptar</u>

52.6 Sin dar una respuesta concreta

I'm not sure what I'm doing that night, but I'll let you know later

no estoy <u>seguro</u> de

It all depends on whether I can get a sitter for Rosie at short notice

<u>depende</u> de si

I'm afraid I can't really make any definite plans until I know when Alex will be able to take her holidays

el problema es que no puedo <u>planear</u> nada definitivamente

53 Redacción

53.1 El argumento en líneas generales

Para introducir un tema

De manera impersonal

It is often said *o* **claimed that** teenagers get pregnant in order to get council accommodation
se suele afirmar que

It is a cliché *o* **a commonplace (to say) that** American accents are infinitely more glamorous than their British counterparts
es un tópico (decir) que

It is undeniably true that Gormley helped to turn his union members into far more sophisticated workers
es innegable que

It is a well-known fact that in this age of technology, it is computer screens which are responsible for many illnesses
es un hecho de sobra conocido que

It is sometimes forgotten that much Christian doctrine comes from Judaism
a veces se olvida que

It would be naïve to suppose that in a radically changing world these 50-year-old arrangements can survive
sería ingenuo suponer que

It would hardly be an exaggeration to say that the friendship of both of them with Britten was among the most creative in the composer's life
se puede decir sin temor a exagerar que

It is hard to open a newspaper nowadays without reading that TV is going to destroy reading and that electronic technology has made the written word obsolete
hoy en día resulta difícil abrir un periódico en el que no leamos que

First of all, it is important to try to understand some of the systems and processes involved in order to create a healthier body
en primer lugar, es importante intentar comprender

It is in the nature of sociological theory **to** make broad generalizations about such things as the evolution of society
es un rasgo característico de

It is often the case that early interests lead on to a career
suele suceder que

De manera personal

By way of introduction, let me summarize the background to this question
a modo de introducción, voy a

I would like to start with a very sweeping statement which can be easily challenged
comenzaré con

Before going specifically into the issue of criminal law, **I wish first to summarize** how Gewirth derives his principles of morality and justice
antes de entrar en el tema concreto de ... quisiera resumir

Let us look at what self-respect in your job actually means
examinemos

We commonly think of people **as** isolated individuals but, in fact, few of us ever spend more than an hour or two of our waking hours alone
normalmente consideramos a ... como

What we are mainly concerned with here is the conflict between what the hero says and what he actually does
nuestra principal preocupación aquí es

We live in a world in which the word "equality" is liberally bandied about
en el mundo en que vivimos

Para incluir conceptos y problemas

The concept of controlling harmful insects by genetic means isn't new
el concepto de

The idea of getting rich without too much effort has universal appeal
la idea de

The question of whether Hamlet was really insane has long occupied critics
que ... es una cuestión que

Why they were successful where their predecessors had failed **is a question that has been much debated**
es una cuestión muy debatida

One of the most striking aspects of this issue is the way (in which) it arouses strong emotions
uno de los aspectos más notables de este tema

There are a number of issues on which China and Britain openly disagree
hay una serie de puntos

Para hacer generalizaciones

People who work outside the home **tend to believe that** parenting is an easy option
la gente que ... tiende a creer que

There's always **a tendency for people to** exaggerate their place in the world
hay una tendencia entre la gente a

Many gardeners **have a tendency to** treat plants like humans
tienen tendencia a

Viewed psychologically, it would seem that **we all have the propensity for** such traits
todos somos propensos a

For the (vast) majority of people, literature is a subject which is studied at school but which has no relevance to life as they know it
para la (inmensa) mayoría de la gente

For most of us, housework is a necessary but boring task
para la mayoría de nosotros

History **provides numerous examples** *o* **instances of** misguided national heroes who did more harm than good in the long run
aporta numerosos ejemplos

Para ser más preciso

The impact of these theories on the social sciences, and economics **in particular**, was extremely significant	*en concreto*
One particular issue raised by Butt was, suppose Hughes at the time of his conviction had been old enough to be hanged, what would have happened?	*un punto en concreto*
A more specific point relates to using this insight as a way of challenging our hidden assumptions about reality	*un aspecto más concreto*
More specifically, he accuses Western governments of continuing to supply weapons and training to the rebels	*más en concreto*

53.2 Para presentar una tesis

Para introducirla

First of all, let us consider the advantages of urban life	*en primer lugar, consideremos*
Let us begin with an examination of the social aspects of this question	*comencemos con un examen de*
The first thing that needs to be said is that the author is presenting a one-sided view	*lo primero que hay que decir es que*
What should be established at the very outset is that we are dealing here with a practical issue rather than a philosophical one	*antes de nada debemos dejar claro que*

Para delimitar el debate

In the next section, I will pursue the question of whether the expansion of the Dutch prison system can be explained by Box's theory	*en la próxima sección me centraré en la cuestión de*
I will then deal with the question of whether or not the requirements for practical discourse are compatible with criminal procedure	*a continuación me ocuparé de la cuestión de*
We must distinguish between the psychic and the spiritual, and **we shall see how** the subtle level of consciousness is the basis for the spiritual level	*veremos cómo*
I will confine myself to giving an account of certain decisive facts in my militant career with Sartre	*me limitaré a*
In this chapter, **I shall largely confine myself to** a consideration of those therapeutic methods that use visualization as a part of their procedures	*me limitaré en gran medida a*
We will not concern ourselves here with the Christian legend of St James	*no nos vamos a ocupar aquí de*
Let us now consider to what extent the present municipal tribunals differ from the former popular tribunals in the above-mentioned points	*pasemos a considerar ahora*
Let us now look at the ideal types of corporatism that neo-corporatist theorists developed to clarify the concept	*pasemos a examinar*

Para exponer los puntos

The main issue under discussion is how the party should re-define itself if it is to play any future role in Hungarian politics	*el principal punto de debate es*
A second, related problem is that business ethics has mostly concerned itself with grand theorizing	*otro problema relacionado con esto es*
The basic issue at stake is this: is research to be judged by its value in generating new ideas?	*el punto básico en cuestión es éste:*
An important aspect of Milton's imagery **is** the play of light and shade	*un aspecto importante de ... es*
It is worth mentioning here that when this was first translated, the opening reference to Heidegger was entirely deleted	*cabe mencionar aquí que*
Finally, there is the argument that watching too much television may stunt a child's imagination	*por último, está el argumento de que*

Para poner un argumento en duda

World leaders appear to be taking a tough stand, but **is there any real substance in what's been agreed**?	*¿se ha decidido algo concreto?*
This is a question which **merits close(r) examination**	*merece un estudio (más) detallado*
The unity of the two separate German states **has raised fundamental questions** for Germany's neighbours	*ha planteado interrogantes fundamentales para*
The failure to protect our fellow Europeans in Bosnia **raises fundamental questions on** the role of the armed forces	*plantea problemas fundamentales sobre*
This raises once again the question of whether a government's right to secrecy should override the public's right to know	*... lo que plantea, una vez más, la cuestión de*
This poses the question of whether these measures are really helping the people they were intended to help	*la cuestión que esto plantea es*

Para ofrecer un análisis de la cuestión

It is interesting to consider why this scheme has been so successful — *es interesante examinar porqué*

On the question of whether civil disobedience is likely to help end the war, Chomsky is deliberately diffident — *en lo que concierne a*

We are often faced with the choice between our sense of duty **and** our own personal inclinations — *solemos vernos ante la necesidad de escoger entre ... y*

When we speak of realism in music, **we do not at all have in mind** the illustrative bases of music — *al hablar de ..., no tenemos presente en absoluto*

It is reasonable to assume that most people living in industrialized societies are to some extent contaminated by environmental poisons — *está dentro de lo razonable suponer que*

Para aportar un argumento

An argument in support of this approach **is that** it produces ... — *un argumento a favor de ... es que*

In support of his theory, Dr Gold notes that most oil contains higher-than-atmospheric concentrations of helium-3 — *para apoyar su teoría*

This is the most telling argument in favour of an extension of the right to vote — *éste es el argumento más convincente a favor de*

The second reason for advocating this course of action **is that** it benefits the community at large — *la segunda razón para mostrarse partidario de ... es que*

The third, more fundamental, reason for looking to the future **is that** even the angriest investors realize they need a successful market — *la tercera razón, más fundamental, para ... es que*

Despite communism's demise, confidence in capitalism seems to be at an all-time low. **The fundamental reason for** this contradiction seems to me quite simple — *la razón fundamental de*

53.3 Para presentar una antítesis

Para criticar u oponerse a algo

In actual fact, the idea of there being a rupture between a so-called old criminology and an emergent new criminology **is somewhat misleading** — *de hecho, la idea de ... es en cierto modo engañoso*

In order to argue this, **I will show that** Wyeth's position is, in actual fact, **untenable** — *voy a demostrar que la postura de ... es ... insostenible*

It is claimed, however, that the strict Leboyer method is not essential for a less traumatic birth experience — *se afirma, sin embargo,*

This need not mean that we are destined to suffer for ever. **Indeed, the opposite may be true** — *esto no significa que .... De hecho quizá sea lo contrario*

Many observers, though, **find it difficult to share his opinion that** it could mean the end of the Tamil Tigers — *les resulta difícil compartir su opinión de que*

On the other hand, there are more important factors that should be taken into consideration — *por otra parte*

The judgement made **may well be true but** the evidence given to sustain it is unlikely to convince the sceptical — *bien puede ser cierto pero*

Reform **is all very well, but** it is pointless if the rules are not enforced — *está muy bien, pero*

The case against the use of drugs in sport rests primarily on the argument that .... **This argument is weak,** for two reasons — *este argumento carece de solidez*

According to one theory, the ancestors of vampire bats were fruit-eating bats. But **this idea does not hold water** — *esta idea no se sostiene*

Their claim to be a separate race **does not stand up to** historical scrutiny — *no resiste*

This view does not stand up if we examine the known facts about John — *esta opinión no se sostiene*

The trouble with this idea is not that it is wrong, **but rather that** it is uninformative — *el problema no es que esta idea ... sino que*

The difficulty with this view is that he bases the principle on a false premise — *el problema que plantea esta opinión radica en que*

The snag with such speculations **is that** too much turns on one man or event — *la pega de ... es que*

But removing healthy ovaries **is entirely unjustified in my opinion** — *no tiene, en mi opinión, justificación alguna*

Para proponer una alternativa

Another approach may be to develop substances capable of blocking the effects of the insect's immune system — *otro planteamiento posible es*

Another way to reduce failure is to improve vocational education — *otra forma de*

However, the other side of the coin is the fact that an improved self-image really can lead to prosperity — *sin embargo, la otra cara de la moneda es*

It is more accurate to speak of a plurality of new criminologies rather than of a single new criminology	*es más <u>preciso</u> hablar de*
Paradoxical as it may seem, computer models of mind can be positively humanizing	*aunque parezca <u>paradójico</u>*

53.4 Para presentar la <u>síntesis</u> argumental

Para evaluar los argumentos expuestos

How can we reconcile these two apparently contradictory viewpoints?	*¿cómo reconciliar ...?*
On balance, making money honestly is more profitable than making it dishonestly	*al fin y al cabo*
Since such vitamins are more expensive, **one has to weigh up the pros and cons**	*hay que <u>sopesar</u> los <u>pros</u> y los <u>contras</u>*
We need to look at the pros and cons of normative theory as employed by Gewirth and Phillips	*es necesario <u>examinar</u> los <u>pros</u> y <u>contras</u> de*
The benefits of partnership in a giant trading market **will** almost certainly **outweigh the disadvantages**	*los <u>beneficios</u> de ... pesarán más que los <u>inconvenientes</u>*
The two perspectives are not mutually exclusive	*las dos perspectivas no se <u>excluyen</u> mutuamente*

Para decantarse por uno de los argumentos

Dr Meaden's theory **is the most convincing explanation**	*es la explicación más <u>convincente</u>*
The truth o **fact of the matter is that** in a free society you can't turn every home into a fortress	*lo <u>cierto</u> es que*
But **the truth is that** Father Christmas has a rather mixed origin	*lo <u>cierto</u> es que*
Although this operation sounds extremely dangerous, **in actual fact** it is extremely safe	*en <u>realidad</u>*
When all is said and done, it must be acknowledged that a purely theoretical approach to social issues is sterile	*a fin de cuentas, se debe <u>reconocer</u> que*

Para resumir los argumentos

In this chapter, **I have demonstrated** o **shown that** the Cuban alternative has been undergoing considerable transformations	*he <u>demostrado</u> que*
This shows how, in the final analysis, adhering to a particular theory on crime is at best a matter of reasoned choice	*esto <u>demuestra</u> cómo*
The overall picture shows that prison sentences were relatively frequent, but not particularly severe	*la visión de conjunto <u>demuestra</u> que*
To recap o **To sum up, then, (we may conclude that)** there are in effect two possible solutions to this problem	*en <u>resumen</u>, (se puede <u>concluir</u> que)*
To sum up this chapter I will offer two examples ...	*para <u>resumir</u> este capítulo*
To summarize, we have seen that the old staple industries in Britain had been hit after the First World War by a deteriorating international competitive position	*en <u>resumen</u>*
Habermas's argument, **in a nutshell**, is as follows	*en <u>suma</u>*
But **the key to the whole argument is** a single extraordinary paragraph	*la clave del problema ... se encuentra en*
To round off this section on slugs, gardeners may be interested to hear that there are three species of predatory slugs in the British Isles	*para <u>terminar</u> esta sección sobre*

Para extraer conclusiones

From all this, it follows that it is impossible to extend those kinds of security measures to all potential targets of terrorism	*de todo esto se <u>deduce</u> que*
This, of course, **leads to the logical conclusion that** those who actually produce do have a claim to the results of their efforts	*nos lleva a la <u>conclusión</u> lógica de que*
There is only one logical conclusion we can reach, which is that we ask our customers what is the Strategic Reality that they perceive in our marketing programme	*sólo podemos llegar a una <u>conclusión</u> lógica*
The inescapable conclusion is that the criminal justice system does not simply reflect the reality of crime; it helps create it	*la <u>conclusión</u> ineludible es que*
We must conclude that there is no solution to the problem of defining crime	*debemos decir, a modo de <u>conclusión</u>, que*
In conclusion, because interpersonal relationships are so complex, there can be no easy way of preventing conflict	*en <u>conclusión</u>*
The upshot of all this is that treatment is unlikely to be available	*la consecuencia de todo esto es que*
So it would appear that butter is not significantly associated with heart disease after all	*parece, pues, que*

This only goes to show that a good man is hard to find — *esto demuestra*

The lesson to be learned from this **is that** you cannot hope to please everyone all of the time — *la lección que se puede aprender es*

At the end of the day, the only way the drug problem will be beaten is when people are encouraged not to take them — *al fin y al cabo*

Ultimately, then, while we may have some sympathy for these young criminals, we must do our utmost to protect society from them — *en definitiva*

53.5 La estructura del párrafo

Para añadir información

In addition, the author does not really empathize with his hero — *además*

This award-winning writer, **in addition to** be**ing** a critic, biographer and poet, has written 26 crime novels — *además de ser*

But this is only part of the picture. **Added to this are** fears that a major price increase would cause riots — *hay que añadir*

An added complication **is that** the characters are not aware of their relationship to one another — *una ... más es*

Also, there is the question of language — *además*

The question also arises as to how this idea can be put into practice — *también se plantea la cuestión de*

Politicians, **as well as** academics and educationalists, tend to feel strongly about the way history is taught — *al igual que*

But, **over and above that**, each list contains fictitious names and addresses — *además de eso*

Furthermore, ozone is, like carbon dioxide, a greenhouse gas — *además*

Para comparar

Compared with the heroine, Alison is an insipid character — *comparada con*

In comparison with the Czech Republic, the culture of Bulgaria is less westernized — *en comparación con*

This is a high percentage for the English Midlands but low **by comparison with** some other parts of Britain — *si se compara con*

On the one hand, there is no longer a Warsaw Pact threat. **On the other (hand)**, the positive changes could have negative side-effects — *por una parte ... por otra*

Similarly, a good historian is not obsessed by dates — *del mismo modo*

There can only be one total at the bottom of a column of figures and **likewise** only one solution to any problem — *del mismo modo*

What others say of us will translate into reality. **Equally**, what we affirm as true of ourselves will likewise come true — *de igual manera*

There will now be a change in the way we are regarded by our partners, and, **by the same token**, the way we regard them — *del mismo modo*

There is a fundamental difference between adequate nutrient intake **and** optimum nutrient intake — *hay una diferencia fundamental entre ... y*

Para unir dos elementos

First of all o **Firstly**, I would like to outline the benefits of the system — *en primer lugar*

In music we are concerned **first and foremost** with the practical application of controlled sounds relating to the human psyche — *ante todo*

In order to understand the conflict between the two nations, **it is first of all necessary to** know something of the history of the area — *para comprender ... es necesario ante todo*

Secondly, it might be simpler to develop chemical or even nuclear warheads for a large shell than for a missile — *en segundo lugar*

In the first/second/third place, the objectives of privatization were contradictory — *en primer/segundo/tercer lugar*

Finally, there is the argument that watching too much television may stunt a child's imagination — *por último*

Para expresar una opinión personal

In my opinion, the government is underestimating the scale of the epidemic — *en mi opinión*

My personal opinion is that the argument lacks depth — *mi opinión personal es que*

This is a popular viewpoint, but **speaking personally**, I cannot understand it — *yo personalmente*

Personally, I think that no one can appreciate ethnicity more than black or African people themselves — *yo personalmente*

For my part, I cannot agree with the leadership on this question — *por mi parte*

My own view is that what largely determines the use of non-national workers are economic factors rather than political ones — *mi opinión personal es que*

In my view, it only perpetuates the very problem that it sets out to address — *a mi parecer*

Although the author argues the case for patriotism, **I feel that** he does not do it with any great personal conviction — *creo que*

I believe that people do understand that there can be no quick fix for Britain's economic problems — *yo creo que*

It seems to me that what we have is a political problem that needs to be solved at a political level — *a mi parecer*

I would maintain that we have made a significant effort to ensure that the results are made public — *yo afirmaría que*

Para expresar la opinión de otra persona

He claims o **maintains that** intelligence is conditioned by upbringing — *mantiene que*

Bukharin **asserts that** all great revolutions are accompanied by destructive internal conflict — *afirma que*

The communiqué **states that** some form of nuclear deterrent will continue to be needed for the foreseeable future — *manifiesta que*

What he is saying is that the time of the old, highly structured political party is over — *lo que dice es que*

His admirers **would have us believe that** watching this film is more like attending a church service than having a night at the pictures — *quieren hacernos creer*

According to the report, poverty creates a climate favourable to violence — *según*

Para dar un ejemplo

To take another example: many thousands of people have been condemned to a life of sickness and pain because ... — *para poner otro ejemplo*

Let us consider, **for example** o **for instance**, the problems faced by immigrants arriving in a strange country — *por ejemplo*

His meteoric rise **is the most striking example yet of** voters' disillusionment with the record of the previous government — *es el ejemplo más claro de ... hasta ahora*

The case of Henry Howey Robson **serves to illustrate** the courage exhibited by young men in the face of battle — *sirve para ilustrar*

Just consider, **by way of illustration**, the difference in amounts accumulated if interest is paid gross, rather than having tax deducted — *a modo de ejemplo*

A case in point is the decision to lift the ban on contacts with the republic — *un ejemplo que viene al caso es*

Take the case of the soldier returning from war — *tomemos el caso de*

As the Prime Minister **remarked** recently, the Channel Tunnel will greatly benefit the whole of the European Community — *tal y como ha señalado ...*

53.6 Los mecanismos del debate

Para presentar una suposición

They have telephoned the president to put pressure on him. **And that could be interpreted as** trying to gain an unconstitutional political advantage — *y eso se podría interpretar como*

Retail sales rose sharply last month. This was higher than expected and **could be taken to mean that** inflationary pressures remain strong — *podría hacernos suponer*

In such circumstances, **it might well be prudent** to diversify your investments — *quizá sería prudente*

These substances do not remain effective for very long. **This is possibly because** they work against the insects' natural instinct to feed — *posiblemente se deba a que*

His wife had become an embarrassment to him and therefore **it is not beyond the bounds of possibility that** he may have contemplated murdering her — *no está fuera de lo posible que*

Mr Fraser's assertion **leads one to suppose that** he is in full agreement with Catholic teaching as regards marriage — *nos lleva a suponer*

It is probably the case that all long heavy ships are vulnerable — *probablemente*

After hearing nothing from the taxman for so long, most people **might reasonably assume that** their tax affairs were in order — *podría suponerse lógicamente que*

One could be forgiven for thinking that because the substances are chemicals they'd be easy to study — *es comprensible que se piense que*

I venture to suggest that very often when people like him talk about love, they actually mean lust — *me atrevo a sugerir que*

Para expresar certeza

<u>Véase también la sección 42 CERTEZA</u>

It is clear that any risk to the human foetus is very low	está <u>claro</u> que
Benn is **indisputably** a fine orator, one of the most compelling speakers in politics today	<u>indiscutiblemente</u>
British universities are **undeniably** good, but they are not turning out enough top scientists	no se puede <u>negar</u> que
There can be no doubt that the Earth underwent a dramatic cooling which destroyed the environment and life style of these creatures	no cabe <u>duda</u> alguna de que
It is undoubtedly true that over the years there has been a much greater emphasis on safer sex	es <u>indudable</u> que
As we all know, adultery is far from uncommon, particularly in springtime	como todos sabemos
One thing is certain: the party is far from united	lo que es <u>cierto</u> es que
It is (quite) certain that unless peace can be brought to this troubled land no amount of aid will solve the long-term problems of the people	está (muy) <u>claro</u> que

Para expresar dudas

<u>Véase también la sección 43 DUDAS</u>

It is doubtful whether, in the present repressive climate, anyone would be brave or foolish enough to demonstrate publicly	es <u>dudoso</u> que
It remains to be seen whether the security forces will try to intervene	queda por ver si
I have a few reservations about the book	tengo ciertas <u>reservas</u> acerca de
The judges are expected to endorse the recommendation, but **it is by no means certain that** they will make up their minds today	no hay ninguna <u>seguridad</u> de que
It is questionable whether media coverage of terrorist organizations actually affects terrorism	es <u>discutible</u> que
This raises the whole question of exactly when men and women should retire	esto <u>plantea</u> la cuestión de
The crisis **puts a question mark against** the Prime Minister's stated commitment to intervention	abre un <u>interrogante</u> acerca de
Both these claims are true up to a point and they need to be made. But they are limited in their significance	ambas <u>afirmaciones</u> son <u>ciertas</u> hasta cierto punto

Para mostrarse de acuerdo

<u>Véase también la sección 38 ACUERDO</u>

I agree wholeheartedly with the opinion that smacking should be outlawed	<u>coincido</u> <u>totalmente</u> con
One must acknowledge that their history will make change more painful	hay que <u>reconocer</u> que
It cannot be denied that there are similarities between the two approaches	no se puede <u>negar</u> que
Courtney - **rightly in my view** - is strongly critical of the snobbery and élitism that is all too evident in these circles	<u>pienso</u> que con toda la <u>razón</u>
Preaching was considered an important activity, **and rightly so** in a country with a high illiteracy rate	y con mayor <u>razón</u>
You may dispute the Pope's right to tell people how to live their lives, **but it is hard to disagree with** his picture of modern society	pero es <u>difícil</u> no <u>coincidir</u> con

Para mostrarse en desacuerdo

<u>Véase también la sección 39 DESACUERDO</u>

I must disagree with Gordon's article on criminality: it is dangerous to suggest that to be a criminal one must look like a criminal	debo mostrar mi <u>desacuerdo</u> con
As a former teacher **I find it hard to believe that** there is no link at all between screen violence and violence on the streets	me <u>cuesta</u> creer que
The strength of their feelings **is scarcely credible**	es poco verosímil
Her claim to have been the first to discover the phenomenon **lacks credibility**	<u>carece</u> de toda <u>credibilidad</u>
Nevertheless, **I remain unconvinced by** Milton	... sigue sin <u>convencerme</u>
Many do not believe that water contains anything remotely dangerous. Sadly, **this is far from the truth**	dista mucho de ser <u>cierto</u>
To say that everyone requires the same amount of a vitamin is as stupid as saying we all have blonde hair and blue eyes. **It simply isn't true**	sencillamente no es <u>cierto</u>
His remarks **were** not only highly offensive to black and other ethnic minorities but **totally inaccurate**	<u>totalmente</u> erróneos

Stomach ulcers are often associated with good living and a fast-moving lifestyle. **(But) in reality** there is no evidence to support this theory   *pero en <u>realidad</u>*

This version of a political economy **does not stand up to close scrutiny**   *no resiste un análisis pormenorizado*

Para resaltar uno de los argumentos

Nowadays, **there is clearly** less stigma attached to unmarried mothers   *está <u>claro</u> que hay*

Evidence shows that ..., so once again **the facts speak for themselves**   *los hechos hablan por sí solos*

Few will argue with the principle that such a fund should be set up   *apenas hay quien <u>discuta</u> el <u>principio</u>*

Hyams **supports this claim** by looking at sentences produced by young children learning German   *apoya esta <u>afirmación</u>*

The most important thing is to reach agreement from all sides   *lo más <u>importante</u> es*

Perhaps **the most important aspect of** cognition is the ability to manipulate symbols   *el aspecto más <u>importante</u> de*

Para destacar un punto en concreto

It would be impossible to exaggerate the importance of these two volumes for anyone with a serious interest in the development of black gospel music   *no se puede exagerar la <u>importancia</u> de*

The symbolic importance of Jerusalem for both Palestinians and Jews **is almost impossible to overemphasize**   *nunca se insistirá demasiado en*

It is important to be clear that Jesus does not identify himself with Yahweh   *es <u>importante</u> dejar claro que*

It is significant that Mandalay seems to have become the central focus in this debate   *<u>resulta</u> <u>revelador</u> que*

It should not be forgotten that many of those now in exile were close to the centre of power until only one year ago   *no hay que olvidar que*

It should be stressed that the only way pet owners could possibly contract such a condition from their pets is by eating them   *habría que <u>recalcar</u> que*

There is a very important point here and that is that the accused claims that he was with Ms Martins all evening on the night of the crime   *lo que resulta <u>importante</u> aquí es que*

At the beginning of his book Mr Stone **makes a telling point**. The Balkan peoples, he notes, are for the first time ...   *hace un comentario <u>revelador</u>*

Suspicion is **the chief feature of** Britain's attitude to European theatre   *el rasgo <u>primordial</u> de*

In order to focus attention on Hobson's distinctive contributions to macroeconomics, these wider issues are neglected here   *con objeto de <u>centrarnos</u> en*

These statements are interesting in that they illustrate different views   *estas <u>afirmaciones</u> son <u>interesantes</u> porque*

Language in Use

Contents

Spanish-English

Lengua y Uso

Índice de materias

Inglés-Español

ENGLISH~SPANISH DICTIONARY

DICCIONARIO INGLÉS~ESPAÑOL

A

A¹, a¹ [eɪ] N **(a)** (*letter*) A, a *f.* **(b)** (*Mus*) A la *m*; **A minor** la *m* menor; **No. 32ᴬ** (*house*) núm. 32 bis, núm. 32 duplicado; **to know a subject from A to Z** saber un tema de cabo a rabo; **to get from A to B** ir de A a B; **A for Andrew, A for Able** (*US*) A de Antonio. **(c) A Level** *V* advanced (b); **A-line dress** vestido *m* de línea trapezoide; **A road** ≈ carretera *f* nacional; **'A' shares** acciones *fpl* de clase A; **A-side** cara *f* A; **A-test** prueba *f* de bomba atómica. **(c)** (*Scol*) sobresaliente.

A. ABBR of **answer** respuesta *f.*

a² [eɪ, ə], **an** [æn, ən, n] (*before words starting with a vowel sound*) INDEF ART **(a)** un, una.
(b) (*omitted in translation*) **half an hour** media hora; **a fine excuse!** ¡bonita disculpa!; **have you a passport?** ¿tiene Vd pasaporte?; **he is an engineer** es ingeniero; **what an idiot!** ¡qué idiota!; (*negative uses*) **I am not a doctor** yo no soy médico; **I haven't got a car** no tengo coche; **you don't stand a chance** no tienes posibilidad alguna; **without a doubt** sin duda; **without saying a word** sin decir palabra; (*apposition*) **the Duero, a Spanish river** el Duero, río de España.
(c) (*a certain*) **a Mr Smith called to see you** vino a verle un tal Sr Smith.
(d) (*distributive*) **2 apples a head** 2 manzanas por persona.
(e) (*rate*) **50 kilometres an hour** 50 kilómetros por hora; **£80 a week** 80 libras por semana; **3 times a month** 3 veces al mes; **she reads 3 books a week** lee 3 libros cada semana; **3 dollars a dozen** 3 dólares la docena.

a... PREF a...; **atonal** atonal; **atypical** atípico.

a- (*†† or dialectal*): **everyone came a-running** todos acudieron corriendo; **it was a-snowing hard** estaba nevando mucho.

A1 [ˈeɪˈwʌn] ADJ de primera clase, de primera categoría; excelente; **to be ~ at Lloyd's** estar en excelentes condiciones, (*fig*) tener la máxima garantía; **to feel ~** estar muy bien.

A3 [ˈeɪˈθriː] ADJ: **~ size** (*paper*) papel *m* tamaño A3, doble folio *m.*

A4 [ˈeɪˈfɔːʳ] ADJ: **~ size** (*paper*) papel *m* tamaño A4, folio *m.*

A&E [ˌeɪənˈdiː] N ABBR of **Accident and Emergency** ≈ Urgencias *fpl.*

AA N **(a)** (*Brit*) ABBR of **Alcoholics Anonymous** Alcohólicos *mpl* Anónimos, A.A. **(b)** (*Brit Aut*) ABBR of **Automobile Association** ≈ RACE *m*, Real Automóvil Club *m* de España. **(c)** (*US Univ*) ABBR of **Associate in** (*or* of) **Arts** Profesor *m* numerario de letras. **(d)** (*Mil*) ABBR of **anti-aircraft** antiaéreo.

AAA N **(a)** ABBR of **Amateur Athletics Association** Asociación *f* de Atletismo Amateur. **(b)** (*US Aut*) ABBR of **American Automobile Association** ≈ Real Automóvil Club *m* de España, RACE *m.*

Aachen [ˈɑːxən] N Aquisgrán *m.*

AAF N ABBR of **American Air Force** Fuerzas *fpl* Aéreas Americanas.

AAIB N (*Brit*) ABBR of **Air Accident Investigation Branch.**

AAM N ABBR of **air-to-air missile.**

AAR ABBR of **against all risks** contra todo riesgo.

Aaron [ˈɛərən] NM Aarón.

AAUP N (*US Univ*) ABBR of **American Association of University Professors.**

AB **(a)** (*Naut*) ABBR of **able-bodied seaman** marinero *m* de primera. **(b)** (*US Univ*) ABBR of **Bachelor of Arts** Lic. en Fil. y Let. **(c)** (*Canada*) ABBR of **Alberta.**

ABA N **(a)** ABBR of **Amateur Boxing Association** Asociación *f* de Boxeo Amateur. **(b)** (*US*) ABBR of **American Bankers Association.** **(c)** (*US*) ABBR of **American Bar Association.**

aback [əˈbæk] ADV: **to take ~** desconcertar, coger de improviso; **to be taken ~** quedar desconcertado; **I was quite taken ~ by the news** la noticia me causó gran sorpresa, la noticia me cogió de improviso.

abacus [ˈæbəkəs] N, PL **abacuses** *or* **abaci** [ˈæbəsaɪ] ábaco *m.*

abaft [əˈbɑːft] **1** ADV a popa, en popa.
2 PREP detrás de.

abalone [ˌæbəˈləʊnɪ] N (*US*) oreja *f* marina.

abandon [əˈbændən] **1** VT **(a)** (*leave*) abandonar, desamparar; salir de; descuidar; **old car etc** dejar tirado; **to ~ sb to his fate** abandonar a uno a su suerte; **~ ship!** ¡evacuar el barco!, ¡todos a los botes!
(b) (*give up*) renunciar a, abandonar; **the attempt had to be ~ed** hubo que renunciar a la tentativa; **the game was ~ed after 20 minutes' play** después de 20 minutos de juego se anuló el partido; **~ hope all ye who ...** abandonad la esperanza todos los que ...
2 VR: **to ~ o.s. to** abandonarse a, entregarse a.
3 N abandono *m*; libertad *f*, desenfado *m*, desenfreno *m*; **to dance with wild ~** abandonarse al éxtasis del baile, bailar desenfrenadamente; **to talk with gay ~** hablar con el mayor desenfado (*or* desparpajo).

abandoned [əˈbændənd] ADJ **(a)** (*deserted*) abandonado; desierto; *child* desamparado. **(b)** (*uninhibited*) libre, desenfadado; **in an ~ fashion** con abandono, desenfrenadamente. **(c)** (*vicious*) vicioso, entregado a los vicios. **(d) an ~ woman** una mujer perdida, una mujer de conducta dudosa.

abandonment [əˈbændənmənt] N **(a)** (*state*) desamparo *m*, abandono *m*; (*act*) acto *m* de desamparar, el abandonar (*etc*). **(b)** (*moral*) = **abandon 3.**

abase [əˈbeɪs] **1** VT humillar, rebajar, degradar; envilecer, despreciar.
2 VR: **to ~ o.s.** humillarse; envilecerse.

abasement [əˈbeɪsmənt] N humillación *f*, rebajamiento *m*, degradación *f*; envilecimiento *m.*

abashed [əˈbæʃt] ADJ avergonzado, confuso, corrido, desconcertado; **to be ~** quedar confuso; **to be ~ at** avergonzarse de; quedar desconcertado por; **he carried on not a bit ~** siguió sin dar la menor señal de vergüenza, siguió como si tal cosa.

abate [əˈbeɪt] **1** VT disminuir, reducir; acabar con; (*Jur*) suprimir; *price* rebajar; *violence* mitigar, suavizar; *energy* debilitar; *enthusiasm* moderar; *pride* abatir.
2 VI disminuir, reducirse; ceder, menguar; (*violence, enthusiasm*) moderarse; (*wind*) calmarse, amainar; (*pain*) ceder; (*fever, flood, price*) bajar; (*courage*) desfallecer.

abatement [əˈbeɪtmənt] N disminución *f*, reducción *f*; moderación *f*; (*Jur*) supresión *f*; (*of pain*) alivio *m.*

abattoir [ˈæbətwɑːʳ] N matadero *m*, camal *m* (*And*), picadero *m* (*And*).

abbacy [ˈæbəsɪ] N abadía *f.*

abbé [ˈæbeɪ] N abate *m.*

abbess [ˈæbɪs] N abadesa *f.*

abbey [ˈæbɪ] N abadía *f*; monasterio *m*, convento *m*, cenobio *m*; **~ church** iglesia *f* abacial; **Westminster A~** Abadía *f* de Westminster.

abbot [ˈæbət] N abad *m.*

abbr., abbrev. ABBR of **abbreviation, abbreviated.**

abbreviate [əˈbriːvɪeɪt] VT abreviar.

abbreviation [əˌbriːvɪˈeɪʃən] N (*short form*) abreviatura *f*; (*act*) abreviación *f.*

ABC [ˈeɪbiːˈsiː] N **(a)** abecé *m*; abecedario *m*; (*fig*) abecé *m*; **~ of Politics** (*as title*) Introducción *f* a la política. **(b)** ABBR of **Australian Broadcasting Commission. (c)** (*US*) ABBR of **American Broadcasting Company.**

abdicate [ˈæbdɪkeɪt] **1** VT *throne* abdicar; *responsibility, rights* renunciar a; *principles* abdicar de.
2 VI abdicar (*in favour of* en, en favor de).

abdication [ˌæbdɪˈkeɪʃən] N abdicación *f*; renuncia *f.*

abdomen [ˈæbdəmen, (*Med*) æbˈdəʊmen] N abdomen *m.*

abdominal [æbˈdɒmɪnl] ADJ abdominal.

abducent [æbˈdjuːsənt] ADJ abductor.

abduct [æbˈdʌkt] VT raptar, secuestrar, plagiar (*LAm*).

abduction [æbˈdʌkʃən] N rapto *m*, secuestro *m*, plagio *m* (*LAm*).

abductor [æbˈdʌktəʳ] N raptor *m*, secuestrador *m.*

abed†† [əˈbed] ADV en cama, acostado.

Aberdonian [ˌæbəˈdəʊnɪən] **1** ADJ de Aberdeen.
2 N nativo *m*, -a *f* (*or* habitante *mf*) de Aberdeen.

aberrant [əˈberənt] ADJ aberrante; (*Bio etc*) anómalo, anormal.

aberration [ˌæbeˈreɪʃən] N (*all senses*) aberración *f*.
abet [əˈbet] VT *criminal* incitar; ayudar; *crime* instigar; **to ~ sb in a crime** ser cómplice de uno en un crimen; **X, aided and ~ted by Y** X, persuadido y ayudado por Y; **accused of aiding and ~ting** acusado de ser cómplice en un crimen.
abetment [əˈbetmənt] N incitación *f*, instigación *f*; (*Jur*) complicidad *f*.
abetter, abettor (*esp Jur*) [əˈbetəʳ] N instigador *m*, -ora *f*; fautor *m*, -ora *f*; (*esp Jur*) cómplice *mf*.
abeyance [əˈbeɪəns] N: **to be in ~** estar en suspenso; estar pendiente de aplicación; **to fall into ~** caer en desuso.
abhor [əbˈhɔːʳ] VT aborrecer, abominar (de), detestar, odiar.
abhorrence [əbˈhɒrəns] N (**a**) aborrecimiento *m*, detestación *f*; **violence fills me with ~** aborrezco la violencia; **to hold in ~** detestar. (**b**) (*object*) abominación *f*.
abhorrent [əbˈhɒrənt] ADJ aborrecible, detestable, repugnante; **a thought ~ to common sense** un concepto repugnante al sentido común.
abide [əˈbaɪd] (*irr*: PRET AND PTP **abode** *or* **abided**) **[1]** VT aguantar, soportar; **I can't ~ him** no le puedo ver; **I can't ~ a coward** aborrezco los cobardes; **I can't ~ tea** me da asco el té.
[2] VI (†† *dwell*) morar; (*stay*) permanecer, continuar; **to ~ by** atenerse a, obrar de acuerdo con, guiarse por; *decision* respetar, atenerse a; *promise* cumplir; *rules of competition* ajustarse a, aceptar.
abiding [əˈbaɪdɪŋ] ADJ permanente, perdurable.
ability [əˈbɪlɪtɪ] N habilidad *f*, capacidad *f*; talento *m*, aptitud *f*; **~ to pay** solvencia *f*, recursos *mpl*; **a boy of ~** un chico de talento; **he has great ~** tiene un gran talento (*for* para); **his ~ in French** su aptitud para el francés; **to the best of my ~** lo mejor que yo pueda (*or* sepa); **my ~ to do it depends on ...** el que yo lo haga depende de ...; **abilities** talento *m*, dotes *fpl*.
ab initio [ˌæbɪˈnɪʃiəu] **[1]** ADV ab initio, desde el principio.
[2] ADJ: **~ learner** principiante *mf*.
abiotic [ˌeɪbaɪˈɒtɪk] ADJ abiótico.
abject [ˈæbdʒekt] ADJ abyecto, vil; servil; abatido; *apology* rastrero; humilde; **an ~ liar** un mentiroso redomado; **to live in ~ poverty** vivir en la mayor miseria.
abjectly [ˈæbdʒektlɪ] ADV abatidamente, vilmente; humildemente.
abjectness [ˈæbdʒektnɪs] N abyección *f*, vileza *f*; lo humilde.
abjure [əbˈdʒʊəʳ] VT renunciar (a), abjurar.
Abkhaz [æbˈkɑːz], **Abkhazi** [æbˈkɑːzɪ], **Abkhazian** [æbˈkɑːzɪən] **[1]** ADJ abjaso.
[2] N (**a**) abjaso *m*, -a *f*. (**b**) (*Ling*) abjaso *m*.
Abkhazia [æbˈkɑːzɪə] N Abjazia *f*.
ablative [ˈæblətɪv] **[1]** ADJ ablativo; **~ case = 2.**
[2] N ablativo *m*; **~ absolute** ablativo *m* absoluto.
ablaze [əˈbleɪz] ADV AND PRED ADJ en llamas, ardiendo; **the cinema was ~ in 5 minutes** en 5 minutos el cine estuvo envuelto en llamas; **the palace was ~ with light** brillaban todas las luces del palacio; **the garden was ~ with colour** resplandecía el jardín con sus flores multicolores; **to be ~ with excitement** estar emocionadísimo; **to be ~ with indignation** estar indignadísimo, estar encolerizado.
able [ˈeɪbl] ADJ (**a**) (*capable*) hábil, capaz, talentoso, competente; **~ to pay** solvente; **he's a very ~ man** es un hombre de mucho talento; **it's an ~ piece of work** es un trabajo sólido, es un trabajo competente; **~ seaman** marinero *m* de primera, marinero *m* patentado.
(**b**) (*in verb phrase*) **to be ~ to** + *infin* poder + infin; (*of acquired skills*) saber + *infin*, *eg* **you can go when you are ~ to swim** te permitiré ir cuando sepas nadar; **the child is nearly ~ to talk** el niño casi sabe hablar; **I was eventually ~ to escape** por fin pude escaparme, por fin logré escaparme; **come as soon as you are ~** ven en cuanto puedas.
-able SUFFIX -able.
able-bodied [ˈeɪblˈbɒdɪd] ADJ sano, robusto; **~ seaman** marinero *m* de primera, marinero *m* patentado.
ablution [əˈbluːʃən] N (**a**) ablución *f*; **to perform one's ~s** (*hum*) lavarse; **to be at one's ~s** (*hum*) estar en el lavabo. (**b**) **~s** (*Mil*ʳ) servicios *mpl*.
ably [ˈeɪblɪ] ADV hábilmente, con mucha habilidad.
ABM N ABBR *of* **anti-ballistic missile**.
abnegate [ˈæbnɪgeɪt] VT *responsibility* eludir, evitar, rehuir; *one's religion* abjurar; **to ~ one's rights** renunciar a los derechos de uno.
abnegation [ˌæbnɪˈgeɪʃən] N abnegación *f*.
abnormal [æbˈnɔːməl] ADJ anormal; anómalo; irregular; deforme, mal formado.
abnormality [ˌæbnɔːˈmælɪtɪ] N anormalidad *f*; irregularidad *f*; deformidad *f*.
abnormally [æbˈnɔːməlɪ] ADV anormalmente, de modo anormal; **an ~ formed bone** un hueso de formación anormal; **an ~ large sum** una cantidad descomunal.
Abo* [ˈæbəʊ] N (*Australia*) = **aboriginal**.
aboard [əˈbɔːd] **[1]** ADV a bordo; **to go ~** embarcarse, ir a bordo; **to**

take ~ tomar a bordo, embarcar, cargar; **all ~!** (*Rail etc*) ¡señores viajeros, al tren! (*etc*); **life ~ is pleasant** es agradable la vida de a bordo.
[2] PREP: **~ the ship** a bordo del barco; **~ the train** en el tren.

┌─ **ABLE, CAN** ──────────────── *see also main entries* ─┐

Poder and *saber* can both translate *to be able to*, *can* and *could*.
Skills
● Use *saber* when *to be able to*, *can* and *could* mean "know how to":
  Can you type?
  ¿Sabes escribir a máquina?
  His wife couldn't drive
  Su mujer no sabía conducir
Other contexts
● Generally, use *poder*:
  He can stay here
  Puede quedarse aquí
  We have not been able to persuade them
  No hemos podido convencerles
NOTE: When *can* and *could* are followed by *find* or a verb of perception - *see, hear, feel, taste* or *smell* - they are usually not translated:
  I can't find it
  No lo encuentro
  What can you see?
  ¿Qué ves?
Alternatives to "poder"
● When *to be able* means "to be capable of", you can often use *ser capaz de* as an alternative to *poder*:
  I don't think he'll be able to resist it
  No creo que sea capaz de or pueda resistirlo
For further uses and examples, see main entries at **able** and **can**.

└──┘

abode [əˈbəʊd] **[1]** PRET AND PTP *of* **abide**.
[2] N domicilio *m*, morada *f*; **place of ~** domicilio *m*; **right of ~** derecho *m* a domiciliarse; **of no fixed ~** sin domicilio fijo; **to take up one's ~** domiciliarse, establecerse.
abolish [əˈbɒlɪʃ] VT suprimir, abolir; anular, revocar; eliminar.
abolishment [əˈbɒlɪʃmənt] N, **abolition** [ˌæbəʊˈlɪʃən] N supresión *f*, abolición *f*; anulación *f*.
abolitionist [ˌæbəʊˈlɪʃənɪst] N abolicionista *mf*.
A-bomb [ˈeɪbɒm] N ABBR *of* **atom bomb** bomba *f* atómica.
abominable [əˈbɒmɪnəbl] ADJ abominable; execrable; *taste, workmanship etc* detestable, pésimo; **the ~ snowman** el abominable hombre *m* de las nieves.
abominably [əˈbɒmɪnəblɪ] ADV abominablemente; detestablemente, pésimamente; **to behave ~** comportarse de una manera detestable; **to be ~ rude to sb** ponerse sumamente grosero con uno; **he writes ~** escribe pésimamente.
abominate [əˈbɒmɪneɪt] VT abominar (de), detestar.
abomination [əˌbɒmɪˈneɪʃən] N abominación *f*.
aboriginal [ˌæbəˈrɪdʒənl] **[1]** ADJ aborigen, indígena.
[2] N aborigen *mf*, indígena *mf*.
aborigine [ˌæbəˈrɪdʒɪnɪ] N aborigen *mf*.
abort [əˈbɔːt] **[1]** VT abortar; (*Comput*) interrumpir, detener prematuramente.
[2] VI abortar, malparir; (*fig*) malograrse; (*Comput*) interrumpir el programa.
abortifacient [əˌbɔːtɪˈfeɪʃənt] **[1]** ADJ abortivo.
[2] N abortivo *m*.
abortion [əˈbɔːʃən] N (**a**) (*Med*) aborto *m* provocado, aborto *m* (criminal); **illegal ~** aborto *m* ilegal; **to have an ~** hacerse abortar; **to procure an ~** hacer abortar a una mujer; **~ clinic** clínica *f* de abortos; **~ law** ley *f* del aborto; **~ pill** píldora *f* abortiva. (**b**) (*creature*) engendro *m*; (*fig*) malogro *m*, fracaso *m*.
abortionist [əˈbɔːʃənɪst] N abortista *mf*.
abortive [əˈbɔːtɪv] ADJ (**a**) (*gen*) abortivo. (**b**) (*fig*) ineficaz, fracasado; malogrado; **to prove ~** fracasar, no dar resultado, malograrse.
abortively [əˈbɔːtɪvlɪ] ADV (*try etc*) en vano; **the negotiations ended ~** las negociaciones fracasaron.
abound [əˈbaʊnd] VI abundar (*in, with* de, en).
about [əˈbaʊt] **[1]** ADV (**a**) (*approximately*) alrededor de, más o menos; aproximadamente; **~ 20** unos 20, 20 más o menos; (*esp LAm*) como (unos) 20; **~ 7 years ago** hace unos 7 años; **~ 2 o'clock** a eso de las 2, sobre las 2; **~ a month** un mes poco más o menos, cosa de un mes; **he must be ~ 40** tendrá alrededor de 40 años; **it's ~ time you stopped** ya es hora de que lo dejes; **~ half** alrededor de la mitad; **it's just ~ finished** está casi terminado; **he's ~ the same** sigue más o menos igual; **that's ~ it, that's ~ right** eso es (más o menos); **that's ~ all I could find** eso es más o menos todo lo que podía encontrar.
(**b**) (*place*) **all ~** por todas partes; **to run ~** correr, correr por todas

partes; **to walk ~** pasearse; ir y venir; *V* **play, turn** *etc.*

(c) (*with verb* to be) **to be ~ again** (*after illness*) estar levantado; **we were ~ early** nos levantamos temprano; **is anyone ~?** ¿hay alguien?; **is Mr Brown ~?** ¿está por aquí el Sr Brown?; **he must be ~ somewhere** debe de andar por aquí; **there's a thief ~** por aquí anda un ladrón; **there's a lot of measles ~** está dando el sarampión; **there isn't much money ~** hay poco dinero, la gente tiene poco dinero; **to be ~ to** + *infin* estar a punto de + *infin*, estar para + *infin*, estar por + *infin* (*LAm*); **nobody is ~ to sell it** nadie tiene la más mínima intención de venderlo.

2 PREP **(a)** (*place*) alrededor de; **all ~ the house** (*outside*) por todos los alrededores de la casa, (*inside*) por todas partes de la casa; **~ the fire** junto a la lumbre; **to walk ~ the house** andar por la casa; **to wander ~ the town** pasearse sin rumbo fijo por la ciudad; **you're ~ the house all day** pasas todo el día en casa; **to do jobs ~ the house** hacer las faenas domésticas; **he looked ~ him** miró a su alrededor; **I have no money ~ me** no llevo dinero encima.

(b) (*place: fig*) **he had a mysterious air ~ him** había algo misterioso en él; **there's sth ~ him** (*that I like*) tiene un no sé qué (que me gusta); **there's sth odd ~ it** aquí hay algo raro; **while you're ~ it** mientras lo estés haciendo; **and while I'm ~ it I'll talk to your father** y de paso charlaré con tu padre; **you've been a long time ~ it** has tardado bastante en hacerlo; **to be ~ one's business** atender a su negocio.

(c) (*relating to*) de, acerca de, sobre, con respecto a, respecto de; **a book ~ travel** un libro de viajes, un libro sobre los viajes; **I can tell you nothing ~ him** no le puedo decir nada acerca de él; **they fell out ~ money** riñeron por cuestión de dinero; **how ~ me?** ¿y yo?; **how ~ that book?** ¿y el libro ese?; **how ~ that?** ¿qué te parece?; **how ~ that!** (*amazement*) ¡toma!, ¡vaya!; **what ~ that book?** ¿y el libro ese?; **what ~ it?** (*what's your answer*) ¿quieres?; (*what of it*) ¿y qué?; **what ~ a song?** ¿queréis que os cante algo?; ¿por qué no nos cantas algo?; **what's that book ~?** ¿de qué trata ese libro?; **what's it all ~?** ¿de qué se trata?, ¿qué pasa?; **what are you ~?** ¿qué haces ahí?; ¿qué pretendes con eso?; **what did he talk ~?** ¿de qué habló?

about-face [ə'baʊt'feɪs], **about-turn** [ə,baʊt't3:n] **1** N **(a)** (*Mil*) media vuelta *f*. **(b)** (*fig*) cambio *m* radical de postura, giro *m* (brusco).

2 VI **(a)** (*Mil*) dar media vuelta. **(b)** (*fig*) cambiar radicalmente de postura.

above [ə'bʌv] **1** ADV encima, por encima, arriba; (*in text*) arriba; **as ~** según lo dicho antes; **as set out ~** según lo arriba expuesto; **as I said ~** según dije ya; **from ~** desde encima, desde arriba; de lo alto; del cielo, de Dios; **orders from ~** órdenes *fpl* superiores, órdenes *fpl* de fuente superior; **the flat ~** el piso de arriba; **the air ~** el aire por encima; **those ~** (*superiors*) los de categoría superior; (*dead*) los que están en el cielo; (*gods*) los dioses.

2 PREP **(a)** (*place*) encima de; **~ my head** encima de mi cabeza; **~ ground** sobre la tierra; **the Tagus ~ Toledo** el Tajo más arriba de Toledo; **2000 metres ~ sea level** 2000 metros sobre el nivel del mar.

(b) (*place: fig*) **he is ~ me in rank** tiene categoría superior a la mía; **to marry ~ one's class** casarse por encima de su clase; **I couldn't hear ~ the din** no podía oír con tanto ruido; **we are ~ that sort of thing** nosotros quedamos por encima de aquello; **it is ~ criticism** queda por encima de toda crítica; **it's ~ me** no lo entiendo, soy incapaz de entenderlo; **he is not ~ a bit of blackmail** es capaz de hacer un poco de chantaje.

(c) (*number*) más de; superior a; **~ 100** más de 100; **there were not ~ 40 people** no había más de 40 personas; **any number ~ 12** cualquier número superior a 12; **she can't count ~ 10** no sabe contar más allá de 10; **those now ~ 21** los ahora mayores de 21 años; **temperatures well ~ normal** temperaturas muy superiores a las normales.

3 ADJ susodicho, citado, arriba escrito, antedicho.

above-board [ə'bʌv'bɔːd] **1** ADV abiertamente, sin rebozo.

2 ADJ legítimo, honrado.

above-mentioned [ə'bʌv'menʃənd] ADJ sobredicho, susodicho.

above-named [ə'bʌv'neɪmd] ADJ arriba mencionado.

Abp ABBR *of* **Archbishop** arzobispo *m*.

abracadabra [,abrəkə'dæbrə] N abracadabra *f*.

abrade [ə'breɪd] VT raer, raspar; desgastar.

Abraham ['eɪbrəhæm] NM Abrahán, Abraham.

abrasion [ə'breɪʒən] N raedura *f*, raspadura *f*; desgaste *m*; (*Med*) abrasión *f*.

abrasive [ə'breɪzɪv] ADJ **(a)** (*gen*) abrasivo. **(b)** (*fig*) *personality* difícil, agresivo, brusco; *tone* áspero, hiriente.

abrasiveness [ə'breɪzɪvnɪs] N **(a)** lo abrasivo. **(b)** (*fig*) agresividad *f*, brusquedad *f*; aspereza *f*.

abreaction [,æbrɪ'ækʃən] N abreacción *f*.

abreast [ə'brest] ADV de frente, de fondo; **to march 4 ~** marchar 4 de frente; marchar en columna de 4 en fondo; **he was walking ~ of**

the last two caminaba a la par de los dos últimos; **to come ~ of** llegar a la altura de; **to be ~ of** (*fig*) estar al corriente de; **to keep ~ of** mantenerse al corriente de; **to keep ~ of the times** mantenerse al día.

abridge [ə'brɪdʒ] VT *book* compendiar, resumir, condensar; (*cut short*) abreviar, acortar.

abridged [ə'brɪdʒd] ADJ resumido, en resumen; abreviado.

abridgement [ə'brɪdʒmənt] N compendio *m*, resumen *m*; abreviación *f*.

abroad [ə'brɔːd] ADV **(a)** (*in foreign parts*) en el extranjero, fuera; **to be ~** estar en el extranjero; **our army ~** nuestro ejército en el extranjero; **our debts ~** nuestras deudas en el exterior; **when the minister is ~** cuando el ministro está fuera del país; **to go ~** ir al extranjero; **he had to go ~** (*fleeing*) tuvo que salir del país; **troops brought in from ~** tropas traídas de fuera.

(b) (*outside*) fuera, fuera de casa; **there were not many ~ at that hour** había poca gente por las calles a aquella hora; **there is a rumour ~ that ...** corre un rumor de que ...; **it has got ~ that ...** se tiene noticia de que ..., (*falsely*) corre la voz de que ..., se ha divulgado la especie de que ...; **how did the news get ~?** ¿cómo se divulgó la noticia?

abrogate ['æbrəʊɡeɪt] VT abrogar.

abrogation [,æbrəʊ'ɡeɪʃən] N abrogación *f*.

abrupt [ə'brʌpt] ADJ **(a)** (*sudden*) repentino, brusco; precipitado; *terrain* abrupto, escarpado; *style* cortado, lacónico; entrecortado; *manner of person* áspero, brusco; **he was very ~ with me** me trató sin miramientos.

abruptly [ə'brʌptlɪ] ADV repentinamente, bruscamente; precipitadamente; **a cliff rose ~ before them** delante de ellos se alzaba un risco cortado a pico; **to leave ~** salir repentinamente; **everything changed ~** de pronto cambió todo.

abruptness [ə'brʌptnɪs] N brusquedad *f*; precipitación *f*; lo escarpado; lo cortado.

ABS N ABBR *of* **antilock braking system** sistema *m* de frenos ABS, ABS *m*.

abscess ['æbsɪs] N absceso *m*.

abscond [əb'skɒnd] VI fugarse, huir (de la justicia), irse a hurtadillas; **to ~ with** alzarse con.

absconder [əb'skɒndəʳ] N (*from prison*) fugitivo *m*, -a *f*, evadido *m*, -a *f*.

absconding [əb'skɒndɪŋ] ADJ en fuga.

abseil ['æbseɪl] VI (*also* **to ~ down**) hacer rappel, bajar en la cuerda; **he ~ed down the rock** hizo rappel bajando de la roca.

abseiling ['æbseɪlɪŋ] N rappel *m*.

absence ['æbsəns] N (*of person*) ausencia *f*; (*of thing*) falta *f*, carencia *f*; **in the ~ of** *person* en ausencia de; *thing* a falta de; **to be sentenced in one's** ser condenado en ausencia; **signed in his ~** firmado por ausencia; **to be conspicuous by one's ~** brillar por su ausencia; **~ of mind** distracción *f*, despiste *m*.

absent **1** ['æbsənt] ADJ ausente (*from* de); (*fig*) distraído; **~ without leave** ausente sin permiso; **where liberty is ~** donde falta la libertad; **why were you ~ from class?** ¿por qué has faltado a la clase?

2 [æb'sent] VR: **to ~ o.s.** ausentarse (*from* de).

absentee [,æbsən'tiː] N ausente *mf*; **~ ballot** (*US*) voto *m* por correo; **~ landlord** absentista *mf*; **~ rate** nivel *m* de absentismo.

absenteeism [,æbsən'tiːɪzəm] N absentismo *m*.

absently ['æbsəntlɪ] ADV distraídamente.

absent-minded ['æbsənt'maɪndɪd] ADJ distraído, despistado, volado (*LAm*).

absent-mindedly ['æbsənt'maɪndɪdlɪ] ADV distraídamente, por distracción.

absent-mindedness ['æbsənt'maɪndɪdnɪs] N distracción *f*, despiste *m*.

absinth(e) ['æbsɪnθ] N (*Bot*) ajenjo *m*; (*drink*) absenta *f*.

absolute ['æbsəluːt] ADJ (*Gram, Math*) absoluto; *majority, monarch, power, zero etc* absoluto; *government* absolutista; *certainty, confidence etc* completo, total, pleno; *support* incondicional; *need* ineludible; *prohibition* terminante, total; *statement* tajante, categórico; *denial* rotundo; *alcohol* puro; *liar* redomado; **the ~** (*Philos*) lo absoluto; **the man's an ~ idiot** es un puro imbécil; **it's ~ rubbish!** ¡es puro disparate!; **it's the ~ end!** ¡es el colmo!; **~ monopoly** monopolio *m* total; **it's an ~ scandal** es simplemente escandaloso.

absolutely ['æbsəluːtlɪ] ADV *rule etc* absolutamente; (*wholly*) completamente, totalmente; **~!** ¡perfectamente!, ¡eso es!; **~ not!** ¡de ninguna manera!; **that is ~ untrue** eso es totalmente falso; **it is ~ forbidden to** + *infin* queda terminantemente prohibido + *infin*; **I deny it ~** lo niego rotundamente (*LAm*: positivamente).

absolution [,æbsə'luːʃən] N absolución *f*; **to give ~ to sb** dar la absolución a uno, absolver a uno.

absolutism ['æbsəluːtɪzəm] N absolutismo *m*.

absolutist ['æbsəluːtɪst] **1** ADJ absolutista.

2 N absolutista *mf*.

absolve [əbˈzɒlv] VT absolver (*from* de), perdonar.

absorb [əbˈzɔːb] VT absorber; *shock etc* amortiguar; **the business ~s a lot of my time** el negocio me lleva mucho tiempo, el negocio me trae ocupadísimo; **she ~s chemistry readily** la química le entra con facilidad; **the country ~ed 1000 refugees** el país dio entrada a 1000 refugiados, el país acogió a 1000 refugiados; **the parent company ~s the losses made by the subsidiary** la compañía matriz absorbe las pérdidas de la filial; **to be ~ed in** (*fig*) estar absorto en, ensimismarse en; **to get ~ed in** (*fig*) engolfarse en, empaparse de, dedicarse de lleno al estudio de.

absorbable [əbˈzɔːbəbl] ADJ absorbible.

absorbency [əbˈzɔːbənsɪ] N absorbencia *f*.

absorbent [əbˈzɔːbənt] ADJ absorbente; **~ cotton** (*US*) algodón *m* hidrófilo.

absorbing [əbˈzɔːbɪŋ] ADJ absorbente, interesantísimo; **I find history very ~** me apasiona la historia.

absorption [əbˈzɔːpʃən] N absorción *f* (*also fig, Comm*); **~ costing** cálculo *m* del costo de absorción.

abstain [əbˈsteɪn] VI abstenerse (*from* de); (*not vote*) abstenerse de votar; (*not drink*) abstenerse de las bebidas alcohólicas; **to ~ from comment** no ofrecer comentario.

abstainer [əbˈsteɪnəʳ] N (*also total ~*) abstemio *m*, -a *f*, abstinente *mf*, persona *f* que no bebe alcohol.

abstemious [əbˈstiːmɪəs] ADJ sobrio, abstemio, moderado.

abstemiousness [əbˈstiːmɪəsnɪs] N sobriedad *f*, moderación *f*.

abstention [əbˈstenʃən] N abstención *f*; (*Parl*) abstención *f* de votar.

abstinence [ˈæbstɪnəns] N abstinencia *f* (*from* de); **total ~** abstinencia *f* total (*esp* de bebidas alcohólicas); **~ syndrome** síndrome *m* de abstinencia.

abstinent [ˈæbstɪnənt] ADJ abstinente.

abstract **1** [ˈæbstrækt] ADJ abstracto; **~ art** arte *m* abstracto; **~ noun** nombre *m* abstracto; **in the ~** en abstracto.
   2 [ˈæbstrækt] N resumen *m*, sumario *m*.
   3 [æbˈstrækt] VT (*remove*) extractar, quitar, separar; (*steal*) sustraer, robar; (*Chem*) extraer; *research publication* resumir, abstractar; *book* resumir, compendiar.
   4 [æbˈstrækt] VR: **to ~ o.s.** abstraerse, ensimismarse.

abstracted [æbˈstræktɪd] ADJ distraído, ensimismado.

abstractedly [æbˈstræktɪdlɪ] ADV: **she listened ~** escuchaba distraída.

abstraction [æbˈstrækʃən] N abstracción *f*; robo *m*; distraimiento *m*, ensimismamiento *m*.

abstruse [æbˈstruːs] ADJ recóndito, abstruso.

abstruseness [æbˈstruːsnɪs] N lo recóndito, carácter *m* abstruso.

▼ **absurd** [əbˈsɜːd] ADJ absurdo, ridículo, disparatado; **how ~!** ¡qué ridículo!; **don't be ~!** ¡no digas tonterías!; **you look ~ in that hat** se te ve ridículo con ese sombrero, con ese sombrero pareces ridículo; **the ~ thing is that ...** lo absurdo es que ...

absurdist [əbˈsɜːdɪst] ADJ *play, novel* del absurdo.

absurdity [əbˈsɜːdɪtɪ] N (**a**) (*an ~*) absurdo *m*, disparate *m*; locura *f*; **it would be an ~ to try** sería una locura intentarlo. (**b**) (*quality*) absurdidez *f*, absurdidad *f*, lo absurdo.

absurdly [əbˈsɜːdlɪ] ADV absurdamente, ridículamente, desproporcionadamente.

ABTA [ˈæbtə] N ABBR *of* **Association of British Travel Agents** ≃ Asociación *f* Empresarial de Agencias de Viajes Españolas, AEDAVE *f*.

Abu Dhabi [ˌæbuˈdɑːbɪ] N Abu Dhabi *m*.

abulia [əˈbuːlɪə] N abulia *f*.

abundance [əˈbʌndəns] N abundancia *f*; **in ~** en abundancia, abundantemente, a granel; **we had an ~ of rain** llovió copiosamente; **we have a great ~ of plums** tenemos ciruelas en abundancia; **out of the ~ of his heart** de la plenitud de su corazón.

abundant [əˈbʌndənt] ADJ abundante (*in* en); copioso.

abundantly [əˈbʌndəntlɪ] ADV abundantemente; copiosamente; **to make it ~ clear that ...** hacer constar con toda claridad que ...

abuse **1** [əˈbjuːs] N (**a**) (*insults*) improperios *mpl*, injurias *fpl*; **to heap ~ on sb** llenar a uno de injurias.
   (**b**) (*misuse*) abuso *m*; (*physical*) malos tratos *mpl*; **~ of confidence, ~ of trust** abuso *m* de confianza; **child ~** maltrato *m* de los hijos; **sexual ~** abuso *m* sexual.
   2 [əˈbjuːz] VT (**a**) (*revile*) maltratar (de palabra), injuriar, llenar de injurias; ultrajar (de palabra); **he roundly ~d the government** dijo mil improperios contra el gobierno.
   (**b**) (*misuse*) abusar de; **he ~d his daughter** abusaba de su hija.
   (**c**) (*mistreat*) maltratar.

abuser [əˈbjuːzəʳ] N (*physical*) culpable de malos tratos; (*sexual*) culpable de abusos deshonestos; **child ~** pederasta *mf*; **she killed her ~** mató al que la maltrataba; *see also* **drug ~**.

Abu Simbel [ˌæbuˈsɪmbl] N Abu Simbel *m*.

abusive [əˈbjuːsɪv] ADJ (**a**) (*insulting*) ofensivo, injurioso, insultante; **to be ~ to sb** decir cosas injuriosas a uno; **to become ~** empezar a

soltar injurias (*to* contra). (**b**) *practice etc* abusivo.

abut [əˈbʌt] VI confinar, estar contiguo; **to ~ against, to ~ on** confinar con, lindar con; (*penthouse etc*) apoyarse en.

abutment [əˈbʌtmənt] N (*Archit*) estribo *m*, contrafuerte *m*; (*Carp*) empotramiento *m*.

abutting [əˈbʌtɪŋ] ADJ colindante, contiguo.

abuzz [əˈbʌz] ADJ: **the whole office was ~ with the news** toda la oficina comentaba la noticia.

abysmal [əˈbɪzməl] ADJ (*gen, liter*) abismal; (*fig*) profundo; **the most ~ ignorance** la ignorancia más profunda; **an ~ result** un malísimo resultado; **an ~ performance** una pésima actuación; **the play was ~** la obra fue una catástrofe; **to live in ~ poverty** vivir en la mayor miseria.

abysmally [əˈbɪzməlɪ] ADV (*fig*) malísimamente, terriblemente; **~ bad** terriblemente malo.

abyss [əˈbɪs] N abismo *m*, sima *f*.

Abyssinia [ˌæbɪˈsɪnɪə] N Abisinia *f*.

Abyssinian [ˌæbɪˈsɪnɪən] **1** ADJ abisinio.
   2 N abisinio *m*, -a *f*.

a/c (**a**) ABBR *of* **account** cuenta *f*, cta. (**b**) (*US*) ABBR *of* **account current** cuenta *f* corriente, c/c.

AC N (**a**) (*Elec*) ABBR *of* **alternating current** corriente *f* alterna. (**b**) (*Aer*) ABBR *of* **aircraftman** cabo *m* segundo de las fuerzas aéreas. (**c**) (*US Sport*) ABBR *of* **Athletic Club** ≃ Club *m* Atlético, C.A.

acacia [əˈkeɪʃə] N acacia *f*.

academe [ˈækədiːm] N centro *m* de erudición, universidad *f*; (*fig*) vida *f* tranquila.

academia [ˌækəˈdiːmɪə] N el mundo erudito, el mundo de la erudición, (*esp*) la universidad.

academic [ˌækəˈdemɪk] **1** ADJ (**a**) (*Univ etc*) académico; universitario; escolar, docente; **~ advisor** (*US*) jefe *mf* de estudios; **~ dean** (*US*) decano *m*, -a *f*; **~ dress** vestidura *f* universitaria; **~ freedom** libertad *f* de cátedra; **~ interests** intereses *mpl* eruditos; **~ journal** revista *f* erudita; **~ officers** (*US*) personal *m* docente de centros de enseñanza; **~ rank** (*US*) rango *m* académico, jerarquía *f* académica; **~ staff** profesorado *m*, personal *m* docente; **~ year** año *m* universitario; **the boy is highly ~** el chico tiene gran aptitud intelectual; **he is an ~ painter** es un pintor académico. (**b**) (*gen pej*) *question* puramente teórico, sin trascendencia práctica; *argument* bizantino, poco provechoso, estéril; **the point is purely ~** la cuestión no tiene aplicación práctica.
   2 N universitario *m*, -a *f*, catedrático *m*, -a *f* (*or* profesor *m*, -ora *f*) (de universidad).

academically [ˌækəˈdemɪkəlɪ] ADV (**a**) **an ~ sound argument** un argumento intelectualmente sólido; **an ~ gifted child** un niño con altas dotes intelectuales; **~ the boy is below average** en los estudios el chico no llega al promedio. (**b**) **to argue ~** (*gen pej*) razonar de manera puramente teórica.

academicals [ˌækəˈdemɪkəlz] NPL vestidura *f* universitaria.

academician [əˌkædəˈmɪʃən] N académico *m*, -a *f*.

academy [əˈkædəmɪ] N academia *f*; (*Scot*) instituto *m* (de segunda enseñanza), colegio *m*; **military ~** academia *f* militar; **naval ~** escuela *f* naval; **~ of music** (*Brit*) conservatorio *m*; **~ for young ladies** colegio *m* para señoritas; **secretarial ~** escuela *f* de secretarias; **Royal A~** (*of Arts*) Real Academia *f* (de Bellas Artes); **the Spanish A~** la Real Academia Española.

acanthus [əˈkænθəs] N acanto *m*.

ACAS [ˈeɪkæs] N (*Brit*) ABBR *of* **Advisory Conciliation and Arbitration Service** ≃ Instituto *m* de Mediación, Arbitraje y Conciliación, IMAC *m*.

acc. (**a**) (*Fin*) ABBR *of* **account** cuenta *f*. (**b**) (*Ling*) ABBR *of* **accusative** acusativo *m*.

accede [ækˈsiːd] VI (**a**) **to ~ to** (*assent to*) *request* consentir en, acceder a; *suggestion* aceptar. (**b**) **to ~ to** (*gain, enter into*) *office, post* tomar posesión de, entrar en; *party* adherirse a; *throne* subir a; *treaty* firmar, adherirse a.

accelerate [ækˈseləreɪt] **1** VT acelerar; impulsar, apresurar; **~d depreciation** depreciación *f* acelerada; **~d program** (*US Univ*) curso *m* intensivo.
   2 VI acelerar.

acceleration [ækˌseləˈreɪʃən] N aceleración *f*; **~ clause** provisión *f* para el vencimiento anticipado de una deuda.

accelerator [ækˈseləreɪtəʳ] N (*Brit*) acelerador *m*, chancleta *f* (*Carib*), hierro *m* (*SC*); **to step on the ~** pisar el acelerador.

accent **1** [ˈæksənt] N (**a**) acento *m*; énfasis *m*; **~ mark** acento *m* ortográfico; **with a strong provincial ~** con fuerte acento de provincia; **in ~s of some surprise** en cierto tono de asombro. (**b**) **to put the ~ on** (*fig*) subrayar (la importancia de), recalcar; **this year the ~ is on bright colours** este año están de moda los colores vivos; **the minister put the ~ on exports** el ministro recalcó la importancia de la exportación.
   2 [ækˈsent] VT acentuar.

accented [æk'sentɪd] ADJ *syllable* acentuado.

accentual [æk'sentjʊəl] ADJ acentual.

accentuate [æk'sentjʊeɪt] VT (a) (*gen*) acentuar. (b) (*fig*) subrayar (la importancia de), recalcar, dar énfasis a; aumentar.

accentuation [æk,sentjʊ'eɪʃən] N acentuación *f*.

▼ **accept** [ək'sept] ① VT aceptar (*also Comm*); aprobar; admitir; reconocer; recibir, acoger, dar acogida a; **the Academy ~s the word** la Academia aprueba la palabra; **the Academy ~ed the word in 1970** la Academia admitió la palabra en 1970; **to ~ orders** (*Comm*) admitir pedidos; **I do not ~ that way of doing it** no apruebo ese modo de hacerlo; **it is ~ed that ...** se reconoce que ...; **he was ~ed as one of us** pasaba por ser uno de nosotros, le acogieron como a uno de nosotros mismos.

② VI aceptar, asentir.

acceptability [ək,septə'bɪlətɪ] N admisibilidad *f*.

acceptable [ək'septəbl] ADJ aceptable; admisible; adecuado, satisfactorio; (*welcome*) grato, oportuno; **tea is always ~** el té siempre agrada; **that would be most ~** eso me gustaría muchísimo; **that would not be ~ to the government** eso no le sería grato al gobierno; **that policy is not ~** esa política no es admisible; **it is not easy to find an ~ gift** no es fácil encontrar un regalo adecuado.

▼ **acceptance** [ək'septəns] N aceptación *f* (*also Comm*); aprobación *f*; (buena) acogida *f*; **~ credit** crédito *m* de aceptación; **to meet with general ~** ser bien recibido por todos; **to win ~** lograr la aprobación.

acceptation [,æksep'teɪʃən] N acepción *f*.

accepted [ək'septɪd] ADJ aceptado; admisible; *fact, idea etc* corriente, reconocido, establecido; **it's the ~ thing** es la norma general, es cosa corriente; **he's an ~ expert** es un experto reconocido (como tal); **it is not a socially ~ habit** es costumbre no admisible en la buena sociedad.

acceptor [ək'septər] N aceptador *m*, -ora *f*; (*Comm*) aceptante *mf*.

access ['ækses] ① N (a) (*entry etc*) acceso *m*, entrada *f*; (*Comput*) acceso *m*; **~ road** vía *f* de acceso; **of easy ~** asequible, de fácil acceso; *person* abordable, tratable; **to give ~ to a room** comunicar con una habitación; **this gives ~ to the garden** por aquí se sale al jardín; **to have ~ to the minister** poder libremente hablar con el ministro, tener libre acceso al ministro; **to obtain legal ~ to a property** conseguir una autorización legal para entrar en una propiedad; **he had ~ to the family papers** pudo leer los papeles de la familia, se le facilitaron los papeles de la familia.

(b) (*fig, Med*) acceso *m*, ataque *m*; **in an ~ of rage** en un arranque de cólera; **he had a sudden ~ of generosity** tuvo un repentino impulso de generosidad.

② VT (*Comput*) entrar.

③ ATTR: **~ code** código *m* de acceso; **~ time** tiempo *m* de acceso.

accessibility [æk,sesɪ'bɪlɪtɪ] N accesibilidad *f*; lo asequible; carácter *m* abordable.

accessible [æk'sesəbl] ADJ accesible, asequible (*to* a); obtenible; *person* tratable, abordable; **he is not ~ to reason** no escucha la razón, hace oídos sordos a la razón; **she is not ~ to compassion** no es capaz de mostrar compasión; **the duke is not ~ to visitors** el duque no recibe visitas.

accession [æk'seʃən] N (a) (*entry etc*) acceso *m*, entrada *f* en posesión (*to* de); (*of king*) subida *f*, ascenso *m* (*to the throne* al trono); **~ to power** ascenso *m* al poder. (b) (*increase*) aumento *m*; (*new library book, exhibit etc*) (nueva) adquisición *f*; **a sudden ~ of strength** un aumento inesperado de fuerzas. (c) (*consent*) accesión *f*, adherencia *f* (*to a treaty* a un tratado).

accessorize [æk'sesə,raɪz] VT: **to ~ a dress** comprar el bolso y los zapatos a juego; **I need to ~ the bathroom** necesito comprar los accesorios del baño.

accessory [æk'sesərɪ] ① ADJ accesorio; secundario; **~ to** (*Jur*) cómplice *mf* de.

② N (a) (*object*) accesorio *m*; **accessories** accesorios *mpl*; (*Aut etc, also of dress*) complementos *mpl*; **toilet accessories** artículos *mpl* de tocador.

(b) (*Jur*) cómplice *mf*; **~ after the fact** cómplice *mf* encubridor, -ora *f*; **~ before the fact** cómplice *mf* instigador, -ora *f*.

accidence ['æksɪdəns] N accidentes *mpl*.

▼ **accident** ['æksɪdənt] N (a) (*mishap*) accidente *m*; percance *m*; **A~ (and Emergency) Unit** (*Aut*) puesto *m* de ayuda en carretera; (*road*) **~ figures** (*or statistics*) cifras *fpl* (*or estadísticas fpl*) de accidentes (en carretera *etc*); **~ insurance** seguro *m* contra accidentes; **~ prevention** prevención *f* de accidentes; **~s will happen** hay accidentes que no se pueden prever; **to have an ~, to meet with an ~** sufrir un accidente.

▼ (b) (*unforeseen event*) accidente *m*; **by ~** (*by chance*) por casualidad; (*unintentionally*) accidentalmente, sin querer, por descuido; **by some ~ I found myself there** me encontré allí sin saber cómo; **more by ~ than by design** más por casualidad que por intención; **I'm sorry, it was an ~** lo siento, lo hice sin querer.

(c) (*Geol, Philos*) accidente *m*.

accidental [,æksɪ'dentl] ① ADJ (a) (*casual*) accidental, fortuito; **~ death** muerte *f* por accidente. (b) (*incidental*) secundario, incidente. ② N (*Mus*) accidente *m*.

accidentally [,æksɪ'dentəlɪ] ADV (a) (*lit*) accidentalmente, por accidente; **he was ~ killed** fue muerto en accidente. (b) (*by chance*) por casualidad; sin querer, por descuido, por inadvertencia; **we met quite ~** nos encontramos por pura casualidad; **the liquids were ~ mixed** los líquidos se mezclaron por descuido.

accident-prone ['æksɪdənt,prəʊn] ADJ con tendencia a sufrir (*or* causar) ... accidentes.

acclaim [ə'kleɪm] ① VT aclamar; (*applaud*) vitorear, ovacionar; **he was ~ed king** le aclamaron rey; **he was ~ed (as) the winner** le aclamaron por vencedor; **the play was ~ed** la obra fue muy aplaudida, la obra recibió muchos aplausos.

② N aclamación *f*, aplausos *mpl*; **the book was met with ~** el libro tuvo una acogida entusiasta.

acclamation [,æklə'meɪʃən] N aclamación *f*, aplausos *mpl*; **amid the ~s of the crowd** entre los vítores de la multitud; **to be chosen by ~** ser elegido por aclamación.

acclimate [ə'klaɪmət] (*US*) = **acclimatize**.

acclimatization [ə,klaɪmətaɪ'zeɪʃən] N, (*US*) **acclimation** [,æklaɪ'meɪʃən] N aclimatización *f*, aclimatación *f*.

acclimatize [ə'klaɪmətaɪz] ① VT aclimatar (*to* a).

② VI, VR: **to ~ o.s., to become ~d** aclimatarse (*to* a).

acclivity [ə'klɪvɪtɪ] N subida *f*, cuesta *f*.

accolade ['ækəʊleɪd] N (a) premio *m*; honor *m*; galardón *m*; elogio *m* entusiasta. (b) (*Hist*) acolada *f*, espaldarazo *m*.

accommodate [ə'kɒmədeɪt] ① VT (a) (*lodge, have room for*) *person* alojar, hospedar; *thing* tener espacio para, tener cabida para, contener; **can you ~ 4 people in July?** ¿tiene Vd habitaciones para 4 personas en julio?; **can you ~ 2 more in your car?** ¿caben 2 más en tu coche?; **this car ~s 6** este coche tiene 6 asientos.

(b) (*reconcile*) *differences* acomodar, concertar; *quarrel* componer, arreglar; *quarrelers* reconciliar.

(c) (*adapt*) acomodar, adaptar (*to* a), ajustar, ataviar (*LAm*).

(d) (*supply*) proveer (*with* de); **to ~ sb with a loan** facilitar un préstamo a uno.

(e) (*oblige*) complacer, hacer un favor a.

② VI (*eye*) adaptarse (*to* a).

accommodating [ə'kɒmədeɪtɪŋ] ADJ servicial, complaciente, atento; (*pej*) acomodadizo, que a todo se aviene fácilmente.

accommodation [ə,kɒmə'deɪʃən] N (a) (*lodging: also* **~s** (*US*)) alojamiento *m*; (*rooms*) habitaciones *fpl*; **'~ to let'** 'se alquila habitación'; **have you any ~ available?** ¿tiene Vd habitación disponible?; **to book ~ in a hotel** reservar una habitación en un hotel; **~ address** dirección *f* por donde uno pasa a recoger cartas; **~ bureau** oficina *f* de hospedaje.

(b) (*space*) espacio *m*, sitio *m*; cabida *f*; **seating ~** plazas *fpl*, asientos *mpl*; **~ train** (*US*) tren *m* de cercanías; **there is standing ~ only** hay sitio solamente para estar de pie; **there is ~ for 20 passengers** hay sitio para 20 pasajeros; **the plane has limited ~** el avión tiene un número fijo de plazas.

(c) (*agreement*) acuerdo *m*, convenio *m*; **to reach an ~ with creditors** llegar a un acuerdo con los acreedores.

(d) (*adaptation*) acomodación *f*, adaptación *f*.

(e) (*loan*) crédito *m*, préstamo *m*; **~ bill, ~ note** (*Comm*) pagaré *m* de favor.

accompaniment [ə'kʌmpənɪmənt] N acompañamiento *m* (*also Mus*).

accompanist [ə'kʌmpənɪst] N acompañante *m*, -a *f*.

accompany [ə'kʌmpənɪ] ① VT acompañar (*by, with* de; *also Mus, on* con, de); (*attach, enclose*) adjuntar, enviar adjunto; **he accompanied this with a grimace** al decir esto hizo una mueca.

② VR: **to ~ o.s. on the piano** acompañarse del (*or* al, con el) piano.

accomplice [ə'kʌmplɪs] N cómplice *mf*.

accomplish [ə'kʌmplɪʃ] VT (*finish*) acabar, concluir; (*carry out*) llevar a cabo, hacer; (*bring about*) efectuar, lograr; *one's design* realizar; *prophecy* cumplir.

accomplished [ə'kʌmplɪʃt] ADJ (a) *person* experto, consumado, hábil, diestro. (b) *fact* consumado.

accomplishment [ə'kʌmplɪʃmənt] N (a) (*act*) conclusión *f*; efectuación *f*, logro *m*; realización *f*; cumplimiento *m*; **difficult of ~** de difícil consecución. (b) (*result*) logro *m*; triunfo *m*, hazaña *f*; **a great ~** una auténtica hazaña; **it's quite an ~ to + infin** exige mucho talento + infin; **her ~ in finishing the film although ill** su triunfo al terminar la película a pesar de estar enferma. (c) (*skill etc*) talento *m*; habilidad *f*; **~s** talentos *mpl*, prendas *fpl*, dotes *fpl*, méritos *mpl*.

accord [ə'kɔːd] ① N (a) (*harmony*) acuerdo *m*, armonía *f*; **of one's own ~** espontáneamente, voluntariamente, por impulso propio; **with one ~** de común acuerdo; **to be in ~** estar de acuerdo (*with* con), estar en armonía (*with* con).

➤ LANGUAGE IN USE: accept: 1 → 11.2, 25.2 acceptance → 19.5, 20.3 accident: b → 18.4

(b) (*treaty*) acuerdo *m*, convenio *m*.
2 VT conceder, otorgar (*to* a); *welcome* dar (*to* a).
3 VI concordar (*with* con), armonizar (*with* con).
accordance [əˈkɔːdəns] N: **in ~ with** conforme a, de conformidad con, con arreglo a, de acuerdo con.
according [əˈkɔːdɪŋ] ADV **(a)** **~ as** según que, a medida que. **(b)** **~ to** según; (*in accordance with*) con arreglo a, conforme a; **~ to what he told me** según me dijo; **everything went ~ to plan** todo salió bien, todo resultó como se había previsto. **(c)** **it's all ~** * según, eso depende.
accordingly [əˈkɔːdɪŋlɪ] ADV en conformidad, de acuerdo con esto; **(and) ~** así pues, por consiguiente, por lo tanto.
accordion [əˈkɔːdɪən] N acordeón *m*.
accordionist [əˈkɔːdɪənɪst] N acordeonista *mf*.
accost [əˈkɒst] VT abordar, dirigirse a, entablar conversación con; (*prostitute*) abordar (con fines deshonestos); **he ~ed me in the street** se dirigió a mí en la calle; **he ~ed me for a light** se acercó a mí para pedir fuego.
accouchement [əˈkuːʃmɑ̃ːŋ] N parto *m*.
▼ **account** [əˈkaʊnt] 1 N **(a)** (*Comm, Fin, fig*) cuenta *f*; computación *f*; (*invoice*) factura *f*; albarán *m*; (*statement of ~*) estado *m* de cuenta; **the A~** (*St Ex*) período *m* (de 15 días) al fin del cual se ajustan las cuentas; **~ balance** saldo *m* de una cuenta; **~s department** sección *f* de contabilidad; **~ payable** cuenta *f* a (*or* por) pagar; **~ receivable** cuenta *f* por cobrar; **~ rendered** cuenta *f* pasada; **(is it) cash or ~?** ¿en metálico o a cuenta?; **on ~** a cuenta; **payment on ~** pago *m* a cuenta; **could I have £50 on ~?** ¿puede Vd darme 50 libras anticipadas?; **on his ~** por él, por causa de él; de su parte; **on his own ~** por cuenta propia; **on ~ of** por, por causa de, por motivo de, debido a; *as conj* (*esp US**) porque, debido a que, *eg* **I couldn't do it on ~ of my back's sore** no he podido hacerlo porque me duele la espalda; **on that ~** por eso; **on no ~, not on any ~** de ninguna manera, bajo ningún concepto; **to bring sb to ~, to call sb to ~** pedir cuentas a uno; **to charge sth to sb's ~** cargar algo en cuenta a uno; **to close an ~** liquidar una cuenta; **they have the Blotto ~** ellos hacen la publicidad de Blotto; **to keep the ~s** llevar las cuentas; **to open an ~** abrir una cuenta; **to render an ~, to send an ~** pasar factura; **to settle an ~** liquidar una cuenta; **to settle ~s with sb** (*fig*) ajustar cuentas con uno; **to turn sth to ~** aprovechar algo, sacar provecho de algo; *V* **current, joint** *etc*.
(b) (*estimation*) importancia *f*; **of no ~, of little ~, of small ~** de poca importancia; **of some ~** de cierta importancia, de alguna consideración.
(c) (*report*) relato *m*, relación *f* (*of* de), informe *m* (*of* sobre); **by (*or* from) all ~s** a decir de todos, por lo que dicen todos; según todas las informaciones; **by (*or* according to) her own ~** por lo que dice ella; **to give an ~ of** dar cuenta de, informar sobre; **to give an ~ of o.s.** justificar su conducta; **to give a good ~ of o.s.** dar buena cuenta de sí; **to leave sth out of ~** no tomar algo en consideración;
▼ **to take sth into ~, to take ~ of sth** tener algo en cuenta, tener algo presente; **to take no ~ of** no tomar en cuenta, desestimar, desatender.
2 VT considerar, creer; **I ~ him a fool** considero que es tonto; **I ~ myself lucky** creo que tengo suerte; **he is ~ed an expert** se le considera un experto; **I should ~ it a favour if** ... agradecería que ...
◆ **account for** VT **(a)** (*answer for*) responder de; (*explain*) dar cuenta de, dar razón de, justificar; representar; **that ~s for it** ésa es la razón, ha sido por eso; **I cannot ~ for it** no me lo explico; **how do you ~ for it?** ¿cómo lo explica Vd?; **everything is now ~ed for** todo está completo ya; **many are still not ~ed for** todavía no sabemos qué suerte han tenido muchos, seguimos ignorando lo que ha pasado a muchos; **there is no ~ing for tastes** sobre gustos no hay nada escrito; **children ~ for 5% of the audience** los niños representan el 5 por ciento de la audiencia.
(b) (*kill*) acabar con, matar; liquidar; **they ~ed for 3 stags** mataron 3 ciervos; **the ship ~ed for 3 enemy aircraft** el barco derribó 3 aviones enemigos; **one bomb ~ed for the power-station** una bomba acabó con la central eléctrica.
accountability [əˌkaʊntəˈbɪlətɪ] N responsabilidad *f*.
accountable [əˈkaʊntəbl] ADJ responsable (*for* de, *to* ante); explicable; **not ~ for one's actions** no responsable de los propios actos; **he is ~ only to himself** no reconoce más responsabilidad que ante sí mismo.
accountancy [əˈkaʊntənsɪ] N contabilidad *f*.
accountant [əˈkaʊntənt] N contable *mf*, contador *m*, -ora *f* (*esp LAm*); asesor *m*, -ora *f* fiscal (*or* de cuentas); (*in bank etc*) economista *mf*; **~'s office** contaduría *f*.
account-book [əˈkaʊntbʊk] N libro *m* de cuentas.
account-day [əˈkaʊntdeɪ] N día *m* de ajuste de cuentas.
accounting [əˈkaʊntɪŋ] N contabilidad *f*; teneduría *f* de libros; **~ period** período *m* contable, ejercicio *m* financiero.
accounting machine [əˈkaʊntɪŋməˌʃiːn] N máquina *f* de

contabilidad, calculadora *f*.
account number [əˈkaʊnt,nʌmbəʳ] N (*at bank etc*) número *m* de cuenta.
accoutred, (*US*) **accoutered** [əˈkuːtəd] PTP AND ADJ equipado (*with* de).
accoutrements [əˈkuːtrəmənts] NPL, (*US*) **accouterments** [əˈkuːtəmənts] NPL equipo *m*, avíos *mpl*, arreos *mpl*.
accredit [əˈkredɪt] VT **(a)** (*credit*) atribuir (*to* a); **to ~ a quality to sb, to ~ sb with a quality** atribuir una cualidad a uno. **(b)** (*recognize*) reconocer (oficialmente); certificar, autorizar. **(c)** (*appoint*) acreditar (*an ambassador to a government*) un embajador cerca de un gobierno).
accreditation [ə,kredɪˈteɪʃən] N reconocimiento *m* (oficial); autorización *f*; (*US Scol, Univ*) habilitación *f* de enseñanza; **~ officer** (*US Scol*) inspector *m*, -ora *f* de enseñanza.
accredited [əˈkredɪtɪd] ADJ autorizado, acreditado; **~ agent** agente *m* acreditado.
accretion [əˈkriːʃən] N aumento *m*, acrecentamiento *m*.
accrual [əˈkruəl] N acumulación *f*.
accrue [əˈkruː] VI (*grow*) aumentar, acumularse; **to ~ from** proceder de; derivarse de; **to ~ to** corresponder a; **some benefit will ~ to you from this** de esto resultará algo a beneficio de Vd; **~d charges** gastos *mpl* vencidos; **~d income** renta *f* acumulada; **~d interest** interés *m* acumulado.
ACCT N ABBR of **Association of Cinematograph, Television and Allied Technicians**.
acct ABBR of **account** cuenta *f*, cta.
acculturate [əˈkʌltʃə,reɪt] VT aculturar.
acculturation [ə,kʌltʃəˈreɪʃən] N aculturación *f*.
accumulate [əˈkjuːmjʊleɪt] 1 VT acumular, amontonar; acopiar, juntar.
2 VI acumularse, amontonarse; **~d depreciation** depreciación *f* acumulada.
accumulation [ə,kjuːmjʊˈleɪʃən] N **(a)** (*act*) acumulación *f*, amontonamiento *m*. **(b)** (*mass*) montón *m*, acopio *m*.
accumulative [əˈkjuːmjʊlətɪv] ADJ acumulativo.
accumulator [əˈkjuːmjʊleɪtəʳ] N acumulador *m*.
accuracy [ˈækjʊrəsɪ] N exactitud *f*, precisión *f*; esmero *m*.
accurate [ˈækjʊrɪt] ADJ *number, observation etc* exacto, preciso, correcto; *copy* fiel; *answer* correcto, acertado; *shot* certero; *worker* exacto, esmerado; **to be strictly ~** ... para decirlo con toda exactitud ...
accurately [ˈækjʊrɪtlɪ] ADV exactamente, correctamente; fielmente; acertadamente; certeramente; con esmero.
accursed, accurst [əˈkɜːst] ADJ (*liter*) maldito; (*ill-fated*) infausto, desventurado; **~ be he who ...!** ¡maldito sea quien ...!, ¡mal haya quien ...!
accusal [əˈkjuːzl] N (*Jur*) acusación *f*.
accusation [,ækjʊˈzeɪʃən] N acusación *f*, cargo *m*; denuncia *f*, delación *f*.
accusative [əˈkjuːzətɪv] 1 ADJ acusativo; **~ case = 2**.
2 N acusativo *m*.
accusatorial [ə,kjuːzəˈtɔːrɪəl] ADJ, **accusatory** [əˈkjuːzətərɪ] ADJ acusador.
accuse [əˈkjuːz] VT acusar (*of* de); denunciar, delatar; echar la culpa a, inculpar; **he stands ~d of** ... se le acusa de ...
accused [əˈkjuːzd] N acusado *m*, -a *f*.
accuser [əˈkjuːzəʳ] N acusador *m*, -ora *f*, delator *m*, -ora *f*.
accusing [əˈkjuːzɪŋ] ADJ acusador, lleno de reproches.
accusingly [əˈkjuːzɪŋlɪ] ADV: **she spoke ~** habló con tono acusador; **she looked at me ~** me lanzó una mirada acusadora.
accustom [əˈkʌstəm] 1 VT acostumbrar, habituar (*to* a); **to be ~ed to + infin** acostumbrar + *infin*, soler + *infin*; estar hecho a + *infin*; **I'm not really ~ed to + ger** en realidad no tengo la costumbre de + *infin*, no estoy realmente acostumbrada a + *infin*; **to get ~ed to sth** acostumbrarse a algo, habituarse a algo; **to get ~ed to + ger** acostumbrarse a + *infin*; **don't worry, you'll get ~ed** no te preocupes, ya te acostumbrarás a esto.
2 VR: **to ~ o.s. to** acostumbrarse a; **to ~ o.s. to + ger** acostumbrarse a + *infin*.
accustomed [əˈkʌstəmd] ADJ acostumbrado, usual.
AC/DC [,eɪsiːˈdiːsiː] 1 N ABBR of **alternating current/direct current** corriente *f* alterna/corriente *f* continua.
2 ADJ: **he's ~*** es bisexual.
ACE N (*US*) ABBR of **American Council on Education**.
ace [eɪs] 1 N **(a)** (*all senses*) as *m*; **to be (*or* come) within an ~ of** estar a dos dedos de, estar a pique de; **to keep an ~ up one's sleeve, to have an ~ in the hole** (*US**) guardar un triunfo en la manga; guardarse un as en la manga; **to play one's ~** (*fig*) jugar su triunfo; **A~ bandage** (*US*) ® venda *f* elástica. **(b)** **he's ~s** (*US**) es fenomenal*.
2 ADJ (*) estupendo*, de aúpa*; **~ player** *etc* as *m*.
acephalous [əˈsefələs] ADJ acéfalo.
acerbic [əˈsɜːbɪk] ADJ acre, áspero (*also fig*).

acerbity [ə'sɜːbɪtɪ] N acritud f, aspereza f; (fig) aspereza f.
acetate ['æsɪteɪt] N acetato m.
acetic [ə'siːtɪk] ADJ acético; ~ **acid** ácido m acético.
acetone ['æsɪtəun] N acetona f.
acetylene [ə'setɪliːn] N acetileno m; ~ **burner**, ~ **lamp**, ~ **torch** soplete m oxiacetilénico; ~ **welding** soldadura f oxiacetilénica.
ache [eɪk] [1] N dolor m (also fig); achaque m; **I have an** ~ **in my side** me duele el costado; **full of** ~**s and pains** lleno de goteras; **with an** ~ **in one's heart** con dolor del corazón.
  [2] VI (a) (tooth etc) doler; **my head** ~**s** me duele la cabeza; **it makes my head** ~ me da un dolor de cabeza; **I** ~ **all over** tengo dolores por todas partes. (b) (fig) **it was enough to make your heart** ~ era para romperle a uno el alma; **my heart** ~**s for you** lo siento en el alma; **I am aching for you** suspiro por ti; **I am aching to see you again** quiero tantísimo volver a verte; **I** ~**d to help him** quería con todo mi ser acudir en su auxilio, ansiaba tanto poder ayudarle, hubiera dado lo que fuera por ayudarle.
achievable [ə'tʃiːvəbl] ADJ alcanzable, realizable, factible; **an aim readily** ~ un propósito fácil de alcanzar.
▼ **achieve** [ə'tʃiːv] [1] VT lograr, conseguir, alcanzar, realizar; llevar a cabo; acabar; **he will never** ~ **anything** él no hará nunca nada; **what can you hope to** ~ **by that?** ¿qué esperas lograr con eso?
  [2] VI ir adelante, hacer progresos; realizar todo su potencial; **here is a man who has** ~**d** he aquí un hombre que ha llegado muy alto; **the children are not achieving as they should** los niños no hacen los progresos que debieran.
achievement [ə'tʃiːvmənt] N (a) (act) consecución f, realización f. (b) (thing achieved) éxito m, logro m; hazaña f; proeza f; conquista f; **that's quite an** ~, **that is no mean** ~ eso representa un éxito nada despreciable; **among his many** ~**s** entre las muchas hazañas en su haber; ~ **test** (Brit Scol) examen m de consecución.
achiever [ə'tʃiːvəʳ] N (also **high** ~) persona f que realiza su potencial; persona f que llega muy alto.
Achilles [ə'kɪliːz] NM Aquiles; ~' **heel** talón m de Aquiles; ~' **tendon** tendón m de Aquiles.
aching ['eɪkɪŋ] [1] ADJ tooth etc dolorido, que duele. (b) (fig) heart etc afligido.
  [2] N dolor m.
achromatic [ˌækrəu'mætɪk] ADJ acromático.
achy* ['eɪkɪ] ADJ dolorido; **to feel** ~ sentirse dolorido; **I feel** ~ **all over** me duele todo.
acid ['æsɪd] [1] ADJ (a) (Chem) ácido; ~ **drops** (Brit) caramelos mpl ácidos; ~ **rain** lluvia f ácida; ~ **test** (fig) prueba f de fuego, prueba f decisiva; ~ **test ratio** razón f de prueba de fuego; **to stand the** ~ **test** resistir a la prueba de fuego. (b) (fig) comment etc mordaz, punzante, áspero.
  [2] N (Chem) ácido m; (*: drug) ácido* m; ~ **(house) music** música f acid*; ~ **house party** fiesta f acid*.
acidhead* ['æsidhed] N adicto m, -a f al ácido.
acidic [ə'sɪdɪk] ADJ ácido.
acidifier [ə'sɪdɪfaɪəʳ] N acidulante m.
acidify [ə'sɪdɪfaɪ] [1] VT acidificar.
  [2] VI acidificarse.
acidity [ə'sɪdɪtɪ] N acidez f; (of stomach) acidez f de estómago, acedía f.
acidly ['æsɪdlɪ] ADV comment etc mordazmente, ásperamente.
acidophilous [ˌæsɪ'dɒfɪləs] ADJ acidófilo.
acid-proof ['æsɪdpruːf] ADJ, **acid-resisting** ['æsɪdrɪ'zɪstɪŋ] ADJ a prueba de ácidos.
acidulant [ə'sɪdjulənt] N acidulante m.
acidulous [ə'sɪdjuləs] ADJ acídulo.
ack-ack* ['æk'æk] N (fire) fuego m antiaéreo; (guns) artillería f antiaérea; ~ **fire** fuego m antiaéreo; ~ **gun** cañón m antiaéreo.
▼ **acknowledge** [ək'nɒlɪdʒ] [1] VT reconocer; truth etc confesar; claim admitir; crime confesarse culpable de; favour agradecer; letter acusar recibo de; present dar las gracias por; greeting contestar a; **to** ~ **defeat** darse por vencido; **to** ~ **receipt** acusar recibo (of de); **I** ~ **that ...** reconozco que ...; **to** ~ **sb as leader** reconocer a uno como jefe; **to** ~ **that sb is superior, to** ~ **sb as superior** reconocer que alguien es mejor.
  [2] VR: **to** ~ **o.s. beaten** darse por vencido, reconocer que uno ha perdido; **I** ~ **myself the loser** reconozco que he perdido; **she** ~**d herself in the wrong** reconoció que estaba equivocada (or era culpable).
acknowledged [ək'nɒlɪdʒd] ADJ: **an** ~ **expert** un experto reconocido como tal; **a generally** ~ **fact** un hecho generalmente admitido.
acknowledgement [ək'nɒlɪdʒmənt] N reconocimiento m; confesión f; agradecimiento m; contestación f (of a greeting a un saludo); (Comm) acuse m de recibo; ~**s** (in preface etc) agradecimientos mpl; **in** ~ **of sb's help** en reconocimiento de la ayuda de uno, agradeciendo la ayuda de uno; **to make** ~**s** expresar su agradecimiento; **I wish to make public** ~ **of the help** quiero agradecer públicamente la ayuda; **to quote sb without** ~ citar a uno sin mencionar la fuente.

ACLU N ABBR of **American Civil Liberties Union.**

┌─ *ACLU - AMERICAN CIVIL LIBERTIES UNION* ─┐

🛈 *La* **American Civil Liberties Union** *o* **ACLU** *es una organización no partidista que se fundó en 1920 para proteger los derechos de los ciudadanos estadounidenses tal y como lo establece la Constitución. La* **ACLU** *presta su apoyo en los tribunales cuando se trata de casos de violación de las libertades del ciudadano, especialmente en circunstancias de discriminación por motivos de religión, raza, color o sexo, o en casos relacionados con la libertad de expresión. Esta organización jugó un papel importante en la lucha contra la segregación racial. Sin embargo, debido a su defensa de la libertad total, también ha apoyado marchas del Partido Nazi Americano y del Ku Klux Klan, decisiones que han creado mucha polémica.*

acme ['ækmɪ] N colmo m, cima f; ~ **of perfection** la suma perfección; **he is the** ~ **of good taste** es el buen gusto en persona.
acne ['æknɪ] N acné f.
acolyte ['ækəulaɪt] N (Rel) acólito m, monaguillo m; (fig) seguidor m.
aconite ['ækənaɪt] N acónito m.
acorn ['eɪkɔːn] N bellota f.
acoustic [ə'kuːstɪk] ADJ acústico; ~ **coupler** acoplador m acústico.
acoustics [ə'kuːstɪks] N SING AND PL acústica f.
ACPO ['ækpəu] N (Brit) ABBR of **Association of Chief Police Officers.**
acquaint [ə'kweɪnt] [1] VT (a) (inform) **to** ~ **sb with** avisar a uno de, informar a uno sobre; poner a uno al corriente de.
  (b) (know) **to be** ~**ed** conocerse; **to be** ~**ed with** person conocer, fact saber, situation estar enterado de, estar al corriente de; **to become** ~**ed with** person (llegar a) conocer, fact saber, situation ponerse al tanto de.
  [2] VR: **to** ~ **o.s. with** informarse sobre, enterarse de, averiguar.
acquaintance [ə'kweɪntəns] N (a) (knowledge) conocimiento m (with de); familiaridad f (with con); trato m (with con); **a plumber of my** ~ un fontanero que conozco; **I have not the honour of his** ~ no tengo el honor de conocerle; **to have a nodding** ~ **with** conocer ligeramente; **it improves on** ~ parece mejor después de conocido; **on closer** (or further) ~ **it seems less attractive** al conocerlo mejor tiene menos atracción; **to make sb's** ~ conocer a uno; **I am very glad to make your** ~ tengo mucho gusto en conocerle; **he scraped** ~ **with Lord X** se las arregló para hacerse presentar a Lord X.
  (b) (person) conocido m, -a f; ~**s** personas fpl que uno conoce, relaciones fpl, amistades fpl; **an** ~ **of mine** una persona que yo conozco; **we're just** ~**s** nos conocemos ligeramente nada más; **we're old** ~**s** nos conocemos desde hace tiempo; **to have a wide circle of** ~**s** conocer a muchas personas.
acquaintanceship [ə'kweɪntənsʃɪp] N (a) (knowledge) conocimiento m (with de), familiaridad f (with con). (b) (between two persons) relaciones fpl.
acquiesce [ˌækwɪ'es] VI consentir (in en), asentir (in a), conformarse (in con); (unwillingly) someterse, doblegarse.
acquiescence [ˌækwɪ'esns] N consentimiento m (in en), asentimiento m (in a), conformidad f (in con); (state) aquiescencia f, resignación f.
acquiescent [ˌækwɪ'esnt] ADJ condescendiente, conforme; aquiescente; **he is** ~ **by nature** por su naturaleza se conforma con todo; **he was perfectly** ~ se mostró completamente conforme.
acquire [ə'kwaɪəʳ] VT adquirir; obtener; conseguir; proporcionarse; language etc aprender; territory, property tomar (from a), tomar posesión de; colour, tint adquirir, tomar; habit contraer; **I seem to have** ~**d a strange umbrella** parece que he tomado el paraguas de otro; **he got a fine tan** se dio un espléndido bronceado; **where did you** ~ **that?** ¿dónde conseguiste eso?; **she** ~**d many followers** se le pegaron muchos pretendientes; **to** ~ **a name for honesty** crearse una reputación de honrado; **to** ~ **a taste for** tomar gusto a, cobrar afición a.
acquired [ə'kwaɪəd] ADJ character(istic), taste adquirido.
acquirement [ə'kwaɪəmənt] N (a) adquisición f; obtención f, consecución f. (b) ~**s** (of knowledge) conocimientos mpl.
acquirer [ə'kwaɪərəʳ] N (Fin) adquirente mf.
acquisition [ˌækwɪ'zɪʃən] N adquisición f.
acquisitive [ə'kwɪzɪtɪv] ADJ codicioso.
acquisitiveness [ə'kwɪzɪtɪvnɪs] N codicia f.
acquit [ə'kwɪt] [1] VT absolver (of de), exonerar (of de), exculpar (of de); **he was** ~**ted on all charges** le absolvieron de todas las acusaciones.
  [2] VR: **to** ~ **o.s.** portarse; **how did he** ~ **himself?** ¿cómo se portó?, ¿cómo desempeñó el cometido?; **to** ~ **o.s. well** tener éxito, hacerlo bien, salir airoso; **to** ~ **o.s. of** duty desempeñar.
acquittal [ə'kwɪtl] N absolución f, exculpación f.
acre ['eɪkəʳ] N (= 40,47 áreas, 4047m²) acre m; **God's** ~ camposanto m; **the family's broad** (or **rolling**) ~**s** las extensas fincas de la familia; **there are** ~**s of space for you to play in*** hay la mar de espacio para que juguéis; **I've got** ~**s of weeds*** tengo un montón

de malas hierbas*.

acreage ['eɪkərɪdʒ] N superficie f (or extensión f) medida en *acres*; **the 1990 wheat** ~ el área sembrada de trigo en 1990; **what ~ have you here?** ¿cuánto miden estos terrenos?, ¿qué extensión tiene esta tierra?; **they farm a large** ~ cultivan unos terrenos muy extensos.

acrid ['ækrɪd] ADJ **(a)** *smell etc* acre, punzante. **(b)** *(fig)* áspero, desapacible.

Acrilan ['ækrɪlæn] ® N acrilán *m*.

acrimonious [,ækrɪ'məʊnɪəs] ADJ *remark etc* áspero, cáustico, mordaz; *argument* amargo, reñido.

acrimoniously [,ækrɪ'məʊnɪəslɪ] ADV ásperamente, mordazmente; amargamente.

acrimony ['ækrɪmənɪ] N aspereza *f*, acrimonia *f*, acritud *f*; lo amargo, lo reñido.

acrobat ['ækrəbæt] N acróbata *mf*.

acrobatic [,ækrəʊ'bætɪk] **1** ADJ acrobático.
2 ~**s** NPL acrobacia *f*; *(as profession)* acrobatismo *m*; *(Aer)* vuelo *m* acrobático.

acronym ['ækrənɪm] N sigla(s) *f(pl)*, acrónimo *m*.

acropolis [ə'krɒpəlɪs] N acrópolis *f*.

across [ə'krɒs] **1** ADV **(a)** *(gen)* a través, al través, de través; **don't go round, go** ~ no des la vuelta, ve al través; **shall I go** ~ **first?** ¿paso yo el primero?; **it's** ~ **from the post-office** está enfrente de Correos.
(b) *(from one side to the other)* de una parte a otra, de un lado a otro; **we shall have to cut it** ~ tendremos que cortarlo por medio; **a plank had been laid** ~ habían colocado una tabla encima; **he helped an old lady** ~ ayudó a una señora mayor a cruzar la calle *(etc)*.
(c) *(measurements)* **the plank is 10 cm** ~ la tabla tiene 10 cm de ancho; **it's not very far** ~ es corta la travesía; **how far is it** ~? *(river etc)* ¿cuántos metros tiene de ancho?; **how far is it** ~ **to the lighthouse?** ¿qué distancia hay desde aquí al faro?
(d) *(crossways)* a través, en cruz, transversalmente.
2 PREP **(a)** *(gen)* a través de, al través de; **to go** ~ **a bridge** pasar un puente; **the bridge** ~ **the Tagus** el puente sobre el Tajo; **with arms folded** ~ **his chest** con los brazos cruzados sobre el pecho; **a tree had fallen** ~ **the road** había caído un árbol a través de la carretera.
(b) *(on the other side of)* al otro lado de, del otro lado de; ~ **the seas** allende el mar; **from** ~ **the sea** desde más allá del mar; **the lands** ~ **the sea** las tierras más allá del mar; ~ **the street from our house** en el otro lado de la calle enfrente de nuestra casa; **he'll be** ~ **the water by now** ya estará al otro lado del mar.
(c) *(measurements)* **it is 12 km** ~ **the strait** el estrecho tiene 12 km de ancho.

across-the-board [ə'krɒsðə'bɔːd] ADJ *increase etc* global, general.

acrostic [ə'krɒstɪk] N acróstico *m*.

acrylic [ə'krɪlɪk] ADJ acrílico; ~ **fibre** fibra *f* acrílica.

acrylonitrile [,ækrɪləʊ'naɪtraɪl] N acrilonitrilo *m*.

ACT *(US)* ABBR *of* **American College Test** *examen que se hace al término de los estudios secundarios.*

act [ækt] **1** N **(a)** *(gen, liter)* acto *m*, acción *f*; obra *f*; **A~s of the Apostles** Hechos *mpl* de los Apóstoles; ~ **of contrition** acto *m* de contrición; ~ **of faith** acto *m* de fe; ~ **of God** *(caso m* de) fuerza *f* mayor; ~ **of justice** acción *f* de justicia; ~ **of war** acción *f* de guerra; **an** ~ **of folly** una locura; **an** ~ **of treason** una traición; **we need** ~**s not words** queremos hechos no palabras; **I was in the** ~ **of writing to him** precisamente le estaba escribiendo (a él); **to catch sb in the** ~ coger a uno en flagrante, coger a uno con las manos en la masa.
(b) *(Parl)* ley *f*; **A~ of Parliament** ley *f* *(aprobada por el Parlamento)*.
(c) *(Theat: division)* acto *m*.
(d) *(Theat: turn)* número *m*; **it's a hard** ~ **to follow** este número es tan bueno que será difícil repetirlo; **to get into** *(or* **in on)** **the** ~* introducirse en el asunto, lograr tomar parte; **to get one's** ~ **together*** organizarse, arreglárselas; **to put on an** ~ *(fig)* fingir (el asco, el enojo *etc)*.
2 VT *play* representar; *part* hacer; **to** ~ **the part of** hacer el papel de; **when I** ~**ed the Comendador** cuando yo hice (el papel) de Comendador; **to** ~ **the fool** hacer el tonto.
3 VI **(a)** *(Theat)* actuar, trabajar, representar; **I** ~**ed in my youth** de joven fui actor; **she's away** ~**ing in the provinces** está actuando en provincias; **never** ~ **with children or animals** no salgas nunca a escena con niños o animales; **to** ~ **in a film** tener un papel en una película; **have you ever** ~**ed?** ¿has hecho algún papel?; **who's** ~**ing in it?** ¿quién actúa?
(b) *(fig)* fingir; **he's only** ~**ing** lo está fingiendo nada más; **to** ~ **ill** hacerse enfermo.
(c) *(function: machine)* funcionar, marchar; *(person)* actuar; **the brakes did not** ~ no funcionaron los frenos; ~**ing in my capacity as chairman** de acuerdo con las funciones atribuidas a mi cargo de presidente; **he declined to** ~ se negó a servir; **to** ~ **as** actuar de, hacer de, servir de; **it** ~**s as a safety valve** funciona como (una)

válvula de seguridad; **he was** ~**ing as ambassador** estaba de embajador; **to** ~ **for sb** representar a uno; hablar por uno; hacer las veces de uno.
(d) *(behave)* actuar, obrar, comportarse; **he is** ~**ing strangely** se está comportando de una manera rara; **to** ~ **with caution** obrar con precaución; **she** ~**ed as if she was unwell** hacía como si estuviese enferma; **to** ~ **up to a principle** obrar con arreglo a un principio, seguir fiel a un principio.
(e) *(take action)* obrar, tomar medidas; **he** ~**ed to stop it** tomó medidas para impedirlo; **now is the time to** ~ es hora ya de ponerse en acción; **he** ~**ed for the best** hizo lo que mejor le parecía; **to** ~ **on a suggestion** seguir una indicación; **to** ~ **on the evidence** obrar de acuerdo con los hechos.
(f) *(take effect)* surtir efecto, dar resultados; **the medicine is slow to** ~ la medicina tarda en surtir efecto.
(g) *(affect)* **to** ~ **on** *(Mech)* impulsar, accionar; **to** ~ **on, to** ~ **upon** afectar (a), obrar sobre, tener resultados en; **the drug** ~**s upon the brain** la droga afecta al cerebro; **acids** ~ **upon metals** los ácidos atacan los metales.
◆**act out** VT representar; expresar; **to** ~ **out a macabre drama** *(fig)* representar (hasta el final) un drama macabro; **she is given to** ~**ing out her fantasies** tiene tendencia a hacer vivir sus fantasías en la realidad.
◆**act up*** VI *(person)* travesear, hacer de las suyas; *(car, machine)* funcionar mal, fallar.

┌─ **ACT OF PARLIAMENT** ─┐

A una ley ya aprobada por el Parlamento británico se la denomina **Act of Parliament**. *Antes, cuando todavía es un proyecto de ley* (**bill**), *puede ser modificado tanto por la Cámara de los Comunes como por la de los Lores. Si ambas cámaras lo aprueban, se envía al monarca para que dé su aprobación* (**Royal Assent**), *aunque esto es una mera formalidad. Tras ello la ley ya es oficialmente un* **Act of Parliament**, *y pasa a formar parte de la legislación británica, reemplazando cualquier ley consuetudinaria* (**common law**) *que hubiera sobre ese asunto.*
⇨ *Ver también* | COMMON LAW |

actable ['æktəbl] ADJ representable.

acting ['æktɪŋ] **1** ADJ interino, suplente; provisional; en funciones.
2 N **(a)** *(Theat: of play)* representación *f*; *(by actor)* desempeño *m*, actuación *f*; interpretación *f*; **what was his** ~ **like?** ¿qué tal hizo el papel?; **this is** ~ **as it should be** esto se llama realmente ser actor *(or* actriz), así es el teatro de verdad.
(b) *(as profession)* profesión *f* de actor; ~ **is not in my line** yo no soy actor; **she has done some** ~ tiene alguna experiencia como actriz, ella ha hecho algunos papeles; **to go in for** ~ hacerse actor.

actinic [æk'tɪnɪk] ADJ actínico.

actinium [æk'tɪnɪəm] N actinio *m*.

action ['ækʃən] N **(a)** *(gen)* acción *f*, acto *m*, hecho *m*; actuación *f*; ~! ¡vamos!, ¡a ello!; **man of** ~ hombre *m* de acción; ~**-packed film** película *f* de acción; ~ **painting** tachismo *m*; ~ **replay** *(Brit TV)* repetición *f* (de la jugada *etc)*; **he likes to be where the** ~ **is** le gusta estar en medio del bullicio; **I want to see some** ~ **here** quiero que todos pongan manos a la obra; **when shall we get some** ~ **on this?** ¿cuándo se hará algo en este asunto?; ~**s speak louder than words** dicho sin hecho no trae provecho; **to judge sb by his** ~**s** juzgar a uno por sus hechos; **to suit the** ~ **to the word** unir la acción a la palabra; **to bring** *(or* **put)** **into** ~ poner en movimiento; desplegar, poner en juego; **to go into** ~ entrar en acción; empezar a funcionar; **to be out of** ~ *(Mech)* no funcionar, estar parado, estar averiado; *(person)* estar inactivo, quedar fuera del juego; **'out of** ~' 'no funciona'; **to put out of** ~ inutilizar, parar, destrozar; **the illness put him out of** ~ la enfermedad le dejó fuera de combate; **he was out of** ~ **for months** durante meses estuvo sin poder hacer nada; **to take** ~ tomar medidas; **to take no** ~ no hacer nada.
(b) a piece of the ~ *(*: Comm)* una parte de las ganancias, una tajada*.
(c) *(*: merry activity)* actividad *f*; bullicio *m*, animación *f*, diversión *f*; vida *f* alegre; **where's the** ~ **in this town?** ¿dónde hay vida en este lugar?; **there's hardly any** ~ **before dark** antes de la noche apenas hay animación.
(d) *(Mil)* acción *f*, batalla *f*; **killed in** ~ muerto en acción, muerto en acto de servicio; **to see** ~ servir, luchar; ~ **stations!** ¡a sus puestos!; **to go to** ~ **stations** ir a sus puestos; **to go into** ~ entrar en batalla.
(e) *(Mech etc)* mecanismo *m*; funcionamiento *m*; movimiento *m*; *(of horse)* marcha *f*.
(f) *(Jur)* demanda *f*, proceso *m*; **civil** ~ demanda *f* civil; **to bring an** ~ entablar demanda *(against* contra).
(g) *(Theat: of play)* argumento *m*, acción *f*.

actionable ['ækʃnəbl] ADJ justiciable, procesable.

action man ['ækʃən,mæn] N *(gen hum)* hombre *m* de acción.

activate ['æktɪveɪt] VT activar.

activator [ˈæktɪˌveɪtəʳ] N activador m.

active [ˈæktɪv] ADJ activo (also Comm, Gram, Comput); personality etc enérgico, vigoroso; **~ assets** bienes mpl activos; **~ balance** saldo m activo; **~ duty (AD)** (US) servicio m activo; (Mil) **~ list** escala f activa; **~ partner** socio mf activo; **~ population** población f activa; **~ service** servicio m activo; **to be on ~ service** estar en activo; **to die on ~ service** morir en acto de servicio; **~ volcano** volcán m en actividad; **we are giving it ~ consideration** lo estamos estudiando en serio; **to play an ~ part in** colaborar activamente en; **to take an ~ interest in** interesarse vivamente por.

actively [ˈæktɪvlɪ] ADV activamente; enérgicamente, vigorosamente; vivamente.

activism [ˈæktɪvɪzəm] N activismo m.

activist [ˈæktɪvɪst] N activista mf.

activity [ækˈtɪvɪtɪ] N actividad f; (of personality) energía f, vigor m; (of busy scene) movimiento m, bullicio m; **activities** actividades fpl; **all his business activities** todos sus intereses comerciales; **social activities** vida f social; **his activities were wide** tuvo una ancha esfera de actividad; **to be in full ~** estar en pleno vigor; **~ holiday** vacaciones fpl activas; **~ method** (Scol) método m de actividades.

actor [ˈæktəʳ] N actor m.

actress [ˈæktrɪs] N actriz f.

ACTT N (Brit) ABBR of **Association of Cinematographic, Television and Allied Technicians**.

actual [ˈæktjʊəl] ADJ verdadero, real, efectivo; **~ loss** (Comm) pérdida f efectiva; **~ total loss** pérdida f total efectiva; **in ~ fact** en realidad; **let's take an ~ case** tomemos un caso concreto; **what were his ~ words?** ¿cuáles fueron sus palabras exactas?, ¿qué es lo que dijo, concretamente?; **is this the ~ book?** ¿es éste el mismo libro?; **what was the ~ price?** ¿cuál fue el precio real?; **there is no ~ contract** no hay contrato propiamente dicho; **there is a church but no ~ village** hay iglesia pero en realidad no hay pueblo.

actuality [ˌæktjʊˈælɪtɪ] N realidad f; **in ~** en realidad.

actualize [ˈæktjʊəlaɪz] VT (a) (make real) realizar. (b) (represent) representar de manera realista, describir con realismo.

actually [ˈæktjʊəlɪ] ADV (a) (really) realmente, en realidad, en efecto, efectivamente; **~ I am her husband** en realidad soy su marido; **those ~ present did not see it** los que en efecto asistían no lo vieron; **I wasn't ~ there** en realidad yo no estuve allí; **did you ~ see him?** ¿le vieron Vds realmente?; **what did he ~ say?** ¿qué es lo que dijo, exactamente?; **~, no** pues no.
(b) (even) **he ~ hit her** incluso llegó a pegarla; **we ~ caught a fish** hasta cogimos un pez.
(c) **that's not true ~** eso no es verdad, que digamos; **as for ~ working, he didn't** pues trabajar, como trabajar, no lo hizo; la verdad es que no trabajó nada.

actuarial [ˌæktjʊˈɛərɪəl] ADJ actuarial; **~ tables** tablas fpl actuariales.

actuary [ˈæktjʊərɪ] N actuario m, -a f de seguros.

actuate [ˈæktjʊeɪt] VT (a) person etc mover, animar; estimular; **a statement ~d by malice** una declaración motivada por el rencor; **he was ~d by envy** la envidia le movió a ello. (b) (Mech) impulsar, accionar.

acuity [əˈkjuːɪtɪ] N acuidad f, agudeza f.

acumen [ˈækjʊmen] N perspicacia f, tino m, agudeza f.

acupressure [ˌækjəˌpreʃəʳ] N acupresión f, digitopuntura f.

acupuncture [ˈækjʊpʌŋktʃəʳ] N acupuntura f.

acupuncturist [ˌækjʊˈpʌŋktʃərɪst] N acupuntor m, -ora f, acupunturista mf.

acute [əˈkjuːt] ADJ (in most senses) agudo; **~ accent** acento m agudo; **~ angle** ángulo m agudo; **~ appendicitis** apendicitis f aguda; **~ anxiety exists** existe una honda preocupación; **he has an ~ sense of the ridiculous** tiene un sentido agudo del ridículo; **that was very ~ of you** te has mostrado muy perspicaz.

acutely [əˈkjuːtlɪ] ADV agudamente; **I am ~ aware that ...** me doy cuenta cabal de que ...; **I feel my position ~** no se me oculta que es muy difícil mi situación.

acuteness [əˈkjuːtnɪs] N agudeza f, perspicacia f.

AD (a) ADV ABBR of **Anno Domini** = in the year of our Lord año m de Cristo, A.C., después de Jesucristo, d. de J.C. (b) N (US Mil) ABBR of **active duty** servicio m activo.

ad* [æd] N ABBR of **advertisement**.

a.d. ABBR of **after date** a partir de la fecha ...

adage [ˈædɪdʒ] N adagio m, refrán m.

adagio [əˈdɑːʒɪəʊ] N adagio m.

Adam [ˈædəm] NM Adán; **~'s ale** agua f; **~'s apple** nuez f (de la garganta or de Adán); **the old ~** la inclinación al pecado; **I don't know him from ~** no le conozco en absoluto.

adamant [ˈædəmənt] ADJ firme, inexorable, inflexible; **he was ~** se mostró inflexible; **he was ~ in his refusal** reiteró inexorablemente su denegación; **we must remain totally ~** tenemos que mantenernos totalmente firmes.

adamantine [ˌædəˈmæntaɪn] ADJ adamantino.

adapt [əˈdæpt] [1] VT (a) adaptar (to a); acomodar, ajustar (to a); **it is perfectly ~ed to its environment** se ajusta perfectamente a su ambiente. (b) text arreglar, refundir; **a novel ~ed by X** una novela en versión de X; **a novel ~ed as a play** una novela en versión dramática; **~ed from the Spanish** basado en una obra española.
[2] VI AND VR: **to ~ (o.s.) to** adaptarse a, ajustarse a, conformarse con.

adaptability [əˌdæptəˈbɪlɪtɪ] N adaptabilidad f; capacidad f para acomodarse (or ajustarse).

adaptable [əˈdæptəbl] ADJ adaptable; person capaz de acomodarse; **he's very ~** se acomoda en seguida a las circunstancias.

adaptation [ˌædæpˈteɪʃən] N adaptación f; (of text) arreglo m, versión f, refundición f.

adapter, adaptor [əˈdæptəʳ] N (Brit) adaptador m.

adaption [æˈdəpʃən] N = **adaptation**.

adaptive [əˈdæptɪv] ADJ: **the human body is remarkably ~** el cuerpo humano tiene una gran capacidad de adaptación; **an ~ reaction to an intolerable situation** una reacción de adaptación a una situación intolerable.

ADC N (a) ABBR of **aide-de-camp** edecán m. (b) (US) ABBR of **Aid to Dependent Children** ayuda a niños dependientes.

add [æd] VT (a) (Math) sumar.
(b) (join) añadir, agregar (to a); (to drink etc) añadir, echar, sumar (to a); **we gave £100 and he ~ed the rest** nosotros dimos 100 libras y él contribuyó lo demás; **'~ salt to taste'** 'echar sal al gusto'.
(c) (say further) añadir, agregar; **he ~ed that ...** añadió que ...; **there's nothing to ~** no hay nada más que decir.

◆**add in** VT añadir, incluir.

◆**add on** VT añadir; poner además; **we ~ed two rooms on** hicimos construir dos habitaciones más; **you have to ~ 15 dollars on for the service** hay que poner 15 dólares más de servicio.

◆**add to** VI aumentar, acrecentar; realzar; **it only ~ed to our problems** no hizo sino aumentar nuestros problemas; **then to ~ to our troubles ...** luego para colmo de desgracias ...

◆**add together** VT sumar.

◆**add up** 1 VT sumar.
[2] VI sumar; **it doesn't ~ up** (Math) no se puede sumar correctamente; (fig) no tiene sentido, no tiene pies ni cabeza; **it all ~s up*** es lógico, tiene sentido; **it's beginning to ~ up*** la cosa nos deja ya entrever una solución, ya podemos empezar a atar cabos.

◆**add up to** VI (Math) sumar, ascender a; (fig) venir a ser, equivaler a, querer decir; **it doesn't ~ up to much*** es poca cosa, no tiene gran importancia.

added [ˈædɪd] ADJ (a) añadido, adicional; **~ value** valor m añadido; **with ~ emphasis** con mayor énfasis, con más énfasis aún; **it's an ~ problem** es un problema más; **there is nothing ~** no hay nada añadido. (b) **~ to which ...** y además ...

addendum [əˈdendəm] N, PL **addenda** [əˈdendə] ad(d)enda f, adición f, artículo m suplementario.

adder [ˈædəʳ] N víbora f.

addict [ˈædɪkt] N partidario m, -a f, entusiasta mf, fanático m, -a f (of de); (Med) adicto m, -a f (and V drug ~); **I'm a guitar ~** me apasiona la guitarra; **I'm a detective story ~** yo soy un apasionado de la novela policíaca.

addicted [əˈdɪktɪd] ADJ: **to be ~ to sth** ser adicto a algo; (viciously) estar enviciado con algo; **to be ~ to drugs** ser drogadicto; **to be ~ to + ger** ser apasionado de + infin, ser fanático de + infin; (viciously) tener el vicio de + infin; **to become ~ to sth** enviciarse con algo, entregarse a algo.

addiction [əˈdɪkʃən] N afición f; (pej) vicio m, dependencia f, hábito m morboso; (to drugs) adicción f, drogadicción f, drogodependencia f.

addictive [əˈdɪktɪv] ADJ adictivo, que conduce al hábito morboso, que crea dependencia.

adding machine [ˈædɪŋməˌʃiːn] N sumadora f.

Addis Ababa [ˈædɪsˈæbəbə] N Addis Abeba m.

▼ **addition** [əˈdɪʃən] N (a) (Math) suma f, adición f; cálculo m; **~ sign** signo m de sumar; **if my ~ is correct** si he hecho bien el cálculo; **to do ~** hacer sumas.
(b) (thing added) adición f, añadidura f; adquisición f; **we made ~s to our stocks** aumentamos nuestras existencias; **these are our new ~s** éstas son nuestras nuevas adquisiciones; **this is a welcome ~ to our books on Ruritania** éste aumenta valiosamente nuestros libros sobre Ruritania; **there's been an ~ to the family** hay uno más en la ▼ familia; **in ~** además; **in ~ to** además de.

additional [əˈdɪʃənl] ADJ adicional; complementario, supletorio; añadido; **we need ~ men** necesitamos más hombres; **it is an ~ reason to + infin** es razón de más para + infin; **this gave him ~ confidence** esto aumentó su confianza.

additionality [əˌdɪʃəˈnælɪtɪ] N adicionalidad f.

additionally [əˈdɪʃənlɪ] ADV adicionalmente; por añadidura; **and ~** y además; **this makes it ~ difficult for me** esto aumenta (aún) mis dificultades.

additive ['ædɪtɪv] N aditivo *m*.

additive-free ['ædɪtɪv'friː] ADJ sin aditivos.

addled ['ædld] ADJ huero, podrido; *brain* confuso, débil.

add-on ['ædɒn] N adicional *m*.

▼ **address** [ə'dres] **1** N (a) *(of house etc)* señas *fpl*, dirección *f*; **business ~** dirección *f* profesional, dirección *f* de la oficina *(etc)* de uno; **home ~** dirección *f* particular; **~ commission** *(Comm)* comisión *f* que se paga al agente fletador por su tarea de embarque; **she isn't at this ~ any more** ya no vive en esta casa; **they left no forwarding ~** no dejaron dirección a la que pudiésemos hacer seguir las cartas.
(b) *(style)* tratamiento *m*, título *m*; **what form of ~ should I use?** ¿qué tratamiento debo darle?
(c) *(speech)* discurso *m*; *(lecture)* conferencia *f*; **election ~, electoral ~** carta *f* electoral; **public ~ system** sistema *m* amplificador.
(d) *(Parl etc)* petición *f*, memorial *m*.
(e) (†: *skill)* destreza *f*, habilidad *f*.
(f) (†: *behaviour)* modales *mpl*; conducta *f*, comportamiento *m*.
(g) **to pay one's ~es to** hacer la corte a, pretender a.
(h) *(Comput)* dirección *f*; **absolute ~** dirección *f* absoluta; **relative ~** dirección *f* relativa.
2 VT (a) *letter, parcel, protest* dirigir *(to* a); **I ~ed it to your home** lo mandé a tu casa; **I haven't ~ed it yet** todavía no he puesto la dirección; **this is ~ed to you** esto viene con el nombre de Vd; **this letter is wrongly ~ed** en esta carta han puesto mal la dirección.
(b) *person* dirigirse a, dirigir la palabra a; *meeting* pronunciar un discurso ante; **to ~ the House** pronunciar un discurso en el Parlamento; **he ~ed us on politics** nos habló de política; **are you ~ing me?** ¿habla Vd conmigo?
(c) **to ~ sb as** dar a uno el tratamiento de; **to ~ sb by his proper title** dar el debido tratamiento a uno; **to ~ sb as 'tú'** tratar a uno de 'tú', tutear a uno.
(d) *problem etc* estudiar; aplicarse a.
3 VR : **to ~ o.s. to** *person* dirigirse a; *problem, task* aplicarse a.

address-book [ə'dresbʊk] N librito *m* de direcciones, agenda *f*.

addressee [ædre'siː] N destinatario *m*, -a *f*; *(Comm)* consignatario *m*, -a *f*; **postage will be paid by the ~** a franquear en destino.

addressing [ə'dresɪŋ] N *(Comput)* direccionamiento *m*; **~ machine** máquina *f* de direcciones.

Addressograph [ə'dresəʊgrɑːf] ® N máquina *f* de direcciones, máquina *f* para dirigir sobres.

adduce [ə'djuːs] VT alegar, aducir, presentar.

adductor [ə'dʌktər] N aductor *m*.

Adelaide ['ædeleɪd] N Adelaida *f*.

Aden ['eɪdn] N Adén *m*; **Gulf of ~** Golfo *m* de Adén.

adenoidal ['ædɪnɔɪdl] ADJ adenoideo; **the child is ~** el niño padece inflamación adenoidea; **he has an ~ tone** tiene una voz gangosa.

adenoids ['ædɪnɔɪdz] NPL vegetaciones *fpl* adenoideas; (*) inflamación *f* adenoidea.

adept ['ædept] **1** ADJ experto, hábil, ducho *(at, in* en).
2 N experto *m*, -a *f*, perito *m*, -a *f*; **to be an ~ at** ser maestro en, ser ducho en; **he's an ~ at thieving** es un ladrón consumado.

adequacy ['ædɪkwəsɪ] N suficiencia *f*; idoneidad *f*, propiedad *f*.

adequate ['ædɪkwɪt] ADJ suficiente, adecuado; proporcionado; idóneo, propio; **to feel ~ to a task** sentirse con fuerzas para una tarea.

adequately ['ædɪkwɪtlɪ] ADV suficientemente.

ADGA N *(US)* ABBR of **Age Discrimination in Employment Act**.

adhere [əd'hɪər] VI (a) *(glue)* pegarse *(to* a). (b) **to ~ to** *(fig) party, policy* adherirse a; *promise* cumplir; *rule* observar, atenerse a.

adherence [əd'hɪərəns] N adherencia *f*, adhesión *f (to* a); observancia *f (to a rule* de una regla).

adherent [əd'hɪərənt] **1** ADJ adhesivo.
2 N partidario *m*, -a *f*.

adhesion [əd'hiːʒən] N = **adherence**.

adhesive [əd'hiːzɪv] **1** ADJ adhesivo, pegajoso; **~ plaster** esparadrapo *m*; **~ tape** *(Brit: stationery)* cinta *f* adhesiva; *(Med)* esparadrapo *m*, scotch *m*.
2 N adhesivo *m*.

ad hoc [æd'hɒk] ADJ ad hoc; **~ committee** comité *m* ad hoc.

adieu [ə'djuː] **1** INTERJ ¡adiós!
2 N (PL **~s** or **~x**) adiós *m*; **to bid ~ to** *person* despedirse de; *thing* renunciar a, separarse de, abandonar; **to make one's ~x** despedirse.

ad infinitum [ˌædɪnfɪ'naɪtəm] ADV ad infinitum, a lo infinito, hasta el infinito; hasta la saciedad; **it just carries on ~** es inacabable, es cosa de nunca acabar; **it varies ~** tiene un sinfín de variaciones; **and so (on) ~** y así hasta el infinito.

ad interim ['æd'ɪntərɪm] **1** ADV en el ínterin, interinamente.
2 ADJ interino.

adipose ['ædɪpəʊs] ADJ adiposo.

adiposity [ˌædɪ'pɒsɪtɪ] N adiposidad *f*.

adjacent [ə'dʒeɪsənt] ADJ contiguo, inmediato *(to* a); *angle* adyacente.

adjectival [ˌædʒek'taɪvəl] ADJ adjetivo, adjetival.

adjectivally [ˌædʒek'taɪvəlɪ] ADV adjetivamente.

adjective ['ædʒektɪv] N adjetivo *m*.

adjoin [ə'dʒɔɪn] **1** VT estar contiguo a, lindar con.
2 VI estar contiguo, colindar.

adjoining [ə'dʒɔɪnɪŋ] ADJ contiguo, vecino, colindante; **two ~ countries** dos países vecinos; **the ~ house** la casa de al lado; **in an ~ room** en un cuarto inmediato.

adjourn [ə'dʒɜːn] **1** VT *(postpone)* aplazar; prorrogar, diferir; *session* suspender, levantar; *(US: end)* terminar; **to ~ a discussion for a week** aplazar un debate por ocho días; **I declare the meeting ~ed** se levanta la sesión.
2 VI (a) *(meeting)* suspenderse; **the house then ~ed** luego se suspendió la sesión; **to stand ~ed** estar en suspenso.
(b) **to ~ to** trasladarse a, pasar a; **so we ~ed to the pub** así que nos trasladamos al bar.

adjournment [ə'dʒɜːnmənt] N *(postponement)* aplazamiento *m*; *(period of time)* suspensión *f*, clausura *f*.

Adjt. ABBR of **adjutant**.

adjudge [ə'dʒʌdʒ] VT *matter* juzgar, decidir; *(award juridically)* adjudicar; **to ~ that ...** estimar que ..., considerar que ...; **he was ~d the winner** se le decretó ganador, se le concedió la victoria; **to ~ sb guilty** declarar culpable a uno.

adjudicate [ə'dʒuːdɪkeɪt] **1** VT *claim* decidir, juzgar.
2 VI ser juez, sentenciar; **to ~ on a matter** fallar un asunto, ser árbitro en un asunto.

adjudication [ə,dʒuːdɪ'keɪʃən] N juicio *m*, sentencia *f*, decisión *f*; *(Comm)* adjudicación *f*; **~ of bankruptcy** adjudicación *f* de quiebra; **~ order** *(Jur)* orden *f* de adjudicación.

adjudicator [ə'dʒuːdɪkeɪtər] N juez *mf*, árbitro *mf*.

adjunct ['ædʒʌŋkt] N adjunto *m*, accesorio *m*.

adjure [ə'dʒʊər] VT ordenar solemnemente *(to do* hacer); suplicar, implorar.

adjust [ə'dʒʌst] **1** VT *(change)* modificar, cambiar; corregir; *(arrange)* arreglar; *machine* ajustar, graduar, regular; *differences* concertar, componer, resolver; *insurance claim* liquidar.
2 VI AND VR: **to ~ to, to ~ o.s. to** adaptarse a; **we shall have to ~** tendremos que adaptarnos; **the boy is having trouble in ~ing** el niño tiene dificultad en adaptarse.

adjustability [ə,dʒʌstə'bɪlɪtɪ] N adaptabilidad *f*.

adjustable [ə'dʒʌstəbl] ADJ ajustable, graduable, regulable; **~ spanner** llave *f* inglesa; **the date is ~** podemos cambiar la fecha.

adjuster, adjustor [ə'dʒʌstər] N ajustador *m*, tensor *m*.

adjustment [ə'dʒʌstmənt] N modificación *f*, cambio *m*; arreglo *m*; reajuste *m*; *(Mech)* ajuste *m*, regulación *f*; *(of differences)* composición *f*; resolución *f*; *(personal)* adaptación *f*; *(Comm)* ajuste *m*, reajuste *m*; **~ of prices** ajuste *m* de precios; **~ of wages** reajuste *m* salarial; **financial ~** arreglo *m* financiero; **social ~** adaptación *f* social; **after ~ for inflation** después de tomar en cuenta la inflación; **we can always make an ~** siempre podemos cambiarlo; **to make a small ~ in one's plans** modificar ligeramente sus proyectos.

adjutant ['ædʒətənt] N ayudante *m*; **A~ General** general responsable del aparato administrativo.

Adlerian [ˌæd'lɪərɪən] ADJ adleriano.

ad-lib [æd'lɪb] **1** ADV a voluntad, a discreción.
2 ADJ *comment etc* espontáneo; hecho sin pensar.
3 VT improvisar; decir *(etc)* espontáneamente.
4 VI improvisar, expresarse espontáneamente.

Adm. ABBR of **Admiral** almirante *m*.

adman ['ædmæn] N, PL **admen** ['ædmen] profesional *m* de la publicidad, publicista *m*.

admass ['ædmæs] N *parte de la población que está considerada como fácilmente influida por los actuales medios de la publicidad o propaganda comercial, conjunto de consumidores que tiene poco sentido crítico*.

admin. ['ædmɪn] *(Brit)* ABBR of **administration** administración *f*.

administer [əd'mɪnɪstər] VT (a) administrar; dirigir, regir, gobernar; **~ed price** precio *m* fijado por el fabricante *(y que no puede ser variado por el detallista)*. (b) *shock etc* dar, proporcionar; *punishment* aplicar. (c) **to ~ an oath to sb** tomar juramento a uno.

adminstrate [əd'mɪnɪstreɪt] VT administrar, dirigir.

administration [əd,mɪnɪs'treɪʃən] N (a) administración *f*; gobierno *m*, dirección *f*; gerencia *f*. (b) *(ministry)* gobierno *m*.

administrative [əd'mɪnɪstrətɪv] ADJ administrativo; **~ assistant** ayudante *m* administrativo, ayudante *f* administrativa; **~ court** *(US Jur)* tribunal *m* administrativo; **~ expenses** gastos *mpl* administrativos; **~ machinery** *(US Jur)* maquinaria *f* administrativa, aparato *m* administrativo; **~ staff** personal *m* de administración.

administrator [əd'mɪnɪstreɪtər] N administrador *m*, -ora *f*; *(Jur)* albacea *mf*.

admirable ['ædmərəbl] ADJ admirable, digno de admiración, excelente; **~!** ¡muy bien!

admirably ['ædmərəblɪ] ADV admirablemente, de una manera digna de admiración.

admiral ['ædmərəl] N almirante m.

Admiralty ['ædmərəltɪ] N (Brit) Ministerio m de Marina, Almirantazgo m; **First Lord of the ~** Ministro m de Marina; **a~ court** (US) tribunal m marítimo.

admiration [ˌædmə'reɪʃən] N admiración f.

admire [əd'maɪəʳ] VT admirar; (express admiration for) manifestar su admiración por, elogiar; **she was admiring herself in the mirror** se estaba mirando satisfecha en el espejo.

admirer [əd'maɪərəʳ] N admirador m, -ora f; (suitor) enamorado m, pretendiente m.

admiring [əd'maɪərɪŋ] ADJ look etc admirativo, de admiración.

admiringly [əd'maɪərɪŋlɪ] ADV con admiración; **he looked at her ~** le lanzó una mirada llena de admiración; **to speak ~ of** hablar en términos elogiosos de.

admissibility [ədˌmɪsə'bɪlɪtɪ] N admisibilidad f.

admissible [əd'mɪsəbl] ADJ admisible, aceptable.

admission [əd'mɪʃən] N **(a)** (entry) entrada f (to a, en); (to academy, club etc) ingreso m (to en); **~ is free on Sundays** la entrada es gratuita los domingos; **'~ free'** 'entrada gratis'; **'no ~'** 'se prohíbe la entrada'; **we gained ~ by a window** logramos entrar por una ventana; **~ fee** cuota f de entrada; **~s form** (US Univ) impreso m de matrícula; **~s office** (US Univ) secretaría f.
(b) (acknowledgement) confesión f (of de); **on his own ~** por confesión propia; **it would be an ~ of defeat** sería reconocer nuestra derrota; **he made an ~ of guilt** se confesó culpable.

▼ **admit** [əd'mɪt] VT **(a)** (allow to enter) dejar entrar, dar entrada a, hacer pasar (LAm); (fig) admitir, aceptar; **'children not ~ted'** 'no se admiten menores'; **ticket which ~s two** entrada f para dos personas; **to be ~ted to the Academy** ingresar en la Academia; **to be ~ted to hospital** ingresar en el hospital; **~ting office** (US Med) oficina f de ingresos.
▼ **(b)** (acknowledge) reconocer, confesar; **it must be ~ted that** hay que reconocer que; **I ~ nothing!** ¡no tengo nada que confesar!; **it is hard, I ~** es difícil, lo reconozco; **he ~ted himself beaten** reconoció que había sido vencido.
◆ **admit of** VT admitir, dar lugar a, permitir; **it ~s of no other explanation** no cabe otra explicación.
◆ **admit to** VT crime confesarse culpable de; **she ~s to doing it** confiesa haberlo hecho; **I ~ to feeling a bit ill** confieso que me siento algo mal.

admittance [əd'mɪtəns] N entrada f; derecho m de entrada; **he was refused ~** se le negó la entrada; **I gained ~ by the window** logré entrar por la ventana; **'no ~'** 'se prohíbe la entrada'.

admittedly [əd'mɪtɪdlɪ] ADV se reconoce que, es verdad que, de acuerdo que; **an ~ serious crime** un crimen que se reconoce como grave.

admixture [əd'mɪkstʃəʳ] N mezcla f, adición f; (fig) dosis f.

admonish [əd'mɒnɪʃ] VT (reprimand) reprender, amonestar; (warn) amonestar, prevenir; (advise) aconsejar (to do hacer).

admonition [ˌædməʊ'nɪʃən] N (reproof) represión f; (warning) amonestación f, advertencia f; (advice) consejo m, recomendación f.

admonitory [əd'mɒnɪtərɪ] ADJ admonitorio.

ad nauseam [ˌæd'nɔ:sɪæm] ADV hasta la saciedad; **he repeated it ~** no se hartó de repetirlo, lo repitió incansablemente; **you've told me that ~** ya me lo has dicho mil veces.

adnominal [ˌæd'nɒmɪnəl] 1 ADJ adnominal.
2 N adnominal m.

ado [ə'du:] N: **much ~ about nothing** mucho ruido y pocas nueces, nada entre dos platos; **without further ~, without more ~** sin más (ni más).

adobe [ə'dəʊbɪ] N adobe m.

adolescence [ˌædəʊ'lesns] N adolescencia f.

adolescent [ˌædəʊ'lesnt] 1 ADJ adolescente.
2 N adolescente mf; joven mf.

Adolf, Adolph ['ædɒlf], **Adolphus** [ə'dɒlfəs] NM Adolfo.

Adonis [ə'dəʊnɪs] NM Adonis.

adopt [ə'dɒpt] VT adoptar; candidate, report, motion aprobar; child adoptar, prohijar; suggestion seguir, aceptar.

adopted [ə'dɒptɪd] ADJ child adoptivo, adoptado (Mex).

adoption [ə'dɒpʃən] N adopción f; **they have two children by ~** tienen dos hijos adoptivos; **country of ~** patria f adoptiva.

adoptive [ə'dɒptɪv] ADJ adoptivo.

adorable [ə'dɔ:rəbl] ADJ adorable; encantador, mono*.

adoration [ˌædɔ:'reɪʃən] N adoración f.

adore [ə'dɔ:ʳ] VT adorar.

adoring [ə'dɔ:rɪŋ] ADJ look lleno de adoración; parent etc cariñoso.

adoringly [ə'dɔ:rɪŋlɪ] ADV con adoración.

adorn [ə'dɔ:n] VT adornar, ornar, embellecer, engalanar.

adornment [ə'dɔ:nmənt] N adorno m, decoración f.

ADP N ABBR of Automatic Data Processing proceso m automático de datos.

adrenal [ə'dri:nl] ADJ suprarrenal; **~ gland** glándula f suprarrenal.

adrenalin(e) [ə'drenəlɪn] N (Brit) adrenalina f; **I feel the ~ rising** siento que me sube la adrenalina.

Adriatic (Sea) [ˌeɪdrɪ'ætɪk (si:)] N (Mar m) Adriático m.

adrift [ə'drɪft] ADV a la deriva, al garete; **to be all ~** (fig) ir a la deriva; estar desorientado; **to break ~** (accidentally) perder las anclas, romper las amarras; (deliberately) cortar las amarras; **to come ~** (fig) soltarse, desprenderse; **to cut a boat ~** cortar las amarras de una barca; **something has gone ~** algo ha fallado; **my bike has gone ~** mi bici se ha extraviado; **to turn sb ~** abandonar a uno a su suerte.

adroit [ə'drɔɪt] ADJ diestro, hábil, mañoso.

adroitly [ə'drɔɪtlɪ] ADV diestramente, hábilmente.

adroitness [ə'drɔɪtnɪs] N destreza f, habilidad f.

ADT N (US) ABBR of **Atlantic Daylight Time**.

adulate ['ædjʊleɪt] VT adular.

adulation [ˌædjʊ'leɪʃən] N adulación f.

adulatory ['ædjʊleɪtərɪ] ADJ adulador.

adult ['ædʌlt] 1 ADJ adulto; maduro; mayor de edad, mayor; (Cine etc) apto para adultos; **~ education** educación f de adultos.
2 N adulto m, -a f; persona f mayor (de edad); **'~s only'** (exhibition etc) '(sólo para) mayores'; (Cine) 'autorizada para los mayores de 18 años'.

adulterate [ə'dʌltəreɪt] VT adulterar.

adulteration [əˌdʌltə'reɪʃən] N adulteración f.

adulterer [ə'dʌltərəʳ] N adúltero m.

adulteress [ə'dʌltərɪs] N adúltera f.

adulterous [ə'dʌltərəs] ADJ adúltero.

adultery [ə'dʌltərɪ] N adulterio m.

adulthood [ə'dʌlthʊd] N adultez f, mayoría f de edad, edad f adulta.

adumbrate ['ædʌmbreɪt] VT bosquejar; (foreshadow) presagiar, anunciar.

adumbration [ˌædʌm'breɪʃən] N bosquejo m; presagio m, anuncio m.

ad val. ABBR of **ad valorem**.

ad valorem [ædvə'lɔ:rəm] ADV conforme a su valor, por avalúo; **~ tax** impuesto m según valor.

▼ **advance** [əd'vɑ:ns] 1 N **(a)** (Mil) avance m; (progress) avance m, progreso m, adelanto m; **an important scientific ~** un importante adelanto científico.
(b) (loan) anticipo m; préstamo m; **to get an ~ on one's salary** conseguir un anticipo de sueldo.
(c) (in price, value) alza f, aumento m; **any ~ on £5?** ¿alguien ofrece más de 5 libras?
(d) **~s** primeros pasos mpl; insinuaciones fpl; (amorous) requerimiento m amoroso; **to accept** (or **respond favourably to**) **sb's ~s** aceptar las intenciones de uno; **to make ~s to a woman** requerir de amores a una mujer; **to make the first ~s** dar los primeros pasos.
▼ **(e)** (phrases with in) **in ~** por adelantado, de antemano; **to arrive in ~ of sb** llegar antes que uno; **to be in ~ of one's times** adelantarse a su época; **to book in ~** reservar con anticipación; **to let sb know a week in ~** avisar a uno con ocho días de anticipación; **to pay in ~** pagar por adelantado; **to thank sb in ~** anticipar las gracias a uno; **thanking you in ~** dándole anticipadas gracias.
2 ADJ anticipado, adelantado; **~ booking** reserva f anticipada; **~ booking office** (Brit) despacho m de venta anticipada; **~ copy** anticipo m editorial; **~ deposit** paga y señal f; **~ freight** flete m pagado; **~ guard** avanzada f; **~ man** (US Pol) responsable m de una campaña política; **~ notice** previo aviso m; **~ party** grupo m avanzado; (Mil) brigada f móvil; **~ payment** anticipo m; **~ post** puesto m de vanguardia; **~ warning** = **~ notice**.
3 VT **(a)** (move forward) avanzar, adelantar; person (in rank) ascender (to a).
(b) (encourage) promover, fomentar, ayudar.
(c) (put forward) idea, opinion, theory proponer (para la discusión), propugnar, exponer; suggestion hacer; claim presentar, formular.
(d) money anticipar; loan prestar; **he ~d me £50** me anticipó 50 libras.
4 VI **(a)** (move forward) avanzar, adelantarse; **she ~d across the room** avanzó a través del cuarto; **to ~ on sb** acercarse (de modo amenazador) a uno; **to ~ on a town** avanzar sobre una ciudad.
(b) (fig) avanzar, adelantarse; **the work is advancing quickly** el trabajo se está adelantando rápidamente.
(c) (in rank) ascender (to a).
(d) (price) subir.

advanced [əd'vɑ:nst] ADJ **(a)** (gen) ideas etc avanzado; machine etc muy moderno; student adelantado; study superior, alto; **~ maths** matemáticas fpl avanzadas; **~ in years** de edad avanzada, entrado en años; **the corn is well ~** el trigo está muy avanzado; **the season is well ~** la estación está avanzada; **~ gas-cooled reactor** reactor m refrigerado por gas de tipo avanzado.
(b) (Brit Scol) **A~ Level** ≃ bachillerato m; **to take 3 A~ Levels** presentarse como candidato en 3 asignaturas de Advanced Level; **she has**

an **A~ Level in chemistry** tiene un título de *Advanced Level* en química.

┌─ ⌐**ADVANCED LEVELS**───────────────────────────────┐

ⓘ *Al terminar la educación secundaria obligatoria, los estudiantes de Inglaterra, Gales e Irlanda del Norte pueden estudiar otros dos años para preparar dos o tres asignaturas más y examinarse de ellas a los 18 años. Estos exámenes se conocen con el nombre de* **Advanced levels** *o* **A levels***. Cada universidad determina el número de* **A levels** *y la calificación necesaria para acceder a ella.*

En Escocia los exámenes equivalentes son los **Highers** *o* **Higher Grades***, que se hacen de unas cinco asignaturas tras un año de estudios. Después se puede optar entre entrar en la universidad directamente o estudiar otro año más, bien para hacer el mismo examen de otras asignaturas, o para sacar los* **CSYS's***, abreviatura de* **Certificate of Sixth Year Studies***.*
⇨ *Ver también* |GCSE|

advancement [əd'vɑːnsmənt] N **(a)** adelantamiento *m*, progreso *m*; fomento *m*. **(b)** (*in rank*) ascenso *m*.

advantage [əd'vɑːntɪdʒ] N **(a)** ventaja *f*; **it's no ~ to play first** el jugar primero no da ventaja; **to be to sb's ~** ser ventajoso para uno; **to have the ~ of sb** llevar ventaja a uno; **I'm sorry, you have the ~ of me** lo siento, pero no recuerdo su nombre; **to have the ~ in numbers** llevar ventaja en cuanto al número; **to show to ~** (VI) lucir, aparecer bajo una luz favorable; **to show sth off to best ~** hacer que algo se vea bajo la luz más favorable; **to take ~ of** aprovechar(se de); sacar partido de; *kindness etc* abusar de; (*euph*) seducir; **to turn sth to (one's) ~** sacar buen partido de algo; **'languages and shorthand an ~'** (*job advert*) 'serán méritos (*or* se valorarán) idiomas y taquigrafía'.
(b) (*Tennis*) ventaja *f*; (*Soccer*) **~ rule** ley *f* de la ventaja.

advantaged [əd'vɑːntɪdʒd] NPL: **the ~** los privilegiados, los favorecidos.

advantageous [ˌædvən'teɪdʒəs] ADJ ventajoso, provechoso.

advantageously [ˌædvən'teɪdʒəslɪ] ADV ventajosamente, provechosamente.

advent ['ædvənt] N advenimiento *m*, venida *f*, llegada *f*; **A~** (*Rel*) Adviento *m*.

adventitious [ˌædven'tɪʃəs] ADJ adventicio.

adventure [əd'ventʃər] N aventura *f*; **~ playground** parque *m* infantil.

adventurer [əd'ventʃərər] N aventurero *m*.

adventuress [əd'ventʃərɪs] N aventurera *f*.

adventurism [əd'ventʃərɪzəm] N aventurismo *m*.

adventurist [əd'ventʃərɪst] **1** ADJ aventurista.
2 N aventurista *mf*.

adventurous [əd'ventʃərəs] ADJ *person, character* aventurero, emprendedor; atrevido; *enterprise* peligroso, arriesgado, difícil; **we had a very ~ time getting here** las hemos pasado negras al venir aquí; **we need a more ~ slogan** necesitamos un eslogan más llamativo.

adventurously [əd'ventʃərəslɪ] ADV con espíritu aventurero (*or* emprendedor); atrevidamente.

adverb ['ædvɜːb] N adverbio *m*.

adverbial [əd'vɜːbɪəl] ADJ adverbial.

adversarial [ˌædvɜː'sɛərɪəl] ADJ: **~ procedure** procedimiento *m* de confrontación.

adversary ['ædvəsərɪ] N adversario *m*, -a *f*, contrario *m*, -a *f*.

adverse ['ædvɜːs] ADJ adverso, contrario, hostil (*to* a); desfavorable (*to* para); *balance* negativo, deudor; *effect, result* adverso.

adversely ['ædvɜːslɪ] ADV desfavorablemente, negativamente; **to affect ~** perjudicar.

adversity [əd'vɜːsɪtɪ] N infortunio *m*, desgracia *f*; **in times of ~** en tiempos difíciles; **he knew ~ in his youth** de joven conoció la miseria; **companion in ~** compañero *m* de desgracias.

advert¹ [əd'vɜːt] VI: **to ~ to** referirse a.

advert²* ['ædvɜːt] N (*Brit*) = **advertisement**.

advertise ['ædvətaɪz] **1** VT **(a)** publicar, anunciar; *weakness etc* exponer, revelar públicamente.
(b) (*Comm etc*) anunciar; **'as ~d on TV'** 'anunciado en TV'.
2 VI hacer publicidad, hacer propaganda; poner un anuncio (*in a paper* en un periódico; *for sth* solicitando algo); **to ~ for** buscar por medio de anuncios, solicitar; **it pays to ~** la publicidad siempre rinde.

advertisement [əd'vɜːtɪsmənt] N anuncio *m*; **~ column** columna *f* de anuncios, sección *f* de anuncios; **~ rates** tarifas *fpl* de anuncios; **small ~s** (*Brit*) anuncios *mpl* por palabras, anuncios *mpl* económicos; **it's not much of an ~ for the place*** no dice mucho en favor de la ciudad (*etc*).

advertiser ['ædvətaɪzər] N anunciante *mf*.

advertising ['ædvətaɪzɪŋ] **1** N publicidad *f*, propaganda *f*; (*adverts collectively*) anuncios *mpl*; **my brother's in ~** mi hermano trabaja en la publicidad.

2 ATTR: **~ agency** agencia *f* de publicidad; **~ campaign** campaña *f* publicitaria; **~ man** empresario *m* de publicidad; **~ manager** jefe *m*, -a *f* de publicidad; **~ matter** material *m* de publicidad; **~ medium** medio *m* de publicidad; **~ rates** tarifa *f* de anuncios.

▼ **advice** [əd'vaɪs] N consejo *m*; (*report*) informe *m*, noticia *f*; (*Comm*) aviso *m*, notificación *f*; **~ column** consultorio *m* sentimental; **~ note** aviso *m* de mercancías, albarán *m*; **~ of dispatch** nota *f* de consignación; **a piece of ~** un consejo; **technical ~** asesoramiento *m* técnico; **my ~ to you is** + *infin* te aconsejo + *infin*; **to ask for ~, to seek ~** pedir consejos; **to take sb's ~** seguir los consejos de uno; **to take legal ~** consultar a un abogado; **to take medical ~** consultar a un médico.

advisability [əd,vaɪzə'bɪlɪtɪ] N conveniencia *f*, prudencia *f*.

▼ **advisable** [əd'vaɪzəbl] ADJ aconsejable, conveniente, prudente; **it would be ~ to** + *infin* sería aconsejable + *infin*; **if you think it ~** si te parece bien, si crees que es recomendable.

▼ **advise** [əd'vaɪz] **1** VT **(a)** (*counsel*) aconsejar (*to do* hacer); (*as paid adviser, also technically*) asesorar; **what do you ~ me to do?** ¿qué me aconsejas (que haga)?
▼ **(b)** (*recommend*) aconsejar, recomendar; **he ~s caution** él recomienda la prudencia; **the doctor ~s complete rest** el médico recomienda el descanso total.
▼ **(c)** (*inform*) avisar, informar; advertir; (*Comm*) notificar; **to ~ sb of an event** informar a uno de un suceso; **to keep sb ~d of sth** tener a uno al corriente de algo; **keep me ~d** manténgame al corriente; **please ~ us of a convenient date** (*Comm*) ruego nos notifique una fecha conveniente; **we will ~ you of delivery in due course** les notificaremos la entrega en su momento.
2 VI: **he ~s against the plan** él aconseja en contra del plan; **he ~s against going** aconseja que no vayamos; **to ~ on** ser asesor en.

advised [əd'vaɪzd] ADJ: **well-~** prudente; **you would be well ~ to** + *infin* sería aconsejable + *infin*, harías bien en + *infin*; V **ill-~**.

advisedly [əd'vaɪzɪdlɪ] ADV deliberadamente; **to speak ~** hablar con conocimiento de causa; **I say so ~** lo digo después de pensarlo bien.

advisement [əd'vaɪzmənt] N (*US*) consulta *f*, deliberación *f*; **~ counseling** guía *f* vocacional.

adviser, advisor [əd'vaɪzər] N consejero *m*, -a *f*; (*eg business ~, technical ~*) asesor *m*, -ora; *f* **legal ~** abogado *mf*, asesor *m* jurídico, asesora *f* jurídica; **spiritual ~** confesor *m*.

advisory [əd'vaɪzərɪ] ADJ consultivo; **~ board** junta *f* consultiva; **~ body** cuerpo *m* consultivo; **~ committee** (*US Pol*) comité *m* consultivo; **~ opinion** (*US Jur*) opinión *f* consultiva, opinión *f* asesoria; **~ service** servicio *m* consultivo; **in an ~ capacity** en calidad de asesor.

advocacy ['ædvəkəsɪ] N apoyo *m* (activo); (*Jur etc*) defensa *f*.

advocate **1** ['ædvəkɪt] N defensor *m*, -ora *f*, partidario *m*, -a *f*; (*Scot Jur*) abogado *mf*; **devil's ~** abogado *m* del diablo; *ver también* |LAWYERS|, |QC/KC|.
2 ['ædvəkeɪt] VT abogar por, recomendar; ser partidario de; **what do you ~?** ¿qué nos aconsejas?; **I ~ doing nothing** yo recomiendo no hacer nada.

advt ABBR *of* **advertisement**.

adze, (*US*) **adz** [ædz] N azuela *f*.

AEA (a) N (*Brit*) ABBR *of* **Atomic Energy Authority** Consejo *m* de Energía Nuclear.
(b) N ABBR *of* **Association of European Airlines** Asociación *f* de Aerolíneas Europeas, AAE *f*.

AEC N (*US*) ABBR *of* **Atomic Energy Commission**.

AEF N (*US*) ABBR *of* **American Expeditionary Forces**.

Aegean Sea [iː'dʒiːən siː] N Mar *m* Egeo.

aegis ['iːdʒɪs] N égida *f*; **under the ~ of** (*protection*) bajo la tutela de; (*patronage*) patrocinado por.

aegrotat [iː'grəʊtæt] N (*Brit*) *título universitario que se concede al candidato que por enfermedad no ha podido presentarse a los exámenes.*

Aeneas [iː'niːæs] NM Eneas.

Aeneid ['iːnɪɪd] N Eneida *f*.

aeon, (*US*) **eon** ['iːən] N eón *m*; (*fig*) eternidad *f*.

aerate ['ɛəreɪt] VT airear; ventilar, oxigenar.

aerated ['ɛəreɪtɪd] ADJ: **~ water** gaseosa *f*.

aeration [ɛə'reɪʃən] N aireación *f*.

aerial ['ɛərɪəl] **1** ADJ aéreo; **~ beacon** aerofaro *m*; **~ cableway** teleférico *m*; **~ input*** (*US*) mensaje *m* recibido por antena; **~ ladder** (*US*) escalera *f* de bomberos; **~ photograph** aerofoto *f*; **~ photography** fotografía *f* aérea; **~ survey** reconocimiento *m* aéreo; **~ tanker** transportador *m* aéreo.
2 N (*esp Brit*) antena *f*; (*mast*) torre *f* de antena.

aerie ['ɛərɪ] N (*US*) = **eyrie**.

aero... ['ɛərəʊ] PREF aero...

aerobatics [ˌɛərəʊ'bætɪks] NPL acrobacia *f* aérea.

aerobic [ɛə'rəʊbɪk] ADJ *shoes, dances* de aerobic, para aerobic.

aerobics [ɛə'rəʊbɪks] N SING aeróbica *f*, aerobic *m*, aerobismo *m* (*SC*).

aerodrome ['ɛərədrəʊm] N (*Brit*) aeródromo *m*.

aerodynamic ['ɛərəʊdaɪ'næmɪk] ADJ aerodinámico.
aerodynamics ['ɛərəʊdaɪ'næmɪks] NPL aerodinámica *f.*
aero-engine ['ɛərəʊ,endʒɪn] N motor *m* de aviación.
aerofoil ['ɛərəʊfɔɪl] N plano *m* aerodinámico.
aerogram(me) ['ɛərəʊgræm] N (*air-letter*) aerograma *m*; (*radio message*) radiograma *m.*
aerolite ['ɛərəlaɪt] N aerolito *m.*
aeromodelling ['ɛərəʊ'mɒdlɪŋ] N aeromodelismo *m.*
aeronaut ['ɛərənɔːt] N aeronauta *mf.*
aeronautic(al) [,ɛərə'nɔːtɪk(əl)] ADJ aeronáutico.
aeronautics [,ɛərə'nɔːtɪks] NPL aeronáutica *f.*
aeroplane ['ɛərəpleɪn] N (*Brit*) avión *m*; **model ~** aeromodelo *m.*
aerosol ['ɛərəsɒl] N aerosol *m.*
aerospace ['ɛərəʊspeɪs] ATTR aeroespacial; **the ~ industry** la industria aeroespacial; **the ~ minister** el ministro encargado de asuntos aeroespaciales.
Aertex ['ɛəteks] ® N *tejido ligero de algodón usado esp. para prendas deportivas.*
Aeschylus ['iːskɪləs] NM Esquilo.
Aesop ['iːsɒp] NM Esopo; **~'s Fables** Fábulas *fpl* de Esopo.
aesthete, (*US*) **esthete** ['iːsθiːt] N esteta *mf.*
aesthetic(al), (*US*) **esthetic(al)** [iːs'θetɪk(əl)] ADJ estético.
aesthetically, (*US*) **esthetically** [iːs'θetɪkəlɪ] ADV estéticamente.
aestheticism, (*US*) **estheticism** [iːs'θetɪsɪzəm] N esteticismo *m.*
aesthetics, (*US*) **esthetics** [iːs'θetɪks] NPL estética *f.*
AEU N (*Brit*) ABBR *of* **Amalgamated Engineering Union** Sindicato *m* Mixto de Ingeniería.
a.f. N (a) ABBR *of* **audio frequency** audiofrecuencia *f.* (b) (*Comm*) ABBR *of* **advance freight** flete *m* pagado.
AFA N (*Brit*) ABBR *of* **Amateur Football Association** Asociación *f* de Fútbol Amateur.
afar [ə'fɑːʳ] ADV (*also ~ off*) lejos, en lontananza; **from ~** desde lejos.
AFB N (*US Mil*) ABBR *of* **Air Force Base** Base *f* Aérea.
AFC N (a) (*Brit*) ABBR *of* **Amateur Football Club** *or* **Association Football Club**. (b) ABBR *of* **automatic frequency control** control *m* automático de frecuencia.
AFDC N (*US Admin*) ABBR *of* **Aid to Families with Dependent Children** Ayuda *f* a familias con hijos menores de edad, Ayuda *f* familiar.
affability [,æfə'bɪlɪtɪ] N afabilidad *f*, amabilidad *f.*
affable ['æfəbl] ADJ afable, amable.
affably ['æfəblɪ] ADV afablemente.
affair [ə'fɛəʳ] N (a) (*event*) acontecimiento *m*; episodio *m*; caso *m*; **The Falklands ~** el asunto de las Malvinas, aquello (*or* lo) de las Malvinas; **the Irangate ~** el caso Irangate, el episodio de Irangate; **it was a strange ~** fue un asunto raro; **it will be a big ~** será un acontecimiento importante; **I have no liking for such ~s** no me gustan estas cosas.
(b) (*concern*) asunto *m*; **current ~s** actualidades *fpl*; **foreign ~s** asuntos *mpl* (*or* relaciones *fpl* (*LAm*)) exteriores; **~ of honour** lance *m* de honor; **~s of state** asuntos *mpl* de estado; **how are your ~s?** ¿qué tal van tus cosas?; **that's my ~** ésa es cosa mía, eso me toca únicamente a mí; **that's his ~** es asunto suyo, que se las arregle él; **to put one's ~s in order** arreglar sus asuntos personales.
(c) (*business*) **~s** negocios *mpl*; **man of ~s** hombre *m* de negocios.
(d) (*love ~*: *also* **affaire**) aventura *f* amorosa; amorío *m*, lío *m*, enredo *m*; (*more serious*) amor *m*, amores *mpl*; (*considered poetically*) idilio *m*; (*seen as vulgar*) plan* *m*, ligue* *m*; **~ of the heart** aventura *f* sentimental; **to have an ~ with sb** andar en relaciones con uno; **he's always having ~s with his secretaries** siempre tiene plan con la secretaria de turno; **she ended the ~** ella terminó las relaciones.
affect [ə'fekt] VT (a) (*concern*) afectar (a), tener que ver con, influir en; (*harm*) perjudicar; (*Med*) interesar, afectar; **this will ~ everybody** esto afectará a todos; **it did not ~ my decision** no influyó en mi decisión; **it ~s me considerably** para mí tiene gran importancia; **a wound ~ing the right leg** una herida que interesa la pierna derecha; **his whole side was ~ed** todo su costado estaba afectado.
(b) (*move*) conmover, enternecer; **he seemed much ~ed** pareció muy emocionado, se conmovió mucho.
(c) (*like*) **she ~s bright colours** a ella le gustan los colores claros.
(d) (*feign*) **he ~s the rebel** se las echa de rebelde; **he ~ed indifference** afectó indiferencia; hizo ostentación de su indiferencia, fingió ser indiferente; **she ~ed to cry** ella fingió llorar.
affectation [,æfek'teɪʃən] N afectación *f*; amaneramiento *m.*
affected [ə'fektɪd] ADJ afectado; amanerado.
affectedly [ə'fektɪdlɪ] ADV de manera afectada, en tono afectado, con afectación.
affecting [ə'fektɪŋ] ADJ conmovedor, enternecedor.
affection [ə'fekʃən] N afecto *m* (*for* a, *towards* hacia), cariño *m*; inclinación *f* (*for* a, hacia); **to have an ~ for** tener cariño a; **to transfer one's ~s** dar su amor a otro (*or* otra).
affectionate [ə'fekʃənɪt] ADJ cariñoso, afectuoso; **with ~ greetings** (*formula in letter*) afectuosamente; **your ~ nephew** con abrazos de tu

sobrino, tu sobrino que te quiere.
affectionately [ə'fekʃənɪtlɪ] ADV afectuosamente, cariñosamente; **~ yours, yours ~** (*formula in letter*) un abrazo cariñoso.
affective [ə'fektɪv] ADJ afectivo.
affectivity [,æfek'tɪvətɪ] N afectividad *f.*
affiance [ə'faɪəns] († *or hum*) **1** VT prometer en matrimonio (*to* a); **to be ~d** estar prometido (*to* a).
2 VR: **to ~ o.s.** to prometerse a.
affidavit [,æfɪ'deɪvɪt] N declaración *f* jurada, testificata *f*, afidávit *m*; **to swear an ~ (to the effect that)** (*Jur*) hacer una declaración jurada (que).
affiliate **1** [ə'fɪlɪeɪt] VI: **to ~ to, to ~ with** afiliarse a.
2 [ə'fɪlɪt] N afiliado *m*, filial *f.*
affiliated [ə'fɪlɪeɪtɪd] ADJ *company* filial, subsidiario; *member, society* afiliado.
affiliation [ə,fɪlɪ'eɪʃən] N (a) afiliación *f*; **political ~s** afiliaciones *fpl* políticas, relaciones *fpl* políticas; **the painting's ~s are with this school** el cuadro está relacionado con esta escuela.
(b) (*Jur*) paternidad *f*; **~ order** decreto *m* relativo a la paternidad; **~ proceedings** proceso *m* para determinar la paternidad.
affinity [ə'fɪnɪtɪ] N afinidad *f*; **A has certain affinities with B** entre A y B existe cierta afinidad; **I feel no ~ whatsoever with him** no nos une ningún lazo de simpatía.
affirm [ə'fɜːm] VT afirmar, asegurar, aseverar.
affirmation [,æfə'meɪʃən] N afirmación *f*, aseveración *f.*
affirmative [ə'fɜːmətɪv] ADJ afirmativo; **to answer in the ~** dar una respuesta afirmativa, contestar afirmativamente; **~ action** (*US Pol*) medidas *fpl* a favor de las minorías.

AFFIRMATIVE ACTION

Affirmative action es el término estadounidense que hace referencia al tratamiento privilegiado que reciben las minorías étnicas y las mujeres en lo que concierne al empleo o la educación. La Administración del presidente Kennedy puso en marcha esta política en los años sesenta, estableciendo cuotas para asegurar más puestos de trabajo y plazas universitarias a aquellos colectivos con baja representación, lo cual se garantizó gracias a la Ley de Igualdad de Oportunidades Laborales (**Equal Employment Opportunities Act**) de 1972. Esta discriminación positiva fue para muchos la causa de que fueran a su vez discriminados los colectivos no minoritarios, por ejemplo, los hombres de raza blanca, por lo que la aplicación estricta de los cupos se ha relajado un tanto desde entonces.

---

affirmatively [ə'fɜːmətɪvlɪ] ADV afirmativamente.
affix **1** ['æfɪks] N afijo *m.*
2 [ə'fɪks] VT *signature etc* poner, añadir; *stamp* poner, pegar; *seal* imprimir; **to ~ a notice to the wall** pegar un anuncio en la pared.
afflict [ə'flɪkt] VT afligir; **the ~ed** los afligidos; **to be ~ed with** (*or* **by**) sufrir de, estar aquejado de.
affliction [ə'flɪkʃən] N (a) (*state*) aflicción *f*, congoja *f*; pena *f*; (*event etc*) mal *m*, infortunio *m*, desgracia *f.* (b) (*Med*) mal *m*; **the ~s of old age** los achaques de la vejez.
affluence ['æfluəns] N riqueza *f*, opulencia *f*; prosperidad *f*; **to live in ~** vivir con lujo.
affluent ['æfluənt] **1** ADJ rico, opulento, acaudalado; próspero; **the ~ society** la sociedad opulenta.
2 N (a) **the ~** los ricos. (b) (*Geog*) afluente *m.*
afflux ['æflʌks] N afluencia *f*; (*Med*) aflujo *m.*
afford [ə'fɔːd] VT (a) (*provide*) dar, proporcionar; **this ~s me a chance to speak** esto me da la oportunidad de hablar; **that ~ed me some relief** eso me proporcionó cierto alivio; **it ~s shade** da sombra.
(b) (*pay for*) **we can ~ it** tenemos con que comprarlo, podemos permitírnoslo; **can we ~ it?** ¿podemos hacer este gasto?, ¿tenemos bastante dinero (para comprarlo *etc*)?; **we can't ~ such things** tales cosas no están a nuestro alcance.
(c) (*spare, risk*) **I can't ~ the time to go** no tengo bastante tiempo para ir; **how much can you ~?** ¿cuánto estás dispuesto a gastar (*or* invertir *etc*)?; **we can ~ to wait** nos conviene esperar, bien podemos esperar; **an opportunity you cannot ~ to miss** una ocasión que no es para desperdiciar; **I can't ~ to be idle** no puedo permitirme el lujo de no hacer nada; **can we ~ the risk?** ¿podemos arriesgarlo?
affordable [ə'fɔːdəbl] ADJ *price* razonable; *purchase* posible, dentro de los medios del comprador.
afforest [æ'fɒrɪst] VT repoblar (de *or* con árboles).
afforestation [æ,fɒrɪs'teɪʃən] N repoblación *f* forestal.
afforested [æ'fɒrɪstɪd] ADJ *land* repoblado de árboles.
affray [ə'freɪ] N refriega *f*, reyerta *f*, riña *f.*
affreightment [ə'freɪtmənt] N fletamiento *m.*
affricate ['æfrɪkət] **1** ADJ africado.
2 N africada *f.*
affright† [ə'fraɪt] VT asustar, espantar.
affront [ə'frʌnt] **1** N afrenta *f*, ofensa *f*; **to offer an ~ to** afrentar a.
2 VT afrentar, ofender; **he was much ~ed** se ofendió mucho.

Afghan ['æfgæn] [1] ADJ afgano.
[2] N (a) afgano *m*, -a *f*. (b) (*dog*) perro *m* afgano.
Afghanistan [æf'gænɪstæn] N Afganistán *m*.
aficionado [ə,fɪsjə'nɑːdəʊ] N aficionado *m*, -a *f*.
afield [ə'fiːld] ADV: **far ~** muy lejos; **countries further ~** países *mpl* más lejanos; **you'll have to go further ~ for that** para eso hará falta buscar más lejos; **we are exploring further ~ all the time** exploramos cada vez más lejos.
afire [ə'faɪəʳ] ADV AND PRED ADJ: **to be ~** arder, quemar, estar en llamas; **to be ~ to help** anhelar ardientemente ayudar; *see also* **ablaze.**
aflame [ə'fleɪm] ADV AND PRED ADJ en llamas; *V* **ablaze, afire.**
AFL-CIO N (*US*) ABBR *of* **American Federation of Labor and Congress of Industrial Organizations.**
afloat [ə'fləʊt] ADV a flote; en el mar; **the oldest ship ~** el barco más viejo que sigue a flote; **the largest navy ~** la mayor marina del mundo; **by a miracle we were still ~** por maravilla quedamos a flote; **to get a business ~** lanzar un negocio; **to keep ~** mantener(se) a flote (*also fig*); **to spend one's life ~** pasar toda la vida a bordo.
aflutter [ə'flʌtəʳ] ADJ: **to set sb's heart ~** hacer que el corazón de uno se acelere.
afoot [ə'fʊt] ADV: **there is sth ~** algo se está tramando; **what's ~?** ¿qué están tramando?; **there is a plan ~ to remove him** existe un proyecto para apearle; **to set a scheme ~** poner un proyecto en práctica, poner una idea en movimiento.
afore [ə'fɔːr] CONJ (*esp Scot*: †) antes (de) que.
aforementioned [ə,fɔː'menʃənd] ADJ, **aforenamed** [ə'fɔːneɪmd] ADJ, **aforesaid** [ə'fɔːsed] ADJ susodicho, mencionado, ya dicho.
aforethought [ə'fɔːθɔːt] ADJ: **with malice ~** con premeditación.
afoul [ə'faʊl] ADV (*esp US*): **to run ~ of sb** enredarse con uno, indisponerse con uno; **to run ~ of a ship** chocar con un barco.
AFP N ABBR *of* **alpha-fetoprotein** alfafetoproteína *f*, AFP *f*.
▼ **afraid** [ə'freɪd] ADJ (a) **to be ~** tener miedo; **everyone was very ~** todos tenían mucho miedo, todos se espantaron mucho; **don't be ~** no tengas miedo, no temas; **to make sb ~** infundir miedo a uno; **to be ~ for sb** temer por uno; **to be ~ of** *person* tener miedo a; *thing* tener miedo de; **I'm ~ of hurting him** temo hacerle daño; **to be ~ to** + *infin* tener miedo de + *infin*, temer + *infin*; **he was ~ to speak** no se atrevía a hablar.
▼ (b) (*polite regret*) **I'm ~ he's out** lo siento, pero no está; **I'm ~ I have to go now** siento tener que irme ahora; **I'm ~ he won't come** me temo que no venga; **I'm ~ not** lo siento pero no; **I'm ~ so!** lo siento, pero es así; **my car is not available, I'm ~** lamento que no disponga ahora de mi coche.
afresh [ə'freʃ] ADV de nuevo, otra vez; **to do sth ~** volver a hacer algo; **to start ~** empezar de nuevo, reempezar, recomenzar.
Africa ['æfrɪkə] N África *f*.
African ['æfrɪkən] [1] ADJ africano.
[2] N africano *m*, -a *f*.
African-American [,æfrɪkənə'merɪkən] ADJ afroamericano.
Afrikaans [,æfrɪ'kɑːns] N africaans *m*.
Afrikaner [,æfrɪ'kɑːnəʳ] **1** ADJ africánder.
[2] N africánder *mf*.
Afro ['æfrəʊ] ADJ, PREF afro; **~ hairstyle** peinado *m* afro; **to go ~** africanizarse.
Afro-American [,æfrəʊə,merɪkən] ADJ afroamericano.
Afro-Asian ['æfrəʊ'eɪʃən] ADJ afroasiático.
Afro-Caribbean ['æfrəʊkærɪ'biːən] [1] ADJ afrocaribeño.
[2] N afrocaribeño *m*, -a *f*.
AFT N (*US*) ABBR *of* **American Federation of Teachers.**
aft [ɑːft] ADV (*Naut*) (*be*) en popa; (*go*) a popa.
after ['ɑːftəʳ] [1] ADV (a) (*time, order*) después; **for weeks ~** durante varias semanas después; **long ~** mucho tiempo después; **soon ~** poco después.
(b) (*place*) detrás.
[2] PREP (a) (*time, order*) después de; **it was 20 ~ 3** eran las 3 y 20; **soon ~ eating it** poco después de comerlo; **do you put Lope ~ Calderón?** ¿crees que Lope le es inferior a Calderón?
(b) (*place, order*) detrás de; tras; **day ~ day** día tras día; **excuse ~ excuse, one excuse ~ another** excusas y más excusas; **one ~ the other** uno tras otro; **he ran ~ me with my umbrella** corrió tras de mí con mi paraguas; **~ you!** ¡pase Vd!, ¡Vd primero!; **~ you with the salt*** ¿me das la sal?
(c) (*in the manner of*) **this is ~ Goya** esto se pintó según el estilo de Goya; **~ the English fashion** a la (manera) inglesa; *V* **heart.**
(d) (*on account of*) **he is named ~ Churchill** se le llamó así por Churchill.
(e) (*idioms with* to be): **the police are ~ him** la policía le está buscando; la policía está detrás de él; **I have been ~ that for years** eso lo busco desde hace años; **what are you ~?** ¿qué pretendes con eso?; **they're all ~ the same thing** todos van a por lo mismo; **I see what you're ~** ya caigo; ya comprendo lo que quieres decir; (*hostile*)

ya te he calado; **she's ~ a husband** va en pos de un marido; **she's ~ a special dress** busca un vestido especial.
[3] CONJ después (de) que; una vez que.
[4] ADJ *part* posterior, trasero, de atrás; (*Naut*) de popa; **in ~ years** en los años siguientes, años después.
[5] NPL: **~s** (*Brit**) postre *m*.

┌───┐
│ **AFTER** *see also main entry* │

Time
Preposition
• You can usually translate *after* referring to a point in time using *después de*:
    Please ring after six
    Por favor, llama después de las seis
    I'll phone you after the match
    Te llamaré después del partido
    ...Francoism after Franco...
    ...el franquismo después de Franco...
• To translate *after* + PERIOD OF TIME, you can also use *al cabo de* in more formal Spanish:
    After a year in the army, he had had enough
    Después de (estar) un año en el ejército or *Al cabo de un año en el ejército, no lo soportaba más*
! Use *más tarde que* or *después que* with names of people and personal pronouns when they stand in for a verb:
    He got there half an hour after us or after we did
    Llegó allí media hora más tarde que nosotros or *después que nosotros*
• Translate *after* + -ING using *después de* + INFINITIVE:
    Don't go swimming immediately after eating
    No te bañes justo después de comer
Conjunction
• When the action in the *after* clause has already happened, and the subjects of the two clauses are different, you can generally translate *after* using *después de que*. This can be followed either by the *indicative* or, especially in formal or literary Spanish, by the *subjunctive*:
    I met her after she had left the company
    La conocí después de que dejó or *dejara la empresa*
• When the action in the *after* clause has not happened yet or had not happened at the time of speaking, *cuando* is more common than *después de que*, though both translations are possible. In both cases, use the *subjunctive*:
    We'll test the brakes after you've done another thousand miles
    Comprobaremos los frenos cuando or *después de que haya recorrido mil millas más*
• If the subject of both clauses is the same, *después de* + INFINITIVE is usually used rather than *después de que*:
    He wrote to me again after he retired
    Me volvió a escribir después de jubilarse
NOTE: This construction is also sometimes used in colloquial Spanish even when the subjects are different:
    After you left, the party ended
    Después de irte tú, se terminó la fiesta
For further uses and examples, see main entry.
└───┘

afterbirth ['ɑːftəbɜːθ] N placenta *f*, secundinas *fpl*.
afterburner ['ɑːftə,bɜːnəʳ] N dispositivo *m* de poscombustión.
aftercare ['ɑːftəkeəʳ] N (*Med*) asistencia *f* postoperatoria; (*of prisoners*) asistencia *f* para ex-prisioneros.
afterdeck ['ɑːftədek] N cubierta *f* de popa.
after-dinner ['ɑːftə'dɪnəʳ] ADJ de sobremesa; **~ drink** copa *f* de después de la cena; **~ speech** discurso *m* de sobremesa.
after-effect ['ɑːftərɪfekt] N consecuencia *f*; secuela *f*; **~s** efectos *mpl*, repercusiones *fpl*.
afterglow ['ɑːftəgləʊ] N (*in sky*) arrebol *m*, resplandor *m* crepuscular; (*bodily*) sensación *f* de bienestar.
after-hours ['ɑːftə'aʊəz] **1** ADV fuera de horas.
[2] ADJ: **~ dealings** transacciones *fpl* fuera de horas.
afterlife ['ɑːftəlaɪf] N (*after death*) vida *f* futura; (*on earth*) vida *f* posterior, resto *m* de la vida.
aftermath ['ɑːftəmæθ] N consecuencias *fpl*, resultados *mpl*, secuelas *fpl*; resaca *f*; **in the ~ of the war** en las condiciones que resultaron de la guerra.
afternoon ['ɑːftə'nuːn] N tarde *f*; **good ~!** ¡buenas tardes!; **~ performance** función *f* de la tarde; **~ tea** el té de las cinco; **~s he's generally out** por las tardes en general no está; *ver también* TEA.
afterpains ['ɑːftə,peɪnz] NPL dolores *mpl* de posparto.
after-sales service ['ɑːftəseɪlz'sɜːvɪs] N (*Brit*) servicio *m* posventa.
after-shave (lotion) ['ɑːftəʃeɪv('ləʊʃən)] N loción *f* para después del afeitado.

aftershock ['ɑːftəʃɒk] N (*of earthquake*) réplica *f.*
aftertaste ['ɑːftəteɪst] N dejo *m,* resabio *m,* gustillo *m.*
after-tax ['ɑːftə'tæks] ADJ después del impuesto; **~ profits** beneficios *mpl* postimpositivos.
afterthought ['ɑːftəθɔːt] N ocurrencia *f* tardía, idea *f* adicional.
after-treatment ['ɑːftətriːtmənt] N tratamiento *m* postoperatorio.
afterwards, (*esp US*) **afterward** ['ɑːftəwəd(z)] ADV después, más tarde; **immediately ~** acto seguido; **long ~** mucho tiempo después; **shortly ~, soon ~** poco después.
afterword ['ɑftə'wɜːd] N epílogo *m.*
afterworld ['ɑːftəwəːld] N mundo *m* más allá.
A.G. ABBR *of* **Attorney General;** *V* **attorney.**
again [ə'gen] ADV (a) otra vez, nuevamente, de nuevo; *often translated by* volver a + *infin, eg* **he climbed up ~** volvió a subir; **would you do it all ~?** ¿lo volverías a hacer?; **~ and ~** una y otra vez, repetidas veces; **I've told you ~ and ~** te lo he dicho mil veces; **what was that joke ~?** ¿cómo era el chiste aquel (que acabas de contar)?; **never ~** nunca más; **I won't do it ever ~** no lo haré nunca más; **as much ~** otro tanto; **as many ~** otros tantos; **he is as old ~ as I am** me dobla la edad; **oh no, not ~!** ¡Dios mío, otra vez!; **what, you ~?** ¿tú otra vez (por aquí)?
(b) (*emphatic: besides, moreover*) además; por otra parte; **and ~, then ~** y además; **~, we just don't know** por otra parte, realmente no sabemos; **~, it may not be true** por otra parte, puede no ser verdad; **these are different ~** también éstos son distintos.
▼ **against** [ə'genst] **1** PREP (a) (*next to*) contra; (*close to*) al lado de, junto a, cerca de; **over ~ the church** enfrente de la iglesia; **~ the light** contra la luz, a contra sol; **he hit his head ~ the wall** se dio la cabeza contra la pared; **the hills stood out ~ the sunset** las colinas se destacaban sobre la puesta del sol; **to lean ~ a table** apoyarse en una mesa; **he leant the ladder ~ the wall** apoyó la escalera contra la pared.
(b) (*contrast*) **~ that, as ~ that** en contraste con eso; por otra parte; **6 today as ~ 7 yesterday** 6 hoy en comparación con 7 ayer.
(c) (*for*) **everything is ready ~ his arrival** todo está listo para su llegada.
▼ (d) (*fig*) contra, en contra de; **he was ~ it** estaba en contra, se opuso a ello; **I see nothing ~ it** no veo nada en contra; **I spoke ~ the plan** hablé en contra del proyecto; **I know nothing ~ him** yo no sé nada que le sea desfavorable; **what have you got ~ me?** ¿por qué me guarda Vd rencor?; **it's ~ the law** lo prohíbe la ley; **it's ~ the rules** no lo permiten las reglas; **conditions are ~ us** las condiciones nos son desfavorables; **luck was ~ him** la suerte le era contraria; **to be up ~ it** estar en un aprieto; **now we're really up ~ it!** ¡ahora sí tenemos problemas!
(e) **refund available ~ this voucher** se devuelve el precio al presentar este comprobante.
2 ADV en contra; **well, I'm ~** bueno, yo estoy en contra; **there were twenty votes ~** hubo veinte votos en contra.
Agamemnon [ˌægə'memnən] NM Agamenón.
agape [ə'geɪp] ADJ AND ADV boquiabierto.
agar-agar [ˌeɪgə'eɪgəʳ] N gelatina *f,* agar-agar *m.*
agate ['ægət] N ágata *f.*
agave [ə'geɪvɪ] N pita *f,* pita *f,* maguey *m* (*LAm*).
age [eɪdʒ] **1** N (a) (*gen*) edad *f;* (*old ~*) vejez *f,* senectud *f;* **~ of consent** edad *f* núbil; **~ of discretion** edad *f* del juicio; **he is 20 years of ~** tiene 20 años; **when I was your ~** cuando yo era de su edad; **what ~ are you?** (*Brit*) ¿cuántos años tienes?; **be your ~!** ¡compórtate de acuerdo con tu edad!, ¡no seas niño!; **60 is no ~ at all** los sesenta no son nada; **to feel one's ~** sentirse viejo; **she doesn't look her ~** no representa los años que tiene; **~ is beginning to tell on him** los años empiezan a pesar sobre él; **at the ~ of 7** a la edad de 7 años; **at my ~** a la edad que yo tengo; **of ~** mayor de edad; **to be of an ~ to go alone** ser de edad para ir solo; **they are both of an ~** los dos tienen la misma edad; **to come of ~** llegar a la mayoría de edad; **over ~** demasiado viejo; **under ~** menor de edad; demasiado joven.
(b) (*period*) época *f,* era *f,* siglo *m;* **this is the ~ of the car** éste es el siglo del coche; **the ~ we live in** el siglo en que vivimos; **in the ~ of Queen Elizabeth** en la época (*or* en tiempos) de la reina Isabel; **atomic ~** era *f* atómica; **A~ of Enlightenment** Siglo *m* de las Luces; **A~ of Reason** Siglo *m* de la Razón; *V* **bronze, dark, middle** *etc.*
(c) (*: long time*) siglo *m,* eternidad *f,* muchísimo tiempo *m;* **we waited an ~, we waited (for) ~s** esperamos una eternidad; **it's ~s since I saw him** hace años que no le veo.
2 ATTR etario; **~ discrimination** discriminación *f* por edad; **~ factor** factor *m* edad; **~ structure** estructura *f* etaria.
3 VT envejecer; **wine** criar, añejar.
4 VI envejecer(se); (*wine etc*) madurar, añejarse.
age-bracket ['eɪdʒˌbrækɪt] N grupo *m* etario.
aged ADJ (a) ['eɪdʒɪd] (*old*) viejo, anciano. (b) [eɪdʒd]: **~ 15** de 15 años, que tiene 15 años.

ageful ['eɪdʒfəl] ADJ (*US: euph*) viejo, de edad.
age-group ['eɪdʒgruːp] N grupo *m* etario, grupo *m* de personas de la misma edad; **the 40 to 50 ~** el grupo que comprende los de 40 a 50 años; **children of the same ~** niños *mpl* de la misma edad; **to arrange people by ~s** clasificar las personas según su edad.
ag(e)ing ['eɪdʒɪŋ] **1** ADJ viejo, que envejece, que va para viejo.
2 N envejecimiento *m,* el envejecer; senescencia *f;* **the ~ process** el proceso de envejecer.
ageism ['eɪdʒɪzəm] N prejuicio *m* contra los viejos.
ageless ['eɪdʒlɪs] ADJ eternamente joven; perenne, inmemorial.
age-limit ['eɪdʒlɪmɪt] N edad *f* mínima *or* máxima; edad *f* tope; (*for retirement*) edad *f* de jubilación.
age-long ['eɪdʒlɒŋ] ADJ multisecular.
agency ['eɪdʒənsɪ] N (a) (*office*) agencia *f;* V **advertising** *etc.*
(b) (*of UN etc*) organismo *m,* oficina *f;* **A~ for International Development** Agencia *f* para el Desarrollo Internacional.
(c) (*Comm, Fin*) agencia *f;* V **sole** *etc.*
(d) **through the ~ of** por medio de, por la mediación de.
agenda [ə'dʒendə] N orden *m* del día, asuntos *mpl* a tratar, agenda *f.*
agent ['eɪdʒənt] N (a) (*representative*) representante *mf,* delegado *m,* agenciero *m,* -a *f* (*SC*); intermediario *m;* (*Jur*) apoderado *m;* (*Comm*) agente *m,* representante *m,* gestor *m;* (*Police etc*) agente *mf;* (*US*) jefe *m* de estación; V **publicity, sole** *etc.*
(b) (*Chem*) agente *m;* **chemical ~** agente *m* químico.
agentive ['eɪdʒəntɪv] N agentivo *m.*
agent provocateur [ˈæʒɑ:prɒvɒkaˈtɜːʳ] N agente *m* provocador.
age-old ['eɪdʒəʊld] ADJ secular, multisecular, antiquísimo.
age-range ['eɪdʒˌreɪndʒ] N: **the ~ of the group is wide** en el grupo hay personas de diversas edades; **children in the ~ 12 to 14** niños en edades comprendidas entre los 12 y los 14 años.
agglomeration [əˌglɒmə'reɪʃən] N aglomeración *f.*
agglutinate [ə'gluːtɪneɪt] **1** VT aglutinar.
2 VI aglutinarse.
agglutination [əˌgluːtɪ'neɪʃən] N aglutinación *f.*
agglutinative [ə'gluːtɪnətɪv] ADJ aglutinante.
aggrandize [ə'grændaɪz] VT agrandar, ampliar; aumentar; engrandecer.
aggrandizement [ə'grændɪzmənt] N agrandamiento *m,* ampliación *f;* engrandecimiento *m.*
aggravate ['ægrəveɪt] VT (a) agravar, empeorar. (b) (*) irritar, sacar de quicio.
aggravating ['ægrəveɪtɪŋ] ADJ (a) (*Jur*) agravante. (b) (*) irritante, molesto; **it's very ~** es para volverse loco; **don't be so ~** no seas pesado*; **he's an ~ child** es un niño molesto.
aggravation [ˌægrə'veɪʃən] N (a) agravación *f,* empeoramiento *m;* (*Jur*) circunstancia *f* agravante; **robbery with ~** robo *m* agravado. (b) (*) irritación *f.*
aggregate **1** ['ægrɪgɪt] ADJ total, global; **~ corporation** corporación *f* global.
2 ['ægrɪgɪt] N (a) agregado *m,* conjunto *m;* **in the ~** en conjunto, en total; **Barataria won 5-4 on ~** ganó Barataria por 5 a 4 en conjunto.
(b) (*Geol etc*) agregado *m.*
3 ['ægrɪgeɪt] VT agregar, juntar, reunir.
4 ['ægrɪgeɪt] VI ascender a, sumar.
aggression [ə'greʃən] N agresión *f.*
aggressive [ə'gresɪv] ADJ (a) agresivo. (b) (*zealous etc*) dinámico, enérgico, emprendedor.
aggressively [ə'gresɪvlɪ] ADV (a) de manera agresiva. (b) con dinamismo, enérgicamente, con empuje.
aggressiveness [ə'gresɪvnɪs] N (a) agresividad *f.* (b) dinamismo *m,* energía *f,* empuje *m.*
aggressor [ə'gresəʳ] N agresor *m,* -ora *f.*
aggrieved [ə'griːvd] ADJ ofendido; apenado; **the ~ husband** el marido ofendido; **in an ~ tone** en un tono de queja; **he was much ~** se ofendió mucho; **to feel ~** ofenderse, resentirse (*at* por).
aggro* ['ægrəʊ] N (*Brit*) (a) (*violence*) violencia *f,* conducta *f* violenta; agresión *f;* (*hooliganism*) gamberrismo *m.* (b) (*hassle*) líos *mpl,* problemas *mpl;* **I'm not going, it's too much ~** no voy, es mucha lata*.
aghast [ə'gɑːst] ADJ horrorizado, pasmado; **to be ~** horrorizarse, pasmarse (*at* de); **we were all ~** todos quedamos pasmados.
agile ['ædʒaɪl] ADJ ágil.
agility [ə'dʒɪlɪtɪ] N agilidad *f.*
agin [ə'gɪn] PREP (*Scot or hum*) = **against (d);** **to be** (*or* **take**) **~ a plan** oponerse a un proyecto.
aging ['eɪdʒɪŋ] = **ag(e)ing.**
agitate ['ædʒɪteɪt] **1** VT (a) (*shake*) agitar.
(b) (*perturb*) inquietar, perturbar; alborotar.
(c) *question* discutir acaloradamente.
2 VI: **to ~ against** hacer propaganda contra, hacer una campaña en contra de; **to ~ for** hacer propaganda por, hacer una campaña en pro de.
agitated ['ædʒɪteɪtɪd] ADJ inquieto, perturbado; **in an ~ tone** en tono

➤ LANGUAGE IN USE: **against: 1d** → 12.1

inquieto; **to be very ~** estar muy inquieto (*about* por), estar en ascuas.

agitation [ˌædʒɪ'teɪʃən] N **(a)** (*state*) inquietud *f*, perturbación *f*; nerviosismo *m*. **(b)** (*Pol etc*) agitación *f*; propaganda *f*, campaña *f*.

agitator ['ædʒɪteɪtə'] N **(a)** agitador *m*, -ora *f*; alborotador *m*, -ora *f*, elemento *m* revoltoso. **(b)** (*Chem*) agitador *m*.

agitprop ['ædʒətprɒp] N propaganda *f* política de izquierdas.

aglow [ə'gləʊ] ADV AND PRED ADJ radiante, brillante; **to be ~ with** brillar de; **to be ~ with happiness** irradiar felicidad; *see also* **ablaze, afire.**

AGM N ABBR *of* **annual general meeting** junta *f* anual.

Agnes ['ægnɪs] NF Inés.

agnostic [æg'nɒstɪk] ⬚1 ADJ agnóstico.
⬚2 N agnóstico *m*, -a *f*.

agnosticism [æg'nɒstɪsɪzəm] N agnosticismo *m*.

ago [ə'gəʊ] ADV: **a week ~** hace una semana; **just a moment ~** hace un momento nada más; **a little while ~** hace poco; **long ~** hace mucho tiempo; **how long ~ was it?** ¿hace cuánto tiempo?; **no longer ~ than yesterday** ayer solamente, ayer nada más; **as long ~ as 1978** ya en 1978.

agog [ə'gɒg] ADJ: **to be ~** estar ansioso, sentir gran curiosidad; **the country was ~** el país estaba emocionadísimo, el país estaba pendiente de lo que pudiera pasar; **he was ~ to hear the news** tenía enorme curiosidad por saber las noticias; **to set ~** emocionar, infundir gran curiosidad a.

agonize ['ægənaɪz] ⬚1 VT atormentar.
⬚2 VI: **to ~ over** sufrir muchísimo a causa de, atormentarse con motivo de, experimentar grandes angustias por.

agonized ['ægənaɪzd] ADJ angustioso.

agonizing ['ægənaɪzɪŋ] ADJ *pain* atroz, muy agudo; *indecision, suspense* angustioso; *moment* de angustia; *reappraisal* agonizante, doloroso.

agonizingly ['ægənaɪzɪŋlɪ] ADV (*V adj*) atrozmente; angustiosamente; dolorosamente; **~ slow** terriblemente lento.

agony ['ægənɪ] N **(a)** (*pain*) dolor *m* agudo, dolor *m* punzante; **I was in ~** sufría unos dolores horrorosos. **(b)** (*last ~, death ~*) agonía *f*. **(c)** (*mental anguish*) angustia *f*, aflicción *f*, congoja *f*; **to be in an ~ of impatience** impacientarse mucho; **to suffer agonies of doubt** ser atormentado por las dudas; **it was ~!*** ¡fue fatal!*; **the play was sheer ~*** la obra era una birria*; **~ aunt** (*Brit*) columnista *f* de la consulta sentimental; **~ column** sección *f* de anuncios personales; consultorio *m* sentimental.

agoraphobe ['ægərəfəʊb] N agorafóbico *m*, -a *f*.

agoraphobia [ˌægərə'fəʊbɪə] N agorafobia *f*.

agoraphobic [ˌægərə'fəʊbɪk] ⬚1 ADJ agorafóbico.
⬚2 N agorafóbico *m*, -a *f*.

AGR N ABBR *of* **Advanced Gas-Cooled Reactor** reactor *m* refrigerado por gas de tipo avanzado.

agrammatical [ˌeɪgrə'mætɪkəl] ADJ agramatical.

agrarian [ə'greərɪən] ADJ agrario; **~ reform** reforma *f* agraria; **~ revolution** revolución *f* agraria.

agrarianism [ə'greərɪənɪzəm] N agrarismo *m*.

▼ **agree** [ə'griː] ⬚1 VT **(a)** (*consent*) **to ~ to do sth** consentir en hacer algo, quedar en hacer algo; **it was ~d to** + *infin* (*Parl etc*) se acordó + *infin.*
(b) (*admit*) reconocer; **I ~ I was too hasty** reconozco que lo hice con precipitación; **I ~ (that) it was foolish** reconozco que era tonto.
▼ **(c)** (*have same opinion*) **everyone ~s it is so** todos están de acuerdo en que es así; **they ~d among themselves to do it** (todos) se pusieron de acuerdo para hacerlo; **it was ~d that** se resolvió que; (*Parl*) se acordó que; **it is ~d that ...** (*legal contracts*) se acuerda que ...; **we ~d to differ** aceptamos (amistosamente) la diferencia de opiniones.
(d) *plan, report, statement etc* aceptar, ponerse de acuerdo en, estar de acuerdo con; *price etc* convenir; **the plan was speedily ~d** el proyecto fue aceptado sin demora; **we ~d that yesterday** quedamos en eso ayer; **at a date to be ~d** en una fecha que queda por determinar; **'salary to be ~d'** 'sueldo a convenir'.
▼ ⬚2 VI **(a)** (*have same opinion*) estar de acuerdo (*with* con, *that* en que); **to ~ with** *plan, policy* aprobar, estar de acuerdo con; **they ~d in finding the film a bore*** convinieron en que la película era una lata*; **I ~ estoy conforme; I quite ~** estoy completamente de acuerdo; **he's an idiot, don't you ~?** es un imbécil, ¿no crees?; **I don't ~ with women playing football** no apruebo que las mujeres jueguen al fútbol, no acepto el fútbol femenino.
(b) (*come to terms*) ponerse de acuerdo (*with* con); consentir, asentir; **eventually he ~d** por fin consintió; **'it's impossible', she ~d** 'es imposible', asintió; **you'll never get him to ~** no lograrás nunca su consentimiento; **to ~ about, to ~ on** convenir en.
▼ **(c) to ~ to** *plan, proposal* convenir en, aprobar; **I ~ to your marrying my niece** convengo en que Vd se case con mi sobrina; **he'll ~ to anything** se aviene a todo.
(d) (*be in harmony*) concordar, coincidir (*with* con); corresponder (*with* a); **these statements do not ~** estas declaraciones no

concuerdan (*with each other* mutuamente); **his reasoning ~s with mine** su razonamiento concuerda con el mío.
(e) (*be in harmony*: *persons*) llevarse bien, entenderse; **we simply don't ~, that's all** es que no existe simpatía entre nosotros, no congeniamos.
(f) (*Gram*) concordar (*with* con).
(g) (*suit*) sentar bien a; **this heat does not ~ with me** este calor no me sienta bien; **garlic never ~s with me** el ajo nunca me sienta bien.

agreeable [ə'griːəbl] ADJ **(a)** (*pleasing*) agradable; *person* simpático, amable; **is that ~ to everybody?** ¿estamos de acuerdo todos?; **he was more ~ this morning** esta mañana se mostró más simpático. **(b)** (*willing*) **if you are ~** si estás de acuerdo, si quieres; **he was ~ to that** estaba conforme con eso, lo aprobó; **he is ~ to help** está dispuesto a ayudar.

agreeably [ə'griːəblɪ] ADV agradablemente.

▼ **agreed** [ə'griːd] ADJ *plan etc* convenido; **as ~** según lo convenido; **at the ~ time** a la hora convenida; **~!** ¡de acuerdo!, ¡conforme(s)!

▼ **agreement** [ə'griːmənt] N **(a)** (*treaty etc*) acuerdo *m*, pacto *m*, convenio *m*; (*Comm*) contrato *m*; **~ to differ** desacuerdo *m* amistoso; **by mutual ~** de común acuerdo, por acuerdo mutuo; **to come to** (*or* **reach**) **an ~** ponerse de acuerdo, llegar a un acuerdo; **to enter into an ~** firmar un contrato (*to* + *infin* para + *infin*); *V* **gentleman.**
▼ **(b)** (*harmony*) concordancia *f*; correspondencia *f*; (*between persons*) conformidad *f*, armonía *f*; **in ~ with** de acuerdo con; **conforme a; to be in ~ on a plan** estar conformes en un proyecto; **to be in ~ with** estar de acuerdo con.
(c) (*Gram*) concordancia *f*.

agribusiness ['ægrɪˌbɪznɪs] N (*esp US*) comercio *m* en productos agrícolas, industria *f* agropecuaria.

agricultural [ˌægrɪ'kʌltʃərəl] ADJ agrícola; agropecuario; **~ college** escuela-granja *f* agrícola, escuela *f* de peritos agrícolas; **~ expert** (perito *m*, -a *f*) agrónomo *m*, -a *f*; **~ show** feria *f* agrícola, feria *f* de campo; **~ subsidy** subvención *f* agrícola.

agriculture ['ægrɪkʌltʃər] N agricultura *f*; **Minister/Ministry of A~** (*Brit*), **Secretary/Department of A~** (*US*) Ministro *m*/Ministerio *m* de Agricultura.

agricultur(al)ist [ˌægrɪ'kʌltʃər(əl)ɪst] N (*farmer*) agricultor *m*, -ora *f*; (*professional expert*) (perito *m*, -a *f*) agrónomo *m*, -a *f*.

agrobiologist [ˌægrəʊbaɪ'ɒlədʒɪst] N agrobiólogo *m*, -a *f*.

agrobiology [ˌægrəʊbaɪ'ɒlədʒɪ] N agrobiología *f*.

agrochemical [ˌægrəʊ'kemɪkəl] ⬚1 ADJ agroquímico.
⬚2 N sustancia *f* agroquímica.

agronomist [ə'grɒnəmɪst] N agrónomo *m*, -a *f*.

agronomy [ə'grɒnəmɪ] N agronomía *f*.

agroproduct [ˌægrəʊ'prɒdʌkt] N agroproducto *m*.

aground [ə'graʊnd] ADV: **to be ~** estar encallado, estar varado; **to run ~** (VI) encallar, varar, embarrancar; **to run a ship ~** varar un barco, hacer que encalle un barco.

agt (*Comm*) ABBR *of* **agent** agente *m*.

ague ['eɪgjuː] N fiebre *f* intermitente.

AH ABBR *of* **anno Hegirae**, = *from the year of the Hegira* desde el año de la Hégira, a.h.

ah [ɑː] EXCL ¡ah!

aha [ɑː'hɑː] EXCL ¡ajá!

ahead [ə'hed] ⬚1 ADV **(a)** (*in space, order*) delante; **to be ~** estar delante; (*in race*) ir delante, ir ganando, llevar ventaja; **can you see who is ~?** ¿ves quién va al frente?; **straight ~** todo seguido; **full speed ~!** ¡avante a toda máquina!; **to draw ~, to pull ~** adelantarse (*of* a); **to get ~** (*fig*) adelantar, hacer progresos, abrirse camino; **she's keen to get ~** tiene ganas de ir adelante; **to go ~, to press ~, to push ~** ir adelante (*also fig*); continuar, avanzar; **to go ~ with one's plans** seguir adelante con sus proyectos; **this put Barataria 3 points ~** esto dio a Barataria 3 puntos de ventaja; **to send sb ~** enviar a uno por delante.
(b) (*in time*) hacia delante; **there's trouble ~** han de sobrevenir disgustos; ya se prevén dificultades; **there's a busy time ~** tendremos mucha tarea; **to look ~** tener en cuenta el futuro, mirar el futuro; **to plan ~** hacer proyectos para el futuro; **to think ~** pensar en el futuro.
⬚2 **(a) ~ of** PREP (*in space, order*) delante de; **to be ~ of** llevar ventaja a; **to get ~ of sb** adelantarse a uno; **you'll get there ~ of us** llegarás antes de nosotros.
(b) (*in time*) **to arrive ~ of time** llegar antes de la hora prevista; **to be 2 hours ~ of the next competitor** llevar 2 horas de ventaja sobre el rival más próximo; **we are 3 months ~ of schedule** llevamos 3 meses de adelanto sobre la fecha prevista; **to be ~ of one's time** anticiparse a su época; **the plane is ~ of its time** el avión va por delante de su tiempo; **Wagner was 2 centuries ~ of his time** Wagner se anticipó en 2 siglos a su época; **share prices rose ~ of the annual report** la cotización subió en anticipación del informe anual.

➤ LANGUAGE IN USE: **agree: 1c** → 26.1, 26.3 **2a** → 11.1, 12.1, 26.2 **2c** → 11.2, 11.3, 12.2, 12.3 **agreed** → 11.2, 13 **agreement: b** → 11.1

ahem [əˈhem] EXCL ¡ejem!

ahold [əˈhəʊld] N (*esp US*) **(a)**: **to get ~ of sb/sth** (*get in touch with*) contactar con uno/algo; (*find*) localizar a uno/algo. **(b)**: **to get ~ of o.s.** tranquilizarse.

ahoy [əˈhɔɪ] EXCL: **~!**, **~ there!** ¡oiga!; **~!** (*Naut*) ¡ah del barco!; **ship ~!** ¡barco a la vista!

AHQ N ABBR *of* **Army Headquarters** cuartel *m* general del ejército.

AI N **(a)** ABBR *of* **Amnesty International** Amnistía *f* Internacional. **(b)** ABBR *of* **artificial insemination** inseminación *f* artificial. **(c)** ABBR *of* **artificial intelligence** inteligencia *f* artificial, I.A. *f*.

aid [eɪd] **1** N **(a)** ayuda *f*, auxilio *m*, socorro *m*; asistencia *f*; **by** (*or* **with**) **the ~ of** con la ayuda de; **in ~ of** (*charity etc*) a beneficio de, pro; **what's all this in ~ of?** (*Brit*) ¿qué motivo tiene esto?, ¿para qué sirve esto?; ¿a qué viene todo esto?; **to come to the ~ of** acudir en ayuda de, (*in argument*) salir en defensa de; **to give ~** prestar ayuda; **to give medical ~** dar asistencia médica; **to go to the ~ of a sinking ship** ir en auxilio de un barco que se hunde; *V* **economic**, **mutual** *etc*.
(b) (*person*) asistente *mf*.
(c) (*object*) ayuda *f*.
2 VT ayudar, auxiliar, socorrer; **~ed by darkness** al amparo de la noche; *V* **abet**.

A.I.D. N **(a)** (*US*) ABBR *of* **Agency for International Development** Agencia *f* Internacional para el Desarrollo, AID *f*.
(b) ABBR *of* **artificial insemination by donor** inseminación *f* artificial por donante anónimo.

aide [eɪd] N (*Mil*) edecán *m*; (*Pol etc*) hombre *m* de confianza.

aide-de-camp [ˌeɪddəˈkɑ̃ːŋ] N, PL **aides-de-camp** edecán *m*.

aide-mémoire [ˈeɪdmeɪˈmwɑː] N, PL **aides-mémoire**, *often* **aide-mémoires**, memorándum *m*.

AIDS, Aids [eɪdz] N ABBR *of* **acquired immune** *or* **immuno- deficiency syndrome** síndrome *m* de inmuno-deficiencia adquirida, SIDA *m*; **~ campaign** campaña *f* anti-SIDA; **~ clinic** sidatorio *m*; **~ sufferer** sidoso *m*, -a *f*; **~ test** test *m* de SIDA, prueba *f* anti-SIDA; **~ victim** víctima *f* del SIDA.

AIDS-related [ˈeɪdzrɪˌleɪtɪd] ADJ relacionado con el SIDA.

aid station [ˈeɪdˌsteɪʃən] N (*US*) puesto *m* de socorro.

AIH N ABBR *of* **artificial insemination by husband** inseminación *f* artificial por donante (esposo).

ail [eɪl] **1** VT afligir; **what ~s you?** ¿qué tienes?, ¿qué te pasa?
2 VI (*gen* **to be ~ing**) estar enfermo, estar sufriendo.

aileron [ˈeɪlərɒn] N alerón *m*.

ailing [ˈeɪlɪŋ] ADJ enfermo, achacoso; *industry etc* decadente, debilitado.

ailment [ˈeɪlmənt] N enfermedad *f*, achaque *m*, dolencia *f*.

▼ **aim** [eɪm] **1** N **(a)** (*of weapon*) puntería *f*; **to have a good ~** tener buena puntería; **to miss one's ~** errar el tiro; **to take ~** apuntar (**at** a).
▼ **(b)** (*fig*) propósito *m*, intención *f*, meta *f*, blanco *m*; **with the ~ of** + *ger* con miras a + *infin*, con la intención de + *infin*; **his one ~ is to** + *infin* su único propósito es de + *infin*; **to have no ~ in life** no saber qué hacer con su vida.
2 VT *gun* apuntar (**at** a); *missile, remark* dirigir (**at** a); *blow* asestar (**at** a); **he ~ed the pistol at me** me apuntó con la pistola.
3 VI **(a)** (*with weapon*) apuntar (**at** a).
(b) (*fig*) **to ~ at** apuntar a, aspirar a, pretender, ambicionar; tener la mira puesta en; **what are you ~ing at?** ¿qué intentas?, ¿qué es lo que pretendes?; **to ~ high** picar muy alto; **to ~ to** + *infin* aspirar a + *infin*, pretender + *infin*, tener la intención de + *infin*.

aimless [ˈeɪmlɪs] ADJ sin propósito fijo, sin objeto; *wandering etc* sin rumbo.

aimlessly [ˈeɪmlɪslɪ] ADV a la ventura; a la buena de Dios; *wander etc* sin rumbo.

aimlessness [ˈeɪmlɪsnɪs] N falta *f* de propósito fijo, carencia *f* de objeto.

ain't [eɪnt] = am not, is not, are not; has not, have not.

air [ɛəʳ] **1** N **(a)** aire *m*; **foul ~** aire *m* viciado; **fresh ~** aire *m* fresco; **he's a breath of fresh ~** es una persona con ideas nuevas; **to get some fresh ~** (salir a) respirar aire limpio; **to let in some fresh ~** airear la atmósfera; (*fig*) aclarar las cosas; **in the open ~** al aire libre; **by ~** en avión; (*Post*) por avión, por vía aérea; **war in the ~** guerra *f* aérea; **spring is in the ~** se presiente ya la llegada de la primavera, corren aires de primavera; **to throw sth into the ~** lanzar algo al aire; **to vanish into thin ~** evaporarse, desaparecer por completo; **one can't live on ~** no se vive de aire solo; **to clear the ~** airear la atmósfera; (*fig*) aclarar las cosas; **to fly through the ~** volar por los aires; **to have a change of ~** mudar de aires; **so we let the ~ out of his tyres** así que desinflamos sus neumáticos; **to take the ~** dar un paseo; **to take to the ~** (*bird*) alzar el vuelo; (*plane*) despegar.
(b) (*further fig phrases*) **to be in the ~** estar en el aire, estar en proyecto; **it's still very much in the ~** está todavía en el aire, queda todavía por resolver; **there's sth in the ~** algo se está tramando; **to give sb the ~** (*US**) despedir a uno, dar calabazas a uno*; **to go up**

in the ~* (*angry*) ponerse negro*, subirse por las paredes*, (*excited*) no caber en sí de alegría; **to hang in the ~** estar en el aire, estar pendiente; **to leave sth in the ~** dejar algo en el aire, dejar algo en suspenso; **to walk on ~** no caber en sí de alegría; **it appeared out of thin ~** salió de la nada, apareció de no se sabe dónde; **he produces money out of thin ~** saca dinero de los aires.
(c) (*Rad, TV*) **to be on the ~** estar en el aire, hablar por radio; (*TV*) estar en antena; **we are on the ~ from 6 to 7** emitimos de 6 a 7; **to go on the ~** comenzar la emisión; **to go off the ~** cerrar la emisión; **to go out on the ~** salir al aire; **to put a programme on the ~** emitir un programa.
(d) (*Mus*) aire *m*, tonada *f*.
(e) (*appearance*) aire *m*, aspecto *m*; (*manner, mien*) porte *m*, ademán *m*; **~s and graces** afectación *f*, melindres *mpl*; **with an ~** con toda confianza, con aplomo, con garbo; **with an ~ of surprise** con aire de sorpresa; **he has a distinguished ~**, **he has an ~ of distinction about him** tiene un no sé qué de distinguido; **to give o.s. ~s**, **to put on ~s** presumir, darse tono.
2 ATTR aéreo; aeronáutico; atmosférico; **~ attack** ataque *m* aéreo; **~ cargo** carga *f* aérea; **~ carrier** aerolínea *f*; **~ consignment note** talón *m* de expedición por vía aérea; **~ express** (*US*) avión *m* de carga; **~ mass** masa *f* de aire; **~ pollution** contaminación *f* del aire, polución *f* de la atmósfera.
3 VT **(a)** *room etc* airear, ventilar; (*fig*) *idea, grievance* airear; **to ~ one's knowledge** lucir sus conocimientos, hacer alarde de sus conocimientos.
(b) (*US: Rad, TV*) *programme* emitir, radiar, radiodifundir.
(c) (*US: transport*) transportar por avión, aerotransportar.

air-alert [ˈɛərəˌlɜːt] N alerta *f* aérea.

airbag [ˈɛəbæg] N (*Aut*) bolsa *f* de aire.

airbase [ˈɛəbeɪs] N base *f* aérea.

airbed [ˈɛəbed] N (*Brit*) colchón *m* neumático.

air-bladder [ˈɛəblædəʳ] N (*Zool*) vejiga *f* natatoria.

airborne [ˈɛəbɔːn] ADJ **(a)** aerotransportado (*also Mil*); *germ* transmitido por el aire; *seed* llevado por el aire; **~ troops** tropas *fpl* aerotransportadas.
(b) **to become ~** elevarse en los aires, subir; **we shall soon be ~** el avión despegará pronto; **suddenly we were ~** de pronto nos vimos en el aire; **we were ~ for 8 hours** volamos durante 8 horas.

airbrake [ˈɛəbreɪk] N freno *m* neumático; (*Aer*) freno *m* aerodinámico.

airbrick [ˈɛəbrɪk] N ladrillo *m* ventilador.

airbrush [ˈɛəbrʌʃ] N aerógrafo *m*.

air-bubble [ˈɛəˌbʌbl] N burbuja *f* de aire.

airbus [ˈɛəbʌs] N aerobús *m*; **~ service** puente *m* aéreo.

air-chamber [ˈɛəˌtʃeɪmbəʳ] N cámara *f* de aire.

air chief marshal [ˌɛətʃiːfˈmɑːʃəl] N (*Brit*) comandante *m* supremo de las Fuerzas Aéreas.

air commodore [ˌɛəˈkɒmədɔːʳ] N (*Brit*) general *m* de brigada aérea.

air-condition [ˈɛəkənˌdɪʃən] VT climatizar, refrigerar.

air-conditioned [ˈɛəkənˌdɪʃənd] ADJ climatizado, refrigerado, con aire acondicionado, con clima artificial.

air-conditioner [ˈɛəkənˌdɪʃənəʳ] N aparato *m* acondicionador del aire, acondicionador *m* del aire.

air-conditioning [ˈɛəkənˌdɪʃənɪŋ] N climatización *f*, refrigeración *f* (del aire), acondicionamiento *m* de aire; **cinema with ~** cine *m* climatizado.

air-cooled [ˈɛəkuːld] ADJ refrigerado por aire.

air-corridor [ˈɛəˌkɒrɪdɔːʳ] N pasillo *m* aéreo.

air-cover [ˈɛəkʌvəʳ] N (*Mil*) cobertura *f* aérea.

aircraft [ˈɛəkrɑːft] N avión *m*; **~ industry** industria *f* aeronáutica.

aircraft-carrier [ˈɛəkrɑːftˌkærɪəʳ] N porta(a)viones *m*.

aircraftman [ˈɛəkrɑːftmən] N, PL **aircraftmen** [ˈɛəkrɑːftmen] (*Brit*) cabo *m* segundo (de las fuerzas aéreas).

aircrew [ˈɛəkruː] N tripulación *f* de avión.

air-current [ˈɛəˌkʌrənt] N corriente *f* de aire.

air-cushion [ˈɛəkuʃən] N cojín *m* de aire, almohada *f* neumática; (*Aer*) colchón *m* de aire.

airdrome [ˈɛəˌdrəʊm] N (*US*) aeródromo *m*.

airdrop [ˈɛədrɒp] N entrega *f* (de víveres *etc*) por paracaídas.

airduct [ˈɛədʌkt] N tubo *m* de aire; tubo *m* de ventilación.

Airedale [ˈɛədeɪl] N (*also* **~ dog**) perro *m* Airedale.

air-fare [ˈɛəfɛəʳ] N precio *m* del billete (por avión); tarifa *f* aérea.

airfield [ˈɛəfiːld] N campo *m* de aviación, aeródromo *m*.

airflow [ˈɛəfləʊ] N corriente *f* de aire.

airfoil [ˈɛəˌfɔɪl] N (*US*) = **aerofoil**.

air force [ˈɛəfɔːs] N aviación *f*, fuerzas *fpl* aéreas; **~ base** (*Mil*) base *f* aérea; **A~ One** (*US*) avión *m* presidencial.

airframe [ˈɛəfreɪm] N armazón *f* de avión.

air-freight [ˈɛəfreɪt] N flete *m* por avión; mercancías *fpl* aerotransportadas; **~ terminal** terminal *f* de mercancías.

air-freshener [ˈɛəfreʃnəʳ] N ambientador *m*.

airgun [ˈɛəgʌn] N escopeta *f* de aire comprimido.

airhead: ['ɛə,hɛd] N cabeza f de serrín*, chorlito* m.

airhole ['ɛəhəʊl] N respiradero m.

air-hostess ['ɛə,həʊstɪs] N (Brit) auxiliar f de vuelo, azafata f, aeromoza f (LAm).

airily ['ɛərɪlɪ] ADV say etc muy a la ligera, sin dar importancia a la cosa; (behave) de manera confiada, con aire satisfecho.

airiness ['ɛərɪnɪs] N (of room etc) (buena) ventilación f.

airing ['ɛərɪŋ] N (a) ventilación f; (of clothes) oreo m; **to go for an ~, to take an ~** dar un paseo (para tomar el fresco). (b) (fig) ventilación f; **to give a matter an ~** ventilar un asunto.

airing-cupboard ['ɛərɪŋ,kʌbəd] N (Brit) cámara f de aire caliente (para secar la ropa).

air-intake ['ɛər,ɪnteɪk] N toma f de aire, admisión f de aire.

airlane ['ɛəleɪn] N vía f aérea, pasillo m aéreo.

airless ['ɛəlɪs] ADJ room mal ventilado; day sin viento; **it's very ~ in here** aquí no hay aire.

airletter ['ɛəletər] N carta f por correo aéreo, aerograma m.

airlift ['ɛəlɪft] 1 N puente m aéreo.
2 VT aerotransportar, transportar por avión.

airline ['ɛəlaɪn] N línea f aérea, aerolínea f, compañía f de aviación.

airliner ['ɛəlaɪnər] N avión m de pasajeros.

airlock ['ɛəlɒk] N (Mech) esclusa f de aire; compartimiento m estanco; (accidental) bola f de aire.

▼ **airmail** ['ɛəmeɪl] 1 N correo m aéreo, aeroposta f (LAm); **by ~** por avión, por vía aérea; **~ edition** edición f aérea; **~ letter** carta f por correo aéreo, aerograma m; **~ paper** papel m para avión; **~ stamp** sello m para correo aéreo; **~ sticker** etiqueta f de correo aéreo.
2 VT enviar por avión, enviar por correo aéreo.
3 AS ADV: **to send a letter ~** mandar una carta por avión.

airman ['ɛəmən] N, PL **airmen** ['ɛəmən] aviador m, piloto m.

air marshal ['ɛə'mɑ:ʃəl] N (Brit) mariscal m de aire.

air-mattress ['ɛə,mætrɪs] N colchón m neumático.

air miles ['ɛəmaɪlz] puntos acumulados que dan derecho a vuelos gratis.

air-miss [,ɛə'mɪs] N incidente m aéreo, air-miss m, aproximación f peligrosa entre dos aviones.

airplane ['ɛəpleɪn] N (US) avión m.

airplay ['ɛəpleɪ] N cobertura f radiofónica.

air-pocket ['ɛə,pɒkɪt] N bache m (aéreo).

airport ['ɛəpɔːt] N aeropuerto m; **~ taxes** impuestos mpl de aeropuerto.

air-power ['ɛə,paʊər] N poderío m aéreo.

air-pressure ['ɛə,preʃər] N presión f atmosférica.

airproof ['ɛəpruːf] ADJ hermético.

air-pump ['ɛəpʌmp] N bomba f de aire.

air-purifier ['ɛə,pjʊərɪfaɪər] N purificador m de aire.

air-raid ['ɛəreɪd] N ataque m aéreo; **~ precautions** precauciones fpl contra ataques aéreos; **~ shelter** refugio m antiaéreo; **~ warden** vigilante m contra ataques aéreos; **~ warning** alarma f antiaérea.

air-rifle ['ɛəraɪfl] N escopeta f de aire comprimido.

airscrew ['ɛəskruː] N (Brit) hélice f de avión.

air-sea ['ɛə'siː] ADJ: **~ base** base f aeronaval; **~ rescue** rescate m aeronaval.

air-shaft ['ɛəʃɑːft] N pozo m de ventilación.

airship ['ɛəʃɪp] N aeronave f, dirigible m.

air-show ['ɛəʃəʊ] N (commercial) feria f aérea; (air display) exhibición f aeronáutica.

air-shuttle ['ɛəʃʌtl] N puente m aéreo.

airsick ['ɛəsɪk] ADJ: **to be ~, to get ~** marearse (en un avión).

airsickness ['ɛəsɪknɪs] N mareo m (en un avión).

airspace ['ɛəspeɪs] N espacio m aéreo.

airspeed ['ɛəspiːd] N velocidad f aérea; **~ indicator** anemómetro m.

air-steward ['ɛə,stjʊəd] N auxiliar m de vuelo.

airstream ['ɛəstriːm] N corriente f de aire.

airstrike ['ɛəstraɪk] N ataque m aéreo.

airstrip ['ɛəstrɪp] N pista f de aterrizaje.

air-suspension [,ɛəsə'spenʃən] N (Aut) suspensión f neumática.

air-taxi ['ɛətæksɪ] N aerotaxi m.

air terminal ['ɛə,tɜːmɪnl] N terminal f (de aeropuerto).

airtight ['ɛətaɪt] ADJ hermético, estanco al aire.

airtime ['ɛə,taɪm] N (Rad, TV) tiempo m en antena.

air-to-air ['ɛətə,ɛər] ADJ missile aire-aire.

air-to-sea ['ɛətə,siː] ADJ missile aire-mar.

air-to-surface ['ɛətə,sɜːfɪs] ADJ missile de aire a superficie, aire-tierra.

air-traffic ['ɛətræfɪk] N tráfico m aéreo; **~ control** control m de tráfico aéreo; **~ controller** controlador m, -ora f de tráfico aéreo.

air-valve ['ɛəvælv] N respiradero m.

air vent ['ɛəvent] N (in building) respiradero m; (on dryer) tobera f de aire caliente.

air vice marshal [,ɛəvaɪs'mɑːʃəl] N (Brit) general m de división de las Fuerzas Aéreas.

air-waves ['ɛəweɪvz] NPL ondas fpl hertzianas (or radiofónicas).

airway ['ɛəweɪ] N (a) (company) línea f aérea, aerolínea f. (b) (route)

ruta f aérea. (c) (Anat) vía f respiratoria. (d) (Tech) conducto m de ventilación.

air waybill ['ɛəweɪbɪl] N hoja f de ruta aérea.

airwoman ['ɛə,wʊmən] N, PL **airwomen** ['ɛə,wɪmɪn] aviadora f.

airworthiness ['ɛə,wɜːðɪnɪs] N aeronavegabilidad f.

airworthy ['ɛəwɜːðɪ] ADJ en condiciones de vuelo, aeronavegable.

airy ['ɛərɪ] ADJ (a) place de mucho viento; ventilado; (large) amplio, espacioso. (b) cloth etc ligero, diáfano; (unsubstantial) etéreo. (c) step ligero, alegre; remark etc dicho a la ligera, hecho sin dar importancia a la cosa; behaviour confiado, satisfecho.

airy-fairy [,ɛərɪ'fɛərɪ] ADJ (Brit: light) superficial; (fanciful) tontamente romántico, tontamente idealista; (insubstantial) sin sustancia; (pretentious) pretencioso, vacío.

aisle [aɪl] N nave f lateral; pasadizo m; (Theat, also US) pasillo m; **it had them rolling in the ~s*** los hizo desternillarse de risa*; **to lead one's bride up the ~** conducir a su novia al altar.

AISP N ABBR of **Agricultural Income Subsidies Programme** Programa m de Ayudas a la Renta Agraria, PARA m.

aitch [eɪtʃ] N nombre de la h inglesa; **to drop one's ~es** no pronunciar las haches (indicio clasista o de habla dialectal).

Aix-la-Chapelle ['eɪkslæʃə'pel] N Aquisgrán m.

Ajaccio [ə'jætʃɪəʊ] N Ajaccio m.

ajar [ə'dʒɑːr] ADV entreabierto, entornado; **to leave the door ~** no cerrar completamente (Mex: entrecerrar) la puerta.

Ajax ['eɪdʒæks] NM Áyax.

AK (US) ABBR of **Alaska.**

a.k.a. ABBR of **also known as** por otro nombre.

akimbo [ə'kɪmbəʊ] ADV: **with arms ~** en jarras.

akin [ə'kɪn] ADJ (a) (related by blood) consanguíneo; **they are not ~** no tienen parentesco consanguíneo. (b) (similar to) relacionado (to con), análogo (to a), semejante (to a).

AL (US) ABBR of **Alabama.**

ALA (US) ABBR of **American Library Association.**

Ala. (US) ABBR of **Alabama.**

alabaster ['æləbɑːstər] 1 N alabastro m.
2 ADJ alabastrino.

alabastrine [,ælə'bæstraɪn] ADJ alabastrino.

à la carte [ælæ'kɑːt] ADV a la carta.

alacrity [ə'lækrɪtɪ] N prontitud f, presteza f; **with ~** con la mayor prontitud.

Aladdin [ə'lædɪn] NM Aladino; **~'s lamp** lámpara f de Aladino.

Alans ['ælənz] NPL alanos mpl.

Alaric ['ælərɪk] NM Alarico.

alarm [ə'lɑːm] 1 N (a) (warning) alarma f; **false ~** falsa alarma f; **~ call** voz f de alarma; **~ system** sistema m de alarma; **~s and excursions** sobresaltos mpl; **to give** (or **raise, sound**) **the ~** dar la alarma. (b) (emotion) alarma f, sobresalto m; inquietud f, temor m; **~ and despondency** confusión f y desconcierto; **there was general ~** hubo una alarma general; **there was some ~ at this** esto produjo cierta inquietud, esto sobresaltó a la gente; **to cry out in ~** gritar alarmado; **to take ~** alarmarse, sobresaltarse. (c) (*) (clock) despertador m; (bell) timbre m del despertador.
2 VT alarmar, sobresaltar; inquietar, asustar; **to be ~ed at** alarmarse de; **don't be ~ed** no te asustes, no te inquietes.

alarm-bell [ə'lɑːmbel] N timbre m de alarma.

alarm-clock [ə'lɑːmklɒk] N despertador m.

alarmed [ə'lɑːmd] ADJ voice etc sobresaltado, asustado.

alarming [ə'lɑːmɪŋ] ADJ alarmante.

alarmingly [ə'lɑːmɪŋlɪ] ADV de modo alarmante; **~ high numbers** cifras fpl alarmantes.

alarmist [ə'lɑːmɪst] 1 ADJ alarmista, catastrofista. 2 N alarmista mf, catastrofista mf.

alarm-signal [ə'lɑːm,sɪgnəl] N señal f de alarma.

alarum [ə'lærəm] N (††, hum) = **alarm 1.**

alas [ə'læs] EXCL ¡ay!, ¡ay de mí!; **~, it is not so** desafortunadamente, no es así; **I must tell you, ~, that ...** tengo que decirte, y lo siento, que ...; **I have no money, ~** no tengo dinero, y esto es triste; **~ for Slobodia!** ¡ay de Eslobodia!

Alas. (US) ABBR of **Alaska.**

Alaska [ə'læskə] N Alaska f; **~ Highway** carretera f de Alaska; **~ Range** Cordillera f de Alaska.

Alaskan [ə'læskən] 1 ADJ de Alaska.
2 N nativo m, -a f (or habitante mf) de Alaska.

alb [ælb] N (Rel) alba f.

Albania [æl'beɪnɪə] N Albania f.

Albanian [æl'beɪnɪən] 1 ADJ albanés.
2 N (a) albanés m, -esa f. (b) (Ling) albanés m.

albatross ['ælbətrɒs] N (a) (Orn) albatros m. (b) (Golf) albatros m, menos tres m.

albeit [ɔːl'biːɪt] CONJ aunque, no obstante (que).

Albert ['ælbət] NM Alberto.

Albigenses [,ælbɪ'dʒensiːz] NPL albigenses mpl.

Albigensian [ˌælbɪ'dʒensɪən] ADJ albigense.
albinism ['ælbɪnɪzəm] N albinismo *m*.
albino [æl'biːnəʊ] ①ADJ albino.
  ②N albino *m*, -a *f*.
Albion ['ælbɪən] N Albión *f*.
album ['ælbəm] N álbum *m*.
album cover ['ælbəm,kʌvəʳ] N portada *f* de disco.
albumen ['ælbjʊmɪn] N (Bot) albumen *m*; (Chem) albúmina *f*.
albumin ['ælbjʊmɪn] N albúmina *f*.
albuminous [æl'bjuːmɪnəs] ADJ albuminoso.
alchemical [æl'kemɪkəl] ADJ alquímico, de alquimia.
alchemist ['ælkɪmɪst] N alquimista *m*.
alchemy ['ælkɪmɪ] N alquimia *f*.
alcohol ['ælkəhɒl] N alcohol *m*.
alcohol-free ['ælkəhɒl,friː] ADJ sin alcohol.
alcoholic [ˌælkə'hɒlɪk] ①ADJ alcohólico.
  ②N alcohólico *m*, -a *f*, alcoholizado *m*, -a *f*.
alcoholism ['ælkəhɒlɪzəm] N alcoholismo *m*; **to die of ~** morir alcoholizado.
alcove ['ælkəʊv] N hueco *m*, nicho *m*.
Ald. ABBR *of* **alderman**.
alder ['ɔːldəʳ] N aliso *m*.
alderman ['ɔːldəmən] N, PL **aldermen** ['ɔːldəmen] concejal *m*, -ala *f* (de categoría superior).
aldosterone [æl'dɒstə,rəʊn] N aldosterona *f*.
aldrin ['ɔːldrɪn] N aldrina *f*.
ale [eɪl] N cerveza *f*; *ver también* BEER .
aleatoric [ˌælɪə'tɒrɪk] ADJ, **aleatory** ['eɪlɪətərɪ] ADJ aleatorio.
Alec ['ælɪk] NM *familiar form of* **Alexander**.
alehouse* ['eɪl,haʊs] N (†) taberna *f*.
alert [ə'lɜːt] ①ADJ alerta (*invariable*: *eg* estaban alerta); vigilante; *character* listo; (*wide-awake*) despierto, despabilado; *expression* vivo.
  ②N alerta *m*, alarma *f*; **bomb ~** aviso *m* de bomba; **to be on the ~** estar alerta, estar sobre aviso; **to put troops on the ~** poner las tropas sobre aviso.
  ③VT alertar, poner sobre aviso, avisar; **he ~ed us to the possibility** nos avisó acerca de la posibilidad; **we are now ~ed to the dangers** ahora estamos sobre aviso en cuanto a los peligros.
alertness [ə'lɜːtnɪs] N vigilancia *f*; listeza *f*; lo despierto, lo despabilado; viveza *f*.
Aleutian [ə'luːʃən] ADJ: **~ Islands** Islas *fpl* Aleutianas.
Alex ['ælɪks] NM *familiar form of* **Alexander**.
Alexander [ˌælɪg'zɑːndəʳ] NM Alejandro; **~ the Great** Alejandro Magno.
Alexandria [ˌælɪg'zɑːndrɪə] N Alejandría *f*.
alexandrine [ˌælɪg'zændraɪn] N alejandrino *m*.
Alf [ælf] NM *familiar form of* **Alfred**.
alfalfa [æl'fælfə] N alfalfa *f*.
Alfred ['ælfrɪd] NM Alfredo.
alfresco [æl'freskəʊ] ①ADV al aire libre.
  ②ADJ de aire libre, al aire libre.
alga ['ælgə] N, PL **algae** ['ældʒɪ] alga *f*.
algal ['ælgəl] ADJ de algas, algal.
Algarve [æl'gɑːv] N: **the ~** el Algarve.
algebra ['ældʒɪbrə] N álgebra *f*.
algebraic [ˌældʒɪ'breɪɪk] ADJ algebraico.
Algeria [æl'dʒɪərɪə] N Argelia *f*.
Algerian [æl'dʒɪərɪən] ①ADJ argelino.
  ②N argelino *m*, -a *f*.
algicide ['æld zɪsaɪd] N algicida *m*.
Algiers [æl'dʒɪəz] N Argel *m*.
algorithm ['ælgə,rɪðəm] N algoritmo *m*.
algorithmic [ˌælgə'rɪðmɪk] ADJ algorítmico.
alias ['eɪlɪæs] ①ADV alias, por otro nombre.
  ②N alias *m*; nombre *m* ficticio, seudónimo *m*.
alibi ['ælɪbaɪ] ①N coartada *f*; (*excuse*) excusa *f*, pretexto *m*.
  ②VT: **to ~ sb** (US) proveer de una coartada a uno.
  ③VI (US) buscar excusas (*for doing sth* por haber hecho algo).
Alice ['ælɪs] NF Alicia; **~ in Wonderland** Alicia en el país de las maravillas; **~ through the Looking-Glass** Alicia en el país del espejo.
Alice band ['ælɪs,bænd] N diadema *f*.
alien ['eɪlɪən] ①ADJ (a) (*strange*) ajeno (*to* a), extraño (*to* a); **~ being** ser *m* extraterrestre. (b) (*of foreign country*) extranjero.
  ②N extranjero *m*, -a *f*; (*fig*) extraño *m*, -a *f*.
alienate ['eɪlɪəneɪt] VT (a) (*Jur*) *property* enajenar, traspasar. (b) *friend* indisponerse con, alejar, ofender; apartar; *other people* ganarse la antipatía de; *sympathies* perder, enajenar. (c) (*Pol etc*) alienar, enajenar.
alienation [ˌeɪlɪə'neɪʃən] N (a) (*Jur*) enajenación *f*, traspaso *m*. (b) (*of friend*) alejamiento *m*. (c) (*Med*) enajenación *f* mental. (d) (*Pol etc*) enajenación *f*, alienación *f*; **feelings of ~** (*from society*)

sentimientos *mpl* de enajenación (social).
alienist ['eɪlɪənɪst] N (US) alienista *mf*.
alight¹ [ə'laɪt] ADJ (a) **to be ~** (*fire*) arder, estar ardiendo, estar quemando; (*light*) estar encendido (*LAm*: prendido); **to keep a fire ~** mantener un fuego ardiendo; **to set ~** pegar fuego a, incendiar. (b) **~ with** (*fig*) encendido de, que brilla de.
alight² [ə'laɪt] VI bajar, apearse (*from* de); (*from air*) posarse (*on* sobre); (*Aer*) aterrizar.
◆**alight on** VT *fact, idea* caer en la cuenta de, darse cuenta de.
align [ə'laɪn] ①VT alinear.
  ②VR: **to ~ o.s. with** ponerse al lado de, alinearse con.
alignment [ə'laɪnmənt] N alineación *f* (*also fig*); **to be in ~** estar alineados, estar en línea recta; **to be out of ~** estar fuera de alineación.
▼ **alike** [ə'laɪk] ①ADJ semejante, parecido, igual; **it's all ~ to me** todo me es igual; **you're all ~!** ¡todos sois iguales!; **to look ~** parecerse; **they all look ~ to me** yo no veo diferencia entre ellos, para mí todos son iguales.
  ②ADV del mismo modo, igualmente; **winter and summer ~** tanto en invierno como en verano, lo mismo en invierno como en verano; **to dress ~** vestir de modo idéntico; **to think ~** pensar del mismo modo.
alimentary [ˌælɪ'mentərɪ] ADJ alimenticio; **~ canal, ~ tract** tubo *m* digestivo.
alimony ['ælɪmənɪ] N alimentos *mpl*, pensión *f* alimenticia.
alive [ə'laɪv] ADJ (a) vivo; **to be ~** estar vivo, vivir; **to be still ~** vivir todavía, estar todavía con vida; **~ and kicking** vivito y coleando; **dead or ~** vivo o muerto; **man ~!** (EXCL) ¡hombre!; **while ~ he did no harm** en vida no hizo daño a nadie; **he's the best footballer ~** es el mejor futbolista del mundo; **no man ~ could do better** no lo podría hacer mejor nadie; **she plays as well as any pianist ~** toca tan bien como cualquier pianista del mundo; **it's good to be ~!** ¡qué bueno es vivir!; **the scene came ~ as she described it** la escena se animaba (*or* vivificaba) al describirla ella; **to be buried ~** ser enterrado vivo; **to burn sb ~** quemar a uno vivo; **to bring a story ~** animar una narración; **to keep sb ~** conservar a uno con vida; **to keep a tradition ~** conservar una tradición; **to keep a memory ~** guardar fresco un recuerdo, hacer perdurar una memoria; **he managed to stay ~ on fruit** logró sobrevivir comiendo frutas.
  (b) **~ with** (*insects etc*) lleno de, hormigueante en, rebosante de; **a book ~ with interest** un libro lleno de interés.
  (c) (*fig*) activo, enérgico; **look ~!** ¡menearse!, ¡apúrate! (*LAm*).
  (d) (*fig*) **~ to** sensible a, consciente de; **I am ~ to the danger** estoy consciente del peligro, me doy cuenta del peligro; **I am fully ~ to the fact that ...** no se me escapa que ..., no ignoro que ...; **I am fully ~ to the honour you do me** soy plenamente consciente del honor que se me hace.
alkali ['ælkəlaɪ] N álcali *m*.
alkaline ['ælkəlaɪn] ADJ alcalino.
alkalinity [ˌælkə'lɪnɪtɪ] N alcalinidad *f*.
alkaloid ['ælkəlɔɪd] ①ADJ alcaloideo.
  ②N alcaloide *m*.
alkie: ['ælkɪ] N ABBR *of* **alcoholic** borrachín *m*, -ina *f*.
all [ɔːl] ①ADJ (*sing*) todo, (*pl*) todos; **~ day** todo el día; **~ the time** todo el tiempo; **is that ~ the time it is!** ¡es ésa la hora tan sólo!; **~ (the) women** todas las mujeres; **~ Spain** toda España; **with ~ due speed** con toda prontitud; **books of ~ kinds** libros de todo tipo, libros de todos los tipos; **~ four of them were there** los cuatro estaban todos; **they chose him, of ~ people** le eligieron a él, como si no hubiera otros; **to choose this of ~ cars!** ¡elegir éste entre tantísimos coches!; **it's ~ done** todo está hecho; **he ate it ~** se lo comió todo; **and ~ that** y cosas así, y otras cosas por el estilo; **with bands and banners and ~ that** con bandas y banderas y qué sé yo qué más; **it's not as bad as ~ that** no es para tanto; **for ~ that** con todo, así y todo; **on ~ fours** a cuatro patas.
  ②PRON (a) (*sing*) todo *m*; **~ or nothing** todo o nada; **~ (that) I can tell you is ...** lo único que puedo decirte es ...; **~ is lost, it's ~ up** se acabó; **it's ~ up with him** no hay remedio para él; **that's ~** eso es todo, nada más; **is that ~?** ¿eso es todo?, ¿nada más?; **it cost him ~ of 50 dollars** le costó 50 dólares largos; **what with the rain and ~** con la lluvia y todo; **it was ~ I could do not to laugh** apenas pude contener la risa; **I did ~ that I could to stop him** hice lo posible para impedirle; **when ~ is said and done** en fin de cuentas.
  (b) (*pl*) todos *mpl*, todas *fpl*; **~ of us** todos nosotros, nosotros todos; **~ of the women** todas las mujeres; **we are ~ going** vamos todos; **they were ~ present** todos estaban presentes.
  (c) (*phrases with prep*) **above ~** sobre todo; **after ~** con todo, después de todo; al fin y al cabo; **did you speak at ~?** ¿dijiste algo?; **if I go at ~** si es que voy; **if it's at ~ possible** si hay la menor posibilidad; **not at ~** de ninguna manera, nada de eso; **not at ~!** (*answer to thanks*) ¡de nada!, ¡no hay de qué!; **not at ~ nice** nada agradable; **I'm not at ~ tired** no estoy cansado en lo más mínimo;

if she can sing at ~ si sabe cantar de alguna manera; **it rarely rains here if at ~** aquí llueve rara vez o nunca; **you mean she didn't sing at ~?** ¿quieres decir que no cantó siquiera?; **I don't know him at ~** no le conozco en absoluto; **for ~ I know** que yo sepa, quizá; **for ~ his boasting** a pesar de toda su jactancia; **50 men in ~** 50 hombres en total; **~ in ~** con todo, en resumen; **most of ~** más que nada, sobre todo; V **best, once** etc.

3 N: **my ~** todo lo que tengo, todo lo que es mío; **I would give my ~ to see it back** daría todo lo que tengo a cambio de verlo aquí; **to stake one's ~** arriesgar el todo por el todo.

4 ADV (**a**) (*entirely*) completamente, enteramente, del todo; **dressed ~ in black** vestido enteramente de negro; **it's ~ dirty** está todo sucio; **~ along the street** todo a lo largo de la calle, por toda la calle; **~ of a sudden** de repente; **the time went ~ too quickly** pasó el tiempo demasiado rápidamente; **it's ~ too true** por desgracia es la misma verdad; **he ~ but died** casi murió, por poco se nos murió; **it's ~ but impossible** es casi imposible; **~ but 7** todos menos 7; V **over, same,** etc.

(**b**) (*in comparisons*) V **better, more.**

(**c**) (*in games*) **to draw 2-~** empatar a 2; **the score stands at 3-~** están empatados a 3 (goles), el marcador está a 3-3.

all- [ɔːl] PREF: **~American** típicamente americano, americano cien por cien; **~leather** todo cuero; **with an ~Chinese cast** con un reparto totalmente chino; **there will be an ~Spanish final** en la final figurarán únicamente españoles; **it's an ~woman show** es un espectáculo enteramente femenino.

```
┌──────ALL-AMERICAN┐
```
ⓘ *El término all-American se usa para referirse a los deportistas universitarios que son seleccionados por su habilidad en un deporte determinado para formar parte de un equipo nacional, equipo que no compite como tal, ya que es sólo un título honorífico. De estos equipos, el que recibe mayor publicidad es el de fútbol americano.*

Este término se usa también para hacer referencia a una persona que representa el ideal de la clase media norteamericana, como cuando se dice, por ejemplo **he is a fine, upstanding all-American boy.**

Allah ['ælə] NM Alá.
all-around ['ɔːlə'raʊnd] ADJ (*US*) = **all-round.**
allay [ə'leɪ] VT *pain* aliviar; *fears, suspicion* aquietar, disipar.
all clear ['ɔːl'klɪə] N (*also ~ signal*) cese *m* (*or* fin *m*) de alarma; (*fig*) visto *m* bueno, luz *f* verde; **~!** ¡fin del alerta!
all-consuming ['ɔːlkən'sjuːmɪŋ] ADJ *passion, interest* absorbente.
allegation [,æle'geɪʃən] N aseveración *f*, aserto *m*; alegato *m*; acusación *f*.
allege [ə'ledʒ] VT declarar, afirmar, pretender (*that* que); (*with n*) alegar, pretextar; **he is ~d to be wealthy** se pretende que es rico; **he is ~d to be the leader** se dice que él es el jefe; **he absented himself alleging illness** se ausentó pretextando una enfermedad.
alleged [ə'ledʒd] ADJ supuesto, pretendido; presunto.
allegedly [ə'ledʒɪdlɪ] ADV supuestamente, según se afirma.
allegiance [ə'liːdʒəns] N lealtad *f*; fidelidad *f*; **to owe ~ to** deber lealtad a; **to swear ~ to** jurar su lealtad a; **oath of ~** (*Brit*) juramento *m* de fidelidad.
allegoric(al) [,ælɪ'gɒrɪk(əl)] ADJ alegórico.
allegorically [,ælɪ'gɒrɪkəlɪ] ADV alegóricamente.
allegorize ['ælɪgəraɪz] VT alegorizar.
allegory ['ælɪgərɪ] N alegoría *f*.
allegro [ə'legrəʊ] N alegro *m*.
alleluia [,ælɪ'luːjə] N aleluya *f*.
all-embracing ['ɔːlɪm'breɪsɪŋ] ADJ comprensivo, universal, global, general.
Allen key ['ælən,kiː], (*US*) **Allen wrench** ['ælən,rentʃ], N llave *f* (de) Allen.
allergen ['ælədʒən] N alérgeno *m*.
allergenic ['ælə,dʒenɪk] ADJ alergénico.
allergic [ə'lɜːdʒɪk] ADJ alérgico (*to* a); **to be ~ to** tener alergia a.
allergist ['ælədʒɪst] N alergista *mf*, alergólogo *m*, -a *f*.
allergy ['ælədʒɪ] N alergia *f* (*to* a); **~ clinic** clínica *f* de alergias; **total ~ syndrome** síndrome *m* de alergia total.
alleviate [ə'liːvɪeɪt] VT aliviar, mitigar.
alleviation [ə,liːvɪ'eɪʃən] N alivio *m*, mitigación *f*.
alley ['ælɪ] N callejuela *f*, callejón *m*; (*in park*) paseo *m*; (*Sport*) bolera *f*; **~ cat** gato *m* callejero, gata *f* callejera (*also *fig*); V **blind.**
alleyway ['ælɪweɪ] N = **alley.**
all-fired* ['ɔːlfaɪəd] (*US*) **1** ADJ excesivo; extremado; **in an ~ hurry** con muchísima prisa.
2 ADV a más no poder.
All Fools' Day ['ɔːl'fuːlzdeɪ] N día *m* de inocentes (*en Inglaterra el 1 abril, en España el 28 diciembre*).
All Hallows' (Day) ['ɔːl'hæləʊz(deɪ)] N Día *m* de Todos los Santos (*1 noviembre*).

alliance [ə'laɪəns] N alianza *f*; **to enter into an ~ with** aliarse con.
allied ['ælaɪd] ADJ (**a**) (*Mil, Pol*) aliado; **the ~ nations** las naciones aliadas. (**b**) (*similar*) afín, conexo, parecido; **languages and ~ subjects** los idiomas y temas afines; **and other subjects ~ to this** y otros temas relacionados con éste.
alligator ['ælɪgeɪtə] N caimán *m*.
all-important ['ɔːlɪm'pɔːtənt] ADJ sumamente importante, importantísimo.
all-in ['ɔːlɪn] ADJ (*Brit*) sum, *figure* global; *charge* todo incluido; *insurance policy* contra todo riesgo; **~ wrestling** lucha *f* libre.
all-inclusive ['ɔːlɪn'kluːsɪv] ADJ todo incluido; global; **~ insurance policy** póliza *f* de seguro completa.
alliteration [ə,lɪtə'reɪʃən] N aliteración *f*.
alliterative [ə'lɪtərətɪv] ADJ aliterado.
all-metal ['ɔːl'metl] ADJ enteramente metálico.
all-night ['ɔːl'naɪt] ADJ *café, garage, etc* (que está) abierto toda la noche; *journey, party, vigil* que dura toda la noche; **~ pass** (*Mil*) permiso *m* de pernocta; **~ service** servicio *m* nocturno, servicio *m* que funciona toda la noche; **~ showing** (*Cine*) sesión *f* continua nocturna.
all-nighter* ['ɔːl'naɪtə] N *espectáculo o fiesta etc que dura hasta la madrugada.*
allocate ['æləʊkeɪt] VT (**a**) (*allot*) asignar, señalar (*to* a). (**b**) (*apportion*) repartir, distribuir.
allocation [,æləʊ'keɪʃən] N (**a**) (*act: allotting*) asignación *f* (*also Comput*). (**b**) (*act: apportioning*) reparto *m*; distribución *f*. (**c**) (*share, amount*) ración *f*, cupo *m*, cuota *f*.
allomorph ['æləʊmɔːf] N alomorfo *m*.
allopathic [,æləʊ'pæθɪk] ADJ alopático.
allopathy [æ'lɒːpəθɪ] N alopatía *f*.
allophone ['æləʊfəʊn] N alófono *m*.
allot [ə'lɒt] VT (**a**) (*assign*) asignar, adjudicar, dar, destinar (*to* a); **the space ~ted to each contributor** el espacio asignado a cada colaborador; **we finished in the time ~ted** hemos terminado en el tiempo previsto; **to ~ funds for a purpose** asignar (*or* destinar) fondos para un propósito; **he was ~ted the role of villain** le dieron el papel de malo. (**b**) (*share out*) repartir, distribuir.
allotment [ə'lɒtmənt] N (**a**) (*act*) asignación *f*; reparto *m*, distribución *f*. (**b**) (*share*) ración *f*, porción *f*, cuota *f*. (**c**) (*Brit: land*) parcela *f* (alquilada para el cultivo); ≈ huerto *m*.
all-out ['ɔːl'aʊt] **1** ADJ *supporter* acérrimo, incondicional; *effort* máximo, supremo; **to make an ~ attack on a problem** atacar un problema de frente; **~ effort** esfuerzo *m* máximo; **~ strike** huelga *f* general; **~ war** guerra *f* total.
2 ADV con todas sus fuerzas; a fondo; (*of speed*) a máxima velocidad; **to go ~** tirar la casa por la ventana; (*Sport*) emplearse a fondo; **to go ~ for the prize** volcarse por conseguir el premio; **we must go ~ to ensure it** hemos de desplegar todas nuestras fuerzas para asegurarlo.
all-over ['ɔːl'əʊvə] **1** ADJ que tiene un diseño repetido sobre toda la superficie.
2 N (tela *f* con) diseño *m* repetido sobre toda la superficie.
▼ **allow** [ə'laʊ] **1** VT (**a**) (*with n object*) permitir; (*grant*) dar, conceder; asignar; *discount* aplicar, dar; *allowance* pagar, dar; **you should ~ more space** conviene dejar más espacio; **~ yourself 3 hours for the journey** cuenta con 3 horas para el viaje; **~ 5 cm for shrinkage** tener en cuenta 5 cm perdidos por encogimiento; **how much should I ~ for expenses?** ¿cuánto debo prever para los gastos?; **it ~s very little time for meals** deja muy poco tiempo para comer; **the judge ~ed him £1000 costs** el juez le asignó 1000 libras en concepto de costas; **~ me!** ¡permítame!
▼ (**b**) (*permit*) **to ~ sb to + infin** permitir a uno + infin, dejar a uno + infin, permitir que uno + subj; **smoking is not ~ed here** aquí no se permite fumar; **'no dogs ~ed'** 'se prohíbe dejar entrar a los perros'.
(**c**) *claim, request* admitir, aceptar; **to ~ that ...** reconocer que ..., confesar que ...; **he is ~ed to be strong** se reconoce que es fuerte; **even ~ing that to be so** aun admitiendo eso.
2 VR: **to ~ o.s. to be persuaded** dejarse persuadir; **she finally ~ed herself to say that ...** por fin se permitió decir que ...
◆ **allow for** VT tener en cuenta, tomar en consideración; prever; **after ~ing for his costs** cuenta habida de sus gastos; **we should ~ for all possibilities** debemos tener presentes todas las posibilidades.
◆ **allow in** VT: **to ~ sb in** dejar entrar a uno, permitir que uno entre.
◆ **allow of** VT permitir; admitir; **the situation ~s of no delay** la situación no permite demora; **this ~s of no excuse** esto no admite disculpa.
◆ **allow out** VT: **to ~ sb out** permitir que uno salga.
allowable [ə'laʊəbl] ADJ permisible; admisible; tolerable; lícito; *expense* deducible; **~ against tax** desgravable.
allowance [ə'laʊəns] N (**a**) (*money etc assigned*) subsidio *m*, subvención *f*, pago *m*; paga *f*; pensión *f*; (*food*) ración *f*; (*esp US: pocket money*) dinero *m* de bolsillo; (*subsistence ~*) dietas *fpl*; **he has an ~ of**

£100 a month tiene una subvención de 100 libras mensuales; **he makes his mother an ~** le concede una pensión a su madre.

(b) (*Comm, Fin: discount*) descuento *m*, rebaja *f*; **tax ~** desgravación *f* fiscal.

(c) (*concession*) concesión *f*; **one must make ~s** hay que hacer concesiones; hay que ser indulgente (*for him* con él); **to make ~s for the weather** tener en cuenta el tiempo.

(d) (*Mech*) tolerancia *f*.

(e) (*volume, weight*) margen *m*.

alloy¹ ['ælɔɪ] N aleación *f*, liga *f*; (*fig*) mezcla *f*; **~ wheels** llantas *fpl* de aleación.

alloy² [ə'lɔɪ] VT alear, ligar.

all-party ['ɔːl'pɑːtɪ] ADJ *group, talks* multipartidista.

all-pervading [,ɔːlpə'veɪdɪŋ] ADJ, **all-pervasive** [,ɔːlpə'veɪsɪv] ADJ omnipresente.

all-points bulletin [,ɔːlpɔɪnts'bʊlɪtɪn] N *boletín difundido por la policía para la búsqueda y captura de un sospechoso.*

all-powerful ['ɔːl'paʊəfʊl] ADJ omnipotente, todopoderoso.

all-purpose ['ɔːl'pɜːpəs] ADJ universal, para todo uso, de uso múltiple.

all right [,ɔːl'raɪt] **1** ADJ **(a)** (*satisfactory*) **it's ~** todo está bien, todo va bien; **yes, that's ~** sí, de acuerdo; sí, vale; **it's ~ with me** yo, de acuerdo; **it's ~ for you** no tienes de qué quejarte, tú no tienes problemas; **it's ~ for you to smile** tú bien puedes sonreír; **it will be ~ on the night** todo estará listo para el estreno; **I made it ~ with the cabby** lo arreglé con el taxista; **is it ~ for me to smoke?** ¿puedo fumar?; **is he ~ with the girls?** ¿se comporta bien con las chicas?; **is it ~ for me to take the dog?** ¿se me permite llevar al perro?; **are you ~ for Tuesday?** ¿estás libre (*or* podrás jugar, podrás venir, *etc*) el martes?; **he's ~ as a goalkeeper (but a lousy forward)** como portero vale (pero como delantero es un desastre); **well, he's ~** (*doubtful*) bueno, es regular; **let me tell you, our Joe is ~!** ¡te digo que Pepe es tremendo!*; **she's a bit of ~:** está buenísima*.

(b) (*safe, well*) **she's ~ again now** está mejor, se ha repuesto ya; **it's ~, you can come out now** está bien, puedes salir ya.

(c) (*prosperous*) **we're ~ for the rest of our lives** no tendremos problema económico en el resto de la vida; **are you ~ for cigarettes?** ¿tienes buena cantidad de tabaco?

2 ADV: **I can see ~, thanks** veo bien, gracias; **you'll get your money back ~** se te devolverá el dinero, eso es seguro; **he complained ~!** ¡ya lo creo que se quejó!; **'You say I was wrong. A~, but ...'** 'Dices que me equivoqué. Bien, pero ...'

3 EXCL (*approval*) ¡bueno!, ¡muy bien!; (*agreement*) ¡de acuerdo!; (*that's enough*) ¡basta ya!; (*exasperation*) ¡se acabó!

all-risks ['ɔːl'rɪsks] ATTR: **~ insurance** seguro *m* contra todo riesgo.

all-round ['ɔːl'raʊnd] ADJ *success etc* completo; *improvement* general, en todos los aspectos; *view* amplio; *person* que hace de todo, hábil para todo, con talentos para todo.

all-rounder ['ɔːl'raʊndər] N persona *f* (*esp* jugador *m*, -ora *f*) que hace de todo.

All Saints' Day ['ɔːl'seɪntsdeɪ] N Día *m* de Todos los Santos (*1 noviembre*).

All Souls' Day ['ɔːl'səʊlzdeɪ] N Día *m* de (los) Difuntos (*2 noviembre*).

allspice ['ɔːlspaɪs] N pimienta *f* inglesa, pimienta *f* de Jamaica.

all-star ['ɔːlstɑː] ADJ *cast* todo estelar; **~ performance, show with an ~ cast** función *f* de primeras figuras, función *f* estelar.

all-terrain vehicle [,ɔːltə,reɪn'viːɪkl] N vehículo *m* todo terreno.

all-the-year-round [,ɔːlðə,jɪə'raʊnd] ADJ *sport* que se practica todo el año; *resort* abierto todo el año.

all-time ['ɔːl'taɪm] ADJ sin precedentes, inaudito, nunca visto; **an ~ record** un récord nunca igualado; **exports have reached an ~ high** las exportaciones han alcanzado cifras nunca conocidas antes; **the pound is at an ~ low** la libra ha caído a su punto más bajo.

allude [ə'luːd] VI: **to ~** referirse a, aludir a.

allure [ə'ljʊər] **1** N atractivo *m*, encanto *m*, fascinación *f*; aliciente *m*.

2 VT atraer, captarse la voluntad de, tentar; fascinar.

alluring [ə'ljʊərɪŋ] ADJ atractivo, seductor, tentador; fascinante.

allusion [ə'luːʒən] N alusión *f*, referencia *f* (*to* a); **he said in ~ to** dijo refiriéndose a.

allusive [ə'luːsɪv] ADJ **(a)** alusivo, referente (*to* a). **(b)** *style* lleno de alusiones.

alluvial [ə'luːvɪəl] ADJ aluvial.

alluvium [ə'luːvɪəm] N aluvión *m*, depósito *m* aluvial.

all-weather ['ɔːl'weðər] ADJ para todo tiempo.

ally¹ **1** ['ælaɪ] N aliado *m*; **the Allies** los Aliados.

2 [ə'laɪ] VR: **to ~ o.s. to** (*or* **with**) aliarse con; (*by marriage*) emparentar con.

ally² ['ælɪ] N bolita *f*, canica *f*.

alma mater ['ælmə'meɪtər] N alma máter *f*.

almanac ['ɔːlmənæk] N almanaque *m*.

almighty [ɔːl'maɪtɪ] **1** ADJ **(a)** omnipotente, todopoderoso; **A~ God, God A~** Dios Todopoderoso.

(b) (***) terrible, imponente, enorme de grande*; **they made an ~ fuss** armaron un tremendo lío*; **he really is an ~ idiot** realmente es un terrible idiota; **I foresee ~ problems** preveo unos enormes problemas.

2 N: **the A~** el Todopoderoso.

3 ADV (***) terriblemente, la mar de*; **an ~ loud bang** un estallido terriblemente fuerte; **that was ~ silly of you** en eso has sido la mar de tonto*.

almond ['ɑːmənd] **1** N (*fruit*) almendra *f*; (*tree*) almendro *m*; V **sugar**.

2 ATTR de almendra(s); **an ~ taste** un sabor a almendra.

almond-eyed ['ɑːmənd'aɪd] ADJ de ojos almendrados.

almond oil ['ɑːmənd,ɔɪl] N aceite *m* de almendra.

almond-shaped ['ɑːmənd,ʃeɪpt] ADJ almendrado.

almond tree ['ɑːməndtriː] N almendro *m*.

almoner ['ɑːmənər] N (*Hist*) limosnero *m*; (*Brit Med*) oficial *mf* de asistencia social (adscrito a un hospital).

almost ['ɔːlməʊst] ADV casi; **an ~ complete failure** un fracaso casi total; **we're ~ there** ya estamos al llegar, nos falta poco para llegar; **he ~ died on us** casi se nos murió, por poco se nos murió.

alms [ɑːmz] N SING AND PL limosna *f*.

almsbox ['ɑːmzbɒks] N cepillo *m* para los pobres.

almshouse ['ɑːmzhaʊs] N, PL **almshouses** ['ɑːmz,haʊzɪz] hospicio *m*, asilo *m* para los pobres; casa *f* de beneficencia.

aloe ['æləʊ] N áloe *m*; **~s** (*juice*) acíbar *m*.

aloe vera ['æləʊ'vɪərə] N aloe vera *m*.

aloft [ə'lɒft] ADV (*also* **up ~**) arriba, en lo alto; en vuelo; (*Naut*) en la arboladura.

alone [ə'ləʊn] **1** ADJ **(a)** solo; **to be ~** estar solo, estar a solas; **to be all** (*or* **quite**) **~** estar completamente solo; **am I ~ in thinking so?** ¿soy yo el único en pensar así?; **to go it ~** hacerlo solo, hacerlo sin ayuda de nadie.

(b) **to leave sb ~** dejar a uno solo; **we must not leave them ~ together** no hay que dejarlos solos; **to leave** (*or* **let**) **sb ~** (*fig*) no molestar a uno, dejar de molestar a uno, dejar a uno tranquilo; **leave me ~!** ¡déjame en paz!, ¡déjame estar! (*LAm*); **to leave** (*or* **let**) **sth ~** no tocar algo; **leave it ~!** ¡déjalo!, ¡no toques!; **just leave the plant ~ so that it will grow** deja la planta sin tocar para que crezca; **I advise you to leave that severely ~** te aconsejo no meterte de ninguna manera en eso.

(c) **let ~** (*as prep etc*) sin mencionar, sin tomar en cuenta; y no digamos; **he can't read, let ~ write** nada de escribir, no sabe leer siquiera; **one can't get into Slobodia, let ~ Ruritania** no se puede entrar en Eslobodia, ni menos en Ruritania.

2 ADV solamente, sólo, únicamente; **it is mine ~** es todo mío; **a charm which is hers ~** un encanto que es únicamente suyo; **man cannot live by bread ~** no sólo de pan vive el hombre; **you ~ can do it** sólo tú puedes hacerlo.

along [ə'lɒŋ] **1** ADV: **all ~** desde el principio, todo el tiempo; **~ with** junto con; **I'll be ~ in a moment** ahora voy; **she'll be ~ tomorrow** vendrá mañana; V **come** etc.

2 PREP a lo largo de; por; **~ the river** a lo largo del río; **all ~ the street** todo lo largo de la calle; **we went ~ the tunnel** pasamos por el túnel; **it's ~ here** es por aquí; **somewhere ~ the way it fell off** en alguna parte del camino se cayó; **please sign ~ this line** por favor firme en este renglón; **we acted ~ the lines suggested** hemos obrado de acuerdo con las indicaciones que nos hicieron.

alongside [ə'lɒŋ'saɪd] **1** ADV (*Naut*) al costado, costado con costado; **to bring a ship ~** acostar un buque; **to come ~** atracarse al costado.

2 PREP junto a, al lado de; (*Naut*) al costado de; **to come ~ a ship** atracarse al costado de un buque; **the car stopped ~ me** el coche se paró a mi lado; **there's a stream ~ the garden** hay un arroyo al lado del jardín; **they have to work ~ each other** tienen que trabajar juntos; **how can these systems work ~ each other?** ¿cómo estos sistemas pueden funcionar en colaboración?

aloof [ə'luːf] **1** ADJ *character* reservado, frío; **he was very ~ with me** conmigo se mostró muy reservado; **she has always been somewhat ~** ella siempre ha guardado las distancias.

2 ADV: **to keep ~, stand ~** mantenerse a distancia, mantenerse apartado (*from* de), guardar las distancias.

aloofness [ə'luːfnɪs] N reserva *f*, frialdad *f*.

alopecia [,æləʊ'piːʃə] N alopecia *f*.

aloud [ə'laʊd] ADV en voz alta, alto.

alpaca [æl'pækə] N alpaca *f*.

alpenhorn ['ælpənhɔːn] N trompa *f* de los Alpes.

alpenstock ['ælpɪnstɒk] N alpenstock *m*, bastón *m* montañero.

alpha ['ælfə] N alfa *f*; (*Brit: Scol, Univ*) sobresaliente *m*; **~ particle** partícula *f* alfa.

alphabet ['ælfəbet] N alfabeto *m*.

alphabetic(al) [,ælfə'betɪk(əl)] ADJ alfabético.

alphabetically [,ælfə'betɪkəlɪ] ADV alfabéticamente, en (*or* por) orden alfabético.

alphabetize ['ælfəbətaɪz] VT alfabetizar, poner en orden alfabético.

alphanumeric [,ælfənjuː'merɪk] ADJ alfanumérico; **~ character**

carácter *m* alfanumérico; **~ field** campo *m* alfanumérico.

Alphonso [æl'fɒnsəʊ] NM Alfonso.

alpine ['ælpaɪn] ① ADJ alpino, alpestre.
② N planta *f* alpestre.

alpinist ['ælpɪnɪst] N alpinista *mf*.

Alps [ælps] NPL Alpes *mpl*.

already [ɔːl'redɪ] ADV ya; **that's enough ~!** (*US**) ¡basta!, ¡vale ya!, ¡ya está bien!

alright* [ˌɔːl'raɪt] = **all right.**

Alsace ['ælsæs] N Alsacia *f*.

Alsace-Lorraine ['ælsæslə'reɪn] N Alsacia-Lorena *f*.

Alsatian [æl'seɪʃən] ① ADJ alsaciano.
② N alsaciano *m*, -a *f*; (*Brit: dog*) perro *m* lobo, (perro *m*) pastor *m* alemán.

▼ **also** ['ɔːlsəʊ] ADV también, además.

also-ran ['ɔːlsəʊræn] N (**a**) (*Sport*) caballo *m* (*or* competidor *m* etc) que no logra colocarse. (**b**) (*: *person*) fracasado *m*, -a *f*, cero *m* a la izquierda, perdedor *m*.

alt. ABBR *of* **altitude** altura *f*.

Alta. (*Canada*) ABBR *of* **Alberta.**

Altamira [ˌæltə'miːrə] N: **the ~ caves** las cuevas de Altamira.

altar ['ɒltəʳ] N altar *m*; (*pagan*) ara *f*; **high ~** altar *m* mayor; **to lead a girl to the ~** conducir a su novia al altar; **he sacrificed all on the ~s of his ambition** lo sacrificó todo en aras de su ambición.

altar-boy ['ɒltəbɔɪ] N acólito *m*, monaguillo *m*.

altar-cloth ['ɒltəklɒθ] N sabanilla *f*, paño *m* de altar.

altarpiece ['ɒltəpiːs] N retablo *m*.

altar-rail ['ɒltəˌreɪl] N comulgatorio *m*.

alter ['ɒltəʳ] ① VT (**a**) (*change*) cambiar, modificar, (*esp for the worse*) alterar; *painting, speech etc* retocar; (*Archit*) reformar; *opinion, course etc* cambiar de; **then that ~s things** entonces la cosa cambia; **it has ~ed things for the better** ha mejorado las cosas, ha cambiado las cosas en sentido positivo; **circumstances ~ cases** el caso depende de las circunstancias; **I see no need to ~ my view** no veo ninguna necesidad de cambiar mi opinión.
(**b**) (*falsify*) *evidence etc* falsificar; *text* alterar.
(**c**) (*US: castrate*) castrar.
② VI cambiar(se), mudarse; **I find him much ~ed** le veo muy cambiado; **to ~ for the better** mejorar, cambiarse en sentido positivo; **to ~ for the worse** empeorar, cambiarse en sentido negativo.

alteration [ˌɒltə'reɪʃən] N cambio *m*, modificación *f*, (*esp for the worse*) alteración *f* (*in, to* de); **~s** (*Archit*) reformas *fpl*; (*to text, painting, speech etc*) retoques *mpl*; (*Sew*) arreglo *m* (*to* de).

altercation [ˌɒltə'keɪʃən] N altercado *m*.

alter ego ['æltər'iːgəʊ] N álter ego *m*.

alternate ① [ɒl'tɜːnɪt] ADJ (**a**) (*Bot, Math, Tech etc*) alterno; *movement* alternativo.
(**b**) (*every second*) alterno; **on ~ days** un día sí y otro no, cada dos días, los días alternos.
(**c**) (*US*) = **alternative.**
② [ɒl'tɜːnɪt] N (*US*) suplente *mf*.
③ ['ɒltɜːneɪt] VTI alternar.

alternately [ɒl'tɜːnɪtlɪ] ADV alternativamente; por turno.

alternating ['ɒltɜːneɪtɪŋ] ADJ alterno; **~ current** corriente *f* alterna.

alternation [ˌɒltɜː'neɪʃən] N alternación *f*; **in ~** alternativamente.

▼ **alternative** [ɒl'tɜːnətɪv] ① ADJ alternativo; otro; **the only ~ system** el único otro sistema; **have you any ~ candidate?** ¿no tienes otro candidato?; **~ energy** energías *fpl* alternativas; **~ medicine** medicina *f* alternativa; **the ~ society** la sociedad alternativa.
▼② N alternativa *f*; posibilidad *f*; **I have no ~** no tengo más remedio, no puedo hacer otra cosa; no me queda otra (*LAm*); **you have no ~ but to go** no tienes más remedio que ir; **what ~s are there?** ¿qué opciones hay?; **she chose the first ~** optó por la primera alternativa.

alternatively [ɒl'tɜːnətɪvlɪ] ADV por otra parte, en cambio; si no ...; otra solución sería ...

alternator ['ɒltɜːneɪtəʳ] N (*Brit*) alternador *m*.

▼ **although** [ɔːl'ðəʊ] CONJ aunque; si bien; a pesar de que.

altimeter ['æltɪmiːtəʳ] N altímetro *m*.

altitude ['æltɪtjuːd] N altura *f*, altitud *f*; **at these ~s** en estas alturas; **~ sickness** mal *m* de altura, soroche *m* (*LAm*).

alto ['æltəʊ] ① ADJ alto; **~ saxophone** saxofón *m* alto; **to sing the ~ part** cantar la parte de contralto.
② N contralto *mf*.

altocumulus [ˌæltəʊ'kjuːmjʊləs] N, PL **altocumuli** [ˌæltəʊ'kjuːmjʊlaɪ] altocúmulo *m*.

altogether [ˌɔːltə'geðəʳ] ① ADV (**a**) (*with everything included*) en conjunto, en total; **how many are there ~?** ¿cuántos hay en total?
(**b**) (*wholly*) enteramente; del todo; **we haven't ~ finished** no hemos terminado del todo; **I'm not ~ sure** no estoy del todo seguro; **this is ~ too hard** esto es demasiado difícil con mucho; **you're ~ wrong**

Vd está completamente equivocado; **I'm not ~ satisfied with it** no estoy satisfecho del todo con ello, no me acaba de convencer.
(**c**) (*on the whole*) en general, en resumidas cuentas; en conjunto; **~ it was a good show** en general ha sido un éxito.
② N: **in the ~*** desnudo, en cueros*, en pelota picada*.

altoist ['æltəʊɪst] N saxofón *m* alto, saxofonista *mf* alto.

altostratus [ˌæltəʊ'streɪtəs] N, PL **altostrati** [ˌæltəʊ'streɪtaɪ] altostrato *m*.

altruism ['æltrʊɪzəm] N altruismo *m*.

altruist ['æltrʊɪst] N altruista *mf*

altruistic [ˌæltrʊ'ɪstɪk] ADJ altruista.

ALU N ABBR *of* **Arithmetical Logic Unit** unidad *f* lógica aritmética, ULP *f*.

alum ['æləm] N alumbre *m*.

aluminium [ˌæljʊ'mɪnɪəm] N (*Brit*), **aluminum** [ə'luːmɪnəm] N (*US*) aluminio *m*; **~ foil** aluminio *m* doméstico.

alumnus [ə'lʌmnəs] N, PL **alumni** [ə'lʌmnaɪ]; **alumna** [ə'lʌmnə] N, PL **alumnae** [ə'lʌmniː] (*esp US*) graduado *m*, -a *f*; **~ association** asociación *f* de graduados.

alveolar [æl'vɪələʳ] ADJ alveolar.

alveolus [æl'vɪələs] N, PL **alveoli** [æl'vɪəlaɪ] alvéolo *m*, alveolo *m*.

always ['ɔːlweɪz] ADV siempre.

Alzheimer's disease ['ælts,haɪməzdɪziːz] N enfermedad *f* de Alzheimer.

AM N (**a**) ABBR *of* **Amplitude Modulation** amplitud *f* modulada, AM. (**b**) (*US*) ABBR *of* **Artium Magister**; *V* **MA.**

am [æm] *V* **be.**

Am. (**a**) ABBR *of* **America** América *f*. (**b**) ABBR *of* **American** americano.

a.m. ADV ABBR *of* **ante meridiem** antes del mediodía, de la mañana.

AMA N (*US*) ABBR *of* **American Medical Association** Colegio *m* Oficial de Médicos de América.

amalgam [ə'mælgəm] N amalgama *f*.

amalgamate [ə'mælgəmeɪt] ① VT amalgamar; *companies etc* unir.
② VI amalgamarse; unirse.

amalgamation [ə,mælgə'meɪʃən] N amalgamación *f*; unión *f*; (*Comm*) fusión *f*.

amanita [ˌæmə'naɪtə] N amanita *f*.

amanuensis [ə,mænjʊ'ensɪs] N, PL **amanuenses** [ə,mænju'ensiːz] amanuense *mf*.

Amaryllis [ˌæmə'rɪlɪs] NF Amarilis.

amass [ə'mæs] VT amontonar, acumular.

amateur ['æmətəʳ] ① N amateur *mf*, aficionado *m*, -a *f* (*also pej*), no profesional *mf*.
② ADJ (**a**) **~ dramatics** teatro *m* no profesional; **A~ Football Association** Asociación *f* de Fútbol Amateur; **~ status** condición *f* de amateur; **~ tennis** tenis *m* amateur, tenis *m* para aficionados; **I have an ~ interest in pottery** me interesa como aficionado la cerámica.
(**b**) (*pej*) = **amateurish.**

amateurish ['æmətərɪʃ] ADJ (*pej*) de (mero) aficionado; superficial, inexperto, torpe, chapucero.

amateurism ['æmətərɪzəm] N amateurismo *m*, estado *m* de aficionado; **~ in sport** deportes *mpl* para los no profesionales, deportes *mpl* de aficionados.

amatory ['æmətərɪ] ADJ amatorio, erótico.

amaze [ə'meɪz] VT asombrar, pasmar; **to be ~d** quedar estupefacto, quedar atónito; **to be ~d at** asombrarse de; **you ~ me!** ¡me admiras!, ¡me dejas patidifuso!

amazed [ə'meɪzd] ADJ *glance, expression* asombrado, lleno de estupor; **to be ~ at (seeing) sth** quedar asombrado de (ver) algo.

amazement [ə'meɪzmənt] N asombro *m*, sorpresa *f*, estupefacción *f*; **they looked on in ~** miraron asombrados; **the news caused general ~** la noticia causó un asombro general.

amazing [ə'meɪzɪŋ] ADJ asombroso, pasmoso; extraordinario.

amazingly [ə'meɪzɪŋlɪ] ADV milagrosamente, por maravilla; extraordinariamente; **~ enough** aunque parece mentira; **she is ~ generous** es extraordinariamente generosa; **~, nobody was killed** por milagro, no hubo víctimas; **he did ~ well** tuvo un éxito formidable; **he is ~ fit for his age** su estado físico es extraordinario para un hombre de su edad.

Amazon¹ ['æməzən] N (**a**) (*Myth*) amazona *f*. (**b**) (*fig: also* **a~**) mujer *f* fuerte, atleta *f* (fuerte); (*US pej*) marimacho *m*.

Amazon² ['æməzən] N (*Geog*) Amazonas *m*; **~ basin** cuenca *f* del Amazonas; **~ jungle** selva *f* de Amazonas.

Amazonia [ˌæmə'zəʊnɪə] N Amazonia *f*.

Amazonian [ˌæmə'zəʊnɪən] ADJ amazónico.

ambassador [æm'bæsədəʳ] N embajador *m*, -ora *f*; **the Spanish ~** el embajador de España.

ambassadorial [æm,bæsə'dɔːrɪəl] ADJ de embajador.

ambassadorship [æm'bæsədəʃɪp] N embajada *f*.

ambassadress [æm'bæsədrɪs] N embajadora *f*.

amber ['æmbəʳ] ① N ámbar *m*.
② ADJ de ámbar; ambarino, color de ámbar; **~ light** (*Brit Aut*) luz *f*

► LANGUAGE IN USE: **also** → 26.2, 26.3   **alternative: 2** → 18.4   **although** → 26.3

amarilla; **at ~** (*Aut*) en el amarillo.
ambergris ['æmbəgriːs] N ámbar *m* gris.
ambi... ['æmbɪ] PREF ambi...
ambiance ['æmbɪəns] = **ambience**.
ambidextrous [ˌæmbɪ'dekstrəs] ADJ ambidextro.
ambience ['æmbɪəns] N ambiente *m*, atmósfera *f*.
ambient ['æmbɪənt] ADJ ambiente.
ambiguity [ˌæmbɪ'gjuːtɪ] N ambigüedad *f*.
ambiguous [æm'bɪgjuəs] ADJ ambiguo.
ambiguously [æm'bɪgjuəslɪ] ADV ambiguamente, de forma ambigua.
ambiguousness [æm'bɪgjuəsnɪs] N ambigüedad *f*.
ambit ['æmbɪt] N ámbito *m*.
ambition [æm'bɪʃən] N ambición *f*; **to have an ~ for sth** ambicionar algo; **to have an ~ to be a doctor** ambicionar ser médico.
ambitious [æm'bɪʃəs] ADJ ambicioso; **to be ~ for sth** ambicionar algo; **they are very ~ for their children** planean cosas grandes para sus hijos; **he was ~ to be the boss** ambicionaba llegar a ser el jefe.
ambitiously [æm'bɪʃəslɪ] ADV ambiciosamente.
ambivalence [æm'bɪvələns] N ambivalencia *f*.
ambivalent [æm'bɪvələnt] ADJ ambivalente.
amble ['æmbl] [1] N (*of horse*) ambladura *f*, portante *m*, paso *m* de andadura; **to walk at an ~** (*person*) andar muy despacio, pasearse despacio.
[2] VI (*horse*) amblar; ir a paso de andadura; (*person*) andar muy despacio; **to ~ along** pasearse despacio, caminar sin prisa; **the bus ~s along at 40 kph** el autobús va tranquilamente a 40 kph; **he ~d into my office at 10 o'clock** entró tranquilamente en mi oficina a las 10; **he ~d up to me** se me acercó despacio.
Ambrose ['æmbrəuz] NM Ambrosio.
ambrosia [æm'brəuzɪə] N ambrosía *f*.
ambulance ['æmbjuləns] N ambulancia *f*; **~ driver, ~ man** ambulanciero *m*.
ambulatory [ˌæmbju'leɪtərɪ] ADJ (*US Med*) no encamado.
ambush ['æmbuʃ] [1] N emboscada *f*; **troops in ~** tropas *fpl* emboscadas; **to fall into an ~** caer en una emboscada; **to lay an ~ for** tender una emboscada a; **to lie in ~** estar emboscado (*for* para coger).
[2] VT tender una emboscada a, coger (*LAm*: agarrar) por sorpresa; **to be ~ed** caer en una emboscada, ser cogido por sorpresa.
ameba [ə'miːbə] N (*US*) = **amoeba**.
ameliorate [ə'miːlɪəreɪt] [1] VT mejorar.
[2] VI mejorar(se).
amelioration [əˌmiːlɪə'reɪʃən] N mejora *f*, mejoramiento *m*, mejoría *f*.
amen ['ɑː'men] [1] INTERJ amén; **~ to that** así sea, ojalá sea así.
[2] N amén *m*.
amenable [ə'miːnəbl] ADJ (a) (*responsive, tractable*) sumiso, dócil, tratable; **~ to argument** flexible, que se deja convencer; **~ to discipline** sumiso, dispuesto a dejarse disciplinar; **~ to reason** que se deja convencer por la razón; **~ to treatment** (*Med*) susceptible de ser curado, curable. (b) (*Jur*) responsable (*for* de).
amend [ə'mend] VT enmendar; rectificar, corregir; modificar; reformar.
amendment [ə'mendmənt] N enmienda *f*; rectificación *f*, corrección *f*; **the Fifth A~** la Quinta Enmienda (a la Constitución de los Estados Unidos); **to invoke** (*or* **plead, take**) **the Fifth (A~)** negarse a dar testimonio bajo la protección de la Quinta Enmienda (*relativa a la autoincriminación*).

┌─── **FIFTH AMENDMENT** ─────────────────────────┐

ⓘ *La Quinta Enmienda a la Constitución de los Estados Unidos establece varios principios legales fundamentales que protegen al ciudadano frente al poder del Estado. Entre estos derechos están el de que una persona no sea encarcelada o sus bienes sean embargados sin juicio previo, así como el derecho a no ser procesada dos veces por el mismo delito, o a no ser obligada a aportar pruebas contra sí misma. Al hecho de negarse a aportar pruebas autoincriminatorias se le conoce como **taking the fifth** (acogerse a la quinta) y, durante las investigaciones anticomunistas que el senador McCarthy realizó en la década de los años 50, aquéllos que se acogían a esta quinta enmienda eran generalmente acusados de llevar a cabo actividades antiamericanas.*

└───┘

amends [ə'mendz] NPL: **to make ~** dar cumplida satisfacción, compensarlo, enmendarlo; **to make ~ for sth** dar satisfacción por algo, enmendar algo, remediar algo; **I'll try to make ~ in future** trataré de dar satisfacción en el futuro.
amenity [ə'miːnɪtɪ] N (a) (*pleasantness*) amenidad *f*. (b) (*pleasant feature*) atractivo *m*, cosa *f* agradable, ventaja *f*; **amenities** PL atractivos *mpl*, conveniencias *fpl*, comodidades *fpl*; **the amenities of life** las cosas agradables de la vida; **a house with all amenities** una casa con todo confort; **we are trying to improve the city's amenities** nos esforzamos por mejorar las instalaciones de la ciudad; **~ bed** (*Brit*) habitación *f* privada; **~ society** asociación *f* para la conservación del medio ambiente.

amenorrhoea, (*US*) **amenorrhea** [eɪˌmenə'rɪə] N amenorrea *f*.
America [ə'merɪkə] N América *f*; (*ie USA*) Estados *mpl* Unidos; V **north** etc.
American [ə'merɪkən] [1] ADJ americano; (*ie of USA*) norteamericano, estadounidense; **~ cloth** hule *m*; **the ~ dream** el sueño americano; **~ English** inglés *m* americano; **football** fútbol *m* americano; **~ Indian** amerindio *m*, -a *f*; **~ leather** cuero *m* artificial; **~ Legion** organización de veteranos de las dos guerras mundiales; **~ plan** (*US*) (habitación *f* con) pensión *f* completa; **~ Spanish** español *m* de América; *ver también* LEGION - AMERICAN LEGION/BRITISH LEGION .
[2] N americano *m*, -a *f*; (*ie of USA*) norteamericano *m*, -a *f*, estadounidense *mf*.

┌─── **AMERICAN DREAM** ───────────────────────────┐

ⓘ *El término **American Dream**, (el sueño americano), se refiere a los valores y creencias que para muchos estadounidenses son característicos de su modo de entender la vida como nación y que encuentran su materialización en la Declaración de Independencia de 1776. Con este término se pone especial énfasis en el individualismo, la importancia de trabajar duro, el hecho de que todos podemos mejorar y que la libertad y la justicia han de ser universales. Para muchos el "sueño americano" era una oportunidad para hacer fortuna.*
El término también se usa de forma irónica para referirse al contraste entre estos ideales y las actitudes materialistas que caracterizan a la sociedad estadounidense actual.

└───┘

Americana [əˌmerɪ'kɑːnə] N (*US*) objetos, documentos etc pertenecientes a la herencia cultural norteamericana.
americanism [ə'merɪkənɪzəm] N americanismo *m*.
americanization [əˌmerɪkənər'zeɪʃən] N americanización *f*.
americanize [ə'merɪkənaɪz] VT americanizar; **to become ~d** americanizarse.
americium [ˌæmə'rɪsɪəm] N americio *m*.
Amerind [ˌæmərɪnd] N amerindio *m*, -a *f*.
Amerindian [ˌæmə'rɪndɪən] [1] ADJ amerindio.
[2] N amerindio *m*, -a *f*.
amethyst ['æmɪθɪst] N amatista *f*.
Amex ['æmeks] N (*US*) ABBR of **American Stock Exchange**.
amiability [ˌeɪmɪə'bɪlɪtɪ] N afabilidad *f*, amabilidad *f*.
amiable ['eɪmɪəbl] ADJ afable, amable, simpático; bonachón; **he's an ~ idiot** es un imbécil simpático.
amiably ['eɪmɪəblɪ] ADV afablemente, amablemente.
amicable ['æmɪkəbl] ADJ amistoso, amigable; **to reach an ~ settlement** llegar a un arreglo amistoso.
amicably ['æmɪkəblɪ] ADV amistosamente, amigablemente.
amid [ə'mɪd] PREP en medio de, entre.
amidships [ə'mɪdʃɪps] ADV en medio del barco.
amidst [ə'mɪdst] PREP = **amid**.
amino-acid [ə'miːnəʊˌæsɪd] N aminoácido *m*.
Amish ['ɑːmɪʃ] N: **the ~** los amish (*secta religiosa menonita*).
amiss [ə'mɪs] [1] ADV mal, fuera de lugar, fuera de propósito; **a little politeness would not come ~** no le vendría mal un poco de cortesía; **a cup of coffee would not come ~** me gustaría mucho una taza de café; **to take sth ~** llevar algo a mal; **don't take it ~, will you?** ¿no te vas a ofender, eh?; **don't take it ~ if I come too** no te ofendas si yo vengo también; **but he took it very ~** pero él se ofendió mucho.
[2] ADJ malo; **there's sth ~** pasa algo malo, no va todo bien, (*with machine etc*) esto no marcha bien, esto funciona mal; **sth is ~ in your calculations** algo está mal en tu cálculo; **what's ~ with you?** ¿qué te pasa?; **is anything ~?** ¿pasa algo?; **we found nothing ~** no encontramos nada fuera de lugar; **to say sth ~** decir algo que no está bien, decir algo inoportuno; **it would not be ~ for him to say thank you** no le estaría mal dar las gracias.
amity ['æmɪtɪ] N concordia *f*, amistad *f*.
AMM N ABBR of **antimissile missile** misil *m* antimisil.
Amman [ə'mɑːn] N Ammán *m*.
ammeter ['æmɪtəʳ] N amperímetro *m*.
ammo* ['æməʊ] N = **ammunition**.
ammonal ['æmənəl] N amonal *m*.
ammonia [ə'məʊnɪə] N amoniaco *m*, amoníaco *m*; **liquid ~** amoníaco *m* líquido.
ammonium [ə'məʊnɪəm] N: **~ hydroxide** hidróxido *m* amónico; **~ sulphate** sulfato *m* amónico.
ammunition [ˌæmjʊ'nɪʃən] N (a) municiones *fpl*; **~ belt** cinturón *m* de municiones; **~ dump, ~ store** depósito *m* de municiones; **~ pouch** cartuchera *f*. (b) (*fig*) argumentos *mpl*, razones *fpl*.
amnesia [æm'niːzɪə] N amnesia *f*.
amnesiac [æm'niːzɪæk] ADJ amnésico.
amnesty ['æmnɪstɪ] [1] N amnistía *f*, indulto *m* general; **to give** (*or* **grant**) **an ~ to sb** amnistiar a uno; **A~ International** Amnistía *f*

Internacional.

[2] VT amnistiar, indultar.

amniocentesis [ˌæmnɪəʊsenˈtiːsɪs] N amniocéntesis f.

amniotic [ˈæmnɪˈɒtɪk] ADJ: ~ **fluid** líquido m amniótico.

amoeba, (US) **ameba** [əˈmiːbə] N, PL **amoebas** (US **amebas**), **amoebae** amiba f, ameba f.

amoebic [əˈmiːbɪk] ADJ amébico; ~ **dysentery** disentería f amébica.

amok [əˈmɒk] ADV = **amuck**.

among(st) [əˈmʌŋ(st)] PREP entre, en medio de; **from ~** de entre; ~ **the Ruritanians it is deemed a virtue** entre ruritanios se considera como una virtud; **he is ~ those who know** es de los que saben; **it is not ~ the names I have** no figura entre los nombres que tengo; **this is ~ the possibilities** esto figura en las posibilidades; **they quarrelled ~ themselves** riñeron entre sí; **one can say that ~ friends** eso se puede decir entre amigos.

amoral [eɪˈmɒrəl] ADJ amoral.

amorality [ˌeɪmɒˈrælɪtɪ] N amoralidad f.

amorous [ˈæmərəs] ADJ enamorado, enamoradizo; cariñoso; (pej: man) mujeriego; **he made ~ advances to his secretary** requebró de amores a su secretaria; **after two drinks she became quite ~** después de dos tragos se puso algo caliente*.

amorously [ˈæmərəslɪ] ADV amorosamente.

amorphous [əˈmɔːfəs] ADJ amorfo.

amortizable [əˈmɔːtɪzəbl] ADJ amortizable; ~ **loan** préstamo m amortizable.

amortization [əˌmɔːtɪˈzeɪʃən] N amortización f.

amortize [əˈmɔːtaɪz] VT amortizar.

amount [əˈmaʊnt] N (a) (total) suma f, importe m; **to the ~ of** hasta un total de; por la suma de, por el valor de; **debts to the ~ of £100** deudas fpl que suman 100 libras; **check in the ~ of $50** (US) cheque m por valor de 50 dólares.

(b) (quantity) cantidad f; **in small ~s** en pequeñas cantidades; **there is quite an ~ left** queda bastante; **I have any ~ of time** tengo mucho tiempo; **we used to drink any ~ of that** bebíamos grandes cantidades de eso; **we have had any ~ of trouble** hemos tenido un sinnúmero de problemas; **no ~ of arguing will help** es totalmente inútil discutir.

▼◆**amount to** VT (a) ascender a, sumar, subir a.

(b) (fig) equivaler a, significar, venir a ser; **it ~s to the same thing** es igual, viene a ser lo mismo; **this ~s to a refusal** esto equivale a una negativa; **it doesn't ~ to much** apenas es significativo, viene a ser poca cosa; **he'll never ~ to much** siempre será una nulidad, es un pobre hombre.

amour [əˈmʊər] N amorío m, aventura f amorosa.

amour-propre [ˈæmʊəˈprɒpr] N amor m propio.

amp [æmp] N, **ampere** [ˈæmpeər] N amperio m; **ampere-hour** amperio-hora m (PL: amperios-hora mpl); **a 13 amp plug** una clavija de 13 amperios.

amperage [ˈæmpərɪdʒ] N amperaje m.

ampersand [ˈæmpəsænd] N el signo & (que significa and).

amphetamine [æmˈfetəmiːn] N anfetamina f.

amphibia [æmˈfɪbɪə] NPL anfibios mpl.

amphibian [æmˈfɪbɪən] [1] ADJ anfibio.

[2] N anfibio m.

amphibious [æmˈfɪbɪəs] ADJ anfibio.

amphitheatre, (US) **amphitheater** [ˈæmfɪˌθɪətər] N anfiteatro m.

Amphitryon [æmˈfɪtrɪən] NM Anfitrión.

amphora [ˈæmfərə] N, PL **amphorae** [ˈæmfəriː] ánfora f.

ample [ˈæmpl] ADJ (a) (large) room etc amplio, ancho, espacioso, extenso; garment amplio, grande. (b) (enough and to spare) bastante, suficiente; **there is ~ room for it** hay más que suficiente espacio para él; **there was an ~ supply of food** había comida abundante; **she has ~ means** tiene medios más que suficientes; **we have ~ reason to believe that ...** tenemos razones sobradas para creer que ...; **thanks, I have ~** gracias, tengo bastante.

amplification [ˌæmplɪfɪˈkeɪʃən] N amplificación f (also Tech); explicación f; desarrollo m.

amplifier [ˈæmplɪfaɪər] N amplificador m.

amplify [ˈæmplɪfaɪ] VT sound amplificar (also Rad), aumentar; statement etc explicar, añadir comentarios a; argument desarrollar; **he refused to ~ his remarks** se negó a dar más comentarios.

amplitude [ˈæmplɪtjuːd] N amplitud f.

amply [ˈæmplɪ] ADV ampliamente; bastante, suficiente; abundantemente; **you were ~ justified** tuviste razón de sobra; **the room is ~ big enough** el cuarto es más que suficientemente grande; **we are ~ supplied with food** tenemos abundancia de comida.

ampoule, (US) **ampule** [ˈæmpuːl] N ampolla f.

amputate [ˈæmpjʊteɪt] VT amputar.

amputation [ˌæmpjʊˈteɪʃən] N amputación f.

amputee [ˌæmpjʊˈtiː] N persona f cuya pierna (or cuyo brazo) ha sido amputada (amputado).

Amsterdam [ˈæmstəˈdæm] N Amsterdam m.

amt ABBR of **amount** importe m, impte.

Amtrak [ˈæmtræk] N (US) empresa nacional de ferrocarriles de los EEUU.

amuck [əˈmʌk] ADV: **to run ~** enloquecer, desbocarse, desmandarse; (fig) conducirse como un loco, hacer locuras, mostrarse violento, atacar a ciegas.

amulet [ˈæmjʊlɪt] N amuleto m.

amuse [əˈmjuːz] [1] VT (a) (cause mirth to) divertir, hacer reír; **this ~d everybody** hizo reír a todos; **we are not ~d** no nos cae en gracia; **to be ~d at** (or by) divertirse con, reírse con; **with an ~d expression** con gesto risueño. (b) (entertain) divertir, entretener, distraer; **to keep sb ~d** entretener a uno; **this should keep them ~d for years** esto deberá ocupar su atención por muchos años.

[2] VR: **to ~ o.s.** distraerse (doing haciendo); **run along and ~ yourselves** idos a jugar; **you'll have to ~ yourselves for a while** tendréis que entreteneros (a vosotros mismos) por un rato; **we ~d ourselves a good deal** lo pasamos muy bien.

amusement [əˈmjuːzmənt] N (a) (amusing thing) diversión f, entretenimiento m; ~**s** (in fairground) máquinas fpl electrónicas, máquinas fpl tragaperras; ~ **arcade** galería f de atracciones; ~ **park** parque m de atracciones; **place of ~** sitio m de recreo.

(b) (pastime) pasatiempo m, recreo m; **a town with plenty of ~s** una ciudad que ofrece muchas diversiones; **it is for ~ only** es una diversión nada más; **they do it for ~ only** lo hacen sólo para divertirse, es un pasatiempo nada más.

(c) (laughter) risa f, regocijo m; **with a look of ~** con mirada risueña; **there was general ~ at this** al oír esto se rieron todos; **much to my ~** con gran regocijo mío; **to conceal one's ~** ocultar sus ganas de reír, aguantarse la risa.

amusing [əˈmjuːzɪŋ] ADJ divertido, gracioso, entretenido.

amusingly [əˈmjuːzɪŋlɪ] ADV de modo divertido, graciosamente.

an [æn, ən, n] INDEF ART = **a²**.

ANA N (US) (a) ABBR of **American Newspaper Association**. (b) ABBR of **American Nurses' Association**.

anabolic [ænəˈbɒlɪk] ADJ: ~ **steroid** esteroide m anabolizante.

anachronism [əˈnækrənɪzəm] N anacronismo m.

anachronistic [əˌnækrəˈnɪstɪk] ADJ anacrónico.

anacoluthon [ˌænəkəˈluːθɒn] N anacoluto m.

anaconda [ˌænəˈkɒndə] N anaconda f.

Anacreon [əˈnækrɪən] NM Anacreonte.

anaemia, (US) **anemia** [əˈniːmɪə] N anemia f.

anaemic, (US) **anemic** [əˈniːmɪk] ADJ (Med) anémico; (fig) soso, fofo, insípido, débil.

anaerobic, (US) **anerobic** [ˌænɛəˈrəʊbɪk] ADJ anaerobio.

anaesthesia, (US) **anesthesia** [ˌænɪsˈθiːzɪə] N anestesia f.

anaesthetic, (US) **anesthetic** [ˌænɪsˈθetɪk] [1] ADJ anestésico.

[2] N anestésico m; **to be under an ~** estar anestesiado; **to give sb an ~**, **to put sb under an ~** anestesiar a uno.

anaesthetist, (US) **anesthetist** [æˈniːsθɪtɪst] N anestesista mf.

anaesthetize, (US) **anesthetize** [æˈniːsθɪtaɪz] VT anestesiar.

anagram [ˈænəgræm] N anagrama m.

anal [ˈeɪnəl] ADJ anal.

analgesia [ˌænælˈdʒiːzɪə] N analgesia f.

analgesic [ˌænælˈdʒiːsɪk] [1] ADJ analgésico.

[2] N analgésico m.

analog [ˈænəlɒg] N (US) = **analogue**.

analogical [ˌænəˈlɒdʒɪkəl] ADJ analógico.

analogous [əˈnæləgəs] ADJ análogo (to, with a); afín, semejante.

analogue, (US) **analog** [ˈænəlɒg] N cosa f (or palabra f etc) análoga; ~ **computer** ordenador m analógico.

analogy [əˈnælədʒɪ] N analogía f; afinidad f, semejanza f; **by ~ with**, **on the ~ of** por analogía con; **to argue from** (or by) ~ razonar por analogía; **to draw an ~ between** aducir una analogía entre.

analysand [əˈnælɪˌsænd] N sujeto m analizado, analizando m.

analyse, (US) **analyze** [ˈænəlaɪz] VT (a) analizar. (b) (esp US) psicoanalizar.

analyser, (US) **analyzer** [ˈænəlaɪzər] N (Tech) analizador m.

▼**analysis** [əˈnæləsɪs] N, PL **analyses** [əˈnælɪsiːz] (a) análisis m; **in the final** (or last) ~ en último término, en fin de cuentas. (b) (esp US) psicoanálisis m.

analyst [ˈænəlɪst] N (a) analista mf; **public ~** jefe mf del laboratorio municipal. (b) (esp US) psicoanalista mf.

analytic(al) [ˌænəˈlɪtɪk(əl)] ADJ analítico.

analyze [ˈænəlaɪz] VT (US) = **analyse**.

analyzer (US) = **analyser**.

anapaest, (US) **anapest** [ˈænəpiːst] N anapesto m.

anaphoric [ˌænəˈfɒrɪk] ADJ anafórico.

anarchic(al) [æˈnɑːkɪk(əl)] ADJ anárquico.

anarchism [ˈænəkɪzəm] N anarquismo m.

anarchist [ˈænəkɪst] [1] ADJ anarquista.

[2] N anarquista mf.

anarchistic [ˌænəˈkɪstɪk] ADJ anarquista.

anarcho- [æˈnɑːkəʊ] PREF anarco-; ~**syndicalism** anarcosindicalismo *m*.

anarchy ['ænəkɪ] N anarquía *f*.

anathema [ə'næθɪmə] N (*Rel, fig*) anatema *m*; (*fig*) abominación *f*; **he is ~ to me** no le puedo ver, para mí es inaguantable; **the idea is ~ to her** para ella la idea es una abominación, la idea le resulta odiosa.

anathematize [ə'næθɪmətaɪz] VT anatematizar.

anatomical [,ænə'tɒmɪkəl] ADJ anatómico.

anatomist [ə'nætəmɪst] N anatomista *mf*.

anatomize [ə'nætəmaɪz] VT anatomizar; (*fig*) analizar minuciosamente.

anatomy [ə'nætəmɪ] N (**a**) anatomía *f*, estructura *f*. (**b**) (*surface of body*) cuerpo *m* humano; carnes *fpl*; (**: bottom*) nalgas *fpl*, posaderas *fpl*.

ANC N ABBR *of* **African National Congress** Congreso *m* Nacional Africano.

ancestor ['ænsɪstər] N antepasado *m*, -a *f*; **~s** PL antepasados *mpl*, abuelos *mpl*, ascendientes *mpl*.

ancestral [æn'sestrəl] ADJ ancestral, hereditario; **~ home** casa *f* solariega, solar *m*.

ancestress ['ænsɪstrɪs] N antepasada *f*.

ancestry ['ænsɪstrɪ] N ascendencia *f*, abolengo *m*, linaje *m*, estirpe *f*.

anchor ['æŋkər] ① N ancla *f*, áncora *f*; **to be** (*or* **lie, ride**) **at ~** estar al ancla, estar anclado; **to cast** (*or* **drop**) **~** echar anclas; **to weigh ~** levar anclas.
② VT poner sobre el ancla; (*fig*) sujetar (*to* a), asegurar.
③ VI anclar, fondear.

anchorage ['æŋkərɪdʒ] N ancladero *m*, fondeadero *m*; **~ dues**, **~ fee** anclaje *m*.

anchorite ['æŋkəraɪt] N anacoreta *mf*.

anchor-man ['æŋkəmæn] N, PL **anchor-men** ['æŋkəmen] (*TV*) hombre *m* ancla, presentador *m*; (*fig*) hombre *m* clave.

anchovy ['æntʃəvɪ] N (*live, fresh*) boquerón *m*; (*salted, tinned*) anchoa *f*.

ancient ['eɪnʃənt] ① ADJ (**a**) antiguo; **in ~ days** en la antigüedad, hace muchísimo tiempo; **~ Greek** griego *m* antiguo; **~ history** historia *f* antigua; **that's ~ history!*** ¡eso pertenece a la historia!; **~ monument** (*Brit*) monumento *m* histórico; **~ Rome** Roma *f* clásica; **remains of ~ times** restos *mpl* de la antigüedad.
(**b**) (*hum*) *person* viejo, anciano; *clothing, object* muy viejo, anticuado, totalmente pasado de moda; **we went in his ~ car** fuimos en su antiquísimo coche; **he's getting pretty ~** va para viejo.
② N (*hum*) viejo *m*, vejete *m*; **the ~s** los antiguos; *see also* OLD .

ancillary [æn'sɪlərɪ] ADJ subordinado (*to* a), ancilar, secundario; auxiliar; **~ staff** (*Brit Scol*) personal *m* auxiliar; **~ workers** personal *m* auxiliar.

and [ænd, ənd, nd, ən] CONJ (**a**) y, (*before i-, hi-*) e, *eg* franceses e ingleses, padre e hijo; **~?** ¿y después?, ¿y qué más?; **~/or** y/o; **better ~ better** cada vez mejor; **more ~ more** cada vez más.
(**b**) (*in numbers*) **a hundred ~ one** ciento uno; **two hundred ~ ten** doscientos diez; **five hours ~ twenty minutes** cinco horas veinte minutos; **ten dollars ~ fifty cents** diez dólares y (*or* con) cincuenta centavos.
(**c**) (*negative sense*) ni; **you can't buy ~ sell here** aquí no se permite comprar ni vender.
(**d**) (*repetition, continuation*) **she cried ~ cried** no dejaba de llorar, lloraba sin parar; **I rang ~ rang** llamé repetidas veces; **he talked ~ talked without effect** habló incansablemente pero sin lograr nada, por mucho que hablase no logró nada.
(**e**) (*before infins*) **come ~ see me** ven a verme; **try ~ do it** trata de hacerlo, hazlo si puedes; **wait ~ see** espera y verás.

┌─ AND ──────────── *see also main entry* ─┐

In order to avoid two "i" sounds coming together, *and* is translated by *e* not *y* before words beginning with *i* and *hi* and before the letter *y* used on its own:
...Spain and Italy...
...*España e Italia*...
...grapes and figs...
...*uvas e higos*...
...words ending in S and Y...
...*palabras terminadas en S e Y*...
NOTE: Words beginning with *hie* are preceded by *y*, since *hie* is not pronounced "i":
...coal and iron mines...
...*minas de carbón y hierro*...

└──┘

Andalusia [,ændə'luːzɪə] N Andalucía *f*.

Andalusian [,ændə'luːzɪən] ① ADJ andaluz.
② N (**a**) andaluz *m*, -uza *f*. (**b**) (*Ling*) andaluz *m*.

Andean ['ændɪən] ADJ andino, de los Andes.

Andes ['ændiːz] NPL Andes *mpl*.

andiron ['ændaɪən] N morillo *m*.

Andorra [,æn'dɔːrə] N Andorra *f*.

Andorran [,æn'dɔːrən] ① ADJ andorrano.
② N andorrano *m*, -a *f*.

Andrew ['ændruː] NM Andrés.

androcentric [,ændrəʊ'sentrɪk] ADJ androcéntrico.

androcentricity [,ændrəʊsen'trɪsɪtɪ] N androcentrismo *m*.

androgen ['ændrədʒən] N andrógeno *m*.

androgenic ['ændrə'dʒenɪk] ADJ androgénico.

androgynous [æn'drɒdʒɪnəs] ADJ andrógino.

androgyny [æn'drɒdʒɪnɪ] N androginia *f*.

android ['ændrɔɪd] N androide *m*.

Andromache [æn'drɒməkɪ] NF Andrómaca.

Andromeda [æn'drɒmɪdə] NF Andrómeda *f*.

androsterone [æn'drɒstə,rəʊn] N androsterona *f*.

Andy ['ændɪ] N *familiar form of* **Andrew**.

anecdotal [,ænɪk'dəʊtəl] ADJ anecdótico.

anecdote ['ænɪkdəʊt] N anécdota *f*.

anemia [ə'niːmɪə] N (*US*) = **anaemia**.

anemic [ə'niːmɪk] ADJ (*US*) = **anaemic**.

anemone [ə'nemənɪ] N (*Bot, Zool*) anemone *f*, anémona *f*, anemona *f*.

anaerobic [,æneə'rəʊbɪk] ADJ (*US*) = **anaerobic**.

aneroid ['ænərɔɪd] ADJ aneroide; **~ barometer** barómetro *m* aneroide.

anesthesia [,ænɪs'θiːzɪə] N (*US*) = **anaesthesia**.

anesthesiologist [,ænɪs,θiːzɪ'ɒlədʒɪst] N (*US*) anestesista *mf*.

anesthetic [,ænɪs'θetɪk] ADJ, N (*US*) = **anaesthetic**.

anesthetist [æ'niːsθɪtɪst] N (*US*) = **anaesthetist**.

anesthetize [æ'niːsθɪtaɪz] VT (*US*) = **anaesthetize**.

aneurism, aneurysm ['ænjə,rɪzəm] N aneurisma *m*.

anew [ə'njuː] ADV de nuevo, otra vez; **to begin ~** comenzar de nuevo, volver a comenzar, recomenzar.

angel ['eɪndʒəl] N (**a**) ángel *m*; **A~ of Darkness** ángel *m* de tinieblas; **I'm on the side of the ~s** yo estoy de parte de los ángeles; **talk of ~s!** hablando del ruin de Roma, por la puerta asoma; **V guardian**.
(**b**) (**: person*) **yes, ~!** ¡sí, querida!, ¡sí, mi amor!; **she's an ~** es un ángel; **be an ~ and give me a cigarette** ¿me das un pitillo, amor?
(**c**) (*Fin*: esp Theat*) caballo *m* blanco*, promotor *m*, -ora *f*.

angel dust ['eɪndʒəl'dʌst] N (*esp US*) polvo *m* de ángel.

Angeleno [,ændʒə'liːnəʊ] N habitante *mf* de Los Angeles.

angelfish ['eɪndʒəlfɪʃ] N angelote *m*, pez *m* ángel.

angelic(al) [æn'dʒelɪk(əl)] ADJ angélico.

angelica [æn'dʒelɪkə] N angélica *f*.

angelus ['ændʒɪləs] N ángelus *m*.

anger ['æŋgər] ① N cólera *f*, ira *f*, furia *f*; **words spoken in ~** palabras *fpl* furiosas; **to move** (*or* **rouse**) **sb to ~** provocar a uno a cólera, encolerizar a uno; **to speak in ~** hablar indignado, hablar coléricamente.
② VT enojar, provocar, encolerizar.

angina [æn'dʒaɪnə] N angina *f*; **~ pectoris** angina *f* del pecho.

angiogram ['ændʒɪəʊgræm] N angiograma *m*.

angiosperm ['ændʒɪə,spɜːm] N angiosperma *f*.

angle¹ ['æŋgl] ① N (**a**) ángulo *m* (*also Math*); **~ of climb** (*Aer*) ángulo *m* de subida; **it is leaning at an ~ of 80°** está ladeado en un ángulo de 80°; **to be at an ~ to** formar ángulo con; **to cut a pipe at an ~** cortar un tubo al sesgo; **to look at a building from a different ~** contemplar un edificio desde otro sitio, tener de un edificio una nueva perspectiva.
(**b**) (*fig*) punto *m* de vista; opinión *f*; criterio *m*; aspecto *m*; **look at it from my ~** considere la cosa desde mi punto de vista; **he has a different ~** tiene otro modo de enfocar la cuestión, en este asunto su criterio es distinto; **what's your ~ on this?** ¿tú qué opinas de esto?; **that's a new ~ to the problem** ése es un aspecto nuevo del problema; **to look at a problem from all ~s** estudiar un problema en todos sus aspectos.
② VT (**a**) (*Sport*) *shot* ladear, sesgar, jugar en diagonal.
(**b**) *report etc* presentar bajo una luz especial; ajustar de acuerdo con intereses concretos; **this article is ~d towards non-specialists** este artículo se dirige preferentemente a los no especializados.

angle² ['æŋgl] VI (**a**) pescar (con caña) (*for trout* truchas). (**b**) **to ~ for** (*fig*) ir a la caza de, tratar de pescar, intrigar para conseguir.

angle-iron ['æŋgl,aɪən] N hierro *m* angular.

Anglepoise ['æŋglpɔɪz] ® N: **~ lamp** lámpara *f* de estudio.

angler ['æŋglər] N pescador *m*, -ora *f* (de caña).

anglerfish ['æŋgləfɪʃ] N rape *m*.

Angles ['æŋglz] NPL anglos *mpl*.

Anglican ['æŋglɪkən] ① ADJ anglicano.
② N anglicano *m*, -a *f*.

Anglicanism ['æŋglɪkənɪzəm] N anglicanismo *m*.

anglicism ['æŋglɪsɪzəm] N anglicismo *m*, inglesismo *m*.

anglicist ['æŋglɪsɪst] N anglicista *mf*.

anglicize ['æŋglɪsaɪz] VT dar forma inglesa a.

angling ['æŋglɪŋ] N pesca *f* (con caña).

Anglo* ['æŋgləʊ] N (*US*) blanco *m*, -a *f*, americano *m*, -a *f* (*de origen no hispano*).

Anglo... ['æŋgləʊ] PREF anglo...; **~-American relations** relaciones *fpl* angloamericanas; **an ~-French project** un proyecto anglofrancés.
Anglo-American ['æŋgləʊə'merɪkən] [1] ADJ angloamericano.
[2] N angloamericano *m*, -a *f*.
Anglo-Asian ['æŋgləʊ'eɪʃn] [1] ADJ angloasiático.
[2] N angloasiático *m*, -a *f*.
Anglo-Catholic ['æŋgləʊ'kæθlɪk] [1] ADJ anglocatólico.
[2] N anglocatólico *m*, -a *f*.
Anglo-Catholicism ['æŋgləʊkə'θɒlɪsɪzəm] N anglocatolicismo *m*.
Anglo-Indian ['æŋgləʊ'ɪndɪən] [1] ADJ angloindio.
[2] N angloindio *m*, -a *f*.
Anglo-Irish ['æŋgləʊ'aɪərɪʃ] ADJ anglo-irlandés.
Anglo-Norman [,æŋgləʊ'nɔːmən] [1] ADJ anglonormando.
[2] N **(a)** anglonormando *m*, -a *f*. **(b)** (*Ling*) anglonormando *m*.
anglophile ['æŋgləʊfaɪl] N anglófilo *m*, -a *f*.
anglophobe ['æŋgləʊfəʊb] N anglófobo *m*, -a *f*.
anglophobia [,æŋgləʊ'fəʊbjə] N anglofobia *f*.
anglophone ['æŋgləʊfəʊn] [1] ADJ anglófono.
[2] N anglófono *m*, -a *f*.
Anglo-Saxon ['æŋgləʊ'sæksən] [1] ADJ anglosajón.
[2] N **(a)** anglosajón *m*, -ona *f*. **(b)** (*Ling*) anglosajón *m*.

ANGLO-SAXON

ⓘ *La lengua anglosajona, **Anglo-Saxon**, también llamada **Old English**, se extendió en Inglaterra tras las invasiones de pueblos germánicos en el siglo V y continuó usándose hasta la conquista normanda de la isla. Hoy en día sigue siendo una parte importante del idioma inglés. Como ejemplos de palabras de origen anglosajón que aún se usan tenemos **man, child, eat, love** o **harvest**. Muchas de las palabras obscenas corrientes también son de origen anglosajón, por ejemplo **shit** o **bollocks**.*
El término se usa también para describir el mundo angloparlante, sobre todo si tiene su origen o está muy influido por costumbres inglesas, si bien hay personas de origen escocés, irlandés, galés o de minorías étnicas que prefieren no usarlo.

Angola [æŋ'gəʊlə] N Angola *f*.
Angolan [æŋ'gəʊlən] [1] ADJ angoleño.
[2] N angoleño *m*, -a *f*.
angora [æŋ'gɔːrə] N angora *mf*.
angostura [,æŋgə'stjʊərə] N angostura *f*: **~ bitters** ® bíter *m* de angostura.
Angoulême [ɑːŋguˈlɛm] N Angulema *f*.
angrily ['æŋgrɪlɪ] ADV coléricamente, airadamente; **he protested ~** protestó colérico.
angry ['æŋgrɪ] [1] ADJ **(a)** enfadado, enojado, airado; **in an ~ voice** en tono colérico; **she gave me an ~ look** me miró enfadada; **~ young man** (*Brit*) joven *m* airado; **to be ~** estar enfadado (*LAm*: enojado) (*about* por; *at, with* con); **you won't be ~ if I tell you?** no te vayas a ofender si te lo digo; **to get ~** enfadarse, ponerse furioso, indignarse; **this sort of thing makes me ~** estas cosas me sacan de quicio.
(b) (*fig*) *sea* bravo; *sky* tormentoso, borrascoso, que amenaza tormenta.
(c) (*Med*) inflamado.
[2] NPL **the angries** los airados *mpl*.
angst [æŋst] N angustia *f*, congoja *f*.
angstrom ['æŋstrʌm] N angstrom *m*.
anguish ['æŋgwɪʃ] N (*bodily*) dolor *m* agudo, tormentos *mpl*; (*mental*) angustia *f*, congoja *f*; **to be in ~** padecer tormentos, sufrir lo indecible.
anguished ['æŋgwɪʃt] ADJ acongojado, afligido, angustiado.
angular ['æŋgjʊləʳ] ADJ angular; *face etc* anguloso.
angularity [,æŋgjʊ'lærətɪ] N angularidad *f*; angulosidad *f*.
aniline ['ænɪliːn] N anilina *f*; **~ dyes** colorantes *mpl* de anilina.
anima ['ænɪmə] N ánima *f*, alma *f*.
animal ['ænɪməl] [1] ATTR animal; **~ fats** grasas *fpl* de animal; **~ husbandry** cría *f* de animales; **~ instinct** instinto *m* animal; **~ kingdom** reino *m* animal; **~ rights movement** movimiento *m* pro derechos de los animales; **~ spirits** vitalidad *f*.
[2] N animal *m*; (*horse etc*) bestia *f*; (*insect etc*) bicho *m*; **you ~!** ¡animal!*, ¡bestia!*
animalcule [,ænɪ'mælkjuːl] N animálculo *m*.
animality [,ænɪ'mælətɪ] N animalidad *f*.
animate [1] ['ænɪmɪt] ADJ vivo, que tiene vida.
[2] ['ænɪmeɪt] VT animar, infundir vida a (*or* en); vivificar, estimular; alentar.
animated ['ænɪmeɪtɪd] ADJ animado; vivo, vivaz, vigoroso; *discussion* vivo; **~ cartoon** dibujos *mpl* animados; **to become ~** animarse.
animatedly ['ænɪmeɪtɪdlɪ] ADV *talk etc* animadamente.
animation [,ænɪ'meɪʃən] N animación *f*; vivacidad *f*, viveza *f*.
animator ['ænɪmeɪtəʳ] N (*Cine*) animador *m*, -ora *f*.
animatronics [,ænɪmə'trɒnɪks] NPL animación *f* por ordenador, animatronics *mpl*.

animism ['ænɪmɪzəm] N animismo *m*.
animist ['ænɪmɪst] [1] ADJ animista.
[2] N animista *mf*.
animosity [,ænɪ'mɒsɪtɪ] N animosidad *f*, rencor *m*, hostilidad *f*.
animus ['ænɪməs] N odio *m*, rencor *m*.
anise ['ænɪs] N anís *m*.
aniseed ['ænɪsiːd] N anís *m*; (*strictly*) grano *m* de anís; **~ ball** bombón *m* de anís.
anisette [,ænɪ'zet] N anisete *m*, anís *m* .
Anjou [ɑːŋ'ʒuː] N Anjeo *m*.
Ankara ['æŋkərə] N Ankara *f*.
ankle ['æŋkl] N tobillo *m*.
anklebone ['æŋklbəʊn] N hueso *m* del tobillo, taba *f*, astrágalo *m*.
ankle-deep ['æŋkl'diːp] ADV: **to be ~ in water** estar metido hasta los tobillos en el agua; **the water is only ~** el agua llega a los tobillos nada más.
ankle joint ['æŋkldʒɔɪnt] N articulación *f* del tobillo.
ankle sock ['æŋklsɒk] N (*Brit*) escarpín *m*.
ankle strap ['æŋklstræp] N tirita *f* tobillera.
anklet ['æŋklɪt] N brazalete *m* para el tobillo, ajorca *f* para el pie; (*US*) calcetín *m* corto.
ankylosis [,æŋkɪ'ləʊsɪs] N anquilosis *f*.
Ann [æn] NF Ana; **~ Boleyn** Ana Bolena.
ann. **(a)** ABBR *of* **annual**. **(b)** (*Fin*) ABBR *of* **annuity**.
annalist ['ænəlɪst] N analista *mf*, cronista *mf*.
annals ['ænəlz] NPL anales *mpl*, crónica *f*; **in all the ~ of crime** en toda la historia del crimen; **never in the ~ of human endeavour** nunca en la historia de los esfuerzos humanos.
Anne [æn] NF Ana; **Queen ~'s dead!*** eso no es noticia, eso lo tenemos archisabido.
anneal [ə'niːl] VT recocer; templar.
annex [ə'neks] VT **(a)** *territory* anexar. **(b)** *document* adjuntar, añadir (*to* a).
annexation [,ænek'seɪʃən] N anexión *f*.
annexe, (*US*) **annex** ['æneks] N **(a)** (*building*) pabellón *m* separado, dependencia *f*, edificio *m* anexo. **(b)** (*to document*) apéndice *m*, anejo *m*.
annihilate [ə'naɪəleɪt] VT aniquilar.
annihilation [ə,naɪə'leɪʃən] N aniquilación *f*, aniquilamiento *m*.
anniversary [,ænɪ'vɜːsərɪ] N aniversario *m*; **the Góngora ~ dinner** el banquete para festejar el aniversario de Góngora.
Anno Domini ['ænəʊ'dɒmɪnaɪ] N (*gen abbr* AD) **(a)** **~ 43** el año 43 después de Jesucristo; **the third century ~** el siglo tercero de Cristo. **(b)** (*·*) vejez *f*, edad *f*.
annotate ['ænəʊteɪt] VT anotar, comentar.
annotation [,ænəʊ'teɪʃən] N anotación *f*, apunte *m*, comentario *m*.
▼ **announce** [ə'naʊns] VT anunciar; informar; proclamar; declarar; hacer saber, comunicar; **then he ~d 'I won't'** luego declaró 'No quiero'; **it is ~d from London that ...** se comunica desde Londres que ...; **we regret to ~ the death of X** lamentamos tener que participar la muerte de X.
announcement [ə'naʊnsmənt] N anuncio *m*; informe *m*; proclama *f*; notificación *f*; declaración *f*; aviso *m*; **~ of birth** (aviso *m*) natalicio *m*; **~ of death** (nota *f*) necrológica *f*.
announcer [ə'naʊnsəʳ] N (*Rad, TV*) locutor *m*, -ora *f*, presentador *m*, -ora *f*, speaker *mf*; (*at airport etc*) el (*or* la) que hace anuncios.
▼ **annoy** [ə'nɔɪ] VT molestar, fastidiar, irritar; **to be ~ed** estar enfadado (*about* por; *at, with* con); **don't be ~ed if I can't come** no te enfades si no puedo venir; **is this man ~ing you, madam?** ¿le está molestando este hombre, señora?; **to get ~ed** enfadarse, molestarse, incomodarse; **it's no good getting ~ed with me** de nada sirve enfadarte conmigo.
annoyance [ə'nɔɪəns] N **(a)** (*state*) enojo *m*, irritación *f*; contrariedad *f*; disgusto *m*; **to my ~ I find that ...** con gran disgusto mío descubro que ... **(b)** (*cause, thing*) molestia *f*.
annoying [ə'nɔɪɪŋ] ADJ molesto, fastidioso, engorroso; *person* pesado, importuno; **how very ~!** ¡qué fastidio!; **it's ~ to have to +** *infin* me molesta tener que + *infin*, es una lata* tener que + *infin*.
annoyingly [ə'nɔɪɪŋlɪ] ADV de modo fastidioso; pesadamente, importunamente; **and then, ~ enough ...** y luego, para fastidiarnos ...; **the radio was ~ loud** la radio nos molestó con su ruido; **he has an ~ loud voice** tiene una voz tan fuerte que molesta.
annual ['ænjʊəl] [1] ADJ anual; **~ general meeting** (*Brit*) junta *f* general (anual); **~ income** ingresos *mpl* anuales; **~ leave** vacaciones *fpl* (anuales); **~(ized) percentage rate** tasa *f* de interés anual; **~ premium** prima *f* anual; **~ rate** tipo *m* anual; **~ report** informe *m* anual, memoria *f* anual; **~ return** (*for tax*) declaración *f* anual; (*report*) informe *m* anual; **~ ring** anillo *m* anual, cerco *m* anual; **~ statement** informe *m* anual.
[2] N **(a)** (*Bot*) planta *f* anual, anual *m*. **(b)** (*book*) anuario *m*.
annually ['ænjʊəlɪ] ADV anualmente, cada año; **£500 ~** 500 libras al

► LANGUAGE IN USE: **announce** → 24.1, 24.2, 24.4, 24.5 **annoy** → 7.3

año.

annuity [ə'njuːɪtɪ] N (also life ~) renta f vitalicia, pensión f vitalicia; anualidad f.

annul [ə'nʌl] VT anular, invalidar; cancelar; *marriage* anular; *law* revocar, abrogar.

annulment [ə'nʌlmənt] N anulación f, invalidación f, cancelación f; revocación f, abrogación f.

annum ['ænəm] N V **per**.

Annunciation [ə,nʌnsɪ'eɪʃən] N Anunciación f.

anode ['ænəʊd] N ánodo m.

anodize ['ænədaɪz] VT anodizar.

anodyne ['ænəʊdaɪn] ① ADJ anodino.
② N anodino m.

anoint [ə'nɔɪnt] VT untar; (Eccl) ungir.

anointing [ə'nɔɪntɪŋ] N: ~ **of the sick** (Rel) unción f de los enfermos.

anomalous [ə'nɒmələs] ADJ anómalo.

anomaly [ə'nɒməlɪ] N anomalía f.

anon¹ [ə'nɒn] ADV (a) luego, dentro de poco; **I'll see you** ~ nos veremos luego. (b) (††) **ever and** ~ a menudo, de vez en cuando.

anon² [ə'nɒn] ABBR = **anonymous**.

anonymity [,ænə'nɪmɪtɪ] N (in general) anonimia f, anonimato m; (particular case) anónimo m; **to preserve one's** ~ conservar el anónimo.

anonymous [ə'nɒnɪməs] ADJ anónimo; ~ **letter** anónimo m; **he wishes to remain** ~ no quiere que se publique su nombre, quiere conservar el anónimo.

anonymously [ə'nɒnɪməslɪ] ADV anónimamente; **the book came out** ~ salió el libro sin nombre de autor; **he gave £100** ~ dio 100 libras sin revelar su nombre.

anorak ['ænəræk] N anorac m, anorak m.

anorectic [,ænə'rektɪk] = **anorexic**.

anorexia [,ænə'reksɪə] N anorexia f; ~ **nervosa** anorexia f nerviosa.

anorexic [,ænə'reksɪk] ① ADJ anoréxico.
② N anoréxico m, -a f.

▼ **another** [ə'nʌðəʳ] ① ADJ (a) (additional) otro (no art needed, eg ~ **man** otro hombre); ~ **glass?** ¿otra copita?; **take** ~ **5** toma 5 más; **in** ~ **10 years** en otros 10 años; **we need** ~ **2 men** necesitamos 2 hombres más; **not** ~ **minute!** ¡ni un minuto más!; **there are** ~ **2 months to go** faltan todavía 2 meses; **without** ~ **word** sin decir una palabra más, sin más palabras.
(b) (similar) otro; **he's** ~ **Hitler** es otro Hitler, es un segundo Hitler; **there's not** ~ **painting like it** no hay otro cuadro como éste.
(c) (different) **come** ~ **day** venga otro día; **that is** ~ **matter altogether** eso es un asunto totalmente distinto.
② PRON otro m, otra f; **just such** ~ otro tal; **many** ~ **would hate it** otros muchos lo detestarían; ~ **would have done it this way** cualquier otro lo hubiera hecho de este modo; **taking one with** ~ **they're not bad** tomándolos en conjunto no son nada malos; **if not this time then** ~ si no esta vez, pues otra.
③ REFLEXIVE PRON: **they love one** ~ (2 persons) se quieren (uno a otro), (more than 2 persons) se quieren unos a otros; **they don't speak to one** ~ no se hablan.

A.N. Other [,eɪ,en'ʌðəʳ] N fulano* m, un tipo cualquiera*; **'~'** (in list) 'a concretar'.

anoxia [ə'nɒksɪə] N anoxia f.

anoxic [ə'nɒksɪk] ADJ anóxico.

Ansaphone ['ɑːnsəfəʊn] ® N contestador m automático.

ANSI N (US) ABBR of **American National Standards Institute**.

▼ **answer** ['ɑːnsəʳ] ① N (a) (to question etc) contestación f, respuesta f (to a); (Jur) contestación f a la demanda, réplica f; **in** ~ **to** contestando a; **he smiled in** ~ contestó con una sonrisa; **his only** ~ **was to smile** por toda respuesta, se sonrió; **I knocked but there was no** ~ llamé pero no contestaron; **she's always got an** ~ siempre tiene la respuesta pronta; **to know all the** ~**s** saberlo todo, ser una hacha*; **he's not exactly the** ~ **to a maiden's prayer** no es precisamente el hombre soñado.
(b) (to problem) solución f (to de); **what do you make the** ~? ¿qué solución tienes?; **my** ~ **is to do nothing** mi solución es no hacer nada, yo me propongo no hacer nada; **there is no easy** ~ esto no se resuelve fácilmente; **it's the poor man's** ~ **to champagne** es lo que se sirve el pobre en lugar de champán.
(c) (defence, reason) **there must be an** ~ debe de haber una razón, debe de haber una explicación; **he has an** ~ **to everything** lo justifica todo; **he has a complete** ~ **to the charges** puede probar su inocencia; **there is no** ~ **to the H-bomb** contra la bomba H no hay defensa posible.
▼ ② VT (a) (charge, question etc) contestar a, responder a; *letter* contestar (a); **he** ~**ed not a word** no dijo palabra; **that should** ~ **your question** eso debe resolver (or satisfacer) sus dudas; **God will** ~ **our prayers** Dios escuchará nuestras oraciones; **our prayers have been** ~**ed** nuestras súplicas han sido oídas; **to** ~ **the bell, to** ~ **the door** acudir a la puerta, atender la puerta (LAm); **to** ~ **the telephone** contestar el teléfono; **to** ~ **one's name** contestar a su nombre; **to** ~ **a call for help** acudir a una llamada de socorro.
(b) description, expectations corresponder a, cuadrar con; purpose convenir para; dream realizar.
(c) **to** ~ **the helm** obedecer al timón.
③ VI (a) contestar, responder.
(b) **to** ~ **to** description corresponder a, cuadrar con; **the dog** ~**s to the name of Cipion** el perro atiende por Cipión.
(c) (suffice) servir, convenir.
◆**answer back** VI replicar; (habitually) ser respondón; **don't** ~ **back!** ¡no repliques!
◆**answer for** VT thing responder de, ser responsable de, person responder por; **I'll not** ~ **for the consequences** no me responsabilizo de las consecuencias; **he's got a lot to** ~ **for** tiene la culpa de muchas cosas.

answerable ['ɑːnsərəbl] ADJ (a) question que tiene contestación, problem que admite solución; **the question is not readily** ~ la pregunta no tiene contestación fácil.
(b) (responsible) responsable; **to be** ~ **to sb for sth** ser responsable ante uno de algo; **he's not** ~ **to anyone** no tiene que dar cuentas a nadie.

answer-back ['ɑːnsə,bæk] N: ~ (**code**) código m de respuesta.

answering ['ɑːnsərɪŋ] ATTR: ~ **machine** contestador m automático; ~ **service** servicio m de contestación automática.

ant [ænt] N hormiga f; **to have** ~**s in one's pants*** tener avispas en el culo*.

ANTA N (US) ABBR of **American National Theater and Academy**.

antacid ['ænt'æsɪd] ① ADJ antiácido.
② N antiácido m.

antagonism [æn'tægənɪzəm] N antagonismo m; oposición f, hostilidad f (to a); rivalidad f (between entre).

antagonist [æn'tægənɪst] N adversario m, -a f, antagonista mf.

antagonistic [æn,tægə'nɪstɪk] ADJ antagónico; contrario, opuesto (to a); **I am not in the least** ~ **to the idea** yo no me opongo en lo más mínimo a la idea.

antagonize [æn'tægənaɪz] VT enemistarse con, provocar la enemistad de; **I don't want to** ~ **him** no quiero contrariarle; **he managed to** ~ **everybody** logró ponerse a malas con todos, logró suscitar el antagonismo de todos.

Antarctic [ænt'ɑːktɪk] ① ADJ antártico; ~ **Ocean** Océano m Antártico.
② N: **the** ~ el Antártico.

Antarctica [ænt'ɑːktɪkə] N Antártida f.

Antarctic Circle [ænt'ɑːktɪk'sɜːkl] N Círculo m Polar Antártico.

ante ['æntɪ] (esp US) ① N apuesta f, tanto m; **to raise** (or **up**) **the** ~ aumentar las apuestas.
② VT apostar.
③ VI poner su apuesta.
◆**ante up** VI (US*) pagar, apoquinar*.

ante... ['æntɪ] PREF ante...

anteater ['ænt,iːtəʳ] N oso m hormiguero.

antebellum ['æntɪ'beləm] ADJ prebélico (particularmente referido a la guerra civil norteamericana).

antecedent [,æntɪ'siːdənt] ① ADJ antecedente.
② N antecedente m; ~**s** antecedentes mpl.

antechamber ['æntɪ,tʃeɪmbəʳ] N antecámara f, antesala f.

antedate ['æntɪ'deɪt] VT (a) (in time) preceder, ser anterior a; **text A** ~**s B by 50 years** el texto A es anterior a B en 50 años; **this building** ~**s the Norman conquest** este edificio se construyó antes de la conquista normanda.
(b) cheque etc antedatar, poner fecha anticipada a.

antediluvian [,æntɪdɪ'luːvɪən] ADJ antediluviano; (fig) viejísimo.

antelope ['æntɪləʊp] N antílope m.

antenatal ['æntɪ'neɪtl] ADJ prenatal, antenatal; ~ **care** asistencia f prenatal; ~ **clinic** clínica f de asistencia prenatal; ~ **examination** reconocimiento m prenatal.

antenna [æn'tenə] N, PL **antennae** [æn'teniː] (all senses) antena f.

antepenult [,æntɪpɪ'nʌlt] N sílaba f antepenúltima.

antepenultimate ['æntɪpɪ'nʌltɪmɪt] ADJ antepenúltimo.

anterior [æn'tɪərɪəʳ] ADJ anterior (to a).

anteroom ['æntɪrʊm] N antesala f, antecámara f.

anthem ['ænθəm] N (Eccl) motete m; **national** ~ himno m nacional.

anther ['ænθəʳ] N antera f.

ant-hill ['ænthɪl] N hormiguero m.

anthologist [æn'θɒlədʒɪst] N antologista mf.

anthologize [æn'θɒlədʒaɪz] VT works hacer una antología de; poem, author incluir en una antología.

anthology [æn'θɒlədʒɪ] N antología f.

Anthony ['æntənɪ] NM Antonio.

anthracite ['ænθrəsaɪt] N antracita f.

anthrax ['ænθræks] N ántrax m.

anthropo... [,ænθrəʊpɒ] PREF antropo...

anthropocentric [,ænθrəʊpəʊ'sentrɪk] ADJ antropocéntrico.

➤ LANGUAGE IN USE: **another:** 1a → 26.2   **answer:** 1a → 21.1   2a → 26.1

anthropoid ['ænθrəʊpɔɪd] ① ADJ antropoide.
② N antropoideo *m*.
anthropological [ˌænθrəpə'lɒdʒɪkəl] ADJ antropológico.
anthropologist [ˌænθrə'pɒlədʒɪst] N antropólogo *m*, -a *f*.
anthropology [ˌænθrə'pɒlədʒɪ] N antropología *f*.
anthropometry [ˌænθrə'pɒmɪtrɪ] N antropometría *f*.
anthropomorphic [ˌænθrəpəʊ'mɔːfɪk] ADJ antropomórfico.
anthropomorphism [ˌænθrəʊpə'mɔːfɪzəm] N antropomorfismo *m*.
anthropomorphist [ˌænθrəpəʊ'mɔːfɪst] ADJ, N antropomorfista *mf*.
anthropomorphous [ˌænθrəʊpə'mɔːfəs] ADJ antropomorfo.
anthropophagi [ˌænθrəʊ'pɒfəgaɪ] NPL antropófagos *mpl*.
anthropophagous [ˌænθrəʊ'pɒfəgəs] ADJ antropófago.
anthropophagy [ˌænθrəʊ'pɒfədʒɪ] N antropofagia *f*.
anti... ['æntɪ] (a) *in compounds*: anti... (b) **he's rather ~*** está más bien opuesto; **she is ~ the whole idea*** ella está completamente en contra de la idea.
anti-abortion [ˌæntɪə'bɔːʃən] ADJ: **~ campaign** campaña *f* en contra del aborto, campaña *f* antiabortista.
anti-abortionist [ˌæntɪə'bɔːʃənɪst] N antiabortista *mf*.
anti-aircraft ['æntɪ'eəkrɑːft] ADJ antiaéreo; **~ gun** cañón *m* antiaéreo.
anti-apartheid ['æntɪə'pɑːteɪt] ADJ anti-apartheid.
anti-authority ['æntɪɔː'θɒrɪtɪ] ADJ *speeches, attitude* antiautoritario, contestatario.
antibacterial ['æntɪbæk'tɪərɪəl] ADJ bactericida.
antiballistic ['æntɪbə'lɪstɪk] ADJ: **~ missile** mísil *m* antibalístico.
antibiotic ['æntɪbaɪ'ɒtɪk] ① ADJ antibiótico.
② N antibiótico *m*.
antibody ['æntɪˌbɒdɪ] N anticuerpo *m*.
antic ['æntɪk] N *V* antics.
Antichrist ['æntɪkraɪst] N Anticristo *m*.
anticipate [æn'tɪsɪpeɪt] VT (a) *(forestall) person* anticiparse a, adelantarse a; *event* anticiparse a, prevenir.
(b) *(foresee)* prever; **~d cost** *(Comm)* coste *m* previsto; **~d profit** beneficios *mpl* previstos; **as ~d** de acuerdo con lo previsto, según se había previsto; **you have ~d my wishes** Vd se ha anticipado (*or* adelantado) a mis deseos; **you have ~d my orders** Vd se ha anticipado a mis órdenes, *(wrongly)* Vd ha actuado sin esperar mis órdenes.
(c) *(expect)* esperar; contar con; *(look forward to)* prometerse; *pleasure* disfrutar de antemano; *pain* sufrir anticipadamente; **this is more than I ~d** esto es más de lo que esperaba; **the police ~d trouble** la policía contaba con algunos disturbios; **the ~d audience did not materialize** no apareció el público con que se había contado; **I ~ seeing her tomorrow** cuento con verla mañana; **to ~ that ...** prever que ..., calcular que ...; **do you ~ that this will be easy?** ¿crees que esto va a resultar fácil?; **we ~ that he will come in spite of everything** esperamos que venga a pesar de todo.
anticipation [ænˌtɪsɪ'peɪʃən] N (a) *(forestalling)* anticipación *f*, prevención *f*.
(b) *(foresight)* previsión *f*, prevención *f*; **to act with ~** proceder con anticipación, obrar con previsión.
(c) *(foretaste)* anticipo *m*, anticipación *f*.
(d) *(expectation)* esperanza *f*, esperanzas *fpl*; **in ~ of a fine week** esperando una semana de buen tiempo; **it did not come up to our ~s** no correspondió a nuestras esperanzas, no alcanzó el nivel esperado; **I bought it in ~ of her visit** lo compré en previsión de su visita; **I thank you in ~** le doy las gracias anticipadas.
(e) *(advance excitement)* expectación *f*, ilusión *f*; **we waited with growing ~** esperábamos con creciente ilusión; **we waited in great ~** esperábamos muy ilusionados.
anticipatory [æn'tɪsɪpeɪtərɪ] ADJ anticipador; **~ breach of contract** violación *f* anticipadora de contrato.
anticlerical ['æntɪ'klerɪkl] **1** ADJ anticlerical.
② N anticlerical *mf*.
anticlericalism ['æntɪ'klerɪklɪzəm] N anticlericalismo *m*.
anticlimactic ['æntɪklaɪ'mæktɪk] ADJ que marca un descenso de la emoción *etc*; decepcionante.
anticlimax ['æntɪ'klaɪmæks] N acontecimiento *m* (*etc*) que marca un descenso de la emoción *etc*; decepción *f*, chasco *m*; *(Rhetoric)* anticlímax *m*; **what an ~!** ¡qué decepción!; **the book ends in ~** la emoción desfallece hacia el fin de la novela, la novela termina de modo decepcionante; **the game came as an ~** el partido no correspondió con las esperanzas, el partido no alcanzó el nivel esperado.
anticlockwise ['æntɪ'klɒkwaɪz] *(Brit)* ① ADJ sinistrorso.
② ADV sinistrórsum, en dirección contraria a la de las agujas del reloj.
anticoagulant ['æntɪkəʊ'ægjʊlənt] ① ADJ anticoagulante.
② N anticoagulante *m*.
anticorrosive ['æntɪkə'rəʊzɪv] ADJ anticorrosivo.
antics ['æntɪks] NPL *(of clown)* bufonadas *fpl*, payasadas *fpl*; *(of child, animal)* gracias *fpl*, travesuras *fpl*; **he's up to his ~ again** ha vuelto a hacer de las suyas; **all his ~** todas sus payasadas.

anticyclone [ˌæntɪ'saɪkləʊn] N anticiclón *m*.
anticyclonic [ˌæntɪsaɪ'klɒnɪk] ADJ anticiclónico, anticiclonal.
anti-dandruff [ˌæntɪ'dændrəf] ADJ anticaspa.
anti-dazzle ['æntɪ'dæzl] ADJ antideslumbrante.
antidepressant [ˌæntɪdɪ'presnt] ① ADJ antidepresivo.
② N antidepresivo *m*.
antidote ['æntɪdəʊt] N antídoto *m* (*against, for, to* contra).
anti-dumping ['æntɪ'dʌmpɪŋ] ATTR: **~ duty** arancel *m* anti-dumping; **~ measures** medidas *fpl* anti-dumping.
anti-Establishment ['æntɪs'tæblɪʃmənt] ADJ en contra del sistema.
antifeminism [ˌæntɪ'femɪnɪzəm] N antifeminismo *m*.
antifeminist [ˌæntɪ'femɪnɪst] ① ADJ antifeminista.
② N antifeminista *mf*.
antifreeze ['æntɪ'friːz] ① ADJ anticongelante.
② N anticongelante *m*.
anti-friction ['æntɪ'frɪkʃən] ADJ antifriccional, contrafricción (ATTR).
antigen ['æntɪdʒən] N antígeno *m*.
anti-glare ['æntɪ'gleəʳ] ADJ antideslumbrante.
Antigone [æn'tɪgənɪ] NF Antígona.
Antigua [æn'tiːgə] N Antigua *f*.
anti-hero ['æntɪˌhɪərəʊ] N antihéroe *m*.
anti-heroine ['æntɪ'herəʊɪn] N antiheroína *f*.
antihistamine [ˌæntɪ'hɪstəmɪn] ① ADJ antihistamínico.
② N antihistamínico *m*.
anti-inflammatory ['æntɪɪn'flæmətərɪ] ADJ, N antiinflamatorio *m*.
anti-inflationary [ˌæntɪɪn'fleɪʃnərɪ] ADJ antiinflacionista.
anti-knock ['æntɪ'nɒk] ADJ antidetonante.
Antilles [æn'tɪliːz] NPL Antillas *fpl*.
anti-lock ['æntɪ'lɒk] ADJ: **~ device** (Aut) dispositivo *m* antibloque.
antilogarithm [ˌæntɪ'lɒgərɪθəm] N antilogaritmo *m*.
antimacassar ['æntɪmə'kæsəʳ] N antimacasar *m*.
antimagnetic [ˌæntɪmæg'netɪk] ADJ antimagnético.
antimalarial [ˌæntɪmə'leərɪəl] ADJ antipalúdico.
anti-marketeer ['æntɪˌmɑːkə'tɪəʳ] N (*Brit Pol*) persona *f* contraria al Mercado Común.
antimatter ['æntɪˌmætəʳ] N antimateria *f*.
antimissile ['æntɪ'mɪsaɪl] ADJ antimisil.
antimony ['æntɪmənɪ] N antimonio *m*.
antinomy [æn'tɪnəmɪ] N antinomia *f*.
antinuclear ['æntɪ'njuːklɪəʳ] ADJ antinuclear.
anti-nuke* [ˌæntɪ'njuːk] ADJ antinuclear.
Antioch ['æntɪɒk] N Antioquía *f*.
antioxidant ['æntɪ'ɒksədənt] N antioxidante *m*.
antiparasitic [ˌæntɪˌpaerə'sɪtɪk] ADJ antiparasitario.
antipathetic [ˌæntɪpə'θetɪk] ADJ antipático (*to* a); hostil (*to* a).
antipathy [æn'tɪpəθɪ] N (a) *(feeling)* antipatía *f* (*between* entre; *to* por, hacia). (b) *(thing disliked)* aversión *f*, cosa *f* aborrecida.
antipersonnel ['æntɪpɜːsə'nel] ADJ destinado a causar bajas.
antiperspirant [ˌæntɪ'pɜːspərənt] ① ADJ antiperspirante.
② N antiperspirante *m*.
antiphon ['æntɪfən] N antífona *f*.
antiphony [æn'tɪfənɪ] N canto *m* antifonal.
antipodean [ænˌtɪpə'diːən] ① ADJ de las antípodas; (*hum*) australiano.
② N habitante *mf* de las antípodas; (*hum*) australiano *m*, -a *f*.
antipodes [æn'tɪpədiːz] NPL antípodas *mpl*; **the A~** (*esp hum*) Australia *f* (y Nueva Zelanda *f*).
antipope ['æntɪpəʊp] N antipapa *m*.
antiprotectionist [ˌæntɪprə'tekʃənɪst] ADJ antiproteccionista.
antiquarian [ˌæntɪ'kweərɪən] ① ADJ anticuario; **~ bookseller** librero *m* especializado en libros antiguos; **~ bookshop** librería *f* anticuaria; **~ collection** colección *f* de antigüedades.
② N (*collector*) aficionado *m*, -a *f* a las antigüedades, coleccionista *mf* de antigüedades; (*dealer*) anticuario *m*, -a *f*.
antiquary ['æntɪkwərɪ] N = **antiquarian 2**.
antiquated ['æntɪkweɪtɪd] ADJ anticuado.
antique [æn'tiːk] ① ADJ antiguo, viejo; (*pej*) anticuado; decimonónico, caduco; *furniture etc* de época.
② N antigüedad *f*, antigualla *f* (*also pej*); **~ dealer** anticuario *m*, -a *f*, comerciante *mf* en antigüedades; **~ shop** tienda *f* de antigüedades.
antiqued [æn'tiːkt] ADJ *furniture* envejecido.
antiquity [æn'tɪkwɪtɪ] N *(all senses)* antigüedad *f*; **antiquities** antigüedades *fpl*; **high ~** remota antigüedad *f*; **in ~** en la antigüedad, en el mundo antiguo.
anti-racism ['æntɪ'reɪsɪzəm] N antirracismo *m*.
antiracist ['æntɪ'reɪsɪst] ① ADJ antirracista.
② N antirracista *mf*.
antireligious ['æntɪrɪ'lɪdʒəs] ADJ antirreligioso.
anti-riot ['æntɪ'raɪət] ADJ: **~ police** policía *f* antidisturbios.
anti-roll ['æntɪ'rəʊl] ADJ: (*Brit*) **~ bar** barra *f* estabilizadora, barra *f* antivuelco, estabilizador *m*; **~ device** estabilizador *m*.
antirrhinum [ˌæntɪ'raɪnəm] N antirrino *m*.

anti-rust [ˈæntɪˈrʌst] ADJ antioxidante, anticorrosión (ATTR).

antisegregationist [ˈæntɪsegrəˈgeɪʃənɪst] ADJ antisegregacionista.

anti-semite [ˈæntɪˈsiːmaɪt] N antisemita *mf*.

anti-semitic [ˈæntɪsɪˈmɪtɪk] ADJ antisemítico.

anti-semitism [ˈæntɪˈsemɪtɪzəm] N antisemitismo *m*.

antiseptic [ˌæntɪˈseptɪk] ①ADJ antiséptico. ② N antiséptico *m*.

anti-skid [ˈæntɪˈskɪd] ADJ antideslizante.

antislavery [ˈæntɪˈsleɪvərɪ] ADJ en contra de la esclavitud.

anti-smoking [ˈæntɪˈsməʊkɪŋ] ADJ antitabaco.

antisocial [ˈæntɪˈsəʊʃəl] ADJ antisocial.

antistatic [ˈæntɪˈstætɪk] ADJ antiestático.

anti-strike [ˈæntɪˈstraɪk] ADJ antihuelga.

anti-submarine [ˈæntɪsʌbməˈriːn] ADJ antisubmarino.

anti-tank [ˈæntɪˈtæŋk] ADJ antitanque.

anti-terrorist [ˈæntɪˈterərɪst] ADJ: **~ brigade** brigada *f* antiterrorista.

anti-theft [ˌæntɪˈθeft] ADJ: **~ device** sistema *m* anti-robo.

antithesis [ænˈtɪθɪsɪs] N, PL **antitheses** [ænˈtɪθɪsiːz] antítesis *f*.

antithetic(al) [ˌæntɪˈθetɪk(əl)] ADJ antitético.

antitoxic [ˈæntɪˈtɒksɪk] ADJ antitóxico.

antitoxin [ˈæntɪˈtɒksɪn] N antitoxina *f*.

anti-trust [ˈæntɪˈtrʌst] ADJ antimonopolista; **~ law** ley *f* anti-monopolios; **~ legislation** legislación *f* antimonopolios.

antivivisection [ˈæntɪˌvɪvɪˈsekʃən] N: **~ campaign/movement** anti-viviseccionismo *m*.

antivivisectionism [ˈæntɪˌvɪvɪˈsekʃənɪzəm] N antiviviseccionismo *m*.

antivivisectionist [ˈæntɪˌvɪvɪˈsekʃənɪst] N antiviviseccionista *mf*.

anti-war [ˌæntɪˈwɔːʳ] ADJ antibelicista, antiguerra, pacifista.

anti-wrinkle [ˈæntɪˈrɪŋkl] ADJ antiarrugas.

antler [ˈæntləʳ] N cuerna *f*; **~s** cuernas *fpl*, cornamenta *f*.

Antony [ˈæntənɪ] NM Antonio.

antonym [ˈæntənɪm] N antónimo *m*.

antonymy [ænˈtɒnɪmɪ] N antonimia *f*.

antsy: [ˈæntsɪ] ADJ (*US*) nervioso, inquieto.

Antwerp [ˈæntwɜːp] N Amberes *m*.

anus [ˈeɪnəs] N ano *m*.

anvil [ˈænvɪl] N yunque *m*.

anxiety [æŋˈzaɪətɪ] N (a) (*worry*) inquietud *f*, preocupación *f*, ansiedad *f*; **some ~ is felt about it** existe cierta inquietud sobre esto; **it is a great ~ to me** me preocupa muchísimo; **that child is a perpetual ~** ese niño me trae loco.
(b) (*eagerness*) ansia *f*, anhelo *m* (*for* de; *to do* de hacer, por hacer); **in his ~ to be off he forgot his case** tanto ansiaba partir que olvidó la maleta.
(c) (*Med*) ansiedad *f*; angustia *f*; **~ neurosis** neurosis *f* de ansiedad.

anxious [ˈæŋkʃəs] ADJ (a) (*worried*) inquieto, preocupado, angustiado; **to be ~ about, to be ~ for** inquietarse por; **I'm very ~ about you** me tienes muy preocupado; **in an ~ voice** en un tono angustiado; **with an ~ glance** con una mirada inquieta, con una mirada llena de inquietud.
(b) (*causing worry*) **it is an ~ time** es un período de gran ansiedad; **you gave me some ~ moments** a ratos me causaste gran inquietud; **it was an ~ moment** fue un momento de ansiedad.
(c) (*eager*) deseoso (*for* de; *to do* de hacer); **he is ~ for success** ansía el triunfo, ambiciona el triunfo; **to be ~ to do** anhelar hacer, tener ganas de hacer, tener empeño en hacer; **I am very ~ that he should go** quiero a toda costa que vaya; **I'm not very ~ to go** tengo pocas ganas de ir; **she is ~ to see you before you go** se empeña en verte antes de que te vayas.

anxiously [ˈæŋkʃəslɪ] ADV (a) con inquietud, de manera angustiada, con ansiedad. (b) con impaciencia.

anxiousness [ˈæŋkʃəsnɪs] N = **anxiety**.

any [ˈenɪ] ①ADJ (a) algún, alguna; **if there are ~ tickets left** si queda alguna entrada; **he'll do it if ~ man can** lo hará si lo puede alguno.
(b) (*partitive: gen not translated*) **have you ~ money?** ¿tienes dinero?; **have you ~ bananas?** ¿hay plátanos?; **is there ~ man who ...?** ¿hay hombre que ...?
(c) (*any ... you like*) cualquier; **~ day now** cualquier día; **~ farmer will tell you** te lo dirá cualquier agricultor; **wear ~ hat (you like)** ponte el sombrero que quieras, ponte sombrero (no importa cuál); **he's not just ~ golfer** no es un golfista cualquiera; **~ person who breaks the rules will be expelled** se expulsará a toda persona que viole las reglas; **take ~ two children** tome dos niños al azar, tome dos niños cualesquiera; **he should arrive at ~ moment now** deberá llegar de un momento a otro.
(d) (*negative sense*) ningún, ninguna; **I haven't ~ money** no tengo dinero; **I don't see ~ cows** no veo vaca alguna, no veo ninguna vaca.
② PRON (a) alguno, alguna; **if there are ~ who ...** si hay algunos que ...; **if ~ of you knows how to drive** si alguno de vosotros sabe conducir; **few, if ~** pocos, si es que los hay; pocos, si acaso alguno.
(b) (*any ... you like*) cualquiera; **take ~ you like** tome cualquier; **~**

but her would have protested cualquier persona que no fuera ella hubiera protestado.
(c) (*negative sense*) ninguno, ninguna; **I haven't ~ of them** no tengo ninguno de ellos; **I have hardly ~ left** apenas me queda (alguno), ninguno apenas me queda.
③ADV (a) (*gen not translated*) **~ more** más; **don't wait ~ longer** no esperes más tiempo; **are there ~ others?** ¿hay otros?; **is he ~ better?** ¿está algo mejor?; **they didn't sing ~ too well** no han cantado bien que digamos; **I couldn't do that ~ more than I could fly** yo haría eso igual que podría volar.
(b) (*esp US*) **it doesn't help us ~** eso no nos ayuda para nada; **does she sing ~?** ¿sabe cantar de alguna manera?

anybody [ˈenɪbɒdɪ] PRON (a) alguien, alguno; **did you see ~?** ¿vio a alguien?; **~ would have said he was mad** se hubiera dicho que estaba loco; **if ~ can manage it, he can** si lo puede alguno lo podrá él; **~ who wants to go back should go now** si alguno quiere volver que vuelva ahora; **I'll shoot ~ who moves** al primero que se mueva le mato.
(b) (*~ ... you like*) cualquiera; **~ will tell you the same** cualquiera te dirá lo mismo; **~ who invests in this** todo el que invierta en esto; **~ else would have laughed** cualquier otro se hubiera reído; **it's ~'s guess!** ¡nadie lo sabe!; **it's ~'s race** esta carrera la podría ganar cualquiera; **he's not just ~, he's the boss** no es un cualquiera, es el jefe.
(c) (*negative sense*) nadie, ninguno; **I can't see ~** no veo a nadie; **hardly ~ came** apenas vino nadie.
(d) (*person of importance*) **is he ~?** ¿es una persona de importancia?; **he isn't ~ in this town** en este pueblo no es nadie, en este pueblo no cuenta para nada; **you must work harder if you want to be ~** tienes que trabajar más si quieres llegar a ser algo.

anyhow [ˈenɪhaʊ] ADV (a) (*at any rate*) de todas formas, de todos modos, con todo; **~ it's not my fault** de todas formas yo no tengo la culpa.
(b) (*in spite of everything*) **I shall go ~** voy a pesar de todo, sin embargo voy.
(c) (*haphazard: also* **any old how**) **he leaves things just ~** deja sus cosas de cualquier modo; **I came in late and finished my essay off ~** volví tarde y terminé mi ensayo sin pensarlo mucho.
(d) (*in any way whatever*) no importa cómo; **do it ~ you like** hazlo del modo que quieras; **the door was locked and I couldn't get in ~** la puerta estaba cerrada y no había manera de entrar.
(e) (*by the way*) a propósito; **why are you going, ~?** por cierto, ¿por qué te vas?

anyone [ˈenɪwʌn] PRON = **anybody**.

anyplace [ˈenɪpleɪs] ADV (*US*) = **anywhere**.

anything [ˈenɪθɪŋ] PRON (a) algo, alguna cosa; **is there ~ inside?** ¿hay algo dentro?; **are you doing ~ tonight?** ¿tienes compromiso para esta noche?; **have you heard ~ of them?** ¿tienes alguna noticia de ellos?; **it's as clean as ~** está pero muy limpio, está requetelimpio; **~ else?** (*in shop etc*) ¿algo más?, ¿alguna cosita más?; **is there ~ in this idea?** ¿tiene algún valor esta idea?; **if ~ it's much better** es mucho mejor si cabe; **if ~ it's larger** si acaso, es algo más grande.
(b) (*~ you like*) cualquier cosa; **he will give you ~ you ask for** te dará lo que pidas; **sing ~ you like** canta lo que quieras, canta cualquier cosa; **~ but that** todo menos eso; **~ but!** (*reply to question*) ¡nada de eso!; **~ else is ruled out** todo lo demás está excluido; **I'll read ~** leeré cualquier otra cosa; **I'm not buying just ~** yo no compro una cosa cualquiera; **it was ~ but pleasant** era todo menos que agradable; **I'd give ~ to know** daría cualquier cosa por saberlo.
(c) (*negative sense*) nada; **I can't see ~** no veo nada; **you haven't seen ~ yet** todavía no has visto nada; **he's not a minister or ~** no es ministro ni nada por el estilo; **can't ~ be done?** ¿no se puede hacer nada?; **we can't do ~ else** no podemos hacer otra cosa; **hardly ~** casi nada; **not for ~ in the world** por nada del mundo.
(d) **like ~** hasta más no poder.

anytime [ˈenɪtaɪm] ADV V **time**.

anyway [ˈenɪweɪ] ADV = **anyhow**.

anywhere [ˈenɪwɛəʳ] ADV (a) en todas partes, en (*or a*) cualquier parte, dondequiera; **~ in the world** en todas partes del mundo; en cualquier parte del mundo; **go ~ you like** vaya adonde quiera; **~ you go you'll see the same** dondequiera que vayas verás lo mismo; **~ else** en cualquier otra parte; **I'm not going to live just ~** yo no voy a vivir en un sitio cualquiera; **it's miles from ~** está en el quinto infierno; **it's not ~ near Castroforte** está bastante lejos de Castroforte; **do you see him ~?** ¿le ves en alguna parte?; **she leaves her things just ~** deja sus cosas en cualquier parte; **~ from 200 to 300** (*US*) entre 200 y 300.
(b) (*negative sense*) en (*or a*) ninguna parte; **I'm not going ~** yo no voy a ninguna parte; **he was first and the rest didn't come ~** él se

clasificó primero y los demás quedaron muy por debajo; **that won't get you ~** así no llegas a ninguna parte; **we didn't go ~ special** no fuimos a ningún sitio especial.

Anzac ['ænzæk] N ABBR of **Australia-New Zealand Army Corps** Fuerzas *fpl* Armadas de Australia y Nueva Zelanda.

A.O.(C.)B. ABBR of **any other (competent) business** ruegos *mpl* y preguntas.

AONB ABBR of **Area of Outstanding Natural Beauty** ≈ Paraje *m* Natural.

aorist ['ɛərɪst] N aoristo *m*.

aorta [eɪ'ɔːtə] N aorta *f*.

aortic [eɪ'ɔːtɪk] ADJ aórtico.

AP N ABBR of **Associated Press** agencia de prensa.

apace [ə'peɪs] ADV aprisa, rápidamente.

apache [ə'pætʃɪ] N apache *m*.

apart [ə'pɑːt] 1 ADV **(a)** (*separated*) aparte, separadamente; **with one's feet ~** con los pies apartados; **posts set equally ~** postes *mpl* espaciados con regularidad, postes *mpl* colocados a intervalos iguales; **they stood a long way ~** estaban muy apartados (el uno del otro); **we live only three doors ~** vivimos a tres puertas de ellos; **the deaths were only three days ~** murieron con sólo tres días de diferencia; **they are living ~ now** ahora viven separados; **he lives ~ from his wife** vive separado de su mujer; **the house stands somewhat ~** la casa está algo aislada; **to hold o.s. ~** mantenerse aparte; **to keep ~** separar, mantener aislado (*from* de); **to tell ~** distinguir.
(b) (*aside*) **that ~** aparte de eso; **but joking ~** pero bromas aparte, pero en serio; **to set ~** guardar, reservar (*for* para), poner aparte.
(c) (*in pieces*) **to come ~, to fall ~** romperse, deshacerse; **to tear ~** hacer trizas, destrozar (*and V tear*[1]); *V* **tear** *etc*.
2 **~ from** PREP aparte de; **but quite ~ from that** pero aparte de eso.

apartheid [ə'pɑːteɪt] N apartheid *m*, segregación *f* racial.

aparthotel [ə'pɑːthəʊˌtel] N apart(a)hotel *m*.

apartment [ə'pɑːtmənt] N **(a)** (*Brit: room*) cuarto *m*, aposento *m*; **~s** piso *m*, apartamento *m* (en una casa), departamento *m* (*LAm*).
(b) (*esp US*) piso *m*, apartamento *m*; **~ hotel** (*US*) pisos *mpl* con personal de servicio; **~ house** (*US*) casa *f* de pisos.

apathetic [ˌæpə'θetɪk] ADJ apático, indiferente; **to be ~ towards** ser indiferente a, no mostrar interés alguno en.

apathetically [ˌæpə'θetɪkəlɪ] ADV con apatía, con indiferencia, sin entusiasmo.

apathy ['æpəθɪ] N apatía *f*, indiferencia *f* (*towards* a), falta *f* de interés (*towards* en).

APB N (*US*) ABBR of **all points bulletin** frase usada por la policía por *'descubrir y aprehender'*.

APC N ABBR of **armoured personnel carrier**.

ape [eɪp] 1 N **(a)** mono *m* (*esp* los antropomorfos), simio *m*, antropoideo *m*; **you (great) ~!*** ¡bestia!*; **to go ~** (*US*) volverse loco, enloquecer. **(b)** (*fig*) mono *m* de imitación, imitador *m*, -ora *f*.
2 VT imitar, remedar.

APEC N ABBR of **Asia Pacific Economic Co-operation** Foro *m* de Cooperación Económica del Asia-Pacífico.

Apennines ['æpɪnaɪnz] NPL Apeninos *mpl*.

aperient [ə'pɪərɪənt] 1 ADJ laxante.
2 N laxante *m*.

apéritif [ə'perɪtɪv] N aperitivo *m*.

aperture ['æpətʃʊər] N abertura *f*, rendija *f*, resquicio *m*; (*Phot etc*) abertura *f*.

apeshit ['eɪpʃɪt] ADJ (*esp US*): **to go ~** (*lose one's temper*) ponerse como un energúmeno*, ponerse hecho una fiera*; (*go wild*) dislocarse*, ponerse como una moto*.

APEX ['eɪpeks] N **(a)** (*Brit*) ABBR of **Association of Professional, Executive, Clerical and Computer Staff** Asociación *f* de Profesionales, Ejecutivos, Auxiliares Administrativos y Personal de Informática. **(b)** (*also* **apex**) ABBR of **Advance Purchase Excursion: ~ fare** precio *m* APEX; **~ ticket** billete *m* APEX.

apex ['eɪpeks] N, PL **apices** ['eɪpɪsiːz] ápice *m*; (*fig*) cumbre *f*.

aphasia [æ'feɪzɪə] N afasia *f*.

aphid ['eɪfɪd] N áfido *m*.

aphis ['eɪfɪs] N, PL **aphides** ['eɪfɪdiːz] áfido *m*.

aphonic [ˌeɪ'fɒnɪk] ADJ afónico.

aphorism ['æfərɪzəm] N aforismo *m*.

aphoristic [ˌæfə'rɪstɪk] ADJ aforístico.

aphrodisiac [ˌæfrəʊ'dɪzɪæk] 1 ADJ afrodisíaco.
2 N afrodisíaco *m*.

Aphrodite [ˌæfrəʊ'daɪtɪ] NF Afrodita.

API N (*US*) ABBR of **American Press Institute**.

apiarist ['eɪpɪərɪst] N apicultor *m*, -ora *f*.

apiary ['eɪpɪərɪ] N colmenar *m*.

apiculture ['eɪpɪkʌltʃər] N apicultura *f*.

apiece [ə'piːs] ADV cada uno; por persona, por cabeza; *eg* **they had a gun ~** tenía cada uno un revólver; **he gave them an apple ~** dio una manzana a cada uno; **the rule is a dollar ~** la regla es un dólar

por persona.

aplastic anaemia, (*US*) **aplastic anemia** [eɪ'plæstɪkə'niːmɪə] N anemia *f* aplástica.

aplenty [ə'plentɪ] ADV: **there was food ~** había comida abundante, había abundancia de comida.

aplomb [ə'plɒm] N aplomo *m*, sangre *f* fría, serenidad *f*; **with the greatest ~** con la mayor serenidad, tan tranquilo.

APO N (*US*) ABBR of **Army Post Office**.

Apocalypse [ə'pɒkəlɪps] N Apocalipsis *m*.

apocalyptic [əˌpɒkə'lɪptɪk] ADJ apocalíptico.

apocopate [ə'pɒkəpeɪt] VT apocopar.

apocope [ə'pɒkəʊpɪ] N apócope *f*.

Apocrypha [ə'pɒkrɪfə] NPL libros *mpl* apócrifos de la Biblia.

apocryphal [ə'pɒkrɪfəl] ADJ apócrifo.

apodosis [ə'pɒdəʊsɪs] N apódosis *f*.

apogee ['æpəʊdʒiː] N apogeo *m*.

apolitical [ˌeɪpə'lɪtɪkəl] ADJ apolítico.

Apollo [ə'pɒleʊ] NM Apolo.

apologetic [əˌpɒlə'dʒetɪk] 1 ADJ **(a)** (*contrite*) lleno de disculpas; apenado, que tiene además de pedir perdón, que se deshace en disculpas; **with an ~ air** como si viniera a pedir perdón; **he was very ~ about it** dijo que lo sentía profundamente; **he was very ~ about his dress** se disculpó mucho por su traje. **(b)** (*vindicatory*) apologético.
2 **~s** NPL apologética *f*.

apologetically [əˌpɒlə'dʒetɪkəlɪ] ADV con aire del que pide perdón, en tono apenado; con muchas excusas, excusándose; **he said ~** dijo apenado.

apologia [ˌæpə'leʊdʒɪə] N apología *f*.

apologist [ə'pɒlədʒɪst] N apologista *mf*.

▼ **apologize** [ə'pɒlədʒaɪz] VI disculparse (*for* de; *to* con), pedir perdón (*to* a); (*for absence etc*) presentar sus excusas; **never ~!** disculpas, ¡nunca!

apologue ['æpəlɒg] N apólogo *m*.

▼ **apology** [ə'pɒlədʒɪ] N **(a)** disculpa *f*, excusa *f*; **letter of ~** carta *f* de disculpa; **please accept my apologies** le ruego me disculpe; **I demand an ~** reclamo una satisfacción, insisto en que Vd se disculpe; **to make** (*or* **offer**) **an ~** disculparse, presentar sus excusas (*for* por); **to send an ~** (*at meeting*) presentar sus excusas; **there are apologies from X and Y** se han excusado X y Y.
(b) (*Liter etc*) apología *f*.
(c) (*pej*) **an ~ for a house** una birria de casa*; **this ~ for a letter** ésta que apenas se puede llamar carta.

apophthegm ['æpəʊθem] N apotegma *m*.

apoplectic [ˌæpə'plektɪk] ADJ apopléctico; (*fig*) furioso; **to get ~** (*fig*) enfurecerse.

apoplexy ['æpəpleksɪ] N apoplejía *f*; **to have ~** (*fig*) reventar (de rabia *etc*).

apostasy [ə'pɒstəsɪ] N apostasía *f*.

apostate [ə'pɒstɪt] N apóstata *mf*.

apostatize [ə'pɒstətaɪz] VI apostatar (*from* de).

a posteriori ['ɑːpɒsˌterɪ'ɔːraɪ] ADJ, ADV a posteriori.

apostle [ə'pɒsl] N apóstol *m*; (*fig*) apóstol *m*, paladín *m*.

apostolate [ə'pɒstəlɪt] N apostolado *m*.

apostolic [ˌæpəs'tɒlɪk] ADJ apostólico; **~ succession** sucesión *f* apostólica.

apostrophe [ə'pɒstrəfɪ] N **(a)** (*sign*) apóstrofo *m*. **(b)** (*address*) apóstrofe *gen m*.

apostrophize [ə'pɒstrəfaɪz] VT apostrofar.

apothecary [ə'pɒθɪkərɪ] N (†) boticario *m*.

apotheosis [əˌpɒθɪ'əʊsɪs] N, PL **apotheoses** [əˌpɒθɪ'əʊsiːz] apoteosis *f*.

appal, (*US*) **appall** [ə'pɔːl] VT horrorizar, aterrar; repugnar; **everyone was ~led** se horrorizaron todos, todos quedaron consternados; **I was ~led by the news** me horrorizó la noticia.

Appalachia [ˌæpə'leɪtʃɪə] N *la región de los Apalaches*.

Appalachians [ˌæpə'leɪʃənz] NPL (Montes *mpl*) Apalaches *mpl*.

appalling [ə'pɔːlɪŋ] ADJ espantoso, horroroso; *taste etc* detestable, pésimo.

appallingly [ə'pɔːlɪŋlɪ] ADV espantosamente, horrorosamente; detestablemente; **it was quite ~ bad** fue del todo horrible; **he's ~ self-centred** es terriblemente egocéntrico.

apparatchik [ˌæpə'rættʃɪk] N (*in Communist country*) miembro *m* del aparato del partido comunista, apparatchik *m*; (*in organization*) funcionario *m*, -a *f*, burócrata *mf*.

apparatus [ˌæpə'reɪtəs] N aparato *m*.

apparel [ə'pærəl] 1 N ropa *f*, vestidos *mpl*; indumentaria *f*; (*hum*) atavío *m*.
2 VT vestir (*in* de); (*hum*) trajear, ataviar (*in* de).

apparent [ə'pærənt] ADJ **(a)** (*seeming*) aparente; **more ~ than real** más aparente que real.
(b) (*clear*) claro, evidente, manifiesto; *heir* forzoso; **it is ~ that ...** está

claro que ...; **it is becoming ~ that ...** ya se está viendo que ...; **their weakness became ~** se hizo patente su debilidad.

apparently [əˈpærəntlɪ] ADV (*evidently*) por lo visto; (*seemingly*) según parece, al parecer.

apparition [ˌæpəˈrɪʃən] N **(a)** (*act*) aparición *f*. **(b)** (*ghost*) fantasma *m*, aparecido *m*.

▼ **appeal** [əˈpiːl] ⃞1 N **(a)** (*call*) llamamiento *m*; **a national ~ for funds** un llamamiento a todo el país para que contribuya dinero; **~ for charity** cuestación *f* para obras benéficas; **he made an ~ for calm** hizo un llamamiento para que se mantuviera la calma.
(b) (*petition*) súplica *f*, ruego *m*, petición *f*; **deaf to all ~s** impasible; **an ~ for help** una petición de socorro.
(c) (*Jur*) apelación *f*, recurso *m* (de casación); **~ committee** (*Sport etc*) comité *m* de apelación; **~ court** tribunal *m* de apelación; **~s procedure** procedimiento *m* de apelación; **without ~** inapelable; **there is no ~ against his decision** su fallo es inapelable; **to give notice of ~** entablar apelación; **to lodge an ~** apelar (*against* de).
(d) (*attraction*) atractivo *m*, encanto *m*, interés *m*; **the ~ of children** el encanto de los niños; **a book of general ~** un libro de interés para todos.
⃞2 VT (*Jur*) **to ~ a case** apelar de una sentencia.
⃞3 VI **(a)** (*call, beg*) **to ~ for** suplicar, reclamar; **I ~ for its return** ruego que se me devuelva; **he ~ed for silence** rogó que se callasen todos; **the authorities ~ed for calm** las autoridades hicieron un llamamiento para que se mantuviera la calma; **to ~ to sb for sth** suplicar algo a uno; **I ~ to you!** ¡se lo ruego!; **it's no good ~ing to me** de nada sirve acudir a mí; **to ~ to arms** recurrir a las armas; **to ~ to the country** (*Pol*) apelar al arbitrio de las urnas; **to ~ to sb's finer feelings** apelar a los sentimientos nobles de uno.
(b) (*Jur*) apelar (*against* de; *to* a), recurrir (*against* contra).
▼ **(c)** (*attract*) atraer, tener atractivo para, interesar, gustar; **jazz does not ~ to me** el jazz no me gusta; **it ~s to the imagination** estimula la imaginación; **I don't think this will ~ much to the public** no creo que esto tenga atractivo para el público.

appealing [əˈpiːlɪŋ] ADJ **(a)** (*begging*) suplicante. **(b)** (*attractive*) atrayente, atractivo, encantador, sugestivo.

appealingly [əˈpiːlɪŋlɪ] ADV de modo suplicante.

appear [əˈpɪər] VI **(a)** (*present o.s.*) aparecer, mostrarse, presentarse; **he ~ed from behind a tree** salió de detrás de un árbol; **he ~ed without a tie** se presentó sin corbata; **the plane ~ed out of a cloud** el avión salió de una nube; **when the sun ~s** cuando se muestra el sol, cuando sale el sol; **the ghost ~s at midnight** el fantasma aparece a medianoche; **he ~ed from nowhere** salió de la nada; **as will ~ in due course** según se verá luego; **she ~ed as Ophelia** hizo el papel de Ofelia; **she ~ed in 'Fuenteovejuna'** hizo un papel en 'Fuenteovejuna'; **when are you going to ~ on TV?** ¿cuándo te vas a presentar en TV?; **¿cuándo vas a salir por la tele?***; **to ~ to sb** (*as vision*) aparecerse a uno.
(b) (*book etc*) salir a luz, publicarse, aparecer.
(c) (*Jur*) comparecer (*before* ante); **to ~ on a charge of murder** comparecer acusado de homicidio; **to ~ on behalf of sb, to ~ for sb** representar a uno.
(d) (*seem*) parecer; **he ~s tired** parece cansado; **how does it ~ to you?** ¿qué le parece esto?; **it ~s that ...** resulta que ..., parece que ...; **so it ~s, so it would ~** así parece; **in daylight it ~s red** a la luz del día se muestra rojo.

appearance [əˈpɪərəns] N **(a)** (*act of appearing*) aparición *f*; **~ money** pago *m* por presentarse; **to make an ~** aparecer, presentarse, dejarse ver; **to make one's first ~** aparecer por primera vez; estrenarse; **to make a personal ~** aparecer en persona; **to put in an ~** hacer acto de presencia.
(b) (*Jur*) comparecencia *f*; **to make an ~ in court** comparecer ante el tribunal.
(c) (*of book etc*) publicación *f*.
(d) (*Theat etc*) actuación *f*; presentación *f*; **his ~ in 'Don Mendo'** su actuación en 'Don Mendo'; **his ~ as Don Mendo** su actuación en el papel de Don Mendo; **cast in order of ~** personajes *mpl* en orden de aparición en escena.
(e) (*aspect*) apariencia *f*, aspecto *m*; **to have a dignified ~** tener aspecto solemne.
(f) **~s** (*seeming*) apariencias *fpl*; **~s are deceptive** las apariencias engañan; **to (or by) all ~s** al parecer, según todos los indicios; **it had all the ~s of a rabbit** se parecía en todo a un conejo; **you shouldn't go by ~s** no hay que juzgar por las apariencias.
(g) (*face*) apariencias *fpl*; **for the sake of ~s** para salvar las apariencias; **to keep up ~s, save ~s** salvar las apariencias.

appease [əˈpiːz] VT apaciguar; aplacar; *hunger* satisfacer, saciar; *passion* mitigar; *person* satisfacer, dar satisfacción a; *angry person* desenojar, apaciguar; (*Pol*) apaciguar, contemporizar con.

appeasement [əˈpiːzmənt] N apaciguamiento *m*, pacificación *f*; (*Pol*) apaciguamiento *m*, contemporización *f*.

appellant [əˈpelənt] N apelante *mf*.

appellate [əˈpelɪt] ADJ: **~ court** (*US*) tribunal *m* de apelación; *ver también* ⃞COURTS⃞.

appellation [ˌæpeˈleɪʃən] N nombre *m*, título *m*; (*of wine*) denominación *f* de origen.

append [əˈpend] VT (*add*) añadir; (*attach, enclose*) adjuntar, enviar adjunto; *signature* poner; (*Comput*) anexionar (al final).

appendage [əˈpendɪdʒ] N añadidura *f*, apéndice *m*; (*fig*) pegote *m*.

appendectomy [ˌæpenˈdektəmɪ] N apendectomía *f*.

appendicitis [əˌpendɪˈsaɪtɪs] N apendicitis *f*.

appendix [əˈpendɪks] N, PL **appendices** [əˈpendɪsiːz] apéndice *m*.

apperception [ˌæpəˈsepʃən] N percepción *f*; **~ test** (*US*) test *m* de percepción.

appertain [ˌæpəˈteɪn] VI: **to ~ to** relacionarse con, tener que ver con.

appetite [ˈæpɪtaɪt] N **(a)** apetito *m*; **~ depressant** inhibidor *m* del apetito; **to eat with an ~** comer con buen apetito; **to have no ~** no tener apetito, no tener ganas; **to whet one's ~** abrir el apetito, despertar el apetito.
(b) (*fig*) deseo *m*, anhelo *m* (*for* de), ganas *fpl*; **they had no ~ for further fighting** ya no les apetecía seguir luchando, no tenían más ganas de luchar; **to spoil one's ~ for** quitar a uno las ganas de.

appetizer [ˈæpɪtaɪzəʳ] N aperitivo *m*; tapa *f*.

appetizing [ˈæpɪtaɪzɪŋ] ADJ apetitoso.

Appian Way [ˈæpɪənˈweɪ] N Vía *f* Apia.

applaud [əˈplɔːd] ⃞1 VT aplaudir; (*fig*) aplaudir, celebrar, elogiar.
⃞2 VI aplaudir, palmotear.

applause [əˈplɔːz] N aplausos *mpl*, aplauso *m*; (*fig*) aplausos *mpl*, aprobación *f*; **a round of ~ for X!** ¡un aplauso para X!; **there was loud ~** sonaron fuertes aplausos; **to win the ~ of** ganarse la aprobación de.

apple [ˈæpl] N (*fruit*) manzana *f*; (*tree*) manzano *m*; **~ of discord** manzana *f* de la discordia; **the ~ of one's eye** la niña de los ojos; **~s and pears** (*Brit*⁑) escalera *f*; **the (Big) A~** (*US**) Nueva York *f*.

apple-blossom [ˈæpl,blɒsəm] N flor *f* del manzano.

apple-brandy [ˌæplˈbrændɪ] N aguardiente *m* de manzana.

applecart [ˈæplkɑːt] N: **to upset the ~** echarlo todo a rodar, desbaratar los planes.

apple-core [ˈæplkɔːʳ] N corazón *m* de manzana.

apple dumpling [ˌæplˈdʌmplɪŋ] N *postre a base de manzana asada y masa*.

apple fritter [ˌæplˈfrɪtəʳ] N manzana *f* rebozada.

apple-green [ˈæplgriːn] ⃞1 ADJ verde manzana.
⃞2 N verde *m* manzana.

applejack [ˈæpldʒæk] N (*US*) aguardiente *m* de manzana.

apple-orchard [ˈæpl,ɔːtʃəd] N manzanar *m*, pomar *m*.

apple-pie [ˈæplˈpaɪ] N tarta *f* de manzanas; **in ~ order** en perfecto orden; **to make sb an ~ bed** (*Brit*) hacerle la petaca a uno.

apple-sauce [ˈæplˈsɔːs] N **(a)** compota *f* de manzanas. **(b)** (*US**) coba *f*.

apple-tart [ˌæplˈtɑːt] N tarta *f* de manzana.

apple tree [ˈæpl,triː] N manzano *m*.

appliance [əˈplaɪəns] N aparato *m*, instrumento *m*, dispositivo *m*; (*Brit: fire ~*) coche *m* de bomberos; **electrical ~** (aparato *m*) electrodoméstico *m*.

applicability [ˌæplɪkəˈbɪlɪtɪ] N aplicabilidad *f*.

applicable [əˈplɪkəbl] ADJ aplicable (*to* a); **a rule ~ to all** una regla que se aplica a todos; **this is not ~ to you** esto no se refiere a Vd; **delete what is not ~** táchese lo que no sea pertinente.

applicant [ˈæplɪkənt] N aspirante *mf*, candidato *m*, -a *f* (*for a post* a un puesto); suplicante *mf*, solicitante *mf*.

application [ˌæplɪˈkeɪʃən] N **(a)** (*in most senses*) aplicación *f*; **for external ~ only** para uso externo.
(b) (*request*) solicitud *f*, petición *f* (*for* de, por); **~ form** hoja *f* de solicitud, formulario *m* de inscripción; **~(s) package, ~(s) software** paquete *m* de aplicación (*or* aplicaciones); **~(s) program** programa *m* de aplicaciones; **prices on ~** los precios, a solicitud; **~s in triplicate** las solicitudes por triplicado; **~ for shares** solicitud *f* de acciones; **are you going to put in an ~?** ¿te vas a presentar?; **to make an ~ for** solicitar; **to make an ~ to** dirigirse a; **to submit one's ~** presentar su solicitud; **details may be had on ~ to Z** para los detalles dirigirse a Z.

applicator [ˈæplɪkeɪtəʳ] N aplicador *m*.

applied [əˈplaɪd] ADJ aplicado **~ linguistics** lingüística *f* aplicada; **~ mathematics** matemáticas *fpl* aplicadas; **~ science** ciencias *fpl* aplicadas.

appliqué [æˈpliːkeɪ] N (*also ~ lace, ~ work*) encaje *m* de aplicación.

apply [əˈplaɪ] ⃞1 VT (*gen*) aplicar; *ointment, paint etc* aplicar; *brakes* poner, echar; *rule* emplear, recurrir a; (*Jur*) poner en vigor; **to ~ heat to a surface** (*Tech*) exponer una superficie al calor; (*Med*) calentar una superficie; **to ~ a match to** poner fuego (con una cerilla) a; **to ~ pressure** ejercer presión, presionar; **how can we best ~ this money?** ¿cómo podemos utilizar mejor este dinero?; **he applied his mind to the problem** se dedicó a resolver el problema.

2 VI **(a)** (*refer to*) ser aplicable, interesar, ser pertinente; **cross out what does not** ~ táchese lo que no interese, táchese lo que no sea pertinente.
(b) (*request*) presentarse, ser candidato; **are you ~ing?** ¿te vas a presentar?; **please ~ at the office** diríjanse a la oficina, (*on notice*) dirigirse a la oficina; **to ~ to sb** dirigirse a uno, acudir a uno; **to ~ to sb for sth** dirigirse a uno pidiendo algo.
3 VR: **to ~ o.s. to** aplicarse a, dedicarse a.
▼♦**apply for** VT solicitar, pedir; *post* solicitar, presentarse a; **'Patent applied for'** 'Patente en trámite'.
♦**apply to** VT tener que ver con, ser aplicable a, referirse a; **the law applies to all** la ley comprende a todos.
appoggiatura [ə,pɒdʒə'tʊərə] N apoyatura f.
appoint [ə'pɔɪnt] VT **(a)** (*fix*) fijar, señalar (*for* para); **at the ~ed time** a la hora señalada.
(b) (*nominate*) nombrar (*to* a); **they ~ed him chairman** le nombraron presidente; **they ~ed him to do it** le nombraron para hacerlo.
(c) **well ~ed** bien amueblado.
appointee [əpɔɪn'tiː] N persona f nombrada.
appointive [ə'pɔɪntɪv] ADJ (*US*): ~ **position** puesto m que se cubre por nombramiento.
appointment [ə'pɔɪntmənt] N **(a)** (*act of appointing*) nombramiento m (*to* a); **'By ~ to HRH'** 'Proveedores de S.A.R.'
(b) (*engagement*) cita f, compromiso m; (*at dentist's, hairdresser's etc*) hora f; **I have an ~ at 10** tengo una cita a las 10; **have you an ~ tonight?** ¿tienes compromiso para esta noche?; **have you an ~?** (*to caller*) ¿tiene Vd hora?; **to keep an ~** acudir a una cita; **to make an ~** (*2 or more persons*) darse una cita, citarse (*with* con); **to make an ~ for 3 o'clock** citarse para las 3; **to meet sb by ~** reunirse con uno de acuerdo con lo convenido.
(c) (*post*) puesto m, empleo m, colocación f; **~s board, ~s service** (*Univ etc*) oficina f de colocación; **~s bureau** agencia f de colocaciones; **'A~s Vacant'** 'ofrecen empleos'.
(d) **~s** (*furniture etc*) mobiliario m, moblaje m, equipo m.
apportion [ə'pɔːʃən] VT prorratear; repartir, distribuir; desglosar; **the blame is to be ~ed equally** todos tienen la culpa por partes iguales.
apportionment [ə'pɔːʃənmənt] N prorrateo m; repartición f, distribución f, desglose m; (*US Pol*) delimitación f de distritos (*or* condados).
apposite ['æpəzɪt] ADJ apropiado (*to* a); a propósito, oportuno.
apposition [,æpə'zɪʃən] N **(a)** (*of position*) yuxtaposición f. **(b)** (*Gram*) aposición f; **in ~** en aposición.
appositional [,æpə'zɪʃənl] ADJ aposicional.
appraisal [ə'preɪzəl] N tasación f, valoración f, evaluación f; (*fig*) estimación f, apreciación f.
appraise [ə'preɪz] VT tasar, valorar, evaluar; (*Comm, Fin*) tasar; *staff* evaluar; (*fig*) estimar, apreciar.
appraiser [ə'preɪzəʳ] N apreciador m, -ora f, evaluador m, -ora f; (*Comm, Fin*) tasador m, -ora f.
appraising [ə'preɪzɪŋ] ADJ *look etc* apreciativo.
appreciable [ə'priːʃəbl] ADJ sensible, perceptible; (*large*) considerable, importante; **an ~ sum** una cantidad importante; **an ~ loss** una pérdida sensible.
appreciably [ə'priːʃəblɪ] ADV sensiblemente, perceptiblemente.
appreciate [ə'priːʃɪeɪt] **1** VT **(a)** (*estimate worth of*) apreciar, valorar, aquilatar.
(b) (*estimate correctly*) apreciar, saber valorar en su justo precio.
(c) (*esteem*) apreciar, tener en mucho, tener un alto concepto de; **he does not ~ music** no sabe apreciar la música, no entiende de música; **I am not ~d here** aquí no me estiman; **we much ~ your work** tenemos un alto concepto de su trabajo.
(d) (*understand*) comprender; hacerse cargo de; **I ~ your wishes** comprendo sus deseos; **yes, I ~ that** sí, lo comprendo; **to ~ that ...** comprender que ...; **we fully ~ that ...** comprendemos perfectamente que ...
(e) (*be grateful for*) agradecer; **I ~ the gesture** agradezco el detalle; **we should much ~ it if ...** agradeceríamos mucho que ... + *subj*.
(f) (*be sensitive to*) percibir; **the smallest change can be ~d on this machine** en esta máquina se percibe el más leve cambio.
2 VI aumentar(se) en valor, subir.
appreciation [ə,priːʃɪ'eɪʃən] N **(a)** (*estimation*) aprecio m, apreciación f, estimación f; (*report*) aprecio m, informe m; (*obituary*) (nota f) necrológica f; (*praise*) elogio m; (*Liter etc*) crítica f.
(b) (*esteem*) aprecio m; **you have no ~ of art** no sabes apreciar el arte, no entiendes de arte.
(c) (*gratitude*) reconocimiento m, agradecimiento m; **as a token of my ~** en señal de agradecimiento; **she smiled her ~** sonrió agradecida.
(d) (*rise in value*) aumento m en valor, subida f.
appreciative [ə'priːʃɪətɪv] ADJ agradecido; *audience* atento, apreciativo; *comment* elogioso, de aprobación; **an ~ look** (*grateful*) una mirada

llena de agradecimiento; (*admiring*) una mirada admirativa; **he was very ~ of what I had done** agradeció mucho lo que yo había hecho; **he is ~ of good wine** estima el buen vino.
appreciatively [ə'priːʃɪətɪvlɪ] ADV (*V adj*) agradecidamente, con gratitud; atentamente; con aprobación; con admiración.
apprehend [,æprɪ'hend] VT **(a)** (*arrest*) prender, detener. **(b)** (*perceive*) percibir; comprender. **(c)** (*fear*) recelar.
apprehension [,æprɪ'henʃən] N **(a)** (*arrest*) prendimiento m, detención f.
(b) (*perception*) percepción f; comprensión f.
(c) (*fear*) recelo m, aprensión f; **my chief ~ is that ...** sobre todo me temo que ... + *subj*.
apprehensive [,æprɪ'hensɪv] ADJ aprensivo, inquieto; **to be ~ about, to be ~ for** temer por, inquietarse por; **to be ~ of danger** temer el peligro; **to be ~ that ...** recelar que ..., temer que ... + *subj*; **to grow ~** inquietarse.
apprehensively [,æprɪ'hensɪvlɪ] ADV con aprensión.
apprentice [ə'prentɪs] **1** N aprendiz m, -iza f; (*fig*) novicio m, -a f, principiante mf, aprendiz m, -iza f; **~ electrician** aprendiz m de electricista.
2 VT poner de aprendiz (*to* con); **to be ~d to** estar de aprendiz con.
apprenticeship [ə'prentɪʃɪp] N aprendizaje m; **to serve one's ~** hacer su aprendizaje.
apprise [ə'praɪz] VT informar, avisar (*of* de); **I will ~ him of it** se lo diré; **I was never ~d of your decision** no se me comunicó nunca su decisión; **to be ~d of** estar al corriente de.
appro* ['æprəʊ] (*Comm*) ABBR of **approval**; **on ~** a prueba.
▼ **approach** [ə'prəʊtʃ] **1** VT **(a)** *place* acercarse a; aproximarse a.
(b) *subject etc* abordar, enfocar; **we must ~ the matter with care** tenemos que abordar el asunto con mucho cuidado; **it all depends on how we ~ it** depende de cómo enfocamos la cuestión; **I ~ it with an open mind** me lo planteo sin prejuicios.
(c) *person* abordar, dirigirse a; **a man ~ed me in the street** un hombre me abordó en la calle; **you should ~ the boss about that** Vd debiera dirigirse al jefe sobre aquello; **have you ~ed him yet?** ¿has hablado ya con él?; **he is difficult to ~** no es fácil abordarle.
(d) (*approximate to*) aproximarse a; parecerse a, ser semejante a; **here the colour ~es blue** aquí el color tira a azul; **she must be ~ing 50** debe de tener cerca de los 50, debe de ser casi cincuentona; **it was ~ing midnight** era casi medianoche; **the performance ~ed perfection** la interpretación era casi perfecta.
2 VI acercarse.
3 N **(a)** (*act*) acercamiento m; (*Golf*) aproximación f; **~ light** (*Aer*) baliza f de aproximación; **~ shot** (*Golf*) golpe m de aproximación; **we observed his ~** le vimos acercarse; **at the ~ of the enemy** al acercarse el enemigo; **at the ~ of night** al entrar la noche; **at the ~ of Easter** al acercarse la Pascua.
▼**(b)** (*to subject etc*) aproximación f (*to* a), enfoque m (*to* de), modo m de enfocar una cuestión, método m de abordar un problema; orientación f, actitud f; planteamiento m; **an ~ to Spanish history** una aproximación a la historia de España; **I don't like your ~ to this matter** no me gusta su modo de enfocar esta cuestión; **we must think of a new ~** tenemos que inventar otro método.
(c) (*access*) acceso m (*to* a); (*Aut*) carril m de aceleración; **~es accesos** mpl, (*Mil*) aproches mpl; **~ road** vía f de acceso; **the station ~es** las vías de acceso a la estación; **the northern ~es to Madrid** las rutas de acceso a Madrid por el norte; **easy of ~** asequible, de fácil acceso.
(d) (*advance*) propuesta f, proposición f; oferta f; **to make ~es to** dirigirse a, tratar de hablar con; hacer gestiones ante; **to make amorous ~es to** requerir de amores a.
approachable [ə'prəʊtʃəbl] ADJ *place* asequible; *person* abordable, tratable, accesible.
approaching [ə'prəʊtʃɪŋ] ADJ próximo, venidero; *car etc* que se acerca, que viene en dirección opuesta.
approbation [,æprə'beɪʃən] N aprobación f.
appropriate **1** [ə'prəʊprɪɪt] ADJ apropiado, conveniente, a propósito; adecuado; correspondiente; *moment etc* oportuno; *authority etc* competente; **~ for, ~ to** apropiado para; **whichever seems more ~** el que te parezca más apropiado; **would it be ~ for me to wear it?** ¿convendría que (yo) me lo pusiera?; **A, and where ~, B** A, y en su caso, B.
2 [ə'prəʊprɪeɪt] VT **(a)** (*take*) apropiarse.
(b) (*assign*) asignar, destinar (*for* a).
appropriately [ə'prəʊprɪɪtlɪ] ADV apropiadamente, convenientemente; **he was ~ named Flint** tuvo el nombre apropiado de Flint; **in an ~ designed house** en una casa convenientemente distribuida; **~ respectful** con el debido respeto.
appropriateness [ə'prəʊprɪɪtnɪs] N propiedad f, conveniencia f.
appropriation [ə,prəʊprɪ'eɪʃən] N **(a)** apropiación f. **(b)** (*Comm, Fin*) apropiación f, asignación f; fondos mpl; (*US*) crédito m; **~ account** cuenta f de apropiaciones; (*US*) **~ bill** ley f financiera; **A~ Committee** (*US Pol*) Comité m de gastos de la Cámara de Representantes; **~**

fund fondo *m* de asignación.

approval [ə'pruːvəl] N aprobación *f*; consentimiento *m*; (*formal OK*) visto *m* bueno; **on ~** (*Comm*) a prueba; previa aceptación; **a look of ~** una mirada aprobatoria; **has this your ~?** ¿Vd ha aprobado esto?; **to meet with sb's ~** obtener la aprobación de uno; **he nodded his ~** asintió con la cabeza.

▼ **approve** [ə'pruːv] ① VT aprobar; **read and ~d** visto bueno. ② VI: **she ~s** ella lo aprueba; **yes, I heartily ~** sí, estoy totalmente de acuerdo.

▼♦**approve of** VT *plan* aprobar, dar por bueno; *person* tener un buen concepto (*or* buena concepción de); *behaviour, idea* aprobar, ser partidario de; **they don't ~ of my fiancé** no les cae bien mi novio, mi novio no les resulta simpático; **we ~ of our new neighbours** nos agradan (*or* nos gustan) los nuevos vecinos; **I cannot ~ of your going** no puedo consentir en que vayas; **grandma doesn't ~ of women smoking** a la abuela no le gusta que fumen las mujeres; **she ~s of being punctual** estima la puntualidad; **I don't ~ of his conduct** no estoy de acuerdo con su conducta; **I don't ~ of your decision** no estoy de acuerdo con tu decisión; **he doesn't ~ of smoking or drinking** está en contra del tabaco y del alcohol.

approved [ə'pruːvd] ADJ aprobado, acreditado; **in the ~ fashion** del modo acostumbrado; **~ school** (*Brit*) correccional *m*, reformatorio *m*.

approving [ə'pruːvɪŋ] ADJ de aprobación, aprobatorio.

approvingly [ə'pruːvɪŋlɪ] ADV con aprobación.

approx ABBR of **approximately** aprox.

approximate ① [ə'prɒksɪmɪt] ADJ aproximado. ② [ə'prɒksɪmeɪt] VI aproximarse (*to* a).

approximately [ə'prɒksɪmətlɪ] ADV aproximadamente, poco más o menos.

approximation [ə,prɒksɪ'meɪʃən] N aproximación *f*.

appt. (*US*) ABBR of **appointment**.

appurtenance [ə'pɜːtɪnəns] N (*frec pl*) (*appendage*) dependencia *f*; (*accessory*) accesorio *m*; **the house and its ~s** la casa con sus dependencias.

Apr. ABBR of **April** abril *m*, abr.

APR, apr N ABBR of **annual(ized) percentage rate** tasa *f* de interés anual.

après-ski [,æpreɪ'skiː] ① N après-ski *m*. ② ATTR de après-ski.

apricot ['eɪprɪkɒt] N (*fruit*) albaricoque *m*, chabacano *m* (*Mex*), damasco *m* (*LAm*); (*tree*) albaricoquero *m*, chabacano *m* (*Mex*), damasco *m* (*LAm*).

April ['eɪprəl] N abril *m*; **~ Fool** inocente; **~ Fools' Day** día *m* de los inocentes (*en Inglaterra el 1 abril*); **to make an ~ fool of sb** hacer una inocentada a uno; **~ showers** lluvias *fpl* de abril.

> **APRIL FOOLS' DAY**
>
> *ⓘ El 1 de abril es **April Fools' Day** en la tradición anglosajona. En ese día se les gastan bromas a los desprevenidos, quienes reciben la denominación de **April Fool** (inocente), y tanto la prensa escrita como la televisión difunden alguna historia falsa con la que sumarse al espíritu del día.*

a priori [eɪpraɪ'ɔːraɪ] ① ADV a priori. ② ADJ apriorístico.

apron ['eɪprən] N (a) (*garment*) delantal *m*; (*workman's, mason's etc*) mandil *m*. (b) (*Aer*) pista *f*. (c) (*Theat*) proscenio *m*; **~ stage** escena *f* saliente.

apron strings ['eɪprən'strɪŋz] NPL: **to be tied to the ~ of** estar cosido a las faldas de.

apropos [,æprə'pəʊ] ① ADV a propósito. ② PREP: **~ of** a propósito de. ③ ADJ oportuno.

apse [æps] N ábside *m*.

APT N (*Brit*) ABBR of **Advanced Passenger Train** ≈ tren *m* de gran velocidad, TGV *m*.

apt¹ [æpt] ADJ (a) (*suitable*) apropiado, conveniente; *remark, reply* acertado, oportuno; *description* exacto, atinado, apto. (b) (*tending*) **to be ~ to** + *infin* tener tendencia a + *infin*, ser propenso a + *infin*, ser susceptible de **~ infin**; **to be rather ~ to** + *infin* tener cierta tendencia a + *infin*; **I am ~ to be out on Mondays** por regla general no estoy los lunes; **we are ~ to forget that ...** a menudo nos olvidamos que ..., es fácil que olvidemos que ...; **only children are ~ to be spoiled** a los hijos únicos casi siempre se les mima; **it is ~ to cause trouble** es probable que cause molestias. (c) (*gifted*) talentoso, inteligente; **to be an ~ pupil** ser un alumno aprovechado.

apt² ABBR of **apartment** apartamento *m*.

▼ **aptitude** ['æptɪtjuːd] N aptitud *f* (*for, in* para), capacidad *f*, habilidad *f*; **~ test** test *m* de aptitud.

aptly ['æptlɪ] ADV oportunamente, acertadamente; **an ~ named plant** una planta de nombre apropiado.

aptness ['æptnɪs] N lo apropiado, propiedad *f*; lo acertado, oportunidad *f*, exactitud *f*.

Apuleius [,æpjə'lɪəs] NM Apuleyo.

aquafarming ['ækwə,fɑːmɪŋ] N piscicultura *f*.

aqualung ['ækwəlʌŋ] N escafandra *f* autónoma.

aquamarine [,ækwəmə'riːn] ① ADJ (de color) verde mar. ② N aguamarina *f*.

aquanaut ['ækwənɔːt] N submarinista *mf*.

aquaplane ['ækwəpleɪn] N hidroavión *m*.

Aquarian [ə'kweərɪən] N acuario *mf*.

aquarium [ə'kweərɪəm] N, PL **aquariums** or **aquaria** [ə'kweərɪə] acuario *m*.

Aquarius [ə'kweərɪəs] N (*Zodiac*) Acuario *m*.

aquatic [ə'kwætɪk] ① ADJ acuático. ② N (a) (*Bot*) planta *f* acuática; (*Zool*) animal *m* acuático. (b) **~s** (*Sport*) deportes *mpl* acuáticos.

aquatint ['ækwətɪnt] N acuatinta *f*.

aqueduct ['ækwɪdʌkt] N acueducto *m*.

aqueous ['eɪkwɪəs] ADJ ácueo, acuoso.

aquifer ['ækwɪfəʳ] N acuífero *m*.

aquiferous [ə'kwɪfərəs] ADJ acuífero.

aquiline ['ækwɪlaɪn] ADJ aguileño, aquilino.

Aquinas [ə'kwaɪnəs] NM Aquino; **St Thomas ~** Santo Tomás Aquino.

AR (a) (*Comm*) ABBR of **account rendered** cuenta *f* girada. **(b)** (*for tax*) ABBR of **annual return** declaración *f* anual. **(c)** (*report*) ABBR of **annual return** informe *m* anual. **(d)** (*US*) ABBR of **Arkansas**.

ARA N (*Brit*) ABBR of **Associate of the Royal Academy**.

A/R ABBR of **against all risks** contra todo riesgo.

Arab ['ærəb] ① ADJ árabe. ② N (a) árabe *mf*; V **street.** (b) (*horse*) caballo *m* árabe.

arabesque [,ærə'besk] N arabesco *m*.

Arabia [ə'reɪbɪə] N Arabia *f*.

Arabian [ə'reɪbɪən] ① ADJ árabe, arábigo; **~ Desert** Desierto *m* Arábigo; **~ Gulf, ~ Sea** Mar *m* de Omán; **The ~ Nights** Las mil y una noches. ② N árabe *mf*.

Arabic ['ærəbɪk] ① ADJ árabe, arábigo; **~ numeral** número *m* arábigo. ② N árabe *m*.

Arabist ['ærəbɪst] N arabista *mf*.

arabization [,ærəbaɪ'zeɪʃən] N arabización *f*.

arabize ['ærəbaɪz] VT arabizar.

arable ['ærəbl] ① ADJ cultivable, arable (*esp LAm*); **~ farm** granja *f* agrícola; **~ farming** agricultura *f*; **~ land = 2.** ② N tierra *f* de labrantío.

arachnid [ə'ræknɪd] N arácnido *m*.

Aragon ['ærəgən] N Aragón *m*.

Aragonese [,ærəgə'niːz] ① ADJ aragonés. ② N (a) aragonés *m*, -esa *f*. (b) (*Ling*) aragonés *m*.

ARAM N (*Brit*) ABBR of **Associate of the Royal Academy of Music**.

Aramaic [,ærə'meɪɪk] N arameo *m*.

arbiter ['ɑːbɪtəʳ] N árbitro *m*.

arbitrage [,ɑːbɪ'trɑːʒ] N arbitraje *m*.

arbitrageur [,ɑːbɪtræ'ʒɜː] N arbitrajista *m*.

arbitrarily ['ɑːbɪtrərɪlɪ] ADV arbitrariamente.

arbitrariness ['ɑːbɪtrərɪnɪs] N arbitrariedad *f*.

arbitrary ['ɑːbɪtrərɪ] ADJ arbitrario; subjetivo; artificial.

arbitrate ['ɑːbɪtreɪt] ① VT resolver, juzgar. ② VI arbitrar (*in* en, *between* entre).

arbitration [,ɑːbɪ'treɪʃən] N arbitraje *m*; **we want the claim to go to ~** queremos que la reclamación pase a una comisión de arbitraje; **the question was referred to ~** se confió el asunto a un juez árbitro (*or* a una comisión de arbitraje).

arbitrator ['ɑːbɪtreɪtəʳ] N juez árbitro *mf*.

arboreal [ɑː'bɔːrɪəl] ADJ arbóreo.

arboretum [,ɑːbə'riːtəm] N arboleda *f*.

arboriculture ['ɑːbərɪ,kʌltʃəʳ] N arboricultura *f*.

arbour, (*US*) **arbor** ['ɑːbəʳ] N cenador *m*, pérgola *f*, glorieta *f*.

arbutus [ɑː'bjuːtəs] N madroño *m*.

ARC N (a) ABBR of **American Red Cross** Cruz *f* Roja Norteamericana. (b) (*Med*) ABBR of **AIDS-related complex**.

arc [ɑːk] ① N arco *m*. ② VI arquearse, formar un arco.

arcade [ɑː'keɪd] N (*series of arches*) arcada *f*; (*round public square*) soportales *mpl*; (*with shops*) galería *f*.

Arcadia [ɑː'keɪdɪə] N Arcadia *f*.

Arcadian [ɑː'keɪdɪən] ① ADJ árcade; arcádico. ② N árcade *mf*.

Arcady ['ɑːkədɪ] N Arcadia *f*.

arcane [ɑː'keɪn] ADJ arcano; secreto, misterioso.

arch¹ [ɑːtʃ] ① N (a) (*Archit*) arco *m*; (*vault*) bóveda *f*. (b) (*Anat*) empeine *m*; (*dental*) arcada *f*, arco *m*; **fallen ~es** pies *mpl* planos.

➤ LANGUAGE IN USE: **approve:** 1 → 11.2   **approve of** → 14   **aptitude** → 15.4, 16.4

2 VT (a) *back, body etc* arquear; *eyebrows* enarcar.
(b) to ~ over (*Archit*) abovedar.
3 VI arquearse, formar un arco; formar una bóveda.

arch² [ɑ:tʃ] ADJ (*cunning*) astuto; (*roguish*) zumbón, picaruelo; *look, remark etc* malicioso, lleno de malicia; de complicidad; *woman* coqueta.

arch³ [ɑ:tʃ] (*gen in compounds, see also below*) principal; consumado; archi-; *eg* **the ~criminal** el mayor de los criminales; **an ~hypocrite** un consumado hipócrita, un hipócrita de primer orden.

archaeological, (*esp US*) **archeological** [ˌɑ:kɪə'lɒdʒɪkəl] ADJ arqueológico.

archaeologist, (*esp US*) **archeologist** [ˌɑ:kɪ'ɒlədʒɪst] N arqueólogo *m*, -a *f*.

archaeology, (*esp US*) **archeology** [ˌɑ:kɪ'ɒlədʒɪ] N arqueología *f*.

archaic [ɑ:'keɪɪk] ADJ arcaico.

archaism ['ɑ:keɪɪzəm] N arcaísmo *m*.

archangel ['ɑ:k,eɪndʒəl] N arcángel *m*.

archbishop ['ɑ:tʃ'bɪʃəp] N arzobispo *m*.

┌─── *ARCHBISHOP* ───┐

ⓘ En la Iglesia anglicana (**Church of England**) existen dos arzobispos: **Archbishop of York** y **Archbishop of Canterbury**, siendo éste el jefe espiritual de la Iglesia. Ambos arzobispos, que ocupan un escaño en la Cámara de los Lores, son nombrados por el monarca con el asesoramiento del Primer Ministro y los representantes de la Iglesia anglicana. El Arzobispo de Canterbury es quien corona al nuevo monarca británico en la ceremonia de la coronación (**Coronation Ceremony**) y oficia en las bodas reales. Los dos arzobispos ejercen autoridad administrativa sobre el clero en sus respectivos arzobispados (**provinces**). El de York comprende catorce diócesis y el de Canterbury treinta, más otra que abarca las congregaciones anglicanas en el resto de Europa.

⇨ *Ver también* CHURCH OF ENGLAND, CHURCH OF SCOTLAND

archbishopric [ɑ:tʃ'bɪʃəprɪk] N arzobispado *m*.

archdeacon ['ɑ:tʃ'di:kən] N arcediano *m*.

archdiocese ['ɑ:tʃ'daɪəsɪs] N archidiócesis *f*.

archduke ['ɑ:tʃ'dju:k] N archiduque *m*.

arched [ɑ:tʃt] ADJ en forma de arco(s); arqueado; abovedado.

arch-enemy ['ɑ:tʃ'enɪmɪ] N archienemigo *m*, -a *f*; (*devil*) el enemigo malo.

archeological [ˌɑ:kɪə'lɒdʒɪkəl] ADJ (*esp US*) = **archaeological**.

archeologist [ˌɑ:kɪ'ɒlədʒɪst] N (*esp US*) = **archaeologist**.

archeology [ˌɑ:kɪ'ɒlədʒɪ] N (*esp US*) = **archaeology**.

archer ['ɑ:tʃər] N arquero *m*.

archery ['ɑ:tʃərɪ] N tiro *m* con arco.

archetypal [ɑ:kɪ'taɪpl] ADJ arquetípico.

archetypally [ˌɑ:kɪ'taɪpəlɪ] ADV arquetípicamente.

archetype ['ɑ:kɪtaɪp] N arquetipo *m*.

archetypical [ˌɑ:kɪ'tɪpɪkəl] = **archetypal**.

Archimedes [ˌɑ:kɪ'mi:di:z] NM Arquímedes; **~' screw** rosca *f* de Arquímedes.

archipelago [ˌɑ:kɪ'pelɪɡəʊ] N archipiélago *m*.

archiphoneme ['ɑ:kɪ,fəʊni:m] N archifonema *m*.

architect ['ɑ:kɪtekt] N (a) arquitecto *mf* (*also* -a *f*). (b) (*fig*) artífice *m*; **the ~ of victory** el artífice de la victoria.

architectonic [ˌɑ:kɪtek'tɒnɪk] ADJ arquitectónico.

architectural [ˌɑ:kɪ'tektʃərəl] ADJ arquitectónico.

architecturally [ˌɑ:kɪ'tektʃərəlɪ] ADV arquitectónicamente; **an ~ striking building** un edificio impresionante desde el punto de vista arquitectónico.

architecture ['ɑ:kɪtektʃər] N arquitectura *f*.

architrave ['ɑ:kɪtreɪv] N arquitrabe *m*.

archive ['ɑ:kaɪv] **1** N (*gen, Comput*) archivo *m*; **~ file** fichero *m* archivado.
2 VT archivar.

archivist ['ɑ:kɪvɪst] N archivero *m*, -a *f*, archivista *mf* (*LAm*).

archness ['ɑ:tʃnɪs] N astucia *f*; picardía *f*; malicia *f*; coquetería *f*.

archpriest ['ɑ:tʃ'pri:st] N arcipreste *m*.

archway ['ɑ:tʃweɪ] N arco *m*, arcada *f*.

arc lamp ['ɑ:klæmp] N lámpara *f* de arco; (*in welding*) arco *m* voltaico.

ARCM N (*Brit*) ABBR *of* **Associate of the Royal College of Music**.

arctic ['ɑ:ktɪk] **1** ADJ ártico; (*fig*) glacial; **A~ Circle** Círculo *m* Polar Ártico; **A~ Ocean** Océano *m* Glacial Ártico.
2 N: **the A~** el Ártico.

arc-welding ['ɑ:k,weldɪŋ] N soldadura *f* por arco.

ARD N (*US*) ABBR *of* **acute respiratory disease**.

Ardennes [ɑ:'denz] NPL Ardenas *fpl*.

ardent ['ɑ:dənt] ADJ ardiente, vehemente, apasionado; *supporter* fervoroso; *desire* ardiente; *lover* apasionado.

ardently ['ɑ:dəntlɪ] ADV ardientemente, con vehemencia, apasionadamente; fervorosamente.

ardour, (*US*) **ardor** ['ɑ:dər] N ardor *m*; fervor *m*; vehemencia *f*;

---

pasión *f*.

arduous ['ɑ:djʊəs] ADJ arduo, fuerte, riguroso; *climb, journey* penoso, arduo; *task* difícil, trabajoso.

arduously ['ɑ:djʊəslɪ] ADV rigurosamente; penosamente; con dificultad.

arduousness ['ɑ:djʊəsnɪs] N rigor *m*, lo riguroso; lo penoso; lo arduo; dificultad *f*.

are [ɑ:r] *V* be.

area ['ɛərɪə] N (a) (*Math, surface extent*) área *f*, superficie *f*; extensión *f*.
(b) (*Geog, space*) región *f*, zona *f*; (*Sport, eg goal ~*) área *f*; (*Comm*) zona *f*; **the London ~** la región londinense; **~ code** (*Brit Post*) código *m* postal; (*US Telec*) código *m* territorial, prefijo *m* (local); **~ manager** gerente *m* de zona; **~ office** oficina *f* regional; **~ representative** representante *mf* de (la) zona.
(c) (*Archit*) corral *m*, patio *m* (de sótano); **dining ~** comedor *m*.
(d) (*fig*) región *f*, zona *f*; ámbito *m*; terreno *m*, campo *m*; **I am not a specialist in this ~** no soy especialista en este campo; **~ of concern** motivo *m* de preocupación; **~ of disagreement** zona *f* de discrepancia; **~ of knowledge** sector *m* del saber; **~ of study** campo *m* de estudio.

arena [ə'ri:nə] N anfiteatro *m*, redondel *m*, arena *f*; palenque *m*; (*Taur*) plaza *f*, ruedo *m*; (*Circus*) pista *f*; **the political ~** el ruedo político.

aren't [ɑ:nt] = **are not**.

areola [ə'rɪələ] N, PL **areolas** *or* **areolae** aureola *f*.

Argentina [ˌɑ:dʒən'ti:nə] N la Argentina.

Argentine ['ɑ:dʒəntaɪn] **1** ADJ argentino.
2 N (a) (*person*) argentino *m*, -a *f*. (b) **the ~** la Argentina.

Argentinian [ˌɑ:dʒən'tɪnɪən] **1** ADJ argentino.
2 N argentino *m*, -a *f*.

Argie* ['ɑ:dʒɪ] N (*pej*) = **Argentine**.

argon ['ɑ:ɡɒn] N argón *m*.

Argonaut ['ɑ:ɡənɔ:t] N argonauta *m*.

argot ['ɑ:ɡəʊ] N argot *m*.

arguable ['ɑ:ɡjʊəbl] ADJ discutible; sostenible; defensible; **it is ~ whether** ... es dudoso si ...; **it is ~ that** ... se puede decir que ...

arguably ['ɑ:ɡjʊəblɪ] ADV: **it is ~ the best** se puede sostener que es el mejor.

▼ **argue** ['ɑ:ɡju:] **1** VT (a) *case* sostener; *matter* razonar acerca de; *point* discutir; **a well ~d case** un argumento razonado; **how will you ~ the case?** ¿cómo va Vd a presentar el pleito?; **to ~ one's way out of a jam** salir de un apuro a fuerza de argumentos.
(b) (*point to*) argüir, indicar; **it ~s his untrustworthiness** esto sugiere que es poco confiable; **it ~s him to be untrustworthy** hace creer que es poco confiable.
(c) to ~ that ... sostener que ...; **I have heard it ~d that** ... he oído sostener que ...
(d) to ~ sb into + *ger* persuadir a uno a + *infin*; **to ~ sb out of** + *ger* disuadir a uno de + *infin*; **to ~ sb out of an idea** persuadir a uno a abandonar una idea.
2 VI (a) (*two persons*) discutir, disputar, polemizar, pelear(se) (*LAm*) (*about* acerca de, *with* con); **we ~d all night** pasamos toda la noche discutiendo; **don't ~!** ¡no discutas!, ¡no repliques!
▼ **(b)** (*reason*) razonar, argüir, discurrir; **I ~ this way** yo pienso de este modo, yo razono así; **he ~s well** razona bien, presenta sus argumentos de modo convincente; **this ~s in his favour** esto habla en su favor; **it ~s well for him** es un indicio a su favor; **to ~ against** *person* hablar en contra de, *thing* alegar razones contra, combatir por argumentos; **to ~ for** abogar por.
◆ **argue out** VT *problem* debatir a fondo, discutir a fondo.

argufy* ['ɑ:ɡjʊfaɪ] VI discutir.

▼ **argument** ['ɑ:ɡjʊmənt] N (a) (*reason*) argumento *m* (*against* en contra de, *for* en pro de); **his ~ is that** ... él sostiene que ...; **there is a strong ~ in favour of** + *ger* hay un fuerte argumento para + *infin*; **I don't follow your ~** no comprendo su razonamiento; **to be open to ~** estar dispuesto a dejarse convencer.
(b) (*debate*) discusión *f*, disputa *f*, debate *m*; **there was a heated ~** hubo una discusión acalorada; **it is beyond ~** es indiscutible, queda fuera de toda duda; **for the sake of ~** ... pongamos por caso ..., pongamos como hipótesis ...; **the conclusion is open to ~** la conclusión es discutible; **to have the better of an ~** salir airoso de un debate; **he had an ~ with a wall** (*hum*) tuvo un asunto con un muro; **let's not have any ~, I don't want any ~ about it** no discutamos; **you've heard only one side of the ~** te han contado solamente un lado del asunto.
(c) (*Jur*) alegato *m*.
(d) (*synopsis*) argumento *m*, resumen *m*.

argumentation [ˌɑ:ɡjʊmən'teɪʃən] N argumentación *f*, argumentos *mpl*.

argumentative [ˌɑ:ɡjʊ'mentətɪv] ADJ discutidor.

Argus ['ɑ:ɡəs] NM Argos.

argy-bargy* ['ɑ:dʒɪ'bɑ:dʒɪ] N (*Brit*) discusión *f*, tiquismiquis *m*, dimes *mpl* y diretes.

► LANGUAGE IN USE: **argue: 2b** → 11.1   **argument: a** → 26.1, 26.2

aria [ˈɑːrɪə] N aria f.
Arian [ˈɛərɪən] [1] ADJ arriano.
[2] N arriano m, -a f.
Arianism [ˈɛərɪənɪzəm] N arrianismo m.
ARIBA [əˈriːbə] N (Brit) ABBR of **Associate of the Royal Institute of British Architects** socio del instituto de arquitectos.
arid [ˈærɪd] ADJ árido (also fig).
aridity [əˈrɪdɪtɪ] N aridez f.
Aries [ˈɛəriːz] N (Zodiac) Aries m.
aright [əˈraɪt] ADV correctamente, acertadamente; **if I heard you ~** si le oí bien; **if I understand you ~** si le entiendo correctamente; **to set ~** rectificar.
arise [əˈraɪz] (irr: PRET **arose**, PTP **arisen**) VI (a) (†, liter) levantarse, alzarse; **~!** (slogan) ¡arriba!
(b) (fig) surgir; presentarse, producirse; **matters arising (from the last meeting)** asuntos mpl pendientes (de la última reunión); **difficulties have ~n** han surgido dificultades; **should the occasion ~** si se presenta la ocasión; **should need ~** si fuera preciso, si nos vemos en el caso; **a storm arose** se desencadenó un temporal; **a great clamour arose** se produjo un tremendo clamor; **the question does not ~** no hay tal, no existe ese problema; **the question ~s whether ...** se plantea el problema de si ...
(c) (result) **to ~ from** provenir de, resultar de; originarse en; **arising from this, can you say ...?** partiendo de esta base, ¿puede Vd decir ...?
arisen [əˈrɪzn] PTP of **arise**.
aristo* [ˈærɪstəʊ] N aristócrata mf.
aristocracy [ˌærɪsˈtɒkrəsɪ] N aristocracia f.
aristocrat [ˈærɪstəkræt] N aristócrata mf.
aristocratic [ˌærɪstəˈkrætɪk] ADJ aristocrático.
Aristophanes [ˌærɪsˈtɒfəniːz] NM Aristófanes.
Aristotelian [ˌærɪstəˈtiːlɪən] ADJ aristotélico.
Aristotelianism [ˌærɪstəˈtiːlɪənɪzəm] N aristotelismo m.
Aristotle [ˈærɪstɒtl] NM Aristóteles.
arithmetic [əˈrɪθmətɪk] N aritmética f; **~ mean** media f aritmética.
arithmetical [ˌærɪθˈmetɪkəl] ADJ aritmético; **~ progression** progresión f aritmética.
arithmetician [əˌrɪθməˈtɪʃən] N aritmético mf.
Ariz. (US) ABBR of **Arizona**.
Ark. (US) ABBR of **Arkansas**.
ark [ɑːk] N arca f; **A~ of the Covenant** Arca f de la Alianza; **Noah's A~** Arca f de Noé; **it's out of the A~** viene del año de la nana.
arm¹ [ɑːm] N (a) (Anat, fig) brazo m; **~ in ~** del brazo, de bracete, cogidos del brazo; **with folded ~s** con los brazos cruzados; **with open ~s** con los brazos abiertos; **within ~'s reach** al alcance del brazo; **with his coat over his ~** con el abrigo sobre el brazo; **she came in on her father's ~** entró del brazo de su padre; **to chance one's ~** arriesgarse, aventurarse; **I'd give my right ~ to own it** daría todo lo que tengo por poseerlo; **to give sb one's ~** dar el brazo a uno; **he held it at ~'s length** lo tenía en la mano con el brazo extendido; **to keep sb at ~'s length** mantener a uno a distancia; **to pay an ~ and a leg for sth*** dar un ojo de la cara por algo; **this pushed them into the ~s of the Ruritanians** esto les obligó a buscar el apoyo de los ruritanios; esto les obligó a aliarse con los ruritanios; **to put one's ~ round sb** rodear a uno del brazo; **to put the ~ on sb** (US*) presionar a uno; **to take sb in one's ~s** abrazar a uno; **please take my ~** toma el brazo; **to twist sb's ~** convencer a uno a la fuerza, presionar a uno; **the long ~ of the law** el brazo de la ley.
(b) (of chair, crane, etc) brazo m; (of coat) manga f; **~ of the sea** brazo m de mar.
(c) (Comm etc) sección f, división f, departamento m; **technical ~** sección f técnica, servicio m técnico.
arm² [ɑːm] [1] N (a) (Mil) arma f; **~s control** control m de armamento(s); **~s dealer** traficante m en armas; **~s factory** fábrica f de armas; **~s limitation** limitación f armamentística (or de armamentos); **~s manufacturer** fabricante m de armas; **~s race** carrera f de armamentos; **to be under ~s** estar sobre las armas; **to be up in ~s** poner el grito en el cielo (about a causa de); **to lay down one's ~s** rendir las armas; **to rise up in ~s** alzarse en armas; **to take up ~s** tomar las armas; **present ~s!** ¡presenten armas!; **order ~s!** ¡descansen armas!; **shoulder ~s!, slope ~s!** ¡armas al hombro!
(b) **~s** (Her) escudo m, blasón m.
[2] VT (a) person, nation armar.
(b) missile cebar.
[3] VR: **to ~ o.s.** armarse; **to ~ o.s. with arguments** pertrecharse de argumentos; **to ~ o.s. with patience** armarse de paciencia.
armada [ɑːˈmɑːdə] N flota f, armada f; **the A~** la Invencible.
armadillo [ˌɑːməˈdɪləʊ] N armadillo m.
Armageddon [ˌɑːməˈgedn] N Armagedón m, lucha f suprema.
armament [ˈɑːməmənt] N armamento m.
armature [ˈɑːmətjʊəʳ] N (Bot, Elec, Zool) armadura f; (of dynamo)

inducido m; (supporting framework) armazón f.
armband [ˈɑːmbænd] N brazal m, brazalete m.
armchair [ˈɑːmtʃɛəʳ] [1] N sillón m, butaca f.
[2] ATTR: **~ general** general m de salón; **~ strategist** estratega m de gabinete, estratega m de café.
armed [ɑːmd] [1] PRET AND PTP of **arm²**.
[2] ADJ armado; provisto de armas; **~ to the teeth** armado hasta los dientes; **~ conflict** conflicto m armado; **~ forces, ~ services** fuerzas fpl armadas; **~ neutrality** neutralidad f armada; **~ robbery** robo m a mano armada.
-armed [ɑːmd] ADJ ending in compounds de brazos ..., eg **strong~** de brazos fuertes; **one~** manco.
Armenia [ɑːˈmiːnɪə] N Armenia f.
Armenian [ɑːˈmiːnɪən] [1] ADJ armenio.
[2] N (a) armenio m, -a f. (b) (Ling) armenio m.
armful [ˈɑːmfʊl] N brazado m, brazada f.
armhole [ˈɑːmhəʊl] N sobaquera f, sisa f.
armistice [ˈɑːmɪstɪs] N armisticio m.
armlet [ˈɑːmlɪt] N brazal m.
armlock [ˈɑːmˈlɒk] N llave f de brazo; **to hold sb in an ~** inmovilizar a uno con una llave.
armor [ˈɑːməʳ] N (US) = **armour**.
armorial [ɑːˈmɔːrɪəl] ADJ heráldico; **~ bearings** escudo m de armas.
armour, (US) armor [ˈɑːməʳ] [1] N (a) (Mil, Zool, fig) armadura f; (steel plates) blindaje m. (b) (tank forces) tanques mpl, fuerzas fpl blindadas.
[2] VT blindar, acorazar.
armour-clad, (US) armor-clad [ˈɑːməklæd] ADJ, **armoured, (US) armored** [ˈɑːməd] ADJ blindado, acorazado; **~ car** (carro m) blindado m; **~ column** columna f blindada; **~ personnel carrier** vehículo m blindado para el transporte de tropas.
armourer, (US) armorer [ˈɑːmərəʳ] N armero m.
armour-piercing, (US) armor-piercing [ˈɑːmə.pɪəsɪŋ] ADJ shell perforante.
armour-plate, (US) armor-plate [ˈɑːmə.pleɪt] N blindaje m.
armour-plated, (US) armor-plated [ˈɑːməˈpleɪtɪd] ADJ blindado, acorazado.
armour-plating, (US) armor-plating [ˈɑːməˈpleɪtɪŋ] N blindaje m.
armoury, (US) armory [ˈɑːmərɪ] N armería f; arsenal m.
armpit [ˈɑːmpɪt] N sobaco m, axila f.
armrest [ˈɑːmrest] N apoyo m para el brazo, apoyabrazos m; (of chair) brazo m.
arm-twisting* [ˈɑːmˈtwɪstɪŋ] N tira y afloja m, persuasión f.
arm-wrestling [ˈɑːmˌreslɪŋ] N lucha f a pulso.
army [ˈɑːmɪ] N ejército m; (fig) ejército m, multitud f; **~ chaplain** capellán m castrense; **~ corps** cuerpo m de ejército; **~ doctor** médico m militar; **~ life** vida f militar; **A~ list** lista f de oficiales del ejército; **~ of occupation** ejército m de ocupación; **~ slang** argot m militar; **to join the ~** hacerse soldado, engancharse, alistarse.
arnica [ˈɑːnɪkə] N árnica f.
aroma [əˈrəʊmə] N aroma m (of a).
aromatherapist [əˈrəʊməˈθerəpɪst] N aromaterapeuta mf.
aromatherapy [əˈrəʊməˈθerəpɪ] N aromaterapia f.
aromatic [ˌærəʊˈmætɪk] ADJ aromático.
arose [əˈrəʊz] PRET of **arise**.
around [əˈraʊnd] [1] ADV (a) (round about) alrededor; a la redonda, eg **for 5 miles ~** en 5 millas a la redonda; **all ~** por todas partes, por todos lados.
(b) (nearby) cerca; por aquí; **is he ~?** ¿está por aquí?; **he must be somewhere ~** debe de andar por aquí; **he'll be ~ soon** estará dentro de poco; **there's a lot of flu ~** hay mucha gripe.
(c) **she's been ~*** (travelled) ha viajado mucho, ha visto mucho mundo; (experienced) tiene mucha experiencia; (pej) tiene historia.
[2] PREP (esp US) (a) (round) alrededor de, en torno de; **all ~ me** por todas partes alrededor de mí; **it's just ~ the corner** está a la vuelta de la esquina; **to go ~ the world** dar la vuelta al mundo; see also **about, round**.
(b) (inside) **to wander ~ the town** pasearse por la ciudad; **there were books all ~ the house** había libros en todas partes de la casa.
(c) (approximately) alrededor de; **~ 50** unos 50, 50 más o menos, alrededor de 50; **~ 2 o'clock** a eso de las 2; **~ 1950** alrededor de 1950.
arousal [əˈraʊzəl] N despertamiento m; (sexual) **~** excitación f (sexual), calentura f.
arouse [əˈraʊz] VT (a) (wake up) despertar. (b) (fig) mover, incitar, estimular, despertar; **it ~d great interest** despertó mucho interés; **it should ~ you to greater efforts** deberá incitarle a esforzarse más.
ARP NPL ABBR of **air-raid precautions** servicios mpl de defensa contra ataques aéreos.
arpeggio [ɑːˈpedʒɪəʊ] N arpegio m.
arr. ABBR of **arrives** llega.
arrack [ˈærək] N arac m, aguardiente m de palma (or caña etc).
arraign [əˈreɪn] VT procesar, acusar (before ante).

arrange [əˈreɪndʒ] ① vт (a) (*put in order*) arreglar, ordenar, disponer, organizar; **to ~ one's hair** arreglarse el pelo; **to ~ one's affairs** poner sus asuntos en orden; **how did we ~ matters last time?** ¿cómo lo organizamos la última vez?
(b) (*draw up*) disponer; **how is the room ~d?** ¿qué disposición tienen los muebles?
(c) (*Mus*) arreglar, adaptar.
(d) (*fix on, agree*) fijar, señalar; decidir, resolver; acordar; *meeting* organizar; *date* fijar; *plan, programme* acordar; **'to be ~d'** 'por determinar'; **I have ~d a surprise for tonight** he preparado una sorpresa para esta noche; **have you anything ~d for tomorrow?** ¿tienes planes para mañana?, ¿tienes compromiso mañana?; **a marriage has been ~d between ...** se ha concertado la boda de ...; **what did you ~ with him?** ¿cómo quedaron Vds con él?; **it was ~d that ...** se decidió que ...
② vı (a) **to ~ for** prevenir, disponer; **I have ~d for you to go** he hecho los arreglos para que vaya Vd; **can you ~ for my luggage to be sent up?** por favor, que me suban los equipajes; **I ~d to meet him at the station** me cité con él en la estación; **I have ~d to see him tonight** quedamos en vernos esta noche, nos hemos dado una cita para esta noche; **can you ~ for him to replace you?** ¿te puedes hacer sustituir por él?
(b) **to ~ with sb to +** *infin* ponerse de acuerdo con uno para que **+** *subj*; **to ~ with sb that ...** convenir con uno en que ... **+** *subj*.
arranged [əˈreɪndʒd] ADJ *marriage* concertado (por los padres).
arrangement [əˈreɪndʒmənt] N (a) (*order, ordering*) arreglo *m*, orden *m*, disposición *f*; ordenación *f*; **flower ~** arreglo *m* floral.
(b) (*Mus*) arreglo *m*, adaptación *f*.
(c) (*agreement*) acuerdo *m*, convenio *m*; **to come to an ~** llegar a un acomodo; **we have an ~ with them** existe un acuerdo con ellos; **larger orders by ~** los pedidos de mayor cantidad previo arreglo; **salary by ~** (*advert*) sueldo a convenir; **by ~ with Covent Garden** con permiso de Covent Garden.
(d) (*plan, line of action*) plan *m*, medida *f*; **~s** (*preparations*) preparativos *mpl*; (*order of events*) programa *m*; **what are the ~s for your holiday?** ¿qué plan tienes para las vacaciones?; **we must make ~s to help them** tenemos que tomar medidas para ayudarles; **to make one's own ~s** obrar por cuenta propia; **if she doesn't like the idea she must make her own ~s** si no le gusta la idea que se las arregle sola; **all the ~s are made** todo está arreglado; **if this ~ doesn't suit you** si este plan no te conviene; **he has an ~ with his secretary** se entiende con su secretaria.
arranger [əˈreɪndʒəʳ] N (*Mus*) arreglador *m*, -ora *f*, arreglista *mf*.
arrant [ˈærənt] ADJ *knave, liar etc* consumado, de siete suelas; **~ nonsense** puro disparate *m*.
array [əˈreɪ] ① N (a) (*Mil*) orden *m*, formación *f*; **in battle ~** en orden de batalla; **in close ~** en filas apretadas.
(b) (*fig*) serie *f* impresionante, colección *f* imponente; **a fine ~ of flowers** un bello conjunto de flores; **a great ~ of hats** una magnífica colección de sombreros.
(c) (*dress*) adorno *m*, atavío *m*.
(d) (*Comput*) matriz *f*, tabla *f*.
② vт (*dress*) ataviar, engalanar (*in* de).
arrears [əˈrɪəz] NPL (*sometimes sing*) atrasos *mpl*; **~ of rent** atrasos *mpl* de alquiler; **in ~** moroso, atrasado en pagos; **to be in ~ with one's correspondence** tener atrasos de correspondencia; **to get into ~** atrasarse en los pagos; **to pay one month in ~** pagar con un mes de retraso.
arrest [əˈrest] ① N detención *f*; (*of goods*) secuestro *m*; **to be under ~** estar detenido; **you're under ~** queda Vd detenido; **to make an ~** hacer una detención.
② vт (a) (*Jur*) *criminal* detener, arrestar, capturar; *judgement* prorrogar.
(b) *attention* llamar.
(c) *growth, progress etc* detener, parar; atajar; (*hinder*) obstaculizar; **measures to ~ inflation** medidas *fpl* para detener la inflación; **~ed development** atrofia *f*, desarrollo *m* atrofiado.
arresting [əˈrestɪŋ] ADJ llamativo, impresionante.
arrest warrant [əˈrestˈwɒrənt] N orden *f* de arresto.
arrival [əˈraɪvəl] N (a) llegada *f*; (*fig*) advenimiento *m*; **'A~s'** (*Aer*) 'Llegadas'; **~ platform** andén *m* de llegada; **on ~** al llegar.
(b) (*person*) persona *f* que llega; **new ~** recién llegado *m*, -a *f*, persona *f* que acaba de llegar; (*baby*) recién nacido *m*, -a *f*.
arrive [əˈraɪv] vı (a) llegar (*at, in* a); **to ~ (up)on the scene** llegar, aparecer, presentarse. (b) (*succeed*) triunfar, llegar (a ser alguien).
♦**arrive at** vт *decision, solution* llegar a; *perfection* lograr, alcanzar; **we finally ~d at a price** por fin convenimos en un precio; **they finally ~d at the idea of doing ...** finalmente llegaron a la decisión de hacer ...; **how did you ~ at this figure?** ¿cómo has llegado a esta cifra?
arriviste [ˌærɪˈviːst] N arribista *mf*.
arrogance [ˈærəgəns] N arrogancia *f*, prepotencia *f* (*LAm*).
arrogant [ˈærəgənt] ADJ arrogante, prepotente (*LAm*).

arrogantly [ˈærəgəntlɪ] ADV arrogantemente, con arrogancia, con prepotencia (*LAm*).
arrogate [ˈærəʊgeɪt] vт: **to ~ sth to o.s.** arrogarse algo; *quality* atribuirse, apropiarse.
arrow [ˈærəʊ] N flecha *f*.
arrowhead [ˈærəʊhed] N punta *f* de flecha.
arrowroot [ˈærəʊruːt] N arrurruz *m*.
arse⁑ [ɑːs] (*esp Brit*) ① N culo⁑ *m*; **he can't tell his ~ from his elbow** confunde el culo con las témporas⁑; **get off your ~!** ¡menearse!; **move** (*or* **shift**) **your ~** córrete para allá.
② vı: **to ~ about, ~ around** hacer el oso*.
arsehole⁑ [ˈɑːshəʊl] N (*esp Brit*) culo⁑ *m*; (*person*) gilipollas⁑ *m*.
arsenal [ˈɑːsɪnl] N arsenal *m*.
arsenic [ˈɑːsnɪk] N arsénico *m*.
arsenical [ɑːˈsenɪkl] ADJ arsénico, arsenical.
arson [ˈɑːsn] N incendio *m* doloso, incendio *m* provocado, incendiarismo *m*.
arsonist [ˈɑːsənɪst] N incendiario *m*, -a *f*, pirómano *m*, -a *f*.
art¹ [ɑːt] N (a) (*artistic*) arte *m* (*gen f in pl*); **~ for ~'s sake** el arte por el arte; **~ collection** colección *f* de arte; **~ college** escuela *f* de Bellas Artes; **~ deco** arte *m* deco; **~ exhibition** exposición *f* de arte; **~ gallery** museo *m* de pintura, pinacoteca *f*; **~ nouveau** art *m* nouveau; **~ paper** papel *m* cuché; **~ school** escuela *f* de arte; **~ student** estudiante *mf* de Bellas Artes.
(b) (*skill*) arte *m*; técnica *f*; (*quality*) habilidad *f*, destreza *f*; **~s and crafts** artes *fpl* y oficios; **A~s Council** (*Brit*) ≃ Consejería *f* de Cultura; **he's got it down to a fine ~** ha perfeccionado su método.
(c) (*Univ*) **A~s** Filosofía *f* y Letras; **Faculty of A~s** Facultad *f* de Filosofía y Letras; **Bachelor of A~s** (ABBR **BA**) Licenciado *m*, -a *f* en Filosofía y Letras; **Master of A~s** (ABBR **MA**) Maestro *m*, -a *f* en Artes; **A~s degree** licenciatura *f* en Letras; **A~s student** estudiante *mf* de Letras.
(d) (*cunning*) arte *m*; astucia *f*; (*trick*) ardid *m*, maña *f*; **all her ~ of persuading** todo su arte de persuadir.

┌─ **ARTS COUNCILS** ─┐

*Las organizaciones británicas denominadas **Arts Councils**, de financiación pública, tienen como finalidad subvencionar compañías de teatro y danza, artistas y orquestas, además de financiar exposiciones de arte y la educación y formación artísticas. Uno de sus principales objetivos es también hacer que el arte sea menos elitista y más accesible al público.*

art²†† [ɑːt] V *be*.
artefact, (*esp US*) **artifact** [ˈɑːtɪfækt] N artefacto *m*.
arterial [ɑːˈtɪərɪəl] ADJ arterial; **~ road** carretera *f* nacional.
arteriosclerosis [ɑːˈtɪərɪəʊsklɪəˈrəʊsɪs] N arteriosclerosis *f*.
artery [ˈɑːtərɪ] N arteria *f* (*also fig*).
artesian [ɑːˈtiːzɪən] ADJ: **~ well** pozo *m* artesiano.
art-form [ˈɑːtfɔːm] N medio *m* de expresión artística.
artful [ˈɑːtfʊl] ADJ mañoso, artero, astuto; (*skilful*) ingenioso.
artfully [ˈɑːtfʊlɪ] ADV con mucha maña, astutamente; ingeniosamente.
artfulness [ˈɑːtfʊlnɪs] N maña *f*, astucia *f*; ingenio *m*, artificio *m*.
art-house [ˈɑːthaʊs] ADJ *film* de autor, de arte y ensayo.
arthritic [ɑːˈθrɪtɪk] ADJ artrítico.
arthritis [ɑːˈθraɪtɪs] N artritis *f*.
arthropod [ˈɑːθrəpɒd] N artrópodo *m*.
Arthur [ˈɑːθəʳ] NM Arturo; **King ~** el Rey Artús, el Rey Arturo.
Arthurian [ɑːˈθjʊərɪən] ADJ arturiano, artúrico.
artichoke [ˈɑːtɪtʃəʊk] N alcachofa *f*.
article [ˈɑːtɪkl] ① N (a) (*object*) artículo *m*, objeto *m*, cosa *f*; **~ of clothing** prenda *f* de vestir; **~s of value** objetos *mpl* de valor.
(b) (*Press etc*) artículo *m*; colaboración *f*; reportaje *m*; (*learned*) artículo *m*.
(c) (*Jur etc*) artículo *m*; **~s of apprenticeship** contrato *m* de aprendizaje; **~s of association** (*Brit*) estatutos *mpl* de fundación (de una sociedad anónima); estatutos *mpl* sociales, escritura *f* social; **~ of faith** artículo *m* de fe; **~s of incorporation** (*US*) carta *f* constitucional; **~ of partnership** contrato *m* de asociación; **~s of war** (*US Mil Hist*) código *m* militar.
(d) (*Gram*) artículo *m*.
② vт *apprentice* pactar, comprometer por contrato; **to be ~d to** estar de aprendiz con, servir bajo contrato a; **~d clerk** pasante *m*.
articulate ① [ɑːˈtɪkjʊlɪt] ADJ (a) *limb* articulado. (b) *speech* claro, distinto; *person* capaz de hablar; que se expresa bien, elocuente; **at 2 a child is hardly ~** a los 2 años el niño es apenas capaz de hablar claramente; **he's not very ~** no se expresa bien, no habla con confianza.
② [ɑːˈtɪkjʊleɪt] vт articular; *plan, goal* expresar claramente.
articulated [ɑːˈtɪkjʊleɪtɪd] ADJ: **~ lorry** camión *m* con remolque.
articulately [ɑːˈtɪkjʊlɪtlɪ] ADV fluidamente, con facilidad.
articulation [ɑːˌtɪkjʊˈleɪʃən] N articulación *f*.
articulatory [ɑːˈtɪkjʊlətərɪ] ADJ articulatorio.

artifact ['ɑːtɪfækt] N (*esp US*) = **artefact**.

artifice ['ɑːtɪfɪs] N (*quality*) artificio *m*; (*ruse*) artificio *m*, ardid *m*, estratagema *f*.

artificial [,ɑːtɪ'fɪʃəl] ADJ (a) artificial; *hair, teeth etc* postizo; ~ **insemination** inseminación *f* artificial; ~ **intelligence** inteligencia *f* artificial; ~ **light** luz *f* artificial; ~ **manure** abono *m* químico; ~ **respiration** respiración *f* artificial; ~ **silk** seda *f* artificial, rayón *m*.
(b) *person* afectado; *smile* forzado; *manner* artificial, poco natural; *grief etc* fingido, fabricado.

artificiality [,ɑːtɪfɪʃɪ'ælɪtɪ] N artificialidad *f*; afectación *f*.

artificially [,ɑːtɪ'fɪʃəlɪ] ADV artificialmente; afectadamente, con afectación.

artillery [ɑː'tɪlərɪ] N artillería *f*.

artilleryman [ɑː'tɪlərɪmən], N, PL **artillerymen** [ɑː'tɪlərɪmen] artillero *m*.

artisan ['ɑːtɪzæn] N artesano *m*.

artisanal [ɑː'tɪzənəl] ADJ *skills, groups, clothes* artesanal.

artist ['ɑːtɪst] N artista *mf*.

artiste [ɑː'tiːst] N (*Theat etc*) artista *mf* (de teatro *etc*); (*Mus*) intérprete *mf*.

artistic [ɑː'tɪstɪk] ADJ artístico; **she is very ~** tiene mucho talento para el arte.

artistically [ɑː'tɪstɪkəlɪ] ADV artísticamente; **to be ~ gifted** tener talento para el arte.

artistry ['ɑːtɪstrɪ] N arte *m*; talento *m* artístico, habilidad *f* artística, maestría *f*.

artless ['ɑːtlɪs] ADJ (a) natural, sencillo; ingenuo. (b) (*pej*) torpe, desmañado.

artlessly ['ɑːtlɪslɪ] ADV ingenuamente.

artlessness ['ɑːtlɪsnɪs] N (a) naturalidad *f*, sencillez *f*; ingenuidad *f*. (b) desmaña *f*.

art-lover ['ɑːt,lʌvəʳ] N aficionado *m*, -a *f* al arte.

artsy* ['ɑːtsɪ] (*esp US*) = **arty**.

artwork ['ɑːtwɜːk] N material *m* gráfico.

arty* ['ɑːtɪ] ADJ *style etc* ostentosamente artístico; seudoartístico; *clothing* afectado, extravagante; *person* de gusto muy afectado, que se las da de muy artista, repipi*.

arty-crafty* ['ɑːtɪ'krɑːftɪ] ADJ, (*US*) **artsy-craftsy*** ['ɑːtsɪ'krɑːftsɪ] ADJ ostentosamente artístico, afectadamente artístico.

arty-farty* ['ɑːtɪ'fɑːtɪ], (*US*) **artsy-fartsy*** ['ɑːtsɪfɑːtsɪ] ADJ pretencioso, con pretensiones artísticas.

A.R.V. N (*US*) ABBR of **American Revised Version** *versión norteamericana de la Biblia*.

Aryan ['ɛərɪən] ⬚1 ADJ ario.
⬚2 N ario *m*, -a *f*.

AS (*US*) (a) N ABBR of **Associate in** (*or* of) **Science**. (b) ABBR of **American Samoa**.

▼**as** [æz, əz] ADV, CONJ AND PREP (a) (*comparisons*) como: **he does ~ I do** hace como yo; **~ ... ~** tan ... como, *eg* **~ tall ~** tan alto como; **~ quickly ~** tan rápidamente como; **is it ~ big ~ all that?** ¿es en verdad tan grande?; **the same ~** el (*or* la, lo) mismo que; **such countries ~ France** países tales como Francia; **large books (such) ~ dictionaries** los libros grandes tales como los diccionarios; **he is not so silly ~ to do that** no es tan tonto como para hacer eso.
(b) (*comparisons: intensifying similes*) (~) **pale ~ death** pálido como un muerto; **~ dead ~ a doornail** más muerto que mi abuela.
(c) (*comparisons: as if etc*) **~ if**, **~ though** como si + *subj*: **~ if (he were) drunk** como si estuviera borracho; **it isn't ~ if he were poor** no es que sea pobre; **it isn't ~ if I didn't care** no es que me trajera sin cuidado; **he was — ~ it were — tired and emotional** estaba — por decirlo de alguna manera — cansado y exaltado; **~ if to +** *infin* como para + *infin*.
(d) (*concessive*) **interesting ~ the book is** por interesante que sea el libro; **stupid ~ he is** aunque es estúpido; **be that ~ it may** sea como sea; **try ~ she would she couldn't lift it** por más que se esforzara no pudo levantarlo.
(e) (*in the capacity of*) como; **~ a husband and father** como marido y padre; **Chaplin ~ Hitler** Charlot en el papel de Hitler; **I don't think much of him ~ an actor** no le estimo como (*or* en cuanto, en tanto que) actor; **she was often ill ~ a child** a menudo estuvo enferma de niña; **it's spelled with V ~ in Valencia** se escribe con V de Valencia; **we're going ~ tourists** vamos en plan de turismo; **he was there ~ adviser** estuvo en calidad de asesor.
(f) (*after certain verbs*) **to act ~** actuar de, estar de; **to be dressed ~** estar vestido de; *see also the verbs*.
(g) (*concerning*) **~ for that**, **~ to that**, **~ regards that** en cuanto a eso, por lo que se refiere a eso, en lo que a eso atañe.
▼(h) (*manner*) como; **~ often happens** como ocurre a menudo; **do ~ you wish** haz lo que quieras, haz como quieras; **to leave things ~ they are** dejar las cosas tal como están; **just ~ you are an engineer,**

(so) **I am a doctor** como Vd es ingeniero yo soy médico; **her door is the first ~ you go up** su puerta es la primera según se sube; **you've got plenty ~** it is tiene ya bastantes; **~ it is we can do nothing** como están las cosas no podemos hacer nada.
(i) (*time*) **he came in ~ I was leaving** entró cuando yo salía, entró al salir yo; **~ I was sitting there he came up** mientras yo estaba sentado allí él vino; **~ she got older she got deafer** a medida que (*or* conforme) envejecía ensordecía más; **~ I was passing the house** al pasar yo delante de la casa; **~ from tomorrow** a partir de mañana; **~ of last week** a partir de la semana pasada.
(j) (*result*) **he did it in such a way ~ to please everyone** lo hizo de tal modo que logró contentar a todos; *V* **so**.
▼(k) (*since*) **~ I don't speak Arabic** como yo no hablo árabe; **I can't come ~ I have an appointment** no puedo venir pues (*or* ya que, porque) tengo un compromiso; **~ we hadn't heard from you** al no tener noticias tuyas.

┌───┐
│ **AS**   see also main entry │
└───┘

Time clauses

● You can usually use *cuando* when the *as* clause simply tells you *when* an event happened. Alternatively, use *al* + INFINITIVE:
   As the car drew level with us, I realized Isabel was driving
   Cuando el coche llegó a nuestra altura or *Al llegar el coche a nuestra altura, me di cuenta de que lo conducía Isabel*
   He tripped as he was coming out of the bank
   Tropezó cuando salía or *al salir del banco*

● Translate *as* using *mientras* for longer actions which are happening at the same time:
   As we walked, we talked about the future
   Mientras caminábamos, hablábamos del futuro

● In the context of two closely linked actions involving progression, translate *as* using *a medida que* or *conforme*. Alternatively, use *según va etc* + GERUND:
   As one gets older, life gets more and more difficult
   A medida que se envejece or *Conforme se envejece* or *Según va uno envejeciendo, la vida se hace cada vez más difícil*

! Don't use *como* in time clauses.

Reason clauses

● When *as* means "since" or "because" and tells you *why*, you can generally use *como*, provided you put it at the beginning of the sentence. Alternatively, use the more formal *puesto que* either at the beginning of the sentence or between the clauses. *Porque* and *pues* between the clauses are further possibilities:
   As you're here, I'll tell you
   Como estás aquí or *Puesto que estás aquí* or *Ya que estás aquí, te lo diré*
   He didn't mention it as he didn't want to worry you
   Como no quería preocuparte, no lo mencionó ◊ *No lo mencionó puesto que* or *porque* or *pues no quería preocuparte*
   For further uses and examples, see main entry.

ASA N (*Brit*) (a) ABBR of **Advertising Standards Authority** Asociación *f* de Normas Publicitarias. (b) ABBR of **Amateur Swimming Association** *federación amateur de natación*. (c) (*US*) ABBR of **American Standards Association** Asociación *f* Norteamericana de Normalización.

a.s.a.p. ADV ABBR of **as soon as possible**.

asbestos [æz'bestəs] N asbesto *m*, amianto *m*.

asbestosis [,æzbes'təusɪs] N asbestosis *f*.

ascend [ə'send] ⬚1 VT *stairs, river* subir; *mountain* escalar, subir a; *throne* subir a, ascender a.
⬚2 VI subir, ascender; (*soar*) elevarse, encaramarse.

ascendancy [ə'sendənsɪ] N ascendiente *m*, dominio *m* (*over* sobre).

ascendant [ə'sendənt] N: **to be in the ~** predominar, tener una influencia cada vez mayor, subir.

ascending [ə'sendɪŋ] ADJ ascendente; **in ~ order** en orden ascendente.

ascension [ə'senʃən] N ascensión *f*; **A~ Day** (Día *m* de) la Ascensión; **A~ Island** Isla *f* Ascensión.

ascent [ə'sent] N (*act*) subida *f*, ascensión *f*; (*slope*) cuesta *f*, pendiente *f*.

ascertain [,æsə'teɪn] VT averiguar, determinar, descubrir, indagar.

ascertainable [,æsə'teɪnəbl] ADJ averiguable, comprobable.

ascertainment [,æsə'teɪnmənt] N averiguación *f*, comprobación *f*.

ascetic [ə'setɪk] ⬚1 ADJ ascético.
⬚2 N asceta *mf*.

asceticism [ə'setɪsɪzəm] N ascetismo *m*.

ASCII N ABBR of **American Standard Code for Information Interchange** código *m* estándar norteamericano para el intercambio de información.

ascorbic [ə'skɔːbɪk] ADJ: **~ acid** ácido *m* ascórbico.

┌─── ASCOT ──┐

ℹ️ **Ascot** o **Royal Ascot** es una competición de carreras de caballos que
dura cuatro días y se celebra en junio en el hipódromo de Ascot, cerca
del castillo de Windsor, en el sur de Inglaterra. Es uno de los
acontecimientos más importantes en el calendario hípico británico, y
también lo es a nivel social, pues a él acuden miembros de la realeza y la
clase alta británica. La familia real hace acto de presencia en carruajes, y
sigue las carreras desde una zona reservada llamada **Royal Enclosure**. Se
considera un gran honor ser invitado a ella y los invitados han de observar
estrictas normas de etiqueta. En el día conocido como **Ladies Day** (el Día de
las Damas), es tradicional que las mujeres vayan a las carreras luciendo
sombreros y vestidos espectaculares.

└──┘

ascribable [əˈkraɪbəbl] ADJ atribuible (to a).
ascribe [əˈskraɪb] VT atribuir (to a).
ascription [əˈskrɪpʃən] N atribución f.
ASCU N (US) ABBR of **Association of State Colleges and Universities**.
ASE N (US) ABBR of **American Stock Exchange**.
ASEAN N ABBR of **Association of South-East Asian Nations** Asociación
f de Naciones del Sureste Asiático.
aseptic [eɪˈseptɪk] ADJ aséptico.
asexual [eɪˈseksjʊəl] ADJ asexual.
ASH [æʃ] N ABBR of **Action on Smoking and Health** organización antitabaco.
ash¹ [æʃ] ① N (also ~ **tree**) fresno m.
　② ATTR de fresno.
ash² [æʃ] N ceniza f; **~es** cenizas fpl (also of dead); **A~ Wednesday**
Miércoles m de Ceniza; **the A~es** trofeo imaginario de los partidos de
críquet Australia-Inglaterra; **to burn** (or **reduce**) **sth to ~es** reducir algo
a cenizas.
ashamed [əˈʃeɪmd] ADJ: **to be ~, to feel ~** avergonzarse, estar
avergonzado, apenarse (LAm) (at, of de; for por; of being de ser); **I am
~ of you** me das vergüenza; **I was ~ to ask for money** me daba
vergüenza pedir dinero; **I am ~ to say that ...** me avergüenza decir
que ...; **your generosity makes me feel ~** su generosidad me
produce vergüenza; **to be ~ of o.s.** tener vergüenza de sí; **you
ought to be ~ of yourself!** ¿no te da vergüenza?, ¿no tienes
vergüenza?
ashbin [ˈæʃbɪn] N cubo m de la basura, tarro m de basura (LAm).
ash blond(e) [æʃˈblɒnd] ① ADJ rubio ceniza.
　② N rubia f ceniza.
ashcan [ˈæʃkæn] N (US) = ashbin.
ash-coloured, (US) **ash-colored** [ˈæʃkʌləd] ADJ ceniciento; color
ceniza; face pálido.
ashen [ˈæʃn] ADJ (a) (pale) pálido, ceniciento. (b) (Bot: of ash wood) de
fresno.
Ashkenazi [ˌæʃkəˈnɑːzɪ] ① ADJ askenazí.
　② N, PL **Ashkenazim** [ˌæʃkəˈnɑːzɪm] askenazí mf.
ashlar [ˈæʃləʳ] N sillar m; (also ~ **work**) sillería f.
ashman [ˈæʃmæn] N, PL **ashmen** [ˈæʃmen] (US) basurero m.
ashore [əˈʃɔːʳ] ADV en tierra; **to be ~** estar en tierra; **to come ~, to go
~** desembarcar; **to put sb ~** desembarcar a uno, poner a uno en tierra.
ashpan [ˈæʃpæn] N cenicero m, cajón m de la ceniza.
ashram [ˈæʃrəm] N ashram m.
ashtray [ˈæʃtreɪ] N cenicero m.
ashy [ˈæʃɪ] ADJ cenizoso.
Asia [ˈeɪʃə] N Asia f; **~ Minor** Asia f Menor.
Asian [ˈeɪʃn] ① ADJ asiático; **~ flu** gripe f asiática.
　② N asiático m, -a f.
Asian-American [ˈeɪʃnəˈmerɪkən] ① ADJ asiático-americano.
　② N asiático-americano m, -a f.
Asiatic [ˌeɪsɪˈætɪk] ① ADJ asiático.
　② N asiático m, -a f.
aside [əˈsaɪd] ① ADV aparte, a un lado; V put, set etc.
　② PREP (esp US) **~ from** aparte de.
　③ N (Theat) aparte m; **to say sth in an ~** decir algo aparte.
asinine [ˈæsɪnaɪn] ADJ asnal; (fig) estúpido.
▼ **ask** [ɑːsk] ① VT (a) (inquire, inquire of) preguntar; **to ~ sb sth** preguntar
algo a uno; **to ~ sb a question** hacer una pregunta a uno; **they ~ed
me about my passport** me hicieron preguntas acerca de mi
pasaporte; **they ~ed me about the new missile** me interrogaron sobre el nuevo mísil; **if you ~ me ...** para mí que ..., en mi opinión ...;
don't ~ me! ¡yo qué sé!; **I ~ you!** (despairing) ¡vaya por Dios!; ¡lo que
faltaba!; **~ed if this was true, she replied ...** preguntada si esto era
cierto, contestó ...
　(b) (request, demand) pedir; **to ~ sb a favour, to ~ a favour of sb**
pedir un favor a uno; **I don't ~ much from you** lo que te pido es
poco; **that's ~ing the impossible** eso es pedir lo imposible; **that's
~ing a lot** eso es mucho pedir; **to ~ that ...** pedir que ... + subj,
rogar que ... + subj; **to ~ sb to do sth** pedir a uno que haga algo.

(c) (invite) invitar, convidar (LAm); **have they ~ed you?** ¿te han
invitado?; **to ~ sb to dinner** invitar a uno a cenar.
　② VI (inquire) preguntar; (request, demand) pedir; **I was only ~ing**
solamente era una simple pregunta; **it's ours for the ~ing** si lo
pedimos nos lo dan, es nuestro con solo pedir; **~ing price** precio m
a que se ofrece; **this is the third time of ~ing** (ésta) es la tercera vez
que te lo pido; **now you're ~ing!** (iro) ¡vaya pregunta!
◆ **ask about** VT preguntar por; pedir noticias de.
◆ **ask after** VT person preguntar por, interesarse por; **to ~ after sb's
health** interesarse por la salud de uno.
◆ **ask along** VT invitar.
◆ **ask back** VT (for second visit) volver a invitar; **to ~ sb back** (on re, reciprocal visit) invitar a uno a que devuelva la visita.
◆ **ask for** VT (a) (inquire) preguntar por.
　(b) (request) pedir, reclamar; solicitar; **to ~ sb for sth** pedir algo a
uno; **he ~ed for it*** se la buscó, bien merecido lo tiene; **to ~ for sth
back** pedir que se devuelva algo; **how much are they ~ing for it?**
¿cuánto piden por él?; **to write ~ing for help** escribir pidiendo
ayuda; V trouble.
◆ **ask in** VT invitar a entrar, invitar a pasar.
◆ **ask out** VT: **they never ~ her out** no le invitan nunca a salir (con
ellos); **I'm ~ed out** estoy invitado; **the first time he ~ed her out** la
primera vez que la invitó a salir con él; **I never dared to ~ her out**
nunca me atreví a pedirle una cita.
◆ **ask round** VT invitar.

┌─── ASK ──────────────────────── see also main entry ──┐

● Translate **ask** by **preguntar** only in contexts where information is
being sought:
　　I'll ask him
　　Voy a preguntárselo
　　Ask her what she thinks
　　Pregúntale qué le parece
　　We asked everyone
　　Preguntamos en todas partes
● Use **pedir** when **ask** means "request" or "demand":
　　No one asked to see my passport
　　Nadie me pidió el pasaporte
　　We asked them to be here before 5 pm
　　Les pedimos que estuviesen or **estuvieran aquí antes de las 5**
　　He was asked to explain his behaviour
　　Le pidieron que explicara su comportamiento
! **Pedir que** is followed by the subjunctive.
　For further uses and examples, see main entries at **ask, ask about** and
　ask for etc.

└──┘

askance [əˈskɑːns] ADV: **to look ~** mirar de soslayo, mirar con recelo.
askew [əˈskjuː] ADV sesgado, ladeado; oblicuamente; **the picture is ~**
el cuadro está torcido.
aslant [əˈslɑːnt] ① ADV a través, oblicuamente.
　② PREP a través de.
asleep [əˈsliːp] ADJ dormido; **to be ~** estar dormido; **to be fast ~, to
be sound ~** estar profundamente dormido; **to fall ~** dormirse,
quedar dormido.
ASLEF [ˈæzlef] N (Brit) ABBR of **Associated Society of Locomotive Engineers and Firemen** sindicato de maquinistas y fogoneros.
ASM N ABBR of **air-to-surface missile** misil m aire-tierra.
asocial [eɪˈsəʊʃl] ADJ (solitary) asocial, insociable; (antisocial) antisocial.
ASP ABBR of **American Selling Price** precio m de venta en América.
asp [æsp] N áspid(e) m.
asparagus [əsˈpærəgəs] N (plant) esparraguera f, espárrago m; (as food)
espárragos mpl.
ASPCA N (US) ABBR of **American Society for the Prevention of Cruelty to Animals**.
▼ **aspect** [ˈæspekt] N aspecto m (also Gram); apariencia f; **to study all ~s
of a question** estudiar una cuestión bajo todos sus aspectos; **seen
from this ~** visto desde este lado; **a house with a southerly ~** una
casa orientada hacia el sur.
aspen [ˈæspən] N álamo m temblón.
asperity [æsˈperɪtɪ] N aspereza f.
aspersion [əsˈpɜːʃən] N calumnia f; **to cast ~s on** difamar,
calumniar.
asphalt [ˈæsfælt] ① N (material) asfalto m; (place) pista f asfaltada,
recinto m asfaltado; **~ jungle** desierto m de asfalto.
　② VT asfaltar.
asphyxia [æsˈfɪksɪə] N asfixia f.
asphyxiate [æsˈfɪksɪeɪt] ① VT asfixiar.
　② VI morir asfixiado.
asphyxiation [æsˌfɪksɪˈeɪʃən] N asfixia f.
aspic [ˈæspɪk] N gelatina f.
aspidistra [ˌæspɪˈdɪstrə] N aspidistra f.
aspirant [ˈæspɪrənt] N aspirante mf, candidato m, -a f (to a).

┌───┐
│ ➤ LANGUAGE IN USE:　**ask: 1a** → 26.1　**aspect** → 26.1, 26.3 │
└───┘

aspirate [1] ['æspərɪt] ADJ aspirado.
[2] ['æspərɪt] N aspirada *f*.
[3] ['æspəreɪt] VT aspirar; **~d H H** *f* aspirada.
aspiration [,æspə'reɪʃən] N (*all senses*) aspiración *f*.
aspirational [,æspə'reɪʃənl] ADJ *person, product* que viste mucho, que queda muy bien.
aspire [əs'paɪər] VI: **to ~ to** aspirar a; ambicionar, anhelar; **we can't ~ to that** no aspiramos a tanto, nuestras pretensiones son más modestas; **he ~s to a new car** anhela tener un coche nuevo; **to ~ to** + *infin* aspirar a + *infin*, anhelar + *infin*, ambicionar + *infin*.
aspirin ['æspɪn] N aspirina *f*.
aspiring [əs'paɪərɪŋ] ADJ ambicioso; en ciernes.
ass¹ [æs] N (**a**) asno *m*, burro *m*, -a *f*. (**b**) (* *fig*) burro *m*, imbécil *m*; **the man's an ~** es un imbécil; **don't be an ~!** ¡no seas imbécil!; **what an ~ I am!** ¡soy un imbécil!; **to make an ~ of o.s.** ponerse en ridículo.
ass²⁑ [æs] N (*US*) culo⁑ *m*; **to bust one's ~** ir de culo⁑; **to fall on one's ~** (*fig*) hacer el ridi⁑; **kiss my ~!** ¡vete a la mierda!⁑; ¡vete al carajo!⁑
assail [ə'seɪl] VT acometer, atacar; *task* acometer, emprender; **doubts began to ~ him** las dudas empezaron a asaltarle; **he was ~ed by critics** le atacaron los críticos; **a sound ~ed my ear** un ruido penetró en mis oídos.
assailant [ə'seɪlənt] N asaltador *m*, -ora *f*, agresor *m*, -ora *f*; **she did not recognize her ~s** no reconoció a los que la agredieron; **there were 4 ~s** eran 4 los agresores.
Assam [æ'sæm] N Assam *m*.
assassin [ə'sæsɪn] N asesino *m*.
assassinate [ə'sæsɪneɪt] VT asesinar.
assassination [ə,sæsɪ'neɪʃən] N asesinato *m*.
assault [ə'sɔ:lt] [1] N (**a**) (*Mil etc*) asalto *m* (**on** sobre), ataque *m* (**on** a, **contra**); **~ course** pista *f* americana; **~ craft** barcaza *f* de asalto; **~ troops** tropas *fpl* de asalto; **to make** (*or* **mount**) **an ~ on** asaltar, hacer un ataque a.
(**b**) (*Jur etc*) atentado *m* (**on** a, **contra**), agresión *f*; violencia *f*; **~ and battery** maltrato *m* de palabra y obra, vías *fpl* de hecho; V **indecent, sexual.**
[2] VT (**a**) (*Mil*) asaltar, atacar.
(**b**) (*Jur etc*) agredir; *woman* (tratar de) violar, atentar contra el pudor de.
assay [ə'seɪ] [1] N ensaye *m*; (*of gold*) ensaye *m*, aquilatamiento *m*; **~ mark** señal *f* de ensaye; **~ office** oficina *f* de ensaye.
[2] VT (**a**) *metal etc* ensayar; *gold* ensayar, aquilatar; (*fig*) intentar, probar. (**b**) **to ~ to** + *infin* (*try*) intentar + *infin*.
assemblage [ə'semblɪdʒ] N (**a**) reunión *f*; colección *f*. (**b**) (*Mech*) montaje *m*; ensambladura *f*.
assemble [ə'sembl] [1] VT reunir, juntar; (*Parl*) convocar; (*Mech*) montar; ensamblar.
[2] VI reunirse, juntarse; celebrar una sesión; **the ~d dignitaries** las dignidades reunidas, la reunión de dignidades.
assembler [ə'semblər] N ensamblador *m*.
assembly [ə'semblɪ] N (**a**) (*meeting*) reunión *f*; (*Pol etc*) asamblea *f*; (*people present*) concurrencia *f*, asistentes *mpl*; (*Brit Scol*) reunión *f* general de todos los alumnos. (**b**) (*Mech*) montaje *m*; ensamblaje *m*, ensamblado *m*. (**c**) (*Comput*) **~ language** lenguaje *m* ensamblador.
assembly-line [ə'semblɪlaɪn] N línea *f* de montaje, cadena *f* de montaje; **~ worker** trabajador *m*, -ora *f* en línea de montaje.
assemblyman [ə'semblɪmən] N, PL **assemblymen** [ə'semblɪmen] (*US*) miembro *m* de una asamblea.
assembly-plant [ə'semblɪ,plɑ:nt] N planta *f* de montaje.
assembly-room [ə'semblɪrʊm] N sala *f* de fiestas.
assembly-shop [ə'semblɪʃɒp] N taller *m* de montaje.
assemblywoman [ə'semblɪwʊmən] N, PL **assemblywomen** (*US*) miembro *m* (*femenino*) de una asamblea.
assent [ə'sent] [1] N asentimiento *m*, consentimiento *m*, aprobación *f*; **royal ~** aprobación *f* real; **to nod one's ~** asentir con la cabeza.
[2] VI consentir (**to** en), asentir (**to** a).
assert [ə'sɜ:t] [1] VT afirmar, declarar; *claim* sostener, defender; *rights* hacer valer; *innocence* afirmar.
[2] VR: **to ~ o.s.** imponerse, hacer valer sus derechos.
▼ **assertion** [ə'sɜ:ʃən] N aserto *m*, afirmación *f*, declaración *f*.
assertive [ə'sɜ:tɪv] ADJ asertivo.
assertively [ə'sɜ:tɪvlɪ] ADV de manera asertiva.
assertiveness [ə'sɜ:tɪvnɪs] N asertividad *f*.
assess [ə'ses] VT valorar, apreciar; tasar, calcular (**at** en); enjuiciar, juzgar; *damages, tax* fijar (**at** en); (*Univ etc*) evaluar; *situation* apreciar; *amount* calcular; **how did you ~ this candidate?** ¿qué juicio formó sobre este candidato?; **how do you ~ your chances now?** ¿cómo evalúa sus posibilidades ahora?
assessable [ə'sesəbl] ADJ tasable, calculable; **~ income** ingresos *mpl* imponibles; **a theory not readily ~** una teoría difícil de enjuiciar.
assessment [ə'sesmənt] N (**a**) (*act*) valoración *f*; tasación *f*; enjuiciamiento *m*; (*opinion*) aprecio *m*, juicio *m*; evaluación *f*; **in my**

~ a mi juicio; **continuous ~** evaluación *f* continua; **what is your ~ of the situation?** ¿cómo ve la situación? (**b**) (*for tax etc*) tasación *f*, imposición *f*; cálculo *m* del valor imponible, cálculo *m* de los ingresos imponibles.
assessor [ə'sesər] N asesor *m*, -ora *f*; (*US: of taxes etc*) tasador *m*, -ora *f*; **~'s office** oficina *f* municipal.
asset ['æset] N (**a**) (*advantage*) ventaja *f*; plus *m*, factor *m* positivo; **she is a great ~ in the department** es una persona valiosísima en el departamento.
(**b**) (*Fin etc*) posesión *f*; (*book-keeping item*) partida *f* del activo; **~s** activo *m*, haber *m*; fondos *mpl*; (**personal**) **~s** bienes *mpl* muebles; **~s in hand** activo *m* disponible, bienes *mpl* disponibles; **~s and liabilities** activo *m* y pasivo.
asset-stripper ['æset,strɪpər] N (*Fin*) persona que compra empresas en crisis para vender sus bienes.
asset-stripping ['æset,strɪpɪŋ] N (*Fin*) compra de empresas en crisis para vender sus bienes.
asseverate [ə'sevəreɪt] VT aseverar.
asseveration [ə,sevə'reɪʃən] N aseveración *f*.
asshole⁑ ['æshəʊl] N (*US*) culo⁑ *m*; (*person*) gilipollas⁑ *m*.
assiduity [,æsɪ'djʊɪtɪ] N asiduidad *f*, diligencia *f*.
assiduous [ə'sɪdjʊəs] ADJ asiduo, diligente.
assiduously [ə'sɪdjʊəslɪ] ADV asiduamente, diligentemente.
assign [ə'saɪn] [1] VT (**a**) (*allot*) asignar; *reason etc* señalar, indicar; *share, task* asignar, señalar; *date* señalar, fijar (**for** para); *room etc* destinar, señalar; *literary work etc* atribuir; *property* traspasar, ceder; **which is the room ~ed to me?** ¿qué habitación es la que me destinan a mí?; **the event is to be ~ed to 1600** hemos de referir el suceso al año 1600.
(**b**) *person* nombrar, destinar; designar; **they ~ed him to the Paris embassy** le nombraron para la embajada de París.
[2] N (*Jur*) cesionario *m*, -a *f*.
assignation [,æsɪg'neɪʃən] N (**a**) (*act*) asignación *f*; traspaso *m*; atribución *f*; nombramiento *m*, designación *f*. (**b**) (*task*) = **assignment** (**b**). (**c**) (*appointment*) cita *f* (*esp* amorosa).
assignee [,æsaɪ'ni:] N (*Jur*) = **assign 2.**
assignment [ə'saɪnmənt] N (**a**) (*act*) asignación *f* etc (V **assignation**). (**b**) (*task*) cometido *m*, tarea *f*; misión *f*; (*Scol etc*) trabajo *m*.
assignor [,æsaɪ'nɔ:r] N (*Jur*) cedente *mf*.
assimilate [ə'sɪmɪleɪt] [1] VT asimilar.
[2] VI asimilarse.
assimilation [ə,sɪmɪ'leɪʃən] N asimilación *f*.
Assisi [ə'si:zɪ] N Asís *m*.
assist [ə'sɪst] [1] VT ayudar; asistir; *development, progress etc* favorecer, estimular, fomentar; **~ed passage** pasaje *m* subvencionado; **to ~ sb out** ayudar a uno a salir; **we ~ed him to his car** le ayudamos a llegar a su coche.
[2] VI ayudar; **to ~ in** tomar parte en, participar en; **to ~ in** + *ger* ayudar a + *infin*, contribuir a + *infin*.
assistance [ə'sɪstəns] N (**a**) ayuda *f*, auxilio *m*; **to be of ~ to**, **to give ~ to** ayudar a, prestar ayuda a; **can I be of ~?** ¿puedo ayudarle?; **to come to sb's ~** acudir en auxilio de uno, socorrer a uno.
(**b**) (*also* **national ~**, **public ~**) subsidio *m* (al necesitado).
assistant [ə'sɪstənt] [1] ADJ auxiliar; **~ manager** subdirector *m*; **~ master** profesor *m* de instituto; **~ mistress** profesora *f* de instituto; **~ principal** subdirector *m*, -ora *f*; **~ professor** (*US*) profesor *m* agregado, profesora *f* agregada; **~ secretary** vicesecretario *m*, -a *f*.
[2] N ayudante *mf*, auxiliar *mf*; (*language ~*) auxiliar *mf* de conversación; V **laboratory.**
assistantship [ə'sɪstəntʃɪp] N (*Brit: at school*) lectorado *m*; (*US: at college*) ayudantía *f*, puesto *m* de profesor ayudante.
assizes [ə'saɪzɪz] NPL (*Brit*) sesiones *fpl* jurídicas (regionales).
assn ABBR of **association** asociación *f*.
assoc. (**a**) ABBR of **association** asociación *f*. (**b**) ABBR of **associate(d)** asociado.
associate [1] [ə'səʊʃɪɪt] ADJ asociado; **~ director** subdirector *m*, -ora *f*; **A~ Justice** (*US*) juez *mf* asociado; **~ member** miembro *mf* correspondiente; **~ producer** (*TV etc*) productor *m* asociado, productora *f* asociada; **~ professor** (*US*) profesor *m* adjunto, profesora *f* adjunta.
[2] [ə'səʊʃɪt] N asociado *m*, -a *f*, colega *mf*; compañero *m*, -a *f*; (*in crime*) cómplice *mf*; (*member*) miembro *mf* correspondiente; (*Comm*) asociado *m*, -a *f*, socio *mf*, consocio *mf*; **Fred Bloggs and A~s** Fred Bloggs y Asociados; **~'s degree** (*US*) licenciatura *f*.
[3] [ə'səʊʃɪeɪt] VT asociar; relacionar; juntar, unir; **I don't wish to be ~d with it** no quiero tener nada que ver con ello; **was he ~d with that scandal?** ¿estuvo mezclado en ese escándalo?; **to be ~d with a plot** participar en un complot.
[4] [ə'səʊʃɪeɪt] VI asociarse (**with** con); juntarse, unirse; **to ~ in** participar juntamente en; **to ~ with** ir con, tratar con, frecuentar (la compañía de).
[5] [ə'səʊʃɪeɪt] VR: **to ~ o.s. with sb in a venture** participar con uno

en una empresa, colaborar con uno en un proyecto; **I should like to ~ myself with that** quiero hacerme eco de aquello.

associated [ə'səʊʃɪeɪtɪd] ADJ asociado; conexo, relacionado; *company* afiliado.

association [ə,səʊsɪ'eɪʃən] N **(a)** (*relation*) asociación *f*; (*with person*) relación *f*, conexión *f*; **A in ~ with B** A conjuntamente con B; **to form an ~ with** relacionarse con, entrar en relaciones con; **by ~ of ideas** por asociación de ideas.
(b) (*body*) asociación *f*; **~ football** (*Brit*) fútbol *m*.
(c) **~s** (*memories*) recuerdos *mpl*; sugestiones *fpl*, connotaciones *fpl*; **the town has historic ~s** la ciudad es rica en recuerdos históricos; **the word has nasty ~s** la palabra tiene connotaciones feas.

associative [ə'səʊʃɪətɪv] ADJ: **~ storage** almacenamiento *m* asociativo.

assonance ['æsənəns] N (*system*) asonancia *f*; (*word*) asonante *m*; **words in ~** palabras *fpl* asonantadas.

assonant ['æsənənt] [1] ADJ asonante.
[2] N asonante *f*.

assonate ['æsəneɪt] VI asonar.

assort [ə'sɔːt] VI concordar (*with* con), convenir (*with* a); **it ~s ill with his character** no cuadra con su carácter; **this does not ~ with what you said** esto no concuerda con lo que dijo.

assorted [ə'sɔːtɪd] ADJ surtido, variado; **he dined with ~ ministers** (*hum*) cenó con este y con el otro ministro.

assortment [ə'sɔːtmənt] N variedad *f*, colección *f* variada; (*Comm*) surtido *m*; **quite an ~!** ¡aquí hay de todo!; **there was an ~ of guests** los invitados eran de lo más variado; **Peter was there with an ~ of girlfriends** estaba Pedro con una colección de amigas.

asst (a) ABBR *of* **assistant** ayudante *mf*. **(b)** (*as ADJ*) auxiliar.

assuage [ə'sweɪdʒ] VT *feelings* calmar; *pain* aliviar; *passion* mitigar, suavizar; *desire* satisfacer; *appetite* saciar; *person* apaciguar, sosegar; **he was not easily ~d** no era fácil apaciguarle.

▼ **assume** [ə'sjuːm] VT **(a)** *aspect, name, possession, importance, large proportions* tomar; *air* darse; *attitude* adoptar; *authority* (*unjustly*) apropiarse, arrogarse; *burden, control, responsibility* asumir; *power* tomar, ocupar.
▼ **(b)** (*suppose*) suponer, dar por sentado; **to ~ that ...** suponer que ...; imaginar que ...; **let us ~ that ...** pongamos por caso que ...; **you resigned, I ~** dimitió Vd, me imagino; **you are assuming a lot** Vd supone demasiado, eso es mucho suponer; **assuming that ...** (*as conj*) en el supuesto de que ...

assumed [ə'sjuːmd] ADJ **(a)** *name etc* falso, fingido. **(b)** (*supposed*) presunto; **the ~ culprit** el presunto culpable.

assumption [ə'sʌmpʃən] N **(a)** (*act*) asunción *f*; el tomar, adopción *f*, apropiación *f*; **the A~** (*Rel*) la Asunción.
(b) (*supposition*) suposición *f*, supuesto *m*; presunción *f*; **we cannot make that ~** no podemos dar eso por sentado; **on the ~ that ...** suponiendo que ...; **to start from a false ~** partir de una base falsa.
(c) (*arrogance*) presunción *f*.

assurance [ə'ʃʊərəns] N **(a)** (*guarantee*) garantía *f*, promesa *f*; **you have my ~ that ...** les aseguro que ...; **I can give you no ~ about that** no les puedo garantizar nada.
(b) (*confidence*) confianza *f*; aplomo *m*, serenidad *f*.
(c) (*certainty*) certeza *f*, seguridad *f*; **with the ~ that ...** con la seguridad de que ...; **to make ~ doubly sure** para mayor seguridad.
(d) (*Brit Fin*) seguro *m*; **~ company** compañía *f* de seguros.

assure [ə'ʃʊər] VT **(a)** (*make certain*) asegurar, garantizar.
(b) (*Brit Fin*) asegurar; **his life is ~d for £500,000** su vida está asegurada en 500.000 libras.
(c) (*reassure*) asegurar; **I ~d him of my support** le afirmé mi apoyo; **you may rest ~d that ...** tenga la seguridad de que ...; **let me ~ you that ...** permita que le asegure que ...; **it is so, I ~ you** es así, se lo garantizo.
[2] VR: **to ~ o.s. of sth** asegurarse de algo.

assured [ə'ʃʊəd] [1] ADJ **(a)** (*self~*) confiado, sereno.
(b) (*certain*) seguro; **you have an ~ future** tienes un porvenir seguro.
[2] N: **the ~** (*Fin*) el asegurado, la asegurada.

assuredly [ə'ʃʊərɪdlɪ] ADV seguramente, sin duda.

ass-wipe ['æswaɪp] N (*US*) papel *m* de wáter*.

Assyria [ə'sɪrɪə] N Asiria *f*.

Assyrian [ə'sɪrɪən] [1] ADJ asirio.
[2] N asirio *m*, -a *f*.

AST N ABBR *of* **Atlantic Standard Time** hora oficial de Nueva Escocia.

aster ['æstər] N aster *f*.

asterisk ['æstərɪsk] [1] N asterisco *m*.
[2] VT señalar con un asterisco, poner un asterisco a.

astern [ə'stɜːn] **1** ADV a popa, por la popa; **to fall ~** quedarse atrás; **to go ~** ciar, ir hacia atrás; **to make a boat fast ~** amarrar un barco por la popa.
[2] PREP: **~ of** detrás de.

asteroid ['æstərɔɪd] N asteroide *m*.

asthma ['æsmə] N asma *f*.

asthmatic [æs'mætɪk] [1] ADJ asmático.

[2] N asmático *m*, -a *f*.

astigmatic [,æstɪg'mætɪk] ADJ astigmático.

astigmatism [æs'tɪgmətɪzəm] N astigmatismo *m*.

astir [ə'stɜːr] ADV, ADJ: **to be ~** estar activo, estar en movimiento; (*up and about*) estar levantado; **we were ~ early** nos levantamos temprano; **nobody was ~ at that hour** a tal hora todos estaban todavía en cama.

ASTM N (*US*) ABBR of **American Society for Testing Materials**.

ASTMS N (*Brit*) ABBR of **Association of Scientific, Technical and Managerial Staff** sindicato de personal científico, técnico y directivo.

astonish [ə'stɒnɪʃ] VT asombrar, pasmar; sorprender; **you ~ me!** ¡esto es asombroso!; **to be ~ed** asombrarse (*at* de), maravillarse (*at* de, con), quedarse asombrado (*at* de); **I am ~ed that ...** me asombra que + *subj*.

astonished [ə'stɒnɪʃt] ADJ estupefacto, pasmado.

astonishing [ə'stɒnɪʃɪŋ] ADJ asombroso, pasmoso; sorprendente; **I find it ~ that ...** me asombra que + *subj*.

astonishingly [ə'stɒnɪʃɪŋlɪ] ADV: **~ easy** increíblemente fácil; **it was an ~ lovely scene** la escena era de una belleza totalmente inesperada; **~ enough** por milagro, por maravilla; **but, ~, he did not** pero, por maravilla, no lo hizo.

astonishment [ə'stɒnɪʃmənt] N asombro *m*, sorpresa *f*, estupefacción *f*; **to my ~** con gran sorpresa mía.

astound [ə'staʊnd] VT *etc* = **astonish** *etc*.

astounded [ə'staʊndɪd] ADJ pasmado, estupefacto; **I am ~** estoy pasmado.

astounding [ə'staʊndɪŋ] ADJ asombroso, pasmoso; **~!** ¡esto es asombroso!; **I find it ~ that ...** me asombra que + *subj*.

astoundingly [ə'staʊndɪŋlɪ] ADV V **astonishingly**.

astrakhan [,æstrə'kæn] N astracán *m*.

astral ['æstrəl] ADJ astral.

astray [ə'streɪ] ADV: **to go ~** extraviarse; (*fig: make a mistake*) equivocarse, (*morally*) descarriar, ir por mal camino; **to lead ~** llevar por mal camino; **I was led ~ by his voice** su voz me despistó.

astride [ə'straɪd] [1] ADV a horcajadas.
[2] PREP a caballo sobre, a horcajadas sobre.

astringency [əs'trɪndʒənsɪ] N astringencia *f*; (*fig*) adustez *f*, austeridad *f*.

astringent [əs'trɪndʒənt] ADJ astringente; (*fig*) adusto, austero.

astro... [æstrəʊ] PREF astro...

astrolabe ['æstrəʊleɪb] N astrolabio *m*.

astrologer [əs'trɒlədʒər] N astrólogo *m*, -a *f*.

astrological [,æstrə'lɒdʒɪkəl] ADJ astrológico.

astrologist [əs'trɒlədʒɪst] N astrólogo *m*, -a *f*.

astrology [əs'trɒlədʒɪ] N astrología *f*.

astronaut ['æstrənɔːt] N astronauta *mf*.

astronautical [,æstrəʊ'nɔːtɪkəl] ADJ astronáutico.

astronautics [,æstrəʊ'nɔːtɪks] N astronáutica *f*.

astronomer [əs'trɒnəmər] N astrónomo *m*, -a *f*.

astronomical [,æstrə'nɒmɪkəl] ADJ astronómico (*also fig*).

astronomically [,æstrə'nɒmɪkəlɪ] ADV *rise, grow, increase* astronómicamente, exageradamente; **lobster is ~ expensive** la langosta está a precios astronómicos; **they set ~ high standards for their employees** exigen un nivel exageradamente alto a sus empleados.

astronomy [əs'trɒnəmɪ] N astronomía *f*.

astrophysicist [,æstrəʊ'fɪzɪsɪst] N astrofísico *mf*.

astrophysics ['æstrəʊ'fɪzɪks] N astrofísica *f*.

Astroturf ['æstrəʊtɜːf] ® N césped *m* artificial.

Asturian [æ'stʊərɪən] [1] ADJ asturiano.
[2] N **(a)** asturiano *m*, -a *f*. **(b)** (*Ling*) asturiano *m*.

Asturias [æ'stʊərɪæs] N Asturias *f*.

astute [əs'tjuːt] ADJ listo, inteligente; sagaz; **that was very ~ of you** en eso has sido muy inteligente; **an ~ choice** una elección acertada.

astutely [əs'tjuːtlɪ] ADV inteligentemente, sagazmente.

astuteness [əs'tjuːtnɪs] N inteligencia *f*; sagacidad *f*.

asunder [ə'sʌndər] ADV: **to put ~** separar; **to tear ~** hacer pedazos, romper en dos.

ASV N (*US*) ABBR of **American Standard Version**.

Aswan [æs'wɑːn] N Asuán *f*; **~ High Dam** Presa *f* de Asuán.

asylum [ə'saɪləm] N **(a)** asilo *m*; **to afford** (*or* **give**) **~ to** (*place*) servir de asilo a, (*person*) dar asilo a; **to ask for political ~** pedir asilo político. **(b)** (*mental ~*) manicomio *m*, hospital *m* psiquiátrico.

asylum seeker [ə'saɪləm'siːkər] N demandante *m* de asilo (político); **fewer than 7% of ~s are accepted as political refugees** menos del 7% de los solicitantes de asilo o de las peticiones de asilo pasan a ser refugiados políticos.

asymmetric(al) [,eɪsɪ'metrɪk(əl)] ADJ asimétrico.

asymmetry [eɪ'sɪmətrɪ] N asimetría *f*.

asymptomatic [æ,sɪmptə'mætɪk] ADJ asintomático.

asynchronous [æ'sɪŋkrənəs] ADJ asíncrono.

AT N ABBR of **automatic translation** traducción *f* automática, TA *f*.

at [æt] PREP **(a)** (*position*) en; **~ the edge** en el borde; **~ the top** en la cumbre; **~ Toledo** en Toledo; **~ school** en la escuela; **~ sea** en el mar; **~ peace** en paz; **~ John's** en casa de Juan; **~ the hairdresser's** en la peluquería; **~ table** en la mesa; **to dry o.s. ~ the fire** secarse junto a la lumbre; **to stand ~ the door** estar a la puerta; **to be ~ the window** estar junto a la ventana; **he came in ~ the window** entró por la ventana; **to find a gap to go in ~** buscar un resquicio por donde entrar; **this is where it's ~*** aquí es donde tiene lugar (la reunión *etc*); aquí es lo importante, aquí es un buen rollo*.
(b) (*time, order, frequency*) **~ 4 o'clock** a las 4; **~ midday** a mediodía; **~ night** de noche, por la noche; **~ this season** en esta época del año; **~ Christmas** por Navidades; **~ a time like this** en un momento como éste; **two ~ a time** de dos en dos; **~ my time of life** con los años que tengo.
(c) (*price, rate*) **~ 5 dollars a pound** a 5 dólares la libra; **~ 4% interest** al 4 por 100 de interés; **~ a high price** a un precio elevado; **to go ~ 100 km an hour** ir a 100 km por hora.
(d) (*following, concerning*) **~ my request** a petición mía; **to awaken ~ the least sound** despertarse al menor ruido; **~ her cries** al escuchar sus gritos; **~ his suggestion** siguiendo su sugerencia, de acuerdo con su sugerencia; **boys ~ play** muchachos que juegan, los muchachos cuando juegan; **he's good ~ games** es bueno para los juegos; **I'm no good ~ that** no valgo para eso.
(e) (*with verb to be*) **to be ~ work** estar en el trabajo; **to be hard ~ it** estar trabajando con ahinco; **I've been ~ it for 3 hours** estoy ocupado en esto desde hace 3 horas; **what are you ~?** ¿qué haces ahí?; **while we're ~ it** mientras lo estamos haciendo; de paso; **you've been ~ me all day** has estado persiguiéndome todo el día; **she's ~ it again** está siempre con la misma canción, sigue con el mismo tema.

┌─ **AT** ─────────────────── *see also main entry* ─┐

Place
• When referring to *location*, *at* should usually be translated by *en*:
    We'll meet at the station, shall we?
    Nos vemos en la estación, ¿vale?
    He was waiting for me at the bus stop
    Me estaba esperando en la parada de autobús
    He wasn't at school
    No estaba en el colegio
• When *at* follows a verb and indicates *movement* or *direction*, it may sometimes be translated by *a*. However VERB + *at* is often translated by one word in Spanish, so check the relevant dictionary entry:
    She glanced at the door
    Echó un vistazo a la puerta
    It was getting dark when they arrived at the port
    Anochecía cuando llegaron al puerto
    He was looking at photos
    Estaba mirando fotos

Time
• Translate *at* + HOUR using *a*:
    We'll see you at 2 o'clock
    Te veremos a las dos
    The telephone rang at midnight
    El teléfono sonó a medianoche
• Translate *at* + MOMENT using *en*:
    At that moment the bomb went off
    En aquel momento estalló la bomba
    At that moment a shot rang out
    En ese instante sonó un disparo
    For further uses and examples, see main entry.

└──┘

atavism ['ætəvɪzəm] N atavismo *m*.
atavistic [ˌætə'vɪstɪk] ADJ atávico.
ataxia [ə'tæksɪə] N ataxia *f*.
ataxic [ə'tæksɪk] ADJ atáxico.
ATC N ABBR of **Air Training Corps** *cuerpo militar para la formación de aviadores*.
ate [eɪt] PRET of **eat**.
atheism ['eɪθɪɪzəm] N ateísmo *m*.
atheist ['eɪθɪɪst] N ateo *m*, -a *f*.
atheistic [ˌeɪθɪ'ɪstɪk] ADJ ateo, ateísta.
Athenian [ə'θiːnɪən] **1** ADJ ateniense.
    2 N ateniense *mf*.
Athens ['æθɪnz] N Atenas *f*.
athirst [ə'θɜːst] ADJ: **to be ~ for** (*fig*) tener sed de.
athlete ['æθliːt] N atleta *mf*; **~'s foot** (*Med*) pie *m* de atleta.
athletic [æθ'letɪk] ADJ atlético; **~ coach** (*US*) profesor *m*, -ora *f* de Educación Física; **~ supporter** (*US*) hincha *mf*.
athleticism [æθ'letsɪzəm] N atletismo *m*.

athletics [æθ'letɪks] N SING (*Brit*) atletismo *m*; (*US*) deportes *mpl*.
at-home [ət'həum] N recepción *f* (en casa particular).
athwart [ə'θwɔːt] **1** ADV de través, al través.
    2 PREP a través de.
atishoo [ə'tɪʃuː] INTERJ ¡(h)achís!
Atlanticism [ət'læntɪsɪzəm] N atlantismo *m*.
Atlanticist [ət'læntɪsɪst] ADJ, N atlantista *mf*.
Atlantic (Ocean) [ət'læntɪk('əuʃən)] N (Océano *m*) Atlántico *m*.
Atlantis [ət'læntɪs] N Atlántida *f*.
atlas ['ætləs] N atlas *m*; **A~** Atlas *m*, Atlante *m*; **A~ Mountains** el Atlas.
ATM N ABBR of **automated teller machine** cajero *m* automático; **~ card** tarjeta *f* de cajero automático.
atmosphere ['ætməsfɪə^r] N atmósfera *f*; (*fig*) ambiente *m*; clima *m*, atmósfera *f*.
atmospheric [ˌætməs'ferɪk] ADJ atmosférico; ambiental; **~ pollution** contaminación *f* atmosférica; **~ pressure** presión *f* atmosférica.
atmospherics [ˌætməs'ferɪks] NPL (*Rad*) interferencias *fpl* atmosféricas, parásitos *mpl*.
atoll ['ætɒl] N atolón *m*.
atom ['ætəm] N átomo *m*; **there is not an ~ of truth in it** eso no tiene ni pizca de verdad; **if you had an ~ of sense** si tuvieras una gota de sentido común; **to smash sth to ~s** hacer algo añicos.
atom-bomb ['ætəm,bɒm] N bomba *f* atómica.
atomic [ə'tɒmɪk] ADJ atómico; **~ age** edad *f* atómica; **~ bomb** bomba *f* atómica; **~ clock** reloj *m* atómico; **~ energy** energía *f* nuclear; **A~ Energy Authority** Consejo *m* de Energía Nuclear; **~ nucleus** núcleo *m* atómico; **~ number** número *m* atómico; **~ particle** partícula *f* atómica; **~ physicist** físico *m*; **~ physics** física *f* atómica; **~ pile** pila *f* atómica; **~ power** (*nation*) potencia *f* atómica; **~ power station** central *f* nuclear; **~ structure** estructura *f* atómica; **~ theory** teoría *f* de los átomos; **~ warfare** guerra *f* atómica; **~ warhead** cabeza *f* atómica; **~ weight** peso *m* atómico.
atomic-powered [ə'tɒmɪk'pauəd] ADJ impulsado por energía atómica.
atomize ['ætəmaɪz] VT atomizar, pulverizar.
atomizer ['ætəmaɪzə^r] N atomizador *m*, pulverizador *m*.
atom-smasher ['ætəm,smæʃə^r] N acelerador *m* de partículas atómicas, rompeátomos *m*.
atonal [æ'təunl] ADJ atonal.
atone [ə'təun] VI: **to ~ for** expiar.
atonement [ə'təunmənt] N expiación *f*; **Day of A~** Día *m* de la Expiación.
atonic [æ'tɒnɪk] ADJ átono.
atop [ə'tɒp] **1** ADV encima.
    2 PREP encima de; sobre; en la cumbre de.
A to Z [ˌeɪtə'zed] ® N callejero *m*.
ATP N ABBR of **Association of Tennis Professionals**.
at-risk [æt'rɪsk] ADJ **group** en peligro.
atrium ['eɪtrɪəm] N, PL **atria** or **atriums** atrio *m*.
atrocious [ə'trəuʃəs] ADJ atroz.
atrociously [ə'trəuʃəslɪ] ADV atrozmente.
atrocity [ə'trɒsɪtɪ] N atrocidad *f*.
atrophy ['ætrəfɪ] **1** N atrofia *f*.
    2 VT atrofiar.
    3 VI atrofiarse.
att. (*Comm*) ABBR of **attached** adjunto, anexo.
attaboy* ['ætə,bɔɪ] INTERJ (*esp US*) ¡bravo!, ¡dale!
attach [ə'tætʃ] **1** VT **(a)** (*fasten*) sujetar; (*stick*) pegar; (*tie*) atar, liar; (*with pin etc*) prender; (*join*) unir; *seal* poner; *trailer etc* acoplar, enganchar; **he's ~ed*** (*married etc*) no está libre.
(b) (*in letter*) adjuntar; **the document is ~ed** enviamos adjunto el documento; **the ~ed letter** la carta adjunta; **please find ~ed details of ...** les adjuntamos detalles de ...
(c) (*fig*) *importance, value* dar, conceder (*to* a); **the salary ~ed to the post is ...** el sueldo que corresponde al puesto es ...; **to be ~ed to an embassy** estar agregado a una embajada; **there are no strings ~ed to this** esto es sin compromiso alguno, esto es libre de condiciones; **commission ~ed to the Ministry of ...** comisión *f* que depende del Ministerio de ...
(d) (*Jur*) *property* incautar, embargar.
(e) **to be ~ed to** *person etc* tener cariño a; *theory etc* estar apegado a; **they are very ~ed** (*to each other*) se quieren mucho.
    2 VI: **to ~** corresponder a, pertenecer a; ser inherente en; **no blame ~es to you** no tienes culpa alguna; **certain duties ~ to this post** ciertas responsabilidades corresponden a este puesto.
    3 VR: **to ~ o.s. to** *group* agregarse a, unirse a, entrar a formar parte de, (*pej*) pegarse a.
attaché [ə'tæʃeɪ] N agregado *m*, -a *f*; **V cultural** *etc*.
attaché case [ə'tæʃeɪkeɪs] N portafolio *m*, cartera *f*; maletín *m*.
attachment [ə'tætʃmənt] N **(a)** (*act*) atadura *f*; unión *f* *etc*.
(b) (*device*) accesorio *m*, dispositivo *m*; (*coupling*) acoplamiento *m*.
(c) (*affection*) cariño *m*, apego *m* (*to* a); (*loyalty*) adhesión *f*.

(d) (*Jur*) incautación *f*, embargo *m*.

attack [əˈtæk] **1** N **(a)** (*Mil etc*) ataque *m* (*on* a, contra, sobre), asalto *m*; (*criminal, on person*) atentado *m*, agresión *f*; **~ on sb's life** atentado *m* contra la vida de uno; **~ on the security of the state** atentado *m* contra la seguridad del estado; **~ is the best form of defence** la mejor defensa está en el ataque; **to be under ~** ser atacado; **to launch an ~** lanzar un ataque; **to leave o.s. open to ~** dejarse expuesto al ataque; **to return to the ~** volver al ataque.
(b) (*Med*) ataque *m*, acceso *m*; crisis *f*; dolencia *f* repentina; **an ~ of pneumonia** una pulmonía; **an ~ of nerves** una crisis nerviosa.
2 VT **(a)** (*Mil etc*) atacar; acometer; (*criminally*) agredir, asaltar; atentar contra; (*bull etc*) embestir; (*gratuitously*) emprenderla con; (*Med*) atacar, afectar; *opinion, theory* impugnar; **he was ~ed by doubts** le asaltaron dudas.
(b) (*fig*) *problem* acometer, tratar de resolver; *task* emprender, lanzarse a; **we must ~ poverty** debemos combatir la pobreza.
(c) (*Chem*) atacar; (*Med*) atacar, minar.
3 VI atacar.
attackable [əˈtækəbl] ADJ atacable, expuesto al ataque.
attack dog [əˈtækˈdɒg] N perro *m* de presa.
attacker [əˈtækər] N agresor *m*, -ora *f*, asaltante *mf*, atacante *mf*.
attain [əˈteɪn] **1** VT alcanzar, lograr, conseguir.
2 VI: **to ~ to** llegar a.
attainable [əˈteɪnəbl] ADJ alcanzable, realizable.
attainder [əˈteɪndər] N extinción *f* de los derechos civiles de un individuo.
attainment [əˈteɪnmənt] N **(a)** (*act*) logro *m*, consecución *f*, obtención *f*; **difficult of ~** de difícil consecución, de difícil realización. **(b)** ~s dotes *fpl*, talento *m* (*in* para), conocimientos *mpl* (*in* de).
attempt [əˈtempt] **1** N **(a)** tentativa *f*, intento *m*, conato *m*; **at the first ~** en el primer intento; **to make an ~ to** + *infin* hacer una tentativa de + *infin*, intentar + *infin*; **he made two ~s** at it trató dos veces de lograrlo; **to make an ~ on the record** tratar de batir el récord; **to make an ~ on the summit** tratar de llegar a la cumbre; **we'll do it or die in the ~** lo haremos o moriremos en la demanda; **it was a good ~** fue un esfuerzo digno de alabanza; **this is my first ~** es la primera vez que lo intento; **we had to give up the ~** tuvimos que renunciar a la empresa.
(b) (*attack*) atentado *m* (*on sb's life* contra la vida de uno).
2 VT **(a)** probar, ensayar, intentar; tratar de efectuar (*or* conseguir *etc*); (*undertake*) emprender.
(b) **to ~ to** + *infin* intentar + *infin*, tratar de + *infin*.
attempted [əˈtemptɪd] ADJ: **~ murder** tentativa *f* de asesinato, homicidio *m* frustrado; **~ suicide** intento *m* de suicidio.
attend [əˈtend] **1** VT **(a)** (*assist at*) asistir a; **a well-~ed meeting** una reunión muy concurrida.
(b) (*serve*) servir; (*accompany*) acompañar; (*Med*) atender, asistir; **a method ~ed by many risks** un método que comporta muchos riesgos; **the policy was ~ed by many difficulties** la política tropezó con muchas dificultades.
2 VI **(a)** (*pay attention*) prestar atención, poner atención (*LAm*).
(b) (*be present*) asistir.
◆**attend to** VT (*Comm*) *order* ejecutar; *one's task, one's business* ocuparse de, atender; *words, work, lesson, speech* prestar atención a, poner atención en (*LAm*); *advice* seguir; **to ~ to a customer** atender a un cliente; **are you being ~ed to?** (*in a shop*) ¿le atienden?, ¿le atiende alguien?; **I'll ~ to you in a moment** un momentito y estoy con Vd; **I'll ~ to you later** (*threatening*) luego me las arregla con Vd.
◆**attend up(on)** VT *person* servir, estar al servicio de.
attendance [əˈtendəns] **1** N **(a)** (*act*) asistencia *f* (*at* a), presencia *f* (*at* en); **is my ~ necessary?** ¿debo asistir?, ¿es preciso que asista yo?; **to be in ~** asistir; estar de servicio; **to be in ~ on the minister** acompañar al ministro, formar parte del séquito del ministro; **to dance ~ on sb** esforzarse por complacer a uno, desvivirse por uno.
(b) (*Med*) asistencia *f*.
(c) (*those present*) concurrencia *f*, asistentes *mpl*; **what was the ~ at the meeting?** ¿cuántos asistieron a la reunión?; **we need an ~ of 1000** hace falta atraer a un público de 1000.
2 ATTR: **~ centre** (*Brit*) centro *m* (*or* prisión *f*) de régimen abierto; **~ fee** honorarios *mpl* por asistencia; **~ money** pago *m* por asistencia; **~ officer** (*Scol*) encargado *m*, -a *f* del control de asistencia; **~ order** (*Brit*) orden que exige a los padres la asistencia de sus hijos en la escuela; **~ sheet** lista *f* de clase.
attendant [əˈtendənt] **1** ADJ relacionado, concomitante; **the ~ crowd** la gente que asistía; **the ~ difficulties** las dificultades intrínsecas; **the ~ circumstances** las circunstancias concomitantes; **old age and its ~ ills** la vejez y los achaques correspondientes.
2 N acompañante *m*; (*servant*) sirviente *m*, -a *f*; (*Theat*) acomodador *m*, -ora *f*; (*in carpark, museum*) celador *m*, encargado *m*; **the prince and his ~s** el príncipe y su séquito.
attendee [əˌtenˈdiː] N (*esp US*) asistente *mf*.

attention [əˈtenʃən] N **(a)** atención *f*; **~ span** capacidad *f* de concentración; **(your) ~ please!** ¡su atención por favor!; **it requires daily ~** hay que atenderlo a diario; **it shall have my earliest ~** lo atenderé lo más pronto posible; **for the ~ of Mr X** a la atención del Sr X; **we were all ~** todos estábamos muy atentos; **to attract** (*or* **catch**) **sb's ~** llamar la atención de uno; **to call** (*or* **draw**) **sb's ~ to** llamar la atención de uno sobre; **to come to sb's ~** hacérsele presente a uno; **it has come to my ~ that ...** me han informado que ...; **to give** (*or* **pay**) **~** prestar atención (*to* a); **he paid no ~** no hizo caso (*to that* de eso); **to pay special ~ to** fijarse de modo especial en; destacar; **to turn one's ~ to** pasar a considerar, pasar a estudiar.
(b) (*Mil*) **~!** ¡firme(s)!; **to come to ~** ponerse firme(s), cuadrarse; **to stand at** (*or* **to**) **~** estar firme(s).
(c) **~s** (*kindnesses*) atenciones *fpl*, cortesías *fpl*.
attention-seeking [əˈtenʃənˌsiːkɪŋ] ADJ que busca (*or* intenta llamar) la atención.
attentive [əˈtentɪv] ADJ **(a)** (*heedful*) atento (*to* a). **(b)** (*polite*) atento, cortés, obsequioso (*to* con).
attentively [əˈtentɪvlɪ] ADV atentamente; cortésmente.
attentiveness [əˈtentɪvnɪs] N atención *f*; cortesía *f*.
attenuate [əˈtenjʊeɪt] VT atenuar.
attenuating [əˈtenjʊeɪtɪŋ] ADJ atenuante.
attenuation [əˌtenjʊˈeɪʃən] N atenuación *f*, disminución *f*.
attest [əˈtest] **1** VT atestiguar (*that* que); dar fe de; *signature* confirmar, autenticar; **~ed herd** (*Brit*) ganado *m* certificado.
2 VI: **to ~ to** dar fe de.
attestation [ˌætesˈteɪʃən] N atestación *f*, testimonio *m*; confirmación *f*, autenticación *f*.
attic [ˈætɪk] N desván *m*, ático *m*, buhardilla *f*.
Attila [ˈætɪlə] NM Atila.
attire [əˈtaɪər] **1** N traje *m*, vestido *m*; (*hum*) atavío *m*.
2 VT vestir (*in* de); (*hum*) ataviar (*in* de).
attitude [ˈætɪtjuːd] N **(a)** (*of body*) actitud *f*, postura *f*; (*Art*) además *m*.
(b) (*of mind*) actitud *f*; postura *f*; disposición *f* de ánimo; **the government's ~ is negative** la postura del gobierno es negativa; **what is your ~ to this?** ¿cuál es su posición con respecto a esto?; **if that's your ~** si te pones en ese plan; **I don't like your ~** no me gusta su manera de enfocar esta cuestión (*or* su tono de voz *etc*); **to adopt** (*or* **strike, take up**) **an ~** adoptar una actitud, tomar una postura (estudiada). **(c)** (*: bad ~*) **don't give me ~, girl!** ¡no te me pongas de morros, guapa!*.
attitudinal [ˌætɪˈtjuːdɪnəl] ADJ *change, difference* de actitud.
attitudinize [ˌætɪˈtjuːdɪnaɪz] VI tomar posturas afectadas (*or* teatrales).
Attn., attn. ABBR *of* **attention** (*esp on letters, documents*) a la atención de.
attorney [əˈtɜːnɪ] N **(a)** (*representative*) apoderado *m*, -a *f*. **(b)** (*US: also* **~-at-law**) abogado *mf*; **V district**. **(c)** **A~ General** (*Brit*) fiscal *mf* general del Estado; (*US*) ≃ ministro *m*, -a *f* de justicia, procurador *m*, -ora *f* general (*LAm*).

┌─────────────┐
│   *ATTORNEY* │
└─────────────┘

🛈 *En Estados Unidos un **attorney** puede defender a sus clientes tanto en las cortes federales como en las estatales. En ocasiones sólo cobran sus honorarios si ganan el caso (**no win, no fee**), lo cual les permite representar a clientes con pocos recursos sin cobrarles, si se trata de casos de gran repercusión social, con la esperanza de obtener beneficios considerables si lo ganan. Ésta es la razón por la que las compensaciones que se piden por daños y perjuicios suelen ser tan altas y llegan tantos casos a los tribunales. También existe la figura del abogado de oficio, que recibe el nombre de **public defender**.*
⇨ *Ver también* LAWYERS

attract [əˈtrækt] VT atraer; *attention* llamar.
attraction [əˈtrækʃən] N atracción *f*; (*attractive feature*) atractivo *m*; (*inducement*) aliciente *m*; **the ~ of the plan is that ...** el aspecto positivo del plan es que ...; **the film has the special ~ of featuring X** la película tiene la atracción especial de presentar a X; **the main ~ at the party was Y** el interés de la fiesta se cifraba en Y; **one of the ~s of the quiet life** uno de los encantos de la vida retirada; **spring ~s in Madrid** las diversiones de la primavera madrileña.
attractive [əˈtræktɪv] ADJ atractivo; agradable; (*interesting*) atrayente, interesante; *idea, plan* sugestivo; *offer, price, salary* interesante; *prospect* halagüeño; *child, girl* mono, guapo, atractivo, lindo (*LAm*); **~ power** fuerza *f* atractiva.
attractively [əˈtræktɪvlɪ] ADV atractivamente; en forma atractiva; de modo atrayente; de modo sugestivo; de modo halagüeño; **an ~ designed garden** un jardín de trazado atractivo.
attractiveness [əˈtræktɪvnɪs] N atracción *f*, atractivo *m*, atractividad *f*.
attributable [əˈtrɪbjʊtəbl] ADJ: **~ to** atribuible a, imputable a.
▼ attribute **1** [ˈætrɪbjuːt] N atributo *m*.
▼ 2 [əˈtrɪbjuːt] VT atribuir (*to* a); achacar (*to* a); **to what would you ~ this?** ¿cómo explicas esto?

attribution [ˌætrɪˈbjuːʃən] N atribución f.
attributive [əˈtrɪbjʊtɪv] ADJ atributivo.
attrit [əˈtrɪt] VT, **attrite** [əˈtraɪt] VT desgastar, agotar.
attrition [əˈtrɪʃən] N desgaste m; rozadura f, roce m; **war of ~** guerra f de agotamiento.
attune [əˈtjuːn] VT (fig): **to ~ to** armonizar con; **to be ~d to** estar en armonía con.
atty (US) ABBR of **attorney**.
Atty Gen. ABBR of **Attorney General**.
ATV N ABBR of **all-terrain vehicle** vehículo m todo terreno.
atypical [ˌeɪˈtɪpɪkəl] ADJ atípico.
atypically [ˌeɪˈtɪpɪklɪ] ADV atípicamente, de manera atípica.
aubergine [ˈəʊbəʒiːn] N (esp Brit) berenjena f.
auburn [ˈɔːbən] ADJ castaño rojizo.
auction [ˈɔːkʃən] [1] N subasta f, almoneda f, licitación f, remate m (esp LAm); (Bridge) subasta f; **~ bridge** bridge-remate m; **~ sale** subasta f; **to put up for ~, to sell at ~** subastar, poner (or vender) en pública subasta.
[2] VT (also **to ~ off**) subastar, licitar (LAm), rematar (esp LAm).
auctioneer [ˌɔːkʃəˈnɪə^r] N subastador m, -ora f, licitador m, -ora f (LAm), rematador m, -ora f (esp LAm).
auction house [ˈɔːkʃənhaʊs] N casa f de subastas.
auction-room [ˈɔːkʃənrʊm] N sala f de subastas.
aud. ABBR of **audit, auditor**.
audacious [ɔːˈdeɪʃəs] ADJ audaz, atrevido; (pej) descarado.
audaciously [ɔːˈdeɪʃəslɪ] ADV audazmente, atrevidamente; (pej) descaradamente.
audacity [ɔːˈdæsɪtɪ] N audacia f, atrevimiento m; (pej) descaro m; **and you have the ~ to say that!** ¡y te atreves a decir eso!, ¡y me lo dices tan fresco!
audibility [ˌɔːdɪˈbɪlɪtɪ] N audibilidad f.
audible [ˈɔːdɪbl] ADJ audible, perceptible, que se puede oír; **the speech was barely ~** apenas se podía oír el discurso; **there was an ~ gasp** se oyó un grito sofocado.
audibly [ˈɔːdɪblɪ] ADV de modo que se puede oír, de modo audible.
audience [ˈɔːdɪəns] N (a) (gathering) auditorio m, público m, audiencia f; **it's got ~ appeal** tiene gancho con el público; **~ participation** participación f del público; **~ rating** (TV) índice m de audiencia; **~ research** sondeo m de opiniones; **there was a big ~** asistió un público numeroso; **those in the ~** los que formaban parte de la audiencia.
(b) (interview) audiencia f (of, with con); **~ chamber** sala f de audiencia; **to have an ~ of** (or **with**) ser recibido en audiencia por; **to receive sb in ~** recibir a uno en audiencia.
audio [ˈɔːdɪəʊ] [1] ADJ de audio; **~ book** audiolibro m, libro m de audio; **~ equipment** equipo m de audio; **~ recording** grabación f en audio; **~ system** sistema m audio, audiosistema m.
[2] N audio m.
audio... [ˈɔːdɪəʊ] PREF audio...
audio-cassette [ˌɔːdɪəʊkəˈset] N cassette f, cinta f de audio, cinta f de cassette.
audiofrequency [ˌɔːdɪəʊˈfriːkwənsɪ] N audiofrecuencia f.
audiometer [ˌɔːdɪˈɒmɪtə^r] N audiómetro m.
audiotronic [ˌɔːdɪəʊˈtrɒnɪk] ADJ audio-electrónico.
audiotyping [ˈɔːdɪəʊˌtaɪpɪŋ] N mecanografía f por dictáfono.
audiotypist [ˈɔːdɪəʊˌtaɪpɪst] N mecanógrafo m, -a f de dictáfono.
audio-visual [ˌɔːdɪəʊˈvɪzjʊəl] ADJ audiovisual; **~ aid** ayuda f audiovisual; **~ equipment** equipo m audiovisual; **~ method** método m audiovisual.
audit [ˈɔːdɪt] [1] N revisión f de cuentas, intervención f; auditoría f.
[2] VT (a) (Fin) revisar, intervenir, auditar. (b) **to ~ a course** (US) asistir a un curso como oyente.
auditing [ˈɔːdɪtɪŋ] N: **~ of accounts** auditoría f, censura f de cuentas.
audition [ɔːˈdɪʃən] [1] N audición f.
[2] VT dar audición a; **he was ~ed for the part** le hicieron una audición para el papel.
[3] VI: **he ~ed for the part** hizo una audición para el papel.
auditor [ˈɔːdɪtə^r] N (a) (Fin) censor m, -ora f de cuentas, interventor m, -ora f; (internal) auditor m, -ora f; **~'s report** informe m del auditor. (b) (US Univ) estudiante mf libre, oyente mf.
auditorium [ˌɔːdɪˈtɔːrɪəm] N auditorio m, sala f.
auditory [ˈɔːdɪtərɪ] ADJ auditivo.
Audubon [ˈɔːdəbɒn] N: **~ Society** (US) sociedad para la conservación de la naturaleza, ≃ ICONA m, ≃ ADENA f.
AUEW N (Brit) ABBR of **Amalgamated Union of Engineering Workers** sindicato mixto de trabajadores de ingeniería.
au fait [əʊˈfeɪ] ADJ: **to be ~ with sth** estar al corriente de algo, estar al tanto de algo, estar al día de algo.
Aug. ABBR of **August** agosto m, ag.
Augean Stables [ɔːˈdʒiːənˈsteɪblz] NPL establos mpl de Augias.
aught [ɔːt] N (†, liter) algo, alguna cosa f; (with negation) nada; **if there is ~ I can do** si puedo hacer algo, si puedo ayudarles de algún

modo; **for ~ I care he can ...** igual me da si él ...; **for ~ I know** que yo sepa.
augment [ɔːgˈment] [1] VT aumentar.
[2] VI aumentar(se).
augmentation [ˌɔːgmenˈteɪʃən] N aumento m.
augmentative [ɔːgˈmentətɪv] ADJ aumentativo.
au gratin [əʊˈgrætɛ̃] ADJ gratinado.
augur [ˈɔːgə^r] [1] VT augurar, pronosticar, anunciar; **it ~s no good** esto no nos promete nada bueno.
[2] VI: **it ~s ill** es de mal agüero; **it ~s well** es de buen agüero (for para).
augury [ˈɔːgjʊrɪ] N augurio m; presagio m; **to take the auguries** consultar los augurios.
August [ˈɔːgəst] N agosto m.
august [ɔːˈgʌst] ADJ augusto.
Augustan [ɔːˈgʌstən] ADJ augustal; **the ~ age** (Rome) el siglo de Augusto, (English) la época neoclásica (del siglo XVIII).
Augustine [ɔːˈgʌstɪn] NM Agustín.
Augustinian [ɔːgəˈstɪnɪən] [1] ADJ agustino.
[2] N agustino m, -a f.
Augustus [ɔːˈgʌstəs] NM Augusto.
auk [ɔːk] N alca f; **little ~** mérgulo m marino.
auld [ɔːld] ADJ (Scot = old) **~ lang syne** tiempos mpl antiguos, los buenos tiempos de antaño; **A~ Reeky** Edimburgo.

┌─ **AULD LANG SYNE** ─┐

ⓘ **Auld Lang Syne** *es el título de una canción tradicional escocesa que se canta en todo el Reino Unido y en EE.UU. al final de algunas fiestas y celebraciones sociales, y en especial para dar la bienvenida al Año Nuevo, a las doce de la noche de fin de año. Con la canción se intenta hacernos recordar los tiempos pasados para que se tengan presentes en esos momentos. Los primeros versos son: **Should auld acquaintance be forgot, And never brought to mind, We'll drink a cup o' kindness yet, For the sake of auld lang syne.***
⇨ Ver también HOGMANAY

---

aunt [ɑːnt] N tía f; **my ~ and uncle** mis tíos; **A~ Sally** blanco m (de insultos, críticas etc).
auntie*, aunty* [ˈɑːntɪ] N tía f; **A~** (Brit hum) la BBC.
au pair [ˈəʊˈpeə] [1] ADV au pair.
[2] ADJ: **~ girl = 3.**
[3] N, PL **au pairs** chica f au pair.
aura [ˈɔːrə] N emanación f; (atmosphere) atmósfera f; **a mystic ~** un halo místico; **an ~ of doom** un halo fatídico.
aural [ˈɔːrəl] ADJ aural, auditivo.
aureole [ˈɔːrɪəʊl] N aureola f.
au revoir [ˌəʊrəˈvwɑː^r] ADV hasta la vista.
auricle [ˈɔːrɪkl] N aurícula f.
aurochs [ˈɔːrɒks] N uro m, aurochs m.
aurora borealis [ɔːˈrɔːrəbɔːrɪˈeɪlɪs] N aurora f boreal.
auspices [ˈɔːspɪsɪz] NPL: **under the ~ of** bajo los auspicios de, auspiciado por.
auspicious [ɔːsˈpɪʃəs] ADJ propicio, favorable, de buen augurio; **to make an ~ start** comenzar felizmente (or favorablemente).
auspiciously [ɔːsˈpɪʃəslɪ] ADV propiciamente, favorablemente; **to start ~** comenzar felizmente (or favorablemente).
Aussie* [ˈɒzɪ] = **Australian**.
austere [ɒsˈtiːə^r] ADJ austero.
austerely [ɒsˈtɪəlɪ] ADV austeramente.
austerity [ɒsˈterɪtɪ] N austeridad f.
Australasia [ˌɒːstrəˈleɪzɪə] N Australasia f.
Australasian [ˌɒːstrəˈleɪzɪən] [1] N australasiano.
[2] ADJ australasiano m, -a f.
Australia [ɒsˈtreɪlɪə] N Australia f.
Australian [ɒsˈtreɪlɪən] [1] ADJ australiano; **~ Rules Football** fútbol m australiano. [2] N australiano m, -a f.

┌─ **AUSTRALIAN RULES FOOTBALL** ─┐

ⓘ **Australian Rules Football** *es un deporte más parecido al rugby que al fútbol. Se juega en un campo ovalado, con dos equipos de dieciocho jugadores y una pelota ovalada de gran tamaño. En cada extremo del campo hay una portería con cuatro postes: por cada gol marcado entre los postes interiores se obtienen seis puntos y sólo uno por cada gol marcado entre un poste interior y uno exterior, lo que se denomina* **behind***. Los jugadores pueden golpear la pelota con las manos y los pies, pero no pueden lanzarla, y para correr con ella deben hacerla botar cada diez metros. La mayoría de los estados australianos tienen sus propias ligas de fútbol australiano.*

Austria [ˈɒstrɪə] N Austria f.
Austrian [ˈɒstrɪən] [1] ADJ austríaco. [2] N austríaco m, -a f.
Austro-Hungarian [ˈɒstrəʊhʌŋˈgeərɪən] ADJ austro-húngaro.

AUT N (*Brit*) ABBR of **Association of University Teachers** *sindicato de profesores de universidad.*

autarchy [ˈɔːtɑːkɪ] N autarquía *f.*

authentic [ɔːˈθentɪk] ADJ auténtico.

authentically [ɔːˈθentɪkəlɪ] ADV auténticamente, genuinamente.

authenticate [ɔːˈθentɪkeɪt] VT autenticar; autentificar.

authentication [ɔːˌθentɪˈkeɪʃn] N autenticación *f.*

authenticity [ˌɔːθenˈtɪsɪtɪ] N autenticidad *f.*

author [ˈɔːθəʳ] **1** N autor *m*, -ora *f*; ~! ~! (*Theat*) ¡que salga el autor!; ~'s copy ejemplar *m* autógrafo, (*book*) ejemplar *m* del autor.
2 VT (*esp US*) escribir, componer.

authoress [ˈɔːθərɪs] N autora *f.*

authorial [ɔːˈθɔːrɪəl] ADJ autorial.

authoritarian [ˌɔːθɒrɪˈtɛərɪən] **1** ADJ autoritario.
2 N autoritario *m*, -a *f.*

authoritarianism [ˌɔːθɒrɪˈtɛərɪənɪzəm] N autoritarismo *m.*

authoritative [ɔːˈθɒrɪtətɪv] ADJ *version etc* autorizado, autoritativo; *manner etc* autoritario.

authoritatively [ɔːˈθɒrɪtətɪvlɪ] ADV autoritativamente; autoritariamente.

authority [ɔːˈθɒrɪtɪ] N (a) (*power*) autoridad *f*; those in ~ los que tienen la autoridad; who is in ~ here? ¿quién manda aquí?; in ~ over al mando de; on one's own ~ por su propia autoridad; to do sth without ~ hacer algo sin tener autorización; to give sb ~ to + *infin* autorizar a uno para que + *subj*; he had no ~ to do that no tenía autoridad para hacer eso.
(b) (*competence*) autoridad *f*; on the ~ of Plato con la autoridad de Platón; I have it on good ~ that ... sé de buena tinta que ...; to speak with ~ hablar con conocimiento de causa.
(c) (*person*) autoridad *f*; (*book*) obra *f* autoritaria, obra *f* clásica; he is the greatest living ~ es la máxima autoridad actual; he is an ~ on the subject es un experto en la materia.
(d) (*official body*) autoridad *f*; the authorities las autoridades; health ~ administración *f* sanitaria; regional ~ autoridad *f* regional; to apply to the proper authorities dirigirse a la autoridad competente.

▼ **authorization** [ˌɔːθəraɪˈzeɪʃn] N autorización *f.*

▼ **authorize** [ˈɔːθəraɪz] VT autorizar; to ~ sb to + *infin* autorizar a uno para que + *subj*; to be ~d to + *infin* estar autorizado para + *infin*, tener autorización para + *infin.*

authorized [ˈɔːθəraɪzd] ADJ autorizado; ~ agent agente *m* oficial; ~ capital capital *m* autorizado, capital *m* social; ~ distributor distribuidor *m* autorizado; A~ Version Versión *f* Autorizada (de la Biblia).

authorship [ˈɔːθəʃɪp] N (a) profesión *f* de autor. (b) (*of book etc*) autoría *f*, paternidad *f* literaria; of unknown ~ de autor desconocido.

autism [ˈɔːtɪzəm] N autismo *m.*

autistic [ɔːˈtɪstɪk] ADJ autístico, autista.

auto[1]... [ˈɔːtəʊ] PREF auto...

auto[2] [ˈɔːtəʊ] N (*US*) coche *m*, automóvil *m*, carro *m* (*LAm*); ~ repair reparación *f* de automóviles; A~ Show Salón *m* del Automóvil; ~ worker trabajador *m*, -ora *f* de la industria automovilística (*or* del automóvil).

autobank [ˈɔːtəʊbæŋk] N cajero *m* automático.

autobiographic(al) [ˈɔːtəʊˌbaɪəʊˈɡræfɪk(əl)] ADJ autobiográfico.

autobiography [ˌɔːtəʊbaɪˈɒɡrəfɪ] N autobiografía *f.*

autocade [ˈɔːtəʊkeɪd] N caravana *f* de automóviles.

autochthonous [ɔːˈtɒkθənəs] ADJ autóctono.

autocracy [ɔːˈtɒkrəsɪ] N autocracia *f.*

autocrat [ˈɔːtəʊkræt] N autócrata *mf.*

autocratic [ˌɔːtəʊˈkrætɪk] ADJ autocrático.

autocross [ˈɔːtəʊkrɒs] N auto-cross *m.*

autocue [ˈɔːtəʊkjuː] N (*Brit TV*) autocue *m*, chuleta* *f.*

autocycle [ˈɔːtəʊsaɪkl] N velomotor *m*, ciclomotor *m.*

auto-da-fe, auto-da-fé [ˈɔːtəʊdɑːˈfeɪ] N, PL **autos-da-fe, autos-da-fé** auto *m* de fe.

autogiro [ˈɔːtəʊˈdʒaɪərəʊ] N autogiro *m.*

autograph [ˈɔːtəɡrɑːf] **1** ADJ autógrafo; ~ album álbum *m* de autógrafos; ~ hunter cazaautógrafos *mf.*
2 N (*manuscript*) autógrafo *m*; (*signature*) firma *f*, autógrafo *m.*
3 VT (*sign*) firmar; *book, photo etc* dedicar.

autohypnosis [ˌɔːtəʊhɪpˈnəʊsɪs] N autohipnosis *f.*

autoimmune [ˌɔːtəʊɪˈmjuːn] ADJ autoinmune.

automat [ˈɔːtəmæt] N (a) (*Brit*) máquina *f* expendedora. (b) (*US*) restaurante *m* de autoservicio.

automata [ɔːˈtɒmətə] NPL of **automaton.**

automate [ˈɔːtəmeɪt] VT automatizar.

automated [ˈɔːtəmeɪtɪd] ADJ automatizado; ~ teller, ~ telling machine cajero *m* automático.

automatic [ˌɔːtəˈmætɪk] **1** ADJ automático; ~ data processing proceso *m* automático de datos; ~ pilot piloto *m* automático; ~ transmission (*Aut*) transmisión *f* automática.

2 N (*pistol*) automática *f*; (*Brit Aut*) automático *m.*

automatically [ˌɔːtəˈmætɪkəlɪ] ADV automáticamente.

automation [ˌɔːtəˈmeɪʃn] N automatización *f.*

automatism [ɔːˈtɒmətɪzəm] N automatismo *m.*

automaton [ɔːˈtɒmətən] N, PL **automata** [ɔːˈtɒmətə] autómata *m.*

automobile [ˈɔːtəməbiːl] N (*esp US*) coche *m*, carro *m* (*LAm*), automóvil *m*; ~ industry industria *f* del automóvil.

automotive [ɔːtəˈməʊtɪv] ADJ automotor.

autonomous [ɔːˈtɒnəməs] ADJ autónomo; autonómico.

autonomy [ɔːˈtɒnəmɪ] N autonomía *f.*

autonymous [ɔːˈtɒnɪməs] ADJ autónimo.

autopilot [ˈɔːtəʊpaɪlət] N piloto *m* automático.

autopsy [ˈɔːtɒpsɪ] N autopsia *f*, necropsia *f* (*LAm*).

autoreverse [ˈɔːtəʊrɪˈvɜːs] N auto-reverse *m.*

autosuggestion [ˈɔːtəʊsəˈdʒestʃən] N (auto)sugestión *f.*

auto-teller [ˈɔːtəʊˌteləʳ] N cajero *m* automático.

autotimer [ˈɔːtəʊˌtaɪməʳ] N programador *m* automático.

autumn [ˈɔːtəm] N otoño *m.*

autumnal [ɔːˈtʌmnəl] ADJ otoñal, de(l) otoño.

Auvergne [əʊˈveən] N Auvernia *f.*

auxiliary [ɔːɡˈzɪljərɪ] **1** ADJ auxiliar; ~ police (*US*) cuerpo *m* de policía auxiliar; ~ staff (*Brit Scol*) profesores *mpl* sustitutos, profesores *mpl* auxiliares; ~ verb verbo *m* auxiliar.
2 N (*Gram*) verbo *m* auxiliar; (*Med etc*) ayudante *mf*; (*Mil*) **auxiliaries** tropas *fpl* auxiliares.

AV (a) ABBR of **Authorized Version** (*of the Bible*). **(b)** ABBR of **audiovisual.**

Av., Ave ABBR of **Avenue** avenida *f*, Av., Avda.

av. ABBR of **average** promedio *m*, prom.

a.v., a/v ABBR of **ad valorem.**

avail [əˈveɪl] (*liter*) **1** N: it is of no ~ es inútil; to no ~ en vano, sin resultado; to be of little ~ ser de poco provecho; of what ~ is it to? + *infin* ¿de qué sirve? + *infin.*
2 VT aprovechar, valer.
3 VI: it ~s nothing to + *infin* de nada sirve + *infin.*
4 VR: to ~ o.s. of aprovechar(se de), valerse de; acogerse a.

availability [əˌveɪləˈbɪlɪtɪ] N (a) disponibilidad *f.* (b) (*US*) validez *f.*

available [əˈveɪləbl] ADJ (a) disponible; asequible, aprovechable; ~ exclusively from Smith's sólo se puede conseguir en Smith's; further details are ~ from the secretary puede obtenerse más información en secretaría; is your latest catalogue ~? ¿está listo su último catálogo?; to make sth ~ to sb poner algo a la disposición de uno; is the manager ~? ¿está libre el gerente?, ¿puedo pasar a ver al gerente?; are you ~ next Thursday? ¿estás libre el jueves que viene?; the Minister is not ~ for comment el Ministro no se ofrece a hacer comentarios; this item is not ~ at the moment no tenemos este artículo por el momento; I am not ~ to visitors no estoy para las visitas; I'd like a seat on the first ~ flight quiero una plaza en el primer vuelo que haya. (b) (*US: valid*) válido.

avalanche [ˈævəlɑːnʃ] N alud *m*, avalancha *f*; (*fig*) torrente *m*, avalancha *f.*

avant-garde [ˈævɑːˌŋˈɡɑːd] **1** ADJ de vanguardia, nueva ola, ultramoderno.
2 N vanguardia *f*, nueva ola *f.*

avarice [ˈævərɪs] N avaricia *f.*

avaricious [ˌævəˈrɪʃəs] ADJ avaro, avariento.

avatar [ˈævətɑːʳ] N (*Rel*) avatar *m.*

avdp. ABBR of **avoirdupois.**

Ave. ABBR of **avenue** avenida *f*, Av., Avda.

avenge [əˈvendʒ] **1** VT vengar.
2 VR: to ~ o.s. vengarse (*on* en).

avenger [əˈvendʒəʳ] N vengador *m*, -ora *f.*

avenging [əˈvendʒɪŋ] ADJ vengador.

avenue [ˈævənjuː] N avenida *f*; (*fig*) vía *f*, camino *m*; to explore every ~ tentar todas las vías.

aver [əˈvɜːʳ] VT afirmar, declarar, aseverar.

average [ˈævərɪdʒ] **1** ADJ (a) (*Math*) medio, de término medio; ~ (daily) balance saldo *m* medio (diario); ~ (due) date fecha *f* media de vencimiento; ~ price precio *m* medio; ~ quality calidad *f* media; wines of above ~ quality vinos *mpl* de calidad superior; of ~ height de regular estatura; the ~ height of players el promedio de talla de los jugadores (*or* por jugador).
(b) (*fig*) mediano, regular, corriente; the ~ man el hombre medio; your ~ Ruritanian el ruritanio corriente; of ~ ability de capacidad regular.
2 N (a) (*Math etc*) promedio *m*, término *m* medio; on (the) ~, on an ~ por término medio; por regla general; above ~ superior al promedio; below ~ inferior al promedio; to do an ~ of 150 kph ir a un promedio de 150 kph; to take an (*or* the) ~ of tomar el promedio de, calcular el promedio de. (b) (*Comm*) avería *f*; ~ adjuster tasador *m* de averías; ~ bond fianza *f* de averías; ~ statement declaración *f* del tasador de averías.

3 VT **(a)** (*also to ~ out*: *find average of*) calcular el término medio de; prorratear.

(b) we ~ 8 hours a day trabajamos (*etc*) por regla general 8 horas diarias; **he ~d 140 all the way** hizo un promedio de 140 kph por todo el recorrido; **the sales ~ 200 a week** la venta media es de 200 ejemplares cada semana.

4 VI ser por término medio, resultar por término medio; ser por regla general.

◆**average down** VT promediar hacia abajo.

◆**average out** **1** VT calcular el término medio de.

2 VI: **our working hours ~ out at 8 per day** trabajamos un promedio de 8 horas al día.

◆**average up** VT promediar hacia arriba.

AVERAGE, HALF	*see also main entries*

Position of "medio"
You should generally put *medio* after the noun when you mean "average" and before the noun when you mean "half":
...the average citizen...
...el ciudadano medio...
...the average salary...
...el salario medio...
...half a kilo of tomatoes...
...medio kilo de tomates...
For further uses and examples, see main entries at **average** and **half**.

---

averse [ə'vɜːs] ADJ: **to be ~ to** sentir repugnancia por, tener antipatía a; **to be ~ to +** *ger* tener pocas ganas de + *infin*, no estar dispuesto a + *infin*; **I am ~ to getting up early** soy enemigo de levantarme temprano; **I am not ~ to an occasional drink** no me repugna tomar algo de vez en cuando.

aversion [ə'vɜːʃən] N **(a)** (*feeling*) aversión *f* (*for, from, to* hacia), repugnancia *f* (*for, from, to* por); **~ therapy** terapia *f* por aversión, terapia *f* aversiva; **to feel an ~ for** sentir repugnancia por; **I have an ~ to him** me resulta antipático; **I took an ~ to it** empezó a repugnarme.

(b) (*hated thing*) cosa *f* aborrecida; **it is one of my ~s** es una de las cosas que me repugnan; **V pet.**

avert [ə'vɜːt] VT *eyes, thoughts* apartar (*from* de); *suspicion* desviar (*from* de); *possibility* evitar, quitar; *blow* impedir, desviar; *accident, illness, rebellion* prevenir.

aviary ['eɪvɪərɪ] N pajarera *f*, avería *f*.

aviation [,eɪvɪ'eɪʃən] N aviación *f*; **~ industry** industria *f* de la aviación; **~ spirit** gasolina *f* de aviación.

aviator ['eɪvɪeɪtə'] N aviador *m*, -ora *f*.

avid ['ævɪd] ADJ ávido, ansioso (*for, of* de).

avidity [ə'vɪdɪtɪ] N avidez *f*, ansia *f*.

avidly ['ævɪdlɪ] ADV ávidamente, ansiosamente; **to read ~** leer con avidez.

Avignon ['ævɪnjɒ] N Aviñón *m*.

avionics [,eɪvɪ'ɒnɪks] N SING aviónica *f*.

avocado [ævə'kɑːdəʊ] N (*Brit also ~ pear*) aguacate *m*, palta *f* (*LAm*); **~ tree** aguacate *m*, palto *m* (*LAm*).

avocation [,ævəʊ'keɪʃən] N diversión *f*, distracción *f*, ocupación *f* accesoria; (*loosely*) vocación *f*.

avoid [ə'vɔɪd] VT evitar; guardarse de; *duty etc* eludir; *danger* salvarse de; **to ~ +** *ger* evitar + *infin*; **he managed to ~ (hitting) the tree** evitó chocar con el árbol; **to ~ being seen** procurar no ser visto; **are you trying to ~ me?** ¿estás tratando de evitar hablar conmigo?; **I try to ~ him** procuro no tener nada que ver con él; **he ~s all his friends** huye de todos sus amigos; **it's to be ~ed like the plague** esto hay que evitarlo como la peste; **this way we ~ London** por esta ruta evitamos pasar por Londres; **to ~ sb's eye** evitar cambiar miradas con uno; **to ~ tax** (*legally*) evitar pagar impuestos, (*illegally*) defraudar al fisco.

avoidable [ə'vɔɪdəbl] ADJ evitable, eludible.

avoidance [ə'vɔɪdəns] N el evitar (*etc*), evitación *f*.

avoirdupois [,ævədə'pɔɪz] N **(a)** *sistema de pesos usado en países de habla inglesa* (1 *libra* = 16 *onzas* = 453,50 *gramos*). **(b)** (*: overweight*) peso *m*, gordura *f*.

avow [ə'vaʊ] **1** VT reconocer, confesar, admitir.

2 VR: **he ~ed himself beaten** admitió que había perdido.

avowal [ə'vaʊəl] N confesión *f*; declaración *f*.

avowed [ə'vaʊd] ADJ declarado, abierto.

avowedly [ə'vaʊɪdlɪ] ADV declaradamente, abiertamente.

AVP N (*US*) ABBR *of* **assistant vice-president**.

avuncular [ə'vʌŋkjʊlə'] ADJ como de tío; **~ advice** consejos *mpl* amistosos.

aw [ɔː] EXCL ¡ay!

AWACS [ˈeɪwæks] N ABBR *of* **airborne warning and control system** AWACS *m*.

▼**await** [ə'weɪt] VT esperar, aguardar; **the fate that ~s him** la suerte que le espera; **we ~ your instructions** esperamos sus instrucciones; **we ~ your reply with interest** nos interesa mucho saber su respuesta; **a long ~ed event** un acontecimiento largamente esperado.

awake [ə'weɪk] **1** ADJ despierto; **to lie ~** quedar despierto, estar sin poder dormir; **to stay ~ all night** pasar toda la noche en vela; **the noise kept me ~** el ruido me impidió dormir; **coffee keeps me ~** el café me desvela.

2 (*irr*: PRET **awoke**, PTP **awoken** *or* **awaked**) VT despertar.

3 VI despertar(se).

awaken [ə'weɪkən] **1** VT despertar (*also fig*); **to ~ sb to a danger** alertar a uno de un peligro.

2 VI (*also to ~ from sleep*) despertar(se); **to ~ from one's illusions** desilusionarse, quitarse las ilusiones; **to ~ to a danger** darse cuenta de un peligro.

awakening [ə'weɪknɪŋ] **1** ADJ (*fig*) naciente.

2 N el despertar, despertamiento *m*; **a rude ~** una sorpresa desagradable.

award [ə'wɔːd] **1** N **(a)** (*prize*) premio *m*; galardón *m*; (*Jur*) sentencia *f*, fallo *m*; (*Mil*) condecoración *f*.

(b) (*act of ~ing*) adjudicación *f*, concesión *f*; **pay ~** adjudicación *f* de aumento de salarios.

2 VT conceder, otorgar; *prize, damages etc* adjudicar, decretar; *medal* dar; (*Sport*) *penalty* decretar, señalar; **the prize is not being ~ed this year** este año el premio se ha declarado desierto.

award-winning [ə'wɔːd,wɪnɪŋ] ADJ premiado.

aware [ə'weə'] ADJ **(a)** (*alert*) enterado; despierto; **politically ~** politizado; **sexually ~** enterado de lo sexual; **socially ~** educado en lo social.

(b) (*knowledgeable*) **to be ~ of** saber, estar enterado de, ser consciente de; **not that I am ~ of** (no) que yo sepa; **our employees are ~ of this advertisement** los empleados de la empresa han sido informados de este anuncio; **to be ~ that ...** saber que ..., ser consciente que ...; **I am fully ~ that ...** sé perfectamente que ...; **to become ~ of** darse cuenta de, enterarse de; **to make sb ~ of sth** hacer que uno se dé cuenta de algo.

awareness [ə'weənɪs] N conciencia *f*, conocimiento *m*; **sexual ~ in the young** los conocimientos sexuales de los jóvenes.

awash [ə'wɒʃ] ADJ: **the deck is ~** la cubierta está a flor de agua; **the house was ~** la casa estaba inundada; **we are ~ with applicants** estamos inundados de solicitudes.

away [ə'weɪ] **1** ADV **(a)** (*at a distance*) **3 km ~** a 3 km (de aquí *or* de allí *or* de distancia); **X won with Y only 2 strokes ~** ganó X con Y a sólo 2 golpes de distancia; **~ in the distance** allá a lo lejos; **~ from the noise** lejos del ruido; **~ back in 1066** allá en 1066; **~!, ~ with you!** ¡vete!, ¡fuera de aquí!; **~ with him!** ¡fuera!, ¡que le lleven de aquí!; **~ with taxes!** ¡abajo los impuestos!; **to play ~** (*Sport*) jugar fuera de casa, jugar en campo ajeno; **they have won only 2 games ~** han ganado solamente dos partidos fuera (de casa).

(b) (*absent*) **to be ~ (from home)** estar fuera, estar ausente; **he's ~ for a week** pasa ocho días fuera; **he's ~ in Bognor** está en Bognor; **she was ~ before I could shout** se fue antes de que yo pudiese gritar; **I must ~** (*liter or hum*) tengo que marcharme.

(c) (*continuously*) sin parar; (*earnestly*) con ahínco; (*persistently*) con empeño; **he was grumbling ~** seguía quejándose; **to talk ~** hablar mucho, no parar de hablar; **talk ~!** ¡di lo que quieras!; **to work ~** seguir trabajando, trabajar sin parar.

(d) *V* **die, get** *etc*.

2 ADJ: **the ~ team** el equipo de fuera; **~ match** partido *m* fuera de casa; **~ win** victoria *f* fuera de casa.

awe [ɔː] **1** N temor *m* reverencial, pavor *m* y respeto; **to go** (*or* **be**) **in ~ of, hold in ~, stand in ~ of** tener temor reverencial a.

2 VT imponer respeto a; atemorizar; **in an ~d tone** con un tono de respeto y temor.

awe-inspiring ['ɔːɪn,spaɪərɪŋ] ADJ, **awesome** ['ɔːsəm] ADJ imponente, pasmoso.

awe-struck ['ɔːstrʌk] ADJ pasmado, atemorizado.

▼**awful** ['ɔːfəl] ADJ **(a)** (*awesome*) tremendo, imponente, terrible, pasmoso.

▼**(b)** (*nasty etc*) horrible, malísimo, fatal; **how ~!** ¡qué horror!; **how ~ for you!** ¡lo que habrás sufrido!; **it was just ~** fue francamente horrible; **what ~ weather!** ¡qué tiempo más feo!; **his English is ~** tiene un inglés fatal*; **he's an ~ fool** es tonto de remate; **there were an ~ lot of people** había la mar de gente; **to feel ~** sentirse molesto, estar sobrecogido, (*ill*) sentirse muy mal; **I felt ~ about what had happened** sentía muchísimo lo que había ocurrido; **you are ~!*** ¡eres una bestia!*

awfully ['ɔːflɪ] ADV **(a)** (*badly*) terriblemente; pasmosamente; **she sings ~** canta terriblemente mal. **(b)** (*intensifying*) terriblemente; **it's ~ hard** es terriblemente difícil; **it's ~ funny** es divertidísimo, es la mar de divertido; **I'm ~ sorry** lo siento muchísimo; **thanks ~!** ¡muchísimas gracias!; **an ~ big car** un coche la mar de grande.

awfulness ['ɔːfʊlnɪs] N horror *m*, atrocidad *f*.
awhile [ə'waɪl] ADV un rato, algún tiempo; **not yet** ~ todavía no.
awkward ['ɔːkwəd] ADJ **(a)** (*inconvenient*) *problem, question* difícil; *situation* violento, difícil; *time* inoportuno; *task* delicado, desagradable; *shape* incómodo; *corner* peligroso; **it's** ~ **for me** es difícil para mí; **it's all a bit** ~ todo esto es un poco violento (*or* molesto); **to come at an** ~ **time** llegar en un momento difícil; **to feel** ~ sentirse molesto; **to make things** ~ **for sb** plantear problemas a uno, crear dificultades para uno.
(b) (*obstinate*) terco, difícil; (*unhelpful*) poco amable; **he's being** ~ se muestra poco dispuesto a ayudar; está poniendo peros; **he's an** ~ **customer*** es un tipo difícil, es un sujeto de cuidado.
(c) (*clumsy*) desmañado, desgarbado, torpe; *phrasing* poco elegante; **the** ~ **squad** la sección de los bisoños; **to be at the** ~ **age** estar en la edad del pavo.
awkwardly ['ɔːkwədlɪ] ADV *move, speak* con dificultad; **he expresses himself** ~ se expresa mal, se expresa con poca elegancia; **he dances** ~ baila torpemente; **we are** ~ **placed** estamos en una situación molesta.
awkwardness ['ɔːkwədnɪs] N (*V adj*) **(a)** dificultad *f*; violencia *f*; incomodidad *f*; molestia *f*. **(b)** terquedad *f*. **(c)** desmaña *f*, torpeza *f*.
awl [ɔːl] N lezna *f*, subilla *f*.
awning ['ɔːnɪŋ] N toldo *m*; (*of cart*) entalamadura *f*; (*Naut*) toldilla *f*; (*over window, at entrance*) marquesina *f*.
awoke [ə'wəʊk] PRET AND PTP *of* **awake**.
awoken [ə'wəʊkən] PTP *of* **awake**.
AWOL ['eɪwɒl] (*Mil*) ABBR *of* **absent without leave** ausente sin permiso.
awry [ə'raɪ] ADV: **with his hat on** ~ con el sombrero torcido, con el sombrero ladeado; **to be** ~ estar de través, estar al sesgo, estar puesto mal; **to go** ~ salir mal, fracasar.
axe, (US) ax [æks] ① N **(a)** hacha *f*; (*fig: blow*) golpe *m*; (*cut-back*) recorte *m*, reducción *f*; **when the** ~ **fell** cuando se descargó el golpe; **to have an** ~ **to grind** tener un interés creado; **I have no** ~ **to grind** no tengo ningún interés personal.
(b) to give sb the ~ *employee* despedir a uno; *boyfriend* dejar plantado a uno; **I got the** ~ (*employee*) me despidieron; (*boyfriend*) me dejó plantado.
② VT (*fig*) *costs etc* reducir, recortar; *person* despedir; *staff* recortar.
axes ['æksiːz] NPL *of* **axis**.
axial ['æksɪəl] ADJ axial.
axiom ['æksɪəm] N axioma *m*.
axiomatic [ˌæksɪəʊ'mætɪk] ADJ axiomático.
axis ['æksɪs] N, PL **axes** ['æksiːz] eje *m*; (*Anat*) axis *m*; **the A~** (*Pol*) el Eje.
axle ['æksl] N eje *m*, árbol *m*, cardán *m* (*CAm*), flecha *f* (*Mex*).
ay(e) [aɪ] ① ADV (*esp Scot, N. England*) sí; ~ ~ **sir!** sí mi capitán (*etc*).
② N sí *m*; **to vote** ~ votar sí; **the** ~**s have it** se ha aprobado la moción; **there were 50** ~**s and 3 noes** votaron 50 a favor y 3 en contra.
ayatollah [aɪə'tɒlə] N imam *m*, ayatolá *m*, ayatollah *m*.
aye [eɪ] ADV: **for ever and** ~ (*Scot*) para siempre jamás.
AYH N (*US*) ABBR *of* **American Youth Hostels**.
Aymara [ˌaɪmə'rɑː] ① ADJ aimará.
② N **(a)** aimará *mf*. **(b)** (*Ling*) aimará *m*.
AZ (*US*) ABBR *of* **Arizona**.
azalea [ə'zeɪlɪə] N azalea *f*.
Azerbaijan [ˌæzəbaɪ'dʒɑːn] N Azerbaiyán *m*.
Azerbaijani [ˌæzəbaɪ'dʒɑːnɪ] ① ADJ azerbaiyaní.
② N azerbaiyaní *mf*.
Azeri [ə'zeərɪ] ① ADJ azerí.
② N **(a)** azerí *mf*. **(b)** (*Ling*) azerí *m*.
Azores [ə'zɔːɪz] NPL Azores *fpl*.
AZT N ABBR *of* **azidothymidine** azidotimidina *f*, AZT *m*.
Aztec ['æztek] ① ADJ azteca.
② N azteca *mf*.
azure ['eɪʒəʳ] ① ADJ azul celeste.
② N azul *m* celeste; (*Her*) azur *m*.

B

B, b [biː] N **(a)** (*letter*) B, b *f* (*Esp*), B larga, b larga (*LAm*). **(b)** **B** (*Mus*) si *m*; **B major** si *m* mayor; **B road** ≃ carretera *f* secundaria. **(c)** **B for Baker** B de Burgos; **number 7b** (*in house numbers*) séptimo segunda; **B-girl** (*US**) camarera *f* de barra. **(d)** (*Scol*) notable *m*. **(e)** (*Cine: also* **B-movie**) película *f* de la serie B.

b. ABBR *of* **born** nacido, n.

B & B N ABBR *of* **bed and breakfast** cama *f* con desayuno, alojamiento *m* y desayuno.

BA (a) N (*Univ*) ABBR *of* **Bachelor of Arts** Lic. en Fil. y Let; *ver también* DEGREE .
  (b) N ABBR *of* **British Academy**.
  (c) N ABBR *of* **British Association (for the Advancement of Science)**.
  (d) (*Geog*) ABBR *of* **Buenos Aires** Bs. As.
  (e) N (*Brit Aer*) ABBR *of* **British Airways**.

BAA N ABBR *of* **British Airports Authority**.

baa [bɑː] [1] N balido *m*.
  [2] INTERJ ¡bee!
  [3] VI balar.

baa-lamb* [ˈbɑːlæm] N corderito *m*, borreguito *m*.

babble [ˈbæbl] [1] N parloteo *m*; barboteo *m*; (*of stream*) murmullo *m*; **a ~ of voices arose** se oyó un ruido confuso de voces.
  [2] VT decir balbuceando.
  [3] VI barbullar, barbotear; (*talk to excess*) parlotear; (*tell secrets*) hablar indiscretamente; (*stream*) murmurar.
  ◆ **babble away, babble on** VI hablar sin parar.

babbling [ˈbæblɪŋ] [1] ADJ *person* hablador; *baby* balbuceante; *stream* que murmura, músico.
  [2] N = **babble 1**.

babe [beɪb] N (*liter or hum*) criatura *f*; (*US**) chica *f*, (*in direct address*) ricura *f*, nena *f*; **~ in arms** niño *m*, -a *f* de pecho.

babel [ˈbeɪbəl] N babel *m or f*; **Tower of B~** Torre *f* de Babel.

baboon [bəˈbuːn] N mandril *m*.

Babs [bæbz] NF *familiar form of* **Barbara**.

baby [ˈbeɪbɪ] [1] N niño *m*, -a *f*, guagua *mf* (*LAm*); (*more sentimental*) bebé *mf*, crío *m*, -a *f*, rorro *m*, -a *f*, nene *m*, -a *f*; (*US**) chica *f*, (*in direct address*) ricura *f*, nena *f*; **she's having a ~ in May** va a tener un niño en mayo; **she's having the ~ in hospital** va a dar a luz en el hospital; **~ of the family** benjamín *m*; **don't be such a ~!** ¡no seas niño!; **that's not my ~*** eso no me toca a mí; **to be left holding the ~*** (tener que) pagar el pato*, cargar con el muerto*; **to throw out the ~ with the bathwater** actuar con un exceso de celo; **that ~ cost me a fortune** (*US**) ese chisme me costó una fortuna*.
  [2] ATTR AND ADJ: **~ bonds** (*US*) bonos *mpl* depreciados; **~ boy** nene *m*; **~ break** interrupción *f* de las actividades profesionales por maternidad; **~ car** coche *m* pequeño; **~ clothes**, **~ linen** ropita *f* de niño; **~ face** cara *f* de niño; **~ food(s)** comida *f* para niños, potitos* *mpl*; **~ girl** nena *f*; **~ hedgehog** cría *f* de erizo; **~ rabbit** conejito *m*; **~ seat** (*Aut*) sillita *f* (*or asiento m*) de seguridad para niños; **~ tender** (*US*) canguro *mf*; **~ tooth*** diente *m* de leche; **~ wipe** toallita *f* húmeda.

baby-batterer [ˈbeɪbɪˌbætərəʳ] N persona *f* que maltrata a sus hijos.

baby-battering [ˈbeɪbɪˌbætərɪŋ] N maltrato *m* de los hijos.

baby bed [ˈbeɪbɪˌbed] N (*US*) cuna *f*.

baby-boom [ˈbeɪbɪbuːm] N boom *m* de natalidad, boom *m* de nacimientos; explosión *f* demográfica.

baby-boomer [ˈbeɪbɪˌbuːməʳ] N niño *m* nacido (*or niña f nacida*) en época de un boom de natalidad (*esp de los años 60*).

Baby bouncer [ˈbeɪbɪˌbaʊnsəʳ] ® N columpio *m* para bebés.

baby buggy [ˈbeɪbɪˌbʌgɪ] N (*US*), **baby carriage** [ˈbeɪbɪˌkærɪdʒ] N (*esp US*) cochecito *m* de niño.

baby-doll pyjamas [ˌbeɪbɪdɒlpɪˈdʒɑːməz] N picardía *f*, camisón corto con pantalones a juego.

baby-faced [ˈbeɪbɪˌfeɪst] ADJ *person* con cara aniñada.

baby grand [ˈbeɪbɪˈgrænd] N piano *m* de media cola.

babygrow [ˈbeɪbɪˌgrəʊ] N pijama *m* de una pieza.

babyhood [ˈbeɪbɪhʊd] N infancia *f*.

babyish [ˈbeɪbɪʃ] ADJ infantil.

Babylon [ˈbæbɪlən] N, **Babylonia** [ˌbæbɪˈləʊnɪə] N Babilonia *f*.

Babylonian [ˌbæbɪˈləʊnɪən] [1] ADJ babilónico; *person* babilonio.
  [2] N babilonio *m*, -a *f*.

baby-minder [ˈbeɪbɪˌmaɪndəʳ] N niñera *f*.

baby-sit [ˈbeɪbɪsɪt] (*irr: V* **sit**) VI hacer de canguro, estar de canguro.

baby-sitter [ˈbeɪbɪˌsɪtəʳ] N canguro *mf*.

baby-sitting [ˈbeɪbɪˌsɪtɪŋ] N hacer *m* de canguro; **I can't pay for ~** no puedo pagar un canguro; **I hate ~** detesto hacer canguros.

baby-snatcher [ˈbeɪbɪˌsnætʃəʳ] N mujer *f* que roba un bebé.

baby talk [ˈbeɪbɪtɔːk] N habla *f* infantil.

baby-walker [ˈbeɪbɪˌwɔːkəʳ] N tacataca* *m*, andador *m*.

baccalaureate [ˌbækəˈlɔːrɪɪt] N (*US*) bachillerato *m*.

baccarat [ˈbækərɑː] N bacará *m*, bacarrá *m*.

bacchanalia [ˌbækəˈneɪlɪə] NPL bacanales *fpl*; (*fig*) bacanal *f*.

bacchanalian [ˌbækəˈneɪlɪən] ADJ bacanal, báquico.

Bacchic [ˈbækɪk] ADJ báquico.

Bacchus [ˈbækəs] NM Baco.

baccy* [ˈbækɪ] N tabaco *m*.

bachelor [ˈbætʃələʳ] N **(a)** (*unmarried man*) soltero *m*; **confirmed ~, old ~** solterón *m*; **~ flat** piso *m* (*LAm: departamento m*) de soltero; **~ girl** soltera *f* (*que se dedica a una carrera*); **~ party** guateque *m* para hombres solos.
  (b) (*Univ*) licenciado *m*, -a *f* (*of en*); **B~ of Science** Licenciado *m*, -a *f* en Ciencias; **~'s degree** licenciatura *f*; *ver también* DEGREE .

bachelorhood [ˈbætʃələhʊd] N soltería *f*, estado *m* de soltero, celibato *m*.

bacillary [bəˈsɪlərɪ] ADJ bacilar.

bacillus [bəˈsɪləs] N, PL **bacilli** [bəˈsɪlaɪ] bacilo *m*.

▼ **back** [bæk] [1] ADJ **(a)** (*not front*) trasero, de atrás; posterior; *view* desde atrás; **~ boiler** (*Brit*) caldera *f* pequeña (*detrás de una chimenea*); **~ burner** hornillo *m* trasero; **to put a problem on the ~ burner** (*fig*) dejar un problema para después, relegar un problema al segundo plano; **~ door** puerta *f* trasera; **~ door methods** métodos *mpl* poco ortodoxos; **by the ~ door** (*fig*) por enchufe, gracias al amiguismo; **~ garden** (*Brit*) jardín *m* detrás de la casa, huerto *m*; **~ matter** apéndices *mpl*; **~ pass** pase *m* atrás; **~ passage** (*euph*) recto *m*; **~ row** última fila *f*; **~ somersault** salto *m* mortal hacia atrás; **~ tooth** muela *f*; **~ wheel** rueda *f* trasera.
  (b) (*overdue*) *issue, number* atrasado; *payment* retrasado; **~ rent** atrasos *mpl* de alquiler; **~ tax** impuestos *mpl* atrasados.
  [2] ADV **(a)** (*place*) atrás, hacia atrás; **~!** ¡atrás!; **~ and forth** de acá para allá, de una parte a otra; **a house standing ~ from the road** una casa algo retirada de la carretera; **to make one's way ~** regresar; **to fly to Madrid and ~** ir en avión a Madrid y volver del mismo modo.
  (b) (*time*) **~ in the 12th century** allá en el siglo XII; **as far ~ as 1900** ya en 1900; **some months ~** hace unos meses.
  (c) (*with verb to be*) **to be ~** estar de vuelta; **when will he be ~?** ¿cuándo volverá?
  [3] PREP: **~ of** (*US*) = **behind**.
  [4] N **(a)** (*Anat*) espalda *f*; (*of animal*) lomo *m*; **~ to ~** espalda con espalda; **~ to front** al revés; **at the ~ of** tras, detrás de; **what's at the ~ of it?** (*fig*) ¿qué motivo oculto tendrá esto?; **who's at the ~ of it?** ¿quién está detrás de esto?; **behind one's ~** a espaldas de uno, detrás de uno; **she wears her hair down her ~** el pelo le cae por la espalda; **with one's ~ to** de espaldas a; **his ~ is broad** (*fig*) es capaz de soportarlo; **to be on one's ~** (*Med*) estar postrado (*en la cama*); **to carry sth on one's ~** llevar algo a cuestas; **he lay on his ~** estaba tumbado boca arriba; **to break one's ~** deslomarse; **to break the ~**

of the work terminar lo más difícil (*or* pesado) del trabajo, superar lo más difícil; **to get** (*or* put) **sb's ~ up** picar a uno; **to get off sb's ~*** dejar de fastidiar a uno*; **to have one's ~ to the wall** estar entre la espada y la pared; **to live off sb's ~** vivir a costa de uno; **to put one's ~ into it** arrimar el hombro; **put your ~s into it!** ¡dale!; **to scratch sb's ~*** hacer un favor a uno; **if you scratch my ~ I'll scratch yours*** favor con favor se paga; **to see the ~ of sb** librarse de uno; **we were glad to see the ~ of him** nos alegramos de que se fuera; **to shoot sb in the ~** matar a uno por la espalda; **to turn one's ~** volver las espaldas (*on* a).

(b) (*of chair*) respaldo *m*; (*spine of book*) lomo *m*; (*end of book*) final *m*; (*of coin*) reverso *m*; (*of knife*) lomo *m*; (*of cheque, document, hand, page*) dorso *m*; **I know Bognor like the ~ of my hand** conozco Bognor como la palma de la mano; **to sign on the ~** firmar al dorso; **the ship broke its ~** el barco se rompió por medio.

(c) (*furthest part*) fondo *m*; (*rear part*) parte *f* trasera; **at the ~ of the hall** en el fondo de la sala, al fondo de la sala; **at the ~ of beyond*** en el quinto pino*, en los quintos infiernos*; **in the ~ of the car** en la parte trasera del coche; **you'll have to sit in the ~** tendrás que ponerte detrás; **in ~ of the house** (*US*) detrás de la casa; **they keep the car round** (*or* out) **the ~** dejan el coche detrás de la casa (*etc*); **you'll have to ask round the ~** tendrás que preguntar ahí detrás.

(d) (*Sport: area*) defensa *f*; **the team is weak at the ~** el equipo es débil defensivamente.

(e) (*Sport: person*) defensa *mf*.

▼**5** VT **(a)** (*support*) apoyar, respaldar; defender; favorecer.

(b) (*bet on*) apostar a.

(c) (*reverse*) *vehicle* dar marcha atrás a; *horse* recular; **she ~ed the car into the garage** hizo entrar el coche en el garaje marcha atrás; **he ~ed the car into a wall** al dar marcha atrás chocó con el muro.

6 VI **(a)** (*move backwards*) moverse atrás, retroceder; (*vehicle*) dar marcha atrás.

(b) (*wind*) cambiar, girar (en dirección contraria a las agujas del reloj).

◆**back away** VI retroceder, dar un paso (*or* varios pasos *etc*) hacia atrás.

◆**back down** VI volverse atrás, echarse atrás, rajarse*.

◆**back off** VI dar marcha atrás; (*US: withdraw*) retirarse; **~ off!** ¡lárgate!, ¡déjame estar!

◆**back on to** VT: **the house ~s on to the park** la parte trasera de la casa da al parque.

◆**back out** **1** VT *vehicle* hacer salir marcha atrás.

2 VI (*vehicle*) salir marcha atrás; (*person*) salir reculando; (*fig*) retirarse, volverse atrás; **to ~ out of** (*fig*) retirarse de, renunciar a; no cumplir.

◆**back up** **1** VT **(a)** *vehicle* dar marcha atrás a. **(b)** (*support*) apoyar, respaldar; defender. **(c)** (*US: delay*) demorar, retrasar. **(d)** (*Comput*) hacer una copia de apoyo de.

2 VI **(a)** dar marcha atrás, retroceder. **(b)** (*Comput*) hacer una copia de apoyo.

backache ['bækeɪk] N dolor *m* de espalda.

backbench [bæk'bentʃ] **1** N: **~es** (*seats*) escaños *mpl* (*de los diputados sin cartera en el gobierno o en la oposición*); (*MPs*) diputados *mpl* (*sin cartera en el gobierno o en la oposición*).

2 ATTR: **~ opinions** opiniones *fpl* de los diputados (*sin cartera en el gobierno o en la oposición*).

backbencher [bæk'bentʃəʳ] N (*Brit*) diputado *m*, -a *f* (*sin cartera en el gobierno o en la oposición*).

┌─────────────────────┐
│ **BACKBENCHER** │
└─────────────────────┘

ⓘ *Se conoce como* **backbencher** *al parlamentario británico que no se sienta en los escaños (**benches**) de las primeras filas de la Cámara de los Comunes (**House of Commons**) junto al líder de su partido, por no pertenecer al Gobierno o a su equivalente en la oposición. Al no ser titulares de ningún cargo, les resulta más fácil hablar o votar en contra de la política oficial del partido. Se les conoce también colectivamente como los* **backbenches.**

⇨ *Ver también* FRONT BENCH

backbite ['bækbaɪt] **1** VT maldecir (*an absent person* de un ausente), hablar mal de.

2 VI murmurar.

backbiting ['bækbaɪtɪŋ] N murmuración *f*, maledicencia *f*.

backboard ['bækbɔːd] N (*US Sport*) tablero *m*.

backbone ['bækbəʊn] N espinazo *m*; (*fig*) (*guts*) firmeza *f*, agallas *fpl*; (*chief support*) espina *f* dorsal, piedra *f* angular; **a patriot to the ~** patriota hasta los tuétanos.

back-breaking ['bækbreɪkɪŋ] ADJ deslomador, matador.

backchat ['bæktʃæt] N réplicas *fpl*.

backcloth ['bækklɒθ] N (*Brit*) telón *m* de fondo.

backcomb ['bækkəʊm] VT *hair* cardar.

backdate ['bæk'deɪt] VT *cheque etc* antedatar; *measure* dar efecto retroactivo a; **a pay rise ~d to April** un aumento salarial con efecto

desde abril, un aumento retroactivo desde abril.

backdrop ['bækdrɒp] N telón *m* de foro.

-backed [bækt] ADJ *ending in compounds* **(a) low~ chair** silla *f* de respaldo bajo. **(b) rubber~ carpet** alfombra *f* con refuerzo de caucho.

backer ['bækəʳ] N (*Pol*) partidario *m*, -a *f*; (*Comm*) promotor *m*, impulsor *m*, caballo *m* blanco; (*Sport*) apostador *m*, -ora *f*.

backfire ['bæk'faɪəʳ] **1** N (*Aut*) petardeo *m*.

2 VI (*Aut*) petardear; (*fig*) salir el tiro por la culata; **the idea ~d** la idea perjudicó a sus propios inventores.

back-formation ['bækfɔː,meɪʃən] N derivación *f* regresiva.

backgammon ['bæk,gæmən] N backgamon *m*.

background ['bækgraʊnd] **1** N **(a)** (*gen*) fondo *m*; (*Art*) fondo *m*, último término *m*; **in the ~** al fondo, en el fondo, en último término; **against a dim ~** sobre un fondo oscuro; **to stay in the ~** mantenerse en segundo plano, no buscar la luz de la publicidad.

(b) (*of person*) antecedentes *mpl*, historial *m*, educación *f*; **what is his ~?** ¿cuáles son sus antecedentes?

(c) (*information*) antecedentes *mpl*; información *f* previa; **the ~ to the crisis** los antecedentes de la crisis; **to fill in the ~ for sb** poner a uno en antecedentes.

2 ATTR: **~ music** música *f* de fondo; **~ noise** ruido *m* de fondo; **~ reading** lecturas *fpl* preparatorias; **~ studies** estudios *mpl* del ambiente histórico (*etc*) (en que vivió un autor *etc*); **~ task** (*Comput*) tarea *f* secundaria.

backhand(ed) ['bæk'hænd(ɪd)] ADJ dado con la vuelta de la mano; (*fig*) irónico, equívoco; **~ drive, ~ shot, ~ stroke** revés *m*; **~ volley** (*Sport*) volea *f* de revés.

backhander ['bæk'hændəʳ] N (*Brit*) **(a)** (*Sport*) revés *m*. **(b)** (*) soborno *m*, coima *f* (*LAm*).

backing ['bækɪŋ] N apoyo *m*; garantía *f*; (*Comm*) respaldo *m*; (*funds*) reserva *f*; (*Mus*) apoyo *m*; **~ store** memoria *f* auxiliar.

backlash ['bæklæʃ] N reacción *f*, contragolpe *m*; (*Pol*) reacción *f* violenta; **the white ~** la resaca blanca.

backless ['bæklɪs] ADJ *dress* sin espalda, muy escotado por detrás.

back-line player ['bæklaɪn,pleɪəʳ] N (*US*) defensa *m*.

backlist ['bæklɪst] N fondo *m* editorial.

backlog ['bæklɒg] N atrasos *mpl*; (*Comm*) reserva *f* de pedidos pendientes; (*work*) volumen *m* de trabajo acumulado.

back number ['bæk'nʌmbəʳ] N número *m* atrasado (de revista *etc*); (*fig*) cero *m* a la izquierda, nulidad *f*.

back-pack ['bækpæk] (*esp US*) **1** N mochila *f*.

2 VI viajar con mochila.

back-packer ['bæk,pækəʳ] N mochilero *m*, -a *f*, persona *f* que viaja con mochila.

back-packing ['bæk,pækɪŋ] N: **to go ~** viajar de mochila.

back pain ['bæk,peɪn] N dolor *m* de espalda, dolor *m* lumbar.

back pay ['bækpeɪ] N atrasos *mpl* (de sueldo).

back-pedal ['bæk'pedl] VI contrapedalear; volverse atrás, echarse atrás; (*fig*) dar marcha atrás.

back-pedalling ['bæk,pedəlɪŋ] N: **~ is his speciality** dar marcha atrás es su especialidad.

back-rest ['bækrest] N respaldo *m*.

back room ['bæk'rʊm] N cuarto *m* interior, cuarto *m* trasero; (*fig*) lugar *m* donde se hacen investigaciones secretas; **~ boy** investigador *m*, inventor *m* (que hace el trabajo preliminar sin reclamar ningún reconocimiento público); (*Pol*) fontanero *m*.

backscratching* ['bæk,skrætʃɪŋ] N compadreo *m*.

back seat ['bæk'siːt] N asiento *m* trasero; **~ driver** pasajero *m*, -a *f* que molesta al conductor dándole consejos *etc*; **to take a ~** ceder su puesto, pasar a segundo plano.

backshift ['bækʃɪft] N turno *m* de tarde.

backside ['bæk'saɪd] N trasero *m*, culo *m*.

backslapping ['bæk,slæpɪŋ] N espaldarazos *mpl*; **mutual ~** bombo *m* mutuo.

backslash ['bækslæʃ] N barra *f* inversa.

backslide ['bæk'slaɪd] (*irr: V* **slide**) VI reincidir, volver a las andadas.

backslider ['bæk'slaɪdəʳ] N reincidente *mf*.

backsliding ['bæk'slaɪdɪŋ] N reincidencia *f*.

backspace [,bæk'speɪs] **1** VT retroceder.

2 N retroceso *m*, tecla *f* de retroceso.

backspin ['bækspɪn] N efecto *m* de retroceso.

backstage ['bæk'steɪdʒ] **1** N (*off-stage*) bastidores *mpl*, espacio *m* entre bastidores; (*dressing-rooms*) camarines *mpl*.

2 ADJ de bastidores.

3 ADV entre bastidores.

backstairs ['bæk'steəz] **1** NPL escalera *f* de servicio; **by the ~** (*fig*) por enchufe.

2 ATTR clandestino.

backstitch ['bækstɪtʃ] **1** N pespunte *m*.

2 VT pespuntar.

backstreet ['bækstriːt] **1** N: **the ~s** (*quiet*) las calles tranquilas, las calles apartadas del centro; (*poor*) las calles de los barrios bajos.

2 ATTR: ~ **abortion** aborto *m* clandestino; ~ **abortionist** curandero *m*, -a *f* abortista, abortista *m* clandestino, abortista *f* clandestina.

backstroke ['bækstrəʊk] N braza *f* de espalda, crol *m* de espalda; **the 100 metres ~** los 100 metros espalda.

back talk ['bæktɔ:k] N (*US*) = **backchat**.

back-to-back ['bæktə'bæk] **1** ADJ: ~ **credit** créditos *mpl* contiguos; ~ **houses** casas *fpl* adosadas.

2 ADV: **to sit ~** sentarse (*or* estar sentados) espalda con espalda.

backtrack ['bæktræk] VI volver pies atrás; volverse atrás, echarse atrás.

back-up ['bækʌp] N (**a**) (*support*) apoyo *m*, respaldo *m*; reserva *f*; ~ **document** (*Comput*) copia *f* de seguridad, copia *f* de respaldo; ~ **lights** (*US*) luces *fpl* de marcha atrás; ~ **operation** operación *f* de apoyo; ~ **services** servicios *mpl* auxiliares. (**b**) (*Aut*) embotellamiento *m*, retención *f*.

backward ['bækwəd] ADJ (**a**) *motion etc* hacia atrás; ~ **and forward movement** movimiento *m* de vaivén. (**b**) (*retarded*) atrasado; (*shy*) tímido; **he's not ~ in coming forward** no peca de tímido; **he was not ~ in taking the money** no vaciló en tomar el dinero.

backwardation [ˌbækwə'deɪʃən] N retraso *m* en la entrega de acciones; (*fee*) prima *f* pagada por retraso en la entrega de acciones.

backward(s) ['bækwəd(z)] ADV atrás, hacia atrás; (*back to front*) al revés; **to walk ~** andar de espaldas; **to read sth ~** leer algo para atrás; **to go ~ and forward** ir de acá para allá; **to know a subject ~** saber un tema al dedillo; **I know this poem ~** este poema lo tengo archisabido.

backward(s)-compatible ['bækwəd(z)kəm'pætɪbl] ADJ (*Comput, Audio etc*) compatible con el modelo, sistema etc anterior.

backward-looking ['bækwəd,lʊkɪŋ] ADJ nostálgico; reaccionario.

backwardness ['bækwədnɪs] N atraso *m*, estado *m* atrasado; timidez *f*.

backwash ['bækwɒʃ] N agua *f* de rechazo; (*fig*) reacción *f*, consecuencias *fpl*.

backwater ['bækwɔ:təʳ] N brazo *m* de río estancado, remanso *m*; (*fig*) lugar *m* atrasado, lugar *m* de agradable tranquilidad.

backwoods ['bækwʊdz] NPL región *f* apartada (*freq* = Las Batuecas *in Spain*); ~ **community** comunidad *f* rústica.

backwoodsman ['bækwʊdzmən] N, PL **backwoodsmen** ['bækwʊdzmen] patán *m*, rústico *m*; (*Pol*) miembro de la Cámara de los Lores que rara vez asiste al Parlamento.

backyard ['bæk'jɑːd] N (*Brit*) patio *m* trasero, corral *m*, traspatio *m* (*LAm*); (*US*) jardín *m* trasero; **'Not in my ~'** (*slogan*) 'no lo [*residuos tóxicos etc*] quiero en mi patio'.

bacon ['beɪkən] N tocino *m* (entreverado, de panceta); ~ **and eggs** tocino *m* con huevos; **to bring home the ~*** sacarse el gordo; lograrlo, tener éxito; **to save one's ~*** salvar el pellejo.

bacteria [bæk'tɪərɪə] NPL *of* **bacterium** bacterias *fpl*.

bacterial [bæk'tɪərɪəl] ADJ bacteriano.

bacteriological [bæk,tɪərɪə'lɒdʒɪkəl] ADJ bacteriológico.

bacteriologist [bæk,tɪərɪ'ɒlɒdʒɪst] N bacteriólogo *m*, -a *f*.

bacteriology [bæk,tɪərɪ'ɒlədʒɪ] N bacteriología *f*.

bacteriosis [ˌbæktɪərɪ'əʊsɪs] N bacteriosis *f*.

bacterium [bæk'tɪərɪəm] N, PL **bacteria** [bæk'tɪərɪə] bacteria *f*.

bad [bæd] **1** ADJ (**a**) (*wicked*) *person* malo, malvado; *habit* malo; *language* indecente; **he's a ~ one** es un mal sujeto; **he's not as ~ as he looks** es mejor persona de lo que parece; **you ~ boy!** ¡eres un niño malo!; **you ~ dog!** ¡qué asco de perro!; **it was very ~ of him to say that** ha hecho muy mal en decir eso.

(**b**) (*inferior etc*) malo; (*ill*) malo, enfermo; (*rotten*) podrido, dañado, pasado; (*harmful*) nocivo, dañoso; *accident, mistake, wound* grave; *air* viciado; *headache, pain* agudo, intenso; *smell* malo; *cheque* descubierto, sin fondos; *coin* falso; *debt* incobrable; *joke* de mal gusto, nada divertido; *law, treatment* injusto; *shot* errado; *tooth* cariado; *voting-paper* inválido; **my ~ leg** mi pierna lisiada; **it's not so ~** no está tan mal; **I'm ~ about getting up** soy lento para levantarme; **to be ~ at French** ser malo en francés; **business is ~** el negocio va mal; **not ~** bastante bueno, nada malo; (*less enthusiastic*) regular; **not ~!** ¡muy bien!; **that's too ~** es una pena; **it's really too ~ of you** te has comportado muy mal; **it would be ~ for you to** + *infin* sería poco aconsejable que tú + *subj*; **it's ~ for you** te hace daño; **what's ~ about it?** ¿qué hay de malo en ello?; **I feel ~** me siento mal; **I feel ~ about it** lo lamento; **to go ~** (*food etc*) echarse a perder, pasarse, alterarse; **to go from ~ to worse** ir de mal en peor; **she's got a ~ cold** tiene un resfriado muy fuerte; **I've got a ~ head** tengo un fuerte dolor de cabeza; **he looks ~** tiene mal aspecto; **this is beginning to look ~** esto se está poniendo feo; **to be taken ~*** caer enfermo; **to talk ~ Spanish** hablar mal el español; **to have a ~ trip** (*Drugs‡*) tener un mal viaje.

(**c**) (*esp US‡*: *great*; COMP **~der**, SUPERL **~dest**) guay‡.

2 ADV (*****) **he's got it ~** (*hobby*) está obsesionado; (*love*) está enamorado como un tonto.

3 N lo malo; **I'm £5 to the ~** he perdido 5 libras; **to be in ~ with sb** (*US*) estar a malas con uno, estar en la lista negra de uno; **to go to the ~** echarse a perder, arruinarse; **to take the ~ with the good** aceptar lo malo con lo bueno.

┌─ BAD ─┐   **◄ see also main entry**

"Malo" shortened to "mal"

● *Malo* must be shortened to *mal* before a masculine singular noun:

> He was in a bad mood
> *Estaba de mal humor*

Position of "malo"

● *Mal/Mala etc* precedes the noun in general comments. Here, there is no comparison, implied or explicit, with something better:

> I'm afraid I have some bad news for you
> *Me temo que traigo malas noticias para usted*
> I've had a bad day today
> *Hoy he tenido un mal día*

● *Malo/Mala etc* follows the noun when there is an implicit or explicit comparison with something good:

> ...the difference between good and bad cholesterol...
> *...la distinción entre el colesterol bueno y el malo...*
> ...his only bad day in the race...
> *...su único día malo en la carrera...*

Ser/Estar malo

● Use *malo* with *ser* to describe inherent qualities and characteristics:

> Smoking is bad for your health
> *Fumar es malo para la salud*
> This is a very bad film
> *Esta película es malísima*

● Use *malo* with *estar* to describe unpleasant food or else to mean "unwell":

> The food was really bad
> *La comida estaba malísima*
> He's been unwell lately
> *Ha estado malo últimamente*

Estar mal

● Use *estar* with the adverb *mal* to give a general comment on a situation that seems bad or wrong:

> Cheating in your exams is really bad
> *Está muy mal que copies en los exámenes*
> In the space of an hour I've signed fifty books. Not bad
> *En una hora he firmado cincuenta libros. No está mal*
> I managed to come second, which wasn't bad
> *He conseguido acabar segundo, lo que no estuvo mal*

---

baddie*, baddy* ['bædɪ] N (*Cine etc*; *often hum*) malo *m*.

baddish ['bædɪʃ] ADJ bastante malo, más bien malo.

bade [bæd] PRET *of* **bid**.

badge [bædʒ] N divisa *f*, insignia *f*; (*worn on coat*) distintivo *m*; (*metal disc*) chapa *f*, placa *f*; (*fig*) señal *f*, indicio *m*; ~ **of office** distintivo *m*, insignia *f* de su función.

badger ['bædʒəʳ] **1** N tejón *m*.

2 VT acosar, atormentar (*for* para obtener); **stop ~ing me!** ¡no me fastidies!; **to ~ sb into doing sth** acosar a uno hasta que haga algo.

badinage ['bædɪnɑːʒ] N chanzas *fpl*, bromas *fpl*.

badlands ['bædlændz] NPL (*US*) tierras *fpl* malas, tierras *fpl* desgastadas por la erosión (*región yerma, esp en los estados de Nebraska y Dakota del Sur*).

badly ['bædlɪ] ADV (**a**) (*gen*) mal; **things are going ~** las cosas van mal; **we came off ~ in the deal** salimos mal del negocio; **to be ~ off** andar (*or* estar) mal de dinero; **we are ~ off for coal** andamos mal de carbón; **how did he take it?** ... **~** ¿qué efecto le produjo la noticia? ... malísimo. (**b**) (*seriously*) **the ~ disabled** los severamente minusválidos; ~ **wounded** gravemente herido; **to be ~ beaten** sufrir una grave derrota; **to be ~ mistaken** equivocarse gravemente. (**c**) (*very much*) **it ~ needs painting** hace mucha falta pintarlo; **I need money ~** tengo mucha necesidad de dinero, necesito urgentemente dinero; **I want it ~** lo deseo muchísimo; **we ~ need another assistant** nos hace gran falta otro ayudante.

badman ['bædmæn] N, PL **badmen** ['bædmen] (*esp US*) gángster *m*.

bad-mannered ['bæd'mænəd] ADJ sin educación, grosero.

badminton ['bædmɪntən] N bádminton *m*, (*juego m del*) volante *m*.

badmouth* ['bæd,maʊθ] VT (*US*) criticar, insultar; murmurar de.

badness ['bædnɪs] N (**a**) (*wickedness*) maldad *f*. (**b**) (*bad quality*) lo malo, mala calidad *f*.

bad-tempered ['bæd'tempəd] ADJ (*permanently*) de mal genio; (*temporarily*) de mal humor; *argument* fuerte; *tone etc* áspero, malhumorado.

BAe ABBR *of* **British Aerospace**.

Baffin ['bæfɪn] N: **~ Bay** Bahía f de Baffin; **~ Island** Tierra f de Baffin.
baffle ['bæfl] ☐ N (also **~ plate**) deflector m; (Rad) pantalla f acústica.
☐ VT progress impedir, estorbar; mind etc desconcertar; person dejar perplejo; searchers confundir; **at times you ~ me** a veces no te comprendo; **the problem ~s me** al problema no le veo solución alguna; **the police are ~d** la policía no tiene pista alguna; **the crime ~d the police for months** durante meses el crimen dejó perpleja a la policía; **it ~s description** es imposible describirlo.
bafflement ['bæflmənt] N perplejidad f; desconcierto m, confusión f.
baffling ['bæflɪŋ] ADJ crime de solución nada fácil, misterioso; action desconcertante, incomprensible; problem dificilísimo.
BAFTA ['bæftə] N (Brit) ABBR of **British Academy of Film and Television Arts** academia británica para la promoción del cine y la televisión.
bag [bæg] ☐ N (a) saco m; talega f; (large sack) costal m; (handbag) bolso m, cartera f (LAm); (suitcase) maleta f, valija f (LAm), veliz m (Mex); (carried over shoulder) zurrón m, mochila f; (in dress) bolsa f; (in trousers) rodillera f; **~s under the eyes** ojeras fpl; **it's a mixed ~** (* fig) es una mezcla de todo; **the whole ~ of tricks*** todo el rollo*; **he was like a ~ of bones** estaba como un saco de huesos; **it's in the ~*** es cosa segura, está en la talega; **we had the game nearly in the ~*** teníamos el partido casi en la mochila*; **it's not his ~** (US*) no es de su gusto; **to be left holding the ~** (US*) cargar con el mochuelo*; **to pack one's ~s** hacer las maletas; **to pack ~ and baggage** liar el petate; **they threw him out ~ and baggage** le pusieron de patitas en la calle con todo lo suyo.
(b) (Hunting) cacería f, caza f; **a good day's ~** una buena cacería.
(c) **~s*** (baggage) equipaje m.
(d) **~s** (Brit*: trousers) pantalones mpl.
(e) (Brit*) **~s of** la mar de*, un montón de*; **we've ~s of time** tenemos tiempo de sobra.
(f) (*) **old ~** bruja f, arpía f.
☐ VT (a) (also **to ~ up**) ensacar; (Hunting) cazar, coger, capturar; (shoot down) derribar; (⁜) birlar. (b) (Brit*) tomar, apropiarse; reservar para sí; **I ~s that** eso pa' mí.
☐ VI (also **to ~ out**) hacer bolsa.
bagatelle [ˌbægə'tel] N bagatela f.
bagel ['beɪgl] N (Culin) pan m ácimo; (US) especie de bollo.
bagful ['bægful] N saco m (lleno).
baggage ['bægɪdʒ] N (a) (luggage) equipaje m; (Mil) bagaje m; **~ allowance** (Aer) límite m de equipaje; **~ car** (US) furgón m de equipajes; **~ check** talón m de equipaje; **~ (check)room** (US) consigna f; **~ claim** = **~reclaim**; **~ handler** despachador m de equipaje; **~ locker** consigna f automática; **~ reclaim** recogida f de equipajes; **~ train** tren m de equipajes. (b) (*: ††) mujercilla f.
baggy ['bægɪ] ADJ muy holgado; que hace bolsa; trousers con rodilleras; abombachado.
Baghdad [ˌbæg'dæd] N Bagdad m.
bag lady* ['bæg,leɪdɪ] N indigente f, mujer f que vive con lo puesto*.
bagpiper ['bægpaɪpəʳ] N gaitero m.
bagpipes ['bægpaɪps] NPL gaita f.
bag-snatcher ['bæg,snætʃəʳ] N ladrón m de bolsos, tironista* m.
bag-snatching ['bæg,snætʃɪŋ] N tirón m (de bolsos).
baguette [bæ'get] N baguette f, barrita f de pan.
bah [bɑː] INTERJ ¡bah!
Bahamas [bə'hɑːməz] NPL Islas fpl Bahamas, las Bahamas.
Bahrain [bɑː'reɪn] N Bahrein m.
Bahraini [bɑː'reɪnɪ] ☐ ADJ bahreiní.
☐ N bahreiní mf.
bail[1] [beɪl] (Jur) ☐ N caución f, fianza f; **on ~** bajo fianza; **he's out on ~** está libre bajo fianza; **to be** (or **go, stand**) **~ for** salir fiador por; **to jump one's ~*** fugarse estando bajo fianza; **to be released on ~** ser puesto en libertad bajo fianza.
☐ VT afianzar.
♦**bail out** VT: **to ~ sb out** obtener la libertad de uno bajo fianza; (fig) echar un cable a uno.
bail[2] [beɪl] N (Cricket) palito m corto.
bail[3] [beɪl] VT (Naut) achicar.
♦**bail out** ☐ VI (Aer) lanzarse en paracaídas.
☐ VT (Naut) = **bail**[3].
bail bandit* ['beɪl,bændɪt] N (Brit) persona que comete un delito estando en libertad bajo fianza.
bail-bond [ˌbeɪl'bɒnd] N caución f, fianza f.
bailiff ['beɪlɪf] N (Jur) alguacil m, corchete m; (steward) administrador m.
bailiwick ['beɪlɪwɪk] N (frm) ámbito m de actuación.
bain-marie [bɛ̃mə'ri] N baño m de María.
bairn [bɛən] N (Scot, N Eng) niño m, -a f.
bait [beɪt] ☐ N cebo m, carnada f; (fig) aliciente m, añagaza f; **he wouldn't rise to the ~** no quería picar; **to swallow the ~** tragar el anzuelo.
☐ VT hook, trap cebar, poner cebo en; (fig) acosar, atormentar.
baize [beɪz] N bayeta f; **green ~** tapete m verde.

bake [beɪk] ☐ VT cocer al horno; bricks etc cocer; (harden) endurecer; **it's baking hot** hace un calor terrible; **a baking hot day** un día de calor asfixiante; **to ~ one's own bread** hornear su propio pan.
☐ VI: **we were baking in the heat** estábamos asfixiados del calor.
baked [beɪkt] ADJ cocido al horno; **~ beans** judías fpl en salsa de tomate; (US) judías fpl guisadas con carne; **~ potatoes** patatas fpl (LAm: papas fpl) al horno.
bakehouse ['beɪkhaʊs] N, PL **bakehouses** ['beɪkhaʊzɪz] tahona f, panadería f.
Bakelite ['beɪkəlaɪt] ® N baquelita f.
baker ['beɪkəʳ] N panadero m; **~'s (shop)** panadería f; **~'s dozen** docena f del fraile.
bakery ['beɪkərɪ] N tahona f, panadería f.
bakeware ['beɪkwɛəʳ] N fuentes fpl de horno.
Bakewell tart [ˌbeɪkwəl'tɑːt] N tarta hecha a base de almendras, mermelada y azúcar en polvo.
baking ['beɪkɪŋ] N cocción f; (batch) hornada f.
baking-chocolate ['beɪkɪŋ,tʃɒklɪt] N (US) chocolate m fondant.
baking-dish ['beɪkɪŋ,dɪʃ] N fuente f de hornear.
baking-pan ['beɪkɪŋ,pæn] N = **baking-tin**.
baking-powder ['beɪkɪŋ,paʊdəʳ] N polvos mpl de levadura, polvo m de hornear.
baking-sheet ['beɪkɪŋ,ʃiːt] N = **baking-tray**.
baking-soda ['beɪkɪŋ,səʊdə] N bicarbonato m de sosa.
baking-tin ['beɪkɪŋ,tɪn] N lata f para hornear.
baking-tray ['beɪkɪŋ,treɪ] N bandeja f de horno.
baksheesh ['bækʃiː] N propina f.
bal. ABBR of **balance** balance m.
Balaclava [ˌbælə'klɑːvə] N (Brit: also **~ helmet**) pasamontañas m.
balalaika [ˌbælə'laɪkə] N balalaica f.
balance ['bæləns] ☐ N (a) (state) equilibrio m; **~ of power** equilibrio m político; distribución f de fuerzas; **~ of terror** equilibrio m del terror, equilibrio m armamentístico; **in ~** en equilibrio, equilibrado; **when the ~ of his mind was disturbed** en un momento de obcecación; **to keep one's ~** mantener el equilibrio; **to lose one's ~** perder el equilibrio; **to throw sb off ~** hacer que uno pierda el equilibrio, (fig) desconcertar a uno.
(b) (scales) balanza f; **to be** (or **hang**) **in the ~** estar pendiente de un hilo; **to hold the ~** tener una influencia decisiva.
(c) (Comm) balance m; (statement) balance m, estado m de cuentas; (remainder) resto m, saldo m; (still to be paid over) remanente m; (credit ~) saldo m; **~ due** saldo m deudor; **~ in hand** alcance m, sobrante m; **~ of payments** balance m (or balanza f) de pagos; **~ of trade** balance m (or balanza f) de comercio; **on ~** pensándolo bien; **to strike a proper ~** encontrar el punto medio.
(d) (good sense) buen sentido m, juicio m; serenidad f.
☐ VT (a) equilibrar; (make up for) contrapesar (with con); **this has to be ~d against that** hay que pesar esto contra aquello.
(b) account saldar; budget nivelar; **to ~ the books** hacer balance, cerrar los libros.
☐ VI equilibrarse.
(b) (Comm) **now the account ~s** ahora está bien el balance de esta cuenta; **to make the budget ~** nivelar el presupuesto.
☐ VR: **to ~ o.s.** equilibrarse (on en).
♦**balance out** ☐ VT (fig) compensar.
☐ VI: **the profits and losses ~ out** las ganancias y las pérdidas se compensan.
♦**balance up** VT finiquitar, saldar.
balanced ['bælənst] ADJ equilibrado.
balance-sheet ['bælənsʃiːt] N balance m, avanzo m.
balancing ['bælənsɪŋ] N (a) (equilibrium) **~ on a high wire is not easy** mantener el equilibrio en la cuerda floja no es fácil; **to do a ~ act** (Theat) andar en la cuerda floja; (fig) hacer malabarismos (between con). (b) (Comm, Fin) **~ of accounts** balance m de cuentas; **~ of the books** balance m de los libros.
balcony ['bælkənɪ] N balcón m; (covered) mirador m; (of block of flats) galería f, terraza f; (Theat) paraíso m; **first** (or **second**) **~** (US) galería f superior.
bald [bɔːld] ADJ (a) calvo; tyre desgastado; **~ patch** claro m; **as ~ as a coot** pelado como bola de billar; **to go ~** quedarse calvo. (b) (fig) style escueto, desnudo; statement franco y sencillo.
balderdash ['bɔːldədæʃ] N tonterías fpl.
bald-headed ['bɔːld'hedɪd] ADJ calvo; **to go ~ into*** lanzarse ciegamente a.
balding ['bɔːldɪŋ] ADJ parcialmente calvo.
baldly ['bɔːldlɪ] ADV escuetamente, desnudamente.
baldness ['bɔːldnɪs] N (a) calvicie f. (b) (fig) lo escueto, desnudez f.
baldy* ['bɔːldɪ] N calvo m.
bale [beɪl] ☐ N bala f; (Agr) paca f, fardo m.
☐ VT (also **to ~ up**) embalar; (Agr) empacar.
♦**bale out** VI (Aer) lanzarse en paracaídas.
Bâle [bɑːl] N Basilea f.

Balearic [ˌbælɪ'ærɪk] **1** ADJ balear. **2**: **the ~s, ~ Islands** NPL los Baleares, Islas *fpl* Baleares.

baleful ['beɪlfʊl] ADJ *influence* funesto, siniestro; *look* ceñudo, hosco.

balefully ['beɪlfəlɪ] ADV *look* tristemente; *say* funestamente, siniestramente.

baler ['beɪlər] N (*Agr*) empacadora *f*, enfardadora *f*.

balk [bɔːk] **1** N (*Agr*) lomo *m*, caballón *m*; (*Billiards*) cabaña *f*; (*of timber*) viga *f*.
2 VT (*thwart*) burlar, impedir; (*miss*) perder, no aprovechar; **we were ~ed of the chance to see it** perdimos la oportunidad para verlo.
3 VI (*stop*) detenerse bruscamente; (*horse*) plantarse, repropiarse (*at* al ver); **he ~ed at this** se resistió a considerarlo, lo rechazó.

Balkan ['bɔːlkən] **1** ADJ balcánico.
2 NPL: **the ~s** los Balcanes.

balkanization ['bɔːlkənaɪ'zeɪʃən] N balcanización *f*.

ball¹ [bɔːl] N **(a)** (*gen*) bola *f*; globo *m*, esfera *f*; (*eg tennis ball*) pelota *f*; (*eg football*) balón *m*; (*Mil*) bala *f*; (*of wool*) ovillo *m*; ~ **(and socket) joint** junta *f* articulada; **he's a real ~ of fire** es muy dinámico; **he's not exactly a ~ of fire** no se le nota exceso de dinamismo; **behind the eight ~** (*US* *fig*) en apuros; **that's the way the ~ bounces** (*US*) así es la vida, así son las cosas; **the ~ is with you** (*or* **in your court**) (*Brit* *fig*) ahora te toca a ti; **to be on the ~** ser un hacha, estar al tanto; **you have to be on the ~ for this** para esto hay que fijarse mucho; **to have a lot on the ~** (*US*) tener mucho talento; **to keep one's eye on the ~** (*fig*) no perder de vista lo principal del asunto; **to play ~** jugar a la pelota, (*fig*) cooperar (*with* con), ser acomodadizo; **to roll up into a ~** hacerse un ovillo; **to start** (*or* **set**) **the ~ rolling** empezar, hablar (*etc*) primero; poner las cosas en marcha.
(b) (*Anat*⁑) cojón *m*⁑, huevo⁑ *m*; **~s!** ¡cojones!; **~s** (*Brit: nonsense*) tonterías *fpl*, pavadas *fpl*.
◆ **ball up**⁑ VT = **balls up**⁑.

ball² [bɔːl] N (*dance*) baile *m* (*gen* de etiqueta); **we had a ~** (*US*⁎) lo pasamos en grande⁎, nos divertimos una barbaridad⁎.

ballad ['bæləd] N balada *f*, (*Spanish*) romance *m*, corrido *m* (*LAm*).

ballade [bæ'lɑːd] N (*Mus*) balada *f*.

ballast ['bæləst] **1** N (*Naut and fig*) lastre *m*; (*Rail*) balasto *m*; **in ~** en lastre.
2 VT (*Naut*) lastrar; (*Rail*) balastar.

ball-bearing [bɔːl'bɛərɪŋ] N bola *f*, cojinete *m* a (*or* de) bolas, rodamiento *m* a bolas, balero *m* (*Mex*), rulemán *m* (*Cono Sur*).

ballboy ['bɔːlbɔɪ] N recogedor *m* de pelotas.

ballcock ['bɔːlkɒk] N llave *f* de bola, llave *f* de flotador.

ballerina [ˌbælə'riːnə] N bailarina *f* (de ballet); **prima ~** primera bailarina *f*.

ballet ['bæleɪ] N ballet *m*, baile *m*.

ballet-dancer ['bæleɪˌdɑːnsər] N bailarín *m*, -ina *f* (de ballet).

balletic [bæ'letɪk] ADJ *grace, movements* de bailarina de ballet.

ballet-shoes ['bæleɪˌʃuːz] NPL zapatillas *fpl* de ballet.

ballet-skirt ['bæleɪˌskɜːt] N falda *f* de bailarina (*or* de ballet).

ball game ['bɔːlgeɪm] N (*US*) partido *m* de béisbol; (*fig*) **this is a different ~** esto es otro cantar, esto es algo muy distinto; **it's a whole new ~** todo ha cambiado; *ver también* BASEBALL .

ball girl ['bɔːlgɜːl] N recogedora *f* de pelotas.

ballgown ['bɔːlgaʊn] N traje *m* de fiesta, vestido *m* de gala.

ballistic [bə'lɪstɪk] ADJ balístico; ~ **missile** misil *m* balístico; **to go ~**⁎ subirse por las paredes⁎.

ballistics [bə'lɪstɪks] N SING balística *f*.

balloon [bə'luːn] **1** N globo *m*, bomba *f* (*And*); (*in cartoons*) bocadillo *m*, globo *m*; **then the ~ went up**⁎ luego se armó la gorda⁎; **that went down like a lead ~**⁎ eso cayó como un jarro de agua fría.
2 VI subir en un globo; (*swell*) dispararse; (*sail etc: also* **to ~ out**) hincharse como un globo.

balloonist [bə'luːnɪst] N ascensionista *mf*, aeronauta *mf*.

ballot ['bælət] **1** N (*voting*) votación *f*; (*paper*) papeleta *f* (para votar); **to take a ~ on sth** someter algo a votación; **there will be a ~ for the remaining places** se sortearán las plazas restantes; **to vote by secret ~** votar en secreto.
2 VT *members etc* invitar a votar.
3 VI votar; **to ~ for** elegir (*or* determinar *etc*) por votación; **to ~ for** *tickets* rifar, sortear; **to ~ for a place** sortear un puesto.

ballot-box ['bælətbɒks] N urna *f* electoral; ~ **stuffing** (*US*) fraude *m* electoral, pucherazo⁎ *m*.

balloting ['bælətɪŋ] N votación *f*.

ballot-paper ['bælətpeɪpər] N papeleta *f* (para votar), boleta *f* (*LAm*).

ballpark ['bɔːlpɑːk] N (*US*) estadio *m* de béisbol; ~ **estimate** cálculo *m* aproximado; ~ **figure,** ~ **number** cifra *f* aproximada; **it's in the same ~** está en la misma categoría, se trata de lo mismo; *ver también* BASEBALL .

ballplayer, ball player ['bɔːlˌpleɪər] N (*esp US: Sport*) jugador *m*, -ora *f* (de béisbol, fútbol americano *etc*).

ball-point (pen) ['bɔːlpɔɪnt(pen)] N bolígrafo *m*, pluma *f* esferográfica (*LAm*), birome *f* (*Cono Sur*).

ballroom ['bɔːlrʊm] N salón *m* de baile; ~ **dance,** ~ **dancing** baile *m* de salón.

balls-up⁑ ['bɔːlzʌp] N (*Brit*) lío *m*; **he made a ~ of the job** la pifió en el trabajo⁎, lo escoñó todo⁎; *see also* **cock-up**.
◆ **balls up**⁑ VT estropear, joder⁑.

ballsy⁑ ['bɔːlzɪ] ADJ con (un par de) cojones⁑, de bandera⁎.

ball-up⁑ ['bɔːlʌp] N (*US*) = **balls-up**⁑.

bally⁑ ['bælɪ] ADJ (*Brit*) puñetero⁑.

ballyhoo⁎ [ˌbælɪ'huː] N (*advertising*) propaganda *f* estrepitosa; (*noise*) ruido *m*, jaleo *m*, conmoción *f*.

balm [bɑːm] N bálsamo *m* (*also fig*).

balmy ['bɑːmɪ] ADJ **(a)** (*liter*) (*soothing*) balsámico; *breeze etc* suave, fragante. **(b)** (*Brit*⁑) = **barmy**.

baloney⁑ [bə'ləʊnɪ] N chorradas⁎ *fpl*.

BALPA ['bælpə] N ABBR *of* **British Airline Pilots' Association** ≃ Sindicato *m* Español de Pilotos de Líneas Aéreas, SEPLA *m*.

balsa ['bɔːlsə] N balsa *f*.

balsam ['bɔːlsəm] N bálsamo *m*.

balsa wood ['bɔːlsəˌwʊd] N madera *f* de balsa.

balti ['bɔːltɪ] N *especialidad de comida india con verduras o carne cocinadas en una sartén de fondo cóncavo*.

Baltic ['bɔːltɪk] ADJ: ~ **Sea** Mar *m* Báltico; **the ~ states** los estados bálticos; **one of the ~ ports** uno de los puertos del Mar Báltico.

balustrade [ˌbæləs'treɪd] N balaustrada *f*, barandilla *f*.

bamboo [bæm'buː] N bambú *m*; ~ **shoots** brotes *mpl* de bambú; **the B~ Curtain** el Telón de Bambú.

bamboozle⁎ [bæm'buːzl] VT embaucar, capear; **she was ~d into buying it** se la engatusó para que lo comprara.

ban [bæn] **1** N prohibición *f* (*on* de); veda *f* (de caza); **to be under a ~** estar prohibido; **to put a ~ on** prohibir (el uso de), proscribir; **to raise the ~ on** levantar el entredicho a.
2 VT prohibir, proscribir; vedar; *person* excluir (*from* de); **B~ the Bomb Campaign** Campaña *f* contra la bomba; **he was ~ned from driving for life** le retiraron el carné de por vida; **the bullfighter was ~ned for 3 months** el torero fue inhabilitado para ejercer la profesión durante 3 meses.

banal [bə'nɑːl] ADJ banal, vulgar.

banality [bə'nælɪtɪ] N banalidad *f*, vulgaridad *f*.

banana [bə'nɑːnə] N plátano *m*, banana *f* (*esp LAm*); ~ **boat** barco *m* bananero; ~ **republic** república *f* bananera; **to be ~s**⁎ estar chalado⁎; **to go ~s**⁎ perder la chaveta (*over* por).

banana-skin [bə'nɑːnəskɪn] N piel *f* de plátano; (*fig*) problema *m* no previsto, peligro *m* no sospechado.

banana tree [bə'nɑːnəˌtriː] N plátano *m*, banano *m*.

band¹ [bænd] N **(a)** (*strip of material*) banda *f*, tira *f*, faja *f*; (*ribbon*) cinta *f*; (*edging*) cenefa *f*, franja *f*; (*of cigar*) vitola *f*, faja *f*; (*of wheel*) fleje *m*; (*armband*) brazalete *m*; (*hatband*) cintillo *m*; (*of harness*) correa *f*; (*stripe*) lista *f*, raya *f*, (*of territory*) faja *f*, zona *f*.
(b) (*Rad*) banda *f*.
(c) (*of statistics, tax etc*) banda *f*, categoría *f*, clase *f*.

band² [bænd] N **(a)** (*Mus*) orquesta *f*; (*Mil Mus*) banda *f*, música *f*; (*brass ~*) charanga *f*, banda *f*; **then the ~ played**⁎ (*US*) y se armó la gorda⁎.
(b) (*group*) grupo *m*; cuadrilla *f*; (*gang*) gavilla *f*, pandilla *f*.
◆ **band together** VI juntarse, asociarse; (*pej*) apandillarse.

bandage ['bændɪdʒ] **1** N venda *f*, vendaje *m*.
2 VT (*also* **to ~ up**) vendar; **with a ~d hand** con una mano en vendas.

Band-Aid ['bændeɪd] ® N tirita *f*.

bandan(n)a [bæn'dænə] N pañuelo *m* de cabeza.

b. and b. N ABBR *of* **bed and breakfast** cama *f* con desayuno, alojamiento *m* y desayuno; *ver también* BED AND BREAKFAST .

bandbox ['bændbɒks] N sombrerera *f*.

banding ['bændɪŋ] N (*Brit Scol*) calificaciones *fpl* por letras.

bandit ['bændɪt] N bandido *m*.

banditry ['bændɪtrɪ] N bandolerismo *m*, bandidismo *m*.

bandleader ['bændliːdər] N líder *mf* de un grupo musical.

bandmaster ['bændmɑːstər] N director *m* de banda.

bandolier [ˌbændə'lɪər] N bandolera *f*.

band-saw ['bændsɔː] N sierra *f* de cinta.

bandsman ['bændzmən] N, PL **bandsmen** ['bændzmen] músico *m* (de banda).

bandstand ['bændstænd] N quiosco *m* de música.

bandwagon ['bændˌwægən] N: **to climb** (*or* **jump**) **on the ~** subirse al carro.

bandy¹ ['bændɪ] VT *words, stories* cambiar; **don't ~ words with me!** ¡no replique Vd!
◆ **bandy about** VT: **the story was bandied about that ...** se rumoreaba que ...; **his name was being bandied about** su nombre estaba en boca de todos.

bandy² ['bændɪ] ADJ, **bandy-legged** ['bændɪ'legd] ADJ estevado.

bane [beɪn] N (††) veneno *m*; (*fig*) plaga *f*, azote *m*; **it's the ~ of my**

life será mi ruina.
baneful ['beɪnfʊl] ADJ nocivo; funesto, fatal.
banefully ['beɪnfəlɪ] ADV nocivamente; funestamente, fatalmente.
bang [bæŋ] **1** INTERJ ¡pum!; (of a blow) ¡zas!; **to go (off)** ~ hacer explosión, estallar; **~ went £5!** se acabaron ¡pum! las 5 libras.
2 ADV (*) precisamente, exactamente; **~ in the middle** justo en el centro; **I ran ~ into a traffic-jam** me encontré de repente en un embotellamiento; **it hit him ~ on the ear** le dio en la oreja precisamente; **~ on!** ¡acertado!; **the answer was ~ on** (Brit) la respuesta era muy acertada; **she came ~ on time** (Brit) llegó a la hora exacta; **it was ~ on target** (Brit) dio en el mismo centro del blanco.
3 N **(a)** (explosion) estallido m, detonación f; (of door) portazo m; (any loud noise) golpe m, estrépito m; **the door closed with a ~** la puerta se cerró de golpe; **not with a ~ but a whimper** no con un estallido sino con un sollozo; **it started off with a ~*** empezó con muchísimo ímpetu; **it all went with a ~*** todo fue a las mil maravillas.
(b) (blow) golpe m (violento).
(c) (also **~s**) (US) flequillo m.
4 VT **(a)** (explode) volar, hacer estallar; door cerrar de golpe; table etc dar golpes en; (strike) golpear; **to ~ one's fist on the table** dar un puñetazo en la mesa; **I ~ed his head on the table** di con su cabeza en la mesa.
(b) (⁑) joder⁑.
5 VI hacer explosión, estallar; hacer estrépito; **the balloons were ~ing** estallaban los globos; **to ~ on a door** dar golpes en una puerta; **downstairs a door ~ed** abajo se cerró de golpe una puerta.
6 VR: **he ~ed himself against the wall** dio consigo contra la pared.
◆**bang about, bang around** VI moverse ruidosamente.
◆**bang away** VI (guns) disparar estrepitosamente; (workman) martillear, dar martillazos; **she was ~ing away on the piano** aporreaba el piano.
◆**bang down** VT receiver colgar de golpe; **he ~ed it down on the table** lo arrojó violentamente sobre la mesa.
◆**bang into** VT chocar (violentamente) con; (meet) tropezar con, topar con.
◆**bang out** VT tune tocar ruidosamente.
◆**bang together** VT heads hacer chocar; **I'll ~ your heads together!** ¡voy a dar un coscorrón a los dos!; **the leaders should have their heads ~ed together** hay que obligar a los jefes a que lleguen a un acuerdo.
◆**bang up*** VT **(a)** (ruin) estropear. **(b)** (prisoner) encerrar (en su celda).
banger ['bæŋəʳ] N **(a)** (firework) petardo m.
(b) (Brit⁑: Aut) cacharro m, coche m destartalado.
(c) (Brit⁑: Culin) = **sausage**.
Bangkok [bæŋ'kɒk] N Bangkok m.
Bangladesh [,bæŋglə'deʃ] N Bangladesh m.
Bangladeshi [,bæŋglə'deʃɪ] **1** ADJ bangladesí.
2 N bangladesí mf.
bangle ['bæŋgl] N ajorca f, brazalete m, esclava f (LAm).
bang-up: ['bæŋʌp] ADJ (US) tope, guay⁑.
banish ['bænɪʃ] VT desterrar (also fig); **to ~ a topic from one's conversation** proscribir un tema de su conversación.
banishment ['bænɪʃmənt] N destierro m.
banisters ['bænɪstəz] NPL barandilla f, pasamanos m.
banjax⁑ ['bændʒæks] VT (US) dar una paliza a.
banjo ['bændʒəʊ] N, PL **banjos** or **banjoes** banjo m.
bank¹ [bæŋk] **1** N **(a)** (of river etc) ribera f, orilla f, ribo m (And); (small hill) loma f; (of earth) terraplén m; (sandbank) banco m; (of snow, clouds) montón m; (rise in road) cuesta f; (escarpment) escarpa f; (Rail) terraplén m; (of switches) batería f, serie f; (of phones etc) equipo m, batería f; (of oars) hilera f.
(b) (Aer) inclinación f lateral.
2 VT **(a)** (also freq to ~ up) (pile) amontonar; fire cubrir.
(b) (Aer) ladear.
3 VI **(a)** (Aer) ladearse. **(b)** **to ~ up** (clouds etc) amontonarse.
bank² [bæŋk] (Comm, Fin) **1** N banco m; (in games) banca f; **B~ of England** Banco m de Inglaterra; **B~ of International Settlements** (US) Banco m Internacional de Pagos; **B~ of Spain** Banco m de España; **to break the ~** hacer saltar (or quebrar) la banca.
2 ATTR bancario; **~ acceptance** letra f de cambio; **~ account** cuenta f bancaria, cuenta f de banco; **~ balance** saldo m; **this won't be good for my ~ balance** esto no será bueno para mi situación financiera; **~ bill** (Brit) letra f de cambio, (US) billete m de banco; **~ charges** (Brit) comisión f por servicio bancario; **~ credit** crédito m bancario; **~ deposits** depósitos mpl bancarios; **~ draft** letra f de cambio; **~ giro** giro m bancario; **~ holiday** (Brit) día m festivo (en que están cerrados los bancos y el comercio en general); **~ loan** préstamo m bancario; **~ manager** director m, -ora f de banco; **~ rate** tipo m bancario, tasa f de descuento bancario; **~ run** (US) asedio m de un banco; **~ statement** estado m de cuentas; **~ transfer** transferencia f bancaria.

3 VT depositar, ingresar.
4 VI: **we ~ with Smith** tenemos la cuenta en el banco Smith.
◆**bank on** VT contar con; **don't ~ on it** sería prudente no contar con eso, no puedes estar tan seguro de eso.
◆**bank up** VT earth, sand amontonar, apilar; fire alimentar (con mucha leña o carbón).

┌─────────────────────┐
│ **BANK HOLIDAY** │
└─────────────────────┘

*ℹ El término **bank holiday** se aplica en el Reino Unido a todo día festivo oficial en el que cierran bancos y comercios, que siempre cae en lunes. Los más destacados coinciden con Navidad, Semana Santa, finales de mayo y finales de agosto. Al contrario que en los países de tradición católica, no se celebran las festividades dedicadas a los santos.*

bankable ['bæŋkəbl] ADJ idea etc válido, valedero.
bank-book ['bæŋkbʊk] N libreta f (de depósitos); (in savings bank) cartilla f.
bank-card ['bæŋkkɑːd] N tarjeta f bancaria.
bank-clerk ['bæŋkklɑːk] N (Brit) empleado m, -a f de banco.
banker ['bæŋkəʳ] N banquero m; **~'s draft** letra f bancaria; **~'s order** (Brit) orden f bancaria; **~'s reference** referencia f bancaria; **to be ~** (at games) tener la banca.
banking¹ ['bæŋkɪŋ] N (of earth) terraplén m, rampas fpl.
banking² ['bæŋkɪŋ] **1** N (Comm, Fin) banca f.
2 ATTR bancario; **~ account** cuenta f bancaria; **~ hours** horas fpl bancarias.
banking-house ['bæŋkɪŋhaʊs] N, PL **banking-houses** ['bæŋkɪŋhaʊzɪz] casa f de banca.
banknote ['bæŋknəʊt] N (Brit) billete m de banco.
bank-robber ['bæŋk,rɒbəʳ] N ladrón m de banco.
bankroll ['bæŋkrəʊl] (US) **1** N fortuna f.
2 VT financiar.
bankrupt ['bæŋkrʌpt] **1** ADJ quebrado, insolvente; **to be ~** estar en quiebra; **to be ~ of ideas** estar totalmente falto de ideas; **to be declared ~** declararse en quiebra; **to go ~** quebrar, (esp fraudulently) hacer bancarrota.
2 N quebrado m; **~'s estate** activo m (or masa f) de la quiebra.
3 VT hacer quebrar, arruinar.
4 VR: **to ~ o.s. buying pictures** arruinarse comprando cuadros.
bankruptcy ['bæŋkrəptsɪ] N quiebra f, insolvencia f, (esp fraudulent) bancarrota f; (fig) falta f (of de); **~ court** (Brit) tribunal m de quiebras; **~ proceedings** juicio m de insolvencia; **moral ~** insolvencia f moral.
banner ['bænəʳ] N bandera f, estandarte m; (carried in demonstration) pancarta f; **~ headlines** titulares mpl sensacionales.
bannisters ['bænɪstəz] NPL = **banisters**.
banns [bænz] NPL amonestaciones fpl, banas fpl (Mex); **to call** (or **put up**) **the ~** correr (or leer) las amonestaciones.
banquet ['bæŋkwɪt] **1** N banquete m.
2 VT festejar, banquetear.
3 VI banquetear.
banqueting-hall ['bæŋkwɪtɪŋ,hɔːl] N comedor m de gala, sala f de banquetes.
banquette [bæŋ'ket] N banqueta f alargada.
banshee [bæn'ʃiː] N (Ir) hada que anuncia una muerte en la familia.
bantam ['bæntəm] N gallinilla f de Bantam.
bantam-weight ['bæntəmweɪt] N peso m gallo.
banter ['bæntəʳ] **1** N burlas fpl, zumba f; comentarios mpl sin importancia.
2 VT chancearse con, tomar el pelo a.
3 VI chancearse, bromear.
bantering ['bæntərɪŋ] **1** ADJ tone de chanza.
2 N = **banter 1**.
Bantu [,bæn'tuː] ADJ, N bantú mf.
BAOR N ABBR of **British Army of the Rhine**.
bap [bæp] N (Brit) bollo m pequeño de pan.
baptism ['bæptɪzəm] N (in general) bautismo m; (act) bautizo m; **~ of fire** bautismo m de fuego.
baptismal [bæp'tɪzməl] ADJ bautismal.
Baptist ['bæptɪst] N bautista mf; **the ~ Church** la Iglesia Bautista; **St John the ~** San Juan Bautista.
baptize [bæp'taɪz] VT bautizar (also fig); **he was ~d John** le bautizaron con el nombre de Juan.
bar [bɑːʳ] **1** N **(a)** (gen, of metal, in harbour, Her) barra f; (on door) tranca f; (lever) palanca f; (of soap) pastilla f; (of chocolate) pastilla f, tableta f; (tavern) bar m, cantina f (CAm, Mex); (counter) bar m, barra f, mostrador m; (of public opinion) tribunal m; (Mus) compás m; (Jur) **the B~** (persons) el colegio de abogados, (profession) el foro, la Barra (Mex), la abogacía; **prisoner at the ~** acusado m, -a f; **to be called to the B~** (Brit) recibirse de abogado; **to be behind ~s** estar entre rejas; **to put sb behind ~s** meter a uno entre rejas; **to spend 3 years behind ~s** pasar 3 años entre rejas. **(b)** (hindrance) obstáculo m, impedimento m (to para); (ban) prohibición f (on de); **it is a ~ to**

progress es un obstáculo para el progreso.
[2] VT (a) *door* atrancar; *road* obstruir. (b) (*fig*) *progress* impedir; (*ban*) prohibir; (*exclude*) excluir (*from* de); **to ~ sb from doing sth** prohibir a uno hacer algo; **to be ~red from a club** ser excluido de un club.
[3] PREP excepto, con excepción de; **all ~ 2** todos con excepción de 2; **~ none** sin excluir a ninguno, sin excepción; **it was all over ~ the shouting** con eso terminaba en efecto el asunto.

barb [bɑːb] N (a) (*of arrow, hook*) lengüeta *f*; (*of feather*) barba *f*; (*Zool*) púa *f*. (b) (*fig*) flecha *f*, dardo *m*; observación *f* mordaz.

Barbadian [bɑːˈbeɪdɪən] [1] ADJ de Barbados.
[2] N nativo *m*, -a *f* (*or* habitante *mf*) de Barbados.

Barbados [bɑːˈbeɪdɒs] N Barbados *m*.

barbarian [bɑːˈbeərɪən] [1] ADJ bárbaro.
[2] N bárbaro *m*, -a *f*.

barbaric [bɑːˈbærɪk] ADJ bárbaro, barbárico; de ruda magnificencia.

barbarism [ˈbɑːbərɪzəm] N barbarie *f*; (*Gram*) barbarismo *m*.

barbarity [bɑːˈbærɪtɪ] N barbaridad *f*.

barbarous [ˈbɑːbərəs] ADJ bárbaro.

barbarously [ˈbɑːbərəslɪ] ADV bárbaramente.

Barbary [ˈbɑːbərɪ] N Berbería *f*; **~ ape** macaco *m*.

barbecue [ˈbɑːbɪkjuː] [1] N barbacoa *f*, asado *m* (*LAm*); **~ sauce** salsa *f* para barbacoa.
[2] VT preparar en barbacoa.

barbed [bɑːbd] ADJ *arrow etc* armado de lengüetas; *criticism* incisivo, mordaz.

barbed wire [ˈbɑːbdˈwaɪəʳ] N alambre *m* de espino, (*Mil*) alambre *m* de púas; **barbed-wire entanglement** alambrada *f*; **barbed-wire fence** cercado *m* de alambrado (*or* de alambre de espino).

barbel [ˈbɑːbəl] N (*Anat*) barbilla *f*, cococha *f*; (*Fish*) barbo *m*.

barbell [ˈbɑːbel] N (*US Sport*) haltera *f*, pesas *fpl*.

barber [ˈbɑːbəʳ] N peluquero *m*, barbero *m*; **~'s** peluquería *f*; **The B~ of Seville** El barbero de Sevilla.

barbershop [ˈbɑːbəʃɒp] N (*US*) barbería *f*; **~ quartet** cuarteto *m* vocal armónico.

barbican [ˈbɑːbɪkən] N barbacana *f*.

Barbie doll [ˈbɑːbɪdɒl] ® N muñeca *f* Barbie ®.

bar billiards [ˈbɑːˈbɪlɪədz] N (*Brit*) billar *m* americano.

barbitone [ˈbɑːbɪtəʊn] N barbitúrico *m*.

barbiturate [bɑːˈbɪtjʊrɪt] N barbitúrico *m*.

barbs‡ [bɑːbz] NPL (*Drugs*) barbitúricos *mpl*.

barcarol(l)e [ˌbɑːkəˈrəʊl] N barcarola *f*.

Barcelona [ˌbɑːsəˈləʊnə] N Barcelona *f*.

bar-chart [ˈbɑːˌtʃɑːt] N cuadro *m* de barras.

bar-code [ˈbɑːˌkəʊd] N código *m* de barras.

bard [bɑːd] N bardo *m*; **the B~** (*Shakespeare*) el Vate; **the B~ of Avon** el Cisne del Avon.

bare [beəʳ] [1] ADJ desnudo; *head* descubierto; *landscape* pelado; *ground* raso; *room* (casi) desprovisto de muebles; *style* escueto, desnudo; **~ to the waist** desnudo hasta la cintura; **in one's ~ skin** en la misma piel; **with one's head ~** sin sombrero; **with the breasts ~** con los senos al desnudo; **with one's ~ hands** con las manos desnudas; **~ of** desprovisto de; **the trees are ~** los árboles están sin hojas; **the pantry is ~** la despensa está vacía; **the ~ bones (of a matter)** los puntos esenciales, lo esencial, el mínimo esencial; **to earn a ~ living** ganar lo justo para vivir; **the ~ minimum** lo justo, lo indispensable; **the ~ necessities** las cosas más indispensables; **there's a ~ chance** hay una remota posibilidad; **by a ~ majority** por una mayoría escasa; **the ~ thought frightens me** me horroriza sólo pensar en ello; **to lay ~** poner al descubierto, poner al desnudo.
[2] VT desnudar; descubrir; **to ~ one's head** descubrirse; **the dog ~d its teeth** el perro mostró los dientes.

bareback [ˈbeəbæk] ADV a pelo, sin montura; **to ride ~** montar a pelo.

bare-bones [ˈbeəˈbəʊnz] ADJ (*US*) muy limitado.

barefaced [ˈbeəfeɪst] ADJ descarado, fresco; **a ~ lie** una mentira descarada; **it's ~ robbery** es un robo descarado.

barefoot(ed) [ˈbeəˈfʊt(ɪd)] ADJ, ADV descalzo, con los pies desnudos.

bareheaded [ˈbeəˈhedɪd] ADJ descubierto, con la cabeza descubierta, sin sombrero.

barelegged [ˈbeəˈlegɪd] ADJ en pernetas.

barely [ˈbeəlɪ] ADV (a) (*scarcely*) apenas; **~ possible** apenas posible; **it was ~ enough** casi no bastaba. (b) **a ~ furnished room** un cuarto escasamente amueblado.

bareness [ˈbeənɪs] N desnudez *f*.

Barents Sea [ˈbærənts siː] N: **the ~** el Mar de Barents.

barf‡ [bɑːf] VI (*US*) arrojar*.

barfly* [ˈbɑːflaɪ] N (*US*) ≃ culo *m* de café*.

bargain [ˈbɑːgɪn] [1] N (a) (*agreement*) pacto *m*, trato *m*; (*business deal*) negocio *m*; (*advantageous deal*) negocio *m* ventajoso; **into the ~** por añadidura, además, y encima; **it's a ~!** ¡trato hecho!; **to drive a good ~** hacer un buen trato; **you drive a hard ~** Vd sabe regatear; **to make** (*or* **strike**) **a ~** cerrar un trato; **I'll make a ~ with you**

hagamos un pacto.
(b) (*cheap thing*) ganga *f*; **~s** (*Comm*) artículos *mpl* de ocasión, oportunidades *fpl*; **it's a real ~** es una verdadera ganga.
[2] ATTR de ocasión; **~ basement**, **~ counter** sección *f* de rebajas; **~ offer** oferta *f* especial; **~ price** precio *m* de ganga, precio *m* de saldo; **~ sale** saldo *m*.
[3] VT: **to ~ away** malvender, malbaratar.
[4] VI negociar (*about* sobre, *for* para obtener, *with* con); (*haggle*) regatear; **I wasn't ~ing for that** yo no contaba con eso; **I wouldn't ~ on it** es mejor no contar con eso; **he got more than he ~ed for** le resultó peor de lo que esperaba.

bargain-hunter [ˈbɑːgɪnˌhʌntəʳ] N cazador *m*, -ora *f* de rebajas; **she's a real ~** siempre va a por saldos.

bargain-hunting [ˈbɑːgɪnˌhʌntɪŋ] N caza *f* de rebajas; **I enjoy ~** me gusta ir de rebajas.

bargaining [ˈbɑːgɪnɪŋ] N negociación *f*; (*haggling*) regateo *m*; **~ power** fuerza *f* en el negocio; **~ table** mesa *f* de negociaciones.

barge [bɑːdʒ] [1] N barcaza *f*; (*towed*) lancha *f* a remolque, gabarra *f*; (*ceremonial*) falúa *f*.
[2] VT (*) empujar; (*Sport*) atajar.
◆**barge about** VI moverse pesadamente, dar tumbos.
◆**barge in** VI entrar sin pedir permiso, irrumpir; (*fig*) entrometerse; **to ~ in on a conversation** entrometerse en una conversación.
◆**barge into** VT *person* chocar contra, dar contra; *room* irrumpir en.

bargee [bɑːˈdʒiː] N (*Brit*) gabarrero *m*.

bargepole [ˈbɑːdʒpəʊl] N bichero *m*; **I wouldn't touch it with a ~** no lo quiero ver ni de lejos.

bargirl* [ˈbɑːgɜːl] N (*US*) camarera *f* de barra.

barhopping [ˈbɑːˌhɒpɪŋ] N (*US*): **to go ~** ir de bar en bar, ir de copeo*.

baritone [ˈbærɪtəʊn] N barítono *m*.

barium [ˈbeərɪəm] N bario *m*; **~ meal** sulfato *m* de bario.

bark¹ [bɑːk] [1] N (*Bot*) corteza *f*.
[2] VT *tree* descortezar; *skin* raer, raspar.

bark² [bɑːk] [1] N ladrido *m*; (*) tos *f* fuerte, tos *f* molesta; **his ~ is worse than his bite** perro que ladra no muerde.
[2] VT: **to ~** (**out**) *order* escupir, dar en un tono muy brusco.
[3] VI ladrar (*at* a); (*) toser; *V* **tree**.

bark³ [bɑːk] N (*liter, Poet*) barco *m*.

barkeeper [ˈbɑːˌkiːpəʳ] N (*US*) tabernero *m*, -a *f*.

barker [ˈbɑːkəʳ] N voceador *m*, -ora *f*, charlatán *m*, -ana *f* de feria.

barking [ˈbɑːkɪŋ] N ladridos *mpl*, ladrar *m*.

barley [ˈbɑːlɪ] N cebada *f*.

barleyfield [ˈbɑːlɪfiːld] N cebadal *m*.

barley-sugar [ˈbɑːlɪˌʃʊgəʳ] N azúcar *m* cande.

barley-water [ˈbɑːlɪˌwɔːtəʳ] N (*esp Brit*) hordiate *m*.

barmaid [ˈbɑːmeɪd] N camarera *f*, moza *f* de taberna (*LAm*).

barman [ˈbɑːmən] N, PL **barmen** [ˈbɑːmen] barman *m*.

Bar Mitzvah, bar mitzvah [bɑːˈmɪtsvə] N Bar Mitzvah *m*.

barmy‡ [ˈbɑːmɪ] ADJ (*Brit*) lelo, gili*; **you must be ~!** ¿estás loco?

barn [bɑːn] N granero *m*, troje *f*; (*US*) establo *m*, cuadra *f*; (*US: for buses etc*) parque *m*, garaje *m*; **a great ~ of a house** una casa enorme, un caserón.

barnacle [ˈbɑːnəkl] N percebe *m*.

barndance [ˈbɑːnˌdɑːns] N (*esp US*) baile *m* campesino.

barndoor [ˈbɑːnˈdɔːʳ] N puerta *f* de granero; **~ fowls** aves *fpl* de corral.

barney [ˈbɑːnɪ] N (*Brit*) bronca *f*.

barn-owl [ˈbɑːnˌaʊl] N lechuza *f*.

barnstorm [ˈbɑːnstɔːm] VI (*US*) hacer una campaña electoral por el campo.

barnyard [ˈbɑːnjɑːd] N corral *m*; **~ fowls** aves *fpl* de corral.

barometer [bəˈrɒmɪtəʳ] N barómetro *m*.

barometric [ˌbærəʊˈmetrɪk] ADJ barométrico; **~ pressure** presión *f* barométrica.

baron [ˈbærən] N (a) barón *m*; (*fig*) magnate *m*, potentado *m*. (b) **~ of beef** solomillo *m*.

baroness [ˈbærənɪs] N baronesa *f*.

baronet [ˈbærənɪt] N baronet *m*.

baronetcy [ˈbærənɪtsɪ] N dignidad *f* del baronet.

baronial [bəˈrəʊnɪəl] ADJ baronial.

barony ['bærənɪ] N baronía f.
baroque [bə'rɒk] [1] ADJ barroco; (fig) complicado; grotesco.
[2] N barroco m.
barrack ['bærək] VT abuchear, dar bronca a; lanzar improperios a.
barracking ['bærəkɪŋ] N abucheo m, bronca f; improperios mpl.
barrack-room ['bærəkrʊm] [1] N dormitorio m de tropa.
[2] ADJ cuartelero; **~ ballad** canción f cuartelera; **~ lawyer** protestón m, -ona f.
barracks ['bærəks] NPL (a) (Mil) cuartel m; **to be confined to ~** estar bajo arresto en el cuartel, ser acuartelado.
(b) (house) caserón m; **a great ~ of a place** (Brit) una casa enorme, un caserón.
barrack-square ['bærək'skweər] N plaza f de armas.
barracuda [,bærə'kju:də] N barracuda f.
barrage ['bærɑːʒ] N presa f; (Mil) cortina f de fuego, barrera f (de artillería); (of balloons etc) barrera f; **a ~ of noise** un estrépito; **a ~ of questions** un aluvión de preguntas; **there was a ~ of protests** estallaron ruidosamente las protestas.
barrage-balloon ['bærɑːʒbə,lu:n] N globo m de barrera.
barred [bɑːɾd] ADJ window etc enrejado, con reja.
barrel ['bærəl] N (a) tonel m, cuba f, barril m; (of oil) barril m; (Tech) cilindro m, tambor m; **to have sb over a ~*** tener a uno con el agua al cuello; **to scrape the (bottom of the) ~** rebañar las últimas migas.
(b) (of gun, pen) cañón m.
barrel-chested ['bærəl'tʃestɪd] ADJ de pecho fuerte y grueso.
barrel-organ ['bærəl,ɔːgən] N organillo m.
barrel-vault ['bærəl,vɔːlt] N bóveda f de cañón.
barren ['bærən] ADJ estéril, árido; woman estéril; **~ of** falto de, desprovisto de.
barrenness ['bærənnɪs] N esterilidad f, aridez f.
barrette [bə'ret] N (US) pasador m (para el pelo).
barricade [,bærɪ'keɪd] [1] N barricada f.
[2] VT barrear, cerrar con barricadas.
[3] VR: **to ~ o.s. in a house** hacerse fuerte en una casa.
barrier ['bærɪər] N barrera f (also fig: to a, para); **~ cream** crema f protectora.
barring ['bɑːrɪŋ] PREP excepto, salvo; **we shall be there ~ accidents** iremos si Dios quiere.
barrio ['bɑːrɪəʊ] N (esp US) barrio m hispano.
barrister ['bærɪstər] N (Brit) abogado mf (que tiene derecho a alegar en los tribunales superiores); ver también [LAWYERS], [QC/KC].
bar-room ['bɑː,rʊm] N (US) bar m, taberna f; **~ brawl** pendencia f de taberna.
barrow¹ ['bærəʊ] N (Hist) túmulo m.
barrow² ['bærəʊ] N carretilla f, carretón m de mano.
barrow-boy ['bærəʊbɔɪ] N vendedor m callejero.
barstool ['bɑː,stu:l] N taburete m (de bar).
Bart [bɑːt] (Brit) ABBR of **Baronet**.
bartender ['bɑːtendər] N barman m.
barter ['bɑːtər] [1] N permuta f, trueque m.
[2] VT permutar, trocar (for por, con); **to ~ away** malvender.
[3] VI hacer negocios de trueque, cambiar unos géneros por otros.
Bartholomew [bɑː'θɒləmjuː] NM Bartolomé.
barytone ['bærɪtəʊn] N viola f de bordón.
basal ['beɪsl] ADJ (lit, fig) fundamental, básico, esencial; (Physiol) basal.
basalt ['bæsɔːlt] N basalto m.
base¹ [beɪs] [1] N base f; (Archit) basa f; (⁑) cocaína f (para fumar); **to get to first ~** (fig) alcanzar la primera meta, dar el primer paso; **he's way off ~** (US*) está totalmente equivocado.
[2] ATTR base; **~ camp** campamento m de base; **~ coat** (of paint) primera capa f, capa f selladora; **~ form** (Ling) base f derivativa; **~ (lending) rate** tipo m de interés base; **~ period** período m base.
[3] VT basar, fundar (on en); **to be ~d on** estar basado en, fundarse en; (Mil) **we were ~d on Malta** tuvimos nuestra base en Malta; **the post will be ~d in Barcelona** la base del empleo será en Barcelona; **where are you ~d now?** ¿dónde estás establecido ahora?
[4] VR: **I ~ myself on the following facts** me apoyo en los hechos siguientes.
base² [beɪs] ADJ bajo, infame, vil; metal bajo de ley, de baja ley.
baseball ['beɪsbɔːl] N béisbol m.

┌─ BASEBALL ─────────────────────────

ⓘ *El baseball es el deporte nacional norteamericano. Dos equipos de nueve jugadores se enfrentan en un campo de cuatro bases que forman un rombo. El bateador (batter) intenta dar a la pelota que le ha tirado el lanzador (pitcher) y enviarla fuera del alcance de los fildeadores (fielders) para después correr alrededor del rombo de base en base y volver a su punto inicial. Existen dos ligas importantes en los Estados Unidos: la National League y la American League. Los equipos ganadores de estas dos ligas juegan después otra serie de partidos que se denominan World Series. Algunos aspectos de este deporte, tales como la camaradería y el espíritu de*

competición tanto entre equipos como entre miembros de un mismo equipo, se usan a menudo en el cine como metáforas del modo de vida americano. Culturalmente el béisbol ha aportado, además de conocidas prendas de vestir como las botas o las gorras de béisbol, ciertas expresiones idiomáticas como a ballpark figure (una cifra aproximada) o a whole new ball game (una situación completamente distinta).

─────────────────────────────────────

baseball cap ['beɪsbɔːl'kæp] N gorra f de béisbol.
baseboard ['beɪsbɔːd] N (US) rodapié m.
-based [beɪst] in compounds: eg **a London~ company** una compañía con base en Londres; **shore~** con base en tierra.
Basel ['bɑːzəl] N Basilea f.
baseless ['beɪslɪs] ADJ infundado.
baseline ['beɪslaɪn] N (Survey) línea f de base; (Tennis) línea f de saque, línea f de fondo.
basely ['beɪslɪ] ADJ (V ADJ) despreciablemente, bajamente, ruínmente.
baseman ['beɪsmən] N, PL **basemen** ['beɪsmen] (Baseball) hombre m de base.
basement ['beɪsmənt] N sótano m.
baseness ['beɪsnɪs] N bajeza f, vileza f.
bases ['beɪsiːz] NPL of **basis**.
bash* [bæʃ] [1] N (a) golpe m, palo m.
(b) (fig) intento m; **to have a ~ at** probar, intentar, echar un tiento a; **go on, have a ~!** ¡vamos, trátalo tú!
(c) (party) fiesta f, juerga f.
[2] VT golpear; aporrear; person pegar, (also **to ~ about, to ~ up**) dar una paliza a.
[3] VI: **to ~ away = to bang away**.
♦ **bash in*** VT door echar abajo; hat, car abollar; lid, cover forzar a golpes, cargarse a golpes*; **to ~ sb's head in** aporrear a uno, mamporrear* a uno.
♦ **bash on*** VI continuar (a pesar de todo); **~ on!** ¡adelante!
bashful ['bæʃfʊl] ADJ tímido, vergonzoso, apenado (LAm).
bashfully ['bæʃfʊlɪ] ADV tímidamente.
bashfulness ['bæʃfʊlnɪs] N timidez f, vergüenza f.
bashing* ['bæʃɪŋ] N tunda f, paliza f; **to give sb a ~** dar una paliza a uno; **the team took a real ~** el equipo recibió una paliza.
basic¹ ['beɪsɪk] [1] ADJ básico (also Chem), fundamental; **~ airman** (US) soldado m raso de la aviación; **~ pay** sueldo m básico; **~ rate** (Fin) interés m base; **~ slag** escoria f básica; **~ training** entrenamiento m básico; **~ turn** (ski) giro m básico, giro m elemental; **~ wage** salario m básico.
[2] N: **the ~s** los fundamentos, los elementos básicos.
basically ['beɪsɪklɪ] ADV fundamentalmente, en el fondo, esencialmente.
basil ['bæzl] N albahaca f.
basilica [bə'zɪlɪkə] N basílica f.
basilisk ['bæzɪlɪsk] N basilisco m.
basin ['beɪsn] N (in kitchen) bol m, tazón m, cuenco m; (washbasin) jofaina f, palangana f; (large fixed washbasin) lavabo m; (of fountain) taza f; (Geog) cuenca f; (of port) dársena f.
basis ['beɪsɪs] N, PL **bases** ['beɪsiːz] base f; **on a daily ~** a base diaria; **on the ~ of** a base de; partiendo de una base de.
bask [bɑːsk] VI asolearse; **to ~ in the sun** tomar el sol; **to ~ in the heat** disfrutar del calor; **he ~s in flattery** le encantan los elogios.
basket ['bɑːskɪt] N cesta f; (big) cesto m; (two-handled) canasta f; (hamper) banasta f, capacho m; (two-handled, for earth etc) espuerta f; (pannier) sera f, serón m; (of balloon) barquilla f; **~ case** (US) caso m desahuciado; **~ chair** silla f de mimbre; **~ of currencies** cesta f de monedas, canasta f de divisas.
basketball ['bɑːskɪtbɔːl] N baloncesto m, básket m.
basketball player ['bɑːskɪt,bɔːl,pleɪər] N jugador m, -ora f de baloncesto.
basketwork ['bɑːskɪtwɜːk] N cestería f.
Basle [bɑːl] N Basilea f.
basmati rice [bəz'mætɪ'raɪs] N arroz m basmati (arroz de grano largo con aromatizantes).
Basque [bæsk] [1] ADJ vasco.
[2] N (a) vasco m, -a f. (b) (Ling) vasco m, vascuence m, euskera m.
Basque Country ['bæsk'kʌntrɪ] N País m Vasco, Euskadi m.
Basque Provinces ['bæsk'prɒvɪnsɪz] NPL las Vascongadas.
bas-relief ['bæsrɪ,liːf] N bajorrelieve m.
bass¹ [beɪs] (Mus) [1] ADJ bajo; **~ baritone** barítono m bajo; **~ clef** clave f de fa; **~ drum** bombo m; **~ flute** flauta f contralto; **~ guitar** bajo m; **~ horn** trompa f baja; **~ strings** instrumentos mpl bajos de cuerda; **~ trombone** trombón m bajo; **~ tuba** tuba f; **~ viol** viola f de gamba baja.
[2] N (voice, note, guitar) bajo m; (double bass) contrabajo m.
bass² [bæs] N (Fish) róbalo m.
basset ['bæsɪt] N perro m basset.
basset hound [bæsɪt'haʊnd] N basset m.
bassist ['beɪsɪst] N (Mus) bajista mf, bajo m.

bassoon [bəˈsuːn] N fagot *m*.

bassoonist [bəˈsuːnɪst] N fagot *mf*, fagotista *mf*.

basso profundo [ˌbæsəʊprəˈfʊndəʊ] N bajo *m* profundo.

bastard [ˈbɑːstəd] [1] ADJ bastardo.

[2] N bastardo *m*, -a *f*; **you ~!**‡ ¡cabrón!‡; **you old ~!**‡ ¡eh, hijoputa!‡; **that silly ~**‡ ese memo‡; **all Slobodians are ~s**‡ todos los eslobodios son cabrones‡; **this job is a real ~**‡ esta faena es la monda‡.

bastardized [ˈbɑːstədaɪzd] ADJ *language* corrupto.

bastardy [ˈbɑːstədɪ] N bastardía *f*.

baste¹ [beɪst] VT (*Culin*) pringar.

baste² [beɪst] VT (a) (*Sew*) hilvanar. (b) (*: beat*) dar de palos a.

basting [ˈbeɪstɪŋ] N (a) (*Sew*) hilván *m*. (b) (*: beating*) paliza *f*, zurra *f*.

bastion [ˈbæstɪən] N bastión *m*, baluarte *m* (*also fig*).

Basutoland [bəˈsuːtəʊlænd] N (*Hist*) Basutolandia *f*.

BASW N ABBR *of* **British Association of Social Workers** *sindicato de empleados de los servicios sociales*.

bat¹ [bæt] N (*Zool*) murciélago *m*; **old ~*** bruja* *f*; **to be ~s***, **to have ~s in the belfry*** estar chiflado; **to go like a ~ out of hell*** ir como alma que lleva el diablo.

bat² [bæt] [1] N (a) (*eg cricket ~*) maza *f*, paleta *f*; (*Baseball*) bate *m*; **off one's own ~** por sí solo, por iniciativa propia; **right off the ~** (*US*) de repente, sin deliberación. (b) (*: blow*) golpe *m*.

[2] VT (*) golpear, apalear; (*US*: fig*) **to ~ sth around** (*discuss*) discutir acerca de algo; **to ~ sth out** hacer algo a toda leche‡.

[3] VI (*Baseball*) batear.

bat³ [bæt] [1] N: **in the ~ of an eyelid** en un santiamén.

[2] VT: **without ~ting an eyelid** (*Brit*), **without ~ting an eye** (*US*) sin inmutarse.

batch [bætʃ] N (a) colección *f*, serie *f*, grupo *m*, cantidad *f*, lote *m*, montoncito *m*; (*of papers*) lío *m*; (*Culin*) hornada *f*; **~ production** producción *f* por lotes. (b) (*Comput*) lote *m*; **in ~ mode** en tratamiento por lotes; **~ processing** tratamiento *m* por lotes, proceso *m* por lotes.

bated [ˈbeɪtɪd] ADJ: **with ~ breath** con aliento entrecortado.

bath [bɑːθ] [1] N, PL **baths** [bɑːðz] (a) (*container*) baño *m*, bañera *f*, tina *f* (*LAm*); (*swimming pool*) piscina *f*. (b) (*act*) baño *m*; **to have (or take) a ~** tomar un baño, bañarse.

[2] VT (*Brit*) bañar, dar un baño a.

[3] VI (*Brit*) tomar un baño.

bathchair [ˈbɑːtʃɛəʳ] N silla *f* de ruedas.

bathcube [ˈbɑːθkjuːb] N cubo *m* de sales para el baño.

bathe [beɪð] [1] N baño *m* (en el mar *etc*); **to go for a ~**, **to have a ~** ir a bañarse.

[2] VT bañar; **to ~ the baby** (*US*) bañar al niño; **~d in tears** bañado en lágrimas.

[3] VI bañarse.

bather [ˈbeɪðəʳ] N bañista *mf*.

bathetic [bəˈθetɪk] ADJ que pasa de lo sublime a lo trivial.

bathhouse [ˈbɑːθhaʊs] N, PL **bathhouses** [ˈbɑːθhaʊzɪz] baño *m*.

bathing [ˈbeɪðɪŋ] N baños *mpl* (de mar *etc*), el bañarse; **'no ~'** 'prohibido bañarse'.

bathing-beauty [ˈbeɪðɪŋˌbjuːtɪ] N sirena *f* (*or* belleza *f*) de la playa.

bathing-cap [ˈbeɪðɪŋˌkæp] N gorro *m* de baño.

bathing-costume [ˈbeɪðɪŋˌkɒstjuːm] N (*Brit*) traje *m* de baño, bañador *m*.

bathing-hut [ˈbeɪðɪŋˌhʌt] N caseta *f* de playa.

bathing-machine [ˈbeɪðɪŋməˌʃiːn] N (*Hist*) caseta *f* de playa movible.

bathing-suit [ˈbeɪðɪŋˌsuːt] N traje *m* de baño, bañador *m*.

bathing-trunks [ˈbeɪðɪŋˌtrʌŋks] N (*Brit*) taparrabo *m*, bañador *m*.

bathing-wrap [ˈbeɪðɪŋˌræp] N albornoz *m*.

bathmat [ˈbɑːθmæt] N estera *f* de baño.

bathos [ˈbeɪθɒs] N paso *m* de lo sublime a lo trivial.

bathrobe [ˈbɑːθrəʊb] N albornoz *m*, bata *f* de baño.

bathroom [ˈbɑːθrʊm] N cuarto *m* de baño, baño *m*; **~ cabinet** armario *m* de aseo; **~ fittings** aparatos *mpl* sanitarios; **~ scales** báscula *f* de baño; *ver también* TOILET .

bath-salts [ˈbɑːθsɒlts] NPL sales *fpl* de baño.

bath-sheet [ˈbɑːθʃiːt] N toalla *f* de baño.

bath-towel [ˈbɑːθtaʊəl] N toalla *f* de baño.

bathtub [ˈbɑːθtʌb] N (*esp US*) bañera *f*, baño *m*, bañadera *f* (*LAm*), tina *f* (*Mex*).

bathwater [ˈbɑːθwɔːtəʳ] N agua *f* del baño.

bathysphere [ˈbæθɪsfɪəʳ] N batisfera *f*.

batik [bəˈtiːk] N (*process, cloth*) batik *m*.

batiste [bæˈtiːst] N batista *f*.

batman [ˈbætmən] N, PL **batmen** [ˈbætmen] (*Brit*) ordenanza *m*.

baton [ˈbætən] N (*Mil*) bastón *m*; (*Mus*) batuta *f*; (*in race*) testigo *m*; **~ charge** carga *f* con bastones; **~ round** bala *f* de goma.

batrachian [bəˈtreɪkɪən] N batracio *m*.

batsman [ˈbætsmən] N, PL **batsmen** [ˈbætsmen] (*Cricket*) bateador *m*.

battalion [bəˈtælɪən] N batallón *m*.

batten [ˈbætn] [1] N alfarjía *f*, lata *f*, listón *m*; (*Naut*) junquillo *m*, sa-

ble *m*.

[2] VT: **to ~ down the hatches** atrancar las escotillas (*also fig*).

♦**batten on** VT vivir (*etc*) a costa de, explotar, cebarse en.

batter¹ [ˈbætəʳ] N (*Culin*) batido *m* (para rebozar).

batter² [ˈbætəʳ] [1] N (*Baseball, Cricket*) bateador *m*, -ora *f*; *ver también* BASEBALL .

[2] VT *person* apalear; (*of boxer*) magullar; (*of the elements*) embravecerse contra; (*Mil*) cañonear, bombardear; (*verbally etc*) criticar ásperamente, poner como un trapo.

♦**batter (away) at** VT dar grandes golpes en.

♦**batter down, batter in** VT derribar a palos.

battered [ˈbætəd] ADJ (*bruised*) magullado; (*damaged*) estropeado; maltrecho, malparado; *hat etc* ajado; **~ baby** niño *m* golpeado, niña *f* golpeada; **~ wife** mujer *f* maltratada.

batterer [ˈbætərəʳ] N persona que maltrata físicamente a su mujer o marido e hijos; **wife-batterer** marido *m* violento.

battering [ˈbætərɪŋ] N (*blows*) paliza *f*; (*Mil*) bombardeo *m*; **the ~ of the waves** el golpear de las olas; **he got a ~ from the critics** los críticos le pusieron como un trapo.

battering-ram [ˈbætərɪŋræm] N ariete *m*.

battery [ˈbætərɪ] N (a) (*Mil*) batería *f*; **~ fire** fuego *m* de batería. (b) (*Elec*) (*dry*) pila *f*; (*wet*) batería *f*. (c) (*series*) serie *f*; (*of lights*) batería *f*, equipo *m*; (*of questions*) descarga *f*. (d) (*Agr*) batería *f*; **~ farming** cría *f* intensiva, cría *f* en batería; **~ hen** gallina *f* de criadero. (e) (*Jur*) violencia *f*, agresión *f*.

battery-charger [ˈbætərɪˌtʃɑːdʒəʳ] N cargador *m* de baterías.

battery-operated [ˌbætərɪˈɒpəreɪtɪd] ADJ a pilas.

battery-set [ˈbætərɪˌset] N (*Rad*) radio *f* de pilas, transistor *m*.

battle [ˈbætl] [1] N (a) batalla *f*; **in ~ array, in ~ order** en formación (or en orden) de batalla; **to do ~** librar batalla (**with** con); **to do ~ for** luchar por; **to fight a ~** luchar; **the ~ was fought in 1346** se libró la batalla en 1346; **to join ~** trabar batalla.

(b) (*fig*) lucha *f* (*for control of* por el control de, *to control* por controlar); **~ royal** batalla *f* campal; (*among women*) pelotera *f*; **~ of wills** lucha *f* de voluntades; **~ of wits** duelo *m* de inteligencias; **confidence is half the ~** la confianza vale por la mitad de la batalla; **to fight a losing ~** ir perdiendo poco a poco, ir de vencida.

[2] VI luchar (*against* contra, *for* por, *to do* por hacer); **the two armies ~d all day** los dos ejércitos se batieron todo el día; **to ~ against the wind** luchar contra el viento; **to ~ for breath** esforzarse por respirar; **to ~ on** seguir luchando.

battle-axe, (*US*) **battle-ax** [ˈbætlæks] N hacha *f* de combate; **old ~*** arpía *f*.

battlecruiser [ˈbætlˌkruːzəʳ] N crucero *m* de batalla.

battlecry [ˈbætlkraɪ] N grito *m* de combate; (*fig*) lema *m*, consigna *f*.

battledore [ˈbætldɔːʳ] N raqueta *f* de bádminton; **~ and shuttlecock** antiguo juego predecesor del bádminton.

battledress [ˈbætldres] N traje *m* de campaña.

battlefield [ˈbætlfiːld] N, **battleground** [ˈbætlgraʊnd] N campo *m* de batalla.

battle fleet [ˈbætlˌfliːt] N flota *f* de guerra.

battle-hardened [ˈbætlˌhɑːdənd] ADJ endurecido por la lucha.

battlements [ˈbætlmənts] NPL almenas *fpl*.

battle-scarred [ˈbætlˌskɑːd] ADJ (*gen hum*) marcado por la lucha; deteriorado.

battleship [ˈbætlʃɪp] N acorazado *m*.

battle zone [ˈbætlˌzəʊn] N zona *f* de batalla.

Battn ABBR *of* **battalion** Bón, batallón *m*.

batty* [ˈbætɪ] ADJ lelo.

bauble [ˈbɔːbl] N chuchería *f*.

baud [bɔːd] N baudio *m*.

baudrate [ˈbɔːdreɪt] N velocidad *f* de transmisión.

baulk [bɔːlk] = **balk**.

bauxite [ˈbɔːksaɪt] N bauxita *f*.

Bavaria [bəˈveərɪə] N Baviera *f*.

Bavarian [bəˈveərɪən] [1] ADJ bávaro.

[2] N bávaro *m*, -a *f*.

bawbee [bɔːˈbiː] N (*Scot and hum*) medio penique *m*.

bawd†† [bɔːd] N alcahueta *f*.

bawdiness [ˈbɔːdɪnɪs] N lo verde.

bawdy [ˈbɔːdɪ] ADJ verde.

bawdyhouse†† [ˈbɔːdɪhaʊs] N, PL **bawdyhouses** [ˈbɔːdɪhaʊzɪz] mancebía *f*.

bawl [bɔːl] [1] VT: **to ~ out** *song etc* cantar (*etc*) en voz muy fuerte; **to ~ sb out** echarle un rapapolvo a uno.

[2] VI gritar, vocear, desgañitarse; hablar (*or* cantar *etc*) muy fuerte; **to ~ at** reñir en voz alta.

bay¹ [beɪ] N (*Bot*) laurel *m*.

bay² [beɪ] N (*Geog*) bahía *f*; (*small*) abra *f*; (*very large*) golfo *m*; **B~ of Biscay** Golfo *m* de Vizcaya.

bay³ [beɪ] N (*Archit*) intercolumnio *m*; crujía *f*; (*Rail*) nave *f*; (*of window*) parte *f* saediza.

bay⁴ [beɪ] **1** N (*bark*) ladrido *m*, aullido *m*; **at ~** acorralado; **to bring to ~** acorralar; **to keep at ~** mantener a raya.
2 VI ladrar, aullar.
bay⁵ [beɪ] **1** ADJ *horse* bayo.
2 N caballo *m* bayo.
bayleaf ['beɪliːf] N, PL **bayleaves** ['beɪliːvz] (hoja *f* de) laurel *m*.
bayonet ['beɪənɪt] **1** N bayoneta *f*; **~ charge** carga *f* a la bayoneta; **~ practice** ejercicios *mpl* con bayoneta, prácticas *fpl* de bayoneta; **at ~ point** a punta de bayoneta; **with fixed ~s** con las bayonetas caladas.
2 VT herir (*or* matar) con la bayoneta.
Bayonne [baɪ'jɒn] N Bayona *f*.
bayou ['baɪjuː] N (*US*) pantanos *mpl*.
bay rum ['beɪˈrʌm] N ron *m* de laurel, ron *m* de malagueta.
bay window ['beɪˈwɪndəʊ] N **(a)** ventana *f* saylediza, mirador *m*. **(b)** (*US**) barriga *f*.
bazaar [bə'zɑːʳ] N bazar *m*.
bazooka [bə'zuːkə] N bazuca *f*.
B.B. N **(a)** ABBR of **Boys' Brigade** *organización parecida a los Boy Scouts*. **(b)** **~ gun** (*US*) carabina *f* de aire comprimido.
B.B.A. N (*US*) ABBR of **Bachelor of Business Administration**.
BBB N (*US*) ABBR of **Better Business Bureau**.
BBC N ABBR of **British Broadcasting Corporation** la BBC; *ver también* ITV , OPEN UNIVERSITY .

┌─── BBC ───────────────────────────────

ⓘ *La BBC (**British Broadcasting Corporation**), fundada en 1927, es el ente público británico de radio y televisión, autónomo en cuanto a su programación pero regulado por un estatuto (**BBC Charter**) que tiene que ser aprobado por el Parlamento. Tiene dos cadenas nacionales de televisión (**BBC1** y **BBC2**), cinco cadenas nacionales de radio, numerosas cadenas locales y una mundial (**World Service**). No tiene publicidad, por lo que se financia a través de operaciones comerciales paralelas y el cobro de una licencia anual (**TV licence**), obligatoria para todo aquél con un aparato de televisión.*
*Los términos **BBC English** y **BBC accent** hacen referencia a la idea que se tiene de sus locutores: de clase media, lenguaje culto y sin acento regional.*
⇨ *Ver también* ITV , ENGLISH

BBFC N ABBR of **British Board of Film Classification**.
bbl ABBR of **barrels**.
BC **(a)** ADV ABBR of **Before Christ** a. de C. **(b)** N (*Canada*) ABBR of **British Columbia**. **(c)** *n* (*Brit*) ABBR of **British Coal**. **(d)** N ABBR of **Bachelor of Commerce**.
BCD N (*Comput*) ABBR of **binary-coded decimal** código *m* decimal binario.
BCG N ABBR of **Bacillus Calmette-Guérin** *vacuna de la tuberculosis*.
BC-NET [ˌbiːsiːˈnet] N ABBR of **Business Cooperation Network** Red *f* de Cooperación de Empresas.
B.Com. [ˌbiːˈkɒm] N ABBR of **Bachelor of Commerce** Licenciado *m*, -a *f* en Comercio.
B/D ABBR of **bank draft**.
b/d (*Fin*) ABBR of **brought down** suma *f* parcial anterior.
BD N **(a)** (*Univ*) ABBR of **Bachelor of Divinity** Licenciado *m*, -a *f* en Teología. **(b)** (*Fin*) ABBR of **bills discounted** efectos *mpl* descontados.
bd (*Fin*) ABBR of **bond** bono *m*, obligación *f*.
BDS N (*Univ*) ABBR of **Bachelor of Dental Surgery** Licenciado *m*, -a *f* en Odontología.
B/E **(a)** (*Fin*) ABBR of **bill of exchange** letra *f* de cambio. **(b)** (*Fin*) ABBR of **Bank of England**.
be [biː] (*irr*: PRES **am, is, are**; PRET **was, were**; PTP **been**) **1** (*absolute*) **to ~ or not to ~** ser o no ser; **as things are** tal como están las cosas; **you're busy enough as it is** estás bastante ocupado ya; **some are and some aren't** algunos lo son y otros no; **let it ~!** ¡déjalo!; **let me ~!** ¡déjame en paz!
2 (*with noun, pronoun, numeral or verb complement* [*but see also 7, 8, 9, 10 below*]) ser; **I am a man** soy hombre; **he's a pianist** es pianista; **he was a communist** era comunista; **he will be pope** será papa; **I was a bullfighter for 2 days** durante 2 días fui torero; **it's a fact** es un hecho; **it is I, it's me** soy yo; **it's 8 o'clock** son las 8; **it's the 3rd of May** es el 3 de mayo; **seeing is believing** ver y creer.
3 (*with ADJ complement*) **(a)** (*when a permanent or essential quality is expressed*) **I'm English** soy inglés; **she's tall** es alta; **it was very bad** fue malísimo; **I used to be poor but now I'm rich** antes era pobre pero ahora soy rico; **when I was young** cuando era joven; **when I'm old** cuando sea viejo.
(b) (*when a temporary or reversible state is indicated, also fig*) estar; **it's dirty** está sucio; **he's ill** está enfermo; **they're tired** están cansados; **the glass is empty** el vaso está vacío; **the pond is always full** el estanque siempre está lleno; **the symphony is full of tunes** la sinfonía está llena de melodías.
(c) (*of persons*, ser + ADJ *indicates a permanent quality of character*, estar + ADJ *indicates a more temporary mood or state*): **he's a cheerful sort** es

alegre, **he's very cheerful** (*about sth*) está alegre; **he's always very smart** siempre es muy elegante, **you're very smart** (*today, for once*) ¡qué guapo estás!; **they're very happy together** son muy felices, **are you happy in your work?** ¿estás contento con tu trabajo?
(d) (+ ADJ, *impersonal*) ser; **it is possible that ...** es posible que ...; **is it certain that ...?** ¿es cierto que ...?
4 (*expressions of authorship, origin, possession, construction*) ser: **it's a Picasso** es de Picasso; **I'm from the south** soy del Sur; **it's mine** es mío; **it's of gold, it's a gold one** es de oro.
5 (*place, geographical location, temporary circumstances*) estar: **he's here** está aquí; **it's on the table** está en la mesa; **Burgos is in Spain** Burgos está en España; **the issue was in doubt** el resultado estaba en duda; **I'm in a jam** estoy en un aprieto; **to ~ on a journey** estar de viaje; **to ~ in a hurry** tener prisa; **to ~ in mourning** estar de luto.
6 (*health*) **how are you?** ¿cómo estás?; **how are you now?** ¿qué tal te encuentras ahora?; **I'm very well, thanks** estoy muy bien, gracias.
7 (*age*) **I'm 8** tengo 8 años; **how old are you?** ¿cuántos años tienes?
8 (*weather, temperatures, certain adjs*) **it is hot** (*weather*) hace calor; **I'm hot** tengo calor; **the water is hot** el agua está caliente; **it's sunny** hay sol; **it's foggy** hay niebla; **it's windy** hace viento; **to ~ hungry** tener hambre; **to ~ afraid** tener miedo.
9 (*certain expressions of time*) **we've been here a year** hace un año que estamos aquí, llevamos un año aquí; **it's a long time since I saw him** hace mucho tiempo que no le veo.
10 **there is, there are** hay; **there was, there were** había, hubo; **there has been, there have been** ha habido; **there may not ~ any** puede no haber ninguno.
11 (*idioms*) **so ~ it** si así sea; **~ that as it may** sea como fuere; **what is it to you?** ¿a ti qué te importa?; **mother to ~** futura madre *f*; **my wife to ~** mi prometida, mi futura esposa; **what's it to ~?** (*in bar etc*) ¿qué vas a tomar?
12 (*call, come*) **has the postman been?** ¿ha venido el cartero?; **you've been and done it now!*** ¡la has hecho buena!; **that dog of yours has been and dug up my flowers!*** ¡el perro ese ha destrozado mis flores!
13 V AUX **(a)** (*conditional sentences*) **if I were to say so** si dijera eso; **if I were you** yo en tu lugar, yo que tú.
(b) (*obligation*) **I am to do it** he de hacerlo; **he was to have come** tenía que venir; **what am I to say?** ¿qué he de decir?
(c) (*continuous tenses*) **to be** + *ger* estar + *ger, eg* **I was singing** estaba cantando, **were you waiting for me?** ¿me estabas esperando?; (*but a simple tense is used in such cases as*) **he is coming tomorrow** viene (*or* vendrá) mañana, **what are you doing?** ¿qué haces?, **I shall ~ seeing him** voy a verle, **will you ~ wanting more?** ¿vas a necesitar más?
(d) (**to be** + PTP, *passive*) ser + PTP: **the window was opened by the servant** la ventana fue abierta por el criado; **it is being studied** está siendo estudiado; (*but the passive is often replaced by a reflexive or active construction*) **the window was opened by the servant** la ventana la abrió el criado; **it is being studied** se está estudiando, está al estudio; **it is said that** se dice que, dicen que; **he was nowhere to ~ seen** no se le veía en ninguna parte; **what's to ~ done?** ¿qué hay que hacer?; **it is to ~ regretted that** es de lamentar que; **it is to ~ hoped that** es de esperar que; **it's a film not to ~ missed** es una película que no hay que perder.
(e) (**to be** + PTP, *state*) estar + PTP: **the window was open** la ventana estaba abierta; **it's made of wood** está hecho de madera; **the book is bereft of ideas** el libro está desprovisto de ideas.
beach [biːtʃ] **1** N playa *f*.
2 VT varar; *whale* embarrancar, encallar.
beachball ['biːtʃbɔːl] N pelota *f* de playa.
beach-buggy ['biːtʃˌbʌgɪ] N buggy *m* (de playa).
beach bum* ['biːtʃbʌm] N playero *m*, -a *f* (de mucho cuidado).
beach-chair ['biːtʃtʃeəʳ] N (*US*) tumbona *f*.
beachcomber ['biːtʃˌkəʊməʳ] N raquero *m*; (*US**) vago *m*, desocupado *m*.
beach-head ['biːtʃhed] N cabeza *f* de playa.
beach-hut ['biːtʃhʌt] N caseta *f* de playa.
beach pyjamas ['biːtʃpɪˌdʒɑːməz] NPL pijama *m* de playa.
beach umbrella ['biːtʃʌmˌbrelə] N sombrilla *f*, parasol *m*, quitasol *m*.
beach volleyball ['biːtʃˈvɒlɪbɔːl] N voley-playa *m*, voleibol-playa *m*.
beachwear ['biːtʃweəʳ] N traje(s) *m(pl)* de playa.
beach-wrap ['biːtʃˌræp] N bata *f*, batín *m* (de playa).
beacon ['biːkən] N almenara *f*; (*in port*) faro *m*, fanal *m*; (*on aerodrome*) baliza *f*, aerofaro *m*; (*Rad*) radiofaro *m*; (*hill*) hacho *m*; **~ light** luz *f* de faro.
bead [biːd] N cuenta *f*; (*of glass*) abalorio *m*; (*of dew, sweat*) gota *f*; (*of gun*) mira *f* globular; **~s** sarta *f* de cuentas, collar *m*, (*Eccl*) rosario *m*; **to draw a ~ on** apuntar a; **to tell one's ~s** rezar el rosario.
beaded ['biːdɪd] ADJ *dress, cushion, curtain* bordado con pedrería, de pedrería; **his forehead was ~ with sweat** su frente estaba salpicada

con gotas de sudor.

beading ['biːdɪŋ] N (*Archit*) astrágalo *m*, contero *m*.

beadle ['biːdl] N (*Brit*) bedel *m*; (*Eccl*) pertiguero *m*.

beady ['biːdɪ] ADJ *eyes* parecidos a dos gotas brillantes; pequeños y brillantes.

beady-eyed ['biːdɪ'aɪd] ADJ de ojos pequeños y brillantes.

beagle ['biːgl] N sabueso *m*, beagle *m*.

beak [biːk] N (a) pico *m*; (*: nose*) nariz *f* (corva); (*Naut*) rostro *m*; ~ **of land** promontorio *m*. (b) (*Brit**) magistrado *m*.

beaked [biːkt] ADJ picudo.

beaker ['biːkəʳ] N (*cup*) taza *f* alta; (*prehistoric*) vaso *m*; (*Chem*) vaso *m* de precipitación.

be-all [biː'ɔːl] N (*also* ~ **and end-all**) único objeto *m*, única cosa *f* que importa; **he is the ~ of her life** él es lo único que le importa en la vida; **money is not the ~** el dinero no es lo único que vale, hay cosas que valen tanto como el dinero.

beam [biːm] **1** N (a) (*Archit*) viga *f*; travesaño *m*; (*of plough*) timón *m*; (*of balance*) astil *m*; (*Mech*) balancín *m*.

(b) (*Naut*) (*timber*) bao *m*; (*width*) manga *f*; **broad in the ~** ancho de caderas, nalgudo; **on the port ~** a babor.

(c) (*of light*) rayo *m*; (*from beacon, lamp*) haz *m* de luz; (*from radio beacon*) haz *m* de radiofaro; (*smile*) sonrisa *f*, mirada *f* alegre, mirada *f* brillante; ~ **lights** (*Aut*) luces *fpl* largas; **with a ~ of pleasure** con

una sonrisa de placer; **to be on the ~*** seguir el buen camino; **to be off the ~*** estar despistado, estar equivocado.

2 VT *light, signal* emitir; **she ~ed her thanks at me** me lanzó una mirada agradecida.

3 VI (*shine*) brillar; (*smile*) sonreírse alegremente (*at* a).

beam-ends ['biːm'endz] NPL (*Naut*) cabezas *fpl* de los baos (de un buque); **she was on her ~** (*Naut*) el buque escoraba peligrosamente; **they are on their ~** (*fig*) están en un grave aprieto, no tienen donde caerse muertos.

beaming ['biːmɪŋ] ADJ sonriente, radiante.

bean [biːn] N (a) (*plant*) (**broad**) ~ haba *f* gruesa; (**dwarf**) ~ judía *f*, enana *f*, fríjol *m*; (**runner**) ~ judía *f*, habichuela *f*.

(b) (*served as food*) ~**s** judías *fpl*; (*broad, haricot*) habas *fpl*; (*of coffee*) granos *mpl*.

(c) (*US**: head, brain*) coco* *m*; **I haven't a ~** (*Brit**) no tengo un céntimo; **not a ~!*** ¡nada en absoluto!; **I didn't make a ~ on the deal** no saqué ni un céntimo del negocio; **he doesn't know ~s about it** (*US**) no tiene ni zorra idea*; **to be full of ~s*** rebosar de vitalidad; **to spill the ~s*** (*improperly*) tirar de la manta; (*tell all*) contarlo todo.

beanbag ['biːnbæg] N (*for throwing*) saquito que se usa para realizar ejercicios gimnásticos; (*chair*) almohadón *m*, cojín *m*.

bean curd ['biːnkɜːd] N tofu *m*, tofú *m*.

---

            see also main entry

"Ser" or "estar"?

You can use "ser":
- when defining or identifying by linking two nouns or noun phrases:
  Paris is the capital of France
  París es la capital de Francia
  He was the most hated man in the village
  Era el hombre más odiado del pueblo
- to describe essential or inherent characteristics (e.g. colour, material, nationality, race, shape, size *etc*):
  His mother is German
  Su madre es alemana
  She was blonde
  Era rubia
- with most impersonal expressions not involving past participles:
  It is important to be on time
  Es importante llegar a tiempo
  NOTE: *Está claro que* is an exception:
  It is obvious you don't understand
  Está claro que no lo entiendes
- when telling the time or talking about time or age:
  It is ten o'clock
  Son las diez
  It's very late. Let's go home
  Es muy tarde. Vamos a casa
  He lived in the country when he was young
  Vivió en el campo cuando era joven
- to indicate possession or duty:
  It's mine
  Es mío
  This is your responsibility
  Este asunto es responsabilidad tuya
- with events in the sense of "take place":
  The 1992 Olympic Games were in Barcelona
  Los Juegos Olímpicos de 1992 fueron en Barcelona
  "Where is the exam?" - "It's in Room 1"
  "¿Dónde es el examen?" - "Es en el Aula Número 1"
  ! Compare this usage with that of *estar (see below)* to talk about location of places, objects and people.

You can use "estar":
- to talk about location of places, objects and people:
  "Where is Zaragoza?" - "It's in Spain"
  "¿Dónde está Zaragoza?" - "Está en España"
  Your glasses are on the bedside table
  Tus gafas están en la mesilla de noche
  ! But use *ser* with events in the sense of "take place" (*see above*).
- to talk about changeable state, condition or mood:
  The teacher is ill
  La profesora está enferma
  The coffee's cold
  El café está frío
  How happy I am!
  ¡Qué contento estoy!
  ! *Feliz*, however, which is seen as more permanent than *contento*, is generally used with *ser*.

- to form progressive tenses:
  We're having lunch. Is it ok if I call you later?
  Estamos comiendo. Te llamaré luego, ¿vale?

Both "ser" and "estar" can be used with past participles
- Use *ser* in *passive* constructions:
  This play was written by Lorca
  Esta obra fue escrita por Lorca
  He was shot dead (by a terrorist group)
  Fue asesinado a tiros (por un grupo terrorista)
  ! The passive is not used as often in Spanish as it is in English.
- Use *estar* with past participles to describe the *results* of a previous action or event:
  We threw them away because they were broken
  Los tiramos a la basura porque estaban rotos
  He's dead
  Está muerto
- Compare the use of *ser* + PAST PARTICIPLE which describes *action* and *estar* + PAST PARTICIPLE which describes *result* in the following:
  The window was broken by the firemen
  La ventana fue rota por los bomberos
  The window was broken
  La ventana estaba rota
  It was painted around 1925
  Fue pintado hacia 1925
  The floor is painted a dark colour
  El suelo está pintado de color oscuro
- *Ser* and *estar* are both used in impersonal expressions with past participles. As above, the use of *ser* implies *action* while the use of *estar* implies *result*:
  It is understood that the work was never finished
  Es sabido que el trabajo nunca se llegó a terminar
  It is a proven fact that vaccinations save many lives
  Está demostrado que las vacunas salvan muchas vidas

"Ser" and "estar" with adjectives
- Some adjectives can be used with both *ser* and *estar* but the meaning changes completely depending on the verb:
  Es listo
  He's clever
  ¿Estás listo?
  Are you ready?
  La química es aburrida
  Chemistry is boring
  Estoy aburrido
  I'm bored
- Other adjectives can also be used with both verbs but the use of *ser* describes a *characteristic* while the use of *estar* implies a *change*:
  Es muy guapo
  He's very handsome
  Estás muy guapa con ese vestido
  You look great in that dress!
  Es delgado
  He's slim
  ¡Estás muy delgada!
  You're (looking) very slim

beanfeast* ['bi:nfi:st] N, **beano*** ['bi:nəʊ] N (Brit: party) fiesta f, juerga f; (meal) comilona f.

beanpole ['bi:npəʊl] N emparrado m; (*) espárrago m; **he's a real ~** está como un espárrago*.

beanshoots ['bi:nʃu:ts] NPL, **beansprouts** ['bi:nspraʊts] NPL (Culin) brotes mpl de soja, soja f germinada.

beanstalk ['bi:nstɔ:k] N judía f.

bear¹ [bɛəʳ] **1** N (a) oso m; **Great B~** Osa f Mayor; **Little B~** Osa f Menor; **to be like a ~ with a sore head** estar de un humor de perros. **(b)** (Fin) bajista m; **~ market** mercado m bajista.
2 VT: **to ~ the market** hacer bajar el mercado vendiendo acciones especulativamente.

▼ **bear²** [bɛəʳ] (irr: PRET **bore**, PTP **borne**) **1** VT **(a)** (carry) llevar; arms, date, inscription etc llevar; character, name, relation, responsibility tener; weight sostener; fruit dar, producir; interest devengar; child parir, tener; cost pagar, correr con; love etc sentir, tener (for para); grudge, ill will guardar, tener (against a).
(b) (stand up to) inspection etc sufrir, resistir a; **it doesn't ~ close examination** no resiste a la inspección de cerca; **it doesn't ~ thinking about** da horror sólo pensar en ello; **the film will ~ a second viewing** la película vale la pena de verse por segunda vez.
▼ **(c)** (endure) soportar, aguantar, resistir; **I can't ~ delays** yo no aguanto los retrasos; **I can't ~ him** no le puedo ver; **I can't ~ spiders** odio las arañas; **I can't ~ to look!** ¡no puedo mirar!; **can you ~ me to look at it?** ¿puedes dejarme verlo?; **I could ~ it no longer** ya no resistía más.
2 VI **(a) a tree that ~s well** un árbol que rinde bien.
(b) the ship ~s north el barco lleva dirección norte; **to ~ left** torcer a la izquierda.
(c) it ~s hard on the old esto pesa bastante sobre los viejos.
(d) to bring a gun to ~ on apuntar a; **to bring pressure to ~ on** ejercer presión sobre.
3 VR: **to ~ o.s.** comportarse, portarse.
◆ **bear away** VT llevarse.
◆ **bear down** VT: **borne down by adversity** derrotado por la adversidad.
◆ **bear down upon** VT **(a)** (ship) correr sobre; (person) avanzar hacia, acercarse majestuosamente (or de manera amenazadora etc) a. **(b)** (press) pesar sobre.
◆ **bear in** VT: **it was borne in on me that ...** iba comprendiendo que ...
◆ **bear off** VT = **bear away**.
◆ **bear on** VT person interesar; subject tener que ver con, referirse a.
◆ **bear out** VT **(a)** (carry) llevar. **(b)** (confirm) confirmar, corroborar; **I can ~ that out** yo confirmo eso; **you will ~ me out that ...** estarás de acuerdo conmigo para decir que ...
◆ **bear up** VI animarse; **~ up!** ¡ánimo!; **I'm ~ing up, thanks** estoy regular, gracias.
◆ **bear with** VT tener paciencia con, ser indulgente con.

bearable ['bɛərəbl] ADJ soportable, aguantable.

béar-cub ['bɛəkʌb] N osezno m.

beard [bɪəd] **1** N barba f; (Bot) arista f; **to have (or wear) a ~** llevar barba.
2 VT desafiar.

bearded ['bɪədɪd] ADJ barbado; (heavily) barbudo.

beardless ['bɪədlɪs] ADJ barbilampiño, lampiño; youth imberbe.

bearer ['bɛərəʳ] N (servant) mozo m; (Comm) portador m, -ora f; (of credentials, office, passport) poseedor m, -ora f; **~ cheque** cheque m al portador.

bear-garden ['bɛə,gɑ:dn] N (fig) manicomio m, guirigay m, casa f de locos.

bear-hug ['bɛəhʌg] N: **he gave me a great ~** me dio un abrazo de oso.

bearing ['bɛərɪŋ] N **(a)** (of person) porte m, comportamiento m; **soldierly ~** porte m militar.
(b) (relationship) relación f (on con); **this has no ~ on the matter** esto no tiene que ver con el asunto.
(c) (Mech) cojinete m.
(d) (Naut) marcación f; **to get one's ~s** orientarse; **to lose one's ~s** desorientarse; **to take a ~** marcarse; **to take one's ~s** orientarse.
(e) (Her) blasón m.
(f) beyond all ~ del todo inaguantable.

bearish ['bɛərɪʃ] ADJ pesimista; (Fin) (de tendencia)bajista.

bearskin ['bɛəskɪn] N piel f de oso; (Mil) gorro m militar (de piel de oso).

beast [bi:st] N **(a)** bestia f; **~ of burden** bestia f de carga; **wild ~** fiera f; **the king of ~s** el rey de los animales. **(b)** (person) animal m, bruto m, salvaje m; (thing) cosa f muy difícil; **you ~!** ¡animal!; **that ~ of a policeman** aquel bruto de policía; **what a ~ he is!** ¡qué bruto!; **this is a ~** esto es horrible; **it's a ~ of a day** es un día horrible.

beastliness ['bi:stlɪnɪs] N bestialidad f.

beastly ['bi:stlɪ] **1** ADJ **(a)** bestial. **(b)** (*) detestable, horrible;

condenado, maldito; **that was a ~ thing to do** aquello sí que fue cruel; **you were ~ to me** fuiste cruel conmigo; **where's that ~ book?** ¿dónde está el maldito libro ese?
2 ADV (Brit*): **it's ~ awkward** es terriblemente difícil; **it's ~ cold** hace un frío bestial.

beat [bi:t] **1** N **(a)** (of heart) latido m.
(b) (Mus) compás m, ritmo m; (of drum) redoble m; **music with a ~** música f de ritmo fuerte.
(c) (of policeman) ronda f; **to be on the ~** estar de ronda; **it's off my ~** (fig) no es de mi competencia.
(d) (Hunting) batida f.
(e) (‡) beatnik mf; **~ generation** generación f de los beatniks.
2 (irr: PRET **beat**, PTP **beaten**) VT **(a)** (strike) golpear; table, door dar golpes en; metal etc batir, martillar; person pegar, (as punishment) dar una paliza a, mondar (LAm); carpet sacudir; (Culin) batir; drum tocar; path abrir; **to ~ time** (Mus) marcar el compás, llevar el compás; **he ~ him on the head** le dio un golpe en la cabeza; **he ~ him about the head** le dio una serie de golpes por la cabeza; **to ~ sb to death** matar a uno a palos; **the bird ~ its wings** el pájaro batió las alas; **to ~ it*** poner pies en polvorosa; **~ it!*** ¡lárgate!
(b) (Hunting) ojear.
(c) (defeat) vencer, derrotar; record batir, superar, mejorar; **to ~ sb to it** ganar por la mano a uno, llegar antes que uno; **to ~ sb hollow (or hands down** (Brit) or **into a cocked hat)** cascar a uno, vencer a uno fácilmente; **he didn't know when he was ~en** en ningún momento quería darse por vencido; **to ~ the system** explotar el sistema.
(d) (be better than) sobrepasar, superar; **if you can't ~ them join them** si no puedes superarlos únete a ellos; **can you ~ that?** ¿has visto cosa igual?; **that ~s everything!** ¡eso es el colmo!
(e) (mystify) confundir; **the police confess themselves ~en** la policía confiesa no tener pista alguna; **the problem has me ~en** el problema me deja totalmente perplejo; **it ~s me how ...** no llego a comprender cómo ...
3 VI (heart) latir, pulsar; **the drums were ~ing** redoblaban los tambores; **to ~ on a door** dar golpes en una puerta; **the waves ~ on the shore** las olas azotaban la playa.
4 ADJ (*) hecho polvo*; see also **beaten**.
◆ **beat about** VI (Naut) barloventear.
◆ **beat back** VT rechazar.
◆ **beat down 1** VT **(a)** abatir, derribar a golpes; corn acamar; opponent, resistance vencer. **(b)** price conseguir rebajar (regateando); seller persuadir a que venda a precio más bajo.
2 VI (sun) picar, calentar mucho; (rain) llover con violencia.
◆ **beat off** VT rechazar.
◆ **beat out** VT metal martillar, formar a martillazos; tune tocar (con fuerte ritmo); fire apagar (a golpes).
◆ **beat up** VT **(a)** (Culin) batir. **(b)** (*) person aporrear, dar una paliza a. **(c)** (recruit) persons reclutar; customers atraer; help asegurar.
◆ **beat up on*** VT (US: hit) golpear a, pegar a; (bully) intimidar a; (criticize) arremeter contra.

beatbox ['bi:t,bɒks] N caja f de ritmos.

beaten ['bi:tn] **1** PTP of **beat**.
2 ADJ **(a)** metal etc batido, martillado; **~ track** camino m trillado (also fig); **a village off the ~ track** un pueblo apartado; **to get off the ~ track** apartarse del camino trillado. **(b)** team etc derrotado, vencido.

beaten-up* [bi:tnʌp] ADJ: **a ~ car** un cacharro*, una birria de coche*.

beater ['bi:təʳ] N **(a)** (Hunting) ojeador m, batidor m. **(b)** (Culin) batidor m, batidora f (eléctrica).

beatific [,bi:ə'tɪfɪk] ADJ beatífico; **with a ~ smile** con una sonrisa de puro contento.

beatification [bi:,ætɪfɪ'keɪʃən] N beatificación f.

beatify [bi:'ætɪfaɪ] VT beatificar.

beating ['bi:tɪŋ] N **(a)** (blows) golpes mpl, golpeo m; (of waves) el batir, el azotar; (punishment) paliza f; **to get a ~** recibir una paliza.
(b) (of heart) latido m, pulsación f.
(c) (Hunting) ojeo m, batida f.
(d) (defeat) derrota f; **to take a ~** salir derrotado (from por), recibir una paliza (at the hands of a manos de); **that score will take some ~** será difícil superar ese total de puntos (etc).

beating-up [,bi:tɪŋ'ʌp] N paliza f.

beatitude [bi:'ætɪtju:d] N beatitud f; **the B~s** las Bienaventuranzas.

beatnik ['bi:tnɪk] N beatnik mf.

Beatrice ['bɪətrɪs] NF Beatriz.

beat-up* ['bi:tʌp] ADJ viejo, destartalado, ruinoso.

beau [bəʊ] **1** ADJ: **~ ideal** lo bello ideal; (person) tipo m ideal.
2 N, PL **beaux** [bəʊ] (fop) petimetre m, dandy m; (ladies' man) galán m; (suitor) pretendiente m; (sweetheart) novio m.

Beaufort scale ['bəʊfət'skeɪl] N escala f de Beaufort.

beaut* [bju:t] N: **it's a ~** es pistonudo*, es de primera.

beauteous ['bju:tɪəs] ADJ (poet) bello.

beautician [bju:'tɪʃən] N esteticista mf.

▶ LANGUAGE IN USE: **bear²**: 1c → 7.3

beautiful ['bjuːtɪfʊl] ADJ hermoso, bello; precioso; **the ~ people** la gente guapa.

beautifully ['bjuːtɪflɪ] ADV (*fig*) maravillosamente, perfectamente; **that will do ~** así sirve perfectamente; **she plays ~** toca a la perfección.

beautify ['bjuːtɪfaɪ] VT embellecer.

beauty ['bjuːtɪ] [1] N (**a**) (*in general*) belleza *f*, hermosura *f*; (*concrete*) belleza *f*, *eg* **the beauties of Majorca** las bellezas de Mallorca; **the ~ of it is that ...** (*fig*) lo genial es que ...
(**b**) (*person*) belleza *f*, beldad *f*; (*thing, specimen*) ejemplar *m* hermoso; **it's a ~** es maravilloso; **that was a ~!** (*stroke etc*) ¡qué golpe más fino!; **isn't he a little ~?** (*child*) ¡mira qué rico está el niño!; **B~ and the Beast** la Bella y la Bestia.
[2] ATTR de belleza; **~ editor** directora *f* de la sección de belleza; **~ products** productos *mpl* para la belleza.

beauty competition ['bjuːtɪ,kɒmpɪ,tɪʃən] N, **beauty contest** ['bjuːtɪ,kɒntest] N concurso *m* de belleza.

beauty consultant ['bjuːtɪkən,sʌltənt] N esteticista *mf*.

beauty-cream ['bjuːtɪkriːm] N crema *f* de belleza.

beauty-parlour ['bjuːtɪ,pɑːlə'] N salón *m* de belleza.

beauty-queen ['bjuːtɪkwiːn] N reina *f* de la belleza, miss *f*.

beauty-salon ['bjuːtɪ,sælɒn] N = **beauty-parlour**.

beauty-sleep ['bjuːtɪsliːp] N primer sueño *m*; **to lose one's ~** (*hum*) perder el tiempo en que uno debiera estar dormido.

beauty-spot ['bjuːtɪspɒt] N (**a**) (*on face*) lunar *m* postizo. (**b**) (*in country*) sitio *m* pintoresco, lugar *m* de excepcional belleza natural.

beaver ['biːvə'] [1] N castor *m*.
[2] VI: **to ~ away** (*Brit*) trabajar diligentemente (*at* en).

bebop ['biːbɒp] N bebop *m*.

becalm [bɪ'kɑːm] VT: **to be ~ed** estar encalmado.

became [bɪ'keɪm] PRET *of* **become**.

▼ **because** [bɪ'kɒz] [1] CONJ porque; **~ I don't want to** porque no quiero; **~ he was ill he couldn't go** por estar enfermo no podía ir; **~ he has two cars he thinks he's somebody** como tiene dos coches se cree un personaje.
▼ [2] PREP: **~ of** a causa de, debido a, por motivo de.

bechamel [,beɪʃə'mel] N (*also* **~ sauce**) besamel *f*.

beck[1] [bek] N: **to be at the ~ and call of** estar a disposición de, estar sometido a la voluntad de.

beck[2] [bek] N (*prov, NEng*) arroyo *m*, riachuelo *m*.

beckon ['bekən] [1] VT llamar con señas; (*fig*) llamar, atraer.

[2] VI: **to ~ to** hacer señas a.

become [bɪ'kʌm] (*irr*: *V* **come**) [1] VT (*of clothes etc*) sentar a, favorecer; (*action etc*) convenir a; **that thought does not ~ you** ese pensamiento es indigno de ti.
[2] VI (**a**) (*absolute*) **what has become of him?** ¿qué es de él?; **what will ~ of me?** ¿qué será de mí?; **what can have become of that book?** ¿adónde diablos se habrá metido aquel libro?
(**b**) (*followed by n: entering profession etc*) hacerse, (*by promotion etc*) llegar a ser, (*of material things*) transformarse en, convertirse en; **to ~ a soldier** hacerse soldado; **to ~ professor** llegar a ser catedrático; **he became king in 1911** subió al trono en 1911; **later this lady became his wife** después esta dama fue su esposa; **to ~ a father** ser padre; **the gas ~s liquid** el gas se convierte en líquido; **the building has become a cinema** el edificio se ha transformado en cine.
(**c**) (*followed by adj*) ponerse, volverse, (*by effort*) hacerse; **this is becoming difficult** esto se está poniendo difícil; **to ~ rich** hacerse rico; **to ~ mad** volverse loco; (*freq to become +* ADJ *is translated by a reflexive verb*) **to ~ red** ponerse rojo, enrojecerse; **to ~ ill** ponerse enfermo, enfermar; **to ~ angry** enfadarse; **he became quite blind** quedó totalmente ciego; **to ~ accustomed to** acostumbrarse a; **it became known that** se supo que, llegó a saberse que; **we became very worried** empezamos a inquietarnos muchísimo.
(**d**) (*of age*) **when he ~s 21** cuando llegue a tener 21 años, cuando cumpla los 21 años.

becoming [bɪ'kʌmɪŋ] ADJ *clothes* favorecedor, que sienta bien, que le va bien a uno; *action* decoroso, conveniente.

becomingly [bɪ'kʌmɪŋlɪ] ADV de modo favorecedor; elegantemente; decorosamente, convenientemente; **~ dressed** elegantemente vestido.

becquerel [,bekə'rel] N becquerelio *m*.

BECTU ['bektu] N (*Brit*) ABBR *of* **Broadcasting, Entertainment, Cinematographic and Theatre Union**.

B.Ed. [,biː'ed] N ABBR *of* **Bachelor of Education** licenciado *m*, -a *f* en pedagogía.

bed [bed] [1] N (**a**) cama *f*; (*of animal*) lecho *m*; **~ and board** comida *f* y casa, pensión *f* completa; **~ and breakfast** (*Brit*) cama *f* con desayuno, alojamiento *m* y desayuno; **~ of roses** lecho *m* de rosas; **life isn't exactly a ~ of roses** la vida no es ningún lecho de rosas; **to get out of ~ on the wrong side, to get up on the wrong side of the ~** (*US**) levantarse por los pies de la

---

BECOME, GO, GET

The translation of *become/go/get/turn* depends on the context and the type of change involved and how it is regarded. Very often there is more than one possible translation, or even a special verb to translate *get +* ADJECTIVE (e.g. *get angry - enfadarse*), but here are some general hints.

Become *etc* + adjective

• Use *ponerse* to talk about temporary but normal changes:
  I got quite ill
  Me puse muy malo
  He went pale
  Se puso pálido
  You've got very brown
  Te has puesto muy morena
  He got very angry
  Se puso furioso

• Use *volverse* to refer to sudden, longer-lasting and unpredictable changes, particularly those affecting the mind:
  He has become very impatient in the last few years
  Se ha vuelto muy impaciente estos últimos años
  She went mad
  Se volvió loca

• Use *quedar(se)* especially when talking about changes that are permanent, involve deterioration and are due to external circumstances. Their onset may or may not be sudden:
  He went blind
  (Se) quedó ciego
  Goya went deaf
  Goya (se) quedó sordo
  NOTE: *Quedarse* is also used to talk about pregnancy:
  She became pregnant
  (Se) quedó embarazada

• Use *hacerse* for states resulting from effort or from a gradual, cumulative process:
  They became very famous
  Se hicieron muy famosos
  The pain became unbearable
  El dolor se hizo insoportable

• Use *llegar a ser* to suggest reaching a peak:
  The heat became stifling
  El calor llegó a ser agobiante

Become *etc* + noun

• Use *hacerse* for career goals and religious or political persuasions:
  He became a lawyer
  Se hizo abogado
  I became a Catholic in 1990
  Me hice católico en 1990
  He became a member of the Green Party
  Se hizo miembro del Partido Verde

• Use *llegar a +* NOUN and *llegar a ser +* PHRASE for reaching a peak after a period of gradual change. This construction is often used to talk about professional accomplishments:
  If you don't make more effort, you'll never get to be a teacher
  Si no te esfuerzas más, no llegarás a profesor
  Castelar became one of the most important politicians of his time
  Castelar llegó a ser uno de los políticos más importantes de su época
  Football became an obsession for him
  El fútbol llegó a ser una obsesión para él

• Use *convertirse en* for long-lasting changes in character, substance and kind which take place gradually:
  Those youngsters went on to become delinquents
  Aquellos jóvenes se convirtieron después en delincuentes
  Over the years I have become a more tolerant person
  Con los años me he convertido en una persona más tolerante
  Water turns into steam
  El agua se convierte en vapor

• Use *quedar(se) +* ADJECTIVE to talk about changes particularly when they are permanent, for the worse and due to external circumstances. Their onset may or may not be sudden:
  She became a widow
  (Se) quedó viuda

• To translate *have turned into* or *have become etc +* NOUN in emphatic phrases particularly about people, you can use *estar hecho un(a) +* NOUN:
  Juan has become a fully-fledged concert pianist
  Juan está hecho todo un pianista

see also main entries

---

cama, levantarse con el pie izquierdo; **to get into** ~ meterse en la cama; **to give sb a** ~ **for the night** hospedar a uno una noche; **to go to** ~ acostarse (*with* con); **to make the** ~ hacer la cama; **you've made your** ~ **and you must lie on it** quien mala cama hace en ella se yace; **to put a child to** ~ acostar a un niño; **to put a paper to** ~ terminar la redacción de un número; **to stay in** ~ (*ill*) guardar cama, (*lazy*) seguir en la cama; **to take to one's** ~ encamarse.
(b) (*Geol*) capa *f*, estrato *m*, yacimiento *m*.
(c) (*Archit, Tech*) base *f*.
(d) (*of sea*) fondo *m*; (*of river*) cauce *m*, lecho *m*.
(e) (*of flowers*) macizo *m*, cuadro *m*, arriate *m*.
[2] VT **(a)** (*Archit etc*) fijar, engastar.
(b) (*) *woman* llevar a la cama, acostarse con.
◆**bed down** [1] VT **(a)** (*Archit*) = **bed 2 (a)**. **(b)** *children* acostar; *animals* hacer un lecho para.
[2] VI hacerse una cama, acostarse.
◆**bed out** VT *plants* plantar en un macizo.

BED AND BREAKFAST
---

*Ⓘ Se llama **Bed and Breakfast** a una casa particular de hospedaje tanto en el campo como en la ciudad, que ofrece cama y desayuno a tarifas inferiores a las de un hotel. El servicio se suele anunciar con carteles colocados en las ventanas del establecimiento, en el jardín o en la carretera y en ellos aparece a menudo únicamente el símbolo **B&B**.*

bedaub [bɪ'dɔːb] VT embadurnar.
bedazzle [bɪ'dæzəl] VT deslumbrar, encandilar; **many people are ~d by fame** mucha gente está deslumbrada por la fama.
bedbath ['bedbɑːθ] N, PL **bedbaths** ['bedbɑːðz]: **they gave him a ~** le lavaron en la cama.
bedbug ['bedbʌg] N chinche *gen f*.
bedchamber ['bed,tʃeɪmbəʳ] N (†) cámara *f*, aposentos *mpl*.
bedclothes ['bedkləʊðz] NPL ropa *f* de cama.
bedcover ['bedkʌvəʳ] N = **bedspread**; ~**s** ropa *f* de cama.
-bedded ['bedɪd] ADJ *ending in compounds:* **twin~ room** habitación *f* doble.
bedding ['bedɪŋ] N ropa *f* de cama; (*for animal*) lecho *m*.
Bede [biːd] NM Beda; **the Venerable ~** el venerable Beda.
bedeck [bɪ'dek] VT adornar, engalanar.
bedevil [bɪ'devəl] VT endiablar; (*dog*) acosar; (*trouble*) fastidiar; **the problem is ~led by several factors** hay diversos factores que complican el problema; **the team has been ~led by injuries** el equipo ha sufrido mucho de lesiones.
bedfellow ['bedfeləʊ] N compañero *m*, -a *f* de cama; **they make strange ~s** hacen una pareja rara.
bedhead ['bedhed] N testero *m*, cabecera *f*.
bedjacket ['beddʒækɪt] N mañanita *f*.
bedlam ['bedləm] N (†† *or fig*) manicomio *m*; **it was sheer ~** la confusión era total; ~ **broke out** se armó una algarabía espantosa.
bedlinen ['bedlɪnɪn] N ropa *f* de cama, sábanas *fpl*.
Bedouin ['beduɪn] [1] ADJ beduino.
[2] N beduino *m*, -a *f*.
bedpan ['bedpæn] N chata *f*, silleta *f*, cuña *f*.
bedpost ['bedpəʊst] N columna *f* (*or* pilar *m*) de cama.
bedraggled [bɪ'drægld] ADJ ensuciado, mojado.
bedridden ['bedrɪdn] ADJ postrado en cama, encamado.
bedrock ['bedrɒk] N lecho *m* de roca, roca *f* sólida; (*fig*) fondo *m* de la cuestión; **to get down to ~** ir a lo fundamental.
bedroll ['bedrəʊl] N petate *m*.
bedroom ['bedrʊm] N dormitorio *m*, alcoba *f*, habitación *f*, recámara *f* (*LAm*); ~ **eyes** * ojos *mpl* seductores; ~ **farce** farsa *f* de dormitorio; ~ **slippers** pantuflas *fpl*; ~ **suburb** (*US*) ciudad *f* colmena; ciudad *f* dormitorio; ~ **suite** juego *m* de muebles para dormitorio; **3-~ flat** piso *m* de 3 habitaciones.
-bedroomed ['bed,rʊmd] ADJ: *eg* **a 5~ house** una casa con 5 dormitorios.
Beds [bedz] N ABBR *of* **Bedfordshire**.
bed-settee [,bedse'tiː] N sofá-cama *m*.
bedside ['bedsaɪd] [1] N: **to wait at the ~ of** esperar a la cabecera de.
[2] ATTR: ~ **lamp** lámpara *f* de noche; ~ **rug** alfombrilla *f* de cama; ~ **table** mesa *f* de noche; **to have a good ~ manner** tener mucho tacto con los enfermos.
bedsit * ['bedsɪt] N, **bedsitter** ['bed'sɪtəʳ] N, **bedsitting room** ['bed'sɪtɪŋrʊm] N (*Brit*) habitación *f* con cocina.
bedsocks ['bedsɒks] NPL calcetines *mpl* de cama.
bedsore ['bedsɔːʳ] N úlcera *f* de decúbito.
bedspread ['bedspred] N sobrecama *m*, cobertor *m*, cubrecama *f*.
bedstead ['bedsted] N cuja *f*, armazón *m or f* de cama.
bedstraw ['bedstrɔː] N (*Bot*) cuajaleche *m*, amor *m* de hortelano.
bedtime ['bedtaɪm] N hora *f* de acostarse; ~ **story** cuento *m* (para hacer dormir a un niño).
bedwetting ['bedwetɪŋ] N enuresis *f*.

bedworthy * ['bed,wɜːðɪ] ADJ atractivo.
bee [biː] N **(a)** abeja *f*; **to have a ~ in one's bonnet** tener una idea fija, tener algo metido entre ceja y ceja; **he thinks he's the ~'s knees** * se cree el mar de listo (*or* de elegante *etc*). **(b)** (*esp US*) reunión *f* social de vecinos, círculo *m* social.
Beeb * [biːb] N: **the ~** (*Brit*) la BBC.
beech [biːtʃ] N haya *f*.
beech-grove ['biːtʃ,grəʊv] N hayal *m*.
beechmast ['biːtʃmɑːst] N hayucos *mpl*.
beechnut ['biːtʃnʌt] N hayuco *m*.
beech-tree ['biːtʃtriː] N haya *f*.
beechwood ['biːtʃwʊd] N **(a)** (*group of trees*) hayedo *m*, hayal *m*. **(b)** (*material*) (madera *f* de) haya *f*.
bee-eater ['biː,iːtəʳ] N (*Orn*) abejaruco *m*.
beef [biːf] [1] N **(a)** carne *f* de vaca, carne *f* de res (*LAm*), vaca *f*. **(b)** (*) fuerza *f* muscular, corpulencia *f*. **(c)** (*US* *) queja *f*.
[2] ATTR: ~ **cattle** ganado *m* vacuno de carne; ~ **olive** picadillo envuelto en una lonja de carne y cocinado en salsa; ~ **sausage** salchicha *f* de carne de vaca; ~ **tea** caldo *m* de carne (para enfermos).
[3] VI (*) quejarse (*about* de).
◆**beef up** * VT *essay, speech* reforzar, fortalecer.
beefburger ['biːf,bɜːgəʳ] N hamburguesa *f*.
beefcake * ['biːf,keɪk] N despliegue *m* de fuerza muscular masculina (*esp en fotos*).
beefeater ['biːf,iːtəʳ] N (*Brit*) alabardero *m* de la Torre de Londres.
beefsteak ['biːf'steɪk] N biftec *m*, bistec *m*, bife *m* (*SC*).
beefy * ['biːfɪ] ADJ fornido, corpulento.
beehive ['biːhaɪv] N colmena *f*.
beekeeper ['biː,kiːpəʳ] N apicultor *m*, -ora *f*, colmenero *m*, -a *f*.
beekeeping ['biː,kiːpɪŋ] N apicultura *f*.
beeline ['biːlaɪn] N: **to make a ~ for** ir en línea recta hacia, salir disparado hacia.
Beelzebub [biː'elzɪbʌb] NM Belcebú.
been [biːn] PTP *of* **be**.
beep [biːp] N bip *m*.
beeper ['biːpəʳ] N (*US*) localizador *m*, busca* *m*.
beer [bɪəʳ] N cerveza *f*; **small ~** (*fig*) cosa *f* sin importancia, bagatela *f*; **we're only here for the ~** venimos en plan de diversión; **life isn't all ~ and skittles** (*Brit*) la vida no es un lecho de rosas.

BEER
---

*Ⓘ La cerveza es la bebida alcohólica más popular en el Reino Unido. La que se sirve en los **pubs** británicos es tradicionalmente de barril (**on draught**) y se bebe en medidas de pinta (**pint**) (0,475 l.) o media pinta (**half a pint**). En Inglaterra y Gales el tipo más común de cerveza se denomina **bitter**, debido a su sabor ligeramente amargo. El equivalente escocés es conocido como **heavy** y es algo más dulce. Otras variedades son **stout**, cerveza negra, **mild**, suave, parecida a la **bitter** pero con menos gas, y **lager**, ligera, rubia y con más gas, al estilo europeo. **Ale** era el término original para referirse a la cerveza elaborada sin gas, aunque ahora también hace referencia a la cerveza en general. Algunas variedades son **light ale** o **pale ale**, de tono pálido y sabor suave, y **brown ale**, más oscura, fuerte y con más sabor.*
*En los Estados Unidos la cerveza es normalmente rubia. Los bares suelen servir sólo cerveza embotellada, por lo que se suele pedir diciendo únicamente **a beer** o la marca concreta.*

beer-barrel ['bɪə,bærəl] N barril *m* de cerveza.
beer-belly * ['bɪə,belɪ] N, **beer-gut** * ['bɪə,gʌt] N curva *f* de la felicidad.
beer-bottle ['bɪə,bɒtl] N botella *f* de cerveza.
beer-can ['bɪə,kæn] N lata *f* de cerveza, bote *m*.
beerfest ['bɪə,fest] N (*US*) festival *m* cervecero.
beer garden ['bɪə'gɑːdn] N terraza *f* de verano, jardín *m* de un bar.
beer-glass ['bɪə,glɑːs] N jarra *f* de cerveza.
beer-mat ['bɪə,mæt] N posavasos *m* (de taberna).
beery ['bɪərɪ] ADJ *smell* a cerveza; *person* muy aficionado a la cerveza; *party* donde se bebe mucha cerveza; **it was a ~ affair** allí se bebió una barbaridad.
beeswax ['biːzwæks] N cera *f* (de abejas).
beet [biːt] N = **beetroot**.
beetle ['biːtl] N escarabajo *m*, coleóptero *m*.
◆**beetle off** * VI marcharse.
beetle-browed ['biːtl'braʊd] ADJ cejialto, de cejas muy espesas.
beetroot ['biːtruːt] N (*Brit*) (raíz *f* de) remolacha *f*, betabel *m* (*LAm*), betarraga *f* (*LAm*).
beet sugar ['biːt'ʃʊgəʳ] N azúcar *m* de remolacha.
befall [bɪ'fɔːl] (*irr:* V **fall**) [1] VT acontecer a.
[2] VI acontecer; **whatever may ~** pase lo que pase.
befallen [bɪ'fɔːlən] PTP *of* **befall**.
befell [bɪ'fel] PRET *of* **befall**.
befit [bɪ'fɪt] VT convenir a, venir bien a, corresponder a.

befitting [bɪˈfɪtɪŋ] ADJ conveniente, decoroso.
befog [bɪˈfɒg] VT (*fig*) *issue etc* entenebrecer; *person* ofuscar, confundir.
before [bɪˈfɔːʳ] ① ADV (**a**) (*place*) delante, adelante; **~ and behind** por delante y por detrás; **that chapter and the one ~** ese capítulo y el anterior.
(**b**) (*time*) antes; anteriormente; **a moment ~** un momento antes; **the day ~** el día anterior; **on this occasion and the one ~** en esta ocasión y la anterior.
② PREP (**a**) (*place*) delante de; (*in the presence of, faced with*) ante, en presencia de; **we still have 2 hours ~ us** tenemos todavía 2 horas por delante; **the problem ~ us** el problema que se nos plantea; **the task ~ us** la tarea que tenemos por delante.
(**b**) (*time*) antes de; **income ~ tax** renta *f* bruta; **profits ~ tax** beneficios *mpl* preimpositivos.
(**c**) (*rather than*) **I should choose this one ~ that** yo escogería éste antes que aquél; **death ~ dishonour!** ¡antes la muerte que el deshonor!
(**d**) (*with verb*) **~ going out** antes de salir.
③ CONJ antes de que.
beforehand [bɪˈfɔːhænd] ADV de antemano, con anticipación; (*esp Liter, Admin*) con antelación.
befoul [bɪˈfaʊl] VT ensuciar.
befriend [bɪˈfrend] VT ofrecer amistad a; amparar, favorecer.
befuddle [bɪˈfʌdl] VT (*confuse*) atontar, confundir; (*make tipsy*) atontar.
befuddled [bɪˈfʌdld] ADJ aturdido; **~ with drink** atontado por la bebida.
beg [beg] ① VT (**a**) pedir, suplicar, rogar (*from, of* a); **to ~ sb for sth** pedir algo a uno; **he ~ged my help** suplicó mi ayuda; **he ~ged me to help him** me suplicó que le ayudara; **he ~ged the book from me** rogó que le diese el libro; **I ~ you!** ¡se lo suplico!; *V* **question.**
(**b**) (*as beggar*) mendigar; pedir; **he ~ged a pound** pidió una libra.
② VI (**a**) pedir, rogar; **to ~ for** pedir, solicitar; **I ~ to inform you that ...** tengo el gusto de informarle que ...
(**b**) (*as beggar*) mendigar, pedir por Dios, pedir limosna; **it's going ~ging** no hay candidato (*or* comprador), nadie lo quiere; **there's some cake going ~ging** hay un poco de tarta por terminar.
◆**beg off*** VI (*US*) pedir dispensa, escabullirse*.
began [bɪˈgæn] PRET *of* begin.
beget [bɪˈget] (*irr*: PRET **begot**, (*arch*) **begat**, PTP **begotten**) VT engendrar (*also fig*).
begetter [bɪˈgetəʳ] N (*frm*) creador *m*, -ora *f*, instigador *m*, -ora *f*.
beggar [ˈbegəʳ] ① N (**a**) mendigo *m*, -a *f*, pordiosero *m*; **~s can't be choosers** a quien dan no escoge, los pobres no escogen. (**b**) (*) tío* *m*, sujeto* *m*; **lucky ~!*** ¡qué chorra tiene el tío!*.

② VT (**a**) empobrecer, arruinar, reducir a la miseria. (**b**) (*fig*) excederse a; **it ~s description** supera toda descripción; **it ~s belief** resulta totalmente inverosímil.
beggarly [ˈbegəlɪ] ADJ indigente; (*fig*) miserable, mezquino.
beggary [ˈbegərɪ] N mendicidad *f*; miseria *f*; **to reduce to ~** reducir a la miseria.
begging [ˈbegɪŋ] N mendicidad *f*; **~ letter** carta *f* en que se pide dinero.
▼**begin** [bɪˈgɪn] (*irr*: PRET **began**, PTP **begun**) ① VT comenzar, empezar; iniciar; (*undertake*) emprender; **the work will be begun tomorrow** mañana se iniciará el trabajo, mañana se dará principio al trabajo; **I was foolish ever to ~ it** hice mal en emprenderlo.
▼② VI comenzar, empezar; **to ~ to** + *infin* comenzar (*or* empezar) a + *infin*; **to ~ talking** empezar a hablar; **it doesn't ~ to be possible** dista mucho de ser posible; **to ~ by saying** comenzar diciendo; **to ~ on emprender**, comenzar; **to ~ with sth** comenzar por (*or* con) algo; **to ~ with** (*as phrase*) en primer lugar, para empezar; **~ning from Monday** a partir del lunes.
beginner [bɪˈgɪnəʳ] N principiante *mf*; novato *m*, -a *f*.
beginning [bɪˈgɪnɪŋ] N (**a**) (*of speech, book, film etc*) principio *m*, comienzo *m*; **at the ~ of** al principio de; **at the ~ of the century** a principios del siglo; **from the ~** desde el principio; **from ~ to end** desde el principio hasta el final, de cabo a rabo; **in the ~** al principio; **the ~ of the end** el comienzo del fin; **to make a ~** empezar.
(**b**) (*origin*) origen *m*; **from small ~s** de orígenes modestos, de antecedentes humildes; **he had the ~s of a beard** tenía un asomo de barba.
begone†† [bɪˈgɒn] INTERJ ¡fuera de aquí!
begonia [bɪˈgəʊnɪə] N begonia *f*.
begot [bɪˈgɒt] PRET *of* beget.
begotten [bɪˈgɒtn] PTP *of* beget; **the only B~ Son** el Unigénito.
begrime [bɪˈgraɪm] VT tiznar, ensuciar.
begrudge [bɪˈgrʌdʒ] VT (*give*) dar de mala gana; (*envy*) tener envidia a; **I don't ~ him his success** no le envidio su éxito.
begrudgingly [bɪˈgrʌdʒɪŋlɪ] ADV de mala gana, a regañadientes.
beguile [bɪˈgaɪl] VT (*delude*) engañar; (*charm away*) seducir, engatusar; *time etc* entretener; **to ~ sb into doing sth** persuadir (*or* engatusar) a uno a hacer algo.
beguiling [bɪˈgaɪlɪŋ] ADJ seductor, persuasivo, atractivo.
begun [bɪˈgʌn] PTP *of* begin.
behalf [bɪˈhɑːf] N: **on ~ of** de parte de; **on ~ of everybody** en nombre de todos; **a collection on ~ of orphans** una colecta en beneficio de los huérfanos, una colecta por huérfanos; **I interceded on his ~**

BEFORE   *see also main entry*

Time

Adverb

● When *before* is an *adverb*, you can usually translate it using *antes*:
  Why didn't you say so before?
  ¿Por qué no lo has dicho antes?
  I had spoken to her before
  Había hablado con ella antes

● But the *before* in *never before* and *ever before* is often not translated:
  I've never been to Spain before
  Nunca he estado en España
  I had never been to a police station before
  Nunca había estado (antes) en una comisaría
  It's not true that the working class is earning more money than ever before
  No es cierto que la clase obrera gane más dinero que nunca

● The *day/night/week etc before* should usually be translated using *el día/la noche/la semana anterior*:
  The night before, he had gone to a rock concert
  La noche anterior había ido a un concierto de rock

● In more formal contexts, where *before* could be substituted by *previously*, *anteriormente* is another option:
  As I said before...
  Como he dicho antes or *anteriormente...*

● When *before* is equivalent to *already*, translate using *ya* (*antes*) or, in questions about whether someone has done what they are doing now before, using *¿es la primera vez que...?*:
  "How about watching this film?" - "Actually, I've seen it before"
  "¿Vemos esa película?" - "Es que ya la he visto"
  I had been to Glasgow a couple of times before
  Ya había estado (antes) en Glasgow un par de veces
  Have you been to Spain before?
  ¿Has estado ya en España? or *¿Es la primera vez que vienes a España?*

● Translate PERIOD OF TIME + *before* using *hacía* + PERIOD OF TIME:
  They had married nearly forty years before
  Se habían casado hacía casi cuarenta años
  ! *Hacía* is invariable in this sense.

Preposition

● When *before* is a *preposition*, you can usually translate it using *antes de*:
  Please ring before seven
  Por favor, llama antes de las siete
  Shall we go for a walk before dinner?
  ¿Nos vamos a dar un paseo antes de cenar?

● But use *antes que* with names of people and personal pronouns when they stand in for a verb:
  If you get there before me or before I do, wait for me in the bar
  Si llegas antes que yo, espérame en el bar

● Translate *before* + -ING using *antes de* + INFINITIVE:
  He said goodbye to the children before leaving
  Se despidió de los niños antes de irse

Conjunction

● When *before* is a *conjunction*, you can usually translate it using *antes de que* + SUBJUNCTIVE:
  I'll ask Peter about it before he goes away on holiday
  Se lo preguntaré a Peter antes de que se vaya de vacaciones
  We reached home before the storm broke
  Llegamos a casa antes de que empezara la tormenta

● If the subject of both clauses is the same, *antes de* + INFINITIVE is usually used rather than *antes de que*:
  Give me a ring before you leave the office
  Llámame antes de salir de la oficina
  NOTE: This construction is also sometimes used in colloquial Spanish when the subjects are different:
  Before you arrived she was very depressed
  Antes de llegar tú, estaba muy deprimida

➤ LANGUAGE IN USE: **begin:** 2 → 26.1

intercedí por él; **don't worry on my ~** no te preocupes por mí.

behave [bɪ'heɪv] **1** vi (*person*) portarse (*to, towards* con), comportarse, conducirse; (*Mech etc*) comportarse, funcionar.

2 vr: **to ~ o.s.** (*esp of or to child*) portarse bien; **~ yourself!** ¡estáte formal!, ¡pórtate bien!; **if you ~ yourself (properly)** si te conduces debidamente.

behaviour, (*US*) **behavior** [bɪ'heɪvjəʳ] N conducta *f*, comportamiento *m*; (*Mech etc*) comportamiento *m*, funcionamiento *m*; **good ~** buena conducta *f*; **to be on one's best ~** portarse del mejor modo posible; **you must be on your best ~** tienes que portarte pero muy bien.

behavioural, (*US*) **behavioral** [bɪ'heɪvjərəl] ADJ conductual, conductista, behaviorístico.

behaviourism, (*US*) **behaviorism** [bɪ'heɪvjərɪzəm] N conductismo *m*, behaviorismo *m*.

behaviourist, (*US*) **behaviorist** [bɪ'heɪvjərɪst] **1** ADJ conductista, behaviorista.

2 N conductista *mf*, behaviorista *mf*.

behead [bɪ'hed] VT decapitar, descabezar.

beheld [bɪ'held] PRET AND PTP *of* **behold**.

behemoth [bɪ'hi:mɒθ] N (*liter: monster*) gigante *m*.

behest [bɪ'hest] N (*liter*): **at the ~ of** por orden de.

behind [bɪ'haɪnd] **1** ADV (**a**) (*in or at the rear*) detrás, por detrás; atrás; **to come from ~** venir desde atrás; **to follow close ~** seguir muy de cerca; **to attack sb from ~** atacar a uno por la espalda; **Pepe won with Paco only 2 strokes ~** ganó Pepe con Paco a sólo 2 golpes de distancia.

(**b**) (*with verb* to be) **to be a bit ~** estar algo atrasadillo; **to be ~ with one's work** estar atrasado en su trabajo, tener atrasos de trabajo.

2 PREP (*at the back of, also fig*) detrás de; **what's ~ all this?** ¿qué hay detrás de todo esto?; **he has all of us ~ him** (*fig*) tiene el apoyo de todos nosotros; **we are much ~ them in technology** les somos muy inferiores en tecnología; **with his hands ~ his back** las manos en la espalda; **X is 9 points ~ Y** X tiene 9 puntos menos que Y; **Ruritania is well ~ Slobodia in production** Ruritania queda muy a la zaga de Eslobodia en la producción; **she has 4 novels ~ her** tiene 4 novelas en el haber; **it's all ~ us now** todo eso ha quedado ya detrás.

3 N (*) trasero *m*, culo *m*.

behindhand [bɪ'haɪndhænd] ADV atrasado, con retraso; **to be ~ with the rent** tener atrasos de alquiler.

behold [bɪ'həʊld] (*irr: V* **hold**) VT (†† *or liter*) contemplar; **~!** ¡fíjese bien!; **~ the results!** ¡he aquí los resultados!; *V* **lo.**

beholden [bɪ'həʊldən] ADJ: **to be ~ to** estar bajo una obligación a; estar agradecido a; **I don't want to be ~ to anybody** yo no quiero tener obligaciones con nadie.

beholder [bɪ'həʊldəʳ] N espectador *m*, -ora *f*, observador *m*, -ora *f*.

behove [bɪ'həʊv], (*US*) **behoove** [bɪ'hu:v] VT: **it ~s him to** + *infin* le incumbe + *infin*.

beige [beɪʒ] **1** ADJ (color de) beige.

2 N beige *m*.

Beijing ['beɪ'dʒɪŋ] N Pekín *m*.

being ['bi:ɪŋ] N ser *m*; **in ~** existente; **to come** (*or* **be called** *or* **be brought**) **into ~** nacer, empezar a existir.

Beirut [beɪ'ru:t] N Beirut *m*.

bejewelled, (*US*) **bejeweled** [bɪ'dʒu:əld] ADJ enjoyado.

belabour, (*US*) **belabor** [bɪ'leɪbəʳ] VT apalear; (*fig*) criticar, dar un palo a.

Belarus [belə'rʊs] N Bielorrusia *f*.

Belarussian [ˌbelə'rʌʃən] **1** ADJ bielorruso.

2 N (**a**) bielorruso *m*, -a *f*. (**b**) (*Ling*) bielorruso *m*.

belated [bɪ'leɪtɪd] ADJ atrasado, tardío.

belatedly [bɪ'leɪtɪdlɪ] ADV con retraso.

belay [bɪ'leɪ] VT amarrar (dando vueltas en una cabilla).

belch [beltʃ] **1** N eructo *m*.

2 VT (*fig: also* **to ~ out**) vomitar, arrojar.

3 VI eructar.

beleaguered [bɪ'li:gəd] ADJ sitiado, asediado, cercado.

Belfast ['belfɑ:st] N Belfast *m*.

belfry ['belfrɪ] N campanario *m*.

Belgian ['beldʒən] **1** ADJ belga.

2 N belga *mf*.

Belgium ['beldʒəm] N Bélgica *f*.

Belgrade [bel'greɪd] N Belgrado *m*.

belie [bɪ'laɪ] VT desmentir, contradecir; *hopes etc* defraudar.

▼ **belief** [bɪ'li:f] N (**a**) (*conviction*) creencia *f* (*that* de que); opinión *f*; **a man of strong ~s** un hombre de opiniones firmes; **contrary to popular ~** ... al contrario de lo que muchos creen ...; **to the best of my ~** según mi leal saber y entender; **I did it in the ~ that** ... lo hice creyendo que ...; **it is my firm ~ that** ... creo firmemente que ...; **it passes ~, it is beyond ~** es increíble (*that* que).

(**b**) (*Rel etc*) fe *f*; **his ~ in God** su fe en Dios.

believable [bɪ'li:vəbl] ADJ creíble.

▼ **believe** [bɪ'li:v] **1** VT creer; *ears, story* dar crédito a; **don't you ~ it!** ¡no lo creas!; **~ it or not, she bought it** aunque parece mentira, lo compró; **it was hot, ~ (you)** me hacía calor ¡y cómo!; **he is ~d to be abroad** se cree que está en el extranjero; **I couldn't ~ my eyes** no pude dar crédito a mis ojos; **do you really ~ the threat?** ¿crees de veras en la amenaza?; **I would never have ~d it of him** no le creía capaz de eso.

2 VI creer; **to ~ in God** creer en Dios; **we don't ~ in drugs** no aprobamos (el uso de) las drogas; **I ~ so** creo que sí; **I ~ not** creo que no.

believer [bɪ'li:vəʳ] N (*Rel*) creyente *mf*, fiel *mf*; (*supporter*) partidario *m*, -a *f*; **I am a ~ in letting things take their course** yo soy partidario de dejar que las cosas se desarrollen por sí mismas.

Belisha beacon [bɪˌli:ʃə'bi:kən] N poste *m* luminoso (*de cruce de peatones*).

belittle [bɪ'lɪtl] VT despreciar, minimizar, conceder poca importancia a.

Belize [be'li:z] N Belice *m*.

Belizean [be'li:zɪən] **1** ADJ beliceño.

2 N beliceño *m*, -a *f*.

bell [bel] N (*church ~*) campana *f*; (*hand ~*) campanilla *f*; (*animal's*) cencerro *m*; (*on toy, dress etc*) cascabel *m*; (*electric*) timbre *m*; (*of trumpet*) pabellón *m*; **2, 8** (*etc*) **~s** las medias horas de cada guardia marítima; **I'll give you a ~** (*Telec**) te llamaré; **that rings a ~** eso me suena; **it doesn't ring a ~ with me** no me suena; **he was saved by the ~** (*fig*) se salvó por los pelos.

belladonna [ˌbelə'dɒnə] N (*Bot, Med*) belladona *f*; **~ lily** azucena *f* rosa.

bell-bottomed ['bel'bɒtəmd] ADJ acampanado, abocinado.

bell-bottoms ['belbɒtəmz] NPL pantalones *mpl* de campana.

bellboy ['belbɔɪ] N botones *m*.

bellbuoy ['belbɔɪ] N boya *f* de campana.

belle [bel] N belleza *f*, beldad *f*; **the ~ of the ball** la reina del baile.

belles-lettres ['bel'letr] NPL bellas letras *fpl*.

bellglass ['belglɑ:s] N campana *f* de cristal.

bellhop ['belhɒp] N (*US*) botones *m*.

bellicose ['belɪkəʊs] ADJ belicoso.

bellicosity [ˌbelɪ'kɒsɪtɪ] N belicosidad *f*.

belligerence [bɪ'lɪdʒərəns] N, **belligerency** [bɪ'lɪdʒərənsɪ] N beligerancia *f*; agresividad *f*.

belligerent [bɪ'lɪdʒərənt] **1** ADJ beligerante; *person, tone* agresivo.

2 N beligerante *m*.

belljar ['beldʒɑ:ʳ] N campana *f* de vidrio.

bellow ['beləʊ] **1** N bramido *m*; (*of person*) rugido *m*.

2 (*also* **to ~ out**) VT gritar, vociferar.

3 VI bramar; (*person*) rugir.

bellows ['beləʊz] NPL fuelle *m*; **a pair of ~** un fuelle.

bellpull ['bel,pʊl] N campanilla *f*.

bellpush ['belpʊʃ] N botón *m* del timbre.

bellringer ['bel,rɪŋəʳ] N campanero *m*; (*as hobby*) campanólogo *m*, -a *f*.

bell-ringing ['bel,rɪŋɪŋ] N campanología *f*.

bellrope ['belrəʊp] N cuerda *f* de campana.

bell-shaped ['belʃeɪpt] ADJ acampanado, campaniforme.

bell-tent ['beltent] N pabellón *m*.

bell-tower ['bel,taʊəʳ] N campanario *m*.

belly ['belɪ] **1** N vientre *m*; (*with offensive connotations*) barriga *f*, panza *f*, guata *f* (*And*); (*of vessel*) barriga *f*; **to go ~ up*** quebrar.

2 VI (*sail: also* **to ~ out**) hacer bolso, llenarse de viento.

bellyache ['belɪeɪk] **1** N dolor *m* de barriga, dolor *m* de tripas.

2 VI (‡) quejarse constantemente (*about* de).

bellyaching: ['belɪ,eɪkɪŋ] N quejas *fpl* constantes.

belly-button* ['belɪ,bʌtn] N ombligo *m*.

belly-dance ['belɪdɑ:ns] N danza *f* del vientre.

belly-dancer ['belɪ,dɑ:nsəʳ] N danzarina *f* del vientre.

bellyflop ['belɪ,flɒp] N panzazo *m*; **to do a ~** dar (*or* darse) un panzazo.

bellyful ['belɪfʊl] N panzada *f*; **I've had a ~** estoy harto ya (*of* de).

belly-landing ['belɪ,lændɪŋ] N aterrizaje *m* de panza.

belly-laugh ['belɪlɑ:f] N carcajada *f* (*grosera*), risotada *f*.

belong [bɪ'lɒŋ] VI (**a**) (*be the possession of*) pertenecer (*to* a); **who does this ~ to?** ¿a quién pertenece esto?, ¿de quién es esto?; **the countryside ~s to everyone** el campo es de todos.

(**b**) (*be incumbent on*) **that duty ~s to me** ese deber me corresponde.

(**c**) (*of membership etc*) **to ~ to a club** ser socio de un club; **to ~ to a party** ser miembro de un partido; **why don't you ~?** ¿por qué no te haces (*or* eres) socio?

(**d**) (*have rightful place*) **this ~s with that** éste va con aquél; **that card ~s under K** esa ficha debiera estar en la K; **where does this ~?** ¿esto dónde lo pongo?; **it ~s on the shelf** tiene un puesto en el estante; **it doesn't ~ here** aquí no está mal colocado.

(e) *(be resident, be at ease)* **I ~ here** yo soy de aquí; **I feel I ~ here** aquí me siento cómodo, aquí me siento como en casa; **that feeling of not ~ing** esa sensación de estar fuera de su ambiente natural.

belongings [bɪ'lɒŋɪŋz] NPL pertenencias *fpl*, bártulos *mpl*, cosas *fpl*; **personal ~** efectos *mpl* personales.

Belorussia [ˌbeləʊ'rʌʃə] N Bielorrusia *f*.

Belorussian [ˌbeləʊ'rʌʃən] ADJ, N = **Belarussian**.

beloved [bɪ'lʌvɪd] **1** ADJ querido *(by, of* de).
2 N querido *m*, amada *f*.

below [bɪ'ləʊ] **1** ADV abajo, (por) debajo; **that flat ~** ese piso de abajo; **the passage quoted ~** el pasaje abajo citado; **here ~** aquí abajo; **en este mundo; 'see ~'** 'véase más abajo'; **it was 5 ~** la temperatura era de 5 grados bajo cero.
2 PREP bajo, debajo de; *(fig)* inferior a; **temperatures ~ normal** temperaturas inferiores a las normales.

Belshazzar [bel'ʃæzəʳ] NM Baltasar; **~'s Feast** la Cena de Baltasar.

belt [belt] **1** N cinturón *m*, fajo *m (Mex)*; *(Mech)* correa *f*, cinta *f*; *(Geog and fig)* zona *f*, región *f*; faja *f*; **a blow below the ~** un golpe bajo; **he has 3 novels under his ~** tiene 3 novelas en su haber; **to tighten one's ~** *(fig)* apretarse el cinturón; **it was a ~-and-braces job*** se tomaron todas las precauciones posibles.
2 VT (*) zurrar, dar una paliza a.
◆**belt along*** VI ir como una bala.
◆**belt down*** VT *(US) drink* cepillarse*.
◆**belt out*** **1** VT *(radio)* emitir muy fuerte; *song* cantar a todo pulmón, cantar a voz en grito; *(band)* tocar muy fuerte.
2 VI *(also* **to come ~ing out**) salir disparado.
◆**belt past** VI pasar como un rayo.
◆**belt up** VI **(a)** *(Aut)* abrocharse el cinturón.
(b) *(Brit*✲*)* callarse, cerrar el pico; **~ up!** ¡calla la boca!

belt bag ['beltbæg] N riñonera *f*.

beltway ['beltweɪ] N *(US)* carretera *f* de circunvalación.

bemoan [bɪ'məʊn] VT lamentar.

bemuse [bɪ'mjuːz] VT aturdir, confundir.

Ben [ben] NM *familiar form of* **Benjamin**.

ben [ben] N *(Scot)* montaña *f*; *(room)* cuarto *m* interior.

bench [bentʃ] N banco *m*; *(Sport)* banquillo *m*; *(court)* tribunal *m*; *(persons)* judicatura *f*; **to be on the ~** *(Jur)* ser juez, ser magistrado; **he's on the ~ today** hoy forma parte del tribunal; **on the Labour ~es** en los escaños laboristas.

benchmark ['bentʃmɑːk] N cota *f*, punto *m* topográfico; **~ price** precio *m* de referencia.

benchwarmer ['bentʃˌwɔːməʳ] N *(US)* calientabanquillos *m*.

bend [bend] **1** N curva *f*; recodo *m*, vuelta *f*; ángulo *m*; *(Her)* banda *f*; *(Naut)* gaza *f*; **~s** *(Med)* apoplejía *f* por cambios bruscos de presión; **to be round the ~** *(Brit*✲*)* estar chiflado; **to go round the ~** *(Brit*✲*)* volverse loco.
2 *(irr: PRET AND PTP* **bent**) VT encorvar; *(buckle)* doblar, torcer; *(cause to sag)* combar; *body, head* inclinar; *knee* doblar; *sail* envergar; *efforts, steps etc* dirigir *(to* a); **to ~ the rule for sb** ajustar la regla a beneficio de uno; **to ~ one's mind to a problem** aplicarse a un problema; **to ~ sb to one's will** doblar a uno a su voluntad.
3 VI encorvarse; *(buckle)* doblarse, torcerse; *(sag)* combarse; *(road)* torcer(se) *(to the left* a la izquierda).
◆**bend back** VT doblar hacia atrás.
◆**bend down 1** VT doblar hacia abajo; *head* inclinar.
2 VI *(person)* encorvarse, inclinarse, agacharse.
◆**bend over** **1** VT doblar.
2 VI *(person)* inclinarse, encorvarse, doblarse *(LAm)*; **to ~ over backwards** *(fig)* hacer lo imposible *(to + infin* por + *infin)*.

bender✲ ['bendəʳ] N: **to go on a ~** ir de juerga, ir de borrachera.

beneath [bɪ'niːθ] ADV AND PREP **(a)** = **below. (b)** *(fig)* **it is ~ him** es indigno de él; **it is ~ him to do such a thing** él es incapaz de hacer tal bajeza; **she married ~ her** se casó con un hombre de clase inferior.

Benedict ['benɪdɪkt] NM Benito; *(pope)* Benedicto.

Benedictine [ˌbenɪ'dɪktɪn] **1** ADJ benedictino.
2 N benedictino *m*.

benediction [ˌbenɪ'dɪkʃən] N bendición *f*.

benefaction [ˌbenɪ'fækʃən] N *(gift)* beneficio *m*.

benefactor ['benɪfæktəʳ] N bienhechor *m*, benefactor *m*.

benefactress ['benɪfæktrɪs] N bienhechora *f*, benefactora *f*.

benefice ['benɪfɪs] N beneficio *m*.

beneficence [bɪ'nefɪsəns] N beneficencia *f*.

beneficent [bɪ'nefɪsənt] ADJ benéfico.

beneficial [ˌbenɪ'fɪʃəl] ADJ provechoso, beneficioso.

beneficially [ˌbenɪ'fɪʃəlɪ] ADV provechosamente, beneficiosamente.

beneficiary [ˌbenɪ'fɪʃərɪ] N beneficiario *m*, -a *f*; *(Eccl)* beneficiado *m*.

benefit ['benɪfɪt] **1** N beneficio *m*; provecho *m*, utilidad *f*; *(payment)* subsidio *m*; *(Theat, Sport)* beneficio *m*; **~ association, ~ society** *(esp US)* sociedad *f* de socorro mutuo, mutualidad *f*; **~ match** partido homenaje *m*, (partido *m* de) beneficio *m*; **~s package** paquete *m* de beneficios; **~ performance** función *f* benéfica; (función *f* de)

beneficio *m*; **for the ~ of** a beneficio de; **(I may say) for your ~ that ...** (y agrego) para tu gobierno que ...; **to be to the ~ of** ser provechoso a; **to give sb the ~ of the doubt** dar a uno el beneficio de la duda; **to have the ~ of** tener la ventaja de; **to marry without ~ of clergy** casarse por lo civil; **to reap the ~ of** sacar el fruto de.
2 VT beneficiar, aprovechar.
3 VI aprovecharse; **to ~ by, to ~ from** sacar provecho de.

Benelux ['benɪlʌks] N Benelux *m*; **the ~ countries** los países del Benelux.

benevolence [bɪ'nevələns] N benevolencia *f*.

benevolent [bɪ'nevələnt] ADJ benévolo; *society* de socorro mutuo; **~ fund** fondos *mpl* benéficos.

benevolently [bɪ'nevələntlɪ] ADV benévolamente, con benevolencia.

B.Eng. [ˌbiː'eŋ] N ABBR *of* **Bachelor of Engineering** licenciado *m*, -a *f* en Ingeniería.

Bengal [beŋ'gɔːl] N Bengala *f*; **~ tiger** tigre *m* de Bengala.

Bengali [beŋ'gɔːlɪ] **1** ADJ bengalí. **2** N bengalí *mf*.

Benghazi [ben'gɑːzɪ] N Bengasi *m*.

benighted [bɪ'naɪtɪd] ADJ *(fig)* ignorante.

benign [bɪ'naɪn] ADJ benigno *(also Med)*.

benignant [bɪ'nɪgnənt] ADJ benigno *(also Med)*; *(healthy)* saludable.

benignly [bɪ'naɪnlɪ] ADV benignamente.

Benjamin ['bendʒəmɪn] NM Benjamín.

benny ['benɪ] N *(Drugs*✲*)* benzedrina *f*.

bent¹ [bent] ADJ, PRET AND PTP *of* **bend**; **(a)** *(curved, twisted)* encorvado; doblado, torcido.
(b) on pleasure ~ empeñado en divertirse; **to be ~ on +** *ger* estar resuelto a + *infin*, estar empeñado en + *infin*; **to be ~ on a quarrel** estar resuelto a provocar una riña.
(c) (✲: *dishonest*) sospechoso; de tendencias criminales; (✲: *perverted*) pervertido; (✲: *homosexual*) invertido.

bent² [bent] N inclinación *f* *(to, towards, for* a); **to follow one's ~** seguir su inclinación; **to have a ~ towards** estar inclinado a.

benumb [bɪ'nʌm] VT entumecer; *(fig)* entorpecer; *mind etc* paralizar.

benumbed [bɪ'nʌmd] ADJ *(cold)* person, fingers entumecido; *(frightened, shocked)* paralizado.

Benzedrine ['benzɪdriːn] ® N benzedrina ® *f*.

benzene ['benziːn] N benceno *m*.

benzine ['benziːn] N bencina *f*.

bequeath [bɪ'kwiːð] VT legar.

bequest [bɪ'kwest] N legado *m*.

berate [bɪ'reɪt] VT censurar; reñir, regañar.

Berber ['bɜːbəʳ] **1** ADJ bereber. **2** N bereber *mf*.

bereave [bɪ'riːv] *(irr: PRET AND PTP* **bereft**) VT privar *(of* de).

bereaved [bɪ'riːvd] ADJ afligido; **the ~** los afligidos; **with the thanks of his ~ family** con el agradecimiento de su desconsolada familia.

bereavement [bɪ'riːvmənt] N aflicción *f* (por la muerte de un pariente); pérdida *f*; luto *m*, duelo *m*.

bereft [bɪ'reft] PTP: **to be ~ of** *(act)* ser privado de, *(state)* estar desprovisto de.

beret ['bereɪ] N boina *f*; **The Red B~s** *(Mil)* los boinas rojas.

bergamot ['bɜːgəmɒt] N bergamota *f*.

beriberi ['berɪˌberɪ] N beriberi *m*.

Bering Sea ['beɪrɪŋ'siː] N Mar *m* de Bering.

berk✲ [bɜːk] N tipo* *m*, tío* *m*; memo* *m*.

berkelium [bɜː'kiːlɪəm] N berkelio *m*.

Berks [bɑːks] N ABBR *of* **Berkshire**.

Berlin [bɜː'lɪn] N Berlín *m*; *(ATTR)* berlinés; **the ~ Wall** el Muro *m* de Berlín; **East ~** Berlín Este; **West ~** Berlín Oeste.

Berliner [bɜː'lɪnəʳ] N berlinés *m*, -esa *f*.

berm [bɜːm] N *(US)* arcén *m*.

Bermuda [bɜː'mjuːdə] N Islas *fpl* Bermudas, las Bermudas; **~ shorts** bermudas *mpl*; **the ~ Triangle** el Triángulo *m* de las Bermudas.

Bern [bɜːn] N Berna *f*.

Bernard ['bɜːnəd] NM Bernardo.

Bernese [bɜː'niːz] ADJ bernés; **~ Alps, ~ Oberland** Alpes *mpl* Berneses.

berry ['berɪ] N baya *f*; *(of coffee)* grano *m*.

berserk [bə'sɜːk] ADJ: **to go ~** perder los estribos; ponerse como una fiera; volverse loco.

Bert [bɜːt] NM *familiar form of* **Albert, Herbert** etc.

berth [bɜːθ] **1** N *(place at wharf)* amarradero *m*; *(place in marina etc)* punto *m* de atraque; *(cabin)* camarote *m*; *(bunk)* litera *f*; (*) puesto *m*, lugar *m*; **to give sb a wide ~** evitar el encuentro de uno, huir el trato de uno.
2 VTI atracar.

beryl ['berɪl] N berilo *m*.

beryllium [be'rɪlɪəm] N berilio *m*.

beseech [bɪ'siːtʃ] *(irr: PRET AND PTP* **besought**) VT suplicar *(for sth* algo, *to do* hacer).

beseeching [bɪ'siːtʃɪŋ] ADJ suplicante.

beseechingly [bɪ'siːtʃɪŋlɪ] ADV en tono *(etc)* de súplica.

beset [bɪ'set] *(irr:* V **set**) VT *person* acosar, perseguir; *road* obstruir, dificultar; **a policy ~ with dangers** una política llena de peligros; **a way ~ with difficulties** un camino erizado de dificultades; **to be ~ by doubts** estar acosado por las dudas.

besetting [bɪ'setɪŋ] ADJ obsesionante; *sin dominante.*

beside [bɪ'saɪd] PREP **(a)** (*at the side of*) cerca de, junto a, al lado de; **to be ~ o.s.** (*with anger*) estar fuera de sí, (*with anxiety*) volverse loco de inquietud. **(b)** (*fig*) **whom can we set ~ him?** ¿con quién podemos compararle?; **what is that ~ victory?** y eso ¿qué importa en comparación con la victoria?

besides [bɪ'saɪdz] **1** ADV además.
2 PREP además de; (*with negation*) excepto, fuera de.

besiege [bɪ'siːdʒ] VT asediar, sitiar; **we are ~d with calls** nos están llamando incesantemente; **we were ~d with inquiries** hubo un torrente de preguntas.

besieger [bɪ'siːdʒər] N sitiador *m.*

besmear [bɪ'smɪər] VT embarrar, embadurnar.

besmirch [bɪ'smɜːtʃ] VT (*fig*) manchar, mancillar.

besom ['biːzəm] N escoba *f.*

besotted [bɪ'sɒtɪd] ADJ entontecido; **~ with alcohol** embrutecido por el alcohol; **~ with love** amartelado, atortolado; encaprichado, encalabrinado; **he is ~ with her** anda loco por ella.

besought [bɪ'sɔːt] PRET AND PTP *of* **beseech.**

bespatter [bɪ'spætər] VT salpicar (*with* de).

bespeak [bɪ'spiːk] (*irr: V* **speak**) VT **(a)** (*engage*) apalabrar; *goods etc* encargar, reservar. **(b)** (*be evidence of*) indicar.

bespectacled [bɪ'spektɪkld] ADJ con gafas, que lleva gafas.

bespoke [bɪ'spəʊk] **1** PRET AND PTP *of* **bespeak.**
2 ADJ (*Brit*): **~ clothing** ropa *f* hecha a la medida; **~ tailor** sastre *m* que confecciona a medida.

bespoken [bɪ'spəʊkən] PTP *of* **bespeak.**

besprinkle [bɪ'sprɪŋkl] VT salpicar, rociar (*with* de); espolvorear (*with* de).

Bess [bes], **Bessie, Bessy** ['besɪ] NF *familiar forms of* **Elizabeth** (Isabelita); **Good Queen Bess** (*Brit*) la buena reina Isabel.

best [best] **1** ADJ SUPERL (el, la) mejor; **the ~ one of all** el mejor de todos; **to know what is ~ for sb** saber lo que más le conviene a uno; **'~ by 31 May'** 'consumir de preferencia antes del 31 mayo', 'consumir preferentemente antes del 31 mayo'; **'~ before date'** fecha *f* de consumo preferente.
2 ADV SUPERL (lo) mejor; **as ~ I could** lo mejor que pude; **she did ~ of all in the test** ella hizo el test mejor que nadie; **I had ~ go** más vale que yo vaya; **I had ~ see him at once** sería aconsejable verle en seguida; **you know ~** Vd sabe mejor que yo; **Mummy knows ~** estas cosas las decide mamá, mamá sabe lo que más conviene; **when it comes to hotels I know ~** yo soy el más experto en asunto de hoteles; **to come off ~** salir ganando.
3 N **(a)** lo mejor; **the ~ of it is that ...** lo mejor del caso es que ...; **is that the ~ you can do?** y eso ¿es todo lo que Vd puede hacer?; **we have had the ~ of the day** el buen tiempo se acabó por hoy; **'my ~'** (*US: ending letter*), **'all the ~'** 'un abrazo'; **all the ~!** (*as farewell*) ¡que tengas suerte!; **all the ~ to Jim!** ¡recuerdos para Jim!
(b) (*phrases with prep*) **at ~, at the ~** a lo más, en el mejor de los casos; **the garden is at its ~ in June** es en junio cuando el jardín luce más; **he wasn't at his ~** no estuvo en forma; **it's boring at the ~ of times** en el mejor de los casos es aburrido; **it's all for the ~** todo conduce al bien a la larga; **I acted for the ~** obré con la mejor intención; **we drank of the ~** bebimos el mejor vino (*etc*); **I can sing with the ~ (of them)** yo canto como el que más.
(c) (*phrases with verb*) **to do one's ~** hacer todo lo posible, hacerlo lo mejor posible; **to do one's ~ to + *infin*** hacer todo lo posible para (*or* por) + *infin*; **I'll do it as ~ I can** lo haré lo mejor que pueda; **to get the ~ of it** salir ganando, imponerse; **to get the ~ of the bargain** llevarse la mejor parte, salir ganando; **in order to get the ~ out of the car** para obtener el máximo rendimiento del coche; **to have the ~ of both worlds** tenerlo todo, tener ventajas por ambas partes; **to look one's ~** mostrarse en todo su esplendor; **she's not looking her ~** está algo desmejorada; **to make the ~ of it** salir de un mal negocio lo mejor posible; **to play ~ of three** jugar al mejor de tres; **I try to think the ~ of him** procuro conservar mi buena opinión de él.
4 VT vencer.

best boy ['best'bɔɪ] N (*Cine*) ayudante *mf* (*de rodaje*), meritorio *m*, -a *f.*

bestial ['bestɪəl] ADJ bestial.

bestiality [ˌbestɪ'ælɪtɪ] N bestialidad *f.*

bestir [bɪ'stɜːr] VR: **to ~ o.s.** menearse.

best man [ˌbest'mæn] N, PL **best men** [ˌbest'men] (*at wedding*) ≃ padrino *m* de boda, testigo *m* del novio.

┌─ *BEST MAN* ─┐

ⓘ *En una boda tradicional el novio (**bridegroom**) va acompañado del **best man**, un amigo íntimo o un pariente cercano que tiene la responsabilidad de asegurarse de que todo marche bien en el día de la boda*

(**wedding-day**). *No hay pues, madrina. El **best man** se encarga, entre otras cosas, de llevar al novio a la iglesia a tiempo, de dar la bienvenida a los invitados y de los anillos de boda. En el banquete de boda (**wedding reception**) lee los telegramas enviados por los que no han podido asistir, presenta los discursos que vayan a dar algunos invitados, da su propio discurso, casi siempre en clave de humor y sobre el novio, y propone un brindis por la pareja de recién casados (**newly-weds**).*

bestow [bɪ'stəʊ] VT (*grant*) otorgar (*on* a); (*give*) conceder, dar (*on* a); *affections* ofrecer (*on* a); *compliment* hacer (*on* a).

bestowal [bɪ'stəʊəl] N otorgamiento *m*; donación *f*; ofrecimiento *m.*

bestraddle [bɪ'strædl] VT montar a horcajadas, estar a horcajadas sobre; (*fig*) estar a caballo sobre.

bestrew [bɪ'struː] (*irr: V* **strew**) VT *things* desparramar, esparcir; *surface* sembrar, cubrir (*with* de).

bestridden [bɪ'strɪdn] PTP *of* **bestride.**

bestride [bɪ'straɪd] (*irr: V* **stride**) VT *horse* montar a horcajadas; *stream etc* cruzar de un tranco; (*fig*) dominar.

bestrode [bɪ'strəʊd] PRET *of* **bestride.**

best-seller ['best'selər] N bestseller *m*, éxito *m* de librería.

best-selling ['best'selɪŋ] ADJ: **our ~ line** nuestro producto de mayor venta, nuestro campeón de ventas; **for years it was the ~ car** durante años fue el coche que más se vendió.

bet [bet] **1** N apuesta *f*; (*sum*) postura *f*; **to lay** (*or* **make, put**) **a ~ on** apostar a; **it's a good ~ that he'll come** seguramente vendrá, es casi seguro que vendrá; **your best ~ is to come today** lo mejor que puedes hacer es venir hoy.
2 (*irr:* PRET AND PTP **bet** *or* **betted**) VT apostar (*on* a); **I ~ you a fiver that ...** te apuesto 5 libras a que ...; **I'll ~ you anything you like!** ¡apuesto lo que quieras!; **you ~ (your life)!** ¡ya lo creo!
3 VI apostar, jugar; **I ~ you can't!** ¡a que no puedes!; **I ~ it isn't!** ¡a que no!; **I don't ~** yo no juego; **don't ~ on it, I wouldn't ~ on it** eso no es tan seguro, no hay que contar con eso.

beta ['biːtə] N beta *f.*

betake [bɪ'teɪk] (*irr: V* **take**) VR: **to ~ o.s. to** dirigirse a, trasladarse a, acudir a.

betaken [bɪ'teɪkən] PTP *of* **betake.**

betel ['biːtəl] N betel *m.*

bête noire ['beɪt'nwɑːr] N bestia *f* negra, pesadilla *f.*

bethink [bɪ'θɪŋk] (*irr: V* **think**) VR: **to ~ o.s. of** acordarse de.

Bethlehem ['beθlɪhem] N Belén *m.*

bethought [bɪ'θɔːt] PRET AND PTP *of* **bethink.**

betide [bɪ'taɪd] VTI acontecer; *V* **woe.**

betimes [bɪ'taɪmz] ADV (*liter*) (*early*) temprano, al alba; (*quickly*) rápidamente; (*in good time*) a tiempo.

betoken [bɪ'təʊkən] VT presagiar, anunciar.

betook [bɪ'tʊk] PRET *of* **betake.**

betray [bɪ'treɪ] VT **(a)** *person, country* traicionar; **to ~ sb to the enemy** vender a uno al enemigo; **his accent ~s him** su acento le traiciona; **his accent ~s him as a foreigner** su acento le acusa de extranjero. **(b)** (*reveal*) *plot etc* revelar, delatar; *ignorance etc* hacer patente. **(c)** (*show signs of*) dejar ver, dar muestras de, descubrir; **his face ~ed a certain surprise** su cara acusó cierto asombro.

betrayal [bɪ'treɪəl] N **(a)** traición *f*; **~ of trust** abuso *m* de confianza. **(b)** revelación *f*. **(c)** descubrimiento *m.*

betrayer [bɪ'treɪər] N traidor *m*, -ora *f*; **she killed her ~** mató a quien la traicionó.

betroth [bɪ'trəʊð] VT (*liter*) prometer en matrimonio (*to* a); **to be ~ed** (*act*) desposarse, (*state*) estar desposado.

betrothal [bɪ'trəʊðəl] N (*liter*) desposorios *mpl*, esponsales *mpl.*

betrothed [bɪ'trəʊðd] (*liter, hum*) **1** ADJ prometido.
2 N, PL INVAR prometido *m*, -a *f.*

▼ **better**[1] ['betər] **1** ADJ COMP mejor; **~ and ~** cada vez mejor; **that's ~** eso va mejor, más vale así; **that's ~!** ¡bien!; **he's much ~** (*Med*) está mucho mejor; **it couldn't be ~** no podría ser mejor; **it is ~ to + *infin*** más vale + *infin*; **it would be ~ to + *infin*** más valdría + *infin*, sería aconsejable + *infin*; **she's no ~ than she ought to be** es una mujer que tiene historia; **to get ~** mejorar(se), (*Med*) mejorar(se), reponerse; **to go one ~** hacer mejor todavía (*than* que).
2 ADV COMP mejor; **all the ~, so much the ~** tanto mejor (*for* para); **to be all the ~ for** haber mejorado mucho a consecuencia de; **it would be all the ~ for a drop of paint** no le vendría mal una mano de pintura; **they withdrew the ~ to resist** se retiraron para poder resistir mejor; **they are ~ off than we are** son más acomodados que nosotros; **I had ~ go** más vale que yo vaya; **but he knew ~** pero él cree que se lo sabe todo; **he thinks he knows ~** él cree que se lo sabe todo; **at his age he ought to know ~** a la edad que tiene debiera saberlo; **he knows ~ than the experts** él sabe más que los expertos; **to think ~ of it** mudar de parecer, cambiar de idea.
3 N **(a) my ~s** mis superiores.
(b) it's a change for the ~ es un cambio beneficioso; **for ~ or**

worse en la fortuna como en la adversidad; **to get the ~ of** vencer, quedar por encima de.
　4 VT mejorar; *record, score* superar.
　5 VR: **to ~ o.s.** mejorar su posición.
better² ['betə^r] N apostador *m*, -ora *f*.
betterment ['betəmənt] N mejora *f*, mejoramiento *m*.
betting ['betɪŋ] 1 ADJ aficionado al juego; **I'm not a ~ man** yo no juego.
　2 N juego *m*, el apostar.
betting-shop ['betɪŋˌʃɒp] N (*Brit*) agencia *f* de apuestas.
betting-slip ['betɪŋslɪp] N (*Brit*) boleto *m* de apuestas.
betting-tax ['betɪŋˌtæks] N impuesto *m* sobre las apuestas.
bettor ['betə^r] N (*US*) apostante *mf*.
Betty ['betɪ] NF *familiar form of* **Elizabeth** (Isabelita).
between [bɪ'twiːn] 1 ADV (*also* **in ~**) en medio.
　2 PREP entre; **~ ourselves** entre nosotros; **~ you and me** entre tú y yo; **we bought it ~ 4 of us** lo compramos entre los 4; **they shared it ~ them** se lo repartieron; **~ now and May** de ahora a mayo; **the shops are shut ~ 2 and 4** las tiendas están cerradas de 2 a 4.
betweentimes [bɪ'twiːntaɪmz] ADV, **betweenwhiles** [bɪ'twiːnwaɪlz] ADV mientras, entretanto.
betwixt [bɪ'twɪkst] 1 ADV en medio; **~ and between** entre lo uno y lo otro.
　2 PREP entre; en medio de.
bevel ['bevəl] 1 ADJ biselado.
　2 N (*tool: also* **~ edge**) cartabón *m*, escuadra *f* falsa; (*surface*) bisel *m*.
　3 VT biselar.
bevel-edged [ˌbevl'edʒd] ADJ biselado.
beverage ['bevərɪdʒ] N bebida *f*.
bevvy* ['bevɪ] N trago* *m*.
bevy ['bevɪ] N (*birds*) bandada *f*; (*women etc*) grupo *m*.
bewail [bɪ'weɪl] VT lamentar.
beware [bɪ'weə^r] VI (a) tener cuidado; **to ~ of** precaverse de, tener cuidado con, guardarse de.
　(b) **~!** ¡cuidado!, ¡atención!, ¡ojo!; **~ of the dog!** ¡ojo con el perro!, (*as notice*) 'perro peligroso'; **~ of pickpockets!** ¡ojo con los carteristas!; **~ of imitations** desconfíe de las imitaciones.
bewhiskered [bɪ'wɪskəd] ADJ bigotudo.
bewilder [bɪ'wɪldə^r] VT aturdir, dejar perplejo, aturrullar, desconcertar.
bewildered [bɪ'wɪldəd] ADJ *person* desconcertado, perplejo, aturdido; **he gave me a ~ look** me miró perplejo.
bewildering [bɪ'wɪldərɪŋ] ADJ desconcertante.
bewilderingly [bɪ'wɪldərɪŋlɪ] ADV de modo desconcertante; **a ~ complicated matter** un asunto tan complicado que desconcierta.
bewilderment [bɪ'wɪldəmənt] N aturdimiento *m*, perplejidad *f*.
bewitch [bɪ'wɪtʃ] VT hechizar (*also fig*).
bewitching [bɪ'wɪtʃɪŋ] ADJ hechicero, encantador.
bewitchingly [bɪ'wɪtʃɪŋlɪ] ADV encantadoramente; **~ beautiful** encantadoramente hermoso.
beyond [bɪ'jɒnd] 1 ADV más allá, más lejos; **next year and ~** el año que viene y después.
　2 PREP (a) (*in space, time*) más allá de; **~ the seas** allende los mares; **we can't see ~ 2010** no podemos ver más allá de 2010.
　(b) (*over and above*) además de, fuera de.
　(c) (*fig*) **the task is ~ him** la tarea es superior a sus fuerzas; **it's ~ me** está fuera de mi alcance, no lo entiendo; **it's ~ me to see how** no alcanzo a ver cómo; **this is getting ~ me** se me está haciendo imposible esto; **it's ~ a doubt** está fuera de toda duda; **it's ~ praise** queda por encima de todo elogio; **to go ~ one's authority** exceder a su autoridad.
　3 N: **the great ~** el más allá.
bezique [bɪ'ziːk] N *juego de cartas que se juega con dos mazos*.
BF* N (*euph*) ABBR *of* **bloody fool**.
b/f ABBR *of* **brought forward** suma *f* del anterior.
BFPO N (*Brit Mil*) ABBR *of* **British Forces Post Office**.
b/fwd = **b/f**.
b.h.p. N ABBR *of* **brake horsepower** potencia *f* al freno.
Bhutan [buː'tɑːn] N Bután *m*.
bi... [baɪ] PREF bi...
Biafra [bɪ'æfrə] N Biafra *f*.
Biafran [bɪ'æfrən] 1 ADJ de Biafra.
　2 N nativo *m*, -a *f* (*or* habitante *mf*) de Biafra.
biannual [baɪ'ænjʊəl] ADJ semestral.
biannually ['baɪ'ænjʊəlɪ] ADV semestralmente, dos veces al año.
bias ['baɪəs] 1 N (a) (*Sew*) sesgo *m*, diagonal *f*; **to cut sth on the ~** cortar algo al sesgo.
　(b) (*inclination*) propensión *f*, predisposición *f* (*to, towards* a); **to have a ~ towards** tener propensión a, estar inclinado a.
　(c) (*prejudice*) pasión *f*, prejuicio *m* (*against* contra).
　2 VT (*fig*) influir en, torcer; **to ~ sb against sth** predisponer a uno en contra de algo; **to be ~sed** tener prejuicio (*against* contra), ser

partidario (*in favour of* de).
bias(s)ed ['baɪəst] ADJ parcial.
biathlon [baɪ'æθlən] N biatlón *m*.
bib [bɪb] N babero *m*, babador *m*; **in one's best ~ and tucker** acicalado, engalanado.
Bible ['baɪbl] N Biblia *f*; **the Holy ~** la Santa Biblia; **~ Belt** (*US*) Estados del Sur ultraprotestantes; **~ class** (*for confirmation etc*) catecismo *m*; **~ college** (*US*) colegio *m* evangelista; **~ school** (*US*) escuela *f* de enseñanza de la Biblia; **~ stories** historias *fpl* de la Biblia; **~ study** estudio *m* de la Biblia; **~ thumper** (*) fanático *m* religioso, fundamentalista *mf*.
Biblical ['bɪblɪkəl] ADJ bíblico.
biblio... ['bɪblɪəʊ] PREF biblio...
bibliographer [ˌbɪblɪ'ɒɡrəfə^r] N bibliógrafo *m*, -a *f*.
bibliographic(al) [ˌbɪblɪəʊ'ɡræfɪk(əl)] ADJ bibliográfico.
bibliography [ˌbɪblɪ'ɒɡrəfɪ] N bibliografía *f*.
bibliomania [ˌbɪblɪəʊ'meɪnɪə] N bibliomanía *f*.
bibliometric [ˌbɪblɪəʊ'metrɪk] ADJ bibliométrico.
bibliometry [ˌbɪblɪ'ɒmɪtrɪ] N bibliometría *f*.
bibliophile ['bɪblɪəʊfaɪl] N bibliófilo *m*, -a *f*.
bibulous ['bɪbjʊləs] ADJ bebedor, borrachín.
bicameral [baɪ'kæmərəl] ADJ bicameral.
bicarb* [baɪ'kɑːb] N, **bicarbonate of soda** [baɪ'kɑːbənɪtəv'səʊdə] N bicarbonato *m* sódico.
bicentenary [ˌbaɪsen'tiːnərɪ], (*US*) **bicentennial** [baɪsen'tenɪəl] 1 ADJ (de) bicentenario; **~ celebrations** celebraciones *fpl* de(l) bicentenario.
　2 N bicentenario *m*.
biceps ['baɪseps] N, PL INVAR bíceps *m*.
bicker ['bɪkə^r] VI reñir, altercar; (*stream*) murmurar.
bickering ['bɪkərɪŋ] N riñas *fpl*, altercados *mpl*.
bicuspid [baɪ'kʌspɪd] 1 ADJ bicúspide.
　2 N bicúspide *m*.
bicycle ['baɪsɪkl] 1 N bicicleta *f*.
　2 VI ir en bicicleta; **to ~ to Dover** ir en bicicleta a Dover.
　3 ATTR: **~ chain** cadena *f* de bicicleta; **~ clip** pinza *f* para ir en bicicleta; **~ kick** chilena *f*, tijereta *f*; **~ lane**, **~ track** carril *m* para ciclistas; **~ pump** bomba *f* de bicicleta; **~ rack** soporte *m* para bicicleta; **~ shed** cobertizo *m* para bicicletas; **~ touring** turismo *m* en bicicleta.
bicyclist ['baɪsɪklɪst] N (†) ciclista *mf*.
bid [bɪd] 1 N (a) (*at auction*) oferta *f*, postura *f*; (*Fin*) oferta *f*; **~ price** precio *m* de oferta; **highest ~** mejor postura *f*.
　(b) (*Cards*) marca *f*; apuesta *f*, declaración *f*; **no ~** paso.
　(c) (*fig*) tentativa *f*, conato *m*; **to make a ~ for control of** tratar de asegurar el control de; **to make a ~ to** + *infin* hacer una tentativa de + *infin*.
　2 (*irr*: PRET **bade**, **bid**, PTP **bidden**, **bid**) VT (a) (*order*) ordenar, mandar; **to ~ sb to do sth** mandar a uno hacer algo.
　(b) (*at auction*) licitar, ofrecer; **to ~ £10 for** ofrecer 10 libras por; **to ~ sb up to £12** hacer que uno siga haciendo posturas hasta 12 libras.
　(c) (*Cards*) marcar, pujar, declarar.
　(d) (*say*) **to ~ sb good-day** dar a uno los buenos días; **to ~ defiance to** desafiar a; **V adieu**.
　3 VI (a) (*at auction*) **to ~ for** pujar por, hacer una oferta por; **to ~ up** pujar.
　(b) **to ~ fair to** + *infin* prometer + *infin*, dar esperanzas de + *infin*.
biddable ['bɪdəbl] ADJ (a) obediente, sumiso. (b) (*Cards*) marcable.
bidden ['bɪdn] PTP *of* **bid**.
bidder ['bɪdə^r] N (a) (*at auction*) postor *m*, -ora *f*; (*Fin*) ofertante *mf*; postor *m*, -ora *f*; **highest ~** mejor postor *m*. (b) (*Cards*) declarante *mf*.
bidding ['bɪdɪŋ] N (a) (*order*) orden *f*, mandato *m*; **they did it at her ~** lo hicieron cumpliendo su orden; **to do sb's ~** cumplir el mandato de uno.
　(b) (*at auction*) licitación *f*, ofertas *fpl*; **the ~ opened at £5** la primera oferta fue de 5 libras; **there was keen ~ for the picture** hubo una rápida serie de ofertas por el cuadro; **to raise** (*or* **up**) **the ~** aumentar la licitación.
　(c) (*Cards*) remate *m*, declaración *f*; **to open the ~** abrir la declaración.
　(d) (*Eccl; also* **~ prayers**) oraciones *fpl* de los fieles.
biddy ['bɪdɪ] N († *or dial*) vieja bruja *f*.
bide [baɪd] VT: **to ~ one's time** esperar la hora propicia.
bidet ['biːdeɪ] N bidet *m*, bidé *m*.
bidirectional [baɪdɪ'rekʃənl] ADJ bidireccional.
biennial [baɪ'enɪəl] 1 ADJ bienal; (*Bot*) bianual.
　2 N planta *f* bienal, bianual *m*.
biennially [baɪ'enɪəlɪ] ADV bienalmente, cada dos años.
bier [bɪə^r] N féretro *m*, andas *fpl*.
biff* [bɪf] 1 N bofetada *f*.

2 VT dar una bofetada a.

bifocal ['baɪ'fəukəl] 1 ADJ bifocal.
2 N lente *m* bifocal; **~s** bifocales *mpl*.

bifurcate ['baɪfəkeɪt] VI bifurcarse.

big [bɪg] 1 ADJ (a) grande; abultado, voluminoso; importante; **the B~ Apple** la Gran Manzana, *Nueva York*; **~ band** orquesta *f*, big band *f*; **the ~ bang** (*Fin, Phys*) el big bang *m*, la gran explosión *f*; **~ bang theory** teoría *f* de la gran explosión; **B~ Ben** Big Ben *m*; **my ~ brother** mi hermano mayor; **B~ Brother is watching you** el Gran Hermano te vigila; **~ cat** felino *m* mayor; **~ city** ciudad *f* grande; **~ city problems** problemas *mpl* de las grandes urbes; **the B~ Easy** Nueva Orleans; **the B~ Eight/Ten** (*US*) las ocho/diez grandes universidades del Centro-Oeste; **~ end** (*Aut*) cabeza *f* (or pie *m*) de biela; **the B~ Four** (*Pol*) las cuatro Grandes (Potencias), (*Fin*) los cuatro Grandes (Bancos); **~ game** (*Brit*) caza *f* mayor; **~ game hunter** cazador *m*, -ora *f* de caza mayor; **the ~ house** la casa principal (de un pueblo *etc*); **the ~ match** el partido principal; **Mr B~** Número *m* Uno; **~ noise, ~ shot** (*Brit***)** pez *m* gordo**;** **a ~ one** (*US***:**) un billete de 1.000 dólares; **~ top** carpa *f*; **it's a ~ shame** es una terrible lástima; **that's ~ money** eso es mucho dinero; **when you're ~** cuando seas mayor; **to earn ~ money** ganar mucho dinero; **to have ~ ideas** tener ideas grandiosas; **boots are ~ this year*** las botas están de moda este año; **to be ~ with child** estar encinta; *ver también* [CITY NICKNAMES] . **(b)** (**:** *generous*) amable; generoso; **that's very ~ of you** eres muy amable; *V* **dipper²**, **name 1 (c)** *etc*.
2 ADV (*) **to go over ~** tener un exitazo*; **to talk ~** darse mucha importancia, fanfarronear, darse bombo; **to think ~** hacer proyectos de gran envergadura.

bigamist ['bɪgəmɪst] N bígamo *m*, -a *f*.

bigamous ['bɪgəməs] ADJ bígamo.

bigamy ['bɪgəmɪ] N bigamia *f*.

big-boned [,bɪg'bəund] ADJ de huesos grandes, huesudo.

biggie* ['bɪgɪ] N (*song, film*) gran éxito *m*; (*outstanding person, company*) uno *m*, -a *f* de los grandes; **some ~ in drugs** uno de los grandes en lo de las drogas.

biggish ['bɪgɪʃ] ADJ bastante grande.

bighead* ['bɪghed] N orgulloso *m*, -a *f*, engreído *m*, -a *f*.

bigheaded* ['bɪg'hedɪd] ADJ engreído.

big-hearted ['bɪg'hɑːtɪd] ADJ generoso.

bight [baɪt] N (a) (*Geog*) ensenada *f*, cala *f*; (*bend*) recodo *m*. (b) (*of rope*) gaza *f*, laza *f*.

bigmouth: ['bɪgmauθ] N, PL **bigmouths** ['bɪgmauðz] (*talkative*) bocazas**:** *mf*; (*gossipy*) chismoso *m*, -a *f*; (*treacherous*) soplón *m*.

big-mouthed ['bɪg'mauθt] ADJ (a) de boca grande, de boca ancha, bocudo. (b) (**:**) bocón; chismoso; soplón.

bigot ['bɪgət] N fanático *m*, -a *f*, intolerante *mf*.

bigoted ['bɪgətɪd] ADJ fanático, intolerante.

bigotry ['bɪgətrɪ] N fanatismo *m*, intolerancia *f*.

big-ticket ['bɪg,tɪkɪt] ADJ (*US*): **~ item** artículo de lujo.

big-time* ['bɪg'taɪm] ADJ de rumbo, de muchas campanillas; importante, poderoso.

bigwig ['bɪgwɪg] N pez *m* gordo, señorón *m*.

bijou ['biːʒuː] *as* ADJ: '**~ residence for sale**' (*Brit*) 'residencia coquetona en venta'.

bike* [baɪk] 1 N bici* *f*; **~ rack** (*US*) soporte *m* para bicicletas; **on your ~!*** ¡largo de aquí!*, ¡andando!*
2 VI ir en bicicleta, ir en moto.

biker* ['baɪkər] N motorista *mf*.

bikeshed ['baɪkʃed] N cobertizo *m* para bicicletas.

bikeway ['baɪkweɪ] N (*lane*) carril *m* de bicicletas; (*track*) pista *f* de ciclismo.

bikini [bɪ'kiːnɪ] N bikini *m*, biquini *m*.

bilabial [baɪ'leɪbɪəl] ADJ, N bilabial *f*.

bilateral [baɪ'lætərəl] ADJ bilateral.

bilberry ['bɪlbərɪ] N arándano *m*.

bile [baɪl] N bilis *f*; (*fig*) mal genio *m*, displicencia *f*.

bilge [bɪldʒ] N (a) (*Naut*) pantoque *m*; (*water*) aguas *fpl* de pantoque. (b) (**:**) tonterías *fpl*.

bilge-water ['bɪldʒwɔːtər] N aguas *fpl* de pantoque.

bilharzia [bɪl'hɑːzɪə] N, **bilharziasis** [,bɪlhɑː'zaɪəsɪs] N bilharciasis *f*, bilarciasis *f*.

bilingual [baɪ'lɪŋgwəl] ADJ bilingüe.

bilingualism [baɪ'lɪŋgwəlɪzəm] N bilingüismo *m*.

bilious ['bɪlɪəs] ADJ bilioso (*also fig*); **~ attack** trastorno *m* biliar; **to be (or feel) ~** tener un trastorno biliar.

biliousness ['bɪlɪəsnɪs] N trastornos *mpl* biliares.

bilk [bɪlk] VT estafar, defraudar.

bill¹ [bɪl] 1 N (a) (*bird's*) pico *m*; (*of anchor*) uña *f*, (*Agr*) podadera *f*, podón *m*; (*Geog*) promontorio *m*.
2 VI: **to ~ and coo** besuquearse, acariciarse.

bill² [bɪl] 1 N (a) (*esp Brit*) (*account*) cuenta *f*, adición *f* (*SC*); (*invoice*) factura *f*; **wages ~** (*in industry*) coste *m* de salarios; **~s discounted**

efectos *mpl* descontados; **~s payable** efectos *mpl* a pagar; **~s receivable** efectos *mpl* a cobrar; **to foot the ~** pagar la cuenta; correr con los gastos.
(b) (*Parl*) proyecto *m* de ley; **~ of rights** declaración *f* de derechos, ley *f* fundamental; **to fill the ~** llenar los requisitos, servir; **the ~ passed the Commons** (*Brit*) el proyecto de ley fue aprobado en la Cámara de los Comunes.
(c) (*US: banknote*) billete *m*; **~ (of exchange)** letra *f* de cambio.
(d) (*notice*) cartel *m*; '**stick no ~s**' 'prohibido fijar carteles'.
(e) **~ of fare** lista *f* (de platos), menú *m*; **clean ~ of health** (*Naut, fig*) patente *f* de sanidad; **~ of lading** conocimiento *m* de embarque; **~ of sale** escritura *f* de venta.
2 VT (a) (*Theat*) anunciar; **he is ~ed to appear next week** figura en el programa de la semana que viene.
(b) (*Comm*) **to ~ sb for sth** extender (*or* pasar) a uno la factura de algo; **you've ~ed me for 5 instead of 4** Vd ha puesto 5 y no 4 en la factura.

┌─ **BILL OF RIGHTS** ─────────────────────────────────┐

*El conjunto de las diez enmiendas (**amendments**) originales a la Constitución de los Estados Unidos, en vigor desde 1791, recibe el nombre de Bill of Rights. Aquí se enumeran los derechos que tiene todo ciudadano norteamericano y se definen algunos de los poderes de los gobiernos estatales y federal. Se incluyen, por ejemplo, el derecho a la libertad de culto, de asociación y de prensa (**First Amendment**), el derecho a llevar armas (**Second Amendment**) y el derecho a un juicio justo (**Sixth Amendment**). Entre las enmiendas hechas a la Constitución después de 1791 están el derecho a la igualdad de protección legal para todos los ciudadanos (**Fourteenth Amendment**) y el derecho al voto (**Fifteenth Amendment**).*

⇨ Ver también [AMENDMENT - FIFTH AMENDMENT]

└──┘

Bill [bɪl] NM *familiar form of* **William**; **the (Old) ~** (*Brit***:**) la pasma**:**, la policía; **~ shop:** comisaría *f*.

billboard ['bɪlbɔːd] N (*esp US*) cartelera *f*, valla *f* publicitaria.

billet¹ ['bɪlɪt] 1 N alojamiento *m*; (*) colocación *f*, puesto *m*.
2 VT alojar (*on* en casa de, a, con).

billet² ['bɪlɪt] N (*wood*) leño *m*.

billet-doux ['bɪleɪ'duː] N, PL **billets-doux** ['bɪleɪ'duː] carta *f* amorosa.

billeting ['bɪlətɪŋ] N acantonamiento *m*; **~ officer** oficial *m* de acantonamiento.

billfold ['bɪlfəuld] N (*US*) billetero *m*, cartera *f*.

billhook ['bɪlhuk] N podadera *f*, podón *m*.

billiard-ball ['bɪlɪəd,bɔːl] N bola *f* de billar.

billiard-cue ['bɪlɪəd,kjuː] N taco *m*.

billiards ['bɪlɪədz] N SING billar *m*.

billiard(s) saloon ['bɪlɪəd(z)sə,luːn] N (*Brit*) salón *m* de billar, billares *mpl*.

billiard-table ['bɪlɪəd,teɪbl] N mesa *f* de billar.

billing¹ ['bɪlɪŋ] N: **to get top/second ~** (*Theat*) ser primero/segundo de cartel.

billing² ['bɪlɪŋ] N: **~ and cooing** besuqueo *m*, caricias *fpl*.

billion ['bɪlɪən] N billón *m*, (*US, now frequent in Britain*) mil millones *mpl*; **I've told you a ~ times** te lo he dicho infinidad de veces.

billionaire [,bɪlɪə'nɛər] N billonario *m*, -a *f*.

billow ['bɪləu] 1 N oleada *f*; **~s** las olas, el mar.
2 VI ondular, ondear.
◆ **billow out** VI hincharse (de viento *etc*).

billowy ['bɪləuɪ] ADJ ondoso; hinchado.

billposter ['bɪl,pəustər] N, **billsticker** ['bɪl,stɪkər] N cartelero *m*, pegador *m* de carteles.

Billy ['bɪlɪ] NM *familiar form of* **William**.

billy ['bɪlɪ] N (*US: also* **~ club**) porra *f*.

billy-can ['bɪlɪ,kæn] N cazo *m*.

billy goat ['bɪlɪgəut] N macho *m* cabrío.

billy-ho* ['bɪlɪhəu] ADV: **like ~** hasta más no poder.

billy-o(h)* ['bɪlɪəu] ADV (*Brit*): **like ~** a todo tren*, a más no poder*; **it's raining like billy-o** llueve a más no poder.

BIM N ABBR *of* **British Institute of Management**.

bimbo: ['bɪmbəu] N jai**:** *f*, gachí**:** *f*, (*pej*) putilla *f*.

bimonthly ['baɪ'mʌnθlɪ] 1 ADJ (*every 2 months*) bimestral; (*twice monthly*) bimensual, quincenal.
2 ADV bimestralmente; bimensualmente, quincenalmente.
3 N revista *f* bimestral; revista *f* bimensual, revista *f* quincenal.

bin [bɪn] 1 N hucha *f*, arcón *m*; (*for bread*) caja *f*; (*Brit: for rubbish*) cubo *m*, tacho *m* (*LAm*); (*for litter*) papelera *f*.
2 VT tirar.

binary ['baɪnərɪ] ADJ binario; **~ code** código *m* binario; **~ notation** notación *f* binaria; **~ number** número *m* binario; **~ system** sistema *m* binario.

bind [baɪnd] (*irr:* PRET AND PTP **bound**) 1 VT (a) (*tie*) atar, liar (*to* a); *hands* atar; *wound* vendar; (*Sew*) ribetear; *corn* agavillar; *book*

encuadernar; (*Med*) estreñir; (*encircle*) rodear (*with* de), ceñir (*with* con, de); (*fig*) liar (*to* a), unir (*to* con).
(b) (*force*) obligar; **to ~ sb to do sth** obligar a uno a hacer algo; **to ~ sb to a promise** obligar a uno a cumplir su promesa; **to ~ sb apprentice to** poner a uno de aprendiz con; V *also* **bound**[1].
2 VI (*cement etc*) endurecerse; cuajarse; adherirse; (*parts of machine*) trabarse.
3 N (*Brit**) (*difficulty*) apuro *m*; situación *f* difícil; (*problem*) pega *f*, problema *m*; **the ~ is that ...** el problema es que ...; **it's a ~** es una lata*; **what a ~!** ¡qué lata!*; **to be in a ~** estar en apuros.
◆ **bind on** VT prender.
◆ **bind over** VT obligar a comparecer ante el magistrado; **to ~ sb over for 6 months** conceder a uno la libertad bajo fianza durante 6 meses; **to ~ sb over to +** *infin* imponer a uno el deber legal de + *infin*.
◆ **bind together** VT atar, liar; (*fig*) vincular.
◆ **bind up** VT *wound* vendar; V **bound**.
binder ['baɪndəʳ] N (*Agr*) agavilladora *f*; (*file*) carpeta *f*; (*of book*) encuadernador *m*, -ora *f*.
bindery ['baɪndərɪ] N taller *m* de encuadernación.
binding ['baɪndɪŋ] **1** ADJ **(a)** *rule etc* obligatorio (*on* a, para); *promise* que hay que cumplir; *decision* vinculante (*on* para); **legally ~** de obligatoriedad jurídica. **(b)** (*Med*) que estriñe.
2 N (*of book*) encuadernación *f*; (*Sew*) ribete *m*.
bindweed ['baɪndwiːd] N convólvulo *m*, enredadera *f*.
binge* [bɪndʒ] N (*drunken*) borrachera *f*; (*of eating*) comilona* *f*, exceso *m* gastronómico; **to go on a ~** ir de juerga.
bingo ['bɪŋgəʊ] **1** N (*game*) bingo *m*.
2 EXCL ¡premio!
bingo-hall ['bɪŋgəʊˌhɔːl] N bingo *m*.
bin-liner ['bɪnlaɪnəʳ] N bolsa *f* de la basura.
binnacle ['bɪnəkl] N bitácora *f*.
binocular [bɪ'nɒkjʊləʳ] **1** ADJ binocular.
2 NPL: **~s** gemelos *mpl*, binoculares *mpl*, prismáticos *mpl*, (*Mil*) anteojo *m* de campaña.
binomial [baɪ'nəʊmɪəl] **1** ADJ de dos términos.
2 N binomio *m*.
bint‡ [bɪnt] N jai‡ *f*.
binuclear [baɪ'njuːklɪəʳ] ADJ binuclear.
bio... ['baɪəʊ] PREF bio...
bioactive ['baɪəʊ'æktɪv] ADJ bioactivo.
biochemical ['baɪəʊ'kemɪkəl] ADJ bioquímico.
biochemist ['baɪəʊ'kemɪst] N bioquímico *mf*.
biochemistry ['baɪəʊ'kemɪstrɪ] N bioquímica *f*.
biodegradable [ˌbaɪədɪ'greɪdəbl] ADJ biodegradable.
biodegradation [ˌbaɪəʊˌdegrə'deɪʃən] N biodegradación *f*.
biodegrade [ˌbaɪədɪ'greɪd] **1** VT biodegradar.
2 VI biodegradarse.
biodiversity [ˌbaɪəʊdaɪ'vɜːsətɪ] N biodiversidad *f*.
biodynamic ['baɪəʊdaɪ'næmɪk] ADJ biodinámico.
bioengineering [ˌbaɪəʊˌendʒɪ'nɪərɪŋ] N bioingeniería *f*.
biofeedback [ˌbaɪəʊ'fiːdbæk] N biofeedback *m*.
biofuel ['baɪəʊfjʊəl] N combustible *m* biológico.
biogas ['baɪəʊgæs] N biogás *m*.
biogenesis [ˌbaɪəʊ'dʒenɪsɪs] N biogénesis *f*.
biographee [baɪˌɒgrəˌfiː] N biografiado *m*, -a *f*.
biographer [baɪ'ɒgrəfəʳ] N biógrafo *m*, -a *f*.
biographic(al) [ˌbaɪəʊ'græfɪk(əl)] ADJ biográfico.
biography [baɪ'ɒgrəfɪ] N biografía *f*.
biological [ˌbaɪə'lɒdʒɪkəl] ADJ biológico; **~ clock** reloj *m* biológico; **~ warfare** guerra *f* biológica.
biologically [ˌbaɪə'lɒdʒɪkəlɪ] ADV *active, programmed, determined* biológicamente; *different* desde el punto de vista biológico; **~ speaking it provides a source of variation** desde el punto de vista biológico facilita el origen de la variación.
biologist [baɪ'ɒlədʒɪst] N biólogo *m*, -a *f*.
biology [baɪ'ɒlədʒɪ] N biología *f*.
biomass ['baɪəʊˌmæs] N biomasa *f*.
biome ['baɪəʊm] N biomedio *m*.
biomedical [ˌbaɪəʊ'medɪkl] ADJ biomédico.
biometrics [ˌbaɪə'metrɪks] N SING, **biometry** [baɪ'ɒmətrɪ] N biometría *f*.
bionic [baɪ'ɒnɪk] ADJ biónico.
bionics [baɪ'ɒnɪks] N SING electrónica *f* biológica.
bioorganic [ˌbaɪəʊɔː'gænɪk] ADJ bioorgánico; **~ chemistry** química *f* bioorgánica.
biophysical [ˌbaɪəʊ'fɪzɪkəl] ADJ biofísico.
biophysicist [ˌbaɪəʊ'fɪzɪsɪst] N biofísico *m*, -a *f*.
biophysics [ˌbaɪəʊ'fɪzɪks] N SING biofísica *f*.
biopic* ['baɪəʊˌpɪk] N biografía *f* cinematográfica.
biopsy ['baɪɒpsɪ] N biopsia *f*.
biorhythm ['baɪəʊrɪðəm] N bioritmo *m*.

bioscopy [baɪ'ɒskəpɪ] N bioscopia *f*.
biosensor ['baɪəʊ'sensəʳ] N biosensor *m*.
biosphere ['baɪəˌsfɪəʳ] N biosfera *f*.
biostatistics ['baɪəʊstə'tɪstɪks] NPL bioestadística *f*.
biosynthesis [ˌbaɪəʊ'sɪnθɪsɪs] N biosíntesis *f*.
biosynthetic [ˌbaɪəʊˌsɪn'θetɪk] ADJ biosintético.
biotechnological [ˌbaɪəˌteknə'lɒdʒɪkəl] ADJ biotecnológico.
biotechnologist [ˌbaɪəʊtek'nɒlədʒɪst] N biotecnólogo *m*, -a *f*.
biotechnology [ˌbaɪəʊtek'nɒlədʒɪ] N biotecnología *f*.
biotic [baɪ'ɒtɪk] ADJ biótico.
biotope ['baɪəˌtəʊp] N biotopo *m*.
biotype ['baɪəˌtaɪp] N biotipo *m*.
biowarfare ['baɪəʊ'wɔːfeəʳ] N guerra *f* bacteriológica.
bipartisan [ˌbaɪ'pɑːtɪzæn] ADJ *policy etc* que tienen en común los dos partidos, bipartido.
bipartite [baɪ'pɑːtaɪt] ADJ bipartido; *treaty etc* bipartito.
biped ['baɪped] N bípedo *m*.
biplane ['baɪpleɪn] N biplano *m*.
bipolar [baɪ'pəʊləʳ] ADJ bipolar.
bipolarize [baɪ'pəʊləraɪz] VT bipolarizar.
birch [bɜːtʃ] **1** N abedul *m*; (*for punishment*) palo *m*, férula *f*.
2 VT castigar con el palo.
birching ['bɜːtʃɪŋ] N flagelación *f*, azotamiento *m*.
birch-tree ['bɜːtʃtriː] N abedul *m*.
birchwood ['bɜːtʃwʊd] N bosque *m* de abedules.
bird [bɜːd] N **(a)** ave *f*, (*gen small*) pájaro *m*; **~ of ill omen** pájaro *m* de mal agüero; **~ of paradise** ave *f* del paraíso; **~ of passage** ave *f* de paso (*also fig*); **~ of prey** ave *f* de rapiña; **a little ~ told me** me lo ha dicho un pajarito; **they haven't yet told her about the ~s and the bees** todavía no le han explicado las cosas de la vida; **the ~s have flown** (*fig*) los pájaros han volado; **strictly for the ~s*** trivial, de poca monta, pal gato*.
(b) (*Theat**) **to get the ~** ganarse un abucheo, ser pateado; **to give sb the ~** abuchear a uno, patear a uno.
(c) (*proverbs*) **the early ~ catches the worm** al que madruga Dios le ayuda; **a ~ in the hand is worth two in the bush** más vale pájaro en mano que ciento volando; **~s of a feather flock together** Dios los cría y ellos se juntan; **they're ~s of a feather** son lobos de una camada; **to kill two ~s with one stone** matar dos pájaros de un tiro.
(d) (*: man*) tío* *m*, tipo* *m*; (*‡: girl*) chica *f*, jai‡ *f*; (*girlfriend*) amiguita *f*.
(e) (‡) **to do 2 years ~** pasar 2 años a la sombra‡.
bird-bath ['bɜːdbɑːθ] N, PL **bird-baths** ['bɜːdbɑːðz] pila *f* para pájaros.
birdbrain* ['bɜːdbreɪn] N casquivano *m*, -a *f*.
bird-brained* ['bɜːdbreɪnd] ADJ casquivano.
birdcage ['bɜːdkeɪdʒ] N jaula *f* de pájaro; (*large, outdoor*) pajarera *f*.
bird-call ['bɜːdkɔːl] N reclamo *m*.
bird-dog ['bɜːddɒg] N (*US*) perro *m* de caza.
bird-fancier ['bɜːd,fænsɪəʳ] N pajarero *m*.
birdie ['bɜːdɪ] N (*Golf*) birdie *m*, menos uno *m*.
birdlike ['bɜːdlaɪk] ADJ como un pajarito.
birdlime ['bɜːdlaɪm] N liga *f*.
bird-nesting ['bɜːdˌnestɪŋ] N: **to go ~** ir a buscar nidos.
bird-sanctuary ['bɜːdˌsæŋktjʊərɪ] N reserva *f* para las aves.
birdseed ['bɜːdsiːd] N alpiste *m*.
bird's-eye view ['bɜːdzaɪ'vjuː] N vista *f* de pájaro.
birdshot ['bɜːdʃɒt] N perdigones *mpl*.
bird's-nest ['bɜːdznest] **1** N nido *m* de pájaro.
2 VI (*esp to go ~ing*) ir a buscar nidos.
bird-table ['bɜːdˌteɪbl] N mesita de jardín para poner comida a los pájaros.
bird-watcher ['bɜːdwɒtʃəʳ] N ornitólogo *m*, -a *f*, observador *m*, -a *f* de aves.
bird-watching ['bɜːdˌwɒtʃɪŋ] N ornitología *f*, observación *f* de aves.
biretta [bɪ'retə] N birrete *m*.
Biro ['baɪrəʊ] ® N (*Brit*) (marca *f* de) bolígrafo *m*.
▼ **birth** [bɜːθ] N nacimiento *m*; (*Med*) parto *m*; (*fig*) nacimiento *m*, origen *m*, comienzo *m*; **the ~ of an idea** el origen de una idea; **by ~** de nacimiento; **of humble ~** de origen humilde; **the village of his ~** el pueblo donde nació, su pueblo natal; **to give ~ to** dar a luz, parir, (*fig*) dar lugar a, ser el origen de; **to be in at the ~ of** (*fig*) asistir al nacimiento de.
birth-certificate ['bɜːθsə'tɪfɪkɪt] N partida *f* de nacimiento, fe *f* de bautismo.
birth-control ['bɜːθkən'trəʊl] N control *m* de natalidad; **method of ~** método *m* anticonceptivo; **~ pill** píldora *f* anticonceptiva.
birthdate ['bɜːθdeɪt] N fecha *f* de nacimiento.
▼ **birthday** ['bɜːθdeɪ] N cumpleaños *m*; (*of event etc*) aniversario *m*; (*the Spaniard more commonly celebrates his*) día *m* del santo de uno, fiesta *f* onomástica; **on my 21st ~** cuando cumplí los 21 años; **in one's ~ suit** en cueros.
birthday-cake ['bɜːθdeɪˌkeɪk] N tarta *f* de cumpleaños.

birthday-card ['bɜːθdeɪˌkɑːd] N tarjeta f de cumpleaños.
birthday-party ['bɜːθdeɪˌpɑːtɪ] N fiesta f de cumpleaños.
birthday-present ['bɜːθdeɪˈpreznt] N regalo m de cumpleaños.
birthing ['bɜːθɪŋ] N pool, centre etc de partos, para el parto.
birthmark ['bɜːθmɑːk] N rosa f, antojo m, marca f de nacimiento.
birth mother ['bɜːθˈmʌðəʳ] N madre f biológica.
birth-pill ['bɜːθˌpɪl] N píldora f anticonceptiva.
birthplace ['bɜːθpleɪs] N lugar m de nacimiento.
birth-rate ['bɜːθreɪt] N natalidad f.
birthright ['bɜːθraɪt] N derechos mpl de nacimiento; primogenitura f; (fig) patrimonio m, herencia f; **it is the ~ of every Englishman** pertenece por derecho natural a todo inglés, es el patrimonio de todo inglés; **to sell one's ~ for a mess of potage** vender su primogenitura por un plato de lentejas.
birthstone ['bɜːθstəʊn] N piedra f natalicia.
BIS N (US) ABBR of **Bank of International Settlements** Banco m Internacional de Pagos, BIP m.
Biscay ['bɪskeɪ] N Vizcaya f.
biscuit ['bɪskɪt] N (a) (Brit) galleta f. (b) (US) bizcocho m; **that takes the ~!** ¡eso es el colmo!
biscuit-barrel ['bɪskɪtˌbærəl] N galletero m.
bisect [baɪˈsekt] VT bisecar.
bisection [baɪˈsekʃən] N (Math) bisección f, división f en dos partes; (angle) bisección f.
bisector [baɪˈsektəʳ] N bisector m.
bisexual ['baɪˈseksjʊəl] ① ADJ bisexual.
　② N bisexual mf.
bisexuality [baɪˌseksjʊˈælɪtɪ] N bisexualidad f.
bishop ['bɪʃəp] N obispo m, -a f; (Chess) alfil m; **yes, B~** sí, Ilustrísima.
bishopric ['bɪʃəprɪk] N obispado m.
bismuth ['bɪzməθ] N bismuto m.
bison ['baɪsən] N bisonte m.
bisque [bɪsk] N (Culin) sopa f de mariscos; (Sport) ventaja f; (Pottery) bizcocho m, biscuit m.
bistable [baɪˈsteɪbl] ADJ (Comput) biestable.
bistro ['biːstrəʊ] N bistro(t) m.
bit¹ [bɪt] N (horse's) freno m, bocado m; (of drill) broca f; (tool) barrena f; **to get the ~ between one's teeth** desbocarse, rebelarse.
bit² [bɪt] ① N (a) (piece) trozo m, pedacito m, porción f.
　(b) (noun phrases) **a ~ of advice** un consejo; **a ~ of news** una noticia; **I had a ~ to eat** tomé un bocado; **I'll have a ~ of cake** tomaré un poco de tarta; **they have a ~ of money** tienen dinerillos; **to blow sth to ~s** hacer algo añicos; **to come to ~s** hacerse pedazos, romperse, desmontarse; **to do one's ~** contribuir, hacer la debida contribución, servir como se debe (a la patria etc); **he did his ~ in the war** durante la guerra aportó su granito de arena; **~s and pieces** trocitos mpl, retazos mpl; (elements) elementos mpl dispersos; (Mech etc) piezas fpl, componentes mpl; **my ~s and pieces** mis cosas, mis bártulos; **he tore the argument to ~s** hizo el argumento pedazos.
　(c) (adjectival uses) **he's a ~ of a liar** es algo mentiroso; **I'm a ~ of a musician** yo sé algo de música; **I'm a ~ of a socialist** yo soy socialista hasta cierto punto; **it was a ~ of a shock** fue un golpe bastante duro; **I've a ~ of a cold** estoy ligeramente acatarrado; **it cost quite a ~ of money** costó bastante dinero; **it takes quite a ~ of my time** ocupa bastante tiempo; **this is a ~ of all right!** ¡esto está muy bien!; **not a ~ of it!** ¡ni hablar!, ¡nada, nada!; **it's not a ~ of use** no sirve para nada en absoluto; **every ~ as good as** de ningún modo inferior a; **every ~ a man** todo un hombre; **to enjoy every ~ of sth** disfrutar algo totalmente.
　(d) (adverbial uses) **~ by ~** poco a poco; **by** (or **in**) **~s and pieces** a retazos; **it's a ~ awkward** es un poco difícil; **it's a ~ much when ...** es intolerable cuando ...; **that's a ~ much!** ¡eso pasa de castaño oscuro!; **a ~ later** poco después, un poco más tarde; **wait a ~!** ¡espere un momento!, ¡un momento, por favor!; **I waited quite a ~** esperé bastante tiempo; **so I waited a ~** así que esperé un ratito; **it's a good ~ further than we thought** queda bastante más lejos de lo que creíamos; **a good ~ bigger** bastante más grande; **are you tired? ... not a ~!** ¿estás cansado? ... ¡en absoluto!; **she was thrilled to ~s** se extasió, se emocionó muchísimo.
　(e) (Comput) bit m, bitio m, unidad f de información.
　(f) **two ~s** (US) 25 centavos.
　(g) (‡) tía* f, jai‡ f.
　② ADJ (Theat): **~ part** papel m pequeño.
bit³ [bɪt] PRET of **bite**.
bitch [bɪtʃ] ① N (a) perra f.
　(b) (‡: woman) lagarta f, zorra f; **you ~!** ¡lagarta!; **this car is a ~** este coche la es la monda*; **it's a ~ of a problem** es un problema cojonudo*.
　(c) (US‡) queja f; **what's your ~?** ¿de qué coño te quejas?‡
　② VI (‡) quejarse (about de).
bitchy* ['bɪtʃɪ] ADJ maldiciente, malicioso; de mal genio; rencoroso; re-

mark etc malintencionado, horrible; **to be ~ to sb** tratar a uno con malevolencia.
bite [baɪt] ① N (a) mordedura f; mordisco m; (toothmark) dentellada f; (of bird, insect) picadura f; **he wants another** (or **a second**) **~ at the cherry** quiere otra oportunidad, quiere probar otra vez; **to put the ~ on sb** (US*) hacer cerrar el pico a uno*.
　(b) (food) bocado m; (snack) bocado m, piscolabis m; **I've not had a ~ to eat** no he probado bocado; **will you have a ~ to eat?** ¿le traigo algo de comer?; **I'll get a ~ on the train** tomaré algo en el tren.
　(c) **are you getting any ~s?** (Fishing) ¿están picando?
　(d) (fig) mordacidad f, penetración f; garra f; **a novel with ~** una novela penetrante; **a speech with ~** un discurso tajante; **without any ~** sin garra.
　② (irr: PRET **bit**, PTP **bitten**) VT morder; (bird, fish, insect) picar; (acid) corroer; (Mech) asir, trabar; **what's biting you?*** ¿qué mosca te ha picado?; **once bitten twice shy** el gato escaldado del agua fría huye; **to be bitten with*** estar contagiado con.
　③ VI morder; picar; (fish) picar; (fig) tragar el anzuelo; (fig) hacer mella, surtir efecto, hacerse sentir; **the strike is beginning to ~** la huelga empieza a hacer mella; **to ~ at** tratar de morder; **to ~ into earth** etc devorar, tragar.
◆**bite back** ① VT words tragar, dejar sin decir.
　② VI: **but the dog bit back** pero el perro mordió a su vez.
◆**bite off** VT arrancar con los dientes; **to ~ off more than one can chew** abarcar más de lo que se puede apretar, abarcar mucho.
◆**bite on** VT morder; afirmar los dientes en.
◆**bite through** VT string, thread cortar; tongue, tip morderse; **he fell and bit through his tongue** al caerse se cortó la lengua de un mordisco.
biter ['baɪtəʳ] N: **the ~ bit** el cazador, cazado.
bite-size(d) ['baɪtˈsaɪz(d)] ADJ (a) food cortado a taquitos, cortado en dados; **bite-sized pieces of ham** taquitos de jamón. (b) (fig) information en cantidades digeribles, en pequeñas dosis.
biting ['baɪtɪŋ] ADJ cold, wind penetrante, cortante; criticism etc mordaz.
bit-player ['bɪtˌpleɪəʳ] N actor m secundario, actriz f secundaria.
bitten ['bɪtn] PTP of **bite**.
bitter ['bɪtəʳ] ① ADJ amargo; cold penetrante, cortante; battle encarnizado; enemy, hatred implacable; disappointment agudo; protest amargo; person resentido; **~ aloes** amargante m para uñas, líquido m para no morderse las uñas; **~ lemon** limonada f ácida; **~ orange** naranja f amarga; **to carry on to the ~ end** continuar hasta el final (cueste lo que cueste); **to feel ~ about sth** resentirse por algo, tener rencor por motivo de algo.
　② N (Brit) cerveza f amarga; ver también BEER .
bitterly ['bɪtəlɪ] ADV amargamente; **it's ~ cold** hace un frío cortante; **he protested ~** se quejó amargamente; **I was ~ disappointed** sufrí una terrible decepción; **she spoke ~ of her experiences** habló con mucho rencor de sus experiencias.
bittern ['bɪtɜːn] N avetoro m (común).
bitterness ['bɪtənɪs] N (taste) amargor m; (feelings) amargura f; encarnizamiento m; implacabilidad f; agudeza f; **there is great ~ between them** entre ellos existe un odio implacable; **I accepted it without ~** lo acepté sin rencor; **I have no ~ towards you** no le guardo rencor.
bitters ['bɪtəz] NPL bíter m.
bittersweet ['bɪtəswiːt] ADJ agridulce.
bitty ['bɪtɪ] ADJ (a) (Brit) poco coherente, descosido; en pedacitos. (b) (US) pequeñito.
bitumen ['bɪtjʊmɪn] N betún m.
bituminous [bɪˈtjuːmɪnəs] ADJ bituminoso.
bivalent ['baɪˈveɪlənt] ADJ bivalente.
bivalve ['baɪvælv] ① ADJ bivalvo.
　② N (molusco m) bivalvo m.
bivouac ['bɪvʊæk] ① N vivaque m, vivac m.
　② VI vivaquear.
bi-weekly ['baɪˈwiːklɪ] ① ADJ (every 2 weeks) quincenal; (twice weekly) bisemanal.
　② ADV quincenalmente; bisemanalmente.
　③ N revista f quincenal; revista f bisemanal.
biz* [bɪz] N ABBR of **business**; V show.
bizarre [bɪˈzɑːʳ] ADJ event extraño, raro; appearance etc estrafalario.
bk (a) ABBR of **book** libro m, l. (b) ABBR of **bank** Banco m, Bco.
bkcy ABBR of **bankruptcy**.
bkg ABBR of **banking**.
bkpt ABBR of **bankrupt**.
B/L ABBR of **bill of lading** conocimiento m de embarque.
BL N (a) ABBR of **British Leyland**. (b) ABBR of **British Library**. (c) ABBR of **Bachelor of Law(s)** licenciado m, -a f en Leyes.
blab [blæb] ① VT (also **to ~ out**) divulgar, soltar.
　② VI chismear; (to police etc) soplar.
blabber* ['blæbəʳ] VI (also **~ on**) charlotear, parlar.
blabbermouth* ['blæbəˌmaʊθ] N (pej) bocazas* mf, cotilla mf.
black [blæk] ① ADJ (a) negro; **~ arts** magia f negra; **~ ball** bola f ne-

gra; **~ bass** perca *f*; **~ belt** (*Sport*) cinturón *m* negro; **~ box** (*Aer*) caja *f* negra; **~ coffee** café *m* solo; **~ comedy** comedia *f* negra; **B~ Country** *región industrial de Birmingham y su comarca* (*Inglaterra*); **B~ Death** peste *f* negra; **~ economy** economía *f* sumergida, economía *f* negra; **~ eye** ojo *m* amoratado, ojo *m* a la funerala; **B~ Forest** Selva *f* Negra; **B~ Forest gâteau** *pastel de chocolate, nata y guindas*; **~ grouse** = **blackcock**; **~-headed gull** gaviota *f* de cabeza negra; **~ hole** (*Astron*) agujero *m* negro; **~ humour** humor *m* negro; **~ ice** *hielo invisible en la carretera*; **~ line** raya *f* en negro; **~ magic** magia *f* negra; **B~ Maria** (*Brit*) coche *m* celular, furgón *m* celular; **~ mark** señal *f* roja; (*fig*) nota *f* adversa, punto *m* negativo; **~ market** estraperlo *m*, mercado *m* negro; **~ marketeer** estraperlista *mf*; **~ pepper** pimienta *f* negra; **~ pudding** (*Brit*) morcilla *f*, moronga *f* (*Mex*); **B~ Rod** (*Brit Parl*) *dignatario de la Cámara de los Lores encargado de reunir a los Comunes en la apertura del Parlamento*; **~ sheep** (**of the family**) oveja *f* negra, garbanzo *m* negro; (*accident*) **~ spot** (*Aut*) punto *m* negro; **~ tie** corbata *f* de lazo, corbata *f* de smoking; '**~ tie**' (*on invitation*) 'de etiqueta'; **B~ Watch** (*Brit Mil*) *regimiento escocés*; **~ and white photo** foto *f* en blanco y negro; **~ and white TV** TV *f* monocromo; **with a face as ~ as thunder** con cara de pocos amigos; **his face was ~ and blue** tenía la cara amoratada; **to swear ~ and blue** jurar por todo lo más santo (*that* que).

(**b**) (*negro*) **~ man** negro *m*; **~ woman** negra *f*; **B~ Africa** el África negra; **the ~ belt** (*US*) zona *f* negra; **~ college** (*US*) *universidad para gente de color*; **B~ English** (*US*) *inglés hablado por los negros americanos*; **B~ Moslem** musulmán *m* negro; **B~ Nationalism** nacionalismo *m* negro; **B~ Panthers** Panteras *fpl* negras; **B~ Power** poder *m* negro; **B~ Studies** (*US*) *estudios de la cultura negra americana*.

(**c**) (*dark*) oscuro, tenebroso; **as ~ as pitch, as ~ as your hat** oscuro como boca de lobo.

(**d**) (*dirty*) sucio; (*with smoke*) negro, ennegrecido.

(**e**) (*Brit: trade union parlance*) **~ goods** géneros *mpl* sujetos a boicoteo; **to declare a product ~** boicotear un producto.

(**f**) (*fig*) (*wicked*) negro; (*angry*) furioso; (*ominous*) negro, ominoso; *thought* malévolo; *rage* negro; *look* ceñudo, de desaprobación; *day, event* negro, funesto, aciago; *outlook* negro; *forecast* pesimista; **a ~ day on the roads** una jornada negra en las carreteras; **he is not as ~ as he is painted** no es tan malo como se cree; **things look pretty ~** la situación es desconsoladora; **things were looking ~ for him** la situación se le presentaba muy difícil.

2️⃣ N (**a**) (*colour*) negro *m*, color *m* negro; **a film in ~ and white** un film en blanco y negro; **I should like it in ~ and white** quisiera tenerlo por escrito; **there it is in ~ and white!** ¡ahí lo tiene en letras de molde!

(**b**) (*person*) negro *m*, -a *f*.

(**c**) (*mourning*) luto *m*; **to be in ~, to wear ~** estar de luto.

(**d**) (*darkness*) oscuridad *f*, noche *f*.

(**e**) **to stay in the ~** (*banking*) estar en números negros.

3️⃣ VT (**a**) ennegrecer; *shoes* limpiar, lustrar; **to ~ sb's eye** ponerle a uno el ojo a la funerala.

(**b**) (*Brit: trade union parlance*) boicotear.

◆**black out** 1️⃣ VT: **to ~ out a house** apagar las luces de una casa, hacer que no sean visibles por fuera las luces de una casa; **the screen was ~ed out by the strike** (*TV*) debido a la huelga no había programas en la pantalla; **the storm ~ed out the city** la tormenta causó un apagón en la ciudad.

2️⃣ VI (*faint*) desmayarse, perder el conocimiento.

blackball ['blækbɔːl] VT dar bola negra a.

blackberry ['blækbəri] N (*fruit*) zarzamora *f*, mora *f*; (*plant*) zarza *f*.

blackberrying ['blæk,beriɪŋ] N: **to go ~** ir a coger zarzamoras.

blackbird ['blækbɜːd] N mirlo *m*.

blackboard ['blækbɔːd] N pizarra *f*, encerado *m*.

blackcap ['blækkæp] N cucurra *f* capirotada.

black-coated ['blæk'kəutɪd] ADJ: **~ worker** oficinista *mf*.

blackcock ['blækkɒk] N gallo *m* lira.

blackcurrant [blæk'kʌrənt] N (*fruit*) casis *m*, grosella *f* negra; (*bush*) grosellero *m* negro.

blacken ['blækən] 1️⃣ VT ennegrecer; (*by fire*) calcinar; *face* tiznar de negro; (*fig*) denigrar, desacreditar.

2️⃣ VI ennegrecerse.

blackguard ['blægɑːd] 1️⃣ N pillo *m*, canalla *m*.

2️⃣ VT vilipendiar.

blackguardly ['blægɑːdlɪ] ADJ vil, canallesco.

blackhead ['blækhed] N comedón *m*, espinilla *f*.

black-hearted ['blæk'hɑːtɪd] ADJ malvado, perverso.

blacking ['blækɪŋ] N betún *m*.

blackish ['blækɪʃ] ADJ negruzco; (*wine parlance*) aguindado.

blackjack ['blækdʒæk] N (*esp US*) (**a**) (*truncheon*) cachiporra *f* (*con puño flexible*). (**b**) (*flag*) bandera *f* pirata. (**c**) (*game*) veintiuna *f*.

blackleg ['blækleg] (*Brit*) 1️⃣ N esquirol *m*.

2️⃣ VI ser esquirol, trabajar durante una huelga.

blacklegging ['blæk,legɪŋ] N esquirolaje *m*.

blacklist ['blæklɪst] 1️⃣ N lista *f* negra.

2️⃣ VT poner en la lista negra.

blackmail ['blækmeɪl] 1️⃣ N chantaje *m*; **it's sheer ~!** ¡es un chantaje!

2️⃣ VT chantajear, sacar dinero por chantaje a; **to ~ sb into doing sth** chantajear a uno para que haga algo; **he was ~ed into it** lo hizo obligado por el chantaje.

blackmailer ['blækmeɪlə'] N chantajista *mf*.

blackness ['blæknɪs] N negrura *f*; (*darkness*) oscuridad *f*.

blackout ['blækaut] N (**a**) (*electrical*) apagón *m*. (**b**) (*Med*) amnesia *f* temporal, desmayo *m*. (**c**) (*of news*) bloqueo *m* informativo, apagón *m* informativo; **there was a media ~ at the request of the police** hubo un bloqueo informativo en los medios de comunicación a petición de la policía.

Black Sea ['blæk'siː] N Mar *m* Negro.

blackshirt ['blækʃɜːt] N camisa negra *mf*, fascista *mf*.

blacksmith ['blæksmɪθ] N herrero *m*; **~'s** (**forge**) herrería *f*.

blackthorn ['blækθɔːn] N endrino *m*.

blacktop ['blæktɒp] (*US*) 1️⃣ N (*substance, road*) asfalto *m*.

2️⃣ VT asfaltar.

black widow ['blæk'wɪdəu] N viuda *f* negra.

bladder ['blædə'] N vejiga *f*.

blade [bleid] N (*of weapon etc*) hoja *f*; (*cutting edge*) filo *m*; (*sword*) espada *f*; (*of propeller*) paleta *f*, aleta *f*; (*of oar, hoe*) pala *f*; **a ~ of grass** una brizna de hierba.

blaeberry ['bleɪbəri] N arándano *m*.

blag [blæg] 1️⃣ N robo *m* a mano armada.

2️⃣ VT robar a mano armada.

blah* [blɑː] 1️⃣ ADJ (*US*) poco apetitoso.

2️⃣ N (*words*) paja *f*, palabrería *f*; **and there was a lot more ~, ~, ~** y hubo mucho más bla, bla, bla. (**b**) **the ~s** (*US*) la depre*.

blamable ['bleɪməbl] ADJ censurable, culpable.

blame [bleim] 1️⃣ N culpa *f*; **to bear the ~** tener la culpa; **to lay** (*or* **put**) **the ~ for sth on sb** echar a uno la culpa de algo.

2️⃣ VT culpar, echar la culpa a; **to ~ sb for sth** echar a uno la culpa de algo; **to be to ~ for** tener la culpa de; **I am not to ~** yo no tengo la culpa; **who's to ~?** ¿quién tiene la culpa?; **you have only yourself to ~** tú eres el único culpable; **and I don't ~ him** y lo comprendo perfectamente.

blameless ['bleimlɪs] ADJ *person* inocente (*of* de); *action* intachable, irreprochable.

blamelessly ['bleimlɪslɪ] ADV inocentemente, intachablemente.

blameworthy ['bleimwɜːðɪ] ADJ censurable, culpable.

blanch [blɑːntʃ] 1️⃣ VT blanquear.

2️⃣ VI palidecer.

blancmange [blə'mɒnʒ] N ≃ crema *f* (de vainilla *etc*).

bland [blænd] ADJ suave.

blandish ['blændɪʃ] VT engatusar, halagar.

blandishments ['blændɪʃmənts] NPL halagos *mpl*, lisonjas *fpl*.

blandly ['blændlɪ] ADV suavemente.

blank [blæŋk] 1️⃣ ADJ *paper, space, cheque etc* en blanco; *tape* sin grabar, virgen; *wall* liso, sin adorno; *verse* suelto, blanco; *cartridge* sin bala, *shell* de fogueo; **to give sb a ~ cheque** dar a uno un cheque en blanco; (*fig*) dar carta blanca a uno (**to** + *infin* para + *infin*); **a ~ look** una mirada sin expresión, una mirada de incomprensión; **a ~ stare** una mirada vaga; **when I asked him he looked ~** cuando se lo pregunté puso la mirada en el vacío; **a look of ~ amazement** una mirada de profundo asombro; **in a state of ~ despair** en un estado de desesperación total; **my mind went ~** no pude recordar nada.

2️⃣ N (*space*) blanco *m*, espacio *m* en blanco; (*form*) formulario *m*, hoja *f*; (*coin*) cospel *m*; (*Mil*) cartucho *m* sin bala, granada *f* de fogueo; **to fire ~s** usar municiones de fogueo; **my mind was a complete ~** no pude recordar nada; **to draw a ~** no encontrar nada, no tener éxito alguno.

blanket ['blæŋkɪt] 1️⃣ N manta *f*, frazada *f* (*LAm*); (*fig*) manto *m*, capa *f*; **a ~ of snow** una manta de nieve; **~ bath** = **bedbath**; **~ stitch** punto *m* de aguja.

2️⃣ ADJ comprensivo, general; **~ agreement** acuerdo *m* comprensivo, acuerdo *m* general; **this insurance policy gives ~ cover** esta póliza de seguro es a todo riesgo.

3️⃣ VT (*fig*) cubrir (**in, with** de), envolver (**by, in, with** en).

blankly ['blæŋklɪ] ADV: **he looked at me ~** me miró sin comprender.

blare [bleə'] 1️⃣ N estrépito *m*, sonido *m* fuerte; (*of trumpet*) trompetazo *m*.

2️⃣ VT: **to ~ out** vociferar, anunciar a gritos; *music* tocar muy fuerte.

3️⃣ VI resonar, sonar muy fuerte.

blarney ['blɑːnɪ] 1️⃣ N coba *f*; labia *f*.

2️⃣ VT dar coba a.

blasé ['blɑːzeɪ] ADJ hastiado; de vuelta de todo; **he's very ~ about it** habla de ello en términos de hastío, habla con indiferencia de ello.

blaspheme [blæs'fiːm] VI blasfemar.

blasphemer [blæs'fiːmə'] N blasfemador *m*, -ora *f*.

blasphemous ['blæsfiməs] ADJ blasfemo.

blasphemously ['blæsfıməslı] ADV blasfemamente.
blasphemy ['blæsfımı] N blasfemia f.
blast [blɑːst] 1 N **(a)** (of wind) ráfaga f; (of air) soplo m; (of sand, water) chorro m.
(b) (sound) trompetazo m; (of whistle etc) toque m.
(c) (explosive) explosión f; onda f explosiva, onda f expansiva.
(d) (of criticism etc) tempestad f, oleada f.
(e) (US*) fiesta f; **to have a ~*** organizar una fiesta; **to get a ~ out of sth*** pasárselo chachi con algo*.
2 VT (with explosive) volar; (by lightning) derribar, destruir; (Mil) bombardear; (Bot) marchitar, (with blight) añublar; (fig) arruinar; criticar duramente; (US: verbally) atacar verbalmente; **to ~ open** abrir con carga explosiva; **~ (it)!*** ¡maldición!
◆**blast away** 1 VT volar; quitar con explosivos.
2 VI (gun) seguir disparando; **they were ~ing away at the town** seguían bombardeando el pueblo.
◆**blast off** VI (rocket) (also US*) despegar.
◆**blast out** VT radio message etc emitir a toda potencia; tune tocar (etc) a máximo volumen.
blasted* ['blɑːstɪd] ADJ condenado*, maldito.
blast-furnace ['blɑːst'fɜːnɪs] N alto horno m.
blasting ['blɑːstɪŋ] N (Tech) explosión f controlada; '**~ in progress**' 'explosión controlada en curso'; **to give sb a ~ for (having done) sth** dar una bronca a uno (or abroncar a uno) por (haber hecho) algo.
blast-off ['blɑːstɒf] N lanzamiento m, despegue m.
blatant ['bleɪtənt] ADJ (shameless) descarado; agresivo; (noisy) estrepitoso, vocinglero; colour etc chillón.
blatantly ['bleɪtəntlı] ADV descaradamente.
blather ['blæðəʳ] 1 N disparates mpl.
2 VI charlatanear, decir tonterías.
blaze¹ [bleɪz] 1 N **(a)** (with flames) llamarada f, (steady glow) resplandor m; (fire) incendio m; (bonfire) hoguera f; **the garden is a ~ of colour** el jardín está radiante de color; **in a ~** en llamas; **in a ~ of anger** en un arranque de cólera; **in a ~ of publicity** bajo los focos de la publicidad, a bombo y platillo. **(b)** (*) **like ~s** hasta más no poder, con todas sus fuerzas; **what the ~s ...?** ¿qué diablos ...?; **go to ~s!** ¡vete al diablo!, ¡vete a la porra!*
2 VT: **the news was ~d across the front page** la noticia venía con grandes titulares en la primera plana.
3 VI arder en llamas; (fig) brillar, resplandecer; **all the lights were blazing** brillaban todas las luces; **to ~ with anger** estar furioso, echar chispas.
◆**blaze abroad** VT (liter) news etc difundir.
◆**blaze away** VI (soldiers) seguir disparando rápidamente.
◆**blaze down** VI: **the sun was blazing down** brillaba implacable el sol, picaba muy fuerte el sol.
◆**blaze forth** VI (liter, sun) aparecer súbitamente; (anger) estallar.
◆**blaze out** VI (fire) llamear; (sun) resplandecer, relucir; (light) relucir; (anger, hatred) estallar.
◆**blaze up** VI (volver a) encenderse vivamente; (fig) estallar.
blaze² [bleɪz] 1 N (on animal) mancha f, estrella f; (on tree) señal f (hecha para servir de guía).
2 VT: **to ~ a trail** abrir un camino (also fig).
blazer ['bleɪzəʳ] N chaqueta f (de deporte, de colegio etc), chaquetilla f, blázer m.
blazing ['bleɪzɪŋ] ADJ sun abrasador; light brillante; anger irreprimible; row violento.
blazon ['bleɪzn] 1 N blasón m.
2 VT (fig) proclamar.
bldg ABBR of **building**.
bleach [bliːtʃ] 1 N lejía f.
2 VT blanquear.
3 VI blanquearse.
bleached [bliːtʃt] ADJ (hair) decolorado, (teñido de) rubio platino; (clothes) descolorido.
bleachers ['bliːtʃəz] NPL (US) gradas fpl.
bleaching-agent ['bliːtʃɪŋ,eɪdʒənt] N decolorante m.
bleaching-powder ['bliːtʃɪŋ,paʊdəʳ] N polvos mpl de blanqueo.
bleak¹ [bliːk] N (fish) breca f, albur m.
bleak² [bliːk] ADJ landscape desierto, desolador, inhóspito; (treeless) pelado; weather crudo; smile triste, adusto; welcome inhospitalario; prospect nada prometedor.
bleakly ['bliːklı] ADV look desoladamente; speak tristemente, descorazonadoramente.
bleakness ['bliːknıs] N (of landscape) desolación f; (of room, furnishings) frialdad f; (of weather) crudeza f, desapacibilidad f.
bleary ['blıərı] ADJ eye legañoso.
bleary-eyed ['blıərıaıd] ADJ de ojos legañosos; semidormido.
bleat [bliːt] 1 N balido m; (*) queja f.
2 VI balar; (fig) quejarse tristemente (about de), gimotear.
bled [bled] PRET AND PTP of **bleed**.

bleed [bliːd] (irr. PRET AND PTP **bled**) 1 VT (Med) sangrar; (fig) desangrar; **to ~ sb white** desangrar a uno, sacarle el jugo a uno; **to ~ a country white** explotar despiadadamente un país.
2 VI sangrar; (tree) exudar; **to ~ to death** morir desangrado, morir de desangramiento; **to ~ for** sangrar de dolor por; **those who have bled for England** los que han vertido su sangre por Inglaterra; **my heart ~s for you** te compadezco mucho.
bleeder ['bliːdəʳ] N (Med*) hemofílico m; (Brit‡) cabrón‡ m.
bleeding ['bliːdɪŋ] 1 ADJ **(a)** wound etc sangrante, sangriento, que sangra; heart dolorido; **~-heart liberal** (US) liberal m de gran corazón.
(b) (‡) puñetero‡, pijotero‡.
2 ADV (‡) **~ awkward** condenadamente difícil‡.
3 N (Med) sangría f; desangramiento m, hemorragia f.
bleep [bliːp] 1 N bip m.
2 VI hacer bip, dar un bip.
bleeper ['bliːpəʳ] N localizador m, busca* m.
blemish ['blemıʃ] 1 N tacha f, mancha f.
2 VT manchar.
blench [blentʃ] VI cejar, recular; palidecer.
blend [blend] 1 N mezcla f, combinación f; (of drinks) mezcla f (de varias cosechas).
2 VT mezclar, combinar, armonizar; colours casar.
3 VI combinarse, armonizarse; **to ~ in with** armonizarse con, formar un conjunto armonioso con; **to ~ into** transformarse poco a poco en.
blended ['blendıd] ADJ mezclado.
blender ['blendəʳ] N **(a)** (person) catador m, -a f; **tea ~** catador m, -ora f de té. **(b)** (Culin) licuadora f.
bless [bles] VT bendecir; **to ~ o.s.** persignarse, santiguarse; **~ you!** (on sneezing) ¡Jesús!; **God ~ you!** ¡Dios te bendiga!; **well I'm ~ed!, God ~ my soul!** ¡caramba!; **I'm ~ed if I know** que me maten si lo sé; **they were ~ed with children** Dios les dio la bendición de los hijos; **she is ~ed with every virtue** la adornan mil virtudes; **I ~ the day I bought it** bendigo el día que lo compré.
blessed ['blesıd] 1 ADJ **(a)** (holy) bendito, bienaventurado; (beatified) beato; **the B~ Virgin** la Santísima Virgen; **the B~ Sacrament** el Santísimo Sacramento; **~ be Thy Name** bendito sea Tu Nombre; **a day of ~ calm** un día de bendita tranquilidad.
(b) (*) santo; **the whole ~ day** todo el santo día; **where's that ~ book?** ¿dónde diablos estará el libro ese?; **we didn't find a ~ thing** encontramos maldita la cosa.
2 NPL: **the B~** los bienaventurados.
blessedness ['blesıdnıs] N (Rel) bienaventuranza f, beatitud f, bendición f; (happiness) felicidad f.
blessing ['blesıŋ] N **(a)** (Rel) bendición f.
(b) (advantage) beneficio m, ventaja f; **the ~s of electricity** los beneficios de la electricidad; **the ~s of science** los adelantos de la ciencia; **to count one's ~s** apreciar lo que uno tiene; **it's a ~ in disguise** no hay mal que por bien no venga; **it's a mixed ~** tiene su pro y su contra.
blest [blest] ADJ AND PTP (poet) of **bless**.
blether ['bleðəʳ] = **blather**.
blew [bluː] PRET of **blow**.
blight [blaıt] 1 N (Bot) añublo m, tizón m, roya f, polvillo m (LAm); (fig) plaga f, infortunio m; desperfecto m, mancha f; **urban ~** desertización f urbana; **to cast a ~ on** (or over) arruinar.
2 VT **(a)** (Bot) añublar, atizonar. **(b)** (fig) arruinar, destruir; hopes arruinar; urban scene desertizar.
blighter‡ ['blaıtəʳ] N (Brit) tío* m, sujeto* m; (hum) **you ~!** ¡cacho cabrón!‡; **(what a) lucky ~!** ¡es un chorrón!*
Blighty* ['blaıtı] N (Brit Mil ††) Inglaterra f.
blimey‡ ['blaımı] INTERJ (Brit) ¡caray!
blimp [blımp] N **(a)** (Aer) globo m. **(b)** (Brit) (person) reaccionario m, militarista m, patriotero m; **a (Colonel) B~** ≃ un carpetovetónico.
blimpish ['blımpıʃ] ADJ reaccionario, militarista, patriotero.
blind [blaınd] 1 ADJ ciego (also fig, Archit; to a, para; with de); corner sin visibilidad; **~ alley** callejón m sin salida (also fig); **~ date** cita f a ciegas; **~ spot** (Anat) punto m ciego; (fig) debilidad f, punto m flojo; **~ in one eye** tuerto; **as ~ as a bat** más ciego que un topo; **a ~ man** un ciego; **it's a case of the ~ leading the ~** tan ciego el uno como el otro; **to be ~ to** no ver, (deliberately) hacer la vista gorda a; **he is ~ to all dangers** no comprende en absoluto los peligros; **he is ~ to her true character** se le oculta su verdadero carácter; **he took not a ~ bit of notice*** no hizo caso alguno, no le concedió la más mínima importancia; **to come up on the ~ side** (Aut) avanzar por el lado donde el conductor tiene la vista impedida; **to go ~** quedar ciego.
2 N **(a) the ~** PL los ciegos, los invidentes (euph).
(b) (also **Venetian ~**) persiana f; (outside window) toldo m.
(c) (pretence) pretexto m, subterfugio m; **it's all a ~** no es más que un pretexto.
(d) to go on a ~‡ ir de juerga*.

3 ADV: **to fly ~** volar a ciegas; **to be ~ drunk*** estar como una cuba*; **he swore ~ that ...*** juró por todo lo más sagrado que ...
4 VT cegar; (*dazzle*) deslumbrar; **to be ~ed in an accident** quedar ciego después de un accidente; **to be ~ed by anger** estar cegado por la ira, estar ciego de ira.

blinder ['blaɪndəʳ] N **(a) to play a ~ (of a match)*** jugar maravillosamente. **(b) ~s** (US) anteojeras *fpl*.

blindfold ['blaɪndfəʊld] **1** ADJ con los ojos vendados; *game of chess* a la ciega; **I could do it ~** sé hacerlo con los ojos cerrados.
2 N venda *f*.
3 VT vendar los ojos a.

blinding ['blaɪndɪŋ] ADJ *light* intenso, cegador, deslumbrante.

blindingly ['blaɪndɪŋlɪ] ADV: **a ~ obvious fact** un hecho de meridiana claridad; **it is ~ obvious that ...** es meridianamente claro que ...

blindly ['blaɪndlɪ] ADV a ciegas (*also fig*), ciegamente.

blind-man's buff ['blaɪndmænz'bʌf] N gallina *f* ciega.

blindness ['blaɪndnɪs] N ceguera *f*, ceguedad *f*.

blindworm ['blaɪndwɜːm] N lución *m*.

blini(s) ['blɪnɪ(z)] N panqueque *m* ruso.

blink [blɪŋk] **1** N parpadeo *m*; (*gleam*) destello *m*; **to be on the ~*** funcionar mal, no pitar*.
2 VT guiñar, cerrar momentáneamente; **to ~ one's eyes** parpadear; **there is no ~ing the fact that ...** es imposible soslayar el hecho de que ...
3 VI parpadear, pestañear; (*light*) oscilar.

blinkered ['blɪŋkəd] ADJ (*fig*) ignorante; de miras estrechas, de cabeza cuadrada.

blinkers ['blɪŋkəz] NPL **(a)** (*Brit*) anteojeras *fpl*. **(b)** (*Aut*) (luces *fpl*) intermitentes *mpl*.

blinking* ['blɪŋkɪŋ] ADJ maldito.

blip [blɪp] N **(a)** = **bleep**.
(b) (*fig*) irregularidad *f* momentánea; interrupción *f* temporal; **this is just a ~** esto es un mal momento que pasará pronto.

bliss [blɪs] N (*Rel*) bienaventuranza *f*; (*happy state*) felicidad *f*; (*fig*) éxtasis *m*, arrobamiento *m*; **the concert was ~!** ¡el concierto fue una gloria!; **what ~!** ¡qué dicha!, ¡qué encanto!; **isn't he ~?** ¡qué hombre más estupendo!

blissful ['blɪsfʊl] ADJ bienaventurado; (*happy*) feliz; (*fig*) deleitoso; (*) maravilloso, estupendo.

blissfully ['blɪsfəlɪ] ADV felizmente *etc*; **to be ~ ignorant** vivir en la luna; **to be ~ ignorant** (or **unaware**) **of** estar completamente ajeno a, estar totalmente inconsciente de.

blister ['blɪstəʳ] **1** N ampolla *f*.
2 VT ampollar, causar ampollas en.
3 VI ampollarse.

blistering ['blɪstərɪŋ] ADJ *heat* abrasador; *criticism* feroz, devastador.

blister-pack ['blɪstə,pæk] N envase *m* en lámina al vacío.

blister-packed ['blɪstə,pækt] ADJ envasado en lámina al vacío.

blithe [blaɪð] ADJ alegre.

blithely ['blaɪðlɪ] ADV alegremente.

blithering* ['blɪðərɪŋ] ADJ: **~ idiot** imbécil *mf*.

B.Lit(t) [,biː'lɪt] N ABBR of **Bachelor of Letters**.

blitz [blɪts] **1** N guerra *f* relámpago; (*Aer*) bombardeo *m* aéreo; (*fig*) campaña *f* (*on contra*); **the B~** el bombardeo alemán de Gran Bretaña en 1940-42; **to have a ~ on** hacer campaña contra.
2 VT bombardear.

blitzkrieg ['blɪtskriːg] N guerra *f* relámpago.

blizzard ['blɪzəd] N ventisca *f*.

BLM N (US) ABBR of **Bureau of Land Management**.

bloated ['bləʊtɪd] ADJ hinchado (*also fig*; *with* de), abotagado.

bloater ['bləʊtəʳ] N arenque *m* ahumado.

blob [blɒb] N (*drop*) gota *f*; (*blot*) borrón *m*; (*stain*) mancha *f*.

bloc [blɒk] N bloque *m*; **en ~** en bloque.

block [blɒk] **1** N **(a)** (*stone*) bloque *m*; (*wood*) zoquete *m*, tarugo *m*; (*for paving*) adoquín *m*; (*butcher's, executioner's*) tajo *m*; (*child's toy*) cubo *m*; (*of brake*) zapata *f*; (*of cylinder*) bloque *m*; (*Brit Typ*) molde *m*; (*Brit: writing pad*) bloc *m*; **~s** (*Sport*) taco *m* de salida; **on the ~** (US*) a tocateja*; **~ (and tackle**) aparejo *m* de polea; **~ diagram** diagrama *m* de bloques; **to knock sb's ~ off*** romper la crisma a uno.
(b) (*buildings*) manzana *f*, cuadra *f* (*LAm*); **~ of flats** (*Brit*) edificio *m* de pisos, bloque *m* de viviendas; **it's 5 ~s away** (US) eso queda a 5 calles (*LAm*: cuadras) de aquí; **to take a stroll round the ~** dar un paseo alrededor de la manzana (*LAm*: cuadra).
(c) (*quantity*) bloque *m*; **~ booking** reserva *f* en bloque; **~ grant** subvención *f* en bloque; **~ of seats** grupo *m* de asientos; **~ of shares** bloque *m* de acciones; **~ release** (*Brit Scol*) exención *f* (or descargo *m*) por estudios; **~ vote** voto *m* por representación.
(d) (*obstruction*) obstáculo *m*, estorbo *m*; **writer's ~** bloqueo *m* de escritor; **to have a mental ~** tener un bloqueo mental.
(e) (*Comput*) bloque *m*.
2 ADJ: **~ letter** mayúscula *f*, letra *f* de molde; **please write in ~ letters** escribir por favor en caracteres de imprenta.

3 VT obstruir, cerrar, atorar (*LAm*); *traffic, progress* estorbar, impedir; (*Parl*) *bill* bloquear; (*Comm*) *account* bloquear; (*Comput*) agrupar; **'road ~ed'** 'cerrado (por obras)'; **the line is ~ed in 4 places** la vía está cortada en 4 lugares; **my nose is ~ed** tengo la nariz taponada.
4 VI obstruirse, cerrarse.
◆ **block in** VT (*sketch roughly*) esbozar.
◆ **block off** VT *road etc* cortar; (*accidentally*) bloquear.
◆ **block out** VT (*sketch roughly*) esbozar; (*suppress*) suprimir, tachar.
◆ **block up** VT tapar, cegar; **his nose is all ~ed up** tiene la nariz congestionada.

blockade [blɒ'keɪd] **1** N bloqueo *m*; **to run the ~** forzar (or burlar) el bloqueo.
2 VT (*also US: traffic*) bloquear.

blockage ['blɒkɪdʒ] N obstrucción *f*; obstáculo *m*, estorbo *m*.

blockbuster ['blɒk,bʌstəʳ] N (*Mil*) bomba *f* revientamanzanas; (*fig*) suceso *m* (*etc*) fulminante; bomba *f*.

blockhead ['blɒkhed] N zopenco *m*, -a *f*; **you ~!** ¡imbécil!

blockhouse ['blɒkhaʊs] N, PL **blockhouses** ['blɒkhaʊzɪz] blocao *m*.

bloke* [bləʊk] N (*Brit*) tío* *m*, sujeto *m*; (*boyfriend*) amigo *m*.

blond(e) [blɒnd] **1** ADJ rubio, güero (*CAm, Mex*).
2 N rubio *m*, -a *f*, güero *m*, -a *f* (*CAm, Mex*).

blood [blʌd] **1** N **(a)** sangre *f*; (*family*) sangre *f*, linaje *m*; raza *f*; parentesco *m*; **~ royal** estirpe *f* regia; **bad ~** mala *f* leche, mala *f* uva; **this created** (or **made**) **bad ~ between them** esto causó rencores entre ellos; **in cold ~** a sangre fría; **that man of ~** aquel monstruo; **~ is thicker than water** la sangre es más espesa que el océano; **it's in the ~** lo lleva la masa de la sangre; **they're out for ~** están dispuestos a verter sangre; **he's after my ~** me tiene un odio mortal, (*hum*) quiere darme una paliza; **when my ~ is up** cuando me encolerizo; **to donate** (or **give**) **~** dar su sangre; **to draw ~** hacer que sangre uno, herir, (*fig*) herir en lo vivo; **he has X's ~ on his hands** tiene las manos manchadas con la sangre de X; **it makes my ~ boil** hace que se me queme la sangre, me saca de quicio; **we need new ~ in the company** hace falta gente nueva en la compañía; **my ~ ran cold** se me heló la sangre; **to scent ~**, **to smell ~** oler la sangre; **to shed one's ~** verter su sangre; **to shed** (or **spill**) **the ~ of** derramar la sangre de; **without shedding ~** sin efusión de sangre; **it's like trying to get ~ out of a stone** es como sacar agua de las piedras.
(b) (††: *person*) galán *m*.
2 VT *hound* iniciar; *new talent* fomentar, criar.

blood-and-thunder ['blʌdən'θʌndəʳ] **1** ADJ aparatosamente violento, intencionadamente cruel; melodramático.
2 N violencia *f* aparatosa, crueldad *f* intencionada; melodrama *m*.

bloodbank ['blʌdbæŋk] N banco *m* de sangre.

bloodbath ['blʌdbɑːθ] N, PL **bloodbaths** ['blʌdbɑːðz] carnicería *f*, baño *m* de sangre.

blood-blister ['blʌd,blɪstəʳ] N ampolla *f* de sangre.

blood brother ['blʌd,brʌðəʳ] N hermano *m* de sangre.

blood-cell ['blʌdsel] N célula *f* sanguínea.

blood-clot ['blʌdklɒt] N coágulo *m* sanguíneo.

blood corpuscle ['blʌd,kɔːpʌsl] N glóbulo *m* sanguíneo.

bloodcount ['blʌdkaʊnt] N recuento *m* sanguíneo.

bloodcurdling ['blʌd,kɜːdlɪŋ] ADJ espeluznante, horripilante.

blood-donor ['blʌd,dəʊnəʳ] N donante *mf* de sangre.

blood-feud ['blʌdfjuːd] N odio *m* de sangre, enemistad *f* mortal (entre clanes, familias).

blood-group ['blʌdgruːp] N grupo *m* sanguíneo.

blood-grouping ['blʌd,gruːpɪŋ] N grupo *m* sanguíneo.

blood-heat ['blʌdhiːt] N temperatura *f* de la sangre.

bloodhound ['blʌdhaʊnd] N **(a)** sabueso *m*. **(b)** (*) policía *m*, sabueso *m*.

bloodied ['blʌdɪd] ADJ ensangrentado; **~ but unbowed** (*fig*) incólume, con una voluntad a prueba de bombas.

bloodily ['blʌdɪlɪ] ADV sangrientamente, con efusión de sangre; violentamente.

bloodiness ['blʌdɪnɪs] N (*lit*) lo sangriento *etc*.

bloodless ['blʌdlɪs] ADJ exangüe; (*lacking spirit*) soso; *revolt etc* incruento, sin efusión de sangre.

bloodlessly ['blʌdlɪslɪ] ADV sin efusión de sangre.

blood-letting ['blʌd,letɪŋ] N (*Med*) efusión *f* de sangre, sangría *f*; (*fig*) sangría *f*, carnicería *f*.

bloodlust ['blʌdlʌst] N sed *f* de sangre.

blood-money ['blʌd,mʌnɪ] N dinero *m* manchado de sangre; precio *m* de la sangre.

blood-orange ['blʌd,ɒrɪndʒ] N naranja *f* sanguina.

blood-plasma ['blʌd,plæzmə] N plasma *m* sanguíneo.

blood-poisoning ['blʌd,pɔɪznɪŋ] N envenenamiento *m* de la sangre.

blood-pressure ['blʌd,preʃəʳ] N presión *f* sanguínea, tensión *f* arterial; **high ~** hipertensión *f*.

blood-pudding [,blʌd'pʊdɪŋ] N (US) morcilla *f*.

blood-red ['blʌd'red] ADJ sanguíneo, sanguinolento.

blood-relation ['blʌdrɪ'leɪʃən] N pariente *m* consanguíneo, parienta *f* consanguínea.
blood-relationship [ˌblʌdrɪ'leɪʃənʃɪp] N consanguinidad *f*; lazo *m* de parentesco.
blood-sausage [ˌblʌd'sɒsɪdʒ] N (*US*) = **blood-pudding**.
bloodshed ['blʌdʃed] N efusión *f* de sangre; mortandad *f*.
bloodshot ['blʌdʃɒt] ADJ inyectado en (or de) sangre, sanguinolento.
blood-sports ['blʌdspɔːts] NPL caza *f*.
bloodstain ['blʌdsteɪn] N mancha *f* de sangre.
bloodstained ['blʌdsteɪnd] ADJ manchado de sangre.
bloodstock ['blʌdstɒk] N caballos *mpl* de raza.
bloodstone ['blʌdstəʊn] N restañasangre *m*; sanguinaria *f*.
bloodstream ['blʌdstriːm] N corriente *f* sanguínea, sangre *f*.
bloodsucker ['blʌdsʌkər] N (*fig*) sanguijuela *f*.
blood sugar ['blʌd'ʃʊgər] ① N azúcar *m* en sangre.
② ATTR: ~ **level** nivel *m* de azúcar en sangre.
blood-test ['blʌdtest] N análisis *m* de sangre.
blood-thirstiness ['blʌd,θɜːstɪnɪs] N (*of person, animal*) sed *f* (or avidez *f*) de sangre; (*of book, of story*) violencia *f*.
bloodthirsty ['blʌdθɜːstɪ] ADJ sanguinario.
blood-transfusion ['blʌdtrænz'fjuːʒən] N transfusión *f* de sangre.
blood-type ['blʌdtaɪp] N grupo *m* sanguíneo.
blood-vessel ['blʌd,vesl] N vaso *m* sanguíneo.
bloody ['blʌdɪ] ① ADJ *a battle* sangriento, cruento; *steak* sanguinolento; *hands, dress* ensangrentado, manchado de sangre; **B~ Mary** María la Sangrienta, María Tudor; ~ **mary** bloody mary *m*, vodka *m* con zumo de tomate.
(**b**) (*Brit*⁑) puñetero⁑, condenado*; **shut the ~ door!** ¡cierra la puerta, coño!⁑; **that ~ dog!** ¡ese puñetero perro!⁑; **you ~ idiot!** ¡gran imbécil!
② ADV (*Brit*⁑) muy, terriblemente, condenadamente; **not ~ likely!** ¡ni hablar!; **he can ~ well do it himself** que lo haga él, ¡coño!⁑
③ VT manchar de sangre; **with bloodied hands** con las manos ensangrentadas; **he was bloodied but unbowed** (*fig*) había sufrido pero no se daba por vencido.
bloody-minded ['blʌdɪ'maɪndɪd] ADJ (*Brit*) malintencionado, de mal genio, de malas pulgas; **to be ~ about a matter** mostrarse poco dispuesto a ayudar en un asunto, crear dificultades para la solución de un problema; **don't be so ~!** ¡no seas malintencionado!, ¡qué mala idea!
bloody-mindedness⁑ ['blʌdɪ'maɪndɪdnɪs] N mala intención *f*; mal genio *m*; mala disposición *f* (para ayudar *etc*); **it's just ~ (on his part)** son ganas de joder⁑.
bloom [bluːm] ① N flor *f*; floración *f*; (*fig*) perfección *f*; lozanía *f*; (*on fruit*) vello *m*; **in ~** en flor; **in full ~** en plena floración; **in the full ~ of youth** en la flor de la edad; **to come into ~** florecer.
② VI florecer; (*fig*) prosperar, lozanear.
bloomer* ['bluːmər] N plancha* *f*.
bloomers ['bluːməz] NPL pantalones *mpl* (de señora), bombachos *mpl*.
blooming ['bluːmɪŋ] (**a**) ADJ floreciente; lleno de salud. (**b**) (*euph**) = **bloody 1** (b).
blooper⁑ ['bluːpər] N (*US*) metedura *f* de pata.
blossom ['blɒsəm] ① N flor *f*; **in ~** en flor.
② VI florecer; **to ~ into** transformarse en, convertirse (algo inesperado) en; **to ~ out** alcanzar su plenitud, florecer, hacer eclosión.
blot [blɒt] ① N borrón *m* (*also fig*); **a ~ on the family escutcheon** una mancha en el honor de la familia; **a ~ on the landscape** una cosa que afea el paisaje.
② VT (*with ink*) manchar, emborronar; (*with blotter*) secar; *reputation* desacreditar.
③ VI (*pen*) echar borrones; (*ink*) correrse.
◆**blot out** VT oscurecer, tapar, hacer desaparecer; (*fig*) aniquilar; borrar (el recuerdo de).
◆**blot up** VT *ink* secar; *mist* beber, absorber.
blotch [blɒtʃ] N mancha *f*; (*on skin*) erupción *f*, rojez *f*.
blotchy ['blɒtʃɪ] ADJ manchado, lleno de manchas; *skin* lleno de manchas.
blotter ['blɒtər] N secante *m* tipo rodillo, secafirmas *m*; (*sheet*) hoja *f* de papel secante.
blotting-pad ['blɒtɪŋ,pæd] N secante *m*.
blotting-paper ['blɒtɪŋ,peɪpər] N papel *m* secante.
blotto⁑ ['blɒtəʊ] ADJ: **to be ~** estar mamado⁑.
blouse [blaʊz] N blusa *f*.
blouson ['bluːzɒn] N cazadora *f*.
blow¹ [bləʊ] N (**a**) golpe *m*; bofetada *f*; (**a ~ with** *may often be translated by the suffix -azo, eg*) **a ~ with a hammer** un martillazo, **a ~ with the fist** un puñetazo; **a ~ by ~ account** una narración pormenorizada; **at one ~** de un solo golpe; **to cushion** (or **soften**) **the ~** amortiguar el golpe; (*fig*) disminuir los efectos de un desastre (*etc*), hacer menos severo un impacto; **to deal** (or **strike**) **sb a ~** dar (or asestar) un golpe a uno; **to strike a ~ for freedom** dar un golpe por

la libertad; **without striking a ~** sin violencia; **to come to ~s** venir a las manos.
(**b**) (*fig*) golpe *m*; **at one ~** de un golpe; de repente; **that's a ~!** ¡qué lástima!; **it is a cruel ~ for everybody** es un golpe cruel para todos; **the news came as a great ~** la noticia me *etc* causó un gran disgusto; **the affair was a ~ to his pride** la cosa le hirió en el amor propio; **it was a final ~ to our hopes** esto acabó de arruinar nuestras esperanzas; **on Monday the ~ fell** el lunes se descargó el golpe.
blow² [bləʊ] ① N soplo *m*, soplido *m*.
② (*irr*: PRET **blew**, PTP **blown**) VT (**a**) (*of wind*) llevar; **the wind blew the ship towards the coast** el viento llevó el barco hacia la costa; **the wind has blown dust all over it** el viento lo ha cubierto todo de polvo; **to ~ open** *door* abrir de golpe, *safe* abrir con explosivos; **the wind blew the door shut** el viento cerró la puerta de golpe; **to ~ a matter wide open** destapar un asunto.
(**b**) (*make by blowing*) *glass* soplar; *bubble* hacer, formar.
(**c**) *trumpet etc* tocar, sonar; *nose* sonarse; *kiss* tirar, enviar con la mano; *egg* vaciar (soplando); *organ* dar viento a; *whistle* pitar.
(**d**) (*destroy*) *fuse* fundir, quemar; *safe* abrir (con explosivos); **he blew a gasket** or (*US*) **his cork** or (*US*) **his stack** (*fig*) estaba que trinaba; **to ~ sb's cover** quitar la cobertura de uno; **to ~ sb's mind⁑** barrer la mente de uno*, dejar a uno alucinado*; **to ~ it⁑** cagarla⁑; **now you've blown it!⁑** ¡ya la has cagado!⁑
(**e**) (*) *money* tirar, despilfarrar.
(**f**) (*) ~ **me!**, ~ **it!**, **well I'm ~ed!** ¡caramba!; **I'll be ~ed if ...** que me cuelguen si ...; ~ **the expense!** ¡al diablo con el gasto!
(**g**) **to ~ grass** (*Drugs⁑*) fumar hierba.
③ VI (**a**) (*wind, whale*) soplar; (*siren etc*) sonar; (*puff and* ~) jadear, resoplar; **it's ~ing a gale** hace muchísimo viento; **to ~ on one's fingers** soplarse los dedos; **to ~ on one's soup** enfriar la sopa soplando; **to ~ open** abrirse de golpe; **the referee blew for a foul** el árbitro pitó para señalar falta.
(**b**) (*fuse*) fundirse, quemarse.
(**c**) (*: leave*) irse; pirarla*; **I must ~** tengo que largarme*.
◆**blow about** VT *leaves etc* llevar de acá para allá.
◆**blow away** ① VT llevarse; arrancar; hacer desaparecer.
② VI ser llevado (por el viento); ser arrancado (por el viento).
◆**blow down** ① VT derribar.
② VI ser derribado (por el viento).
◆**blow in*** VI entrar de sopetón; llegar (inesperadamente).
◆**blow off** VT quitar, arrebatar; **to ~ the dust off a table** quitar el polvo de una mesa soplando.
◆**blow out** ① VT (**a**) *candle* apagar. (**b**) *cheeks* henchir. (**c**) **it blew out the window** rompió la ventana.
② VI (**a**) (*candle etc*) apagarse. (**b**) (*tyre*) reventar; (*window*) romperse (con la fuerza del viento *etc*).
③ VR: **next day the storm had blown itself out** al día siguiente la tormenta se había calmado.
◆**blow over** ① VT derribar, volcar.
② VI pasar; pasar al olvido, quedar olvidado; no tener consecuencias de importancia; (*storm*) pasar, calmarse.
◆**blow up** ① VT (**a**) *tyre* inflar. (**b**) *photo* ampliar. (**c**) (*with explosive*) volar, hacer saltar, explotar. (**d**) (*) (*with publicity*) dar bombo a; **to ~ sb up into a great novelist** hacer creer que alguien es gran novelista. (**e**) (*) **the boss blew the boy up** el jefe puso al chico como un trapo*.
② VI (**a**) (*explosive*) estallar, explotar, explosionar; (*container*) estallar, reventar; (*) reventar (de ira). (**b**) **it's ~ing up for rain** con este viento tendremos lluvia; **now sth else has ~n up** ahora ha surgido otra cosa.
blow-drier ['bləʊ,draɪər] N secador *m* de pelo.
blow-dry ['bləʊ,draɪ] VT secar con secador.
blower⁑ ['bləʊər] N teléfono *m*.
blowfly ['bləʊflaɪ] N moscarda *f*, mosca *f* azul.
blowgun ['bləʊ,gʌn] N (*US*) cerbatana *f*.
blowhole ['bləʊhəʊl] N (*of whale*) orificio *m* nasal; (*Tech*) sopladura *f*, venteadura *f*.
blow job⁑ ['bləʊdʒɒb] N francés⁑ *m*, felacio *f*.
blowlamp ['bləʊlæmp] N soplete *m*, lámpara *f* de soldar.
blown [bləʊn] ① PTP of **blow²**.
② ADJ (**a**) *flower* marchito. (**b**) *bridge etc* volado, destruido.
blow-out ['bləʊaʊt] N (**a**) (*Aut*) pinchazo *m*, pinchadura *f* (*Mex*); (*Elec*) quemadura *f*; (*of oil-well*) erupción *f*. (**b**) (⁑: *meal*) banquetazo* *m*, comilona* *f*.
blowpipe ['bləʊpaɪp] N cerbatana *f*.
blowsy ['blaʊzɪ] = **blowzy**.
blow-torch ['bləʊtɔːtʃ] N soplete *m*.
blow-up ['bləʊʌp] N (**a**) (*Phot*) ampliación *f*. (**b**) (*) explosión *f* de ira; riña *f*, pelea *f* (*between* entre).
blowy ['bləʊɪ] ADJ ventoso; de mucho viento; **on a ~ day in March** un día de marzo de mucho viento; **it's ~ here** aquí hay mucho viento.

blowzy ['blauzɪ] ADJ desaliñado; de aspecto muy ordinario; (*red in face*) coloradote.
BLS N (*US*) ABBR *of* **Bureau of Labor Statistics**.
BLT N ABBR *of* **bacon, lettuce and tomato** (**sandwich**).
blub* [blʌb] VI lloriquear.
blubber¹ ['blʌbər] N grasa *f* de ballena.
blubber² ['blʌbər] ① VT decir lloriqueando.
 ② VI lloriquear, llorar a lágrima viva.
blubbery ['blʌbərɪ] ADJ (*fat*) fláccido, fofo; ~ **lips** labios *mpl* carnosos.
bludgeon ['blʌdʒən] ① N cachiporra *f*.
 ② VT aporrear; **to ~ sb into doing sth** (*fig*) coaccionar (*or* forzar) a uno a hacer algo.
blue [bluː] ① ADJ (a) azul; *body, bruise* amoratado; (*Pol*) conservador; *blood* azul, noble; ~ **with cold** amoratado de frío; **you can talk till you're ~ in the face*** puedes hablar hasta que revientes; **to go like a ~ streak** ir como un rayo; **to talk like a ~ streak*** hablar muy rápidamente; ~ **baby** niño *m*, -a *f* azul, niño *m* cianótico, niña *f* cianótica; ~ **beret** (*UN*) casco *m* azul; ~ **blood** sangre *f* azul; ~ **book** (*US Scol*) cuaderno *m* de exámenes; ~ **cheese** queso *m* de tipo Roquefort, queso *m* de gusanos*; ~ **chips, ~-chip securities** fianzas *fpl* fiables; ~ **grass** (*US*) hierba norteamericana usada como forraje; ~ **grass music** (*US*) música folk de Kentucky; ~ **jeans** tejanos *mpl*, vaqueros *mpl*; ~ **pencil** lápiz *m* negro (en la censura); **B~ Peter** (*Naut*) bandera *f* de salida; ~ **shark** tiburón *m* azul; ~ **whale** ballena *f* azul; ~ **whiting** bacaladilla *f*.
 (b) (*sad*) triste, deprimido, melancólico; **to feel ~** estar melancólico; **to look ~** tener aspecto triste.
 (c) (*obscene*) verde, colorado (*LAm*); ~ **film** película *f* porno.
 ② N (a) azul *m*; (*Chem*) añil *m*; **the ~** (*sky*) el cielo, (*sea*) el mar; **to come out of the ~** venir como cosa llovida del cielo, bajar del cielo; (*bad news*) caer como una bomba; **he said out of the ~** dijo de repente, dijo inesperadamente.
 (b) (*Pol*) conservador *m*, -ora *f*; V **true-blue**.
 (c) **~s** melancolía *f*, murrias *fpl*, morriña *f*; (*Mus*) blues *m*.
 (d) **Dark/Light B~** (*Brit Univ*) deportista *mf* representante de Oxford/de Cambridge.
 ③ VT (a) azular; *washing* añilar, dar azulete a. (b) (*Brit*) despilfarrar.
Bluebeard ['bluːbɪəd] NM Barba Azul.
bluebell ['bluːbel] N jacinto *m* silvestre; (*Scot: harebell*) campanilla *f*.
blueberry ['bluːberɪ] N (*US*) arándano *m*.
bluebird ['bluːbɜːd] N pájaro *m* azul, azulejo *m* (de América).
blue-blooded ['bluːˈblʌdɪd] ADJ de sangre noble, linajudo.
bluebottle ['bluːˌbɒtl] N moscarda *f*, mosca *f* azul.
blue-chip ['bluːˈtʃɪp] ATTR: ~ **company** empresa *f* que gestiona con inversión muy segura; ~ **investment** inversión *f* en acciones de mucha demanda; inversión *f* asegurada.
blue-collar ['bluːˌkɒlər] ATTR: ~ **worker** manual *mf*.
blue-eyed ['bluːˌaɪd] ADJ de ojos azules; ~ **boy*** (*Brit*) favorito *m*, ojo *m* derecho.
bluejacket ['bluːˌdʒækɪt] N marinero *m* (de buque de guerra).
bluejay ['bluːdʒeɪ] N (*US*) arrendajo *m* azul.
blueness ['bluːnɪs] N azul *m*, lo azul.
blue-pencil ['bluːˈpensl] VT (*US*) tachar con lápiz negro (en la censura).
blueprint ['bluːprɪnt] N cianotipo *m*, ferroprusiato *m*; (*fig*) anteproyecto *m* (*for* de).
blue-sky ['bluːskaɪ] ATTR (*US*): ~ **laws** legislación *f* para regular la emisión y venta de valores.
bluestocking ['bluːˌstɒkɪŋ] N literata *f*, marisabidilla *f*.
bluesy ['bluːzɪ] ADJ (*Mus*) de blues.
bluetit ['bluːtɪt] N herrerillo *m* (común).
blue-water ['bluːˌwɔːtər] ADJ (*Naut*) *navy, ship* de altura, pelágico.
bluey ['bluːɪ] ADJ azulado.
bluff¹ [blʌf] ① ADJ (a) *cliff etc* escarpado. (b) *person* brusco, francote.
 ② N (*Geog*) risco *m*, peñasco *m*.
bluff² [blʌf] ① N bluff *m*, blof *m* (*LAm*), farol *m*; **to call sb's ~** descubrirle a uno la fanfarronada, pillar a uno en un farol, coger a uno la palabra (*Sp*).
 ② VT hacer un bluff a, engañar, intimidar con amenazas que no se pueden cumplir.
 ③ VI hacer un bluff, farolear, tirarse un farol.
bluffer ['blʌfər] N farolero *m*.
bluish ['bluːɪʃ] ADJ azulado, azulino.
blunder ['blʌndər] ① N patochada *f*, metedura *f* de pata; error *m* garrafal.
 ② VI hacer una patochada, tirarse una plancha.
 ◆ **blunder about** VI andar a ciegas, andar a tontas y a locas.
 ◆ **blunder into** VT chocar con.
 ◆ **blunder out** VT descolgarse con.
 ◆ **blunder upon** VT tropezar con.
blunderbuss ['blʌndəbʌs] N trabuco *m*.
blunderer ['blʌndərər] N torpe *m*, metelapata* *m*.

blundering ['blʌndərɪŋ] ① ADJ *person* torpe, que mete la pata; *words, act* torpe.
 ② N torpeza *f*.
blunt [blʌnt] ① ADJ (a) *edge* embotado, desafilado; *point* despuntado; **with a ~ instrument** con un instrumento contundente. (b) *manner* directo, franco, abrupto; *statement* terminante, franco; *person* francote; **I will be ~ with you** voy a hablar con franqueza; **he was very ~ with me** conmigo no se mordió la lengua.
 ② VT embotar (*also fig*), desafilar, despuntar.
bluntly ['blʌntlɪ] ADV francamente; de modo terminante.
bluntness ['blʌntnɪs] N (a) embotadura *f*. (b) (*fig*) franqueza *f*, brusquedad *f*.
blur [blɜːr] ① N contorno *m* borroso, impresión *f* imprecisa; **my mind was a ~** no me podía acordar claramente, todo se había vuelto borroso en mi mente.
 ② VT hacer borroso, oscurecer, empañar, desdibujar; **a ~red photo** una foto desenfocada; **a ~red image** una imagen borrosa; **my eyes were ~red with tears** las lágrimas enturbiaban mi vista.
 ③ VI desdibujarse, hacerse borroso.
blurb [blɜːb] N anuncio *m* efusivo (de un libro), propaganda *f* publicitaria.
blurred [blɜːd] ADJ (a) *outline, photo etc* borroso, poco nítido. (b) *speech* incoherente, poco claro; *memory* borroso.
blurt [blɜːt] VT: **to ~ out** descolgarse con; *secret* revelar, dejar escapar impulsivamente.
blush [blʌʃ] ① N rubor *m*, sonrojo *m*; (*glow*) color *m* de rosa; (*US: make-up*) colorete *m*; **the first ~ of dawn** la primera luz del alba; **in the first ~ of youth** en la inocencia de la edad juvenil; **at first ~** a primera vista; **it should not bring a ~ to the face of a bishop** no haría sonrojar a una hermana de la caridad; **to spare sb's ~es** (dejar de contar algo para) no ofender a uno.
 ② VI ruborizarse, sonrojarse, ponerse colorado (*at* por, *with* de); **to ~ like a lobster** (*or* **tomato**) ponerse colorado como un pavo; **I ~ for you** me das vergüenza; **I ~ to +** *infin* me avergüenzo de + *infin*; **to make sb ~** sofocar a uno, hacer que uno se ruborice.
blusher ['blʌʃər] N colorete *m*.
blushing ['blʌʃɪŋ] ADJ ruboroso; *bride* candoroso.
bluster ['blʌstər] ① N jactancia *f*; fanfarronadas *fpl*, bravatas *fpl*.
 ② VT: **to ~ it out** defenderse echando bravatas, baladronear.
 ③ VI fanfarronear, echar bravatas.
blusterer ['blʌstərər] N fanfarrón *m*.
blustering ['blʌstərɪŋ] ADJ *person* jactancioso, fanfarrón.
blustery ['blʌstərɪ] ADJ *wind* tempestuoso; *day* de mucho viento.
Blvd ABBR *of* **boulevard** Bulevar *m*, Blvr.
BM N (a) ABBR *of* **British Museum**. (b) ABBR *of* **Bachelor of Medicine** licenciado *m*, -a *f* en medicina.
BMA N ABBR *of* **British Medical Association**.
BMC N ABBR *of* **British Medical Council**.
BMJ N ABBR *of* **British Medical Journal**.
B.Mus. [ˌbiːˈmʌs] N ABBR *of* **Bachelor of Music**.
BMX N ABBR *of* **bicycle motorcross** ciclocross *m*; ~ **bike** bicicleta *f* de ciclocross.
bn ABBR *of* **billion**.
BNFL N ABBR *of* **British Nuclear Fuels Limited**.
BNP N (*Pol*) ABBR *of* **British National Party** *partido político de la extrema derecha*.
B/O (*Fin*) ABBR *of* **brought over** suma *f* anterior.
BO N (a) (*euph*) ABBR *of* **body odour** olor *m* a sudor. (b) (*US*) ABBR *of* **box-office**.
b.o. (*Comm*) ABBR *of* **buyer's option** opción *f* del comprador.
boa ['bəʊə] N (*snake, fur etc*) boa *f*; ~ **constrictor** boa *f*.
Boadicea [ˌbəʊədɪˈsɪə] NF Boadicea.
boar [bɔːr] N verraco *m*, cerdo *m* (padre); **wild ~** jabalí *m*, coche *m* de monte (*Mex*).
board [bɔːd] ① N (a) (*of wood*) tabla *f*, tablero *m*, tablón *m*; (*notice ~*) tablón *m*, tablero *m*; (*table*) mesa *f*; (*in bookbinding*) cartón *m*; (*for chess etc*) tablero *m*; (*Comput*) placa *f*, tarjeta *f*; **the ~s** (*Theat*) las tablas; **increase across the ~** aumento *m* global (*or* general *or* lineal); **in ~s** *book* en cartoné; **to sweep the ~** ganar todas las bazas, (*in election*) copar todos los escaños; **to tread the ~s** (*as profession*) ser actor, ser actriz, (*action*) salir a escena.
 (b) (*provision of meals*) pensión *f*; **full ~** pensión *f* (completa); ~ **and lodging** (*Brit*) comida *f* y casa, (*as advert*) comidas *fpl* y camas.
 (c) (*Naut*) **on ~** a bordo; en el tren, en el autobús *etc*; **on ~ (the) ship** a bordo del barco; **to go on ~** embarcarse, ir a bordo; **to go by the ~** ser abandonado; **to take on ~** *idea etc* adoptar, asimilar.
 (d) (*persons*) junta *f*, consejo *m* de administración; ~ **of directors** junta *f* directiva; ~ **of governors** (*Brit Scol*) consejo *m* (de escuela); ~ **of inquiry** comisión *f* investigadora; **B~ of Trade** (*Brit*) Departamento *m* de Comercio y Exportación, (*US*) Cámara *f* de Comercio; ~ **meeting** reunión *f* de la junta directiva.
 ② VT (a) *ship* ir a bordo de, embarcarse en; *enemy ship* abordar; *bus,*

train subir a. **(b)** *person* hospedar, dar pensión (completa) a.
[3] VI: **to ~ with** hospedarse en casa de.
◆ **board in** VT = **board up.**
◆ **board out** VT *person* buscar alojamiento a; **he is ~ed out with rela-tives** vive con unos parientes (pagando la pensión).
◆ **board up** VT *door, window* entablar.
boarder ['bɔːdəʳ] N huésped *m*, -eda *f*; (*Brit Scol*) interno *m*, -a *f*.
board-game ['bɔːdgeɪm] N juego *m* de mesa.
boarding ['bɔːdɪŋ] N entablado *m*.
boarding-card ['bɔːdɪŋ,kɑːd] N tarjeta *f* de embarque.
boarding-house ['bɔːdɪŋhaʊs] N, PL **boarding-houses** ['bɔːdɪŋ,haʊzɪz] pensión *f*, casa *f* de huéspedes.
boarding-party ['bɔːdɪŋ,pɑːtɪ] N pelotón *m* de abordaje.
boarding-pass ['bɔːdɪŋ,pɑːs] N tarjeta *f* de embarque, pase *m* de embarque (*LAm*).
boarding-school ['bɔːdɪŋskuːl] N internado *m*.
boardroom ['bɔːdrʊm] N sala *f* de juntas.
boardwalk ['bɔːdwɔːk] N paseo *m* entablado.
boast [bəʊst] [1] N fanfarronada *f*, alarde *m*; **it is his ~ that ...** se jacta de que ...
[2] VT enorgullecerse de poseer, ostentar.
[3] VI jactarse; **to ~ about, to ~ of** jactarse de, hacer alarde de; **that's nothing to ~ about** eso no es motivo para vanagloriarse.
boasted ['bəʊstɪd] ADJ alardeado, cacareado.
boaster ['bəʊstəʳ] N jactancioso *m*, -a *f*, fanfarrón *m*, -ona *f*, pre-sumido *m*, -a *f*.
boastful ['bəʊstfʊl] ADJ jactancioso, fanfarrón, presumido.
boastfully ['bəʊstfʊlɪ] ADV jactanciosamente.
boastfulness ['bəʊstfʊlnɪs] N jactancia *f*.
boasting ['bəʊstɪŋ] N jactancia *f*, fanfarronadas *fpl*.
boat [bəʊt] N (*gen*) barco *m*; (*large ship*) buque *m*, navío *m*; (*small*) barca *f*, embarcación *f*; (*racing eight, ship's ~*) bote *m*; **we're all in the same ~** todos estamos embarcados en la misma nave, todos remamos en la misma galera; **to burn one's ~s** quemar las naves, **to go by ~** ir en barco; **to launch** (*or* **lower**) **the ~s** botar los botes al agua; **to miss the ~** (*fig*) perder el tren; **to push the ~ out*** celebrar dispendiosamente; ir de parranda; tirar la casa por la ventana; **to rock the ~** (*fig*) hacer olas, perturbar el equilibrio.
boatbuilder ['bəʊt,bɪldəʳ] N constructor *m* de barcos; **~'s** (**yard**) asti-llero *m*.
boatbuilding ['bəʊt,bɪldɪŋ] N construcción *f* de barcos.
boat-deck ['bəʊt,dek] N cubierta *f* de botes.
boater ['bəʊtəʳ] N canotier *m*, canotié *m*.
boatful ['bəʊtfʊl] N (*goods*) cargamento *m*; **the refugees arrived in ~s** llegaron barcos llenos de refugiados.
boat-hook ['bəʊthʊk] N bichero *m*.
boathouse ['bəʊthaʊs] N, PL **boathouses** ['bəʊthaʊzɪz] cobertizo *m* para botes.
boating ['bəʊtɪŋ] N canotaje *m*; **~ holiday/trip** vacaciones *fpl*/paseo *m* en barca.
boatload ['bəʊtləʊd] N barcada *f*.
boatman ['bəʊtmən] N, PL **boatmen** ['bəʊtmen] barquero *m*.
boat people ['bəʊt,piːpl] NPL *refugiados que huyen en barco* (*esp de Vietnam*).
boat-race ['bəʊtreɪs] N regata *f*; **the B~ Race** *carrera anual de remo en-tre Oxford y Cambridge*.
boatswain ['bəʊsn] N contramaestre *m*.
boat-train ['bəʊttreɪn] N tren *m* que enlaza con un barco, tren *m* del barco.
boatyard ['bəʊtjɑːd] N astillero *m*.
Bob [bɒb] NM *familiar form of* **Robert;** **~'s your uncle!*** (*Brit*) ¡ya está!, ¡y se acabó!
bob¹ [bɒb] [1] N (*of hair*) pelo *m* a lo garçon.
[2] VT *hair* cortar a lo garçon.
bob²* [bɒb] N, PL INVAR (*Brit*) chelín *m*.
bob³ [bɒb] [1] N (*jerk*) sacudida *f*, meneo *m*, movimiento *m* brusco; (*curtsy*) reverencia *f* (breve).
[2] VI menearse, agitarse.
◆ **bob about** VI (*in wind etc*) bailar; (*on water*) fluctuar.
◆ **bob down** VI agacharse; esconderse.
◆ **bob to** VI: **to ~ to sb** hacer una reverencia a uno.
◆ **bob up** VI levantarse; aparecer; (*fig*) surgir, presentarse inesperadamente; **to ~ up and down** subir y bajar; (*person*) levantarse y sentarse repetidas veces.
bob⁴ [bɒb] N (*also* **bobsleigh**) bob *m*, bobsleigh *m*.
bobbin ['bɒbɪn] N carrete *m*, bobina *f* (*also Elec*); (*Sew*) canilla *f*.
bobble ['bɒbl] [1] N (**a**) borla *f*. (**b**) (*US**) pifia *f*.
[2] VT (*US**) pifiar.
Bobby ['bɒbɪ] NM *familiar form of* **Robert.**
bobby* ['bɒbɪ] N guili* *m*, poli* *m*.
bobby pin ['bɒbɪ,pɪn] N (*US*) horquilla *f*, prendedor *m*.
bobbysocks* ['bɒbɪsɒks] NPL (*US*) escarpines *mpl*.

bobbysoxer* ['bɒbɪsɒksəʳ] N (*US*) tobillera *f*.
bobcat ['bɒbkæt] N (*US*) lince *m*.
bobsled ['bɒbsled] N, **bobsleigh** ['bɒbsleɪ] N bob *m*, bobsleigh *m*.
bobtail ['bɒbteɪl] N cola *f* corta; animal *m* de cola corta, animal *m* rabón.
bobtailed ['bɒbteɪld] ADJ rabicorto.
Boccaccio [bɒˈkætʃɪəʊ] NM Bocacio.
Boche [bɒʃ] [1] ADJ (*pej*) alemán, tudesco.
[2] N (*pej*) boche *m*, alemán *m*; **the ~** los alemanes.
bock beer ['bɒk,bɪəʳ] N (*US*) cerveza *f* alemana.
bod* [bɒd] N (*Brit*) tío* *m*, individuo *m*.
bode [bəʊd] [1] VT presagiar; **it ~s no good** esto no nos promete nada bueno.
[2] VI: **this ~s ill for** es mala señal para, es de mal agüero para.
bodega [bəʊˈdeɪgə] N (*grocery shop*) almacén *m*, tienda *f* de ul-tramarinos.
bodge* [bɒdʒ] VT = **botch.**
bodice ['bɒdɪs] N corpiño *m*, almilla *f*.
bodice-ripping ['bɒdɪsrɪpɪŋ] ADJ *film, novel* romanticón.
-bodied ['bɒdɪd] *ending in compounds* de cuerpo ..., *eg* **small~** de cuerpo pequeño; **full~** *cry* fuerte, *wine* de mucho cuerpo.
bodily ['bɒdɪlɪ] [1] ADJ corpóreo, corporal; **~ harm** daños *mpl* corporales; **~ needs** necesidades *fpl* corporales.
[2] ADV (*in person*) en persona; (*as a whole*) en conjunto; **to lift sb ~** levantar a uno en peso.
bodkin ['bɒdkɪn] N (*Sew*) aguja *f* de jareta; (*Typ*) punzón *m*; (*for hair:* ††) espadilla *f* ††.
body ['bɒdɪ] N (**a**) cuerpo *m*; (*corpse*) cadáver *m*; (*) persona *f*; (*frame*) armazón *f*, bastidor *m*; (*Aut*) caja *f*, carrocería *f*; (*Astron, Chem*) cuerpo *m*; **~ and soul** (*as adv*) de todo corazón, con el alma; **the ~ politic** el estado; **~ repairs** (*Aut*) reparación *f* de la carrocería; **~ (repair) shop** taller *m* de reparaciones; **over my dead ~!** ¡sobre mi cadáver!; ¡bajo ningún concepto!; **to keep ~ and soul together** vivir justo, seguir viviendo; **her salary hardly keeps ~ and soul together** apenas si gana para vivir.
(b) (*corporation etc*) corporación *f*, cuerpo *m*.
(c) (*group*) grupo *m*, conjunto *m*; **a considerable ~ of evidence** una colección importante de datos; **there is a ~ of opinion that ...** hay quienes opinan que ...; **a large ~ of people** un nutrido grupo de personas; **main ~** grueso *m*; **the main ~ of his speech** la parte principal de su discurso; **in a ~** todos juntos, en bloque.
(d) (*of wine*) cuerpo *m*, volumen *m*.
body armour, (*US*) **body armor** ['bɒdɪ,ɑːməʳ] N *equipo de protección corporal.*
body-bag ['bɒdɪ,bæg] N bolsa *f* para restos humanos.
body-blow ['bɒdɪ,bləʊ] N (*fig*) golpe *m* duro.
body-builder ['bɒdɪ,bɪldəʳ] N culturista *mf*.
body-building ['bɒdɪ,bɪldɪŋ,] N culturismo *m*.
body clock ['bɒdɪ'klɒk] N reloj *m* biológico.
body count ['bɒdɪ,kaʊnt] N (*US*) número *m* de muertos; **to do a ~** (*of those present*) hacer un recuento de la asistencia; (*of dead*) hacer un recuento de los muertos.
body double ['bɒdɪ'dʌbl] N (*Cine, TV*) doble *m*.
bodyguard ['bɒdɪgɑːd] N (*man*) guardaespaldas *m*; (*royal*) guardia *f* de corps; (*men*) guardia *f* personal.
body-language ['bɒdɪ,læŋgwɪdʒ] N lenguaje *m* gestual, gestualidad *f*.
body-lotion ['bɒdɪ,ləʊʃən] N loción *f* corporal.
body-mike* ['bɒdɪmaɪk] N micrófono *m* escondido, micro* *m* de solapa.
body-odour, (*US*) **body-odor** ['bɒdɪ,əʊdəʳ] N olor *m* a sudor.
body-scanner ['bɒdɪ,skænəʳ] N escáner *m*.
body-search ['bɒdɪsɜːtʃ] [1] N registro *m* de la persona.
[2] VT registrar (la persona de).
body-snatcher ['bɒdɪ,snætʃəʳ] N (*Hist*) ladrón *m* de cadáveres.
body stocking ['bɒdɪ,stɒkɪŋ] N, **body suit** ['bɒdɪ,suːt] N body *m*, bodi *m*.
body warmer ['bɒdɪ,wɔːməʳ] N chaleco *m* acolchado.
bodywork ['bɒdɪwɜːk] N (*Aut*) carrocería *f*.
Boer ['bəʊəʳ] [1] ADJ bóer.
[2] N bóer *mf*.
Boer War ['bəʊə,wɔːʳ] N Guerra *f* Bóer, Guerra *f* del Transvaal.
B. of E. N ABBR *of* **Bank of England.**
boffin ['bɒfɪn] N (*Brit*) científico *m*, inventor *m*.
bog [bɒg] [1] N (**a**) pantano *m*, ciénaga *f*. (**b**) (*Brit‡*) meadero‡ *m*; *ver también* TOILET .
[2] VT: **to get ~ged down** quedar atascado en el lodo, hundirse en el lodo; (*fig*) empantanarse, atrancarse (*in* en).
bogey ['bəʊgɪ] N (**a**) (*goblin*) duende *m*, trasgo *m*; (*bugbear*) pesadilla *f*; **that is our ~ team** ése es un equipo gafe para nosotros.
(b) (*Brit‡: policeman*) bofia‡ *m*.
(c) (*Rail*) bogie *m*, boga *f*.
(d) (*Golf*) bogey *m*, más uno *m*.

bogeyman ['bəʊgɪ,mæn] N, PL **bogeymen** ['bəʊgɪ,men] coco *m*.

boggle ['bɒgl] **1** VI sobresaltarse, pasmarse; **don't just stand and ~** no te quedes ahí parado con la boca abierta; **the imagination ~s** la imaginación es incapaz de representárselo; **the mind ~s** nos quedamos pasmados; **to ~ at** vacilar ante, titubear ante.
2 VT: **to ~ the mind*** dejar alucinado.

boggy ['bɒgɪ] ADJ pantanoso.

bogie ['bəʊgɪ] N = **bogey**.

Bogotá [,bɒgəʊ'tɑː] N Bogotá *m*.

bog-paper; ['bɒg,peɪpəʳ] N (*Brit*) papel *m* higiénico, papel *m* de wáter.

bog-roll; ['bɒgrəʊl] N (*Brit*) rollo *m* de papel de wáter.

bog-standard* ['bɒg'stændəd] ADJ (*Brit*) normalito, nada del otro mundo.

bogtrotter; ['bɒg,trɒtəʳ] N (*pej*) irlandés *m*, -esa *f*.

bogus ['bəʊgəs] ADJ falso, fraudulento; *person* fingido; (*of person's character*) artificial, afectado.

bogy ['bəʊgɪ] N = **bogey, bogie**.

Bohemia [bəʊ'hiːmɪə] N Bohemia *f*.

Bohemian [bəʊ'hiːmɪən] **1** ADJ bohemo; (*fig*) bohemio.
2 N bohemo *m*, -a *f*; (*fig*) bohemio *m*, -a *f*.

Bohemianism [bəʊ'hiːmɪənɪzəm] N bohemia *f*, vida *f* bohemia.

boho* ['bəʊhəʊ] **1** ADJ bohemio.
2 N bohemio *m*, -a *f*.

boil¹ [bɔɪl] N (*Med*) divieso *m*, furúnculo *m*, chupón *m* (*And*), postema *f* (*Mex*).

boil² [bɔɪl] **1** N: **to be on the ~** estar hirviendo; (*fig*) (*situation*) estar a punto de estallar, (*person*) estar furioso; **to bring to the** (*US*: **a**) **~** calentar hasta que hierva, llevar a ebullición; **to come to the** (*US*: **a**) **~** comenzar a hervir, (*fig*) entrar en ebullición; **to go off the ~** dejar de hervir.
2 VT hervir, hacer hervir, calentar hasta que hierva; (*Culin*) *liquid* hervir; *vegetables, meat* herventar, cocer; *salcochar*; *egg* pasar por agua.
3 VI (**a**) hervir; **to ~ dry** hervir hasta que se consume el caldo. (**b**) (*fig*) **it makes me ~** me hace rabiar; **to ~ with rage** estar furioso; **to ~ with indignation** estar indignado.
♦**boil away** VI (*evaporate completely*) evaporarse, reducirse (por ebullición).
♦**boil down** **1** VT *sauce etc* reducir por cocción; (*fig*) reducir a forma más sencilla.
2 VI: **~ down to** reducirse a; **it all ~s down to this** la cosa se reduce a lo siguiente.
♦**boil over** VI (**a**) (*liquid*) irse, rebosar. (**b**) (*fig*) desbordarse.
♦**boil up** VI (*lit: milk*) hervir, subir; **anger was ~ing up in him** estaba a punto de estallar de ira; **they are ~ing up for a real row** se están enfureciendo de verdad.

boiled [bɔɪld] ADJ hervido; **~ egg** huevo *m* pasado por agua; **~ potatoes** patatas *fpl* cocidas al agua; **~ shirt** camisa *f* de pechera; **~ sweet** (*Brit*) caramelo *m* con sabor a frutas.

boiler ['bɔɪləʳ] N (**a**) caldera *f*; (*Brit: for washing clothes*) caldero *m*, calefón *m* (*SC*). (**b**) (*Culin*) pollo *m* viejo (*que sólo sirve para hervir*).

boilerhouse ['bɔɪləhaʊs] N, PL **boilerhouses** ['bɔɪləhaʊzɪz] edificio *m* de la caldera.

boilermaker ['bɔɪlə,meɪkəʳ] N calderero *m*.

boiler-room ['bɔɪlərʊm] N sala *f* de calderas.

boilersuit ['bɔɪləsuːt] N (*Brit*) mono *m*.

boiling ['bɔɪlɪŋ] **1** ADJ hirviendo (*invariable*), en ebullición.
2 ADV: **it's ~ hot** (*weather*) hace un calor terrible; **on a ~ hot day** un día de mucho calor.

boiling-point ['bɔɪlɪŋpɔɪnt] N punto *m* de ebullición.

boil-in-the-bag ['bɔɪlɪnðə'bæg] ADJ: **~ meals** platos que se cuecen en su misma bolsa.

boisterous ['bɔɪstərəs] ADJ *wind* borrascoso; *behaviour* ruidoso, turbulento; *child* bullicioso, revoltoso; (*in high spirits*) muy alegre, de excelente humor; *meeting* nada tranquilo, alborotado; *welcome* tumultuoso.

boisterously ['bɔɪstərəslɪ] ADV (V ADJ) bulliciosamente; ruidosamente.

bold [bəʊld] ADJ (*courageous*) valiente, audaz; (*excessively ~*) atrevido, osado, temerario; (*shameless*) descarado; *move, stroke* enérgico; *relief, contrast* fuerte; *headland* escarpado; *line* claro, vigoroso; **~ face** (*Typ*) negrita *f*; **~ type** (*Typ*) (caracteres *mpl* en) negrita *f*; **he came up as ~ as brass** se acercó tan fresco; **if I may make so ~** si Vd me lo permite; **if I may make so ~ as to** + *infin* si se me permite + *infin*.

boldly ['bəʊldlɪ] ADV (V ADJ) audazmente; atrevidamente, con temeridad; descaradamente; enérgicamente; vigorosamente.

boldness ['bəʊldnɪs] N (V ADJ) audacia *f*, osadía *f*; temeridad *f*; descaro *m*; energía *f*; fuerza *f*, lo marcado.

bole [bəʊl] N tronco *m*.

bolero [bə'lɛərəʊ] N bolero *m*.

boletus [bəʊ'liːtəs] N seta *f*.

Bolivia [bə'lɪvɪə] N Bolivia *f*.

Bolivian [bə'lɪvɪən] **1** ADJ boliviano.

2 N boliviano *m*, -a *f*.

boll [bəʊl] N (*Bot*) cápsula *f*.

bollard ['bɒləd] N (*Brit*) (*at wharf*) bolardo *m*, noray *m*; (*Aut*) poste *m*.

bollocking; ['bɒləkɪŋ] N: **to give sb a right ~** poner a uno como un trapo*.

bollocks; ['bɒləks] NPL (*Brit*) = **ball¹ (b)**.

Bollywood* ['bɒlɪwʌd] N (*hum*) la industria cinematográfica de la India.

Bologna [bə'ləʊnjə] N Bolonia *f*.

bolognese [bɒlə'njeɪz] ADJ: **~ sauce** salsa *f* boloñesa.

boloney; [bə'ləʊnɪ] N (*US: sausage*) tipo de salchicha; (*nonsense*) chorradas; *fpl*; = **baloney**.

Bolshevik ['bɒlʃəvɪk] **1** ADJ bolchevique.
2 N bolchevique *mf*.

Bolshevism ['bɒlʃəvɪzəm] N bolchevismo *m*, bolcheviquismo *m*.

Bolshevist ['bɒlʃəvɪst] **1** ADJ bolchevista.
2 N bolchevista *mf*.

bolshie*, bolshy* ['bɒlʃɪ] **1** N bolchevique *mf*.
2 ADJ (*Pol*) bolchevique; (*fig*) revoltoso; difícil; protestón*, contestón*.

bolster ['bəʊlstəʳ] **1** N travesero *m*, cabezal *m*; (*Tech*) cojín *m*.
2 VT (*also to ~ up*) reforzar; (*fig*) alentar, dar aliento a.

bolt [bəʊlt] **1** N (**a**) (*of door, rifle*) cerrojo *m*; (*of crossbow*) cuadrillo *m*; (*of cloth*) rollo *m*; (*Tech*) perno *m*, tornillo *m*; (*of thunder*) rayo *m*; **~ from the blue** suceso *m* inesperado, sorpresa *f* desagradable; **like a ~ from the blue** como una bomba; **he has shot his ~** ha quemado su último cartucho.
(**b**) (*dash*) fuga *f* precipitada, salida *f* repentina; **to make a ~ for it** evadirse corriendo, fugarse repentinamente; **he made a ~ for the door** se precipitó hacia la puerta.
2 as ADV: **~ upright** rígido, erguido; **to sit ~ upright** (*action*) incorporarse de golpe.
3 VT (**a**) *door* echar el cerrojo a; (*Tech*) sujetar con tornillos, empernar; **to ~ together** unir con pernos.
(**b**) *food* engullir, comer rapidísimamente.
4 VI (*escape*) fugarse; (*horse*) desbocarse, dispararse; (*rush*) precipitarse; (*US Pol*) separarse del partido; **to ~ past** pasar como un rayo.
♦**bolt in** **1** VT (*lock in*) encerrar echando el cerrojo (*or* bajo cerrojo).
2 VI (*rush in*) entrar precipitadamente.
♦**bolt on** VT (*Tech*) asegurar con perno.
♦**bolt out** **1** VT (*lock out*) **to ~ sb out** dejar fuera a uno echando el cerrojo.
2 VI (*rush out*) salir de golpe.

bolt-hole ['bəʊlthəʊl] N refugio *m*.

bomb [bɒm] **1** N bomba *f*; **~ alert**, **~ warning** aviso *m* de bomba; **~ attack** atentado con bomba; **~ scare** amenaza *f* con bomba; **this car goes like a ~** (*Brit**) este coche corre a toda pastilla (*or* va a toda hostia;); **it all went like a ~*** (*Brit*) todo fue sobre ruedas*, todo fue a las mil maravillas*; **it costs a ~*** (*Brit*) cuesta un ojo de la cara*; **he made a ~*** se ganó un fortunón*.
2 VT bombardear; (*US: fail*) suspender.
3 VI (*US*) fracasar.
♦**bomb along*** VI ir como el demonio, ir muy rápido; **we were ~ing along at 150** corríamos a 150.
♦**bomb out** VT *house* volar; **the family was ~ed out** (*by terrorists*) a la familia les volaron la casa; (*by planes*) a la familia les bombardearon la casa.

bombard [bɒm'bɑːd] VT bombardear; (*fig*) asediar, llenar (*with* de); **I was ~ed with questions** me acribillaron a preguntas.

bombardier [,bɒmbə'dɪəʳ] N bombardero *m*.

bombardment [bɒm'bɑːdmənt] N bombardeo *m*.

bombast ['bɒmbæst] N ampulosidad *f*, rimbombancia *f*; (*words*) palabras *fpl* altisonantes; (*boasts*) bravatas *fpl*.

bombastic [bɒm'bæstɪk] ADJ altisonante, ampuloso, rimbombante; *person* jactancioso, farolero.

bombastically [bɒm'bæstɪklɪ] ADV altilocuentemente, ampulosamente, rimbombantemente.

Bombay [bɒm'beɪ] N Bombay *m*; **~ duck** (*Culin*) pescado seco utilizado en la elaboración del curry.

bomb-bay ['bɒm,beɪ] N compartimento *m* de bombas.

bomb-crater ['bɒm,kreɪtəʳ] N cráter *m* de bomba.

bomb-disposal ['bɒmdɪs'pəʊzəl] N desactivación *f* de bombas, neutralización *f* de bombas; **~ expert** técnico *m* de desactivación de bombas, artificiero *m*; **~ squad**, **~ unit** brigada *f* de bombas.

bomber ['bɒməʳ] N bombardero *m*; **~ command** jefatura *f* de bombardeo; **~ jacket** cazadora *f* de aviador; **~ pilot** piloto *m* de bombardero.

bomb factory ['bɒm'fæktərɪ] N local clandestino de fabricación de bombas.

bombing ['bɒmɪŋ] N bombardeo *m*.

bombproof ['bɒmpruːf] ADJ a prueba de bombas.

bombshell ['bɒmʃel] N obús *m*, granada *f*; **it fell like a ~** cayó como una bomba; **she was a real ~** era algo excepcional; **a blond ~** una rubia despampanante*.

bomb-shelter ['bɒmˌʃeltər] N refugio m antiaéreo.

bombsight ['bɒmsaɪt] N mira f de bombardeo, visor m de bombardeo.

bomb-site ['bɒmsaɪt] N lugar m donde ha estallado una bomba; solar m arrasado por una bomba.

bona fide ['bəʊnə'faɪdɪ] ADJ genuino, auténtico, de fiar, fiable.

bona fides ['bəʊnə'faɪdɪz] N buena fe f; autenticidad f.

bonanza [bə'nænzə] N (US Min, fig) bonanza f.

bonce: [bɒns] N coco* m.

bond [bɒnd] ⓵ N (a) (link) lazo m, vínculo m; **~s of friendship** lazos mpl de amistad; **the marriage ~** el vínculo del matrimonio.
(b) (Fin) bono m, obligación f; (bail, customs) fianza f; **in ~** en depósito bajo fianza; **~ washing** lavado m de bonos; **to put goods into ~** poner mercancías en el almacén aduanero; **to take goods out of ~** retirar mercancías del almacén aduanero.
(c) (Chem etc) enlace m.
(d) **~s** (fetters) cuerdas fpl, cadenas fpl.
⓶ VT (also **to ~ together**) liar, vincular.

bondage ['bɒndɪdʒ] N esclavitud f, cautiverio m; (as fetish) bondage m.

bonded ['bɒndɪd] ADJ: **~ goods** mercancías fpl en depósito de Aduanas; **~ warehouse** almacén m aduanero.

bondholder ['bɒndˌhəʊldər] N obligacionista mf, titular mf de bonos.

bonding ['bɒndɪŋ] N vinculación f.

bone [bəʊn] ⓵ N hueso m; (of fish) espina f; **~s** (of dead) huesos mpl, (more respectfully) restos mpl mortales; **~ of contention** manzana f de la discordia; **close to the ~** joke verde, arriesgado; **to feel sth in one's ~s** tener una corazonada con respecto a algo, tener un presentimiento de algo; **to work one's fingers to the ~** trabajar como un esclavo; **to have a ~ to pick with sb** tener que arreglar cuentas con uno; **to make no ~s about** + ger no vacilar en + infin; **to make no ~s about sth** no tener reparos en algo, no andarse con rodeos en (el asunto de) algo; **he won't make old ~s** no llega a viejo.
⓶ VT (a) meat deshuesar, fish quitar las espinas a. (b) (:) birlar:.
⓷ VI (*) **to ~ up** quemarse las cejas (on estudiando), empollar (on sobre).

bone china ['bəʊn'tʃaɪnə] N porcelana f fina.

boned [bəʊnd] ADJ meat deshuesado; fish sin espinas; corset de ballenas.

bone-dry ['bəʊn'draɪ] ADJ enteramente seco.

bonehead* ['bəʊnhed] N tonto m, -a f.

boneheaded* ['bəʊn'hedɪd] ADJ estúpido.

bone-idle ['bəʊn'aɪdl] ADJ muy gandul.

boneless ['bəʊnlɪs] ADJ (a) (Anat) sin hueso(s), deshuesado. (b) (fig) sin carácter, débil.

bone-marrow ['bəʊnˌmærəʊ] N médula f ósea.

bonemeal ['bəʊnmiːl] N harina f de huesos.

boner* ['bəʊnər] N (US) plancha f, patochada f; **to pull a ~** meter el cuezo*.

bone-shaker* ['bəʊnˌʃeɪkər] N (Aut etc) armatoste m, rácano m.

bonfire ['bɒnfaɪər] N hoguera f, fogata f; **B~ Night** (Brit) fiesta que se celebra en la noche del 5 noviembre en toda Gran Bretaña.

bongo ['bɒŋɡəʊ] N (also **~ drum**) bongó m.

bonhomie ['bɒnɒmiː] N afabilidad f.

bonk¹* [bɒŋk] ⓵ N (blow) golpe m.
⓶ VT golpear, pegar.

bonk²* [bɒŋk] N: **it went ~** hizo ¡pum!, se oyó un ruido sordo; **things that go ~ in the night** cosas que hacen ruidos misteriosos en la noche.

bonk³: [bɒŋk] VTI joder:.

bonkers: ['bɒŋkəz] ADJ (Brit): **to be ~** estar chalado*; **to go ~** chalarse*.

bonking: ['bɒŋkɪŋ] N joder: m.

bon mot ['bɒn'məʊ] N dicho m agudo, chiste m, agudeza f.

Bonn [bɒn] N Bona m, Bonn m.

bonnet ['bɒnɪt] N (a) (woman's) gorra f, cofia f; (large, showy) papalina f, toca f; (baby's) gorro m; (Scot's) gorra f escocesa. (b) (Brit Aut) capó m.

bonny ['bɒnɪ] ADJ (esp Scot) bonito, rollizo.

bonsai ['bɒnsaɪ] N bonsai m.

bonus ['bəʊnəs] ⓵ N plus m; (on wages) sobrepaga f, bonificación f, prima f, suplemento m, abono m (LAm); (insurance etc) prima f; (to shareholders) dividendo m adicional.
⓶ ADJ adicional, extra; **~ scheme** plan m de incentivos; **~ shares, ~ stock** (US) acciones fpl gratuitas.

bony ['bəʊnɪ] ADJ huesudo; (like bone) óseo, huesoso; (thin) descarnado, flaco.

boo [buː] ⓵ N (equivalents in Spain etc) silbido m, rechifla f, pateo m; **he couldn't say ~ to a goose*** no dice ni mu.
⓶ VT abuchear, silbar, rechiflar, patear; **to ~ an actor** patear a un

actor; **he was ~ed off the stage** tuvo que abandonar la escena a fuerza de pateo.
⓷ VI silbar.

boob* [buːb] ⓵ N (mistake) patochada f.
⓶ VI tirar una plancha.

boobies: ['buːbɪz] NPL (US), **boobs:** [buːbz] NPL tetas* fpl.

booboo* ['buːbuː] N (US) patochada f.

boobtube ['buːbtjuːb] N (US: TV set) televisor m; (sun top) camiseta-tubo f.

booby ['buːbɪ] N bobo m.

booby hatch ['buːbɪˌhætʃ] N (US:) casa f de locos.

booby-prize ['buːbɪpraɪz] N premio m al peor competidor.

booby-trap ['buːbɪtræp] ⓵ N trampa f; (bomb) trampa f explosiva, trampa f cazabobos, bomba f trampa.
⓶ VT poner trampa explosiva a; **the house had been ~ped** habían puesto una trampa explosiva en la casa.

booby-trapped ['buːbɪtræpt] ADJ: **~ car** coche-bomba m; **~ door** puerta f con sorpresa.

boogie* ['buːɡɪ] ⓵ N (dance) baileteo* m; **to go for a ~** irse de marcha*, darle marcha (al cuerpo):.
⓶ VI bailotear*, dar marcha (al cuerpo):.

boogie-woogie ['buːɡɪˌwuːɡɪ] N bugui-bugui m.

boo-hoo* [ˌbuːˈhuː] ⓵ VI lloriquear, berrear*.
⓶ EXCL ¡bua!

booing ['buːɪŋ] N abucheo m, silbos mpl, rechifla f.

book [bʊk] ⓵ N (a) (gen) libro m; (notebook) libreta f, librito m; (exercise book) cuaderno m; (of cheques, tickets) (libro m) talonario m; (of members) registro m; (of stamps) taco m; **it's a closed ~ to me** para mí es un asunto misterioso; **the good ~** la Biblia; **in my ~** (fig) a mi modo de ver, en mi concepto; **to be in sb's good ~s** estar bien con uno; **to be in sb's bad** (or **black**) **~s** estar mal con uno, estar en la lista negra de uno; **there's no such name on our ~s** no existe ese nombre en nuestro registro, no consta tal nombre en nuestros registros; **to bring sb to ~** pedir cuentas a uno, llamar a uno a capítulo; **to go by the ~** proceder según las reglas (or normas); **to make a ~ on** aceptar apuestas sobre; **to read sb like a(n open) ~** conocer a uno a fondo; conocer a uno como la palma de la mano; **to suit sb's ~** convenir a uno; **to throw the ~ at sb** acusar a uno de todo lo posible; castigar a uno con todo rigor; **that's one for the ~s** (or **for the ~** (US)) es digno de ser enmarcado. (b) (Comm, Fin) **the ~s** los libros, las cuentas; el balance; **to close the ~s** cerrar los libros; **to cook the ~s*** falsificar las cuentas; **to keep the ~s** llevar las cuentas, llevar los libros; **~ debts** deudas fpl contabilizadas; **~ entry** apunte m en los libros de contabilidad; **~ value** valor m en libros.
⓶ VT (note down) apuntar; (Comm) asentar (to en la cuenta de), order anotar; room, place reservar; (Brit) ticket sacar; performer contratar; suspect fichar*, reseñar; (Sport) player reseñar; **please ~ us in for Tuesday** le ruego reservarnos una habitación para el martes; **the hotel is ~ed up** todas las habitaciones del hotel están reservadas; **we are ~ed up all summer** no tenemos nada libre en todo el verano, lo tenemos todo reservado para todo el verano; **are you ~ed up for tonight?** ¿tienes compromiso para esta noche?
⓷ VI: **to ~ in** firmar el registro; tomar una habitación; reservar una habitación; **~ well in advance** es aconsejable reservar con mucha anticipación; **to ~ through to** sacar un billete hasta.

bookable ['bʊkəbl] ADJ seat etc que se puede reservar (de antemano); (Sport) offence sujeto a tarjeta amarilla.

bookbinder ['bʊkˌbaɪndər] N encuadernador m, -ora f.

bookbinding ['bʊkˌbaɪndɪŋ] N encuadernación f.

bookcase ['bʊkkeɪs] N librería f, estante m para libros, librero m (Carib).

book-club ['bʊkklʌb] N club m de lectores.

book-ends ['bʊkendz] NPL sujetalibros mpl, soportalibros mpl.

ⓘ **BOOKER PRIZE**

Booker Prize es el nombre de un premio literario que se concede anualmente a una obra de ficción en inglés publicada en el Reino Unido, Irlanda o cualquier otro país de la **Commonwealth**. El premio, que viene otorgándose desde 1969, es de 15.000 libras esterlinas y está financiado por la empresa **Booker McConnell**. La entrega de premios, en la que se anuncia el ganador, provoca un considerable interés en los medios de comunicación y se televisa en directo. La decisión de los jueces, normalmente escritores, catedráticos y críticos, suele generar bastante polémica.

---

book-fair ['bʊkfeər] N feria f de libros.

bookie* ['bʊkɪ] N = **bookmaker**.

▼ **booking** ['bʊkɪŋ] N (esp Brit) reserva f; contratación f; **he had 9 ~s last year** (Sport) el año pasado se le tomó el nombre 9 veces, el año pasado recibió tarjeta amarilla 9 veces.

booking-clerk ['bʊkɪŋˌklɑːk] N (Brit) taquillero m, -a f.

booking-office ['bʊkɪŋˌɒfɪs] N (Rail) despacho m de billetes (LAm:

boletos); (*Theat*) taquilla *f*.

bookish ['bʊkɪʃ] ADJ *learning* libresco; *person* estudioso, (*pej*) pedantesco.

book-jacket ['bʊk,dʒækɪt] N sobrecubierta *f*.

book-keeper ['bʊk,kiːpəʳ] N contable *mf*, contador *m*, -ora *f*, tenedor *m*, -ora *f* de libros.

book-keeping ['bʊk,kiːpɪŋ] N teneduría *f* de libros; **~ by double entry** contabilidad *f* por partida doble; **~ by single entry** contabilidad *f* por partida simple.

book-learning ['bʊk,lɜːnɪŋ] N saber *m* libresco, erudición *f*.

booklet ['bʊklɪt] N folleto *m*; (*learned*) opúsculo *m*; (*of tickets*) bono *m*.

book-lover ['bʊk,lʌvəʳ] N bibliófilo *m*, -a *f*.

bookmaker ['bʊkmeɪkəʳ] N corredor *m* de apuestas, apostador *m* profesional; *ver también* GREYHOUND RACING .

bookmaking ['bʊkmeɪkɪŋ] N apuestas *fpl*, correduría *f* de apuestas; **a ~ firm** una casa de apuestas.

bookmark ['bʊkmɑːk] N señal *f*, registro *m* (de libro).

bookmobile ['bʊkməʊ,biːl] N (*US*) bibliobús *m*.

bookplate ['bʊkpleɪt] N ex libris *m*.

book-post ['bʊkpəʊst] N correo *m* de libros; tarifa *f* especial para libros.

bookrest ['bʊkrest] N atril *m*.

bookseller ['bʊk,seləʳ] N librero *m*, -a *f*; **~'s** librería *f*.

bookshelf ['bʊkʃelf] N, PL **bookshelves** ['bʊkʃelvz] anaquel *m* para libros, estantería *f*; **~shelves** estante *m* para libros.

bookshop ['bʊkʃɒp] N librería *f*.

bookstall ['bʊkstɔːl] N (*Brit*) quiosco *m* de libros.

bookstore ['bʊkstɔːʳ] N (*US*) librería *f*.

book-token ['bʊk,təʊkən] N (*Brit*) vale *m* para comprar libros.

bookworm ['bʊkwɜːm] N polilla *f*; (*fig*) ratón *m* de biblioteca.

Boolean ['buːlɪən] ADJ booleano; **~ algebra** álgebra *f* de Boole; **~ logic** lógica *f* booleana.

boom¹ [buːm] N (**a**) (*Naut*) (*of jib*) botalón *m*, (*of mainsail*) botavara *f*; (*of crane*) aguilón *m*, brazo *m* (de grúa). (**b**) (*across harbour*) barrera *f*.

boom² [buːm] ① N estampido *m*, trueno *m*.
② VT (*also* **~ out**) tronar; anunciar (*etc*) muy fuerte.
③ VI (*also* **~ out**) hacer estampido, tronar; (*voice, radio, organ*) resonar, retumbar; (*gun*) retumbar.

boom³ [buːm] ① N boom *m*; alza *f* rápida (*in prices* de los precios); prosperidad *f* repentina (*in an industry* de una industria).
② ADJ: **~ economy** economía *f* de alza; **~ market** mercado *m* de alza; **~ town** ciudad *f* boom, ciudad *f* que disfruta de una prosperidad repentina; **in ~ conditions** en condiciones de prosperidad repentina.
③ VI (*prices*) estar en alza; (*commodity*) tener mucha demanda; (*industry, town*) gozar de boom, disfrutar de gran prosperidad.

boomerang ['buːməræŋ] ① N bumerang *m*.
② ADJ contraproducente, contrario a lo que se esperaba.
③ VI tener un resultado contraproducente (*on* para); **it ~ed on him** le salió el tiro por la culata.

booming¹ ['buːmɪŋ] ADJ *voice* resonante, retumbante.

booming² ['buːmɪŋ] ADJ (*Comm etc*) próspero, que goza de boom, floreciente.

boon¹ [buːn] N favor *m*; ventaja *f*, beneficio *m* (*to* para); **it would be a ~ if he went** nos alegraríamos si se fuera; **the new machine is a great ~** la nueva máquina representa un gran adelanto; **the servant is a ~ to me** la criada me ayuda muchísimo; **it should be a ~ to humanity** ha de ser un beneficio para el género humano.

boon² [buːn] ADJ: **~ companion** compañero *m*, -a *f* inseparable.

boondocks* ['buːndɒks] NPL (*US*): **out in the ~** en el quinto pino.

boondoggle* ['buːndɒgl] VI (*US*) enredar*.

boons* [buːnz] NPL (*US*) = **boondocks**.

boor [bʊəʳ] N patán *m*, hombre *m* grosero.

boorish ['bʊərɪʃ] ADJ palurdo, grosero.

boorishly ['bʊərɪʃlɪ] ADV *behave, speak* groseramente.

boorishness ['bʊərɪʃnɪs] N grosería *f*.

boost [buːst] ① N (**a**) (*thrust etc*) empuje *m*, empujón *m*, estímulo *m*, ayuda *f*; **to give a ~ to** = 2. (**b**) (*rise: esp US*) aumento *m*, subida *f*.
② VT empujar (hacia arriba); *price, sales, total* aumentar; *product* hacer publicidad por; *person* dar bombo a; *morale* reforzar; *process* estimular, fomentar, dar ímpetu a; (*Elec*) elevar.

booster¹ ['buːstəʳ] ① N (*Elec*) elevador *m* de tensión, elevador *m* de voltaje; (*Aer*) impulsor *m*, impulsador *m*; (*Mech*) aumentador *m* de presión; (*Rad*) repetidor *m*.
② ATTR auxiliar; **~ injection** revacunación *f*.

booster² ['buːstəʳ] N, **booster rocket** ['buːstə,rɒkɪt] N cohete *m* acelerador (*or* lanzador).

booster station ['buːstə,steɪʃən] N repetidor *m*.

boot¹ [buːt] ① N (**a**) bota *f*; **now the ~ is on the other foot** (*Brit*) los papeles están trastrocados; **to die with one's ~s on** morir con las botas puestas; **to get** (*or* **be given**) **the ~*** ser despedido; **he's get-**

ting too big for his **~s** tiene muchos humos; **to give sb the ~*** poner a uno de patitas en la calle; **to lick sb's ~s** hacer la pelotilla a uno; **to put the ~ in*** emplear la violencia; (*fig*) obrar decisivamente.
(**b**) (*Brit Aut*) maletero *m*, baúl *m* (*LAm*), maletera *f* (*LAm*).
(**c**) (*: *blow*) puntapié *m*.
(**d**) (*US Aut; also* **Denver ~**) cepo *m*.
② VT (**a**) (*kick*) dar un puntapié a; **to ~ out** poner de patitas en la calle.
(**b**) (*Comput*) arrancar, cebar, inicializar.
③ VI (*Comput*) arrancar, cebar, inicializar.

boot² [buːt] ADV: **to ~** (*liter*) además, por añadidura.

bootblack ['buːtblæk] N limpiabotas *m*.

boot camp ['buːtkæmp] N (*in army*) campamento *m* militar; (*prison*) *prisión civil con régimen militar*.

bootee [buː'tiː] N borceguí *m*, bota *f* de lana.

booth [buːð] N (*in market*) puesto *m*; (*at fair*) barraca *f*; (*Telec, interpreter's, voting*) cabina *f*.

booting-up [,buːtɪŋ'ʌp] N (*Comput*) operación *f* de cargo, iniciación *f*; **~ switch** tecla *f* de iniciación.

bootlace ['buːtleɪs] N cordón *m*.

bootleg ['buːtleg] (*US*) ① ADJ: **~ whisky** whisky *m* de contrabando, whisky *m* ilegal.
② VI contrabandear en licores (*etc*).

bootlegger ['buːt,legəʳ] N (*US*) contrabandista *m* en licores.

bootlicker* ['buːt,lɪkəʳ] N lameculos‡ *m*.

bootlicking* ['buːt,lɪkɪŋ] ① ADJ pelotillero*.
② N pelotilleo* *m*.

bootmaker ['buːtmeɪkəʳ] N zapatero *m* que hace botas.

boot-polish ['buːt,pɒlɪʃ] N betún *m*, crema *f* para botas.

boots [buːts] N SING (*Brit*) limpiabotas *m* (de un hotel).

bootstrap ['buːtstræp] N oreja *f*; **to pull oneself up by one's ~s** reponerse gracias a sus propios esfuerzos.

booty ['buːtɪ] N botín *m*, presa *f*.

booze* [buːz] ① N (**a**) (*in general*) bebida *f*, alcohol *m*; (*in particular*) vino *m*, cerveza *f* etc; **to go on the ~** darse a la bebida.
(**b**) (*outing*) borrachera *f*; **to go on a ~** ir de juerga.
② VT beber.
③ VI beber; emborracharse.

boozer‡ ['buːzəʳ] N (**a**) (*person*) bebedor *m*, tomador *m* (*LAm*). (**b**) (*Brit: pub*) bar *m*, taberna *f*.

booze-up‡ ['buːz,ʌp] N (*Brit*) bebezona‡ *f*.

boozy‡ ['buːzɪ] ADJ *person* borracho, aficionado a la bebida; *party* donde se bebe bastante; *song etc* tabernario.

bop¹* [bɒp] (*Mus*) ① N bop *m*.
② VI bailar.

bop²* [bɒp] VT (*US: hit*) cascar*.

bo-peep [bəʊ'piːp] N: **to play ~** jugar tapándose la cara y descubriéndola de repente; **Little B~** *personaje de una poesía infantil, famoso por haber perdido sus ovejas*.

boracic [bə'ræsɪk] ADJ bórico.

borage ['bɒrɪdʒ] N borraja *f*.

borax ['bɔːræks] N bórax *m*.

Bordeaux [bɔː'dəʊ] N Burdeos *m*; **b~** (*wine*) burdeos *m*.

bordello [bɔː'deləʊ] N (*US*) casa *f* de putas.

border ['bɔːdəʳ] ① N borde *m*, margen *m*; (*Sew*) orla *f*, orilla *f*, cenefa *f*; (*Pol*) frontera *f*; (*Hort*) arriate *m*; **the B~** (*Brit*) *la frontera entre Inglaterra y Escocia*.
② ATTR *area, town, ballad* fronterizo; *guard* de la frontera; **~ dispute** disputa *f* fronteriza; **~ incident** incidente *m* fronterizo; **~ patrol** (*US*) patrulla *f* de fronteras; **~ post** puesto *m* fronterizo.
③ VT (*Sew*) ribetear, orlar; **it is ~ed on the north by ...** confina en el norte con ...
◆ **border on** VT lindar con, confinar con; (*fig*) rayar en, aproximarse a.

bordering ['bɔːdərɪŋ] ADJ contiguo.

borderland ['bɔːdəlænd] N zona *f* fronteriza.

borderline ['bɔːdəlaɪn] ① N línea *f* divisoria; (*Pol and fig*) frontera *f*.
② ADJ *case etc* dudoso, incierto; **~ case** caso *m* dudoso.

bore¹ [bɔːʳ] ① N (**a**) (*tool*) taladro *m*, barrena *f*; (*Geol*) sonda *f*.
(**b**) (*hole*) agujero *m*, barreno *m*; (*of gun*) calibre *m*, alma *f*; (*of cylinder*) alesaje *m*; (*for oil*) perforación *f*.
② VT taladrar, perforar, agujerear, barrenar; **to ~ a hole in** practicar un agujero en; **to ~ one's way through** abrirse un camino por; **wood ~d by insects** madera *f* carcomida.
③ VI: **to ~ for oil** hacer perforaciones en busca de petróleo.

bore² [bɔːʳ] ① N (**a**) (*person*) pelmazo *m*, pesado *m*, -a *f*; **what a ~ he is!** ¡qué hombre más pesado!
(**b**) (*thing*) lata* *f*, rollo* *m*; **what a ~!** ¡qué rollo!*; **it's such a ~** es una lata*.
② VT aburrir; fastidiar, molestar, dar la lata a*; **to be ~d, to get ~d** aburrirse; **to be ~d to death** (*or* **to tears, stiff**) aburrirse como una ostra; **to be ~d with** estar harto de.

bore³ [bɔːʳ] PRET of **bear²**.

bore⁴ [bɔːʳ] N (*tidal wave*) marea f.

boredom ['bɔːdəm] N aburrimiento m, fastidio m.

borehole ['bɔːhəʊl] N perforación f.

Borgia ['bɔːdʒjə] N Borja m.

boric ['bɔːrɪk] ADJ: ~ **acid** ácido m bórico.

boring ['bɔːrɪŋ] ADJ aburrido, pesado, latoso.

born [bɔːn] 1 PTP of **bear²**; **to be ~** nacer; **I was ~ in 1927** nací en 1927; **a daughter was ~ to them** les nació una hija; **he wasn't ~ yesterday** es perro viejo; **evil is ~ of idleness** la pereza es madre de todos los vicios; **to be ~ again** renacer, volver a nacer.
2 ADJ actor, artist etc nato; liar innato; **a Londoner ~ and bred** londinense de casta y cuna; **in all my ~ days** en mi vida.

-born [-bɔːn] ADJ ending in compounds: **British~** británico de nacimiento.

born-again ['bɔːnə,gen] ADJ renacido, vuelto a nacer.

borne [bɔːn] PTP of **bear²**.

-borne [-bɔːn] SUFFIX llevado por, traído por; V **water~** etc.

Borneo ['bɔːnɪəʊ] N Borneo m.

boron ['bɔːrɒn] N boro m.

borough ['bʌrə] N (Brit) municipio m; (US) distrito m municipal.

borrow ['bɒrəʊ] VT pedir prestado, tomar prestado (from, of a); idea etc adoptar, apropiarse; word tomar (from de); **may I ~ your car?** ¿me prestas tu coche?; **you can ~ it till I need it** te lo presto hasta que yo lo necesite.

borrower ['bɒrəʊəʳ] N él (la) que toma prestado; (in library) usuario m, -a f; (Comm) prestatario m, -a f.

borrowing ['bɒrəʊɪŋ] N préstamo(s) m(pl) (from de); ~ **power(s)** capacidad f de endeudamiento.

borstal ['bɔːstl] N (Brit) reformatorio m de menores; ~ **boy** joven m delincuente (que ha pasado por el reformatorio).

borzoi ['bɔːzɔɪ] N galgo m ruso.

Bosch [bɒʃ] NM El Bosco.

bosh* [bɒʃ] N tonterías fpl.

bo's'n ['bəʊsən] N = **boatswain**.

Bosnia ['bɒznɪə] N Bosnia f.

Bosnia Herzegovina ['bɒznɪə,hɜːtsəgəʊ'viːnə] N Bosnia f Herzegovina.

Bosnian ['bɒznɪən] 1 ADJ bosnio.
2 N bosnio m, -a f.

bosom ['bʊzəm] 1 N seno m, pecho m; (of garment) pechera f; **in the ~ of the family** en el seno de la familia; **to take sb to one's ~** acoger amorosamente a uno.
2 ATTR friend íntimo, inseparable.

bosomy ['bʊzəmɪ] ADJ tetuda*, de pecho abultado.

Bosphorus ['bɒsfərəs] N Bósforo m.

boss¹ [bɒs] N (bulge) protuberancia f; (stud) clavo m, tachón m; (of shield) ombligo m; (Archit) llave f de bóveda.

boss² [bɒs] 1 N jefe m; (owner, employer) patrón m, amo m; (foreman) capataz m; (manager) gerente m; (US Pol) cacique m; **I like to be my own ~** quiero mandar en mis asuntos, quiero controlar mis propias cosas; **I'm the ~ here** aquí mando yo; **OK, you're the ~** vale, tú mandas.
2 VT (also **to ~ about**) regentar, dar órdenes a, dominar.
3 ADJ (US*) chulo*.
◆**boss around*** VT person mandonear.

boss-eyed [,bɒs'aɪd] ADJ bizco.

bossiness ['bɒsɪnɪs] N carácter m mandón, tiranía f.

bossy ['bɒsɪ] ADJ mandón, tiránico.

Bostonian [bɒs'təʊnɪən] N bostoniano m, -a f.

bosun ['bəʊsən] N = **boatswain**.

botanic(al) [bə'tænɪk(əl)] ADJ botánico.

botanist ['bɒtənɪst] N botánico mf, botanista mf.

botanize ['bɒtənaɪz] VI herborizar.

botany ['bɒtənɪ] N botánica f.

botch [bɒtʃ] 1 N chapuza f; **to make a ~ of** = 2.
2 VT chapucear, chafullar; **to ~ it** arruinarlo, estropearlo; **to ~ up** remendar (chapuceramente).

both [bəʊθ] 1 ADJ AND PRON los dos, ambos; **I bought ~ books** compré ambos libros; ~ **of them are nice** uno y otro son agradables; **we ~ went** fuimos los dos; ~ **of them** los dos; ~ **of us** nosotros dos.
2 ADV AND CONJ: ~ **A and B** tanto A como B; **he ~ plays and sings** canta y toca además; **I find it ~ impressive and vulgar** encuentro que es impresionante y vulgar a la vez.

bother ['bɒðəʳ] 1 N (a) molestia f, lata* f; **it's no ~** no es molestia; **it's such a ~ to clean** me molesta tener que limpiarlo, es muy incómodo limpiarlo; **I went to the ~ of finding one** me tomé la molestia de buscar uno; **what a ~!** ¡qué lata!*
(b) **he had a spot of ~ with the police** tuvo una dificultad con la policía; **do you have much ~ with your car?** ¿tienes muchas dificultades con el coche?

Pronoun and adjective

● When *both* is a pronoun or adjective you can usually translate it using *los/las dos*:
    We're both climbers, Both of us are climbers
    Los dos somos alpinistas
    I know both of them or I know them both
    Los conozco a los dos
    Both (of) sisters were blind
    Las dos hermanas eran ciegas

● Alternatively, in more formal speech, use *ambos/ambas*:
    We both liked it
    Nos gustó a ambos
    Both (of the) regions are autonomous
    Ambas regiones son autónomas
! Don't use the article with *ambos*.

"Both ... and"

● *Both ... and* can be translated in a variety of ways, depending on what is referred to. If it relates to 2 individuals, you can usually use the invariable *tanto ... como*. Alternatively, you can often use *los/las dos*, though this may involve changing the syntax:
    Both Mary and Peter will be very happy here
    Tanto Mary como Peter van a ser muy felices aquí ◊ Mary y Peter van a ser los dos muy felices aquí
    Both Mike and Clare could see something was wrong
    Tanto Mike como Clare veían que algo iba mal

● When talking about 2 groups or things use *tanto ... como* or, if *both* is equivalent to "at one and the same time", use *a la vez*:
    The course is directed at both piano and violin teachers
    El curso está dirigido a profesores tanto de piano como de violín ◊ El curso está dirigido a la vez a profesores de piano y de violín

● *Tanto ... como* can also be used with adverbs:
    He was a weak man both physically and mentally
    Era un hombre débil, tanto física como mentalmente
    NOTE: When adverbs ending in *-mente* are linked together with a conjunction as here, only the last retains the *-mente*.

● When *both ... and* relates to verbs, you can usually use *y además*:
    He both paints and sculpts
    Pinta y además hace esculturas

● Use *a la vez* to comment on descriptions which are both true at the same time:
    The book is both interesting and depressing
    El libro es interesante y deprimente a la vez

---

2 VT molestar, fastidiar, incomodar; poner nervioso; **does the noise ~ you?** ¿le molesta el ruido?; **does it ~ you if I smoke?** ¿le molesta que fume?; **stop ~ing me!** ¡no fastidies!; **please don't ~ me about it now** le ruego no molestarme con eso ahora; **I can't be ~ed** no quiero tomarme el trabajo (to + infin de + infin), no me da la gana (to go ir); **to get ~ed** desconcertarse, ponerse nervioso, perder la calma.
3 VI: **to ~ about, to ~ with** molestarse con, preocuparse por; **to ~ to + infin** tomarse la molestia de + infin.
4 EXCL: ~ **(it)** ¡porras!; ~ **that child!** ¡caray con el niño!

botheration [,bɒðə'reɪʃən] INTERJ ¡porras!

bothersome ['bɒðəsəm] ADJ molesto.

Bothnia ['bɒθnɪə] N: **Gulf of ~** Golfo m de Botnia.

Botswana [bɒ'tswɑːnə] N Botsuana f.

bottle ['bɒtl] 1 N (a) botella f; (of ink, scent) frasco m; (baby's) biberón m, tetero m (LAm); **to hit the ~** beber mucho; **to take to the ~** darse a la bebida. (b) (*) valor m; descaro m; **to lose one's ~** rajarse*; **it takes a lot of ~ to + infin** hay que tener mucho valor para + infin.
2 VT embotellar; enfrascar.
◆**bottle out*** VI rajarse*; **they ~d out of doing it** se rajaron y no lo hicieron*.
◆**bottle up** VT embotellar; emotion reprimir, contener.

bottle-bank ['bɒtl,bæŋk] N banco m de botellas.

bottle-brush ['bɒtl,brʌʃ] N escobilla f, limpiabotellas m; (Bot) calistemon m.

bottled ['bɒtld] ADJ: ~ **beer** cerveza f de botella; ~ **water** agua f embotellada.

bottle-fed ['bɒtlfed] ADJ alimentado con biberón.

bottle-feed ['bɒtl,fiːd] VT (irr: V **feed**) criar con biberón.

bottle-green ['bɒtl'griːn] 1 ADJ verde botella.
2 N verde m botella.

bottleneck ['bɒtlnek] N (fig) cuello m de botella.

bottle-opener ['bɒtl,əʊpnəʳ] N abrebotellas m, destapador m de botellas, descapsulador m.

bottle-party ['bɒtl,pɑːtɪ] N guateque m al que cada invitado lleva su botella.

bottler ['bɒtlə^r] N (*person*) embotellador *m*, -ora *f*; (*company*) embotelladora *f*.

bottling ['bɒtlɪŋ] N embotellado *m*.

bottom ['bɒtəm] **1** N (*of cup, river, sea, box, garden*) fondo *m*; (*of stairs, hill, page*) pie *m*; (*of chair*) asiento *m*; (*of ship*) quilla *f*, casco *m*; (*Anat*) trasero *m*, culo *m*; **~s up!** ¡salud y pesetas!; **at ~** en el fondo; **at the ~ of the garden** en el fondo del jardín; **he's at the ~ of the class** es el último de la clase; **to be at the ~ of sth** (*fig: thing*) ser el motivo de algo, (*person*) ser el causante oculto de algo; **from the ~ of one's heart** de todo corazón; **the ~ has fallen out of the market** se han derrumbado los precios; **to get to the ~ of a matter** llegar al fondo de un asunto, desentrañar un asunto; **to go to the ~** (*Naut*) irse a pique; **to knock the ~ out of** desfondar; **to send a ship to the ~** hundir un buque; **to touch ~** (*lit*) tocar fondo; (*fig*) tocar fondo, llegar al punto más bajo.

2 ADJ *part* más bajo, inferior; (*last*) último; **~ drawer** (*Brit*) ajuar *m* (de novia); **~ floor** planta *f* baja; **~ gear** primera *f* (velocidad *f*); **~ half** mitad *f* de abajo, mitad *f* inferior; **~ line** (*minimum*) mínimo *m* aceptable; (*essential point*) punto *m* fundamental; **the ~ line is he has to go** al fin y al cabo tenemos que despedirle; **~ price** precio *m* más bajo; **~ step** primer peldaño *m*; **~ team** colista *m*.

♦**bottom out** VI (*figures etc*) tocar fondo.

bottomless ['bɒtəmlɪs] ADJ sin fondo, insondable.

bottommost ['bɒtəmməʊst] ADJ (el) más bajo; último.

botulism ['bɒtjʊlɪzəm] N botulismo *m*.

bouclé [buːˈkleɪ] **1** N lana *f* rizada, ropa *f* rizada.

2 ADJ de lana rizada.

boudoir ['buːdwɑːʳ] N tocador *m*.

bouffant ['buːfɔːŋ] ADJ *hairdo* crepado.

bougainvillea [ˌbuːgənˈvɪlɪə] N buganvilla *f*.

bough [baʊ] N rama *f*.

bought [bɔːt] PRET AND PTP *of* buy; **~ ledger** libro *m* de compras.

bouillon ['buːjɔːŋ] N caldo *m*; **~ cube** cubito *m* de caldo.

boulder ['bəʊldəʳ] N canto *m* rodado.

boulevard ['buːləvɑːʳ] N bulevar *m*, zócalo *m* (*Mex*).

bounce [baʊns] **1** N (a) (re)bote *m*; **to catch a ball on the ~** coger una pelota de rebote.

(b) (*fig: swagger*) fanfarronería *f*, presunción *f*; (*energy*) energía *f*, dinamismo *m*; (*resilience*) capacidad *f* de recuperación.

2 VT (a) hacer (re)botar.

(b) (*: eject*) plantar en la calle, poner de patitas en la calle.

(c) **I will not be ~d into it** no lo voy a hacer bajo presión, no permito que me presionen para hacerlo.

3 VI (a) (re)botar; **to ~ back, come bouncing back** (*fig*) recuperarse (de repente); **to ~ in** (*fig*) irrumpir (alegremente).

(b) (*: cheque*) ser incobrable.

bouncer* ['baʊnsəʳ] N forzudo *m*, gorila *m*, sacabullas *m* (*Mex*) (*que echa a los alborotadores de un café etc*).

bouncing ['baʊnsɪŋ] ADJ robusto, fuerte.

bouncy ['baʊnsɪ] ADJ (a) *ball* de mucho rebote, que rebota fuertemente. (b) *person* enérgico; bullicioso, muy activo.

bouncy castle ['baʊnsɪˈkɑːsl] ® N castillo *m* inflable.

bound¹ [baʊnd] PRET AND PTP *of* bind.

2 ADJ (a) **to be ~ for** (*Naut*) navegar con rumbo a, tener ... como puerto de destino, (*fig*) dirigirse a; **where are you ~ for?** ¿adónde se dirige Vd?

(b) (*obliged*) **to be ~ to** + *infin* (*sure*) estar seguro de + *infin*, (*must*) tener que + *infin*; **we are ~ to win** estamos seguros de ganar; **he's ~ to come** es seguro que vendrá, no puede dejar de venir; **it's ~ to happen** tiene forzosamente que ocurrir; **you're not ~ to go** no es que tengas que ir; **I am ~ to say that** ... tengo el deber de decir que ...; **I feel ~ to tell you that** ... no tengo la necesidad de decirte que ...; **they'll regret it, I'll be ~** se arrepentirán de ello, estoy seguro; **to be ~ by contract to sb** estar ligado por contrato a uno; **I feel ~ to him by gratitude** el agradecimiento me liga a él.

(c) (*linked*) **the problems are ~ together** existe una estrecha relación entre estos problemas; **they are ~ by close ties** entre ellos existen vínculos muy fuertes; **to be ~ up with** tener que ver con; estar estrechamente vinculado con; **they are ~ up in each other** están absortos el uno en el otro.

bound² [baʊnd] **1** N límite *m*; **out of ~s** fuera de los límites; **out of ~s to civilians** prohibido el paso a los civiles; **to put a place out of ~s** prohibir la entrada a un lugar; **it is within the ~s of possibility** cabe dentro de lo posible; **to keep sth within ~s** tener algo a raya; **to set ~s to one's ambitions** poner límites a sus ambiciones; **his ambition knows no ~s** su ambición no tiene límite.

2 VT limitar, deslindar; **a field ~ed by woods** un campo rodeado de bosque; **on one side it is ~ed by the park** por un lado confina con el parque.

bound³ [baʊnd] **1** N (*jump*) salto *m*; **at a ~, in one ~** de un salto.

2 VT saltar por encima de.

3 VI saltar; (*ball*) (re)botar; **to ~ forward** avanzar a saltos; **his heart ~ed with joy** su corazón daba brincos de alegría; **the number is ~ing up** el número aumenta rápidamente.

-bound [-baʊnd] ADJ *ending in compounds*: **to be London~** ir rumbo a Londres; **the south~ carriageway** la autopista dirección sur.

boundary ['baʊndərɪ] N límite *m*, lindero *m*; (*Sport*) banda *f*; (*Pol etc*) frontera *f*; **to make ~ changes** (*Brit Pol*) hacer cambios en las circunscripciones.

boundary-line ['baʊndərɪˌlaɪn] N límite *m*, frontera *f*.

boundary-stone ['baʊndərɪˌstəʊn] N mojón *m*.

bounden ['baʊndən] ADJ: **~ duty** obligación *f* ineludible.

bounder*† ['baʊndəʳ] N (*esp Brit*) sinvergüenza *m*, granuja *m*.

boundless ['baʊndlɪs] ADJ ilimitado.

bounteous ['baʊntɪəs] ADJ, **bountiful** ['baʊntɪfʊl] ADJ *crop etc* abundante; *person* liberal, generoso.

bounty ['baʊntɪ] N (a) (*generosity*) munificencia *f*, liberalidad *f*. (b) (*Mil*) premio *m* de enganche; (*Comm*) prima *f*, subvención *f*.

bounty hunter ['baʊntɪˌhʌntəʳ] N cazarrecompensas *mf invar*.

bouquet ['bʊkeɪ] N (a) (*of flowers*) ramo *m*, ramillete *m*. (b) (*of wine*) buqué *m*, nariz *f*.

Bourbon ['bʊəbən] **1** N Borbón *m*; **b~ (whiskey)** (*US*) whisky *m* americano.

2 ADJ borbónico.

bourgeois ['bʊəʒwɑː] **1** ADJ burgués.

2 N burgués *m*, -esa *f*.

bourgeoisie [ˌbʊəʒwɑːˈziː] N burguesía *f*.

bout [baʊt] N (*spell*) turno *m*, rato *m*; (*Med*) ataque *m*; (*Fencing*) asalto *m*; (*fight in general*) lucha *f*, combate *m*; (*boxing fixture*) encuentro *m*, match *m*; (*of drinking*) juerga *f* de borrachera.

boutique [buːˈtiːk] N boutique *f*; **~ furniture** muebles *mpl* artesano.

bovine ['bəʊvaɪn] ADJ bovino; (*fig*) lerdo, estúpido.

bovver⣉ ['bɒvəʳ] N (*Brit*) desorden *m*, alboroto *m*; violencia *f*; gamberrismo *m*; **~ boots** botas de suela gruesa usadas por los punkis.

bow¹ [bəʊ] N (*Mil, Mus*) arco *m*; (*tie, knot*) lazo *m*; **~ and arrow** arco *m* y flechas.

bow² [baʊ] **1** N inclinación *f*, reverencia *f*; **to make a ~** inclinarse (*to* delante de), hacer una reverencia (*to* a); **to make one's ~** presentarse, debutar; **to take a ~** salir a recibir aplausos.

2 VT *head etc* inclinar, (*in shame*) bajar; (*fig: also* **to ~ down**) agobiar; **to ~ one's thanks** inclinarse en señal de agradecimiento.

3 VI inclinarse (*to* delante de), hacer una reverencia (*to* a); **to ~ and scrape** hacer zalamerías; **to ~ beneath** estar agobiado por; **to ~ to** inclinarse a, ceder ante, transigir con, someterse a; **to ~ to the inevitable** resignarse a lo inevitable.

♦**bow down** **1** VT (*lit, fig*) doblegar.

2 VI doblegarse.

♦**bow out** **1** VT: **to ~ sb out** despedir con cortesía al que sale.

2 VI retirarse.

bow³ [baʊ] N (*Naut*) proa *f*; **~s** proa *f*; **on the port ~** a babor; **shot across the ~s** cañonazo *m* de advertencia.

Bow Bells [ˌbəʊˈbelz] NPL *famoso campanario de Londres*; **born within the sound of ~** nacido en la zona alrededor de Bow Bells (*definición del puro cockney londinense*).

bowdlerization [ˌbaʊdlərəˈzeɪʃən] N expurgación *f*.

bowdlerize ['baʊdləraɪz] VT expurgar.

bowel ['baʊəl] N intestino *m*; **~s** intestinos *mpl*, vientre *m*, (*fig*) entrañas *fpl*; **~s of the earth** entrañas *fpl* de la tierra; **~s of compassion** compasión *f*; **~ movement** evacuación *f* del vientre.

bower ['baʊəʳ] N emparrado *m*, enramada *f*; cenador *m*.

bowing ['bəʊɪŋ] N (*Mus*) técnica *f* del arco; (*marked on score*) inicio *m* del golpe de arco; **his ~ was sensitive** su uso del arco era sensible; **to mark the ~** indicar (*or* marcar) los movimientos del arco.

bowl¹ [bəʊl] N (*Culin*) escudilla *f*, tazón *m*; (*for washing*) jofaina *f*, palangana *f*; (*of spoon*) cuenco *m*; (*of fountain*) tazón *m*; (*of pipe*) hornillo *m*, cazoleta *f*; (*of WC*) taza *f* (de retrete); (*US Sport*) estadio *m*; (*Geog*) cuenca *f*.

bowl² [bəʊl] **1** N bola *f*, bocha *f*; **~s** (*Brit*) juego *m* de las bochas, (*US*) boliche *m*.

2 VT rodar; (*Sport*) arrojar, lanzar, tirar (*LAm*).

3 VI (*Sport*) arrojar la pelota; jugar a las bochas.

♦**bowl along** VI correr, rodar rápidamente.

♦**bowl over** VT (a) tumbar, derribar, echar a rodar. (b) (*fig*) desconcertar, dejar atónito; **we were quite ~ed over by the news** la noticia nos desconcertó, la noticia nos sorprendió; **she ~ed him over** ella le dejó patidifuso.

bow-legged ['bəʊˌlegɪd] ADJ estevado, patiestevado; (*stance*) con las piernas en arco.

bowlegs [ˌbəʊˈlegz] NPL piernas *fpl* arqueadas.

bowler¹ ['bəʊləʳ] N (*Brit Sport*) lanzador *m*, -ora *f*; (*US Sport*) jugador *m*, -ora *f* de bolos; *ver también* ⟨CRICKET⟩ .

bowler² ['bəʊləʳ] N (*Brit: also* **~ hat**) hongo *m*, bombín *m*.

bowline ['bəʊlɪn] N bolina *f*.

bowling ['bəʊlɪŋ] N (US) bolos mpl, boliche m (LAm).
bowling-alley ['bəʊlɪŋ,ælɪ] N bolera f, boliche m (LAm).
bowling-green ['bəʊlɪŋ,griːn] N pista f para bochas.
bowling-match ['bəʊlɪŋ,mætʃ] N (Brit) concurso m de bochas.
bowman ['bəʊmən] N, PL **bowmen** ['bəʊmen] arquero m, (cross-~) ballestero m.
bowsprit ['bəʊsprɪt] N bauprés m.
bowstring ['bəʊstrɪŋ] N cuerda f de arco.
bow-tie ['bəʊ'taɪ] N corbata f de lazo, pajarita f.
bow-window ['bəʊ'wɪndəʊ] N mirador m, ventana f saslediza.
bow-wow ['baʊ'waʊ] INTERJ ¡guau!
box¹ [bɒks] **1** N caja f, (large) cajón m; (for money etc) cofre m, arca f; (for jewels etc) estuche m; (Racing, Theat) palco m; (Brit: road junction) parrilla f; (Typ) recuadro m; (on form, to be filled in) casilla f; **the ~*** la caja boba*, la tele*; **we saw it on the ~*** lo hemos visto en la tele*; **~ of matches** caja f de cerillas; **(post-office) ~** apartado m de correos, casilla f (de correos) (LAm).
2 VT encajonar, poner en una caja; (capture) encerrar en una caja; **to ~ the compass** cuartear la aguja.
◆ **box in** VT **(a)** pipe etc tapar, revestir (de madera etc).
(b) (fig) **to ~ sb in** encerrar a uno; cortar los vuelos a uno; **to feel ~ed in** sentirse encerrado; **to get ~ed in** (Sport) encontrarse tapado.
◆ **box off** VT compartimentar.
◆ **box up** VT poner en una caja; (fig) constreñir.
box² [bɒks] N (Bot) boj m.
box³ [bɒks] **1** N: **~ on the ear** cachete m.
2 VT boxear contra; **to ~ sb's ear** dar un cachete a uno.
3 VI boxear.
box camera ['bɒks'kæmərə] N cámara f de cajón.
boxcar ['bɒks,kɑːʳ] N (US) furgón m.
boxer ['bɒksəʳ] N boxeador m; (dog) boxer m; **~ shorts** calzones mpl.
box file ['bɒks'faɪl] N archivador m.
box-girder ['bɒks,gɜːdəʳ] N viga f en forma de cajón, vigas fpl gemelas.
boxing ['bɒksɪŋ] N boxeo m.
Boxing Day ['bɒksɪŋdeɪ] N (Brit) día de fiesta después de Navidad (26 diciembre).

──┤ **BOXING DAY** ├──

ⓘ *El día después de Navidad es **Boxing Day**, fiesta en todo el Reino Unido, aunque si el 26 de diciembre cae en domingo el día de descanso se traslada al lunes. El nombre proviene de una costumbre del siglo XIX, cuando en dicho día se daba un aguinaldo o pequeño regalo (**Christmas box**) a los comerciantes, carteros, etc. En la actualidad es una fecha en la que se celebran importantes encuentros deportivos.*

boxing-gloves ['bɒksɪŋglʌvz] NPL guantes mpl de boxeo.
boxing-match ['bɒksɪŋ,mætʃ] N partido m de boxeo.
boxing-ring ['bɒksɪŋ,rɪŋ] N cuadrilátero m (de boxeo).
box junction ['bɒks,dʒʌnkʃən] N (Brit) cruce m con parrilla.
box-number ['bɒks,nʌmbəʳ] N apartado m, casilla f (LAm).
box-office ['bɒks,ɒfɪs] **1** N taquilla f; boletería f (LAm); **to be good ~** ser taquillero, estar seguro de obtener un éxito.
2 ATTR taquillero; **~ receipts** ingresos mpl de taquilla; **~ success** éxito m de taquilla.
box-pleat ['bɒks,pliːt] N tablón m.
boxroom ['bɒksrʊm] N (Brit) trastero m.
box-seat ['bɒks,siːt] N (US: Theat) asiento m de palco.
box-spring ['bɒks'sprɪŋ] N muelle m.
boxwood ['bɒkswʊd] N boj m.
boxy ['bɒksɪ] ADJ (gen pej) building amazacotado; car cuadrado.
boy [bɔɪ] N (small) niño m; (older, also apprentice etc, and affectionately of adult) muchacho m, chico m; (son) hijo m; (servant) criado m; (boyfriend) amigo m, amiguito m; **García and his ~s in the national team** García y sus muchachos del equipo nacional; **the ~s in blue** (Brit*) los policías, los marrones; **oh ~!** ¡vaya, vaya!; **old ~** (Brit: of school) antiguo alumno m; (*) vejete m; **old ~!** ¡chico!; **old ~ network** (sistema m de) amiguismo m; **that's the ~!, that's my ~!** ¡bravo el chico!; **but my dear ~!** ¡pero hijo!; **I have known him from a ~** le conozco desde chico; **~s will be ~s** así son los chicos; **my husband's out with the ~s** mi marido ha salido con sus amigotes; **he's one of the ~s now** ahora es un personaje; **it's all jobs for the ~s** ahora todo es puestos para los amigotes, todo es amiguismo; **to send a ~ to do a man's job** mandar un chico para hacer un trabajo de hombre.
boycott ['bɔɪkɒt] **1** N boicoteo m.
2 VT boicotear.
boyfriend ['bɔɪfrend] N amigo m, amiguito m; compañero m.
boyhood ['bɔɪhʊd] N juventud f, muchachez f.
boyish ['bɔɪɪʃ] ADJ juvenil, muchachil, de muchacho.
boy scout [,bɔɪ'skaʊt] N (muchacho m or niño m) explorador m.
B/P, b/p (Comm) ABBR of **bills payable**.

BP N ABBR of **British Petroleum**.
Bp ABBR of **Bishop** obispo m, obpo.
bpi N (Comput) ABBR of **bits per inch**.
BPOE N (US) ABBR of **Benevolent and Protective Order of Elks** organización benéfica.
BPS NPL ABBR of **bits per second** bits mpl por segundo.
B/R N ABBR of **bills receivable** obligaciones fpl por cobrar.
BR N ABBR of **British Rail**.
Br ABBR of **Brother** hermano m. **(b)** ABBR of **British**.
bra* [brɑː] N sostén m, sujetador m.
brace [breɪs] **1** N **(a)** (strengthening piece) abrazadera f, refuerzo m; (Archit) riostra f, tirante m; (for teeth) banda f, corrector m; (Naut) braza f; (tool) berbiquí m; **~s** (Brit) tirantes mpl, tiradores mpl (LAm); (US) corrector m; **~ and bit** berbiquí m y barrena.
(b) (Mus) corchete m; (Typ) corchete m ({).
(c) (pair) par m; **in a ~ of shakes*** en un decir Jesús.
2 VT asegurar, reforzar.
3 VR: **to ~ o.s.** prepararse para resistir (una sacudida etc); (fig) fortalecer su ánimo; **we ~d ourselves for bad news** nos preparamos para aguantar una noticia mala.
bracelet ['breɪslɪt] N pulsera f, brazalete m.
bracing ['breɪsɪŋ] ADJ tónico, vigorizante.
bracken ['brækən] N helecho m.
bracket ['brækɪt] **1** N **(a)** (holding) abrazadera f; (supporting) soporte m, puntal m; (angle) escuadra f; (Archit) ménsula f, repisa f; (for gas) mechero m.
(b) (Typ) **round ~s** () paréntesis mpl curvos; **square ~s** [] corchetes mpl rectos, paréntesis mpl cuadrados; **angled ~s** <> corchetes mpl agudos; {} corchetes mpl, llaves fpl; **in ~s** entre paréntesis.
(c) (fig) clase f, categoría f; **he's in the £200,000 a year ~** pertenece a la categoría de los que ganan 200,000 libras al año.
2 VT **(a)** (join by brackets) asegurar con ménsulas (etc).
(b) (Typ) poner entre paréntesis; **to ~ sth with sth else** agrupar algo con otra cosa.
◆ **bracket off** VT excluir; poner aparte, separar; aislar.
◆ **bracket together** VT agrupar, poner juntos.
brackish ['brækɪʃ] ADJ salobre, semisalado.
brad [bræd] N puntilla f, clavito m.
brae [breɪ] N (Scot) ladera f de monte, pendiente f.
brag [bræg] **1** N fanfarronada f, bravata f.
2 VI jactarse (about, of de; that de que), fanfarronear.
braggart ['brægət] N fanfarrón m, jactancioso m.
bragging ['brægɪŋ] N fanfarronadas fpl.
Brahman ['brɑːmən], **Brahmin** ['brɑːmɪn] N brahamán m, -ana f; bracmán m, -ana f.
Brahmaputra ['brɑːmə,puːtrə] N Brahmaputra m.
braid [breɪd] **1** N **(a)** (of hair) trenza f. **(b)** (Mil) galón m; **(gold) ~** galón m de oro.
2 VT trenzar; dress galonear.
Braille [breɪl] **1** N Braille m.
2 ATTR: **~ library** biblioteca f Braille.
brain [breɪn] **1** N **(a)** (Anat) cerebro m; **~s** (Anat, Culin) sesos mpl; **to blow one's ~s out** pegarse un tiro, levantarse la tapa de los sesos.
(b) (fig) **~s** inteligencia f, cabeza f; capacidad f; **to beat one's ~s out*** romperse el coco*; **to cudgel (or rack) one's ~s** devanarse los sesos; **to get sth on the ~** dejarse obsesionar por algo; **to have sth on the ~** estar obsesionado por algo, no poder quitar algo de la cabeza; **to have ~s** ser inteligente; **to pick sb's ~s** exprimir a uno, explotar los conocimientos de uno; **to turn sb's ~** volver loco a uno.
2 VT (*) romper la crisma a.
brainchild ['breɪntʃaɪld] N parto m del ingenio, invento m.
brain-damage ['breɪn,dæmɪdʒ] N lesión f cerebral, lesión f medular.
brain-damaged ['breɪn,dæmɪdʒd] ADJ: **he was permanently ~ by meningitis** sufrió lesiones cerebrales por la meningitis; **the child was ~ for life** el niño quedó con lesiones medulares de por vida.
brain-dead ['breɪn,ded] ADJ clínicamente muerto.
brain-death ['breɪn,deθ] N muerte f clínica, muerte f cerebral.
brain-drain ['breɪn,dreɪn] N fuga f de cerebros.
brainless ['breɪnlɪs] ADJ estúpido, insensato.
brainpower ['breɪn,paʊəʳ] N fuerza f intelectual.
brain-scan ['breɪn,skæn] N exploración f cerebral mediante escáner.
brain-scanner ['breɪn,skænəʳ] N escáner m cerebral.
brainstorm ['breɪnstɔːm] N frenesí m; (*) idea f genial, idea f luminosa.
brainstorming ['breɪnstɔːmɪŋ] N puesta f en común, brainstorming m; **a ~ session** una reunión para hacer una puesta en común.
brains-trust ['breɪnz,trʌst] N, (US) **brain trust** ['breɪn,trʌst] N consultorio m intelectual; grupo m de peritos; (TV etc) jurado m de expertos.
brain-teaser ['breɪn,tiːzəʳ] N rompecabezas m.
brain-tumour, (US) **braintumor** ['breɪn,tjuːməʳ] N tumor m cere-

bral.

brainwash ['breɪnwɒʃ] VT lavar el cerebro a; **he was ~ed into believing that ...** le lavaron el cerebro para hacerle creer que ...

brainwashing ['breɪn,wɒʃɪŋ] N lavado *m* de cerebro.

brainwave ['breɪnweɪv] N idea *f* luminosa.

brainwork ['breɪnwɜːk] N trabajo *m* intelectual.

brainy ['breɪnɪ] ADJ muy inteligente, talentudo.

braise [breɪz] VT brasear.

brake¹ [breɪk] ⊡ N freno *m* (*also fig*); **to apply the ~s, put the ~s on** echar los frenos, frenar; **to put a ~ on** (*fig*) frenar, detener el progreso de.
⊡ VTI frenar.

brake² [breɪk] N (*vehicle*) break *m*; (*estate car*) rubia *f*.

brake³ [breɪk] N (*Bot*) helecho *m*; (*thicket*) soto *m*.

brake-block ['breɪkblɒk] N pastilla *f* de freno.

brake-drum ['breɪkdrʌm] N tambor *m* de freno.

brake-fluid ['breɪk,fluɪd] N líquido *m* para frenos.

brake-horsepower ['breɪk'hɔːspaʊəʳ] N potencia *f* al freno.

brake-lever ['breɪk,liːvəʳ] N palanca *f* de freno.

brake-lights ['breɪklaɪts] N = **braking-lights**.

brake-lining ['breɪk,laɪnɪŋ] N forro *m* del freno, guarnición *f* del freno.

brake-pad ['breɪkpæd] N pastilla *f* de frenos.

brake-pedal ['breɪk,pedl] N pedal *m* de freno.

brake-shoe ['breɪkʃuː] N zapata *f* del freno.

brakesman ['breɪksmən] N, PL **brakesmen** ['breɪksmen] encargado *m* del montacargos de la mina.

brake-van ['breɪkvæn] N furgón *m* de cola.

braking ['breɪkɪŋ] ⊡ N frenar *m*, frenaje *f*.
⊡ ATTR de frenar, de frenaje.

braking-distance ['breɪkɪŋ,dɪstəns] N distancia *f* recorrida después de frenar.

braking-lights ['breɪkɪŋ,laɪts] NPL luces *fpl* de stop, luces *fpl* de frenado.

braking-power ['breɪkɪŋ,paʊəʳ] N potencia *f* al freno.

bramble ['bræmbl] N zarza *f*.

bran [bræn] N salvado *m*; **~ tub** (*Brit*) sorteo *m* de regalos.

branch [brɑːntʃ] ⊡ N (*Bot*) rama *f*; (*fig*) ramo *m*, división *f*, sección *f*; (*Comm*) sucursal *f*; (*road, Rail*) ramal *m*; (*of river*) brazo *m*; (*US: of stream*) arroyo *m*; (*of family*) ramo *m*.
⊡ VI (*also to ~ out*) ramificarse, echar ramas.

◆**branch off** VI salir, separarse (*from* de); **we ~ed off at Medina** salimos de la carretera principal en Medina.

◆**branch out** VI (*fig*) extenderse, ensanchar el campo de sus operaciones (*etc*).

branch-line ['brɑːntʃlaɪn] N ramal *m*, línea *f* secundaria.

branch-manager ['brɑːntʃ'mænɪdʒəʳ] N director *m*, -ora *f* de sucursal.

branch-office ['brɑːntʃ,ɒfɪs] N sucursal *f*.

brand [brænd] ⊡ N (*mark*) marca *f*; (*iron*) hierro *m* (de marcar). **(b)** (*Comm*) marca *f*; **~ awareness** conciencia *f* de una marca; **~ image** imagen *f* de marca; **~ loyalty** fidelidad *f* a una marca; **~ name** nombre *m* de marca. **(c)** (*fire*) tizón *m*, tea *f*.
⊡ VT **(a)** marcar (con hierro candente), ventear (*Mex*). **(b)** (*fig*) **to ~ sb as** motejar a uno de, estigmatizar a uno de; **to ~ sth as** calificar algo de; **to be ~ed a liar** quedar por mentiroso; **it is ~ed in my memory** lo tengo grabado en la memoria. **(c)** **~ed goods** (*Comm*) artículos *mpl* de marca.

branding-iron ['brændɪŋ,aɪən] N hierro *m* (de marcar).

brandish ['brændɪʃ] VT blandir.

brand-new ['brænd'njuː] ADJ flamante, completamente nuevo, novísimo.

brandy ['brændɪ] N coñac *m*, brandy *m*; aguardiente *m*; **~ butter** mantequilla *f* al coñac.

brash [bræʃ] ADJ (*rough*) inculto, tosco; (*cheeky*) descarado, respondón; (*rash*) impetuoso; (*unwise*) indiscreto; (*know-all*) presuntuoso.

brashly ['bræʃlɪ] ADV (*V ADJ*) incultamente, toscamente; descaradamente, respondonamente; impetuosamente; indiscretamente; presuntuosamente.

brashness ['bræʃnɪs] N (*V ADJ*) incultura *f*, tosquedad *f*; descaro *m*; impetuosidad *f*; indiscreción *f*; presunción *f*.

Brasilia [brə'zɪljə] N Brasilia *f*.

brass [brɑːs] ⊡ N **(a)** (*metal*) latón *m*; **to get down to ~ tacks** ir al grano; **it's not worth a ~ farthing** no vale un ardite. **(b)** (*plate*) placa *f* conmemorativa; (*Eccl*) plancha *f* sepulcral (de latón). **(c)** (*Mus*) **the ~** el cobre, el bronce; **~ band** banda *f*, charanga *f*. **(d)** (**: money*) pasta* *f*. **(e)** **the top ~** (*Mil*) los jefazos*. **(f)** (**: nerve*) cara* *f*; **he had the ~ to ask me for it** tuvo la cara de pedírmelo.

brassed off: ['brɑːst,ɒf] ADJ (*fed up*) quemado (*with* de); **I'm really ~ with this damn essay** de verdad, estoy quemado de este maldito trabajo.

brasserie ['brɑːsərɪ] N brasserie *f*.

brass hat* ['brɑːs'hæt] N (*Mil*) jefazo* *m*.

brassica ['bræsɪkə] N brassica *f*, crucífera *f*.

brassière ['bræsɪəʳ] N sostén *m*, sujetador *m*.

brass knuckles [,brɑːs'nʌklz] NPL (*US*) nudilleras *fpl*.

brass-rubbing [,brɑːs'rʌbɪŋ] N (*art, object*) calco *m* de plancha sepulcral (de latón).

brassy ['brɑːsɪ] ADJ de latón; *sound* desapacible, metálico; *person etc* descarado.

brat [bræt] N mocoso *m*, crío *m*; **~ pack** (*actors etc*) generación *f* de jóvenes artistas con éxito, (*pej*) niños *mpl* pijos*.

bravado [brə'vɑːdəʊ] N bravatas *fpl*, baladronadas *fpl*; **a piece of ~** una bravata; **out of sheer ~** de puro bravucón.

brave [breɪv] ⊡ ADJ **(a)** (*valiant*) valiente, valeroso; esforzado; bizarro; **as ~ as a lion** más fiero que un león. **(b)** (*splendid*) magnífico, vistoso, garboso; **B~ New World** El nuevo mundo feliz.
⊡ N valiente *m*; (*Indian*) guerrero *m* indio.
⊡ VT desafiar, arrostrar; **to ~ the storm** aguantar la tempestad; **to ~ sb's anger** no amilanarse ante la ira de uno; **to ~ it out** defenderse sin confesarse culpable.

bravely ['breɪvlɪ] ADV valientemente, con valor; (*fig*) vistosamente, airosamente.

bravery ['breɪvərɪ] N valor *m*, valentía *f*.

bravo ['brɑː'vəʊ] INTERJ ¡bravo!

bravura [brə'vʊərə] N **(a)** arrojo *m*, brío *m*. **(b)** (*Mus*) virtuosismo *m*.

brawl [brɔːl] ⊡ N pendencia *f*, reyerta *f*; alboroto *m*.
⊡ VI armar pendencia, alborotar.

brawling ['brɔːlɪŋ] ⊡ ADJ pendenciero, alborotador.
⊡ N alboroto *m*.

brawn [brɔːn] N (*Brit*) carne *f* en gelatina; (*fig*) fuerza *f* muscular.

brawny ['brɔːnɪ] ADJ fornido, musculoso.

bray [breɪ] ⊡ N rebuzno *m*; (*laugh*) carcajada *f*.
⊡ VI rebuznar; (*trumpet*) sonar con estrépito.

braze [breɪz] VT soldar.

brazen ['breɪzn] ⊡ ADJ (*fig*) descarado, cínico; **~ lie** mentira *f* descarada.
⊡ VT: **to ~ it out** defenderse con argumentos descarados.

brazenly ['breɪznlɪ] ADV descaradamente, con cinismo.

brazenness ['breɪzənnɪs] N descaro *m*, desvergüenza *f*.

brazier ['breɪzɪəʳ] N brasero *m*.

Brazil [brə'zɪl] N el Brasil; **~ nut** nuez *f* del Brasil.

Brazilian [brə'zɪlɪən] ⊡ ADJ brasileño.
⊡ N brasileño *m*, -a *f*.

BRCS N ABBR of **British Red Cross Society**.

breach [briːtʃ] ⊡ N **(a)** (*gap*) abertura *f*, brecha *f*; (*Mil*) brecha *f*. **(b)** (*fig*) violación *f*, infracción *f*; (*between friends: act*) rompimiento *m* de relaciones, (*state*) desavenencia *f*; (*Pol*) ruptura *f*; **~ of confidence** abuso *m* de confianza; **~ of contract** incumplimiento *m* de contrato; **~ of faith** (or **trust**) abuso *m* de confianza, infidencia *f*; **~ of the law** violación *f* de la ley; **~ of the peace** perturbación *f* del orden público; **~ of privilege** (*Parl*) abuso *m* del privilegio parlamentario; **~ of promise** incumplimiento *m* de la palabra de casamiento; **~ of security** fallo *m* de seguridad; **to be in ~ of a rule** incumplir una regla; **to fill the ~, to step into the ~** llenar el vacío; **to heal the ~** hacer las paces.
⊡ VT romper; (*Mil*) abrir brecha en.

bread [bred] N **(a)** pan *m* (*also fig*); **~ grains** granos *mpl* panificables; **to be on ~ and water** estar a pan y agua; **to break ~ with** sentarse a la mesa con; **to cast one's ~ on the waters** hacer el bien sin mirar a quién; **to earn one's daily ~** (or **one's ~ and butter**) ganarse el pan; **to know which side one's ~ is buttered** saber dónde aprieta el zapato; **man cannot live by ~ alone** no sólo de pan vive el hombre; **to take the ~ out of sb's mouth** quitar el pan de la boca de uno.
(b) (‡) guita‡ *f*, pasta* *f*, plata *f* (*LAm*).

bread-and-butter ['bredən'bʌtəʳ] ⊡ N pan *m* con mantequilla; (*) pan *m* de cada día; **~ pudding** pudín *m* de pan y mantequilla.
⊡ ADJ corriente (y moliente), normal, regular; prosaico; de uso general; **~ letter** carta *f* de agradecimiento (*a una señora en cuya casa el invitado ha pasado varios días*).

breadbasket ['bred,bɑːskɪt] N cesto *m* para el pan; (‡) tripa* *f*.

breadbin ['bredbɪn] N caja *f* del pan, panera *f*.

breadboard ['bredbɔːd] N (*in kitchen*) tablero *m* para cortar el pan; (*Comput*) circuito *m* experimental.

breadbox ['bredbɒks] N (*US*) = **breadbin**.

bread-crumb ['bredkrʌm] N migaja f; ~s (Culin) pan m rallado; **in ~s** empanado.

breaded ['bredɪd] ADJ empanado.

breadfruit ['bredfruːt] N fruto m del pan; ~ **tree** árbol m del pan.

breadknife ['brednaɪf] N, PL **breadknives** ['brednaɪvz] cuchillo m para cortar el pan.

breadline ['bredlaɪn] N (US) cola f del pan; **to be on the ~** (fig) vivir en la mayor miseria.

bread-pudding [,bred'pʊdɪŋ] N pudín m de leche y pan.

bread stick ['bredstɪk] N piquito m, palito m.

breadth [bretθ] N anchura f; (Naut) manga f; (fig) amplitud f, extensión f; **to be 2 metres in ~** tener 2 metros de ancho.

breadthwise ['bretθwaɪz] ADV de lado a lado.

breadwinner ['bred,wɪnər] N mantenedor m, -ora f de la familia.

break [breɪk] **1** N (a) (breakage) ruptura f, rompimiento m; (between friends) ruptura f; (in voice) quiebro m; sollozo m; (in register of voice) gallo m; (in weather) cambio m; **two ~s of service** (Tennis) dos servicios rotos; **at ~ of day** al amanecer; **to make a ~ with** cortar con; romper relaciones con.
(b) (gap) abertura f; (crack) grieta f; (on paper etc) espacio m, blanco m; (of time) intervalo m; (in process) interrupción f; (in clouds) claro m; (holiday) vacación f, (one day) asueto m; (rest) descanso m; (at school) período m de recreo; ~ **in continuity** solución f de continuidad; **without a ~** sin interrupción, sin descansar; **to take a ~** descansar; **to take a weekend ~** ir a pasar el fin de semana fuera, hacer una escapada de fin de semana.
(c) (vehicle) break m, volanta f (LAm).
(d) (chance) oportunidad f; **lucky ~** chiripa f, racha f de suerte; **to give sb a ~** dar una oportunidad a uno, dejar de presionar a uno; **give me a ~!** ¡déjame un momento respirar!
(e) (break-out) evasión f, fuga f; **to make a ~ for it** tratar de evadirse.
(f) (Billiards, Snooker) tacada f; serie f.
2 (irr: PRET **broke**, PTP **broken**) VT (a) (smash, tear) romper; ground roturar; heart partir; record batir, superar, mejorar; code descifrar; conspiracy, ring deshacer; **to ~ one's leg** romperse la pierna; V back, heart etc.
(b) (fail to observe) appointment no acudir a; promise, word faltar a, incumplir; law, treaty violar, infringir, quebrantar.
(c) (weaken, vanquish) rebellion, strike vencer; acabar con; horse domar, amansar; rival arruinar; health quebrantar; bank (in gambling) quebrar, hacer quebrar; (morally) abatir, vencer; **to ~ sb of a habit** lograr que uno abandone una costumbre, quitar a uno una costumbre.
(d) (interrupt) silence, spell romper; custom romper con; journey interrumpir; (Elec) interrumpir, cortar; **to ~ sb's service** (Tennis) romper el servicio del otro.
(e) (leave) cover abandonar, salir de; jail fugarse de; ranks salir de; camp ausentarse de.
(f) (soften) impact, fall amortiguar.
(g) news comunicar (to a).
(h) (Naut) flag desplegar.
(i) (US) **can you ~ me a 100-dollar bill?** ¿me puede cambiar un billete de 100 dólares?
3 VI (a) (fall apart) romperse, quebrarse, hacerse pedazos; (machine) estropearse; (boil) reventar; (heart) partirse; (ranks, wave) romperse.
(b) **to ~ free** soltarse; liberarse; V loose.
(c) (news) saberse, llegar a saberse; (story) revelarse; (storm) desencadenarse.
(d) (weaken) acabarse; debilitarse; (voice) mudar, cambiar, (singing voice) cascarse; (heat wave) terminar; (weather) cambiar (bruscamente); (bank) quebrar; (health) decaer (de repente).
(e) (Boxing) separarse.
(f) (dawn) romper; (day) apuntar.
(g) **to ~ even** salir sin ganar ni perder.
(h) (Sport: ball) torcerse, desviarse.

♦**break away** VI (a) (piece) desprenderse, separarse. (b) (runner) despegarse, salir del pelotón; (at games) escapar; ~ **away from** guard evadirse de; party romper con.

♦**break down** **1** VT (a) (shatter) derribar, romper, echar abajo; resistance acabar con, vencer; alibi probar la falsedad de. (b) figures analizar, descomponer, desglosar; clasificar.
2 VI (a) (Med) perder la salud, sufrir un colapso; (Aut) averiarse, descomponerse (LAm); (machine) estropearse, dañarse, descomponerse (LAm); dejar de funcionar; (negotiation, plan) fracasar; (person) perder el control; romper a llorar.

♦**break forth** VI (light, water) surgir; (storm) estallar; **to ~ forth into song** romper a cantar.

♦**break in** **1** VT (a) (shatter) forzar, romper.
(b) recruit desbastar, acostumbrar a la vida militar (etc); horse domar.
2 VI (burglar) forzar una entrada; (in conversation) cortar, interrumpir.

♦**break into** VT (a) **to ~ into a house** allanar una morada; **to ~ into the market** introducirse en el mercado, establecerse en el mercado.

(b) **to ~ into a run** echar a correr, empezar a correr; **to ~ into tears** romper a llorar.

♦**break off** **1** VT (a) piece separar, desgajar. (b) engagement, relations romper; (Mil) action terminar.
2 VI (a) (piece) separarse, desprenderse, desgajarse.
(b) (cease) pararse repentinamente; dejar de hablar, interrumpirse; suspender el trabajo (etc).

♦**break out** VI (a) (from prison) escaparse, evadirse.
(b) (fire, war, riot, argument) estallar; (noise) hacerse oír; (Med) declararse; (exclaim) exclamar, gritar.
(c) **she broke out in spots** le salieron granos en la piel; **he broke out in a sweat** quedó cubierto de sudor.

♦**break through** **1** VT barrier penetrar, atravesar, romper.
2 VI (a) (water etc) abrirse paso, abrirse (un) camino; **to ~ through to** miners llegar a, abrirse un camino hasta.
(b) (inventor) hacer un descubrimiento importante; abrirse paso, empezar a tener éxito.

♦**break up** **1** VT (a) (shatter) romper, deshacer; ship desguazar; estate parcelar; industry desconcentrar; camp levantar; meeting, organization disolver; gang desarticular; marriage deshacer; ~ **it up!** ¡no quiero más follón!; **it's time we broke it up** es hora de irnos, es hora de terminar; **they broke the place up** destrozaron el local.
(b) (divide) dividir; separar.
(c) (US*) hacer reír a carcajadas.
2 VI (a) (shatter) romperse, hacerse pedazos; desmenuzarse; (ice) romperse; (in disorder) disolverse; (marriage) deshacerse, romperse; (federation, group) desmembrarse, disgregarse; (partnership) romperse; (weather) cambiar; (crowd) dispersarse.
(b) (Brit: end) (school) terminar el curso, cerrarse (para las vacaciones); (session) levantarse, terminar.
(c) (divide) dividirse, desglosarse (into en).
(d) (US*) reír a carcajadas.

♦**break with** VT romper con.

breakable ['breɪkəbl] ADJ frágil, quebradizo.

breakage ['breɪkɪdʒ] N rotura f.

breakaway ['breɪkəweɪ] **1** ADJ group etc disidente, separatista; ~ **state** (Pol) estado m independizado.
2 N (Sport) escapada f.

break-dancer ['breɪk,dɑːnsər] N bailarín m, -ina f de break.

break-dancing ['breɪk,dɑːnsɪŋ] N break m.

breakdown ['breɪkdaʊn] N (a) interrupción f; (failure) fracaso m, mal éxito m; (Med) colapso m, crisis f nerviosa; (Aut etc) avería f, pana f, descompostura f (LAm); ~ **gang** (Brit Aut) equipo m de asistencia en carretera; ~ **service** (Brit Aut) asistencia f en carretera, servicio m de averías; ~ **truck**, ~ **van** (Brit) grúa f, camión m grúa.
(b) (of numbers etc) análisis m, descomposición f; desglose m; (report) informe m detallado.

breaker ['breɪkər] N ola f grande, cachón m.

break-even [,breɪk'iːvən] ATTR: ~ **chart** gráfica f del punto de equilibrio; ~ **point** punto m de indiferencia.

breakfast ['brekfəst] **1** N desayuno m; ~ **cereals** cereales mpl para el desayuno; ~ **cup** taza f de desayuno; ~ **room** habitación f del desayuno; ~ **TV** televisión f matinal.
2 VI desayunar(se) (off eggs, on eggs huevos).

break-in ['breɪk,ɪn] N escalamiento m, (loosely) robo m.

breaking ['breɪkɪŋ] N rotura f, rompimiento m; ~ **and entering** allanamiento m de morada.

breaking-point ['breɪkɪŋpɔɪnt] N punto m de ruptura, carga f de rotura; **to reach ~** llegar a la crisis, llegar al límite.

breaking-up [,breɪkɪŋ'ʌp] N (meeting etc) disolución f, levantamiento m (de la sesión); (school, college) fin m de las clases, fin m de curso.

breakneck ['breɪknek] ADJ: **at ~ speed** como alma que lleva el diablo.

breakout ['breɪkaʊt] N evasión f, fuga f.

break-point ['breɪkpɔɪnt] N (Tennis) punto m de break; (Comput) punto m de interrupción.

breakthrough ['breɪkθruː] N (Mil) ruptura f; (fig) avance m, adelanto m, invento m decisivo; **to achieve a ~** hacer grandes progresos, hacer un descubrimiento importante.

break-up ['breɪkʌp] N disolución f, desintegración f, desmembración f; ~ **value** (Comm) valor m en liquidación.

breakwater ['breɪk,wɔːtər] N rompeolas m, espigón m.

bream [briːm] N (sea) besugo m.

breast [brest] **1** N (Anat) pecho m; (woman's) pecho m, seno m; (of bird) pechuga f; (fig) corazón m; ~ **cancer** cáncer m de mama; **to beat one's ~** darse golpes de pecho; **to make a clean ~ of** confesar con franqueza; **to make a clean ~ of it** confesarlo todo, desembuchar.
2 VT (a) waves etc hacer cara a, arrostrar. (b) **to ~ the tape** romper la cinta, (fig) llegar a la meta.

breastbone ['brestbəʊn] N esternón m.

breast-fed ['brestfed] ADJ criado a pecho.

breast-feed ['brestfiːd] (irr: V feed) VT criar a los pechos; amamantar,

dar el pecho a.
breast-feeding ['brest,fiːdɪŋ] N cría *f* a los pechos, amamantamiento *m*.
breast-high ['brest'haɪ] ADV a la altura del pecho.
breast milk ['brestmɪlk] N leche *f* materna.
breastplate ['brestpleɪt] N peto *m*.
breast-pocket ['brest,pɒkɪt] N bolsillo *m* de pecho.
breast-stroke ['breststrəʊk] N braza *f* (de pecho).
breastwork ['brestwɜːk] N parapeto *m*.
breath [breθ] N aliento *m*, respiración *f*; (*esp visible in air*) hálito *m*; **bad ~** halitosis *f*; **the first ~ of spring** el primer viento suave que anuncia la primavera; **the least ~ of scandal** la más ligera sospecha de escándalo; **there's not a ~ of air stirring** no hay ni un soplo de aire; **the theatre was the ~ of life to her** el teatro era la misma vida para ella; **to bring a ~ of fresh air to** traer un soplo de aire refrescante a; **all in the same ~** de una tirada, todo al mismo tiempo; **in the very next ~** a renglón seguido; **out of ~** sofocado, jadeante, sin aliento; **to get out of ~** quedar sin aliento; **short of ~** corto de resuello; **under one's ~** a media voz, en voz baja; **to catch one's ~** suspender la respiración; **it made me catch my ~** (*fig*) me dejó pasmado; **to draw a deep ~** respirar a fondo; **to draw one's last ~** tomar el último aliento; **the best that ever drew ~** el mejor que se conoció jamás; **to gasp for ~** luchar por respirar; **to get one's ~ back** recuperar el aliento; **to go out for a ~ of air** salir a tomar el fresco; **to hold one's ~** contener la respiración; **to save one's ~** ahorrar las palabras; **to take a deep ~** respirar a fondo; **it took my ~ away** me dejó pasmado; **to waste one's ~** perder el tiempo (*on* hablando con), predicar en el desierto.
breathable ['briːðəbl] ADJ *air* respirable, que se puede respirar.
breathalyse, (*US*) **breathalyze** ['breθəlaɪz] VT someter a la prueba del alcoholímetro (*or* del alcohol).
Breathalyser, (*US*) **Breathalyzer** ['breθəlaɪzəʳ] ® N alcoholímetro *m*.
breathe [briːð] **1** VT respirar; *sigh* dar; *prayer* decir en voz baja; **to ~ air into a balloon** inflar un globo soplando; **it ~s the spirit of late** por todas partes el espíritu de.
2 VI respirar; (*noisily*) resollar; **to ~ again** respirar.
◆**breathe in** VTI aspirar, respirar.
◆**breathe out 1** VT exhalar.
2 VI espirar.
breather* ['briːðəʳ] N respiro *m*, descanso *m*; **to give sb a ~** dejar que uno tome una pausa; **to go out for a ~** salir a descansar un momento.
breathing ['briːðɪŋ] N respiración *f*; **heavy ~** resuello *m*; **~ apparatus** respirador *m*.
breathing-space ['briːðɪŋspeɪs] N respiro *m*.
breathing-tube ['briːðɪŋtjuːb] N tubo *m* de respiración.
breathless ['breθlɪs] ADJ (a) falto de aliento, jadeante; **~ with excitement** sin aliento por la emoción; **a ~ confession** una confesión apresurada.
(b) **a ~ silence** un silencio lleno de expectación.
breathlessly ['breθlɪslɪ] ADV: **to say ~** decir jadeante.
breathlessness ['breθlɪsnɪs] N falta *f* de aliento, dificultad *f* respiratoria.
breathtaking ['breθ,teɪkɪŋ] ADJ *sight* imponente, pasmoso; *speed* vertiginoso; *effrontery* pasmoso; **the view is ~** la vista corta la respiración.
breathtakingly ['breθ,teɪkɪŋlɪ] ADV: **~ beautiful** tan hermoso que corta la respiración; **to go ~ fast** ir a una velocidad vertiginosa.
breath-test ['breθtest] **1** N prueba *f* del alcoholímetro (*or* del alcohol).
2 VT someter a la prueba del alcoholímetro.
breathy ['breθɪ] ADJ *voice* entrecortado.
bred [bred] PRET AND PTP *of* **breed**.
breech [briːtʃ] N recámara *f*.
breeches ['briːtʃɪz] NPL calzones *mpl*; (**riding**) **~** pantalones *mpl* de montar; **~ buoy** boya *f* pantalón; **to wear the ~** llevar los pantalones, llevar los calzones.
breechloader ['briːtʃ,ləʊdəʳ] N arma *f* de retrocarga.
breed [briːd] **1** N raza *f*, casta *f*.
2 (*irr*: PRET AND PTP **bred**) VT criar, engendrar; (*as farmer*) criar; (*fig*) engendrar, producir; **town bred** criado en la ciudad; **they are bred for show** se crían para las exposiciones; **we ~ them for hunting** los criamos para la caza.
3 VI reproducirse, procrear; **they ~ like flies** (*or* **rabbits**) se multiplican como conejos.
breeder ['briːdəʳ] N (a) (*person*) criador *m*, -ora *f*; (*of cattle*) ganadero *m*. (b) (*animal*) criadero *m*, paridera *f*.
breeder reactor ['briːdəɪ;æktəʳ] N reactor *m* reproductor.
breeding ['briːdɪŋ] N (a) (*Bio*) reproducción *f*. (b) (*of stock*) cría *f*. (c) (*of person*) crianza *f*, educación *f*; **bad ~, ill ~** mala crianza *f*, falta *f* de educación; **good ~** educación *f*, cultura *f*; **he has (good) ~** es

una persona educada; **it shows bad ~** indica una falta de educación.
breeding-ground ['briːdɪŋ,graʊnd] N tierra *f* de cría; (*fig*) caldo *m* de cultivo (*of, for* de).
breeding-season ['briːdɪŋ,siːzn] N época *f* de reproducción.
breeks [briːks] NPL (*Scot*) pantalones *mpl*.
breeze [briːz] **1** N brisa *f*; **to do sth in a ~** (*US**) hacer algo con los ojos cerrados; **to shoot the ~** (*US**) charlar; **it's a ~** (*US**) esto es coser y cantar.
2 VI: **to ~ in** entrar como Pedro por su casa; **to ~ through sth** (*US**) hacer algo con los ojos cerrados.
breeze-block ['briːzblɒk] N (*Brit*) bloque *m* de cemento; bovedilla *f*.
breezily ['briːzɪlɪ] ADV jovialmente, despreocupadamente.
breezy ['briːzɪ] ADJ (a) *day, place* de mucho viento; **it is ~** hace viento. (b) *person's manner* animado, jovial, despreocupado.
Bren [bren] N: **~ gun** fusil *m* ametrallador; **~ (gun) carrier** vehículo *m* de transporte ligero (con fusil ametrallador).
brethren ['breðrɪn] NPL (*irr* PL *of* **brother**: *esp Rel*) hermanos *mpl*.
Breton ['bretən] **1** ADJ bretón.
2 N (a) bretón *m*, -ona *f*. (b) (*Ling*) bretón *m*.
breve [briːv] N (*Mus, Typ*) breve *f*.
breviary ['briːvɪərɪ] N breviario *m*.
brevity ['brevɪtɪ] N brevedad *f*.
brew [bruː] **1** N (*hum*) poción *f*, brebaje *m*.
2 VT *beer* hacer, elaborar; *tea* hacer; (*fig: also* **to ~ up**) urdir, tramar.
3 VI (*fig*) prepararse; (*storm*) amenazar; **there's sth ~ing** algo se está tramando; **there's trouble ~ing** soplan vientos de fronda.
◆**brew up** VI preparar el té.
brewer ['bruːəʳ] N cervecero *m*.
brewery ['bruːərɪ] N cervecería *f*, fábrica *f* de cerveza.
brew-up ['bruːʌp] N: **let's have a ~** (*Brit**) vamos a tomar un té.
briar ['braɪəʳ] N (a) (*rose*) escaramujo *m*, rosa *f* silvestre; (*hawthorn*) espino *m*; (*bramble*) zarza *f*; (*heather*) brezo *m*. (b) (*pipe*) pipa *f* de brezo.
bribable ['braɪbəbl] ADJ sobornable.
bribe [braɪb] **1** N soborno *m*, cohecho *m*, mordida *f* (*Mex*), coima *f* (*LAm*); **to take a ~** dejarse sobornar (*from* por).
2 VT sobornar, cohechar, mojar (*LAm*), aceitar (*LAm*).
bribery ['braɪbərɪ] N soborno *m*, cohecho *m*, coima *f* (*LAm*).
bric-à-brac ['brɪkəbræk] N chucherías *fpl*, curiosidades *fpl*.
brick [brɪk] **1** N ladrillo *m*, tabique *m* (*LAm*); (*of ice cream*) bloque *m*; (*Brit: child's*) cubo *m*; **a ~ wall** una pared de ladrillos; **~s and mortar** (*fig*) construcción *f*, edificios *mpl*; (*fig*) inversión *f* sólida; **resultados** *mpl* tangibles; **he's a ~** (**†*) es un buen chico; **be a ~ and lend it to me** (**†*) préstamelo como buen amigo; **he came down on us like a ton of ~s** nos echó una bronca fenomenal; **to drop a ~*** (*Brit*) tirarse una plancha; **you can't make ~s without straw** sin paja ho hay ladrillos.
2 ATTR de ladrillo(s).
3 VT (*also* **to ~ up**) cerrar con ladrillos, tapar con ladrillos.
brickbat ['brɪkbæt] N trozo *m* de ladrillo; (*fig*) palabra *f* hiriente, crítica *f*.
brick-built ['brɪk,bɪlt] ADJ construido de ladrillos.
brickie* ['brɪkɪ] N albañil *m*.
brick-kiln ['brɪk,kɪln] N horno *m* de ladrillos.
bricklayer ['brɪkleɪəʳ] N albañil *m*.
bricklaying ['brɪk,leɪɪŋ] N albañilería *f*.
brick-red ['brɪkred] **1** ADJ rojo ladrillo.
2 N rojo *m* ladrillo.
brickwork ['brɪkwɜːk] N enladrillado *m*, ladrillos *mpl*.
brickworks ['brɪkwɜːks] N, **brickyard** ['brɪk,jɑːd] N ladrillar *m*.
bridal ['braɪdl] ADJ nupcial.
bride [braɪd] N novia *f*; **the ~ and groom** los novios.
bridegroom ['braɪdgrʊm] N novio *m*; *ver también* ⟨BEST MAN⟩.
bridesmaid ['braɪdzmeɪd] N dama *f* de honor.
bridge¹ [brɪdʒ] **1** N puente *m* (*also Mus*); (*Naut*) puente *m* de mando; (*of nose*) caballete *m*; **to burn one's ~s** quemar las naves; **we'll cross that ~ when we come to it** nos enfrentaremos con ese problema en su momento; **don't cross your ~s before you come to them** no adelantes los acontecimientos; **much water has flowed under the ~ since then** mucho ha llovido desde entonces; **we must rebuild our ~s** (*fig*) tenemos que restablecer las relaciones.
2 VT tender un puente sobre; *gap* llenar, salvar.
bridge² [brɪdʒ] N (*Cards*) bridge *m*.
bridge-building ['brɪdʒ,bɪldɪŋ] N construcción *f* de puentes; (*fig*) restablecimiento *m* de relaciones.
bridgehead ['brɪdʒhed] N cabeza *f* de puente (*also fig*).
bridge-party ['brɪdʒ,pɑːtɪ] N reunión *f* de bridge.
bridge-player ['brɪdʒ,pleɪəʳ] N jugador *m*, -ora *f* de bridge.
bridge-roll [,brɪdʒ'rəʊl] N tipo de bollo.
Bridget ['brɪdʒɪt] NF Brígida.
bridging-loan ['brɪdʒɪŋ,ləʊn] N (*Brit*) crédito *m* puente.
bridle ['braɪdl] **1** N brida *f*, freno *m*.

2 VI: **to ~ at** picarse por, ofenderse por.

bridle-path ['braɪdlpɑ:θ] N, PL **bridle-paths** ['braɪdlpɑ:ðz] camino *m* de herradura.

brief [bri:f] 1 ADJ breve, corto; *(fleeting)* fugaz, pasajero; *style* lacónico; **well, to be ~** ... bueno, en resumen ...; bueno, para decirlo con pocas palabras ...; **please be as ~ as possible** explíquese con la mayor brevedad.

2 N **(a)** *(Eccl: papal)* breve *m*.
(b) *(Jur)* escrito *m*; **to go beyond one's ~** exceder las instrucciones; **to hold a ~ for** representar a; **to hold a watching ~ for sb** representar a un cliente a quien no interesa directamente un juicio; **to hold no ~ for** no aprobar, no apoyar; **to stick to one's ~** atenerse a las órdenes dadas.
(c) *(Brit*: barrister)* abogado *mf*.
(d) **in ~** en resumen.
(e) **~s** *(man's)* calzoncillos *mpl*, *(woman's)* bragas *fpl*.
3 VT *(Mil etc)* dar órdenes a, dar instrucciones a; informar (de antemano); *barrister, lawyer* constituir; **she had been well ~ed** estaba bien informada.

briefcase ['bri:fkeɪs] N cartera *f*, maletín *m*, portafolio *m* *(LAm)*.

briefing ['bri:fɪŋ] N reunión *f* en que se dan las órdenes (a la tripulación de un avión militar); órdenes *fpl*, instrucciones *fpl*; *(to press)* informe *m*, sesión *f* informativa; *(heading in press)* informaciones *fpl*.

briefly ['bri:flɪ] ADV brevemente; en resumen, en pocas palabras; **he was ~ ambassador in Lima** por poco tiempo fue embajador en Lima.

briefness ['bri:fnɪs] N brevedad *f*.

brier ['braɪəʳ] N = **briar**.

brig [brɪg] N *(Naut)* bergantín *m*.

Brig. ABBR of **Brigadier** general *m* de brigada.

brigade [brɪ'geɪd] N brigada *f*; *(fire etc)* cuerpo *m*; **one of the old ~** un veterano.

brigadier [ˌbrɪgə'dɪəʳ] N *(Brit)* general *m* de brigada.

brigand ['brɪgənd] N bandido *m*, bandolero *m*.

brigandage ['brɪgəndɪdʒ] N bandidaje *m*, bandolerismo *m*.

bright [braɪt] ADJ 1 **(a)** claro, brillante, luminoso; *day* luminoso, de sol; *eyes* claro; *sun* brillante; *surface* lustroso; *colour* subido; *smile* radiante; **~ interval** período *m* de sol; **~ lights** *(US Aut)* luces *fpl* largas.
(b) *(clever)* listo, inteligente; ocurrente; *idea* luminoso; *conversation, remark* ingenioso; **that was ~ of you** en eso anduviste muy listo; **you're a ~ one!** ¡qué despiste tienes!; **the child's as ~ as a button** el niño es más listo que el hambre.
(c) *(cheerful)* alegre, animado, optimista.
(d) *prospect etc* prometedor, esperanzador; *hope* vivo, firme.
2 ADV: **to get up ~ and early** levantarse tempranito.

brighten ['braɪtn] 1 VT *(also* **to ~ up) (a)** *(make shine)* abrillantar, lustrar. **(b)** *house* hacer más alegre, poner colores en; *(cheer)* alegrar.
2 VI *(also* **to ~ up) (a)** *(person)* animarse, alegrarse. **(b)** *(weather)* despejarse; *(prospect)* mejorar.

bright-eyed ['braɪt'aɪd] ADJ de ojos vivos.

brightly ['braɪtlɪ] ADV **(a)** brillantemente; **the sun shone ~** el sol lucía brillantemente; **the fire burned ~** el fuego resplandecía. **(b)** ingeniosamente; *smile, look* radiantemente; *say, answer* con prontitud.

brightness ['braɪtnɪs] N *(V adj)* **(a)** claridad *f*; brillantez *f*, luminosidad *f*; lustre *m*; lo subido; **~ control** botón *m* de ajuste del brillo. **(b)** inteligencia *f*; viveza *f* de ingenio.

brill[1] [brɪl] N rodaballo *m* menor.

brill[2]⚓ [brɪl] ADJ = **brilliant**; tremendo*, fantástico*; **~!** ¡fantástico!*

brilliance ['brɪljəns] N, **brilliancy** ['brɪljənsɪ] N brillo *m*, brillantez *f*.

brilliant ['brɪljənt] 1 ADJ brillante; *idea* genial, luminoso; *student etc* brillante, sobresaliente; *success* clamoroso, resonante, brillante; *wine* completamente límpido; (*) tremendo*, fantástico*; **~!** ¡fantástico!
2 N brillante *m*.

brilliantine [ˌbrɪljən'ti:n] N brillantina *f*.

brilliantly ['brɪljəntlɪ] ADV brillantemente *(also fig)*.

Brillo pad ['brɪləʊˌpæd] ® N estropajo *m* de aluminio.

brim [brɪm] 1 N borde *m*; *(of hat)* ala *f*.
2 VI: **to ~ over** desbordarse, rebosar; **to ~ with** rebosar de.

brimful ['brɪm'fʊl] ADJ lleno hasta el borde; **~ of, ~ with** rebosante de.

brimstone ['brɪmstəʊn] N azufre *m*.

brindled ['brɪndld] ADJ manchado, mosqueado.

brine [braɪn] N salmuera *f*; *(fig)* mar *m or f*.

bring [brɪŋ] *(irr: PRET AND PTP* **brought)** 1 VT **(a)** *person, object, news, luck etc* traer; *person* llevar, conducir; **to ~ a matter to a conclusion** concluir un asunto, llevar un asunto a su desenlace; **it brought us to the verge of disaster** nos llevó al borde del desastre; **this brought him to his feet** esto hizo que se pusiera de pie, con esto se levantó; **he brought it upon himself** se lo buscó; **~ it over here** tráelo para acá; **~ it closer** acércalo; *V* **house, light, sense** *etc.*

(b) *(cause)* causar; traer, provocar; *profit etc* dar, producir; **you ~ nothing but trouble** no haces más que causarme molestias; **it brought tears to her eyes** con esto se le llenaron los ojos de lágrimas; **to ~ sth to happen** hacer que algo ocurra.
(c) *(Jur)* *charge* hacer, formular; *suit* entablar; **no charges will be brought** no se hará ninguna acusación; **the case was brought before the judge** la causa fue vista por el juez.
(d) **to ~ sb to do sth** inducir a uno a hacer algo, hacer que uno haga algo; **he was brought to see his error** le convencieron de su error; **it brought me to realize that ...** me hizo comprender que ...
2 VR: **to ~ o.s. to** + *infin* convencerse para + *infin*; cobrar suficiente ánimo para + *infin*; resignarse a + *infin*.

◆**bring about** VT ocasionar, producir, causar; *change* efectuar.

◆**bring along** VT traer consigo, llevar consigo.

◆**bring away** VT llevarse.

◆**bring back** VT **(a)** volver a traer; volver con, traer de vuelta; *monarchy etc* restaurar; *thing borrowed* devolver; *(to life)* devolver la vida a.
(b) *memory* recordar, traer a la memoria.

◆**bring down** VT **(a)** *luggage etc* bajar.
(b) *(Mil, Hunting)* abatir, derribar; *government* derribar, derrocar.
(c) *price* rebajar, reducir.

◆**bring forth** VT *child* parir, dar a luz; *(fig)* producir.

◆**bring forward** VT **(a)** *proposal* proponer, presentar, suscitar.
(b) *date* adelantar.
(c) *(Comm)* pasar a otra cuenta; **brought forward** suma *f* del anterior.

◆**bring in** VT **(a)** *(carry in)* entrar, traer, introducir; *meal* servir; *harvest* recoger; *person* introducir, hacer entrar; *suspect* detener, llevar a la comisaría; **to ~ in the police** llamar a la policía; pedir la intervención de la policía; **~ him in!** ¡que entre!, ¡que pase!; **I was not brought into the matter at any stage** no me dieron voz en este asunto en ningún momento.
(b) *fashion, custom* introducir; *(Parl)* *bill* presentar.
(c) *(attract)* atraer; **this should ~ in the masses** esto deberá atraer a las masas.
(d) *(Fin)* *income* dar, producir.
(e) *(Jur)* *verdict* dar, pronunciar.

◆**bring off** VT lograr, conseguir; *success* obtener, realizar; *plan* llevar a cabo.

◆**bring on** VT **(a)** *(cause)* causar, acarrear.
(b) *growth* estimular, favorecer; *plant* hacer acelerar el desarrollo de.
(c) *(Theat)* presentar, introducir; hacer salir a la escena.

◆**bring out** VT **(a)** *(take out)* sacar; *argument* sacar a relucir; *product* lanzar, lanzar al mercado; *book* publicar, sacar a luz.
(b) *(emphasize)* subrayar, recalcar; *colour* hacer resaltar.
(c) *person* hacer menos reservado, ayudar a adquirir confianza.

◆**bring over** VT **(a)** *person* ir a buscar. **(b)** *(convert)* *person* convertir, convencer.

◆**bring round** VT **(a)** *(win over)* ganarse la voluntad de; convencer, convertir.
(b) *(Med)* hacer volver en sí.

◆**bring to** VT **(a)** *(Naut)* pairear, poner al pairo. **(b)** *unconscious person* reanimar.

◆**bring together** VT reunir; *enemies* reconciliar.

◆**bring under** VT *(fig)* someter.

◆**bring up** VT **(a)** *(carry)* subir; *person* hacer subir.
(b) *subject* sacar a colación, sacar a relucir; llamar la atención sobre.
(c) *person* criar, educar; **she was badly brought up** la criaron de manera poco satisfactoria; **he was brought up to believe that ...** le educaron en la creencia de que ...; **where were you brought up?** *(iro)* ¡cómo se ve que no has ido a colegios de pago!
(d) (*) arrojar, vomitar.
(e) **to ~ sb up short** parar a uno en seco.
(f) **to ~ up the rear** *(Mil)* cerrar la marcha.
(g) **to ~ sb up in court** *(Jur)* hacer que uno comparezca ante el magistrado.
(h) *V* **date.**

bring-and-buy sale [ˌbrɪŋənd'baɪseɪl] N *(Brit)* tómbola *f* de beneficencia.

brink [brɪŋk] N borde *m*; **on the ~ of** *(fig)* + N en la antesala de + N; + *ger* a punto de + *infin*.

brinkmanship ['brɪŋkmənʃɪp] N política *f* de la cuerda floja, política *f* del borde del abismo.

briny ['braɪnɪ] 1 ADJ salado, salobre.
2 N: **the ~** (†, *hum*) el mar.

briquette [brɪ'ket] N briqueta *f*.

brisk [brɪsk] ADJ enérgico, vigoroso; *pace, sales* rápido; *trade etc* activo; *wind* fuerte; **business is ~** el negocio va bien; estos géneros *(etc)* se venden bien.

brisket ['brɪskɪt] N carne *f* de pecho (para asar).

briskly ['brɪsklɪ] ADV enérgicamente; rápidamente; activamente.

briskness ['brɪsknɪs] N energía *f*; rapidez *f*; actividad *f*.

brisling ['brɪzlɪŋ] N espadín *m* (noruego).
bristle ['brɪsl] [1] N cerda *f*; (*pure*) ~ **brush** cepillo *m* de púas.
[2] VI (a) (*hair etc*) erizarse; (*animal*) erizar las cerdas; **to ~ with** (*fig*) estar erizado de. (b) (*fig*) ofenderse, irritarse (*at* por).
bristly ['brɪslɪ] ADJ cerdoso; **to have a ~ chin** tener la barba crecida.
Bristol ['brɪstəl] N (a) ~ **board** cartulina *f*. (b) **b~s:** tetas* *fpl*.
Brit* [brɪt] N británico *m*, -a *f*, (*loosely*) inglés *m*, -esa *f*.
Britain ['brɪtən] N Gran Bretaña *f*, (*loosely*) Inglaterra *f*.

┌─── BRITAIN ───────────────────────────────────────┐

*A veces se usa el término **England** para referirse a la totalidad del país, aunque no es un término usado con precisión; sin embargo, mucha gente confunde a menudo los nombres **Britain, Great Britain, United Kingdom** y **British Isles** .*
*Se denomina **Great Britain** a la isla que comprende Inglaterra, Escocia y Gales. Desde el punto de vista administrativo, el término también incluye las islas menores cercanas, a excepción de la Isla de Man (**Isle of Man**) y las Islas Anglonormandas o Islas del Canal de la Mancha (**Channel Islands**).*
***United Kingdom (of Great Britain and Northern Ireland),** o **UK,** es la unidad política que comprende Gran Bretaña e Irlanda del Norte.*
***British Isles** es el término geográfico que abarca Gran Bretaña, Irlanda, la Isla de Man y las Islas Anglonormandas. En lo político, el término comprende dos estados soberanos: el Reino Unido y la República de Irlanda. El término **Britain** se utiliza fundamentalmente para referirse al Reino Unido, y en algunas ocasiones también a la isla, a Gran Bretaña.*

└──┘

Britannia [brɪ'tænɪə] N Britania *f*, *figura que representa simbólicamente a Gran Bretaña; ver también* RULE BRITANNIA .
Britannic [brɪ'tænɪk] ADJ: **His** (*or* **Her**) ~ **Majesty** su Majestad *f* Británica.
britches ['brɪtʃəz] = **breeches**.
briticism ['brɪtɪsɪzəm] N (*US*) modismo *m* (*or* vocablo *m etc*) del inglés de Inglaterra.
British ['brɪtɪʃ] [1] ADJ británico, (*loosely*) inglés; ~ **Council** Consejo *m* Británico; ~ **English** inglés *m* hablado en Gran Bretaña, inglés *m* británico; ~ **Legion** organización de veteranos de las dos guerras mundiales; ~ **Museum** Museo *m* Británico; **the best of ~** (*luck*)! ¡y un cuerno!:; *ver también* LEGION - AMERICAN LEGION/BRITISH LEGION .
[2] N: **the ~** los británicos, (*loosely*) los ingleses.

┌─── BRITISH COUNCIL ───────────────────────────────┐

*El **British Council** se creó en 1935 para fomentar la cultura británica en el extranjero y actualmente tiene delegaciones en más de 100 países. Sus principales cometidos son la organización de actividades culturales, tales como exposiciones y conferencias, con el fin de dar a conocer el arte, la ciencia y la literatura del país, así como la enseñanza del inglés, además de ayudar a aquellos que desean estudiar en el Reino Unido.*

└──┘

Britisher ['brɪtɪʃər] N (*US*) británico *m*, -a *f*, natural *mf* de Gran Bretaña.
British Isles ['brɪtɪʃ'aɪlz] NPL Islas *fpl* Británicas.
Briton ['brɪtən] N británico *m*, -a *f*, (*loosely*) inglés *m*, -esa *f*.
Brittany ['brɪtənɪ] N Bretaña *f*.
brittle ['brɪtl] ADJ frágil, quebradizo.
brittleness ['brɪtlnɪs] N fragilidad *f*, lo quebradizo.
Bro. N ABBR *of* **Brother** hermano *m*.
broach [brəʊtʃ] VT *cask* espitar; *bottle etc* abrir; *subject* comenzar a hablar de, mencionar por primera vez, abordar; **he didn't ~ the subject** no mencionó el punto, no sacó el tema a colación.
broad [brɔːd] [1] ADJ (a) ancho; extenso, amplio; ~ **bean** haba *f* gruesa; ~ **jump** (*US*) salto *m* de longitud; **3 metres ~** ancho de 3 metros; **it's as ~ as it is long** (*fig*) lo mismo da.
(b) (*fig*) ancho; *view* comprensivo; *mind* tolerante, liberal; *hint* claro, inconfundible; *accent* marcado, cerrado, fuerte; *story* verde; *sense of word* ancho, lato; *grin, smile* jovial; *range, spectrum* amplio, extenso; ~ **daylight** plena luz *f* de día; **in ~ daylight** en (*or* a) pleno día.
[2] N (*US*:) tía* *f*.
broad-brimmed ['brɔːd'brɪmd] ADJ *hat* de ala ancha.
broadcast ['brɔːdkɑːst] [1] ADJ (*Agr*) sembrado a voleo; (*Rad*) radiodifundido, de (la) radio.
[2] ADV por todas partes.
[3] N emisión *f*, programa *m*.
[4] VT (*Agr*) sembrar a voleo; (*fig*) diseminar, divulgar; (*Rad*) emitir, radiar.
[5] VI hablar (*or* tocar *etc*) por la radio.
broadcaster ['brɔːdkɑːstər] N conferenciante *mf* (*or* cronista *mf*) de radio; (*announcer*) locutor *m*, -ora *f*.
broadcasting ['brɔːdkɑːstɪŋ] [1] N radiodifusión *f*.
[2] ATTR de radiodifusión.
broadcasting station ['brɔːdkɑːstɪŋ,steɪʃən] N emisora *f*.
broadcloth ['brɔːdklɒθ] N velarte *m*.

broaden ['brɔːdn] (*also* **to ~ out**) [1] VT ensanchar; **travel ~s the mind** los viajes edifican el entendimiento.
[2] VI ensancharse.
broadleaved [,brɔːd'liːvd] ADJ de hoja ancha.
broadloom ['brɔːdluːm] ADJ: ~ **carpet** alfombra *f* sin costuras.
broadly ['brɔːdlɪ] ADV extensamente; *smile* de modo jovial; **it is ~ true that ...** es en general verdad que ...; ~ **speaking** grosso modo, en general, hablando en términos generales.
broadly-based ['brɔːdlɪ,beɪst] ADJ que cuenta con una base amplia, apoyado por sectores muy diversos; **a ~ coalition** una coalición que representa gran diversidad de intereses.
broad-minded ['brɔːd'maɪndɪd] ADJ de amplias miras, de criterio amplio, tolerante, liberal.
broad-mindedness ['brɔːd'maɪndɪdnɪs] N amplitud *f* de criterio, tolerancia *f*.
broadness ['brɔːdnɪs] N anchura *f*, extensión *f*; (*of accent*) lo cerrado.
broadsheet ['brɔːdʃiːt] N periódico *m* de gran formato; *ver también* TABLOIDS AND BROADSHEETS .
broad-shouldered ['brɔːd'ʃəʊldəd] ADJ ancho de espaldas.
broadside ['brɔːdsaɪd] N (*side*) costado *m*; (*shots*) andanada *f*; (*abuse etc*) andanada *f* verbal; ~ **on** de costado; **to fire a ~** soltar (*or* disparar) una andanada (*also fig*).
broadsword ['brɔːd,sɔːd] N sable *m*.
Broadway ['brɔːd,weɪ] [1] N Broadway *m* (*calle de Nueva York famosa por sus teatros*).
[2] ATTR *musical, theatre* de Broadway; *ver también* OFF-BROADWAY .
broadways ['brɔːdweɪz] ADV a lo ancho, por lo ancho; con la parte ancha por delante; ~ **on to the waves** de costado a las olas.
brocade [brəʊ'keɪd] N brocado *m*.
broccoli ['brɒkəlɪ] N brécol *m*, bróculi *m*, broculí *m*.
brochure ['brəʊʃjʊər] N folleto *m*.
brock [brɒk] N (*Brit*) tejón *m*.
brogue¹ [brəʊg] N (*shoe*) abarca *f*, zapato *m* de estilo inglés picado.
brogue² [brəʊg] N (*Ling*) acento *m* irlandés.
broil [brɔɪl] VT asar a la parrilla.
broiler ['brɔɪlər] N (a) (*chicken*) pollo *m* para asar. (b) (*US: grill*) parrilla *f*, grill *m*.
broiler-house ['brɔɪlə,haʊs] N, PL **broiler-houses** ['brɔɪlə,haʊzɪz] batería *f* de engorde.
broiling ['brɔɪlɪŋ] ADJ: **it's ~ hot** hace un calor sofocante.
broke [brəʊk] PRET *of* **break**; **to be ~*** no tener un céntimo, estar sin blanca; **to go ~*** quebrar; **to go for ~*** echar el resto*, ir al límite.
broken ['brəʊkən] [1] PTP *of* **break**.
[2] ADJ *ground* accidentado, quebrado; *tone* de desesperación; ~ **in health** deshecho, muy decaído; **in ~ Spanish** en castellano chapurreado; ~ **home** familia *f* desestructurada, familia *f* en la que se han divorciado (*or* separado) los padres; ~ **man** hombre *m* que no vale para nada; hombre *m* arruinado; ~ **reed** (*fig*) persona *f* quemada.
broken-down ['brəʊkən'daʊn] ADJ agotado; *machine* destartalado, desvencijado.
broken-hearted ['brəʊkən'hɑːtɪd] ADJ traspasado de dolor; **to be ~** tener el corazón partido.
brokenly ['brəʊkənlɪ] ADV *say etc* en tono angustiado, con palabras entrecortadas.
broker ['brəʊkər] N corredor *m*, bolsista *m*; agente *m* de negocios.
brokerage ['brəʊkərɪdʒ] N, **broking** ['brəʊkɪŋ] N corretaje *m*.
brolly* ['brɒlɪ] N (*Brit*) paraguas *m*.
bromide ['brəʊmaɪd] N (a) (*Typ*) bromuro *m*. (b) (*fig: platitude*) perogrullada *f*.
bromine ['brəʊmiːn] N bromo *m*.
bronchial ['brɒŋkɪəl] ADJ bronquial; ~ **asthma** asma *f* bronquial; ~ **tubes** bronquios *mpl*.
bronchitic [brɒŋ'kɪtɪk] ADJ bronquítico.
bronchitis [brɒŋ'kaɪtɪs] N bronquitis *f*.
bronchopneumonia [,brɒŋkəʊnjuː'məʊnɪə] N bronconeumonía *f*.
broncho-pulmonary ['brɒŋkəʊ'pʌlmənərɪ] ADJ broncopulmonar.
bronchus ['brɒŋkəs] N, PL **bronchi** ['brɒŋkaɪ] bronquio *m*.
bronco ['brɒŋkəʊ] N (*US*) potro *m* cerril.
broncobuster* ['brɒŋkəʊ,bʌstər] N (*US*) domador *m* de potros cerriles, domador *m* de caballos.
brontosaurus [,brɒntə'sɔːrəs] N brontosauro *m*.
Bronx [brɒŋks] N: ~ **cheer** (*US**) pedorreta *f*.
bronze [brɒnz] [1] N bronce *m*.
[2] ADJ de bronce; **B~ Age** Edad *f* de(l) Bronce; ~ **medal** medalla *f* de bronce; ~ **medallist** medallero *m*, -a *f* de bronce.
[3] VT broncear.
[4] VI broncearse.
bronzed [brɒnzd] ADJ bronceado.
bronzing ['brɒnzɪŋ] ADJ *powder, gel* bronceador.
brooch [brəʊtʃ] N alfiler *m* (de pecho), prendedor *m*; (*ancient*) fíbula *f*.
brood [bruːd] [1] N camada *f*, cría *f*; (*of chicks*) nidada *f*; (*of insects, first etc*) generación *f*; (*fig*) familia *f*, progenie *f*, (*pej*) prole *f*.

2 ADJ: ~ **mare** yegua f de cría.

3 VI (*also* **to ~ on:** *eggs*) empollar; (*fig*) meditar tristemente; **to ~ on**, **to ~ over** meditar tristemente; **you mustn't ~ over it** no debes dejarte obsesionar con eso; **disaster ~ed over the town** se cernía el desastre sobre la ciudad.

brooding ['bruːdɪŋ] ADJ *evil, presence etc* siniestro, amenazador.

broodings ['bruːdɪŋs] NPL meditaciones fpl.

broody ['bruːdɪ] ADJ clueca; (*fig*) triste, melancólico.

brook¹ [brʊk] N arroyo m.

brook² [brʊk] VT (*liter*) aguantar, permitir.

brooklet ['brʊklɪt] N arroyuelo m.

broom [brʊm] N **(a)** escoba f, pichana f (*And*); **new ~** (*fig*) escoba f nueva. **(b)** (*Bot*) hiniesta f, retama f.

broomstick ['brʊmstɪk] N palo m de escoba.

Bros ABBR *of* **Brothers** Hermanos mpl, Hnos.

broth [brɒθ] N caldo m.

brothel ['brɒθl] N prostíbulo m, casa f de putas, quilombo m (*LAm*).

brother ['brʌðəʳ] N hermano m (*also Eccl*); compañero m, camarada m; **hey, ~!*** ¡oye, amigo!*; **oh, ~!*** ¡santo cielo!; **X and his ~ teachers** X y sus colegas profesionales; **they're ~s under the skin** debajo de la piel son hermanos.

brotherhood ['brʌðəhʊd] N fraternidad f; (*religious, group*) hermandad f; cofradía f.

brother-in-arms ['brʌðəɪn'ɑːmz] N compañero m de armas.

brother-in-law ['brʌðərɪnlɔː] N, PL **brothers-in-law** cuñado m, hermano m político.

brotherly ['brʌðəlɪ] ADJ fraternal.

brought [brɔːt] PRET AND PTP *of* **bring**.

brouhaha [bruːhɑːhɑː] N barullo m.

brow [braʊ] N ceja f; (*forehead*) frente f; (*of hill*) cresta f, cumbre f, (*of cliff*) borde m; **to knit one's ~** fruncir las cejas.

browbeat ['braʊbiːt] VT intimidar (con amenazas) (*into doing sth* para que haga algo).

brown [braʊn] **1** ADJ moreno; marrón; *hair* castaño; (*tanned*) moreno, bronceado; **as ~ as a berry** muy moreno, muy bronceado; **to get ~** (*in sun*) ponerse moreno, morenearse, broncearse; **~ ale** cerveza f negra; **~ bread** pan m moreno; **~ egg** huevo m moreno; **~ paper** papel m de embalar, papel m de estraza; **~ rice** arroz m integral; **~ shoes** zapatos mpl marrones; **~ sugar** azúcar f negra, azúcar f terciada.

2 N color m moreno (*etc*).

3 VT poner moreno *etc*; *skin* broncear; (*Culin*) dorar.

4 VI ponerse moreno (*etc*); (*skin*) ponerse moreno, morenearse, broncearse; (*Culin*) dorarse.

◆**brown off:** VT (*Brit*): **to ~ sb off** fastidiar a uno; **I'm ~ed off** estoy hasta las narices (**with** de).

brownie ['braʊnɪ] N **(a)** (*fairy*) duende m; (*person*) miembro joven de las *Girl Guides*; **to earn** (*or* **get, win**) **~ points** apuntarse un tanto a favor, merecerse una notita favorable. **(b)** (*US: cookie*) pastelillo m de chocolate y nueces.

browning ['braʊnɪŋ] N (*Brit Culin*) aditamento m colorante.

brownish ['braʊnɪʃ] ADJ pardusco, que tira a moreno.

brownnose: ['braʊnˌnəʊz] (*US*) **1** N lameculos* mf.

2 VT lamer el culo a**:**

Brownshirt ['braʊnʃɜːt] N *soldado de las SA en la Alemania nazi*.

brownstone ['braʊnstəʊn] N (*US*) (casa f construida con) piedra f caliza de color rojizo.

browse [braʊz] **1** N: **to have a ~** (**around**) curiosear; pasearse para ver cosas.

2 VT *grass* pacer, rozar; *trees* ramonear.

3 VI pacer; (*fig*) leer ociosamente; curiosear; **to spend an hour browsing in a bookshop** pasar una hora hojeando los libros en una librería.

◆**browse on** VT pacer.

BRS N (*Brit*) ABBR *of* **British Road Services** *empresa británica de transportes por carretera*.

brucellosis [ˌbruːsəˈləʊsɪs] N brucelosis f.

Bruges [bruːʒ] N Brujas f.

bruise [bruːz] **1** N contusión f, cardenal m, magulladura f, magullón m, moretón m (*esp LAm*).

2 VT contundir, magullar; *fruit* estropear.

bruiser* ['bruːzəʳ] N boxeador m.

bruising ['bruːzɪŋ] ADJ *experience* doloroso, penoso; *match* durísimo, violento.

bruit [bruːt] VT: **to ~ about** (††, *US*) rumorear.

Brum* [brʌm] N (*Brit*) ABBR *of* **Birmingham.**

Brummie* ['brʌmɪ] N nativo m, -a f (*or* habitante mf) de Birmingham.

brunch* [brʌntʃ] N desayuno-almuerzo m.

brunette [bruːˈnet] **1** ADJ moreno.

2 N morena f.

brunt [brʌnt] N: **the ~ of the attack** lo más fuerte del ataque; **the ~ of the work** la mayor parte del trabajo; **to bear the ~ of** aguantar

lo más recio de, llevar el peso de.

brush [brʌʃ] **1** N **(a)** (*act of brushing*) cepilladura f, cepillado m; **to give a coat a ~** cepillar un abrigo; **let's give it a ~** vamos a pasar el cepillo.

(b) (*implement*) cepillo m; (*large*) escoba f; (*shaving ~*) brocha f; (*currying ~, scrubbing ~*) bruza f; (*artist's*) pincel m; (*housepainter's*) brocha f; (*Elec*) escobilla f.

(c) (*fox's*) rabo m, hopo m; *ver también* [FOXHUNTING].

(d) (*Bot*) broza f; maleza f, monte m bajo.

(e) (*Mil*) escaramuza f; (*fig*) encuentro m; **to have a ~ with sb** tener un roce con uno.

2 VT cepillar; *shoes etc* limpiar; (*in passing*) rozar al pasar.

◆**brush against** VT rozar al pasar.

◆**brush aside** VT rechazar, no hacer caso de; quitar importancia a.

◆**brush away** VT quitar (con un cepillo, con la mano *etc*).

◆**brush down** VT cepillar, limpiar; *horse* almohazar.

◆**brush off** VT **(a)** quitar (con un cepillo, con la mano *etc*). **(b) to ~ sb off*** mandar a uno a paseo; deshacerse de uno, zafarse de uno.

◆**brush past** **1** VT pasar muy cerca de; rozar al pasar.

2 VI pasar muy cerca.

brush-off ['brʌʃɒf] N: **to give sb the ~** mandar a uno a paseo*.

brush-stroke ['brʌʃstrəʊk] N pincelada f.

brush-up ['brʌʃʌp] N: **to have a ~** lavarse y peinarse, arreglarse.

brushwood ['brʌʃwʊd] N maleza f, monte m bajo; (*faggots*) broza f, leña f menuda.

brushwork ['brʌʃwɜːk] N pincelada f, técnica f del pincel; **Turner's ~** la pincelada de Turner, la técnica del pincel de Turner.

brusque [bruːsk] ADJ *comment, manner etc* brusco, abrupto, áspero; *person* malhumorado; **he was very ~ with me** me trató con poca cortesía.

brusquely ['bruːsklɪ] ADV bruscamente, abruptamente, ásperamente.

brusqueness ['bruːsknɪs] N brusquedad f, aspereza f; mal humor m; falta f de cortesía.

Brussels ['brʌslz] N Bruselas f; **~ sprouts** coles fpl de Bruselas.

brutal ['bruːtl] ADJ brutal.

brutality [bruːˈtælɪtɪ] N brutalidad f.

brutalize ['bruːtəlaɪz] VT brutalizar.

brutally ['bruːtəlɪ] ADV de manera brutal.

brute [bruːt] **1** ADJ brutal; (*unthinking*) bruto; **by ~ force** a fuerza bruta.

2 N bruto m; (*person*) bestia f, hombre m bestial; **you ~!** ¡bestia!; **it's a ~ of a problem** es un problema de los más feos.

brutish ['bruːtɪʃ] ADJ bruto.

Brutus ['bruːtəs] NM Bruto.

Brylcreem ['brɪlkriːm] ® **1** N gomina f, fijador m (*de pelo*).

2 VT engominar, echarse gomina en.

BS N **(a)** (*Brit*) ABBR *of* **British Standard(s)**. **(b)** (*US*) ABBR *of* **Bachelor of Science**; *ver también* [DEGREE].

bs (a) (*Comm*) ABBR *of* **bill of sale**. **(b)** (*Comm, Fin*) ABBR *of* **balance sheet**.

BSA N (*US*) ABBR *of* **Boy Scouts of America**.

BSB N ABBR *of* **British Sky Broadcasting**.

BSC N ABBR *of* **Broadcasting Standards Council**.

BSc N ABBR *of* **Bachelor of Science**; *ver también* [DEGREE].

BSE N ABBR *of* **bovine spongiform encephalopathy** encefalopatía f espongiforme bovina.

BSI N (*Brit*) ABBR *of* **British Standards Institution**.

BST N (*Brit*) ABBR *of* **British Summer Time**.

Bt ABBR *of* **Baronet** baronet m.

BTA N ABBR *of* **British Tourist Authority**.

bt fwd ABBR *of* **brought forward** suma f del anterior.

BTU N ABBR *of* **British Thermal Unit** Unidad f térmica británica.

bubble ['bʌbl] **1** N burbuja f, ampolla f; (*under paint etc*) ampolla f; (*in cartoon*) bocadillo m, globo m; **to blow ~s** hacer pompas; **the ~ burst** se deshizo la burbuja.

2 VI burbujear, borbotar.

◆**bubble over** VI desbordarse; **to ~ over with** rebosar de.

◆**bubble up** VI (*liquid*) burbujear, borbotear; (*excitement etc*) rebosar.

bubble and squeak [ˌbʌbləndˈskwiːk] N (*Brit*) *carne picada frita con patatas y col*.

bubble-bath ['bʌblˌbɑːθ] N, PL **bubble-baths** ['bʌblˌbɑːðz] baño m de espuma, baño m de burbujas.

bubble-car ['bʌblkɑːʳ] N coche-cabina m, huevo m.

bubble-gum ['bʌblgʌm] N chicle m de globo, chicle m de burbuja.

bubblejet printer ['bʌbldʒetˈprɪntəʳ] N impresora f de inyección de burbujas.

bubble-memory ['bʌblˌmeməɪ] N memoria f de burbuja.

bubble-pack ['bʌblˌpæk] N, **bubble-package** ['bʌblˌpækɪdʒ] N envasado m en lámina.

bubble-store ['bʌblˌstɔːʳ] N memoria f de burbuja.

bubbly ['bʌblɪ] **1** ADJ burbujeante, gaseoso.

2 N (*) champaña m.

bubonic [bjuːˈbɒnɪk] ADJ: **~ plague** N peste f bubónica.

buccaneer [ˌbʌkə'nɪər] 1 N bucanero m.
2 VI piratear.
buccaneering [ˌbʌkə'nɪərɪŋ] ADJ (fig) aventurero.
Bucharest [ˌbuːkə'rest] N Bucarest m.
buck [bʌk] 1 ADJ (male) macho; ~ **nigger** (Hist) negrazo m; ~ **private** (US) soldado m raso; ~ **rabbit** conejo m (macho); ~ **sergeant** (US) sargento m chusquero.
2 N (a) (male) macho m; (deer) gamo m; (goat) macho m cabrío; (rabbit) conejo m macho.
(b) (††) galán m, dandy m.
(c) (US*) dólar m; **to make a fast** (or **quick**) ~ hacer pasta rápidamente*.
(d) (*) **to pass the** ~ echar a uno el muerto, escurrir el bulto; **the** ~ **stops here** yo soy el responsable.
3 VT (esp US) rider desarzonar; system vencer, desbaratar; **to** ~ **the market** (Fin) ir en contra del mercado; **to** ~ **the system** (US) oponerse al sistema; **to** ~ **the trend** ir en contra de la tendencia.
4 VI (a) (horse) corcovear, ponerse de manos.
(b) **to** ~ **for sth** (US*) buscar algo.
◆ **buck up*** 1 VT (a) (hurry) dar prisa a. (b) (cheer) animar, dar ánimos a; V idea.
2 VI (a) (hurry) darse prisa; ~ **up!** ¡date prisa!; ¡espabílate!
(b) (cheer up) animarse, cobrar ánimos; ~ **up!** ¡ánimo!; **we were very ~ed up** nos alegramos mucho.
bucket ['bʌkɪt] 1 N cubo m, balde m; (child's) cubito m; (of waterwheel etc) cangilón m; **to kick the ~:** estirar la pata; **to rain ~s*** llover a cántaros; **to weep ~s*** llorar a mares.
2 VI: **it was ~ing down** llovía a cántaros.
bucketful ['bʌkɪtfʊl] N cubo m (lleno), balde m (lleno); **by the** ~ a cubos, (fig) a montones, en grandes cantidades.
bucket-shop ['bʌkɪtʃɒp] N agencia f de viajes que vende barato.

buckle ['bʌkl] 1 N hebilla f.
2 VT (a) abrochar con hebilla.
(b) (deform) torcer, combar, encorvar.
3 VI torcerse, combarse, doblarse.
◆ **buckle down to** VT dedicarse con empeño a, emprender en serio.
◆ **buckle in** VT: **to** ~ **a baby** abrochar el cinturón de un niño; **I was ~d in my seat** estaba en mi asiento con el cinturón abrochado.
◆ **buckle on** VT armour, sword ceñirse.
◆ **buckle to*** VI empezar a trabajar.
◆ **buckle up** VI (US) ponerse el cinturón de seguridad.
buckra ['bʌkrə] N (US pej) blanco m.
buckram ['bʌkrəm] N bucarán m.
Bucks [bʌks] N ABBR of **Buckinghamshire**.
bucksaw ['bʌksɔː] N sierra f de arco.
buckshee [bʌk'ʃiː] (Brit‡) 1 ADJ gratuito.
2 ADV gratis.
buckshot ['bʌkʃɒt] N perdigón m zorrero, posta f.
buckskin ['bʌkskɪn] N cuero m de ante.
buckthorn ['bʌkθɔːn] N espino m cerval.
buck-tooth ['bʌk'tuːθ] N diente m saliente.
buck-toothed ['bʌk'tuːθt] ADJ de dientes salientes, dentón, dentudo.
buckwheat ['bʌkwiːt] N alforfón m, trigo m sarraceno.
bucolic [bjuː'kɒlɪk] 1 ADJ bucólico.
2 N: **the B~s** las Bucólicas.
bud¹ [bʌd] 1 N brote m, yema f, (containing flower) capullo m; **in** ~ en brote; **to nip in the** ~ cortar de raíz, salir al paso a.
2 VT injertar de escudete.
3 VI brotar, echar brotes.
bud² [bʌd] N (US*) = **buddy**.
Budapest [ˌbjuːdə'pest] N Budapest m.
Buddha ['bʊdə] NM Buda.
Buddhism ['bʊdɪzəm] N budismo m.
Buddhist ['bʊdɪst] 1 ADJ budista.
2 N budista mf.
budding ['bʌdɪŋ] ADJ (fig) en ciernes, en embrión.
buddleia ['bʌdlɪə] N budleia f.
buddy ['bʌdɪ] N (esp US) compañero m, amigote m, compadre m (esp LAm), compinche m; (in direct address) chico, hijo; **they use the** ~ **system*** emplean el amiguismo, se ayudan mutuamente.
budge [bʌdʒ] 1 VT mover, hacer que se mueva; **I couldn't** ~ **him an inch** no pude hacerle cambiar de opinión en lo más mínimo.
2 VI moverse; bullir; menearse; **he didn't dare to** ~ no osaba bullir; **he won't** ~ **an inch** no nos ofrece la más pequeña concesión.

◆ **budge up** VI moverse un poco (para dejar espacio), correrse un poco a un lado (etc).
budgerigar ['bʌdʒərɪgɑːr] N periquito m (australiano).
budget ['bʌdʒɪt] 1 N presupuesto m; **the B~** los Presupuestos Generales del Estado; ver también TREASURY .
2 ATTR presupuestario; ~ **account** cuenta f presupuestaria; ~ **day** día m de la presentación de los Presupuestos Generales del Estado; ~ **plan** plan m presupuestario; ~ **speech** discurso m en el que se presentan los Presupuestos Generales del Estado.
◆ **budget for** VT presupuestar; (fig) tener en cuenta, contar con.

-budget ['bʌdʒɪt] ADJ ending in compounds: **low~** de bajo presupuesto; **big~** de alto presupuesto.
budgetary ['bʌdʒɪtrɪ] ADJ presupuestario; ~ **control** control m presupuestario; ~ **deficit** déficit m presupuestario; ~ **policy** política f presupuestaria; ~ **year** año m presupuestario.
budgeted ['bʌdʒɪtɪd] ADJ: ~ **costs** costos mpl presupuestados.
budgeting ['bʌdʒɪtɪŋ] N elaboración f de un presupuesto, presupuesto m; **with careful** ~ con buena administración.
budgie* ['bʌdʒɪ] N = **budgerigar**.
Buenos Aires [ˌbwenəs'aɪərɪz] N Buenos Aires m sing.
buff¹ [bʌf] 1 ADJ color de ante.
2 N piel f de ante; **in the ~*** en cueros.
3 VT pulir, pulimentar.
buff²* [bʌf] N aficionado m, -a f; entusiasta mf; **film** ~ cinéfilo m, -a f.
buffalo ['bʌfələʊ] N, PL **buffaloes** búfalo m; (esp US) bisonte m.
buffer¹ ['bʌfər] N amortiguador m (de choques); (Rail: on carriage) tope m, (fixed) parachoques m; (US Aut) parachoques m; (Comput) memoria f intermedia, buffer m; ~ **state** estado m tapón; ~ **zone** espacio m amortiguador; **the plan suddenly hit the ~s** de pronto el plan chocó con los topes.
buffer² ['bʌfər] N: **old** ~ (Brit) mastuerzo m, carca* m.
buffering ['bʌfərɪŋ] N (Comput) almacenamiento m en memoria intermedia.
buffet¹ ['bʌfɪt] 1 N bofetada f; (of sea, wind etc) golpe m.
2 VT abofetear; (of sea, wind etc) golpear, llevar de aquí para allá, combatir.
buffet² ['bʊfeɪ] N aparador m; (Rail) cantina f, cafetería f; ~ **lunch** buffet m libre, bufé m libre; ~ **meal** comida f buffet, comida f fría; ~ **supper** cena f fría.
buffet-car ['bʊfeɪkɑːr] N (Brit) coche-comedor m.
buffeting ['bʌfɪtɪŋ] N (of sea etc) el golpear; **to get a** ~ **from** sufrir los golpes de.
buffoon [bə'fuːn] N bufón m, chocarrero m, payaso m.
buffoonery [bə'fuːnərɪ] N bufonadas fpl.
bug [bʌg] 1 N (a) (Ent) chinche f (also m); (any insect) bicho m, sabandija f; **big ~*** señorón* m, pez m gordo.
(b) (Med*) microbio m, bacilo m; **flu** ~ virus m de la gripe; **to get the travel** ~ entusiasmarse por los viajes, coger la manía de viajar; **he's got the painting** ~ le ha dado por la pintura.
(c) (*: defect, snag: esp US) estorbo m, traba f, pega f; problema m; (Comput) duende m*, fallo m, error m.
(d) (*: Telec) micrófono m oculto, aparato m auditivo escondido; (Tech) indicador m de posición.
2 VT (a) (*: annoy: esp US) molestar, fastidiar*; **what's ~ging you?** ¿qué mosca te ha picado?
(b) (*: Telec) phone intervenir, pinchar*; room poner un micrófono oculto en; person escuchar clandestinamente a, pinchar el teléfono de*; **this phone is ~ged** este teléfono está pinchado*; **do you think this room is ~ged?** ¿crees que en esta habitación hay un micro oculto?*
◆ **bug out‡** VI (US) largarse.
bugaboo ['bʌgəbuː] N (US) espantajo m, coco m.
bugbear ['bʌgbeər] N pesadilla f, obsesión f.
bug-eyed* [ˌbʌg'aɪd] ADJ: **to be** ~ mirar con los ojos saltones.
bug-free* ['bʌg'friː] ADJ (Comput) sin errores, libre de duendes*.
bugger ['bʌgər] 1 N (a) (Jur) sodomita m.
(b) (‡‡) mierda m‡‡, coño‡‡ m; **that silly** ~ ese mierda‡‡; **some poor** ~ algún pobre hombre; **I don't give a** ~! ¡me importa un rábano!
2 EXCL ~ **it!‡‡** ¡mierda!‡‡
3 VT (a) (Jur) cometer sodomía con. (b) (well) **I'll be ~ed!** ¡coño!‡‡; **lawyers be ~ed!** ¡que se jodan los abogados!‡‡; **I'll be ~ed if I will**

que me cuelguen si lo hago.

◆**bugger about, bugger around** (*Brit*) 1 VT: **to ~ sb about** fastidiar a uno.

2 VI perder el tiempo, no hacer nada; ocuparse en tonterías.

◆**bugger off** VI (*Brit*) largarse*; **~ off!** ¡vete a hacer puñetas!*

◆**bugger up*** VT: **to ~ sth up** joder algo*.

bugger-all* ['bʌgə,ɔːl] = **damn-all**.

buggery ['bʌgərɪ] N sodomía *f*.

bugging* ['bʌgɪŋ] N (*Telec*) intervención *f*; **~ device** micrófono *m* oculto.

buggy ['bʌgɪ] N calesa *f*; (*US*) cochecito *m* (de niño); (**baby**) **~** (*Brit*) cochecito *m* de niño; (*Golf*) cochecito *m*.

bughouse* ['bʌghaʊs] N, PL **bughouses** ['bʌg,haʊzɪz] (*US*) casa *f* de locos, manicomio *m*.

bug-hunter* ['bʌghʌntəʳ] N entomólogo *m*, -a *f*.

bugle ['bjuːgl] N corneta *f*, clarín *m*.

bugler ['bjuːgləʳ] N corneta *m*.

bug-ridden ['bʌg,rɪdn] ADJ: **this house is ~** esta casa está llena de bichos; **this program is ~** este programa está lleno de errores.

build [bɪld] 1 N talle *m*, tipo *m*; **of powerful ~** fornido.

2 (*irr*: PRET AND PTP **built**) VT construir, edificar, hacer (*in, of* de); *ship* construir; *fire* preparar; *nest* hacer.

◆**build in** VT *cupboard etc* empotrar; (*Mech*) incorporar.

◆**build on** 1 VT (*add*) añadir; **to ~ a garage on to a house** añadir un garaje a una casa; **the garage is built on to the house** la casa tiene un garaje anexo.

2 VI (*construct*) edificar sobre; **to ~ on a site** construir casas (*etc*) en un solar; **now we have a base to ~ on** ahora tenemos base en la que podemos construir.

◆**build up** 1 VT (*Mech etc*) montar, armar; (*Med*) fortalecer; *company* fomentar, desarrollar; *sales, numbers* acrecentar; *reputation* crear para sí; *impression* crear; *stocks* acumular, formar; **the area was built up years ago** la zona fue urbanizada hace años.

2 VI desarrollarse; (*pressure*) aumentar; (*excitement*) crecer; (*picture*) perfilarse, formarse.

builder ['bɪldəʳ] N constructor *m* (*also fig*); (*contracting firm*) contratista *m*; aparejador *m*.

building ['bɪldɪŋ] N (a) edificio *m*; (*at exhibition*) pabellón *m*; **the Ruritanian B~** el pabellón de Ruritania.

(b) (*act*) construcción *f*; **~ block** (*toy*) bloque *m* de construcción; (*fig*) elemento *m* esencial, componente *m* básico; **~ contractor** contratista *m*; **~ industry** industria *f* de la construcción; **~ land** tierra *f* para construcción, terrenos *mpl* edificables; **~ lot**, **~ plot** solar *m* (para construcción); **~ materials** material *m* de construcción; **~ permit** permiso *m* de obras; **~ site** solar *m* (para construcción), obra *f* (*LAm*); **~ society** (*Brit*) sociedad *f* de crédito hipotecario; **the ~ trade** (la industria de) la construcción; **~ worker** obrero *m* (*or* trabajador *m*) de la construcción; **~ works** obras *fpl* de construcción.

┌─── **BUILDING SOCIETY** ───┐

ⓘ *Las* **Building societies** *(sociedades de crédito hipotecario) se fundaron en el Reino Unido con el objeto de atraer inversiones, normalmente mediante préstamos hipotecarios para adquirir una vivienda. Aunque éste sigue siendo su papel principal, desde 1986 se les ha permitido extender sus servicios financieros, compitiendo así con las entidades bancarias. En contrapartida, estas sociedades ya no tienen el monopolio de las cuentas de ahorros e hipotecas y los bancos acaparan buena parte de este sector. Algunas de las sociedades mayores han optado por convertirse en bancos debido a los cambios en la normativa.*

build-up ['bɪldʌp] N (a) (*of pressure*) aumento *m*; (*of gas*) acumulación *f*, concentración *f*; (*of forces*) concentración *f*. (b) (*fig*) propaganda *f* previa; bombo *m*.

built [bɪlt] PRET AND PTP of **build**.

-built ADJ *ending in compounds*: **American~** de construcción americana; **brick~** construido de ladrillos.

built-in ['bɪlt'ɪn] ADJ (*Archit*) empotrado; (*Mech, Rad etc*) interior, incorporado; **~ obsolescence** caducidad *f* programada, caducidad *f* calculada.

built-up ['bɪlt'ʌp] ADJ: **~ area** zona *f* edificada.

bulb [bʌlb] N (*Bot*) bulbo *m*, camote *m* (*Mex*); (*Elec*) bombilla *f*, foco *m* (*LAm*), bombillo *m* (*And*), bujía *f* (*CAm*); (*of thermometer*) ampolleta *f*.

bulbous ['bʌlbəs] ADJ bulboso.

Bulgaria [bʌl'gɛərɪə] N Bulgaria *f*.

Bulgarian [bʌl'gɛərɪən] 1 ADJ búlgaro.

2 N (a) búlgaro *m*, -a *f*. (b) (*Ling*) búlgaro *m*.

bulge [bʌldʒ] 1 N bombeo *m*, pandeo *m*; protuberancia *f*; (*in statistics*) protuberancia *f*; **the ~ in the birth rate** el aumento (súbito y transitorio) de la natalidad.

2 VI bombearse, pandearse; sobresalir; (*pocket etc*) hacer bulto; **his pockets ~d with apples** sus bolsillos estaban atestados de manzanas; **their eyes ~d at the sight** se les saltaron los ojos al

verlo.

bulging ['bʌldʒɪŋ] ADJ: **~ eyes** ojos *mpl* saltones; **~ pocket** bolsillo *m* muy lleno; **~ suitcase** maleta *f* que está para reventar.

bulimia [bjuːˈlɪmɪə] N bulimia *f*.

bulimic [bjuːˈlɪmɪk] 1 ADJ bulímico.

2 N bulímico *m*, -a *f*.

bulk [bʌlk] 1 N (a) bulto *m*, volumen *m*; masa *f*, mole *f*; **the enormous ~ of the ship** la enorme mole del buque; **he set his full ~ down in a chair** dejó caer todo el peso de su cuerpo en un sillón.

(b) (*Comm*) **in ~** a granel; (*unpackaged*) suelto; **to buy in ~** comprar en grandes cantidades.

(c) (*main part*) **the ~ of** la mayor parte de; **the ~ of those present** la mayor parte de los presentes; **the ~ of the army** el grueso del ejército.

2 ADJ: **~ goods** mercancías *fpl* a granel; **~ purchase** compra *f* de cantidad grande.

3 VI: **to ~ large** tener un puesto importante, ocupar un lugar importante.

bulk-buying ['bʌlk'baɪɪŋ] N compra *f* en grandes cantidades.

bulk carrier ['bʌlk,kærɪəʳ] N (buque *m*) granelero *m*.

bulkhead ['bʌlkhed] N (*Brit*) mamparo *m*.

bulkiness ['bʌlkɪnɪs] N volumen *m*, lo abultado.

bulky ['bʌlkɪ] ADJ voluminoso, abultado, grueso; *goods* de gran bulto.

bull[1] [bʊl] 1 N (a) (*Zool*) toro *m*; (*of elephant, whale*) macho *m*; **to be like a ~ in a china shop** comportarse como un elefante en una tienda de porcelana; **to take the ~ by the horns** coger (*LAm*: agarrar) el toro por los cuernos.

(b) (*Fin*) alcista *m*.

(c) (*Mil*) trabajos *mpl* rutinarios.

(d) (*: nonsense*) tonterías *fpl*; **to shoot the ~** decir chorradas*.

2 ADJ (a) (*Zool*) macho.

(b) (*Fin*) *market* alcista.

3 VT (*Fin*): **to ~ the market** hacer subir el mercado comprando acciones especulativamente.

bull[2] [bʊl] N (*Eccl*) bula *f*.

bull-calf ['bʊl,kaːf] N, PL **bull-calves** ['bʊl,kaːvz] becerro *m*.

bulldog ['bʊldɒg] N bul(l)dog *m*, (perro *m*) dogo *m*; **the ~ breed** los ingleses (*bajo su aspecto heroico y porfiado*); **~ clip** (*Brit*) pinza *f*.

bulldoze ['bʊldəʊz] VT *site* nivelar (con motoniveladora); *building* arrasar (con motoniveladora); *opposition* arrollar.

bulldozer ['bʊldəʊzəʳ] N motoniveladora *f*, aplanadora *f*, bulldozer *m*.

bull-dyke* ['bʊldaɪk] N (*pej*) camionera* *f*.

bullet ['bʊlɪt] N bala *f*; **to bite (on) the ~** resolverse, tomar una decisión heroica; **to go by like a ~** pasar como un rayo.

bullet-hole ['bʊlɪt,həʊl] N agujero *m* de bala.

bulletin ['bʊlɪtɪn] N anuncio *m*, parte *m*; (*journal*) boletín *m*.

bulletin board ['bʊlɪtɪnbɔːd] N (*US*) tablón *m* de anuncios; (*Comput*) tablero *m* de noticias.

bulletproof ['bʊlɪtpruːf] ADJ a prueba de balas; **~ glass** vidrio *m* antibalas.

bullet train ['bʊlɪt,treɪn] N tren *m* de gran velocidad (*japonés*).

bullet-wound ['bʊlɪtwuːnd] N balazo *m*.

bullfight ['bʊlfaɪt] N corrida *f* (de toros).

bullfighter ['bʊlfaɪtəʳ] N torero *m*, matador *m* de toros.

bullfighting ['bʊlfaɪtɪŋ] N toreo *m*; arte *m* de torear, tauromaquia *f*; **do you like ~?** ¿le gustan los toros?

bullfinch ['bʊlfɪntʃ] N camachuelo *m*.

bullfrog ['bʊlfrɒg] N rana *f* toro.

bullhorn ['bʊlhɔːn] N (*US*) megáfono *m*.

bullion ['bʊljən] N oro *m* en barras, plata *f* en barras.

bullish ['bʊlɪʃ] ADJ optimista; (*Fin*) (de tendencia) alcista.

bull-neck [,bʊl'nek] N cuello *m* de toro.

bull-necked [,bʊl'nekt] ADJ de cuello de toro.

bullock ['bʊlək] N toro *m* castrado, novillo *m* castrado.

bullring ['bʊlrɪŋ] N plaza *f* de toros.

bull's-eye ['bʊlzaɪ] N (*of target*) centro *m* del blanco, diana *f*; (*lantern*) linterna *f* sorda; (*Naut*) ojo *m* de buey; (*sweet*) tipo de dulce; **to score a ~** dar en el blanco, (*fig*) acertar.

bullshit* ['bʊlʃɪt] N = **bull 1 (c), (d)**.

bullshitter * ['bʊlʃɪtəʳ] N fanfarrón *m*, -ona *f*.

bull terrier [,bʊl'terɪəʳ] N bulterrier *m*.

bully[1] ['bʊlɪ] 1 N (a) matón *m*, valentón *m*. (b) (*Brit Hockey: also* **~-off**) saque *m*.

2 VT intimidar, tiranizar; **to ~ sb into** + *ger* forzar a uno con amenazas a + *infin*.

◆**bully off** VI (*Brit Hockey*) sacar.

bully[2] ['bʊlɪ] 1 ADJ de primera.

2 INTERJ: **~ for you!** ¡bravo!

bully-beef ['bʊlɪ'biːf] N carne *f* de vaca conservada en lata.

bully-boy ['bʊlɪ,bɔɪ] N matón *m*, esbirro *m*; **~ tactics** táctica *f* de matón.

bullying ['bʊlɪɪŋ] 1 ADJ *person* abusón, matón, valentón; *attitude* amenazador; tiránico; propio de matón.

  2 N intimidación f, abuso m.

bulrush ['bʊlrʌʃ] N (rush) junco m; (reedmace) anea f, espadaña f.

bulwark ['bʊlwək] N (Mil and fig) baluarte m; (Naut) macarrón m.

bum¹ [bʌm] N (Brit Anat) culo m.

bum² [bʌm] (US) 1 N (idler) holgazán m; (tramp) vagabundo m; (scrounger) gorrón m; (as term of general disapproval) vago m; **you poor ~!** ¡tío tonto!; **to give sb the ~'s rush** expulsar violentamente a uno; **to go** (or **live**) **on the ~** vivir de gorra, vagabundear.

  2 ADJ (US) falso; **~ deal** negocio m turbio; **~ rap** acusación f falsa; **~ steer** bulo m, noticia f falsa.

  3 VT (:) mendigar, gorronear; **he ~med a cigarette off me** me gorroneó un pitillo.

  4 VI (also **to ~ around**) holgazanear, vagabundear.

bumbag ['bʌmbæg] N (Ski) riñonera f.

bumble ['bʌmbl] VI (walk unsteadily) andar de forma vacilante, andar a tropezones; (fig) trastabillar.

bumblebee ['bʌmblbiː] N abejorro m.

bumbling ['bʌmblɪŋ] 1 ADJ (inept) inepto, inútil; (muttering) que habla a tropezones, que se atropella al hablar.

  2 N divagación f.

bumf [bʌmf] N (Brit) (a) papel m higiénico. (b) (fig) papeles mpl, papeleo m.

bummer ['bʌmər] N (esp US) (nuisance) lata* f; (bore) rollo* m; (disaster) desastre m; **what a ~!** ¡qué desastre!, ¡qué horror!

bump [bʌmp] 1 N (a) (blow) golpe m, topetazo m; choque m; (jolt of vehicle) sacudida f; (Aer) rebote m; (in falling) batacazo m; **things that go ~ in the night** cosas que hacen ruidos misteriosos en la noche. (b) (swelling) bollo m, abolladura f, protuberancia f; (on skin) chichón m, hinchazón f; (on road) bache m; **to have a ~ for** tener el don de, tener un sentido especial de.

  2 VT chocar contra, topetar; **to ~ one's head** darse un golpe en la cabeza; **to ~ one's head on a door** dar con su cabeza contra una puerta.

  3 VI (vehicle) dar sacudidas.

♦**bump against** VT chocar contra, topetar, dar contra.

♦**bump along** VI avanzar dando sacudidas.

♦**bump into** VT chocar contra, tropezar con; person topar; **fancy ~ing into you!** ¡qué casualidad encontrarle a Vd!

♦**bump off** VT cargarse a*.

♦**bump up** VT price subir, aumentar.

♦**bump up against** VT tropezar con.

bumper ['bʌmpər] 1 N (a) (Aut) parachoques m; **~ car** auto m de choque; **~ sticker** pegatina f de parachoques; **traffic is ~ to ~ as far as the airport** hay una caravana hasta el aeropuerto. (b) (glass) copa f llena.

  2 ADJ: **~ crop** cosecha f abundante, cosechón m.

bumph [bʌmf] N = bumf.

bumpkin ['bʌmpkɪn] N (gen **country ~**) patán m.

bump-start ['bʌmpstaːt] 1 N: **to give a car a ~** empujar un coche para que arranque.

  2 VT V 1.

bumptious ['bʌmpʃəs] ADJ engreído, presuntuoso.

bumpy ['bʌmpɪ] ADJ surface desigual; road accidentado, lleno de baches; air agitado; journey de muchas sacudidas.

bun [bʌn] N (a) (bread) bollo m; (Brit: cake) pastel m; **to have a ~ in the oven** estar en estado. (b) (hair) rodete m, moño m.

bunch [bʌntʃ] 1 N manojo m, puñado m; (of flowers) ramo m, ramillete m; (of grapes) racimo m, cacho m; (of bananas) racimo m, cacho m; (of keys) manojo m; (set of people) grupo m, (pej) pandilla f; **a ~ of times** (US) varias veces, muchas veces; **the best of a bad ~** el menos malo de una serie de malos; **they're an odd ~** son gente rara; **they're a ~ of traitors** son unos traidores; **to wear one's hair in ~es** (Brit) llevar coletas.

  2 VT agrupar, juntar; **to be ~ed together** estar muy juntos unos a otros.

♦**bunch up** 1 VT (a) dress, skirt arremangar. (b) **they sat ~ed up on the bench** se apretujaban en el banco.

  2 VI apretujarse; ponerse más cerca unos de otros.

bundle ['bʌndl] 1 N (a) (sticks) lío m, bulto m, fardo m; (of sticks) haz f; (of papers) legajo m; **he's a ~ of nerves** es un manojo de nervios, está hipertenso. (b) **to go a ~ on** entusiasmarse mucho por; **to make a ~** ganarse un pastón.

  2 VT: **~ it all into the case** póngalo todo en la maleta no importa cómo.

♦**bundle off** VT person despachar; **he was ~d off to Australia** le despacharon para Australia.

♦**bundle out** VT: **to ~ sb out** botar a uno; **they ~d him out into the street** le pusieron de patitas en la calle.

♦**bundle up** VT liar, atar, envolver.

bun-fight ['bʌn‚faɪt] N té m (servido para mucha gente); merienda f.

bung [bʌŋ] 1 N tapón m.

  2 VT (a) tapar con bitoque; (gen) cerrar, tapar; **to be ~ed up** estar obturado, estar obstruido; (eye) estar hinchado. (b) (Brit) (throw) tirar, lanzar; **~ it over** tíralo para acá. (c) (*: put) poner, meter.

♦**bung in** VT (include) añadir.

♦**bung out** VT tirar, botar.

bungalow ['bʌŋgələʊ] N casa f de un solo piso, chalet m, bungalow m.

bungee jumping, bungy jumping ['bʌndʒiː'dʒʌmpɪŋ] N bungee m; (from bridge) puenting m, puentismo m; **to go bungee** or **bungy jumping** hacer bungee or puenting or puentismo.

bunghole ['bʌŋhəʊl] N piquera f, boca f (de tonel).

bungle ['bʌŋgl] 1 N chapuza f.

  2 VT work chapucear, hacer con los pies; **to ~ it** hacerlo malísimamente; desperdiciar la ocasión.

bungled ['bʌŋgld] ADJ: **a ~ job** una chapuza; **a ~ operation** una operación mal ejecutada.

bungler ['bʌŋglər] N chapucero m.

bungling ['bʌŋglɪŋ] ADJ torpe, desmañado.

bunion ['bʌnjən] N juanete m.

bunk¹ [bʌŋk] N (Naut) litera f, camastro m; (Rail, child's) litera f; (*) cama f.

bunk² [bʌŋk] 1 N: **to do a ~** (Brit) = 2. 2 VI huir, poner pies en polvorosa.

bunk³ [bʌŋk] N tonterías fpl, música f celestial; **~!** ¡tonterías!; **history is ~** la historia es un absurdo.

bunk-bed ['bʌŋk'bed] N litera f.

bunker ['bʌŋkər] 1 N (a) (for coal) carbonera f; (Naut) pañol m del carbón. (b) (Mil) refugio m, búnker m. (c) (Golf) búnker m, arena f.

  2 VT (a) (Naut) proveer de carbón. (b) **to be ~ed** (fig) estar en un atolladero.

bunkhouse ['bʌŋk‚haʊs] N, PL **bunkhouses** ['bʌŋk‚haʊzɪz] (US) casa f de dormitorios (para trabajadores de hacienda).

bunkum ['bʌŋkəm] N = bunk³.

bunk-up [‚bʌŋk'ʌp] N: **to give sb a ~** ayudar a uno a subir.

bunny ['bʌnɪ] N (a) conejito m. (b) (girl) tía f buena; **~ girl** conejita f.

Bunsen ['bʌnsn] N: **~ burner** mechero m Bunsen.

bunting¹ ['bʌntɪŋ] N (Orn) escribano m.

bunting² ['bʌntɪŋ] N (decoration) banderas fpl, empavesado m; (cloth) lanilla f.

buoy [bɔɪ, US buːɪ] 1 N boya f.

  2 VT channel aboyar, señalar con boyas.

♦**buoy up** VT person mantener a flote; (fig) animar, alentar.

buoyancy ['bɔɪənsɪ] N lo boyante, capacidad f para flotar; (Aer) fuerza f ascensional; (fig) confianza f, optimismo m.

buoyant ['bɔɪənt] ADJ boyante, capaz de flotar; (fig) ilusionado, optimista; (Comm) con tendencia al alza.

buoyantly ['bɔɪəntlɪ] ADV de modo boyante; (fig) de modo ilusionado, con optimismo.

BUPA ['buːpə] N ABBR of **British United Provident Association** seguro médico privado.

buppie*, buppy* ['bʌpɪ] N ABBR of **black upwardly mobile professional** yuppie m negro, yuppie f negra.

bur(r) [bɜːʳ] N erizo m.

burble ['bɜːbl] VI (bubble) burbujear, hervir; (talk) parlotear.

burbot ['bɜːbət] N lota f.

burbs*, 'burbs* [bɜːbz] (US) = suburbs.

burden ['bɜːdn] 1 N (a) carga f; (weight) peso m. (b) (Naut) arqueo m. (c) (fig) carga f; fardo m; **~ of proof** peso m de la prueba; **to be a ~ to sb** ser una responsabilidad molesta para uno; **he carries a heavy ~** tiene que cargar con una gran responsabilidad; **to make sb's life a ~** amargar la vida a uno. (d) (of speech etc) tema m principal; (of song) estribillo m.

  2 VT cargar (with de); **to be ~ed with** tener que cargar con; **don't ~ me with your troubles** no me vengas a mí con tus problemas.

burdensome ['bɜːdnsəm] ADJ gravoso, oneroso.

burdock ['bɜːdɒk] N (Bot) bardana f.

bureau [bjʊə'rəʊ] N, PL **bureaux** [bjʊ'rəʊz] (a) (esp Brit: desk) escritorio m, buró m. (b) (US: chest of drawers) cómoda f. (c) (office) oficina f, agencia f, departamento m; (of congress) oficina f, mesa f; **~ de change** caja f de cambio; **B~ of Indian Affairs** (US) Departamento m de Asuntos Indios; **~ of standards** (US) oficina f de pesos y medidas. (d) **Federal B~** (US) Departamento m de Estado.

┌─ **BUREAU OF INDIAN AFFAIRS** ─┐

*La agencia del gobierno estadounidense denominada **Bureau of Indian Affairs** (Departamento de Asuntos Indios) se encarga de todos los asuntos relacionados con los indios nativos norteamericanos. Este organismo, fundado en 1824 como parte del Ministerio de Guerra, llevaba en un principio la gestión de las reservas indias. Hoy en día trabaja conjuntamente con los indios para tratar de mejorar su situación,* *elaborando programas de salud y bienestar social y dando facilidades para la educación y el empleo. Desde la década de los sesenta viene proporcionando también asistencia técnica y formación para que puedan gestionar sus tierras y recursos.*

bureaucracy [bjʊəˈrɒkrəsɪ] N burocracia *f*.
bureaucrat [ˈbjʊərəʊkræt] N burócrata *mf*.
bureaucratic [ˌbjʊərəʊˈkrætɪk] ADJ burocrático.
burg [bɜːɡ] N (*US, often hum*) burgo *m*.
burgeon [ˈbɜːdʒən] VI (*Bot*) retoñar; (*fig*) empezar a prosperar (rápidamente); (*trade etc*) florecer.
burgeoning [ˈbɜːdʒənɪŋ] ADJ que empieza a prosperar (*or* florecer), en vías de expansión.
burger [ˈbɜːɡəʳ] N (*US*) hamburguesa *f*.
burgess [ˈbɜːdʒɪs] N (*Brit*) ciudadano *m*, -a *f*; (*Parl* ††) diputado *m*, -a *f*.
burgh [ˈbʌrə] N (*Scot*) villa *f*.
burgher [ˈbɜːɡəʳ] N (*Hist*) burgués *m*, -esa *f*; ciudadano *m*, -a *f*.
burglar [ˈbɜːɡləʳ] N ladrón *m*, escalador *m*.
burglar-alarm [ˈbɜːɡlərə,lɑːm] N alarma *f* antirrobo.
burglarize [ˈbɜːɡləraɪz] VT (*US*) = **burgle**.
burglar-proof [ˈbɜːɡləpruːf] ADJ a prueba de ladrones.
burglary [ˈbɜːɡlərɪ] N robo *m* en una casa, robo *m* con escalamiento, (*Jur*) allanamiento *m* de morada.
burgle [ˈbɜːɡl] VT robar, escalar, allanar, desvalijar.
Burgundian [bɜːˈɡʌndɪən] ① ADJ borgoñón.
② N borgoñón *m*, -ona *f*.
Burgundy [ˈbɜːɡəndɪ] N Borgoña *f*; **b~** vino *m* de Borgoña.
burial [ˈberɪəl] N entierro *m*.
burial-ground [ˈberɪəlɡraʊnd] N cementerio *m*, camposanto *m*.
burial-mound [ˈberɪəl,maʊnd] N túmulo *m*.
burial-place [ˈberɪəl,pleɪs] N lugar *m* de sepultura.
burial service [ˈberɪəl,sɜːvɪs] N funerales *mpl*.
burial-vault [ˈberɪəl,vɔːlt] N panteón *m* familiar, cripta *f*.
Burkina Faso [bɜːˈkiːnəˈfæsəʊ] N Burkina Faso *f*.
burlap [ˈbɜːlæp] N arpillera *f*.
burlesque [bɜːˈlesk] ① ADJ burlesco, festivo, paródico; **~ show** (*US*) revista *f* de estriptise.
② N parodia *f*; (*US*) revista *f* de estriptise.
③ VT parodiar.
burly [ˈbɜːlɪ] ADJ fornido, membrudo, corpulento, anchote.
Burma [ˈbɜːmə] N Birmania *f*.
Burmese [bɜːˈmiːz] ① ADJ birmano.
② N birmano *m*, -a *f*.
burn¹ [bɜːn] ① N (a) quemadura *f*. (b) (‡) tabaco *m*, cigarrillos *mpl*.
② (*irr:* PRET AND PTP **burned** *or* **burnt**) VT quemar; *house etc* incendiar; *corpse* incinerar; *plants* (*by sun*) abrasar; *almonds etc* tostar; *fuel* funcionar con, utilizar como combustible; *mouth, tongue* quemar, escaldar; **to ~ one's hand** quemarse la mano; **to ~ a hole in sth** hacer un agujero en algo quemándolo; **to ~ sth to ashes** reducir algo a cenizas; **to ~ a house to the ground** incendiar y arrasar una casa; **to be ~ed alive** ser quemado vivo; **to be ~ed to death** morir abrasado; **with a face ~ed by the sun** con una cara tostada al sol; **it has a burnt taste** sabe a quemado.
③ VI (a) quemar(se), arder; (*catch fire*) incendiarse; (*light, gas*) estar encendido; (*smart*) escocer; **to ~ to death** morir abrasado.
(b) (*fig*) arder (*with* de, en); **to ~ to + infin** desear ardientemente + *infin*; **to ~ with desire for** desear ardientemente; **to ~ with impatience** consumirse de impaciencia.
◆**burn away** ① VT quemar, consumir.
② VI (a) (*be consumed*) consumirse. (b) (*go on burning*) seguir ardiendo, arder bien.
◆**burn down** ① VT incendiar; destruir por incendio, quemar totalmente.
② VI quedar destruido en un incendio, quemarse hasta los cimientos.
◆**burn off** VT *paint etc* quitar con la llama; *weeds* quemar.
◆**burn out** ① VT (a) (*criminally*) incendiar; *person* incendiar la casa de.
(b) (*destroy*) reducir a cenizas, destruir con fuego.
(c) (*Elec*) fundir, quemar.
② VI (a) (*go out*) consumirse, apagarse; (*Elec*) fundirse.
(b) (*fig*) apagarse.
③ VR: **to ~ o.s. out** quemarse.
◆**burn up** ① VT (a) quemar, consumir.
(b) *crop* abrasar.
(c) *person* indignar, sacar de quicio.
② VI (a) consumirse.
(b) (*burn brighter*) arder más.
③ VR: **to ~ o.s. up** (*fig*) quemarse.
burn² [bɜːn] N (*Scot*) arroyo *m*, riachuelo *m*.
burner [ˈbɜːnəʳ] N mechero *m*; (*on stove etc*) hornillo *m*, quemador *m*, fuego *m*.
burning [ˈbɜːnɪŋ] ① ADJ (a) ardiente (*also fig*); **it's ~ hot** está que

quema, hace un calor sofocante, el sol pica mucho. (b) *question* candente, palpitante.
② N el quemar; **the ~ of the embassy during the riots** el incendio de la embajada durante los disturbios; **a smell of ~** un olor a quemado.
burnish [ˈbɜːnɪʃ] VT bruñir.
burnoose, burnous(e) [bɜːˈnuːz] N albornoz *m*.

┌─── **BURNS' NIGHT** ───┐

ⓘ *En la noche del 25 de enero,* **Burns' Night,** *se celebra el aniversario del nacimiento del poeta escocés Robert Burns (1759-1796). Los escoceses de todo el mundo se reúnen para celebrar su vida y obra haciendo una cena en su honor (***Burns' Supper***), en la que, al son de la gaita, se sirve* **haggis** *(asaduras de cordero, avena y especias cocidas en las tripas del animal) con patatas y puré de nabos. Después de la cena se cantan canciones de Burns, se leen sus poemas y se hacen discursos de carácter festivo relacionados con ellos.*

burnt [bɜːnt] PRET AND PTP of **burn¹**; **~ almonds** almendras FPL dulces tostadas; **~ offering** holocausto *m*.
burnt-out [ˌbɜːntˈaʊt] ADJ *person* quemado.
burp* [bɜːp] ① N eructo *m*.
② VI eructar.
burr [bɜːʳ] N (*Bot*) erizo *m*.
burrow [ˈbʌrəʊ] ① N madriguera *f*; (*rabbit's*) conejera *f*.
② VT hacer madrigueras en; (*and undermine*) socavar, minar; **to ~ one's way into** abrirse camino cavando en, (*fig*) insinuarse en.
③ VI amadrigarse, hacer una madriguera; **to ~ into** hacer madrigueras en, horadar; (*fig*) investigar minuciosamente.
bursar [ˈbɜːsəʳ] N (*Univ etc*) tesorero *m*; (*of school*) administrador *m*, -ora *f*.
bursary [ˈbɜːsərɪ] N (*Univ*) beca *f*.
burst [bɜːst] ① N (*explosion*) estallido *m*, explosión *f*; (*of shots*) serie *f* de tiros, ráfaga *f* de tiros; **a ~ of applause** una salva de aplausos; **a ~ of speed** una arrancada; **a ~ of activity** un frenesí repentino de actividad; **in a ~ of anger** en un arranque de cólera.
② (*irr:* PRET AND PTP **burst**) VT *balloon etc* reventar; *bubble* deshacer; *tyre* pinchar; *banks, dam, pipe* romper; **to ~ open a door** abrir de golpe una puerta.
③ VI (*balloon, boil, boiler*) reventar(se); (*bubble*) deshacerse; (*tyre*) pincharse; (*dam, pipe*) romperse; (*bomb etc*) estallar; (*heart*) partirse; (*storm*) desencadenarse; **he was ~ing to tell me** reventaba por decírmelo; **he was ~ing with impatience** reventaba de impaciencia; **I'm ~ing for the loo*** necesito urgentemente ir al wáter; **to ~ with laughter** reventar de risa; **London is ~ing with young people** Londres está que bulle de juventud; **to be full to ~ing** estar lleno a reventar; estar apretado a presión.
◆**burst forth** VI brotar, salir a chorro.
◆**burst in** VI entrar violentamente; **he ~ in on the meeting** irrumpió en la reunión.
◆**burst into** VT (a) **to ~ into a room** irrumpir en un cuarto.
(b) **to ~ into flames** estallar en llamas; **to ~ into song** romper a cantar; **to ~ into tears** deshacerse en lágrimas.
◆**burst out** VI (a) **to ~ out of a room** salir repentinamente de un cuarto; **to be ~ing out of a dress** no caber en un vestido.
(b) **to ~ out laughing** soltar la carcajada; **'No!', he ~ out** '¡No!', gritó con pasión.
◆**burst through** VT *barrier* romper (violentamente); **the sun ~ through the clouds** el sol brilló repentinamente por entre las nubes.
bursting [ˈbɜːstɪŋ] N (*Comput*) separación *f* de hojas.
burton [ˈbɜːtn] N: **it's gone for a ~*** (*broken etc*) se ha fastidiado*; (*lost*) se ha perdido; **he's gone for a ~** (*Brit Aer‡*) la palmó*.
Burundi [bəˈrʊndɪ] N Burundi *m*.
bury [ˈberɪ] ① VT enterrar (*also fig*); *body* enterrar, sepultar; *memory, matter* echar tierra sobre; (*Sport**) *opponents* cascar*; **to ~ a dagger in sb's heart** clavar un puñal en el corazón de uno; **to ~ one's face in one's hands** ocultar el rostro en las manos; **it's buried away in the library** está no sabemos dónde en la biblioteca, está en algún rincón de la biblioteca; **to be buried in thought** estar absorto en la meditación.
② VR: **to ~ o.s. in the country** enterrarse en el campo; **the bullet buried itself in a tree** la bala se empotró en un árbol; **she buried herself in her book** se ensimismó con su lectura, se enfrascó en su libro.
bus [bʌs] ① N (a) autobús *m*, colectivo *m* (*SC*), camión *m* (*Mex*); (*coach*) autocar *m*; **to go by ~** ir en autobús; **to miss the ~** perder el tren; **the house is (not) on a ~ route** la casa (no) se halla en el recorrido de un autobús. (b) (*) (*car*) cacharro* *m*; (*plane*) avión *m* viejo. (c) (*Comput*) bus *m*.
② VT llevar en autobús.
③ VI (a) ir en autobús. (b) (*US:* clear away dishes) quitar los platos de

la mesa.

busbar [ˈbʌzbɑːʳ] N **(a)** (*Comput*) bus *m*. **(b)** (*Tech*) barra *f* ómnibus.

busboy [ˈbʌsbɔɪ] N (*US*) ayudante *m* de camarero.

busby [ˈbʌzbɪ] N (*Brit*) gorro *m* alto de piel negra.

bus-conductor [ˈbʌskənˌdʌktəʳ] N cobrador *m*.

bus-conductress [ˈbʌskənˌdʌktrɪs] N cobradora *f*.

bus-depot [ˈbʌsˌdepəʊ] N cochera *f* de autobuses.

bus-driver [ˈbʌsˌdraɪvəʳ] N chófer *m*.

bush¹ [bʊʃ] N (*Bot*) arbusto *m*; **the ~** (*Australia*) el monte, el despoblado; **to beat about the ~** andarse por las ramas, ir con rodeos.

bush² [bʊʃ] N (*Tech*) cojinete *m*.

bush-baby [ˈbʊʃˌbeɪbɪ] N (*Zool*) lemúrido *m*.

bushed [bʊʃt] ADJ **(a)** (‡) (*puzzled*) perplejo, pasmado; (*exhausted*) agotado, hecho polvo*. **(b)** (*Australia*) perdido en la maleza.

bushel [ˈbʊʃl] N *medida de áridos: British = 36,36 litros, US = 35,24 litros*.

bush-fire [ˈbʊʃfaɪəʳ] N incendio *m* de monte.

bush-league [ˈbʊʃˌliːg] ADJ de calidad mediocre.

bushman [ˈbʊʃmən] N, PL **bushmen** [ˈbʊʃmen] bosquimano *m*, bosquimán *m*.

bushranger [ˈbʊʃˌreɪndʒəʳ] N (*Australia*) bandido *m*.

bush telegraph* [ˈbʊʃˈtelɪgrɑːf] N teléfono *m* árabe*.

bushwhack [ˈbʊʃˌwæk] VI (*US*) abrirse camino por el bosque.

bushwhacker [ˈbʊʃˌwækəʳ] N (*US*) pionero *m*, -a *f*, explorador *m*, -ora *f*.

bushy [ˈbʊʃɪ] ADJ *plant* arbustivo; parecido a un arbusto; *ground* lleno de arbustos; *beard* poblado, espeso.

busily [ˈbɪzɪlɪ] ADV activamente; enérgicamente; **everyone was ~ writing** todos escribían con ahínco; **he was ~ engaged in painting it** se ocupaba enérgicamente en pintarlo.

business [ˈbɪznɪs] ① N **(a)** (*commerce in general*) comercio *m*, negocios *mpl*; **~ is ~** la cuenta es la cuenta, el comercio es una cosa seria; **~ before pleasure** primero es la obligación que la devoción; **~ as usual** (*general slogan*) los negocios como de costumbre; (*notice outside shop*) 'continúa la venta al interior'; **big ~** comercio *m* en gran escala; **kidnapping is big ~** los secuestros son un gran negocio; **~ is good at the moment** el negocio va bien por el momento; **he's in ~** se dedica al comercio; **he's in ~ in London** trabaja en una empresa comercial de Londres; **we're not in ~ to** + *infin* no es nuestro propósito + *infin*; **if we can find a car we're in ~*** si encontramos un coche todo empieza a rodar; **to be (away) on ~** estar (en viaje) de negocios; **to carry on ~ as** tener un negocio de; **to do ~ with** comerciar con; **to get down to ~** ir al grano, ir derecho a lo esencial; **to go into ~** dedicarse al comercio; **to go abroad on ~** ir al extranjero en viaje de negocios; **to go out of ~** quebrar; **the shop is losing ~** la tienda pierde clientela; **to put sb out of ~** hacer que uno quiebre; **to mean ~** hablar (*etc*) en serio; **to send sb about his ~** echar a uno con cajas destempladas; **to set up in ~** montar un negocio de; **to set sb up in ~** proveer a uno de un capital explotable.

(b) (*firm*) empresa *f*, casa *f*; **it's a family ~** es una empresa familiar.

(c) (*task, duty*) **that's my ~** eso me toca únicamente a mí; **it is my ~ to** + *infin* me corresponde + *infin*; **it's no ~ of mine** yo no tengo nada que ver con eso; **the dog did its ~*** el perro hizo sus necesidades; **you had no ~ to** + *infin* Vd no tenía ningún derecho a + *infin*; **what ~ have you to intervene?** ¿con qué derecho interviene Vd?; **they're working away like nobody's ~** están trabajando como demonios; **I will make it my ~ to tell him** yo me propongo decírselo, yo les aseguro que se lo diré; **mind your own ~** no se meta Vd donde no le llaman.

(d) (*one's trade, profession*) oficio *m*, ocupación *f*; **what ~ are you in?** ¿a qué se dedica Vd?; **he's got the biggest laugh in the ~** tiene la risa más fuerte que hay por aquí.

(e) (*affair*) cosa *f*, asunto *m*, cuestión *f*; **the Suez ~** el asunto de Suez, la cuestión Suez; **the ~ before the meeting** los asuntos a tratar; **I have ~ with the minister** tengo asuntos que tratar con el ministro; **it's a nasty ~** es un asunto desagradable; **did you hear about that ~ yesterday?** ¿le dijeron algo de lo que pasó ayer?; **what a ~ this is!** ¡qué lío!; **I can't stand this ~ of doing nothing** no puedo con este plan de no hacer nada; **any other ~** (*agenda*) ruegos *mpl* y preguntas.

(f) (*Theat*) acción *f*, gag *m*.

② ADJ, ATTR *connection, deal, quarter* comercial; *house* de comercio; *cycle* económico; **his ~ address** su dirección *f* profesional; **~ administration** (*as course*) administración *f* de empresas; **~ agent** agente *m* de negocios; **~ associate** socio *m*, -a *f*, asociado *m*, -a *f*; **~ card** tarjeta *f* comercial, tarjeta *f* de visita; **~ centre** centro *m* financiero; **~ class** (*Aer*) clase *f* preferente; **~ college** escuela *f* de comercio; **~ consultancy** empresología *f*; **~ consultant** empresólogo *m*, -a *f*; **~ deal** trato *m* comercial; **~ end*** punta *f*; **~ expenses** gastos *mpl* del negocio, gastos *mpl* comerciales; **~ hours** horas *fpl* de oficina; **~ language** lenguaje *m* comercial; **~ lunch** comida *f* de negocios; **~ machines** máquinas *fpl* para la empresa; **~ management** dirección *f*

empresarial; **~ manager** (*Theat*) secretario *m*, -a *f*; **~ park** parque *m* industrial; **~ people** empresarios *mpl*, gente *f* de negocios; **~ premises** local *m* comercial; **~ school = business college**; **~ sense** olfato *m* para los negocios; **~ Spanish** español *m* comercial, español *m* para el comercio; **~ suit** traje *m* de oficina, traje *m* de calle; **(Faculty of) B~ Studies** (Facultad *f* de) Estudios *mpl* de la Empresa, (Facultad *f* de) Estudios *mpl* Empresariales; **~ trip** viaje *m* de negocios.

businesslike [ˈbɪznɪslaɪk] ADJ formal, metódico, serio, práctico.

businessman [ˈbɪznɪsmæn] N, PL **businessmen** [ˈbɪznɪsmen] hombre *m* de negocios, empresario *m*; **small ~** pequeño empresario *m*.

businesswoman [ˈbɪznɪsˌwʊmən] N, PL **businesswomen** [ˈbɪznɪsˌwɪmɪn] mujer *f* de negocios, mujer *f* empresaria.

busk [bʌsk] VI (*Brit*) tocar música (en la calle).

busker [ˈbʌskəʳ] N (*Brit*) músico *m*, -a *f* ambulante.

bus lane [ˈbʌsˌleɪn] N (*Brit*) carril *m* de autobús.

busload [ˈbʌsləʊd] N autobús *m* (lleno, completo); **they came by the ~** (*fig*) vinieron en masa, vinieron en tropel.

busman [ˈbʌsmən] N, PL **busmen** [ˈbʌsmen] conductor *m* (*or* cobrador *m*) de autobús; **~'s holiday** ocupación *f* del ocio parecida a la del trabajo diario.

bus-service [ˈbʌsˌsɜːvɪs] N servicio *m* de autobús.

bus-shelter [ˈbʌsˌʃeltəʳ] N refugio *m* de espera, parada *f* cubierta, marquesina *f*.

bus(s)ing [ˈbʌsɪŋ] N (*US*) transporte *m* escolar.

bus-station [ˈbʌsˌsteɪʃən] N estación *f* de autobuses.

bus-stop [ˈbʌsstɒp] N parada *f* de autobús.

bust¹ [bʌst] N (*Anat: Art*) busto *m*; (*bosom*) pecho *m*, pechos *mpl*.

bust² [bʌst] ① (*) PTP *of* **burst**; roto; inservible; **to go ~** (*Comm*) quebrar.

② VT **(a)** (*) romper, estropear. **(b)** (‡) arrestar, detener; **the police ~ed him for drugs** la policía le detuvo por uso de drogas; **the police ~ed the place** la policía registró el local.

③ VI (*) romperse, estropearse.

④ N (*US**) pifia *f*.

◆ **bust up:** ① VT *marriage, friendship* romper.

② VI (*friends*) reñir, pelearse.

bustard [ˈbʌstəd] N avutarda *f*.

buster* [ˈbʌstəʳ] N (*in direct address*) macho*, tío*.

bus-ticket [ˈbʌsˌtɪkɪt] N billete *m* de autobús.

bustier [ˈbuːstɪeɪ] N bustier *m*.

bustle¹ [ˈbʌsl] N (*Hist: dress*) polisón *m*.

bustle² [ˈbʌsl] ① N movimiento *m*, actividad *f*; bullicio *m*, animación *f*; (*haste*) prisa *f*.

② VI (*gen* **to ~ about**) menearse, apresurarse, ir y venir.

bustling [ˈbʌslɪŋ] ADJ activo, hacendoso; *crowd* apresurado, animado, bullicioso.

bust-up* [ˈbʌstʌp] N riña *f*.

busty* [ˈbʌstɪ] ADJ tetuda*.

busway [ˈbʌsweɪ] N (*US*) carril *m* de autobús.

busy [ˈbɪzɪ] ① ADJ **(a)** *person* ocupado; atareado; activo; (*pej*) entrometido; **as ~ as a bee** muy activo, ocupadísimo; **are you ~?** ¿está ocupado?; **to be ~ at** (*or* **on, with**) estar ocupado en; **to be ~ doing sth** estar ocupado en hacer algo; **to get ~** empezar a trabajar, (*hurry*) menearse, darse prisa; **let's get ~!** ¡vamos!; **to keep ~** estar siempre ocupado; **to keep sb ~** ocupar a uno.

(b) *day* de muchas ocupaciones; ajetreado; **the busiest season is the autumn** la época de mayor actividad es el otoño.

(c) *place* (muy) concurrido, de mucho movimiento; *scene* animado, lleno de movimiento.

(d) (*esp US Telec*) **~ signal** señal *f* de comunicando; **to be ~** estar comunicando.

② VT ocupar.

③ VR: **to ~ o.s. at** (*or* **in, with**) ocuparse en, estar ocupado con; **she busied herself with the children** ella se ocupó de los niños.

busybody [ˈbɪzɪbɒdɪ] N entrometido *m*, -a *f*, metijón *m*, -ona *f*.

but [bʌt] (*see also* BUT) ① ADV (*only*) sólo, solamente, no más que; **all ~** casi; **nothing ~** nada más que; **he is ~ a servant** no es más que un criado; **he talks ~ little** habla muy poco; **if I could ~ speak to him** si solamente pudiese hablar con él; **had I ~ known** si lo hubiera sabido; **you can ~ try** en todo caso vale probarlo.

② PREP (*except*) excepto, menos; salvo; **all ~ him** todos excepto él, todos salvo él; **the last ~ one** el penúltimo; **the last ~ three** el tercero antes del último; **for a no ser por, si no fuera por; **there is nothing for it ~ to pay up** no hay más remedio que pagar; **one cannot ~ admire him** no se puede sino admirarle; **I'll do anything ~ sing** lo hago todo menos cantar.

③ CONJ **(a)** pero; **she was poor ~ she was honest** era pobre pero honrada; **~ it does move!** ¡pero sí se mueve!; **it never rains ~ it pours** llueve sobre mojado; **I never go there ~ I think of you** nunca voy allá sin pensar en ti.

(b) (*in statements of direct contradiction*) sino, *eg* **he's not English ~ Irish** no es inglés sino irlandés; **he didn't sing ~ he shouted** no cantó sino que gritó.

4 N pero *m*, objeción *f*; **there are no ~s about it** no hay pero que valga.

┌─ BUT ──────────────── see also main entry ─┐

There are three main ways of translating the conjunction *but*: *pero*, *sino* and *sino que*.

Contrasting

• To introduce a contrast or a new idea, use *pero*:
  Strange but interesting
  Extraño pero interesante
  I thought he would help me but he refused
  Creí que me ayudaría, pero se negó

• In informal language, *pero* can be used at the start of a comment:
  But where are you going to put it?
  Pero ¿dónde lo vas a poner?

! In formal language, *sin embargo* or *no obstante* may be preferred:
  But, in spite of the likely benefits, he still opposed the idea
  Sin embargo or *No obstante, a pesar de las probables ventajas, todavía se oponía a la idea*

Correcting a previous negative

• When *but* or *but rather* introduces a noun phrase, prepositional phrase or verb in the infinitive which corrects a previous negative, translate *but* using *sino*:
  Not wine, but vinegar
  No vino, sino vinagre
  They aren't from Seville, but from Bilbao
  No son de Sevilla, sino de Bilbao
  His trip to London was not to investigate the case but to hush it up
  Su viaje a Londres no fue para investigar el caso sino para taparlo

• When *but* or *but rather* introduces a verb clause (or requires a verb clause in Spanish) which corrects a previous negative, translate using *sino que*:
  He's not asking you to do what he says but (rather) to listen to him
  No te pide que hagas lo que él dice, sino que le escuches

Not only ... but also

• When the *but also* part of this construction contains SUBJECT + VERB, translate using *no sólo* or *no solamente ... sino que también* or *sino que además*:
  It will not only cause tension, but it will also damage the economy
  No sólo or *No solamente provocará tensiones, sino que además* or *sino que también dañará la economía*

• When the *but also* part does not contain SUBJECT + VERB, translate using *no sólo* or *no solamente ... sino también* or *sino además*:
  Not only rich but also powerful
  No sólo or *No solamente rico sino también* or *sino además poderoso*
  We don't only want to negotiate but also to take decisions
  No queremos sólo or *solamente negociar, sino también tomar decisiones*

└──┘

butane ['bjuːteɪn] N butano *m*; (*US: for camping*) camping gas *m*; **~ gas** gas *m* butano.

butch‡ [bʊtʃ] **1** ADJ *woman* marimacho; *man* macho.
  2 N (*woman*) marimacho *m*; (*man*) macho *m*.

butcher ['bʊtʃəʳ] **1** N (a) carnicero *m* (*also fig*); **~'s** (*shop*) carnicería *f*. (b) (*US*) vendedor *m* de dulces. (c) **let's have a ~'s** (*Brit‡*) déjame verlo; *ver también* [RHYMING SLANG].
  2 VT matar; (*fig*) dar muerte a, hacer una carnicería con.

butchery ['bʊtʃərɪ] N matanza *f*, carnicería *f*.

butler ['bʌtləʳ] N mayordomo *m*.

butt¹ [bʌt] N (*barrel*) tonel *m*; (*for rainwater*) tina *f*.

butt² [bʌt] N (*end*) cabo *m*, extremo *m*; extremo *m* más grueso; (*of gun*) culata *f*; (*of cigarette*) colilla *f*; (*US: cigarette*) colilla *f*, pito* *m*; (*US*: *Anat*) culo *m*; **to work one's ~ off** romperse los cuernos*.

butt³ [bʌt] N (*target*) blanco *m*; **~s** campo *m* de tiro al blanco; **to be a ~ for** ser el blanco de, ser el objeto de.

butt⁴ [bʌt] **1** N (*push with head*) cabezada *f*, topetada *f*.
  2 VT dar cabezadas contra, topetar; **to ~ one's head against** dar con la cabeza contra; **to ~ one's way through** abrirse paso dando cabezadas.

◆**butt in** VI interrumpir; (*meddle*) entrometerse, meter baza, meter su cuchara.

◆**butt into** VT *conversation* meterse en; *meeting* interrumpir.

butt-end ['bʌtend] N = **butt²**.

butter ['bʌtəʳ] **1** N mantequilla *f*; **~ wouldn't melt in his mouth** es una mosquita muerta.
  2 VT untar con mantequilla.

◆**butter up** VT (*Brit*) dar coba a*.

butterball ['bʌtəbɔːl] N (*US*) gordo *m*.

butter-bean ['bʌtə,biːn] N (*Bot*) judía *f* valenciana.

buttercup ['bʌtəkʌp] N ranúnculo *m*.

butter-dish ['bʌtə,dɪʃ] N mantequillera *f*.

butter-fingered ['bʌtə,fɪŋgəd] ADJ desmañado en coger la pelota (*etc*).

butterfingers* ['bʌtə,fɪŋgəz] N SING manos *m* de trapo, manos *m* de mantequilla; **~!** ¡premio!

butterfly ['bʌtəflaɪ] N mariposa *f*; **~ mind** mentalidad *f* frívola; **to have butterflies in the stomach** estar muy nervioso.

butterfly-knot ['bʌtəflaɪ,nɒt] N nudo *m* de lazo.

butterfly-net ['bʌtəflaɪ,net] N manga *f* de mariposas.

butterfly-nut ['bʌtəflaɪ,nʌt] N tuerca *f* de mariposa.

butterfly-stroke ['bʌtəflaɪ,strəʊk] N braza *f* de mariposa.

butter-icing [,bʌtər'aɪsɪŋ] N cobertura *f* de mantequilla.

butter-knife ['bʌtə,naɪf] N, PL **butter-knives** ['bʌtə,naɪvz] cuchillo *m* de mantequilla.

buttermilk ['bʌtəmɪlk] N suero *m* de leche, suero *m* de manteca.

butterscotch ['bʌtəskɒtʃ] N *dulce de azúcar terciado con mantequilla*.

buttery ['bʌtərɪ] N despensa *f*.

buttocks ['bʌtəks] NPL nalgas *fpl*, cachas *fpl*.

button ['bʌtn] **1** N (*all senses*) botón *m*; **~s** (*esp Brit: person*) botones *m*; **on the ~*** *arrive* en punto; (*absolutely exact*) exacto.
  2 VT (*also to ~ up*) abotonar, abrochar; **to ~ one's lip*** no decir ni mu.
  3 VI: **it ~s in front** se abrocha por delante.

button-down ['bʌtndaʊn] ADJ: **~ shirt** camisa *f* con cuello de botones; **~ collar** cuello *m* de botones.

buttoned-up* ['bʌtnd,ʌp] ADJ reservado.

buttonhole ['bʌtnhəʊl] **1** N ojal *m*; (*Brit: flower*) flor *f* que se lleva en el ojal.
  2 VT obligar a escuchar, abordar; **I was ~d by X** me vi obligado a detenerme en conversación con X.

buttonhook ['bʌtnhʊk] N abotonador *m*.

button mushroom [,bʌtn'mʌʃrʊm] N champiñón *m* pequeño.

button-through dress [,bʌtn,θruː'dres] N vestido *m* abrochado por delante.

buttress ['bʌtrɪs] **1** N contrafuerte *m* (*also Geog*); (*fig*) apoyo *m*, sostén *m*.
  2 VT poner contrafuerte a; (*fig*) apoyar, reforzar.

butty* ['bʌtɪ] N bocadillo *m*.

buxom ['bʌksəm] ADJ rollizo, frescachón; tetuda*.

buy [baɪ] **1** N compra *f*; **a good ~** un buen negocio, una ganga, una buena compra; **this month's best ~** la ganga del mes.
  2 (*irr*: PRET AND PTP **bought**) VT (a) comprar (*from, off* a); **money couldn't ~ it** no se puede comprar con dinero.
  (b) (*bribe*) comprar, sobornar.
  (c) (*: believe*) creer, tragar; **he won't ~ that** eso no lo va a tragar; **all right, I'll ~ it** bueno, dime.
  (d) **he bought it‡** la palmó‡.

◆**buy back** VT volver a comprar.

◆**buy forward** VI comprar con antelación.

◆**buy in** VT (*Brit*) *foods* aprovisionarse de; (*Stock Exchange*) comprar; (*Fin*) comprar por cuenta del dueño.

◆**buy into** VT (a) *company* comprar acciones de. (b) (*fig*) *idea* apoyar.

◆**buy off** VT comprar la benevolencia de; (*bribe*) sobornar.

◆**buy out** VT *partner* comprar la parte de.

◆**buy up** VT comprar todas las existencias de, acaparar.

buy-back ['baɪ,bæk] ADJ: **~ option** opción *f* de recompra.

buyer ['baɪəʳ] N comprador *m*, -ora *f*; (*in store*) encargado *m* de compras; **~'s market** mercado *m* de compradores, mercado *m* de signo favorable al comprador.

buying ['baɪɪŋ] N compra *f*; **~ power** poder *m* adquisitivo.

buy-out ['baɪaʊt] N compra *f* (de la totalidad de las acciones); **management ~** compra *f* (de acciones) por los gerentes; **workers' ~** compra *f* de una empresa por los trabajadores de la misma.

buzz [bʌz] **1** N (a) zumbido *m*. (b) (*: rumour*) rumor *m*. (c) (*Telec*) llamada *f* (telefónica); **I'll give you a ~** te llamaré.
  2 VT (a) (*US Telec*) llamar. (b) (*Aer*) zumbar.
  3 VI zumbar; **my ears are ~ing** me zumban los oídos; **the school ~ed with the news** todo el colegio comentaba la noticia.

◆**buzz about, buzz around** VI ir zumbando de acá para allá; (*fig*) ser muy activo, correr a todas partes.

◆**buzz off*** VI (*Brit*) largarse*, rajarse*; **~ off!** ¡largo de aquí!*

buzzard ['bʌzəd] N ratonero *m* común, águila *f* ratonera.

buzz-bomb ['bʌzbɒm] N bomba *f* volante.

buzzer ['bʌzəʳ] N timbre *m*.

buzzing ['bʌzɪŋ] N zumbido *m*, zumbar *m*.

buzz-saw ['bʌz,sɔː] N (*US*) sierra *f* circular.

buzz-word ['bʌz,wɜːd] N palabra *f* que está de moda, cliché *m*.

b.v. ABBR *of* **book value** valor *m* en libros.

B.V.M. N ABBR *of* **Blessed Virgin Mary.**

by [baɪ] **1** ADV: ~ **and** ~ más tarde, luego; ~ **and large** en general, por lo general.

2 PREP **(a)** *(agent, by means of)* por; **a house built** ~ **X** una casa construida por X; ~ **one's own efforts** por sus propios esfuerzos; ~ **God** por Dios; **made** ~ **hand** hecho a mano; **to divide** ~ **5** dividir por 5; **he had 3 children** ~ **his first wife** tuvo 3 hijos con su primera mujer; **he is known** ~ **the name of** se le conoce con *(of pseudonym:* bajo) el nombre de; **he did it** ~ **himself** lo hizo por sí solo, lo hizo por sí mismo.

(b) *(manner)* ~ **air** en avión; por avión; ~ **cheque** por cheque; ~ **easy stages** en cortas etapas; ~ **leaps and bounds** a pasos agigantados; ~ **moonlight** a la luz de la luna; ~ **train** *(come)* en tren, *(send)* por ferrocarril; **to be** ~ **o.s.** estar solo.

(c) *(rate)* **hour** ~ **hour** hora tras hora, cada hora; ~ **the dozen** a docenas, por docenas; **2** ~ **2** de 2 en 2; **little** ~ **little** poco a poco; **to buy sth** ~ **the kilo** comprar algo por kilos; **to reduce sth** ~ **a third** reducir algo en una tercera parte; **we pay** ~ **the month** pagamos cada mes.

(d) *(in accordance with)* según, de acuerdo con; ~ **what you say** según lo que dices; **to be cautious** ~ **nature** ser de naturaleza cauteloso.

(e) *(time)* ~ **2 o'clock** para las 2; ~ **nightfall** antes del anochecer; ~ **then** para entonces, antes de eso; ~ **day** de día.

(f) *(place: next)* junto a, cerca de, al lado de; ~ **me** a mi lado; **north** ~ **west** norte por oeste; *(through, along)* por; **he came in** ~ **the window** entró por la ventana.

(g) *(measurement)* **6 metres** ~ **4** 6 metros por 4; **it's too short** ~ **a foot** falta un pie; **he missed** ~ **an inch** erró el tiro en una pulgada.

(h) *(with gerund)* ~ **working hard** trabajando mucho; **he ended** ~ **saying that** ... terminó diciendo que ...

3 N: ~ **the** ~ a propósito.

bye¹ [baɪ] N **1** *(Golf etc)* bye *m*; **to have a** ~ pasar a la segunda eliminatoria por sorteo; **by the** ~ por cierto, a propósito.

2: bye-election = by-election; bye-law = by-law.

bye²* [baɪ] INTERJ = **bye-bye.**

bye-bye* ['baɪ'baɪ] **1** INTERJ ¡adiós!, ¡hasta luego!

2 N: **to go** ~**s** dormirse, quedar dormido; **it's time to go** ~**s** es hora de acostarte.

by-election ['baɪˌlekʃən] N elección *f* parcial; *ver también* CONSTITUENCY, MARGINAL SEAT .

CONSTITUENCY, MARGINAL SEAT

---

i ┌─ **BY-ELECTION** ─────────────────────────────────┐

*Se denomina **by-election** en el Reino Unido y otros países de la **Commonwealth** a las elecciones convocadas con carácter excepcional cuando un escaño queda desierto por fallecimiento o dimisión de un parlamentario (**Member of Parliament**). Dichas elecciones tienen lugar únicamente en el área electoral representada por el citado parlamentario, su **constituency**.*

└───┘

Byelorussia [ˌbjeləʊˈrʌʃə] N Bielorrusia *f*.

Byelorussian [ˌbjeləʊˈrʌʃən] **1** ADJ bielorruso.

2 N **(a)** bielorruso *m*, -a *f*. **(b)** *(Ling)* bielorruso *m*.

bygone ['baɪgɒn] **1** ADJ pasado.

2 N: **let** ~**s be** ~**s** lo pasado pasado está.

by-law ['baɪlɔː] N *(Brit)* estatuto *m*, reglamento *m* local *(or* suplementario).

by-line ['baɪlaɪn] N *(Press)* pie *m* de autor.

by-name ['baɪneɪm] N sobrenombre *m*; *(nickname)* apodo *m*, mote *m*.

BYOB* ABBR *of* **bring your own bottle** trae botella.

bypass ['baɪpɑːs] **1** N *(Aut)* carretera *f* de circunvalación; *(Elec)* desviación *f*; ~ **operation** by-pass *m*, operación *f* de by-pass; ~ **surgery** cirugía *f* de by-pass.

2 VT evitar, evitar el contacto con; prescindir de; *town* evitar entrar en, pasar de largo; *lower official etc* puentear.

by-play ['baɪpleɪ] N *(Theat)* acción *f* aparte, escena *f* muda.

by-product ['baɪˌprɒdəkt] N subproducto *m*; *(Chem)* derivado *m*; *(fig)* consecuencia *f*.

byre ['baɪər] N *(Brit)* establo *m*, vaquería *f*.

by-road ['baɪrəʊd] N camino *m* vecinal, carretera *f* secundaria.

bystander ['baɪˌstændər] N espectador *m*, -ora *f*, circunstante *mf*; curioso *m*, -a *f*, mirón *m*, -ona *f*.

byte [baɪt] N byte *m*, octeto *m*.

byway ['baɪweɪ] N camino *m* apartado, camino *m* poco frecuentado; **the** ~**s of history** los aspectos poco conocidos de la historia.

byword ['baɪwɜːd] N: **to be a** ~ **for** *(Brit)* ser conocidísimo por, ser ... por antonomasia.

by-your-leave [ˌbaɪjɔːˈliːv] N: **without so much as a** ~ sin pedir permiso; sin decir nada, así por las buenas, sin más ni más.

Byzantine [baɪˈzæntaɪn] **1** ADJ bizantino.

2 N bizantino *m*, -a *f*.

Byzantium [baɪˈzæntɪəm] N Bizancio *m*.

C

C, c [siː] N **(a)** (*letter*) C, c *f*; **C for Charlie** C de Carmen. **(b)** C (*Mus*) do *m*; **C major** do *m* mayor.

C. (a) (*Liter*) ABBR of **chapter** capítulo *m*, cap. **(b)** (*Geog*) ABBR of **Cape** cabo *m*. **(c)** ABBR of **centigrade** termómetro *m* centígrado. **(d)** (*Pol*) ABBR of **Conservative** conservador *m*, -ora *f*.

c (a) (*US Fin*) ABBR of **cent** centavo *m*. **(b)** ABBR of **century** siglo *m*, S. **(c)** ABBR of **circa, about** hacia, h. **(d)** (*Math*) ABBR of **cubic** cúbico.

C4 N (*Brit: TV*) ABBR of **Channel Four** *cadena de TV británica que ofrece programas dedicados a sectores minoritarios y regionales, con especial atención a la cultura.*

C & W N ABBR of **Country and Western**; V **country**.

CA (*US Post*) ABBR of **California**.

C.A. N **(a)** ABBR of **chartered accountant**; V **chartered**. **(b)** ABBR of **Central America** Centroamérica *f*.

C/A (a) ABBR of **current account** cuenta *f* corriente, cta. cte. **(b)** ABBR of **credit account** cuenta *f* a crédito.

CAA N (*Brit*) ABBR of **Civil Aviation Authority** ≃ Aviación *f* Civil.

C.14 N ABBR of **carbon 14**; **~ dating** datación *f* por C-14.

CAB N (*Brit*) ABBR of **Citizens' Advice Bureau** Oficina *f* de Información al Ciudadano; *ver también* CITIZENS' ADVICE BUREAU .

cab [kæb] N (*taxi*) taxi *m*; (††) cabriolé *m*, coche *m* de alquiler; (*of lorry etc*) cabina *f*.

cabal [kəˈbæl] N cábala *f*; camarilla *f*; cabildeo *m*.

cabaret [ˈkæbəreɪ] N cabaret *m*.

cabbage [ˈkæbɪdʒ] N **(a)** col *f*, berza *f*, repollo *m*; **~ white** (*butterfly*) mariposa *f* de la col. **(b)** (*person*) vegetal *m*.

cab(b)ala [kəˈbɑːlə] N cábala *f*.

cabbalistic [ˌkæbəˈlɪstɪk] ADJ cabalístico.

cabbie, cabby* [ˈkæbɪ] N, **cabdriver** [ˈkæbdraɪvəʳ] N taxista *m*; (††) cochero *m*.

caber [ˈkeɪbəʳ] N (*Scot*) tronco *m*; *ver también* HIGHLAND GAMES .

cabin [ˈkæbɪn] N (*hut*) cabaña *f*, barraca *f*; (*Naut*) camarote *m*; (*of lorry, plane*) cabina *f*; **~ class** clase *f* de cámara; **~ crew** tripulación *f* de pilotaje.

cabin-boy [ˈkæbɪnbɔɪ] N grumete *m*.

cabin-cruiser [ˈkæbɪnˌkruːzəʳ] N yate *m* de motor, motonave *f*.

cabinet [ˈkæbɪnɪt] N **(a)** (*cupboard*) armario *m*; (*for display*) vitrina *f*; (*Rad, TV*) caja *f*; **medicine ~** botiquín *m*. **(b)** (*Pol*) consejo *m* de ministros, gabinete *m*, ministros *mpl*; **~ crisis** crisis *f* del gobierno; **~ meeting** consejo *m* de ministros; **~ minister** ministro *m*, -a *f*; *ver también* SHADOW CABINET .

─ CABINET ─

ⓘ *El Consejo de Ministros británico (**Cabinet**) se compone de unos veinte ministros, escogidos por el Primer Ministro (**Prime Minister**). Su función es la de planificar la legislación importante y defender la política del Gobierno en los debates.*
*En Estados Unidos el **Cabinet** tiene meramente carácter consultivo, su función es aconsejar al Presidente. Sus miembros, escogidos por él y nombrados con el consentimiento del Senado (**Senate**), son jefes de departamentos ejecutivos o altos cargos del gobierno, pero no pueden ser miembros del Congreso (**Congress**). Existe otro grupo de asesores del Presidente, que actúan a un nivel menos oficial, que se conoce como **kitchen cabinet**.*

cabinetmaker [ˈkæbɪnɪtˌmeɪkəʳ] N ebanista *m*.

cabinetmaking [ˈkæbɪnɪtˌmeɪkɪŋ] N ebanistería *f*.

cable [ˈkeɪbl] 1 N (*Naut, Elec, Telec*) cable *m*; (*message*) cablegrama *m*; **~ address** dirección *f* cablegráfica; **~ television** televisión *f* por cable; **~ transfer** transferencia *f* por cable, transferencia *f* cablegráfica.
2 VTI cablegrafiar.

cable-car [ˈkeɪblkɑːʳ] N coche *m* de teleférico.

cablecast [ˈkeɪblˌkɑːst] 1 N emisión *f* de televisión por cable.

2 VT emitir por cable.

cablegram [ˈkeɪblɡræm] N cablegrama *m*.

cable-railway [ˈkeɪblˈreɪlweɪ] N teleférico *m*, funicular *m* aéreo.

cable-stitch [ˈkeɪblstɪtʃ] N punto *m* de trenza.

cableway [ˈkeɪblweɪ] N teleférico *m*, funicular *m* aéreo.

cabling [ˈkeɪblɪŋ] N (*cables*) red *f* de cables, cableado *m*; (*process*) cableado *m*.

cabman [ˈkæbmən] N, PL **cabmen** [ˈkæbmən] taxista *m*; (††) cochero *m*.

caboodle* [kəˈbuːdl] N: **the whole ~** todo el rollo*.

caboose [kəˈbuːs] N (*US*) furgón *m* de cola.

cabrank [ˈkæbræŋk] N, **cabstand** [ˈkæbstænd] N parada *f* de taxis.

cacao [kəˈkɑːəʊ] N cacao *m*.

cache [kæʃ] 1 N (*hiding-place*) escondite *m*, escondrijo *m*; (*stores*) víveres *mpl* (*etc*) escondidos; (*of contraband, arms*) alijo *m*; **~ memory** cache *m*, submemoria *f* ultrarrápida.
2 VT esconder, ocultar; acumular.

cachet [ˈkæʃeɪ] N caché *m*, cachet *m*.

cack-handed* [ˌkækˈhændɪd] ADJ (*Brit*) zurdo; (*fig*) torpe, desmañado.

cackle [ˈkækl] 1 N cacareo *m*; (*laughter*) risotada *f*; (*talk*) parloteo *m*; **cut the ~!*** ¡corta el rollo!*; ¡basta de cháchara!
2 VI cacarear; (*laugh*) reírse agudamente, desternillarse de risa; parlotear.

CACM N ABBR of **Central American Common Market** Mercado *m* Común Centroamericano, MCCA *m*.

cacophonous [kəˈkɒfənəs] ADJ cacofónico.

cacophony [kæˈkɒfənɪ] N cacofonía *f*.

cactus [ˈkæktəs] N, PL **cacti** [ˈkæktaɪ] cactus *m*, cacto *m*.

CAD N ABBR of **computer-aided design** diseño *m* asistido por ordenador, DAO *m*.

cad [kæd] N (*Brit*) sinvergüenza *m*, caradura *m*, canalla *m*; **you ~!** ¡canalla!

cadaster, cadastre [kəˈdæstəʳ] N catastro *m*.

cadaver [kəˈdeɪvəʳ] N (*esp US*) cadáver *m*.

cadaverous [kəˈdævərəs] ADJ cadavérico.

CADCAM [ˈkædˌkæm] N ABBR of **computer-aided design and manufacture**.

caddie [ˈkædɪ] N caddie *mf*.

caddis fly [ˈkædɪsflaɪ] N frígano *m*.

caddish*† [ˈkædɪʃ] ADJ desvergonzado, canallesco; **~ trick** canallada *f*.

caddy¹ [ˈkædɪ] N **(a)** cajita *f* para té. **(b)** (*US: shopping trolley*) carrito *m* de la compra.

caddy² [ˈkædɪ] N = **caddie**.

cadence [ˈkeɪdəns] N cadencia *f*; **the ~s of prose** el ritmo de la prosa.

cadenza [kəˈdenzə] N cadencia *f*.

cadet [kəˈdet] N (*Mil etc*) cadete *mf*; (*younger son*) hijo *m* menor.

cadet corps [kəˈdetˌkɔːʳ] N (*Brit: in school*) cuerpo *m* de alumnos que reciben entrenamiento militar; (*Police*) cuerpo *m* de cadetes.

cadet school [kəˈdetˌskuːl] N escuela *f* en la que se ofrece instrucción militar.

cadge [kædʒ] (*Brit*) 1 VT sacar de gorra, obtener mendigando, gorronear (*off* a); **he tried to ~ a lift** trató de conseguir que le llevaran gratis (en coche).
2 VI gorronear, vivir de gorra, sablear; **you can't ~ off me** es inútil pedirme cosas a mí.

cadger [ˈkædʒəʳ] N (*Brit*) gorrón *m*, -ona *f*, sablista *mf*.

Cadiz [kəˈdɪz] N Cádiz *m*.

cadmium [ˈkædmɪəm] N cadmio *m*.

cadre [ˈkɑːdə] N (*Mil etc*) cuadro *m*.

CAE N ABBR of **computer-assisted engineering** ingeniería *f* asistida por computadora, IAC *f*.

caecum, (US) cecum [ˈsiːkəm] N (*intestino m*) ciego *m*.

Caesar ['si:zər] NM César.
Caesarean, (*US*) **Cesarean** [si:'zɛəriən] ① N = **2.**
  ② ADJ cesariano, cesáreo; **~ operation, ~ section** (operación *f*) cesárea *f*.
caesium, (*US*) **cesium** ['si:zɪəm] N cesio *m*.
caesura [sɪ'zjʊərə] N cesura *f*.
CAF, c.a.f. N ABBR *of* **cost and freight** coste y flete *m*, C. y F.
café ['kæfeɪ] N café *m*, cafetería *f*.
cafeteria [ˌkæfɪ'tɪərɪə] N (restaurante *m* de) autoservicio *m*.
caff‡ [kæf] N = **café.**
caffein(e) ['kæfi:n] N cafeína *f*.
caftan ['kæftæn] N caftán *m*.
cage [keɪdʒ] ① N jaula *f*.
  ② VT enjaular; **a ~d bird** un pájaro en jaula; **like a ~d tiger** como una fiera enjaulada.
cage bird ['keɪdʒbɜːd] N pájaro *m* de jaula.
cagey* ['keɪdʒɪ] ADJ cauteloso, reservado, reservón*; **he was very ~ about it** en eso anduvo con mucha reserva.
cagily* ['keɪdʒɪlɪ] ADV cautelosamente, con reserva.
caginess* ['keɪdʒɪnɪs] N cautela *f*, reserva *f*.
cagoule [kə'gu:l] N canguro *m*.
cahoots* [kə'hu:ts] N: **to be in ~ with sb** obrar de acuerdo con uno; confabularse con uno; **to go ~** entrar por partes iguales.
CAI N ABBR *of* **computer-aided instruction** instrucción *f* asistida por ordenador, IAO *f*.
caiman ['keɪmən] N caimán *m*.
Cain [keɪn] NM Caín; **to raise ~** armar la gorda, protestar enérgicamente.
cairn [keən] N mojón *m*, montón *m* de piedras (*puesto en una cumbre o sobre una sepultura, etc*).
Cairo ['kaɪərəʊ] N el Cairo.
caisson ['keɪsən] N (*Mech*) cajón *m* hidráulico; (*Naut*) cajón *m* de suspensión; (*of dry-dock*) puerta *f* de dique; (*Mil*) cajón *m* de municiones.
cajole [kə'dʒəʊl] VT halagar, camelar; **to ~ sb into doing sth** halagar (*or* engatusar) a uno para que haga algo.
cajolery [kə'dʒəʊlərɪ] N halagos *mpl*, marrullería *f*, engatusamiento *m*.
Cajun ['keɪdʒən] ① ADJ cajún; **~ cookery** cocina *f* tipo cajún.
  ② N (a) cajún *mf*. (b) (*Ling*) cajún *m*.

┌─── *CAJUN* ──────────────────────────────┐

ⓘ *A los habitantes del sur de Luisiana que hablan un dialecto francés se les llama* **Cajuns.** *Son los descendientes de los canadienses franceses expulsados de Nueva Escocia por los británicos en 1755, llamada entonces Acadia (***Cajun*** es la forma acortada de* **Acadian***). El dialecto combina francés arcaico con inglés y español, junto con algunas palabras y frases hechas indias. Tanto su comida picante como su música se conocen hoy en el mundo entero.*

└───────────────────────────────────────┘

cake [keɪk] ① N (*large*) pastel *m*; tarta *f*; (*small*) pasta *f*, pastelillo *m*, queque *m* (*LAm*); (*sponge*) bizcocho *m*; (*of soap*) pastilla *f*; **it's a piece of ~*** es pan comido*, está tirado; **to want to have one's ~ and eat it** querer nadar y guardar la ropa; **the way the national ~ is divided** el modo de repartir la tarta (*or* el pastel) nacional; **to go** (*or* **sell**) **like hot ~s** venderse como pan bendito; **that takes the ~!*** ¡es el colmo!
  ② VT endurecer; **a tyre ~d with mud** un neumático incrustado de lodo.
  ③ VI endurecerse, apelmazarse.
caked [keɪkt] ① PRET AND PTP *of* **cake.**
  ② ADJ endurecido.
cake-mix ['keɪkmɪks] N polvos *mpl* para hacer pasteles.
cakeshop ['keɪkʃɒp] N pastelería *f*.
cake-tin ['keɪktɪn] N (*Culin*) molde *m* para pastel; (*for keeping*) caja *f* de pastel.
Cal. ABBR *of* **California.**
cal. N ABBR *of* **calorie.**
calabash ['kæləbæʃ] N calabaza *f*.
calaboose* ['kæləbu:s] N (*US*) jaula *f**, cárcel *f*.
calamine ['kæləmaɪn] N calamina *f*.
calamitous [kə'læmɪtəs] ADJ calamitoso, desastroso.
calamity [kə'læmɪtɪ] N calamidad *f*, desastre *m*.
calcareous [kæl'keərɪəs] ADJ calcáreo.
calcicole ['kælsɪˌkəʊl] N calcícola *f*.
calcicolous [kæl'sɪkələs] ADJ calcícola.
calcification [ˌkælsɪfɪ'keɪʃən] N calcificación *f*.
calcifugous [kæl'sɪfjəgəs] ADJ calcífugo.
calcify ['kælsɪfaɪ] ① VT calcificar.
  ② VI calcificarse.
calcium ['kælsɪəm] N calcio *m*; **~ carbonate** carbonato *m* de calcio; **~ chloride** cloruro *m* de calcio.
calculable ['kælkjʊləbl] ADJ calculable.
calculate ['kælkjʊleɪt] ① VT calcular; **~d to +** *infin* aprestado para **+** *infin*; **this is ~d to give him a jolt** esto tiene el propósito de

darle una sacudida; **it is hardly ~d to help us** esto apenas será ventajoso para nosotros.
  ② VI calcular; **to ~ on** contar con.
calculated ['kælkjʊleɪtɪd] ADJ *risk etc* calculado, premeditado, estudiado.
calculating ['kælkjʊleɪtɪŋ] ADJ astuto.
calculating machine ['kælkjʊleɪtɪŋməˌʃi:n] N máquina *f* de calcular, calculadora *f*.
calculation [ˌkælkjʊ'leɪʃən] N cálculo *m*, cómputo *m*.
calculator ['kælkjʊleɪtər] N (*machine*) calculadora *f*; (*small*) minicalculadora *f*.
calculus ['kælkjʊləs] N cálculo *m*.
Calcutta [kæl'kʌtə] N Calcuta *f*.
Caledonia [ˌkælə'dəʊnɪə] N Caledonia *f*.
Caledonian [ˌkælɪ'dəʊnɪən] (*liter*) ① ADJ caledoniano.
  ② N caledoniano *m*, -a *f*.
calendar ['kæləndər] N (a) calendario *m*; (*Jur*) lista *f* (de pleitos); **university ~** (*Brit*) calendario *m* universitario; **~ month** mes *m* civil; **~ year** año *m* civil. (b) (‡) condena *f* de un año de prisión.
calf¹ [kɑ:f] N, PL **calves** [kɑ:vz] (*Zool*) ternero *m*, -a *f*, becerro *m*, -a *f*; (*of elephant*) cría *f*; (*of whale*) ballenato *m*; (*of seal etc*) cría *f*; (*skin*) piel *f* de becerro; **the cow is in** (*or* **with**) **~** la vaca está preñada; **to kill the fatted ~** festejar con mucho rumbo a un recién llegado, celebrar una fiesta de bienvenida.
calf² [kɑ:f] N, PL **calves** [kɑ:vz] (*Anat*) pantorrilla *f*.
calf love ['kɑ:flʌv] N amor *m* juvenil.
calfskin ['kɑ:fskɪn] N piel *f* de becerro.
caliber ['kælɪbər] N (*US*) = **calibre.**
calibrate ['kælɪbreɪt] VT calibrar.
calibrated ['kælɪbreɪtɪd] ADJ calibrado.
calibration [ˌkælɪ'breɪʃən] N calibración *f*.
calibre, (*US*) **caliber** ['kælɪbər] N calibre *m*; (*fig*) capacidad *f*, aptitud *f*, carácter *m*, valor *m*; **a man of his ~** un hombre de su calibre; **then he showed his real ~** luego demostró su verdadero valor.
calico ['kælɪkəʊ] N calicó *m*, indiana *f*.
Calif. ABBR *of* **California.**
California [ˌkælɪ'fɔ:nɪə] N California *f*.
Californian [ˌkælɪ'fɔ:nɪən] ① ADJ californiano.
  ② N californiano *m*, -a *f*.
californium [ˌkælɪ'fɔ:nɪəm] N californio *m*.
calipers ['kælɪpəz] NPL (*US*) = **callipers.**
caliph ['keɪlɪf] N califa *m*.
caliphate ['keɪlɪfeɪt] N califato *m*.
calisthenics [ˌkælɪs'θenɪks] N (*US*) = **callisthenics.**
CALL [kɔ:l] N ABBR *of* **computer-assisted language learning** enseñanza *f* de lenguas asistida por ordenador.

▼ **call** [kɔ:l] ① N (a) (*gen*) llamada *f* (*also Mil*); (*cry*) grito *m*; (*of bird*) canto *m*, reclamo *m*; (*imitating bird's cry*) reclamo *m*, (*imitating animal's cry*) chilla *f*; (*Theat: summons to actor*) llamamiento *m*, (*curtain ~*) salida *f*; **~ loan** préstamo *m* cobrable a la vista; **~ of nature** (*euph*) necesidad *f* fisiológica; **~ option** opción *f* de compra a precio fijado; **the ~ of the unknown** la atracción de lo desconocido; **on ~** disponible, a su disposición; **money on** (*or* **at**) **~** dinero *m* a la vista; **within ~** al alcance de la voz; **they came at my ~** acudieron a mi llamada; **please give me a ~ at 7** hágame el favor de llamarme a las 7; **he's had a ~ to the Palace** le han llamado a palacio; **to have a close ~** escapar por un pelo, salvarse de milagro.

▼ (b) (*Telec etc*) llamada *f*, llamado *m* (*LAm*); **to give sb a ~** llamar a uno; **to make a ~** llamar, hacer una llamada.
  (c) (*visit*) visita *f*; **port of ~** puerto *m* de escala; **the boat makes a ~ at Vigo** el barco hace escala en Vigo; **to pay a ~ on sb** hacer una visita a uno.
  (d) (*appeal, summons, invitation*) llamamiento *m*; **a ~ went to the fire brigade** se llamó a los bomberos; **the boat sent out a ~ for help** el barco emitió una llamada de socorro; **the minister sent out a ~ to the country to remain calm** el ministro hizo un llamamiento al país para que conservara la calma; **~ for a strike** convocatoria *f* de huelga; **~ for congress papers** convocatoria *f* de ponencias para un congreso; **to answer the ~** acudir al llamamiento; **to be on ~** estar de turno, (*doctor*) estar de guardia localizable, (*nurse*) estar de retén.
  (e) (*need etc*) (*Comm*) demanda *f* (*for, on* de); **there isn't much ~ for these now** éstos tienen poca demanda ahora; **you had no ~ to say that** no había razón para que dijeras eso; **what ~ was there for you to intervene?** ¿qué necesidad había para que tú te entrometieras?
  (f) (*claim*) **there are many ~s on my attention** son muchas las cosas que reclaman mi atención; **he has many ~s on his purse** tiene muchas obligaciones financieras.
  (g) (*Bridge*) marca *f*, voz *f*; **whose ~ is it?** ¿a quién le toca?
  ② VT (a) (*gen*) llamar; **did you ~?** ¿me llamaste?; **they ~ed me to see it** me llamaron para que lo viese; **please ~ me at 8** hágame el favor de llamarme a las 8.

▼ **(b)** (*Telec*) llamar (por *or* al teléfono), telefonear (*esp LAm*); **London ~ed you this morning** esta mañana le llamaron (al teléfono) desde Londres; **I'll ~ you again tomorrow** volveré a llamarle mañana; **don't ~ us, we'll ~ you** no se moleste en llamar, nosotros le llamaremos.

(c) (*name*) llamar; **I'm ~ed Peter** me llamo Pedro; **what are you ~ed?** ¿cómo te llamas?; **what are they ~ing him?** ¿qué nombre le van a poner?; **they're ~ing the boy John** al niño le van a dar el nombre de Juan; **I ~ it an insult** yo digo que es un insulto; **I ~ed him a liar** le califiqué de mentiroso; **are you ~ing me a liar?** ¿dice Vd que yo soy un mentiroso?; **shall we ~ it £50?** ¿ponemos 50 libras?; **what time do you ~ this?** (*iro*) ¿qué hora crees que es?

(d) (*special uses*) *attention* llamar (*to* sobre); *meeting* convocar; *roll* pasar; *strike* declarar, convocar; *election* convocar; (*Bridge*) marcar; (*US*) *game* suspender; **to be ~ed to the Bar** (*Brit Jur*) recibirse de abogado; **to ~ sb as a witness** citar a uno como testigo; **he felt ~ed to do it** se creó llamado a hacerlo, se creó obligado a hacerlo; *V* **halt, name, question** *etc.*

③ VI **(a)** (*cry out*) llamar, dar voces, dar gritos.

▼ **(b)** (*Telec*) llamar; **who is it ~ing?** ¿quién llama?; ¿de parte de quién?; (*Rad*) **Madrid ~ing!** ¡aquí Radio Madrid!

(c) (*visit*) venir, hacer una visita.

◆ **call aside** VT llamar aparte.

◆ **call at** VT *house* visitar, pasar por; *port* hacer escala en.

◆ **call away** VT: **he was ~ed away** tuvo que salir (*or* partir); se vio obligado a ausentarse (*from* de); **he was ~ed away on business** tuvo que ir a atender un negocio.

▼◆ **call back** ① VT hacer volver; (*Telec*) llamar, volver a llamar.

▼ ② VI volver, regresar (*LAm*); (*Telec*) volver a llamar.

◆ **call down** VT **(a)** *blessings etc* pedir (*on* para); *curses* lanzar (*on* contra).
(b) (*US**) poner verde*.

◆ **call for** VT **(a)** *person* venir por, venir a recoger.
(b) (*demand, require*) pedir, requerir, exigir; *food* pedir; **to ~ for help** pedir socorro (a voces); **this ~s for firm measures** esto exige unas medidas contundentes.
(c) (*US*) pronosticar, prever.

◆ **call forth** VT sacar; *remark* inspirar; *protest* motivar, provocar.

◆ **call in** ① VT **(a)** hacer entrar; *expert etc* llamar, hacer intervenir, pedir la ayuda de; *V* **receiver**.
(b) *old notes* retirar de la circulación; *book, loan* pedir la devolución de.
② VI entrar, venir; dar un vistazo.

◆ **call off** VT cancelar, suspender; *meeting, strike* desconvocar; *search* dar por terminado, suspender, abandonar; *dog* llamar.

◆ **call out** ① VT *workers* llamar a la huelga; *rescue services* llamar.
② VI **(a)** gritar, dar voces. **(b)** (*fig*) **this ~s out for universal condemnation** esto pide a gritos la condena de todos.

◆ **call over** VT llamar; *names* pasar la lista de.

◆ **call round** VI: **to ~ round to see sb** ir de visita a casa de uno, ir a ver a uno; **I'll ~ round in the morning** pasaré por ahí por la mañana.

◆ **call together** VT convocar, reunir.

◆ **call up** VT **(a)** hacer subir.
(b) (*esp US: Telec*) llamar.
(c) *memory* evocar; traer a la memoria.
(d) (*Mil*) llamar a filas, llamar al servicio militar.

◆ **call (up)on** VT **(a)** (*visit*) *person* visitar, ir a ver.
(b) (*for a speech*) invitar a hablar; (*invoke*) invocar; **to ~ (up)on sb to do** (*invite*) convidar a uno a hacer; (*demand*) reclamar a uno que haga; **I now ~ (up)on Mr X to speak** ahora cedo la palabra al Sr. X; **to ~ (up)on sb for help** pedir ayuda a uno, acudir a uno pidiendo ayuda; **he ~ed (up)on the nation to be strong** hizo un llamamiento a la nación para que se mostrara fuerte.

callable ['kɔːləbəl] ADJ redimible, amortizable.

callback ['kɔːlbæk] N reclamación *f* (*de productos con defecto de origen*).

callbox ['kɔːlbɒks] N (*Brit*) cabina *f* telefónica.

callboy ['kɔːlbɔɪ] N (*Theat*) traspunte *m*; (*hotel*) botones *m*.

called-up ['kɔːldʌp] ADJ: **~ capital** capital *m* desembolsado.

caller ['kɔːlər] N visita *f*; (*Brit Telec*) comunicante *mf*; **~, please wait** espere por favor; **the first ~ at the shop** el primer cliente de la tienda.

callgirl ['kɔːlgɜːl] N prostituta *f*, chica *f* de cita.

calligrapher [kəˈlɪgrəfər] N calígrafo *m*, -a *f*.

calligraphic [ˌkælɪˈgræfɪk] ADJ caligráfico.

calligraphy [kəˈlɪgrəfɪ] N caligrafía *f*.

call-in ['kɔːlɪn] N (*also* **~ program**: *US*) (programa *m*) coloquio *m* (por teléfono).

calling ['kɔːlɪŋ] N vocación *f*, profesión *f*.

calling card ['kɔːlɪŋkɑːd] N (*US*) tarjeta *f* de visita, tarjeta *f* comercial.

callipers ['kælɪpəz] NPL calibrador *m*; (*Med*) soporte *m*, corrector *m*.

callisthenics [ˌkælɪsˈθenɪks] N SING calistenia *f*.

call letters ['kɔːlˌletəz] NPL (*US: Telec*) letras *fpl* de identificación, indicativo *m*.

call money ['kɔːlmʌnɪ] N dinero *m* a la vista.

call-number ['kɔːlˌnʌmbər] N número *m* de catalogación.

callosity [kæˈlɒsɪtɪ] N callo *m*, callosidad *f*.

callous ['kæləs] ADJ **(a)** insensible, cruel. **(b)** (*Med*) calloso.

calloused ['kæləsd] ADJ calloso, con callos.

callously ['kæləslɪ] ADV cruelmente.

callousness ['kæləsnɪs] N insensibilidad *f*, crueldad *f*.

callow ['kæləʊ] ADJ inexperto, novato; *youth* imberbe.

call-sign ['kɔːlsaɪn] N (*Rad*) (señal *f* de) llamada *f*.

call-signal ['kɔːlˌsɪgnəl] N (*Telec*) codigo *m* de llamada.

call-up ['kɔːlʌp] N (*of reserves*) movilización *f*; (*conscription*) servicio *m* militar obligatorio; (*act of calling*) llamamiento *m* (a filas); **~ papers** notificación *f* de llamada a filas.

callus ['kæləs] N callo *m*.

callused ['kæləst] ADJ *fingers, hands* encallecido, calloso.

calm [kɑːm] ① ADJ *person, mind* tranquilo, sosegado; *weather* calmoso, sin viento; *sea* liso, en calma; **to keep ~** no emocionarse, conservar la tranquilidad; **keep ~, everybody!** ¡todos tranquilos!; ¡no se pongan nerviosos!; **to grow ~** calmarse, sosegarse.
② N calma *f*, tranquilidad *f*; **the ~ before the storm** la calma antes de la tormenta.
③ VT (*also* **to ~ down**) calmar, tranquilizar.
④ VI (*also* **to ~ down**) calmarse, tranquilizarse; **~ down!** ¡cálmese!, (*to excited child*) ¡estáte quieto!
⑤ VR: **~ yourself!** ¡cálmese!

calming ['kɑːmɪŋ] ADJ calmante.

calmly ['kɑːmlɪ] ADV con calma, tranquilamente.

calmness ['kɑːmnɪs] N calma *f*, tranquilidad *f*, sosiego *m*.

Calor gas ['kæləˌgæs] ® N (*Brit*) butano *m*.

caloric [ˌkəˈlɒrɪk] ADJ calórico, térmico; **~ energy** energía *f* calórica, energía *f* térmica.

calorie ['kælərɪ] N caloría *f*; **~-conscious** cuidadoso con la línea.

calorific [ˌkælərˈɪfɪk] ADJ calorífico; **~ value** valor *m* calorífico.

calque [kælk] N calco *m* (*on* de).

calumniate [kəˈlʌmnɪeɪt] VT calumniar.

calumny ['kæləmnɪ] N calumnia *f*.

Calvados ['kælvəˌdɒs] N Calvados *m*.

Calvary ['kælvərɪ] N Calvario *m*.

calve [kɑːv] VI parir (*la vaca*).

calves [kɑːvz] NPL of **calf**[1] *and* **calf**[2].

Calvin ['kælvɪn] NM Calvino.

Calvinism ['kælvɪnɪzəm] N calvinismo *m*.

Calvinist ['kælvɪnɪst] ① ADJ calvinista.
② N calvinista *mf*.

Calvinistic [ˌkælvɪˈnɪstɪk] ADJ calvinista.

calypso [kəˈlɪpsəʊ] N calipso *m*.

calyx ['keɪlɪks] N, PL **calyces** ['keɪlɪsiːz] cáliz *m*.

CAM N ABBR of **computer-aided manufacture** fabricación *f* asistida por ordenador, FAO *f*.

cam[1] [kæm] N leva *f*.

cam[2]* [kæm] N ABBR of **camera**.

camaraderie [ˌkæməˈrɑːdərɪ] N compañerismo *m*, camaradería *f*.

camber ['kæmbər] ① N combadura *f*; convexidad *f*; (*of road*) peralte *m*.
② VT combar, arquear.
③ VI combarse, arquearse.

Cambodia [kæmˈbəʊdɪə] N Camboya *f*.

Cambodian [kæmˈbəʊdɪən] ① ADJ camboyano.
② N camboyano *m*, -a *f*.

cambric ['keɪmbrɪk] N batista *f*.

Cambs ABBR of **Cambridgeshire**.

camcorder ['kæmkɔːdər] N cámara *f* de vídeo y audio, cámcorder *m*.

came [keɪm] PRET of **come**.

camel ['kæməl] N camello *m*.

camel-hair ['kæməlˌheər] N, **camel's-hair** ['kæməlzˌheər] N pelo *m* de camello.

camellia [kəˈmiːlɪə] N camelia *f*.

cameo ['kæmɪəʊ] N camafeo *m*.

camera ['kæmərə] N **(a)** máquina *f* (fotográfica); (*Cine, TV*) cámara *f*; **~ crew** equipo *m* de cámara; **to be on ~** estar enfocado; **we shall be on ~ in 30 seconds** entramos en cámara dentro de 30 segundos. **(b)** (*Jur*) **in ~** en secreto, a puerta cerrada.

cameraman ['kæmərəmæn] N, PL **cameramen** ['kæmərəmen] cámara *m*.

camera-ready ['kæmərəˌredɪ] ADJ: **~ copy** material *m* preparado para la cámara.

camera-shy ['kæmərəˌʃaɪ] ADJ: **to be ~** cohibirse en presencia de la cámara.

camerawork ['kæmərəˌwɜːk] N (*Cine*) uso *m* de la cámara.

Cameroon [ˌkæməˈruːn] N Camerún *m*.

Cameroonian [ˌkæməˈruːnɪən] ① ADJ camerunés, camerunense.
② N camerunés *m*, -esa *f*, camerunense *mf*.

➤ LANGUAGE IN USE: **call: 2b** → 27.3, 27.5, 27.7 **3b** → 27.2, 27.3, 27.4, 27.5 **call back: 1** → 27.4, 27.6 **2** → 27.4

camiknickers ['kæmɪ,nɪkəz] NPL conjunto *m* de camiseta y bragas.
camisole ['kæmɪsəʊl] N camisola *f*.
camomile ['kæməʊmaɪl] N camomila *f*; ~ **tea** (infusión *f* de) manzanilla *f*.
camouflage ['kæməflɑ:ʒ] 1 N camuflaje *m*.
2 VT camuflar.
camp[1] [kæmp] 1 N (a) campamento *m*, campo *m*; **to make ~, to pitch ~** poner el campamento, armar la tienda, acampar(se); **to break ~, to strike ~** levantar el campamento.
(b) (*Pol etc*) grupo *m*, facción *f*; **to have a foot in both ~s** tener intereses en ambos partidos (*etc*).
2 VI acampar(se); (*) alojarse temporalmente; **to go ~ing** hacer camping, ir a veranear (*etc*) con la tienda; **to ~ out on the beach** pasar la noche en la playa.
camp[2]* [kæmp] 1 ADJ (a) (*affected*) afectado (y divertido), exagerado; (*intencionadamente*) teatral; sensible, elegante; (*Liter etc*) afectado, amanerado.
(b) (*effeminate*) afeminado; (*openly gay*) (abiertamente) homosexual.
2 N (a) afectación *f* divertida, exageración *f*, teatralidad *f* intencionada; (*Liter etc*) amaneramiento *m*.
(b) afeminación *f*; homosexualidad *f* (abierta).
3 VT: **to ~ it up** parodiarse a sí mismo; comportarse ostentosamente de modo raro; guasearse, hacer el tonto.
campaign [kæm'peɪn] 1 N campaña *f*; ~ **trail** recorrido *m* electoral; ~ **worker** colaborador *m*, -ora *f* en una campaña política.
2 VI (*Mil*) luchar; servir; hacer campaña; **to ~ against** hacer campaña en contra de; **to ~ for** hacer campaña a favor de.
campaigner [kæm'peɪnəʳ] N (*fig*) paladín *m*, partidario *m*, -a *f* (for de), propagandista *mf* (for por); **old ~** veterano *m*, -a *f*.
campanile [,kæmpə'ni:lɪ] N campanario *m*.
campanologist [,kæmpə'nɒlədʒɪst] N campanólogo *m*, -a *f*.
campanology [,kæmpə'nɒlədʒɪ] N campanología *f*.
campbed ['kæmp'bed] N (*Brit*) cama *f* de campaña, cama *f* plegable, catre *m* (*LAm*).
camp-chair ['kæmp'tʃeəʳ] N silla *f* plegadiza.
camper ['kæmpə] N (a) (*person*) campista *mf*. (b) (*Aut: esp US*) autocaravana *f*, campero *m* (*LAm*).
campfire ['kæmp'faɪə] N hoguera *f* de campamento; (*of scouts*) reunión *f* alrededor de la hoguera.
camp-follower ['kæmp,fɒləʊəʳ] N (*fig*) simpatizante *mf*; (*Mil†: prostitute*) prostituta *f*; (*civilian worker*) trabajador *m* civil.
campground ['kæmpgraʊnd] N (*US*) cámping *m*.
camphor ['kæmfəʳ] N alcanfor *m*.
camphorated ['kæmfəreɪtɪd] ADJ alcanforado.
camping ['kæmpɪŋ] N cámping *m*.
Camping gas ['kæmpɪŋ,gæs] ® N (*Brit: gas*) gas *m* butano; (*US: stove*) cámping gas ® *m*.
camping-ground ['kæmpɪŋgraʊnd] N, **camping-site** ['kæmpɪŋsaɪt] N (terreno *m* de) cámping *m*.
camping-van ['kæmpɪŋ,væn] N camioneta-casa *f*.
campion ['kæmpɪən] N colleja *f*.
campsite ['kæmpsaɪt] N cámping *m*; campamento *m*.
camp-stool ['kæmpstu:l] N taburete *m* plegable.
camp-stove ['kæmp'stəʊv] N hornillo *m* de campista.
campus ['kæmpəs] N campus *m*.
CAMRA ['kæmrə] (*Brit*) ABBR of **Campaign for Real Ale** organización de defensa y promoción de la cerveza tradicional.
camshaft ['kæmʃɑ:ft] N árbol *m* de levas.
▼ **can**[1] [kæn] (*irr*: CONDITIONAL AND PRET **could**; *defective*) VI (a) (*be able to*) poder; **if I ~** si puedo; **we can't go swimming today** hoy no podemos ir a bañarnos; **that cannot be!** ¡eso no puede ser!, ¡es imposible!; **he will do all he ~** hará lo posible (to + *infin* por + *infin*); **I could have screamed** estuve para lanzar un grito; **it could have been a wolf** pudo ser un lobo; **I reckon you could have got a job last year** creo que podías obtener un trabajo el año pasado; **'have another helping'** — **'I really couldn't'** '¿otra ración?' — 'no puedo'.
(b) (*with verbs of perception, not translated*) **I ~ hear it** lo oigo; **I couldn't see it anywhere** no lo veía en ninguna parte; **I can't understand why** no comprendo por qué.
▼ (c) (*of acquired skills, know how to*) saber, *eg* ~ **you swim?** ¿sabes nadar?
▼ (d) (*have permission to*) poder, *eg* ~ **I go now?** ¿puedo irme ahora?
▼ (e) (*with emphasis*) **you cannot be serious!** ¿lo dices en serio?; **but he can't be dead!** ¡pero no es posible que esté muerto!; **he can't possibly have been wrong** no es posible que se haya equivocado; **he can't have said that** no puede haber dicho eso; **you could have told me!** ¡podías habérmelo dicho!; **how ~ you say that?** ¿cómo te atreves a decir eso?; **where ~ she be?** ¿dónde demonios puede estar?
(f) (*comparisons*) **I'm doing it as well as I ~** lo hago lo mejor que puedo; **as cheap as ~ be** lo más barato posible; **as big as big ~ be**

lo más grande posible; *see also* ABLE, CAN .
can[2] [kæn] 1 N lata *f*, bote *m*; (*for petrol etc*) bidón *m*; (*of film*) lata *f*, cartucho *m*; (*US: toilet*) wáter *m*; (*US: prison*) chirona: *f*; (*US: buttocks*) culo: *m*; ~ **of worms** problema *m* (*etc*) peliagudo; **it's in the ~** está en el bote*; (**to be left**) **to carry the ~** pagar el pato*; *ver también* TOILET .
2 VT conservar en lata; enlatar, envasar; (*US:*) *employee* despedir; ~ **it!** (*US:*) ¡cállate!; *see also* **canned**.
Canaan ['keɪnən] N Canaán *m*.
Canaanite ['keɪnənaɪt] N canaanita *mf*.
Canada ['kænədə] N el Canadá.
Canadian [kə'neɪdɪən] 1 ADJ canadiense.
2 N canadiense *mf*.
canal [kə'næl] N canal *m*; (**alimentary ~**) tubo *m* digestivo; **the C~ Zone** (*Brit: Suez*) la zona del Canal de Suez; (*US: Panama*) la zona del Canal de Panamá.
canalization [,kænəlaɪ'zeɪʃən] N canalización *f*.
canalize ['kænəlaɪz] VT canalizar.
canapé ['kænəpeɪ] N (*Culin*) canapé *m*.
canard [kæ'nɑ:d] N filfa *f*, bulo *m*, noticia *f* falsa.
Canaries [kə'neərɪz] NPL Las Canarias.
canary [kə'neərɪ] N canario *m*.
Canary Islands [kə'neərɪ,aɪləndz] NPL Islas *fpl* Canarias.
canary seed [kə'neərɪ,si:d] N alpiste *m*.
canary yellow [kə,neərɪ'jeləʊ] ADJ amarillo canario.
canasta [kə'næstə] N canasta *f*.
Canberra ['kænbərə] N Canberra *f*.
cancan ['kænkæn] N cancán *m*.
▼ **cancel** ['kænsəl] 1 VT cancelar; suprimir; *flight, holiday, party* suspender; *permission etc* retirar; *stamp* matar, inutilizar; **they ~ each other out** se anulan mutuamente.
2 VI (*Math*) **to ~ out** destruirse, anularse.
cancel key ['kænsəlki:] N teclado *m* de anulación.
cancellation [,kænsə'leɪʃən] N cancelación *f*; supresión *f*; suspensión *f*; el retirar; (*Post: mark*) matasellos *m*, (*act*) inutilización *f*.
Cancer ['kænsəʳ] N (*Zodiac*) Cáncer *m*.
cancer ['kænsəʳ] N cáncer *m*; ~ **causing** cancerígeno; ~ **patient** canceroso *m*, -a *f*; ~ **research** investigación *f* del cáncer; ~ **specialist** cancerólogo *m*, -a *f*, oncólogo *m*, -a *f*; ~ **stick** (*Brit:*) pito* *m*, fumata: *m*.
cancerous ['kænsərəs] ADJ canceroso; **to become ~** cancerarse.
candelabra [,kændɪ'lɑ:brə] N candelabro *m*.
C and F (*Comm*) ABBR of **Cost and Freight** costo *m* y flete.
candid ['kændɪd] ADJ franco, sincero, abierto; ~ **camera** cámara *f* indiscreta; **to be quite ~** hablando con franqueza.
candida ['kændɪdə] N (*Med*) afta *f*.
candidacy ['kændɪdəsɪ] N (*esp US*) candidatura *f*.
candidate ['kændɪdeɪt] N (*applicant*) aspirante *mf* (for a), solicitante *mf* (for de); (*for election, examinee, Pol, etc*) candidato *m*, -a *f* (for a); (*in competitive exams*) opositor *m*, -ora *f* (for a post a un puesto).
candidature ['kændɪdətʃəʳ] N (*Brit*) candidatura *f*.
candidly ['kændɪdlɪ] ADV francamente, con franqueza.
candidness ['kændɪdnɪs] N franqueza *f*.
candied ['kændɪd] ADJ azucarado; ~ **fruits** frutas *fpl* escarchadas; ~ **peel** piel *f* almibarada, cascas *fpl* almibaradas.
candle ['kændl] N vela *f*, cera *f* (*And*); candela *f*; (*Eccl*) cirio *m*; **to burn the ~ at both ends** consumir la vida, hacer de la noche día; **you can't hold a ~ to him** no llegas a la suela de su zapato.
candle-end ['kændl,end] N cabo *m* de vela.
candle-grease ['kændlgri:s] N cera *f* derretida.
candle holder ['kændl'həʊldəʳ] N = **candlestick**.
candlelight ['kændllaɪt] N luz *f* de una vela; **by ~** a la luz de una vela.
candlelit ['kændllɪt] ADJ alumbrado por velas; **a ~ supper for two** una cena para dos con velas.
Candlemas ['kændlmæs] N Candelaria *f* (2 febrero).
candlepower ['kændl,paʊəʳ] N bujía *f*.
candlestick ['kændlstɪk] N (*single*) candelero *m*; (*low*) palmatoria *f*; (*large, ornamental*) candelabro *m*; (*processional*) cirial *m*.
candlewick ['kændlwɪk] N (a) pabilo *m*, mecha *f* (de vela). (b) (*cloth*) tela *f* de algodón afelpada, chenille *f*.
can-do[*] [,kæn'du:] ADJ (*US*) dinámico.
candour, (*US*) **candor** ['kændəʳ] N franqueza *f*.
candy ['kændɪ] 1 N azúcar *m* cande; (*US*) caramelo *m*, bombón *m*, dulce *m*, golosina *f* (*LAm*).
2 VT azucarar, garapiñar.
candy bar ['kændɪ,bɑ:ʳ] N (*US*) barrita *f* de caramelo, chocolatina *f*.
candy-floss ['kændɪflɒs] N (*Brit*) algodón *m* azucarado.
candy store ['kændɪstɔ:ʳ] N (*US*) bombonería *f*, confitería *f*.
candy-striped ['kændɪ,straɪpt] ADJ a rayas multicolores.
cane [keɪn] 1 N (*Bot*) caña *f*; (*sugar~*) caña *f* de azúcar; (*stick*) bastón *m*; (*for punishment*) palmeta *f*, vara *f*; (*in furnishings*) mimbre *m* or

f; **~ sugar** azúcar *m* de caña.

[2] VT castigar con palmeta, azotar.

canine ['kænaɪn] [1] ADJ canino; **~ tooth** diente *m* canino, colmillo *m*.
[2] N (*dog*) perro *m*, can *m*; (*tooth*) canino *m*, colmillo *m*.

caning ['keɪnɪŋ] N castigo *m* con palmeta; **to give sb a ~** castigar a uno con la palmeta, (*fig*) dar una paliza a uno.

canister ['kænɪstər] N lata *f*, bote *m*; (*of gas*) bombona *f*; (*smoke-bomb*) bote *m* (de humo).

canker ['kæŋkər] [1] N (*Med*) llaga *f* gangrenosa; úlcera *f* en la boca; (*Bot*) cancro *m*; (*fig*) cáncer *m*.
[2] VT ulcerar; (*fig*) corromper.
[3] VI ulcerarse; (*fig*) corromperse.

cankerous ['kæŋkərəs] ADJ ulceroso.

cannabis ['kænəbɪs] N (*Bot*) cáñamo *m* (índico); (*drug*) canabis *m*.

canned ['kænd] ADJ *food* en lata, de lata; *music* grabado, enlatado; **~ foods** conservas *fpl* alimenticias; **to be ~:** estar ajumado*, estar tomado* (*LAm*).

cannelloni [ˌkænɪ'ləʊnɪ] NPL canelones *mpl*.

cannery ['kænərɪ] N fábrica *f* de conservas.

cannibal ['kænɪbəl] [1] ADJ antropófago.
[2] N caníbal *mf*, antropófago *m*.

cannibalism ['kænɪbəlɪzəm] N canibalismo *m*.

cannibalistic [ˌkænɪbə'lɪstɪk] ADJ canibalesco.

cannibalization [ˌkænɪbəlaɪ'zeɪʃən] N (*fig: of machine, product*) canibalización *f*.

cannibalize ['kænɪbəlaɪz] VT (*fig*) canibalizar.

canning ['kænɪŋ] N enlatado *m*; **~ factory** fábrica *f* de conservas; **~ industry** industria *f* conservera.

cannon ['kænən] [1] N (**a**) cañón *m*; (*collectively*) artillería *f*. (**b**) (*Brit Billiards*) carambola *f*.
[2] VI (*Brit Billiards*) hacer carambola.

◆**cannon into** VT chocar violentamente con.

◆**cannon off** VT rebotar contra.

cannonade [ˌkænə'neɪd] N cañoneo *m*.

cannonball ['kænənbɔːl] N bala *f* de cañón.

cannon-fodder ['kænən,fɒdər] N carne *f* de cañón.

cannon-shot ['kænənʃɒt] N cañonazo *m*, tiro *m* de cañón; (*ammunition*) bala *f* de cañón; **within ~** al alcance de un cañón.

cannot ['kænɒt] *negative of* **can**[1].

canny ['kænɪ] ADJ (*esp Scot*) astuto.

canoe [kə'nuː] [1] N canoa *f*, chalupa *f* (*LAm*); (*sporting*) piragua *f*.
[2] VI ir en canoa.

canoeing [kə'nuːɪŋ] N piragüismo *m*.

canoeist [kə'nuːɪst] N piragüista *mf*.

canon ['kænən] N (**a**) canon *m*; criterio *m*; **~ law** derecho *m* canónico.
(**b**) (*person*) canónigo *m*.

canonical [kə'nɒnɪkəl] ADJ canónico.

canonization [ˌkænənaɪ'zeɪʃən] N canonización *f*.

canonize ['kænənaɪz] VT canonizar.

canonry ['kænənrɪ] N canonjía *f*.

canoodle* [kə'nuːdl] VI besuquearse*.

can-opener ['kænəʊpnər] N abrelatas *m*.

canopy ['kænəpɪ] N dosel *m*, toldo *m*; (*over bed*) cielo *m*; (*Archit*) baldaquín *m*; (*over tomb*) doselete *m*; **the ~ of heaven** la bóveda celeste.

cant[1] [kænt] [1] N (*slope*) inclinación *f*, sesgo *m*; (*of crystal etc*) bisel *m*.
[2] VT inclinar, sesgar.
[3] VI inclinarse, ladearse.

◆**cant over** VI volcar.

cant[2] [kænt] [1] N (**a**) (*special language*) jerga *f*. (**b**) (*hypocritical talk*) hipocresías *fpl*, camándulas *fpl*; tópicos *mpl*; gazmoñería *f*.
[2] VI camandulear.

can't [kɑːnt] = **cannot**.

Cantab [kæn'tæb] ADJ (*Brit*) ABBR of **Cantabrigiensis**, *of* **Cambridge**.

Cantabrian [kæn'tæbrɪən] ADJ cantábrico.

cantaloup ['kæntəluːp] N cantalupo *m*.

cantankerous [kæn'tæŋkərəs] ADJ arisco, malhumorado, irritable.

cantata [kæn'tɑːtə] N cantata *f*.

canteen [kæn'tiːn] N (**a**) (*restaurant*) cantina *f*, comedor *m*. (**b**) (*bottle*) cantimplora *f*. (**c**) (*of cutlery*) juego *m*.

canter ['kæntər] [1] N medio galope *m*; **to go for a ~** pasearse a caballo; **to win in a ~** (*Brit fig*) ganar fácilmente.
[2] VI ir a medio galope.

Canterbury ['kæntəbərɪ] N Cantórbery *m*; **~ Tales** Cuentos *mpl* de Cantórbery.

cantharides [kæn'θærɪdiːz] NPL polvo *m* de cantárida.

canticle ['kæntɪkl] N cántico *m*; **the C~s** el Cantar de los Cantares.

cantilever ['kæntɪliːvər] N viga *f* voladiza; **~ bridge** puente *m* voladizo.

canting ['kæntɪŋ] ADJ hipócrita.

canto ['kæntəʊ] N canto *m*.

canton ['kæntɒn] N cantón *m*.

cantonal ['kæntənl] ADJ cantonal.

Cantonese [ˌkæntə'niːz] [1] ADJ cantonés.
[2] N (**a**) cantonés *m*, -esa *f*. (**b**) (*Ling*) cantonés *m*.

cantonment [kən'tuːnmənt] N acantonamiento *m*.

Canuck: [kə'nʌk] N (*a Canadian, pej a French Canadian*) canuck *mf*.

Canute [kə'njuːt] NM Canuto.

canvas ['kænvəs] N (**a**) lona *f*; (*Naut*) velamen *m*, velas *fpl*; **~ chair** silla *f* de lona; **~ shoes** calzado *m* de lona; (*rope-soled*) alpargatas *fpl*; **under ~** en tiendas de campaña. (**b**) (*Art*) lienzo *m*.

canvass ['kænvəs] [1] N (**a**) (*inquiry*) sondeo *m*.
(**b**) (*for votes*) solicitación *f*; **to make a door-to-door ~** ir solicitando votos de puerta en puerta.
[2] VT (**a**) *possibility, question* discutir, hacer que se discuta, someter a una discusión pública.
(**b**) *opinion* sondear; hacer una encuesta de.
(**c**) *votes* solicitar; *voter* solicitar el voto de; *district* hacer campaña en; *orders* solicitar; *purchaser* solicitar pedidos de.
(**d**) (*US*) *votes* escudriñar.
[3] VI: **to ~ for** solicitar votos por, hacer campaña a favor de; **to go out ~ing** salir a solicitar votos.

canvasser ['kænvəsər] N (*Pol*) representante *mf* electoral; (*Comm*) corredor *m*, -ora *f*.

canvassing ['kænvəsɪŋ] N solicitación *f* (de votos).

canyon ['kænjən] N cañón *m*.

CAP N ABBR of **Common Agricultural Policy** Política *f* Agraria Común, PAC *f*.

cap [kæp] [1] N (**a**) (*hat*) gorra *f*; (*Univ*) bonete *m*; (*servant's etc*) cofia *f*; **~ and gown** toga *f* y bonete; **to come ~ in hand to sb** venir a uno con el sombrero en la mano; **if the ~ fits wear it** el que se pica ajos come; **to put on one's thinking ~** calarse las gafas, ponerse a pensar; **to set one's ~ at sb** proponerse conquistar a uno; **he's got his ~ for England, he's an England ~** (*Brit*) es miembro de la selección nacional inglesa.
(**b**) (*lid*) tapa *f*, tapón *m*; (*of gun*) cápsula *f*; (*of pen*) capuchón *m*; (*on chimney*) caballete *m*; (*Mech*) casquete *m*; (*contraceptive*) diafragma *m*.
(**c**) (*percussion ~*) cápsula *f* (fulminante).
[2] VT (**a**) *hill etc* coronar; *work* terminar, poner remate a; *oil-well* encapuchar, tapar.
(**b**) (*surpass*) exceder, superar; **see if you can ~ that story** a ver si cuentas un chiste mejor que ése; **I can ~ that** yo sé algo mejor sobre el mismo asunto; **to ~ it all** para colmo de desgracias.
(**c**) *expenditure* restringir, imponer un límite a; *council etc* restringir los gastos de, imponer un límite presupuestario a.
(**d**) **to be ~ped for Ruritania** jugar en el equipo nacional de Ruritania.

cap. (*Typ*) ABBR of **capital** mayúscula *f*, may.

capability [ˌkeɪpə'bɪlɪtɪ] N capacidad *f*, aptitud *f*.

capable ['keɪpəbl] ADJ capaz, competente; **to be ~ of** ser capaz de; **it's ~ of some improvement** se puede mejorar en algo.

capably ['keɪpəblɪ] ADV competentemente.

capacious [kə'peɪʃəs] ADJ *room* grande, extenso, espacioso; *container* de mucha cabida, grande, capaz; *dress* ancho, holgado.

capacitance [kə'pæsɪtəns] N (*Elec*) capacitancia *f*.

capacitor [kə'pæsɪtər] N capacitor *m*.

▼**capacity** [kə'pæsɪtɪ] N (**a**) (*ability to contain*) capacidad *f*; cabida *f*; (*Aut*) cilindrada *f*; (*carrying ~*) capacidad *f* de cargo; **filled to ~** totalmente lleno, lleno a rebosar; **~ audience** lleno *m*; **~ booking** reserva *f* total; **there was a ~ crowd** hubo un lleno completo; **what is the ~ of this hall?** ¿cuántos caben en esta sala?; **to work at full ~** dar el pleno rendimiento.
▼(**b**) (*ability*) capacidad *f*; aptitud *f*; **her capacities** su talento, su aptitud; **her ~ for research** su aptitud para la investigación; **it is beyond my capacities now** supera ya a mis fuerzas; **to the extent of my ~** hasta donde yo pueda, en la medida de mis fuerzas.
(**c**) (*status*) calidad *f*; **in my ~ as treasurer** en mi calidad de tesorero, como tesorero que soy; **in what ~ were you there?** ¿en calidad de qué estabas allí?

caparison [kə'pærɪsn] [1] N caparazón *m*, gualdrapa *f*; (*of person*) vestido *m* rico, galas *fpl*; (*harness etc*) equipo *m*.
[2] VT engualdrapar; **gaily ~ed** brillantemente enjaezado, (*fig*) brillantemente vestido.

cape[1] [keɪp] N (*Geog*) cabo *m*, promontorio *m*; **the C~** (*esp*) el Cabo de Buena Esperanza; **~ honeysuckle** madreselva *f* siempreviva, bignonia *f* del Cabo.

cape[2] [keɪp] N (*cloak*) capa *f*; (*short*) capotillo *m*, esclavina *f*; (*oilskin*) chubasquero *m*; (*Taur*) capote *m*.

Cape Canaveral [ˌkeɪp'kænəvərəl] N Cabo *m* Cañaveral.

Cape Coloureds ['keɪp'kʌlədz] NPL *personas de padres racialmente mixtos* (*que habitan en la provincia del Cabo*).

Cape Horn ['keɪp'hɔːn] N Cabo *m* de Hornos.

Cape of Good Hope ['keɪpəvgʊd'həʊp] N Cabo *m* de Buena Esperanza.

Cape Province ['keɪp'prɒvɪns] N Provincia f del Cabo.

caper¹ ['keɪpəʳ] N (*Bot*) alcaparra f.

caper² ['keɪpəʳ] ① N (a) (*of horse*) cabriola f; **to cut ~s** hacer cabriolas. (b) (*fig*) (*prank*) travesura f; (*) lío m, embrollo m; **that was quite a ~** eso sí que fue un número*; **I don't bother with taxes and all that ~** no me molesto con contribuciones y cosas así; **how did your Spanish ~ go?** ¿qué tal el viajecito por España?

② VI (a) (*horse*) hacer cabriolas; (*other animal*) brincar, corcovear; (*child*) juguetear, correr y brincar; **to ~ about** brincar, juguetear. (b) (*) ir, correr; **he went ~ing off to Paris** se marchó a París como si tal cosa.

capercaillie [ˌkæpəˈkeɪlɪ] N urogallo m.

Cape Town ['keɪptaʊn] N El Cabo, Ciudad f del Cabo.

Cape Verde Islands ['keɪp'vɜːd'aɪləndz] NPL Islas fpl de Cabo Verde.

capful ['kæpfʊl] N: **one ~ to 4 litres of water** un tapón por cada cuatro litros de agua.

capillarity [ˌkæpɪˈlærɪtɪ] N capilaridad f.

capillary [kəˈpɪlərɪ] ① ADJ capilar.
② N vaso m capilar.

capital ['kæpɪtl] ① ADJ (a) (*Jur*) capital; **~ offence** delito m capital; **~ punishment** pena f de muerte; **~ sentence** condena f a la pena de muerte. (b) (*essential*) capital, primordial; **of ~ importance** de importancia primordial. (c) (*chief*) capital; **~ city** capital f; **~ letter** mayúscula f; **~ Q** Q f mayúscula; **~ ship** acorazado m; **it was farce with a ~ F** fue una farsa con F mayúscula. (d) (*) magnífico, estupendo; **~!** ¡magnífico!

② N (a) (*money*) capital m; **~ account** (*Fin, Econ etc*) cuenta f de capital; **~ allowances** amortización fpl; **~ assets** activo m fijo, activo m inmovilizado; **~ expenditure** inversiones fpl; **~ gain(s)** plusvalía f; **~ gains tax** impuesto m sobre la plusvalía; **~ goods** bienes mpl de equipo, bienes mpl de capital; **~ intensive** intensivo de capital; **~ investment** inversión f de capital; **~ levy** impuesto m sobre el capital; **~ outlay** desembolso m de capital; **~ reserves** reservas fpl de capital; **~ spending** capital m adquisitivo; **~ stock** (*capital*) capital m social, (*shares*) acciones fpl de capital; **~ sum** capital m; **~ transfer tax** impuesto m sobre plusvalía de cesión; **to make ~ out of** (*fig*) aprovechar, sacar partido de. (b) (*city*) capital f. (c) (*Archit*) capitel m. (d) (*Typ*) mayúscula f; **~s** (*large*) versales fpl, (*small*) versalitas fpl; **please write in ~s** escribir en letras de imprenta.

capitalism ['kæpɪtəlɪzəm] N capitalismo m.

capitalist ['kæpɪtəlɪst] ① ADJ capitalista.
② N capitalista mf.

capitalistic [ˌkæpɪtəˈlɪstɪk] ADJ capitalista.

capitalization [kəˌpɪtəlaɪˈzeɪʃən] N capitalización f.

capitalize [kəˈpɪtəlaɪz] ① VT (a) capitalizar. (b) (*Typ*) *word* escribir (*or* imprimir) con mayúscula; *letter* convertir en mayúscula.
② VI: **to ~ on** aprovechar, sacar partido de, capitalizar.

capitation [ˌkæpɪˈteɪʃən] N capitación f; impuesto m por cabeza; **~ grant** subvención f por capitación.

Capitol ['kæpɪtɒl] N (*US*) Capitolio m.

ⓘ El Capitolio (Capitol) es el edificio en el que se reúne el Congreso de los Estados Unidos (Congress), situado en la ciudad de Washington. Al estar situado en la colina llamada Capitol Hill, también se suele hacer referencia a él con ese nombre en los medios de comunicación.
Por otra parte, a menudo se llama Capitol, por extensión, al edificio en el que tienen lugar las sesiones parlamentarias de la cámara de representantes de muchos estados.

capitulate [kəˈpɪtjʊleɪt] VI capitular (*to* ante), rendirse, entregarse (*to* a); (*fig*) ceder, conformarse.

capitulation [kəˌpɪtjʊˈleɪʃən] N capitulación f, rendición f.

capon ['keɪpən] N capón m.

cappuccino [ˌkæpəˈtʃiːnəʊ] N capuchino m.

caprice [kəˈpriːs] N capricho m.

capricious [kəˈprɪʃəs] ADJ caprichoso, caprichudo.

capriciously [kəˈprɪʃəslɪ] ADV caprichosamente.

Capricorn ['kæprɪkɔːn] N (*Zodiac*) Capricornio m.

caps [kæps] NPL (*Typ*) ABBR *of* **capital letters** mayúsculas fpl, may.

capsicum ['kæpsɪkəm] N pimiento m.

capsize [kæp'saɪz] ① VT volcar; (*Naut*) hacer zozobrar, tumbar.
② VI volcarse, dar una vuelta de campana; (*Naut*) zozobrar.

capstan ['kæpstən] N cabrestante m.

capsule ['kæpsjuːl] N (*all senses*) cápsula f.

Capt. ABBR *of* **Captain** capitán m.

captain ['kæptɪn] ① N capitán m; (*Sport*) capitán m, -ana f; **~ of industry** gran industrial m, magnate m.

② VT capitanear, ser el capitán de; **a team ~ed by Grace** un equipo capitaneado por Grace.

captaincy ['kæptənsɪ] N capitanía f.

caption ['kæpʃən] ① N (*heading*) encabezamiento m, título m; (*to cartoon etc*) leyenda f, pie m; (*to photo*) pie m de foto; (*in film*) subtítulo m.
② VT titular; poner un pie a.

captious ['kæpʃəs] ADJ criticón, reparón.

captivate ['kæptɪveɪt] VT cautivar, encantar.

captivating ['kæptɪveɪtɪŋ] ADJ cautivante, encantador, delicioso.

captive ['kæptɪv] ① ADJ cautivo; **~ audience** público m cautivo; **~ balloon** globo m cautivo; **~ market** mercado m cautivo.
② N cautivo m, -a f.

captivity [kæpˈtɪvɪtɪ] N cautiverio m; cautividad f; **bred in ~** criado en cautividad.

captor ['kæptəʳ] N apresador m, -ora f.

capture ['kæptʃəʳ] ① N (a) (*act*) apresamiento m, captura f; (*of city etc*) toma f, conquista f; (*Comput*) captura f, recogida f. (b) (*thing captured*) presa f.
② VT *person* prender; apresar; *specimen etc* capturar; *animal* coger; *city etc* tomar, conquistar; (*Comm*) *market* conquistar, acaparar; (*fig*) captar; *attention* llamar, atraer; *interest* ocupar; (*Art etc*) captar, reproducir, representar fielmente; (*Comput*) capturar, recoger.

capuchin ['kæpjʊʃɪn] N (a) (*cowl*) capucho m. (b) (*Zool*) mono m capuchino. (c) **C~** (*Eccl*) capuchino m.

car [kɑːʳ] N (*Aut*) coche m, automóvil m, carro m (*LAm*), máquina f (*Carib*); (*tramcar*) tranvía m; (*US Rail*) vagón m, coche m; (*of cable railway*) coche m; (*of lift*) caja f; (*of balloon etc*) barquilla f; **~ accident** accidente m de circulación; **~ allowance** extra m por uso de coche propio; **~ boot sale** (*Brit*) mercadillo que se organiza en un aparcamiento y en el que se exponen las mercancías en el maletero del coche; **~ industry** industria f del automóvil; **~ insurance** seguro m del automóvil; **~ journey** viaje m en coche; **~ licence** permiso m de circulación; **~ number** (*Brit*) matrícula f; **~ radio** radio f de coche, autorradio f; **~ rental** alquiler m de coches; **~ sleeper** (*Rail*) tren coche-cama que transporta automóviles; **~ worker** trabajador m, -ora f de la industria del automóvil.

ⓘ En los mercadillos británicos llamados car boot sales la gente vende todo tipo de objetos usados de los que quiere deshacerse, como ropa, muebles, libros, etc, que exhiben en los maleteros de sus coches.
Normalmente tienen lugar en aparcamientos u otros espacios abiertos y los propietarios de los vehículos han de pagar una pequeña tarifa por aparcar. Los mercadillos más importantes atraen también a comerciantes y en ellos se venden tanto artículos usados como nuevos. En otras ocasiones se organizan para recaudar dinero con fines benéficos.

Caracas [kəˈrækəs] N Caracas m.

carafe [kəˈræf] N jarro m.

caramel ['kærəməl] N caramelo m; azúcar m quemado; **~ cream** flan m.

caramelize ['kærəməlaɪz] ① VT caramelizar.
② VI caramelizarse.

carapace ['kærəpeɪs] N carapacho m.

carat ['kærət] N quilate m; **18-~ gold** oro m de 18 quilates.

caravan ['kærəvæn] ① N (a) (*gipsies'*) carricoche m, carromato m; (*Brit Aut*) caravana f, remolque m, tráiler m (*LAm*); (*Aut: camper*) autocaravana f; (*of camels*) caravana f; **~ site** cámping m para caravanas. (b) (*US*) = **convoy 1**.
② VI: **to go ~ing** ir de vacaciones en caravana, viajar en caravana.

caravanette [ˌkærəvəˈnet] N (*Brit*) caravana f pequeña, rulota f pequeña.

caravanserai, caravansary [ˌkærəˈvænsəraɪ, ˌkærəˈvænsəraɪ] N caravasar m.

caravel ['kærəvel] N carabela f.

caraway ['kærəweɪ] N alcaravea f; **~ seed** carvi m.

carbide ['kɑːbaɪd] N carburo m.

carbine ['kɑːbaɪn] N carabina f.

carbohydrate ['kɑːbəʊˈhaɪdreɪt] N hidrato m de carbono; (*starch in food*) fécula f.

carbolic [kɑːˈbɒlɪk] ADJ: **~ acid** ácido m carbólico, ácido m fénico.

car-bomb ['kɑːˌbɒm] N coche-bomba m.

carbon ['kɑːbən] N (*Chem*) carbono m; (*Elec, paper*) carbón m; **~ copy** copia f al carbón; **he's a ~ copy of my uncle** está calcado a mi tío; **~-date** datar mediante la prueba del carbono 14; **~ dating** datación f por C-14; **~ dioxide** dióxido m de carbono; **~ fibre** fibra f de carbono; **~ monoxide** monóxido m de carbono; **~ ribbon** cinta f mecanográfica de carbón; **~ tetrachloride** tetracloruro m de carbono.

carbonaceous [ˌkɑːbəˈneɪʃəs] ADJ carbonoso.

carbonate ['kɑːbənɪt] N carbonato m.

carbonated ['kɑːbəneɪtɪd] ADJ: ~ **drink** gaseosa *f*; ~ **water** agua *f* mineral.

carbonic [kɑː'bɒnɪk] ADJ: ~ **acid** ácido *m* carbónico.

carboniferous [ˌkɑːbə'nɪfərəs] ADJ carbonífero.

carbonization [ˌkɑːbənaɪ'zeɪʃən] N carbonización *f*.

carbonize ['kɑːbənaɪz] [1] VT carbonizar.
[2] VI carbonizarse.

carbonless paper ['kɑːbənlɪs'peɪpəʳ] N papel *m* autocopiativo.

carbon-paper ['kɑːbən,peɪpəʳ] N papel *m* carbón, papel *m* carbónico (*LAm*).

carborundum [ˌkɑːbə'rʌndəm] N carborundo *m*.

carboy ['kɑːbɔɪ] N bombona *f*, garrafón *m*, damajuana *f*.

carbuncle ['kɑːbʌŋkl] N **(a)** (*ruby*) carbúnculo *m*, carbunco *m*. **(b)** (*Med*) carbunc(l)o *m*, grano *m*.

carburation [ˌkɑːbjʊ'reɪʃən] N carburación *f*.

carburettor, (*US*) **carburetor** [ˌkɑːbjʊ'retəʳ] N carburador *m*.

carcass ['kɑːkəs] N cadáver *m* de animal, res *f* muerta; (*frame*) armazón *f*; (*) cuerpo *m*.

car-chase ['kɑːtʃeɪs] N persecución *f* de (*or* por) un coche; **there followed a ~ along the motorway** se persiguió luego al coche por la autopista.

carcinogen [kɑː'sɪnədʒen] N carcinógeno *m*.

carcinogenic [ˌkɑːsɪnə'dʒenɪk] ADJ cancerígeno, carcinogénico.

carcinoma [ˌkɑːsɪ'nəʊmə] N, PL **carcinomas** *or* **carcinomata** [ˌkɑːsɪ'nəʊmətə] carcinoma *m*.

card¹ [kɑːd] (*Tech*) [1] N carda *f*.
[2] VT cardar.

card² [kɑːd] [1] N **(a)** (*playing ~*) carta *f*, naipe *m*; (*Post*) tarjeta *f* (postal), postal *f*; (*visiting ~*) tarjeta *f* (de visita); (*index ~*) ficha *f*; (*member's, press ~*) carnet *m*, carné *m*; (*at dance, race*) programa *m*; (*piece of cardboard*) cartulina *f*; **to play ~s** jugar a las cartas; **to lose money at ~s** perder el dinero jugando a las cartas.
(b) (*idioms*) **isn't he a ~?** ¡qué gracia tiene el tío!, ¡qué tipo más salado! **like a house of ~s** como un castillo de naipes; **it is quite on** (*or* (*US*) **in) the ~s that ...** es perfectamente posible que ... + *subj*; **to ask for one's ~s** (*Brit*) dejar su puesto, renunciar; **to get one's ~s** (*Brit*) ser despedido; **to have a ~ up one's sleeve** quedar a uno todavía un recurso; **to hold all the ~s** tener los triunfos en la mano; **to lay one's ~s on the table** poner las cartas boca arriba; **if you play your ~s properly** si obras con el debido cuidado.
[2] VT (*US*): **to ~ sb*** verificar los papeles de identidad de uno.

cardamom ['kɑːdəməm] N cardamomo *m*.

cardboard ['kɑːdbɔːd] N cartón *m*, cartulina *f*; ~ **box** caja *f* de cartón.

card-carrying member [ˌkɑːd,kærɪŋ'membəʳ] N miembro *mf* de (*or* con) carnet.

card-catalogue ['kɑːd,kætəlɒg] N catálogo *m* de fichas, fichero *m*.

card-game ['kɑːdgeɪm] N juego *m* de naipes, juego *m* de cartas.

cardholder ['kɑːd,həʊldəʳ] N (*political party, organization*) miembro *mf* de carnet; (*library*) socio *mf* (de una biblioteca); (*restaurant etc*) asiduo *m*; (*credit card*) titular *mf* (de tarjeta de crédito).

cardiac ['kɑːdɪæk] ADJ cardíaco; ~ **arrest** paro *m* cardíaco.

cardie* ['kɑːdɪ] N (*Brit*) ABBR of **cardigan**.

cardigan ['kɑːdɪgən] N rebeca *f*; cárdigan *m*.

cardinal ['kɑːdɪnl] [1] ADJ cardinal; ~ **number** número *m* cardinal; ~ **points** puntos *mpl* cardinales; ~ **sin** pecado *m* capital.
[2] N cardenal *m*.

card-index [1] ['kɑːd,ɪndeks] N fichero *m* (de tarjetas).
[2] [ˌkɑːd'ɪndeks] VT fichar, catalogar.

cardio... ['kɑːdɪəʊ] PREF cardio....

cardiogram ['kɑːdɪəʊ,græm] N cardiograma *m*.

cardiograph ['kɑːdɪəʊ,græf] N cardiógrafo *m*.

cardiological [ˌkɑːdɪə'lɒdʒɪkəl] ADJ cardiológico.

cardiologist [ˌkɑːdɪ'ɒlədʒɪst] N cardiólogo *m*, -a *f*.

cardiology [ˌkɑːdɪ'ɒlədʒɪ] N cardiología *f*.

cardiopulmonary ['kɑːdɪəʊ'pʌlmənərɪ] ADJ cardiopulmonar.

cardiorespiratory ['kɑːdɪəʊ'respərətɔːrɪ] ADJ cardiorrespiratorio.

cardiovascular ['kɑːdɪəʊ'væskjʊləʳ] ADJ cardiovascular.

card-phone ['kɑːd,fəʊn] N (*Brit*) cabina que funciona con una tarjeta de crédito telefónico.

card-reader ['kɑːd,riːdəʳ] N lector *m* de fichas.

Cards N (*Brit*) ABBR of **Cardiganshire**.

card-sharp ['kɑːd,ʃɑːp] N, **card-sharper** ['kɑːd,ʃɑːpəʳ] N fullero *m*, tahur *m*.

card-stacker ['kɑːd,stækəʳ] N depósito *m* de descarga de fichas.

card-table ['kɑːd,teɪbl] N mesa *f* de baraja, tapete *m* verde.

card-trick ['kɑːd,trɪk] N truco *m* de naipes.

card-vote ['kɑːd,vəʊt] N voto *m* por delegación, voto *m* de grupo.

CARE [keəʳ] N (*US*) ABBR of **Cooperative for American Relief Everywhere**.

care [keəʳ] [1] N **(a)** (*anxiety*) cuidado *m*; inquietud *f*, solicitud *f*; **full of ~s** lleno de inquietudes; **he has many ~s** son muchas las cosas que

le preocupan; **he hasn't a ~ in the world** no tiene problema alguno; **the ~s of State** las responsabilidades de un cargo oficial, las preocupaciones y fatigas del gobierno.
(b) (*carefulness*) cuidado *m*, esmero *m*, atención *f*; (*gingerliness*) delicadeza *f*; **'with ~!'** '¡atención!', '¡cuidado!'; **convicted of driving without due ~ and attention** declarado culpable de conducir sin la debida precaución; **have a ~, sir!** ¡mire Vd lo que está diciendo!; **to take ~** tener cuidado; **be ~!** ¡(ten) cuidado!, ¡ojo!; (*as farewell*) ¡cuídate!; **to take ~ of** cuidar de, *valuable object* guardar, custodiar, *thing to be done* encargarse de; **I'll take ~ of him*** yo me encargo de él; **that can take ~ of itself** eso se resolverá por sí mismo; **that takes ~ of that** con eso todo queda arreglado; **she can take ~ of herself** ella sabe cuidar a sí misma; **I'll take ~ of this** (*bill etc*) esto corre de mi cuenta; **to take good ~ of o.s.** cuidarse mucho; **to take ~ to** + *infin* cuidar de que + *subj*, asegurarse de que + *subj*; **he doesn't take enough ~ to** + *infin* no pone bastante cuidado en + *infin*; **to take ~ not to** + *infin* guardarse de + *infin*; **take ~ not to drop it!** ¡ten cuidado, no lo dejes caer!
(c) (*charge*) cargo *m*, custodia *f*; (*Med etc*) asistencia *f*; ~ **of** (*on letter*) en casa de; **to be in the ~ of** estar bajo la custodia de; **he is in the ~ of Dr X** le asiste el doctor X, le atiende el doctor X; **the child was taken into ~** el niño fue internado en un centro de protección de menores.
[2] VI **(a)** (*feel interest, anxiety etc*) interesarse, preocuparse; **we need more people who ~** necesitamos más gente que se preocupe por los demás, necesitamos más personas que se interesen por los prójimos; **to ~ about** preocuparse de (*or* por), tener interés en, interesarse por; **to ~ deeply about sb's fate** preocuparse hondamente por la suerte de uno; **that's all he ~s about** es lo único que le interesa; **what do I ~ ?** ¿qué se me da a mí?, ¡maldito lo que me importa!; **as if I ~d!** y a mí ¿qué?; **I couldn't ~ less!** (*Brit*) eso me trae sin cuidado; **I could ~ less** (*US*) eso me trae sin cuidado; **for all I ~ you can take it** por mí te lo puedes llevar; **I don't ~** me es igual, no me importa; **I don't ~ twopence!** (*or* **a fig, hoot, jot, rap** *etc*) ¡me importa un comino!; **I don't ~ either way** me da lo mismo; **I don't ~ what people say** me trae sin cuidado lo que diga la gente; **who ~s?** ¿qué más da?
(b) (*like, want*) **to ~ to** + *infin* querer + *infin*, tener ganas de + *infin*; **if you ~ to** si quieres; **would you ~ to tell me?** ¿quieres decírmelo?; **would you ~ to take a walk?** ¿te apetece dar un paseo?; **would you ~ to take your hat off?** ¿tendrías inconveniente en quitarte el sombrero?

◆**care for** VT **(a)** (*like*) tener afecto a, sentir cariño por; (*amorously*) sentirse atraído por; **I don't much ~ for him** no me resulta simpático; **I know he ~s for you a lot** sé que te tiene mucho cariño; **I don't ~ for the idea** no me hace gracia la idea; **I don't ~ for coffee** no me gusta el café; **would you ~ for a walk?** ¿te apetece dar un paseo?; **would you ~ for a drink?** ¿quieres tomar algo?
(b) (*look after*) cuidar; atender; **well ~d for** (bien) cuidado, bien atendido.

careen [kə'riːn] [1] VT carenar.
[2] VI inclinarse, escorar.

career [kə'rɪəʳ] [1] N profesión *f*, carrera *f* (profesional); ~**s adviser** (*or* **officer**) (*Brit*), ~**(s) counselor** (*US*), ~**s teacher** (*Brit Scol*) persona encargada de la guía vocacional de los alumnos; ~ **diplomat** diplomático *m*, -a *f* de carrera; ~ **girl** mujer *f* dedicada a su profesión; ~**s guidance** (*Brit*) guía *f* vocacional; ~**s office** oficina *f* de guía vocacional; ~ **prospects** perspectivas *fpl* de futuro; ~**s service** servicio *m* de consejería profesional.
[2] VI (*also* **to ~ along**) correr a toda velocidad; **to ~ down the street** correr calle abajo; **to ~ into a wall** estrellarse contra un muro.

careerist [kə'rɪərɪst] N ambicioso *m*, -a *f*, arribista *mf*.

carefree ['keəfriː] ADJ despreocupado, libre de preocupaciones, alegre, inconsciente.

careful ['keəfʊl] ADJ **(a)** cuidadoso; cauteloso, prudente; ~**!** ¡cuidado!, ¡ojo!; **to be ~** tener cuidado; **be ~!** ¡ten cuidado!; **one can't be too ~** nunca se peca por demasiado cuidadoso; **we must be very ~ here** en esto conviene andar con pies de plomo; **be ~ what you say to him** ten cuidado con lo que le dices; **we shall lose it if we're not ~** lo perderemos si no tenemos cuidado; **to be ~ of** tener cuidado con; **to be ~ to** + *infin* poner diligencia en + *infin*, asegurarse cuidadosamente de que + *subj*; **he was ~ to say that ...** dijo de modo particular que ...
(b) (*painstaking*) esmerado, cuidadoso; competente, concienzudo.
(c) (*with money*) económico, ahorrativo; (*pej*) tacaño.

carefully ['keəfəlɪ] ADV (*V* ADJ) **(a)** con cuidado, cuidadosamente; **we must go ~ here** en esto conviene andar con pies de plomo; **I have to spend ~** tengo que pensar mucho en lo que gasto; **he replied ~** contestó con cautela. **(b)** con esmero, esmeradamente; competentemente, concienzudamente.

carefulness ['keəfəlnɪs] N (*V* ADJ) **(a)** cuidado *m*; prudencia *f*, cautela *f*. **(b)** esmero *m*, cuidado *m*. **(c)** economía *f*; (*pej*) tacañería *f*.

care-giver ['keə,gɪvəʳ] N (*professional*) asistente *mf* social, cuidador *m*,

-ora f; (relative, friend) persona que cuida de un incapacitado.

care label ['kɛə,leɪbl] N (on garment) etiqueta f de instrucciones de lavado.

careless ['kɛəlɪs] ADJ descuidado; negligente; (inattentive) poco atento; (thoughtless) irreflexivo, imprudente; stroke hecho a la ligera; appearance descuidado, desaliñado; (~ of others) indiferente, insensible (of a); ~ **driving** conducción f negligente; **that was very ~ of you** en eso fuiste muy imprudente.

carelessly ['kɛəlɪslɪ] ADV descuidadamente; a la ligera.

carelessness ['kɛəlɪsnɪs] N descuido m; falta f de atención; desaliño m; indiferencia f (of a); **through sheer ~** por simple descuido, por simple falta de atención.

carer ['kɛərəʳ] N (professional) asistente mf social, cuidador m, -ora f; (relative, friend) persona que cuida de un incapacitado.

caress [kə'res] [1] N caricia f.
[2] VT acariciar.

caret ['kærət] N signo m de intercalación (^).

caretaker ['kɛə,teɪkəʳ] N (Brit) vigilante m; (in museum etc) guardián m; (of flats) portero m, conserje m, celador m, curador m; ~ **government** gobierno m de transición.

care-worker ['kɛə,wɜːkəʳ] N asistente mf social, cuidador m, -ora f.

careworn ['kɛəwɔːn] ADJ person agobiado de preocupaciones; face, frown preocupado, lleno de ansiedad.

carfare ['kɑːfɛəʳ] N (US) pasaje m, precio m (del billete).

car-ferry ['kɑː,ferɪ] N transbordador m para coches, ferry m.

cargo ['kɑːgəʊ] N cargamento m, carga f.

cargo-boat ['kɑːgəʊbəʊt] N barco m de carga, carguero m.

cargo-plane ['kɑːgəʊ,pleɪn] N avión m de carga.

car-hire ['kɑːhaɪəʳ] N alquiler m de coches; ~ **firm** empresa f de alquiler de coches.

carhop ['kɑːhɒp] N (US) camarero m, -a f de un restaurante 'drive-in'.

Caribbean [,kærɪ'biːən] ADJ caribe, caribeño.

Caribbean Sea [,kærɪ'biːən'siː] N Mar m Caribe.

caribou ['kærɪbuː] N caribú m.

caricature ['kærɪkətjʊəʳ] [1] N caricatura f; (in newspaper) dibujo m cómico; **it was a ~ of a ceremony** fue una parodia de ceremonia.
[2] VT caricaturizar.

caricaturist [,kærɪkə'tjʊərɪst] N caricaturista mf, dibujante mf.

CARICOM ['kærɪ,kɒm] N ABBR of **Caribbean Community and Common Market** Comunidad f y Mercado Común del Caribe, CMCC f.

caries ['kɛəriːz] N caries f.

carillon [kə'rɪljən] N carillón m.

caring ['kɛərɪŋ] [1] ADJ afectuoso, bondadoso; humanitario; **the ~ professions** las profesiones de dedicación humanitaria; **the ~ society** la sociedad humanitaria.
[2] N (care) cuidado m; (affection) afecto m, cariño m; (help) ayuda f, auxilio m.

carious ['kɛərɪəs] ADJ cariado.

carjacker ['kɑːdʒækəʳ] N persona que asalta a los automovilistas.

carjacking ['kɑːdʒækɪŋ] N asalto a automovilistas.

Carlism ['kɑːlɪzəm] N carlismo m.

Carlist ['kɑːlɪst] [1] ADJ carlista.
[2] N carlista mf.

Carmelite ['kɑːməlaɪt] [1] ADJ carmelita.
[2] N carmelita mf.

carmine ['kɑːmaɪn] [1] ADJ carmín, de carmín.
[2] N carmín m.

carnage ['kɑːnɪdʒ] N carnicería f, mortandad f, matanza f.

carnal ['kɑːnl] ADJ carnal; **to have ~ knowledge of** tener ayuntamiento carnal con.

carnation [kɑː'neɪʃən] N clavel m.

carnival ['kɑːnɪvəl] N carnaval m; fiesta f, feria f; (US) parque m de atracciones; ~ **queen** reina f de la fiesta.

carnivore ['kɑːnɪvɔːʳ] N carnívoro m.

carnivorous [kɑː'nɪvərəs] ADJ carnívoro.

carob ['kærəb] N (bean) algarroba f; (tree) algarrobo m.

carol ['kærəl] [1] N villancico m.
[2] VI cantar alegremente.

Carolingian [kærə'lɪndʒɪən] ADJ carolingio.

carotene ['kærətiːn] N caroteno m.

carotid [kə'rɒtɪd] N (also ~ **artery**) carótida f.

carousal [kə'raʊzəl] N jarana f, parranda f, juerga f.

carouse [kə'raʊz] VI jaranear, estar de parranda, estar de juerga.

carousel [,kæru:'sel] N (merry-go-round) caballitos mpl, tiovivo m, carrusel m; (Phot) bombo m de diapositivas; (at airport) cinta f de equipajes.

carp¹ [kɑːp] N carpa f.

carp² [kɑːp] VI criticar (sin motivo); **to ~ at, to ~ about** quejarse (sin motivo) de, murmurar de.

car-park ['kɑːpɑːk] N (Brit) aparcamiento m, parking m, estacionamiento m (LAm).

Carpathians [kɑː'peɪθɪənz] NPL Montes mpl Cárpatos.

carpenter ['kɑːpɪntəʳ] N carpintero m.

carpentry ['kɑːpɪntrɪ] N carpintería f.

carpet ['kɑːpɪt] [1] N alfombra f; moqueta f; ~ **square**, ~ **tile** loseta f; **to be on the ~*** tener que aguantar un rapapolvo*; **to roll out the red ~ for sb** recibir a uno con todos los honores debidos; **they tried to sweep it under the ~** trataron de ocultar los trapos sucios, quisieron echar tierra sobre el asunto.
[2] VT alfombrar; (fig) alfombrar, cubrir, revestir (with de); **to ~ sb*** echar un rapapolvo a uno*.

carpet-bag ['kɑːpɪt,bæg] N (US) maletín m, morral m.

carpetbagger ['kɑːpɪt,bægəʳ] N (US) aventurero m político, explotador m político (venido de fuera).

carpet-bomb ['kɑːpɪt,bɒm] VT arrasar con bombas.

carpet-bombing ['kɑːpɪt,bɒmɪŋ] N bombardeo m de arrasamiento.

carpeted ['kɑːpɪtɪd] ADJ floor alfombrado, enmoquetado; ~ **with** (fig) cubierto de.

carpet-slippers ['kɑːpɪt,slɪpəz] NPL zapatillas fpl.

carpeting ['kɑːpɪtɪŋ] N alfombrado m, tapizado m; moqueta f.

carpet-sweeper ['kɑːpɪt,swiːpəʳ] N (mechanical) máquina f para barrer alfombras; (vacuum-cleaner) aspiradora f.

car-phone ['kɑːfəʊn] N teléfono m móvil (de coche).

carping ['kɑːpɪŋ] ADJ criticón, reparón.

carpool ['kɑːpuːl] N (US) coches mpl de uso compartido, uso m compartido de coches.

carport ['kɑːpɔːt] N garaje m abierto, cobertizo m para coche.

carriage ['kærɪdʒ] N (a) (Brit Rail) vagón m, coche m; (horse-drawn) carruaje m, coche m; (gun ~) cureña f; (of typewriter etc) carro m; ~ **return** retorno m del carro.
(b) (bearing) andares mpl, modo m de andar, porte m.
(c) (Brit: act of carrying) transporte m; (Comm) porte m; ~ **forward** al precio de cotización (el comprador paga el coste del porte); ~ **free** franco de porte; ~ **inwards** pagos mpl por porte de mercancías compradas; ~ **outwards** flete m de ida; ~ **paid** porte pagado.

carriage-drive ['kærɪdʒdraɪv] N calzada f.

carriage trade ['kærɪdʒ,treɪd] N (US) sector m de transporte de mercancías.

carriageway ['kærɪdʒweɪ] N (Brit) carretera f; calzada f.

carrier ['kærɪəʳ] N (a) (person) transportista m; (company) empresa f de transportes; (Aer) aerotransportista m, aerolínea f.
(b) (Med) portador m, -ora f (de enfermedad).
(c) (basket etc) portaequipajes m; (on cycle) parrilla f.
(d) (Naut) portaaviones m.

carrier-bag ['kærɪə'bæg] N (Brit) saco m (de plástico), bolsa f.

carrier-pigeon ['kærɪə,pɪdʒən] N paloma f mensajera.

carrion ['kærɪən] N carroña f; inmundicia f; ~ **crow** corneja f negra.

carrot ['kærət] N zanahoria f.

carrot-and-stick ['kærətənd'stɪk] ADJ: ~ **policy** la política del palo y la zanahoria.

carroty ['kærətɪ] ADJ pelirrojo.

carrousel [,kæru:'sel] N (US) = **carousel**.

carry ['kærɪ] [1] N (of ball, shot) alcance m.
[2] VT (a) (transport) llevar; traer; transportar, acarrear; disease transmitir, ser portador de; (in mind) retener; authority etc tener, revestir; **as fast as his legs could ~ him** lo más rápidamente posible, a todo correr; **this bus carries 60 passengers** este autobús tiene asientos para 60 personas; **he carries our lives in his hands** lleva nuestras vidas en sus manos; **to ~ one's audience with one** (fig) captarse al auditorio.
(b) (have on one's person) llevar encima, tener consigo.
(c) (involve) consequence acarrear, tener como consecuencia; (Fin) interest llevar, producir; guarantee tener, llevar; responsibility conllevar; interpretation encerrar, llevar implícito; meaning tener; **the offence carries a fine of £100** el delito es castigado por una multa de 100 libras.
(d) (support) burden sostener; crop producir, llevar.
(e) (Comm) stock tener en existencia; article tener, tratar en; ~**ing charge** costo m de géneros no en venta (almacenados etc).
(f) (extend) extender, prolongar; **to ~ sth too far** llevar algo al exceso.
(g) (win) position tomar, conquistar; (Parl) seat ganar; proposition hacer aceptar; motion aprobar; **to ~ all before one** triunfar, vencer todos los obstáculos, arrollarlo todo.
(h) (newspaper etc) story llevar, imprimir; informar sobre; **this journal does not ~ reviews** esta revista no tiene reseñas.
(i) (Math) llevar.
(j) child estar encinta de.
[3] VI (reach) alcanzar, llegar; (sound) oírse; **she has a voice which carries** tiene una voz que se oye bastante lejos.
[4] VR: **to ~ o.s.** portarse; **to ~ o.s. well** andar con garbo, tener buena presencia.

◆**carry about** VT llevar consigo; llevar de acá para allá.

◆**carry along** VT llevar; (*flood, water*) arrastrar.

◆**carry away** VT (**a**) llevarse; (*kidnap*) secuestrar.
(**b**) (*fig*) arrebatar, inspirar, entusiasmar; **to get carried away** exaltarse, emocionarse (demasiado), entusiasmarse (demasiado); extralimitarse.

◆**carry back** VT (*lit*) *things* traer; (*Fin*) cargar (sobre cuentas anteriores); **that music carries me back to the 60s** esa música me hace recordar los 60.

◆**carry down** VT bajar.

◆**carry forward** VT (*Comm*) pasar a cuenta nueva; **carried forward** suma y sigue.

◆**carry off** VT (**a**) llevarse; llevar a la fuerza; *prize* alzarse con, arramblar con; *election* ganar; **she carried it off splendidly** salió muy airosa de la prueba.
(**b**) (*kill*) matar, llevar a la tumba.

◆**carry on** ① VT *work* continuar, proseguir; *business* poseer, llevar, ser dueño de.
② VI (**a**) (*continue*) continuar; seguir adelante; **we ~ on somehow** vamos tirando; **if you ~ on like that** si sigues así; **~ on!** ¡adelante!, ¡sigue!, (*in talking*) ¡prosigue!
(**b**) (*) (*complain*) quejarse, protestar; murmurar (*about* de); (*protest*) protestar amargamente (*about* de, por).
(**c**) (*) (*insist*) insistir, machacar; (*argue*) discutir; armar un follón*; **you do ~ on!** ¡dale que dale!; **don't ~ on so!** ¡no machaques!
(**d**) **to ~ on with sb*** (*lovers*) tener un plan con uno*.

◆**carry out** VT (**a**) *order, promise, threat* cumplir; *intention* realizar; *plan* llevar a cabo, poner por obra.
(**b**) *repair* hacer; *test* verificar; *work* realizar, llevar a cabo.

◆**carry over** VT (**a**) posponer; guardar para después.
(**b**) (*Comm*) pasar a cuenta nueva.

◆**carry through** VT (**a**) *plan* llevar a cabo, ejecutar.
(**b**) *person* sostener hasta el fin; **to ~ sb through a crisis** ayudar a uno a superar una crisis; **the stock will ~ us through the winter** las existencias nos bastarán durante todo el invierno.

◆**carry up** VT subir.

carryall ['kærɪɔːl] N (*US*) cesto *m* grande; = **hold-all**.

carry-back ['kærɪbæk] N (*Fin*) traspaso *m* al período anterior.

carrycot ['kærɪkɒt] N (*Brit*) cuna *f* portátil, capazo *m*.

carrying-on ['kærɪŋ'ɒn] N (**a**) continuación *f*; prosecución *f*.
(**b**) (*) plan *m*, relaciones *fpl* amorosas (ilícitas).

carry-on* [,kærɪ'ɒn] N aspaviento *m*, conmoción *f*, alharaca *f*; lío* *m*; riña *f*, pelea *f*; **what a ~!** ¡qué follón!*; **there was a great ~ about the tickets** se armó un tremendo lío a causa de los billetes*; **did you ever see such a ~?** ¿se ha visto un embrollo igual?

carry-out ['kærɪˌaʊt] ① ADJ *meal etc* para llevar.
② N (*food*) comida *f* para llevar; (*drink*) bebida *f* para llevar.

carry-over ['kærɪ'əʊvər] N (*surplus*) sobrante *m*; resto *m*, remanente *m*; (*Comm*) suma *f* anterior (para traspasar), suma *f* que pasa de una página (de cuenta) a la siguiente; (*St Ex*) aplazamiento *m* de pago hasta el próximo día de ajuste de cuentas.

car-sick ['kɑːˌsɪk] ADJ: **to be ~, to get ~** marearse (en el coche).

car-sickness ['kɑːˌsɪknɪs] N mareo *m* (*al ir en coche*); **to suffer ~** marearse (en el coche).

cart [kɑːt] ① N carro *m*, carreta *f*; (*heavy*) carretón *m*; (*hand~*) carretilla *f*, carro *m* de mano; (*US*) carrito *m* de la compra, carrito *m* de supermercado; **to be in the ~*** estar en un atolladero; **to put the ~ before the horse** poner el carro delante de los bueyes.
② VT llevar, acarrear, carretear; (*) llevar (con gran dificultad).

◆**cart away, cart off** VT llevarse.

cartage ['kɑːtɪdʒ] N acarreo *m*, porte *m*.

carte blanche ['kɑːt'blɑːnʃ] N carta *f* blanca; **to give sb ~** dar carta blanca a uno.

cartel [kɑːˈtel] N cartel *m*.

carter ['kɑːtər] N carretero *m*.

Cartesian [kɑːˈtiːzɪən] ① ADJ cartesiano.
② N cartesiano *m*.

Carthage ['kɑːθɪdʒ] N Cartago *f*.

Carthaginian [,kɑːθəˈdʒɪnɪən] ① ADJ cartaginés.
② N cartaginés *m*, -esa *f*.

cart-horse ['kɑːthɔːs] N caballo *m* de tiro.

Carthusian [kɑːˈθjuːzɪən] ① ADJ cartujo.
② N cartujo *m*.

cartilage ['kɑːtɪlɪdʒ] N cartílago *m*.

cartilaginous [,kɑːtɪˈlædʒɪnəs] ADJ cartilaginoso.

cartload ['kɑːtləʊd] N carretada *f* (*also fig*); **by the ~** a carretadas, a montones.

cartographer [kɑːˈtɒɡrəfər] N cartógrafo *m*, -a *f*.

cartographic(al) [,kɑːtəʊˈɡræfɪk(əl)] ADJ cartográfico.

cartography [kɑːˈtɒɡrəfɪ] N cartografía *f*.

cartomancy ['kɑːtəmænsɪ] N cartomancia *f*.

carton ['kɑːtən] N envase *m*, caja *f* de cartón, cartón *m*.

cartoon [kɑːˈtuːn] N (*newspaper*) dibujo *m* cómico, caricatura *f*; (*Art*) cartón *m*; (*film*) dibujos *mpl* animados; (*strip*) tira *f* cómica.

cartoonist [,kɑːˈtuːnɪst] N dibujante *mf*, caricaturista *mf*.

cartridge ['kɑːtrɪdʒ] N cartucho *m* (*also Comput*); (*for pen*) recambio *m*.

cartridge-belt ['kɑːtrɪdʒbelt] N cartuchera *f*, canana *f*.

cartridge-case ['kɑːtrɪdʒkeɪs] N cartucho *m*.

cartridge-paper ['kɑːtrɪdʒ,peɪpər] N papel *m* guarro (de acuarela).

cartridge-player ['kɑːtrɪdʒ,pleɪər] N lector *m* de cartucho.

cart-track ['kɑːttræk] N (*rut*) carril *m*, rodada *f*; (*road*) camino *m* (para carros).

cartwheel ['kɑːtwiːl] N rueda *f* de carro; (*fig*) voltereta *f* lateral, rueda *f*.

cartwright ['kɑːtraɪt] N carretero *m*.

carve [kɑːv] VT *meat* trinchar; *stone* esculpir, tallar, labrar; *name on tree etc* grabar; **to ~ one's way through** abrirse a la fuerza un camino por.

◆**carve out** VT *piece of wood* tallar; *piece of land* limpiar; *statue, figure* esculpir; *tool* tallar; **to ~ out a career for o.s.** labrarse un porvenir.

◆**carve up** VT *country* dividir, repartir entre los vencedores; desmembrar; *person* (*) coser a puñaladas.

carver ['kɑːvər] N (**a**) (*person*) (*Culin*) trinchador *m*; (*Art*) escultor *m*, -ora *f*, tallista *mf*. (**b**) **~s** cubierto *m* de trinchar.

carvery ['kɑːvərɪ] N restaurante *m* que se especializa en asados.

carve-up* ['kɑːvˌʌp] N división *f*, repartimiento *m*; (*Pol etc*) arreglo *m*.

carving ['kɑːvɪŋ] N (*Culin*) arte *m* de trinchar; (*Art*) escultura *f*, obra *f* de talla.

carving-knife ['kɑːvɪŋnaɪf] N, PL **carving-knives** ['kɑːvɪŋnaɪvz] trinchante *m*.

car-wash ['kɑːwɒʃ] N tren *m* (*or* túnel *m*) de lavado (de coches).

caryatid [,kærɪˈætɪd] N cariátide *f*.

Casablanca [,kæsəˈblæŋkə] N Casablanca *f*.

Casanova [,kæsəˈnəʊvə] N (*fig*) casanova *m*, conquistador *m*.

cascade [kæsˈkeɪd] ① N cascada *f*, salto *m* de agua; (*fig*) chorro *m*; torrente *m*.
② VI caer en cascada.

cascara [kæsˈkɑːrə] N (*Pharm*) cáscara *f* sagrada.

case¹ [keɪs] ① N (**a**) (*container*) caja *f*; (*packing~*) cajón *m*; (*Brit: suitcase*) maleta *f*, valija *f* (*LAm*), veliz *m* (*Mex*); (*for jewels, spectacles etc*) estuche *m*; (*for scissors etc*) vaina *f*; (*of watch*) caja *f*; (*for guitar etc*) funda *f*; (*of window*) marco *m*, bastidor *m*; (*of cartridge*) cartucho *m*, vaina *f*, cápsula *f*; (*showcase*) vitrina *f*.
(**b**) (*Typ*) caja *f*; **lower ~** caja *f* baja; **upper ~** caja *f* alta.
② VT (**a**) encajonar; enfundar; **~d in concrete** revestido de hormigón.
(**b**) (‡) *house etc* estudiar la situación de (con intención de robar).

case² [keɪs] N (**a**) (*instance*) caso *m* (*also Med*); asunto *m*; **a fever ~** un caso de fiebre; **a hospital ~** un caso para el hospital, un enfermo que tendrá que ser trasladado al hospital; **a ~ in point** un ejemplo que hace al caso; **it's a sad ~** es un caso triste; **it's a hopeless ~** (*Med*) es un caso desahuciado; **it's a ~ for the police** éste es asunto para la policía; **it's a ~ of ...** se trata de ...; **it's a clear ~ of murder** es un claro caso de homicidio; **he's working on the train-robbery ~** está haciendo investigaciones sobre el robo del tren; **he's a ~*** es un caso, es un tipo raro*.
(**b**) (*argument, reasoning*) **there seems to be a ~ for reform** parece que hay razones para reformarlo; **there is a ~ for saying that ...** puede decirse razonablemente que ...; **there is a ~ for that attitude** hay argumentos en favor de esa actitud; **that alters the ~** eso cambia la cosa; **I understand that is not the ~** tengo entendido que no es así; **if that is the ~, such being the ~** si las cosas son así; **as the ~ may be** según el caso.
(**c**) (*with prep*) **in ~ he comes** por si viene, (en) caso de que venga; **in ~ of** en caso de; **in your ~** en tu caso; **as in the ~ of** como en el caso de; **in most ~s** en la mayoría de los casos; **in any ~** en todo caso, de todas formas; **just in ~** por si acaso, por lo que pueda ocurrir, por si las moscas; **in such a ~** en tal caso; **in that ~** en ese caso.
(**d**) (*Jur*) causa *f*, pleito *m*, proceso *m*; **the ~ for the defence** la defensa, el conjunto de razones alegadas por el acusado; **the ~ for the prosecution** la acusación, el conjunto de acusaciones alegadas por el fiscal; **the Dreyfus ~** el proceso de Dreyfus, (*more loosely*) el asunto Dreyfus; **there is no ~ to answer** no hay acusación para contestar; **to have a good** (*or* **strong**) **~** tener argumentos fuertes (*for* para); **to make the ~ for doing nothing** exponer las razones para no hacer nada; **to make out a ~** exponer un argumento; **to make out a good ~** presentar argumentos convincentes (*for* para); **all right, you have made your ~** bien, Vd ha justificado su posición; **to put** (*or* **state**) **one's ~** presentar sus argumentos; **to rest one's ~** terminar la presentación de su alegato.
(**e**) (*Gram*) caso *m*.

casebook ['keɪsbʊk] N diario *m*, registro *m*.

case-file ['keɪsfaɪl] N historial *m*.

case grammar ['keɪs,græmər] N gramática *f* de caso.

case-hardened ['keɪs,hɑːdnd] ADJ cementado; (*fig*) insensible, poco compasivo.

case-history ['keɪs'hɪstərɪ] N historia f, historial m, antecedentes mpl; **what is the patient's ~?** ¿cuál es la historia médica del enfermo?; **I'll give you the full ~** le contaré la historia con todos los detalles.

case law ['keɪs'lɔ:] N jurisprudencia f.

casement ['keɪsmənt] N ventana f a bisagra; (frame) marco m de ventana.

case-study ['keɪs,stʌdɪ] N estudio m de casos (prácticos).

case-system ['keɪs,sɪstəm] N sistema m de casos.

casework ['keɪswɜ:k] N asistencia f social individualizada, trabajo m social con individuos.

caseworker ['keɪs,wɜ:kər] N asistente mf social.

cash [kæʃ] **1** N dinero m contante; efectivo m, metálico m; (*) dinero m, plata f (LAm); (cashdesk) caja f; ~ **account** cuenta f de caja; ~ **advance** adelanto m; ~ **card** tarjeta f de dinero; ~ **crop** cultivo m comerciale; ~ **deficit** déficit m de caja; ~ **discount** descuento m por pronto pago (or por pago al contado); ~ **down, for** ~ al contado; ~ **income** ingresos mpl al contado; ~ **offer** oferta f de pago al contado; ~ **order** pedido m al contado; ~ **payment, ~ terms** pago m al contado; ~ **price** precio m al contado; ~ **prize** premio m en metálico; ~ **ratio** coeficiente m de caja; ~ **receipts** total m cobrado; ~ **reduction** = ~ **discount**; ~ **reserves** reservas fpl en metálico; ~ **sale** venta f al contado; ~ **squeeze** restricciones fpl económicas; ~ **transaction** transacción f al contado; ~ **in hand** (in till) efectivo m en caja; ~ **on delivery** entrega f contra reembolso; '~ **with order**' 'enviar dinero con pedido'; **in** ~ en metálico, en efectivo; **to be out of** ~ estar sin blanca; **I haven't any** ~ **on me** no llevo dinero conmigo; **to pay** ~ **for** pagar al contado.
2 VT cheque cobrar, hacer efectivo; coupon (also **to** ~ **in**) canjear; **to** ~ **sb a cheque** pagar a uno en metálico a cambio de su cheque, cambiarle a uno un cheque.

◆**cash in** VT bonds, savings certificates vender.

◆**cash in on*** VT sacar partido de, aprovechar.

◆**cash up** VI contar el dinero recaudado (al cerrar la tienda etc).

cash-and-carry ['kæʃən'kærɪ] **1** N almacén m de venta al por mayor.
2 ADJ goods, business de venta al por mayor.

cashbook ['kæʃbʊk] N libro m de caja.

cashbox ['kæʃbɒks] N caja f.

cashdesk ['kæʃdesk] N caja f.

cash-dispenser ['kæʃdɪs,pensər] N (Brit) cajero m automático.

cashew [kæ'ʃu:] N (also ~ **nut**) anacardo m, marañón m.

cash-flow ['kæʃ,fləʊ] N flujo m de fondos, cash-flow m; ~ **problems** problemas mpl de cash-flow.

cashier [kæ'ʃɪər] **1** N cajero m, -a f.
2 VT (Mil) separar del servicio, degradar, destituir.

cashless ['kæʃlɪs] ADJ: **the** ~ **society** la sociedad sin dinero.

cashmere [kæʃ'mɪər] N cachemir m, cachemira f.

cashpoint ['kæʃ,pɔɪnt] N cajero m automático.

cash-register ['kæʃ,redʒɪstər] N caja f registradora.

casing ['keɪsɪŋ] N caja f, cubierta f, envoltura f; revestimiento m, carcasa f reforzada.

casino [kə'si:nəʊ] N casino m (de juego).

cask [kɑ:sk] N tonel m, barril m, barrica f.

casket ['kɑ:skɪt] N cajita f, cofrecito m, estuche m, arquilla f; (US) ataúd m, féretro m.

Caspian Sea ['kæspɪən,si:] N Mar m Caspio.

Cassandra [kə'sændrə] NF Casandra.

cassava [kə'sɑ:və] N mandioca f, tapioca f.

casserole ['kæsərəʊl] N (Brit) cacerola f; (food) cazuela f.

cassette [kæ'set] N casete f, cassette f.

cassette-deck [kə'set,dek] N platina f a cassette.

cassette-player [kæ'set,pleɪər] N casete m, cassette m, tocacasete m, tocacintas m.

cassette-recorder [kə'setrɪ,kɔ:dər] N cassette f grabadora.

cassette tape [kæ'set,teɪp] = **cassette**.

cassis [kæ'si:s] N cassis m.

Cassius ['kæsɪəs] NM Casio.

cassock ['kæsək] N sotana f.

cassowary ['kæsəweərɪ] N casuario m.

cast [kɑ:st] **1** N (a) (throw) echada f.
(b) (Tech) pieza f fundida.
(c) (mould) forma f, molde m; (plaster ~) vaciado m; escayola f; ~ **of features** facciones fpl, fisonomía f; ~ **of mind** temperamento m; genio m; **leg in** ~ pierna f enyesada, pierna f escayolada.
(d) (Theat) reparto m; ~ **(and credits)** (US: Cine, TV) reparto m.
(e) (in eye) estrabismo m.
2 VT (a) (throw) echar, lanzar, arrojar; anchor, net echar.
(b) (throw: fig) blame, glance, lots echar; eyes volver (on a, hacia); light arrojar (on sobre); shadow proyectar; doubt suscitar (on acerca de); vote dar, emitir; horoscope hacer; spell echar.
(c) (shed) skin mudar; (lose) perder.
(d) (Tech: in mould) vaciar; (Metal) fundir.

(e) (Theat) parts repartir; part asignar; **to** ~ **an actor in the part of** dar a un actor el papel de; **he was** ~ **as the fool** le dieron el papel del gracioso; **we shall** ~ **the play on Tuesday** repartiremos los papeles de la obra el martes.
3 VI (Fishing) lanzar, arrojar.

◆**cast about, cast around** VI: **to** ~ **about for** buscar, andar buscando.

◆**cast aside** VT desechar.

◆**cast away** VT desechar, tirar; abandonar; **to be** ~ **away** (Naut) naufragar; quedar desamparado; **to be** ~ **away on an island** naufragar y arribar en una isla.

◆**cast back** **1** VT: **to** ~ **one's thoughts back to** rememorar.
2 VI volver.

◆**cast down** VT (a) derribar; eyes bajar.
(b) (fig) desanimar; **to be** ~ **down** estar deprimido.

◆**cast in** VT, VI: **to** ~ **in** (one's lot) **with sb** compartir el destino de uno.

◆**cast off** **1** VT (a) desechar, abandonar; burden deshacerse de, quitarse de encima; clothing quitarse; wife repudiar; mistress dejar.
(b) (Knitting) terminar, cerrar los puntos de.
2 VI (a) (Naut) soltar las amarras, desamarrar.
(b) (Knitting) rematar.

◆**cast on** VT (Knitting) echar los puntos de.

◆**cast out** VT arrojar, echar fuera de sí, expulsar.

◆**cast up** VT (a) echar; vomitar. (b) account sumar.

castanet [,kæstə'net] N castañuela f.

castaway ['kɑ:stəweɪ] N náufrago m, -a f.

caste [kɑ:st] N casta f; **to lose** ~ desprestigiarse.

castellated ['kæstəleɪtɪd] ADJ almenado.

caster ['kɑ:stər] N = **castor¹ and castor²**.

castigate ['kæstɪgeɪt] VT reprobar, condenar, censurar.

castigation [,kæstɪ'geɪʃən] N reprobación f, censura f.

Castile [kæs'ti:l] N Castilla f.

Castilian [kæs'tɪlɪən] **1** ADJ castellano.
2 N (a) castellano m, -a f. (b) (Ling) castellano m.

casting ['kɑ:stɪŋ] **1** ADJ: ~ **vote** voto m de calidad.
2 N (a) (Tech) pieza f fundida, pieza f de fundición. (b) (Theat) reparto m.

casting-couch ['kɑ:stɪŋ,kaʊtʃ] N (Cine: hum) diván m del director (del reparto).

cast-iron ['kɑ:st'aɪən] **1** ADJ hecho de hierro fundido; (fig) fuerte, duro; will férreo, inflexible; case sólido, convincente; excuse inatacable.
2 N hierro m colado, hierro m fundido.

castle ['kɑ:sl] **1** N castillo m; (Chess) torre f, roque m; **to build ~s in the air** construir castillos en el aire.
2 VI (Chess) enrocar.

castling ['kɑ:slɪŋ] N enroque m.

cast-off ['kɑ:stɒf] **1** ADJ clothing etc de desecho.
2 N persona f (or cosa) abandonada, persona f (or cosa) desechada, plato m de segunda mesa; ~s ropa f de desecho.

castor¹ ['kɑ:stər] N (at table: sugar) azucarero m; (salt) salero m; ~s convoy m, vinagreras fpl.

castor² ['kɑ:stər] N (wheel) ruedecilla f, castor m.

castor-oil ['kɑ:stər'ɔɪl] N aceite m de ricino; ~ **plant** ricino m.

castor sugar ['kɑ:stə'ʃʊgər] N (Brit) azúcar m extrafino.

castrate [kæs'treɪt] VT castrar.

castration [kæs'treɪʃən] N castración f.

castrato [kæs'trɑ:təʊ] N, PL **castrati** castrato m.

Castroism ['kæstrəʊɪzəm] N castrismo m.

Castroist ['kæstrəʊɪst] ADJ, N castrista mf.

casual ['kæʒjʊəl] **1** ADJ (a) (happening by chance) fortuito, accidental, casual; **a** ~ **glance** una mirada al azar; **a** ~ **stroll** un paseo sin rumbo fijo; **in a** ~ **conversation I had with him** en una conversación sin trascendencia que tuve con él, en una conversación que por casualidad tuve con él; **a** ~ **meeting** un encuentro fortuito.
(b) (offhand) despreocupado; **a** ~ **remark** una observación hecha a la ligera; **in a** ~ **manner** con afectada indiferencia; **he tried to sound** ~ se esforzó por parecer tranquilo; **to assume a** ~ **air** hacer como si nada; **he was very** ~ **about it** no daba importancia a la cosa.
(c) clothing informal; corriente; de sport.
(d) labour temporero, eventual; ~ **earnings** ingresos mpl ocasionales; ~ **worker** jornalero m, temporero m.
2 N hincha m violento que viste ropa cara.
3 ~s NPL traje m de sport, ropa f de estar por casa.

casually ['kæʒjʊəlɪ] ADV (a) (by chance) por casualidad, de manera fortuita.
(b) (offhandedly) de manera despreocupada; con aire de indiferencia, con aire de naturalidad; **he said** ~ dijo con mucha tranquilidad; **I was** ~ **watching them** los miraba un poco distraído; **I said it quite** ~ lo dije sin darle importancia.

casualness ['kæʒjʊəlnɪs] N despreocupación f.

casualty ['kæʒjʊəltɪ] N (a) (Mil) baja f; ~ **list** lista f de bajas; **casualties** pérdidas fpl; **there were heavy casualties** hubo muchas bajas.
(b) (in accident) víctima f, herido m, muerto m; **casualties** víctimas fpl; **fortunately there were no casualties** por fortuna no hubo víctimas; **a ~ of modern society** una víctima de la sociedad moderna; ~ **department** sección f de accidentes; ~ **list** lista f de víctimas; ~ **ward** sala f de accidentes.
casuist ['kæzjʊɪst] N casuista mf; (pej) sofista mf.
casuistry ['kæzjʊɪstrɪ] N casuística f; (pej) sofismas mpl, razonamiento m falaz.
CAT N (a) ABBR of **computer-assisted translation** traducción f asistida por ordenador, TAO f. (b) ABBR of **College of Advanced Technology**. (c) ABBR of **computerized tomography scanner** tomografía f axial computerizada, TAC m o f; ~ **scan** escáner m TAC; **to have a ~ scan: I'm going to have a ~ scan** me van a hacer un (escáner) TAC.
cat [kæt] N (a) gato m, (she-~) gata f; **to be like a ~ on hot bricks** estar como gato sobre ascuas; **to fight like ~ and dog** pelearse como gato y perro; **he hasn't a ~ in hell's chance** no tiene la más mínima posibilidad; **to lead a ~ and dog life** vivir como perros y gatos; **to let the ~ out of the bag** descubrir el pastel, tirar de la manta; **he looked like something the ~ had brought in** estaba hecho un desastre; **to rain ~s and dogs** llover a cántaros; **to see which way the ~ jumps** esperar a ver de qué lado caen las peras; **to set the ~ among the pigeons** meter los perros en danza; **there isn't room to swing a ~** aquí no cabe un alfiler; **he thinks he's the ~'s pyjamas** (or whiskers)* se cree la mar de listo*; **when the ~'s away the mice will play** cuando el gato no está bailan los ratones. (b) (US*) tío* m, tipo* m. (c) (††Naut) azote m.
cataclysm ['kætəklɪzəm] N cataclismo m.
cataclysmic [ˌkætə'klɪzmɪk] ADJ de cataclismo.
catacombs ['kætəkuːmz] NPL catacumbas fpl.
catafalque ['kætəfælk] N catafalco m.
Catalan ['kætələn] 1 ADJ catalán.
2 N (a) catalán m, -ana f. (b) (Ling) catalán m.
catalepsy ['kætlepsɪ] N catalepsia f.
cataleptic [ˌkætə'leptɪk] 1 ADJ cataléptico.
2 N cataléptico m, -a f.
catalogue, (US) **catalog** ['kætəlɒg] 1 N catálogo m; (of cards) fichero m; (US: pamphlet, also prospectus (Scol)) folleto m; **a whole ~ of complaints** toda una serie de quejas.
2 VT catalogar, poner en un catálogo; **it is not catalog(u)ed** no consta en el catálogo.
Catalonia [ˌkætə'ləʊnɪə] N Cataluña f.
Catalonian [ˌkætə'ləʊnɪən] = **Catalan**.
catalyse, (US) **catalyze** ['kætəlaɪz] VT catalizar.
catalysis [kə'tælɪsɪs] N catálisis f.
catalyst ['kætəlɪst] N catalizador m.
catalytic [ˌkætə'lɪtɪk] ADJ catalítico; ~ **converter** catalizador m.
catamaran [ˌkætəmə'ræn] N catamarán m.
cat-and-mouse ['kætn'maʊs]: **to play a ~ game with sb** jugar al gato y ratón con uno.
catapult ['kætəpʌlt] 1 N (Hist and Aer) catapulta f; (boy's) tirador m, tiragomas m, tirachinas m.
2 VT (a) (Aer) catapultar. (b) (fig) **he was ~ed into fame** le llegó muy súbitamente la fama.
cataract ['kætərækt] N (Geog and Med) catarata f.
catarrh [kə'tɑːʳ] N catarro m.
catastrophe [kə'tæstrəfɪ] N catástrofe f.
catastrophic [ˌkætə'strɒfɪk] ADJ catastrófico.
catatonic [ˌkætə'tɒnɪk] 1 ADJ catatónico.
2 N catatónico m, -a f.
cat-basket ['kæt,bɑːskɪt] N (for carrying) cesto m para llevar el gato; (for sleeping) cesto m del gato.
catbird ['kætbɜːd] ATTR: **to be in the ~ seat** (US*) sentirse seguro.
cat-burglar ['kætbɜːgləʳ] N (ladrón m) balconero m.
catcall ['kætkɔːl] 1 N silbo m, silbido m, rechifla f.
2 VI silbar.
catch [kætʃ] 1 N (a) (act of catching) cogida f.
(b) (thing caught) presa f, captura f; (fish: quantity caught) pesca f, captura f, cantidad f de peces cogidos; **he's a good ~*** (in marriage) es un buen partido; **he's a good ~ for the team** es un buen recluta para el equipo.
(c) (Brit: of lock, on door) pestillo m; (Brit: of box, window) cerradura f; (small flange) fiador m.
(d) (Mus) canon m.
(e) (trick) trampa f; **there must be a ~ here somewhere** aquí debe de haber trampa; **the ~ is that ...** la dificultad es que ...; **a question with a ~ to it,** ~ **question** pregunta f de pega, pregunta f tramposa; ~ **22 situation** situación f de callejón sin salida, círculo m vicioso.
(f) (Sport) catch-can m, lucha f.
(g) **with a ~ in one's voice** con la voz entrecortada.
2 (irr: PRET AND PTP **caught**) VT (a) (capture) coger (Sp), agarrar, atrapar;

(grasp) asir; ball recoger (Sp), coger (Sp), parar, agarrar (LAm); attention captar; cold coger (Sp); ~! ¡cógelo! (Sp), ¡toma!; **to be caught like a rat in a trap** estar en una trampa sin salida; **I tried to ~ you on the phone** traté de hablar contigo por teléfono; **you've caught me at a bad moment** me has pillado en un mal momento; **when can I ~ you next?** ¿cuándo te convendrá hablar de esto?, ¿me das hora para volver a hablar de esto?
(b) (surprise) sorprender, coger (Sp); coger en una falta (Sp); **they caught him stealing apples** le pillaron mientras robaba manzanas; **you'll not ~ me doing it** no hay peligro de que yo lo haga; **we never caught them at it** no los sorprendimos nunca en flagrante; **we were caught by the snow** nos sorprendió la nieve; **we'll not be caught like this again** no volveremos a caer en esta trampa; **he was caught off stride** (US*) le cogieron (LAm: agarraron) con la guardia baja.
(c) bus, train etc coger (Sp), tomar.
(d) (be in time for) **to ~ the post** llegar antes de la recogida del correo; **we only just caught the train** por poco perdimos el tren; **hurry if you want to ~ it** date prisa si quieres llegar a tiempo.
(e) (entangle) **I caught my fingers in the door** pillé los dedos en la puerta; **I caught my coat on that nail** mi chaqueta se enganchó en ese clavo; **I caught my head on that beam** di con la cabeza contra esa viga.
(f) (Med) coger (Sp), contagiarse de; habit adquirir, adoptar.
(g) (perceive) likeness captar; meaning comprender; flavour percibir; (hear) oír, llegar a oír; **I didn't quite ~ you** no oí bien lo que dijiste; **to ~ the mood of the times** definir el espíritu de la época; **the painter has caught her expression** el pintor ha sabido captar su gesto.
(h) **to ~ sb a blow** pegar un golpe a uno; **the stone caught him on the ear** la piedra le dio en la oreja; **she caught me one on the nose** me pegó en la nariz.
(i) breath suspender.
(j) (*) **to ~ it** merecerse una regañina (from de); **you'll ~ it!** ¡las vas a pagar!; **he caught it good and proper** todo se le vino encima, se le cargaron por las buenas.
(k) (receive) **this room ~es the morning sun** este cuarto recibe el sol de la mañana; **the light was ~ing her hair** la luz brillaba en su pelo.
3 VI (a) (fire) encenderse, prenderse; (Culin) quemarse.
(b) (entangle) engancharse (on en); (Tech) engranar, (improperly) rozar, ludir (on con), prender (on en).
◆ **catch at** VT tratar de coger (LAm: agarrar), asir.
◆ **catch on** VI (a) (see the joke) caer, percibir lo gracioso del cuento; (tumble to) caer en la cuenta; (get the knack) coger el truco; **to ~ on to comprender**.
(b) (become popular) hacerse popular, alcanzar gran popularidad, afirmarse en el gusto del público; **it never really caught on** no logró establecerse de verdad.
◆ **catch out** VT (esp Brit) sorprender, pillar, cazar; coger en una falta (Sp); **we were caught out by the rise in the dollar** nos cogió desprevenidos la subida del dólar; **you won't ~ me out again like that** no me vas a pillar así otra vez.
◆ **catch up** 1 VT (a) person etc alcanzar, llegar al nivel de.
(b) weapon etc asir.
(c) **we were caught up in the traffic** nos vimos bloqueados por el tráfico; **a society caught up in change** una sociedad afectada por cambios.
2 VI ponerse al día; hacer los atrasos de trabajo (etc); ponerse al nivel de los demás; **to ~ up on one's sleep** recuperar los atrasos de sueño; **to ~ up with** person alcanzar; news etc ponerse al corriente de; work poner al día, cubrir los atrasos de.
catch-all ['kætʃ,ɔːl] 1 ADJ regulation, clause etc general; ~ **phrase** frase f para todo.
2 N algo que sirve para todo.
catcher ['kætʃəʳ] N (Baseball) apañador m, receptor m.
catching ['kætʃɪŋ] ADJ (Med) contagioso; (fig) pegajoso, atrayente, cautivador.
catchment ['kætʃmənt] N: ~ **area** zona f de captación; ~ **basin** cuenca f.
catchpenny ['kætʃ,penɪ] ADJ llamativo (y barato); hecho para venderse al instante; ~ **solution** solución f atractiva (pero poco recomendable).
catch-phrase ['kætʃfreɪz] N tópico m; muletilla f; slogan m; (Rad etc) frase f típica.
catchword ['kætʃwɜːd] N (Typ) reclamo m; (Theat) pie m; (catch-phrase) tópico m.
catchy ['kætʃɪ] ADJ (a) (Mus) pegadizo, atractivo, fácil de recordar. (b) question tramposo.
catechism ['kætɪkɪzəm] N (manual) catecismo m; (instruction) catequismo m, catequesis f.
catechist ['kætɪkɪst] N catequista mf.

catechize ['kætıkaız] VT catequizar.
categoric(al) [,kætı'gɒrık(əl)] ADJ categórico, terminante; *refusal* rotundo.
categorically [,kætı'gɒrıkəlı] ADV *state etc* de modo terminante; *refuse* rotundamente.
categorization [,kætıgəraı'zeıʃən] N categorización *f*.
categorize ['kætıgəraız] VT clasificar; **to ~ sth as** calificar algo de, clasificar algo como.
category ['kætıgərı] N categoría *f*.
cater ['keıtəʳ] VI (a) **to ~ for** abastecer a, proveer comida a; *(fig)* atender a, proveer a; satisfacer; servir, ofrecer servicios a; **we ~ for group bookings** atendemos a las reservas de grupos; **this magazine ~s for the under-21s** esta revista se dirige a los sub-21; **to ~ for all tastes** atender a todos los gustos.
(b) *(US)* **to ~ to** transigir con, hacer concesiones a.
cater-cornered ['keıtə'kɔ:nəd] *(US)* [1] ADJ diagonal.
[2] ADV diagonalmente.
caterer ['keıtərəʳ] N abastecedor *m*, -ora *f*, proveedor *m*, -ora *f*.
catering ['keıtərıŋ] N abastecimiento *m*; servicio *m* de comidas, servicio *m* de comedor; **~ company** empresa *f* de hostelería; **~ industry**, **~ trade** restaurantería *f*, hostelería *f*; **a career in ~** una carrera en la hostelería.
caterpillar ['kætəpıləʳ] N oruga *f*, gusano *m*; **~ track**, **~ tread** (rodado *m* de) oruga *f*; **~ tractor** tractor *m* oruga.
caterwaul ['kætəwɔ:l] VI chillar, aullar, maullar.
caterwauling ['kætə,wɔ:lıŋ] N chillidos *mpl*, aullidos *mpl*.
catfish ['kætfıʃ] N, PL INVAR siluro *m*, bagre *m*, perro *m* del norte.
catflap ['kætflæp] N gatera *f*.
catgut ['kætgʌt] N cuerda *f* de tripa; *(Med)* catgut *m*.
Cath. (a) ABBR *of* **Cathedral** catedral *f*. (b) ABBR *of* **Catholic** católico *m*.
Catharine ['kæθərın] NF Catalina.
catharsis [kə'θɑ:sıs] N catarsis *f*.
cathartic [kə'θɑ:tık] [1] ADJ *(Med)* catártico, purgante; *(Liter)* catártico.
[2] N purgante *m*.
cathedral [kə'θi:drəl] N catedral *f*; **~ city** ciudad *f* episcopal; **~ church** iglesia *f* catedral.
Catherine ['kæθərın] NF Catalina; **~ wheel** *(firework)* rueda *f* catalina.
catheter ['kæθıtəʳ] N catéter *m*.
catheterize ['kæθıtə,raız] VT *bladder, person* entubar.
cathode ['kæθəʊd] N cátodo *m*; **~ rays** rayos *mpl* catódicos; **~ ray tube** tubo *m* de rayos catódicos.
Catholic ['kæθəlık] [1] ADJ católico.
[2] N católico *m*, -a *f*.
catholic ['kæθəlık] ADJ (a) católico. (b) *(fig)* liberal, de amplias miras; de gustos eclécticos; *taste* amplio.
Catholicism [kə'θɒlısızəm] N catolicismo *m*.
cathouse: ['kæthaʊs] N, PL **cathouses** ['kæthaʊzız] *(US)* casa *f* de putas.
Cathy ['kæθı] NF *familiar form of* **Catharine, Catherine**.
catkin ['kætkın] N amento *m*, candelilla *f*.
cat-lick* ['kætlık] N mano *f* de gato; **to give o.s. a ~** lavarse a lo gato.
catlike ['kætlaık] ADJ felino, gatuno.
catmint ['kætmınt] N, *(US)* **catnip** ['kætnıp] N hierba *f* gatera, nébeda *f*.
catnap ['kætnæp] N siestecita *f*, sueñecito *m*.
Cato ['keıtəʊ] NM Catón.
cat-o'nine-tails ['kætə'naınteılz] N azote *m* (con nueve ramales).
cat's-cradle ['kæts,kreıdl] N (juego *m* de la) cuna *f*.
cat's-eyes ['kæts,aız] NPL *(Brit Aut)* catafotos *mpl*.
cat's-paw ['kætspɔ:] N instrumento *m*.
catsuit ['kætsu:t] N traje *m* de gato.
catsup ['kætsəp] N *(US)* salsa *f* de tomate, catsup *m*.
cat's whisker [,kæts'wıskəʳ] N *(Rad)* cable *m* antena.
cattery ['kætərı] N residencia *f* para gatos.
cattiness ['kætınıs] N malicia *f*, rencor *m*.
cattle ['kætl] NPL ganado *m*, ganado *m* vacuno, vacas *fpl*.
cattle-breeder ['kætl,bri:dəʳ] N criador *m*, -ora *f* de ganado.
cattle-breeding ['kætl,bri:dıŋ] N crianza *f* de ganado.
cattle-crossing ['kætl,krɒsıŋ] N paso *m* de ganado.
cattle drive ['kætl,draıv] N *(US)* recogida *f* de ganado.
cattle egret ['kætl'i:grıt] N garcilla *f* bueyera.
cattle-grid ['kætl,grıd] N *(Brit)* rejilla *f* de retención (de ganado).
cattleman ['kætlmæn] N, PL **cattlemen** ['kætlmen] ganadero *m*.
cattle-market ['kætl,mɑ:kıt] N mercado *m* ganadero (*or* de ganado); *(also fig)* feria *f* de ganado.
cattle prod ['kætl,prɒd] N picana *f*.
cattle-raising ['kætl,reızıŋ] N ganadería *f*.
cattle rustler ['kætl,rʌsləʳ] N *(US)* ladrón *m* de ganado, cuatrero *m*.
cattle-shed ['kætl,ʃed] N establo *m*.
cattle-show ['kætl,ʃəʊ] N feria *f* de ganado.
cattle-truck ['kætltrʌk] N *(Aut)* camión *m* ganadero; *(Brit Rail)* vagón *m* para ganado.

catty ['kætı] ADJ malicioso, rencoroso.
Catullus [kə'tʌləs] NM Catulo.
CATV N ABBR *of* **community antenna television**.
catwalk ['kætwɔ:k] N pasadizo *m*, pasarela *f*.
Caucasian [kɔ:'keızıən] [1] ADJ *(by race)* caucásico; *(Geog)* caucasiano.
[2] N *(by race)* caucásico *m*, -a *f*; *(Geog)* caucasiano *m*, -a *f*.
Caucasus ['kɔ:kəsəs] N Cáucaso *m*.
caucus ['kɔ:kəs] N *(Brit Pol)* camarilla *f* (política), junta *f* secreta; *(US Pol)* reunión *f* de un partido; jefes *mpl* de un partido, comité *m* directivo.
caudal ['kɔ:dl] ADJ caudal.
caught [kɔ:t] PRET AND PTP *of* **catch**.
cauldron ['kɔ:ldrən] N caldera *f*, calderón *m*.
cauliflower ['kɒlıflaʊəʳ] N coliflor *f*; **~ cheese** coliflor *f* con queso; **~ ear** oreja *f* deformada por los golpes.
caulk [kɔ:k] VT calafatear.
causal ['kɔ:zəl] ADJ causal.
causality [kɔ:'zælıtı] N causalidad *f*.
causally ['kɔ:zəlı] ADV causalmente; **they are ~ related** guardan una relación de causa-efecto.
causation [kɔ:'zeıʃən] N causalidad *f*.
causative ['kɔ:zətıv] ADJ causativo.
▼ **cause** [kɔ:z] [1] N (a) causa *f*, motivo *m*, razón *f*; **lost ~** causa *f* perdida, causa *f* imposible; **with good ~** con razón; **to be the ~ of** ser causa de, causar, motivar; **there's no ~ for alarm** no hay por qué asustarse; **in the ~ of liberty** por la libertad; **it's all in a good ~** todo esto tiene un propósito noble; **to die in a good ~** morir por una causa noble; **to give ~ for complaint** dar motivo de queja; **you have ~ to be worried** Vd tiene buen motivo para inquietarse; **to make common ~ with** hacer un frente común con, hacer causa común con; **to show ~** aducir argumentos convincentes; **to take up sb's ~** apoyar la campaña de uno, acudir a la defensa de uno.
(b) *(Jur)* causa *f*, pleito *m*.
▼[2] VT causar, motivar, provocar; originar; **to ~ an accident** causar un accidente; **to ~ sb to do sth** hacer que uno haga algo.
cause célèbre [,kɔ:zseı'lebrə] N pleito *m* célebre, caso *m* célebre.
causeway ['kɔ:zweı] N calzada *f* elevada; carretera *f* elevada; *(in sea)* arrecife *m*.
caustic ['kɔ:stık] ADJ cáustico; **~ soda** sosa *f* cáustica.
cauterize ['kɔ:təraız] VT cauterizar.
caution ['kɔ:ʃən] [1] N (a) cautela *f*, prudencia *f*; **'~!'** *(Aut)* '¡cuidado!', '¡precaución!'; **to throw ~ to the winds** abandonar la prudencia.
(b) *(warning)* advertencia *f*, amonestación *f*.
(c) (*) **he's a ~** *(odd)* es un tío muy raro, *(amusing)* es un tío divertidísimo.
[2] VT amonestar *(against* contra).
cautionary ['kɔ:ʃənərı] ADJ *tale* de escarmiento, aleccionador.
cautious ['kɔ:ʃəs] ADJ cauteloso, prudente, precavido; cauto; **to make a ~ statement** hacer una declaración prudente; **to play a ~ game** jugar con mucha prudencia.
cautiously ['kɔ:ʃəslı] ADV cautelosamente, con cautela.
cautiousness ['kɔ:ʃəsnıs] N cautela *f*, prudencia *f*.
cavalcade [,kævəl'keıd] N cabalgata *f*; *(fig)* desfile *m*.
cavalier [,kævə'lıəʳ] [1] ADJ arrogante, desdeñoso; *treatment* sin miramientos.
[2] N caballero *m*; (††) galán *m*; *(Brit Hist)* partidario del Rey en la Guerra Civil inglesa (1641-49).
cavalierly [,kævə'lıəlı] ADV arrogantemente, desdeñosamente; sin miramientos.
cavalry ['kævəlrı] N caballería *f*; **~ charge** carga *f* de caballería; **~ officer** oficial *m* de caballería; **~ twill** tela asargada utilizada para confeccionar pantalones.
cavalryman ['kævəlrımən] N, PL **cavalrymen** ['kævəlrımen] soldado *m* de caballería.
cave¹ [keıv] [1] N cueva *f*, caverna *f*.
[2] VI: **to ~ in** derrumbarse, hundirse; *(fig)* ceder, rendirse.
cave² ['keıvı] INTERJ: **~!** *(Brit Scol:*)* ¡ojo!, ¡ahí viene!; **to keep ~** estar a la mira.
caveat ['kævıæt] N advertencia *f*; *(Jur)* advertencia *f* de suspensión; **to enter a ~** hacer una advertencia.
cave-dweller ['keıv,dweləʳ] N cavernícola *mf*, troglodita *mf*.
cave-in ['keıvın] N *(of roof etc)* derrumbe *m*, derrumbamiento *m*; *(of pavement etc)* socavón *m*.
caveman ['keıvmæn] N, PL **cavemen** ['keıvmen] cavernícola *m*, troglodita *m*; hombre *m* de las cavernas; *(vaguely)* hombre *m* prehistórico; *(hum and iro)* machote *m*.
cave-painting ['keıv,peıntıŋ] N pintura *f* rupestre.
caver ['keıvəʳ] N espeleólogo *m*, -a *f*.
cavern ['kævən] N caverna *f*.
cavernous ['kævənəs] ADJ cavernoso.
caviar(e) ['kævıɑ:ʳ] N caviar *m*.
cavil ['kævıl] [1] N reparo *m*.

2 VI sutilizar, critiquizar; **to ~ at** poner peros a, critiquizar sin motivo.

caving ['keɪvɪŋ] N espeleología f.

cavity ['kævɪtɪ] N cavidad f, hueco m, hoyo m; (of tooth) caries f; **nasal cavities** fosas fpl nasales; **~ wall** doble pared f.

cavort [kə'vɔːt] VI dar cabrioladas; (fig) divertirse ruidosamente.

cavy ['keɪvɪ] N conejillo m de Indias, cobaya m.

caw [kɔː] 1 N graznido m.
2 VI graznar.

cawing ['kɔːɪŋ] N graznidos mpl, el graznar.

cayenne ['keɪen] N (also **~ pepper**) pimienta f de chile.

cayman ['keɪmən] N caimán m.

Cayman Islands ['keɪmən,aɪləndz] NPL: **the ~** las Islas Caimán.

CB (a) N ABBR of **Companion (of the Order) of the Bath** título honorífico británico. (b) (Mil) ABBR of **confined to barracks** (men) arresto m menor en cuartel; (officers) arresto m en banderas. (c) ATTR: **~ Radio** ABBR of **Citizens' Band Radio** banda f ciudadana.

CBC N ABBR of **Canadian Broadcasting Corporation.**

CBE N ABBR of **Commander of the Order of the British Empire** título honorífico británico.

CBI N ABBR of **Confederation of British Industry** ≃ Confederación f Española de Organizaciones Empresariales, CEOE f; ver también TRADE UNIONS.

CBS N (US) ABBR of **Columbia Broadcasting System.**

CC N ABBR of **County Council.**

c.c. (a) NPL (Math) ABBR of **cubic centimetres** centímetros mpl cúbicos. (b) (Comm) ABBR of **carbon copy.**

CCA N (US) ABBR of **Circuit Court of Appeals** tribunal m de apelación itinerante.

CCC N (US) ABBR of **Commodity Credit Corporation.**

CCTV N ABBR of **closed-circuit television.**

CCU N (US) ABBR of **coronary care unit** unidad f de cuidados cardiológicos.

CD N (a) ABBR of **Corps Diplomatique** Cuerpo m Diplomático, CD. (b) ABBR of **Civil Defence (Corps)** defensa f civil. (c) (US Pol) ABBR of **congressional district.** (d) ABBR of **compact disk** disco m compacto. (e) (Pol) ABBR of **Conference on Disarmament.**

CDC N (US) ABBR of **Centers for Disease Control.**

CDC - CENTERS FOR DISEASE CONTROL

ⓘ *El organismo federal estadounidense conocido como **the CDC**, abreviatura de **Centers for Disease Control**, con sede en Atlanta, controla muchos aspectos de la sanidad pública del país. Además de establecer y hacer cumplir las normas de salud medioambiental y laboral, se encarga de recoger y analizar información sobre la salud, y es responsable de la prevención y el control de las enfermedades infecciosas. De hecho, es especialmente conocido en el extranjero por ser pionero en el control del virus del Sida y la identificación de sus vías de contagio.*

CDI ADJ ABBR of **compact disk interactive.**

Cdr (Brit Naut, Mil) ABBR of **commander** Comandante m; **~ R. Thomas** (on envelope) Cdte. R. Thomas.

CD-ROM [,siːdiːˈrɒm] N ABBR of **compact disk read-only memory** CD-ROM m; **~ drive** unidad f de CD-ROM.

CDT N (US) ABBR of **Central Daylight Time.**

CDTV N ABBR of **compact disc television.**

CDV N ABBR of **compact disk video.**

CE N ABBR of **Church of England** Iglesia f Anglicana.

cease [siːs] 1 VT suspender, cesar; **to ~ work** suspender el trabajo, terminar de trabajar.
2 VI cesar; **to ~ (from)** + ger, **to ~ to** + infin dejar de + infin, cesar de + infin.

ceasefire [,siːsˈfaɪəʳ] N cese m de hostilidades, alto m el fuego; **~ line** línea f del alto el fuego.

ceaseless ['siːslɪs] ADJ incesante, continuo.

ceaselessly ['siːslɪslɪ] ADV incesantemente, sin cesar.

Cecil ['sesl] NM Cecilio.

Cecily ['sɪsɪlɪ] NF Cecilia.

cecum ['siːkəm] N (US) = **caecum.**

CED N (US) ABBR of **Committee for Economic Development.**

cedar ['siːdəʳ] N cedro m; **~ wood** madera f de cedro.

cede [siːd] VT ceder (to a).

cedilla [sɪ'dɪlə] N cedilla f.

CEEB N (US) ABBR of **College Entry Examination Board.**

ceilidh ['keɪlɪ] N baile con música y danzas tradicionales escocesas o irlandesas.

ceiling ['siːlɪŋ] N techo m (also Aer); cielo m raso; (fig) límite m, punto m más alto; **~ price** precio m tope; **to fix a ~ for, to put a ~ on** fijar el límite de, señalar el punto más alto de; **to hit the ~*** subirse por las paredes*; **he has not yet reached his ~** se desarrollará todavía algo más, ha de ser mejor aún.

celandine ['seləndaɪn] N celidonia f.

celeb* [sɪ'leb] N famoso m, -a f.

celebrant ['selɪbrənt] N celebrante m.

▼ **celebrate** ['selɪbreɪt] 1 VT celebrar; festejar; marriage solemnizar; happy event celebrar, señalar con una fiesta; anniversary etc conmemorar; **we're celebrating his arrival** estamos celebrando su llegada; **what are you celebrating?** ¿qué festejáis?, ¿qué motivo tiene esta fiesta?; **he ~d his birthday by scoring 2 goals** celebró su cumpleaños marcando 2 goles.
2 VI divertirse, estar (or ir) de parranda.

celebrated ['selɪbreɪtɪd] ADJ célebre, famoso.

celebration [,selɪ'breɪʃən] N celebración f; (party) fiesta f, guateque m; (public rejoicing) festividad f; **~s** (of anniversary etc) conmemoraciones fpl; **in ~ of** en conmemoración de.

celebratory [,selɪ'breɪtərɪ] ADJ event etc de celebración; **let's have a ~ dinner** vamos a ofrecer una cena para celebrarlo.

celebrity [sɪ'lebrɪtɪ] N (all senses) celebridad f.

celeriac [sə'lerɪæk] N apio m nabo.

celerity [sɪ'lerɪtɪ] N celeridad f.

celery ['selərɪ] N apio m, panil m (SC).

celestial [sɪ'lestɪəl] ADJ celestial.

celibacy ['selɪbəsɪ] N celibato m.

celibate ['selɪbɪt] 1 ADJ célibe.
2 N célibe mf.

cell [sel] N (of prison, monastery) celda f; (Bio, Pol) célula f; (of bees) celda f, celdilla f; (Elec) elemento m, vaso m, pila f; (Pol, of terrorists etc) célula f; **~ biology** biología f celular.

cellar ['seləʳ] N sótano m; (for wine) bodega f; **to keep a good ~** tener buena bodega.

cellist ['tʃelɪst] N violonchelista mf.

cellmate ['selmeɪt] N compañero m de celda, compañera f de celda.

cello ['tʃeləʊ] N violonchelo m.

Cellophane ['seləfeɪn] ® N celofán m.

cellphone ['sel,fəʊn] N = **cellular telephone.**

cellular ['seljʊləʳ] ADJ celular; **~ telephone** teléfono m celular.

cellulite ['seljəlaɪt] N celulitis f.

cellulitis [,selju'laɪtɪs] N celulitis f.

celluloid ['seljʊlɔɪd] N celuloide m.

cellulose ['seljʊləʊs] N celulosa f.

Celsius ['selsɪəs] ADJ celsius, centígrado.

Celt [kelt, selt] N celta mf.

Celtiberia [,keltaɪ'bɪərɪ] N Celtiberia f.

Celtiberian [,keltaɪ'bɪərɪən] 1 ADJ celtibérico.
2 N celtíbero m, -a f.

Celtic ['keltɪk, 'seltɪk] 1 ADJ celta, céltico.
2 N (Ling) céltico m.

cembalo ['tʃembələʊ] N clavicordio m, clave m.

cement [sə'ment] 1 N cemento m; (glue) cola f, pegamento m; **~ mixer** hormigonera f.
2 VT cementar; cubrir (or revestir etc) de cemento; (fig) fortalecer, reforzar, consolidar.

cementation [,siːmen'teɪʃən] N cementación f.

cemetery ['semɪtrɪ] N cementerio m.

cenotaph ['senətɑːf] N cenotafio m.

censer ['sensəʳ] N incensario m.

censor ['sensəʳ] 1 N censor m, -ora f.
2 VT censurar; (delete) tachar, suprimir.

censorious [sen'sɔːrɪəs] ADJ hipercrítico, criticón.

censorship ['sensəʃɪp] N censura f.

censurable ['senʃərəbl] ADJ censurable.

censure ['senʃəʳ] 1 N censura f.
2 VT censurar.

census ['sensəs] N censo m; empadronamiento m; **to take a ~ of** levantar el censo de.

cent [sent] N (Canada, US) centavo m; **I haven't a ~** no tengo un céntimo.

cent. (a) ABBR of **centigrade.** (b) ABBR of **central.** (c) ABBR of **century.**

centaur ['sentɔːʳ] N centauro m.

centenarian [,sentɪ'neərɪən] 1 ADJ centenario.
2 N centenario m, -a f.

centenary [sen'tiːnərɪ] N centenario m; **the ~ celebrations for ...** las festividades para celebrar el centenario de ...

centennial [sen'tenɪəl] (esp US) 1 ADJ centenario.
2 N centenario m.

center ['sentəʳ] etc (US) = **centre** etc.

centesimal [sen'tesɪməl] ADJ centesimal.

centigrade ['sentɪgreɪd] ADJ centígrado; **30 degrees ~** 30 grados centígrados.

centigram(me) ['sentɪgræm] N centigramo m.

centilitre, (US) centiliter ['sentɪ,liːtəʳ] N centilitro m.

centime ['sɑːntiːm] N céntimo m.

centimetre, (US) centimeter ['sentɪ,miːtəʳ] N centímetro m.

centipede ['sentɪpiːd] N ciempiés m.

central ['sentrəl] ADJ central; (*in town etc*) céntrico; ~ **bank** banco *m* central; ~ **government** gobierno *m* central; ~ **heating** calefacción *f* central; ~ **locking** cierre *m* centralizado; ~ **processing unit** unidad *f* procesadora central, unidad *f* central de proceso; ~ **reservation** (*Brit Aut*) mediana *f*; **of** ~ **importance** de la mayor importancia, primordial; **it is** ~ **to our policy** es un punto clave de nuestra política.

Central African Republic [,sentrəl,æfrɪkənrɪ'pʌblɪk] N República *f* Centroafricana.

Central America ['sentrələ'merɪkə] N Centroamérica *f*.

Central American ['sentrələ'merɪkən] ① ADJ centroamericano.
② N centroamericano *m*, -a *f*.

Central Asian ['sentrəl'eɪʃn] ADJ centroasiático.

Central Europe ['sentrəl'jʊərəp] N Europa *f* Central.

Central European ['sentrəl,jʊərə'piːən] ① ADJ centroeuropeo.
② N centroeuropeo *m*, -a *f*.

centralism ['sentrəlɪzm] N (*Pol*) centralismo *m*.

centralist ['sentrəlɪst] ADJ centralista.

centrality [sen'trælɪtɪ] N (*frm*) centralidad *f*.

centralization [,sentrəlaɪ'zeɪʃən] N centralización *f*.

centralize ['sentrəlaɪz] VT centralizar; concentrar, reunir en un centro.

centralized ['sentrəlaɪzd] ADJ centralizado.

centrally ['sentrəlɪ] ADV *organize etc* centralmente; ~**-heated** con calefacción central; ~ **planned economy** economía *f* de planificación central.

centre, (*US*) **center** ['sentər] ① N centro *m*; núcleo *m*; (*of chocolate*) relleno *m*; (*Sport*) centro *m* (*also kick*); ~ **of attraction** centro *m* de atracción; ~ **of gravity** centro *m* de gravedad; ~ **of intrigue** centro *m* de intrigas.
② ATTR central; del centro; ~ **court** pista *f* central; ~ **parties** partidos *mpl* centristas, partidos *mpl* del centro; ~ **spread** artículo *m* de doble página central; ~ **vowel** vocal *f* media.
③ VT centrar; *ball* pasar al centro; (*fig*) concentrar (*on* en).
④ VI: **to** ~ **(a)round, to** ~ **in, to** ~ **on** concentrarse en, estar concentrado en, tener por centro, (*hopes etc*) cifrarse en.

centre-back ['sentə'bæk] N defensa *m* centro, escoba *m*.

centre-board, (*US*) **center-board** ['sentəbɔːd] N orza *f* de deriva.

-centred, (*US*) **-centered** ['sentəd] *in compounds* centrado en, basado en; *eg* home~ centrado en el hogar.

centrefold, (*US*) **centerfold** ['sentə,fəʊld] N entrepágina *f*.

centre-forward ['sentə'fɔːwəd] N delantero *m* centro.

centre-half ['sentə'hɑːf] N, PL **centre-halves** ['sentə'hɑːvz] medio *m* centro.

centrepiece, (*US*) **centerpiece** ['sentəpiːs] N centro *m* de mesa; (*fig*) atracción *f* principal, objeto *m* (*etc*) de mayor interés.

centrifugal [sen'trɪfjʊgəl] ADJ centrífugo.

centrifuge ['sentrɪfjuːʒ] ① N centrífuga *f*.
② VT centrifugar.

centripetal [sen'trɪpɪtl] ADJ centrípeto.

centrism ['sentrɪzəm] N centrismo *m*.

centrist ['sentrɪst] ① ADJ centrista.
② N centrista *mf*.

centuries-old ['sentjʊrɪz,əʊld] ADJ secular.

centurion [sen'tjʊərɪən] N centurión *m*.

century ['sentjʊrɪ] N siglo *m*; (*cricket etc*) cien carreras *fpl* (*etc*); **in the 20th** ~ en el siglo veinte.

CEO N (*US*) = ABBR *of* **Chief Executive Officer.**

ceramic [sɪ'ræmɪk] ADJ cerámico.

ceramics [sɪ'ræmɪks] N SING cerámica *f*.

cereal ['sɪərɪəl] ① ADJ cereal.
② N cereal *m*; ~**s** (*crops, cornflakes*) cereales *mpl*.

cerebellum [serɪ'beləm] N cerebelo *m*.

cerebral ['serɪbrəl] ADJ cerebral; intelectual; ~ **palsy** parálisis *f* cerebral.

cerebration [,serɪ'breɪʃən] N meditación *f*, actividad *f* mental.

cerebrum ['serəbrəm] N cerebro *m*.

ceremonial [,serɪ'məʊnɪəl] ① ADJ de ceremonia, de gala.
② N ceremonial *m*.

ceremonially [,serɪ'məʊnɪəlɪ] ADV con ceremonia.

ceremonious [,serɪ'məʊnɪəs] ADJ ceremonioso.

ceremoniously [,serɪ'məʊnɪəslɪ] ADV ceremoniosamente.

▼ **ceremony** ['serɪmənɪ] N ceremonia *f*; **to stand on** ~ hacer ceremonias, ser etiquetero, estar de cumplido; **let's not stand on** ~ dejémonos de cumplidos.

cerise [sə'riːz] ① ADJ (de) color de cereza.
② N cereza *f*.

CERN [sɜːn] N ABBR *of* **Conseil Européen pour la Recherche Nucléaire** Consejo *m* Europeo para la Investigación Nuclear.

cert* [sɜːt] N (*Brit*) ABBR *of* **certainty**; **it's a (dead)** ~ es cosa segura; **he's a (dead)** ~ **for the job** sin duda le darán el puesto.

cert. ABBR *of* **certified** certificado.

▼ **certain** ['sɜːtən] ADJ (**a**) (*of things*) seguro, cierto; **it is** ~ **that ...** es seguro que ..., es cierto que ...; **it is** ~ **death to go there** ir allí es buscarse una muerte segura.

▼(**b**) (*of person*) seguro; **are you** ~? ¿estás seguro?; **I am** ~ **of it** estoy seguro de ello; **I am** ~ **that...** estoy seguro de que...; **we are** ~ **of his support** estamos seguros de tener su apoyo; **he is** ~ **to be there** es seguro que estará allí; **be** ~ **to call on him** no dejes de visitarle; **you don't sound very** ~ no pareces estar muy seguro.

(**c**) (*a particular*) cierto; **to quote a** ~ **book** citar cierto libro; **to see a** ~ **man** ver a cierto hombre; **a** ~ **Mr Smith** un tal Sr Smith; **on a** ~ **day in May** cierto día de mayo; **he left on a** ~ **Tuesday** se marchó uno de tantos martes; ~ **of our leaders** algunos de nuestros líderes.

▼(**d**) (*phrases*) **we don't know for** ~ no sabemos a ciencia cierta; **to make** ~ **of** asegurarse de; **I'll make** ~ lo averiguaré; **I'll make it as** ~ **as I can** lo haré todo lo seguro que pueda ser; **this should make victory** ~ esto ha de asegurarnos la victoria; **you should make** ~ **of your facts** conviene comprobar los datos.

▼ **certainly** ['sɜːtənlɪ] ADV (**a**) ~**!** ¡desde luego!, ¡por supuesto!, ¡naturalmente!; ~ **madam!** ¡con mucho gusto, señora!, ¡cómo Vd quiera, señora!; ~ **not!** ¡de ninguna manera!, ¡ni hablar!

▼(**b**) **it is** ~ **true that...** desde luego es verdad que...; **you may** ~ **take the car** desde luego que puedes tomar el coche; **I shall** ~ **be there** es seguro que asistiré, estaré allí sin falta; **you** ~ **did that well** eso sí que lo hiciste bien; **the meat is** ~ **tough** la carne sí es dura; **and** ~ **the Germans had more planes** y por cierto los alemanes tenían más aviones.

certainty ['sɜːtəntɪ] N certeza *f*, certidumbre *f*; seguridad *f*; **in the** ~ **of being able to go** con la certeza de poder ir; **there is no** ~ **about it** sobre esto no hay seguridad alguna; **his** ~ **was alarming** su convicción era desconcertante; **faced with the** ~ **of disaster** ante la inevitabilidad del desastre; **it's a** ~ es cosa segura; **we know for a** ~ **that ...** sabemos a ciencia cierta que ...; **we can't know with complete** ~ no lo podemos saber a ciencia cierta.

Cert. Ed. N ABBR *of* **Certificate of Education.**

certifiable [,sɜːtɪ'faɪəbl] ADJ (**a**) certificable. (**b**) (*Med*) demente, que padece tal demencia que hay que encerrarle en un manicomio.

certificate [sə'tɪfɪkɪt] N certificado *m*; (*academic etc*) título *m*; (*of birth etc*) partida *f*, acta *f* (*Mex*); ~ **of airworthiness** certificado *m* de aeronavegabilidad; ~ **of baptism** partida *f* de bautismo; ~ **of birth** partida *f* de nacimiento; ~ **of death** partida *f* de defunción; ~ **of deposit** certificado *m* de depósito; ~ **of incorporation** escritura *f* de constitución (de una sociedad anónima); ~ **of marriage** partida *f* de casamiento; ~ **of origin** certificado *m* de origen; **C~ of Secondary Education** (*Brit Scol*) ≃ Título *m* de BUP.

certificated [sə'tɪfɪkeɪtɪd] ADJ titulado, diplomado.

certification [,sɜːtɪfɪ'keɪʃən] N certificación *f*.

certified ['sɜːtɪfaɪd] ADJ *document* certificado, atestiguado; (*in profession*) titulado, diplomado; ~ **copy** copia *f* certificada; ~ **mail** (*US*) correo *m* certificado; ~ **public accountant** experto *m*, -a *f* contable.

certify ['sɜːtɪfaɪ] VT certificar; atestiguar, dar fe de; **certified as a true copy** confirmada como copia auténtica; **to** ~ **that...** declarar que...; **to** ~ **sb insane** declarar loco a uno.

certitude ['sɜːtɪtjuːd] N certidumbre *f*.

cerumen [sɪ'ruːmen] N cerumen *m*.

cervical ['sɜːvɪkəl] ADJ cervical; ~ **cancer** cáncer *m* cervical; ~ **smear test** diagnosis *f* citológica del cuello uterino, frotis *m* cervical.

cervix ['sɜːvɪks] N, PL **cervices** ['sɜːvɪsiːz] cuello *m* del útero.

Cesarean (*US*) = **Caesarean.**

cesium ['siːzɪəm] (*US*) = **caesium.**

cessation [se'seɪʃən] N cesación *f*, suspensión *f*; ~ **of hostilities** cese *m* de hostilidades.

cession ['seʃən] N cesión *f*.

cesspit ['sespɪt], **cesspool** ['sespuːl] N pozo *m* negro; (*fig*) sentina *f*.

CET N ABBR *of* **Central European Time.**

cetacean [sɪ'teɪʃən] ① ADJ cetáceo.
② N cetáceo *m*.

Cetnik ['setnɪk] ADJ, N chetnik *mf*.

Ceylon [sɪ'lɒn] N (*Hist*) Ceilán *m*.

Ceylonese [sɪlɒ'niːz] (*Hist*) ① ADJ ceilanés.
② N ceilanés *m*, -esa *f*.

CF, cf N ABBR *of* **cost and freight** costo *m* y flete.

C/F ABBR *of* **carried forward** suma y sigue.

cf. ABBR *of* **confer, compare** confróntese, cfr.

c/f, c/fwd ABBR *of* **carried forward** suma y sigue.

CFC N ABBR *of* **chlorofluorocarbon** clorofluorocarbono *m*, CFC *m*.

CG N (*US*) ABBR *of* **coastguard.**

cg ABBR *of* **centigram(s), centigramme(s)** centigramo(s) *m(pl)*, cg.

CGA N (*Comput*) ABBR *of* **colour graphics adaptor** adaptador *m* gráfico de colores.

CH N (*Brit*) ABBR *of* **Companion of Honour** título honorífico.

ch ABBR *of* **central heating** calefacción *f* central, cal. cen.

ch. (**a**) (*Liter*) ABBR *of* **chapter** capítulo *m*, cap. (**b**) (*Fin*) ABBR *of* **cheque**

► LANGUAGE IN USE: **ceremony** → 25.1   **certain:** a → 16.1, 26.3 b → 16.1 d → 15.1, 16.1   **certainly:** b → 15.1

cheque *m*, ch. (**c**) (*Rel*) ABBR of **church** iglesia *f*.

cha-cha-(cha) ['tʃɑː'tʃɑː('tʃɑː)] N cha-cha-cha *m*.

Chad [tʃæd] **1** N Chad *m*; **Lake ~** Lago *m* Chad.
2 ADJ chadiano.

chador ['tʃʌdər] N chador *m*.

chafe [tʃeɪf] **1** VT (**a**) (*rub*) rozar, raer.
(**b**) (*warm*) calentar frotando.
2 VI desgastarse (*against, on* contra); (*fig*) irritarse, impacientarse; **to ~ at, to ~ under** (*fig*) impacientarse por, irritarse debido a.

chaff [tʃɑːf] **1** N barcia *f*, ahechaduras *fpl*, paja *f* menuda; (*waste*) desperdicios *mpl*; (*fig*) zumbas *fpl*, chanzas *fpl*, burlas *fpl*; (*Mil*) paja *f* metálica.
2 VT zumbarse de, tomar el pelo a.

chaffinch ['tʃæfɪntʃ] N pinzón *m* (vulgar).

chafing-dish ['tʃeɪfɪŋdɪʃ] N calientaplatos *m*.

chagrin ['ʃægrɪn] **1** N mortificación *f*, desazón *f*, disgusto *m*; **to my ~** con gran disgusto mío.
2 VT mortificar, disgustar.

chain [tʃeɪn] **1** N cadena *f* (*also fig*); **~ of command** cadena *f* de mando; **~ of mountains** cordillera *f*; **in ~s** en cadenas; **to pull the ~** tirar del cordón.
2 VT encadenar.
◆ **chain up** VT *animal* encadenar.

chain-gang ['tʃeɪngæn] N grupo *m* de prisioneros encadenados.

chain-letter ['tʃeɪn,letər] N carta *f* que circula en cadena (*con promesa de una ganancia cuantiosa para los que la hacen seguir según las indicaciones*).

chain lightning ['tʃeɪn'laɪtnɪŋ] N (*US*) relámpagos *mpl* en zigzag.

chain-link fence ['tʃeɪnlɪŋk,fens] N valla *f* de tela metálica.

chainmail ['tʃeɪn'meɪl] N cota *f* de malla.

chainpump ['tʃeɪnpʌmp] N bomba *f* de cangilones.

chain-reaction ['tʃeɪnriː'ækʃən] N reacción *f* en cadena, reacción *f* eslabonada.

chainsaw ['tʃeɪn,sɔː] N sierra *f* de cadena.

chain-smoke ['tʃeɪn,sməʊk] VI fumar un pitillo tras otro.

chain-smoker ['tʃeɪnsməʊkər] N fumador *m*, -ora *f* que fuma un pitillo tras otro.

chain-stitch ['tʃeɪnstɪtʃ] N (*Sew*) punto *m* de cadeneta, cadeneta *f*.

chain-store ['tʃeɪnstɔːr] N tienda *f* (*or* sucursal *f*) de una cadena.

chair [tʃeər] **1** N (**a**) silla *f*; (*Univ*) cátedra *f*; (*of meeting*) presidencia *f*; **to address the ~** dirigirse al presidente; **to be in the ~, to take the ~** presidir (*at a meeting* una reunión); **won't you take a ~?** ¿quiere sentarse?; **the ~** (*US: electric ~*) la silla eléctrica.
(**b**) (*person*) presidente *m*, -a *f*.
2 VT (**a**) *person* llevar a hombros; **they ~ed him off the ground** le sacaron a hombros del campo.
(**b**) *meeting* presidir.

chairback ['tʃeəbæk] N respaldo *m*.

chairbound ['tʃeəbaʊnd] ADJ en silla de ruedas.

chairlift ['tʃeəlɪft] N telesilla *m*.

chairman ['tʃeəmən] N, PL **chairmen** ['tʃeəmen] presidente *m*, -a *f*; **~'s report** informe *m* del presidente.

chairmanship ['tʃeəmənʃɪp] N (*post*) presidencia *f*; (*art*) arte *m* de presidir reuniones.

chairoplane ['tʃeərəʊ,pleɪn] N silla *f* colgante.

chairperson ['tʃeə,pɜːsn] N presidente *m*, -a *f*.

chairwarmer* ['tʃeə,wɔːməʳ] N (*US*) calientasillas *mf*.

chairwoman ['tʃeə,wʊmən] N, PL **chairwomen** ['tʃeə,wɪmɪn] presidenta *f*.

chaise longue ['ʃeɪz'lɔ̃ːŋ] N tumbona *f*.

chakra ['tʃækrə] N chakra *m*.

chalet ['ʃæleɪ] N chalet *m*, chalé *m*.

chalice ['tʃælɪs] N cáliz *m*.

chalk [tʃɔːk] **1** N (*Geol*) creta *f*; (*for writing*) tiza *f*, gis *m* (*LAm*); **by a long ~** (*Brit fig*) de lejos; **not by a long ~** (*Brit fig*) ni con mucho; **they're as different as ~ and cheese** (*persons*) se parecen (*or* son) como el día y la noche.
2 VT marcar (*or* dibujar *etc*) con tiza.
◆ **chalk up** VT apuntar, anotar; atribuir (*to* a).

chalkboard ['tʃɔːkbɔːd] N (*US*) pizarra *f*.

chalkface ['tʃɔːkfeɪs] N: **the teacher at the ~** el maestro en su clase, el profesor delante de la pizarra; **those at the ~** los que enseñan.

chalkpit ['tʃɔːkpɪt] N cantera *f* de creta.

chalktalk* ['tʃɔːktɔːk] N (*US*) charla *f* ilustrada en la pizarra.

chalky ['tʃɔːkɪ] ADJ cretáceo; gredoso, cretoso.

challenge ['tʃælɪndʒ] **1** N reto *m*, desafío *m*, reto *m*; (*of sentry*) quién vive *m*; (*Jur*) recusación *f*; **the ~ of new ideas** el reto de las nuevas ideas; **the ~ of the 21st century** el reto del siglo XXI, las posibilidades del siglo XXI; **Vigo's ~ for the league leadership** la tentativa que hace el Vigo para tomar el liderato de la liga; **this is a ~ to us all** esto es un reto a todos nosotros; **to issue a ~ to sb** desafiar a uno; **to take up a ~** aceptar un desafío.

2 VT (*to duel*) desafiar, retar; (*sentry*) dar el quién vive a; (*Jur*) recusar; *fact, point* poner en duda, cuestionar, expresar dudas acerca de; contestar; *speaker* hablar en contra de; **to ~ sb to + infin** desafiar a uno a que + *subj*; **I ~ you to name her** a ver si Vd se atreve a decir su nombre; **I ~ that conclusion** creo que esa conclusión no es acertada.

-challenged ['tʃælɪndʒd] ADJ *ending in compounds* (*gen hum*): **vertically~** no muy alto; **intellectually~** no muy listo.

challenger ['tʃælɪndʒəʳ] N desafiador *m*, -ora *f*; (*competitor*) aspirante *mf*, concursante *mf*; (*opponent*) contrincante *mf*.

challenging ['tʃælɪndʒɪŋ] ADJ desafiante; *tone* de desafío; *speech etc* estimulante, provocador; *book* sugestivo, lleno de sugestiones; *task* arduo; **it's a ~ job** es un puesto que constituye un reto.

chamber ['tʃeɪmbəʳ] N (**a**) (*room*) cámara *f*; aposento *m*, sala *f*; (*Pol*) cámara *f*; **~s** (*Jur*) despacho *m*, bufete *m*; (*Brit: lodgings*) aposentos *mpl*; **~ of commerce** cámara *f* de comercio. (**b**) (*of gun*) recámara *f*. (**c**) (*Mus*) **~ concert** concierto *m* de cámara; **~ music** música *f* de cámara; **~ orchestra** orquesta *f* de cámara.

chamberlain ['tʃeɪmbəlɪn] N chambelán *m*, gentilhombre *m* de cámara.

chambermaid ['tʃeɪmbəmeɪd] N camarera *f*, sirvienta *f*, recamarera *f* (*Mex*).

chamberpot ['tʃeɪmbəpɒt] N orinal *m*, vaso *m* de noche.

chambray ['tʃæmbreɪ] N (*US*) = **cambric**.

chameleon [kə'miːlɪən] N camaleón *m*.

chamfer ['tʃæmfəʳ] **1** N chaflán *m*, bisel *m*.
2 VT chaflanar, biselar.

chammy ['ʃæmɪ] N gamuza *f*.

chamois N (**a**) ['ʃæmwɑː] (*Zool*) gamuza *f*. (**b**) ['ʃæmɪ] (*also ~ leather*) gamuza *f*.

chamomile ['kæməʊmaɪl] N = **camomile**.

champ¹ [tʃæmp] VT (*also* VI: **to ~ at**) morder, mordiscar; *bit* tascar, morder; **to be ~ing at the bit** (*fig*) estar impaciente por algo, morirse por algo.

champ²* [tʃæmp] N = **champion**.

Champagne [ʃæm'peɪn] N Champaña *f*.

champagne [ʃæm'peɪn] N champán *m*, champaña *m*; **~ breakfast** desayuno *m* con champán; **~ cup**, **~ glass** copa *f* de champán.

champers* ['ʃæmpəz] N (†) champán *m*.

champion ['tʃæmpɪən] **1** ADJ (**a**) campeón; **a ~ athlete** un atleta campeón.
(**b**) (*) magnífico; **~!** ¡estupendo!
2 N (**a**) campeón *m*, -ona *f*.
(**b**) (*of a cause*) defensor *m*, -ora *f*, paladín *m*.
3 VT defender, apoyar, abogar por.

championship ['tʃæmpɪənʃɪp] N (**a**) campeonato *m*. (**b**) (*of cause*) defensa *f*.

▼ **chance** [tʃɑːns] **1** ADJ fortuito, casual; imprevisto; (*random*) aleatorio.
2 N (**a**) (*luck, fortune, fate*) casualidad *f*; azar *m*; suerte *f*; **game of ~** juego *m* de azar; **the ~s of war** la fortuna de la guerra; **~ was against him** la suerte se le fue contraria; **~ ordained that ... un** la suerte quiso que ...; **it cannot have been a matter of ~** esto no habrá tenido nada de casual; **by ~** por casualidad; **by sheer ~** por pura casualidad; **do you by any ~ have a pen?** ¿tienes por casualidad una pluma?; **to leave things to ~** dejar las cosas al azar; **to leave nothing to ~** obrar con la mayor previsión, no dejar nada imprevisto.

▼(**b**) (*opportunity*) ocasión *f*, oportunidad *f*; **now's our ~!** ya nos toca el turno, nos ha llegado la vez; **~ would be a fine thing!** ¡ojalá tuviera la oportunidad!; **this is my big ~** ésta es la oportunidad que venía esperando; **you'll never get another ~ like this** la suerte nunca te deparará otra ocasión como ésta; **give me a ~ to show what I can do** déme la oportunidad de mostrar si soy capaz; **give me a ~ won't you?** ¡déjame un momento en paz!; **to give sb another ~** darle otra oportunidad a uno; **he has had every ~** le hemos dado todas las oportunidades posibles; **to have an eye for the main ~** mirar por su propio provecho; **to let the ~ slip by** perder la ocasión; **to waste one's ~s** desperdiciar las ocasiones.

▼(**c**) (*possibility*) posibilidad *f*, probabilidad *f*; **the ~s are that ...** lo más probable es que + *subj*; **there is no ~ of that** eso es imposible; **there's one ~ in ten** hay una posibilidad sobre diez; **it's a long ~** eso es poco probable; **to be in with a ~** tener algunas posibilidades; **to have a fair ~ of + ger** tener buenas probabilidades de + *infin*; **he hasn't a ~** no tiene posibilidad alguna; **I never had a ~ in life** la suerte no me ha favorecido jamás en la vida; **to stand a ~** tener posibilidades; **you don't stand a ~** no tienes posibilidad alguna.
(**d**) (*risk*) riesgo *m*; **to take a ~** arriesgarse, probar fortuna; **to take no ~s** obrar con la mayor previsión, no dejar nada imprevisto; **that's a ~ we shall have to take** tendremos que tomar ese riesgo.
3 VT (**a**) (*risk*) arriesgar; probar; **to ~ it** probarlo, aventurarse; **shall we ~ it?** ¿probaremos?; V **arm¹**.
(**b**) (*happen*) **it ~d that ...** aconteció que ...; **if it ~s that ...** si resulta

que ...; **I ~d to see him** le vi por casualidad.

[4] VI: **to ~ upon** encontrar por casualidad, tropezar con, topar con.

chancel ['tʃɑːnsəl] N coro m y presbiterio.

chancellery ['tʃɑːnsərɪ] N cancillería f.

chancellor ['tʃɑːnsələ'] N canciller m; **C~ of the Exchequer** (Brit) Ministro m, -a f de Economía y Hacienda; **Lord C~** jefe de la administración de la justicia en Inglaterra y Gales, y presidente de la Cámara de los Lores; ver también TREASURY.

chancer* ['tʃænsə'] N (Brit) trepa* mf.

chancery ['tʃɑːnsərɪ] N (Jur) chancillería f (††), tribunal m de equidad; **ward in ~** pupilo m, -a f bajo la protección del tribunal.

chancre ['ʃæŋkə'] N chancro m.

chancy* ['tʃɑːnsɪ] ADJ arriesgado; dudoso.

chandelier [ˌʃændə'lɪə'] N araña f (de luces).

chandler ['tʃɑːndlə'] N velero m.

change [tʃeɪndʒ] [1] N (a) cambio m; modificación f; transformación f; (of skin etc) muda f; **~ of address** cambio m de domicilio; **~ of clothes** cambio m (or muda f LAm) de ropa; **~ of front** cambio m de frente; **~ of heart** cambio m de sentimiento, cambio m de idea; **~ of horses** relevo m de los tiros; **~ of life** menopausia f; **~ of ownership** cambio m de dueño; **~ of scene** (Theat) mutación f; **for a ~** para variar un poco; **it's a ~ for the better** es una mejora; **to get no ~ out of sb** no conseguir sacar nada a uno; **to make a ~ of direction** cambiar de dirección; **the day out made a refreshing ~** el día fuera de casa nos dio un buen cambio de aire; **to resist ~** resistirse a las innovaciones; **to ring the ~s on sth** hacer algo de diversas maneras. (b) (money) (small coins) moneda f suelta, suelto m, sencillo m (LAm), feria f (Mex); (for a larger coin) cambio m; (money returned) vuelta f, vuelto m (LAm); **to give sb ~ for a £10 note** cambiar a uno un billete de 10 libras; **(you may) keep the ~** quédese con la vuelta (LAm: el vuelto).

[2] VT cambiar (for por), trocar; reemplazar; modificar; transformar (into en); clothes, colour, gear, mind etc cambiar de, mudar de; **to ~ pounds into dollars** cambiar libras en dólares; **can you ~ this note for me?** ¿me hace el favor de cambiar este billete?; **I find him much ~d** le veo muy cambiado; **to ~ a baby, to ~ a nappy** cambiar el pañal de un bebé.

[3] VI cambiar(se), mudar; transformarse (into en); (Rail etc) hacer transbordo, cambiar de tren (etc); **all ~!** ¡cambio de tren!; **you haven't ~d a bit!** ¡no has cambiado en lo más mínimo!

♦**change down** VI (Aut) cambiar a una velocidad inferior.

♦**change over** [1] VT cambiar, trocar. [2] VI cambiar (to a).

♦**change up** VI (Aut) cambiar a una velocidad superior.

changeability [ˌtʃeɪndʒə'bɪlɪtɪ] N lo cambiable, mutabilidad f; inconstancia f, lo cambiadizo; variabilidad f.

changeable ['tʃeɪndʒəbl] ADJ cambiable, mudable; inconstante, cambiadizo; weather variable.

changeless ['tʃeɪndʒlɪs] ADJ inmutable.

changeling ['tʃeɪndʒlɪŋ] N niño m sustituido por otro, niña f sustituida por otra.

change machine ['tʃeɪndʒməˌʃiːn] N máquina f de cambio.

changeover ['tʃeɪndʒˌəʊvə'] N cambio m.

change purse ['tʃeɪndʒpɜːs] N (US) monedero m.

changing ['tʃeɪndʒɪŋ] [1] ADJ cambiante; mudable, variable; **a ~ world** un mundo en perpetua evolución. [2] N: **~ of the guard** relevo m de la guardia.

changing-room ['tʃeɪndʒɪŋrʊm] N (Brit) vestuario m.

channel ['tʃænl] [1] N canal m (also TV); (of a river) cauce m; (strait) estrecho m; (fig) conducto m, medio m; (irrigation ~) acequia f, canal m de riego; **~ of distribution** vía f de distribución, canal m de distribución; **the (English) C~** el Canal (de la Mancha); **the C~ Tunnel** el túnel del Canal de la Mancha; **by the usual (or proper) ~s** por las vías de costumbre, por los conductos normales; **green ~** (Customs) pasillo m verde; **red ~** (Customs) pasillo m rojo. [2] VT acanalar; (fig) encauzar, dirigir (into a, por).

♦**channel off** VT (lit, fig) water, energy, resources canalizar.

| CHANNEL FOUR |

(i) ***Channel Four*** *es una de las cadenas nacionales de televisión en el Reino Unido, que comenzó a emitir en 1982 y se financia únicamente a través de la publicidad. Sus programas están enfocados hacia grupos con preferencias o intereses más bien minoritarios, que no tienen cabida en otros canales nacionales. También emite teleseries innovadoras que a veces resultan bastante polémicas, así como programas musicales y magazines dirigidos a los jóvenes. Una de sus características principales es su apoyo a la industria cinematográfica británica.*

channel-hop ['tʃænlhɒp] VI (Brit) hacer zapping.

channel-hopping ['tʃænl'hɒpɪŋ] N (Brit) zapping m.

Channel Islands ['tʃænl,aɪləndz] NPL, **Channel Isles** ['tʃænəl,aɪlz] NPL Islas fpl Normandas, Islas fpl Anglonormandas, Islas fpl del Canal

(de la Mancha).

channel-surf ['tʃænl,sɜːf] (US) = **channel-hop**.

channel-surfing ['tʃænl,sɜːfɪŋ] (US) = **channel-hopping**.

chant [tʃɑːnt] [1] N canto m; (Rel: plain ~) canto m llano; (fig) sonsonete m; (by demonstrators etc) grito m, eslogan m. [2] VT cantar (el canto llano); praises cantar; slogan gritar (rítmicamente), corear, entonar; (fig) salmodiar, recitar en tono monótono. [3] VI (Rel) cantar (el canto llano); (at demonstration etc) gritar (rítmicamente).

chantey ['ʃɑːntɪ] N (US) saloma f.

chaos ['keɪɒs] N caos m, desorden m.

chaos theory ['keɪɒs'θɪərɪ] N teoría f del caos.

chaotic [keɪ'ɒtɪk] ADJ caótico, desordenado.

chap¹ [tʃæp] [1] N grieta f, hendedura f. [2] VT agrietar. [3] VI agrietarse.

chap² [tʃæp] N (Anat) mandíbula f; (cheek) mejilla f.

chap³* [tʃæp] N tío* m, tipo* m, pájaro* m; **a ~ I know** un tío que conozco; **he's a nice ~** es buen chico, es buena persona; **he's very deaf, poor ~** es muy sordo, el pobre; **how are you, old ~?** ¿qué tal, amigo?; **be a good ~ and say nothing** sé buen chico y no digas nada.

chap. ABBR of **chapter** capítulo m, cap.

chapat(t)i [tʃə'pætɪ, tʃə'paːtɪ] N, PL **~ or ~s or ~es** chapatti m, en la cocina india, pan de forma achatada, sin levadura.

chapel ['tʃæpəl] [1] N capilla f; (Protestant etc) templo m; (Typ) personal m de una imprenta. [2] as ADJ: **people here are very ~** la gente aquí son metodistas (etc) muy firmes; **I'm not ~ myself** yo mismo no soy practicante.

chaperon(e) ['ʃæpərəʊn] [1] N acompañanta f (de señorita), carabina f*. [2] VT acompañar (a una señorita).

chaplain ['tʃæplɪn] N capellán m.

chaplaincy ['tʃæplɪnsɪ] N capellanía f.

chaplet ['tʃæplɪt] N guirnalda f, corona f de flores; (necklace) collar m; (Eccl) rosario m.

chapped [tʃæpt] ADJ skin agrietado.

chappy* ['tʃæpɪ] N = **chap³**.

chaps [tʃæps] NPL (US) zahones mpl, chaparreras fpl.

chapter ['tʃæptə'] N (a) capítulo m; **~ of accidents** serie f de desgracias; **with ~ and verse** con pelos y señales, con todo lujo de detalles; **he can quote you ~ and verse** él lo sabe citar con todos sus pelos y señales. (b) (Eccl) cabildo m.

chapterhouse ['tʃæptəhaʊs] N, PL **chapterhouses** ['tʃæptəhaʊzɪz] sala f capitular.

char¹ [tʃɑː'] VT carbonizar, chamuscar.

char² [tʃɑː'] N (Brit*) té m.

char³ [tʃɑː'] [1] N (Brit*) = **charlady**. [2] VI limpiar, trabajar como asistenta.

char-à-banc ['ʃærəbæŋ] N (†) autocar m.

character ['kærɪktə'] N (a) (nature of thing) carácter m, naturaleza f, índole f, calidad f; (moral ~ of person) carácter m; **~ assassination** defamación f, asesinato m moral; **~ reference** informe m, referencia f; **to be in ~** ser característico, ser conforme al tipo; **to be out of ~ with** disonar de, desentonar con; **to bear a good ~** tener una buena reputación; **to have a bad ~** tener mala fama; **to give sb a good ~** dar a uno una recomendación satisfactoria. (b) (personage in novel, play etc) personaje m; (rôle) papel m; 'Six C~s in Search of an Author' 'Seis personajes en busca de autor'; **the play has 8 ~s** la obra tiene 8 personajes; **chief ~** protagonista mf; **~ actor** actor m de carácter; **~ actress** característica f; **in the ~ of** en el papel de; **that is more in ~** eso es más característico; **~ part** papel m de carácter; **~ sketch** esbozo m de carácter. (c) (energy, determination) carácter m; **a man of ~** un hombre de carácter; **he lacks ~** le falta carácter. (d) (*) tipo* m, sujeto* m; **a ~ I know** un tipo que yo conozco; **he's quite a ~** es un tipo pintoresco, es un original; **he's a very odd ~** es un tipo muy raro. (e) (Bio, Comput, Typ etc) carácter m; **~ code** código m de caracteres; **~ set** juego m de caracteres; **~ space** espacio m (de carácter).

characterful ['kærɪktəfʊl] ADJ wine, singer con (mucho) carácter.

characteristic [ˌkærɪktə'rɪstɪk] [1] ADJ característico (of de). [2] N característica f, carácter m; peculiaridad f; distintivo m, señal f distintiva.

characteristically [ˌkærɪktə'rɪstɪkəlɪ] ADV característicamente, de modo característico.

characterization [ˌkærɪktəraɪ'zeɪʃən] N caracterización f.

characterize ['kærɪktəraɪz] VT caracterizar.

characterless ['kærɪktəlɪs] ADJ sin carácter.

charade [ʃə'rɑːd] N (game: also ~s) charada f; (fig) payasada f, farsa f, comedia *f.*

charcoal [ˈtʃɑːkəʊl] N carbón *m* vegetal; (*Art*) carboncillo *m*; ~ **drawing** dibujo *m* al carbón, dibujo *m* al carboncillo.

charcoal-burner [ˈtʃɑːkəʊlˌbɜːnəʳ] N carbonero *m.*

charcoal-grey [ˌtʃɑːkəʊlˈgreɪ] ADJ gris marengo.

charge [tʃɑːdʒ] **1** N (a) (*explosive, electrical*) carga *f.*
(b) (*attack*) carga *f*, ataque *m*, asalto *m*; (*of bull*) embestida *f*; (*Sport*) placaje *m*, atajo *m.*
(c) (*Jur etc*) acusación *f*, cargo *m*; **to appear on a ~ of** comparecer acusado de; **to beat the ~*** ser absuelto; **to bring** (*or* **lay**) **~s against** hacer acusaciones contra, levantar expediente contra (*LAm*); **to give sb in ~** entregar a uno a la policía; **to lay o.s. open to the ~ of ...** dejarse expuesto a la acusación de ...; **to return to the ~** volver al cargo, repetir la acusación.
(d) (*price*) precio *m*, coste *m*; (*professional*) honorarios *mpl*; ~ **account** cuenta *f* para compras a crédito, cuenta *f* abierta; ~ **card** tarjeta *f* de cuenta; **free of ~** gratis; ~ **for admission** precio *m* de entrada; 'no ~ for admission' 'entrada gratis', 'entrada gratuita'; **there's no ~** esto no se cobra, esto es gratuito; **is there a ~ for delivery?** ¿se paga el transporte?; **to be a ~ upon** cargarse en cuenta a; **to make a ~ for sth** cobrar por algo; **to reverse the ~s** (*Telec*) cobrar al número llamado, llamar a cobro revertido.
(e) (*responsibility*) responsabilidad *f*; (*office*) cargo *m*; (*task*) encargo *m*, cometido *m*; **the person in ~** la persona responsable; **to be in ~** mandar; **who is in ~ here?** ¿quién manda aquí?; **to be in ~ of** estar encargado de; **to be in the ~ of** correr a cargo de; **to take ~ of** hacerse cargo de, encargarse de; **men, expedition etc** asumir el mando de.
(f) (*person etc cared for*) **the teacher and her ~s** la maestra y sus alumnos; **the nurse and her ~s** la enfermera y sus enfermos.
(g) (*order*) orden *f*, instrucción *f.*
(h) (*Her*) blasón *m.*
2 VT (a) (*fill*) cargar (*also Mil, Elec*; **with** de).
(b) (*attack*) atacar, cargar contra; (*bull etc*) embestir; atajar.
(c) (*Jur etc*) acusar (**with** de).
(d) *price* pedir; *price, person* cobrar (a); **to ~ 3% commission** cobrar un 3 por cien de comisión; **what are they charging for it?** ¿cuánto piden por él?; **what did they ~ you for it?** ¿cuánto te cobraron?.
(e) (*record as debt: also* **to ~ up**) **to ~ sth** (**up**) **to sb, to ~ sth** (**up**) **to sb's account** cargar algo en cuenta a uno; ~ **it to my card** cárguelo a mi tarjeta; **cash or ~?** (*US*) ¿al contado o a crédito?
(f) (*order*) **to ~ sb to do sth** ordenar a uno hacer algo; **to ~ sb with a mission** confiar una misión a uno; **I am ~d with the task of** + *ger* me han encargado el deber de + *infin.*
3 VI (a) (*Mil*) atacar, cargar; (*bull*) embestir; **to ~ down upon** cargar sobre, precipitarse sobre; **to ~ into** *wall* chocar contra; *crowd, meeting* irrumpir en; *fray* lanzarse a (participar en).
(b) (*make pay*) cobrar, (*a lot*) cobrar mucho.

◆**charge up** VT (a) = **charge 2** (e). (b) *battery* cargar.

chargeable [ˈtʃɑːdʒəbl] ADJ (a) ~ **with** (*Jur*) *person* acusable de. (b) ~ **to** a cargo de.

charge-cap [ˈtʃɑːdʒkæp] VT (*Brit*) *local authority* fijar un tope a los impuestos de.

charged [tʃɑːdʒd] ADJ (*Elec*) cargado, con carga.

chargé d'affaires [ˈʃɑːʒeɪdæˈfeəʳ] N encargado *m* de negocios.

chargehand [ˈtʃɑːdʒhænd] N (*Brit*) capataz *m.*

charge-nurse [ˈtʃɑːdʒˌnɜːs] N (*Brit*) enfermero *m*, -a *f* jefe.

charger [ˈtʃɑːdʒəʳ] N (*horse*) corcel *m*, caballo *m* de guerra; (*Elec*) cargador *m.*

charge-sheet [ˈtʃɑːdʒˌʃiːt] N ≈ hoja *f* (*or* impreso *m*) de cargos.

char-grilled [ˈtʃɑːˈgrɪld] ADJ a la brasa.

charily [ˈtʃɛərɪlɪ] ADV cuidadosamente, cautelosamente; parcamente, con parquedad.

chariot [ˈtʃærɪət] N carro *m* (romano, de guerra *etc*).

charioteer [ˌtʃærɪəˈtɪəʳ] N auriga *m.*

charisma [kæˈrɪzmə] N carisma *m.*

charismatic [ˌkærɪzˈmætɪk] ADJ carismático.

charitable [ˈtʃærɪtəbl] ADJ (a) *person* caritativo; *remark, view* comprensivo, compasivo. (b) *purpose, trust, society* benéfico; ~ **institution** institución *f* benéfica, institución *f* de beneficencia.

charitably [ˈtʃærɪtəblɪ] ADV caritativamente; con caridad; con compasión.

charity [ˈtʃærɪtɪ] N (a) caridad *f*; (*sympathy*) comprensión *f*, compasión *f*; **out of ~** por caridad; ~ **begins at home** la caridad bien entendida empieza por uno mismo; **to live on ~** vivir de limosnas.
(b) (*organization*) sociedad *f* benéfica; ~ **appeal** cuestación *f* para obras benéficas; **to raffle sth for ~** rifar algo para fines benéficos; **all proceeds go to ~** todo el importe se destina a obras de beneficencia; **most of it goes to ~** la mayor parte está destinada a obras de beneficencia.
(c) (*act*) **it would be a ~ if ...** sería una obra de caridad si ...

charlady [ˈtʃɑːleɪdɪ] N (*Brit*) asistenta *f*, mujer *f* de la limpieza.

charlatan [ˈʃɑːlətən] N charlatán *m*; (*Med*) charlatán *m*, curandero *m.*

Charlemagne [ˈʃɑːləmeɪn] NM Carlomagno.

Charles [tʃɑːlz] NM Carlos.

charleston [ˈtʃɑːlstən] N charlestón *m.*

charley horse* [ˈtʃɑːlɪhɔːs] N (*US*) calambre *m.*

Charlie [ˈtʃɑːlɪ] NM (a) Carlitos; ~ **Chaplin** Charlot. (b) ~*: imbécil *m*; **he must have looked a proper ~!** (*Brit*) ¡debía parecer un verdadero gilipollas!‡; **I felt a right ~!** (*Brit*) me sentí como un gilipollas‡.

Charlotte [ˈʃɑːlət] NF Carlota.

charm [tʃɑːm] **1** N (a) (*gen*) encanto *m*, atractivo *m*, hechizo *m*; ~**s** (*of woman*) atractivo *m*, hechizos *mpl*; **he has great ~** tiene mucho encanto, tiene un fuerte atractivo; **typical Spanish ~** la típica simpatía española; **to turn on the ~** ponerse fino, deshacerse en finuras.
(b) (*spell*) hechizo *m*, (*recited*) ensalmo *m.*
(c) (*object*) amuleto *m*; dije *m.*
2 VT hechizar, encantar, seducir; **we were ~ed by Granada** nos encantó Granada.

◆**charm away** VT hacer desaparecer como por magia, llevarse misteriosamente.

charm bracelet [ˈtʃɑːmˌbreɪslɪt] N brazalete *m* amuleto.

charmed circle [ˈtʃɑːmdˈsɜːkl] N (*liter*) círculo *m* privilegiado.

charmer [ˈtʃɑːməʳ] N hombre *m* (*etc*) encantador.

charming [ˈtʃɑːmɪŋ] ADJ encantador; *person* encantador, simpático; *present, remark etc* fino, gentil; ~**!** (*iro*) ¡qué simpático!; **how ~ of you!** ¡qué detalle!

charmingly [ˈtʃɑːmɪŋlɪ] ADV de modo encantador; con finura; **a ~ simple dress** un vestido sencillo pero muy mono.

charmless [ˈtʃɑːmlɪs] ADJ *place* sin encanto; *person* sin atractivo, sin chispa*.

charm offensive [ˈtʃɑːməˈfensɪv] N ofensiva *f* amistosa; **to launch a ~** lanzar una ofensiva amistosa.

charm-school* [ˈtʃɑːmˌskuːl] N = **finishing school.**

charnel-house [ˈtʃɑːnlhaʊs] N, PL **charnel-houses** [ˈtʃɑːnlhaʊzɪz] osario *m.*

charred [tʃɑːd] ADJ carbonizado, chamuscado.

chart [tʃɑːt] **1** N tabla *f*, cuadro *m*, esquema *m*, gráfico *m*; (*graph*) gráfica *f*; (*of discs*) lista *f*; (*Naut*) carta *f* de navegación; **the ~s*** los cuarenta (principales); ~ **topper*** éxito *m* discográfico.
2 VT (*record*) poner en una carta; (*outline*) explorar; (*on graph etc*) mostrar, representar, registrar; **the diagram ~s the company's progress** el diagrama muestra el progreso de la compañía; **to ~ a course** trazar un derrotero, planear una ruta.

charter [ˈtʃɑːtəʳ] **1** N (a) (*city, bill of rights*) fuero *m*; (*of company*) carta *f* de privilegio; **royal ~** cédula *f* real.
(b) (*hire*) alquiler *m*; fletamiento *m*; ~ **flight** vuelo *m* chárter; ~ **plane** avión *m* chárter.
2 VT (a) estatuir; dar carta de privilegio a.
(b) *bus etc* alquilar; *plane, ship* fletar.

chartered [ˈtʃɑːtəd] ADJ *person* diplomado; *company* legalmente constituido; ~ **accountant** (*Brit, Canada*) censor *m* jurado de cuentas, censora *f* jurada de cuentas, contador *m* público, contadora *f* pública (*LAm*).

Chartism [ˈtʃɑːtɪzəm] N (*Hist*) cartismo *m.*

Chartist [ˈtʃɑːtɪst] N: **the ~s** (*Hist*) los cartistas.

charwoman [ˈtʃɑːˌwʊmən] N, PL **charwomen** [ˈtʃɑːˌwɪmɪn] = **charlady.**

chary [ˈtʃɛərɪ] ADJ cuidadoso, cauteloso, reservado; **to be ~ of** + N ser avaro de + N, ser parco en + N; **to be ~ of** + *ger* evitar + *infin*, no prestarse de buena gana a + *infin.*

chase¹ [tʃeɪs] **1** N persecución *f*; (*hunt*) caza *f*; **to give ~ to** dar caza a, perseguir; **to join in the ~ for sth** unirse a los que buscan algo.
2 VT (*follow*) perseguir; (*hunt*) cazar; *girl etc* perseguir, dar caza a; **to ~ sb for money** reclamar dinero a uno.
3 VI correr, precipitarse.

◆**chase after** VT ir tras, (*fig*) correr tras.

◆**chase away** VT ahuyentar.

◆**chase down** VT (*US*) = **chase up.**

◆**chase off** VT ahuyentar.

◆**chase out** VT echar fuera.

◆**chase up** VT buscar, tratar de localizar; investigar, tratar de aclarar; **I'll ~ him up** se lo voy a recordar.

chase² [tʃeɪs] VT *metal* grabar, adornar grabando, cincelar.

chaser [ˈtʃeɪsəʳ] N bebida *f* tomada inmediatamente después de otra distinta, *p.ej.* copita *f* de licor.

chasm [ˈkæzəm] N (*Geog*) sima *f*, abismo *m*, grieta *f*; (*fig*) abismo *m*, fosa *f.*

chassis [ˈʃæsɪ] N chasis *m.*

chaste [tʃeɪst] ADJ casto.

chastely [ˈtʃeɪstlɪ] ADV castamente.

chasten [ˈtʃeɪsn] VT castigar, corregir, escarmentar.

chastened [ˈtʃeɪsnd] **1** PRET AND PTP of **chasten.** **2** ADJ (*by experience* *etc*) escarmentado; *tone etc* sumiso; **they seemed much ~** parecían haberse arrepentido.

chasteness ['tʃeɪstnɪs] N castidad *f*.

chastening ['tʃeɪsnɪŋ] ADJ *experience etc* aleccionador.

chastise [tʃæs'taɪz] VT castigar.

chastisement ['tʃæstɪzmənt] N castigo *m*.

chastity ['tʃæstɪtɪ] N castidad *f*.

chasuble ['tʃæzjʊbl] N casulla *f*.

chat [tʃæt] **1** N charla *f*, plática *f* (*LAm*); **to have a ~ with** charlar con; **I'll have a ~ with him** hablaré con él.
  2 VI charlar, platicar (*LAm*) (*to, with* con).
◆ **chat up** VT (*Brit**) *girl* ligar*, enrollarse con*; *influential person* dar jabón a*.

chatline ['tʃætlaɪn] N teléfono *m* del placer.

chat-show ['tʃætʃəʊ] N (*Brit TV*) programa *m* de entrevistas (informales), tertulia *f* (de TV); **~ host/hostess** presentador *m*, -ora *f* de programa de entrevistas.

chattels ['tʃætlz] NPL bienes *mpl* muebles; (*loosely*) cosas *fpl*, enseres *mpl*.

chatter ['tʃætər] **1** N (*talk*) charla *f*, parloteo *m*; (*of birds*) parloteo *m*; (*of teeth*) castañeteo *m*.
  2 VI (*person*) charlar, parlotear; (*birds*) parlotear; (*monkeys*) chillar; (*teeth*) castañetear; **she does ~ so** es muy habladora; **stop ~ing!** ¡silencio!

chatterbox ['tʃætəbɒks] N, **chatterer** ['tʃætərər] N parlanchín *m*, -ina *f*, charlatán *m*, -ana *f*, platicón *m*, -ona *f* (*Mex*), tarabilla *mf*.

chattering ['tʃætərɪŋ] **1** N charloteo *m*, parloteo *m*.
  2 ATTR (*Brit: pej*): **the ~ classes*** los intelectualoides*.

chatty ['tʃætɪ] ADJ *person* hablador, locuaz; *style* familiar; *letter* afectuoso y lleno de noticias; *article* de tono familiar.

chat-up line ['tʃætʌp,laɪn] N: **a good ~** una buena frase para entrarle a uno*.

chauffeur ['ʃəʊfər] **1** N chófer *m*, chofer *m* (*LAm*).
  2 VT llevar en coche (*to the station* a la estación); actuar de chófer para.

chauffeur-driven ['ʃəʊfə,drɪvən] ADJ: **~ car** coche *m* con chófer.

chauvinism ['ʃəʊvɪnɪzəm] N chauvinismo *m*, patriotería *f*; **male ~** machismo *m*, falocracia *f*.

chauvinist ['ʃəʊvɪnɪst] **1** ADJ chauvinista, patriotero; **male ~ pig** falócrata *m*, cerdo *m* machista.
  2 N chauvinista *mf*, patriotero *m*, -a *f*.

chauvinistic [ˌʃəʊvɪ'nɪstɪk] ADJ (*of race, sex etc*) chauvinista; (*jingoistic*) patriotero.

Ch.E. (*esp US*) **(a)** ABBR *of* **Chemical Engineer. (b)** ABBR *of* **Chief Engineer.**

cheap [tʃiːp] **1** ADJ barato; *ticket etc* económico; (*fig*) de mal gusto, cursi, chabacano; *trick* malo; **~ labour** mano *f* de obra barata; **~ money** préstamos *mpl* obtenidos a bajo interés, créditos *mpl* a tipos de interés bajos; **~ shot** golpe *m* bajo; **it's ~ at the price** a ese precio resulta económico; **that's pretty ~** eso es poco recto, eso se llama no jugar limpio; **to feel ~** sentirse humillado, sentir vergüenza; **to hold ~** tener en poco; **to make o.s. ~** hacer cosas indignas de sí, aplebeyarse; **to make a product ~er** abaratar un producto.
  2 ADV barato; V **cheaply**.
  3 N (*) **on the ~** barato; **to do sth on the ~** hacer algo con el mínimo de gastos, hacer algo en plan económico; **to get sth on the ~** obtener algo a precio reducido.

cheapen ['tʃiːpən] **1** VT abaratar.
  2 VI abaratarse.
  3 VR: **to ~ o.s.** hacer cosas indignas de sí, aplebeyarse.

cheapie* ['tʃiːpɪ] **1** ADJ de barato*.
  2 N (*ticket, meal etc*) ganga *f*.

cheap-jack ['tʃiːpdʒæk] **1** ADJ de bajísima calidad, malísimo; muy mal hecho.
  2 N baratillero *m*.

cheaply ['tʃiːplɪ] ADV barato; a precio económico; **you got off ~** te has librado barato, podía haberte sido peor.

cheapness ['tʃiːpnɪs] N lo barato, baratura *f*.

cheapo* ['tʃiːpəʊ] **1** ADJ baratejo, de (a) perrona, perronero.
  2 N perronero* *m*.

cheapshot‡ ['tʃiːpʃɒt] VT: **to ~ sb** (*US*) hablar mal de uno.

cheapskate* ['tʃiːpskeɪt] N (*US*) canalla *m*; tacaño *m*, roñoso *m*.

cheat [tʃiːt] **1** N (a) trampa *f*, fraude *m*; **it was a ~** fue un timo, hubo trampa; **there's a ~ in it somewhere** aquí hay trampa.
  (b) (*person*) tramposo *m*, -a *f*, petardista *mf*; (*at cards*) fullero *m*.
  2 VT *person* defraudar, timar, embaucar; **to ~ sb out of sth** estafar algo a uno; **to feel ~ed** sentirse defraudado.
  3 VI (*in exam etc*) hacer trampas.
◆ **cheat on** VT (*esp US*) engañar.

cheater ['tʃiːtər] N (*esp US: person*) = **cheat 1(b)**.

cheating ['tʃiːtɪŋ] N trampa *f*, fraude *m*; (*at cards*) fullerías *fpl*.

Chechen [tʃɪ'tʃen] **1** ADJ checheno.

---

  2 N checheno *m*, -a *f*.

Chechnya [tʃɪtʃ'nɪə] N Chechenia *f*.

check¹ [tʃek] **1** N **(a)** (*halt, setback*) parada *f* (súbita); (*Mil*) repulsa *f*; (*to plans*) contratiempo *m*, revés *m*; (*restraint*) restricción *f* (*on* de); (*obstacle*) impedimento *m* (*on* para), estorbo *m* (*on* a); **~s and balances** (*US: Pol*) mecanismo de equilibrio de poderes; **to act as a ~ on** (*restrain*) refrenar, (*impede*) ser un estorbo a; **to hold** (*or* **keep**) **in ~** contener, tener a raya; **to suffer a ~** sufrir un revés.
  (b) (*Chess*) jaque *m*; **in ~** en jaque; **continuous ~** tablas *fpl* por jaque continuo.
  (c) (*check-up*) control *m*, inspección *f*, verificación *f* (*on* de); (*Mech etc*) repaso *m*; (*Med*) chequeo *m*, reconocimiento *m* general; **~ digit** dígito *m* de control; **to keep a ~ on** controlar.
  (d) (*token*) (*counterfoil*) talón *m*; (*at cloakroom*) número *m*, billete *m*, boleto *m*; (*in games*) ficha *f*; (*US: invoice*) factura *f*; (*US: cheque*) cheque *m*; (*bill for food*) nota *f*, cuenta *f*; **to cash** (*or* **hand**) **in one's ~s** (*US*‡) estirar la pata, palmarla*.
  2 INTERJ **(a) ~!** (*Chess*) ¡jaque! **(b)** (*US*: O.K.) ¡vale!
  3 VT **(a)** *motion* parar, detener; *spread etc* restringir, tener a raya, refrenar; (*be an obstacle to*) impedir, estorbar; *attack* rechazar.
  (b) (*Chess*) dar jaque a.
  (c) (*also* **to ~ out**) (*examine*) controlar, examinar, inspeccionar; *facts* comprobar; *document* compulsar, revisar; (*count*) llevar la cuenta de, contar; (*Mech*) revisar, repasar; *baggage* (*US*) facturar; *tickets, passports* comprobar; **to ~ a copy against the original** cotejar una copia con el original; '**~ against delivery**' (*on text of speech*) 'comprobar el texto definitivo'; **~ the state of him!** ¡mira cómo viene!
  4 VI **(a)** (*make sure*) = **~ up. (b)** (*agree*) concordar, estar de acuerdo (*with* con); **that ~s with our results here** eso concuerda con nuestros resultados aquí.
  5 VR: **to ~ o.s.** detenerse, refrenarse.
◆ **check in** **1** VT *baggage* facturar, chequear (*LAm*).
  2 VI (*Aer*) presentarse, facturar el equipaje; (*hotel*) firmar el registro, (*fig*) llegar, entrar.
◆ **check off** VT *list* marcar; (*count*) contar; **to ~ items off on a list** comprobar artículos en una lista.
◆ **check on** VT *information, time etc* verificar; **to ~ on sb** investigar a uno.
◆ **check out** **1** VT **(a)** *accounts etc* verificar, chequear (*LAm*). **(b)** *luggage* recoger, llevar (fuera). **(c)** (*look at, inspect*) mirar, controlar.
  2 VI **(a)** pagar y marcharse, (*loosely*) salir, marcharse.
  (b) = **check¹ 4 (b)**.
◆ **check over** VT revisar, escudriñar.
◆ **check up** VI comprobar; hacer una investigación; informarse; **to ~ up on** comprobar, verificar; investigar; investigar los antecedentes (*or* la lealtad *etc*) de.
◆ **check with** VI consultar a.

CHECKS AND BALANCES

ⓘ *El sistema de* **checks and balances** *es uno de los principios de gobierno de Estados Unidos, cuyo objetivo es prevenir abusos de poder por parte de uno de los tres poderes del Estado. Para garantizar la libertad dentro del marco constitucional, los padres de la Constitución estadounidense crearon un sistema por el que tanto el poder del Presidente, como el del Congreso, el de los Tribunales o el de los gobiernos de cada estado puede ser sometido a debate o, si fuera necesario, controlado por el resto de los poderes.*

---

check² [tʃek] **1** N (*in pattern*) cuadro *m*; (*cloth*) paño *m* a cuadros.
  2 ADJ a cuadros; **~ suit** traje *m* a cuadros.

checkbook ['tʃekbʊk] N (*US*) = **chequebook.**

checked [tʃekt] ADJ, **checkered** ['tʃekəd] ADJ (*US*) a cuadros; = **chequered.**

checker ['tʃekər] N verificador *m*; (*US: in supermarket*) cajero *m*, -a *f*; (*in cloakroom*) encargado *m*, -a *f* de guardarropa.

checkerboard ['tʃekəbɔːd] N (*US*) tablero *m* de damas.

checkers ['tʃekəz] N (*US: game*) damas *fpl*.

check-in ['tʃekɪn] **1** N (*Aer: also* **~ desk**) mostrador *m* de facturación, mostrador *m* de embarque.
  2 ATTR: **~ desk** (*Aer*) mostrador *m* de facturación, mostrador *m* de embarque; **your ~ time is an hour before departure** su hora de facturación es una hora antes de la salida.

checking ['tʃekɪŋ] N control *m*, comprobación *f*; **~ account** (*US*) cuenta *f* corriente.

checking-in [ˌtʃekɪŋ'ɪn] N (*Aer*) facturación *f*.

checklist ['tʃeklɪst] N lista *f* de chequeo, catálogo *m*.

checkmate ['tʃek'meɪt] **1** N mate *m*, jaque *m* mate; (*fig*) callejón *m* sin salida, situación *f* irresoluble.
  2 VT dar mate a; **to be ~d** (*fig*) estar en un callejón sin salida.

check-out ['tʃekaʊt] **1** N (*Comm*) caja *f*.
  2 ATTR: **~ counter** caja *f* (de supermercado); **~ girl** cajera *f* (de supermercado); **~ time** hora *f* de salida (de un hotel).

checkpoint ['tʃekpɔɪnt] N (punto *m* de) control *m*.

checkroom ['tʃekrʊm] N (US) guardarropa m; (Rail) consigna f; (euph) lavabo m.

check-up ['tʃekʌp] N comprobación f, verificación f; examen m; (Med) chequeo m, reconocimiento m general.

cheddar ['tʃedər] N queso m Cheddar.

> **CHEDDAR**

> *(i) El queso cheddar, hecho con leche de vaca, se denomina así por la región del suroeste de Inglaterra donde se elaboraba originariamente y es, sin duda, el queso más vendido en el Reino Unido. A pesar de que hay queserías tradicionales que todavía lo hacen de forma casera, hoy en día se produce normalmente en fábricas repartidas por las Islas Británicas, Canadá, Estados Unidos y Australia.*

---

cheek [tʃiːk] ① N (a) mejilla f, carrillo m; (*: buttock) nalga f; ~ by jowl codo a codo, codo con codo (with con); they were dancing ~ to ~ bailaban muy apretados; to turn the other ~ poner la otra mejilla.
(b) (*) descaro m, frescura* f, impertinencia f; what a ~!, of all the ~! ¡qué caradura!*, ¡qué frescura!*; to have the ~ to + infin tener el valor de + infin, descararse a + infin.
② VT (Brit*) decir cosas descaradas a, portarse como un fresco con*.

cheekbone ['tʃiːkbəʊn] N pómulo m.

cheekily* ['tʃiːkɪlɪ] ADV descaradamente, con frescura*.

cheekiness* ['tʃiːkɪnɪs] N descaro m, frescura f, impertinencia f.

cheeky* ['tʃiːkɪ] ADJ descarado, fresco*, impertinente.

cheep [tʃiːp] ① N pío m; we couldn't get a ~ out of him no dijo ni pío.
② VI piar.

cheer [tʃɪər] ① N (a) (applause) grito m de entusiasmo; ~s aplausos mpl, aclamaciones fpl, vítores mpl, vivas fpl; there were loud ~s at this en esto hubo fuertes aplausos; to give three ~s for vitorear a, aclamar a; three ~s for the general! ¡viva el general!
(b) (state of mind) humor m; what ~? ¿qué tal?; ~s! (esp Brit*) (thanks) ¡gracias!; (toast) ¡salud y pesetas!; be of good ~! (liter) ¡ánimo!
② VT (a) (also to ~ up) alegrar, animar; I was much ~ed by the news me alegró mucho la noticia.
(b) (applaud) aplaudir, aclamar, vitorear.
③ VI aplaudir, gritar con entusiasmo.
♦ **cheer on** VT animar con aplausos.
♦ **cheer up** ① VT alegrar, animar.
② VI cobrar ánimo, alegrarse; ~ up! ¡anímate!

cheerful ['tʃɪəfʊl] ADJ alegre; de buen humor.

cheerfully ['tʃɪəfʊlɪ] ADV alegremente.

cheerfulness ['tʃɪəfʊlnɪs] N alegría f; buen humor m.

cheerily ['tʃɪərɪlɪ] ADV alegremente, jovialmente; de modo acogedor.

cheering ['tʃɪərɪŋ] ① ADJ news etc bueno, esperanzador.
② N aplausos mpl, aclamaciones fpl, vítores mpl, vivas fpl.

cheerio ['tʃɪərɪ'əʊ] INTERJ (esp Brit) ¡hasta luego!; (toast) ¡salud y pesetas!

cheer-leader ['tʃɪə,liːdər] N (esp US) animador m, -ora f; organizador m, -ora f de los aplausos.

cheerless ['tʃɪəlɪs] ADJ triste, sombrío.

cheery ['tʃɪərɪ] ADJ alegre, jovial; room etc acogedor.

cheese [tʃiːz] ① N (a) queso m; hard ~!‡ ¡mala pata! (b) (‡) big ~, head ~ (person) pez m gordo, jefazo m, -a f, personaje m.
② VT (a) (‡) dejar, poner fin a; ~ it! (US) ¡déjalo!; ¡ojo, que viene gente!; let's ~ it dejémoslo; vámonos.
(b) to ~ sb off‡ fastidiar a uno*; I'm ~d off (Brit‡) estoy hasta las narices* (with this con esto).

cheeseboard ['tʃiːzbɔːd] N plato m de quesos.

cheeseburger ['tʃiːz,bɜːgər] N hamburguesa f con queso.

cheesecake ['tʃiːzkeɪk] N quesadilla f; (*) fotos, dibujos etc de chicas atractivas en traje o actitud incitante.

cheesecloth ['tʃiːzklɒθ] N estopilla f.

cheesedish ['tʃiːzdɪʃ] N quesera f.

cheeseparing ['tʃiːz,peərɪŋ] ① ADJ tacaño.
② N economías fpl pequeñas.

cheesy ['tʃiːzɪ] ADJ (a) caseoso, como queso; que huele (or sabe) a queso. (b) (US‡) horrible, sin valor. (c) grin de hiena.

cheetah ['tʃiːtə] N leopardo m cazador.

chef [ʃef] N jefe m de cocina, (primer) cocinero m.

chef-d'œuvre [ʃedœvrə] N, PL **chefs-d'œuvre** [ʃedœvrə] obra f maestra.

Chekhov ['tʃekɒf] NM Chejov.

chemical ['kemɪkəl] ① ADJ químico; ~ agent agente m químico; ~ engineer ingeniero m químico; ~ warfare guerra f química; ~ weapon arma f química.
② N sustancia f química, producto m químico.

chemically ['kemɪkəlɪ] ADV químicamente, por medios químicos.

chemise [ʃə'miːz] N camisa f de señora.

chemist ['kemɪst] N (scientist) químico mf (also -a f); (Brit: pharmacist) farmacéutico m, -a f; ~'s (shop) (Brit) farmacia f; all-night ~'s farmacia f de guardia, farmacia f de turno.

chemistry ['kemɪstrɪ] N química f; ~ laboratory laboratorio m de química; ~ set juego m de química; the ~ between them is right (fig) tienen buena química.

chemotherapy ['kemoʊ'θerəpɪ] N quimioterapia f.

chenille [ʃə'niːl] N (Textiles) felpa f, chenille m.

▼**cheque,** (US) **check** [tʃek] N cheque m, talón m (bancario); bad ~ cheque m sin fondos, cheque m sin provisión; to make out a ~, to write a ~ extender un cheque (for £100 de 100 libras, por 100 libras; to Rodríguez a favor de Rodríguez); to pay by ~ pagar por (or con) cheque.

chequebook, (US) **checkbook** ['tʃekbʊk] N talonario m (de cheques), libreta f de cheques; ~ journalism periodismo m por talonario.

cheque-card ['tʃek,kɑːd] N (Brit) (also **cheque guarantee card**) tarjeta f de identidad bancaria.

chequered, (US) **checkered** ['tʃekəd] ADJ cloth etc a cuadros; aje-drezado; (fig) career accidentado, lleno de vicisitudes, lleno de altibajos; collection variado.

chequers, (US) **checkers** ['tʃekəz] N damas fpl.

cherish ['tʃerɪʃ] VT querer, apreciar; cuidar, proteger; mimar; hope etc abrigar, acariciar.

cherished ['tʃerɪʃt] ADJ memory etc precioso, entrañable; privilege apreciado.

cheroot [ʃə'ruːt] N puro m (cortado en los dos extremos).

cherry ['tʃerɪ] ① ADJ (de) color rojo cereza.
② N (fruit) cereza f; (tree, wood) cerezo m; (colour) rojo m cereza; ~ brandy aguardiente m de cerezas; ~ laurel laurel m cerezo.

cherry-red ['tʃerɪ'red] ADJ (de) color rojo cereza.

cherry-tree ['tʃerɪtriː] N cerezo m.

cherub ['tʃerəb] N (a) querubín m, angelito m. (b) (Rel) PL **cherubim** ['tʃerəbɪm] querubín m.

cherubic [tʃe'ruːbɪk] ADJ querúbico.

chervil ['tʃɜːvɪl] N perifollo m.

Ches N (Brit) ABBR of **Cheshire**.

Cheshire cat ['tʃeʃə'kæt] N: to grin like a ~ sonreír de oreja a oreja.

chess [tʃes] N ajedrez m; ~ tournament torneo m de ajedrez.

chessboard ['tʃesbɔːd] N tablero m de ajedrez.

chessman ['tʃesmæn] N, PL **chessmen** ['tʃesmen] pieza f, trebejo m, ficha f.

chessplayer ['tʃespleɪər] N ajedrecista mf.

chess-set ['tʃes,set] N (juego m de) ajedrez m.

chest [tʃest] N (a) (Anat) pecho m; tórax m; ~ trouble enfermedad f del pecho; to get sth off one's ~* desahogarse, confesar algo de una vez; to have a cold on the ~ tener el pecho resfriado.
(b) (box) cofre m, arca f, cajón m; ~ of drawers cómoda f.

chest cold ['tʃest,kəʊld] N resfriado m de pecho.

chesterfield ['tʃestəfiːld] N (esp US) sofá m.

chest expander ['tʃestɪk,spændər] N tensor m, extensor m.

chest freezer ['tʃest'friːzər] N congelador m de arcón.

chest infection ['tʃestɪn,fekʃən] N infección f bronquial.

chest measurement ['tʃest'meʒəmənt] N anchura f de pecho.

chestnut ['tʃesnʌt] ① ADJ (also ~ brown) castaño.
② N (a) (fruit) castaña f; (tree, wood) castaño m.
(b) (horse) caballo m castaño.
(c) (*) (joke) chiste m viejo.

chestnut-tree ['tʃesnʌtriː] N castaño m.

chest pain ['tʃest,peɪn] N dolor m de pecho.

chest size ['tʃest,saɪz] N anchura f de pecho; (of clothes) talla f (de chaqueta etc).

chest specialist ['tʃest,speʃəlɪst] N especialista mf de pecho.

chesty ['tʃestɪ] ADJ (Brit) person que tiene el pecho resfriado (or congestionado); (permanently) enfermizo del pecho; ~ cough tos f que afecta al pecho.

Chetnik ['tʃetnɪk] ADJ, N chetnik mf.

cheval glass [ʃə'vælglɑːs] N psique f.

chevron ['ʃevrən] N (Mil) galón m; (Her) cheurón m.

chew [tʃuː] VT mascar, masticar.
♦ **chew** VT (fig) facts, problems rumiar.
♦ **chew out** VT (US) = **chew up** (b).
♦ **chew over** VT: to ~ sth over rumiar algo.
♦ **chew up** VT (a) (damage) estropear. (b) (‡) person echar una bronca a.

chewing-gum ['tʃuː,ɪŋgʌm] N chicle m, goma f de mascar.

chewy ['tʃuːɪ] ADJ fibroso, correoso.

chiaroscuro [kɪ,ɑːrəs'kʊərəʊ] N claroscuro m.

chic [ʃiːk] ① ADJ elegante.
② N chic m, elegancia f.

chicanery [ʃɪ'keɪnərɪ] N embustes mpl, sofismas mpl; a piece of ~ un sofisma, una superchería, una triquiñuela.

Chicano [tʃɪ'kɑːnəʊ] ① ADJ chicano.
② N chicano m, -a f.

chichi ['ʃiːʃiː] ADJ afectado, extravagante.

chick [tʃɪk] N pollito *m*, polluelo *m*; (*US**) chavala *f*.

chickadee ['tʃɪkədiː] N carbonero *m*.

chicken ['tʃɪkɪn] **1** N gallina *f*, pollo *m*; (*as food*) pollo *m*; **to be ~*** dejarse intimidar, acobardarse, cejar; **to play ~*** jugar a quién es más valiente; **she's no ~** ya no es pollita, ya no es tan pichona; **it's a ~ and egg situation** es aquello de la gallina y el huevo; **the ~s are coming home to roost** ahora se ven las consecuencias; **don't count your ~s before they're hatched** no hagas las cuentas de la lechera. **2** VI: **to ~ out*** amedrentarse, rajarse; dejarse intimidar; **to ~ out of** retirarse miedoso de, zafarse de.

chicken-farmer ['tʃɪkɪn,fɑːməʳ] N avicultor *m*, -ora *f*.

chicken-farming ['tʃɪkɪn,fɑːmɪŋ] N avicultura *f*.

chickenfeed ['tʃɪkɪnfiːd] N pienso *m* para gallinas; (*) minucias *fpl*, bagatelas *fpl*; **it's ~ to him** para él es una bagatela.

chicken-hearted ['tʃɪkɪn,hɑːtɪd] ADJ cobarde, gallina.

chicken liver ['tʃɪkɪn,lɪvəʳ] N hígado *m* de pollo.

chickenpox ['tʃɪkɪnpɒks] N varicela *f*.

chicken-run ['tʃɪkɪnrʌn] N corral *m*, gallinero *m*.

chicken-wire ['tʃɪkɪn,waɪəʳ] N tela *f* metálica, alambrada *f*.

chickpea ['tʃɪkpiː] N garbanzo *m*.

chickweed ['tʃɪkwiːd] N pamplina *f*.

chicory ['tʃɪkərɪ] N (*in coffee*) achicoria *f*; (*in salad*) escarola *f*.

chide [tʃaɪd] (*irr*: PRET **chid**, PTP **chidden** *or* **chid**) VT (*liter*) reprender.

chief [tʃiːf] **1** ADJ principal, primero, mayor, capital; **~ constable** (*Brit*) jefe *m* de policía; **C~ Executive** (*Brit*: *local government*) director *m*, -ora *f*; (*US Pol*) jefe *m* del Ejecutivo; primer mandatario *m*; **~ inspector** (*Brit Police*) inspector *m* jefe; **~ justice** (*US*) presidente *m*, inspectora *f* jefe del Tribunal Supremo; **~ superintendent** (*Brit Police*) comisario *m* jefe. **2** N jefe *m*; jerarca *m*; (*of tribe*) jefe *m*, cacique *m*; (*: *boss*) jefe *m*; **yes, ~!** ¡sí, patrón!; **~ of staff** jefe *m* del estado mayor; **~ of state** jefe *m* de estado; **... in ~** ... en jefe.

chiefly ['tʃiːflɪ] ADV principalmente, sobre todo.

chieftain ['tʃiːftən] N jefe *m*, cacique *m*.

chiffchaff ['tʃɪftʃæf] N mosquitero *m* común.

chiffon ['ʃɪfɒn] N gasa *f*.

chignon ['ʃiːnjɔ̃ːŋ] N moño *m*.

chihuahua [tʃɪ'wɑːwɑː] N chihuahua *m*.

chilblain ['tʃɪlbleɪn] N sabañón *m*.

child [tʃaɪld] N, PL **children** ['tʃɪldrən] niño *m*, -a *f*; (*as offspring*) hijo *m*, -a *f*; **~ abuse** abuso *m* (sexual) de niños; **~ battering** maltrato *m* de los hijos; **~ benefit** *ayuda familiar por hijos*; **~ guidance** psicopedagogía *f*; **~ guidance centre** centro *m* psicopedagógico; **~ labour** trabajo *m* de menores; **~ lock** (*on door*) seguro *m* para niños; **~ prodigy** niño *m*, -a *f* prodigio; **~ welfare** asistencia *f* infantil, protección *f* a la infancia; **children's home** asilo *m* de niños; **children's literature** literatura *f* infantil; **to be with ~** estar encinta; **to get sb with ~** dejar a una encinta; **I have known him from a ~** le conozco desde niño.

┌─── **CHILDREN IN NEED** ───┐

ⓘ *La organización benéfica* **Children in Need** *(Niños Necesitados), fundada por la* **BBC** *en 1972, recauda dinero en beneficio de los niños necesitados en el Reino Unido y en el extranjero. Se la conoce sobre todo por los* **telethons** *(telemaratones) que organiza anualmente: los programas de TV en los que se invita a los televidentes a llamar para hacer donativos y a organizar sus propias campañas de ayuda para niños enfermos, minusválidos, pobres, etc.*
⇨ *Ver también* **BBC**

childbearing ['tʃaɪld,beərɪŋ] **1** ATTR: **~ women** las mujeres fecundas, las mujeres que producen hijos; **women of ~ age** las mujeres de edad para tener hijos. **2** N (*act*) parto *m*; (*as statistic*) natalidad *f*.

childbed ['tʃaɪldbed] N parturición *f*.

childbirth ['tʃaɪldbɜːθ] N parto *m*; alumbramiento *m*; **to die in ~** morir de sobreparto.

childcare ['tʃaɪldkeəʳ] N cuidado *m* de los niños; **~ services** servicios *mpl* de asistencia al niño.

childhood ['tʃaɪldhʊd] N niñez *f*, infancia *f*; **to be in one's second ~** estar en su segunda infancia; **from ~** desde niño.

childish ['tʃaɪldɪʃ] ADJ (**a**) (*slightly pej*) pueril, aniñado; infantil, achiquillado (*Mex*); **don't be so ~!** ¡no seas niño! (**b**) *disease etc* infantil; **~ ailment** enfermedad *f* de la infancia.

childishly ['tʃaɪldɪʃlɪ] ADV de modo pueril; **she behaved ~** se portó como una niña.

childishness ['tʃaɪldɪʃnɪs] N puerilidad *f*.

childless ['tʃaɪldlɪs] ADJ sin hijos.

childlike ['tʃaɪldlaɪk] ADJ como de niño, infantil.

child-minder ['tʃaɪld,maɪndəʳ] N (*Brit*) niñera *f*.

child-minding ['tʃaɪld,maɪndɪŋ] N cuidado *m* de niños.

child-proof ['tʃaɪld,pruːf] ADJ a prueba de niños; **~ (door) lock** cerradura *f* de seguridad para niños.

children ['tʃɪldrən] NPL *of* **child**.

child-resistant ['tʃaɪld,rɪzɪstənt] ADJ = **child-proof**.

child's-play ['tʃaɪldzpleɪ] N (*fig*): **it's ~** es cosa de coser y cantar (*to para*).

Chile ['tʃɪlɪ] N Chile *m*.

Chilean ['tʃɪlɪən] **1** ADJ chileno. **2** N chileno *m*, -a *f*.

chili ['tʃɪlɪ] N (*Brit*) chile *m*, ají *m* (*SC*); **~ powder** polvos *mpl* de chile; **~ sauce** salsa *f* de ají.

chill [tʃɪl] **1** ADJ frío. **2** N (**a**) frío *m*; **a ~ of horror** un estremecimiento de horror; **to cast a ~ over** enfriar el ambiente de; verter un jarro de agua fría sobre; **to take the ~ off** *liquid, room* calentar un poco. (**b**) (*Med*) escalofrío *m*; resfriado *m*; **to catch a ~** resfriarse. **3** VT enfriar; (*with fear etc*) helar; *meat etc* congelar; **to be ~ed to the bone** estar helado hasta los huesos.
◆**chill out*** VI (*esp US*) descansarse, relajarse; **~ out, man!** ¡tranqui tronco!*

chill(i)ness ['tʃɪl(ɪ)nɪs] N frío *m*; (*fig*) frialdad *f*.

chilling ['tʃɪlɪŋ] ADJ (*fig*) escalofriante.

chill-out* ['tʃɪlaʊt] ADJ *music* relajante.

chilly ['tʃɪlɪ] ADJ (**a**) frío; (*fig*) frío, glacial; **it is (very) ~** hace (mucho) frío; **I am feeling ~** tengo frío. (**b**) (*sensitive to cold*) friolento, friolero.

chime [tʃaɪm] **1** N (*set*) juego *m* de campanas, carillón *m*; (*peal*) repique *m*, campanada *f*; **~ clock** (*US*) reloj *m* de carillón. **2** VT repicar; **to ~ six** dar las seis. **3** VI repicar, sonar; **to ~ in** hablar inesperadamente, (*pej*) entrometerse; **to ~ in with** decir inesperadamente; (*harmonize*) estar en armonía con.

chimera [kaɪ'mɪərə] N quimera *f*.

chimerical [kaɪ'merɪkəl] ADJ quimérico.

chiming ['tʃaɪmɪŋ] **1** ADJ: **~ clock** reloj *m* de carillón. **2** N repiqueteo *m*, campanadas *fpl*.

chimney ['tʃɪmnɪ] N chimenea *f*; (*of lamp*) tubo *m* de lámpara; (*Mountaineering*) olla *f*, chimenea *f*.

chimney-breast ['tʃɪmnɪ,brest] N manto *m* de chimenea.

chimney-corner ['tʃɪmnɪ,kɔːnəʳ] N rincón *m* de la chimenea.

chimneypiece ['tʃɪmnɪ,piːs] N repisa *f* de chimenea.

chimneypot ['tʃɪmnɪpɒt] N (cañón *m* de) chimenea *f*.

chimney-stack ['tʃɪmnɪstæk] N fuste *m* de chimenea.

chimney-sweep ['tʃɪmnɪswiːp] N deshollinador *m*, limpiachimeneas *m*.

chimp* [tʃɪmp] N = **chimpanzee**.

chimpanzee [,tʃɪmpæn'ziː] N chimpancé *m*.

chin [tʃɪn] **1** N barba *f*, barbilla *f*, mentón *m*; **to keep one's ~ up** no desanimarse; **keep your ~ up!** ¡ánimo!; **to take it on the ~** (* *fig*) encajar el golpe. **2** VT (*) (*punch*) dar una hostia a*; (*reprimand*) echar un rapapolvo a*. **3** VI (*US**) charlar.

China ['tʃaɪnə] N China *f*; **~ Sea** Mar *m* de China; **~ tea** té *m* de China.

china¹ ['tʃaɪnə] N porcelana *f*, (*loosely*) loza *f*; **~ cabinet** vitrina *f* de la porcelana; **~ clay** coalín *m*, barro *m* de porcelana, arcilla *f* figulina.

china²‡ ['tʃaɪnə] N amigo *m*, compinche *m*; **here you are, my old ~** toma, macho*.

Chinaman ['tʃaɪnəmən] N, PL **Chinamen** ['tʃaɪnəmen] (*pej in US*) chino *m*.

Chinatown ['tʃaɪnətaʊn] N (*US*) barrio *m* chino.

chinaware ['tʃaɪnəweəʳ] N porcelana *f*.

chinch (bug) ['tʃɪntʃ(bʌg)] N (*US*) chinche *m or f* de los cereales.

chinchilla [tʃɪn'tʃɪlə] N chinchilla *f*.

chin-chin* [,tʃɪn'tʃɪn] EXCL ¡chin-chin!

Chinese ['tʃaɪ'niːz] **1** ADJ chino; **~ lantern** farolillo *m*; **~ leaves** (*US*) col *f* china; **~ puzzle** (*fig*) rompecabezas *m*. **2** N chino *m*, -a *f*. (**b**) (*Ling*) chino *m*.

Chink* [tʃɪŋk] N (‡ *in US*) chino *m*, -a *f*.

chink¹ [tʃɪŋk] N (*slit*) grieta *f*, hendedura *f*, resquicio *m*; **~ in one's armour** punto *m* débil, talón *m* de Aquiles.

chink² [tʃɪŋk] **1** N (*sound*) sonido *m* metálico, tintineo *m*. **2** VT hacer sonar. **3** VI sonar (a metal), tintinear.

chinless ['tʃɪnlɪs] ADJ (*fig*: *spineless*) apocado.

chintz [tʃɪnts] N cretona *f*.

chintzy ['tʃɪntsɪ] ADJ (**a**) *style* de oropel. (**b**) (*US*‡: *mean*) garrapo‡.

chin-ups ['tʃɪnʌps] NPL: **to do ~** hacer contracciones.

chinwag* ['tʃɪnwæg] N charla *f*; **to have a ~** charlar, echar un párrafo.

chip [tʃɪp] **1** N (**a**) (*splinter*) astilla *f*, pedacito *m*; (*of stone*) lasca *f*; **he's a ~ off the old block** de tal palo tal astilla; **to have a ~ on one's shoulder** ser un resentido.

(b) ~**s** (*Culin*) (*Brit*) patatas *fpl* fritas, papas *fpl* (*LAm*) fritas (a la española); (*US: also* **potato** ~) patatas *fpl* fritas, papas *fpl* (*LAm*) fritas (a la inglesa).
(c) (*break, mark*) saltadura *f*; (*on rim of vessel*) desportilladura *f*.
(d) (*Cards*) ficha *f*; **to hand in one's** ~**s*** palmarla*; **he's had his** ~**s*** se acabó para él; **when the** ~**s are down** en la hora de la verdad.
(e) (*Comput*) chip *m*, micropastilla *f*, pastilla *f*, microplaquete *m*, circuito *m* integrado.
(f) (*Golf*) chip *m*.
2 VT **(a)** astillar, desportillar; *surface* picar; *sculpture* cincelar.
(b) (*) tomar el pelo a.
3 VI astillarse; (*surface*) picarse, desconcharse.
♦ **chip away** **1** VT *paint etc* desconchar.
2 VI (*paint etc*) caer a pedazos; **to** ~ **away at** *authority, lands* ir usurpando; *law, decision* reducir paulatinamente el alcance de.
♦ **chip in*** VI **(a)** (*interrupt*) cortar, interrumpir (**with** diciendo). **(b)** (*contribute*) contribuir (**with** con).
♦ **chip off** VT = **chip away**.
chip-based ['tʃɪp,beɪst] ADJ: ~ **technology** tecnología *f* a base de micropastillas.
chipboard ['tʃɪpbɔːd] N cartón-madera *m*.
chipmunk ['tʃɪpmʌŋk] N ardilla *f* listada.
chipolata [,tʃɪpə'lɑːtə] N (*Brit*) salchicha *f* pequeña.
chipper* ['tʃɪpəʳ] ADJ (*US*) alegre, contento.
chippings ['tʃɪpɪŋz] NPL gravilla *f*; **'loose** ~**'** 'gravilla suelta'.
chippy* ['tʃɪpɪ] N **(a)** (*US*) tía* *f*, fulana* *f*. **(b)** (*Brit*) = **chip shop**.
chip shop ['tʃɪpʃɒp] N (*esp Brit*) tienda de comida rápida, principalmente de pescado rebozado y patatas fritas.

┌─ *CHIP SHOP* ─┐

ⓘ *Las tiendas de comida rápida llamadas* **chip shops**, **fish-and-chip shops** *o incluso* **chippies** *son toda una institución en las Islas Británicas. Su nombre procede de uno de los platos más populares que se venden en ellas: pescado rebozado y patatas fritas* **fish and chips**, *aunque también se sirven otros, casi siempre fritos. Mucha gente acude a ellas regularmente y la afluencia de gente a las* **chip shops** *al cierre de los* **pubs** *es una imagen ya tradicional. Para muchos son la imagen por antonomasia de la dieta británica.*

chiromancer ['kaɪərəmænsəʳ] N quiromántico *m*, -a *f*, quiromante *mf*.
chiropodist [kɪ'rɒpədɪst] N (*Brit*) pedicuro *m*, -a *f*, podólogo *m*, -a *f*.
chiropody [kɪ'rɒpədɪ] N (*Brit*) pedicura *f*, podología *f*.
chiropractic [,kaɪərəʊ'præktɪk] **1** ADJ quiropráctico.
2 N quiropráctica *f*.
chiropractor ['kaɪrəʊ,præktəʳ] N quiropráctico *m*.
chirp [tʃɜːp] **1** N pío *m*, gorjeo *m*; (*of cricket*) chirrido *m*.
2 VI piar, gorjear; (*cricket*) chirriar.
chirpy* ['tʃɜːpɪ] ADJ alegre, animado.
chirrup ['tʃɪrəp] = **chirp**.
chisel ['tʃɪzl] **1** N (*for wood*) formón *m*, escoplo *m*; (*for stone*) cincel *m*.
2 VT **(a)** escoplear; cincelar. **(b)** (*) timar, estafar.
chiseller, (*US*) **chiseler** ['tʃɪzləʳ] N gorrón *m*.
chit¹ [tʃɪt] N: **a** ~ **of a girl** una muchachita no muy crecida.
chit² [tʃɪt] N nota *f*, esquela *f*; vale *m*.
chitchat ['tʃɪttʃæt] N chismes *mpl*, habladurías *fpl*.
chitlings ['tʃɪtlɪŋz] NPL, **chitlins** ['tʃɪtlɪnz] NPL, **chitterlings** ['tʃɪtəlɪŋz] NPL menudos *mpl* de cerdo (comestibles); *ver también* ⌐SOUL FOOD⌐ .
chitty ['tʃɪtɪ] N = **chit²**.
chiv* [tʃɪv] N chori* *m*, navaja *f*.
chivalresque [ʃɪvəl'resk] ADJ, **chivalric** [ʃɪ'vælrɪk] ADJ caballeresco.
chivalrous ['ʃɪvəlrəs] ADJ caballeroso.
chivalrously ['ʃɪvəlrəslɪ] ADV caballerosamente.
chivalry ['ʃɪvəlrɪ] N (*institution*) caballería *f*; (*spirit*) caballerosidad *f*.
chive [tʃaɪv] N cebollino *m*.
chivvy ['tʃɪvɪ] VT (*Brit**) perseguir, atormentar, acosar; **to** ~ **sb into doing sth** no dejar en paz a uno hasta que haga algo.
♦ **chivvy up** VT *person* espabilar.
chloral ['klɔːrəl] N cloral *m*.
chlorate ['klɔːreɪt] N clorato *m*.
chloric ['klɔːrɪk] ADJ clórico; ~ **acid** ácido *m* clórico.
chloride ['klɔːraɪd] N cloruro *m*; ~ **of lime** cloruro *m* de cal.
chlorinate ['klɒrɪneɪt] VT clorinar, clorar, tratar con cloro.
chlorinated ['klɒrɪneɪtɪd] ADJ: ~ **water** agua *f* clorinada.
chlorination [,klɒrɪ'neɪʃən] N cloración *f*, tratamiento *m* con cloro.
chlorine ['klɔːriːn] N cloro *m*; ~ **monoxide** monóxido *m* de cloro; ~ **nitrate** nitrato *m* de cloro.
chlorofluorocarbon ['klɔːrəʊ'flʊərəʊ'kɑːbən] N clorofluorocarbono *m*.
chloroform ['klɒrəfɔːm] **1** N cloroformo *m*.
2 VT cloroformizar, cloroformar (*LAm*).
chlorophyl(l) ['klɒrəfɪl] N clorofila *f*.
choc* [tʃɒk] N = **chocolate**.

chocaholic* [,tʃɒkə'hɒlɪk] N adicto *m*, -a *f* al chocolate.
choc-ice ['tʃɒkaɪs] N helado *m* de chocolate.
chock [tʃɒk] **1** N calzo *m*, cuña *f*.
2 VT calzar, acuñar; poner calzos a.
chock-a-block ['tʃɒkə'blɒk] ADJ, **chock-full** ['tʃɒk'fʊl] ADJ de bote en bote; ~ **of**, ~ **with** atestado de, totalmente lleno de.
chocker* ['tʃɒkəʳ] ADJ: **to be** ~ estar harto (**with** de).
chocolate ['tʃɒklɪt] N **1** (*in bar, for drinking*) chocolate *m*; **a** ~ una chocolatina, un bombón; **a box of** ~**s** una caja de bombones (*or* chocolatinas).
2 ATTR de chocolate; ~ **biscuit** galleta *f* de chocolate; ~ **éclair** relámpago *m* de chocolate.
3 ADJ color (de) chocolate.
chocolate-box ['tʃɒklɪt,bɒks] ADJ *look, picture* de postal de Navidad.
choice [tʃɔɪs] **1** ADJ selecto, escogido; *quality, wine etc* fino.
2 N (*act of choosing*) elección *f*, selección *f*; (*thing chosen*) preferencia *f*; (*between 2 or more possibilities*) opción *f*, alternativa *f*; (*range to choose from*) surtido *m*, serie *f* de posibilidades; **for** ~ preferentemente; **he did it but not from** ~ lo hizo pero de mala gana; **the house of my** ~ mi casa predilecta; **the prince married the girl of his** ~ el príncipe se casó con la joven que había elegido; **it's your** ~, **the** ~ **is yours** Vd elige; **it was not a free** ~ no estuvo libre para elegir a su gusto; **we have a wide** ~ (*Comm*) tenemos un gran surtido; **you have a wide** ~ tienes muchas posibilidades; **to have no** ~ no tener alternativa, no tener opción; **he had no** ~ **but to go** no tuvo más remedio que ir; **to take one's** ~ elegir; **take your** ~! ¡lo que quieras!
choir ['kwaɪəʳ] N **(a)** coro *m*; coros *mpl*; orfeón *m*; coral *f*. **(b)** (*Archit*) coro *m*.
choirboy ['kwaɪəbɔɪ] N niño *m* de coro.
choirmaster ['kwaɪə,mɑːstəʳ] N director *m* de coro, maestro *m* de coros.
choir-practice ['kwaɪə,præktɪs] N ensayo *m* de coro.
choirschool ['kwaɪə,skuːl] N *escuela primaria para niños cantores*.
choir-stall ['kwaɪəstɔːl] N silla *f* de coro.
choke [tʃəʊk] **1** N (*Mech*) obturador *m*, cierre *m*; (*Aut*) estárter *m*, ahogador *m* (*Mex*), chok(e) *m* (*LAm*).
2 VT *pipe etc* atascar, tapar, obstruir; *person* (*to death*) estrangular, ahogar, sofocar; **a** ~**d cry** un grito ahogado; **in a voice** ~**d with emotion** en una voz embargada (*or* empañada) por la emoción; **a street** ~**d with traffic** una calle atestada de tráfico; **a canal** ~**d with weeds** un canal atascado de hierbas.
3 VI (*also to* ~ **to death**) sofocarse; (*over food*) atragantarse; no poder respirar; **to** ~ **on a bone** atragantarse con un hueso; **to** ~ **with laughter** desternillarse de risa.
♦ **choke back** VT contener, ahogar.
♦ **choke down** VT *rage, sobs* ahogar.
♦ **choke off** VT *supply, suggestions etc* cortar; *discussion* cortar por lo sano; *person* cortar; **to** ~ **sb off*** echar un rapapolvo a uno*; hacer callar a uno; desanimar a uno, disuadir a uno.
♦ **choke up** **1** VT *pipe, drain* obstruir.
2 VI **(a)** (*pipe, drain*) atascarse. **(b)** (*person*) quedarse sin habla.
choked* ['tʃəʊkt] ADJ cortado.
choker ['tʃəʊkəʳ] N **(a)** (*Mech*) obturador *m*. **(b)** (*necklace*) gargantilla *f*; (*hum*) cuello *m* alto.
choking ['tʃəʊkɪŋ] **1** ADJ asfixiador, asfixiante.
2 N ahogo *m*, asfixia *f*.
choky* ['tʃəʊkɪ] N (*prison*) trena* *f*; (*cell*) unidad *f* de aislamiento.
cholera ['kɒlərə] N cólera *m*.
choleric ['kɒlərɪk] ADJ colérico.
cholesterol [kə'lestərɒl] N colesterol *m*.
chomp* [tʃɒmp] VTI mascar.
Chomskyan ['tʃɒmskɪən] ADJ de Chomsky, chomskiano.
choo-choo* ['tʃuː'tʃuː] N (*Brit: child's language*) chu-chú *m*, tren *m*.
choose [tʃuːz] (*irr:* PRET **chose**, PTP **chosen**) **1** VT **(a)** elegir, escoger; *candidate* elegir; *team etc* seleccionar; **he was chosen leader** fue elegido caudillo.
(b) to ~ **to** + *infin* optar por + *infin*; **if I don't** ~ si no quiero; **I'll do it when I** ~ (**to**) lo haré cuando me dé la gana; **he cannot** ~ **but (to) go** no tiene más remedio que ir; **you cannot** ~ **but admire it** no puedes menos de admirarlo; **there is nothing to** ~ **between them** no les veo diferencia alguna.
2 VI: **to** ~ **between** elegir entre; **there are 5 kinds to** ~ **from** a elegir entre 5 tipos, hay 5 clases de las que se puede elegir.
choos(e)y* ['tʃuːzɪ] ADJ melindroso, delicado; **he's a bit** ~ **about it** en esto es algo difícil de contentar; **I'm** ~ **about whom I go out with** yo no salgo con un cualquiera; **in his position he can't be** ~ en su posición no le permite darse el lujo de escoger.
chop¹ [tʃɒp] **1** N **(a)** (*Culin*) chuleta *f*. **(b)** (*blow*) golpe *m* cortante; **he's for the** ~***** le van a despedir; **this programme is for the** ~***** este programa se va a suprimir; **to get the** ~***** ser despedido; **to give sb the** ~***** despedir a uno.
2 VT **(a)** (*cut*) cortar, tajar; **to** ~ **one's way through** abrirse camino a

tajadas. **(b)** *person* despedir. **(c)** *ball* cortar.
◆**chop at** VT tratar de tajar.
◆**chop down** VT talar.
◆**chop off** VT tronchar, separar; *(fig)* recortar, reducir.
◆**chop up** VT desmenuzar; *meat* picar.

chop² [tʃɒp] VI: **to ~ and change** *(person)* cambiar constantemente de opinión *(etc)*.

chopper ['tʃɒpər] N **(a)** *(for cutting)* hacha *f*; *(butcher's)* tajadera *f*, cuchilla *f*. **(b)** *(Aer*)* helicóptero *m*. **(c)** *(US*: motorbike)*, *(Brit: cycle)* chópper *f*.

chopping-block ['tʃɒpɪŋblɒk] N, **chopping board** ['tʃɒpɪŋ,bɔːd] N tajadera *f*, tajo *m*.

chopping-knife ['tʃɒpɪŋ,naɪf] N, PL **chopping-knives** ['tʃɒpɪŋ,naɪvz] tajadera *f*.

choppy ['tʃɒpɪ] ADJ *sea* picado, agitado.

chops [tʃɒps] NPL *(Anat)* boca *f*, labios *mpl*; **to lick one's ~** relamerse, chuparse los dedos.

chopsticks ['tʃɒpstɪks] NPL palillos *mpl* (de los chinos).

chop suey [,tʃɒp'suɪ] N chop suey *m*.

choral ['kɔːrəl] ADJ coral; **~ society** orfeón *m*.

chorale [kɔ'rɑːl] N coral *m*.

chord [kɔːd] N *(string, Anat, Math)* cuerda *f*; *(group of notes, sound)* acorde *m*; **we must strike a common ~** tenemos que encontrar un punto común; **this struck a responsive ~ with everyone** esto produjo una reacción positiva de todos; **to strike the right ~** acertar el tono.

chore [tʃɔːr] N faena *f*, tarea *f*, tarea *f* necesaria pero falta de interés, trabajo *m* rutinario; **~s** *(at home)* quehaceres *mpl* domésticos.

choreograph ['kɔrɪə,græf] VT coreografiar.

choreographer [,kɒrɪ'ɒgrəfər] N coreógrafo *m*, -a *f*.

choreographic [,kɒrɪəʊ'græfɪk] ADJ coreográfico.

choreography [,kɒrɪ'ɒgrəfɪ] N coreografía *f*.

chorister ['kɒrɪstər] N corista *mf*; *(US)* director *m*, -a *f* de un coro.

chortle ['tʃɔːtl] ① N risa *f* alegre.
② VI reírse alegremente; *(pej)* reírse satisfecho *(over* por*)*.

chorus ['kɔːrəs] ① N *(Mus)* coro *m*; *(of chorus girls)* conjunto *m*; *(repeated words)* estribillo *m*; **~ line** línea *f* de coro; **a ~ of praise greeted the book** el libro recibió la aprobación de todos, el libro se mereció las alabanzas de todos; **a ~ of shouts greeted this** todos gritaron a la vez al oír esto; **in ~** en coro; **to sing in ~** cantar en coro; **to join in the ~** cantar el estribillo.
② VT cantar *(etc)* en coro; *(answer)* contestar todos con una voz.

chorus-girl ['kɔːrəsgɜːl] N corista *f*, conjuntista *f*, chica *f* de conjunto.

chose [tʃəʊz] PRET *of* **choose**.

chosen ['tʃəʊzn] ① PTP *of* **choose**. ② ADJ preferido, predilecto; **the ~ people** el pueblo escogido; **one of the ~** uno de los elegidos; **their ~ representative** su representante elegido.

chough [tʃʌf] N chova *f* (piquirroja).

choux pastry ['ʃuː'peɪstrɪ] N masa *f* de profiteroles.

chow¹ [tʃaʊ] N *(dog)* chow-chow *m*, perro *m* chino.

chow²* [tʃaʊ] N comida *f*.

chowder ['tʃaʊdər] N *(US)* estofado *m* con almejas y pescado; *(soup)* sopa *f* de pescado.

chow mein [tʃaʊ'meɪn] N *plato de la cocina china de tallarines rehogados con carne o verduras.*

Chris [krɪs] NM *familiar form of* **Christopher**.

Christ [kraɪst] NM Cristo; **~!** ¡Dios mío!

christen ['krɪsn] VT bautizar *(also fig)*.

Christendom ['krɪsndəm] N cristiandad *f*.

▼ **christening** ['krɪsnɪŋ] N bautizo *m*, bautismo *m*; **~ gown, ~ robe** faldón *m* bautismal.

Christian ['krɪstɪən] ① ADJ cristiano; **name** de pila, de bautismo. ② N cristiano *m*, -a *f*.

Christianity [,krɪstɪ'ænɪtɪ] N cristianismo *m*.

Christianize ['krɪstɪənaɪz] VT cristianizar.

Christlike ['kraɪstlaɪk] ADJ como Cristo.

▼ **Christmas** ['krɪsməs] ① N Navidad *f*; *(ie ~ period)* Navidades *fpl*; **at ~** por Navidades; **merry ~!** ¡felices Pascuas!
② ATTR navideño, de Navidad; **~ box** *(Brit)* aguinaldo *m*; **~ cake** tarta *f* de Reyes; **~ card** crisma *m*, tarjeta *f* de Navidad; **~ carol** villancico *m*; **~ club** club *m* de ahorros (que los reparte por Navidades); **~ Day** día *m* de Navidad; **~ dinner** comida *f* de Navidad; **~ Eve** Nochebuena *f*; **~ Island** Isla *f* Christmas; **~ party** fiesta *f* de Navidad; **~ present** regalo *m* de Navidad; **~ pudding** pudín *m* de Navidad; **~ rose** eléboro *m* negro; **~ stocking** ≈ zapatos *mpl* de Reyes; **~ time** Navidades *fpl*, Pascua *f* de Navidad; **~ tree** árbol *m* de Navidad.

┌─ **CHRISTMAS DINNER** ─┐

ⓘ *La comida de Navidad* (**Christmas dinner**) *que se celebra en familia el día 25, es un momento central de las celebraciones navideñas. En ella se suele comer pavo relleno asado* (**roast turkey with stuffing**) *acompañado*

de coles de Bruselas y patatas asadas. En el Reino Unido el postre tradicional es **Christmas pudding**, *un pastel hecho a base de frutas secas, especias y brandy al que se le añade* **brandy butter**, *una mezcla de mantequilla, azúcar y brandy.*

Christmassy* ['krɪsməsɪ] ADJ navideño, propio de Navidad.

Christopher ['krɪstəfər] NM Cristóbal.

chromatic [krə'mætɪk] ADJ cromático.

chromatogram [krəʊ'mætə,græm] N cromatograma *m*.

chromatography [,krəʊmə'tɒgrəfɪ] N cromatografía *f*.

chrome [krəʊm] N cromo *m*; **~ steel** acero *m* al cromo, acerocromo *m*; **~ yellow** amarillo *m* de cromo.

chromium ['krəʊmɪəm] N cromo *m*.

chromium-plated ['krəʊmɪəm,pleɪtɪd] ADJ cromado.

chromium-plating ['krəʊmɪəm,pleɪtɪŋ] N cromado *m*.

chromosomal [,krəʊmə'səʊməl] ADJ cromosomático, cromosómico.

chromosome ['krəʊməsəʊm] N cromosoma *m*.

chronic ['krɒnɪk] ADJ **(a)** crónico; *(fig)* constante, permanente. **(b)** *(*)* horrible, malísimo; insufrible; **I had toothache something ~** me dolían las muelas horriblemente.

chronically ['krɒnɪkəlɪ] ADV: **to be ~ sick** sufrir una enfermedad crónica; **beer is ~ scarce** hay una escasez permanente de cerveza.

chronicle ['krɒnɪkl] ① N crónica *f*; **C~s** *(Bib)* Crónicas *fpl*.
② VT historiar; registrar, describir.

chronicler ['krɒnɪklər] N cronista *mf*.

chronological [,krɒnə'lɒdʒɪkəl] ADJ cronológico.

chronologically [,krɒnə'lɒdʒɪkəlɪ] ADV por orden cronológico.

chronology [krə'nɒlədʒɪ] N cronología *f*.

chronometer [krə'nɒmɪtər] N cronómetro *m*.

chrysalis ['krɪsəlɪs] N crisálida *f*.

chrysanthemum [krɪ'sænθəməm] N crisantemo *m*.

chub [tʃʌb] N cacho *m*.

chubby ['tʃʌbɪ] ADJ rechoncho, gordinflón, regordete; *face* mofletudo.

chuck¹ [tʃʌk] ① N **(a)** *(throw)* tiro *m*, echada *f*. **(b)** **~ under the chin** mamola *f*. **(c)** *(ⱡ)* **to get the ~** ser despedido.
② VT **(a)** *(throw)* lanzar, arrojar; *(pass, hand)* echar. **(b)** *(give up)* abandonar; **~ it!** ¡basta ya!, ¡déjalo!; **I'm thinking of ~ing it (in)** estoy pensando en dejarlo todo; **so I had to ~ it** así que tuve que abandonarlo. **(c) to ~ sb under the chin** dar la mamola a uno.
◆**chuck away** VT *old clothes, books* tirar, botar *(LAm)*; *money* despilfarrar; *chance* desperdiciar.
◆**chuck in*** VT **= chuck up 1.**
◆**chuck out** VT *rubbish* tirar, botar *(LAm)*; *person* poner de patitas en la calle; *person from work etc* despedir, dar el pasaporte a*.
◆**chuck up** ① VT *(*)* abandonar, renunciar a.
② VI *(USⱡ: vomit)* arrojar*.

chuck² [tʃʌk] **= chock**.

chuck³ [tʃʌk] N **(a)** *(also ~ steak)* bistec *m* de pobre. **(b)** *(USⱡ)* manduca‡ *f*; **~ wagon** carromato *m* de provisiones; *ver también* ⌐DUDE RANCH⌐ .

chucker-out* ['tʃʌkər'aʊt] N *(Brit)* forzudo *m* *(que echa a los alborotadores de un café etc)*.

chuckle ['tʃʌkl] ① N risita *f*, risa *f* sofocada; **we had a good ~ over that** nos reímos bastante con eso.
② VI reírse entre dientes, soltar una risita; **to ~ at, to ~ over** reírse con.

chuddar ['tʃʌdər] N chador *m*.

chuffed [tʃʌft] ADJ *(Brit*)* contento, alegre; **he was pretty ~ about it** estaba la mar de contento por eso.

chug [tʃʌg] VI hacer ruidos explosivos repetidos; *(Rail)* resoplar; **the train ~ged past** pasó el tren resoplando.
◆**chug along** VI *(car, train)* avanzar haciendo chuf-chuf.

chukker, chukka ['tʃʌkər] N tiempo *m* de un partido de polo.

chum* [tʃʌm] ① N compinche *m*, compañero *m*, cuate *m* *(Mex)*; *(child)* amiguito *m*, -a *f*; *(in direct address)* amigo; **to be great ~s** ser íntimos amigos; **to be ~s with sb** ser amigo de uno.
② VI: **to ~ up** hacerse amigos; **to ~ up with sb** hacerse amigo de uno.

chummy* ['tʃʌmɪ] ADJ familiar, muy afable; **they're very ~** son muy amigos; **he's very ~ with the boss** es muy amigo del jefe; **he got ~ with the boss** se hizo amigo del jefe.

chump* [tʃʌmp] N **(a)** *(head)* cabeza *f*; **to be off one's ~** estar chiflado. **(b)** *(idiot)* imbécil *m*, melón *m*; **you ~!** ¡imbécil!

chump chop ['tʃʌmp'tʃɒp] N *(Brit)* chuleta gruesa con hueso.

chunk [tʃʌŋk] N *(of bread, cheese etc)* pedazo *m*, trozo *m*; pedazo *m* grueso; *cantidad f* considerable.

chunky* ['tʃʌŋkɪ] ADJ *person* fornido; *object* sólido, macizo.

Chunnel ['tʃʌnl] N *(hum)* túnel *m* bajo el Canal de la Mancha.

chunter* ['tʃʌntər] VI murmurar; *(complain)* quejarse; **to ~ on about** seguir quejándose de.

church [tʃɜːtʃ] N iglesia *f*; *(esp non-Catholic)* templo *m*; **C~ of England** Iglesia *f* anglicana; **C~ of Scotland** Iglesia *f* presbiteriana escocesa; **C~ and State** Iglesia *f* y Estado; **~ fathers** Padres *mpl* de la Iglesia; **~**

hall sacristía *f*; **~ service** oficio *m*, culto *m*, servicio *m*; **to go to ~** (*Protestant*) ir al oficio, asistir al culto, (*Catholic*) ir a misa; **to go into the ~** hacerse cura (*or* pastor *etc*); *ver también* MONARCHY .

CHURCH OF ENGLAND, CHURCH OF SCOTLAND

ⓘ *La Iglesia anglicana* (**Church of England**) *es la iglesia oficial de Inglaterra. Tiene su origen en la ruptura de Enrique VIII con la Iglesia católica en el siglo XVI. En ella se unen aspectos de la tradición católica y de la protestante. Su dirigente oficial es el monarca y su jefe espiritual el Arzobispo de Canterbury. Al clero se le permite contraer matrimonio y, desde 1992, las mujeres pueden ejercer el sacerdocio, cambio al que se opuso radicalmente la corriente conservadora.*

La Iglesia Presbiteriana Escocesa (**Church of Scotland**) *es la iglesia nacional de Escocia, pero no depende de ninguna autoridad civil. Sigue la doctrina calvinista y se rige según las normas presbiterianas, lo que significa que está gobernada a nivel local, por* **ministers** *y dirigentes laicos* (**elders**). *Tanto hombres como mujeres pueden ejercer el sacerdocio. Hay una reunión anual* (**General Assembly**) *en la que se discuten asuntos nacionales, presidida por un* **Moderator**, *que es elegido anualmente.*

⇨ *Ver también* ARCHBISHOP

churchgoer ['tʃɜ:tʃ,gəʊəʳ] N fiel *mf* (que practica una religión).
churchman ['tʃɜ:tʃmən] N, PL **churchmen** ['tʃɜ:tʃmən] (a) (*priest*) sacerdote *m*, eclesiástico *m*. (b) (*member*) fiel *m* practicante.
churchwarden ['tʃɜ:tʃwɔ:dn] N capillero *m*.
churchwoman ['tʃɜ:tʃ,wʊmən] N, PL **churchwomen** ['tʃɜ:tʃ,wɪmɪn] fiel *f* practicante.
churchy* ['tʃɜ:tʃɪ] ADJ beato; que va mucho a la iglesia, que toma muy en serio las cosas de la iglesia.
churchyard ['tʃɜ:tʃjɑ:d] N cementerio *m*, camposanto *m*.
churl [tʃɜ:l] N (*fig*) patán *m*.
churlish ['tʃɜ:lɪʃ] ADJ *person* poco afable, grosero, hosco; *remark* nada amistoso; **it would be ~ not to thank him** sería muy maleducado no darle las gracias.
churlishly ['tʃɜ:lɪʃlɪ] ADV groseramente, sin educación.
churlishness ['tʃɜ:lɪʃnɪs] N grosería *f*, hosquedad *f*; conducta *f* (*etc*) poco amistosa; mala educación *f*.
churn [tʃɜ:n] **1** N (*for milk*) lechera *f*; cántara *f* de leche; (*for butter*) mantequera *f*.
2 VT *butter* batir (*or* hacer) en una mantequera; (*fig: also* to **~ up**) revolver, agitar, remover.
3 VI revolverse, agitarse; **my stomach ~ed** se me revolvió el estómago.
♦**churn out** VT producir en serie, producir en masa.
chute [ʃu:t] N (a) (*Tech*) tolva *f*, vertedor *m*, rampa *f* de caída; (*Brit: in playground, swimming-pool*) tobogán *m*. (b) (*: *Aer*) paracaídas *m*.
chutney ['tʃʌtnɪ] N chutney *m* (*condimento a base de frutas de la India*).
chutzpa(h)* ['xʊtspə] N (*US*) cara *f* dura.
CI ABBR *of* **Channel Islands** Islas *fpl* del Canal (de la Mancha).
C.I. N ABBR *of* **Consular Invoice** factura *f* consular.
CIA N (*US*) ABBR *of* **Central Intelligence Agency.**
ciao* [tʃaʊ] INTERJ ¡chao!
cicada [sɪ'kɑ:də] N cigarra *f*.
Cicero ['sɪsərəʊ] NM Cicerón.
Ciceronian [,sɪsə'rəʊnɪən] ADJ ciceroniano.
CID N (*Brit*) ABBR *of* **Criminal Investigation Department**; **~ man, ~ officer** policía *m* (*or* oficial *m*) del Departamento de Investigación Criminal.
cider ['saɪdəʳ] N sidra *f*; **~ apple** manzana *f* de sidra; **~ vinegar** vinagre *m* de sidra.
cider-press ['saɪdəpres] N lagar *m* para hacer sidra.
CIF, c.i.f. N ABBR *of* **cost, insurance and freight** coste, seguro y flete, c.s.f.
cig* [sɪg] N = **cigarette.**
cigar [sɪ'gɑ:ʳ] N puro *m*, cigarro *m*.
cigar-case [sɪ'gɑ:keɪs] N cigarrera *f*.
cigarette [,sɪgə'ret] N cigarrillo *m*, pitillo *m*, cigarro *m*.
cigarette-ash [sɪgə'ret,æʃ] N ceniza *f* de cigarrillo.
cigarette-card [,sɪgə'retkɑ:d] N cromo *m* (coleccionable).
cigarette-case [,sɪgə'ret,keɪs] N pitillera *f*, petaca *f*.
cigarette-end [,sɪgə'ret,end] N colilla *f* (de cigarrillo).
cigarette-holder [,sɪgə'ret,həʊldəʳ] N boquilla *f*.
cigarette-lighter [,sɪgə'ret,laɪtəʳ] N mechero *m*, encendedor *m*.
cigarette machine [sɪgə'retməʃi:n] N máquina *f* de tabaco.
cigarette-paper [,sɪgə'ret,peɪpəʳ] N papel *m* de fumar.
cigar-holder [sɪ'gɑ:,həʊldəʳ] N boquilla *f* de puro.
cigar-lighter [sɪ'gɑ:,laɪtəʳ] N (*Aut*) encendedor *m* de puro.
cigar-shaped [sɪ'gɑ:ʃeɪpt] ADJ en forma de puro.
ciggy* ['sɪgɪ] N = **cigarette.**
CIM N (*Comput*) ABBR *of* **computer-integrated manufacturing** fabricación *f* integrada por ordenador.
C.-in-C. N ABBR *of* **Commander-in-Chief.**

cinch: [sɪntʃ] N: **it's a ~** es facilísimo, está chupado:, es un chollo:.
cinchona [sɪŋ'kəʊnə] N quino *m*; **~ bark** quina *f*.
cinder ['sɪndəʳ] N carbonilla *f*; **~s** cenizas *fpl*; **to be burned to a ~** quedar carbonizado.
cinder block ['sɪndəblɒk] N (*US*) ladrillo *m* de cenizas.
Cinderella [,sɪndə'relə] NF la Cenicienta; **it's the ~ of the arts** es la hermana pobre de las artes.
cinder track ['sɪndətræk] N pista *f* de ceniza.
cinéaste ['sɪnɪæst] N cinéfilo *m*, -a *f*.
cine-camera ['sɪnɪ'kæmərə] N (*Brit*) cámara *f* cinematográfica.
cine-film ['sɪnɪ,fɪlm] N (*Brit*) película *f* de cine.
cinema ['sɪnəmə] N cine *m* multisalas.
cinema-going ['sɪnəmə,gəʊɪŋ] **1** N: **~ is very popular among the young** el ir al cine es muy popular entre los jóvenes.
2 ADJ: **the ~ public** el público aficionado al cine.
Cinemascope ['sɪnəməskəʊp] ® N Cinemascope ® *m*.
cinematic [,sɪnɪ'mætɪk] ADJ cinemático.
cinematograph [,sɪnɪ'mætəgrɑ:f] N (*Brit*) cinematógrafo *m*.
cinematographer [,sɪnəmə'tɒgrəfəʳ] N (*US*) cinematógrafo *m*, -a *f*.
cinematography [,sɪnəmə'tɒgrəfɪ] N cinematografía *f*.
cine-projector [,sɪnɪprə'dʒektəʳ] N (*Brit*) proyector *m* de películas.
cinerary ['sɪnərərɪ] ADJ cinerario.
cinnabar ['sɪnəbɑ:ʳ] N cinabrio *m*.
cinnamon ['sɪnəmən] N canela *f*.
cipher ['saɪfəʳ] **1** N (a) (o, *zero*) cero *m*; (*any number, initials*) cifra *f*; (*Arabic numeral*) cifra *f*, número *m*; **he's a mere ~** (*fig*) es un cero a la izquierda. (b) (*secret writing*) cifra *f*, código *m*; **in ~** cifrado, en cifra, en clave. (c) (*monogram*) monograma *m*.
2 VT *code, calculations, communications* cifrar; (*Math*) calcular.
circa ['sɜ:kə] PREP hacia; **~ 1500** hacia (el año) 1500.
circadian [sə'keɪdɪən] ADJ circadiano; **~ cycle** ciclo *m* circadiano.
circle ['sɜ:kl] **1** N (a) círculo *m*; (*Brit Theat*) anfiteatro *m*; (*set of people*) círculo *m*, grupo *m*; **an inner ~ of ministers** un grupo interior de ministros; **John and his ~** Juan y sus amigos, Juan y su peña; **the wheel has come full ~** la rueda ha dado una vuelta completa; **we're going round in ~s** (*fig*) estamos en un círculo vicioso.
(b) **~s** (*fig*): **in certain ~s** en ciertos medios; **in business ~s** en círculos comerciales; **to move in fashionable ~s** frecuentar la buena sociedad; **to go round in small ~s** perderse en detalles nimios; **it had us running round in ~s** nos hizo dar vueltas sin orden ni concierto.
2 VT (*be round*) cercar, rodear; (*move round*) girar alrededor de, dar la vuelta a; *part of body* ceñir, rodear; **the lion ~d its prey** el león se movió alrededor de la presa; **the cosmonaut ~d the earth** el cosmonauta dio la vuelta al mundo; **the aircraft ~d the town twice** el avión dio dos vueltas sobre la ciudad.
3 VI dar vueltas.
circlet ['sɜ:klɪt] N anillo *m*; adorno *m* en forma de círculo.
circuit ['sɜ:kɪt] **1** N (*Elec etc*) circuito *m*; (*tour*) gira *f*; (*track*) pista *f*; (*lap by runner*) vuelta *f*; (*Brit Jur, approx*) distrito *m*.
2 ATTR: **~ board** tarjeta *f* de circuitos; **~ court** (*US*) tribunal *m* superior; **~ switching network** red *f* de conmutación de circuito.
circuit-breaker ['sɜ:kɪt,breɪkəʳ] N cortacircuitos *m*.
circuitous [sɜ:'kjʊɪtəs] ADJ tortuoso, indirecto.
circuitry ['sɜ:kɪtrɪ] N circuitería *f*, sistema *m* de circuitos.
circuit-training ['sɜ:kɪt,treɪnɪŋ] N circuito *m* de entrenamiento.
circular ['sɜ:kjʊləʳ] **1** ADJ circular; **~ saw** sierra *f* circular; **~ tour** viaje *m* redondo. **2** N circular *f*.
circularity [,sɜ:kjʊ'lærɪtɪ] N circularidad *f*.
circularize ['sɜ:kjʊləraɪz] VT enviar circulares a.
circulate ['sɜ:kjʊleɪt] **1** VT poner en circulación; *letter, papers etc* hacer circular; *news* anunciar por circular.
2 VI circular.
circulating ['sɜ:kjʊleɪtɪŋ] ADJ circulante; **~ assets** activo *m* circulante; **~ capital** capital *m* circulante; **~ library** (*US*) biblioteca *f* circulante; **~ medium** medios *mpl* monetarios.
circulation [,sɜ:kjʊ'leɪʃən] N circulación *f*; (*number of papers printed*) tirada *f*; **~ of the blood** circulación *f* de la sangre; **he's in ~ again**, **he's back in ~** ha vuelto a circular; **to put into ~** poner en circulación.
circulatory [,sɜ:kjʊ'leɪtərɪ] ADJ circulatorio.
circum... PREF circun..., circum...
circumcise ['sɜ:kəmsaɪz] VT circuncidar.
circumcision [,sɜ:kəm'sɪʒən] N circuncisión *f*.
circumference [sə'kʌmfərəns] N circunferencia *f*.
circumflex ['sɜ:kəmfleks] N circunflejo *m*; **~ accent** acento *m* circunflejo.
circumlocution [,sɜ:kəmlə'kju:ʃən] N circunloquio *m*, rodeo *m*.
circumnavigate [,sɜ:kəm'nævɪgeɪt] VT circunnavegar.
circumnavigation ['sɜ:kəm,nævɪ'geɪʃən] N circunnavegación *f*.
circumscribe ['sɜ:kəmskraɪb] VT circunscribir; limitar, restringir.
circumspect ['sɜ:kəmspekt] ADJ circunspecto, prudente.

circumspection [ˌsɜːkəmˈspekʃən] N circunspección f, prudencia f.

circumspectly [ˈsɜːkəmspektlɪ] ADV prudentemente.

▼ **circumstance** [ˈsɜːkəmstəns] N **(a)** circunstancia f; **in** (or **under**) **the ~s** en las circunstancias; **in no ~s, under no ~s** de ninguna manera, bajo ningún concepto; **owing to ~s beyond our control** debido a circunstancias ajenas a nuestra voluntad; **~s alter cases** las circunstancias cambian los casos; **were it not for the ~ that ...** si no fuera por la circunstancia de que ...; V **pomp**.
(b) (economic situation) **to be in easy ~s** estar acomodado; **to be in narrow** (or **reduced**) **~s** estar estrecho; **what are your ~s?** ¿cuál es su situación económica?; **if the family ~s allow it** si lo permite la situación económica de la familia.

circumstantial [ˌsɜːkəmˈstænʃəl] ADJ report detallado, circunstanciado; **~ evidence** prueba f indiciaria.

circumstantiate [ˌsɜːkəmˈstænʃɪeɪt] VT probar refiriendo más detalles, corroborar, confirmar.

circumvent [ˌsɜːkəmˈvent] VT burlar; difficulty, obstacle salvar, evitar.

circumvention [ˌsɜːkəmˈvenʃən] N acción f de burlar (or salvar); **the ~ of this obstacle will not be easy** no va a ser fácil salvar este obstáculo.

circus [ˈsɜːkəs] N circo m; (in town) plaza f redonda, glorieta f.

cirrhosis [sɪˈrəusɪs] N cirrosis f.

cirrocumulus [ˌsɪrəʊˈkjuːmjʊləs] N, PL **cirrocumuli** [ˌsɪrəʊˈkjuːmjʊlaɪ] cirrocúmulo m.

cirrostratus [ˌsɪrəʊˈstrɑːtəs] N, PL **cirrostrati** [ˌsɪrəʊˈstrɑːtaɪ] cirrostrato m.

cirrus [ˈsɪrəs] N, PL **cirri** [ˈsɪraɪ] cirro m.

CIS N ABBR of **Commonwealth of Independent States** Comunidad f de Estados Independientes, CEI f.

cissy* [ˈsɪsɪ] N = **sissy**.

Cistercian [sɪsˈtɜːʃən] 1 ADJ cisterciense; **~ Order** Orden f del Císter. 2 N cisterciense m.

cistern [ˈsɪstən] N tanque m, depósito m; (of WC) cisterna f, depósito m; (for hot water) termo m; (for rainwater) aljibe m, cisterna f.

citadel [ˈsɪtədl] N ciudadela f; (in Spain, freq) alcázar m; (fig) reducto m.

citation [saɪˈteɪʃən] N cita f; (Jur) citación f; (Mil) mención f, citación f; **~ index** índice m de citación.

cite [saɪt] VT citar; (Mil) mencionar, citar.

citizen [ˈsɪtɪzn] N ciudadano m, -a f; (in counting inhabitants etc) habitante mf, vecino m, -a f; (national) súbdito m, -a f; **~'s arrest** arresto realizado por un ciudadano normal; **C~s' Band** (Rad) banda f ciudadana.

citizenry [ˈsɪtɪznrɪ] N ciudadanos mpl, ciudadanía f.

Citizens' Advice Bureau [ˈsɪtɪznzəˈdˈvaɪsbjʊəˈrəʊ] N (Brit) organización voluntaria británica que asesora legal o financieramente.

┌─ **CITIZENS' ADVICE BUREAU** ─┐

*ⓘ Las oficinas de información al ciudadano, **Citizens' Advice Bureaux** o **CABs**, se crearon en 1939 para asesorar al pueblo británico sobre las normas que había que cumplir en tiempos de guerra. Después pasaron a ser un servicio de asesoramiento general al público, ofreciendo información gratuita y ayuda en problemas de carácter diverso. Actualmente se encargan de aconsejar en lo concerniente a la vivienda, problemas económicos, prestaciones y servicios sociales y derechos del consumidor. Existen unas 900 oficinas por todo el país, financiadas con dinero público y en las que trabajan normalmente voluntarios dirigidos por una persona que cobra por su trabajo.*

---

citizenship [ˈsɪtɪznʃɪp] N ciudadanía f.

citrate [ˈsɪtreɪt] N citrato m.

citric [ˈsɪtrɪk] ADJ: **~ acid** ácido m cítrico.

citron [ˈsɪtrən] N (fruit) cidra f; (tree) cidro m.

citrus [ˈsɪtrəs] N: **~ fruits** agrios mpl, cítricos mpl.

city [ˈsɪtɪ] 1 N ciudad f; **the C~** (Brit: London) el centro bursátil y bancario.
2 ATTR municipal, de la ciudad; **~ center** (US), **~ centre** centro m de la ciudad; **~ council** concejo m municipal, ayuntamiento m; **~ desk** (Brit) sección f de noticias financieras (de un periódico); (US) sección f de noticias de la ciudad (de un periódico); **~ dweller** ciudadano m, -a f; **~ editor** redactor m encargado de las noticias financieras, redactora f encargada de las noticias financieras; **~ fathers** prohombres mpl de la ciudad; **~ hall** palacio m municipal; (US) ayuntamiento m; **~ limits** perímetro m urbano; **~ manager** administrador m, -ora f municipal; **~ news** (Brit) noticias fpl financieras; (US) noticias fpl de la ciudad; **~ plan** (US) plano m de la ciudad; **~ planner** (US) urbanista mf; **~ planning** (US) urbanismo m; **~ slicker*** capitalino m.

┌─ **CITY NICKNAMES** ─┐

*ⓘ Las ciudades estadounidenses a menudo tienen apodos por los que se las conoce informalmente. Por ejemplo, a Nueva York se la llama **Big Apple**, ya que apple en argot significa gran ciudad. Chicago es **Windy City***

*debido a los fuertes vientos que vienen del lago Michigan. A Nueva Orleans la llaman **Big Easy**, por la tranquilidad con la que se lo toman todo sus habitantes. Detroit tiene el apelativo de **Motown**, que es un compuesto de **Motor** y **Town**, por las fábricas de coches que hay en ella; Boston es **Bean Town** por las famosas alubias llamadas **Boston baked beans**. Philadelphia es la **City of Brotherly Love** (ciudad del amor fraterno), que es una traducción de la palabra griega. Denver tiene el nombre de **Mile High City** porque está a una milla por encima del nivel del mar, y Birmingham es **Magic City**, porque creció tan rápidamente que parecía que había surgido de la nada. A otras ciudades estadounidenses se las conoce por sus iniciales, como por ejemplo, Los Angeles, **LA** y Dallas, **Big D** o por una parte de su nombre como **Vegas**, en lugar de **Las Vegas** o **Corpus** por **Corpus Christi**, en Texas. También hay veces en las que se usa una versión acortada del nombre, como ocurre en los casos de San Francisco y Philadelphia, a las que se llama **Frisco** y **Philly** respectivamente.*

---

cityscape [ˈsɪtɪskeɪp] N (US) paisaje m urbano.

city-state [ˈsɪtɪˌsteɪt] N ciudad-estado f.

City Technology College [ˈsɪtɪtekˈnɒlədʒɪˈkɒlɪdʒ] N (Brit) ≈ Centro m de formación profesional.

civet [ˈsɪvɪt] N algalia f.

civic [ˈsɪvɪk] ADJ cívico; municipal; **~ centre** (Brit) conjunto m de edificios municipales.

civics [ˈsɪvɪks] NPL cívica f; (as course) educación f cívica.

civies* [ˈsɪvɪz] NPL (US) = **civvies**.

civil [ˈsɪvl] ADJ **(a)** civil; **~ defence** protección f civil; **~ disobedience** resistencia f pasiva; **~ engineer** ingeniero m de caminos, canales y puertos; **~ engineering** ingeniería f civil; **~ law** derecho m civil; **~ liberties** libertades fpl civiles; **C~ List** (Brit) presupuesto de la casa real aprobado por el parlamento; **~ marriage** matrimonio m civil; **~ rights** derechos mpl civiles; **~ servant** funcionario m, -a f (del Estado); **C~ Service** cuerpo m de funcionarios (del Estado); **~ status** estado m civil; **~ war** guerra f civil; ver también [MONARCHY]. **(b)** (polite) cortés, atento; amable; **he was very ~ to me** fue muy cortés conmigo; **that's very ~ of you** es Vd muy amable; **be more ~ !** ¡hable con más educación!

civilian [sɪˈvɪlɪən] 1 ADJ (de) paisano; civil. 2 N civil mf, paisano m, -a f.

civility [sɪˈvɪlɪtɪ] N **(a)** (politeness) cortesía f; urbanidad f; amabilidad f; **lack of ~** falta f de educación. **(b)** (polite remark) cortesía f, cumplido m.

civilization [ˌsɪvɪlaɪˈzeɪʃən] N civilización f.

civilize [ˈsɪvɪlaɪz] VT civilizar.

civilized [ˈsɪvɪlaɪzd] ADJ civilizado.

civilizing [ˈsɪvɪlaɪzɪŋ] ADJ influence etc civilizador.

civilly [ˈsɪvɪlɪ] ADV cortésmente, atentamente.

civism [ˈsɪvɪzəm] N civismo m.

civvies* [ˈsɪvɪz] NPL traje m civil; **in ~** vestido de civil.

civvy* [ˈsɪvɪ] ADJ: **~ street** (Brit) la vida civil.

CJD N ABBR of **Creutzfeldt-Jakob disease** enfermedad f de Creutzfeldt-Jakob.

CKD ADJ ABBR of **completely knocked down**; V **knock down**.

cl ABBR of **centilitre(s)** centilitro(s) m(pl), cl.

clack [klæk] VI (chatter) charlar, chismear; **this will make the tongues ~** esto será tema para los chismosos.

clad [klæd] (††) 1 PRET AND PTP of **clothe**. 2 ADJ: **~ in** vestido de.

cladding [ˈklædɪŋ] N (Tech) revestimiento m.

claim [kleɪm] 1 N **(a)** (gen, demand) reclamación f; (formally stated) petición f; (wage ~) reivindicación f salarial; **to have a ~ on sb** tener motivo para reclamar contra uno; **I think this has a ~ on your attention** creo que esto merece su atención; **I have many ~s on my time** son muchas las cosas que ocupan el tiempo de que dispongo; **to lay ~ to** reclamar; **he put in a ~ for a rise** pidió un aumento de sueldo.
(b) (Jur) demanda f (for de); (insurance ~) demanda f, reclamación f; **to put in a ~ for** entablar demanda de; **to state a ~** presentar una demanda; **you have no legal ~** Vd no tiene derecho legal alguno.
(c) (pretension) pretensión f; afirmación f, declaración f; **his ~ turned out to be untrue** su declaración resultó ser falsa; **that's a big ~ to make** eso es mucho decir; **to make large ~s for an invention** pretender que un invento tiene grandes ventajas.
(d) (Min) pertenencia f, concesión f.
2 VT **(a)** (demand as one's due) reclamar, exigir; benefit solicitar; **to ~ the right to vote** reclamar (or reivindicar) el derecho de votar; **to ~ sth from sb** reclamar algo a uno; **sth else ~ed her attention** otra cosa mereció su atención; **death ~ed him** se lo llevó la muerte.
(b) (Jur) demandar; **to ~ damages from sb** reclamar a uno por daños y perjuicios.
(c) (profess, assert) pretender; reivindicar; **XYZ has ~ed responsibility for the bomb** XYZ ha reivindicado la colocación de la bomba; **to ~ kinship with sb** afirmar ser pariente de uno; **he ~s to be her son** afirma ser su hijo; **he ~s to have seen her** afirma haberla visto;

to ~ that ... sostener que ..., afirmar que ...; **that's ~ing a lot** eso es mucho decir.

3 VI presentar una reclamación, presentar una demanda (*for* de).

claimant ['kleɪmənt] N (*of benefit etc*) solicitante *mf*; (*Jur*) demandante *mf*; (*to throne*) pretendiente *m*, -a *f*.

claim form ['kleɪm.fɔːm] N (*Admin*) (*for benefit*) impreso *m* de solicitud; (*for expenses*) impreso *m* de demanda de gastos.

clairvoyance [kleə'vɔɪəns] N clarividencia *f*.

clairvoyant(e) [kleə'vɔɪənt] N clarividente *mf*, vidente *mf*.

clam [klæm] 1 N (**a**) almeja *f*; **~ chowder** (*US*) sopa *f* de almejas. (**b**) (*US*: *dollar*) dólar *m*.
2 VI: **to ~ up*** callarse como un muerto.

clambake ['klæmbeɪk] N (*US*) merienda *f* en la playa (*or* en el campo); (*) fiesta *f*.

clamber ['klæmbəʳ] 1 N subida *f*.
2 VI trepar, subir gateando (*over* sobre, *up* a).

clammy ['klæmɪ] ADJ frío y húmedo, pegajoso.

clamorous ['klæmərəs] ADJ clamoroso, vociferante, ruidoso.

clamour, (*US*) **clamor** ['klæməʳ] 1 N clamor *m*, clamoreo *m*, griterío *m*.
2 VI clamorear, vociferar; **to ~ for** clamar por, pedir a voces.

clamp [klæmp] 1 N (**a**) (*brace*) abrazadera *f*; (*Aut*: *on parked car*) cepo *m*; (*in laboratory etc*) grapa *f*; (*Carp*) tornillo *m* de banco, cárcel *f*. (**b**) (*Agr*) ensilado *m*, montón *m*.
2 VT (**a**) (*secure*) afianzar (*or* sujetar *etc*) con abrazadera; **he ~ed it in his hand** lo agarró con la mano; **he ~ed his hand down on it** lo sujetó firmemente con la mano. (**b**) *car* poner un cepo en.
3 VI: **to ~ down on** (*fig*) tratar de acabar con, restringir, reprimir; apretar los tornillos a.

clamp-down ['klæmpdaʊn] N restricción *f* (*on* de); prohibición *f* (*on* de).

clan [klæn] N clan *m* (*also fig*).

clandestine [klæn'destɪn] ADJ clandestino.

clang [klæŋ] 1 N sonido *m* metálico fuerte, estruendo *m*.
2 VT hacer sonar.
3 VI sonar, hacer estruendo; **the gate ~ed shut** la puerta se cerró ruidosamente.

clanger‡ ['klæŋəʳ] N (*Brit*) plancha* *f*, metida *f* de pata* (*LAm*); **to drop a ~** tirarse una plancha*, meter la pata*.

clangorous ['klæŋgərəs] ADJ estrepitoso, estruendoso.

clangour, (*US*) **clangor** ['klæŋgəʳ] N estruendo *m*.

clank [klæŋk] 1 N sonido *m* metálico seco, golpeo *m* metálico.
2 VT hacer sonar.
3 VI sonar, hacer estruendo, rechinar metálico; **the train went ~ing past** pasó el tren con estruendo.

clannish ['klænɪʃ] ADJ exclusivista, con fuerte sentimiento de tribu.

clansman ['klænzmən] N, PL **clansmen** ['klænzmen] miembro *m* del clan.

clap[1] [klæp] 1 N (*on shoulder*) palmoteo *m*; (*of the hands*) palmada *f*; **~ of thunder** trueno *m* (seco), estampido *m* (seco) de trueno.
2 VT (**a**) (*with hands*) *person, play, announcement* aplaudir; **to ~ one's hands** batir las manos, dar palmadas, batir palmas; **to ~ sb on the back** dar a uno una palmada en la espalda.
(**b**) (*place*) poner; **he ~ped his hat on** se encasquetó el sombrero; **to ~ eyes on** clavar la vista en; **to ~ a hand over sb's mouth** tapar a uno la boca con la mano; **to ~ sth shut** cerrar algo de golpe; **to ~ sb in jail** encarcelar a uno, meter a uno en la cárcel.
3 VI aplaudir.

clap[2]‡ [klæp] N (*Med*) gonorrea *f*.

clapboard ['klæpbɔːd] N (*US*) chilla *f*, tablilla *f*.

clapped-out* [ˌklæpt'aʊt] ADJ *car etc* anticuado; desvencijado; inútil; *mine* agotado.

clapper ['klæpəʳ] N badajo *m*; **to go like the ~s** (*Brit**) correr como un loco.

clapperboard ['klæpə.bɔːd] N (*Cine*) claqueta *f*.

clapping ['klæpɪŋ] N aplausos *mpl*.

claptrap* ['klæptræp] N pavadas* *fpl*, burradas* *fpl*.

claque [klæk] N claque *f*.

claret ['klærət] N vino *m* tinto (*esp* de Burdeos); (*colour*) burdeos *m*.

clarification [ˌklærɪfɪ'keɪʃən] N aclaración *f*.

clarify ['klærɪfaɪ] VT aclarar.

clarinet [ˌklærɪ'net] N clarinete *m*.

clarinettist [ˌklærɪ'netɪst] N clarinetista *mf*.

clarion ['klærɪən] N (*toque m de*) trompeta *f*; **~ call** llamada *f* fuerte y sonora.

clarity ['klærɪtɪ] N claridad *f*.

clash [klæʃ] 1 N (**a**) (*noise*) estruendo *m*, fragor *m*.
(**b**) (*conflict*) choque *m*; enfrentamiento *m*; (*Mil*) encuentro *m*; (*of opinions etc*) desacuerdo *m*, conflicto *m*; **~ of dates** coincidencia *f* de fechas; **~ of wills** lucha *f* de voluntades; **timetable ~** incompatibilidad *f* de horas.
2 VT batir, golpear.

3 VI (*Mil*) encontrarse, batirse; (*be opposed*) pugnar (con), estar en pugna, chocar; (*persons*) pelearse, reñir; enfrentarse (uno con otro); (*colours*) desentonar; (*dates*) coincidir; (*opinions*) estar en desacuerdo.

clasp [klɑːsp] 1 N (*fastener*) broche *m*, corchete *m*; (*of box, necklace etc*) cierre *m*; (*of book*) broche *m*, manecilla *f*; **with a ~ of the hand** con un apretón de manos.
2 VT (*fasten*) abrochar; (*embrace*) abrazar; *hand* apretar, estrechar; (*in one's hand*) tener asido, agarrar; **to ~ sb to one's bosom** estrechar a uno contra el pecho.

claspknife ['klɑːspnaɪf] N, PL **claspknives** ['klɑːspnaɪvz] navaja *f*.

class [klɑːs] 1 N clase *f*; **first ~** primera clase *f*; **lower ~es** clase *f* baja; **middle ~es** clase *f* media; **upper ~** clase *f* alta; **~ of degree** (*Brit Univ*) categoría *f* del título; **~ of '92** (*esp US*) promoción *f* del '92; **a good ~ novel** una novela de buena calidad; **it's just not in the same ~** no hay comparación entre los dos; **it's in a ~ by itself** no tiene igual, es único en su género; **she's certainly got ~** ella sí que tiene clase.
2 ATTR clasista, de clase(s); **~ distinction** distinción *f* de clases; **~ list** (*Scol*) lista *f* de clase; (*Univ*) lista *f* de estudiantes aprobados para la licenciatura; **~ society** (*Pol*) sociedad *f* clasista; **~ struggle** lucha *f* de clases; **~ system** sistema *m* de clases sociales; **~ teacher** (*Brit*) tutor *m*, -a *f*; **~ war(fare)** = **~ struggle**.
3 VT clasificar.

class-conscious ['klɑːs'kɒnʃəs] ADJ que tiene conciencia de clase.

class-consciousness ['klɑːs'kɒnʃəsnɪs] N conciencia *f* de clase.

classic ['klæsɪk] 1 ADJ clásico.
2 N (*person*) autor *m* clásico; (*work*) obra *f* clásica; (*Sport*) carrera *f* clásica; **the ~s** los clásicos, las obras clásicas; **~s** (*Univ etc*) clásicas *fpl*.

classical ['klæsɪkəl] ADJ clásico; **~ scholar** erudito *m*, -a *f* en lenguas clásicas.

classically ['klæsɪkəlɪ] ADV *styled, beautiful* clásicamente; *educated, trained* en la tradición clásica.

classicism ['klæsɪsɪzəm] N clasicismo *m*.

classicist ['klæsɪsɪst] N clasicista *mf*.

classifiable ['klæsɪfaɪəbl] ADJ clasificable.

classification [ˌklæsɪfɪ'keɪʃən] N clasificación *f*.

classified ['klæsɪfaɪd] ADJ (**a**) *information* secreto, reservado. (**b**) **~ advertisement** anuncio *m* por palabras.

classify ['klæsɪfaɪ] VT (**a**) clasificar (*in, into* en; *under letter B* en la B). (**b**) *information* clasificar como secreto, reservar.

classism ['klæsɪzm] N clasismo *m*.

classist ['klɑːsɪst] ADJ clasista.

classless ['klɑːslɪs] ADJ *society* sin clases.

classmate ['klɑːsmeɪt] N (*Brit*) compañero *m*, -a *f* de clase, condiscípulo *m*, -a *f*.

classroom ['klɑːsrʊm] N aula *f*, clase *f*.

classy* ['klɑːsɪ] ADJ de buen tono, muy pera*.

clatter ['klætəʳ] 1 N ruido *m*, estruendo *m*; (*of plates*) choque *m*; (*of hooves*) chacoloteo *m*; (*of train*) triquitraque *m*; (*hammering*) martilleo *m*.
2 VI hacer ruido, hacer estruendo; (*hooves, feet*) chacolotear; **to come ~ing down** caer ruidosamente; **to ~ down the stairs** bajar ruidosamente la escalera.

Claudius ['klɔːdɪəs] NM Claudio.

clause [klɔːz] N cláusula *f*; (*Gram*) oración *f*; cláusula *f*.

claustrophobia [ˌklɔːstrə'fəʊbɪə] N claustrofobia *f*.

claustrophobic [ˌklɔːstrə'fəʊbɪk] 1 ADJ claustrofóbico.
2 N claustrófobo *m*, -a *f*.

clavichord ['klævɪkɔːd] N clavicordio *m*.

clavicle ['klævɪkl] N clavícula *f*.

claw [klɔː] 1 N (*Zool*) garra *f*, zarpa *f*, (*of cat*) uña *f*, (*of lobster*) pinza *f*; (*Tech*) garfio *m*, gancho *m*; **~s** (*) dedos *mpl*, mano *f*; **to get one's ~s into** (*attack*) atacar con rencor; (*dominate*) dominar, tener los sesos sorbidos a; **to get one's ~s on** agarrarse de (*or* a); **get your ~s off that!** ¡fuera las manos!; **to show one's ~s** sacar las uñas.
2 VT arañar; (*tear*) desgarrar.
◆ **claw at** VT arañar; (*tear*) desgarrar.
◆ **claw back** VT volver a tomar, tomar otra vez para sí.

clawback ['klɔːbæk] N (*Econ*) desgravación fiscal obtenida por devolución de impuestos.

claw-hammer ['klɔːˌhæməʳ] N martillo *m* de orejas, martillo *m* de carpintero.

clay [kleɪ] N arcilla *f*; **~ court** pista *f* de lodo, pista *f* de tierra batida; **~ pigeon** plato *m* de barro; (*fig*: *victim*) víctima *f*; **~ pigeon shooting** tiro *m* al plato; **~ pipe** pipa *f* de cerámica; **~ pit** pozo *m* de arcilla.

clayey ['kleɪɪ] ADJ arcilloso.

clean [kliːn] 1 ADJ (**a**) (*not dirty*) limpio; aseado; (*unobstructed*) despejado; **as ~ as a new pin** tan limpio como un espejo; **he's ~** (*US*‡) no lleva arma; **to come ~**‡ confesarlo todo, desembuchar*.
(**b**) (*pure etc*) limpio, decente; inocente; *life* sano; *joke etc* que no

ofende; *reputation* bueno, sin tacha; *game* limpio; *player* honrado; **to do a ~ copy** hacer una copia en limpio; **to have a ~ record** no tener nota adversa (en su historial); **'must have ~ driving licence'** 'imprescindible tener carnet de conducir sin nota de sanción'; **Mr C~** Señor Manos Limpias; V **bill² 1 (e)**, **party 1 (c)**.

(c) (*clear-cut*) neto, distinto, bien definido; (*shapely*) bien formado, elegante; (*adroit*) diestro, elegante; **~ lines** contornos *mpl* elegantes.

2 ADV enteramente; **he cut ~ through it** lo cortó de un golpe; **it cuts ~ across tradition** esto corta netamente con la tradición; **to get ~ away** escaparse sin dejar rastro; **I ~ forgot** se me olvidó por completo; **the fish jumped ~ out of the net** el pez saltó fuera de la red.

3 N limpia *f*, limpieza *f*; **to give the car a ~** limpiar el coche.

4 VT limpiar; asear; *streets* barrer; (*dry-clean*) limpiar en seco.

◆**clean down** VT limpiar.

◆**clean off** VT *surface etc* limpiar; *dirt* quitar limpiando.

◆**clean out** VT **(a)** limpiar; **to ~ out a box** limpiar (el interior de) una caja.
(b) (*: in robbery*) limpiar.
(c) (*: fleece*) **we were ~ed out** nos dejaron sin blanca, quedamos limpios*.

◆**clean up** **1** VT **(a)** *room* limpiar, asear.
(b) (*morally*) limpiar; reformar; *act, play* suprimir los pasajes verdes de; **they're trying to ~ up TV** tratan de hacer más decentes los programas de TV.
(c) **we ~ed up £500*** sacamos 500 libras de ganancia.
2 VI **(a)** **to ~ up after sb** limpiar lo que ha dejado (*or* ensuciado) otro; **to ~ up after a party** limpiar después de un party.
(b) (***) hacer una pingüe ganancia, ponerse las botas*; **he ~ed up on that deal** sacó una buena ganancia de ese negocio.

clean-break divorce [ˌkliːnˌbreɪkdɪˈvɔːs] N divorcio en el que se renuncia a la pensión alimenticia por un bien capitalizable.

clean-cut [ˈkliːnˈkʌt] **(a)** claro, bien definido, preciso; *outline* nítido. **(b)** *person* de buen parecer; de tipo elegante.

cleaner [ˈkliːnəʳ] N **(a)** (*person*) limpiador *m*, -ora *f*, asistenta *f*, mujer *f* de la limpieza; **~'s** (**shop**) tintorería *f*, lavandería *f*; **we'll take them to the ~'s*** les dejaremos sin blanca, les dejaremos limpios*. **(b)** (*household ~*) producto *m* para la limpieza.

cleaning [ˈkliːnɪŋ] N limpia *f*, limpieza *f*; **~ fluid** líquido *m* de limpieza; **~ lady**, **~ woman** asistenta *f*, mujer *f* de la limpieza, limpiadora *f*.

clean-limbed [ˌkliːnˈlɪmd] ADJ bien proporcionado.

cleanliness [ˈklenlɪnɪs] N limpieza *f* (habitual), aseo *m*.

clean-living [ˌkliːnˈlɪvɪŋ] ADJ de vida sana.

cleanly¹ [ˈklenlɪ] ADJ limpio, aseado.

cleanly² [ˈkliːnlɪ] ADV limpiamente; (*adroitly*) diestramente, con destreza.

cleanness [ˈkliːnnɪs] N limpieza *f*, aseo *m*.

clean-out [ˈkliːnaʊt] N limpieza *f*.

cleanse [klenz] VT limpiar (*of* de).

cleanser [ˈklenzəʳ] N agente *m* de limpieza, producto *m* (químico) para la limpieza.

clean-shaven [ˈkliːnˈʃeɪvn] ADJ sin barba ni bigote, todo afeitado.

cleansing [ˈklenzɪŋ] **1** ADJ (*for complexion*) limpiador; (*fig*) purificador; **~ cream** crema *f* desmaquilladora; **~ department** departamento *m* de la limpieza; **~ lotion** loción *f* limpiadora.
2 N limpieza *f*.

clean-up [ˈkliːnʌp] N limpia *f*, limpieza *f*.

▼**clear** [klɪəʳ] **1** ADJ **(a)** (*transparent, audible, distinct, unambiguous, obvious*) claro; *sky, surface* despejado; *air* transparente; *conscience* limpio, tranquilo; *mind* penetrante, despejado; *majority* absoluto, neto; *round* (*Sport*) sin penalizaciones; **as ~ as crystal** más claro que el agua; **as ~ as day** más claro que el sol; **as ~ as mud*** nada claro; **it ... está claro que ...; is that ~?** ¿comprendido?; **to make o.s. ~** explicarse bien, explicarse claramente; **do I make myself ~?** ¿entiende?, ¿estamos?; **I think I've got it pretty ~** creo que lo entiendo bastante bien; **I wish to make it ~ that ...** quiero subrayar que ..., quiero dejar bien sentado que ...; **a ~ case of murder** un caso evidente de homicidio.
(b) (*certain*) **I'm not ~ whether** yo no sé a punto fijo si; **I'm not very ~ about this** no tengo una idea muy clara de esto; **he was perfectly ~ that he did not intend to go** dijo de modo tajante que no pensaba ir; **are we ~ that we want this?** ¿estamos seguros de que queremos esto?
(c) (*complete*) entero, completo; **3 ~ days** 3 días completos; **£3 ~ profit** una ganancia neta de 3 libras; **to win by a ~ head** ganar por una cabeza larga.
(d) (*free*) **~ of** libre de; **to be ~ of debt** estar libre de deudas.
2 ADV claramente; **I can hear you loud and ~** te oigo perfectamente; **to get ~ away** escaparse sin dejar rastro alguno; **to jump ~** quitarse de en medio de un salto; **to get ~ of** deshacerse de; **when we get ~ of London** cuando estemos fuera de Londres; **to**

steer ~ of evitar cualquier contacto con; **stand ~ of the doors!** ¡atención a las puertas!

3 N **(a)** **to be in the ~** (*of debt*) estar libre de deudas; (*of suspicion*) quedar fuera de toda sospecha; (*of danger*) estar fuera de peligro. **(b)** **message in ~** mensaje *m* no cifrado.

4 VT **(a)** (*remove obstacles from*) *place, road* despejar, limpiar; desescombrar; *pipe* desatascar; *wood* desmontar; *land* despejar; *court, hall* desocupar, desalojar (de público *etc*); *postbox* recoger las cartas de; (*Sport*) *ball* despejar; **to ~ the table** quitar la mesa; **to ~ a space for** hacer sitio para; V **way**.
(b) (*clarify*) *liquid* aclarar, clarificar; *blood* purificar; *bowels* purgar; *head* despejar; **to ~ one's throat** carraspear, aclarar la voz.
(c) (*find innocent*) absolver (*of* de); demostrar la inocencia de; **you will have to be ~ed by Security** será preciso que le acredite la Seguridad; **the plan will have to be ~ed with the director** el plan tendrá que ser aprobado por el director; **we've already ~ed it with him** hemos obtenido ya su visto bueno.
(d) (*jump over*) salvar, saltar por encima de; (*avoid touching*) pasar sin rozar; **to ~ 2 metres** saltar 2 metros; **the plane just ~ed the roof** el avión por poco no tocó el tejado; **this part has to ~ that by at least 1 centimetre** entre esta pieza y aquélla tiene que haber un espacio de 1 centímetro al menos.
(e) *cheque* pasar por un banco, (*in clearing-house*) compensar; *account, stock, debt* liquidar; *profit* sacar (una ganancia de); *conscience* descargar; (*of Customs*) despachar, dejar pasar; **he ~ed £50 on the deal** ganó 50 libras en el negocio; **we have just about ~ed our costs** estamos a punto de cubrir los gastos; **she ~s £500 a week** se saca 500 libras a la semana; **'half-price to ~'** 'liquidación a mitad de precio'.
(f) (*Comput*) despejar.

5 VI (*liquid*) aclararse, clarificarse; (*weather*) despejarse; (*Sport*) despejar.

6 VR: **to ~ o.s. of a charge** probar su inocencia de una acusación.

◆**clear away** **1** VT quitar (de en medio); *dishes* retirar.
2 VI **(a)** (*dishes*) quitar los platos, quitar la mesa.
(b) (*mist*) disiparse.

◆**clear off** **1** VT *debt* pagar, liquidar.
2 VI (***) irse, largarse*; desaparecer; **~ off!** ¡lárgate!, ¡fuera de aquí!

◆**clear out** **1** VT *place* limpiar; vaciar; desescombrar; *objects* quitar.
2 VI (***) = **clear off 2**.

◆**clear up** **1** VT **(a)** *crime* esclarecer; *mystery* aclarar; *doubt* resolver, aclarar, disipar; *difficulty* aclarar; *business* despachar.
(b) (*tidy*) limpiar, asear; (*arrange*) arreglar, poner en orden.
2 VI **(a)** (*weather*) aclararse, despejarse; (*problem*) resolverse; (*illness*) curarse, terminar.
(b) (*tidy*) limpiar, ordenar las cosas.

clearance [ˈklɪərəns] N **(a)** (*of road etc; also Sport*) despeje *m*; (*of land*) desmonte *m*, roza *f*.
(b) (*Tech*) espacio *m* (libre), espacio *m* muerto; separación *f*, holgura *f*; (*distance above ground*) luz *f* libre.
(c) (*by Customs*) despacho *m* de aduana; (*by Security*) acreditación *f*; (*Fin*) compensación *f*; **~ for take-off** autorización *f* para despegar; **~ sale** liquidación *f*, realización *f* (*LAm*).

clear-cut [ˈklɪəˈkʌt] ADJ claro, bien definido, neto, nítido.

clear-eyed [ˌklɪːˈraɪd] ADJ de ojos claros; (*fig*) clarividente.

clear-headed [ˈklɪəˈhedɪd] ADJ de mentalidad lógica, perspicaz, inteligente, sereno.

clear-headedness [ˈklɪəˈhedɪdnɪs] N mentalidad *f* lógica, perspicacia *f*, inteligencia *f*, serenidad *f*.

clearing [ˈklɪərɪŋ] **1** N **(a)** (*in wood*) claro *m*; *see also* **clearance**. **(b)** (*Fin*) liquidación *f*.
2 ATTR: **~ account** cuenta *f* de compensación; **~ cheque** cheque *m* de compensación.

clearing-bank [ˈklɪərɪŋbæŋk] N, **clearing-house** [ˈklɪərɪŋhaʊs] N, PL **clearing-houses** [ˈklɪərɪŋˌhaʊzɪz] (*Brit*) cámara *f* (*or* banco *m*) de compensación.

clearly [ˈklɪəlɪ] ADV **(a)** claramente. **(b)** (*at start of sentence*) desde luego; (*as answer*) sin duda, naturalmente.

clearness [ˈklɪənɪs] N claridad *f*.

clear-out [ˈklɪəraʊt] N: **to have a good ~** limpiarlo todo, despejarlo todo.

clear-sighted [ˈklɪəˈsaɪtɪd] ADJ clarividente, perspicaz.

clear-sightedness [ˈklɪəˈsaɪtɪdnɪs] N clarividencia *f*, perspicacia *f*.

clearway [ˈklɪəweɪ] N (*Brit*) carretera *f* en la que está prohibido parar.

cleat [kliːt] N abrazadera *f*, listón *m*, fiador *m*.

cleavage [ˈkliːvɪdʒ] N escisión *f*, división *f*; (*in dress*) escote *m*.

cleave¹ [kliːv] (*irr*: PRET **clove** *or* **cleft**, PTP **cloven** *or* **cleft**) VT partir, hender, abrir por medio; *water* surcar.

cleave² [kliːv] VI: **to ~ to** adherirse a, no separarse de; **to ~ together** ser inseparables.

cleaver [ˈkliːvəʳ] N cuchilla *f* de carnicero.

clef [klef] N clave *f*.

cleft [kleft] **1** PRET AND PTP *of* **cleave¹**.
2 ADJ: ~ **palate** fisura *f* del paladar, palatosquisis *f*.
3 N grieta *f*, hendedura *f*.
cleg [kleg] N tábano *m*.
clematis ['klemətɪs] N clemátide *f*.
clemency ['klemənsɪ] N clemencia *f*.
Clement ['klemənt] NM Clemente.
clement ['klemənt] ADJ clemente, benigno.
clementine ['kleməntaɪn] N clementina *f*.
clench [klentʃ] VT *teeth, fist* apretar, cerrar; **the ~ed fist** el puño cerrado; = **clinch**.
Cleopatra [ˌkliːə'pætrə] NF Cleopatra.
clerestory ['klɪə,stɔːrɪ] N triforio *m*.
clergy ['klɜːdʒɪ] N clero *m*.
clergyman ['klɜːdʒɪmən] N, PL **clergymen** ['klɜːdʒɪmen] clérigo *m*; (*specifically Anglican*) sacerdote *m* anglicano; (*Protestant minister*) pastor *m*.
clergywoman ['klɜːdʒɪ,wʊmən] N, PL **clergywomen** (*Anglican*) pastora *f* anglicana; (*Protestant*) pastora *f* protestante.
cleric ['klerɪk] N eclesiástico *m*, clérigo *m*.
clerical ['klerɪkəl] ADJ (a) oficinista, oficinesco, de oficina; ~ **error** error *m* de pluma, error *m* de copia; ~ **grades** (*Civil Service etc*) oficinistas *mpl*; ~ **staff** personal *m* de oficina; ~ **work** trabajo *m* de oficina; ~ **worker** oficinista *mf*. (b) (*Eccl*) clerical; ~ **collar** alzacuello(s) *m*.
clericalism ['klerɪkə,lɪzəm] N clericalismo *m*.
clerihew ['klerɪhjuː] N *estrofa inglesa de 4 versos, de carácter festivo*.
clerk [klɑːk, (*US*) klɜːrk] **1** N (a) oficinista *mf*, empleado *m*, -a *f*, secretario *m*, -a *f*; (*in bank*) funcionario *m*, -a *f*; (*in hotel*) recepcionista *mf*; (*esp US*) dependiente *m*, -a *f*, vendedor *m*, -ora *f*; (*Jur*) escribano *m*; ~ **of works** maestro *m* de obras. (b) (*Eccl: also* ~ **in holy orders**) clérigo *m*.
2 VI (*US*) trabajar como dependiente.
clerkship ['klɑːkʃɪp, (*US*) 'klɜːrkʃɪp] N empleo *m* de oficinista; (*Jur*) escribanía *f*.
clever ['klevər] ADJ inteligente, listo; *move, speech etc* hábil; *invention, parody, trick, etc* ingenioso; **to be ~ at** ser listo en, tener aptitud para; **he is very ~ with his fingers** es muy hábil con los dedos, tiene mucha destreza manual; **she is very ~ with cars** entiende de coches, tiene mano para los coches; **that was ~ of you** lo hiciste muy bien, (*you were right*) has acertado; **that's ~, isn't it?** ¿es ingenioso, eh?; **to be too ~ by half** pasarse de listo; **he was too ~ for us** fue demasiado astuto para nosotros; **he tries to be too ~** se esfuerza por parecer ingenioso; ~ **Dick*** sabelotodo *m*.
clever-clever* ['klevə,klevər] ADJ sabihondo; **he's very ~** es un siete ciencias.
cleverly ['klevəlɪ] ADV hábilmente; ingeniosamente; con destreza.
cleverness ['klevənɪs] N inteligencia *f*; habilidad *f*; ingenio *m*; destreza *f*.
clew [kluː] N (*US*) = **clue**.
cliché ['kliːʃeɪ] N cliché *m*, tópico *m*, frase *f* hecha, lugar *m* común.
cliched, clichéd ['kliːʃeɪd] ADJ *image, view, argument* manido, muy visto; *song* de siempre.
click [klɪk] **1** N golpecito *m* seco; (*of gun*) piñoneo *m*; (*of heels*) taconeo *m*; (*of tongue*) chasquido *m*; (*of typewriter etc*) tecleo *m*.
2 VT *tongue etc* chasquear; **to ~ one's heels** taconear, hacer sonar los talones.
3 VI (a) (*gun*) piñonear; sonar con un golpecito seco; (*typewriter etc*) teclear.
(b) (*) (*succeed*) tener suerte, lograrlo; (*2 persons*) congeniar, gustarse inmediatamente; (*sexually*) ligar; (*product, invention*) tener éxito.
(c) **suddenly it ~ed** de repente caí en la cuenta, de repente me di cuenta.
(d) (*Comput*) hacer click.
♦**click on** **1** VI (*: *understand*) = **3** (c).
2 VT (*Comput*) hacer click en.
clicking ['klɪkɪŋ] N chasquido *m*.
client ['klaɪənt] N cliente *mf*; **my ~** (*in court*) mi defendido.
clientèle [ˌkliːɑ̃ːn'tel] N clientela *f*.
client state ['klaɪənt,steɪt] N (*Pol*) estado *m* satélite, estado *m* cliente.
cliff [klɪf] N risco *m*, precipicio *m*; (*sea* ~) acantilado *m*.
cliff-dweller* ['klɪf,dwelər] N (*US*) *persona que habita en un bloque*.
cliff-hanger ['klɪf,hæŋər] N película *f* (*etc*) melodramática, película *f* (*etc*) de suspense; **the election was a ~** el resultado de la elección siguió muy incierto hasta el final.
cliff-hanging ['klɪf,hæŋɪŋ] ADJ muy emocionante (por su final dudoso y apasionado), que tiene a todos pendientes de su resultado; *drama* de suspense.
climacteric [klaɪ'mæktərɪk] **1** ADJ climactérico.
2 N período *m* climactérico.
climactic [klaɪ'mæktɪk] ADJ culminante.
climate ['klaɪmɪt] N clima *m*; (*fig*) ambiente *m*; ~ **of opinion** opinión *f*

general.
climatic [klaɪ'mætɪk] ADJ climático; ~ **change** cambio *m* climático.
climatological [ˌklaɪmətə'lɒdʒɪkəl] ADJ climatológico.
climatologist [ˌklaɪmə'tɒlədʒɪst] N climatólogo *m*, -a *f*.
climatology [ˌklaɪmə'tɒlədʒɪ] N climatología *f*.
climax ['klaɪmæks] **1** N punto *m* culminante, colmo *m*, apogeo *m*, (*of play etc*) clímax *m*; (*sexual*) orgasmo *m*; **to reach a ~** llegar a su punto álgido, alcanzar una cima de intensidad.
2 VI llegar a un (*or* su) clímax.
climb [klaɪm] **1** N subida *f*, escalada *f*, ascenso *m*; **it was a stiff ~** la subida fue penosa.
2 VT *tree, wall etc* trepar a; *staircase* subir, subir por; *mountain* subir a, escalar.
3 VI (a) subir, trepar; (*aircraft, price, road, sun*) subir; **the path ~s higher yet** la senda sigue subiendo todavía; **to ~ to power** subir al poder.
♦**climb down** **1** VT: **to ~ down a tree** bajar de un árbol; **to ~ down a cliff** bajar por un precipicio.
2 VI (a) bajar. (b) (*fig*) volverse atrás, rajarse, desdecirse; darse por vencido.
♦**climb into** VT: **to ~ into an aircraft** subir a un avión; **to ~ into a tree** trepar a un árbol.
♦**climb out** VI salir trepando.
♦**climb out of** VT salir trepando de.
♦**climb over** VT: **to ~ over a wall** franquear una tapia.
♦**climb up** **1** VT: **to ~ up a rope** trepar por una cuerda; **to ~ up a cliff** trepar por un precipicio.
2 VI subir, trepar.
climb-down ['klaɪmdaʊn] N vuelta *f* atrás, retroceso *m*.
climber ['klaɪmər] N montañista *mf*, alpinista *mf*, escalador *m*, -ora *f*, andinista *mf* (*LAm*); (*fig*) arribista *mf*, trepador *m*, -ora *f*; (*Bot*) trepadora *f*, enredadera *f*.
climbing ['klaɪmɪŋ] **1** N montañismo *m*, alpinismo *m*, andinismo *m* (*LAm*).
2 ADJ (*Bot*) trepador.
climbing-frame ['klaɪmɪŋ,freɪm] N *estructura metálica en la cual los niños juegan trepando*.
climbing-irons ['klaɪmɪŋaɪənz] NPL garfios *mpl*.
clime [klaɪm] N (*liter*) clima *m*; región *f*.
clinch [klɪntʃ] **1** N abrazo *m*; (*Boxing*) clinch *m*; **to go into a ~** abrazarse.
2 VT (a) (*secure*) afianzar; *nail* remachar, roblar.
(b) (*fig*) resolver de una vez, decidir; *argument* remachar; *deal* cerrar; **to ~ matters** para remacharlo todavía; **that ~es it** eso es concluyente; ¡ni una palabra más!; = **clench**.
clincher ['klɪntʃər] N: **that was the ~** eso fue el punto clave, eso fue el argumento irrebatible.
clinching ['klɪntʃɪŋ] ADJ *argument* decisivo, irrebatible.
cling [klɪŋ] (*irr*: PRET AND PTP **clung**) VI: **to ~ to** adherirse a, pegarse a, quedar pegado a; *life* aferrarse a; *person* agarrarse a, abrazarse a, quedar abrazado a; *person pursued* no separarse de; *opinion* seguir fiel a, aferrarse a; **they clung to one another** quedaron abrazados; **a dress that ~s to the figure** un vestido que se pega al cuerpo.
Clingfilm ['klɪŋfɪlm] ® N, **clingwrap** ['klɪŋræp] N plástico *m* para envolver.
clinging ['klɪŋɪŋ] ADJ *dress* ceñido, muy ajustado; *person* pegajoso; *odour* tenaz; ~ **vine** (*US fig*) lapa* *mf*.
clingy ['klɪŋɪ] ADJ (a) *person* pegajoso. (b) *clothes* ceñido.
clinic ['klɪnɪk] N clínica *f*; centro *m* médico (privado); (*of hospital*) dispensario *m*.
clinical ['klɪnɪkəl] ADJ (a) clínico; ~ **thermometer** termómetro *m* clínico. (b) (*fig*) clínico, aséptico, frío.
clinically ['klɪnɪkəlɪ] ADV (a) clínicamente; ~ **dead** clínicamente muerto. (b) (*fig*) de manera clínica, de manera aséptica, fríamente.
clinician [klɪ'nɪʃən] N médico *m*, -a *f* de clínica.
clink¹ [klɪŋk] **1** N tintín *m*, sonido *m* metálico; (*of glasses*) choque *m*.
2 VT hacer sonar, hacer tintinar; *glasses* chocar.
3 VI tintinar.
clink²* [klɪŋk] N trena* *f*.
clinker ['klɪŋkər] N escoria *f* de hulla.
clinker-built ['klɪŋkə,bɪlt] ADJ (*Naut*) de tingladillo.
clip¹ [klɪp] **1** N (a) (*cut with scissors*) tijeretada *f*; (*shearing*) esquila *f*, esquileo *m*; (*wool*) cantidad *f* de lana esquilada; (*Cine*) fotograma *m*.
(b) (*blow*) golpe *m*, cachete *m*; **at a** (**fast**) ~ (*US*) a toda pastilla.
2 VT (a) (*cut*) cortar; (*cut to shorten*) acortar; *wool* trasquilar, esquilar; *coin* cercenar; *ticket* picar; *wings* cortar; *words* comerse, abreviar; (*US*) *news story etc* recortar.
(b) (*hit*) golpear, dar un cachete a.
♦**clip off** VT cortar, quitar cortando.
♦**clip out** VT recortar.
clip² [klɪp] **1** N (*clamp*) grapa *f*; (*for papers*) sujetapapeles *m*, broche *m* (*LAm*); (*of pen*) sujetador *m*; (*of cyclist*) pinza *f*; (*for hair*) prendido *m*,

horquilla *f*, clip *m*; (*brooch*) alfiler *m* de pecho, clip *m*, abrochador *m* (*LAm*).
  2 VT sujetar.
♦ **clip on** 1 VT *brooch* sujetar; *document etc* sujetar con un clip.
  2 VI: **it ~s on here** se fija aquí (con clip).
♦ **clip together** VT unir.
clipboard ['klɪp,bɔːd] N tablilla *f* con sujetapapeles.
clip-clop ['klɪp'klɒp] N ruido *m* de los cascos del caballo.
clip-joint* ['klɪp,dʒɔɪnt] N (*US*) bar *m* (muy caro).
clip-on ['klɪpɒn] ADJ *badge etc* para prender, con prendedor.
clipped [klɪpt] ADJ *accent* abrupto; *style* sucinto; *hair* corto.
clipper ['klɪpə'] N (*Naut*) clíper *m*.
clippers ['klɪpəz] NPL (*for hair*) maquinilla *f* (para el pelo); (*Hort*) tijeras *fpl* podadoras.
clippie* ['klɪpɪ] N (*Brit*) cobradora *f* (de autobús).
clipping ['klɪpɪŋ] N (*from newspaper*) recorte *m*; (*of cloth*) retazo *m*.
clique [kliːk] N pandilla *f*, camarilla *f*, peña *f*.
cliquey ['kliːkɪ] ADJ, **cliquish** ['kliːkɪʃ] ADJ exclusivista.
cliquishness ['kliːkɪʃnɪs] N exclusivismo *m*.
cliterodectomy [,klɪtərɪ'dektəmɪ] N clitoridectomía *f*.
clitoral ['klɪtərəl] ADJ del clítoris.
clitoris ['klɪtərɪs] N clítoris *m*.
Cllr ABBR *of* **Councillor**.
cloak [kləʊk] 1 N capa *f*, manto *m*; (*fig*) pretexto *m*; **under the ~ of** so capa de, al amparo de.
  2 VT encapotar; (*cover*) cubrir (*in, with* de); (*fig*) encubrir, disimular.
cloak-and-dagger ['kləʊkən'dægə'] ADJ clandestino, propio de agente secreto; *play* de capa y espada; *story* de agentes secretos, de espías.
cloakroom ['kləʊkrʊm] N guardarropa *m*; (*Brit Rail*) consigna *f*; (*Brit euph*) aseos *mpl*, lavabo *m*, servicios *mpl*, baño *m* (*LAm*).
clobber‡ ['klɒbə'] 1 N (*dress*) ropa *f*, traje *m*; (*Brit: gear*) bártulos *mpl*, trastos *mpl*.
  2 VT (*defeat*) cascar*; (*beat up*) dar una paliza a.
cloche [klɒʃ] N campana *f* de cristal.
clock [klɒk] 1 N (**a**) reloj *m*; (*dial*) esfera *f*, cuadrante *m*; (*of taxi*) taxímetro *m*; (*Aut: speedometer*) velocímetro *m*, (*milometer*) cuentakilómetros *m*; **it's only got 60 miles on the ~** este coche ha hecho solamente 60 millas; **this will put the ~ back 50 years** esto nos hará retroceder a la situación de hace 50 años; **you can't put the ~ back** no se puede detener el progreso; **against the ~** contra (el) reloj; **we have surveillance round the ~** tenemos vigilancia de veinticuatro horas, tenemos vigilancia permanente; **to sleep round the ~** dormir doce horas seguidas; **the garage is open around the ~** el garaje está abierto las veinticuatro horas; **to do sth by the ~** hacer algo con precisión de reloj; **to keep one's eyes on** (*or* **watch**) **the ~** mirar mucho el reloj (ansiando abandonar el trabajo).
  (**b**) (‡) jeta *f*.
  2 VT (**a**) registrar; **she ~ed 4 minutes for the mile** hizo la milla en 4 minutos; **we ~ed 80 m.p.h.** alcanzamos una velocidad de 80 millas por hora.
  (**b**) (*Brit‡: hit*) **he ~ed him one** le dió un bofetón*.
  (**c**) (*Brit‡: see*) guipar‡, calar‡.
♦ **clock in** VI fichar, picar, (*loosely*) llegar al trabajo.
♦ **clock off** VI fichar la salida, (*loosely*) terminar el trabajo.
♦ **clock on** VI = **clock in**.
♦ **clock out** VI = **clock off**.
♦ **clock up** VT acumular; **he ~ed up 250 miles** (*Aut*) recorrió 250 millas.
clockface ['klɒkfeɪs] N esfera *f* de reloj.
clockmaker ['klɒk,meɪkə'] N relojero *m*.
clock radio [,klɒk'reɪdɪəʊ] N radio-despertador *m*.
clock repairer ['klɒkrɪ,peərə'] N relojero *m*.
clocktower ['klɒk,taʊə'] N torre *f* de reloj.
clock-watcher ['klɒk,wɒtʃə'] N persona *f* que mira mucho el reloj (ansiando abandonar el trabajo).
clockwise ['klɒkwaɪz] 1 ADJ dextrorso.
  2 ADV dextrórsum, en la dirección de las agujas del reloj.
clockwork ['klɒkwɜːk] 1 N aparato *m* de relojería; **to go like ~** ir como un reloj.
  2 ATTR de cuerda; **~ train** tren *m* de cuerda; **C~ Orange** La Naranja Mecánica.
clod [klɒd] N (**a**) terrón *m*. (**b**) (*person*) patán *m*; **you ~!** ¡bestia!
clodhopper ['klɒd,hɒpə'] N patán *m*.
clodhopping ['klɒdhɒpɪŋ] ADJ *person* torpón, desgarbado; *boots* basto, pesado.
clog [klɒg] 1 N zueco *m*, chanclo *m*.
  2 VT (*also* **to ~ up**) atascar, obstruir.
  3 VI (*also* **to ~ up**) atascarse, obstruirse.
cloister ['klɔɪstə'] N claustro *m*.
cloistered ['klɔɪstəd] ADJ conventual; **to live a ~ life** (*fig*) llevar una vida de ermitaño.

clonal ['kləʊnəl] ADJ clónico.
clone [kləʊn] 1 N clon *m*; (*Comput*) clónico *m*.
  2 VT clonar.
cloning ['kləʊnɪŋ] N clonación *f*, clonaje *m*.
clonk [klɒnk] 1 N (*sound*) ruido *m* hueco.
  2 VI (*make sound*) hacer un ruido hueco.
close¹ [kləʊs] 1 ADV cerca; **~ by** muy cerca; **~ by sth**, **~ to sth** cerca de algo; **to be ~ together** estar muy juntos, estar muy cerca uno(s) de otro(s); **to come ~** acercarse; **that comes ~ to an insult** eso equivale casi a un insulto; **the runners finished very ~** llegaron los atletas casi a la par; **to fit ~** ajustarse al cuerpo (*etc*); **to follow ~ behind sb** seguir muy de cerca a uno; **to keep ~ to the wall** ir arrimado a la pared; **to look at sth ~ up** (*or* **to**) mirar algo de cerca; **it's ~ on 6 o'clock** son casi las 6; **he must be ~ on 50** estará frisando en los 50; **according to sources ~ to the police** según fuentes allegadas a la comisaría.
  2 ADJ (**a**) (*near*) cercano, próximo; (**~ together**) apretados, arrimados unos a otros; densos; *connection, contact, friendship* estrecho, íntimo; *friend* íntimo; *relation* cercano; *resemblance* casi completo, muy estrecho; *imitation* arrimado; **a ~ circle of friends** un estrecho círculo de amigos; **~ combat** combate *m* cuerpo a cuerpo; **they are very ~** son muy amigos; **he was the ~st thing to a real worker among us** entre nosotros él tenía más visos de ser un obrero auténtico.
  (**b**) (*compact*) *weave* compacto, tupido; *print* compacto; *formation* cerrado.
  (**c**) (*strict*) *control* estricto, rígido; *confinement, watch* estricto, severo; *attention* concienzudo; *argument, questioning, study* detallado, minucioso; *translation* fiel, exacto; **to keep a ~ eye** (*or* **watch**) **on sth** vigilar algo con mucho cuidado.
  (**d**) (*airless*) *atmosphere* sofocante; *weather* pesado, bochornoso; *room* mal ventilado.
  (**e**) (*nearly equal*) *election, finish, result* muy reñido; *scores* casi iguales.
  (**f**) (*secretive*) reservado; (*mean*) tacaño.
  (**g**) **~ season** veda *f*.
  (**h**) (*Ling*) *vowel* cerrado.
  (**i**) (*Fin*) **~ company** (*Brit*), **~ corporation** (*US*) sociedad *f* exclusiva, compañía *f* propietaria.
  3 N recinto *m*.
close² [kləʊz] 1 N fin *m*, final *m*, conclusión *f*; **at the ~** al final; **at the ~ of day** a la caída de la tarde; **at the ~ of the year** al fin del año; **to bring sth to a ~** terminar algo, concluir algo; **to draw to a ~** tocar a su fin, estar terminando.
  2 VT (*shut*) cerrar; (*end*) concluir, terminar; *hole etc* tapar, obstruir; *breach, gap* cerrar; *deal, list, sale* cerrar; *ceremony, debate* clausurar; *account* (*Comm*) saldar; *bank account* cerrar, finiquitar; *ranks* apretar; **'road ~d'** 'carretera cerrada', 'cerrado el paso'.
  3 VI (*shut*) cerrarse; (*end*) concluir(se), terminar(se); **Pooleys ~d \$2 up** los Pooley habían subido \$2 al cierre; **the crowd ~d round him** se agolpó la multitud en torno suyo; **the clouds ~d round the peak** las nubes envolvieron la cumbre; **the waters ~d round it** lo rodearon las aguas.
♦ **close down** 1 VT cerrar (definitivamente), clausurar.
  2 VI cerrarse (definitivamente); (*Brit Rad*) cerrar la emisión.
♦ **close in** 1 VT cercar, rodear.
  2 VI (*person*) acercarse, ir acercándose; **the days are closing in** los días son cada vez más cortos; **night was closing in** se cerraba ya la noche; **to ~ in on sb** rodear a uno, cercar a uno.
♦ **close off** VT *road etc* cerrar; *supply* cortar; *access* bloquear.
♦ **close on** VT (**a**) (*get nearer to*) acercarse a. (**b**) (*US*) = **close in on**; V **close in 1**.
♦ **close out** VT (*US: Fin*) liquidar.
♦ **close up** 1 VT cerrar del todo.
  2 VI (*flower*) cerrarse del todo; (*people*) arrimarse más, ponerse más cerca unos de otros; (*ranks*) apretarse; (*wound*) cicatrizarse.
♦ **close with** VT: **to ~ with sb** cerrar con uno.
close-cropped ['kləʊs'krɒpt] ADJ (*cortado*) al rape, rapado.
closed [kləʊzd] 1 PRET AND PTP *of* **close**. 2 ADJ *car, circuit etc* cerrado; *mind* de miras estrechas; *society* exclusivista, cerrado; *session, hearing* a puerta cerrada; **~ primary** (*US Pol*) elección primaria reservada a los miembros de un partido; **~ season** (*US*) veda *f*; **~ shop** coto *m* cerrado; V **book** *etc*.
closed-circuit ['kləʊzd'sɜːkɪt] ADJ: **~ television** circuito *m* interno de televisión, televisión *f* por circuito cerrado.
closed-door ['kləʊzd,dɔː'] ADJ (*US*) *meeting, session* a puerta cerrada.
close-down ['kləʊzdaʊn] N (*Brit Rad*) cierre *m*; (*by strike etc*) cierre *m*, paralización *f*.
close-fisted ['kləʊs'fɪstɪd] ADJ tacaño.
close-fitting ['kləʊs'fɪtɪŋ] ADJ ceñido, ajustado.
close-grained [,kləʊs'greɪnd] ADJ *wood* tupido.
close-harmony singing [,kləʊs,hɑːmənɪ'sɪŋɪŋ] N canto *m* en estrecha armonía.
close-knit ['kləʊsnɪt] ADJ muy unido, bien ensamblado, homogéneo.

closely ['kləʊslɪ] ADV (exactly) fielmente, exactamente; (carefully) atentamente; ~ **packed** case atestado.

closeness ['kləʊsnɪs] N (a) (nearness) proximidad f; cercanía f; (of connection) intimidad f. (b) (of translation) fidelidad f. (c) (of room) mala ventilación f; (of weather) pesantez f, lo bochornoso. (d) (of election etc) lo muy reñido. (e) (secretiveness) reserva f; (meanness) tacañería f.

close-run [,kləʊs'rʌn] ADJ: ~ **race** carrera f muy reñida.

close-set ['kləʊs,set] ADJ eyes muy juntos.

closet ['klɒzɪt] ① N (a) wáter m, lavabo m; (US: cupboard) armario m, (for clothes) ropero m. (b) **to come out of the ~** (US) anunciarse públicamente, hacerse público, darse a conocer. ② ATTR (esp US) secreto, tapado; ~ **gay** gay m de tapada. ③ VT: **to be ~ed with** estar encerrado con.

close-up ['kləʊsʌp] N primer plano m; ~ **lens** teleobjetivo m.

closing ['kləʊzɪŋ] ① N cierre m; clausura f. ② ADJ, ATTR: ~ **date** fecha f tope, fecha f límite; ~ **entry** (in account) asiento m de cierre; ~ **price** (Fin) cotización f de cierre; ~ **speech** discurso m de clausura; **in the ~ stages** en las últimas etapas; ~ **time** (Brit) hora f de cerrar; **his ~ words were ...** sus palabras finales eran ...

closing-down ['kləʊzɪŋ'daʊn] N cierre m; ~ **sale** venta f de liquidación.

closure ['kləʊʒər] N (close-down) cierre m; (end) fin m, conclusión f; (Parl) clausura f.

clot [klɒt] ① N (a) (Culin etc) grumo m, cuajarón m; (Med) embolia f; ~ **of blood** coágulo m sanguíneo; ~ **on the brain** embolia f cerebral. (b) (Brit*) papanatas* m; **you ~!** ¡bobo! ② VI cuajarse, coagularse; **~ted cream** nata f espesa, nata f cuajada.

cloth [klɒθ] N, PL **cloths** [klɒθs, klɒðz] (material) paño m, tela f; (for cleaning) trapo m; (table-) mantel m; **the ~** (Eccl) el clero; **a man of the ~** un clérigo; ~ **cap** (Brit) gorra f de paño; **bound in ~** encuadernado en tela; **to lay the ~** poner la mesa.

clothbound ['klɒθ,baʊnd] ADJ: ~ **book** libro m en tela.

clothe [kləʊð] VT vestir (in, with de); (fig) cubrir, revestir (in, with de).

cloth-eared ['klɒθɪəd] ADJ sordo como una tapia.

clothed [kləʊðd] ADJ vestido.

clothes [kləʊðz] NPL ropa f, vestidos mpl.

clothes-basket ['kləʊðz,bɑːskɪt] N canasta f de la ropa sucia.

clothes-brush ['kləʊðzbrʌʃ] N cepillo m de la ropa.

clothes-drier, clothes-dryer ['kləʊðz,draɪər] N secadora f.

clothes-hanger ['kləʊðz,hæŋər] N percha f.

clothes-horse ['kləʊðz,hɔːs] N (a) (also fig) tendedero m; (US*: model) modelo mf; **she's a ~** (US*) está obsesionada con sus trapos*.

clothes-line ['kləʊðzlaɪn] N (cuerda f de) tendedero m, tendedera f (LAm).

clothes-moth ['kləʊðzmɒθ] N polilla f.

clothespeg ['kləʊðzpeg] N, (US) **clothespin** ['kləʊðzpɪn] N pinza f.

clothespole ['kləʊðzpəʊl] N, **clothesprop** ['kləʊðzprɒp] N palo m de tendedero.

clothes-rack ['kləʊðz,ræk] N tendedero m.

clothes-rope ['kləʊðzrəʊp] N = **clothes-line.**

clothes-shop ['kləʊðzʃɒp] N tienda f de modas.

clothier ['kləʊðɪər] N ropero m, (tailor) sastre m; ~'**s** (shop) pañería f, ropería f, (tailor's) sastrería f.

clothing ['kləʊðɪŋ] ① N ropa f, vestidos mpl; **article of ~** prenda f de vestir. ② ATTR: ~ **industry** industria f textil; ~ **shop** pañería f, ropería f, (tailor's) sastrería f; **the ~ trade** la industria de la confección.

clotting agent ['klɒtɪŋ,eɪdʒənt] N agente m coagulante.

cloture ['kləʊtʃər] N (US: Pol) clausura f; ~ **rule** control del tiempo de intervención (en un debate).

cloud [klaʊd] ① N nube f (also fig); (storm-~) nubarrón m; **to be under a ~** estar desacreditado; **to leave under a ~** ser despedido bajo sospecha; **to be up in the ~s** estar en las nubes; **every ~ has a silver lining** no hay mal que por bien no venga; **to be on ~ 9** estar en el séptimo cielo. ② VT anublar (also fig). ③ VI (also **to ~ over**) nublarse (also fig).

cloudberry ['klaʊdbərɪ] N (US) camemoro m.

cloudburst ['klaʊdbɜːst] N chubasco m (violento), aguacero m fuerte.

cloud-cuckoo land [,klaʊd'kuːkuː,lænd] N, (US) **cloudland** ['klaʊdlænd] N: **to be in ~** estar en Babia, estar en las Batuecas, vivir en la luna.

cloudiness ['klaʊdɪnɪs] N lo nublado, lo nuboso; lo turbio.

cloudless ['klaʊdlɪs] ADJ sin nubes, despejado.

cloudy ['klaʊdɪ] ADJ nublado, nuboso; liquid turbio; glass empañado; **partly ~** con nubes alternas; **it is ~** el cielo está nublado.

clout¹ [klaʊt] ① N (a) (blow) tortazo m. (b) (*) influencia f, fuerza f (política etc). ② VT dar un tortazo a.

clout² [klaʊt] N: **ne'er cast a ~ till May be out** hasta el cuarenta de

mayo no te quites el sayo.

clove¹ [kləʊv] N (spice) clavo m de especia; ~ **of garlic** diente m de ajo.

clove² [kləʊv] PRET of **cleave¹.**

clove-hitch ['kləʊvhɪtʃ] N ballestrinque m.

cloven ['kləʊvn] PTP of **cleave²;** ~ **hoof** pata f hendida.

cloven-footed [,kləʊvn'fʊtɪd] ADJ animal de pezuña hendida; devil con pezuña.

clover ['kləʊvər] N trébol m; **to be in ~** estar en Jauja, vivir a cuerpo de rey.

cloverleaf ['kləʊvəliːf] N, PL **cloverleaves** ['kləʊvəliːvz] hoja f de trébol; (Aut) cruce m en trébol.

clown [klaʊn] ① N payaso m, clown m; (boor) patán m; **to make a ~ of o.s.** hacer el ridículo. ② VI (also **to ~ about, to ~ around**) hacer el payaso; **stop ~ing!** ¡déjate de tonterías!

clowning ['klaʊnɪŋ] N payasadas fpl.

clownish ['klaʊnɪʃ] ADJ clownesco.

cloy [klɔɪ] VTI empalagar.

cloying ['klɔɪɪŋ] ADJ empalagoso.

cloyingly ['klɔɪɪŋlɪ] ADV de manera empalagosa; ~ **sweet** tan dulce que empalaga.

C.L.U. N (US) ABBR of **Chartered Life Underwriter.**

club [klʌb] ① N (a) (stick) porra f, cachiporra f, garrote m; (golf~) palo m. (b) (Cards) ~**s** tréboles mpl, (in Spanish pack) bastones mpl. (c) (association) club m; (for gaming etc) casino m; ~ **car** (US: Rail) coche m club; ~ **class** clase f club; ~ **member** socio m, -a f; ~ **sandwich** bocadillo vegetal con pollo y bacón; ~ **soda** (US) agua f de sifón; ~ **steak** (US) bistec m culer; **to be in the ~** (hum) estar en estado; **he put her in the ~** él la dejó encinta. ② VT aporrear; **to ~ sb to death** matar a uno a porrazos. ③ VI: **to ~ together** pagar a escote; **we ~bed together to buy it for him** entre todos se lo compramos.

clubbable* ['klʌbəbl] ADJ sociable.

clubber ['klʌbər] N discotequero m, -a f.

clubbing* ['klʌbɪŋ] N (Brit) ir de discotecas; **to go ~** ir de discotecas.

club-foot ['klʌb'fʊt] N pie m zopo.

club-footed ['klʌb,fʊtɪd] ADJ con el pie zopo.

clubhouse ['klʌbhaʊs] N, PL **clubhouses** ['klʌb,haʊzɪz] (Golf etc) chalet m, chalé m, casa f (de) club.

clubland ['klʌblænd] N (esp Brit) zona de las discotecas de moda.

clubroom ['klʌbrʊm] N salón m, sala f de reuniones.

cluck [klʌk] ① N (a) (of hen) cloqueo m. (b) (with tongue) chasquido m (de la lengua). ② VI (a) cloquear. (b) chasquear con la lengua.

◆ **cluck over** VT: **she ~ed over the children** con los niños estaba como la gallina con sus polluelos.

clue [kluː] ① N indicio m; (in a crime etc) pista f; (of crossword) indicación f; **I haven't a ~*** no tengo ni idea; **he hasn't a ~*** es un pobre hombre, tiene un tremendo despiste; **can you give me a ~?** ¿me das una pista? ② VT (:) **to ~ sb up** (US: in) informar a uno; poner a uno al tanto; **to be all ~d up** (US: in) estar bien informado, estar al tanto.

clueless* ['kluːlɪs] ADJ (Brit) estúpido; despistado; desorientado.

clump¹ [klʌmp] N (of trees) grupo m; (of plant) mata f, macizo m.

clump² [klʌmp] ① N (noise of feet) pisadas fpl fuertes. ② VI pisar fuerte, ir pisando fuerte.

clumpy ['klʌmpɪ] ADJ shoes grandón, grandote.

clumsily ['klʌmzɪlɪ] ADV torpemente; pesadamente; toscamente, chapuceramente.

clumsiness ['klʌmzɪnɪs] N torpeza f, desmaña f; tosquedad f.

clumsy ['klʌmzɪ] ADJ torpe, desmañado; (in movement) desgarbado, pesado; (inartistic) tosco, chapucero.

clung [klʌŋ] PRET AND PTP of **cling.**

Cluniac ['kluːnɪæk] ① ADJ cluniacense. ② N cluniacense m.

clunk [klʌŋk] ① N (a) (sound) sonido m metálico sordo. (b) (US:) cabezahueca mf. ② VI (make sound) sonar a hueco.

clunker: ['klʌŋkər] N (US) cacharro* m.

clunky ['klʌŋkɪ] ADJ macizo.

cluster ['klʌstər] ① N grupo m; (Bot) racimo m. ② VI agruparse, apiñarse; (Bot) arracimarse; **to ~ round sb** reunirse en torno de uno, apiñarse alrededor de uno.

cluster-bomb ['klʌstə,bɒm] N bomba f de dispersión, bomba f de racimo.

clutch¹ [klʌtʃ] ① N (a) (grasp) apretón m; **to make a ~ at sth** tratar de agarrar algo. (b) **to fall into sb's ~es** caer en las garras de uno; **to get sth out of sb's ~es** hacer que uno ceda la posesión (or se desprenda) de algo. (c) (Aut) embrague m, cloche m (LAm); (pedal) pedal m de embrague;

to disengage the ~ desembragar; **to let in** (*or* **engage**) **the ~** embragar.

(d) (*US*: crisis*) crisis *f*.

2 VT tener asido en la mano; sujetar, apretar, empuñar; **he ~ed her to his heart** la estrechó contra el pecho.

3 VI: **to ~ at** agarrarse a, tratar de asir; **he ~ed at my hand** trató de coger mi mano; **to ~ at a hope** aferrarse a una esperanza.

clutch² [klʌtʃ] N (*of eggs*) nidada *f*.

clutter ['klʌtəʳ] 1 N desorden *m*, confusión *f*; **a ~ of shoes** un montón de zapatos.

2 VT llenar desordenadamente, atestar; **to be ~ed up with** estar atestado de.

CM (*US Post*) ABBR *of* **North Mariana Islands**.

cm ABBR *of* **centimetre(s)** centímetro(s) *m(pl)*, cm.

Cmdr ABBR *of* **Commander**.

CNAA N (*Brit*) ABBR *of* **Council for National Academic Awards**.

CND N ABBR *of* **Campaign for Nuclear Disarmament** Campaña *f* pro Desarme Nuclear.

CNN N (*US*) ABBR *of* **Cable News Network**.

CO (a) N (*Brit*) (V **Commonwealth**) ABBR *of* **Commonwealth Office** *Ministerio de relaciones con la Commonwealth*. **(b)** N (*Mil*) ABBR *of* **Commanding Officer**. **(c)** N ABBR *of* **conscientious objector** objetor *m* de conciencia. **(d)** (*US Post*) ABBR *of* **Colorado**.

Co. (a) [kəʊ] N (*Comm*) ABBR *of* **company** compañía *f*, Cía, S.A.; **Mrs Thatcher and ~** (*pej*) La Thatcher y compañía. **(b)** ABBR *of* **county** condado *m*.

c/o (a) ABBR *of* **care of** en casa de, c/d; al cuidado de, a/c. **(b)** (*Comm*) ABBR *of* **cash order** orden *f* de pago al contado.

co... PREF CO...

coach [kəʊtʃ] 1 N **(a)** (*gen*) coche *m*; (††: *stage~*) diligencia *f*; (*ceremonial*) carroza *f*; (*Rail*) coche *m*, vagón *m*; (*Aut*) autocar *m*, coche *m* de línea, camión *m* (*Méx*), autobús *m* (*LAm*).

(b) (*Sport*) entrenador *m*, -ora *f*, preparador *m*, -ora *f*, instructor *m*, -ora *f*; (*Golf*) maestro *m*, -a *f*; (*tutor*) profesor *m*, -ora *f* particular.

2 VT *team* entrenar, preparar; *student* enseñar, preparar; **to ~ sb in French** enseñar francés a uno; **to ~ sb in a part** ensayar un papel a uno.

coachbuilder ['kəʊtʃ,bɪldəʳ] N (*Brit Aut*) carrocero *m*.

coachbuilding ['kəʊtʃ,bɪldɪŋ] N (*Brit*) construcción *f* de carrocerías.

coach-driver ['kəʊtʃ,draɪvəʳ] N conductor *m*, -ora *f* de autocar.

coaching ['kəʊtʃɪŋ] N (*Sport*) entrenamiento *m*; (*esp US: tuition*) enseñanza *f* particular.

coachload ['kəʊtʃləʊd] N autocar *m* (lleno); **they came by the ~** vinieron en masa, vinieron hordas de ellos.

coachman ['kəʊtʃmən] N, PL **coachmen** ['kəʊtʃmen] cochero *m*.

coach-operator ['kəʊtʃ,ɒpəreɪtəʳ] N compañía *f* de autocares.

coach station ['kəʊtʃ,steɪʃən] N estación *f* de autocares.

coach-trip ['kəʊtʃtrɪp] N excursión *f* en autocar, viaje *m* en autocar.

coachwork ['kəʊtʃwɜːk] N (*Brit*) carrocería *f*.

coagulant [kəʊ'ægjʊlənt] N coagulante *m*.

coagulate [kəʊ'ægjʊleɪt] 1 VT coagular.

2 VI coagularse.

coagulation [kəʊ,ægjʊleɪʃən] N coagulación *f*.

coal [kəʊl] 1 N carbón *m*; hulla *f*; **a ~** un pedazo de carbón; **to carry ~s to Newcastle** ir a vendimiar y llevar uvas de postre; **to haul sb over the ~s** echar una bronca a uno; **to heap ~s of fire on sb's head** avergonzar a uno devolviéndole bien por mal.

2 ATTR: **~ industry** industria *f* del carbón; **~ measures** depósitos *mpl* de carbón.

3 VI (*Naut*) tomar carbón.

coal-black ['kəʊl'blæk] ADJ negro como el carbón.

coal-bunker ['kəʊl,bʌŋkəʳ] N carbonera *f*.

coal-burning ['kəʊl,bɜːnɪŋ] ADJ que quema carbón.

coal-cellar ['kəʊl,seləʳ] N carbonera *f*.

coaldust ['kəʊldʌst] N polvillo *m* de carbón, cisco *m*.

coalesce [kəʊə'les] VI fundirse; unirse, incorporarse.

coalescence [kəʊə'lesəns] N fusión *f*; unión *f*, incorporación *f*.

coalface ['kəʊlfeɪs] N frente *m* de (arranque de) carbón.

coalfield ['kəʊlfiːld] N yacimiento *m* de carbón; (*large area*) cuenca *f* minera, cuenca *f* carbonífera.

coal fire [,kəʊl'faɪəʳ] N hogar *m* de carbón.

coal-fired [,kəʊl'faɪəd] ADJ que quema carbón.

coalgas ['kəʊlgæs] N gas *m* de hulla.

coal-hod ['kəʊlhɒd] N cubo *m* de carbón.

coalition [,kəʊə'lɪʃən] N coalición *f*; **~ government** gobierno *m* de coalición.

coalman ['kəʊlmən] N, PL **coalmen** ['kəʊlmən], **coal merchant** ['kəʊl,mɜːtʃənt] N carbonero *m*.

coalmine ['kəʊlmaɪn] N mina *f* de carbón.

coalminer ['kəʊl,maɪnəʳ] N minero *m* de carbón.

coalmining ['kəʊl,maɪnɪŋ] N minería *f* de carbón.

coal oil ['kəʊl,ɔɪl] N (*US*) parafina *f*.

coalpit ['kəʊlpɪt] N mina *f* de carbón, pozo *m* de carbón.

coal-scuttle ['kəʊl,skʌtl] N cubo *m* para carbón.

coal strike ['kəʊl,straɪk] N huelga *f* de mineros.

coal-tar ['kəʊl'tɑːʳ] N alquitrán *m* mineral.

coaltit ['kəʊltɪt] N carbonero *m* garrapinos.

coalyard ['kəʊljɑːd] N patio *m* del carbón.

coarse [kɔːs] ADJ **(a)** (*of texture*) basto, burdo; *sand etc* grueso; (*badly-made*) tosco, torpe; *hands* calloso, poco elegante, *skin* áspero, poco fino. **(b)** *character, laugh, remark* ordinario, grosero; *joke* verde; **~ fishing** pesca *f* de agua dulce (excluyendo salmón y trucha).

coarse-grained ['kɔːsgreɪnd] ADJ de grano grueso; (*fig*) tosco, basto.

coarsely ['kɔːslɪ] ADV toscamente; groseramente.

coarsen ['kɔːsn] 1 VT *person* volver basto, poner grosero, embastecer.

2 VI embastecerse.

coarseness ['kɔːsnɪs] N **(a)** basteza *f*; tosquedad *f*; falta *f* de finura, falta *f* de elegancia. **(b)** ordinariez *f*, grosería *f*; lo verde.

coast [kəʊst] 1 N costa *f*; litoral *m*; **the ~ is clear** ya no hay peligro.

2 VI (*Aut etc*) llanear; (*on sledge, cycle etc*) deslizarse cuesta abajo; **to ~ along** (*Aut*) llanear; (*fig*) avanzar sin esfuerzo, (*pej*) gandulear.

coastal ['kəʊstəl] ADJ costero, costanero; **~ defences** defensas *fpl* costeras; **~ traffic** (*Naut*) cabotaje *m*.

coaster ['kəʊstəʳ] N **(a)** (*Naut*) buque *m* costero, barco *m* de cabotaje; (*US*) trineo *m*. **(b)** (*dripmat*) posavasos *m*.

coastguard ['kəʊstgɑːd] N guardacostas *m*; **~ station** puesto *m* de guardacostas; **~ vessel** guardacostas *m*.

coastline ['kəʊstlaɪn] N litoral *m*.

coat [kəʊt] 1 N **(a)** (*jacket*) chaqueta *f*, americana *f*, saco *m* (*LAm*); (*overcoat*) abrigo *m*; (*chemist's etc*) bata *f*; **~ of arms** escudo *m* (de armas); **~ of mail** cota *f* de malla; **to cut one's ~ according to one's cloth** adaptarse a las circunstancias; **to turn one's ~** chaquetear, cambiar de chaqueta.

(b) (*animal's*) pelo *m*, lana *f*.

(c) (*layer*) capa *f*; **~ of paint** mano *f* de pintura.

2 VT cubrir, revestir (*with* de); (*with a liquid*) bañar (*with* en); **to ~ sth with paint** dar una mano de pintura a algo.

coated ['kəʊtɪd] ADJ *tongue* saburral.

coat-hanger ['kəʊt,hæŋəʳ] N percha *f*, colgador *m*, gancho *m* (*LAm*).

coating ['kəʊtɪŋ] N capa *f*, baño *m*; (*of paint etc*) mano *f*.

coatstand ['kəʊtstænd] N perchero *m*.

coat-tails ['kəʊlteɪlz] NPL faldón *m*; **to ride on sb's ~** salir adelante gracias al favor de uno, lograr el éxito a la sombra de uno.

co-author ['kəʊ,ɔːθəʳ] 1 N coautor *m*, -ora *f*.

2 VT (*US*) escribir conjuntamente, componer en colaboración.

coax [kəʊks] VT halagar, mimar; **to ~ sth out of sb** sonsacar algo a uno; **to ~ sb into doing sth** halagar a uno para que haga algo; **she likes to be ~ed** se hace rogar; **to ~ sb along** mimar a uno.

coaxial [,kəʊ'æksɪəl] ADJ coaxial; **~ cable** cable *m* coaxial.

coaxing ['kəʊksɪŋ] 1 ADJ mimoso.

2 N mimos *mpl*, halagos *mpl*.

coaxingly ['kəʊksɪŋlɪ] ADV mimosamente.

cob [kɒb] N **(a)** (*swan*) cisne *m* macho. **(b)** (*horse*) jaca *f* fuerte. **(c)** (*loaf*) pan *m* redondo. **(d)** (*nut*) avellana *f*. **(e)** (*maize*) mazorca *f*.

cobalt ['kəʊbɒlt] N cobalto *m*; **~ blue** azul *m* de cobalto; (*colour*) azul *m* cobalto; **~ bomb** bomba *f* de cobalto.

cobber* ['kɒbəʳ] N (*Australia*) amigo *m*, compañero *m*; (*in direct address*) amigo.

cobble ['kɒbl] VT **(a)** (*also* **to ~ up**) *shoes* remendar. **(b)** *street* empedrar con guijarros, enguijarrar.

♦**cobble together** VT (*pej*) ensamblar, juntar (de modo poco satisfactorio); arreglar (provisionalmente).

cobbled ['kɒbld] ADJ: **~ street** calle *f* adoquinada.

cobbler ['kɒbləʳ] N zapatero *m* remendón.

cobblers ['kɒbləz] NPL (*Brit*) **(a)** (*Anat‡*) cojones‡ *mpl*. **(b)** (*fig‡*) chorradas‡ *fpl*.

cobbles ['kɒblz] NPL, **cobblestones** ['kɒblstəʊnz] NPL guijarros *mpl*, enguijarrado *m*.

COBOL ['kəʊbɒl] N (*Comput*) COBOL *m*.

cobra ['kəʊbrə] N cobra *f*.

cobweb ['kɒbweb] N telaraña *f*; **to blow** (*or* **clear**) **the ~s away** (*fig*) despejar la mente.

cobwebbed ['kɒbwebd] ADJ cubierto de telarañas, lleno de telarañas.

coca ['kəʊkə] N coca *f*.

cocaine [kə'keɪn] N cocaína *f*; **~ addict** cocainómano *m*, -a *f*; **~ addiction** cocainomanía *f*.

coccyx ['kɒksɪks] N cóccix *m*.

cochineal [kɒtʃɪniːl] N cochinilla *f*.

cochlea ['kɒklɪə] N, PL **cochleae** ['kɒkliːi] cóclea *f*, caracol *m* óseo.

cock [kɒk] 1 N **(a)** (*cockerel*) gallo *m*; (*other male bird*) macho *m*; **~ of the walk** gallito *m* del lugar; **old ~!*** ¡amigo!, ¡viejo!

(b) (*tap*) grifo *m*, espita *f*; (*Anat‡*) polla‡ *f*.

(c) (*of gun*) martillo *m*; **to go off at half ~** (*plan*) ponerse por obra sin la debida preparación.

2 VT (a) *gun* amartillar; *head* ladear; *ears* aguzar; **to ~ one's eye at** mirar con intención a, guiñar el ojo a; **to keep one's ears ~ed** mantenerse alerta, aguzar las orejas.

(b) **to ~ sth up:** joder algo:.

cockade [kɒˈkeɪd] N escarapela *f*.

cock-a-doodle-doo [ˈkɒkəduːdlˈduː] INTERJ ¡quiquiriquí!

cock-a-hoop [ˈkɒkəˈhuːp] ADJ: **to be ~** estar jubiloso, estar más contento que unas pascuas.

cockamamie* [ˌkɒkəˈmeɪmɪ] ADJ (*US*) pijotero*.

cock-and-bull [ˈkɒkənˈbʊl] ADJ: **~ story** cuento *m*, camelo *m*, cuento *m* chino.

cockatoo [ˌkɒkəˈtuː] N cacatúa *f*.

cockchafer [ˈkɒkˌtʃeɪfəʳ] N abejorro *m*.

cockcrow [ˈkɒkkrəʊ] N canto *m* del gallo; **at ~** al amanecer.

cocked [kɒkt] ADJ: **~ hat** sombrero *m* de tres picos; **to knock sth into a ~ hat** ser netamente superior a algo, dar quince y raya a algo.

cocker [ˈkɒkəʳ] N (*also* **~ spaniel**) cocker *m*.

cockerel [ˈkɒkrəl] N gallito *m*, gallo *m* joven.

cock-eyed* [ˈkɒkaɪd] ADJ (a) (*squinting*) bizco. (b) (*fig*) incomprensible; estúpido, estrafalario.

cockfight [ˈkɒkfaɪt] N, **cockfighting** [ˈkɒkˌfaɪtɪŋ] N pelea *f* de gallos.

cockiness* [ˈkɒkɪnɪs] N engreimiento *m*, presunción *f*.

cockle [ˈkɒkl] N (*Zool*) berberecho *m*; **to warm the ~s of the heart** dar grandísimo contento a uno.

cockleshell [ˈkɒklʃel] N concha *f* de berberecho; (*boat*) cascarón *m* de nuez.

cockney [ˈkɒknɪ] N (*person*) cockney *mf, habitante del este de Londres*; (*dialect*) cockney *m, dialecto del este de Londres*; *ver también* RHYMING SLANG .

COCKNEY
---

i *Se llama* **cockneys** *a las personas de la zona este de Londres conocida como* **East End**, *un barrio tradicionalmente obrero, aunque según la tradición un* **cockney** *auténtico ha de haber nacido dentro del área en la que se oye el repique de las campanas de la iglesia de* **Mary-Le-Bow**, *en la* **City** *londinense. Este término también hace referencia al dialecto que se habla en esta parte de Londres, aunque a veces también se aplica a cualquier acento de la clase trabajadora londinense. El actor* **Michael Caine** *es un* **cockney** *famoso.*

⇨ *Ver también* RHYMING SLANG

---

cockpit [ˈkɒkpɪt] N (*Aer*) cabina *f* (del piloto); carlinga *f*; (*for cockfight*) cancha *f*, reñidero *m* de gallos, palenque *m* (*LAm*); (*fig*) ruedo *m*, campo *m* de batalla; **the ~ of Europe** Bélgica *f* (*escenario de muchos combates*).

cockroach [ˈkɒkrəʊtʃ] N cucaracha *f*.

cockscomb [ˈkɒkskəʊm] N cresta *f* de gallo.

cock sparrow [ˌkɒkˈspærəʊ] N gorrión *m* macho.

cocksucker: [ˈkɒkˌsʌkəʳ] N cabrón: *m*, mamón: *m*.

cocksure [ˈkɒkˈʃʊəʳ] ADJ presumido, presuntuoso.

cocktail [ˈkɒkteɪl] N combinado *m*, copetín *m*, cóctel *m* (*also fig*); **~ bar** bar *m*; **~ dress** vestido *m* de cóctel; **~ lounge** salón *m* de cóctel; **~ onion** cebolla *f* perla; **~ sausage** salchichita *f* de aperitivo.

cocktail-cabinet [ˈkɒkteɪlˌkæbɪnɪt] N mueble-bar *m*.

cocktail-party [ˈkɒkteɪlˌpɑːtɪ] N cóctel *m*.

cocktail-shaker [ˈkɒkteɪlˌʃeɪkəʳ] N coctelera *f*.

cock-teaser: [kɒkˌtiːzəʳ] N calientapollas:• *f*.

cock-up: [ˈkɒkʌp] N lío* *m*, embrollo *m*; **there's been a ~ over my passport** me han armado un follón con el pasaporte*; **to make a ~ of sth** joder algo:.

cocky* [ˈkɒkɪ] ADJ engreído, hinchado.

cocoa [ˈkəʊkəʊ] N cacao *m*; (*drink*) chocolate *m*; **~ bean** grano *m* de cacao.

coconut [ˈkəʊkənʌt] N coco *m*; **~ matting** estera *f* de hojas de cocotero; **~ oil** aceite *m* de coco; **~ palm**, **~ tree** cocotero *m*; **~ shy** tiro *m* al coco.

cocoon [kəˈkuːn] **1** N capullo *m*.

2 VT envolver.

COD ABBR *of* **cash on delivery** (*Brit*), **collect on delivery** (*US*) contra reembolso.

cod [kɒd] N bacalao *m*.

coda [ˈkəʊdə] N coda *f*.

coddle [ˈkɒdl] VT mimar, hacer mimos a.

code [kəʊd] **1** N (a) (*Jur etc*) código *m*; (*Telec*) prefijo *m*, código *m*; (*Comput*) código *m*; **~ of practice** código *m* de práctica. (b) (*cypher*) clave *f*, cifra *f*; (*of Morse etc*) alfabeto *m*; **in ~** en cifra.

2 VT cifrar, poner en cifra, poner en clave.

codebook [ˈkəʊdbʊk] N libro *m* de códigos.

coded [ˈkəʊdɪd] ADJ en cifra, en clave (*also fig*).

code-dating [ˈkəʊdˌdeɪtɪŋ] N fechación *f* en código.

codeine [ˈkəʊdiːn] N codeína *f*.

code-letter [ˈkəʊdˌletəʳ] N letra *f* de código.

code-name [ˈkəʊdneɪm] **1** N nombre *m* en clave.

2 VT dar nombre en clave a; **the operation was ~d Clavileño** la operación tuvo el nombre en clave de Clavileño.

code-number [ˈkəʊdˌnʌmbəʳ] N (*Tax*) índice *m* de desgravación fiscal.

codeword [ˈkəʊdwɜːd] N palabra *f* en clave.

codex [ˈkəʊdeks] N, PL **codices** [ˈkɒdɪsiːz] códice *m*.

codfish [ˈkɒdfɪʃ] N, PL INVAR bacalao *m*.

codger* [ˈkɒdʒəʳ] N: **old ~** sujeto *m*, vejete *m*.

codices [ˈkɒdɪˌsiːz] NPL *of* **codex**.

codicil [ˈkɒdɪsɪl] N codicilo *m*.

codify [ˈkəʊdɪfaɪ] VT codificar.

coding [ˈkəʊdɪŋ] N (*of telegram, message*) codificación *f*; (*Comput*) codificación *f*; **~ sheet** hoja *f* de programación.

cod-liver oil [ˈkɒdlɪvəʳɒɪl] N aceite *m* de hígado de bacalao.

codpiece [ˈkɒdpiːs] N (*Hist*) bragueta *f*.

co-driver [ˈkəʊdraɪvəʳ] N copiloto *mf*.

codswallop: [ˈkɒdzwɒləp] N (*Brit*) chorradas: *fpl*.

coed* [ˈkəʊed] **1** ADJ mixto.

2 N alumna *f* de un colegio mixto.

3 ADJ ABBR *of* **coeducational**.

co-edition [ˈkəʊɪˌdɪʃən] N edición *f* conjunta.

coeducation [ˈkəʊˌedjʊˈkeɪʃən] N coeducación *f*, educación *f* mixta.

coeducational [ˈkəʊˌedjʊˈkeɪʃənl] ADJ mixto.

coefficient [ˌkəʊɪˈfɪʃənt] N coeficiente *m*.

coelacanth [ˈsiːləkænθ] N celacanto *m*.

coerce [kəʊˈɜːs] VT forzar, obligar (*into doing sth* a hacer algo), coaccionar.

coercion [kəʊˈɜːʃən] N coacción *f*, coerción *f*, compulsión *f*; **under ~** obligado a ello, a la fuerza.

coercive [kəʊˈɜːsɪv] ADJ coactivo, coercitivo.

coeval [kəʊˈiːvəl] **1** ADJ coetáneo (*with de*), contemporáneo (*with* de), coevo.

2 N coetáneo *m*, -a *f*, contemporáneo *m*, -a *f*.

coexist [ˈkəʊɪgˈzɪst] VI coexistir (*with* con), convivir (*with* con).

coexistence [ˈkəʊɪgˈzɪstəns] N coexistencia *f*, convivencia *f*.

coexistent [ˈkəʊɪgˈzɪstənt] ADJ coexistente.

co-extensive [ˌkəʊɪkˈstensɪv] ADJ de la misma extensión (*with* que).

C of C N ABBR *of* **Chamber of Commerce**.

C of E N ABBR *of* **Church of England** Iglesia *f* anglicana; **to be ~*** ser anglicano.

coffee [ˈkɒfɪ] N café *m*; **white ~** (*Brit*), **~ with milk** (*or* **cream**) (*US*) café *m* con leche.

coffee-bar [ˈkɒfɪbɑːʳ] N (*Brit*) cafetería *f*, café *m*.

coffee-bean [ˈkɒfɪbiːn] N grano *m* de café.

coffee-break [ˈkɒfɪˌbreɪk] N tiempo *m* del bocadillo.

coffee-cake [ˈkɒfɪˌkeɪk] N (*Brit*) pastel *m* de café.

coffee-coloured, (*US*) **coffee-colored** [ˈkɒfɪˌkʌləd] ADJ (de) color café.

coffee-cup [ˈkɒfɪkʌp] N taza *f* para café.

coffee-filter [ˈkɒfɪˌfɪltəʳ] N filtro *m* de café.

coffee-grounds [ˈkɒfɪgraʊndz] NPL poso *m* de café.

coffee-house [ˈkɒfɪhaʊs] N, PL **coffee-houses** [ˈkɒfɪˌhaʊzɪz] café *m*.

coffee-machine [ˈkɒfɪməˌʃiːn] N (*small*) máquina *f* de café, cafetera *f*; (*vending machine*) máquina *f* expendedora de café.

coffee-maker [ˈkɒfɪˌmeɪkəʳ] N máquina *f* de café, cafetera *f*.

coffee-mill [ˈkɒfɪmɪl] N molinillo *m* de café.

coffee morning [ˈkɒfɪˌmɔːnɪŋ] N tertulia *f* formada para tomar el café por la mañana.

coffee percolator [ˈkɒfɪˌpɜːkəleɪtəʳ] N = **coffee-maker**.

coffee plantation [ˈkɒfɪplɑːnˌteɪʃən] N cafetal *m*.

coffeepot [ˈkɒfɪpɒt] N cafetera *f*.

coffee-service [ˈkɒfɪˌsɜːvɪs] N, **coffee-set** [ˈkɒfɪˌset] N servicio *m* de café.

coffee shop [ˈkɒfɪʃɒp] N (*shop*) tienda *f* especializada en variedades de café; (*café*) café *m*.

coffee-spoon [ˈkɒfɪspuːn] N cucharilla *f* de café.

coffee-table [ˈkɒfɪˌteɪbl] N mesita *f* baja; **~ book** libro *m* de gran formato (*bello e impresionante*).

coffee-whitener [ˈkɒfɪˌwaɪtnəʳ] N leche *f* en polvo.

coffer [ˈkɒfəʳ] N cofre *m*, arca *f*; (a) **~s** (*fig*) tesoro *m*, fondos *mpl*; reservas *fpl*. (b) (*Archit*) artesón *m*.

cofferdam [ˈkɒfədæm] N ataguía *f*.

coffin [ˈkɒfɪn] N ataúd *m*, cajón *m* (*SC*).

C of I N ABBR *of* **Church of Ireland**.

co-founder [ˈkəʊˈfaʊndəʳ] N cofundador *m*, -ora *f*.

C of S N ABBR *of* **Church of Scotland**.

cog [kɒg] N diente *m*; (*wheel*) rueda *f* dentada; **to be just a ~ in a machine** ser solamente una pieza de un mecanismo.

cogency [ˈkəʊdʒənsɪ] N fuerza *f*, lógica *f*, convicción *f*.

cogent [ˈkəʊdʒənt] ADJ fuerte, lógico, convincente, sólido.

cogently [ˈkəʊdʒəntlɪ] ADV lógicamente, de modo convincente, con argumentos sólidos.

cogitate ['kɒdʒɪteɪt] VTI meditar, reflexionar.

cogitation [,kɒdʒɪ'teɪʃən] N meditación *f*, reflexión *f*.

cognac ['kɒnjæk] N coñac *m*.

cognate ['kɒgneɪt] 1 ADJ cognado (*with* con); afín.
2 N cognado *m*.

cognition [kɒg'nɪʃən] N cognición *f*.

cognitive ['kɒgnɪtɪv] ADJ cognitivo, cognoscitivo; **~ modelling** modelización *f* cognoscitiva.

cognizance ['kɒgnɪzəns] N conocimiento *m*; **to be within one's ~** ser de la competencia de uno; **to take ~ of** tener en cuenta.

cognizant ['kɒgnɪzənt] ADJ: **to be ~ of** saber, estar enterado de.

cognoscenti [,kɒnəʊ'ʃenti] NPL expertos *mpl*, peritos *mpl*.

cogwheel ['kɒgwiːl] N rueda *f* dentada.

cohabit [kəʊ'hæbɪt] VI cohabitar.

cohabitation [,kəʊhæbɪ'teɪʃən] N cohabitación *f*.

cohere [kəʊ'hɪəʳ] VI adherirse, pegarse; (*ideas etc*) formar un conjunto sólido, ser consecuentes.

coherence [kəʊ'hɪərəns] N coherencia *f*.

coherent [kəʊ'hɪərənt] ADJ coherente; lógico, comprensible.

coherently [kəʊhɪərəntlɪ] ADV coherentemente; lógicamente, comprensiblemente.

cohesion [kəʊ'hiːʒən] N cohesión *f*.

cohesive [kəʊ'hiːsɪv] ADJ cohesivo; unido.

cohesiveness [kəʊ'hiːsɪvnɪs] N cohesión *f*.

cohort ['kəʊhɔːt] N cohorte *f*.

COHSE ['kəʊzɪ] N (*Brit*) ABBR *of* **Confederation of Health Service Employees** confederación *de trabajadores de la seguridad social*.

COI N (*Brit*) ABBR *of* **Central Office of Information.**

coif [kɔɪf] N cofia *f*.

coiffed ['kwɑːft] ADJ (*frm*) peinado.

coiffeur [kwɒ'fɜːʳ] N peluquero *m*.

coiffure [kwɒ'fjʊəʳ] N peinado *m*.

coiffured [kwɒ'fjʊəd] ADJ (*frm*) peinado.

coil [kɔɪl] 1 N rollo *m*; (*of rope etc*) aduja *f*; (*of snake*) anillo *m*; (*of smoke*) espiral *f*; (*of still etc*) serpentín *m*; (*Elec*) bobina *f*, carrete *m*; (*contraceptive*) espiral *f* (intrauterina).
2 VT arrollar, enrollar; *rope* (*Naut*) adujar.
3 VI arrollarse, enrollarse.
◆**coil up** 1 VT arrollar, enrollar.
2 VI (*snake*) enroscarse; (*smoke*) subir en espiral.

coiled [kɔɪld] ADJ arrollado, enrollado.

coin [kɔɪn] 1 N moneda *f*; **to pay sb back in his own ~** pagar a uno en (*or* con) la misma moneda; **to toss a ~** echar a cara o cruz.
2 VT *money* acuñar; *word etc* acuñar, inventar, idear; **he must be ~ing money** debe de estar acuñando dinero, el negocio ha de ser un río de oro para él.

coinage ['kɔɪnɪdʒ] N (*system*) moneda *f*, sistema *m* monetario; (*act*) acuñación *f*; (*word etc*) invención *f*.

coinbox ['kɔɪnbɒks] N (*Telec*) depósito *m* de monedas.

coincide [,kəʊɪn'saɪd] VI coincidir (*with* con); (*agree*) estar de acuerdo (*with* con).

coincidence [kəʊ'ɪnsɪdəns] N coincidencia *f*; (*chance*) casualidad *f*; **what a ~!** ¡qué casualidad!

coincident [kəʊ'ɪnsɪdənt] ADJ (*simultaneous, identical*) coincidente; **~ with her marriage...** al mismo tiempo que su boda...; **to be ~ with** coincidir con.

coincidental [kəʊ,ɪnsɪ'dentl] ADJ coincidente; (*by chance*) fortuito, casual.

coincidentally [,kəʊɪnsɪ'dentəlɪ] ADV por casualidad, casualmente; **not ~, we ...** no es una casualidad que nosotros ... + *subj*.

coin-op* ['kɔɪn,ɒp] N ABBR *of* **coin-operated laundry** lavandería *f* que funciona con monedas.

coin-operated ['kɔɪn'ɒpəreɪtɪd] ADJ que funciona con monedas.

coinsurance [,kəʊɪn'ʃʊərəns] N coaseguro *m*, seguro *m* copartícipe.

coinsurer [,kəʊɪn'ʃʊərəʳ] N coasegurador *m*.

coital ['kɔɪtəl] ADJ (*frm*) coital; *see also* **postcoital.**

coitus ['kɔɪtəs] N coito *m*.

Coke* [kəʊk] ® N Coca-Cola ® *f*, cola* *f*, colas* *fpl*.

coke¹ [kəʊk] N coque *m*.

coke²‡ ['kəʊk] N (*Drugs*) coca‡ *f*.

Col. ABBR (**a**) *of* **Colonel** coronel *m*. (**b**) (*US*) ABBR *of* **Colorado.**

col. ABBR *of* **column** columna *f*, col.

COLA N (*US*) ABBR *of* **cost-of-living adjustment** reajuste *m* salarial de acuerdo con el costo de la vida.

colander ['kʌləndəʳ] N colador *m*, escurridor *m*.

cold [kəʊld] 1 ADJ (**a**) frío (*also fig*); **as ~ as charity** frío como un mármol; **my feet are ~ as ice** tengo los pies helados; **to be ~** (*person*) tener frío, (*thing*) estar frío, (*weather*) hacer frío; **to be very ~** (*person*) tener mucho frío, (*thing*) estar muy frío, (*weather*) hacer mucho frío; **to get ~** (*thing*) enfriarse, (*weather*) empezar a hacer frío; **he's got them ~*** (*audience*) los tiene en el bolsillo; **he's got three**

tricks ~* tiene tres bazas segurísimas; **to knock sb (out) ~*** dejar a uno sin conocimiento; **it leaves me ~** no me produce emoción alguna, me deja frío. (**b**) **~ cream** crema *f*; **~ cuts** (*US*) fiambres *mpl*; **~ duck** (*US**) vino *m* gaseado barato; **~ frame** vivero *m* de plantas; **~ front** frente *m* frío; **~ room** = **~ store**; **~ selling** venta *f* en frío, venta *f* directa; **~ sore** herpes *m* labial, pupas* *fpl*; **~ start, ~ starting** (*US*) arranque *m* en frío; **~ storage** almacenaje *m* frigorífico; **to put a plan into ~ storage** archivar un proyecto, dejar un proyecto en suspenso; **~ store** cámara *f* frigorífica; **he broke into a ~ sweat** le entró un sudor frío; **~ turkey** (*Drugs*‡) mono‡ *m*, síndrome *m* de abstinencia; **~ war** guerra *f* fría; **~ wave** ola *f* de frío.

2 N (**a**) frío *m*; **to catch ~** coger frío; **to leave sb out in the ~** dejar a uno al margen, dejar a uno colgado.
(**b**) (*Med, also* **common ~**) resfriado *m*, catarro *m*; **to catch a ~** resfriarse, acatarrarse; **to have a ~** estar resfriado, estar acatarrado, estar constipado.

3 ADV (*US**) (*completely*) totalmente; (*unexpectedly*) en frío; **to do sth ~** hacer algo en frío; **to know sth ~** conocer algo a fondo (*or* como la palma de la mano).

cold-blooded ['kəʊld'blʌdɪd] ADJ (*Zool*) de sangre fría, poiquilotérmico; (*fig*) insensible; (*cruel*) desalmado.

cold-bloodedly ['kəʊld'blʌdɪdlɪ] ADV a sangre fría.

cold-hearted ['kəʊld'hɑːtɪd] ADJ insensible, cruel.

coldly ['kəʊldlɪ] ADV fríamente (*also fig*).

coldness ['kəʊldnɪs] N (*lit, fig*) frialdad *f*.

cold-shoulder ['kəʊld'ʃəʊldəʳ] VT dar (*or* volver) la espalda a.

coleslaw ['kəʊlslɔː] N ensalada *f* de col.

coley ['kəʊlɪ] N abadejo *m*.

colic ['kɒlɪk] N cólico *m*.

Coliseum [,kɒlɪ'siːəm] N Coliseo *m*.

colitis [kɒ'laɪtɪs] N colitis *f*.

collaborate [kə'læbəreɪt] VI colaborar (*in, on* en; *with* con).

collaboration [kə,læbə'reɪʃən] N colaboración *f*; (*Pol: pej*) colaboracionismo *m*; **in ~** en colaboración (*with* con).

collaborationist [kə,læbə'reɪʃənɪst] ADJ colaboracionista.

collaborative [kə'læbərətɪv] ADJ: **by a ~ effort** por un esfuerzo común, ayudándose unos a otros; **it's a ~ work** es un trabajo de colaboración.

collaboratively [kə'læbərətɪvlɪ] ADV en colaboración.

collaborator [kə'læbəreɪtəʳ] N colaborador *m*, -ora *f*; (*Pol: pej*) colaboracionista *mf*.

collage [kɒ'lɑːʒ] N collage *m*.

collagen ['kɒlədʒən] N colágeno *m*.

collapse [kə'læps] 1 N (*Med*) colapso *m*; (*of building*) hundimiento *m*, derrumbamiento *m*, desplome *m*; (*of roadway etc*) socavón *m*; (*of plans*) fracaso *m*; (*of prices*) desplome *m*.
2 VI (**a**) (*Med*) sufrir un colapso; **to ~ with laughter** (*fig*) morirse de risa.
(**b**) (*building*) hundirse, derrumbarse, desplomarse; (*fig*) fracasar; **hood that ~s** capota *f* plegable; **the deal ~d** el negocio fracasó; **the company ~d** la compañía se vino abajo, la compañía se hundió.

collapsible [kə'læpsəbl] ADJ plegable; *steering-wheel* articulado.

collar ['kɒləʳ] 1 N cuello *m*; (*of animal, Tech*) collar *m*; (*Med*) collarín *m*; **~ size** medida *f* del cuello; **to get hot under the ~** sulfurarse.
2 VT prender por el cuello; (*) apropiarse, pisar.

collarbone ['kɒləbəʊn] N clavícula *f*.

collar-stud ['kɒləstʌd], (*US*) **collar-button** ['kɒləbʌtən] N botón *m* de camisa.

collate [kɒ'leɪt] VT cotejar.

collateral [kɒ'lætərəl] 1 ADJ colateral; **~ loan** préstamo *m* colateral; préstamo *m* pignoraticio; **~ security** garantía *f* colateral.
2 N (**a**) (*Fin*) seguridad *f* subsidiaria, garantía *f* subsidiaria. (**b**) (*person*) colateral *mf*.

collation [kə'leɪʃən] N (*meal*) colación *f*; (*of texts*) cotejo *m*.

colleague ['kɒliːg] N colega *m*.

collect¹ ['kɒlekt] N (*Eccl*) colecta *f*.

collect² [kə'lekt] 1 VT reunir, acumular; *people* reunir; *stamps etc* coleccionar; *fares, wages* cobrar; *taxes* recaudar; *money for charity* recaudar, colectar; (*pick up, also Brit Post*) recoger; *dust, water etc* retener; **I'll go and ~ the mail** voy por el correo; **I'll ~ you at 8** vengo a recogerte (*or* buscarte: *esp LAm*) a las 8; **I must ~ my bags from the station** tengo que recoger mi equipaje en la estación; **~ on delivery** (*US*) entrega *f* contra reembolso.
2 VI reunirse, acumularse; (*people*) reunirse, congregarse; (*be a collector*) ser coleccionista, coleccionar; (*water*) estancarse; (*dust*) acumularse; **when do we ~?** ¿cuándo cobramos?; **to ~ for charity** hacer una colecta con fines benéficos.
3 VR: **to ~ o.s.** reponerse, sosegarse.
4 ADV: **to call ~** (*US*) llamar a cobro revertido.
◆**collect up** VT recoger, volver a tomar.

collectable [kə'lektəbl] N coleccionable *m*.

collect call [kə'lektkɔːl] N (*US*) llamada *f* a cobro revertido.

collected [kə'lektɪd] [1] PRET AND PTP of **collect²**.
[2] ADJ (cool) sosegado, tranquilo; ~ **works** obras fpl completas.
collectible [kə'lektəbl] N coleccionable m.
collecting [kə'lektɪŋ] N coleccionismo m, el coleccionar.
collecting-tin [kə'lektɪŋ,tɪn] N bote m de cuestación, lata f petitoria.
collection [kə'lekʃən] N acumulación f, montón m; (of people) grupo m; (of pictures, stamps etc) colección f; (of fares, wages) cobro m; (of taxes) recaudación f; (Eccl) colecta f; (for charity) cuestación f; (Brit Post) recogida f; **to make a ~ for** hacer una colecta a beneficio de; ~ **charges** (Fin, Comm) gastos mpl de cobro; ~ **plate** platillo m.
collective [kə'lektɪv] [1] ADJ colectivo; ~ **bargaining** trato m colectivo, negociaciones fpl colectivas; ~ **farm** granja f colectiva; ~ **noun** nombre m colectivo; ~ **ownership** propiedad f colectiva; ~ **security** seguridad f colectiva; ~ **unconscious** inconsciente m colectivo.
[2] N colectivo m.
collectively [kə'lektɪvlɪ] ADV colectivamente.
collectivism [kə'lektɪvɪzə] N colectivismo m.
collectivist [kə'lektɪvɪst] ADJ colectivista.
collectivization [kə,lektɪvaɪ'zeɪʃən] N colectivización f.
collectivize [kə'lektɪvaɪz] VT colectivizar.
collector [kə'lektər] N (of folktales etc) recolector m, -ora f; (of stamps etc) coleccionista mf; (tax-~) recaudador m, -ora f; **it's a real ~'s item** es una verdadera pieza de colección (or para coleccionista).
colleen [kɒ'liːn] N (Ir) muchacha f.
college ['kɒlɪdʒ] N **(a)** (eg of Oxford) colegio m universitario; (eg of art) escuela f; (US: of university) ≃ facultad f; **C~ of Advanced Technology** (Brit) ≃ politécnico m; **C~ of Education** Escuela f Normal (Superior); **C~ of Further Education** ≃ Escuela f de Formación Profesional; **to go to ~** seguir estudios superiores. **(b)** (body) colegio m.

| COLLEGE |

ⓘ En el Reino Unido **college** es un término muy general que designa cualquier institución de estudios no primarios. Puede hacer referencia a centros que otorgan un título de licenciado en materias específicas como arte o música o a centros de formación profesional. También algunas universidades como Oxford y Cambridge se componen de **colleges** en los que los estudiantes, además de estudiar tienen alojamiento, aunque es la universidad la que otorga las titulaciones. El **King's College** de Cambridge o el **Balliol College** de Oxford son ejemplos muy conocidos.
En los Estados Unidos también hay tipos distintos de **colleges**. En la universidad un **college** es normalmente una división administrativa, semejante a una facultad, por ejemplo **College of Arts and Science** o **College of Medicine**. En ellos se pueden estudiar carreras de cuatro años tras las que se obtiene el título de **bachelor's degree**. Los cursos de postgrado se imparten en **graduate schools**. Por otra parte, en los centros denominados **junior colleges** o **community colleges** se otorga un diploma llamado **associate degree** después de dos años de estudio y también se imparten clases de formación profesional a gente que está ya trabajando.
⇨ Ver también | DEGREE |

---

collegiate [kə'liːdʒɪt] ADJ **(a)** (Eccl) colegial, colegiado; ~ **church** iglesia f colegial. **(b)** (Univ) que tiene colegios, organizado a base de colegios.
collide [kə'laɪd] VI chocar (with con; also fig), colisionar (with con).
collie ['kɒlɪ] N perro m pastor escocés, collie m, coli m.
collier ['kɒlɪər] N minero m (de carbón); (ship) barco m carbonero.
colliery ['kɒlɪərɪ] N mina f de carbón.
collision [kə'lɪʒən] N choque m (also fig), colisión f; **to be on a ~ course** ir rumbo al enfrentamiento; **to come into ~ with** chocar con.
collocate ['kɒlə,keɪt] VI: **to ~ with** colocarse con.
collocation [,kɒlə'keɪʃən] N colocación f (also Ling).
colloquial [kə'ləʊkwɪəl] ADJ familiar, coloquial.
colloquialism [kə'ləʊkwɪəlɪzəm] N palabra f (or expresión f) familiar; (style) estilo m familiar.
colloquially [kə'ləʊkwɪəlɪ] ADV coloquialmente.
colloquium [kə'ləʊkwɪəm] N coloquio m.
colloquy ['kɒləkwɪ] N coloquio m.
collude [kə'luːd] VI confabularse (with con).
collusion [kə'luːʒən] N confabulación f; connivencia f; (Jur) colusión f; **to be in ~ with** estar de connivencia con, confabularse con.
collusive [kə'luːsɪv] ADJ (frm) behaviour colusivo, connivente.
collywobbles* ['kɒlɪ,wɒblz] NPL (Anat) ruido m de tripas; (fig) nerviosismo m, ataque m de nervios; **she had the ~** le sonaban las tripas.
Colo. (US) ABBR of **Colorado**.
Cologne [kə'ləʊn] N Colonia f.
Colombia [kə'lɒmbɪə] N Colombia f.
Colombian [kə'lɒmbɪən] [1] ADJ colombiano.
[2] N colombiano m, -a f.
colon¹ ['kəʊlən] N (Anat) colon m.

colon² ['kəʊlən] N (Typ) dos puntos mpl.
colonel ['kɜːnl] N coronel m.
colonial [kə'ləʊnɪəl] [1] ADJ colonial.
[2] N colono m.
colonialism [kə'ləʊnɪəlɪzəm] N colonialismo m.
colonialist [kə'ləʊnɪəlɪst] N colonialista mf.
colonic [kəʊ'lɒnɪk] ADJ de colon; ~ **irrigation** lavado m de colon.
colonist ['kɒlənɪst] N colonizador m, -ora f, colono m.
colonization [,kɒlənaɪ'zeɪʃən] N colonización f.
colonize ['kɒlənaɪz] VT colonizar.
colonnade [,kɒlə'neɪd] N columnata f, galería f.
colony ['kɒlənɪ] N colonia f.
colophon ['kɒləfən] N colofón m, pie m de imprenta.
color ['kʌlər] etc (US) = **colour** etc; ~ **line** barrera f de color.
Colorado [,kɒlə'rɑːdəʊ] N: ~ **beetle** escarabajo m de la patata, dorífora f.
colorant ['kʌlərənt] (US) = **colourant**.
coloration [,kʌlə'reɪʃən] N colorido m, colores mpl, coloración f.
coloratura [,kɒlərə'tʊərə] N (passage) coloratura f; (singer) soprano f de coloratura.
colorcast ['kʌləkɑːst] (US) [1] N programa m de TV en color.
[2] VT transmitir en color.
colorist ['kʌlərɪst] (US) = **colourist**.
colossal [kə'lɒsl] ADJ colosal.
colossally [kə'lɒsəlɪ] ADV colosalmente, inmensamente.
colossus [kə'lɒsəs] N coloso m.
colostomy [kə'lɒstəmɪ] N colostomía f.
colostrum [kə'lɒstrəm] N colostro m, calostro m.
colour, (US) **color** ['kʌlər] [1] N **(a)** color m; (~s, combination) colorido m; ~ **code** código m de colores; ~ **film** película f en colores; ~ **photograph** fotografía f en color; ~ **photography** fotografía f en colores; ~ **problem** problema m racial; ~ **slide** diapositiva f en color; ~ **supplement** (Brit) suplemento m en color; ~ **television** (set) televisor m en color; ~ **TV** TV f en colores; (US) **people of ~** personas fpl de color; **it's a blue ~, it's blue in ~** es de color azul; **what ~ is it?** ¿de qué color es?; **in full ~** a todo color; **to be off ~** estar indispuesto; **to change** ~ mudar de color; **to lend ~ to a story** hacer que un cuento parezca más verosímil; **let's see the ~ of your money!** ¡a ver si te retratas!, ¡a ver el dinero!; **to take all the ~ out of sth** quitar todo el colorido de algo.
(b) ~**s** (flag) bandera f; ~ **sergeant** (Brit) sargento m abanderado; **to call to the ~s** llamar a filas, llamar al servicio militar; **to come out with flying ~s** salir airoso, triunfar; **to nail one's ~s to the mast** proclamar su lealtad; mantenerse firme; **to sail under false ~s** encubrir su verdadera lealtad; **to show o.s. in one's true ~s** quitarse la máscara.
[2] VT (also **to ~ in**) color(e)ar; (paint) pintar; (dye) teñir (red de rojo); drawing colorear; adornar, embellecer.
[3] VI (also **to ~ up**) sonrojarse.
colourant, (US) **colorant** ['kʌlərənt] N colorante m.
colour-bar ['kʌləbɑːr] N (Brit) barrera f racial.
colour-blind, (US) **color-blind** ['kʌləblaɪnd] ADJ daltoniano.
colour-blindness, (US) **color-blindness** ['kʌlə,blaɪndnɪs] N daltonismo m.
colour-coded, (US) **color-coded** ['kʌlə'kəʊdɪd] ADJ con código de colores.
coloured, (US) **colored** ['kʌləd] [1] PRET AND PTP of **colour**. 2 ADJ person († in US), pencil de color; **a highly ~ tale** un cuento de los más pintorescos.
[3] N: ~**s** (US, Brit) personas fpl de color; (in South Africa) personas de padres racialmente mixtos.
-coloured, (US) **-colored** [,kʌləd] ADJ: eg rust~ de color de orín, color orín.
colourfast, (US) **colorfast** ['kʌləfɑːst] ADJ no desteñible.
colour-filter, (US) **color-filter** ['kʌlə'fɪltər] N (Phot) filtro m de color.
colourful, (US) **colorful** ['kʌləfəl] ADJ lleno de color; scene vivo, animado; person etc pintoresco.
colourfully ['kʌləfʊlɪ] ADV decorated, painted con colores muy vivos; describe con mucho color.
colouring, (US) **coloring** ['kʌlərɪŋ] N colorido m; (substance) colorante m; (of complexion) colores mpl; tez f; ~ **(-in) book** libro m para colorear; **high** ~ sonrojamiento m; **'no artificial ~'** 'sin colores artificiales'.
colourist, (US) **colorist** ['kʌlərɪst] N (artist) colorista mf; (hairdresser) peluquero especializado en tintes.
colourless, (US) **colorless** ['kʌləlɪs] ADJ sin color, incoloro; (fig) soso, insípido.
colour-scheme, (US) **color-scheme** ['kʌlə,skiːm] N combinación f de colores.
colourway ['kʌləweɪ] N (Brit) combinación f de colores.
colt [kəʊlt] N potro m, potranco m (LAm).
coltish ['kɒltɪʃ] ADJ juguetón, retozón.

coltsfoot ['kəʊltsfʊt] N uña *f* de caballo, fárfara *f*.

Columbia [kə'lʌmbɪə] N: **(District of)** ~ (*US*) Distrito *m* de Columbia; V **British**.

Columbine ['kɒləmbaɪn] NF Columbina.

columbine ['kɒləmbaɪn] N aguileña *f*.

Columbus [kə'lʌmbəs] NM Colón; ~ **Day** Día *m* de la Raza.

column ['kɒləm] N (*all senses*) columna *f*; **they gave the news only 2 ~ inches** dieron sólo 2 pulgadas de columna a la noticia; **to dodge the ~*** ponerse al socaire.

columnist ['kɒləmnɪst] N columnista *mf*, articulista *mf*.

colza ['kɒlzə] N colza *f*.

coma ['kəʊmə] N coma *m*; **to be in a ~** estar en estado de coma.

comatose ['kəʊmətəʊs] ADJ comatoso.

comb [kəʊm] **1** N **(a)** peine *m*; (*ornamental*) peineta *f*; (*for horse*) almohaza *f*; (*Tech*) carda *f*; **to give one's hair a ~** peinarse (el pelo). **(b)** (*of fowl*) cresta *f*. **(c)** (*honeycomb*) panal *m*.

2 VT peinar; *wool* cardar; *countryside etc* peinar, registrar con minuciosidad (*for* en busca de); **to ~ one's hair** peinarse; **we've been ~ing the town for you** te hemos buscado por toda la ciudad.

◆**comb out** VT *hair* desenmarañar; **they ~ed out the useless members of the staff** se deshicieron de los miembros del personal inútiles.

combat ['kɒmbæt] **1** N combate *m*; ~ **duty** servicio *m* de frente; ~ **jacket** guerrera *f*; ~ **troops** tropas *fpl* de combate; ~ **zone** zona *f* de combate.

2 VT combatir, luchar contra.

combatant ['kɒmbətənt] N combatiente *mf*.

combative ['kɒmbətɪv] ADJ combativo.

combe [kuːm] N = **coomb**.

combination [ˌkɒmbɪ'neɪʃən] N **(a)** (*gen*) combinación *f*; ~ **lock** cerradura *f* de combinación. **(b)** ~**s** (*undergarment*) combinación *f*.

combinatory [ˌkɒmbɪ'neɪtərɪ] ADJ combinacional.

combine 1 ['kɒmbaɪn] N **(a)** (*Comm*) asociación *f*, (*pej*) monopolio *m*. **(b)** (*Agr*) cosechadora *f*.

2 [kəm'baɪn] VT combinar; *qualities etc* reunir, conjugar; **expertise ~ed with charm** la pericia combinada con la simpatía, pericia y simpatía conjuntamente.

3 [kəm'baɪn] VI combinarse; (*companies etc*) asociarse, fusionarse.

combined [kəm'baɪnd] **1** PRET AND PTP of **combine**. **2** ADJ *operation* coordinado, conjunto.

combine-harvester [kɒmbaɪn'hɑːvɪstəʳ] N cosechadora *f*.

combings ['kəʊmɪŋz] NPL peinaduras *fpl*.

combo ['kɒmbəʊ] N (*Mus*) grupo *m*, conjunto *m*; (*: *clothes*) conjunto *m*.

combs* [kɒmz] NPL combinación *f*.

combustible [kəm'bʌstɪbl] **1** ADJ combustible. **2** N combustible *m*.

combustion [kəm'bʌstʃən] N combustión *f*; ~ **chamber** cámara *f* de combustión.

come [kʌm] (*irr:* PRET **came**, PTP **come**) VI **(a)** (*gen*) venir; **coming!** ¡voy!; **I'll ~ for you at 8** vengo a recogerte a las 8; **oh ~!**, **now!**, ~, ~! ¡vamos!; ¡no es para tanto!; **it ~s in 3 sizes** se hace en 3 tamaños; **to ~ and go** ir y venir; **the pain ~s and goes** el dolor es intermitente; **the picture ~s and goes** (*TV*) un momento tenemos imagen y al siguiente no; **to ~ running** llegar corriendo; **when did he ~?** ¿cuándo llegó?; **we came to a river** llegamos a un río; **then the rains came** luego llegaron las lluvias; **the time will ~ when ...** tiempo habrá que + *subj*; **it never came into my mind** no pasó siquiera por mi mente; **it came as a shock** fue un golpe, nos asombró; **when your turn ~s** cuando llegue tu turno; **when it ~s to Latin** por lo que se refiere al latín, en cuanto al latín; **when it ~s to deciding** cuando se trata de decidir.

(b) (*have its place*) **the harvest ~s in August** la cosecha es en agosto; **May ~s before June** mayo es antes de junio; **it ~s on the next page** está en la página siguiente; **the adjective ~s before the noun** el adjetivo precede al sustantivo.

(c) (*happen*) pasar; ~ **what may** pase lo que pase; **recovery came slowly** la recuperación fue lenta; **no harm will ~ to him** no le pasará nada; **nothing came of it** no dio resultados; **no good will ~ of it** no dará nada bueno; **no tendrá consecuencias beneficiosas; that's what ~s of trusting him** es la consecuencia de fiarnos de él.

(d) ~ **to** + *infin* llegar a *infin*; **I came to admire her** llegué a admirarla; **he came to admit he was wrong** por fin reconoció que se había equivocado; **now I ~ to think of it** ahora que me doy cuenta; **it came to pass that ...** (*liter*) aconteció que ....

(e) (⁎⁎) correrse (*Sp*⁎⁎), acabar (*LAm*⁎⁎).

(f) (*phrases*) **you could see that coming** eso se veía venir; **how ~?*** ¿cómo es eso?, ¿por qué?; **how ~ you don't know?*** ¿cómo es que no lo sabes?; ~ **again?*** ¿cómo?; **if it ~s to that** en cuanto a eso; si llegamos a ese punto; **it will be 2 years ~ March** en marzo hará 2 años; **a week ~ Monday** ocho días a partir del lunes; **I like my tea just as it ~s** me gusta el té hecho de cualquier modo; **I don't know whether I'm coming or going** no sé lo que me hago, no sé si coger

muchacha o ponerme a servir; **he had it coming to him** bien merecido lo tenía; **she's as pretty as they ~** más guapa no la hay; **they don't ~ any better than that** mejores no los hay; **cars like that don't ~ cheap** los coches así no son baratos; **don't ~ that game with me!*** ¡no me vengas con esos cuentos!; **that's coming it a bit strong** eso me parece algo exagerado, no es para tanto.

◆**come about** VI ocurrir, suceder; **it came about that ...** sucedió que ...; **how did this ~ about?** ¿cómo ha sido esto?

◆**come across 1** VT dar con, topar (con), encontrar(se con). **2** VI **(a)** (*cross*) cruzar.

(b) (*meaning*) ser entendido; (*message*) llegar (al público *etc*); surtir efecto; **to ~ across as** dar la impresión de ser, dar una imagen de; **it didn't ~ across like that** no lo entendimos en ese sentido, no es ésa la impresión que nos produjo.

(c) (*US*: keep one's word*) cumplir la palabra.

◆**come across with*** VT *money* apoquinar*; **to ~ across with the information** soltar prenda.

◆**come along** VI **(a)** venir también; **are you coming along?** ¿vienes?, ¿nos acompañas?; **you'll have to ~ along with me to the station** Vd me acompaña a la comisaría.

(b) ~ **along!** ¡vamos!, ándale (*LAm*); (*hurrying*) ¡date prisa!

(c) (*develop*) hacer progresos; **it's coming along nicely** va bien; **how's the book coming along?** ¿qué tal va el libro?

(d) (*chance etc*) presentarse.

◆**come apart** VI romperse.

◆**come at** VT **(a)** *solution* llegar a.

(b) (*attack*) atacar, precipitarse sobre.

◆**come away** VI **(a)** (*depart*) marcharse; salir de casa (*etc*).

(b) (*fall off*) separarse, desprenderse, soltarse.

◆**come back** VI **(a)** (*person: return*) volver, regresar (*LAm*) (*for* para); (*to mind*) volver a la memoria; **it all ~s back to money** todo viene a ser cuestión de dinero; **to ~ back to what I was saying** para volver a mi tema.

(b) **to ~ back with** (*reply*) replicar; responder diciendo; **when accused, he came back with a counter-accusation** cuando le acusaron, respondió con una contraacusación.

◆**come before** VT (*Jur*) *person* comparecer ante; **his case came before the courts** su caso llegó a los tribunales.

◆**come between** VT interponerse entre; dividir, separar; **nothing can ~ between us** no hay nada que sea capaz de separarnos.

◆**come by 1** VT **(a)** (*pass*) pasar.

(b) (*obtain*) conseguir, adquirir; **how did she ~ by that name?** ¿cómo adquirió ese nombre?

2 VI **(a)** (*pass*) pasar; **could I ~ by, please?** ¿me permite?

(b) (*visit*) visitar; entrar a ver; **next time you ~ by** la próxima vez que vengas por aquí.

◆**come down** VI **(a)** (*descend*) bajar (*from* de); (*rain*) caer; (*Aer*) aterrizar, (*crash*) estrellarse, (*in sea*) amarar; (*heirloom*) pasar, (*tradition*) ser transmitido; **to ~ down on sb's side** tomar partido por uno; **to ~ down against a policy** declararse en contra de una política; **if it ~s down heads** si sale cara; **so it ~s down to this** así que se reduce a esto; **to ~ down hard on sb** ser duro con uno, castigar severamente a uno.

(b) (*roof etc*) caerse, desplomarse, venirse abajo; (*be demolished*) ser derribado.

(c) (*price, temperature*) bajar.

◆**come down with** VT **(a)** (*become ill from*) enfermar de, caer enfermo de, contraer.

(b) (*: *pay out*) apoquinar.

◆**come for** VT venir por.

◆**come forward** VI **(a)** avanzar, moverse hacia adelante.

(b) (*present o.s.*) presentarse, ofrecerse (*to* + *infin* a + *infin*); **to ~ forward with a suggestion** ofrecer una sugerencia.

◆**come from** VT **(a)** (*stem from*) venir de, proceder de; resultar de.

(b) (*person*) ser de; **I ~ from Wigan** soy de Wigan.

(c) **I can't get behind where you're coming from** (*US**) no alcanzo a comprender la base de tu argumento.

◆**come in** VI entrar; (*train etc*) llegar; (*tide*) subir, crecer; (*Pol*) acceder al poder; (*fashion*) imponerse, ponerse de moda; ~ **in!** ¡adelante!, ¡pase!; **this is where we came in** (*fig*) estamos de vuelta de todo esto; **he came in last** (*in race*) llegó el último; **he has £100 coming in each week** tiene ingresos (*or* entradas *LAm*) de 100 libras por semana; **where do I ~ in?** (*fig*) ¿qué voy a pintar yo aquí?; ¿qué papel me dais a mí?; **to ~ in on a deal** tomar parte en un negocio.

◆**come in for** VT: **he came in for a lot of criticism** fue blanco de muchas críticas.

◆**come into** VT **(a)** (*inherit*) **he came into a fortune** heredó una fortuna, le correspondió una fortuna. **(b)** (*have relevance*) **melons don't ~ into it** los melones no tienen que ver, los melones no hacen al caso.

◆**come of** VT: **to ~ of a good family** ser de buena familia, venir de buena familia.

◆**come off 1** VT **(a)** (*separate from*) desprenderse de; **the label came**

off the bottle la etiqueta se desprendió de la botella; **the car came off the road** el coche salió de la carretera; **she came off her bike** se cayó de la bici.
(b) ~ off it!* ¡vaya!; ¡vamos, anda!; ¡no te lo creo!; **I told him to ~ off it** le dije que dejase de hacer el tonto.
(c) (*give up*) dejar; **it's time you came off the pill** es hora de dejar la píldora.
2 VI **(a)** (*become detached*) desprenderse; soltarse; caerse; **does this lid ~ off?** ¿se puede quitar esta tapa?
(b) (*take place*) tener lugar, verificarse.
(c) (*succeed*) tener éxito, dar resultados; **to ~ off best** salir ganando; **to ~ off badly** salir malparado, salir perdiendo.
(d) (*cease*) **the play came off in January** la obra dejó de figurar en la cartelera en enero.
(e) (**⁎**) dejarlo ir⁎.
◆**come on** 1 VT encontrar, descubrir.
2 VI **(a)** (*advance*) avanzar; (*rain etc*) empezar; (*illness*) aparecer; (*night*) acercarse; **~ on!** ¡vamos!, (*hurrying*) ¡date prisa!, (*to runner*) ¡ánimo!; **winter was coming on** entraba el invierno; **I have a cold coming on** siento que me voy a acatarrar; **I'm coming on to that next** de eso hablo en seguida.
(b) (*progress*) hacer progresos; (*plant*) crecer, desarrollarse; **how is the book coming on?** ¿qué tal va el libro?
(c) (*actor*) salir a la escena.
(d) (*light*) encenderse.
(e) (*US fig*) **he came on sincere** fingía ser sincero.
◆**come on to*** VT (*esp US*) tirar los tejos a*, insinuarse a.
◆**come out** VI (*emerge*) salir (*of* de); mostrarse; (*sun*) salir; (*book*) salir (a luz); (*novelty*) aparecer, estrenarse; (*debutante*) ser presentada en sociedad, ponerse de largo; (*homosexual*) hacerse conocer, declararse; (*news*) revelarse, publicarse; (*flower*) florecer; (*photo*) salir (bien); (*stain*) salir, quitarse; **the idea came out of an experiment** la idea se originó en un experimento; (*Brit Ind: also* **to ~ out on strike**) ponerse en huelga; **it ~s out at £5 a head** sale a 5 libras por cabeza; **it all came out all right** todo salió bien; **to ~ out against** declararse en contra de; **to ~ out for** declararse a favor de; **she came out in spots** le salieron erupciones (en la piel); **I came out in a sweat** empecé a sudar, me cubrí de sudor; **he came out of it with credit** salió con honor.
◆**come out with** VT *remark* soltar, descolgarse con.
◆**come over** 1 VT apoderarse de, invadir; **sleep came over her** la invadió el sueño; **what's ~ over you?** ¿qué te pasa?; **I don't know what came over me** no sé lo que me pasó.
2 VI **(a)** (*visit*) visitar, venir a ver.
(b) (**⁎**: *be transformed*) volverse, ponerse, sentirse; **she came over quite ill** se puso bastante mala; **he came over all religious** se puso muy devoto.
(c) (*give impression*) **how did he ~ over?** ¿qué impresión produjo?; **the speech didn't ~ over at all well** el discurso produjo una impresión bastante mala.
◆**come round** VI **(a)** (*visit*) visitar, venir a ver.
(b) (*agree*) asentir; dejarse convencer; cambiar de idea; **he came round to our view** adoptó nuestra opinión.
(c) (*Med*) volver en sí.
(d) (*anniversary etc*) llegar.
◆**come through** 1 VT (*survive*) sobrevivir a; *illness* recuperarse de; *test* superar.
2 VI **(a)** (*survive*) sobrevivir; (*illness*) recuperarse.
(b) (*message*) ser recibido, llegar.
◆**come through with** VT (*US*) = **come up with (b).**
◆**come to** VI **(a)** (*Naut*) fachear.
(b) (*Med*) volver en sí.
(c) *sum* ascender a; **how much does it ~ to?** ¿a cuánto sube?, ¿cuánto es?
(d) **so it ~s to this** así que viene a ser esto; **what are we coming to?** ¿adónde va a parar todo esto?
◆**come together** VI **(a)** (*assemble*) reunirse, juntarse; **great qualities ~ together in his work** en su obra se dan cita grandes cualidades.
(b) (*agree*) reconciliarse; arreglar las diferencias.
◆**come under** VT *person* ser de la competencia de, incumbir a; estar bajo la jurisdicción de; *heading* estar comprendido en, pertenecer a; **to ~ under attack** sufrir un ataque, verse atacado.
◆**come up** VI subir (*also fig*); (*sun*) salir; (*plant*) aparecer; (*light*) encenderse; (*difficulty*) surgir; (*in talk*) salir, surgir, ser mencionado; (*lucky number*) salir; (*Univ*) matricularse; **he came up to Oxford last year** (*Brit*) se matriculó en la universidad de Oxford el año pasado; **he has ~ up in the world** ha subido mucho en la escala social; **to ~ up before the judge** comparecer ante el juez; **his case ~s up tomorrow** su proceso se verá mañana; se presenta su pleito mañana; **to ~ up for sale** ponerse a la venta.
◆**come up against** VT *problem* tropezar con; *enemy* tener que habérselas con; *opposition* chocar con.

◆**come up to** VT subir a; (*reach*) llegar hasta; (*approach*) acercarse a, aproximarse a, (*in street*) abordar; (*fig*) estar a la altura de, corresponder a; *standard* llegar a, satisfacer.
◆**come up with** VT **(a)** *person* alcanzar, llegar a la altura de. **(b)** *proposal* presentar, proponer; *solution* ofrecer, sugerir; *surprise* salir con; **eventually he came up with the money** por fin ofreció el dinero.
◆**come upon** = **come on 1.**

┌───┐
│ COME, GO   *see also main entries* │
└───┘
Although *come* and *venir* usually imply motion towards the speaker while *go* and *ir* imply motion away from them, there are some differences between the two languages. In English we sometimes describe movement as if from the other person's perspective. In Spanish, this is not the case.
● For example when someone calls you:
  I'm coming
  Ya voy
● Making arrangements over the phone or in a letter:
  I'll come and pick you up at 4
  Iré a recogerte a las 4
  Can I come too?
  ¿Puedo ir yo también?
  Shall I come with you?
  ¿Voy contigo?
● So, use *ir* rather than *venir* when going towards someone else or when joining them to go on somewhere else.
● Compare:
  Are you coming with us? (*viewed from the speaker's perspective*)
  ¿(Te) vienes con nosotros?
For further uses and examples, see main entries at **come** *and* **go**.

comeback ['kʌmbæk] N **(a)** (*restoration*) restablecimiento *m*, rehabilitación *f*; esfuerzo *m* por volver a su antigua posición; **to make a ~** restablecerse, rehabilitarse; volver a resurgir; presentarse de nuevo.
(b) (*response*) reacción *f*; (*US*) réplica *f*; (*witty*) respuesta *f* aguda.
Comecon ['kɒmɪkɒn] N ABBR *of* **Council for Mutual Economic Aid** Consejo *m* para la Mutua Ayuda Económica, COMECON *m*.
comedian [kə'miːdɪən] N cómico *m*.
comedic [kə'miːdɪk] ADJ (*frm*) *moment, performance* cómico.
comedienne [kə,miːdɪ'en] N cómica *f*.
comedown* ['kʌmdaʊn] N revés *m*, humillación *f*.
comedy ['kɒmɪdɪ] N comedia *f*; (*humour of event*) comicidad *f*; **~ of manners** comedia *f* de costumbres.
come-hither ['kʌm'hɪðəʳ] ADJ *look* incitante, provocativo.
comely ['kʌmlɪ] ADJ (*liter*) gentil; lindo.
come-on* [kʌm,ɒn] N **(a)** (*enticement*) insinuación *f*, invitación *f*; aliciente *m*; **to give sb the ~** poner ojos tiernos a uno. **(b)** (*Comm*) truco *m*, señuelo *m*.
comer ['kʌməʳ] N: **all ~s** todos los contendientes; **the first ~** el primero en llegar.
comestible [kə'mestɪbl]† 1 ADJ comestible.
2 N (*gen pl*) **~s** comestibles *mpl*.
comet ['kɒmɪt] N cometa *m*.
comeuppance [,kʌm'ʌpəns] N: **to get one's ~** recibir el justo castigo.
COMEX ['kɒmeks] N (*US*) ABBR *of* **Commodities Exchange.**
comfort ['kʌmfət] 1 N **(a)** (*solace*) consuelo *m*; (*from pain*) alivio *m*; **that's cold** (*or small*) **~, that's no ~ at all** eso no me consuela nada; **you're a great ~ to me** eres un gran consuelo; **the exam is too close for ~** el examen está demasiado cerca para que me sienta tranquilo; **to give ~ to the enemy** dar aliento al enemigo.
(b) (*bodily*) confort *m*, comodidad *f*; bienestar *m*; **the ~s of life** las cosas agradables de la vida diaria; **with every modern ~** con todo confort, con toda comodidad; **to live in ~** vivir cómodamente.
2 VT (*solace*) consolar; *pain* aliviar; (*bodily*) confortar; (*encourage*) alentar.
comfortable ['kʌmfətəbl] ADJ *house, chair, shoes etc* cómodo, confortable; *income* adecuado; *majority* suficiente, adecuado; *living* holgado; **to feel ~** encontrarse a gusto; **I don't feel altogether ~ about it** la cosa me trae algo preocupado; **he came closer to the truth than was ~** se acercó de manera incómoda a la verdad; **to have a ~ win over sb** vencer a uno fácilmente; **to make o.s. ~** acomodarse a su gusto; (*euph*) ir al baño; **make yourself ~!** ¡póngase cómodo!, ¡acomódese bien!
comfortably ['kʌmfətəblɪ] ADV *sit etc* cómodamente; *live* holgadamente; *win* fácilmente; **to be ~ off** tener unos ingresos adecuados, vivir holgadamente.
comfort eating ['kʌmfət,iːtɪŋ] N *comida como terapia contra la depresión.*
comforter ['kʌmfətəʳ] N **(a)** (*scarf*) bufanda *f*; (*US*) cobertor *m* acol-

chado, edredón *m*. **(b)** (*baby's*) chupete *m*, chupón *m* (*LAm*).

comforting ['kʌmfətɪŋ] ADJ consolador, (re)confortante.

comfortless ['kʌmfətlɪs] ADJ incómodo, sin comodidad.

comfort station ['kʌmfət,steɪʃən] N (*US*) urinario *m* público, servicios *mpl*.

comfrey ['kʌmfrɪ] N consuelda *f*.

comfy* ['kʌmfɪ] ADJ = **comfortable**.

comic ['kɒmɪk] ① ADJ cómico; divertido; ~ **book** libro *m* de cómics; ~ **opera** ópera *f* bufa, ópera *f* cómica; ~ **strip** historieta *f*, tira *f* cómica, banda *f* de dibujos; ~ **verses** poesías *fpl* jocosas, poesías *fpl* festivas.

② N **(a)** (*person*) cómico *m*, -a *f*. **(b)** (*paper*) cómic *m*, (*child's*) tebeo *m*; ~**s** (*US*) = ~ **strip**.

┌─── ▯ **COMIC RELIEF** ──────────────────────────────────┐

🛈 *Comic Relief es una campaña con fines benéficos organizada por actores y humoristas para recaudar dinero y paliar así la pobreza, especialmente en África. La cadena de televisión **BBC** le dedica cada dos años una noche entera y en el programa actores, humoristas y famosos hacen números cómicos, informando a la vez sobre proyectos para luchar contra la pobreza e invitando al público a que llame y haga donativos. Como muestra de apoyo mucha gente lleva narices rojas de plástico (**red noses**) o las ponen en la parte frontal del coche.*

  ⇨ *Ver también* ▯BBC▯

└──┘

comic(al) ['kɒmɪk(əl)] ADJ cómico; divertido, entretenido.

comically ['kɒmɪkəlɪ] ADV de manera cómica; graciosamente.

coming ['kʌmɪŋ] ① ADJ *year etc* que viene; (*future*) venidero; (*promising*) prometedor; **it's the ~ thing** es la moda del futuro.

② N venida *f*, llegada *f*; (*of Christ*) advenimiento *m*; ~**(s) and going(s)** ir y venir *m*, trajín *m*, ajetreo *m*.

coming-of-age ['kʌmɪŋəv'eɪdʒ] N (llegada *f* a la) mayoría *f* de edad.

coming-out ['kʌmɪŋ'aʊt] N presentación *f* en sociedad.

Comintern ['kɒmɪntɜːn] N (*Pol*) ABBR of **Communist International** Comintern *f*.

comm. ABBR **(a)** of **commerce**. **(b)** of **commercial**. **(c)** of **committee**.

comma ['kɒmə] N coma *f*.

command [kə'mɑːnd] ① N **(a)** (*order*) orden *f*; mandato *m*; (*Comput*) comando *m*; ~ **language** lenguaje *m* de órdenes; ~ **line** orden *f*; **at the ~ of, by (the) ~ of** por orden de; **by royal ~** por real orden; ~ **performance** (*Brit Theat*) representación *f* a petición del monarca; **to be at the ~ of** estar a la disposición de.

(b) (*control*) mando *m*, dominio *m*; ~ **module** módulo *m* de mando; ~ **post** puesto *m* de mando; **his ~ of English** su dominio del inglés; ~ **of the seas** dominio *m* de los mares; **under the ~ of** bajo el mando de; **to be in ~ of** estar al mando de; **to be in ~ of one's faculties** seguir en control de sus facultades; **who is in ~ here?** ¿quién manda aquí?; **to have at one's ~** *men* mandar; **to have good resources at one's ~** disponer de muchos recursos; **to take ~ of** asumir el mando de.

(c) (*authority, Mil, Naut*) comandancia *f*; jefatura *f*; **second in ~** segundo *m*, subjefe *m*, (*Naut*) comandante *m* segundo de a bordo.

② VT **(a)** (*order*) mandar, ordenar (*that* que, *to do* hacer).

(b) (*be in command of*) mandar, comandar.

(c) (*have at one's disposal*) disponer de, tener a su disposición; *attention* llamar poderosamente; *resources* tener.

(d) *respect etc* imponer; *sympathy* merecerse; *price* venderse a (or por).

(e) (*overlook*) *area* dominar; *view* tener, disfrutar de.

commandant [,kɒmən'dænt] N comandante *m*.

commandeer [,kɒmən'dɪər] VT *stores, ship etc* requisar, expropiar; *men* reclutar por fuerza; (*) tomar, apropiarse.

commander [kə'mɑːndər] N (*gen*) comandante *m*, jefe *m*; (*Brit Police*) comandante *m*; (*Hist: of chivalric order*) comendador *m*; (*rank*) capitán *m* de fragata.

commander-in-chief [kə'mɑːndərɪn'tʃiːf] N jefe *m* supremo, comandante *m* en jefe.

commanding [kə'mɑːndɪŋ] ADJ *position* dominante; *appearance* imponente; *lead, advantage* abrumador; ~ **officer** jefe *m*, comandante *m*; **in a ~ tone** con voz de mando.

commandingly [kə'mɑːndɪŋlɪ] ADV *speak etc* con voz de mando.

commandment [kə'mɑːndmənt] N mandamiento *m*; **the Ten C~s** los diez mandamientos.

commando [kə'mɑːndəʊ] N (*man, group*) comando *m*.

commemorate [kə'meməreɪt] VT conmemorar.

commemoration [kə,memə'reɪʃən] N conmemoración *f*; **in ~ of** en conmemoración de.

commemorative [kə'memərətɪv] ① ADJ conmemorativo.

② N (*stamp*) conmemorativo *m*.

commence [kə'mens] ① VT comenzar, empezar.

② VI **to ~ to** + *infin*, **to ~** + *ger* empezar a + *infin*.

commencement [kə'mensmənt] N comienzo *m*, principio *m*; (*mainly US: Univ*) ceremonia *f* de entrega de diplomas.

commend [kə'mend] VT **(a)** (*praise*) alabar, elogiar; **to ~ sb for his action** alabar la acción de uno.

(b) (*recommend*) **I ~ him to you** se lo recomiendo; **I ~ it to your attention** creo que merece su atención; **the plan does not ~ itself to me** el proyecto no me resulta aceptable; **it has little to ~ it** poco hay que decir a su favor.

(c) (*entrust*) encomendar (*to* a).

commendable [kə'mendəbl] ADJ recomendable, encomiable, loable.

commendably [kə'mendəblɪ] ADV de manera loable; **it was ~ short** tuvo el mérito de ser breve; **you have been ~ prompt** le felicito por la prontitud.

commendation [,kɒmen'deɪʃən] N **(a)** (*praise*) elogio *m*, encomio *m*; (*Mil*) felicitación *f*. **(b)** (*recommendation*) recomendación *f*.

commensurable [kə'menʃərəbl] ADJ conmensurable, comparable (*with* con).

commensurate [kə'menʃərɪt] ADJ proporcionado; ~ **with** equivalente a, que corresponde a.

▼ **comment** ['kɒment] ① N comentario *m*; observación *f*; **no ~** sin comentarios, no hay comentarios; **it seems to call for ~** sobre eso convendría hacer algún comentario; **to make the ~ that ...** observar que ...

② VT *text* comentar; **to ~ that ...** observar que ...

③ VI hacer comentarios, hacer una observación; **to ~ on** *text* comentar; *subject etc* hacer observaciones acerca de; **to ~ unfavourably on sth** criticar algo.

commentary ['kɒməntərɪ] N comentario *m*; reportaje *m*.

commentate ['kɒmenteɪt] (*Rad, TV*) ① VT hacer un reportaje sobre.

② VI hacer un reportaje.

commentator ['kɒmənteɪtər] N comentador *m*, -ora *f*, comentarista *mf*; (*Rad, TV*) comentarista *mf*, locutor *m*, -ora *f*.

commerce ['kɒmɜːs] N comercio *m*.

commercial [kə'mɜːʃəl] ① ADJ comercial; ~ **art** arte *m* comercial; ~ **artist** artista *mf* comercial; ~ **attaché** agregado *m*, -a *f* comercial; ~ **bank** banco *m* comercial; ~ **break** espacio *m* publicitario; ~ **centre** centro *m* comercial; ~ **college** escuela *f* para secretarias; ~ **law** derecho *m* mercantil; ~ **paper** (*esp US*) letras *fpl* comerciables; ~ **property** propiedad *f* comercial; ~ **radio** emisora *f* comercial; ~ **television** televisión *f* comercial; ~ **traveller** viajante *m*; ~ **value** valor *m* comercial; **'no ~ value'** 'sin valor comercial'; ~ **vehicle** vehículo *m* comercial.

② N **(a)** (*Rad, TV*) anuncio *m*, emisión *f* publicitaria. **(b)** ~**s** (*St Ex*) (acciones *fpl* de) empresas *fpl* comerciales.

commercialism [kə'mɜːʃəlɪzəm] N mercantilismo *m*.

commercialization [kə,mɜːʃəlaɪ'zeɪʃən] N comercialización *f*.

commercialize [kə'mɜːʃəlaɪz] VT comercializar, convertir en comercial.

commercialized [kə'mɜːʃəlaɪzd] ADJ (*pej*) comercializado.

commercially [kə'mɜːʃəlɪ] ADV comercialmente.

commie* ['kɒmɪ] ADJ, N = **communist**.

commiserate [kə'mɪzəreɪt] VI expresar su sentimiento; **to ~ with** compadecerse de, condolerse de.

commiseration [kə,mɪzə'reɪʃən] N conmiseración *f*.

commissar ['kɒmɪsɑːr] N comisario *m*.

commissariat [,kɒmɪ'seərɪət] N comisaría *f*.

commissary ['kɒmɪsərɪ] N **(a)** comisario *m*, -a *f*. **(b)** (*US: shop*) economato *m*.

commission [kə'mɪʃən] ① N (*order, fee*) comisión *f*; (*committee*) comisión *f*, comité *m*; (*of crime*) perpetración *f*; (*Mil*) graduación *f* de oficial, despacho *m* de oficial, (*warrant*) nombramiento *m*; ~ **agent** comisionista *mf*; **on ~, on a ~ basis** a comisión; **to be out of ~** estar fuera de servicio; **to charge 10% ~** cobrar una comisión del 10 por cien; **to put out of ~** inutilizar; **to put into ~** poner en servicio activo.

② VT *officer* nombrar (*in a regiment* a un regimiento); *ship* poner en servicio activo; *architect etc* nombrar, hacer un encargo a; *picture* comisionar, encargar; *article* encargar; **to ~ sb to do sth** encargar a uno que haga algo.

commissionaire [kə,mɪʃə'neər] N (*Brit, Canada*) portero *m*, conserje *m*.

commissioned [kə'mɪʃnd] ADJ: ~ **officer** oficial *mf*.

commissioner [kə'mɪʃənər] N comisario *m*, -a *f*; ~ **for oaths** notario *m* público; ~ **of police** (*Brit*) jefe *m* de policía.

commissioning editor [kə'mɪʃənɪŋ'edɪtər] N jefe *m*, -a *f* de sección, responsable *mf* de departamento.

commit [kə'mɪt] ① VT **(a)** *crime* cometer; *error* hacer, *perjury* incurrir en; **to ~ suicide** suicidarse.

(b) (*involve*) *troops* enviar a la batalla; *resources* empeñar.

(c) (*entrust*) entregar (*to* a); (*Parl*) *bill* someter a una comisión; **to ~ sth to sb's charge** confiar algo a uno; **to ~ sth to the flames** entregar algo a las llamas; **to ~ sth to memory** aprender algo de memoria; **to ~ sb to prison** encarcelar a uno; **to ~ sb to a mental hospital** internar a uno en un manicomio; **to ~ sb for trial** remitir a uno al tribunal; **to ~ sth to paper** (*or* **writing**) poner algo por

┌───┐
│ ➤ LANGUAGE IN USE: **comment: 1 → 26.1, 26.2** │
└───┘

escrito.

2 VR: **to ~ o.s.** hacer una promesa, declararse; comprometerse; **to ~ o.s. to** comprometerse a, declararse a favor de; **without ~ing myself** sin compromiso por mi parte; **I am ~ted to help him** me he comprometido a ayudarle; **we are deeply ~ted to this policy** nos hemos declarado firmemente a favor de esta política.

commitment [kə'mɪtmənt] N (a) (*obligation*) compromiso *m*, obligación *f*, cometido *m*. (b) (*quality*) entrega *f*, devoción *f*.

committal [kə'mɪtl] N comisión *f*; compromiso *m*, cometido *m*; (*burial*) entierro *m*; **~ to prison** (auto *m* de) prisión *f*.

committed [kə'mɪtɪd] ADJ comprometido.

committee [kə'mɪtɪ] N comisión *f*, comité *m*; **~ of management** consejo *m* de administración; **~ meeting** reunión *f* de(l) comité; **~ member** miembro *mf* de(l) comité; **to be** (or **sit**) **on a ~** ser miembro de un comité.

commode [kə'məʊd] N (*with chamberpot*) silla con orinal; (*chest of drawers*) cómoda *f*.

commodious [kə'məʊdɪəs] ADJ grande, espacioso.

commodity [kə'mɒdɪtɪ] N artículo *m* (de consumo *or* de comercio), mercancía *f*, mercadería *f*, producto *m*; **commodities** mercancías *fpl*, géneros *mpl*; productos *mpl* de base; **~ exchange** bolsa *f* de artículos de consumo; **~ markets** mercados *mpl* de mercancías; **~ trade** comercio *m* de mercancías.

commodore ['kɒmədɔːr] N comodoro *m*.

common ['kɒmən] **1** ADJ (a) (*belonging to many*) común (*also Math, Gram*); **~ ground** puntos *mpl* en común; **~ land** campo *m* común, ejido *m*; **C~ Market** Mercado *m* Común; **~ sense** sentido *m* común; **~ sense tells us that ...** el sentido común nos dice que ...; **surely it's ~ sense that ...?** ¿no es lógico que ...?; **it is ~ to all men** es común a todos; **A has nothing in ~ with B** A no tiene nada en común con B; **we have nothing in ~** no tenemos ningún interés en común; **we have a lot in ~** tenemos muchos intereses en común; **I, in ~ with everybody else** yo, al igual que todos los demás; **to work for a ~ aim** cooperar todos a un mismo fin; V **knowledge.**
(b) (*public*) público.
(c) (*frequent*) común, frecuente; **this butterfly is ~ in Spain** esta mariposa es común en España.
(d) (*usual, ordinary*) corriente, usual; **belief** vulgar; **~ crab** cangrejo *m* común; **~ cold** catarro *m*, resfriado *m*; **~ law** derecho *m* consuetudinario; **~ noun** nombre *m* común; **~ or garden** ordinario, normal y corriente; **~ prisoner** preso *m* común, preso *m* social; **~ soldier** soldado *m* raso; **~ stock** (*US Fin*) acciones *fpl* ordinarias; **the ~ man** el hombre medio; **in ~ use** de uso corriente; **it is no more than ~ courtesy to write** no es más que una cortesía elemental escribir; **it is ~ to see such things now** ahora es frecuente ver tales cosas.
(e) (*vulgar*) ordinario, vulgar (*esp LAm*); **she's very ~** es muy ordinaria; **as ~ as dirt** de lo más ordinario.

2 N (a) (*land*) campo *m* común, ejido *m*.
(b) **~s** (*Pol*) estado *m* llano; **the C~s** los Comunes.
(c) **short ~s** ración *f* escasa; **to be on short ~s** comer mal.
(d) **~s** (*US Univ*) comedor *m*.

┌─── **COMMON LAW** ───┐

ⓘ Se llama common law o case law (derecho consuetudinario o jurisprudencia), al conjunto de leyes basadas en el fallo de los tribunales, a diferencia de las leyes establecidas por escrito en el Parlamento. El derecho consuetudinario inglés se desarrolló después de la conquista normanda, cuando los jueces basaban sus decisiones en la tradición o en el precedente judicial. La jurisprudencia sigue usándose como base del sistema legal anglosajón, aunque va perdiendo vigencia por el desarrollo del derecho escrito.
⇨ *Ver también* ACT OF PARLIAMENT , CONSTITUTION

commonality ['kɒmənælɪtɪ], **commonalty** ['kɒmənəltɪ] N (*commonness*) común *m*; **the ~** (*ordinary people*) el común de la gente, la plebe.

common core ['kɒmən'kɔːr] N (*Scol: also* **common-core syllabus**) asignaturas *fpl* comunes, tronco *m* común.

common currency [ˌkɒmən'kʌrənsɪ] N: **to become/be ~** *idea, belief* convertirse en/ser moneda corriente.

Common Entrance ['kɒmən'entrəns] N (*Brit Scol*) examen de entrada en la enseñanza privada.

commoner ['kɒmənər] N plebeyo *m*, -a *f*; (*Univ*) estudiante *m* que no tiene beca del colegio.

common-law ['kɒmən,lɔː] ATTR: **~ marriage** unión *f* consensual; **~ wife** mujer *f* en una unión consensual.

commonly ['kɒmənlɪ] ADV comúnmente, frecuentemente; generalmente; **it is ~ believed that ...** se cree vulgarmente que ...

commonness ['kɒmənnɪs] N (a) (*frequency*) frecuencia *f*. (b) (*vulgarity*) ordinariez *f*.

commonplace ['kɒmənpleɪs] **1** ADJ vulgar, trivial; **it is ~ to see**

that ... es frecuente ver que ...
2 N (a) (*ordinary thing*) cosa *f* común, cosa *f* corriente.
(b) (*Liter etc*) lugar *m* común, tópico *m*, perogrullada *f*.

common-room ['kɒmənrʊm] N salón *m* (de un colegio *etc*).

commons ['kɒmənz] NPL (*Pol*) V **common 2** (b).

commonsense ['kɒmən,sens] ADJ racional, lógico; **the ~ thing to do is ...** lo lógico es ...

commonwealth ['kɒmənwelθ] N república *f*; **the (British) C~** la Commonwealth, la Comunidad Británica de Naciones; **Minister of State** (or **Secretary of State**) **for C~ Affairs** Ministro *m* (or Secretario *m*) de Estado para los Asuntos de la Commonwealth; **the C~** (*Brit Hist*) la república de Cromwell; **the C~ of Kentucky** el estado de Kentucky; **the C~ of Puerto Rico** el estado de Puerto Rico; *ver también* MONARCHY .

┌─── **COMMONWEALTH** ───┐

ⓘ La Commonwealth (Comunidad Británica de Naciones) es una asociación de estados soberanos, la mayoría de los cuales eran colonias británicas en el pasado, establecida para fomentar el comercio y los lazos de amistad entre ellos. Actualmente se compone de 51 estados miembros, entre los cuales se encuentran el Reino Unido, Australia, Canadá, India, Jamaica, Kenia, Nueva Zelanda, Nigeria, Pakistán y Sudáfrica. Los países miembros reconocen al soberano británico como Head of the Commonwealth y se reúnen anualmente para debatir asuntos políticos y económicos. Además, cada cuatro años uno de los países miembros es el anfitrión de la competición deportiva conocida como Commonwealth Games.

commotion [kə'məʊʃən] N tumulto *m*, confusión *f*; alboroto *m*; (*civil*) disturbio *m*, perturbación *f* del orden público; **to cause a ~** armar un lío; **to make a ~** (*noise*) provocar (*or* causar) un alboroto; **there was a ~ in the crowd** se armó un lío entre los espectadores; **what a ~!** ¡qué alboroto!

communal ['kɒmjuːnl] ADJ comunal.

communally ['kɒmjuːnəlɪ] ADV comunalmente; **to act ~** obrar como comunidad; **the property is held ~** la propiedad la posee la comunidad.

commune 1 ['kɒmjuːn] N (*all senses*) comuna *f*.
2 [kə'mjuːn] VI (a) (*Eccl: esp US*) comulgar. (b) **to ~ with** conversar con, comunicarse con.

communicable [kə'mjuːnɪkəbl] ADJ comunicable; *disease* transmisible.

communicant [kə'mjuːnɪkənt] N comulgante *mf*.

communicate [kə'mjuːnɪkeɪt] **1** VT comunicar.
2 VI (a) (*Eccl*) comulgar. (b) (*buildings etc*) comunicarse. (c) (*speak*) comunicarse (*with* con).

communicating [kə'mjuːnɪkeɪtɪŋ] ADJ: **~ rooms** cuartos *mpl* comunicados.

communication [kə,mjuːnɪ'keɪʃən] N comunicación *f*; **~ breakdown** malentendido *m*; **~ cord** (*Brit Rail*) timbre *m* de alarma; **~ gap** falta *f* de entendimiento; **~ problem** problema *m* de expresión; **~s program** programa *m* de comunicación; **~ satellite** satélite *m* de comunicaciones; **~ science** telecomunicaciones *fpl*; **~ skills** destrezas *fpl* comunicativas; **~s software** paquete *m* de comunicación; **~s technology** tecnología *f* para las comunicaciones; **to be in ~ with** estar en contacto con; **to get into ~ with** ponerse en contacto con.

communicative [kə'mjuːnɪkətɪv] ADJ comunicativo, expansivo.

communicator [kə'mjuːnɪkeɪtər] N (*person*) comunicador *m*, -ora *f*.

communion [kə'mjuːnɪən] N comunión *f*; **to take ~** comulgar; **~ service** comunión *f*; **~ table** mesa *f* de comunión.

communiqué [kə'mjuːnɪkeɪ] N comunicado *m*, parte *m*.

communism ['kɒmjʊnɪzəm] N comunismo *m*.

communist ['kɒmjʊnɪst] **1** ADJ comunista; **C~ Party** Partido *m* Comunista.
2 N comunista *mf*.

community [kə'mjuːnɪtɪ] **1** N comunidad *f*; (*people at large*) colectividad *f*, sociedad *f*; (*local inhabitants*) vecindario *m*; **the C~** (*EC*) la Comunidad; **the black ~** la población negra, los habitantes negros; **the artistic ~** el mundillo artístico; **the Ruritanian ~ in Rome** la colonia ruritania de Roma.
2 ATTR comunitario; **~ bodies** organismos *mpl* comunitarios; **~ budget** presupuesto *m* comunitario; **~ care** (*Brit*) política de integración social de enfermos y ancianos; **~ centre** centro *m* social; **~ charge** (*Brit formerly*) (contribución *f* de) capitación *f*, impuesto *m* municipal; **~ chest** (*US*) fondo *m* para beneficencia social; **~ college** (*US*) centro universitario donde se imparten cursos de dos años; **~ health centre** clínica *f* comunitaria; **C~ law** derecho *m* comunitario; **~ life** vida *f* social; **~ medicine** medicina *f* de familia; **~ policing** política policial de acercamiento a la comunidad; **C~ policy** (*EC*) política *f* comunitaria; **C~ regulations** normas *fpl* comunitarias; **~ service** servicio *m* comunitario; **~ singing** canto *m* colectivo; **~ spirit** sentimiento *m* de comunidad; civismo *m*; **~ worker** asistente *mf* social (del barrio).

COMMUNITY CARE

i *La expresión* **Community Care** *hace referencia a la política del Gobierno británico para la integración en la comunidad de aquellos que necesitan cuidados especiales, como ancianos o enfermos mentales, es decir, se intenta que puedan vivir en sus casas o en residencias pequeñas. La puesta en marcha de esta política ha terminado con las largas estancias en hospitales u otras instituciones de gran tamaño y ha transferido recursos y fondos a los servicios de asistencia social o domiciliaria y a centros de día. La opinión pública no ha sido muy favorable a un recorte de recursos que puede dar lugar a una atención inadecuada de los más necesitados.*

---

communize ['kɒmjuːnaɪz] VT comunizar.
commutable [kəˈmjuːtəbl] ADJ (*gen, Jur*) conmutable.
commutation ['kɒmjuˈteɪʃən] N conmutación *f* (*also Fin*); (*US Rail etc*) uso *m* de un billete de abono; **~ ticket** billete *m* de abono.
commute [kəˈmjuːt] **1** VT *payment* conmutar (*into* en, *for* por); *sentence* conmutar (*to* en, por).
2 VI viajar a diario, ir y venir regularmente (*to work* al trabajo); **I work in London but I ~** (*Brit*) trabajo en Londres pero tengo que viajar cada día.
commuter [kəˈmjuːtəʳ] N viajero *m* diario, viajera *f* diaria (*desde los barrios exteriores etc de una ciudad al centro*); **~ belt** (*Brit*), **~ country** (*Brit*) zona *f* de los barrios exteriores; **~ services** servicios *mpl* de cercanías; **~ train** tren *m* de cercanías.
commuting [kəˈmjuːtɪŋ] N: **~ is very stressful** el viajar para ir al trabajo provoca mucho estrés.
compact **1** ['kɒmpækt] N (**a**) (*agreement*) pacto *m*, convenio *m*. (**b**) (*powder ~*) polvera *f*. (**c**) (*US Aut*) utilitario *m*.
2 [kəmˈpækt] ADJ compacto; *material* apretado, sólido; *style* breve, conciso; **~ car** (*US*) utilitario *m*; **~ disk** disco *m* compacto.
3 [kəmˈpækt] VT *material* comprimir (*into* en); condensar; **to be ~ed of** consistir en.
compactly [kəmˈpæktlɪ] ADV de modo compacto; apretadamente, sólidamente; brevemente, concisamente.
compactness [kəmˈpæktnɪs] N compacidad *f*, compresión *f*; (*of style*) concisión *f*.
companion [kəmˈpænɪən] **1** N (**a**) compañero *m*, -a *f*; (*lady's*) señora *f* de compañía; (*euph: lover*) compañero *m*, -a *f*. (**b**) (*Naut*) lumbrera *f*; (*~way*) escala *f* (*que conduce a los camarotes*). (**c**) (*handbook*) manual *m*.
2 ATTR: **~ volume** libro de tema relacionado.
companionable [kəmˈpænɪənəbl] ADJ sociable, simpático.
companionship [kəmˈpænɪənʃɪp] N compañerismo *m*.
companionway [kəmˈpænjənweɪ] N escalerilla *f*.
company ['kʌmpənɪ] N (**a**) (*gen*) compañía *f* (*also Mil, Theat*); (*ship's ~*) tripulación *f*; **~ commander** capitán *m* de compañía; **~ sergeant-major** sargento *m* mayor de una compañía; **he's good ~** es un compañero divertido; **they are in good ~** están en buena compañía; **two's ~ but three's a crowd** con dos basta y sobra uno; **to do sth in ~** hacer algo en colaboración; **present ~ excepted** mejorando lo presente, salvando a los presentes; **we have ~** tenemos visita; **to join ~ with** reunirse con; **to keep sb ~** acompañar a uno, hacerle compañía a uno; **to keep ~** (*lovers*) andar en relaciones; **to keep bad ~** tener malas compañías; **a man is known by the ~ he keeps** dime con quién andas y te diré quién eres; **to part ~** separarse (*with* de), (*fig*) desprenderse, soltarse.
(**b**) (*Comm*) sociedad *f*, compañía *f*, empresa *f*; **Smith and C~** Smith y Compañía; **Wilson and ~** (*pej*) Wilson y compañía; **~ car** (*Brit*) coche *m* de la empresa; **~ director** director *m*, -ora *f* de empresa; **~ law** derecho *m* de compañías (*or* de sociedades); **~ lawyer** (*Brit Jur*) abogado *mf* empresarial; (*working within company*) abogado *mf* de la compañía; **~ man** empleado *m* que se desvive por su empresa; **~ policy** normas *fpl* de la empresa; **~ secretary** (*Brit*) apoderado *m*; **~ time** horario *m* del trabajo; **~ union** (*US*) sindicato *m* de empresa.
comparability [kɒmpərəˈbɪlɪtɪ] N comparabilidad *f*.
comparable ['kɒmpərəbl] ADJ comparable; **a ~ case** un caso análogo; **they are not ~** no se les puede comparar.
comparably ['kɒmpərəblɪ] ADV de manera comparable.
comparative [kəmˈpærətɪv] **1** ADJ relativo; (*Gram etc*) comparativo; *study* comparado, contrastado; **~ literature** literatura *f* comparada.
2 N comparativo *m*.
▼ **comparatively** [kəmˈpærətɪvlɪ] ADV relativamente.
▼ **compare** [kəmˈpɛəʳ] **1** N: **beyond ~, past ~, without ~** sin comparación, impar.
▼ **2** VT (**a**) comparar (*to, with* con); (*put side by side: esp texts*) cotejar; **as ~d with** comparado con; **they are not to be ~d** no se les puede comparar. (**b**) (*Gram*) formar los grados de comparación de.
3 VI poderse comparar; **he can't ~ with you** no se le puede comparar con Vd; **it ~s favourably with the other** no pierde por comparación con el otro, supera al otro; **it ~s poorly with the other** es inferior al otro; **how do they ~?** ¿cuáles son sus cualidades

respectivas?; **how do they ~ for speed?** ¿cuál tiene mayor velocidad?
▼ **comparison** [kəmˈpærɪsn] N (**a**) comparación *f*; cotejo *m*; **in ~ with** en comparación con; **there's no ~** no hay comparación (posible); **this one is large in ~** comparando los dos éste es más grande; **it will bear** (*or* **stand**) **~ with the best** se puede comparar con los mejores. (**b**) (*Gram*) comparación *f*.
compartment [kəmˈpɑːtmənt] N compartimiento *m*; (*Rail, of case etc*) departamento *m*.
compartmentalization [ˌkɒmpɑːtˌmentəlaɪˈzeɪʃən] N compartimentación *f*.
compartmentalize [ˌkɒmpɑːtˈmentəlaɪz] VT dividir en categorías; aislar en categorías, compartimentar.
compass ['kʌmpəs] **1** N (**a**) (*Naut etc*) brújula *f*.
(**b**) (*range*) alcance *m*, extensión *f*; (*area*) ámbito *m*; **beyond my ~** fuera de mi alcance; **in a small ~** en un espacio reducido.
(**c**) (*esp US*) compás *m*.
(**d**) **~es** (*Math*) compás *m*; **a pair of ~es** un compás.
2 VT (*contrive*) conseguir, (*pej*) tramar; (*grasp mentally*) comprender; (*surround*) rodear; **to be ~ed about by** estar rodeado de.
compass card ['kʌmpəs,kɑːd] N (*Naut*) rosa *f* de los vientos.
compass course ['kʌmpəs,kɔːs] N ruta *f* magnética.
compass rose ['kʌmpəs'rəʊz] N = **compass card**.
compassion [kəmˈpæʃən] N compasión *f*; **to have ~ on** tener piedad de; **to move sb to ~** mover a uno a compasión.
compassionate [kəmˈpæʃənɪt] ADJ compasivo; **~ leave** baja *f* por razones familiares; **on ~ grounds** por compasión.
compassionately [kəmˈpæʃənɪtlɪ] ADV compasivamente, con compasión.
compatibility [kəmˌpætəˈbɪlɪtɪ] N compatibilidad *f* (*also Comput*).
compatible [kəmˈpætɪbl] ADJ compatible (*also Comput*), conciliable.
compatriot [kəmˈpætrɪət] N compatriota *mf*.
compel [kəmˈpel] VT obligar; *admiration, respect* imponer; *surrender* exigir, hacer inevitable; **to ~ sb to do sth** forzar a uno a hacer algo; **I feel ~led to say** me veo obligado a decir.
compelling [kəmˈpelɪŋ] ADJ *argument etc* irresistible, apremiante, convincente; *curiosity etc* compulsivo.
compellingly [kəmˈpelɪŋlɪ] ADV de modo convincente.
compendious [kəmˈpendɪəs] ADJ compendioso.
compendium [kəmˈpendɪəm] N compendio *m*.
compensate ['kɒmpənseɪt] **1** VT compensar; (*reward*) recompensar; (*for loss etc*) indemnizar, resarcir (*for* de).
2 VI: **to ~ for sth** compensar algo.
compensation [ˌkɒmpənˈseɪʃən] N compensación *f*; (*reward*) recompensa *f*; (*for loss etc*) indemnización *f*, resarcimiento *m*; **~ fund** fondo *m* de compensación.
compensatory [kɒmpənˈseɪtərɪ] ADJ compensatorio; **~ finance** financiación *f* compensatoria.
compère ['kɒmpɛəʳ] (*Brit*) **1** N presentador *m*, animador *m*.
2 VT *show* presentar.
3 VI actuar de presentador.
compete [kəmˈpiːt] VI (*as rivals*) competir, hacer competencia (*against, with* con, *for* por); (*in a race*) tomar parte (*in* en), presentarse (*in* a), concurrir (*in* a); **to ~ in a market** concurrir a un mercado.
competence ['kɒmpɪtəns], (*esp US*) **competency** ['kɒmpɪtənsɪ] N (**a**) aptitud *f*, capacidad *f*, competencia *f*; (*of court etc*) competencia *f*, incumbencia *f*; **that is not within my ~** eso está fuera de mi competencia. (**b**) (*Fin*) ingresos *mpl* (suficientes); **to have a modest ~** tener suficiente para vivir.
competent ['kɒmpɪtənt] ADJ (**a**) (*capable*) competente, capaz; **to be ~ to do sth** ser competente para hacer algo. (**b**) (*adequate*) adecuado, suficiente; **a ~ knowledge of the language** un conocimiento suficiente del idioma.
competently ['kɒmpɪtəntlɪ] ADV de modo adecuado, competentemente.
competing [kəmˈpiːtɪŋ] ADJ *claim, product* en competencia, rival.
competition [ˌkɒmpɪˈtɪʃən] N (**a**) (*spirit*) competencia *f*, rivalidad *f*; **in ~ with** en competencia con; **there was keen ~ for the prize** se disputó reñidamente el premio.
(**b**) (*Comm*) competencia *f*; **unfair ~** competencia *f* desleal.
(**c**) (*contest*) concurso *m*; (*eg for Civil Service posts*) oposiciones *fpl*; **60 places to be filled by ~** 60 vacantes a cubrir por oposiciones.
competitive [kəmˈpetɪtɪv] ADJ *spirit* competidor, de competencia; *exam* de concurso, de 'numerus clausus'; *market, price, product* competitivo; **we must make ourselves more ~** tenemos que hacernos más competitivos; **we must improve our ~ position** tenemos que mejorar nuestras posibilidades de competir.
competitively [kəmˈpetɪtɪvlɪ] ADV *do etc* con espíritu competidor; **a ~ priced product** un producto de precio competitivo.
competitiveness [kəmˈpetɪtɪvnɪs] N competitividad *f*.
competitor [kəmˈpetɪtəʳ] N (**a**) (*rival*) competidor *m*, -ora *f*, rival *mf*; (*Comm*) competidor *m*; (*Sport*) competidor *m*, -ora *f*, participante *mf*.

➤ LANGUAGE IN USE: **comparatively** → 5.1   **compare: 2a** → 5.1   **comparison: a** → 5.1, 5.5, 26.3

(b) (*in contest*) concursante *mf*; aspirante *mf*; (*eg for Civil Service post*) opositor *m*, -ora *f*.

compilation [ˌkɒmpɪˈleɪʃən] N compilación *f*, recopilación *f*.

compile [kəmˈpaɪl] VT compilar (*also Comput*), recopilar.

compiler [kəmˈpaɪləʳ] N **(a)** compilador *m*, -ora *f*, recopilador *m*, -ora *f*. **(b)** (*Comput*) compilador *m*.

complacence [kəmˈpleɪsəns] N, **complacency** [kəmˈpleɪsnsɪ] N suficiencia *f*, satisfacción *f* de sí mismo (*or consigo*); falso sentimiento *m* de seguridad.

complacent [kəmˈpleɪsənt] ADJ suficiente, satisfecho de sí mismo (*or consigo*), autosatisfecho.

complacently [kəmˈpleɪsəntlɪ] ADV suficientemente, de modo satisfecho; **he looked at me** ~ me miró complacido.

complain [kəmˈpleɪn] VI quejarse (*about, of* de, *that* de que, *to* a); reclamar (*about* contra, *to* ante); (*in shop etc, formally*) formular una queja; **to ~ of** (*Med*) presentar síntomas de, sufrir de; **you should ~ to the police** hay que denunciarlo a la policía; **I can't ~** yo no me quejo.

complainant [kəmˈpleɪnənt] N (*Jur*) demandante *mf*, querellante *mf*.

complaint [kəmˈpleɪnt] N **(a)** queja *f*; reclamación *f*; (*to police*) denuncia *f*; (*Jur*) querella *f*, demanda *f*; **~s department** sección *f* de reclamaciones; **~s procedure** procedimiento *m* para presentar reclamaciones; **~s book** libro *m* de reclamaciones; **to have cause for ~** tener motivo de queja; **to lodge** (*or* **make**) **a ~** formular una queja, hacer una reclamación.
(b) (*Med*) enfermedad *f*, mal *m*, dolencia *f*.

complaisance [kəmˈpleɪzəns] N (*liter*) complacencia *f*, sumisión *f*.

complaisant [kəmˈpleɪzənt] ADJ servicial, cortés; *husband* consentido.

-complected [kəmˈplektɪd] *in compounds* (*US*) = **-complexioned**.

complement [1] [ˈkɒmplɪmənt] N **(a)** (*gen*) complemento *m*. **(b)** (*staff*) personal *m*, dotación *f* (*also Naut*).
[2] [ˈkɒmplɪment] VT complementar.

complementary [ˌkɒmplɪˈmentərɪ] ADJ complementario; **they are ~** se complementan.

complete [kəmˈpliːt] [1] ADJ entero, completo; total; (*finished*) acabado; (*accomplished*) consumado; **my happiness is ~** mi dicha es completa; **tell me the ~ story** cuéntamelo todo; **it is a ~ mistake to think that ...** es totalmente erróneo pensar que ...; **it's a ~ disaster** es un desastre total; **it was not a ~ success** (*iro*) no obtuvo un éxito rotundo que digamos; **my report is still not quite ~** mi informe todavía no está terminado del todo; **are we ~?** ¿estamos todos?; **it comes ~ with instructions** se sirve con sus instrucciones correspondientes; **he arrived ~ with equipment** llegó con su equipo y todo.
[2] VT completar; (*finish*) terminar, acabar, concluir; *years* cumplir; *form* rellenar, llenar; **to ~ my happiness** para colmo de dicha.

completely [kəmˈpliːtlɪ] ADV completamente, enteramente; totalmente; por completo; a fondo.

completeness [kəmˈpliːtnɪs] N integridad *f*, perfección *f*; lo completo *etc*; **for the sake of ~** para completar.

completion [kəmˈpliːʃən] N terminación *f*, conclusión *f*; (*of contract etc*) realización *f*; **on ~** en cuanto se termine; **to be nearing ~** estar para terminarse; **~ date** (*Jur: for work*) fecha *f* de cumplimiento; (*in house-buying*) fecha *f* de firma del contrato.

complex [ˈkɒmpleks] [1] ADJ complejo, complicado.
[2] N **(a)** (*Psych*) complejo *m*; **he's got a ~ about it** aquello le acompleja, se siente acomplejado de (*or* con) eso.
(b) (*Tech*) complejo *m*; (*industrial ~*) complejo *m* industrial; **shopping ~** complejo *m* comercial.

complexion [kəmˈplekʃən] N tez *f*, cutis *m*; (*in terms of colour*) tez *f*, piel *f*; (*fig*) cariz *m*, aspecto *m*; **that puts a different ~ on it** entonces la cosa cambia de aspecto.

-complexioned [kəmˈplekʃnd] ADJ *ending in compounds* de piel ...; **dark~** de piel morena; **light~** de piel blanca.

complexity [kəmˈpleksɪtɪ] N complejidad *f*, lo complicado.

compliance [kəmˈplaɪəns] N sumisión *f* (*with* a); (*agreement*) conformidad *f*; **in ~ with** de acuerdo con, obedeciendo a, conforme a.

compliant [kəmˈplaɪənt] ADJ sumiso.

complicate [ˈkɒmplɪkeɪt] VT complicar.

complicated [ˈkɒmplɪkeɪtɪd] ADJ complicado.

complication [ˌkɒmplɪˈkeɪʃən] N complicación *f*; lo complicado; **~s** dificultades *fpl*; **it seems there are ~s** parece que han surgido dificultades.

complicity [kəmˈplɪsɪtɪ] N complicidad *f* (*in* en).

compliment [1] [ˈkɒmplɪmənt] N **(a)** (*polite expression, of praise*) cumplido *m*; (*flirtatious*) piropo *m*; **what a nice ~!** ¡qué detalle!; **that was meant as a ~** lo dije con buena intención; **to pay a ~ to** hacer cumplidos a, (*flirtatiously*) piropear a; **I take that as a ~** agradezco la cortesía; **I take it as a ~ that ...** para mí es un honor que + *subj*; **they did me the ~ of coming along** me hicieron el honor de asistir.
(b) **~s** (*greetings*) saludos *mpl*; **~s slip** hoja *f* de cumplido; **'with ~s'**

'con un atento saludo'; **with the ~s of Mr X** con un atento saludo de X, de parte del Sr X; **with the ~s of the season** deseándole felices Pascuas (*etc*); **with the ~s of the management** obsequio *m* de la casa; **with the author's ~s** homenaje *m* del autor, obsequio *m* del autor; **to return the ~** devolver el cumplido; **to send one's ~s to** enviar saludos a.
[2] [ˈkɒmplɪment] VT: **to ~ sb on sth** felicitar a uno por algo.

complimentary [ˌkɒmplɪˈmentərɪ] ADJ *remark etc* lisonjero; favorable; *ticket* de favor; ~ *copy* ejemplar *m* obsequio; **he was very ~ about the play** habló en términos muy favorables de la obra.

complin(e) [ˈkɒmplɪn] N completas *fpl*.

comply [kəmˈplaɪ] VI obedecer; acceder; **to ~ with** conformarse con, ajustarse a, *order* obedecer, *law* acatar.

component [kəmˈpəʊnənt] [1] ADJ componente; **its ~ parts** las piezas que lo integran.
[2] N componente *m*; (*Tech*) pieza *f*, componente *m*; **~s factory** fábrica *f* de componentes.

comport [kəmˈpɔːt] [1] VI: **to ~ with** concordar con.
[2] VR: **to ~ o.s.** comportarse.

comportment [kəmˈpɔːtmənt] N comportamiento *m*.

compose [kəmˈpəʊz] [1] VTI componer; **to be ~d of** constar de, componerse de.
[2] VR: **to ~ o.s.** calmarse, tranquilizarse; **I ~d myself to play** me dispuse a tocar.

composed [kəmˈpəʊzd] ADJ sosegado, tranquilo, sereno.

composedly [kəmˈpəʊzɪdlɪ] ADV sosegadamente.

composer [kəmˈpəʊzəʳ] N compositor *m*, -ora *f*.

composite [ˈkɒmpəzɪt] [1] ADJ compuesto; ~ **motion** propuesta *f*.
[2] N propuesta *f*.

composition [ˌkɒmpəˈzɪʃən] N **(a)** (*gen*) composición *f*. **(b)** (*Jur*) acomodamiento *m*, arreglo *m*.

compositional [ˌkɒmpəˈzɪʃənl] ADJ de composición.

compositor [kəmˈpɒzɪtəʳ] N cajista *m*.

compos mentis [ˈkɒmpɒsˈmentɪs] ADJ: **to be ~** estar en su sano (*or* entero) juicio.

compost [ˈkɒmpɒst] N abono *m* (vegetal).

compost-heap [ˈkɒmpɒsthiːp] N montón *m* de abono (vegetal).

composting [ˈkɒmpɒstɪŋ] N compostación *f*.

composure [kəmˈpəʊʒəʳ] N serenidad *f*, calma *f*; **to recover one's ~** serenarse.

compote [ˈkɒmpəʊt] N compota *f*.

compound [1] [ˈkɒmpaʊnd] ADJ compuesto; *fracture* complicado; ~ **interest** interés *m* compuesto; ~ **sentence** oración *f* compuesta.
[2] [ˈkɒmpaʊnd] N **(a)** (*Chem*) compuesto *m*; (*Gram*) vocablo *m* compuesto. **(b)** (*enclosure*) recinto *m*.
[3] [kəmˈpaʊnd] VT **(a)** componer, mezclar; *difficulty, offence* agravar; *debt* ajustar, componer; **to ~ a felony** aceptar dinero para no entablar juicio. **(b)** **it is ~ed of X and Z** consiste en X y Z.
[4] [kəmˈpaʊnd] VI: **to ~ with** capitular con.

compounding [ˈkɒmpaʊndɪŋ] N composición *f*.

comprehend [ˌkɒmprɪˈhend] [1] VT **(a)** (*understand*) comprender, entender. **(b)** (*include*) comprender, abarcar.
[2] VI comprender.

comprehensible [ˌkɒmprɪˈhensəbl] ADJ comprensible.

comprehensibly [ˌkɒmprɪˈhensəblɪ] ADV comprensiblemente, de modo comprensible.

comprehension [ˌkɒmprɪˈhenʃən] N comprensión *f*; ~ **test** test *m* de comprensión; **it is past ~** es incomprensible; **it passes my ~ that ...** para mí resulta incomprensible que ...

comprehensive [ˌkɒmprɪˈhensɪv] [1] ADJ completo, exhaustivo; de gran alcance, de máximo alcance; *knowledge, study* extenso; *report* global; *account, view* de conjunto; ~ **insurance** seguro *m* a todo riesgo; ~ **school** (*Brit*) = **2**.
[2] N (*Brit*) instituto *m* (de segunda enseñanza).

┌─ **COMPREHENSIVE SCHOOLS** ─────────────────┐

ⓘ La mayoría de las escuelas de educación secundaria en el Reino Unido se conocen como **comprehensive schools** *y ofrecen una gran variedad de asignaturas para cubrir las necesidades educativas de alumnos con diferentes aptitudes. Fueron creadas en los años sesenta en un intento de fomentar la igualdad de oportunidades y acabar con la división tradicional entre los centros selectivos de enseñanzas teóricas* (**grammar schools**) *y otros de enseñanza básicamente profesional* (**secondary modern schools**).
⇨ *Ver también* GRAMMAR SCHOOL , EDUCATION

└───┘

compress [1] [ˈkɒmpres] N compresa *f*.
[2] [kəmˈpres] VT comprimir (*into* en) (*also Comput*); *text etc* reducir (*into* a), condensar.

compressed [kəmˈprest] ADJ comprimido; ~ **air** aire *m* comprimido; ~ **charge** (*US*) precio *m* inclusivo.

compression [kəmˈpreʃən] N compresión *f*.

compressor [kəmˈpresəʳ] N compresor *m* (*also Comput*); ~ **unit** unidad *f* de compresor.

comprise [kəm'praɪz] VT (*include*) comprender; (*consist of*) constar de, componerse de; (*range*) abarcar; **to be ~d within certain limits** estar incluido dentro de ciertos límites.

compromise ['kɒmprəmaɪz] ① N (*spirit, art of ~*) transigencia *f*; contemporización *f*; (*agreement*) transacción *f*, avenencia *f*, arreglo *m*; concesiones *fpl* recíprocas; (*midway point*) término *m* medio; solución *f* intermedia; **we shall have to make a ~** tendremos que hacer una concesión; **there can be no ~ with treason** no transigimos con la traición; **to reach a ~** llegar a un arreglo.
② VT *person* comprometer; *thing* poner en peligro.
③ VI transigir, ceder un poco para llegar a un acuerdo; contemporizar; hacerse concesiones recíprocas; llegar a un acuerdo; **I agreed to ~** consentí en que la cosa quedase en un término medio, convine en transigir; **so we ~d on 7** así que convinimos en el término medio de 7; **to ~ with** transigir con, avenirse con.
④ VR: **to ~ o.s.** comprometerse.

compromising ['kɒmprəmaɪzɪŋ] ADJ *situation* comprometedor; *mind, spirit* acomodaticio.

comptometer [kɒmp'tɒmɪtər] N máquina *f* de calcular; **~ operator** operador *m*, -ora *f* de máquina de calcular.

comptroller [kən'trəʊlər] N interventor *m* -ora *f*.

compulsion [kəm'pʌlʃən] N obligación *f*, fuerza *f* mayor, coacción *f*; **under ~** por fuerza; **you are under no ~** nadie le obliga a ello.

compulsive [kəm'pʌlsɪv] ADJ compulsivo.

compulsively [kəm'pʌlsɪvlɪ] ADV compulsivamente.

compulsorily [kəm'pʌlsərɪlɪ] ADV por fuerza, forzosamente.

▼ **compulsory** [kəm'pʌlsərɪ] ADJ obligatorio; preceptivo, de precepto; **~ liquidation** liquidación *f* obligatoria; **~ purchase** (*Brit*) expropiación *f*; **~ purchase order** orden *f* de expropiación; **~ redundancy** despido *m* forzoso.

compunction [kəm'pʌŋkʃən] N remordimiento *m*; compunción *f*; **without ~** sin escrúpulo.

computation [ˌkɒmpjʊ'teɪʃən] N (a) (*gen*) cómputo *m*, cálculo *m*. (b) (*Comput*) computación *f*.

computational [ˌkɒmpjʊ'teɪʃənl] ADJ computacional; **~ linguistics** lingüística *f* computacional.

compute [kəm'pju:t] VT computar, calcular (*at* en).

computer [kəm'pju:tər] ① N ordenador *m*, computadora *f*; **we do it by ~ now** ahora lo hacemos con el ordenador; **the records have all been put on ~** todos los registros han entrado en (el) ordenador.
② ATTR de ordenador; informático; **~ animation** animación *f* por ordenador; **~ crime** delitos *mpl* informáticos; **~ dating service** agencia *f* matrimonial por ordenador; **~ expert** experto *m*, -a *f* en ordenadores; **~ game** vídeojuego *m*; **~ graphics** gráficas *fpl* por ordenador; **~ language** lenguaje *m* de ordenador; **~ literacy** competencia *f* en la informática; **~ literate** competente en la informática; **~ model** modelo *m* informático; **~ operator** operador *m*, -ora *f* de ordenador; **~ printout** impresión *f* (de ordenador); **~ program** programa *m* de ordenador; **~ programmer** programador *m*, -ora *f* de ordenadores; **~ programming** programación *f* de ordenadores; **~ science** informática *f*, ciencias *fpl* de la computación; **~ scientist** informático *m*, -a *f*; **~ simulation** simulación *f* por ordenador; **~ skills** conocimientos *mpl* de informática; **~ studies** = **~ science**; **~ time** tiempo *m* máquina; **~ typesetting** composición *f* por ordenador; **~ user** usuario *m*, -a *f* de ordenador.

computeracy [ˌkəmpjʊ'terəsɪ] N competencia *f* en la informática.

computer-aided [kəm'pju:tə'eɪdɪd] ADJ, **computer-assisted** [kəm'pju:təˈsɪstɪd] ADJ asistido por ordenador.

computerate [kəm'pju:tərɪt] ADJ competente en la informática.

computer-controlled [kəm'pju:təkən'trəʊld] ADJ controlado por ordenador.

computerese [kəmˌpju:tə'ri:z] N jerga *f* informática.

computer-generated [kəmˌpju:tə'dʒenəreɪtɪd] ADJ *graphics, images* realizado por ordenador, creado por ordenador.

computerization [kəmˌpju:təraɪ'zeɪʃən] N computerización *f*.

computerize [kəm'pju:təraɪz] VT *information* computerizar, informatizar; *office* instalar ordenadores en; **we're ~d now** ahora tenemos ordenador.

computer-operated [kəm'pju:tə'ɒpəreɪtɪd] ADJ operado por ordenador, computerizado.

computing [kəm'pju:tɪŋ] N informática *f*; **~ problem** problema *m* de cómputo; **~ task** tarea *f* de computar.

comrade ['kɒmrɪd] N camarada *mf* (*also Pol*), compañero *m*, -a *f*.

comrade-in-arms ['kɒmrɪdɪn'ɑ:mz] N compañero *m* de armas.

comradely ['kɒmreɪdlɪ] ADJ de camarada(s); **we did it in a ~ spirit** lo hicimos como camaradas; **I gave him some ~ advice** le di unos consejos de camarada.

comradeship ['kɒmrɪdʃɪp] N compañerismo *m*, camaradería *f*.

COMSAT ['kɒmsæt] ® N ABBR *of* **communications satellite** satélite *m* de comunicaciones, COMSAT ® *m*.

con¹ (††) [kɒn] VT (*also* **to ~ over**) estudiar, repasar.

con² [kɒn] ① N timo *m*, estafa *f*.
② VT timar, estafar; **to ~ sb into doing sth** lograr con engaños que uno haga algo; **I was ~ned into it** me camelaron para que lo hiciera* (*or* aceptara *etc*); **he ~ned them into thinking that ...** logró con mañas que pensaran que ...
③ ATTR: **~ artist** estafador *m*, engañabobos *m*.

con³ [kɒn] N *V* pro.

con⁴ [kɒn] N (: *prisoner*) preso *m*, -a *f*.

Con. (*Brit*) ABBR *of* **constable**.

conc. ABBR *of* **concessions**.

concatenate [kɒn'kætɪˌneɪt] VT concatenar.

concatenation [kɒnˌkætɪ'neɪʃən] N concatenación *f*.

concave ['kɒn'keɪv] ADJ cóncavo.

concavity [kɒn'kævɪtɪ] N concavidad *f*.

conceal [kən'si:l] VT ocultar (*from* a); *emotion* disimular; (*Jur*) encubrir.

concealed [kən'si:ld] ADJ oculto; *emotion* disimulado; *lighting* indirecto.

concealment [kən'si:lmənt] N ocultación *f*; encubrimiento *m* (*also Jur*); (*of emotion*) disimulación *f*; **place of ~** escondrijo *m*.

concede [kən'si:d] VT conceder; *match* ceder, entregar; **I ~ that ...** confieso que ...; **to ~ victory** darse por vencido.

conceit [kən'si:t] N (a) (*pride*) presunción *f*, engreimiento *m*, vanidad *f*. (b) (*Liter*) concepto *m*.

conceited [kən'si:tɪd] ADJ presumido, engreído, vanidoso, creído (*LAm*); **to be ~ about** envanecerse con (*or* de, por).

conceitedly [kən'si:tɪdlɪ] ADV vanidosamente, envanecidamente.

conceivable [kən'si:vəbl] ADJ concebible.

conceivably [kən'si:vəblɪ] ADV posiblemente; **it cannot ~ be true** no es concebible que sea verdad; **more than one could ~ need** más de lo que se podría imaginar como necesidad.

conceive [kən'si:v] ① VT (a) *child* concebir.
(b) (*imagine*) imaginar, formarse un concepto de; *idea* tener; *plan* idear; **I ~ it to be my duty** creo que es mi deber; **I cannot ~ why** no me explico por qué; **~d in plain terms** formulado en lenguaje sencillo.
(c) *affection, dislike etc* tomar, cobrar (*for* a).
② VI concebir; **to ~ of** formarse un concepto de; **I cannot ~ of anything worse** no me puedo imaginar nada peor.

concelebrant [kən'selɪˌbrənt] N concelebrante *m*.

concelebrate [kən'selɪbreɪt] VT *mass* concelebrar.

concentrate ['kɒnsəntreɪt] ① N (*Chem*) concentrado *m*, sustancia *f* concentrada.
② VT concentrar; *troops etc* concentrar, reunir; *hopes* cifrar (*on* en); **it ~s the mind wonderfully** hace reflexionar profundamente, da lugar a una maravillosa toma de conciencia.
③ VI concentrarse; (*troops etc*) concentrarse, reunirse; **to ~ on** concentrarse en, concentrar la atención en; **to ~ on doing sth** concentrarse para hacer algo; **he can't ~** no sabe concentrarse.

concentrated ['kɒnsən,treɪtɪd] ADJ concentrado.

concentration [ˌkɒnsən'treɪʃən] N concentración *f*; **~ camp** campo *m* de concentración.

concentric [kən'sentrɪk] ADJ concéntrico.

concept ['kɒnsept] N concepto *m*.

concept album ['kɒnsept'ælbəm] N disco *m* monográfico.

conception [kən'sepʃən] N (a) (*of child*) concepción *f*. (b) (*idea*) idea *f*, concepto *m*; **a bold ~** un concepto grandioso; **he has not the remotest ~ of** no tiene la menor idea de.

conceptual [kən'septjʊəl] ADJ conceptual.

conceptualization [kən,septjʊəlaɪ'zeɪʃən] N conceptualización *f*.

conceptualize [kən'septjʊəlaɪz] VT conceptualizar.

conceptually [kən'septjʊəlɪ] ADV conceptualmente, como concepto; **~, the idea made sense** como concepto, la idea podía funcionar.

▼ **concern** [kən'sɜ:n] ① N (a) (*matter*) asunto *m*; **that's my ~** eso es asunto mío; **it's no ~ of yours** no tiene nada que ver con Vd, no le atañe a Vd; **that's your ~!** ¡allá Vd!
(b) (*interest*) interés *m*; **it is of some ~ to us all** nos interesa a todos; **it's of no ~** no tiene importancia.
(c) (*anxiety*) preocupación *f* (*for, with* por), inquietud *f*; **it is a matter for ~ that ...** es inquietante que ...; **he showed his ~** se mostró preocupado; **with growing ~** con creciente alarma.
(d) (*firm*) empresa *f*; **going ~** empresa *f* próspera, empresa *f* en pleno funcionamiento; **the whole ~*** el asunto entero, todo el negocio.
▼② VT tener que ver con, interesar, concernir; **as ~s** respecto de; **that does not ~ me** eso no tiene que ver conmigo, eso no me atañe; **it ~s me closely** me toca de cerca; **the book ~s a family** el libro trata de una familia; **my question ~s money** mi pregunta se refiere al dinero; **those ~ed** los interesados; **where** (*or* **as far as**) **women are ~ed** por lo que se refiere a las mujeres; **please contact the department ~ed** sírvase contactar con la sección correspondiente; **to whom it may ~** (*reference*) a quien interese, a quien le corresponda; **as far as I am ~ed** en cuanto a mí, por lo que a mí se

---

refiere; **to be ~ed in** tomar parte en, intervenir en; estar involucrado en; **were you ~ed in this?** ¿tú estabas metido en esto?; **to be ~ed with others in a crime** estar implicado con otros en un crimen; **I am ~ed to ...** me preocupa + *infin*, me interesa + *infin*; **we are ~ed with facts** a nosotros nos interesan los hechos.

3 VR: **to ~ o.s. about sb** preocuparse por uno; **to ~ o.s. with** interesarse por, ocuparse de.

▼ **concerned** [kən'sɜːnd] ADJ preocupado; inquieto; **to be very ~** inquietarse mucho (*about* por); **he sounded very ~** parecía estar muy preocupado; **I am ~ about you** me traes preocupado; **I am ~ to find that ...** me inquieta descubrir que ...

concerning [kən'sɜːnɪŋ] PREP sobre, acerca de.

concert **1** ['kɒnsət] N concierto *m*; **in ~ with** conjuntamente con; **to act in ~** obrar de común acuerdo; **'The Crotch' are in ~ at the Palace** el grupo 'The Crotch' aparece en persona en el Teatro Palace.

2 ['kɒnsət] ATTR: **~ grand** piano *m* de cola larga; **~ party** (*Theat*) grupo *m* de artistas de revista; (*Fin*) confabulación *f* para adquirir acciones individualmente con intención de reunirlas en bloque; **~ performance** presentación *f* (de una ópera) en concierto, versión *f* concertante; **~ performer** concertista *mf*; **~ pianist** pianista *mf* de concierto; **~ pitch** diapasón *m* normal; **~ tour** gira *f* de conciertos.

3 [kən'sɜːt] VT concertar; *policy* coordinar, armonizar.

concerted [kən'sɜːtɪd] ADJ *action etc* coordinado, conjunto; **we made a ~ effort** coordinamos los esfuerzos (*to* + *infin* por + *infin*).

concertgoer ['kɒnsət,gəʊər] N aficionado *m*, -a *f* a los conciertos; **we are regular ~s** vamos con regularidad a los conciertos; **the ~s are an odd lot** los que asisten al concierto son gente rara.

concert-hall ['kɒnsəthɔːl] N sala *f* de conciertos.

concertina [,kɒnsə'tiːnə] **1** N concertina *f*; **~ crash** (*Aut*) choque *m* de acordeón.

2 VI: **the vehicles ~ed into each other** los vehículos colisionaron en acordeón.

concertmaster ['kɒnsət,mɑːstər] N (*US*) primer violín *m*.

concerto [kən'tʃeətəʊ] N concierto *m*.

concession [kən'seʃən] N concesión *f*; privilegio *m*; (*of tax*) desgravación *f*, exención *f*.

concessionaire [kən,seʃə'neər] N concesionario *m*, -a *f*.

concessionary [kən'seʃənərɪ] **1** ADJ *fare* reducido; *ticket* de favor.

2 N concesionario *m*, -a *f*.

conch [kɒntʃ] N (*shell*) concha; (*Archit*) cóclea *f*.

concierge [,kɔ̃:nsɪ'eəʒ] N conserje *m*.

conciliate [kən'sɪlɪeɪt] VT conciliar.

conciliation [kən,sɪlɪ'eɪʃən] N conciliación *f*; **~ service** servicio *m* de conciliación (*and see* **ACAS**).

conciliator [kən'sɪlɪeɪtər] N conciliador *m*, -ora *f*; (*Ind*) árbitro *mf*.

conciliatory [kən'sɪlɪətərɪ] ADJ conciliador, conciliatorio.

concise [kən'saɪs] ADJ conciso.

concisely [kən'saɪslɪ] ADV concisamente, con concisión.

conciseness [kən'saɪsnɪs] N, **concision** [kən'sɪʒən] N concisión *f*.

conclave ['kɒnkleɪv] N cónclave *m*.

▼ **conclude** [kən'kluːd] **1** VT (a) (*end*) concluir, terminar; **'to be ~d'** (*serial*) 'terminará con el próximo episodio'.

(b) (*arrange*) *treaty* hacer, firmar, pactar; *agreement* llegar a, concertar; *deal* cerrar.

▼ (c) (*infer*) colegir, concluir; **I ~ that ...** saco la consecuencia de que ...; **what are we to ~ from that?** ¿qué consecuencia se saca de eso?; **it was ~d that ...** se concluyó que ..., se decidió que ...

(d) (*US: decide*) decidir (*to do* hacer).

▼ **2** VI terminar(se); **he ~d with this remark** terminó haciendo esta observación; **the judge ~d in his favour** el juez decidió a su favor.

concluding [kən'kluːdɪŋ] ADJ final.

▼ **conclusion** [kən'kluːʒən] N (a) (*end*) conclusión *f*, terminación *f*; **in ~** en conclusión, para terminar; **to bring sth to a ~** concluir un asunto, llevar un asunto a su desenlace.

(b) (*of treaty etc*) el firmar *etc*.

▼ (c) (*inference*) conclusión *f*, consecuencia *f*; **foregone ~** resultado *m* inevitable; **to come to the ~ that ...** llegar a la conclusión de que ...; **draw your own ~s** extraiga Vd las conclusiones oportunas; **to jump to ~s** sacar conclusiones precipitadas; **to try ~s with** medirse con.

conclusive [kən'kluːsɪv] ADJ concluyente, decisivo; *evidence* decisivo.

conclusively [kən'kluːsɪvlɪ] ADV concluyentemente.

concoct [kən'kɒkt] VT confeccionar; *lie, story* inventar; *plot* tramar.

concoction [kən'kɒkʃən] N (a) (*act*) confección *f*; (*of story*) invención *f*. (b) (*substance*) mezcla *f*; (*drink*) brebaje *m*.

concomitant [kən'kɒmɪtənt] **1** ADJ concomitante.

2 N concomitante *m*.

concord ['kɒŋkɔːd] N concordia *f*, armonía *f*; (*Mus, Gram*) concordancia *f*.

concordance [kən'kɔːdəns] N concordancia *f*; (*index, book*) concordancias *fpl*.

concordant [kən'kɔːdənt] ADJ concordante.

concordat [kɒn'kɔːdæt] N concordato *m*.

Concorde ['kɒŋkɔːd] N Concorde *m*; **to fly by ~** volar en Concorde.

concourse ['kɒŋkɔːs] N (*of people*) muchedumbre *f*, concurrencia *f*; (*of rivers*) confluencia *f*; (*Comm, Rail*) explanada *f*.

concrete ['kɒnkriːt] **1** ADJ (a) concreto; específico; **~ music** música *f* concreta; **~ noun** nombre *m* concreto. (b) (*Tech*) de hormigón; **~ jungle** jungla *f* de asfalto.

2 N hormigón *m*, gorgón *m* (*And*).

3 VT revestir de hormigón.

concrete-mixer ['kɒnkriːt,mɪksər] N hormigonera *f*, revolvedora *f* (*LAm*).

concretion [kən'kriːʃən] N concreción *f*.

concretize ['kɒnkrɪtaɪz] VT (*US*) concretar.

concubine ['kɒŋkjʊbaɪn] N concubina *f*, barragana *f*, manceba *f*.

concupiscence [kən'kjuːpɪsəns] N concupiscencia *f*.

concupiscent [kən'kjuːpɪsənt] ADJ concupiscente.

concur [kən'kɜːr] VI (a) (*happen together*) concurrir, coincidir. (b) (*agree*) asentir; **to ~ in** convenir en; **to ~ with** estar de acuerdo con.

concurrence [kən'kʌrəns] N acuerdo *m*, conformidad *f*.

concurrent [kən'kʌrənt] ADJ concurrente; **~ processing** procesamiento *m* concurrente.

concurrently [kən'kʌrəntlɪ] ADV al mismo tiempo.

concuss [kən'kʌs] VT producir una conmoción cerebral a.

concussion [kən'kʌʃən] N conmoción *f* cerebral.

▼ **condemn** [kən'dem] VT condenar (*to* a); (*blame*) censurar; *building* declarar ruinoso; *bad food* confiscar; **~ed cell** celda *f* de los condenados a muerte; **the ~ed man** el reo de muerte; **such conduct is to be ~ed** tal conducta es censurable.

▼ **condemnation** [,kɒndem'neɪʃən] N condena *f*, condenación *f*; (*blaming*) censura *f*.

condemnatory [,kɒndem'neɪtərɪ] ADJ condenatorio.

condensation [,kɒnden'seɪʃən] N condensación *f*; (*of text*) forma *f* abreviada.

condense [kən'dens] **1** VT condensar; *text* abreviar; **~d milk** leche *f* condensada.

2 VI condensarse.

condenser [kən'densər] N condensador *m*.

condescend [,kɒndɪ'send] VI: **to ~ to** + *infin* dignarse + *infin*.

condescending [,kɒndɪ'sendɪŋ] ADJ superior, lleno de superioridad; desdeñoso, altivo; **he's very ~** se cree muy superior, mira por encima del hombro a los demás.

condescendingly [,kɒndɪ'sendɪŋlɪ] ADV con aire de superioridad, con desdén.

condescension [,kɒndɪ'senʃən] N aire *m* de superioridad, aire *m* protector.

condiment ['kɒndɪmənt] N condimento *m*.

condition [kən'dɪʃən] **1** N (a) (*stipulation*) condición *f*; **on this ~** con esta condición; **on no ~** de ninguna manera; **on ~ (that)** a condición de que + *subj*.

(b) (*state*) condición *f*, estado *m*; **in a bad ~** en malas condiciones; **he has a heart ~** tiene una afección cardíaca; **to be in no ~ to +** *infin* no estar en condiciones de + *infin*; **to be out of ~** estar en mal estado; (*person*) no estar en forma; **to keep o.s. in ~** mantenerse en forma.

(c) **~s** (*circumstances*) condiciones *fpl*; **under existing ~s** en las circunstancias actuales.

(d) (*social*) clase *f*; **of humble ~** de clase humilde.

2 VT condicionar, determinar.

conditional [kən'dɪʃənl] **1** ADJ condicional; **~ offer** oferta *f* condicional; **to be ~ upon** depender de.

2 N potencial *m*.

conditionally [kən'dɪʃnəlɪ] ADV condicionalmente, con reservas.

conditioned [kən'dɪʃənd] ADJ condicionado; **~ reflex** reflejo *m* condicionado.

conditioner [kən'dɪʃənər] N (*for hair*) suavizante *m* de cabello; (*for skin*) crema *f* suavizante; (*fabric ~*) suavizante *m*.

conditioning [kən'dɪʃənɪŋ] N acondicionamiento *m*.

condo* ['kɒndəʊ] N (*US*) = **condominium**.

condole [kən'dəʊl] VI: **to ~ with sb** condolerse de uno; dar el pésame a uno.

condolences [kən'dəʊlənsɪz] NPL pésame *m*; **please accept my ~** le acompaño en el sentimiento; **to send one's ~** dar el pésame.

condom ['kɒndəm] N condón *m*, preservativo *m*.

condominium ['kɒndə'mɪnɪəm] N condominio *m*; (*US*) apartamento *m*, piso *m*, condominio *m* (*LAm*) (*que es propiedad del que lo habita*); propiedad *f* horizontal.

condone [kən'dəʊn] VT condonar; *abuse* tolerar.

condor ['kɒndɔːr] N cóndor *m*.

conduce [kən'djuːs] VI: **to ~ to** conducir a.

conducive [kən'djuːsɪv] ADJ: **~ to** conducente a, propicio para, que favorece.

conduct **1** ['kɒndʌkt] N conducta *f*, comportamiento *m*; (*of business* *etc*) manejo *m*, dirección *f*, administración *f*; **~ report** (*Scol*) informe *m* de conducta.

2 [kən'dʌkt] VT conducir (*also Phys*); *business, negotiations, campaign etc* llevar, dirigir; *one's case* presentar; *orchestra* dirigir; **to ~ a correspondence with** estar en correspondencia con, cartearse con; **we were ~ed through a passage** nos hicieron pasar por un pasillo; **we were ~ed round by Lord X** actuó de guía Lord X.

3 [kən'dʌkt] VI (*Mus*) llevar la batuta.

4 [kən'dʌkt] VR: **to ~ o.s.** comportarse.

conducted [kən'dʌktɪd] ADJ: **~ tour** (*Brit*) (*of building*) visita *f* guiada, (*of country*) viaje *m* acompañado.

conduction [kən'dʌkʃən] N conducción *f*.

conductive [kən'dʌktɪv] ADJ conductivo.

conductivity [ˌkɒndʌk'tɪvɪtɪ] N conductibilidad *f*, conductividad *f*.

conductor [kən'dʌktəʳ] N (a) (*Mus*) director *m*; (*of bus*) cobrador *m*; (*US Rail*) revisor *m*. (b) (*lightning ~*) pararrayos *m*; (*Phys*) conductor *m*.

conductress [kən'dʌktrɪs] N cobradora *f*.

conduit ['kɒndɪt] N conducto *m*.

cone [kəʊn] N (*Geom*) cono *m*; (*Bot*) cono *m*, piña *f*; (*ice cream*) cucurucho *m*, pirucho *m* (*CAm*), cambucho *m* (*SC*).

◆**cone off** VT *road* cerrar con conos, cortar con conos.

coney ['kəʊnɪ] N (*US*) conejo *m*.

confab* ['kɒnfæb] N = **confabulation**.

confabulate [kən'fæbjʊleɪt] VI conferenciar.

confabulation [kənˌfæbjʊ'leɪʃən] N conferencia *f*.

confection [kən'fekʃən] N (a) confección *f*, hechura *f*. (b) (*Culin*) dulce *m*, confite *m*.

confectioner [kən'fekʃənəʳ] N pastelero *m*, -a *f*, repostero *m*, -a *f*; **~'s** (**shop**) pastelería *f*, repostería *f*, confitería *f*, dulcería *f* (*LAm*); **~'s sugar** (*US*) azúcar *m* glas(eado).

confectionery [kən'fekʃənərɪ] N (*Brit*) pasteles *mpl*; (*sweets*) dulces *mpl*, confites *mpl*, golosinas *fpl* (*LAm*), confitería *f*.

confederacy [kən'fedərəsɪ] N confederación *f*; (*plot*) complot *m*; **the C~** (*US*) los Estados Confederados.

confederate **1** [kən'fedərɪt] ADJ confederado.

2 [kən'fedərɪt] N confederado *m*; (*Jur*) cómplice *m*; (*US Hist*) confederado *m*, -a *f*.

3 [kən'fedəreɪt] VT confederar.

4 [kən'fedəreɪt] VI confederarse.

confederation [kənˌfedə'reɪʃən] N confederación *f*.

confer [kən'fɜːʳ] **1** VT conceder, otorgar (*on* a).

2 VI conferenciar (*about* sobre, *with* con).

conferee [ˌkɒnfɜː'riː] N (*US*) congresista *mf*.

conference ['kɒnfərəns] N (*assembly*) congreso *m*, conferencia *f*; (*business meeting*) conferencia *f*, reunión *f*; **~ call** conferencia *f*; **~ centre** (*town*) ciudad *f* de congresos; (*building*) palacio *m* de congresos; (*in institution*) centro *m* de conferencias; **~ member** congresista *mf*; **~ room** sala *f* de conferencias; **~ table** mesa *f* negociadora; **he's in ~ right now** precisamente ahora está conferenciando.

conferencing ['kɒnfərənsɪŋ] N (*Comput*) conferencia *f*; **~ system** sistema *m* de conferencias.

conferment [kən'fɜːmənt] N, **conferral** [kən'fɜːrəl] N concesión *f*, otorgamiento *m* (*on* a).

▼ **confess** [kən'fes] **1** VT confesar.

2 VI (*Eccl*) confesarse; **to ~ to a crime** confesarse culpable de un crimen; **to ~ to a liking for** confesar tener afición a; **I was wrong, I ~** me equivoqué, lo confieso.

3 VR: **I ~ myself wholly ignorant** confieso que no sé nada en absoluto de eso.

confessed [kən'fest] ADJ declarado.

confession [kən'feʃən] N confesión *f*; **~ of faith** profesión *f* de fe, credo *m*; **to go to ~** confesarse; **to hear sb's ~** confesar a uno; **to make a full ~** confesarlo todo, confesar de plano.

confessional [kən'feʃənl] N confesonario *m*.

confessor [kən'fesəʳ] N confesor *m*.

confetti [kən'fetiː] N confeti *m*.

confidant [ˌkɒnfɪ'dænt] N confidente *m*.

confidante [ˌkɒnfɪ'dænt] N confidenta *f*.

confide [kən'faɪd] **1** VT confiar (*to* a, en).

2 VI: **to ~ in** confiar en, fiarse de; **please ~ in me** puedes fiarte de mí; **to ~ to** hacer confidencias a; **he ~d to me that ...** me dijo en confianza que ...

▼ **confidence** ['kɒnfɪdəns] N (a) (*gen*) confianza *f* (*in* en, *that* en que); (*secrecy*) confidencialidad *f*, reserva *f*; **in ~** en confianza; '(**write**) **in strict ~**' 'absoluta reserva'; '**please apply in strict ~ to ...**' 'las solicitudes bajo reserva absoluta a ...'; **to be in sb's ~**, **to enjoy sb's ~** disfrutar de la intimidad de uno; **to gain ~** adquirir confianza; **to give sb ~** infundir confianza a uno; **we have every ~ in you** tenemos entera confianza en Vd; **I have every ~ that ...** estoy totalmente seguro de que ...; **to put one's ~ in** confiar en; **to take sb into one's ~** revelar un secreto a uno, hacer confidencias a uno. (b) (*revelation*) confidencia *f*.

confidence man ['kɒnfɪdənsmæn] N, PL **confidence men** ['kɒnfɪdənsmen] timador *m*, estafador *m*.

confidence trick ['kɒnfɪdənstrɪk] N, (*US*) **confidence game** ['kɒnfɪdənsgeɪm] N timo *m*, estafa *f*.

confidence trickster ['kɒnfɪdənsˌtrɪkstəʳ] N timador *m*, estafador *m*.

confident ['kɒnfɪdənt] ADJ seguro de sí mismo, lleno de confianza; (*over~*) confiado; **to be ~ about, to be ~ of** estar seguro de; **to be ~ that ...** estar seguro de que ...

confidential [ˌkɒnfɪ'denʃəl] ADJ *information, letter, report etc* confidencial; *secretary, tone* de confianza.

confidentiality [ˌkɒnfɪˌdenʃɪ'ælɪtɪ] N confidencialidad *f*.

confidentially [ˌkɒnfɪ'dənʃəlɪ] ADV en confianza.

confidently ['kɒnfɪdəntlɪ] ADV: **he said ~** dijo lleno de confianza; **we ~ expect that ...** creemos con toda confianza que ...

confiding [kən'faɪdɪŋ] ADJ: (**too**) **~** confiado; crédulo; **in a ~ tone** en tono de confianza.

configuration [kənˌfɪgjʊ'reɪʃən] N configuración *f* (*also Comput*).

configure [kən'fɪgəʳ] VT (*Comput*) configurar.

confine [kən'faɪn] **1** VT (*enclose*) encerrar (*to* en), confinar; (*fig*) limitar (*to* a); **to be ~d** (*woman*) estar de parto; **to be ~d to** limitarse a; **the damage is ~d to this part** el daño afecta únicamente esta parte; **this bird is ~d to Spain** esta ave existe únicamente en España; **to be ~d to bed** tener que guardar cama; **to be ~d to one's room** no poder dejar su cuarto.

2 VR: **to ~ o.s. to** limitarse a; **please ~ yourself to the facts** le ruego se limite a exponer los hechos.

confined [kən'faɪnd] ADJ reducido.

confinement [kən'faɪnmənt] N (*enclosure*) encierro *m* (*to* en); confinamiento *m*, confinación *f*; (*imprisonment*) prisión *f*, reclusión *f*; (*Med*) parto *m*, sobreparto *m*; **~ to barracks** arresto *m* en cuartel.

confines ['kɒnfaɪnz] NPL confines *mpl*.

▼ **confirm** [kən'fɜːm] VT confirmar; *treaty* ratificar; (*Eccl*) confirmar.

confirmation [ˌkɒnfə'meɪʃən] N confirmación *f*; ratificación *f*; (*Eccl*) confirmación *f*.

confirmed [kən'fɜːmd] ADJ inveterado.

confiscate ['kɒnfɪskeɪt] VT confiscar, incautarse de, requisar (*esp LAm*).

confiscation [ˌkɒnfɪs'keɪʃən] N confiscación *f*, incautación *f*, requisa *f* (*esp LAm*).

conflagration [ˌkɒnflə'greɪʃən] N conflagración *f*, incendio *m*.

conflate [kən'fleɪt] VT combinar.

conflation [kən'fleɪʃn] N combinación *f*.

conflict **1** ['kɒnflɪkt] N conflicto *m*; **~ of evidence** contradicción *f* de testimonios; **~ of interests** incompatibilidad *f*; **the theories are in ~** las teorías están reñidas; **to be in ~ with** estar en pugna con, estar reñido con; **to come into ~ with** chocar con.

2 [kən'flɪkt] VI estar en pugna (*with* con), estar reñido (*with* con).

conflicting [kən'flɪktɪŋ] ADJ *report* contradictorio; *interest* opuesto.

confluence ['kɒnflʊəns] N confluencia *f*.

conform [kən'fɔːm] VI conformarse; **to ~ to, to ~ with** ajustarse a, estar de acuerdo con, cuadrar con.

conformation [ˌkɒnfə'meɪʃən] N conformación *f*, estructura *f*.

conformism [kən'fɔːmɪzəm] N conformismo *m*.

conformist [kən'fɔːmɪst] **1** ADJ conformista.

2 N conformista *mf*.

conformity [kən'fɔːmɪtɪ] N conformidad *f*; **in ~ with** conforme a (*or* con).

confound [kən'faʊnd] VT confundir; **~ it!** ¡demonio!; **~ the man!** ¡maldito sea éste!

confounded [kən'faʊndɪd] ADJ condenado.

confront [kən'frʌnt] VT (*face squarely*) hacer frente a, encararse con; (*face defiantly*) enfrentarse con; *texts* confrontar; **the problems which ~ us** los problemas que se nos plantean; **we were ~ed by the river** estaba delante el río; **to ~ sb with sth** confrontar a uno con algo; **to ~ the accused with witnesses** confrontar al acusado con los testigos, carear a los testigos con el acusado; **to ~ sb with the facts** exponer delante de uno los hechos.

confrontation [ˌkɒnfrən'teɪʃən] N confrontación *f*; careo *m*.

confrontational [ˌkɒnfrən'teɪʃənəl] ADJ *approach, attitude, style* confrontacional, agresivo.

Confucian [kən'fjuːʃən] **1** ADJ de Confucio.

2 N confuciano *m*, -a *f*.

Confucianism [kən'fjuːʃənɪzəm] N confucionismo *m*.

Confucius [kən'fjuːʃəs] NM Confucio.

confuse [kən'fjuːz] VT (a) (*mix up*) confundir (*with* con); *issue etc* complicar, embarullar, (*deliberately*) embrollar, entenebrecer; **to ~ A and B** confundir A con B.

(b) (*perplex*) desconcertar, dejar confuso a, aturdir; **to get ~d** desorientarse, aturrullarse, desconcertarse.

confused [kən'fjuːzd] ADJ *situation etc* confuso; *person* perplejo, despistado; **my mind is ~** tengo la cabeza trastornada.

confusedly [kən'fjuːzɪdlɪ] ADV confusamente.

confusing [kən'fjuːzɪŋ] ADJ confuso, desconcertante; **it's all very ~**

todo ello es muy difícil de comprender.

confusingly [kən'fjuːzɪŋlɪ] ADV **(a)** confusamente; de manera confusa. **(b)** ~, **two of them had the same name** para despistar a la gente, dos de ellos tenían el mismo nombre.

confusion [kən'fjuːʒən] N **(a)** (*disorder*) confusión *f*, desorden *m*; **to be in** ~ estar en desorden; **to retire in** ~ retirarse en desorden. **(b)** (*perplexity*) confusión *f*, perplejidad *f*, desorientación *f*, despiste *m*; (*embarrassment*) confusión *f*, humillación *f*; **to be in** ~ estar desorientado; **to be covered in** ~ estar avergonzado.

confute [kən'fjuːt] VT refutar.

conga ['kɒŋgə] N **(a)** (*dance*) conga *f*. **(b)** (*also* ~ **drum**) congas *fpl*.

congeal [kən'dʒiːl] **1** VT congelar, cuajar, coagular; **2** VI congelarse, cuajarse, coagularse.

congenial [kən'dʒiːnɪəl] ADJ simpático, agradable, compatible.

congenital [kən'dʒenɪtl] ADJ congénito.

congenitally [kən'dʒenɪtlɪ] ADV congénitamente.

conger (eel) ['kɒŋgər('iːl)] N congrio *m*.

congested [kən'dʒestɪd] ADJ *area* congestionado, superpoblado; *building etc* lleno, de bote en bote; **to get** ~ **with** llenarse de, atestarse de; **it's getting very** ~ **in here** esto se nos está poniendo muy apretado.

congestion [kən'dʒestʃən] N congestión *f* (*also Med*), aglomeración *f*.

congestive [kən'dʒestɪv] ADJ (*Med*) congestivo; ~ **heart failure** insuficiencia *f* cardíaca congestiva.

conglomerate 1 [kən'glɒmərɪt] N conglomerado *m*. **2** [kən'glɒməreɪt] VT conglomerar, aglomerar. **3** [kən'glɒməreɪt] VI conglomerarse, aglomerarse.

conglomeration [kən,glɒmə'reɪʃən] N conglomeración *f*.

Congo ['kɒŋgəʊ] N: **the** ~ el Congo; **Republic of the** ~ República *f* del Congo.

Congolese [,kɒŋgəʊ'liːz] **1** ADJ congoleño. **2** N congoleño *m*, -a *f*.

congrats‡ [kən'græts] EXCL (*esp Brit*) enhorabuena, felicidades.

congratulate [kən'grætjuleɪt] VT felicitar, dar la enhorabuena a (*on* por).

▼ **congratulations** [kən,grætjʊ'leɪʃənz] NPL felicitaciones *fpl*; ~! ¡enhorabuena!, ¡felicidades!

congratulatory [kən'grætjʊlətərɪ] ADJ de felicitación.

congregate ['kɒŋgrɪgeɪt] VI congregarse.

congregation [,kɒŋgrɪ'geɪʃən] N (*assembly*) reunión *f*; (*Eccl: present in church*) fieles *mpl*, (*parishioners*) feligreses *mpl*; (*society of religious*) congregación *f*.

congregational [,kɒŋgrɪ'geɪʃnl] ADJ congregacionalista.

congregationalist [,kɒŋgrɪ'geɪʃənəlɪst] N congregacionalista *mf*.

congress ['kɒŋgres] N congreso *m*; **C~** (*US*) Congreso *m*; ~ **member** miembro *mf* del congreso, congresista *mf*; *ver también* CABINET, CAPITOL.

CONGRESS

ℹ️ *En el Congreso de Estados Unidos (***Congress***) se elaboran y aprueban las leyes federales. Consta de dos cámaras: la Cámara de Representantes (***House of Representatives***), cuyos 435 miembros son elegidos cada dos años por voto popular directo y en número proporcional a los habitantes de cada estado, y el Senado (***Senate***), con 100 senadores (***senators***), 2 por estado, de los que un tercio se elige cada dos años y el resto cada seis.*

congressional [kɒŋ'greʃənl] ADJ del congreso.

congressman ['kɒŋgresmən] N, PL **congressmen** ['kɒŋgresmən] (*US*) diputado *m*, miembro *m* del Congreso.

congresswoman ['kɒŋgres,wʊmən] N, PL **congresswomen** ['kɒŋgres,wɪmɪn] (*US*) diputada *f*, miembro *f* del Congreso.

congruence ['kɒŋgrʊəns] N, **congruency** ['kɒŋgrʊənsɪ] N congruencia *f*.

congruent ['kɒŋgrʊənt] ADJ congruente.

congruity [kɒŋ'gruːɪtɪ] N congruencia *f* (*with* con).

congruous ['kɒŋgrʊəs] ADJ congruo (*with* con).

conic(al) ['kɒnɪk(əl)] ADJ cónico; **conic section** sección *f* cónica.

conifer ['kɒnɪfər] N conífera *f*.

coniferous [kə'nɪfərəs] ADJ conífero.

conjectural [kən'dʒektʃərəl] ADJ conjetural.

conjecture [kən'dʒektʃər] **1** N conjetura *f*. **2** VT conjeturar (*from* de, por, *that* que).

conjoin [kən'dʒɔɪn] **1** VT aunar, unir. **2** VI aunarse, unirse.

conjoint [kɒn'dʒɔɪnt] ADJ aunado, asociado.

conjointly ['kɒn'dʒɔɪntlɪ] ADV conjuntamente.

conjugal ['kɒndʒʊgəl] ADJ conyugal.

conjugate ['kɒndʒʊgeɪt] VT conjugar.

conjugation [,kɒndʒʊ'geɪʃən] N conjugación *f*.

conjunct [kən'dʒʌŋkt] ADJ (*Astron*) en conjunción.

conjunction [kən'dʒʌŋkʃən] N conjunción *f*; **in** ~ **with** conjuntamente con; **in** ~ **with this** (*as ADV*) con relación a esto, con respecto

a esto.

conjunctive [kən'dʒʌŋktɪv] ADJ conjuntivo.

conjunctivitis [kən,dʒʌŋktɪ'vaɪtɪs] N conjuntivitis *f*.

conjuncture [kən'dʒʌŋktʃər] N coyuntura *f*.

conjure¹ [kən'dʒʊər] VT suplicar (*to do sth* hacer algo).

conjure² ['kʌndʒər] VI hacer juegos de manos; **he ~s with handkerchiefs** hace un truco con pañuelos; **a name to** ~ **with** un nombre prestigioso.

◆ **conjure away** VT conjurar, hacer desaparecer.

◆ **conjure up** VT hacer aparecer; (*fig*) evocar, hacer pensar en.

conjurer ['kʌndʒərər] N prestidigitador *m*, mago* *m*.

conjuring ['kʌndʒərɪŋ] N juegos *mpl* de manos, ilusionismo *m*, prestidigitación *f*.

conjuring trick ['kʌndʒərɪŋ,trɪk] N juego *m* de manos.

conjuror ['kʌndʒərər] N = **conjurer**.

conk¹‡ [kɒŋk] N **(a)** (*Brit: nose*) narigón *m*, napias‡ *fpl*. **(b)** (*blow*) golpe *m*. **(c)** (*US: head*) cholla‡ *f*, coco‡ *m*.

conk²‡ [kɒŋk] VI: **to** ~ **out*** escoñarse‡, fallar, averiarse; pararse.

conker* ['kɒŋkər] N (*Brit*) castaña *f* de Indias; ~**s** (*game*) juego *m* de las castañas.

con man* ['kɒnmæn] N, PL **con men** ['kɒnmen] timador *m*, estafador *m*.

Conn. (*US*) ABBR = **Connecticut**.

connect [kə'nekt] **1** VT (*join*) juntar, unir (*to* con); (*Elec*) conectar (*to* con); (*relate*) relacionar, asociar (*with* con); **to** ~ **sb with** poner a uno al habla con; **I'm trying to** ~ **you** (*Telec*) trato de ponerle, trato de comunicarle (*LAm*); **are these matters ~ed?** ¿tienen alguna relación entre sí estas cuestiones?; **to be well ~ed** estar bien relacionado; **the Jones are ~ed with the Smiths** los Jones están emparentados con los Smith; **what firm are you ~ed with?** ¿con qué empresa trabajas?; **I never ~ed you with that** nunca creía que tuvieras que ver con eso. **2** VI (*join*) unirse, (*Elec*) conectarse; **to** ~ **with** (*Rail etc*) enlazar con.

connected [kə'nektɪd] ADJ *languages* relacionado; (*Bot, Jur*) conexo; (*fig*) *argument etc* conexo; ~ **speech** discurso *m* conexo.

connecting [kə'nektɪŋ] ADJ *rooms etc* comunicado; *part, wire* conectable; ~ **flight** vuelo *m* de enlace; **bedroom with** ~ **bathroom** habitación *f* comunicada con el baño.

connecting-rod [kə'nektɪŋrɒd] N biela *f*.

connection, connexion [kə'nekʃən] N **(a)** (*joint*) juntura *f*, unión *f*; (*Mech, Elec*) conexión *f*; (*Rail etc*) enlace *m*, correspondencia *f* (*with* con); **our ~s with the town are poor** son malas nuestras comunicaciones con la ciudad; **'we've got a bad ~'** (*Telec*) 'no se oye bien la línea'. **(b)** (*fig*) relación *f* (*between* entre, *with* con); nexo *m*, enlace *m*; **we have ~s everywhere** tenemos relaciones con todas partes; **you have to have ~s** hay que tener buenas relaciones; **no** ~ **with any other firm** ésta es una firma independiente; **in** ~ **with** a propósito de; **in this** ~ con respecto a esto.

connective [kə'nektɪv] **1** ADJ conjuntivo; ~ **tissue** tejido *m* conjuntivo. **2** N conjunción *f*.

connectivity [,kɒnek'tɪvɪtɪ] N conectividad *f*.

connector [kə'nektər] N (*Elec*) conector *m*.

conning-tower ['kɒnɪŋ,taʊər] N (*submarine*) torrecilla *f*, (*other warship*) torre *f* de mando.

connivance [kə'naɪvəns] N connivencia *f*; (*agreement*) consentimiento *m*.

connive [kə'naɪv] VI: **to** ~ **at** hacer la vista gorda a; **to** ~ **with sb to do sth** confabularse con uno para hacer algo.

conniving [kə'naɪvɪŋ] ADJ muy dado a intrigas; mañoso, tramposo.

connoisseur [,kɒnə'sɜːr] N entendido *m*, -a *f* (*of* en), conocedor *m*, -ora *f* (*of* de), experto *m*, -a *f* (*of* en).

connotation [,kɒnəʊ'teɪʃən] N connotación *f*.

connotative ['kɒnə,teɪtɪv] ADJ connotativo.

connote [kɒ'nəʊt] VT connotar.

connubial [kə'njuːbɪəl] ADJ conyugal, connubial.

conquer ['kɒŋkər] **1** VT *territory* conquistar; *enemy, habit etc* vencer. **2** VI triunfar.

conquering ['kɒŋkərɪŋ] ADJ victorioso, triunfador.

conqueror ['kɒŋkərər] N conquistador *m*; vencedor *m*.

conquest ['kɒŋkwest] N conquista *f*.

conquistador [kɒn'kwɪstədɔː] N conquistador *m*.

Cons. ABBR of **Conservative** conservador *m*, -ora *f*.

consanguinity [,kɒnsæŋ'gwɪnɪtɪ] N consanguinidad *f*.

conscience ['kɒnʃəns] N conciencia *f*; **bad** ~ mala conciencia *f*; **in all** ~ en verdad; **with a clear** ~ con la conciencia tranquila; **I have a clear** ~ **about it** no creo tener culpa alguna por ello; **I have a guilty** ~ **about it, I have it on my** ~ me está remordiendo la conciencia por ello; **I would not have the** ~ **to** + *infin* no me atrevería a + *infin*; **I could not in** ~ **say that** en conciencia no podría decir eso.

conscience money ['kɒnʃəns,mʌnɪ] N dinero *que se paga para descar-*

gar la conciencia (*p. ej., atrasos de impuestos*).

conscience-raising ['kɒnʃəns,reɪzɪŋ] N concienciación *f*.

conscience-stricken ['kɒnʃəns,strɪkən] ADJ lleno de remordimientos.

conscientious [,kɒnʃɪ'enʃəs] ADJ concienzudo; **~ objector** objetor *m* de conciencia.

conscientiously [,kɒnʃɪ'enʃəslɪ] ADV concienzudamente.

conscientiousness [,kɒnʃɪ'enʃəsnɪs] N diligencia *f*, escrupulosidad *f*.

conscious ['kɒnʃəs] [1] ADJ (a) (*aware*) **to be ~ of** ser consciente de, saber, hacerse cargo de; **to be ~ that** ... saber (perfectamente) que ...; **to become ~ of** darse cuenta de; **to become ~ that** ... darse cuenta de que ....
(b) (*deliberate*) intencional, expreso.
(c) (*Med*) **to be ~** tener conocimiento, estar consciente; **to become ~** volver en sí.
[2] N: **the ~** el consciente.

-conscious [-,kɒnʃəs] *in compounds*: *eg* **security~** consciente de los problemas relativos a la seguridad.

consciously ['kɒnʃəslɪ] ADV conscientemente, a sabiendas.

consciousness ['kɒnʃəsnɪs] N (a) conciencia *f*. (b) (*Med*) conocimiento *m*; **to lose ~** perder el conocimiento; **to regain ~** recobrar el conocimiento, volver en sí.

consciousness-raising ['kɒnʃəsnɪs,reɪzɪŋ] N concienciación *f*.

conscript [1] ['kɒnskrɪpt] N recluta *m*, quinto *m*, conscripto *m*, -a *f* (*LAm*).
[2] [kən'skrɪpt] VT (*Mil*) llamar al servicio militar; *labourer etc* reclutar a la fuerza.

conscripted [kən'skrɪptɪd] ADJ *labourer etc* reclutado a la fuerza, forzado.

conscription [kən'skrɪpʃən] N servicio *m* militar obligatorio; (*act*) llamada *f* al servicio militar, conscripción *f* (*LAm*).

consecrate ['kɒnsɪkreɪt] VT consagrar.

consecration [,kɒnsɪ'kreɪʃən] N consagración *f*.

consecutive [kən'sekjʊtɪv] ADJ sucesivo, seguido; (*Gram etc*) consecutivo; **on 3 ~ days** 3 días seguidos.

consecutively [kən'sekjʊtɪvlɪ] ADV sucesivamente.

consensual [kən'sensjʊəl] ADJ *approach, decision etc* consensuado; *sex* consentido.

consensus [kən'sensəs] N consenso *m*.

consent [kən'sent] [1] N consentimiento *m* (*to* a); **by common ~** según la opinión general, de común acuerdo; **by mutual ~** de común acuerdo; **divorce by mutual ~** divorcio *m* por acuerdo mutuo.
[2] VI consentir (*to* en, *to* + *infin* en + *infin*).

consenting [kən'sentɪŋ] ADJ: **~ party** parte *f* que da su consentimiento; **between ~ adults** entre personas de edad para consentir.

▼ **consequence** ['kɒnsɪkwəns] N consecuencia *f*; resultado *m*; **in ~** por consiguiente; **in ~ of** de resultas de; **it is of no ~** no tiene importancia; **to put up with** (*or* **take**) **the ~s** aceptar las consecuencias.

consequent ['kɒnsɪkwənt] ADJ consiguiente.

consequential [,kɒnsɪ'kwenʃəl] ADJ (a) (*resulting*) consiguiente, resultante; **the moves ~ upon this decision** las medidas que resultan de esta decisión.
(b) (*important*) importante, con consecuencias importantes.

consequently ['kɒnsɪkwəntlɪ] ADV por consiguiente.

conservancy [kən'sɜːvənsɪ] N conservación *f*; *V* **nature 2**.

conservation [,kɒnsə'veɪʃən] N conservación *f* (*esp* de recursos naturales), preservación *f*; **~ area** (*Brit*) zona *f* perteneciente al patrimonio artístico.

conservationism [,kɒnsə,veɪʃənɪzəm] N conservacionismo *m*.

conservationist [,kɒnsə'veɪʃənɪst] N conservacionista *mf*.

conservatism [kən'sɜːvətɪzəm] N conservadurismo *m*.

conservative [kən'sɜːvətɪv] [1] ADJ (a) (*Pol*) conservador; **C~ Party** (*Brit*) Partido *m* Conservador. (b) *estimate etc* prudente, cauteloso, moderado.
[2] N conservador *m*, -ora *f*.

conservatoire [kən'sɜːvətwɑːʳ] N conservatorio *m*.

conservatory [kən'sɜːvətrɪ] N invernadero *m*.

conserve [kən'sɜːv] [1] N conserva *f*.
[2] VT conservar; **to ~ one's strength** reservarse.

▼ **consider** [kən'sɪdəʳ] [1] VT (a) (*deem*) considerar; **I ~ that** ... considero que ...; **I ~ it an honour** lo tengo a mucha honra; **I ~ him to be clever** le considero inteligente, creo que es inteligente; **I ~ the matter closed** para mí el asunto está concluido; **he is ~ed to be the best** se le considera el mejor.
(b) (*realize*) **when one ~s that** ... cuando uno se da cuenta de que ...
▼(c) (*think over*) considerar, pensar, meditar; **~ how much you owe him** considera cuánto le debes; **all things ~ed** considerándolo bien, todo bien mirado; **my ~ed opinion is that** ... estoy convencido de que ....
▼(d) (*study*) estudiar, examinar; **we are ~ing the matter** estamos estudiando el asunto; **he is being ~ed for the post** le están considerando para el puesto.

▼(e) (*entertain*) **have you ever ~ed going by train?** ¿has pensado alguna vez en ir en tren?; **would you ~ buying it?** ¿te interesa comprarlo?; **I wouldn't ~ it for a moment** no quiero pensarlo siquiera; **he refused even to ~ it** se negó a pensarlo siquiera.
(f) (*take into account*) tomar en cuenta; **you must ~ others' feelings** hay que tomar en cuenta los sentimientos de los demás.
[2] VR: **I ~ myself happy** me considero feliz; **~ yourself lucky** puedes considerarte afortunado; **~ yourself dismissed** considérese despedido.

considerable [kən'sɪdərəbl] ADJ importante, apreciable, cuantioso; *sum etc* importante; *loss* sensible; **we had ~ difficulty** tuvimos bastante dificultad.

considerably [kən'sɪdərəblɪ] ADV bastante, mucho, considerablemente.

considerate [kən'sɪdərɪt] ADJ considerado, atento, comedido; **it's most ~ of you** es muy amable de su parte.

considerately [kən'sɪdərɪtlɪ] ADV con consideración.

consideration [kən,sɪdə'reɪʃən] N (a) (*thoughtfulness*) consideración *f*; **as a mark of my ~** en señal de mi consideración; **in ~ of** en consideración a; **out of ~ for** por respeto a; **without due ~** sin reflexión; **that is a ~** eso hay que tenerlo en cuenta; **it is under ~** lo estamos estudiando; **we are giving the matter our ~** estamos estudiando la cuestión; **to take into ~** tener en cuenta.
(b) (*payment*) retribución *f*; **for a ~** previo pago, mediante pago.
(c) (*importance*) importancia *f*, consideración *f*; **to be of no** (*or* **little**) **~** no tener importancia.

considering [kən'sɪdərɪŋ] [1] ADV (*) teniendo en cuenta todas las circunstancias, a pesar de todo.
[2] PREP en consideración a, teniendo en cuenta ...

consign [kən'saɪn] VT consignar (*also Comm*); enviar; (*entrust*) confiar (*to* a); **to ~ to oblivion** sepultar en el olvido.

consignee [,kɒnsaɪ'niː] N consignatario *m*, -a *f*.

consigner, consignor [kən'saɪnəʳ] N consignador *m*, -ora *f*.

consignment [kən'saɪnmənt] N consignación *f*; envío *m*, remesa *f*; **~ note** (*Brit*) talón *m* de expedición; **goods on ~** mercancías *fpl* en consignación.

consist [kən'sɪst] VI: **to ~ of** consistir en, constar de, componerse de.

consistency [kən'sɪstənsɪ] N (*of person, action*) consecuencia *f*, lógica *f*; coherencia *f*; (*density*) consistencia *f*.

consistent [kən'sɪstənt] ADJ *person, action, argument* consecuente, lógico; coherente; *pupil, results* constante; (*dense*) consistente; **to be ~ with** ser consecuente con, estar de acuerdo con, ser compatible con.

consistently [kən'sɪstəntlɪ] ADV (*logically*) consecuentemente; (*all the time*) constantemente; **to act ~** obrar con consecuencia.

consolation [,kɒnsə'leɪʃən] N consuelo *m*; (*act*) consolación *f*; **~ goal** tanto *m* del honor; **~ prize** premio *m* de consolación, (*academic etc*) accésit *m*; **it is some ~ to know that** ... me reconforta saber que ...; **if it's any ~ to you** si te consuela de algún modo.

consolatory [kən'sɒlətərɪ] ADJ consolador.

console¹ [kən'səʊl] VT consolar.

console² ['kɒnsəʊl] N (*Mus, Tech etc*) consola *f*.

consolidate [kən'sɒlɪdeɪt] [1] VT consolidar; concentrar; fortalecer.
[2] VI consolidarse.

consolidated [kən'sɒlɪdeɪtɪd] ADJ consolidado; **~ accounts** cuentas *fpl* consolidadas; **~ balance sheet** hoja *f* de balance consolidado; **~ fund** fondo *m* consolidado.

consolidation [kən,sɒlɪ'deɪʃən] N consolidación *f*; concentración *f*; fortalecimiento *m*.

consoling [kən'səʊlɪŋ] ADJ consolador, reconfortante.

consols ['kɒnsɒlz] NPL valores *mpl* consolidados.

consommé [kən'sɒmeɪ] N consomé *m*, caldo *m*.

consonance ['kɒnsənəns] N consonancia *f*.

consonant ['kɒnsənənt] [1] ADJ consonante; **~ with** de acuerdo con, conforme a.
[2] N consonante *f*.

consonantal [,kɒnsə'næntl] ADJ consonántico.

consort [1] ['kɒnsɔːt] N consorte *mf*; **prince ~** príncipe *m* consorte *m*.
[2] [kən'sɔːt] VI: **to ~ with** ir con, asociarse con; (*agree*) concordar con.

consortium [kən'sɔːtɪəm] N consorcio *m*.

conspectus [kən'spektəs] N vista *f* general, ojeada *f* general; resumen *m*.

conspicuous [kən'spɪkjʊəs] ADJ visible, llamativo, que sobresale; (*fig*) destacado, sobresaliente; notable; **~ consumption** consumo *m* ostentoso; **to be ~** destacar(se); **to make o.s. ~** llamar la atención; singularizarse; *V* **absence**.

conspicuously [kən'spɪkjʊəslɪ] ADV visiblemente, claramente; de modo que llama la atención; (*fig*) notablemente.

conspiracy [kən'spɪrəsɪ] N conspiración *f*, conjuración *f*, complot *m*; **~ of silence** conspiración *f* de silencio.

conspiracy theory [kən'spɪrəsɪ'θɪərɪ] N teoría *f* conspiratoria, teoría *f* conspiracional.

➤ LANGUAGE IN USE: **consequence** → 2.3 **consider: 1c** → 26.1 **1d** → 26.1 **1e** → 8.4

conspirator [kən'spɪrətəʳ] N conspirador *m*, -ora *f*.
conspiratorial [kən,spɪrə'tɔːrɪəl] ADJ de conspirador.
conspiratorially [kən,spɪrə'tɔːrɪəlɪ] ADV *behave* con complicidad.
conspire [kən'spaɪəʳ] VI conspirar (*against* contra, *with* con, *to* + *infin* para + *infin*).
constable ['kʌnstəbl] N (*Brit*) policía *m*, guardia *m*.
constabulary [kən'stæbjʊlərɪ] N (*Brit*) policía *f*.
Constance ['kɒnstəns] NF Constanza.
constancy ['kɒnstənsɪ] N constancia *f*; fidelidad *f*.
constant ['kɒnstənt] [1] ADJ (**a**) (*unending*) constante, continuo, incesante. (**b**) (*faithful*) constante; fiel, leal; *reader etc* asiduo.
   [2] N constante *f*.
Constantine ['kɒnstəntaɪn] NM Constantine.
Constantinople [,kɒnstæntɪ'nəʊpl] N Constantinopla *f*.
constantly ['kɒnstəntlɪ] ADV constantemente.
constellation [,kɒnstə'leɪʃən] N constelación *f*.
consternation [,kɒnstə'neɪʃən] N consternación *f*; **in ~** consternado; **there was general ~** se consternaron todos.
constipate ['kɒnstɪpeɪt] VT estreñir; **to be ~d** estar estreñido.
constipation [,kɒnstɪ'peɪʃən] N estreñimiento *m*.
constituency [kən'stɪtjʊənsɪ] N distrito *m* electoral, circunscripción *f*.

┌─── **CONSTITUENCY** ───┐

ⓘ **Constituency** *es la denominación que recibe un distrito o circunscripción electoral y el grupo de electores registrados en ella, en el sistema electoral británico. Cada circunscripción elige a un diputado (**Member of Parliament**), que se halla disponible para las consultas y peticiones de sus electores durante ciertas horas a la semana, tiempo que se llama* **surgery***.*
⇨ *Ver también* MARGINAL SEAT , BY-ELECTION

constituency party [kən'stɪtjʊənsɪ'pɑːtɪ] N partido *m* local.
constituent [kən'stɪtjʊənt] [1] ADJ constitutivo, integrante; **~ assembly** cortes *fpl* constituyentes.
   [2] N constitutivo *m*, componente *m*; (*Pol*) elector *m*, -ora *f*.
constitute ['kɒnstɪtjuːt] [1] VT constituir; (*make up*) componer, integrar.
   [2] VR: **to ~ o.s. a judge** constituirse en juez.
constitution [,kɒnstɪ'tjuːʃən] N constitución *f*.

┌─── **CONSTITUTION** ───┐

ⓘ *El Reino Unido no tiene una constitución escrita. La Constitución británica está compuesta por el derecho legislado en el Parlamento (**statute law**) y por el derecho consuetudinario (**common law**), además de aquellas normas y prácticas necesarias para el funcionamiento del Gobierno. Las leyes constitucionales pueden ser modificadas o derogadas por el Parlamento como cualquier otra ley.*
⇨ *Ver también* ACT OF PARLIAMENT , COMMON LAW

constitutional [,kɒnstɪ'tjuːʃənl] [1] ADJ constitucional; **~ law** derecho *m* político.
   [2] N paseo *m*.
constitutionality [,kɒnstɪtjuːʃə'nælɪtɪ] N constitucionalidad *f*.
constitutionally [,kɒnstɪ'tjuːʃənəlɪ] ADV según la constitución.
constrain [kən'streɪn] VT: **to ~ sb to do sth** obligar a uno a hacer algo; **to feel ~ed to do sth** verse en la necesidad de hacer algo.
constrained [kən'streɪnd] ADJ *atmosphere* constrictivo; *voice, manner, smile* constreñido.
constraint [kən'streɪnt] N (*compulsion*) fuerza *f*; (*confinement*) encierro *m*; (*restraint*) reserva *f*, (*of atmosphere*) frialdad *f*; **budgetary ~s** restricciones *fpl* presupuestarias; **under ~** obligado (a ello); **to feel a certain ~** sentirse algo cohibido.
constrict [kən'strɪkt] VT apretar, estrechar.
constricted [kən'strɪktɪd] ADJ *space* limitado, reducido; *freedom, movement* restringido; (*Phon*) constrictivo; **to feel ~** (*by clothes etc*) sentirse constreñido; **I feel ~ by these regulations** me siento constreñido por estas reglas.
constricting [kən'strɪktɪŋ] ADJ *dress, ideology* estrecho.
constriction [kən'strɪkʃən] N constricción *f*.
constrictive [kən'strɪktɪv] = **constricting**.
constrictor [kən'strɪktəʳ] N constrictor *f*.
construct [1] [kən'strʌkt] VT construir.
   [2] ['kɒnstrʌkt]
construction [kən'strʌkʃən] N (**a**) (*act*) construcción *f*; (*building*) construcción *f*, edificio *m*; **~ company** compañía *f* constructora; **~ engineer** ingeniero *m* de construcción; **~ industry** industria *f* de la construcción; **in course of ~, under ~** en construcción. (**b**) (*interpretation*) interpretación *f*; **to put a wrong ~ on sth** interpretar algo mal; **it depends what ~ one places on his words** depende de cómo se interpreten sus palabras. (**c**) (*Gram*) construcción *f*.
constructional [kən'strʌkʃənl] ADJ estructural; **~ toy** juguete *m* con que se construyen modelos.

constructive [kən'strʌktɪv] ADJ constructivo; positivo.
constructively [kən'strʌktɪvlɪ] ADV constructivamente.
constructivism [kən'strʌktɪvɪzəm] N constructivismo *m*.
constructivist [kən'strʌktɪvɪst] [1] ADJ constructivista.
   [2] N constructivista *mf*.
constructor [kən'strʌktəʳ] N constructor *m*.
construe [kən'struː] VT interpretar; (*Gram*) construir; analizar.
consul ['kɒnsəl] N cónsul *mf*; **~ general** cónsul *mf* general.
consular ['kɒnsjʊləʳ] ADJ consular.
consulate ['kɒnsjʊlɪt] N consulado *m*.
consulship ['kɒnsəlʃɪp] N consulado *m*.
consult [kən'sʌlt] [1] VT consultar; *one's interests* tener en cuenta.
   [2] VI: **people should ~ more** la gente debiera consultar más entre sí; **to ~ together** (*US*) consultar entre sí; **to ~ with** (*US*) consultar con, aconsejarse con.
consultancy [kən'sʌltənsɪ] N (*Comm*) consultoría *f*, asesoría *f*; (*Med*) puesto *m* de especialista; **~ fees** (*Comm*) derechos *mpl* de asesoría; (*Med*) derechos *mpl* de consulta.
consultant [kən'sʌltənt] N consultor *m*, -ora *f*; asesor *m*, -ora *f*; (*Tech*) consejero *m* técnico, consejera *f* técnica; (*Brit Med*) especialista *mf*; **to act as ~** asesorar; **~ engineer** ingeniero *m* consejero; **~ physician** médico *mf* especialista; **~ psychiatrist** psiquiatra *mf* especialista.
consultation [,kɒnsəl'teɪʃən] N (*act*) consulta *f*; (*meeting*) consulta *f*, consultación *f*.
consultative [kən'sʌltətɪv] ADJ consultivo; **~ document** documento *m* consultivo; **I was there in a ~ capacity** yo estuve en calidad de asesor.
consulting-hours [kən'sʌltɪŋ,aʊəz] NPL (*Brit*) horas *fpl* de consulta.
consulting-room [kən'sʌltɪŋrʊm] N (*Brit*) consultorio *m*, consulta *f*.
consumable [kən'sjuːməbl] ADJ (*Econ etc*) consumible; **~ goods** bienes *mpl* consumibles, artículos *mpl* de consumo.
consumables [kən'sjuːməblz] NPL artículos *mpl* de consumo.
consume [kən'sjuːm] VT (*eat*) comer(se), (*drink*) beber(se); (*use*) consumir, utilizar; (*by fire etc*) consumir; **the house was ~d by fire** la casa quedó arrasada por el fuego; **to be ~d with** *envy etc* estar muerto de.
consumer [kən'sjuːməʳ] [1] N consumidor *m*, -ora *f*.
   [2] ATTR consumista; **~ behavior** (*US*), **~ behaviour** comportamiento *m* del consumidor; **~ choice** libertad *f* del consumidor para elegir; **~ credit** crédito *m* al consumidor; **~ demand** demanda *f* de consumo; **~ durables** artículos *mpl* de equipo; **~ goods** bienes *mpl* de consumo; **~ price index** índice *m* de precios al consumo, IPC *m*; **~ product** producto *m* al consumidor; **~ protection** protección *f* al consumidor; **~ research** estudio *m* de mercado; **~ resistance** resistencia *f* por parte del consumidor; **~ rights** derechos *mpl* del consumidor; **~ sampling** muestreo *m* del consumidor; **~ sector** sector *m* consumista; **~ society** sociedad *f* de consumo; **~ survey** encuesta *f* sobre consumidores.
consumerism [kən'sjuːmərɪzəm] N consumismo *m*; defensa *f* del consumidor.
consuming [kən'sjuːmɪŋ] ADJ arrollador, apasionado; *passion* dominante, avasallador.
consummate [1] [kən'sʌmɪt] ADJ consumado, completo; *skill* sumo.
   [2] ['kɒnsʌmeɪt] VT consumar.
consummation [,kɒnsʌ'meɪʃən] N consumación *f*.
consumption [kən'sʌmpʃən] N (**a**) consumo *m*. (**b**) (*Med*) tisis *f*.
consumptive [kən'sʌmptɪv] [1] ADJ tísico.
   [2] N tísico *m*, -a *f*.
cont. ABBR *of* **continued** continuación *f*, sigue.
▼ **contact** ['kɒntækt] [1] N contacto *m*; **business ~s** relaciones *fpl* comerciales; **he rang up one of his business ~s** llamó a uno de sus colegas comerciales; **he has a lot of ~s** tiene muchas relaciones, (*pej*) tiene muchos enchufes, tiene buenas aldabas; **you have to have a ~ in the business** hay que tener un buen enchufe en el negocio; **to come into ~ with** tocar, (*violently*) chocar con, (*fig*) tener que ver con, tratar; **to get into ~ with** ponerse en contacto con; **to lose ~ with sb** perder el contacto con uno; **to make ~ with sb** lograr contactar con uno; **I seem to make no ~ with him** me resulta imposible comunicar con él.
▼ [2] VT contactar (con), ponerse en contacto con, comunicar con.
contact-breaker ['kɒntækt,breɪkəʳ] N (*Elec*) interruptor *m*.
contact-lens ['kɒntækt,lenz] N lente *f* de contacto, (micro)lentilla *f*.
contact-man ['kɒntæktmæn] N, PL **contact-men** ['kɒntæktmen] intermediario *m*.
contact-print ['kɒntæktprɪnt] N contact *m*.
contagion [kən'teɪdʒən] N contagio *m*.
contagious [kən'teɪdʒəs] ADJ contagioso.
contain [kən'teɪn] [1] VT contener; (*Math*) ser exactamente divisible por.
   [2] VR: **to ~ o.s.** contenerse, contener la risa (*etc*).
container [kən'teɪnəʳ] N (**a**) recipiente *m*, receptáculo *m*; (*box*) caja *f*; (*wrapper etc*) envase *m*. (**b**) (*Naut, Rail etc*) contenedor *m*, contáiner *m*; **~ depot, ~ terminal** terminal *f* para portacontenedores; **~ ship** bu-

que *m* contenedor, portacontenedores *m*; ~ **train** tren *m* de contenedores; ~ **transport** transporte *m* por contenedor.

containerization [kən,teɪnəraɪˈzeɪʃən] N contenerización *f*.

containerize [kənˈteɪnəraɪz] VT contenerizar, transportar en contenedores.

containment [kənˈteɪnmənt] N (*Pol*) contención *f*.

contaminant [kənˈtæmɪnənt] N contaminante *m*.

contaminate [kənˈtæmɪneɪt] VT contaminar; **to be ~d by** contaminarse con (*or* de).

contamination [kən,tæmɪˈneɪʃən] N contaminación *f*.

contango [kənˈtæŋgəʊ] N (*St Ex*) aplazamiento *m* de pago hasta el próximo día de ajuste de cuentas.

contd ABBR *of* **continued** continuación *f*, sigue.

contemplate [ˈkɒntempleɪt] VT (a) (*gaze on*) contemplar; **I ~ the future with misgiving** el futuro lo veo dudoso.
(b) (*expect*) contar con.
(c) (*intend*) pensar, intentar, proyectar; **he ~d suicide** pensó suicidarse; **we ~ a holiday in Spain** proyectamos unas vacaciones en España; **when do you ~ doing it?** ¿cuándo se propone hacerlo?, ¿cuándo tiene intención de hacerlo?

contemplation [,kɒntemˈpleɪʃən] N contemplación *f*.

contemplative [kənˈtemplətɪv] ADJ contemplativo.

contemplatively [kənˈtemplətɪvlɪ] ADV pensativamente.

contemporaneous [kən,tempəˈreɪnɪəs] ADJ contemporáneo.

contemporaneously [kən,tempəˈreɪnɪəslɪ] ADV contemporáneamente.

contemporary [kənˈtempərərɪ] [1] ADJ contemporáneo, coetáneo. [2] N contemporáneo *m*, -a *f*, coetáneo *m*, -a *f*.

contempt [kənˈtempt] N desprecio *m*; ~ **of court** desacato *m* al juez (*or* al tribunal), rebeldía *f*; **beneath** ~ despreciable; **to bring into** ~ desprestigiar, envilecer; **to hold in** ~ despreciar, (*Jur*) declarar en rebeldía.

contemptible [kənˈtemptəbl] ADJ despreciable, vil.

contemptuous [kənˈtemptjʊəs] ADJ desdeñoso, despectivo; **to be ~ of** desdeñar, menospreciar.

contemptuously [kənˈtemptjʊəslɪ] ADV desdeñosamente, con desprecio.

contend [kənˈtend] [1] VT afirmar, sostener (*that* que). [2] VI contender, luchar; **to ~ with sb for sth** contender con uno sobre algo; **we have many problems to ~ with** se nos plantean muchos problemas.

contender [kənˈtendər] N contendiente *mf*.

contending [kənˈtendɪŋ] ADJ rival, opuesto.

content¹ [kənˈtent] [1] ADJ contento (*with* con), satisfecho (*with* de); **to be ~** estar contento; **he was ~ to stay there** estaba contento de seguir allí. [2] N contento *m*, satisfacción *f*; **to one's heart's** ~ a gusto, a más no poder, hasta quedarse satisfecho. [3] VT contentar, satisfacer. [4] VR: **to ~ o.s.** contentarse (*with sth* con algo, *with saying* con decir).

content² [ˈkɒntent] N contenido *m*; **~s** contenido *m*; (*of book: heading*) índice *m* de materias.

contented [kənˈtentɪd] ADJ satisfecho, contento.

contentedly [kənˈtentɪdlɪ] ADV con satisfacción, contentamente.

contentedness [kənˈtentɪdnɪs] N contento *m*.

contention [kənˈtenʃən] N (a) (*strife*) contienda *f*; **teams in** ~ equipos *mpl* rivales. (b) (*point*) argumento *m*, aseveración *f*, pretensión *f*; **it is our ~ that ...** pretendemos que ..., sostenemos que ....

contentious [kənˈtenʃəs] ADJ contencioso, conflictivo, discutible.

contentment [kənˈtentmənt] N contento *m*.

contest [1] [ˈkɒntest] N (*struggle*) contienda *f*, lucha *f*; (*competition*) concurso *m*, prueba *f*. [2] [kənˈtest] VT (*dispute*) impugnar, atacar; *legal suit* defender; *election* ser candidato en; *seat* disputar, presentarse como candidato a; **I your right to do that** niego que Vd tenga el derecho de hacer eso; **the seat was not ~ed** en las elecciones se presentó un solo candidato. [3] [kənˈtest] VI: **to ~ against** contender con; **they are ~ing for a big prize** se disputan un premio importante.

contestant [kənˈtestənt] N contendiente *mf*, contrincante *m*; (*Sport, competition etc*) concursante *mf*, aspirante *mf*.

context [ˈkɒntekst] N contexto *m*; **to put sth in** ~ explicar el contexto de algo; **we must see this in** ~ tenemos que ver esto en su contexto; **it was taken out of** ~ fue arrancado de su contexto.

contextual [kɒnˈtekstjʊəl] ADJ contextual.

contextualize [kənˈtekstjʊəlaɪz] VT contextualizar.

contiguity [ˈkɒntɪgjuːɪtɪ] N contigüidad *f*.

contiguous [kənˈtɪgjʊəs] ADJ contiguo (*to* a).

continence [ˈkɒntɪnəns] N continencia *f*.

continent [ˈkɒntɪnənt] [1] ADJ continente. [2] N continente *m*; **the C~** (*Brit*) el continente europeo; **on the C~** (*Brit*) en Europa (continental).

continental [,kɒntɪˈnentl] [1] ADJ continental; ~ **breakfast** desayuno *m* continental; ~ **climate** clima *m* continental; ~ **drift** deriva *f* continental; ~ **quilt** edredón *m*; ~ **shelf** plataforma *f* continental. [2] N (*Brit*) europeo *m*, -a *f* (continental).

contingency [kənˈtɪndʒənsɪ] N contingencia *f*; ~ **fund** fondo *m* para imprevistos; ~ **planning** planificación *f* para una eventual emergencia; ~ **plans** medidas *fpl* de prevención; **should the ~ arise** por si acaso; **to provide for every** ~ tener en cuenta todas las posibilidades; **£50 for contingencies** 50 libras para gastos imprevistos.

contingent [kənˈtɪndʒənt] [1] ADJ contingente, eventual; **to be ~ upon** depender de. [2] N contingente *m*.

continual [kənˈtɪnjʊəl] ADJ continuo, constante.

continually [kənˈtɪnjʊəlɪ] ADV constantemente.

continuance [kənˈtɪnjʊəns] N continuación *f* (*also St Ex*); (*stay*) permanencia *f*.

continuation [kən,tɪnjʊˈeɪʃən] N continuación *f*; (*lengthening*) prolongación *f*.

continue [kənˈtɪnjuː] [1] VT continuar; seguir; *story etc* proseguir; (*retain*) mantener (*in a post* en un puesto); (*lengthen*) prolongar; **~d on page 10** sigue en la página 10; **'to be ~d'** (*serial*) 'continuará', 'seguirá'. [2] VI continuar; seguir; (*extend*) prolongarse; **to ~ talking, to ~ to talk** seguir hablando; **to ~ on one's way** seguir su camino; **to ~ in office** seguir en su puesto; **to ~ in a place** seguir en un sitio.

continuing [kənˈtɪnjʊɪŋ] ADJ *argument* irresoluto; *correspondence* continuado; ~ **education** cursos de enseñanza para adultos.

continuity [,kɒntɪˈnjuːɪtɪ] N continuidad *f* (*also Cine*); ~ **girl**, ~ **man** secretaria *f*, -o *m* de continuidad.

continuo [kənˈtɪnjʊəʊ] N continuo *m*.

continuous [kənˈtɪnjʊəs] ADJ continuo; ~ **assessment** evaluación *f* continua; ~ **inventory** inventario *m* continuo; ~ **(feed) paper**, ~ **stationery** papel *m* continuo.

continuously [kənˈtɪnjʊəslɪ] ADV continuamente.

continuum [kənˈtɪnjʊəm] N continuo *m*.

contort [kənˈtɔːt] VT retorcer, deformar.

contortion [kənˈtɔːʃən] N contorsión *f*.

contortionist [kənˈtɔːʃənɪst] N contorsionista *mf*.

contour [ˈkɒntʊər] N contorno *m*; ~ **flying** vuelo *m* rasante; ~ **line** isohipsa *f*, curva *f* de nivel; ~ **map** mapa *m* hipsométrico, plano *m* acotado.

contoured [ˈkɒntʊəd] ADJ *surface* contorneado.

contra... [ˈkɒntrə] PREF contra...

contraband [ˈkɒntrəbænd] [1] N contrabando *m*. [2] ATTR de contrabando.

contrabass [,kɒntrəˈbeɪs] N contrabajo *m*.

contrabassoon [,kɒntrəbəˈsuːn] N contrafagot *m*.

contraception [,kɒntrəˈsepʃən] N contracepción *f*.

contraceptive [,kɒntrəˈseptɪv] [1] ADJ anticonceptivo, anticoncepcional, contraceptivo; ~ **pill** píldora *f* anticonceptiva. [2] N anticonceptivo *m*, contraceptivo *m*.

contract [1] [ˈkɒntrækt] N contrato *m* (*for* de); (*for public works, Theat, etc*) contrata *f*; ~ **bridge** bridge-contrato *m*; ~ **of employment** contrato *m* de trabajo; ~ **killer** asesino *m* contratado, asesino *m* a sueldo; ~ **price** precio *m* contractual; ~ **work** trabajo *m* bajo contrato; **they are under** ~ **to X** tienen contrato con X, tienen obligaciones contractuales con X; **to enter into a** ~ hacer un contrato (*with* con); **to place a** ~ **with** dar un contrato a; **to put work out to** ~ ofrecer trabajo bajo contrato fuera de la empresa; **there's a ~ out for him*** le han puesto precio a su cabeza. [2] [kənˈtrækt] VT contraer. [3] [kənˈtrækt] VI (a) (*become smaller*) contraerse, encogerse. (b) **to ~ to do sth** comprometerse por contrato a hacer algo; **to ~ for** contratar.
◆**contract in** VI optar por tomar parte.
◆**contract out** [1] VT: **this work is ~ed out** este trabajo se hace fuera de la empresa bajo contrato. [2] VI optar por no tomar parte (*of* en).

contracting [kənˈtræktɪŋ] ADJ: ~ **party** contratante *mf*.

contraction [kənˈtrækʃən] N contracción *f* (*in, of* de).

contractor [kənˈtræktər] N contratista *mf*.

contractual [kənˈtræktʃʊəl] ADJ contractual; ~ **liability** responsabilidad *f* contractual; ~ **obligation** obligación *f* contractual.

contractually [kənˈtræktʃʊəlɪ] ADV contractualmente, por contrato; **a ~ binding agreement** un acuerdo vinculante según contrato; **we are ~ bound to finish it** estamos obligados por contrato a terminarlo.

▼ **contradict** [,kɒntrəˈdɪkt] VT contradecir; (*deny*) desmentir; **don't ~ me!** ¡no repliques!

contradiction [,kɒntrəˈdɪkʃən] N contradicción *f*; ~ **in terms** contradicción *f* en los términos.

contradictory [,kɒntrəˈdɪktərɪ] ADJ contradictorio.

contradistinction [,kɒntrədɪsˈtɪŋkʃən] N: **in ~ to** a diferencia de.

➤ LANGUAGE IN USE: **contradict** → 12.1

contraflow ['kɒntrəfləʊ] N: ~ **system** sistema *m* de contracorriente.
contraindication [,kɒntrə,ɪndɪ'keɪʃən] N contraindicación *f*.
contralto [kən'træltəʊ] [1] N (*person*) contralto *f*; (*voice*) contralto *m*. [2] ADJ de contralto.
contraption [kən'træpʃən] N dispositivo *m*, ingenio *m*, artilugio *m*; (*vehicle*) armatoste *m*.
contrapuntal [,kɒntrə'pʌntl] ADJ de contrapunto.
contrarian [kən'treəriən] (*frm*) [1] ADJ inconformista. [2] N inconformista *mf*.
contrarily [kən'treərɪlɪ] ADV tercamente.
contrariness [kən'treərɪnɪs] N terquedad *f*.
contrariwise [kən'treərɪwaɪz] ADV al contrario; por otra parte; a la inversa.
contrary¹ ['kɒntrərɪ] [1] ADJ contrario (*to* a); **in a ~ direction** en dirección contraria.
[2] ADV: ~ **to** contrario a; ~ **to what we had thought** al contrario de lo que habíamos pensado.
[3] N contrario *m*; **the ~ seems to be the case** parece que es al revés; **he holds the ~** él sostiene lo contrario; **quite the ~** muy al contrario; **on the ~** al contrario; **I know nothing to the ~** yo no sé nada en contrario; **unless we hear to the ~** a no ser que nos digan lo contrario.
contrary² [kən'treərɪ] ADJ terco, que siempre lleva la contraria.
▼ **contrast** [1] ['kɒntrɑːst] N contraste *m* (*between* entre, *to, with* con); **in ~** por contraste; **in ~ to** por contraste con, a diferencia de; **to form a ~ to** (*or* **with**) contrastar con.
[2] [kən'trɑːst] VT poner en contraste (*with* con), comparar.
[3] [kən'trɑːst] VI contrastar (*with* con), hacer contraste (*with* con).
contrasting [kən'trɑːstɪŋ] ADJ opuesto.
contravene [,kɒntrə'viːn] VT *law* contravenir a; (*dispute*) oponerse a.
contravention [,kɒntrə'venʃən] N contravención *f*.
contretemps ['kɔ̃ːntrətɑ̃ːŋ] N contratiempo *m*, revés *m*.
contribute [kən'trɪbjuːt] [1] VT contribuir, aportar (*esp LAm*) (*to* a); *article* escribir (*to* para); *aid* prestar; *facts, information etc* aportar.
[2] VI contribuir (*to, towards* a); **to ~ to** + *ger* contribuir + *infin*; **to ~ to a journal** colaborar en una revista; **to ~ to a discussion** intervenir en una discusión; **it all ~d to the muddle** todo sirvió para aumentar la confusión.
contribution [,kɒntrɪ'bjuːʃən] N contribución *f*; (*money*) donativo *m*, cuota *f*; (*salary deduction*) cotización *f*; (*to journal*) artículo *m*, colaboración *f*; (*to discussion*) intervención *f*; (*of information etc*) aportación *f*.
contributor [kən'trɪbjʊtər] N donante *mf*; (*to journal*) colaborador *m*, -ora *f* (*to* en).
contributory [kən'trɪbjʊtərɪ] ADJ contributivo; *factor, negligence* que contribuye; ~ **pension** pensión *f* contributiva; ~ **pension scheme** plan *m* cotizable de jubilación.
contrite ['kɒntraɪt] ADJ arrepentido, contrito.
contritely ['kɒntraɪtlɪ] ADV *say etc* en tono arrepentido.
contrition [kən'trɪʃən] N arrepentimiento *m*.
contrivance [kən'traɪvəns] N (*scheme*) treta *f*, estratagema *f*; (*invention*) invención *f*; (*Mech*) aparato *m*, invento *m*, dispositivo *m*, artilugio *m*.
contrive [kən'traɪv] [1] VT (*invent*) inventar, idear; (*bring about*) efectuar; (*plot*) tramar.
[2] VI: **to ~ to** + *infin* lograr que + *subj*, ingeniárselas a + *infin* (*or* para + *infin*).
contrived [kən'traɪvd] ADJ artificial; efectista.
control [kən'trəʊl] [1] N (**a**) (*command*) control *m*, mando *m*, gobierno *m*, dirección *f*; (*of car etc*) control *m*, conducción *f*; ~ **of the seas** dominio *m* de los mares; **for reasons beyond** (*or* **outside**) **our ~** por causas ajenas a nuestra voluntad; **to be in ~** mandar, tener el mando; **to be out of ~** estar fuera de control; **to be under ~** estar bajo control; **to be under private ~** estar en manos de particulares; **to get out of ~** desmandarse; **to get under ~** conseguir dominar; **she has no ~ over the children** no tiene autoridad sobre los niños; **causes over which the vendor has no ~** causas respecto a las cuales nada puede el vendedor, causas ajenas a la voluntad del vendedor; **to lose ~ of** perder el control de; **to lose ~ of o.s.** perder el control, perder los estribos.
(**b**) (*Mech*) control *m*; ~**s** (*Aer etc*) mando *m*, aparatos *mpl* de mando; **the Prince is at the ~s** el Príncipe está a los mandos.
(**c**) (*check*) freno *m* (*on* para).
(**d**) (*self-restraint*) dominio *m* de (*or* sobre) sí mismo.
(**e**) (*in experiment*) grupo *m* (de) control, norma *f* de comprobación.
[2] ATTR: ~ **column** palanca *f* de mando; ~ **engineering** ingeniería *f* de control; **he's a total ~ freak*** tiene la manía de controlarlo todo; ~ **group** grupo *m* (de) control; ~ **key** tecla *f* de control; ~ **knob** botón *m* de mando; ~ **panel** tablero *m* de mando; ~ **point** punto *m* de control; ~ **room** sala *f* de control, sala *f* de mando; ~ **system** sistema *m* de control; ~ **tower** torre *f* de control; ~ **unit** unidad *f* de control.

[3] VT (*command*) controlar, mandar, gobernar; *traffic, business* dirigir; *price* controlar; (*Mech*) regular, controlar; *car etc* manejar; *immigration* regular; *outbreak of disease, fire* dominar; *animal* hacerse obedecer por, imponer su autoridad a; *emotion* contener; *temper* dominar, refrenar.
[4] VR: **to ~ o.s.** dominarse, sobreponerse; ~ **yourself!** ¡domínese!, ¡cálmese!
controlled [kən'trəʊld] ADJ *emotion* contenido; *voice* sereno, que no revela la emoción; ~ **drugs** medicamentos que se expiden únicamente con receta médica; ~ **economy** economía *f* controlada; ~ **explosion** explosión *f* controlada.
-controlled [kən'trəʊld] ADJ: *eg* **a Labour~ council** un ayuntamiento laborista; **a government~ organization** una organización bajo control gubernamental; **computer~ equipment** equipo *m* computerizado.
controller [kən'trəʊlər] N director *m*, -ora *f*; inspector *m*, -ora *f*; (*Comm*) interventor *m*, -ora *f*; (*Aer*) controlador *m*, -ora *f*.
controlling [kən'trəʊlɪŋ] ADJ *interest* controlador, mayoritario.
▼ **controversial** [,kɒntrə'vɜːʃəl] ADJ discutido, debatido, polémico, controvertido, conflictivo.
controversy [kən'trɒvəsɪ] N controversia *f*.
controvert ['kɒntrəvɜːt] VT contradecir.
contumacious [,kɒntjʊ'meɪʃəs] ADJ contumaz.
contumaciously [,kɒntjʊ'meɪʃəslɪ] ADV contumazmente.
contumacy ['kɒntjʊməsɪ] N contumacia *f*.
contumely ['kɒntjʊmɪlɪ] N contumelia *f*.
contusion [kən'tjuːʒən] N contusión *f*.
conundrum [kə'nʌndrəm] N acertijo *m*, adivinanza *f*; (*fig*) problema *m*; enigma *m*.
conurbation [,kɒnɜː'beɪʃən] N conurbación *f*.
convalesce [,kɒnvə'les] VI convalecer.
convalescence [,kɒnvə'lesəns] N convalecencia *f*.
convalescent [,kɒnvə'lesənt] [1] ADJ convaleciente.
[2] N convaleciente *mf*; ~ **home** clínica *f* de reposo.
convection [kən'vekʃən] N convección *f*.
convector [kən'vektər] N (*also* ~ **heater**) convector *m*, calentador *m* de convección.
convene [kən'viːn] [1] VT convocar.
[2] VI reunirse.
convener, convenor [kən'viːnər] N (*of meeting*) organizador *m*, -ora *f*; (*of committee*) presidente *mf* (de comisión); (*of shop stewards*) jefe *mf*, presidente *mf*.
convenience [kən'viːniəns] N (**a**) comodidad *f*; conveniencia *f*; (*advantage*) ventaja *f*; ~ **foods** platos *mpl* preparados; comidas *fpl* en el acto; **at your ~** cuando te venga bien; **at your earliest ~** con la mayor brevedad, tan pronto como le sea posible; **for your ~ an envelope is enclosed** para facilitar su contestación adjuntamos un sobre; **it is a great ~ to be so close** resulta muy práctico estar tan cerca; **to make a ~ of** abusar de (la amabilidad de).
(**b**) (*Brit*) (**public**) ~(s) aseos *mpl* públicos; **a house with all modern** ~s una casa con todas las comodidades; '**all mod. cons**' 'todo confort'.
convenient [kən'viːniənt] ADJ (**a**) cómodo; *tool etc* práctico, útil; *place* accesible, céntrico; **it is ~ to live here** resulta práctico vivir aquí; **her death was certainly ~ for him** es cierto que su muerte fue oportuna para él; **we looked for a ~ place to stop** buscamos un sitio apropiado para parar; **he put it on a ~ chair** lo puso en una silla que estaba a mano.
(**b**) (*of time*) oportuno; **at a ~ moment** en un momento oportuno; **when it is ~ for you** cuando te venga bien; **would tomorrow be ~?** ¿te conviene mañana?
conveniently [kən'viːniəntlɪ] ADV con comodidad, cómodamente; oportunamente; **the house is ~ situated** la casa está en un sitio muy práctico; **it fell ~ close** cayó muy cerca; **when you ~ can do so** cuando puedas hacerlo sin inconveniente.
convenor [kən'viːnər] N = **convener**.
convent ['kɒnvənt] N convento *m* (de monjas); ~ **school** ≃ escuela *f* de monjas.
convention [kən'venʃən] N (*agreement*) convenio *m*, convención *f*; (*meeting*) asamblea *f*, congreso *m*.
conventional [kən'venʃənl] ADJ convencional.
conventionalism [kən'venʃənəlɪzəm] N convencionalismo *m*.
conventionally [kən'venʃənəlɪ] ADV de manera convencional, de manera tradicional; **they went back to more ~ acceptable ways of life** retornaron a estilos de vida más aceptables desde el punto de vista tradicional; ~ **educated students** los estudiantes educados a la manera tradicional.
conventioneer [kən,venʃə'nɪər] N (*esp US*) asistente *mf* a un congreso, congresista *mf*.
converge [kən'vɜːdʒ] VI convergir (*on* en); **to ~ on** (*persons*) dirigirse todos a.
convergence [kən'vɜːdʒəns] N convergencia *f*.
convergent [kən'vɜːdʒənt] ADJ, **converging** [kən'vɜːdʒɪŋ] ADJ

convergente.

conversant [kən'vɜːsənt] ADJ: ~ **with** versado en, enterado de; **to become ~ with** familiarizarse con, informarse sobre.

conversation [ˌkɒnvə'seɪʃən] N conversación f; ~ **piece** (Art) cuadro m de conversación; (Liter) conversación f, diálogo m; **I said it just to make ~** lo dije sólo por decir algo; **that was a ~ stopper*** aquello dejó a todos sin habla*.

conversational [ˌkɒnvə'seɪʃənl] ADJ tone conversacional, familiar; person locuaz, hablador; **he's not very ~** no es amigo de la conversación; ~ **mode** modo m de conversación.

conversationalist [ˌkɒnvə'seɪʃnəlɪst] N: **to be a good ~** brillar en la conversación, resultar simpático charlando; **he's not much of a ~** tiene poco que decir, no le gusta hablar mucho en las conversaciones.

conversationally [ˌkɒnvə'seɪʃnəlɪ] ADV en tono familiar.

converse¹ ['kɒnvɜːs] [1] ADJ contrario, inverso; (Logic) recíproco.
[2] N (Math) inversa f; (Logic) teorema m recíproco; **but the ~ is true** pero la verdad es al revés.

converse² [kən'vɜːs] VI conversar, hablar (with con); **to ~ by signs** hablar por señas.

conversely [kɒn'vɜːslɪ] ADV a la inversa.

conversion [kən'vɜːʃən] N conversión f (into en, to a); (industrial) reconversión f; (Jur) apropiación f ilícita; (Rugby) transformación f; ~ **kit** equipo m de conversión; ~ **(loan) stock** obligaciones fpl convertibles; ~ **table** tabla f de equivalencias.

convert [1] ['kɒnvɜːt] N converso m, -a f; **to become a ~** convertirse.
[2] [kən'vɜːt] VT convertir (also Eccl, Fin; into a, en, to a), transformar (into en); industry reconvertir; house reformar, modificar; (Jur) apropiarse ilícitamente (to one's own use para uso propio); (Sport) penalty, try transformar.
[3] [kən'vɜːt] VI convertirse (to a).

converter [kən'vɜːtəʳ] N (Elec, Metal) convertidor m.

convertibility [kənˌvɜːtə'bɪlɪtɪ] N convertibilidad f.

convertible [kən'vɜːtəbl] [1] ADJ convertible; car descapotable; ~ **debenture** obligación f convertible; ~ **loan stock** obligaciones fpl convertibles.
[2] N (US) descapotable m.

convertor [kən'vɜːtəʳ] N = **converter**.

convex ['kɒn'veks] ADJ convexo.

convexity [kɒn'veksɪtɪ] N convexidad f.

convey [kən'veɪ] VT goods transportar, llevar; person llevar; sound, smell llevar; current transmitir; news comunicar; (Jur) traspasar, transferir; meaning tener, expresar (to para); **I am trying to ~ that** ... quiero dar a entender que ..., quiero sugerir que ...; **the name ~s nothing to me** el nombre no me dice nada; **what does this music ~ to you?** ¿qué es lo que esta música evoca para ti?

conveyance [kən'veɪəns] N (a) (act) transporte m; transmisión f (etc); (Jur) compra f y venta.
(b) (Jur: deed) compra f y venta.
(c) (vehicle) vehículo m, medio m de transporte; **public ~** vehículo m de servicio público.

conveyancer [kən'veɪənsəʳ] N (Brit) persona que formaliza el traspaso de la propiedad de inmuebles, ≃ notario m, -a f.

conveyancing [kən'veɪənsɪŋ] N (Jur) redacción f de escrituras de compra y venta.

conveyor [kən'veɪəʳ] N portador m, transportador m; (belt) cinta f transportadora.

conveyor-belt [kən'veɪəbelt] N cinta f transportadora.

convict [1] ['kɒnvɪkt] N presidiario m, recluso m; ~ **settlement** colonia f de presidiarios.
[2] [kən'vɪkt] VT condenar; **a ~ed murderer** un asesino convicto como tal; **to ~ sb of a crime** declarar a uno culpable de un crimen; **he was ~ed of drunken driving** fue condenado por conducir en estado de embriaguez; **to ~ sb of an error** coger a uno en una falta.

conviction [kən'vɪkʃən] N (a) (Jur) condena f; **there were 12 ~s for theft** hubo 12 condenas por robo; **to have no previous ~s** no tener antecedentes penales.
(b) (belief) creencia f, convicción f, artículo m de fe; convencimiento m; **it is my ~ that** ... tengo el convencimiento de que ...; **he said with ~** dijo con convicción.
(c) **I am open to ~** estoy dispuesto a dejarme convencer; **it carries ~** convence, es convincente.

▼ **convince** [kən'vɪns] VT convencer (of de, that de que); **I am not ~d** no estoy convencido, no me convenzo.

convinced [kən'vɪnst] ADJ Christian etc convencido, fiel, firme.

convincing [kən'vɪnsɪŋ] ADJ convincente.

convincingly [kən'vɪnsɪŋlɪ] ADV convincentemente; **to prove sth ~** probar algo de modo concluyente.

convivial [kən'vɪvɪəl] ADJ person sociable; evening alegre, festivo, atmosphere alegre.

conviviality [kənˌvɪvɪ'ælɪtɪ] N alegría f, buen humor m; compañerismo m alegre; **there was a certain amount of ~** nos divertimos

bastante, (pej) se bebió una barbaridad.

convocation [ˌkɒnvə'keɪʃən] N (act) convocación f; (meeting) asamblea f.

convoke [kən'vəuk] VT convocar.

convoluted ['kɒnvə,luːtɪd] ADJ route serpentino, lleno de recovecos; argument complicado.

convolution [ˌkɒnvə'luːʃən] N circunvolución f.

convolvulus [kən'vɒlvjuləs] N convólvulo m.

convoy ['kɒnvɔɪ] [1] N convoy m; escolta f.
[2] VT convoyar; escoltar.

convulse [kən'vʌls] VT (fig) convulsionar, sacudir; (joke etc) hacer morir de risa; **his face was ~d with pain** el dolor le crispó la cara; **to be ~d with laughter** desternillarse de risa.

convulsion [kən'vʌlʃən] N convulsión f; ~**s of laughter** paroxismo m de risa.

convulsive [kən'vʌlsɪv] ADJ convulsivo.

convulsively [kən'vʌlsɪvlɪ] ADV shake, jerk convulsivamente.

cony ['kəunɪ] N (US) conejo m.

coo¹ [kuː] VI arrullar.

coo²* [kuː] INTERJ (Brit) ¡toma!, ¡vaya!

co-occur [ˌkəuə'kɜːʳ] VI coocurrir.

co-occurrence [ˌkəuə'kʌrəns] N coocurrencia f.

cooing ['kuːɪŋ] N arrullos mpl.

cook [kuk] [1] N cocinero m, -a f; **too many ~s spoil the broth** demasiadas cocineras estropean el caldo.
[2] VT (a) (Culin) guisar, cocer, cocinar; meal preparar. (b) accounts (Brit*) falsificar.
[3] VI (food) cocer; (person) cocinar; **what's ~ing?*** ¿qué pasa?
◆ **cook up** VT (Culin) preparar; (*) excuse inventar; plan tramar.

cookbook ['kukbuk] N (US) libro m de cocina.

cooked [kukt] ADJ meats etc preparado.

cooker ['kukəʳ] N (a) (Brit: stove) cocina f; (US) olla f para cocinar. (b) (fruit) fruta f para cocer.

cookery ['kukərɪ] N cocina f, arte m de cocinar; gastronomía f; **French ~** la cocina francesa; ~ **course** curso m de cocina; **her ~ is a delight** sus platos son un encanto; **I'm no good at ~** yo no sé nada de cocina.

cookery-book ['kukərɪbuk] N libro m de cocina.

cookhouse ['kukhaus] N, PL **cookhouses** ['kuk,hauzɪz] cocina f; (Mil) cocina f móvil de campaña.

cookie ['kukɪ] N (US) (a) (biscuit) galleta f, bizcocho m (LAm); **that's the way the ~ crumbles** (US*) así es la vida; **to wait to see which way the ~ crumbles*** esperar a ver por dónde van los tiros.
(b) (‡) tipo* m, tío* m, tía* f; **she's a smart ~** es una chica lista; **a tough ~** un tío duro*.

cooking ['kukɪŋ] [1] N (a) (art) cocina f, arte m culinario; **typical Galician ~** la típica cocina gallega. (b) (act) cocción f.
[2] ATTR: ~ **apple** manzana f para cocer; ~ **foil** papel m de aluminio; ~ **salt** sal f de cocina; ~ **time** tiempo m de cocción.

cookout ['kukaut] N (US) barbacoa f, comida f al aire libre.

cookware ['kukweəʳ] N batería f de cocina.

cool [kuːl] [1] ADJ (a) (rather cold) fresco; (~ enough to drink etc) tibio, bastante frío; **it is ~** (weather) hace fresco, (object) está fresco; **to get ~(er)** refrescarse; **'to be kept in a ~ place'** 'guárdese en un sitio fresco'.
(b) (calm) tranquilo, imperturbable; **as ~ as a cucumber** más fresco que una lechuga; **to keep ~** tomarlo con la calma; **keep ~!** ¡no se alarme!
(c) (lacking zeal) frío, indiferente; **to be ~ towards a plan** acoger un proyecto con poco entusiasmo; **to be ~ towards sb** tratar a uno con frialdad.
(d) (calmly audacious) fresco, descarado; **he's a ~ customer** es un caradura; **he answered me as ~ as you please** me contestó tan fresco.
(e) **a ~ £100*** nada menos que 100 libras, la bonita suma de 100 libras.
(f) (‡) fabuloso*, de aúpa*; **it was real ~, man** fue fenómeno, tío*.
[2] ADV: **to play it ~** no dejarse emocionar, no exagerar.
[3] N (a) fresco m; **in the ~ of the evening** en el aire fresco de la tarde. (b) (‡) **to keep one's ~** no dejarse emocionar; **to lose one's ~** ponerse nervioso; perder los estribos.
[4] VT (also to ~ down) enfriar; refrescar; engine refrigerar; (fig) calmar, moderar el entusiasmo (etc) de; ~ **it!*** ¡tranqui!*
[5] VI (also to ~ down) enfriarse; (weather etc) refrescarse; (person) tener menos calor; (fig) calmarse.
◆ **cool down** [1] VT V **cool 4**.
[2] VI (a) V **cool 5**. (b) (fig) calmarse; ~ **down!** ¡cálmese!
◆ **cool off** VI (fig) perder su entusiasmo, entibiarse; (relations) enfriarse.

coolant ['kuːlənt] N refrigerante m.

cool box ['kuːl,bɒks] N nevera f portátil.

cooler ['kuːləʳ] N (a) (US) nevera f portátil. (b) (‡) trena‡ f.

cool-headed ['kuːl,hedɪd] ADJ imperturbable.

coolie ['ku:lɪ] N cooli *m*, culi *m*.
cooling ['ku:lɪŋ] ① ADJ refrescante; (*Tech*) refrigerante.
  ② N refrigeración *f*.
cooling-fan ['ku:lɪŋˌfæn] N ventilador *m*.
cooling-off [ˌku:lɪŋ'ɒf] ATTR: ~ **period** plazo *m* para que se entablen
  negociaciones.
cooling-tower ['ku:lɪŋtaʊəʳ] N torre *f* de refrigeración.
coolly ['ku:lɪ] ADV (*calmly*) con tranquilidad; (*unenthusiastically*) con
  poco entusiasmo; (*boldly*) descaradamente.
coolness ['ku:lnɪs] N (a) (*coldness*) frescura *f*, lo fresco.
  (b) (*calmness*) tranquilidad *f*, imperturbabilidad *f*; (*in battle etc*) sangre *f* fría.
  (c) (*lack of zeal*) tibieza *f*, falta *f* de entusiasmo; (*of welcome, between
  persons*) frialdad *f*.
  (d) (*audacity*) frescura *f*.
coomb [ku:m] N garganta *f*, desfiladero *m*.
coon⁑ [ku:n] N (*esp US*) negro *m*, -a *f*.
coop [ku:p] N gallinero *m*.
♦ **coop up** VT encerrar, enjaular.
co-op⁎ ['kəʊ'ɒp] N (*Brit*) ABBR of **cooperative society** cooperativa *f*.
cooper ['ku:pəʳ] N tonelero *m*.
cooperage ['ku:pərɪdʒ] N tonelería *f*.
cooperate [kəʊ'ɒpəreɪt] VI cooperar, colaborar (*in* en, *with* con, *to* +
  infin para + *infin*).
cooperation [kəʊˌɒpə'reɪʃən] N cooperación *f*, colaboración *f*.
cooperative [kəʊ'ɒpərətɪv] ① ADJ cooperativo; *person* servicial, dispuesto a ayudar; ~ **society** cooperativa *f*.
  ② N cooperativa *f*.
cooperatively [kəʊ'ɒpərətɪvlɪ] ADV (*jointly*) en cooperación, en colaboración, conjuntamente; (*obligingly*) servicialmente.
coopt [kəʊ'ɒpt] VT nombrar por cooptación, cooptar (*on to* a).
cooption [kəʊ'ɒpʃən] N cooptación *f*.
coordinate ① [kəʊ'ɔːdnɪt] N coordenada *f*.
  ② [kəʊ'ɔːdɪneɪt] VT coordinar.
coordinating [kəʊ'ɔːdɪneɪtɪŋ] ADJ: ~ **committee** comité *m*
  coordinador.
coordination [kəʊˌɔːdɪ'neɪʃən] N coordinación *f*.
coordinator [kəʊ'ɔːdɪneɪtəʳ] N coordinador *m*.
coot [ku:t] N (*Orn*) focha *f* (común), fúlica *f*; (⁎) bobo *m*, -a *f*.
coowner [ˌkəʊ'əʊnəʳ] N copropietario *m*, -a *f*.
coownership [ˌkəʊ'əʊnəʃɪp] N copropiedad *f*.
cop⁎ [kɒp] ① N (a) (*policeman*) poli⁎ *m* (*Sp*), guindilla⁑ *m* (*Sp*); guarura⁑
  m (*Méx*), cana⁑ *m* (*SC*), tira⁑ *m* (*LAm*); **the ~s** la pasma⁑ (*Sp*), la bofia⁑
  (*Sp*), la jara⁑ (*Mex*), la cana⁑ (*SC*); **~s and robbers** (*game*) justicias y
  ladrones; ~ **shop** (*Brit*⁑) comisaría *f*.
  (b) (*Brit*) **it's a fair ~!** ¡está bien!; **it's not much ~** es poca cosa, no
  vale gran cosa.
  ② VT (a) (*Brit: capture*) coger, prender.
  (b) **he ~ped 6 months** se cargó 6 meses; **you'll ~ it!** (*Brit*) ¡las vas a
  pagar!; **I ~ped it from the head** el director me puso como un trapo;
  ~ **this!** ¡hay que ver esto!; ~ **hold of this** coge esto, toma esto.
  (c) (*US*) *drugs* comprar.
♦ **cop out** VI resbalarse⁑, escabullirse, rajarse⁎.
copartner ['kəʊ'pɑːtnəʳ] N consocio *mf*, copartícipe *mf*.
copartnership ['kəʊ'pɑːtnəʃɪp] N asociación *f*, cogestión *f*,
  coparticipación *f*.
cope¹ [kəʊp] N (*Eccl*) capa *f* pluvial.
cope² [kəʊp] VI (a) arreglárselas; **he's coping pretty well** se las está
  arreglando bastante bien; **we shall be able to ~ better next year**
  podremos arreglarnos mejor el año que viene; **can you ~ ?** ¿tú
  puedes con esto?; **how are you coping?** ¿cómo te va esto?; **he can't
  ~ any more** ya no aguanta más, ya no puede más.
  (b) **to ~ with** poder con; *problem* hacer frente a; *difficulty* contender
  con; *situation* enfrentarse con.
Copenhagen [ˌkəʊpn'heɪgən] N Copenhague *m*.
Copernicus [kə'pɜːnɪkəs] NM Copérnico.
copestone ['kəʊpstəʊn] N (piedra *f* de) albardilla *f*.
copier ['kɒpɪəʳ] N copiadora *f*.
co-pilot ['kəʊ'paɪlət] N copiloto *mf*.
coping ['kəʊpɪŋ] N albardilla *f*, mojinete *m*; **~stone** = **copestone**.
copious ['kəʊpɪəs] ADJ copioso, abundante.
copiously ['kəʊpɪəslɪ] ADV copiosamente, en abundancia.
cop-out⁑ ['kɒpaʊt] N evasión *f* de responsabilidad.
copper ['kɒpəʳ] ① N (a) (*material*) cobre *m*.
  (b) (*utensil*) caldera *f* de lavar.
  (c) (*money*) calderilla *f*, monedas *fpl* de poco valor; **it costs a few ~s**
  vale unos peniques.
  (d) (⁎: *policeman*) poli⁎ *m* (*Sp*), guindilla⁑ *m* (*Sp*); *see also* **cop**.
  ② ADJ, ATTR de cobre, cobreño; (*colour*) cobrizo; ~ **sulphate** sulfato *m*
  de cobre.
copper-beech ['kɒpə'bi:tʃ] N haya *f* roja, haya *f* de sangre.
copper-bottomed [ˌkɒpə'bɒtəmd] ADJ con fondo de cobre; (*fig*) to-

talmente fiable, de máxima seguridad.
copper-coloured, (*US*) **copper-colored** ['kɒpə,kʌləd] ADJ cobrizo.
copperhead ['kɒpəhed] N víbora *f* cobriza.
copperplate ['kɒpəpleɪt] ATTR: ~ **writing** letra *f* caligrafiada, caligrafía
  f.
coppersmith ['kɒpəsmɪθ] N cobrero *m*.
coppery ['kɒpərɪ] ADJ cobreño; (*colour*) cobrizo.
coppice ['kɒpɪs] N soto *m*, bosquecillo *m*.
copra ['kɒprə] N copra *f*.
copresidency [kəʊ'prezɪdənsɪ] N copresidencia *f*.
copresident [kəʊ'prezɪdənt] N copresidente *m*, -a *f*.
coprocessor ['kəʊ'prəʊsesəʳ] N coprocesador *m*; **graphics ~** coprocesador *m* de gráficos.
coproduce [ˌkəʊprə'dju:s] VT coproducir.
coproduction [ˌkəʊprə'dʌkʃən] N coproducción *f*.
copse [kɒps] N soto *m*, bosquecillo *m*.
Copt [kɒpt] N copto *m*, -a *f*.
´copter⁎, copter⁎ ['kɒptəʳ] N ABBR of **helicopter** helicóptero *m*.
Coptic ['kɒptɪk] ADJ copto; **the ~ Church** la Iglesia Copta.
copula ['kɒpjʊlə] N cópula *f*.
copulate ['kɒpjʊleɪt] VI copularse (*with* con).
copulation [ˌkɒpjʊ'leɪʃən] N cópula *f*.
copulative ['kɒpjʊlətɪv] ADJ copulativo.
copy ['kɒpɪ] ① N (a) (*reproduction*) copia *f*.
  (b) (*book*) ejemplar *m*; (*journal*) número *m*.
  (c) (*Typ*) material *m*, original *m*; **there's plenty of ~ here** tenemos
  aquí un material abundante; **a murder is always good ~** un asesinato es siempre un buen tema.
  ② ATTR: ~ **typist** mecanógrafo *m*, -a *f*.
  ③ VT (a) (*also* **to ~ down, to ~ out**) copiar; imitar; **to ~ from** copiar
  de.
  (b) (*send a copy to*) enviar una copia a.
copybook ['kɒpɪbʊk] ① N cuaderno *m* de escritura; **to blot one's ~**
  tirarse una plancha⁎, manchar la reputación.
  ② ADJ perfecto; **the pilot made a ~ landing** el piloto aterrizó perfectamente.
copy-boy ['kɒpɪˌbɔɪ] N chico *m* de los recados de la redacción.
copycat⁎ ['kɒpɪkæt] N imitador *m*, -ora *f*, copión *m*, -ona *f*; ~ **crime**
  crimen *m* de imitación.
copy-edit ['kɒpɪ'edɪt] VT editar y corregir.
copy-editor ['kɒpɪ'edɪtəʳ] N editor *m*, -ora *f* corrector *m*, -ora *f* de
  manuscritos (*or de material etc*).
copying-ink ['kɒpɪɪŋ,ɪŋk] N tinta *f* de copiar.
copying-machine ['kɒpɪɪŋməˌʃiːn] N copiadora *f*.
copyist ['kɒpɪɪst] N copista *mf*.
copy-machine ['kɒpɪməˌʃiːn] N fotocopiadora *f*.
copyreader ['kɒpɪˌriːdəʳ] N corrector *m*, -ora *f*.
copyright ['kɒpɪraɪt] ① ADJ protegido por los derechos de(l) autor.
  ② N derechos *mpl* de(l) autor, copyright *m*, propiedad *f* literaria;
  (derechos *mpl* de) propiedad *f* intelectual; '~ **reserved**' 'es propiedad', 'reservados todos los derechos', 'copyright'; **the book is still
  in ~** siguen vigentes los derechos del autor de este libro; **it will be
  out of ~ in 2020** los derechos del autor terminarán en 2020.
  ③ VT registrar como propiedad literaria.
copywriter ['kɒpɪ,raɪtəʳ] N escritor *m*, -ora *f* de material publicitario.
coquetry ['kɒkɪtrɪ] N coquetería *f*.
coquette [kə'ket] N coqueta *f*.
coquettish [kə'ketɪʃ] ADJ coqueta.
coquettishly [kə'ketɪʃlɪ] ADV con aire (*or tono etc*) coqueta.
cor⁑ [kɔːʳ] INTERJ (*Brit*) ¡caramba!; ~ **blimey!** ¡coño!⁑
coracle ['kɒrəkl] N barquilla *f* de cuero.
coral ['kɒrəl] ① N coral *m*.
  ② ADJ coralino, de coral; ~ **island** isla *f* coralina; ~ **reef** barrera *f*
  coralina, arrecife *m* de coral; **C~ Sea** Mar *m* del Coral.
cor anglais ['kɔːr'ɑ̃ŋgleɪ] N corno *m* inglés.
corbel ['kɔːbəl] N ménsula *f*, repisa *f*.
cord [kɔːd] ① N (a) cuerda *f*; (*US Elec*) cordón *m*; (**umbilical**) ~ cordón
  m umbilical. (b) (*cloth*) pana *f*; **~s** pantalones *mpl* de pana.
  ② VT encordar, atar con cuerdas.
cordage ['kɔːdɪdʒ] N cordaje *m*, cordería *f*.
cordial ['kɔːdɪəl] ① ADJ cordial, afectuoso.
  ② N cordial *m*.
cordiality [ˌkɔːdɪ'ælɪtɪ] N cordialidad *f*, afecto *m*.
cordially ['kɔːdɪəlɪ] ADV cordialmente, afectuosamente; **I ~ detest him**
  le odio cordialmente.
cordite ['kɔːdaɪt] N cordita *f*.
cordless ['kɔːdlɪs] ADJ *iron, kettle, tools* sin cable; ~ **telephone** teléfono
  m móvil, teléfono *m* sin hilos.
cordon ['kɔːdn] ① N cordón *m*.
  ② VT: **to ~ off** acordonar.
cordon bleu [ˌkɔːdɔ̃'blɜː] ① N cordón *m* azul; (*Culin*) cocinero *m*, -a
  f de primera clase.

2 ADJ, ATTR de primera clase.

cordon sanitaire ['kɔːdɔ̃,sænɪ'teɪ] N, PL **cordons sanitaires** (Pol) cordón m sanitario.

Cordova ['kɔːdəvə] N Córdoba f.

Cordovan ['kɔːdəvən] 1 ADJ cordobés.
2 N cordobés m, -esa f; (leather) cordobán m.

corduroy ['kɔːdərɔɪ] N pana f; ~s pantalones mpl de pana; ~ **road** (US) camino m de troncos.

CORE [kɔːʳ] N (US) ABBR of **Congress of Racial Equality**.

core [kɔːʳ] 1 N centro m, núcleo m; (of fruit) corazón m; (of cable) alma f; (of group etc) centro m; elementos mpl centrales; (fig, of problem etc) lo esencial, esencia f; **a hard ~ of resistance** un foco de dura resistencia; **the hard ~ of unemployment** el núcleo duro del paro; **English to the ~** inglés hasta los tuétanos; **rotten to the ~** (fig) corrompido hasta la médula; **shocked to the ~** profundamente afectado.
2 ATTR: ~ **curriculum** (programa m de) estudios mpl troncales, asignaturas fpl comunes; ~ **memory** memoria f de núcleos; ~ **subject** asignatura f común; ~ **time** período m nuclear.
3 VT apple quitar el corazón de.

co-religionist ['kəʊrɪ'lɪdʒənɪst] N correligionario m, -a f.

corer ['kɔːrəʳ] N (Culin) despepitadora f.

co-respondent ['kəʊrɪs'pɒndənt] N codemandado m, -a f (en casos de divorcio).

Corfu [kɔː'fuː] N Corfú m.

corgi ['kɔːgɪ] N perro m galés.

coriander [,kɒrɪ'ændəʳ] N culantro m.

Corinth ['kɒrɪnθ] N Corinto m.

Corinthian [kə'rɪnθɪən] ADJ corintio.

cork [kɔːk] 1 N corcho m.
2 ATTR de corcho.
3 VT (also **to ~ up**) tapar con corcho, taponar; **the wine is ~ed** el vino sabe a corcho.

corkage ['kɔːkɪdʒ] N precio m que se cobra en un restaurante por una botella traída de fuera.

corked [kɔːkt] ADJ wine que sabe a corcho.

corker‡ ['kɔːkəʳ] N (lie) bola* f, trola* f; (story) historia f absurda; (Sport: shot, stroke) golpe m de primera; (player) crac* m; (girl) tía f buena*; **that's a ~!** ¡es cutre!‡

cork-oak [,kɔːk'əʊk] N = **cork-tree**.

corkscrew ['kɔːkskruː] 1 N sacacorchos m.
2 ATTR movement en espiral.
3 VI subir en espiral.

cork-tree ['kɔːktriː] N alcornoque m.

corm [kɔːm] N (Bot) bulbo m.

cormorant ['kɔːmərənt] N cormorán m (grande).

corn[1] [kɔːn] N (a) (Bot) granos mpl, cereales mpl; (Brit: wheat) trigo m; (US, also **Indian ~**) maíz m; ~ **bread** (US) pan m de maíz; ~ **meal** (US) harina f de maíz; ~ **on the cob** mazorca f. (b) (*) cosas fpl rancias, historia f (etc) vieja; sentimentalismo m, sensiblería f.

corn[2] [kɔːn] N (Med) callo m; **to tread on sb's ~s** (Brit) herir los sentimientos de uno.

cornball* ['kɔːnbɔːl] N (US) paleto* m, -a f.

corncob ['kɔːnkɒb] N (US) mazorca f de maíz.

corncrake ['kɔːnkreɪk] N guión m de codornices.

cornea ['kɔːnɪə] N córnea f.

corneal ['kɔːnɪəl] ADJ corneal.

corned ['kɔːnd] ADJ: ~ **beef** (Brit) carne f de vaca acecinada (enlatada).

cornelian [kɔː'niːlɪən] N cornalina f.

corner ['kɔːnəʳ] 1 N ángulo m; (outside ~) esquina f, (inside ~) rincón m; (bend in road) curva f, recodo m; (Sport) córner m, esquina f; (kick) córner m, saque m de esquina; (Comm) monopolio m (in de); ~ **house** casa f en una esquina, casa f esquinera; ~ **shop** tienda f de esquina; **a picturesque ~ of Soria** un rincón pintoresco de Soria; **the four ~s of the earth** las cinco partes del mundo; **out of the ~ of one's eye** con el rabillo del ojo; **it's round the ~** está a la vuelta de la esquina; **prosperity is just around the ~** la prosperidad está precisamente a la vuelta de la esquina; **to be in a tight ~** estar en un aprieto; **to cut ~s** atajar; **to drive sb into a ~** (fig) arrinconar a uno, acorralar a uno, poner a uno entre la espada y la pared; **to go round the ~** doblar la esquina; **he made a ~ in peanuts** se hizo con el monopolio de cacahuetes, acaparó el mercado de cacahuetes; **to paint o.s. into a ~** verse acorralado; **to turn the ~** doblar la esquina, (fig) ir saliendo del apuro.
2 VT acorralar, arrinconar; person abordar, detener; fugitive cazar; market acaparar.
3 VI (Aut) tomar una curva.

corner-flag ['kɔːnəflæg] N banderola f de esquina.

cornering ['kɔːnərɪŋ] N: **the new suspension allows much safer ~** (Aut) la nueva suspensión proporciona un mayor agarre en las curvas.

corner-kick ['kɔːnəkɪk] N córner m, saque m de esquina.

corner-seat ['kɔːnəsiːt] N asiento m del rincón, rinconera f.

cornerstone ['kɔːnəstəʊn] N piedra f angular (also fig).

cornet ['kɔːnɪt] N (a) (Mus) corneta f. (b) (Brit: ice cream) cucurucho m.

corn exchange ['kɔːnɪks'tʃeɪndʒ] N bolsa f de granos.

cornfield ['kɔːnfiːld] N (Brit) trigal m, campo m de trigo; (US) maizal m, milpa f.

cornflakes ['kɔːnfleɪks] NPL copos mpl de maíz (tostado), (loosely) cereales mpl.

cornflour ['kɔːnflaʊəʳ] N (Brit) harina f de maíz.

cornflower ['kɔːnflaʊəʳ] N aciano m, azulina f; ~ **blue** azul aciano.

cornice ['kɔːnɪs] N, **corniche** ['kɔːnɪʃ] N cornisa f.

Cornish ['kɔːnɪʃ] 1 ADJ de Cornualles; ~ **pasty** empanada f de Cornualles.
2 N córnico m.

corn-oil ['kɔːnɔɪl] N aceite m de maíz.

corn-poppy ['kɔːn,pɒpɪ] N amapola f.

cornstarch ['kɔːnstɑːtʃ] N (US) almidón m de maíz, maicena f.

cornucopia [,kɔːnjʊ'kəʊpɪə] N cuerno m de la abundancia.

Cornwall ['kɔːnwəl] N Cornualles m.

corny* ['kɔːnɪ] ADJ viejo, gastado, rancio; sentimental, sensiblero.

corolla [kə'rɒlə] N corola f.

corollary [kə'rɒlərɪ] N corolario m.

corona [kə'rəʊnə] N (Anat, Astron) corona f; (Elec) descarga f de corona; (Archit) corona f, alero m.

coronary ['kɒrənərɪ] 1 ADJ coronario; ~ **thrombosis** = 2.
2 N infarto m de miocardio, trombosis f coronaria.

coronation [,kɒrə'neɪʃən] N coronación f.

coroner ['kɒrənəʳ] N (approx) juez m de primera instancia e instrucción (que establece las causas de defunción).

coronet ['kɒrənɪt] N corona f (de marqués etc); (lady's) diadema f.

Corp. (a) (Comm, Fin) ABBR of **Corporation** sociedad f anónima, S.A. (b) (Pol) ABBR of **Corporation** ayuntamiento m, municipio m. (c) (Mil) ABBR of **Corporal** cabo m.

corpora ['kɔːpərə] NPL of **corpus**.

corporal ['kɔːpərəl] 1 ADJ corporal; ~ **punishment** castigo m corporal.
2 N cabo m.

corporate ['kɔːpərɪt] ADJ corporativo, colectivo; ~ **car** (US) coche m de la compañía; ~ **growth** crecimiento m corporativo; ~ **identity** identidad f corporativa; ~ **image** imagen f corporativa; ~ **name** nombre m social; ~ **planning** planificación f corporativa; ~ **strategy** estrategia f de la compañía.

corporately ['kɔːpərɪtlɪ] ADV corporativamente, como corporación.

corporation [,kɔːpə'reɪʃən] 1 N (a) (Comm, Fin) corporación f; (esp US Comm) sociedad f anónima. (b) (Brit: of city) ayuntamiento m. (c) (Brit*) panza f.
2 ATTR: ~ **tax** (Brit) impuesto m sobre sociedades.

corporatism ['kɔːpərətɪzəm] N corporacionismo m.

corporatist ['kɔːpərətɪst] ADJ theory, tendencies corporativista.

corporeal [kɔː'pɔːrɪəl] ADJ corpóreo.

corps [kɔːʳ] N, PL **corps** [kɔːz] cuerpo m; ~ **de ballet** cuerpo m de baile; ~ **diplomatique** cuerpo m diplomático.

corpse [kɔːps] N cadáver m.

corpulence ['kɔːpjʊləns] N gordura f.

corpulent ['kɔːpjʊlənt] ADJ gordo.

corpus ['kɔːpəs] N cuerpo m; ~ **delicti** cuerpo m del delito; **C~ Christi** Corpus m.

corpuscle ['kɔːpʌsl] N glóbulo m, corpúsculo m.

corral [kə'rɑːl] (US) 1 N corral m.
2 VT acorralar.

correct [kə'rekt] 1 ADJ (a) (accurate) correcto, exacto, justo; ~! ¡exacto!; **you are perfectly ~** tienes toda la razón, estás en lo cierto; **am I ~ in saying that ...?** ¿me equivoco al decir que ...?, ¿no es cierto que ...?
(b) (proper) correcto.
2 VT corregir; rectificar, enmendar; exam corregir, calificar; ~ **me if I'm wrong** me dirás si tengo razón o no; **I stand ~ed** confieso que me equivoqué.

correcting [kə'rektɪŋ] ADJ: ~ **fluid** corrector m.

correction [kə'rekʃən] N corrección f; rectificación f; (erasure) tachadura f; **I speak under ~** puede que me equivoque.

corrective [kə'rektɪv] 1 ADJ correctivo; ~ **glasses** gafas fpl correctoras.
2 N correctivo m.

correctly [kə'rektlɪ] ADV correctamente.

correctness [kə'rektnɪs] N (accuracy) exactitud f; (properness) corrección f.

correlate ['kɒrɪleɪt] 1 VT correlacionar.
2 VI tener correlación.

correlation [,kɒrɪ'leɪʃən] N correlación f.

correlative [kɒ'relətɪv] 1 ADJ correlativo.
2 N correlativo m.

correspond [,kɒrɪs'pɒnd] vi (a) (agree) corresponder (to, with a). (b) (by letter) escribirse; **to ~ with** estar en correspondencia con, cartearse con.

correspondence [,kɒrɪs'pɒndəns] 1 N (a) (agreement) correspondencia f.
(b) (by letter) correspondencia f; **to be in ~ with sb** estar en correspondencia con uno.
(c) (collected letters) epistolario m.
2 ATTR: ~ **college** escuela f de enseñanza por correspondencia; ~ **column** sección f de cartas; ~ **course** curso m por correspondencia.

correspondent [,kɒrɪs'pɒndənt] N correspondiente mf; (of paper) corresponsal mf.

corresponding [,kɒrɪs'pɒndɪŋ] ADJ correspondiente.

correspondingly [,kɒrɪs'pɒndɪŋlɪ] ADV igualmente, equivalentemente.

corridor ['kɒrɪdɔːʳ] N pasillo m (also Rail), corredor m (also Pol); ~**s of power** pasillos mpl del poder.

corroborate [kə'rɒbəreɪt] vt corroborar, confirmar.

corroboration [kə,rɒbə'reɪʃən] N corroboración f, confirmación f.

corroborative [kə'rɒbərətɪv] ADJ corroborativo, confirmatorio.

corrode [kə'rəʊd] 1 vt corroer.
2 vi corroerse.

corroded [kə'rəʊdɪd] ADJ corroído.

corrosion [kə'rəʊʒən] N corrosión f.

corrosive [kə'rəʊzɪv] ADJ corrosivo.

corrugated ['kɒrəgeɪtɪd] ADJ ondulado, corrugado; ~ **cardboard** cartón m ondulado; ~ **iron** hierro m ondulado, calamina f (LAm); ~ **paper** papel m ondulado.

corrupt [kə'rʌpt] 1 ADJ corrompido; text viciado; taste depravado, estragado; person venal; ~ **practices** corrupción f.
2 vt corromper; (bribe) sobornar; (Comput) data degradar.

corruptible [kə'rʌptəbl] ADJ corruptible.

corruption [kə'rʌpʃən] N corrupción f.

corsage [kɔː'sɑːʒ] N (of dress) cuerpo m; (flowers) ramillete m (para el pecho).

corsair ['kɔːsɛəʳ] N corsario m.

cors anglais ['kɔːz'ɑːŋgleɪ] NPL of **cor anglais**.

corset ['kɔːsɪt] N faja f, (old-style) corsé m.

corseted ['kɔːsɪtɪd] ADJ encorsetado.

Corsica ['kɔːsɪkə] N Córcega f.

Corsican ['kɔːsɪkən] 1 ADJ corso.
2 N corso m, -a f.

cortège [kɔː'teɪʒ] N (procession) cortejo m, comitiva f; (train) séquito m; (funeral ~) cortejo m fúnebre.

cortex ['kɔːteks] N, PL **cortices** ['kɔːtɪsiːz] córtex m, corteza f.

corticoids ['kɔːtɪkɔɪdz] NPL, **corticosteroids** ['kɔːtɪkəʊ'stɪərɔɪdz] NPL corticoides mpl, corticosteroides mpl.

cortisone ['kɔːtɪzəʊn] N cortisona f.

Corunna [kə'rʌnə] N La Coruña.

coruscating ['kɒrəskeɪtɪŋ] ADJ humour chispeante.

corvette [kɔː'vet] N corbeta f.

COS (Comm) ABBR of **cash on shipment** pago m al embarcar; V **cash 1**.

cos [kɒs] ABBR of **cosine** coseno m.

´cos* [kɒs] CONJ = **because**.

cosh [kɒʃ] (Brit) 1 N cachiporra f.
2 vt golpear con una cachiporra.

cosignatory ['kəʊ'sɪgnətərɪ] N cosignatario m, -a f.

cosily ['kəʊzɪlɪ] ADV (V ADJ) cómodamente, agradablemente; amistosamente; íntimamente.

cosine ['kəʊsaɪn] N coseno m.

cosiness ['kəʊzɪnɪs] N comodidad f; lo acogedor.

COSLA ['kɒzlə] N (Scot) ABBR of **Convention of Scottish Local Authorities**.

cos lettuce ['kɒs'letɪs] N (Brit) lechuga f romana.

cosmetic [kɒz'metɪk] 1 ADJ cosmético; ~ **surgery** cirugía f estética; **the changes are merely ~** los cambios son puramente cosméticos.
2 N cosmético m.

cosmetician [kɒzmɪ'tɪʃən] N cosmetólogo m, -a f.

cosmic ['kɒzmɪk] ADJ cósmico; ~ **rays** rayos mpl cósmicos.

cosmogony [kɒz'mɒgənɪ] N cosmogonía f.

cosmographer [kɒz'mɒgrəfəʳ] N cosmógrafo m, -a f.

cosmography [kɒz'mɒgrəfɪ] N cosmografía f.

cosmology [kɒz'mɒlədʒɪ] N cosmología f.

cosmonaut ['kɒzmənɔːt] N cosmonauta mf.

cosmopolitan [,kɒzmə'pɒlɪtən] 1 ADJ cosmopolita.
2 N cosmopolita mf.

cosmos ['kɒzmɒs] N cosmos m.

co-sponsor ['kəʊ'spɒnsəʳ] N (esp Advertising) copatrocinador m, -ora f.

Cossack ['kɒsæk] 1 ADJ cosaco.
2 N cosaco m, -a f.

cosset ['kɒsɪt] vt mimar.

cossie* ['kɒzɪ] N (Brit) bañador m.

cost [kɒst] 1 N (a) precio m; coste m, costo m, costa f; ~**s** (in industry etc) costes mpl; ~ **analysis** análisis m de costos; ~ **centre** centro m de costos; ~ **control** control m de costos; ~ **of living** coste m de vida; ~**-of-living allowance** subsidio m por coste de vida; ~**-of-living bonus** plus m de carestía de vida, prima f por coste de vida; ~**-of-living increase** incremento m según el coste de la vida; ~**-of-living index** índice m de coste de vida; ~ **of sales** coste m de la campaña de ventas; **at ~** a (precio de) costa; **at the ~ of his health** a costa de su salud; **at the ~ of his life** pagó con la vida; **at all ~s, at any ~** a todo trance, a toda costa; **at great ~** tras grandes esfuerzos, tras grandes pérdidas; **at little ~ to himself** con poco riesgo para sí mismo; **to my ~** a mis expensas; **without counting the ~** sin pensar en los riesgos; **whatever the ~** cueste lo que cueste;
(b) (Jur) ~**s** costas fpl, litisexpensas fpl; **he was ordered to pay ~s** se le condenó con costas.
2 vt (a) (Comm) calcular el coste de, preparar el presupuesto de; **the job was ~ed at £5000** se calculó el coste del trabajo en 5000 libras; **it has not been properly ~ed** no se ha calculado detalladamente el coste de esto.
(b) (irr: PRET AND PTP **cost**) (gen) costar, valer; **it ~ £2** costó 2 libras; **how much does this ~?** ¿cuánto vale esto?, ¿cuánto es?; **what does it ~ to go?** ¿cuánto cuesta el viaje?; **it'll ~ you*** te costará algo caro; **~ what it may** cueste lo que cueste; **it ~ him his life** le costó la vida; **it ~ him a lot of trouble** le causó muchas molestias.
◆**cost out** vt presupuestar.

cost accountant ['kɒstə,kaʊntənt] N contable mf de costos.

cost accounting ['kɒstə,kaʊntɪŋ] N contabilidad f de costos.

co-star ['kəʊstɑːʳ] 1 N coestrella f.
2 vt: **the film ~s A and B** le película presenta como coestrellas A y B.
3 vi: **to ~ with sb** hacer de coestrella con uno.

Costa Rica ['kɒstə'riːkə] N Costa f Rica.

Costa Rican ['kɒstə'riːkən] 1 ADJ costarricense.
2 N costarricense mf.

cost-benefit analysis [,kɒst,benəfɪtə'næləsɪs] N análisis m costes-ventajas (or de costos-beneficios).

cost-conscious ['kɒst,kɒnʃəs] ADJ consciente de (los) costos.

cost-cutting ['kɒst,kʌtɪŋ] N recorte m de costos.

cost-effective [,kɒstɪ'fektɪv] ADJ rentable, beneficioso.

cost-effectiveness [,kɒstɪ'fektɪvnɪs] N rentabilidad f, relación f costo-eficacia (or costo-rendimiento).

coster ['kɒstəʳ] N, **costermonger** ['kɒstə,mʌŋgəʳ] N (Brit) vendedor m ambulante.

costing ['kɒstɪŋ] N cálculo m del coste; fijación f del precio.

costive ['kɒstɪv] ADJ estreñido.

costliness ['kɒstlɪnɪs] N (dearness) alto precio m; lo caro; (great value) suntuosidad f.

costly ['kɒstlɪ] ADJ (dear) costoso; caro; (valuable) suntuoso.

cost-plus [,kɒst'plʌs] N precio m de coste más beneficio; **on a ~ basis** a base de precio de coste más beneficio.

cost-price ['kɒst'praɪs] (Brit) 1 N precio m de coste; **at ~ = 2**
2 ADV al precio de coste.

costume ['kɒstjuːm] N traje m; (fancy-dress) disfraz m; ~ **ball** baile m de trajes; ~ **designer** (Cine, TV) encargado m, -a f de vestuario; figurinista mf; ~ **jewelry** (US), ~ **jewellery** (Brit) joyas fpl de fantasía, bisutería f; ~ **party** (US) baile m de disfraces; ~ **piece**, ~ **play** obra f de época.

costumier [kɒs'tjuːmɪəʳ] N, (esp US) **costumer** [kɒs'tjuːmə] N sastre m de teatro.

cosy, (US) **cozy** ['kəʊzɪ] 1 ADJ cómodo, agradable; atmosphere acogedor, amistoso; chat íntimo, amistoso; life holgado.
2 N cubierta f para tetera.

cot [kɒt] N (Brit) cuna f, camita f de niño; (US) cama f plegable; ~ **death** muerte m en la cuna.

coterie ['kəʊtərɪ] N grupo m; tertulia f; (clique) peña f, camarilla f.

Cotswolds ['kɒtswəʊldz] NPL: **the ~** región f de lomas del suroeste de Inglaterra.

cottage ['kɒtɪdʒ] N casita f de campo; (US) vivienda f campestre, quinta f; (labourer's etc) choza f, barraca f; ~ **cheese** requesón m; ~ **hospital** (Brit) pequeño hospital m local; ~ **industry** industria f artesanal, industria f casera; ~ **loaf** (Brit) ≃ pan m de payés.

cottage pie ['kɒtɪdʒ'paɪ] N (Brit) pastel de carne cubierto con puré de patatas.

cottager ['kɒtɪdʒəʳ] N (Brit) aldeano m, -a f; (US) veraneante mf (que vive en una casita de campo).

cotter ['kɒtəʳ] N chaveta f.

cotton ['kɒtn] 1 N algodón m; (plant) algodonero m; (Brit: sewing thread) hilo m de coser; (US Med) algodón m hidrófilo (en rama).
2 ATTR de algodón; algodonero; ~ **belt** (US) zona f algodonera; ~ **bud**, ~ **swab** (US) bastoncillo m de algodón; ~ **candy** (US) algodón m azucarado; **the ~ industry** la industria algodonera; ~ **waste** borra f de algodón.
◆**cotton on*** vi caer en la cuenta; **to ~ on to** entender, caer en la

cuenta de.

cottongrass ['kɒtngrɑːs] N algodonosa f, algodoncillo m (silvestre).

cotton-mill ['kɒtnmɪl] N fábrica f de algodón.

cotton-picking* ['kɒtn‚pɪkɪŋ] ADJ (US) condenado.

cottonseed-oil ['kɒtnsiːdɔɪl] N aceite m de algodón.

cottontail ['kɒtnteɪl] N (US) conejo m (de cola blanca).

cottonwood ['kɒtnwʊd] N (US) álamo m de Virginia.

cotton-wool ['kɒtn'wʊl] N (Brit) algodón m hidrófilo (en rama).

cotyledon [‚kɒtɪ'liːdən] N cotiledón m.

couch [kaʊtʃ] **1** N canapé m, sofá m; (psychiatrist's) diván m; ~ **pota-to*** haragán m, -ana f del sofá; **to be on the** ~ (US) ir al psicoanalista.
   2 VT (liter) expresar; **~ed in jargon** redactado en jerigonza.

couchette [kuː'ʃet] N (Rail) litera f.

couch-grass ['kaʊtʃgrɑːs] N hierba f rastrera, grana f del norte, agropiro m.

cougar ['kuːgəʳ] N puma f.

cough [kɒf] **1** N tos f.
   2 VI toser; (‡) cantar.

◆**cough up** **1** VT (a) (lit) escupir, arrojar.
   (b) (*fig) money desembolsar, pagar.
   2 VI (*) desdinerarse*, pagar.

cough-drop ['kɒfdrɒp] N pastilla f para la tos.

coughing ['kɒfɪŋ] N toser m, toses fpl; **fit of** ~ acceso m de tos; **you couldn't hear the symphony for** ~ el público tosía tanto que apenas se oía la sinfonía.

cough-lozenge ['kɒf‚lɒzɪndʒ] N pastilla f para la tos.

cough-mixture ['kɒf‚mɪkstʃəʳ] N, **cough-syrup** ['kɒf‚sɪrəp] N jarabe m para la tos.

could [kʊd] PRET AND CONDITIONAL of can¹; see also ABLE, CAN .

couldn't ['kʊdnt] = **could not.**

could've ['kʊdəv] = **could have**; V can¹.

coulomb ['kuːlɒm] N culombio m.

council ['kaʊnsl] N (a) (meeting, body) consejo m, junta f; (Eccl) concilio m; **C~ of Europe** Consejo m de Europa; ~ **of war** consejo m de guerra.
   (b) (town ~) concejo m; (loosely) municipio m, ayuntamiento m; ~ **flat** (Brit) ≈ piso m de protección oficial; ~ **house** (Brit) vivienda f protegida (alquilada del municipio); ~ **housing** (Brit) viviendas fpl de protección oficial; ~ **housing estate** zona f urbanística de viviendas de protección oficial; ~ **tax** (Brit) impuesto municipal; ~ **tenant** inquilino m, -a f de una vivienda protegida; **you should write to the** ~ **about it** deberás escribir al Ayuntamiento acerca de eso; **the** ~ **should move the rubbish** les cumple a los servicios municipales recoger la basura.

councillor, (US) **councilor** ['kaʊnsɪləʳ] N (also town ~) concejal m, -ala f.

councilman ['kaʊnsɪlmən] N, PL **councilmen** ['kaʊnsɪlmən] (US) concejal m.

councilwoman ['kaʊnsl‚wʊmən] N, PL **councilwomen** (US) concejala f.

counsel ['kaʊnsəl] **1** N (a) consejo m; **a** ~ **of perfection** un ideal imposible; **to keep one's own** ~ guardar silencio; **to take** ~ **with** aconsejarse con.
   (b) (Jur) abogado mf; ~ **for the defence** (Brit) abogado m defensor, abogado f defensora; ~ **for the prosecution** (Brit) fiscal mf.
   2 VT person aconsejar; (Med etc) orientar; prudence etc recomendar; **to** ~ **sb to do sth** aconsejar a uno hacer algo.

counselling, (US) **counseling** ['kaʊnsəlɪŋ] **1** N (gen: advice) asesoramiento m; (Psych) asistencia f sociopsicológica; (Brit Scol) ayuda f psicopedagógica.
   2 ATTR: ~ **service** servicio m de orientación; (Univ) servicio m de orientación universitaria.

counsellor, (US) **counselor** ['kaʊnsələʳ] N (gen) asesor m, -ora f, consejero m, -a f; (Psych) consejero m, -a f; (US Scol) consejero m, -a f, asesor m, -ora f; (Ireland, US Jur: also ~-at-law) abogado mf.

count¹ [kaʊnt] **1** N (a) (act of counting) cuenta f, cálculo m; (of words etc) recuento m; (of votes) recuento m; (Boxing) cuenta f; **at the last** ~ la última vez que los (etc) contamos; **to be out for the** ~ estar K.O.; **to keep** ~ **of** contar; **to lose** ~ **of** perder la cuenta de.
   (b) (total) suma f, total m.
   (c) (Jur) cargo m, acusación f.
   2 VT (a) (Math) contar; calcular.
   (b) (include) incluir; **not ~ing** sin contar, además de, con exclusión de.
   (c) (deem) creer, considerar; **I don't** ~ **him among my friends** no le considero como amigo; **I** ~ **it an honour** lo considero un honor; **will you** ~ **it against me if ...?** ¿vas a pensar mal de mí si ...?
   3 VI (a) (Math) contar; **to** ~ **on one's fingers** contar con los dedos; **he ~s as 2** él cuenta por 2.
   (b) **that doesn't** ~ (be valid) eso no vale, (in games) eso no puntúa.

(c) (be important) **every second ~s** cada segundo es importante; **he doesn't** ~ él no vale para esto; **he doesn't** ~ **for much** él apenas si vale, pinta poco; **ability ~s for little here** aquí la aptitud sirve para muy poco.
   4 VR: **I** ~ **myself fortunate** me considero feliz.

◆**count down** VI contar atrás, contar al revés.

◆**count in** VT incluir; ~ **me in** cuenta conmigo.

▼◆**count on** VT contar con; **to** ~ **on** + ger contar con + infin; **he is not to be ~ed on** no podemos confiar en él.

◆**count out** VT (a) money etc ir contando.
   (b) (Boxing) declarar vencido.
   (c) excluir; ~ **me out** no cuentes conmigo.

◆**count towards** VT contar para, ser válido para.

◆**count up** VT contar.

count² [kaʊnt] N (noble) conde m.

countable ['kaʊntəbl] ADJ contable.

countdown ['kaʊntdaʊn] N cuenta f atrás, cuenta f al revés.

countenance ['kaʊntɪnəns] **1** N semblante m, rostro m; **to be out of** ~ estar desconcertado; **to give** (or **lend**) ~ **to** news acreditar; **to keep one's** ~ contener la risa; **to lose** ~ desconcertarse; **to put sb out of** ~ desconcertar a uno.
   2 VT aprobar, tolerar, sancionar.

counter¹ ['kaʊntəʳ] N (a) (of shop) mostrador m; ~ **staff** personal m de ventas, cajeras fpl; **to pay over the** ~ pagar al contado; **over the** ~ **purchases** compras fpl al contado; **over the** ~ **market** (St Ex) mercado m de acciones no cotizadas en la bolsa; **you can buy it over the** ~ (Med) esto se compra sin receta obligatoria; **under the** ~ por la trastienda. **(b)** (in games) ficha f. **(c)** (Tech) contador m.

counter² ['kaʊntəʳ] **1** ADJ contrario, de sentido opuesto (to a).
   2 ADV: **to run** ~ **to** oponerse a, ser contrario a.
   3 VT contrarrestar; blow parar; devolver; attack contestar a.
   4 VI: **to** ~ **with** contestar con.

counter... ['kaʊntəʳ] PREF contra...

counteract [‚kaʊntə'rækt] VT contrarrestar; neutralizar.

counter-argument ['kaʊntər‚ɑːgjʊmənt] N contraargumento m.

counter-attack ['kaʊntərə‚tæk] **1** N contraataque m.
   2 VT contraatacar.

counter-attraction ['kaʊntərə‚trækʃən] N atracción f rival.

counterbalance ['kaʊntə‚bæləns] **1** N contrapeso m; compensación f.
   2 VT contrapesar; compensar.

counterbid **1** ['kaʊntə‚bɪd] N contraoferta f; **to make** or **launch a** ~ hacer or presentar una contraoferta.
   2 VT, VI contraofertar.

counterblast ['kaʊntəblɑːst] N respuesta f vigorosa (to a).

counterblow ['kaʊntəbləʊ] N contragolpe m.

countercharge ['kaʊntətʃɑːdʒ] N recriminación f; contraataque m.

countercheck ['kaʊntətʃek] **1** N segunda comprobación f.
   2 VT comprobar por segunda vez.

counterclaim ['kaʊntəkleɪm] N reconvención f.

counter-clockwise ['kaʊntə'klɒkwaɪz] ADV en sentido contrario al de las agujas del reloj, sinistrórsum.

counter-culture ['kaʊntə‚kʌltʃəʳ] N contracultura f.

counter-espionage ['kaʊntə'respɪɑnɑːʒ] N contraespionaje m.

counterexample ['kaʊntərɪg‚zɑːmpl] N contraejemplo m.

counterfeit ['kaʊntəfiːt] **1** ADJ falso, falsificado, contrahecho.
   2 N falsificación f; (coin) moneda f falsa, (note) billete m falso.
   3 VT falsificar, contrahacer.

counterfoil ['kaʊntəfɔɪl] N (Brit) talón m, matriz f.

counterhand ['kaʊntə‚hænd] N (in shop) dependiente m, -a f; (in snack bar) camarero m, -a f.

counter-indication ['kaʊntər‚ɪndɪ'keɪʃən] N contraindicación f.

counter insurgency ['kaʊntərɪn'sɜːdʒənsɪ] N medidas fpl antiin-surrectivas.

counterinsurgent ['kaʊntərɪn'sɜːdʒənt] N contrainsurgente mf.

counterintelligence ['kaʊntərɪn‚telɪdʒəns] N contraespionaje m.

countermand ['kaʊntəmɑːnd] VT revocar, cancelar.

counter-measure ['kaʊntəmeʒəʳ] N contramedida f.

counter-move ['kaʊntəmuːv] N contrajugada f; (fig) contraataque m; contramaniobra f.

counter-offensive ['kaʊntərə'fensɪv] N contraofensiva f.

counter-order ['kaʊntər‚ɔːdəʳ] N contraorden f.

counterpane ['kaʊntəpeɪn] N sobrecama m, colcha f, cobertor m.

counterpart ['kaʊntəpɑːt] N (person) homólogo m, -a f; (thing) equivalente m.

counterpoint ['kaʊntəpɔɪnt] N contrapunto m.

counterpoise ['kaʊntəpɔɪz] **1** N contrapeso m; compensación f.
   2 VT contrapesar; compensar.

counter-productive [‚kaʊntəprə'dʌktɪv] ADJ contraproducente.

counter-proposal ['kaʊntəprə‚pəʊzəl] N contrapropuesta f.

counterpunch ['kaʊntəpʌntʃ] N contragolpe m.

Counter-Reformation ['kaʊntə‚refə'meɪʃən] N Contrarreforma f.

counter-revolution ['kaʊntərevə'lu:ʃən] N contrarrevolución f.
counter-revolutionary ['kaʊntəreva'lu:ʃənrɪ] [1] ADJ contra-rrevolucionario.
[2] N contrarrevolucionario m, -a f.
countersign ['kaʊntəsaɪn] [1] N (Mil) contraseña f.
[2] VT refrendar.
countersink ['kaʊntəsɪŋk] VT avellanar.
counter-stroke ['kaʊntəstraʊk] N contragolpe m.
countersunk ['kaʊntəsʌŋk] ADJ screws encastrado, avellanado.
countertenor ['kaʊntə,tenəʳ] N contratenor m; ~ **voice** voz f de contratenor.
countervailing ['kaʊntə,veɪlɪŋ] ADJ compensatorio; ~ **duties** aranceles mpl compensatorios.
counterweigh [,kaʊntə'weɪ] VT contrapesar; compensar.
counterweight ['kaʊntəweɪt] N contrapeso m.
countess ['kaʊntɪs] N condesa f.
counting ['kaʊntɪŋ] N cálculo m.
countless ['kaʊntlɪs] ADJ incontable, innumerable; ~ **times** infinitas veces.
count-noun ['kaʊntnaʊn] N sustantivo m contable.
countrified ['kʌntrɪfaɪd] ADJ rústico.
country ['kʌntrɪ] [1] N (political) país m; (regarded more sentimentally) patria f; (countryside) campo m; (region) región f, tierra f; **love of** ~ amor m a la patria; **there's some good** ~ **to the north** hacia el norte hay buena tierra; **this is good fishing** ~ ésta es buena tierra para la pesca; **we had to leave the road and go across** ~ tuvimos que dejar la carretera e ir a través del campo; **to go to the** ~ (Brit Pol) apelar al país, convocar elecciones generales; **to live off the** ~ vivir del país.
[2] ATTR: ~ **bumpkin** patán m; ~ **club** club m campestre; ~ **cousin** pariente m pueblerino, parienta f pueblerina; ~ **cottage** casita f (en el campo); ~ **dance** contradanza f; baile m regional, baile m campestre; ~ **dancing** baile m folklórico; ~ **dweller** persona f que vive en el campo; ~ **folk** gente f del campo; ~ **gentleman** hacendado m; ~ **house** quinta f, finca f; ~ **life** vida f del campo, vida f campestre; ~ **music, ~ and western** (US Mus) música f country; ~ **park** parque m; ~ **people** gente f del campo; ~ **road** camino m vecinal; ~ **seat** finca f, casa f solariega; ver también GRAND OLE OPRY.
country-born [,kʌntrɪ'bɔ:n] ADJ nacido en el campo.
country-bred [,kʌntrɪ'bred] ADJ criado en el campo.
countryman ['kʌntrɪmən] N, PL **countrymen** ['kʌntrɪmən] campesino m; (fellow ~) compatriota m.
countryside ['kʌntrɪsaɪd] N campo m.
country-wide [,kʌntrɪ'waɪd] ADJ por todo el país, a escala nacional, de todo el país.
countrywoman ['kʌntrɪ,wʊmən] N, PL **countrywomen** ['kʌntrɪ,wɪmɪn] campesina f.
county ['kaʊntɪ] [1] N condado m.
[2] ADJ, ATTR: ~ **clerk's office** (US) registro m civil; ~ **commission** (US), ~ **council** (Brit) ≃ diputación f provincial; ~ **court** (Brit) juzgado m municipal; ~ **cricket** (Brit) partidos de cricket entre los condados; ~ **family** (Brit) familia f aristocrática rural; ~ **recorder's office** (US) ≃ registro m de la propiedad; ~ **road** (US) ≃ carretera f secundaria; ~ **seat** (US) cabeza f de partido; ~ **town** (esp Brit) capital f de condado; ver también COURTS.
coup [ku:] N golpe m; ~ **d'état** golpe m de estado; ~ **de grâce** golpe m de gracia; ~ **de théâtre** golpe m de teatro, golpe m de efecto; **to bring off a** ~ obtener un éxito inesperado.
coupé ['ku:peɪ] N cupé m.
couple ['kʌpl] [1] N (of things) par m; (of persons) pareja f; (married ~) matrimonio m; **young** ~ matrimonio m joven; **just a** ~ **of minutes** dos minutos nada más; **we had a** ~ **in a bar*** tomamos algo en un bar; **when he's had a** ~ **he starts to shout*** cuando ha bebido más de la cuenta se pone a gritar.
[2] VT names etc unir, juntar; ideas asociar; (Mech) acoplar, enganchar.
[3] VI (Zool) copularse.
coupledom* ['kʌpldəm] N convivencia f en pareja.
coupler ['kʌpləʳ] N (Comput) acoplador m; (US Rail) enganche m; **acoustic** ~ acoplador m acústico.
couplet ['kʌplɪt] N pareado m.
coupling ['kʌplɪŋ] N (Mech) acoplamiento m; (Rail, Aut) enganche m.
coupon ['ku:pɒn] N cupón m; vale m; (Fin) cupón m; (football-pool ~) boleto m.
courage ['kʌrɪdʒ] N valor m, valentía f; ~! ¡ánimo!; **to have the** ~ **of one's convictions** tener el valor de sus convicciones; **to pluck up one's** ~ hacer de tripas corazón; **to screw up one's** ~ **to** + infin cobrar bastante ánimo como para + infin; **we may take** ~ **from the fact that ...** es alentador el hecho de que ...; **take** ~! ¡ánimo!; **to take one's** ~ **in both hands** armarse de valor.
courageous [kə'reɪdʒəs] ADJ valiente, valeroso.
courageously [kə'reɪdʒəslɪ] ADV valientemente.
courgette [kʊə'ʒet] N (Brit) calabacín m, calabacita f.

courier ['kʊrɪəʳ] N estafeta f, mensajero m; correo m diplomático; (travel ~) guía mf de turismo.
▼ **course** [kɔ:s] [1] N (a) (movement, direction) dirección f, ruta f; (of bullet etc) trayectoria f; (of road) dirección f; (of river, star) curso m; (of illness) desarrollo m; (Naut) rumbo m, derrota f, (marked on chart) derrotero m; **we are on** ~ vamos por buen camino, esta ruta es la buena; **we are on** ~ **for victory** nos encaminamos al triunfo; **to change** ~ cambiar de rumbo (also fig); **to set** ~ **for** hacer rumbo a; **to steer a** ~ **for** ir rumbo a.
(b) (mode of action) proceder m, camino m; ~ **of action** línea f de conducta, línea f de acción, proceder m; ~ **of conduct** línea f de conducta; ~ **of events** marcha f de los acontecimientos; **in the ordinary** ~ **of events** normalmente; **the** ~ **of true love** el camino del verdadero amor; **your best** ~ **is to say nothing** lo mejor es no decir nada; **there was no** ~ **open to me but to go** no tuve más remedio que ir; **what** ~ **do you suggest?** ¿qué es lo que me aconsejas?; **the affair has run its** ~ el asunto ha terminado; **we will let things take their** ~ dejaremos que las cosas sigan su curso normal, dejaremos correr los acontecimientos; **to take a middle** ~ evitar los extremos.
(c) (Golf) campo m, cancha f (LAm); (for races) pista f, (for horse-races) hipódromo m; **to stay the** ~ no cejar, continuar hasta el fin.
(d) (in meal) plato m.
(e) (Archit) hilada f.
(f) (series) curso m; (of injections) serie f; (Univ etc) curso m, asignatura f; **I failed the chemistry** ~ me suspendieron en química; **what** ~ **do you take?** ¿qué asignatura haces?; **a French** ~ un curso de francés; **I bought a French grammar** ~ compré una gramática francesa; **a** ~ **of lectures** un ciclo de conferencias; ~ **of treatment** tratamiento m, cura f; **to take a** ~ **with** seguir un curso con.
(g) (phrases) **in the** ~ **of** durante, en el curso de; durante el desarrollo de; **in** ~ **of construction** en vías de construcción; **it is in** ~ **of being applied** está en trance de ser aplicado; **in (the)** ~ **of time, in due** ~ andando el tiempo, a su debido tiempo; **we shall inform you**
▼ **in due** ~ se lo comunicaremos en su momento; **of** ~ desde luego,
▼ naturalmente; **of ~!** ¡por supuesto!, ¡naturalmente!, ¡claro!; **of ~ it's not true** claro que no es cierto; **it is of ~ true that ...** bien es verdad que ...; **he takes it all as a matter of** ~ para él todo esto no tiene nada de especial; **he took it as a matter of ~ that ...** para él era de cajón que ....
[2] VT hares cazar (con perros).
[3] VI (Sport) correr; **it sent the blood coursing through my veins** me hizo hervir la sangre.
coursing ['kɔ:sɪŋ] N caza f con perros.
court [kɔ:t] [1] N (a) (Archit) patio m.
(b) (Sport) pista f, cancha f.
(c) (royal) corte f; **at** ~ en la corte; ~ **circular** noticiario m de la corte; ~ **shoe** (Brit) escarpín m; **to hold** ~ dar audiencia, recibir en audiencia.
(d) **to pay** ~ **to** hacer la corte a.
(e) (Jur) tribunal m, juzgado m; ~ **of appeal** (Brit) tribunal m de apelación; ~ **of inquiry** comisión f de investigación; ~ **of justice,** ~ **of law** tribunal m de justicia; **C~ of Session** (Scot) Tribunal m Supremo de Escocia; ~ **order** (Jur) mandato m judicial; **in open** ~ en pleno tribunal; **to laugh sth out of** ~ rechazar algo poniéndolo en ridículo; **to rule sth out of** ~ desestimar algo; **to settle out of** ~ negociar una solución al margen de los tribunales, arreglar una disputa de modo privado; **to take sb to** ~ demandar a uno; recurrir a la vía judicial, llevar a uno ante los tribunales.
[2] VT woman cortejar, hacer la corte a, (less formally) tener relaciones con; favour solicitar; danger, trouble buscar; disaster correr hacia.
[3] VI estar en relaciones, ser novios; **they've been ~ing 3 years** llevan 3 años de relaciones; **are you ~ing?** ¿tienes novio?; **~ing couple** pareja f de novios.

COURTS

ⓘ En Inglaterra, Gales e Irlanda del Norte, los delitos graves y los juicios en los que el acusado se declara inocente en la vista preliminar se resuelven en el Tribunal de la Corona (**Crown Court**), ante un juez y un jurado compuesto por doce personas. Los delitos menores se juzgan en los tribunales de primera instancia, llamados **magistrate's courts**, sin jurado. La mayoría de los casos de lo civil se juzgan en los tribunales locales. Los casos más serios o complejos se resuelven en el Tribunal Supremo (**High Court**). Las apelaciones, tanto civiles como penales, se pueden remitir al Tribunal de Apelación (**Court of Appeal**) y en última instancia a la Cámara de los Lores (**House of Lords**).
En el sistema judicial escocés, el Tribunal Superior (**High Court of Justiciary**) se encarga de la mayoría de los delitos penales, mientras que los tribunales de distrito (**sheriff courts**) se ocupan de los casos menores. El Tribunal Supremo es el llamado **Court of Session**.
En Estados Unidos, los tribunales federales se ocupan de los asuntos relativos a las leyes federales o que competen a más de un estado, mientras que los tribunales estatales se ocupan de los casos concernientes a las leyes

---

*específicas de cada estado. Éstos tienen su propio sistema legal y competencias para dictar sus propias leyes, siempre y cuando éstas no se opongan a la Constitución o a las leyes federales. No existe ninguna distinción entre tribunales de lo penal y lo civil, ni a nivel federal ni estatal. La mayoría de los asuntos federales se resuelven en tribunales de distrito (**district courts**) mientras que doce tribunales de apelación (**courts of appeal**) se ocupan de las apelaciones que provienen de los tribunales federales menores. El tribunal federal más importante es el Tribunal Supremo (**Supreme Court**), el mismo nombre que recibe el más alto tribunal estatal. Por debajo de éste se encuentran los tribunales con competencia de apelación (**appellate courts**) y los tribunales de cada condado (**county court**) y ciudad (**city courts**), que se encargan de temas de jurisdicción general.*
⇨ *Ver también* MAGISTRATE

court card ['kɔːtkɑːd] N (*esp Brit*) figura *f*.
Courtelle [kɔː'tel] ® N Courtelle *f* ®.
courteous ['kɜːtɪəs] ADJ cortés, fino, correcto.
courteously ['kɜːtɪəslɪ] ADV cortésmente.
courtesan [ˌkɔːtɪ'zæn] N cortesana *f*.
courtesy ['kɜːtɪsɪ] [1] N cortesía *f*; atención *f*; gentileza *f*; **by ~ of** con permiso de; gracias a; **to exchange courtesies** cambiar cumplidos (de etiqueta); **I'll do it out of ~** lo haré por cortesía; **you might have had the ~ to tell me** el no decírmelo fue una falta de educación; **he did me the ~ of reading it** tuvo la gentileza de leérmelo.
[2] ATTR: **~ bus** autobús *m* de cortesía; **~ call, ~ visit** visita *f* de cumplido; **~ car** coche *m* de cortesía; **~ card** (*US*) tarjeta *f* (de visita); **~ coach** (*Brit*) autocar *m* de cortesía al aeropuerto; **~ light** (*Aut*) luz *f* interior; **~ title** título *m* de cortesía.
courthouse ['kɔːthaʊs] N, PL **courthouses** ['kɔːtˌhaʊzɪz] palacio *m* de justicia.
courtier ['kɔːtɪəʳ] N cortesano *m*.
courtly ['kɔːtlɪ] ADJ cortés, elegante, fino; **~ love** amor *m* cortés.
court-martial ['kɔːt'mɑːʃəl], PL **courts-martial** [1] N consejo *m* de guerra, tribunal *m* militar.
[2] VT someter a consejo de guerra.
courtroom ['kɔːtrʊm] N sala *f* de justicia, sala *f* de tribunal.
courtship ['kɔːtʃɪp] N (*act*) cortejo *m*; (*period*) noviazgo *m*.
courtyard ['kɔːtjɑːd] N patio *m*.
cousin ['kʌzn] N primo *m*, -a *f*; **first ~** primo *m* carnal, prima *f* carnal; **second ~** primo *m* segundo, prima *f* segunda.
couth [kuːθ] N (*US*) buenos modales *mpl*.
couture [kuː'tjʊə] N alta costura *f*.
couturier [kuː'tʊərɪˌeɪ] N modisto *m*.
cove¹ [kəʊv] N (*Geog*) cala *f*, ensenada *f*; (*US: valley*) valle *m*.
cove²*† [kəʊv] N tío* *m*.
coven ['kʌvən] N aquelarre *m*, asamblea *f* de brujas.
covenant ['kʌvɪnənt] [1] N pacto *m*, convenio *m*; (*Bible*) **C~** Alianza *f*; (**tax**) **~** (*Brit*) sistema *m* de contribuciones caritativas con beneficios fiscales para el recipiente.
[2] VI: **to ~ with sb for sth** pactar algo con uno; **to ~ £500** contribuir 500 libras bajo 'covenant'.
Coventry ['kɒvəntrɪ] N (*Brit*) **to send sb to ~** hacer el vacío a uno.
cover ['kʌvəʳ] [1] N (a) (*gen*) cubierta *f*; (*lid*) tapa *f*, tapadura *f*; (*on bed*) cobertor *m*, colcha *f*; (*of chair, typewriter*) funda *f*; **~s** (*bedclothes*) ropa *f* de cama, mantas *fpl*.
(b) (*envelope*) sobre *m*; **first-day ~** sobre *m* de primer día; **under separate ~** por (envío) separado.
(c) (*of book*) forro *m*, cubierta *f*; (*of magazine*) portada *f*; **to read a book from ~ to ~** leer un libro desde el principio hasta el fin.
(d) (*at table*) cubierto *m*.
(e) (*fig*) protección *f*; (*shelter*) abrigo *m*; (*Brit: insurance*) cobertura *f*; (*pretext*) pretexto *m*; (*Fin*) cobertura *f*, (*of spy*) cobertura *f*, tapadera *f*; **under ~** al abrigo, (*indoors*) bajo techo; **under ~ of** al abrigo de, bajo, (*fig*) so capa de; **under the ~ of night** al amparo de la noche; **to break ~** salir a campo raso; **to take ~** abrigarse, ponerse al abrigo, (*Mil*) refugiarse (*from* de).
[2] VT (a) (*gen*) cubrir (*with* de); revestir (*with* de); (*with lid*) tapar (*with* con); *book* forrar; (*shelter*) cubrir, proteger, abrigar; *eyes, face* tapar; **to be ~ed in confusion** estar lleno de confusión; **to be ~ed in glory** estar cubierto de gloria.
(b) (*protect*) proteger; *advance, retreat* cubrir, proteger.
(c) (*with gun*) apuntar; **I've got you ~ed** te tengo apuntado.
(d) (*Sport*) cubrir.
(e) (*distance*) cubrir, recorrer, salvar.
(f) (*include*) incluir, abarcar, comprender; (*be enough for*) cubrir; *problem* abarcar; *points in discussion* tratar, discutir; (*in speech*) tratar, exponer; dar razón de; *costs, insurance risk* cubrir; **to ~ all possibilities** abarcar todas las posibilidades; **to ~ one's expenses** cubrir los gastos; **to ~ a loss** cubrir una pérdida; **£50 will ~ everything** 50 libras lo cubrirá todo.
(g) *story* cubrir, hacer un reportaje sobre, escribir una crónica de;

news item informar acerca de.
[3] VR: **to ~ o.s.** protegerse a sí mismo; **to ~ o.s. with glory** cubrirse de gloria.
◆**cover in** VT cubrir; (*roof*) poner un techo a, techar.
◆**cover over** VT cubrir, revestir (*with* de).
◆**cover up** [1] VT *object* cubrir completamente, tapar; *truth, facts* correr un velo sobre, ocultar, encubrir; *emotion* disimular.
[2] VI (a) **to ~ up for sb** encubrir a uno.
(b) (*with clothes*) abrigarse, taparse bien; (*in bed*) taparse.
coverage ['kʌvərɪdʒ] N (a) alcance *m*; espacio *m* cubierto, cantidad *f* cubierta; (*of news*) cobertura *f*, reportaje *m*. (b) (*Fin*) cobertura *f*, conjunto *m* de los riesgos que cubre una póliza de seguros.
coveralls ['kʌvərɔːlz] NPL (*US*) = overalls.
cover-charge ['kʌvətʃɑːdʒ] N precio *m* del cubierto.
covered wagon [ˌkʌvəd'wægən] N carreta *f* entoldada.
covergirl ['kʌvəgɜːl] N modelo *f* de portada.
covering ['kʌvərɪŋ] [1] N (*wrapping*) cubierta *f*, envoltura *f*; (*dress etc*) abrigo *m*; (*Sport*) cobertura *f*; **a ~ of snow** una capa de nieve.
[2] ADJ: **~ letter** carta *f* adjunta.
coverlet ['kʌvəlɪt] N sobrecama *m*, colcha *f*, cobertor *m*.
cover-letter ['kʌvəˌletəʳ] N carta *f* (adjunta) de explicación.
cover-note ['kʌvəˌnəʊt] N (*Brit*) ≃ seguro *m* provisional.
cover price ['kʌvəˌpraɪs] N precio *m* de cubierta.
cover-story ['kʌvəˌstɔːrɪ] N (*Press*) noticia *f* de primera página; (*in espionage etc*) tapadera *f*; **our ~ this week** nuestra noticia de primera página de esta semana.
covert ['kʌvət] [1] ADJ secreto, disimulado.
[2] N soto *m*, matorral *m*.
cover-up ['kʌvərʌp] N encubrimiento *m*; **there's been a ~** están tratando de encubrir el escándalo (*etc*).
covet ['kʌvɪt] VT codiciar.
covetous ['kʌvɪtəs] ADJ codicioso.
covetousness ['kʌvɪtəsnɪs] N codicia *f*.
covey ['kʌvɪ] N (*Orn*) nidada *f* (de perdices); (*fig*) grupo *m*.
cow¹ [kaʊ] N (a) vaca *f*; (*of elephant etc*) hembra *f*; **till the ~s come home** hasta que la rana críe pelo. (b) (*: *also* **old ~**) bruja* *f*.
cow² [kaʊ] VT intimidar, acobardar.
coward ['kaʊəd] N cobarde *m*.
cowardice ['kaʊədɪs] N, **cowardliness** ['kaʊədlɪnɪs] N cobardía *f*.
cowardly ['kaʊədlɪ] ADJ cobarde.
cowbell ['kaʊbel] N cencerro *m*.
cowboy ['kaʊbɔɪ] N vaquero *m*; (*Cine etc*) cowboy *m*; **~s and Indians** (*game*) cowboys y pieles rojas; **the ~s of the building trade** los piratas de la construcción.
cowboy boots ['kaʊbɔɪˌbuːts] NPL botas *fpl* camperas.
cowboy hat ['kaʊbɔɪˌhæt] N sombrero *m* de cowboy.
cowcatcher ['kaʊˌkætʃəʳ] N rastrillo *m* delantero, quitapiedras *m*.
cower ['kaʊəʳ] VI encogerse (de miedo), empequeñecerse (preso del terror); **the servants were ~ing in a corner** los criados se habían refugiado medrosos en un rincón.
cowgirl ['kaʊgɜːl] N vaquera *f*.
cowherd ['kaʊhɜːd] N pastor *m*, -ora *f* de ganado, vaquero *m*, -a *f*.
cowhide ['kaʊhaɪd] N cuero *m*.
cow-house ['kaʊhaʊs] N, PL **cow-houses** ['kaʊhaʊzɪz] establo *m*.
cowl [kaʊl] N (*hood*) capucha *f*; (*garment*) cogulla *f*; (*of chimney*) sombrerete *m*.
cowlick ['kaʊlɪk] N (*US*) chavito *m*, mechón *m*.
cowling ['kaʊlɪŋ] N cubierta *f*.
cowman ['kaʊmən] N, PL **cowmen** ['kaʊmən] (*Brit*) pastor *m* de ganado, vaquero *m*; (*US*) ganadero *m*.
co-worker ['kəʊ'wɜːkəʳ] N colaborador *m*, -ora *f*.
cow-parsley [ˌkaʊ'pɑːslɪ] N perejil *m* de monte.
cowpat ['kaʊpæt] N cagada *f* de vaca, boñiga *f*.
cowpoke* ['kaʊpəʊk] N (*US*) vaquero *m*.
cowpox ['kaʊpɒks] N vacuna *f*.
cowrie ['kaʊrɪ] N cauri *m*.
cowshed ['kaʊʃed] N establo *m*.
cowslip ['kaʊslɪp] N primavera *f*, prímula *f*.
cow town* ['kaʊtaʊn] N (*US*) pueblucho *m* de mala muerte.
cox [kɒks] [1] N timonel *m*.
[2] VT gobernar.
[3] VI hacer (*or* actuar) de timonel.
coxcomb ['kɒkskəʊm] N cresta *f* de gallo.
coxless pairs [ˌkɒkslɪs'peəz] N dos *m* sin timonel.
coxswain ['kɒksn] N timonel *m*.
Coy (*Mil*) ABBR *of* **company**.
coy [kɔɪ] ADJ tímido; evasivo, reservado; (*roguish*) coquetón.
coyly ['kɔɪlɪ] ADV tímidamente; con coquetería.
coyness ['kɔɪnɪs] N timidez *f*; coquetería *f*.
coyote [kɔɪ'əʊtɪ] N coyote *m*.
coypu ['kɔɪpuː] N coipo *m*.
'coz* [kɒz] = **because**.

coz* [kɒz] = **cousin**.
coziness ['kəʊzɪnɪs] N (US) = **cosiness**.
cozy ['kəʊzɪ] ADJ (US) = **cosy**.
cozzie* ['kɒzɪ] = **cossie**.
CP (a) N (Pol) ABBR of **Communist Party** Partido m Comunista, PC m. (b) (Comm) ABBR of **carriage paid** porte m pagado, P.P.
c/p ABBR of **carriage paid** porte pagado, P.P.
cp. ABBR of **compare** compárese, comp.
CPA (a) (US) ABBR of **Certified Public Accountant**. (b) ABBR of **critical path analysis**.
CPI N (US) ABBR of **Consumer Price Index** Indice m de precios al consumo, IPC.
Cpl ABBR of **Corporal** cabo m.
CP/M N ABBR of **Central Program for Microprocessors** CP/M m.
CPO (a) N ABBR of **Chief Petty Officer** suboficial mf jefe de marina. (b) N ABBR of **Crime Prevention Officer** agente mf de prevención del delito.
CPR N ABBR of **cardiopulmonary resuscitation** reanimación f cardio-pulmonar.
cps NPL abbr of **characters per second** caracteres mpl por segundo, cps.
CPSA N ABBR of **Civil and Public Services Association** sindicato de funcionarios.
CPU N ABBR of **central processing unit** unidad f central de proceso, UPC f.
Cr (a) (Comm) ABBR of **credit** haber m. (b) (Comm) ABBR of **creditor** acreedor m. (c) (Pol) ABBR of **councillor** concejal m, -ala f.
crab [kræb] [1] N (a) cangrejo m; **C~** (Astron) Cáncer m; **to catch a ~** (fig) fallar con el remo, dar una calada. (b) **~s** (Med) ladillas fpl.
[2] VI: **to ~** (about)* quejarse (acerca de).
crabapple ['kræb‚æpl] N (fruit) manzana f silvestre; (tree) manzano m silvestre.
crabbed ['kræbd] ADJ writing apretado, indescifrable; temperament de miras estrechas; mood malhumorado, hosco.
crabby ['kræbɪ] ADJ malhumorado, hosco, gruñón.
crab grass ['kræbgrɑːs] N garranchuelo m.
crab louse ['kræblaʊs] N, PL **crab lice** ['kræblaɪs] ladilla f.
crabmeat ['kræbmiːt] N carne f de cangrejo.
crabwise ['kræb‚waɪz] [1] ADJ movement como de cangrejo, lateral.
[2] ADV move como cangrejo, lateralmente.
crack [kræk] [1] N (a) (noise) crujido m; (of whip) chasquido m; (shot) estallido m; **to get a fair ~ of the whip** recibir un trato equitativo, ser tratado lo mismo que otros. (b) (blow) golpe m (on en). (c) (fissure) grieta f, hendedura f; (slit) rendija f; **at the ~ of dawn** al romper el alba; **to open the window a ~** abrir la ventana un poquito; **to paper over the ~s** disimular las grietas (also fig). (d) (*: joke) chiste m, chanza f, cuchufleta f; **to make ~s about person** tomar el pelo a, burlarse de, thing poner en ridículo. (e) (*: attempt) **to have a ~ at sth** intentar algo, probar algo. (f) (*: drug) crack m, cocaína f dura.
[2] ADJ team etc de primera categoría; **~ driver, shot** etc as m.
[3] VT (a) (cause to sound) whip, fingers chasquear; knuckles etc crujir. (b) (break) agrietar, hender, romper; nut cascar; safe forzar; (*) bottle abrir (with para festejar a); oil craquear; **to ~ one's head on the wall** dar con la cabeza contra la pared; **to ~ sb over the head** golpear a uno en la cabeza. (c) (*) joke contar. (d) code descifrar; case, mystery resolver, aclarar; **I think we've ~ed the problem** creo que hemos resuelto el problema.
[4] VI (a) (make noise) chasquear; crujir; (shot) estallar. (b) (break) agrietarse, henderse, rajarse, romperse; (burst) reventar; (voice) cascarse; (resistance etc) desplomarse; **to ~ under the strain** romperse bajo el peso, (person) sufrir un colapso bajo la presión. (c) **to get ~ing** (Brit*) ponerse a trabajar (etc), poner manos a la obra; **let's get ~ing!** ¡a ello!, ¡manos a la obra!
♦**crack down on** VT castigar severamente; tomar medidas enérgicas contra; suprimir.
♦**crack up** [1] VT dar bombo a; **it's not all it's ~ed up to be** no es tan bueno como la gente dice.
[2] VI (esp US: plane) estrellarse; (car etc) averiarse; (business etc) derrumbarse, venirse abajo; fallar; no poder soportarlo más; (Med) sufrir un colapso nervioso; (get angry) enfadarse, ponerse furioso.
crackajack ['krækədʒæk] N, ADJ (US) = **crackerjack**.
crack-brained ['krækbreɪnd] ADJ loco.
crackdown ['krækdaʊn] N campaña f (on contra); medidas fpl enérgicas (on contra); supresión f (on de); período m de aplastamiento.
cracked [krækt] ADJ (a) voice cascado. (b) (mad) chiflado, tarado (LAm).
cracker ['krækər] N (a) (firework) buscapiés m; (Brit: Christmas ~) sorpresa f. (b) (biscuit) galleta f de soda, galleta f para queso; (US) galleta f. (c) **a ~ of a game*** un partido fenomenal*.
crackerjack, (US) **crackajack** ['krækədʒæk] [1] N (person) as* m;

(thing) bomba* f.
[2] ADJ bomba*, súper*.
crackers: ['krækəz] ADJ (Brit) lelo, chiflado.
crackhead* ['kræk‚hed] N adicto m, -a f al crack.
crack house ['krækhaʊs] N lugar donde se vende crack.
cracking ['krækɪŋ] [1] N (petroleum) cracking m; (cracks) grietas fpl, agrietamiento m.
[2] ADJ (Brit) cutre*; **at a ~ speed** (or **pace**) a toda pastilla*.
[3] ADV (Brit*) tope*.
crackle ['krækl] [1] N (of wood, bacon) crepitación f, chisporroteo m; (of dry leaves) crujido m; (of shots) traqueteo m.
[2] VI crepitar, chisporrotear; crujir; traquetear.
crackling ['kræklɪŋ] N (a) (Culin) chicharrón m. (b) (sound) V **crackle**.
crackly ['krækəlɪ] ADJ phone line, noise chirriante, chisporroteante.
crackpot ['krækpɒt] [1] ADJ tonto, estrafalario, excéntrico.
[2] N chiflado m, -a f, excéntrico m, -a f.
crack-up ['krækʌp] N crisis f nerviosa; (Fin etc) derrumbamiento m, quiebra f; (Med) colapso m nervioso.
cradle ['kreɪdl] [1] N cuna f (also fig); (for house-painting etc) plataforma f colgante; **from the ~ to the grave** de la cuna a la tumba; **she's a ~ snatcher*** siempre va detrás de jovencitos; **to rob the ~** (US*) casarse con una persona mucho más joven.
[2] VT: **to ~ a child in one's arms** mecer un niño en los brazos.
cradlesong ['kreɪdlsɒŋ] N canción f de cuna.
craft [krɑːft] [1] N (a) (skill in general) destreza f, habilidad f; (craftiness) astucia f. (b) (special skill) arte m; (trade) oficio m; **~ union** sindicato m de obreros especializados; **~ work** artesanía f. (c) (Naut) barco m, embarcación f.
[2] VT hacer (a mano); **~ed products** productos mpl de artesanía.
craftily ['krɑːftɪlɪ] ADV astutamente.
craftiness ['krɑːftɪnɪs] N astucia f.
craftsman ['krɑːftsmən] N, PL **craftsmen** ['krɑːftsmən] artesano m.
craftsmanship ['krɑːftsmənʃɪp] N artesanía f.
craftsperson ['krɑːfts‚pɜːsn] N, PL **craftspeople** artesano m, -a f.
craftswoman ['krɑːfts‚wʊmən] N, PL **craftswomen** artesana f.
crafty ['krɑːftɪ] ADJ (a) person, move etc astuto. (b) (*) gadget etc ingenioso.
crag [kræg] N peñasco m, risco m.
craggy ['krægɪ] ADJ peñascoso, escarpado; face de facciones marcadas.
cram [kræm] [1] VT (a) hen cebar; subject empollar, aprender apresuradamente; pupil preparar apresuradamente para un examen. (b) **to ~ food into one's mouth** llenarse la boca de comida; **to ~ things into a case** ir metiendo cosas apretadamente en una maleta; **we can't ~ any more in** es imposible meter más. (c) **to ~ sth with** llenar algo de, henchir algo de; **the hall is ~med** la sala está de bote en bote; **the room is ~med with furniture** el cuarto está atestado de muebles; **he had his head ~med with odd ideas** tenía la cabeza cargada de ideas raras.
[2] VI (a) **to ~ in, come ~ming in** entrar en masa, amontonarse; **7 of us ~med into the Mini** los 7 logramos encajarnos en el Mini; **can I ~ in here?** ¿quepo yo aquí? (b) (for exam) empollar. (c) = **3**.
[3] VR: **to ~ o.s. with food** darse un atracón; **to ~ o.s. with cakes** atracarse de pastas.
cram-full ['kræm'fʊl] ADJ atestado (of de), de bote en bote.
crammer ['kræmər] N (Scol: pupil) empollón m, -ona f; (teacher) profesor m, -ora f que prepara rapidísimamente a sus alumnos para los exámenes.
cramp¹ [kræmp] N (Med) calambre m.
cramp² [kræmp] [1] N (Tech) grapa f; (Archit) pieza f de unión, abrazadera f.
[2] VT (hamper) estorbar, restringir; **to ~ sb's style** cortar los vuelos a uno, cohibir a uno.
cramped [kræmpt] ADJ room etc estrecho; writing menudo, apretado; position nada cómodo; **we are very ~ for space here** estamos muy estrechos aquí.
crampon ['kræmpən] N garfio m; (Mountaineering) crampón m.
cramponning ['kræmpənɪŋ] N uso m de crampones.
cranberry ['krænbərɪ] N arándano m (agrio).
crane [kreɪn] [1] N (Orn) grulla f; (Tech) grúa f.
[2] VT (also **to ~ up**) levantar con grúa; **to ~ one's neck** estirar el cuello.
♦**crane forward** VI inclinarse estirando el cuello; **to ~ forward to look at sth** estirar el cuello para mirar algo.
crane-driver ['kreɪn‚draɪvər] N gruista mf.
cranefly ['kreɪnflaɪ] N típula f.
crane operator ['kreɪn‚ɒpəreɪtər] N = **crane-driver**.
cranial ['kreɪnɪəl] ADJ craneal.
cranium ['kreɪnɪəm] N, PL **crania** ['kreɪnɪə] cráneo m.
crank¹ [kræŋk] [1] N manivela f, manubrio m; cigüeñal m.
[2] VT engine (also **to ~ up**) dar vuelta a, hacer arrancar con la

manivela.
◆**crank out*** VT (US) producir penosamente.
crank²* [kræŋk] N (Brit: person) maniático m, -a, f, chiflado m, -a f, excéntrico m, -a f; (US: person) gruñón m, -ona f.
crankcase ['kræŋkkeɪs] N cárter m (del cigüeñal).
crankshaft ['kræŋkʃɑːft] N (eje m del) cigüeñal m, árbol m del cigüeñal.
cranky* ['kræŋkɪ] ADJ person maniático, chiflado, excéntrico; idea raro, estrafalario.
cranny ['krænɪ] N grieta f.
crap** [kræp] [1] N (a) (lit) mierda**. (b) (fig): to be ~ ser una mierda**; that's ~ eso es una chorrada*; to talk ~ decir chorradas*.
[2] ATTR malísimo.
[3] VI cagar**.
◆**crap out**** VI (US) (a) (back down) rajarse*. (b) (fail) fracasar.
crape [kreɪp] N crespón m.
crappy** ['kræpɪ] ADJ (esp US) asqueroso.
craps [kræps] NPL (US) dados mpl; to shoot ~ jugar a los dados.
crapulous ['kræpjʊləs] ADJ (frm) crapuloso, ebrio.
crash [kræʃ] [1] N (a) (noise) estruendo m, estrépito m; (explosion) estallido m.
(b) (collision) accidente m, colisión f; choque m, encontronazo m; (Aer) accidente m de aviación.
(c) (ruin) fracaso m, ruina f; (Comm) quiebra f; crac m; the 1929 ~ la crisis económica de 1929.
(d) (*: drug) mono** m, síndrome m de abstinencia.
[2] VT car, aircraft estrellar (into contra); estropear; he ~ed the plate to the ground echó el plato por tierra; he ~ed the plate into her face le dio con el plato en la cara; to ~ a party* colarse, entrar de rondón*.
[3] VI (a) (fall noisily: also to ~ down, to come ~ing down) caer con estrépito; (shatter) romperse, hacerse añicos.
(b) (have accident) tener un accidente; (2 cars etc) colisionar, chocar; (Aer) estrellarse, caer a tierra; to ~ into chocar con, estrellarse contra.
(c) (fail) fracasar, hundirse; derrumbarse; (Comm) quebrar; when the stock market ~ed cuando la bolsa se derrumbó.
(d) (*) dormir, pasar la noche.
[4] ADV: he went ~ into a tree dio de lleno consigo contra un árbol.
[5] INTERJ ¡zas!, ¡pum!
[6] ADJ: ~ course curso m acelerado, curso m concentrado; ~ programme programa m de urgencia.
◆**crash out**** [1] VT: to be ~ed out estar hecho polvo.
[2] VI caer redondo, dormirse, apalancar**.
crash-barrier ['kræʃ,bærɪər] N (Brit) valla f protectora.
crash dive ['kræʃ,daɪv] N (of submarine) inmersión f de emergencia.
crash-helmet ['kræʃ,helmɪt] N casco m protector.
crashing ['kræʃɪŋ] ADJ: a ~ bore una paliza*, un muermo*.
crashingly ['kræʃɪŋlɪ] ADV dull, boring tremendamente.
crash-land ['kræʃlænd] [1] VT aircraft poner forzosamente en tierra.
[2] VI aterrizar forzosamente.
crash-landing ['kræʃ,lændɪŋ] N aterrizaje m forzado.
crash-pad** ['kræʃ,pæd] N guarida f, lugar m donde dormir.
crass [kræs] ADJ craso, estúpido.
crassly ['kræslɪ] ADV estúpidamente, tontamente.
crassness ['kræsnɪs] N estupidez f.
crate [kreɪt] [1] N (a) cajón m de embalaje, jaula f. (b) (*: car etc) armatoste m, cacharro* m.
[2] VT (also to ~ up) embalar (en cajones).
crater ['kreɪtər] N cráter m.
cravat(e) [krə'væt] N corbata f de fantasía, fular m, foulard m.
crave [kreɪv] [1] VT suplicar, implorar; attention reclamar.
[2] VI: to ~ for ansiar, anhelar.
craven ['kreɪvən] ADJ (liter) cobarde.
cravenly ['kreɪvənlɪ] ADV de manera cobarde, con cobardía.
cravenness ['kreɪvənnɪs] N (liter) cobardía f.
craving ['kreɪvɪŋ] N deseo m vehemente, ansia f, sed f (for de); (during pregnancy) antojo m; to get a ~ for sth encapricharse por algo.
craw [krɔː] N: to stick in one's ~*: it really sticks in my ~ that she thinks... no trago con que ella piense que....
crawfish ['krɔːfɪʃ] N (US: freshwater) cangrejo m de río; (saltwater) cigala f.
crawl [krɔːl] [1] N (action) arrastramiento m; (journey) camino m a gatas; (Swimming) crol m; the traffic went at a ~ la circulación avanzaba a paso de tortuga; the ~ to the coast el viaje a una lentitud desesperante hacia la costa.
[2] VI (a) (drag o.s.) arrastrarse; avanzar a rastras; (child) andar a gatas, gatear; to ~ in entrar a gatas; the fly ~ed up the window la mosca subió despacio el cristal; the cars were ~ing along los coches avanzaban a paso de tortuga.
(b) to ~ to sb humillarse ante uno, ir humildemente a pedir perdón a uno.

(c) to ~ with, to be ~ing with estar cuajado de, estar plagado de, hervir en (or de).
crawler ['krɔːlər] N (Mech) tractor m de oruga; ~ lane (Brit Aut) carril m (de autopista) para vehículos lentos.
crayfish ['kreɪfɪʃ] N (freshwater) cangrejo m de río; (saltwater) cigala f.
crayon ['kreɪən] [1] N (Art) pastel m, lápiz m de tiza; (child's) lápiz m de color.
[2] VT dibujar al pastel (etc).
craze [kreɪz] N manía f (for por); (fashion) moda f (for de); to be the ~ estar en boga.
crazed [kreɪzd] ADJ loco (with de), demente.
crazily ['kreɪzɪlɪ] ADV locamente; lean etc de modo peligroso.
craziness ['kreɪzɪnɪs] N locura f, chifladura f.
crazy ['kreɪzɪ] ADJ (a) person loco, chiflado, tarado (LAm), zafado (LAm); idea disparatado, estrafalario; to be ~ about person estar chiflado por, thing andar loco por; to be ~ with worry estar loco de inquietud; to drive sb ~ volver loco a uno; it's enough to drive you ~ es para volverse loco; to go ~ volverse loco; everyone shouted like ~ todos gritaron como locos; ~ house (US*) casa f de locos*.
(b) building destartalado; to lean at a ~ angle inclinarse de modo peligroso.
(c) ~ paving enlosado m (de diseño) irregular.
(d) (US**) tope*.
crazy-bone ['kreɪzɪ,bəʊn] N (US) hueso m de la alegría.
CRC N (US) ABBR of **Civil Rights Commission.**
CRE N (Brit) ABBR of **Commission for Racial Equality** comisión f para la no discriminación racial.
creak [kriːk] [1] N (of wood, shoe etc) crujido m; (of hinge etc) chirrido m, rechinamiento m.
[2] VI crujir; chirriar, rechinar.
creaky ['kriːkɪ] ADJ rechinador; (fig) poco sólido, inestable, nada firme.
cream [kriːm] [1] N (a) (on milk) nata f; single ~ (Brit) crema f de leche; double ~ (Brit) nata f.
(b) (gen) crema f; ~ of tartar crémor m tártaro; ~ of wheat (US) sémola f.
(c) (fig) flor f y nata, crema f, lo mejor y más selecto; the ~ of society la crema de la sociedad; the ~ of the joke was that lo más gracioso fue que.
[2] ADJ color de crema.
[3] ATTR: ~ cake pastel m de nata; ~ cheese requesón m, queso m de nata; ~ cracker galleta f de soda, galleta f para queso; ~ puff petisú m; ~ of tomato soup crema f de sopa de tomate.
[4] VT (a) milk desnatar; butter batir. (b) (US*) arrollar, aplastar.
◆**cream off** VT (fig) quitar lo mejor de, tomarse lo mejor de.
creamery ['kriːmərɪ] N (a) (on farm) lechería f; (butter factory) fábrica f de productos lácteos. (b) (small shop) lechería f.
creaminess ['kriːmɪnɪs] N cremosidad f.
creamy ['kriːmɪ] ADJ cremoso.
crease [kriːs] [1] N (fold) pliegue m; (in trousers) raya f; (wrinkle) arruga f.
[2] VT paper plegar, doblar; clothes arrugar; to ~ one's trousers (press ~ in) hacer la raya a los pantalones.
[3] VI plegarse, doblarse; arrugarse.
◆**crease up** VT hacer morirse de risa.
creaseless ['kriːslɪs] ADJ, **crease-resisting** ['kriːsɪ,zɪstɪŋ] ADJ inarrugable.
crease-resistant ['kriːsɪ,zɪstənt] ADJ inarrugable.
create [kriː'eɪt] [1] VT crear (also Comput); (produce) producir, motivar; character inventar; rôle encarnar; (appoint) nombrar.
[2] VI (Brit*) protestar, armar un lío*.
creation [kriː'eɪʃən] N creación f; (appointment) nombramiento m; (dress etc) modelo m.
creationism [kriː'eɪʃənɪzəm] N creacionismo m.
creationist [kriː'eɪʃənɪst] N creacionista mf.
creative [kriː'eɪtɪv] ADJ creativo; work original; ~ accounting maquillaje m contable, artificios mpl contables; ~ writing creación f literaria.
creatively [kriː'eɪtɪvlɪ] ADV de manera original, con originalidad.
creativity [,kriːeɪ'tɪvɪtɪ] N creatividad f.
creator [krɪ'eɪtər] N creador m, -ora f; the C~ el Criador.
creature ['kriːtʃər] N (a) (animal) criatura f; animal m, bicho m; poor ~! ¡pobre animal!, (to human) ¡pobrecito!; ~ comforts bienestar m material.
(b) (person) to be sb's ~ ser la criatura de uno; wretched ~! ¡desgraciado!; he's a poor ~ es un infeliz; pay no attention to that ~ no hagas caso de esa individua.
crèche [kreɪʃ] N (Brit) guardería f infantil.
cred* [kred] N = **credibility.**
credence ['kriːdəns] N: to give ~ to prestar fe a.
credentials [krɪ'denʃəlz] NPL documentos mpl (de identidad etc); referencias fpl; (of diplomat) cartas fpl credenciales; what are his ~ for the post? ¿qué méritos alega para el puesto?

credibility [ˌkredəˈbɪlətɪ] N credibilidad *f*; **~ gap** margen *m* de credibilidad; **~ rating** índice *m* de credibilidad.

credible [ˈkredɪbl] ADJ creíble, fidedigno, verosímil.

credibly [ˈkredɪblɪ] ADV creíblemente, verosímilmente.

credit [ˈkredɪt] **1** N **(a)** *(belief)* crédito *m*; **to give ~ to** creer.
   (b) *(reputation)* buena fama *f*, reputación *f*.
   (c) *(honour)* honor *m*, mérito *m*; **to his ~ he confessed** dicho sea a su honor confesó la verdad; **he is a great ~ to the family** le hace mucho honor a la familia; **to come out of sth with ~** salir airoso de algo; **the only people to emerge with any ~** los únicos que salen con honor; **to pass a test with ~** salir bien de una prueba; **it does you ~** puedes enorgullecerte de ello; **he did himself great ~** se honró mucho; **to take the ~** atribuirse el mérito *(for* de); **to give ~ to** *(US: in film, book)* reconocer.
   (d) *(Comm)* crédito *m*; *(side of account)* haber *m*; **'~ terms available'** 'ventas a plazos'; **to be in ~** *(account, person)* tener saldo acreedor, estar en números negros; **on ~** a crédito, al fiado; **on the ~ side** en el haber; *(fig)* en el aspecto positivo; **you have £10 to your ~** tiene 10 libras en el haber; **to give sb ~** abrir crédito a uno; **I gave you ~ for more sense** te creía con *(or* de) más inteligencia.
   (e) **~s** *(Cine, TV)* títulos *mpl* de crédito, rótulos *mpl* de crédito.
   (f) *(US: Scol etc)* unidad *f* de crédito.
   2 ATTR crediticio; **~ account** cuenta *f* a crédito, credicuenta *f*; **~ agency** agencia *f* de créditos; **~ arrangements** facilidades *fpl* de pago; **~ balance** saldo *m* positivo, saldo *m* acreedor; **~ charges** interés *m* de crédito; **~ control** control *m* de créditos; **~ entry** abono *m*, asiento *m* al haber; **~ facilities** facilidades *fpl* crediticias; **~ freeze** congelación *f* de crédito; **~ limit** límite *m* de crédito; **~ line** línea *f* de crédito; **~ note** *(Brit)* nota *f* de crédito; **~ rating** valoración *f* crediticia; **~ regulations** *(US)*, **~ restrictions**, **~ squeeze** restricciones *fpl* de crédito; **~ sales** ventas *fpl* a crédito; **~ side** haber *m* *(also fig)*; **~ transfer** transferencia *f* bancaria.
   3 VT **(a)** *(believe)* creer, prestar fe a; **would you ~ it?** *(iro)* ¿te parece posible?; **you wouldn't ~ it** parece mentira.
   (b) *(Comm)* **to ~ sb with £5, to ~ £5 to sb** abonar 5 libras en cuenta a uno; **please ~ this to my account** abone *(or* cargue) esto en mi cuenta.
   (c) *(attribute)* **I ~ed you with more sense** le creía con *(or* de) más inteligencia; **we must ~ him with charm at least** por lo menos hay que reconocer que tiene gran atractivo personal; **to be ~ed with having done sth** pasar por haber hecho algo; **he ~ed them with the victory** les atribuyó (el mérito de) la victoria; **they had less drawing power than they were ~ed with** no tenían tanta fuerza atractiva como se les suponía.

creditable [ˈkredɪtəbl] ADJ loable, estimable.

creditably [ˈkredɪtəblɪ] ADV de modo loable.

credit-card [ˈkredɪtkɑːd] N tarjeta *f* de crédito.

creditor [ˈkredɪtəʳ] N acreedor *m*, -ora *f*.

credit-worthiness [ˈkredɪtˌwɜːðɪnɪs] N solvencia *f*.

credit-worthy [ˈkredɪtˌwɜːðɪ] ADJ solvente.

credo [ˈkreɪdəʊ] N credo *m*.

credulity [krɪˈdjuːlɪtɪ] N credulidad *f*.

credulous [ˈkredjʊləs] ADJ crédulo.

creed [kriːd] N credo *m*; **the C~** el Credo.

creek [kriːk] N *(esp Brit: inlet)* cala *f*, ensenada *f*; *(US: stream)* riachuelo *m*; **to be up the ~ (without a paddle)‡** estar en un apuro, estar jodido‡.

creel [kriːl] N nasa *f*, cesta *f* (de pescador).

creep [kriːp] **1** N **(a)** (*) *(toady)* cobista* *mf*, pelotillero* *m*, -a *f*; *(rotter)* canalla *m*.
   (b) **it gives me the ~s** me horripila, me da escalofríos.
   2 *(irr: PRET AND PTP* **crept**) VI **(a)** *(animal etc)* arrastrarse, reptar, deslizarse, moverse muy despacio por el suelo.
   (b) *(person etc)* arrastrarse, andar a gatas; *(stealthily)* ir cautelosamente; *(slowly)* ir despacito, ir a paso de tortuga; **to ~ about on tiptoe** andar a *(or* de) puntillas; **to ~ along** *(traffic)* avanzar a paso de tortuga; **to ~ in** entrar sin ser sentido; **to ~ out** salir silenciosamente; **to ~ up on sb** acercarse sigilosamente a uno.
   (c) *(fig)* **it's enough to make your flesh ~** es para poner carne de gallina; **doubts began to ~ in** las dudas empezaron a insinuarse; **an error crept in** se deslizó un error; **old age is ~ing on** se está acercando a la vejez; **fear crept over him** le invadió el terror; **to ~ to s.o.*** hacer la pelotilla a uno*, dar jabón a uno*.

creeper [ˈkriːpəʳ] N *(Bot)* enredadera *f*; **~s** *(US: shoes)* zapatillas *fpl* de goma; *(US: babywear)* pelele *m*.

creeping [ˈkriːpɪŋ] ADJ *(Med etc)* progresivo; *barrage* móvil; **~ inflation** inflación *f* progresiva.

creepy [ˈkriːpɪ] ADJ horripilante, escalofriante.

creepy-crawly* [ˈkriːpɪˈkrɔːlɪ] N *(Brit)* bicho *m*.

cremate [krɪˈmeɪt] VT incinerar.

cremation [krɪˈmeɪʃən] N incineración *f* (de cadáveres), cremación *f*.

crematorium [ˌkreməˈtɔːrɪəm] N, PL **crematoria** [ˌkreməˈtɔːrɪə],

(US) **crematory** [ˈkremətərɪ] N horno *m* crematorio.

crème caramel [ˈkremˈkærəməl] N flan *m*.

crème de la crème [ˈkremdəlɑːˈkrem] N: **the ~** la crème de la crème, la flor y nata.

crème de menthe [ˈkremdəmɒːnθ] N licor *m* de crema de menta.

crenellated [ˈkrenɪleɪtɪd] ADJ almenado.

crenellations [ˌkrenɪˈleɪʃənz] NPL almenas *fpl*.

Creole [ˈkriːəʊl] **1** ADJ criollo.
   2 N criollo *m*, -a *f*.

creosote [ˈkrɪəsəʊt] **1** N creosota *f*, chapote *m* *(Mex)*.
   2 VT pintar con creosota; dar un baño de creosota a.

crepe, crêpe [kreɪp] N crespón *m*; *(rubber)* crep *m*, crepé *m*; **~ bandage** envoltura *f* de crepé *(or* crep); **~ paper** papel *m* crep; **~-soled shoes** zapatos *mpl* de suela de crepé.

crept [krept] PRET AND PTP of **creep**.

crepuscular [krɪˈpʌskjʊləʳ] ADJ *(liter)* crepuscular.

crescendo [krɪˈʃendəʊ] N crescendo *m*.

crescent [ˈkresnt] **1** ADJ creciente; **~ moon** media luna *f*.
   2 N *(shape)* media luna *f*; *(street)* calle *f* en forma de arco, medialuna *f*.

cress [kres] N mastuerzo *m*, berro *m*.

crest [krest] **1** N *(of bird, wave)* cresta *f*; *(of turkey)* moco *m*; *(on helmet)* cimera *f* *(also Her)*; *(of hill)* cima *f*, cumbre *f*, cresta *f*; *(Her)* blasón *m*.
   2 VI *(US)* llegar al máximo, alcanzar su punto más alto; **the flood ~ed at 2 meters** las aguas llegaron a 2 metros sobre su nivel normal.

crested [ˈkrestɪd] ADJ *bird etc* crestado, con cresta; *notepaper* con escudo.

crestfallen [ˈkrestˌfɔːlən] ADJ alicaído, cabizbajo.

cretaceous [krɪˈteɪʃəs] ADJ cretáceo.

Cretan [ˈkriːtən] **1** ADJ cretense.
   2 N cretense *mf*.

Crete [kriːt] N Creta *f*.

cretin [ˈkretɪn] N cretino *m*, -a *f*.

cretinous [ˈkretɪnəs] ADJ cretino; *(fig)* imbécil.

cretonne [kreˈtɒn] N cretona *f*.

crevasse [krɪˈvæs] N grieta *f* de glaciar.

crevice [ˈkrevɪs] N grieta *f*, hendedura *f*.

crew [kruː] **1** N *(Naut, Aer)* tripulación *f*; *(Mil, number of ~, ~ members)* dotación *f*; personal *m*, equipo *m*; *(gang)* banda *f*, pandilla *f*; **three ~ were drowned** perecieron ahogados tres tripulantes; **they looked a sorry ~** daba lástima verlos.
   2 VT tripular.

crew-cut [ˈkruːkʌt] N corte *m* de pelo al rape.

crewman [ˈkruːmən] N, PL **crewmen** [ˈkruːmen] *(Naut)* tripulante *m*; *(TV etc)* miembro *m* del equipo (de cámara *etc)*.

crew-neck [ˈkruːnek] N cuello *m* de barco; **~ sweater** suéter *m* con cuello de barco.

crib [krɪb] **1** N **(a)** *(Brit: for infant)* pesebre *m*; *(US: for toddler)* cuna *f*; **~ death** *(US)* muerte *f* en la cuna; **portable ~** *(US)* cuna *f* portátil. **(b)** (*) *(translation)* traducción *f*; *(thing copied)* plagio *m*; *(in exam)* chuleta* *f*.
   2 VT *(Brit*) plagiar, tomar *(from* de).
   3 VI (*) usar una chuleta.

cribbage [ˈkrɪbɪdʒ] N juego de cartas que se juega utilizando un tablero de puntuación.

crick [krɪk] **1** N: **~ in the neck** tortícolis *f*.
   2 VT: **to ~ one's neck** darse una tortícolis.

cricket¹ [ˈkrɪkɪt] N *(Zool)* grillo *m*.

cricket² [ˈkrɪkɪt] **1** N críquet *m*, cricket *m*; **that's not ~** eso no es jugar limpio.
   2 ATTR: **~ ball** pelota *f* de críquet; **~ bat** bate *m* de críquet; **~ match** partido *m* de críquet; **~ pavilion** caseta *f* de críquet; **~ pitch** terreno *m* de juego de críquet.

┌─ CRICKET ─┐

ⓘ *El críquet se practica en todo el Reino Unido y los países de la Commonwealth, aunque se considera un juego típicamente inglés. Se juega sobre todo en verano al aire libre, sobre hierba y se puede reconocer inmediatamente porque todos los jugadores van vestidos de blanco. Tiene unas reglas un tanto complejas: hay dos equipos de 11 jugadores. En el primer equipo todos los jugadores batean por turnos, mientras que en el otro equipo hay un boleador (**bowler**) y diez fildeadores (**fielders**) en puntos estratégicos del campo. El boleador lanza la pelota al bateador (**batsman**). Éste intenta a su vez lanzarla lo más lejos posible y así tener tiempo para correr de un poste (**wicket**) a otro conseguir puntos, llamados por ello **runs**. Los fildeadores del equipo contrario intentan atrapar la pelota lanzada por el bateador para evitar que consiga más puntos. Si atrapan la pelota en el aire o si dan en el **wicket** con ella, el bateador es eliminado. Cuando todos los bateadores del primer equipo han sido eliminados, se cambian los papeles. Un partido puede durar varios días seguidos.*

Como ocurre con el béisbol en Estados Unidos, algunas expresiones de críquet han pasado a la lengua cotidiana, entre otras, **a sticky wicket** *(una situación difícil).*

cricketer ['krɪkɪtə'] N criquetero *m*, -a *f*, jugador *m*, -ora *f* de críquet.

crier ['kraɪə'] N: **town ~** pregonero *m* público.

crikey: ['kraɪkɪ] INTERJ *(Brit)* ¡caramba!

crime [kraɪm] N crimen *m*, delito *m*; **it's the ~ capital of Slobodia** es la capital del crimen de Eslobodia; **~ prevention** prevención *f* del crimen; **C~ Squad** ≃ Brigada *f* de Investigación Criminal; **~ statistics** estadísticas *fpl* del crimen; **~ wave** ola *f* delictiva; **~ writer** autor *m*, -ora *f* de novelas policíacas.

Crimea [kraɪ'mɪə] N Crimea *f*.

Crimean War [kraɪ'mɪən'wɔː'] N Guerra *f* de Crimea.

criminal ['krɪmɪnl] ① ADJ criminal; *act, intent* delictivo; *code, law* penal; **it would be ~ to let her go out** sería un crimen dejarla salir; **~ damage** *(Jur)* delito *m* de daños; **C~ Investigation Department** *(Brit)* ≃ Brigada *f* de Investigación Criminal; **~ law** derecho *m* penal; **~ lawyer** abogado *m*, -a *f* criminalista; **~ negligence** imprudencia *f* criminal; **~ record** antecedentes *mpl* delictivos.
② N criminal *mf*, delincuente *mf*.

criminality [ˌkrɪmɪ'nælɪtɪ] N criminalidad *f*.

criminalization [ˌkrɪmɪnəlaɪ'zeɪʃən] N criminalización *f*.

criminalize ['krɪmɪnəlaɪz] VT criminalizar.

criminally ['krɪmɪnəlɪ] ADV de manera criminal; **~ insane** incapacitado legal; **the pay was ~ poor** el sueldo era tan pobre que era un crimen.

criminologist [ˌkrɪmɪ'nɒlədʒɪst] N criminalista *mf*.

criminology [ˌkrɪmɪ'nɒlədʒɪ] N criminología *f*.

crimp [krɪmp] VT rizar, encrespar.

crimped [krɪmpt] ADJ rizado, con rizos, encrespado.

Crimplene ['krɪmpliːn] ® N ≃ crepé *m* de poliéster.

crimson ['krɪmzn] ① ADJ carmesí.
② N carmesí *m*.

cringe [krɪndʒ] VI agacharse, encogerse; *(fig)* reptar; **to ~ with fear** encogerse de miedo.

cringing ['krɪndʒɪŋ] ADJ servil, rastrero.

crinkle ['krɪŋkl] ① N arruga *f*.
② VT arrugar.
③ VI arrugarse.

crinkle-cut ['krɪŋkl,kʌt] ADJ *chips* ondulado.

crinkly ['krɪŋklɪ] ① ADJ arrugado; *hair* rizado, crespo.
② N (*) viejo *m*, -a *f*.

crinoline ['krɪnəliːn] N miriñaque *m*, crinolina *f*.

cripes: [kraɪps] INTERJ ¡coño!:.

cripple ['krɪpl] ① N lisiado *m*, -a *f*, mutilado *m*, -a *f*, cojo *m*, -a *f*; *(from birth)* minusválido *m*, -a *f*.
② VT lisiar, tullir, mutilar; *ship* inutilizar; *(fig)* paralizar, estropear.

crippled ['krɪpld] ① ADJ *person* tullido, lisiado; *(from birth)* minusválido; *(fig) plane, vehicle* averiado; *(after bomb etc) factory* paralizado; **~ with rheumatism** paralizado por reumatismo.
② NPL: **the ~** los tullidos; los minusválidos.

crippling ['krɪplɪŋ] ADJ *disease* que conduce a la parálisis; *blow, defect* muy grave, muy severo; *taxes, debts* abrumador, agobiante, demoledor.

crisis ['kraɪsɪs] N, PL **crises** ['kraɪsiːz] crisis *f*; **~ management** manejo *m* de crisis.

crisis centre, *(US)* **crisis center** ['kraɪsɪs,sentə'] N *(for disaster)* ≃ centro *m* coordinador de rescate; *(for personal help)* ≃ teléfono *m* de la esperanza; *(for battered women)* centro *m* de ayuda a las mujeres maltratadas.

crisp [krɪsp] ① ADJ duro pero quebradizo; *(after cooking)* crujiente, tostado; *hair* crespo; *air* vivificante, vigorizante; *manner, tone* resuelto, seco; *style* conciso, nervioso.
② **~s** NPL *(Brit)* patatas *fpl* (*LAm*: papas *fpl*) fritas (a la inglesa).

crispbread ['krɪspbred] N pan *m* tostado (escandinavo).

crisply ['krɪsplɪ] ADV *say etc* secamente.

crispness ['krɪspnɪs] N *(V ADJ)* naturaleza *f* dura pero quebradiza; lo crujiente, lo vivificante, lo vigorizante; resolución *f*, sequedad *f*; concisión *f*, nerviosidad *f*.

crispy ['krɪspɪ] ADJ *food* crujiente.

crisscross ['krɪskrɒs] ① ADJ entrecruzado.
② N: **a ~ of paths** veredas *fpl* entrecruzadas.
③ VI entrecruzarse.

criss-crossed ['krɪskrɒst] ADJ entrelazado; **~ by** surcado de.

crit [krɪt] N crítica *f*.

criterion [kraɪ'tɪərɪən] N, PL **criteria** [kraɪ'tɪərɪə] criterio *m*.

critic ['krɪtɪk] N crítico *mf* *(also* -a *f).*

critical ['krɪtɪkəl] ADJ (a) *(grave)* crítico, grave; *illness, injury* muy grave, de gravedad; **~ juncture, ~ moment** coyuntura *f* crítica; **~ mass** masa *f* crítica; **~ path analysis** análisis *m* del camino crítico; **to go ~** llegar a la coyuntura crítica.
(b) *(faultfinding)* crítico; severo; *(hyper~)* criticón; **to be ~ of** criticar.

(c) *(Art, Liter etc)* crítico; **~ edition** edición *f* crítica; **~ essays** ensayos *mpl* de crítica.

critically ['krɪtɪkəlɪ] ADV críticamente; **to be ~ ill** estar gravemente enfermo.

criticism ['krɪtɪsɪzəm] N crítica *f*.

criticize ['krɪtɪsaɪz] VT criticar; censurar.

critique [krɪ'tiːk] ① N crítica *f*.
② VT: **to ~ a paper** evaluar una ponencia.

croak [krəʊk] ① N *(of raven)* graznido *m*; *(of frog)* canto *m*; *(of person)* gruñido *m*.
② VI (a) *(raven)* graznar; *(frog)* croar; *(person)* gruñir, refunfuñar. (b) (:) espicharla:.

croaky ['krəʊkɪ] ADJ *voice* ronco.

Croat ['krəʊæt] N croata *mf*.

Croatia [krəʊ'eɪʃɪə] N Croacia *f*.

Croatian [krəʊ'eɪʃɪən] ① ADJ croata.
② N croata *mf*.

crochet ['krəʊʃeɪ] ① N croché *m*, labor *f* de ganchillo.
② VT hacer en croché, hacer de ganchillo.
③ VI hacer croché, hacer labor de ganchillo.

crochet-hook ['krəʊʃɪhʊk] N ganchillo *m*.

crock [krɒk] ① N vasija *f* de barro; **old ~** *(person)* carcamal *m*; *(esp Brit: car etc)* cacharro *m*; **old ~s' race** rallye *m* de coches clásicos.
② VT lisiar, incapacitar.

crockery ['krɒkərɪ] N loza *f*, vajilla *f*, los platos.

crocodile ['krɒkədaɪl] N cocodrilo *m*; *(Brit Scol)* doble fila *f*; **to walk in a ~** andar en doble fila; **~ tears** lágrimas *fpl* de cocodrilo.

crocus ['krəʊkəs] N azafrán *m*.

Croesus ['kriːsəs] NM Creso.

croft [krɒft] N *(Scot)* granja *f* pequeña, parcela *f*.

crofter ['krɒftə'] N *(Scot)* arrendatario *m* de una granja pequeña.

crofting ['krɒftɪŋ] *(Scot)* ① N minifundismo *m*.
② ATTR minifundista *mf*.

croissant [krwʌsãː.ŋ] N croissant *m*, cruasán *m*, medialuna *f*.

crone [krəʊn] N vieja *f*, arpía *f*, bruja *f*.

crony ['krəʊnɪ] N compinche *mf*, amigote *m*.

cronyism ['krəʊnɪɪzəm] N amiguismo *m*.

crook [krʊk] ① N (a) *(staff)* cayado *m*; *(Eccl)* báculo *m*.
(b) *(bend)* curva *f*; **~ of the arm** pliegue *m* del codo.
(c) (*: *person)* criminal *m*, estafador *m*, ladrón *m*, maleante *mf*; **you ~!** *(hum)* ¡animal!
② VT encorvar.
③ VI encorvarse.

crooked ['krʊkɪd] ADJ (a) curvo, encorvado, torcido; *path* tortuoso; *smile* torcido. (b) (*) *deal, means* poco limpio; *person* criminal, nada honrado.

crookedly ['krʊkɪdlɪ] ADV *smile* de manera torcida.

crookedness ['krʊkɪdnɪs] N *(lit)* sinuosidad *f*; *(fig)* criminalidad *f*.

croon [kruːn] VT canturrear, cantar en voz baja.

crooner ['kruːnə'] N vocalista *mf* (sentimental), canzonetista *mf*.

crooning ['kruːnɪŋ] N canturreo *m*, tarareo *m*.

crop [krɒp] ① N (a) *(Agr) (species grown)* cultivo *m*; *(produce)* cosecha *f*; **~ rotation** rotación *f* de cultivos.
(b) *(Orn)* buche *m*.
(c) *(whip)* látigo *m* (mocho), fusta *f*.
(d) *(hair-style)* corte *m* a lo garçon.
② VT *(cut)* cortar; *(trim)* recortar; *animal's ears* desorejar, *tail* cortar; *(graze)* pacer.
③ VI: **a tree which ~s well** un árbol que rinde bien.

◆**crop out** VI *(Geol)* aflorar.

◆**crop up** VI (a) *(Geol)* aflorar.
(b) *(fig)* surgir, producirse inesperadamente; **sth must have ~ped up** habrán tenido alguna dificultad; **now another problem has ~ped up** ahora se ha planteado otro problema.

crop-dusting ['krɒp,dʌstɪŋ] N, **crop-spraying** ['krɒp,spreɪɪŋ] N fumigación *f* aérea, aerofumigación *f* (de las cosechas).

cropper: ['krɒpə'] N: **to come a ~** coger una liebre:; *(fig)* fracasar; tirarse una plancha:.

crop-sprayer ['krɒp,spreɪə'] N *(device)* sulfatadora *f*; *(plane)* avión *m* fumigador.

croquet ['krəʊkeɪ] N croquet *m*.

croquette [krəʊ'ket] N croqueta *f*.

crosier ['krəʊʒə'] N báculo *m* (pastoral).

cross [krɒs] ① ADJ (a) *(crossed)* cruzado; *(diagonal etc)* transversal, oblicuo.
(b) *(fig)* malhumorado; **to be ~** estar de mal humor; **to be ~ with sb** estar enfadado con uno, estar enojado con uno *(LAm)*; **don't be ~ with me** no te vayas a enfadar *(or* enojar *LAm)* conmigo; **to get ~** enfadarse, enojarse *(about* de, por, *with* con).
② N (a) *(mark, emblem: also fig)* cruz *f*; **the C~** la Cruz; **to make the sign of the C~** hacer la señal de la Cruz *(over* sobre).
(b) *(Bio)* cruce *m*; *(hybrid)* cruce *m*, híbrido *m*; *(fig)* mezcla *f*; **it's a ~**

between A and B es una mezcla de A y B, tiene algo de A y algo de B.
(c) to cut sth on the ~ (*Sew etc*) cortar algo al sesgo.
3 VT **(a)** (*place crosswise*) cruzar; **to ~ one's arms** cruzarse de brazos; **to ~ sb's hand with silver** dar una moneda de plata a uno; **the lines are ~ed** (*Brit Telec*) hay un cruce en las líneas, la conferencia está atravesada.
(b) (*draw line across*) *cheque* cruzar, rayar; **~ed cheque** (*Brit*) cheque *m* cruzado.
(c) (*go across*) cruzar, pasar, atravesar; *river* (*as obstacle*) salvar.
(d) (*meet and pass*) cruzarse.
(e) (*Bio*) cruzar.
(f) (*thwart*) contrariar, ir contra; **to be ~ed in love** sufrir un fracaso sentimental.
4 VI **(a)** cruzar, ir al otro lado.
(b) (*letters*) cruzarse.
5 VR: **to ~ o.s.** santiguarse.
◆ **cross off** VT tachar.
◆ **cross out** VT tachar; '**~ out what does not apply**' 'táchese lo que no proceda'.
◆ **cross over** VI = **cross 4.**
crossbar ['krɒsbɑːʳ] N travesaño *m*; (*Sport*) larguero *m*, travesaño *m*.
crossbeam ['krɒsbiːm] N viga *f* transversal.
crossbencher ['krɒs'bentʃəʳ] N diputado *m*, -a *f* independiente.
crossbill ['krɒsbɪl] N piquituerto *m* común.
crossbones ['krɒsbəʊnz] NPL tibias *fpl* cruzadas; V **skull.**
cross-border ['krɒs'bɔːdəʳ] ATTR transfronterizo; **~ security** seguridad *f* a través de la frontera; **~ travel** viajes *mpl* a través de la frontera.
crossbow ['krɒsbəʊ] N ballesta *f*.
crossbred ['krɒsbred] ADJ cruzado, híbrido.
crossbreed ['krɒsbriːd] **1** N cruce *m*, híbrido *m*, -a *f*.
2 VT (*irr V* **breed**) cruzar.
cross-Channel ['krɒs'tʃænl] ADJ: **~ services** servicios *mpl* a través del Canal (de la Mancha); **~ steamer** barco *m* que hace la travesía del Canal (de la Mancha).
cross-check ['krɒstʃek] **1** N comprobación *f* hecha al revés, comprobación *f* adicional; verificación *f* mediante un cotejo con otras fuentes.
2 VT comprobar al revés; comprobar una vez más (*or* por otro sistema); verificar cotejando con otras fuentes.
cross-compiler ['krɒskəm'paɪləʳ] N compilador *m* cruzado.
cross-country ['krɒs'kʌntrɪ] ADJ *route, walk* a campo traviesa; **~ race** cross *m*, campo *m* a través; **~ running** cross *m*; **~ skiing** esquí *m* nórdico.
cross-cultural ['krɒs'kʌltʃərəl] ADJ transcultural.
cross-current ['krɒs'kʌrənt] N contracorriente *f*.
cross-disciplinary [ˌkrɒs'dɪsɪplɪnərɪ] ADJ multidisciplinario.
cross-dress ['krɒsdres] VI travestirse.
cross-dresser ['krɒsdresəʳ] N travesti *mf*, travestido *m*, -a *f*.
cross-dressing ['krɒs'dresɪŋ] N travestismo *m*.
cross-examination ['krɒsɪgˌzæmɪ'neɪʃən] N (*Jur*) segunda pregunta *f*, repregunta *f*; (*fig*) interrogatorio *m* severo.
cross-examine ['krɒsɪg'zæmɪn] VT (*Jur*) repreguntar; (*fig*) interrogar severamente.
cross-eyed ['krɒsaɪd] ADJ bizco.
cross-fertilize ['krɒs'fɜːtɪlaɪz] VT fecundar por fertilización cruzada.
crossfire ['krɒsfaɪəʳ] N fuego *m* cruzado; **we were caught in the ~** estábamos inmovilizados en el fuego cruzado; (*fig*) nos veíamos atacados por ambos lados.
cross-grained ['krɒsgreɪnd] ADJ de fibras cruzadas.
crossing ['krɒsɪŋ] N **(a)** (*intersection*) cruce *m*; (*Rail*) paso *m* a nivel; (*on road*) paso *m* para peatones; (*journey*) travesía *f*; **~ guard** (*US*) persona encargada de ayudar a los niños a cruzar la calle. **(b)** (*Bio*) cruce *m*.
cross-legged ['krɒs'legd] ADJ con las piernas cruzadas.
crossly ['krɒslɪ] ADV con mal humor.
crossover ['krɒsəʊvəʳ] N (*Aut etc*) paso *m*.
cross-party ['krɒs'pɑːtɪ] ADJ: **~ support** apoyo *m* multilateral.
crosspatch ['krɒspætʃ] N cascarrabias *mf*, gruñón *m*, -ona *f*.
crosspiece ['krɒspiːs] N travesaño *m*.
cross-ply ['krɒsplaɪ] ADJ (*Aut*) a carcasa diagonal.
cross-pollination ['krɒsˌpɒlɪ'neɪʃən] N polinización *f* cruzada.
cross-purposes ['krɒs'pɜːpəsɪz] NPL: **to be at ~** no comprenderse uno a otro; **we're at ~** aquí hay un malentendido, hay un error de interpretación.
cross-question ['krɒs'kwestʃən] VT (*Jur*) repreguntar; (*fig*) interrogar.
cross-questioning ['krɒs'kwestʃənɪŋ] N (*Jur*) repregunta *f*, segunda pregunta *f*; (*fig*) interrogación *f*.
cross-refer [ˌkrɒsrɪ'fɜːʳ] VT remitir (*to* a), reenviar (*to* a).
cross-reference ['krɒs'refərəns] **1** N reenvío *m*, referencia *f* cruzada, remisión *f* (*to* a).
2 VT poner referencia cruzada a; **to ~ A to Q** poner en A una nota que remite al usuario (*etc*) a Q.

crossroads ['krɒsrəʊdz] N (*Brit*) cruce *m*, encrucijada *f*; (*fig*) encrucijada *f*; **to be at a ~** (*fig*) estar en una encrucijada.
cross-section ['krɒs'sekʃən] N corte *m* transversal, sección *f* transversal, perfil *m*; (*fig*) sección *f* representativa, selección *f* característica.
cross-stitch ['krɒsstɪtʃ] **1** N punto *m* de cruz.
2 VT coser en punto de cruz.
crosstalk ['krɒstɔːk] N (*Brit*) réplicas *fpl* agudas; **~ act** (*Theat*) diálogo *m* ágil salpicado de humor.
cross-tie ['krɒs,taɪ] N (*US*) durmiente *m*, traviesa *f*.
cross-vote [ˌkrɒs'vəʊt] VI votar en contra del partido.
crosswalk ['krɒs,wɔːk] N (*US*) paso *m* de peatones.
crosswind ['krɒswɪnd] N viento *m* de costado.
crosswise ['krɒswaɪz] ADV al través; en cruz.
crossword ['krɒswɜːd] N (*also* **~ puzzle**) crucigrama *m*.
crotch [krɒtʃ] N (*Anat*) horcajadura *f*; (*of dress*) entrepiernas *fpl*.
crotchet ['krɒtʃɪt] N (*Brit*) negra *f*, capricho *m*.
crotchety ['krɒtʃɪtɪ] ADJ áspero, arisco, antojadizo.
crouch [kraʊtʃ] VI agacharse, acurrucarse, ponerse en cuclillas; **men ~ing in trenches** hombres agazapados en trincheras.
croup[1] [kruːp] N (*Med*) crup *m*, garrotillo *m*.
croup[2] [kruːp] N (*of horse*) grupa *f*.
croupier ['kruːpɪeɪ] N crupier *m*, crupié *m*.
croûton ['kruːtɒn] N cuscurro *m*.
crow[1] [krəʊ] N **(a)** (*Orn*) cuervo *m*, grajo *m*, corneja *f*; **as the ~ flies** en línea recta; **stone the ~s!⁀** ¡coño!⁀. **(b)** (*cry*) canto *m*, cacareo *m*.
2 VI (*cock*) cantar, cacarear; (*child*) gorjearse; (*fig*) jactarse, exultar; pavonearse; **it's nothing to ~ about** no hay motivo para sentirse satisfecho.
◆ **crow over** VT: **to ~ over sth** jactarse de algo, felicitarse por algo.
crowbar ['krəʊbɑːʳ] N palanca *f*.
crowd [kraʊd] **1** N multitud *f*; muchedumbre *f*, gentío *m*; agolpamiento *m*; (*esp disorderly*) tropel *m*; (*Sport etc*) público *m*, espectadores *mpl*; (*Theat: on stage*) comparsa *f*; (***) grupo *m*, peña *f*; **the ~** (*common herd*) el vulgo; **a (whole) ~ of,** (***) of una multitud de; **there was quite a ~** había bastante gente; **how big was the ~?** ¿cuántas personas había?; **~ control** control *m* de muchedumbres; **~ scene** escena *f* con muchas comparsas; **in a ~** en tropel, todos juntos; **to follow the ~** dejarse llevar por los demás; **to rise above the ~** destacar(se).
2 VT **(a)** (*collect*) amontonar; apretar unos contra otros.
(b) (*US**: *jostle*) codear; **to ~ the streets** llenar las calles; **to ~ a place with** llenar un sitio de; **to ~ things in** ir metiendo cosas apretadamente; **to ~ on sail** hacer fuerza de vela; **he was ~ed off the pavement** había tanta gente que tuvo que bajar de la acera.
3 VI reunirse, congregarse (*into* en); **to ~ around, to ~ together** agolparse, apiñarse; **to ~ round sb** apiñarse (*or* agruparse) en torno de uno; **to ~ in** entrar en tropel; **to ~ into a car** entrar todos apretadamente en un coche; **memories ~ed in upon me** me inundaron muchísimos recuerdos.
◆ **crowd out** VT excluir; dejar fuera.
crowded ['kraʊdɪd] ADJ lleno, atestado (*with* de); *meeting, event etc* muy concurrido; **it's very ~ here** aquí hay muchísima gente; **the place was ~ out** el local estaba de bote en bote; **the houses are ~ together** las casas están apretadas unas contra otras; **one ~ hour** una sola hora llena de actividad; **it's a very ~ profession** es una profesión en la que sobra gente.
crowd-puller ['kraʊd,pʊləʳ] N (*show*) gran atracción *f*; función *f* (*etc*) muy taquillera; (*person*) orador *m*, -ora *f* muy popular.
crowfoot ['krəʊfʊt] N ranúnculo *m*.
crowing ['krəʊɪŋ] N (*of cock*) canto *m*, cacareo *m*; (*of child*) gorjeo *m*; (*fig*) cacareo *m*.
crown [kraʊn] **1** N corona *f*; (*of hat*) copa *f*; (*of hill*) cumbre *f*; (*of head*) coronilla *f*; **the ~ of the road** el centro de la calzada; **C~** (*Brit Jur, witness, evidence*) Estado *m*; **the C~** (*monarch*) la Corona.
2 ATTR: **~ colony** (*Brit*) colonia *f*; **~ court** ≈ Audiencia *f* provincial; **~ jewels** joyas *fpl* reales; **~ lands** propiedad *f* de la corona; **~ prince** príncipe *m* heredero; **~ princess** princesa *f* heredera;
ver también COURTS ;
3 VT **(a)** coronar; (*fig*) completar, rematar; **to ~ it all** para completarlo todo, (*misfortune*) para colmo de desgracias; **to ~ sth with success** coronar algo con éxito.
(b) (***) golpear en la cabeza.
crowning ['kraʊnɪŋ] **1** ADJ supremo.
2 N coronación *f*.
crow's-foot ['krəʊzfʊt] N (*eye*) pata *f* de gallo.
crow's-nest ['krəʊznest] N cofa *f* de vigía de tope.
CRT N ABBR *of* **cathode ray tube** tubo *m* de rayos catódicos, TRC *m*.
crucial ['kruːʃəl] ADJ decisivo, crítico, crucial; (⁀) guay*, de vicio*.
crucially ['kruːʃəlɪ] ADV: **~ important** de importancia crucial.
crucible ['kruːsɪbl] N crisol *m* (*also fig*).
crucifix ['kruːsɪfɪks] N crucifijo *m*.

crucifixion [,kru:sɪ'fɪkʃən] N crucifixión f.
cruciform ['kru:sɪfɔ:m] ADJ cruciforme.
crucify ['kru:sɪfaɪ] VT crucificar (*also fig*).
crud* [krʌd] N (*esp US*) porquería f.
cruddy* ['krʌdɪ] ADJ asqueroso.
crude [kru:d] ☐1 ADJ *oil etc* crudo, *steel etc* bruto; *object, workmanship* tosco; (*vulgar*) ordinario.
☐2 N crudo m.
crudely ['kru:dlɪ] ADV toscamente; ordinariamente.
crudeness ['kru:dnɪs] N, **crudity** ['kru:dɪtɪ] N tosquedad f; ordinariez f.
crudités ['kru:dɪ'teɪ] NPL crudités *mpl*.
cruel ['kruəl] ADJ cruel.
cruelly ['kruəlɪ] ADV cruelmente.
cruelty ['kruəltɪ] N crueldad f; **society for the prevention of ~ to animals** sociedad f protectora de los animales.
cruet ['kru:ɪt] N (*one vessel*) vinagrera f, salvilla f (*SC*); (*set*) vinagreras *fpl*; vinajeras *fpl*; (*stand*) angarillas *fpl*.
cruise [kru:z] ☐1 N crucero m, viaje m por mar; **~ control** control m de crucero; **~ missile** misil m de crucero.
☐2 VI (a) cruzar, navegar. (b) (*fig*) ir, andar; (*Aut etc*) ir a velocidad de crucero, llanear.
◆**cruise around** VI (*US*) pasear en coche.
cruiser ['kru:zə'] N crucero m.
cruiser-weight ['kru:zəweɪt] N peso m semipesado.
cruising speed ['kru:zɪŋspi:d] N velocidad f de crucero.
cruller ['krʌlə'] N (*US*) buñuelo m.
crumb [krʌm] N migaja f; (*not crust*) miga f; **a ~ of comfort** una migaja de consolación.
crumble ['krʌmbl] ☐1 VT desmenuzar, desmigajar.
☐2 VI (*material*) desmenuzarse, desmigajarse; (*building etc*) desmoronarse, derrumbarse.
crumbly ['krʌmblɪ] ADJ desmenuzable; (*US*) *pastry* sobado.
crummy* ['krʌmɪ] ADJ (*bad*) ínfimo, de mala muerte, miserable; (*unwell*) fatal.
crumpet ['krʌmpɪt] N (a) bollo m blando (para tostar). (b) (‡) (*girl*) jai‡ f; (*girls*) las jais‡ (*colectivamente*); (*sex*) vida f sexual, actividad f sexual; **a bit of ~** (*Brit*) una jai‡.
crumple ['krʌmpl] ☐1 VT deshacer; *paper* estrujar; (*wrinkle*) arrugar.
☐2 VI deshacerse; arrugarse; plegarse; (*fig, also* **to ~ up**) hundirse, derrumbarse; (*person*) desplomarse.
crumple zone ['krʌmpl,zəʊn] N zona f de deformación absorbente.
crunch [krʌntʃ] ☐1 N crujido m; (*fig*) crisis f, punto m decisivo; **when the ~ comes, when it comes to the ~** en el momento de la verdad.
☐2 VT (*with teeth*) mascar, ronzar; *ground etc* hacer crujir; *numbers* devorar.
☐3 VI crujir.
crunchy ['krʌntʃɪ] ADJ crujiente, que cruje.
crupper ['krʌpə'] N (*of horse*) anca f, grupa f; (*part of harness*) baticola f.
crusade [kru:'seɪd] ☐1 N cruzada f.
☐2 VI participar en una cruzada; **to ~ for** hacer campaña en pro de.
crusader [kru:'seɪdə'] N cruzado m.
crush [krʌʃ] ☐1 N (a) (*of people*) agolpamiento m; aglomeración f; (*of cars etc*) masa f; **there was an awful ~** hubo la mar de gente; **there's always a ~ in the tube** el metro va siempre atestado de gente; **I lost my handbag in the ~** perdí el bolso en la aglomeración; **two died in the ~** dos murieron aplastados.
(b) (*) amartelamiento m; **to have a ~ on sb** andar amartelado por una, perder la chaveta por uno*.
(c) **orange ~** (*Brit*) naranjada f.
☐2 VT (a) aplastar; *paper etc* estrujar; *stones* triturar, moler; *grapes etc* prensar, exprimir; **to ~ sth into a case** meter algo a la fuerza en una maleta.
(b) (*fig*) *country* aplastar; *enemy, opposition* aniquilar, destruir; *person in argument* confundir, aplastar.
◆**crush in** VI meterse apretadamente en; **can we all ~ in?** ¿cabemos todos?
crush-barrier ['krʌʃ,bærɪə'] N (*Brit*) barrera f de seguridad.
crusher ['krʌʃə'] N (*for paper etc*) prensador m; (*for food*) trituradora f.
crushing ['krʌʃɪŋ] ADJ *blow, defeat, reply* aplastante; *grief etc* abrumador; *argument* decisivo; *burden* agobiador.
crushingly ['krʌʃɪŋlɪ] ADV *dull, familiar* terriblemente; *beautiful* conmovedoramente.
crush-resistant [,krʌʃrɪ'zɪstənt] ADJ inarrugable.
crust [krʌst] ☐1 N (*of bread, Geol*) corteza f; (*old bread*) mendrugo m; (*Med*) costra f; (*of wine*) depósito m, poso m.
☐2 VT: **~ed with** con una costra de; con un depósito de.
crustacean [krʌs'teɪʃən] N crustáceo m.
crusty ['krʌstɪ] ADJ (a) *bread* con corteza (apetitosa). (b) (*fig*) malhumorado, irritable.
crutch [krʌtʃ] N (a) muleta f. (b) (*Anat*) = **crotch**.

crux [krʌks] N: **the ~ of the matter** lo esencial del caso, el quid, el punto capital.
cry [kraɪ] ☐1 N (a) grito m; (*of peddler, town crier*) pregón m; **it's a far ~ from that** esto tiene poco que ver con aquello; **the hounds were in full ~** los perros seguían de cerca la presa; **the crowd was in full ~ after him** la multitud le perseguía con gritos.
(b) (*watchword*) lema m, slogan m.
(c) (*weep*) lloro m, llanto m; **to have a good ~** dejarse llorar, aliviarse llorando.
☐2 VT (*also* **to ~ out**) gritar; *wares* pregonar; *V* **eye** *etc*.
☐3 VI (a) (*call*) gritar; **to ~ for** clamar por; **to ~ for help** pedir socorro a voces.
(b) (*weep*) llorar (*for, with* de).
☐4 VR: **to ~ o.s. to sleep** dormirse llorando.
◆**cry down** VT despreciar, desacreditar.
◆**cry off** VI retirarse, rajarse.
◆**cry out** VI gritar; **it's ~ing out for reform** (*fig*) pide la reforma a gritos, necesita urgentemente reformarse; **for ~ing out loud!*** ¡por Dios!; **to ~ out against** protestar contra, poner el grito en el cielo por.
◆**cry over** VT lamentarse de (*or* por), llorar.
crybaby ['kraɪ,beɪbɪ] N llorón m, -ona f.
crying ['kraɪɪŋ] ☐1 ADJ atroz, enorme; **it's a ~ shame*** es una verdadera vergüenza.
☐2 N lloro m, llanto m.
cryogenics [,kraɪə'dʒenɪks] N criogenia f.
cryonics [kraɪ'ɒnɪks] N criogenética f.
cryosurgery [,kraɪəʊ'sɜ:dʒərɪ] N criocirugía f.
crypt [krɪpt] N cripta f.
cryptic ['krɪptɪk] ADJ misterioso, secreto, enigmático.
cryptically ['krɪptɪkəlɪ] ADV misteriosamente.
crypto- ['krɪptəʊ] PREF cripto-.
crypto-communist ['krɪptəʊ'kɒmjʊnɪst] N criptocomunista *mf*.
cryptogram ['krɪptəʊɡræm] N criptograma m.
cryptographer [krɪp'tɒɡrəfə'] N criptógrafo m, -a f.
cryptographic(al) [,krɪptəʊ'ɡræfɪk(əl)] ADJ criptográfico.
cryptography [krɪp'tɒɡrəfɪ] N criptografía f.
crystal ['krɪstl] ☐1 N cristal m.
☐2 ADJ cristalino; **~ ball** bola f de cristal; **~ set** (*Rad*) receptor m de cristal.
crystal-clear ['krɪstl'klɪə'] ADJ transparente como el cristal; (*fig*) evidente, más claro que el agua.
crystal-gazing ['krɪstl,ɡeɪzɪŋ] N (*fig*) adivinación f del futuro en la bola de cristal.
crystalline ['krɪstəlaɪn] ADJ cristalino.
crystallize ['krɪstəlaɪz] ☐1 VT cristalizar.
☐2 VI cristalizarse; (*fig*) cuajarse, resolverse.
crystallized ['krɪstəlaɪzd] ADJ *fruit* escarchado.
crystallographer [,krɪstə'lɒɡrəfə'] N cristalógrafo m, -a f.
crystallography [,krɪstə'lɒɡrəfɪ] N cristalografía f.
CSA (a) N (*Brit*) ABBR of **Child Support Agency**. (b) N (*US*) ABBR of **Confederate States of America**.
CSC N ABBR of **Civil Service Commission**.
CSE N (*Brit Scol: formerly*) ABBR of **Certificate of Secondary Education**.
CSEU N (*Brit*) ABBR of **Confederation of Shipbuilding and Engineering Unions** *sindicato de trabajadores de construcción naval*.
CS gas [,si:,es'ɡæs] N (*Brit*) gas m lacrimógeno.
CST N (*US*) ABBR of **Central Standard Time** *hora central estándar*.
CSU N (*Brit*) ABBR of **Civil Service Union** *sindicato de funcionarios*.
CT (a) (*Fin*) ABBR of **cable transfer**. (b) (*US Post*) ABBR of **Connecticut**.
Ct. (*US*) ABBR of **Connecticut**.
ct ABBR of **carat** *quilate m*.
CTC N ABBR of **City Technology College**.
CTT N ABBR of **Capital Transfer Tax**.
cu. ABBR of **cubic** cúbico.
cub [kʌb] N cachorro m; (*boy; also* **~ scout**) niño m explorador; **~ reporter** periodista m novato.
Cuba ['kju:bə] N Cuba f.
Cuban ['kju:bən] ☐1 ADJ cubano.
☐2 N cubano m, -a f.
cubbyhole ['kʌbɪhəʊl] N chiribitil m.
cube [kju:b] ☐1 N cubo m; (*of sugar*) terrón m; **~ root** (*Math*) raíz f cúbica.
☐2 VT cubicar.
cubic ['kju:bɪk] ADJ cúbico; **~ measure** medida f cúbica; **~ metre** metro m cúbico.
cubicle ['kju:bɪkəl] N cubículo m; (*at swimming pool etc*) caseta f.
cubism ['kju:bɪzəm] N cubismo m.
cubist ['kju:bɪst] ☐1 ADJ cubista.
☐2 N cubista *mf*.
cubit ['kju:bət] N codo m.
cuckold ['kʌkəld] ☐1 N cornudo m.

2 VT poner los cuernos a.

cuckoo ['kʊkuː] 1 N cuco *m*, cuclillo *m*.

2 ADJ (*) lelo.

cuckoo-clock ['kʊkuːklɒk] N reloj *m* de cuclillo.

cuckoopint [,kʊkuː'paɪnt] N aro *m*.

cucumber ['kjuːkʌmbəʳ] N pepino *m*.

cud [kʌd] N: **to chew the ~** (*lit*, *fig*) rumiar.

cuddle ['kʌdl] 1 N abrazo *m* (amoroso).

2 VT abrazar (amorosamente).

3 VI (*2 persons*) abrazarse, estar abrazados.

◆ **cuddle down** VI (*child in bed*) acurrucarse (en la cama); **~ down now!** ¡a dormir!

◆ **cuddle up** VI: **to ~ up to sb** arrimarse (amorosamente) a uno.

cuddly ['kʌdlɪ] ADJ mimoso; *toy* blando.

cudgel ['kʌdʒəl] 1 N porra *f*; **to take up the ~s for sb** salir en defensa de uno, sacar la cara por uno.

2 VT aporrear.

cue [kjuː] N (a) (*Billiards*) taco *m*. (b) (*Theat*) pie *m*, apunte *m*, entrada *f*; **that gave me my ~** eso me sirvió de indicación; **to take one's ~ from** seguir el ejemplo de; **to come in on ~** entrar en el momento justo.

◆ **cue in** VT (*Rad*, *TV*) dar la entrada a; **to ~ sb in on sth** (*US**) poner a uno al tanto (*or* al corriente) de algo.

cuff¹ [kʌf] 1 N bofetada *f*.

2 VT abofetear.

cuff² [kʌf] N (*of shirt*) puño *m*; (*US*) vuelta *f* (de pantalón); **~s** esposas *fpl*; **to say sth off the ~** decir algo sin pensarlo, decir algo de improviso, sacar algo de la manga.

cufflinks ['kʌflɪŋks] NPL gemelos *mpl*, broches *mpl* (*LAm*), mellizos *mpl* (*LAm*).

cu.ft ABBR *of* **cubic foot, cubic feet** pie *m* cúbico, pies *mpl* cúbicos.

cu.in ABBR *of* **cubic inch(es)** pulgada *f* cúbica, pulgadas *fpl* cúbicas.

cuisine [kwɪ'ziːn] N cocina *f*.

cul-de-sac ['kʌldə'sæk] N (*esp Brit*) callejón *m* sin salida.

culinary ['kʌlɪnərɪ] ADJ culinario.

cull [kʌl] 1 N (*of deer, seals*) matanza *f* (selectiva).

2 VT *flowers* coger; (*select*) entresacar; *deer, seals* matar (selectivamente).

culminate ['kʌlmɪneɪt] VI culminar (*in* en).

culminating ['kʌlmɪneɪtɪŋ] ADJ culminante.

culmination [,kʌlmɪ'neɪʃən] N (*fig*) culminación *f*, punto *m* culminante, colmo *m*; **it is the ~ of much effort** es la culminación de grandes esfuerzos.

culotte(s) [kjuː'lɒt(s)] N(PL) falda-pantalón *f*.

culpability [,kʌlpə'bɪlɪtɪ] N culpabilidad *f*.

culpable ['kʌlpəbl] ADJ culpable; **~ homicide** homicidio *m* sin premeditación.

culprit ['kʌlprɪt] N persona *f* culpable, culpado *m*, -a *f*, delincuente *mf*; (*of accident etc*) causa *f*, elemento *m* responsable.

cult [kʌlt] N culto *m* (*of* a).

cult figure ['kʌlt,fɪgəʳ] N figura *f* de culto.

cultivable ['kʌltɪvəbl] ADJ cultivable.

cultivar ['kʌltɪvaːʳ] N (*Bot*) variedad *f* cultivada; planta *f*, cosecha *f*.

cultivate ['kʌltɪveɪt] VT cultivar (*also fig*).

cultivated ['kʌltɪveɪtɪd] ADJ (*fig*) culto; **~ land** tierras *fpl* cultivadas.

cultivation [,kʌltɪ'veɪʃən] N (*Agr*) cultivo *m*; (*fig*) cultura *f*.

cultivator ['kʌltɪveɪtəʳ] N (a) (*person*) cultivador *m*, -ora *f*. (b) (*machine*) cultivador *m*.

cultural ['kʌltʃərəl] ADJ cultural; **~ attaché** agregado *m*, -a *f* cultural.

culturally ['kʌltʃərəlɪ] ADV *diverse* culturalmente, desde el punto de vista cultural; **to be ~ aware/sensitive** estar pendiente de/sensibilizado con la cultura; **~, they have much in common with their neighbours** culturalmente hablando, tienen mucho en común con sus vecinos.

culture ['kʌltʃəʳ] 1 N (*Agr, Bio*) cultivo *m*; (*fig*) cultura *f*; **~ clash** choque *m* de culturas; **~ shock** choque *m* cultural.

2 VT *tissue etc* cultivar.

cultured ['kʌltʃəd] ADJ culto; **~ pearl** perla *f* cultivada.

culture fluid ['kʌltʃə,fluːɪd] N caldo *m* de cultivo.

culture gap ['kʌltʃə,gæp] N vacío *m* cultural.

culture medium ['kʌltʃə,miːdɪəm] N, PL **culture media** ['kʌltʃə,miːdɪə] caldo *m* de cultivo.

culture-vulture ['kʌltʃə,vʌltʃəʳ] N (*hum**) persona *f* excesivamente ávida de cultura.

culvert ['kʌlvət] N alcantarilla *f* (debajo de una carretera).

cum [kʌm] PREP con; **it's a sort of kitchen-~-library** es algo así como cocina y biblioteca combinadas; **I was butler-~-gardener to Lady Z** yo fui mayordomo y jardinero a la vez en el servicio de Lady Z.

cumbersome ['kʌmbəsəm] ADJ, **cumbrous** ['kʌmbrəs] ADJ molesto, incómodo, engorroso, de mucho bulto.

cumin ['kʌmɪn] N comino *m*.

cum laude [kʊm'laʊdeɪ] ADJ (*Univ*) cum laude.

cummerbund ['kʌməbʌnd] N faja *f*.

cumulative ['kjuːmjʊlətɪv] ADJ cumulativo.

cumulonimbus [,kjuːmjʊləʊ'nɪmbəs] N, PL **cumulonimbi** [,kjuːmjʊləʊ'nɪmbaɪ] cumulonimbo *m*.

cumulus ['kjuːmələs] N, PL **cumuli** ['kjuːmjʊlaɪ] cúmulo *m*.

cuneiform ['kjuːnɪfɔːm] ADJ cuneiforme.

cunnilingus [,kʌnɪ'lɪŋgəs] N cunnilingus *m*.

cunning ['kʌnɪŋ] 1 ADJ (a) (*clever*) astuto, (*sly*) taimado. (b) (*skilfully made*) artificioso, ingenioso. (c) (*US**) precioso, mono.

2 N astucia *f*.

cunt⁣ [kʌnt] N (a) coño⁣ *m*, concha⁣ *f* (*LAm*). (b) (*person*) mierda *m*⁣; **you ~!** ¡coño!⁣.

CUP N ABBR *of* **Cambridge University Press.**

cup [kʌp] 1 N taza *f*; (*Eccl, Bot*) cáliz *m*; (*Brit: trophy*) copa *f*; (*in ground*) hoyo *m*, hondonada *f*; (*of bra*) copa *f*; **to be in one's ~s** estar borracho; **his ~ of sorrow was full** le agobiaba el dolor; **it's not quite my ~ of tea** no es plato de mi gusto; **he's not my ~ of tea** no es de mi agrado, no es santo de mi devoción; **how's your ~?** ¿quieres más té?

2 VT: **to ~ one's hands** (*for shouting*) formar bocina con las manos; (*for drinking*) ahuecar las manos.

cup-bearer ['kʌp,bɛərəʳ] N copero *m*.

cupboard ['kʌbəd] N (*esp Brit*) armario *m*; (*on wall*) alacena *f*; **~ love** (*Brit*) amor *m* interesado.

cup final ['kʌpfaɪnl] N (*Brit*) final *f* de copa.

cupful ['kʌpfʊl] N taza *f*, contenido *m* de una taza; **two ~s of milk** dos tazas de leche.

Cupid ['kjuːpɪd] NM Cupido.

cupidity [kjuː'pɪdɪtɪ] N codicia *f*.

cupola ['kjuːpələ] N cúpula *f*.

cuppa* ['kʌpə] N (*Brit*) taza *f* (de té).

cup-tie ['kʌptaɪ] N (*Brit*) partido *m* de copa.

cur [kɜːʳ] N perro *m* de mala raza; (*person*) canalla *m*.

curable ['kjʊərəbl] ADJ curable.

curaçao [kjʊərə'səʊ] N curaçao *m*.

curacy ['kjʊərəsɪ] N curato *m*; coadjutoría *f*.

curare [kjʊə'raːrɪ] N curare *m*.

curate ['kjʊərɪt] N (*parish priest*) cura *m*; (*assistant*) coadjutor *m*; **it's like the ~'s egg** (*Brit*) tiene su lado bueno y su lado malo.

curative ['kjʊərətɪv] ADJ curativo.

curator [kjʊə'reɪtəʳ] N (*of museum*) director *m*, -ora *f*, conservador *m*, -ora *f*.

curatorial [,kjʊərə'tɔːrɪəl] ADJ (*frm*) de conservadores, de conservación; **the museum's ~ team** el equipo de conservadores del museo; **valuable ~ expertise** valiosos conocimientos de conservación.

curb [kɜːb] 1 N (*fig*) freno *m*, estorbo *m* (*on* para); (*US*) bordillo *m*; **to put a ~ on** refrenar; = **kerb**.

2 VT (*fig*) refrenar, reprimir, limitar; *expenditure* restringir; *temper* dominar.

curb service ['kɜːb,sɜːvɪs] N (*US*) servicio *m* drive-in.

curbstone ['kɜːbstəʊn] N (*US*) = **kerbstone**.

curd [kɜːd] N (*freq pl*) cuajada *f*, requesón *m*.

curdle ['kɜːdl] 1 VT cuajar; **to ~ one's blood** helar la sangre de uno.

2 VI cuajarse.

cure [kjʊəʳ] 1 N (a) (*Med: process*) cura *f*, curación *f*; (*remedy*) remedio *m*; **there is no known ~** no existe remedio. (b) (*Eccl: also ~ of souls*) curato *m*, cura *f* de almas.

2 VT curar (*of* de).

cure-all ['kjʊərɔːl] N panacea *f*, sanalotodo *m*.

curettage [,kjʊəre'tɪdʒ] N legrado *m*, raspado *m*.

curfew ['kɜːfjuː] N (toque *m* de) queda *f*.

curie ['kjʊərɪ] N curie *m*.

curing ['kjʊərɪŋ] N curación *f*; V **cure 2**.

curio ['kjʊərɪəʊ] N curiosidad *f*.

curiosity [,kjʊərɪ'ɒsɪtɪ] N curiosidad *f*.

curious ['kjʊərɪəs] ADJ curioso; **I am ~ to see Granada** tengo ganas de ver Granada.

curiously ['kjʊərɪəslɪ] ADV curiosamente; **~ made** ingenioso, artificioso; **~ enough** aunque parece mentira.

curl [kɜːl] 1 N (*of hair*) rizo *m*, bucle *m*; (*of smoke etc*) penacho *m*, espiral *f*.

2 VT *hair* rizar, ensortijar; *paper etc* arrollar; *lip* fruncir.

3 VI (*hair*) rizarse, ensortijarse, formar bucles; (*paper etc*) arrollarse; (*leaf*) abarquillarse; (*waves*) encresparse.

◆ **curl up** VI arrollarse; (*smoke*) subir en espiral; (*animal*) apelotonarse; (*person*) hacerse un ovillo; (*) morirse de risa; **to ~ up in an armchair** hacerse un ovillo en una butaca; **to ~ up into a ball** hacerse un ovillo; **to ~ up with a book** acurrucarse con un libro.

curler ['kɜːləʳ] N (*for hair*) bigudí *m*, chicho *m*, rulo *m*.

curlew ['kɜːluː] N zarapito *m*.

curlicue ['kɜːlɪkjuː] N floritura *f*, floreo *m*.

curling ['kɜːlɪŋ] N (*Sport*) *deporte que se juega sobre hielo*.

curling-iron ['kɜːlɪŋ,aɪən] N, **curling-tongs** ['kɜːlɪŋtɒŋz] NPL tenaci-

llas *fpl* de rizar.
curl-paper ['kɜːl,peɪpəʳ] N papillote *m*.
curly ['kɜːlɪ] ADJ rizado, ensortijado.
curly-haired [,kɜːlɪ'hɛəd] ADJ, **curly-headed** [kɜːlɪ'hedɪd] ADJ de pelo rizado.
curmudgeon [kɜː'mʌdʒən]† N cascarrabias *mf*.
curmudgeonly [kɜː'mʌdʒənlɪ]† ADJ de viejo cascarrabias.
currant ['kʌrənt] N (*dried*) pasa *f* de Corinto; *V* **black** *etc*.
currency ['kʌrənsɪ] [1] N (a) (*money*) moneda *f*.
  (b) (*fig*) uso *m*; **it had a certain ~** se usó bastante.
  [2] ATTR: **~ market** mercado *m* monetario; **~ note** pagaré *m* fiscal (*or* de tesorería); **~ restrictions** restricciones *fpl* monetarias; **~ snake** serpiente *f* monetaria; **~ unit** unidad *f* monetaria.
current ['kʌrɪ] [1] ADJ corriente, actual; *price, account etc* corriente; **~ account** (*Brit*) cuenta *f* corriente; **~ assets** activo *m* corriente; **~ liabilities** pasivo *m* corriente; **the ~ month** el mes que corre; **the ~ year** el año presente; **the ~ number of a magazine** el último número de una revista; **the ~ opinion is that ...** se cree actualmente que ...; **it is still quite ~** se usa bastante todavía; **to be in ~ use** estar en uso corriente.
  [2] N (*most senses*) corriente *f*; (*Elec*) flúido *m*, corriente *f*.
currently ['kʌrəntlɪ] ADV actualmente, en la actualidad.
curriculum [kə'rɪkjʊləm] N, PL **curricula** [kə'rɪkjʊlə] plan *m* de estudios, programa *m* de estudios, currículo *m*; **~ vitae** curriculum *m* (vitae), historial *m* (profesional).

┌─ **CURRICULUM - NATIONAL CURRICULUM** ─────────┐

🛈 *El* **National Curriculum** *es el conjunto de asignaturas obligatorias para todos los alumnos de los colegios de Inglaterra y Gales, que son: lengua inglesa, matemáticas, ciencias, tecnología, historia, geografía, música, arte, educación física e idioma extranjero; en los centros de Gales se enseña además el idioma galés. Las pruebas de lengua, matemáticas y ciencias se evalúan a nivel nacional cuando el alumno tiene 7, 11 y 14 años. Los centros de primaria y secundaria cuentan como asignatura opcional con religión y en los de secundaria además se imparte educación sexual, aunque son los padres quienes deciden si sus hijos recibirán estas enseñanzas o no. En Irlanda del Norte el contenido curricular es muy parecido, mientras que en Escocia es responsabilidad de la administración local y de cada colegio.*

curried ['kʌrɪd] ADJ (preparado) con curry.
curry[1] ['kʌrɪ] (*Culin*) [1] N curry *m*.
  [2] VT preparar con curry.
curry[2] ['kʌrɪ] VT *horse* almohazar; *V* **favour**.
currycomb ['kʌrɪkəʊm] N almohaza *f*.
curry-powder ['kʌrɪ,paʊdəʳ] N polvo *m* de curry.
curse [kɜːs] [1] N (a) maldición *f*; **~s!** ¡maldición!; **a ~ on it!** ¡maldito sea!
  (b) (*oath*) palabrota *f*, taco *m*.
  (c) (*bane*) calamidad *f*; azote *m*; **the ~ (of Eve)** el período, la regla, la cuenta*; **the dampness is a ~ here** aquí la humedad es una calamidad; **drought is the ~ of Spain** la sequía es el azote de España; **it's been the ~ of my life** me ha amargado la vida, siempre me ha afligido; **the ~ of it is that ...** lo peor es que ...
  [2] VT maldecir; echar pestes de; **to ~ sb with** castigar a uno con; **to be ~d with** padecer de, tener que aguantar, sufrir la aflicción de; **~ it!** ¡maldito sea!
  [3] VI blasfemar, echar pestes, soltar palabrotas; **to ~ and swear** echar sapos y culebras, echar tacos.
  [4] VR: **to ~ o.s.** maldecirse (*for being a fool* por tonto).
cursed ['kɜːsɪd] ADJ maldito.
cursive ['kɜːsɪv] ADJ cursivo.
cursor ['kɜːsəʳ] N cursor *m*; **~ key** tecla *f* del cursor.
cursorily ['kɜːsərɪlɪ] ADV rápidamente, de modo superficial.
cursory ['kɜːsərɪ] ADJ rápido, superficial.
curt [kɜːt] ADJ brusco, seco, lacónico.
curtail [kɜː'teɪl] VT acortar, abreviar; restringir.
curtailment [kɜː'teɪlmənt] N acortamiento *m*, abreviación *f*; restricción *f*.
curtain ['kɜːtn] [1] N cortina *f* (*also Mil*); (*small*) visillo *m*; (*Theat*) telón *m*; **~ wall** paneles *mpl*; **when the final ~ came down** cuando el telón bajó por última vez; **it was ~s for him*** para él fue el fin.
  [2] VT proveer de cortina.
◆**curtain off** VT separar con cortinas.
curtain-call ['kɜːtnkɔːl] N llamada *f* a escena.
curtained ['kɜːtənd] ADJ *door etc* con cortina(s).
curtain-hook ['kɜːtn,hʊk] N gancho *m* de cortina.
curtain-pole ['kɜːtn,pəʊl] N, **curtain-rail** ['kɜːtn,reɪl] N palo de las cortinas.
curtain-raiser ['kɜːtn,reɪzəʳ] N pieza *f* preliminar.
curtain-ring ['kɜːtnrɪŋ] N anilla *f*.
curtain-rod ['kɜːtnrɒd] N barra *f* de cortina.
curtly ['kɜːtlɪ] ADV bruscamente, secamente.

curtness ['kɜːtnɪs] N brusquedad *f*, laconismo *m*.
curtsy ['kɜːtsɪ] [1] N reverencia *f*; **to drop a ~ = 2**.
  [2] VI hacer una reverencia (*to* a).
curvaceous* [kɜː'veɪʃəs] ADJ *girl* de buen tipo, curvilínea.
curvature ['kɜːvətʃəʳ] N curvatura *f*; **~ of the spine** escoliosis *f*.
curve [kɜːv] [1] N curva *f*; combadura *f*.
  [2] VT encorvar, torcer; combar.
  [3] VI encorvarse, torcerse; combarse; (*road etc*) torcerse, hacer una curva; (*through air*) volar en curva.
curved [kɜːvd] ADJ curvo, encorvado.
curvy ['kɜːvɪ] ADJ curvo, encorvado; *road etc* serpentino, con muchas curvas.
cushion ['kʊʃən] [1] N cojín *m*; (*Billiards*) banda *f*; (*fig*) colchón *m*.
  [2] VT *blow etc* amortiguar.
cushy‡ ['kʊʃɪ] ADJ (*Brit*) fácil, agradable; **~ job** chollo‡ *m*.
cusp [kʌsp] N (*Bot, Astron*) cúspide *f*; (*tooth*) corona *f*; (*moon*) cuerno *m*.
cuspidor ['kʌspɪdɔːʳ] N (*US*) escupidera *f*.
cuss* [kʌs] [1] N (*US*) tipo* *m*, tío* *m*.
  [2] VT *etc V* **curse**.
cussed* ['kʌsɪd] ADJ (a) terco, cabezón. (b) = **cursed**.
cussedness* ['kʌsɪdnɪs] N terquedad *f*; **out of sheer ~** de puro terco.
custard ['kʌstəd] [1] N natillas *fpl*; crema *f* instantánea (en polvo).
  [2] ATTR: **~ apple** (*Bot*) chirimoya *f*; **~ pie** (*missile*) torta *f* de crema; **~ powder** polvos *mpl* de natillas; **~ tart** pastel *m* de crema.
custodial [kʌs'təʊdɪəl] ADJ (a) **~ sentence** condena *f* de prisión. (b) **~ staff** (*museum etc*) personal *m* de vigilancia.
custodian [kʌs'təʊdɪən] N custodio *m*, guardián *m*; (*museum*) conservador *m*, -ora *f*.
custody ['kʌstədɪ] N custodia *f*; **in safe ~** en buenas manos; **to be in ~** estar detenido; **to take sb into ~** detener a uno.
custom ['kʌstəm] [1] N (a) costumbre *f*.
  (b) (*Brit Comm*) clientela *f*, parroquia *f*; (*total sales*) caja *f*, ventas *fpl*; **to attract ~** atraer clientela; **we've not had much ~ today** hoy hemos tenido pocos clientes.
  (c) **~s** aduana *f*; (*duty*) derechos *mpl* de aduana; **C~s and Excise** (*Brit*) Aduanas *fpl* y Arbitrios; **to go through the ~s** pasar por la aduana.
  [2] ATTR (a) = **custom-built, custom-made**. (b) **~s** aduanero, aduanal, de aduana; **~ clearance** despacho *m* aduanal; **~ declaration** declaración *f* aduanera; **~ duty** derechos *mpl* de aduana; **~ inspection** revisión *f* aduanera; **~ inspector** aduanero *m*, -a *f*; **~ invoice** factura *f* de aduana; **~ service** servicio *m* aduanero; **~ union** unión *f* aduanera; **~ warehouse** depósito *m* aduanero.
customarily ['kʌstəmərɪlɪ] ADV por regla general, normalmente.
customary ['kʌstəmərɪ] ADJ acostumbrado, de costumbre; normal; **it is ~ to** + *infin* es costumbre + *infin*, se suele + *infin*.
custom-built ['kʌstəm,bɪlt] ADJ hecho de encargo.
customer ['kʌstəməʳ] N (a) cliente *m*, -a *f*; **~ liaison, ~ relations** relaciones *fpl* con los clientes; **~ profile** perfil *m* de la clientela; **~ service** servicio *m* de asistencia posventa; **~ services** servicios *mpl* para los clientes. (b) (*) tipo* *m*.
customhouse ['kʌstəmhaʊs] N (*US*) aduana *f*.
customize ['kʌstəmaɪz] VT hacer al gusto del consumidor, adaptar en razón de un cliente particular, personalizar.
customized ['kʌstəmaɪzd] ADJ hecho de encargo; **~ software** software *m* a medida del usuario.
custom-made ['kʌstəm'meɪd] ADJ (*US*) hecho a la medida, hecho para un cliente específico; fuera de serie.
customs-house ['kʌstəmzhaʊs] N, PL **customs-houses** ['kʌstəmz,haʊzɪz] aduana *f*.
customs-officer ['kʌstəmz,ɒfɪsəʳ] N aduanero *m*, -a *f*.
customs-post ['kʌstəmzpəʊst] N puesto *m* aduanero.
cut [kʌt] [1] ADJ cortado; **~ flowers** flores *fpl* cortadas; **~ glass** vidrio *m* tallado; **~ prices** precios *mpl* reducidos; **~ and dried** rutinario; seguro; preparado de antemano; convenido de antemano; **~ off** aislado (*from* de).
  [2] N (a) (*incision*) corte *m*; (*in skin*) cortadura *f*.
  (b) (*slash with sword*) tajo *m*, (*with knife*) cuchillada *f*, (*with whip*) latigazo *m*; (*insult, offence*) corte *m*; **the ~ and thrust of politics** la esgrima política; **the unkindest ~ of all** el golpe más duro; **whose ~ is it?** (*Cards*) ¿quién corta?
  (c) (*deletion*) corte *m*, trozo *m* suprimido.
  (d) **short ~** atajo *m*; **there is no short ~ to success** no se alcanza el éxito por ningún camino fácil; **to take a short ~** atajar, ir por el atajo, (*fig*) echar por el atajo.
  (e) (*of clothes, diamond*) corte *m*; **to be a ~ above the rest** ser algo superior a los demás.
  (f) (*woodcut*) grabado *m*; (*US*) foto *f*, diagrama *m*, dibujo *m*.
  (g) (*kind of meat*) clase *f* de carne; (*slice*) tajada *f*; (*share*) parte *f*, tajada *f*.
  (h) (*reduction*) reducción *f*, rebaja *f* (*in* de); corte *m*, recorte *m*; (*Elec*) apagón *m*; **to take a ~ in salary** sufrir una reducción de sueldo.

(i) (*share*) parte *f*; tajada* *f*; **the manager gets a ~ of 5%** el gerente recibe su parte de 5 por ciento.

3 (*irr*. PRET AND PTP **cut**) VT **(a)** (*gen*) cortar; *cards, communications, hair, hedge, drug etc* cortar; *corn* segar; *meat* trinchar; (*of wind*) cortar; *engine* parar; (*divide*) cortar, partir, dividir (*into 2* en 2); **to ~ one's finger** cortarse el dedo; **to get one's hair ~** cortarse el pelo; **to ~ sb free** cortar las cuerdas que lían a uno.

(b) (*shape*) *glass, stone* tallar; *disc* grabar; *hole* practicar, hacer.

(c) (*ignore*) no hacer caso a; fingir no ver; negar el saludo a; *class etc* ausentarse de, no asistir a.

(d) (*intersect*) cruzar, cortar.

(e) (*Aut*) *corner* tomar muy cerrado.

(f) (*reduce*) recortar, rebajar, reducir; *price* reducir (*by 5%* en un 5 por cien); *staff* recortar; (*delete*) cortar, suprimir; **she ~ 2 seconds off the record** mejoró la marca en 2 segundos.

(g) he's ~ting a tooth le está saliendo un diente.

4 VI **(a)** (*gen*) cortar; (*material*) cortarse; **this ~s both ways** esto tiene doble fila; **to ~ and run** largarse*; rajarse*; claudicar.

(b) (*Math etc: lines*) cortarse.

(c) (*Cine, TV*) **~!** ¡corten!; **they ~ from the palace to the castle scene** pasan (*or* cambian) del palacio a la escena del castillo.

(d) (*Cards*) cortar; **to ~ for deal** cortar para determinar el repartidor.

◆ **cut across** VT **(a)** **to ~ wood across** cortar una madera a través; cortar una madera completamente.

(b) atajar, tomar un atajo; **to ~ across a field** atajar por un campo, atravesar un campo.

(c) **this ~s across the usual categories** (*fig*) esto rebasa (*pej*: no respeta) las categorías establecidas.

◆ **cut along** VI irse de prisa.

◆ **cut away** VT cortar, separar cortando.

◆ **cut back** **1** VT acortar, recortar, reducir; *expenditure, production* recortar, reducir; *staff etc* recortar.

2 VI **(a)** volver (*to* a).

(b) = **cut down 2.**

(c) **to ~ back on** = **cut back 1.**

◆ **cut down** **1** VT **(a)** *tree etc* talar, derribar, cortar; *enemy* matar.

(b) *price* rebajar; *costs* reducir (*by 5%* en un 5 por cien); *size, majority* reducir (*by* en).

2 VI economizar; **to ~ down on** economizar con, reducir el consumo de.

◆ **cut in** **1** VT: **to ~ sb in on a deal** permitir que uno participe en un negocio (*esp poco limpio*).

2 VI **(a)** (*Aut*) pasar peligrosamente, meterse delante (de modo peligroso).

(b) (*in conversation*) interrumpir, cortar; **to ~ in on a conversation** interrumpir una conversación.

◆ **cut into** VT: **to ~ into one's holiday** interrumpir sus vacaciones; **this will ~ into our holiday** esto quitará una parte de las vacaciones; **we shall have to ~ into savings** tendremos que usar una parte de los ahorros.

◆ **cut off** VT **(a)** cortar; (*Elec, Telec etc*) cortar, interrumpir; desconectar; *limb* amputar; **we were ~ off** nos desconectaron; **to ~ sb's life off in its prime** tronchar una vida joven.

(b) *troops* cercar, copar; *retreat* cortar, impedir; (*of flood, snow*) aislar; dejar incomunicado; bloquear; **we were ~ off by the snow** quedamos bloqueados por la nieve.

(c) (*disinherit*) desheredar.

◆ **cut out** **1** VT **(a)** recortar; *hole etc* practicar, hacer; *diseased part* extirpar.

(b) (*exclude*) excluir, dejar fuera; *opposition* eliminar; *harmful substance* dejar (de tomar), suprimir (el uso de); **he ~ his nephew out of his will** borró de su testamento la mención del sobrino; **~ it out!** ¡basta ya!, ¡déjalo!; **~ out the singing!** ¡basta ya de cantar!; **you can ~ that out for a start** en primer lugar puedes olvidar eso.

(c) (*delete*) suprimir, tachar, cortar.

(d) **he's not ~ out to be a poet** no tiene madera de poeta, no tiene talento de poeta.

(e) **he had his work ~ out to finish it** tuvo que trabajar duro para terminarlo; **you'll have your work ~ out to manage it** vas a sudar la gota gorda para lograrlo.

2 VI **(a)** (*engine*) pararse; (*Elec*) cortarse, interrumpirse.

(b) (*US*: *leave*) pirarla*.

◆ **cut through** VI abrirse camino, abrirse paso (a la fuerza).

◆ **cut up** **1** VT **(a)** cortar (en pedazos); desmenuzar; dividir; *meat* picar; (*wound*) herir, acuchillar.

(b) (*Brit**) **to be ~ up** afligirse (*about* por); **he's very ~ up** está muy deshinchado; **he was very ~ up by the death of his son** estaba muy afectado por la muerte de su hijo.

2 VI **(a)** **he'll ~ up for several millions*** dejará varios millones.

(b) **to ~ up rough** (*Brit**) cabrearse*.

(c) (*US*) (*clown around*) hacer tonterías, hacer el bobo.

cutaneous [kjuːˈteɪnɪəs] ADJ cutáneo.

cutback [ˈkʌtbæk] N recorte *m*, corte *m*, reducción *f*; economía *f*.

cute [kjuːt] ADJ **(a)** (*nice*) mono, lindo; (*shrewd*) cuco, astuto, listo. **(b)** (*esp US: affecting prettiness etc*) presumido.

cutesy* [ˈkjuːtsɪ] ADJ (*pej*) *person, painting, clothes* cursi.

cut-glass [ˈkʌtˈɡlɑːs] ADJ de vidrio tallado.

cuticle [ˈkjuːtɪkl] N cutícula *f*.

cutie* [ˈkjuːtɪ] N (*US*) chica *f*.

cutie pie* [ˈkjuːtɪpaɪ] N (*US*) monada *f*, ricura *f*.

cutlass [ˈkʌtləs] N alfanje *m*, chafarote *m*.

cutler [ˈkʌtlər] N cuchillero *m*.

cutlery [ˈkʌtlərɪ] N cubiertos *mpl*, cuchillería *f*; **~ cabinet** caja *f* de cuchillería.

cutlet [ˈkʌtlɪt] N chuleta *f*.

cut-off [ˈkʌtɒf] N (*Mech*) cieɪre *m*, corte *m*; (*Elec*) desconectador *m*; (*US*) atajo *m*; **~ point** punto *m* de corte.

cutoffs* [ˈkʌtɒfs] NPL tejanos *mpl* cortados.

cut-out [ˈkʌtaʊt] N **(a)** (*child's*) recorte *m*, diseño *m* para recortar, recortable *m*. **(b)** (*Elec*) cortacircuito *m*, disyuntor *m*; (*Mech*) válvula *f* de escape.

cut-price [ˈkʌtpraɪs] ADJ (*Brit*) a precio reducido; **~ shop, ~ store** tienda *f* de saldos.

cut-rate [ˌkʌtˈreɪt] ADJ barato.

cutter [ˈkʌtər] N **(a)** (*Sew etc*) cortador *m*, -ora *f*. **(b)** (*Mech*) cortadora *f*; **~s** (*for wire etc*) cizallas *fpl*, cortaalambres *m*. **(c)** (*Naut*) cúter *m*; patrullero *m*, guardacostas *m*.

cut-throat [ˈkʌtθrəʊt] **1** ADJ *competition* encarnizado, despiadado, intenso; **~ razor** (*Brit*) navaja *f* (de afeitar).

2 N asesino *m*.

cutting [ˈkʌtɪŋ] **1** ADJ cortante; *remark* mordaz; **~ board** plancha *f* para cortar; **~ edge** filo *m*, (*fig*) vanguardia *f*; **~ room** (*Cine*) sala *f* de montaje.

2 N **(a)** (*from paper*) recorte *m*. **(b)** (*Rail*) desmonte *m*, trinchera *f*. **(c)** (*Bot*) esqueje *m*.

cuttlefish [ˈkʌtlfɪʃ] N jibia *f*, sepia *f*.

cut-up* [ˌkʌtˈʌp] ADJ **(a)** (*Brit*) V **cut up**. **(b)** (*US*) gracioso.

CV N ABBR *of* **curriculum vitae** curriculum *m* vitae.

CW N **(a)** ABBR *of* **chemical weapons**. **(b)** ABBR *of* **chemical warfare**.

c.w.o. ABBR *of* **cash with order** pago *m* al contado.

CWS N ABBR *of* **Cooperative Wholesale Society**.

cwt ABBR *of* **hundredweight(s)**.

cyanide [ˈsaɪənaɪd] N cianuro *m*; **~ of potassium** cianuro *m* de potasio.

cyanose [ˈsaɪənəʊz] N cianosis *f*.

cybernetic [ˌsaɪbəˈnetɪk] ADJ cibernético.

cybernetics [ˌsaɪbəˈnetɪks] N SING AND PL cibernética *f*.

cyberpunk [ˈsaɪbəpʌŋk] N (*Liter*) ciberpunk *m*.

cybersex [ˈsaɪbəseks] N cibersexo *m*.

cyberspace [ˈsaɪbəspeɪs] N ciberespacio *m*.

cyborg [ˈsaɪbɔːɡ] N ciborg *m*, organismo *m* cibernético.

cyclamate [ˈsɪkləmeɪt] N ciclamato *m*.

cyclamen [ˈsɪkləmən] N ciclamen *m*, ciclamino *m*.

cycle [ˈsaɪkl] **1** N **(a)** ciclo *m*; **life ~** ciclo *m* vital; **menstrual ~** ciclo *m* menstrual. **(b)** (*bicycle*) bicicleta *f*.

2 VI ir (*or* montar) en bicicleta; **we ~d to the coast** fuimos en bicicleta a la costa.

cycle-bell [ˈsaɪkl,bel] N timbre *m* de bicicleta.

cycle-clip [ˈsaɪkl,klɪp] N pinza *f* para ir en bicicleta.

cycle-lane [ˈsaɪkl,leɪn] N pista *f* para ciclistas.

cycle-path [ˈsaɪkl,pɑːθ] N carril *m* de bicicleta.

cycler [ˈsaɪklər] N (*US*) ciclista *mf*.

cycle race [ˈsaɪklreɪs] N carrera *f* ciclista.

cycle-rack [ˈsaɪkl,ræk] N soporte *m* para bicicletas; (*on car roof*) baca *f* para transportar bicicletas.

cycle-shed [ˈsaɪkl,ʃed] N cobertizo *m* para bicicletas.

cycle-track [ˈsaɪkl,træk] N (*Sport*) pista *f* de ciclismo.

cycleway [ˈsaɪklweɪ] N carril *m* bici.

cyclic(al) [ˈsaɪklɪk(əl)] ADJ cíclico.

cycling [ˈsaɪklɪŋ] **1** N ciclismo *m*.

2 ATTR: **~ holiday** vacaciones *fpl* en bicicleta; **~ tour** vuelta *f* ciclista; **~ track** velódromo *m*.

cyclist [ˈsaɪklɪst] N ciclista *mf*.

cyclone [ˈsaɪkləʊn] N ciclón *m*.

Cyclops [ˈsaɪklɒps] N cíclope *m*.

cyclostyle [ˈsaɪkləʊstaɪl] **1** N ciclostil(o) *m*.

2 VT ciclostilar, reproducir en ciclostil(o).

cyclostyled [ˈsaɪkləstaɪld] ADJ en ciclostil(o).

cyclotron [ˈsaɪklɒtrɒn] N ciclotrón *m*.

cygnet [ˈsɪɡnɪt] N pollo *m* de cisne, cisnecito *m*.

cylinder [ˈsɪlɪndər] N cilindro *m*.

cylinder-block [ˈsɪlɪndəblɒk] N bloque *m* de cilindros.

cylinder capacity [ˈsɪlɪndəˈpæsɪtɪ] N cilindrada *f*.

cylinder-head [ˈsɪlɪndəhed] N culata *f* de cilindro; **~ gasket** junta *f*

de culata.
cylindrical [sɪ'lɪndrɪkəl] ADJ cilíndrico.
cymbal ['sɪmbəl] N (freq pl) platillo m, címbalo m.
cynic ['sɪnɪk] N cínico m, -a f.
cynical ['sɪnɪkəl] ADJ cínico; despreciativo, desengañado.
cynically ['sɪnɪklɪ] ADV con cinismo.
cynicism ['sɪnɪsɪzəm] N cinismo m; desprecio m, desengaño m.
cynosure ['saɪnəʃʊəʳ] N: ~ **of every eye** blanco m de todas las miradas.
CYO N (US) ABBR of **Catholic Youth Organization**.
cypher ['saɪfəʳ] = **cipher**.
cypress ['saɪprɪs] N ciprés m.
Cypriot ['sɪprɪət] 1 ADJ chipriota.
    2 N chipriota mf.
Cyprus ['saɪprəs] N Chipre f.
Cyrillic [sɪ'rɪlɪk] 1 ADJ cirílico.
    2 N cirílico m.
cyst [sɪst] N quiste m.

cystic ['sɪstɪk] ADJ cístico; ~ **fibrosis** fibrosis f cística.
cystitis [sɪs'taɪtɪs] N cistitis f.
cytological [,saɪtə'lɒdʒɪkəl] ADJ citológico.
cytology [saɪ'tɔlədʒɪ] N citología f.
cytoplasm ['saɪtəʊplæzm] N citoplasma m.
cytotoxic [,saɪtəʊ'tɒksɪk] ADJ citotóxico.
CZ (US) ABBR of **Canal Zone**.
czar [zɑːʳ] N zar m; (person in authority, chief) jefe m.
czarina [zɑː'riːnə] N zarina f.
czarism ['zɑːrɪzəm] N zarismo m.
czarist ['zɑːrɪst] ADJ, N zarista mf.
Czech [tʃek] 1 ADJ checo; **the ~ Republic** la República Checa.
    2 N (a) checo m, -a f. (b) (Ling) checo m.
Czechoslovak ['tʃekəʊ'sləʊvæk] 1 ADJ checoslovaco.
    2 N checoslovaco m, -a f.
Czechoslovakia ['tʃekəʊsləʊ'vækɪə] N Checoslovaquia f.
Czechoslovakian ['tʃekəʊslə'vækɪən] 1 ADJ checoslovaco.
    2 N checoslovaco m, -a f.

D

D, d [diː] N **(a)** (*letter*) D, d *f*; **D for David, D for Dog** (*US*) D de Dolores. **(b) D** (*Mus*) re *m*; **D major** re mayor.

D (a) N (*Scol: mark around 50%*) aprobado *m*, suficiente *m*. **(b)** (*US Pol*) ABBR of **Democrat(ic)**.

d. N **(a)** ABBR of **date** fecha *f*. **(b)** ABBR of **daughter** hija *f*. **(c)** ABBR of **died** murió, m. **(d)** (*Rail etc*) ABBR of **depart(s)** sale. **(e)** († *Brit*) ABBR of **penny** penique *m*.

DA N (*US*) ABBR of **District Attorney**.

D/A ABBR of **deposit account**.

dab¹ [dæb] [1] N (*blow*) golpe *m* ligero; (*small amount*) pequeña cantidad *f*; (*of paint*) brochazo *m*; (*of liquid*) gota *f*; **~s** (*esp Brit*: *hands*) manos *fpl*; (*fingerprints*) huellas *fpl* dactilares.

[2] VT (*strike*) golpear ligeramente, tocar ligeramente; (*with sponge etc*) tocar; frotar suavemente; (*moisten*) mojar ligeramente; **to ~ a stain off** quitar una mancha mojándola ligeramente; **to ~ paint on a wall** embadurnar una pared de pintura.

[3] VI: **to ~ at one's eyes with a handkerchief** llevar repetidas veces un pañuelo a los ojos.

dab² [dæb] N (*Fish*) lenguado *m*.

dab³* [dæb] [1] ADJ: **to be a ~ hand at** (*Brit*) tener buena mano para, ser un hacha en.

[2] N as* *m*, hacha *m* (*at en*).

[3] ADV: **~ in the middle** (*US*) en el mismo centro.

dabble ['dæbl] [1] VT salpicar, mojar; **to ~ one's feet** chapotear los pies.

[2] VI: **to ~ in sth** interesarse en algo por pasatiempo, ser ligeramente aficionado a algo, trabajar superficialmente en algo; **I only ~ in it** para mí es un pasatiempo nada más; **to ~ in politics** jugar a la política; **to ~ in shares** jugar a la bolsa.

dabbler ['dæbləʳ] N (*pej*) aficionado *m*, -a *f* (*in a*), diletante *mf*; **he's just a ~** es un simple aficionado, para él es un pasatiempo nada más.

dabchick ['dæbtʃɪk] N somorgujo *m* menor.

Dacca ['dækə] N Dacca *f*.

dace [deɪs] N albur *m*.

dacha ['dætʃə] N dacha *f*.

dachshund ['dækshʊnd] N perro *m* tejonero.

Dacron ['dækrɒn] ® N (*US*) terylene *m*.

dactyl ['dæktɪl] N dáctilo *m*.

dactylic [dæk'tɪlɪk] ADJ dactílico.

dad* [dæd] N, **daddy*** ['dædɪ] N papá *m*, papaíto *m*.

Dada ['dɑːdɑː] [1] N dada *m*, dadaísmo *m*.

[2] ATTR *movement* dadaísta.

dadaism ['dɑːdɑːɪzəm] N dadaísmo *m*.

dadaist ['dɑːdɑːɪst] [1] ADJ dadaísta.

[2] N dadaísta *mf*.

daddy-long-legs ['dædɪ'lɒŋlegz] N (*Brit*) típula *f*.

dado ['deɪdəʊ] N dado *m*; friso *m*.

daemon ['diːmən] N demonio *m*.

daff* [dæf] N (*Brit*) ABBR of **daffodil** narciso *m*.

daffodil ['dæfədɪl] N narciso *m* (trompón).

daffy* ['dæfɪ] ADJ (*US*) chiflado*.

daft [dɑːft] ADJ bobo, tonto.

dagger ['dægəʳ] N puñal *m*, daga *f*; (*Typ*) cruz *f*, obelisco *m*; **to be at ~s drawn** odiarse a muerte; **to look ~s at** apuñalar con la mirada, fulminar (con la mirada).

dago ['deɪgəʊ] N *término peyorativo aplicado a españoles, portugueses e italianos*.

daguerrotype [də'gɛrəʊˌtaɪp] N daguerrotipo *m*.

dahlia ['deɪlɪə] N dalia *f*.

Dáil [dɔɪl] N (*also* ~ **Éireann**) *Cámara baja del Parlamento de la República de Irlanda*.

daily ['deɪlɪ] [1] ADJ diario, cotidiano; **our ~ bread** el pan nuestro de cada día; **~ dozen** ejercicios *mpl* matinales; **~ paper** diario *m*; **the ~ round** la rutina cotidiana.

[2] ADV a diario, cada día.

[3] N **(a)** (*paper*) diario *m*.

(b) (*Brit*: *also* ~ **help**, ~ **woman**) asistenta *f*, chacha* *f*.

daintily ['deɪntɪlɪ] ADV delicadamente; elegantemente, primorosamente; melindrosamente.

daintiness ['deɪntɪnɪs] N **(a)** delicadeza *f*; elegancia *f*, primor *m*. **(b)** melindres *mpl*.

dainty ['deɪntɪ] [1] ADJ **(a)** (*delicate*) delicado, fino; (*tasteful*) elegante, primoroso, precioso. **(b)** (*fastidious*) delicado, melindroso.

[2] N bocado *m* exquisito, golosina *f*.

daiquiri ['daɪkɪrɪ] N daiquiri *m*.

dairy ['dɛərɪ] [1] N (*shop*) lechería *f*; (*on farm*) quesería *f*, vaquería *f*.

[2] ATTR lechero; lácteo; ~ **butter** mantequilla *f* de granja; ~ **cattle** vacas *fpl* lecheras; ~ **farm** granja *f* especializada en producción de leche; ~ **farming** industria *f* lechera; ~ **herd** ganado *m* lechero; ~ **ice cream** helado *m* hecho con leche; ~ **produce** productos *mpl* lácteos.

dairymaid ['dɛərɪmeɪd] N lechera *f*.

dairyman ['dɛərɪmən] N, PL **dairymen** ['dɛərɪmen] lechero *m*.

dais [deɪs] N estrado *m*.

daisy ['deɪzɪ] N maya *f*, margarita *f*; **to be pushing up the daisies*** criar malvas*.

daisy-chain ['deɪzɪˌtʃeɪn] N (*US fig*) serie *f*.

daisy-wheel ['deɪzɪˌwiːl] N margarita *f*; ~ **printer** impresora *f* de margarita.

Dakar ['dækəʳ] N Dakar *m*.

Dalai Lama ['dælaɪ'lɑːmə] N Dalai Lama *m*.

dale [deɪl] N (*N Eng*) valle *m*; **the (Yorkshire) D~s** los valles de Yorkshire.

dalliance ['dælɪəns] N (*play*) juegos *mpl*, diversiones *fpl*; (*time-wasting*) frivolidad *f*; **amorous** ~ coquetería *f*, flirteo *m*.

dally ['dælɪ] VI (*delay*) tardar, perder el tiempo; (*amuse o.s.*) divertirse; **to ~ with** *lover* coquetear con, entretenerse en amores con; *idea* entretenerse con.

Dalmatia [dæl'meɪʃə] N Dalmacia *f*.

dalmatian [dæl'meɪʃən] N (*dog*) perro *m* dálmata.

daltonism ['dɔːltənɪzəm] N daltonismo *m*.

dam¹ [dæm] [1] N presa *f*; (*small*) dique *m*.

[2] VT represar; construir una presa sobre.

◆ **dam up** VT cerrar, tapar; *overflowing water* contener con un dique.

dam²* [dæm] ADJ = **damn 3, damned**.

dam³ [dæm] N (*Zool*) madre *f*.

damage ['dæmɪdʒ] [1] N **(a)** daño *m*, perjuicio *m*; (*Mech*) avería *f*; (*visible, eg on car*) desperfectos *mpl*; ~ **limitation exercise** campaña *f* para contener los daños; **what's the ~?*** ¿cuánto te debo?

(b) ~**s** (*Jur*) daños *mpl* y perjuicios, indemnización *f*.

[2] VT dañar, perjudicar; (*Mech*) averiar, estropear; *chances, reputation* perjudicar; **to be ~d in a collision** sufrir daños en un choque.

damaging ['dæmɪdʒɪŋ] ADJ perjudicial.

damascene ['dæməsiːn] [1] ADJ damasquinado, damasquino.

[2] VT damasquinar.

Damascus [də'mɑːskəs] N Damasco *m*.

damask ['dæməsk] [1] ADJ *cloth* adamascado; *steel* damasquino.

[2] N (*cloth*) damasco *m*; (*steel*) acero *m* damasquino.

[3] VT *cloth* adamascar; *steel* damasquinar.

dame [deɪm] N **(a)** (*esp Brit*) dama *f*, señora *f*; (*Brit Theat*) vieja dama *f*; *ver también* PANTOMIME. **(b) D~** (*Brit: in titles*) título que lleva una mujer condecorada con una orden de caballería. **(c)** (*esp US**) tía* *f*, chica *f*.

damfool* ['dæm'fuːl] ADJ (*Brit*) estúpido, tonto; **some ~ driver** algún imbécil de conductor; **that's a ~ thing to say!** ¡qué tontería!

dammit* ['dæmɪt] EXCL (*Brit*) ¡córcholis!*; **as near as ~** casi; por un pelo.

damn [dæm] **1** VT condenar (*also Eccl*); maldecir; ~!, ~ it! ¡condenación!; ~ **this car!** ¡al diablo con este coche!; **the effort was** ~**ed from the start** desde el principio el esfuerzo estaba condenado a fracasar; **his arrogance** ~**ed him** su arrogancia le perdió; **the critics** ~**ed the book** los críticos dieron una paliza al libro; **well I'm** ~**ed!** ¡mecachis!; **I'll see him** ~**ed first** antes le veré colgado; **I'll be** ~**ed if ...** que me cuelguen si ...
2 N: **I don't give a** ~ maldito lo que me importa.
3 ADJ (*) maldito; ~ **Yankee** (*US‡*) sucio yanqui *m*.
damnable ['dæmnəbl] ADJ detestable.
damnably ['dæmnəblɪ] ADV terriblemente.
damn-all‡ ['dæm'ɔːl] **1** ADJ: **it's** ~ **use** no sirve para nada en absoluto.
2 N: **he does** ~ no hace absolutamente nada; **I know** ~ **about it** (*Brit*) no sé absolutamente nada de eso.
damnation [dæm'neɪʃən] N condenación *f*; perdición *f*; ~! ¡condenación!; **to go down to** ~ ir a la perdición.
damned [dæmd] **1** ADJ (a) *soul* condenado, maldito. (b) (*damnable*) detestable, abominable; **that** ~ **book** ese maldito libro; **to do one's** ~**est to** + *infin* hacer lo imposible para + *infin*; **it's a** ~ **shame** es una terrible vergüenza.
2 ADV muy, extraordinariamente; **it's** ~ **awkward** es terriblemente difícil; **it's** ~ **hot** hace un calor terrible.
3 N: **the** ~ las almas en pena.
damn-fool*, damnfool* ['dæmfuːl] ADJ tonto.
damning ['dæmɪŋ] ADJ *evidence* irrecusable.
Damocles ['dæməkliːz] NM Damocles.
damp [dæmp] **1** ADJ húmedo; mojado; **that was a** ~ **squib** (*Brit**) resultó ser un rollo*.
2 N humedad *f*; (*Min*) mofeta *f*.
3 VT (*also* **dampen** ['dæmpən]) (a) (*wet*) mojar, humedecer. (b) (*fig*) *person* desalentar; *hopes* ahogar; *excitement* calmar; *zeal* enfriar, moderar.
♦ **damp down** VT amortiguar; *fire* cubrir; *demand* reducir.
dampcourse ['dæmpkɔːs] N (*Brit*) cortahumedades *m*, aislante *m* hidrófugo.
dampen ['dæmpən] VT = **damp 3.**
damper ['dæmpər] N (*Mus*) apagador *m*, sordina *f*; (*of fire*) regulador *m* de tiro; **to put a** ~ **on** (*fig*) acabar con, parar; disminuir; verter un jarro de agua fría sobre.
dampish ['dæmpɪʃ] ADJ algo húmedo.
dampness ['dæmpnɪs] N humedad *f*.
damp-proof ['dæmppruːf] ADJ a prueba de humedad.
damsel ['dæmzəl] N damisela *f*, doncella *f*.
damson ['dæmzən] N (*fruit*) ciruela *f* damascena; (*tree*) ciruelo *m* damasceno.
Dan [dæn] NM *familiar form of* **Daniel.**
dan [dæn] N (*Sport*) dan *m*.
dance [dɑːns] **1** N baile *m*; ~ **of death** danza *f* de la muerte; **to lead sb a** ~ (*Brit*) traerle a uno al retortero.
2 VT bailar.
3 VI bailar; (*artistically*) danzar; (*fig*) danzar, saltar, brincar; **to** ~ **for joy** brincar de alegría; **shall we** ~? ¿quieres bailar?
dance-band ['dɑːnsbænd] N orquesta *f* de baile.
dance class ['dɑːnsˌklɑːs] N clase *f* de baile.
dance-floor ['dɑːnsflɔːr] N pista *f* de baile.
dance-hall ['dɑːnshɔːl] N salón *m* de baile, sala *f* de fiestas.
dance-music ['dɑːnsˌmjuːzɪk] N música *f* de baile.
dancer ['dɑːnsər] N bailador *m*, -ora *f*; (*professional*) bailarín *m*, -ina *f*.
dancing ['dɑːnsɪŋ] **1** N baile *m*.
2 ATTR de baile.
dancing-girl ['dɑːnsɪŋgɜːl] N bailarina *f*.
dancing-partner ['dɑːnsɪŋˌpɑːtnər] N pareja *f* de baile.
dancing-shoes ['dɑːnsɪŋˌʃuːz] NPL zapatillas *fpl*.
D and C ['diːəndˈsiː] N ABBR *of* **dilation and curettage.**
dandelion ['dændɪlaɪən] N diente *m* de león.
dander ['dændər] N: **to get sb's** ~ **up** sacar a uno de sus casillas.
dandified ['dændɪfaɪd] ADJ guapo, acicalado.
dandle ['dændl] VT hacer saltar sobre las rodillas.
dandruff ['dændrəf] N caspa *f*; ~ **shampoo** champú *m* anticaspa.
dandy ['dændɪ] **1** N dandy *m*, dandi *m*, currutaco *m*.
2 ADJ (*esp US**) mono, de primera.
Dane [deɪn] N danés *m*, -esa *f*.
dang* [dæŋ] EXCL (*euph*) V **damn.**
danger ['deɪndʒər] N peligro *m*; riesgo *m*; '~!' (*sign*) '¡peligro!'; **there is a** ~ **of** hay riesgo de; **to be in** ~ estar en peligro, peligrar; **to be in** ~ **of** + *ger* correr riesgo de + *infin*; **to be out of** ~ estar fuera de peligro.
danger-area ['deɪndʒərˌeərɪə] N zona *f* de peligro.
danger-list ['deɪndʒəlɪst] N: **to be on the** ~ estar de cuidado.
danger-money ['deɪndʒəˌmʌnɪ] N prima *f* por trabajos peligrosos, plus *m* de peligrosidad.

dangerous ['deɪndʒrəs] ADJ peligroso, arriesgado; *animal* peligroso; *substance* nocivo; **convicted of** ~ **driving** culpable de conducir con imprudencia temeraria.
dangerously ['deɪndʒrəslɪ] ADV peligrosamente; arriesgadamente; **to come** ~ **close to** acercarse de modo peligroso a; **he likes to live** ~ le gusta arriesgar la vida.
danger-point ['deɪndʒə,pɔɪnt] N punto *m* crítico.
danger-signal ['deɪndʒə,sɪgnl] N señal *f* de peligro.
danger-zone ['deɪndʒə,zəun] N zona *f* de peligro.
dangle ['dæŋgl] **1** VT colgar, dejar colgado; **to** ~ **the prospect of sth before sb** ofrecer a uno la posibilidad de algo.
2 VI estar colgado, pender; bambolearse; **to** ~ **after** ir tras de; **she kept him dangling for 3 months** ella le tuvo suspenso durante 3 meses.
Daniel ['dænjəl] NM Daniel.
Danish ['deɪnɪʃ] **1** ADJ danés, dinamarqués; ~ **blue cheese** queso *m* mohoso danés; ~ **pastry** pasta rellena de manzana, pasta de almendras *etc*.
2 N (a) **the** ~ los daneses. (b) (*Ling*) danés *m*. (c) (*US: cake*) = ~ **pastry.**
dank [dæŋk] ADJ húmedo y malsano.
Dante ['dæntɪ] NM Dante.
Danube ['dænjuːb] N Danubio *m*.
Daphne ['dæfnɪ] NF Dafne.
dapper ['dæpər] ADJ apuesto, pulcro.
dapple ['dæpl] VT motear a colores.
dappled ['dæpld] ADJ moteado, salpicado de manchas; *horse* rodado.
DAR N ABBR *of* **Daughters of the American Revolution**; *ver también* DAUGHTERS OF THE AMERICAN REVOLUTION.
Darby and Joan ['dɑːbɪənˈdʒəun] NPL el matrimonio ideal, de ancianos que siguen viviendo en la mayor felicidad; ~ **club** (*Brit*) club *m* para personas de la tercera edad.
Dardanelles [,dɑːdəˈnelz] NPL Dardanelos *mpl*.
dare [dɛər] **1** N: **to do sth for a** ~ hacer algo en desafío.
2 VT (a) (*attempt*) arriesgar; *sb's anger* hacer frente a.
(b) **to** ~ **sb to do sth** desafiar a uno a hacer algo, provocar a uno a hacer algo; **I** ~ **you!** ¡a que no eres capaz!, ¡a ver si te atreves!; **to** ~ (**to**) **do sth** atreverse a hacer algo, osar hacer algo.
(c) **I** ~ **say** quizá; (*iro*) es muy posible; **I** ~ **say that ...** no me sorprendería que + *subj*; **I** ~ **say you're tired** sin duda estás cansado.
3 VI: **how** ~ **you!** ¡cómo te atreves!, ¡qué fresco!; **just you** ~ !, **you wouldn't** ~! ¡ya te guardarás de hacerlo!
daredevil ['dɛə,devl] **1** ADJ temerario.
2 N temerario *m*, -a *f*, atrevido *m*, -a *f*.
daren't ['dɛənt] = **dare not.**
Dar-es-Salaam [,dɑːressəˈlɑːm] N Dar-es-Salaam *m*.
daring ['dɛərɪŋ] **1** ADJ atrevido, osado.
2 N atrevimiento *m*, osadía *f*.
daringly ['dɛərɪŋlɪ] ADV atrevidamente, osadamente.
Darius [dəˈraɪəs] NM Darío.
dark [dɑːk] **1** ADJ (a) (*unilluminated*) oscuro; tenebroso; **to get** ~ hacerse de noche, anochecer; **as** ~ **as a dungeon** oscuro como boca de lobo.
(b) (*in colour*) oscuro; ~ **glasses** gafas *fpl* negras; ~ **horse** incógnita *f*, figura *f* misteriosa; (*in race*) contendiente *m* desconocido; (*US: in election*) candidato *m* poco conocido; (*winner*) vencedor *m* inesperado.
(c) *complexion, hair* moreno.
(d) (*cheerless*) triste, sombrío; ~ **days** días *mpl* funestos, días *mpl* negros.
(e) (*secret*) secreto, escondido; *doings* misterioso, sospechoso; **the D~ Continent** el Continente Negro; **to keep sth** ~ tener algo secreto; **keep it** ~! ¡de esto no digas ni pío!
(f) (*unenlightened*) ignorante; **D~ Ages** Edades *fpl* bárbaras, primera parte *f* de la Edad Media.
2 N oscuridad *f*; tinieblas *fpl*; **after** ~ después del anochecer; **to grope about in the** ~ ir buscando algo a oscuras; **we are all in the** ~ **about it** no sabemos nada en absoluto de ello; **to keep sb in the** ~ ocultar algo a uno, no revelar a uno cierta noticia; **to be left in the** ~ quedar sin saber nada de algo.
darken ['dɑːkən] **1** VT oscurecer; (*colour*) hacer más oscuro; **in a** ~**ed room** en un cuarto oscuro.
2 VI oscurecerse; (*sky*) anublarse.
dark-eyed [,dɑːkˈaɪd] ADJ de ojos oscuros.
darkie‡ ['dɑːkɪ] N negro *m*, -a *f*.
darkish ['dɑːkɪʃ] ADJ oscuro; *hair etc* algo moreno.
darkly ['dɑːklɪ] ADV misteriosamente.
darkness ['dɑːknɪs] N oscuridad *f*; tinieblas *fpl*; **the house was in** ~ la casa estaba a oscuras; **to cast sb into outer** ~ condenar a uno a las penas infernales.
darkroom ['dɑːkrum] N cuarto *m* oscuro.
dark-skinned [,dɑːkˈskɪnd] ADJ de piel morena.

darling ['dɑːlɪŋ] [1] N querido m, -a f; (in direct address) querido, querida, mi vida, mi cielo; **the ~ of the muses** el querido de las musas; **yes ~** sí querida; **she's a little ~** (child) es un encanto. [2] ADJ muy querido; **a ~ little hat*** un sombrerito que es un encanto; **a ~ little house*** una casita adorable.

darn¹• [dɑːn] EXCL: **~!, ~ it!** ¡condenación!

darn² [dɑːn] [1] N zurcido m, zurcidura f. [2] VT zurcir.

darned• [dɑːnd] ADJ condenado, maldito.

darning ['dɑːnɪŋ] N (act) zurcidura f; (garments) cosas fpl por zurcir.

darning-needle ['dɑːnɪŋ,niːdl] N aguja f de zurcir.

darning-wool ['dɑːnɪŋ,wʊl] N hilo m de zurcir.

dart [dɑːt] [1] N (a) (Mil) dardo m, saeta f.
(b) (in game) rehilete m, dardo m, flecha f; **to play ~s** jugar a los dardos.
(c) (Sew) sisa f.
(d) (movement) movimiento m rápido; **to make a ~ for** precipitarse hacia.
[2] VT look lanzar.
[3] VI lanzarse, precipitarse (for, to hacia).
♦**dart away, dart off** VI salir disparado.

dartboard ['dɑːtbɔːd] N diana f, blanco m (en el juego de dardos).

Darwinian [dɑːˈwɪnɪən] ADJ darwiniano.

Darwinism ['dɑːwɪnɪzəm] N darwinismo m.

Darwinist ['dɑːwɪnɪst] [1] ADJ darwinista.
[2] N darwinista mf.

dash [dæʃ] [1] N (a) (small quantity) pequeña cantidad f, poquito m; **a ~ of colour** una nota de color; **with a ~ of soda** con dos gotitas de sifón.
(b) (with pen) rasgo m, plumada f; (Morse, Typ) raya f.
(c) (rush) carrera f; **to make a ~ for** precipitarse hacia; **to make a ~ for it** huir precipitadamente; **we shall have to make a ~ for it** tendremos que correr.
(d) brío m; **to cut a ~** hacer gran papel, destacar.
(e) (Aut) = **dashboard**.
[2] VT (a) (shatter) romper, estrellar (against contra); **to ~ sth to pieces** hacer algo pedazos; **to ~ sth to the ground** tirar algo al suelo.
(b) hopes defraudar, acabar con.
[3] VI ir de prisa, precipitarse; **we shall have to ~** tendremos que correr; **I must ~** tengo que marcharme; **the waves are ~ing against the rock** las olas se rompen contra la roca.
[4] EXCL (*: euph): **~!, ~ it!** ¡porras!*
♦**dash away** = **dash off 1**.
♦**dash in** VI entrar precipitadamente.
♦**dash off** [1] VT letter escribir de prisa; sketch dibujar rápidamente.
[2] VI salir corriendo, marcharse apresuradamente.
♦**dash out** VI salir precipitadamente.
♦**dash past** VI pasar como un rayo.
♦**dash up** VI (person) llegar corriendo; (car) llegar a toda velocidad.

dashboard ['dæʃbɔːd] N cuadro m de mandos, tablero m de instrumentos.

dashed• [dæʃt] ADJ (euph) = **damned**.

dashing ['dæʃɪŋ] ADJ bizarro, gallardo, arrojado; elegante.

dashingly ['dæʃɪŋlɪ] ADV behave gallardamente, arrojadamente; dress garbosamente.

dastardly ['dæstədlɪ] ADJ ruin, vil, miserable; cobarde.

DAT N ABBR of **digital audio tape**.

data ['deɪtə] NPL (a) datos mpl. (b) (Comput) datos mpl; **~ capture** formulación f de datos; **~ dictionary, ~ directory** guía f de datos; **~ entry** entrada f de datos; **~ management** gestión f de datos; **~ preparation** preparación f de datos; **~ processing** proceso m de datos; **~ processor** procesador m de datos; **~ protection** protección f de datos; **~ transmission** transmisión f de datos, telemática f.

databank ['deɪtəbæŋk] N banco m de datos.

database ['deɪtəbeɪs] N base f de datos.

database manager ['deɪtəbeɪs,mænɪdʒəʳ] N (Comput) gestor m de base de datos.

datable ['deɪtəbl] ADJ datable, fechable (to en).

datafile ['deɪtə,faɪl] N archivo m de datos.

datalink ['deɪtəlɪŋk] N medio m de transmisión de datos.

dataphone ['deɪtəfəʊn] N datáfono m.

Datapost ['deɪtəpəʊst] ® N (Brit) correo m urgente.

date¹ [deɪt] [1] N (a) fecha f; **~ of birth** fecha f de nacimiento; **~ of issue** fecha f de emisión; **what's the ~?, what ~ is it today?** ¿qué día es hoy?; **closing ~, last ~** fecha f tope; **at a later ~** en una fecha posterior; **at some future ~** en alguna fecha futura; **at an early ~** en fecha próxima; dentro de poco; **out of ~** anticuado, (person) atrasado de noticias; (expired) caducado; **to go out of ~** quedar anticuado; **to ~** hasta la fecha; **up to ~** (ADV) hasta la fecha; **to be up to ~** (building etc) tener aspecto moderno; **to be up to ~ in one's thinking** tener ideas modernas; **to be up to ~ in one's studies** estar al

día en los estudios; **to bring sth up to ~** modernizar algo, poner algo al día, actualizar algo; **to bring sb up to ~** poner a uno al corriente.
(b) (Fin) plazo m.
(c) (with girl, boy) cita f; (with friend) compromiso m; **to have a ~ with sb** tener cita con uno; **have you got a ~ tonight?** ¿tienes compromiso para esta noche?; **to make a ~ with sb** citar a uno; **they made a ~ for 8 o'clock** se citaron para las 8.
(d) (esp US) pareja f, acompañante mf, novio m, -a f.
[2] VT (a) (put ~ on) fechar, poner la fecha en.
(b) (assign ~ to) fechar (to en), asignar una fecha a; situar en una época.
(c) (esp US*) citar; salir con.
[3] VI (a) (become old-fashioned) ir quedando anticuado, pasar de moda.
(b) **to ~ back to** remontarse a; **to ~ from** datar de, ser de la época de.

date² [deɪt] N (fruit) dátil m; (tree) palmera f datilera.

dated ['deɪtɪd] ADJ anticuado, pasado de moda.

dateline ['deɪtlaɪn] N línea f de cambio de fecha.

date-palm ['deɪtpɑːm] N palmera f datilera.

date rape ['deɪtreɪp] N violación a manos de un conocido.

date-stamp ['deɪtstæmp] [1] N fechador m.
[2] VT estampar la fecha en.

dating ['deɪtɪŋ] N (a) (Archeology) datación f. (b) **~ agency** agencia f matrimonial.

dating agency ['deɪtɪŋ,eɪdʒənsɪ] N agencia f de contactos.

dating service ['deɪtɪŋ,sɜːvɪs] N servicio m de contactos.

dative ['deɪtɪv] [1] ADJ dativo; **~ case = 2**.
[2] N dativo m.

datum ['deɪtəm] N, PL **data** dato m; V **data**.

daub [dɔːb] [1] N (smear) mancha f; (bad painting) pintarrajo m.
[2] VT (smear) manchar (with de); untar (with de); **to ~ a wall with paint, to ~ paint on to a wall** embadurnar una pared de pintura.
[3] VI pintarrajear.

dauber ['dɔːbəʳ] N, **daubster** ['dɔːbstəʳ] N pintor m de brocha gorda, mal pintor m.

daughter ['dɔːtəʳ] N hija f.

DAUGHTERS OF THE AMERICAN REVOLUTION

*La organización **Daughters of the American Revolution** o **DAR**, fundada en 1890, está formada por mujeres que descienden de familias que lucharon para defender las colonias contra los británicos durante la Revolución americana (1775-1783). Sus miembros han trabajado mucho para fomentar el patriotismo y preservar los lugares históricos.*
Políticamente, es una organización muy conservadora que incluso se ha opuesto a la existencia de las Naciones Unidas.

---

daughterboard ['dɔːtə,bɔːd] N placa f hija.

daughter-in-law ['dɔːtərɪnlɔː] N, PL **daughters-in-law** nuera f, hija f política.

daunt [dɔːnt] VT acobardar, intimidar, desalentar; **nothing ~ed** sin inmutarse.

daunting ['dɔːntɪŋ] ADJ desalentador, amedrentador.

dauntless ['dɔːntlɪs] ADJ impávido, intrépido.

dauntlessly ['dɔːntlɪslɪ] ADV impávidamente; **to carry on ~** continuar impávido.

dauphin ['dɔːfɪn] N (Hist) delfín m.

Dave [deɪv] NM familiar form of **David**.

davenport ['dævnpɔːt] N (Brit: desk) escritorio m pequeño; (US) sofá m, sofá-cama m.

David ['deɪvɪd] NM David.

davit ['dævɪt] N pescante m.

Davy Jones ['deɪvɪ'dʒəʊnz] N: **~' locker** el fondo del mar (tumba de los marineros ahogados).

dawdle ['dɔːdl] [1] VT: **to ~ away** malgastar.
[2] VI perder el tiempo, holgazanear; (in walking etc) andar muy despacio, ir muy despacio.

dawdler ['dɔːdləʳ] N holgazán m, -ana f, ocioso m, -a f; persona f que anda despacio, rezagado m, -a f.

dawdling ['dɔːdlɪŋ] [1] ADJ que pierde el tiempo, que holgazanea.
[2] N pérdida f de tiempo.

dawn [dɔːn] [1] N alba f, amanecer m; (fig) aurora f, nacimiento m; **~ chorus** coro m del alba; **at ~** al alba; **from ~ to dusk** de sol a sol; **to get up with the ~** madrugar.
[2] VI (a) amanecer, alborear, romper el día; **a new epoch has ~ed** ha nacido una época nueva.
(b) **it ~ed on me that ...** caí en la cuenta de que ..., empecé a comprender que ...

dawning ['dɔːnɪŋ] [1] ADJ hope etc naciente.
[2] N = **dawn 1**.

day [deɪ] N (a) día m; (working period etc) jornada f; **an 8-hour ~** una jornada de 8 horas.

(b) *(with prep etc)* **~ after ~, ~ in ~ out** día a día, día tras día; **~ and night** día y noche; **the ~ after** el día siguiente, al día siguiente; **the ~ after tomorrow** pasado mañana; **the ~ before** el día anterior; **the ~ before yesterday** anteayer; **two ~s before this** dos días antes de esto; **the ~ before the coronation** la víspera de la coronación; **~ off** día *m* libre; **~ by ~** día por día, de día a día *(LAm)*; **by ~** de día; **by the ~** diariamente, día a día, cada día, al día; **every other ~** un día sí y otro no; **from ~ to ~** de día en día; **in this ~ and age** en estos tiempos nuestros; **in my ~** en mis tiempos; **in the ~s of Queen Elizabeth, in Queen Elizabeth's ~** en tiempos de la reina Isabel; **on the ~** everything will be all right para el día en cuestión todo estará en orden; **these ~s** estos días; **to this ~** hasta el día de hoy; **it's a year to the ~ since she died** murió precisamente hoy hace un año; **this ~ week** de hoy en ocho días.

(c) *(with adj etc)* **D~ of Judgement** día *m* del Juicio Final; **~ of reckoning** *(fig)* día *m* de ajustar cuentas; **it was a black ~ for the country** fue un día negro *(or* aciago*)* para el país; **it's early ~s yet** todavía es pronto; **one ~, some ~** algún día; **one fine ~, one of these ~s** el día menos pensado; **good ~!** ¡buenos días!; **the good old ~s** los buenos tiempos pasados; **any old ~** el mejor día; **until my dying ~** hasta la muerte.

(d) *(with verb)* **that'll be the ~** me gustaría verlo, habría que verlo; **she's 40 if she's a ~** tiene a lo menos 40 años; **to call it a ~** dejar de trabajar *(etc)*, suspender el trabajo *(etc)*; darlo por acabado; **let's call it a ~** terminemos ya; **to carry the ~** ganar la victoria; **to give sb his ~ in court** *(US*)* darle a uno la oportunidad de explicarse; **it has had its ~** ha dejado ya de ser útil, ya pasó aquello; **you don't look a ~ older** no pasan por ti los días, no pareces un día más viejo; **it made my ~** hizo que el día fuese feliz para mí; **it has seen better ~s** ya no vale lo que antes; **to take a ~ off** darse un día libre, no presentarse en el trabajo *(etc)*.

day-bed ['deɪbed] N *(US)* meridiana *f*.

day-boarder ['deɪ'bɔːdəʳ] N *(Scol)* alumno *m*, -a *f* de media pensión.

daybook ['deɪbʊk] N diario *m*; *(US)* agenda *f*.

dayboy ['deɪbɔɪ] N *(Brit Scol)* externo *m*.

daybreak ['deɪbreɪk] N amanecer *m*; **at ~** al amanecer.

day-care ['deɪkeəʳ] ATTR: **~ centre** guardería *f*; **~ services** *(Brit)* servicios *mpl* de guardería.

day-centre ['deɪ,sentəʳ] N *(Brit)* centro *m* de día.

daydream ['deɪdriːm] **1** N ensueño *m*, ilusión *f*.

2 VI soñar despierto.

daygirl ['deɪgɜːl] N *(Brit Scol)* externa *f*.

Day-glo ['deɪgləʊ] ® ATTR *colours etc* fosforito, fosforescente.

day job ['deɪdʒɒb] N trabajo *m* habitual, ocupación *f* habitual **don't give up the ~!** *(hum)* ¡sigue en lo tuyo!

day-labourer, *(US)* **day-laborer** ['deɪ'leɪbərəʳ] N jornalero *m*.

daylight ['deɪlaɪt] N luz *f*, luz *f* del día; **it's ~ robbery*** es una extorsión; **to beat** *(or* knock*)* **the living ~s out of sb*** dar una tremenda paliza a uno; **to scare the ~(s) out of sb*** dar un susto de muerte a uno; **to see ~** empezar a ver el final de un trabajo *(etc)*.

daylight-saving ['deɪlaɪt,seɪvɪŋ] N cambio *m* de hora; **~ time** hora *f* de verano.

daylong ['deɪlɒŋ] *(liter)* **1** ADJ que dura todo el día.

2 ADV todo el día.

day-nurse ['deɪ,nɜːs] N enfermera *f* diurna.

day-nursery ['deɪ,nɜːsəri] N guardería *f* infantil.

day-old ['deɪ'əʊld] ADJ *chick* de un día.

day-release course [,deɪrɪ'liːs,kɔːs] N *(Brit: Comm, Ind)* curso *m* no recuperable.

day-return ['deɪrɪ'tɜːn] N *(Brit: also ~ ticket)* billete *m* barato de ida y vuelta en un día.

dayroom ['deɪruːm] N *(in hospital etc)* sala de estar para los internos de un hospital.

day-school ['deɪ,skuːl] N: **to go to ~** *(Scol)* ir a un colegio sin internado.

day-shift ['deɪʃɪft] N turno *m* de día.

daytime ['deɪtaɪm] N día *m*; **in the ~** de día.

day-to-day ['deɪtə'deɪ] ADJ cotidiano, rutinario; **on a ~ basis** día por día.

day-trip ['deɪtrɪp] N excursión *f* de ida y vuelta en un día.

day-tripper ['deɪ,trɪpəʳ] N excursionista *mf*.

daze [deɪz] **1** N: **to be in a ~** estar aturdido.

2 VT aturdir; *(dazzle)* deslumbrar.

dazed [deɪzd] ADJ aturdido.

dazzle ['dæzl] **1** N lo brillante, brillo *m*.

2 VT deslumbrar *(also fig)*; **to be ~d by** *(fig)* quedar deslumbrado por.

dazzling ['dæzlɪŋ] ADJ deslumbrante, deslumbrador.

dazzlingly ['dæzlɪŋli] ADV *shine* deslumbradoramente; **~ beautiful** deslumbrantemente hermoso.

DB ABBR *of* **database**.

dB ABBR *of* **decibel** decibelio *m*, db *m*.

DBMS N ABBR *of* **database management system** sistema *m* de manejo de base de datos.

DBS N ABBR *of* **direct broadcasting by satellite**.

DC N **(a)** *(Elec)* ABBR *of* **direct current**. **(b)***(US)* ABBR *of* **District of Columbia**.

DC - DISTRICT OF COLUMBIA

District of Columbia es el distrito donde se encuentra el gobierno de Estados Unidos. No forma parte de ningún estado, sino que es un distrito autónomo que comprende únicamente la capital del país, Washington. Se halla en el este de los Estados Unidos y tiene un área de unos 180 kilómetros cuadrados, donados por los estados de Maryland y Virginia. Normalmente se hace referencia a este distrito mediante sus siglas, *DC*, y se usa después del nombre de la capital: **Washington DC**.

DCC ® N ABBR *of* **digital compact cassette** ca(s)se(t)te *m* digital compacto.

DCF N ABBR *of* **discounted cash-flow**.

D.D. N **(a)** *(Univ)* ABBR *of* **Doctor of Divinity** Doctor *m* en Teología. **(b)** *(US Mil)* ABBR *of* **dishonorable discharge** licencia *f* deshonrosa.

D-day ['diːdeɪ] N día *m* de la invasión aliada de Normandía *(6 junio 1944)*; *(fig)* día *m* 'D'.

DDS N *(US)* ABBR *of* **Doctor of Dental Science** *(or* Surgery*)*.

DDT N ABBR *of* **dichlorodiphenyltrichloroethane** diclorodifeniltricloroetano *m*, DDT.

DE (a) *(US)* ABBR *of* **Delaware**. **(b)** *(Brit)* ABBR *of* **Department of Employment**.

de... [diː] PREF de...

DEA N *(US)* ABBR *of* **Drug Enforcement Administration** *departamento para la lucha contra la droga*.

deacon ['diːkən] N diácono *m*.

deaconess ['diːkənes] N diaconisa *f*.

deactivate [diːˈæktɪveɪt] VT desactivar.

dead [ded] **1** ADJ **(a)** muerto; **~ man** muerto *m*; *(*)* botella *f* vacía; **~ march** marcha *f* fúnebre; **the ~ king** el difunto rey; **as ~ as the dodo, as ~ as a doornail, as ~ as mutton** más muerto que mi abuela; **to be ~** estar muerto; **he has been ~ 3 years** hace 3 años que murió; **to be ~ on arrival** *(in hospital)* ingresar cadáver; **to drop ~** caer muerto, morir de repente; **drop ~!*** ¡vete al cuerno!*; **to flog** *(Brit)* **or beat** *(US)* **a ~ horse** machacar en hierro frío; **I wouldn't be seen ~ in a hat like that!** ¡ese sombrero, ni para un apuro!; **~ men tell no tales** los muertos no hablan; *V* **set 1 (f)**.

(b) *(inactive etc)* *limb* sin sentido; *town* muerto, desierto; *language* muerto; *leaf* marchito, seco; *ball* parado, fuera de juego; *colour, fire* apagado; *wire* sin corriente; **~ matter** materia *f* inanimada; **~ season** estación *f* muerta.

(c) *(obsolete)* anticuado; **~ letter** letra *f* muerta; **all that stuff's pretty ~ now** todo eso ya no tiene interés.

(d) *(absolute, exact)* *silence* profundo; *stop* en seco, repentino; **~ calm** calma *f* chicha; **~ centre** *(Mech)* punto *m* muerto; **~ certainty** seguridad *f* completa; **~ level** superficie *f* completamente plana; **a ~ ringer for** el doble de, la viva imagen de.

(e) to cut sb ~ hacer el vacío a uno, no hacer caso alguno a uno.

2 ADV *(Brit)* completamente, totalmente; **~ drunk** borracho como una cuba; **~ easy** facilón, chupado*; **~ level** completamente plano; **~ slow** muy despacio; **~ straight** completamente recto; **~ tired** hecho polvo, muerto de cansancio; **~ between the eyes** justo entre los ojos; **~ on the target** exactamente en el blanco, en el mismo blanco; **we got there ~ on time** llegamos a la hora exacta, llegamos con toda puntualidad; **to be ~ against sth** estar totalmente opuesto a algo; **to be ~ certain** estar completamente seguro; **to be ~ set on doing sth** estar decidido a hacer algo; **to stop ~** parar(se) en seco.

3 N **(a) the ~** los muertos.

(b) at ~ of night, in the ~ of night en plena noche, en las altas horas; **in the ~ of winter** en lo más recio del invierno.

dead-and-alive ['dedənə'laɪv] ADJ aburrido, monótono.

dead-beat ['ded'biːt] **1** ADJ rendido; **to be ~** estar hecho polvo.

2 N *(US*)* gorrón *m*, vagabundo *m*.

deadbolt ['dedbəʊlt] N *(US)* cerrojo *m* de seguridad.

deaden ['dedn] VT *noise etc* amortiguar; *pain* aliviar.

dead end ['ded'end] N callejón *m* sin salida; **to reach a ~** *(fig)* llegar a un punto muerto; **~ job** trabajo *m* sin futuro; **~ kids** *(US)* chicos *mpl* de la calle.

deadening ['dednɪŋ] ADJ *boredom etc* de mala muerte.

dead hand ['ded'hænd] N *(of state, bureaucracy)* peso *m* muerto.

dead heat ['ded'hiːt] **1** N empate *m*.

2 VI empatar *(with con)*.

deadline ['dedlaɪn] N fecha *f* tope, fecha *f* límite, plazo *m*; hora *f* de cierre; **we cannot meet the government's ~** no podemos terminarlo *(etc)* antes de la fecha señalada por el gobierno.

deadliness ['dedlɪnɪs] N *(of poison)* letalidad *f*; *(of aim)* certeza *f*;

(*boredom*) tedio *m*, esplín *m*.

deadlock ['dedlɒk] ①︎ N parálisis *f*; callejón *m* sin salida; **the ~ is complete** la parálisis es total, no se ve salida alguna; **to reach ~** llegar a un punto muerto.
②︎ VT: **to be ~ed** estar en un punto muerto.

deadly ['dedlɪ] ①︎ ADJ (a) mortal (*also fig*); *aim* exacto, certero; *criticism* devastador; **~ sin** pecado *m* capital; **with ~ accuracy** con la más absoluta exactitud.
(b) (*) fatal*, malísimo.
②︎ ADV: **~ dull** terriblemente aburrido, aburridísimo.

deadness ['dednɪs] N inercia *f*, falta *f* de vida.

deadnettle ['ded,netl] N ortiga *f* muerta.

deadpan ['ded,pæn] ADJ sin expresión, inexpresivo.

dead reckoning ['ded'rekɪŋ] N estima *f*.

Dead Sea ['ded'si:] N Mar *m* Muerto; **the ~ Scrolls** los manuscritos del Mar Muerto.

deadstock [,ded'stɒk] N aperos *mpl*.

dead weight [,ded'weɪt] N peso *m* muerto; (*of vehicle*) tara *f*; (*fig*) lastre *m*, carga *f* inútil.

deadwood ['ded'wʊd] N (*fig*) persona *f* inútil, gente *f* inútil, cosas *fpl* inútiles.

deaf [def] ①︎ ADJ sordo (**to** a); **as ~ as a post** sordo como una tapia; **~ to all appeals** sordo a todos los ruegos; **the plea fell on ~ ears** escucharon el ruego como quien oye llover; **to turn a ~ ear to** hacer oídos sordos a.
②︎ N: **the ~** los sordos *mpl*.

deaf-aid ['defeɪd] N aparato *m* del oído, audífono *m*.

deaf-and-dumb ['defən'dʌm] ADJ sordomudo; **~ alphabet** alfabeto *m* de los sordomudos.

deafen ['defn] VT ensordecer, asordar.

deafening ['defnɪŋ] ADJ ensordecedor.

deaf-mute ['def'mju:t] N sordomudo *m*, -a *f*.

deafness ['defnɪs] N sordera *f*.

deal[1] [di:l] N (a) (*wood*) madera *f* de pino (*or* abeto) (b) (*plank*) tablón *m*; (*beam*) viga *f*.

▼ **deal**[2] [di:l] ①︎ N (a) (*Comm*) transacción *f*, negocio *m*, trato *m*; **big ~** negocio *m* importante; **big ~!** (*iro*) ¡gran cosa!; **don't make such a big ~ out of it!*** ¡no hagas una montaña de un grano de arena!
▼ (b) (*agreement*) pacto *m*, convenio *m*; (*secret*) pacto *m* secreto; **it's a ~!** ¡trato hecho!; **to do a ~ with** hacer un trato con; **we might do a ~** podríamos llegar a un acuerdo; **we fear A might do a ~ with B** tememos que A pudiera hacer una componenda con B.
(c) (*arrangement, treatment*) trato *m*; **New D~** (*US*) Nueva Política *f*, Nuevo Programa *m*, Nuevo Trato *m*; **a new ~ for the miners** un nuevo arreglo de salarios para los mineros; **he got a very bad ~** recibió un trato muy injusto, le trataron muy injustamente; **we're looking for a better ~** buscamos un arreglo más equitativo.
(d) (*Cards*) reparto *m*; **whose ~ is it?** ¿a quién le toca dar?
(e) (*amount*) **a good ~** bastante, mucho; **a great ~** muchísimo; **a great ~ of** gran cantidad de; **to make a great ~ of** *person* estimar mucho a, *thing* dar importancia a.
②︎ (*irr*: PRET AND PTP **dealt**) VT (a) *cards* dar.
(b) *blow* dar, descargar; **to ~ a blow to** (*fig*) destruir de un golpe; **to ~ a blow for freedom** librar una batalla en pro de la libertad.
③︎ VI (a) (*Comm etc*) comerciar; comprar y vender; cerrar un trato. (b) (*Cards*) ser mano.
◆**deal in** VI tratar en, comerciar en.
◆**deal out** VT repartir.
◆**deal with** VT (a) *person* tratar con, tener relaciones con; **he dealt very fairly with me** se portó muy bien conmigo; **he dealt cleverly with the ambassador** se las arregló inteligentemente con el embajador; **I'll ~ with him** yo me ocuparé de él; **he is used to ~ing with criminals** está acostumbrado a tratar con criminales.
(b) *problem* ocuparse de; hacer frente a; **how should we ~ with this problem?** ¿qué hemos de hacer con este problema?; **the matter has been dealt with** el asunto está concluido; **how will the government ~ with coal?** ¿qué política tiene el gobierno para el carbón?
(c) *subject in book etc* tratar de, versar sobre, tener por tema; **he dealt with Africa in his speech** en su discurso se ocupó de África; **the book ~s with war** el libro versa sobre la guerra.
(d) (*punish*) castigar; **the offenders will be dealt with** se castigará a los delincuentes; **they were dealt with severely** se les castigó de modo ejemplar.
(e) (*finish off*) *work* terminar, concluir; *person* despachar.
(f) (*in shop*) **which shop do you ~ with?** ¿en qué tienda compras tus cosas?

dealer ['di:lə'] N comerciante *m*, tratante *m* (**in** en); concesionario *m*, -a *f*; (*in drugs*) traficante *mf*; (*retail*) distribuidor *m* (**in** de), proveedor *m*; (*Cards*) repartidor *m*, -ora *f*, dador *m*, -ora *f*.

dealership ['di:ləʃɪp] N (*US*) representación *f*, concesión *f*.

dealing ['di:lɪŋ] N (a) (*also* **~ out**) reparto *m*, distribución *f*; (*Cards*) reparto *m*. (b) (*St Ex*) comercio *m*; V **wheel**.

dealings ['di:lɪŋz] NPL (a) (*Fin*) transacciones *fpl*. (b) (*relations*) trato *m*, relaciones *fpl*; **to have ~ with** tratar con, tener relaciones con; **I wish to have no ~ with him** no quiero tener nada que ver con él.

dealt [delt] PRET AND PTP of **deal**[2].

dean [di:n] N (*Eccl*) deán *m*; (*Brit Univ etc*) decano *m*; **D~'s List** (*US Univ*) lista de honor académica.

┌─ **DEAN'S LIST** ─┐

🛈 *Se llama* **Dean's List** *(lista del decano), a la relación honorífica de alumnos que se hace en muchas universidades estadounidenses al final de cada año académico o al final de la carrera. En algunas universidades, para figurar en ella se ha de haber obtenido A o B en todas las asignaturas, aunque normalmente la lista se basa en la nota media, conocida como* **grade-point average**. *Los estudiantes que han recibido la máxima puntuación, A, en todo, aparecen a veces en otra lista, llamada* **scholars's list** *o* **president's list**. *En algunas escuelas también se publican listas similares, conocidas como* **honor roll**.
⇨ *Ver también* GRADE-POINT AVERAGE

dear [dɪə'] ①︎ ADJ (a) *person etc* querido; **a very ~ friend of mine** un amigo mío muy querido; **my ~est friend** mi más íntimo amigo; **he was very ~ to all of us** fue querido de todos nosotros; **because your country is very ~ to me** por el mucho amor que le tengo a vuestra patria.
(b) (*in letters*) **D~ John, D~ Mr White** mi querido amigo; **D~ Dr Green** (*from colleague*) mi querido amigo y colega; (*Comm etc*) **D~ Sir** muy señor mío, **D~ Sirs** muy señores míos; **D~ Miss Brown** estimada Señorita; **D~ Mrs Black** estimada Señora de Black; **D~ Madam** estimada Señora; **D~ Sir or Madam** estimado Señor, estimada Señora; **D~ John letter** carta *f* de ruptura.
(c) (*expensive*) caro, costoso; *shop* carero.
②︎ N (*direct address*) **my ~** querido, querida; **come along, ~** (*to child*) ven, pequeño; **be a ~ and pass the salt** ¿me das la sal, querido?; **be a ~ and phone him** sé amable y llámale; **he's a ~** es simpatiquísimo; **he's a little ~** es un niño precioso.
③︎ EXCL: **oh ~!, ~ me!** (*dismay*) ¡ay!, ¡Dios mío!; (*pity*) ¡qué lastima!, ¡qué pena! (*LAm*).
④︎ ADV *sell etc* caro.

dearie* ['dɪərɪ] N querido* *m*, -a *f*; **yes ~** sí, cariño; **~ me!** ¡ay!

dearly ['dɪəlɪ] ADV (a) tiernamente; **to love sb ~** querer muchísimo a uno; **I would ~ like to know why** quisiera muchísimo saber por qué.
(b) **to pay ~ for sth** (*fig*) pagar algo caro; **it cost him ~** le costó caro.

dearness ['dɪənɪs] N alto precio *m*, carestía *f*.

dearth [dɜ:θ] N escasez *f*; falta *f*, ausencia *f*.

▼ **death** [deθ] ①︎ N muerte *f*; (*euph*) fallecimiento *m*, defunción *f*; **~ to traitors!** ¡mueran los traidores!; **it will be the ~ of me** acabará conmigo, me matará; **this is ~ to our hopes** esto acaba con nuestras esperanzas; **it was ~ to the company** arruinó la sociedad; **to be in at the ~** ver el final de la caza (*etc*); **to be at ~'s door** estar a la muerte, estar in extremis; **to catch one's ~** (*of cold*) coger un catarro de muerte; **to do** (*or* **put**) **to ~** matar, dar muerte a, (*Jur*) ajusticiar; **to fight to the ~** luchar a muerte; **it frightens me to ~** me da un miedo espantoso; **to hold on like grim ~** estar firmemente agarrado, (*fig*) resistir con la mayor firmeza; **he's working himself to ~** trabaja tanto que se está estropeando la salud; **he works his men to ~** a sus hombres los mata trabajando; **it worries me to ~** me preocupa muchísimo.
②︎ ATTR: **~ benefit** (*Insurance*) indemnización *f* (*or* beneficio *m*) por muerte; **~ blow** golpe *m* mortal; **~ camp** campo *m* de exterminación; **~ cell** celda *f* de los condenados a muerte; **~ certificate** partida *f* de defunción; **~ duties** (*Brit*) derechos *mpl* de herencia, derechos *mpl* reales; **~ house** pabellón *m* de los condenados a muerte; **~ march** marcha *f* fúnebre; **~ mask** mascarilla *f*; **~ penalty** pena *f* de muerte; **~ rate** mortalidad *f*; **~ rattle** estertor *m*; **~ ray** rayo *m* mortal; **~ roll** número *m* de víctimas, lista *f* de víctimas; **~ row** (*US*) celdas *fpl* de los condenados a muerte, corredor *m* de la muerte; **~ sentence** (condena *f* a la) pena *f* de muerte; **~ squad** escuadrón *m* de la muerte; **~ threat** amenaza *f* de muerte; **~ throes** agonía *f*; **~ toll** número *m* de víctimas; **~ warrant** sentencia *f* de muerte; **~ wish** deseo *m* de muerte.

deathbed ['deθbed] N lecho *m* de muerte; **~ confession** confesión *f* en el lecho de muerte; **~ conversion** conversión *f* a última hora; **~ repentance** arrepentimiento *m* de última hora.

death-dealing ['deθdi:lɪŋ] ADJ (*liter*) *blow, missile* mortífero, letal.

death knell ['deθnel] N toque *m* de difuntos, doble *m*; **it sounded the ~ of the empire** anunció el fin del imperio, presagió la caída del imperio.

deathless ['deθlɪs] ADJ inmortal.

deathlike ['deθlaɪk] ADJ como de muerto, cadavérico.

deathly ['deθlɪ] ①︎ ADJ mortal; de muerte; *silence* profundo.

2 ADV como la muerte; **~ pale** pálido como la muerte.
death's-head ['deθshed] N calavera *f*; **~ moth** mariposa *f* de la muerte.
deathtrap ['deθtræp] N sitio *m* muy peligroso.
deathwatch ['deθwɒtʃ] ATTR: **~ beetle** reloj *m* de la muerte.
deb*** [deb] N = **débutante**.
débâcle [deɪ'bɑːkl] N debacle *f*, fracaso *m*; (*Mil*) derrota *f*.
debag [diː'bæg] VT (*Brit hum*) quitar (violentamente) los pantalones a.
debar [dɪ'bɑːʳ] VT excluir (*from* de); **to ~ sb from doing sth** prohibir a uno hacer algo.
debark [dɪ'bɑːk] VI (*US*) desembarcar.
debarkation [diːbɑː'keɪʃən] N (*US*) desembarco *m*.
debase [dɪ'beɪs] VT degradar, envilecer; *coinage* alterar, falsificar.
debasement [dɪ'beɪsmənt] N degradación *f*, envilecimiento *m*; alteración *f*, falsificación *f*.
▼ **debatable** [dɪ'beɪtəbl] ADJ discutible.
debate [dɪ'beɪt] **1** N discusión *f*; (*Parl etc*) debate *m*; **that is in ~, that is open to ~** ése es un tema discutido.
2 VT discutir, debatir.
3 VI discutir (*with* con); **to ~ with o.s.** pensar, deliberar; **I am debating whether to do it** estoy dudando si hacerlo o no.
debater [dɪ'beɪtəʳ] N persona *f* que toma parte en un debate; polemista *mf*; **he was a brilliant ~** brillaba en los debates.
debating [dɪ'beɪtɪŋ] N: **~ is a difficult skill to learn** el saber debatir es una habilidad difícil de adquirir; **~ society** sociedad *f* de debates.
debauch [dɪ'bɔːtʃ] VT *youth* corromper; *woman* seducir.
debauched [dɪ'bɔːtʃt] ADJ vicioso.
debaucher [dɪ'bɔːtʃəʳ] N (*of person, taste, morals*) corruptor *m*, (*of woman*) seductor *m*.
debauchery [dɪ'bɔːtʃərɪ] N libertinaje *m*, corrupción *f*.
debenture [dɪ'bentʃəʳ] N vale *m*, bono *m*, obligación *f*.
debenture bond [dɪ'bentʃə,bɒnd] N obligación *f*.
debenture capital [dɪ'bentʃə'kæpɪtl] N capital *m* hipotecario.
debenture holder [dɪ'bentʃə,həʊldəʳ] N obligacionista *mf*.
debenture stock [dɪ'bentʃə,stɒk] N obligaciones *fpl*.
debilitate [dɪ'bɪlɪteɪt] VT debilitar.
debilitating [dɪ'bɪlɪteɪtɪŋ] ADJ debilitante, que debilita.
debility [dɪ'bɪlɪtɪ] N debilidad *f*.
debit ['debɪt] **1** N debe *m*; **~ balance** saldo *m* deudor, saldo *m* negativo; **~ card** tarjeta *f* de cobro automático; **~ entry** débito *m*; **~ note** nota *f* de cargo; **~ side** debe *m*; **on the ~ side** en el lado deudor (*also fig*).
2 VT: **to ~ sth to sb, to ~ sb's account** cargar algo en cuenta a uno; **to ~ an account directly** domiciliar una cuenta.
debonair [debə'nɛəʳ] ADJ elegante, gallardo.
debone [diː'bəʊn] VT *meat* deshuesar; *fish* quitar las espinas a.
Deborah ['debərə] NF Débora.
debouch [dɪ'baʊtʃ] (*frm*) VI: **to ~ into** *river* desembocar en.
Debrett [də'bret] N *libro de referencia de la aristocracia del Reino Unido*, (*loosely*) anuario *m* de la nobleza.
debrief [diː'briːf] VT tomar informes de (al terminarse una operación *etc*).
debriefing [diː'briːfɪŋ] N informe *m* sobre una operación (*etc*).
debris ['debriː] N escombros *mpl*; (*Geol*) rocalla *f*.
debt [det] N deuda *f*; **bad ~** deuda *f* incobrable, droga *f* (*LAm*); **~ collection** cobro *m* de morosos; **~ collector** cobrador *m*, -ora *f* de deudas; **~ of honour** deuda *f* de honor; **~ ratio** razón *f* de deudas; **~ service** (*US*), **~ servicing** servicio *m* de la deuda; **to be in ~** tener deudas (*to* con); **to be £5 in ~** deber 5 libras (*to* a); **to be in sb's ~** (*fig*) sentirse bajo una obligación a uno; **to be out of ~** estar libre de deudas, no tener deudas; **to get into ~, to run into ~, to run up ~s** contraer deudas.
debtor ['detəʳ] N deudor *m*, -ora *f*; **~ nation** nación *f* deudora.
debt-ridden ['det,rɪdn] ADJ agobiado por las deudas.
debug [diː'bʌg] VT (*Tech*) resolver los problemas de, superar (*or* suprimir) las pegas de; (*remove mikes from*) quitar los micrófonos escondidos de; (*Comput*) depurar, quitar el duende de.
debugger [diː'bʌgəʳ] N programa *m* de depuración.
debugging [diː'bʌgɪŋ] N (*Comput*) depuración *f*.
debunk [diː'bʌŋk] VT quitar lo falso y legendario de; desacreditar, demoler; *person* desenmascarar.
début ['deɪbuː] N debú *m*, presentación *f*; **to make one's ~** (*Theat*) hacer su presentación, estrenarse; (*in society*) presentarse en la sociedad, ponerse de largo.
débutante ['debjuːtãːnt] N joven *f* que se presenta en la sociedad, debutante *f*.
Dec. ABBR of **December** diciembre *m*, dic.
dec. ABBR of **deceased**.
decade ['dekeɪd] N década *f*, decenio *m*.
decadence ['dekədəns] N decadencia *f*.
decadent ['dekədənt] ADJ decadente.
de-caff*** ['diːkæf] N ABBR of **decaffeinated** descafeinado *m*.

decaffeinated [diː'kæfɪneɪtɪd] ADJ descafeinado.
decagram(me) ['dekəgræm] N decagramo *m*.
decal [dɪ'kæl] N (*US*) pegatina *f*.
decalcification ['diː,kælsɪfɪ'keɪʃən] N descalcificación *f*.
decalcify [diː'kælsɪfaɪ] VT descalcificar.
decalitre, (*US*) **decaliter** ['dekə,liːtəʳ] N decalitro *m*.
Decalogue ['dekəlɒg] N: **the ~** el Decálogo.
decametre, (*US*) **decameter** ['dekə,miːtəʳ] N decámetro *m*.
decamp [dɪ'kæmp] VI (*Mil*) decampar; (*fig*) largarse, fugarse, rajarse (*LAm*).
decant [dɪ'kænt] VT decantar.
decanter [dɪ'kæntəʳ] N jarra *f*.
decapitate [dɪ'kæpɪteɪt] VT decapitar, degollar, descabezar.
decapitation [dɪ,kæpɪ'teɪʃən] N decapitación *f*, degollación *f*.
decarbonization ['diː,kɑːbənaɪ'zeɪʃən] N (*Aut*) descarburación *f*; (*of steel*) descarbonación *f*.
decarbonize [diː'kɑːbənaɪz] VT descarburar; descarbonar.
decasyllable ['dekəsɪləbl] N decasílabo *m*.
decathlete [dɪ'kæθliːt] N decatlonista *mf*, decatleta *mf*.
decathlon [dɪ'kæθlən] N decatlón *m*.
decay [dɪ'keɪ] **1** N decadencia *f*, decaimiento *m*; (*rotting*) pudrición *f*; (*of teeth*) caries *f*; (*of building*) desmoronamiento *m*.
2 VT deteriorar, pudrir.
3 VI decaer, desmoronarse; (*rot*) pudrirse; (*teeth*) cariarse; (*building*) desmoronarse, arruinarse.
decayed [dɪ'keɪd] ADJ *wood etc* podrido; *teeth* cariado; *family* venido a menos.
decaying [dɪ'keɪɪŋ] ADJ *food* en estado de putrefacción; *vegetation etc* podrido, pútrido; *flesh* en descomposición; *tooth* cariado; *building* deteriorado, en ruinas; *stone* que se descompone; *civilization* decadente.
decease [dɪ'siːs] **1** N fallecimiento *m*.
2 VI fallecer.
deceased [dɪ'siːst] **1** ADJ difunto.
2 N: **the ~** el difunto, la difunta.
deceit [dɪ'siːt] N engaño *m*, fraude *m*; (*lying*) mentira *f*.
deceitful [dɪ'siːtfʊl] ADJ engañoso, falso, fraudulento; (*lying*) mentiroso.
deceitfully [dɪ'siːtfəlɪ] ADV engañosamente; falsamente.
deceitfulness [dɪ'siːtfʊlnɪs] N falsedad *f*.
deceive [dɪ'siːv] **1** VT engañar; *hopes* defraudar; **if my memory does not ~ me** si mal no recuerdo; **I was ~d into buying it** me engañaron para que lo comprara; **I was ~d into thinking it was new** me engañé al pensar que era nuevo; **let nobody be ~d by this** que nadie padezca engaño en este asunto.
2 VR: **to ~ o.s.** engañarse, equivocarse.
deceiver [dɪ'siːvəʳ] N impostor *m*, -ora *f*, embustero *m*, -a *f*; (*of woman*) seductor *m*.
decelerate [diː'seləreɪt] VT aminorar la marcha de, desacelerar, decelerar.
deceleration ['diː,selə'reɪʃən] N desaceleración *f*, deceleración *f*, disminución *f* de velocidad.
December [dɪ'sembəʳ] N diciembre *m*.
decency ['diːsənsɪ] N (a) decencia *f*; **offence against ~** atentado *m* contra el pudor; **it is no more than common ~ to** + *infin* la más mínima educación exige que + *subj*.
(b) **decencies** buenas costumbres *fpl*.
(c) (*kindness*) bondad *f*, amabilidad *f*.
decent ['diːsənt] ADJ (a) (*seemly*) decente; **are you ~?** (*hum*) ¿estás visible?
(b) (*kind*) simpático, amable, bueno; **he's a ~ sort** es buena persona; **he was very ~ to me** fue muy amable conmigo.
(c) (*passable*) bastante bueno; (*US***: *great*) cutre*****; **a ~ sum** una cantidad considerable.
decently ['diːsəntlɪ] ADV (a) decentemente. (b) amablemente, con amabilidad; **he very ~ offered it to me** muy amablemente me lo ofreció.
decentralization [diː,sentrəlaɪ'zeɪʃən] N descentralización *f*.
decentralize [diː'sentrəlaɪz] VT descentralizar.
decentre, (*US*) **decenter** [diː'sentəʳ] VT descentrar.
deception [dɪ'sepʃən] N engaño *m*, fraude *m*.
deceptive [dɪ'septɪv] ADJ engañoso.
deceptively [dɪ'septɪvlɪ] ADV: **the village looks ~ near** el pueblo parece engañosamente cerca; **he was ~ obedient/still** *etc* estaba engañosamente obediente/quieto *etc*.
deceptiveness [dɪ'septɪvnɪs] N carácter *m* engañoso.
decibel ['desɪbel] N decibel(io) *m*.
decide [dɪ'saɪd] **1** VT decidir, determinar; **that ~d me** eso me decidió.
2 VI decidir, resolver; **to ~ to do sth** decidir hacer algo, decidirse a hacer algo, resolverse a hacer algo; **to ~ against sth** optar por no hacer (*etc*) algo; **to ~ in favour of sb** decidir a favor de uno.

◆**decide on** VT: **to ~ on sth** decidir por algo, optar por algo, quedar en algo.

decided [dɪ'saɪdɪd] ADJ *person* decidido, resuelto; *difference etc* marcado, acusado; (*unquestionable*) indudable.

decidedly [dɪ'saɪdɪdlɪ] ADV decididamente; **he said ~** dijo con resolución; **it is ~ difficult** indudablemente es difícil.

decider [dɪ'saɪdə^r] N (*Sport*) (partido *m* de) desempate *m*; partido *m* decisivo; gol *m* (*etc*) decisivo.

deciding [dɪ'saɪdɪŋ] ADJ *factor etc* decisivo, concluyente; *vote* de calidad, decisivo.

deciduous [dɪ'sɪdjʊəs] ADJ de hoja caduca.

decile ['desɪl] N decil *m*.

decilitre, (*US*) **deciliter** ['desɪ,liːtə^r] N decilitro *m*.

decimal ['desɪməl] ① ADJ decimal; **~ currency** moneda *f* decimal; **~ fraction** fracción *f* decimal; **~ point** coma *f* decimal, coma *f* de decimales; **~ system** sistema *m* métrico; **I've worked it out to two ~ places** lo he calculado hasta centésimas.
② N decimal *m*.

decimalization [,desɪməlaɪ'zeɪʃən] N decimalización *f*.

decimalize ['desɪməlaɪz] VT decimalizar.

decimate ['desɪmeɪt] VT diezmar (*also fig*).

decimation [,desɪ'meɪʃən] N diezmamiento *m*.

decimetre, (*US*) **decimeter** ['desɪ,miːtə^r] N decímetro *m*.

decipher [dɪ'saɪfə^r] VT descifrar.

decipherable [dɪ'saɪfərəbl] ADJ descifrable.

decision [dɪ'sɪʒən] N (a) (*a resolve*) decisión *f*; (*Jur*) fallo *m*; **~ table** (*Comput*) tabla *f* de decisiones; **to make** (*or* **come to, take**) **a ~** tomar una decisión. (b) (*resoluteness*) resolución *f*, firmeza *f*.

decision-maker [dɪ'sɪʒən,meɪkə^r] N persona *f* que toma decisiones.

decision-making [dɪ'sɪʒən,meɪkɪŋ] ① ATTR: **~ process** proceso *m* decisorio; **~ unit** unidad *f* de adopción de decisiones.
② N: **he's good at ~** es bueno tomando decisiones.

decisive [dɪ'saɪsɪv] ADJ (a) *factor etc* decisivo, concluyente.
(b) (*conclusive*) terminante; *manner* tajante, categórico, firme.

decisively [dɪ'saɪsɪvlɪ] ADV con decisión, con resolución; **to be ~ beaten** ser derrotado de modo decisivo.

decisiveness [dɪ'saɪsɪvnɪs] N carácter *m* tajante; firmeza *f*.

deck [dek] ① N (a) cubierta *f*; (*of bus*) piso *m*; (*·*) suelo *m*, superficie *f*; (*US*✱: *drugs*) saquito *m* de heroína; **~ cargo** carga *f* de cubierta; **top ~, upper ~** (*of bus*) piso *m* de arriba; **to clear the ~s** (*fig*) despejar la mesa (*etc*); **he hit the ~** ✱ cayó al suelo.
(b) (*esp US: of cards*) baraja *f*.
(c) (*of record player*) platina *f*.
② VT (a) (*also* **to ~ out**) engalanar, adornar (**with** de); **all ~ed out** muy ataviado, de punta en blanco.
(b) (*US*✱) derribar de un golpe.

deck cabin ['dek,kæbɪn] N cabina *f* de cubierta.

deckchair ['dek,tʃɛə^r] N tumbona *f*, perezosa *f* (*LAm*).

-decker ['dekə^r] N *ending in compounds*: **single~** (*bus*) autobús *m* de un piso; **three~** (*Naut*) barco *m* de tres cubiertas; V **double-decker**.

deckhand ['dekhænd] N marinero *m* de cubierta.

deckhouse ['dekhaʊs] N, PL **deckhouses** ['dek,haʊzɪz] camareta *f* alta.

declaim [dɪ'kleɪm] VT declamar.

declamation [,deklə'meɪʃən] N declamación *f*.

declamatory [dɪ'klæmətərɪ] ADJ declamatorio.

declaration [,deklə'reɪʃən] N declaración *f*.

declare [dɪ'klɛə^r] ① VT declarar, afirmar; *dividend* anunciar; *war* declarar; **to ~ sth to the customs** declarar algo en la aduana; **have you anything to ~?** ¿tiene algo que declarar?; **to ~ sb to be a traitor** dar a uno por traidor.
② VI: **to ~ for, to ~ in favour of** pronunciarse a favor de; **well I ~!** ¡vaya por Dios!
③ VR: **to ~ o.s.** declararse; **to ~ o.s. surprised** confesar su sorpresa; **he ~d himself beaten** se dio por vencido; **to ~ o.s. against** afirmar su oposición a, pronunciarse en contra de.

declared [dɪ'klɛəd] ADJ declarado, abierto.

declarer [dɪ'klɛərə^r] N (*Bridge*) declarante *mf*.

déclassé [deɪ'klæseɪ] ADJ desprestigiado, empobrecido; que ha perdido su categoría social.

declassify [diː'klæsɪfaɪ] VT *information* levantar el secreto de.

declension [dɪ'klenʃən] N declinación *f*.

declinable [dɪ'klaɪnəbl] ADJ declinable.

▼**decline** [dɪ'klaɪn] ① N (*lessening*) declinación *f*, descenso *m*, disminución *f* (*in* de); (*in price*) baja *f*; (*decay*) decaimiento *m*, decadencia *f*; (*of sun, empire*) ocaso *m*; (*Med*) debilitación *f*; **to be on the ~** ir disminuyendo; **to go into a ~** ir debilitándose.
▼② VT (a) rehusar, negarse a aceptar.
(b) (*Gram*) declinar.
③ VI (a) (*go down*) declinar, disminuir; (*in price*) bajar; (*decay*) decaer; (*Med*) debilitarse; **to ~ in importance** ir perdiendo importancia.
(b) (*refuse*) rehusar; **to ~ to do sth** rehusar hacer algo, negarse a

hacer algo.

declining [dɪ'klaɪnɪŋ] ADJ: **~ industry** industria *f* en decadencia; **~ interest** pérdida *f* de interés; **in my ~ years** en mis últimos años.

declivity [dɪ'klɪvɪtɪ] N declive *m*.

declutch ['diː'klʌtʃ] VI desembragar.

decoction [dɪ'kɒkʃən] N decocción *f*.

decode ['diː'kəʊd] VT descifrar; (*Ling, TV*) descodificar.

decoder [diː'kəʊdə^r] N (*Comput, TV*) descodificador *m*.

decoding ['diː'kəʊdɪŋ] N (*Comput*) descodificación *f*.

decoke (*Brit Aut*) ① ['diː'kəʊk] N descarburación *f*.
② [diː'kəʊk] VT descarburar.

decollate [,diːkə'leɪt] VT separar, alzar.

décolletage [deɪˈkɒlɑːʒ] N escote *m*.

décolleté(e) [deɪ'kɒlteɪ] ADJ *dress* escotado; *woman* en traje escotado.

decolonization [diː,kɒlənaɪ'zeɪʃən] N descolonización *f*.

decolonize [diː'kɒlənaɪz] VT descolonizar.

decommission [,diːkə'mɪʃən] VT (a) *nuclear power station* cerrar, desmantelar. (b) *warship, aircraft* desmantelar. (c) *weapons* retirar de la circulación.

decommissioning [,diːkə'mɪʃənɪŋ] N (*of nuclear power station*) demolición *f*; (*of warship, aircraft*) desguace *m*; (*of weapons*) destrucción *f*.

decompartmentalization [,diːkɒmpɑːt,mentəlaɪ'zeɪʃən] N descompartimentación *f*.

decompartmentalize [,diːkɒmpɑː't mentəlaɪz] VT descompartimentar.

decompose [,diːkəm'pəʊz] ① VT descomponer.
② VI descomponerse.

decomposition [,diːkɒmpə'zɪʃən] N descomposición *f*.

decompress [,diːkəm'pres] VT descomprimir.

decompression [,diːkəm'preʃən] N descompresión *f*; **~ chamber** cámara *f* de descompresión; **~ sickness** enfermedad *f* de la descompresión.

decongestant [,diːkən'dʒestənt] N descongestivo *m*.

decongestion [,diːkən'dʒestʃən] N descongestión *f*.

deconstruct [,diːkən'strʌkt] VT deconstruir.

deconstruction [,diːkən'strʌkʃən] N deconstrucción *f*.

decontaminate [,diːkən'tæmɪneɪt] VT descontaminar.

decontamination ['diːkən,tæmɪ'neɪʃən] N descontaminación *f*.

decontextualize [diːkən'tekstjʊəlaɪz] VT descontextualizar.

decontrol [,diːkən'trəʊl] ① N descontrol *m*, supresión *f* del control; liberalización *f*.
② VT suprimir el control de; liberalizar.

décor ['deɪkɔː^r] N decoración *f*; (*Theat*) decorado *m*, decoración *f*.

decorate ['dekəreɪt] VT (a) adornar, decorar (**with** de); *room* empapelar, pintar; *house* pintar. (b) (*Mil etc*) condecorar.

decorating ['dekəreɪtɪŋ] N: **interior ~** decoración *f* del hogar.

decoration [,dekə'reɪʃən] N (a) adorno *m*, ornato *m*; (*act*) decoración *f*. (b) (*Mil etc*) condecoración *f*.

decorative ['dekərətɪv] ADJ (*in function*) de adorno, decorativo; (*pleasant*) hermoso, elegante; **~ arts** artes *fpl* decorativas.

decorator ['dekəreɪtə^r] N (*esp Brit*) decorador *m*; pintor *m* decorador.

decorous ['dekərəs] ADJ decoroso, correcto.

decorously ['dekərəslɪ] ADV decorosamente, correctamente.

decorum [dɪ'kɔːrəm] N decoro *m*, corrección *f*.

decouple [dɪ'kʌpl] VT (*frm*) escindir, separar.

decoy ['diːkɔɪ] ① N señuelo *m*; (*bird*) cimbel *m*, reclamo *m*; (*person*) entruchón *m*; (*fig*) señuelo *m*, trampa *f*; **~ duck** pato *m* de reclamo.
② VT atraer (*or* apartar) con señuelo (*or* mediante una estratagema), entruchar; **to ~ sb away** lograr mediante una estratagema que uno se aparte de un sitio.

decrease [diː'kriːs] ① N disminución *f* (*in* de); **to be on the ~** ir disminuyendo.
② VT disminuir, reducir.
③ VI disminuirse, reducirse.

decreasing [diː'kriːsɪŋ] ADJ decreciente.

decreasingly [diː'kriːsɪŋlɪ] ADV decrecientemente.

decree [dɪ'kriː] ① N decreto *m*; **~ absolute** fallo *m* absoluto (de divorcio); **~ nisi** fallo *m* provisional (de divorcio).
② VT decretar.

decrepit [dɪ'krepɪt] ADJ decrépito.

decrepitude [dɪ'krepɪtjuːd] N decrepitud *f*.

decriminalization [,dɪ:'krɪmɪnəlaɪ'zeɪʃən] N despenalización *f*.

decriminalize [diː'krɪmɪnəlaɪz] VT despenalizar.

decry [dɪ'kraɪ] VT desacreditar, rebajar, censurar.

dedicate ['dedɪkeɪt] ① VT dedicar, consagrar; (*US*) *official building* inaugurar oficialmente.
② VR: **to ~ o.s. to** dedicarse a.

dedicated ['dedɪkeɪtɪd] ADJ totalmente entregado, de mucha entrega, dedicado; (*Comput*) dedicado, especializado.

dedication [,dedɪ'keɪʃən] N (a) dedicación *f*. (b) (*in book*) dedicatoria *f*. (c) (*quality*) dedicación *f*, entrega *f*, devoción *f*.

deduce [dɪ'djuːs] VT deducir; **I ~ that** ... me imagino que ..., supongo que ...; **what do you ~ from that?** ¿qué conclusión sacas de eso?; **as can be ~d from** según se colige de, según se desprende de.

deducible [dɪ'djuːsɪbl] ADJ deducible (*from* de).

deduct [dɪ'dʌkt] VT restar (*also Math*; *from* de), descontar, rebajar; *tax etc* deducir (*from* de).

deductible [dɪ'dʌktəbl] ADJ deducible, descontable.

deduction [dɪ'dʌkʃən] N (**a**) (*inference*) deducción *f*, conclusión *f*; **what are your ~s?** ¿cuáles son sus conclusiones? (**b**) (*amount*) descuento *m*, rebaja *f*; retención *f*.

deductive [dɪ'dʌktɪv] ADJ deductivo.

deed [diːd] **1** N (**a**) (*act*) hecho *m*, acto *m*, acción *f*; (*brave etc*) hazaña *f*. (**b**) (*Jur*) escritura *f*; **~ of covenant** escritura *f* de 'covenant'; **~ of partnership** contrato *m* de sociedad; **~ of transfer** escritura *f* de traspaso.
2 VT (*US Jur*) *property* transferir por acto notarial.

deed-poll ['diːd,pəʊl] N: **to change one's name by ~** cambiar su apellido por escritura legal.

deejay* ['diːdʒeɪ] N pinchadiscos* *mf*.

deem [diːm] VT juzgar, creer; **I ~ it a mistake** creo que es un error; **I ~ him a fool** considero que es tonto; **I ~ it to be my duty** considero que es mi deber.

deep [diːp] **1** ADJ (**a**) (*far down*) profundo, hondo; **to be 6 metres ~** tener una profundidad de 6 metros, tener 6 metros de hondo; **~ end** parte *f* honda; **to go off the ~ end*** subirse por las paredes*; **I was thrown in at the ~ end** (*fig*) de entrada me enfrenté con graves problemas; desde el principio tuve que trabajar (*etc*) muy en serio; no me dieron tiempo para aprender el oficio; **the streets were half a metre ~ in snow** las calles tenían medio metro de nieve; **to be ~ in debt** estar lleno de deudas; **to be ~ in thought** estar absorto en la meditación; **he's pretty ~ in it** está muy metido en el asunto; **to be in ~ trouble** estar en grandes apuros; **these are ~ waters, Watson** querido Watson, aquí hay honduras.
(**b**) (*far back*) ancho; **a plot 30 m ~** un terreno de 30 m de fondo; **the ~ South** (*US*) los estados de más al sur.
(**c**) (*Mus*) bajo, grave.
(**d**) *colour* intenso, subido, (*and dark*) oscuro; *tan* intenso.
(**e**) (*fig*) profundo; *emotion* profundo, hondo; *mystery* profundo; *breath* profundo, a pleno pulmón; *mind* penetrante; *mourning* riguroso; *person* (*reserved*) muy reservado, insondable; (*pej*) astuto, taimado; **~ grammar** gramática *f* profunda; **~ structure** estructura *f* profunda; **he's a ~ one** la procesión le va por dentro; **it's too ~ for me** no lo entiendo, no alcanzo a entenderlo.
2 ADV: **don't go in too ~** no te metas en la parte profunda; **the miners are ~ underground** los mineros están a una gran profundidad; **the snow lay ~** había una profunda capa de nieve; **~ in his heart** en lo más hondo del corazón; **he thrust his hand ~ into his pocket** metió la mano hasta el fondo del bolsillo; **~ into the night** hasta las altas horas de la noche; **to form up 6 ~** formarse de 6 en fondo.
3 N: **the ~** (*liter*) el piélago.

deep-breathing ['diːp'briːðɪŋ] N gimnasia *f* respiratoria, ejercicios *mpl* respiratorios.

deep-chested ['diːp'tʃestɪd] ADJ ancho de pecho.

deepen ['diːpən] **1** VT *hole etc* ahondar, profundizar, hacer más profundo; *voice* ahuecar; *colour, emotion* intensificar; *study* ahondar en.
2 VI (*water etc*) hacerse más profundo; (*colour, emotion*) intensificarse; (*gloom*) aumentar.

deepening ['diːpənɪŋ] ADJ (**a**) que se hace más profundo.
(**b**) *meaning, mystery etc* que se vuelve más oscuro.

deep-felt ['diːp'felt] ADJ hondamente sentido.

deep-freeze ['diːp'friːz] **1** N (ultra)congelador *m*.
2 VT (ultra)congelar.

deep-freezing [,diːp'friːzɪŋ] N ultracongelación *f*.

deep-frozen [,diːp'frəʊzn] ADJ ultracongelado.

deep-fry ['diːp'fraɪ] VT freír en aceite abundante.

deep-laid ['diːp'leɪd] ADJ *plan* bien preparado.

deeply ['diːplɪ] ADV profundamente, hondamente; intensamente; **to breathe ~** respirar a pleno pulmón.

deep-rooted ['diːp'ruːtɪd] ADJ muy arraigado.

deep-sea ['diːp'siː] ADJ de altura, de alta mar; **~ diving** buceo *m* de altura; **~ fishing** pesca *f* de gran altura; **~ tug** remolcador *m* de altura.

deep-seated ['diːp'siːtɪd] ADJ profundamente arraigado.

deep-set ['diːp'set] ADJ *eyes* hundido.

deep-six* [,diːp'sɪks] VT (*US*) (*throw out*) tirar; (*kill*) cargarse*.

deer [dɪə^r] N ciervo *m*, venado *m*.

deerhound ['dɪəhaʊnd] N galgo *m* (para cazar venados); galgo *m* escocés (de pelo lanoso).

deerskin ['dɪəskɪn] N piel *f* de ciervo, gamuza *f*.

deerstalker ['dɪə,stɔːkə^r] N (**a**) (*person*) cazador *m* de ciervos al ace-

cho. (**b**) (*hat*) gorro *m* de cazador (de ciervos).

deerstalking ['dɪə,stɔːkɪŋ] N caza *f* de venado.

de-escalate [,diː'eskəleɪt] VT desescalar.

de-escalation [diː,eskə'leɪʃən] N (*Mil, Pol*) desescalada *f*; (*in industrial relations*) descrispación *f*.

def* [def] ADJ fantástico*, súper*.

deface [dɪ'feɪs] VT desfigurar, mutilar.

de facto [deɪ'fæktəʊ] ADJ, ADV de facto.

defalcation [,diːfæl'keɪʃən] N desfalco *m*.

defamation [,defə'meɪʃən] N difamación *f*.

defamatory [dɪ'fæmətərɪ] ADJ difamatorio.

defame [dɪ'feɪm] VT difamar, calumniar.

default [dɪ'fɔːlt] **1** N: (**a**) **in ~ of** a falta de, en ausencia de; **judgement by ~** juicio *m* en rebeldía; **he won by ~** ganó en ausencia de su adversario; **we must not let it go by ~** no debemos permitir que lo perdamos por descuido (*or* sin hacer nada). (**b**) (*Comput*) **~ options** opciones *fpl* por defecto; **~ values** valores *mpl* por defecto.
2 VI (**a**) (*not pay*) no pagar, ponerse en mora; **to ~ on one's payments** no pagar los plazos (*etc*).
(**b**) (*Sport*) perder por incomparecencia.
(**c**) (*Comput*) **it always ~s to drive C** siempre va a la unidad de disco C por exclusión.

defaulter [dɪ'fɔːltə^r] N (*on payments*) moroso *m*, -a *f*; (*Mil*) delincuente *m*.

defaulting [dɪ'fɔːltɪŋ] ADJ (**a**) (*Stock Exchange*) moroso. (**b**) (*Jur*) en rebeldía.

defeat [dɪ'fiːt] **1** N derrota *f*; **eventually he admitted ~** por fin reconoció que había sido vencido.
2 VT vencer, derrotar; *plan* estorbar, frustrar; *hopes* defraudar; (*Parl*) *bill etc* rechazar; **this will ~ its own ends** esto será contraproducente; **the problem ~s me** el problema me trae perplejo; **it ~ed all our efforts** burló todos nuestros esfuerzos.

defeated [dɪ'fiːtɪd] ADJ *army, team, player* derrotado.

defeatism [dɪ'fiːtɪzəm] N derrotismo *m*.

defeatist [dɪ'fiːtɪst] **1** ADJ derrotista.
2 N derrotista *mf*.

defecate ['defəkeɪt] VTI defecar.

defecation [,defə'keɪʃən] N defecación *f*.

defect **1** ['diːfekt] N defecto *m*.
2 [dɪ'fekt] VI desertar (*from* de, *to* a).

defection [dɪ'fekʃən] N deserción *f*, defección *f*.

defective [dɪ'fektɪv] **1** ADJ defectuoso; (*Gram*) defectivo; *child* anormal, retrasado.
2 N persona *f* anormal, retrasado *m*, -a *f* mental; (*Gram*) defectivo *m*.

defector [dɪ'fektə^r] N desertor *m*, -ora *f*, tránsfuga *mf*.

defence, (*US*) **defense** [dɪ'fens] **1** N (*all senses*) defensa *f*; **Secretary (of State) for** (*or* **Minister of**) **D~** (*Brit*), **Secretary of Defense** (*US*) Secretario *m* (de Estado) (*or* Ministro *m*) de Defensa; **Department** (*or* **Ministry**) **of D~** (*Brit*), **Department of Defense** (*US*) Departamento *m* (*or* Ministerio *m*) de Defensa; **to come out in ~ of** salir en defensa de; **what have you to say in your own ~?** ¿qué tiene Vd que decir en defensa propia?
2 ATTR: **~ counsel** abogado *mf* defensor; **~ forces** fuerzas *fpl* defensivas; **~ mechanism** mecanismo *m* de defensa; **~ spending** presupuesto *m* de las fuerzas armadas, gastos *mpl* de defensa.

defenceless, (*US*) **defenseless** [dɪ'fenslɪs] ADJ indefenso; (*fig*) inocente, inofensivo.

defencelessness, (*US*) **defenselessness** [dɪ'fenslɪsnɪs] N indefensión *f*.

defend [dɪ'fend] VT defender (*against* contra, *from* de).

defendant [dɪ'fendənt] N (*civil*) demandado *m*, -a *f*; (*criminal*) acusado *m*, -a *f*.

defender [dɪ'fendə^r] N defensor *m*, -ora *f*; (*Sport*) defensa *mf*.

defending [dɪ'fendɪŋ] ADJ *champion* titular; **~ counsel** (*Jur*) abogado *mf* defensor.

defense [dɪ'fens] N (*US*) = **defence**.

defensible [dɪ'fensɪbl] ADJ defendible; *action etc* justificable.

defensive [dɪ'fensɪv] **1** ADJ defensivo; **~ works** fortificaciones *fpl*.
2 N defensiva *f*; **to be on the ~** estar a la defensiva.

defensively [dɪ'fensɪvlɪ] ADV *say etc* en tono defensivo.

defensiveness [dɪ'fensɪvnɪs] N tono *m* (*etc*) defensivo, actitud *f* defensiva.

defer¹ [dɪ'fɜː^r] VT aplazar, diferir, postergar (*LAm*); *conscript* dar una prórroga a.

defer² [dɪ'fɜː^r] VI: **to ~ to sb, to ~ to sb's opinion** acatar la opinión de uno, someterse al punto de vista de uno; **in this I gladly ~ to you** en esto acepto gustoso su opinión.

deference ['defərəns] N deferencia *f*, respeto *m*; **in ~ to, out of ~ to** por deferencia hacia.

deferential [,defə'renʃəl] ADJ respetuoso.

deferentially [,defə'renʃəlɪ] ADV deferentemente, respetuosamente.

deferment [dɪˈfɜːmənt] N, **deferral** [dɪˈfɜːrəl] N aplazamiento *m*; (*Mil*) prórroga *f*.

deferred [dɪˈfɜːd] ADJ: **~ annuity** cuota *f* de pensión; **~ credit** crédito *m* diferido; **~ liabilities** pasivo *m* diferido; **~ payment** pago *m* a plazos.

defiance [dɪˈfaɪəns] N desafío *m* (*of* a); oposición *f* terca (*of* a); **in ~ of** en contra de, con infracción de; **to bid ~ to** desafiar a.

defiant [dɪˈfaɪənt] ADJ provocativo, insolente; *tone* desafiante, retador.

defiantly [dɪˈfaɪəntlɪ] ADV de modo provocativo, insolentemente; en tono retador, en son de reto.

defibrillator [dɪˈfaɪbrɪˌleɪtər] N desfibrilador *m*.

deficiency [dɪˈfɪʃənsɪ] N (*lack*) falta *f*; (*defect*) defecto *m*, deficiencia *f*; (*Comm*) déficit *m*, descubierto *m*; **~ disease** mal *m* carencial.

deficient [dɪˈfɪʃənt] ADJ deficiente; (*in quantity*) insuficiente; (*incomplete*) incompleto; (*defective*) defectuoso; (*mentally*) retrasado, anormal; **to be ~ in** carecer de, estar falto de.

deficit [ˈdefɪsɪt] N déficit *m*; **to be in ~** estar en déficit, tener déficit.

defile¹ [ˈdiːfaɪl] N desfiladero *m*.

defile² [dɪˈfaɪl] VT manchar, deshonrar; *flag* ultrajar; *sacred thing* profanar.

defilement [dɪˈfaɪlmənt] N deshonra *f*; ensuciamiento *m*, corrupción *f*; profanación *f*.

definable [dɪˈfaɪnəbl] ADJ definible.

define [dɪˈfaɪn] VT definir (*also Comput*), determinar.

definite [ˈdefɪnɪt] ADJ claro, categórico; positivo; concreto; *date etc* determinado; (*Gram*) definido; **he was very ~ about it** nos lo dijo sin dejar lugar a dudas; **we have no ~ record of it** no nos consta de manera clara; **the plan is not yet ~** todavía el proyecto no se ha aprobado de modo definitivo.

definitely [ˈdefɪnɪtlɪ] ADV claramente, categóricamente; **oh, ~!, yes, ~!** sí, desde luego; **did he say so ~?** ¿lo dijo claramente?; **we are ~ not going** es seguro que no vamos; **it is ~ impossible** es francamente imposible; **the plan is not yet ~ fixed** todavía el proyecto no se ha aprobado de modo definitivo.

definition [ˌdefɪˈnɪʃən] N (a) definición *f*; **by ~** por definición. (b) (*Phot*) nitidez *f*, claridad *f*.

definitive [dɪˈfɪnɪtɪv] ADJ definitivo.

definitively [dɪˈfɪnɪtɪvlɪ] ADV en definitiva, con toda seguridad, definitivamente.

deflate [diːˈfleɪt] VT desinflar; *person* quitar los humos a; quitar los ánimos (*or* esperanzas) a; *reputation* rebajar, desacreditar; (*Fin*) causar (la) deflación en; **at this news he felt very ~d** con esta noticia se desanimó por completo.

deflation [diːˈfleɪʃən] N desinflamiento *m*; (*Fin*) deflación *f*.

deflationary [diːˈfleɪʃənərɪ] ADJ (*Fin*) deflacionista, deflacionario.

deflationist [diːˈfleɪʃənɪst] ADJ deflacionista.

deflator [diːˈfleɪtər] N medida *f* deflacionista.

deflect [dɪˈflekt] VT desviar (*from* de).

deflection [dɪˈflekʃən] N desviación *f*.

deflector [dɪˈflektər] N deflector *m*.

defloration [ˌdiːflɔːˈreɪʃən] N desfloración *f*.

deflower [diːˈflaʊər] VT desflorar.

defog [diːˈfɒg] VT desempañar.

defogger [diːˈfɒgər] N (*US*) dispositivo *m* antivaho.

defoliant [diːˈfəʊlɪənt] N defoliante *m*.

defoliate [diːˈfəʊlɪeɪt] VT defoliar.

defoliation [ˌdiːfəʊlɪˈeɪʃən] N defoliación *f*.

deforest [diːˈfɒrɪst] VT deforestar, despoblar de árboles.

deforestation [diːˌfɒrəˈsteɪʃən] N deforestación *f*, despoblación *f* forestal.

deform [dɪˈfɔːm] VT deformar.

deformation [ˌdiːfɔːˈmeɪʃən] N deformación *f*.

deformed [dɪˈfɔːmd] ADJ deforme, mutilado.

deformity [dɪˈfɔːmɪtɪ] N deformidad *f*.

defraud [dɪˈfrɔːd] VT defraudar (*of* de); estafar; **to ~ sb of sth** estafar algo a uno.

defrauder [dɪˈfrɔːdər] N defraudador *m*, -ora *f*.

defray [dɪˈfreɪ] VT sufragar, pagar, costear; **to ~ sb's expenses** sufragar los gastos de uno.

defrayal [dɪˈfreɪəl] N, **defrayment** [dɪˈfreɪmənt] N pago *m*.

defreeze [diːˈfriːz] VT descongelar.

defrock [diːˈfrɒk] VT apartar del sacerdocio.

defrost [diːˈfrɒst] VT deshelar, descongelar.

defroster [diːˈfrɒstər] N (*US*) dispositivo *m* antivaho; (*Aut*) esprai *m* antihielo.

deft [deft] ADJ diestro, hábil.

deftly [ˈdeftlɪ] ADV diestramente, hábilmente.

deftness [ˈdeftnɪs] N destreza *f*, habilidad *f*.

defunct [dɪˈfʌŋkt] ADJ difunto; *company etc* que ya no existe; *idea, theory* que ya no tiene validez; *scheme* que no se realizó nunca.

defuse [diːˈfjuːz] VT *bomb* desactivar; *tensions* calmar, apaciguar; *situation* reducir la tensión de.

defy [dɪˈfaɪ] VT (a) (*challenge*) desafiar; **to ~ sb to do sth** desafiar a uno a hacer algo.

(b) (*resist*) oponerse tercamente a; *order* contravenir a; *bad weather* resistir a; **it defies definition** se escapa a la definición; **it defies description** resulta imposible describirlo.

degeneracy [dɪˈdʒenərəsɪ] N degeneración *f*, depravación *f*.

degenerate ⟨1⟩ [dɪˈdʒenərɪt] ADJ degenerado.

⟨2⟩ [dɪˈdʒenərɪt] N degenerado *m*, -a *f*.

⟨3⟩ [dɪˈdʒenəreɪt] VI degenerar (*into* en); **to ~ into** (*end up being*) degenerar en, terminar siendo, terminar en; **the essay ~d into jottings** el ensayo terminó siendo meros apuntes.

degeneration [dɪˌdʒenəˈreɪʃən] N degeneración *f*.

degenerative [dɪˈdʒenərətɪv] ADJ *disease etc* degenerativo.

deglamourize [diːˈglæməˌraɪz] VT quitar el atractivo de.

degradable [dɪˈgreɪdəbl] ADJ degradable; **biologically ~** biodegradable.

degradation [ˌdegrəˈdeɪʃən] N degradación *f*, envilecimiento *m*.

degrade [dɪˈgreɪd] ⟨1⟩ VT degradar, envilecer.

⟨2⟩ VR: **to ~ o.s.** degradarse, aplebeyarse.

degrading [dɪˈgreɪdɪŋ] ADJ degradante, envilecedor.

▼ **degree** [dɪˈgriː] N (a) (*Math, Astron, Gram etc*) grado *m*; **10 ~s below freezing** 10 grados bajo cero.

(b) (*stage in process*) etapa *f*, punto *m*; **things have reached such a ~ that ...** las cosas han llegado a tal extremo que ...; **by ~s** poco a poco, gradualmente, progresivamente; **in no ~** de ninguna manera; **in some ~, to a certain ~** hasta cierto punto; **to the highest ~** en sumo grado; **he is superstitious to a ~** (*esp Brit*) es sumamente supersticioso.

▼ (c) (*Univ*) título *m*; licenciatura *f*; **~ day** día *m* de concesión de títulos; **to get a ~** sacar un título; **to take one's ~** graduarse, licenciarse, recibir un título; **to take a ~ in** licenciarse en; **to do a ~ course** (*Brit Univ*) hacer una licenciatura.

(d) (*social*) rango *m*, condición *f* social; **people of ~** personas *fpl* de cierto rango social.

(e) **third ~** interrogación *f* brutal; **to give sb the third ~** interrogar a uno brutalmente, sacudir a uno*.

┌─── **DEGREE** ───┐

ⓘ *Al título universitario equivalente a la licenciatura se le conoce como* **Bachelor's degree**, *que se obtiene normalmente tras tres años de estudios. Las titulaciones más frecuentes son las de Letras:* **Bachelor of Arts** *o* **BA** *y Ciencias:* **Bachelor of Science** *o* **BSc** *en el Reino Unido,* **BS** *en Estados Unidos.*

En el Reino Unido, la mayoría de los estudiantes reciben un **honours degree**, *cuyas calificaciones, en orden descendente son:* **first** *(1) la nota más alta, seguida de* **upper second** *(2-1),* **lower second** *(2-2) y* **third** *(3). En algunas ocasiones se recibe un* **ordinary degree**, *por ejemplo en el caso de que no se aprueben los exámenes para obtener el título pero los examinadores consideren que a lo largo de la carrera se han tenido unos resultados mínimos satisfactorios.*

*En Estados Unidos los estudiantes no reciben calificaciones en sus titulaciones de fin de carrera, pero sí existe la matrícula de honor (***honours***), que puede ser, de menor a mayor importancia:* **cum laude, magna cum laude** *y* **summa cum laude.**

Master's degree *es normalmente un título que se recibe tras estudios de postgrado, en los que se combinan horas lectivas o investigación con una tesina final, conocida como* **dissertation***. Las titulaciones más frecuentes son las de Master of Arts o* **MA***, Master of Science o* **MSc** *y Master of Business Administration o* **MBA***. El título se concede con la única calificación de apto. En algunas universidades, como las escocesas, el título de* **master's degree** *no es de postgrado, sino que corresponde a la licenciatura.*

El título universitario más alto es el de doctorado, **doctorate** *o* **doctor's degree**, *abreviado normalmente como* **PhD** *o* **DPhil.**

dehumanization [diːˌhjuːmənaɪˈzeɪʃən] N deshumanización *f*.

dehumanize [diːˈhjuːmənaɪz] VT deshumanizar.

dehumanizing [diːˈhjuːmənaɪzɪŋ] ADJ deshumanizante.

dehumidifier [ˌdiːhjuːˈmɪdɪfaɪər] N (*US*) deshumedecedor *m*.

dehumidify [ˌdiːhjuːˈmɪdɪfaɪ] VT (*US*) deshumedecer.

dehydrate [diːˈhaɪdreɪt] VT deshidratar.

dehydrated [ˌdiːhaɪˈdreɪtɪd] ADJ deshidratado.

dehydration [ˌdiːhaɪˈdreɪʃən] N deshidratación *f*.

de-ice [diːˈaɪs] VT deshelar, descongelar.

de-icer [ˈdiːˈaɪsər] N deshelador *m*, descongelador *m*.

de-icing [diːˈaɪsɪŋ] N descongelación *f*.

deictic [ˈdaɪktɪk] N deíctico *m*.

deification [ˌdiːɪfɪˈkeɪʃən] N deificación *f*.

deify [ˈdiːɪfaɪ] VT deificar.

deign [deɪn] VI: **to ~ to** + *infin* dignarse + *infin*.

deism [ˈdiːɪzəm] N deísmo *m*.

deist [ˈdiːɪst] N deísta *mf*.

deity ['diːɪtɪ] N deidad *f*; divinidad *f*; **the D~** Dios *m*.
deixis ['daɪksɪs] N deixis *f*.
déjà vu [deɪʒɑː'vuː] N déjà vu *m*.
dejected [dɪ'dʒektɪd] ADJ abatido, desanimado.
dejectedly [dɪ'dʒektɪdlɪ] ADV *say* con tono de abatimiento.
dejection [dɪ'dʒekʃən] N abatimiento *m*, desaliento *m*.
de jure [,deɪ'dʒʊərɪ] ADJ, ADV de iure.
dekko: ['dekəʊ] N (*Brit*) vistazo *m*; **let's have a ~** déjame verlo.
Del. (*US*) ABBR of **Delaware**.
del. ABBR of **delete**.
delay [dɪ'leɪ] **1** N (*gen*) dilación *f*; (*a ~*) retraso *m*, demora *f*; **without ~** sin demora, sin dilación.
2 VT (a) (*postpone*) aplazar, demorar; **~ed broadcast** (*US*) transmisión *f* diferida; **~ed effect** efecto *m* retardado.
(b) (*person*) entretener; (*obstruct*) impedir; (*make slow, eg train*) retrasar, retardar; **what ~ed you?** ¿por qué has tardado tanto?; **the train was ~ed by fog** el tren se retrasó por la niebla.
3 VI tardar, demorarse; **don't ~!** (*in doing sth*) ¡date prisa!, ¡cuanto antes mejor!; (*on the way*) ¡no te entretengas!, ¡no tardes!
delayed-action [dɪ'leɪd'ækʃən] ADJ de acción retardada.
delayering [diː'leɪərɪŋ] N reducción *f* de niveles jerárquicos.
delaying [dɪ'leɪɪŋ] ADJ: **~ tactics** tácticas *fpl* retardatorias.
delectable [dɪ'lektəbl] ADJ delicioso, deleitable.
delectation [,diːlek'teɪʃən] N deleite *m*, deleitación *f*.
delegate 1 ['delɪgɪt] N delegado *m*, -a *f*, diputado *m*, -a *f* (*to* a).
2 ['delɪgeɪt] VT delegar, diputar; **I was ~d to do it** me dieron autoridad para hacerlo, me nombraron para hacerlo; **that task cannot be ~d** ese cometido no se puede delegar a otro.
delegation [,delɪ'geɪʃən] N (a) (*act*) delegación *f*. (b) (*body*) delegación *f*, diputación *f*.
delete [dɪ'liːt] VT suprimir, tachar; (*Comput*) cancelar; **~ key** tecla *f* de borrado.
deleterious [,delɪ'tɪərɪəs] ADJ nocivo, perjudicial.
deletion [dɪ'liːʃən] N supresión *f*, tachadura *f*; (*Comput*) cancelación *f*.
delft [delft] N porcelana *f* de Delft.
Delhi ['delɪ] N Delhi *m*.
deli* ['delɪ] N = **delicatessen**.
deliberate 1 [dɪ'lɪbərɪt] ADJ (a) (*intentional*) intencionado, premeditado.
(b) (*cautious*) prudente; (*unhurried*) pausado, lento.
2 [dɪ'lɪbəreɪt] VT meditar; **I ~d what to do** medité lo que debiera hacer.
3 [dɪ'lɪbəreɪt] VI deliberar (*on* sobre); **I ~d whether to do it** dudaba si hacerlo o no.
deliberately [dɪ'lɪbərɪtlɪ] ADV (a) (*intentionally*) adrede, con intención, de propósito. (b) (*cautiously*) prudentemente; (*slowly*) pausadamente.
deliberation [dɪ,lɪbə'reɪʃən] N (a) (*consideration*) deliberación *f*, reflexión *f*; **after due ~** después de meditarlo bien. (b) (*discussion*: *freq ~s*) debates *mpl*, discusiones *fpl*. (c) (*slowness*) lentitud *f*; (*caution*) prudencia *f*; **to proceed with due ~** proceder con la debida prudencia.
deliberative [dɪ'lɪbərətɪv] ADJ deliberativo.
delicacy ['delɪkəsɪ] N (a) delicadeza *f*; fragilidad *f*. (b) (*titbit*) manjar *m* exquisito, golosina *f*.
delicate ['delɪkɪt] ADJ (a) delicado; *workmanship* fino, exquisito; escrupuloso; (*fragile*) frágil; *flavour, food* exquisito; *situation* difícil. (b) (*Med*) algo débil, enfermizo.
delicately ['delɪkɪtlɪ] ADV delicadamente; finamente, exquisitamente; frágilmente.
delicatessen [,delɪkə'tesn] N delicatessen *m*.
delicious [dɪ'lɪʃəs] ADJ delicioso, exquisito, rico.
deliciously [dɪ'lɪʃəslɪ] ADV deliciosamente, exquisitamente, ricamente.
▼ **delight** [dɪ'laɪt] **1** N (*feeling*) placer *m*, deleite *m*; (*pleasurable thing*) encanto *m*, delicia *f*; **a ~ to the eye** un gozo para los ojos, un placer para la vista; **one of the ~s of Majorca** uno de los encantos de Mallorca; **it has been the ~ of many children** ha hecho las delicias de muchos niños; **the book is sheer ~** el libro es un verdadero encanto; **to take ~ in sth** deleitarse con algo; **much to her ~** con gran regocijo de su parte; **to take ~ in** + *ger* deleitarse en + *infin*, (*pej*) gozarse en + *infin*.
▼ **2** VT encantar, deleitar; **~ed!** ¡encantado!; **the play ~ed everyone** la obra encantó a todos; **we are ~ed with it** estamos encantados con él; **(I'm) ~ed to meet you** (estoy) encantado de conocerle, mucho gusto de conocerle (*LAm*); **we shall be ~ed to come** tendremos muchísimo gusto en venir.
3 VI: **to ~ in sth** deleitarse con algo; **to ~ in** + *ger* deleitarse en + *infin*, (*pej*) gozarse en + *infin*.
delightedly [dɪ'laɪtɪdlɪ] ADV alegremente, con alegría; **she smiled ~** sonrió encantada, sonrió contentísima.
delightful [dɪ'laɪtfʊl] ADJ encantador, delicioso, precioso.
delightfully [dɪ'laɪtfəlɪ] ADV deliciosamente; **to be ~ vague** tener un despiste delicioso.

Delilah [dɪ'laɪlə] NF Dalila.
delimit [diː'lɪmɪt] VT delimitar.
delimitation [,diːlɪmɪ'teɪʃən] N delimitación *f*.
delineate [dɪ'lɪnɪeɪt] VT delinear; (*portray*) bosquejar, pintar; (*delimit*) definir.
delineation [dɪ,lɪnɪ'eɪʃən] N delineación *f*.
delinquency [dɪ'lɪŋkwənsɪ] N delincuencia *f*; (*guilt*) culpa *f*.
delinquent [dɪ'lɪŋkwənt] **1** ADJ delincuente.
2 N delincuente *mf*.
delirious [dɪ'lɪrɪəs] ADJ delirante; **to be ~** delirar, desvariar; **to be ~ with joy** estar loco de contento, estar delirante de alegría.
deliriously [dɪ'lɪrɪəslɪ] ADV con delirio; **to be ~ happy** estar loco de contento.
delirium [dɪ'lɪrɪəm] N delirio *m*; **~ tremens** delírium *m* tremens.
deliver [dɪ'lɪvər] **1** VT (a) (*distribute*) repartir, entregar; (*Comm*) entregar; *mail* repartir; **'we ~'** (*Comm*) 'servicio a domicilio'.
(b) (*hand over*: *also* **to ~ over, to ~ up**) entregar (*to* a).
(c) *message* llevar, comunicar; *sermon, speech, judgement* pronunciar; *lecture* dar; *ball, missile* lanzar; *blow* dar.
(d) (*save*) librar (*from* de); **~ us from evil** líbranos del mal.
(e) (*Med*) **she was ~ed of a child** dio a luz un niño; **to ~ a woman** asistir a un parto; **the doctor ~ed her of twins** el médico la asistió en el nacimiento de gemelos.
2 VI (*) cumplir lo prometido, hacer lo pactado.
3 VR (a) **to ~ o.s. of** *speech* pronunciar, *remark* hacer (con solemnidad), *opinion* expresar.
(b) **to ~ o.s. up** entregarse (*to* a).
deliverance [dɪ'lɪvərəns] N liberación *f*, rescate *m* (*from* de).
deliverer [dɪ'lɪvərər] N (*saviour*) libertador *m*, -ora *f*, salvador *m*, -ora *f*.
▼ **delivery** [dɪ'lɪvərɪ] N (a) (*distribution*) distribución *f*, entrega *f*, repartido *m*; (*Comm*) entrega *f*; (*of mail*) reparto *m*; **~ charge** gastos *mpl* de entrega; **~ date** fecha *f* de entrega; **~ man** repartidor *m*; **~ note** nota *f* de entrega; **~ order** orden *f* de entrega; **~ service** servicio *m* de entrega; (*to home*) servicio *m* a domicilio; **~ time** plazo *m* de entrega; **~ truck** (*US*), **~ van** (*Brit*) camioneta *f* de reparto.
(b) (*handing over*) entrega *f*.
(c) (*of speech*) pronunciación *f*; (*manner of speaking etc*) declamación *f*; presentación *f*, estilo *m*.
(d) (*saving*) liberación *f*, rescate *m* (*from* de).
(e) (*Med*) parto *m*, alumbramiento *m*; **~ room** sala *f* de alumbramiento.
dell [del] N vallecito *m*.
delouse ['diː'laʊs] VT despiojar, espulgar.
Delphi ['delfaɪ] N Delfos *m*.
Delphic ['delfɪk] ADJ délfico.
delphinium [del'fɪnɪəm] N espuela *f* de caballero.
delta ['deltə] N (*Geog*) delta *m*; (*letter*) delta *f*.
delta-winged ['deltə'wɪŋd] ADJ con alas en delta.
deltoid ['deltɔɪd] **1** ADJ deltoideo.
2 N deltoides *m*.
delude [dɪ'luːd] **1** VT engañar.
2 VR: **to ~ o.s.** engañarse.
deluded [dɪ'luːdɪd] ADJ iluso, engañado.
deluge ['deljuːdʒ] **1** N diluvio *m*; (*fig*) diluvio *m*, inundación *f*; **a ~ of protests** un torrente de protestas.
2 VT inundar (*with* de); **he was ~d with gifts** quedó inundado de regalos, le llovieron los regalos encima; **we are ~d with work** tenemos trabajo hasta encima de las cabezas.
delusion [dɪ'luːʒən] N engaño *m*, error *m*, ilusión *f*; **~s of grandeur** ilusiones *fpl* de grandeza; **to labour under a ~** estar equivocado.
delusive [dɪ'luːsɪv] ADJ engañoso, ilusorio.
de luxe [dɪ'lʌks] ADJ de lujo.
delve [delv] **1** VT cavar.
2 VI cavar; (*fig*) **to ~ into** investigar, ahondar en; **we must ~ deeper** tenemos que ahondar todavía más.
Dem. (*US Pol*) **1** N ABBR of **Democrat**.
2 ADJ ABBR of **Democratic**.
demagnetize [diː'mægnɪtaɪz] VT desimantar.
demagogic [,demə'gɒgɪk] ADJ demagógico.
demagogue, (*US sometimes*) **demagog** ['deməgɒg] N demagogo *m*.
demagoguery [demə'gɒgərɪ] N (*US*) demagogia *f*.
demagogy ['deməgɒgɪ] N demagogia *f*.
de-man [,diː'mæn] VT (*Brit*: *reduce manpower in*) reducir el personal en.
demand [dɪ'mɑːnd] **1** N (a) (*request*) petición *f*, solicitud *f* (*for* de); **by popular ~** a petición del público; **on ~** a solicitud; **abortion on ~** aborto *m* a petición (de la interesada).
(b) (*urgent claim*) exigencia *f*; requerimiento *m*; (*for payment*) reclamación *f*, aviso *m*, intimación *f*; (*Pol, Ind*) reivindicación *f*; **the ~s of duty** las exigencias del deber; **there is a pressing ~ for** hay una urgente necesidad de; **I have many ~s on my time** mis asuntos me tienen ocupadísimo; **it makes great ~s on my resources** exige mucho dinero; **he resisted the pressing ~s made on him** resistió a los

apremiantes requerimientos que se le habían dirigido. **(c)** *(Comm)* demanda *f (for* de); **~ bill, ~ draft** letra *f* a la vista; **~ curve** curva *f* de la demanda; **~ management** control *m* de la demanda; **~ note** solicitud *f* de pago; **there is a ~ for** existe demanda de; **to be in ~** tener demanda, *(fig)* ser muy solicitado, ser muy popular.

② VT **(a)** exigir *(from, of* a), reclamar, solicitar perentoriamente; **I ~ my rights** yo reclamo mis derechos; **the job ~s care** el trabajo exige cuidado.

(b) I ~ed to know why insistí en saber por qué.

demanding [dɪ'mɑːndɪŋ] ADJ *(person)* exigente; *(task)* absorbente; **physically ~** duro, agotador.

de-manning [ˌdiː'mænɪŋ] N *(Brit: Industry)* reducción *f* de personal, despidos *mpl.*

demarcate ['diːmɑːkeɪt] VT demarcar.

demarcation [ˌdiːmɑː'keɪʃən] N demarcación *f;* **~ dispute** conflicto *m* de demarcación; **~ line** línea *f* de demarcación.

démarche ['deɪmɑːʃ] N gestión *f,* diligencia *f.*

dematerialize [ˌdiːmə'tiːərɪəlaɪz] VI desmaterializarse.

demean [dɪ'miːn] VR: **to ~ o.s.** degradarse.

demeaning [dɪ'miːnɪŋ] ADJ degradante.

demeanour, *(US)* **demeanor** [dɪ'miːnər] N porte *m,* conducta *f.*

demented [dɪ'mentɪd] ADJ demente; *(fig)* loco.

dementedly [dɪ'mentɪdlɪ] ADV *(fig)* como un loco.

dementia [dɪ'menʃɪə] N demencia *f.*

demerara [ˌdemə'rɛərə] N *(Brit: also* **~ sugar)** azúcar *m* terciado.

demerit [diː'merɪt] N demérito *m,* desmerecimiento *m.*

demesne [dɪ'meɪn] N heredad *f;* tierras *fpl* solariegas.

demi... ['demɪ] PREF semi..., medio...

demigod ['demɪɡɒd] N semidiós *m.*

demijohn ['demɪdʒɒn] N damajuana *f.*

demilitarization ['diːmɪlɪtərəɪ'zeɪʃən] N desmilitarización *f.*

demilitarize ['diː'mɪlɪtəraɪz] VT desmilitarizar.

demilitarized zone [diː'mɪlɪtəraɪzd'zəʊn] N zona *f* desmilitarizada.

demimonde [ˌdemɪ'mɒːnd] N mujeres *fpl* mundanas.

demise [dɪ'maɪz] N fallecimiento *m.*

demisemiquaver ['demɪsemɪˌkweɪvər] N *(Brit)* fusa *f.*

demist [diː'mɪst] VT eliminar el vaho de, desempañar.

demister [diː'mɪstər] N *(Brit Aut)* desempañador *m.*

demisting [diː'mɪstɪŋ] N eliminación *f* del vaho.

demitasse ['demɪtæs] N *(US)* taza *f* pequeña, tacita *f.*

demi-vegetarian [ˌdemɪvedʒɪ'tɛərɪən] N semi-vegetariano *m,* -a *f.*

demo* ['deməʊ] N **(a)** *(Brit Pol)* mani* *f,* manifestación *f,* protesta *f* callejera. **(b)** *(Comm)* modelo *m* de demostración; **~ disk** disquete *m* de demostración; **~ tape** maqueta *f.*

demob* ['diː'mɒb] *(Brit)* ABBR *of* **demobilization, demobilize.**

demobilization ['diːˌməʊbɪləɪ'zeɪʃən] N desmovilización *f.*

demobilize [diː'məʊbɪlaɪz] VT desmovilizar.

democracy [dɪ'mɒkrəsɪ] N democracia *f.*

democrat ['deməkræt] N demócrata *mf.*

democratic [ˌdemə'krætɪk] ADJ democrático.

democratically [ˌdemə'krætɪklɪ] ADV democráticamente.

democratization [dɪˌmɒkrətə'zeɪʃən] N democratización *f.*

democratize [dɪ'mɒkrətaɪz] VT democratizar.

démodé [deɪ'mɒdeɪ] ADJ pasado de moda.

demographer [dɪ'mɒɡrəfər] N demógrafo *m,* -a *f.*

demographic [ˌdemə'ɡræfɪk] ADJ demográfico.

demographics [ˌdemə'ɡræfɪks] NPL estadísticas *fpl* sobre población, perfil *m* demográfico.

demography [dɪ'mɒɡrəfɪ] N demografía *f.*

demolish [dɪ'mɒlɪʃ] VT derribar, demoler; *argument* destruir; *food* devorar, zamparse.

demolisher [dɪ'mɒlɪʃər] N *(lit, fig)* demoledor *m,* -ora *f.*

demolition [ˌdemə'lɪʃən] N derribo *m,* demolición *f;* **~ area, ~ zone** zona *f* de demolición; **~ squad** pelotón *m* de demolición.

demon ['diːmən] ① N demonio *m.*

② ADJ **(a) the ~ drink** la bebida infernal, el alcohol del demonio. **(b)** (*) **he's a ~ squash-player** es un as en el squash*, jugando al squash es fabuloso*.

demonetization [diːˌmʌnɪtaɪ'zeɪʃən] N desmonetización *f.*

demonetize [diː'mʌnɪtaɪz] VT desmonetizar.

demoniac [dɪ'məʊnɪæk] ADJ, N demoníaco *m,* -a *f.*

demoniacal [ˌdiːmə'naɪəkəl] ADJ demoníaco, demoníaco.

demonic [dɪ'mɒnɪk] ADJ *(lit) forces, possession, influence* demoníaco; *(fig) energy, laughter* demoníaco, diabólico.

demonize ['diːmənaɪz] VT demonizar.

demonology [ˌdiːmə'nɒlədʒɪ] N demonología *f.*

demonstrable ['demənstrəbl] ADJ demostrable.

demonstrably ['demənstrəblɪ] ADV manifiestamente, obviamente; **a ~ false statement** una afirmación manifiestamente falsa.

demonstrate ['demənstreɪt] ① VT demostrar.

② VI manifestarse, hacer una manifestación *(against* para protestar contra, *in favour* a favor de).

demonstration [ˌdemən'streɪʃən] N **(a)** demostración *f,* prueba *f;* manifestación *f;* **~ model** modelo *m* de demostración. **(b)** *(Pol)* manifestación *f.*

demonstrative [dɪ'mɒnstrətɪv] ① ADJ **(a)** *(Gram)* demostrativo. **(b)** *person* exagerado, exaltado; **not very ~** más bien reservado.

② N demostrativo *m.*

demonstrator ['demənstreɪtər] N *(Pol)* manifestante *mf;* *(Univ etc)* ayudante *mf* (en un laboratorio).

demoralization [dɪˌmɒrəlaɪ'zeɪʃən] N desmoralización *f.*

demoralize [dɪ'mɒrəlaɪz] VT desmoralizar.

demoralizing [dɪ'mɒrəlaɪzɪŋ] ADJ desmoralizador.

Demosthenes [dɪ'mɒsθəniːz] NM Demóstenes.

demote [dɪ'məʊt] VT degradar.

demotic [dɪ'mɒtɪk] ADJ demótico.

demotion [dɪ'məʊʃən] N degradación *f.*

demur [dɪ'mɜːr] ① N: **without ~** sin reparo, sin poner reparos.

② VI objetar, poner reparos.

demure [dɪ'mjʊər] ADJ grave, solemne; *(modest)* recatado; *(coy)* modoso, de una coquetería disimulada; **in a ~ little voice** en tono dulce y algo coqueta.

demurely [dɪ'mjʊəlɪ] ADV gravemente, solemnemente; recatadamente; con una coquetería disimulada; en tono dulce y algo coqueta.

demureness [dɪ'mjʊənɪs] N gravedad *f,* solemnidad *f;* recato *m;* modosidad *f.*

demurrage [dɪ'mʌrɪdʒ] N *(Naut)* estadía *f.*

demurrer [dɪ'mʌrər] N *(Jur)* ≈ excepción *f* perentoria.

demystification [diːˌmɪstɪfɪ'keɪʃən] N desmistificación *f.*

demystify [diː'mɪstɪfaɪ] VT desmistificar.

demythification [diːˌmɪθɪfɪ'keɪʃən] N desmitificación *f.*

demythify [diː'mɪθɪfaɪ] VT desmitificar.

demythologize [ˌdiːmɪ'θɒlədʒaɪz] VT desmitificar.

den [den] N *(animal's)* madriguera *f,* guarida *f;* *(private room)* estudio *m,* gabinete *m;* **~ of iniquity, ~ of vice** templo *m* del vicio; **~ of thieves** ladronera *f.*

denationalization ['diːˌnæʃnəlaɪ'zeɪʃən] N desnacionalización *f.*

denationalize [diː'næʃnəlaɪz] VT desnacionalizar.

denatured [diː'neɪtʃəd] ADJ: **~ alcohol** *(US)* alcohol *m* desnaturalizado.

dendrochronology [ˌdendrəʊkrə'nɒlədʒɪ] N dendrocronología *f.*

dengue ['deŋɡɪ] N dengue *m.*

denial [dɪ'naɪəl] N *(of request)* denegación *f,* negativa *f;* *(of report etc)* desmentido *m,* desmentimiento *m;* *(self~)* abnegación *f.*

denier ['deniər] N **(a)** *(weight)* denier *m;* **25 ~ stockings** medias *fpl* de 25 denier. **(b)** *(coin)* denario *m.*

denigrate ['denɪɡreɪt] VT denigrar.

denigration [ˌdenɪ'ɡreɪʃən] N denigración *f.*

denigratory [ˌdenɪ'ɡreɪtərɪ] ADJ denigratorio.

denim ['denɪm] N dril *m* (de algodón); tela *f* vaquera; **~ jacket** chaqueta *f* vaquera, saco *m* vaquero *(LAm);* **~s** pantalón *m* de dril, vaqueros *mpl.*

denizen ['denɪzn] N habitante *mf;* vecino *m,* -a *f,* morador *m,* -ora *f.*

Denmark ['denmɑːk] N Dinamarca *f.*

denominate [dɪ'nɒmɪneɪt] VT denominar.

denomination [dɪˌnɒmɪ'neɪʃən] N **(a)** *(name)* denominación *f.* **(b)** *(class)* clase *f,* categoría *f;* *(of coin etc)* valor *m;* *(of measure, weight)* unidad *f;* *(Eccl)* secta *f,* confesión *f.*

denominational [dɪˌnɒmɪ'neɪʃənl] ADJ *(Eccl)* sectario; *(US) school* confesional.

denominator [dɪ'nɒmɪneɪtər] N: **(lowest) common ~** (mínimo) denominador *m* común.

denotation [ˌdiːnəʊ'teɪʃən] N **(a)** *(gen, also Ling, Philos)* denotación *f;* *(meaning)* sentido *m.* **(b)** *(symbol)* símbolo *m,* señal *f.*

denotative [dɪ'nəʊtətɪv] ADJ *(Ling)* denotativo.

denote [dɪ'nəʊt] VT denotar; indicar, significar; *(Ling, Philos)* denotar; **what does this ~?** ¿qué quiere decir esto?

dénouement [deɪ'nuːmɒn] N desenlace *m.*

denounce [dɪ'naʊns] VT *(to police etc)* denunciar; *treaty* denunciar, abrogar; *(inveigh against)* censurar.

denouncement [dɪ'naʊnsmənt] = **denunciation.**

denouncer [dɪ'naʊnsər] N denunciante *mf.*

dense [dens] ADJ **(a)** denso; espeso, compacto, tupido. **(b)** (*) *person* duro de mollera.

densely ['denslɪ] ADV densamente; espesamente; **~ populated** con gran densidad de población.

denseness ['densnɪs] N, **density** ['densɪtɪ] N densidad *f;* lo espeso, lo compacto, lo tupido.

dent [dent] ① N abolladura *f;* *(in edge)* mella *f;* **to make a ~ in*** afectar malamente, hacer estragos en.

② VT abollar; mellar; **his reputation was somewhat ~ed** su reputación quedaba algo deslustrada.

dental ['dentl] ① ADJ dental; **~ nurse** enfermero *m,* -a *f* dental; **~ sci-**

ence odontología f; ~ **surgeon** dentista mf, odontólogo m, -a f.
2 N dental f.
dental floss ['dentl,flɒs] N hilo m de higiene dental.
dented ['dentɪd] ADJ abollado, con abolladuras.
dentifrice ['dentɪfrɪs] N dentífrico m.
dentine ['dentiːn] N dentina f, esmalte m dental.
dentist ['dentɪst] N dentista mf, odontólogo m, -a f; ~'s **surgery**, ~'s **office** (US) consultorio m dental.
dentistry ['dentɪstrɪ] N odontología f, dentistería f.
dentition [den'tɪʃən] N dentición f.
denture ['dentʃər] N dentadura f; (false teeth, also ~s) dentadura f postiza.
denuclearize [diː'njuːklɪəraɪz] VT desnuclearizar.
denude [dɪ'njuːd] VT (Geol etc) denudar; (strip) despojar (of de).
denuded [dɪ'njuːdɪd] ADJ terrain denudado; ~ **of** despojado de.
denunciation [dɪ,nʌnsɪ'eɪʃən] N denuncia f, denunciación f; (inveighing) censura f.
denunciator [dɪ'nʌnsɪeɪtər] N denunciante mf.
Denver ['denvər] ATTR: ~ **boot**, ~ **clamp** cepo m.
▼ **deny** [dɪ'naɪ] 1 VT possibility, truth of statement etc negar; request denegar; charge rechazar; report desmentir; faith renegar de; **he denies me his help** me niega su ayuda; **he denies that he said it, he denies having said it** niega haberlo dicho; **I don't ~ it** no lo niego; **there's no ~ing it** es innegable; **he was not to be denied** no se conformaba con la negativa; no iba a quedar en menos; **he was not going to be denied his revenge** nada iba a impedir su venganza.
2 VR: **to ~ o.s.** privarse; **to ~ o.s. sth** privarse de algo, no permitirse algo.
deodorant [diː'əʊdərənt] N desodorante m.
deodorize [diː'əʊdəraɪz] VT desodorizar.
deontology [,diːɒn'tɒlədʒɪ] N deontología f.
deoxidize [diː'ɒksɪdaɪz] VT desoxidar.
deoxygenate [,diː'ɒksɪdʒəneɪt] VT deoxigenar.
deoxyribonucleic [dɪ'ɒksɪ,raɪbəʊnjuː'kleɪɪk] ADJ: ~ **acid** ácido m desoxirribonucleico.
dep. (Rail etc) ABBR of **departs** sale.
depart [dɪ'pɑːt] 1 VT: **to ~ this life** partir de esta vida.
2 VI partir, irse, marcharse (from de); (train etc) salir (at a, for para, from de); **to ~ from** custom, truth etc apartarse de, desviarse de.
departed [dɪ'pɑːtɪd] N: **the ~** el difunto, la difunta.
department [dɪ'pɑːtmənt] 1 N departamento m; (of business) sección f; (of learning, activity) ramo m, especialidad f; (US Pol) ministerio m; **D~ of State** (US) Ministerio m de Asuntos Exteriores; **in that ~ of the game** en ese aspecto del juego.
2 ATTR: ~ **store** (grandes) almacenes mpl, tienda f por departamento (Carib).
departmental [,diːpɑːt'mentl] ADJ departamental; ~ **policy** política f del departamento; ~ **head** jefe m de sección.
departmentalization [,diːpɑːt,mentəlaɪ'zeɪʃən] N división f en departamentos, compartimentación f.
departmentalize [,diːpɑːt'mentə,laɪz] VT dividir en departamentos, compartimentar.
departure [dɪ'pɑːtʃər] 1 N (a) partida f, ida f; (of train etc) salida f; **'D~s'** (Aer) 'Salidas'; **to take one's ~** marcharse.
(b) (fig) desviación f (from de); **new ~** rumbo m nuevo, nueva orientación f; novedad f; **this is a ~ from the norm** esto se aparta de lo normal; **this is a ~ from the truth** esto no representa la verdad.
2 ATTR: ~ **board** (Aer, Rail) tablón m de salidas; ~ **gate** (Aer) puerta f de embarque; ~ **language** (Ling) lengua f de origen; ~ **lounge** (Aer) sala f de embarque; ~ **platform** andén m de salida; ~ **time** hora f de salida.
depend [dɪ'pend] VI: **it ~s** eso depende, según; **it ~s what you mean** depende de lo que Vd quiera decir.
♦ **depend on** VT circumstances, result etc depender de; (rely on) contar con, confiar en; **can we ~ on you?** ¿podemos contar contigo?; **can we ~ on you to do it?** ¿podemos contar contigo para hacerlo?, ¿podemos confiar en que tú lo hagas?; **she ~s on her own resources** ella cuenta con sus propios recursos; **he has to ~ on his pen** tiene que vivir de su pluma; **you may ~ (up)on it** es cosa segurísima; **~ing on the weather, we can go either way** según el tiempo que haga, podemos ir por una ruta o por la otra; **~ing on the individual, there may be problems** según el individuo, puede haber problemas.
dependability [dɪ,pendə'bɪlɪtɪ] N seguridad f; seriedad f, formalidad f.
dependable [dɪ'pendəbl] ADJ thing seguro; person serio, formal.
dependance [dɪ'pendəns] = **dependence**.
dependant [dɪ'pendənt] N familiar mf dependiente; **have you any ~s?** ¿tiene personas a su cargo?
dependence [dɪ'pendəns] N (depending) dependencia f (on de); (reliance) confianza f (on en); (subordination) subordinación f (on a); ~

on drugs drogodependencia f.
dependency [dɪ'pendənsɪ] N (a) (Pol) posesión f. (b) (Ling) dependencia f.
dependent [dɪ'pendənt] 1 ADJ dependiente (on de); (subordinate: also Gram) subordinado (on a); **to be ~ on** depender de.
2 N familiar mf dependiente.
depersonalize [diː'pɜːsənəlaɪz] VT despersonalizar.
depict [dɪ'pɪkt] VT representar, pintar.
depiction [dɪ'pɪkʃən] N representación f.
depilatory [dɪ'pɪlətərɪ] 1 ADJ depilatorio.
2 N (also ~ **cream**) depilatorio m.
deplane [diː'pleɪn] VI (US) salir del avión, desembarcar.
deplenish [dɪ'plenɪʃ] VT (reduce) reducir; (empty) vaciar.
deplete [dɪ'pliːt] VT agotar; mermar, reducir.
depletion [dɪ'pliːʃən] N agotamiento m; merma f, reducción f.
▼ **deplorable** [dɪ'plɔːrəbl] ADJ lamentable, deplorable; **it would be ~ if** sería lamentable que + subj.
deplorably [dɪ'plɔːrəblɪ] ADV lamentablemente, deplorablemente; **in ~ bad taste** de un mal gusto lamentable; **it has been ~ exaggerated** ha sido exagerado de un modo lamentable.
deplore [dɪ'plɔːr] VT lamentar, deplorar; **it is to be ~d** es de lamentar, es deplorable.
deploy [dɪ'plɔɪ] 1 VT desplegar.
2 VI desplegarse.
deployment [dɪ'plɔɪmənt] N despliegue m.
depolarization [diː,pəʊləraɪ'zeɪʃən] N despolarización f.
depolarize [diː'pəʊlə,raɪz] VT despolarizar.
depoliticize [,diːpə'lɪtɪsaɪz] VT despolitizar.
depopulate [diː'pɒpjʊleɪt] VT despoblar, desertizar.
depopulation ['diː,pɒpjʊ'leɪʃən] N despoblación f.
deport [dɪ'pɔːt] 1 VT deportar.
2 VR: **to ~ o.s.** comportarse.
deportation [,diːpɔː'teɪʃən] N deportación f.
deportation order [,diːpɔː'teɪʃən,ɔːdər] N orden f de deportación.
deportee [,diːpɔː'tiː] N deportado m, -a f.
deportment [dɪ'pɔːtmənt] N conducta f, comportamiento m; (carriage) porte m, modo m de andar.
depose [dɪ'pəʊz] 1 VT deponer; destituir.
2 VI declarar, deponer.
deposit [dɪ'pɒzɪt] 1 N (a) (Geol) depósito m, yacimiento m; (Chem, dregs) poso m, sedimento m.
(b) (Fin etc) depósito m; entrada f; fianza f; (pledge) señal f; (act of ~ing money in account) imposición f, ingreso m; (on hire purchase, car) depósito m, abono m (LAm); (on house) desembolso m inicial; **to have £50 on ~** tener 50 libras en cuenta de ahorros; **to leave £50 ~** hacer un desembolso inicial de 50 libras; **to lose one's ~** (Brit Pol) perder el depósito.
2 VT (a) (place, lay) depositar; eggs poner.
(b) (entrust etc) depositar (in en).
(c) (leave) depositar (with en), dejar (with con).
(d) (Geol, Chem) depositar, sedimentar.
(e) (Fin) depositar; (pledge) dar para señal; (money in account) depositar, ingresar (in en), (esp savings account) imponer (in en); **to ~ £X on a house** hacer un desembolso inicial de X libras para una casa, dar una entrada de X libras por una casa.
3 ATTR: (Brit) ~ **account** cuenta f de depósitos a plazo, cuenta f a plazo fijo; ~ **slip** hoja f de ingreso.
depositary [dɪ'pɒzɪtərɪ] N (a) (person) depositario m, -a f. (b) = **depository**.
deposition [,diːpə'zɪʃən] N (a) deposición f. (b) (Jur) declaración f, deposición f.
depositor [dɪ'pɒzɪtər] N depositante mf, impositor m, -ora f, imponente mf; cuentacorrentista mf.
depository [dɪ'pɒzɪtərɪ] N depositaría f, almacén m; (fig) pozo m; ~ **library** (US) biblioteca f de depósito.
depot ['depəʊ] N (storehouse) depósito m, almacén m; (Mil HQ) depósito m; (Brit: for vehicles) parque m, cochera f; (buses, US Rail) estación f.
depot ship ['depəʊ'ʃɪp] N buque m nodriza.
depravation [,deprə'veɪʃən] N depravación f.
deprave [dɪ'preɪv] VT depravar.
depraved [dɪ'preɪvd] ADJ depravado, perverso, vicioso.
depravity [dɪ'prævɪtɪ] N depravación f, perversión f.
deprecate ['deprɪkeɪt] VT desaprobar, lamentar.
deprecating ['deprɪkeɪtɪŋ] ADJ tone etc de desaprobación.
deprecatingly ['deprɪkeɪtɪŋlɪ] ADV con desaprobación.
deprecatory ['deprɪkətərɪ] ADJ de desaprobación.
depreciate [dɪ'priːʃɪeɪt] 1 VT depreciar; (fig) desestimar.
2 VI depreciarse, perder valor, bajar de precio.
depreciation [dɪ,priːʃɪ'eɪʃən] N depreciación f; (of value) amortización f; ~ **account** cuenta f de amortización; ~ **allowance** reservas fpl para depreciaciones.

depredations [ˌdeprɪˈdeɪʃənz] NPL estragos *mpl*.

depress [dɪˈpres] VT (*push down*) presionar, deprimir; *status* rebajar; *trade* paralizar; *price* hacer bajar; (*dispirit*) deprimir, abatir, desalentar.

depressant [dɪˈpresnt] 1 ADJ (*Med*) deprimente, sedante.

2 N (*Med*) deprimente *m*, sedante *m*.

depressed [dɪˈprest] ADJ *area* deprimido, de elevado paro obrero; *person* abatido, desalentado, pesimista; *market* deprimido; *period* de depresión; **to feel ~ about** sentirse pesimista por.

depressing [dɪˈpresɪŋ] ADJ triste, deprimente.

depressingly [dɪˈpresɪŋlɪ] ADV tristemente, en tono pesimista; **it was a ~ familiar story** era la triste historia de siempre.

depression [dɪˈpreʃən] N (*Fin, Met etc*) depresión *f*; (*slump*) crisis *f* económica, depresión *f*, bache *m*; (*in ground, road*) bache *m*, hoyo *m*; (*dejection*) depresión *f*, desaliento *m*, abatimiento *m*.

depressive [dɪˈpresɪv] 1 ADJ depresivo.

2 N depresivo *m*, -a *f*.

depressurization [dɪˌpreʃəraɪˈzeɪʃən] N descompresión *f*.

depressurize [diːˈpreʃəˌraɪz] VT despresurizar.

deprivation [ˌdeprɪˈveɪʃən] N privación *f*; **a great ~** una gran pérdida.

deprive [dɪˈpraɪv] 1 VT: **to ~ sb of sth** privar a uno de algo.

2 VR: **to ~ o.s. of sth** privarse de algo; **don't ~ yourself!** ¡no te vayas a quedar sin nada!

deprived [dɪˈpraɪvd] ADJ *child* desventajado, desvalido.

deprogramme, (*US, also freq Comput*) **deprogram** [diːˈprəʊgræm] VT desprogramar.

dept ABBR *of* **department** departamento *m*.

depth [depθ] N (**a**) profundidad *f* (*also fig*); (*of room*) fondo *m*; (*width*) ancho *m*; (*of colour, feeling*) intensidad *f*; **~ of field** (*Phot*) profundidad *f* del campo; **defence in ~** defensa *f* en profundidad; **investigation in ~** investigación *f* en profundidad; **to be 5 metres in ~** tener una profundidad de 5 metros; **to study a subject in ~** estudiar un tema a fondo; **he was out of his ~** (*lit*) le cubría el agua; **I'm out of my ~ with physics** (*fig*) no entiendo nada de física; **to get out of one's ~** (*lit*) meterse donde le cubre a uno, perder pie; (*fig*) meterse en honduras, salirse de su terreno.

(**b**) **~s: in the ~s of the sea** en los abismos del mar; **from the ~s of the mine** desde lo más hondo de la mina; **the ~s of degradation** (*fig*) la mayor degradación; **the ~s of despair** la mayor desesperación; **in the ~s of one's heart** en lo más hondo del corazón; **in the ~s of winter** en lo más crudo del invierno.

depth charge [ˈdepθtʃɑːdʒ] N carga *f* de profundidad.

deputation [ˌdepjʊˈteɪʃən] N diputación *f*, delegación *f*.

depute [dɪˈpjuːt] VT diputar, delegar; **to ~ sb to do sth** diputar a uno para que haga algo.

deputize [ˈdepjʊtaɪz] VI: **to ~ for sb** sustituir a uno, desempeñar las funciones de uno.

deputy [ˈdepjʊtɪ] 1 ADJ suplente; **~ chairman** vicepresidente *m*, -a *f*; **~ director** vicerrector *m*, -ora *f*; **~ head, ~ manager** subdirector *m*, -ora *f*; **~ minister** viceministro *m*, -a *f*.

2 N sustituto *m*, -a *f*; suplente *mf*; (*Pol*) diputado *m*, -a *f*; (*agent*) representante *mf*.

derail [dɪˈreɪl] VT hacer descarrilar.

derailment [dɪˈreɪlmənt] N descarrilamiento *m*.

derange [dɪˈreɪndʒ] VT desarreglar, descomponer; *person* volver loco, desquiciar; **to be ~d** estar desquiciado, padecer un trastorno mental.

derangement [dɪˈreɪndʒmənt] N desarreglo *m*; (*Med*) trastorno *m* mental.

Derby, derby[1] [ˈdɑːbɪ] N (*Brit Sport*) (**a**) Derby *m* (*importante carrera de caballos en Inglaterra*). (**b**) **local d~** derby *m*, encuentro *m* entre dos equipos locales.

derby[2] [ˈdɑːbɪ] N (*US: also ~ hat*) hongo *m* (*sombrero*).

Derbys N (*Brit*) ABBR *of* **Derbyshire**.

deregulate [diːˈregjʊleɪt] VT desregular.

deregulation [diːˌregjʊˈleɪʃən] N desregulación *f*.

derelict [ˈderɪlɪkt] 1 ADJ abandonado.

2 N derelicto *m*.

dereliction [ˌderɪˈlɪkʃən] N abandono *m*; **~ of duty** negligencia *f*.

deride [dɪˈraɪd] VT ridiculizar, mofarse de.

de rigueur [dərɪˈgɜːr] ADV de rigor.

derision [dɪˈrɪʒən] N irrisión *f*, mofas *fpl*; **this was greeted with ~** en esto hubo risas.

derisive [dɪˈraɪsɪv] ADJ burlón, mofador, irónico.

derisively [dɪˈraɪsɪvlɪ] ADV burlonamente.

derisory [dɪˈraɪsərɪ] ADJ *quantity etc* irrisorio, ridículo.

derivation [ˌderɪˈveɪʃən] N derivación *f*.

derivative [dɪˈrɪvətɪv] 1 ADJ (*gen, Ling*) derivado; *work* poco original.

2 N derivado *m*.

derive [dɪˈraɪv] 1 VT derivar (*from* de); *profit, advantage* sacar, obtener (*from* de); **~d demand** demanda *f* derivada.

2 VI derivar(se) (*from* de); **to ~ from, to be ~d from** (*fig*) proceder

de, provenir de.

dermatitis [ˌdɜːməˈtaɪtɪs] N dermatitis *f*.

dermatologist [ˌdɜːməˈtɒlədʒɪst] N dermatólogo *m*, -a *f*.

dermatology [ˌdɜːməˈtɒlədʒɪ] N dermatología *f*.

dermis [ˈdɜːmɪs] N dermis *f*.

derogatory [dɪˈrɒgətərɪ] ADJ despectivo.

derrick [ˈderɪk] N grúa *f*; (*of oil well*) derrick *m*, torre *f* de perforación.

derring-do [ˈderɪŋˈduː] N (*liter*) gestas *fpl*, hazañas *fpl*.

derringer [ˈderɪndʒər] N pistola *f* de cañón corto y calibre ancho.

derv [dɜːv] N (*Brit*) gas-oil *m*.

dervish [ˈdɜːvɪʃ] N derviche *m*; (*fig*) salvaje *m*.

DES N (*Brit*) ABBR *of* **Department of Education and Science**.

desalinate [diːˈsælɪneɪt] VT desalinar.

desalination [diːˌsælɪˈneɪʃən] N desalinación *f*; **~ plant** planta *f* potabilizadora (de agua de mar).

descale [diːˈskeɪl] VT desincrustar; **descaling agent** agente *m* desincrustante; **descaling product** producto *m* desincrustante.

descant [ˈdeskænt] 1 N discante *m*.

2 VI: **to ~ on** disertar largamente sobre.

descend [dɪˈsend] 1 VT descender, bajar.

2 VI descender, bajar (*from de*); **to ~ from** *ancestors etc* descender de; **to ~ on** caer sobre; (*as visitors*) invadir; **to ~ to** (*as inheritance*) pasar a; (*lower o.s.*) rebajarse a; **to ~ to** + *ger* rebajarse a + *infin*.

descendant [dɪˈsendənt] N descendiente *mf*; **to leave no ~s** no dejar descendencia.

descending [dɪˈsendɪŋ] ADJ descendente; **in ~ order** en orden descendente.

descent [dɪˈsent] N (**a**) (*Geog*) pendiente *f*, declive *m*; (*coming down*) descendimiento *m* (*also Rel*), bajada *f*; (*fall*) descenso *m* (*in* de).

(**b**) (*raid*) ataque *m* (*on* sobre), incursión *f*.

(**c**) (*origin*) origen *m*, familia *f*; **of Italian ~** de ascendencia italiana.

descramble [ˈdiːˈskræmbl] VT (*TV*) descodificar.

descrambler [ˈdiːˈskræmblər] N (*TV*) descodificador *m*.

describe [dɪsˈkraɪb] VT describir (*also Geom*); **to ~ sb as** calificar a uno de.

description [dɪsˈkrɪpʃən] N (**a**) descripción *f*; **it was beyond** (*or* **past**) **~** superaba toda descripción. (**b**) (*sort*) clase *f*, género *m*.

descriptive [dɪsˈkrɪptɪv] ADJ descriptivo.

descriptivism [dɪsˈkrɪptɪvɪzəm] N descriptivismo *m*.

descriptivist [dɪsˈkrɪptɪvɪst] N descriptivista *mf*.

descry [dɪsˈkraɪ] VT divisar.

Desdemona [ˌdezdɪˈməʊnə] NF Desdémona.

desecrate [ˈdesɪkreɪt] VT profanar.

desecration [ˌdesɪˈkreɪʃən] N profanación *f*.

deseed [ˌdiːˈsiːd] VT *fruit* despepitar.

desegregate [diːˈsegrəgeɪt] VT desegregar.

desegregation [ˈdiːˌsegrəˈgeɪʃən] N desegregación *f*.

deselect [ˌdiːsɪˈlekt] VT no renovar la candidatura de, revocar el nombramiento de.

deselection [diːsɪˈlekʃən] N no renovación *f* de la candidatura, revocación *f* del nombramiento.

desensitize [diːˈsensɪtaɪz] VT desensibilizar, insensibilizar; (*Phot*) hacer insensible a la luz.

desert[1] [ˈdezət] 1 ADJ desierto; **~ island** isla *f* desierta; **~ rat** rata *f* del desierto.

2 N desierto *m*.

desert[2] [dɪˈzɜːt] 1 VT (*Mil, Jur etc*) desertar de; *person* abandonar, desamparar, dejar; **his luck ~ed him** la suerte le abandonó.

2 VI (*Mil*) desertar (*from* de, *to* a).

desert boots [ˈdezətˌbuːts] NPL botines *mpl* de ante.

deserted [dɪˈzɜːtɪd] ADJ *road, place* desierto; *wife etc* abandonado.

deserter [dɪˈzɜːtər] N (*Mil*) desertor *m*; (*Pol*) tránsfuga *mf*.

desertification [ˌdezəˌtɪfɪˈkeɪʃən] N desertización *f*.

desertify [deˈzɜːtɪfaɪ] VT desertizar.

desertion [dɪˈzɜːʃən] N deserción *f* (*also Mil*), abandono *m*.

deserts [dɪˈzɜːts] NPL lo merecido; **to get one's (just) ~** llevar su merecido.

deserve [dɪˈzɜːv] 1 VT merecer, ser digno de; **he got what he ~d** llevó su merecido.

2 VI: **to ~ well of** merecer ser bien tratado por; **to ~ to** + *infin* merecer + *infin*.

deservedly [dɪˈzɜːvɪdlɪ] ADV merecidamente.

deserving [dɪˈzɜːvɪŋ] ADJ meritorio; **to be ~ of** merecer, ser digno de.

déshabillé [ˌdeɪzæˈbiːeɪ] N desabillé *m*.

desiccant [ˈdesɪkənt] N secante *m*.

desiccate [ˈdesɪkeɪt] VT desecar.

desiccated [ˈdesɪkeɪtɪd] ADJ (**a**) (*lit*) deshidratado; **~ coconut** coco rallado y seco. (**b**) (*fig*) *person* marchito, mustio.

desiccation [ˌdesɪˈkeɪʃən] N desecación *f*.

desideratum [dɪˌzɪdəˈrɑːtəm] N, PL **desiderata** [dɪˌzɪdəˈrɑːtə] desiderátum *m*.

design [dɪˈzaɪn] 1 N (**a**) (*Tech etc*) diseño *m*; (*pattern of cloth, wallpaper*

etc) dibujo *m*; (*of car etc*) diseño *m*; estilo *m*, líneas *fpl*; (*preliminary sketch*) bosquejo *m*; proyecto *m*; (*Theat, Cine*) boceto *m*; (*of building etc*) estilo *m*; (*ground plan*) distribución *f*; (*art of* ~) dibujo *m*; **~ department** sección *f* de proyectos; **~ studio** estudio *m* de diseños.
(b) (*aim*) intención *f*, propósito *m*; (*plan*) plan *m*, proyecto *m*; **~s** (*pej*) malas intenciones *fpl* (*on* con respecto a); **grand ~** plan *m* general, (*Mil*) estrategia *f* general; **by ~** adrede, intencionalmente; **to have (one's) ~s on** tener sus proyectos sobre, tener la mira puesta en.
2 VT (*contrive*) idear; (*plan*) proyectar; (*Tech*) diseñar, proyectar; *pattern* dibujar; (*sketch*) bosquejar; **a well ~ed house** una casa bien distribuida; **a well ~ed programme** un programa bien concebido; **to be ~ed to** + *infin* estar diseñado para + *infin*, estar proyectado para + *infin*; (*fig*) tener la intención de + *infin*, ir encaminado a + *infin*; **it was not ~ed for that** no fue proyectado con esa finalidad.
3 VI: **to ~ to** + *infin* proponerse + *infin*.
designate 1 ['dezɪgnɪt] ADJ designado, nombrado.
2 ['dezɪgneɪt] VT (*name*) denominar; (*appoint*) nombrar (*to* + *infin* para que + *subj*); (*point to*) señalar; (*destine*) designar.
designation [,dezɪg'neɪʃən] N (*name*) denominación *f*; (*appointment*) nombramiento *m*, designación *f*.
designedly [dɪ'zaɪnɪdlɪ] ADV de propósito.
design engineer [dɪ'zaɪn,endʒɪ'nɪəʳ] N ingeniero *m* diseñador, ingeniera *f* diseñadora.
designer [dɪ'zaɪnəʳ] 1 N (*Tech*) diseñador *m*, proyectista *mf*; (*draughtsman*) delineante *m*; (*Art*) dibujante *mf*; (*dress* ~) modisto *m*, -a *f*; (*Theat*) escenógrafo *m*, -a *f*; (*TV*) diseñador *m*, -ora *f*.
2 ATTR: **~ clothes** ropa *f* de diseño; **~ drug** droga *f* de laboratorio; **~ jeans** vaqueros *mpl* de marca; **~ stubble** barba *f* con 'look' de tres días.
designing [dɪ'zaɪnɪŋ] 1 ADJ intrigante.
2 N diseño *m*, el diseñar.
desirability [dɪ,zaɪərə'bɪlɪtɪ] N lo apetecible, lo atractivo, carácter *m* atractivo; deseabilidad *f*, conveniencia *f*; **the ~ of the plan is not in question** que el proyecto en sí es deseable nadie lo duda.
desirable [dɪ'zaɪərəbl] ADJ (*arousing desire*) apetecible, atractivo; (*proper*) deseable, conveniente; **oh ~ creature!** ¡oh prenda de mi corazón!; **I don't think it ~ to** + *infin* no creo que sea conveniente + *infin*.
desirably [dɪ'zaɪərəblɪ] ADV: **~ located** con una situación ideal; **~ priced** a un precio ideal.
desire [dɪ'zaɪəʳ] 1 N deseo *m* (*for* de, *to* + *infin* de + *infin*); **I haven't the least ~ to go** no tengo el menor deseo de ir; **to meet sb's ~** satisfacer los deseos de uno.
2 VT (a) (*want*) desear; querer tener; **to ~ to do** desear hacer; **what does madam ~?** ¿qué manda la señora?; **it leaves much to be ~d** deja mucho que desear.
(b) to ~ sb to do sth (*wish*) rogar a uno hacer algo; (*order*) mandar a uno hacer algo.
desirous [dɪ'zaɪərəs] ADJ: **~ of** deseoso de; **to be ~ that** querer que + *subj*; **to be ~ to** + *infin* desear + *infin*.
desist [dɪ'zɪst] VI: **to ~ from sth** desistir de algo; **to ~ from** + *ger* dejar de + *infin*; **we begged him to ~** le rogamos dejarlo, le rogamos no continuar.
desk [desk] 1 N (*in office, study etc*) mesa *f* de trabajo; (*Scol*) pupitre *m*; (*bureau*) escritorio *m*; (*of ministry, newspaper*) sección *f*; (*Brit: in shop, restaurant*) caja *f*.
2 ATTR: **~ clerk** (*US*) recepcionista *mf*; **~ diary** agenda *f* de mesa, diario *m* de escritorio; **~ job** trabajo *m* de escritorio; **~ lamp** lámpara *f* de escritorio; **~ pad** bloc *m* de notas; **~ study** estudio *m* sobre el papel.
desk-bound ['deskbaʊnd] ADJ sedentario.
desktop ['desktɒp] ATTR de sobremesa, de oficina, de escritorio; **~ publishing** autoedición *f*.
desolate 1 ['desəlɪt] ADJ (*lonely*) solitario; (*deserted*) desierto, deshabitado; (*ruinous*) arruinado; (*barren*) desolado, yermo, desierto; (*dreary*) triste; *person* triste, afligido.
2 ['desəleɪt] VT asolar, arrasar; *person* afligir; **we were utterly ~d** quedamos profundamente afligidos.
desolately ['desəlɪtlɪ] ADV *say etc* tristemente.
desolation [,desə'leɪʃən] N (a) (*act*) arrasamiento *m*. (b) (*state*) desolación *f*, lo desierto *etc*; soledad *f*; (*of person*) aflicción *f*.
despair [dɪs'pɛəʳ] 1 N (a) desesperación *f*; **to be in ~** estar desesperado.
(b) he is the ~ of his parents les trae locos a sus padres.
2 VI perder la esperanza, desesperar(se) (*of* de); **his life is ~ed of** se desespera de su vida; **don't ~!** ¡ánimo!
despairing [dɪs'pɛərɪŋ] ADJ desesperado.
despairingly [dɪs'pɛərɪŋlɪ] ADV desesperadamente.
despatch [dɪs'pætʃ] = **dispatch**.
desperado [,despə'rɑːdəʊ] N criminal *m*, bandido *m*.
desperate ['despərɪt] ADJ (a) (*hopeless*) desesperado; *plight, situation* desesperado, muy grave; *urgency* apremiante; *need* extremo; *measure*

arriesgado; *resistance* heroico; *effort* furioso, violento; (*reckless from despair*) dispuesto a arriesgarlo todo; capaz de hacer cualquier locura; **he was ~ for money** necesitaba dinero con urgencia; **we are getting ~** empezamos a perder la esperanza; **he's a ~ man** es un hombre sumamente peligroso; **I was ~ to see her** quería a toda costa verla, moría por verla.
(b) (*) atroz, fatal*.
desperately ['despərɪtlɪ] ADV desesperadamente; *fight etc* furiosamente, heroicamente; **we ~ need it** lo necesitamos urgentemente; **~ bad** terriblemente malo; **~ ill** gravemente enfermo.
desperation [,despə'reɪʃən] N desesperación *f*; **in ~** desesperado.
despicable [dɪs'pɪkəbl] ADJ vil, despreciable.
despicably [dɪs'pɪkəblɪ] ADV despreciablemente.
despise [dɪs'paɪz] VT despreciar, desdeñar.
despite [dɪs'paɪt] PREP a pesar de.
despoil [dɪs'pɔɪl] VT despojar (*of* de).
despondence [dɪs'pɒndəns] N, **despondency** [dɪs'pɒndənsɪ] N abatimiento *m*, desaliento *m*, pesimismo *m*.
despondent [dɪs'pɒndənt] ADJ abatido, deprimido; *letter etc* de tono triste, pesimista; **he was very ~ about our chances** habló en términos pesimistas de nuestras posibilidades.
despot ['despɒt] N déspota *m*.
despotic [des'pɒtɪk] ADJ despótico.
despotically [des'pɒtɪkəlɪ] ADV despóticamente.
despotism ['despətɪzəm] N despotismo *m*.
des. res.* ['dez'rez] N = **desirable residence**.
dessert* [dɪ'zɜːt] N postre *m*; **what is there for ~?** ¿qué hay de postre?
dessert apple [dɪ'zɜːt,æpl] N manzana *f* para repostería.
dessert plate [dɪ'zɜːt,pleɪt] N plato *m* de postre.
dessertspoon [dɪ'zɜːtspuːn] N (*Brit*) cuchara *f* de postre.
destabilization [diː,steɪbɪlaɪ'zeɪʃən] N desestabilización *f*.
destabilize [diː'steɪbɪlaɪz] VT desestabilizar.
destination [,destɪ'neɪʃən] N destino *m* (*also Rail etc*).
destine ['destɪn] VT destinar (*for, to* para); **to be ~d to** + *infin* estar llamado a + *infin*; **it was ~d to fail** estuvo condenado a fracasar; **it was ~d to happen this way** forzosamente tuvo que ocurrir así.
destiny ['destɪnɪ] N destino *m*.
destitute ['destɪtjuːt] ADJ (a) (*poverty-stricken*) indigente, desamparado; necesitado; **to be ~** estar en la miseria.
(b) ~ of desprovisto de.
destitution [,destɪ'tjuːʃən] N indigencia *f*, miseria *f*.
destroy [dɪs'trɔɪ] VT destruir; (*kill*) matar; *pet* sacrificar; *vermin* exterminar; (*finish*) aniquilar, acabar con, anular.
destroyer [dɪs'trɔɪəʳ] N destructor *m*.
destruct [dɪ'strʌkt] 1 VT destruir.
2 VI destruirse.
3 ATTR: **~ button** botón *m* de destrucción; **~ mechanism** mecanismo *m* de destrucción.
destructible [dɪs'trʌktəbl] ADJ destructible.
destruction [dɪs'trʌkʃən] N destrucción *f*; (*fig*) ruina *f*, perdición *f*; **to test a machine to ~** someter una máquina a pruebas límite.
destructive [dɪs'trʌktɪv] ADJ destructivo, destructor; *animal* dañino; **to be ~ of** ser nocivo a, ser peligroso para, ser perjudicial para.
destructively [dɪs'trʌktɪvlɪ] ADV destructivamente.
destructiveness [dɪ'strʌktɪvnɪs] N destructividad *f*.
destructor [dɪs'trʌktəʳ] N (*Brit: also* **refuse ~**) incinerador *m* (*or* quemador *m*) de basuras.
desuetude [dɪ'sjʊɪtjuːd] N desuso *m*; **to fall into ~** caer en desuso.
desulphurization [,diːsʌlfəraɪ'zeɪʃən] N desulfurización *f*.
desultory ['desəltərɪ] ADJ *way of working etc* poco metódico; esporádico; *fire etc* intermitente, irregular; (*disconnected*) inconexo.
det. (a) ABBR *of* **detached**. (b) ABBR *of* **detective**.
detach [dɪ'tætʃ] VT separar (*from* de); desvincular (*from* de); (*unstick*) despegar; (*Mil*) destacar.
detachable [dɪ'tætʃəbl] ADJ separable; (*Tech*) desprendible; desmontable.
detached [dɪ'tætʃt] ADJ (a) separado, suelto; *collar* postizo; *house* independiente; (*Brit*) **~ house** casa *f* independiente, hotelito *m*, chalet *m*; **~ retina** desprendimiento *m* de la retina; **to become ~** separarse, desprenderse; **they live ~ from everything** viven desligados de todo.
(b) (*unbiased*) imparcial, objetivo; indiferente, desinteresado; **to take a ~ view of** considerar objetivamente.
detachment [dɪ'tætʃmənt] N (a) (*act*) separación *f*. (b) (*Mil*) destacamento *m*. (c) (*fig*) imparcialidad *f*, objetividad *f*.
▼ **detail** ['diːteɪl] 1 N (a) detalle *m*, pormenor *m*; **in ~** en detalle, detalladamente; **to go into ~s** entrar en detalles, pormenorizar; **they planned it down to the last ~** lo planearon todo hasta en los menores detalles.
(b) (*Mil*) destacamento *m*.
2 VT (a) detallar, referir con sus pormenores.
(b) (*Mil*) destacar (*to* + *infin* para + *infin*).

detailed ['di:teɪld] ADJ detallado, pormenorizado.

detain [dɪ'teɪn] VT **(a)** (*arrest*) detener. **(b)** (*keep waiting*) retener; **I was ~ed at the office** me demoré en la oficina; **I was ~ed by fog** el retraso se debe a la niebla.

detainee [,di:teɪ'ni:] N detenido *m*, -a *f*.

detect [dɪ'tekt] VT descubrir; (*perceive*) percibir; *crime* resolver, *criminal* identificar; (*Tech, by radar etc*) detectar.

detectable [dɪ'tektəbl] ADJ perceptible, detectable.

detection [dɪ'tekʃən] N descubrimiento *m*; percepción *f*; resolución *f*, identificación *f*; detección *f*.

detective [dɪ'tektɪv] ☐ N detective *mf*.
☐ ADJ *attr* detectivesco; **~ chief inspector** (*Brit*) ≃ comisario *m*; **~ chief superintendent** (*Brit*) ≃ superintendente *m* general; **~ constable** (*Brit*) ≃ agente *m*; **~ inspector** (*Brit*) ≃ inspector *m*; **~ sergeant** (*Brit*) ≃ cabo *m*; **~ superintendent** (*Brit*) ≃ comisario *m* jefe; **~ story** novela *f* policíaca; **~ work** (*fig*) trabajo *m* detectivesco, trabajo *m* de investigación.

detector [dɪ'tektər] N detector *m*; **~ van** (*Brit*) camioneta *f* detectora.

détente ['deɪtɑ̃:nt] N distensión *f*.

detention [dɪ'tenʃən] ☐ N detención *f*, arresto *m*.
☐ ATTR: **~ centre** (*Brit*) centro *m* de detención; **~ home** (*US*) centro *m* de rehabilitación.

deter [dɪ'tɜ:r] VT (*discourage*) desalentar; (*dissuade*) disuadir (*from* + *ger* de + *infin*); (*prevent*) impedir (*from doing* hacer); *enemy etc* refrenar; **I was ~red by the cost** el precio me hizo abandonar la idea; **a weapon which ~s nobody** un arma que no refrena a nadie, un arma sin fuerza disuasoria; **don't let the weather ~ you** no dejes de hacerlo por el mal tiempo.

detergent [dɪ'tɜ:dʒənt] ☐ ADJ detergente.
☐ N detergente *m*.

deteriorate [dɪ'tɪərɪəreɪt] VI empeorar, deteriorarse, degradarse.

deterioration [dɪ,tɪərɪə'reɪʃən] N deterioro *m*, empeoramiento *m* (*in* de), degradación *f*.

determinable [dɪ'tɜ:mɪnəbl] ADJ determinable.

determinant [dɪ'tɜ:mɪnənt] ☐ ADJ determinante.
☐ N determinante *m*.

determinate [dɪ'tɜ:mɪnɪt] ADJ **(a)** (*frm: fixed*) determinado. **(b)** (*Jur*) *sentence* definitivo.

determination [dɪ,tɜ:mɪ'neɪʃən] N **(a)** (*act*) determinación *f*. **(b)** (*resolve*) resolución *f*; **he set off with great ~** partió muy resuelto; **in his ~ to do it** estando resuelto a hacerlo.

determinative [dɪ'tɜ:mɪnətɪv] ☐ ADJ determinativo.
☐ N determinativo *m*.

determine [dɪ'tɜ:mɪn] ☐ VT **(a)** (*ascertain, define*) determinar; *date etc* señalar, fijar; *scope, limits, boundary* definir; *future course, person's fate* decidir; *dispute* determinar, resolver; (*be the deciding factor in*) determinar; **to ~ what is to be done** decidir lo que hay que hacer; **to ~ whether sth is true** decidir si algo es verdad; **we couldn't ~ who it was** no podíamos decidir quién era; **demand ~s supply** la demanda determina la oferta; **to be ~d by** depender de.
(b) (*impel*) **this ~d him to go** esto le determinó a ir.
(c) (*resolve*) **to ~ to do sth** decidir hacer algo, resolverse a hacer algo.
☐ VI: **to ~ on** optar por.

▼ **determined** [dɪ'tɜ:mɪnd] ADJ *person* resuelto; *effort* resuelto, enérgico; **he's very ~ about it** está muy empeñado en ello; **to be ~ to do sth** estar resuelto a hacer algo.

determiner [dɪ'tɜ:mɪnər] N determinador *m*.

determining [dɪ'tɜ:mɪnɪŋ] ADJ decisivo, determinante; **~ factor** factor *m* determinante.

determinism [dɪ'tɜ:mɪnɪzəm] N determinismo *m*.

determinist [dɪ'tɜ:mɪnɪst] ☐ ADJ determinista.
☐ N determinista *mf*.

deterministic [dɪ,tɜ:mɪ'nɪstɪk] ADJ determinista.

deterrence [dɪ'terəns] N disuasión *f*.

deterrent [dɪ'terənt] ☐ ADJ disuasivo, disuasorio.
☐ N freno *m*, impedimento *m* (*on, to* para); medida *f* represiva; (*Mil*) fuerza *f* disuasiva, fuerza *f* disuasoria, contraamenaza *f*; (**nuclear**) **~** fuerza *f* disuasiva (nuclear); **to act as a ~** to servir como un freno para, ser una amenaza a, refrenar.

detest [dɪ'test] VT detestar, aborrecer.

detestable [dɪ'testəbl] ADJ detestable, aborrecible, odioso.

detestation [,di:tes'teɪʃən] N detestación *f*, aborrecimiento *m*; **to hold in ~** aborrecer, odiar.

dethrone [di:'θrəʊn] VT destronar.

dethronement [di:'θrəʊnmənt] N destronamiento *m*.

detonate ['detəneɪt] ☐ VT hacer detonar.
☐ VI detonar, estallar.

detonation [,detə'neɪʃən] N detonación *f*.

detonator ['detəneɪtər] N detonador *m*, cápsula *f* fulminante.

detour ['di:tʊər] ☐ N rodeo *m*, vuelta *f*; desviación *f*; (*Aut*) desvío *m*; **to make a ~** desviarse, hacer un rodeo.

☐ VT (*US*) desviar.
☐ VI (*US*) desviarse, hacer un rodeo.

detox* ['di:tɒks] ABBR *of* **detoxicate, detoxication, detoxification, detoxify.**

detoxicate [di:'tɒksɪkeɪt] VT, **detoxify** [di:'tɒksɪfaɪ] VT desintoxicar.

detoxication [di:,tɒksɪ'keɪʃən] N, **detoxification** [di:,tɒksɪfɪ'keɪʃən] N desintoxicación *f*.

detract [dɪ'trækt] VI: **to ~ from** quitar mérito (*or* atractivo *etc*) a, desvirtuar, restar valor a.

detraction [dɪ'trækʃən] N detracción *f*.

detractor [dɪ'træktər] N detractor *m*, -ora *f*.

detriment ['detrɪmənt] N perjuicio *m*; **to the ~ of** en perjuicio de, en detrimento de; **without ~ to** sin perjuicio de, sin perjudicar (a).

detrimental [,detrɪ'mentl] ADJ perjudicial (*to* a, para).

detritus [dɪ'traɪtəs] N detrito *m*, detritos *mpl*.

de trop [də'trəʊ] ADV: **to be ~** estar de más, sobrar.

deuce¹ [dju:s] ADV (*Tennis*) deuce, cuarenta iguales.

deuce² [dju:s] N: **a ~ of a row** un tremendo jaleo; **a ~ of a mess** una terrible confusión; **the ~ it is!** ¡qué demonio!; **what the ...?** ¿qué demonios ...?; **where the ~ ...?** ¿dónde demonios ...?; **to play the ~ with** estropear, echar a perder; *see also* **devil.**

deuced [dju:st] ☐ ADJ maldito.
☐ ADV diabólicamente, terriblemente.

Deuteronomy [,dju:tə'rɒnəmɪ] N Deuteronomio *m*.

deuterium [dju:'tɪərɪəm] N deuterio *m*; **~ oxide** óxido *m* deutérico.

deutschmark ['dɔɪtʃmɑ:k] N marco *m* alemán.

devaluate [di:'væljʊeɪt] VT desvalorizar, desvalorar.

devaluation [,dɪvæljʊ'eɪʃən] N desvalorización *f*, devaluación *f*.

devalue ['di:'vælju:] VT desvalorizar, devaluar.

devastate ['devəsteɪt] VT devastar, asolar; *person* hundir en la tristeza; **we were simply ~d** nos quedamos anonadados con la noticia.

devastating ['devəsteɪtɪŋ] ADJ devastador; (*fig*) *argument etc* arrollador; *news* pasmoso; *defeat* contundente; *wit* muy agudo; *charm* irresistible.

devastatingly ['devəsteɪtɪŋlɪ] ADJ *beautiful, funny* devastadoramente; arrolladoramente.

devastation [,devə'steɪʃən] N **(a)** (*act*) devastación *f*. **(b)** (*state*) devastación *f*, ruinas *fpl*.

develop [dɪ'veləp] ☐ VT desarrollar (*also Math*); idear, crear; desenvolver; (*encourage*) fomentar; *process* perfeccionar; *plan* elaborar; *land* urbanizar; *resources, mine etc* explotar; *site* ampliar; (*Phot*) revelar; *engine trouble* empezar a tener; *disease* coger, empezar a sufrir de, mostrar los síntomas de; *tendency* coger, dar en; *liking* mostrar, acusar; *power* producir, desarrollar.
☐ VI **(a)** desarrollarse; progresar, avanzar; evolucionar; **how is the book ~ing?** ¿qué tal te va el libro?; **to ~ into** transformarse en. **(b)** (*symptoms etc*) aparecer, mostrarse.

developed [dɪ'veləpt] ADJ **(a)** *country, world* desarrollado. **(b)** *sense of humour, of justice* profundo.

developer [dɪ'veləpər] N **(a)** (*also* **property ~**) promotor *m* inmobiliario, promotora *f* inmobiliaria, promotor *m*, -ora *f* de construcciones. **(b)** (*Phot*) revelador *m*.

developing [dɪ'veləpɪŋ] ☐ ADJ *country* en (vías de) desarrollo.
☐ ATTR: **~ bath** baño *m* de revelado.

development [dɪ'veləpmənt] ☐ N **(a)** (*gen*) desarrollo *m*; progreso *m*; evolución *f*; (*encouragement*) promoción *f*, fomento *m*; (*of resources*) explotación *f*. **(b)** (*of land*) urbanización *f*; ensanche *m*, ampliación *f*; (*as housing*) colonia *f*. **(c)** (*Phot*) revelado *m*. **(d)** (*also* **new ~**) hecho *m* nuevo, nueva situación *f*; cambio *m*; novedad *f*; adelanto *m*, avance *m*; **what is the latest ~?** ¿hay alguna novedad?; **there are no new ~s to report** no hay cambios que registrar.
☐ ATTR: **~ agency** agencia *f* de promoción; **~ area** polo *m* de promoción; **~ bank** banco *m* de desarrollo; **~ company** compañía *f* de explotación; **~ corporation** (*of new town*) corporación *f* de desarrollo, corporación *f* de promoción; **~ officer** director *m*, -ora *f* de promoción; **~ plan** plan *m* de desarrollo.

developmental [dɪ,veləp'mentl] ADJ relativo al desarrollo; **~ economics** ciencias *fpl* económicas relativas a los países en desarrollo.

deviance ['di:vɪəns] N, **deviancy** N ['di:vɪənsɪ] (*gen, also Psych*) desviación *f*; (*sexual*) perversión *f*.

deviant ['di:vɪənt] ☐ ADJ desviado; pervertido; (*Ling*) desviado.
☐ N pervertido *m*, -a *f*.

deviate ['di:vɪeɪt] VI desviarse (*from* de).

deviation [,di:vɪ'eɪʃən] N desviación *f* (*also Med*).

deviationism [,di:vɪ'eɪʃənɪzəm] N desviacionismo *m*.

deviationist [,di:vɪ'eɪʃənɪst] ☐ ADJ desviacionista.
☐ N desviacionista *mf*.

device [dɪ'vaɪs] N **(a)** (*Mech*) aparato *m*, mecanismo *m*, dispositivo *m*; (*explosive*) artefacto *m*; **nuclear ~** ingenio *m* nuclear.
(b) (*scheme*) estratagema *f*, recurso *m*.
(c) (*emblem*) emblema *m*; (*motto*) lema *m*.
(d) to leave sb to his own ~s dejar a uno hacer lo que le dé la gana; dejar que uno se las arregle por sí solo.

devil ['devl] **1** N **(a)** diablo *m*, demonio *m*; **little ~** diablillo *m*; **a poor ~** un pobre diablo; **you ~!** ¡eres el demonio!; **be a ~ and drink it** a ver si te atreves a beberlo; **~'s advocate** abogado *m* del diablo.
(b) *(Jur)* aprendiz *m* (de abogado); *(Typ)* aprendiz *m* de imprenta.
(c) *(intensifier)* **a ~ of a mess** una terrible confusión; **a ~ of a noise** un ruido de todos los demonios; **we had the ~ of a job, we had the ~'s own job** nos costó un ojo de la cara *(to get* obtener); **it's a ~ of a problem** un problema diabólico; **why the ~ didn't you say so?** ¿por qué demonios no me lo has dicho?
(d) *(phrases)* **the ~!** ¡demonio!; **the ~ it is!** ¡qué demonio!; **what the ~?** ¿qué demonios ...?; **like the ~** como el demonio; **the ~ take it!** ¡que se lo lleve el diablo!; **go to the ~!** ¡vete al diablo!; **he's going to the ~** se está arruinando; **to be between the ~ and the deep blue sea** estar entre la espada y la pared; **better the ~ we know** vale más lo malo conocido que lo bueno por conocer; **the ~ finds work for idle hands** cuando el diablo no tiene que hacer con el rabo mata moscas; **to give the ~ his due** para ser justo hasta con el diablo; **there'll be the ~ to pay** esto nos va a costar muy caro, ahí será el diablo; **to play the ~ with** arruinar, estropear; **to raise the ~** armar la gorda; **talk of the ~!** ¡hablando del ruin de Roma por la puerta asoma!
(e) *(fire etc)* arrojo *m*, energía *f*.
2 VT **(a)** *meat* asar con mucho picante.
(b) *(US*)* fastidiar.
3 VI: **to ~ for** *(Jur)* trabajar de aprendiz para.
devilfish ['devlfɪʃ] N raya *f*, manta *f*.
devilish ['devlɪʃ] **1** ADJ diabólico.
2 ADV a la mar de; **~ cunning** la mar de ingenioso.
devilishly ['devlɪʃlɪ] ADV *behave* endemoniadamente.
devil-may-care ['devlmeɪ'kɛəʳ] ADJ despreocupado; *(rash)* temerario, arriesgado.
devilment ['devlmənt] N diablura *f*; = **devilry**.
devilry ['devlrɪ] N *(wickedness)* maldad *f*, crueldad *f*; *(mischief)* diablura *f*, travesura *f*, pillería *f*.
devious ['diːvɪəs] ADJ *path* tortuoso, sinuoso; *means, method, plan* intrincado, enrevesado; *person* taimado.
deviously ['diːvɪəslɪ] ADV *act, behave* taimadamente.
deviousness ['diːvɪəsnɪs] N carácter *m* taimado.
devise [dɪ'vaɪz] VT idear, inventar, imaginar.
deviser [dɪ'vaɪzəʳ] N *(of scheme, plan)* inventor *m*, -ora *f*, maquinador *m*, -ora *f*.
devitalize [diː'vaɪtəlaɪz] VT debilitar, privar de vitalidad, desvitalizar.
devoid [dɪ'vɔɪd] ADJ: **~ of** desprovisto de.
devolution [ˌdiːvə'luːʃən] N delegación *f* (de poderes); *(Pol)* traspaso *m* de competencias.

┌─ **DEVOLUTION** ─┐

ⓘ *En el Reino Unido se usa el término* **devolution** *para referirse al proceso de traspaso de competencias de la Administración central a las regiones, especialmente a Escocia y Gales. Pero éste es un tema muy polémico, puesto que hay distintas opiniones respecto al nivel de descentralización al que se quiere llegar. Algunos abogan por la creación de asambleas legislativas autónomas para Escocia y Gales, pero dentro del Reino Unido, mientras que los movimientos nacionalistas rechazan la transferencia de competencias y reclaman una independencia total.*

devolve [dɪ'vɒlv] **1** VT delegar.
2 VI: **to ~ upon** incumbir a, corresponder a; **it ~s upon me to +** *infin* me toca a mí + *infin*.
Devonian [de'vəʊnɪən] ADJ *(Geol)* devónico.
devote [dɪ'vəʊt] **1** VT dedicar *(to* a; *to* + *ger* a + *infin)*; **he is ~d to her** la quiere con verdadera devoción; **this room is ~d to Goya** esta sala está dedicada a Goya; **this chapter is ~d to politics** este capítulo trata de la política.
2 VR: **to ~ o.s. to** dedicarse a.
devoted [dɪ'vəʊtɪd] ADJ leal, fiel, dedicado.
devotedly [dɪ'vəʊtɪdlɪ] ADV con devoción.
devotee [ˌdevəʊ'tiː] N devoto *m*, -a *f* (of de); partidario *m*, -a *f* (of de).
devotion [dɪ'vəʊʃən] N **(a)** devoción *f* (to a); *(to studies etc)* dedicación *f* (to a); entrega *f*; *(of friend etc)* lealtad *f*. **(b)** **~s** *(Rel)* oraciones *fpl*.
devotional [dɪ'vəʊʃənl] ADJ piadoso, devoto.
devour [dɪ'vaʊəʳ] VT devorar *(also fig)*, comerse; **to be ~ed with curiosity** no caber en sí de curiosidad; **to be ~ed with envy** morirse de envidia.
devouring [dɪ'vaʊərɪŋ] ADJ *(fig)* absorbente.
devout [dɪ'vaʊt] ADJ devoto, piadoso.
devoutly [dɪ'vaʊtlɪ] ADV con devoción, piadosamente.
dew [djuː] N rocío *m*.
dewdrop ['djuːdrɒp] N gota *f* de rocío.
dewlap ['djuːlæp] N papada *f*.
dewpond ['djuːpɒnd] N charca *f* formada por el rocío.
dewy ['djuːɪ] ADJ rociado; lleno de rocío; *eyes* húmedo.

dewy-eyed ['djuːɪ'aɪd] ADJ ingenuo.
dexterity [deks'terɪtɪ] N destreza *f*.
dexterous ['dekstrəs] ADJ, **dextrous** ['dekstrəs] ADJ diestro; **by the ~ use of** por el diestro uso de.
dexterously ['dekstrəslɪ] ADV, **dextrously** ['dekstrəslɪ] ADV diestramente, hábilmente.
dextrose ['dekstrəʊs] N dextrosa *f*.
DG N ABBR *of* **Director General.**
dg ABBR *of* **decigram(s)** decigramo(s) *m(pl)*.
DH N *(Brit)* ABBR *of* **Department of Health.**
DHSS N *(Brit, formerly)* ABBR *of* **Department of Health and Social Security.**
DI N ABBR *of* **Donor Insemination.**
Di [daɪ] NF *familiar form of* **Diana.**
di... [daɪ] PREF di....
diabetes [ˌdaɪə'biːtiːz] N diabetes *f*.
diabetic [ˌdaɪə'betɪk] **1** ADJ diabético.
2 N diabético *m*, -a *f*.
diabolic(al) [ˌdaɪə'bɒlɪk(əl)] ADJ diabólico.
diabolically [ˌdaɪə'bɒlɪkəlɪ] ADV *behave etc* diabólicamente, endemoniadamente; **~ difficult** endemoniadamente difícil; **it was ~ hot** hacía un calor de infierno.
diachronic [ˌdaɪə'krɒnɪk] ADJ diacrónico.
diacritic [ˌdaɪə'krɪtɪk] **1** ADJ *(also ~al)* diacrítico.
2 NM signo *m* diacrítico.
diadem ['daɪədem] N diadema *f*.
diaeresis, *(US)* **dieresis** [daɪ'erɪsɪs] N diéresis *f*.
diagnose ['daɪəgnəʊz] VT diagnosticar.
diagnosis [ˌdaɪəg'nəʊsɪs] N, PL **diagnoses** [ˌdaɪəg,nəʊsiːz] *(of patient)* diagnóstico *m*; *(science)* diagnosis *f*.
diagnostic [ˌdaɪəg'nɒstɪk] ADJ diagnóstico.
diagnostics [ˌdaɪəg'nɒstɪks] N diagnóstica *f*.
diagonal [daɪ'ægənl] **1** ADJ diagonal.
2 N diagonal *f*.
diagonally [daɪ'ægənəlɪ] ADV diagonalmente.
diagram ['daɪəgræm] N esquema *m*, diagrama *m*, gráfico *m*.
diagrammatic [ˌdaɪəgrə'mætɪk] ADJ esquemático.
▼ **dial** ['daɪəl] **1** N esfera *f*, cuadrante *m*, cara *f* *(LAm)*; *(Aut: on dashboard)* reloj *m*; *(Telec)* disco *m*; **(‡)** jeta* *f*, cara *f*; **~ code** *(US)* prefijo *m*; **~ tone** *(US Telec)* tono *m* de marcar.
▼ **2** VT marcar.
dialect ['daɪəlekt] **1** N dialecto *m*.
2 ATTR dialectal; **~ atlas** atlas *m* lingüístico; **~ survey** estudio *m* de geografía lingüística.
dialectal [ˌdaɪə'lektl] ADJ dialectal.
dialectic [ˌdaɪə'lektɪk] ADJ dialéctico.
dialectical [ˌdaɪə'lektɪkəl] ADJ dialéctico.
dialectic(s) [ˌdaɪə'lektɪk(s)] N dialéctica *f*.
dialectology [ˌdaɪəlek'tɒlədʒɪ] N dialectología *f*.
dialling, *(US)* **dialing** ['daɪəlɪŋ] N marcación *f*, discado *m*; **~ code** prefijo *m*; **~ tone** *(Brit)* tono *m* de marcar.
dialogue, *(US)* **dialog** ['daɪəlɒg] **1** N diálogo *m*.
2 VI dialogar.
dial-up service ['daɪəl,ʌp'sɜːvɪs] N servicio *m* de enlace entre cuadrantes.
dialysis [daɪ'æləsɪs] N diálisis *f*.
diamanté [diːə'mɑːnteɪ] ADJ de strass.
diameter [daɪ'æmɪtəʳ] N diámetro *m*.
diametrical [ˌdaɪə'metrɪkəl] ADJ diametral.
diametrically [ˌdaɪə'metrɪkəlɪ] ADV: **~ opposed to** diametralmente opuesto.
diamond ['daɪəmənd] N diamante *m*; *(Archit etc, Baseball)* losange *m*; **~s** *(Cards)* diamantes *mpl*, *(in Spanish pack)* oros *mpl*; **~ cut ~** tal para cual; **~ jubilee** sexagésimo aniversario *m*; **~ merchant** tratante *mf* en diamantes; **~ necklace** collar *m* de diamantes; **~ wedding** bodas *fpl* de diamante.
diamond-cutter ['daɪəmənd,kʌtəʳ] N diamantista *m*.
diamond-shaped ['daɪəmənd,ʃeɪpt] ADJ de forma de losange (or rombo), romboidal.
diamorphine [ˌdaɪə'mɔːfiːn] N diamorfina *f*.
Diana [daɪ'ænə] NF Diana.
diapason [ˌdaɪə'peɪzən] N diapasón *m*.
diaper ['daɪəpəʳ] N *(US)* pañal *m*; **~ pin** imperdible *m*, seguro *m* *(LAm)*; **~ service** servicio *m* de pañales a domicilio.
diaphanous [daɪ'æfənəs] ADJ diáfano.
diaphragm ['daɪəfræm] N diafragma *m*.
diarist ['daɪərɪst] N diarista *mf*.
diarrhoea, *(US)* **diarrhea** [ˌdaɪə'riːə] N diarrea *f*.
diary ['daɪərɪ] N diario *m*; *(engagement ~)* agenda *f*, diario *m*, calendario *m* *(US)*.
diaspora [daɪ'æspərə] N diáspora *f*.
diastole [daɪ'æstəlɪ] N diástole *f*.

diatonic [ˌdaɪə'tɒnɪk] ADJ diatónico; **~ scale** escala f diatónica.

diatribe ['daɪətraɪb] N diatriba f.

dibble ['dɪbl] ① N plantador m.

② VT (also **to ~ in**) plantar con plantador.

dibs [dɪbz] N (a) (Brit‡†) parné‡ m. (b) (US*) **to have ~ on sth** tener derechos sobre algo; **~ on the cookies!** ¡las galletas pa' mí!

dice [daɪs] ① N dado m; (as pl) dados mpl; (shapes) cubitos mpl, cuadritos mpl; **no ~!*** (US) ¡ni hablar!, nada de eso.

② VT vegetables cortar en cubitos; hacer macedonia de; **~d vegetables** macedonia f de legumbres.

③ VI jugar a los dados; **to ~ with death** jugar con la muerte.

dicey* ['daɪsɪ] ADJ (Brit) incierto, dudoso; peligroso; difícil, problemático.

dichotomy [dɪ'kɒtəmɪ] N dicotomía f.

Dick [dɪk] NM familiar form of **Richard.**

dick [dɪk] N (US) (a) (ṽ) polla‡ f. (b) (US‡) detective m.

dickens ['dɪkɪnz] (euph) en muchas frases = **devil.**

Dickensian [dɪ'kenzɪən] ADJ dickensiano.

dicker ['dɪkər] VI (a) vacilar, titubear. (b) (US Comm) regatear, cambalachear.

dickey*, dicky¹* ['dɪkɪ] N (a) (baby talk; also **dicky bird**) pajarito m. (b) (shirt front) pechera f postiza. (c) (Brit: also **~ seat**) spider m.

dickhead‡ ['dɪkhed] N bobo m.

dicky²* ['dɪkɪ] ADJ (Brit) poco firme, inestable; (Med) **to feel ~** sentirse algo indispuesto; **to have a ~ heart** tener una debilidad cardíaca.

dicta ['dɪktə] NPL of **dictum.**

Dictaphone ['dɪktəfəʊn] ® N dictáfono ® m.

dictate ① ['dɪkteɪt] N mandato m; **~s** dictados mpl, preceptos mpl.

② [dɪk'teɪt] VT (a) (say aloud) dictar; (order) mandar, disponer; terms imponer.

(b) **I will not be ~d to** yo no estoy a las órdenes de nadie, a mí no me manda nadie.

③ [dɪk'teɪt] VI: **to ~ to one's secretary** dictar a su secretaria.

dictation [dɪk'teɪʃən] N (a) dictado m; **at ~ speed** a velocidad de dictado; **to take ~** tomar dictado; **to write at the ~ of** escribir al dictado de. (b) (order) mandato m.

dictator [dɪk'teɪtər] N dictador m, -ora f.

dictatorial [ˌdɪktə'tɔːrɪəl] ADJ dictatorio; manner etc dictatorial, imperioso.

dictatorially [ˌdɪktə'tɔːrɪəlɪ] ADV dictatorialmente.

dictatorship [dɪk'teɪtəʃɪp] N dictadura f.

diction ['dɪkʃən] N dicción f; lengua f, lenguaje m.

dictionary ['dɪkʃənrɪ] N diccionario m.

dictum ['dɪktəm] N, PL **dicta** ['dɪktə] sentencia f, aforismo m; (Jur) dictamen m.

did [dɪd] PRET of **do¹.**

didactic [daɪ'dæktɪk] ADJ didáctico.

didactically [dɪ'dæktɪkəlɪ] ADV didácticamente.

diddle* ['dɪdl] VT (Brit) estafar, embaucar; **to ~ sb out of sth** estafar algo a uno.

diddly-squat‡ ['dɪdlɪ'skwɒt] N (US) nada de nada.

didn't ['dɪdənt] = **did not.**

Dido [daɪdəʊ] NF Dido.

die¹ [daɪ] VI morir (from, of de; for por); (wither) marchitarse; (disappear) desvanecerse, desaparecer; (light) palidecer, extinguirse; **to ~ like flies** morir como chinches; **we nearly died!*** (laughter) para morirse de risa, (embarrassment) ¡cómo nos sofocamos!, ¡qué bochorno!; (fear) ¡qué susto!; **never say ~!** ¡ánimo!, ¡mientras hay vida hay esperanza!; **he died a hero** murió como héroe; **the secret died with her** llevó el secreto a la tumba; **the custom dies hard** la costumbre tarda bastante en desaparecer; **to be dying for sth** morirse por algo, perecerse por algo; **to be dying to** + infin morirse por + infin; **to ~ a violent death** tener una muerte violenta, morir de manera violenta.

◆**die away** VI apagarse gradualmente; disminuir; desaparecer; desvanecerse; (sound) dejar poco a poco de oírse, alejarse hasta perderse.

◆**die back** VI (Bot) secarse.

◆**die down** VI (fire) apagarse; (wind) perder su fuerza, amainar; (battle etc) hacerse menos violento; (discontent, excitement, protests) calmarse, sosegarse.

◆**die off** VI morirse, (family, race) irse extinguiendo.

◆**die out** VI extinguirse, desaparecer; (custom) caer en desuso; (of showers etc) desaparecer.

die² [daɪ] N (a) (PL **dice** [daɪs]) dado m; **the ~ is cast** la suerte está echada. (b) (PL **dies** [daɪz]) cuño m, troquel m; matriz f.

die-casting ['daɪˌkɑːstɪŋ] N pieza f fundida a troquel.

diectic [daɪ'ektɪk] N diéctico m.

diehard ['daɪhɑːd] ① ADJ intransigente, empedernido, acérrimo.

② N incondicional mf, intransigente mf.

dieldrin ['diːldrɪn] N dieldrina f.

dielectric [ˌdaɪə'lektrɪk] ① ADJ dieléctrico.

② N dieléctrico m.

diesel ['diːzəl] ① N (a) diesel m. (b) (‡) té m.

② ATTR: **~ engine** motor m diesel; **~ fuel, ~ oil** gasóleo m, gas-oil m; **~ train** tren m diesel.

diesel-electric ['diːzəlɪ'lektrɪk] ADJ dieseleléctrico.

die-sinker ['daɪˌsɪŋkər] N grabador m de troqueles.

die-stamp ['daɪˌstæmp] VT grabar.

diet¹ ['daɪət] ① N régimen m, dieta f; **to be on a ~** estar a régimen; **to go on a ~** ponerse a régimen; **to put sb on a ~** poner a uno a régimen.

② VI estar a régimen.

diet² ['daɪət] N (Pol) dieta f.

dietary ['daɪətərɪ] ADJ dietético; **~ fibre** fibra f dietética.

dieter ['daɪətər] N persona f que está a dieta.

dietetic [ˌdaɪɪ'tetɪk] ① ADJ dietético.

② **~s** N dietética f.

dietician [ˌdaɪɪ'tɪʃən] N dietético m, -a f.

differ ['dɪfər] VI (a) **they ~** (things) son distintos, (persons) no están de acuerdo; **the texts ~** los textos discrepan.

(b) **to ~ from** ser distinto de, diferenciarse de, discrepar de; **how does this ~ from that?** ¿en qué se diferencia éste de aquél?

(c) (personal subject) **I beg to ~** siento tener que disentir; **we ~ed about it** no estábamos de acuerdo sobre ello; **I ~ from you** no estoy de acuerdo contigo; **I ~ from your opinion** discrepo de tu opinión, no comparto tu opinión.

▼ **difference** ['dɪfrəns] N diferencia f; **~ of opinion** desacuerdo m, (euph) controversia f, (euph: quarrel) riña f; **a novel with a ~** una novela que tiene algo distintivo; **it makes no ~** lo mismo da; **as near as makes no ~** con tan poca diferencia que no se nota; **it makes a lot of ~** importa mucho; **what ~ does it make?** ¿qué más da?; **it will make no ~ to us** no nos afectará en lo más mínimo; **that makes all the ~** eso cambia totalmente la cosa; **I'll pay the ~** yo pago la diferencia; **I see no ~ between them** no les veo diferencia alguna; **to split the ~** partir la diferencia.

▼ **different** ['dɪfrənt] ADJ diferente, distinto (from de); **to be as ~ as chalk from cheese** parecerse como día y noche.

differential [ˌdɪfə'renʃəl] ① ADJ diferencial; **~ calculus** cálculo m diferencial.

② N (Math, Aut) diferencial m.

differentiate [ˌdɪfə'renʃɪeɪt] ① VT diferenciar, distinguir (from de).

② VI diferenciarse (also Bio); **to ~ between two things** distinguir entre dos cosas.

differentiation [ˌdɪfərenʃɪ'eɪʃən] N diferenciación f.

differently ['dɪfrəntlɪ] ADV de modo distinto, de otro modo.

difficult ['dɪfɪkəlt] ADJ difícil; **to make life ~ for sb** hacer la vida imposible a uno; see also **EASY, DIFFICULT, IMPOSSIBLE**.

difficulty ['dɪfɪkəltɪ] N dificultad f; (jam) apuro m, aprieto m; **to get into difficulties** hacerse un lío, meterse en apuros, (eg while swimming) encontrarse sin fuerzas para continuar, (ship) encontrarse en peligro; **to have ~ in breathing** tener la respiración penosa; **he's having difficulties with his wife** tiene problemas con su mujer; **we have ~ in getting enough staff** es difícil encontrar bastante personal; **I find ~ in walking** encuentro difícil el andar; **to make difficulties for sb** poner estorbos a uno; **I see no ~ in admitting that ...** no hay dificultad para reconocer que...

diffidence ['dɪfɪdəns] N timidez f, falta f de confianza en sí mismo.

diffident ['dɪfɪdənt] ADJ tímido, falto de confianza en sí mismo.

diffidently ['dɪfɪdəntlɪ] ADV tímidamente, con timidez.

diffract [dɪ'frækt] VT difractar.

diffraction [dɪ'frækʃən] N difracción f.

diffuse ① [dɪ'fjuːs] ADJ difuso; (long-winded) prolijo.

② [dɪ'fjuːz] VT difundir.

③ [dɪ'fjuːz] VI difundirse.

diffused [dɪ'fjuːzd] ADJ difuso.

diffuseness [dɪ'fjuːsnɪs] N prolijidad f.

diffusion [dɪ'fjuːʒən] N difusión f.

dig [dɪg] ① N (a) (archaeological etc) excavación f.

(b) (prod) empujón m; (with elbow) codazo m.

(c) (*: remark) indirecta f, zumba f; **to have a ~ at** aludir irónicamente a, tomar el pelo a.

② (irr: PRET AND PTP **dug**) VT (a) cavar, excavar; (of animals) escarbar; garden cultivar, patch of earth remover con laya; coal extraer, sacar; teeth, nails hincar (into en).

(b) (prod) empujar, dar un codazo a; **to ~ sb in the ribs** dar a uno un codazo en las costillas.

(c) (‡) **I don't ~ jazz** no me gusta el jazz, el jazz no me dice nada; **I really ~ that** eso me chifla*; **~ this!** ¡mira esto!

③ VI cavar; **to ~ deeper into a subject** ahondar en un tema; **to ~ for gold** cavar en busca de oro.

◆**dig in** ① VT manure añadir al suelo.

② VI (a) (Mil) atrincherarse; hacerse fuerte.

(b) (*) empezar a comer, hincar el diente; **~ in!** ¡a comer!

➤ LANGUAGE IN USE: **difference** → 5.3, 26.3 **different** → 5.3

◆**dig into** VT *reserves etc* consumir, usar; **he dug into his pocket** metió la mano en el bolsillo, buscó en el bolsillo; **to ~ into a meal*** empezar a zamparse una comida.

◆**dig out** VT *hole* excavar; *buried object* sacar cavando, extraer; (*from rubble*) desescombrar; *thorn in flesh* extraer; (*fig*) sacar, extraer.

◆**dig over** VT *earth* voltear; *garden* recavar.

◆**dig up** VT desenterrar (*also fig*), descubrir; *flowerbed* remover la tierra de; *potatoes* sacar; *plant* desarraigar; *roadway etc* levantar.

digest [1] ['daɪdʒest] N resumen *m*; (*Jur*) digesto *m*.
[2] [daɪ'dʒest] VT *food* digerir; (*think over*) meditar, digerir; *knowledge, territory* asimilar; *insult* tragarse; *opinion* aceptar.

digestible [dɪ'dʒestəbl] ADJ digerible; **easily ~** fácil de digerir.

digestion [dɪ'dʒestʃən] N digestión *f*.

digestive [dɪ'dʒestɪv] ADJ digestivo; **~ juices** jugos *mpl* digestivos; **~ system** aparato *m* digestivo; **~ tract** canal *m* digestivo.

digger ['dɪgəʳ] N (a) cavador *m*, -ora *f*; (*archaeological*) excavador *m*, -ora *f*; (*Mech*) excavadora *f*. (b) (*) australiano *m*, -a *f*.

digging ['dɪgɪŋ] N (a) (*with spade, of hole etc*) cava *f*; (*Min*) excavación *f*. (b) **~s** (*Min*) material *m* excavado; (*Archaeology*) excavaciones *fpl*.

digit ['dɪdʒɪt] N cifra *f*, número *m*, dígito *m*.

digital ['dɪdʒɪtəl] ADJ digital; **~ clock, ~ watch** reloj *m* digital; **~ computer** ordenador *m* digital; **~ mapping** cartografía *f* digital; **~ network** red *f* digital; **~ recording** grabación *f* digital.

digitalis [ˌdɪdʒɪ'teɪlɪs] N digital *f*.

digitalize ['dɪdʒɪtə,laɪz] VT, **digitize** ['dɪdʒɪtaɪz] VT digitalizar.

digitally ['dɪdʒɪtlɪ] ADV *scan, record, store* digitalmente; **~ remastered** reprocesado digitalmente.

digitizer ['dɪdʒɪtaɪzəʳ] N digitalizador *m*.

diglossia [daɪ'glɒsɪə] N diglosia *f*.

dignified ['dɪgnɪfaɪd] ADJ grave, solemne; *gait etc* majestuoso; *action, ceremony* decoroso; **it's not ~ to** + *infin* no es elegante + *infin*.

dignify ['dɪgnɪfaɪ] VT dignificar; dar un título altisonante a.

dignitary ['dɪgnɪtərɪ] N dignatario *m*, dignidad *f*.

dignity ['dɪgnɪtɪ] N dignidad *f*; **it would be beneath my ~ to** + *infin* desmerecería de mi dignidad + *infin*; **to stand on one's ~** ponerse en su lugar, ponerse tan alto.

digress [daɪ'gres] VI hacer una digresión; (*pej*) divagar; **to ~ from** apartarse de; **but I ~** pero vamos al grano.

digression [daɪ'greʃən] N digresión *f*.

digressive [daɪ'gresɪv] ADJ que se aparta del tema principal.

digs [dɪgz] NPL (*Brit**) pensión *f*, alojamiento *m*.

dike¹ [daɪk] N (*embankment: also fig*) dique *m*; (*ditch*) canal *m*, acequia *f*.

dike²‡ [daɪk] N lesbiana *f*, tortillera‡ *f*.

diktat [dɪk'tɑːt] N diktat *m*, dictamen *m*.

dilapidated [dɪ'læpɪdeɪtɪd] ADJ *building etc* desmoronado, ruinoso; *vehicle etc* desvencijado.

dilapidation [dɪ,læpɪ'deɪʃən] N estado *m* ruinoso; lo desvencijado.

dilate [daɪ'leɪt] [1] VT dilatar.
[2] VI dilatarse; extenderse; **to ~ upon** dilatarse sobre.

dilation [daɪ'leɪʃən] N dilatación *f*.

dilatoriness ['dɪlətərɪnɪs] N tardanza *f*, lentitud *f*.

dilatory ['dɪlətərɪ] ADJ tardo, lento; **to be ~ in replying** tardar mucho en contestar.

dildo ['dɪldəʊ] N consolador *m*.

dilemma [daɪ'lemə] N dilema *m*; **to be in a ~** estar en un dilema.

dilettante [ˌdɪlɪ'tæntɪ] N, PL **dilettanti** [ˌdɪlɪ'tæntɪ] diletante *mf*.

dilettantism [ˌdɪlə'tæntɪzəm] N diletantismo *m*.

diligence ['dɪlɪdʒəns] N diligencia *f*.

diligent ['dɪlɪdʒənt] ADJ diligente.

diligently ['dɪlɪdʒəntlɪ] ADV diligentemente.

dill [dɪl] N eneldo *m*.

dilly* ['dɪlɪ] N (*US*): **she's a ~** (*girl*) está muy bien*; **it's a ~** (*problem*) es un rompecabezas.

dilly-dally ['dɪlɪdælɪ] VI vacilar; titubear; (*loiter*) perder el tiempo.

dilly-dallying ['dɪlɪdælɪŋ] N vacilación *f*; titubeo *m*; pérdida *f* de tiempo.

dilute [daɪ'luːt] [1] ADJ diluido.
[2] VT diluir; (*fig*) adulterar.

dilution [daɪ'luːʃən] N dilución *f*; (*fig*) adulteración *f*.

dim [dɪm] [1] ADJ (a) *light* débil; *sight* turbio; *room etc* oscuro, sombrío; *object, outline* indistinto, confuso; **in the ~ and distant past** en un pasado remoto.
(b) (*) *opinion* poco favorable; **to take a ~ view of sth** ver algo con malos ojos, desaprobar algo.
(c) (*Brit**) *person* lerdo.
[2] VT *light* reducir la intensidad de; *headlamps* bajar; (*fig*) *splendour* ofuscar, oscurecer; *memory* borrar; **to ~ one's lights** (*US Aut*) poner luces de cruce.
[3] VI (*colour, light*) apagarse; (*memory*) difuminarse; (*glory*) empañarse.

dime [daɪm] N (*Canada, US*) moneda de 10 centavos; (*Drugs sl: also ~ bag*) saquito *m* de marijuana de diez dólares; **~ novel** (*US*) novela *f* de cinco duros, novelucha *f*; **~ store** tienda *f* que vende mercadería

barata; **a ~ a dozen** muy barato, (*fig*) a montones.

dimension [dɪ'menʃən] N dimensión *f*.

-dimensional [daɪ'menʃənl] ADJ *ending in compounds*: **two~** bidimensional.

diminish [dɪ'mɪnɪʃ] [1] VT disminuir.
[2] VI disminuir(se).

diminished [dɪ'mɪnɪʃt] ADJ *numbers, speed, strength* reducido; *character, reputation* oscurecido; *value* (*Mus*) disminuido; **a ~ staff** una plantilla reducida; **~ responsibility** (*Jur*) responsabilidad *f* reducida.

diminishing [dɪ'mɪnɪʃɪŋ] ADJ menguante; **law of ~ returns** ley *f* de rendimiento decreciente.

diminuendo [dɪ,mɪnjʊ'endəʊ] [1] N (*Mus*) diminuendo *m*.
[2] VI hacer un diminuendo.

diminution [ˌdɪmɪ'njuːʃən] N disminución *f*.

diminutive [dɪ'mɪnjʊtɪv] [1] ADJ diminuto; (*Gram*) diminutivo.
[2] N diminutivo *m*.

dimly ['dɪmlɪ] ADV *shine etc* débilmente; *see* confusamente; **one could ~ make out forms** se veían indistintamente unos bultos.

dimmer ['dɪməʳ] N regulador *m* de intensidad; (*US Aut*) interruptor *m*; **~ switch** botón *m* de regulación de la intensidad.

dimming ['dɪmɪŋ] N (*of light*) oscurecimiento *m*; (*of mirror, reputation*) empañamiento *m*; (*of headlights*) cambio *m* a cortas.

dimness ['dɪmnɪs] N (*V adj*) debilidad *f*; lo turbio; oscuridad *f*, semioscuridad *f*, lo sombrío; lo indistinto, lo confuso; lo lerdo.

dimple ['dɪmpl] [1] N hoyuelo *m*.
[2] VT formar hoyuelos en; *water* rizar.
[3] VI formarse hoyuelos; (*water*) rizarse.

dimpled ['dɪmpld] ADJ *cheek, chin* con hoyuelo; *hand, arm* con hoyuelos.

dimwit* ['dɪmwɪt] N imbécil *mf*.

dim-witted* ['dɪm'wɪtɪd] ADJ lerdo, imbécil.

din [dɪn] [1] N estruendo *m*, estrépito *m*.
[2] VT: **to ~ sth into sb** meter algo a la fuerza en la cabeza de uno; **I had it ~ned into me as a child** lo aprendí de niño a fuerza de repeticiones.
[3] VI: **it ~s in my ears** me taladra el oído.

dinar ['diːnɑː] N dinar *m*.

din-dins* ['dɪndɪns] NPL (*child's language*) cenita *f*.

dine [daɪn] [1] VT dar de cenar (*or* comer) a; **they ~d me very well** me dieron muy bien de cenar.
[2] VI cenar.

◆**dine in** VI cenar en casa.

◆**dine off** VT cenar.

◆**dine on** VT cenar.

◆**dine out** VI cenar fuera; **he ~d out on the story** le invitaron por el cuento.

diner ['daɪnəʳ] N (a) (*person*) comensal *m*. (b) (*Rail*) coche-comedor *m*; (*US*) restaurante *m* económico; (*US Aut*) cafetería *f* de carretera.

dinero* [dɪ'neərəʊ] N (*US*) plata *f*.

dinette [daɪ'net] N comedor *m* pequeño, comedorcito *m*.

ding-a-ling [ˌdɪŋə'lɪŋ] N (a) (*of bell, telephone*) tilín *m*. (b) (*US*‡) bobo *m*.

dingbat‡ ['dɪŋbæt] N gilipollas‡ *m*.

ding-dong ['dɪŋ'dɒŋ] [1] N: **~!** ¡din dan!, ¡din don!
[2] ADJ *battle* furioso, muy reñido.

dinghy ['dɪŋgɪ] N dingui *m*, bote *m*; (*rubber ~*) lancha *f* neumática.

dinginess ['dɪndʒɪnɪs] N lo deslustrado, deslucimiento *m*; color *m* oscuro; lo sombrío, oscuridad *f*; lo sucio.

dingo ['dɪŋgəʊ] N, PL **dingoes** ['dɪŋgəʊz] dingo *m*.

dingy ['dɪndʒɪ] ADJ (*dull*) deslustrado, deslucido; (*dark in colour*) de color oscuro; *room etc* sombrío, oscuro; (*dirty*) sucio.

dining-car ['daɪnɪŋkɑːʳ] N (*Brit*) coche-comedor *m*, vagón *m* restaurante.

dining-hall ['daɪnɪŋ,hɔːl] N comedor *m*, refectorio *m*.

dining-room ['daɪnɪŋrʊm] N comedor *m*.

dining-table ['daɪnɪŋ,teɪbl] N mesa *f* de comedor.

dink‡ [dɪŋk] N (*US*) tontorrón* *m*, -ona *f*.

dinkie ['dɪŋkɪ] = **dinky** 2.

dinky* ['dɪŋkɪ] [1] ADJ (*Brit*) (*small*) pequeñito *m*; (*nice*) mono, precioso.
[2] N ABBR *of* **double** (*or* **dual**) **income no kids**.

▼ **dinner** ['dɪnəʳ] N (*evening meal*) cena *f*, (*in some regions*) comida *f*; (*lunch*) comida *f*, (*in some regions*) almuerzo *m*; (*public feast*) cena *f*, banquete *m*; (*to mark retirement etc*) cena *f* homenaje; **we were at ~ with the minister** estábamos cenando con el ministro; **can you come to ~?** ¿puedes venir a cenar?; **to have ~** cenar, comer; **when he retired they gave him a ~** cuando se jubiló le obsequiaron con una cena; **we sat down to ~ at 10.30** nos sentamos a cenar a las 10.30.

dinner-bell ['dɪnə,bel] N campana *f* de la cena.

dinner-dance ['dɪnə,dɑːns] N cena *f* seguida de baile.

dinner-duty ['dɪnə,djʊtɪ] N (*Scol*) supervisión *f* de comedor.

dinner-jacket ['dɪnə,dʒækɪt] N (*Brit*) smoking *m*, esmoquin *m*.

dinner-knife ['dɪnə,naɪf] N, PL **dinner-knives** ['dɪnə,naɪvz] cuchillo *m* grande.

dinner-lady ['dɪnə,leɪdɪ] N ayudanta *f* (*en el servicio de comidas en las escuelas*).

dinner-party ['dɪnə,pɑːtɪ] N cena *f*.

dinner-plate ['dɪnə,pleɪt] N plato *m* grande.

dinner-roll ['dɪnə,rəʊl] N panecillo *m*.

dinner-service ['dɪnə,sɜːvɪs] N vajilla *f*, servicio *m* de mesa.

dinner-table ['dɪnə,teɪbl] N mesa *f* de comedor.

dinner-time ['dɪnətaɪm] N hora *f* de cenar (*or* comer).

dinner-trolley ['dɪnə,trɒlɪ] N, **dinner-wagon** ['dɪnə,wægən] N carrito *m* de la comida.

dinosaur ['daɪnəsɔːr] N dinosaurio *m*.

dint¹ [dɪnt] N: **by ~ of** a fuerza de.

dint² [dɪnt] = **dent**.

diocesan [daɪ'ɒsɪsən] ADJ diocesano.

diocese ['daɪəsɪs] N diócesis *f*.

diode ['daɪəʊd] N diodo *m*.

Dionysian [,daɪə'nɪzɪən] ADJ dionisiaco.

Dionysius [,daɪə'nɪsɪəs] NM Dionisio.

dioxide [daɪ'ɒksaɪd] N dióxido *m*.

dioxin [daɪ'ɒksɪn] N dioxina *f*.

dip [dɪp] **1** N (a) (*bath, bathe*) baño *m*; **to go for a ~, to have a ~** darse un chapuzón, darse un remojón, ir a bañarse.
(b) (*Geol*) buzamiento *m*; (*of horizon*) depresión *f*; (*slope*) pendiente *f*; inclinación *f*; (*to one side*) ladeo *m*.
(c) V **lucky**.
(d) (*) **~s** luces *fpl* cortas, luces *fpl* de cruce.
2 VT (a) (*put into liquid*) bañar, mojar (*in, into* en); *pen* mojar; *ladle, scoop etc* meter; *sheep* lavar; **she ~ped her hand into her pocket** metió la mano en el bolsillo.
(b) **to ~ water out with a bucket** sacar agua con un cubo.
(c) *flag* bajar, saludar con; (*Aer*) *wings* saludar con; **to ~ one's lights** (*Brit Aut*) bajar los faros, poner las luces cortas, poner luces de cruce.
3 VI (a) (*slope down*) inclinarse hacia abajo; (*Geol*) buzar; **the road ~s into the valley** la carretera baja hacia el valle.
(b) (*move down: bird, plane*) bajar de picada; **the sun ~ped below the hill** el sol desapareció tras la colina.
(c) **to ~ into one's pocket** meter la mano en el bolsillo; **to ~ into a book** hojear un libro, leer distraídamente un libro.

Dip. ABBR *of* **Diploma**.

Dip Ed ['dɪped] N (*Brit*) ABBR *of* **Diploma in Education** título *de magisterio*.

diphtheria [dɪf'θɪərɪə] N difteria *f*.

diphthong ['dɪfθɒŋ] N diptongo *m*.

diphthongize ['dɪfθɒŋaɪz] **1** VT diptongar.
2 VI diptongarse.

diploma [dɪ'pləʊmə] N diploma *m*.

diplomacy [dɪ'pləʊməsɪ] N diplomacia *f*.

diplomat ['dɪpləmæt] N diplomático *m*, -a *f*.

diplomatic [,dɪplə'mætɪk] **1** ADJ diplomático; **~ bag, ~ pouch** (*US*) valija *f* diplomática; **~ corps, ~ service** cuerpo *m* diplomático; **~ immunity** inmunidad *f* diplomática.
2 N: **the D~*** el cuerpo diplomático.

diplomatically [,dɪplə'mætɪkəlɪ] ADV diplomáticamente.

diplomatist [dɪ'pləʊmətɪst] N diplomático *m*, -a *f*.

dipole ['daɪ,pəʊl] N bipolo *m*.

dipped [dɪpt] ADJ: **~ headlights** luces *fpl* cortas, luces *fpl* de cruce.

dipper¹ ['dɪpər] N (*Orn*) mirlo *m* acuático.

dipper² ['dɪpər] N: **big ~** montaña *f* rusa; **Big D~** (*US Astron*) Osa *f* Mayor.

dipper³ ['dɪpər] N (*Culin*) cazo *m*, cucharón *m*.

dipping ['dɪpɪŋ] N (*Agr*) lavado *m*.

dippy* ['dɪpɪ] ADJ chiflado*.

dipso* ['dɪpsəʊ] = **dipsomaniac**.

dipsomania [,dɪpsəʊ'meɪnɪə] N dipsomanía *f*.

dipsomaniac [,dɪpsəʊ'meɪnɪæk] N dipsomaníaco *m*, -a *f*, dipsómano *m*, -a *f*.

dipstick ['dɪpstɪk] N (a) (*Aut*) varilla *f* (para comprobar el nivel del aceite), cala *f*. (b) (:) gili:: *mf*.

dipswitch ['dɪpswɪtʃ] N (*Brit Aut*) interruptor *m*.

diptych ['dɪptɪk] N díptico *m*.

dir. ABBR *of* **director**.

dire [daɪər] ADJ (a) *event* horrendo, calamitoso. (b) (*: film, book etc*) horrible, fatal*.

direct [daɪ'rekt] **1** ADJ directo; *current* continuo; *answer* claro, inequívoco; *manner, character* abierto, franco; **~ access** (*Comput*) acceso *m* directo; **~ action** acción *f* directa; **~ advertising** publicidad *f* directa; **~ cost** costo *m* directo; **~ current** corriente *f* continua; **~ debit** pago *m* a la orden; **~ debiting** domiciliación *f*; **~ dialling** servicio *m* (telefónico) automático; **~ free kick** golpe *m* libre directo; **~ grant school** (*Brit* †) escuela *f* subvencionada; **~ method** método

m directo; **~ object** complemento *m* directo; **~ rule** gobierno *m* directo; **~ selling** ventas *fpl* directas; **~ speech** oración *f* directa; **~ tax** impuesto *m* directo; **~ taxation** tributación *f* directa.
2 ADV (*in a ~ manner*) directamente; (*straight*) derecho, en línea recta.
3 VT (a) *letter, remark, gaze, attention, film etc* dirigir (*at, to* a).
(b) **can you ~ me to the shop?** ¿me hace el favor de decirme dónde está la tienda?, ¿podría indicarme la dirección de la tienda?
(c) (*control*) dirigir, gobernar, controlar.
(d) (*order*) mandar; **to ~ that ...** mandar que ...; **to ~ sb to do sth** mandar a uno hacer algo.

direction [dɪ'rekʃən] N (a) (*act of managing, also Theat etc*) dirección *f*.
(b) (*course*) dirección *f*; **~ finder** radiogoniómetro *m*; **~ indicator** (*Aut*) intermitente *m*; **in the ~ of** en dirección a, en la dirección de, hacia; **in the opposite ~** en sentido contrario; **in all ~s** por todos lados; **they ran off in different ~s** salieron corriendo cada uno por su lado.
(c) **~s** órdenes *fpl*, instrucciones *fpl*; **~s for use** modo *m* de empleo.

directional [dɪ'rekʃənl] ADJ direccional; **~ aerial** antena *f* dirigida; **~ light** (*Aut*) intermitente *m*.

directionless [dɪ'rekʃənlɪs] ADJ *activity* sin dirección, que no conduce a ninguna parte; **to be/feel ~** andar/sentirse perdido o sin rumbo.

directive [dɪ'rektɪv] N directiva *f*, directriz *f*.

directly [dɪ'rektlɪ] **1** ADV (*in a direct manner*) directamente; (*in a straight line*) derecho, en línea recta; (*Brit: at once*) en seguida; **~ opposite** exactamente enfrente (de).
2 CONJ: **~ you hear it** (*esp Brit*) en cuanto lo oigas.

directness [daɪ'rektnɪs] N franqueza *f*.

director [dɪ'rektər] N director *m* -ora *f*; **~ general** director *m*, -ora *f* general; **D~ of Education** (*Brit*) ≃ Jefe *m* de la Delegación del Ministerio de Educación; **D~ of Public Prosecutions** (*Brit Jur*) ≃ Fiscal *m* General del Estado.

directorate [daɪ'rektərɪt] N (a) (*post*) dirección *f*, cargo *m* de director.
(b) (*body*) junta *f* directiva, consejo *m* de administración.

directorial [daɪrek'tɔːrɪəl] ADJ directivo, directorial; **~ responsibilities** obligaciones *fpl* directivas; responsabilidades *fpl* de administración.

directorship [dɪ'rektəʃɪp] N cargo *m* de director.

▼ **directory** [dɪ'rektərɪ] N (*Telec*) guía *f* telefónica; (*of streets*) guía *f* de calles; (*Comput*) directorio *m*; **~ inquiries** (*Brit*), **~ assistance** (*US*) información *f*.

dirge [dɜːdʒ] N endecha *f*, canto *m* fúnebre.

dirigible ['dɪrɪdʒəbl] **1** ADJ dirigible.
2 N dirigible *m*.

dirk [dɜːk] N (*Scot*) puñal *m*.

dirndl ['dɜːndl] N falda *f* acampanada.

dirt [dɜːt] N (*unclean matter*) suciedad *f*, mugre *f*, (*litter*) basura *f*; (*earth*) tierra *f*; (*mud*) lodo *m*; (*obscenity*) suciedad *f*, inmundicia *f*; (*worthless stuff*) porquería *f*; **~ farmer** (*US**) pequeño granjero *m* (sin obreros); **the book is just ~** el libro es una inmundicia nada más; **to treat sb like ~** tratar a uno como una basura; **to do sb ~*, to do the ~ on sb*** (*US*) hacerle una putada a uno*.

dirt-cheap ['dɜːt'tʃiːp] ADJ tirado, regalado, muy barato.

dirtily ['dɜːtɪlɪ] ADV *eat, live* míseramente; (*fig*) *act, behave* bajamente; *play, fight* suciamente.

dirtiness ['dɜːtɪnɪs] N suciedad *f*.

dirt road ['dɜːt'rəʊd] N (*US*) camino *m* sin firme, camino *m* de tierra.

dirt track ['dɜːt'træk] N pista *f* de ceniza.

dirty ['dɜːtɪ] **1** ADJ sucio; (*grubby*) mugriento; (*stained*) manchado; *trick, play etc* sucio; *novel, story, joke* verde, indecente, sucio; *weather* horrible, feo; **~ old man** viejo *m* verde; **~ tricks department** sección *f* de trampas; **~ war** guerra *f* sucia; **~ weekend*** (*hum*) fin de semana de lujuria; **~ word** palabra *f* fea, palabrota *f*; **to do sb's ~ work for him** hacer los trabajos sucios de uno; **there's been ~ work (at the crossroads)** ha habido trampa, aquí no han jugado limpio.
2 ADV (*) *play etc* sucio*.
3 N: **to do the ~ on sb** (*Brit*) hacer una mala pasada a uno.
4 VT ensuciar; (*stain*) manchar.

dirty-minded [,dɜːtɪ'maɪndɪd] ADJ de mente sucia, de imaginación malsana.

disability [,dɪsə'bɪlɪtɪ] N (a) (*state*) incapacidad *f*; (*physical*) invalidez *f*, minusvalidez *f*, discapacidad *f*; **~ allowance, ~ benefit** subsidio *m* por incapacidad; **~ pension** pensión *f* por incapacidad laboral. (b) (*feature*) impedimento *m*, estorbo *m*, desventaja *f*.

disable [dɪs'eɪbl] VT (*cripple*) estropear, mutilar; *ship etc* inutilizar; (*disqualify etc*) incapacitar, inhabilitar (*for* para).

disabled [dɪs'eɪbld] ADJ *person* minusválido, discapaz.

disablement [dɪs'eɪblmənt] N inhabilitación *f*; (*Med*) minusvalidez *f*; *see also* **disability**.

disabuse [,dɪsə'bjuːz] VT desengañar (*of* de).

disadvantage [,dɪsəd'vɑːntɪdʒ] **1** N desventaja *f*, inconveniente *m*; **to the ~ of** con detrimento de; **to be at a ~** estar en una situación desventajosa; **this put him at a ~** esto le dejó en situación desventajosa; **to be taken at a ~** encontrarse en una situación violenta. [2] VT perjudicar.

disadvantaged [ˌdɪsədˈvɑːntɪdʒd] [1] ADJ desventajado; no privilegiado, marginado; perjudicado. [2] NPL: **the ~** los no privilegiados, los marginados.

disadvantageous [ˌdɪsædvɑːnˈteɪdʒəs] ADJ desventajoso.

disaffected [ˌdɪsəˈfektɪd] ADJ desafecto (*towards* hacia).

disaffection [ˌdɪsəˈfekʃən] N descontento m, desafección f.

disaffiliate [ˌdɪsəˈfɪlɪˌeɪt] VI desafiliarse (*from* de).

▼ **disagree** [ˈdɪsəˈɡriː] VI **(a)** no estar de acuerdo (*about, on* sobre, *with* con), discrepar (*with* de); **I ~ with you** no estoy de acuerdo contigo, discrepo de ti, no comparto esa opinión; **I ~ with bullfighting** yo no apruebo el toreo, no me gustan los toros; **their findings ~** discrepan sus conclusiones.
(b) to ~ with (*of food etc*) sentar mal a, hacer daño a.

disagreeable [ˌdɪsəˈɡriːəbl] ADJ *experience, task* desagradable; (*bad-tempered*) displicente, de mal genio; antipático; *tone of voice etc* malhumorado, áspero; **he was very ~ to me** me trató con bastante aspereza; **I'm rather ~ in the mornings** por la mañana estoy de bastante mal humor.

disagreeableness [ˌdɪsəˈɡriːəblnɪs] N (*of work, experience*) desagrado m; (*of person*) antipatía f.

disagreeably [ˌdɪsəˈɡriːəblɪ] ADV con desagrado.

▼ **disagreement** [ˌdɪsəˈɡriːmənt] N **(a)** desacuerdo m, disconformidad f (*with* con); discrepancia f (*with* de); **so we were in ~** así que discrepamos. **(b)** (*quarrel*) riña f, altercado m.

disallow [ˈdɪsəˈlaʊ] VT no aceptar, no sancionar, rechazar; *goal* anular.

disambiguate [ˌdɪsæmˈbɪɡjʊeɪt] VT *term etc* despejar la ambigüedad de.

disappear [ˌdɪsəˈpɪəʳ] [1] VT (*) hacer desaparecer. [2] VI desaparecer.

disappearance [ˌdɪsəˈpɪərəns] N desaparición f.

▼ **disappoint** [ˌdɪsəˈpɔɪnt] VT decepcionar, desilusionar; *hopes* defraudar; **we were ~ed with the book** el libro nos decepcionó; **we shall be ~ed if you don't come** sentiremos mucho que no vengas; **her daughter ~ed her** su hija la defraudó.

disappointing [ˌdɪsəˈpɔɪntɪŋ] ADJ decepcionante, desilusionante; **it is ~ that ...** es triste que ... + *subj*.

disappointingly [ˌdɪsəˈpɔɪntɪŋlɪ] ADV de manera decepcionante; **it was ~ brief** fue tan breve que decepcionó; **~, nothing happened** a nuestro pesar no pasó nada.

disappointment [ˌdɪsəˈpɔɪntmənt] N **(a)** decepción f, desilusión f; **to our ~** a nuestro pesar. **(b)** (*event*) contratiempo m; decepción f; **~ in love** fracaso m sentimental; **he is a big ~ to us** nos ha decepcionado muchísimo.

disapproval [ˌdɪsəˈpruːvəl] N desaprobación f.

disapprove [ˌdɪsəˈpruːv] VI: **to ~ of** desaprobar; **he ~s of gambling** no le gusta el juego, está en contra del juego; **I think he ~s of me** creo que me tiene poca simpatía; **I strongly ~** yo estoy firmemente en contra; **but father ~d** pero papá no quiso permitirlo; **your mother would ~** tu madre estaría en contra.

disapproving [ˌdɪsəˈpruːvɪŋ] ADJ *look etc* de desaprobación.

disapprovingly [ˌdɪsəˈpruːvɪŋlɪ] ADV con desaprobación.

disarm [dɪsˈɑːm] [1] VT desarmar; *bomb* desactivar. [2] VI desarmarse.

disarmament [dɪsˈɑːməmənt] N desarme m.

disarmer [dɪsˈɑːməʳ] N partidario m, -a f del desarme.

disarming [dɪsˈɑːmɪŋ] ADJ *smile etc* encantador; *speech* conciliador.

disarmingly [dɪsˈɑːmɪŋlɪ] ADV encantadoramente.

disarrange [ˌdɪsəˈreɪndʒ] VT desarreglar, descomponer.

disarranged [ˌdɪsəˈreɪndʒd] ADJ *bed* deshecho; *hair, clothes* desarreglado.

disarray [ˌdɪsəˈreɪ] N desorden m, confusión f; desarreglo m; (*of dress*) desaliño m; **in ~** desordenado, en confusión; **the plan was thrown into ~ by the storm** la tormenta dio al traste con el proyecto.

disassemble [ˌdɪsəˈsembl] VT desmontar.

disassociate [ˌdɪsəˈsəʊʃɪˌeɪt] VT separar, desligar (*from* de).

disaster [dɪˈzɑːstəʳ] N desastre m; **~ area** región f devastada; **~ fund** fondo m de ayuda para casos de desastres; **to court ~** correr al desastre.

disastrous [dɪˈzɑːstrəs] ADJ catastrófico, desastroso, funesto, nefasto.

disastrously [dɪˈzɑːstrəslɪ] ADV catastróficamente.

disavow [ˈdɪsəˈvaʊ] VT desconocer, rechazar.

disavowal [ˌdɪsəˈvaʊəl] N negativa f, rechazo m.

disband [dɪsˈbænd] [1] VT *army* licenciar; *organization* desmantelar, disolver. [2] VI desbandarse; disolverse.

disbar [dɪsˈbɑːʳ] VT *barrister* excluir del ejercicio de la abogacía, prohibir ejercer; **he was ~red** le prohibieron ejercer la abogacía.

disbarment [dɪsˈbɑːmənt] N inhabilitación m (*para el ejercicio de la abogacía*).

disbelief [ˈdɪsbəˈliːf] N incredulidad f.

disbelieve [ˈdɪsbəˈliːv] [1] VT no creer, desconfiar de. [2] VI no creer (*in* en).

disbeliever [ˈdɪsbəˈliːvəʳ] N incrédulo m, -a f; (*Eccl*) descreído m, -a f.

disbelieving [ˈdɪsbɪˈliːvɪŋ] ADJ incrédulo; desconfiado.

disburden [dɪsˈbɜːdn] [1] VT descargar. [2] VR: **to ~ o.s. of** descargarse de.

disburse [dɪsˈbɜːs] VT desembolsar.

disbursement [dɪsˈbɜːsmənt] N desembolso m.

disc [dɪsk] N disco m; (*Med*) vértebra f; (*Comput*) = **disk**.

discard [1] [ˈdɪskɑːd] N descarte m (*also Cards*), desecho m. [2] [dɪsˈkɑːd] VT descartar; (*Cards*) descartarse de; rechazar, desechar; *clothing* dejar de llevar; *unwanted thing* tirar; *habit* renunciar a. [3] [dɪsˈkɑːd] VI descartar(se).

disc brakes [ˈdɪskbreɪks] NPL (*Brit*) frenos *mpl* de disco.

discern [dɪˈsɜːn] VT percibir, discernir.

discernible [dɪˈsɜːnəbl] ADJ perceptible.

discernibly [dɪˈsɜːnəblɪ] ADV sensiblemente, visiblemente.

discerning [dɪˈsɜːnɪŋ] ADJ perspicaz.

discernment [dɪˈsɜːnmənt] N perspicacia f, discernimiento m.

discharge [1] [ˈdɪstʃɑːdʒ] N **(a)** (*of weapon, Elec: unloading*) descarga f; (*of debt*) pago m, descargo m; (*of duty*) desempeño m, ejecución f; (*Mil*) licenciamiento m; (*of worker*) despedida f; (*of bankrupt*) rehabilitación f.
(b) (*Med*) secreción f; (*vaginal ~*) flujo m.
[2] [dɪsˈtʃɑːdʒ] VT **(a)** *weapon, current, cargo, ship* descargar; *shot, arrow* disparar.
(b) *debt* pagar, descargar; *duty* desempeñar, cumplir; *task* ejecutar.
(c) *troops* licenciar; *worker* despedir; *person from duty* dispensar, exonerar (*from* de); *prisoner* poner en libertad; *patient* dar de alta; *bankrupt* rehabilitar; **to be ~d from the army** ser licenciado del ejército; **they ~d him from hospital on Monday** le dieron de alta el lunes.
[3] [dɪsˈtʃɑːdʒ] VI (*river, Elec*) descargar (*into* en); (*Med*) supurar.

disciple [dɪˈsaɪpl] N discípulo m, -a f.

disciplinarian [ˌdɪsɪplɪˈnɛərɪən] N ordenancista mf.

disciplinary [ˈdɪsɪplɪnərɪ] ADJ disciplinario; **~ action, ~ measure** medida f de disciplina.

discipline [ˈdɪsɪplɪn] [1] N disciplina f. [2] VT disciplinar.

disc-jockey [ˈdɪskˌdʒɒkɪ] N pinchadiscos mf.

disclaim [dɪsˈkleɪm] VT negar, rechazar; desconocer; (*Jur*) renunciar a; **he ~ed all knowledge of it** dijo que no sabía nada en absoluto de ello.

disclaimer [dɪsˈkleɪməʳ] N negación f; (*Jur*) renuncia f; **to put in a ~** negarlo, rechazarlo.

disclose [dɪsˈkləʊz] VT revelar.

disclosure [dɪsˈkləʊʒəʳ] N revelación f.

disco [ˈdɪskəʊ] N disco(teca) f.

disco-dancing [ˈdɪskəʊˌdɑːnsɪŋ] N baile m disco.

discography [dɪsˈkɒɡrəfɪ] N discografía f.

discolour, (*US*) **discolor** [dɪsˈkʌləʳ] [1] VT de(s)colorar. [2] VI de(s)colorarse.

discolouration, (*US*) **discoloration** [ˌdɪsˌkʌləˈreɪʃən] N de(s)coloramiento m.

discoloured, (*US*) **discolored** [dɪsˈkʌləd] ADJ de(s)colorado.

discombobulate [ˌdɪskəmˈbɒbjʊˌleɪt] VT (*US*) *person, plans* dislocar.

discomfit [dɪsˈkʌmfɪt] VT desconcertar.

discomfiture [dɪsˈkʌmfɪtʃəʳ] N desconcierto m, confusión f.

discomfort [dɪsˈkʌmfət] N (*lack of comfort*) incomodidad f, falta f de comodidades; (*physical*) malestar m; (*uneasiness*) inquietud f.

discomposure [ˌdɪskəmˈpəʊʒəʳ] N desconcierto m, confusión f.

disconcert [ˌdɪskənˈsɜːt] VT desconcertar.

disconcerting [ˌdɪskənˈsɜːtɪŋ] ADJ desconcertante.

disconcertingly [ˌdɪskənˈsɜːtɪŋlɪ] ADV de modo desconcertante; **he spoke in a ~ frank way** desconcertó a todos hablando con tanta franqueza.

disconnect [ˈdɪskəˈnekt] VT separar, desacoplar; (*Elec*) desconectar.

disconnected [ˈdɪskəˈnektɪd] ADJ (*fig*) inconexo.

disconnection [ˌdɪskəˈnekʃən] N desconexión f.

disconsolate [dɪsˈkɒnsəlɪt] ADJ inconsolable.

disconsolately [dɪsˈkɒnsəlɪtlɪ] ADV inconsolablemente.

discontent [ˈdɪskənˈtent] N descontento m.

discontented [ˈdɪskənˈtentɪd] ADJ descontento, disgustado.

discontentment [ˈdɪskənˈtentmənt] N descontento m.

discontinuance [ˌdɪskənˈtɪnjʊəns] N, **discontinuation** [ˌdɪskənˌtɪnjʊˈeɪʃən] N (*of production etc*) cesación f, interrupción f.

discontinue [ˈdɪskənˈtɪnjuː] VT suspender, descontinuar, interrumpir, terminar; *payment* suspender; *newspaper etc* anular el abono de; **'D~d'** (*Comm*) 'Fin de serie'.

discontinuity [ˌdɪskɒntɪˈnjuːɪtɪ] N discontinuidad f; interrupción f.

discontinuous [ˈdɪskənˈtɪnjʊəs] ADJ discontinuo; interrumpido.

discord [ˈdɪskɔːd] N discordia f; (*Mus*) disonancia f; **to sow ~ among**

sembrar la discordia entre, sembrar cizaña entre.
discordant [dɪs'kɔːdənt] ADJ discorde; (*Mus*) disonante.
discothèque ['dɪskəʊtek] N discoteca *f*.
▼ **discount** [1] ['dɪskaʊnt] N descuento *m*, rebaja *f*; ~ **house** (*US*) tienda *f* de rebajas; ~ **rate** tasa *f* de descuento; ~ **store** (*US*) economato *m*; **to be at a** ~ (*fig*) no valorarse en su justo precio; **to give a** ~ **of 10%** dar un descuento del 10 por cien; **to sell at a** ~ vender con descuento, vender a precio reducido.
[2] [dɪs'kaʊnt] VT **(a)** descontar, rebajar; ~**ed cash-flow** cashflow *m* actualizado.
(b) (*leave out of account*) dejar a un lado, descartar, desechar; *report etc* considerar exagerado.
discourage [dɪs'kʌrɪdʒ] VT **(a)** (*dishearten*) desalentar, desanimar.
(b) (*advise against*) *development etc* oponerse a, desaprobar; *offer, advances* rechazar; *tendency* resistir; **to** ~ **sb from doing sth** disuadir a uno de hacer algo; **smoking is** ~**d** se recomienda no fumar.
discouragement [dɪs'kʌrɪdʒmənt] N **(a)** (*depression*) desaliento *m*. **(b)** (*act*) oposición *f*; desaprobación *f*; disuasión *f*; (*obstacle*) estorbo *m*; **it's a real** ~ **to progress** es un verdadero estorbo para el progreso.
discouraging [dɪs'kʌrɪdʒɪŋ] ADJ desalentador; **he was** ~ **about it** habló de ello en tono pesimista.
discourse [1] ['dɪskɔːs] N discurso *m*; (*talk*) plática *f*; (*essay*) tratado *m*; ~ **analysis** análisis *m* del discurso.
[2] [dɪs'kɔːs] VI: **to** ~ **upon** (*converse*) platicar sobre, (*make a speech*) disertar sobre.
discourteous [dɪs'kɜːtɪəs] ADJ descortés, desatento.
discourteously [dɪs'kɜːtɪəslɪ] ADV descortésmente.
discourtesy [dɪs'kɜːtɪsɪ] N descortesía *f*.
discover [dɪs'kʌvəʳ] VT descubrir.
discoverer [dɪs'kʌvərəʳ] N descubridor *m*, -ora *f*.
discovery [dɪs'kʌvərɪ] N descubrimiento *m*.
discredit [dɪs'kredɪt] [1] N descrédito *m*; **it was to the general's** ~ **that ...** fue un descrédito para el general que ....
[2] VT desacreditar, deshonrar; (*disbelieve*) poner en duda; **that theory is now** ~**ed** esa teoría ya está desacreditada; **all his evidence is thus** ~**ed** por lo tanto se pone en duda todo su testimonio.
discreditable [dɪs'kredɪtəbl] ADJ deshonroso, vergonzoso.
discreet [dɪs'kriːt] ADJ discreto, circunspecto, prudente.
discrepancy [dɪs'krepənsɪ] N discrepancia *f*, diferencia *f*.
discrete [dɪs'kriːt] ADJ discreto.
discretion [dɪs'kreʃən] N discreción *f*, circunspección *f*, prudencia *f*; **at one's** ~ a discreción; **at the chairman's** ~ **the meeting may ... le** incumbe al presidente decidir si la junta ...; **he may at his** ~ **allow ...** puede discrecionalmente permitir ...; **it is within his** ~ **to** + *infin* es de su competencia + *infin*; **to use one's own** ~ juzgar una cosa por sí mismo, obrar como mejor le parezca a uno; ~ **is the better part of valour** una retirada a tiempo es una victoria; **to reach years of** ~ llegar a la edad del discernimiento.
discretionary [dɪs'kreʃənərɪ] ADJ discrecional.
discriminate [dɪs'krɪmɪneɪt] [1] VT distinguir (*from* de).
[2] VI: **to** ~ **against** discriminar a (*or* contra), hacer una distinción en perjuicio de; **to** ~ **between** distinguir entre.
discriminating [dɪs'krɪmɪneɪtɪŋ] ADJ perspicaz, discernidor; *taste etc* fino.
discrimination [dɪsˌkrɪmɪ'neɪʃən] N **(a)** (*discernment*) discernimiento *m*, perspicacia *f*; (*good taste*) buen gusto *m*, finura *f*. **(b)** (*distinction*) distinción *f* (*between* entre); (*partiality*) parcialidad *f*, discriminación *f* (*against* a, contra); **racial** ~ discriminación *f* racial.
discriminatory [dɪs'krɪmɪnətərɪ] ADJ *duty etc* discriminatorio.
discursive [dɪs'kɜːsɪv] ADJ divagador, prolijo; (*Ling*) discursivo.
discus ['dɪskəs] N disco *m*.
▼ **discuss** [dɪs'kʌs] VT discutir, hablar de, tratar de, estudiar, comentar; *theme* tratar.
discussant [dɪs'kʌsənt] N (*US*) miembro *mf* de la mesa (de la sección de un congreso).
discussion [dɪs'kʌʃən] N discusión *f*; **it is under** ~ lo están estudiando; **to come up for** ~ someterse a discusión.
disdain [dɪs'deɪn] [1] N desdén *m*.
[2] VT desdeñar.
[3] VI: **to** ~ **to** + *infin* no dignarse + *infin*.
disdainful [dɪs'deɪnfʊl] ADJ desdeñoso.
disdainfully [dɪs'deɪnfəlɪ] ADV desdeñosamente.
disease [dɪ'ziːz] N enfermedad *f*; (*liter*) morbo *m*; dolencia *f*; (*fig*) mal *m*.
diseased [dɪ'ziːzd] ADJ *person* enfermo; *tissue* contagiado; *mind* enfermo, morboso.
disembark [ˌdɪsɪm'baːk] VTI desembarcar.
disembarkation [ˌdɪsembaː'keɪʃən] N (*of goods*) desembarque *m*; (*by person*) desembarco *m*.
disembodied [ˌdɪsɪm'bɒdɪd] ADJ incorpóreo.
disembowel [ˌdɪsɪm'baʊəl] VT desentrañar, destripar.
disenchanted ['dɪsɪn'tʃɑːntɪd] ADJ: **to be** ~ **with sb** quedar des-

encantado (*or* desengañado) con uno; **to be** ~ **with Slobodia** quedar desencantado (*or* desengañado) de Eslobodia.
disenchantment [ˌdɪsɪn'tʃɑːntmənt] N desencanto *m*.
disenfranchise ['dɪsɪn'fræntʃaɪz] VT = **disfranchise**.
disengage [ˌdɪsɪn'geɪdʒ] [1] VT (*free*) soltar, desasir; (*Mech*) desacoplar, desenganchar; *clutch* desembragar.
[2] VI (*Mil*) retirarse, romper el contacto.
disengaged [ˌdɪsɪn'geɪdʒd] ADJ libre, desocupado.
disengagement [ˌdɪsɪn'geɪdʒmənt] N retirada *f*, rompimiento *m* de contacto.
disentangle ['dɪsɪn'tæŋgl] [1] VT desenredar, desenmarañar (*also fig; from* de).
[2] VR: **to** ~ **o.s.** desenredarse (*from* de), librarse (*from* de).
disequilibrium [ˌdɪsiːkwɪ'lɪbrɪəm] N (*esp Fin*) desequilibrio *m*.
disestablish ['dɪsɪs'tæblɪʃ] VT (*Eccl*) separar del Estado.
disestablishment [ˌdɪsɪs'tæblɪʃmənt] N (*Eccl*) separación *f* del Estado.
disfavour, (*US*) **disfavor** [dɪs'feɪvəʳ] N desaprobación *f*; **to fall into** ~ (*custom*) dejar de usarse, caer en desuso, (*person*) caer en desgracia; **to look with** ~ **on sth** desaprobar algo.
disfigure [dɪs'fɪgəʳ] VT desfigurar; afear.
disfigured [dɪs'fɪgəd] ADJ desfigurado.
disfigurement [dɪs'fɪgəmənt] N desfiguración *f*; afeamiento *m*.
disfranchise ['dɪs'fræntʃaɪz] VT privar de los derechos civiles, (*esp*) privar del derecho de votar.
disgorge [dɪs'gɔːdʒ] VT vomitar, arrojar; (*bird*) desembuchar; (*fig*) devolver, restituir.
disgrace [dɪs'greɪs] [1] N **(a)** (*state of shame*) ignominia *f*, deshonra *f*; **there is no** ~ **in being poor** no es vergonzoso ser pobre; **to be in** ~ estar desacreditado, (*pet, child*) estar castigado; **to bring** ~ **on** deshonrar; **to fall into** ~ caer en desgracia.
(b) (*downfall*) caída *f*.
(c) (*shameful thing*) vergüenza *f*; escándalo *m*; **it's a** ~ es una vergüenza; **what a** ~**!** ¡qué vergüenza!; **she's a** ~ **to her family** es la vergüenza de su familia.
[2] VT deshonrar, desacreditar; **he was** ~**d and banished** le destituyeron de sus cargos y le desterraron.
[3] VR: **to** ~ **o.s.** deshonrarse.
disgraceful [dɪs'greɪsfʊl] ADJ vergonzoso, deshonroso; *behaviour* escandaloso; ~**!** ¡qué vergüenza!
disgracefully [dɪs'greɪsfəlɪ] ADV vergonzosamente; escandalosamente.
disgruntled [dɪs'grʌntld] ADJ disgustado (*at, with* de), contrariado, malhumorado; **to look** ~ poner mala cara.
disguise [dɪs'gaɪz] [1] N disfraz *m*; **to be in** ~ estar disfrazado.
[2] VT disfrazar (*as* de).
[3] VR: **to** ~ **o.s. as** disfrazarse de.
disgust [dɪs'gʌst] [1] N repugnancia *f*, aversión *f*; **it fills me with** ~ me da asco.
[2] VT repugnar, inspirar aversión a, dar asco a; (*disappointment etc*) disgustar; **the thought** ~**s me** el pensamiento me repugna; **you** ~ **me** me das asco; **he was** ~**ed by his failure** se enfureció contra sí mismo por su fracaso; **I am** ~**ed with you** me das vergüenza; **I was** ~**ed with the referee** el árbitro me dio asco.
disgusted [dɪs'gʌstɪd] ADJ asqueado, lleno de asco; **in a** ~ **voice** en tono disgustado.
disgustedly [dɪs'gʌstɪdlɪ] ADV asqueadamente, con asco; **... he said** ~ ... dijo con asco.
disgusting [dɪs'gʌstɪŋ] ADJ repugnante, asqueroso; ~**!** ¡qué asco!
disgustingly [dɪs'gʌstɪŋlɪ] ADV asquerosamente; **they are** ~ **rich** son tan ricos que da asco.
dish [dɪʃ] [1] N **(a)** plato *m*; (*large, for serving etc*) fuente *f*; (*food*) plato *m*; platillo *m* (*Mex*); **a typical Spanish** ~ un plato típico español; **to wash the** ~**es** fregar los platos.
(b) (*Astron*) reflector *m*; (*TV*) antena *f* parabólica.
(c) (*: girl, boy*) bombón* *m*; **this is not my** ~* esto no me gusta; yo no sé nada de esto.
[2] VT *hopes, chances* confundir, burlar.
◆ **dish out** VT (*fig*) (*gen*) distribuir; repartir; *criticism* difundir.
◆ **dish up** VT (*fig*) servir; ofrecer, producir; sacar; **he** ~**ed up the same old arguments** repitió los argumentos de siempre.
dishabille [ˌdɪsæ'biːl] N desabillé *m*.
dish aerial ['dɪʃeərɪəl] N, (*US*) **dish antenna** ['dɪʃæn'tenə] N antena *f* parabólica.
disharmony ['dɪs'hɑːmənɪ] N discordia *f*; (*Mus*) disonancia *f*.
dishcloth ['dɪʃklɒθ] N, PL **dishcloths** ['dɪʃklɒðz] trapo *m* (de fregar), paño *m* de cocina, bayeta *f*.
dishearten [dɪs'hɑːtn] VT desalentar, desanimar; **don't be** ~**ed!** ¡ánimo!
disheartening [dɪs'hɑːtnɪŋ] ADJ desalentador.
dishevelled, (*US*) **disheveled** [dɪ'ʃevəld] ADJ despeinado, desmelenado.
dishmop ['dɪʃmɒp] N fregona *f* para lavar los platos.
dishonest [dɪs'ɒnɪst] ADJ *person* nada honrado, falso, tramposo; *means*

fraudulento.

dishonestly [dɪs'ɒnɪstlɪ] ADV fraudulentamente; **to act ~** obrar con poca honradez.

dishonesty [dɪs'ɒnɪstɪ] N falta *f* de honradez, falsedad *f*; *(of means)* fraude *m*.

dishonour, *(US)* **dishonor** [dɪs'ɒnəʳ] **1** N deshonra *f*, deshonor *m*.
2 VT deshonrar; *cheque etc* negarse a aceptar, no pagar; *promise* faltar a, no cumplir.

dishonourable, *(US)* **dishonorable** [dɪs'ɒnərəbl] ADJ deshonroso.

dishonourably, *(US)* **dishonorably** [dɪs'ɒnərəblɪ] ADV deshonrosamente; **to be ~ discharged** ser licenciado con deshonor.

dishrack ['dɪʃræk] N escurridera *f* de platos.

dishrag ['dɪʃræg] N trapo *m* para fregar los platos.

dish soap ['dɪʃsəʊp] N *(US)* lavavajillas *m.*

dishtowel ['dɪʃtaʊəl] N trapo *m* de secar los platos.

dishware ['dɪʃweəʳ] N *(US)* loza *f*, vajilla *f.*

dishwasher ['dɪʃˌwɒʃəʳ] N *(person)* friegaplatos *mf*; *(machine)* (máquina *f*) lavaplatos *m*, lavavajillas *m.*

dishwashing liquid ['dɪʃˌwɒʃɪŋˌlɪkwɪd] N *(US)* lavavajillas *m.*

dishwater ['dɪʃwɔːtəʳ] N agua *f* de lavar platos; *(fig)* agua *f* sucia.

dishy ['dɪʃɪ] ADJ *(Brit)* mono, apetitoso.

disillusion [ˌdɪsɪ'luːʒən] **1** N desilusión *f*, desengaño *m.*
2 VT desilusionar, desengañar; **to be ~ed with sb** quedar desilusionado con uno; **to be ~ed with Paris** quedar desilusionado de París.

disillusionment [ˌdɪsɪ'luːʒənmənt] N desilusión *f.*

disincentive [ˌdɪsɪn'sentɪv] N desincentivo *m.*

disinclination [ˌdɪsɪnklɪ'neɪʃən] N aversión *f (for* a, hacia, por).

disinclined ['dɪsɪn'klaɪnd] ADJ: **to be ~ to do sth** estar poco dispuesto a hacer algo, tener pocas ganas de hacer algo; **I feel very ~** no me siento con ganas.

disinfect [ˌdɪsɪn'fekt] VT desinfectar.

disinfectant [ˌdɪsɪn'fektənt] N desinfectante *m.*

disinfection [ˌdɪsɪn'fekʃən] N desinfección *f.*

disinflation [ˌdɪsɪn'fleɪʃən] N desinflación *f.*

disinflationary [ˌdɪsɪn'fleɪʃənərɪ] ADJ desinflacionista.

disinformation [ˌdɪsɪnfə'meɪʃən] N desinformación *f.*

disingenuous [ˌdɪsɪn'dʒenjʊəs] ADJ doble, poco sincero.

disingenuousness [ˌdɪsɪn'dʒenjʊəsnɪs] N falsedad *f*, insinceridad *f.*

disinherit ['dɪsɪn'herɪt] VT desheredar.

disintegrate [dɪs'ɪntɪgreɪt] VI disgregarse, desagregarse, desintegrarse.

disintegration [dɪsˌɪntɪ'greɪʃən] N disgregación *f*, desagregación *f*, desintegración *f.*

disinter ['dɪsɪn'tɜːʳ] VT desenterrar.

disinterest [dɪs'ɪntrəst] N desinterés *m*, apatía *f.*

disinterested [dɪs'ɪntrɪstɪd] ADJ desinteresado.

disinterestedly [dɪs'ɪntrɪstɪdlɪ] ADV *act etc* de manera desinteresada.

disinterment [ˌdɪsɪn'tɜːmənt] N exhumación *f*, desenterramiento *m.*

disinvest [ˌdɪsɪn'vest] VT desinvertir.

disinvestment [ˌdɪsɪn'vestmənt] N desinversión *f.*

disjointed [dɪs'dʒɔɪntɪd] ADJ *(fig)* inconexo, descosido, desarticulado.

disjunctive [dɪs'dʒʌŋktɪv] ADJ disyuntivo.

disk [dɪsk] N *(esp US)* = **disc**; *(Comput)* disco *m*; **~ drive** unidad *f* de disco, disk drive *m*; **~ operating system** sistema *m* operativo de discos; **~ pack** paquete *m* de discos; **~ unit** unidad *f* de disco.

diskette [dɪs'ket] N disquete *m*, diskette *m*, disco *m* flexible.

diskless ['dɪsklɪs] ADJ sin disco(s).

▼ **dislike** [dɪs'laɪk] **1** N aversión *f*, antipatía *f (for, of* a, hacia); **to take a ~ to** coger *(LAm:* agarrar*)* antipatía a, tomar hincha a.
2 VT **(a)** *(object: person)* tener aversión a, tener antipatía a; **I ~ him** me resulta antipático; **it's not that I ~ him** no es que yo le tenga aversión.
(b) *(object: thing)* **I ~ that** eso no me gusta, eso me desagrada; **I ~ flying** no me gusta ir en avión.

dislocate ['dɪsləʊkeɪt] VT *bone* dislocarse, descoyuntar; *traffic* interceptar, interrumpir; *plans* trastornar, dar al traste con.

dislocation [ˌdɪsləʊ'keɪʃən] N dislocación *f*; interceptación *f*; trastorno *m*; confusión *f.*

dislodge [dɪs'lɒdʒ] VT *enemy etc* desalojar *(from* de); *object etc* desprender; hacer caer.

disloyal ['dɪs'lɔɪəl] ADJ desleal.

disloyalty ['dɪs'lɔɪəltɪ] N deslealtad *f.*

dismal ['dɪzməl] ADJ *(dark)* sombrío, tenebroso; *(depressing)* triste, tétrico; *(depressed)* abatido; *tone* lúgubre; *failure* catastrófico; *(very bad)* malísimo, fatal.

dismally ['dɪzməlɪ] ADV *(sadly)* tristemente; **to fail ~** tener un fracaso catastrófico; **the play was ~ bad** la obra fue fatal.

dismantle [dɪs'mæntl] VT *machine* desarmar, desmontar; *fort, ship* desmantelar.

dismast [dɪs'mɑːst] VT desarbolar.

dismay [dɪs'meɪ] **1** N consternación *f*; **there was general ~** se consternaron todos; **in ~** consternado; **to my ~** para mi

consternación; **to fill sb with ~** consternar a uno.
2 VT consternar; **I am ~ed to hear that ...** me da pena saber que ...; **don't look so ~ed!** ¡no te aflijas!

dismember [dɪs'membəʳ] VT desmembrar.

dismemberment [dɪs'membəmənt] N desmembramiento *m*, desmembración *f.*

dismiss [dɪs'mɪs] **1** VT **(a)** *(discharge) worker* despedir, *official* destituir *(from* de), *(Mil)* licenciar; *(send away)* mandar ir; dar permiso para irse a; *assembly* disolver; **to be ~ed from the service** ser separado del servicio.
(b) *thought* rechazar, apartar de sí; *request* rechazar; *possibility* descartar, desechar; **to ~ a subject briefly** hablar brevemente de un asunto; **with that he ~ed the matter** con eso dio por concluido el asunto.
(c) *(Jur) appeal* rechazar; **the case was ~ed** el tribunal absolvió al acusado.
2 VI *(Mil)* romper filas; **~!** ¡rompan filas!

dismissal [dɪs'mɪsəl] N despedida *f*; destitución *f.*

dismissive [dɪs'mɪsɪv] ADJ: **he said in a ~ tone** dijo como quien no quería tomar la cosa en serio; **he was very ~ about it** parecía no tomar la cosa en serio.

dismount [dɪs'maʊnt] **1** VT desmontar.
2 VI desmontarse, apearse, bajar *(from* de).

Disneyland ['dɪznɪˌlænd] N Disneylandia *f (also fig).*

disobedience [ˌdɪsə'biːdɪəns] N desobediencia *f.*

disobedient [ˌdɪsə'biːdɪənt] ADJ desobediente.

disobey ['dɪsə'beɪ] VTI desobedecer.

disobliging ['dɪsə'blaɪdʒɪŋ] ADJ poco servicial.

disorder [dɪs'ɔːdəʳ] **1** N **(a)** *(confusion)* desorden *m*; desarreglo *m*; **to be in ~** estar en desorden; **to retreat in ~** retirarse a la desbandada.
(b) *(commotion)* disturbio *m*, tumulto *m*; **there were ~s in the streets** hubo disturbios en las calles.
(c) *(Med) (upset)* trastorno *m*; *(illness)* enfermedad *f*; **mental ~** trastorno *m* mental.
2 VT desordenar; *(Med)* trastornar.

disordered [dɪs'ɔːdəd] ADJ desordenado; desarreglado; *(Med)* trastornado.

disorderly [dɪs'ɔːdəlɪ] ADJ **(a)** *(untidy)* desordenado; *person* poco metódico.
(b) *(unruly)* turbulento, indisciplinado; *youth* revoltoso; *meeting* alborotado; **the meeting became ~** la reunión se alborotó.
(c) *conduct* escandaloso; **~ house** *(euph)* burdel *m.*

disorganization [dɪsˌɔːgənaɪ'zeɪʃən] N desorganización *f*; confusión *f*, falta *f* de organización.

disorganize [dɪs'ɔːgənaɪz] VT desorganizar; *communications etc* interrumpir.

disorganized [dɪs'ɔːgənaɪzd] ADJ *person* poco metódico.

disorient [dɪs'ɔːrɪənt], **disorientate** [dɪs'ɔːrɪənteɪt] VT desorientar.

disown [dɪs'əʊn] VT rechazar, desconocer; *belief etc* renegar de, repudiar.

disparage [dɪs'pærɪdʒ] VT menospreciar, denigrar, hablar mal de.

disparagement [dɪs'pærɪdʒmənt] N denigración *f.*

disparaging [dɪs'pærɪdʒɪŋ] ADJ *person* despreciativo; *remark etc* despectivo.

disparagingly [dɪs'pærɪdʒɪŋlɪ] ADV: **to speak ~ of** hablar en términos despreciativos de.

disparate ['dɪspərɪt] ADJ dispar.

disparity [dɪs'pærɪtɪ] N disparidad *f.*

dispassionate [dɪs'pæʃnɪt] ADJ desapasionado, imparcial.

dispassionately [dɪs'pæʃnɪtlɪ] ADV de modo desapasionado.

▼ **dispatch** [dɪs'pætʃ] **1** N **(a)** *(act of sending) (of person)* envío *m*, *(of goods)* consignación *f*, envío *m*; *(killing)* ejecución *f*, muerte *f*; **~ documents** documentos *mpl* de envío; **~ note** aviso *m* de envío.
(b) *(speed)* prontitud *f.*
(c) *(message)* mensaje *m*, despacho *m*, informe *m*; *(Mil)* parte *m*, comunicado *m.*
▼ **2** VT **(a)** *(send) person* enviar, *goods* consignar, enviar, remitir.
(b) *(kill)* despachar.
(c) *(transact)* despachar.
(d) *food* despachar, despabilar.

dispatch-box [dɪs'pætʃbɒks] N *(Brit)* cartera *f.*

dispatch-case [dɪs'pætʃˌkeɪs] N portafolios *m.*

dispatcher [dɪs'pætʃəʳ] N transportista *m.*

dispatch-rider [dɪs'pætʃˌraɪdəʳ] N correo *m*; *(Mil)* correo *m* militar.

dispel [dɪs'pel] VT disipar, dispersar; *doubts* disipar, barrer; *(fig)* desvanecer.

dispensable [dɪs'pensəbl] ADJ prescindible, innecesario.

dispensary [dɪs'pensərɪ] N *(Brit)* dispensario *m*, farmacia *f.*

dispensation [ˌdɪspen'seɪʃən] N *(distribution, exemption)* dispensación *f*; *(of justice)* administración *f*; *(Eccl)* dispensa *f*; *(ruling)* decreto *m*; **~ of Providence** designio *m* divino.

dispense [dɪs'pens] VT **(a)** *(issue)* dispensar, repartir; *(Pharm)* preparar;

justice administrar. **(b) to ~ sb from** dispensar a uno de, eximir a uno de.

◆**dispense with** VT prescindir de; deshacerse de.

dispenser [dɪsˈpensəʳ] N (Brit) **(a)** (person) farmacéutico m, -a f. **(b)** (device) dosificador m; distribuidor m automático, máquina f expendedora.

dispensing [dɪsˈpensɪŋ] ATTR: **~ chemist** farmacéutico m, -a f.

dispersal [dɪsˈpɜːsəl] N dispersión f; (of light) descomposición f.

dispersant [dɪsˈpɜːsənt] N (Chem) dispersante m.

disperse [dɪsˈpɜːs] **1** VT dispersar; light descomponer.
2 VI dispersarse; **they ~d to their homes** fue cada uno a su casa.

dispersion [dɪsˈpɜːʃən] N dispersión f.

dispirit [dɪsˈpɪrɪt] VT desalentar, desanimar.

dispirited [dɪsˈpɪrɪtɪd] ADJ abatido, deprimido, desanimado.

dispiritedly [dɪsˈpɪrɪtɪdlɪ] ADV desalentadamente, desanimadamente.

dispiriting [dɪsˈpɪrɪtɪŋ] ADJ deprimente, desalentador.

displace [dɪsˈpleɪs] VT **(a)** (shift) desplazar, sacar de su sitio. **(b)** (remove from office) destituir; (oust) quitar el puesto a, reemplazar. **(c)** (Phys, Naut) desplazar; (Chem) reemplazar.

displaced [dɪsˈpleɪst] ADJ: **~ person** desplazado m, -a f.

displacement [dɪsˈpleɪsmənt] N **(a)** (shift) cambio m de sitio. **(b)** (removal from office) destitución f; (ousting) reemplazo m. **(c)** (Phys, Naut) desplazamiento m; (Chem) reemplazo m. **(d) ~ activity** (Psych) actividad f de sustitución.

display [dɪsˈpleɪ] **1** N **(a)** (act of ~ing) exhibición f; (showing) exposición f; (Comput) visualización f, despliegue m; (of goods for sale) exposición f, presentación f; (of emotion) manifestación f, demostración f; (of energy, quality) despliegue m; (Mil) alarde m, demostración f militar; **to make a ~ of** hacer alarde de; **to be on ~** estar expuesto.
(b) (showiness) aparato m, pompa f, ostentación f.
2 VT (put on view) exponer, presentar; (Comput) desplegar; emotion etc acusar, manifestar, demostrar; quality, energy desplegar; (show ostentatiously) ostentar, hacer gala de, lucir.

display advertising [dɪsˈpleɪˌædvətaɪzɪŋ] N (Press) pancartas fpl publicitarias, publicidad f gráfica.

display unit [dɪsˈpleɪjuːnɪt] N (Comput) monitor m.

display window [dɪsˈpleɪˌwɪndəʊ] N escaparate m.

displease [dɪsˈpliːz] VT (be disagreeable to) desagradar; (offend) ofender; (annoy) enojar, enfadar; **to be ~d at** (or **with**) estar disgustado con (or de).

displeasing [dɪsˈpliːzɪŋ] ADJ desagradable.

displeasure [dɪsˈpleʒəʳ] N desagrado m, enojo m, indignación f, disgusto m; **to incur sb's ~** ofender a uno.

disport [dɪsˈpɔːt] VR: **to ~ o.s.** retozar, jugar; divertirse.

disposable [dɪsˈpəʊzəbl] ADJ **(a)** napkin etc de usar y tirar, desechable; **~ goods** productos mpl no reutilizables. **(b)** (available) disponible; **~ income** renta f disponible.

▼**disposal** [dɪsˈpəʊzəl] N **(a)** (placing, arrangement) disposición f, colocación f, orden m.
(b) (sale) venta f; (of house etc) traspaso m; (of rights) enajenación f; (rubbish ~) recogida f de basuras.
▼**(c) to have at one's ~** disponer de, tener a su disposición; **I am at your ~** estoy a su disposición.

dispose [dɪsˈpəʊz] VT **(a)** (place, arrange) disponer, colocar, poner en orden.
(b) (determine) determinar, decidir.
(c) (persuade) inclinar, mover; **to ~ sb to help** mover a uno a ayudar; **to be ~d to do sth** estar dispuesto a hacer algo; **to be well ~d towards sth** estar bien dispuesto hacia algo.

◆**dispose of** VT **(a)** (have at one's command) disponer de.
(b) (get rid of) deshacerse de; eliminar; rubbish tirar, botar (LAm); depositar; rights enajenar, ceder; (sell) vender; house etc traspasar; (give away) regalar; food comerse, despachar; (finish) terminar, concluir; problem resolver; argument echar por tierra; business despachar; (kill) matar, despachar.

disposer [dɪsˈpəʊzəʳ] N (also **waste ~**) equipo m de destrucción de basuras.

disposition [ˌdɪspəˈzɪʃən] N **(a)** (placing) disposición f, colocación f; orden m.
(b) ~s preparativos mpl; plan m; **to make one's ~s** hacer preparativos.
(c) to be at the ~ of estar a la disposición de.
(d) (temperament) natural m, temperamento m.
(e) (inclination) propensión f (to a); **I have no ~ to help him** no estoy dispuesto a ayudarle.

dispossess [ˈdɪspəˈzes] VT tenant desahuciar; **to ~ sb of** desposeer a uno de, privar a uno de.

disproportion [ˌdɪsprəˈpɔːʃən] N desproporción f.

disproportionate [ˌdɪsprəˈpɔːʃnɪt] ADJ desproporcionado.

disproportionately [ˌdɪsprəˈpɔːʃnɪtlɪ] ADV desproporcionadamente.

disprove [dɪsˈpruːv] VT refutar, confutar.

disputable [dɪsˈpjuːtəbl] ADJ discutible.

disputation [ˌdɪspjuːˈteɪʃən] N disputa f.

disputatious [ˌdɪspjuːˈteɪʃəs] ADJ discutidor, disputador.

dispute [dɪsˈpjuːt] **1** N disputa f; (spoken) discusión f, altercado m; (labour ~) conflicto m laboral; (Jur) contencioso m; **beyond ~** indiscutible, incuestionable; **it is beyond ~ that ...** es indudable que ...; **territory in ~** territorio m en litigio.
2 VT disputar; cuestionar, expresar dudas acerca de; protestar de; **I ~ that** lo dudo; **I do not ~ the fact that ...** no niego que ...; **to ~ possession of a house with sb** contender con uno sobre la posesión de una casa; **the final will be ~d between A and B** se disputarán la final A y B.
3 VI discutir (about, over sobre, whether si).

disputed [dɪsˈpjuːtɪd] ADJ discutible; territory etc en litigio; **a ~ matter** un asunto contencioso, un asunto en litigio; **a ~ decision** una decisión discutida.

disqualification [dɪsˌkwɒlɪfɪˈkeɪʃən] N (act, effect) inhabilitación f; (Sport) descalificación f; (thing that disqualifies) impedimento m, desventaja f.

disqualify [dɪsˈkwɒlɪfaɪ] VT inhabilitar, incapacitar (for para); (Sport) descalificar.

disquiet [dɪsˈkwaɪət] **1** N inquietud f, desasosiego m.
2 VT inquietar.

disquieting [dɪsˈkwaɪətɪŋ] ADJ inquietante.

disquietude [dɪsˈkwaɪɪtjuːd] N inquietud f, intranquilidad f.

disquisition [ˌdɪskwɪˈzɪʃən] N disquisición f.

disregard [ˈdɪsrɪˈgɑːd] **1** N indiferencia f (for a); (neglect) descuido m (of de); despreocupación f; **with complete ~ for** sin atender en lo más mínimo a; **with complete ~ for his own safety** sin considerar un momento su propia salvación.
2 VT desatender, descuidar; (ignore) no hacer caso de, hacer caso omiso de, pasar por alto.

disrepair [ˈdɪsrɪˈpeəʳ] N mal estado m; **to fall into ~** (house) desmoronarse; (machinery etc) deteriorarse, descomponerse.

disreputable [dɪsˈrepjʊtəbl] ADJ de mala fama; (shameful) vergonzoso, escandaloso; clothing etc horrible, asqueroso.

disreputably [dɪsˈrepjʊtəblɪ] ADV vergonzosamente.

disrepute [ˈdɪsrɪˈpjuːt] N: **to bring into ~** desacreditar, desprestigiar.

disrespect [ˈdɪsrɪsˈpekt] N falta f de respeto, desacato m; **I meant no ~** no quería ofenderle.

disrespectful [ˌdɪsrɪsˈpektfʊl] ADJ irrespetuoso.

disrespectfully [ˌdɪsrɪsˈpektfʊlɪ] ADV irrespetuosamente; **... he said ~** ... dijo de forma irrespetuosa.

disrobe [ˈdɪsˈrəʊb] **1** VT desnudar, desvestir.
2 VI desnudarse.

disrupt [dɪsˈrʌpt] VT romper; (fig) communications etc desorganizar, interrumpir; plans desbaratar, dar al traste con, trastornar.

disruption [dɪsˈrʌpʃən] N rompimiento m; (fig) desorganización f, interrupción f; desbaratamiento m.

disruptive [dɪsˈrʌptɪv] ADJ que tiende a romper la unidad; destructivo, subversivo, perjudicial.

dissatisfaction [ˈdɪsˌsætɪsˈfækʃən] N descontento m, insatisfacción f; disgusto m.

dissatisfied [ˈdɪsˈsætɪsfaɪd] ADJ descontento, insatisfecho; **everyone was ~ with the result** el resultado no gustó a nadie, el resultado dejó insatisfechos a todos.

dissect [dɪˈsekt] VT hacer la disección de; anatomizar, seccionar; (fig) analizar minuciosamente.

dissection [dɪˈsekʃən] N disección f; (fig) análisis m minucioso.

dissemble [dɪˈsembl] **1** VT disimular, encubrir.
2 VI fingir, ser hipócrita.

disseminate [dɪˈsemɪneɪt] VT diseminar, difundir, divulgar.

dissemination [dɪˌsemɪˈneɪʃən] N diseminación f, difusión f.

dissension [dɪˈsenʃən] N disensión f, discordia f.

dissent [dɪˈsent] **1** N disentimiento m; (Eccl) disidencia f.
2 VI disentir (from de); (Eccl) disidir.

dissenter [dɪˈsentəʳ] N (Eccl) disidente mf.

dissentient [dɪˈsenʃɪənt] **1** ADJ (also **dissenting**) disidente, disconforme, discrepante; **there was one ~ voice** hubo una voz en contra.
2 N disidente mf.

dissenting [dɪˈsentɪŋ] ADJ voice disidente; **a long ~ tradition** una larga tradición de disidencia.

dissertation [ˌdɪsəˈteɪʃən] N disertación f; (US Univ) tesis f; (Brit Univ) tesina f.

disservice [ˈdɪsˈsɜːvɪs] N deservicio m; **to do a ~ to** perjudicar a.

dissidence [ˈdɪsɪdəns] N disidencia f.

dissident [ˈdɪsɪdənt] **1** ADJ disidente.
2 N disidente mf.

dissimilar [ˈdɪˈsɪmɪləʳ] ADJ distinto, diferente (to de).

dissimilarity [ˌdɪsɪmɪˈlærɪtɪ] N desemejanza f, disimilitud f.

dissimulate [dɪˈsɪmjʊleɪt] VT disimular.

dissimulation [dɪˌsɪmjʊ'leɪʃən] N disimulación f.

dissipate ['dɪsɪpeɪt] VT disipar; *fear, doubt etc* desvanecer; *(waste)* derrochar, desperdiciar.

dissipated ['dɪsɪpeɪtɪd] ADJ disoluto.

dissipation [ˌdɪsɪ'peɪʃən] N *(act)* disipación f; *(waste)* derroche m, desperdicio m; *(moral)* disipación f, disolución f, libertinaje m, vicio m.

dissociate [dɪ'səʊʃɪeɪt] 1 VT separar, desligar *(from* de).
2 VR: **to ~ o.s. from** hacerse insolidario de, separarse de, desligarse de.

dissociation [dɪˌsəʊsɪ'eɪʃən] N disociación f.

dissoluble [dɪ'sɒljʊbl] ADJ disoluble.

dissolute ['dɪsəluːt] ADJ disoluto.

dissolution [ˌdɪsə'luːʃən] N disolución f *(also Pol)*.

dissolvable [dɪ'zɒlvəbl] ADJ soluble.

dissolve [dɪ'zɒlv] 1 VT disolver *(also fig, Pol etc)*, desleír.
2 VI disolverse; desleírse; *(fade)* desvanecerse; **to ~ into tears** deshacerse en lágrimas.

dissonance ['dɪsənəns] N disonancia f.

dissonant ['dɪsənənt] ADJ disonante.

dissuade [dɪ'sweɪd] VT disuadir *(from* de); **to ~ sb from doing sth** disuadir a uno de hacer algo.

dissuasion [dɪ'sweɪʒən] N disuasión f.

dissuasive [dɪ'sweɪsɪv] ADJ *(gen) voice, person* disuasivo; *powers* disuasorio.

distaff ['dɪstɑːf] N rueca f; **the ~ side** la rama femenina; **on the ~ side** por parte de la madre.

distance ['dɪstəns] 1 N distancia f *(also fig)*; *(difference)* diferencia f; **it's a good ~** está bastante lejos, *(journey)* es mucho camino; **what ~ is it to London?** ¿cuánto hay de aquí a Londres?; **~ learning** enseñanza f a distancia, enseñanza f por correspondencia; **~ race** carrera f de larga distancia; **within speaking ~** al alcance de la voz; **within easy ~** a poca distancia, no muy lejos *(of* de); **to be within striking ~ of** estar al alcance de; **at a ~ of 60 km** a una distancia de 60 km; **at this ~** a esta distancia; **at this ~ of time** después de tanto tiempo; **from a ~** desde lejos; **in the ~** a lo lejos; **in the middle ~** en segundo término; **to keep one's ~** mantenerse a distancia, *(fig)* guardar las distancias; **to keep sb at a ~** guardar las distancias con uno.
2 VR: **to ~ o.s. from** distanciarse de.

distancing ['dɪstənsɪŋ] N: **~ o.s. from others is sometimes necessary** a veces es necesario guardar las distancias con los demás.

distant ['dɪstənt] ADJ **(a)** distante, lejano, remoto *(from* de); **it is 12 km ~** dista 12 km, está a 12 km; **is it very ~?** ¿dista mucho?, ¿está muy lejos?; **in some far ~ land** en algún país lejano; **we had a ~ view of the sea** vimos el mar a lo lejos; **in some ~ future** en un futuro remoto.
(b) *relation, resemblance* lejano.
(c) *(fig)* reservado, frío; **to be ~ with sb** tratar a uno con frialdad.

distantly ['dɪstəntlɪ] ADV **(a) we are ~ related** somos parientes lejanos; **it ~ resembles the one we had before** tiene una ligera semejanza con el que teníamos antes. **(b) he treated me ~** *(fig)* me trató con frialdad.

distaste ['dɪs'teɪst] N aversión f, repugnancia f *(for* por).

distasteful [dɪs'teɪstfʊl] ADJ desagradable, repugnante; *task* nada grato; **it is ~ to me to have to +** *infin* me es poco grato tener que + *infin*.

Dist. Atty. *(US)* ABBR *of* **District Attorney**.

distemper¹ [dɪs'tempər] 1 N pintura f al temple.
2 VT pintar al temple.

distemper² [dɪs'tempər] N *(Vet)* moquillo m; *(fig)* mal m, destemplanza f.

distend [dɪs'tend] 1 VT dilatar, hinchar.
2 VI dilatarse, hincharse.

distension [dɪs'tenʃən] N distensión f, dilatación f, hinchazón f.

distich ['dɪstɪk] N dístico m.

distil, *(US)* **distill** [dɪs'tɪl] VT destilar; **distilled water** agua f destilada.

distillation [ˌdɪstɪ'leɪʃən] N destilación f.

distiller [dɪs'tɪlər] N destilador m.

distillery [dɪs'tɪlərɪ] N destilería f.

distinct [dɪs'tɪŋkt] ADJ **(a)** *(different)* distinto *(from* de); **~ as ~ from** a diferencia de. **(b)** *(clearly perceptible)* claro, inconfundible, visible; *(unmistakable)* inequívoco; **a ~ French accent** un marcado acento francés; **there is a ~ chance that ...** existe una clara posibilidad de que + *subj*.

distinction [dɪs'tɪŋkʃən] N **(a)** *(difference)* distinción f; **to draw a ~ between** hacer una distinción entre.
(b) *(eminence)* distinción f; **a man of ~** un hombre distinguido; **an artist of ~** un artista destacado; **to gain** *(or* **win)** **~** distinguirse *(as* como); **you have the ~ of being the first** a Vd le corresponde el honor de ser el primero.
(c) *(Univ etc)* sobresaliente m.

distinctive [dɪs'tɪŋktɪv] ADJ distintivo, característico.

distinctively [dɪs'tɪŋktɪvlɪ] ADV indiscutiblemente, típicamente; **~**

English/masculine *etc* típicamente inglés/masculino *etc*; **~ patterned** con un diseño muy particular.

distinctiveness [dɪs'tɪŋktɪvnɪs] N peculiaridad f; **the cultural ~ of these groups** la singularidad cultural de estos grupos.

distinctly [dɪs'tɪŋktlɪ] ADV claramente; inconfundiblemente; **it is ~ possible** bien podría ser *(that* que + *subj)*; **it is ~ awkward** es sumamente difícil.

distinguish [dɪs'tɪŋgwɪʃ] 1 VT distinguir *(from* de).
2 VI: **to ~ between** distinguir entre.
3 VR: **to ~ o.s.** distinguirse *(as* como); *(iro)* señalarse, lucirse.

distinguishable [dɪs'tɪŋgwɪʃəbl] ADJ distinguible.

distinguished [dɪs'tɪŋgwɪʃt] ADJ distinguido *(for* por), eminente, destacado.

distinguishing [dɪs'tɪŋgwɪʃɪŋ] ADJ distintivo.

distort [dɪs'tɔːt] VT deformar; *(fig)* deformar, torcer, tergiversar; distorsionar.

distorted [dɪs'tɔːtɪd] ADJ *(lit, fig)* distorsionado; **he gave us a ~ version of the events** nos dio una versión distorsionada de los hechos.

distortion [dɪs'tɔːʃən] N deformación f; *(of sound)* distorsión f; *(fig)* deformación f, torcimiento m, tergiversación f; distorsión f.

distr. ABBR *of* **distribution; distributor**.

distract [dɪs'trækt] VT distraer; *attention* distraer, apartar *(from* de); *(bewilder)* aturdir, confundir.

distracted [dɪs'træktɪd] ADJ alocado, aturdido; **like one ~** como un loco; **she is easily ~** se distrae fácilmente; **to be ~ with anxiety** estar loco de inquietud.

distractedly [dɪs'træktɪdlɪ] ADV locamente, como un loco.

distracting [dɪs'træktɪŋ] ADJ que distrae la atención, molesto.

distraction [dɪs'trækʃən] N **(a)** *(being distracted)* distracción f. **(b)** *(bewilderment)* aturdimiento m, confusión f; **to drive sb to ~** volver loco a uno. **(c)** *(amusement)* diversión f.

distrain [dɪs'treɪn] VI: **to ~ upon** secuestrar, embargar.

distraint [dɪs'treɪnt] N secuestro m, embargo m.

distrait [dɪs'treɪ] ADJ distraído.

distraught [dɪs'trɔːt] ADJ muy turbado, loco de inquietud *(etc)*; **in a ~ voice** en una voz embargada por la emoción.

distress [dɪs'tres] 1 N *(pain)* dolor m; *(mental anguish)* angustia f, pena f, aflicción f; *(misfortune)* desgracia f; *(want)* miseria f; *(danger)* peligro m; *(Med)* agotamiento m; **to be in ~** estar en un apuro, *(Med)* estar con dolor, *(ship etc)* estar en peligro; **to be in financial ~** pasar apuros.
2 VT *(pain)* doler; *(cause anguish to)* apenar, afligir; *(Med)* agotar, fatigar; **I am ~ed to hear that ...** me da pena saber que ...; **I am very ~ed at the news** estoy afligidísimo por la noticia.

distressed [dɪs'trest] ADJ afligido, angustiado.

distressing [dɪs'tresɪŋ] ADJ doloroso, penoso, que da pena.

distressingly [dɪs'tresɪŋlɪ] ADV dolorosamente, penosamente; **a ~ bad picture** un cuadro tan malo que daba pena.

distress-rocket [dɪs'tres,rɒkɪt] N cohete m de señales.

distress-signal [dɪs'tres,sɪgnəl] N señal f de socorro.

distribute [dɪs'trɪbjuːt] VT distribuir, repartir.

distribution [ˌdɪstrɪ'bjuːʃən] N distribución f, reparto m, repartimiento m; *(Ling)* distribución f; **~ network** red f de distribución; **~ rights** derechos mpl de distribución.

distributional [ˌdɪstrɪ'bjuːʃənəl] ADJ distribucional.

distributive [dɪs'trɪbjʊtɪv] 1 ADJ distributivo; **~ trade** comercio m de repartimiento.
2 N *(Ling)* adjetivo m distributivo.

distributor [dɪs'trɪbjʊtər] N **(a)** repartidor m, -ora f, distribuidor m, -ora f; *(Comm)* concesionario m, -a f, distribuidor m; *(firm)* (compañía f) distribuidora f; *(Cine)* distribuidor m. **(b)** *(Elec, Mech)* distribuidor m; *(Aut)* delco ® m.

distributorship [dɪs'trɪbjʊtəʃɪp] N distribución f *(en)* exclusiva.

district ['dɪstrɪkt] 1 N zona f, región f; *(of town)* barrio m; *(of country)* comarca f; *(Pol)* distrito m; *(postal ~)* distrito m postal.
2 ATTR: **~ attorney** *(US)* fiscal m de un distrito judicial; **~ commissioner** *(Brit)* jefe m de policía de distrito; **~ council** *(Brit)* ≈ ayuntamiento m; **~ court** tribunal m de distrito; **~ manager** gerente mf regional; **~ nurse** enfermera f de la Seguridad Social encargada de una zona determinada.

DISTRICT COUNCIL

*En Inglaterra y Gales, con la excepción de Londres, la administración local corre a cargo del **district council**, responsable de los servicios municipales como vivienda, urbanismo, recolección de basuras, salud medioambiental, etc. La mayoría de sus miembros son elegidos a nivel local cada cuatro años. Hay un total de 369 distritos (**districts**), repartidos en 53 condados (**counties**), que se financian a través de las contribuciones municipales y partidas presupuestarias del Estado. Éste controla sus gastos a través de una comisión independiente.*

---

distrust [dɪs'trʌst] 1 N desconfianza f, recelo m.

2 VT desconfiar de, recelar.

distrustful [dɪs'trʌstful] ADJ desconfiado, receloso.

disturb [dɪs'tɜːb] VT *peace, order, meeting etc* perturbar, alterar; *process, course* interrumpir; *(Psych) balance of mind* trastornar; *(disarrange)* desordenar; *person (disquiet)* perturbar, inquietar, *(bother)* molestar; **don't ~ yourself!** ¡no se moleste!; **do not ~!** por favor no molestar; **sorry to ~ you!** ¡perdone la molestia!; **I am seriously ~ed** estoy muy preocupado.

disturbance [dɪs'tɜːbəns] N *(act, state)* perturbación *f*; alteración *f*; *(outbreak of violence)* tumulto *m*, alboroto *m*; *(to service)* interrupción *f* *(to* de); *(Pol)* disturbio *m*; *(of mind)* trastorno *m*; **~ of the peace** alteración *f* del orden público; **there was a ~ in the crowd** se alborotaron algunos de los espectadores; **the ~s in Slobodia** los disturbios en Eslobodia.

disturbed [dɪs'tɜːbd] ADJ *state* alborotado, nada tranquilo; *(Psych)* trastornado; **to have a ~ night** dormir mal.

disturbing [dɪs'tɜːbɪŋ] ADJ *influence, thought* perturbador; *event* inquietante, preocupante; **it is ~ that** ... es inquietante que ...

disturbingly [dɪs'tɜːbɪŋlɪ] ADV de manera inquietante; **a ~ large number** un número tan grande que resulta inquietante; **the bomb fell ~ close** la bomba cayó tan cerca que causó inquietud.

disunited ['dɪsju'naɪtɪd] ADJ desunido.

disunity [,dɪs'juːnɪtɪ] N desunión *f*.

disuse ['dɪs'juːs] N desuso *m*; **to fall into ~** caer en desuso.

disused ['dɪs'juːzd] ADJ abandonado.

disyllabic [,dɪsɪ'læbɪk] ADJ disílabo.

ditch [dɪtʃ] 1 N zanja *f*; *(at roadside)* cuneta *f*, arroyo *m*; *(irrigation channel)* acequia *f*; *(defensive)* foso *m*; **to die in the last ~** luchar hasta quemar el último cartucho.
2 VT *(*) (get rid of)* deshacerse de, zafarse de, sacudirse a; *car etc* abandonar; **to ~ a plane** hacer un amaraje forzoso.

ditching ['dɪtʃɪŋ] N **(a)** abertura *f* de zanjas; **hedging and ~** mantenimiento *m* de setos y zanjas. **(b)** *(Aer)* amaraje *m*.

ditchwater ['dɪtʃ,wɔːtəʳ] N (†) **to be as dull as ~** ser muy soso, no tener gracia ninguna.

dither ['dɪðəʳ] *(esp Brit)* 1 N: **to be all of a ~**, **to be in a ~** *(fig)* = **2**.
2 VI estar nerviosísimo; *(be undecided)* no saber qué hacer, vacilar.

ditherer ['dɪðərəʳ] N *(Brit)* indeciso *m*, -a *f*; **don't be such a ~!** ¡no seas tan indeciso!

dithery ['dɪðərɪ] ADJ *(fig)* nervioso; indeciso, vacilante; *(from old age)* chocho.

ditto ['dɪtəʊ] ADJ ídem, lo mismo; **~ marks**, **~ sign** comillas *fpl*; **I say ~** yo digo lo mismo; **'~', he said** dijo 'yo también'.

ditty ['dɪtɪ] N cancioneta *f*.

diuretic [,daɪjʊə'retɪk] 1 ADJ diurético.
2 N diurético *m*.

diurnal [daɪ'ɜːnl] ADJ diurno.

diva ['diːvə] N, PL **~s** or **dive** ['diːve] diva *f*.

divan [dɪ'væn] N diván *m*, cama *f* turca.

dive [daɪv] 1 N **(a)** zambullida *f*; *(artistic, from board etc)* salto *m*; *(by professional diver, of submarine)* inmersión *f*; *(Aer)* picado *m*, picada *f* *(LAm)*; **his reputation has taken a ~** su reputación ha caído en picado. **(b)** (‡) tasca *f*.
2 VI *(US: irr: PRET dove, PP dived)* **(a)** *(duck etc)* zambullirse; *(from bank etc: also* **to ~ in**) tirarse al agua, saltar al agua, zambullirse; *(artistically)* saltar; *(professional diver)* bucear, sumergirse; *(submarine)* sumergirse; **the kids were diving for coins** los niños se tiraban al agua para recoger monedas; **to ~ for pearls** pescar perlas; **to ~ into the water** tirarse al agua.
(b) *(Aer)* picar.
(c) to ~ for cover *(fig)* meterse precipitadamente en un abrigo, buscar cobijo precipitadamente; **the goalkeeper ~d for the ball** el portero se lanzó a parar el balón; **to ~ into the undergrowth** meterse en la maleza; **to ~ into one's pocket** meter la mano en el bolsillo; **to ~ into a bar** entrar de prisa en un bar; **I ~d into the shop for a paper*** pasé corriendo por la tienda a por un periódico.
(d) *(prices etc)* bajar de golpe, caer en picado.

dive-bomb ['daɪvbɒm] VT bombardear en picado.

dive-bomber ['daɪv,bɒməʳ] N bombardero *m* en picado.

dive-bombing ['daɪv,bɒmɪŋ] N bombardeo *m* en picado.

diver ['daɪvəʳ] N **(a)** *(professional)* buzo *m*, buceador *m*; *(sporting)* saltador *m*, -ora *f*. **(b)** *(Orn)* colimbo *m*.

diverge [daɪ'vɜːdʒ] VI divergir *(from* de); **to ~ from** apartarse de.

divergence [daɪ'vɜːdʒəns] N divergencia *f*.

divergent [daɪ'vɜːdʒənt] ADJ divergente.

divers ['daɪvɜːz] ADJ PL *(liter)* diversos, varios.

diverse [daɪ'vɜːs] ADJ diverso, variado.

diversification [daɪ,vɜːsɪfɪ'keɪʃən] N diversificación *f*.

diversify [daɪ'vɜːsɪfaɪ] 1 VT diversificar
2 VI diversificarse.

diversion [daɪ'vɜːʃən] N *(pastime, Mil)* diversión *f*; *(Brit: of route)* desviación *f*, desvío *m*; **'D~'** *(road sign)* 'Desvío'.

diversionary [daɪ'vɜːʃnərɪ] ADJ de diversión.

diversity [daɪ'vɜːsɪtɪ] N diversidad *f*.

divert [daɪ'vɜːt] VT *(amuse)* divertir; *(turn aside)* desviar; *(Brit) traffic* desviar.

diverting [daɪ'vɜːtɪŋ] ADJ divertido.

divest¹ [daɪ'vest] 1 VT: **to ~ sb of sth** despojar a uno de algo.
2 VR: **to ~ o.s. of one's rights** renunciar a sus derechos; **he ~ed himself of his coat** se quitó el abrigo.

divest² [daɪ'vest] VTI *(US Fin)* desinvertir.

divestment [daɪ'vestmənt] N *(US Fin)* desinversión *f*.

divide [dɪ'vaɪd] 1 N *(Geog: esp US)* divisoria *f*.
2 VT dividir *(by* por, *from* de, *into* en); partir; separar; **to ~ the House** *(Brit Parl)* hacer que la Cámara proceda a la votación.
3 VI dividirse *(into* en); separarse; *(road etc)* bifurcarse; **~ and rule** divide y vencerás; **the House ~d** *(Brit Parl)* la Cámara procedió a la votación.
♦ **divide off** 1 VT dividir.
2 VI dividirse.
♦ **divide out** VT repartir.
♦ **divide up** VT dividir, partir.

divided [dɪ'vaɪdɪd] ADJ dividido; **~ highway** *(US)* carretera *f* de doble calzada.

dividend ['dɪvɪdend] N dividendo *m*; *(fig)* beneficio *m*; **~ warrant** cédula *f* de dividendo; **this should pay handsome ~s** *(fig)* esto ha de proporcionar grandes beneficios.

dividers [dɪ'vaɪdəz] NPL compás *m* de puntas.

dividing [dɪ'vaɪdɪŋ] ADJ *wall, fence* divisorio.

dividing-line [dɪ'vaɪdɪŋlaɪn] N línea *f* divisoria.

divination [,dɪvɪ'neɪʃən] N adivinación *f*.

divine¹ [dɪ'vaɪn] 1 ADJ divino; *(fig)* sublime; (*) estupendo*, maravilloso; **~ right** derecho *m* divino; **~ service** culto *m*, oficio *m* divino.
2 N teólogo *m*.

divine² [dɪ'vaɪn] VT adivinar.

divinely [dɪ'vaɪnlɪ] ADV divinamente; *(fig)* sublimemente; (*) divinamente, maravillosamente.

diviner [dɪ'vaɪnəʳ] N adivinador *m*, -ora *f*; *(water ~)* zahorí *m*.

diving ['daɪvɪŋ] N *(professional)* el bucear, buceo *m*; *(sporting)* salto *m*.

diving-bell ['daɪvɪŋbel] N campana *f* de buzo.

diving-board ['daɪvɪŋbɔːd] N trampolín *m*.

diving-suit ['daɪvɪŋsuːt] N escafandra *f*, traje *m* de buceo.

divining rod [dɪ'vaɪnɪŋrɒd] N varilla *f* de zahorí.

divinity [dɪ'vɪnɪtɪ] N **(a)** *(deity)* divinidad *f*. **(b)** *(as study)* teología *f*.

divisible [dɪ'vɪzəbl] ADJ divisible.

division [dɪ'vɪʒən] N división *f* *(also Math, Mil, Brit Police)*; separación *f*; *(sharing out)* repartimiento *m*; *(within company etc)* sección *f*; *(disagreement)* discordia *f*; *(Brit Parl)* votación *f*; **approved without a ~** aprobado por unanimidad; **there is a ~ of opinion about this** sobre esto hay diversos pareceres; **upper-~ student** *(US)* estudiante *mf* de tercer *(or* cuarto*)* año; **~ of labour** repartimiento *m* del trabajo; **~ sign** signo *m* de división.

divisional [dɪ'vɪʒənl] ADJ de división, divisional.

divisive [dɪ'vaɪsɪv] ADJ divisivo, divisionista.

divisiveness [dɪ'vaɪsɪvnɪs] N: **the ~ of this decision** las disensiones causadas *(o* que serán causadas*)* por esta decisión.

divisor [dɪ'vaɪzəʳ] N divisor *m*.

divorce [dɪ'vɔːs] 1 N divorcio *m*; *(fig)* separación *f* *(from* de); **~ court** tribunal *m* de pleitos matrimoniales; **~ proceedings** pleito *m* de divorcio; **to get a ~** divorciarse *(from* de).
2 VT divorciarse de; *(fig)* divorciar, separar *(from* de).
3 VI divorciarse.

divorcé [də'vɔːseɪ] N divorciado *m*.

divorced [dɪ'vɔːst] ADJ divorciado.

divorcee [dɪ,vɔː'siː] N divorciado *m*, -a *f*.

divot ['dɪvɪt] N terrón *m*; *(Golf)* chuleta *f*.

divulge [daɪ'vʌldʒ] VT divulgar, revelar.

divvy ['dɪvɪ] 1 N *(Brit*)* ABBR of **dividend** dividendo *m*.
2 VT *(US‡: also* **to ~ up**) dividir.

Dixie ['dɪksɪ] N *el sur de los Estados Unidos*.

| DIXIE |

(i) *Dixie* o *Dixieland* es el sobrenombre con el que se conoce de forma global a los estados sureños de EE.UU., en especial a los once estados que formaron los Estados Confederados de América durante la Guerra Civil: Alabama, Arkansas, Georgia, Florida, Louisiana, Mississippi, Carolina del Norte, Carolina del Sur, Tennessee, Texas y Virginia. También se usa como un adjetivo para describir características de los estados sureños y de sus habitantes, así como el jazz que surgió en ellos. Se supone que el nombre *Dixie* proviene de Louisiana, donde los billetes de diez dólares llevaban impreso en el anverso la palabra francesa *dix*. Para otros la palabra proviene de la línea simbólica *Mason-Dixon*, que separa el norte del sur.
⇨ *Ver también* MASON-DIXON LINE

dixie ['dɪksɪ] N (*Brit Mil*) olla *f*, marmita *f*.
DIY ABBR of **do-it-yourself** bricolaje *m*.
dizzily ['dɪzɪlɪ] ADV vertiginosamente.
dizziness ['dɪzɪnɪs] N vértigo *m*, vértigos *mpl*.
dizzy ['dɪzɪ] ADJ (a) *speed* vertiginoso; *height* que produce vértigo.
  (b) *feeling* de vértigo; (*dazed*) mareado, aturdido; **to feel ~, to get ~** marearse, estar mareado, tener vértigos; **I'm feeling rather ~** me está dando vueltas la cabeza.
  (c) (*esp US**) alelado, cascabelero, casquivano.
DJ N (a) ABBR of **disc-jockey** pinchadiscos *m*. (b) ABBR of **dinner-jacket** smoking *m*.
Djakarta [dʒə'kɑːtə] N Yakarta *f*.
djellabah ['dʒeləbə] N chilaba *f*.
DJIA N (*US St Ex*) ABBR of **Dow Jones Industrial Average**.
Djibouti [dʒɪ'buːtɪ] N Yibuti *f*.
dl ABBR of **decilitre(s)** decilitro(s) *m(pl)*, dl.
D Lit(t) [,diː'lɪt] N (a) ABBR of **Doctor of Letters**. (b) ABBR of **Doctor of Literature**.
DLO N ABBR of **dead-letter office** oficina de Correos que se encarga de las cartas que no llegan a su destino.
DM ABBR of **Deutschmark** marco *m* alemán.
dm ABBR of **decimetre(s)** decímetro(s) *m(pl)*, dm.
D-mark ['diːmɑːk] N ABBR of **Deutschmark** marco *m* alemán.
DMU N ABBR of **decision-making unit**.
D Mus [,diː'mʌz] N ABBR of **Doctor of Music** Doctor *m*, -ora *f* en Música.
DMZ N ABBR of **demilitarized zone**.
DNA N ABBR of **deoxyribonucleic acid** ácido *m* desoxirribonucleico, ADN.
DNA fingerprinting [,diːen'eɪ'fɪŋɡəprɪntɪŋ], **DNA profiling** = genetic fingerprinting.
DNB N ABBR of **Dictionary of National Biography**.
DNF (*Athletics*) ABBR of **did not finish**.
DNS (*Athletics*) ABBR of **did not start**.
do. ABBR of **ditto** lo mismo, ídem, íd.
do¹ [duː] (*irr*: PRET **did**, PTP **done**) **1** VT hacer; (*Culin*) guisar, preparar; (*Theat*) *play* representar, poner, *rôle* hacer, *personaje* hacer de, hacer el papel de; *duty* cumplir, hacer; *homage* rendir, tributar (*to* a); *problem* resolver; *dishes* lavar; *room* limpiar; *hair* peinar, (*wash and set*) arreglar; (*Univ etc*) *subject* estudiar, cursar; *distance* cubrir, recorrer, salvar; *speed* alcanzar, ir a; (*) *town etc* hacer la visita de, recorrer los monumentos de, (*) *country* visitar, recorrer, viajar por; (*Brit**: *cheat*) estafar, timar; **they ~ you very well in this hotel** en este hotel la comida es muy buena; **what's to ~?*** ¿qué pasa?; **that does it!** ¡no aguanto más!; ¡es el colmo!; **now what can I ~ for you?** ¿en qué puedo ayudarle?; **there's nothing to be done about it** no hay nada que hacer; **to have one's hair done** arreglarse el pelo; **he was done for speeding** le multaron por exceso de velocidad; **she was done for pilfering** la procesaron por ladrona; **to ~ again** rehacer, repetir, volver a hacer.
  2 VI (a) (*act, proceed*) hacer; obrar, actuar, proceder; **you did well** hiciste muy bien; **you would ~ well to draw with him** sería muy honroso lograr un empate con él; **to ~ better** mejorar, hacer progresos; **you can ~ better than that** eres capaz de hacerlo mejor; **you would ~ better to accept** sería aconsejable aceptar; **~ as you are told!** ¡haz lo que te digo!; **~ as you think best** haga lo que mejor le parezca; **~ as you would be done by** trata como quieres ser tratado.
  (b) (*fare*) **how is he ~ing?** ¿qué tal le va esto?; **how did you ~ at school?** ¿qué tal te fue en el colegio?; **how do you ~?** tengo mucho gusto en conocerle, (*less formally*) encantado, mucho gusto; **to ~ badly** sufrir reveses, ir perdiendo, fracasar, (*in exam*) salir mal; **you didn't ~ so badly** no has hecho del todo mal; **to ~ well** tener éxito, prosperar, (*in exam*) salir bien; **her son's ~ing well** su hijo tiene una buena posición; **business is ~ing well** los negocios van bien; **the crops are ~ing well** la cosecha se muestra buena.
  (c) (*cook*) cocer.
  (d) (*answer purpose*) servir; (*be suitable*) convenir, venir al caso, ser a propósito; **this one will ~** me quedo con éste; **will this ~?** ¿qué te parece éste?; (*suffice*) bastar; **will that ~?** ¿te basta eso?; **that will ~** con eso basta; está bien así; **that will have to ~** tendremos que conformarnos con eso; **that will ~!** ¡basta ya!, ¡cállate!, ¡déjate de eso!; **that won't ~** eso no vale; eso no se hace; **that will never ~** eso no resultará, eso no saldrá bien; eso no puede ser, eso no se puede consentir; **it would never ~ to** + *infin* sería inconcebible + *infin*, sería intolerable que + *subj*; **to make ~** arreglárselas por su cuenta; **to make ~ with** contentarse con, conformarse con.
  3 V AUX (a) (*emphatic*) **DO tell me** dígamelo, por favor; **I DO feel better** ciertamente me encuentro mejor; **I DO hope so** así lo espero; **I DO so wish I could** ¡ojalá pudiera!; **but I DID ~ it** pero yo sí lo hice.
  (b) (*with inversion*) **rarely does it happen that...** rara vez ocurre que ...
  (c) (*in questions*) **~ you know him?** ¿le conoces?

  (d) (*negation with* not) **you ~ not earn enough** Vd no gana bastante.
  4 VERB SUBSTITUTE: **I spoke before you did** yo hablé antes que tú; **he talks to servants as others ~ to their dogs** habla a los criados como otros a sus perros; **~ as I ~** haz tú como yo; **so ~ I** yo también, yo hago lo mismo; **did you see him? ... I did** ¿le viste? ... yo sí; **but I didn't** pero yo no; **you didn't see him but I did** tú no le viste pero yo sí; **he spoke as he often did** habló como lo había hecho muchas veces.
  5 VR: **to ~ o.s. proud** (*or* **well**) darse buena vida, vivir a cuerpo de rey.
  6 N (*) (a) (*gathering*) reunión *f*; (*Brit: ceremony*) ceremonia *f*, acto *m*; (*Brit: party*) fiesta *f*, guateque *m*.
  (b) (*trouble*) lío *m*; **that was quite a ~** eso sí que fue un lío; **he had a ~ with the police** tuvo un lío con la policía.
  (c) **~s and don'ts** reglas *fpl*; **he gave us a series of ~s and don'ts** nos dio una serie de cosas que hacer y que evitar hacer.
  (d) (*phrases*) **it's a poor ~ when ...** mala cosa cuando ...; **fair ~s!** ¡seamos justos!; **fair ~s all round** la parte justa para cada uno.
◆**do away with** VT suprimir, eliminar; acabar con; abolir; *pet* sacrificar.
◆**do down*** VT (a) (*Brit: cheat*) timar, estafar; (*play false*) hacer una mala pasada a.
  (b) (*denigrate*) hablar mal de, denigrar; dejar en mal lugar.
◆**do for** VT (a) (‡) acabar con.
  (b) (*: *as servant*) ser asistenta de, hacer la limpieza (en casa) de; llevar la casa a.
◆**do in‡** VT apiolar‡, cargarse a‡.
◆**do into** VT: **to ~ a book into English** (*Liter*) traducir un libro al inglés.
◆**do out** VT (a) *room* (*decorate*) renovar, pintar, decorar; (*clean*) limpiar.
  (b) **to ~ sb out of sth** estafar algo a uno; **they did me out of my big chance** me pisaron mi gran oportunidad; **nobody can ~ you out of that** nadie puede hacer que pierdas eso.
◆**do over** VT (a) (*repeat*) rehacer, volver a hacer.
  (b) (‡) dar una paliza a.
◆**do up** VT (a) (*tie*) liar, atar; *buttons* abotonar, *clasp* abrochar, *fastener etc* cerrar; *parcel* envolver.
  (b) *room* renovar, decorar.
◆**do with** VT (a) (*need etc*) **I could really ~ with a beer** no me iría mal una cerveza; **I could ~ with another** necesito otro además; **we could ~ with more money** no nos vendría mal más dinero; **we could have done with you there** nos hacías gran falta.
  (b) (*concern*) **it's nothing to ~ with me** no tiene que ver conmigo; **she won't have anything to ~ with him** no quiere tener nada que ver con él; **we have nothing to ~ with the neighbours** no tenemos contacto alguno con los vecinos.
  (c) **I can't be ~ing with pop‡** no aguanto la música pop.
◆**do without** VT pasarse sin, prescindir de; **one can't ~ without money** es imprescindible tener dinero.
do² [dəʊ] N (*Mus*) do *m*.
DOA ADJ ABBR of **dead on arrival** ingresó cadáver.
d.o.b. N ABBR of **date of birth** fecha *f* de nacimiento.
Doberman ['dəʊbəmən] N (*also* **~ pinscher**) dóberman *m*.
doc* [dɒk] N (*US*) = **doctor**; (*in direct address*) doctor.
docile ['dəʊsaɪl] ADJ dócil.
docility [dəʊ'sɪlɪtɪ] N docilidad *f*.
dock¹ [dɒk] N (*Bot*) acedera *f*, romaza *f*.
dock² [dɒk] VT *animal* descolar; *hair, tail* recortar; (*Brit*) *pay etc* reducir, rebajar; **I've been ~ed £1** me han rebajado la paga en una libra.
dock³ [dɒk] **1** N (*Naut*) dársena *f*, muelle *m*; (*with gates*) dique *m*; **~s** muelles *mpl*, puerto *m*; **~ warrant** conocimiento *m* de almacén; resguardo *m* de entrega; **to be in ~** (*Brit**: *car*) estar en el taller.
  2 VT *ship* poner en dique, hacer entrar en dique; *spacecraft* atracar, acoplar.
  3 VI (a) (*Naut*) entrar en dique, atracar al muelle, (*loosely*) llegar; **we ~ed at 5** llegamos a las 5, entramos en el puerto a las 5; **when we ~ed at Vigo** cuando llegamos a Vigo.
  (b) (*spacecraft*) atracar (*with* con), acoplarse (*with* a).
dock⁴ [dɒk] N (*Brit Jur*) banquillo *m* (de los acusados).
docker ['dɒkər] N trabajador *m* portuario, estibador *m*.
docket ['dɒkɪt] N (*Brit*) certificado *m*; (*label*) etiqueta *f*, marbete *m*; (*bill*) factura *f*.
docking ['dɒkɪŋ] N (*spacecraft*) atraque *m*, acoplamiento *m*; **~ manoeuvre** maniobra *f* de atraque.
dock labourer ['dɒk,leɪbərər] N, **dock worker** ['dɒk,wɜːkər] N, (*US*) **dock walloper*** ['dɒk,wɒləpər] N trabajador *m* portuario.
dockland(s) ['dɒklænd(z)] N(PL) zona *f* del puerto, zona *f* portuaria.
dockyard ['dɒkjɑːd] N astillero *m*, (*naval*) arsenal *m*.
doctor ['dɒktər] **1** N (a) (*Med*) médico *m*, -a *f*; **to be under the ~** estar bajo tratamiento médico; **to go to the ~'s** ir al médico; **it was just what the ~ ordered*** fue mano de santo; **~'s line, ~'s note**

(*Brit*), **~'s excuse** (*US*) baja *f*.
(**b**) (*Univ*) doctor *m*, -ora *f* (*of* en); **~'s degree** doctorado *m*; *ver también* DEGREE.
2 VT (**a**) (*Med*) medicinar, tratar, curar.
(**b**) (*Brit*) cat *etc* castrar.
(**c**) *drink, food* adulterar; *text* ajustar, manipular.
(**d**) **to ~ up** *machine etc* remendar, arreglar de cualquier modo.
3 VR: **to ~ o.s.** tomar medicinas, curarse.

doctoral ['dɒktərəl] ADJ doctoral; **~ thesis** (*Brit*), **~ dissertation** (*US*) tesis *f* doctoral.

doctorate ['dɒktərɪt] N doctorado *m*; *ver también* DEGREE .

doctrinaire [ˌdɒktrɪ'neəʳ] 1 ADJ doctrinario.
2 N doctrinario *m*, -a *f*.

doctrinal [dɒk'traɪnl] ADJ doctrinal.

doctrine ['dɒktrɪn] N doctrina *f*.

docudrama ['dɒkjuˌdrɑːmə] N docudrama *m*.

document 1 ['dɒkjʊmənt] N documento *m*.
2 ['dɒkjʊment] VT documentar.

documentary [ˌdɒkjʊ'mentərɪ] 1 ADJ documental; (*Comm, Fin*) documentario; **~ bill of exchange** letra *f* de cambio documentaria; **~ (letter of) credit** crédito *m* documentario; **~ evidence** prueba *f* documental.
2 N documental *m*.

documentation [ˌdɒkjumen'teɪʃən] N documentación *f*.

document case ['dɒkjumənt ˌkeɪs] N portadocumentos *m*.

document reader ['dɒkjumənt ˌriːdəʳ] N (*Comput*) lector *m* de documentos.

DOD N (*US*) ABBR *of* **Department of Defense** Ministerio *m* de Defensa.

do-dad* ['duːdæd] N (*US*) = **doodad**.

dodder ['dɒdəʳ] VI chochear.

dodderer ['dɒdərəʳ] N chocho *m*.

doddering ['dɒdərɪŋ] ADJ, **doddery** ['dɒdərɪ] ADJ chocho.

doddle: ['dɒdl] N: **it's a ~** (*Brit*) es un chollo:.

Dodecanese [ˌdəʊdɪkə'niːz] N: **the ~** el Dodecaneso.

dodecaphonic [ˌdəʊdekə'fɒnɪk] ADJ dodecafónico.

dodge [dɒdʒ] 1 N (**a**) (*of body*) regate *m*, esguince *m*, evasión *f*.
(**b**) (*) truco *m*; maniobra *f*; (*Mech*) dispositivo *m*.
2 VT (*elude*) evadir, *blow* esquivar, *pursuer* dar esquinazo a; **to ~ the issue** esquivar la cuestión; andar con rodeos; **to ~ work** gandulear.
3 VI hurtar el cuerpo, dar un esguince; (*fig*) escurrir el bulto; **to ~ into a shop** entrar de repente en una tienda; **to ~ round a corner** doblar una esquina (y desaparecer); **to ~ behind a tree** ocultarse tras un árbol.
◆**dodge about** VI ir de aquí para allá.

dodgem ['dɒdʒəm] N (*Brit*) coche *m* de choque, chocón *m*.

dodger ['dɒdʒəʳ] N gandul *mf*; **artful ~** trampista *mf*, tunante *m*.

dodgy* ['dɒdʒɪ] ADJ (*Brit*) = **dicey**.

dodo ['dəʊdəʊ] N (**a**) dodó *m*. (**b**) (*US*) bobo *m*.

DOE N (**a**) (*Brit*) ABBR *of* **Department of the Environment** Departamento *m* del Medio Ambiente. (**b**) (*US*) ABBR *of* **Department of Energy** Departamento *m* de Energía.

doe [dəʊ] N (*deer*) gama *f*; (*rabbit*) coneja *f*; (*hare*) liebre *f*.

doer ['duːəʳ] N (**a**) (*author of deed*) hacedor *m*, -ora *f*; agente *m*; **he's a great ~ of crosswords** adora los crucigramas. (**b**) (*active person*) persona *f* enérgica, persona *f* dinámica.

does [dʌz] V do[1].

doeskin ['dəʊskɪn] N ante *m*, piel *f* de ante.

doesn't ['dʌznt] = **does not**.

doff [dɒf] VT (*liter*) quitarse.

dog [dɒg] 1 N (**a**) perro *m*; (*fox*) zorro *m*; **the ~s** (*Brit*: *greyhounds*) carreras *fpl* de galgos, canódromo *m*; *ver también* GREYHOUND RACING .
(**b**) (*term of abuse etc*) tunante *m*, bribón *m*; (:: *unattractive girl*) callo: *m*; **~'s breakfast*** revoltijo *m*; **you ~!** ¡canalla!; (*hum*) ¡tunante!; **dirty ~*** tío *m* sucio*, tipo *m* asqueroso*; **gay ~*** tío *m* alegre*; **you lucky ~!*** ¡qué suerte tienes!; **he's a lucky ~*** es un tío suertudo.
(**c**) (*Telec*) teléfono *m*; **~s:** (*feet*) tachines: *mpl*.
(**d**) (*phrases*) **to be a ~ in the manger** ser el perro del hortelano; **to be top ~** ser el gallo del lugar, triunfar; **she was dressed up like a ~'s dinner** estaba hecha un adefesio; **~ eats ~ in this place** aquí los perros se comen unos a otros; **to go to the ~s** echarse a perder, arruinarse; **you haven't a ~'s chance** no tienes la más remota posibilidad, no tienes ni esperanza; **to lead a ~'s life** llevar una vida de perros; **let sleeping ~s lie** vale más no meneallo; **to put on the ~*** (*US*) vestirse de punta en blanco.
2 VT seguir los pasos de, seguir la pista de; **he was ~ged by ill luck** le persiguió la mala suerte.

dog-basket ['dɒgˌbɑːskɪt] N cesto *m* del perro.

dog-biscuit ['dɒgˌbɪskɪt] N galleta *f* de perro.

dog-breeder ['dɒgˌbriːdəʳ] N criador *m*, -ora *f* de perros.

dogcart ['dɒgkɑːt] N dócar *m*.

dog-collar ['dɒgˌkɒləʳ] N collar *m* de perro; (*Eccl*: *hum*) gola *f*, alzacuello(s) *m*, cuello *m* de cura.

dog-days ['dɒgdeɪz] NPL canícula *f*, caniculares *mpl*.

doge [dəʊdʒ] N dux *m*.

dog-eared ['dɒgɪəd] ADJ sobado, muy manoseado.

dog-end: ['dɒgend] N colilla *f*, toba: *f*.

dog-fancier ['dɒgˌfænsɪəʳ] N (*connoisseur*) entendido *m*, -a *f* en perros; (*breeder*) criador *m*, -ora *f* de perros.

dogfight ['dɒgfaɪt] N (*Aer*) combate *m* aéreo (reñido y confuso); (*fig*) batalla *f* muy reñida.

dogfish ['dɒgfɪʃ] N perro *m* marino, cazón *m*.

dog food ['dɒgfuːd] N comida *f* para perros.

dog fox ['dɒgˌfɒks] N zorro *m* macho.

dogged ['dɒgɪd] ADJ tenaz, obstinado.

doggedly ['dɒgɪdlɪ] ADV tenazmente.

doggedness ['dɒgɪdnɪs] N tenacidad *f*.

doggerel ['dɒgərəl] N versos *mpl* ramplones, malos versos *mpl*, coplas *fpl* de ciego.

doggie ['dɒgɪ] N = **doggy**.

doggo* ['dɒgəʊ] ADV: **to lie ~** (*Brit*) no bullir; estar escondido.

doggone* [ˌdɒg'gɒn] (*US*) 1 EXCL ¡maldición!
2 ADJ condenado, maldito.

dog-guard ['dɒgˌgɑːd] N (*Aut*) reja *f* separadora.

doggy ['dɒgɪ] N perrito *m*; **~ bag** bolsita *f* para el perro.

dog-handler ['dɒgˌhændləʳ] N (*Police etc*) entrenador *m* de perros.

doghouse ['dɒghaʊs] N, PL **doghouses** ['dɒgˌhaʊzɪz] (*US*) perrera *f*; **to be in the ~** estar en desgracia.

dog Latin ['dɒg'lætɪn] N latín *m* macarrónico, latinajo *m*.

dogleg ['dɒgleg] N (*in road etc*) codo *m*, ángulo *m* abrupto.

dog-licence ['dɒgˌlaɪsəns] N permiso *m* para perro.

doglike ['dɒglaɪk] ADJ canino; de perro.

dogma ['dɒgmə] N dogma *m*.

dogmatic [dɒg'mætɪk] ADJ dogmático.

dogmatically [dɒg'mætɪkəlɪ] ADV dogmáticamente.

dogmatism ['dɒgmətɪzəm] N dogmatismo *m*.

dogmatist ['dɒgmətɪst] N dogmático *m*, -a *f*.

dogmatize ['dɒgmətaɪz] VI dogmatizar.

do-gooder* ['duː'gʊdəʳ] N *persona bien intencionada*; (*pej*) bienhechor candoroso *y* entrometido.

dog-paddle ['dɒgˌpædl] 1 N braza *f* de perro.
2 VI nadar como los perros.

dog-rose ['dɒgrəʊz] N escaramujo *m*, rosal *m* silvestre.

dogsbody* ['dɒgzbɒdɪ] N: **to be a ~** hacer de todo; **to be the general ~** ser el burro de carga para todos.

dogshow ['dɒgʃəʊ] N exposición *f* canina.

Dog Star ['dɒgˌstɑːʳ] N Sirio *m*.

dog tag ['dɒgtæg] N (*US*) placa *f* de identidad (*or* de identificación).

dog-tired ['dɒg'taɪəd] ADJ: **to be ~** estar rendido.

dogtrack ['dɒgtræk] N canódromo *f*.

dogtrot ['dɒgtrɒt] N trote *m* lento.

dog-watch ['dɒgwɒtʃ] N (*Naut*) guardia *f* de cuartillo.

doily ['dɔɪlɪ] N pañito *m* de adorno.

doing ['duːɪŋ] 1 PRES PART of **do**; **there's not much ~** hay poca animación; **nothing ~!** ¡de ninguna manera!, ¡ni hablar!; **this is your ~** eres tú quien ha hecho esto; **it was none of my ~** no he tenido que ver; **it takes some ~** no es nada fácil, exige bastante esfuerzo (*or* fuerza *etc*).
2 N (**a**) **~s** (*deeds*) hechos *mpl*; acciones *fpl*; (*conduct*) conducta *f*, actuación *f*; (*happenings*) sucesos *mpl*; **there were great ~s in the house** hubo muchísima actividad en la casa.
(**b**) (*: Mech etc*) **~s** chisme *m*; **that ~s with two knobs** (*Brit*) aquel chisme con dos botones.

do-it-yourself ['duːɪtjə'self] ATTR hágalo Vd mismo; (*as n*) bricolaje *m*; **~ enthusiast, ~ expert** bricolador *m*, -ora *f*, bricolero *m*, -a *f*, aficionado *m*, -a *f* al bricolaje; **~ kit** juego *m* de montar; **~ shop** tienda *f* de bricolaje.

do-it-yourselfer [ˌduːɪtjə'selfəʳ] N aficionado *m*, -a *f* al bricolaje.

Dolby ['dɒlbɪ] ® N Dolby *m* ®.

doldrums ['dɒldrəmz] NPL (*Naut*) zona *f* de las calmas ecuatoriales; **to be in the ~** (*fig*: *person*) estar abatido, (*business*) estar encalmado, (*St Ex*) estar en calma.

dole [dəʊl] N limosna *f*; (*of unemployed*) subsidio *m* de paro; **~ queue** cola *f* de los parados; **to be on the ~** (*Brit*) estar parado; **love on the ~** el amor en la miseria.
◆**dole out** VT repartir (parcamente), distribuir (con parsimonia).

doleful ['dəʊlfʊl] ADJ triste, lúgubre, lastimero.

dolefully ['dəʊlfəlɪ] ADV tristemente.

doll [dɒl] N muñeca *f*; (*esp US:*) gachí: *f*, jai: *f*.
◆**doll up*** 1 VT adornar, ataviar.
2 VI = **3**.
3 VR: **to ~ o.s. up** emperejilarse, ataviarse.

dollar ['dɒləʳ] N dólar *m*; **you can bet your bottom ~ that ...** es completamente seguro que ...; **it's ~s to doughnuts that ...*** es tan cierto como hay Dios que ...*.

dollar area ['dɒlər,eəriə] N zona f en que se emplea el dólar.
dollar bill ['dɒlə'bɪl] N billete m de un dólar.
dollar diplomacy ['dɒlədɪ'pləʊməsɪ] N diplomacia f a golpe de dólar.
dollar rate ['dɒləreɪt] N cambio m del dólar.
dollar sign ['dɒlə,saɪn] N signo m del dólar.
dollop ['dɒləp] N porción f, masa f.
doll's house ['dɒlzhaʊs] N, PL **doll's houses** ['dɒlzhaʊzɪz] casa f de muñecas.
Dolly ['dɒlɪ] NF familiar form of **Dorothy**.
dolly ['dɒlɪ] N (a) (doll) muñequita f. (b)(*: girl) chica f, jovencita f; **you're a ~ to help me*** eres un ángel por ayudarme. (c) (US) carretilla f. (d) (Cine, TV) travelín m, plataforma f rodante.
dolly bird: ['dɒlɪbɜ:d] N (Brit) niña f mona*.
dolomite ['dɒləmaɪt] N dolomía f, dolomita f.
Dolomites ['dɒləmaɪts] NPL Dolomitas fpl, Alpes mpl Dolomíticos.
dolphin ['dɒlfɪn] N delfín m.
dolphinarium [,dɒlfɪ'neərɪəm] N delfinario m.
dolt [dəʊlt] N imbécil m, mastuerzo m; **you ~!** ¡bobalicón!
domain [dəʊ'meɪn] N (lands) heredad f, propiedad f; (empire) dominio m; (sphere) campo m, competencia f; **the matter is now in the public ~** el asunto es ya del dominio público.
dome [dəʊm] N cúpula f; bóveda f (also fig); (Geog) colina f redonda.
domed [dəʊmd] ADJ forehead, building abovedado.
Domesday Book ['du:mzdeɪ,bʊk] N: **the ~** el Domesday Book (libro del registro catastral realizado en Inglaterra en 1086).
domestic [də'mestɪk] ① ADJ doméstico; appliance de uso doméstico; industry, product nacional; trade interior; strife interno, intestino; (home-loving) casero, hogareño; **~ flight** vuelo m nacional; **~ market** mercado m nacional, mercado m interior; **~ science** (esp Brit) ciencia f del hogar; **~ staff** personal m de servicio; criados mpl, servidumbre f; **~ trade** comercio m interior; **~ work** trabajo m de casa, labor f doméstica.
② N doméstico m.
domestically [dəʊ'mestɪkəlɪ] ADV: **a ~ produced article** un artículo producido en el país; **she is not ~ inclined** no tiene inclinación doméstica.
domesticate [də'mestɪkeɪt] VT domesticar.
domesticated [də'mestɪkeɪtɪd] ADJ domesticado; person casero, hogareño.
domestication [dəʊ,mestɪ'keɪʃən] N domesticación f.
domesticity [,dəʊmes'tɪsɪtɪ] N domesticidad f.
domicile ['dɒmɪsaɪl] (Brit) ① N domicilio m.
② VT: **to be ~d in** domiciliarse en.
domiciliary [,dɒmɪ'sɪlɪərɪ] ADJ domiciliario.
dominance ['dɒmɪnəns] N dominación f.
dominant ['dɒmɪnənt] ADJ dominante.
dominate ['dɒmɪneɪt] VTI dominar.
dominating ['dɒmɪneɪtɪŋ] ADJ dominante, dominador.
domination [,dɒmɪ'neɪʃən] N dominación f.
dominatrix [,dɒmɪ'neɪtrɪks] N ama f (prostituta especializada en servicios sadomasoquistas).
domineer [,dɒmɪ'nɪə'] VI dominar, tiranizar (over sb a alguien).
domineering [,dɒmɪ'nɪərɪŋ] ADJ dominante, dominador, tiránico.
Dominic ['dɒmɪnɪk] NM Domingo.
Dominica [,dɒmɪ'ni:kə] N Dominica f.
Dominican [də'mɪnɪkən] ① ADJ dominicano.
② N (Pol) dominicano m, -a f; (Eccl) dominico m, dominicano m.
Dominican Republic [də'mɪnɪkənɪr'pʌblɪk] N República f Dominicana.
dominion [də'mɪnɪən] N dominio m; (Brit Pol) dominio m.
domino ['dɒmɪnəʊ] N, PL **dominoes** ['dɒmɪnəʊz] (dress) dominó m; (in game) ficha f de dominó; **~ effect** (Pol) reacción f en cadena; **~ theory** (Pol) teoría f de la reacción en cadena.
dominoes ['dɒmɪnəʊz] NPL dominó m.
Domitian [də'mɪʃɪən] NM Domiciano.
don¹ [dɒn] VT ponerse.
don² [dɒn] N (Brit Univ) profesor m, -ora f (esp en Oxford y Cambridge).
donate [dəʊ'neɪt] VT donar.
donation [dəʊ'neɪʃən] N donativo m.
done [dʌn] ① PTP of **do¹**.
② ADJ (a) **~!** ¡trato hecho!; **well ~!** ¡muy bien!, ¡bravo!
(b) (Culin) **I like my meat well ~** me gusta la carne muy hecha; **is it ~ yet?** ¿está hecho ya?
(c) **it's not ~** no se hace, es mal visto; **it's not ~ to yawn** no es elegante bostezar, es de mal gusto bostezar.
(d) **have you ~?** ¿has terminado?; **I've ~ with travelling** he terminado de viajar, he renunciado a los viajes; **I've ~ with him** he roto con él.
(e) **I'm ~ for** (tired) estoy rendido; **if we don't leave now we shall be ~ for** si no nos vamos ahora estamos perdidos; **the car is ~ for** el coche está estropeado del todo; **as a musician he's ~ for** ya no vale para músico.

(f) **to feel ~ in***, **to be ~ up*** estar rendido.
dong: [dɒŋ] N badajo: m, polla: f.
Don Juan [dɒn'hwɑ:n] N (fig) Don Juan.
donkey ['dɒŋkɪ] N burro m, burra f; **it went on for ~'s years*** (Brit) continuó durante muchísimos años; **I haven't seen him for ~'s years*** (Brit) hace siglos que no le he visto.
donkey derby ['dɒŋkɪ,dɑ:bɪ] N carrera f de burros.
donkey-engine ['dɒŋkɪ,endʒɪn] N pequeña máquina f de vapor, motor m auxiliar.
donkey-jacket ['dɒŋkɪ,dʒækɪt] N chaqueta f de lanilla de trabajo.
donkey-work ['dɒŋkɪ,wɜ:k] N trabajo m duro y aburrido.
donnish ['dɒnɪʃ] ADJ de erudito, de profesor; de aspecto erudito; (pej) profesoril; pedantesco; **he looks very ~** tiene aspecto de muy erudito.
donor ['dəʊnə'] N donante mf.
donor card ['dəʊnə,kɑ:d] N carnet m de donante de órganos.
Don Quixote [dɒn'kwɪksət] NM Don Quijote.
don't [dəʊnt] ① = **do not**.
② N prohibición f, consejo m negativo.
don't knows [,dəʊnt'nəʊz] NPL V **know 3 (b)**.
donut ['dəʊnʌt] N (US) buñuelo m, rosquilla f.
doodad* ['du:dæd] N (US) artilugio m.
doodah* ['du:dɑ:] N (a) (Brit: gadget) = **doodad***. (b) **to go all of a ~** ponerse a temblar; ponerse muy nervioso.
doodle ['du:dl] ① N garabatos mpl (or dibujos etc) que hace uno para distraerse.
② VI garrapatear, borronear, borrajear (para distraerse).
doodlebug ['du:dlbʌg] N (Brit) bomba f volante.
doohickey* [,du:'hɪkɪ] N trasto m.
doolally: [,du:'lælɪ] ADJ tarumba*.
doom [du:m] ① N (fate) suerte f, hado m; (death) perdición f, muerte f; (Rel) juicio m final; **a sense of ~** una sensación de desastre; **it's all ~ and gloom here** aquí reina el catastrofismo.
② VT condenar (a muerte etc); predestinar (a la perdición etc); **to be ~ed to die** estar sentenciado a muerte; **the plan was ~ed to fail** el proyecto tenía fatalmente que fracasar, el proyecto estaba llamado a fracasar; **the ~ed ship** el buque fatalmente siniestrado.
doom-laden ['du:m,leɪdn] ADJ warning, prophecy aciago.
doomsday ['du:mzdeɪ] N día m del juicio final; **the ~ scenario** los resultados más catastróficos.
doomwatcher ['du:m,wɒtʃə'] N cataclismista mf, catastrofista mf.
doomwatching ['du:m,wɒtʃɪŋ] N cataclismismo m, catastrofismo m.
door [dɔ:'] N puerta f; entrada f; (of vehicle) portezuela f; **3 ~s up from us** 3 puertas arriba de nosotros; **behind closed ~s** a puerta cerrada; **from ~ to ~** de puerta en puerta; **next ~** en la casa de al lado; **at the table next ~*** en la mesa de al lado; **my next ~ neighbour** mi vecino de (la casa de) al lado; **this is next ~ to lunacy** esto raya en la locura; **he was on the ~ at the club** hacía de portero (or echador etc) en el club; **she was on the ~ at the theatre** hacía de acomodadora en el teatro; **to be out of ~s** estar al aire libre; **to be at death's ~** estar a la muerte; **to bang the ~** dar un portazo; **it closed the ~ on negotiations** cerró la puerta de las negociaciones; **never darken my ~ again** no vuelva nunca por aquí; **to lay the blame (or sth) at sb's ~** echar a uno la culpa; **to leave the ~ open for** (fig) dejar la puerta abierta para; **a name like that opens ~s** un apellido así abre muchas puertas; **this opened the ~ to further progress** esto facilitó los progresos ulteriores; **to pay at the ~** pagar a la entrada; **to show sb to the ~** acompañar a uno a la puerta; **to show sb the ~** enseñar la puerta a uno; **to shut the ~ on a proposal** negarse a considerar una propuesta; **to slam the ~** dar un portazo; **to slam the ~ in sb's face** dar con la puerta en las narices de uno; **to slam the ~ on negotiations** terminar de modo concluyente las negociaciones.
doorbell ['dɔ:bel] N timbre m (de llamada).
doorchain ['dɔ:tʃeɪn] N cadena f de la puerta.
do-or-die ['du:ə'daɪ] ADJ effort extraordinario; **it's ~** es todo o nada.
doorframe ['dɔ:freɪm] N marco m de la puerta.
door-handle ['dɔ:,hændl] N tirador m (de puerta), puño m; (of car) manija f.
door-jamb ['dɔ:dʒæm] N jamba f de la puerta.
doorkeeper ['dɔ:,ki:pə'] N conserje m, portero m.
doorknob ['dɔ:nɒb] N pomo m (de puerta), tirador m (de puerta).
door-knocker ['dɔ:,nɒkə'] N aldaba f, llamador m.
doorman ['dɔ:mən] N, PL **doormen** ['dɔ:mən] portero m.
doormat ['dɔ:mæt] N felpudo m, estera f, alfombrilla f.
doornail ['dɔ:neɪl] N V **dead**.
doorpost ['dɔ:pəʊst] N jamba f (de puerta).
doorstep ['dɔ:step] N umbral m, peldaño m de la puerta; **we don't want an airport on our ~** no queremos un aeropuerto aquí tan cerca.
doorstop ['dɔ:stɒp] N tope m (de puerta).
door-to-door ['dɔ:tədɔ:'] ADJ: **~ salesman** vendedor m de puerta en

puerta, vendedor *m* a domicilio; ~ **selling** ventas *fpl* a domicilio.

doorway ['dɔ:weɪ] N puerta *f*, entrada *f*; portal *m*.

dope [dəʊp] ① N **(a)** (*varnish*) barniz *m*.
(b) (*Drugs*‡) droga *f*, narcótico *m*; **to do** ~ (*US**) doparse, drogarse.
(c) (‡: *information*) informes *mpl*, información *f*; **give me the** ~ dime, desembucha*; **what's the** ~ **on him?** ¿qué es lo que se sabe de él?
(d) (*: *person*) mastuerzo* *m*, idiota *mf*; **you** ~! ¡bobo!
② ATTR **(a)** (*Drugs*‡) ~ **fiend** drogata‡ *mf*; ~ **peddler**, ~ **pusher** camello* *m*; ~ **test** prueba *f* contra drogas.
(b) ~ **sheet*** periódico *m* de carreras de caballos.
③ VT narcotizar, drogar.
♦**dope up*** VT: **to be ~d up on/with Valium** ir ciego a Valium*.

dopehead* ['dəʊphed] N porrero* *m*, -a *f*.

dopey* ['dəʊpɪ] ADJ (*dazed*) aturdido, mareado; (*silly*) imbécil.

doping ['dəʊpɪŋ] N drogado *m*, doping *m*.

Doppler effect ['dɒplɑːˌfekt] N efecto *m* Doppler.

dopy ['dəʊpɪ] = **dopey**.

Dordogne [dɔːˈdɔɪn] N (*region*) Dordoña *f*; (*river*) Dordoña *m*.

dorf‡ [dɔːf] N (*US*) borde* *mf*.

Doric ['dɒrɪk] ADJ (*Archit*) dórico.

dork* [dɔːk] N (*esp US*) zumbado *m*, -a *f*.

dorm* [dɔːm] N = **dormitory**.

dormancy ['dɔːmənsɪ] N *of volcano* inactividad *f*; *of virus* estado *m* latente; *of plant* reposo *m* (vegetativo).

dormant ['dɔːmənt] ADJ **(a)** inactivo; **to be** ~, **to lie** ~ dormir. **(b)** (*fig*) inactivo, latente, en estado latente.

dormer ['dɔːməʳ] N (*also* ~ **window**) buhardilla *f*.

dormice ['dɔːmaɪs] NPL of **dormouse**.

dormitory ['dɔːmɪtrɪ] N (*Brit*) dormitorio *m*; (*US Univ*) colegio *m* mayor; ~ **suburb** (*esp Brit*) barrio *m* dormitorio; ~ **town** (*esp Brit*) pueblo *m* dormitorio.

Dormobile ['dɔːməbiːl] ® N (*Brit*) combi *f*.

dormouse ['dɔːmaʊs] N, PL **dormice** ['dɔːmaɪs] lirón *m*.

Dorothy ['dɒrəθɪ] NF Dorotea.

Dors N (*Brit*) ABBR of **Dorset**.

dorsal ['dɔːsl] ADJ dorsal.

dory¹ ['dɔːrɪ] N (*Fish*) gallo *m*, pez *m* de San Pedro.

dory² ['dɔːrɪ] N (*boat*) arenera *f*.

DOS [dɒs] N ABBR of **disk operating system** sistema *m* operativo de discos.

dosage ['dəʊsɪdʒ] N dosificación *f*, dosis *f*.

dose [dəʊs] ① N dosis *f*.
② VT (*also* **to** ~ **up**) administrar una dosis a; medicinar; *wine* adulterar.
③ VR: **to** ~ **o.s.** (*also* **to** ~ **o.s. up**) medicinarse (*with* de).

dosh‡ [dɒʃ] N guita‡ *f*, dinero *m*.

doss‡ [dɒs] VI **(a)** (*sleep*) dormir; **to** ~ **down** echarse. **(b) to** ~ **around** gandulear, no hacer nada.

dosser‡ ['dɒsəʳ] N (*Brit*) gandul* *m*, vago *m*; *persona que vive en pensiones de mala muerte*.

dosshouse* ['dɒshaʊs] N, PL **dosshouses** ['dɒsˌhaʊzɪz] refugio *m* nocturno para pobres.

dossier ['dɒsɪeɪ] N expediente *m*, do(s)sier *m*.

DOT N (*US*) ABBR of **Department of Transportation**.

Dot [dɒt] NF *familiar form of* **Dorothy**.

dot [dɒt] ① N punto *m*; **three** ~**s** (*Typ*) puntos *mpl* suspensivos; ~**s and dashes** puntos *mpl* y rayas; **at 7 o'clock on the** ~ a las 7 en punto; **to pay on the** ~ pagar puntualmente; **in the year** ~ (*Brit*) en tiempos de Maricastaña; ~ **command** orden *f* con punto (inicial); ~ **prompt** indicación *f* de punto.
② VT **(a)** *letter* poner el punto sobre; **to** ~ **the i's and cross the t's** (*fig*) poner los puntos sobre las íes.
(b) (*speckle*) puntear, motear, salpicar de puntos.
(c) (*scatter*; *also* **to** ~ **about**) esparcir, desparramar; **to be ~ted with** estar salpicado de; **they are ~ted about the country** se encuentran esparcidos por el país.
(d) (*) **to** ~ **sb a blow** dar un golpe a uno; **he ~ted him one** le pegó, le pegó un porrazo.

dotage ['dəʊtɪdʒ] N chochez *f*; **to be in one's** ~ chochear.

dote [dəʊt] VI: **to** ~ **on** adorar, idolatrar.

doting ['dəʊtɪŋ] ADJ chocho, tontamente cariñoso; **her** ~ **parents** sus padres que la adoran, sus complacientes padres.

dot-matrix printer [ˌdɒtˌmeɪtrɪksˈprɪntəʳ] N impresora *f* matricial (*or* de matriz) de puntos.

dotted ['dɒtɪd] ADJ: ~ **line** línea *f* de puntos; **to sign on the** ~ **line** (*fig*) aprobar algo maquinalmente.

dotty* ['dɒtɪ] ADJ (*Brit*) chiflado*, disparatado; *idea, scheme* estrafalario, tonto; **you must be** ~! ¿estás loco o qué?; **it's driving me** ~ esto me trae loco.

double ['dʌbl] ① ADJ doble; *sense* doble, ambiguo; **the** ~ **6** el 6 doble; ~ **9** (*Telec*) nueve nueve; **the word has** ~ **'m'** la palabra se escribe

con dos 'm'(emes); ~ **the sum**, **a** ~ **sum** el doble, una cantidad doble; **it is** ~ **what it was** es el doble de lo que era; **my income is** ~ **that of my neighbour** gano dos veces más que mi vecino; **he's** ~ **your age** te dobla la edad; **to be bent** ~ estar encorvado; ~ **act** (*Theat*) número *m* doble; ~ **bed** cama *f* de matrimonio; ~ **bend** (*Brit Aut*) curva *f* en S; ~ **bluff** engaño *m* doble; ~ **bogey** más dos *m*; ~ **chin** papada *f*; ~ **density disk** disco *m* de doble densidad; ~ **Dutch*** (*Brit*) galimatías *m*; **it's** ~ **Dutch to me*** (*Brit*) para mí es chino; **to talk** ~ **Dutch*** (*Brit*) hablar chino; **in** ~ **figures** 10 o más; ~ **helix** hélice *f* doble; ~ **pay** paga *f* doble; **it's** ~ **pay on Sundays** los domingos se paga el doble; ~ **room** habitación *f* doble; **to do a** ~ **take** quedarse quedado (*or* atónito); ~ **time** *V* ~ **pay**; **in** ~ **time** (*Mil*) a paso ligero; ~ **track** (*Rail*) vía *f* doble; **a** ~ **whisky** un whisky doble.
② ADV: ~ **or quits** doble o nada; **to cost** ~ costar el doble; **to fold sth** ~ doblar algo; **to pay** ~ pagar el doble; **to see** ~ ver doble.
③ N **(a)** (*quantity*) doble *m*; (*person*) doble *mf*.
(b) ~**s** (*Tennis*) juego *m* de dobles.
(c) (*Bridge*) doble *m*, contra *f*.
(d) at the ~ corriendo, (*Mil*) a paso ligero.
(e) (*drink*) doble *m*.
④ VT doblar; *money, quantity etc* doblar, duplicar; *efforts* redoblar; (*Theat, Bridge*) doblar.
⑤ VI doblarse; (*quantity etc*) doblarse, duplicarse.
♦**double back** VI volver sobre sus pasos.
♦**double for** VT sustituir, hacer las veces de (*also Theat*).
♦**double over** VT doblar.
♦**double up** ① VT: **to be ~d up with laughter** troncharse de risa; **to be ~d up with pain** doblarse de dolor.
② VI (*lodgers*) compartir la misma habitación.

double-acting [ˌdʌblˈæktɪŋ] ADJ de doble acción.

double agent ['dʌblˈeɪdʒənt] N agente *m* doble.

double bar [ˌdʌblˈbɑːʳ] N (*Mus*) barra *f* doble.

double-barrelled ['dʌblˌbærəld] ADJ de dos cañones; (*Brit**) *name* de dos apellidos (unidos con guión).

double bass ['dʌblˈbeɪs] N contrabajo *m*.

double bassoon [ˌdʌblbəˈsuːn] N contrafagot *m*.

double bill [ˌdʌblˈbɪl] N (*Cine*) programa *m* doble.

double bind [ˌdʌblˈbaɪnd] N callejón *m* sin salida*.

double-blind [ˌdʌblˌblaɪnd] ADJ: ~ **experiment** experimento en el que ni el analizador ni el sujeto conoce las características; ~ **method** método según el cual ni el analizador ni el sujeto conoce las características del producto.

double boiler [ˌdʌblˈbɔɪləʳ] N (*US*) baño *m* de María.

double-book [ˌdʌblˈbʊk] VT: **we were ~ed** habíamos hecho dos citas distintas; (*in hotel*) **we found we were ~ed** encontramos que habían reservado la habitación para dos parejas distintas.

double booking [ˌdʌblˈbʊkɪŋ] N doble reserva *f*.

double-breasted ['dʌblˈbrestɪd] ADJ cruzado, con botonadura doble.

double-check ['dʌblˈtʃek] ① VTI verificar dos veces.
② N doble verificación *f*.

double-click ['dʌblˌklɪk] (*Comput*) ① VI hacer doble click.
② VT hacer doble click en.

double cream [ˌdʌblˈkriːm] N (*Brit*) nata *f* enriquecida.

double-cross ['dʌblˈkrɒs] ① N engaño *m*, trampa *f*, traición *f*.
② VT engañar, traicionar.

double-date [ˌdʌblˈdeɪt] ① VT engañar con otro/otra.
② VI (*US*) salir dos parejas.

double dealer [ˌdʌblˈdiːləʳ] N traidor *m*, -ora *f*.

double-dealing ['dʌblˈdiːlɪŋ] N trato *m* doble, juego *m* doble, duplicidad *f*.

double-decker ['dʌblˈdekəʳ] N (*Aut*) autobús *m* de dos pisos; (*Culin*) sándwich *m* doble.

double declutch [ˌdʌbldiːˈklʌtʃ] VI hacer un doble desembragaje.

double-digit [ˌdʌblˈdɪdʒɪt] ADJ de dos dígitos.

double door [ˌdʌblˈdɔːʳ] N puerta *f* partida.

double eagle [ˌdʌblˈiːgl] N doble eagle *m*.

double-edged ['dʌblˈedʒd] ADJ de doble filo.

double entendre ['duːblɑːnˈtɑːndr] N equívoco *m*, frase *f* ambigua.

double entry ['dʌblˈentrɪ] N partida *f* doble; ~ **book-keeping** contabilidad *f* por partida doble.

double exposure [ˌdʌblɪksˈpəʊʒəʳ] N doble exposición *f*.

double-faced [ˌdʌblˈfeɪst] ADJ *material* reversible; (*pej*) *person* de dos caras.

double fault [ˌdʌblˈfɔːlt] ① N falta *f* doble.
② VI cometer doble falta.

double feature [ˌdʌblˈfiːtʃəʳ] N (*Cine*) sesión *f* doble, programa *m* doble.

double-figure [ˌdʌblˈfɪgəʳ] ADJ = **double-digit**.

double flat [ˌdʌblˈflæt] N doble bemol *m*.

double-glaze [ˌdʌblˈgleɪz] VT: **to** ~ **a window** termoaislar una ventana.

double-glazed [ˌdʌblˈgleɪzd] ADJ con doble acristalamiento.

double glazing [ˌdʌblˈgleɪzɪŋ] N (*Brit*) doble acristalamiento *m*.

double-header [ˈdʌblˌhedəʳ] N (*US: Sport*) dos encuentros consecutivos entre los mismos o diferentes equipos.

double indemnity [ˌdʌblɪnˈdemnɪtɪ] N doble indemnización *f*; ~ **coverage** seguro *m* de doble indemnización.

double jeopardy [ˌdʌblˈdʒepədɪ] N (*esp US*) procesamiento *m* por segunda vez.

double-jointed [ˈdʌblˈdʒɔɪntɪd] ADJ con articulaciones muy flexibles.

double knit(ting) [ˈdʌblˈnɪt(ɪŋ)] ① N (*wool*) lana *f* gruesa. ② ADJ de lana gruesa.

double knot [ˈdʌblnɒt] N doble lazo *m*.

double lock [ˌdʌblˈlɒk] ① VT cerrar con dos vueltas. ② N cerradura *f* doble.

double marking [ˌdʌblˈmɑːkɪŋ] N doble corrección *f*.

double negative [ˌdʌblˈnegətɪv] N doble negación *f*.

double-page [ˈdʌblpeɪdʒ] ADJ: ~ **spread** doble página *f*.

double-park [ˌdʌblˈpɑːk] VTI aparcar en doble fila.

double-parking [ˌdʌblˈpɑːkɪŋ] N aparcamiento *m* en doble fila.

double pneumonia [ˈdʌblnjuːˈməʊnɪə] N pulmonía *f* doble.

double-quick [ˈdʌblˈkwɪk] ADV rapidísimamente, con toda prontitud, (*Mil*) a paso ligero.

double sharp [ˌdʌblˈʃɑːp] N doble sostenido *m*.

double-sided disk [ˌdʌblˌsaɪdɪdˈdɪsk] N disco *m* de dos caras.

double-space [ˌdʌblˈspeɪs] VT escribir a doble espacio.

double-spaced [ˈdʌblˈspeɪst] ADV a doble espacio.

double spacing [ˈdʌblˈspeɪsɪŋ] N: **in** ~ a doble espacio.

doublespeak [ˈdʌblspiːk] N (*pej*) doble lenguaje *m*.

double standards [ˌdʌblˈstændədz] NPL: **to have** ~ medir a dos raseros.

double star [ˌdʌblˈstɑːʳ] N estrella *f* binaria.

double stopping [ˌdʌblˈstɒpɪŋ] N doble cuerda *f*.

doublet [ˈdʌblɪt] N (a) (††) jubón *m*. (b) (*Ling*) doblete *m*.

double-take [ˈdʌblteɪk] N: **to do a** ~ reaccionar tarde.

double-talk [ˈdʌblˌtɔːk] N palabras *fpl* insinceras.

double-think [ˈdʌblθɪŋk] N: **a piece of** ~ pasaje *m* (*etc*) lleno de contradicciones, ejemplo *m* (*etc*) de hipocresía.

doubleton [ˈdʌbltən] N dubletón *m*.

double windows [ˌdʌblˈwɪndəʊz] NPL doble acristalado *m*.

double vision [ˈdʌblˌvɪʒən] N doble visión *f*, diplopía *f*.

doubling [ˈdʌblɪŋ] N (*number*) multiplicación *f* por dos; (*letter*) duplicación *f*.

doubly [ˈdʌblɪ] ADV doblemente.

▼ **doubt** [daʊt] ① N (a ~) duda *f*; (*state*) duda *f*, incertidumbre *f*; **no** ~! ¡sin duda!; **beyond** ~, **past all** ~, **without** (a) ~ fuera de toda duda, indudablemente; **beyond all reasonable** ~ más allá de toda duda; **when in** ~ en caso de duda; **the matter is still in some** ~ el caso sigue dudoso; **she was in** ~ **whether to ...** dudaba si ...; **there is some** ~ **about it** sobre esto existen dudas; **there is no** ~ **that ...** es indudable que ..., no cabe duda de que ...; **I have no** ~ **that it is true** no dudo que es verdad; **to begin to have one's** ~**s** empezar a dudar; **to clear up sb's** ~**s** sacar a uno de dudas; **to cast** (*or* **throw**) ~ **on** poner en duda; **let there be no** ~ **about it** que nadie dude de esto; **the marks left no** ~ **about how he died** las señales no dejaban lugar a dudas sobre cómo murió.

▼ ② VT dudar; (*distrust*) dudar de; **I** ~ **it** lo dudo; **to** ~ **sb's loyalty** dudar de la lealtad de uno; **she** ~**ed whether to go** dudaba si iría; **I greatly** ~ **whether he will accept** dudo mucho que acepte; **I never** ~**ed you** nunca tuve dudas acerca de ti.

③ VI dudar; ~**ing Thomas** Tomás el incrédulo.

doubter [ˈdaʊtəʳ] N escéptico *m*, -a *f*.

▼ **doubtful** [ˈdaʊtfʊl] ADJ dudoso, incierto; *character, place* sospechoso; **I am** ~ **whether ...** dudo si ...; **he remained** ~ **about it** tenía todavía sus dudas sobre ello; **of** ~ **efficacy** de eficacia incierta.

doubtfully [ˈdaʊtfʊlɪ] ADV inciertamente; **he said** ~ dijo nada convencido.

doubtfulness [ˈdaʊtfʊlnɪs] N (*hesitation*) vacilación *f*, duda *f*; (*uncertainty*) incertidumbre *f*; (*suspicious quality*) carácter *m* sospechoso.

▼ **doubtless** [ˈdaʊtlɪs] ADV sin duda; a no dudar(lo), a buen seguro.

douceur [duːˈsɜːʳ] N (*frm: gift, tip etc*) gratificación *f*.

douche [duːʃ] ① N ducha *f*; (*Med*) jeringa *f*. ② VT duchar. ③ VI ducharse.

dough [dəʊ] N masa *f*, pasta *f*; (✝) pasta *f*.

doughboy [ˈdəʊbɔɪ] N (*US*) soldado *m* de infantería; (*Hist*) soldado de la Primera Guerra Mundial.

doughnut [ˈdəʊnʌt] N (*Brit*) buñuelo *m*, rosquilla *f*.

doughty [ˈdaʊtɪ] ADJ *person* valiente, esforzado; *deed* hazañoso.

doughy [ˈdəʊɪ] ADJ pastoso.

dour [ˈdʊəʳ] ADJ (*grim*) austero, severo; (*obstinate*) terco; **a** ~ **Scot** un escocés cerrado; **a** ~ **struggle** una batalla muy reñida.

Douro [ˈdʊərəʊ] N Duero *m*.

douse [daʊs] VT *fire, light* apagar; (*with water*) mojar, lavar (*with* de).

dove¹ [dʌv] N paloma *f* (*also Pol*).

dove² [dəʊv] (*US*) PRET *of* dive.

dovecote [ˈdʌvkɒt] N palomar *m*.

dove-grey [ˌdʌvˈgreɪ] ADJ gris paloma.

Dover [ˈdəʊvəʳ] N Dover *m*.

dovetail [ˈdʌvteɪl] ① N cola *f* de milano. ② VT ensamblar a cola de milano. ③ VI (*fig*) encajar (con), ajustarse; **to** ~ **in with** encajar perfectamente con.

dovish [ˈdʌvɪʃ] ADJ (*Pol etc*) blando.

dowager [ˈdaʊədʒəʳ] N viuda *f* de un título; ~ **duchess** duquesa *f* viuda.

dowdiness [ˈdaʊdɪnɪs] N falta *f* de elegancia.

dowdy [ˈdaʊdɪ] ADJ poco elegante, poco atractivo.

dowel [ˈdaʊəl] N clavija *f*.

Dow-Jones average [ˌdaʊˌdʒəʊnzˈævərɪdʒ] N (*US Fin: also* **Dow-Jones index**) índice *m* Dow-Jones.

down¹ [daʊn] N (*Orn*) plumón *m*, flojel *m*; (*fluff*) pelusa *f*; (*on face*) bozo *m*; (*on body*) vello *m*; (*on fruit*) pelusilla *f*; (*Bot*) vilano *m*.

down² [daʊn] N (*Geog*) colina *f*; **the D~s** (*Brit*) las Downs (*colinas del sur de Inglaterra*).

down³ [daʊn] ① ADV (a) (*downwards*) abajo, hacia abajo, para abajo; (*to the ground*) por tierra, en tierra; (*to the south*) hacia el sur; **to fall** ~ caerse; **I ran all the way** ~ bajé toda la distancia corriendo; **there was snow all the way** ~ estaba nevando durante todo el recorrido.

(b) ~ **below** allá abajo; ~ **by the river** abajo en la ribera; ~ **on the shore** abajo en la playa; ~ **to** hasta; ~ **under** en Australia (*or* en Nueva Zelanda); **to go** ~ **under** ir a Australia *etc*.

(c) **to be** ~ (*price, temperature, etc*) haber bajado; (*Aer*) haber aterrizado, estar en tierra; (*person*) haber caído, estar en tierra; **you're** ~ **for Tuesday** te hemos apuntado para el martes; **she's** ~ **with the flu** está en cama con gripe; **the computer is** ~ el ordenador no funciona, el ordenador tiene una avería; **to be** ~ **from college** haber terminado el curso universitario; **he's not** ~ **yet** (*eg for breakfast*) todavía no ha bajado, sigue en cama; **to be** ~ **and out** no tener donde caerse muerto, estar sin un cuarto; **to be 3 goals** ~ tener 3 goles menos; **one** ~, **five to go** uno en el bote y quedan cinco; tenemos uno y faltan cinco; **I'm £20** ~ he perdido 20 libras, me faltan 20 libras; **to be** ~ **on sb** (*esp US*) tener inquina a uno; **I'm** ~ **to my last cigarette** me queda un cigarrillo nada más; **it's** ~ **to him** le toca a él, le incumbe a él; **it's all** ~ **to us now** ahora nosotros somos los únicos responsables.

(d) (*Fin*) **to pay £50** ~ pagar un depósito de 50 libras, hacer un desembolso inicial de 50 libras.

② PREP: ~ **the hill** cuesta abajo; ~ **river** río abajo (*from* de); **to walk** ~ **the street** bajar la calle, ir por la calle; **the rain was running** ~ **the trunk** la lluvia corría por el tronco.

③ INTERJ: ~! ¡abajo!; ~!, ~ **boy!** (*to dog*) ¡quieto!; ~ **with the tyrant!** ¡abajo el tirano!, ¡muera el tirano!

④ ADJ (a) (*Brit*) *train, stroke* descendente.

(b) **to feel** ~ estar triste, estar deprimido.

⑤ VT *food* devorar; *drink* beberse (de un trago), tragarse; *person* derribar, echar por los suelos; *plane* derribar, abatir; V **tool**.

⑥ N: **to have a** ~ **on sb** (*Brit*) tener inquina a uno; V **up**.

down-and-out [ˈdaʊnənˌaʊt] ① ADJ derrotado, pobrísimo. ② N pobre *mf*, vagabundo *m*.

down-at-heel(s) [ˈdaʊnətˈhiːl(z)] ADJ decaído, venido a menos; *appearance* desastrado.

downbeat [ˈdaʊnˌbiːt] ADJ (*gloomy*) pesimista, deprimido; (*unemphatic*) apático, callado; de tono menor.

down-bow [ˈdaʊnˌbəʊ] N descenso *m* de arco.

downcast [ˈdaʊnkɑːst] ADJ abatido, alicaído.

down-cycle [ˈdaʊnˌsaɪkl] N ciclo *m* de caída.

downer [ˈdaʊnəʳ] N (*tranquilizer*) tranquilizante *m*; (*depressing experience*) experiencia *f* deprimente; (*fig*) jarro *m* de agua fría.

downfall [ˈdaʊnfɔːl] N caída *f*, ruina *f*; **it will be his** ~ será su perdición.

downgrade ① [ˈdaʊngreɪd] N: **to be on the** ~ ir cuesta abajo, estar en plena decadencia. ② [daʊnˈgreɪd] VT degradar, asignar a un grado más bajo.

downhearted [ˈdaʊnˈhɑːtɪd] ADJ desanimado; **don't be** ~ no te dejes desanimar.

downhill [ˈdaʊnˈhɪl] ① ADV cuesta abajo; **to go** ~ ir cuesta abajo, (*fig*) ir de capa caída; estar en franca decadencia. ② ADJ en declive.

down-home [ˌdaʊnˈhəʊm] (*US*) ADJ (*from the South*) del sur; (*narrow-minded*) cerrado de miras.

Downing Street [ˈdaʊnɪŋˌstriːt] N Downing Street (*calle de Londres en que están las residencias oficiales del ministro de Hacienda y del primer ministro británicos*).

---

down-in-the-mouth ['daʊnɪnðə'maʊθ] ADJ decaído, deprimido.
download [,daʊn'ləʊd] VT (Comput) descargar.
downloading [,daʊn'ləʊdɪŋ] N descarga f.
down-market [,daʊn'mɑːkɪt] 1 ADJ product inferior, para la sección popular del mercado (or de la clientela).
2 ADV: **to go ~** buscar clientela en la sección popular.
down payment ['daʊn,peɪmənt] N (Fin) entrada f, pago m al contado; (deposit) desembolso m inicial.
downpipe ['daʊn,paɪp] N (Brit) (canal f) bajante f.
downplay* ['daʊn'pleɪ] VT (US) minimizar la importancia de, quitar importancia a.
downpour ['daʊnpɔːʳ] N aguacero m, chaparrón m.
downright ['daʊnraɪt] 1 ADJ person franco; lie abierto, patente, manifiesto; (obvious) notorio, evidente; (out-and-out) abierto, declarado.
2 ADV completamente, rotundamente.
down-river ['daʊn'rɪvəʳ] ADV = **downstream**.
down side ['daʊn,saɪd] N lo malo (of de), pega f, desventaja f.
downsize [,daʊn'saɪz] VT (euph) hacer recortes de plantilla en.
Down's syndrome ['daʊnz,sɪndrəʊm] 1 N mongolismo m.
2 ATTR: **a ~ baby** un niño mongólico.
downstairs ['daʊn'stɛəz] 1 ADV abajo; (in lower flat) en el piso de abajo; **to fall ~** caer escaleras abajo; **he went slowly ~** bajó despacio la escalera.
2 ADJ de abajo; **a ~ window** una ventana de la planta baja.
3 N: **the ~** el piso inferior, la parte de abajo.
downstream ['daʊn'striːm] ADV aguas abajo, río abajo (from de); **to go ~** ir río abajo; **to swim ~** nadar con la corriente; **a town ~ from Soria** una ciudad más abajo de Soria; **about 5 km ~ from Zamora** unos 5 km más abajo de Zamora.
downstroke ['daʊnstrəʊk] N (with pen) pierna f; (by child when learning) palote m; (Mech) carrera f descendente.
downswept ['daʊnswept] ADJ wings con caída posterior.
downswing ['daʊnswɪŋ] N (fig) recesión f, caída f.
downtime ['daʊn,taɪm] N tiempo m de inactividad, tiempo m muerto.
down-to-earth ['daʊntʊ'ɜːθ] ADJ práctico, realista.
downtown ['daʊn'taʊn] 1 ADV go hacia el centro (de la ciudad), be en el centro (de la ciudad).
2 ADJ del centro (de la ciudad), céntrico; **~ Bognor** el centro de Bognor.
downtrend ['daʊn,trend] N (Econ) tendencia f a la baja; **in** or **on a ~** en baja.
downtrodden ['daʊn,trɒdn] ADJ oprimido, pisoteado.
downturn ['daʊntɜːn] N descenso m, bajada f, disminución f.
downward ['daʊnwəd] ADJ curve, movement etc descendente; slope en declive; tendency a la baja.
downward(s) ['daʊnwəd(z)] ADV hacia abajo.
downwind ['daʊn,wɪnd] ADV a favor del viento.
downy ['daʊnɪ] ADJ velloso; (and soft) blando, suave.
dowry ['daʊrɪ] N dote f.
dowse [daʊz] VT = **douse**.
dowser ['daʊzəʳ] N zahorí m.
doyen ['dɔɪən] N decano m.
doyenne ['dɔɪen] N decana f.
doz. N ABBR of **dozen** docena f.
doze [daʊz] 1 N sueño m ligero; sueño m breve; **to have a ~** (after meal) echar una siestecita.
2 VI dormitar; **to ~ off** quedarse medio dormido, dormirse.
dozen ['dʌzn] N docena f; **three ~ oranges** tres docenas de naranjas; **they arrived in (their) ~s, they arrived by the ~** llegaron a docenas.
dozy* ['dəʊzɪ] ADJ amodorrado; soñoliento.
DP N ABBR of **data processing**.
DPh, DPhil [,diː'fɪl] N ABBR of **Doctor of Philosophy**; ver también DEGREE.
DPM N ABBR of **Diploma in Psychological Medicine**.
DPP N (Brit) ABBR of **Director of Public Prosecutions**.
DPT N ABBR of **diphtheria, pertussis, tetanus** vacuna f trivalente.
dpt ABBR of **department** departamento m, dto.
DPW N (US) ABBR of **Department of Public Works** ≃ Ministerio m de obras Públicas y Urbanismo.
DQ (Athletics) ABBR of **Disqualified**.

Dr (a) (Med) ABBR of **Doctor** doctor m, Dr. (b) (Fin) ABBR of **debtor** deudor m. (c) (street) ABBR of **Drive**.
dr (Fin) ABBR of **debtor** deudor m.
drab [dræb] ADJ (fig) gris, monótono, triste.
drabness ['dræbnɪs] N monotonía f, tristeza f.
drachm [dræm] N (a) (measure, Pharm) dracma f. (b) = **drachma**.
drachma ['drækmə] N dracma m (sometimes f).
draconian [drə'kəʊnɪən] ADJ draconiano, severo, riguroso.
Dracula ['drækjʊlə] N Drácula f.
draft [drɑːft] 1 N (a) (Comm) giro m, letra f de cambio; orden f de pago.
(b) (Mil) destacamento m; (reinforcements) refuerzos mpl; (conscription) quinta f; (US) llamada f a filas, leva f (LAm).
(c) (preliminary study: also **first ~, rough ~**) borrador m; **third ~** tercera versión f; V **draught**.
(d) (Comput) borrador m, impresión f tenue de puntos.
2 ATTR (a) (US Mil) **~ board** junta f de reclutamiento; **~ card** cartilla f militar; **~ dodger** prófugo m.
(b) **~ agreement** proyecto m de (un) acuerdo; **~ bill, ~ law** anteproyecto m de estatuto; **~ letter** borrador m de carta, (more formal) proyecto m de carta; **~ version** versión f preliminar.
3 VT (a) document redactar; scheme preparar; (rough out) hacer un borrador de, preparar una versión de.
(b) (Mil) destacar, (send) mandar (to a); (US: conscript) quintar, llamar al servicio militar; (fig) forzar, obligar.
draftee [drɑːf'tiː] N (US) recluta mf.
draftsman ['drɑːftsmən] etc (US) = **draughtsman** etc.
drag [dræg] 1 N (a) (net etc) rastra f, red f barredera; (sledge) narria f.
(b) (Aer etc) resistencia f al avance.
(c) (fig) obstáculo m, estorbo m (on a, para); (boring thing) cosa f pesada, lata f.
(d) (*: on cigarette) chupada f, fumada f, calada* f.
(e) (*: Theat etc) travesti m; **in ~** en travesti.
(f) **to have a ~** (US*) tener un enchufe*.
(g) **the main ~** (US*) la calle mayor.
2 VT object arrastrar, llevar arrastrado; sea bed, river etc dragar, rastrear, efectuar obras de dragado en; **to ~ the anchor** garrar; **to ~ a secret out of sb** arrancar un secreto a uno.
3 VI arrastrarse por el suelo; (go very slowly) moverse muy despacio; (time) pasar lentamente; **the book begins to ~** el libro empieza a cansar; **how that afternoon ~ged!** ¡cómo nos aburrimos aquella tarde!; **to ~ for** rastrear en busca de.
◆**drag about** 1 VT arrastrar de un lado a otro.
2 VI arrastrarse de un lado a otro.
3 VR: **to ~ o.s. about** (in pain etc) arrastrarse (de dolor etc).
◆**drag along** 1 VT: **to ~ sth along** arrastrar algo tras sí, arrastrar algo con mucha dificultad.
2 VR: **to ~ o.s. along** arrastrarse.
◆**drag apart** VT separar por la fuerza.
◆**drag away** VT arrancar; **she ~ged him away from the television** le arrancó de la televisión.
◆**drag down** VT arrastrar hacia abajo; **to ~ sb down to one's level** (fig) hacer bajar a uno al nivel de uno; **his illness is ~ging him down** su enfermedad le está debilitando mucho.
◆**drag in** VT reference traer por los pelos, hacer entrar a la fuerza; person implicar, involucrar.
◆**drag on** VI: **to ~ on and on** continuar como si nunca fuera a acabarse; ser interminable, ir para largo.
◆**drag out** 1 VT story etc ir alargando, hacer interminable.
2 VI = **drag on**.
◆**drag up** VT sacar a luz, sacar a relucir.
draglift ['dræglɪft] N (Ski) arrastre m.
dragnet ['drægnet] N (a) rastra f, red f barredera; (fig) emboscada f. (b) (US Pol) dragadora f.
dragon ['drægən] N dragón m; (woman) fiera f.
dragonfly ['drægənflaɪ] N libélula f, caballito m del diablo.
dragoon [drə'guːn] 1 N dragón m.
2 VT tiranizar; **to ~ sb into doing sth** obligar a uno (por intimidación) a hacer algo, forzar a uno a hacer algo.
drag queen* ['drægkwiːn] N travestí m.
drag race ['drægreɪs] N (US Aut) carrera f de coches trucados de salida parada.
drag show* ['drægʃəʊ] N espectáculo m de travestismo m.
dragster ['drægstəʳ] N coche m trucado.
drain [dreɪn] 1 N (a) (outlet) desaguadero m; (in street) boca f de alcantarilla, sumidero m; (Agr) zanja f de drenaje; **the ~s** (sewage system) las alcantarillas, el alcantarillado; **it's money down the ~** es dinero tirado, eso es tirar el dinero; **to go down the ~*** perderse, echarse a perder.
(b) (fig) (source of loss) desaguadero m, sumidero m, desagüe m; (loss) pérdida f, disminución f; **to be a ~ on** energies, resources consumir, agotar; **they are a great ~ on our reserves** constituyen el gran

1031   **drain away → draw together**

sumidero de nuestras reservas.
(c) there's just a ~ **left** quedan unas gotitas.
[2] VT **(a)** desaguar; *(Agr, Med)* drenar; *(Mech)* purgar, drenar; *glass* apurar; *last drops* apurar, beberse, tragarse; *lake* desangrar, desecar.
(b) *(fig)* agotar, consumir; **the country is being ~ed of wealth** el país está siendo empobrecido; **to feel ~ed of energy** estar agotado, sentirse sin fuerzas.
[3] VI *(washed dishes)* escurrirse.
♦**drain away** [1] VT vaciar.
    [2] VI *(water etc)* irse.
♦**drain into** VT *river etc* desaguar en.
♦**drain off** VT desangrar; vaciar.
drainage ['dreinidʒ] N *(act)* desagüe *m*; *(Agr, Med)* drenaje *m*; *(of marsh)* desecación *f*; *(sewage system)* alcantarillado *m*.
drainage area ['dreinidʒ,eəriə] N, **drainage basin** ['dreinidʒ,beisn] N *(Geol)* cuenca *f* hidrográfica.
drainage channel ['dreinidʒ,tʃænl] N zanja *f* de drenaje.
drainage tube ['dreinidʒ,tju:b] N *(Med)* tubo *m* de drenaje.
drainer ['dreinəʳ] N escurridor *m*.
draining-board ['dreiniŋ,bɔːd] N, *(US)* **drainboard** ['dreinbɔːd] N escurreplatos *m*, escurridera *f*, escurridor *m*.
drainpipe ['dreinpaip] [1] N tubo *m* de desagüe.
    [2] ATTR: ~ **trousers** *(Brit)* pantalones *mpl* pitillo.
Drake [dreik] NM Draque.
drake [dreik] N pato *m* (macho).
Dralon ['dreilɒn] ® N Dralón *m* ®.
dram [dræm] N *(Brit)* *(Pharm)* dracma *f*; *(of drink)* trago *m*.
drama ['drɑːmə] [1] N drama *m*.
    [2] ATTR: ~ **critic** crítico *mf* de teatro.
drama-doc* ['drɑːmədɒk], **drama-documentary** N ['drɑːmə-,dɒkjʊ'mentərı] docudrama *m*.
drama queen ['drɑːmə,kwiːn] (*) N *(pej)* peliculero *m*, -a *f*; **you're such a ~** eres demasiado peliculero.
dramatic [drə'mætɪk] ADJ dramático; espectacular, sensacional; *example* elocuente; *décor etc* de gran efecto.
dramatically [drə'mætɪkəlɪ] ADV dramáticamente; de manera espectacular *etc*.
dramatics [drə'mætɪks] NPL *(Theat)* arte *m* dramático; (*) teatro *m*; V **amateur**.
dramatis personae ['dræmətɪspɜː'səʊnaɪ] N personajes *mpl* (del drama *etc*).
dramatist ['dræmətɪst] N dramaturgo *mf* *(also* -a *f)*.
dramatization [,dræmətaɪ'zeɪʃən] N dramatización *f*.
dramatize ['dræmətaɪz] VT **(a)** *(Theat)* adaptar al teatro, escenificar, dramatizar; **X ~d by Y** X en versión dramática de Y.
(b) *(show quality of)* poner de manifiesto, demostrar palpablemente.
(c) *(exaggerate)* exagerar.
Drambuie [dræm'bjuːɪ] ® N Drambuie *m* ®.
drank [dræŋk] PRET *of* drink.
drape [dreip] [1] N colgadura *f*; *(Brit: hangings)* cortinas *fpl*; **~s** *(US)* cortinas *fpl*.
    [2] VT *object* adornar con colgaduras, cubrir *(in, with* de), vestir *(with* de); *cloth, clothing* arreglar los pliegues de; **~ this round your shoulders** ponte esto sobre las espaldas; **he ~d a towel about himself** se cubrió con una toalla; **he ~d an arm about my shoulders** me ciñó el hombro con su brazo.
draper ['dreipəʳ] N *(Brit)* pañero *m*, mercero *m* *(LAm)*, *(linen)* lencero *m*.
drapery ['dreipərɪ] N **(a)** *(hangings)* colgaduras *fpl*, ropaje *m*; *(as merchandise)* pañería *f*, mercería *f* *(LAm)*, bonetería *f* *(Mex)*. **(b)** *(Brit: also* **draper's shop)** pañería *f*, tienda *f* de paños, mercería *f* *(LAm)*, bonetería *f* *(Mex)*.
drastic ['dræstɪk] ADJ drástico; enérgico, fuerte; *measure* draconiano, severo; *reduction etc* importante; *change* radical.
drastically ['dræstɪkəlɪ] ADV drásticamente; enérgicamente; severamente; **to be ~ reduced** sufrir una reducción importante; **he ~ revised his ideas** cambió radicalmente de ideas.
drat* [dræt] VT: ~!, ~ **it!** ¡maldición!
dratted* ['drætɪd] ADJ maldito.
draught, *(US)* **draft** [drɑːft] [1] N **(a)** *(drink)* trago *m*; *(Med)* dosis *f*; **at one ~** de un trago; **on ~** *(beer)* de barril.
(b) *(Naut)* calado *m*.
(c) *(of air)* corriente *f* de aire; *(breeze)* viento *m*, brisa *f*; **to feel the ~** *(fig)* tener dificultades, sufrir las consecuencias, resentirse de los efectos.
(d) **~s** *(Brit: game)* juego *m* de damas.
    [2] ATTR *horse* de tiro; **~ beer** cerveza *f* de barril; *see also* **draft**.
draughtboard ['drɑːftbɔːd] N *(Brit)* tablero *m* de damas.
draught excluder, *(US)* **draft excluder** ['drɑːftɪks'kluːdəʳ] N burlete *m*.
draught horse, *(US)* **draft horse** ['drɑːfthɔːs] N caballo *m* de tiro.
draughtiness, *(US)* **draftiness** ['drɑːftɪnɪs] N corriente *f* de aire.
draught-proof, *(US)* **draft-proof** ['drɑːftpruːf] ADJ a prueba de co-

rrientes de aire.
draught-proofing, *(US)* **draft-proofing** ['drɑːft,pruːfɪŋ] N burlete *m*.
draughtsman, *(US)* **draftsman** ['drɑːftsmən] N, PL **draughtsmen**, *(US)* **draftsmen** ['drɑːftsmən] **(a)** delineante *m*, proyectista *m*. **(b)** *(Brit: in game)* dama *f*, pieza *f*.
draughtsmanship, *(US)* **draftsmanship** ['drɑːftsmənʃɪp] N *(skill)* arte *m* del delineante; *(quality)* habilidad *f* para el dibujo.
draughty, *(US)* **drafty** ['drɑːftɪ] ADJ *room* que tiene corrientes de aire, lleno de corrientes de aire; *day, place* de mucho viento.
draw [drɔː] [1] N **(a)** *(Sport)* empate *m*, *(Chess)* tablas *fpl*.
(b) *(lottery)* sorteo *m* *(for de)*; **it's the luck of the ~** así es la suerte.
(c) *(attraction)* atracción *f*; *(Theat)* función *f* taquillera, obra *f* de mucho éxito.
(d) **to beat sb to the ~** *(lit)* desenfundar más rápido que uno; *(fig)* adelantarse a uno; **to be quick on the ~** ser rápido en sacar la pistola; *(fig)* ser muy listo.
(e) *(of chimney)* tiro *m*.
    [2] *(irr*: PRET **drew**, PTP **drawn)** VT **(a)** *(pull along)* tirar; arrastrar; *(pull at)* tirar de; *bow* tender; *curtains* correr; **to ~ one's hand over one's eyes** pasar la mano por los ojos; **to ~ one's hat over one's eyes** bajar el sombrero sobre los ojos; **I drew her to me** tiré de ella hacia mí; **I drew her to the window** la llevé a la ventana; **his shouts ~ me to the place** sus gritos me llevaron al lugar, fui al lugar siguiendo sus gritos; **we ~ him into the plan** le persuadimos a que participara en el proyecto.
(b) *(extract)* sacar, extraer; *cork, gun, sword, confession, tooth* sacar; *(pluck out)* arrancar; *card* robar; *trumps* arrastrar; *(Med)* *boil* hacer reventar; *money* retirar; *lots* echar; *number, prize* sacarse; *wages* cobrar; *salary* ganar, percibir, cobrar; *cheque* girar *(on a cargo de, for* por); *blood* hacer manar, derramar; *breath* tomar, respirar; *inspiration etc* sacar.
(c) *(attract, cause)* atraer; provocar; *attention* llamar *(to* sobre); *laughter* causar, provocar; *applause* despertar, motivar; *criticism* provocar; **it drew no reply** no hubo contestación a esto; **he refuses to be ~n** se niega a hablar de ello, se guarda de hacer comentario alguno; **to feel ~n to** sentirse atraído por, sentir la atracción de; *person* tener simpatía por.
(d) *(Art etc)* *drawing, scene* dibujar; *line* trazar, tirar; *(Liter)* *character* trazar.
(e) *(formulate)* *conclusion* sacar; *comparison, distinction* hacer.
(f) **the boat ~s 2 metres** el barco tiene un calado de 2 metros.
(g) **to ~ a game** *(Sport)* lograr el empate, empatar *(with* con); *(Chess)* entablar.
(h) *(Culin)* *fowl* destripar.
(i) *(Tech)* *wire* estirar.
    [3] VI **(a)** *(move)* **to ~ to one side** moverse a un lado, apartarse; **the train drew into the station** el tren entró en la estación; **the car drew into the kerb** el coche paró junto a la acera; **we could ~ in here** podríamos parar aquí; *V* **ahead, level, near**.
(b) *(chimney)* tirar (bien).
(c) *(Art)* dibujar.
(d) *(Sport)* empatar; *(Chess)* entablar.
(e) *(tea)* prepararse.
♦**draw aside** [1] VT *covering* apartar; *curtain* descorrer; *person* apartar, llamar aparte, llevar aparte.
    [2] VI ir aparte, apartarse.
♦**draw away** [1] VT apartar, llevar aparte.
    [2] VI irse, apartarse, retirarse; alejarse; *(in race)* adelantarse (a los otros), dejar atrás a los otros.
♦**draw back** [1] VT retirar; *curtain* descorrer.
    [2] VI retroceder; dar un paso hacia atrás; *(fig)* volverse atrás, cejar; **to ~ back from doing sth** no atreverse a hacer algo.
♦**draw down** VT *blind* bajar; *(fig)* *blame, ridicule* atraer.
♦**draw forth** VT *comment etc* motivar, provocar, dar lugar a.
♦**draw in** [1] VT tirar hacia dentro, retirar; *breath* tomar, aspirar; *(attract)* atraer.
    [2] VI **(a)** *(train etc)* llegar, entrar.
(b) *(days)* acortarse, hacerse más cortos.
♦**draw off** VT **(a)** *gloves* quitarse.
(b) *liquid* vaciar, trasegar.
(c) *pursuers* apartar, desviar.
♦**draw on** [1] VT **(a)** *gloves* ponerse.
(b) **to ~ sb on** engatusar a uno.
(c) = **draw upon**.
    [2] VI *(night etc)* acercarse.
♦**draw out** [1] VT **(a)** *(take out)* sacar.
(b) *(lengthen)* alargar, estirar; *wire* tirar.
(c) *person* hacer hablar, hacer menos reservado; *(pej)* sonsacar.
    [2] VI **(a)** *(train etc)* arrancar, ponerse en marcha, salir de la estación.
(b) *(days)* hacerse más largos.
♦**draw together** [1] VT reunir, juntar.

2 VI reunirse, juntarse; (*fig*) hacerse más unidos.
◆**draw up** **1** VT (**a**) (*raise*) levantar, alzar; *water from well* sacar.
(**b**) (*move*) *chair* acercar.
(**c**) (*form up*) *men* formar; *army* ordenar para el combate.
(**d**) *report etc* redactar, preparar.
2 VI pararse, acercarse y parar.
3 VR: **to ~ o.s.** VI erguirse, estirarse.
◆**draw (up)on** VT *source* inspirarse en; *text* poner a contribución; *resources* usar, hacer uso de, explotar, recurrir a; *experience* beneficiarse de, aprovechar; *bank account* retirar dinero de.
drawback ['drɔːbæk] N inconveniente *m*, desventaja *f* (*of, to* de).
drawbridge ['drɔːbrɪdʒ] N puente *m* levadizo.
drawee [drɔː'iː] N girado *m*, librado *m*.
drawer[1] ['drɔːəʳ] N (*Comm*) girador *m*.
drawer[2] [drɔːʳ] N cajón *m*; gaveta *f*; **out of the top ~** de primera calidad, de categoría superior; **bien nacido**.
drawers [drɔːz] NPL (*man's*) calzoncillos *mpl*, (*woman's*) bragas *fpl*.
drawing[1] ['drɔːɪŋ] N (*Art*) dibujo *m*.
drawing[2] ['drɔːɪŋ] ATTR (*Fin*): **~ account** cuenta *f* de anticipos; fondo *m* para gastos; **~ rights** derechos *mpl* de giro.
drawing-board ['drɔːɪŋbɔːd] N tablero *m* de delineante; (*Art*) tablero *m* de dibujo; **back to the ~!** ¡a recomenzar!
drawing-office ['drɔːɪŋ,ɒfɪs] N sección *f* de delineantes.
drawing-paper ['drɔːɪŋ,peɪpəʳ] N papel *m* de dibujo.
drawing-pen ['drɔːɪŋ,pen] N tiralíneas *m*.
drawing-pin ['drɔːɪŋpɪn] N (*Brit*) chinche *f*.
drawing power ['drɔːɪŋ,paʊəʳ] N fuerza *f* de atracción, poder *m* de convocatoria, capacidad *f* de arrastre.
drawing-room ['drɔːɪŋrʊm] N salón *m*, sala *f* (*LAm*).
drawl [drɔːl] **1** N habla *f* lenta y pesada.
2 VT pronunciar lenta y pesadamente, arrastrar.
3 VI hablar lenta y pesadamente.
drawn [drɔːn] **1** PTP *of* **draw**.
2 ADJ (**a**) *game* empatado. (**b**) *face* cansado, ojeroso. (**c**) **long ~ out** larguísimo, interminable. (**d**) **with ~ sword** con la espada en la mano. (**e**) **~ butter** (*US*) mantequilla *f* derretida.
drawstring ['drɔːstrɪŋ] N cordón *m*.
dray [dreɪ] N carro *m* pesado.
dread [dred] **1** N pavor *m*, terror *m*; **to go in ~ of** tener pavor a; **to fill sb with ~** infundir terror a uno.
2 ADJ espantoso.
3 VT tener miedo a, temer; **I ~ what may happen when he comes** me horroriza lo que pueda pasar cuando venga; **I ~ to think of it** el pensamiento me horroriza.
dreadful ['dredfʊl] ADJ terrible, espantoso; (*fig*) horrible, fatal, malísimo; **how ~!** ¡qué barbaridad!, qué horror!; **I feel ~** me siento muy mal; **I feel ~ about it** la cosa me da vergüenza, me da muchísima pena.
dreadfully ['dredfəlɪ] ADV terriblemente; (*fig*) malísimamente; **I'm ~ sorry** lo siento muchísimo; **it's ~ difficult** es terriblemente difícil.
dreadlocks ['dredlɒks] NPL rizos *mpl* de estilo rastafari.
dreadnought ['drednɔːt] N (*Hist*) acorazado *m*.
▼**dream** [driːm] **1** N sueño *m*; (*daydream*) ensueño *m*; (*ideal*) ideal *m*; (*fond hope*) ilusión *f*; **bad ~** pesadilla *f*; **sweet ~s!** ¡duerme bien!; **the house of my ~s** mi casa ideal, la casa soñada, la casa de mis ilusiones; **isn't it a ~?*** es un sueño, ¿verdad?; **to see sth in a ~** ver algo en sueños; **she goes about in a ~** parece que está soñando; **my fondest ~ is to ~ + infin** el sueño de mi vida es + *infin*, mi mayor ilusión es + *infin*; **to be rich beyond one's ~s** ser más rico de lo que jamás se soñara; **to succeed beyond one's wildest ~s** tener muchísimo más éxito de lo que se esperaba; **it went like a ~** fue a las mil maravillas.
2 ATTR ideal; **~ boat*** sueño* *m*; **it's/he's a ~ boat*** es un sueño*; **my ~ house** mi casa ideal; **~ ticket** (*Pol etc*) equipo *m* ideal, equipo *m* perfecto; **~ world** mundo *m* de ensueño; **to live in a ~ world** vivir en un mundo de sueños, vivir de pura fantasía.
3 (PRET AND PTP **dreamed** *or* **dreamt**) VTI soñar (*of* con, *that* que); **you must have ~ed it** lo habrás imaginado; **I wouldn't ~ of it!** ¡ni hablar!; **I wouldn't ~ of going** no iría ni soñando, ¿ir? ¡ni soñarlo!
◆**dream away** VT: **to ~ away the day** pasar el día soñando.
◆**dream up** VT inventar, idear; **who ~ed this one up?** ¿a quién debemos esta idea?
dreamer ['driːməʳ] N soñador *m*, -ora *f*, fantaseador *m*, -ora *f*; visionario *m*, -a *f*.
dreamily ['driːmɪlɪ] ADV distraídamente, como si estuviera soñando.
dreamland ['driːmlænd] N reino *m* del ensueño, país *m* de los sueños; utopía *f*.
dreamless ['driːmlɪs] ADJ sin sueños.
dreamlike ['driːmlaɪk] ADJ de ensueño, como de sueño.
dreamt [dremt] PRET AND PTP *of* **dream**.
dreamy ['driːmɪ] ADJ (**a**) *character* soñador, distraído, muy en las nubes. (**b**) *tone etc* del que fantasea, distraído; *music* soñador, de

sueño. (**c**) (*) precioso, maravilloso.
dreariness ['drɪərɪnɪs] N tristeza *f*, monotonía *f*; lo aburrido.
dreary ['drɪərɪ] ADJ triste, monótono; *book etc* aburrido.
dredge[1] [dredʒ] **1** N draga *f*, rastra *f*.
2 VT *channel* dragar, limpiar (*etc*) con draga; *mud etc* dragar; **to ~ up** pescar; (*fig*) sacar a luz.
dredge[2] [dredʒ] N (*Culin*) espolvoreador *m*.
dredger[1] ['dredʒəʳ] N draga *f*.
dredger[2] ['dredʒəʳ] N (*Culin*) espolvoreador *m*.
dredging[1] ['dredʒɪŋ] N dragado *m*, obras *fpl* de dragado.
dredging[2] ['dredʒɪŋ] N (*Culin*) espolvoreado *m*.
dregs [dregz] NPL heces *fpl*, sedimento *m*; (*fig*) hez *f*; **the ~ of society** la hez de la sociedad; **to drain a glass to the ~** apurar un vaso hasta las heces.
drench [drentʃ] **1** N (*Vet*) poción *f*.
2 VT mojar (*in, with* de), empapar (*in, with* en); **to get ~ed** mojarse hasta los huesos.
drenching ['drentʃɪŋ] **1** ADJ *rain* torrencial.
2 N: **to get a ~** mojarse hasta los huesos.
Dresden ['drezdən] N Dresde *m*; **~ china** loza *f* de Dresde.
dress [dres] **1** N (*in general*) vestido *m*, indumentaria *f*; (*clothing*) ropa *f*; (*frock*) vestido *m*.
2 ATTR: **~ shirt** camisa *f* de frac; **~ shop** casa *f* de modas; **~ suit** traje *m* de etiqueta.
3 VT (**a**) (*clothe*) vestir (*in* de, *in green* de verde); **to be ~ed in** vestir, llevar, ir vestido de; **to get ~ed** vestirse; V *also* **dressed**.
(**b**) (*Theat*) *play* hacer los trajes para.
(**c**) (*decorate*) *hair* peinar; *shop window* poner, decorar; *Christmas tree* arreglar, adornar.
(**d**) (*Culin*) aderezar, aliñar.
(**e**) (*Agr*) abonar (*with* de).
(**f**) *skins* adobar, curtir; *stone* labrar; *wood* desbastar.
(**g**) (*Mil*) *troops* formar.
(**h**) *wound* curar, vendar.
4 VI (**a**) vestirse; **to ~ for dinner** (*man*) ponerse smoking; (*woman*) ponerse traje de noche.
(**b**) (*Mil*) formar, alinearse.
◆**dress down*** VT (*Brit*) poner como un trapo.
◆**dress up** **1** VT ataviar, engalanar (*in* de); **to ~ sb up as** disfrazar a uno de; **they ~ed the setback up as a triumph** hicieron creer que el revés era un triunfo.
2 VI ataviarse, engalanarse (*in* de); (*formally*) vestirse de etiqueta; **to ~ up as** disfrazarse de.
dressage ['dresɑːʒ] N doma y monta *f*, doma *f* artística.
dress circle ['dres'sɜːkl] N (piso *m*) principal *m*.
dress coat ['dres'kəʊt] N frac *m*.
dress code ['dres,kəʊd] N *regulaciones en materia de indumentaria o uniforme*.
dress designer ['dresdɪ'zaɪnəʳ] N modisto *m*, -a *f*.
dressed [drest] ADJ vestido; **well-~** bien vestido; **to be ~ for the country** (*or* **town** *or* **tennis**) ir vestido para ir al campo (*or* a la ciudad *or* al tenis); **~ as a man** vestido de hombre; **~ in black** vestido de negro.
dresser ['dresəʳ] N (**a**) (*furniture*) aparador *m* (con estantes), rinconera *f*; (*US*) cómoda *f* con espejo. (**b**) (*Theat*) camarero *m*, -a *f*; (*Cine, TV*) tocadorista *mf*. (**c**) **he's an elegant ~** se viste elegantemente.
dressing ['dresɪŋ] N (**a**) (*act*) el vestir(se). (**b**) (*Med*) vendaje *m*. (**c**) (*Culin*) salsa *f*, aliño *m*. (**d**) (*Agr*) abono *m*.
dressing-case ['dresɪŋkeɪs] N neceser *m*.
dressing-down* ['dresɪŋ'daʊn] N rapapolvo* *m*; **to give sb a ~** echar un rapapolvo a uno*.
dressing-gown ['dresɪŋgaʊn] N (*Brit*) (*woman's*) bata *f*, salto *m* de cama; (*man's*) batín *m*.
dressing-room ['dresɪŋrʊm] N vestidor *m*; (*Theat*) camarín *m*, camerino *m*.
dressing-station ['dresɪŋ,steɪʃən] N puesto *m* de socorro.
dressing-table ['dresɪŋ,teɪbl] N tocador *m*.
dress length ['dres,leŋθ] N (*material*) largo *m* de vestido.
dressmaker ['dresmeɪkəʳ] N costurera *f*, modista *f*.
dressmaking ['dresmeɪkɪŋ] N costura *f*, corte *m* y confección *f*.
dress parade ['drespə'reɪd] N desfile *m* de gala.
dress rehearsal ['dresrɪ'hɜːsəl] N ensayo *m* general.
dress uniform ['dres'juːnɪfɔːm] N uniforme *m* de gala.
dressy ['dresɪ] ADJ *person, clothing* elegante.
drew [druː] PRET *of* **draw**.
dribble ['drɪbl] **1** N (**a**) (*water etc*) gotitas *fpl*.
(**b**) (*Sport*) regate *m*.
2 VT (**a**) dejar caer gota a gota.
(**b**) (*Sport*) regatear, driblar.
3 VI (**a**) gotear, caer gota a gota (*down* por); (*from mouth*) babear.
(**b**) (*Sport*) regatear, driblar (*past* a).
dribbler ['drɪbləʳ] N (*Sport*) driblador *m*.

driblet ['drɪblɪt] N adarme *m*; **in ~s** por adarmes.

dribs [drɪbz] NPL: **~ and drabs** cantidades *fpl* pequeñísimas; **in ~ and drabs** gota a gota; **the money came in in ~ and drabs** el dinero llegó por adarmes (*or* por gotas).

dried [draɪd] ADJ seco; *fruit* desecado, paso.

dried out [,draɪd'aʊt] ADJ *alcoholic* seco.

drier ['draɪəʳ] N = **dryer**.

drift [drɪft] **1** N **(a)** (*Naut*) impulso *m* de la corriente, velocidad *f* de la corriente; (*amount off course*) deriva *f*; (*fig*) tendencia *f*, movimiento *m*; (*Ling*) evolución *f*; **the ~ of events** la tendencia de los acontecimientos; **the ~ from the land** la despoblación del campo, el éxodo rural; **the ~ to the city** el movimiento hacia la ciudad.
(b) (*fig: lack of drive*) inacción *f*.
(c) (*of sand, snow*) montón *m*; (*of clouds, leaves*) banco *m*; (*Geol*) terrenos *mpl* de acarreo.
(d) (*fig*) (*sense*) significado *m*; (*purpose*) intención *f*, propósito *m*; **to catch sb's ~** caer en la cuenta de lo que uno quiere decir; **I don't get your ~** no te entiendo.
2 VT (*carry*) impeler, llevar; (*pile up*) amontonar.
3 VI **(a)** (*Naut*) ir a la deriva, decaer; (*on water, in air etc*) flotar, dejarse llevar por la corriente (*or* el viento); (*be off course*) derivar; (*snow*) amontonarse.
(b) (*fig*) vivir sin rumbo, no tener propósito fijo; **to ~ into war** dejarse llevar a la guerra; **to ~ from job to job** cambiar a menudo de trabajo sin propósito fijo; **he just lets things ~** deja que sus cosas vayan a la deriva.
◆**drift apart** VI irse separando poco a poco, irse separando sin quererlo.
◆**drift away** VI dejarse llevar por la corriente.
◆**drift off** VI = **drift away**; (*doze off*) dormirse, quedarse medio dormido.

drifter ['drɪftəʳ] N **(a)** (*Naut*) trainera *f*. **(b)** (*person*) vago *m*.

drift-ice ['drɪftaɪs] N hielo *m* flotante.

drifting ['drɪftɪŋ] N nieve *f* acumulada (*después de una tormenta*).

drift-net ['drɪftnet] N traíña *f*.

driftwood ['drɪftwʊd] N madera *f* de deriva, madera *f* de playa.

drill¹ [drɪl] **1** N **(a)** (*Mech*) taladro *m*; (*part of brace and bit*) broca *f*; (*bench machine*) fresadora *f*; (*dentist's*) fresa *f*; (*in mining*) perforadora *f*, barrena *f*; (*in roadmending: also* **pneumatic ~**) martillo *m* picador, taladradora *f*.
(b) (*Mil etc*) instrucción *f*; (*Scol*) ejercicios *mpl*, educación *f* física; (*for fire*) simulacro *m* de incendio; **you all know the ~*** todos sabéis lo que habéis de hacer; **what's the ~?*** ¿qué es lo que tenemos que hacer?
2 VT **(a)** *metal etc* perforar, taladrar, barrenar; *hole* practicar; **to ~ sb full of holes*** agujerear a uno como a un colador*.
(b) (*Mil*) enseñar instrucción a; (*Sport etc*) entrenar, adiestrar; **to ~ a class in French verbs** hacer ejercicios de los verbos franceses con una clase; **to ~ sb to do sth** enseñar metódicamente a uno a hacer algo; **I had it ~ed into me as a boy** me lo hicieron comprender a la fuerza siendo chico.
3 VI **(a)** perforar (*for* en busca de).
(b) (*Mil*) hacer instrucción; (*Sport etc*) entrenarse, adiestrarse.

drill² [drɪl] **1** N (*Agr*) **(a)** (*machine*) sembradora *f*. **(b)** (*row*) hilera *f*, surco *m*.
2 VT (*Agr*) sembrar con sembradora.

drill³ [drɪl] N (*cloth*) dril *m*.

drilling¹ ['drɪlɪŋ] N (*for oil etc*) perforación *f*; **~ platform** plataforma *f* de perforación; **~ rig** torre *f* de perforación, cabria *f* de perforación.

drilling² ['drɪlɪŋ] N (*Mil*) instrucción *f*.

drily, dryly ['draɪlɪ] ADV secamente; **he said ~** dijo guasón, dijo con su humorismo peculiar.

drink [drɪŋk] **1** N (*gen, alcohol*) bebida *f*; (*a draught*) trago *m*; **the ~:** el mar, el agua; **~s cupboard** mueble-bar *m*; **~s trolley** carrito *m* de bebidas; **I need a ~ of water** necesito un trago de agua; **could I have a ~ of water?** ¿puedes darme un poco de agua?; **to have a ~** tomar algo; **will you have a ~?** ¿quieres tomar algo?; **we had a ~ or two** tomamos unas copas (*LAm*: unos tragos); **to take to ~** darse a la bebida; **she has a ~ problem** tiene problema alcohólico; **to ask friends round for ~s** invitar a los amigos a tomar algo en casa; **he's a long ~ of water** (*US: tall*) es más alto que un espárrago.
2 (*irr*: PRET **drank**, PTP **drunk**) VT beber; tomar; **what will you ~?**, **what are you ~ing?** ¿qué quieres tomar?; **to ~ sb under the table** beber hasta tumbar a uno.
3 VI (*ie ~ alcohol*) beber; **thanks, I don't ~** gracias, yo no bebo; **to ~ like a fish** beber como una esponja; **to ~ to sb** brindar por uno, beber a la salud de uno; **to ~ to the success of** brindar por el éxito de.
4 VR: **to ~ o.s. to death** morir alcoholizado; **to ~ o.s. silly** beber hasta emborracharse.
◆**drink down** VT beber de un trago.
◆**drink in** VT (*fig*) beber, embeberse en; *words* estar pendiente de.

◆**drink off** VT beber de un trago.
◆**drink out of** VT beber de.
◆**drink up** **1** VT beberse, terminar de beber.
2 VI terminar de beber; **~ up, we're going** termina ya, que nos vamos.

drinkable ['drɪŋkəbl] ADJ *water* potable; *coffee, wine etc* bebible; **it's quite a ~ wine** es un vino nada malo.

drink-driving ['drɪŋk'draɪvɪŋ] ATTR: **~ campaign** campaña *f* contra el alcohol en carretera; **~ offence** delito *m* de conducir en estado de embriaguez.

drinker ['drɪŋkəʳ] N bebedor *m*, -ora *f*.

drinking ['drɪŋkɪŋ] N el beber; (*drunkenness*) bebida *f*; **~ too much alcohol can be dangerous** beber demasiado alcohol es peligroso; **eating and ~** comer y beber; **he wasn't used to ~** no estaba acostumbrado a beber; **there was a lot of heavy ~** se bebía mucho; **his problem was ~** la bebida era su problema; **his ~ caused his marriage to break up** la bebida fue la causa de la ruptura de su matrimonio; **I don't object to ~ in moderation** no me opongo a que se beba con moderación; **~ by the under-18s must be stopped** se ha de impedir que beban los menores de 18 años beban.

drinking-bout ['drɪŋkɪŋbaʊt] N juerga *f* de borrachera.

drinking chocolate ['drɪŋkɪŋ,tʃɒklɪt] N chocolate *m* (*bebida*).

drinking companion ['drɪŋkɪŋkəm,pænjən] N compañero *m*, -a *f* de bar.

drinking fountain ['drɪŋkɪŋ,faʊntɪn] N fuente *f* (de agua potable).

drinking session ['drɪŋkɪŋ,seʃən] N juerga *f* de borrachera; **they went out for a ~** se fueron de copas.

drinking-song ['drɪŋkɪŋsɒŋ] N canción *f* de taberna.

drinking-trough ['drɪŋkɪŋtrɒf] N abrevadero *m*, camellón *m*.

drinking-up ['drɪŋkɪŋʌp] ATTR: **~ time** tiempo *m* permitido para terminar de beber (en el pub).

drinking-water ['drɪŋkɪŋ,wɔːtəʳ] N agua *f* potable.

drip [drɪp] **1** N **(a)** (*act*) goteo *m*, el gotear. **(b)** (*one drop*) gota *f*; (*from roof, inside house*) gotera *f*. **(c)** (*Med: also* **~ feed**) gota a gota *m*. **(d)** (:) pelmazo* *m*.
2 VT dejar caer gota a gota.
3 VI gotear, caer gota a gota (*down* por).

drip-dry ['drɪp'draɪ] ADJ de lava y pon.

drip-feed: ['drɪp,fiːd] **1** N (alimentación *f*) gota a gota *m*; **to be on a ~** recibir alimentación gota a gota.
2 VT (*irr: V* **feed**) alimentar gota a gota.

dripmat ['drɪpmæt] N posavasos *m*.

dripping ['drɪpɪŋ] **1** ADJ *tap etc* que gotea; *clothes* chorreantes, que chorrean agua; **to be ~ wet** estar calado.
2 N pringue *m*, grasa *f*.

drippy* ['drɪpɪ] ADJ *person, idea, book, music* ñoño.

drivability [,draɪvə'bɪlɪtɪ] N manejabilidad *f*, capacidad *f* de maniobras.

drive [draɪv] **1** N **(a)** (*outing*) paseo *m* (en coche *etc*); (*journey*) viaje *m* (en coche *etc*); **to go for a ~** dar un paseo (or una vuelta) en coche; **to take sb for a ~** llevar a uno de paseo en coche; **it's a long ~** es un trayecto largo.
(b) (*Hunting*) batida *f*; (*Mil*) ataque *m*, avance *m*; (*fig*) campaña *f* (*against*, *on* contra, para suprimir).
(c) (*stroke*) golpe *m* fuerte, golpe *m* directo; (*Golf, Tennis*) drive *m*.
(d) (*energy*) energía *f*, vigor *m*; dinamismo *m*; (*driving force*) impulso *m*; **the ~ to power** el empuje hacia el poder; **the sex ~** el instinto sexual, la líbido; **the strongest of man's ~s** el más fuerte de los instintos humanos.
(e) (*carriageway*) calzada *f*, avenida *f*.
(f) (*Mech*) mecanismo *m* de transmisión; (*Comput*) unidad *f* de disco.
2 (*irr*: PRET **drove**, PTP **driven**) VT **(b)** (*urge in a direction*) empujar, impeler, *game* batir; *cattle* guiar, llevar.
(b) (*urge on*) hacer trabajar, hacer sudar; **he drove us to victory** él nos condujo a la victoria.
(c) (*steer*) *car, carriage etc* conducir, manejar (*LAm*); *plough* manejar; **he ~s a taxi** es taxista; **Pepe ~s a Shark** Pepe tiene un Tiburón.
(d) (*power*) mover, actuar; *vehicle etc* impulsar; (*Comput*) controlar, accionar; **the wind ~s the boat along** el viento empuja el barco; **a car ~n by steam** un coche impulsado por vapor, un coche que funciona con vapor.
(e) *ball etc* golpear con fuerza; *furrow* hacer; *hole* perforar, practicar; *tunnel* abrir, construir; *road* construir; *nail* clavar (*into* en); *teeth etc* hincar (*into* en); *object* introducir a la fuerza (*into* en); (*fig*) *bargain* hacer; **to ~ a post into the ground** hincar un poste en el suelo a martillazos (*etc*); **to ~ a way through** abrirse paso por; *V* **home 3 (b)**.
(f) (*carry*) *passenger* llevar en coche; **I'll ~ you home** te llevo (a casa).
(g) (*force*) **to ~ sb to do** (or **into doing**) **sth**, forzar a uno a hacer algo; **to ~ sb mad** volver a uno loco; **to ~ sb to despair** hacer des-

esperar a uno; **to ~ people to revolt** provocar a la gente a que se subleve.

3 VI **(a)** (*steer*) conducir, manejar (*LAm*); '**~ slowly**' 'marcha moderada'; **to ~ on the left** circular por la izquierda.

(b) (*go etc*) pasearse en coche, dar un paseo en coche; **to ~ to London** ir en coche a Londres; **he drove alone** hizo el viaje solo; **he drove 50 miles in an hour** recorrió 50 millas en una hora; **he had been driving all day** había pasado todo el día al volante; **she drove into the garage** entró en el garaje; **he drove into a wall** chocó con un muro; **next time we'll ~ here** la próxima vez vamos en coche.

(c) **the rain is driving down** está lloviendo a chuzos.

(d) to let ~ at asestar un golpe a; (*fig*) denunciar, atacar.

◆**drive along** **1** VT (*wind, current*) empujar.

2 VI (*vehicle*) circular; (*person*) conducir.

◆**drive at** VT insinuar, querer decir; **what are you driving at?** ¿qué quieres decir?, ¿qué pretendes?

◆**drive away** **1** VT **(a)** (*chase away*) ahuyentar; *person* alejar; *cares* alejar, quitarse de encima.

(b) (*in car*) llevarse (en coche).

2 VI = **drive off 2.**

◆**drive back** **1** VT rechazar; *defenders* obligar a ceder terreno; *crowd* obligar a retroceder.

2 VI volver (en coche).

◆**drive in** **1** VT *nail* clavar.

2 VI entrar (en coche).

◆**drive off** **1** VT = **drive away 1.**

2 VI irse, marcharse (en coche) partir; (*car*) arrancar y partir.

◆**drive on** **1** VT empujar, llevar adelante.

2 VI seguir adelante; **~ on!** ¡adelante!

◆**drive on to** VT *ferry* embarcar en.

◆**drive out** **1** VT expulsar; obligar a salir (*of* de).

2 VI dar un paseo en coche.

◆**drive over** **1** VT **(a)** (*convey*) llevar en coche.

(b) (*crush*) aplastar.

2 VI venir (*or* ir) en coche; **we drove over in 2 hours** vinimos en 2 horas; **we drove over to see them** fuimos a verlos (en coche).

◆**drive up** **1** VT *price etc* hacer subir.

2 VI llegar (en coche); acercarse; **to ~ up to town** ir (en coche) a la ciudad.

driveability [ˌdraɪvəˈbɪlɪtɪ] = **drivability.**

drive-by ['draɪvbaɪ] N (*also* **~ shooting**) tiroteo *m* desde el coche.

drive-in ['draɪv.ɪn] (*US*) **1** N restaurante *m* donde se sirve al cliente en su automóvil; (*cinema*) autocine *m*.

2 ATTR *bank etc* dispuesto para el uso del automovilista en su coche; **~ cinema** autocine *m*.

drivel ['drɪvl] **1** N tonterías *fpl*.

2 VI decir tonterías.

driven ['drɪvn] PTP *of* **drive.**

-driven ['drɪvn] ADJ *ending in compounds* que funciona con, accionado por; **electricity~** que funciona con electricidad, accionado por electricidad; **steam~** impulsado por vapor, a vapor.

driver ['draɪvə^r] N (*Aut*) conductor *m*, -ora *f*; chófer *mf*, chofer *mf* (*LAm*); (*Brit Rail*) maquinista *m*; (*of coach*) cochero *m*; **~'s licence**, (*US*) **~'s license** carnet *m* de conducir; *V* **racing 2.**

driveshaft ['draɪvʃɑːft] N árbol *m* motor.

drive-through, drive-thru ['draɪvθruː] N (*US*) = **drive-in.**

drive-up window [draɪvʌp'wɪndəʊ] N (*US*) taquilla *f* para automovilistas.

driveway ['draɪvweɪ] N camino *m* de entrada, avenida *f*.

drive-yourself ['draɪvjɔː'self] ATTR: **~ service** servicio *m* de alquiler sin chófer.

driving ['draɪvɪŋ] **1** ADJ *rain* torrencial.

2 ATTR *power* motor; (*fig*) impulsor; (*Aut*) de conducción, para conductor *etc*.

3 N conducción *f*, el conducir, el manejar (*LAm*).

driving belt ['draɪvɪŋbelt] N correa *f* de transmisión.

driving instructor ['draɪvɪŋɪn'strʌktə^r] N instructor *m*, -ora *f* de conducción.

driving lesson ['draɪvɪŋ.lesn] N clase *f* de conducción.

driving licence (*Brit*), (*US*) **driver's license** ['draɪvəs.laɪsəns] N

carnet *m* de conducir; **provisional/full ~** carnet *m* de conducir provisional/definitivo.

driving mirror ['draɪvɪŋˌmɪrə^r] N retrovisor *m*.

driving range ['draɪvɪŋˌreɪndʒ] N *zona de un campo de golf para practicar tiros de salida*.

driving school ['draɪvɪŋskuːl] N autoescuela *f*, escuela *f* automovilista, academia *f* de conductores.

driving seat ['draɪvɪŋˌsiːt] N asiento *m* del conductor; **he's in the ~ now** (*fig*) ahora él es quien manda, ahora él es el jefe.

driving test ['draɪvɪŋtest] N examen *m* de conducción.

driving wheel ['draɪvɪŋˌwiːl] N rueda *f* motriz.

drizzle ['drɪzl] **1** N llovizna *f*, garúa *f* (*LAm*).

2 VI lloviznar.

drizzly ['drɪzlɪ] ADJ lloviznoso.

droll [drəʊl] ADJ (*funny*) divertido, gracioso; (*odd*) raro.

dromedary ['drɒmɪdərɪ] N dromedario *m*.

drone [drəʊn] **1** N **(a)** (*Ent, fig*) zángano *m*. **(b)**(*noise*) zumbido *m*; (*of voice*) tono *m* monótono.

2 VI zumbar; (*voice*) hablar monótonamente; **he ~d on and on** hablaba interminablemente en tono monótono.

drool [druːl] VI babear; **to ~ over** (*fig*) caérsele a uno la baba por.

droop [druːp] **1** VT inclinar; dejar caer (*over* por).

2 VI (*slope*) inclinarse; (*fall*) caer, colgar; (*flower*) marchitarse; (*fig: spirit*) decaer, (*person*) desanimarse.

drooping ['druːpɪŋ] ADJ caído; *flower* marchito; *ears* gacho; *movement* lánguido, desmayado.

droopy ['druːpɪ] ADJ **(a)** *moustache, tail, breasts* colgón. **(b)** (*hum: tired*) mustio.

drop [drɒp] **1** N **(a)** (*of liquid*) gota *f* (*also Med*); (*sweet*) pastilla *f*; **just a ~** dos gotitas nada más; sólo una pizca; **there's just a ~ left** quedan unas gotas; **with a ~ of soda** con un poquitín de sifón; **I haven't touched a ~** no he probado una sola gota; **in 3 weeks we didn't have a ~ of rain** no cayó ni una gota en 3 semanas; **it's a ~ in the ocean** es una gota de agua en el mar; **he's had a ~ too much** lleva una copa de más.

(b) (*fall*) caída *f*; (*by parachute*) lanzamiento *m*; (*in price*) baja *f*; (*of temperature etc*) descenso *m*; (*in number, demand*) disminución *f*, reducción *f* (*in* de); **~ shipment** remesa *f* directa; **at the ~ of a hat** con cualquier pretexto; en seguida.

(c) (*slope*) bajada *f*, declive *m*, pendiente *f*; (*cliff*) precipicio *m*; (*for secret mail etc*) escondrijo *m* (para correo secreto); **there's a ~ of 6 metres** está a una altura de 6 metros sobre el suelo; **to have the ~ on sb** (*US**) llevar la delantera a uno, tener ventaja sobre uno.

(d) (*Theat*) telón *m* de boca.

2 VT **(a)** (*let fall*) (*deliberately*) dejar caer; (*accidentally*) caérsele a uno; (*let go of*) soltar; *bomb, parachutist* lanzar; *anchor* echar; *letter in pillar box* echar; *note* poner (*to* a); *curtsy* hacer; *hint* soltar; *passenger* dejar (*at* en); *eyes, voice* bajar; *price* reducir; *charge* retirar; (*allow to drip*) verter a gotas.

(b) *game, enemy* derribar, tumbar.

(c) (*lose*) perder; **Bivar ~ped a point at home** Bivar empató en casa; **they say he ~ped a packet*** dicen que perdió un dineral.

(d) (*Sew*) *hem* alargar, extender hacia abajo.

(e) (*omit*) omitir; *letter H* no pronunciar; *syllable* comerse.

(f) (*abandon*) *claim, plan* renunciar a, abandonar; *condition etc* suprimir; *habit* dejar; *subject* dejar, cambiar de; *friend* romper con; **~ that!** ¡déjese de eso!; **we had to ~ what we were doing** tuvimos que dejar lo que estábamos haciendo; **they ~ped him like a hot brick** le abandonaron como a perro sarnoso; **I've been ~ped from**

the team ya no formo parte del equipo.

(g) to ~ acid (*Drugs*‡) tomar ácido.

③ VI **(a)** (*fall*) caer; caer a tierra; (*terrain*) bajar; (*drip*) gotear; (*crouch*) agacharse; **to ~ with fatigue** caer rendido; **I feel ready to ~** estoy que no me tengo; **he let it ~ that ...** reveló que ...; dio a entender que ...; **so we let the matter ~** así que dejamos el asunto.

(b) (*decrease*) (*wind*) calmarse, amainar; (*price, temperature*) bajar; (*demand, number*) disminuir.

♦**drop across*** VI: **we ~ped across to see him** nos dejamos caer por su casa*; **he ~ped across to see us** se dejó caer por casa*.

♦**drop away** VI (*attendance etc*) disminuir.

♦**drop back, drop behind** VI quedarse atrás, rezagarse; (*rate etc*) bajar.

♦**drop by** VI = **drop in.**

♦**drop down** VI caer; (*crouch*) agacharse; **we ~ped down to the coast** bajamos hacia la costa.

♦**drop in** VI entrar un momento; entrar de paso, entrar de sopetón; **to ~ in on** visitar inesperadamente; **do ~ in any time** ven a vernos cuando quieras (sin ceremonia).

♦**drop off** ① VT *passenger* dejar.
② VI **(a)** (*part*) desprenderse, separarse.
(b) (*decrease*) bajar, disminuir.
(c) (*sleep*) quedarse dormido.
(d) (*passenger*) apearse, bajar.

♦**drop out** VI **(a)** (*part*) desprenderse, separarse.
(b) (*person*) darse de baja; retirarse; (*Univ etc*) abandonar los estudios, ahorcarse los libros; (*socially*) marginarse; **to ~ out of** *course etc* dejar de asistir a, *team* dejar de ser miembro de, *race* abandonar; **he ~ped out of my life** no volví a saber nada de él.

♦**drop round** ① VT: **I'll ~ it round to you** pasaré por casa para dártelo. ② VI = **drop in.**

drop goal ['drɒp,gəʊl] N (*Rugby*) drop *m.*

drop handlebars ['drɒp,hændlbɑːz] NPL manillar *m* de (bicicleta de) carreras.

drop-kick ['drɒpkɪk] N puntapié *m* de botepronto.

drop-leaf table [drɒpliːfˈteɪbl] N mesa *f* de ala abatible.

droplet ['drɒplɪt] N gotita *f.*

drop-off ['drɒpɒf] N disminución *f.*

drop-out ['drɒpaʊt] N **(a)** automarginado *m,* -a *f;* (*Univ etc*) persona *f* que ha abandonado los estudios (*etc*). **(b)** (*Rugby*) puntapié *m* de saque.

dropper ['drɒpəʳ] N (*Med etc*) cuentagotas *m.*

dropping-out [,drɒpɪŋˈaʊt] N automarginación *f;* (*Univ*) abandono *m* de los estudios.

droppings ['drɒpɪŋz] NPL excremento *m* (de animales).

dropshot ['drɒpʃɒt] N dejada *f.*

dropsical ['drɒpsɪkəl] ADJ hidrópico.

dropsy ['drɒpsɪ] N hidropesía *f.*

drop zone ['drɒp,zəʊn] N (*Aer*) zona *f* de salto.

dross [drɒs] N (*Brit*) escoria *f* (*also fig*).

drought [draʊt] N sequía *f.*

drove [drəʊv] ① PRET *of* **drive.**
② N (*Agr*) rebaño *m,* manada *f;* (*of people*) multitud *f;* **people came in ~s** la gente acudió en tropel.

drover ['drəʊvəʳ] N boyero *m,* pastor *m.*

drown [draʊn] ① VT (*kill*) anegar; *kittens etc* ahogar; (*inundate*) anegar, inundar; *sound* apagar; *cry* ahogar; *sorrows* olvidar emborrachándose; **his cries were ~ed by the noise of the waves** sus gritos se perdieron en el estruendo de las olas; **he came in like a ~ed rat** entró mojado hasta los huesos.
② VI (*also* **to be ~ed**) perecer ahogado, ahogarse.
③ VR: **to ~ o.s.** ahogarse.

♦**drown out** VT *sound* ahogar.

drowning ['draʊnɪŋ] N ahogo *m.*

drowse [draʊz] VI dormitar, quedar medio dormido; **to ~ off** adormecerse.

drowsily ['draʊzɪlɪ] ADV soñolientamente, soporíferamente.

drowsiness ['draʊzɪnɪs] N somnolencia *f;* (*sluggishness*) modorra *f.*

drowsy ['draʊzɪ] ADJ (*sleepy*) soñoliento; (*sluggish*) amodorrado; (*lulling*) soporífero; **to be ~, to feel ~** tener sueño.

drub [drʌb] VT apalear, vapulear; (*fig*) derrotar, cascar.

drubbing ['drʌbɪŋ] N paliza *f;* (*fig*) paliza *f,* derrota *f.*

drudge [drʌdʒ] ① N esclavo *m* del trabajo; (*in home*) esclava *f* de la cocina.
② VI trabajar como un esclavo.

drudgery ['drʌdʒərɪ] N trabajo *m* penoso, faena *f* monótona; **to take the ~ out of work** hacer el trabajo menos penoso.

drug [drʌg] ① N (*Med*) droga *f,* medicamento *m,* fármaco *m;* (*eg heroin*) droga *f,* estupefaciente *m;* **to be a ~ on the market** ser invendible.
② VT *person* drogar, administrar narcóticos a; narcotizar; *wine etc* echar un narcótico a; **to be ~ged with sleep** estar muerto de sueño.

③ VR: **to ~ o.s.** drogarse.

drug abuse ['drʌgəˈbjuːs] N toxicomanía *f.*

drug abuser ['drʌgəˌbjuːzəʳ] N toxicómano *m,* -a *f.*

drug-addict ['drʌgˈædɪkt] N drogadicto *m,* -a *f,* toxicómano *m,* -a *f.*

drug-addiction ['drʌgəˌdɪkʃən] N drogadicción *f,* drogodependencia *f,* toxicomanía *f.*

drug-check ['drʌgtʃek] N prueba *f* anti-doping.

drug dealer ['drʌg,diːləʳ] N vendedor *m,* -ora *f* de drogas.

drug dependency ['drʌgdɪˈpendənsɪ] N drogodependencia *f.*

druggist ['drʌgɪst] N farmacéutico *m;* **~'s** (*shop*) farmacia *f.*

druggy‡ ['drʌgɪ] N, **drugster‡** ['drʌgstəʳ] N drogata‡ *mf,* drogota‡ *mf.*

drug-habit ['drʌg,hæbɪt] N adicción *f* (a las drogas).

drug-peddler ['drʌg,pedləʳ] N, **drug-pusher** ['drʌg,pʊʃəʳ] N droguero *m,* traficante *mf* en drogas, camello* *mf.*

drug-related ['drʌgrɪˌleɪtɪd] ADJ relacionado con la droga; **~ crime** drogodelincuencia *f.*

drug-runner ['drʌg,rʌnəʳ] N narcotraficante *mf.*

drug-squad ['drʌgskwɒd] N brigada *f* antidrogas, grupo *m* de estupefacientes.

drugstore ['drʌgstɔːʳ] N (*US*) farmacia *f* (*donde se venden comestibles, revistas, etc*).

drug-taker ['drʌg,teɪkəʳ] N consumidor *m,* -ora *f* de drogas, el (*or* la) que se droga.

drug-taking ['drʌg,teɪkɪŋ] N consumo *m* de drogas.

drug-traffic ['drʌg'træfɪk] N narcotráfico *m,* tráfico *m* de narcóticos.

drug trafficker ['drʌg,træfɪkəʳ] N traficante *mf* de drogas, narcotraficante *mf.*

drug trafficking ['drʌg,træfɪkɪŋ] N tráfico *m* de drogas, narcotráfico *m.*

drug-user ['drʌg,juːzəʳ] N consumidor *m,* -ora *f* de drogas, drogadicto *m,* -a *f.*

druid ['druːɪd] N druida *m.*

drum [drʌm] ① N (*Mus*) tambor *m,* (*large*) timbal *m,* bombo *m;* (*Mech*) tambor *m;* (*for oil*) bidón *m;* (*of gas*) bombona *f;* (*of ear*) tímpano *m;* **~s** (*in band*) batería *f;* **to beat a ~ for a product** (*US*) hacer publicidad de un producto.
② VT: **to ~ one's fingers on the table** tabalear, tamborilear con los dedos en la mesa; **to ~ sth into sb** hacer que uno aprenda algo a fuerza de repetírselo.
③ VI (*Mus*) tocar el tambor; (*with fingers*) tabalear, tamborilear, teclear; (*with heels*) zapatear; **the noise is ~ming in my ears** el ruido me está taladrando los oídos; **his words ~med in my mind** sus palabras se repetían incansablemente en mi cabeza.

♦**drum into** VT: **I had that ~med into me years ago** hace años que me hicieron comprender eso a la fuerza (*or* a fuerza de repetírmelo).

♦**drum out** VT: **to ~ sb out** expulsar a uno.

♦**drum up** VT *support* tratar de conseguir; reunir, organizar; *trade* fomentar.

drumbreat ['drʌm,biːt] N redoble *m.*

drum brake ['drʌmbreɪk] N (*Aut*) freno *m* de tambor.

drumhead ['drʌmhed] N parche *m* de tambor; **~ court-martial** consejo *m* de guerra sumarísimo.

drumkit ['drʌmkɪt] N batería *f.*

drum-machine ['drʌmməˈʃiːn] N caja *f* de ritmos.

drum-major [,drʌm'meɪdʒəʳ] N (*Brit*) tambor *m* mayor.

drum-majorette [,drʌmmeɪdʒəˈret] N (*esp US*) batonista *f.*

drummer ['drʌməʳ] N tambor *m;* (*in pop group*) batería *m.*

drumming ['drʌmɪŋ] N tamborileo *m.*

drumroll ['drʌm,rəʊl] N redoble *m.*

drumstick ['drʌmstɪk] N palillo *m,* baqueta *f;* (*Culin*) pierna *f* de pavo (*etc*).

drunk [drʌŋk] ① PTP *of* **drink.**
② ADJ: **to be ~** estar borracho; **to get ~** emborracharse (*on* con); **to get sb ~** emborrachar a uno; **as ~ as a lord** (*or* **sailor** *US*) más borracho que una cuba; **to be ~ with joy** estar ebrio de alegría; **he was charged with being ~ and disorderly** se le acusó de estar borracho y alterar el orden público.
③ N (*) borracho *m,* -a *f.*

drunkard ['drʌŋkəd] N borracho *m,* -a *f.*

drunken ['drʌŋkən] ADJ borracho; **a ~ brawl** una reyerta de borrachos; **in a ~ voice** en una voz de borracho; **charged with ~ driving** acusado de conducir en estado de embriaguez.

drunkenly ['drʌŋkənlɪ] ADV *quarrel* embriagadamente; *sing* con voz de borracho; *walk* con pasos de borracho.

drunkenness ['drʌŋkənnɪs] N embriaguez *f.*

drupe [druːp] N drupa *f.*

druthers* ['drʌðəz] N (*US*): **if I had my ~** si por mí fuera.

dry [draɪ] ① ADJ **(a)** (*gen*) seco; *climate* árido, seco; *weather* seco, sin lluvia; *bread* sin mantequilla, (*stale*) viejo; **as ~ as a bone** completamente seco; **I'm very ~** tengo mucha sed; **the river ran ~** se secó el río; **to wipe sth ~** secar algo (con un paño *etc*); **~ dock** dique *m* seco; **~ fly** (*Fishing*) mosca *f* seca; **~ goods, ~ goods store**

(US) mercería *f*; **~ ice** nieve *f* carbónica; **~ land** (*Agr*) tierras *fpl* de secano; (*not sea*) tierra *f* firme; **~ measure** medida *f* para áridos; **~ rot** podredumbre *f* seca; **~ run** viaje *m* (*etc*) de ensayo, prueba *f*; **~ shampoo** champú *m* en polvo; **~ ski-slope** pista *f* de esquí artificial; **~ stone wall** muro *m* seco.
(b) *wine etc* seco.
(c) *state* seco, prohibicionista.
(d) *humour* agudo; lacónico.
(e) (*dull*) aburrido, pesado; **as ~ as dust** de lo más aburrido.
2 N: **to be in the ~** estar bajo techo.
3 VT secar; (*wipe*) enjugar, secar; *tears* enjugarse.
4 VI secarse.

◆**dry off** 1 VT secar.
2 VI secarse.

◆**dry out** 1 VT **(a)** secar.
(b) *alcoholic* desalcoholizar.
2 VI **(a)** secarse.
(b) (*alcoholic*) desalcoholizarse.

◆**dry up** 1 VT secar.
2 VI **(a)** (*spring etc*) secarse, agotarse; (*supply*) agotarse.
(b) (*Met*) dejar de llover.
(c) (*dry the dishes*) secar los platos.
(d) (**: be silent*) callarse; (*in speech etc*) cortarse, atascarse, enmudecer; **oh do ~ up!** ¡cállate por Dios!

dry-as-dust ['draɪəz'dʌst] ADJ de lo más seco, de lo más aburrido.
dry-clean ['draɪ'kliːn] VT limpiar en seco.
dry cleaner's ['draɪ'kliːnəz] N tintorería *f*.
dry cleaning ['draɪ'kliːnɪŋ] N limpieza *f* en seco.
dryer ['draɪər] N (*for hair*) secador *m*.
dry-eyed ['draɪ'aɪd] ADJ sin lágrimas.
drying ['draɪɪŋ] ADJ *wind* secante; **~ cupboard** armario *m* de tender; **~ room** habitación *f* de tender.
drying-up ['draɪɪŋ'ʌp] N secamiento *m*; deshidratación *f*.
dryly ['draɪlɪ] = **drily**.
dryness ['draɪnɪs] N sequedad *f*, lo seco; (*of climate*) aridez *f*; (*of wit*) agudeza *f*; laconismo *m*.
dry-shod ['draɪ'ʃɒd] ADV a pie enjuto.
D/s ABBR of **days after sight a ... días vista.**
DSC N (*Brit*) ABBR of **Distinguished Service Cross** ≃ cruz *f* al mérito militar.
D.Sc. ABBR of **Doctor of Science.**
DSM N (*Brit*) ABBR of **Distinguished Service Medal** ≃ medalla *f* al mérito militar.
DSO N (*Brit*) ABBR of **Distinguished Service Order.**
DSS N (*Brit*) ABBR of **Department of Social Security.**
DST N (*US*) ABBR of **Daylight Saving Time.**
DT N (*Comput*) ABBR of **data transmission** transmisión *f* de datos.
DTI N (*Brit*) ABBR of **Department of Trade and Industry.**
DTP N ABBR of **desktop publishing.**
DTs NPL *abbr* of **delirium tremens** delírium *m* tremens.
dual ['djʊəl] ADJ doble; (*Gram*) dual; **~ carriageway** (*Brit*) autovía *f*; **~ control** doble mando *m*; **~ nationality** nacionalidad *f* doble; **~ ownership** condominio *m*; **~ personality** conciencia *f* doble.
dualism ['djʊəlɪzəm] N dualismo *m*.
dualist ['djʊəlɪst] 1 ADJ dualista.
2 N dualista *mf*.
duality [djʊ'ælɪtɪ] N dualidad *f*.
dual-purpose ['djʊəl'pɜːpəs] ADJ que sirve para dos cosas, de doble finalidad, de doble uso.
dub¹ [dʌb] VT *knight* armar caballero a; (*with name*) apodar.
dub² [dʌb] VT *film* doblar.
Dubai [duː'baɪ] N Dubai *m*.
dubbin ['dʌbɪn] N adobo *m* impermeable, cera *f*.
dubbing ['dʌbɪŋ] N (*Cine*) doblaje *m*; **~ mixer** mezclador *m*, -ora *f* de sonido.
dubiety [djuː'baɪətɪ] N incertidumbre *f*.
dubious ['djuː'bɪəs] ADJ dudoso; *compliment* equívoco; *character* sospechoso; **to be ~ about** tener dudas sobre; **I am ~ whether ...** dudo si ...
dubiously ['djuː'bɪəslɪ] ADV *look etc* con duda; *act* de manera sospechosa.
Dublin ['dʌblɪn] 1 N Dublín *m*.
2 ATTR: **~ Bay prawn** langostina *f*.
Dubliner ['dʌblɪnər] N dublinés *m*, -esa *f*.
ducal ['djuː'kəl] ADJ ducal.
ducat ['dʌkɪt] N ducado *m* (*moneda*).
duchess ['dʌtʃɪs] N duquesa *f*.
duchy ['dʌtʃɪ] N ducado *m* (*territorio*).
duck¹ [dʌk] N (*Orn*) pato *m*, -a *f*; ánade *m*; (*domestic*) pato *m*; (*Cricket*) cero *m*; **yes, ~(s)** (*Brit**) sí, cariño; **like water off a ~'s back** sin producir efecto alguno; **he's a dead ~** está quemado; **that issue is a dead ~** esa cuestión ya no tiene interés; **to play ~s and drakes**

hacer saltar una piedra plana sobre el agua; **to play ~s and drakes with** despilfarrar; **to take to sth like a ~ to water** encontrarse en seguida en su elemento; **to make a ~, to be out for a ~** (*Brit Cricket*) ser eliminado a cero.
duck² [dʌk] 1 N **(a)** (*under water*) chapuz *m*.
(b) (*to escape*) agachada *f*, (*Boxing*) esquiva *f*.
2 VT **(a)** (*in water*) chapuzar.
(b) (*to escape*) agachar (la cabeza *etc*), bajar.
(c) *problem* eludir, esquivar; *question* esquivar.
3 VI **(a)** (*in water*) chapuzarse, sumergirse.
(b) (*to escape*) agachar la cabeza, agacharse, hurtar el cuerpo.
◆**duck out of** VT (*fig*) escabullirse de.
duck³ [dʌk] N (*US*) dril *m*.
duckbill ['dʌkbɪl] N, **duck-billed platypus** ['dʌkbɪld'plætɪpəs] N ornitorrinco *m*.
duckboard ['dʌkbɔːd] N pasadera *f*.
duckie* ['dʌkɪ] N: **~!** (*Brit*) ¡cariño!
ducking ['dʌkɪŋ] N chapuz *m*, inmersión *f*; **to give sb a ~** meter la cabeza en el agua a uno.
ducking-and-diving* [,dʌkɪŋən'daɪvɪŋ] N **(a) he did a lot of ~ in London's drug-world** estuvo metido en muchos trapicheos en el mundo de la droga de Londres*. **(b) ~ is all part of political life** los políticos saben siempre cómo escaquearse*.
duckling ['dʌklɪŋ] N patito *m*, anadón *m*.
duckpond ['dʌkpɒnd] N estanque *m* de patos.
duck soup* [,dʌk'suːp] N (*US: fig*): **it's just ~** es cosa de coser y cantar.
duckweed ['dʌkwiːd] N lenteja *f* de agua.
ducky* ['dʌkɪ] 1 N: **~!** ¡cariño!
2 ADJ (*US*) muy mono.
duct [dʌkt] N conducto *m*, canal *m*.
ductile ['dʌktaɪl] ADJ dúctil.
ductless ['dʌktlɪs] ADJ endocrino; **~ gland** glándula *f* endocrina.
dud* [dʌd] 1 ADJ *coin etc* falso; *shell* que no estalla; *merchandise* invendible; *cheque* sin fondos.
2 N (*coin*) moneda *f* falsa; (*shell*) obús *m* que no estalla; (*machine*) filfa *f*; (*person*) persona *f* inútil.
dude* [dju:d] N (*US*) petimetre *m*, gomoso *m*; tió* *m*, individuo *m*; **~ ranch** rancho *m* para turistas.

│ DUDE RANCH │

ⓘ Se llama dude ranch a un rancho del oeste de Estados Unidos que se abre a los turistas para ofrecerles el sabor de la vida del oeste al aire libre. Puede ser un rancho que funciona como tal en la realidad o uno que recrea la atmósfera tradicional de los vaqueros. Los turistas pueden montar a caballo, ayudar en las tareas del rancho o probar la comida hecha en el carromato (chuck-wagon) alrededor de la hoguera. Dude es una palabra que pertenece al argot americano, usada para referirse a una persona de ciudad muy bien vestida o a alguien del este.

---

dudgeon ['dʌdʒən] N: **in high ~** enojadísimo.
duds [dʌdz] NPL (*US**) prendas *fpl* de vestir, trapos* *mpl*; pertenencias *fpl*.
▼**due** [dju:] 1 ADJ **(a)** (*owing*) debido; **to be ~** (*Fin*) ser pagadero; **I have £50 ~ to me** me deben 50 libras; **our thanks are ~ to her** le estamos muy agradecidos; **to fall ~** (*Fin*) vencer; **he's ~ a salary raise** (*US*) le corresponde un aumento de sueldo; **I'm ~ for a holiday next week** en principio voy de vacaciones la semana que viene.
(b) (*proper*) conveniente, oportuno; debido; **with all ~ care** con todo el debido cuidado.
(c) (*of timing etc*) **~ date** fecha *f* de vencimiento; fecha *f* de pago; **the train is ~ at 6** el tren debe llegar a las 6; **when is the plane ~ (in)?** ¿cuándo debe aterrizar el avión?; **I'm ~ in Chicago tomorrow** mañana me esperan en Chicago; **it was ~ to happen yesterday** se esperaba para ayer; **when is it ~ to happen?** ¿para cuándo se prevé?; **it is ~ to be demolished** se proyecta su demolición.
▼**(d) ~ to** debido a, por causa de; **it is all ~ to** todo se debe a; **what is this ~ to?** ¿a qué se debe esto?
2 ADV: **to go ~ east** ir derecho hacia el este; **~ east of the town** exactamente al este del pueblo.
3 N **(a)** (*debt*) deuda *f*; (*desert*) lo que merece uno; **to get one's ~** recibir lo que merece uno, (*in bad sense*) llevar su merecido; **to give him his ~** hay que reconocer la razón (*or* las cualidades *etc*) que tiene; **to give him his ~, I ...** para ser justo con él, yo ...
(b) ~s (*fees*) derechos *mpl*.
duel ['djʊəl] 1 N duelo *m*; **to fight a ~ = 2.**
2 VI batirse en duelo.
duellist, (*US*) **duelist** ['djʊəlɪst] N duelista *m*.
duet [dju:'et] N dúo *m*.
duff¹* [dʌf] ADJ (*Brit*) (*poor quality*) soso, insípido, sin valor; (*useless*) inútil.
duff²* [dʌf] VT: **to ~ sb up** dar una paliza a uno.

duff³ [dʌf] N (Culin) budín m, pudín m.

duff⁴: [dʌf] N culo: m; **he just sits on his ~ all day** pasa el día sin hacer nada; **get off your ~!** ¡no te quedes ahí sentado y haz algo!

duffel-bag, duffle-bag [ˈdʌfəlbæg] N (Mil) talego m para efectos de uso personal; bolsa f de lona.

duffel-coat, duffle-coat [ˈdʌfəlkəut] N comando m, abrigo m tres cuartos.

duffer [ˈdʌfəʳ] N zoquete m.

dug¹ [dʌg] N (Zool) teta f, ubre f.

dug² [dʌg] PRET AND PTP of **dig**.

dugout [ˈdʌgaut] N (Mil) refugio m subterráneo.

duke [djuːk] N duque m.

dukedom [ˈdjuːkdəm] N ducado m (título).

dukes: [djuːks] NPL puños mpl.

dulcet [ˈdʌlsɪt] ADJ dulce, suave.

dulcimer [ˈdʌlsɪməʳ] N dulcémele m.

dull [dʌl] **1** ADJ colour, gleam apagado; light sombrío, pálido; surface deslustrado, mate; sound, pain sordo; edge embotado; day, weather gris; stock market inactivo, flojo; person (slow) lerdo, torpe; (uninteresting) soso, insípido, pesado; **as ~ as ditchwater** de lo más aburrido; **I feel ~ today** hoy me siento desanimado, hoy me encuentro sin fuerzas.
2 VT edge embotar; surface deslustrar; pain aliviar; person entorpecer; enthusiasm etc enfriar.

dullard [ˈdʌləd] N zoquete m.

dullness [ˈdʌlnɪs] N lo deslustrado; lo sombrío; inactividad f, flojedad f; torpeza f; lo soso, insipidez f.

dullsville [ˈdʌlzvɪl] N (US): **it's ~ here** esto es un muermo*.

dully [ˈdʌlɪ] ADV de modo apagado, con brillo apagado; pálidamente; sordamente, con ruido sordo.

duly [ˈdjuːlɪ] ADV (properly) debidamente; (punctually) a su debido tiempo; **he ~ arrived at 3** llegó en efecto a las 3; **he ~ protested** protestó de la manera que se había previsto; **everybody was ~ shocked** se escandalizaron todos según era de esperar.

dumb [dʌm] ADJ **(a)** mudo; **the ~ millions** los millones que no tienen voz; **~ animal** bruto m; **~ show** pantomima f, espectáculo m de mímica; **in ~ show** por señas; **to become ~** quedar mudo; **to strike sb ~** dejar a uno sin habla.
(b) (*) estúpido; soso; **as ~ as an ox** más bruto que un adoquín; **~ blonde** rubia f boba; **to act ~** hacerse el sueco*.

dumb-ass: [ˈdʌmæs] (US) **1** ADJ burro.
2 N burro m, -a f.

dumbbell [ˈdʌmbel] N **(a)** (Sport) pesa f. **(b)** (US*) bobo m, -a f.

dumbcluck [ˈdʌmklʌk] N borde* mf.

dumbfound [dʌmˈfaund] VT dejar sin habla, pasmar; **we were ~ed** quedamos mudos de asombro.

dumbness [ˈdʌmnɪs] N mudez f; (*) estupidez f.

dumbo [ˈdʌmbəu] N (US) imbécil m.

dumbstruck [ˈdʌmstrʌk] ADJ: **we were ~** quedamos mudos de asombro.

dumbwaiter [dʌmˈweɪtəʳ] N (Brit) estante m giratorio; (US) monta-platos m.

dum-dum [ˈdʌmdʌm] ADJ: **~ bullet** bala f dum-dum.

dummy [ˈdʌmɪ] **1** ADJ falso, postizo; **~ company** empresa f fantasma; **~ number** (Press) número m cero; **~ run** ensayo m, prueba f.
2 N (life-size figure) muñeco m; (tailor's) maniquí m; (packet) envase m vacío; (Brit: baby's) chupete m; (Bridge) muerto m; (Fin) persona f ficticia; hombre m de paja.

dump [dʌmp] **1** N (heap) montón m; (rubbish tip) vertedero m, basurero m, vaciadero m, botadero m (LAm); (Mil) depósito m; (*: hovel) tuguorio m, casucha f; (*: town) pueblucho m, poblachón m; (Comput) vuelco m de memoria; **to be down in the ~s*** tener murria.
2 VT rubbish etc descargar, verter, vaciar; (get rid of) deshacerse de, dejar; goods inundar el mercado de; (Comput) volcar; **to ~ sth down*** poner algo (con mucho ruido); **can I ~ this here?*** ¿puedo dejar esto aquí?

dumper [ˈdʌmpəʳ] N (also **~ truck**) dúmper m.

dumping [ˈdʌmpɪŋ] N (Comm) dúmping m.

dumping-ground [ˈdʌmpɪŋgraund] N vertedero m.

dumpling [ˈdʌmplɪŋ] N pelota f, bola f de masa hervida.

Dumpster [ˈdʌmpstəʳ] ® N (US) contenedor m de escombros o deshechos.

dumptruck [ˈdʌmptrʌk] N (US) dúmper m.

dumpy [ˈdʌmpɪ] ADJ regordete, culibajo.

dun¹ [dʌn] ADJ pardo.

dun² [dʌn] VT: **to ~ sb** apremiar a uno para que pague lo que debe; (fig) dar la lata a uno.

dunce [dʌns] N burro m, -a f, zopenco m, -a f.

dunderhead [ˈdʌndəhed] N zoquete m.

Dundonian [dʌnˈdəuniən] **1** N habitante mf or nativo m -a f de Dundee.

2 ADJ de Dundee.

dune [djuːn] N duna f.

dune buggy [ˈdjuːn‚bʌgɪ] N buggy m, vehículo para terrenos arenosos.

dung [dʌŋ] N excremento m; (as manure) estiércol m.

dungarees [‚dʌŋgəˈriːz] NPL mono m; (Brit: of child, woman) peto m.

dung beetle [ˈdʌŋ‚biːtl] N escarabajo m pelotero.

dungeon [ˈdʌndʒən] N mazmorra f, calabozo m.

dunghill [ˈdʌŋhɪl] N estercolero m.

dunk [dʌŋk] VT (US) **(a)** bread etc mojar, remojar. **(b)** (Basketball: also **slam ~**) machacar.

Dunkirk [dʌnˈkɜːk] N Dunquerque m.

dunno: [dəˈnəu] EXCL = **(I) don't know**; no sé, ni flores*.

dunnock [ˈdʌnək] N acentor m (común).

dunny* [ˈdʌnɪ] N (Australia) retrete m, wáter m.

duo [ˈdjuːəu] N dúo m.

duodecimal [‚djuːəuˈdesiməl] ADJ duodecimal.

duodenal [‚djuːəuˈdiːnl] ADJ duodenal; **~ ulcer** úlcera f duodenal.

duodenum [‚djuːəuˈdiːnəm] N duodeno m.

duopoly [djuˈɒpəli] N duopolio m.

dupe [djuːp] **1** N primo m, inocentón m; **to be the ~ of** ser víctima de.
2 VT engañar, embaucar; (swindle) timar.

duple [ˈdjuːpl] ADJ (gen) doble; (Mus) de dos tiempos; **~ time** (Mus) tiempo m doble.

duplex [ˈdjuːpleks] **1** ADJ doble.
2 N (US house: also **~ house**) casa f semiseparada, casa f para dos familias; (US apartment: also **~ apartment**) dúplex m.

duplicate **1** [ˈdjuːplɪkɪt] ADJ duplicado; **~ key** duplicado m de una llave.
2 [ˈdjuːplɪkɪt] N duplicado m; (copy of letter etc) copia f, doble m; **in ~** por duplicado.
3 [ˈdjuːplɪkeɪt] VT duplicar; repetir; imitar; text hacer a multicopista.

duplicating machine [ˈdjuːplɪkeɪtɪŋməˈʃiːn] N multicopista f.

duplication [‚djuːplɪˈkeɪʃən] N duplicación f; repetición f (incómoda); pluralidad f (innecesaria).

duplicator [ˈdjuːplɪkeɪtəʳ] N multicopista m.

duplicitous [djuːˈplɪsɪtəs] ADJ (liter) tramposo.

duplicity [djuːˈplɪsɪtɪ] N duplicidad f, doblez f.

Dur N (Brit) ABBR of **Durham**.

durability [‚djuərəˈbɪlɪtɪ] N lo duradero, durabilidad f.

durable [ˈdjuərəbl] **1** ADJ duradero; **~ goods** (US) bienes mpl de consumo duraderos.
2 **~s** NPL bienes mpl duraderos; **consumer ~s** artículos mpl de equipo.

duration [djuəˈreɪʃən] N duración f; **for the ~*** mientras dure la guerra.

Dürer [ˈdjuərəʳ] NM Durero.

duress [djuəˈres] N compulsión f; **under ~** por coacción.

Durex [ˈdjuəreks] ® N preservativo m.

during [ˈdjuərɪŋ] PREP durante.

durst†† [dɜːst] PRET of **dare**.

dusk [dʌsk] N crepúsculo m, anochecer m; **at ~** al atardecer; **in the gathering ~** en la creciente oscuridad.

dusky [ˈdʌskɪ] ADJ oscuro; complexion moreno.

dust [dʌst] **1** N polvo m; (sweepings) barreduras fpl; (rubbish) basura f; (of coal) cisco m; **to bite the ~** morder el polvo; **to kick up the ~** levantar una polvareda; **to raise a ~** armarla; **to shake the ~ of a place off one's feet** salir muy ofendido de un lugar; **when the ~ has settled** (fig) cuando se aclare la atmósfera; **to throw ~ in sb's eyes** engañar a uno.
2 VT **(a)** quitar el polvo a, desempolvar, (by beating) sacudir el polvo a; (clean) limpiar.
(b) **to ~ sth with** salpicar algo de; (Culin etc) espolvorear algo de; **~ the insecticide on the surface** espolvoree el insecticida sobre la superficie.

◆ **dust down** VT quitar el polvo a, desempolvar.

◆ **dust off** VT = **dust down**.

◆ **dust out** VT box, cupboard quitar el polvo de.

dustbag [ˈdʌstbæg] N bolsa f de aspiradora.

dustbin [ˈdʌstbɪn] N (Brit) cubo m de (la) basura; balde m (LAm); **~ liner** bolsa f de basura.

dustbowl [ˈdʌstbəul] N terreno m inutilizado por la erosión, zona f desértica.

dustcart [ˈdʌstkɑːt] N (Brit) camión m de la basura.

dustcloud [ˈdʌstklaud] N polvareda f.

dust-cover [ˈdʌst‚kʌvəʳ] N guardapolvo m; (of book) forro m, sobrecubierta f, camisa f.

duster [ˈdʌstəʳ] N **(a)** (Brit) (cloth) paño m, trapo m, sacudidor m, bayeta f; (of feathers) plumero m; (for blackboard) borrador m. **(b)** (US) guardapolvo m.

dustheap [ˈdʌsthiːp] N basurero m.

dusting [ˈdʌstɪŋ] N **(a)** limpieza f. **(b)** (*) paliza f.

dusting powder ['dʌstɪŋ,paʊdəʳ] N polvos *mpl* secantes.

dust-jacket ['dʌst,dʒækɪt] N forro *m*, sobrecubierta *f*, camisa *f*.

dustman ['dʌstmən] N, PL **dustmen** ['dʌstmən] (*Brit*) basurero *m*, recogedor *m* de basura.

dustpan ['dʌstpæn] N cogedor *m*.

dust-proof ['dʌstpruːf] ADJ a prueba de polvo.

dust-sheet ['dʌstʃiːt] N guardapolvo *m*.

dust-storm ['dʌststɔːm] N vendaval *m* de polvo.

dust-up* ['dʌstʌp] N (*Brit*) pelea *f*, reyerta *f*, riña *f*; **to have a ~ with** pelearse con.

dusty ['dʌstɪ] ADJ polvoriento, empolvado; **to get ~** cubrirse de polvo; **not so ~** nada malo; **to give sb a ~ answer** dar a uno una respuesta equívoca.

Dutch [dʌtʃ] [1] ADJ holandés; **~ auction** subasta *f* a la baja; **~ barn** granero de acero con techo curvo; **~ cap** diafragma *m*; **~ cheese** queso *m* de bola; **~ courage** envalentonamiento *m* (del que ha bebido), valentía *f* de botella; **~ elm disease** enfermedad *f* holandesa del olmo, grafiosis *f*; **~ oven** olla *f*; **~ school** (*Art*) escuela *f* holandesa; **~ treat** comida (etc) en la que cada uno paga lo suyo; **to talk to sb like a ~ uncle** decirle cuatro verdades a uno; **to be in ~ with sb** (*US**) estar en la lista negra de uno.
[2] N (**a**) **the ~** los holandeses.
(**b**) (*Ling*) holandés *m*.
[3] (*) as ADV: **to go ~** pagar cada uno su cuota, ir a escote.

Dutchman ['dʌtʃmən] N, PL **Dutchmen** ['dʌtʃmən] holandés *m*; **it's him or I'm a ~** que me maten si no es él.

Dutchwoman ['dʌtʃ,wʊmən] N, PL **Dutchwomen** ['dʌtʃ,wɪmɪn] holandesa *f*.

dutiable ['djuːtɪəbl] ADJ sujeto a derechos de aduana.

dutiful ['djuːtɪfʊl] ADJ obediente, sumiso.

dutifully ['djuːtɪfəlɪ] ADV obedientemente, sumisamente.

▼**duty** ['djuːtɪ] [1] N (**a**) (*gen*) deber *m*, obligación *f*; **out of a sense of ~** por compromiso, cumpliendo con su deber; **it is my ~ to +** *infin* me incumbe **+** *infin*, me corresponde **+** *infin*; **to be in ~ bound to +** *infin* estar obligado a **+** *infin*; **it is no part of my ~ to +** *infin* no me corresponde **+** *infin*; **I feel it to be my ~** creo que es mi deber; **to do one's ~ by** cumplir con; **to fail in one's ~** faltar a su deber; **to make it one's ~ to +** *infin* encargarse de **+** *infin*.
(**b**) **duties** (*of post*) funciones *fpl*; responsabilidad *f*; **to neglect one's duties** no cumplir sus funciones; **to take up one's duties** entrar en funciones.
(**c**) (*Med, Mil etc*) servicio *m*; **an off ~ policeman** un policía franco de servicio; **to be off ~** estar libre, (*Mil*) estar libre (or franco) de servicio; **to be on ~** estar de servicio; **to do ~ as** servir de; **to do ~ for** servir en lugar de; **to go on ~** entrar de servicio.
(**d**) (*Fin*) derechos *mpl* (de aduana); aranceles *mpl*; **to pay ~ on** pagar derechos de aduana por.
[2] ATTR: **~ call** visita *f* de cumplido.

duty-free ['djuːtɪ'friː] ADJ libre de impuestos; **~ shop** tienda *f* libre de impuestos.

duty officer ['djuːtɪ,ɒfɪsəʳ] N oficial *m* de guardia.

duty-paid [,djuːtɪ'peɪd] ADJ con aranceles pagados.

duty roster ['djuːtɪ,rɒstəʳ] N, **duty rota** ['djuːtɪ,rəʊtə] N lista *f* de guardias.

duvet ['duːveɪ] N (*Brit*) edredón *m*.

DV ABBR of **Deo volente**, *God willing* Dios mediante.

DVLA N (*Brit*) ABBR of **Driver and Vehicle Licensing Agency** organismo encargado de la expedición de permisos de conducir y matriculación de vehículos, ≃ DGT *f* (*Sp*).

DVLC N (*Brit*) ABBR of **Driver and Vehicle Licensing Centre** centro de donde se expiden los permisos de conducir y matriculación de vehículos, ≃ DGT *f* (*Sp*).

DVM N (*US*) ABBR of **Doctor of Veterinary Medicine**.

dwarf [dwɔːf] [1] ADJ enano; diminuto, pequeñito; **~ bean** judía *f* enana, fríjol *m*.
[2] N enano *m*, -a *f*.
[3] VT achicar, empequeñecer, hacer que parezca pequeño; (*stunt*) impedir el crecimiento de.

dweeb: [dwiːb] N (*esp US*) memo* *m*, -a *f*.

dwell [dwel] (*irr*: PRET AND PTP **dwelt**) VI morar; **to ~ on** *subject* explicar largamente, explayarse en; insistir en; hacer hincapié en; *thought* meditar; *note, syllable* dar énfasis a, alargar.

dweller ['dweləʳ] N morador *m*, -ora *f*; **~ in** habitante *mf* de; inquilino *m*, -a *f* de.

dwelling ['dwelɪŋ] N morada *f*, vivienda *f*.

dwelling house ['dwelɪŋhaʊs] N, PL **dwelling houses** ['dwelɪŋ,haʊzɪz] casa *f*.

dwelt [dwelt] PRET AND PTP of **dwell**.

dwindle ['dwɪndl] VI (*also* **to ~ away**) disminuir, menguar; ir desapareciendo, ir acabándose; **to ~ to** quedar reducido a.

dwindling ['dwɪndlɪŋ] [1] ADJ que va disminuyendo, menguante.
[2] N disminución *f*.

dye [daɪ] [1] N tinte *m*, colorante *m*; (*hue*) matiz *m*, color *m*; **of (the) deepest ~** de lo más vil, de la peor calaña.
[2] VT teñir (*green* de verde).

dyed-in-the-wool ['daɪdɪnðə'wʊl] ADJ (*fig*) testarudo.

dyeing ['daɪɪŋ] N tinte *m*, tintura *f*.

dyer ['daɪəʳ] N tintorero *m*; **~'s** tintorería *f*.

dyestuff ['daɪstʌf] N tinte *m*, colorante *m*.

dyeworks ['daɪwɜːks] NPL tintorería *f*.

dying ['daɪɪŋ] [1] PRESENT PARTICIPLE of **die**.
[2] ADJ *man* moribundo, agonizante; *moments* final; *words* último.
[3] N: **the ~** los moribundos.

dyke [daɪk] N = **dike¹** and **dike²**.

dynamic [daɪ'næmɪk] [1] ADJ dinámico.
[2] N dinámica *f*.

dynamically [daɪ'næmɪkəlɪ] ADV dinámicamente.

dynamics [daɪ'næmɪks] N dinámica *f*.

dynamism ['daɪnəmɪzəm] N dinamismo *m*.

dynamite ['daɪnəmaɪt] [1] N dinamita *f*; **that issue is ~** ese asunto es dinamita; **the book is ~** el libro es explosivo.
[2] VT dinamitar, volar con dinamita.

dynamo ['daɪnəməʊ] N (*esp Brit*) dinamo *f*, dínamo *f* (*also m in LAm*).

dynastic [daɪ'næstɪk] ADJ dinástico.

dynasty ['dɪnəstɪ] N dinastía *f*.

d'you ['djuː] = **do you**.

dysentery ['dɪsntrɪ] N disentería *f*.

dysfunction [dɪs'fʌŋkʃən] N disfunción *f*.

dysfunctional [dɪs'fʌŋkʃənəl] ADJ disfuncional.

dyslexia [dɪs'leksɪə] N dislexia *f*.

dyslexic [dɪs'leksɪk] [1] ADJ disléxico.
[2] N disléxico *m*, -a *f*.

dysmenorrhoea, (*US*) **dysmenorrhea** [,dɪsmenə'rɪə] N dismenorrea *f*.

dyspepsia [dɪs'pepsɪə] N dispepsia *f*.

dyspeptic [dɪs'peptɪk] ADJ dispéptico.

dysphasia [dɪs'feɪzɪə] N disfasia *f*.

dystrophy ['dɪstrəfɪ] N distrofia *f*; **muscular ~** distrofia *f* muscular.

E

E, e [i:] N (*letter*) E, e *f*; **E** (*Mus*) mi *m*; **E major** mi *m* mayor; **E for Edward, E for Easy** (*US*) E de Enrique; **E number** número *m* E.

E **1** ABBR of **east** este, E.

2 N (*) ABBR of **ecstasy** éxtasis* *m*.

E111 ['iːwʌnɪ'levn] N ABBR (*also form* ~) *impreso para la asistencia sanitaria en el extranjero.*

E&OE ABBR of **errors and omissions excepted** salvo error u omisión, s.e.u.o.

E.A. (*US*) ABBR of **educational age.**

ea. ABBR of **each** cada uno, c/u.

each [iːtʃ] **1** ADJ cada (*invariable*); (~ **and every**, *any*) todo; ~ **one of them** cada uno de ellos; ~ **and every child** todos los niños sin excepción.

2 PRON cada uno; **they help** ~ **other** (*2 persons*) se ayudan (mutuamente), se ayudan uno a otro, se ayudan el uno al otro, (*more than 2 persons*) se ayudan unos a otros; ~ **of us** cada uno de nosotros; ~ **of the countries** cada uno de los países; **a bit of** ~, **please** un poco de cada cosa.

3 ADV (*apiece*) **two sweets** ~ dos dulces por persona, dos dulces para cada uno; **we paid £5** ~ pagamos 5 libras cada uno.

eager ['iːgər] ADJ impaciente; *desire etc* apremiante, vehemente; (*hopeful*) ilusionado; (*ambitious*) ambicioso; **to be** ~ ansiar, anhelar, tener vivo deseo de; **to be** ~ **to** + *infin* ansiar + *infin*, impacientarse por + *infin*; **don't be so** ~! ¡ten paciencia!, ¡no te afanes!; ~ **beaver** entusiasta *mf*.

eagerly ['iːgəlɪ] ADV con impaciencia, con ansia; con ilusión.

eagerness ['iːgənɪs] N impaciencia *f*; afán *m*, ansia *f*, deseo *m* (*for* de); (*hopefulness*) ilusión *f*; **in his** ~ **to get there first** en su ansia por llegar el primero.

EAGGF N ABBR of **European Agricultural Guidance and Guarantee Fund** Fondo *m* Europeo de Orientación y de Garantía Agrícola, FEOGA *m*.

eagle ['iːgl] N águila *f*; (*Golf*) eagle *m*, menos dos *m*; **with** ~ **eye** con ojos de lince.

eagle-eyed ['iːgl'aɪd] ADJ de ojos de lince.

eaglet ['iːglɪt] N aguilucho *m*.

ear¹ [ɪər] N (*Anat*) oreja *f*; (*sense, Mus*) oído *m*; **to bend sb's** ~ (*US**) hinchar la cabeza a uno; **a word in your** ~ una palabra en confianza; **to be all** ~s ser todo oídos; **he's up to his** ~s **in debt** tiene deudas hasta encima de la coronilla; **he could not believe his** ~s no daba crédito a sus oídos; **to give** (*or* **lend**) ~ prestar oído a; **to give sb a thick** ~* darle un cachete a uno; **it goes in one** ~ **and out the other** por un oído le entra y por el otro le sale; **to have a good** ~ tener buen oído; **she has an** ~ **for music** tiene buen oído para la música; **to have one's** ~ **to the ground** (*fig*) mantenerse al corriente; **to have the minister's** ~ poder contar con el interés del ministro; **to play by** ~ tocar de oído; **we're playing it by** ~ (*fig*) obramos por instinto, vamos improvisando; **to prick up one's** ~s aguzar el oído; **he set them by the** ~s sembró la discordia entre ellos, causó desavenencias entre ellos; *V* **deaf, inner** *etc*.

ear² [ɪər] N (*Bot*) espiga *f*; **to come into** ~ espigar.

earache ['ɪəreɪk] N dolor *m* de oídos.

eardrops ['ɪədrɒps] NPL (*Med*) gotas *fpl* para el oído.

eardrum ['ɪədrʌm] N tímpano *m*.

earflap ['ɪəflæp] N orejera *f*.

earful* ['ɪəfʊl] N (a) **I got an** ~ **of Wagner** me llenaron los oídos de Wagner; **get an** ~ **of this** (*Brit*) escucha esto. (b) **to give sb an** ~ regañar a uno; **she gave me an** ~ **of her complaints** me soltó el rollo de sus quejas*.

earhole* ['ɪəhəʊl] N agujero *m* de la oreja.

earl [ɜːl] N conde *m*.

earldom ['ɜːldəm] N condado *m*.

ear lobe ['ɪələʊb] N lóbulo *m* de la oreja.

early ['ɜːlɪ] **1** ADJ temprano (*also Bot*); (*first*) primero, primitivo; *age* tierno; *death* prematuro, temprano; *reply* pronto; *retirement* anticipado, prematuro; *diagnosis* precoz; *book, work etc* juvenil, de primera época; **an** ~ **Victorian table** una mesa victoriana de primera época; ~ **Christian art** arte *m* cristiano primitivo; ~ **bird** (*fig*) madrugador *m*, -ora *f*; ~ **closing is on Mondays** las tiendas se cierran temprano los lunes; ~ **frosts** heladas *fpl* tempranas; ~ **fruits** frutas *fpl* tempranas; ~ **man** el hombre primitivo; ~ **retirement** jubilación *f* anticipada; ~ **stages** (*of insect*) estados *mpl* inmaduros; **an** ~ **summer** un verano precoz; ~ **warning system** sistema *m* de alarma anticipada, sistema *m* de alerta previa; **it's** ~ **in the day** (*or* **it's** ~ **days**) **to say that** (*Brit*) es demasiado pronto para decir eso; **we need two seats on an** ~ **flight** necesitamos dos plazas en el primer vuelo en que las haya; **to be in one's** ~ **forties** tener poco más de 40 años; *V* **date, life** *etc*.

2 ADV (a) (*gen*) temprano; **as** ~ **as possible** lo más pronto posible, cuanto antes; **as** ~ **as 1978** ya en 1978; **a month earlier** un mes antes; **earlier on** antes; ~ **in the morning** muy de mañana, de madrugada; ~ **in the afternoon** a primera hora de la tarde, en las primeras horas de la tarde; ~ **in the week** en los primeros días de la semana; ~ **last century** a principios del siglo pasado; ~ **in his life** en su juventud; ~ **in the twenties** al comienzo de los años veinte, al principio de los años veinte; ~ **in the book** en las primeras páginas del libro; **the earliest I can do it is next Tuesday** lo más pronto que lo podré hacer será el martes que viene.

(b) (*in good time*) con tiempo, con anticipación; **to book** ~ reservar con mucha anticipación; **to come an hour** ~ llegar con una hora de anticipación; **he took his summer holiday** ~ anticipó el veraneo, salió en fecha temprana para veranear.

earmark ['ɪəmɑːk] VT (*fig*) reservar (*for* para), destinar (*for* a); **an** ~**ed grant** una subvención destinada a fines especiales.

earmuff ['ɪəmʌf] N orejera *f*.

earn [ɜːn] VT *salary etc* ganar(se), percibir; *interest* devengar; (*win for o.s.*) merecer(se); adquirir, obtener; ~**ed income** ingresos *mpl* devengados, renta *f* devengada; **it** ~**ed him the nickname of X** le valió el apodo de X.

earner ['ɜːnər] N persona *f* que gana un sueldo; asalariado *m*, -a *f*; **there are 3** ~s **in the family** en la familia hay 3 que ganan un sueldo; **the shop is a nice little** ~ la tienda es una buena fuente de ingresos, la tienda es rentable.

earnest¹ ['ɜːnɪst] ADJ *person, character etc* serio, formal; *wish etc* fervoroso; **it is my** ~ **wish that ...** deseo con fervor que + *subj*; **to be in** ~ hablar con la mayor seriedad; **are you in** ~? ¿esto va de veras?, ¿me lo dices en serio?

earnest² ['ɜːnɪst] N prenda *f*, señal *f*; ~ **money** fianza *f*; **as an** ~ **of** en señal de.

earnestly ['ɜːnɪstlɪ] ADV *speak etc* con la mayor seriedad; **I** ~ **entreat you** se lo suplico de todo corazón.

earnestness ['ɜːnɪstnɪs] N seriedad *f*, formalidad *f*.

earning ['ɜːnɪŋ] **1** ATTR: ~ **potential** potencial *m* ganador; ~ **power** poder *m* adquisitivo.

2 ~s NPL (*of individual*) sueldo *m*, ingresos *mpl*; (*of company etc*) ganancias *fpl*, beneficios *mpl*, utilidades *fpl*; ~s **related benefits** beneficios *mpl* relacionados con los ingresos.

ear, nose and throat [ˌɪəˌnəʊzənˈθrəʊt] ATTR (*Med*): ~ **department** departamento *m* de otorrinolaringología; ~ **specialist** otorrinolaringólogo *m*.

earphone ['ɪəfəʊn] N (*US*) auricular *m*.

earphones ['ɪəfəʊnz] NPL auriculares *mpl*, cascos *mpl*, audífono *m* (*LAm*).

earpiece ['ɪəpiːs] N auricular *m*.

ear-piercing ['ɪəˌpɪəsɪŋ] ADJ penetrante, que taladra el oído.

ear-plug ['ɪəplʌg] N tapón *m* para el oído.

earring ['ɪərɪŋ] N (long) pendiente m; (round) arete m, zarcillo m.

earshot ['ɪəʃɒt] N: **to be within ~** estar al alcance del oído; **to be out of ~** estar fuera del alcance del oído.

ear-splitting ['ɪə,splɪtɪŋ] ADJ que rompe el tímpano, que taladra el oído, ensordecedor.

earth [ɜːθ] **1** N (a) (world) tierra f; **~ sciences** ciencias fpl concernientes a la Tierra; geología f; **here on ~** en este mundo; **to come down to ~**, **to get back to ~** volver a la realidad; **it must have cost the ~** habrá costado un potosí; **to promise the ~** prometer el oro y el moro; **nothing on ~ will stop me now** no lo dejo ahora por nada del mundo; **it tasted like nothing on ~** (good) tenía un sabor como nada de este mundo, (bad) sabía a algo inmundo; **what on ~...?** ¿qué demonios ...?; **why on ~ do it now?** ¿por qué demonios hacerlo ahora?

(b) (soil) tierra f.

(c) (Zool) madriguera f; **to go to ~** (fox) meterse en su madriguera, (person) esconderse, refugiarse; **to run to ~** encontrar finalmente.

(d) (Brit Elec) tierra f; **~ cable**, **~ lead** cable m de toma de tierra.

2 VT (Elec) conectar a tierra.

♦**earth up** VT (Agr) acollar.

earthbound ['ɜːθbaʊnd] ADJ terrestre; (fig) prosaico.

earthen ['ɜːθən] ADJ de tierra; pot de barro.

earthenware ['ɜːθənweəʳ] **1** N loza f de barro.

2 ATTR de barro.

earthling ['ɜːθlɪŋ] N terrícola mf.

earthly ['ɜːθlɪ] ADJ (a) (lit) terrenal, mundano; **~ paradise** paraíso m terrenal.

(b) (fig) **to be of no ~ use** no servir para nada en absoluto; **there is no ~ reason why not** no hay la más pequeña razón en contra; **he hasn't an ~** (Brit) no tiene posibilidad alguna, no tiene ni esperanza.

earth mother ['ɜːθ,mʌðəʳ] N (Mit) la madre tierra; (*: woman) venus f.

earthquake ['ɜːθkweɪk] N terremoto m, seísmo m, temblor m (de tierra) (LAm).

earthscape ['ɜːθskeɪp] N vista de la tierra desde una nave espacial.

earth-shaking ['ɜːθ,ʃeɪkɪŋ] ADJ, **earth-shattering** ['ɜːθ,ʃætərɪŋ] ADJ trascendental.

earthward(s) ['ɜːθwəd(z)] ADV hacia la tierra.

earthwork ['ɜːθwɜːk] N terraplén m.

earthworm ['ɜːθwɜːm] N lombriz f.

earthy ['ɜːθɪ] ADJ terroso; flavour terrero; character práctico; nada espiritual; (coarse) grosero.

eartrumpet ['ɪə,trʌmpɪt] N trompetilla f acústica.

earwax ['ɪəwæks] N cerumen m, cera f de los oídos.

earwig ['ɪəwɪg] N tijereta f, cortaplumas m.

ease [iːz] **1** N (a) (easiness) facilidad f; **with ~** con facilidad, fácilmente.

(b) (relief from pain) alivio m.

(c) (freedom from worry) tranquilidad f; alivio m; **a life of ~** una vida desahogada; **to live a life of ~** vivir con desahogo.

(d) (relaxed state) comodidad f; **to be at (one's) ~** sentirse cómodo, encontrarse a gusto; **to be ill at ~** sentirse molesto; **to put sb at his ~** lograr que uno se sienta cómodo; **to set sb's mind at ~** tranquilizar el ánimo a uno; **stand at ~!** en su lugar ¡descanso!; **to take one's ~** descansar.

(e) (of manner) naturalidad f.

2 VT (a) task facilitar.

(b) pain aliviar; mind tranquilizar, aliviar; (slacken) aflojar; pressure aflojar; weight aligerar; impact suavizar, mitigar.

3 VI (wind) amainar, calmarse; (rain) moderarse; **prices have ~d** han bajado ligeramente los precios.

4 VR: **to ~ o.s. of a burden** quitarse un peso de encima.

♦**ease along** VT: **to ~ a table along** mover una mesa con cuidado.

♦**ease off** **1** VT: **to ~ a lid off** levantar una tapa poco a poco.

2 VI suavizarse, aligerarse; (at work) trabajar menos; (pain) aliviarse; (tension) decrecer.

♦**ease up** **1** VT: **to ~ a weight up** levantar un peso con cuidado.

2 VI (a) = ease off 2.

(b) **to ~ up on sb** tratar a uno con menos rigor.

easel ['iːzl] N caballete m.

easily ['iːzɪlɪ] ADV fácilmente, con facilidad; **to win ~** ganar fácilmente; **it could ~ be** bien podría ser; **the engine is running ~** el motor funciona bien; **it holds 4 litres ~** caben 4 litros largos; **it's ~ the best** es con mucho el mejor, seguramente es el mejor; **to take life ~** no preocuparse por nada.

easiness ['iːzɪnɪs] N facilidad f.

east [iːst] **1** N este m, oriente m; (of Spain) Levante m; **the E~** el Oriente.

2 ADJ del este, oriental; wind del este; **E~ Africa** África f Oriental; **E~ Berlin** (Hist) Berlín Este; **E~ Berliner** (Hist) berlinés m, -esa f oriental (or del Este); **the E~ End** (of London) la zona del Este de Londres; **E~ German** (Hist: N) alemán m, -ana f oriental, (ADJ) germanooriental;

E~ Germany (Hist) Alemania f Oriental; **the E~ Side** (of New York) la zona del Este de Nueva York.

3 ADV al este, hacia el este.

eastbound ['iːstbaʊnd] ADJ traffic que va hacia el este; carriageway dirección este.

Eastender ['iːst'endəʳ] N habitante o nativo del este de Londres.

Easter ['iːstəʳ] **1** N Pascua f de Resurrección; (period, loosely) Semana f Santa.

2 ATTR: **~ bonnet** sombrero m de primavera; **~ Day**, **~ Sunday** Domingo m de Resurrección; **~ egg** huevo m de Pascua; **~ Island** Isla f de Pascua; **~ Monday** lunes m de Pascua de Resurrección; **~ parade** desfile m de Pascua; **~ week** Semana f Santa.

easterly ['iːstəlɪ] ADJ este, oriental; wind del este.

eastern ['iːstən] ADJ del este, oriental.

easterner ['iːstənəʳ] N (esp US) habitante mf del este.

easternmost ['iːstənməʊst] ADJ (el) más oriental, situado más al este.

Eastertide ['iːstətaɪd] N = **Easter**.

east-facing ['iːst,feɪsɪŋ] ADJ con cara al este, orientado hacia el este; **~ slope** vertiente f este.

East Indies ['iːst'ɪndɪz] NPL Indias fpl Orientales.

east-south-east [,iːstsaʊθ'iːst] N estesudeste m.

eastward ['iːstwəd] **1** ADJ advance etc hacia el este, en dirección este.

2 ADV (also ~s) hacia el este, en dirección este.

easy ['iːzɪ] **1** ADJ (a) (simple) fácil; sencillo; **it's ~ to see why** es fácil comprender por qué; **he's ~ to get on with** es muy simpático; **I'm ~** me es igual; **an ~ house** una casa de fácil manejo; **to come in an ~ first** llegar fácilmente el primero; **it's as ~ as pie** (or ABC etc) es facilísimo, más fácil no puede ser; **they made it very ~ for us** nos lo pusieron muy fácil; **'Slobodian made ~'** 'Eslóbode por etapas fáciles'.

(b) (relaxed, comfortable) **to feel ~ in one's mind** estar tranquilo; **you can rest ~** puedes dormir tranquilo.

(c) life, conditions holgado, cómodo; **~ chair** butaca f, sillón m; **to be on ~ street*** vivir en el lujo.

(d) manners natural, sin afectación; style llano, corriente; movement suelto.

(e) money, credit abundante; **~ money** dinero m fácil; **by ~ payments** con facilidades de pago; **steel is easier** el acero tiene menos demanda; **prices are easier** los precios han bajado ligeramente.

(f) pace lento, pausado.

(g) woman fácil; **of ~ virtue** de moral relajada; **she's an ~ lay** (US: make‡) es un coño caliente‡, es una tía fácil*.

2 ADV (*) fácilmente; **~ there!** ¡despacio!; **~ come ~ go** así se viene y así se va; **~ does it!** ¡con calma!; ¡despacito!, ¡no hay prisa!; **to go ~ on sb** tratar a uno con menos rigor; **to go ~ with** moderar; emplear más cuidado con; economizar en; **go ~ with the sugar!** ¡cuidado con el azúcar!; **stand ~!** en su lugar ¡descanso!; **he's got it ~*** lo tiene fácil*; **to take it ~** (rest) descansar; (go slow) ir despacio; **take it ~!** ¡cálmese!, ¡no se ponga nervioso!

┌─ **EASY, DIFFICULT, IMPOSSIBLE** ─┐ ┌─ **see also main entries** ─┐

• Fácil, difícil and imposible are followed directly by the infinitive when they qualify the action itself:

Solving the problem is easy or It's easy to solve the problem
Es fácil resolver el problema
It is sometimes difficult/impossible to control oneself
En ocasiones es difícil/imposible controlarse

• When the adjective qualifies a noun or pronoun rather than the verb, de is inserted before the infinitive:

The problem is easy to solve
El problema es fácil de resolver
That's difficult or hard to believe
Eso es difícil de creer
Semtex is impossible to detect
El Semtex es imposible de detectar

! Remember in this case to make the adjective agree with the noun or pronoun it describes:

Some of his works are difficult to classify
Algunas de sus obras son difíciles de encasillar

For further uses and examples, see main entries at easy, difficult and impossible.

easy-care ['iːzɪkeəʳ] ADJ (Brit) que no necesita cuidados especiales.

easy-going ['iːzɪ'gəʊɪŋ] ADJ acomodadizo, nada severo; (morally) de manga ancha; (lazy) indolente.

easy-peasy* [,iːzɪ'piːzɪ] ADJ (Brit: child's language) tirado*, chupado‡.

eat [iːt] (irr: PRET **ate**, PTP **eaten**) **1** VT comer; meal tomar; (with envy etc) consumir, devorar; **to ~ one's way through the menu** pedir todos los platos en la lista; **I thought he was going to ~ me** creía que iba a comerme vivo; **what's ~ing you?*** ¿qué mosca te ha picado?

2 VI comer; **he always ~s well** siempre tiene buen apetito; **this fish ~s well** este pescado es muy sabroso; **he had them ~ing out of his**

hand los tenía totalmente dominados.

[3] ~s* NPL (*Brit*) comida *f*, comestibles *mpl*; **let's get some ~s** vamos a comer algo.

♦ **eat away** VT corroer; desgastar.

♦ **eat in** VI comer en casa.

♦ **eat into** VT *metal* corroer; *surface etc* desgastar; *reserves etc* mermar; *leisure time etc* reducir.

♦ **eat out** VI comer fuera, comer en un restaurante.

♦ **eat up** VT comerse, acabar; **to ~ up the miles** tragar los kilómetros; **this fire ~s up coal** esta chimenea devora el carbón; **to be ~en up with envy** consumirse de envidia.

eatable ['iːtəbl] [1] ADJ comestible;

[2] ~s NPL comestibles *mpl*.

eaten ['iːtn] PTP of **eat.**

eater ['iːtəʳ] N (a) (*person*) **to be a big ~** tener siempre buen apetito, ser comilón; **I'm not a big ~** yo como bastante poco. (b) (*apple etc*) manzana *f (etc)* de boca.

eatery ['iːtəri] N (*US*) restaurante *m*.

eating ['iːtɪŋ] [1] N (a) (*act*) el comer. (b) **to be good ~** ser sabroso.

[2] ATTR: ~ **apple** manzana *f* de mesa; ~ **olives** aceitunas *fpl* de boca.

eating-house ['iːtɪŋhaʊs] N, PL **eating-houses** ['iːtɪŋ,haʊzɪz] restaurante *m*.

eau de Cologne ['əʊdəkə'ləʊn] N agua *f* de colonia, colonia *f*.

eaves ['iːvz] NPL alero *m*.

eavesdrop ['iːvzdrɒp] VI escuchar a escondidas, orejear (*LAm*) (*on a conversation* una conversación).

eavesdropper ['iːvz,drɒpəʳ] N escuchador *m* escondido.

ebb [eb] [1] N reflujo *m*; **the ~ and flow** el flujo y reflujo; **to be at a low ~** estar decaído; **at a low ~ in his fortunes** en un punto bien bajo de su vida.

[2] ATTR: ~ **tide** marea *f* menguante.

[3] VI bajar; menguar; (*fig*) decaer; **to ~ and flow** fluir y refluir; **life is ~ing from him** le estaba abandonando sus últimas fuerzas.

♦ **ebb away** VI (*fig*) menguar, disminuir.

ebonite ['ebənaɪt] N ebonita *f*.

ebony ['ebəni] [1] N ébano *m*.

[2] ATTR de ébano.

EBU N ABBR of **European Broadcasting Union** Unión *f* Europea de Radiodifusión, UER *f*.

ebullience [ɪ'bʌliəns] N exaltación *f*, entusiasmo *m*, exuberancia *f*, animación *f*.

ebullient [ɪ'bʌliənt] ADJ exaltado, entusiasta, exuberante, animado.

EC N ABBR of **European Community** Comunidad *f* Europea, CE *f*.

eccentric [ɪk'sentrɪk] [1] ADJ excéntrico.

[2] N excéntrico *m*, -a *f*.

eccentrically [ɪk'sentrɪkəli] ADV de manera excéntrica.

eccentricity [,eksən'trɪsɪti] N excentricidad *f*.

Ecclesiastes [ɪ,kliːzi'æstiːz] N (*Bible*): **the Book of ~** el Libro de Eclesiastés.

ecclesiastic [ɪ,kliːzi'æstɪk] N eclesiástico *m*.

ecclesiastical [ɪ,kliːzi'æstɪkəl] ADJ eclesiástico.

ECG N ABBR of **electrocardiogram** electrocardiograma *m*.

ECGD N ABBR of **Export Credits Guarantee Department** Departamento *m* de Garantía de Crédito a la Exportación.

echelon ['eʃəlɒn] [1] N escalón *m*.

[2] VT escalonar.

echo ['ekəʊ] [1] N (PL **echoes** ['ekəʊz]) eco *m*; **to cheer sb to the ~** aplaudir a uno repetidas veces, ovacionar a uno.

[2] VT *sound* repetir; (*imitate*) imitar; *opinion etc* hacerse eco de; **his opinion is ~ed by ...** su opinión es coreada por ...

[3] VI resonar, hacer eco; **the valley ~ed with shouts** resonaban los gritos por el valle.

echo-chamber ['ekəʊ,tʃeɪmbəʳ] N (*Rad, TV*) cámara *f* de eco.

echolocation [,ekəʊləʊ'keɪʃən] N ecolocación *f*.

echo-sounder ['ekəʊ,saʊndəʳ] N sonda *f* acústica.

ECJ N ABBR of **European Court of Justice** Corte *f* Europea de Justicia.

ECLA ['eklə] N ABBR of **Economic Commission for Latin America** CEPAL *f*.

éclair ['eɪkleəʳ] N relámpago *m* de chocolate.

eclampsia [ɪ'klæmpsɪə] N eclampsia *f*.

éclat ['eɪklɑː] N brillo *m*; (*success*) éxito *m* brillante; **with great ~** brillantemente.

eclectic [ɪ'klektɪk] [1] ADJ ecléctico.

[2] N ecléctico *m*, -a *f*.

eclecticism [ɪ'klektɪsɪzəm] N eclecticismo *m*.

eclipse [ɪ'klɪps] [1] N eclipse *m*.

[2] VT eclipsar.

eclogue ['eklɒg] N égloga *f*.

eclosion [ɪ'kləʊʒən] N eclosión *f*.

ECM N (a) ABBR of **electronic counter-measure** contramedida *f* electrónica. (b) (*US*) ABBR of **European Common Market** Mercado *m* Común Europeo, MCE *m*.

eco... ['iːkəʊ] PREF eco...

ecobalance ['iːkəʊ,bæləns] N ecoequilibrio *m*.

ecoclimatic [,iːkəʊklaɪ'mætɪk] ADJ ecoclimático.

eco-friendly ['iːkəʊ'frendlɪ] ADJ amigo de la ecología, ecológicamente puro.

eco-labelling, (*US*) **eco-labeling** [,iːkəʊ'leɪbəlɪŋ] N etiquetado *m* ecologista.

ecological [,iːkəʊ'lɒdʒɪkəl] ADJ ecológico.

ecologically [,iːkəʊ'lɒdʒɪkəli] ADV ecológicamente; **an ~ sound scheme** un plan ecológicamente razonable.

ecologist [ɪ'kɒlədʒɪst] N ecólogo *m*, -a *f*; (*Pol*) ecologista *mf*.

ecology [ɪ'kɒlədʒɪ] [1] N ecología *f*.

[2] ATTR: ~ **movement** movimiento *m* ecologista.

econometric [ɪ,kɒnə'metrɪk] ADJ econométrico.

econometrician [ɪ,kɒnəmə'trɪʃən] N, **econometrist** [ɪ,kɒnə'metrɪst] N econometrista *mf*.

econometrics [ɪ,kɒnə'metrɪks] N econometría *f*.

economic(al) [,iːkə'nɒmɪk(əl)] ADJ económico; *rent* equitativo; (~ *to operate, to run*) rentable; ~ **aid** ayuda *f* económica; ~ **expansion** expansión *f* económica; ~ **forecast** previsiones *fpl* económicas; ~ **growth** crecimiento *m* económico; ~ **indicator** indicador *m* económico; ~ **policy** política *f* económica; ~ **sanctions** sanciones *fpl* económicas; ~ **warfare** guerra *f* económica.

economically [,iːkə'nɒmɪkəli] ADJ económicamente; de modo rentable.

economics [,iːkə'nɒmɪks] NPL economía *f* política; (*Univ*) ciencias *fpl* económicas; **home ~** (*US*) economía *f* doméstica.

economist [ɪ'kɒnəmɪst] N economista *mf*.

economize [ɪ'kɒnəmaɪz] [1] VT economizar, ahorrar.

[2] VI economizar (*on* en).

economy [ɪ'kɒnəmɪ] [1] N (a) (*saving*) economía *f*; ~ **of scale** economía *f* de escala; **to make economies, to practise ~** economizar; **he writes with great ~** escribe con gran economía. (b) (*system*) economía *f*.

[2] ATTR: ~ **class** (*Aer*) clase *f* económica, clase *f* turista; ~ **drive** campaña *f* de economías (presupuestarias); ~ **size** tamaño *m* económico, tamaño *m* familiar.

ecosensitive ['iːkəʊ'sensɪtɪv] ADJ ecosensible.

ecosphere ['iːkəʊ,sfɪəʳ] N ecosfera *f*.

ecosystem ['iːkəʊ,sɪstɪm] N ecosistema *m*, sistema *m* ecológico.

eco-tourism ['iːkəʊ'tʊərɪzəm] N ecoturismo *m*, turismo *m* verde *or* ecológico.

ecotype ['iːkə,taɪp] N ecotipo *m*.

ECS N ABBR of **extended character set** conjunto *m* de caracteres extendido.

ECSC N ABBR of **European Coal and Steel Community** Comunidad *f* Europea del Carbón y del Acero, CECA *f*.

ecstasy ['ekstəsɪ] N (a) éxtasis *m*; **in an ~ of passion** en un arrebato de amor, arrebatado por el amor; **to be in ecstasies** estar en éxtasis; **to go into ecstasies over sth** extasiarse ante algo. (b) (‡: *drug*) éxtasis* *m*, metanfetamina *f*.

ecstatic [eks'tætɪk] ADJ extático.

ecstatically [eks'tætɪkəli] ADV con éxtasis.

ECT N ABBR of **electroconvulsive therapy** terapia *f* de electroshock; V **electroconvulsive.**

ectomorph ['ektəʊ,mɔːf] N ectomorfo *m*.

ectopic [ek'tɒpɪk] ADJ ectópico; ~ **pregnancy** embarazo *m* ectópico.

ectoplasm ['ektəʊplæzəm] N ectoplasma *m*.

ECU ['eɪkjuː] N ABBR of **European Currency Unit** Unidad *f* de Cuenta Europea, UCE *f*.

ecu ['eɪkjuː] N ecu *m*.

Ecuador [,ekwə'dɔːʳ] N El Ecuador.

Ecuador(i)an [,ekwə'dɔːr(i)ən] [1] ADJ ecuatoriano.

[2] N ecuatoriano *m*, -a *f*.

ecumenical [,iːkjʊ'menɪkəl] ADJ ecuménico; ~ **council** concejo *m* ecuménico; ~ **movement** movimiento *m* ecuménico.

ecumenism [ɪ'kjuːmənɪzəm] N ecumenismo *m*.

eczema ['eksɪmə] N eccema *m*, eczema *m*.

Ed [ed], **Eddie** ['edɪ] NM *familiar forms of* **Edward.**

ed. [ed] (a) N ABBR of **edition** edición *f*, ed. (b) N ABBR of **editor**. (c) ABBR of **edited by** en edición de.

Edam ['iːdæm] N (*also* ~ **cheese**) queso *m* de Edam, queso *m* de bola.

eddy ['edɪ] [1] N remolino *m*.

[2] VI arremolinarse.

edelweiss ['eɪdlvaɪs] N edelweiss *m*.

edema [ɪ'diːmə] N (*esp US*) edema *m*.

Eden ['iːdn] N Edén *m*.

EDF N ABBR of **European Development Fund** Fondo *m* Europeo de Desarrollo, FED *m*.

edge [edʒ] [1] N (*cutting*) filo *m*, corte *m*; (*border: of chair, cliff, wood etc*) borde *m*; (*of page, sheet*) margen *m*; (*of coin, table etc*) canto *m*; (*of town*) afueras *fpl*; (*of lake etc*) margen *f*, orilla *f*; (*end*) extremidad *f*;

to be on ~ estar de canto, (fig) tener los nervios de punta; **my nerves are on ~** tengo los nervios de punta; **to be on the ~ of disaster** estar al borde del desastre; **to have the** (or **an**) **~ on** (or **over**) **sb** llevar ventaja a; ganar a uno por los pelos; **to put an ~ on** afilar; **to set sb's teeth on ~** dar dentera a uno; **to smooth the rough ~s** limar las asperezas (also fig); **to take the ~ off** embotar; **to take the ~ off one's appetite** engañar el hambre; **to take the ~ off an argument** quitar fuerza a un argumento.

2 VT **(a)** (Sew) ribetear, orlar (with de); path etc poner un borde a; **~d in**, **~d with** ribeteado de; bordeado de.

(b) to ~ one's way into a room introducirse con dificultad en un cuarto (atestado de gente).

◆**edge along** **1** VT mover algo de canto (poco a poco).

2 VI avanzar de lado poco a poco.

◆**edge away** VI alejarse poco a poco.

◆**edge in** **1** VT introducir de canto.

2 VI abrirse paso poco a poco; colarse.

◆**edge out** **1** VT (defeat) derrotar por muy poco; (ostracize) apartar.

2 VI asomarse con precaución.

◆**edge up** VI **(a)** (price etc) subir poco a poco, aumentar lentamente.

(b) to ~ up to sb acercarse con cautela a uno.

edgeways ['edʒweɪz] ADV de lado, de canto; V **word.**

edgewise ['edʒwaɪz] ADV de canto.

edginess ['edʒɪnɪs] N tirantez f, irritabilidad f.

edging ['edʒɪŋ] N (Sew) ribete m, orla f; (of path etc) borde m.

edgy ['edʒɪ] ADJ nervioso, inquieto.

edibility [,edɪ'bɪlətɪ] N comestibilidad f.

edible ['edɪbl] ADJ comestible.

edict ['iːdɪkt] N edicto m.

edification [,edɪfɪ'keɪʃən] N edificación f.

edifice ['edɪfɪs] N edificio m (esp grande, imponente).

edify ['edɪfaɪ] VT edificar.

edifying ['edɪfaɪɪŋ] ADJ edificante.

Edinburgh ['edɪnbərə] N Edimburgo m.

edit ['edɪt] VT newspaper, magazine, series dirigir, ser director de; text, book preparar una edición de; script preparar para la imprenta, (correct) corregir; (Comput) editar; **~ed by** (newspaper etc) bajo la dirección de, (text, book) prólogo y notas de, a cargo de, (en) edición de; **~ key** tecla f de edición; **to ~ a phrase out** eliminar una frase.

◆**edit out** VT: **to ~ words out** eliminar unas palabras, suprimir unas palabras.

editing ['edɪtɪŋ] N (of magazine) redacción f; (of newspaper, dictionary) dirección f; (of article, series of texts, tape) edición f; (of film) montaje m; (Comput) edición f; (video) editaje m.

edition [ɪ'dɪʃən] N edición f; (Typ: no of copies) tirada f.

editor ['edɪtər] N (of newspaper, magazine, series) director m, -ora f; (staff ~) redactor-jefe m, redactora-jefa f; (of a book) autor m, -ora f de la edición; (TV, Comput, also of critical text) editor m, -ora f; **~'s note** nota f de la redacción.

editorial [,edɪ'tɔːrɪəl] **1** ADJ editorial; de la dirección; **~ board** consejo m de redacción; **~ corrections** ajustes mpl de estilo, ajustes mpl de redacción; **~ staff** redacción f.

2 N editorial m, artículo m de fondo.

editorialist [,edɪ'tɔːrɪəlɪst] N (US) editorialista mf.

editorialize [,edɪ'tɔːrɪəlaɪz] VI editorializar.

editor-in-chief ['edɪtərɪn'tʃiːf] N jefe m, -a f de redacción.

editorship ['edɪtəʃɪp] N dirección f; **under the ~ of** bajo la dirección de.

Edmund ['edmənd] NM Edmundo m.

EDP N ABBR of **electronic data processing** proceso m electrónico de datos, PED m.

EDT N (US) ABBR of **Eastern Daylight Time.**

educability [,edjʊkə'bɪlɪtɪ] N educabilidad f.

educable ['edjʊkəbl] ADJ educable.

educate ['edjʊkeɪt] VT educar; formar; instruir; **where were you ~d?** ¿dónde cursó sus estudios?; **the prince is being privately ~d** el príncipe tiene un preceptor particular.

educated ['edjʊkeɪtɪd] ADJ culto.

education [,edjʊ'keɪʃən] **1** N educación f; enseñanza f; instrucción f; formación f cultural, cultura f; (as Univ department etc) pedagogía f; **I never had much ~** pasé poco tiempo en la escuela; **they paid for his ~** le pagaron los estudios; **Department of E~ and Science** (Brit) ≃ Dirección f General de Educación y Ciencia; **Minister of E~** (Brit) Ministro m, -a f de Educación y Ciencia; V **primary** etc.

2 ATTR: **~ authority** (Brit) ≃ delegación f de educación; **~ department** (Brit: of local authority) ≃ departamento m de educación; **E~ Department** (Ministry) Ministerio m de Educación.

educational [,edjʊ'keɪʃənl] ADJ policy etc educacional, relativo a la educación; function etc, centre docente; film etc instructivo, educativo; **~ television** televisión f escolar.

education(al)ist [,edjʊ'keɪʃn(əl)ɪst] N educacionista mf.

educationally [,edjʊ'keɪʃnəlɪ] ADV (as regards teaching methods) pedagógicamente; (as regards education, schooling) educativamente; **~ subnormal** de inteligencia inferior a la normal.

educative ['edjʊkətɪv] ADJ educativo.

educator ['edjʊkeɪtər] N educador m, -ora f.

educe [ɪ'djuːs] VT educir, sacar.

edutainment [,edjʊ'teɪnmənt] N (esp US) programa informático ameno y educativo.

Edward ['edwəd] NM Eduardo; **~ the Confessor** Eduardo el Confesor.

Edwardian [ed'wɔːdɪən] (Brit) **1** ADJ eduardiano.

2 N eduardiano m, -a f.

EE ABBR of **electrical engineer.**

EEC N ABBR of **European Economic Community** Comunidad f Económica Europea, CEE.

EEG N ABBR of **electroencephalogram** electroencefalograma m.

eel [iːl] N anguila f.

e'en [iːn] (liter) = **even.**

EENT N (US) ABBR of **eye, ear, nose and throat.**

EEOC N (US) ABBR of **Equal Employment Opportunities Commission** comisión que investiga la discriminación racial o sexual en el empleo.

e'er [eər] (liter) = **ever.**

eerie ['ɪərɪ] ADJ misterioso; sound, experience extraño, fantástico, horripilante.

EET N ABBR of **Eastern European Time.**

eff: [ef] VI: **he was ~ing all over the place** soltaba palabrotas por todas partes.

efface [ɪ'feɪs] **1** VT borrar.

2 VR: **to ~ o.s.** retirarse modestamente, lograr pasar inadvertido.

effect [ɪ'fekt] **1** N (result) efecto m, consecuencia f, resultado m; (impression) efecto m, impresión f; **~s** efectos mpl; **pleasing ~** impresión f agradable; **striving after ~** efectismo m; **just for ~** sólo por impresionar; **in ~** en realidad; **to be in ~** (Jur) estar vigente; **to come into ~** entrar en vigor; **of no ~** inútil; **to be of no ~** no tener efecto, no hacer mella; (Jur) no tener fuerza legal; **to no ~** inútilmente; **a message to the ~ that ...** un mensaje en el sentido de que ...; **to the same ~** del mismo tenor, a este tenor, en el mismo sentido; **to this ~** con este propósito; **or words to that ~** o algo parecido; **to good ~** con éxito, con buenos resultados; **an increase with immediate ~** un aumento a partir de hoy; **with ~ from April** a partir de abril; **to feel the ~(s) of** sentir los efectos de, estar resentido de; **to give ~ to** poner en efecto, hacer efectivo; **to have an ~** dejarse sentir, surtir efecto (*on* en); **to put into ~** poner en vigor; **to take ~** (*remedy*) surtir efecto, (*law*) entrar en vigor (*from* a partir de).

   2 VT efectuar, llevar a cabo; *sale* efectuar; *saving* hacer.

effective [ɪ'fektɪv] **1** ADJ eficaz; (*striking*) impresionante, llamativo, logrado; (*real*) efectivo, verdadero; (*Mil*) útil para todos los servicios; **~ capacity** (*Tech*) capacidad *f* útil; **~ date** fecha *f* de vigencia; **~ power** (*Tech*) potencia *f* real; **~ from** en vigor a partir de; **to become ~** entrar en vigor (*from, on* a partir de).

   2 ~s NPL efectivos *mpl*.

effectively [ɪ'fektɪvlɪ] ADV eficazmente; (*strikingly*) de manera impresionante; acertadamente; (*in fact*) en efecto, realmente.

effectiveness [ɪ'fektɪvnɪs] N eficacia *f*, efectividad *f*.

effectual [ɪ'fektjʊəl] ADJ eficaz.

effectually [ɪ'fektjʊəlɪ] ADV (*frm*) eficazmente, con eficacia.

effectuate [ɪ'fektjʊeɪt] VT efectuar, lograr.

effeminacy [ɪ'femɪnəsɪ] N afeminación *f*, afeminamiento *m*.

effeminate [ɪ'femɪnɪt] ADJ afeminado.

effervesce [ˌefə'ves] VI estar en efervescencia, (*begin to ~*) entrar en efervescencia; bullir, hervir; (*fig*) ser muy alegre, ser muy vivo.

effervescence [ˌefə'vesns] N efervescencia *f*.

effervescent [ˌefə'vesnt] ADJ efervescente (*also fig*).

effete [ɪ'fiːt] ADJ decadente; agotado, cansado.

effeteness [ɪ'fiːtnɪs] N decadencia *f*, cansancio *m*.

efficacious [ˌefɪ'keɪʃəs] ADJ eficaz.

efficacy ['efɪkəsɪ] N eficacia *f*.

efficiency [ɪ'fɪʃənsɪ] N eficiencia *f*, eficacia *f*; buena marcha *f*; (*Mech*) rendimiento *m*.

efficient [ɪ'fɪʃənt] ADJ eficiente; *remedy, product* eficaz; (*Mech*) de buen rendimiento; *person* eficiente, eficaz, competente, capaz.

efficiently [ɪ'fɪʃəntlɪ] ADV eficientemente, eficazmente.

effigy ['efɪdʒɪ] N efigie *f*.

effing‡ ['efɪŋ] ADJ (*euph*) = **fucking**.

effloresce [ˌeflə'res] VI (*Chem*) eflorescer.

efflorescence [ˌeflə'resns] N **(a)** (*Chem, Med*) eflorescencia *f*; (*Bot*) floración *f*. **(b)** (*fig: liter*) florecimiento *m*, prosperidad *f*.

efflorescent [ˌeflə'resnt] ADJ eflorescente.

effluent ['efluənt] N efluente *m*, aguas *fpl* residuales.

effluvium [e'fluːvɪəm] N, PL **effluvia** [e'fluːvɪə] efluvio *m*, emanación *f*, tufo *m*.

effort ['efət] N **(a)** esfuerzo *m*; **all his ~ was directed to** todos sus esfuerzos iban dirigidos a; **to make an ~ to + *infin*** esforzarse por + *infin*, hacer un esfuerzo por + *infin*; **to make every ~ to + *infin*, to spare no ~ to + *infin*** no regatear medio para + *infin*.

   (b) (*) resultado *m*, producto *m*; obra *f*; tentativa *f*; **good ~!** ¡bien hecho!; **it was a pretty poor ~** fue una exhibición pobre; **what did you think of his latest ~?** ¿qué opinas de su nueva obra?; **it's not bad for a first ~** siendo su primer intento no es nada malo; **it wasn't worth the ~** no valía la pena.

effortless ['efətlɪs] ADJ sin esfuerzo alguno, fácil.

effortlessly ['efətlɪslɪ] ADV sin esfuerzo alguno, fácilmente.

effrontery [ɪ'frʌntərɪ] N descaro *m*; **what ~!** ¡qué frescura!; **he had the ~ to say** llegó su cinismo hasta decir.

effusion [ɪ'fjuːʒən] N efusión *f*.

effusive [ɪ'fjuːsɪv] ADJ efusivo.

effusively [ɪ'fjuːsɪvlɪ] ADV con efusión.

effusiveness [ɪ'fjuːsɪvnɪs] N efusividad *f*.

EFL N ABBR of **English as a Foreign Language**; V **English**; *ver también* `TEFL/EFL, TESL/ESL, ELT, TESOL/ESOL`.

EFT N ABBR of **electronic funds transfer** transferencia *f* electrónica de fondos.

eft [eft] N tritón *m*.

EFTA ['eftə] N ABBR of **European Free Trade Association** Asociación *f* Europea para el Libre Comercio, AELC *f*.

e.g. ADV ABBR of **exempli gratia** por ejemplo, p.ej.

EGA N ABBR of **enhanced graphics adaptor**.

egalitarian [ɪˌgælɪ'teərɪən] ADJ igualitario.

egalitarianism [ɪˌgælɪ'teərɪənɪzəm] N igualitarismo *m*.

egg¹ [eg] N **(a)** huevo *m*; **~s** (*of some insects*) carrocha *f*; **to lay an ~*** (*esp US*) fracasar totalmente; **as sure as ~s (is ~s)** sin ningún género de dudas; **don't put all your ~s in one basket** no pongas toda la carne en el asador; **we all had ~ on our faces*** todos hemos quedado en ridículo.

   (b) (*) tío* *m*; **bad ~** sinvergüenza *m*.

egg² [eg] VT: **to ~ sb on** animar a uno, incitar a uno; **to ~ sb on to do sth** incitar a uno a hacer algo.

egg-and-spoon race ['egən,spuːn,reɪs] N juego *m* del huevo con la cuchara.

eggbeater ['eg,biːtər] N batidor *m* de huevos; (*US**) helicóptero *m*.

eggcup ['egkʌp] N huevera *f*.

egg custard [ˌeg'kʌstəd] N ≃ natillas *fpl* de huevo.

egg flip ['eg'flɪp] N yema *f* mejida.

egghead* ['eghed] N intelectual *mf*.

eggnog ['eg'nɒg] N yema *f* mejida, ponche *m* de huevo.

eggplant ['egplɑːnt] N berenjena *f*.

egg roll [ˌeg'rəʊl] N paté a base de huevo con carne de cerdo y legumbres.

egg-shaped ['egʃeɪpt] ADJ oviforme.

eggshell ['egʃel] N cáscara *f* de huevo.

egg timer ['eg,taɪmər] N cronómetro *m* para huevos.

egg whisk ['egwɪsk] N batidor *m* de huevos.

egg white ['egwaɪt] N clara *f* (de huevo).

egg yolk ['egjəʊk] N yema *f* (de huevo).

egis ['iːdʒəs] (*US*) = **aegis**.

eglantine ['egləntaɪn] N eglantina *f*.

EGM N ABBR of **extraordinary general meeting**.

ego ['iːgəʊ] **1** N ego *m*, el yo; amor *m* propio; **to boost one's ~*** halagar el yo.

   2 ATTR: **~ trip*** autobombada *f*.

egocentric(al) [ˌegəʊ'sentrɪk(əl)] ADJ egocéntrico.

egoism ['egəʊɪzəm] N egoísmo *m*.

egoist ['egəʊɪst] N egoísta *mf*.

egoistical [ˌegəʊ'ɪstɪkəl] ADJ egoísta.

egomania [ˌiːgəʊ'meɪnɪə] N egomanía *f*.

egomaniac [ˌegəʊ'meɪnɪæk] N ególatra *mf*.

egotism ['egəʊtɪzəm] N egotismo *m*.

egotist ['egəʊtɪst] N egotista *mf*.

egotistic(al) [ˌegəʊ'tɪstɪk(əl)] ADJ egotista.

egregious [ɪ'griːdʒəs] ADJ atroz, enorme; *liar etc* notorio.

egress ['iːgres] N salida *f*.

egret ['iːgret] N garceta *f*.

Egypt ['iːdʒɪpt] N Egipto *m*.

Egyptian [ɪ'dʒɪpʃən] **1** ADJ egipcio.

   2 N egipcio *m*, -a *f*.

Egyptologist [ˌiːdʒɪp'tɒlədʒɪst] N egiptólogo *m*, -a *f*.

Egyptology [ˌiːdʒɪp'tɒlədʒɪ] N egiptología *f*.

eh [eɪ] INTERJ (*please repeat*) ¿cómo?, ¿qué?; (*inviting assent*) ¿no?, ¿verdad?, ¿no es así?

EIB N ABBR of **European Investment Bank** Banco *m* Europeo de Inversiones, BEI *m*.

eider ['aɪdər] N, **eider duck** ['aɪdə'dʌk] N eider *m*, pato *m* de flojel.

eiderdown ['aɪdədaʊn] N edredón *m*.

eidetic [aɪ'detɪk] ADJ *memory, vision* eidético.

Eiffel Tower [ˌaɪfəl'taʊər] N torre *f* Eiffel.

eight [eɪt] **1** ADJ ocho.

   2 N ocho *m*; (*Rowing*) bote *m* de a ocho; **to have had one over the ~** llevar una copa de más.

eighteen ['eɪ'tiːn] ADJ dieciocho.

eighteenth ['eɪ'tiːnθ] ADJ decimoctavo.

eighth [eɪtθ] **1** ADJ octavo; (*US Mus*) **~ note** corchea *f*.

   2 N octavo *m*, octava parte *f*.

eightieth ['eɪtɪθ] ADJ octogésimo; ochenta; **the ~ anniversary** el ochenta aniversario.

eighty ['eɪtɪ] ADJ ochenta; **the eighties** (*eg* 1980s) los años ochenta; **to be in one's eighties** tener más de ochenta años, ser ochentón.

Eire ['eərə] N Eire *m*.

EIS N ABBR of **Educational Institute of Scotland** sindicato de profesores.

Eisteddfod [aɪs'teðvɒd] N *festival galés en el que se celebran concursos de música y poesía*.

┌─────────────┐
│ **EISTEDDFOD** │
└─────────────┘

*ⓘ En Gales un **eisteddfod** es un concurso de poesía, canto, música y danza, en el que las canciones, los poemas y los relatos son mayormente en galés. Cada año tienen lugar muchos de estos **eisteddfodau** por todo Gales y el nivel de competición suele ser muy alto en los concursos más importantes. En Llangollen, al noreste de Gales, se celebra anualmente un concurso internacional en el que hay participantes de todo el mundo, pero el concurso principal, el **National Eisteddfod**, se celebra en un lugar diferente cada año.*

▼ **either** ['aɪðər] **1** ADJ **(a)** (*one or other*) cualquier ... de los dos; **you can do it ~ way** puedes hacerlo de este modo o del otro; (*neg sense*) **I don't like ~ book** no me gusta ninguno de los dos libros, no me gusta ni uno ni otro.

   (b) (*each*) cada; **on ~ side of the street** en cada lado de la calle, en ambos lados de la calle.

   2 PRON cualquiera de los dos, uno u otro; **~ of us** cualquiera de nosotros; (*neg sense*) **I don't want ~ of them** no quiero ninguno de los dos, no quiero ni uno ni otro.

▼ **3** CONJ: **~ come in or stay out** o entras o quedas fuera.

   4 ADV tampoco; **I won't go ~** yo no voy tampoco.

ejaculate [ɪ'dʒækjʊleɪt] VT **(a)** (*cry out*) exclamar; proferir (de repente), lanzar. **(b)** (*Physiol*) eyacular.

ejaculation [ɪˌdʒækjʊ'leɪʃən] N **(a)** (*cry*) exclamación *f*. **(b)** (*Physiol*) eyaculación f.

ejaculatory [ɪ'dʒækjʊlətərɪ] ADJ (Physiol) eyaculador.

eject [ɪ'dʒekt] ① VT expulsar, echar; tenant desahuciar.
② VI (Aer) eyectarse.

ejection [ɪ'dʒekʃən] N expulsión f; desahucio m.

ejector [ɪ'dʒektəʳ] N expulsor m; ~ **seat** asiento m expulsable, asiento m de eyección, asiento m eyectable.

eke [iːk] VT: **to ~ out** suplir las deficiencias de; money etc hacer que llegue; **to ~ out a livelihood** ganarse la vida a duras penas.

EKG N (US) ABBR of **electrocardiogram**.

el* [el] N (US) ABBR of **elevated railroad**.

elaborate ① [ɪ'læbərɪt] ADJ complicado; detallado; meal de muchos platos; work of art primoroso, rebuscado; courtesy exquisito, estudiado.
② [ɪ'læbəreɪt] VT elaborar.
③ [ɪ'læbərɪt] VI explicarse con muchos detalles; **to ~ on** ampliar, dar más explicaciones acerca de; **he refused to ~** se negó a dar más detalles, se negó a ampliar la referencia.

elaborately [ɪ'læbərɪtlɪ] ADV de manera complicada; con muchos detalles; primorosamente.

elaboration [ɪ'læbə'reɪʃən] N elaboración f.

élan [eɪ'lɑːn, eɪ'læn] N (liter) elán m.

elapse [ɪ'læps] VI pasar, transcurrir.

elastic [ɪ'læstɪk] ① ADJ elástico; (fig) elástico, flexible; ~ **band** (Brit) goma f elástica, gomita f.
② N elástico m; (Sew) goma f.

elasticated [ɪ'læstɪkeɪtɪd] ADJ waist, waistband con elástico.

elasticity [ˌiːlæs'tɪsɪtɪ] N elasticidad f; ~ **of demand** elasticidad f de la demanda.

Elastoplast [ɪ'læstəˌplɑːst] ® N esparadrapo m.

elate [ɪ'leɪt] VT regocijar.

elated [ɪ'leɪtɪd] ADJ: **to be ~** alegrarse (at, with de), estar eufórico.

elation [ɪ'leɪʃən] N alegría f, euforia f, júbilo m.

Elba ['elbə] N Elba f.

elbow ['elbəʊ] ① N codo m; (of road etc) recodo m; **at one's ~** a la mano, muy cerca; **out at the ~(s)** raído, descosido.
② VT empujar con el codo; **to ~ sb aside** apartar a uno a codazos; **to ~ one's way through** abrirse paso codeando (por).

elbow grease* ['elbəʊgriːs] N trabajo m duro; energía f; **it's a matter of ~** es a base de puños.

elbow joint ['elbəʊˌdʒɔɪnt] N articulación f del codo.

elbow-rest ['elbəʊˌrest] N (of a chair) brazo m.

elbow-room ['elbəʊrʊm] N espacio m (suficiente); espacio m para moverse; libertad f de acción.

elder¹ ['eldəʳ] ① ADJ mayor; ~ **statesman** estadista m veterano; figura f muy respetada; **Pliny the E~** Plinio el Viejo.
② N (Eccl) dirigente laico de la Iglesia presbiteriana escocesa; **my ~s** mis mayores; **the ~s of the tribe** los jefes de la tribu; ver también CHURCH OF ENGLAND, CHURCH OF SCOTLAND .

elder² ['eldəʳ] N (Bot) saúco m.

elderberry ['eldəˌberɪ] N baya f del saúco; ~ **wine** vino m de saúco.

elderly ['eldəlɪ] ADJ de edad, mayor; **to be getting ~** ir para viejo.

eldest ['eldɪst] ADJ (el, la) mayor; primogénito m, -a f; **my ~ son** mi hijo mayor; **the ~ of the four** el mayor de los cuatro.

Eleanor ['elɪnəʳ] NF Leonor.

elec. ABBR of **electric, electricity**.

elect [ɪ'lekt] ① VT elegir; **to ~ sb a member** elegir a uno socio; **to ~ to + infin** optar por + infin, decidir + infin.
② ADJ electo; **president ~** presidente m electo.
③ N: **the ~** los elegidos, los predestinados.

elected [ɪ'lektɪd] ADJ elegido; ~ **government** gobierno m elegido.

election [ɪ'lekʃən] ① N elección f (for a); **general ~** elecciones fpl generales.
② ATTR: ~ **agent** secretario m, -a f electoral; ~ **campaign** campaña f electoral; ~ **college** colegio m electoral; ~ **expenses** gastos mpl de la campaña electoral; ~ **machine** aparato m electoral.

electioneer [ɪˌlekʃə'nɪəʳ] VI hacer su campaña electoral; (pej) hacer propaganda electoral.

electioneering [ɪˌlekʃə'nɪərɪŋ] N campaña f electoral; (pej) maniobras fpl electorales.

elective [ɪ'lektɪv] ① ADJ electivo; (US: Univ) facultativo, optativo.
② N (also ~ **subject**) asignatura f facultativa (or discrecional).

elector [ɪ'lektəʳ] N elector m, -ora f.

electoral [ɪ'lektərəl] ADJ electoral; ~ **college** (US) colegio m electoral; ~ **register**, ~ **roll** censo m, lista f electoral.

ELECTORAL COLLEGE

ⓘ Los norteamericanos no votan directamente a su Presidente o a su vicepresidente, sino que votan a unos compromisarios (**electors**) que a su vez se comprometen a votar a determinados candidatos. Estos compromisarios conforman el **electoral college**, tal y como se contempla en la Constitución. El número de votos que tiene un estado para elegir al

Presidente es igual al de senadores y diputados. Cada partido político elige a un grupo de compromisarios y en el día de las elecciones presidenciales el pueblo vota al grupo que apoya al candidato de su elección. Como el grupo que gana usa todos los votos del estado para votar a su candidato, podría ocurrir, en teoría, que un candidato ganara el voto popular pero no las elecciones, si le han apoyado colegios electorales con un número pequeño de votos.

electorally [ɪ'lektərəlɪ] ADV: **an ~ damaging incident** un incidente con malas consecuencias electorales; **this was not ~ popular** esto no gustó a los votantes.

electorate [ɪ'lektərɪt] N electorado m; número m de votantes; censo m.

electric [ɪ'lektrɪk] ① ADJ eléctrico; **the atmosphere was ~** la atmósfera estaba cargada de electricidad; ~ **blanket** manta f eléctrica; ~ **blue** azul m eléctrico; ~ **chair** silla f eléctrica; ~ **charge** carga f eléctrica; ~ **clock** reloj m eléctrico; ~ **cooker** cocina f eléctrica; ~ **current** corriente f eléctrica; ~ **eel** anguila f eléctrica; ~ **eye** célula f fotoeléctrica; ~ **fence** cercado m electrificado; ~ **field** campo m eléctrico; ~ **fire** (Brit) estufa f eléctrica, calentador m eléctrico; ~ **guitar** guitarra f eléctrica; ~ **heater** = ~ **fire**; ~ **light** luz f eléctrica; ~ **organ** órgano m eléctrico; ~ **ray** (Zool) torpedo m, tembladera f, temblón m; ~ **shock** electrochoque m; ~ **shock treatment** tratamiento m por electrochoque; ~ **windows** (Aut) elevalunas m eléctrico.
② NPL: **the ~s*** (Brit) el sistema eléctrico.

electrical [ɪ'lektrɪkəl] ADJ eléctrico; ~ **engineer** perito m, -a f electricista, ingeniero m, -a f electricista; ~ **engineering** electrotecnia f; ~ **fittings** accesorios mpl eléctricos; ~ **storm** tronada f, tormenta f eléctrica.

electrically [ɪ'lektrɪkəlɪ] ADV por electricidad.

electrician [ɪlek'trɪʃən] N electricista mf; (Cine, TV) iluminista mf.

electricity [ɪlek'trɪsɪtɪ] ① N electricidad f.
② ATTR: **E~ Board** (Brit) compañía f eléctrica estatal; ~ **dispute** conflicto m del sector eléctrico.

electrification [ɪ'lektrɪfɪ'keɪʃən] N electrificación f.

electrify [ɪ'lektrɪfaɪ] VT electrificar; (fig) electrizar; **electrified fence** cercado m eléctrico.

electrifying [ɪ'lektrɪfaɪɪŋ] ADJ electrizante.

electro... [ɪ'lektrəʊ] PREF electro...

electrocardiogram [ɪ'lektrəʊ'kɑːdɪəgræm] N electrocardiograma m.

electrocardiograph [ɪˌlektrəʊ'kɑːdɪəgræf] N electrocardiógrafo m.

electrochemical [ɪˌlektrəʊ'kemɪkəl] ADJ electroquímico.

electrochemistry [ɪˌlektrəʊ'kemɪstrɪ] N electroquímica f.

electroconvulsive [ɪˌlektrəkən'vʌlsɪv] ADJ electroconvulsivo; ~ **therapy** terapia f electroconvulsiva, electroterapia f.

electrocute [ɪ'lektrəʊkjuːt] VT electrocutar.

electrocution [ɪˌlektrəʊ'kjuːʃən] N electrocución f.

electrode [ɪ'lektrəʊd] N electrodo m.

electrodialysis [ɪˌlektrəʊdaɪ'æləsɪs] N electrodiálisis f.

electrodynamic [ɪˌlektrəʊdaɪ'næmɪk] ADJ electrodinámico.

electrodynamics [ɪˌlektrəʊdaɪ'næmɪks] N electrodinámica f.

electroencephalogram [ɪˌlektrəʊen'sefələˌgræm] N electroencefalograma m.

electroencephalograph [ɪ'lektrəʊɪn'sefələgrɑːf] N electroencefalógrafo m.

electrolyse [ɪ'lektrəʊˌlaɪz] VT electrolizar.

electrolysis [ɪlek'trɒlɪsɪs] N electrólisis f.

electrolyte [ɪ'lektrəʊˌlaɪt] N electrolito m.

electromagnet [ɪ'lektrəʊ'mægnɪt] N electroimán m.

electromagnetic [ɪ'lektrəʊmæg'netɪk] ADJ electromagnético.

electromagnetism [ɪˌlektrəʊ'mægnɪtɪzəm] N electromagnetismo m.

electromechanical [ɪˌlektrəʊmɪ'kænɪkəl] ADJ electromecánico.

electromechanics [ɪˌlektrəʊmɪ'kænɪks] N electromecánica f.

electrometallurgy [ɪˌlektrəʊmɪ'tælədʒɪ] N electrometalurgia f.

electrometer [ɪlek'trɒmɪtəʳ] N electrómetro m.

electromotive [ɪˌlektrəʊ'məʊtɪv] ADJ electromotriz.

electron [ɪ'lektrɒn] ① N electrón m.
② ATTR: ~ **camera** cámara f electrónica; ~ **gun** pistola f de electrones; ~ **microscope** microscopio m electrónico.

electronic [ɪlek'trɒnɪk] ADJ electrónico; ~ **banking** banco m informatizado; ~ **data processing** proceso m electrónico de datos; ~ **fund transfer** transferencia f electrónica de fondos; ~ **keyboard** teclado m electrónico; ~ **mail** correo m electrónico; ~ **mailbox** buzón m electrónico; ~ **publishing** autoedición f electrónica; ~ **shopping** compra f computerizada; ~ **spreadsheet** hoja f electrónica; ~ **surveillance** vigilancia f electrónica; ~ **tag** etiqueta f electrónica de control.

electronically [ɪlek'trɒnɪklɪ] ADV electrónicamente.

electronics [ɪlek'trɒnɪks] N electrónica f.

electrophysiological [ɪˌlektrəʊˌfɪzɪə'lɒdʒɪkəl] ADJ electrofisiológico.

electrophysiology [ɪˌlektrəʊˌfɪzɪ'ɒlədʒɪ] N electrofisiología f.

electroplate [ɪ'lektrəʊpleɪt] VT galvanizar, electrochapar.

electroplated [ɪ'lektrəʊpleɪtɪd] ADJ galvanizado, electrochapado.
electroshock [ɪ'lektrəʊʃɒk] ATTR: ~ **treatment** electrochoque *m*; ~ **therapy** terapia *f* de electrochoque.
electrostatic [ɪ,lektrəʊ'stætɪk] ADJ electrostático.
electrostatics [ɪ,lektrəʊ'stætɪks] N electrostática *f*.
electrosurgery [ɪ,lektrəʊ'sɜːdʒərɪ] N electrocirugía *f*.
electrosurgical [ɪ,lektrəʊ'sɜːdʒɪkəl] ADJ electroquirúrgico.
electrotechnological [ɪ,lektrəʊ,teknə'lɒdʒɪkəl] ADJ electrotecnológico.
electrotechnology [ɪ,lektrəʊtek'nɒlədʒɪ] N electrotecnología *f*.
electrotherapeutic [ɪ,lektrəʊ,θerə'pjuːtɪk] ADJ electroterapéutico.
electrotherapeutics [ɪ,lektrəʊ,θerə'pjuːtɪks] N electroterapia *f*.
electrotherapist [ɪ,lektrəʊ'θerəpɪst] N electroterapeuta *mf*.
electrotherapy [ɪ,lektrəʊ'θerəpɪ] N electroterapia *f*.
elegance ['elɪgəns] N elegancia *f*.
elegant ['elɪgənt] ADJ elegante.
elegantly ['elɪgəntlɪ] ADV elegantemente.
elegiac [,elɪ'dʒaɪək] ADJ elegíaco.
elegy ['elɪdʒɪ] N elegía *f*.
element ['elɪmənt] N elemento *m* (*also Chem, Elec etc*); ~**s** (*rudiments*) elementos *mpl*, primeras nociones *fpl*; **to be in one's ~** estar en su elemento; **to be out of one's ~** estar fuera de su elemento, estar como pez fuera del agua; **to brave the ~s** arrostrar la tempestad, (*go out*) salir a la intemperie; **it's the personal ~ that counts** es el factor personal el que cuenta; **it has an ~ of truth about it** tiene su poquito de verdad.
elemental [,elɪ'mentl] ADJ elemental.
elementary [,elɪ'mentərɪ] ADJ elemental; (*primitive*) rudimentario; ~ **school** escuela *f* primaria; ~ **schooling** primera enseñanza *f*; **~, my dear Watson** elemental, querido Watson; *ver también* EDUCATION .
elephant ['elɪfənt] N elefante *m*, -a *f*.
elephantiasis [,elɪfən'taɪəsɪs] N elefantiasis *f*.
elephantine [,elɪ'fæntaɪn] ADJ (*fig*) elefantino, mastodóntico.
elevate ['elɪveɪt] VT elevar; (*Eccl*) alzar; *person* exaltar; (*in rank*) ascender (*to* a).
elevated ['elɪveɪtɪd] ADJ elevado, sublime; ~ **railway**, ~ **railroad** (*US*) ferrocarril *m* urbano elevado.
elevating ['elɪveɪtɪŋ] ADJ *reading* enriquecedor.
elevation [,elɪ'veɪʃən] N (*act*) elevación *f*; (*of person*) exaltación *f*; (*in rank*) ascenso *m*; (*of style*) sublimidad *f*; (*hill*) altura *f*; (*Aer etc*) altitud *f*; (*Archit*) alzado *m*.
elevator ['elɪveɪtə^r] 1 N (**a**) (*Agr*) almacén *m* de granos, elevador *m* de granos; (*Aer*) timón *m* de profundidad; (*US*) ascensor *m*, (*for goods*) montacargas *m*. (**b**) (*US: also* ~ **shoe**) zapato *m* de tacón alto.
2 ATTR: ~ **car** (*US*) caja *f* de ascensor; ~ **shaft** (*US*) hueco *m* del ascensor.
eleven [ɪ'levn] 1 ADJ once.
2 N once *m* (*also Sport*); **the ~ plus** (*Brit† Scol*) examen selectivo *realizado por niños mayores de 11 años*.
elevenses [ɪ'levnzɪz] NPL (*Brit*): **to have ~** tomar las once(s)*.
eleventh [ɪ'levnθ] ADJ undécimo, onceno; **at the ~ hour** a última hora.
elf [elf] N, PL **elves** [elvz] duende *m*; (*Nordic Myth*) elfo *m*.
elfin ['elfɪn] ADJ de duende(s), mágico; de elfo(s).
Elgin Marbles ['elgɪn'mɑːblz] NPL: **the ~** los mármoles del Partenón.
elicit [ɪ'lɪsɪt] VT sacar, (*lograr*) obtener, provocar.
elide [ɪ'laɪd] VT elidir.
eligibility [,elɪdʒə'bɪlɪtɪ] N elegibilidad *f*.
eligible ['elɪdʒəbl] ADJ elegible; (*desirable*) deseable, atractivo; *bachelor* de partido; **he's the most ~ bachelor in town** es el soltero más cotizado de la ciudad; **to be ~ for** llenar los requisitos para, tener derecho a.
Elijah [ɪ'laɪdʒə] NM Elías.
eliminate [ɪ'lɪmɪneɪt] VT eliminar; suprimir; *suspect, possibility etc* descartar; *person* (*in purge*) eliminar.
elimination [ɪ,lɪmɪ'neɪʃən] 1 N eliminación *f*; supresión *f*.
2 ATTR: ~ **round** eliminatoria *f*.
eliminator [ɪ'lɪmɪneɪtə^r] N (*Boxing*) combate *m* eliminatorio.
Elishah [ɪ'laɪʃə] NM Elíseo.
elision [ɪ'lɪʒən] N elisión *f*.
élite [eɪ'liːt] N élite *f*, elite *f*, minoría *f* selecta.
elitism [ɪ'liːtɪzəm] N elitismo *m*.
elitist [ɪ'liːtɪst] 1 ADJ elitista.
2 N elitista *mf*.
elixir [ɪ'lɪksə^r] N elixir *m*.
Elizabeth [ɪ'lɪzəbəθ] NF Isabel.
Elizabethan [ɪ,lɪzə'biːθən] 1 ADJ isabelino.
2 N isabelino *m*, -a *f*.
elk [elk] N alce *m*, anta *f*.
ellipse [ɪ'lɪps] N elipse *f*.
ellipsis [ɪ'lɪpsɪs] N, PL **ellipses** [ɪ'lɪpsiːz] (*omission*) elipsis *f*; (*dots*) puntos *mpl* suspensivos.

elliptic(al) [ɪ'lɪptɪk(əl)] ADJ elíptico.
elliptically [ɪ'lɪptɪkəlɪ] ADV de manera elíptica.
elm [elm] N (*also* ~ **tree**) olmo *m*.
elocution [,elə'kjuːʃən] N elocución *f*.
elocutionist [,elə'kjuːʃənɪst] N profesor *m*, -ora *f* de elocución; recitador *m*, -ora *f*.
elongate ['iːlɒŋgeɪt] VT alargar, extender.
elongated ['iːlɒŋgeɪtɪd] ADJ alargado, estirado, extendido.
elongation [,iːlɒŋ'geɪʃən] N alargamiento *m*, estiramiento *m*.
elope [ɪ'ləʊp] VI (*1 person*) fugarse con su amante, (*2 persons*) fugarse para casarse; **to ~ with** fugarse con.
elopement [ɪ'ləʊpmənt] N fuga *f*.
eloquence ['eləkwəns] N elocuencia *f*.
eloquent ['eləkwənt] ADJ elocuente.
eloquently ['eləkwəntlɪ] ADV elocuentemente.
El Salvador [el'sælvədɔː^r] N El Salvador.
else [els] ADV (**a**) (*after pron*) **all ~, everything ~** todo lo demás; **everyone ~** todos los demás; **anyone ~ would do it** cualquier otra persona lo haría; **anything ~ is impossible** cualquier otra cosa es imposible; **have you anything ~ to tell me?** ¿tiene algo más que decirme?; **anything ~, madam?** (*in shop*) ¿algo más, señora?, ¿alguna cosita más, señora?; **that was sb ~** fue otra persona; **there's sb ~, isn't there?** hay alguien más, ¿verdad?; **somewhere ~** en otra parte; **it's** (*or* **she's**) **something ~!** ¡es fuera de serie!
(**b**) (*after pron, neg*) **I don't know anyone ~ here** aquí no conozco a nadie más; **nobody ~ knows** no lo sabe ningún otro; **there's nothing ~ I can do** no hay nada más que pueda hacer; **nothing ~, thanks** nada más, gracias.
(**c**) (ADV *of quantity*) **there was little ~ to do** apenas quedaba otra cosa que hacer; **and much ~ besides** y mucho más también.
(**d**) (*after interrog*) **how ~?** ¿de qué otra manera?; **what ~?** ¿qué más?; **where ~?** ¿en qué otro sitio?; **where ~ can he have gone?** ¿a qué otro sitio habrá podido ir?; **who ~?** ¿quién más?; **who ~ could do it as well as you?** ¿qué otra persona podría hacerlo tan bien como Vd?
(**e**) (*standing alone*) **how could I have done it ~?** ¿de qué otro modo hubiera podido hacerlo?; **red or ~ black** rojo o bien negro; **or ~ I'll do it** si no, lo hago yo; **do this, or ~...** haga esto, pues de otro modo ...
elsewhere ['els'weə^r] ADV *be* en otra parte; *go* a otra parte.
ELT N ABBR *of* **English Language Teaching** enseñanza *f* del inglés; V **English**; *ver también* TEFL/EFL, TESL/ESL, ELT, TESOL/ESOL .
elucidate [ɪ'luːsɪdeɪt] VT aclarar, elucidar, esclarecer.
elucidation [ɪ,luːsɪ'deɪʃən] N aclaración *f*, elucidación *f*.
elude [ɪ'luːd] VT *blow etc* eludir, esquivar, evitar; *grasp* escapar de; *pursuer* escaparse de, burlar, zafarse de; *obligation* zafarse de; **the name ~s me** se me escapa el nombre; **the answer has so far ~d us** hasta ahora no hemos encontrado la solución.
elusive [ɪ'luːsɪv] ADJ (**a**) difícil de encontrar. (**b**) (*fig*) esquivo; inaprensible, escurridizo.
elusiveness [ɪ'luːsɪvnɪs] N carácter *m* esquivo.
elusory [ɪ'luːsərɪ] = **elusive**.
elver ['elvə^r] N angula *f*.
elves [elvz] NPL *of* **elf**.
Elysium [ɪ'lɪzɪəm] N Elíseo *m*.
EM ABBR *of* **Engineer of Mines**.
emaciated [ɪ'meɪsɪeɪtɪd] ADJ demacrado; **to become ~** demacrarse.
emaciation [ɪ,meɪsɪ'eɪʃən] N demacración *f*.
email, e-mail ['iːmeɪl] N correo *m* electrónico.
emanate ['eməneɪt] VI emanar, proceder (*from* de).
emanation [,emə'neɪʃən] N emanación *f*.
emancipate [ɪ'mænsɪpeɪt] VT emancipar; *slave* manumitir.
emancipated [ɪ'mænsɪpeɪtɪd] ADJ emancipado; *slave* manumitido; (*fig*) libre.
emancipation [ɪ,mænsɪ'peɪʃən] N emancipación *f*; manumisión *f*; (*fig*) libertad *f*.
emasculate [ɪ'mæskjʊleɪt] VT castrar, emascular; (*fig*) mutilar, estropear.
emasculated [ɪ'mæskjʊleɪtɪd] ADJ castrado, emasculado; (*fig*) mutilado, estropeado; *style* empobrecido.
embalm [ɪm'bɑːm] VT embalsamar.
embalmer [ɪm'bɑːmə^r] N embalsamador *m*.
embalming [ɪm'bɑːmɪŋ] 1 N embalsamamiento *m*.
2 ATTR: ~ **fluid** líquido *m* embalsador.
embankment [ɪm'bæŋkmənt] N terraplén *m*.
embargo [ɪm'bɑːgəʊ] 1 N prohibición *f* (*on* de); (*Jur*) embargo *m*; **to be under an ~** estar prohibido; **there is an ~ on arms** está prohibido comerciar en armas, hay embargo sobre el comercio de armas; **there is an ~ on that subject** está prohibido discutir ese asunto; **to lift an ~** levantar una prohibición; **to put an ~ on sth** prohibir el comercio de algo, (*fig*) prohibir el uso de algo.
2 VT prohibir; (*Jur*) embargar.

embark [ɪm'bɑːk] **1** VT embarcar.
2 VI embarcarse (*for* con rumbo a, *on* en); **to ~ upon** emprender, lanzarse a.
embarkation [ˌembɑː'keɪʃən] N embarco *m*, embarque *m*.
embarrass [ɪm'bærəs] VT desconcertar, turbar, azorar, apenar (*LAm*); (*deliberately*) poner en un aprieto; (*financially*) crear dificultades económicas a; **to be ~ed** sentirse violento, sentirse molesto, estar azorado; **to be financially ~ed** tener dificultades económicas, andar mal de dinero; **I was ~ed by the question** la pregunta me desconcertó; **I feel ~ed about it** me siento algo avergonzado por eso.
embarrassed [ɪm'bærəst] ADJ: **he said with an ~ laugh** dijo riéndose pero evidentemente molesto (*or* incómodo).
embarrassing [ɪm'bærəsɪŋ] ADJ *experience etc* embarazoso, desconcertante; *moment, situation* violento.
embarrassingly [ɪm'bærəsɪŋlɪ] ADV de manera desconcertante; violentamente; **there were ~ few people** había tan pocas personas que resultaba desconcertante.
embarrassment [ɪm'bærəsmənt] N **(a)** (*state*) desconcierto *m*, turbación *f*, azoramiento *m*, pena *f* (*LAm*); **financial ~** apuros *mpl*, dificultades *fpl* económicas; **I am in a state of some ~** mi situación es algo delicada.
(b) (*object*) estorbo *m*; **you are an ~ to us all** eres un estorbo para todos nosotros.
embassy ['embəsɪ] N embajada *f*; **the Spanish E~** la embajada de España.
embattled [ɪm'bætld] ADJ *army* en orden de batalla; *city* sitiado.
embed [ɪm'bed] **1** VT empotrar; *weapon, teeth etc* clavar, hincar (*in* en); (*Ling*) incrustar.
2 VR: **to ~ itself in** empotrarse en.
embedding [ɪm'bedɪŋ] N (*gen, Ling*) incrustación *f*.
embellish [ɪm'belɪʃ] VT embellecer; (*fig, story etc*) adornar (*with* de).
embellishment [ɪm'belɪʃmənt] N embellecimiento *m*; (*fig*) adorno *m*.
embers ['embəz] NPL rescoldo *m*, ascuas *fpl*.
embezzle [ɪm'bezl] VT malversar, desfalcar.
embezzlement [ɪm'bezlmənt] N malversación *f*, desfalco *m*.
embezzler [ɪm'bezlər] N malversador *m*, -ora *f*, desfalcador *m*, -ora *f*.
embitter [ɪm'bɪtər] VT amargar; *relations etc* envenenar, amargar.
embittered [ɪm'bɪtəd] ADJ resentido, rencoroso; **to be very ~** estar muy amargado, estar muy resentido (*about* por, *against* contra).
embittering [ɪm'bɪtərɪŋ] ADJ *experience etc* amargo; que causa resentimiento.
emblazon [ɪm'bleɪzən] VT engalanar (*or* esmaltar) con colores brillantes; (*fig*) escribir de modo llamativo, adornar de modo llamativo; ensalzar.
emblem ['embləm] N emblema *m*.
emblematic [ˌemblɪ'mætɪk] ADJ emblemático.
embodiment [ɪm'bɒdɪmənt] N encarnación *f*, personificación *f*; **to be the very ~ of virtue** ser la misma virtud, ser la misma personificación de la virtud.
embody [ɪm'bɒdɪ] VT **(a)** *spirit, quality* encarnar, personificar; *idea etc* expresar. **(b)** (*include*) incorporar.
embolden [ɪm'bəuldən] VT animar (*to + infin* a + *infin*), envalentonar (*to + infin* para que + *subj*).
embolism ['embəlɪzəm] N embolia *f*.
emboss [ɪm'bɒs] VT realzar; estampar en relieve; **~ed paper** papel *m* con nombre (*etc*) en relieve; **~ed with the royal arms** con el escudo real en relieve.
embouchure [ˌɒmbu'ʃuər] N (*Mus*) boquilla *f*.
embrace [ɪm'breɪs] **1** N abrazo *m*.
2 VT **(a)** (*clasp*) abrazar, dar un abrazo a.
(b) (*include*) abarcar.
(c) *offer* aceptar; *opportunity* aprovechar; *course of action* adoptar; *doctrine, party* adherirse a; *profession* dedicarse a; *religion* convertirse a.
3 VI abrazarse.
embrasure [ɪm'breɪʒər] N (*Archit*) alféizar *m*; (*Mil*) tronera *f*, aspillera *f*.
embrocation [ˌembrəu'keɪʃən] N embrocación *f*.
embroider [ɪm'brɔɪdər] VT bordar, recamar; (*fig*) adornar con detalles ficticios.
embroidery [ɪm'brɔɪdərɪ] **1** N bordado *m*.
2 ATTR: **~ silk** seda *f* de bordar; **~ thread** hilo *m* de bordar.
embroil [ɪm'brɔɪl] VT embrollar, enredar; **to ~ sb with** indisponer a uno con; **to ~ A with B** mezclar a A con B; **to get ~ed in sth** enredarse en algo, hacerse un lío con algo.
embroilment [ɪm'brɔɪlmənt] N embrollo *m*.
embryo ['embrɪəu] **1** N embrión *m*; (*fig*) embrión *m*, germen *m*; **in ~** en embrión.
2 ATTR embrionario.
embryologist [ˌembrɪ'ɒledʒɪst] N embriólogo *m*, -a *f*.
embryology [ˌembrɪ'ɒlədʒɪ] N embriología *f*.
embryonic [ˌembrɪ'ɒnɪk] ADJ embrionario.
emcee* ['em'siː] (*US*) **1** N presentador *m*, animador *m*.
2 *vt* presentar; **to ~ a show** animar un espectáculo.

EMCF N ABBR *of* **European Monetary Cooperation Fund** Fondo *m* Europeo de Cooperación Monetaria, FECOM *m*.
emend [ɪ'mend] VT enmendar.
emendation [ˌiːmen'deɪʃən] N enmienda *f*.
emerald ['emərəld] **1** N esmeralda *f*.
2 ADJ de color esmeralda, esmeraldino; **~ green** verde esmeralda; **the E~ Isle** la verde Irlanda.
emerge [ɪ'mɜːdʒ] VI salir (*from* de; *also fig*), aparecer, dejarse ver; (*problem etc*) surgir; **it ~s that ...** resulta que ...; **what has ~d from this inquiry?** ¿qué se saca de esta investigación?
emergence [ɪ'mɜːdʒəns] N salida *f*, aparición *f*.
emergency [ɪ'mɜːdʒənsɪ] **1** N emergencia *f*; crisis *f*; necesidad *f* urgente, necesidad *f* apremiante; estado *m* de excepción; situación *f* imprevista; **there is a national ~** existe una crisis nacional; **in an ~**, **in case of ~** en caso de urgencia; **to provide for emergencies** prevenirse contra toda eventualidad (*or* contingencia).
2 ATTR de urgencia, de emergencia; **~ blinkers** intermitentes *mpl* de emergencia; **~ brake** freno *m* de mano, freno *m* de auxilio; **~ case** caso *m* de emergencia; **~ centre** centro *m* de emergencia; **~ exit** salida *f* de urgencia, salida *f* de emergencia; **~ flasher** (*US Aut*) señales *fpl* de emergencia; **~ landing** aterrizaje *m* forzoso (*or* forzado); **~ lane** (*US*) andén *m*, arcén *m*; **~ measure** medida *f* de urgencia; **~ meeting** reunión *f* extraordinaria; **~ powers** poderes *mpl* extraordinarios; **~ ration** ración *f* de reserva; **~ service** (*Med*) urgencias *fpl*; **~ services** servicios *mpl* de emergencia; **~ stop** (*Aut*) parada *f* en seco; **~ supply** provisión *f* de reserva; **~ ward** sala *f* para casos de urgencia.
emergent [ɪ'mɜːdʒənt] ADJ, **emerging** [ɪ'mɜːdʒɪŋ] ADJ emergente.
emeritus [ɪ'merɪtəs] ADJ emeritus, jubilado.
emery ['emərɪ] **1** N esmeril *m*.
2 ATTR: **~ board** tabla *f* de esmeril; **~ cloth** tela *f* de esmeril; **~ paper** papel *m* de esmeril.
emetic [ɪ'metɪk] **1** ADJ emético, vomitivo.
2 N emético *m*, vomitivo *m*.
emigrant ['emɪgrənt] **1** ADJ emigrante.
2 N emigrante *mf*.
emigrate ['emɪgreɪt] VI emigrar.
emigration [ˌemɪ'greɪʃən] N emigración *f*.
émigré(e) ['emɪgreɪ] N emigrado *m*, -a *f*.
Emily ['emɪlɪ] NF Emilia.
eminence ['emɪnəns] N eminencia *f*; **His E~** Su Eminencia; **Your E~** Vuestra Eminencia.
eminent ['emɪnənt] ADJ eminente.
eminently ['emɪnəntlɪ] ADJ sumamente.
emir [e'mɪər] N emir *m*.
emirate [e'mɪərɪt] N emirato *m*.
emissary ['emɪsərɪ] N emisario *m*.
emission [ɪ'mɪʃən] N emisión *f*; **~ controls** controles *mpl* de emisiones.
emit [ɪ'mɪt] VT *light, signals etc* emitir; *smoke etc* arrojar; *smell* despedir; *cry* dar; *sound* producir.
emitter [ɪ'mɪtər] N (*Electronics*) emisor *m*.
Emmanuel [ɪ'mænjʊəl] NM Manuel.
Emmy ['emɪ] N (*US TV*) Emmy *m*.
emollient [ɪ'mɒlɪənt] **1** ADJ emoliente.
2 N emoliente *m*.
emolument [ɪ'mɒljʊmənt] N emolumento *m*.
emote* [ɪ'məut] VI actuar de una manera muy emocionada.
emotion [ɪ'məuʃən] N emoción *f*.
emotional [ɪ'məuʃənl] ADJ emocional; afectivo; emotivo; *moment* de honda emoción, muy emotivo; *person* (*warm-hearted*) sentimental, (*taking things too hard*) demasiado sensible, (*showing excessive emotion*) exaltado, exagerado; **~ tension** tensión *f* emocional; **an ~ farewell** una despedida emotiva; **to get ~** emocionarse.
emotionalism [ɪ'məuʃnəlɪzəm] N emoción *f*, emotividad *f*; sentimentalismo *m*; (*in newspaper etc*) sensacionalismo *m*.
emotionally [ɪ'məuʃnəlɪ] ADV con emoción; **~ unstable** emocionalmente inestable.
emotionless [ɪ'məuʃnlɪs] ADJ sin emoción.
emotive [ɪ'məutɪv] ADJ emotivo.
empanel [ɪm'pænl] VT *jury* seleccionar; **to ~ sb for a jury** inscribir a uno para jurado.
empathetic [ˌempə'θetɪk] ADJ, **empathic** ADJ comprensivo, empático.
empathetically [ˌempə'θetɪkəlɪ] ADV, **empathically** ADV con comprensión, con empatía.
empathize ['empəθaɪz] VI sentir empatía (*with* con), empatizar(se) (*with* con).
empathy ['empəθɪ] N empatía *f*.
emperor ['empərər] N emperador *m*.
emphasis ['emfəsɪs] N énfasis *m*; **to lay** (*or* **put**) **~ on** subrayar; **the ~ is on sport** se le concede mucha importancia al deporte; **this year**

the ~ is on femininity este año las modas hacen resaltar la feminidad.

▼ **emphasize** ['emfəsaız] VT (*Gram*) acentuar; (*fig*) dar importancia a, subrayar, recalcar, enfatizar (*LAm*); **I must ~ that ...** tengo que subrayar que ...

emphatic [ɪm'fætɪk] ADJ enfático; *speech, condemnation etc* categórico, enérgico; *person* decidido; **he was most ~ that ...** dijo categóricamente que ...

emphatically [ɪm'fætɪkəlɪ] ADV con énfasis; **yes, ~** sí, sin ningún género de dudas; **the answer is ~ no** bajo ningún concepto.

emphysema [emfɪ'si:mə] N enfisema *m*.

Empire ['empaɪər] ADJ *costume, furniture* estilo Imperio; **the ~ State** (*US*) el estado de Nueva York.

empire ['empaɪər] N imperio *m*.

empire-builder ['empaɪə,bɪldər] N (*fig*) constructor *m* de imperios.

empire-building ['empaɪə,bɪldɪŋ] N (*fig*) construcción *f* de imperios.

empiric(al) [em'pɪrɪk(əl)] ADJ empírico.

empirically [em'pɪrɪkəlɪ] ADV empíricamente.

empiricism [em'pɪrɪsɪzəm] N empirismo *m*.

empiricist [em'pɪrɪsɪst] N empírico *m*.

emplacement [ɪm'pleɪsmənt] N (*Mil*) emplazamiento *m*.

emplane [ɪm'pleɪn] VI (*US*) subir al avión; embarcar (en avión).

employ [ɪm'plɔɪ] **1** N: **to be in the ~ of** trabajar por, (*as servant etc*) estar al servicio de.

2 VT *person* emplear; *thing* emplear, usar; *time* ocupar; **to be ~ed in** emplearse en.

employable [ɪm'plɔɪəbl] ADJ *person* que se puede emplear; *skill* útil, utilizable.

employee [emplɔɪ'i:] N empleado *m*, -a *f*, dependiente *m*, -a *f*; **~ rights** derechos *mpl* de los trabajadores.

employer [ɪm'plɔɪər] N empresario *m*, -a *f*; patrón *m*, -ona *f*; **~s' organization** organización *f* patronal; **my ~** mi amo, mi jefe.

employment [ɪm'plɔɪmənt] N **(a)** (*act*) empleo *m*; uso *m*.
(b) (*job*) empleo *m*, colocación *f*, puesto *m*; ocupación *f*; **to be in ~** tener trabajo; **to give ~ to** emplear a; **to look for ~** buscar empleo, buscar colocación; **conditions of ~** condiciones *fpl* de empleo; **her ~ prospects are poor** tiene pocas posibilidades de colocarse; **~ agency** agencia *f* de colocaciones; **~ exchange** (*Brit*), **~ office** (*US*) bolsa *f* de trabajo.
(c) (*jobs collectively*) empleo *m*; **full ~** pleno empleo *m*; **a high level of ~** un alto nivel de trabajo; **Secretary (of State) for** (or **Minister of) E~** (*Brit*), **Secretary for E~** (*US*) Ministro *m* de Trabajo; **Department of E~** (*Brit*) Ministerio *m* de Trabajo; **~ statistics** estadística *f* del empleo.

emporium [em'pɔ:rɪəm] N emporio *m*.

empower [ɪm'pauər] VT: **to ~ sb to do sth** autorizar a uno a hacer algo.

empress ['emprɪs] N emperatriz *f*.

emptiness ['emptɪnɪs] N vacío *m*, lo vacío; (*of person's life*) vaciedad *f*, vacuidad *f*; **its ~ of moral content** su carencia de todo contenido moral.

empty ['emptɪ] **1** ADJ vacío; *house* desocupado; *place* desierto; *vehicle* vacío, sin carga; *post* vacante; *threat, words* vano, inútil; *phrase* hueco, sin significado real; **I'm ~** tengo hambre.
2 N (*gen pl*) envase *m*, botella *f* (*etc*) vacía; casco *m*; **V returnable**.
3 VT *contents* vaciar, verter; *container* vaciar, descargar; *place, room* dejar vacío; desocupar, desalojar.
4 VI vaciarse; (*vehicle*) quedar vacío; (*room etc*) quedar desocupado; (*place*) quedar desierto; **to ~ into** (*river*) desembocar en.

empty-handed ['emptɪ'hændɪd] ADJ: **to return ~** volver con las manos vacías, volver manivacío.

empty-headed ['emptɪ'hedɪd] ADJ casquivano.

Empyrean [empɪ'ri:ən] N: **the ~** (*liter*) el empíreo.

EMS N ABBR of **European Monetary System** Sistema *m* Monetario Europeo, SME *m*.

EMT N ABBR of **emergency medical technician**.

emu ['i:mju:] N dromeo *m*, emú *m*.

emulate ['emjuleɪt] VT emular (*also Comput*).

emulator ['emjuˌleɪtər] N (*Comput*) emulador *m*.

emulation [emju'leɪʃən] N emulación *f* (*also Comput*).

emulsifier [ɪ'mʌlsɪˌfaɪər] N agente *m* emulsionador, emulsionante *m*.

emulsify [ɪ'mʌlsɪfaɪ] VT emulsionar.

emulsion [ɪ'mʌlʃən] N emulsión *f*; **~ (paint)** pintura *f* emulsionada.

EN N (*Brit*) ABBR of **Enrolled Nurse** ≃ ATS *mf*.

enable [ɪ'neɪbl] VT: **to ~ sb to do sth** permitir a uno hacer algo, capacitar a uno para hacer algo, poner a uno en condiciones para hacer algo; **I am now ~d to go** ahora puedo ir.

enact [ɪ'nækt] VT **(a)** (*Jur*) decretar (*that* que); *law* promulgar. **(b)** (*perform*) *play, scene* representar; *part* hacer.

enactment [ɪ'næktmənt] N **(a)** promulgación *f*. **(b)** representación *f*.

enamel [ɪ'næməl] **1** N esmalte *m*.
2 ATTR: **~ paint** pintura *f* esmaltada.

3 VT esmaltar, pintar al esmalte.

enamelled, (*US*) **enameled** [ɪ'næməld] ADJ esmaltado.

enamelling [ɪ'næməlɪŋ] N esmaltado *m*.

enamelware [ɪ'næməlwɛər] N utensilios *mpl* de hierro esmaltado.

enamour, (*US*) **enamor** [ɪ'næmər] VT: **to be ~ed of** *person* estar enamorado de, *thing* estar entusiasmado con.

enc. ABBR of **enclosure(s)**, **enclosed** adjunto.

encamp [ɪn'kæmp] VI acamparse.

encampment [ɪn'kæmpmənt] N campamento *m*.

encapsulate [ɪn'kæpsjuleɪt] VT (*fig*) resumir, encerrar, encapsular.

encase [ɪn'keɪs] VT encerrar; (*Tech*) revestir; **to be ~d in** estar revestido de.

encash [ɪn'kæʃ] VT cobrar, hacer efectivo.

encashment [ɪn'kæʃmənt] N cobro *m*.

encephalic [ensɪ'fælɪk] ADJ encefálico.

encephalitis [ensefə'laɪtɪs] N encefalitis *f*.

encephalogram [ɪn'sefələgræm] N encefalograma *m*.

enchain [ɪn'tʃeɪn] VT encadenar.

enchant [ɪn'tʃɑ:nt] VT encantar (*also fig*); **we were ~ed with the place** el sitio nos encantó.

enchanter [ɪn'tʃɑ:ntər] N hechicero *m*.

enchanting [ɪn'tʃɑ:ntɪŋ] ADJ encantador.

enchantingly [ɪn'tʃɑ:ntɪŋlɪ] ADV de manera encantadora, deliciosamente.

enchantment [ɪn'tʃɑ:ntmənt] N (*act*) encantamiento *m*; (*charm*) encanto *m*; **it lent ~ to the scene** aumentó el encanto de la escena.

enchantress [ɪn'tʃɑ:ntrɪs] N hechicera *f*.

enchilada [entʃɪ'lædə] N enchilada *f*; **big ~** (*US**) peso pesado.

encircle [ɪn'sɜ:kl] VT rodear (*with* de); (*Mil*) envolver; *waist, shoulders etc* ceñir; **it is ~d by a wall** está rodeado de una tapia.

encirclement [ɪn'sɜ:klmənt] N (*Mil*) envolvimiento *m*.

encircling [ɪn'sɜ:klɪŋ] ADJ *movement* envolvente.

encl. ABBR of **enclosure(s)**, **enclosed** adjunto.

enclave ['enkleɪv] N enclave *m*.

enclitic [ɪn'klɪtɪk] ADJ enclítico.

▼ **enclose** [ɪn'kləuz] VT **(a)** *land, garden* cercar (*with* de); (*put in a receptacle*) meter, encerrar; (*include*) encerrar.
▼ **(b)** (*with letter*) remitir adjunto, adjuntar, acompañar; **~d herewith please find ...** le mandamos adjunto ...; **the ~d letter** la carta adjunta.

enclosure [ɪn'kləuʒər] N **(a)** (*act*) cercamiento *m*; (*place*) cercado *m*, recinto *m*. **(b)** (*in letter*) carta *f* adjunta, carta *f* inclusa.

encode [ɪn'kəud] VT codificar; (*Ling*) cifrar.

encoder [ɪn'kəudər] N (*Comput*) codificador *m*.

encoding [ɪn'kəudɪŋ] N (*Comput, Ling*) codificación *f*.

encomium [ɪn'kəumɪəm] N elogio *m*, encomio *m*.

encompass [ɪn'kʌmpəs] VT **(a)** (*surround*) cercar, rodear (*with* de). **(b)** (*include*) abarcar. **(c)** (*bring about*) lograr; (*pej*) lograr, efectuar.

encore [ɒŋ'kɔ:r] **1** INTERJ ¡otra!, ¡bis!
2 N bis *m*, repetición *f*; **to call for an ~** pedir una repetición; **to give an ~** repetir algo a petición del público, dar un bis; **to sing a song as an ~** bisar una canción.
3 VT *song* pedir la repetición de, *person* pedir una repetición a.

encounter [ɪn'kauntər] **1** N encuentro *m*; **~ group** grupo *m* de encuentro.
2 VT encontrar, encontrarse con; *difficulty etc* tropezar con.

encourage [ɪn'kʌrɪdʒ] VT *person* animar, alentar, dar aliento a; *industry* fomentar, estimular; *growth* estimular; (*in a belief*) fortalecer, reforzar; **to ~ sb to do sth** animar a uno a hacer algo.

encouragement [ɪn'kʌrɪdʒmənt] N (*act*) estímulo *m*, (*of industry*) fomento *m*; (*support*) aliento *m*, ánimo(s) *m(pl)*, aprobación *f*; **to give ~ to** infundir ánimo(s) a, dar aliento a; **to give ~ to the enemy** dar aliento al enemigo.

encouraging [ɪn'kʌrɪdʒɪŋ] ADJ alentador, esperanzador; favorable, halagüeño; **it is not an ~ prospect** es una perspectiva nada halagüeña; **he was always very ~** siempre me daba aliento.

encouragingly [ɪn'kʌrɪdʒɪŋlɪ] ADV favorablemente; *speak etc* en tono alentador.

encroach [ɪn'krəutʃ] VI avanzar; **to ~ on** *rights* usurpar; *land* (*of neighbour*) invadir, pasar los límites de; *land* (*by sea*) hurtar, invadir; *person's subject* invadir; *time* ocupar, quitar, llevar (una parte cada vez mayor de).

encroachment [ɪn'krəutʃmənt] N usurpación *f* (*on* de); invasión *f* (*on* de); abuso *m* (*on* de); **this new ~ on our liberty** esta nueva usurpación de nuestra libertad.

encrust [ɪn'krʌst] VT incrustar (*with* de).

encrustation [ɪnkrʌs'teɪʃən] N incrustación *f*.

encrusted [ɪn'krʌstɪd] ADJ: **~ with** incrustado de.

encrypt [ɪn'krɪpt] VT codificar.

encryption [ɪn'krɪpʃən] N codificación *f*.

encumber [ɪn'kʌmbər] VT *person, movement* estorbar; (*with debts*) gravar, cargar; *place* llenar (*with* de); **to be ~ed with** tener que cargar con, (*debts*) estar gravado de.

encumbrance [ɪnˈkʌmbrəns] N estorbo *m*; (*of debt*) carga *f*, gravamen *m*; **without ~** sin familia.

encyclical [enˈsɪklɪkəl] N encíclica *f*.

encyclopaedia, encyclopedia [en,saɪkləʊˈpiːdɪə] N enciclopedia *f*.

encyclopaedic, encyclopedic [en,saɪkləʊˈpiːdɪk] ADJ enciclopédico.

encyclopaedist, encyclopedist [en,saɪkləʊˈpiːdɪst] N enciclopedista *mf*.

end [end] **1** N **(a)** (*in physical sense*) (*of street etc*) final *m*; (*of line, table etc*) extremo *m*; (*of rope etc*) cabo *m*; (*point*) punta *f*; (*of estate etc*) límite *m*; (*Sport*) lado *m*; (*of town*) parte *f*, zona *f*, barrio *m*; **the ~s of the earth** los confines del mundo; **at the ~** of al cabo de, en el extremo de; al final de; **from one ~ to the other, from ~ to ~** de un extremo a otro; **on ~** de punta, de cabeza, de canto; **~ to ~** juntando los dos extremos; **to be at the ~ of one's tether** estar casi completamente agotado; no poder más; **to change ~s** (*Sport*) cambiar de lado; **to get hold of the wrong ~ of the stick** tomar el rábano por las hojas; **to keep one's ~ up** defenderse bien; **to make both ~s meet** hacer llegar el dinero; poder llegar a fin de mes; **to read a book to the very ~** leer un libro hasta el mismo final; **to stand on ~** (*hair*) erizarse; *object* poner de punta; **to start at the wrong ~** empezar por el fin.

(b) (*of time, process, resources*) fin *m*, final *m*; término *m*, conclusión *f*; límite *m*; (*of book etc*) desenlace *m*, conclusión *f*; **the ~ of the empire** el fin del imperio; **that was the ~ of him** así terminó él; **it's not the ~ of the world** no es ningún desastre; **at the ~ of the day** (*fig*) a la larga; al fin y al cabo; **at the ~ of 3 months** al cabo de 3 meses; **at the ~ of the century** a fines del siglo; **in the ~** al fin, por fin, finalmente; **no ~ of*** la mar de*; **no ~ of an expert** sumamente experto, más experto que nadie; **it caused no ~ of trouble** causó la mar de problemas; **3 days on ~** 3 días seguidos; **for days on ~** día tras día, durante una infinidad de días; **towards the ~ of** hacia el final de, *century etc* hacia fines de; **to be at an ~** estar terminando, (*be all over*) haber terminado ya; **to be at the ~ of one's resources** haber agotado los recursos; **there's no ~ to it all** esto no tiene fin, esto es inacabable; **to bring to an ~** terminar; clausurar; **to come** (*or draw*) **to an ~** terminarse; **to come to a bad ~** tener mal fin, ir a acabar mal; **that's the ~ of the matter, that's an ~ to the matter** asunto concluido; **you'll never hear the ~ of it** esto no se olvidará pronto, esto no es fácil que se olvide; **to make an ~ of, to put an ~ to** acabar con, poner fin a; **to meet one's ~** encontrar la muerte; **we see no ~ to it** no entrevemos posibilidad alguna de que termine; **to think no ~ of sb** tener un muy alto concepto de uno; **that movie is the ~!** (*US*) esa película es el no va más.

(c) (*remnant*) cabo *m*; resto *m*; pedazo *m*.

(d) (*aim*) fin *m*, objeto *m*, propósito *m*, intención *f*; **to this ~, with this ~ in view** con este propósito; **to the ~ that ...** a fin de que + *subj*; **with what ~?** ¿para qué?; **the ~ justifies the means** el fin justifica los medios; **to gain one's ~s** salirse con la suya.

2 ADJ final; **~-all** V **be-all**; **~ game** (*Chess*) fase *f* final; **the ~ house** la última casa; **~ line** (*Basketball*) línea *f* de fondo; **~ note** nota *f* final; **~ product** producto *m* final; **~ result** resultado *m* final.

3 VT terminar, acabar; *abuse etc* acabar con; *book* concluir; **to ~ it all** terminarlo del todo; (*kill o.s.*) suicidarse.

4 VI terminar, acabar; **to ~ by saying** terminar diciendo; **to ~ in** terminar en; **to ~ with** terminar con.

◆**end off** VT poner fin a.

◆**end up** VI terminar, acabar; **to ~ up at** parar en.

endanger [ɪnˈdeɪndʒəʳ] VT poner en peligro; arriesgar; exponer, aventurar; **~ed species** especie *f* en peligro (de extinción).

endear [ɪnˈdɪəʳ] **1** VT: **this did not ~ him to the public** esto no le granjeó las simpatías del público.

2 VR: **to ~ o.s. to** hacerse querer de (*or* por).

endearing [ɪnˈdɪərɪŋ] ADJ simpático, entrañable.

endearingly [ɪnˈdɪərɪŋlɪ] ADV encantadoramente.

endearment [ɪnˈdɪəmənt] N palabra *f* cariñosa, ternura *f*.

endeavour, (US) endeavor [ɪnˈdevəʳ] **1** N (*attempt*) esfuerzo *m* (*to do* por hacer), tentativa *f* (*to do* de hacer); (*striving*) empeño *m*, esfuerzos *mpl*; **in spite of my best ~s** a pesar de todos mis esfuerzos; **to use every ~ to** + *infin* no regatear esfuerzo para + *infin*.

2 VI: **to ~ to do** esforzarse por hacer, procurar hacer.

endemic [enˈdemɪk] ADJ endémico.

ending [ˈendɪŋ] N **(a)** (*gen*) fin *m*, conclusión *f*; (*of book etc*) desenlace *m*; **the tale has a happy ~** el cuento tiene un desenlace feliz. **(b)** (*Ling*) terminación *f*, desinencia *f*.

endive [ˈendaɪv] N escarola *f*, endibia *f*.

endless [ˈendlɪs] ADJ interminable, inacabable; *screw etc* sin fin.

endlessly [ˈendlɪslɪ] ADV interminablemente, sin parar.

endocardium [endəʊˈkɑːdɪəm] N, PL **endocardia** [endəʊˈkɑːdɪə] endocardio *m*.

endocarp [ˈendəkɑːp] N endocarpio *m*.

endocrine [ˈendəʊkraɪn] **1** ADJ endocrino; **~ gland** glándula *f* endo-

crina.

2 N endocrina *f*.

endocrinologist [,endəʊkraɪˈnɒlədʒɪst] N endocrinólogo *m*, -a *f*.

endodontics [,endəʊˈdɒntɪks] N SING endodoncia *f*.

endogenous [,enˈdɒdʒɪnəs] ADJ endógeno.

endomorf [ˈendəʊˌmɔːf] N endomorfo *m*.

endomorph [ˈendəʊmɔːf] N endomorfo *m*, -a *f*.

endorphin [,enˈdɔːfɪn] N endorfina *f*.

endorse [ɪnˈdɔːs] VT endosar; (*Brit*) *licence* poner nota de una sanción en, dejar constancia de sanción en; (*fig*) aprobar, confirmar, ratificar.

endorsee [ɪn,dɔːˈsiː] N endosatario *m*, -a *f*.

endorsement [ɪnˈdɔːsmənt] N endoso *m*; (*Brit: in licence*) nota *f* de sanción; (*fig*) aprobación *f*, confirmación *f*.

endorser [ɪnˈdɔːsəʳ] N endosante *mf*.

endoscope [ˈendəʊˌskəʊp] N endoscopio *m*.

endoscopy [,enˈdɒskəpɪ] N endoscopia *f*.

endow [ɪnˈdaʊ] VT dotar (*with* con, (*fig*) de); *institution* fundar, crear; **to be ~ed with** (*fig*) estar dotado de.

endowment [ɪnˈdaʊmənt] **1** N **(a)** (*act*) dotación *f*; (*creation*) fundación *f*, creación *f*. **(b)** (*amount*) dotación *f*. **(c)** (*fig*) dote *f*, cualidad *f*, talento *m*.

2 ATTR: **~ assurance, ~ insurance** (*US*) seguro *m* dotal; **~ mortgage** hipoteca *f* dotal; **~ policy** seguro *m* mixto.

endpaper [ˈendpeɪpəʳ] N guarda *f*.

endue [ɪnˈdjuː] VT dotar (*with* de).

endurable [ɪnˈdjʊərəbl] ADJ aguantable, tolerable, soportable.

endurance [ɪnˈdjʊərəns] N resistencia *f*, aguante *m*; **beyond ~, past ~** intolerable; **to have great powers of ~** tener gran resistencia; **~ race** carrera *f* de resistencia; **~ test** prueba *f* de resistencia.

endure [ɪnˈdjʊəʳ] **1** VT aguantar, soportar, tolerar; resistir; **I can't ~ him** no le aguanto, no le puedo ver; **I can't ~ it a moment longer** no lo aguanto un momento más; **I can't ~ being corrected** no tolero que me corrijan; **I can't ~ being too hot** no resisto el calor excesivo.

2 VI (*last*) durar, perdurar; (*not give in*) aguantar, resistir, sufrir sin rendirse.

enduring [ɪnˈdjʊərɪŋ] ADJ permanente, perdurable.

end-user [ˈendˈjuːzəʳ] N usuario *m*, -a *f* final.

endways [ˈendweɪz] ADV de punta; de lado, de canto.

ENE ABBR of **east-north-east** estenordeste, ENE.

enema [ˈenɪmə] N enema *f*.

enemy [ˈenɪmɪ] **1** ADJ enemigo; **~ alien** extranjero *m* enemigo, extranjera *f* enemiga.

2 N enemigo *m*, -a *f*; **the ~ within** el enemigo interior; **to be one's own worst ~** ser enemigo de sí mismo.

enemy-occupied [,enəmɪˈɒkjupaɪd] ADJ: **~ territory** territorio *m* ocupado por el enemigo.

energetic [,enəˈdʒetɪk] ADJ enérgico; *person etc* enérgico, activo; *protest* vigoroso.

energetically [,enəˈdʒetɪkəlɪ] ADV enérgicamente; activamente; vigorosamente.

energize [ˈenədʒaɪz] VT activar, energizar, dar energía a.

energizing [ˈenədʒaɪzɪŋ] ADJ *food* energético.

energy [ˈenədʒɪ] **1** N energía *f*; vigor *m*; **Secretary (of State) for** (*or* **Minister of**) **E~** (*Brit*) Secretario *m* (de Estado) (*or* Ministro *m*) de Energía.

2 ATTR energético; **~ conservation** conservación *f* de la energía, ahorro *m* energético; **~ crisis** crisis *f* energética; **~-giving** *food etc* energético; **~-intensive industry** industria *f* consumidora de gran cantidad de energía; **~ level** nivel *m* energético; **~ needs** necesidades *fpl* energéticas, requisitos *mpl* energéticos; **~ policy** política *f* de energía; **~ resources** recursos *mpl* energéticos.

energy-saving [ˈenədʒɪˌseɪvɪŋ] **1** N ahorro *m* de energía.

2 ATTR *device* que ahorra energía; *policy* para ahorrar energía.

enervate [ˈenɜːveɪt] VT enervar, debilitar.

enervating [ˈenɜːveɪtɪŋ] ADJ enervador; deprimente.

enfeeble [ɪnˈfiːbl] VT debilitar.

enfeeblement [ɪnˈfiːblmənt] N debilitación *f*.

enfilade [,enfɪˈleɪd] VT enfilar.

enfold [ɪnˈfəʊld] VT envolver; (*in arms*) abrazar, estrechar (en los brazos).

enforce [ɪnˈfɔːs] VT *law* hacer cumplir, (*from a date*) aplicar, poner en vigor; *claim* hacer valer; *rights* hacer respetar; *demand* insistir en; *sentence* ejecutar; *obedience, will* imponer (*on* a).

enforceable [ɪnˈfɔːsəbl] ADJ *laws, rules* ejecutable, que se puede hacer cumplir.

enforced [ɪnˈfɔːst] ADJ inevitable; forzoso, forzado.

enforcement [ɪnˈfɔːsmənt] N aplicación *f*; ejecución *f*.

enfranchise [ɪnˈfræntʃaɪz] VT (*free*) emancipar; *slave* manumitir; *voter* conceder el derecho de votar a.

enfranchisement [ɪnˈfræntʃɪzmənt] N emancipación *f* (*of* de); concesión *f* del derecho de votar (*of* a).

Eng. (a) ABBR of **England** Inglaterra f. **(b)** ABBR of **English** inglés m and adj.

engage [ɪn'geɪdʒ] **1** VT *attention* llamar, atraer; ocupar; *taxi etc* alquilar; *servant* tomar a su servicio; *person in conversation* abordar (entablando conversación con), *(and delay)* entretener; *workmen* apalabrar, ajustar; *lawyer etc* requerir los servicios de; *enemy* atacar, trabar batalla con; *(Mech)* cog etc engranar con, *coupling* acoplar, *gear meter*; **to ~ to do sth** comprometerse a hacer algo.
2 VI *(Mech)* engranar.
3 VR: **to ~ o.s. to do sth** comprometerse a hacer algo.
◆**engage in** VT dedicarse a, ocuparse en; *sport etc* tomar parte en.
◆**engage with** VT *(Mech)* engranar con.

engagé [ã:ŋgæ'ʒeɪ] ADJ *writer etc* comprometido.

▼**engaged** [ɪn'geɪdʒd] ADJ **(a) to be ~** *(seat)* estar ocupado; *(person)* estar ocupado; tener compromiso; no estar libre; *(Brit: toilet)* estar ocupado.
(b) *(Brit Telec)* **to be ~** estar comunicando, estar ocupado *(LAm)*; **~ signal, ~ tone** señal f de estar comunicando.
(c) to be ~ in estar ocupado en, dedicarse a; **what are you ~ in?** ¿a qué se dedica Vd?
▼**(d) to be ~ (to be married)** estar prometido; *(2 persons)* estar prometidos, ser novios, tener relaciones formales; **they've been ~ for 2 years** llevan 2 años de relaciones formales; **to get ~** prometerse *(to con)*; **the ~ couple** los novios.
(e) *writer etc* comprometido.

▼**engagement** [ɪn'geɪdʒmənt] **1** N **(a)** *(contract)* contrato m; obligación f; **to enter into an ~ to +** infin comprometerse a + infin.
▼**(b)** *(appointment)* compromiso m, cita f; **have you an ~ tonight?** ¿tienes compromiso para esta noche?; **I have an ~ at 10** tengo una cita a las 10; **owing to a previous ~** por tener compromiso anterior.
(c) *(Mil)* combate m, acción f.
▼**(d)** *(to marry)* compromiso m; *(period etc)* noviazgo m; **they have announced their ~** han anunciado su compromiso, se han dado palabra de casamiento; **the ~ is announced of Miss A to Mr B** los señores de A tienen el placer de comunicar que por los señores de B ha sido pedida la mano de su encantadora hija Isabel para su hijo Juan.
2 ATTR: **~ book, ~ diary** dietario m; agenda f de trabajo; **~ party** fiesta f de compromiso; **~ ring** anillo m de prometida, anillo m de compromiso *(note: Spanish equivalent is usually a bracelet,* pulsera f de pedido).

engaging [ɪn'geɪdʒɪŋ] ADJ atractivo, simpático; *enthusiasm etc* contagioso.

engender [ɪn'dʒendər] VT engendrar; *(fig)* engendrar, suscitar, motivar.

engine ['endʒɪn] **1** N **(a)** *(gen)* motor m. **(b)** *(Rail)* máquina f, locomotora f; **back to the ~** de espaldas a la máquina; **facing the ~** de frente a la máquina.
2 ATTR: **~ failure, ~ trouble** avería f del motor.

engine-block ['endʒɪn,blɒk] N *(Aut)* bloque m del motor.

-engined ['endʒɪnd] ADJ *eg* **four~** de cuatro motores, cuatrimotor, tetramotor; **petrol~** propulsado por gasolina.

engine-driver ['endʒɪn,draɪvər] N *(Brit)* maquinista m.

engineer [,endʒɪ'nɪər] **1** N ingeniero m, -a f; mecánico mf; *(US Rail)* maquinista m; V **civil** etc.
2 VT *(pej)* tramar, gestionar, lograr.

engineering [,endʒɪ'nɪərɪŋ] **1** N ingeniería f.
2 ATTR: **~ factory** fábrica f de maquinaria; **~ industry** industria f de ingeniería; **~ works** taller m de ingeniería.

engine-room ['endʒɪnrʊm] N sala f de máquinas.

engine-shed ['endʒɪn,ʃed] N *(Brit Rail)* cochera f de tren.

England ['ɪŋglənd] N Inglaterra f.

English ['ɪŋglɪʃ] **1** ADJ inglés; **~ breakfast** desayuno m inglés, desayuno m a la inglesa; **~ horn** corno m inglés.
2 N **(a) the ~** los ingleses.
(b) *(Ling)* inglés m; **Old ~** inglés m antiguo; **King's ~, Queen's ~** inglés m correcto; **~ speaker** anglófono m, -a f, anglohablante mf; **in plain ~** sin rodeos, en buen romance; **~ as a Foreign Language** inglés m para extranjeros; **~ as a Second Language** inglés m como segunda lengua; **~ for Special Purposes** inglés m para fines específicos; **~ Language Teaching** enseñanza f del inglés.

ENGLISH

*En el Reino Unido, se llama **Received Pronunciation** o **RP** a un tipo de acento no asociado a ninguna región en concreto (si bien tuvo su origen en el inglés hablado en el sur de Inglaterra) que hoy en día usan especialmente las personas educadas en colegios privados, las clases dirigentes y los locutores en los informativos nacionales de la **BBC**. En los medios de comunicación se acepta ya el uso de acentos regionales siempre y cuando se use la norma lingüística, es decir, utilicen un inglés gramaticalmente correcto, el llamado **Standard English**. La pronunciación **RP** suele también tomarse como norma en la enseñanza del inglés británico*

---

como lengua extranjera. Todavía goza de cierto prestigio, aunque la gran mayoría de la población habla con el acento de su región, que puede ser más o menos marcado según su educación o clase social.

*El inglés americano difiere del inglés británico principalmente en la pronunciación, aunque también hay diferencias ortográficas y léxicas. Tiene también una pronunciación estándar, conocida por el nombre de **Network Standard**, que es la que se usa en los medios de comunicación, así como diversas variedades regionales. A diferencia del Reino Unido, la asociación de acento y clase social no es muy evidente.*

English Channel ['ɪŋglɪʃ'tʃænl] N Canal m de la Mancha.

English Heritage [,ɪŋglɪʃ'herɪtɪdʒ] N *(England)* ≃ Patrimonio m Histórico-Artístico.

Englishman ['ɪŋglɪʃmən] N, PL **Englishmen** ['ɪŋglɪʃmən] inglés m.

English-speaking ['ɪŋglɪʃ,spi:kɪŋ] ADJ anglófono, anglohablante, de habla inglesa.

Englishwoman ['ɪŋglɪʃ,wʊmən] N, PL **Englishwomen** ['ɪŋglɪʃ,wɪmɪn] inglesa f.

engorged [ɪn'gɔ:dʒd] ADJ dilatado, hinchado; **to become ~** dilatarse, hincharse.

engrave [ɪn'greɪv] VT grabar *(also fig: on* en); burilar.

engraver [ɪn'greɪvər] N grabador m.

engraving [ɪn'greɪvɪŋ] N grabado m.

engross [ɪn'grəʊs] VT **(a)** *attention, person* absorber; **to be ~ed in** estar entregado a, estar absorto en; **to become ~ed in** dedicarse por completo a. **(b)** *(Jur)* copiar.

engrossing [ɪn'grəʊsɪŋ] ADJ absorbente.

engulf [ɪn'gʌlf] VT tragar; sumergir, hundir; **to be ~ed by** quedar sumergido bajo.

enhance [ɪn'hɑ:ns] VT realzar, intensificar, aumentar; *price etc* aumentar.

enhancement [ɪn'hɑ:nsmənt] N realce m, intensificación f; aumento m, incremento m.

enhancer [ɪn'hɑ:nsər] N potenciador m.

enigma [ɪ'nɪgmə] N enigma m.

enigmatic [,enɪg'mætɪk] ADJ enigmático.

enigmatically [,enɪg'mætɪkəlɪ] ADV enigmáticamente.

enjambement [ɪn'dʒæmmənt] N encabalgamiento m.

enjoin [ɪn'dʒɔɪn] VT: **to ~ sth on sb** imponer algo a uno; **to ~ sb to do sth** ordenar a uno hacer algo; **to ~ sb from doing sth** *(US)* prohibir a uno hacer algo.

▼**enjoy** [ɪn'dʒɔɪ] **1** VT **(a)** *(have use of)* health, possession etc disfrutar de, gozar de; *income, sb's confidence* tener; *advantage* poseer.
▼**(b)** *(take delight in)* meal comer con gusto; *pipe* fumar con fruición; **~ your meal!** ¡que aproveche!; **I ~ed the book** me gustó el libro; **did you ~ the game?** ¿te gustó el partido?, ¿qué tal el partido?; **I ~ reading** me gusta leer, me gusta la lectura; **I hope you ~ your holiday** que lo pases muy bien en las vacaciones; que te diviertas mucho en las vacaciones; **the author did not mean his book to be ~ed exactly** el autor no quería que su libro resultase meramente divertido.
2 VR: **to ~ o.s.** pasarlo bien, divertirse; **~ yourselves!** ¡que lo paséis bien!; **we ~ed ourselves tremendously** lo pasamos en grande, nos divertimos la mar de bien; **he ~ed himself chasing the girls** se divirtió persiguiendo a las chicas.

enjoyable [ɪn'dʒɔɪəbl] ADJ agradable; *(amusing)* divertido.

enjoyment [ɪn'dʒɔɪmənt] N **(a)** *(use)* disfrute m; posesión f. **(b)** *(delight)* placer m, fruición f; **he listened with real ~** escuchó con verdadero placer.

enlarge [ɪn'lɑ:dʒ] **1** VT extender, aumentar, ensanchar; *(Phot)* ampliar; *(Med)* dilatar; *business* extender, ampliar; **~d heart** dilatación f del corazón; **~d edition** edición f aumentada.
2 VI extenderse, aumentarse; **to ~ upon** extenderse sobre, ampliar la referencia a, explicar con más detalles.

enlargement [ɪn'lɑ:dʒmənt] N extensión f, aumento m, ensanche m; *(Phot)* ampliación f.

enlarger [ɪn'lɑ:dʒər] N *(Phot)* ampliadora f.

enlighten [ɪn'laɪtn] VT **(a)** *(inform)* informar, instruir; **can you ~ me?** ¿puede ayudarme?; **I was able to ~ him about it** pude darle informes sobre este asunto. **(b)** *(civilize)* ilustrar, iluminar.

enlightened [ɪn'laɪtnd] ADJ ilustrado, culto; bien informado; *despot* ilustrado; *attitude etc* comprensivo, inteligente.

enlightening [ɪn'laɪtnɪŋ] ADJ informativo, lleno de datos útiles; *experience etc* instructivo.

enlightenment [ɪn'laɪtnmənt] N ilustración f; aclaración f; V **age**.

enlist [ɪn'lɪst] **1** VT *(Mil)* alistar, reclutar; *support etc* conseguir; **~ed man** *(US)* soldado m *(etc)* que no es oficial, soldado m raso.
2 VI alistarse *(in* en).

enlistment [ɪn'lɪstmənt] N alistamiento m.

enliven [ɪn'laɪvn] VT avivar, animar.

en masse [ã:ŋ'mæs] ADV en masa.

enmesh [ɪn'meʃ] VT coger en una red; **to get ~ed in** enredarse en.

▶ LANGUAGE IN USE: **engaged: d →** 24.2   **engagement: 1b →** 25.2 **1d →** 24.2   **enjoy: 1b →** 7.2

enmity ['enmɪtɪ] N enemistad f.

ennoble [ɪ'nəʊbl] VT ennoblecer.

ennui [ãː'nwiː] N tedio m, aburrimiento m.

enology [iː'nɒlədʒɪ] etc (US) = **oenology** etc.

enormity [ɪ'nɔːmɪtɪ] N enormidad f.

enormous [ɪ'nɔːməs] ADJ enorme.

enormously [ɪ'nɔːməslɪ] ADV enormemente.

enough [ɪ'nʌf] **1** ADV bastante, suficientemente; **not big ~** no suficientemente grande; **she sings well ~** canta bastante bien; V **good, sure** etc.

2 ADJ bastante, suficiente; **I hadn't ~ money to buy it** no tuve bastante dinero para comprarlo.

3 PRON: **that's ~, thanks** con eso basta, gracias; ya está bien, gracias; **that's ~ now!** ¡basta ya!; **it is ~ for us to know that ...** nos basta saber que ...; **there's more than ~ for all** hay más que suficiente para todos; **~ is ~** bueno está lo bueno, basta y sobra; **~ is as good as a feast** rogar a Dios por santos mas no por tantos; **it was ~ to drive you mad** era para volverse loco; **as if that weren't ~** por si fuera poco; **we have ~ to live on** tenemos lo suficiente para vivir, tenemos con qué vivir; **one can never have ~ of his music** es imposible escuchar demasiado su música; **I've had ~ of him** estoy harto de él; **tell me when you've had ~** dime en cuanto te empieces a cansar; **I had ~ to do to find one** me costó trabajo encontrar uno.

4 INTERJ: **~ of this!** ¡basta ya!, ¡concluyamos de una vez!

⌐ *ENOUGH*   *see also main entry* ¬

Agreement

• When used as an *adjective* or *pronoun*, *bastante*, like *suficiente*, agrees with the noun it describes or refers to:

  Are there enough potatoes?
  ¿Hay bastantes patatas?
  Eggs? Yes, there are enough
  ¿Huevos? Sí, hay bastantes

• Don't add an "s" to the *adverb bastante* (*i.e.* when it modifies an adjective or verb):

  They're not poor enough to get money from the State
  No son lo bastante pobres como para recibir dinero del Estado
  We've studied these photographs enough
  Ya hemos estudiado bastante estas fotografías

After verbs

• When a purpose is implied or stated, translate using *lo suficiente* or, especially in affirmative phrases, *lo bastante*:

  We know enough to be able to say that these techniques are safe
  Sabemos lo suficiente or lo bastante (como) para afirmar que estas técnicas son seguras

• When no purpose is implied or stated, translate using either *bastante* or *lo suficiente*:

  He says he hasn't had enough to eat
  Dice que no ha comido bastante or no ha comido lo suficiente
  We shall never be able to thank you enough
  Nunca se lo podremos agradecer bastante or lo suficiente

After adjectives and adverbs

• Translate using *lo* + *bastante* + ADJECTIVE/ADVERB or *lo suficientemente* + ADJECTIVE/ADVERB:

  He isn't good enough to take part in the Olympics
  No es lo bastante or lo suficientemente bueno (como) para participar en las Olimpiadas
  She couldn't run fast enough to catch him
  No pudo correr lo bastante or lo suficientemente rápido (como) para atraparlo

To be enough

• *To be enough* can often be translated using *bastar*:

  That's enough!
  ¡Basta ya!
  That's enough to feed an army!
  Con eso basta para dar de comer a un regimiento
  NOTE: As *bastar* is an impersonal verb, it often takes an indirect object:
  Promises are no longer enough for him
  Ya no le bastan las promesas
  That's enough for him
  Con eso le basta
  For further uses and examples, see main entry.

---

enquire [ɪn'kwaɪəʳ] etc = **inquire**.

enrage [ɪn'reɪdʒ] VT enfurecer, hacer rabiar; **to be ~d with pain** rabiar de dolor.

enrapture [ɪn'ræptʃəʳ] VT embelesar, arrebatar, extasiar.

enrich [ɪn'rɪtʃ] VT enriquecer; *soil* fertilizar.

enriched [ɪn'rɪtʃt] ADJ *food* etc enriquecido.

enrichment [ɪn'rɪtʃmənt] N enriquecimiento m; fertilización f.

enrol, (US) **enroll** [ɪn'rəʊl] **1** VT *member* registrar, inscribir; *student* matricular; (*Mil*) alistar.

2 VI inscribirse; matricularse; alistarse; **to ~ for a course** matricularse para un curso.

enrolment, (US) **enrollment** [ɪn'rəʊlmənt] N inscripción f; matrícula f; alistamiento m.

en route ADV en el camino; **to be ~ for** ir camino de, ir con rumbo a, dirigirse a; **it was stolen ~** lo robaron durante el viaje.

ensconce [ɪn'skɒns] VR: **to ~ o.s.** instalarse cómodamente, acomodarse; **to be ~d in** estar cómodamente instalado en.

ensemble [ãː'nsãːmbl] N (*whole*) conjunto m; (*general effect*) impresión f de conjunto; (*dress*) conjunto m; (*Mus*) conjunto m (musical), agrupación f.

enshrine [ɪn'ʃraɪn] VT (*fig*) encerrar, englobar.

enshroud [ɪn'ʃraʊd] VT (*liter, lit*) envolver; **the case remains ~ed in mystery** el caso permanece envuelto en misterio.

ensign ['ensaɪn] N (a) (*flag*) bandera f; **Red E~** (*Brit*) Enseña f Roja (*bandera de la marina mercante británica*); **White E~** (*Brit*) Enseña f Blanca (*bandera de la marina de guerra británica*). (b) (*rank*) alférez m.

enslave [ɪn'sleɪv] VT esclavizar; (*fig*) dominar.

enslavement [ɪn'sleɪvmənt] N esclavitud f.

ensnare [ɪn'sneəʳ] VT entrampar, coger en una trampa (*also fig*).

ensue [ɪn'sjuː] VI (*follow*) seguirse; (*happen*) sobrevenir; (*result*) resultar (*from* de).

ensuing [ɪn'sjuːɪŋ] ADJ consiguiente, subsiguiente, resultante.

en suite [ã'swiːt] ADJ: **with bathroom ~, with an ~ bathroom** con baño adjunto.

▼ **ensure** [ɪn'ʃʊəʳ] VT asegurar.

ENT N (*Med*) ABBR of **ear, nose and throat** otorrinolaringología f.

entail [ɪn'teɪl] **1** N vínculo m.

2 VT (a) (*necessitate*) imponer; (*imply*) suponer; (*bring in its train*) acarrear; **it ~s a lot of work** supone mucho trabajo para nosotros; **it ~ed buying a new car** nos obligó a comprar un nuevo coche; **what does the job ~?** ¿cuáles son las funciones del puesto? (b) (*Jur*) vincular.

entangle [ɪn'tæŋgl] VT enredar, enmarañar; **to get ~d in an affair** quedar enredado en un asunto; **to get ~d with sb** meterse en un lío con uno.

entanglement [ɪn'tæŋglmənt] N enredo m, embrollo m; (*love affair*) aventura f amorosa; (*Mil*) alambrada f; **to keep out of ~s** no meterse en líos.

entente [ãːn'tãːnt] N (*Pol*) entente f, trato m secreto.

enter ['entəʳ] **1** VT (a) (*go into*) entrar en; penetrar en; *hospital* ingresar en; **it never ~ed my head** jamás se me pasó por la cabeza. (b) (*fig*) *society* ingresar en, hacerse socio de; *army* alistarse en; *college, school* matricularse en. (c) (*write down*) *note* anotar, apuntar; *name* etc escribir; *member* inscribir, matricular; *record* asentar, anotar, dar entrada a, registrar; *data* (*Comput*) introducir; *claim, request* presentar, formular; *order* (*Comm*) asentar; *protest* formular; **to ~ a horse for a race** inscribir un caballo para una carrera; **to ~ one's son for Eton** apuntar (*or* inscribir) a su hijo para Eton (*como futuro alumno*); **to ~ a dog for a show** inscribir un perro en un concurso canino.

2 VI (a) entrar; (*Theat*) entrar en escena; **~ Macbeth** sale Macbeth; **'Do not ~'** (US) 'se prohíbe la entrada', (*Aut*) 'dirección prohibida'. (b) **to ~ for** *competition, race* participar en, tomar parte en, presentarse para; *post* presentarse como candidato a, oponerse a.

◆**enter into** VT (a) *agreement* llegar a, firmar; *bargain* cerrar; *contract* hacer, firmar; *obligation* contraer; *explanation* dar; *argument* meterse en, tomar parte en; *conversation* entablar; *negotiations* iniciar; *relations* establecer (*with* con); *marriage* contraer (*with* con). (b) *calculations, plans* formar parte de; **that doesn't ~ into it at all** eso no figura aquí para nada, eso no afecta la cosa en lo más mínimo; **her feelings don't ~ into it** sus sentimientos no tienen que ver; **to ~ into the spirit of the game** tomar parte en el juego con entusiasmo.

◆**enter up** VT *entry* asentar; *ledger* hacer, llevar; *diary* poner al día.

◆**enter (up)on** VT *career* emprender; *office* tomar posesión de; *term of office* empezar; *one's 20th year* empezar.

enteric [en'terɪk] ADJ entérico; **~ fever** fiebre f entérica.

enteritis [ˌentə'raɪtɪs] N enteritis f.

enterprise ['entəpraɪz] **1** N (a) (*firm, undertaking*) empresa f. (b) (*spirit*) iniciativa f; espíritu m emprendedor, empuje m; V **free** etc. **2** ATTR: **the ~ culture** la cultura empresarial; **~ zone** zona f de empresas.

enterprising ['entəpraɪzɪŋ] ADJ *person, spirit* emprendedor; **an ~ thing to do** una cosa que muestra mucha iniciativa; **that was ~ of you** en eso has mostrado mucha iniciativa.

enterprisingly ['entəpraɪzɪŋlɪ] ADV de modo emprendedor, con mucha iniciativa.

entertain [ˌentə'teɪn] **1** VT (a) (*amuse*) divertir, entretener.

(b) *guest* (*at home*) recibir, recibir en casa, alojar consigo; (*make a fuss of*) festejar, agasajar; **they ~ a good deal** reciben mucho; **they ~ed him with a dinner** le invitaron a cenar; (*formally*) le obsequiaron con una cena.

(c) *idea, hope* abrigar, acariciar; *proposal* estudiar, considerar; **I wouldn't ~ it for a moment** tal idea es totalmente inconcebible para mí.

2 VI (*at home*) recibir en casa.

entertainer [‚entə'teɪnər] N artista *mf*, actor *m*, actriz *f*, músico *m* (*etc*).

entertaining [‚entə'teɪnɪŋ] ADJ divertido, entretenido.

entertainingly [‚entə'teɪnɪŋlɪ] ADV de manera divertida, graciosamente.

entertainment [‚entə'teɪnmənt] **1** N **(a)** (*amusement*) diversión *f*; **for your ~** para divertiros.
(b) (*show*) función *f*, espectáculo *m*, fiesta *f*; (*musical ~*) concierto *m*; **to put on an ~** organizar un espectáculo.
2 ATTR: **~ allowance** extra *m* de visita, gastos *mpl* de representación; **~ business** mundo *m* de los espectáculos; **~ expenses** = **~ allowance**; **~ guide** guía *f* del ocio; **~ tax** impuesto *m* sobre los espectáculos.

enthrall, (*US*) **enthral** [ɪn'θrɔːl] VT (*fig*) embelesar, extasiar; captar la atención de; **we listened ~ed** escuchamos embelesados.

enthralling [ɪn'θrɔːlɪŋ] ADJ embelesador, cautivador.

enthrone [ɪn'θrəʊn] VT entronizar.

enthronement [ɪn'θrəʊnmənt] N (*lit*) entronización *f*; (*fig*) consagración *f*.

enthuse [ɪn'θuːz] VI: **to ~ over** entusiasmarse muchísimo por, extasiarse ante.

enthusiasm [ɪn'θuːzɪæzəm] N entusiasmo *m* (*for* por).

enthusiast [ɪn'θuːzɪæst] N entusiasta *mf* (*for* por).

enthusiastic [ɪn‚θuːzɪ'æstɪk] ADJ *person* entusiasta; *cry etc* entusiástico; **to be ~ about** entusiasmarse por, estar lleno de entusiasmo por.

enthusiastically [ɪn‚θuːzɪ'æstɪkəlɪ] ADV con entusiasmo; **he shouted ~** gritó entusiasmado.

entice [ɪn'taɪs] VT tentar, atraer (con maña); (*in bad sense*) seducir; **to ~ sb away from sb** inducir mañosamente a uno a dejar a una persona; **to ~ sb away from a place** inducir mañosamente a uno a abandonar un sitio; **to ~ sb into a room** inducir mañosamente a uno a entrar en un cuarto; **to ~ sb to do sth** tentar a uno a hacer algo.

enticement [ɪn'taɪsmənt] N **(a)** (*act*) tentación *f*, atracción *f*; seducción *f*; persuasión *f* (mañosa). **(b)** (*bait*) atractivo *m*, aliciente *m*, cebo *m*.

enticing [ɪn'taɪsɪŋ] ADJ atractivo, tentador, seductor.

enticingly [ɪn'taɪsɪŋlɪ] ADV atractivamente, seductoramente.

entire [ɪn'taɪər] ADJ entero, completo; total; todo; **the ~ world** el mundo entero; **the ~ trip** todo el viaje; **the ~ stock** todas las existencias.

entirely [ɪn'taɪəlɪ] ADV enteramente, totalmente; **that is not ~ true** eso no es del todo verdad.

entirety [ɪn'taɪərətɪ] N: **in its ~** en su totalidad, enteramente.

entitle [ɪn'taɪtl] VT **(a)** *book etc* titular; **the book is ~d X** el libro se titula X.
(b) to ~ sb to do sth autorizar a uno para hacer algo; **to be ~d to do sth** tener derecho a hacer algo; **to ~ sb to sth** dar a uno derecho a algo; **I think I am ~d to some respect** creo que se me debe cierto respeto.

entitlement [ɪn'taɪtlmənt] N derecho *m*; autorización *f*; **holiday ~** derecho *m* a vacaciones.

entity ['entɪtɪ] N entidad *f*, ente *m*; **legal ~** persona *f* jurídica.

entomb [ɪn'tuːm] VT sepultar.

entombment [ɪn'tuːmmənt] N sepultura *f*.

entomological [‚entəmə'lɒdʒɪkəl] ADJ entomológico.

entomologist [‚entə'mɒlədʒɪst] N entomólogo *m*, -a *f*.

entomology [‚entə'mɒlədʒɪ] N entomología *f*.

entourage [‚ɒntʊ'rɑːʒ] N séquito *m*.

entr'acte ['ɒntrækt] N descanso *m*, intermedio *m*, entreacto *m*.

entrails ['entreɪlz] NPL entrañas *fpl*, tripas *fpl*; (*US*) asadura *f*, menudos *mpl*.

entrain [ɪn'treɪn] VI (*esp Mil*) tomar el tren (*for* a).

entrance[1] ['entrəns] **1** N **(a)** (*place*) entrada *f*.
(b) (*act*) entrada *f* (*into* en); (*into profession etc*) ingreso *m*; (*Theat*) entrada *f* en escena; **to make one's ~** hacer su entrada.
2 ATTR: **~ card** pase *m*; **~ examination** examen *m* de ingreso; **~ fee** (*Brit*) cuota *f* (de entrada); **~ permit** pase *m*; **~ qualifications, ~ requirements** requisitos *mpl* de entrada.

entrance[2] [ɪn'trɑːns] VT encantar, hechizar; **we listened ~d** escuchamos extasiados.

entrance hall ['entrəns‚hɔːl] N hall *m* de entrada.

entrance ramp ['entrəns‚ræmp] N (*US*) rampa *f* de acceso.

entrancing [ɪn'trɑːnsɪŋ] ADJ encantador, cautivador, delicioso.

entrancingly [ɪn'trɑːnsɪŋlɪ] ADV *play etc* maravillosamente, deliciosamente; **it was ~ beautiful** contemplamos extasiados aquella belleza.

entrant ['entrənt] N participante *mf*, concurrente *mf*, concursante *mf*.

entrap [ɪn'træp] VT coger en una trampa; (*fig*) entrampar.

entrapment [ɪn'træpmənt] N acción *f* de entrampar; **he complained of ~** se quejó de que le habían entrampado.

entreat [ɪn'triːt] VT rogar, suplicar; **to ~ sb to do sth** suplicar a uno hacer algo.

entreating [ɪn'triːtɪŋ] **1** ADJ suplicante.
2 N súplica *f*, suplicación *f*.

entreatingly [ɪn'triːtɪŋlɪ] ADV de modo suplicante.

entreaty [ɪn'triːtɪ] N ruego *m*, súplica *f*.

entrée ['ɒntreɪ] N entrada *f*; (*US*) plato *m* fuerte, plato *m* principal.

entrench [ɪn'trentʃ] **1** VT atrincherar; **to be ~ed** (*also fig*) estar atrincherado; (*Pol: clause*) ser artículo inalterable.
2 VR: **to ~ o.s.** atrincherarse.

entrenched [ɪn'trentʃt] ADJ (*Mil*) atrincherado; (*fig*) *person* de ideas fijas; *attitude* inamovible; *clause* inalterable; **~ interests** intereses *mpl* creados.

entrenchment [ɪn'trentʃmənt] N trinchera *f*.

entrepôt ['ɒntrəpəʊ] N centro *m* comercial, centro *m* de distribución; almacén *m*, depósito *m*.

entrepreneur [‚ɒntrəprə'nɜːr] N (*Comm*) empresario *m*, patrón *m*; contratista *m*; (*Fin*) capitalista *m*.

entrepreneurial [‚ɒntrəprə'nɜːrɪəl] ADJ empresarial.

entrepreneurship [‚ɒntrəprə'nɜːʃɪp] N espíritu *m* emprendedor, espíritu *m* empresarial; **to promote ~** promover la iniciativa empresarial.

entropy ['entrəpɪ] N entropía *f*.

entrust [ɪn'trʌst] VT: **to ~ sth to sb, to ~ sb with sth** confiar algo a uno.

entry ['entrɪ] **1** N **(a)** (*place*) entrada *f*; (*passage*) callejuela *f*; (*of street*) bocacalle *f*; **'no ~'** 'se prohíbe la entrada', (*Aut*) 'dirección prohibida'.
(b) (*act*) entrada *f* (*into* en); acceso *m* (*into* a); (*into profession etc*) ingreso *m* (*into* en); (*into office*) toma *f* de posesión (*into, on* de); **~ into the hall had been forbidden** se había prohibido el acceso a la sala; **to make one's ~** hacer su entrada.
(c) (*Sport etc*) (*total*) participación *f*, participantes *mpl*; (*competitor*) participante *mf*, concurrente *mf*.
(d) (*in reference book*) artículo *m*; entrada *f*; (*in diary*) apunte *m*; (*in account*) partida *f*, rubro *m* (*LAm*); (*in record*) apunte *m*, apuntación *f*, entrada *f*.
2 ATTR: **~ fee** cuota *f* (de entrada); **~ form** boleto *m* de inscripción; **~ permit** permiso *m* de entrada; **~ phone** portero *m* automático; **~ qualifications, ~ requirements** requisitos *mpl* de entrada.

entwine [ɪn'twaɪn] VT entrelazar, entretejer.

enumerate [ɪ'njuːməreɪt] VT enumerar.

enumeration [ɪ‚njuːmə'reɪʃən] N enumeración *f*.

enunciate [ɪ'nʌnsɪeɪt] VT *words* pronunciar, articular; *principle* enunciar.

enunciation [ɪ‚nʌnsɪ'eɪʃən] N pronunciación *f*, articulación *f*; enunciación *f*.

enuresis [‚enjʊə'riːsɪs] N enuresis *f*.

enuretic [‚enjʊ'retɪk] ADJ enurético.

envelop [ɪn'veləp] VT envolver (*in* en).

envelop(e) ['envələʊp] N sobre *m*; (*Aer*) envoltura *f*.

enveloping [ɪn'veləpɪŋ] ADJ *movement* envolvente.

envelopment [ɪn'veləpmənt] N envolvimiento *m*.

envenom [ɪn'venəm] VT envenenar.

enviable ['envɪəbl] ADJ envidiable.

envious ['envɪəs] ADJ envidioso; *look etc* de envidia; **to be ~ of** tener envidia de, envidiar; **it makes me ~** me da envidia; **I am ~ of your good luck** te envidio tu suerte.

enviously ['envɪəslɪ] ADV con envidia.

environment [ɪn'vaɪərənmənt] N medio *m* ambiente, ambiente *m*, entorno *m*; (*Comput*) entorno *m*; **Department of the E~** (*Brit*) Ministerio *m* del Medio Ambiente; **Secretary (of State) for** (*or* **Minister of**) **the E~** (*Brit*) Secretario *m* (de Estado) (*or* Ministro *m*) del Medio Ambiente.

environmental [ɪn‚vaɪərən'mentl] ADJ ambiental, medioambiental; **~ concern** preocupación *f* ambiental; **~ pollution** contaminación *f* ambiental.

environmentalism [ɪn‚vaɪərən'mentəlɪzəm] N ambientalismo *m*.

environmentalist [ɪn‚vaɪərən'mentəlɪst] **1** ADJ ambiental; ecologista.
2 N ambientalista *mf*, ecologista *mf*.

environmentally [ɪn‚vaɪərən'mentlɪ] ADV: **an ~ acceptable product** un producto aceptable en lo que concierne al medio ambiente; **it is not ~ safe** ofrece un peligro ambiental.

environment-friendly [ɪn'vaɪərənment'frendlɪ] ADJ que no daña al medio ambiente, ecológico.

environs [ɪn'vaɪərənz] NPL alrededores *mpl,* inmediaciones *fpl.*

envisage [ɪn'vɪzɪdʒ] VT **(a)** *(foresee)* prever; **it is ~d that ...** se prevé que ...; **an increase is ~d next year** está previsto que se aumentará el año que viene.
(b) *(imagine)* concebir, formarse una idea de, representarse; **it is hard to ~ such a situation** es difícil formarse una idea de tal situación.

envision [ɪn'vɪʒən] VT *(US)* **(a)** *(imagine)* imaginar. **(b)** *(foresee)* prever.

envoy ['envɔɪ] N enviado *m.*

envy ['envɪ] **1** N envidia *f;* **it was the ~ of all the neighbours** nos lo envidiaban todos los vecinos.
2 VT envidiar, tener envidia a; **to ~ sb sth** envidiar algo a uno.

enzyme ['enzaɪm] N enzima *f.*

EOC N ABBR *of* **Equal Opportunities Commission.**

Eocene ['iːəʊsiːn] ADJ *(Geol)* eoceno.

eolithic [ˌiːəʊ'lɪθɪk] ADJ eolítico.

eon ['iːən, 'iːɒn] N *(US)* eón *m;* *(loosely)* eternidad *f.*

EP N ABBR *of* **extended play** maxi *m,* maxi-single *m.*

EPA N *(US)* ABBR *of* **Environmental Protection Agency** Agencia *f* para la Protección del Medio Ambiente.

epaulette ['epɔːlet] N charretera *f.*

epee, epée ['epeɪ] N espada *f* de esgrima.

ephedrine ['efɪdrɪn] N efedrina *f.*

ephemera [ɪ'femərə] NPL *(transitory items)* cosas *fpl* efímeras; *(collectables)* objetos *mpl* coleccionables *(sin valor).*

ephemeral [ɪ'femərəl] ADJ efímero.

Ephesians [ɪ'fiːʒjənz] NPL efesios *mpl.*

epic ['epɪk] **1** ADJ épico.
2 N épica *f,* epopeya *f.*

epicene ['episiːn] ADJ epiceno.

epicentre, *(US)* **epicenter** ['episentər] N epicentro *m.*

epicure ['epɪkjʊər] N epicúreo *m,* gastrónomo *m.*

epicurean [ˌepɪkjʊ'riːən] **1** ADJ epicúreo.
2 N epicúreo *m.*

epicureanism [ˌepɪkjʊə'riːənɪzəm] N epicureísmo *m.*

epidemic [ˌepɪ'demɪk] **1** ADJ epidémico.
2 N epidemia *f.*

epidermis [ˌepɪ'dɜːmɪs] N epidermis *f.*

epidural [ˌepɪ'djʊərəl] **1** ADJ: **~ (anaesthetic)** raquianestesis *f.*
2 N = **1.**

epiglottis [ˌepɪ'glɒtɪs] N epiglotis *f.*

epigram ['epɪgræm] N epigrama *m.*

epigrammatic(al) [ˌepɪgrə'mætɪk(əl)] ADJ epigramático.

epigraph ['epɪgrɑːf] N epígrafe *m.*

epigraphy [ɪ'pɪgrəfɪ] N epigrafía *f.*

epilepsy ['epɪlepsɪ] N epilepsia *f,* alferecía *f.*

epileptic [ˌepɪ'leptɪk] **1** ADJ epiléptico; **~ fit** acceso *m* epiléptico.
2 N epiléptico *m,* -a *f.*

epilogue ['epɪlɒg] N epílogo *m.*

Epiphany [ɪ'pɪfənɪ] N Epifanía *f.*

episcopacy [ɪ'pɪskəpəsɪ] N episcopado *m.*

episcopal [ɪ'pɪskəpəl] ADJ episcopal.

episcopalian [ɪˌpɪskə'peɪlɪən] **1** ADJ episcopalista.
2 N episcopalista *mf.*

episcopate [ɪ'pɪskəʊpət] N episcopado *m.*

episode ['epɪsəʊd] N episodio *m;* *(TV)* capítulo *m* (televisivo), entrega *f* (televisiva).

episodic [ˌepɪ'sɒdɪk] ADJ episódico.

epistemological [ɪˌpɪstɪmə'lɒdʒɪkəl] ADJ epistemológico.

epistemology [ɪˌpɪstə'mɒlədʒɪ] N epistemología *f.*

epistle [ɪ'pɪsl] N epístola *f.*

epistolary [ɪ'pɪstələrɪ] ADJ epistolar.

epitaph ['epɪtɑːf] N epitafio *m.*

epithet ['epɪθet] N epíteto *m.*

epitome [ɪ'pɪtəmɪ] N epítome *m,* compendio *m,* resumen *m;* *(fig)* representación *f* en miniatura; **to be the ~ of virtue** ser la misma virtud, ser la virtud en persona.

epitomize [ɪ'pɪtəmaɪz] VT epitomar, compendiar, resumir; *(fig)* personificar; representar en miniatura; **he ~d resistance to the enemy** se cifraba en él la resistencia al enemigo; **he ~d virtue** era la misma virtud, era la virtud en persona.

EPNS N ABBR *of* **electroplated nickel silver.**

epoch ['iːpɒk] N época *f;* **to mark an ~** hacer época.

epochal ['epəkəl] *(frm)* ADJ = **epoch-making.**

epoch-making ['iːpɒkˌmeɪkɪŋ] ADJ que hace época.

eponymous [ɪ'pɒnɪməs] ADJ epónimo.

EPOS ['iːpɒs] N ABBR *of* **electronic point of sale.**

epoxy resin [ɪ'pɒksɪ'rezɪn] N resina *f* epoxídica.

Epsom salts ['epsəm,sɔːlts] NPL epsomita *f,* sal *f* de La Higuera.

EPW N *(US)* ABBR *of* **enemy prisoner of war.**

equable ['ekwəbl] ADJ *climate etc* uniforme, igual; *person,* ecuánime; *tone* tranquilo, afable.

equal ['iːkwəl] **1** ADJ igual *(to* a); *treatment* equitativo; **~ in value** de igual valor; **with ~ ease** con la misma facilidad; **E~ Opportunities Commission** *(Brit)* Comisión *f* para la Igualdad de Oportunidades; **~ opportunities** *(or* **opportunity) employer** empresario *m* no discriminatorio; **~ rights campaign** campaña *f* en pro de la igualdad de derechos; **~ time** *(US Rad, TV)* derecho *m* de respuesta; **~(s) sign** *(Math)* signo *m* de igualdad; **other things being ~** en igualdad de circunstancias; **si todo sigue igual; to be ~ to** *task* tener fuerzas para, *situation* estar a la altura de; **I don't feel ~ to it** no me siento con fuerzas para ello; **he is ~ to every demand made upon him** hace bien cuanto se le pide; **to be ~ to doing sth** tener fuerzas para hacer algo.
2 N igual *mf;* **without ~** sin igual, sin par; **it has no ~ in modern times** no hay nada parecido en los tiempos modernos; **to treat sb as an ~** tratar a uno de igual a igual.
3 VT ser igual a; **6 + 4 ~s 10** 6 más 4 son 10.

equality [ɪ'kwɒlɪtɪ] N igualdad *f;* **~ of opportunity** igualdad *f* de oportunidades.

equalization [ˌiːkwəlaɪ'zeɪʃən] N igualación *f;* nivelación *f;* *(Fin)* compensación *f;* **~ account** cuenta *f* de compensación; **~ fund** fondo *m* de compensación.

equalize ['iːkwəlaɪz] **1** VT igualar; nivelar.
2 VI *(Sport)* lograr el empate, lograr la igualada, igualar.

equalizer ['iːkwəlaɪzər] N **(a)** *(Sport)* igualada *f,* tanto *m* del empate. **(b)** *(US)* pipa‡ *f,* revólver *m.*

▼ **equally** ['iːkwəlɪ] ADV igualmente; *share etc* por igual; *treat etc* equitativamente.

equanimity [ˌekwə'nɪmɪtɪ] N ecuanimidad *f.*

equate [ɪ'kweɪt] VT igualar; equiparar *(to, with* con); considerar equivalente *(to, with* a), comparar *(to, with* con).

equation [ɪ'kweɪʒən] N ecuación *f.*

equator [ɪ'kweɪtər] N ecuador *m.*

equatorial [ˌekwə'tɔːrɪəl] ADJ ecuatorial.

Equatorial Guinea [ˌekwə'tɔːrɪəl'gɪnɪ] N Guinea *f* Ecuatorial.

equerry ['ekwərɪ] N caballerizo *m* del rey.

equestrian [ɪ'kwestrɪən] **1** ADJ ecuestre.
2 N jinete *m,* -a *f.*

equestrianism [ɪ'kwestrɪənɪzm] N equitación *f.*

equi... ['iːkwɪ] PREF equi...

equidistant ['iːkwɪ'dɪstənt] ADJ equidistante.

equilateral ['iːkwɪ'lætərəl] ADJ equilátero.

equilibrium [ˌiːkwɪ'lɪbrɪəm] N equilibrio *m.*

equine ['ekwaɪn] ADJ equino.

equinoctial [ˌiːkwɪ'nɒkʃəl] ADJ equinoccial.

equinox ['iːkwɪnɒks] N equinoccio *m.*

equip [ɪ'kwɪp] VT equipar *(with* de); *person* proveer *(with* de); **to be ~ped with** *(person)* estar provisto de, *(machine etc)* estar dotado de; **to be well ~ped to** + *infin* estar bien dotado para + *infin.*

equipment [ɪ'kwɪpmənt] N equipo *m,* material *m;* *(tools)* avíos *mpl;* *(mental)* aptitud *f,* dotes *fpl.*

equipoise ['iːkwɪpɔɪz] N *(frm)* estabilidad *f.*

equitable ['ekwɪtəbl] ADJ equitativo.

equitably ['ekwɪtəblɪ] ADV equitativamente.

equity ['ekwɪtɪ] N **(a)** equidad *f.* **(b)** *(Fin: also* **~ capital)** capital *m* propio, patrimonio *m* neto; **equities** acciones *fpl.* **(c)** **E~** *(Brit)* sindicato *de actores.*

equivalence [ɪ'kwɪvələns] N equivalencia *f.*

▼ **equivalent** [ɪ'kwɪvələnt] **1** ADJ equivalente *(to* a); **to be ~ to** equivaler a.
2 N equivalente *m.*

equivocal [ɪ'kwɪvəkəl] ADJ equívoco, ambiguo.

equivocate [ɪ'kwɪvəkeɪt] VI usar equívocos, no dar una respuesta clara, soslayar el problema.

equivocation [ɪˌkwɪvə'keɪʃən] N equívoco *m;* evasión *f,* ambigüedad *f.*

E.R. ABBR *of* **Elizabeth Regina** la reina Isabel.

ERA N *(US Pol)* ABBR *of* **Equal Rights Amendment.**

era ['ɪərə] N época *f,* era *f;* **to mark an ~** hacer época.

eradicate [ɪ'rædɪkeɪt] VT desarraigar, extirpar.

eradication [ɪˌrædɪ'keɪʃən] N desarraigo *m,* extirpación *f.*

erase [ɪ'reɪz] VT **(a)** borrar *(also Comput, fig).* **(b)** *(US*)* liquidar*.*

erase head [ɪ'reɪz,hed] N cabezal *m* borrador.

eraser [ɪ'reɪzər] N goma *f* de borrar, borrador *m.*

Erasmism [ɪ'ræzmɪzəm] N erasmismo *m.*

Erasmist [ɪ'ræzmɪst] **1** ADJ erasmista.
2 N erasmista *mf.*

Erasmus [ɪ'ræzməs] NM Erasmo.

erasure [ɪ'reɪʒər] N borradura *f,* raspadura *f;* *(Comput)* borrado *m.*

ERDF N ABBR *of* **European Regional Development Fund** Fondo *m* Europeo de Desarrollo Regional, FEDER *m.*

ere [ɛər] (††) **1** PREP antes de; **~ long** dentro de poco.
2 CONJ antes de que.

erect [ɪ'rekt] **1** ADJ erguido, derecho; vertical.

2 VT (build) erigir, construir, levantar; (assemble) montar; **to ~ sth into a principle** constituir algo en principio.

erectile [ɪ'rektaɪl] ADJ eréctil.

erection [ɪ'rekʃən] N **(a)** (act) erección f, construcción f; (assembly) montaje m. **(b)** (structure) edificio m, construcción f. **(c)** (Physiol) erección f.

erectly [ɪ'rektlɪ] ADV de manera erguida; verticalmente.

erector [ɪ'rektəʳ] ATTR: ~ **set** (US) juego m de construcciones.

erg [ɜːg] N ergio m, erg m.

ergative ['ɜːgətɪv] ADJ ergativo.

ergo ['ɜːgəʊ] CONJ (frm, hum) ergo.

ergonomic [ˌɜːgəʊ'nɒmɪk] ADJ ergonómico.

ergonomics [ˌɜːgəʊ'nɒmɪks] N ergonomía f.

ergonomist [ɜː'gɒnəmɪst] N ergonomista mf, ergónomo m, -a f.

ergot ['ɜːgət] N cornezuelo m (del centeno).

ergotism ['ɜːgətɪzəm] N ergotismo m.

Eric ['erɪk] NM Erico.

Erie ['ɪərɪ] N: **Lake ~** Lago m Erie.

Erin ['ɪərɪn] N Erín m (nombre antiguo y sentimental de Irlanda).

ERISA [ə'rɪsə] N (US) ABBR of **Employee Retirement Income Security Act** ley que regula pensiones de jubilados.

Eritrea [ˌerə'treɪə] N Eritrea f.

Eritrean [erɪ'treɪən] **1** ADJ eritreo.
   2 N (person) eritreo m, -a f.

ERM N ABBR of **Exchange Rate Mechanism**.

ermine ['ɜːmɪn] N armiño m.

Ernest ['ɜːnɪst] NM Ernesto.

ERNIE ['ɜːnɪ] N (Brit) ABBR of **Electronic Random Number Indicator Equipment** computadora que elige al azar los números ganadores de los bonos del Estado.

erode [ɪ'rəʊd] VT (Geol) causar erosión en, erosionar; metal corroer, desgastar; (fig) erosionar, mermar, perjudicar.

erogenous [ɪ'rɒdʒənəs] ADJ erógeno; ~ **zone** zona f erógena.

Eros ['ɪərɒs] NM Eros.

erosion [ɪ'rəʊʒən] N (Geol) erosión f; (of metal) desgaste m.

erosive [ɪ'rəʊzɪv] ADJ erosivo, erosionante.

erotic [ɪ'rɒtɪk] ADJ erótico; erotómano.

erotica [ɪ'rɒtɪkə] NPL literatura f erótica.

eroticism [ɪ'rɒtɪsɪzəm] N erotismo m; erotomanía f.

eroticize [ɪ'rɒtɪsaɪz] VT erotizar.

erotomania [ɪ,rɒtəʊ'meɪnɪə] N erotomanía f.

err [ɜːʳ] VI errar, equivocarse; (sin) pecar; **to ~ is human** de los hombres es errar; **to ~ on the side of** pecar de, pecar por exceso de.

errand ['erənd] N recado m, mandado m; misión f; ~ **of mercy** misión f de caridad; **what ~ brings you here?** ¿qué te trae por aquí?; **to run an ~** llevar un recado, hacer un mandado.

errand-boy ['erəndbɔɪ] N recadero m, mandadero m.

errant ['erənt] ADJ errante; knight andante.

errata [e'rɑːtə] NPL of **erratum**.

erratic [ɪ'rætɪk] ADJ (uncertain) irregular, poco constante; conduct excéntrico; person voluble; record, results etc desigual, poco uniforme; (Geol, Med) errático.

erratically [ɪ'rætɪkəlɪ] ADV de modo irregular (etc).

erratum [e'rɑːtəm] N, PL **errata** [e'rɑːtə] errata f.

erroneous [ɪ'rəʊnɪəs] ADJ erróneo.

erroneously [ɪ'rəʊnɪəslɪ] ADV equivocadamente.

▼ **error** ['erəʳ] N error m, equivocación f; ~ **message** mensaje m de error; **by ~** por equivocación; **~s and omissions excepted** salvo error u omisión; **by some human ~** por algún fallo humano; **to be in ~** estar equivocado; **to see the ~ of one's ways** reconocer las faltas en que uno ha incurrido.

ersatz ['eəzæts] **1** ADJ sucedáneo, sustituto.
   2 N sucedáneo m, sustituto m.

erstwhile ['ɜːstwaɪl] ADJ (liter) antiguo.

erudite ['erʊdaɪt] ADJ erudito.

eruditely ['erʊdaɪtlɪ] ADV eruditamente.

erudition [ˌerʊ'dɪʃən] N erudición f.

erupt [ɪ'rʌpt] VI (volcano) estar en erupción; (begin to ~) entrar en erupción; (Med) hacer erupción; (anger, war etc) estallar; **to ~ into a room** irrumpir en un cuarto.

eruption [ɪ'rʌpʃən] N (Geol, Med) erupción f; (fig) explosión f.

erysipelas [ˌerɪ'sɪpɪləs] N erisipela f.

erythrocyte [ɪ'rɪθrəʊ,saɪt] N eritrocito m.

ESA N ABBR of **European Space Agency** Agencia f Europea del Espacio, AEE f.

Esau ['iːsɔː] NM Esaú.

escalate ['eskəleɪt] **1** VT extender, intensificar, escalar.
   2 VI extenderse, intensificarse, escalarse.

escalation [ˌeskə'leɪʃən] N extensión f, intensificación f, escalamiento m, escalada f; ~ **clause** cláusula f de precio escalonado.

escalator ['eskəleɪtəʳ] **1** N escalera f mecánica.
   2 ATTR: ~ **clause** (Fin) cláusula f de precio escalonado.

escalope [eskə'lɒp] N escalope m.

escapade [ˌeskə'peɪd] N aventura f, travesura f.

escape [ɪs'keɪp] N escape m; fuga f, huida f, evasión f; (leak) fuga f; (from duties etc) escapatoria f; **it was a lucky ~ for him** tuvo suerte al poderse escapar; **to have a narrow ~** escapar por los pelos; **to make one's ~** escapar; **to make good one's ~** escapar y desaparecer.
   2 ATTR: ~ **chute** rampa f de emergencia; ~ **clause** cláusula f de excepción; ~ **hatch** escotilla f de escape (or de salvamento); ~ **key** (Comput) tecla f de escape; ~ **mechanism** mecanismo m de escape; ~ **pipe** tubo m de escape; ~ **route** ruta f de escape; ~ **valve** válvula f de escape; ~ **velocity** (Space) velocidad f de escape.
   3 VT (avoid) evitar, eludir; consequences, death escapar a; vigilance burlar; **the meaning ~s me** se me escapa el significado; **the fact had ~d me for the moment** por el momento el hecho se me escapó; **a cry ~d him** no pudo contener un grito; V notice.
   4 VI escapar(se); evadirse, huir; (leak) fugarse; **to ~ from** person escaparse a, prison escaparse de, clutches librarse de; **to ~ to France** huir a Francia, refugiarse en Francia; **to ~ with a fright** escapar llevándose un susto; **he just ~d being run over** por poco murió atropellado.

escaped [ɪs'keɪpt] ADJ prisoner fugado.

escapee [ɪskeɪ'piː] N (from prison) fugado m, -a f.

escapement [ɪs'keɪpmənt] N (of watch) escape m.

escapism [ɪs'keɪpɪzəm] N escapismo m, evasión f, evasionismo m.

escapist [ɪs'keɪpɪst] **1** ADJ escapista, evasionista; ~ **literature** literatura f de evasión.
   2 N escapista mf, evasionista mf.

escapologist [ˌeskəʳ'pɒlədʒɪst] N rey m de la evasión, evasionista mf.

escarpment [ɪs'kɑːpmənt] N escarpa f.

eschatological [ˌeskətə'lɒdʒɪkəl] ADJ (Rel) escatológico.

eschatology [ˌeskə'tɒlədʒɪ] N (Rel) escatología f.

eschew [ɪs'tʃuː] VT evitar, renunciar a, abstenerse de.

escort **1** ['eskɔːt] N **(a)** (entourage) acompañamiento m; (lady's) acompañante m; (girl supplied by agency) azafata f, señorita f de compañía.
   (b) (Mil) escolta f; (Naut) convoy m, buque m de escolta.
   2 ['eskɔːt] ATTR: ~ **agency** agencia f de azafatas; ~ **vessel** buque m (de) escolta.
   3 [ɪs'kɔːt] VT acompañar; (Mil) escoltar; (Naut) convoyar, escoltar; **to ~ sb home** acompañar a uno a su casa.

escrow ['eskrəʊ] N garantía f; depósito m en fideicomiso; **in ~** en depósito; ~ **account** cuenta f de plica.

escudo [es'kuːdəʊ] N escudo m.

escutcheon [ɪs'kʌtʃən] N escudo m de armas, blasón m; (fig) honor m.

ESE ABBR of **east-south-east** estesudeste, ESE.

-ese ['iːz] SUFFIX: eg biotechese lenguaje m de la biotecnología, (pej) jerga f biotecnológica.

ESF N ABBR of **European Social Fund** Fondo m Social Europeo, FSE m.

Eskimo ['eskɪməʊ] **1** ADJ esquimal.
   2 N **(a)** esquimal mf. **(b)** (Ling) esquimal m.

ESL N ABBR of **English as a Second Language** inglés m como segunda lengua; ver también TEFL/EFL, TESL/ESL, ELT, TESOL/ESOL .

ESN ADJ ABBR of **educationally subnormal** de inteligencia inferior a la normal.

ESOL N ABBR of **English for Speakers of Other Languages**; ver también TEFL/EFL, TESL/ESL, ELT, TESOL/ESOL .

esophagus [ɪ'sɒfəgəs] N (US) = **oesophagus**.

esoteric [ˌesəʊ'terɪk] ADJ esotérico.

ESP N ABBR of **extrasensory perception** percepción f extrasensorial.

esp. ABBR of **especially**.

espadrille [ˌespə'drɪl] N alpargata f.

espalier [ɪ'spæljəʳ] N espaldar m.

esparto [e'spɑːtəʊ] N esparto m.

especial [ɪs'peʃəl] ADJ especial, particular.

especially [ɪs'peʃəlɪ] ADV especialmente; sobre todo, ante todo; en particular; **it is ~ awkward** es especialmente difícil; **you ~ ought to know** tú debieras saberlo más que nadie; **why me ~?** ¿por qué yo y no otro?; **~ when it rains** sobre todo cuando llueve.

Esperantist [ˌespə'ræntɪst] N esperantista mf.

Esperanto [ˌespə'ræntəʊ] N esperanto m.

espionage [ˌespɪə'nɑːʒ] N espionaje m.

esplanade [ˌesplə'neɪd] N paseo m; (by sea) paseo m marítimo; (Mil) explanada f.

espousal [ɪ'spaʊzl] N adherencia f (of a); adopción f (of de).

espouse [ɪs'paʊz] VT cause adherirse a; plan adoptar.

espresso [es'presəʊ] ADJ: ~ **bar** café m donde se sirve café exprés; ~ **coffee** café m exprés.

esprit de corps ['espriːdə'kɔːʳ] N espíritu m de cuerpo.

espy [ɪs'paɪ] VT divisar.

Esq. (Brit) ABBR of **esquire** Don, D.

Esquire [ɪs'kwaɪəʳ] N: **Henry Crun ~** (on envelope) Sr D. Henry Crun.

▼ **essay** **1** ['eseɪ] N ensayo m; (Scol) composición f.

2 [e'seɪ] vt probar, ensayar; *task* intentar; **to ~ to** + *infin* intentar + *infin*.

essayist ['eseɪɪst] N ensayista *mf*; tratadista *mf*.

essence ['esəns] N esencia *f*; **the ~ of the matter is** lo esencial es; **in ~ the book is not about religion** fundamentalmente el libro no tiene que ver con la religión; **speed is of the ~** es esencial hacerlo con la mayor prontitud.

▼ **essential** [ɪ'senʃəl] 1 ADJ esencial; indispensable, fundamental, imprescindible; **it is ~ to** + *infin* es imprescindible + *infin*; **it is ~ that ...** es necesario que + *subj*.
2 N elemento *m* necesario, factor *m* imprescindible; **we have all the ~s** tenemos todo lo necesario; **in all ~s** fundamentalmente.

essentially [ɪ'senʃəlɪ] ADV esencialmente, en su esencia.

EST N (a) (*US*) ABBR of **Eastern Standard Time.** (b) ABBR of **electric shock treatment** terapia *f* de electroshock.

est. (a) ABBR of **estimated.** (b) ABBR of **established; ~ 1888** se fundó en 1888.

▼ **establish** [ɪs'tæblɪʃ] 1 vt establecer, fundar, crear; *assembly etc* constituir, crear; *date* determinar; *facts* verificar; *proof* demostrar, probar; *relations* entablar; *precedent* crear; **to ~ that ...** comprobar que ..., constatar que ...; **his father ~ed him in business** su padre compró el negocio para él; **he ~ed her in a flat** la instaló en un piso; **the book ~ed him as a writer** el libro le consagró como escritor.
2 vr: **to ~ o.s.** crearse una reputación, hacerse un negocio sólido; **to ~ itself** establecerse, consolidarse, (*custom*) arraigar.

established [ɪs'tæblɪʃt] ADJ *person, business* de buena reputación, sólido; *custom* arraigado; *fact* conocido, admitido; *church* oficial, del Estado; *staff* fijo, de plantilla.

establishment [ɪs'tæblɪʃmənt] N (a) (*act, body*) establecimiento *m*, fundación *f*; (*business house*) establecimiento *m*, casa *f*.
(b) (*Mil*) fuerzas *fpl*, efectivos *mpl*; (*servants*) casa *f*, servidumbre *f*; (*staff of company etc*) plantel *m*, personal *m*; **to be on the ~** ser de plantilla; **they have a smaller ~ nowadays** ahora mantienen una casa más modesta, tienen menos servicio ahora.
(c) **the E~** (*Brit Pol*) el sistema (*la clase dirigente*).

┌─ *ESTABLISHMENT* ─┐

ⓘ *En el Reino Unido el término* **Establishment** *hace referencia a la clase dirigente, es decir, al Gobierno, los altos cargos de la Administración pública, la Iglesia, las Fuerzas Armadas y a otras personas en puestos de influencia en organizaciones como la* **BBC**. *Por lo general, se piensa que esta clase dirigente apoya el status quo tanto a nivel político como cultural o social.*
En Estados Unidos, el **Establishment** *se asocia sobre todo con Washington, donde se encuentra el gobierno federal, y en concreto con aquellos que estudiaron en universidades del noreste, especialmente* **Yale** *y* **Harvard**.
⇨ *Ver también* BBC , IVY LEAGUE

estate [ɪs'teɪt] N (a) (*land*) finca *f*, hacienda *f*.
(b) (*property, assets*) propiedad *f*; (*real ~*) bienes *mpl* raíces, inmuebles *mpl* (*LAm*).
(c) (*inheritance*) bienes *mpl* relictos; herencia *f*, heredad *f*; testamentaría *f*; **he left a large ~** dejó una inmensa fortuna.
(d) (*Pol*) estado *m*; **third ~** estado *m* llano; **fourth ~** (*hum*) la prensa.

estate agency [ɪs'teɪt,eɪdʒənsɪ] N (*esp Brit*) agencia *f* inmobiliaria.

estate agent [ɪs'teɪt,eɪdʒənt] N (*esp Brit*) corredor *m*, -ora *f* de fincas, agente *m* inmobiliario, agente *f* inmobiliaria.

estate car [ɪs'teɪtkɑːʳ] N (*Brit*) furgoneta *f*, rubia *f*, camioneta *f* (*LAm*).

estate duty [ɪs'teɪt,djuːtɪ] N (*Brit*) impuesto *m* de sucesión, impuesto *m* sobre los bienes heredados.

esteem [ɪs'tiːm] 1 N estima *f*, estimación *f*; consideración *f*; **to hold sb in high ~** estimar en mucho a uno, tener un alto concepto de uno; **to hold sb in low ~** estimar en poco a uno; **to rise in sb's ~** merecer que uno le estime más.
2 vt estimar, apreciar; **I would ~ it a privilege** lo consideraría un privilegio; **my ~ed colleague** mi estimado colega.

ester ['estəʳ] N (*Chem*) éster *m*.

Esther ['estəʳ] NF Ester.

esthete ['iːsθiːt] N (*US*) *etc* = **aesthete** *etc*.

Esthonia [es'təʊnɪə] = **Estonia.**

Esthonian [es'təʊnɪən] = **Estonian.**

estimable ['estɪməbl] ADJ estimable.

estimate 1 ['estɪmɪt] N (*judgement*) estimación *f*, apreciación *f*; (*approximate assessment*) estimación *f*; tasa *f*, cálculo *m*; (*for work etc*) presupuesto *m* previo; **E~s** (*Parl*) presupuesto *m*; **at a rough ~** aproximadamente.
2 ['estɪmeɪt] vt (*judge*) estimar, apreciar; (*assess*) calcular, computar, tasar (*at en*); **to ~ that ...** calcular que ...
3 ['estɪmeɪt] vi: **to ~ for** *building work etc* presupuestar, hacer un presupuesto de.

estimation [,estɪ'meɪʃən] N (a) (*judgement*) opinión *f*; juicio *m*; **in my ~** a mi juicio; **what is your ~ of him?** ¿qué concepto tienes de él?

(b) (*esteem*) estima *f*, aprecio *m*.

estimator ['estɪmeɪtəʳ] N asesor *m*, -ora *f*.

Estonia [e'stəʊnɪə] N Estonia *f*.

Estonian [e'stəʊnɪən] 1 ADJ estonio.
2 N (a) estonio *m*, -a *f*. (b) (*Ling*) estonio *m*.

estrange [ɪs'treɪndʒ] vt enajenar, apartar (*from* de); **his ~d wife** su mujer que vive separada de él; **to become ~d** enemistarse (*from* con).

estrangement [ɪs'treɪndʒmənt] N enajenación *f*; alejamiento *m*, distanciamiento *m*; separación *f*.

estrogen ['iːstrəʊdʒən] N (*US*) = **oestrogen.**

estrus ['iːstrəs] (*US*) = **oestrus.**

estuary ['estjʊərɪ] N estuario *m*, ría *f*.

ET N (a) (*Brit*) ABBR of **Employment Training.** (b) (*US*) ABBR of **Eastern Time.**

ETA N ABBR of **estimated time of arrival.**

et al [et'æl] ABBR of **et alii** y otros.

etc. ABBR of **etcetera** etcétera, etc.

etcetera [ɪt'setrə] 1 *as* ADV etcétera.
2 **~s** NPL extras *mpl*, adornos *mpl*.

etch [etʃ] vt grabar al aguafuerte.

etching ['etʃɪŋ] N aguafuerte *f*; **he invited her in to see his ~s** la invitó a entrar a ver su colección de sellos.

ETD N ABBR of **estimated time of departure.**

eternal [ɪ'tɜːnl] ADJ eterno; sempiterno; de siempre.

eternally [ɪ'tɜːnəlɪ] ADV eternamente; sempiternamente; siempre.

eternity [ɪ'tɜːnɪtɪ] N eternidad *f*; **it seemed like an ~** parecía un siglo, parecía que no iba a acabar (*etc*) nunca.

ethane ['iːθeɪn] N etano *m*.

ethanol ['eθənɒl] N etanol *m*.

ether ['iːθəʳ] N éter *m*.

ethereal [ɪ'θɪərɪəl] ADJ etéreo (*also fig*).

ethic ['eθɪk] N ética *f*; V **work.**

ethical ['eθɪkəl] ADJ ético; (*honourable*) honrado.

ethically ['eθɪklɪ] ADV *behave* éticamente, con ética; *sound, unacceptable* desde el punto de vista ético.

ethics ['eθɪks] N ética *f*; (*honourableness*) moralidad *f*.

Ethiopia [,iːθɪ'əʊpɪə] N Etiopía *f*.

Ethiopian [,iːθɪ'əʊpɪən] 1 ADJ etíope.
2 N etíope *mf*.

ethnic ['eθnɪk] ADJ étnico; **~ cleansing** limpieza *f* étnica; **~ minority** minoría *f* étnica.

ethnically ['eθnɪklɪ] ADV *pure, diverse* étnicamente, desde el punto de vista étnico; **an ~ mixed region** una región con una gran mezcla de razas.

ethnicity [eθ'nɪsɪtɪ] N etnicidad *f*.

ethnocentric [,eθnəʊ'sentrɪk] ADJ etnocéntrico.

ethnocentrism [,eθnəʊ'sentrɪzəm] N etnocentrismo *m*.

ethnographer [eθ'nɒɡrəfəʳ] N etnógrafo *m*, -a *f*.

ethnographic [,eθnəʊ'ɡræfɪk] ADJ etnográfico.

ethnography [eθ'nɒɡrəfɪ] N etnografía *f*.

ethnolinguistics [,eθnəʊlɪŋ'ɡwɪstɪks] N etnolingüística *f*.

ethnological [,eθnəʊ'lɒdʒɪkl] ADJ etnológico.

ethnologist [eθ'nɒlədʒɪst] N etnólogo *m*, -a *f*.

ethnology [eθ'nɒlədʒɪ] N etnología *f*.

ethnomusicology [,eθnəʊmjuːzɪ'kɒlədʒɪ] N etnomusicología *f*.

ethos ['iːθɒs] N genio *m*, carácter *m* (*nacional*), actitud *f* vital.

ethyl ['iːθaɪl] N etilo *m*.

ethylene ['eθɪliːn] N etileno *m*.

etiology [,iːtɪ'ɒlədʒɪ] N etiología *f*.

etiquette ['etɪket] N etiqueta *f*; (*of profession*) honor *m* profesional; **it is not ~ to** + *infin* no es elegante + *infin*, está mal visto + *infin*.

Eton crop ['iːtn'krɒp] N corte *m* a lo garçon.

Etruscan [ɪ'trʌskən] 1 ADJ etrusco.
2 N (a) etrusco *m*, -a *f*. (b) (*Ling*) etrusco *m*.

et seq. ABBR of **et sequentia** y siguientes, y sigs.

ETU N (*Brit*) ABBR of **Electrical Trades Union** sindicato *m* de electricistas.

ETV N (*US*) ABBR of **Educational Television.**

etymological [,etɪmə'lɒdʒɪkəl] ADJ etimológico.

etymologically [,etɪmə'lɒdʒɪkəlɪ] ADV etimológicamente.

etymologist [,etɪ'mɒlədʒɪst] N etimólogo *m*, -a *f*, etimologista *mf*.

etymology [,etɪ'mɒlədʒɪ] N etimología *f*.

etymon ['etɪmɒn] N, PL **etymons** ['etɪmɒnz] or **etyma** ['etɪmə] étimo *m*.

EU N ABBR of **European Union** Unión *f* Europea, UE *f*.

eucalyptus [,juːkə'lɪptəs] N eucalipto *m*.

Eucharist ['juːkərɪst] N Eucaristía *f*.

Eucharistic [juːkə'rɪstɪk] ADJ de la Eucaristía, eucarístico.

Euclid ['juːklɪd] NM Euclides.

Euclidean [juː'klɪdɪən] ADJ euclidiano.

Eugene [juː'ʒeɪn] NM Eugenio.

eugenic [juː'dʒenɪk] ADJ eugenésico.

eugenics [juːˈdʒenɪks] N eugenismo *m*, eugenesia *f*.
eulogistic [ˈjuːlədʒɪstɪk] ADJ elogioso, ensalzador.
eulogize [ˈjuːlədʒaɪz] VT elogiar, encomiar.
eulogy [ˈjuːlədʒɪ] N elogio *m*, encomio *m*.
eunuch [ˈjuːnək] N eunuco *m*.
euphemism [ˈjuːfɪmɪzəm] N eufemismo *m*.
euphemistic [ˌjuːfɪˈmɪstɪk] ADJ eufemístico.
euphonic [juːˈfɒnɪk], **euphonious** [juːˈfəʊnɪəs] ADJ eufónico.
euphonium [juːˈfəʊnɪəm] N bombardino *m*.
euphony [ˈjuːfənɪ] N eufonía *f*.
euphoria [juːˈfɔːrɪə] N euforia *f*.
euphoric [juːˈfɒrɪk] ADJ eufórico.
Euphrates [juːˈfreɪtiːz] N Eufrates *m*.
Eurasia [jʊəˈreɪʃə] N Eurasia *f*.
Eurasian [jʊəˈreɪʃn] ① ADJ eurasiático.
   ② N eurasiático *m*, -a *f*.
Euratom [jʊəˈrætəm] N ABBR *of* **European Atomic Energy Commission** Comisión *f* Europea de Energía Atómica.
eureka [jʊəˈriːkə] INTERJ ¡eureka!
eurhythmics [juːˈrɪðmɪks] N euritmia *f*.
Euripides [jʊˈrɪpɪdiːz] NM Eurípides.
Euro..., **euro...** [ˈjʊərəʊ] PREF euro...
Eurobonds [ˈjʊərəʊbɒndz] NPL eurobonos *mpl*.
Eurocentric [ˈjʊərəʊsentrɪk] ADJ eurocentrista, centrado en Europa.
Eurocentrism [ˈjʊərəʊˌsentrɪzəm] N eurocentrismo *m*.
Eurocheque [ˈjʊərəʊtʃek] ① N eurocheque *m*.
   ② ATTR: **~ card** tarjeta *f* de eurocheque.
Eurocommunism [ˈjʊərəʊˌkɒmjʊnɪzəm] N eurocomunismo *m*.
Eurocommunist [ˈjʊərəʊˌkɒmjʊnɪst] ① ADJ eurocomunista.
   ② N eurocomunista *mf*.
Eurocrat [ˈjʊərəʊkræt] N (*hum*) eurócrata *mf*.
Eurocredit [ˈjʊərəʊˌkredɪt] N Eurocrédito *m*.
Eurocurrency [ˈjʊərəʊˌkʌrənsɪ] N eurodivisa *f*.
Eurodollar [ˈjʊərəʊˌdɒlər] N eurodólar *m*.
Euromarket [ˈjʊərəʊˌmɑːkɪt] N, **Euromart** [ˈjʊərəʊˌmɑːt] N euromercado *m*, Mercado *m* Común.
Euro-MP [ˈjʊərəʊˌemˌpiː] N ABBR *of* **Member of the European Parliament** eurodiputado *m*, -a *f*.
Europe [ˈjʊərəp] N Europa *f*; **to go into ~**, **to join ~** (*Brit Pol*) entrar en Europa.
European [ˌjʊərəˈpiːən] ① ADJ europeo; **~ (Economic) Community** Comunidad *f* (Económica) Europea; **~ Commission** Comisión *f* Europea; **~ Court of Justice** Tribunal *m* de Justicia Europeo; **~ Currency Unit** Unidad *f* de Cuenta Europea, ECU *m*; **~ Monetary System** Sistema *m* Monetario Europeo; **~ Parliament** Parlamento *m* Europeo; **~ plan** (*US*) habitación *f* (de hotel) con servicios (pero sin comidas); **~ Union** Unión *f* Europea.
   ② N europeo *m*, -a *f*.
europeanization [ˌjʊərəˌpɪənaɪˈzeɪʃən] N europeización *f*.
europeanize [ˌjʊərəˈpɪənaɪz] VT europeizar.
Europhile [ˈjʊərəʊfaɪl] N eurófilo *m*, -a *f*.
Europhobe [ˈjʊərəʊfəʊb] N eurófobo *m*, -a *f*.
Euro-sceptic, **Eurosceptic** [ˈjʊərəʊskeptɪk] N euroescéptico *m*, -a *f*.
Euro-size [ˈjʊərəʊˌsaɪz] N: **~ 1** (*Comm*) talla *f* europea 1.
Eurospeak [ˈjʊərəʊspiːk] N (*hum*) jerga *f* burocrática de la CE.
Eurotunnel [ˈjʊərəʊˌtʌnl] N Eurotúnel *m*.
Eurovision [ˈjʊərəʊvɪʒən] N Eurovisión *f*.
Eurydice [jʊˈrɪdɪsiː] NF Eurídice.
Eustachian [juːˈsteɪʃən] ADJ: **~ tube** trompa *f* de Eustaquio.
euthanasia [juːθəˈneɪzɪə] N eutanasia *f*.
evacuate [ɪˈvækjʊeɪt] VT evacuar; *building etc* desocupar.
evacuation [ɪˌvækjʊˈeɪʃən] N evacuación *f*.
evacuee [ɪˌvækjʊˈiː] N evacuado *m*, -a *f*.
evade [ɪˈveɪd] VT evadir, eludir; *grasp* escaparse de; **to ~ taxes** defraudar impuestos; *V* issue.
evaluate [ɪˈvæljʊeɪt] VT evaluar, calcular (el valor de); tasar.
evaluation [ɪˌvæljʊˈeɪʃən] N evaluación *f*, cálculo *m*.
evaluative [ɪˈvæljʊətɪv] ADJ evaluativo.
evanescent [ˌiːvəˈnesnt] ADJ efímero, evanescente, fugaz.
evangelic(al) [ˌiːvænˈdʒelɪk(əl)] ADJ evangélico.
evangelism [ɪˈvændʒəˌlɪzəm] N evangelismo *m*.
evangelist [ɪˈvændʒəlɪst] N evangelista *mf*; evangelizador *m*, -ora *f*, misionero *m*, -a *f*; **St John the E~** San Juan Evangelista.
evangelize [ɪˈvændʒɪlaɪz] VT evangelizar.
evaporate [ɪˈvæpəreɪt] ① VT evaporar; **~d milk** leche *f* evaporada.
   ② VI evaporarse; (*fig*) desvanecerse, esfumarse.
evaporation [ɪˌvæpəˈreɪʃən] N evaporación *f*.
evasion [ɪˈveɪʒən] N evasiva *f*, evasión *f*.
evasive [ɪˈveɪzɪv] ADJ evasivo; **he was very ~** contestó de manera evasiva.
evasively [ɪˈveɪzɪvlɪ] ADV de manera evasiva.
evasiveness [ɪˈveɪzɪvnɪs] N carácter *m* evasivo.

Eve [iːv] NF Eva.
eve¹ [iːv] N víspera *f*; **on the ~ of** la víspera de, (*fig*) en vísperas de.
eve² [iːv] N (*liter: evening*) tarde *f*.
▼ **even** [ˈiːvən] ① ADJ (a) (*level*) llano; (*smooth*) liso, igual, uniforme; (*on same level*) a nivel.
   (b) (*regular*) *speed* uniforme; *temperature etc* uniforme, constante; *treatment* equitativo; *temper* ecuánime, apacible; *tone* imperturbable.
   (c) (*equal*) *score, teams, match etc* igual; **now we're ~** ahora vamos iguales; **the chances are about ~** las posibilidades son más o menos iguales; **to be ~ with** (*at game*) andar igual con, (*fig*) estar en paz con; **to break ~** salir sin ganar ni perder; **to get ~ with** ajustar cuentas con, desquitarse con; **I'll get ~ with you yet!** ¡me las pagarás!; **that makes us ~** (*at game*) eso iguala el tanteo, (*fig*) tal para cual.
   (d) *number* par.
   ② ADV (a) **~ the priest was there** hasta el cura estuvo allí; **pick them all, ~ the little ones** cógelos todos incluso los pequeños; **~ on Sundays** incluso los domingos; **and he ~ sings** e incluso canta.
   (b) (+ COMP *adj or adv*) **~ more curious** aún más curioso, más curioso aún; **~ faster** aún más rápidamente.
   (c) (*phrases*) **~ I** yo también; **~ as you tricked me** del mismo modo que Vd me engañó; **~ as I went in** en el mismo momento en que
▼ yo entraba; **~ if** aunque + *subj*, aun cuando + *subj*; **~ so** aun así; sin embargo; **~ though** aunque + *indic*, aun cuando + *indic*.
   (d) (+ *neg*) **not ~** ni siquiera; **not ~ a look** ni una mirada siquiera; **he didn't ~ kiss me** ni me besó siquiera; **without ~ reading it** sin leerlo siquiera.
   ③ VT *surface* allanar, nivelar.
◆ **even out** VT *inequalities* igualar, allanar; *distribution* hacer uniforme; *thing distributed* repartir equitativamente.
◆ **even up** ① VT (a) = **even out**.
   (b) *score etc* igualar, nivelar.
   ② VI: **to ~ up with sb** ajustar cuentas con uno.
even-handed [ˈiːvənˈhændɪd] ADJ imparcial; equitativo.
even-handedly [ˈiːvənˈhændɪdlɪ] ADV imparcialmente; equitativamente.
evening [ˈiːvnɪŋ] ① N (*early*) tarde *f*, (*at sunset*) atardecer *m*, (*after dark*) noche *f*; **~ was coming on** atardecía, anochecía; **good ~!** ¡buenas tardes!, ¡buenas noches!
   ② ATTR: **~ class** clase *f* nocturna; **~ dress** (*man's*) traje *m* de etiqueta, (*woman's*) traje *m* de noche; **~ fixture** partido *m* nocturno; **~ institute** escuela *f* nocturna; **~ match = ~ fixture**; **~ paper** periódico *m* de la tarde, vespertino *m*; **~ performance** función *f* de noche; **~ prayers** oraciones *fpl* de la tarde; **~ service** (*Rel*) misa *f* vespertina; **~ star** estrella *f* vespertina, lucero *m* de la tarde.
evenly [ˈiːvənlɪ] ADV (*smoothly*) lisamente; (*uniformly*) de modo uniforme; *distribute etc* igualmente, equitativamente; *speak etc* en el mismo tono, apaciblemente; *look etc* sin alterarse.
evenness [ˈiːvənnɪs] N lisura *f*; uniformidad *f*; igualdad *f*; (*of treatment*) imparcialidad *f*; (*of temper*) serenidad *f*, ecuanimidad *f*.
evensong [ˈiːvənsɒŋ] N vísperas *fpl*.
even-stevens [ˌiːvənˈstiːvənz] ADV: **to be ~ with sb** estar en paz con uno; ir parejo con uno; **they're pretty well ~** están más o menos igualados.
event [ɪˈvent] N suceso *m*, acontecimiento *m*, evento *m*; (*in a programme*) número *m*; (*Sport*) prueba *f*; (*ceremony*) acto *m*; **programme of ~s** (*civic*) programa *m* de actos, (*shows*) programa *m* de atracciones; **coming ~s** sucesos *mpl* venideros, (*shows etc*) atracciones *fpl* venideras; **current ~s** actualidades *fpl*; **this is quite an ~!** ¡esto sí es un acontecimiento!; **the ~ will show** ya lo veremos, ello dirá, veremos qué consecuencias tendrá esto; **at all ~s, in any ~** en todo caso; **in either ~** en cualquiera de los dos casos; **in the ~** tal como resultó después; **in the ~ of** en caso de; **in the ~ of his dying** en caso de que muriese; **in the ~ that ...** caso (de) que + *subj*; **to be expecting a happy ~** estar en estado de buena esperanza; **to be wise after the ~** mostrar sabiduría cuando ya no hay remedio.
even-tempered [ˈiːvənˈtempəd] ADJ ecuánime, apacible.
eventer [ɪˈventər] N (*Horse-riding*) *jinete participante en el concurso completo*.
eventful [ɪˈventfʊl] ADJ *life, journey etc* accidentado, azaroso; *match etc* lleno de incidentes, lleno de emoción, memorable.
eventide home [ˈiːvəntaɪdˌhəʊm] N hogar *m* de ancianos.
eventing [ɪˈventɪŋ] N concurso *m* hípico (de tres días).
eventual [ɪˈventʃʊəl] ADJ final, definitivo; consiguiente.
eventuality [ɪˌventʃʊˈælɪtɪ] N eventualidad *f*; **in that ~** en esa eventualidad; **in the ~ of** en la eventualidad de; **to be ready for any ~** estar dispuesto a aguantar cualquier posibilidad.
eventually [ɪˈventʃʊəlɪ] ADV (*at last*) finalmente, al fin y al cabo, al final (*LAm*); (*given time*) con el tiempo, a la larga; en su día.
eventuate [ɪˈventʃʊeɪt] VI: **to ~ in** (*US*) resultar en.
ever [ˈevər] ADV (a) (*always*) siempre; **~ after**, **~ since** desde entonces, (CONJ) después de que; **as ~** como siempre; **as ~, yours ~** (*ending*

letter) recibe un abrazo de tu amigo ...; **for ~** para siempre; **for ~ and ~, for ~ and a day** por siempre jamás.

(b) (+ *neg*: *at no time*) nunca, jamás; **hardly ~** casi nunca; **better than ~** mejor que nunca; **more than ~** más que nunca; **nothing ~ happens** no pasa nunca nada; **all she ~ does is make jam** lo único que hace en la vida es hacer mermelada; **not often if ~** rara vez si nunca.

(c) (*at any time*) **if you ~ go there** si acaso vas allí alguna vez; **did you ~ find it?** ¿lo encontraste por fin?; **did you ~ meet him?** ¿llegó a conocerle?; **did you ~?** ¿se vio jamás tal cosa?; **a nice man, if ~ I saw one** hombre simpático si los hay.

(d) (*emphasizing question*) **what ~ did he want?** ¿qué demonios quería?; **why ~ did you do it?** ¿por qué demonios lo hiciste?

(e) (*intensive*) **he's ~ so nice** es simpatiquísimo; **it's ~ so cold** hace un frío terrible; **we're ~ so grateful** le estamos profundamente agradecidos; **~ so much** muchísimo; **~ so little** muy poco; **~ so many things** tantísimas cosas, la mar de cosas; **as quickly as ~ you can** lo más pronto posible; **before ~ you were born** antes de que nacieras.

(f) (*after superl*) **the best ~** el mejor que se ha visto jamás; **the coldest night ~** la noche más fría que nunca hemos tenido; **as soon as ~ I can** en cuanto pueda.

ever-changing [evə'tʃeɪndʒɪŋ] ADJ siempre variable, infinitamente mudable.

Everest ['evərɪst] N: **(Mount)** ~ monte *m* Everest, Everest *m*.

everglade ['evəgleɪd] N (*US*) *tierra baja pantanosa cubierta de altas hierbas.*

evergreen ['evəgriːn] **1** ADJ **(a)** *trees, shrubs* de hoja perenne; siempreverde; **~ oak** encina *f.* **(b)** (*fig*) *memory* imperecedero; *song etc* de popularidad perenne. **2** N árbol *m* (*etc*) de hoja perenne.

ever-growing ['evə'grəʊɪŋ] ADJ que va en continuo aumento.

everlasting [,evə'lɑːstɪŋ] ADJ eterno, perdurable, perpetuo; (*pej*) interminable.

everlastingly [,evə'lɑːstɪŋlɪ] ADV eternamente; (*pej*) interminablemente.

evermore ['evə'mɔːr] ADV eternamente; **for ~** por (*or* para) siempre jamás.

every ['evrɪ] ADJ cada (*invariable*); (*each and every, any*) todo; **~ man** cada hombre, todo hombre, todos los hombres; **~ man Jack** todo ser viviente; **~ one** cada uno; **~ one of them** todos ellos; **his ~ effort** todos sus esfuerzos; **I gave you ~ assistance** te ayudé en lo que podía; **she had ~ chance** se le dieron todas las posibilidades; **we wish you ~ success** te deseamos todo el éxito posible; **I have ~ reason to think that ...** tengo sólidas razones para pensar que ...; **~ day** cada día; **~ other month** un mes sí y otro no, cada dos meses; **~ other person has a car** de cada dos personas una tiene coche; **~ 5 years** cada 5 años; **~ now and then, ~ now and again** de vez en cuando; **~ so often** cada cierto tiempo; *V* **bit** *etc.*

everybody ['evrɪbɒdɪ] PRON todos, todo el mundo.

everyday ['evrɪdeɪ] ADJ (*occurring daily*) diario, cotidiano, de todos los días; (*usual*) corriente, acostumbrado; (*commonplace*) vulgar; (*routine*) rutinario; **for ~** (*use*) de diario; **in ~ use** de uso corriente; **~ clothes** ropa *f* para todos los días; **it's an ~ event** es un suceso ordinario.

everyone ['evrɪwʌn] PRON = **everybody**.

everyplace ['evrɪpleɪs] ADV (*US*) = **everywhere**.

everything ['evrɪθɪŋ] PRON **(a)** (*as subject etc*) todo; **~ is ready** todo está dispuesto; **~ nice had been sold** se había vendido todo lo deseable; **time is ~** el tiempo lo es todo; **money isn't ~** el dinero no lo es todo en la vida; **I've argued with him and ~, but he won't listen** he razonado y todo eso con él, pero no quiere escuchar.

(b) (*as object*) **he sold ~** lo vendió todo.

everywhere ['evrɪweər] ADV *be* en todas partes, *go* a todas partes, por todas partes; **I looked ~** busqué por todas partes; **~ in Spain** en todas partes de España; **~ you go you'll find the same** en todas partes encontrarás lo mismo.

evict [ɪ'vɪkt] VT desahuciar, desalojar, expulsar.

eviction [ɪ'vɪkʃən] **1** N desahucio *m*, desalojo *m*, expulsión *f.* **2** ATTR: **~ notice** orden *f* de desahucio (desalojo *LAm*).

evidence ['evɪdəns] **1** N **(a)** (*obviousness*) evidencia *f*; **in ~** bien visible, manifiesto.

(b) (*sign*) prueba *f*, indicios *mpl*; (*testimony*) testimonio *m*; (*facts*) hechos *mpl*, datos *mpl*; **there is ~ to show that ...** hay indicios que demuestran que ...; **what ~ is there for this belief?** ¿qué hechos se alegan a favor de tal creencia?

(c) (*Jur*) testimonio *m*, declaración *f*, deposición *f*; **there is no ~ against him** no hay evidencia en contra suya; **to call sb in ~** llamar a uno como testigo; **to give ~** prestar declaración, (*more formally*) deponer, dar testimonio; **to hold sth in ~** citar algo como prueba; **to turn Queen's** (*or* **King's**) **~** (*Brit*), **to turn state's ~** (*US*) delatar a los cómplices.

2 VT (*make evident*) patentizar; (*prove*) probar; *emotion* dar muestras

de; **as is ~d by the fact that ...** según lo demuestra el hecho de que ....

evident ['evɪdənt] ADJ evidente, manifiesto, claro; **it is ~ that ...** es evidente que ..., se ve que ...; **to be ~ in** manifestarse en; **as is all too ~** como queda bien patente; **as is ~ from her novel** como queda bien claro de su novela.

evidently ['evɪdəntlɪ] ADV: **~!** ¡naturalmente!; **it is ~ difficult** por lo visto es difícil; **~ he cannot come** por lo visto no puede venir.

evil ['iːvl] **1** ADJ malo, pernicioso; *person* malo, malvado, perverso; (*unlucky*) aciago; *influence* funesto; *smell* horrible; **~ eye** aojo *m*, mal *m* de ojo; **~ spirit** espíritu *m* maligno; **he had his ~ way with her** se la llevó al huerto, la sedujo.

2 N mal *m*, maldad *f*; **the lesser of two ~s** el menor de dos males; **to do ~** hacer mal; **to speak ~ of** hablar mal de.

evildoer ['iːvldʊːər] N malhechor *m*, -ora *f.*

evilly ['iːvɪlɪ] ADV malvadamente, perversamente; aciagamente; diabólicamente.

evil-minded ['iːvl'maɪndɪd] ADJ malintencionado, mal pensado.

evil-smelling ['iːvl'smelɪŋ] ADJ fétido, maloliente, hediondo.

evil-tempered ['iːvl'tempəd] ADJ de muy mal genio, de muy mal carácter.

evince [ɪ'vɪns] VT dar señales de, mostrar.

eviscerate [ɪ'vɪsəreɪt] VT destripar.

evocation [,evə'keɪʃən] N evocación *f.*

evocative [ɪ'vɒkətɪv] ADJ sugestivo, evocador, sugerente.

evoke [ɪ'vəʊk] VT evocar.

evolution [,iːvə'luːʃən] N evolución *f* (*also Bio*); desarrollo *m.*

evolutionary [,iːvə'luːʃnərɪ] ADJ evolutivo.

evolve [ɪ'vɒlv] **1** VT desarrollar, producir; *gas, heat etc* desprender. **2** VI evolucionar, desarrollarse.

ewe [juː] N oveja *f.*

ewer ['juːər] N aguamanil *m.*

ex [eks] **1** PREP: **~ dividend** sin dividendo; **price ~ factory** precio *m* en fábrica; *V* **~ officio**.

2 N: **my ~*** mi antiguo marido, mi ex mujer, mi ex novio *etc.*

ex- [eks] PREF (*former*) ex, antiguo: **~ambassador in Moscow** ex embajador en Moscú; **~leader of** antiguo jefe de; **~minister** ex ministro; *V* **ex-husband, ex-serviceman** *etc.*

exacerbate [eks'æsəbeɪt] VT exacerbar.

exact [ɪg'zækt] **1** ADJ exacto; **99, to be ~** concretamente 99, en concreto 99.

2 VT exigir (*from a*); *obedience etc* imponer (*from a*).

exacting [ɪg'zæktɪŋ] ADJ exigente; *conditions* severo, arduo.

exaction [ɪg'zækʃən] N exacción *f.*

exactitude [ɪg'zæktɪtjuːd] N exactitud *f.*

▼ **exactly** [ɪg'zæktlɪ] ADV exactamente; (*of time*) en punto; **~!** ¡exacto!; **what did you tell him ~?** ¿qué le dijiste, en concreto?; **he is not ~ an actor** no es un actor que digamos; **and I'm not ~ a dwarf** y yo tampoco soy un enano precisamente.

exactness [ɪg'zæktnɪs] N exactitud *f.*

exaggerate [ɪg'zædʒəreɪt] VT exagerar.

exaggerated [ɪg'zædʒəreɪtɪd] ADJ exagerado.

exaggeratedly [ɪg'zædʒəreɪtɪdlɪ] ADV exageradamente.

exaggeration [ɪg'zædʒəreɪʃən] N exageración *f.*

exalt [ɪg'zɔːlt] VT (*elevate*) exaltar, elevar; (*praise*) ensalzar.

exaltation [,egzɔːl'teɪʃən] N exaltación *f*, elevación *f*; ensalzamiento *m.*

exalted [ɪg'zɔːltɪd] ADJ exaltado, elevado.

exam* [ɪg'zæm] N = **examination**.

examination [ɪg,zæmɪ'neɪʃən] N (*Scol*) examen *m*; (*Jur*) interrogación *f*; (*inquiry*) investigación *f* (*into* de); (*by Customs etc*) registro *m*; (*of account*) revisión *f*; (*Med*) reconocimiento *m*; **our chemistry ~** nuestro examen de química; **the matter is under ~** el asunto está bajo estudio; **to enter** (*or* **go in for, sit**) **an ~** presentarse a un examen; **to take an ~** in examinarse en.

▼ **examine** [ɪg'zæmɪn] VT examinar; inspeccionar, escudriñar; (*Jur*) interrogar; *baggage etc* registrar; (*Med*) examinar, hacer un reconocimiento médico de; **we are examining whether ...** estamos pensando si ...; **we are examining the question** estamos estudiando la cuestión; **I was ~d in maths** me examinaron de matemáticas.

examinee [ɪg,zæmɪ'niː] N examinando *m*, -a *f*; **to be a bad ~** hacer siempre mal los exámenes.

examiner [ɪg'zæmɪnər] N examinador *m*, -ora *f*; inspector *m*, -ora *f.*

▼ **example** [ɪg'zɑːmpl] N ejemplo *m*; (*copy, specimen*) ejemplar *m*; (*Math*) problema *m*; **for ~** por ejemplo; **following the ~ of** siguiendo el ejemplo de; **to make an ~ of sb** castigar a uno de modo ejemplar; **to set an ~** dar ejemplo.

exasperate [ɪg'zɑːspəreɪt] VT exasperar, irritar, sacar de quicio; **to get ~d** irritarse.

exasperating [ɪg'zɑːspəreɪtɪŋ] ADJ irritante, que le saca a uno de quicio; **it's so ~!** es para volverse loco; **you're an ~ person** eres un hombre imposible.

► LANGUAGE IN USE: **exactly** → 11.1 **examine** → 26.1, 26.2 **example** → 26.2

exasperatingly [ɪgˈzɑːspəreɪtɪŋlɪ] ADV: ~ **slow/stupid** tan lento/estúpido que le saca a uno de quicio.

exasperation [ɪg,zɑːspəˈreɪʃən] N exasperación f, irritación f.

ex cathedra [eksəˈθiːdrə] ADJ, ADV ex cátedra.

excavate [ˈekskəveɪt] VT excavar.

excavation [,ekskəˈveɪʃən] N excavación f.

excavator [ˈekskəveɪtəʳ] N (person) excavador m, -ora f; (machine) excavadora f.

exceed [ɪkˈsiːd] VT exceder (by en); number pasar de, exceder de; limit rebasar; speed limit sobrepasar; rights ir más allá de, abusar de; powers, instructions excederse en; hopes, expectations superar; **a fine not ~ing £50** una multa que no pase de 50 libras.

exceedingly [ɪkˈsiːdɪŋlɪ] ADV sumamente, sobremanera.

excel [ɪkˈsel] ① VT aventajar, superar.
② VI sobresalir (at, in en).
③ VR: **to ~ o.s.** (often iro) lucirse, pasarse (LAm).

excellence [ˈeksələns] N excelencia f.

Excellency [ˈeksələnsɪ] N Excelencia f; **His ~** su Excelencia; **yes, Your ~** sí, Excelencia.

▼ **excellent** [ˈeksələnt] ADJ excelente.

excellently [ˈeksələntlɪ] ADV excelentemente, muy bien; **to do sth ~** hacer algo muy bien.

excelsior [ekˈselsɪɔːʳ] N (US) virutas fpl de embalaje.

except [ɪkˈsept] ① VT exceptuar, excluir.
② PREP (also ~ **for**) excepto, con excepción de, salvo; sin contar; menos; dejando aparte; **all ~ me** todos menos yo; **~ (that)** ... salvo que ...

excepting [ɪkˈseptɪŋ] PREP = **except**.

exception [ɪkˈsepʃən] N excepción f; **with the ~ of** a excepción de; **without ~** sin excepción; **to be an ~ to the rule** ser excepción de la regla; **the ~ proves the rule** la excepción confirma la regla; **to make an ~** hacer una excepción; **to take ~ to** desaprobar, (feel offended) ofenderse por, molestarse por.

exceptionable [ɪkˈsepʃənəbl] ADJ (open to objection) conduct objetable, censurable, contestable; proposal impugnable, refutable.

exceptional [ɪkˈsepʃənl] ADJ excepcional.

exceptionally [ɪkˈsepʃənəlɪ] ADV: ~ **good** excepcionalmente bueno; **it happens ~ that** ... ocurre en casos excepcionales que ...

excerpt [ˈeksɜːpt] N extracto m.

excess [ɪkˈses] ① N (a) exceso m; (Comm) excedente m; **in ~ de** sobra; **in ~ of** superior a; **to carry to ~** llevar al exceso; **to drink to ~** beber en exceso.
(b) (fig) exceso m, desmán m, desafuero m.
② ATTR excedente, sobrante; **~ demand** exceso m de demanda; **~ fare** suplemento m; **~ luggage, ~ baggage** exceso m de equipaje; **~ profits tax** impuesto m sobre las ganancias excesivas; **~ supply** exceso m de oferta; **~ weight** exceso m de peso.

excessive [ɪkˈsesɪv] ADJ excesivo; **with ~ courtesy** con exagerada cortesía.

excessively [ɪkˈsesɪvlɪ] ADV excesivamente; exageradamente; **you are ~ kind** es Vd amable en exceso.

exchange [ɪksˈtʃeɪndʒ] ① N (a) (act) cambio m; (of prisoners, publications, stamps etc) canje m; (of ideas, information) intercambio m; **~ of contracts** intercambio m de escrituras; **~ of shots** tiroteo m; **~ of views** cambio m de impresiones; **~ of words** diálogo m; **in ~ for** a cambio de.
(b) **foreign ~** (Fin) divisas fpl.
(c) (building) (of corn, cotton etc) lonja f; (labour ~) bolsa f de trabajo; (stock ~) bolsa f; (Telec) central f telefónica.
② ATTR: **~ control** (Fin) control m de divisas; **~ rate** (Fin) tipo m de cambio; **E~ Rate Mechanism** (Fin) mecanismo m de paridades (or de cambio) del SME; **~ restrictions** (Fin) restricciones fpl monetarias; **~ value** contravalor m; **~ visit** visita f de intercambio.
③ VT cambiar (for por); prisoners, publications, stamps etc canjear (for por, with con); greetings, shots cambiar; courtesies hacerse; blows darse; **we ~d glances** nos miramos el uno al otro, cruzamos una mirada.

exchangeable [ɪksˈtʃeɪndʒəbl] ADJ cambiable; canjeable.

exchequer [ɪksˈtʃekəʳ] N hacienda f, tesoro m, erario m; **the E~** (Brit) la Hacienda f del Fisco; ver también TREASURY .

excisable [ekˈsaɪzəbl] ADJ tasable.

excise ① [ˈeksaɪz] N impuestos mpl interiores; **the E~** (Brit) organismo recaudador de derechos de aduana y de importación.
② [ˈeksaɪz] ATTR: **~ duties** (Brit) impuestos mpl sobre consumos o ventas.
③ [ekˈsaɪz] VT (cut) cortar, quitar; (fig) suprimir, eliminar.

excision [ekˈsɪʒən] N corte m; supresión f; (Med) excisión f.

excitability [ɪkˈsaɪtəˈbɪlɪtɪ] N excitabilidad f; exaltación f, nerviosismo m.

excitable [ɪkˈsaɪtəbl] ADJ excitable; exaltado, nervioso.

excite [ɪkˈsaɪt] VT (move to emotion) emocionar, llenar de emoción, entusiasmar; (stimulate) excitar, estimular; provocar; revolt instigar; interest despertar, suscitar; **to ~ sb to action** provocar a uno a la acción.

excited [ɪkˈsaɪtɪd] ADJ emocionado, entusiasmado, ilusionado; voice etc lleno de emoción; **to be ~** estar muy emocionado, (and upset) estar agitado; **I'm so ~ about the new house** la nueva casa me da mucha ilusión; **to get ~** emocionarse, entusiasmarse (about, over por); (crowd etc) alborotarse; (discussion) acalorarse; (get upset) agitarse; **don't get so ~!** ¡no te emociones tanto!

excitedly [ɪkˈsaɪtɪdlɪ] ADV con emoción, con entusiasmo; **he said ~** dijo entusiasmadísimo, dijo excitadísimo.

excitement [ɪkˈsaɪtmənt] N emoción f, entusiasmo m; excitación f; ilusión f; agitación f; alboroto m; **his arrival caused great ~** su llegada produjo una enorme emoción; **why all the ~?, what's all the ~ about?** ¿a qué se debe tanta conmoción?

exciting [ɪkˈsaɪtɪŋ] ADJ emocionante, apasionante; excitante; **how ~!** ¡qué ilusión!, ¡qué emocionante!; **it's a most ~ film** es una película llena de emoción.

excl. ABBR of **excluding, exclusive (of)** con exclusión de.

exclaim [ɪksˈkleɪm] VI exclamar.

exclamation [,ekskləˈmeɪʃən] N exclamación f; **~ mark, ~ point** (US) signo m de admiración.

exclamatory [eksˈklæmətərɪ] ADJ exclamatorio.

exclude [ɪksˈkluːd] VT excluir; exceptuar; possibility of error etc evitar.

excluding [ɪksˈkluːdɪŋ] as PREP excepto, con exclusión de; sin contar; **everything ~ the piano** todo excepto el piano.

exclusion [ɪksˈkluːʒən] ① N exclusión f; **to the ~ of** con exclusión de.
② ATTR: **total ~ zone** zona f de exclusión total; **~ clause** cláusula f de exclusión.

exclusionary [ɪksˈkluːʒənrɪ] ADJ (frm) exclusivista; **the club had ~ policies** el club practicaba una política exclusivista.

exclusive [ɪksˈkluːsɪv] ① ADJ (a) (owned by one) exclusivo; único; **~ agency** agencia f exclusiva; **~ policy** política f exclusivista; **~ rights** exclusiva f, derechos mpl exclusivos; **~ story** reportaje m exclusivo; **~ to** privativo de; **they are mutually ~** se excluyen mutuamente.
(b) (select) area, club, gathering selecto; offer de privilegio.
② ADV (not including) **from 13 to 20 ~** del 13 al 20 exclusive; **till 9 January ~** hasta el 9 de enero exclusive; **~ of** excepto, con exclusión de; sin contar.
③ N (story) reportaje m exclusivo, exclusiva f, pisotón m.

exclusively [ɪksˈkluːsɪvlɪ] ADV exclusivamente.

exclusiveness [ɪksˈkluːsɪvnɪs] N exclusividad f.

exclusivity [ɪksˈkluːˈsɪvətɪ] N exclusividad f.

excommunicate [,ekskəˈmjuːnɪkeɪt] VT excomulgar.

excommunication [ˈekskə,mjuːnɪˈkeɪʃən] N excomunión f.

ex-con* [,eksˈkɒn] N ex convicto m.

excoriate [ɪksˈkɔːrɪeɪt] VT (frm) person, organization, idea desprestigiar, vilipendiar.

excrement [ˈekskrɪmənt] N excremento m.

excrescence [ɪksˈkresns] N excrecencia f.

excreta [eksˈkriːtə] NPL excremento m.

excrete [eksˈkriːt] VT excretar.

excretion [eksˈkriːʃən] N excreción f.

excretory [eksˈkriːtərɪ] ADJ excretorio.

excruciating [ɪksˈkruːʃɪeɪtɪŋ] ADJ pain agudísimo, atroz; (very bad) horrible, fatal.

excruciatingly [ɪksˈkruːʃɪeɪtɪŋlɪ] ADV atrozmente; (very badly) horriblemente, fatal; **it was ~ funny** era para morirse de risa.

exculpate [ˈekskʌlpeɪt] VT exculpar.

excursion [ɪksˈkɜːʃən] ① N excursión f.
② ATTR: **~ ticket** billete m de excursión; **~ train** tren m de excursión, tren m de recreo.

excursionist [ɪkˈskɜːʃənɪst] N excursionista mf.

excursus [ekˈskɜːsɪz] N excursus m.

excusable [ɪksˈkjuːzəbl] ADJ perdonable, disculpable, excusable.

▼ **excuse** ① [ɪksˈkjuːs] N disculpa f, excusa f; razón f, defensa f, justificación f; (insincere) pretexto m; **there's no ~ for this** esto no admite disculpa; **it's only an ~** es un pretexto nada más; **to make ~s for sb** presentar excusas de uno; **he's only making ~s** está buscando pretextos; **he gives poverty as his ~** alega su pobreza; **what's your ~ this time?** ¿qué razón me das esta vez?

▼② [ɪksˈkjuːz] VT disculpar, perdonar; **to ~ sb sth** perdonar algo a uno; **to ~ sb from doing sth** dispensar a uno de hacer algo, eximir a uno de hacer algo; **that does not ~ your conduct** eso no justifica su conducta; **~ me!** (in passing sb) ¡perdón!, por favor, con (su) permiso; (on interrupting sb) perdone Vd; (on leaving table) ¡con permiso!; **if you will ~ me I must go** con permiso de Vds tengo que marcharme; **I must ask to be ~d this time** esta vez les ruego dispensarme; **may I be ~d for a moment?** ¿puedo salir un momento?
③ [ɪksˈkjuːz] VR: **to ~ o.s. from doing sth** dispensarse de hacer algo; **after 10 minutes he ~d himself** después de 10 minutos pidió permiso y se fue.

ex-directory [,eksdɪˈrektərɪ] ADJ: **the number is ~** el número no figura en la guía (*por razones de seguridad etc*); **they are ~** su número no figura en la guía; **he had to go ~** tuvo que pedir que su número no figurara en la guía.

ex dividend [ˌeksˈdɪvɪdend] ADJ sin dividendo.

execrable [ˈeksɪkrəbl] ADJ execrable, abominable; *manners* detestable.

execrably [ˈeksɪkrəblɪ] ADV execrablemente.

execrate [ˈeksɪkreɪt] VT execrar, abominar (de).

execration [ˌeksɪˈkreɪʃən] N execración *f*, abominación *f*.

executable [ˈeksɪkjuːtəbl] ADJ ejecutable; **~ file** (*Comput*) fichero *m* ejecutable.

executant [ɪgˈzekjʊtənt] N ejecutante *mf*.

▼ **execute** [ˈeksɪkjuːt] VT (**a**) ejecutar (*also Art, Mus, Comput*); *order* cumplir; *scheme* llevar a cabo, realizar; *document* otorgar. (**b**) *man* ejecutar, ajusticiar.

execution [ˌeksɪˈkjuːʃən] N (**a**) ejecución *f*; cumplimiento *m*; realización *f*; otorgamiento *m*; (*of act, crime*) comisión *f*; **in the ~ of his duties** en el desempeño de sus obligaciones. (**b**) (*killing*) ejecución *f*.

executioner [ˌeksɪˈkjuːʃnəʳ] N verdugo *m*.

executive [ɪgˈzekjʊtɪv] **1** ADJ ejecutivo; **~ assistant** ayudante *m* ejecutivo, ayudante *f* ejecutiva; **~ car** coche *m* de ejecutivo; **~ committee** junta *f* directiva; **~ director** (*Brit*) director *m* ejecutivo, directora *f* ejecutiva; **~ jet** reactor *m* ejecutivo; **~ officer** oficial *m* Ejecutivo; **~ power** poder *m* ejecutivo; **~ privilege** (*US Pol*) inmunidad *f* del ejecutivo; **~ producer** (*TV*) productor *m* ejecutivo, productora *f* ejecutiva; **~ vice-president** vicepresidente *m* ejecutivo, vicepresidenta *f* ejecutiva.

2 N (**a**) (*power*) poder *m* ejecutivo, autoridad *f* suprema. (**b**) (*person*) ejecutivo *m*, gerente *mf*, directivo *m*, director *m*, -ora *f*.

┌─ **EXECUTIVE PRIVILEGE** ─┐

ⓘ *Se conoce como **executive privilege** el derecho que tiene el Presidente de Estados Unidos a no revelar cierta información al Congreso o a la judicatura en lo que se refiere a las actividades de su oficina. Suelen alegarse normalmente motivos de seguridad nacional o la necesidad de no desvelar ciertas conversaciones privadas del gobierno, pero no puede pedirse por razones personales. Varios presidentes han pedido durante su mandato que se les concediera este derecho de forma absoluta, pero los tribunales se lo han denegado. Durante el escándalo Watergate, el presidente Richard Nixon intentó acogerse a este derecho para no revelar ciertas grabaciones de conversaciones telefónicas de la Comisión de Investigación del Senado, pero le fue denegado por el Tribunal Supremo.*

executor [ɪgˈzekjʊtəʳ] N albacea *m*, testamentario *m*.

executrix [ɪgˈzekjʊtrɪks] N albacea *f*, ejecutora *f* testamentaria.

exegesis [ˌeksɪˈdʒiːsɪs] N exégesis *f*.

exemplar [ˈɪgzemplɑː] (*frm*) N (**a**) (*example*) ejemplar *m*. (**b**) (*model*) ejemplo *m*.

exemplary [ɪgˈzemplərɪ] ADJ ejemplar.

exemplification [ɪgˌzemplɪfɪˈkeɪʃən] N ejemplificación *f*.

exemplify [ɪgˈzemplɪfaɪ] VT ejemplificar; ilustrar, demostrar; **as exemplified by X** según lo demuestra X.

exempt [ɪgˈzempt] **1** ADJ exento, libre (*from* de); **to be ~ from paying** estar dispensado de pagar.

2 VT exentar, eximir, dispensar (*from* de).

exemption [ɪgˈzempʃən] N exención *f* (*from* de); inmunidad *f* (*from* de).

exercise [ˈeksəsaɪz] **1** N (**a**) ejercicio *m*; **to do (physical) ~s** hacer gimnasia; **to take ~** hacer ejercicio; **in the ~ of my duties** en el ejercicio de mi cargo.

(**b**) **~s** (*US: ceremony*) ceremonias *fpl*.

2 ATTR: **~ bicycle**, **~ bike*** bicicleta *f* de ejercicio, bicicleta *f* estática; **~ book** cuaderno *m*.

3 VT (**a**) (*use*) *authority, influence, option, power* ejercer; *patience, restraint* usar de, emplear; *right* valerse de; **to ~ care** tomar cuidado de, proceder con cautela; tomar precaución.

(**b**) *mind* preocupar; **I am much ~d about it** esto me tiene preocupadísimo.

(**c**) *horse, team* entrenar; *dog* llevar de paseo; *muscle* ejercitar, hacer ejercicios con.

4 VI ejercitarse, hacer ejercicios.

exercycle [ˈeksəsaɪkl] = **exercise bike**.

exert [ɪgˈzɜːt] **1** VT ejercer, emplear.

2 VR: **to ~ o.s.** esforzarse, afanarse (*to do* por hacer); (*overdo things*) trabajar demasiado; **he doesn't ~ himself at all** no hace el más mínimo esfuerzo.

exertion [ɪgˈzɜːʃən] N esfuerzo *m*; (*overdoing things*) esfuerzo *m* excesivo, trabajo *m* excesivo.

exeunt [ˈeksɪʌnt] VI (*Theat*) salen, vánse.

exfoliant [eksˈfəʊlɪənt] N exfoliante *m*.

exfoliate [eksˈfəʊlɪeɪt] **1** VT exfoliar.

2 VI exfoliarse.

exfoliation [eksˌfəʊlɪˈeɪʃən] N exfoliación *f*.

ex gratia [ˌeksˈgreɪʃə] ADJ *payment* ex-gratia, a título gracioso.

exhalation [ˌekshəˈleɪʃən] N exhalación *f*.

exhale [eksˈheɪl] **1** VT *air* espirar, exhalar; *fumes* despedir.

2 VI espirar.

exhaust [ɪgˈzɔːst] **1** N (*fumes*) gases *mpl* de escape; (*Aut etc*) escape *m*; (*Aut: also* **~ pipe**) tubo *m* de escape.

2 ATTR de escape.

3 VT (*all senses*) agotar; **to be ~ed** estar agotado.

exhaustible [ɪgˈzɔːstəbl] ADJ *resource* que se puede agotar, limitado.

exhausting [ɪgˈzɔːstɪŋ] ADJ agotador.

exhaustion [ɪgˈzɔːstʃən] N agotamiento *m*; (*nervous*) postración *f* nerviosa.

exhaustive [ɪgˈzɔːstɪv] ADJ exhaustivo.

exhaustively [ɪgˈzɔːstɪvlɪ] ADV de modo exhaustivo.

exhaustiveness [ɪgˈzɔːstɪvnɪs] N exhaustividad *f*.

exhibit [ɪgˈzɪbɪt] **1** N objeto *m* expuesto; pieza *f* de museo; (*painting etc*) obra *f* expuesta; (*Jur*) documento *m*; **to be on ~** estar expuesto.

2 VT *signs etc* mostrar, manifestar; *emotion* acusar; *exhibit* exponer, presentar al público; *film* presentar.

3 VI (*painter etc*) exponer, hacer una exposición.

exhibition [ˌeksɪˈbɪʃən] **1** N demostración *f*, manifestación *f*; (*by painter, sport etc*) exposición *f*; (*Brit Univ*) beca *f*; **an ~ of bad temper** una demostración de mal genio; **to be on ~** estar expuesto; **to make an ~ of o.s.** ponerse en ridículo.

2 ATTR: **~ game**, **~ match** partido *m* de exhibición.

exhibitionism [ˌeksɪˈbɪʃənɪzəm] N exhibicionismo *m*.

exhibitionist [ˌeksɪˈbɪʃənɪst] **1** ADJ exhibicionista.

2 N exhibicionista *mf*.

exhibitor [ɪgˈzɪbɪtəʳ] N expositor *m*, -ora *f*.

exhilarate [ɪgˈzɪləreɪt] VT levantar el ánimo de, estimular, vigorizar; arrebatar; **to feel ~d** sentirse muy estimulado, estar alegre.

exhilarating [ɪgˈzɪləreɪtɪŋ] ADJ tónico, vigorizador, estimulador.

exhilaration [ɪgˌzɪləˈreɪʃən] N (*effect*) efecto *m* tónico, efecto *m* vigorizador; (*mood*) euforia *f*, júbilo *m*, alegría *f*; **the ~ of speed** lo emocionante de la velocidad.

exhort [ɪgˈzɔːt] VT exhortar (*to do* a hacer).

exhortation [ˌegzɔːˈteɪʃən] N exhortación *f*.

exhumation [ˌekshjuːˈmeɪʃən] N exhumación *f*.

exhume [eksˈhjuːm] VT exhumar, desenterrar.

ex-husband [ˌeksˈhʌzbənd] N ex marido *m*.

exigence [ˈeksɪdʒəns] N, **exigency** [ɪgˈzɪdʒənsɪ] N (*need*) exigencia *f*, necesidad *f*; (*emergency*) caso *m* de urgencia.

exigent [ˈeksɪdʒənt] ADJ exigente; urgente.

exiguous [egˈzɪgjʊəs] ADJ exiguo.

exile [ˈeksaɪl] **1** N (**a**) (*state*) destierro *m*, exilio *m*; **government in ~** gobierno *m* en el exilio. (**b**) (*person*) exilado *m*, -a *f*, exiliado *m*, -a *f*, desterrado *m*, -a *f*.

2 VT desterrar, poner en el exilio, exilar, exiliar.

exiled [ˈeksaɪld] ADJ exiliado.

exist [ɪgˈzɪst] VI existir; vivir.

existence [ɪgˈzɪstəns] N existencia *f*; vida *f*; **to be in ~** existir; **to come into ~** formarse, nacer, fundarse, empezar a tener existencia.

existent [ɪgˈzɪstənt] ADJ existente, actual.

existential [ˌegzɪsˈtenʃəl] ADJ existencial.

existentialism [ˌegzɪsˈtenʃəlɪzəm] N existencialismo *m*.

existentialist [ˌegzɪsˈtenʃəlɪst] **1** ADJ existencialista.

2 N existencialista *mf*.

existing [ɪgˈzɪstɪŋ] ADJ existente, actual.

exit [ˈeksɪt] **1** N salida *f*; (*Theat*) mutis *m*; **to make one's ~** salir, marcharse.

2 ATTR: **~ permit** permiso *m* de salida; **~ poll** encuesta *f* de votantes al salir del centro electoral; **~ ramp** (*US*) vía *f* de acceso; **~ visa** visado *m* de salida.

3 VT (*Comput*) salir de; **if we have to ~ the plane** (*US*) si tenemos que abandonar (*or* salir de) el avión.

4 VI (*Theat*) hacer mutis; (*Comput*) salir (del sistema); **~ Hamlet** váse Hamlet.

ex nihilo [ˌeksˈnɪhɪləʊ] ADV ex nihilo.

exodus [ˈeksədəs] N éxodo *m*; **there was a general ~** salieron todos.

ex officio [ˌeksəˈfɪʃɪəʊ] **1** ADV *act* ex officio, oficialmente.

2 ADJ *member* nato, ex officio.

exonerate [ɪgˈzɒnəreɪt] VT exculpar, disculpar (*from* de).

exoneration [ɪgˌzɒnəˈreɪʃən] N exculpación *f*.

exorbitance [ɪgˈzɔːbɪtəns] N exorbitancia *f*.

exorbitant [ɪgˈzɔːbɪtənt] ADJ excesivo, exorbitante.

exorbitantly [ɪgˈzɔːbɪtəntlɪ] ADV excesivamente.

exorcise [ˈeksɔːsaɪz] VT exorcizar, conjurar.

exorcism [ˈeksɔːsɪzəm] N exorcismo *m*.

exorcist [ˈeksɔːsɪst] N exorcista *mf*.

exotic [ɪgˈzɒtɪk] **1** ADJ exótico.

2 N planta *f* exótica.

exotica [ɪgˈzɒtɪkə] NPL objetos *mpl* exóticos.
exotically [ɪgˈzɒtɪklɪ] ADV *named, dressed, designed* exóticamente, de forma exótica; **an ~ beautiful meal** una comida muy rica y muy exótica.
exoticism [ɪgˈzɒtɪsɪzəm] N exotismo *m*.
exp. ABBR *of* **expenses; expired; export; express.**
expand [ɪksˈpænd] 1 VT extender; ensanchar; dilatar; *number* aumentar; *chest* expandir; *market, operations etc* expandir, expansionar; *wings* abrir, desplegar; *(Math)* desarrollar.
2 VI extenderse; ensancharse; dilatarse; *(number)* aumentarse; *(market etc)* expandirse; *(person)* ponerse más expansivo.
♦**expand (up)on** VT *theme* tratar más extensamente, explayarse en el análisis de.
expanded [ɪksˈpændɪd] ADJ *(Metal, Tech)* dilatado; **~ polystyrene** poliestireno *m* dilatado.
expander [ɪksˈpændər] N ejercitador *m* pectoral; = **chest expander.**
expanding [ɪksˈpændɪŋ] ADJ *metal etc* dilatable; *bracelet* expandible; *market, industry, profession* en expansión; **the ~ universe** el universo en expansión; **~ file** carpeta *f* de acordeón; **a job with ~ opportunities** un empleo con perspectivas de futuro; **a rapidly ~ industry** una industria en rápida expansión.
expanse [ɪksˈpæns] N extensión *f*; *(of wings)* envergadura *f*.
expansion [ɪksˈpænʃən] N extensión *f*; dilatación *f*; *(of town etc)* ensanche *m*; *(of economy, trade etc)* expansión *f*; *(of number)* aumento *m*; *(Math etc)* desarrollo *m*; **~ board** placa *f* de expansión; **~ bottle** (*or* **tank**) *(Aut)* depósito *m* del agua; **~ bus** bus *m* de expansión; **~ card** tarjeta *f* de expansión; **~ slot** ranura *f* para tarjetas de expansión.
expansionary [ɪksˈpænʃənəry] ADJ expansionaria, de expansión.
expansionism [ɪksˈpænʃənɪzəm] N expansionismo *m*.
expansionist [ɪksˈpænʃənɪst] ADJ expansionista.
expansive [ɪksˈpænsɪv] ADJ expansivo *(also fig)*.
expansively [ɪksˈpænsɪvlɪ] ADV *(in detail)* *relate* extensamente, en extensión, ampliamente; *(warmly)* *welcome, say* cálidamente; **to gesture ~** hacer ademanes extravagantes.
expansiveness [ɪkˈspænsɪvnɪs] N expansividad *f*.
expat* = **expatriate.**
expatiate [eksˈpeɪʃɪeɪt] VI: **to ~ on** extenderse en un análisis de, extenderse en alabanzas *(etc)* de.
expatriate [eksˈpætrɪeɪt] 1 ADJ expatriado.
2 N expatriado *m*, -a *f*.
3 VT desterrar.
4 VR: **to ~ o.s.** expatriarse.
expect [ɪksˈpekt] 1 VT **(a)** *(with n)* *storm, defeat, baby etc* esperar; *fun, good time* prometerse; contar con; **it's not what I ~ed** no es lo que yo esperaba; **I ~ed as much, just what I ~ed** ya me lo figuraba; **difficulties are only to be ~ed** es natural que haya dificultades; **as might have been ~ed, as one might ~, as was to be ~ed** como era de esperar, como podía esperarse; **we ~ your help** contamos con su ayuda; **I ~ed nothing less of you** no esperaba menos de ti; **it was not so tough as I ~ed (it to be)** era menos severo de lo que yo esperaba; **when least ~ed** el día menos pensado, a lo mejor; **we ~ you tomorrow** le esperamos mañana; **he is ~ed in Madrid** le esperan en Madrid; **is he ~ing you?** ¿tiene Vd cita con él?, ¿está Vd citado?; **don't ~ me till you see me** no contéis conmigo hasta verme llegar; **you know what to ~** ya sabes a qué atenerte.
(b) *(with verb)* **I ~ to see him** espero verle; **we ~ he will come** contamos con que venga; **I ~ you to be punctual** cuento con que seas puntual; **so you ~ me to pay?** ¿así que esperas que pague yo?; **what do you ~ me to do about it?** ¿qué pretendes que haga yo?; **how do you ~ me to go out like this?** ¿cómo pretendes que salga así?; **she can't be ~ed to know that** no está obligada a saber eso; **it is ~ed that ...** se espera que + *subj*; se prevé que + *indic*; **it is hardly to be ~ed that ...** apenas cabe esperar que + *subj*.
(c) *(think, suppose)* imaginarse; suponer; figurarse; **I ~ so** supongo que sí; **I ~ he's there by now** me imagino que ya habrá llegado.
2 VI: **to be ~ing** estar encinta, estar en estado (interesante).
expectancy [ɪksˈpektənsɪ] N *(state)* expectación *f*; *(hope, chance)* expectativa *f* *(of* de); *(life ~)* esperanza *f* de vida, vida *f* media, índice *m* vital.
expectant [ɪksˈpektənt] ADJ expectante; *(hopeful)* ilusionado; **~ mother** mujer *f* encinta, futura madre *f*.
expectantly [ɪksˈpektəntlɪ] ADV con expectación; **to wait ~** esperar a ver qué sale.
expectation [ˌekspekˈteɪʃən] N **(a)** *(state)* expectación *f*; **in ~ of** en expectativa de, esperando.
(b) *(hope)* esperanza *f*, expectativa *f*; **~s** *(in will)* esperanzas *fpl* de heredar; **~ of life** esperanza *f* de vida, vida *f* media, índice *m* vital; **our ~ is that ...** esperamos que ...; **contrary to ~s** en contra de lo que se esperaba; **it is beyond our ~s** es mejor de lo que esperábamos; **to come up to one's ~s** resultar tan bueno como se esperaba; **to exceed one's ~s** sobrepasar lo que se esperaba; **to fall**

below one's ~s no llegar a lo que se esperaba.
expectorant [eksˈpektərənt] ADJ, N expectorante *m*.
expectorate [eksˈpektəreɪt] VT expectorar.
expedience [ɪksˈpiːdɪəns] N, **expediency** [ɪksˈpiːdɪənsɪ] N conveniencia *f*, oportunidad *f*.
expedient [ɪksˈpiːdɪənt] 1 ADJ conveniente, oportuno.
2 N expediente *m*, recurso *m*.
expedite [ˈekspɪdaɪt] VT *(speed up)* acelerar; *business* despachar (con prontitud); *progress* facilitar.
expedition [ˌekspɪˈdɪʃən] N expedición *f*.
expeditionary [ˌekspɪˈdɪʃənrɪ] ADJ expedicionario; **~ force** fuerza *f* expedicionaria.
expeditious [ˌekspɪˈdɪʃəs] ADJ rápido, pronto.
expeditiously [ˌekspɪˈdɪʃəslɪ] ADV con toda prontitud.
expel [ɪksˈpel] VT arrojar, expeler; *person* expulsar.
expend [ɪksˈpend] VT *money* expender, gastar; *ammunition* usar; *resources* consumir, agotar; *time* pasar; *effort* dedicar *(on* a); *care* poner *(on* en).
expendability [ɪks,pendəˈbɪlətɪ] N prescindibilidad *f*.
expendable [ɪksˈpendəbl] 1 ADJ que se puede sacrificar, que no es insustituible; reemplazable, sustituible.
2 **~s** NPL géneros *mpl* (or elementos *mpl etc*) reemplazables.
expenditure [ɪksˈpendɪtʃər] N *(of money etc)* gasto *m*, desembolso *m*; *(of effort, energy)* despliegue *m*; **after a great ~ of time on it** después de dedicarle mucho tiempo.
expense [ɪksˈpens] 1 N gasto *m*, gastos *mpl*; costa *f*; **~s** gastos *mpl*; **at great ~** gastándose muchísimo dinero; **at my ~** a mi costa, corriendo yo con los gastos; **at the ~ of** *(fig)* a costa de, a expensas de; **regardless of ~** sin parar en gastos, sin escatimar gastos; **with all ~s paid** con todos los gastos pagados; **to be a great ~ to sb** costar a uno mucho dinero; **to go to ~** meterse en gastos *(over* por); **to pay sb's ~s** pagar los gastos a uno; **to put sb to ~** hacer que uno gaste dinero; *V* **business** *etc.*
2 ATTR: **~ account** cuenta *f* de gastos (de representación).
expensive [ɪksˈpensɪv] ADJ caro, costoso; *shop etc* carero.
expensively [ɪksˈpensɪvlɪ] ADV costosamente; *(sparing no expense)* sin pararse en gastos.
expensiveness [ɪksˈpensɪvnɪs] N carestía *f*.
▼**experience** [ɪksˈpɪərɪəns] 1 N experiencia *f*; **to know from bitter ~ that ...** saber por amargas experiencias personales que ...; **to learn by ~, to profit from ~** aprender por la experiencia.
2 VT experimentar; *fate, loss* sufrir; *difficulty* tener, tropezar con.
experienced [ɪksˈpɪərɪənst] ADJ experimentado, perito, experto *(in* en).
experiential [ɪks,pɪərɪˈenʃəl] ADJ *(Philos)* experiencial.
experiment [ɪksˈperɪmənt] 1 N experimento *m*; experiencia *f*; prueba *f*, ensayo *m*; **as an ~, by way of ~** como experimento.
2 VI experimentar, hacer experimentos *(on* en, *with* con).
experimental [eks,perɪˈmentl] ADJ experimental; **the process is still at the ~ stage** el proceso está todavía en prueba.
experimentally [eks,perɪˈmentəlɪ] ADV experimentalmente, como experimento.
experimentation [eks,perɪmenˈteɪʃən] N experimentación *f*.
experimenter [ɪksˈperɪmentər] N investigador *m*, -ora *f*.
expert [ˈekspɜːt] 1 ADJ experto, perito *(at, in* en); *touch etc* hábil; *witness, evidence* pericial; **~ system** sistema *m* experto; **~ valuation** tasación *f* pericial.
2 N experto *m*, -a *f (at, in* en); técnico *m*; especialista *mf*.
expertise [ˌeksˈpɜːtiːz] N pericia *f*; conocimientos *mpl* técnicos; *(of touch etc)* habilidad *f*.
expertly [ˈekspɜːtlɪ] ADV expertamente.
expertness [ˈekspɜːtnɪs] N pericia *f*; habilidad *f*.
expiate [ˈekspɪeɪt] VT expiar.
expiation [ˌekspɪˈeɪʃən] N expiación *f*.
expiatory [ˈekspɪətərɪ] ADJ expiatorio.
expiration [ˌekspaɪəˈreɪʃən] N **(a)** *(ending)* terminación *f*; expiración *f*; *(Comm)* vencimiento *m*, caducidad *f*. **(b)** *(of breath)* espiración *f*.
expire [ɪksˈpaɪər] VI **(a)** *(end)* terminar; *(die)* expirar; *(reach its term)* expirar, cumplirse, *(Comm)* vencer, *(ticket)* caducar, vencerse. **(b)** *(breathe out)* espirar.
expiry [ɪksˈpaɪərɪ] N: **~ date** fecha *f* de caducidad; = **expiration.**
▼**explain** [ɪksˈpleɪn] 1 VT explicar; *plan* exponer; *mystery* aclarar; *conduct* explicar; justificar; **that ~s it** con eso todo queda aclarado.
2 VR: **to ~ o.s.** *(clearly)* hablar más claro, explicarse con más detalles; *(morally)* justificar su conducta; **kindly ~ yourself!** ¡explíquese Vd!
♦**explain away** VT: **to ~ sth away** justificar algo hábilmente, dar razones convincentes de algo, *difficulty* salvar hábilmente; **just you ~ that away!** ¡a ver si logras justificar eso!
explainable [ɪksˈpleɪnəbl] ADJ explicable.
explanation [ˌekspləˈneɪʃən] N explicación *f*; aclaración *f*; **what is the ~ of this?** ¿cómo se explica esto?; **there must be some ~** ha de

haber alguna razón.

explanatory [ɪks'plænətərɪ] ADJ explicativo; aclaratorio.

expletive [eks'pliːtɪv] [1] N (*Gram*) palabra *f* expletiva; (*oath*) palabrota *f*, taco *m*; '~ **deleted**' 'se suprime palabrota'.
[2] ADJ (*Gram*) expletivo.

explicable [eks'plɪkəbl] ADJ explicable.

explicate ['eksplɪkeɪt] VT (*frm*) *poem, painting etc* comentar.

explicit [ɪks'plɪsɪt] ADJ explícito.

explicitly [ɪks'plɪsɪtlɪ] ADV explícitamente.

explicitness [ɪk'splɪsɪtnɪs] N carácter *m* explícito, lo explícito, claridad *f*.

explode [ɪks'pləʊd] [1] VT volar, hacer saltar, explotar, explosionar; *rumour, myth, belief, theory* desacreditar, refutar.
[2] VI estallar, hacer explosión, explotar, explosionar; (*with anger etc*) reventar (*with* de); **the town ~d in revolt** estalló la rebelión en la ciudad; **when I said that he ~d** cuando dije eso se puso furioso.

exploit [1] ['eksplɔɪt] N hazaña *f*, proeza *f*.
[2] [ɪks'plɔɪt] VT explotar.

exploitable [eks'plɔɪtəbl] ADJ explotable.

exploitation [ˌeksplɔɪ'teɪʃən] N explotación *f*.

exploitative [eks'plɔɪtətɪv] ADJ explotador.

exploiter [eks'plɔɪtəʳ] N explotador *m*, -ora *f*.

exploration [ˌeksplɔː'reɪʃən] N exploración *f*.

exploratory [eks'plɒrətərɪ] ADJ exploratorio, preparatorio, de sondaje.

explore [ɪks'plɔːʳ] VT explorar; (*fig*) examinar, sondar, investigar.

explorer [ɪks'plɔːrəʳ] N explorador *m*, -ora *f*.

explosion [ɪks'pləʊʒən] N explosión *f* (*also fig*).

explosive [ɪks'pləʊzɪv] [1] ADJ explosivo (*also fig*).
[2] N explosivo *m*.
[3] ATTR: ~**s expert** artificiero *m*.

explosiveness [ɪk'spləʊzɪvnɪs] N carácter *m* explosivo.

expo ['ekspəʊ] N ABBR *of* **exposition** expo *f*.

exponent [eks'pəʊnənt] N exponente *mf*, partidario *m*, -a *f* (*of* de), intérprete *mf* (*of* de); (*Gram*) exponente *m*.

exponential [ˌekspəʊ'nenʃəl] ADJ exponencial.

exponentially [ˌekspəʊ'nenʃlɪ] ADV de manera exponencial.

export [1] ['ekspɔːt] N exportación *f*, artículo *m* de exportación.
[2] ['ekspɔːt] ATTR: ~ **agent** agente *mf* de exportación; ~ **credit** crédito *m* a la exportación; ~ **duty** derechos *mpl* de exportación; ~ **earnings** ganancias *fpl* por exportación; ~ **invoice** factura *f* de exportación; ~ **licence**, ~ **license** (*US*) permiso *m* de exportación; ~ **manager** director *m*, -ora *f* de exportación; ~**-orientated** (*Brit*), ~**-oriented** (*esp US*) dedicado a la exportación; ~ **sales** ventas *fpl* de exportación; ~ **subsidy** subsidio *m* de exportación; ~ **trade** comercio *m* de exportación.
[3] [eks'pɔːt] VT exportar.

exportable [eks'pɔːtəbl] ADJ exportable.

exportation [ˌekspɔː'teɪʃən] N exportación *f*.

exporter [eks'pɔːtəʳ] N exportador *m*, -ora *f*.

exporting [ek'spɔːtɪŋ] ADJ exportador; ~ **company** empresa *f* exportadora; ~ **country** país *m* exportador.

expose [ɪks'pəʊz] [1] VT exponer (*also Phot*); *weakness* descubrir; *falsity* demostrar; *ignorance, weakness* revelar, descubrir; *fake, plot, imposter* desenmascarar; **to ~ sb to ridicule** exponer a uno al ridículo.
[2] VR to ~ **o.s. to** *risk, danger* exponerse a.
(b) **to ~ o.s.** (*sexually*) practicar el exhibicionismo.

exposé [ek'spəʊzeɪ] N exposición *f*, revelación *f*.

exposed [ɪks'pəʊzd] ADJ expuesto; *land, house* desprotegido; (*Elec*) *wire* al aire; *pipe, beam* al descubierto; **to be ~** (*thing normally hidden*) estar al descubierto; **to be ~** to estar expuesto a.

exposition [ˌekspə'zɪʃən] N exposición *f*, explicación *f*.

expostulate [ɪks'pɒstjʊleɪt] VI protestar; **to ~ with** reconvenir a, discutir con, tratar de convencer a.

expostulation [ɪksˌpɒstjʊ'leɪʃən] N protesta *f*, reconvención *f*.

exposure [ɪks'pəʊʒəʳ] N exposición *f* (*also Phot*); revelación *f*; desenmascaramiento *m*; (*sexual*) exhibición *f*, acto *m* de exhibicionismo; **a house with a southerly ~** una casa orientada hacia el sur; **to die from ~** morir de frío, morir por estar a la intemperie; **he's getting a lot of ~** se le dedica mucha atención (pública, en la prensa *etc*); **to threaten sb with ~** amenazar con desenmascarar a uno.

exposure-meter [ɪks'pəʊʒəˌmiːtəʳ] N fotómetro *m*.

expound [ɪks'paʊnd] VT exponer, explicar; *text* comentar.

ex-president [ˌeks'prezɪdənt] N ex presidente *m*, -a *f*.

express [ɪks'pres] [1] ADJ (a) (*clear*) expreso, explícito, categórico; ~ **warranty** garantía *f* escrita.
(b) (*Brit*) *letter* urgente; *service etc* rápido; ~ **coach** autobús *m* rápido; ~ **delivery** (*Brit*) entrega *f* urgente; ~ **train** rápido *m*.
[2] N rápido *m*.
[3] ADV: **to send sth ~** enviar algo por carta urgente (*etc*).
[4] VT (a) (*make known*) expresar.
(b) (*squeeze out*) *juice* exprimir.
[5] VR: **to ~ o.s.** expresarse.

expression [ɪks'preʃən] N expresión *f*; **as an ~ of thanks** en señal de agradecimiento; **if you'll pardon the ~** hablando con perdón, perdonen la palabra.

expressionism [eks'preʃənɪzəm] N expresionismo *m*.

expressionist [eks'preʃənɪst] [1] ADJ expresionista.
[2] N expresionista *mf*.

expressionless [ɪks'preʃənlɪs] ADJ sin expresión, inexpresivo.

expressive [ɪks'presɪv] ADJ expresivo.

expressively [ɪks'presɪvlɪ] ADV expresivamente.

expressiveness [ɪks'presɪvnɪs] N expresividad *f*.

expressly [ɪks'preslɪ] ADV expresamente; *deny, prohibit etc* terminantemente.

expresso [ɪk'spresəʊ] = **espresso**.

expressway [ɪks'presweɪ] N (*US*) autopista *f*.

expropriate [eks'prəʊprɪeɪt] VT expropiar.

expropriation [eksˌprəʊprɪ'eɪʃən] N expropiación *f*.

expulsion [ɪks'pʌlʃən] N expulsión *f*.

expunge [ɪks'pʌndʒ] VT borrar, tachar.

expurgate ['ekspɜːgeɪt] VT expurgar.

exquisite [eks'kwɪzɪt] [1] ADJ exquisito, primoroso; *pain etc* intenso.
[2] N (††) petimetre *m*, figurín *m*.

exquisitely [eks'kwɪzɪtlɪ] ADV primorosamente, con primor.

ex-service [ˌeks'sɜːvɪs] ADJ (*Brit: Mil*) retirado del ejército.

ex-serviceman ['eks'sɜːvɪsmən] N, PL **ex-servicemen** militar *m* retirado, ex militar *m*.

ex-servicewoman [ˌeks'sɜːvɪsˌwʊmən] N, PL **ex-servicewomen** militar *f* retirada, ex militar *f*.

ex-smoker ['eks'sməʊkəʳ] N (*US*) persona *f* que ha dejado de fumar.

ext. (*Telec*) ABBR *of* **extension** extensión *f*.

extant [eks'tænt] ADJ existente.

extemporaneous [eksˌtempə'reɪnɪəs] ADJ, **extemporary** [ɪks'tempərərɪ] ADJ extemporáneo.

extemporary [ɪks'tempərərɪ] ADJ improvisado, hecho sin preparación.

extempore [eks'tempərɪ] [1] ADV de improviso, sin preparación.
[2] ADJ improvisado, hecho sin preparación.

extemporize [ɪks'tempəraɪz] VTI improvisar.

▼ **extend** [ɪks'tend] [1] VT (a) extender; *hand* tender, alargar; *building etc* ensanchar, ampliar; *road etc* prolongar; (*increase*) aumentar; *term, stay* prolongar, prorrogar.
▼ (b) *thanks, welcome* dar, ofrecer; *invitation* enviar.
(c) *athlete* pedir el máximo esfuerzo a; **the staff is fully ~ed** el personal trabaja al máximo; el personal rinde todo lo que puede; **that child is not sufficiently ~ed** a ese niño no se le exige bastante esfuerzo.
[2] VI extenderse; prolongarse; **to ~ over** abarcar, incluir; **to ~ to** extenderse a, llegar hasta, (*fig*) abarcar, incluir; **does that ~ to me?** ¿eso me incluye a mí?
[3] VR: **to ~ o.s.** trabajar (*etc*) al máximo, esforzarse.

extendable [ɪk'stendɪbl] ADJ extensible.

extended [ɪk'stendɪd] ADJ extendido; ampliado; **during our ~ stay** durante nuestra estancia prolongada; ~ **area network** red *f* de área extendida; ~ **family** familia *f* extendida; ~ **forecast** (*US*) pronóstico *m* a largo plazo, pronóstico *m* para varios días; **to grant sb ~ credit** conceder a uno un crédito ilimitado; **he has been granted ~ leave** se le ha permitido prolongar su permiso.

extended-play [ɪks'tendɪd,pleɪ] ADJ: ~ **single** maxi-single *m*.

extendible [ɪks'tendəbl] = **extendable**.

extensible [ɪks'tensɪbl] ADJ extensible.

extension [ɪks'tenʃən] [1] N extensión *f*; (*of building etc*) ensanche *m*, ampliación *f*; *anejo m*; (*of road*) prolongación *f*; (*of term, stay*) prolongación *f*, prórroga *f*; (*Comm*) prórroga *f*; (*increase*) aumento *m*; (*Telec*) extensión *f*, supletorio *m* (*LAm*), interno *m* (*SC*); **by ~** por extensión.
[2] ATTR: ~ **cable**, ~ **cord** (*Elec*) prolongación *f* eléctrica; ~ **course(s)** *cursos nocturnos organizados por una universidad*; ~ **ladder** escalera *f* extensible; ~ **lead** (*Elec*) extensión *f* de cable.

extensive [ɪks'tensɪv] ADJ extenso; vasto, ancho, dilatado; *use etc* frecuente, general, común.

extensively [ɪks'tensɪvlɪ] ADV extensamente; **to travel ~** viajar por muchos países; **he travelled ~ in Mexico** viajó por muchas partes de Méjico; **it is used ~** se usa comúnmente.

extent [ɪks'tent] N (*space*) extensión *f*; (*scope*) alcance *m*; **the ~ of the problem** el alcance del problema; **to the ~ of** + *ger* hasta el punto de + *infin*; **to a certain ~**, **to some ~** hasta cierto punto; **to the full ~** en toda su extensión; (*fig*) completamente; **to a great** (*or* **large**) ~ en gran parte, en alto grado; **to a lesser ~** en menor grado; **to such an ~ that** hasta tal punto que; **to that ~** hasta ahí; **to what ~?** ¿hasta qué punto?

extenuate [eks'tenjʊeɪt] VT atenuar, mitigar, disminuir (la gravedad de).

extenuating [eks'tenjʊeɪtɪŋ] ADJ *circumstance* atenuante.

exterior [eks'tɪərɪəʳ] [1] ADJ exterior, externo.

2 N exterior *m*; (*appearance*) aspecto *m*.
exteriorize [eks'tɪərɪəraɪz] VT exteriorizar.
exterminate [eks'tɜ:mɪneɪt] VT exterminar.
extermination [eks,tɜ:mɪ'neɪʃən] N exterminio *m*.
exterminator [eks'tɜ:mɪneɪtəʳ] N (*US*) exterminador *m* de plagas.
extern ['ekstɜ:n] N (*US*) externo *m*, -a *f*.
external [eks'tɜ:nl] **1** ADJ externo, exterior; ~ **account** cuenta *f* con el exterior; ~ **audit** auditoría *f* externa; ~ **trade** comercio *m* exterior; **for** ~ **use** para uso externo.
2 ~**s** NPL exterioridad *f*, aspecto *m* exterior.
externalize [ɪks'tɜ:nəlaɪz] VT *ideas, feelings* exteriorizar, manifestar.
externally [eks'tɜ:nəlɪ] ADV externamente, exteriormente; por fuera.
extinct [ɪks'tɪŋkt] ADJ *volcano* extinto, apagado, extinguido; *animal* extinto, desaparecido.
extinction [ɪks'tɪŋkʃən] N extinción *f*.
extinguish [ɪks'tɪŋgwɪʃ] VT extinguir, apagar; *title etc* suprimir.
extinguisher [ɪks'tɪŋgwɪʃəʳ] N (*for fire*) extintor *m*; (*for candle*) apagador *m*, apagavelas *m*.
extirpate ['ekstɜ:peɪt] VT extirpar.
extirpation [,ekstə'peɪʃən] N extirpación *f*.
extn (*Telec*) ABBR of **extension** extensión *f*.
extol, (*US*) **extoll** [ɪks'tɒl] VT ensalzar, alabar.
extort [ɪks'tɔ:t] VT obtener por fuerza (*from* de), exigir por amenazas (*from* a).
extortion [ɪks'tɔ:ʃən] N exacción *f*; (*by public official*) concusión *f*.
extortionate [ɪks'tɔ:ʃənɪt] ADJ *price etc* excesivo, exorbitante.
extortioner [ɪks'tɔ:ʃənəʳ] N desollador *m*; (*official*) concusionario *m*.
extortionist [ɪks'tɔ:ʃənɪst] N extorsionador *m*, -ora *f*.
extra ['ekstrə] **1** ADJ adicional; de más, de sobra; *charge, pay etc* extraordinario; *part* de repuesto; **we need 2** ~ **chairs** necesitamos 2 sillas más; **we seem to have 2** ~ **men** parece que tenemos 2 hombres de sobra; ~ **charge** recargo *m*; suplemento *m*; ~ **pay** sobresueldo *m*; ~ **time** (*Sport*) prórroga *f*; **postage** ~ gastos de franqueo no incluidos; **postage and packing** ~ gastos de envío no incluidos; **5 tons** ~ **to requirements** un excedente de 5 toneladas; **to take** ~ **care** ir con especial cuidado; **for** ~ **security** para mayor seguridad; **you must make an** ~ **effort** tienes que hacer un esfuerzo excepcional; **service is** ~ el servicio no está incluido; **the wine is** ~ el vino no está incluido (en el precio).
2 ADV (**a**) (*with adj, adv, verb*) especialmente, extraordinariamente; ~ **big** más grande que lo normal; ~ **smart** más elegante que de costumbre; **with** ~ **special care** con especial cuidado; **of** ~ **special quality** de calidad superior; **this is** ~ **difficult** esto es extraordinariamente difícil; **to sing** ~ **loud** cantar extraordinariamente fuerte.
(**b**) (*after verb*) **we shall have to work** ~ tendremos que trabajar más; **to pay** ~ pagar más; pagar un suplemento.
3 N (**a**) (*on bill*) extra *m*, suplemento *m*; (*Theat*) extra *mf*, comparsa *mf*; (*of paper*) edición *f* extraordinaria; (*spare part, US*) repuesto *m*; ~**s** (*Aut: also* **optional** ~**s**) accesorios *mpl*, extras *mpl*.
(**b**) **what shall we do with the** ~? ¿qué hacemos con el exceso?, ¿qué hacemos con lo que sobra?
extra... ['ekstrə] PREF extra...
extract **1** ['ekstrækt] N (*Liter*) cita *f*, trozo *m*; (*Pharm*) extracto *m*; (*of beef etc*) extracto *m*, concentrado *m*; ~**s from 'Don Quijote'** (*as book*) selecciones *fpl* del 'Quijote'.
2 [ɪks'trækt] VT sacar (*from* de); extraer (*also Math*); *confession etc* arrancar, sacar, obtener.
extraction [ɪks'trækʃən] N extracción *f*; obtención *f*.
extractor [ɪks'træktəʳ] N extractor *m*.
2 ATTR: ~ **fan** (*Brit*) extractor *m* de olores.
extracurricular [,ekstrəkə'rɪkjʊləʳ] ADJ extracurricular.
extraditable ['ekstrədaɪtəbl] ADJ sujeto a extradición.
extradite ['ekstrədaɪt] VT extraditar.
extradition [,ekstrə'dɪʃən] N extradición *f*.
extradition warrant [,ekstrə'dɪʃən,wɒrənt] N orden *f* de extradición.
extramarital [,ekstrə'mærɪtəl] ADJ extramarital, fuera del matrimonio.
extramural ['ekstrə'mjʊərəl] ADJ *jurisdiction etc* (de) extramuros; *activities* de carácter privado; (*esp US*) *course* para externos; **an** ~ **chapel** una capilla extramuros; **Department of E~ Studies** (*Brit Univ*) Departamento *m* de cursos para externos.
extraneous [eks'treɪnɪəs] ADJ extraño; ~ **to** ajeno a.
extraordinaire [eks,trɔ:dɪ'neəʳ] ADJ sin igual; **he's a film-maker** ~ es un cineasta como no hay otro igual.
extraordinarily [ɪks'trɔ:dnrɪlɪ] ADV extraordinariamente.
extraordinary [ɪks'trɔ:dnrɪ] ADJ extraordinario; (*exceptional*) excepcional, poco común, insólito; (*odd*) raro; (*incredible*) increíble; **how** ~! ¡qué raro!; ~ **general meeting** junta *f* general extraordinaria; ~ **meeting of shareholders** (*Brit*) junta *f* extraordinaria de accionistas; ~ **reserve** (*Fin*) reserva *f* extraordinaria; **it is** ~ **that** ... es increíble que + *subj*.
extrapolate [ɪks'træpəleɪt] VT extrapolar.

extrapolation [ɪks,træpə'leɪʃən] N extrapolación *f*.
extrasensory ['ekstrə'sensərɪ] ADJ: ~ **perception** percepción *f* extrasensorial.
extraspecial [,ekstrə'speʃəl] ADJ muy especial; **to take** ~ **care over sth** tomar extremadas precauciones en algo.
extraterrestrial [,ekstrətə'restrɪəl] ADJ extraterrestre.
extraterritorial ['ekstrə,terɪ'tɔ:rɪəl] ADJ extraterritorial.
extravagance [ɪks'trævəgəns] N (**a**) prodigalidad *f*; derroche *m*; despilfarro *m*; lujo *m* desmedido. (**b**) exorbitancia *f*; lo excesivo; rareza *f*.
extravagant [ɪks'trævəgənt] ADJ (**a**) (*lavish*) pródigo; (*wasteful*) derrochador, despilfarrador; (*luxurious*) muy lujoso. (**b**) *price* exorbitante; *praise, claim etc* exagerado, excesivo; (*odd*) raro, estrafalario.
extravagantly [ɪks'trævəgəntlɪ] ADV *spend etc* profusamente, con gran despilfarro; (*luxuriously*) muy lujosamente; *praise* excesivamente; *behave* de modo raro.
extravaganza [eks,trævə'gænzə] N obra *f* extravagante y fantástica.
extravehicular [,ekstrəvɪ'hɪkjʊləʳ] ADJ fuera de la nave.
extreme [ɪks'tri:m] **1** ADJ extremo; *care, poverty etc* extremado; *case* excepcional.
2 N extremo *m*, extremidad *f*; ~**s of temperature** temperaturas *fpl* extremas; **in the** ~ en sumo grado; **to go from one** ~ **to the other** pasar de un extremo a otro; **to go to** ~**s** ir muy lejos, tomar medidas extremas.
extremely [ɪks'tri:mlɪ] ADV sumamente, extremadamente; sobremanera; **it is** ~ **difficult** es sumamente difícil, es dificilísimo; **we are** ~ **glad** nos alegramos muchísimo.
extremism [ɪks'tri:mɪzəm] N extremismo *m*.
extremist [ɪks'tri:mɪst] **1** ADJ extremista.
2 N extremista *mf*, ultra *mf*.
extremity [ɪks'tremɪtɪ] N (**a**) (*end*) extremidad *f*, punta *f*. (**b**)(*want*) apuro *m*, necesidad *f*; **in this** ~ en tal apuro; **to be driven to** ~ estar muy apurado. (**c**) **extremities** (*Anat*) extremidades *fpl*; (*measures*) medidas *fpl* extremas.
extricate ['ekstrɪkeɪt] **1** VT (*disentangle*) desenredar, soltar; (*fig*) librar, sacar (*from* de).
2 VR: **to** ~ **o.s. from** (*fig*) lograr sacarse de.
extrinsic [eks'trɪnsɪk] ADJ extrínseco.
extrovert ['ekstrəʊvɜ:rt] **1** ADJ extrovertido, extravertido.
2 N extrovertido *m*, -a *f*, extravertido *m*, -a *f*.
extroverted ['ekstrəvɜ:tɪd] ADJ (*esp US*) = **extrovert 1**.
extrude [eks'tru:d] VT sacar; (*force out*) expulsar; (*Tech*) estirar.
extrusion [eks'tru:ʒən] N extrusión *f*, estirado *m*.
exuberance [ɪg'zu:bərəns] N euforia *f*; exuberancia *f*.
exuberant [ɪg'zu:bərənt] ADJ *person, spirit etc* eufórico; *growth, style etc* exuberante.
exuberantly [ɪg'zu:bərəntlɪ] ADV eufóricamente; exuberantemente.
exude [ɪg'zju:d] **1** VT exudar; rezumar, destilar, sudar.
2 VI rezumarse.
exult [ɪg'zʌlt] VI exultar; **to** ~ **in**, **to** ~ **at** regocijarse por; **to** ~ **over** triunfar sobre; **to** ~ **to find** regocijarse al encontrar.
exultant [ɪg'zʌltənt] ADJ regocijado, jubiloso.
exultantly [ɪg'zʌltəntlɪ] ADV jubilosamente, exultantemente.
exultation [,egzʌl'teɪʃən] N exultación *f*, júbilo *m*.
ex-wife [,eks'waɪf] N ex mujer *f*.
ex-works [,eks'wɜ:ks] ADJ (*needle*) *price* franco fábrica, en fábrica.
eye [aɪ] **1** N ojo *m* (*also of needle*); (*Bot*) yema *f*; ~**s right!** ¡vista a la derecha!; **an** ~ **for an** ~ **(and a tooth for a tooth)** ojo por ojo (y diente por diente); **as far as the** ~ **can see** hasta donde alcanza la vista; **it happened before my very** ~**s** ocurrió delante de mis propios ojos; **the grass grows before your very** ~**s** crece la hierba a ojos vistas; **in the** ~**s of** a los ojos de; **with an** ~ **to the future** cara al futuro; **with an** ~ **to a possible job** con miras a un empleo eventual; **with an** ~ **to** + *infin* con la intención de + *infin*; **with the naked** ~ a simple vista; **it's all my** ~!* ¡es puro cuento!; **to be all** ~**s** ser todo ojos; **that's one in the** ~ **for him!** ese golpe va dirigido a él; **there wasn't a dry** ~ **in the house** no había ojos sin lágrimas en todo el teatro; **to be up to one's** ~**s** (*in work*) estar hasta los ojos de trabajo; **to catch the** ~ llamar la atención; atraer las miradas; **to catch sb's** ~ atraer la atención de uno; **to catch the Speaker's** ~ hacer uso de la palabra (con permiso del presidente); **to clap** ~**s on** clavar la vista en; **to close one's** ~**s to** (*fig*) hacer la vista gorda a; **to cock one's** ~ **at** mirar con intención a; **to cry one's** ~**s out** llorar a moco tendido; **he did** (*or* **went into**) **it with his** ~**s open** lo hizo con los ojos abiertos; **to feast one's** ~**s on sth** recrear la vista mirando algo, mirar algo con fruición; **to give sb the glad** ~ lanzar una mirada incitante a uno; **to have an** ~ **for sth** tener afición a algo, saber apreciar algo; saber elegir; **to have an** ~ **to sth** tener algo en cuenta; obrar (*or* actuar *etc*) con miras a algo; **to have good** ~**s** tener buena vista; **to have one's** ~**s on** (*watch*) vigilar, echar una mirada a; (*covet*) echar el ojo a; **she had** ~**s only for me** no dejaba de mirarme a mí; **it hits you in the** ~ salta a la vista; **to keep an** ~

on sth (*watch*) vigilar; (*bear in mind*) tener algo en cuenta; (*follow*) no perder algo de vista; **he couldn't keep his ~s off the girl** se le fueron los ojos tras la chica; **to keep one's ~s peeled** estar alerta; **keep your ~s open for bag-snatchers!** ¡mucho ojo con los del tirón!; **keep an ~ out for snakes** cuidado por si hay culebras; **to make ~s at sb** lanzar una mirada incitante a uno; **there's more in this than meets the ~** esto tiene su miga; **to open sb's ~s to sth** abrir los ojos de uno a algo; **to rub one's ~s** restregarse los ojos; **to run one's ~ over sth** recorrer algo con la vista; echar un vistazo a; **I don't see ~ to ~ with him over that** en eso no estoy completamente de acuerdo con él; **when I first set ~s on him** la primera vez que le puse los ojos encima; **it's 5 years since I set ~s on him** hace 5 años que no le veo; **to shut one's ~s to sth** cerrar los ojos a algo, hacer la vista gorda a (*or* ante) algo; **we must not shut our ~s to this** importa que nos demos cuenta de esto; **he couldn't take his ~s off the girl** se le fueron los ojos tras la joven; **to turn a blind ~ to sth** fingir no ver algo, hacer la vista gorda a (*or* ante) algo.

[2] VT ojear, mirar (detenidamente, sospechosamente *etc*).

◆**eye up** VT: **he was ~ing the girl up** se comía a la joven con los ojos.
eyeball ['aɪbɔːl] N globo *m* del ojo.
eyebath ['aɪbɑːθ] N, PL **eyebaths** ['aɪbɑːðz] (*esp Brit*) ojera *f*, lavaojos *m*.
eyebrow ['aɪbraʊ] [1] N ceja *f*; **to raise one's ~s** levantar las cejas; **he never raised an ~ at it** no se sorprendió en lo más mínimo;
[2] ATTR: **~ pencil** lápiz *m* de cejas; **~ tweezers** pinzas *fpl* para las cejas.
eye-catcher ['aɪˌkætʃəʳ] N cosa *f* que llama la atención.
eye-catching ['aɪˌkætʃɪŋ] ADJ llamativo, vistoso.
eye-contact ['aɪˌkɒntækt] N contacto *m* ocular.
eye-cup ['aɪˌkʌp] N = **eyebath**.
-eyed [aɪd] ADJ de ojos ...; **green~** de ojos verdes; **two~** de dos ojos.
eye doctor ['aɪˌdɒktəʳ] N (*US*) oculista *mf*.
eye-dropper ['aɪˌdrɒpəʳ] N cuentagotas *m*.

eye-drops ['aɪdrɒps] NPL gotas *fpl* para los ojos.
eyeful★ ['aɪfʊl] N: **he got an ~ of mud** el lodo le dio de lleno en el ojo; **get an ~ of this!** ¡echa un vistazo a esto!, ¡mírame esto!; **she's quite an ~!** ¡está buenísima!★
eyeglass ['aɪglɑːs] N lente *m*; (*worn in the eye*) monóculo *m*; **~es** (*esp US*) gafas *fpl*.
eyelash ['aɪlæʃ] N pestaña *f*.
eyelet ['aɪlɪt] N (*Sew*) ojete *m*.
eye-level ['aɪˌlevl] N altura *f* del ojo.
eyelid ['aɪlɪd] N párpado *m*.
eyeliner ['aɪˌlaɪnəʳ] N lápiz *m* de ojos, delineador *m* de ojos.
eye-opener★ ['aɪˌəʊpnəʳ] N (a) revelación *f*, sorpresa *f* grande; **it was an ~ to me** fue una revelación para mí. (b) (*US*) copa *f* para despertarse.
eye-patch ['aɪˌpætʃ] N parche *m*.
eye-pencil ['aɪˌpensl] N lápiz *m* de ojos.
eyepiece ['aɪpiːs] N ocular *m*.
eyeshade ['aɪʃeɪd] N visera *f*.
eyeshadow ['aɪˌʃædəʊ] N sombreador *m* de ojos, sombra *f* de ojos.
eyesight ['aɪsaɪt] N vista *f*; (*extent of ~*) alcance *m* de la vista.
eye-socket ['aɪsɒkɪt] N cuenca *f* del ojo.
eyesore ['aɪsɔːʳ] N monstruosidad *f*, cosa *f* antiestética.
eyestrain ['aɪstreɪn] N vista *f* fatigada; **to get ~** cansar los ojos, cansar la vista; **to suffer from ~** padecer de los ojos.
eye test ['aɪˌtest] N test *m* visual, test *m* de visión; examen *m* de los ojos.
eye-tooth ['aɪtuːθ] N, PL **eye-teeth** ['aɪtiːθ] colmillo *m*; **I'd give my eye-teeth to see it** daría todo lo que tengo por verlo.
eyewash ['aɪwɒʃ] N (*Med*) colirio *m*; (★) música *f* celestial; **it's a lot of ~!** ¡es puro cuento!
eyewitness ['aɪˌwɪtnɪs] N testigo *mf* presencial, testigo *mf* ocular.
eyrie ['aɪərɪ] N aguilera *f*.
Ezekiel [ɪ'ziːkɪəl] NM Ezequiel.

F

F, f [ef] N **(a)** (*letter*) F, f *f*; **F for Frederick, F for Fox** (*US*) F de Francia. **(b)** F (*Mus*) fa *m*; **F major** fa *m* mayor.

F. (a) ABBR of **Fahrenheit** termómetro *m* Fahrenheit. **(b)** (*Eccl*) ABBR of **Father** Padre *m*, Pᵉ.

f. (a) (*Math*) ABBR of **foot, feet. (b)** ABBR of **following** siguiente, sig. **(c)** (*Biol*) ABBR of **female** hembra *f*.

FA N **(a)** (*Brit Sport*) ABBR of **Football Association** ≃ Asociación *f* Futbolística Española, AFE *f*; **~ Cup** Copa *f* de la FA. **(b)** (*) ABBR of **(sweet) Fanny Adams.**

fa [fɑː] N (*Mus*) fa *m*.

FAA N (*US*) ABBR of **Federal Aviation Administration.**

fab: [fæb] ADJ (*Brit*) = **fabulous.**

Fabian ['feɪbɪən] **1** ADJ fabianista; **~ Society** Sociedad *f* Fabiana.
2 N fabianista *mf*.

fable ['feɪbl] N fábula *f*.

fabled ['feɪbld] ADJ fabuloso, legendario.

fabric ['fæbrɪk] **1** N **(a)** (*cloth*) tejido *m*, tela *f*. **(b)** (*Archit*) fábrica *f*; **the upkeep of the ~** la manutención de los edificios; **the ~ of society** la estructura de la sociedad; **the ~ of Church and State** (*freq hum*) los fundamentos de la Iglesia y del Estado.
2 ATTR: **~ ribbon** cinta *f* de tela.

fabricate ['fæbrɪkeɪt] VT *goods etc* fabricar; (*fig*) inventar; *document, evidence* falsificar.

fabrication [,fæbrɪ'keɪʃən] N invención *f*, ficción *f*; **the whole thing is a ~** todo es mentira, todo es un cuento.

fabulous ['fæbjʊləs] ADJ fabuloso; (*) fabuloso*, estupendo*.

fabulously ['fæbjʊləslɪ] ADV fabulosamente; **~ rich** fabulosamente rico; **it was ~ successful** tuvo un éxito fabuloso.

façade [fə'sɑːd] N fachada *f* (*also fig*).

face [feɪs] **1** N **(a)** (*Anat etc*) cara *f*, rostro *m*, semblante *m*; (*of dial, watch*) esfera *f*, cara *f* (*LAm*); (*of sundial*) cuadrante *m*; (*surface*) superficie *f*; (*Min*) cara *f* de trabajo; (*of building*) frente *f*, fachada *f*; **~ of the earth** faz *f* de la tierra; **~ downwards** boca abajo; **~ upwards** boca arriba; **to bring A ~ to ~ with B** confrontar A con B; **to bring two people ~ to ~** poner a dos personas cara a cara; **in the ~ of** ante, en presencia de, en vista de; **in the ~ of this threat** ante esta amenaza; **in the ~ of such difficulties** vistas tantas dificultades; **courage in the ~ of the enemy** valor frente al enemigo; **the wind was blowing in our ~s** el viento nos daba de cara.
(b) (*phrases*) **to fly in the ~ of reason** oponerse abiertamente a la razón; **they laughed in his ~** se le rieron en la cara; **he'll laugh on the other side of his ~** pasará de la risa al llanto; **he didn't dare to look me in the ~** no osaba mirarme a la cara; **I could never look him in the ~ again** yo no tendría valor para mirarle a la cara; **to look sb square in the ~** mirar directamente a los ojos de uno; **to tell sb sth to his ~** decirle algo a uno en su cara; **to say sth to sb's ~** decir algo en la cara de uno; **to set one's ~ against sth** oponerse resueltamente a algo; **to show one's ~** asomar la cara, dejarse ver; **shut your ~!*** ¡cállate ya!, ¡calla la boca!; **to struggle to keep a straight ~** esforzarse por contener la risa.
(c) (*expression*) **(wry ~)** mueca *f*; **to go about with a long ~** andar cariacontecido; **to make ~s, to pull ~s** hacer muecas (*at* a); **to pull a (wry) ~** poner cara de desagrado.
(d) (*effrontery*) cara *f*, cara *f* dura, descaro *m*; **to have the ~ to + *infin*** ser bastante descarado para + *infin*.
(e) (*dignity*) prestigio *m*; **to lose ~** desprestigiarse, perder prestigio; quedar mal; **to save (one's) ~** salvar las apariencias.
(f) (*outward show*) **on the ~ of it** a primera vista, según las apariencias.
2 VT **(a)** (*look towards: of person, object*) estar de cara a; ponerse de cara a; volver la cara hacia; **~ the wall!** ¡póngase de cara a la pared!; **turn it to ~ the fire** gírelo para que esté de cara a la lumbre; **they sat facing each other** estaban sentados uno frente al otro; **to sit**

facing the engine estar sentado de frente a la máquina.
(b) (*of building*) mirar hacia, estar enfrente de, dar a; **the flat ~s the Town Hall** el piso está enfrente del Ayuntamiento; **the house ~s the sea** la casa está frente al mar; **the house ~s the south** la casa está orientada hacia el sur.
(c) (*fig*) *person, enemy, electorate* encararse con, enfrentarse con; *consequences, danger* arrostrar, hacer cara a; *facts* reconocer; *situation* hacer frente a; *problem* afrontar; **we ~ grave problems** afrontamos unos problemas graves; **we are ~d with grave problems** se nos plantean graves problemas; **he ~s a fine of £100** se arriesga a una multa de 100 libras; **we will ~ him with the facts** le expondremos los hechos; **let's ~ it!** ¡seamos realistas!; **we're poor, let's ~ it!** ¡reconozcamos que somos pobres!
(d) (*Tech*) revestir, forrar (*with* de).
3 VI: **to ~ in a direction** estar orientado en una dirección; **which way does it ~?** ¿en qué dirección está orientado?; **~ this way!** ¡vuélvase hacia aquí!

◆**face about** VI (*Mil*) dar media vuelta; (*fig*) cambiar de actitud, cambiar de postura.
◆**face down** VT (*US*) intimidar con la mirada.
◆**face on to** VT mirar hacia, dar a.
◆**face out** VT: **to ~ it out** insistir descaradamente en ello.
◆**face up to** VT: **to ~ up to sth** reconocer la realidad de algo, hacer frente a algo, arrostrar algo; **she ~d up to it bravely** lo aguantó con mucha resolución.

face card ['feɪskɑːd] N (*US*) figura *f*.

facecloth ['feɪsklɒθ] N (*Brit*) manopla *f*, paño *m*.

facecream ['feɪskriːm] N crema *f* (de belleza).

-faced [feɪst] ADJ *ending in compounds* de cara ..., *eg* **brown~** de cara morena, **long~** de cara larga.

face-flannel ['feɪs,flænl] N (*Brit*) manopla *f*, paño *m*.

faceless ['feɪslɪs] ADJ sin cara, sin rostro.

facelift ['feɪslɪft] N **(a)** estirado *m* de piel, estiramiento *m* facial. **(b)** (*fig*) reforma *f* (superficial), modernización *f* (ligera); **to give a ~ to** remozar; mejorar de aspecto.

face-off ['feɪsɒf] N (*US*) confrontación *f*.

facepack ['feɪspæk] N tratamiento *m* facial.

face-powder ['feɪs,paʊdəʳ] N polvos *mpl*.

facer* ['feɪsəʳ] N (*Brit*) problema *m* desconcertante; **that's a ~!** ¡vaya problemazo!*

face-saver ['feɪs,seɪvəʳ] N maniobra *f* para salvar las apariencias.

face-saving ['feɪs,seɪvɪŋ] **1** ADJ: **~ operation** maniobra *f* para salvar las apariencias.
2 N: **~ is important** importa salvar las apariencias; **this is a piece of blatant ~** esto es una maniobra transparente para salvar las apariencias.

facet ['fæsɪt] N faceta *f* (*also fig*).

facetious [fə'siːʃəs] ADJ *person* chistoso; *remark* festivo, gracioso; *speech* divertido, lleno de chistes.

facetiously [fə'siːʃəslɪ] ADV chistosamente; **he said ~** dijo guasón.

facetiousness [fə'siːʃəsnɪs] N carácter *m* festivo (*etc*); chistes *mpl*.

face-to-face [,feɪstə'feɪs] **1** ADJ cara a cara.
2 ADV cara a cara.

face-value ['feɪs'væljuː] N valor *m* nominal; (*of stamp, coin etc*) valor *m* facial; (*fig*) valor *m* aparente, significado *m* literal; **you can't take it at its ~** no se deje engañar por las apariencias; **I took his statement at its ~** tomé lo que dijo en sentido literal.

facia ['feɪʃɪə] = **fascia.**

facial ['feɪʃəl] **1** ADJ de la cara, facial.
2 N tratamiento *m* facial, masaje *m* facial; limpieza *f*.

facile ['fæsaɪl] ADJ fácil, superficial, ligero.

facilitate [fə'sɪlɪteɪt] VT facilitar.

facilitator [fə'sɪlɪteɪtəʳ] N facilitador *m*, -ora *f*.

facility [fə'sɪlɪtɪ] N facilidad *f*; **facilities** (*most senses*) facilidades *fpl*; (*US euph*) servicios *mpl*; **recreational facilities** instalaciones *fpl* recreativas.

facing ['feɪsɪŋ] ① PREP de cara a, frente a.
② *as* ADJ opuesto, de enfrente; **the houses** ~ las casas de enfrente; **on a** ~ **page** en una página de enfrente.
③ N (*Tech*) revestimiento *m*; (*Sew*) vuelta *f*, guarnición *f*; ~**s** (*Sew*) vueltas *fpl*.

-facing ['feɪsɪŋ] ADJ *ending in compounds*: **south~** con orientación sur, orientado hacia el sur.

facsimile [fæk'sɪmɪlɪ] ① ADJ facsímil.
② N facsímil *m*.
③ ATTR: ~ **machine** teleproductor *m* de imágenes; ~ **transmission** telefacsímil *m*.

▼ **fact** [fækt] N hecho *m*; (*real world*) realidad *f*; ~ **and fiction** lo real y lo ficticio; ~**s and figures** hechos *mpl* y números; ~ **sheet** hoja *f* informativa; **the** ~**s of life** los hechos (*or* las realidades) de la vida, (*esp*) las cosas de la vida, los detalles de la reproducción humana; **hard** ~**s** hechos *mpl* innegables; **a film based on** ~ una película basada en hechos verídicos; **it has no basis in** ~ carece de base real; **as a matter of** ~, **in** ~, **in point of** ~ a decir verdad, de hecho; en realidad; **the** ~ **of the matter is** la pura verdad es; **the** ~ **is that** ... el hecho es que ..., ello es que ...; **it is a** ~ **that** ... se ha comprobado que ...; **the** ~ **that I am here** el hecho de que estoy aquí; **is that a** ~? ¿(lo dices) en serio?; **to bow to the** ~**s** reconocer que las cosas son así, doblegarse ante los hechos; **I don't dispute your** ~**s** yo no niego los hechos que alega; **to know for a** ~ **that** ... saber a ciencia cierta que ...; **to stick to the** ~**s** atenerse a los hechos; *V* **accessory.**

fact-finding ['fækt,faɪndɪŋ] ADJ *mission, visit* de investigación, de indagación, de reconocimiento.

faction ['fækʃən] N facción *f*.

factional ['fækʃənl] ADJ *fighting* partidista, entre distintas facciones.

factionalism ['fækʃənəlɪzm] N enfrentamiento *m* entre distintas tendencias.

factionalize ['fækʃənlaɪz] ① VT fragmentar, dividir en facciones.
② VI dividirse en facciones.

factious ['fækʃəs] ADJ faccioso.

factitious [fæk'tɪʃəs] ADJ facticio.

factitive ['fæktɪtɪv] ADJ factivo, causativo.

▼ **factor** ['fæktər] N (a) (*fact*) factor *m*, hecho *m*, elemento *m*; **the Falklands** ~ el factor Malvinas.
(b) (*Math*) factor *m*; **highest common** ~ máximo común divisor *m*.
(c) (*Comm*) agente *m*.

factorial [fæk'tɔːrɪəl] ADJ, N factorial *m*.

factoring ['fæktərɪŋ] N factorización *f*.

factory ['fæktərɪ] ① N (a) fábrica *f*, factoría *f*.
(b) (‡) comisaría *f*.
② ATTR: ~ **farming** agricultura *f* industrializada, cría *f* intensiva; ~ **floor opinion** opinión *f* de las bases sindicales, opinión *f* de los obreros; ~ **inspector** inspector *m*, -ora *f* de fábricas; ~ **ship** buque *m* factoría; ~ **work** trabajo *m* de fábrica; ~ **worker** obrero *m*, -a *f* de fábrica.

factotum [fæk'təʊtəm] N factótum *m*.

factual ['fæktjʊəl] ADJ objetivo, que consta de hechos, basado en datos; de carácter expositivo; ~ **error** error *m* de hecho.

factually ['fæktjʊəlɪ] ADV objetivamente; ~ **speaking, I would say** ... limitándome a los hechos, diría que ...

faculty ['fækltɪ] N (a) facultad *f*. (b) (*Univ*) facultad *f*. (c) (*esp US: Univ*) profesorado *m*.

fad [fæd] N manía *f*; novedad *f*; **it's just a** ~ es una novedad nada más, es una moda pasajera; **he has his** ~**s** tiene sus caprichos; **the** ~ **for Italian clothes** la manía de los trajes italianos.

faddish ['fædɪʃ] ADJ, **faddy** ['fædɪ] ADJ *person* caprichoso, dengoso, que tiene sus manías, difícil de contentar; *distaste, desire* idiosincrático.

fade [feɪd] ① VT *colour, dress* descolorar, desteñir; *flower* marchitar.
② VI (a) (*colour, dress*) descolorarse, desteñirse, perder su color; (*flower*) marchitarse; **guaranteed not to** ~ no se descolora.
(b) (*light*) apagarse gradualmente; (*sound*) desvanecerse; (*memory etc*) desvanecerse; **the daylight was fading fast** anochecía rápidamente; **he saw his chances fading** veía como se estaban acabando sus posibilidades.
◆ **fade away** VI (*sight*) desdibujarse, desvanecerse; (*sound*) apagarse, dejar poco a poco de oírse; **she was fading away** (*dying*) se consumía lentamente, (*slimming*) adelgazaba muchísimo; **this season the team has just** ~**d away** en esta temporada el equipo casi ha dejado de figurar.
◆ **fade in** VT (*Cine*) hacer aparecer gradualmente.
◆ **fade out** VI = **fade away.**
◆ **fade to** VI (*Cine*) fundir a.
◆ **fade up** VT = **fade in.**

faded ['feɪdɪd] ADJ *plant* marchito, seco; *colour, dress* descolorido; *glory* marchito.

fade-in ['feɪdɪn] N (*Cine, TV*) fundido *m*.

fade-out ['feɪdaʊt] N (*Cine*) fundido *m* (de cierre); **to do a** ~* (*US*) desaparecer.

faecal, fecal ['fiːkəl] ADJ fecal.

faeces, (*US*) **feces** ['fiːsiːz] NPL excrementos *mpl*.

Faeroes, Faeroe Islands ['feərəʊz, 'feərəʊ,aɪləndz] = **Faroes.**

faff* [fæf] VI: **to** ~ **about** perder el tiempo, ocuparse en bagatelas; **stop** ~**fing about!** ¡déjate de tonterías!

fag [fæg] ① N (a) (*Brit*: *job*) faena *f*, lata *f* (*LAm*), trabajo *m* penoso; **what a** ~! ¡qué faena!; **it's just too much** ~ la verdad, es mucho trabajo.
(b) (*Brit Scol*) alumno *m* joven que trabaja por otro mayor.
(c) (*Brit*‡: *cigarette*) pitillo *m*, cigarro *m* (*LAm*), pucho *m* (*SC*).
(d) (*esp US*‡) maricón *m*.
② VT (*Brit*) fatigar, cansar; **to be** ~**ged out** estar rendido.
③ VI trabajar como un negro; **to** ~ **for** (*Brit Scol*) trabajar por.

fag-end‡ ['fægend] N colilla *f*; (*fig*) cabo *m*; desperdicios *mpl*.

faggot, (*mainly US*) **fagot** ['fægət] N (a) haz *m* de leña, astillas *fpl*. (b) (*esp US*‡) maricón‡ *m*.

fah [fɑː] N (*Mus*) fa *m*.

Fahrenheit ['færənhaɪt] ATTR: ~ **thermometer** termómetro *m* de Fahrenheit (*grados Fahrenheit menos 32 × 5/9 = grados centígrados*).

FAI N ABBR *of* **Football Association of Ireland.**

fail [feɪl] ① N (a) (*Univ*) suspenso *m* (*in* en).
(b) **without** ~ sin falta.
② VT (a) *person* faltar a, faltar en sus obligaciones a; decepcionar; **his strength** ~**ed him** se sintió desfallecer, le abandonaron sus fuerzas; **his heart** ~**ed him** se encontró sin ánimo; **words** ~ **me** no encuentro palabras para expresarme; **you have** ~**ed me** me has decepcionado.
(b) (*Univ*) *exam* no aprobar, salir mal en; *candidate* suspender.
③ VI (a) (*run short: supply, strength*) acabarse; (*engine*) fallar; (*voice*) irse, debilitarse, desfallecer; (*eyes*) debilitarse; (*light*) acabarse; (*crop*) fallar; perderse; (*electricity supply etc*) cortarse, interrumpirse; (*mechanism*) tener una avería, averiarse; (*patient*) debilitarse, hacerse más débil; **the light was** ~**ing** iba anocheciendo.
(b) (*neglect*) **to** ~ **to do sth** dejar de hacer algo; **he** ~**ed to appear** no se presentó, dejó de presentarse; **don't** ~ **to visit her** no dejes de visitarla; **to** ~ **to keep one's word** faltar a su palabra.
(c) (*be unable*) **I** ~ **to see how** no veo cómo; **I** ~ **to understand why** no puedo comprender por qué; **but she** ~**ed to come** pero no vino.
(d) (*not succeed*) fracasar, no tener éxito; (*remedy*) no surtir efecto; (*hopes*) frustrarse, malograrse; (*Fin*) quebrar; (*Univ etc*) ser suspendido (*in* en); **a** ~**ed painter** un pintor fracasado; **to** ~ **to be elected** no lograr ser elegido; **to** ~ **to win a prize** no obtener un premio; **to** ~ **by 5 votes** perder por 5 votos.
(e) **to** ~ **in one's duty to sb** faltar a uno, faltar en sus obligaciones a uno.

failing ['feɪlɪŋ] ① PREP a falta de; ~ **that** si eso no es posible.
② N falta *f*, defecto *m*; flaqueza *f*; **the plan has numerous** ~**s** el plan tiene muchos defectos; **it is his only** ~ es su único punto débil.
③ ADJ: **he was in** ~ **health** su salud era cada vez más débil, iba desfalleciendo; **we reached the top in** ~ **light** anochecía cuando llegamos a la cumbre; **life in a** ~ **marriage** la vida en un matrimonio que anda mal.

failsafe ['feɪlseɪf] ATTR: ~ **device** mecanismo *m* de seguridad, mecanismo *m* a prueba de fallo.

failure ['feɪljər] ① N (a) (*lack of success*) fracaso *m*; (*of hopes*) malogro *m*; (*failed thing*) fracaso *m*, (*person*) fracasado *m*, -a *f*; (*Mech*) fallo *m*, avería *f*; (*Elec*) corte *m*, interrupción *f*, apagón *m* (*LAm*); (*of crop*) fallo *m*; pérdida *f*; (*Fin*) quiebra *f*; **the crop was a total** ~ el cultivo se perdió por completo.
(b) **your** ~ **to come** el hecho de que no viniste, el dejar de venir (tú); ~ **to pay** incumplimiento *m* en el pago, impago *m*.
(c) (*Univ*) suspenso *m* (*in* en).
② ATTR: ~ **rate** (*in exams*) porcentaje *m* de suspensos; (*of machine*) porcentaje *m* de averías.

fain†† [feɪn] ADV (*used only with 'would'*) de buena gana.

faint [feɪnt] ① ADJ débil; *colour* pálido; *line* tenue; *outline* borroso, indistinto; *trace* apenas perceptible; *sound* casi imperceptible, débil; *voice* débil; *smell* tenue; *hope* nada firme; *idea, memory* vago; *resemblance* ligero; *heart* medroso; **to feel** ~ estar mareado, tener vahidos; **I haven't the** ~**est** (*idea*) no tengo la más remota idea.
② N desmayo *m*; **to be in a** ~ estar desmayado, estar sin conocimiento; **to fall down in a** ~ desmayarse.
③ VI (*also* **to** ~ **away**) desmayarse, perder conocimiento; **to be** ~**ing with tiredness** estar rendido; **to be** ~**ing with hunger** estar muerto de hambre.

fainthearted ['feɪnt'hɑːtɪd] ADJ medroso, pusilánime, apocado.

faintheartedness [,feɪnt'hɑːtɪdnɪs] N pusilanimidad *f*; cobardía *f*.

fainting fit ['feɪntɪŋ,fɪt] N, **fainting spell** ['feɪntɪŋ,spel] N síncope *m*, desvanecimiento *m*.

faintly ['feɪntlɪ] ADV *call, say* débilmente; *breathe, shine* débilmente, ligeramente; *write, mark, scratch* vagamente, débilmente; *(slightly)* ligeramente; **this is ~ reminiscent of ...** esto me recuerda vagamente ...

faintness ['feɪntnɪs] N debilidad *f*; tenuidad *f*; lo indistinto; *(Med)* desmayo *m*, desfallecimiento *m*.

fair¹ [feə^r] **1** ADJ (a) *(beautiful)* bello, hermoso; **the ~ sex** el bello sexo. **(b)** *(blond) hair* rubio; *skin* blanco. **(c)** *(clean) name* honrado; *reputation* bueno; **~ copy** copia *f* en limpio. **(d)** *(just)* justo, equitativo; *hearing, report, summary* imparcial; *comment* acertado; *means* recto; *play* limpio; *competition* leal; *chance, price, warning* razonable; **~ enough!** ¡vale!, ¡muy bien!; **as is only ~** como es justo; **but to be ~** pero en honor a la verdad; **it's not ~!** ¡no hay derecho!; **it's not ~ on the old** afecta injustamente a los viejos; **~ deal** trato *m* equitativo, política *f* equitativa; **~ game** caza *f* legal; *(fig)* objeto *m* legítimo; **it is ~ game for criticism** es un objeto legítimo de la crítica; **to give sb a ~ share*** tratar justamente a uno; **~ trade** comercio *m* legítimo; **~ trade agreement** *(US)* acuerdo *m* por el cual el vendedor promete no vender un producto a un precio inferior al fijado por el fabricante; **~ wage** salario *m* justo; **~ wear and tear** desgaste *m* por uso justo. **(e)** *(middling)* regular, mediano. **(f)** *(promising)* prometedor, favorable, bastante bueno. **(g)** *(Met) sky* sereno, despejado; *day, weather* bueno; **if it's ~ tomorrow** si hace buen tiempo mañana. **2** ADV **(a) to play ~** jugar limpio. **(b) it hit the target ~ and square** dio en el centro del blanco; **so he told me ~ and square** así que me lo dijo sin rodeos. **(c)** *(*: fairly)* **we were ~ terrified** nos asustamos bastante; **then it ~ rained** entonces sí que llovió.

fair² [feə^r] N **(a)** *(Comm etc)* feria *f*. **(b)** *(Brit: funfair)* parque *m* de atracciones; verbena *f*.

STATE FAIR

ℹ️ *En todos los estados de EE.UU. se celebra una feria en otoño llamada* **state fair** *a la que acude gran cantidad de gente de todo el estado. Estas ferias son generalmente agrícolas y en ellas se celebran concursos de animales y productos del campo, de gastronomía y de artesanía. También se organizan juegos y se instalan stands en los que fabricantes y comerciantes hacen demostraciones de sus productos. La feria más grande de todo el país es la Feria de Texas, que se celebra cada octubre en Dallas.*

---

fairground ['feəɡraʊnd] N real *m* (de la feria); parque *m* de atracciones.

fair-haired ['feə'heəd] ADJ, **fair-headed** ['feə'hedɪd] ADJ rubio, pelirrubio.

fairly ['feəlɪ] ADV **(a)** justamente, equitativamente, con imparcialidad; rectamente; limpio, limpiamente. **(b) ~ good** bastante bueno. **(c)** *(utterly)* completamente.

fair-minded ['feə'maɪndɪd] ADJ imparcial, equitativo.

fair-mindedness [,feə'maɪndɪdnɪs] N imparcialidad *f*.

fairness ['feənɪs] N *(V fair¹)* **(a)** hermosura *f*. **(b)** lo rubio; blancura *f*. **(c)** justicia *f*, imparcialidad *f*; **in all ~** para ser justo *(to him* con él).

FAIRNESS DOCTRINE

ℹ️ *La* **Fairness Doctrine** *(Doctrina de la Imparcialidad) es un principio llevado a la práctica en Estados Unidos por la* **Federal Communications Commission** *o* **FCC** *por el que, cuando se trata de noticias importantes de carácter local o nacional, la radio y la televisión deben ofrecer los distintos puntos de vista de forma equilibrada. Este principio, establecido por la* **FCC** *en 1949 con el apoyo del Congreso, no tiene carácter de ley y cuenta entre sus atribuciones con el control equitativo del tiempo en los espacios electorales dedicados a cada uno de los líderes políticos en campaña. También se utilizó en 1967 en la lucha antitabaco, cuando la* **FCC** *estableció que los fabricantes debían dejar claro en sus anuncios los peligros del tabaco, aunque hoy día la* **Fairness Doctrine** *ya ha dejado prácticamente de tener influencia en publicidad.*

⇨ *Ver también* **FCC - FEDERAL COMMUNICATIONS COMMISSION**

---

fair-sized ['feəsaɪzd] ADJ bastante grande.

fair-skinned [,feə'skɪnd] ADJ de tez blanca.

fairway ['feəweɪ] N *(Naut)* canalizo *m*; *(Golf)* calle *f*, fairway *m*.

fair-weather ['feə,weðə^r] ADJ: **~ friend** amigo *m*, -a *f* en la prosperidad, amigo *m*, -a *f* del buen viento.

fairy ['feərɪ] **1** N **(a)** hada *f*. **(b)** (‡) maricón‡ *m*. **2** ATTR feérico, mágico; **~ footsteps** pasos *mpl* ligeros; **~ godmother** hada *f* madrina; **~ queen** reina *f* de las hadas.

fairy cycle ['feərɪ,saɪkl] N bicicleta *f* de niño.

fairyland ['feərɪlænd] N tierra *f* de (las) hadas; *(fig)* país *m* de ensueño; **he must be living in ~** vive en la luna.

fairy-lights ['feərɪlaɪts] NPL bombillas *fpl* de colorines.

fairy-story ['feərɪ,stɔːrɪ] N, **fairy-tale** ['feərɪteɪl] **1** N cuento *m* de hadas; *(fig)* cuento *m*, patraña *f*. **2** ADJ fantástico, de ensueño.

fait accompli [,feɪtə'kɒmplɪ] N hecho *m* consumado.

faith [feɪθ] N fe *f* *(also Eccl)*; *(trust)* confianza *f* *(in* en); *(doctrine)* creencia *f*; *(sect, confession)* religión *f*; **bad ~** mala fe *f*; **in good ~** de buena fe; **what ~ does he belong to?** ¿qué religión tiene?; **to break ~** faltar a su palabra *(with* dada a); **to have ~ in** tener fe en; **to keep ~** cumplir la palabra *(with* dada a); **to pin one's ~ to** cifrar sus esperanzas en.

faithful ['feɪθfʊl] **1** ADJ fiel *(also Eccl)*; *friend, servant* leal; *translation* fiel; *account* exacto. **2** NPL: **the ~** los fieles.

faithfully ['feɪθfəlɪ] ADV fielmente; lealmente; con exactitud; **yours ~** *(Brit)* le saluda atentamente.

faithfulness ['feɪθfʊlnɪs] N fidelidad *f*; lealtad *f*; exactitud *f*.

faith-healer ['feɪθ,hiːlə^r] N curador *m*, -ora *f* por fe.

faith-healing ['feɪθ,hiːlɪŋ] N curación *f* por fe.

faithless ['feɪθlɪs] ADJ desleal, pérfido, infiel.

faithlessness ['feɪθlɪsnɪs] N infidelidad *f*, deslealtad *f*, perfidia *f*.

fake [feɪk] **1** N *(thing)* falsificación *f*, impostura *f*; imitación *f*; *(person)* impostor *m*, -ora *f*, embustero *m*, -a *f*, *(as term of abuse)* farsante *mf*. **2** ADJ falso, fingido, contrahecho. **3** VT contrahacer, falsificar, fingir; *(improvise)* improvisar; **to ~ an illness** fingirse enfermo. **4** VI fingir.

◆**fake up** VT = **fake 3**.

fakir ['faːkɪə^r] N faquir *m*.

falcon ['fɔːlkən] N halcón *m*.

falconer ['fɔːlkənə^r] N halconero *m*.

falconry ['fɔːlkənrɪ] N halconería *f*, cetrería *f*.

Falklander ['fɔːlkləndə^r] N, **Falkland Islander** ['fɔːlklənd,aɪləndə^r] N habitante *mf* de las Islas Malvinas, malvinense *mf*.

Falkland Islands ['fɔːlklənd,aɪləndz] NPL Islas *fpl* Malvinas.

fall [fɔːl] **1** N caída *f*; *(Fin)* baja *f*; *(decrease)* disminución *f*; *(in price, demand, temperature)* descenso *m* *(in* de); *(Mil)* caída *f*, toma *f*, rendición *f*; *(of ground)* declive *m*, desnivel *m*; *(of water, also ~s)* salto *m* de agua, catarata *f*, cascada *f*; *(US)* otoño *m*; **the F~** la Caída; **~ of earth** corrimiento *m* de tierras; **~ of rocks** derrumbamiento *m* de piedras; **~ of snow** nevada *f*; **to have a ~** sufrir una caída; **to be riding for a ~** presumir demasiado. **2** *(irr:* PRET **fell**, PTP **fallen)** VI caer; caerse; *(fig: empire, government, night, hair, drapery, morally etc)* caer; *(decrease)* disminuir; *(price, level, demand, temperature etc)* bajar, descender; *(Mil)* caer, rendirse; *(ground)* estar en declive; *(wind)* amainar; **his face fell** se inmutó; **night was ~ing** anochecía, se hacía de noche; **at a time of ~ing interest rates** en un período cuando bajan los tipos de interés; **to ~ among thieves** ir a parar entre ladrones.

◆**fall about*** VI *(laugh)* desternillarse (de risa)*.

◆**fall apart** VI *(object)* romperse, deshacerse; *(empire)* desmoronarse; *(scheme, marriage)* fracasar.

◆**fall away** VI **(a)** *(ground)* descender, estar en declive *(to* hacia). **(b)** *(plaster etc)* desconcharse; *(cliff)* desmoronarse; *(stage of rocket, part)* desprenderse. **(c)** *(numbers etc)* bajar, disminuir; *(zeal)* enfriarse; *(trade etc)* decaer. **(d)** *(morally)* abandonar sus principios; *(Rel)* apostatar; perder la fe; *(in quality)* empeorar.

◆**fall back** VI **(a)** retroceder; *(Mil)* replegarse *(on* sobre), retirarse. **(b) it fell back into the sea** volvió a caer al mar. **(c)** *(price etc)* bajar. **(d) to ~ back on** *remedy etc* recurrir a, echar mano a.

◆**fall backwards** VI caer de espaldas.

◆**fall behind** VI quedarse atrás, rezagarse; **to ~ behind with one's payments** atrasarse en los pagos.

◆**fall down** VI **(a)** *(fall)* caer, caerse; *(person)* caerse; dar consigo en el suelo; *(building)* hundirse, derrumbarse; venirse abajo; **to ~ down the stairs** caer rodando por la escalera; **to ~ down and worship sb** arrodillarse ante uno; **the rain was ~ing down** llovía a cántaros. **(b)** *(fail)* fracasar; ser frustrado; **that is where you fell down** ésta es la causa de tu fracaso; *V* **job**.

◆**fall for** VT **(a)** *(person)* enamorarse de; *thing* aficionarse a, tomar afición a; *place* apreciar los encantos de. **(b)** *trick* dejarse engañar por; **he fell for it** picó, se la tragó.

◆**fall in** VI **(a)** *(roof)* desplomarse, hundirse. **(b)** *(Mil)* alinearse, formar filas; **~ in!** ¡en filas! **(c)** *(Comm)* vencer; expirar. **(d) to ~ in with** *(meet)* encontrarse con, juntarse con. **(e) to ~ in with** *(agree to)* convenir en, aprobar; aceptar; *opinion* adherirse a.

◆**fall into** VT **(a)** *(river)* desembocar en. **(b)** *error* incurrir en; *conversation* entablar; *habit* adquirir.

(c) it ~s into 4 parts se divide en 4 partes; it ~s into this category está incluido en esta categoría; se puede clasificar en este apartado.

◆**fall off** VI = **fall away** (b) (c) (d).

◆**fall on** VT (a) (*tax etc*) incidir en.

(b) (*accent*) cargar sobre, caer sobre.

(c) (*Mil*) caer sobre.

(d) **to ~ on one's food** caer sobre la comida, atacar las viandas; **people were ~ing on each other in delight** todos se abrazaban de puro contentos.

(e) (*birthday etc*) caer en.

(f) (*find*) tropezar con, dar con; **to ~ on a way of doing sth** topar por casualidad con la forma de hacer algo.

(g) (*duty*) = **fall to**.

(h) **my gaze fell on certain details** quedé mirando ciertos detalles, empecé a estudiar ciertos detalles.

◆**fall out** VI (a) caer; desprenderse.

(b) (*quarrel*) reñir, pelearse, tener un disgusto (*with* con).

(c) (*Mil*) romper filas.

(d) (*come to pass*) **it fell out that ...** resultó que ...; **it fell out as we had expected** pasó como lo habíamos esperado.

◆**fall over** 1 VT *object* tropezar con.

2 VI (a) (*person, object*) caer, caerse.

(b) (*fig*) **to ~ over backwards to help sb** desvivirse por ayudar a uno; **they were ~ing over each other to buy them** se estaban pegando por comprarlos.

◆**fall through** VI (*plans etc*) fracasar.

◆**fall to** VI (a) ponerse a trabajar (*etc*); empezar a comer; **~ to!** ¡a ello!, ¡vamos!; **to ~ to** + *ger* empezar a + *infin*, ponerse a + *infin*.

(b) **to ~ to temptation** sucumbir a la tentación.

(c) (*duty*) corresponder a, incumbir a, tocar a.

◆**fall upon** V **fall on**.

fallacious [fəˈleɪʃəs] ADJ erróneo, engañoso, falaz.

fallacy [ˈfæləsɪ] N error *m*; sofisma *m*; mentira *f*, falacia *f*.

fall-back [ˈfɔːlbæk] ATTR: **~ position** segunda línea *f* de defensa; posición *f* de repliegue.

fallen [ˈfɔːlən] 1 PTP of **fall**; **the ~** los caídos.

2 ADJ (*morally*) perdido.

fall guy* [ˈfɔːlgaɪ] N (*US*) cabeza *f* de turco; víctima *f* (de un truco); víctima *f* predestinada.

fallibility [ˌfælɪˈbɪlɪtɪ] N falibilidad *f*.

fallible [ˈfæləbl] ADJ falible.

falling [ˈfɔːlɪŋ] ADJ *market etc* descendente, decreciente.

falling-off [ˈfɔːlɪŋˈɒf] N (*in quantity*) disminución *f*; (*of price etc*) baja *f*, descenso *m*; (*in quality*) empeoramiento *m*.

falling-out [ˈfɔːlɪŋˈaʊt] N (*esp US*) altercado *m*, pelea *f*.

falling star [ˈfɔːlɪŋˈstɑːr] N estrella *f* fugaz.

Fallopian [fəˈləʊpɪən] ADJ: **~ tube** trompa *f* de Falopio.

fallout [ˈfɔːlaʊt] 1 N (a) polvillo *m* radiactivo, lluvia *f* radiactiva. (b) (*fig*) consecuencias *fpl*, repercusiones *fpl*; beneficios *mpl* secundarios.

2 ATTR: **~ shelter** refugio *m* antiatómico.

fallow [ˈfæləʊ] 1 ADJ barbecho; **to lie ~** estar en barbecho; (*fig*) quedar sin emplear, no ser utilizado.

2 N barbecho *m*.

fallow deer [ˈfæləʊˈdɪər] N gamo *m*.

false [fɔːls] ADJ (a) (*mistaken*) erróneo; **~ alarm** falsa alarma *f*; **~ dawn** (*lit*) resplandor que precede al amaneces; (*fig*) espejismo *m*; **~ friend** falso amigo *m*; **~ move** paso *m* en falso; **~ note** nota *f* falsa; **~ start** (*race*) salida *f* nula; (*fig*) falso comienzo *m*; **~ step** paso *m* en falso.

(b) (*deceitful*) falso, engañoso; *person* desleal, pérfido; **by** (*or* **under, with**) **~ pretences** con fraude, mediante fraude, con engaño; **~ promises** promesas *fpl* falsas; **~ witness** falso testimonio *m*; **to bear ~ witness** jurar en falso, perjurarse; **under ~ colours** bajo pabellón falso; **to be ~ to sb, to play sb's ~** traicionar a uno; **his words rang ~** sus palabras sonaban falsas (*or* a falso).

(c) (*counterfeit*) falso; *hair, jewel, teeth* postizo; **~ bottom** doble fondo *m*; **~ door** puerta *f* falsa.

falsehood [ˈfɔːlshʊd] N (*falseness*) falsedad *f*; (*lie*) mentira *f*.

falsely [ˈfɔːlslɪ] ADV falsamente.

falseness [ˈfɔːlsnɪs] N falsedad *f*; (*of person*) perfidia *f*.

falsetto [fɔːlˈsetəʊ] 1 ADJ *voice* de falsete.

2 ADV *sing* con voz de falsete.

3 N falsete *m*.

falsies* [ˈfɔːlsɪz] NPL rellenos *mpl*.

falsification [ˌfɔːlsɪfɪˈkeɪʃən] N falsificación *f*.

falsify [ˈfɔːlsɪfaɪ] VT falsificar.

falsity [ˈfɔːlsɪtɪ] N falsedad *f*.

falter [ˈfɔːltər] 1 VT decir titubeando

2 VI (*waver*) vacilar, titubear; (*voice*) desfallecer, empañarse (por emoción); **without ~ing** sin vacilar.

faltering [ˈfɔːltərɪŋ] ADJ *step* vacilante; *voice* entrecortado.

falteringly [ˈfɔːltərɪŋlɪ] ADV *say* en voz entrecortada.

fame [feɪm] N fama *f*; **Bader, of 1940 ~** Bader, famoso por lo que hizo en 1940.

famed [feɪmd] ADJ famoso.

familial [fəˈmɪlɪəl] ADJ (*relating to families*) familiar; (*typical of a family*) de familia.

familiar [fəˈmɪlɪər] ADJ (a) (*known, usual*) familiar; (*well-known*) conocido, consabido; (*common*) corriente, común; **it's a ~ feeling** es un sentimiento común, es un sentimiento que conocemos todos; **his voice sounds ~** me parece que conozco su voz; **it doesn't sound ~** no me suena.

(b) (*conversant*) **to be ~ with** estar familiarizado con, conocer; estar enterado de; **to make o.s. ~ with** familiarizarse con.

(c) (*intimate*) íntimo; de confianza; (*pej*) fresco; que presume de amigo; *language etc* familiar; **to be on ~ terms with** tener confianza con; **he got too ~** se tomó demasiadas confianzas.

familiarity [fəˌmɪlɪˈærɪtɪ] N (a) familiaridad *f*; (*knowledge*) conocimiento *m* (*with* de); **~ breeds contempt** lo conocido no se estima. (b) (*of tone*) intimidad *f*; confianza *f*; (*pej*) frescura *f*; **familiarities** familiaridades *fpl*, confianzas *fpl*.

familiarize [fəˈmɪlɪəraɪz] 1 VT familiarizar (*with* con).

2 VR: **to ~ o.s. with** familiarizarse con.

familiarly [fəˈmɪlɪəlɪ] ADV con demasiada confianza.

family [ˈfæmɪlɪ] 1 N familia *f*; **to be one of the ~** ser como de la familia; **to be in the ~ way** estar en estado de buena esperanza; **to get** (*or* **put**) **a girl in the ~ way** dejar encinta a una joven; **to run in the ~** venir de familia.

2 ATTR *gathering etc* familiar; **~ allowance** (*Brit*) subsidio *m* familiar; **~ business** negocio *m* de la familia; **~ butcher** carnicero *m* doméstico; **~ credit** (*Brit*) ≈ suplemento *m* familiar, puntos* *mpl*; **~ doctor** médico *m*, -a *f* de cabecera; **~ friend** amigo *m*, -a *f* de la familia; **~ hotel** hotel *m* familiar; **~ income** ingresos *mpl* familiares; **~ life** vida *f* doméstica; **~ man** (*having family*) padre *m* de familia, (*home-loving*) hombre *m* casero; **~ name** nombre *m* de familia, apellido *m*; **~ pet** animal *m* doméstico; **~ planning** planificación *f* familiar; **~ planning clinic** clínica *f* de planificación familiar; **~-size(d) packet** paquete *m* familiar; **~ tree** árbol *m* genealógico.

famine [ˈfæmɪn] N hambre *f* (general y grave), hambruna *f*; (*of goods*) escasez *f*, carestía *f*.

famished [ˈfæmɪʃt] ADJ hambriento, famélico; **I'm simply ~** tengo un hambre canina.

famous [ˈfeɪməs] ADJ famoso, célebre (*for* por).

famously [ˈfeɪməslɪ] ADV (*fig*) estupendamente bien, a las mil maravillas.

fan¹ [fæn] 1 N abanico *m* (*also fig*); (*Agr*) aventador *m*; (*machine, Aut*) ventilador *m*; (*electric*) abanico *m* eléctrico, ventilador *m*; **when the shit hits the ~*** cuando se arma la gorda*.

2 VT *face* abanicar; (*mechanically*) ventilar; (*Agr*) aventar; *fire* soplar; (*fig*) excitar, atizar.

3 VR: **to ~ o.s.** abanicarse, hacerse aire.

◆**fan out** 1 VT *cards etc* exponer (*or* ordenar) en abanico.

2 VI (*Mil etc*) desparramarse (en abanico), avanzar en abanico; diseminarse, dispersarse.

fan² [fæn] N aficionado *m*, -a *f*, admirador *m*, -ora *f*, entusiasta *mf*, (*Sport*) hincha *mf*; (*of pop music*) fan *mf*; **I am not one of his ~s** no soy de sus admiradores, yo no soy de los que le admiran.

fanatic [fəˈnætɪk] N fanático *m*, -a *f*.

fanatic(al) [fəˈnætɪk(əl)] ADJ fanático.

fanatically [fəˈnætɪklɪ] ADV fanáticamente, hasta el fanatismo; **they were ~ loyal to their Emperor** su lealtad hacia el emperador llegaba al fanatismo.

fanaticism [fəˈnætɪsɪzəm] N fanatismo *m*.

fanbelt [ˈfænbelt] N correa *f* de ventilador.

fanciable* [ˈfænsɪəbl] ADJ (*Brit*) guapo, bueno*.

fancied [ˈfænsɪd] ADJ (*imaginary*) imaginario; (*preferred*) favorito; selecto; **a much ~ possibility** una posibilidad en que muchos creen; **a little ~ team** un equipo que se cree con pocas posibilidades.

fancier [ˈfænsɪər] N V **pigeon-fancier**.

fanciful [ˈfænsɪfʊl] ADJ *temperament* caprichoso; *construction, explanation etc* fantástico; (*unreal*) imaginario.

fan-club [ˈfænklʌb] N club *m* de admiradores; (*Mus*) club *m* de fans.

▼ **fancy** [ˈfænsɪ] 1 N (a) (*delusion*) quimera *f*, suposición *f* arbitraria; **it's just your ~** lo habrás soñado; **it's one of her fancies** son cosas de ella.

(b) (*imaginative capacity*) fantasía *f*, imaginación *f*; **in the realm of ~** en el mundo de la fantasía.

(c) (*whim*) capricho *m*, antojo *m*; **to have a ~ for sth** antojarse algo a uno; **as the ~ takes her** según su capricho.

(d) (*taste*) afición *f*, gusto *m*; **to take a ~ to sth** tomar afición a algo, encapricharse por algo; **to take a ~ to sb** tomar cariño a uno, (*amorously*) prendarse de uno; **to take** (*or* **tickle**) **sb's ~** atraer a uno, cautivar a uno, (*amuse*) caer en gracia a uno.

2 ADJ (a) (*ornamental*) de adorno, de lujo; *jewels etc* de fantasía; **~**

dress disfraz *m*; **~ dress ball** baile *m* de disfraces; baile *m* de trajes; **~ footwork** (*fig*) filigranas *fpl*; **~ goods** géneros *mpl* de fantasía; **~ work** (*Sew*) labor *f*.
(b) (*pej*) *idea* fantástico, estrafalario; *price* excesivo; **her ~ man*** su amante; **his ~ woman*** su querida.
3 VT **(a)** (*picture to o.s.*) imaginarse, figurarse; (*rather think*) creer, suponer; **I ~ he is away** creo (*LAm*: se me hace) que está fuera; **he fancies he knows it all** se cree un pozo de sabiduría; **~!, ~ that!, just ~!** ¡fíjate!, (*doubting*) ¡parece mentira!; ¡lo que son las cosas!; **~ meeting you!** ¡qué casualidad encontrarle a Vd!; **~ him winning!** ¡qué raro que lo ganara él!
▼**(b)** (*want, like*) aficionarse a, encapricharse por; **I don't ~ the idea** no me gusta la idea; **what do you ~?** ¿qué quieres tomar?; **do you ~ a stroll?** ¿te apetece (*LAm*: ¿se te antoja) dar un paseo?; **he fancies her*** (*Brit*) ella le gusta, se siente atraído por ella.
(c) (*have high opinion of*) tener un alto concepto de; **he fancies his game** cree tener muchísima habilidad; **I don't ~ his chances of winning** no le doy mucha esperanza de ganar.
4 VR: **to ~ o.s. (a)** (*imagine o.s.*) creerse, soñar que uno es *etc*; **he fancied himself in Spain** soñó que estaba en España.
(b) (*Brit*) presumir; **you ~ yourself!** ¡eres un presumido!; **he fancies himself as a footballer** las echa de futbolista.
fancydan* [ˌfænsɪˈdæn] N (*US*) chulo *m*.
fancy-free [ˈfænsɪˈfriː] ADJ sin compromiso.
fandango [fænˈdæŋɡəʊ] N, PL **fandangos** fandango *m*.
fanfare [ˈfænfeəʳ] N toque *m* de trompeta, fanfarria *f*.
fanfold paper [ˈfænfəʊldˌpeɪpəʳ] N papel *m* plegado en abanico (*or* en acordeón).
fang [fæŋ] N colmillo *m*.
fan-heater [ˈfænˌhiːtəʳ] N (*Brit*) calefactor *m*, calentador *m* de aire.
fanlight [ˈfænlaɪt] N (montante *m* de) abanico *m*.
fanmail [ˈfænmeɪl] N cartas *fpl* escritas por admiradores.
Fanny [ˈfænɪ] NF **(a)** (*familiar form of* **Frances**. **(b)** **sweet ~ Adams***, (*Brit*) absolutamente nada, nada de nada, na' de na'*.
fanny* [ˈfænɪ] N (*esp US: buttocks*) culo* *m*; (*Brit*: vagina*) coño* *m*.
fan-shaped [ˈfænʃeɪpt] ADJ de (*or* en) abanico.
fantabulous* [fænˈtæbjʊləs] ADJ (*US*) superguay*.
fantasia [fænˈteɪzɪə] N (*Liter, Mus*) fantasía *f*.
fantasist [ˈfæntəzɪst] N fantaseador *m*, -ora *f*.
fantasize [ˈfæntəsaɪz] VI fantasear.
fantastic [fænˈtæstɪk] ADJ (*gen*) fantástico; (**: excellent*) estupendo*, bárbaro* (*LAm*).
fantastical [fænˈtæstɪkl] ADJ (*liter*) mítico, fabuloso, fantástico.
fantastically [fænˈtæstɪkəlɪ] ADV fantásticamente; **~ learned** enormemente erudito.
fantasy [ˈfæntəzɪ] N fantasía *f*.
fan-vaulting [ˈfænˌvɔːltɪŋ] N bóveda *f* de abanico.
fanzine [ˈfænziːn] N fanzine *m*.
FAO N ABBR *of* **Food and Agriculture Organization** Organización *f* para la Alimentación y la Agricultura, OAA *f*.
FAQ ABBR *of* **Frequently Asked Questions**: **~ (file)** fichero *m* de preguntas frecuentes.
faq ABBR *of* **of fair average quality** de calidad estándar.
▼**far** [fɑːʳ] **1** ADV **(a)** (*distance: lit*) lejos, a lo lejos (*also* **~ away**, **~ off**); **not ~ from Dover** no muy lejos de Dover; **is it ~?** ¿está lejos?, ¿dista mucho?; **how ~ is it to Irún?** ¿cuánto hay de aquí a Irún?; **~ and near, ~ and wide** por todas partes; **as ~ as** hasta; **so ~** hasta aquí; **a bridge too ~** un puente de más; **to walk ~ into the hills** penetrar profundamente en los montes.
(b) (*distance: fig*) **how ~ ...?** ¿hasta qué punto ...?; **how ~ have you gone in your work?** ¿a qué punto han llegado tus trabajos?; **~ into the night** hasta las altas horas de la noche; **he's not ~ off 70** tiene casi 70 años, frisa en los 70 años; **she was not ~ off tears** estaba al borde de las lágrimas; **as ~ back as we can recall** hasta donde alcanza la memoria; **so ~** hasta aquí, (*in time*) hasta ahora; **so ~ this year** en lo que va del año; **so ~ so good** hasta aquí, bien; **so ~ and no further** hasta aquí pero ni un paso más.
▼**(c)** (*phrases*) **as ~ as I know**, **as ~ as I can tell** que yo sepa; **I will help you as ~ as I can** te ayudaré en lo que pueda; **as ~ as I am concerned** en cuanto a mí, por lo que a mí se refiere; **in so ~ as ...** en la medida en que ..., en cuanto ...; **~ from approving it, I ...** lejos de aprobarlo, yo ...; **~ from it!** ¡nada de eso!; **~ be it from me to + infin** no permita Dios que yo + *subj*.
(d) (*with adj or adv*) **~ better** mucho mejor; **it is ~ better not to go** más vale no ir; **~ and away the best**, **the best by ~** con mucho el mejor; **~ superior to** muy superior a; **~ faster than** mucho más rápidamente que.
(e) (*with go*) **to go ~** (*plan etc*) ir lejos; **that young man will go ~** ese joven irá lejos, ese joven tiene un brillante porvenir; **it doesn't go ~ enough** no va bastante lejos, no tiene todo el alcance que quisiéramos; **to go too ~** ir demasiado lejos; pasarse, propasarse, excederse; **the theory is good as ~ as it goes** la teoría es buena

dentro de sus límites; **he was pretty ~ gone** (*dying*) se acercaba a la muerte, (*drunk*) estaba muy borracho; **for a white wine you won't go ~ wrong with this** si buscas un vino blanco éste ofrece bastante garantía; **he wasn't ~ wrong** (*or* **off, out**) casi acertada, casi estaba en lo justo; **he's gone too ~ to back out now** ha ido demasiado lejos para retirarse ahora; **to go ~ to + infin** contribuir mucho a + *infin*; **to go so ~ as to + infin** llegar a + *infin*.
2 ADJ lejano, remoto; **at the ~ end** en el otro extremo, (*of room*) en el fondo; **at the ~ side** en el lado opuesto; **the ~ north** el extremo norte.
farad [ˈfærəd] N faradio *m*.
faraway [ˈfɑːrəweɪ] ADJ remoto; *look* preocupado, distraído.
farce [fɑːs] N (*Theat*) farsa *f*; (*fig*) farsa *f*, absurdo *m*, tontería *f*; **this is a ~** esto es absurdo; **what a ~ this is!** ¡qué follón!; **the trial was a ~** el proceso fue una parodia de la justicia.
farcical [ˈfɑːsɪkəl] ADJ absurdo, ridículo.
far-distant [ˈfɑːˈdɪstənt] ADJ lejano, remoto.
fare [feəʳ] **1** N **(a)** (*cost*) precio *m* (del viaje, del billete); (*ticket*) billete *m*, boleto *m* (*LAm*); (*Naut*) pasaje *m*; **~ stage**, **~ zone** (*US*) zona *f* (del recorrido del autobús); **~s please!** ¡billetes, por favor!
(b) (*person*) pasajero *m*, -a *f*.
(c) (*food*) comida *f*.
2 VI: **to ~ badly** pasarlo mal, irle mal a uno; **to ~ well** pasarlo bien, irle bien a uno; **how did you ~?** ¿qué tal le fue?; **to ~ alike** correr la misma suerte.
Far East [ˈfɑːrˈiːst] N Extremo Oriente *m*, Lejano Oriente *m*.
Far Eastern [ˈfɑːrˈiːstən] ADJ del Extremo Oriente.
farewell [feəˈwel] **1** INTERJ ¡adiós!; **it's ~ to all that** ya se acabó todo eso; **you can say ~ to your wallet** puedes considerar tu cartera como perdida.
2 N adiós *m*; (*ceremony*) despedida *f*; **to bid ~ to** despedirse de.
3 ATTR de despedida.
far-fetched [ˈfɑːˈfetʃt] ADJ inverosímil, poco probable; *comparison* traído por los pelos.
far-flung [ˈfɑːˈflʌŋ] ADJ extenso.
farinaceous [ˌfærɪˈneɪʃəs] ADJ farináceo.
farm [fɑːm] **1** N granja *f*; cortijo *m*, quinta *f*, estancia *f* (*LAm*); (*of mink, oysters etc*) criadero *m*; (*house*) cortijo *m*, alquería *f*, casa *f* de labranza.
2 ATTR agrícola; **~ produce** productos *mpl* agrícolas; **~ tractor** tractor *m* agrícola.
3 VT (*till*) cultivar, labrar; **he ~s 300 acres** tiene una finca de 300 acres.
4 VI (*till*) cultivar la tierra; (*as profession*) ser agricultor; **he ~s in Devon** tiene una finca (*or* tierras) en Devon.
◆**farm out** VT arrendar, dar en arriendo; *work* dar fuera, confiar a terceros.
farmer [ˈfɑːməʳ] N agricultor *m*, cultivador *m*, hacendado *m* (*LAm*), granjero *m*; (*peasant ~*) labrador *m*; estanciero *m* (*LAm*).
farmhand [ˈfɑːmhænd] N labriego *m*, mozo *m* de labranza, peón *m*.
farmhouse [ˈfɑːmhaʊs] N, PL **farmhouses** [ˈfɑːmhauzɪz] cortijo *m*, alquería *f*, casa *f* de labranza, casa *f* de hacienda (*LAm*).
farming [ˈfɑːmɪŋ] **1** N (*tilling*) cultivo *m*, labranza *f*; (*in general*) agricultura *f*.
2 ATTR agrícola; **the ~ community** los agricultores; **good ~ practice** técnicas *fpl* agrícolas reconocidas.
farm labourer, (*US*) **farm laborer** [ˈfɑːmˌleɪbərəʳ] N trabajador *m* agrícola.
farmland [ˈfɑːmlænd] N tierras *fpl* de labrantío.
farmstead [ˈfɑːmsted] N alquería *f*.
farm worker [ˈfɑːmˌwɜːkəʳ] N trabajador *m*, -ora *f* agrícola.
farmyard [ˈfɑːmjɑːd] N corral *m*.
Faroes [ˈfeərəʊz] NPL, **Faroe Islands** [ˈfeərəʊˌaɪləndz] NPL Islas *fpl* Feroe.
far-off [ˈfɑːrˈɒf] ADJ lejano, remoto.
far-out* [ˌfɑːrˈaʊt] ADJ **(a)** (*odd*) raro, extraño; estrafalario. **(b)** (*modern*) muy moderno, de vanguardia. **(c)** (*superb*) guai*, fenomenal*, tremendo*. **(d)** (*Pol etc*) extremista.
farrago [fəˈrɑːɡəʊ] N fárrago *m*.
far-reaching [ˈfɑːˈriːtʃɪŋ] ADJ trascendental, de gran alcance, de ancha repercusión.
farrier [ˈfærɪəʳ] N (*esp Brit*) herrador *m*.
farrow [ˈfærəʊ] **1** N lechigada *f* de puercos.
2 VT parir.
3 VI parir (la cerda).
far-seeing [ˈfɑːˈsiːɪŋ] ADJ clarividente, previsor.
far-sighted [ˈfɑːˈsaɪtɪd] ADJ présbita; (*fig*) clarividente, previsor.
far-sightedly [ˈfɑːˈsaɪtɪdlɪ] ADV de modo clarividente, con previsión.
far-sightedness [ˈfɑːˈsaɪtɪdnɪs] N clarividencia *f*, previsión *f*.
fart* [fɑːt] **1** N **(a)** pedo* *m*. **(b)** **he's a boring old ~** es un tío terriblemente pesado*, es un carrozón*.
2 VI pederse*, tirarse un pedo*.

◆**fart about**‡, **fart around**‡ VI = **mess about**.

farther ['fɑːðəʳ] COMP of **far**; = **further**.

farthest ['fɑːðɪst] SUPERL of **far**; = **furthest**.

farthing ['fɑːðɪŋ] N cuarto *m* de penique.

FAS ABBR of **free alongside ship** libre al costado del barco.

fascia ['feɪʃə] N (*on building*) faja *f*; (*Brit Aut*) tablero *m*.

fascicle ['fæsɪkl] N, **fascicule** ['fæsɪkjuːl] N fascículo *m*.

fascinate ['fæsɪneɪt] VT fascinar, encantar.

fascinated ['fæsɪneɪtɪd] ADJ fascinado; **to be ~ with sth** estar fascinado por algo.

fascinating ['fæsɪneɪtɪŋ] ADJ fascinador, encantador, sugestivo.

fascination [,fæsɪ'neɪʃən] N fascinación *f*, encanto *m*, sugestión *f*; **his former ~ with the cinema** la atracción que tuvo para él el cine.

fascism ['fæʃɪzəm] N fascismo *m*.

fascist ['fæʃɪst] 1 ADJ fascista.

2 N fascista *mf*.

fashion ['fæʃən] 1 N (a) (*usage, manner*) uso *m*, manera *f*, estilo *m*; **it is not my ~ to pretend** yo no acostumbro fingir; **after a ~** en cierto modo; medianamente; no muy bien; **I play after a ~** toco algo; **after the ~ of** a la manera de; **in the French ~** a la francesa, a lo francés, al estilo francés; **in one's own ~** a su propio modo.

(b) (*vogue*) moda *f*; **it's all the ~ now** ahora está muy de moda; **it's the ~ to say that ...** es un tópico decir que ...; **to be in ~** estar de moda; **to be out of ~** haber pasado de moda; **to come into ~** empezar a estar de moda; **to dress in the latest ~** vestirse a la última moda; **to go out of ~** pasar de moda; **to set the ~** imponer la moda (*for* de), dictar la moda (*for* de).

(c) (*good taste*) buen tono *m*, buen gusto *m*; **what ~ demands** lo que impone el buen gusto; **a man of ~** un hombre elegante.

2 ATTR **~ designer** modisto *m*, -a *f*; **~ editor** director *m*, -ora *f* de modas; **~ house** casa *f* de modas; **~ magazine** revista *f* de modas; **~ model** modelo *mf*; **~ page** sección *f* de modas; **~ paper** revista *f* de modas; **~ parade** desfile *m* de modelos, presentación *f* de modelos; **~ plate** figurín *m* de moda; **~ show** presentación *f* de modelos.

3 VT formar, labrar, forjar (*on* sobre).

fashionable ['fæʃnəbl] ADJ *dress etc* de moda, elegante; *place, restaurant* de buen tono, elegante; **~ people** gente *f* elegante, gente *f* bien*; **in ~ society** en la buena sociedad; **it is ~ to +** *infin* está de moda + *infin*; **he is hardly a ~ painter now** es un pintor que no está ahora muy de moda.

fashionably ['fæʃnəblɪ] ADV: **to be ~ dressed** estar vestido muy elegantemente, ir vestido de acuerdo con la moda actual.

fashion-conscious ['fæʃən,kɒnʃəs] ADJ pendiente de la moda.

fast¹ [fɑːst] 1 ADJ (a) (*speedy*) rápido, veloz; ligero; (*Sport*) *pitch* seco y firme; *court* rápido; *train* rápido, expreso; **~ lane** (*Aut*) carril *m* de adelantamiento; (*Brit*) carril *m* de la derecha, (*most countries*) carril *m* de la izquierda; **he lives life in the ~ lane** vive deprisa; **he was too ~ for me** corrió más que yo; **to pull a ~ one on sb** jugar una mala pasada a uno, embaucar a uno; **he's a ~ talker*** es un pretencioso.

(b) (*clock*) **to be ~** estar adelantado; **my watch is 5 minutes ~** mi reloj está 5 minutos adelantado.

(c) *woman* cachonda, fresca; *life, set* entregado a los placeres, hedonista; disoluto.

(d) (*firm*) fijo, firme; *friend* leal; *colour* sólido, inalterable; *film* rápido.

2 ADV (a) (*speedily*) rápidamente; de prisa; **~er!** ¡más!; **how ~ can you type?** ¿cuántas palabras haces por minuto?; **I ran as ~ as I could** corrí cuanto pude; **don't speak so ~** habla más despacio; **not so ~!** ¡más despacio!, (*interrupting*) ¡un momento!; **as ~ as I finished them he wrapped them up** a medida que yo los terminaba él los envolvía.

(b) **to play ~ and loose with** jugar con.

(c) (*firmly*) firmemente; **~ asleep** profundamente dormido; **to hold ~** agarrarse bien, (*fig*) mantenerse firme; **hold ~!** ¡agarraos!, (*stop*) ¡para!; **to make sth ~** sujetar algo; **to make a rope ~** atar firmemente una cuerda; **to make a boat ~** amarrar una barca; **to stand ~** mantenerse firme; **to stick ~** quedar bien pegado; **to be stuck ~ in the mud** quedar atascado en el lodo; **to be stuck ~ in a doorway** estar metido por una puerta sin poderse mover.

fast² [fɑːst] 1 N ayuno *m*.

2 VI ayunar.

fast day ['fɑːstdeɪ] N día *m* de ayuno.

fasten ['fɑːsn] 1 VT (a) asegurar, sujetar, fijar; (*with rope*) atar; (*with paste*) pegar; *box, door, window* cerrar; (*with bolt*) echar el cerrojo a; *belt, dress* abrochar; **to ~ two things together** pegar dos cosas.

(b) (*fig*) **to ~ the blame on sb** echar (*or* achacar) la culpa a uno; **to ~ the responsibility on sb** atribuir a uno la responsabilidad; **they're trying to ~ the crime on me** tratan de demostrar que yo fui autor del crimen.

2 VI (*box etc*) cerrarse.

◆**fasten down** VT *blind, flap* cerrar.

◆**fasten on to** VT agarrarse de, pegarse a, (*fig*) fijarse en; **he ~ed on to me at once** se fijó en mí en seguida, (*as companion*) se me pegó a mí

en seguida; **to ~ on to a pretext** echar mano (*or* valerse) de un pretexto.

◆**fasten up** 1 VT *dress, coat* abotonar, abrochar.

2 VI: **it ~s up in front** se abrocha por delante.

◆**fasten (up)on** VT *gaze* fijar en, dirigir a; **to ~ (up)on an excuse** aferrarse a una excusa; **to ~ (up)on the idea of doing** aferrarse a la idea de hacer.

fastener ['fɑːsnəʳ] N, **fastening** ['fɑːsnɪŋ] N (*of door etc*) cerrojo *m*, pestillo *m*; (*on box*) cierre *m*; (*on dress*) broche *m*, corchete *m*; (*for papers*) grapa *f*; (*zip-~*) cremallera *f*.

fast food ['fɑːst'fuːd] N (a) (*snack*) comida *f* rápida, platos *mpl* preparados. (b) (*place*: *also* **~ restaurant**) restaurante *m* fast-food, hamburguesería *f*; fast-food *m*.

fast forward ['fɑːst'fɔːwəd] 1 N (*also* **~ button**) botón *m* de avance rápido.

2 VT hacer avanzar rápidamente.

3 VI avanzar rápidamente.

fastidious [fæs'tɪdɪəs] ADJ delicado, quisquilloso; (*about cleanliness etc*) exigente; *taste* fino; *mind* refinado.

fastidiously [fæs'tɪdɪəslɪ] ADV *examine, clean, check* meticulosamente, quisquillosamente.

fastidiousness [fæs'tɪdɪəsnɪs] N meticulosidad *f*, exigencia *f*.

fast-moving [,fɑːst'muːvɪŋ] ADJ rápido, veloz; *target* que cambia rápidamente de posición; *goods* de venta rápida, que se venden rápidamente; *plot* muy movido, lleno de acciones, que se desarrolla rápidamente.

fastness ['fɑːstnɪs] N (*Mil*) fortaleza *f*; (*of mountain etc*) lo más intrincado; **in their Cuban mountain ~** en las espesuras serranas de Cuba.

fat [fæt] 1 ADJ (a) *person* gordo; (*thick*) grueso; **~ cat*** (*esp US*) pez *m* gordo*, potentado *m*; **~ farm** (*US**) clínica *f* de adelgazamiento; **to get ~** engordar.

(b) *meat* poco magro, que tiene mucha grasa; (*greasy*) grasiento, graso.

(c) *land* fértil; *living* lujoso; *profit* pingüe; *salary* muy grande; **the ~ years** los años de las vacas gordas.

(d) (*) **a ~ lot he knows!** ¡maldito lo que él sabe!; **a ~ chance he's got no time ni chance***; **a ~ lot of good you did us!** ¡menudo provecho que nos has traído!; **a ~ lot of good that is!** y eso ¿para qué sirve?

2 N (*on person*) carnes *fpl*; (*of meat*) grasa *f*; (*for cooking*) manteca *f* (de cerdo); (*lard*) lardo *m*; **to live on the ~ of the land** vivir a cuerpo de rey, nadar en la abundancia; comer opíparamente; **now the ~ is in the fire** aquí se va a armar la gorda.

fatal ['feɪtl] ADJ fatal (*also Comput*); *consequences* funesto (*to* para); *accident, injury* mortal; **~ accident enquiry** (*Scot*) investigación de accidente mortal; **that was ~** eso fue el colmo; **it's ~ to say that** es peligrosísimo decir eso.

fatalism ['feɪtəlɪzəm] N fatalismo *m*.

fatalist ['feɪtəlɪst] N fatalista *mf*.

fatalistic [,feɪtə'lɪstɪk] ADJ fatalista.

fatality [fə'tælɪtɪ] N calamidad *f*, desgracia *f*; fatalidad *f*; (*victim*) víctima *f*, muerto *m*; **luckily there were no fatalities** por fortuna no hubo víctimas.

fatally ['feɪtəlɪ] ADV fatalmente; *injure etc* mortalmente, a muerte.

fate [feɪt] N (a) (*force*) hado *m*, destino *m*, sino *m*; **the F~s** las Parcas; **what ~ has in store for us** lo que la suerte nos va a deparar.

(b) (*person's lot*) suerte *f*; **to leave sb to his ~** dejar a uno a su suerte; **to meet one's ~** encontrar la muerte; **this sealed his ~** esto acabó de perderle.

fated ['feɪtɪd] ADJ *friendship, person* predestinado, condenado; **to be ~ to do** estar predestinado a hacer, tener fatalmente que hacer.

fateful ['feɪtʊl] ADJ fatal, fatídico; decisivo.

fat-free ['fætfriː] ADJ *diet* sin grasa.

fathead* ['fæthed] N imbécil *mf*; **you ~!** ¡imbécil!

fat-headed* ['fæt,hedɪd] ADJ imbécil.

father ['fɑːðəʳ] 1 N padre *m*; **F~s of the Church** Santos Padres *mpl*; **Our F~** Padre nuestro; **to say three Our F~s** rezar tres padrenuestros; **F~ Brown** (*Rel*) (el) padre Brown; **~ confessor** padre *m* confesor, director *m* espiritual; **F~ Christmas** (*Brit*) Papá *m* Noel; **Old F~ Time** el Tiempo; **F~'s Day** Día *m* del Padre; **city ~s** prohombres *mpl* de la ciudad; **my ~ and mother** mis padres; **like ~ like son** de tal palo tal astilla; **a ~ and mother of a row*** una bronca fenomenal*; **the ~ of English poetry** el padre de la poesía inglesa; **to talk to sb like a ~** hablar a uno en tono paternal.

2 VT *child* engendrar; (*fig*) inventar, producir; **to ~ sth on sb** atribuir algo a uno.

father-figure ['fɑːðə,fɪgəʳ] N figura *f* que sirve de padre, persona *f* que se finge (*or* cree *etc*) dotada de las cualidades paternales.

fatherhood ['fɑːðəhʊd] N paternidad *f*.

father-in-law ['fɑːðərɪnlɔː] N, PL **fathers-in-law** suegro *m*, padre *m* político.

fatherland ['fɑːðəlænd] N patria f.
fatherless ['fɑːðəlɪs] ADJ huérfano de padre.
fatherly ['fɑːðəlɪ] ADJ paternal.
fathom ['fæðəm] **1** N braza f; **5 ~s deep** de (or a etc) una profundidad de 5 brazas.
    2 VT (Naut) sond(e)ar; (fig) profundizar, penetrar; mystery desentrañar; **we couldn't ~ it out** no logramos sacar nada en claro; **I can't ~ why** no comprendo por qué.
fathomless ['fæðəmlɪs] ADJ insondable.
fatigue [fə'tiːg] **1** N (a) fatiga f, cansancio m; (Tech) fatiga f.
    (b) (Mil) faena f.
    (c) (Mil: also ~s) uniforme m (or traje m) de faena (or de cuartel), mono m.
    2 ATTR (Mil) ~ **dress = 1 c; ~ duty** servicio m de fajina; **~ party** destacamento m de fajina.
    3 VT fatigar, cansar.
fatigued [fə'tiːgd] ADJ fatigado.
fatiguing [fə'tiːgɪŋ] ADJ fatigoso.
fatless ['fætlɪs] ADJ food sin grasa.
fatness ['fætnɪs] N gordura f.
fatso‡ ['fætsəʊ] N (pej) gordo m, -a f.
fatstock ['fætstɒk] N (Agr) animales mpl de engorde.
fatten ['fætn] **1** VT animal engordar, cebar.
    2 VI engordar.
fattening ['fætnɪŋ] **1** ADJ food que hace engordar.
    2 NM (Agr) engorde m.
fatty ['fætɪ] **1** ADJ graso; tissue, degeneration etc grasoso; **~ acid** ácido m graso.
    2 N (*) gordinflón* m, -ona f; **~!** ¡gordo!
fatuity [fə'tjuːɪtɪ] N fatuidad f, necedad f.
fatuous ['fætjʊəs] ADJ fatuo, necio.
fatuously ['fætjʊəslɪ] ADV neciamente.
fatuousness ['fætjʊəsnɪs] = **fatuity**.
fatwa ['fætwə] N fatwa f.
faucet ['fɔːsɪt] N (US) grifo m, llave f (LAm).
faugh [fɔː] INTERJ ¡fu!
▼**fault** [fɔːlt] **1** N (a) (defect: in character) defecto m; (in manufacture) desperfecto m, imperfección f; (in supply, machine) avería f; **with all his ~s** con todos sus defectos; **her ~ is excessive shyness** peca de demasiado reservada; **generous to a ~** excesivamente generoso, generoso hasta el exceso; **to find ~ with** criticar, poner peros a.
    (b) (Geol) falla f.
    ▼(c) (blame) culpa f; **it's all your ~** tienes toda la culpa; **it's not my ~** yo no tengo la culpa; **whose ~ is it if ...?** ¿quién tiene la culpa si ...?; **you were not at ~** tú no tuviste la culpa; **you were at ~ in not telling me** hiciste mal en no decírmelo; **your memory is at ~** recuerdas mal.
    (d) (mistake) falta f (also Tennis etc); **through no ~ of his own** sin falta alguna de su parte.
    2 VT tachar, encontrar defectos en; **it cannot be ~ed** es intachable; **you cannot ~ him on spelling** no le encontrarás falta alguna en la escritura.
faultfinder ['fɔːlt,faɪndəʳ] N criticón m, -ona f.
faultfinding ['fɔːlt,faɪndɪŋ] **1** ADJ criticón, reparón.
    2 N manía f de criticar.
faultless ['fɔːltlɪs] ADJ impecable, intachable, sin defecto.
faultlessly ['fɔːltlɪslɪ] ADV impecablemente.
faulty ['fɔːltɪ] ADJ defectuoso, imperfecto.
faun [fɔːn] N fauno m.
fauna ['fɔːnə] N fauna f.
Faust [faʊst] NM Fausto.
Faustian ['faʊstɪən] ADJ de Fausto.
faux pas ['fəʊ'pɑː] N (false move) paso m en falso; (gaffe) plancha f, metedura f (LAm: metida f) de pata.
fava bean ['fɑːvəbiːn] N (US) haba f.
▼**favour**, (US) **favor** ['feɪvəʳ] **1** N (a) (approval, regard) favor m; aprobación f; (protection) amparo m; **to be in ~** (thing) tener mucha aceptación, (dress etc) estar de moda; **to be in ~ with** (person) tener el apoyo de, (at court etc) gozar de favor cerca de; **to be out of ~** (thing) no estimarse, (dress etc) estar fuera de moda; **to curry ~** buscar favores; **to curry ~ with sb** tratar de congraciarse con uno; **to find ~ with sb** caer en gracia a uno; **to look with ~ on** favorecer; **to stand high in sb's ~** ser tenido en mucho por uno.
    ▼(b) (kindness) favor m; **~s** (of woman) favores mpl; **to ask a ~ of** pedir un favor a; **to do sb a ~** hacer un favor a uno; **please do me the ~ of + ger** haga el favor de + infin; **do me a ~!**‡ (as answer) ¡nada de eso!; ¿crees que soy tan tonto?; **do me a ~ and clear off!**‡ ¡por Dios, lárgate!*
    (c) **your ~ of the 5th inst** (Comm) su atenta del 5 del corriente.
    (d) (partiality) parcialidad f; **by your ~** con permiso de Vd; **to show ~ to sb** favorecer a uno.

▼(e) (aid, support) apoyo m; **in ~ of** a favor de; **balance in your ~** saldo m a su favor; **that's a point in his ~** es un punto a su favor; **to be in ~ of** person apoyar, estar por; thing aprobar, ser partidario de; **to be in ~ of + ger** apoyar la idea de + infin, ser partidario de + infin.
    (f) (token) prenda f.
    2 VT person favorecer, (unjustly) mostrar parcialidad hacia; idea, scheme aprobar, ser partidario de; party apoyar; (choose to wear) elegir; progress ser propicio a, ayudar; team, horse preferir; **fortune ~s the brave** la fortuna ayuda a los valientes; **he eventually ~ed us with a visit** por fin nos honró con su visita, por fin se dignó visitarnos; **most ~ed nation treatment** trato m de nación más favorecida.
favourable, (US) **favorable** ['feɪvərəbl] ADJ favorable; conditions etc propicio.
favourably, (US) **favorably** ['feɪvərəblɪ] ADV favorablemente.
favoured, (US) **favored** ['feɪvəd] ADJ favorecido; (favourite) predilecto; **~ by nature** dotado por la naturaleza (with de); **one of the ~ few** uno de los pocos afortunados.
▼**favourite**, (US) **favorite** ['feɪvərɪt] **1** ADJ favorito, predilecto; **~ son** (US Pol) hijo m predilecto.
    2 N favorito m, -a f (also Sport); (at court) valido m, privado m; (mistress) querida f.
favouritism, (US) **favoritism** ['feɪvərɪtɪzəm] N favoritismo m.
fawn[1] [fɔːn] **1** N (a) (Zool) cervato m. (b) (colour) beige.
    2 ADJ beige.
fawn[2] [fɔːn] VI: **to ~ on** (animal) acariciar; (fig) adular, lisonjear; congraciarse con.
fawning ['fɔːnɪŋ] ADJ adulador, servil.
fax [fæks] **1** N fax m.
    2 ATTR: **~ message** fax m; **~ number** número m de (tele)fax.
    3 VT faxear.
faze* [feɪz] VT (esp US) perturbar; molestar; marear.
fazed* [feɪzd] ADJ (US) pasmado*.
FBA ABBR of **Fellow of the British Academy**.
FBI N (US) ABBR of **Federal Bureau of Investigation** FBI m.
FC N ABBR of **football club** club m de fútbol, C.F. m.
FCA N (a) ABBR of **Fellow of the Institute of Chartered Accountants**.
    (b) (US) ABBR of **Farm Credit Administration**.
FCC N (US) ABBR of **Federal Communications Commission**; ver también FAIRNESS DOCTRINE

┌─ **FCC - FEDERAL COMMUNICATIONS COMMISSION** ─┐

i La **FCC** o **Federal Communications Commission** es un organismo gubernamental independiente que regula y supervisa las transmisiones de radio, televisión y comunicación por cable y satélite en Estados Unidos. Entre las funciones más importantes de la **FCC** están la de conceder la licencia de emisión a las cadenas de radio y televisión privadas, así como la de asignarles sus frecuencias de transmisión. Además, tiene una gran influencia en la programación de las cadenas de televisión, entre las que ha introducido, por ejemplo, un espacio de dos horas para toda la familia por las noches, un límite a la cantidad de programas nacionales que pueden ser transmitidos por una cadena local y una **Fairness Doctrine** o doctrina de imparcialidad para los asuntos más polémicos. La comisión se compone de cinco miembros nombrados por el Presidente de EE.UU., y es responsable de sus actividades ante el Congreso.
⇨ Ver también FAIRNESS DOCTRINE

FCO N (Brit) ABBR of **Foreign and Commonwealth Office** ≃ Ministerio m de Asuntos Exteriores, Min. de AA EE.
F.D. (US) ABBR of **Fire Department**.
FDA N (US) ABBR of **Food and Drug Administration**.

┌─ **FDA - FOOD AND DRUG ADMINISTRATION** ─┐

i El **FDA** o **Food and Drug Administration** es el organismo de atención al consumidor más antiguo de Estados Unidos. Su función es la de analizar los alimentos, aditivos alimentarios, medicinas y cosméticos para asegurarse de que son aptos para el consumo. El **FDA** es muy conocido en el extranjero por su papel en el análisis de los nuevos productos, de su efectividad y de sus posibles efectos nocivos, así como en el control de su consumo una vez han sido puestos a la venta.

FDIC N (US) ABBR of **Federal Deposit Insurance Corporation**.
FDR initials of **Franklin Delano Roosevelt**.
fealty ['fiːəltɪ] N (Hist) lealtad f (feudal).
▼**fear** [fɪəʳ] **1** N miedo m (of a, de), temor m; aprensión f; **for ~ of** temiendo, por miedo de; **for ~ that ...** por miedo de que + subj; **no ~!** ¡ni hablar!; **there's no ~ of that happening** no hay peligro de que ocurra eso; **without ~ or favour** imparcialmente, sin temor ni favor; **to go in ~ of one's life** temer por su vida; **to put the ~ of God into sb** dar un susto mortal a uno.
    2 VT temer; person tener miedo a, thing tener miedo de.
    3 VI: **to ~ for** temer por; **to ~ to + infin** tener miedo de + infin; **never ~!** ¡no hay cuidado!, ¡no temas!

►   LANGUAGE IN USE: **fault: 1c → 18.3**   **favour: 1b → 4 1e → 6.3, 26.3**   **favourite: 1 → 7.2**   **fear: 1 → 17.1**

fearful ['fɪəfʊl] ADJ (a) (*frightened*) temeroso (*of* de); aprensivo; (*cowardly*) tímido. (b) (*frightening*) pavoroso, horrendo. (c) (*) tremendo*, terrible.

fearfully ['fɪəfəlɪ] ADV *cower etc* con miedo; *say* tímidamente; (*) terriblemente.

fearfulness ['fɪəfʊlnɪs] N (*fear*) medrosidad *f*; (*shyness*) timidez *f*.

fearless ['fɪəlɪs] ADJ intrépido, audaz; ~ **of** sin temor a.

fearlessly ['fɪəlɪslɪ] ADV intrépidamente, audazmente; **he went on** ~ siguió impertérrito.

fearlessness ['fɪəlɪsnɪs] N intrepidez *f*, audacia *f*.

fearsome ['fɪəsəm] ADJ temible, espantoso.

fearsomely ['fɪəsəmlɪ] ADV espantosamente.

feasibility [,fiːzə'bɪlɪtɪ] ① N factibilidad *f*, viabilidad *f*; **to doubt the ~ of a scheme** dudar si un proyecto es factible.
② ATTR: ~ **analysis** análisis *m* de viabilidad; ~ **study** estudio *m* de factibilidad.

▼ **feasible** ['fiːzəbl] ADJ factible, viable, posible; **to make sth ~** posibilitar algo.

feast [fiːst] ① N (a) (*meal*) banquete *m*, festín *m*. (b) (*Eccl*) fiesta *f*.
② VT banquetear; agasajar, festejar.
③ VI banquetear; **to ~ on** regalarse con.

feast-day ['fiːstdeɪ] N fiesta *f*.

feat [fiːt] N hazaña *f*, proeza *f*.

feather ['feðə'] ① N pluma *f*; **in fine ~** de excelente humor; **that is a ~ in his cap** es un triunfo para él; se ha apuntado un tanto; **you could have knocked me down with a ~** casi me caigo patas arriba; **to show the white ~** mostrarse cobarde.
② VT (a) emplumar. (b) *oar* volver horizontal.

feather-bed ['feðə'bed] ① N plumón *m*.
② VT subvencionar (demasiado), dar primas (excesivas) a.

featherbedding ['feðə,bedɪŋ] N subvencionismo *m*.

featherbrain ['feðəbreɪn] N cabeza *f* de chorlito.

featherbrained ['feðəbreɪnd] ADJ cascabelero.

feather duster ['feðə'dʌstə'] N plumero *m*.

feathered ['feðəd] ADJ *bird* plumado, con plumas; **our ~ friends** nuestros amigos plumados, nuestros amigos las aves.

feathering ['feðərɪŋ] N plumaje *m*.

featherweight ['feðəweɪt] N peso *m* pluma.

feathery ['feðərɪ] ADJ *texture* plumoso; (*light*) ligero como pluma.

feature ['fiːtʃə'] ① N (a) rasgo *m* distintivo, característica *f*; (*Ling: also* **distinctive ~**) rasgo *m* distintivo.
(b) (*of face*) facción *f*; **~s** facciones *fpl*, rostro *m*.
(c) (*Theat*) número *m*, (*Cine*) largometraje *m*, película *f* principal.
(d) (*in paper*) artículo *m*, crónica *f*.
② ATTR: ~ **article** crónica *f* especial, reportaje *m* especial; ~ **film** largometraje *m*, película *f* principal.
③ VT (*portray*) delinear, representar; (*in paper etc*) presentar, ofrecer (*como atracción principal*); *actor* presentar; **a film featuring Garbo as ...** una película que presenta a Garbo en el papel de ...
④ VI existir, constar, figurar.

featureless ['fiːtʃəlɪs] ADJ sin rasgos distintivos, monótono.

feature-writer ['fiːtʃə,raɪtə'] N articulista *mf*, cronista *mf*.

Feb. ABBR *of* **February** febrero *m*, feb.

febrile ['fiːbraɪl] ADJ febril.

February ['februərɪ] N febrero *m*.

feces ['fiːsiːz] NPL (*US*) = **faeces**.

feckless ['feklɪs] ADJ irreflexivo; casquivano.

fecund ['fiːkənd] ADJ fecundo.

fecundity [fɪ'kʌndɪtɪ] N fecundidad *f*.

Fed [fed] (a) (*US*) N ABBR *of* **federal officer** federal* *mf*. (b) (*US Banking*) N ABBR *of* **Federal Reserve Board.** (c) (*esp US*) ABBR *of* **federal, federated, federation.**

fed [fed] ① PRET AND PTP *of* **feed.**
② ADJ: **to be ~ up*** estar harto (*with* de).

federal ['fedərəl] ① ADJ federal; **the F~ Republic of Germany** la República Federal de Alemania; **F~ Reserve Bank** (*US*) Banco *m* de Reserva Federal; ~ **tax** impuesto *m* federal; *ver también* FCC – *FEDERAL COMMUNICATIONS COMMISSION*.
② NM (*US Hist*) federal *m*.

federalism ['fedərəlɪzəm] N federalismo *m*.

federalist ['fedərəlɪst] N federalista *mf*.

federalize ['fedərəlaɪz] VT federar, federalizar.

federate ['fedəreɪt] ① VT federar.
② VI federarse.

federation [,fedə'reɪʃən] N federación *f*.

fedora [fə'dɔːrə] N (*US*) sombrero *m* flexible, sombrero *m* tirolés.

fee [fiː] N (*professional*) derechos *mpl*, honorarios *mpl*; (*to club etc*) cuota *f*; (*for admission*) precio *m* (de entrada); (*for doctor's visit*) precio *m* de visita; **~s** (*Univ etc*) (gastos *mpl* de) matrícula *f*; **for a small ~** pagando un poco, por un pequeño reconocimiento.

feeble ['fiːbl] ADJ débil (*also Med*); flojo; *light, sound* tenue; *effort* irresoluto, débil; *argument* poco convincente.

feeble-minded ['fiːbl'maɪndɪd] ADJ imbécil; irresoluto.

feeble-mindedness [,fiːbl'maɪndɪdnɪs] N debilidad *f* mental; irresolución *f*.

feebleness ['fiːblnɪs] N debilidad *f* (*also Med*); flojedad *f*; tenuidad *f*; irresolución *f*.

feebly ['fiːblɪ] ADV débilmente; flojamente.

feed [fiːd] ① N (a) (*food*) comida *f*; (*Agr*) pienso *m*; **to be off one's ~** no tener apetito, estar desganado.
(b) (*) cuchipanda* *f*, comilona* *f*; **to have a good ~** darse un atracón*.
(c) (*Mech*) tubo *m* de alimentación.
② (*irr.* PRET AND PTP **fed**) VT (*nourish*) alimentar, nutrir; (*give meal to*) dar de comer a; (*Brit*) *baby* dar el pecho a, dar de mamar a, (*with bottle*) dar el biberón a; *fire* cebar; (*fig*) alimentar; **they fed us well at the hotel** nos dieron bien de comer en el hotel; **to ~ sth into a machine** ir metiendo algo en una máquina; **to ~ data into the computer** suministrar datos al ordenador, hacer entrar datos en el ordenador; **to ~ sb on sth** dar algo de comer a uno.
③ VI comer; (*Agr*) pacer; **to ~ on** comer, alimentarse de (*also fig*).
◆ **feed back** VT *information, results* proporcionar, facilitar.
◆ **feed in** VT *tape, wire* alimentar; *facts, information* introducir.
◆ **feed up** VT (a) *animal* cebar. (b) (*) **it really ~s me up** me saca totalmente de quicio.

feedback ['fiːdbæk] N (a) (*Rad*) realimentación *f*. (b) (*information etc*) feedback *m*, transmisión *f* en dirección inversa; (*reaction*) efecto *m* recíproco, retroacción *f*, reacción *f*; **we're not getting much ~** casi no se nota reacción alguna.

feeder ['fiːdə'] ① N (a) (*Mech*) alimentador *m*, tubo *m* de alimentación. (b) (*Geog*) afluente *m*; (*Rail*) ramal *m* tributario. (c) (*device: for birds etc*) comedero *m*. (d) (*Brit: bib*) babero *m*.
② ATTR: ~ **primary (school)** (*Scol*) escuela *f* primaria que provee de alumnos a una secundaria; ~ **service** (*US*) servicio *m* secundario (de transportes).

feeding ['fiːdɪŋ] N alimentación *f*; (*meals collectively*) comida *f*, comidas *fpl*.

feeding-bottle ['fiːdɪŋ,bɒtl] N (*esp Brit*) biberón *m*.

feeding-ground ['fiːdɪŋ,graʊnd] N terreno *m* de pasto.

feeding-stuffs ['fiːdɪŋ,stʌfs] NPL piensos *mpl*.

feeding time ['fiːdɪŋ,taɪm] N (*of baby: breast-feeding*) hora *f* del pecho; (*: bottle-feeding*) hora *f* del biberón; (*in zoo*) hora *f* de dar de comer.

feedpipe ['fiːdpaɪp] N tubo *m* de alimentación.

feedstuffs ['fiːdstʌfs] NPL piensos *mpl*.

feel [fiːl] ① N (*sense of touch*) tacto *m*; (*sensation*) sensación *f*; **at the ~ of his skin** al contacto con su piel; **to be rough to the ~** ser áspero al tacto; **to know silk by its ~** conocer la seda al tocarla; **to get the ~ of** acostumbrarse a, (*knack*) coger el tino a.
② (*irr.* PRET AND PTP **felt**) VT (a) (*explore*) tocar, palpar, tentar; *pulse* tomar; (*caress*) acariciar, palpar.
(b) (*perceive*) *blow, pain, heat, need* sentir; experimentar; **I felt it move** lo sentí moverse, sentí que se movió; **I felt it getting hot** sentí como se estaba calentando.
(c) (*be conscious of*) estar consciente de, darse cuenta de; **I ~ my position very much** me doy plenamente cuenta de mi situación.
(d) (*experience*) sentir, experimentar; (*be affected by*) resentirse de; **I ~ no interest in it** no me interesa; **we are beginning to ~ the effects** empezamos a resentirnos de los efectos; **the consequences will be felt next year** se sufrirán las consecuencias el año que viene.
(e) (*think, believe*) **I ~ that ...** creo que ..., siento que (+ *indic*), me parece que ...; **I ~ strongly that ...** estoy convencido de que ....
③ VI (a) (*explore*) **to ~ about in the dark** buscar a tientas en la oscuridad; **to ~ (around) in one's pocket for a key** buscar una llave en el bolsillo; **I can't see but I'll ~ for it** no veo nada pero lo buscaré tanteando.
(b) (*be*) sentirse; **to ~ bad, to ~ ill** sentirse mal; **to ~ old** sentirse viejo; **to ~ cold** (*person*) tener frío; **to ~ hungry** tener hambre; **how do you ~?** ¿qué tal te encuentras?; **she's not ~ing quite herself** no se encuentra del todo bien; **to ~ all the better for sth** sentirse mucho mejor después de algo; **I don't ~ up to it** no me siento con fuerzas para ello.
(c) (*think*) **how do you ~ about this?** ¿qué opinas de esto?; **how does it ~ to go hungry?** ¿cómo le gusta pasar hambre?
(d) (*give impression of*) **it ~s rough** es áspero al tacto; **it ~s like silk** es como la seda al tacto, parece ser seda; **it ~s cold** está frío (al tacto); **it ~s colder out here** aquí fuera hace más frío; **it ~s like rain** parece que va a llover; **how does it ~?** ¿qué impresión te hace?
(e) (*sympathize*) **I ~ for you** lo siento en el alma, te compadezco; **we ~ for you (in your loss)** te acompañamos en el sentimiento.
(f) **to ~ like doing sth** tener ganas de hacer algo; **I ~ like an apple** me apetece una manzana; **do you ~ like a walk?** ¿quieres dar un paseo?, ¿te apetece dar un paseo?; **I go out whenever I ~ like it** salgo siempre cuando quiero; **right now I don't ~ like it** ahora mismo no quiero.

◆**feel out*** VT (*US*) *person* sondear la opinión de; **to ~ out the ground** tantear el terreno, reconocer el terreno.

◆**feel up:** VT: **to ~ sb up** meter mano a una*.

feeler ['fiːlər] N (a) (*Zool*) antena *f*; tentáculo *m*. (b) (*Pol etc*) sondeo *m*, tentativa *f*; **to put out a ~** hacer un sondeo.

feelgood ['fiːlgʊd] ADJ: **the ~ factor** la sensación de bienestar; **a ~ movie** una película que te hace sentir bien.

▼**feeling** ['fiːlɪŋ] N (a) (*sensation*) sensación *f*; **a cold ~** una sensación de frío; **to have no ~ in one's arm** no tener sensibilidad en un brazo.

(b) (*emotion*) sentimiento *m*, emoción *f*; (*tenderness*) ternura *f*; **bad ~** rencor *m*, envidia *f*, hostilidad *f*; **a man of ~** un hombre sensible; **to speak with ~** hablar con convicción, (*angrily*) hablar con pasión; **~s** sentimientos *mpl*; **you can imagine my ~s** puedes suponer cuáles serían mis sentimientos; **to appeal to sb's finer ~s** apelar a los sentimientos nobles de uno; **to hurt sb's ~s** herir los sentimientos de uno; **to relieve one's ~s** desahogarse; **to spare sb's ~s** no herir los sentimientos de uno.

(c) (*appreciation*) **he has no ~ for music** no sabe apreciar la música.

(d) (*opinion*) opinión *f*, parecer *m*; **our ~s do not matter** nuestras opiniones no valen para nada; **my ~ is that ...** creo que ...; **what is your ~?** ¿qué opina Vd?; **the general ~ was that ...** en general se creía que ....

▼(e) (*foreboding*) presentimiento *m*; **I have a ~ that ...** presiento que ..., se me antoja que ..., me barrunto que ....

feelingly ['fiːlɪŋlɪ] ADV con honda emoción.

fee-paying ['fiːˌpeɪɪŋ] ADJ *pupil* que paga pensión; *school* privado.

feet [fiːt] NPL *of* **foot**.

FEFC N (*Brit*) ABBR *of* **Further Education Funding Council** organismo de financiación de la formación profesional.

feign [feɪn] VT fingir, aparentar; *excuse etc* inventar; **to ~ mad(ness)** fingirse loco; **to ~ sleep** fingirse dormido; **to ~ dead** fingirse muerto; **to ~ not to know** fingir no saber.

feigned [feɪnd] ADJ fingido.

feint [feɪnt] **1** N treta *f*, estratagema *f*; (*Fencing*) finta *f*.
  2 VI hacer una finta.

feisty* ['faɪstɪ] ADJ (*US*) (*lively*) animado; (*quarrelsome*) pendenciero.

feldspar ['feldspɑːr] N feldespato *m*.

felicitate [fɪ'lɪsɪteɪt] VT felicitar, congratular.

felicitations [fɪlɪsɪ'teɪʃənz] NPL felicitaciones *fpl*.

felicitous [fɪ'lɪsɪtəs] ADJ feliz, oportuno.

felicity [fɪ'lɪsɪtɪ] N felicidad *f*; (*phrase*) ocurrencia *f* oportuna.

feline ['fiːlaɪn] **1** ADJ felino.
  2 N felino *m*.

fell¹ [fel] PRET *of* **fall**.

fell² [fel] VT derribar (*with a blow* de un golpe); *tree* talar, cortar; *cattle* acogotar.

fell³ [fel] N (*Brit Geog*) (*hill*) montaña *f*; (*moor*) brezal *m*, páramo *m*.

fell⁴ [fel] ADJ (*liter*) cruel, feroz; (*fatal*) funesto; **at one ~ swoop** de un solo golpe.

fell⁵ [fel] N (*hide, pelt*) piel *f*.

fellate [fe'leɪt] VI hacer una felación, practicar la felación.

fellatio [fɪ'leɪʃɪəʊ] N, **fellation** [fɪ'leɪʃən] N felación *f*.

fellow ['feləʊ] N (a) (*comrade*) compañero *m*, -a *f*; (*~-being*) prójimo *m*; **one's ~ animals** sus prójimos los animales; **our ~ Ruritanians** nuestros compatriotas; **'my ~ Americans ...'** (*in speech*) 'queridos compatriotas ...'

(b) (*other half*) pareja *f*; (*equal*) igual *mf*; **it has no ~** no tiene par.

(c) (*Brit Univ etc*) miembro *m* de la junta de gobierno de un colegio; (*of society*) socio *mf*, miembro *mf*; *ver también* ROYAL SOCIETY.

(d) (*chap*) tipo* *m*, sujeto* *m*, tío* *m*; **he's an odd ~** es un tipo raro; **well, this journalist ~** bueno, el tal periodista; **those journalist ~s** los periodistas esos; **a ~ gets no peace** no le dejan a uno en paz; **my dear ~!** ¡hombre!; **nice ~** buen chico *m*, buena persona *f*; **old ~** viejo *m*; **look here, old ~** mira, amigo; **poor ~!** ¡pobrecito!; **some poor ~** algún pobre diablo; **young ~** chico *m*; **I say, young ~** oye, joven.

fellow-being ['feləʊ'biːɪŋ] N prójimo *m*.

fellow-citizen ['feləʊ'sɪtɪzən] N conciudadano *m*, -a *f*.

fellow-countryman ['feləʊ'kʌntrɪmən] N, PL **fellow-countrymen** ['feləʊ'kʌntrɪmən] compatriota *m*; paisano *m*; **'my fellow-countrymen ...'** (*in speech*) 'queridos compatriotas ...'

fellow-countrywoman ['feləʊ'kʌntrɪwʊmən] N, PL **fellow-countrywomen** ['feləʊ'kʌntrɪwɪmɪn] compatriota *f*, paisana *f*.

fellow-creature ['feləʊ'kriːtʃər] N prójimo *m*.

fellow-feeling ['feləʊ'fiːlɪŋ] N simpatía *f*, afinidad *f*.

fellow-member ['feləʊ'membər] N consocio *mf*.

fellow-men ['feləʊ'men] NPL prójimos *mpl*.

fellow-passenger ['feləʊ'pæsɪndʒər] N compañero *m*, -a *f* de viaje.

fellowship ['feləʊʃɪp] N (a) (*companionship*) compañerismo *m*. (b) (*society*) asociación *f*. (c) (*Brit Univ*) dignidad *f* del **fellow**. (d) (*US*) *grant* beca *f*.

fellow-sufferer [ˌfeləʊ'sʌfərər] N persona *f* que tiene la misma enfermedad que uno; compañero *m*, -a *f* en la desgracia.

fellow-traveller, (*US*) **fellow-traveler** ['feləʊ'trævlər] N compañero *m*, -a *f* de viaje; (*Pol*) filocomunista *mf*, comunizante *mf*.

fellow-worker ['feləʊ'wɜːkər] N compañero *m*, -a *f* de trabajo, colega *m*.

felon ['felən] N criminal *m*, delincuente *mf* (de mayor cuantía).

felonious [fɪ'ləʊnɪəs] ADJ criminal, delincuente.

felony ['felənɪ] N crimen *m*, delito *m* mayor, delito *m* grave.

felspar ['felspɑːr] N feldespato *m*.

felt¹ [felt] PRET AND PTP *of* **feel**.

felt² [felt] **1** N fieltro *m*.
  2 ATTR: **~ hat** sombrero *m* de fieltro; **~ tip pen** rotulador *m*.

fem. [fem] ABBR (a) *of* **female** mujer, hembra. (b) *of* **feminine** femenino.

female ['fiːmeɪl] **1** ADJ *animal, plant* hembra; *slave, subject* del sexo femenino; **a ~ voice** una voz de mujer; **the ~ hippopotamus** el hipopótamo hembra; **a ~ friend** una amiga; **the ~ sex** el sexo femenino; **~ labour** trabajo *m* de mujeres, trabajo *m* femenino; **~ suffrage** derecho *m* de las mujeres a votar.
  2 N hembra *f*.

feminine ['femɪnɪn] **1** ADJ femenino (*also Gram*).
  2 N femenino *m*; **in the ~** en femenino.

femininity [ˌfemɪ'nɪnɪtɪ] N feminidad *f*.

feminism ['femɪnɪzəm] N feminismo *m*.

feminist ['femɪnɪst] **1** ADJ feminista.
  2 N feminista *mf*.

feminize ['femɪnaɪz] VT (*frm*) feminizar.

femme fatale ['femfə'tæl] N mujer *f* fatal.

femoral ['femərəl] ADJ femoral.

femur ['fiːmər] N fémur *m*.

fen [fen] N (*Brit*) pantano *m*.

fence [fens] **1** N (a) cerca *f*, cercado *m*, valla *f*; **to mend one's ~s** restablecer la reputación; mejorar las relaciones; **to sit on the ~** ver los toros desde la barrera; no resolverse, estar a ver venir.
(b) (*) perista* *mf*.
  2 VT cercar; *machinery etc* cubrir, proteger.
  3 VI (*Sport*) esgrimir; (*fig*) defenderse con evasivas.

◆**fence in** VT encerrar con cerca.

◆**fence off** VT separar con cerca.

fenced [fenst] ADJ: **~ area** zona *f* cercada con valla.

fencer ['fensər] N esgrimidor *m*, -ora *f*.

fencing ['fensɪŋ] **1** N (a) (*Sport*) esgrima *f*. (b) (*for making fences*) materiales *mpl* para cercas.
  2 ATTR: **~ master** maestro *m* de esgrima.

fend [fend] VI: **to ~ for o.s.** arreglárselas.

◆**fend off** VT *attack* defenderse de, rechazar; *blow* apartar; *trouble etc* mantener a raya.

fender ['fendər] N (*round fire*) guardafuego *m*; (*US Aut*) parachoques *m*; guardafango *m*; (*US Rail*) trompa *f*; (*Naut*) defensa *f*.

fenestration [ˌfenɪs'treɪʃən] N ventanaje *m*.

fenland ['fenlənd] N terreno *m* pantanoso, marisma *f*.

fennel ['fenl] N hinojo *m*.

Fens [fenz] NPL (*Brit*): **the ~** las tierras bajas de Norfolk (*antes zona de marismas*).

FEPC N (*US*) ABBR *of* **Fair Employment Practices Committee**.

feral ['fɪərəl] ADJ (*frm*) silvestre, salvaje.

FERC N (*US*) ABBR *of* **Federal Energy Regulatory Commission**.

Ferdinand ['fɜːdɪnænd] NM Fernando.

ferment **1** ['fɜːment] N (*leaven*) fermento *m*; (*process*) fermentación *f*; (*fig*) agitación *f*, conmoción *f*; **to be in a ~** estar en conmoción, estar en ebullición.
  2 [fə'ment] VT hacer fermentar.
  3 [fə'ment] VI fermentar.

fermentation [ˌfɜːmen'teɪʃən] N fermentación *f*.

fermium ['fɜːmɪəm] N fermio *m*.

fern [fɜːn] N helecho *m*.

ferocious [fə'rəʊʃəs] ADJ feroz, fiero; (*fig*) violento.

ferociously [fə'rəʊʃəslɪ] ADV ferozmente.

ferociousness [fə'rəʊʃəsnɪs] N ferocidad *f*.

ferocity [fə'rɒsɪtɪ] N ferocidad *f*.

ferret ['ferɪt] **1** N hurón *m*.
  2 VI (a) cazar con hurones. (b) **to ~ about** buscar revolviéndolo todo.

◆**ferret out** VT *person* encontrar por fin; *secret* descubrir, lograr saber.

ferric ['ferɪk] ADJ férrico.

Ferris wheel ['ferɪswiːl] N (*US*) noria *f*.

ferrite ['feraɪt] N ferrito *m*, ferrita *f*.

ferro- ['ferəʊ] PREF ferro-.

ferro-alloy ['ferəʊ'ælɔɪ] N ferroaleación *f*.

ferrous ['ferəs] ADJ ferroso.

ferrule ['feruːl] N regatón *m*, contera *f*.

ferry ['ferɪ] [1] N (*small boat*) balsa *f*, barca *f* (de pasaje), embarcadero *m* (*LAm*); (*large, for cars, trains etc*) ferry *m*, transbordador *m*.
[2] VT: **to ~ sb across** llevar a uno a la otra orilla; **to ~ sth across** transportar (*or* pasar) algo a través del río (*etc*).

ferryboat ['ferɪbəʊt] N = **ferry**.

ferryman ['ferɪmən] N, PL **ferrymen** ['ferɪmən] balsero *m*, barquero *m*.

fertile ['fɜːtaɪl] ADJ (*Agr*) fértil (*of, in* en); (*also fig*); (*Bio*) fecundo.

fertility [fə'tɪlɪtɪ] [1] N fertilidad *f*; fecundidad *f*.
[2] ATTR: **~ drug** (*Med*) droga *f* de fecundidad, medicamento *m* contra la infertilidad.

fertilization [ˌfɜːtɪlaɪ'zeɪʃən] N fecundación *f*, fertilización *f*.

fertilize ['fɜːtɪlaɪz] VT fecundar, fertilizar; (*Agr*) abonar.

fertilizer ['fɜːtɪlaɪzər] N fertilizante *m*, abono *m*.

fervent ['fɜːvənt] ADJ, **fervid** ['fɜːvɪd] ADJ fervoroso, ardiente, apasionado.

fervently ['fɜːvəntlɪ] ADV fervorosamente, ardientemente; **we ~ wish that ...** deseamos con fervor que ...

fervour, (*US*) **fervor** ['fɜːvər] N fervor *m*, ardor *m*, pasión *f*.

fest* [fest] N: **film ~** festival *m* de cine; **gore ~** orgía *f* de sangre.

fester ['festər] VI ulcerarse, enconarse; (*fig*) amargarse.

festival ['festɪvəl] N fiesta *f*; (*Mus etc*) festival *m*.

festive ['festɪv] ADJ festivo, regocijado; **the ~ season** las Navidades; **to be in a ~ mood** estar muy alegre.

festivity [fes'tɪvɪtɪ] N (*celebration*) fiesta *f*, festividad *f*; (*joy*) regocijo *m*; **festivities** regocijos *mpl*, festejos *mpl*, fiestas *fpl*.

festoon [fes'tuːn] [1] N guirnalda *f*, festón *m*; (*Sew*) festón *m*.
[2] VT adornar, engalanar, enguirnaldar, festonear (*with* de); **to be ~ed with** estar adornado de.

FET N (*US*) ABBR *of* **Federal Excise Tax**.

fetal ['fiːtl] ADJ (*US*) = **foetal**.

fetch [fetʃ] [1] VT (a) (*bring*) traer; ir por, ir a buscar; (*) atraer; **I'll go and ~ it for you** te lo voy a buscar; **please ~ my coat** ¿me trae el abrigo?; **they're ~ing the doctor** han ido por el médico; **please ~ the doctor** llama al médico; **they ~ed him all that way** le hicieron venir desde tan lejos; **to ~ sb back from Spain** hacer que uno vuelva de España.
(b) *blow, sigh* dar.
(c) *price* venderse por, venderse a; **how much did it ~?** ¿cuánto dieron por él?
[2] VI: **to ~ and carry** ir de acá para allá, trajinar; ocuparse en oficios humildes; **to ~ and carry for sb** ser como el esclavo de uno.
◆**fetch in** VT *person* hacer entrar; *thing* entrar.
◆**fetch out** VT sacar.
◆**fetch up** [1] VT (*Brit**) arrojar, vomitar.
[2] VI ir a parar.

fetching ['fetʃɪŋ] ADJ atractivo.

fête [feɪt] [1] N (*Brit*) fiesta *f*; **to be en ~** estar de fiesta.
[2] VT festejar.

fetid ['fetɪd] ADJ hediondo, fétido.

fetish ['fetɪʃ] N fetiche *m*.

fetishism ['fetɪʃɪzəm] N fetichismo *m*.

fetishist ['fetɪʃɪst] N fetichista *mf*.

fetlock ['fetlɒk] N (*joint*) espolón *m*; (*hair*) cernejas *fpl*.

fetter ['fetər] VT poner grillos a, encadenar; trabar; (*fig*) estorbar.

fetters ['fetəz] NPL grillos *mpl*; (*fig*) trabas *fpl*.

fettle ['fetl] N: **in fine ~** en buenas condiciones; (*of mood*) de excelente humor.

fettuccine [ˌfetə'tʃiːnɪ] N fettuchini *mpl*.

fetus ['fiːtəs] N (*US*) = **foetus**.

feud [fjuːd] [1] N enemistad *f* heredada (entre dos familias *etc*), odio *m* de sangre; disputa *f*.
[2] VI reñir, pelear.

feudal ['fjuːdl] ADJ feudal; **~ system** feudalismo *m*.

feudalism ['fjuːdəlɪzəm] N feudalismo *m*.

fever ['fiːvər] N (*disease*) fiebre *f*; (*high temperature*) fiebre *f*, calentura *f*; **a ~ of excitement** una emoción febril; **the gambling ~** la fiebre del juego; **the excitement was at ~ pitch** la emoción estaba al rojo vivo; **she's in a ~ about the party** está muy agitada por la fiesta.

fevered ['fiːvəd] ADJ = **feverish**.

feverish ['fiːvərɪʃ] ADJ (a) (*Med*) febril, calenturiento; **to be ~** tener fiebre. (b) (*fig*) febril.

feverishly ['fiːvərɪʃlɪ] ADV febrilmente.

feverishness ['fiːvərɪʃnɪs] N (*Med, fig*) febrilidad *f*.

few [fjuː] ADJ pocos; algunos, unos; **a ~, some ~** unos pocos, unos cuantos; **a ~ of us** algunos de nosotros; **quite a ~, not a ~** no pocos, algunos; **a good ~** un buen número (de); **he had had a ~*** llevaba ya una copa de más; **every ~ minutes** cada pocos minutos; **in the next ~ days** un día de éstos que vienen; **the ~** los pocos, la minoría; **the lucky ~** los afortunados (que son pocos); **such men are ~** hay pocos hombres así; **they are ~ and far between** son poquísimos, son contadísimos.

fewer ['fjuːər] ADJ *comp* menos; **~ than 10** menos de 10; **they have ~ than I** tienen menos que yo; **no ~ than 8 goals** nada menos que 8 goles; **the ~ the better** cuantos menos mejor;
ver también LESS THAN, FEWER THAN.

fewest ['fjuːɪst] ADJ *superl* los menos, las menos, el menor número (de).

fewness ['fjuːnɪs] N corto número *m*.

fey [feɪ] ADJ vidente.

fez [fez] N fez *m*.

ff ABBR *of* **following** siguientes, sigs.

FFA N (*US*) ABBR *of* **Future Farmers of America**.

FFV ABBR *of* **First Families of Virginia** *descendientes de los primeros colonos de Virginia*.

FH ABBR *of* **fire hydrant**.

FHA N (*US*) ABBR *of* **Federal Housing Association**.

fiancé [fɪ'ɑːnseɪ] N novio *m*, prometido *m*.

fiancée [fɪ'ɑːnseɪ] N novia *f*, prometida *f*.

fiasco [fɪ'æskəʊ] N fiasco *m*.

fiat ['faɪæt] N fíat *m*, autorización *f*.

fib [fɪb] [1] N mentirilla *f*, bola *f*.
[2] VI decir mentirillas.

fibber ['fɪbər] N mentirosillo *m*, -a *f*.

fibre, (*US*) **fiber** ['faɪbər] N (a) fibra *f*. (b) (*fig*) nervio *m*, carácter *m*.

fibreboard, (*US*) **fiberboard** ['faɪbəbɔːd] N panel *m* de madera conglomerada, fibra *f* vulcanizada.

fibre-glass, (*US*) **fiberglass** ['faɪbəglɑːs] N fibra *f* de vidrio, fibravidrio *m*.

fibre-optic, (*US*) **fiber-optic** [ˌfaɪbər'ɒptɪk] ADJ: **~ cable** cable *m* de fibra óptica.

fibre-optics, (*US*) **fiber-optics** [ˌfaɪbər'ɒptɪks] N transmisión *f* por fibra óptica.

fibre-tip (pen) ['faɪbətɪp('pen)] N (*Brit*) rotulador *m* de punta de fibra.

fibroid ['faɪbrɔɪd] N fibroma *m*.

fibrositis [ˌfaɪbrə'saɪtɪs] N fibrositis *f*.

fibrous ['faɪbrəs] ADJ fibroso.

fibula ['fɪbjʊlə] N peroné *m*.

FIC N (*US*) ABBR *of* **Federal Information Centers**.

FICA N (*US*) ABBR *of* **Federal Insurance Contributions Act**.

fickle ['fɪkl] ADJ inconstante, veleidoso, voluble.

fickleness ['fɪklnɪs] N inconstancia *f*, veleidad *f*, volubilidad *f*.

fiction ['fɪkʃən] N (a) (*invention*) ficción *f*, invención *f*. (b) (*Liter*) ficción *f*, novelística *f*, género *m* novelístico.

fictional ['fɪkʃənl] ADJ novelesco; relativo a la novela (*etc*).

fictionalize ['fɪkʃənəlaɪz] VT novelar.

fictionalized ['fɪkʃənəlaɪzd] ADJ novelado.

fictitious [fɪk'tɪʃəs] ADJ ficticio.

Fid. Def. ABBR *of* **Fidei Defensor** = **Defender of the Faith**; Defensor *m* de la Fe.

fiddle ['fɪdl] [1] N (a) (*Mus*) violín *m*; **to play second ~** desempeñar un papel secundario (*to* después de).
(b) (*esp Brit**) trampa *f*, superchería *f*; **tax ~** defraudación *f* fiscal, evasión *f* fiscal; **it's a ~** aquí hay trampa, son unos tramposos; **to be on the ~** trampear, trapichear*.
[2] VT (*esp Brit**) *results* falsificar; *accounts* manipular, falsificar; *extra money, privilege* agenciarse; *job etc* agenciarse, obtener por enchufe*; **to ~ one's income-tax** defraudar impuestos.
[3] VI (a) (*Mus*) tocar el violín.
(b) (*esp Brit**) hacer trampas; **to ~ with** jugar nerviosamente con, manosear; **sb's been fiddling with it** alguno lo ha estropeado.
◆**fiddle about, fiddle around** VI perder el tiempo.

fiddler ['fɪdlər] N (a) (*Mus*) violinista *mf*. (b) (*esp Brit**) tramposo *m*, -a *f*.

fiddlesticks ['fɪdlstɪks] INTERJ ¡tonterías!

fiddling ['fɪdlɪŋ] [1] ADJ trivial, insignificante.
[2] N (*) trampas *fpl*, trapicheos* *mpl*.

fiddly ['fɪdlɪ] ADJ *task* difícil, complicado; *object* complicado (*or* difícil) de manejar.

FIDE N ABBR *of* **Fédération Internationale des Échecs** Federación *f* Internacional de Ajedrez, FIDE *f*.

fidelity [fɪ'delɪtɪ] N fidelidad *f*; **high ~** (ABBR: **hi-fi**) alta fidelidad *f*.

fidget ['fɪdʒɪt] [1] N (a) persona *f* inquieta, azogado *m*, -a *f*.
(b) **~s** agitación *f* nerviosa; **to have the ~s** ser un azogue, no poder estar quieto.
[2] VT poner nervioso.
[3] VI ser un azogue, agitarse nerviosamente; **don't ~!, stop ~ing!** ¡estáte quieto!; **to ~ about** revolverse nerviosamente; **to ~ with** jugar con.

fidgety ['fɪdʒɪtɪ] ADJ azogado, nervioso; **to be ~** tener azogue, no poder tenerse quieto.

fiduciary [fɪ'djuːʃɪərɪ] ADJ fiduciario.

fie [faɪ] EXCL (††): **~ on him!** ¡al diablo con él!

fief [fi:f] N feudo *m*.

fiefdom ['fi:fdəm] N feudo *m*.

field [fi:ld] **1** N **(a)** (*Agr, Elec, Her, Mil*) campo *m*; (*meadow*) prado *m*; (*Sport*) campo *m*, cancha *f* (*LAm*); (*Geol*) yacimiento *m*; (*Comput*) campo *m*, sector *m*; ~ **of battle** campo *m* de batalla; ~ **of vision** campo *m* visual; **a scientist working in the** ~ un científico que trabaja en el terreno; **to be the first in the** ~ ser el primero en inventar algo (*etc*); **to take the** ~ salir a campaña (*against* contra); (*fig*) salir a (la) palestra.
(b) (*fig*) esfera *f*; especialidad *f*; ~ **of activity** esfera *f* de actividades, ámbito *m* de acción; **in the** ~ **of painting** en la esfera de la pintura, en la pintura; **what's your** ~? ¿qué especialidad tiene Vd?; **it's not my** ~ no es de mi competencia.
(c) (*in race etc*) competidores *mpl*, (*in competition*) concurrentes *mpl*, (*for post*) opositores *mpl*, candidatos *mpl*; **is there a strong** ~? ¿se ha presentado gente buena?; **to lead the** ~ ir en cabeza, llevar la delantera; **to play the** ~ (*US*) alternar con cualquiera.
2 ATTR: ~ **event** prueba *f* de atletismo; ~ **hand** (*US*) jornalero *m*; ~ **hospital** hospital *m* de campaña; ~ **study** estudio *m* de campo; ~ **test**, ~ **trial** (*Agr*) prueba *f* de campo.
3 VT *ball* parar, recoger; *team* presentar.

field day ['fi:lddeɪ] N (*Mil*) día *m* de maniobras; **to have a** ~ (*fig*) obtener un gran éxito, triunfar; divertirse muchísimo.

fielder ['fi:ldər] N fildeador *m*, -ora *f*; *ver también* ⟨BASEBALL⟩, ⟨CRICKET⟩.

fieldfare ['fi:ldfeər] N zorzal *m* real.

fieldglasses ['fi:ld,glɑ:sɪz] NPL gemelos *mpl* (de campo), prismáticos *mpl*.

fieldgun ['fi:ldgʌn] N cañón *m* de campaña.

field-kitchen ['fi:ld'kɪtʃɪn] N cocina *f* de campaña.

field-marshal ['fi:ld'mɑ:ʃəl] N (*Brit*) mariscal *m* de campo; (*Spain*) capitán *m* general del ejército.

fieldmouse ['fi:ldmaʊs] N, PL **fieldmice** ['fi:ldmaɪs] ratón *m* de campo.

field-officer ['fi:ld,ɒfɪsər] N oficial *m* superior.

fieldsman ['fi:ldzmən] N = **fielder**.

field-sports ['fi:ldspɔ:ts] NPL caza *f*.

field-test ['fi:ld,test] VT probar sobre el terreno.

field-trip ['fi:ldtrɪp] N salida *f* (*or* excursión *f*) de estudios.

fieldwork ['fi:ldwɜ:k] N labor *f* de campo, trabajo *m* en el terreno.

field-worker ['fi:ld,wɜ:kər] N investigador *m*, -ora *f* que trabaja en el terreno.

fiend [fi:nd] N **(a)** demonio *m*, diablo *m*; (*fig*) desalmado *m*. **(b)** (*for hobby etc*) fanático *m*, -a *f*, entusiasta *mf* (*for* de).

fiendish ['fi:ndɪʃ] ADJ diabólico.

fiendishly ['fi:ndɪʃlɪ] ADV diabólicamente; ~ **difficult** terriblemente difícil; ~ **expensive** carísimo.

fierce [fɪəs] ADJ *animal etc* feroz, salvaje; *cruel*; *look* feroz; *attack* furioso; *wind* violento; *heat, competition* intenso; *supporter* acérrimo.

fiercely ['fɪəslɪ] ADV ferozmente; furiosamente; intensamente.

fierceness ['fɪəsnɪs] N ferocidad *f*; furia *f*; intensidad *f*.

fiery ['faɪərɪ] ADJ (*burning*) ardiente; (*red*) rojo; *taste* muy picante, picaro (*LAm*); *temperament, speech* apasionado, vehemente; *horse* fogoso; *liquor* ardiente, muy fuerte.

fiesta [fɪ'estə] N fiesta *f*, festejo *m*.

FIFA ['fi:fə] N ABBR *of* **Fédération Internationale de Football Association** FIFA *f*.

fife [faɪf] N pífano *m*.

FIFO ['faɪfəʊ] ABBR *of* **first in first out** primero en entrar, primero en salir.

fifteen [fɪf'ti:n] **1** ADJ quince.
2 N quince *m*.

fifteenth [fɪf'ti:nθ] ADJ decimoquinto.

fifth [fɪfθ] **1** ADJ quinto; ~ **column** quinta columna *f*.
2 N quinto *m*, quinta parte *f*; (*Mus*) quinta *f*; V also **amendment**.

fifth columnist [,fɪfθ'kɒləmnɪst] N quintacolumnista *mf*.

fiftieth ['fɪftɪθ] ADJ quincuagésimo; cincuenta; **the** ~ **anniversary** el cincuenta aniversario.

fifty ['fɪftɪ] ADJ cincuenta; **the fifties** (*eg 1950s*) los años cincuenta; **to be in one's fifties** tener más de cincuenta años, ser cincuentón.

fifty-fifty ['fɪftɪ'fɪftɪ] **1** ADV: **to go** ~ ir a medias, ir mitad y mitad.
2 ADJ: **there is a** ~ **chance** hay un cincuenta por cien de posibilidades; **it's a** ~ **deal** es un acuerdo para repartir los beneficios mitad y mitad; **we'll do it on a** ~ **basis** lo haremos a base de mitad y mitad, iremos por partes iguales.

fiftyish ['fɪftɪʃ] ADJ de unos cincuenta años.

fig [fɪg] N higo *m*; (*early*) breva *f*; (*tree*) higuera *f*; (**I don't give**) **a** ~ **for J.B!** ¡me importa un comino J.B!

fight [faɪt] **1** N **(a)** (*Mil*) combate *m*; (*between 2 persons*) pelea *f*; (*struggle, campaign*) lucha *f* (*for* por); **in fair** ~ en buena lid; **to make a** ~ **of it** no dejarse vencer fácilmente; **to put up a good** ~ defenderse bien, dar buena cuenta de sí.
(b) (*argument*) disputa *f* (*over* sobre); (*quarrel, esp US*) riña *f*, pelea *f*;

to have a ~ **with sb** tener una pelea con uno; **to pick a** ~ **with sb** meterse con uno.
(c) (*fighting spirit*) combatividad *f*, ánimo *m* (de pelear), brío *m*; **to show** ~ enseñar los dientes, mostrarse dispuesto a resistir; **there was no** ~ **left in him** no le quedaba ningún ánimo de luchar más.
2 (*irr*: PRET AND PTP **fought**) VT (*Mil*) *enemy* batirse con, luchar con (*or* contra); *battle* dar, librar; *bull* lidiar; *fire* luchar por sofocar, combatir; *proposal, urge, tendency* combatir, resistir, luchar contra; **to** ~ **a case** negar una acusación; **we shall** ~ **this case all the way** seguiremos luchando por cambiar esta decisión, no nos conformaremos nunca con esta decisión; **to** ~ **one's way out** lograr salir luchando; **to** ~ **one's way to the sea** abrirse paso luchando hacia el mar.
3 VI pelear, luchar (*against* contra, *for* por, *with* con); batirse; **did you** ~ **in the war?** ¿fue Vd soldado cuando la guerra?, ¿desempeñó algún papel en la guerra?; **they were** ~**ing over it** lo estaban disputando a golpes; **we shall have to** ~ tendremos que luchar; **to go down** ~**ing** seguir luchando hasta el fin.
◆**fight back 1** VT: **to** ~ **back one's tears** andar a puñetazos con las lágrimas.
2 VI defenderse, resistir; contraatacar.
◆**fight down** VT reprimir.
◆**fight off** VT *attack* rechazar; *sleep* sacudirse; *illness etc* luchar por no sucumbir ante.
◆**fight on** VI seguir luchando.
◆**fight out** VT: **to** ~ **it out** decidirlo luchando; **they fought it out** siguieron luchando hasta que uno cedió; **leave them to** ~ **it out** deja que se arreglen entre ellos.

fightback ['faɪtbæk] N remontada *f*; resistencia *f*, defensa *f*; contraataque *m*.

fighter ['faɪtər] **1** N **(a)** combatiente *mf*; luchador *m*, -ora *f* (*for* por); (*warrior*) guerrero *m*, soldado *m*; (*boxer*) boxeador *m*; **a bonny** ~ un valiente guerrero. **(b)** (*Aer*) caza *m*.
2 ATTR: ~ **command** jefatura *f* de cazas.

fighter-bomber ['faɪtə'bɒmər] N caza-bombardero *m*.

fighter pilot ['faɪtə'paɪlət] N piloto *m* de caza.

fighting ['faɪtɪŋ] **1** N (*in general*) el luchar, el pelear; (*battle*) combate *m*; **the street** ~ **lasted all day** se luchó todo el día en las calles; **there has been** ~ **in the colony** ha estallado la guerra en la colonia, ha habido disturbios sangrientos en la colonia; **we want no** ~ **here** aquí nada de pendencias; **the Slobodians are fond of** ~ a los eslobodios les gusta pelearse.
2 ATTR: ~ **bull** toro *m* de lidia; ~ **chance** buena posibilidad *f*; ~ **cock** gallo *m* de pelea; ~ **forces** fuerzas *fpl* militares; ~ **line** frente *m* de combate; ~ **man** guerrero *m*, soldado *m*; ~ **spirit** espíritu *m* de lucha, combatividad *f*; ~ **strength** número *m* de soldados (listos para el combate); ~ **talk** palabras *fpl* que provocan a pelea.

figleaf ['fɪgli:f] N, PL **figleaves** ['fɪgli:vz] (*fig*) hoja *f* de parra.

figment ['fɪgmənt] N: ~ **of the imagination** quimera *f*, producto *m* de la imaginación.

fig tree ['fɪgtri:] N higuera *f*.

figurative ['fɪgərətɪv] ADJ *sense etc* figurado; (*Art*) figurativo.

figuratively ['fɪgərətɪvlɪ] ADV figuradamente, en sentido figurado; **he was speaking** ~ hablaba en metáfora; **you should understand this** ~ hay que entender esto en sentido figurado.

figure ['fɪgər] **1** N **(a)** (*statue*) figura *f*, estatua *f*.
(b) (*form of body*) tipo *m*, línea *f*, talle *m*, silueta *f*; **a fine** ~ **of a man** un hombre de físico imponente; **a fine** ~ **of a woman** una real hembra; **she's got a nice** ~ tiene buen tipo, tiene buen físico (*LAm*); **to keep one's** ~ guardar la línea; **to lose one's** ~ perder la línea; **to be** ~**-conscious** ser cuidadoso con la línea.
(c) (*person*) figura *f*; **the central** ~ **in the crisis** la figura más importante de la crisis; **to cut a** ~ hacer papel; **to cut a sorry** ~ parecer ridículo, salir desairado.
(d) (*diagram*) figura *f*, dibujo *m*.
(e) (*Math*) (*numeral*) cifra *f*, número *m*, guarismo *m*; (*quantity*) cifra *f*, cantidad *f*; (*price*) precio *m*; (*sum*) suma *f*; ~ **of eight**, ~ **eight** (*US*) (*in dance etc*) figura *f* de ocho; **in round** ~**s** en números redondos; **to be good at** ~**s** ser fuerte en aritmética; **to have a six-**~ **income** ganar más de 100.000 libras al año; **to reach double** ~**s** llegar a 10; **to reach 3** ~**s** ascender a 100; **we want inflation brought down to single** ~**s** queremos que la inflación baje a menos de 10 por cien.
(f) (*Geom, Dancing, Skating*) figura *f*.
(g) ~ **of speech** figura *f*, tropo *m*.
2 VT (*in diagram*) representar; (*picture mentally*) representarse, figurarse; (*esp US*) imaginar; **I** ~ **it like this** (*US*) yo lo veo del modo siguiente.
3 VI **(a)** (*appear*) figurar (*among* entre, *as* como); constar.
(b) (*esp US*) **it doesn't** ~ no tiene sentido; **that** ~**s** es natural; es comprensible.
◆**figure in*** VT (*US*) contar a.
◆**figure on** VT (*US*) contar con; proyectar; esperar.
◆**figure out 1** VT *person* entender; *problem* resolver; *writing* descifrar;

sum calcular; *means etc* inventar, imaginar; **I can't ~ it out at all** no me lo explico, no lo comprendo.

2 VI: **to ~ out at** venir a ser.

◆**figure up** VT (*US*) calcular.

-figure ['fɪgər] ADJ: **a four~ sum** una suma superior a mil (libras *etc*); **a seven~ number** un número de siete cifras.

figurehead ['fɪgəhed] N mascarón *m* de proa, figurón *m* de proa; (*fig: esp pej*) figura *f* decorativa.

figure-skate ['fɪgə,skeɪt] VI hacer patinaje artístico (sobre hielo).

figure-skating ['fɪgə,skeɪtɪŋ] N patinaje *m* de figuras, patinaje *m* artístico.

figurine [fɪgə'riːn] N figurilla *f*, estatuilla *f*.

Fiji ['fiːdʒiː] N (*also* **the ~ Islands**) las (Islas *fpl*) Fiji; **in ~** en las Fiji.

Fijian [fɪ'dʒiːən] 1 ADJ de (las Islas) Fiji.

2 N (*person*) nativo *m*, -a *f* de (las Islas) Fiji.

filament ['fɪləmənt] N filamento *m*.

filbert ['fɪlbət] N avellana *f*.

filch [fɪltʃ] VT sisar, ratear.

file[1] [faɪl] 1 N (*tool*) lima *f*.

2 VT (*also* **to ~ away, to ~ down, to ~ off**) limar.

file[2] [faɪl] 1 N (*folder*) carpeta *f*; (*dossier*) expediente *m*; (*eg loose-leaf ~*) archivador *m*, clasificador *m*; (*bundle of papers*) legajo *m*; (*cabinet*) fichero *m*, archivo *m*; (*Comput*) fichero *m*; **the ~s** los archivos; **the Lucan ~** el expediente Lucan; **police ~s** archivos *mpl* policíacos; **to close the ~s** cerrar la carpeta; **to have sth on ~** tener algo archivado.

2 VT (a) (*also* **to ~ away**) archivar; clasificar; registrar.

(b) (*Jur*) *suit* entablar, presentar; **to ~ a claim** presentar una reclamación; **to ~ a petition for divorce** entablar pleito de divorcio.

file[3] [faɪl] 1 N (*row*) fila *f*, hilera *f*; **in single ~** en fila de a uno.

2 VI: **to ~ past** desfilar; **they ~d past the general** desfilaron ante el general.

◆**file for** VT (*Jur*) **to ~ for divorce** presentar una demanda de divorcio; **to ~ for bankruptcy** presentar una declaración de quiebra; **to ~ for custody (of children)** reclamar la custodia (de los hijos).

◆**file in** VI entrar en fila.

◆**file out** VI salir en fila.

file name ['faɪlneɪm] N (*Comput*) nombre *m* de fichero.

file server ['faɪl,sɜːvər] N servidor *m* de archivos.

filial ['fɪlɪəl] ADJ filial.

filiation [ˌfɪlɪ'eɪʃən] N filiación *f*.

filibuster ['fɪlɪbʌstər] (*US*) 1 N (*person*) obstruccionista *mf*, filibustero *m*; (*act*) maniobra *f* obstruccionista, filibusterismo *m*.

2 *vi* usar de maniobras obstruccionistas.

filigree ['fɪlɪgriː] N filigrana *f*.

filing ['faɪlɪŋ] N (*of documents*) clasificación *f*; (*of claim etc*) formulación *f*, presentación *f*; **to do the ~** archivar documentos.

filing-cabinet ['faɪlɪŋ,kæbmɪt] N fichero *m*, archivador *m*.

filing-clerk ['faɪlɪŋ,klɑːk] N (*Brit*) archivero *m*, -a *f*.

filings ['faɪlɪŋz] NPL limaduras *fpl*.

Filipino [fɪlɪ'piːnəʊ] 1 ADJ filipino.

2 N (a) (*person*) filipino *m*, -a *f*. (b) (*Ling*) tagalo *m*.

fill [fɪl] 1 VT llenar (*with* de); (*stuff*) rellenar; (*charge, fuel, load*) cargar; *space* llenar completamente, ocupar completamente; *tooth* empastar, obturar; *tyre* inflar; *sail* hinchar; *post, chair* ocupar; *vacancy* cubrir; *requirement* llenar; *order* despachar; **he ~ed the post very well** desempeñó muy bien el cargo.

2 VI (*also* **to ~ up**) llenarse (*with* de); (*sail*) hincharse.

3 N: **to eat one's ~** hartarse de comer; **to have a ~ of tobacco** cargar la pipa; **I've had my ~ of that** estoy harto ya de eso.

◆**fill in** 1 VT (a) llenar; *depression* terraplenar; *form* llenar; *details* añadir; *outline* completar; *time* ocupar. (b) (*) **to ~ sb in** informar a uno, poner a uno en antecedentes; **~ me in on what happened** dime lo que pasó.

2 VI: **to ~ in for sb** hacer las veces de uno, sustituir a uno, suplir a uno.

◆**fill out** 1 VT (*fatten*) engordar; *form* rellenar, llenar.

2 VI echar carnes; (*face*) redondearse.

◆**fill up** 1 VT llenar (hasta el borde), colmar; (*Brit*) *form* rellenar, llenar.

2 VI (a) = **fill 2**.

(b) **to ~ up with fuel** repostar combustible.

3 VR: **to ~ o.s. up with** darse un atracón de, llenarse el estómago de.

filler ['fɪlər] N (a) (*utensil, of bottle*) rellenador *m*; (*funnel*) embudo *m*. (b) (*for cracks in wood etc*) masilla *f*; (*Press*) relleno *m*.

filler-cap ['fɪləkæp] N (*Aut*) tapa *f* del depósito de gasolina, trampilla *f*.

fillet ['fɪlɪt] 1 N (*all senses*) filete *m*.

2 VT *fish* quitar la raspa de, desespinar; cortar en filetes.

fill-in ['fɪlɪn] N sustituto *m*, suplente *mf*.

filling ['fɪlɪŋ] 1 ADJ *food* sólido, que llena el estómago.

2 N relleno *m*; (*Mech*) empaquetadura *f*; (*of tooth*) obturación *f*,

empaste *m*.

filling-station ['fɪlɪŋ,steɪʃən] N gasolinera *f*, estación *f* de servicio.

fillip ['fɪlɪp] N estímulo *m*; **to give a ~ to** estimular.

filly ['fɪlɪ] N potra *f*.

film [fɪlm] 1 N (a) (*thin skin*) película *f*; (*of dust*) capa *f*; (*fig*) velo *m*. (b) (*Phot, Cine*) película *f*, film *m*, filme *m*; **the ~s** el cine; **to make a ~ of** *book* hacer una película de, *event* filmar.

2 ATTR: **~ buff** cineasta *mf*, cinéfilo *m*, -a *f*; **~ camera** cámara *f* cinematográfica; **~ festival** festival *m* de cine (*or* cinematográfico); **~ library** cinemateca *f*; **~ premiere** estreno *m* oficial, premier *f*; **~ rights** derechos *mpl* cinematográficos; **~ script** guión *m*; **~ sequence** secuencia *f*; **~ set** plató *m*; **~ studio** estudio *m* (de cine); **~ test** prueba *f* cinematográfica.

3 VT *book* hacer una película de, *event* filmar; *scene* rodar (*at, in* en).

◆**film over** VI empañarse, cubrirse con película.

film-fan ['fɪlmfæn] N aficionado *m*, -a *f* al cine, cineasta *mf*.

filmic ['fɪlmɪk] ADJ fílmico.

filming ['fɪlmɪŋ] N filmación *f*.

film-maker ['fɪlmmeɪkər] N cineasta *mf*.

film-making ['fɪlmmeɪkɪŋ] N cinematografía *f*.

filmsetting ['fɪlmsetɪŋ] N fotocomposición *f*.

filmstar ['fɪlmstɑːr] N astro *m*, estrella *f* (de cine).

filmstrip ['fɪlmstrɪp] N tira *f* (*or* cinta *f*) de película, tira *f* proyectable.

filmy ['fɪlmɪ] ADJ transparente, diáfano.

Filofax ['faɪləʊfæks] ® N filofax ® *m*.

filter ['fɪltər] 1 N (a) filtro *m*. (b) (*Brit Aut*) semáforo *m* de flecha verde de desvío.

2 ATTR: **~ coffee** café *m* (molido) para filtrar; (*Aut*) **~ lane** ≃ carril *m* de giro; **~ light** semáforo *m* de flecha de desvío.

3 VT filtrar.

4 VI filtrarse.

◆**filter in** VI infiltrarse; (*person etc*) introducirse.

◆**filter out** 1 VT *impurities* quitar filtrando.

2 VI (*news*) trascender, llegar a saberse.

◆**filter through** VI = **filter in**.

filter paper ['fɪltə,peɪpər] N papel *m* de filtro.

filter-tip [ˌfɪltə'tɪp] N filtro *m*; **~ cigarette** cigarrillo *m* con filtro.

filter-tipped ['fɪltə,tɪpt] ADJ con filtro.

filth [fɪlθ] N inmundicia *f*, suciedad *f*, porquería *f*; (*fig*) inmundicias *fpl*.

filthiness ['fɪlθɪnɪs] N (*of language, behaviour*) obscenidad *f*, indecencia *f*.

filthy ['fɪlθɪ] 1 ADJ inmundo, sucio, puerco; (*fig*) inmundo, obsceno.

2 (*) ADV: **they're ~ rich** son tan ricos que dan asco.

filtration [fɪl'treɪʃən] N filtración *f*.

fin [fɪn] N (*all senses*) aleta *f*.

fin. ABBR of **finance**.

final ['faɪnl] 1 ADJ (a) (*last*) último, final; *exam* de fin de curso; **~ demand** demanda *f* final; **~ dividend** dividendo *m* final; **~ instalment** plazo *m* final, último plazo *m*. (b) (*conclusive*) terminante, decisivo, definitivo; **and that's ~** y no hay más que decir, y sanseacabó; **the judges' decisions will be ~** las decisiones de los jueces serán inapelables.

2 N (*Sport*) final *f*; **~s** (*Univ*) examen *m* de fin de curso; **the World Cup ~s** las finales de la Copa Mundial.

finale [fɪ'nɑːlɪ] N (*Mus*) final *m*; **grand ~** (*Theat*) gran escena *f* final; (*fig*) final *m* impresionante, final *m* triunfal.

finalist ['faɪnəlɪst] N (*Sport*) finalista *mf*.

finality [faɪ'nælɪtɪ] N finalidad *f*; (*decision*) resolución *f*; **he said with ~** dijo de modo terminante.

finalization [ˌfaɪnəlaɪ'zeɪʃən] N ultimación *f*, conclusión *f*.

finalize ['faɪnəlaɪz] VT ultimar, completar, concluir, aprobar de modo definitivo; *date etc* decidir, acordar.

▼ **finally** ['faɪnəlɪ] ADV (a) (*lastly*) por último, finalmente; (*eventually*) por fin. (b) (*irrevocably*) de modo definitivo, definitivamente.

finance [faɪ'næns] 1 N (*in general*) finanzas *fpl*, asuntos *mpl* financieros; (*funds*) finanzas *fpl*, fondos *mpl* (*also* **~s**); **~ company** sociedad *f* financiera; **~ director** director *m*, -ora *f* de finanzas; **the country's ~s** la situación económica del país; **Minister of F~** Ministro *m*, -a *f* de Hacienda.

2 VT financiar, proveer fondos para.

financial [faɪ'nænʃəl] ADJ financiero; *policy, resources* económico; **~ accounting** contabilidad *f* financiera; **~ adviser** asesor *m* financiero, asesora *f* financiera; **~ analysis** análisis *m* financiero; **~ backing** respaldo *m* financiero, apoyo *m* económico; **~ director** director *m*, -ora *f* de finanzas; **~ management** administración *f* financiera; **~ statement** estado *m* financiero, balance *m*; **F~ Times Index** índice *m* bursátil del Financial Times; **~ year** (*Brit*) año *m* económico, año *m* fiscal, ejercicio *m*.

financially [faɪ'nænʃəlɪ] ADV: **~ independent** independiente en el aspecto económico; **~ sound** económicamente sólido; **a ~ success-**

ful scheme un plan económicamente satisfactorio; **this is not ~ possible** esto no es posible por razones financieras.

financier [faɪˈnænsɪəʳ] N financiero m.

financing [faɪˈnænsɪŋ] N financiación f.

finch [fɪntʃ] N pinzón m.

find [faɪnd] (*irr*: PRET AND PTP **found**) **1** VT **(a)** (*gen*) encontrar, hallar; descubrir; (*stumble on*) dar con, tropezar con; **where did you ~ it?** ¿dónde lo encontraste?; **how did you ~ him?** (*in health*) ¿qué tal le encontraste?; **it's found all over Spain** se encuentra (*or* existe) en todas partes de España; **it's not to be found** no se encuentra; **I now ~ it is not so** ahora descubro que no es así; **it has been found that ...** se ha comprobado que ...

(b) (*supply, obtain*) facilitar, proporcionar, proveer; **we found him a car** le facilitamos un coche; **if you can ~ the time** si tienes el tiempo; **can you ~ the money?** ¿podrás reunir el dinero?; **they found half the cost** lograron hacerse con la mitad del precio; **all found** todo incluido.

(c) (*with adj*) **you will not ~ it easy** no le será fácil (*to do* hacer); **I found it impossible** me fue imposible (*to go* ir); **I ~ the house small** la casa me resulta pequeña.

(d) (*Jur*) declarar; **V guilty**.

2 VI: **to ~ for the defendant** (*Jur*) fallar a favor del demandado.

3 VR: **to ~ o.s.** encontrarse; verse; **I found myself alone** me encontré solo; **I ~ myself at a loss** me encuentro perplejo; **he found himself** descubrió su verdadera vocación (*or* identidad *etc*).

4 N hallazgo m.

◆**find out** **1** VT (*realize*) darse cuenta de; (*discover*) averiguar, (llegar a) saber; **to ~ sb out** conocer el juego de uno, calar a uno; **his pride found him out** su orgullo le traicionó.

2 VI: **to ~ out about** informarse sobre, buscar detalles acerca de; **we didn't ~ out about it in time** no nos enteramos a tiempo.

finder [ˈfaɪndəʳ] N descubridor m, -ora f, el (la) que encuentra algo.

finding [ˈfaɪndɪŋ] N **(a)** descubrimiento m. **(b)** **~s** (*Jur etc*) fallo m; (*of report etc*) recomendaciones fpl.

▼**fine¹** [faɪn] **1** ADJ **(a)** (*delicate, small*) *thread* fino, sutil; *particle, print* menudo; *line* tenue; *pencil, nib* delgado; *edge* muy afilado; *distinction* delicado, sutil; **the ~r points of the argument** los puntos más sutiles del argumento.

▼**(b)** (*good*) bueno; (*beautiful*) bello, hermoso; (*exquisitely made*) fino, delicado, primoroso; *dress* elegante; (*showy*) vistoso; (*imposing*) magnífico, imponente; (*selected*) escogido; (*pure*) refinado, puro; *ideal* bello; *feeling* elevado, noble; *person* admirable; (*accomplished*) excelente, experto; **~!** ¡magnífico!, ¡estupendo!; **~ arts** bellas artes fpl; **eleven of England's ~st** (*hum*) once de los mejores de Inglaterra; **that's ~ by me** por mí, bien; de acuerdo; **it's a ~ thing to** + *infin* es admirable + *infin*.

(c) (*iro*) bueno, lindo, valiente; **that's all very ~, but ...** todo eso está muy bien, pero ...; **a ~ friend you are!** ¡valiente amigo!, ¡menudo amigo!; **you're a ~ one!** ¡estás tú bueno!, ¡qué tío!

(d) (*weather*) *day etc* bueno; **to be ~** hacer buen tiempo.

▼**2** ADV **(a)** muy bien; **~ and dandy** (*US*) requetebién; **you're doing ~** lo estás haciendo la mar de bien; **to feel ~** estar como un reloj.

(b) **to chop sth up ~** cortar algo en trozos menudos; **to cut** (*or* **run**) **it ~** llegar con muy poco tiempo, llegar justo a tiempo, dejarse muy poco tiempo.

◆**fine down** VTI adelgazar.

fine² [faɪn] **1** N multa f, boleta f (*Carib*).

2 VT multar.

fine-drawn [ˈfaɪnˈdrɔːn] ADJ estirado en un hilo muy delgado; *wire* muy delgado; *distinction etc* sutil, fino.

fine-grained [ˈfaɪnˈɡreɪnd] ADJ de grano fino.

finely [ˈfaɪnlɪ] ADV **(a)** sutilmente; menudamente. **(b)** hermosamente; primorosamente; elegantemente; vistosamente. **(c)** (*iro*) lindamente.

fineness [ˈfaɪnnɪs] N **(a)** fineza f. **(b)** (*Metal*) pureza f.

finery [ˈfaɪnərɪ] N galas fpl, adornos mpl, trajes mpl vistosos; **spring in all its ~** la primavera con todo su esplendor.

fine-spun [ˈfaɪnspʌn] ADJ *yarn etc* fino; (*fig: hair*) fino, sedoso.

finesse [fɪˈnes] **1** N **(a)** (*in judgement*) discriminación f sutil, discernimiento m; (*in action*) diplomacia f, tino m, sutileza f; (*cunning*) astucia f. **(b)** (*Cards*) impase m.

2 VT hacer el impase a.

fine-tooth comb [ˌfaɪnˌtuːˈθkəʊm] N peine m espeso; **to go over** (*or* **through**) **sth with a ~** revisar (*or* examinar) algo a fondo.

fine-tune [ˌfaɪnˈtjuːn] VT poner a punto; (*fig*) hacer más preciso, matizar; poner a punto.

fine-tuning [ˌfaɪnˈtjuːnɪŋ] N matización f; puesta f a punto.

finger [ˈfɪŋɡəʳ] **1** N **(a)** dedo m; **first ~, index ~** dedo m índice; **little ~** dedo m meñique; **middle ~** dedo m del corazón; **his ~s are all thumbs** es terriblemente desmañado; **to burn one's ~s, to get one's ~s burned** (*fig*) cogerse los dedos, pillarse los dedos; **to get** (*or* **pull**) **one's ~ out** espabilarse; **get your ~ out** ¡espabílate!; **to have a green ~s** tener mucha habilidad en jardinería; **to have a ~ in the**

pie meter su cucharada; **to keep one's ~s crossed** tocar madera, esperar que todo salga bien; **and please keep your ~s crossed for me** y te ruego tocar madera; **they never laid a ~ on her** no la tocaron en absoluto; **he didn't lift a ~ to help** no movió un dedo para ayudarnos; **to point the ~ of scorn at sb** señalar a uno con el dedo; **to put one's ~ on** (*fig*) concretar, señalar acertadamente; **to put one's ~ on it** (*or* **on the spot**) poner el dedo en la llaga; **there was nothing you could put your ~ on** no había nada concreto; **he slipped through their ~s** se les escapó entre los dedos; **to snap one's ~s at sb** (*fig*) tratar a uno con desprecio; **to twist sb round one's little ~** hacer que uno baile al son que le tocan; **to put two ~s up at sb** (*Brit*), **to give sb the ~** (*US*) hacer un corte de mangas a uno.

(b) (*Aer*) corredor m de carga y descarga, brazo m.

2 ATTR: **~ exercises** (*for piano etc*) ejercicios mpl de dedos.

3 VT **(a)** (*touch*) manosear, tocar; (*Mus*) tocar (distraídamente).

(b) (*esp US*) (*identify*) señalar; identificar; (*betray*) traicionar, delatar.

fingerboard [ˈfɪŋɡəˌbɔːd] N (*Mus*) diapasón m.

fingerbowl [ˈfɪŋɡəˌbəʊl] N lavafrutas m.

finger food [ˈfɪŋɡəˌfuːd] N (*US*) tapas fpl.

fingering [ˈfɪŋɡərɪŋ] N (*Mus*) digitación f.

fingermark [ˈfɪŋɡəmɑːk] N huella f.

fingernail [ˈfɪŋɡəneɪl] N uña f.

fingerprint [ˈfɪŋɡəprɪnt] **1** N huella f dactilar, huella f digital. **2** VT tomar las huellas dactilares a; (*Med*) identificar genéticamente.

fingerstall [ˈfɪŋɡəstɔːl] N dedil m.

fingertip [ˈfɪŋɡətɪp] N punta f (*or* yema f) del dedo; **to have sth at one's ~s** tener algo a mano, (*fig*) saber(se) algo al dedillo.

finicky [ˈfɪnɪkɪ] ADJ delicado, melindroso, superferolítico*.

finish [ˈfɪnɪʃ] **1** N **(a)** (*end*) fin m, final m, conclusión f; remate m; (*Sport*) poste m de llegada; **to be in at the ~** estar presente en la conclusión; **to fight to a ~** seguir luchando hasta decidir la victoria. **(b)** (*of manufactured article*) acabado m; **gloss(y) ~** acabado m brillo; **to have a rough ~** estar sin pulir.

2 VT **(a)** (*also to ~ off, to ~ up*) terminar, acabar, concluir; completar, llevar a cabo, rematar; dar la última mano a; *person* (*destroy*) quemar, acabar con; **that last kilometre nearly ~ed me** el kilómetro final casi acabó conmigo; **I'm ~ed** (*tired*) estoy rendido; **he's ~ed** (*fig*) está quemado; **as a film star she's ~ed** como estrella está quemada.

(b) (*Tech*) acabar.

3 VI **(a)** terminar, acabar; **to ~ doing sth** terminar de hacer algo; **to ~ by saying that ...** terminar diciendo que ...; **to ~ with** terminar con; **she ~ed with him** rompió con él; **wait till I've ~ed with him!** ¡a ver lo que le voy a hacer!, ¡ya verás cómo le dejo!

(b) (*Sport*) llegar; **to ~ third** llegar el tercero.

◆**finish off** VT **(a)** V finish 2 (a). **(b)** (*kill*) despachar; (*destroy*) acabar con.

◆**finish up** **1** VT *food* terminar, acabar; V finish 2 (a).

2 VI: **to ~ up at** ir a parar a.

finished [ˈfɪnɪʃt] ADJ acabado, terminado; **~ goods** productos mpl acabados; **~ product** producto m acabado.

finishing-line [ˈfɪnɪʃɪŋˌlaɪn] N línea f de meta.

finishing-school [ˈfɪnɪʃɪŋˌskuːl] N escuela f de educación social para señoritas.

finishing touch [ˈfɪnɪʃɪŋˌtʌtʃ] N último toque m, toque m final; **to put** *or* **add the ~** *or* **touches to sth** dar los últimos toques a algo.

finite [ˈfaɪnaɪt] ADJ **(a)** finito, que tiene fin. **(b)** (*Gram*) *mood, verb* conjugado; **~ verb** verbo m finito.

fink* [fɪŋk] N (*US*) (*informer*) soplón* m; (*strikebreaker*) esquirol m.

◆**fink out*** VI acobardarse.

Finland [ˈfɪnlənd] N Finlandia f.

Finn [fɪn] N finlandés m, -esa f.

Finnish [ˈfɪnɪʃ] **1** ADJ finlandés. **2** N finlandés m.

Finno-Ugrian [ˈfɪnəʊˈuːɡrɪən], **Finno-Ugric** [ˈfɪnəʊˈuːɡrɪk] **1** ADJ fino-húngaro. **2** N (*Ling*) fino-húngaro m.

fiord [fjɔːd] N fiordo m.

fir [fɜːʳ] N abeto m.

fircone [ˈfɜːkəʊn] N piña f (de abeto).

fire [faɪəʳ] **1** N **(a)** (*gen*) fuego m; (*accidental, damaging*) incendio m; (*in grate*) fuego m, lumbre f; (*electric*) estufa f eléctrica; **to be on ~** estar ardiendo, estar en llamas; **to catch ~** encenderse, prenderse; **to cook sth on a slow ~** cocer algo a fuego lento; **to hang ~** demorarse, estar en suspenso; **to make up a ~** echar carbón a la lumbre; **to play with ~** jugar con fuego; **to set on ~, to set ~ to** pegar (*or* prender) fuego a, incendiar; **to sit by** (*or* **round**) **the ~** estar sentado al lado de la chimenea, estar sentado al amor de la lumbre; **to take ~** encenderse.

(b) (*Mil*) **to hold one's ~** no disparar; **to open ~** abrir fuego, romper el fuego; **to be under ~** (*fig*) ser criticado.

➤ LANGUAGE IN USE: **fine¹: 1b** → 11.2, 11.3, 13 **2a** → 13

(c) (*fig*) ardor *m*, pasión *f*; entusiasmo *m*; **the ~ of youth** el ardor de la juventud; **men with ~ in their bellies** hombres llenos de celo idealista.

2 ATTR: **it's a ~ hazard, it's a ~ risk** es un peligro de incendio.

3 VT **(a)** (*set ~ to*) encender, incendiar, pegar fuego a, quemar; *bricks, pottery* cocer.

(b) *gun, shot, salute* disparar; *torpedo, rocket* lanzar; **to ~ a question at sb** disparar una pregunta inesperada a uno.

(c) (*fig*) *imagination* excitar, enardecer, exaltar; *interest* despertar; (*inspire*) inspirar.

(d) (*) *person* despedir, echar (*LAm*), rajar* (*SC*); **you're ~d!** ¡queda Vd despedido!

4 VI **(a)** (*catch ~*) encenderse.

(b) (*Mil*) hacer fuego; **to ~ at, to ~ on** hacer fuego sobre, tirar a; **they were firing at each other all day** se estaban tiroteando todo el día; **~!** ¡fuego!; **~ away!** (*fig*) ¡adelante!, ¡siga no más! (*LAm*).

(c) (*Aut*) encenderse; dar explosiones; **the engine is not firing on one cylinder** uno de los cilindros del motor no se enciende (*LAm*: no prende).

◆ **fire off** VT = **fire 3 (b)**.

◆ **fire on** VT = **fire at**.

◆ **fire up*** VI (*fig*) ponerse furioso.

fire-alarm ['faɪərə,lɑ:m] N alarma *f* de incendios.

firearm ['faɪərɑ:m] N arma *f* de fuego.

fireball ['faɪəbɔ:l] N bola *f* de fuego.

Firebird ['faɪəbɜ:d] N: **the ~** (*Mus*) el Pájaro de fuego.

firebomb ['faɪəbɒm] **1** N bomba *f* incendiaria.

2 VT colocar una bomba incendiaria en; (*Aer*) bombardear con bombas incendiarias.

firebrand ['faɪəbrænd] N **(a)** tea *f*. **(b)** (*fig*) partidario *m* violento, partidaria *f* violenta, revoltoso *m*, -a *f*.

firebreak ['faɪəbreɪk] N (línea *f*) cortafuegos *m*.

firebrick ['faɪəbrɪk] N ladrillo *m* refractario.

fire-brigade ['faɪəbrɪ,geɪd] N (*Brit*) cuerpo *m* de bomberos.

firebug ['faɪəbʌg] N (*US*) incendiario *m*, -a *f*, pirómano *m*, -a *f*.

fire chief ['faɪətʃi:f] N (*US*) jefe *mf* del cuerpo de bomberos.

fireclay ['faɪəkleɪ] N (*Brit*) arcilla *f* refractaria.

firecracker ['faɪə,krækər] N (*US*) petardo *m*.

fire-curtain ['faɪə,kɜ:tn] N telón *m* metálico, telón *m* a prueba de incendios.

firedamp ['faɪədæmp] N grisú *m*.

fire-department ['faɪədɪ,pɑ:tmənt] N = **fire-brigade**.

fire dog ['faɪə,dɒg] N morillo *m*.

fire-door ['faɪədɔ:ʳ] N puerta *f* contra incendios.

fire-drill ['faɪə'drɪl] N (ejercicio *m* de) simulacro *m* de incendio.

fire-eater ['faɪər,i:təʳ] N tragafuegos *mf*; (*fig*) matamoros *m*.

fire-engine ['faɪər,endʒɪn] N bomba *f* de incendios, coche *m* de bomberos.

fire-escape ['faɪərɪs,keɪp] N escalera *f* de incendios.

fire-exit ['faɪər,egzɪt] N salida *f* de incendios (*or* de emergencia).

fire-extinguisher ['faɪərɪks,tɪŋgwɪʃəʳ] N extintor *m*.

firefight ['faɪə,faɪt] N (*Mil*) tiroteo *m*.

fire-fighter ['faɪə,faɪtəʳ] N bombero *m*.

fire-fighting ['faɪə,faɪtɪŋ] N lucha *f* por apagar incendios; **~ equipment** equipo *m* contra incendios.

firefly ['faɪəflaɪ] N luciérnaga *f*.

fireguard ['faɪəgɑ:d] N alambrera *f*, guardafuego *m*.

firehouse ['faɪəhaʊs] N, PL **firehouses** ['faɪəhaʊzɪz] (*US*) parque *m* de bomberos.

fire-hydrant ['faɪə,haɪdrənt] N boca *f* de incendios.

fire insurance ['faɪərɪn,ʃʊərəns] N seguro *m* contra incendios.

fire-irons ['faɪər,aɪənz] NPL útiles *mpl* de chimenea.

fire-lane ['faɪəleɪn] N (*US*) (línea *f*) cortafuegos *m*.

firelight ['faɪəlaɪt] N lumbre *f*.

firelighter ['faɪə,laɪtəʳ] N astillas *fpl* (para encender el fuego), tea *f*.

fireman ['faɪəmən] N, PL **firemen** ['faɪəmən] (*of fire service*) bombero *m*; (*Rail*) fogonero *m*.

fireplace ['faɪəpleɪs] N chimenea *f*; (*hearth*) hogar *m*.

fireplug ['faɪəplʌg] N (*US*) boca *f* de incendios.

firepower ['faɪə,paʊəʳ] N (*Mil*) potencia *f* de fuego.

fire practice ['faɪə,præktɪs] = **fire drill**.

fire prevention ['faɪəprɪ'venʃən] N prevención *f* de incendios.

fireproof ['faɪəpru:f] **1** ADJ incombustible, a prueba de fuego; *dish* refractario; *material* ignífugo, ininflamable, incombustible.

2 VT ignifugar.

fire-raiser ['faɪə,reɪzəʳ] N (*Brit*) incendiario *m*, -a *f*, pirómano *m*, -a *f*.

fire-raising ['faɪə,reɪzɪŋ] N (*Brit*) (delito *m* de) incendiar *m*, piromanía *f*.

fire regulations ['faɪə,regjʊ'leɪʃənz] NPL normas *fpl* para la prevención de incendios.

fire-resistant ['faɪərɪ,zɪstənt] ADJ ignífugo.

fire retardant ['faɪərɪ,tɑ:dənt] **1** ADJ resistente al fuego.

2 N ignirretardante *m*.

fire sale ['faɪə,seɪl] N venta *f* de liquidación por incendio.

fire-screen ['faɪəskri:n] N pantalla *f* refractaria.

fire-service ['faɪə,sɜ:vɪs] N cuerpo *m* de bomberos, servicio *m* de extinción de incendios.

fireside ['faɪəsaɪd] **1** N hogar *m*.

2 ATTR hogareño, doméstico, familiar; **~ chair** butaca *f* cerca de la lumbre; **~ chat** charla *f* íntima.

fire-station ['faɪə,steɪʃən] N parque *m* de bomberos.

fire-tender ['faɪə,tendəʳ] N, **firetruck** ['faɪətrʌk] N (*US*) coche *m* de bomberos.

firetower ['faɪə,taʊəʳ] N (*US*) torre *f* de vigilancia contra incendios.

firetrap ['faɪətræp] N lugar *m* (*or* edificio *m* *etc*) con peligro de incendio; **this house is a ~** en caso de incendio esta casa es una trampa.

firewater* ['faɪə,wɔ:təʳ] N (*US*) licor *m*, aguardiente *m*.

firewood ['faɪəwʊd] N leña *f*, astillas *fpl*.

firework ['faɪəwɜ:k] N fuego *m* artificial; petardo *m*; **~s** (*fig*) explosión *f* (de cólera *etc*); **there will be ~s at the meeting** (*fig*) en la reunión se va a armar la gorda.

firing ['faɪərɪŋ] N **(a)** (*Mil*) disparo *m*, (*continuous*) tiroteo *m*, cañoneo *m*. **(b)** (*Aut*) encendido *m*. **(c)** (*of bricks etc*) cocción *f*. **(d)** (*esp US**) despido *m*.

firing-hammer ['faɪərɪŋ,hæməʳ] N martillo *m*.

firing-line ['faɪərɪŋlaɪn] N línea *f* de fuego.

firing-pin ['faɪərɪŋ,pɪn] N = **firing-hammer**.

firing-squad ['faɪərɪŋskwɒd] N pelotón *m* de ejecución.

firm¹ [fɜ:m] **1** ADJ firme; (*Comm*) *offer, order* en firme; **as ~ as a rock** tan firme como una roca; **he was very ~ about it** se mostró muy decidido, lo dijo de modo terminante; **these prices are ~** estos precios son invariables; **to stand ~** mantenerse firme.

2 ADV: **to buy ~** comprar firme.

◆ **firm up** **1** VT fortalecer, reforzar; *proposal etc* redondear.

2 VI fortalecerse, reforzarse.

firm² [fɜ:m] N firma *f*, empresa *f*, casa *f* de comercio; **the old ~** (*hum*) la vieja firma.

firmament ['fɜ:məmənt] N firmamento *m*.

firmly ['fɜ:mlɪ] ADV firmemente; con firmeza.

firmness ['fɜ:mnɪs] N firmeza *f*.

firmware ['fɜ:mweəʳ] N soporte *m* lógico inalterable, software *m* de ROM.

▼ **first** [fɜ:st] **1** ADJ primero; primitivo, original; **~ base** (*Baseball*) primera base *f*; V **cousin**; (*Univ*) **~ degree** licenciatura *f*; **~ edition** primera edición *f*; (*of early or rare book*) edición *f* príncipe; **~ floor** (*Brit*) primer piso *m*; (*US*) planta *f* baja; **~ form** (*Brit Scol*) ≃ primer curso *m* de secundaria; **~ fruits** primicias *fpl*; **~ gear** primera *f* (velocidad *f*); **~ lady** (*US*) primera dama *f*; **the ~ lady of jazz** la primera dama del jazz; **~ language** (*mother tongue*) lengua *f* materna; (*in state etc*) lengua *f* principal; **~ lieutenant** (*US Aer*) teniente *m*; (*Brit Naut*) teniente *m* de navío; **~ mate** primer oficial *m*; **~ name** nombre *m* de pila; **to be on ~ name terms with sb** tutear a uno; **~ night** (*Theat*) estreno *m*; **~ offender** persona *f* que comete un delito por primera vez, persona *f* sin antecedentes penales; **~ officer** primer oficial *m*; **~-past-the-post system** sistema *m* mayoritario; **~ performance** estreno *m*; **~ person** persona *f*; **~ school** escuela *f* primaria; **~ strike** primer golpe *m*; **~ strike weapon** arma *f* de primer golpe; **~ string** (N: *Sport*) crack *mf*; **~-string** (ADJ) de primera; **~ violin** primer violín *m*; **he hadn't the ~ idea how to do it** no tenía la más mínima idea de cómo hacerlo; V **thing (c)**.

▼ **2** ADV primero; (*firstly*) en primer lugar; (*for the first time*) por primera vez; **~ of all, ~ and foremost** ante todo; **head ~** de cabeza; **stern ~** la popa por delante; **ladies ~** las señoras pasan primero; **women and children ~!** ¡primero las mujeres y los niños!; **to come ~** (*in race*) ganar, llegar el primero; (*in league*) ir en cabeza, ocupar el primer puesto; (*have priority*) venir primero, tener la prioridad; **it was done on a ~ come ~ served basis** lo hicieron por riguroso orden de llegada; **to get in ~** (*fig*) madrugar; **to go ~** entrar (*etc*) el primero, (*Rail*) viajar en primera; **you go ~!** ¡Vd primero!, ¡pase Vd!

3 N primero *m*, -a *f*; (*Brit Univ*) primera clase *f*, sobresaliente *m*; **at ~** al principio; **I didn't see them at ~** no les vi de momento; **from the ~** desde el principio; **from ~ to last** desde el principio hasta el fin; **it was a ~ for Pérez** fue el primer triunfo de Pérez; **to be the ~ to do sth** ser el primero en hacer algo; **he came in an easy ~** llegó con mucho el primero, ganó fácilmente; *ver también* DEGREE .

first aid ['fɜ:st'eɪd] **1** N primera curación *f*, primeros auxilios *mpl*.

2 ATTR: **~ box, ~ kit** botiquín *m*; **~ post** puesto *m* de socorro; **~ station** caseta *f* de primeros auxilios.

first-born ['fɜ:st'bɔ:n] N primogénito *m*, -a *f*.

first-class ['fɜ:stklɑ:s] **1** ADJ de primera clase; **~ mail, ~ post** correo *m* de primera clase; **~ ticket** billete *m* de primera clase.

2 ADV: **to send a letter ~** enviar una carta por correo de primera clase; **to travel ~** viajar en primera.

▶ LANGUAGE IN USE: **first:** 1 → 26.1 2 → 26.1, 26.2, 26.3

first-degree ['fɜːstdɪ'griː] ATTR: **~ burns** quemaduras *fpl* de primer grado.

first-ever ['fɜːst,evəʳ] ADJ primerísimo.

first footing [,fɜːst'futɪŋ] N: **to go ~** (*Scot*) *ser el primero en visitar a amigos y familiares tras las doce en Nochevieja*; *ver también* HOGMANAY .

first-generation ['fɜːst,dʒenə'reɪʃən] ADJ: **he's a ~ American** es americano de primera generación.

first-hand ['fɜːst'hænd] ADJ de primera mano; directo, personal; **at ~** directamente.

▼ **firstly** ['fɜːstlɪ] ADV en primer lugar.

first-named [,fɜːst'neɪmd] ADJ: **the ~** el primero, la primera.

first-nighter ['fɜːst'naɪtəʳ] N estrenista *mf*.

first-rate ['fɜːst'reɪt] ADJ de primera clase; magnífico, estupendo; **she is ~ at her work** su trabajo es de primera clase; **~!** ¡magnífico!

first-time ['fɜːst'taɪm] ADJ: **~ buyer** persona *f* que compra su primera vivienda.

first-timer [,fɜːst'taɪməʳ] N novato *m*, -a *f*, principiante *mf*.

firth [fɜːθ] N (*gen Scot*) estuario *m*, ría *f*.

fir-tree ['fɜːtriː] N abeto *m*.

FIS N (*Brit*) ABBR of **Family Income Supplement** *ayuda estatal familiar*.

fiscal ['fɪskəl] ADJ fiscal; monetario; *policy* fiscal, financiero, económico; **~ year** año *m* económico.

fish [fɪʃ] **1** N, PL **fish** (a) pez *m*, (*as food*) pescado *m*; **~ and chips** (*esp Brit*) pescado *m* frito con patatas fritas; **to be like a ~ out of water** estar como pez fuera del agua; **there are other ~ in the sea** hay otros peces en el mar; **to have other ~ to fry** tener cosas más importantes que hacer.
(b) (*) tío *m**; **big ~** pez *m* gordo; **odd ~** tío *m* raro*; **he's a (bit of a) cold ~** es un tipo frío*; **he's a poor ~** es un pobre hombre.
2 ATTR: **~-and-chip shop** (*esp Brit*) *tienda de comida rápida, principalmente de pescado rebozado y patatas fritas*; **~ course** pescado *m*; **~ merchant** (*US*) pescadero *m*, -a *f*; **~ soup** sopa *f* de pescado; *ver también* CHIP SHOP .
3 VT *river* pescar en.
4 VI pescar; (*trawler etc*) faenar; **to ~ for** (*tratar de*) pescar; *compliment etc* andar a la pesca de; **he ~ed in his pocket for it** lo buscó en el bolsillo; **to ~ in troubled waters** (*fig*) pescar en río revuelto; **to go ~ing** ir de pesca.
◆**fish out** VT (a) sacar. (b) **this lake has been ~ed out** en este lago se ha pescado tanto que ya no quedan peces.
◆**fish up** VT sacar.

fishbone ['fɪʃbəʊn] N espina *f* (de pez), raspa *f*.

fishbowl ['fɪʃbəʊl] N pecera *f*.

fishcake ['fɪʃkeɪk] N croqueta *f* de pescado.

fisherman ['fɪʃəmən] N, PL **fishermen** ['fɪʃəmən] pescador *m*; **~'s tale** (*Brit fig*) cuento *m* de pescador.

fishery ['fɪʃərɪ] **1** N pesquería *f*, pesquera *f*.
2 ATTR: **~ policy** política *f* pesquera; **~ protection** protección *f* pesquera.

fish-eye ['fɪʃaɪ] **1** N (*in door*) mirilla *f*.
2 ATTR: **~ lens** (*Phot*) objetivo *m* de ojo de pez.

fish factory ['fɪʃ,fæktərɪ] N fábrica *f* de elaboración de pescado.

fish-farm ['fɪʃfɑːm] N criadero *m* de peces, piscifactoría *f*.

fish-farmer ['fɪʃ,fɑːməʳ] N acuicultor *m*, -ora *f*.

fish-farming ['fɪʃ,fɑːmɪŋ] N cría *f* de peces, piscicultura *f*, acuicultura *f*.

fish-finger [,fɪʃ'fɪŋgəʳ] N (*Brit*) filete *m* de pescado empanado.

fish-glue ['fɪʃgluː] N cola *f* de pescado.

fish-hook ['fɪʃhʊk] N anzuelo *m*.

fishing ['fɪʃɪŋ] **1** N pesca *f*.
2 ATTR pesquero; de pesca; **~ fleet** flota *f* pesquera; **~ industry** industria *f* pesquera; **~ licence, ~ permit** licencia *f* para pescar; **~ port** puerto *m* pesquero; **to go on a ~ expedition** ir de pesca.

fishing-boat ['fɪʃɪŋbəʊt] N barca *f* pesquera.

fishing-grounds ['fɪʃɪŋgraʊndz] NPL pesquería *f*.

fishing-line ['fɪʃɪŋlaɪn] N sedal *m*.

fishing-net ['fɪʃɪŋnet] N red *f* de pesca.

fishing-rod ['fɪʃɪŋrɒd] N caña *f* de pescar.

fishing-tackle ['fɪʃɪŋ,tækl] N aparejo *m* de pescar.

fish-knife ['fɪʃnaɪf] N, PL **fish-knives** ['fɪʃnaɪvz] cuchillo *m* de pescado.

fish-manure ['fɪʃmə,njʊəʳ] N abono *m* de pescado.

fish-market ['fɪʃmɑːkɪt] N mercado *m* de pescado, pescadería *f*.

fishmeal ['fɪʃmiːl] N harina *f* de pescado.

fishmonger ['fɪʃmʌŋgəʳ] N pescadero *m*; **~'s (shop)** pescadería *f*.

fishnet ['fɪʃnet] ATTR: **~ stockings** medias *fpl* de red, medias *fpl* de rejilla; **~ tights** leotardo *m* de red.

fish-paste ['fɪʃpeɪst] N pasta *f* de pescado.

fishplate ['fɪʃpleɪt] N (*Rail*) eclisa *f*.

fishpond ['fɪʃpɒnd] N piscina *f*, vivero *m*.

fishseller ['fɪʃ,seləʳ] (*US*) = **fishmonger**.

fish-shop ['fɪʃʃɒp] N pescadería *f*.

fish-slice ['fɪʃslaɪs] N (*Brit*) pala *f* para el pescado.

fish stick ['fɪʃstɪk] N (*US*) croqueta *f* de pescado.

fishstore ['fɪʃstɔːʳ] N (*US*) pescadería *f*.

fishtank ['fɪʃtæŋk] N acuario *m*.

fishwife ['fɪʃwaɪf] N, PL **fishwives** ['fɪʃwaɪvz] pescadera *f*; (*pej*) verdulera *f*.

fishy ['fɪʃɪ] ADJ (a) *eye* como de pez; (*of taste*) que sabe a pescado, (*of smell*) que huele a pescado. (b) (*) sospechoso; **it's ~** me huele a camelo; **there's sth ~ going on here** aquí hay gato encerrado, me huele a chamusquina.

fissile ['fɪsaɪl] ADJ físil.

fission ['fɪʃən] N (*Phys*) fisión *f*; (*Bio*) escisión *f*.

fissionable ['fɪʃnəbl] ADJ fisionable.

fissure ['fɪʃəʳ] N grieta *f*, hendedura *f*; (*Anat, Geol, Metal*) fisura *f*.

fissured ['fɪʃəd] ADJ agrietado.

fist [fɪst] N (a) puño *m*; **to shake one's ~ at sb** amenazar a uno con el puño; **to make a poor ~ of sth** hacer algo mal. (b) (*) escritura *f*.

fistfight ['fɪst,faɪt] N lucha *f* a puñetazos.

fistful ['fɪstfʊl] N puñado *m*.

fisticuffs ['fɪstɪkʌfs] NPL puñetazos *mpl*.

fistula ['fɪstjʊlə] N, PL **fistulas** or **fistulae** fístula *f*.

fit[1] [fɪt] **1** ADJ (*suitable*) adecuado, conveniente, apto, a propósito, apropiado (*for* para); hábil, capaz; **the ~test** (*Bio*) los mejor dotados; **~ for duty** apto para servicio; **a meal ~ for a king** una comida digna de un rey; **to be ~ for** ser adecuado para; **he's not ~ for the job** no es adecuado para el puesto, no merece que se le dé el puesto; **he's not ~ to teach** no tiene madera de profesor; **he is not ~ to drive** no es apto para conducir; **~ to eat** bueno de comer; **it's not ~ to eat** no se puede comer, es incomible; **it's not ~ to be seen** es indigno de que lo vean las gentes; **is this ~ to wear?** ¿puedo ponerme esto?; **I felt ~ to drop** tuve ganas de caerme rendido; **to see** (*or* **think**) **~ to** + *infin* estimar conveniente + *infin*; **he saw ~ to** + *infin* se vio en el caso de + *infin*; **do as you think ~** haga lo que mejor le parezca.
(b) (*Med*) sano, bien de salud; en buen estado físico; (*Sport*) en forma; **3 players are not ~** 3 jugadores están lesionados; **come when you're ~ again** ven cuando te hayas repuesto del todo; **to be as ~ as a fiddle** andar como un reloj; **are you ~?*** ¿estás listo?, ¿vamos?; **to get ~** (*Sport*) entrenarse, (*Med*) reponerse; **to keep ~** mantenerse en forma, mantenerse en buen estado físico.
2 ADV: **to laugh ~ to burst*** desternillarse de risa*.
3 VT (a) (*make suitable*) ajustar, acomodar, adaptar (*to* a); **to ~ sb for a post** capacitar a uno para un puesto.
(b) (*suit*) *description, facts* cuadrar con, corresponder con, estar de acuerdo con; *colour scheme etc* hacer juego con; (*of dress etc*) sentar bien a, ir bien a.
(c) (*try on*) *clothes* probar (*on* a).
(d) (*fill up, exactly correspond to*) encajar en; **it ~s the space perfectly** encaja perfectamente en el espacio; **the key does not ~ the lock** la llave no entra en la cerradura.
(e) (*put*) **to ~ two things together** unir dos cosas; **I ~ted A into B** encajé A en B; **you ~ it in here** se encaja aquí, se coloca aquí; **to ~ the key into the lock** introducir la llave en la cerradura.
(f) (*supply*) **to ~ sth with** proveer algo de; **~ted with a heater** provisto de un calentador, dotado de un calentador; **I'm having a new door ~ted** me van a colocar una nueva portezuela; *see also* **fitted**.
4 VI (a) (*correspond*) corresponder, estar de acuerdo; **the facts don't ~** los datos no tienen sentido; **it all ~s** todo hace un conjunto lógico.
(b) (*of clothes etc*) entallar; **the suit ~s well** el traje le sienta bien.
(c) (*of space*) encajarse; caber; **it ~s in here, it ~s on here** se encaja aquí; **do they ~?** ¿se encajan uno en otro?; **does it ~?** ¿cabe?; **it won't ~ in here** aquí no cabe; **the key doesn't ~** la llave no sirve; **the key ~s into the lock** la llave encaja en la cerradura.
5 N ajuste *m*, corte *m*; correspondencia *f*; **it's a good ~** le sienta bien; **the suit is a tight ~** el traje me viene bastante estrecho; **it's not a good ~** no se ajusta bien; **there is no ~ between A and B** no hay correspondencia entre A y B.
◆**fit in** **1** VT: **can you ~ me in?** ¿puedes incluirme?, ¿tienes un hueco para mí?; **I'll see if the director can ~ you in** voy a ver si el director tiene tiempo para verle; **I ~ted in a trip to Ávila** logré hacer una excursión a Ávila.
2 VI (*of person*) **he ~s in well here** aquí se lleva bien con todos; **I don't ~ in here** aquí no estoy bien.
◆**fit on** VI: **this bottle top won't ~ on any more** este tapón ya no cabe; **it should ~ on this end somewhere** tendría que ir por esta parte.
◆**fit out** VT *expedition, person* equipar; *ship* armar; **to ~ sb out with** proveer a uno de, equipar a uno con.
◆**fit up** VT (a) equipar, montar, instalar; **to ~ sb up with** proveer a uno de, equipar a uno con; **they have ~ted their house up with all modern conveniences** han equipado su casa con todas las co-

modidades modernas.
(b) (:) incriminar dolosamente.
fit² [fɪt] N (Med) acceso m, ataque m; **~ of anger** arranque m de cólera; **~ of coughing** acceso m de tos; **by ~s and starts** a rachas, a empujones; **we were in ~s (of laughter)** moríamos de risa; **he'd have a ~ if he knew** le daría un ataque si lo supiera.
fitful ['fɪtfʊl] ADJ espasmódico, irregular, intermitente.
fitfully ['fɪtfəlɪ] ADV espasmódicamente, a rachas, por intervalos.
fitment ['fɪtmənt] N (Brit) mueble m.
fitness ['fɪtnɪs] N **(a)** (suitability) conveniencia f, oportunidad f; (for post etc) idoneidad f, capacidad f. **(b)** (Med) (buena) salud f, (buen) estado m físico; **~ activity** (US) ejercicios mpl para mantenerse en forma; **~ classes** clases fpl de gimnasia; **~ fanatic** fanático m, -a f de la buena salud.
fitted ['fɪtɪd] ADJ **(a)** suit, carpet hecho a medida; cupboard empotrado. **(b) to be ~ for sth** tener talento para algo, ser idóneo para algo, ser apto para algo.
fitter ['fɪtər] N (Mech) (mecánico m) ajustador m.
fitting ['fɪtɪŋ] 1 ADJ (suitable) conveniente, adecuado; (worthy) digno; **it is ~ that …** es propio que + subj, es justo que + subj; **it is not ~ that …** no está bien que + subj.
2 N **(a)** (of dress) prueba f; (size) medida f.
(b) ~s (Brit) guarniciones fpl; (for bathroom) aparatos mpl sanitarios; (electrical) accesorios mpl eléctricos.
3 ATTR: **~ room** probador m, vestidor m (LAm).
fittingly ['fɪtɪŋlɪ] ADV convenientemente, adecuadamente; dignamente; **~, it was he who …** según cabía razonablemente esperar, era él quien …
five [faɪv] 1 ADJ cinco.
2 N cinco m; **give me ~!** ¡choquen esos cinco!:.
five-and-ten-cent store [ˌfaɪvən'tensent'stɔːr] N, **five-and-dime** [ˌfaɪvən'daɪm] N, **five-and-ten** [ˌfaɪvən'ten] N (US) almacén m de baratillo.
five-a-side ['faɪvəˌsaɪd] ADJ football, team (outdoors) de futbito; (indoors) de fútbol-sala.
five-day week ['faɪvdeɪˌwiːk] N semana f inglesa.
five-fold ['faɪvˌfəʊld] 1 ADJ quintuplo.
2 ADV cinco veces.
five-o'-clock shadow ['faɪvəklɒk'ʃædəʊ] N barba f crecida.
fiver* ['faɪvər] N (Brit) billete m de 5 libras.
five spot* ['faɪvspɒt] N (US) billete m de cinco dólares.
five-star ['faɪvstɑːr] ATTR: **~ hotel** hotel m de cinco estrellas; **~ restaurant** ≃ restaurante m de cinco estrellas.
five-year ['faɪv'jɪər] ADJ: **~ plan** plan m quinquenal.
fix [fɪks] 1 VT **(a)** (secure) fijar, asegurar, sujetar; bayonet calar; (Phot) fijar; **to ~ sth in one's memory** grabar algo en la memoria.
(b) (direct) attention fijar (on en); eyes clavar (on en); hopes poner (on en); blame echar (on a).
(c) to ~ sb with one's eyes fijar los ojos en uno.
(d) (place) fijar (at en).
(e) (determine position of) fijar, precisar.
(f) (determine) author, date etc fijar, señalar; price fijar, determinar.
(g) (arrange, prepare: also **to ~ up**) arreglar; decidir; organizar, preparar; **it's all ~ed up** todo está arreglado; **there is nothing ~ed yet** todavía no se ha decidido nada; **he ~ed it with the police** lo arregló con la policía; **I'll soon ~ him!*** ¡me lo cargaré!*; **that ought to ~ him*** eso ha de acabar con él, que se apañe con esto.
(h) (esp US) dar, servir, preparar; **can I ~ you a drink?** ¿te preparo algo de beber?; **I'll ~ you some supper** te prepararé algo para cenar.
(i) (repair) componer, arreglar.
(j) (Sport etc) game, jury amañar; **it's been ~ed!** ¡hay tongo!
(k) how are we ~ed for time? ¿cómo vamos de tiempo?; **how are we ~ed for money?** ¿qué tal andamos de dinero?
2 N **(a)** (Aer etc) posición f.
(b) (*) aprieto m; **to be in a ~** estar en un aprieto.
(c) (:) (of drug) dosis f; (shot) pinchazo: m; **to give o.s. a ~** pincharse:.
◆**fix on** VT escoger; date etc fijar, señalar.
◆**fix up** 1 VT **(a)** = fix 1 (g). **(b)** (provide) **to ~ sb up with sth** proveer a uno de algo; **to ~ sb up with a job** conseguir un puesto para uno.
2 VI: **to ~ up with sb** arreglarlo con uno; **to ~ up with sb to +** infin convenir con uno en + infin.
fixate [fɪk'seɪt] 1 VT: **to be ~d on sb/sth** estar obsesionado con uno/algo; **to become** or **get ~d on** or **with sth/sb** obsesionarse con uno/algo.
2 VI: **to ~ on sth/sb** tener una fijación con uno/algo.
fixated [fɪk'seɪtɪd] ADJ: **mother ~** con fijación en la madre, con fijación materna.
fixation [fɪk'seɪʃən] N fijación f.
fixative ['fɪksətɪv] N fijativo m.
fixed [fɪkst] ADJ (all senses) fijo; **~ assets** activo m fijo; **~ capital** capital m fijo; **~ charge** gasto m fijo; **~ costs** costos mpl fijos; **~ debt** deuda

f consolidada; **~ format** formato m fijo; **~ investment** inversión f fija; **~ link** enlace m fijo; **~ price** precio m fijo; **~ star** estrella f fija; **~ wheel** piñón m fijo, rueda f fija; **~ yield securities** valores mpl de renta fija.
fixed-interest ['fɪkstˌɪntrɪst] ADJ a interés fijo.
fixedly ['fɪksɪdlɪ] ADV fijamente.
fixed-rate ['fɪkst,reɪt] ADJ a tipo fijo.
fixed-wing ['fɪkst,wɪŋ] ADJ: **~ aircraft** aeroplano f de ala fija.
fixer* ['fɪksər] N apañador m, -ora* f, amañador m, -ora* f.
fixings ['fɪksɪŋz] NPL (US) accesorios mpl, guarniciones fpl.
Fixit* ['fɪksɪt] N: **Mr ~** Señor m Arreglalotodo*.
fixture ['fɪkstʃər] N **(a)** cosa f fija; (furniture etc) mueble m fijo, instalación f fija; **the house was sold with ~s and fittings** (Brit) la casa se vendió acondicionada. **(b)** (Brit Sport) partido m, encuentro m. **(c)** (person) cliente m fijo.
fixture-list ['fɪkstʃəˌlɪst] N lista f de encuentros.
fizz [fɪz] 1 N **(a)** efervescencia f; (noise) ruido m sibilante. **(b)** (*) champán m; (US: soft drink) gaseosa f.
2 VI estar (or entrar) en efervescencia; hacer un ruido sibilante.
fizzle ['fɪzl] = fizz.
◆**fizzle out** VI apagarse; (fig) no dar resultado, fracasar.
fizzy ['fɪzɪ] ADJ gaseoso, espumoso, efervescente.
fjord [fjɔːd] N = fiord.
FL (US Post) ABBR of **Florida**.
Fla. (US) ABBR of **Florida**.
flab* [flæb] N grasa f, michelín* m.
flabbergast ['flæbəɡɑːst] VT pasmar, dejar sin habla; **I was ~ed by the news** la noticia me causó estupor.
flabbiness ['flæbɪnɪs] N **(a)** (chubbiness) gordura f. **(b)** (fig: of speech, argument etc) flojedad f, debilidad f; **a speech of exceptional ~** un discurso muy poco convincente.
flabby ['flæbɪ] ADJ flojo, fofo, blanducho; (fat) gordo; (fig) débil, soso.
flaccid ['flæksɪd] ADJ fláccido.
flaccidity [flæk'sɪdɪtɪ] N flaccidez f.
flag¹ [flæɡ] N (Bot) falso ácoro m, lirio m.
flag² [flæɡ] N (stone) losa f.
flag³ [flæɡ] 1 N bandera f, pabellón m; (small, charity etc) banderita f; (small, as souvenir, also Sport) banderín m; (Comput) señalizador m, bandera f; **~ of convenience** pabellón m de conveniencia; **~ of truce** bandera f de parlamento; **to keep the ~ flying** seguir defendiéndose, resistir, no rendir la bandera; **to show the ~** hacer acto de presencia.
2 VT **(a)** (signal) hacer señales con una bandera a. **(b)** path etc señalar con banderitas; item, reference señalar, marcar; indicar de manera especial.
◆**flag down** VT: **to ~ sb down** hacer señales a uno para que se detenga.
flag⁴ [flæɡ] VI (strength) acabarse, flaquear, decaer; (enthusiasm etc) enfriarse; (conversation) languidecer.
flag day ['flæɡdeɪ] N (Brit) día m de la banderita, cuestación f; **F~ Day** (US) día m de la Bandera (14 junio).
flagellate ['flædʒəleɪt] VT flagelar.
flagellation [ˌflædʒə'leɪʃən] N flagelación f.
flagging ['flæɡɪŋ] ADJ que flaquea; que se enfría; que languidece.
flag officer ['flæɡˌɒfɪsər] N (Naut) oficial m superior de la marina.
flagon ['flæɡən] N (approx) jarro m; (as measure) botella de unos 2 litros.
flagpole ['flæɡpəʊl] N asta f de bandera.
flagrant ['fleɪɡrənt] ADJ notorio, escandaloso.
flagrantly ['fleɪɡrəntlɪ] ADV notoriamente, escandalosamente; **~ unfair** notoriamente injusto.
flagship ['flæɡʃɪp] N buque m insignia, buque m escuadra, (††) capitana f.
flagstaff ['flæɡstɑːf] N asta f de bandera.
flagstone ['flæɡstəʊn] N losa f.
flag stop ['flæɡstɒp] N (US) parada f a petición.
flag-waving ['flæɡˌweɪvɪŋ] N (fig) patriotismo m de banderita.
flail [fleɪl] 1 N mayal m.
2 VT (Agr) desgranar; (fig) golpear, azotar.
3 VI (arms etc: also **to ~ about**) debatirse.
flair [fleər] N instinto m, aptitud f especial, don m (for para).
flak [flæk] N **(a)** fuego m antiaéreo. **(b)** (*) críticas fpl, comentarios mpl adversos; **to get a lot of ~** ser muy criticado.
flake [fleɪk] 1 N escama f, hojuela f; (of snow) copo m.
2 VT separar en escamas.
3 VI (also **to ~ away**, **to ~ off**) desprenderse en escamas.
◆**flake off** VI **(a)** V flake 3. **(b) ~ off!:** (US) ¡lárgate!*, ¡pírala!*
◆**flake out*** VT: **to be ~d out** (Brit) estar rendido.
2 VI (Brit) caer rendido.
flak-jacket ['flæk,dʒækɪt] N chaleco m antibala.
flaky ['fleɪkɪ] ADJ **(a)** escamoso; desmenuzable; **~ pastry** hojaldre m. **(b)** (US:) chiflado*.
flambé ['flɑːmbeɪ] ADJ flameado.

flamboyance [flæm'bɔɪəns] N (*of person, behaviour*) extravagancia *f*, rimbombancia *f*; (*of colour, design*) vistosidad *f*.

flamboyant [flæm'bɔɪənt] ADJ *dress etc* vistoso, llamativo; *character, speech* extravagante; *style* rimbombante.

flame [fleɪm] **1** N (a) llama *f*; **to be in ~s** arder en llamas; **to burst into ~s** estallar en llamas; **to commit sth to the ~s** entregar algo a las llamas; **to fan the ~s** soplar el fuego; **we watched the house go up in ~s** mirábamos cómo la casa ardía en llamas.
(b) (*) amante *mf*; **old ~** amante *mf* de otros tiempos.
2 VI (*burn*) llamear; (*shine*) brillar.
◆**flame-up** VI (*fig*) estallar, (*person*) inflamarse.

flame-coloured, (*US*) **flame-colored** ['fleɪm,kʌləd] ADJ de un amarillo intenso.

flamenco [flə'meŋkəu] ADJ, N flamenco *m*.

flame-proof ['fleɪmpruːf] ADJ a prueba de fuego.

flame retardant ['fleɪmrɪ,tɑːdənt] = **fire retardant**.

flamethrower ['fleɪm,θrəuəʳ] N lanzallamas *m*.

flaming ['fleɪmɪŋ] ADJ (a) llameante, en llamas. (b) (:) condenado*.

flamingo [flə'mɪŋgəu] N flamenco *m*.

flammable ['flæməbl] ADJ inflamable.

flan [flæn] N (*Brit*) tarta *f* de fruta, tarteleta *f* de fruta.

Flanders ['flɑːndəz] N Flandes *m*.

flange [flændʒ] N pestaña *f*, reborde *m*, resalte *m*, brida *f*.

flanged [flændʒd] ADJ con pestaña.

flank [flæŋk] **1** N (*of person*) costado *m*; (*of animal*) ijada *f*; (*of hill*) lado *m*, falda *f*; (*Mil*) flanco *m*.
2 ATTR: **~ attack** ataque *m* de flanco.
3 VT lindar con, estar contiguo a; (*Mil etc*) flanquear; **it is ~ed by hills** tiene unas colinas a su lado; **he was ~ed by two policemen** iba escoltado por dos guardias.

flannel ['flænl] **1** N (a) (*cloth*) franela *f*; (*Brit: face ~*) manopla *f*, paño *m*; **~s** (*Brit*) (*trousers*) pantalones *mpl* de franela; (*underclothes*) ropa *f* interior de lana.
(b) (*) (*soft soap*) jabón* *m*, coba* *f*; (*Brit: waffle*) paja *f*.
2 ADJ de franela.
3 VT (*Brit*) dar coba a*.
4 VI (*Brit*) llenar muchos renglones (*etc*) sin decir nada de valor.

flannelette [,flænə'let] N muletón *m*.

flap [flæp] **1** N (a) (*on dress*) faldilla *f*; (*of pocket*) cartera *f*; (*of envelope*) solapa *f*; (*of table*) hoja *f* plegadiza; (*of counter*) trampa *f*; (*of skin*) colgajo *m*; (*Aer*) flap *m*.
(b) (*of wing*) aletazo *m*, movimiento *m*.
(c) (*Brit*) (*crisis*) crisis *f*; (*row*) lío* *m*; **there's a big ~ on** hay una crisis; **se ha armado un lío imponente***; **to get into a ~** ponerse nervioso, azorarse.
2 VT *wings* batir; (*shake*) sacudir; *arms* agitar.
3 VI (a) (*wings*) aletear; (*sail*) sacudirse; (*flag etc*) ondear, agitarse.
(b) (*Brit*) ponerse nervioso, azorarse; **don't ~!** ¡con calma!

flapdoodle* ['flæp,duːdl] N chorrada* *f*.

flapjack ['flæpdʒæk] N torta *f* de avena, hojuela *f*, panqueque *m* (*LAm*).

flapper* ['flæpəʳ] N (*Hist*) joven *f* a la moda (*de los 1920*).

flare [fleəʳ] **1** N (a) (*blaze*) llamarada *f*; (*signal*) cohete *m* de señales, (*Mil*) bengala *f*, proyectil *m* de iluminación; (*solar*) erupción *f* solar.
(b) (*Sew*) vuelo *m*.
2 VT (*Sew*) abocinar, acampanar.
3 VI (a) (*blaze*) llamear, resplandecer, fulgurar; (*shine*) brillar.
(b) (*skirt*) acampanarse.
◆**flare up** VI (a) llamear, encenderse. (b) (*fig: person*) encolerizarse; ponerse hecho una fiera (*at* con); (*revolt etc*) estallar; (*epidemic*) declararse.

flared [fleəd] ADJ *skirt* de vuelo amplio; *trousers* de perneras amplias, acampanado.

flarepath ['fleəpɑːθ] N pista *f* iluminada con balizas.

flare-up ['fleəʳʌp] N (*fig*) explosión *f*; (*of anger*) arranque *m* de cólera; (*quarrel*) riña *f*; (*of trouble*) manifestación *f* súbita, estallido *m*.

flash [flæʃ] **1** N (a) (*of light*) relámpago *m*; destello *m*, ráfaga *f*; (*of gun*) fogonazo *m*; **~ of lightning** relámpago *m*; **like a ~** como un relámpago.
(b) (*moment*) instante *m*; **in a ~** en un instante.
(c) **~ of inspiration** ráfaga *f* de inspiración; **~ of wit** rasgo *m* de ingenio; **~ in the pan** esfuerzo *m* abortado, éxito *m* único; chiripa *f*; **it was just a ~ in the pan** eso fue por chiripa.
(d) (*news ~*) flash *m*, noticia *f* de última hora; mensaje *m* urgente.
(e) (*Phot*) flash *m*, magnesio *m*.
2 (*) ADJ: **a really ~ car** un coche realmente fabuloso*.
3 VT (a) *light* despedir, lanzar; *look* dirigir, lanzar (*rápidamente*); *message* transmitir por heliógrafo, transmitir por radio, (*fig*) transmitir rápidamente.
(b) *torch* encender; **~ it this way** proyéctala por aquí; **he ~ed the light in my eyes** hizo brillar la luz en mis ojos, dio con la luz en mis ojos.

(c) **to ~ sth about** sacar algo a relucir, hacer ostentación de algo.
4 VI (a) relampaguear, destellar; (*window, reflection*) brillar; **to ~ on and off** encenderse y apagarse.
(b) **to ~ past** pasar como un rayo.
(c) **to ~ back to** (*Cine*) volver atrás a.
(d) (*) exhibirse, desenfundar*.

flashback ['flæʃbæk] N escena *f* retrospectiva, vuelta *f* atrás (*to* a).

flash bulb ['flæʃbʌlb] N flash *m*, bombilla *f* fusible.

flash card ['flæʃkɑːd] N tarjeta *f*, carta *f*.

flash cube ['flæʃkjuːb] N flash *m* de cubo.

flasher* ['flæʃəʳ] N (*Brit*) exhibicionista *m*.

flash flood ['flæʃflʌd] N riada *f*.

flash gun ['flæʃgʌn] N disparador *m* de flash.

flashily ['flæʃɪlɪ] ADV: **to dress ~** vestirse a lo chulo.

flashing ['flæʃɪŋ] N (*) exhibicionismo *m*.

flashlight ['flæʃlaɪt] N (*Phot*) flash *m*; (*torch*) linterna *f* eléctrica.

flashpoint ['flæʃpɔɪnt] N (a) punto *m* de inflamación. (b) (*fig*) punto *m* de explosión.

flashy ['flæʃɪ] ADJ *jewel etc* de relumbrón; *car etc* ostentoso; *person* charro, chulo.

flask [flɑːsk] N frasco *m*; redoma *f*; (*vacuum ~*) termo *m*, termos *m*; (*Chem*) matraz *m*.

flat [flæt] **1** ADJ (a) (*level*) *countryside etc* llano; *object* plano; horizontal; (*smooth*) liso, igual; *tyre* desinflado; *foot* plano; *painted surface* mate, sin brillo; *rate* uniforme, igual; **400 metres ~** 400 metros lisos; **~ nose** nariz *f* chata; **~ race** carrera *f* lisa; **~ rate** tipo *m* fijo, tipo *m* estándar; **~ roof** azotea *f*; **~ screen** pantalla *f* plana; **as ~ as a pancake** *countryside* totalmente llano, (*after bombing*) desnudo como la palma de la mano; **the town was just ~** la ciudad quedó totalmente arrasada.
(b) (*downright*) terminante, categórico; **and that's ~** no hay más que decir.
(c) (*Mus*) *voice, instrument* desafinado; *key* bemol; **E ~ major** mi bemol mayor.
(d) (*dull, lifeless*) *taste, style* insípido, soso; *drink* muerto; *battery* descargado; *tone* monótono; *lecture etc* aburrido, pesado; *business* flojo; *feeling* de abatimiento; **to be ~*** (*US*) no tener ni un céntimo; **to be feeling rather ~** sentirse algo deprimido.
2 ADV (a) **to fall ~** (*on one's face*) caer de bruces, caer de boca; **to fall ~** (*joke*) caer mal, no hacer gracia a uno, (*suggestion*) caer en el vacío; **to be lying down ~** estar tendido; **to put sth ~ on the table** extender algo sobre la mesa.
(b) (*Mus*) **to sing ~**, **to play ~** desafinar.
(c) **to be ~ broke*** (*Brit*) no tener ni un céntimo; **to go ~ out** ir a máxima velocidad; (*Aut*) ir con el acelerador pisado a fondo; **to go ~ out for sth** tratar de conseguir algo por todos los medios; **to turn sth down ~** rechazar algo de plano.
3 N (a) (*Brit: rooms*) piso *m*, apartamento *m*, departamento *m* (*SC*).
(b) superficie *f* plana, superficie *f* lisa; (*of hand*) palma *f*; (*of sword*) plano *m*; **racing on the ~** carreras *fpl* (de caballos) sin obstáculos; **this car can do 160 km/h on the ~** este coche puede correr a 160 km/h. en superficie plana.
(c) (*Mus*) bemol *m*.
(d) (*Aut, esp US*) pinchazo *m*, neumático *m* pinchado.
(e) (*Geog*) **~s** (*mud*) marisma *f*; (*salt ~*) salinas *fpl*.

flat-bottomed ['flæt'bɒtəmd] ADJ *boat* de fondo plano.

flat-chested ['flæt'tʃestɪd] ADJ de pecho plano.

flatfish ['flætfɪʃ] N, PL **flatfish** pez *m* pleuronecto (*p.ej.* platija, lenguado).

flatfooted ['flæt'fʊtɪd] ADJ de pies planos; (*Brit*) torpe, desmañado.

flatiron ['flæt,aɪən] N plancha *f*.

flatlet ['flætlɪt] N (*Brit*) piso *m* pequeño, pisito *m*, apartamentito *m*.

flatly ['flætlɪ] ADV *refuse etc* de plano; *deny* terminantemente; **we are ~ opposed to** quedamos totalmente opuestos a.

flatmate ['flætmeɪt] N compañero *m*, -a *f* de piso.

flatness ['flætnɪs] N llanura *f*, lo llano; (*fig*) insipidez *f*, monotonía *f*, aburrimiento *m*.

flat-racing ['flæt,reɪsɪŋ] N carreras *fpl* de caballos sin obstáculos.

flatten ['flætn] **1** VT (a) (*also* **to ~ out**) allanar, aplanar; (*smoothe*) alisar; *map etc* extender. (b) *house, city* aplastar. (c) (*fig*) desconcertar, aplastar.
2 VR: **to ~ o.s. against a wall** aplanarse contra una pared.
◆**flatten out** **1** VT = **flatten 1 (a)**.
2 VI (*Aer*) enderezarse; (*road, countryside*) nivelarse, allanarse.

flatter ['flætəʳ] **1** VT adular, lisonjear, halagar; (*photo, clothes etc*) favorecer.
2 VR: **to ~ o.s.** felicitarse, congratularse (*on* de, *that* de que); **you ~ yourself!** ¡presumido!

flatterer ['flætərəʳ] N adulador *m*, -ora *f*.

flattering ['flætərɪŋ] ADJ lisonjero; halagüeño; *photo, clothes etc* que favorece.

flatteringly ['flætərɪŋlɪ] ADV *speak etc* en términos lisonjeros.

flattery ['flætərı] N adulación f, lisonjas fpl, halago(s) m(pl).

flatulence ['flætjuləns] N flatulencia f; (fig) hinchazón f.

flatulent ['flætjulənt] ADJ flatulento; (fig) hinchado.

flatworm ['flætwɜ:m] N platelminto m.

flaunt [flɔ:nt] [1] VT ostentar, lucir; hacer gala de.

  [2] VR: **to ~ o.s.** pavonearse.

flautist ['flɔ:tɪst] N (Brit) flautista mf, flauta m.

flavin ['fleɪvɪn] N flavina f.

flavour, (US) **flavor** ['fleɪvəʳ] [1] N sabor m (of a), gusto m; (flavouring) condimento m; **with a banana ~** con sabor a plátano.

  [2] VT sazonar, condimentar (with con); (fig) dar un sabor característico a; **~ed with** con sabor a.

flavouring, (US) **flavoring** ['fleɪvərɪŋ] N condimento m.

flavourless, (US) **flavorless** ['fleɪvəlɪs] ADJ insípido, soso.

flaw [flɔ:] N desperfecto m, imperfección f; (crack) grieta f; (in character, scheme, case etc) defecto m.

flawed [flɔ:d] ADJ imperfecto, defectuoso.

flawless ['flɔ:lɪs] ADJ intachable, impecable.

flax [flæks] N lino m.

flaxen ['flæksən] ADJ hair muy rubio.

flay [fleɪ] VT (a) desollar. (b) (fig: beat) azotar; (defeat) cascar; (criticize) despellejar.

flea [fli:] [1] N pulga f; **to send sb away with a ~ in his ear** echar a uno la pulga detrás de la oreja.

  [2] ATTR: **~ collar** collar m antipulgas.

fleabag: ['fli:bæg] N (Brit: person) guarro m, -a f; (US: hotel) hotelucho m de mala muerte*.

fleabite ['fli:baɪt] N picadura f de pulga; (fig) pérdida f (etc) insignificante, nada f.

fleabitten ['fli:bɪtn] ADJ infestado de pulgas; (fig) miserable.

flea-market ['fli:,mɑ:kɪt] N mercado m de baratijas y cosas usadas.

fleapit* ['fli:pɪt] N (Brit) cine m de bajísima categoría.

fleck [flek] [1] N punto m, mancha f.

  [2] VT puntear, salpicar (with de).

fled [fled] PRET AND PTP of **flee.**

fledged [fledʒd] ADJ plumado.

fledg(e)ling ['fledʒlɪŋ] [1] N (a) volantón m, pajarito m. (b) (fig) novato m, -a f.

  [2] ADJ en ciernes; nuevo, joven, que acaba de establecerse; **~ poet** poeta mf en ciernes.

flee [fli:] (irr: PRET AND PTP **fled**) [1] VT (escape from) huir de, abandonar; (shun) evitar.

  [2] VI huir (from de), darse a la fuga, fugarse (to a); (vanish) desaparecer.

fleece [fli:s] [1] N vellón m; lana f.

  [2] VT esquilar; (fig) pelar, mondar.

fleece-lined [,fli:s'laɪnd] ADJ forrado de muletón.

fleecy ['fli:sɪ] ADJ lanudo; cloud aborregado.

fleet¹ [fli:t] N (Naut, Aer) flota f; (of cars) parque m; **the British ~** la armada inglesa; **F~ Air Arm** (Brit) Fuerzas fpl Aéreas de la Armada.

fleet² [fli:t], **fleet-footed** ['fli:t'fʊtɪd] ADJ (also **~ of foot**) veloz, ligero, rápido.

fleeting ['fli:tɪŋ] ADJ fugaz, momentáneo, efímero, pasajero; moment, visit breve.

fleetingly ['fli:tɪŋlɪ] ADV fugazmente, momentáneamente.

Fleet Street ['fli:t,stri:t] N (Brit) la prensa británica.

Fleming ['flemɪŋ] N flamenco m, -a f.

Flemish ['flemɪʃ] [1] ADJ flamenco.

  [2] N flamenco m.

flesh [fleʃ] N carne f (also fig); (of fruit) pulpa f; **in the ~** en persona; **of ~ and blood** de carne y hueso; **my own ~ and blood** mi familia, mis parientes, los de mi sangre; **it was more than ~ and blood could stand** era inaguantable, rebasaba el límite de lo soportable; **to go the way of all ~** pagar tributo a la muerte; **to press sb's ~** estrechar la mano a uno; **to put on ~** echar carnes; V **creep.**

◆**flesh out** VT (fig) desarrollar.

flesh colour, (US) **flesh color** ['fleʃ,kʌləʳ] N (gen, Art) color m carne.

flesh-coloured, (US) **flesh-colored** ['fleʃ,kʌləd] ADJ de color del cutis.

flesh-eating ['fleʃi:tɪŋ] ADJ carnívoro.

fleshly ['fleʃlɪ] ADJ (frm) lusts, desires carnal, de la carne.

fleshpots ['fleʃpɒts] NPL (fig) vida f de lujo; **to remember the ~s of Egypt** recordar los ollas de Egipto.

flesh wound ['fleʃwu:nd] N herida f superficial.

fleshy ['fleʃɪ] ADJ (fat) gordo; (Bot etc) carnoso.

flew [flu:] PRET of **fly.**

flex [fleks] [1] N (Brit) cable m, flexible m, hilo m, cordón m (de la luz); prolongación f eléctrica.

  [2] VT doblar; muscle flexionar.

  [3] VI doblarse; flexionarse.

flexibility [,fleksɪ'bɪlɪtɪ] N flexibilidad f (also fig).

flexible ['fleksəbl] ADJ flexible (also fig); **~ working hours** horas fpl de

trabajo flexibles; **we have to be ~ about this** hay que mostrarse flexibles en este asunto.

flexion ['flekʃən] N flexión f.

flexitime ['fleksɪ,taɪm] N horario m flexible.

flexor ['fleksəʳ] [1] N flexor m, músculo m flexor.

  [2] ADJ flexor.

flibbertigibbet ['flɪbətɪ'dʒɪbɪt] N casquivana f.

flick [flɪk] [1] N (a) (blow) golpecito m rápido; (with finger) capirotazo m; (of whip) chasquido m; **with a ~ of the wrist** con un movimiento rápido de la muñeca.

  (b) (Brit*) película f; **the ~s** el cine.

  [2] VT (strike) dar un golpecito a; (touch in passing) rozar levemente; (with finger) dar un capirotazo a; whip chasquear; **to ~ sth with a whip** dar algo ligeramente con el látigo; **to ~ sth away** quitar algo con un movimiento rápido; **to ~ over the pages** hojear rápidamente las páginas.

◆**flick off** VT (a) dust, ash tirar con el dedo. (b) light etc apagar.

◆**flick on** VT light etc encender.

◆**flick out** [1] VT (a) **the snake ~ed its tongue out** la serpiente lengueteaba. (b) light etc apagar.

  [2] VI: **the snake's tongue ~ed out** la serpiente lengueteaba.

◆**flick through** VT pages hojear rápidamente.

flicker ['flɪkəʳ] [1] N parpadeo m; **without a ~ of** sin la menor señal de.

  [2] VI (light) parpadear, (on going out) brillar con luz mortecina; (flame) vacilar; (snake's tongue etc) vibrar; **the candle ~ed out** la vela parpadeó y se apagó.

flickering ['flɪkərɪŋ] ADJ flames, candle tembloroso; (before going out) vacilante; needle oscilante.

flickknife ['flɪknaɪf] N, PL **flickknives** ['flɪknaɪvz] (Brit) navaja f de muelle, navaja f de resorte.

flier ['flaɪəʳ] N (a) aviador m, -ora f. (b) (US) prospecto m, folleto m.

flight [flaɪt] N (a) (flying) vuelo m; (of bullet) trayectoria f; (distance flown) recorrido m; **~ of fancy** sueño m, ilusión f; **to be in the first ~** ser de primera categoría; **to take ~** alzar el vuelo.

  (b) (escape) huida f, fuga f; **~ of capital** evasión f de capitales; **to be in full ~** huir en desorden; **to put to ~** ahuyentar, (Mil) poner en fuga; **to take to ~** darse a la fuga.

  (c) **~ of steps** tramo m, escalera f; **we live 3 ~s up** vivimos en el tercer piso.

  (d) (group of birds) bandada f; (Aer. unit) escuadrilla f.

flight attendant ['flaɪtə'tendənt] N auxiliar mf de vuelo.

flightbag ['flaɪtbæg] N bolso m de bandolera.

flight-crew ['flaɪtkru:] N tripulación f.

flightdeck ['flaɪtdek] N cubierta f de vuelo.

flight engineer ['flaɪt,endʒɪniəʳ] N mecánico m de vuelo, mecánica f de vuelo.

flightless ['flaɪtlɪs] ADJ bird incapaz de volar.

flight-lieutenant ['flaɪtlef'tenənt] N (Brit) teniente m de aviación.

flight-log ['flaɪtlɒg] N (Aer) diario m de vuelo.

flightpath ['flaɪtpɑ:θ] N trayectoria f de vuelo.

flightplan ['flaɪtplæn] N plan m de vuelo, carta f de vuelo.

flight-recorder ['flaɪtrɪ,kɔ:dəʳ] N registrador m de vuelo.

flight-sergeant ['flaɪt'sɑ:dʒənt] N (Brit) sargento m de aviación.

flight-simulator ['flaɪt,sɪmjuleɪtəʳ] N simulador m de vuelo.

flight-test ['flaɪttest] VT probar en vuelo.

flighty ['flaɪtɪ] ADJ frívolo, poco serio; caprichoso, inconstante; travieso; coqueta.

flimsily ['flɪmzɪlɪ] ADV débilmente; muy delgadamente, muy ligeramente; de modo diáfano; **~ covered** ligeramente cubierto.

flimsiness ['flɪmzɪnɪs] N debilidad f, endeblez f; delgadez f, ligereza f; diafanidad f; lo baladí.

flimsy ['flɪmzɪ] [1] ADJ (weak) débil, endeble; (thin) muy delgado, muy ligero; cloth diáfano; excuse baladí.

  [2] N (Brit) papel m de copiar; copia f.

flinch [flɪntʃ] VI acobardarse, arredrarse, retroceder (from ante), encogerse de miedo; **without ~ing** sin cejar, sin vacilar.

fling [flɪŋ] [1] N (a) **to go on a ~** echar una cana al aire; **to have one's ~** correrla; **youth will have its ~** los jóvenes han de correrla; **to have a ~ at sth** intentar algo; **he had a final ~** tuvo una juerga de despedida.

  (b) (*) aventura f amorosa.

  (c) **highland ~** cierto baile escocés.

  [2] (irr: PRET AND PTP **flung**) VT arrojar, tirar, lanzar; rider tirar al suelo; **to ~ sb into jail** echar a uno en la cárcel, encarcelar a uno; **to ~ one's arms round sb** echar los brazos encima a uno; **to ~ open** abrir de golpe.

  [3] VR: **to ~ o.s.** arrojarse, precipitarse; **to ~ o.s. over a cliff** despeñarse por un precipicio.

◆**fling down** [1] VT tirar.

  [2] VR: **to ~ o.s. down** tirarse al suelo.

◆**fling off** VT clothes quitarse (de prisa).

◆**fling on** [1] vt *clothes* ponerse (de prisa).
[2] vr: **to ~ o.s. on sb** echarse sobre uno.
◆**fling out** [1] vt *rubbish* tirar; *remark* lanzar; *person* expulsar.
[2] vi: **she flung out of the room** salió indignada del cuarto.
flint [flɪnt] [1] N (*material*) sílex m; (*one ~*) pedernal m; (*of lighter*) piedra f.
[2] ATTR: **~ axe** hacha f de sílex.
flinty ['flɪntɪ] ADJ (a) *material* de sílex; *soil* que tiene muchas piedras, pedregoso. (b) (*fig*) empedernido, de piedra.
flip¹ [flɪp] [1] N capirotazo m; (*Aer*⁎) vuelo m.
[2] ATTR: **~ side** cara f secundaria, cara f B.
[3] vt (*with fingers*) echar de un capirotazo; (*jerk*) mover de un tirón; *coin* echar a cara o cruz; **to ~ open** abrir de golpe.
[4] vi (⁎) enloquecer, perder la chaveta⁎.
◆**flip off** vt *cigarette ash* quitar de un golpe de dedo (*or* de un capirotazo).
◆**flip out**⁎ vi enloquecer; *see also* **flip¹ 3**.
◆**flip over** vi (*esp US Aut etc*) capotar, dar una vuelta de campana.
◆**flip through** vt: **to ~ through a book** hojear un libro.
flip²⁎ [flɪp] ADJ = **flippant**.
flip³⁎ [flɪp] EXCL ¡porras!
flip-flop ['flɪpflɒp] [1] N (a) **~s** (*sandals*) chancletas fpl. (b) (*Comput*) circuito m basculante (*or* biestable), flip-flop m. (c) (*fig: esp US*) cambio m de chaquetas, golpe m de timón.
[2] vi (*US fig*) cambiar de opinión, cambiarse de chaqueta, dar un golpe de timón.
flippancy ['flɪpənsɪ] N falta f de seriedad, ligereza f.
flippant ['flɪpənt] ADJ poco serio, ligero.
flippantly ['flɪpəntlɪ] ADV con poca seriedad, ligeramente.
flipper ['flɪpə⁎] N aleta f (*also*⁎).
flipping⁎ ['flɪpɪŋ] ADJ (*Brit*) condenado⁎.
flip-top ['flɪptɒp] N *bin, pack* con tapa abatible.
flirt [flɜːt] [1] N mariposón m, coqueta f; **she's a great ~** es terriblemente coqueta.
[2] vi flirtear, coquetear (*with* con), mariposear; **to ~ with** (*fig*) jugar con, entretenerse con; **to ~ with death** jugar con la muerte; **to ~ with an idea** acariciar una idea.
flirtation [flɜːˈteɪʃən] N flirteo m.
flirtatious [flɜːˈteɪʃəs] ADJ *man* mariposón, *woman* coqueta; *glance etc* coqueta.
flirty ['flɜːtɪ] ADJ *person, dress, smile* coqueto.
flit [flɪt] [1] vi (a) revolotear, volar con vuelo cortado; (*before eyes etc*) pasar rápidamente. (b) (*Brit*⁎) mudarse a la chita callando. (c) (*person*) **to ~ in, ~ out** *etc* (*Brit: lightly*) entrar, salir *etc* con ligereza; (*US: affectedly*) entrar/salir a pasitos amanerados.
[2] N: **to do a (moonlight) ~**⁎ (*Brit*) mudarse a la chita callando.
flitch [flɪtʃ] N: **~ of bacon** hoja f de tocino.
flitting ['flɪtɪŋ] N (*N Engl, Scot*) mudanza f.
Flo [fləʊ] NF *familiar form of* **Florence**.
float [fləʊt] [1] N (a) (*Fishing*) corcho m; (*of seaplane etc*) pontón m, flotador m.
(b) (*in procession*) carroza f; (: *Rel*) paso m.
(c) (*Fin: loan*) préstamo m; (*in shop*) dinero m en caja antes de empezar las ventas del día (para cambios *etc*).
[2] vt (a) hacer flotar; (*refloat*) poner a flote.
(b) *company* lanzar, fundar; *share issue, loan* emitir.
(c) **to ~ an idea** sugerir una idea.
(d) **to ~ the pound** (hacer) flotar la libra esterlina.
[3] vi (a) flotar; (*bather*) hacer la plancha; (*flag, hair*) ondear; **it ~ed to the surface** salió a la superficie.
(b) **we shall let the pound ~** dejaremos flotar la libra esterlina.
◆**float (a)round**⁎ vi (*rumour, news*) circular, correr.
◆**float away** vi irse a la deriva.
◆**float off** vi (*wreck etc*) irse a la deriva.
floating ['fləʊtɪŋ] ADJ *object, population etc* flotante; **~ assets** activo m flotante; **~ currency** moneda f flotante; **~ debt** deuda f flotante; **~ dock** dique m flotante; **~ exchange** tipo m de cambio flotante; **~ rib** costilla f flotante; **~ vote** voto m de los indecisos; **~ voter** votante m indeciso, votante f indecisa.
flock¹ [flɒk] [1] N (*Agr etc*) rebaño m; (*of birds*) bandada f; (*Eccl*) grey f; (*of people*) multitud f, tropel m; **they came in ~s** acudieron en tropel.
[2] vi (*also* **to ~ together**) congregarse, reunirse; **to ~ about sb** reunirse en torno de uno; **to ~ to** acudir en tropel a.
flock² [flɒk] N (*wool*) borra f.
floe [fləʊ] N (*also* **ice ~**) témpano m de hielo.
flog [flɒg] vt (a) azotar. (b) (*Brit*⁎) vender.
flogger ['flɒgə⁎] N partidario m, -a f del restablecimiento de la pena de azotes.
flogging ['flɒgɪŋ] N azotaina f, paliza f.
flood [flʌd] [1] N inundación f; (*in river*) avenida f; (*tide*) pleamar f, flujo m; (*fig*) torrente m, diluvio m; **the F~** el Diluvio; **a ~ of letters**

una riada de cartas; **a ~ of light** un torrente de luz; **to be in ~** estar crecido; **to weep ~s of tears** llorar a mares.
[2] vt inundar, anegar; **to ~ the market with sth** inundar (*or* saturar) el mercado de algo; **we are ~ed with applications** tenemos montones de solicitudes.
[3] vi desbordar.
◆**flood in** vi: **to come ~ing in** (*people*) entrar a raudales, (*applications*) llegar a montones.
◆**flood out** vt: **ten families were ~ed out** diez familias tuvieron que abandonar sus casas debido a la inundación.
flood-control ['flʌdkəntrəʊl] N medidas fpl para controlar las inundaciones.
floodgate ['flʌdgeɪt] N compuerta f, esclusa f.
flooding ['flʌdɪŋ] N inundación f.
floodlight ['flʌdlaɪt] [1] N foco m.
[2] (*irr: V* **light**) vt iluminar con focos.
floodlighting ['flʌdlaɪtɪŋ] N iluminación f con focos.
floodlit ['flʌdlɪt] PRET AND PTP *of* **floodlight** ADJ iluminado.
floodplain ['flʌdpleɪn] N llanura f sujeta a inundaciones (de un río).
flood-tide ['flʌdtaɪd] N pleamar f, marea f creciente.
floodwater ['flʌdwɔːtə⁎] N crecida f, riada f.
floor [flɔː⁎] [1] N (a) (*gen*) suelo m; (*of sea etc*) fondo m; (*dance ~*) pista f; (*Cine, TV*) plató m; **the F~** (*St Ex*) el parqué; **to cross the ~** (*of the House*) atravesar la sala; **to have the ~** tener la palabra; **to hold the ~** tener a los asistentes (*etc*) pendientes de su palabra; **to take the ~** salir a bailar, (*fig*) salir a palestra; **to wipe the ~ with**⁎ cascar⁎.
(b) (*storey*) piso m; V **first** *etc*.
[2] ATTR: **~ lamp** (*US*) lámpara f de pie.
[3] vt (a) *room* solar, entarimar (*with* de).
(b) *person* derribar; (*fig*) anonadar, apabullar.
(c) (*US Aut*) *accelerator* pisar.
floor area ['flɔːreərɪə] N área f total.
floorboard ['flɔːbɔːd] N tabla f (del suelo).
floorcloth ['flɔːklɒθ] N bayeta f.
floor-covering ['flɔːkʌvərɪŋ] N recubrimiento m de piso.
floor exercise ['flɔːeksəsaɪz] N (*Gymnastics*) ejercicio m de suelo.
flooring ['flɔːrɪŋ] N suelo m; (*material*) solería f.
floor-manager ['flɔːmænɪdʒə⁎] N jefe mf de plató.
floorplan ['flɔːplæn] N planta f.
floorpolish ['flɔːpɒlɪʃ] N cera f (para suelos).
floor-polisher ['flɔːpɒlɪʃə⁎] N encerador m de piso.
floorshow ['flɔːʃəʊ] N (espectáculo m de) cabaret m, atracciones fpl (en la pista de baile).
floorspace ['flɔːspeɪs] N espacio m útil.
floorwalker ['flɔːwɔːkə⁎] N (*US*) jefe mf de sección (de unos grandes almacenes), vigilante mf.
floosie⁎, floozie⁎ ['fluːzɪ] N putilla f⁎.
flop [flɒp] [1] (⁎) N fracaso m.
[2] vi (a) (*drop etc*) dejarse caer pesadamente (*into* en). (b) (⁎: *fail*) fracasar.
flophouse ['flɒphaʊs] N, PL **flophouses** ['flɒphaʊzɪz] (*US*) pensión f de mala muerte, fonducha f.
floppy ['flɒpɪ] [1] ADJ flojo, colgante; **~ disk** disco m flexible, disquete m, diskette m, floppy m.
[2] N = **~ disk**.
flora ['flɔːrə] N flora f.
floral ['flɔːrəl] ADJ floral; *tribute etc* de flores, floral.
Florence ['flɒrəns] (a) NF Florencia. (b) N (*Geog*) Florencia f.
Florentine ['flɒrəntaɪn] [1] ADJ florentino.
[2] N florentino m, -a f.
florescence [flɔːˈresns] N florescencia f.
floret ['flɒrət] N (*of flower*) flósculo m; (*of cauliflower, broccoli*) grumo m, cabezuela f.
florid ['flɒrɪd] ADJ florido (*also Liter etc*); *complexion* rojizo, subido de color.
Florida ['flɒrɪdə] N Florida f.
florin ['flɒrɪn] N florín m; (*Brit* ††) florín m (*moneda de 2 chelines*).
florist ['flɒrɪst] N florista mf; **~'s (shop)** floristería f, florería f.
floss [flɒs] N (*also* **~ silk**) cadarzo m; seda f floja.
Flossie ['flɒsɪ] NF *familiar form of* **Florence**.
flossy ['flɒsɪ] ADJ *cloud, hair* vaporoso, ahuecado; (*US*⁎: *showy*) llamativo, espectacular, ostentoso.
flotation [fləʊˈteɪʃən] N (*lit: of boat etc*) flotación f; (*Fin*) (*of shares, loan etc*) emisión f; (*of company*) lanzamiento m; **~ tank** tanque m de flotación.
flotilla [fləˈtɪlə] N flotilla f.
flotsam ['flɒtsəm] N pecio(s) m(pl), restos mpl flotantes; **~ and jetsam** (*fig*) restos mpl, desechos mpl.
flounce¹ [flaʊns] N (*Sew*) volante m.
flounce² [flaʊns] vi: **to ~ about** moverse violentamente; **to ~ away, to ~ off** alejarse exagerando los movimientos del cuerpo; **to ~ in** entrar con gesto exagerado; **to ~ out** salir enfadado.

flounced [flaʊnst] ADJ *dress* guarnecido con volantes.

flounder¹ ['flaʊndə'] N (*Fish*) (*especie de*) platija *f*.

flounder² ['flaʊndə'] VI quedar indeciso, no saber qué hacer (*etc*); estar confuso; (*in a speech etc*) tropezar, perder el hilo, no saber qué decir.

◆**flounder about** VI revolcarse, debatirse, forcejear; (*fig*) quedar indeciso.

flour ['flaʊə'] N harina *f*.

flour-bin ['flaʊəbɪn] N harinero *m*.

flourish ['flʌrɪʃ] 1 N (a) (*with pen*) rasgo *m*, plumada *f*; (*on signature*) rúbrica *f*; (*of hand*) movimiento *m*, ademán *m*; **to do sth with a ~** hacer algo con un ademán triunfal; **we like to do things with a ~** nos gusta hacer las cosas con estilo.

(b) (*Mus: on guitar*) floreo *m*, (*fanfare*) toque *m* de trompeta.

2 VT *weapon etc* blandir; *stick etc* agitar, menear; (*fig*) hacer gala de, mostrar orgullosamente.

3 VI florecer, prosperar; (*plant etc*) crecer rápidamente.

flourishing ['flʌrɪʃɪŋ] ADJ floreciente, próspero; (*Bot*) lozano; (*healthy*) como un reloj.

flour-mill ['flaʊəmɪl] N molino *m* de harina.

floury ['flaʊərɪ] ADJ harinoso.

flout [flaʊt] VT mofarse de, no hacer caso de; *law* incumplir.

flow [fləʊ] 1 N (*stream*) corriente *f*; (*jet*) chorro *m*; (*movement*) flujo *m*, movimiento *m*; (*quantity flowing*) caudal *m*, cantidad *f*; (*direction of* ~) curso *m*; (*of words etc*) torrente *m*; (*of dress etc*) movimiento *m* suave, movimiento *m* elegante; (*of music*) lo suave; **to have a ready ~ of words** hablar con soltura; **to maintain a steady ~** mantener un movimiento constante.

2 VI fluir, correr (*along, down* por); (*tide*) subir, crecer; (*hair*) ondear (*in the wind* al viento); (*blood, being shed*) derramarse, (*from wound*) manar, correr; **tears were ~ing down her cheeks** le corrían las lágrimas por las mejillas; **to ~ from** (*fig*) provenir de; **to ~ past** pasar (*delante de*); **to ~ with** abundar en.

◆**flow away** VI irse.

◆**flow back** VI refluir.

◆**flow in** VI entrar; **money is ~ing in** entra el dinero en grandes cantidades; **people are ~ing in** entra la gente a raudales.

◆**flow into** VT *river* desaguar en, desembocar en.

◆**flow over** VI desbordarse.

flowchart ['fləʊtʃɑːt] N flujograma *m*, organigrama *m*; (*Comput*) = **flowsheet**.

flow diagram ['fləʊˌdaɪəgræm] N = **flowsheet**.

flower ['flaʊə'] 1 N flor *f*; (*fig*) flor *f*, flor *f* y nata; **in ~** en flor.

2 ATTR: **~ arrangement** arreglo *m* floral; **~ children** hijos *mpl* de la flor; **~ people** gente *f* de la flor, hippies *mpl*; **~ power** filosofía *f* de la flor; **~ stall** floristería *f*, florería *f*.

3 VI florecer.

flowerbed ['flaʊəbed] N cuadro *m*, macizo *m*, reata *f* (*Mex*).

flowered ['flaʊəd] ADJ *cloth, shirt etc* floreado, de flores.

flower-garden ['flaʊəˌgɑːdn] N jardín *m* (de flores).

flowerhead ['flaʊəˌhed] N cabezuela *f*.

flowering ['flaʊərɪŋ] 1 ADJ floreciente, en flor.

2 N floración *f*.

flowerpot ['flaʊəpɒt] N tiesto *m*, maceta *f*.

flower-seller ['flaʊəˌselə'] N floristo *m*, -a *f*, vendedor *m*, -ora *f* de flores.

flower-shop ['flaʊəʃɒp] N floristería *f*, florería *f*.

flower-show ['flaʊəʃəʊ] N exposición *f* de flores.

flowery ['flaʊərɪ] ADJ florido (*also fig*); *design* floreado.

flowing ['fləʊɪŋ] ADJ *movement, stream* corriente; *hair* suelto; *style* fluido, corriente.

flown [fləʊn] PTP of **fly**.

flowsheet ['fləʊˌʃiːt] N (*Comput*) diagrama *m* de flujo, organigrama *m*, ordinograma *m*; (*Administration*) organigrama *m*.

fl. oz. ABBR of **fluid ounce**.

F/Lt ABBR of **Flight Lieutenant** teniente *m* de aviación.

flu [fluː] 1 N gripe *f*, trancazo *m*.

2 ATTR: **~ vaccine** vacuna *f* antigripal.

fluctuate ['flʌktjʊeɪt] VI fluctuar; variar.

fluctuation [ˌflʌktjʊ'eɪʃən] N fluctuación *f*; variación *f*.

flue [fluː] N humero *m*, cañón *m* de chimenea; (*of lamp, boiler*) tubo *m*.

fluency ['fluːənsɪ] N fluidez *f*; elocuencia *f*, facundia *f*; facilidad *f* de lengua; competencia *f*, soltura *f*, dominio *m*; **his ~ in Russian** su dominio del ruso.

fluent ['fluːənt] ADJ *style* fluido, corriente; *speaker* elocuente, facundo; de lengua fácil; (*in foreign language*) competente, que habla con soltura; **he is ~ in Russian, his Russian is ~** domina el ruso, habla ruso con soltura.

fluently ['fluːəntlɪ] ADV con fluidez, corrientemente; elocuentemente; **he speaks Russian ~** domina el ruso.

fluey* ['fluːiː] ADJ (*Brit*) griposo; **to feel ~** estar griposo.

fluff [flʌf] 1 N pelusa *f*, lanilla *f*.

2 VT (a) (*also* **to ~ out**) *feathers* encrespar. (b) *shot* errar; (*Theat*) *lines* decir mal.

fluffy ['flʌfɪ] ADJ velloso, lanudo; *hair* encrespado; (*feathered*) plumoso; *surface* que tiene mucha pelusa.

fluid ['fluːɪd] 1 ADJ fluido, líquido; *situation* inestable; *plan* flexible; **~ ounce** onza *f* líquida.

2 N fluido *m*, líquido *m*.

fluidity [fluː'ɪdɪtɪ] N fluidez *f*; inestabilidad *f*.

fluke¹ [fluːk] N (*Zool*) trematodo *m*; (*Fish*) (*especie f de*) platija *f*.

fluke² [fluːk] N chiripa *f*, racha *f* de suerte; **to win by a ~** ganar por chiripa.

fluky ['fluːkɪ] ADJ afortunado.

flummox ['flʌməks] VT (*disconcert*) desconcertar, confundir; (*startle*) asombrar; **I was completely ~ed** quedé totalmente despistado.

flung [flʌŋ] PRET AND PTP of **fling**.

flunk* [flʌŋk] (*US*) 1 VT *student* suspender; *course* perder; *exam* no aprobar, salir mal en.

2 VI ser suspendido; **I ~ed** me suspendieron.

◆**flunk out*** VI salir del colegio (*etc*) sin recibir un título.

flunk(e)y ['flʌŋkɪ] N lacayo *m* (*also fig*); adulador *m*, -a *f*.

fluorescence [flʊə'resns] N fluorescencia *f*.

fluorescent [flʊə'resnt] ADJ fluorescente; **~ lamp** lámpara *f* fluorescente.

fluoridate ['flʊərɪˌdeɪt] VT fluorizar.

fluoridation [ˌflʊərɪ'deɪʃən] N fluoración *f*, fluorización *f*.

fluoride ['flʊəraɪd] N fluoruro *m*.

fluorine ['flʊəriːn] N flúor *m*.

flurry ['flʌrɪ] 1 N (a) (*nervous haste*) agitación *f*, estado *m* nervioso; **a ~ of activity** un frenesí de actividad; **to be in a ~** estar agitado, estar nervioso.

(b) (*of snow etc*) ráfaga *f*.

2 VT agitar, hacer nervioso; **to get flurried** ponerse nervioso.

flush¹ [flʌʃ] VT *game* levantar.

◆**flush out** VT *criminal* poner al descubierto; **to ~ sb out** hacer que uno salga, hacer salir a uno.

flush² [flʌʃ] 1 VT (*also* **to ~ out**) limpiar con un chorro de agua; *WC* hacer funcionar.

2 VI (*WC*) funcionar.

◆**flush away** VT (*down sink*) tirar por el fregadero; (*down lavatory*) tirar al retrete; (*down drain*) tirar por la alcantarilla.

flush³ [flʌʃ] 1 N (*on face*) rubor *m*; (*in sky*) arrebol *m*; (*of fever*) calor *m* súbito; **in the first ~ of success** en el momento emocionado del triunfo; **in the first ~ of youth** en la primera juventud; **no longer in the first ~ of youth** ya algo entrado en años.

2 VT: **to be ~ed with success** estar muy emocionado con el triunfo; **a face ~ed with drink** una cara encendida por el alcohol.

3 VI ruborizarse, sonrojarse; (*with anger*) sofocarse, ponerse rojo de ira.

flush⁴ [flʌʃ] ADJ (a) (*Tech*) nivelado, igual, parejo, a ras; **to make two things ~** nivelar dos cosas. (b) **to be ~:** tener dinero.

flush⁵ [flʌʃ] N (*Cards*) flux *m*.

Flushing ['flʌʃɪŋ] N Flesinga *m*.

fluster ['flʌstə'] 1 N confusión *f*, aturdimiento *m*; conmoción *f*; **to be in a ~** estar azacaneado.

2 VT aturdir, poner nervioso, aturrullar; **to get ~ed** aturrullarse.

flute [fluːt] N flauta *f*.

fluted ['fluːtɪd] ADJ (*Archit*) estriado, acanalado.

flutist ['fluːtɪst] N (*US*) flautista *mf*.

flutter ['flʌtə'] 1 N (a) (*of wings*) revoloteo *m*, aleteo *m*, movimiento *m*; (*of eyelashes*) pestañeo *m*.

(b) (*excitement*) emoción *f*, agitación *f*, conmoción *f*; **to cause a ~** agitar los espíritus, causar un revuelo; **to be in a ~** estar muy agitado.

(c) (*Brit**) apuesta *f*; **to have a ~ on a race** apostar a un caballo.

2 VT agitar, menear, mover ligeramente; (*fig*) agitar.

3 VI (*bird etc*) revolotear, aletear; (*butterfly*) mover ligeramente las alas; (*flag*) ondear; (*heart*) palpitar; **a leaf came ~ing down** cayó balanceándose una hoja.

fluty ['fluːtɪ] ADJ *tone* aflautado.

fluvial ['fluːvɪəl] ADJ fluvial.

flux [flʌks] N (*flow*) flujo *m*; **to be in a state of ~** estar continuamente cambiando.

fly¹ [flaɪ] 1 N (a) mosca *f*; **there's a ~ in the ointment** existe una dificultad; **he's the ~ in the ointment** es la única pega, él es el estorbo; **there are no flies on him** no se chupa el dedo, no tiene ni pelo de tonto; **people were dropping like flies** las personas caían como moscas; **to fish with a ~** pescar a mosca; **he wouldn't hurt a ~** sería incapaz de matar una mosca.

(b) (*on trousers: also* **flies**) bragueta *f*.

(c) **flies** (*Theat*) peine *m*, telar *m*.

(d) (*carriage*) calesa *f*.

2 (*irr:* PRET **flew**, PTP **flown**) VT (a) hacer volar; *plane* pilotar, pilotear

fly away → **folder**

(*LAm*), dirigir; *passengers, goods etc* transportar (en avión); *ocean etc* atravesar (en avión); *distance* recorrer (en avión); *flag* enarbolar, llevar, tener izado.

(b) *danger* huir (de); *country* abandonar, salir de.

3 VI (a) volar; (*travel by air*) ir en avión; (*fly a plane*) pilotar un avión; (*flag*) estar izado, ondear; **do you ~ often?** ¿viajas mucho por avión?; **we ~ (with)** Iberia vamos con Iberia; **to send sth ~ing** echar algo a rodar; **to ~ into pieces** hacerse pedazos; **to ~ open** abrirse de repente; **to let ~** (*shoot*) tirar, disparar, hacer fuego; (*emotionally*) desahogarse; (*verbally*) empezar a proferir insultos (*etc*); **to let ~ at** (*shoot*) tirar sobre, disparar contra, (*emotionally*) desahogarse criticando, (*verbally*) empezar a llenar de injurias.

(b) (*rush*) lanzarse, precipitarse; **I must ~** tengo que correr; **to ~ at sb** lanzarse sobre uno, arremeter contra uno, (*fig*) ponerse furioso con uno; **to ~ into a rage** encolerizarse; **to ~ to sb's help** ir volando a socorrer a uno; **to ~ to sb's side** volar hacia el lado de uno.

(c) (*escape*) evadirse, huir (*from* de); (*vanish*) desaparecer; **to ~ for one's life** salvar la vida huyendo.

◆**fly away** VI irse volando.

◆**fly back** VI regresar (en avión).

◆**fly in** VI llegar (en avión).

◆**fly into** VT: **to ~ into London Airport** llegar (en avión) al aeropuerto de Londres.

◆**fly off** VI (a) (*bird, insect*) alejarse volando; (*in plane*) partir (en avión).
(b) (*part*) desprenderse, separarse.

◆**fly out** **1** VT: **we shall ~ supplies out to them** les enviaremos provisiones por avión; **the hostages have been flown out** los rehenes han partido en avión.
2 VI irse, partir (en avión).

◆**fly over** VT sobrevolar.

fly² [flaɪ] ADJ (*esp Brit*) avispado, espabilado.

fly³* [flaɪ] N: **on the ~** a hurtadillas; disimuladamente, sigilosamente.

flyaway ['flaɪəweɪ] ADJ *hair* suelto, lacio; (*frivolous*) frívolo.

fly-blown ['flaɪbləʊn] ADJ lleno de cresas; (*fig*) viejo, gastado.

flybutton ['flaɪ,bʌtn] N botón *m* de bragueta.

flyby ['flaɪ,baɪ] N (*US*) desfile *m* aéreo.

fly-by-night ['flaɪbaɪnaɪt] **1** ADJ informal, de poca confianza, nada confiable.
2 N persona *f* informal, casquivano *m*, -a *f*; persona *f* nada confiable.

flycatcher ['flaɪ,kætʃər] N (*Orn*) papamoscas *m*.

flyer ['flaɪər] = **flier**.

fly-fishing ['flaɪ,fɪʃɪŋ] N pesca *f* a (*or* con) mosca.

fly-half ['flaɪ,hɑːf] N apertura *m*.

flying ['flaɪɪŋ] **1** ADJ volante, volador; (*swift*) rápido, veloz; **~ bomb** bomba *f* volante; **~ buttress** arbotante *m*; **to come out with ~ colours** salir airoso, triunfar; **~ doctor** médico *m* rural aerotransportado; **the F~ Dutchman** el holandés errante; **~ fish** pez *m* volante; **~ fortress** fortaleza *f* volante; **~ fox** zorro *m* volador; **~ jump** salto *m* vigoroso; **~ officer** subteniente *m* de aviación; **~ picket** piquete *m* volante (*or* móvil); **~ saucer** platillo *m* volante; **~ squad** brigada *f* móvil, equipo *m* volante; **~ start** salida *f* lanzada; **to get off to a ~ start** entrar con buen pie; **~ suit** traje *m* de vuelo; **~ trapeze** trapecio *m* volador; **~ visit** visita *f* relámpago.
2 N el volar, el ir en avión; (*as profession, hobby*) aviación *f*.

flying-boat ['flaɪɪŋbəʊt] N hidroavión *m*.

flying-machine ['flaɪɪŋmə,ʃiːn] N avión *m*, máquina *f* de volar.

flying time ['flaɪɪŋtaɪm] N horas *fpl* de vuelo, duración *f* del vuelo.

flyleaf ['flaɪliːf] N, PL **flyleaves** ['flaɪliːvz] hoja *f* de guarda.

flyover ['flaɪ,əʊvər] N (a) (*Brit*) paso *m* superior, paso *m* elevado, paso *m* a desnivel (*LAm*). (b) (*US*) = **flypast**.

flypaper ['flaɪ,peɪpər] N papel *m* matamoscas.

flypast ['flaɪpɑːst] N (*Brit*) desfile *m* aéreo.

fly-posting [,flaɪ'pəʊstɪŋ] N pegada *f* (ilegal) de carteles.

flysheet ['flaɪʃiːt] N (*Brit*) hoja *f* volante.

flyspray ['flaɪspreɪ] N rociador *m* de moscas.

fly-swat(ter) ['flaɪswɒt(ər)] N matamoscas *m*.

fly-tipping [,flaɪ'tɪpɪŋ] N descarga *f* (ilegal) de basura *etc*.

flyweight ['flaɪweɪt] N peso *m* mosca; **light ~** peso *m* mosca ligero.

flywheel ['flaɪwiːl] N volante *m* (de motor).

FM N (a) (*Brit Mil*) ABBR *of* **Field Marshal**. (b) (*Rad*) ABBR *of* **frequency modulation** frecuencia *f* modulada.

FMB N (*US*) ABBR *of* **Federal Maritime Board**.

FMCS N (*US*) ABBR *of* **Federal Mediation and Conciliation Services**.

FO (a) (*Brit Pol*) ABBR *of* **Foreign Office** Ministerio *m* de Asuntos Exteriores, Min. de AA.EE. (b) (*Aer*) ABBR *of* **Flying Officer** subteniente *m* de aviación.

fo. ABBR *of* **folio** folio *m*.

foal [fəʊl] **1** N potro *m*, -a *f*.
2 VI parir (*la yegua*).

foam [fəʊm] **1** N espuma *f*.

2 VI espumar, echar espuma; **to ~ at the mouth** espumajear (de rabia).

foambath ['fəʊmbɑːθ] N, PL **foambaths** ['fəʊmbɑːðz] baño *m* de espuma.

foam-extinguisher [,fəʊmɪk'stɪŋgwɪʃər] N lanzaespumas *m*, extintor *m* de espuma.

foam-rubber ['fəʊm'rʌbər] N espuma *f* de caucho, goma *f* esponjosa, caucho *m* alveolar.

foamy ['fəʊmɪ] ADJ espumoso.

FOB, f.o.b. ABBR *of* **free on board** franco a bordo, f.a.b.

fob [fɒb] **1** VT: **to ~ sb off** apartar a uno de un propósito con excusas; **to ~ sb off with sth** persuadir a uno a aceptar algo (de modo fraudulento).
2 N (††) faltriquera *f* de reloj.

FOC ABBR *of* **free of charge** libre de cargos.

focal ['fəʊkəl] ADJ focal; **~ distance** distancia *f* focal; **~ plane** plano *m* focal; **~ point** punto *m* focal; (*fig*) centro *m* de atención.

focus ['fəʊkəs] **1** N foco *m*; (*of attention etc*) centro *m*; **to be in ~** estar enfocado; **to be out of ~** estar desenfocado.
2 VT enfocar (*on* a); *attention etc* fijar, concentrar (*on* en); **all eyes were ~sed on him** todos le miraban fijamente.
3 VI enfocar(se).

◆**focus on** VT enfocar a.

fodder ['fɒdər] N pienso *m*, forraje *m*; **~ grain** cereales *mpl* forrajeros, cereal-pienso *m*.

FOE N (a) (*Brit*: *also* **FoE**) ABBR *of* **Friends of the Earth**. (b) (*US*) ABBR *of* **Fraternal Order of Eagles** sociedad benéfica.

foe [fəʊ] N (*liter*) enemigo *m*.

foetal, (*US*) **fetal** ['fiːtl] ADJ fetal.

foetus, (*US*) **fetus** ['fiːtəs] N feto *m*.

fog [fɒg] **1** N niebla *f*; (*fig*) confusión *f*.
2 VT (*fig*) *matter* entenebrecer; *person* ofuscar; (*Phot*) velar; *spectacles, window* (*also* **to ~ up**) empañar.
3 VI (*fig*: *also* **to ~ up**) empañarse.

fogbank ['fɒgbæŋk] N banco *m* de niebla.

fogbound ['fɒgbaʊnd] ADJ inmovilizado por la niebla.

fogey* ['fəʊgɪ] N: **old ~** persona *f* de ideas anticuadas, persona *f* chapada a la antigua, carroza* *m*.

foggy ['fɒgɪ] ADJ nebuloso, brumoso; *day* de niebla; (*Phot*) velado; **it is ~** hay niebla; **I haven't the foggiest** (**idea**) no tengo la más remota idea.

foghorn ['fɒghɔːn] N sirena *f* (de niebla).

foglamp ['fɒglæmp] N (*Brit*), **foglight** ['fɒglaɪt] N (*US*) (*Aut*) faro *m* antiniebla.

fog-signal ['fɒg,sɪgnl] N aviso *m* de niebla.

FOIA N (*US*) ABBR *of* **Freedom of Information Act** ley *f* del derecho a la información; *ver también* FREEDOM OF INFORMATION ACT .

foible ['fɔɪbl] N flaco *m*; manía *f*; debilidad *f*.

foil¹ [fɔɪl] N (a) (*metal*) hoja *f*, hojuela *f*; (*Culin*) aluminio *m* doméstico.
(b) (*fig*) contraste *m* (*to* con); **to act as a ~ to sth** servir de contraste con algo, hacer resaltar algo.

foil² [fɔɪl] VT frustrar.

foil³ [fɔɪl] N (*Fencing*) florete *m*.

foist [fɔɪst] **1** VT: **to ~ sth off on sb** encajar algo a uno, lograr con engaño que uno acepte algo; **the job was ~ed on to me** lograron mañosamente que yo me encargara de ello.
2 VR: **to ~ o.s. on sb** insistir en acompañar a uno, pegarse a uno.

fol. ABBR *of* **folio** folio *m*.

fold¹ [fəʊld] N (*Agr*) redil *m*, aprisco *m*; **to return to the ~** (*Eccl*) volver al redil de la Iglesia.

fold² [fəʊld] **1** N pliegue *m*, doblez *m*, arruga *f*; (*Geol*) pliegue *m*.
2 VT plegar, doblar; *wings* recoger; **to ~ one's arms** cruzar los brazos; **to ~ sb in one's arms** abrazar a uno tiernamente, estrechar a uno contra el pecho; **to ~ sth in a wrapper** envolver algo en una envoltura.
3 VI (a) plegarse, doblarse.
(b) (*fig*) fracasar, terminar; (*Comm*) quebrar, entrar en liquidación; (*Theat*) cerrar.

◆**fold away** **1** VT *clothes, newspaper* doblar (*or* plegar) para guardar.
2 VI (*table, bed*) plegarse.

◆**fold back** VT doblar (hacia abajo), plegar.

◆**fold down** **1** VT = **fold back**.
2 VI: **it ~s down at night** de noche se dobla hacia abajo.

◆**fold in** VT (*Culin*) *flour, sugar* mezclar.

◆**fold over** VT *paper* plegar; *blanket* hacer el embozo con.

◆**fold up** **1** VT doblar, *chair etc* plegar.
2 VI (a) doblarse, plegarse; **to ~ up** (**with laughter**)* troncharse de risa*. (b) (*fig*) = **fold 3** (b).

-fold [fəʊld] SUF: *eg* **thirty~** (ADJ) de treinta veces, (ADV) treinta veces.

fold-away ['fəʊldəweɪ] ATTR plegable, plegadizo.

folder ['fəʊldər] N (*file*) carpeta *f*; (*binder*) carpeta *f* de anillas; (*brochure*) folleto *m*, desplegable *m*; (*of matches*) carterita *f*.

folding ['fəʊldɪŋ] ADJ plegable, plegadizo; de tijera; ~ **chair** silla f de tijera; ~ **doors** puertas fpl plegadizas; ~ **money**, ~ **stuff*** billetes mpl (de banco); ~ **rule(r)** metro m plegable; ~ **seat** asiento m plegadizo; ~ **table** mesa f plegable.

fold-up ['fəʊldʌp] ATTR plegable, plegadizo.

foliage ['fəʊlɪɪdʒ] N hojas fpl, follaje m.

foliation [ˌfəʊlɪ'eɪʃən] N foliación f.

folic acid [ˌfəʊlɪk'æsɪd] N ácido m fólico.

folio ['fəʊlɪəʊ] N folio m; (book) infolio m, libro m en folio.

folk [fəʊk] **1** N (a) (tribe) nación f, tribu f, pueblo m.
(b) (people in general; also ~s) gente f; **my** ~**s** mi familia, mis parientes; **the old** ~**s** los viejos; **hullo** ~**s!** ¡hola, amigos!; **they're strange** ~ **here** aquí la gente es algo rara.
2 ADJ folk(lórico), tradicional.

folk-art ['fəʊkɑːt] N arte m folklórico.

folkdance ['fəʊkdɑːns] N baile m popular, danza f tradicional.

folkdancing ['fəʊkˌdɑːnsɪŋ] N baile m folklórico.

folklore ['fəʊklɔːr] N folklore m, foklor m.

folkloric ['fəʊkˌlɔːrɪk] ADJ folklórico, folclórico.

folkmusic ['fəʊkˌmjuːzɪk] N música f folklórica, música f popular típica.

folkrock [ˌfəʊk'rɒk] N folk rock m.

folksinger ['fəʊkˌsɪŋər] N cantante mf folklorista, cantante m típico, cantante f típica.

folksong ['fəʊksɒŋ] N canción f popular, canción f tradicional.

folksy* ['fəʊksɪ] ADJ afectadamente folklorista; que finge ser popular (or tradicional etc), que se esfuerza por parecer que es del pueblo.

folktale ['fəʊkteɪl] N cuento m popular.

folk wisdom ['fəʊk'wɪzdəm] N saber m popular.

foll. ABBR of **following** siguiente(s), sig., sigs.

follicle ['fɒlɪkl] N folículo m.

follow ['fɒləʊ] **1** VT (a) (gen) seguir; suspect vigilar, seguir la pista a; (pursue) perseguir; **there's sb** ~**ing us** alguien nos viene siguiendo; **the road** ~**s the coast** la carretera va por la costa; **to** ~ **sb into a room** entrar en una habitación detrás de uno; **they** ~**ed this with threats** tras esto empezaron a amenazarnos.
(b) advice, example seguir; person imitar el ejemplo de; instructions seguir; news estar al corriente de, estar enterado de; **do you** ~ **football?** ¿te interesa el fútbol?; **we** ~ **Borchester** somos hinchas del Borchester.
(c) profession ejercer.
(d) (understand) person comprender; argument seguir el hilo de.
2 VI (a) (come behind) seguir.
(b) (result) seguirse; resultar; **as** ~**s** como sigue, a saber; **it** ~**s that ...** síguese que ..., resulta que ...; **it doesn't** ~ **at all that ...** no es lógico que ... + subj.
(c) (understand) comprender; **I don't quite** ~ no te comprendo del todo.
◆**follow about, follow around** VT seguir a todas partes.
◆**follow on** VI (a) **we'll** ~ **on behind** nosotros seguiremos, vendremos después. (b) **it** ~**s on from what I said** es la consecuencia lógica de lo que dije.
◆**follow out** VT idea, plan llevar a cabo; order ejecutar, cumplir; instructions seguir.
◆**follow through** VT shot terminar, completar; plan llevar hasta el fin; clue investigar; matter perseguir, obtener más detalles sobre; suggestion adoptar.
◆**follow up** VT = **follow through**; offer reiterar; visit etc repetir, pasar a la segunda etapa de.

follower ['fɒləʊər] N (Pol etc) partidario m, -a f, adherente mf; (Sport) seguidor m, -ora f, hincha mf; (pej) secuaz mf; (Philos etc) discípulo m; (imitator) imitador m, -ora f; ~**s** (of prince etc) séquito m; **all the** ~**s of football** todos los que se interesan por el fútbol; **the** ~**s of fashion** los que siguen la moda.

following ['fɒləʊɪŋ] **1** ADJ siguiente; wind en popa; **the** ~ lo siguiente.
2 N (Pol etc) partidarios mpl, (pej) secuaces mpl; (of prince etc) séquito m; **football has no** ~ **here** aquí nadie se interesa por el fútbol.

follow-my-leader ['fɒləʊmaɪ'liːdər] N juego en el que los participantes hacen lo que alguien manda.

follow-through ['fɒləʊ'θruː] N continuación f.

follow-up ['fɒləʊ'ʌp] **1** N seguimiento m; (Comm etc) continuación f, reiteración f.
2 ADJ: (Telec) ~ **call** llamada f de reiteración; ~ **interview** entrevista f complementaria; ~ **letter** carta f recordativa; ~ **survey** investigación f complementaria; ~ **visit** visita f de reiteración, visita f complementaria.

folly ['fɒlɪ] N (a) locura f. (b) (Archit) disparate m.

foment [fəʊ'ment] VT fomentar (also Med); revolt etc provocar, instigar.

fomentation [ˌfəʊmen'teɪʃən] N fomentación f; fomento m.

▼**fond** [fɒnd] ADJ (loving) cariñoso, afectuoso; (doting) demasiado indulgente; hope fervoroso; **to be** ~ **of** thing ser aficionado a, tener afición a; person tener mucho cariño a; **to be** ~ **of** + ger ser aficionado a + infin; **to become** (or **grow**) ~ **of** thing aficionarse a, person tomar cariño a.

fondant ['fɒndənt] **1** ADJ delicado; ~ **blue** azul m pastel.
2 N glaseado m.

fondle ['fɒndl] VT acariciar.

fondly ['fɒndlɪ] ADV con cariño, afectuosamente; hope fervorosamente; imagine inocentemente.

fondness ['fɒndnɪs] N cariño m; afición f (for a).

fondue [fɒn'duː] N fondue f; ~ **set** fondue f.

font [fɒnt] N pila f (bautismal); (Typ) fundición f; (Comput) fuente f, tipo m de letra.

fontanel(le) [ˌfɒntə'nel] N fontanela f.

food [fuːd] **1** N alimento m, comida f; (edible matter) comestible m; (for animals) pasto m, pienso m; **to buy** ~ comprar víveres, comprar provisiones; **the** ~ **is good here** aquí se come bien; **the cost of** ~ el coste de la alimentación; **she gave him** ~ le dio de comer; **he likes plain** ~ le gustan las comidas sencillas; **to send** ~ **and clothing** enviar comestibles y ropa; **to be off one's** ~ no tener apetito, estar desganado; **to give sb** ~ **for thought** dar a uno en qué pensar, dar motivo de reflexión.
2 ATTR: ~ **additive** aditivo m alimenticio; ~ **chain** cadena f de alimentación; ~ **crop** cosecha f de alimentos; ~ **mixer** mezcladora f, batidora f; ~ **parcel** paquete m de comestibles; ~ **prices** precios mpl alimenticios; ~ **processing** preparación f de alimentos; ~ **processor** robot m de cocina; ~ **rationing** racionamiento m de víveres; ~ **science** ciencia f de la alimentación; ~ **subsidy** subvención f alimenticia; ~ **supply** suministro m de alimentos; ~ **supplies** víveres mpl; ~ **technology** tecnología f de la alimentación; ver también [FDA - FOOD AND DRUG ADMINISTRATION] .

foodie* ['fuːdɪ] N persona que se interesa con entusiasmo en la preparación y consumo de los alimentos; entusiasta mf de la comida saludable.

food poisoning ['fuːdˌpɔɪznɪŋ] N botulismo m, intoxicación f alimenticia, toxinfección f alimentaria.

food stamp ['fuːdˌstæmp] N (US) vale m de comida, cupón m alimenticio.

foodstuffs ['fuːdstʌfs] NPL comestibles mpl, artículos mpl alimenticios.

food-value ['fuːdˌvæljuː] N valor m alimenticio.

fool¹ [fuːl] **1** N (a) tonto m, -a f, imbécil mf, zonzo m, -a f (LAm); **you** ~**!** ¡imbécil!; **some** ~ **of a minister** algún ministro imbécil; **he's nobody's** ~ no le toma el pelo nadie; **to be** ~ **enough to** + infin ser bastante tonto como para + infin; **don't be a** ~**!** ¡no seas tonto!, ¡déjate de tonterías!; **there's no** ~ **like an old** ~ la cabeza blanca y el seso por venir; **to act** (or **play**) **the** ~ hacer el tonto; **to live in a** ~**'s paradise** vivir en un mundo de sueños, imaginarse una novela, hacerse ilusiones; **to make a** ~ **of sb** poner a uno en ridículo, engañar a uno; **to make a** ~ **of o.s.** ponerse en ridículo; **to send sb on a** ~**'s errand** enviar a uno a una misión inútil.
(b) (Hist) bufón m.
2 ADJ (*) tonto.
3 VT (deceive) engañar, embaucar; (puzzle) confundir, dejar perplejo; **you can't** ~ **me** a mí no me engaña nadie; **you could have** ~**ed me!** casi lo creí; **you had me properly** ~**ed there** eso sí que me despistó; **that** ~**ed nobody** no se dejó engañar nadie por eso; **that** ~**ed him!** ¡aquello coló!, ¡se lo tragó!
4 VI chancear, bromear; **no** ~**ing** en serio; **no** ~? ¿en serio?, ¿sin bromas?; **I was only** ~**ing** lo dije en broma; **quit** ~**ing!** ¡déjate de tonterías!
◆**fool about, fool around** VI divertirse, juguetear; hacer el tonto; perder el tiempo neciamente; **to** ~ **about with** jugar con, (and damage) estropear.
◆**fool away** VT time perder ociosamente; money despilfarrar.

fool² [fuːl] N (Brit Culin: also **fruit** ~) puré m de frutas con nata (or natillas); **gooseberry** ~ ≃ puré m de grosella con nata (or natillas).

foolery ['fuːlərɪ] N bufonadas fpl; (nonsense) tonterías fpl.

foolhardiness ['fuːlˌhɑːdɪnɪs] N temeridad f.

foolhardy ['fuːlˌhɑːdɪ] ADJ temerario.

foolish ['fuːlɪʃ] ADJ tonto, necio; imbécil; ridículo; absurdo; estúpido; imprudente; ~ **thing** tontería f; **don't be** ~ no seas tonto; **that was very** ~ **of you** en eso fuiste muy imprudente; **I felt very** ~ creí haberme puesto en ridículo; **to make sb look** ~ hacer que uno parezca ridículo, ridiculizar a uno.

foolishly ['fuːlɪʃlɪ] ADV tontamente, neciamente; ~, **I agreed** como un tonto consentí.

foolishness ['fuːlɪʃnɪs] N tontería f, necedad f; imbecilidad f; ridiculez f; estupidez f; imprudencia f.

foolproof ['fuːlpruːf] ADJ device seguro; a toda prueba, a prueba de impericia; plan etc infalible, que no tiene fallo, a prueba de tontos.

foolscap ['fuːlskæp] **1** N (approx) papel m tamaño folio.
2 ATTR: ~ **envelope** ≃ sobre m tamaño folio; ~ **sheet** ≃ folio m.

foot [fʊt] **1** N, PL **feet** [fiːt] (of animal, furniture) pata f; (of hill, page, stairs etc) pie m; ... **my** ~!* ... y un cuerno*, ... y un jamón*;

lady, my ~!* ¡dama, ni hablar!; **at the ~ of the hill** al pie de la colina; **he's on his feet all day long** está trajinando todo el santo día, no descansa en todo el día; **he's on his feet again** ha vuelto a levantarse y a salir; **it's wet under ~** el suelo está mojado; **to come** (*or* **go**) **on ~** venir (*or* ir) a pie, venir (*or* ir) andando *or* caminando (*LAm*); **to drag one's feet** (*fig*) echarse atrás, hacerse el roncero; **to fall on one's feet** tener suerte, caer de pie; **to find one's feet** acostumbrarse al ambiente; **to get cold feet** perder su entusiasmo (*or* interés *etc*), desanimarse; empezar a tener dudas; **to get one's ~ in the door** abrirse una brecha; **to have one ~ in the grave** estar con un pie en la sepultura; **to have one's feet on the ground** (*fig*) ser realista, ser práctico; **to keep one's feet** mantenerse en pie; **to put one's ~ down** (*Aut*) acelerar, (*fig*) oponerse enérgicamente, adoptar una actitud firme; **to put one's feet up** (*fig*) descansar; **she never put a ~ wrong** lo hizo perfectamente, lo hizo impecablemente; **to put one's ~ in it** meter la pata; **to put one's best ~ forward** animarse a continuar; hacer lo posible por hacer una buena impresión; **to rise to one's feet** ponerse de pie, levantarse; **to set ~ inside sb's door** poner los pies en la casa de uno, pasar el umbral de uno; **to set sth on ~** promover algo, poner algo en marcha; **to set ~ on dry land** poner el pie en tierra firme; **to shoot o.s. in the ~** (*fig*) pegarse un tiro en el pie; **to sit at sb's feet** ser discípulo de uno; **to stand on one's own two feet** volar con sus propias alas; **to start off on the right ~** entrar con buen pie; **it all started off on the wrong ~** todo empezó mal; **to sweep a girl off her feet** enamorar perdidamente a una chica; **to trample sth under ~** pisotear algo; **the children are always under my feet** siempre tengo los niños pegados; *ver también* IMPERIAL SYSTEM .

[2] (*) VT **(a)** bill pagar.

(b) to ~ it* (*walk*) ir andando, (*dance*) bailar.

footage ['fʊtɪdʒ] N **(a)** distancia *f*, extensión *f* (medida en pies). **(b)** (*Cine*) cantidad *f*, extensión *f*; imágenes *fpl*; secuencias *fpl* filmadas.

foot-and-mouth (disease) ['fʊtən'maʊθ(dɪ'ziːz)] N fiebre *f* aftosa, glosopeda *f*.

football ['fʊtbɔːl] [1] N (*Brit: game*) fútbol *m*; (*ball*) balón *m*.
[2] ATTR: **~ coupon** (*Brit*) boleto *m* de quinielas; **~ hooligan** (*Brit*) espectador *m* de fútbol violento; **~ hooliganism** (*Brit*) violencia *f* en las gradas; **~ league** (*Brit*) liga *f* de fútbol; **~ player** futbolista *mf*; **~ season** temporada *f* de fútbol.

footballer ['fʊtbɔːləʳ] N futbolista *mf*.

footballing ['fʊtbɔːlɪŋ] ADJ *career, skills* futbolístico; **~ countries** países en los que se juega al fútbol; **he's got a great ~ brain** tiene una buena cabeza para el fútbol.

football-pool ['fʊtbɔːl,puːl] N quinielas *fpl*.

footboard ['fʊtbɔːd] N estribo *m*.

footbrake ['fʊtbreɪk] N pedal *m* del freno; freno *m* de pie.

footbridge ['fʊtbrɪdʒ] N puente *m* peatonal, pasarela *f*.

-footed ['fʊtɪd] ADJ de ... patas; **four~** de cuatro patas; **light~** ligero (de pies).

footer ['fʊtəʳ] N **(a)** (*Brit**) fútbol *m*. **(b)** (*Typ, Comput*) pie *m* de página.

-footer ['fʊtəʳ] N *ending in compounds*: **he's a six~** mide 6 pies.

footfall ['fʊtfɔːl] N paso *m*, pisada *f*.

foot-fault ['fʊt,fɔːlt] N (*Tennis*) falta *f* de saque.

footgear ['fʊtgɪəʳ] N calzado *m*.

foothills ['fʊthɪlz] NPL estribaciones *fpl*.

foothold ['fʊthəʊld] N pie *m* firme, asidero *m* para el pie; **to gain a ~** ganar pie, lograr establecerse.

footing ['fʊtɪŋ] N **(a)** (*lit*) pie *m*; **to lose** (*or* **miss**) **one's ~** perder el pie.
(b) (*fig*) pie *m*, posición *f*; **on an equal ~** en un mismo pie de igualdad (*with* con); **on a friendly ~** en relaciones amistosas; **on a war ~** en pie de guerra; **to gain a ~** ganar pie, lograr establecerse; **to put a company on a sound financial ~** poner una compañía en un pie financiero firme.

footle ['fuːtl] [1] VT: **to ~ away** malgastar.
[2] VI perder el tiempo, hacer el tonto.

footlights ['fʊtlaɪts] NPL candilejas *fpl*.

footling ['fuːtlɪŋ] ADJ trivial, insignificante.

footloose ['fʊtluːs] ADJ libre; (*wandering*) andariego; **~ and fancy-free** libre como el aire.

footman ['fʊtmən] N, PL **footmen** ['fʊtmən] N lacayo *m*.

footmark ['fʊtmɑːk] N huella *f*, pisada *f*.

footnote ['fʊtnəʊt] N nota *f* (al pie de la página).

foot passengers ['fʊt,pæsəndʒəz] NPL pasajeros *mpl* de a pie.

footpath ['fʊtpɑːθ] N, PL **footpaths** ['fʊtpɑːðz] senda *f*, sendero *m*; (*Brit: pavement*) acera *f*, vereda *f* (*SC*), banqueta *f* (*Mex*).

footplate ['fʊtpleɪt] N (*esp Brit*) plataforma *f* del maquinista.

footprint ['fʊtprɪnt] N huella *f*, pisada *f*.

footpump ['fʊtpʌmp] N bomba *f* de pie.

footrest ['fʊtrest] N apoyapié *m*, reposapiés *m*.

footrot ['fʊtrɒt] N uñero *m*.

Footsie* ['fʊtsɪ] N = **Financial Times Stock Exchange 100 Index**.

footsie* ['fʊtsɪ] N: **to play ~ with** hacer del pie con, acariciar con el pie.

footslog: ['fʊtslɒg] VI andar, marchar.

footslogger* ['fʊtslɒgəʳ] N peatón *m*; (*Mil*) soldado *m* de infantería.

foot-soldier ['fʊt,səʊldʒəʳ] N soldado *m* de infantería.

footsore ['fʊtsɔːʳ] ADJ: **to be ~** tener los pies cansados (*or* doloridos).

footstep ['fʊtstep] N paso *m*, pisada *f*; **to follow in sb's ~s** seguir los pasos de uno.

footstool ['fʊtstuːl] N escabel *m*, banquillo *m*.

footway ['fʊt,weɪ] N acera *f*.

footwear ['fʊtweəʳ] N calzado *m*.

footwork ['fʊtwɜːk] N (*Sport*) juego *m* de piernas.

fop [fɒp] N petimetre *m*, currutaco *m*.

foppish ['fɒpɪʃ] ADJ petimetre, litri*.

FOR ABBR *of free on rail* franco en ferrocarril.

▼ **for** [fɔːʳ] [1] PREP **(a)** (*destined for*) para; **hats ~ women** sombreros para mujeres; **is this ~ me?** ¿es esto para mí?; **a job ~ next week** un trabajo para la semana que viene; **we went to Tossa ~ our holidays** fuimos a pasar nuestras vacaciones a Tossa, las vacaciones las pasamos en Tossa; **it's time ~ dinner** es hora de comer; **'Groucho ~ Mayor'** (*slogan*) 'Groucho Alcalde'; **anyone ~ tennis?** ¿hay quien quiera jugar al tenis?; **to write ~ the papers** escribir en los periódicos; **I have news ~ you** tengo que darte una noticia; **it was ~ your good** era para (*or* por) tu bien.
(b) (*as, representing*) por; **member ~ Hove** diputado por Hove; **M ~ Madrid** M de Madrid; **a cheque ~ £500** un cheque por valor de 500 libras; **agent ~ Ford cars** distribuidor de automóviles Ford; **will you write ~ me?** ¿quieres escribir en mi nombre?; **I'll go ~ you** yo iré en tu lugar; **if not the government will do it ~ them** si no el gobierno lo hará en su lugar; **they shot him ~ a traitor** le fusilaron por traidor.
(c) (*in exchange for*) por; **I'll give you this ~ that** te doy éste por ése; **I sold it ~ £5** lo vendí por 5 libras; **she sold the house ~ several millions** vendió la casa en varios millones; **to exchange one's hat ~ another** cambiar el sombrero por otro; **word ~ word** palabra por palabra; **1 dead ~ every 5 injured** 1 muerto por cada 5 lisiados; **what's the German ~ 'hill'?** ¿cómo se dice en alemán 'colina'?
(d) (*in favour of*) **I'm ~ the government** yo estoy a favor del gobierno; **a collection ~ the poor** una colecta a beneficio de los pobres; **the campaign ~ education** la campaña pro (*or* en pro de la) enseñanza; **I'm all ~ it** lo apruebo sin reserva.
(e) (*because of*) por, a causa de, con motivo de, debido a; **~ this reason** por esta razón; **famous ~ its church** famoso por su iglesia; **the reason ~ not doing it** la razón por no hacerlo; **we chose it ~ its climate** lo escogimos por su clima; **if it were not ~ him** si no fuera por él; **to shout ~ joy** gritar de alegría.
(f) (*purpose*) **what ~?** ¿para qué?, ¿por qué?; **what's this ~?** ¿para qué es esto?, ¿para qué sirve esto?
(g) (*bound for*) **he left ~ Ohio** partió para Ohio; **the ship left ~ Vigo** el buque partió (con) rumbo a Vigo; **the train ~ Madrid** el tren de Madrid; **where are you ~ ?** ¿adónde se dirige Vd?
(h) (*considering*) **tall ~ his age** alto para su edad.
(i) (*in spite of*) **he's nice ~ a policeman** para policía es muy simpático, a pesar de ser policía es muy simpático; **~ all that** pese a todo; *V also* **all.**
(j) **oh ~ a horse!** ¡quién tuviera un caballo!
(k) (*distance*) **there was nothing to be seen ~ miles** no había nada que ver en muchos kilómetros; **the trail led on ~ many kilometres** el camino siguió por muchos kilómetros.
(l) (*time: past*) **he was away ~ 2 years** estuvo ausente (durante) 2 años; **was he away ~ long?** ¿estuvo fuera mucho tiempo?; **it has not rained ~ 3 weeks** hace 3 semanas que no llueve, desde hace 3 semanas no llueve; **we went to the seaside ~ the day** fuimos a pasar el día en la playa; (*future*) **I'm going ~ 3 weeks** voy por 3 semanas; **will it be ~ long?** ¿será mucho tiempo?
(m) **now ~ it!** ¡ahora!; ¡ya viene!; **he'll be ~ it!** ¡le va a tocar la gorda!; **there's nothing ~ it** no hay más remedio; *V* **but.**
(n) (*with verb clause*) **it is ~ you to decide** te toca a ti decidir; **it is best ~ you to go** más vale que vayas; **it is right ~ you to go** es justo que vayas; **it's bad ~ you to smoke so much** te hace daño fumar tanto; **~ this to be possible** para que esto sea posible; **~ him to fail now would be disastrous** sería terrible que fracasara ahora; **he gave orders ~ it to be done** mandó que se hiciera, dio instrucciones para que se hiciera.

▼ [2] CONJ pues, ya que.

forage ['fɒrɪdʒ] [1] N forraje *m*.
[2] VI forrajear; **to ~ for** buscar.

foray ['fɒreɪ] N correría *f*, incursión *f* (*into* en).

forbad(e) [fə'bæd] PRET *of* **forbid.**

forbear [fɔː'beəʳ] (*irr: V* **bear**) VI contenerse; tener paciencia; **to ~ to +** *infin* abstenerse de + *infin*.

forbearance [fɔː'beərəns] N paciencia *f*, dominio *m* sobre sí mismo.

➤ LANGUAGE IN USE: **for: 2 → 17.1**

forbearing [fɔːˈbeərɪŋ] ADJ indulgente.

forbears [ˈfɔːbeəz] NPL antepasados *mpl*.

▼ **forbid** [fəˈbɪd] (*irr*: PRET forbad(e), PTP **forbidden**) VT prohibir; **to ~ sth to sb, to ~ sb sth** prohibir algo a uno; **to ~ sb to do sth** prohibir a uno hacer algo; **that's ~den** eso está prohibido; **'smoking ~den'** 'prohibido fumar'; V **God**.

forbidden [fəˈbɪdn] ① PTP of **forbid**. ② ADJ prohibido.

forbidding [fəˈbɪdɪŋ] ADJ *appearance etc* formidable; imponente; (*dismal*) lúgubre; *person's manner* severo.

forbore [fɔːˈbɔːʳ] PRET of **forbear**.

forborne [fɔːˈbɔːn] PTP of **forbear**.

▼ **force** [fɔːs] ① N (a) (*gen*) fuerza *f*; **~ of gravity** fuerza *f* de gravedad; **I can see the ~ of that** comprendo la fuerza de ese argumento; **to resort to ~** recurrir a la fuerza; **to yield to ~** rendirse a la fuerza; **by ~** a la fuerza; **by ~ of** a fuerza de; **by ~ of circumstances** debido a las circunstancias; **by ~ of habit** por costumbre; **by sheer ~** por fuerza mayor; a viva fuerza; **to be in ~** (*Jur*) ser vigente, estar en vigor, (*price*) regir, imperar; **to come in ~** venir en gran número.
(b) (*persons*) personal *m*; (*Mil*) cuerpo *m*, fuerza *f*, ejército *m*; **the ~** la policía; **a strong ~ of police** un numeroso cuerpo de policía; **~s** (*Brit Mil*) fuerzas *fpl* armadas; **representatives of the three ~s** (*Mil*) representantes de los tres ejércitos; **to join ~s** coligarse, juntar meriendas.
② VT (a) (*compel*) forzar, obligar; *door* forzar, violentar, descerrajar; *pace* apresurar; *plant* hacer madurar temprano; (*cause*) hacer; **to ~ a smile** sonreír forzadamente; **to ~ a country into war** empujar a un país a que declare la guerra; **to ~ sb into a corner** arrinconar a uno, hacer que uno quede arrinconado; **to ~ a car off the road** hacer que uno coche salga de la calzada; **to ~ sb into bankruptcy** hacer que uno quiebre.
▼ (b) **to ~ sb to do sth** forzar a uno a hacer algo; **I am ~d to say** me veo obligado a decir.
(c) **to ~ sth on sb** imponer algo a uno, forzar a uno a aceptar algo; **the decision was ~d on him** se le impuso la decisión; **to ~ open** forzar, abrir por fuerza; **we ~d the secret out of him** logramos por fuerza que nos dijera el secreto; **to ~ a bill through parliament** emplear todos los medios para hacer aprobar por el parlamento un proyecto de ley.
③ VR: **to ~ o.s. to** + *infin* hacer un esfuerzo por + *infin*.

◆ **force back** VT hacer retroceder.

◆ **force down** VT (a) (*gen*) hacer bajar. (b) (*Aer*) obligar a aterrizar. (c) *food* tragar por fuerza; **can you ~ a bit more down?** ¿cabe todavía un poco más?

◆ **force in** VT introducir por fuerza.

◆ **force out** VT (a) (*gen*) hacer salir; empujar hacia fuera; **he was ~d out of office** le obligaron a dimitir el cargo. (b) *words* pronunciar con dificultad.

◆ **force up** VT *prices* hacer subir.

forced [fɔːst] ADJ *smile, laughter* forzado; *landing* forzoso; *march, sale, loan* forzado; *entry* violento, a la fuerza; *error* forzado; **~ saving** ahorros *mpl* forzados.

force-feed [ˈfɔːsfiːd] VT alimentar a la fuerza.

force-feeding [ˈfɔːsˌfiːdɪŋ] N alimentación *f* a la fuerza.

forceful [ˈfɔːsfʊl] ADJ enérgico, vigoroso.

forcefully [ˈfɔːsfʊlɪ] ADV enérgicamente, vigorosamente.

forcefulness [ˈfɔːsfʊlnɪs] N energía *f*, vigor *m*.

force majeure [ˈfɔːsməˈʒɜːʳ] N fuerza *f* mayor.

forcemeat [ˈfɔːsmiːt] N relleno *m* (de carne picada), picadillo *m* de relleno.

forceps [ˈfɔːseps] N SING AND PL fórceps *m*; pinzas *fpl*, tenacillas *fpl*.

forcible [ˈfɔːsəbl] ADJ (a) (*done by force*) a la fuerza, a viva fuerza, por fuerza. (b) (*telling*) enérgico, vigoroso.

forcibly [ˈfɔːsəblɪ] ADV a la fuerza; enérgicamente.

forcing-house [ˈfɔːsɪŋˌhaʊs] N, PL **forcing-houses** [ˈfɔːsɪŋˌhaʊzɪz] (*Agr etc*) maduradero *m*; (*fig*) instituto etc donde se llevan a cabo cursos intensivos.

ford [fɔːd] ① N vado *m*, botadero *m* (*Mex*). ② VT vadear.

fordable [ˈfɔːdəbl] ADJ vadeable.

fore [fɔːʳ] ① ADV: **~ and aft** de popa a proa, por todas partes. ② ADJ anterior, delantero; (*Naut*) de proa. ③ N: **to be at the ~** ir delante; **to come to the ~** empezar a destacar. ④ INTERJ (*Golf*) ¡atención!

forearm [ˈfɔːrɑːm] N antebrazo *m*.

forebears [ˈfɔːbeəz] NPL = **forbears**.

forebode [fɔːˈbəʊd] VT presagiar, anunciar.

foreboding [fɔːˈbəʊdɪŋ] N presagio *m*; presentimiento *m*; **to have a ~ that ...** presentir que ...; **to have ~s** tener una corazonada.

forecast [ˈfɔːkɑːst] ① N pronóstico *m*; previsión *f*; **according to all the ~s** según todas las previsiones; **what is the ~ for the weather?** ¿qué pronóstico hacen del tiempo?

┌─ FOR ────────────────────────────────── **see also main entry** ─┐

Time
- When translating VERB + *for* + PERIOD OF TIME, it is often unnecessary to find a word which translates *for*. Simply give VERB + PERIOD OF TIME:
  She was in Mexico for three months
  Estuvo tres meses en México
  Allow it to simmer for fifteen minutes
  Déjelo hervir a fuego lento quince minutos
  They waited for over two hours
  Estuvieron esperando más de dos horas
- Alternatively, translate *for* using *durante* or, especially when talking about very short periods, using *por*:
  Estuvo en México durante tres meses
  Estuvieron esperando durante más de dos horas
  For a moment, he didn't know what to say
  Por un momento, no supo qué decir
- Use *por* rather than *durante* with *ir* (though again the preposition is usually optional):
  I'm going to the country for a while
  Me voy al campo (por) una temporada
- ! But *por* must be given in questions like the following:
  How long are you going for?
  ¿Por cuánto tiempo vas?
- Use the construction *llevar* (in the *present*) + PERIOD OF TIME + GERUND to translate *have been doing* or *have done sth for X years/weeks/days etc*:
  I have been studying Spanish for four years
  Llevo cuatro años estudiando español
  We have worked here for two months
  Llevamos dos meses trabajando aquí
- Alternatively, use *hace* + PERIOD OF TIME + *que* + VERB (in the *present*):
  Hace cuatro años que estudio español
  Hace dos meses que trabajamos aquí
- Or VERB (in the *present*) + *desde hace* + PERIOD OF TIME:
  Estudio español desde hace cuatro años
  Trabajamos aquí desde hace dos meses
- ! Don't use the perfect tense in Spanish to translate phrases like these with *for*.

- To translate *had been doing* or *had done sth for X years/weeks/days etc*, use *llevar* in the *imperfect* + PERIOD OF TIME + GERUND. Alternatively use *hacía* + PERIOD OF TIME + *que* + VERB (in the *imperfect*) or else VERB (in the *imperfect*) + *desde hacía* + PERIOD OF TIME:
  John had been waiting for an hour when they arrived
  John llevaba una hora esperando cuando llegaron ellos
  Hacía una hora que John esperaba cuando llegaron ellos
  John esperaba desde hacía una hora cuando llegaron ellos
- Translate *for* using *para* when talking about dates or deadlines:
  The meeting was fixed for 10th January
  La reunión quedó fijada para el 10 de enero

"Para" or "por"?
- Use *para* to translate *for* + RECIPIENT, DESTINATION or PURPOSE:
  These flowers are for you
  Estas flores son para ti
  Can you cut some wood for the fire?
  ¿Puedes cortar un poco de madera para el fuego?
  He left for Bilbao this morning
  Salió para Bilbao esta mañana
  Books are for reading
  Los libros son para leerlos
- Use *por* to translate *for* + REASON or when it means "for the sake of", "for the benefit of" or indicates exchange:
  They married for love
  Se casaron por amor
  We'll have to fight for our rights
  Tendremos que luchar por nuestros derechos
  I'll give you fifty pounds for that painting
  Te doy cincuenta libras por ese cuadro
- Note how an *indirect object* construction is often used to talk about actions done *for* people that they might otherwise have to do for themselves:
  She prepared dinner for her parents
  Les preparó la cena a sus padres
  Will you open the door for me, please?
  ¿Me abres la puerta, por favor?
  For further uses and examples, see main entry.

---

2 (*irr*: *V* **cast**) VT pronosticar, prever.

forecaster ['fɔːkɑːstəʳ] N (*Econ, Pol, Sport*) pronosticador *m*, -ora *f*; (*Met*) meteorólogo *m*, -a *f*.

forecastle ['fəʊksl] N camarote *m* de la tripulación; (*Hist*) castillo *m* de proa.

foreclose [fɔːˈkləʊz] VTI extinguir el derecho de redimir (una hipoteca).

foreclosure [fɔːˈkləʊʒəʳ] N extinción *f* del derecho de redimir (una hipoteca).

forecourt ['fɔːkɔːt] N atrio *m*, antepatio *m*; (*of garage*) patio *m*.

foredoomed [fɔːˈduːmd] ADJ: **to be ~ to** + *infin* estar condenado de antemano a + *infin*.

forefathers ['fɔːˌfɑːðəz] NPL antepasados *mpl*.

forefinger ['fɔːˌfɪŋgəʳ] N (dedo *m*) índice *m*.

forefoot ['fɔːfʊt] N, PL **forefeet** ['fɔːfiːt] mano *f*, pie *m* delantero, pata *f* delantera.

forefront ['fɔːfrʌnt] N: **to be in the ~** estar en la vanguardia (*of* de); estar en primer plano.

foregather [fɔːˈgæðəʳ] VI reunirse.

forego [fɔːˈgəʊ] (*irr*: PRET **forewent**, PTP **foregone**) VT pasarse sin, privarse de, renunciar a.

foregoing ['fɔːgəʊɪŋ] ADJ anterior, precedente.

foregone ['fɔːgɒn] ADJ: **~ conclusion** resultado *m* inevitable.

foreground ['fɔːgraʊnd] 1 N primer plano *m*, primer término *m*; **in the ~** en primer término.
2 VT traer al primer plano; destacar, subrayar.

forehand ['fɔːhænd] 1 N directo *m*, derechazo *m*. 2 ATTR directo.

forehead ['fɒrɪd] N frente *f*.

foreign ['fɒrɪn] ADJ (a) extranjero; *relations, trade etc* exterior; **~ agent** agente *m* extranjero, agente *f* extranjera; **~ aid** ayuda *f* exterior; **~ bill** letra *f* sobre el exterior; **~ currency** moneda *f* extranjera, divisas *fpl*; **~ debt** deuda *f* externa; **~ exchange** divisas *fpl*; **~ exchange dealer** tratante *m* de divisas; **~ exchange market** mercado *m* de divisas; **~ investment** inversión *f* extranjera; inversión *f* en el extranjero; **F~ Legion** Legión *f* Extranjera; **F~ Minister, F~ Secretary** Ministro *m*, -a *f* de Asuntos Exteriores; **F~ Ministry, F~ Office** (*Brit*) Ministerio *m* de Asuntos Exteriores; **~ policy** política exterior; **F~ Service** Servicio *m* Exterior (*Sp*); **~ trade** comercio *m* exterior.
(b) *body* extraño; (*belonging to sb else*) ajeno (*to* a); **deceit is ~ to his nature** no cabe en él el engaño, el engaño es ajeno a su modo de ser.

foreigner ['fɒrɪnəʳ] N extranjero *m*, -a *f*.

foreknowledge [fɔːˈnɒlɪdʒ] N presciencia *f*; **to have ~ of sth** saber algo de antemano.

foreland ['fɔːlənd] N cabo *m*, promontorio *m*.

foreleg ['fɔːleg] N pata *f* delantera, brazo *m*.

forelock ['fɔːlɒk] N guedeja *f*; **to take time by the ~** tomar la ocasión por los pelos.

foreman ['fɔːmən] N, PL **foremen** ['fɔːmən] (*of workers*) capataz *m*, caporal *m* (*Mex*); mayoral *m*; (*Jur*) presidente *m* (del jurado).

foremast ['fɔːmɑːst] N (palo *m*) trinquete *m*.

▼ **foremost** ['fɔːməʊst] ADJ primero, delantero; (*outstanding*) primero, principal.

forename ['fɔːneɪm] N nombre *m*, nombre *m* de pila.

forenoon ['fɔːnuːn] N mañana *f*.

forensic [fəˈrensɪk] ADJ forense; *medicine* legal, forense.

forepaw ['fɔːpɔː] N (*of cat, lion*) zarpa *f*; (*of dog, wolf*) uña *f*.

foreplay ['fɔːpleɪ] N caricias *fpl* estimulantes, excitación *f* preliminar.

forequarters ['fɔːˌkwɔːtəz] NPL cuartos *mpl* delanteros.

forerunner ['fɔːˌrʌnəʳ] N precursor *m*, -ora *f*.

foresail ['fɔːseɪl] N trinquete *m*.

foresee [fɔːˈsiː] (*irr*: *V* **see**) VT prever.

foreseeable [fɔːˈsiːəbl] ADJ previsible; **in the ~ future** hasta donde se pueda ver.

foreseeably [fɔːˈsiːəblɪ] ADV previsiblemente.

foreshadow [fɔːˈʃædəʊ] VT prefigurar, anunciar; presagiar; (*person*) prever.

foreshore ['fɔːʃɔːʳ] N playa *f* (entre los límites de pleamar y bajamar).

foreshorten [fɔːˈʃɔːtn] VT escorzar.

foreshortening [fɔːˈʃɔːtnɪŋ] N escorzo *m*.

foresight ['fɔːsaɪt] N previsión *f*; **lack of ~** imprevisión *f*, falta *f* de precaución.

foreskin ['fɔːskɪn] N prepucio *m*.

forest ['fɒrɪst] 1 N bosque *m*; (*large, dense*) selva *f*.
2 ATTR forestal, del bosque; **~ fire** incendio *m* forestal, incendio *m* de bosque; **~ ranger = forester**; **~ track, ~ trail** camino *m* forestal.

forestall [fɔːˈstɔːl] VT anticiparse a, adelantarse a (e impedir).

forested ['fɒrɪstɪd] ADJ arbolado, de bosques; **densely/heavily ~** cubierto de bosques; **only 8 per cent of Britain is ~** las áreas forestales de Gran Bretaña se reducen al 8 por ciento del territorio.

forester ['fɒrɪstəʳ] N (*expert*) ingeniero *m* de montes; (*keeper*) guardabosques *m*.

forestry ['fɒrɪstrɪ] 1 N silvicultura *f*; (*as Univ course*) ciencias *fpl* forestales.
2 ATTR: **F~ Commission** (*Brit*) ≃ Comisión *f* del Patrimonio Forestal.

┌─ **FORESTRY COMMISSION** ─┐

ⓘ El **Forestry Commission** es el organismo británico responsable de la administración de bosques, que asesora al gobierno y pone en marcha su política en materia forestal. Esta comisión, con sede en Edimburgo, administra millones de hectáreas de bosque público en todo el país y concede ayudas a los propietarios de áreas privadas de bosque. Además, es responsable del control de la producción maderera, de la conservación de los bosques y de la adecuación de algunos espacios forestales para acampadas y excursiones campo a través, así como del fomento de la investigación forestal.

En Estados Unidos el organismo equivalente al **Forestry Commission** es el **US Forest Service**, que se encarga del control de cientos de millones de hectáreas de bosque en todo el territorio nacional, tanto de los que son propiedad de los gobiernos federal o estatal como de los bosques privados. También concede ayudas a los terratenientes y ofrece programas de conservación, investigación y desarrollo.

foretaste ['fɔːteɪst] N anticipo *m*, muestra *f*.

foretell [fɔːˈtel] (*irr*: *V* **tell**) VT (*predict*) predecir, pronosticar; (*presage*) presagiar.

forethought ['fɔːθɔːt] N prevención *f*, previsión *f*; (*pej*) premeditación *f*.

forever [fərˈevəʳ] ADV **(a)** (*incessantly*) constantemente, sin cesar. **(b)** (*for always*) para siempre.

forewarn [fɔːˈwɔːn] VT prevenir; **to be ~ed** estar prevenido, precaverse; **~ed is forearmed** hombre prevenido vale por dos.

foreword ['fɔːwɜːd] N prefacio *m*.

forfeit ['fɔːfɪt] 1 N (*loss*) pérdida *f*; (*fine*) multa *f*; (*penalty*) pena *f*; (*in games*) prenda *f*; **~s** juego *m* de prendas.
2 VT perder (el derecho a).

forfeiture ['fɔːfɪtʃəʳ] N pérdida *f*.

forgather [fɔːˈgæðəʳ] VI reunirse.

forgave [fəˈgeɪv] PRET of **forgive**.

forge¹ [fɔːdʒ] 1 N (*fire*) fragua *f*; (*smithy*) herrería *f*; (*ironworks*) fundición *f*, fundidora *f* (*LAm*).
2 VT **(a)** *metal* forjar, fraguar; *friendship, plan, unity etc* fraguar. **(b)** (*falsify*) falsificar, falsear, contrahacer.

forge² [fɔːdʒ] VI: **to ~ ahead** avanzar constantemente; adelantarse muchísimo (*of* a).

forger ['fɔːdʒəʳ] N falsificador *m*, -ora *f*, falsario *m*, -a *f*.

forgery ['fɔːdʒərɪ] N falsificación *f*.

forget [fəˈget] (*irr*: PRET **forgot**, PTP **forgotten**) 1 VT olvidarse de, olvidar; **~ it!** ¡no se preocupe!; ¡no importa!; **and don't you ~ it!** ¡y que no se te olvide esto!; **never to be forgotten** inolvidable; **to ~ to do sth** olvidarse de hacer algo; **I forgot all about it** se me olvidó por completo; **I forgot to tell you why** se me olvidó decirte por qué; **if there's no money, you can ~** (**about**) **the new car** si no hay dinero, puedes olvidarte del nuevo coche.
2 VI olvidarse; **I ~ no** recuerdo, me he olvidado; **but I forgot** pero se me olvidó.
3 VR: **to ~ o.s.** propasarse, olvidar los buenos modales, pasarse (*LAm*); **you ~ yourself, sir!** ¡prudencia, caballero!

◆ **forget about** VT olvidarse de; **let's ~ about it!** ¡pelillos a la mar!

┌─ **FORGET** ─────────── *see also main entry* ─┐

You can use *olvidar* in 3 ways when translating *to forget*: *olvidar*, *olvidarse de* or the impersonal *olvidársele algo a alguien*.

● When *forgetting* is *accidental*, the impersonal construction with *se me*, *se le*, etc is the commonest option - it emphasizes the involuntary aspect. Here, the object of *forget* becomes the subject of *olvidar*:

  I forgot
  Se me olvidó
  I've forgotten what you said this morning
  Se me ha olvidado lo que dijiste esta mañana
  He forgot his briefcase
  Se le olvidó el maletín
  NOTE: *Olvidarse de* and *olvidar* would be more formal alternatives.

● In other contexts, use either *olvidarse de* or *olvidar*.
  Have you forgotten what you promised me?
  ¿Te has olvidado de or *Has olvidado lo que me prometiste?*
  In the end he managed to forget her
  Al final consiguió olvidarse de ella or *consiguió olvidarla*
  Don't forget me
  No te olvides de mí ◊ No me olvides
  For further uses and examples, see main entry.

forgetful [fəˈgetfʊl] ADJ *character* olvidadizo, desmemoriado; descuidado; ~ **of all else** olvidando todo lo demás, sin hacer caso de todo lo demás; **he's terribly** ~ tiene un tremendo despiste, tiene pésima memoria.

forgetfulness [fə'getfʊlnɪs] N olvido *m*, falta *f* de memoria; descuido *m*; (*absentmindedness*) despiste *m*.

forget-me-not [fə'getmɪnɒt] N nomeolvides *f*.

forgettable [fə'getəbl] ADJ olvidable; digno de ser olvidado.

▼ **forgive** [fə'gɪv] (*irr: V* **give**) VT perdonar, disculpar (*LAm*); **to ~ sb (for) sth** perdonar algo a uno, perdonar a uno por algo.

forgiven [fə'gɪvn] PTP *of* **forgive**.

forgiveness [fə'gɪvnɪs] N (*pardon*) perdón *m*; (*compassion*) misericordia *f*.

forgiving [fə'gɪvɪŋ] ADJ perdonador, misericordioso; **to feel ~** estar dispuesto a perdonar.

forgo [fɔː'gəʊ] (*irr: V* **go**) VT = **forego**.

forgot [fə'gɒt] PRET *of* **forget**.

forgotten [fə'gɒtn] PTP *of* **forget**.

fork [fɔːk] [1] N (*at table*) tenedor *m*; (*Agr*) horca *f*, horquilla *f*; (*Mech etc*) horquilla *f*; (*of cycle*) tijera *f*; (*in road*) bifurcación *f*, empalme *m* (*LAm*); (*Anat*) horcajadura *f*, entrepierna *f*; (*in river*) horcajo *m*; (*of tree*) horcadura *f*.

[2] VT cultivar con horquilla.

[3] VI (*road*) bifurcarse, hacer empalme (*LAm*); ~ **right for Oxford** tuerza a la derecha para ir a Oxford.

◆**fork out*** [1] VT desembolsar (de mala gana).

[2] VI aflojar la pasta* (*for* para comprar).

◆**fork over** = **fork 2**.

◆**fork up** VT (a) *soil* remover con la horquilla. (b) = **fork out 1**.

forked [fɔːkt] ADJ ahorquillado, bifurcado; *lightning* en zigzag; *tail* hendido; *tongue* bífido.

fork-lift ['fɔːklɪft] ATTR: ~ **truck** carretilla *f* elevadora, carretilla *f* de horquilla.

forlorn [fə'lɔːn] ADJ abandonado, desamparado; *appearance* de abandono; **to look ~** (*person*) tener aspecto triste; **why so ~?** ¿por qué tan triste?; ~ **hope** empresa *f* desesperada; esperanza *f* que tiene poca probabilidad de verse realizada.

forlornly [fə'lɔːnlɪ] ADV tristemente; con aire de abandono.

form [fɔːm] [1] N (a) (*shape, style, type, method etc; also Liter, Gram*) forma *f*; **a new ~ of government** un nuevo sistema de gobierno; **the same thing in a new ~** la misma cosa bajo una nueva forma; **choose another ~ of words** busque otra expresión; **it took the ~ of a cash prize** consistió en un premio en metálico; **what ~ will the ceremony take?** ¿en qué consistirá la ceremonia?

(b) (*shape vaguely seen*) figura *f*, bulto *m*.

(c) (*Brit Scol*) clase *f*.

(d) (*Brit: bench*) banco *m*.

(e) (*document*) hoja *f*, formulario *m*; **to fill up a ~** llenar una hoja; **has he got any ~?*** ¿tiene antecedentes penales?; *V* **application.**

(f) (*customary method*) forma *f*; **in due ~** en la debida forma, en la forma reglamentaria; **that is common** ~ eso es muy corriente; **what's the ~?** ¿qué es lo que hemos de hacer?

(g) (*formality*) **for ~'s sake** por pura fórmula, para salvar las apariencias.

(h) (*behaviour*) **it's bad ~ to** + *infin* es de mal gusto + *infin*, es de mala educación + *infin*.

(i) (*condition*) estado *m* físico; **to be in good ~, to be on ~** (*Sport*) estar en forma, (*be witty*) estar de vena; **to be out of ~** estar desentrenado.

(j) **to study (the) ~** (*Brit Racing*) estudiar resultados anteriores.

[2] VT formar; *habit* adquirir; *body* formar, integrar, formar parte de; *company* fundar, establecer; *plan* concebir; *idea* hacerse; *impression, opinion* formarse; *queue* hacer; **to ~ the plural** formar el plural; **to ~ a government** formar gobierno; **those who ~ the group** los que integran el grupo.

[3] VI formarse; **an idea ~ed in his mind** una idea tomó forma en su mente; **how do ideas ~?** ¿cómo se forman las ideas?

◆**form up** [1] VT *troops* formar.

[2] VI alinearse, (*Mil*) formar.

formal ['fɔːməl] ADJ formal; *person's manner* ceremonioso, protocolario, estirado; *person's character* etiquetero; *greeting* ceremonioso; *visit* de cumplido, oficial; *education etc* convencional, regular; *proposal* formal, oficial; *function* protocolario; *dance, dress* de etiqueta; (*relating to form*) formal; ~ **acceptance** aceptación *f* formal; ~ **denial** negación *f* formal; **don't be so ~!** ¡no te andes con tantos cumplidos!; **there was no ~ agreement** no hubo contrato en forma.

formaldehyde [fɔː'mældɪhaɪd] N formaldehído *m*.

formalin(e) ['fɔːməlɪn] N formalina *f*.

formalism ['fɔːməlɪzəm] N formalismo *m*.

formalist ['fɔːməlɪst] [1] ADJ formalista.

[2] N formalista *mf*.

formalistic [fɔːmə'lɪstɪk] ADJ formalista.

formality [fɔː'mælɪtɪ] N (a) (*of occasion*) ceremonia *f*, lo ceremonioso; (*of person*) lo etiquetero; (*of dress etc*) etiqueta *f*; **with all due ~** en la debida forma; **it's a mere ~** es pura fórmula.

(b) **formalities** ceremonias *fpl*; formalidades *fpl*; requisitos *mpl*; **first there are certain formalities** primero hay ciertos requisitos; **let's do without the formalities** prescindamos de los trámites de costumbre.

formalize ['fɔːməlaɪz] VT formalizar.

formally ['fɔːməlɪ] ADV *greet etc* ceremoniosamente; *open, visit* oficialmente; *agree etc* en forma.

format ['fɔːmæt] [1] N formato *m*.

[2] ATTR: ~ **line** línea *f* de formato.

[3] VT formatear.

formation [fɔː'meɪʃən] [1] N formación *f*; **in battle ~** en orden de batalla.

[2] ATTR: ~ **flying** vuelo *m* en formación.

formative ['fɔːmətɪv] [1] ADJ formativo.

[2] N formativo *m*.

formatting ['fɔːmætɪŋ] N formateado *m*, formateo *m*, formación *f*.

▼ **former** ['fɔːməʳ] [1] ADJ (a) (*of two*) primero, anterior; **your ~ idea** su primera idea.

(b) (*earlier*) antiguo; **a ~ seat of government** una antigua sede del gobierno.

(c) (*of person*) ex, que fue; ~ **president** ex presidente *m*; **a ~ ambassador in Lima** embajador que fue en Lima.

▼[2] PRON: **the ~** (*... the latter*) aquél *etc* (*... éste etc*); *ver también* OLD .

formerly ['fɔːməlɪ] ADV antes, antiguamente.

form feed ['fɔːm,fiːd] N salto *m* de página.

formic ['fɔːmɪk] ADJ: ~ **acid** ácido *m* fórmico.

Formica [fɔː'maɪkə] ® N formica ® *f*.

formidable ['fɔːmɪdəbl] ADJ formidable.

formless ['fɔːmlɪs] ADJ informe.

form letter ['fɔːm,letəʳ] N (*US*) carta *f* tipo.

formula ['fɔːmjʊlə] N, PL ~**s** *or* **formulae** ['fɔːmjʊliː] fórmula *f*.

formulaic [fɔːmjʊ'leɪɪk] ADJ formulaico, formulario.

formulate ['fɔːmjʊleɪt] VT formular.

formulation [fɔːmjʊ'leɪʃən] N formulación *f*.

fornicate ['fɔːnɪkeɪt] VI fornicar.

fornication [fɔːnɪ'keɪʃən] N fornicación *f*.

forsake [fə'seɪk] (*irr: PRET* **forsook**, *PTP* **forsaken**) VT *person etc* abandonar, dejar, desamparar; *plan* renunciar a; *belief* renegar de; **he forsook Seville for Madrid** abandonó Sevilla y se fue a vivir a Madrid.

forsaken [fə'seɪkən] PTP *of* **forsake**.

forsook [fə'sʊk] PRET *of* **forsake**.

forsooth [fə'suːθ] ADV († *or hum*) en verdad; (EXCL) ~! ¡caramba!

forswear [fɔː'sweəʳ] (*irr: V* **swear**) [1] VT abjurar de, renunciar a.

[2] VR: **to ~ o.s.** perjurarse.

forsythia [fɔː'saɪθɪə] N forsitia *f*.

fort [fɔːt] N fuerte *m*, fortín *m*; **to hold the ~** (*fig*) defenderse, seguir en su puesto, encargarse del trabajo (temporalmente); **hold the ~ till I get back** hazte cargo hasta que yo regrese.

forte ['fɔːtɪ, (*US*) fɔːt] N fuerte *m*; (*Mus*) forte *m*.

forth [fɔːθ] ADV: **and so ~** etcétera; **y así sucesivamente**; **from this day ~** de aquí en adelante; *V* **back** *etc*.

forthcoming [fɔːθ'kʌmɪŋ] ADJ (a) (*approaching*) venidero, próximo; *book etc* de próxima aparición, en preparación.

(b) (*available*) disponible; **if help is ~** si nos mandan socorros, si nos ayudan; **if funds are ~** si nos facilitan fondos; **no answer was ~** no hubo respuesta.

(c) *character* afable, comunicativo; **he's not very ~** no dice mucho; **he's not ~ with strangers** tiene poca confianza con los desconocidos.

forthright ['fɔːθraɪt] ADJ *person* directo, franco; enérgico; *answer etc* terminante; *refusal* rotundo.

forthwith ['fɔːθ'wɪθ] ADV (*then and there*) en el acto; (*without delay*) sin dilación.

fortieth ['fɔːtɪɪθ] ADJ cuadragésimo; cuarenta; **the ~ anniversary** el cuarenta aniversario.

fortification [fɔːtɪfɪ'keɪʃən] N fortificación *f*.

fortified ['fɔːtɪfaɪd] ADJ *wine* encabezado.

fortify ['fɔːtɪfaɪ] VT (*Mil*) fortificar; (*strengthen*) fortalecer; *wine* encabezar; *person* vigorizar, fortalecer; **to ~ sb in a belief** confirmar la opinión que tiene uno.

[2] VR: **to ~ o.s.** (*fig*) fortalecerse.

fortitude ['fɔːtɪtjuːd] N fortaleza *f*, entereza *f*, valor *m*.

Fort Knox [fɔːt'nɒks] N *lugar donde se guardan las reservas de oro de EE.UU.*; **they've turned their house into ~** (*fig*) han convertido su casa en un búnker.

fortnight ['fɔːtnaɪt] N (*esp Brit*) quince días *mpl*, quincena *f*; **today ~** de hoy en quince días.

fortnightly ['fɔːtnaɪtlɪ] [1] ADJ que sale (*etc*) cada quince días, quincenal.

2 ADV cada quince días, quincenalmente.

FORTRAN, Fortran ['fɔːtræn] N (*Comput*) ABBR *of* **formula translator** FORTRAN *m*, Fortran *m*.

fortress ['fɔːtrɪs] N fortaleza *f*, plaza *f* fuerte, alcázar *m*.

fortuitous [fɔː'tjuːɪtəs] ADJ fortuito, casual.

fortuitously [fɔː'tjuːɪtəslɪ] ADV fortuitamente, por casualidad.

fortunate ['fɔːtʃənɪt] ADJ afortunado; (*happy*) dichoso, feliz; **to be ~** (*person*) tener suerte; **that was ~ for you** en eso tuviste suerte.

fortunately ['fɔːtʃənɪtlɪ] ADV afortunadamente.

fortune ['fɔːtʃən] N **(a)** (*luck, fate*) fortuna *f*, suerte *f*; **by good ~** por fortuna; **the ~s of war** las vicisitudes de la guerra, las peripecias de la guerra; **we had the good ~ to find him** tuvimos la suerte de encontrarle; **he restored the company's ~s** restableció la prosperidad de la empresa, devolvió el éxito a la compañía; **to tell sb's ~** decir a uno la buenaventura; **to try one's ~** probar fortuna. **(b)** (*money*) fortuna *f*, caudal *m*; **to come into a ~** heredar una fortuna; **to cost a ~** valer un dineral; **to make a ~** enriquecerse, hacer su pacotilla; **to marry a ~** casarse con una mujer acaudalada.

fortune cookie ['fɔːtʃən,kʊkɪ] N (*esp US*) *galleta china con un mensaje sobre la suerte*.

fortune-hunter ['fɔːtʃən,hʌntəʳ] N (*man*) cazador *m* de dotes, cazadotes *m*; (*woman*) mujer *f* que busca un marido rico.

fortune-teller ['fɔːtʃən,teləʳ] N adivina *f*.

fortune-telling ['fɔːtʃən,telɪŋ] N adivinación *f*.

forty ['fɔːtɪ] ADJ cuarenta; **the forties** (*eg 1940s*) los años cuarenta; **to be in one's forties** tener más de cuarenta años, ser cuarentón.

fortyish ['fɔːtɪɪʃ] ADJ de unos cuarenta años.

forum ['fɔːrəm] N foro *m*; (*fig*) tribunal *m*, foro *m*.

forward ['fɔːwəd] **1** ADJ **(a)** (*front*) delantero; *position* (*Mil etc*) avanzado; (*Naut*) de proa; *movement* progresivo, de avance; *gears* de avance; **~ line** línea *f* delantera; **~ pass** pase *m* adelantado. **(b)** *season, crop* adelantado; precoz. **(c)** *person* atrevido, fresco, descarado. **(d)** (*Comm*) **~ buying** compra *f* a término, compras *fpl* para el futuro; **~ delivery** entrega *f* en fecha futura; **~ market** mercado *m* de futuros, mercado *m* forward; **~ planning** planificación *f*; **~ sales** ventas *fpl* que deben efectuarse en fecha posterior.

2 N (*Sport*) delantero *m*, -a *f*.

3 VT **(a)** (*send*) enviar; (*re-address*) hacer seguir; **'to be ~ed'**, **'please ~'** 'se ruega hacer seguir'; **~ing address** dirección *f* a la que han de hacerse seguir las cartas; **she left no ~ing address** no dejó dirección; **~ing agent** agente *mf* de tránsito, agente *mf* de transporte. **(b)** (*promote*) promover, avanzar; favorecer.

forward-looking ['fɔːwəd,lʊkɪŋ] ADJ **(a)** *plan etc* con miras al futuro. **(b)** *person* previsor; consciente de las posibilidades futuras; (*Pol*) progresista.

forward(s) ['fɔːwəd(z)] ADV adelante, hacia adelante; (*Naut*) hacia la proa; **~!** ¡adelante!; **~ march!** de frente ¡mar!; **the lever is placed well ~** la palanca está colocada bastante hacia adelante; **from that day ~** desde ese día en adelante, a partir de entonces; **to go ~** ir hacia adelante, avanzar; (*fig*) progresar, hacer progresos.

forwardness ['fɔːwədnɪs] N **(a)** (*of crop etc*) precocidad *f*. **(b)** (*pertness*) frescura *f*, descaro *m*.

forward-thinking ['fɔːwəd,θɪŋkɪŋ] ADJ (*Pol*) progresista; **to be ~** ir por delante.

forwent [fɔː'went] PRET *of* **forgo**.

Fosbury flop ['fɒzbərɪ,flɒp] N fosbury-flop *m*.

fossil ['fɒsl] **1** ADJ fósil; **~ fuel** combustible *m* fósil.

2 N fósil *m*.

fossilization [,fɒsɪlaɪ'zeɪʃən] N fosilización *f*.

fossilized ['fɒsɪlaɪzd] ADJ fosilizado.

foster ['fɒstəʳ] VT **(a)** (*encourage*) fomentar, promover; (*aid*) favorecer; *hope* alentar. **(b)** *child* criar, acoger en una familia.

fosterage ['fɒstərɪdʒ] N (*US*), **fostering** ['fɒstərɪŋ] N acogimiento *m* familiar.

foster-brother ['fɒstə,brʌðəʳ] N hermano *m* de leche.

foster-home ['fɒstəhəʊm] N casa *f* cuna, familia *f* adoptiva.

foster-mother ['fɒstə,mʌðəʳ] N madre *f* adoptiva; (*wet-nurse*) ama *f* de leche.

fought [fɔːt] PRET AND PTP *of* **fight**.

foul [faʊl] **1** ADJ (*dirty*) sucio, puerco; (*disgusting*) asqueroso; (*of bad quality*) horrible; (*morally vile*) vil, horrible; *air* viciado; *blow, language* sucio; *breath* fétido; *calumny* vil; *smell* insoportable; *weather* feo, horrible; **to fall ~ of** *person* indisponerse con, ponerse a malas con, *rule* infringir; **to fall ~ of the law** tener un lío con la justicia; **someone is sure to cry '~'** es seguro que alguien dirá que no hemos jugado limpio.

2 N (*Sport*) falta *f* (*on* contra).

3 VT **(a)** (*dirty*) ensuciar; *good name, one's nest* manchar.

(b) (*block*) atascar, obstruir; (*catch up in*) enredarse en; (*hit*) chocar contra.

(c) (*Sport*) cometer una falta contra.

4 VI **(a)** (*Sport*) cometer falta. **(b)** (*rope etc*) enredarse.

◆ **foul up*** VT armar un lío con*, liar*, embrollar; joder‡; *relationship* estropear.

foulmouthed ['faʊl'maʊðd] ADJ malhablado.

foul play ['faʊl,pleɪ] N (*Sport*) mala jugada *f*, jugada *f* sucia; (*Jur*) muerte *f* violenta; intervención *f* siniestra.

foul-smelling ['faʊl'smelɪŋ] ADJ hediondo.

foul-tempered ['faʊl'tempəd] ADJ: **to be ~** (*habitually*) ser un cascarrabias; (*on one occasion*) estar malhumorado.

foul-up* ['faʊlʌp] N (*US*) lío* *m*, embrollo *m*, follón* *m*.

found¹ [faʊnd] PRET AND PTP *of* **find**.

found² [faʊnd] VT fundar, establecer; *fortune* crear; **a statement ~ed on fact** una declaración basada en hechos.

found³ [faʊnd] VT (*Tech*) fundir.

foundation [faʊn'deɪʃən] **1** N **(a)** (*act*) fundación *f*, establecimiento *m*; creación *f*. **(b)** (*basis*) base *f*, fundamento *m*; **statement devoid of ~** declaración *f* que carece de base. **(c)** (*make-up*) maquillaje *m* de fondo, base *f*. **(d)** **~s** (*Archit*) cimientos *mpl*; **to lay the ~s** echar los cimientos (*of* de; *also fig*).

2 ATTR: **~ course** curso *m* de base; **~ cream** crema *f* base; **~ garment** corsé *m*; **~ stone** (*Brit*) primera piedra *f*; (*fig*) piedra *f* angular.

founder¹ ['faʊndəʳ] N fundador *m*, -ora *f*; **~ member** (*Brit*) miembro *m* fundador, miembro *f* fundadora.

founder² ['faʊndəʳ] VI irse a pique, hundirse; (*fig*) fracasar (*on* debido a).

founding ['faʊndɪŋ] **1** ADJ: **F~ Fathers** (*US*) Padres *mpl* Fundadores.

2 N fundación *f*.

foundling ['faʊndlɪŋ] N niño *m* expósito, niña *f* expósita, inclusero *m*, -a *f*; **~ hospital** inclusa *f*.

foundry ['faʊndrɪ] N fundición *f*, fundidora *f* (*LAm*).

fount [faʊnt] N **(a)** (*liter: spring*) fuente *f*, manantial *m*; **~ of justice** (*fig*) fuente *f* de justicia. **(b)** (*Brit Typ*) fundición *f*, familia *f* (de la letra).

fountain ['faʊntɪn] N (*natural*) fuente *f*, manantial *m* (*also fig*); (*artificial*) fuente *f*, surtidor *m*; (*jet*) chorro *m*.

fountainhead ['faʊntɪnhed] N fuente *f*, origen *m*; **to go to the ~** acudir a la propia fuente.

fountain-pen ['faʊntɪnpen] N estilográfica *f*, plumafuente *f* (*LAm*).

four [fɔːʳ] **1** ADJ cuatro.

2 N cuatro *m*; **to be on all ~s with** (*thing*) concordar con, estar en completa armonía con; **to go on all ~s** ir a gatas; **to form ~s** formar a cuatro; **to make up a ~ for bridge** completar los cuatro para bridge; **~-figure debt** deuda *f* de 1000 libras o más; **~-~ time** compás *m* de cuatro por cuatro; **~-minute mile** milla *f* que se corre en cuatro minutos.

four-colour, (*US*) **four-color** ['fɔː,kʌləʳ] ATTR: **~ (printing) process** cuatricromía *f*.

four-cycle ['fɔː,saɪkl] ADJ (*US*) = **four-stroke**.

four-door ['fɔː'dɔːʳ] ADJ *car* de cuatro puertas.

four-engined ['fɔːr'endʒɪnd] ADJ cuatrimotor, tetramotor.

four-eyes* ['fɔːraɪz] N cuatrojos* *mf*.

fourflusher* ['fɔː'flʌʃəʳ] N (*US*) embustero *m*.

fourfold ['fɔːfəʊld] **1** ADJ cuádruple.

2 ADV cuatro veces.

fourfooted ['fɔː'fʊtɪd] ADJ cuadrúpedo.

four-handed ['fɔː'hændɪd] ADJ de cuatro jugadores.

four-letter ['fɔː,letəʳ] ADJ: **~ word** (*lit*) que tiene cuatro letras; (*fig*) taco *m*, palabrota *f*.

four-part ['fɔːpɑːt] ADJ *song* para cuatro voces.

four-ply ['fɔːplaɪ] ADJ *wood* de cuatro capas; *wool* de cuatro hebras.

fourposter ['fɔː,pəʊstəʳ] N (*also* **~ bed**) cama *f* de columnas.

fourscore†† ['fɔː'skɔːʳ] ADJ ochenta.

four-seater [,fɔː'siːtəʳ] N coche *m* (*etc*) con cuatro asientos.

foursome ['fɔːsəm] N grupo *m* de cuatro personas.

foursquare ['fɔː'skweəʳ] **1** ADJ firme; franco, sincero.

2 ADV: **to stand ~ with sb** estar en completa armonía con uno, apoyar a uno incondicionalmente.

four-star ['fɔːstɑːʳ] ATTR: **~ hotel** hotel *m* de cuatro estrellas; **~ petrol** (*Brit*) ≃ gasolina *f* súper.

four-stroke ['fɔːstrəʊk] ADJ (*Aut*) de cuatro tiempos.

fourteen ['fɔː'tiːn] ADJ catorce.

fourteenth ['fɔː'tiːnθ] ADJ decimocuarto.

fourth [fɔːθ] **1** ADJ cuarto; **the F~ of July** (*US*) el cuatro de julio; **~ dimension** cuarta dimensión *f*; **~ estate** (*hum*) la prensa; **~ gear** cuarta *f* (velocidad *f*); **~ note** (*US Mus*) cuarta *f*.

2 N cuarto *m*, cuarta parte *f*; (*Mus*) cuarta *f*; **to make a ~** (*Cards*) unirse a otras tres personas (para que se pueda jugar).

fourthly ['fɔ:θlɪ] ADV en cuarto lugar.

fourth-rate ['fɔ:θ'reɪt] ADJ (*fig*) de cuarta categoría.

four-wheel ['fɔ:wi:l] ATTR: **~ drive** tracción *f* de 4 por 4, tracción *f* a las cuatro ruedas.

fowl [faʊl] N (*bird in general*) ave *f*; (*chicken*) ave *f* de corral, gallina *f*; (*served as food*) pollo *m*; **the ~s of the air** las aves.

fowling-piece ['faʊlɪŋ,pi:s] N escopeta *f*.

fowl pest ['faʊlpest] N peste *f* aviar.

fox [fɒks] **1** N zorra *f*, (*dog-~*) zorro *m*; (*fig*) zorro *m*; **he's an old ~** es un viejo zorro. **2** VT confundir, dejar perplejo; **this will ~ them** esto les ha de despistar; **you had me properly ~ed there** eso me tuvo completamente despistado. **3** VI disimular, fingir.

foxcub ['fɒkskʌb] N cachorro *m* (de zorro).

foxed [fɒkst] ADJ *book* manchado.

fox-fur ['fɒksfɜ:ʳ] N piel *f* de zorro.

foxglove ['fɒksglʌv] N dedalera *f*.

foxhole ['fɒkshəʊl] N madriguera *f* de zorro; (*Mil*) hoyo *m* de protección.

foxhound ['fɒkshaʊnd] N perro *m* raposero.

foxhunt ['fɒkshʌnt] N cacería *f* del zorro.

foxhunting ['fɒks,hʌntɪŋ] N caza *f* del zorro; **to go ~** ir a cazar zorros.

fox-terrier ['fɒks'terɪəʳ] N foxterrier *m*, perro *m* raposero, perro *m* zorrero.

foxtrot ['fɒkstrɒt] N fox *m*.

foxy ['fɒksɪ] ADJ taimado, astuto.

foyer ['fɔɪeɪ] N hall *m*, vestíbulo *m*; (*Theat*) foyer *m*.

FP (**a**) (*US*) ABBR *of* **fireplug** boca *f* de incendio. (**b**) N (*Brit*) ABBR *of* **former pupil**.

FPA N (*Brit*) ABBR *of* **Family Planning Association** Asociación *f* de Planificación Familiar.

Fr (*Rel*) (**a**) ABBR *of* **Father** Padre *m*, P., Pᵉ. (**b**) ABBR *of* **Friar** fray *m*, Fr.

fr. ABBR *of* **franc(s)** franco(s) *m*(*pl*), f.

fracas ['fræka:] N gresca *f*, riña *f*.

fractal ['fræktəl] (*Geometry*) **1** ADJ fractal; **~ geometry** geometría *f* fractal. **2** N fractal *m*.

fraction ['frækʃən] N (*Math*) fracción *f*, quebrado *m*; (*fig*) pequeña porción *f*, parte *f* muy pequeña; **for a ~ of a second** por un instante.

fractional ['frækʃənl] ADJ fraccionario; (*fig*) muy pequeño.

fractionally ['frækʃnəlɪ] ADV ligeramente.

fractious ['frækʃəs] ADJ (*character*) díscolo, displicente; *horse* rebelón; (*mood*) malhumorado.

fracture ['fræktʃəʳ] **1** N fractura *f*. **2** VT fracturar. **3** VI fracturarse.

fragile ['frædʒaɪl] ADJ frágil, quebradizo; *person* delicado.

fragility [frə'dʒɪlɪtɪ] N fragilidad *f*.

fragment **1** ['frægmənt] N fragmento *m*; trozo *m*; **to smash sth to ~s** hacer algo añicos. **2** [fræg'ment] VT fragmentar. **3** [fræg'ment] VI fragmentarse.

fragmentary [fræg'mentərɪ] ADJ fragmentario.

fragmentation [,frægmen'teɪʃən] N fragmentación *f*; **~ grenade** granada *f* de fragmentación.

fragmented [fræg'mentɪd] ADJ fragmentado.

fragrance ['freɪgrəns] N fragancia *f*.

fragrant ['freɪgrənt] ADJ fragante, oloroso; *memory* dulce.

frail [freɪl] ADJ frágil, quebradizo; delicado; (*Med*) débil; (*morally*) flaco, endeble.

frailty ['freɪltɪ] N fragilidad *f*; (*Med*) debilidad *f*; (*moral*) flaqueza *f*.

frame [freɪm] **1** N (**a**) (*framework*) estructura *f*, esqueleto *m*; (*Tech*) armazón *f*, bastidor *m*; (*Sew*) tambor *m*, bastidor *m* para bordar; (*of spectacles*) montura *f*, armadura *f*; (*of bicycle*) cuadro *m*; (*of picture, door, window*) marco *m*; (*Video*) cuadro *m*; **~ of reference** sistema *m* de referencias, sistema *m* de coordenadas; perspectiva *f* intelectual, marco *m* ideológico; **to put sb in the ~*** acusar a uno, delatar a uno. (**b**) (*body*) figura *f*, talle *m*; **his large ~** su cuerpo fornido; **her whole ~ was shaken by sobs** los sollozos sacudían su cuerpo entero. (**c**) **~ of mind** estado *m* de ánimo; **when you're in a better ~ of mind** cuando estés de mejor humor. **2** VT (**a**) (*construct*) construir; (*arrange*) disponer, arreglar; (*contrive*) idear; *sound* articular; *question etc* formular, expresar. (**b**) *picture* poner un marco a, enmarcar; (*fig*) servir de marco a; **he appeared ~d in the doorway** apareció en el marco de la puerta; **she was ~d against the sunset** el ocaso le servía de marco. (**c**) (*: *also* **to ~ up**) encasquetar, incriminar dolosamente; **I've been ~d!** ¡me han hecho trampa! **3** VI (**a**) **how is it framing?** ¿qué tal se está desarrollando?; **he's framing well** hace buenos progresos, promete. (**b**) **to ~ up to sb** ponerse en actitud para defenderse contra uno.

frame house ['freɪm,haʊs] N (*US*), PL **frame houses** ['freɪm,haʊzɪz] casa *f* de madera.

framer ['freɪməʳ] N (*also* **picture ~**) fabricante *mf* de marcos.

frame-up* ['freɪmʌp] N estratagema *f* para incriminar a uno; **it's a ~** aquí hay trampa.

framework ['freɪmwɜ:k] N (*Tech*) armazón *f*, esqueleto *m*; (*fig*) estructura *f*, sistema *m*, organización *f*, marco *m*; **within the ~ of the constitution** dentro del marco de la constitución.

framing ['freɪmɪŋ] N (**a**) (*also* **picture ~**) enmarcado *m*. (**b**) (*Art, Phot*) encuadrado *m*.

Fran [fræn] NF *familiar form of* **Frances**.

franc [fræŋk] N franco *m*.

France [frɑ:ns] N Francia *f*.

Frances ['frɑ:nsɪs] NF Francisca.

franchise ['fræntʃaɪz] N (**a**) (*Pol*) derecho *m* de votar, sufragio *m*. (**b**) (*Comm*) franquicia *f*; **~ holder** franquiciado *m*, -a *f*.

franchisee [,fræntʃaɪ'zi:] N franquiciado *m*, -a *f*, concesionario *m*, -a *f*.

franchising ['fræntʃaɪzɪŋ] N franquiciamiento *m*.

franchisor [,fræntʃaɪ'zɔ:ʳ] N franquiciador *m*, -ora *f*, (*compañía f*) concesionaria *f*.

Francis ['frɑ:nsɪs] NM Francisco.

Franciscan [fræn'sɪskən] **1** ADJ franciscano. **2** N franciscano *m*.

francium ['frænsɪəm] N francio *m*.

franco ['fræŋkəʊ] ADJ: **~ invoice** factura *f* franca.

Franco... ['fræŋkəʊ] PREFIX franco-; **~-British** franco-británico.

francophile ['fræŋkəʊfaɪl] N francófilo *m*, -a *f*.

francophobe ['fræŋkəʊfəʊb] N francófobo *m*, -a *f*.

frangipane ['frændʒɪpeɪn] N, **frangipani** [,frændʒɪ'pɑ:nɪ] N (*perfume, pastry*) frangipani *m*; (*shrub*) flor *f* de cebo, frangipani *m* blanco, jazmín *m* de las Antillas.

franglais ['frɑ̃'gleɪ] N (*hum*) franglés *m*.

Frank¹ [fræŋk] N (*Hist*) franco *m*.

Frank² [fræŋk] NM *familiar form of* **Francis**.

frank¹ [fræŋk] ADJ franco.

frank² [fræŋk] VT *letter* franquear.

Frankenstein ['fræŋkənstaɪn] NM Frankenstein.

frankfurter ['fræŋk,fɜ:təʳ] N salchicha *f*.

frankincense ['fræŋkɪnsens] N incienso *m*.

franking machine ['fræŋkɪŋmə'ʃi:n] N (máquina *f*) franqueadora *f*.

Frankish ['fræŋkɪʃ] **1** ADJ fráncico. **2** N fráncico *m*.

frankly ['fræŋklɪ] ADV francamente.

frankness ['fræŋknɪs] N franqueza *f*.

frantic ['fræntɪk] ADJ frenético, furioso; **to be ~ with worry** andar como loco de inquietud; **to drive sb ~** sacar a uno de quicio.

frantically ['fræntɪkəlɪ] ADV frenéticamente, con frenesí.

frat* [fræt] N (*US*) ABBR *of* **fraternity**; *ver también* SORORITY/FRATERNITY .

fraternal [frə'tɜ:nl] ADJ fraternal, fraterno.

fraternity [frə'tɜ:nɪtɪ] N fraternidad *f*; (*guild*) cofradía *f*; (*US*) club *m* de estudiantes; *ver también* SORORITY/FRATERNITY .

fraternization [,frætənaɪ'zeɪʃən] N fraternización *f*.

fraternize ['frætənaɪz] VI confraternizar (*with* con), fraternizar (*with* con).

fratricide ['frætrɪsaɪd] N (**a**) (*act*) fratricidio *m*. (**b**) (*person*) fratricida *m*.

fraud [frɔ:d] **1** N (**a**) fraude *m*; estafa *f*, trampa *f*. (**b**) (*person*)

impostor *m*, -ora *f*, farsante *m*.
  2 ATTR: **~ squad** grupo *m* de estafas, brigada *f* de delitos monetarios.
fraudster* ['frɔːdstər] N defraudador *m*, -ora *f*.
fraudulence ['frɔːdjʊləns] N fraudulencia *f*, fraude *m*.
fraudulent ['frɔːdjʊlənt] ADJ fraudulento; **~ conversion** apropiación *f* ilícita.
fraught [frɔːt] ADJ **(a)** tenso, lleno de tensión; difícil; **things got a bit ~** la situación se puso difícil. **(b) ~ with** cargado de, lleno de.
fray¹ [freɪ] N combate *m*, lucha *f*; refriega *f*; **to be ready for the ~** tener ganas de pelear; **to gird o.s. for the ~** aprestarse para la lucha.
fray² [freɪ] 1 VT desgastar, raer; *nerves* destrozar, crispar.
  2 VI deshilacharse; **to ~ against, to ~ on** ludir con, rozar.
frayed [freɪd] ADJ raído, dishilachado; *nerves* crispado, de punta; **tempers were getting ~** todos estaban a punto de perder la paciencia.
frazzle* ['fræzl] 1 N: **to beat sb to a ~** (*Sport*) cascar a uno*, derrotar a uno por completo; **it was burned to a ~** quedó carbonizado; **to be worn to a ~** estar hecho un trapo*.
  2 VT (*US*) agotar, rendir; reventar*.
FRB N (*US*) ABBR of **Federal Reserve Bank** Banco *m* de Reserva Federal.
FRCM N (*Brit*) ABBR of **Fellow of the Royal College of Music.**
FRCO N (*Brit*) ABBR of **Fellow of the Royal College of Organists.**
FRCP N (*Brit*) ABBR of **Fellow of the Royal College of Physicians.**
FRCS N (*Brit*) ABBR of **Fellow of the Royal College of Surgeons.**
freak [friːk] 1 N **(a)** (*abnormal specimen*) monstruo *m*, monstruosidad *f*; curiosidad *f*, rareza *f*; ejemplar *m* anormal; (*Bio*) mutación *f*; **the result was a ~** el resultado fue totalmente imprevisible, el resultado se debió a una chiripa.
  (b) (*whim*) capricho *m*.
  (c) (*) (*person*) fenómeno *m*; (*mad*) chalado* *m*, -a *f*, chiflado* *m*, -a *f*; (*oddly dressed*) adefesio *m*; **peace ~*** fanático *m*, -a *f* de la paz; **V Jesus.**
  2 ADJ = **freakish.**
◆**freak out:** 1 VT afectar mucho; impresionar de mala manera, dejar frío.
  2 VI desmadrarse; marginarse; abandonarlo todo; (*on drugs*) ir de viaje*, hacer el viaje*.
freakish ['friːkɪʃ] ADJ **(a)** *specimen* anormal, monstruoso; *result* inesperado, imprevisible, fortuito. **(b)** *person* caprichoso.
freak-out* ['friːkaʊt] N desmadre *m*; (*party*) fiesta *f* loca*; (*on drug*) viaje* *m*.
freaky* ['friːkɪ] ADJ raro, estrafalario.
freckle ['frekl] N peca *f*.
freckled ['frekld] ADJ, **freckly** ['freklɪ] ADJ pecoso, lleno de pecas.
Fred [fred], **Freddie, Freddy** ['fredɪ] NM *familiar forms of* **Frederick.**
Frederick ['fredrɪk] NM Federico.
free [friː] 1 ADJ **(a)** (*at liberty etc*) libre (*from, of* de); (*not fixed*) suelto, libre; (*untied*) libre, desatado; *account, choice, translation, verse* libre; *port* franco; **~ agent** persona *f* independiente; **to be a ~ agent** poder actuar libremente; **F~ Church** (*Brit*) Iglesia *f* libre, Iglesia *f* independiente; **~ collective bargaining** ≈ negociación *f* colectiva entre sindicatos y patronal; **~ composition** ejercicio *m* (de expresión escrita) de carácter libre; **~ enterprise** libre empresa *f*, libertad *f* de empresa; **~-enterprise economy** economía *f* de libre empresa; **~ fall** (*Space*) caída *f* libre; **~ fight** sarracina *f*, riña *f* general; **~ flight** vuelo *m* a motor parado; **~ format** formato *m* libre; **~ hit** tiro *m* (or lanzamiento *m*) directo; **~ kick** golpe *m* franco, golpe *m* libre; **~ labour** trabajadores *mpl* no sindicados; **~ love** amor *m* libre; **~ market** mercado *m* libre (*in* de); **~ pass** permiso *m* para entrada gratuita; **~ period** (*Educ*) hora *f* libre; **~ port** puerto *m* franco; **~ post** correo *m* libre de franqueo; **~ school** escuela *f* libre; **~ speech** libertad *f* de palabra, libertad *f* de expresión; **~ trade** libre cambio *m*; **~ trader** librecambista *mf*; **~-trade zone** zona *f* franca; **~ of duty** libre de derechos de aduana; **~ surface** superficie *f* libre; **~ from dust** una superficie libre de polvo; **the fishing is ~** la pesca está autorizada; **the area is ~ of malaria** no hay paludismo en la región; **to be ~ to + *infin*** poder libremente + *infin*, ser libre de + *infin*; **he is not ~ to act** tiene las manos atadas; **we are ~ of him at last** por fin nos hemos librado de él; **to break ~** soltarse; **to let sb go ~** poner en libertad a uno; **to set ~** *person* poner en libertad, libertar, librar; *slave* manumitir, emancipar; *animal* soltar.
  (b) (*not occupied*) libre; *post* vacante; *premises* desocupado; **is this table ~?** ¿está libre esta mesa?; **are you ~ tomorrow?** ¿estás libre mañana?
  (c) (*improper*) *language etc* libre, desvergonzado; (*insolent*) descarado; **~ and easy** despreocupado, poco ceremonioso.
  (d) (*generous*) **to be ~ with** ser liberal con, no regatear; dar en abundancia; **to be ~ with one's money** gastar libremente, no reparar en gastos; **he's very ~ in blaming others** echa muy fácilmente la culpa a otros; **he's too ~ with his remarks** es demasiado libre en sus comentarios; **to be ~ with one's hands** (*stealing*) ser largo de manos, (*amorously*) ser tocotón; **to make ~ of** (or **with**) usar como si fuera cosa propia.

(e) (*for nothing*) gratuito; *ticket* de favor; **~ of charge** gratis; (*Comm*) gratuito, libre de cargo; **admission ~** entrada gratis; **catalogue ~ on request** el catálogo se envía gratis a petición; **~ on board** (*Comm*) franco a bordo; **to get sth for ~*** obtener algo gratis.
  2 ADV gratis.
  3 VT (*set free*) poner en libertad, libertar; *slave* manumitir; *animal* soltar; (*untie*) desatar, soltar; *knot, tangle* desenredar; *place, surface etc* despejar, desembarazar (*of* de); (*rescue*) librar, salvar (*from* de), rescatar; (*from burden, tax etc*) eximir, exentar (*from* de).
  4 VR: **to ~ o.s.** desatarse, soltarse.
◆**free up** VT *funds, resources* hacer disponible.
-free [friː] ADJ: *e.g.* **additive~** sin aditivos; **duty~** libre de impuestos; **lead~** sin plomo.
freebase* ['friːbeɪs] N (*Drugs*) crack *m*⁑.
freebie* ['friːbɪ] 1 ADJ gratuito.
  2 N comida *f* (or bebida *f* etc) gratuita, ganga *f*; **it's a ~** es gratis.
freebooter ['friːbuːtər] N filibustero *m*.
freedom ['friːdəm] 1 N libertad *f*; exención *f* (*from* de), inmunidad *f* (*from* contra); (*ease*) facilidad *f*, soltura *f*; **~ of a city** ciudadanía *f* de honor; **~ of action** libertad *f* de acción; **~ of association** libertad *f* de asociación; **F~ of Information Act** (*US*) ley *f* del derecho a la información; **~ of the press** libertad *f* de prensa; **~ of speech** libertad *f* de palabra, libertad *f* de expresión; **~ of worship** libertad *f* de cultos.
  2 ATTR: **~ fighter** luchador *m*, -ora *f* por la libertad.

┌─── **FREEDOM OF INFORMATION ACT** ───┐

i   El **Freedom of Information Act** o **FOIA** es la ley estadounidense del derecho a la información, que obliga a los organismos federales a proporcionar información sobre sus actividades a cualquiera que lo solicite, lo que resulta muy útil, sobre todo a los periodistas. Esta información debe ser facilitada por el Estado en un plazo de diez días laborables y, en caso de que no se acceda a la solicitud, esta decisión tiene que ser debidamente justificada. Los motivos para retener la información pueden ser varios, entre ellos el que se ponga en peligro la seguridad nacional, se revelen secretos comerciales o que la información afecte a la vida privada de los ciudadanos. Entre otras noticias, el **FOIA** ha hecho posible la publicación de información anteriormente catalogada como secreta sobre asuntos de extrema importancia, como la guerra de Vietnam y las actividades de espionaje ilegal del **FBI.**

free-floating ['friː'fləʊtɪŋ] ADJ libre, que flota libremente.
freefone ['friːfəʊn] N = **Freephone.**
free-for-all ['friːfə'rɔːl] N sarracina *f*, riña *f* general, refriega *f*, barullo *m*.
free-form ['friːfɔːm] ADJ (*Art, Mus*) de estilo libre.
freehand ['friːhænd] ADJ hecho a pulso.
freehold ['friːhəʊld] (*Brit*) 1 ADJ: **~ property** = **2.**
  2 N feudo *m* franco, alodio *m*, propiedad *f* absoluta.
freeholder ['friː,həʊldər] N (*Brit*) poseedor *m*, -ora *f* de feudo franco.
freeing ['friːɪŋ] N puesta *f* en libertad.
freelance ['friːlɑːns] 1 ADJ independiente, autónomo, de libre dedicación.
  2 N periodista *mf* etc independiente; persona *f* de libre dedicación, informador *m*, -ora *f* etc) por libre, francotirador *m*, -ora *f*.
  3 VI ir por libre, trabajar por libre, trabajar por cuenta propia.
freeloader* ['friːləʊdər] N (*US*) gorrón *m*, invitadizo *m*.
freely ['friːlɪ] ADV libremente; (*generously*) liberalmente; *confess, speak etc* francamente; **you may come and go ~** Vd puede ir y venir con toda libertad.
freeman ['friːmən] N, PL **freemen** ['friːmən] (*Hist*) hombre *m* libre; (*of city*) ciudadano *m* de honor.
freemason ['friː,meɪsn] N masón *m*, francmasón *m*.
freemasonry ['friː,meɪsnrɪ] N masonería *f*, francmasonería *f*; (*fig*) compañerismo *m*, camaradería *f*.
Freephone ['friːfəʊn] ® N (*Brit Telec*) ≈ llamada *f* telefónica sin cargo al usuario.
free-range ['friːreɪndʒ] ATTR: **~ eggs** huevos *mpl* de granja, huevos *mpl* de corral; **~ poultry** aves *fpl* de granja.
free-ranging ['friː'reɪndʒɪŋ] ADJ *discussion* sobre temas muy diversos; sin conclusiones preconcebidas; *role* libre, amplio.
freesia ['friːzɪə] N fresia *f*.
free-standing ['friː'stændɪŋ] ADJ independiente.
freestyle ['friːstaɪl] ADJ: **200 metres ~** 200 metros libres; **~ race** carrera *f* de estilo libre; **~ wrestling** lucha *f* libre.
freethinker ['friː'θɪŋkər] N librepensador *m*, -ora *f*.
freethinking ['friː'θɪŋkɪŋ] 1 ADJ librepensador.
  2 N librepensamiento *m*.
freeway ['friːweɪ] N (*US*) autopista *f*.
freewheel ['friː'wiːl] (*Brit*) 1 N rueda *f* libre.
  2 VI (*cyclist*) andar a rueda libre, (*Aut*) ir en punto muerto.
freewheeling ['friː,wiːlɪŋ] ADJ *discussion* desenvuelto; (*free*) libre,

espontáneo; (*careless*) irresponsable.

freewill ['friː'wɪl] N libre albedrío *m*.

freeze [friːz] (*irr*: PRET **froze**, PTP **frozen**) **1** VT helar; *food, prices, wages etc, video* congelar; **we're simply frozen** estamos francamente helados.

2 VI helarse; congelarse; (*fig*) quedar helado (de miedo *etc*); (*remain motionless*) quedarse rígido, permanecer enteramente inmóvil; **I'm freezing** estoy helado; **it's freezing** hay helada, hiela; (*fig*) hace un frío glacial; **to ~ to death** morir de frío; **the smile froze on his lips** se le heló la sonrisa en los labios; **it will ~ tonight** esta noche habrá helada.

3 N helada *f*; ola *f* de frío; (*of prices, wages etc*) congelación *f*.

◆**freeze out** VT *competitor* marginar.

◆**freeze over** VI helarse; congelarse; **the lake has frozen over** el lago está helado.

◆**freeze up 1** VT helar; **we're frozen up at home** en casa las cañerías están heladas.

2 VI = **freeze over**.

freeze-dried [ˌfriːz'draɪd] ADJ deshidratado por congelación, liofilizado.

freeze-dry [ˌfriːz'draɪ] VT deshidratar por congelación, liofilizar.

freezer ['friːzər] N congelador *m*, (ultra)congelador *m*, congeladora *f* (*LAm*).

freeze-up ['friːzʌp] N helada *f*, ola *f* de frío.

freezing ['friːzɪŋ] **1** ADJ glacial (*also fig*), helado; **~ mixture** mezcla *f* refrigerante.

2 ADV: **it's ~ cold** hace un frío glacial.

3 N (a) (*deep ~*) (ultra)congelación *f*; (*of rents etc*) congelación *f*. (b) = **freezing-point**.

freezing-point ['friːzɪŋpɔɪnt] N punto *m* de congelación; **5 degrees below ~** 5 grados bajo cero.

freight [freɪt] **1** N flete *m*; (*load*) carga *f*; (*goods*) mercancías *fpl*; (*esp Brit: ship's cargo*) flete *m*; **to send sth (by) ~** enviar algo por flete.

2 (*as ADV*) **~ collect** (*US*), **~ forward** flete *m* por cobrar, porte *m* por cobrar; **~ free** franco de porte; **~ inward** flete *m* sobre compras; **~ paid** porte *m* pagado.

3 VT enviar por flete.

freightage ['freɪtɪdʒ] N flete *m*.

freight-car ['freɪtkɑːr] N (*US*) vagón *m* de mercancías.

freight charges ['freɪtˌtʃɑːdʒɪz] NPL gastos *mpl* de transporte.

freighter ['freɪtər] N (a) (*Naut*) buque *m* de carga, nave *f* de mercancías. (b) (*person: carrier*) transportista *m*; (*agent*) fletador *m*.

freight forwarder ['freɪtˌfɔːwədər] N agente *m* expedidor.

freightliner ['freɪtˌlaɪnər] N tren *m* de mercancías de contenedores.

freight-plane ['freɪtˌpleɪn] N avión *m* de transporte de mercancías.

freight terminal ['freɪtˌtɜːmɪnl] N terminal *f* de mercancías, (*Aer*) terminal *f* de carga.

freight-train ['freɪtˌtreɪn] N (*US*) (tren *m*) mercancías *m*.

freight-yard ['freɪtˌjɑːd] N área *f* de carga.

French [frentʃ] **1** ADJ francés *m*; **~ bean** judía *f* enana, fríjol *m*; **~ bread** pan *m* francés; **~ chalk** jaboncillo *m* de sastre, esteatita *f*; **~ door** (*US*) puertaventana *f*; **~ dressing** vinagreta *f*; **~ fried potatoes**, **~ fries** (*US*) patatas *fpl* (*LAm*: papas *fpl*) fritas; **~ horn** trompa *f* de llaves; **~ kiss** beso *m* de tornillo; **~ leave** despedida *f* a la francesa; **~ letter** condón *m*; **~ loaf** barra *f* de pan francés; **~ pastry** pastelito *m* relleno de nata (or frutas); **~ polish** laca *f*; **~ toast** (*Brit: toast*) tostada *f* tostada sólo por un lado; (*bread fried in egg*) torrija *f*; **~ windows** puertaventanas *fpl*.

2 N (a) **the ~** los franceses. (b) (*Ling*) francés *m*; **pardon my ~*** perdona la palabra.

French-Canadian ['frentʃkə'neɪdɪən] **1** ADJ francocanadiense.

2 N (a) francocanadiense *mf*. (b) (*Ling*) francés *m* canadiense.

French Guiana [ˌfrentʃgɑɪ'ænə] N Guayana *f* Francesa.

Frenchified ['frentʃɪfaɪd] ADJ afrancesado.

Frenchman ['frentʃmən] N, PL **Frenchmen** ['frentʃmən] francés *m*.

French-polish [ˌfrentʃ'pɒlɪʃ] VT (*Brit*) laquear.

French Riviera ['frentʃˌrɪvɪ'eərə] N la Riviera *f*.

French-speaking ['frentʃˌspiːkɪŋ] ADJ francófono, francohablante, de habla francesa.

Frenchwoman ['frentʃˌwʊmən] N, PL **Frenchwomen** ['frentʃˌwɪmɪn] francesa *f*.

Frenchy* ['frentʃɪ] N gabacho* *m*, -a *f*, francés *m*, -esa *f*.

frenetic [frɪ'netɪk] ADJ frenético.

frenzied ['frenzɪd] ADJ *effort etc* frenético; *crowd etc* enloquecido.

frenzy ['frenzɪ] N frenesí *m*, delirio *m*.

frequency ['friːkwənsɪ] **1** N frecuencia *f* (*also Elec*); **high ~** alta frecuencia *f*; **low ~** baja frecuencia *f*.

2 ATTR: **~ band** banda *f* de frecuencia; **~ distribution** distribución *f* de frecuencia; **~ modulation** frecuencia *f* modulada; **~ sweeper** barredor *m* de frecuencia.

frequent 1 ['friːkwənt] ADJ frecuente.

2 [frɪ'kwent] VT frecuentar.

frequentative [frɪ'kwentətɪv] **1** ADJ frecuentativo.

2 N frecuentativo *m*.

frequenter [frɪ'kwentər] N frecuentador *m*, -ora *f* (*of* de).

frequently ['friːkwəntlɪ] ADV frecuentemente, con frecuencia, a menudo.

fresco ['freskəʊ] N, PL **fresco(e)s** ['freskəʊz] fresco *m*.

fresh [freʃ] ADJ (a) (*new*) nuevo; **~ paint** (*US*) recién pintado; **to start a ~ life** comenzar una vida nueva; **he has had a ~ attack** ha sufrido un nuevo ataque; **it is ~ in my memory** se conserva muy fresco en mi memoria; **to put ~ courage into sb** reanimar a uno.

(b) (*newly come*) **~ from Spain** recién llegado (*or* importado *etc*) de España; **~ from the oven** acabadito de salir del horno.

(c) (*inexperienced*) nuevo.

(d) (*not stale*) *fruit etc* fresco; *bread* nuevo, tierno; *vegetable* natural; *air* fresco, puro (*and V* **air**); *water* dulce; **as ~ as a daisy** tan fresco como una rosa; **to feel perfectly ~** estar lleno de vigor.

(e) (*: *cheeky*) fresco*, descocado*; **to get ~ with sb** ponerse fresco con uno*.

(f) (*cool*) fresco.

(g) *wind* recio.

(h) *face, complexion* de buen color.

fresh-air fiend* [ˌfreʃ'ɛəˌfiːnd] N: **he's a ~** siempre quiere estar al aire libre.

freshen ['freʃn] **1** VT refrescar.

2 VI (*temperature*) refrescarse; (*wind*) soplar más recio; (*person*) lavarse, arreglarse.

◆**freshen up 1** VT = **freshen 1**.

2 VI (*person*) lavarse, arreglarse.

freshener ['freʃnər] N: **air ~** ambientador *m*; **skin ~** tónico *m* para la piel.

fresher* ['freʃər] N (*Brit*) = **freshman**.

fresh-faced ['freʃfeɪst] ADJ (a) (*youthful-looking*) lozano, saludable. (b) (*inexperienced*) sin experiencia, nuevo.

freshly ['freʃlɪ] ADV nuevamente; recientemente; **~ made** nuevo, recién hecho, acabado de hacer.

freshman ['freʃmən] N, PL **freshmen** ['freʃmən] (a) (*Scol, Univ*) estudiante *mf* de primer año. (b) (*beginner*) novato *m*, -a *f*; *ver también* GRADE.

freshness ['freʃnɪs] N frescura *f*; lozanía *f*; (*newness*) novedad *f*; vigor *m*.

freshwater ['freʃˌwɔːtər] ADJ de agua dulce; **~ fish** pez *m* de agua dulce.

fret¹ [fret] **1** VT (a) (*wear away*) corroer, raer, desgastar.

(b) *person* irritar, molestar.

(c) **to ~ the hours away** pasar las horas consumiéndose de inquietud.

2 VI inquietarse, apurarse; impacientarse (*at* por); **it's ~ting for its mother** se está apurando por la ausencia de su madre; **don't ~!** ¡no te apures!

3 N: **to be in a ~** estar muy inquieto, apurarse.

fret² [fret] N (*for guitar*) traste *m*.

fretful ['fretfʊl] ADJ displicente, quejoso; impaciente; inquieto.

fretfully ['fretfəlɪ] ADV impacientemente; inquietamente.

fretfulness ['fretfʊlnɪs] N displicencia *f*; impaciencia *f*; inquietud *f*.

fretsaw ['fretsɔː] N sierra *f* de calados.

fretwork ['fretwɜːk] N calado *m*.

Freudian ['frɔɪdɪən] ADJ freudiano; **~ slip** desliz *m* freudiano.

FRG N (*Hist*) ABBR *of* **Federal Republic of Germany** República *f* Federal de Alemania, RFA *f*.

Fri. ABBR *of* **Friday** viernes *m*, vier.

friable ['fraɪəbl] ADJ friable, desmenuzable.

friar ['fraɪər] N (a) fraile *m*; **black ~** dominico *m*; **grey ~** franciscano *m*; **white ~** carmelita *m*. (b) (*before name*) fray.

friary ['fraɪərɪ] N monasterio *m*.

fribie* ['friːbɪ] N (*US*) = **freebie**.

fricassee ['frɪkəsiː] N fricandó *m*, fricasé *m*.

fricative ['frɪkətɪv] **1** ADJ fricativo.

2 N fricativa *f*.

friction ['frɪkʃən] **1** N (a) (*Tech*) fricción *f*, rozamiento *m*; (*Med etc*) frote *m*, frotamiento *m*. (b) (*fig*) tirantez *f*, desavenencia *f* (*about, over* con motivo de).

2 ATTR: **~ feed** alimentación *f* por fricción, avance *m* por fricción.

Friday ['fraɪdɪ] N viernes *m*; **Good ~** Viernes *m* Santo.

fridge* [frɪdʒ] N (*Brit*) frigo *m*, nevera *f*, heladera *f* (*SC*), refrigeradora *f* (*LAm*).

fridge-freezer ['frɪdʒˌfriːzər] N frigorífico-congelador *m*.

fried [fraɪd] ADJ frito; **~ egg** huevo *m* frito, huevo *m* estrellado (*LAm*).

friend [frend] N amigo *m*, -a *f*; **F~** (*Rel*) cuáquero *m*, -a *f*; **~s** amigos *mpl*, amistades *fpl*; **~!** (*Mil*) ¡gente de paz!; **a ~ of mine** un amigo mío; **he's no ~ of mine** no es uno de mis amigos; **he is no ~ to violence** no es partidario de la violencia; **we're the best of ~s** somos muy amigos; **to be ~s with sb** ser amigo de uno; **to have a ~ at**

court tener el padre alcalde, tener enchufe; **to make ~s with sb** hacerse amigo de uno, trabar amistad con uno; **he makes ~s easily** hace amigos con facilidad.

friendless ['frendlɪs] ADJ sin amigos.

friendliness ['frendlɪnɪs] N simpatía f; amabilidad f; cordialidad f; lo acogedor.

friendly ['frendlɪ] **1** ADJ **(a)** person simpático; amable; **people here are very ~** aquí la gente es muy simpática; **he's a ~ soul** es simpatiquísimo; **your ~ neighbourhood policeman** el simpático guardia urbano que vigila su barrio; **to be ~ with** ser amigo de; **to get ~** hacerse amigos.
(b) relationship, greeting, tone amistoso, cordial; shout jovial; atmosphere, place acogedor; match amistoso; nation amigo; **~ fire** fuego m amigo; **~ society** (Brit) mutualidad f, sociedad f de socorro mutuo, montepío m; **that wasn't a very ~ thing to do** eso no fue la acción de un amigo.
2 N (Sport) partido m amistoso.

-friendly ['frendlɪ] SUF que no daña, que no perjudica, que no afecta a, eg **environment~** que no daña al medio ambiente, ecológico; V **user~** etc.

friendship ['frendʃɪp] N amistad f; (US) compañerismo m.

Friesian ['friːʒən] = **Frisian**.

Friesland ['friːzlənd] N Frisia f.

frieze [friːz] N friso m.

frig⁑ [frɪg] VI: **to ~ about** or **around** hacer gilipolleces⁑, joder⁑⁑.

frigate ['frɪgɪt] N fragata f.

frigging⁑ ['frɪgɪŋ] **1** ADJ: **do I need to do every ~ thing myself!** ¿por qué porras tengo que hacerlo yo todo?⁑; **it's a ~ nuisance!** ¡es un coñazo!⁑. **2** ADV: **she's so ~ lazy!** ¡es una vaga de la hostia!⁑.

fright [fraɪt] N **(a)** (sudden fear) susto m, sobresalto m; (state of alarm) terror m; **what a ~ you gave me!** ¡qué susto me diste!; **to have a ~** tener un susto, llevarse un susto; **to take ~** asustarse (at de).
(b) (*: person) espantajo m; **doesn't she look a ~?** ¡qué adefesio de mujer!

frighten ['fraɪtn] VT asustar, espantar, sobresaltar; alarmar; **to be ~ed** tener miedo (of a); **don't be ~ed!** ¡no te asustes!; **she is easily ~ed** es asustadiza; **to ~ sb into doing sth** obligar a uno a hacer algo infundiéndole miedo, amenazar a uno para que haga algo.
◆**frighten away, frighten off** VT ahuyentar, espantar.

frighteners⁑ ['fraɪtnəz] NPL: **to put the ~ on sb** meterle a uno el ombligo para dentro*.

frightening ['fraɪtnɪŋ] ADJ espantoso, aterrador.

frighteningly ['fraɪtnɪŋlɪ] ADV thin alarmantemente; ugly espantosamente; expensive, uncertain terriblemente.

frightful ['fraɪtfʊl] ADJ espantoso, horrible, horroroso; (very bad) horrible, malísimo.

frightfully ['fraɪtfəlɪ] ADV (fig) terriblemente, tremendamente; **it's ~ hard** es terriblemente difícil; **it's ~ good** es la mar de bueno; **I'm ~ sorry** lo siento muchísimo, lo siento en el alma.

frightfulness ['fraɪtfʊlnɪs] N horror m.

frigid ['frɪdʒɪd] ADJ frío; (Med) frígido; atmosphere, look etc glacial.

frigidity [frɪ'dʒɪdɪtɪ] N frialdad f; (Med) frigidez f.

frill [frɪl] N lechuga f, volante m; **~s** (fig) adornos mpl; **~s and furbelows** encajes mpl y puntillas fpl; **a package holiday without ~s** unas vacaciones de paquete sin adornos.

frilly ['frɪlɪ] ADJ con volantes, con adornos.

Fringe [frɪndʒ] N (Brit) (also **~ Festival, Festival ~**) festival alternativo de Edimburgo; ver también EDINBURGH FESTIVAL .

fringe [frɪndʒ] **1** N **(a)** (Sew) franja f, orla f, borde m; (Brit: hair) flequillo m.
(b) (edge) margen m; **the outer ~s of the city** las periferias, las partes exteriores de la ciudad; **on the ~s of the lake** en los bordes del lago; **to live on the ~ of society** vivir al margen de la sociedad.
(c) (social) elementos mpl periféricos, elementos mpl marginales.
2 ATTR: **~ benefits** beneficios mpl complementarios, complementos mpl; **~ group** grupo m marginal; **~ organization** organización f marginal, organización f no oficial; **~ theatre** (Brit) teatro m periférico, teatro m experimental.

frippery ['frɪpərɪ] N perifollos mpl, perejiles mpl.

Frisbee ['frɪzbɪ] ® N disco m volador.

Frisian ['frɪʒən] **1** ADJ frisio; **~ Islands** Islas fpl Frisias.
2 N **(a)** frisio m, -a f.
(b) (Ling) frisio m.

frisk [frɪsk] **1** VT cachear, registrar.
2 VI (also **to ~ about**) retozar, juguetear, brincar.

friskiness ['frɪskɪnɪs] N vivacidad f.

frisky ['frɪskɪ] ADJ retozón, juguetón; horse fogoso; **he's pretty ~ still** sigue bastante activo.

frisson ['friːsɒn] N repelús m.

fritter¹ ['frɪtə*] N fruta f de sartén, buñuelo m.

fritter² ['frɪtə*] VT (also **to ~ away**) desperdiciar, disipar.

frivolity [frɪ'vɒlɪtɪ] N frivolidad f, informalidad f, ligereza f.

frivolous ['frɪvələs] ADJ frívolo, poco formal, ligero.

frizz [frɪz], **frizzle** ['frɪzl] **1** N rizos mpl pequeños y muy apretados.
2 VT rizar con rizos pequeños y muy apretados.

frizz(l)y ['frɪz(l)ɪ] ADJ muy ensortijado, crespo, frito*.

fro [frəʊ] ADV: **to and ~** de un lado a otro, de aquí para allá; **to and ~ movement** vaivén m.

frock [frɒk] N vestido m.

frock-coat ['frɒk'kəʊt] N levita f.

Frog* [frɒg] N, **Froggy*** ['frɒgɪ] N gabacho* m, -a f, francés m, -esa f.

frog [frɒg] N rana f; **to have a ~ in one's throat** tener carraspera.

frogging ['frɒgɪŋ] N alamares mpl.

frogman ['frɒgmən] N, PL **frogmen** ['frɒgmən] hombre-rana m, submarinista m.

frog-march ['frɒgmɑːtʃ] VT llevar codo con codo, llevar a la fuerza (cogidos los brazos).

frogspawn ['frɒgspɔːn] N huevas fpl de rana.

frolic ['frɒlɪk] **1** N juego m alegre; (party) fiesta f, holgorio m; (prank) travesura f.
2 VI juguetear, retozar; divertirse (with con).

frolicsome ['frɒlɪksəm] ADJ retozón, juguetón; (mischievous) travieso.

from [frɒm] PREP **(a)** de; **~ A to Z** de A a Z, desde A hasta Z; **~ door to door** de puerta en puerta; **~ £2 upwards** desde 2 libras en adelante; **he had gone ~ home** se había ido de su casa; **to pick sb ~ the crowd** escoger a uno de la multitud.
(b) (time) **~ Friday** a partir del viernes; **~ a child** desde niño; **~ that time** desde aquel momento.
(c) (deprivation) **to take sth ~ sb** quitar algo a uno; **he stole the book ~ me** me robó el libro; **I'll buy it ~ you** te lo compraré.
(d) (against) **to shelter ~ the rain** abrigarse de la lluvia.
(e) (distinguishing) **to know good ~ bad** saber distinguir entre el bien y el mal, saber distinguir el bien del mal.
(f) (originating) **the train ~ Madrid** el tren de Madrid, el tren procedente de Madrid; **he comes ~ Segovia** es de Segovia; **where are you ~?** ¿de dónde es Vd?; **a message ~ him** un mensaje de parte de él; **tell him that ~ me** dile eso de parte mía; **one of the best performances we have seen ~ him** uno de los mejores papeles que le hayamos visto; **to drink ~ a cup** beber de una taza; **we learned it ~ him** lo aprendimos de él; **we learned it ~ a book** lo aprendimos en un libro.
(g) (because of) **~ what he says** por lo que dice, según lo que dice; **to act ~ conviction** obrar por convicción; **~ sheer necessity** por pura necesidad; **to die ~ a fever** morir de una fiebre; **he is tired ~ overwork** está cansado por exceso de trabajo.
(h) **~ above** desde encima; **~ afar** desde lejos; **~ among** de entre.

fromage frais ['frɒmɑːʒ'freɪ] N queso fresco descremado.

frond [frɒnd] N fronda f.

front [frʌnt] **1** ADJ **(a)** (gen) delantero, anterior; (first) primero; **~ bench(es)** (Brit Parl) escaños mpl de los ministros (y del gobierno en la sombra); **~ desk** (US) recepción f de un hotel; **~ door** puerta f principal, puerta f de entrada; **~ garden** jardín m delante de la casa; **~ line** primera línea f; **~ matter** preliminares mpl; **~ money** capital m inicial; **~ page** primera página f, (of newspaper) primera plana f; **~ room** (lit) cuarto m que da a la calle, (freq) salón m; **~ row** primera fila f; **~ runner** corredor m, -ora f que va en cabeza; (candidate) favorito m, -a f; **~ seat** asiento m delantero; **~ tooth** incisivo m; **~ vowel** vocal f frontal; **~ wheel** rueda f delantera.
(b) **~ elevation** alzado m frontal; **~ view** vista f de frente.
2 N **(a)** frente m (also Mil, Pol, Met); (forepart) parte f delantera, parte f anterior; (of house) fachada f; (of book, start) principio m; (of shirt etc) pechera f; (Theat) auditorio m; (Brit: beach) playa f, (promenade) paseo m marítimo; **on Brighton ~** en la playa de Brighton; **cold ~** frente m frío; **popular ~** frente m popular; **at** (or **in**) **the ~ of the book** al principio del libro; **in ~** delante; **in ~ of** delante de; **to be in ~** ir primero, ir delante, (in race) ir en cabeza; **to come to the ~** empezar a destacar; **to push one's way to the ~** abrirse camino a empujones hasta la primera fila (etc); **to send sb on in ~** enviar a uno por delante; see also **up~**.
(b) (fig) apariencias fpl; **it's all just ~ with him** con él no son más que apariencias; **to put on a bold ~** hacer de tripas corazón.
(c) (Pol etc) fachada f; tapadera f (for de); **~ organization** organización f fachada; **it's merely a ~ organization** sólo es una tapadera; **~ for subversion** tapadera f de la subversión.
3 ADV: **eyes ~!** (Mil) ¡ojos al frente!
4 VT (TV etc) programme presentar; organization liderar; illegal body servir de fachada (or tapadera) a; band ser el vocalista principal en.
5 VI **(a)** **to ~ for** illegal body servir de fachada (or tapadera) a. **(b)** **to ~ on** (to) dar a, estar enfrente de.

⌐ FRONT BENCH ¬

(i) *El término genérico* **front bench** *se usa para referirse a los escaños situados en primera fila a ambos lados del Presidente (Speaker) de la Cámara de los Comunes del Parlamento británico. Dichos escaños son*

*ocupados por los parlamentarios que son miembros del gobierno a un lado y por los del gobierno en la sombra (**shadow cabinet**) al otro y, por esta razón, se les conoce como **frontbenchers**.*
⇨ *Ver también* BACKBENCHER , SHADOW CABINET

frontage ['frʌntɪdʒ] N fachada *f*.
frontal ['frʌntl] ADJ frontal; *attack* de frente.
frontbencher ['frʌnt'bentʃəʳ] N (*Brit Parl*) parlamentario *miembro del gobierno o del gobierno en la sombra*; *ver también* FRONT BENCH .
front-end ['frʌnt,end] ATTR: ~ **costs** gastos *mpl* iniciales; ~ **processor** procesador *m* frontal.
frontier ['frʌntɪəʳ] [1] N frontera *f*; **to push back the ~s of knowledge** ampliar los conocimientos (científicos *etc*), ensanchar el horizonte del conocimiento.
[2] ATTR fronterizo; ~ **dispute** conflicto *m* fronterizo; ~ **post** puesto *m* de frontera.
frontiersman [frʌn'tɪəzmən] N, PL **frontiersmen** [frʌn'tɪəzmən] hombre *m* de la frontera.
frontispiece ['frʌntɪspiːs] N frontispicio *m*.
front-line ['frʌntlaɪn] ADJ troops, news de primera línea; *countries, areas* fronterizo a una zona en guerra.
front-loader [,frʌnt'ləʊdəʳ] N (*also* **front-loading washing machine**) lavadora *f* de carga frontal.
front-loading ['frʌnt'ləʊdɪŋ] ATTR de carga frontal.
frontman ['frʌntmæn] N, PL **frontmen** ['frʌntmen] (*TV etc*) presentador *m*.
front-page ['frʌnt'peɪdʒ] ADJ de primera página, de primera plana; ~ **news** noticias *fpl* de primera plana.
frontwards ['frʌntwədz] ADV de frente, con la parte delantera primero.
front-wheel ['frʌntwiːl] ATTR: ~ **drive** tracción *f* delantera.
frost [frɒst] [1] N helada *f*; (*visible, also* **hoar ~, white ~**) escarcha *f*; **4 degrees of ~** (*Brit*) 4 grados bajo cero.
[2] VT (**a**) cubrir de escarcha; **the grass was ~ed over** el césped apareció cubierto de escarcha.
(**b**) *plant* quemar.
(**c**) (*US Culin*) alcorzar, escarchar.
[3] VI: **to ~ over, to ~ up** cubrirse de escarcha, escarcharse.
frostbelt [frɒstbelt] N (*US*) *estados del norte de Estados Unidos caracterizados por su clima frío*; *ver también* SUNBELT .
frostbite ['frɒstbaɪt] N congelación *f*.
frostbitten ['frɒst,bɪtn] ADJ congelado.
frostbound ['frɒstbaʊnd] ADJ helado; bloqueado por la helada.
frosted ['frɒstɪd] ADJ *glass* deslustrado; (*US Culin*) alcorzado, escarchado.
frostily ['frɒstɪlɪ] ADV (*fig*) glacialmente.
frosting ['frɒstɪŋ] N (*US Culin*) azúcar *m* glaseado.
frosty ['frɒstɪ] ADJ (**a**) (*Met*) **in ~ weather** en época de hielo; **on a ~ morning** una mañana de helada; **it was ~ last night** anoche heló.
(**b**) *surface* escarchado, cubierto de escarcha.
(**c**) (*fig*) glacial.
froth [frɒθ] [1] N espuma *f*; (*fig*) bachillerías *fpl*.
[2] VI espumar, echar espuma; **to ~ at the mouth** espumajear.
frothy ['frɒθɪ] ADJ (**a**) espumoso. (**b**) (*fig*) frivolón, superficial, de poca sustancia, vacío.
frown [fraʊn] [1] N ceño *m*; **he said with a ~** dijo frunciendo el entrecejo.
[2] VI fruncir el entrecejo; **to ~ at** mirar con ceño.
◆**frown (up)on** VT desaprobar.
frowning ['fraʊnɪŋ] ADJ (*fig*) ceñudo, amenazador, severo.
frowsy, frowzy ['fraʊzɪ] ADJ (*dirty*) sucio; (*untidy*) desaliñado; (*smelly*) fétido, maloliente; (*neglected*) descuidado.
froze [frəʊz] PRET *of* **freeze**.
frozen ['frəʊzn] [1] PTP *of* **freeze**.
[2] ADJ *food* congelado; ~ **assets** activo *m* congelado.
FRS N (**a**) (*Brit*) ABBR *of* **Fellow of the Royal Society**. (**b**) (*US*) ABBR *of* **Federal Reserve System** banco *m* central de los EE.UU.
fructify ['frʌktɪfaɪ] VI fructificar.
frugal ['fruːgəl] ADJ frugal.
frugality [fruː'gælɪtɪ] N frugalidad *f*.
frugally ['fruːgəlɪ] ADV *give out* en pequeñas cantidades; *live* económicamente, sencillamente.
fruit [fruːt] [1] N SING AND PL (*on the tree etc*) fruto *m* (*also Bio, fig*); (*served as food*) fruta *f*, frutas *fpl*; **to bear ~** (*fig*) dar resultado, dar fruto, fructificar.
[2] VI frutar, dar fruto.
fruit-basket ['fruːt,baːskɪt] N frutero *m*, canasto *m* de la fruta.
fruit-cake ['fruːtkeɪk] N tarta *f* de frutas.
fruit cocktail ['fruːt'kɒkteɪl] N cóctel *m* de frutas.
fruit-cup ['fruːtkʌp] N ≃ sangría *f*.
fruit-dish ['fruːtdɪʃ] N frutero *m*.

fruit-drop [,fruːt'drɒp] N bombón *m* de fruta.
fruiterer ['fruːtərəʳ] N (*Brit*) frutero *m*; ~'**s** (**shop**) frutería *f*.
fruit-farm ['fruːtfɑːm] N granja *f* frutera.
fruit-farmer ['fruːt,fɑːməʳ] N fruticultor *m*, -ora *f*, granjero *m* frutícola.
fruit-farming ['fruːt,fɑːmɪŋ] N fruticultura *f*.
fruitfly ['fruːtflaɪ] N mosca *f* de la fruta.
fruitful ['fruːtfʊl] ADJ ˎfig) fructuoso, provechoso.
fruitfully ['fruːtfəlɪ] ADV (*fig*) fructuosamente, fructíferamente, provechosamente.
fruitfulness ['fruːtfʊlnɪs] N (*of soil*) fertilidad *f*, fecundidad *f*, productividad *f*; (*of plant*) fertilidad *f*, fecundidad; (*of discussion etc*) utilidad *f*.
fruit-grower ['fruːt,grəʊəʳ] N fruticultor *m*, -ora *f*, granjero *m* frutícola.
fruit-growing ['fruːt,grəʊɪŋ] N fruticultura *f*.
fruit-gum ['fruːtgʌm] N (*Brit*) caramelo *m* de goma.
fruition [fruː'ɪʃən] N cumplimiento *m*; (*of plan etc*) realización *f*; **to bring to ~** realizar; **to come to ~** llegar a la madurez, (*plan etc*) verse logrado, realizarse, (*hope*) cumplirse.
fruit juice ['fruːt,dʒuːs] N zumo *m* de fruta, jugo *m* de fruta (*LAm*).
fruit-knife ['fruːtnaɪf] N, PL **fruit-knives** ['fruːtnaɪvz] cuchillo *m* de la fruta.
fruitless ['fruːtlɪs] ADJ infructuoso, inútil.
fruit-machine ['fruːtmə,ʃiːn] N (*Brit*) (máquina *f*) tragaperras *m*.
fruit-salad [,fruːt'sæləd] N macedonia *f* de frutas, ensalada *f* de frutas (*LAm*).
fruit-salts ['fruːtsɒlts] NPL sal *f* de fruta(s).
fruit-tree ['fruːttriː] N (árbol *m*) frutal *m*.
fruity ['fruːtɪ] ADJ (**a**) que sabe a fruta; *wine* afrutado. (**b**) *voice* pastoso. (**c**) *joke etc* verde; *style* de fuerte sabor.
frump [frʌmp] N espantajo *m*, adefesio *m*, mujer *f* desaliñada.
frumpish ['frʌmpɪʃ] ADJ desaliñado.
frustrate [frʌs'treɪt] VT frustrar; **to feel ~d** sentirse frustrado.
frustrating [frʌs'treɪtɪŋ] ADJ frustrante.
frustration [frʌs'treɪʃən] N frustración *f*.
fry¹ [fraɪ] N (*Fish*) pececillos *mpl*; **small ~** gente *f* de poca monta, gente *f* menuda.
fry² [fraɪ] [1] N fritada *f*.
[2] VT freír; **fried fish** pescado *m* frito.
[3] VI freírse.
fryer ['fraɪəʳ] N (*pan*) sartén *f*; (*person*) empleado *m*, -a *f* de una freiduría; **deep-fat ~** freidora *f*.
frying ['fraɪɪŋ] N: **there was a smell of ~** olía a frito.
frying-pan ['fraɪɪŋ,pæn] N, (*US*) **frypan** ['fraɪpæn] N sartén *f*; **to jump out of the ~ into the fire** escaparse del trueno para dar en el relámpago, salir de Guatemala y dar en Guatepeor.
fry-up ['fraɪʌp] N (*Brit*) fritura *f*.
FSLIC N (*US*) ABBR *of* **Federal Savings and Loan Insurance Corporation**.
F/T (*US*) ABBR *of* **full-time**.
F.T. N (*Brit*) ABBR *of* **Financial Times**; V financial.
ft ABBR *of* **foot, feet** pie *m*, pies *mpl*.
FTC N (*US*) ABBR *of* **Federal Trade Commission**.
FTP, ftp (*Comput*) N ABBR *of* **file transfer protocol**; **anonymous ftp** ftp anónimo.
FTSE 100 Index N ABBR *of* **Financial Times Stock Exchange 100 Index**.
fuchsia ['fjuːʃə] N fucsia *f*.
fuck⁑ [fʌk] [1] N polvo⁑ *m*; **to have a ~** echar un polvo⁑, joder⁑; **like ~ he will!** ¡si es por los cojones!⁑
[2] VT joder⁑ (*Sp*), coger⁑ (*LAm*); ~ **it!** ¡¡joder!⁑, ¡carajo!⁑ (*LAm*).
[3] VI joder⁑ (*Sp*), coger⁑ (*LAm*); ~**!** ¡¡joder!⁑, ¡carajo!⁑ (*LAm*).
◆**fuck about**⁑, **fuck around**⁑ VI joder⁑; **to ~ about** (*or* **around**) **with** manosear, estropear.
◆**fuck off**⁑ VI: ~ **off!** ¡vete a la mierda!⁑
◆**fuck up**⁑ VT joder⁑.
fuck-all⁑ [,fʌk'ɔːl] (*Brit*) [1] ADJ: **it's ~ use** no sirve para nada en absoluto.
[2] N: **I know ~ about it** no sé nada en absoluto de eso; **he's done ~ today** hoy no ha hecho nada en absoluto.
fucker⁑ ['fʌkəʳ] N hijoputa⁑ *m*, cabronazo⁑ *m*.
fucking⁑ ['fʌkɪŋ] [1] ADJ maldito, condenado*; jodido⁑.
[2] ADV: **a ~ awful film** una película endiabladamente mala; **it's ~ cold** hace un frío de demonios.
[3] N joder⁑ *m*, jodienda⁑ *f*.
fuck-up⁑ ['fʌkʌp] N lío* *m*, follón* *m*.
fuddled ['fʌdld] ADJ (*drunk*) borracho; (*confused*) aturdido; **to get ~** emborracharse.
fuddy-duddy* ['fʌdɪ,dʌdɪ] [1] ADJ viejo; chapado a la antigua.
[2] N persona *f* chapada a la antigua, vejestorio *m*.
fudge [fʌdʒ] [1] N dulce *m* de azúcar.

2 VT *issue, problem* esquivar, rehuir, dejar sin concretar, dejar en estado confuso.
3 VI quedar indeciso, no resolverse.

fuel [fjʊəl] **1** N combustible *m*, carburante *m*; (*specifically coal*) carbón *m*, (*wood*) leña *f*; (*fig*) pábulo *m*; **to add ~ to the flames** echar leña al fuego.
2 ATTR energético; **~ crisis** crisis *f* energética; **~ needs** necesidades *fpl* energéticas; **~ policy** política *f* energética.
3 VT (**a**) aprovisionar de combustible. (**b**) (*fig*) *speculation etc* estimular, provocar; *dispute* avivar, acalorar.
4 VI aprovisionarse de combustible.

fuel-cap ['fjʊəlkæp] N (*Aut*) tapa *f* del depósito de gasolina, trampilla *f*.

fuel injection ['fjʊəlɪn'dʒekʃən] ATTR de inyección; **~ engine** motor *m* de inyección.

fuel-oil ['fjʊəlɔɪl] N aceite *m* combustible, fuel-oil *m*, mazut *m*.

fuel-pump ['fjʊəlpʌmp] N bomba *f* de combustible.

fuel-saving ['fjʊəl,seɪvɪŋ] ADJ que ahorra combustible.

fuel-tank ['fjʊəltæŋk] N depósito *m* de combustible.

fug [fʌg] N (*esp Brit*) aire *m* viciado (*or* confinado, cargado), tufo *m*; **what a ~!** ¡qué olor!; **there's a ~ in here** aquí huele a encerrado.

fuggy ['fʌgɪ] ADJ (*esp Brit*) *air* viciado, cargado; *room* que huele a encerrado.

fugitive ['fjuːdʒɪtɪv] **1** ADJ fugitivo.
2 N fugitivo *m*, -a *f*; (*refugee*) refugiado *m*, -a *f*; **~ from justice** prófugo *m*, -a *f*.

fugue [fjuːg] N fuga *f*.

┌─ **FULBRIGHT** ─┐

(i) *Las becas **Fulbright** son concedidas por el gobierno de Estados Unidos a licenciados nacionales y extranjeros con el fin de facilitar la ampliación de estudios y el acceso a la investigación o la enseñanza dentro del país. Miles de personas se han beneficiado de estas becas desde que se introdujo el programa **Fulbright** en 1946, como parte de la legislación establecida por el senador J. William Fulbright, un hombre de estado demócrata con gran experiencia en política exterior.*

fulcrum ['fʌlkrəm] N fulcro *m*.

fulfil, (*US*) **fulfill** [fʊl'fɪl] **1** VT *duty, promise* cumplir con; *ambition, norm, plan* realizar; *condition* satisfacer, llenar; *order* ejecutar.
2 VR: **to ~ o.s.** realizarse (plenamente).

fulfilling [fʊl'fɪlɪŋ] ADJ *work etc* que realiza a uno.

fulfilment, (*US*) **fulfillment** [fʊl'fɪlmənt] N cumplimiento *m*; realización *f*; satisfacción *f*; ejecución *f*; (*satisfied feeling*) contento *m*, satisfacción *f*.

full [fʊl] **1** ADJ (**a**) (*filled*) lleno; *vehicle etc* completo (*also* **~ up**); **~ of cares** lleno de cuidados; **~ of hope** lleno de esperanza, ilusionado; **~ to bursting** lleno de bote en bote; **~ to overflowing** lleno hasta los bordes; **house** (*Theat*) lleno *m*; **'~ house'** 'no hay localidades'; **~ measure** medida *f* completa, cantidad *f* completa; **to be ~ of** estar lleno de; **I'm ~ (up)** (*of food*) no puedo más; **we are ~ up for July** no tenemos nada libre para julio; **I've had a ~ day** he estado ocupado todo el día; **he's had a ~ life** ha tenido una vida llena de actividades; **he was very ~ of himself*** estaba la mar de engreído; no paró de hablar de sus cosas.
(**b**) (*fig*) *session* pleno, plenario; *member* de número; *authority, employment, power* pleno.
(**c**) (*complete*) completo; *account* detallado, extenso; *meal* completo; *fare, pay, price* íntegro; sin descuento; *speed, strength* máximo; *text* íntegro; *dress* de etiqueta, *uniform* de gala; **in ~ colour** a todo color; **~ cost** coste *m* total; **~ employment** pleno empleo *m*; **~ house** (*Cards*) full *m*; **~ marks** puntuación *f* máxima; **~ member** socio *mf* numerario; **~ moon** luna *f* llena, plenilunio *m*; **~ name** nombre *m* y apellidos; **he was suspended on ~ pay** se le suspendió sin reducción de sueldo; **~ professor** (*US*) profesor *m*, -ora *f* titular; **with ~ particulars** con todos los detalles; **until we have ~ information** hasta que tengamos todos los datos; **in the ~ sense of the word** en el sentido más amplio de la palabra; **a ~ hour** una hora entera, una hora larga; **a ~ 3 miles** 3 millas largas.
(**d**) *face* redondo; *figure* llenito; holgado; *bosom* abultado, (*euph*) importante; *lips* grueso; *skirt* amplio; *V* **speed** *etc*.
2 ADV (**a**) **~ well** perfectamente, muy bien, sobradamente; **to know ~ well that ...** saber perfectamente que ...; **he understands ~ well that ...** se da cuenta cabal de que ...
(**b**) **it hit him ~ in the face** le dio de lleno en la cara.
3 N: **in ~** sin abreviar, por extenso, sin quitar nada; **name in ~** nombre *m* y apellidos; **text in ~** texto *m* íntegro; **to pay in ~** pagar la deuda entera; **to the ~** completamente, al máximum.

fullback ['fʊlbæk] N defensa *mf*; (*Rugby*) zaguero *m*.

full-beam ['fʊl'biːm] ATTR: **~ headlights** luces *fpl* largas, luces *fpl* de carretera.

full-blast ['fʊl'blɑːst] ADV *work* a máxima capacidad; *travel* a toda velocidad; *play etc* al máximo volumen, a toda potencia.

full-blooded ['fʊl'blʌdɪd] ADJ *character* viril, vigoroso; *attack* vigoroso; *animal* de raza.

full-blown ['fʊl'bləʊn] ADJ (*fig*) hecho y derecho.

full-bodied ['fʊl'bɒdɪd] ADJ *cry* fuerte; *wine* de mucho cuerpo.

full-cream ['fʊl'kriːm] ADJ: **~ milk** leche *f* cremosa, leche *f* sin desnatar.

full-dress ['fʊl'dres] **1** ADJ *function* de etiqueta, de gala.
2 N traje *m* de etiqueta.

fuller ['fʊlə*] N: **~'s earth** tierra *f* de batán.

full-face [,fʊl'feɪs] ADJ *portrait* de rostro entero.

full-fledged ['fʊl'fledʒd] ADJ (*US*) = **fully-fledged**.

full-frontal ['fʊl'frʌntl] ADJ (*unrestrained*) desenfrenado; **~ nude** desnudo *m* visto de frente.

full-grown ['fʊl'grəʊn] ADJ crecido, maduro.

full-length ['fʊl'leŋθ] **1** ADJ *picture* de cuerpo entero; *novel, study* completo, extenso; *pool etc* de tamaño normal; **~ film** cinta *f* de largo metraje, largometraje *m*.
2 ADV: **he was lying ~** estaba tumbado todo lo largo que era.

fullness ['fʊlnɪs] N plenitud *f*; amplitud *f*; **in the ~ of time** a su debido tiempo.

full-page [,fʊl'peɪdʒ] ADJ *advert etc* de plana entera, de página entera.

full-scale ['fʊl'skeɪl] ADJ *study* amplio, extenso; *investigation* de gran alcance; *attack* en gran escala; *plan, model* de tamaño natural.

full-sized ['fʊl'saɪzd] ADJ de tamaño normal.

full stop ['fʊl'stɒp] N (*Brit*) punto *m*; **you failed, ~** te suspendieron, y punto; **to come to a ~** (*fig*) pararse, paralizarse, quedar detenido en un punto muerto.

full-throated ['fʊl'θrəʊtɪd] ADJ *cry etc* fuerte, a pleno pulmón.

full-time ['fʊl'taɪm] **1** ADJ *professional* en plena dedicación, *worker* que trabaja una jornada completa, que trabaja a pleno tiempo; **~ course** curso *m* a dedicación plena; **~ employment**, **~ work** trabajo *m* de jornada completa; **a ~ job** un puesto de plena dedicación.
2 ADV: **to work ~** trabajar en régimen de dedicación exclusiva, trabajar una jornada entera.
3 N (*Sport*) fin *m* del partido.

fully ['fʊlɪ] ADV (**a**) (*completely*) completamente, enteramente; **~ dressed** completamente vestido; **I'm not ~ convinced** no me convenzo del todo; **I don't ~ understand** no lo acabo de comprender. (**b**) (*at least*) **he earns ~ as much as I do** gana sin duda tanto como yo; **it is ~ 3 miles** son lo menos 3 millas; **we waited ~ 3 hours** esperamos 3 horas largas.

fully-fashioned ['fʊlɪ'fæʃnd] ADJ *stocking* menguado, de costura francesa.

fully-fledged ['fʊlɪ'fledʒd] ADJ (*Brit*) *bird* adulto; en edad de volar, capaz de volar; (*fig*) hecho y derecho, con pleno derecho.

fully-paid ['fʊlɪ'peɪd] ADJ: **~ share** acción *f* liberada.

fulminate ['fʊlmɪneɪt] VI: **to ~ against** tronar contra.

fulmination [,fʊlmɪ'neɪʃən] N (*frm*) invectiva *f*, filípica *f* (*against* contra).

fulsome ['fʊlsəm] ADJ exagerado, excesivo; *person* servil, obsequioso.

fumble ['fʌmbl] **1** VT manosear, revolver (*etc*) torpemente; *ball* dejar caer; **to ~ one's way along** ir a tientas.
2 VI: **to ~ for sth** buscar algo con las manos; **to ~ for a word** titubear buscando una palabra; **to ~ in one's pockets** revolver en los bolsillos; **to ~ with sth** manejar (*etc*) algo torpemente; **to ~ with a door** tratar torpemente de abrir una puerta.

fume [fjuːm] VI (**a**) humear. (**b**) (*be furious*) estar furioso, rabiar, echar humo; echar pestes (*at thing* contra, *at person* de).

fumes [fjuːmz] NPL humo *m*, gas *m*, vapor *m*.

fumigate ['fjuːmɪgeɪt] VT fumigar.

fumigation [,fjuːmɪ'geɪʃən] N fumigación *f*.

fun [fʌn] **1** N (*amusement*) diversión *f*; (*merriment*) alegría *f*; (*joke*) broma *f*; **for ~**, **in ~** en broma; **it's great ~** es muy divertido; **he's great ~** es una persona divertidísima; **it's not much ~ for us** no nos divertimos en absoluto; **it's only his ~** está bromeando, te está tomando el pelo; **to do sth for the ~ of it** hacer algo para divertirse, hacer algo sin propósito serio; **to have ~** divertirse; **have ~!** ¡que os divirtáis!, ¡que lo paséis bien!; **what ~ we had!** ¡cómo nos divertimos!; **we had ~ with the passports** nos armamos un lío con los pasaportes; **they had lots of ~ and games at the party** se divirtieron una barbaridad en la fiesta; **he's having ~ and games with the nurse** se entiende con la enfermera; **she's been having ~ and games with the washing-machine** ha tenido muchos líos con la lavadora; **to make ~ of**, **to poke ~ at** burlarse de, ridiculizar; **to spoil the ~** aguar la fiesta.
2 ADJ: **it's a ~ thing** es para divertirse; **she's a ~ person** es una persona divertida; es una persona a quien le gustan las diversiones.

function ['fʌŋkʃən] [1] N función f; **it is no part of my ~ to** + infin no corresponde a mi cargo + infin, no me compete a mí + infin; **to exceed one's ~s** excederse en sus funciones.
[2] VI funcionar.
functional ['fʌŋkʃnəl] ADJ funcional; **~ analysis** análisis m funcional.
functionalism ['fʌŋkʃnəlɪzəm] N funcionalismo m.
functionalist ['fʌŋkʃnəlɪst] (frm) [1] ADJ funcionalista.
[2] N funcionalista mf.
functionary ['fʌŋkʃənərɪ] N funcionario m.
function key ['fʌŋkʃənkiː] N tecla f de función.
function word ['fʌŋkʃənwɜːd] N palabra f funcional.
fund [fʌnd] [1] N fondo m; **~s** fondos mpl; **to be in ~s** estar en fondos; **to have a ~ of stories** saber un montón de chistes.
[2] VT (a) (Fin) financiar; proveer fondos a; debt consolidar. (b) campaign etc pagar, costear, financiar.
▼ **fundamental** [,fʌndə'mentl] [1] ADJ fundamental; **to be ~ to** ser esencial para.
[2] N: **~s** fundamentos mpl.
fundamentalism [,fʌndə'mentəlɪzəm] N fundamentalismo m, integrismo m.
fundamentalist [,fʌndə'mentəlɪst] [1] ADJ fundamentalista, integrista.
[2] N fundamentalista mf, integrista mf.
fundamentally [,fʌndə'mentəlɪ] ADV fundamentalmente, esencialmente.
funding ['fʌndɪŋ] N (a) (funds) fondos mpl, finanzas fpl; (act of ~) financiación f, provisión f de fondos. (b) (of debt) consolidación f.
fund-raiser ['fʌnd,reɪzəʳ] N recogedor m, -ora f de fondos.
fund-raising ['fʌnd,reɪzɪŋ] N recolección f de fondos, recaudación f de fondos.
▼ **funeral** ['fjuːnərəl] [1] ADJ and attr march etc fúnebre; pyre funerario; service de difuntos; **~ cortège** cortejo m fúnebre, comitiva f fúnebre; **~ director** director m de funeraria; **~ march** marcha f fúnebre; **~ oration** oración f fúnebre; **~ parlour** funeraria f; **~ procession** = **~ cortège**; **~ service** exequias fpl.
▼[2] N entierro m, funerales mpl; **that's your ~!** ¡allá te las compongas!, ¡allá tú!, ¡con tu pan te lo comas!
funerary ['fjuːnərərɪ] ADJ (frm) funerario, fúnebre.
funereal [fjuː'nɪərɪəl] ADJ fúnebre, funéreo.
funfair ['fʌnfeəʳ] N parque m de atracciones.
fungal ['fʌŋgl] ADJ infection, disease micótico, de hongos.
fungi ['fʌŋgaɪ] NPL of **fungus**.
fungicide ['fʌŋgɪsaɪd] N fungicida m.
fungoid ['fʌŋgɔɪd] ADJ parecido a un hongo, como un hongo; (Med) fungoide.
fungous ['fʌŋgəs] ADJ fungoso.
fungus ['fʌŋgəs] N, PL **fungi** ['fʌŋgaɪ] hongo m.
funicular [fjuː'nɪkjʊləʳ] N (also **~ railway**) (ferrocarril m) funicular m.
funk* [fʌŋk] [1] N (a) (Brit: state) canguelo* m, jindama* f, mieditis* f; **to be in a (blue) ~** estar muerto de miedo.
(b) (person) gallina* mf, mandria mf.
[2] VT: **to ~ it** rajarse, dejar de hacer algo por miedo, retirarse por miedo; **to ~ doing something** dejar de hacer algo por miedo.
funky* ['fʌŋkɪ] ADJ cobarde, miedoso; **you're ~!** ¡cobarde!
fun-loving ['fʌn,lʌvɪŋ] ADJ amigo de diversiones, amigo de pasarlo bien.
funnel ['fʌnl] [1] N embudo m; (Brit Naut, Rail etc) chimenea f.
[2] VT traffic etc acanalar, canalizar (through por); aid, finance encauzar, dirigir (through por).
funnily ['fʌnɪlɪ] ADV de un modo divertido; **~ enough ...** cosa curiosa ..., cosa más rara ...
funny ['fʌnɪ] [1] ADJ (a) (amusing) divertido, gracioso, cómico; (full of jokes) chistoso; **~ money*** una millonada; **~ story** chiste m; **I thought the film very ~** la película me hizo mucha gracia; **that's not ~** eso no tiene gracia; **I find it ~ that ...**, **it strikes me as ~ that ...** me hace mucha gracia que ...; **he's trying to be ~** quiere hacerse el gracioso; **don't try to be ~** no se haga el gracioso.
(b) (odd) raro, curioso; **a ~ feeling** una sensación rara; **I find it ~ that ...**, **it strikes me as ~ that ...** me extraña que + subj, se me hace extraño que + subj; **the ~ thing about it is that ...** lo curioso es que ...; **he's ~ that way** tiene esa manía.
[2] N: **funnies** (US) sección f de historietas gráficas (del periódico).
funnybone ['fʌnɪbəʊn] N hueso m de la alegría.
funny farm: ['fʌnɪfɑːm] N (hum) loquero* m.
funny man* ['fʌnɪmæn] N comediante mf.
fun-run ['fʌnrʌn] N maratón m (corto, de ciudad, para los no atletas).
fur [fɜːʳ] [1] N piel f; (on tongue) saburra f; (in kettle) sarro m; **~ coat** abrigo m de pieles.
[2] VI (kettle etc: also **to ~ up**) cubrirse de sarro, formar sarro.
furbish ['fɜːbɪʃ] VT: **to ~ up** renovar, restaurar.
furious ['fjʊərɪəs] ADJ furioso; effort etc frenético, violento; pace vertiginoso; **to be ~ with sb** estar muy enfadado con uno; **to get ~** ponerse furioso.

furiously ['fjʊərɪəslɪ] ADV con furia.
furl [fɜːl] VT (Naut) aferrar; wings recoger.
furlong ['fɜːlɒŋ] N estadio m (octava parte de una milla).
furlough ['fɜːləʊ] N (Mil etc) licencia f, permiso m.
furnace ['fɜːnɪs] N horno m; **the town was like a ~** la ciudad era un horno.
furnish ['fɜːnɪʃ] VT (a) (provide) proveer, suministrar, proporcionar (sb with sth algo a uno); opportunity dar, proporcionar, deparar; proof aducir; information facilitar; **we are ~ed with all that is necessary** estamos equipados con todo lo necesario.
(b) room amueblar (with de); **~ed flat** (Brit) piso m amueblado.
furnishings ['fɜːnɪʃɪŋz] NPL muebles mpl, mobiliario m.
furniture ['fɜːnɪtʃəʳ] N muebles mpl, mobiliario m, mueblaje m; (piece of ~) mueble m.
furniture mover ['fɜːnɪtʃ,ə,muːvəʳ] N (US), **furniture remover** ['fɜːnɪtʃərɪ,muːvəʳ] N compañía f de mudanzas.
furniture polish ['fɜːnɪtʃə,pɒlɪʃ] N cera f para muebles.
furniture shop ['fɜːnɪtʃə,ʃɒp] N tienda f de muebles.
furniture van ['fɜːnɪtʃə,væn] N camión m de mudanzas.
furore [fjʊə'rɔːrɪ] N, (US) **furor** ['fjʊərɔːʳ] N ola f de protestas; escándalo m; ola f de entusiasmo.
furrier ['fʌrɪəʳ] N peletero m.
furrow ['fʌrəʊ] [1] N surco m; (on face) arruga f; **to plough a lonely ~** ser el único en estudiar (etc) algo.
[2] VT surcar; arrugar.
[3] VI arrugarse; **his brow ~ed** frunció el ceño.
furrowed ['fʌrəʊd] ADJ: **with ~ brow** con ceño fruncido.
furry ['fɜːrɪ] ADJ peludo; **~ toy** juguete m de felpa.
further ['fɜːðəʳ] COMP of **far**: [1] ADV (a) (place) más lejos, más allá; **move it ~ away** apártalo un poco más; **~ back** más atrás; **~ off** más lejos; **~ on** más adelante; **how much ~ is it?** ¿cuánto camino nos queda?; **have you much ~ to go?** ¿le queda mucho camino por hacer?; **I got no ~ with him** no pude adelantar más con él, no pude hacer más progresos con él; **nothing is ~ from my thoughts** nada más lejos de mi intención.
(b) (more) además; **and I ~ believe that ...** y creo además que ...
(c) **to go ~ into a matter** estudiar una cosa más a fondo; **they questioned us ~** nos hicieron más preguntas; **he heard nothing ~** no le volvieron a decir nada; **don't trouble yourself any ~** no se moleste más.
(d) **~ to that** además de eso; **~ to my letter of the 7th** con relación a mi carta del 7.
[2] ADJ (a) (place) más lejano, más remoto, de más allá; end, side opuesto; **at the ~ end** en el otro extremo.
(b) (additional) nuevo, adicional; complementario, supletorio; education superior; **~ education** educación f postescolar; **~ facts** nuevos datos mpl, más datos mpl; **after ~ consideration** después de considerarlo más detenidamente; **until ~ notice** hasta nuevo aviso; **till ~ orders** hasta nueva orden; **without ~ loss of time** sin más pérdida de tiempo.
[3] VT promover, fomentar, adelantar.
furtherance ['fɜːðərəns] N promoción f, fomento m.
furthermore ['fɜːðə'mɔːʳ] ADV además.
furthermost ['fɜːðəməʊst] ADJ más lejano.
furthest ['fɜːðɪst] SUPERL of **far**: [1] ADV más lejos; **that's the ~ that anyone has gone** es el punto extremo a que han llegado, nadie ha ido más allá.
[2] ADJ más lejano; extremo.
furtive ['fɜːtɪv] ADJ furtivo.
furtively ['fɜːtɪvlɪ] ADV furtivamente.
fury ['fjʊərɪ] N furor m, furia f; violencia f; frenesí m; **the Furies** las Furias; **like ~** a toda furia, (of person) hecho una furia; **to be in a ~** estar furioso; **to work o.s. up into a ~** montar en cólera.
furze [fɜːz] N aulaga f, tojo m.
fuse, (US) **fuze** [fjuːz] [1] N (Elec) plomo m, fusible m; (Mil) mecha f, espoleta f; **he's on a very short ~*** tiene mucho genio.
[2] VT (a) (Brit Elec) fundir. (b) (fig) fusionar.
[3] VI (a) (Elec) fundirse; **the lights ~d** se fundieron los plomos. (b) (fig) fusionarse.
fuse-box ['fjuːzbɒks] N caja f de fusibles.
fused [fjuːzd] ADJ (Elec) con fusible; **~ plug** enchufe m con fusible.
fuselage ['fjuːzəlɑːʒ] N fuselaje m.
fuse-wire ['fjuːzwaɪəʳ] N alambre m de fusible.
fusilier [,fjuːzɪ'lɪəʳ] N (Brit) fusilero m.
fusillade [,fjuːzɪ'leɪd] N descarga f cerrada (also fig).
fusion ['fjuːʒən] N fusión f (also fig), fundición f.
fuss [fʌs] [1] N (a) (noise, bustle) conmoción f, bulla f, alharacas fpl.
(b) (dispute) lío m; protesta f; **that ~ about the money** ese lío con el dinero; **to kick up (or make) a ~** dar cuatro voces, armar un lío; **I think you were quite right to make a ~** creo que hiciste bien en protestar.
(c) (excessive display) aspaviento m, hazañería f; **it's a lot of ~ about**

nothing mucho ruido y pocas nueces; **there's no need to make such a ~** no es para tanto; **to make a ~ of** hacer mimos a, hacer fiestas a.
(d) (*formalities*) ceremonias *fpl*; trámites *mpl*; **such a ~ to get a passport!** ¡tanta lata para conseguir un pasaporte!
2 VT *person* molestar, fastidiar; **don't ~ me!** ¡no fastidies!
3 VI agitarse, preocuparse (por bagatelas); **to ~ over sb** mimar con exceso a uno.
◆**fuss about, fuss around** VI andar azacaneado, andar de acá para allá; preocuparse de menudencias.
fussed* [fʌst] ADJ (*Brit*): **I'm not ~** me da igual, me da lo mismo; **he wasn't ~ about getting back to Belfast that night** no tenía prisa por llegar a Belfast esa noche.
fussily ['fʌsɪlɪ] ADV (*V adj*) exigentemente, puntillosamente.
fusspot* ['fʌspɒt] N quisquilloso *m*, -a *f*.
fussy ['fʌsɪ] ADJ **(a)** *person* (*demanding*) exigente; quisquilloso; (*nervous*) nervioso. **(b)** *details* nimio; *dress* con muchos ringorrangos; *decoration* con muchos adornos.
fusty ['fʌstɪ] ADJ mohoso, rancio; *air, room* que huele a cerrado.
futile ['fjuːtaɪl] ADJ inútil, vano, infructuoso.
futility [fjuː'tɪlɪtɪ] N inutilidad *f*, lo inútil.
futon ['fuːtɒn] N futón *m*.
future ['fjuːtʃəʳ] **1** ADJ futuro; venidero; **in ~ years** en los años

venideros.
2 N **(a)** futuro *m*, porvenir *m*; **in (the) ~** en el futuro, en lo sucesivo; **in the near ~** en fecha próxima; **there's no ~ in it** esto no tiene porvenir; **what does the ~ hold for us?** ¿qué nos tiene reservado el destino?
(b) **~s** (*Comm*) futuros *mpl*; **~s market** mercado *m* de futuros.
futurism ['fjuːtʃərɪzəm] N futurismo *m*.
futurist ['fjuːtʃərɪst] N (*futurologist*) futurólogo *m*, -a *f*; (*Art*) futurista *mf*.
futuristic [ˌfjuːtʃə'rɪstɪk] ADJ futurístico.
futurologist [ˌfjuːtʃəʳ'ɒlədʒɪst] N futurólogo *m*, -a *f*.
futurology [ˌfjuːtʃəʳ'ɒlədʒɪ] N futurología *f*.
fuze [fjuːz] N (*US*) = **fuse.**
fuzz [fʌz] N **(a)** tamo *m*, pelusa *f*; (*on face*) vello *m*. **(b) the ~** (**:**) la pasma**:**, la bofia**:** (*Sp*), la jara**:** (*Mex*), la cana**:** (*SC*).
fuzzily ['fʌzɪlɪ] ADV **(a)** borrosamente. **(b)** confusamente.
fuzzy ['fʌzɪ] ADJ **(a)** (*hairy*) velloso; *hair* muy rizado. **(b)** (*blurred*) borroso. **(c)** *reasoning* confuso, nada claro.
fwd (*esp Comm*) ABBR *of* **forward.**
f-word ['ef,wɜːd] N: **to say the ~** (*euph of 'fuck'*) decir 'jo...roba'.
fwy (*US*) ABBR *of* **freeway.**
FY ABBR *of* **fiscal year.**
FYI ABBR *of* **for your information.**

G

G, g [dʒiː] N **(a)** (letter) G, g f; **G for George** G de Gerona. **(b) G** (Mus) sol m, **G major** sol m mayor; **G-string** (Mus) cuerda f de sol; (hum) tanga f, taparrabo m. **(c)** (Scol: mark) ABBR of **Good** Notable, N. **(d)** (US Cine) ABBR of **general audience** todos los públicos. **(e)** (:) ABBR of **grand** (Brit) mil libras fpl, (US) mil dólares mpl.

g. (a) ABBR of **gram(s)**, **gramme(s)** gramo(s) m(pl), gr. **(b)** N ABBR of **gravity** gravedad f, g.; **G-force** fuerza f de la gravedad.

GA (US Post) ABBR of **Georgia**.

g.a. ABBR of **general average**.

GAB N ABBR of **General Arrangements to Borrow**.

gab* [gæb] ①️ N (chatter) cháchara f; (chat) charla f; **to have the gift of (the) ~** tener mucha labia, tener un pico de oro.
②️ VI parlotear, charlar, cotorrear.

gabardine [ˌgæbəˈdiːn] N gabardina f.

gabble [ˈgæbl] ①️ N torrente m de palabras ininteligibles.
②️ VT decir (or leer etc) atropelladamente, pronunciar de modo ininteligible.
③️ VI hablar atropelladamente; parlotear, cotorrear.
◆**gabble away** VI: **they were gabbling away in French** hablaban atropelladamente en francés, parlaban francés.

gabby* [ˈgæbɪ] ADJ (esp US) hablador, locuaz.

gaberdine [ˌgæbəˈdiːn] N gabardina f.

gable [ˈgeɪbl] ①️ N aguilón m.
②️ ATTR: **~ end** hastial m; **~ roof** tejado m de dos aguas, tejado m de caballete.

gabled [ˈgeɪbld] ADJ houses, roofs (con tejado) a dos aguas.

Gabon [gəˈbɒn] N Gabón m.

Gabriel [ˈgeɪbrɪəl] NM Gabriel.

gad¹ [gæd] VI: **to ~ about** salir mucho, viajar mucho, callejear.

gad² [gæd] INTERJ ¡cáspita!

gadabout [ˈgædəbaʊt] N azotacalles mf, pindonga f.

gadfly [ˈgædflaɪ] N tábano m.

gadget [ˈgædʒɪt] N artilugio m, chisme m, aparato m.

gadgetry [ˈgædʒɪtrɪ] N chismes mpl, aparatos mpl.

gadolinium [ˌgædəˈlɪnɪəm] N gadolinio m.

gadwall [ˈgædwɔːl] N ánade m friso.

Gael [geɪl] N gaélico m, -a f.

Gaelic [ˈgeɪlɪk] ①️ ADJ gaélico.
②️ N (Ling) gaélico m.

gaff¹ [gæf] ①️ N arpón m, garfio m.
②️ VT arponear, enganchar.

gaff²* [gæf] N: **to blow the ~** descubrir el pastel.

gaffe [gæf] N plancha f, patinazo m, metedura f de pata; **to make a ~** tirarse una plancha.

gaffer [ˈgæfəʳ] N **(a)** (old man) vejete m, tío m. **(b)** (Brit: foreman) capataz m; (boss) jefe m; (Cine, TV) iluminista mf.

gag [gæg] ①️ N **(a)** mordaza f; (Parl) clausura f. **(b)** (Theat) morcilla f; (joke) chiste m; (hoax) broma f; (gimmick) truco m publicitario; **is this a ~?** ¿es una broma esto?; **it's a ~ to raise funds** es un truco para reunir fondos.
②️ VT amordazar; (fig) amordazar, hacer callar; (Parl) clausurar; discussion impedir, estorbar.
③️ VI (Theat) meter morcillas; (joke) contar chistes, chunguearse; **I was only ~ging** lo dije en broma.

gaga* [ˈgɑːˈgɑː] ADJ gagá*, lelo, chocho; **to be going ~** chochear; **to go ~** (senile) chochear; (ecstatic) caérsele a uno la baba.

gage [geɪdʒ] N (US) = **gauge**.

gaggle [ˈgægl] N manada f.

gaiety [ˈgeɪtɪ] N alegría f, regocijo m; (of gathering etc) animación f; **gaieties** diversiones fpl alegres; **it contributes to the ~ of nations** alegra al mundo entero.

gaily [ˈgeɪlɪ] ADV alegremente.

gain [geɪn] ①️ N (increase) aumento m (in, of de); (profit, earning) ganancia f, beneficio m; **his loss is our ~** pierde él y ganamos nosotros; **there have been ~s of up to 3 points** ha habido alzas de hasta 3 enteros; **I lost all my ~s** perdí todas mis ganancias.
②️ VT ganar; objective conseguir; possession, territory etc adquirir; approval, respect merecer, captar, conquistar; (reach) llegar a, alcanzar, ganar; time ganar; **my watch has ~ed 5 minutes** mi reloj se ha adelantado 5 minutos; **I've ~ed 3 kilos** he engordado 3 kilos; **the shares have ~ed 4 points** las acciones han subido 4 enteros; **what have you ~ed by it?** ¿qué has ganado con esto?; **what do you hope to ~?** ¿qué provecho vas a sacar?
③️ VI (shares etc) aumentar en valor, subir; (Med) mejorar; (in weight) engordar, poner carnes; (in advantage) ganar terreno; **to ~ in popularity** resultar más popular, adquirir mayor popularidad; **it ~s in contrast with the other picture** gana al compararse con el otro cuadro.
◆**gain (up)on** VT: **to ~ (up)on sb** ir ganando terreno a uno, ir alcanzando a uno; (and outstrip) ir dejando atrás a uno.

gainer [ˈgeɪnəʳ] N: **to be the ~** salir ganando.

gainful [ˈgeɪnfʊl] ADJ employment remunerado, retribuido.

gainfully [ˈgeɪnfʊlɪ] ADV: **to be ~ employed** tener un trabajo retribuido; **there was nothing that could ~ be said** no había nada provechoso que se pudiese decir.

gainsay [ˌgeɪnˈseɪ] (irr: V say) VT (liter) contradecir, negar; **it cannot be gainsaid** es innegable.

gait [geɪt] N modo m de andar, paso m.

gaiter [ˈgeɪtəʳ] N polaina f.

gal* [gæl] N = **girl**.

gal. ABBR of **gallon(s)**.

gala [ˈgɑːlə] ①️ N fiesta f; (Sport) certamen m, concurso m.
②️ ATTR: **~ day** día m de gala.

galactic [gəˈlæktɪk] ADJ (Med) lácteo; (Astron) galáctico.

Galapagos Islands [gəˈlæpəgəsˌaɪləndz] NPL Islas fpl (de los) Galápagos.

Galatians [gəˈleɪʃənz] NPL Galateos mpl.

galaxy [ˈgæləksɪ] N galaxia f; (fig) grupo m brillante, constelación f, pléyade f.

gale [geɪl] N ventarrón m, vendaval m; (storm) tormenta f, tempestad f; **to blow a ~** soplar una galerna, soplar una tempestad.

gale-force [ˈgeɪlfɔːs] ATTR: **~ 10** vendaval m de fuerza 10; **~ winds** vientos mpl de tormenta.

Galen [ˈgeɪlən] NM Galeno.

gale-warning [ˈgeɪlˌwɔːnɪŋ] N aviso m de tormenta.

Galicia [gəˈlɪʃɪə] N **(a)** (Central Europe) Galitzia f. **(b)** (Spain) Galicia f.

Galician [gəˈlɪʃɪən] ①️ ADJ gallego.
②️ N **(a)** gallego m, -a f. **(b)** (Ling) gallego m.

Galilean [ˌgælɪˈliːən] ①️ ADJ (Bible, Geog) galileo; (Astron) galileico.
②️ N galileo m, -a f; **the ~** (Bible) el Galileo.

Galilee [ˈgælɪliː] N Galilea f.

gall¹ [gɔːl] ①️ N **(a)** (Anat) bilis f, hiel f. **(b)** (fig) hiel f; bilis f; (*) descaro m; **she had the ~ to say that** tuvo el descaro de decir eso.
②️ VT mortificar.

gall² [gɔːl] N (Bot) agalla f; (on animal) matadura f.

gallant ①️ ADJ **(a)** [ˈgælənt] (brave) valiente, valeroso, bizarro; (showy) lucido, gallardo; (stately) imponente; **the ~ captain** el intrépido capitán.
(b) [gəˈlænt] (attentive to women) galante; cortés, atento.
②️ N [gəˈlænt] galán m.

gallantly [ˈgæləntlɪ] ADV **(a)** valientemente. **(b)** galantemente; cortésmente.

gallantry [ˈgæləntrɪ] N **(a)** (bravery) valentía f, valor m, heroísmo m, bizarría f. **(b)** (courtesy) galantería f, cortesía f; **gallantries** galanterías fpl.

gall-bladder [ˈgɔːlˌblædəʳ] N vesícula f biliar.

galleon ['gælɪən] N galeón *m*.

gallery ['gælərɪ] N galería *f* (*also Min, Theat*); (*for spectators*) tribuna *f*; (**art**) ~ museo *m* (de bellas artes); **to play to the** ~ actuar para la galería.

galley ['gælɪ] N (**a**) (*ship*) galera *f*. (**b**) (*kitchen*) cocina *f*, fogón *m*. (**c**) (*Typ*) galerada *f*, galera *f*.

galley-proof ['gælɪpruːf] N galerada *f*.

galley-slave ['gælɪsleɪv] N galeote *m*.

Gallic ['gælɪk] ADJ gálico, galo, galicano.

gallicism ['gælɪsɪzəm] N galicismo *m*.

galling ['gɔːlɪŋ] ADJ mortificante.

gallium ['gælɪəm] N galio *m*.

gallivant [,gælɪ'vænt] VI = **gad¹**.

gallon ['gælən] N galón *m* (= 4,546 *litros, US* = 3,785 *litros*); *ver también* IMPERIAL SYSTEM .

gallop ['gæləp] ⃞1 N galope *m*; (*distance covered*) galopada *f*; **at a** ~ a galope; **at full** ~ a galope tendido; **to break into a** ~ echar a galopar.
⃞2 VT hacer galopar.
⃞3 VI galopar; **to** ~ **past** desfilar a galope.
◆**gallop off** VI alejarse a galope.
◆**gallop up** VI llegar a galope.

galloping ['gæləpɪŋ] ADJ (*Med and fig*) galopante.

gallows ['gæləuz] ⃞1 N SING horca *f*.
⃞2 ATTR: ~ **humour** (*fig*) humor *m* negro *or* macabro.

gallstone ['gɔːlstəun] N cálculo *m* biliario.

Gallup poll ['gæləp,pəul] N sondeo *m* Gallup, encuesta *f* Gallup.

galoot [gə'luːt] N (*esp US*) zoquete* *mf*.

galore [gə'lɔːʳ] ADV en abundancia, a porrillo.

galosh [gə'lɒʃ] N chanclo *m* (de goma).

galumph [gə'lʌmf] VI (*hum*) brincar alegre pero torpemente, brincar como un elefante contento.

galvanic [gæl'vænɪk] ADJ galvánico.

galvanism ['gælvənɪzəm] N galvanismo *m*.

galvanize ['gælvənaɪz] VT (**a**) galvanizar. (**b**) (*fig*) galvanizar; **to** ~ **sb into life** sacudir a uno de su abstracción; **to** ~ **sb into doing sth** sacudir a uno para que haga algo.

galvanized ['gælvənaɪzd] ADJ galvanizado.

galvanometer [,gælvə'nɒmɪtəʳ] N galvanómetro *m*.

Gambia ['gæmbɪə] N: (**The**) ~ Gambia *f*.

Gambian ['gæmbɪən] ⃞1 ADJ gambiano.
⃞2 N gambiano *m*, -a *f*.

gambit ['gæmbɪt] N gambito *m*; (*fig*) táctica *f*; **opening** ~ estrategia *f* inicial.

gamble ['gæmbl] ⃞1 N jugada *f* (de resultado imprevisible); empresa *f* arriesgada; **life's a** ~ la vida es una lotería; **I did it as a pure** ~ lo hice para probar suerte nada más; **the** ~ **came off** la tentativa tuvo éxito, la jugada nos salió bien; **to have a** ~ **on** *horse* jugar dinero a, apostar a, *company shares* especular en.
⃞2 VT jugar, aventurar en el juego; **to** ~ **one's future** jugarse el porvenir.
⃞3 VI jugar; (*Fin*) especular; **to** ~ **on the Stock Exchange** jugar a la bolsa; **he ~d on my being there** confiaba en que yo estuviera; **to** ~ **with others' money** especular con el dinero ajeno.
◆**gamble away** VT perder en el juego.

gambler ['gæmbləʳ] N jugador *m*, -ora *f*.

gambling ['gæmblɪŋ] ⃞1 N juego *m*; ~ **on the Stock Exchange** especulación *f* en la bolsa.
⃞2 ATTR: ~ **debts** deudas *fpl* de juego; ~ **losses** pérdidas *fpl* de juego; **I'm not a** ~ **man** yo no juego.

gambling-den ['gæmblɪŋden] N garito *m*, casa *f* de juego.

gambol ['gæmbəl] VI brincar, retozar, juguetear.

game¹ [geɪm] ⃞1 N (**a**) (*gen*) juego *m*; deporte *m*; (*match: with ball etc*) partido *m*, (*of cards, chess, snooker etc*) partida *f*; (*at bridge*) manga *f*; **~s** (*eg Olympic*) juegos *mpl*; ~, **set and match** juego, set y partido; ~ **of chance** juego *m* de azar; ~ **theory** teoría *f* de los juegos; **it's only a** ~ es un juego nada más; **this isn't a** ~ esto no es ninguna broma, esto va de veras; **the** ~ **is not worth the candle** la cosa no vale la pena; **I was no good at ~s at school** en el colegio no tenía talento para los deportes; **to be off one's** ~ no estar en forma, estar desentrenado; **to go to** ~ (*Bridge*) ir a manga; **to have a** ~ **of chess** echar una partida de ajedrez; **to have a** ~ **with** (*tease*) tomar el pelo a, hacer una broma a; **to play the** ~ (*fig*) jugar limpio; **he plays a good** ~ **of football** juega bien al fútbol, es buen futbolista; **two can play at that** ~ donde las dan las toman; **to play a double** ~ jugar doble; **to play a waiting** ~ estar a ver venir, esperar hasta ver qué pasa; **to put sb off his** ~ hacer fallar a uno; **that's what the ~'s all about** es lo más esencial, es lo más importante.
(**b**) (*deception*) **the** ~ **is up** todo se acabó; **they saw the** ~ **was up** comprendieron que ya no había nada que hacer; **what's the ~?** ¿qué hacéis ahí?, ¿qué pretendéis con eso?; **to give the** ~ **away** tirar de la manta; **we know his little** ~ le conocemos el juego, le hemos

calado; **I wonder what his** ~ **is?** ¿qué estará tramando?
(**c**) (*: trouble*) lío* *m*; **I had such a** ~ **getting here** me hice un lío al venir aquí*; **what a** ~ **this is!** ¡qué faena!*
(**d**) (*business*) **how long have you been in this ~?** ¿cuánto tiempo llevas dedicado a esto?; **what's your ~?** ¿a qué te dedicas?
(**e**) (*) prostitución *f*; **to be on the** ~ ser prostituta, hacer la calle*.
(**f**) (*Hunting*) caza *f*; V **big 1**.
⃞2 ATTR: ~ **bird** ave *f* de caza; ~ **fish** salmón *m* *or* trucha *f*; ~ **fishing** pesca *f* de salmón *or* de trucha; ~ **laws** leyes *fpl* relativas a la caza; **~s master** profesor *m* de educación física; **~s mistress** profesora *f* de educación física; ~ **park** parque *m* natural, reserva *f* natural; ~ **plan** (*US: fig*) táctica *f*; ~ **reserve** coto *m* de caza; ~ **show** programa *m* concurso; ~ **warden** guarda *m* de caza, guardamonte *m*.
⃞3 ADJ animoso, valiente; **are you ~?** ¿quieres?, ¿te animas?; **I'm** ~ me apunto, cuenta conmigo; **to be** ~ **for anything** atreverse a todo.
⃞4 VI jugar (por dinero).

game² [geɪm] ADJ (*lame*): **a** ~ **leg** una pierna coja.

gamebag ['geɪmbæg] N morral *m*.

gamecock ['geɪmkɒk] N gallo *m* de pelea.

gamekeeper ['geɪm,kiːpəʳ] N guardabosque *m*.

gamely ['geɪmlɪ] ADV bravamente.

gamesman ['geɪmzmən] N, PL **gamesmen** ['geɪmzmən] jugador *m* astuto.

gamesmanship ['geɪmzmənʃɪp] N arte *m* de ganar astutamente; habilidad *f*; **piece of** ~ truco *m* para ganar.

gamester ['geɪmstəʳ] N jugador *m*, tahur *m*.

gamete ['gæmiːt] N gameto *m*.

gamin ['gæmɛ̃] N golfillo *m*.

gamine [gæ'miːn] ⃞1 N chica *f* provocativa, joven *f* picaruela.
⃞2 ATTR: ~ **haircut** corte *m* a lo garçon.

gaming ['geɪmɪŋ] ⃞1 N juego *m*.
⃞2 ATTR: ~ **laws** leyes *fpl* reguladoras del juego.

gaming-house ['geɪmɪŋhaus] N, PL **gaming-houses** ['geɪmɪŋhauzɪz] casa *f* de juego.

gamma ['gæmə] ⃞1 N gama *f*.
⃞2 ATTR: ~ **rays** rayos *mpl* gama.

gammon ['gæmən] N (*Brit*) jamón *m*.

gammy* ['gæmɪ] ADJ (*Brit*) tullido, lisiado.

gamp* [gæmp] N (*Brit*) paraguas *m*.

gamut ['gæmət] N gama *f*; **to run the whole** ~ **of ...** recorrer toda la gama de ...

gamy ['geɪmɪ] ADJ *meat* faisandé.

gander ['gændəʳ] N (**a**) ganso *m* (macho). (**b**) **to take a ~:** echar un vistazo (*at* a).

gang [gæŋ] N pandilla *f*, cuadrilla *f*, grupo *m*; (*of workmen*) brigada *f*; (*criminal*) pandilla *f*; **G~ Of Four** (*Pol*) Banda *f* de los Cuatro; **he's one of the** ~ **now** ya es uno de los nuestros.
◆**gang together** VI formar un grupo (*or* una pandilla), agruparse.
◆**gang up** VI conspirar, confabularse, obrar de concierto (*against, on* contra).

gang-bang: ['gæŋbæŋ] ⃞1 N violación *f* múltiple, violación *f* colectiva; sexo *m* tribal:.
⃞2 VT violar colectivamente.

ganger ['gæŋəʳ] N (*Brit*) capataz *m*.

Ganges ['gændʒiːz] N Ganges *m*.

gangland ['gæŋlænd] N mundillo *m* del crimen; ~ **murder** asesinato *m* en el mundillo del crimen, asesinato *m* por ajuste de cuentas entre criminales.

gangling ['gæŋglɪŋ] ADJ larguirucho, desgarbado.

ganglion ['gæŋglɪən] N, PL **ganglia** ['gæŋglɪə] ganglio *m*.

gangplank ['gæŋplæŋk] N (*Naut*) plancha *f*.

gangrene ['gæŋgriːn] N gangrena *f*.

gangrenous ['gæŋgrɪnəs] ADJ gangrenoso.

gangster ['gæŋstəʳ] N pistolero *m*, pandillero *m*, gán(g)ster *m*.

gangsterism ['gæŋstərɪzəm] N gan(g)sterismo *m*.

gangway ['gæŋweɪ] N pasillo *m*, pasadizo *m*; (*Naut: on ship*) escalerilla *f*, pasarela *f*; (*from ship to shore*) plancha *f*, pasadera *f*; (*between seats*) pasillo *m*; ~! ¡abran paso!

ganja: ['gændʒə] N maría* *f* (*Sp*), marihuana *f*.

gannet ['gænɪt] N alcatraz *m*.

gantlet ['gæntlɪt] N (*US Rail*) vía *f* traslapada, vía *f* de garganta.

gantry ['gæntrɪ] N caballete *m*; (*on crane, railway signal*) pórtico *m*; (*for rocket*) torre *f* de lanzamiento.

GAO N (*US*) ABBR of **General Accounting Office** oficina general de contabilidad gubernamental.

gaol [dʒeɪl] N, VT (*Brit*) = **jail**.

gaoler ['dʒeɪləʳ] N (*Brit*) = **jailer**.

gap [gæp] N (*natural*) vacío *m*, hueco *m*; (*man-made*) abertura *f*, brecha *f*; (*in wall etc*) boquete *m*; (*between bars etc*) distancia *f*, separación *f*; (*in mountains*) desfiladero *m*; (*in writing*) espacio *m*; (*in text*) laguna *f*; omisión *f*; (*of time*) intervalo *m*, brecha *f*; (*in process*) solución *f* de continuidad; (*in quality*) disparidad *f*; (*maladjustment*) desfase *m*, desajuste *m*; (*in traffic, trees*) claro *m*; (*crack*) hendedura *f*, resquicio *m*; **there is a ~ in the balance of payments** hay un desequilibrio en la balanza de pagos; **we discerned a ~ in the market** vimos una abertura en el mercado; **to close the ~** cerrar la brecha; **he left a ~ which it will be hard to fill** dejó un hueco difícil de llenar; **leave a ~ for the name** deje un espacio para poner el nombre; **without a ~** sin solución de continuidad.

gape [geɪp] VI (a) abrirse (mucho), estar muy abierto; **the chasm ~d before him** se abría delante de él la sima.
(b) (*person*) estar boquiabierto; pensar en las musarañas; **to ~ at** mirar boquiabierto, embobarse con.

gaping ['geɪpɪŋ] ADJ (a) abierto. (b) *person* boquiabierto, embobado.

gappy ['gæpɪ] ADJ *teeth* separado.

gap-toothed ['gæp'tuːθt] ADJ que ha perdido un diente (*or* varios dientes).

garage ['gærɑːʒ] [1] N (*of house*) garaje *m*, cochera *f*; (*for repairs*) taller *m*; (*petrol station*) gasolinera *f*, estación *f* de servicio.
[2] ATTR: **~ mechanic** mecánico *m*; **~ proprietor** propietario *m*, -a *f* de un taller de reparaciones; **~ sale** venta *f* de objetos usados (*en una casa particular*).
[3] VT dejar en garaje.

garageman ['gærɑːʒˌmæn] N, PL **garagemen** ['gærɑːʒmen] garajista *m*.

garaging ['gærɑːʒɪŋ] N plazas *fpl* de garaje.

garb [gɑːb] [1] N traje *m*, vestido *m*; (*of profession etc*) vestido *m* típico; (*iro*) ropaje *m* (*also fig*).
[2] VT vestir (*in* de).

garbage ['gɑːbɪdʒ] [1] N basuras *fpl*, desperdicios *mpl*; (*fig*) basura *f*; (*Comput*) in, **~ out** basura entra, basura sale.
[2] ATTR: **~ bag** (*US*) bolsa *f* de la basura; **~ can** (*US*) cubo *m* de la basura; **~ collector** (*US*), **~ man** (*US*) basurero *m*; **~ disposal unit** triturador *m* de basuras; **~ dump** (*US*) vertedero *m*; **~ truck** (*US*) camión *m* de la basura.

garble ['gɑːbl] VT mutilar, falsear (por selección).

garbled ['gɑːbld] ADJ mutilado, confuso.

Garda ['gɑːdə] N Policía *f* irlandesa.

garden ['gɑːdn] [1] N jardín *m*; **G~ of Eden** Edén *m*; **everything in the ~ is lovely** todo está a las mil maravillas.
[2] ATTR de jardín; **~ center** (*US*), **~ centre** centro *m* de jardinería; **~ city** (*Brit*) ciudad *f* jardín; **~ flat** piso *m* con jardín en planta baja; **~ furniture** muebles *mpl* de jardín, muebles *mpl* de exterior; **~ hose** manguera *f* de jardín; **to lead sb up the ~ path** embaucar a uno; **~ produce** productos *mpl* de jardín; **~ seat** banco *m* de jardín; **~ shears** tijeras *fpl* de jardín; **~ tools** útiles *mpl* de jardinería; **he lives just over the ~ wall from us** vive justo al otro lado de la valla.
[3] VI cultivar un huerto, trabajar en el jardín (*or* huerto).

gardener ['gɑːdnər] N jardinero *m*, -a *f*; (*market*) hortelano *m*; **I'm no ~** no entiendo de jardinería.

gardenia [gɑːˈdiːnɪə] N gardenia *f*.

gardening ['gɑːdnɪŋ] N jardinería *f*, horticultura *f*.

garden-party ['gɑːdnˌpɑːtɪ] N garden-party *m*, recepción *f* (al aire libre).

garfish ['gɑːˌfɪʃ] N aguja *f*.

gargantuan [gɑːˈgæntjʊən] ADJ gargantuesco, colosal, gigantesco.

gargle ['gɑːgl] [1] N (*act*) gárgaras *fpl*; (*liquid*) gargarismo *m*.
[2] VI gargarizar, hacer gárgaras, gargarear (*LAm*).

gargoyle ['gɑːgɔɪl] N gárgola *f*.

garish ['geərɪʃ] ADJ chillón, llamativo, charro.

garland ['gɑːlənd] [1] N guirnalda *f*.
[2] VT enguirnaldar (*with* de).

garlic ['gɑːlɪk] [1] N ajo *m*.
[2] ATTR: **~ press** aparato *m* para machacar ajos; **~ salt** sal *f* de ajo; **~ sausage** salchicha *f* de ajo.

garlicky ['gɑːlɪkɪ] ADJ *food* con ajo; *breath* con olor a ajo.

garment ['gɑːmənt] N prenda *f* (de vestir).

garner ['gɑːnər] [1] N (*liter*) troj *f*, granero *m*; (*fig*) acopio *m*, abundancia *f*; provisión *f*.
[2] VT entrojar, (*fig*) recoger, acumular.

garnet ['gɑːnɪt] N granate *m*.

garnish ['gɑːnɪʃ] [1] N (*Culin*) aderezo *m*.
[2] VT adornar (*with* de); (*Culin*) aderezar (*with* de).

garnishing ['gɑːnɪʃɪŋ] N (*Culin*) aderezo *m*.

Garonne [gəˈrɒn] N Garona *m*.

garotte [gəˈrɒt] = **garrotte**.

garret ['gærɪt] N guardilla *f*, desván *m*.

garrison ['gærɪsən] [1] N guarnición *f*.
[2] ATTR: **~ town** ciudad *f* con guarnición; **~ troops** tropas *fpl* de guarnición.
[3] VT guarnecer.

garrotte [gəˈrɒt] [1] N garrote *m*.
[2] VT agarrotar.

garrulity [gəˈruːlɪtɪ] N garrulidad *f*.

garrulous ['gærʊləs] ADJ gárrulo.

garrulousness ['gærʊləsnɪs] = **garrulity**.

garter ['gɑːtər] N liga *f*; **Order of the G~** Orden *f* de la Jarretera; **Knight of the G~** Caballero *m* de la Orden de la Jarretera.

garter belt ['gɑːtəbelt] N (*US*) portaligas *m*, liguero *m*.

gas [gæs] [1] N (a) gas *m*. (b) (*US: gasoline*) gasolina *f*; = **gasoline**; **to step on the ~*** tumbar la aguja*, acelerar la marcha. (c) (‡: *fun*) **what a ~!** ¡qué estupendo!*; **he's a ~!** ¡es un tío divertidísimo!*
[2] VT asfixiar con gas, gasear.
[3] VI (*) charlar, parlotear.

gasbag ['gæsbæg] N (*Aer*) bolsa *f* de gas; (*) charlatán *m*, -ana *f*.

gas-bracket ['gæs,brækɪt] N brazo *m* de lámpara de gas.

gas-burner ['gæs,bɜːnər] N mechero *m* de gas.

gas can ['gæs,kæn] N (*US*) bidón *m* de gasolina.

gas-canister ['gæs,kænɪstər] N bombona *f* de gas.

gas-chamber ['gæs,tʃeɪmbər] N cámara *f* de gas.

Gascon ['gæskən] [1] ADJ gascón.
[2] N (a) gascón *m*, -ona *f*. (b) (*Ling*) gascón *m*.

Gascony ['gæskənɪ] N Gascuña *f*.

gas-cooker ['gæs'kʊkər] N cocina *f* de (*or* a) gas.

gas-cooled ['gæsku:ld] ADJ: **~ reactor** reactor *m* enfriado por gas.

gas-cylinder ['gæs,sɪlɪndər] N bombona *f* de gas.

gaseous ['gæsɪəs] ADJ gaseoso.

gas fire ['gæs'faɪər] N estufa *f* de gas.

gas-fired ['gæs,faɪəd] ADJ de gas, alimentado por gas.

gas-fitter ['gæs,fɪtər] N gasista *m*, empleado *m* del gas.

gas-fittings ['gæs,fɪtɪŋz] NPL instalación *f* de gas.

gas-guzzler* ['gæs'gʌzlər] N chupagasolina* *m*.

gash [gæʃ] [1] N raja *f*, hendedura *f*; (*wound*) cuchillada *f*.
[2] VT rajar, hender; (*wound*) acuchillar.
[3] ADJ (*Brit‡*) (*spare*) de sobra; (*free*) gratuito.

gas-heater ['gæs,hiːtər] N estufa *f* de gas.

gasholder ['gæs,həʊldər] N gasómetro *m*.

gasification [,gæsɪfɪˈkeɪʃən] N gasificación *f*.

gas-jet ['gæsdʒet] N llama *f* de mechero de gas.

gasket ['gæskɪt] N junta *f*.

gaslight ['gæslaɪt] N luz *f* de gas, alumbrado *m* de gas.

gas lighter ['gæs,laɪtər] N mechero *m* de gas.

gas lighting ['gæs,laɪtɪŋ] N alumbrado *m* de gas.

gaslit ['gæslɪt] ADJ con alumbrado de gas.

gas-main ['gæsmeɪn] N cañería *f* maestra de gas.

gasman ['gæsmæn] N, PL **gasmen** ['gæsmen] gasista *m*, empleado *m* del gas.

gas-mantle ['gæs,mæntl] N manguito *m* incandescente.

gasmask ['gæsmɑːsk] N careta *f* antigás.

gas-meter ['gæs,miːtər] N contador *m* (*LAm*: medidor *m*) de gas.

gasohol ['gæsəʊhɒl] N (*US*) gasohol *m*.

gas-oil ['gæsɔɪl] N gasóleo *m*.

gasoline ['gæsəliːn] N (*US*) gasolina *f*, nafta *f* (*SC*), bencina *f* (*SC*).

gasometer [gæˈsɒmɪtər] N (*Brit*) gasómetro *m*.

gas-oven ['gæs,ʌvn] N cocina *f* de gas.

gasp [gɑːsp] [1] N boqueada *f*; (*cry*) grito *m* sofocado; **last ~** boqueada *f*; **to be at one's last ~** estar dando las boqueadas; **with a ~ of astonishment** con un grito sofocado de asombro.
[2] VI boquear, anhelar, respirar con dificultad; (*pant*) jadear; **to ~ for air** (*or* **breath**) luchar por respirar; **I was ~ing for a smoke** tenía unas tremendas ganas de fumar; **to ~ with astonishment** dar un grito sofocado de asombro.

◆gasp out VT decir con voz entrecortada.

gas pedal ['gæs,pedal] N (*esp US*) acelerador *m*.

gasper‡ ['gɑːspər] N (*Brit*) pito* *m*, pitillo* *m*.

gas-pipe ['gæspaɪp] N tubo *m* de gas.

gas pipeline [,gæs'paɪplaɪn] N gasoducto *m*.

gas pump ['gæs,pʌmp] N (*US*) (*in car*) bomba *f* de gasolina; (*in gas station*) surtidor *m* de gasolina.

gas-ring ['gæsrɪŋ] N hornillo *m* de gas.

gassed‡ [gæst] ADJ (*US*) bebido, enmonado*.

gas station ['gæs,steɪʃən] N (*US*) gasolinera *f*.

gas-stove ['gæs'stəʊv] N cocina *f* de (*or* a) gas.

gassy ['gæsɪ] ADJ gaseoso.

gastank ['gæstæŋk] N (*US*) depósito *m* de gasolina.

gas-tap ['gæstæp] N llave *f* del gas.

gastric ['gæstrɪk] ADJ gástrico; **~ flu** gripe *f* gastrointestinal; **~ juice** jugos *mpl* gástricos; **~ ulcer** úlcera *f* gástrica.

gastritis [gæs'traɪtɪs] N gastritis *f*.

gastro... ['gæstrəʊ] PREF gastro...

gastroenteritis [,gæstrəʊ,entə'raɪtɪs] N gastroenteritis *f*.

gastronome [,gæstrənəʊm] N, **gastronomist** [,gæs'trɒnəmɪst] N gastrónomo *m*, -a *f*.

gastronomic [,gæstrə'nɒmɪk] ADJ gastronómico.

gastronomy [gæs'trɒnəmɪ] N gastronomía *f*.

gastropod ['gæstrəpɒd] N gastrópodo *m*.

gas turbine [ˌgæs'tɜːbaɪn] N turbina f de gas.
gas worker ['gæs,wɜːkəʳ] N trabajador m, -ora f de la compañía de gas.
gasworks ['gæswɜːks] N fábrica f de gas.
gat‡ [gæt] N (US) revólver m, quitapenas‡ m.
gate [geɪt] N (a) puerta f (also of town); (iron) verja f; (Rail) barrera f; (of sluice) compuerta f. (b) (Sport) entrada f, taquillaje m, recaudación f.
-gate [-geɪt] N ending in compounds: **Irangate** Irangate m.
gâteau ['gætəʊ] N, PL **gâteaux** ['gætəʊz] (Brit) tarta f.
gatecrash ['geɪtkræʃ] 1 VT colarse (de gorra) en, asistir sin ser invitado a.
  2 VI colarse (de gorra), asistir sin ser invitado.
gatecrasher ['geɪt,kræʃəʳ] N intruso m, -a f, colado m, -a f.
gatehouse ['geɪthaʊs] N, PL **gatehouses** ['geɪt,haʊzɪz] casa f del guarda (or del portero etc).
gatekeeper ['geɪt,kiːpəʳ] N portero m; (Rail) guardabarrera m.
gate-legged ['geɪtlegd] ADJ: ~ **table** mesa f de alas abatibles.
gate-money ['geɪt,mʌnɪ] N ingresos mpl de entrada, recaudación f.
gatepost ['geɪtpəʊst] N poste m (de una puerta de cercado); **between you, me, and the** ~ en confianza, entre nosotros.
gateway ['geɪtweɪ] N (a) = **gate.** (b) (fig) puerta f, pórtico m (to de).
gather ['gæðəʳ] 1 VT (a) (assemble) reunir, recoger; acumular, acopiar; (harvest) recolectar; flowers, wood coger (Sp), recoger (LAm); (Sew) fruncir.
  (b) (collect) **to** ~ **dust** empolvarse; **to** ~ **speed** ganar velocidad, ir cada vez más rápidamente; **to** ~ **strength** cobrar fuerzas.
  (c) (infer) **to** ~ **that** ... colegir que, sacar la consecuencia que ...; **I** ~ **from him that** ... según lo que él me dice; **what are we to** ~ **from this?** ¿qué consecuencia sacamos de esto?; **as you will have** ~**ed** según habrás comprendido; **as one** ~**s from these reports** según se desprende de estos informes.
  2 VI reunirse, juntarse, congregarse; (clouds) amontonarse; (Med) formar pus; **the** ~**ing storm** la tormenta que amenaza.
  3 N (Sew) frunce m.
♦**gather in** VT recoger; taxes etc recaudar.
♦**gather round** 1 VT: **to** ~ **round sb** agruparse en torno a uno.
  2 VI: ~ **round!** ¡acercaos!
♦**gather together** 1 VT reunir, juntar.
  2 VI reunirse, juntarse, congregarse.
♦**gather up** VT recoger.
gathered ['gæðəd] ADJ (Sew) fruncido.
gatherer ['gæðərəʳ] N (of flowers, nuts) recolector m, -ora f; (of intelligence) recopilador m, -ora f; V also **hunter-gatherer**.
gathering ['gæðərɪŋ] N (a) (meeting) reunión f, asamblea f; (persons present) concurrencia f. (b) (Med) absceso m. (c) (Typ) alzado m.
gator*, **'gator*** ['geɪtəʳ] (US) = **alligator.**
GATT [gæt] N ABBR of **General Agreement on Tariffs and Trade** Acuerdo m General Sobre Aranceles Aduaneros y Comercio, GATT m.
gauche [gəʊʃ] ADJ torpe, desmañado; (socially) falto de confianza, poco seguro de sí mismo.
gaucho ['gaʊtʃəʊ] N gaucho m.
gaudy ['gɔːdɪ] ADJ colour, cloth chillón, llamativo; building etc vulgar y hortera.
gauge [geɪdʒ] 1 N (standard measure) norma f de medida; (of gun etc) calibre m; (test) indicación f, prueba f; (instrument) calibrador m; indicador m, manómetro m; (Rail) ancho m, entrevía f, trocha f (LAm).
  2 VT medir; calibrar; (fig) juzgar, estimar; **to** ~ **the distance with one's eye** medir la distancia con el ojo; **to** ~ **the right moment** elegir el momento propicio.
Gaul [gɔːl] N (a) Galia f. (b) (person) galo m, -a f.
Gaullist ['gəʊlɪst] 1 ADJ gaulista, golista.
  2 N gaulista mf, golista mf.
gaunt [gɔːnt] ADJ flaco, desvaído, chupado; (fig) severo, adusto.
gauntlet ['gɔːntlɪt] N guante m; (armour) guantelete m; **to run the** ~ (Mil Hist) correr baquetas; **to run the** ~ **of** (fig) pasar por los peligros de; salir ileso de; **to throw down the** ~ arrojar el guante.
gauze [gɔːz] N gasa f.
gauzy ['gɔːzɪ] ADJ vaporoso; **a** ~ **nightdress** un vaporoso vestido de noche.
gave [geɪv] PRET of **give.**
gavel ['gævl] N martillo m (de presidente o subastador).
gavotte [gə'vɒt] N gavota f.
Gawd‡ [gɔːd] EXCL (Brit = **God**) ¡Dios mío!
gawk [gɔːk] 1 N papamoscas mf.
  2 VI papar moscas.
gawky ['gɔːkɪ] ADJ desgarbado, torpe.
gawp* [gɔːp] VI papar moscas; **to** ~ **at** mirar boquiabierto.
gay [geɪ] 1 ADJ (a) (US†: cheerful) alegre; appearance brillante, vistoso; colour vivo, brillante; life lleno de placeres. (b) (homosexual) gay, homosexual; ~ **club** club m para gays; ~ **lib(eration)** campaña f pro

derechos de los homosexuales; ~ **movement** movimiento m homosexual; ~ **rights** derechos mpl de los homosexuales.
  2 N gay mf, homosexual mf.
gayness ['geɪnɪs] N homosexualidad f.
Gaza Strip ['gɑːzə'strɪp] N Franja f de Gaza.
gaze [geɪz] 1 N mirada f (fija); **his** ~ **met mine** cruzamos una mirada.
  2 VI (also **to** ~ **at, to** ~ **upon**) mirar (con fijeza), contemplar.
gazebo [gə'ziːbəʊ] N, PL **gazebos** or **gazeboes** cenador m.
gazelle [gə'zel] N gacela f.
gazette [gə'zet] N gaceta f.
gazetteer [ˌgæzɪ'tɪəʳ] N diccionario m geográfico.
gazpacho [gæz'pætʃəʊ] N gazpacho m.
gazump* [gə'zʌmp] (Brit) 1 VT person ofrecer un precio más alto que; **we were** ~**ed** ofrecieron más que nosotros.
  2 VI faltar a una promesa de vender (esp una casa) para aceptar un precio más alto ofrecido por otro.
gazumping* [gə'zʌmpɪŋ] N la subida del precio de una casa una vez que ya ha sido apalabrado.
gazunder* [gə'zʌndəʳ] (Brit) 1 VT person ofrecer un precio más bajo a; **we were** ~**ed** nos ofrecieron menos de lo antes convenido.
  2 VI ofrecer un precio más bajo de lo antes convenido.
  3 N la baja en la oferta para comprar una casa una vez que ya ha sido apalabrada.
GB N ABBR of **Great Britain** Gran Bretaña f.
GBH N (Brit Jur) ABBR of **grievous bodily harm** graves daños mpl corporales.
GBP, gbp ABBR of **Great British Pounds.**
GBS (Brit) ABBR of **George Bernard Shaw.**
GC N (Brit) ABBR of **George Cross** medalla del valor civil.
GCA N ABBR of **ground-controlled approach** aproximación f controlada desde tierra.
GCE N (Brit) ABBR of **General Certificate of Education.**
GCHQ N (Brit) ABBR of **Government Communications Headquarters** entidad gubernamental que recoge datos mediante escuchas electrónicas.
GCSE N (Brit) ABBR of **General Certificate of Secondary Education.**

┌─── GCSE ───┐

ⓘ El **GCSE** o **General Certificate of Secondary Education** es el certificado académico que se expide en el Reino Unido (con la excepción de Escocia, cuyo equivalente es el **Standard Grade**) para cada una de las asignaturas de la Educación Secundaria Obligatoria. Los exámenes tienen lugar cuando el alumno tiene dieciséis años y las calificaciones van de la A a la G, (A es la máxima, G la mínima), y son el resultado de la combinación de una evaluación continua y de la nota de los exámenes finales, que son corregidos por un tribunal ajeno al centro escolar.
⇨ Ver también ADVANCED LEVELS , EDUCATION
└──┘

gdn ABBR of **garden** jardín m.
Gdns ABBR of **Gardens** jardines mpl.
GDP N ABBR of **gross domestic product** producto m interior bruto, PIB m.
GDR N (Hist) ABBR of **German Democratic Republic** República f Democrática Alemana, RDA f.
gear [gɪəʳ] 1 N (a) (equipment) equipo m, herramientas fpl, pertrechos mpl; (fishing) aparejo m; (possessions) cosas fpl, bártulos mpl; (Brit: clothing) ropa f, traje m.
  (b) (apparatus) aparato m, mecanismo m.
  (c) (Mech) engranaje m, rueda f dentada; **in** ~ en juego, engranado; **to be in** ~ **with** engranar con; **to throw out of** ~ desengranar, (fig) dislocar.
  (d) (Aut etc: speed) marcha f, velocidad f, cambio m; **there are 5 forward** ~**s** hay 5 marchas adelante; **high** ~ (US) (fourth) cuarta velocidad f, directa f; (fifth) quinta velocidad f, superdirecta f; **to change** ~ (Brit), **to shift** ~ (US) cambiar de marcha.
  2 ATTR: ~ **ratio** (of cycle) proporción f entre plato y piñón.
  3 VT (Mech) engranar (into, with con); **the programme is** ~**ed in with** (or to) the plan el programa forma parte integral del plan.
  4 VI engranar (into, with con); **it** ~**s in with the plan** concuerda con el plan, se desarrolla al ritmo del plan.
♦**gear down** VT (Mech) desmultiplicar; (fig) reducir, rebajar.
♦**gear up** 1 VT (Mech) multiplicar; (fig) aumentar; intensificar.
  2 VI hacer preparativos, prepararse; **they are** ~**ing up to fight** se están disponiendo para luchar.
gearbox ['gɪəbɒks] N (Brit Aut) caja f de cambios; (Mech) caja f de engranajes.
gear-lever ['gɪə,liːvəʳ] N, **gear-change** ['gɪə,tʃeɪndʒ] N (Brit), (US) **gearshift** ['gɪəʃɪft] N, **gearstick*** ['gɪə,stɪk] N (Brit) palanca f de cambios.
gearwheel ['gɪəwiːl] N rueda f dentada.
gecko ['gekəʊ] N geco m, dragón m.
GED N (US) ABBR of **general educational development.**

geddid* ['gedɪd] = **get it?** (¿entiendes?).
gee¹* [dʒiː] INTERJ (esp US) ¡caramba!; ~ **whiz!*** ¡corcholís!*; ~ **up!** ¡arre!
gee²* [dʒiː] N (also ~-~: baby talk) caballito m, tatán m.
gee-gee* ['dʒiːdʒiː] N (child's language, hum) caballo m, jaca f.
geek* [giːk] N (esp US) cretino m, -a f.
geeky* ['giːkɪ] ADJ (esp US) cretino.
geese [giːs] NPL of **goose**.
geezer* ['giːzəʳ] N (Brit) vejancón* m, tío* m.
Geiger counter ['gaɪɡə,kaʊntəʳ] N contador m Geiger.
geisha ['geɪʃə] N geisha f.
gel [dʒel] [1] N gel m.
[2] VI aglutinarse; (fig) cuajar.
gelatin(e) ['dʒelətiːn] N gelatina f.
gelatinous [dʒɪ'lætɪnəs] ADJ gelatinoso.
geld [geld] VT castrar, capar.
gelding ['geldɪŋ] N caballo m castrado.
gelignite ['dʒelɪɡnaɪt] N gelignita f.
gelt* [gelt] N (US) pasta* f.
gem [dʒem] N joya f (also fig), piedra f preciosa, gema f.
Gemini ['dʒemɪniː] NPL (Zodiac) Géminis m, Gemelos mpl.
gemstone ['dʒemstəʊn] N piedra f preciosa, piedra f semipreciosa.
Gen. (Mil) ABBR of **General** General m, Gen., Gral.
gen. ABBR of **general, generally**.
gen* [dʒen] (Brit) N información f; **to give sb the ~ on sth** poner a uno al corriente de algo.
◆ **gen up*** (Brit) [1] VT: **to ~ sb up** informar a uno; **I'm thoroughly ~ned up now** ahora estoy bien enterado, ahora estoy completamente al tanto.
[2] VI: **to ~ up on sth** informarse acerca de algo.
gendarme ['ʒãːndɑːm] N gendarme m.
gender ['dʒendəʳ] N género m.
gene [dʒiːn] N gene m, gen m.
genealogical [,dʒiːnɪə'lɒdʒɪkəl] ADJ genealógico.
genealogist [,dʒiːnɪ'ælədʒɪst] N genealogista mf.
genealogy [,dʒiːnɪ'ælədʒɪ] N genealogía f.
genera ['dʒenərə] NPL of **genus**.
general ['dʒenərəl] [1] ADJ general; (common) corriente, usual; ~ **anaesthetic**, ~ **anesthetic** (US) anestesia f general; ~ **assembly** asamblea f general; ~ **average** media f general; (Comm) avería f general; ~ **audit** auditoría f general; ~ **cargo** mercancías fpl (de) general, cargamento m mixto; ~ **delivery** (US, Canada) lista f de correos; ~ **expenses** gastos mpl generales; ~ **knowledge** conocimientos mpl generales; ~ **manager** director m, -ora f general; ~ **partnership** sociedad f regular colectiva; ~ **practice** (Med) medicina f general; ~ **practitioner** médico m, -a f de cabecera, médico m, -a f de medicina general; **the ~ public** el público en general, el gran público; ~ **reserve** reserva f general; ~ **staff** estado m mayor general; ~ **store** tienda f (de pueblo) que vende de todo; ~ **strike** huelga f general.
[2] N (Mil) general m, -ala f; (servant) chica f para todo; **in ~** en general, por lo general.
generalissimo [,dʒenərə'lɪsɪməʊ] N generalísimo m.
generality [,dʒenə'rælɪtɪ] N generalidad f.
generalization [,dʒenərəlaɪ'zeɪʃən] N generalización f.
generalize [,dʒenərəlaɪz] VI generalizar.
generally ['dʒenərəlɪ] ADV generalmente, en general, por lo común; ~ **speaking** en términos generales.
general-purpose [,dʒenərəl'pɜːpəs] ADJ tool, dictionary de uso general.
generalship ['dʒenərəlʃɪp] N estrategia f, táctica f; (leadership) dirección f, don m de mando.
generate ['dʒenəreɪt] VT (Elec etc) generar; (fig) producir.
generating ['dʒenəreɪtɪŋ] ATTR: ~ **set** grupo m electrógeno; ~ **station** central f generadora.
generation [,dʒenə'reɪʃən] [1] N (gen, Ling) generación f.
[2] ATTR: ~ **gap** desnivel m generacional, barrera f generacional.
generational [,dʒenə'reɪʃənl] ADJ generacional.
generative ['dʒenərətɪv] ADJ generativo; ~ **grammar** gramática f generativa.
generator ['dʒenəreɪtəʳ] N grupo m electrógeno, generador m.
generic [dʒɪ'nerɪk] ADJ genérico.
generosity [,dʒenə'rɒsɪtɪ] N generosidad f.
generous ['dʒenərəs] ADJ generoso; espléndido, dadivoso; supply, quantity abundante, amplio, liberal.
generously ['dʒenərəslɪ] ADV generosamente; abundantemente.
genesis ['dʒenɪsɪs] N (a) génesis f. (b) G~ Génesis m.
genet ['dʒenɪt] N jineta mf.
genetic [dʒɪ'netɪk] ADJ genético, genésico; ~ **code** código m genético; ~ **engineering** ingeniería f genética; ~ **fingerprint(ing)** huella f genética.
genetically [dʒɪ'netɪkəlɪ] ADV (gen) genéticamente; ~ **engineered** manipulado genéticamente.
geneticist [dʒɪ'netɪsɪst] N geneticista mf; (Med) genetista mf.
genetics [dʒɪ'netɪks] NPL genética f.

Geneva [dʒɪ'niːvə] N Ginebra f; ~ **Convention** Convención f de Ginebra.
genial ['dʒiːnɪəl] ADJ simpático, afable.
geniality [,dʒiːnɪ'ælɪtɪ] N simpatía f, afabilidad f.
genially ['dʒiːnɪəlɪ] ADV afablemente.
genie ['dʒiːnɪ] N genio m.
genital ['dʒenɪtl] [1] ADJ genital; ~ **herpes** herpes m genital.
[2] NPL: ~s genitales mpl.
genitalia [,dʒenɪ'teɪlɪə] NPL genitales mpl.
genitive ['dʒenɪtɪv] [1] ADJ genitivo; ~ **case** = **2**.
[2] N genitivo m.
genius ['dʒiːnɪəs] N genio m; genialidad f; **man of ~** hombre m genial; **he's a ~** es un genio, es genial; **you're a ~!** (iro) ¡eres un hacha!; **he has a ~ for propaganda** es un genio para la propaganda; **you have a ~ for forgetting things** tienes un don especial para olvidar las cosas.
genned up ['dʒend'ʌp] ADJ V **gen up**.
Genoa ['dʒenəʊə] N Génova f.
genocidal [,dʒenəʊ'saɪdl] ADJ genocida.
genocide ['dʒenəʊsaɪd] N genocidio m.
Genoese [dʒenəʊ'iːz] [1] ADJ genovés.
[2] N genovés m, -esa f.
genome ['dʒiːnəʊm] N genoma m.
genotype ['dʒenəʊtaɪp] N genotipo m.
genre [ʒãːŋr] N género m.
gent* [dʒent] N ABBR of **gentleman** caballero m; ~**s'*** wáter m (de caballeros); **what will you have, ~s?** (hum) ¿qué vais a tomar, caballeros?; ver también TOILET .
genteel [dʒen'tiːl] ADJ (iro) fino, elegante; (pej) cursi; accent etc refinado, de buen tono, señorito*.
gentian ['dʒenʃɪən] N genciana f; ~ **violet** violeta f de genciana.
gentile ['dʒentaɪl] [1] ADJ no judío; (pagan) gentil.
[2] N no judío m, -a f; (pagan) gentil mf.
gentility [dʒen'tɪlɪtɪ] N (iro) finura f, elegancia f; buen tono m.
gentle ['dʒentl] ADJ person's character benévolo, amable; apacible; breeze, heat, stop, progress, transition etc suave; rule blando; sound, voice dulce; push, touch ligero; (slow) lento, pausado; hint, reminder discreto; animal etc manso, dócil, apacible; (tender) dulce, tierno; **of ~ birth** bien nacido; ~ **reader** amado lector; **the ~ sex** el sexo débil.
gentleman ['dʒentlmən] [1] N, PL **gentlemen** ['dʒentlmən] (man) señor m; (having gentlemanly qualities) caballero m; (at court) gentilhombre m; ~**'s** ~ ayuda m de cámara; **gentlemen's agreement** pacto m de caballeros; **young** ~ señorito m; **there's a ~ waiting to see you** le espera un señor; **to be a perfect ~** ser un cumplido caballero; **he's no ~** poco caballero es él; **'gentlemen'** (lavatory) 'caballeros'.
[2] ATTR: ~ **farmer** terrateniente m.
gentlemanly ['dʒentlmənlɪ] ADJ caballeroso; cortés, fino.
gentleness ['dʒentlnɪs] N amabilidad f; suavidad f; dulzura f; mansedumbre f; docilidad f; ternura f.
gentlewoman ['dʒentl,wʊmən] N, PL **gentlewomen** ['dʒentl,wɪmɪn] dama f, señora f de buena familia.
gently ['dʒentlɪ] ADV suavemente; dulcemente; (slowly) despacio, pausadamente, poco a poco; apaciblemente; tiernamente; ~!, ~ **now!**, ~ **there!** ¡más despacio!, ¡con cuidado!
gentrification [,dʒentrɪfɪ'keɪʃən] N aburguesamiento m.
gentrified ['dʒentrɪ,faɪd] ADJ area, houses aburguesado.
gentrify ['dʒentrɪfaɪ] VT aburguesar.
gentry ['dʒentrɪ] N (Brit) alta burguesía f, pequeña aristocracia f; (pej) familias fpl bien, gente f bien; (set of people) gente f.
genuflect ['dʒenjʊflekt] VI doblar la rodilla.
genuflexion, (US) **genuflection** [,dʒenjʊ'flekʃən] N genuflexión f.
genuine ['dʒenjʊɪn] ADJ auténtico, legítimo, genuino; person sincero; **this dancer is the ~ article** esta bailarina es un ejemplar auténtico.
genuinely ['dʒenjʊɪnlɪ] ADV prove, originate auténticamente; feel, think sinceramente; sorry, surprised, unable verdaderamente.
genuineness ['dʒenjʊɪnnɪs] N autenticidad f; sinceridad f.
genus ['dʒenəs] N, PL **genera** ['dʒenərə] género m.
geo... ['dʒiːəʊ] PREF geo...
geochemical [,dʒiːəʊ'kemɪkəl] ADJ geoquímico.
geochemist [,dʒiːəʊ'kemɪst] N geoquímico m, -a f.
geochemistry [,dʒiːəʊ'kemɪstrɪ] N geoquímica f.
geodesic [,dʒiː(ː)əʊ'desɪk] ADJ geodésico.
geodesy [dʒiː'ɒdɪsɪ] N geodesia f.
geodetic [,dʒiːəʊ'detɪk] = **geodesic**.
Geoffrey ['dʒefrɪ] NM Geofredo, Godofredo.
geographer [dʒɪ'ɒɡrəfəʳ] N geógrafo m, -a f.

┌─ NATIONAL GEOGRAPHIC SOCIETY ─┐

ⓘ *La **National Geographic Society** es una organización norteamericana de carácter científico y educativo fundada en Washington D.F. en 1888, para el desarrollo y la difusión del estudio de la geografía. Para hacerse* *miembro de esta sociedad basta con subscribirse a su famosa revista mensual, cuyos ejemplares, con el borde amarillo, han pasado a convertirse en objeto de colección para los estadounidenses. Esta sociedad sin ánimo de lucro también publica libros, mapas y material escolar, produce documentales para la televisión y ha patrocinado más de 4.000 exploraciones y proyectos de investigación. En su afán de estimular la enseñanza de la geografía, su Fundación para la Educación concede los premios **Distinguished Geography Educator** y organiza cursos de verano para profesores.*

geographical [dʒɪə'græfɪkəl] ADJ geográfico.

geographically [dʒɪə'græfɪkəlɪ] ADV geográficamente; ~ **speaking** desde el punto de vista geográfico.

geography [dʒɪ'ɒgrəfɪ] N geografía f; **let me show you the ~ of the house** (*euph*) te voy a mostrar dónde están los servicios.

geological [dʒɪə'lɒdʒɪkəl] ADJ geológico.

geologically [dʒɪə'lɒdʒɪkəlɪ] ADV geológicamente; ~ **speaking** desde el punto de vista geológico.

geologist [dʒɪ'ɒlədʒɪst] N geólogo m, -a f.

geology [dʒɪ'ɒlədʒɪ] N geología f.

geomagnetic [ˌdʒɪəʊmæg'netɪk] ADJ geomagnético.

geomagnetism [ˌdʒɪəʊ'mægnɪˌtɪzəm] N geomagnetismo m.

geometric(al) [dʒɪə'metrɪk(əl)] ADJ geométrico; ~ **progression** progresión f geométrica.

geometrically [dʒɪə'metrɪkəlɪ] ADV geométricamente.

geometry [dʒɪ'ɒmɪtrɪ] N geometría f.

geomorphic [ˌdʒɪə'mɔːfɪk] ADJ geomórfico.

geomorphologic(al) [ˌdʒɪəʊmɔːfə'lɒdʒɪk(əl)] ADJ geomorfológico.

geomorphology [ˌdʒɪəʊmɔː'fɒlədʒɪ] N geomorfología f.

geophysical [ˌdʒɪə'fɪzɪkəl] ADJ geofísico.

geophysicist [ˌdʒɪəʊ'fɪzɪsɪst] N geofísico m, -a f.

geophysics [dʒɪəʊ'fɪzɪks] N SING geofísica f.

geopolitical [ˌdʒɪəʊpə'lɪtɪkəl] ADJ geopolítico.

geopolitics [dʒɪəʊ'pɒlɪtɪks] N SING geopolítica f.

Geordie* ['dʒɔːdɪ] N (*Brit*) habitante mf de Tyneside en el NE de Inglaterra.

George [dʒɔːdʒ] NM Jorge.

Georgia ['dʒɔːdʒɪə] N (*US and USSR*) Georgia f.

Georgian ['dʒɔːdʒɪən] ADJ (*Brit*) georgiano.

geoscience [ˌdʒɪəʊ'saɪəns] N geociencia f.

geoscientist [ˌdʒɪəʊ'saɪəntɪst] N geocientífico m, -a f.

geostationary [ˌdʒɪəʊ'steɪʃənərɪ] ADJ geostacionario.

geostrategic [ˌdʒɪəʊstrə'tiːdʒɪk] ADJ geoestratégico.

geostrategy [ˌdʒɪəʊ'strætədʒɪ] N geoestrategia f.

geothermal [ˌdʒɪəʊ'θɜːməl] ADJ geotérmico.

geranium [dʒɪ'reɪnɪəm] N geranio m.

gerbil ['dʒɜːbɪl] N gerbo m, jerbo m.

geriatric [ˌdʒerɪ'ætrɪk] **1** ADJ geriátrico.
2 N geriátrico m, -a f.

geriatrics [ˌdʒerɪ'ætrɪks] N SING geriatría f.

germ [dʒɜːm] N germen m; (*Med*) microbio m, bacilo m, bacteria f; (*Bio, also fig*) germen m; **the ~ of an idea** el germen de una idea.

German ['dʒɜːmən] **1** ADJ alemán; ~ **Democratic Republic** (*Hist*) República f Democrática Alemana; ~ **measles** rubeola f, rubéola f; ~ **shepherd (dog)** (*US*) pastor m alemán, perro m lobo.
2 N (a) alemán m, -ana f. (b) (*Ling*) alemán m.

germane [dʒɜː'meɪn] ADJ relacionado (*to* con); **not ~ to the issue** inoportuno.

Germanic [dʒɜː'mænɪk] ADJ germánico.

germanium [dʒɜː'meɪnɪəm] N germanio m.

germanophile [dʒɜː'mænəfaɪl] N germanófilo m, -a f.

germanophobe [dʒɜː'mænəfəʊb] N germanófobo m, -a f.

German-speaking ['dʒɜːmən,spiːkɪŋ] ADJ de habla alemana.

Germany ['dʒɜːmənɪ] N Alemania f; **East ~** (*Hist*) Alemania f Oriental; **West ~** (*Hist*) Alemania f Occidental.

germ carrier ['dʒɜːm,kærɪəʳ] N portador m, -ora f de microbios (*or* bacterias).

germ cell ['dʒɜːm'sel] N célula f germen.

germ-free [ˌdʒɜːm'friː] ADJ esterilizado.

germicidal [ˌdʒɜːmɪ'saɪdl] ADJ germicida, microbicida, bactericida.

germicide ['dʒɜːmɪsaɪd] N germicida m, bactericida m.

germinate ['dʒɜːmɪneɪt] VI germinar.

germination [ˌdʒɜːmɪ'neɪʃən] N germinación f.

germ-killer ['dʒɜːm,kɪləʳ] N germicida m, bactericida m.

germ plasm ['dʒɜːm'plæzəm] N germen m plasma.

germproof [ˌdʒɜːmpruːf] ADJ a prueba de microbios (*or* bacterias).

germ warfare [dʒɜːm'wɔːfeəʳ] N guerra f bacteriana.

gerontocracy [ˌdʒerɒn'tɒkrəsɪ] N gerontocracia f.

gerontologist [ˌdʒerɒn'tɒlədʒɪst] N gerontólogo m, -a f.

gerontology [ˌdʒerɒn'tɒlədʒɪ] N gerontología f.

Gerry ['dʒerɪ] NM *familiar form of* **Gerald, Gerard**.

gerrymander ['dʒerɪmændəʳ] VI falsificar elecciones.

gerrymandering ['dʒerɪmændərɪŋ] N fraude m electoral, pucherazo* m.

gerund ['dʒerənd] N (*Latin*) gerundio m; (*English*) sustantivo m verbal.

gerundive [dʒə'rʌndɪv] **1** ADJ gerundivo.
2 N gerundio m.

gestalt [gə'ʃtɑːlt] **1** N gestalt m.
2 ATTR: ~ **psychology** psicología f gestalt.

Gestapo [ges'tɑːpəʊ] N Gestapo f.

gestate [dʒes'teɪt] VT (a) (*Bio*) llevar en el útero. (b) (*fig*) *idea* meditar.

gestation [dʒes'teɪʃən] N gestación f.

gesticulate [dʒes'tɪkjʊleɪt] VI accionar, gesticular, manotear.

gesticulation [dʒes,tɪkjʊ'leɪʃən] N gesticulación f, manoteo m.

gestural ['dʒestʃərəl] ADJ *language* gestual.

gesture ['dʒestʃəʳ] **1** N (a) (*lit*) ademán m, gesto m.
(b) (*fig*) demostración f; (*small token*) muestra f, detalle m; **as a ~ of friendship** en señal de amistad; **as a ~ of support** para demostrar nuestro apoyo; **empty ~** pura formalidad f; **what a nice ~!** ¡qué detalle!
2 VI hacer un ademán; **he ~d towards the door** con la mano indicó la puerta.
3 VT expresar con un ademán.

get [get] (*irr.* PRET **got**, PTP **got**, US **gotten**) **1** VT (a) (*obtain*) obtener, adquirir, (*after effort*) lograr, conseguir; (*buy*) comprar; (*find*) encontrar; (*gain*) ganar; *prize* ganar, llevarse; *reputation* granjearse, hacerse; *credit, glory* atribuirse; (*receive*) recibir; *radio station* captar, sintonizar; *wage* cobrar; *benefit, profit* sacar; *goals, points* marcar; **he got it for me** él me lo procuró; **he got me a job** me consiguió un puesto; **that's what got him the rise** eso fue lo que le valió el aumento; **I never got an answer** no me contestaron; **~ me Mr X, please** (*Telec*) póngame (*LAm*: comuníqueme) con el Sr X, por favor; **he got 6 months** le condenaron a 6 meses de prisión; **I don't ~ much from his lectures** saco poco provecho de sus clases; **we shan't ~ anything out of him** no lograremos sacarle nada, no nos dirá nada; **what are you ~ting out of it?** ¿qué vas a sacar de ello?, ¿qué vas a sacar en beneficio propio?; **you may ~ some fun out of it** puede que te resulte divertido; **we got him on the subject of drugs** logramos que hablase de las drogas.
(b) (*arrest*) prender, detener; (*capture, kill*) cazar; **got you at last!** ¡por fin te he cazado!; **I'll ~ him one day!** ¡algún día me lo cargaré!; **I'll ~ you yet!** ¡me las pagarás!; **he got it from the teacher** el profesor le echó un rapapolvo; **they're out to ~ him** andan tras él, se proponen cargárselo.
(c) *disease* coger (*Sp*), agarrar (*LAm*); **to ~ religion** darse a la religión; V **bad 2**.
(d) (*: *irritate*) **that's what ~s me!** ¡eso es lo que más me fastidia!
(e) (*: *attract*) **this tune ~s me** esta melodía me chifla*, esta melodía me apasiona.
(f) (*strike*) dar en; **it got him on the head** le dio en la cabeza; **it ~s me in the throat** me afecta la garganta.
(g) (*: *understand*) comprender; (**do you**) **~ it?** ¿ya caes?*, ¿me entiendes?
(h) (*move*) trasladar, pasar; **we can't ~ it through the door** no lo podemos pasar por la puerta; **to ~ sth past the customs** conseguir pasar algo por la aduana; **how can we ~ it home?** ¿cómo podemos llevarlo a casa?
(i) (*fetch*) buscar, traer, ir a buscar; *person* llamar, ir por; **I'll go and ~ it for you** te lo voy a buscar; **please ~ the doctor** por favor llame al médico; **can I ~ you a drink?** ¿quieres tomar algo?, ¿te traigo algo de beber?
(j) *meal* preparar, hacer.
(k) **to have got** tener, poseer; **what have you got there?** ¿qué tienes ahí?; **there you've got me** eso no te lo puedo decir, no sé nada de eso.
(l) **to have got to** + *infin* tener que + *infin*.
(m) **to ~ sb to do sth** (*persuading*) conseguir que uno haga algo, persuadir a uno a hacer algo; (*ordering*) encargar a uno que haga algo.
(n) **to get** + PTP *or adj*: **to ~ sth done** mandar hacer algo; **to ~ one's hair cut** hacerse cortar el pelo, cortarse el pelo; **to ~ one's feet wet** mojarse los pies; (*often translated by a simple verb, eg*) **to ~ sth ready** preparar algo; **to ~ sb drunk** emborrachar a uno.
(o) **to ~ sth going** poner algo en marcha, hacer que algo empiece a funcionar; **to ~ a plan moving** hacer que se empiece a realizar un proyecto.
2 VI (a) (*become*) ponerse, volverse, hacerse (*for usage, V* **become 2** (c); **to ~** + PTP *or adj is often translated by passive, vi or vr*) **to ~ beaten** ser vencido; **to ~ run over** ser atropellado; **to ~ angry** enfadarse, enojarse (*LAm*); **to ~ dark** hacerse de noche, anochecer; **to ~ drunk** emborracharse; **to ~ excited** emocionarse; **to ~ hurt** hacerse daño; **to ~ married** casarse; **to ~ old** envejecer(se); **to ~ wet** mojarse.
(b) (*reach*) **to ~ from A to B** ir de A a B, trasladarse de A a B; **to ~ to a place** llegar a un lugar; **how did it ~ here?** ¿cómo vino a parar aquí?; **he got there late** llegó tarde; **now we're ~ting somewhere**

ahora empezamos a hacer progresos; **the whisky has got to him*** el whisky le ha afectado.

(c) (**≠**: *go*) largarse*; **~!** ¡lárgate!*

(d) **to ~ +** *ger* empezar a + *infin*; **we got talking** empezamos a charlar; **to ~ going, to ~ moving** ponerse en marcha; **~ going!** ¡menearse!; ¡andando!; **the idea never got going** la idea nunca tuvo consecuencias prácticas.

(e) (+ *infin*) **to ~ to do sth** llegar (con el tiempo) a hacer algo; **to ~ to like sth** tomar afición a algo; **we never got to see him** no logramos verle; **eventually I got to be an expert at it** por fin llegué a hacerlo bastante bien.

3 VR: **to ~ o.s. arrested** hacerse detener; **to ~ o.s. drunk** emborracharse; **to ~ o.s. lost** extraviarse.

◆**get about** VI (a) (*person*) salir mucho, viajar mucho, ir a muchos sitios; (*after illness*) levantarse y salir. (b) (*report*) saberse, divulgarse.

◆**get above** VR: **to ~ above o.s.** engreírse.

◆**get across** **1** VT (a) *load etc* pasar, hacer pasar. (b) *message etc* hacer entender, lograr comunicar. (c) **he got across the manager*** se indispuso con el jefe.

2 VI (a) (*person*) lograr cruzar. (b) (*message etc*) surtir efecto; (*meaning*) ser comprendido; **to ~ across to** lograr comunicar con, hacerse entender por.

◆**get after** VT perseguir, dar caza a.

◆**get along** **1** VT: **we'll try to ~ him along** trataremos de hacerle venir.

2 VI (a) seguir andando; (*depart*) irse; **we must be ~ting along** es hora de irnos ya; **~ along now!** ¡vete ya!; **~ along with you!*** (*Brit*) ¡no digas bobadas! (b) (*manage*) **we ~ along (somehow)** vamos tirando; **to ~ along without sth** pasarse sin algo. (c) (*be on good terms*) V **~ on.** (d) (*progress*) V **~ on.**

◆**get around** VI (a) = **~ about** (a). (b) **to ~ around to sth** llegar por fin a algo; empezar a estudiar (*etc*) algo; **I never seem to ~ around to it** parece que nunca tengo tiempo para eso.

◆**get at** VT (a) (*reach*) llegar a; **a place hard to ~ at** un lugar de difícil acceso; **as soon as he ~s at the drink** en cuanto se pone a beber; **he's not easy to ~ at** es difícil ponerse en contacto con él; **let me ~ at him!** ¡que me dejen llegar a él!

(b) (*ascertain*) descubrir, averiguar.

(c) (*suggest*) apuntar a; **what are you ~ting at?** ¿qué quieres decir con eso?

(d) (*attack*) atacar; (*spoil*) estropear; (*tease*) tomar el pelo a, (*unpleasantly*) meterse con; **are you ~ting at me?** ¿lo dices por mí?

(e) (*: *bribe*) sobornar; (*intimidate*) intimidar; **he's been got at** le han sobornado; le han intimidado.

◆**get away** **1** VT (*remove*) quitar, quitar de en medio; separar; **to ~ sth away from sb** quitar algo a uno; **to get sb away** ayudar a uno a escapar.

2 VI (*leave*) conseguir marcharse; salir, ir fuera; ir de vacaciones; (*escape*) escaparse, evadirse; (*at start of race*) escapar; **~ away!*** ¡no digas bobadas!; **to ~ away from** *place, person* escaparse de; **to ~ away from it all** evadirse del bullicio; dejar atrás los problemas; **to ~ away with** (*steal*) llevarse, alzarse con; **to ~ away with it** (*go unpunished*) salir impune, quedar sin castigo; **you shan't ~ away with it!** ¡me las pagarás!; **there's no ~ting away from it** los hechos son hechos, hay que reconocer la verdad.

◆**get back** **1** VT recobrar, recuperar.

2 VI (a) (*return*) volver, regresar; **to ~ back to sb** (*Telec*) llamar a uno; **~ back!** ¡atrás! (b) **to ~ back at sb** desquitarse con uno.

◆**get behind** VI quedarse atrás.

◆**get by** **1** VT (*pass*) pasar, lograr pasar; *person* (*fig*) eludir, burlar la vigilancia de.

2 VI (a) (*pass*) pasar, lograr pasar. (b) (*manage*) arreglárselas; **we'll ~ by** nos las arreglaremos, nos las apañaremos; **I can ~ by in Dutch** me defiendo en holandés.

◆**get down** **1** VT (a) (*lift down*) bajar; descolgar; (*swallow*) tragar.

(b) (*note*) apuntar; (*put in writing*) poner por escrito.

(c) (*depress*) deprimir; desanimar; **this is ~ting me down** no puedo con esto, apenas aguanto esto; **don't let it ~ you down** no te dejes desanimar.

2 VI (a) bajar; **to ~ down to** llegar a.

(b) **to ~ down to a problem** abordar un problema, empezar a estudiar un problema; **to ~ down to work** ponerse (seriamente) a trabajar; **~ down to it!** ¡a ello!, ¡manos a la obra!

◆**get in** **1** VT *person etc* hacer entrar; *plants etc* plantar; *harvest* recoger; *money* recaudar; *word* decir, lograr decir; *supplies* obtener; *blow* lograr dar.

2 VI (a) (*enter*) (lograr) entrar (en); (*arrive home*) llegar a casa, regresar; (*train etc*) llegar.

(b) (*Pol*) ser elegido.

(c) **to ~ in with sb** (*gain favour*) congraciarse con uno; llegar a tener influencia con uno.

(d) **she got in with a bad crowd** formó unas amistades peligrosas,

alternó con gente de mala fama.

(e) **to ~ in on** lograr introducirse en, lograr tomar parte en; V **act 1** (d).

◆**get into** VT *house etc* lograr entrar en; *vehicle* subir a; *club* ingresar en, hacerse miembro de; *clothes* ponerse; *difficulty* meterse en; *habit* adquirir; **I can't ~ into this dress** no logro encajarme en este vestido, este vestido me está pequeño; **what's got into you?** ¿qué mosca te ha picado?

◆**get off** **1** VT (a) *burden* quitarse de encima; *clothes* quitarse; *stain* sacar, quitar.

(b) *letter* escribir; mandar, despachar (*to* a); *work* despachar, terminar.

(c) (*learn*) aprender.

(d) **to ~ an accused person off** lograr que se absuelva a un acusado.

(e) (*Naut*) *boat* sacar a flote; *persons* desembarcar.

(f) **let's ~ off this subject** cambiemos de tema; **we've rather got off the subject** nos hemos alejado bastante del tema; **she got off washing up** se zafó del deber de lavar los platos.

2 VI (a) (*from vehicle*) apearse (de), bajar (de); **to tell sb where he ~s off*** cantar a uno los cuarenta.

(b) (*depart*) irse, marcharse; (*escape*) escapar; **~ off!** ¡suelta!; **but he got off** pero se libró (del castigo); **he got off with a fine** se libró con una multa; **he got off unharmed** salió indemne; *see also* **~ away.**

(c) (*sleep*) conciliar el sueño, dormirse.

(d) **to ~ off with sb*** liarse con uno*, ligar con uno*.

◆**get off on≠** VT pirrarse por*.

◆**get on** **1** VT poner; *clothes* ponerse.

2 VI (a) (*mount*) subir a; ponerse encima (de).

(b) (*progress, succeed*) hacer progresos; tener éxito; **how did you ~ on?** ¿qué tal te fue?; **how are you ~ting on with him?** ¿cómo te avienes con él?; **I can't ~ on with this child** no hago carrera con este niño; **I can't ~ on with maths** no me entran las matemáticas; **he's keen to ~ on** quiere ir adelante, es ambicioso.

(c) (*with numerals etc*) **he's ~ting on for 70** anda cerca de los 70; **he's ~ting on now** va para viejo; **it's ~ting on for 9** son casi las 9; **there were ~ting on for 50 people** había unas cincuenta personas.

(d) (*continue*) seguir; **time is ~ting on, it's ~ting on** se hace tarde; **~ on, man!** ¡sigue!, ¡adelante!; **let's ~ on with it** vamos; prosigamos; **this will do to be ~ting on with** esto basta por ahora.

(e) (*agree*) **to ~ on with sb** llevarse bien con uno, congeniar con uno; **they ~ on well together** se llevan bien.

◆**get on to** VT (a) (*find, recognize*) *facts, truth* descubrir; encontrar, localizar; (*identify*) identificar; **the police got on to him at once** la policía se puso sobre su pista en seguida.

(b) (*contact*) ponerse en contacto con, contactar con, comunicar con; (*Telec*) llamar; **I'll ~ on to him** hablaré con él.

(c) **she's always ~ting on to me** siempre me está regañando.

◆**get out** **1** VT (a) hacer salir; (*take out*) sacar; *stain* sacar, quitar; *book* (*from library*) sacar.

(b) *book* (*publish*) publicar.

(c) *problem* resolver.

(d) (*prepare*) *plan etc* preparar, hacer.

2 VI (a) (*leave*) salir; irse; **to ~ out of the bus** bajar del autobús; **~ out!** ¡vete!, ¡fuera de aquí!

(b) (*escape*) escaparse; **to ~ out of** *duty* librarse de, zafarse de; *habit* perder; *difficulty* salir de; **there's no ~ting out of it** no hay más remedio.

(c) (*news*) saberse, divulgarse, hacerse público.

◆**get over** **1** VT (a) (*lift over*) hacer pasar por encima de.

(b) (*put across*) comunicar, hacer comprender.

(c) (*finish*) terminar; **let's ~ it over (with)!** ¡vamos a concluir de una vez!

(d) *difficulty* vencer, superar; salir de; *illness* reponerse de; *fright* sobreponerse a; *grief* dominar; *surprise* volverse de; *resentment* olvidar.

2 VI (*cross*) pasar, cruzar.

◆**get round** VT (a) *difficulty* soslayar; *corner etc* dar la vuelta a. (b) *person* persuadir, engatusar; *see also* **~ around.**

◆**get round to** VT: **to ~ round to doing sth** encontrar tiempo para hacer algo; **I never got round to going to see her** no tuve tiempo de ir a verla; **I shan't ~ round to that before next week** no lo podré hacer antes de la semana próxima.

◆**get through** **1** VT (a) conseguir pasar por.

(b) (*Parl*) *bill* hacer aprobar.

(c) *message etc* = **get across 1** (b), **get over 1** (b).

(d) *exam* aprobar.

(e) *time* pasar; *period, work* llegar al final de, terminar; *money* gastar; *food etc* consumir.

2 VI (a) **to ~ through (to)** (*Telec*) (lograr) comunicar con; (*fig*) hacerse comprender por, llegar a.

(b) (*be accepted*) pasar, ser aceptado, ser aprobado.

◆**get together** **1** VT reunir, juntar.

2 VI reunirse; verse; (for celebration) organizar una fiesta.
◆**get under** **1** VT (a) **to ~ under a fence/rope** etc pasar por debajo de una cerca/cuerda etc. (b) (lit) hacer pasar por debajo; (fig: control) fire, revolt controlar.
   2 VI (pass underneath) pasar por debajo.
◆**get up** **1** VT (a) (lift) levantar, alzar; (take up) subir.
(b) (from bed) hacer levantarse; (wake) despertar.
(c) speed etc aumentar.
(d) (learn) aprender; (revise) repasar.
(e) (organize) organizar, preparar.
(f) (dress) ataviar (in de); (disguise) disfrazar (as de).
   2 VI (a) (stand) levantarse, ponerse de pie; (from bed) levantarse; (bird etc) alzar el vuelo; (rise) subir; **~ up!** ¡levántate!, (to horse) ¡arre!
(b) (wind) empezar a soplar recio; (fire) avivarse; (sea) embravecerse.
(c) (be involved in, do) **to ~ up to** llegar a; **to ~ up to mischief** andar en diabluras; **what did you ~ up to in London?** ¿qué diabluras hiciste en Londres?; **you never know what he'll ~ up to next** nunca se sabe qué bobadas hará.
   3 VR: **to ~ o.s. up as** disfrazarse de, vestir de.
get-at-able [get'ætəbl] ADJ accesible.
getaway ['getəweɪ] **1** N escape m, huida f, fuga f; **to make one's ~** escaparse.
   2 ATTR: **the thieves' ~ car** el coche en que los ladrones habían huido.
Gethsemane [geθ'semənɪ] N Getsemaní m.
get-rich-quick* [ˌget.rɪtʃ'kwɪk] ADJ: **~ scheme** plan m para hacer una rápida fortuna.
get-together ['getəˌgeðəʳ] N (meeting) reunión f; (regular social gathering) tertulia f; (party) guateque m.
getup ['getʌp] N atavío m, traje m.
get-up-and-go* [ˌgetʌpənd'gəʊ] N: **he's got lots of ~** tiene mucho empuje.
get-well card [ˌget'wel,kɑːd] N tarjeta f que se envía a uno que está enfermo deseándole que se mejore.
gewgaw ['gjuːgɔː] N (†) baratija f.
geyser ['giːzəʳ] N (Geog) géiser m; (Brit: heater) calentador m de agua.
G-Force N ABBR of **force of gravity**.
Ghana ['gɑːnə] N Ghana f.
Ghanaian [gɑː'neɪən] **1** ADJ ghanés.
   2 N ghanés m, -esa f.
ghastly ['gɑːstlɪ] ADJ (a) horrible; (pale) pálido; (corpselike) cadavérico. (b) (*) horrible, fatal, malísimo; person pesado; **how ~!** ¡qué horror!; **it must be ~ for her** debe ser horrible para ella.
Ghent [gent] N Gante m.
gherkin ['gɜːkɪn] N pepinillo m.
ghetto ['getəʊ] N gueto m; (Hist) judería f.
ghetto-blaster ['getəʊˌblɑːstəʳ] N cassette m portátil con altavoz incorporado.
ghettoization [ˌgetəʊaɪ'zeɪʃən] N confinamiento f en guetos.
ghettoize ['getəʊˌaɪz] VT confinar en guetos.
ghost [gəʊst] **1** N fantasma m, espectro m; (TV) imagen f fantasma; **without the ~ of a smile** sin la más leve sonrisa; **he hasn't the ~ of a chance** no tiene la más remota posibilidad; **to give up the ~** entregar el alma, (fig) perder toda esperanza; **the car finally gave up the ~** por fin el coche se averió definitivamente.
   2 ATTR: **~ edition** edición f inexistente; **~ image** (Cine, TV) imagen f fantasma; **~ story** cuento m de fantasmas; **~ town** ciudad f muerta, pueblo m fantasma; **~ word** palabra f inexistente; **~ writer** negro m, -a f.
   3 VT book escribir por otro; **an autobiography ~ed by X** una autobiografía escrita por el negro X.
ghostly ['gəʊstlɪ] ADJ espectral, fantasmal.
ghost-write ['gəʊstˌraɪt] (irr: V **write**) VT V **ghost 3**.
ghoul [guːl] N demonio m necrófago; (fig) persona f de gustos inhumanos.
ghoulish ['guːlɪʃ] ADJ espantosamente cruel; sádico; macabro.
GHQ N ABBR of **General Headquarters** cuartel m general.
G.I. N (US) ABBR of **Government Issue** propiedad f del Estado. (b) ABBR of soldado m (raso) americano; **~ bride** novia f (or esposa f) de un soldado americano; **~ Joe** ≈ el recluta Pérez.
giant ['dʒaɪənt] **1** N gigante m; **XYZ, the computer ~** XYZ, líder en ordenadores; **he was a ~ among actors** como actor fue un coloso.
   2 ADJ gigantesco, gigante.
giantess ['dʒaɪən'tes] N giganta f.
giant-killer ['dʒaɪənt,kɪləʳ] N matagigantes m.
Gib* [dʒɪb] N = **Gibraltar**.
gibber ['dʒɪbəʳ] VI farfullar, hablar atropelladamente, hablar de una manera ininteligible.
gibbering ['dʒɪbərɪŋ] ADJ farfullador; **I sounded like a ~ idiot** daba la impresión de desvariar.
gibberish ['dʒɪbərɪʃ] N galimatías m, guirigay m.
gibbet ['dʒɪbɪt] N horca f.

gibbon ['gɪbən] N gibón m.
gibe [dʒaɪb] **1** N pulla f, dicterio m.
   2 VI mofarse (at de).
giblets ['dʒɪblɪts] NPL menudillos mpl.
Gibraltar [dʒɪ'brɔːltəʳ] N Gibraltar m.
Gibraltarian [ˌdʒɪbrɔːl'tɛərɪən] **1** ADJ gibraltareño.
   2 N gibraltareño m, -a f.
giddily ['gɪdɪlɪ] ADV (light-heartedly) frívolamente; (heedlessly) despreocupadamente, a la ligera.
giddiness ['gɪdɪnɪs] N vértigo m.
giddy ['gɪdɪ] ADJ speed vertiginoso; character atolondrado, ligero de cascos; (dizzy) mareado; **to feel ~** sentirse mareado; **it makes me ~** me marea, me da vértigo.
GIFT [gɪft] N ABBR of **Gamete In** (or **Intra**) **Fallopian Transfer**.
gift [gɪft] **1** N (a) (present) regalo m; obsequio m; (Eccl) ofrenda f; (Jur) donación f; (bargain) ganga f; **~ tax** impuesto m sobre donaciones; **the office is in the ~ of** la dignidad está en manos de; **it's a ~!*** ¡está tirado!*; **I wouldn't have it as a ~** no lo quiero ni regalado; **don't look a ~ horse in the mouth** a caballo regalado no le mires el dentado.
(b) (faculty, talent) don m, talento m, prenda f; **~ of tongues** don m de las lenguas; **he has a ~ for administration** tiene talento para la administración; **he has artistic ~s** tiene dotes artísticas.
   2 VT dar, donar.
gift certificate ['gɪft,sə'tɪfɪkɪt] N (US) vale-regalo m.
gift-coupon ['gɪft,kuːpɒn] N cupón m de regalo.
gifted ['gɪftɪd] ADJ talentoso.
gift-shop ['gɪft,ʃɒp] N, **gift-store** ['gɪft,stɔːʳ] N (US) tienda f de regalos; (in signs) 'artículos mpl de regalo'.
gift-token ['gɪft,təʊkən] N, **gift-voucher** ['gɪft,vaʊtʃəʳ] N vale-regalo m.
giftwrap ['gɪft,ræp] VT envolver en papel de regalo.
giftwrapped ['gɪft,ræpt] ADJ envuelto para regalo.
giftwrapping ['gɪft,ræpɪŋ] N envoltorio m de regalo, papel m de colores para regalo.
gig [gɪg] N (a) (vehicle) calesín m. (b) (Naut) lancha f, canoa f. (c) (Mus) actuación f; concierto m. (d) (US: job) trabajo m temporal.
gigabyte ['dʒɪgə,baɪt] N gigabyte m.
gigantic [dʒaɪ'gæntɪk] ADJ gigantesco.
gigawatt ['dʒɪgə,wɒt] N gigavatio m.
giggle ['gɪgl] **1** N risilla f sofocada, risilla f tonta; **she got the ~s** le dio la risa tonta; **they did it for a ~** (Brit) lo hicieron para reírse.
   2 VI reírse con una risilla sofocada (or tonta).
giggly ['gɪglɪ] ADJ dado a la risa tonta.
GIGO ['gaɪgəʊ] (Comput) ABBR of **garbage in, garbage out** basura entra, basura sale, BEBS.
gigolo ['ʒɪgələʊ] N gigoló m.
gigot ['ʒɪːgəʊ, 'dʒɪgət] N (Culin) gigot m.
gild [gɪld] (irr: PRET **gilded**, PTP **gilded** or **gilt**) VT dorar; metal dorar, sobredorar; (fig) embellecer, adornar; pill dorar.
gilded ['gɪldɪd] ADJ dorado.
gilding ['gɪldɪŋ] N doradura f, dorado m.
Giles [dʒaɪlz] NM Gil.
gill¹ [dʒɪl] N (Brit) cuarta parte de una pinta (= approx ⅛ litro).
gill² [gɪl] N (Fish) agalla f, branquia f; **to look green about the ~s** tener mala cara.
gillie ['gɪlɪ] N (Scot) ayudante m de cazador (or pescador); (Scot) criado m.
gilt [gɪlt] **1** PTP of **gild**.
   2 ADJ dorado.
   3 N (a) dorado m; (fig) atractivo m. (b) (Fin) **~s** papel m del Estado.
gilt-edged ['gɪlt'edʒd] ADJ: **~ securities** (Brit) papel m del Estado, valores mpl de máxima confianza.
gimbal(s) ['dʒɪmbəl(z)] N (Aut, Naut) cardán m.
gimcrack ['dʒɪmkræk] ADJ furniture de mala calidad.
gimlet ['gɪmlɪt] N barrena f de mano.
gimme* ['gɪmɪ] EXCL = **give me**.
gimmick ['gɪmɪk] N (Theat) truco m característico; (Comm) truco m publicitario; **it's just a sales ~** es un truco para vender más.
gimmickry ['gɪmɪkrɪ] N truquería f.
gimmicky ['gɪmɪkɪ] ADJ truquero.
gimp* [gɪmp] N (US) cojo m, -a f.
gin¹ [dʒɪn] N (drink) ginebra f; **~ and it** (Brit) vermú m con ginebra; **~ and tonic** gin-tonic m.
gin² [dʒɪn] N (trap) trampa f; (Mech) desmotadera f de algodón.
ginger ['dʒɪndʒəʳ] **1** N (a) jengibre m. (b) (fig) energía f, empuje m.
   2 ADJ hair rojo, bermejo; cat de color melado, barcino, amarillento.
◆**ginger up** VT (Brit) espabilar, estimular.
ginger-ale ['dʒɪndʒər'eɪl] N, **ginger-beer** ['dʒɪndʒə'bɪəʳ] N gaseosa f de jengibre.
gingerbread ['dʒɪndʒəbred] N pan m de jengibre.
ginger-group ['dʒɪndʒəgruːp] N (Brit) grupo m de activistas, grupo m de presión.

gingerly ['dʒɪndʒəlɪ] ① ADJ cauteloso.
② ADV con tiento, con pies de plomo.
gingery ['dʒɪndʒərɪ] ADJ *hair* rojo, bermejo.
gingham ['gɪŋəm] N guinga *f*, guingán *m*.
gingivitis [ˌdʒɪndʒɪ'vaɪtɪs] N gingivitis *f*.
Ginny ['dʒɪnɪ] NF *familiar form of* **Virginia**.
ginormous* [dʒaɪ'nɔːməs] ADJ *(hum)* enorme de grande.
ginseng ['dʒɪnseŋ] ① N ginseng *m*.
② ATTR *tea, tablets* de ginseng.
gipsy ['dʒɪpsɪ] ① N gitano *m*, -a *f*.
② ATTR gitano, cíngaro; ~ **moth** lagarta *f*.
giraffe [dʒɪ'rɑːf] N jirafa *f*.
gird [gɜːd] *(irr: PRET AND PTP* **girded** *or* **girt)** ① VT ceñir; rodear *(with* de).
② VR: **to ~ o.s. for the fight** *(or* **fray)** aprestarse para la lucha.
◆**gird on** VT: **to ~ on one's sword** ceñirse la espada.
◆**gird up** VT: **to ~ up one's loins** aprestarse para la lucha.
girder ['gɜːdəʳ] N viga *f*.
girdle ['gɜːdl] ① N cinto *m*, ceñidor *m*; *(belt, also fig)* cinturón *m*; *(woman's)* faja *f*.
② VT ceñir, rodear *(also fig; with* de).
girl [gɜːl] ① N chica *f*, muchacha *f*; *(small)* niña *f*; *(young woman)* chica *f*, joven *f*; *(servant)* criada *f*, chica *f*; *(girlfriend)* amiguita *f*; **best ~** novia *f*; **old ~** *(Brit: of school)* antigua alumna *f*; *(*)* vieja *f*.
② ATTR: ~ **Friday** empleada *f* de confianza; ~ **guide** *(Brit)*, ~ **scout** *(US)* exploradora *f*, muchacha-guía *f*.
girlfriend ['gɜːlfrend] N amiga *f*, amiguita *f*; compañera *f*.
girlhood ['gɜːlhʊd] N juventud *f*, mocedad *f*.
girlie ['gɜːlɪ] ① N *(US*)* nena *f*, chiquilla *f*.
② ATTR: ~ **magazine** revista *f* de desnudos, revista *f* de destape.
girlish ['gɜːlɪʃ] ADJ de niña; juvenil; *(pej)* afeminado.
giro ['dʒaɪrəʊ] *(Brit)* ① N: **National G~** Giro *m* postal.
② ATTR: **bank ~ system** sistema *m* de giro bancario; **by ~ transfer** mediante giro; ~ **cheque** cheque *m* de giro.
Gironde [dʒɪ'rɒnd] N Gironda *m*.
girt [gɜːt] PRET AND PTP *of* **gird**.
girth [gɜːθ] N **(a)** *(strap)* cincha *f*. **(b)** *(measure)* circunferencia *f*; *(stoutness)* gordura *f*, obesidad *f*; **because of its great ~** por su gran tamaño, por lo abultado.
gist [dʒɪst] N esencia *f*, lo esencial, quid *m*; **to get the ~ of a matter** entender lo esencial de una cuestión.
git* [gɪt] N *(Brit)* bobo *m*, -a *f*.
give [gɪv] *(irr: PRET* **gave**, *PTP* **given)** ① VT **(a)** *(bestow free)* dar; *(as present)* regalar; *(hand over)* entregar; *aid* prestar; *life* dar, sacrificar; *party* ofrecer, organizar *(for* en honor de); **to ~ sth to sb, to ~ sb sth** dar algo a uno; **I wouldn't want it if you gave it to me** eso no lo quiero ni regalado; **(God) ~ me strength!** ¡Dios me dé paciencia!; ~ **me the old songs!** ¡para mí las canciones viejas!
(b) *(deliver)* entregar; *regards etc* dar; *one's word* dar, empeñar; *promise* hacer; **to ~ sth into sb's hands** entregar *(or* confiar) algo a uno; **to ~ sb sth to eat** dar de comer a uno.
(c) *(pay)* pagar, dar; **what did you ~ for it?** ¿cuánto pagaste por él?; **I would ~ a lot to know** daría un dineral por saberlo.
(d) *(dedicate)* *energy, time etc* dedicar, consagrar; **he gave his life to it** consagró su vida a ello.
(e) *cry etc* lanzar, proferir, dar; **to ~ a smile** sonreir *(to* a); **to ~ a start** sobresaltarse.
(f) *(state, present, utter)* *particulars* hacer constar; *example* citar; *details etc* dar; *recitation etc* ofrecer; *play* representar, poner; *lecture* dar; *speech* pronunciar; *decision* comunicar, *(by judge etc)* dictar; **he ~s no references** no cita referencias; **it gave no sign of life** no dio señal alguna de vida; ~ **us a song!** ¡cántanos algo!; **I ~ you the Queen** brindemos por la Reina.
(g) *(impart)* comunicar; *(pass on)* transmitir; *disease* contagiar con; **to ~ sb to understand that ...** dar a uno a entender que ...; **I was given to believe that ...** me hicieron creer que ...
(h) *(allot, grant, assign)* dar; conceder, otorgar; *contract, job* dar; *task* imponer; *name* dar, poner, *(formally)* imponer; *punishment* condenar a, castigar con; **in A.D. 500 ~ or take a few years** en el año 500 después de J.C. quitando o poniendo alguno.
(i) *(produce)* *result* dar por resultado, producir, arrojar; **it ~s a total of 80** arroja un total de 80, suman 80; **it ~s 6% a year** rinde un 6 por cien al año; **it ~s an average of 4** da un promedio de 4.
(j) *(cause)* ocasionar, causar; **you gave me much pain** me causaste mucha pena.
(k) *(allow)* permitir; **I gave myself 10 minutes to do it** me permití 10 minutos para hacerlo; **he can ~ you 5 years** él tiene la ventaja de ser 5 años más joven que tú; **how long would you ~ that marriage?** ¿cuánto tiempo crees que durará ese matrimonio?
(l) *(*)* **to ~ it to sb** *(beat)* dar una paliza a uno; *(verbally)* poner a uno como un trapo*; **I gave him what for** le dije cuatro verdades; **I'll ~ him what for!** ¡me las pagará!; **holidays? I'll ~ you holidays!**

¡ni vacaciones ni pollos en vinagre!*
② VI **(a)** *(bestow)* dar; **to ~ and take** hacer concesiones mutuas; **to ~ as good as one gets** devolver golpe por golpe.
(b) *(stretch)* dar de sí; *(break)* romperse; *(door etc)* ceder; *(floor, roof etc)* hundirse.
(c) **what ~s?** *(esp US*)* ¿qué pasa?, ¿qué se cuece por ahí?*
③ N elasticidad *f*.
◆**give away** ① VT **(a)** *(give free)* regalar, obsequiar *(esp LAm)*; *(get rid of)* deshacerse de; *(sell cheap)* regalar, malvender; *(Sport)* *ball* regalar; *bride* conducir al altar. **(b)** *(disclose)* revelar, descubrir; *(betray)* traicionar.
② VR: **to ~ o.s. away** venderse, traicionarse.
◆**give back** VT devolver.
◆**give in** ① VT entregar, dar; *name* poner, dar.
② VI ceder; rendirse, darse por vencido; *(agree)* consentir; **I ~ in!** ¡me rindo!; **to ~ in to** *person* condescender con, ceder a las súplicas de; *threats* rendirse ante, sucumbir ante; **she always ~s in to him** ella hace siempre lo que él quiere.
◆**give off** VT emitir, despedir, arrojar.
◆**give on to** VT dar a.
◆**give out** ① VT **(a)** *(hand out)* distribuir, repartir. **(b)** *(announce)* anunciar; *(reveal)* revelar, divulgar; **to ~ it out that ...** anunciar que ..., *(falsely)* hacer creer que ... **(c)** *smoke etc* emitir, arrojar.
② VI *(supply)* agotarse, acabarse; *(patience)* acabarse; *(engine etc)* fallar.
◆**give over** ① VT **(a)** *(transfer)* traspasar; *(devote)* dedicar. **(b)** *(*: stop)* dejar; ~ **over arguing!** ¡deja de discutir!
② VI *(*)* cesar; ~ **over!** ¡basta ya!
③ VR: **to ~ o.s. over to** entregarse a, darse a.
◆**give up** ① VT **(a)** *(devote)* dedicar; **to ~ up one's life to music** dedicar su vida a la música.
(b) *(renounce)* ceder; renunciar a; *(sacrifice)* sacrificar; *habit* dejar; *idea, interest* abandonar, renunciar a; *seat, place* ceder; *post* dimitir de, renunciar a; **to ~ up smoking** dejar de fumar; **eventually she gave him up** por fin ella rompió con él.
(c) *(hand over, deliver)* entregar; *authority etc* ceder, traspasar.
(d) *(abandon hope for)* *patient* desahuciar; *visitor* no esperar más tiempo; *(for lost)* dar por perdido; *problem* renunciar a resolver; **we'd given you up** creíamos que no ibas a venir; **they gave him up for dead** le dieron por muerto.
② VI **(a)** darse por vencido, rendirse; perder la esperanza, desanimarse; **I ~ up!** ¡me rindo!; **don't ~ up yet!** ¡anímate!
(b) *(Mech)* averiarse, fallar, estropearse; **the car gave up on us** nos falló el coche.
③ VR: **to ~ o.s. up** entregarse *(a la policía etc)*; **to ~ o.s. up to** *vice etc* entregarse a, darse a.
give-and-take ['gɪvən'teɪk] N toma y daca *m*, concesiones *fpl* mutuas.
giveaway ['gɪvəweɪ] ① ADJ: ~ **price** precio *m* obsequio, precio *m* de ruina; ~ **terms** condiciones *fpl* excesivamente generosas.
② N *(gift)* regalo *m*; ganga *f*; *(revelation)* revelación *f* involuntaria; **the exam was a ~** el examen estaba tirado.
given ['gɪvn] ① PTP *of* **give**.
② **(a)** ~ **money one can do anything** con dinero todo es posible.
(b) **on a ~ day** un día determinado; **in a ~ time** en un tiempo dado; ~ **that ...** dado que ...
(c) **to be ~ to** ser dado a, ser adicto a; **to be ~ to +** *ger* ser propenso a + *infin*.
(d) ~ **name** *(Scot, US)* nombre *m* de pila.
③ NPL: ~**s** *(US)* hechos *mpl* reconocidos; datos *mpl*, bases *fpl*.
giver ['gɪvəʳ] N donante *mf*, donador *m*, -ora *f*.
gizmo* ['gɪzməʊ] N *(US)* artilugio *m*, chisme *m*.
gizzard ['gɪzəd] N molleja *f*; **it sticks in my ~** no lo puedo tragar.
glacé ['glæseɪ] ADJ *fruit* escarchado; ~ **icing** azúcar *m* escarchado.
glacial ['gleɪsɪəl] ADJ glacial.
glaciation [ˌgleɪsɪ'eɪʃən] N glaciación *f*.
glacier ['glæsɪəʳ] N glaciar *m*.
glaciology [ˌglæsɪ'ɒlədʒɪ] N glaciología *f*.
glad [glæd] ADJ alegre; *news etc* bueno; ~ **rags*** ropa *f* dominguera; **to be ~ about** alegrarse de; **I'm very ~ for you** me alegro mucho por ti; **to be ~ that ...** alegrarse de que + *subj*; **I am ~ to hear it** me alegro de saberlo; **I shall be ~ to come** tendré mucho gusto en venir; **he seemed ~** se mostró satisfecho.
gladden ['glædn] VT alegrar, regocijar.
glade [gleɪd] N claro *m*.
glad-hand* ['glædhænd] VT *(hum)* estrechar (con entusiasmo fingido) la mano de.
gladiator ['glædɪeɪtəʳ] N gladiador *m*.
gladiatorial [ˌglædɪə'tɔːrɪəl] ADJ de gladiadores.
gladiolus [ˌglædɪ'əʊləs] N, PL **gladioli** [ˌglædɪ'əʊlaɪ] estoque *m*, gladíolo *m*.
gladly ['glædlɪ] ADV alegremente, con satisfacción; **yes, ~** sí, con mucho gusto.
gladness ['glædnɪs] N alegría *f*; satisfacción *f*.

glam: [glæm] **1** VT: **to ~ up** embellecer, adornar; mejorar el aspecto de.
2 ADJ V **glamorous**.
3 N V **glamour**.

glamorize ['glæməraɪz] VT embellecer; hacer más atractivo; **this programme ~s crime** este programa presenta el crimen bajo una luz favorable.

glamorous ['glæmərəs] ADJ encantador, atractivo, hechicero.

glamour, (US) **glamor** ['glæmər] N encanto m, atractivo m, glamour m.

glamour-boy, (US) **glamor-boy** ['glæmə,bɔɪ] N niño m bonito.

glamour-girl, (US) **glamor-girl** ['glæməgɜːl] N belleza f, guapa f.

glam rock* ['glæm'rɒk] N glam rock m.

glance [glɑːns] **1** N ojeada f, vistazo m; mirada f; **at a ~** de un vistazo; **at first ~** a primera vista; **with many a backward ~ at** (fig) pensando con mucha nostalgia en.
2 VI (look) mirar; **she ~d in my direction** miró hacia donde yo estaba; **to ~ at** person etc lanzar una mirada a, object echar un vistazo a, ojear; **to ~ at, to ~ over, to ~ through** book etc hojear, examinar por encima, examinar de paso.
◆**glance away** VI apartar los ojos.
◆**glance down** VI echar un vistazo hacia abajo.
◆**glance off** VT: **to ~ off sth** chocar con algo y rebotar, desviarse al chocar con algo.
◆**glance round** VI (round about) echar un vistazo alrededor; (behind) echar un vistazo atrás.
◆**glance up** VI (raise eyes) elevar la mirada; (look upwards) mirar hacia arriba.

glancing ['glɑːnsɪŋ] ADJ blow oblicuo.

gland [glænd] N (Bio) glándula f; (Mech) prensaestopas m.

glandular ['glændjʊlər] ADJ glandular; **~ fever** mononucleosis f infecciosa.

glans [glænz] N: **~ (penis)** glande m.

glare [gleər] **1** N **(a)** (of light) luz f deslumbradora, reverbero m, brillo m, luminosidad f; (dazzle) deslumbramiento m; **because of the ~ of the light in Spain** debido a lo fuerte de la luz en España; **in the full ~ of publicity** bajo los focos de la publicidad.
(b) (look) mirada f feroz.
2 VI **(a)** (light) relumbrar, deslumbrar.
(b) (person) mirar ferozmente (at a), echar fuego por los ojos.

glaring ['gleərɪŋ] ADJ **(a)** (dazzling) deslumbrador, fuerte.
(b) colour chillón; mistake manifiesto, notorio.

glaringly ['gleərɪŋlɪ] ADV: **~ obvious** totalmente obvio, meridianamente claro.

glasnost ['glæznɒst] N glasnost f.

glass [glɑːs] **1** N **(a)** (material) vidrio m, cristal m; (glassware) artículos mpl de vidrio, cristalería f; (Met) barómetro m; (spyglass) catalejo m; (mirror) espejo m; **under ~** (exhibit) bajo vidrio, en una vitrina, (plant) en invernáculo; **to look at o.s. in the ~** mirarse en el espejo.
(b) (tumbler, also for wine) vaso m; (for beer) caña f; (stemmed; for sherry, champagne etc) copa f; (for liqueur, brandy) copita f.
(c) **~es** (spectacles) gafas fpl, lentes mpl; anteojos mpl (LAm); (binoculars) gemelos mpl.
2 ATTR de vidrio, de cristal; **~ case** vitrina f; **~ ceiling** techo m (or barrera f) invisible (que impide ascender profesionalmente a las mujeres o miembros de minorías étnicas); **~ door** puerta f vidriera, puerta f de cristales; **~ eye** ojo m de cristal; **~ fiber** (US), **~ fibre** (N) fibra f de vidrio; (ATTR) de fibra de vidrio; **~ industry** industria f vidriera; **~ slipper** zapatilla f de cristal; **~ wool** lana f de vidrio.

glassblower ['glɑːs,bləʊər] N soplador m de vidrio.

glassblowing ['glɑːs,bləʊɪŋ] N soplado m de vidrio.

glasscutter ['glɑːs,kʌtər] N (person) cortador m de vidrio.

glassful ['glɑːsfʊl] N vaso m.

glasshouse ['glɑːshaʊs] N, PL **glasshouses** ['glɑːs,haʊzɪz] (Brit Hort) invernáculo m, invernadero m; (Brit;) cárcel f (militar).

glasspaper ['glɑːs,peɪpər] N (Brit) papel m de vidrio.

glassware ['glɑːsweər] N artículos mpl de vidrio, cristalería f.

glassworks ['glɑːswɜːks] N fábrica f de vidrio.

glassy ['glɑːsɪ] ADJ substance vítreo; surface liso; water espejado; eye vidrioso.

glassy-eyed [,glɑːsɪ'aɪd] ADJ de mirada vidriosa; (from drugs, drink) de mirada perdida; (from displeasure) de mirada glacial.

ⓘ **GLASTONBURY**

Glastonbury es una ciudad situada al suroeste de Inglaterra donde, desde 1969, se ha venido celebrando casi todos los veranos un festival de música pop de tres días de duración. El festival es lugar de encuentro para miles de visitantes que acuden a la ciudad para oir a los mejores nombres del pop, y que aprovechan para visitar los lugares que se asocian con la mítica tumba del rey Arturo y con el lugar donde José de Arimatea llevó el Santo Grial.

Glaswegian [glæz'wiːdʒən] **1** ADJ de Glasgow.
2 N nativo m, -a f (or habitante mf) de Glasgow.

glaucoma [glɔː'kəʊmə] N glaucoma m.

glaze [gleɪz] **1** N vidriado m, barniz m, lustre m.
2 VT **(a)** (Brit: put glass in) poner vidrios a, vidriar. **(b)** pottery vidriar; (Culin) glasear; (fig) lustrar.
3 VI: **to ~ over** (eyes) velarse.

glazed [gleɪzd] ADJ **(a)** surface vidriado; paper satinado; eye vidrioso; (Culin) glaseado. **(b)** (Brit) door, window etc con cristal; picture barnizado. **(c)** (US*) achispado*.

glazier ['gleɪzɪər] N (Brit) vidriero m.

GLC N (formerly) ABBR of **Greater London Council** Corporación f Metropolitana de Londres.

gleam [gliːm] **1** N (of light) rayo m, destello m; (of colour) viso m; (in one's eye) chispa f; (fig) vislumbre f; **there is a ~ of hope** hay un rayo de esperanza.
2 VI brillar (in the sun al sol; with de), relucir, destellar.

gleaming ['gliːmɪŋ] ADJ reluciente.

glean [gliːn] **1** VT espigar; (fig) espigar, recoger; **to ~ information about** rebuscar datos sobre; **from what I have been able to ~** de lo que yo he podido saber.
2 VI espigar.

gleaner ['gliːnər] N espigador m, -ora f.

gleanings ['gliːnɪŋz] NPL (fig) fragmentos mpl recogidos.

glebe [gliːb] N terreno m beneficial.

glee [gliː] N alegría f, júbilo m, regocijo m.

glee club ['gliːklʌb] N orfeón m, sociedad f coral.

gleeful ['gliːfəl] ADJ alegre, regocijado.

gleefully ['gliːfəlɪ] ADV con júbilo.

glen [glen] N cañada f, valle m estrecho.

glib [glɪb] ADJ person de mucha labia, poco sincero; speech elocuente pero insincero; explanation fácil.

glibly ['glɪblɪ] ADV con poca sinceridad; elocuentemente pero con poca sinceridad; con una facilidad sospechosa.

glibness ['glɪbnɪs] N labia f; falta f de sinceridad; facilidad f.

glide [glaɪd] **1** N deslizamiento m; (Aer) planeo m; (Mus) ligadura f.
2 VI **(a)** deslizarse; **to ~ away, to ~ off** escurrirse, irse silenciosamente; **she ~s to the door** se desliza hacia la puerta.
(b) (Aer) planear.

glider ['glaɪdər] N planeador m, velero m; (towed) avión m remolcado; (US: swing) columpio m.

gliding ['glaɪdɪŋ] N planeo m.

glimmer ['glɪmər] **1** N luz f trémula, luz f tenue, vislumbre f; **without a ~ of understanding** sin dar el menor indicio de haber comprendido; **there is a ~ of hope** hay un rayo de esperanza.
2 VI brillar con luz trémula (or tenue).

glimpse [glɪmps] **1** N vislumbre f; vista f momentánea; **to catch a ~ of** vislumbrar.
2 VT vislumbrar, entrever, ver por un instante.

glint [glɪnt] **1** N destello m, centelleo m; fulgor m; (in one's eye) chispa f.
2 VI destellar, centellear.

glissando [glɪ'sændəʊ] ADV glisando.

glisten ['glɪsn] VI relucir, brillar.

glitch* [glɪtʃ] N (US) fallo m técnico, fallo m en un sistema electrónico.

glitter ['glɪtər] **1** N brillo m, resplandor m.
2 VI relucir, brillar, rutilar; **all that ~s is not gold** no es oro todo lo que reluce.

glitterati* [,glɪtə'rɑːtiː] NPL (hum) celebridades fpl del mundillo literario y artístico.

glittering ['glɪtərɪŋ] ADJ, **glittery** ['glɪtərɪ] ADJ reluciente, brillante (also fig); **~ prize** premio m de oro.

glitz* [glɪts] N ostentación f, relumbrón m, atractivo m ostentoso.

glitzy* ['glɪtsɪ] ADJ ostentoso, de relumbrón, ostentosamente atractivo.

gloaming ['gləʊmɪŋ] N crepúsculo m; **in the ~** al anochecer.

gloat [gləʊt] VI relamerse; **to ~ over** money etc recrearse contemplando, sight saborear, news refocilarse con, victory manifestar satisfacción maligna por, beaten enemy triunfar jactanciosamente de.

gloating ['gləʊtɪŋ] ADJ: **with a ~ smile** sonriendo satisfecho, con una sonrisa satisfecha.

glob [glɒb] N (US) gotita f, glóbulo m; masa f redonda, masa f pequeña; grumo m.

global ['gləʊbl] ADJ (world-wide) mundial; sum etc global; **~ village** pueblo m global; **~ warming** recalentamiento m global.

globalize ['gləʊbəlaɪz] **1** VI globalizarse.
2 VT globalizar.

globally ['gləʊbəlɪ] ADV mundialmente; globalmente.

globe [gləʊb] N globo m, esfera f; (spherical map) esfera f terrestre, globo m terráqueo.

globe artichoke ['gləʊb'ɑːtɪtʃəʊk] N alcachofa f.

globe-trotter ['gləʊb,trɒtər] N trotamundos mf.

globe-trotting ['gləʊb,trɒtɪŋ] N viajar *m* alrededor del mundo.
globular ['glɒbjʊləʳ] ADJ globular.
globule ['glɒbjuːl] N glóbulo *m*.
glockenspiel ['glɒkənspiːl] N carillón *m*.
gloom [gluːm] N, **gloominess** ['gluːmɪnɪs] N oscuridad *f*, semioscuridad *f*, penumbra *f*, tenebrosidad *f*; (*fig*) pesimismo *m*; melancolía *f*, tristeza *f*; **it's not all gloom and doom here** aquí no todo son pronósticos de desastre.
gloomily ['gluːmɪlɪ] ADV oscuramente, lóbregamente; de modo pesimista, con pesimismo; melancólicamente, tristemente.
gloomy ['gluːmɪ] ADJ oscuro, lóbrego, tenebroso; *atmosphere, character, forecast* pesimista; *outlook* nada prometedor; *day, tone* melancólico, triste.
glorification [,glɔːrɪfɪ'keɪʃən] N glorificación *f*.
glorify ['glɔːrɪfaɪ] VT glorificar; (*praise*) alabar, ensalzar; **it was nothing but a glorified cottage** resultó ser solamente una casita con pretensiones de palacio.
glorious ['glɔːrɪəs] ADJ glorioso; *day, view, stroke etc* magnífico; **it was a ~ muddle** la confusión era mayúscula, resultó un lío colosal.
gloriously ['glɔːrɪəslɪ] ADV gloriosamente; magníficamente; **it was ~ sunny** hacía un sol magnífico.
glory ['glɔːrɪ] **1** N gloria *f*; (*fig*) esplendor *m*; **~ be!** ¡gracias a Dios!; **to be in one's ~** estar en sus glorias; **to go to ~** subir a los cielos.
2 VI: **to ~ in** gloriarse de; **I ~ in the name of Ruritanian** me enorgullezco de ser ruritanio; **the café glories in the name of El Dorado** el café tiene el magnífico nombre de El Dorado.
glory-hole* ['glɔːrɪhəʊl] N cuarto *m* (*or* cajón *etc*) en desorden, leonera* *f*.
Glos N (*Brit*) ABBR *of* **Gloucestershire**.
gloss¹ [glɒs] (*note*) **1** N glosa *f*.
2 VT glosar, comentar.
♦**gloss over** VT (*excuse*) disculpar; (*play down*) paliar, colorear, restar importancia a; (*cover up*) pasar por alto, encubrir.
gloss² [glɒs] **1** N (*shine*) lustre *m*, brillo *m*.
2 ATTR: **~ finish** acabado *m* brillo; **~ paint** pintura *f* esmalte; **~ paper** papel *m* satinado.
3 VT lustrar, pulir.
glossary ['glɒsərɪ] N glosario *m*.
glossily ['glɒsɪlɪ] ADV brillantemente; **~ illustrated** elegantemente ilustrado, ilustrado con lujo.
glossy ['glɒsɪ] **1** ADJ *surface* lustroso, brillante; *hair* liso; *cloth, paper* satinado; *magazine etc* impreso en papel satinado; de lujo, elegante.
2 N: **the glossies*** las revistas elegantes.
glottal ['glɒtl] ADJ glotal; **~ stop** oclusión *f* glotal.
glottis ['glɒtɪs] N glotis *f*.
Gloucs. ABBR *of* **Gloucestershire**.
glove [glʌv] **1** N guante *m*; **to fit sb like a ~** sentar a uno como el anillo al dedo.
2 ATTR: **~ compartment** guantera *f*; **~ puppet** títere *m* de guante.
gloved [glʌvd] ADJ *hand* enguantado.
glove-maker ['glʌv,meɪkəʳ] N, **glover** ['glʌvəʳ] N guantero *m*, -a *f*.
glow [gləʊ] **1** N (*of lamp, sun etc*) luz *f* (difusa); (*of jewel*) brillo *m*; (*of fire*) calor *m* vivo; (*bright colour*) color *m* vivo; (*in sky*) arrebol *m*; (*Tech*) incandescencia *f*; (*warm feeling*) sensación *f* de bienestar; (*of satisfaction etc*) sensación *f* grata, sentimiento *m* de vivo placer.
2 VI (*lamp, sun, jewel etc*) brillar (con luz difusa); (*fire*) arder vivamente; (*Tech*) estar candente; **to ~ with pleasure** experimentar una sensación de bienestar; **to ~ with health** rebosar de salud.
glower ['glaʊəʳ] VI: **to ~ at** mirar con ceño.
glowering ['glaʊərɪŋ] ADJ *person, sky* ceñudo.
glowing ['gləʊɪŋ] ADJ candente, incandescente; *light* brillante; *fire* vivo; *cheek etc* encendido; *colour* intenso; *report etc* entusiasta.
glow-worm ['gləʊwɜːm] N (*Brit*) luciérnaga *f*.
gloxinia [glɒk'sɪnɪə] N gloxínea *f*.
glucose ['gluːkəʊs] N glucosa *f*.
glue [gluː] **1** N cola *f*, goma *f* (de pegar); (*as drug*) pegamento *m*.
2 VT (*also* **to ~ on**, **to ~ together**) encolar, pegar; **her face was ~d to the window** tenía la cara pegada a la ventana.
glue-sniffer ['gluː,snɪfəʳ] N esnifador *m*, -ora *f* de pegamento, persona *f* que inhala (*or* esnifa) pegamento.
glue-sniffing ['gluː,snɪfɪŋ] N inhalación *f* de colas, esnife *m* pegamentoso.
gluey ['gluːɪ] ADJ pegajoso, viscoso.
glum [glʌm] ADJ (*by nature*) taciturno, melancólico; *mood* triste, abatido; *tone* melancólico, sombrío.
glumly ['glʌmlɪ] ADV *walk, shake one's head* sombríamente; *answer* tristemente, sombríamente; *look, inspect* taciturnamente, tristemente.
glut [glʌt] **1** N superabundancia *f*, exceso *m*; exceso *m* de oferta; **to be a ~ on the market** abarrotar el mercado.
2 VT *person* hartar, saciar; *market* abarrotar, inundar; **to be ~ted with fruit** (*person*) haberse atracado de frutas.
3 VR: **to ~ o.s.** atracarse (*with* de).

glutamate ['gluːtəmeɪt] V **monosodium ~**.
glutamic acid [glu:,tæmɪk'æsɪd] N ácido *m* glutámico.
gluteal [glʊ'tiːəl] ADJ glúteo.
gluten ['gluːtən] N gluten *m*; **~-free** sin gluten, libre de gluten.
glutenous ['gluːtənəs] ADJ glutenoso.
gluteus [glʊ'tiːəs] N, PL **glutei** [glʊ'tiːaɪ] glúteo *m*.
glutinous ['gluːtɪnəs] ADJ glutinoso.
glutton ['glʌtn] N glotón *m*, -ona *f*; **to be a ~ for work** trabajar incansablemente.
gluttonous ['glʌtənəs] ADJ glotón, goloso.
gluttony ['glʌtənɪ] N glotonería *f*, gula *f*.
glycerin(e) [,glɪsə'riːn] N glicerina *f*.
glycerol ['glɪsərɒl] N glicerol *m*.
glycin(e) ['glaɪsiːn] N glicina *f*.
glycogen ['glaɪkəʊdʒen] N glicógeno *m*.
glycol ['glaɪkɒl] N glicol *m*.
GM N **(a)** ABBR *of* **general manager** director *m*, -ora *f* general. **(b)** (*Brit*) ABBR *of* **George Medal** *medalla del valor civil*. **(c)** (*US*) ABBR *of* **General Motors**.
gm, gms ABBR *of* **gram(s), gramme(s)** gramo(s) *m(pl)*, g., gr.
G-man ['dʒiːmæn] N, PL **G-men** ['dʒiːmen] (*US*) agente *m* del FBI.
GMAT N (*US*) ABBR *of* **Graduate Management Admissions Test**.
GMB N (*Brit*) ABBR *of* **General, Municipal and Boilermakers** *sindicato*.
GMT N ABBR *of* **Greenwich Mean Time** hora *f* media de Greenwich.
GMWU N (*Brit*) ABBR *of* **General and Municipal Workers' Union** *sindicato de trabajadores autónomos y municipales*.
gnarled [nɑːld] ADJ nudoso, torcido.
gnash [næʃ] VT *teeth* rechinar.
gnashing ['næʃɪŋ] **1** N: **~ of teeth** rechinamiento *m* de dientes.
2 ADJ rechinante.
gnat [næt] N mosquito *m*, jején *m* (*LAm*).
gnaw [nɔː] **1** VT roer; **~ed by doubts** asaltado por dudas; **~ed by hunger** atormentado por el hambre.
2 VI roer; **to ~ at** roer.
♦**gnaw away, gnaw off** VT roer.
gnawing ['nɔːɪŋ] ADJ *sound* mordisqueante; (*fig*) *remorse, anxiety etc* corrosivo; *hunger* con retortijones; *pain* punzante; **I had a ~ feeling that something had been forgotten** tenía el mal presentimiento de que se había olvidado algo.
gneiss [naɪs] N gneis *m*.
gnocchi ['nɒkɪ] NPL ñoquis *mpl*.
gnome [nəʊm] N gnomo *m*; **the G~s of Zurich** (*hum*) los banqueros suizos.
gnomic ['nəʊmɪk] ADJ gnómico.
gnostic ['nɒstɪk] **1** ADJ gnóstico.
2 N gnóstico *m*, -a *f*.
gnosticism ['nɒstɪ,sɪzəm] N gnosticismo *m*.
GNP N ABBR *of* **gross national product** producto *m* nacional bruto, PNB *m*.
gnu [nuː] N ñu *m*.
go [gəʊ] (*irr*: PRET **went**, PTP **gone**) **1** VI **(a)** (*gen*) ir; viajar; andar; **to ~ to London** ir a Londres; **to ~ to England** ir a Inglaterra; **all roads ~ to Rome** todos los caminos van a Roma; **to ~ the shortest way** tomar el camino más corto; **to ~ (at) 90 k.p.h.** ir a 90 k.p.h.; **the numbers that ~ from 6 to 12** los números que van de 6 a 12; **to ~ to sb for sth** acudir a uno a pedir (*or* buscar) algo; **there he ~es!** ¡ahí va!; **here ~es!** ¡vamos a ver!, ¡a ello!; **who ~es there?** ¿quién va?, ¿quién vive?; **what ~es?** (*US**) ¿qué hay de nuevo?; **there you ~ again!** ¡has vuelto a la misma canción!; **there ~es the bell** suena el timbre; **what shall I ~ in?** ¿qué traje me pongo?; **where do we ~ from here?** ¿adónde vamos desde aquí?; **it ~es by seasons** esto va por temporadas; **it ~es by age** varía según la edad, depende de la edad; **promotion ~es by seniority** los ascensos se hacen por orden de antigüedad.
(b) (*progress*) ir, andar; **business is ~ing well** los negocios van (*or* andan) bien; **everything went well** todo salió bien, todo resultó perfecto; **how's it ~ing?, how ~es it?** ¿qué tal?, ¿cómo anda esto?, ¿cómo te va esto?; **how did the exam ~?** ¿qué tal el examen?; **we'll see how things ~** veremos cómo va; **she had so much ~ing for her** tenía tantas cosas a su favor; **to make the party ~** animar la fiesta; V **get, keep** *etc*.
(c) (*purpose etc*) **to ~ and see sb, to ~ to see sb** ir a ver a uno; **he went and bought it** lo compró, por fin se decidió a comprarlo; (*near future*) **I am ~ing to see him** voy a verle.
(d) (*function*) funcionar, marchar, andar; **it won't ~** no funciona; **it ~es on petrol** funciona con gasolina; **it ~es on wheels** marcha sobre ruedas; **to make sth ~** hacer funcionar algo; **to set a machine ~ing** poner en marcha una máquina.
(e) (*depart*) irse, marcharse, salir, partir; (*train etc*) salir, partir; **let's ~!** ¡vamos!, ¡vámonos!; **don't ~ yet** no te vayas tan pronto, quédate un poco más; **be gone!, get you gone!** ¡váyase!; **~!** (*starting race*) ¡ya!; **from the word ~** desde el principio; **when does the train ~?**

¿a qué hora sale el tren?; **200 hamburgers, to ~** (US) 200 hamburguesas para llevar.

(f) (disappear etc) **my hat has gone** ha desaparecido mi sombrero; **my money is all gone** ya no me queda dinero; **the coffee is all gone** se acabó el café; **he'll have to ~** (be dismissed) tendremos que deshacernos de él, tendremos que echarle; **luxuries will have to ~** tendremos que prescindir de las cosas de lujo; **the trees have been gone for years** hace años que se quitaron los árboles; **his mind is ~ing** está perdiendo la cabeza; **all my teeth have gone** he perdido todos mis dientes.

(g) (be sold) venderse; **it went next day** se vendió al día siguiente; **it went for £5** se vendió por 5 libras; **~ing, ~ing, gone!** (auction) ¡a la una ... a las dos ... a las tres!

(h) (time) pasar; **the day went slowly** el día pasó lentamente; **how is the time ~ing?** ¿cuánto tiempo ha pasado ya?; ¿cómo va la hora?

(i) (of the hour) **it has gone 3** ya dieron las 3, son las 3 y pico; **it has gone 8 already** son las 8 dadas.

(j) (pass by descent etc) pasar; **his books went to the college** sus libros pasaron al colegio; **the silver medal went to Slobodia** la medalla de plata fue para Eslobodia.

(k) (extend) **the garden ~es down to the lake** el jardín se extiende hasta el lago; **it's good as far as it ~es** dentro de sus límites es bueno.

(l) (be available) estar disponible; **are there any houses ~ing?** ¿hay casas en venta?; **are there any jobs ~ing?** ¿están ofreciendo empleos?; **anything that's ~ing** lo que haya.

(m) (exist) **as prices ~ that's not dear** considerando los precios que corren eso no es caro; **he's quite nice as professors ~** para profesor, es buena persona.

(n) (text) decir, rezar; **the text ~es ... reza** el texto así ...; **as the saying ~es** como dice el refrán; **how does the song ~?** ¿cómo es la canción?

(o) (be acceptable) **anything ~es with him** se allana a todo; se amolda a todo; hace las cosas de cualquier modo; **what I say ~es** aquí mando yo; **that ~es for me too** yo de acuerdo, yo contigo, yo también; **anything ~es these days** todo se permite hoy; **these colours don't ~ at all** estos colores no se combinan en absoluto; **white ~es with anything** el blanco va con todo.

(p) (fit) **it ~es under the table** cabe debajo de la mesa; **where does this book ~?** ¿dónde pongo este libro?; **this part ~es here** esta pieza se coloca aquí; **3 into 12 ~es 4** 12 entre 3 son 4.

(q) (break etc) romperse, estropearse; (give way) ceder, hundirse; (fall) caer; **a fuse went** se quemó un plomo; **it went at the seams** se deshizo por las juntas; **there ~es another button!** ¡ahí va otro botón!

(r) (help, contribute) **the qualities that ~ to make a king** las cualidades que hacen a un rey; **it ~es to show that** sirve para demostrar que; **the money to help the poor** el dinero se destina a ayudar a los pobres; **the money will ~ towards a deposit on the flat** el dinero aumentará lo que tenemos ahorrado para el depósito del piso.

(s) (+ ger) **to ~ fishing** ir de pesca; **to ~ hunting** ir de caza; **to ~ riding** montar a caballo.

(t) (become) hacerse, volverse, ponerse; (ie ~ bad) pasarse; (milk) cortarse; **to ~ black** ponerse negro; **to ~ mad** volverse loco; **to ~ communist** hacerse comunista; **the country went socialist** el país pasó al socialismo; **to ~ pale** palidecer, ponerse pálido; **suddenly she went all patriotic** de repente se volvió muy patriótica, de golpe le dio el patriotismo; **my tyre's gone flat** se ha pinchado mi neumático.

(u) (let ~) **let me ~!** ¡suelta!, ¡déjame!; **to let an animal ~** soltar un animal, poner un animal en libertad; **to let ~ of sth** soltar algo; **to let o.s. ~** (emotionally) desahogarse, (angrily) perder los estribos, (on a subject) entusiasmarse; (physically) abandonarse, dejar de cuidarse; (relax) relajarse; **they've let the house ~** han dejado de cuidar la casa; **we'll let it ~ at that** dejémoslo ahí.

(v) (make a noise) **he went 'psst'** dijo 'psst'; **the balloon went bang** el globo estalló; **the hooter ~es at 5** la sirena suena a las 5; **cats ~ 'miaow'** los gatos hacen 'miau'.

(w) (remain) **eight down and two to ~** ocho tenemos y faltan dos, ocho hechos y dos por hacer.

(x) (to go and ...) **I'll ~ and see** voy a ver; **he went and shut the door** cerró la puerta, fue a cerrar la puerta; **now you've gone and done it!*** ¡ahora sí la has hecho buena!

(y) (going to + infin) **I'm ~ing to tell him** voy a decírselo; **I'm not ~ing to put up with that** no voy a aguantar eso.

2 VT: **to ~ it** (speed) ir a toda velocidad; (live it up) correrla; **~ it!** ¡a ello!, ¡ánimo!; **to ~ it alone** hacerlo solo, hacerlo sin ayuda de nadie; **to ~ one better** hacer mejor todavía (than que); **to ~ 3 hearts** marcar 3 corazones.

3 N **(a)** (energy) energía f, empuje m; **there's no ~ about him** le falta energía; **it's all ~ here** aquí todo es actividad frenética.

(b) to be on the ~ trajinar, moverse, estar trabajando, estar

viajando; **to have two novels on the ~** tener dos novelas entre manos; **to keep sb on the ~** hacer que uno siga trabajando, no dejar descansar a uno.

(c) (attempt) **at one ~, in one ~** de un solo golpe, de un tirón; **to have a ~** (Brit) intentar, probar suerte; **have a ~!** ¡a ver!; **to have a ~ at sth** intentar algo; **to have a ~ at + ger** intentar + infin.

(d) (attack etc) **to have a ~ at sb** atacar a uno; criticar a uno; emprenderla con uno, tomarla con uno.

(e) (turn) **it's your ~** te toca a ti; **whose ~ is it?** ¿a quién le toca?

(f) (success) **it's all the ~** hace furor; **it's no ~** es inútil, es imposible; **to make a ~ of sth** tener éxito en algo.

(g) (bargain) **it's a ~!** ¡trato hecho!; **is it a ~?** ¿hace?, ¿estamos de acuerdo?

(h) the lights were at ~ la luz estaba en verde, se mostraba luz verde; **all systems are ~** todo está listo; todo funciona perfectamente; **all systems ~!** ¡todo listo!; ver también $\boxed{\text{COME, GO}}$.

◆**go about, go around** **1** VT: **to ~ about one's business** ocuparse de sus asuntos; **to ~ about a task** emprender un trabajo; **he knows how to ~ about it** sabe lo que hay que hacer, sabe cómo hacerlo.

2 VI (move about) andar (de un sitio para otro); **to ~ around barefoot** andar descalzo; **to ~ around stirring up trouble** andar metiendo cizaña; **to ~ about together** ir juntos, salir juntos; **to ~ about with** salir con, alternar con. **(b)** (Naut) virar. **(c)** (rumour) correr.

◆**go across** **1** VT river, road atravesar, cruzar.
2 VI (cross) cruzar; **she went across to Mrs Smith's** cruzó para ir a casa de la Sra de Smith.

◆**go after** VT girl andar tras; (follow) seguir; (seek) buscar; (persecute) cazar, perseguir.

◆**go against** VT **(a)** (oppose) principle ir en contra de, oponerse a; person oponerse a. **(b)** (prove hostile to) ser desfavorable a; **luck went against him** la suerte le fue contraria.

◆**go ahead** VI (also go on ahead) ir adelante; **~ ahead!** (fig) ¡sigue!, ¡adelante!; V ahead 1 (a).

◆**go along** VI **(a)** ir; (go away) marcharse; **to ~ along with** ir con, acompañar a; **I'll tell you as we ~ along** te lo diré de camino; **I'm learning as I ~ along** aprendo mientras lo hago, aprendo poco a poco. **(b)** (fig) **to ~ along with a plan** aprobar un proyecto; **we don't ~ along with that** no estamos de acuerdo con eso.

◆**go at** VT (undertake) emprender; (attack) lanzarse sobre, acometer.

◆**go away** VI (depart) irse, marcharse; (vanish) desaparecer; **don't ~ away with the idea that ...** no vayas a pensar que ...

◆**go back** VI **(a)** (return) volver, regresar; (retreat) retroceder. **(b)** (in time) **it ~es back to Elizabeth I** se remonta a Isabel I; **it ~es back a long way** esto tiene mucha historia, esto es muy antiguo. **(c)** (extend) extenderse; **the path ~es back to the river** la senda se extiende hasta el río; **the cave ~es back 300 metres** la caverna tiene 300 metros de fondo. **(d)** (revert) **I sold the car and went back to a bicycle** vendí el coche y volví a la bicicleta; **he went back to his old habits** volvió a sus antiguas costumbres.

◆**go back on** VT: **to ~ back on one's word** faltar a su palabra.

◆**go before** **1** VT: **the matter has gone before a grand jury** (US) el asunto se ha sometido a un gran jurado.
2 VI ir primero; (in order) anteceder, preceder; **all that has gone before** todo lo que ha pasado (etc) antes.

◆**go below** VI (Naut) bajar.

◆**go by** **1** VT **(a)** place pasar, pasar delante de, pasar cerca de, pasar junto a. **(b)** (be guided by) atenerse a, guiarse por; (base o.s. on) basarse en, fundarse en; **to ~ by appearances** juzgar por las apariencias; **that's nothing to ~ by** eso no es criterio seguro, eso no es nada; **the only thing to ~ by is ...** el único criterio que vale es ...
2 VI (person) pasar; (time) pasar, transcurrir; **in days gone by** en tiempos pasados, antaño; **to let a chance ~ by** perder una oportunidad.

◆**go down** **1** VT bajar, descender; **to ~ down a slope** bajar (por) una pendiente; **to ~ down a mine** bajar a una mina.
2 VI **(a)** (descent) bajar; descender.
(b) (fall) caer, caerse; (temperature etc) bajar, descender; (tide) bajar.
(c) (sink) hundirse.
(d) (Brit Univ) salir de la universidad; marcharse; terminar el curso.
(e) (sun, moon) ponerse.
(f) (be swallowed) tragarse; (fig) ser aceptable; poderse aguantar; **that omelette went down a treat*** esa tortilla era sabrosísima; **that will ~ down well with him** eso le va a gustar; **his speech didn't ~ down at all well** su discurso fue recibido muy mal; **how will this series ~ down in Slobodia?** ¿qué van a pensar de esta serie en Eslobodia?
(g) (lose) ser derrotado (to por), perder (to frente a); **Jaca went down 2-0 to Huesca** el Jaca perdió 2-0 frente al Huesca.
(h) (tyre) desinflarse.
(i) (be remembered) ser recordado; **he went down to posterity as ...** pasó a la posteridad como ...; **it will ~ down as a failure** será recordado como un fracaso.

(j) to **~ down with flu** coger una gripe.

◆**go down on: VT** chupárselo:.

◆**go for VT (a)** (*fetch*) ir por, ir a buscar. **(b)** *price* venderse por. **(c)** (*attack*) atacar, acometer; (*verbally*) meterse con; **~ for him!** (*to dog*) ¡a él!; **~ for it!** ¡a ello!; **(d)** (*: like, admire*) entusiasmarse por; **I really ~ for that film** esa película me chifla de verdad*; **I don't ~ for him at all** me resulta la mar de antipático*. **(e)** (*strive for*) dedicarse a obtener, esforzarse por ganar (*etc*); (*choose*) escoger, optar por.

◆**go forward VI** (*person, vehicle*) avanzar; **they let the suggestion ~ forward that ...** (*fig*) dieron a entender que ...

◆**go in VI (a)** (*enter*) entrar (en); (*fit*) caber (en), poderse colocar (en); (*have a place*) ponerse en, deber colocarse en; (*Sport*) entrar a batear; (*Mil*) atacar. **(b)** (*sun, moon*) esconderse, cubrirse.

◆**go in for VT (a)** (*compete in*) presentarse a; *exam* tomar, presentarse para; *post* solicitar, ser candidato para, presentarse para. **(b)** *hobby* dedicarse a; (*collect*) coleccionar; (*buy*) comprar, adquirir; *style etc* adoptar, seguir; *activity* tomar parte en; **we don't ~ in for such things here** aquí esas cosas no se hacen.

◆**go into VT (a)** (*enter*) entrar en; caber en; **to ~ into politics** entrar en la política, dedicarse a la política; **to ~ into first gear** meter primera velocidad; **he went into a long explanation** se engolfó en una larga explicación; **let's not ~ into all that now** dejamos todo eso por ahora. **(b)** (*investigate*) examinar, investigar.

◆**go in with VT** asociarse con, unirse con; **she went in with her sister to buy the present** entre ella y su hermana compraron el regalo.

◆**go off 1 VT** (*Brit*) perder el gusto por; **I've gone off him lately*** ahora no me chifla tanto*.

2 VI (a) (*leave*) irse, marcharse; **he went off with the au pair** se marchó con la chica au pair. **(b)** (*gun*) dispararse; (*explosive*) estallar, explosionar. **(c)** (*Brit*) (*go bad*) pasarse, deteriorarse; (*lose quality*) perder su calidad, bajar de calidad; (*Sport*) perder forma; (*lose the knack*) perder el tino. **(d)** (*go to sleep*) dormirse, quedar dormido. **(e)** (*happen*) pasar; **how did it ~ off?** ¿qué tal resultó?, ¿qué tal te fue?; **it all went off well** todo salió perfecto.

◆**go on 1 VT (a)** (*be guided by*) guiarse por; basarse en; **there's nothing to ~ on** no hay pista que podamos seguir; **that's nothing to ~ on** no se puede juzgar por eso; **what are you ~ing on?** ¿en qué te basas? **(b)** **I don't ~ much on that*** eso no me gusta.

2 VI (a) (*fit*) **the lid won't ~ on** la tapa no se puede poner; **these shoes won't ~ on** mis pies no caben en estos zapatos. **(b)** (*proceed on one's way*) seguir adelante, seguir su camino; (*progress*) avanzar, ir adelante; **everything is ~ing on normally** todo sigue normal, todo avanza normalmente. **(c)** (*continue*) seguir, continuar; **to ~ on** + *ger* seguir + *ger*, continuar + *ger*; **~ on!** ¡vamos!, (*with narrative*) ¡adelante!, (*surprise*) ¡anda!; **~ on with you!** ¡no digas bobadas!; **that'll do to be ~ing on with** eso basta por ahora. **(d)** (*talk*) **he does ~ on so** habla más que siete, no para de hablar; **don't ~ on so!** ¡no machaques!; **she's always ~ing on about it** siempre está con la misma cantilena; **he's always ~ing on about the government** siempre está echando pestes contra el gobierno; **if you ~ on like that** si sigues en ese plan; **don't ~ on like that!** ¡no te pongas así!; **to ~ on at sb** reñir a uno. **(e)** (*proceed*) **to ~ on to** pasar a; **she went on to learn Arabic** pasó a aprender el árabe; **he went on to say that ...** dijo a continuación que ... **(f)** (*occur*) pasar; **what's ~ing on?** ¿qué pasa?; **it had been ~ing on in her absence** había pasado en su ausencia; **how long will this ~ on for?** ¿cuánto tiempo durará esto? **(g)** (*behave*) conducirse, comportarse; **what a way to ~ on!** ¡qué manera de comportarse! **(h)** (*Theat*) salir (a escena); **to ~ on as substitute** (*Sport*) jugar como suplente. **(i)** (*light*) encenderse, prenderse (*LAm*).

◆**go on for VT** (*with numbers*) **it's ~ing on for 8** son casi las 8; **he's ~ing on for 70** va para los 70.

◆**go out VI (a)** (*depart*) salir; **to ~ out for a meal** ir a comer fuera; **she went out with him for 2 years** salió con él durante 2 años; **the mail has gone out** ha salido el correo; **to ~ out to work** ir al trabajo; **she ~es out to work** trabaja, tiene un trabajo; **my heart went out to him** le compadecí mucho, sentí una gran compasión por él. **(b)** (*fire, light*) apagarse; (*fashion*) pasar de moda, quedar anticuado; (*custom*) dejar de usarse. **(c)** (*tide*) retirarse. **(d)** (*end: year etc*) terminar, acabar.

◆**go over 1 VT (a)** (*examine*) examinar, escudriñar; (*check*) revisar, repasar; (*rehearse*) repasar; **to ~ over a house** visitar una casa, examinar una casa; **to ~ over the ground** estudiar el terreno, reconocer el terreno.

(b) (*cross*) pasar por encima (de); *terrain* recorrer, atravesar. **(c)** (*touch up*) retocar. **2 VI (a) how did it ~ over?** ¿qué tal lo recibió el público? (*etc*). **(b) to ~ over to** (*change party etc*) pasarse a. **(c)** (*overturn*) volcar.

◆**go round 1 VT** *obstacle etc* dar la vuelta a, hacer un rodeo para evitar.

2 VI (a) (*turn*) girar; dar vueltas; **the idea was ~ing round in my head** la idea daba vueltas en mi cabeza. **(b)** (*make a detour*) hacer un rodeo, dar una vuelta. **(c) to ~ round to John's house** ir a casa de Juan. **(d)** (*circulate*) circular, correr; **the word is ~ing round that ...** se dice que ..., corre la voz de que ... **(e)** (*suffice*) ser bastante, alcanzar para todos; **there's enough to ~ round** hay bastante (para todos); **to make the money ~ round** arreglárselas en cuanto al dinero.

◆**go through 1 VT (a)** (*pass*) pasar (por), pasar a través (de); penetrar; **the book went through 8 editions** el libro tuvo 8 ediciones. **(b)** (*undergo*) sufrir, experimentar. **(c)** (*examine*) examinar, estudiar; (*revise*) repasar; **to ~ through sb's pockets** registrar los bolsillos de uno. **(d)** (*use up*) *money* gastar; *supply* usar, gastar.

2 VI (a) (*pass, be approved*) ser aprobado, ser aceptado; (*deal*) concluirse, hacerse; (*motion*) votarse, aprobarse; **it all went through safely** todo se aprobó sin problema. **(b) the bullet went right through** la bala pasó de parte a parte.

◆**go through with VT: to ~ through with a plan** llevar un proyecto a cabo; **I can't ~ through with it!** ¡no puedo seguir con esto!

◆**go to VT: ~ to it!** ¡adelante!, ¡empieza!

◆**go together VI** ir juntos; (*colours etc*) hacer juego, armonizar; (*ideas etc*) complementarse.

◆**go under 1 VT: he now ~es under the name of Moriarty** ahora se conoce por Moriarty.

2 VI (*ship*) hundirse; (*person*) desaparecer debajo del agua; (*fig*) hundirse, fracasar.

◆**go up VI (a)** (*travel*) subir; **to ~ up to London** ir a Londres; **to ~ up to sb** acercarse a uno, abordar a uno. **(b)** (*level, price etc*) subir; **the total ~es up to ...** el total asciende a ... **(c)** (*Brit Univ*) entrar en la universidad; volver a la universidad. **(d)** (*explode*) estallar; explotar; *V* **smoke**.

◆**go with VT (a)** (*accompany*) ir con, acompañar a; (*lovers*) salir con. **(b)** (*match*) armonizar con, hacer juego con.

◆**go without 1 VT** pasarse sin. **2 VI** pasárselas.

goad [gəʊd] **1 N** aguijada *f*, aguijón *m*; (*fig*) estímulo *m*.

2 VT aguijonear, picar; (*fig*) incitar, provocar, (*anger*) irritar, (*taunt*) provocar con insultos; **to ~ sb into fury** provocar a uno hasta la furia; **to ~ sb into doing sth, to ~ sb to do sth** incitar porfiadamente a uno a hacer algo.

◆**goad on VT** pinchar, provocar; **to ~ sb on to doing sth** provocar a uno para que haga algo.

go-ahead ['gəʊəhed] **1 ADJ** emprendedor, enérgico.

2 N luz *f* verde; **to give the ~** dar luz verde (*for, to* a); **to get the ~** recibir luz verde.

▼**goal** [gəʊl] **N (a)** (*purpose*) fin *m*, objeto *m*, meta *f*; (*ambition*) ambición *f*; **to reach one's ~** llegar a la meta, realizar una ambición. **(b)** (*~posts*) meta *f*, portería *f*; **to keep ~, to play in ~** ser portero. **(c)** (*score*) gol *m*, tanto *m*; **~!** ¡gol!; **to score a ~** marcar un gol.

goal-area ['gəʊl,ɛərɪə] **N** área *f* de meta.

goal average ['gəʊl,ævərɪdʒ] **N** promedio *m* de goles, golaverage *m*.

goalie* ['gəʊlɪ] **N** = **goalkeeper**.

goalkeeper ['gəʊl,kiːpəʳ] **N** guardameta *mf*, portero *m*, -a *f*.

goal-kick ['gəʊl'kɪk] **N** saque *m* de portería.

goalless ['gəʊllɪs] **ADJ** sin goles, con empate a cero; **a ~ draw** un empate a cero, un empate a cero goles.

goal-line ['gəʊllaɪn] **N** línea *f* de portería.

goalmouth ['gəʊlmaʊθ] **N** portería *f*.

goalpost ['gəʊlpəʊst] **N** poste *m* de la portería; **to move the ~s** (*fig*) mover los postes, cambiar las reglas del juego.

goal-scorer ['gəʊl,skɔːrəʳ] **N** goleador *m*, -ora *f*.

goat [gəʊt] **N** cabra *f*, macho *m* cabrío; **to get sb's ~*** sacar a uno de quicio.

goat cheese ['gəʊt,tʃiːz] **N**, **goat's cheese** **N** queso *m* de cabra.

goatee [gəʊ'tiː] **N** barbas *fpl* de chivo.

goatherd ['gəʊthɜːd] **N** cabrero *m*.

goatskin ['gəʊtskɪn] **N** piel *f* de cabra.

gob: [gɒb] **1 N (a)** (*spit*) salivazo *m*. **(b)** (*esp Brit: mouth*) boca *f*. **2 VTI** escupir.

gobbet ['gɒbɪt] **N** (*of food etc*) trocito *m*, pequeña porción *f*; **~s of information** pequeños elementos *mpl* de información.

gobble ['gɒbl] **1 N** gluglú *m*.

2 VT engullir; **to ~ up** tragarse, engullirse ávidamente.

3 VI (*turkey*) gluglutear.

gobbledegook, gobbledygook* ['gɒbldɪguːk] N jerigonza *m*, galimatías *m*.

go-between ['gəʊbɪˌtwiːn] N medianero *m*, -a *f*, intermediario *m*, -a *f*, tercero *m*, -a *f*; (*pimp*) alcahuete *m*, -a *f*.

Gobi Desert ['gəʊbɪˈdezət] N desierto *m* del Gobi.

goblet ['gɒblɪt] N copa *f*.

goblin ['gɒblɪn] N duende *m*, trasgo *m*.

gobsmacked: ['gɒbsmækt] ADJ: **I was ~** quedé parado*.

gob-stopper* ['gɒbˌstɒpəʳ] N (*Brit*) caramelo grande y redondo.

go-by* ['gəʊbaɪ] N: **to give sth the ~** pasar algo por alto, omitir algo; **to give a place the ~** dejar de visitar un sitio; **to give sb the ~** desairar a uno (no haciendo caso de él), no hacer caso de uno.

GOC N ABBR of **General Officer Commanding** general *m*, jefe *m*.

go-cart ['gəʊkɑːt] N cochecito *m* de niño.

god [gɒd] N dios *m*; **G~** Dios *m*; **~s** (*Theat*) paraíso *m*, gallinero *m*; **for G~'s sake!** ¡por Dios!; **good G~!, my G~!** ¡Dios mio!, ¡santo Dios!; **G~ forbid!** ¡no lo permita Dios!; **please G~!** ¡plegue a Dios!; **G~ willing** si Dios quiere, Dios mediante; **G~-speed!** †† buena suerte, ande Vd con Dios; **G~ (only) knows** sólo Dios sabe; **I hope to ~ she'll be happy** Dios quiera que sea feliz; **G~ helps those who help themselves** a quien madruga Dios le ayuda; **G~ help them if that's what they think** Dios se la depare buena si piensan así; **he thinks he's G~'s gift to women*** se cree creado para ser la felicidad de las mujeres; **what in G~'s name is he doing?** ¿qué demonios está haciendo?

god-awful: ['gɒdˈɔːfʊl] ADJ horrible, fatal*.

god-botherer* ['gɒdˌbɒðərəʳ] N (*pej*) pesado *m*, -a *f* de la religión.

godchild ['gɒdtʃaɪld] N, PL **godchildren** ['gɒdtʃɪldrən] ahijado *m*, -a *f*.

goddam: ['gɒdˈdæm] (*US*) 1 ADJ (*also* **goddamn(ed)**) maldito, puñetero:.

2 EXCL (*also* **goddammit**) ¡maldición!

goddaughter ['gɒdˌdɔːtəʳ] N ahijada *f*.

goddess ['gɒdɪs] N diosa *f*.

godfather ['gɒdˌfɑːðəʳ] N padrino *m* (*to* de).

god-fearing ['gɒdˌfɪərɪŋ] ADJ temeroso de Dios, timorato.

godforsaken ['gɒdfəˌseɪkn] ADJ *person* dejado de la mano de Dios; *place* triste, remoto, desierto.

Godfrey ['gɒdfrɪ] NM Godofredo.

godhead ['gɒdhed] N divinidad *f*.

godless ['gɒdlɪs] ADJ impío, descreído.

godlike ['gɒdlaɪk] ADJ divino.

godly ['gɒdlɪ] ADJ piadoso.

godmother ['gɒdˌmʌðəʳ] N madrina *f* (*to* de).

godparents ['gɒdˌpeərənts] NPL padrinos *mpl*.

godsend ['gɒdsend] N cosa *f* llovida del cielo; **it was a ~ to us** fue un regalo celestial para nosotros.

godson ['gɒdsʌn] N ahijado *m*.

-goer ['gəʊəʳ] N *ending in compounds*: **cinema~** asiduo *m*, -a *f* del cine; **V opera, theatre** *etc*.

goes [gəʊz] V **go**.

go-faster stripes [gəʊˈfɑːstəstraɪps] NPL bandas *fpl* laterales decorativas.

gofer ['gəʊfəʳ] N (*US*) recadero *m*, -a *f*.

go-getter* ['gəʊgetəʳ] N (*esp US*) (a) persona *f* dinámica, persona *f* emprendedora. (b) (*pej*) arribista *mf*, egoísta *mf*.

go-getting* ['gəʊgetɪŋ] ADJ dispuesto, resuelto.

goggle ['gɒgl] VI salírsele a uno los ojos de las órbitas; **to ~ at** mirar con ojos desorbitados, mirar sin comprender.

goggle-box* ['gɒglbɒks] N (*Brit TV*) caja *f* boba*.

goggle-eyed ['gɒglˌaɪd] ADJ con ojos desorbitados.

goggles ['gɒglz] NPL (*Aut etc*) anteojos *mpl*; (*of skin-diver*) gafas *fpl* submarinas; (*) gafas *fpl*.

go-go ['gəʊgəʊ] ADJ (a) *dancer, dancing* gogó. (b) (*US*) *market, stocks* especulativo. (c) (*US*) *team etc* dinámico.

going ['gəʊɪŋ] 1 N (a) (*departure*) ida *f*, salida *f*, partida *f*.

(b) (*pace*) **good ~!** ¡bien hecho!; **that was good ~** eso fue muy rápido; **it was slow ~** el avance fue lento.

(c) (*state of surface etc*) estado *m* del camino, (*Sport*) estado *m* de la pista; (*Racing*) terreno *m*; **the path is hard ~** el camino está muy malo; **let's cross while the ~ is good** crucemos mientras podamos; **we made money all the while the ~ was good** mientras las condiciones eran favorables ganábamos dinero; **the book was heavy ~** la lectura del libro resultó pesada; **it's heavy ~ talking to her** exige mucho esfuerzo conversar con ella. ▼

2 ADJ *concern* próspero, en pleno funcionamiento; *price, rate, salary etc* actual, existente, corriente.

going-over ['gəʊɪŋˈəʊvəʳ] N (a) (*check*) inspección *f*; **we gave the house a thorough ~** registramos la casa de arriba abajo.

(b) (*fig: beating*) paliza *f*; **they gave him a ~** le dieron una paliza.

goings-on ['gəʊɪŋzˈɒn] NPL actividades *fpl* (sospechosas); conducta *f* (sospechosa); tejemaneje *m*.

goitre, (*US*) **goiter** ['gɔɪtəʳ] N bocio *m*.

go-kart ['gəʊkɑːt] N kart *m*.

go-karting ['gəʊˌkɑːtɪŋ] N karting *m*.

Golan Heights ['gəʊlænˈhaɪts] NPL: **the ~** los Altos del Golán.

gold [gəʊld] 1 N oro *m*.

2 ATTR de oro; **~ bar** barra *f* de oro; **~ braid** galón *m*; **~ disc** (*Mus*) disco *m* de oro; **~ dust** oro *m* en polvo; **Biros are like ~ dust in this office** los bolígrafos parece que se los lleva el viento de esta oficina; **~ fever** fiebre *f* del oro; **~ leaf** pan *m* de oro; **~ medal** medalla *f* de oro; **~ medallist** medallero *m*, -a *f* de oro; **~ miner** minero *m* de oro; **~ mining** minería *f* de oro; **~ plate** vajilla *f* de oro; **~ reserves** reservas *fpl* de oro; **~ standard** patrón *m* oro.

goldbrick* ['gəʊldˈbrɪk] (*US*) 1 N (a) (*swindle*) estafa *f*. (b) (*person*) gandul *m*.

2 VI escurrir el bulto.

Gold Coast ['gəʊldˈkəʊst] N (*Hist*) Costa *f* de Oro.

goldcrest ['gəʊldkrest] N reyezuelo *m* (sencillo).

gold-digger ['gəʊldˌdɪgəʳ] N aventurera *f*.

golden ['gəʊldən] ADJ de oro; dorado; áureo; *deed* meritorio; *hours* dorado; *opportunity* excelente; **~ age** (*Myth*) edad *f* dorada, edad *f* de oro; **G~ Age** (*Sp*) Siglo *m* de Oro; **the ~ boy of boxing** el joven ídolo del boxeo, el niño bonito del boxeo; **~ eagle** águila *f* real; **G~ Fleece** Vellocino *m* de oro, Toisón *m* de oro; **~ goal** (*Ftbl*) gol *m* de oro; **~ handcuffs** prima *f* de lealtad; **~ handshake** pago *m* cuantioso por baja incentivada; **~ hello** prima *f* de ingreso, prima *f* de contratación; **~ jubilee** quincuagésimo aniversario *m*; **~ mean** justo medio *m*; **~ oldie*** melodía *f* del ayer, vieja canción *f*; **~ rule** regla *f* de oro; **~ share** accionariado *m* mayoritario; **the ~ sixties** (*Mus etc*) los dorados sesenta; **~ wedding** bodas *fpl* de oro.

goldenrod ['gəʊldənˈrɒd] N vara *f* de oro.

goldfield ['gəʊldfiːld] N campo *m* aurífero.

gold-filled ['gəʊldˌfɪld] ADJ lleno de oro; (*Tech*) revestido de oro, enchapado en oro; *tooth* empastado de oro.

goldfinch ['gəʊldfɪntʃ] N jilguero *m*.

goldfish ['gəʊldfɪʃ] N pez *m* de colores.

goldfish bowl ['gəʊldfɪʃˌbaʊl] N pecera *f*.

Goldilocks ['gəʊldɪlɒks] NF Rubiales.

gold-mine ['gəʊldmaɪn] N mina *f* de oro; (*fig*) río *m* de oro, potosí *m*.

gold-plated [ˌgəʊldˈpleɪtɪd] ADJ chapado en oro; (*fig**) *deal, contract* de oro.

gold-rimmed [ˌgəʊldˈrɪmd] ADJ *spectacles* con montura de oro.

gold-rush ['gəʊldrʌʃ] N rebatiña *f* del oro.

goldsmith ['gəʊldsmɪθ] N orfebre *m*; **~'s shop** tienda *f* de orfebre.

golf [gɒlf] 1 N golf *m*.

2 VI jugar al golf.

golfball ['gɒlfbɔːl] N (a) pelota *f* de golf. (b) (*Typ*) cabeza *f* de escritura, esfera *f* impresora, bola *f*.

golf-buggy ['gɒlfbʌgɪ] N cochecito *m* de golf.

golf-club ['gɒlfklʌb] N (a) (*society*) club *m* de golf. (b) (*stick*) palo *m* (de golf).

golf-course ['gɒlfkɔːs] N campo *m* (*LAm*: cancha *f*) de golf.

golfer ['gɒlfəʳ] N golfista *mf*.

golfing ['gɒlfɪŋ] N golf *m*, golfismo *m*.

golf-links ['gɒlflɪŋks] NPL campo *m* de golf.

Golgotha ['gɒlgəθə] N Gólgota *m*.

Goliath [gəˈlaɪəθ] NM Goliat.

golliwog ['gɒlɪwɒg] N (*Brit*) negrito *m*, muñeco *m* negrito.

golly¹* ['gɒlɪ] N (*Brit*) = **golliwog**.

golly²* ['gɒlɪ] INTERJ (*Brit*) ¡caramba!

golosh [gəˈlɒʃ] N chanclo *m*, galocha *f*.

Gomorrah [gəˈmɒrə] N Gomorra *f*.

gonad ['gɒnæd] N gónada *f*.

gondola ['gɒndələ] N góndola *f*; (*Aer*) barquilla *f*; **~ car** (*US Rail*) vagón *m* descubierto, batea *f*.

gondolier [ˌgɒndəˈlɪəʳ] N gondolero *m*.

gone [gɒn] PTP of **go**.

goner: ['gɒnəʳ] N: **he's a ~** está muerto, está desahuciado.

gong [gɒŋ] N (a) gong *m*, gongo *m*. (b) (*Brit**) medalla *f*, condecoración *f*; (*in civil service*) cinta* *f*, cintajo* *m*.

gonna* ['gɒnə] (*esp US*) = **going to**; V **go 1** (y).

gonorrhoea, (*US*) **gonorrhea** [ˌgɒnəˈrɪə] N gonorrea *f*.

goo* [guː] N (a) cosa *f* muy pegajosa, sustancia *f* viscosa.

(b) (*sentimentality*) lenguaje *m* sentimental, sentimentalismo *m*.

good [gʊd] 1 ADJ (COMP **better**, SUPERL **best**) (a) (*gen, also of ~ quality, right, morally sound, favourable etc*) bueno, (*before m sing n* buen) **a ~ book** un buen libro; **the G~ Book** la Biblia; **G~ Friday** Viernes *m* Santo; **~!** ¡bueno!, ¡muy bien!; **~ one!** ¡muy bien!; **~ for you!** ¡muy bien tú!; **~ old Peter!** ¡bravo Pedro!

(b) (*sufficient*) **~ enough!** ¡muy bien!; **that's ~ enough for me** eso me basta; **it's just not ~ enough!** ¡esto no se puede consentir!

(c) (*pleasant*) **it's ~ to see you** me alegro de verte; **how ~ it is to know that ...!** ¡cuánto me alegro de saber que ...!; **it's ~ to be here** da gusto estar aquí; **it's as ~ as a holiday to me** esto me vale tanto como unas vacaciones.

(d) (*beneficial*) bueno, provechoso; (*advantageous*) ventajoso; (*wholesome*) sano, saludable; **~ to eat** bueno de comer; **it's ~ for you** es cosa muy sana; **it's ~ for you to swim** la natación es cosa sana; **oil is ~ for burns** el aceite es bueno para las quemaduras; **spirits are not ~ for me** los licores no me sientan bien; **he eats more than is ~ for him** come más de lo que le conviene.

(e) (*useful*) bueno, útil, servible; **the only ~ chair** la única silla servible (*or* sana); **to be ~ for** servir para; **he's ~ for nothing** es completamente inútil; **he's ~ for 10 years yet** tiene todavía por delante 10 años de vida; **he's ~ for £5** seguramente tendrá 5 libras para contribuir; **I'm ~ for another mile** tengo fuerzas para ir otra milla más; **it'll be ~ for some years** durará todavía algunos años; **a ticket ~ for 3 months** un billete valedero para 3 meses.

▼**(f)** (*clever*) **to be ~ at** ser hábil en, tener aptitud para, ser fuerte en; **she's ~ with cats** entiende de gatos; **she's ~ at maths** es buena para matemáticas, se le dan muy bien las matemáticas.

(g) (*kind*) bueno, amable; **he's a ~ sort** es buena persona; **he was ~ to me** fue muy amable conmigo; **he was so ~ as to** + *infin* tuvo la amabilidad de + *infin*; **please be so ~ as to** + *infin* ¿me hace el favor de + *infin*?, (*more formally*) tenga la bondad de + *infin*; **that's very ~ of you** es Vd muy amable.

(h) (*well-behaved*) de buenos modales, educado; **the child has been as ~ as gold** el niño se ha portado como un ángel, el niño ha sido más bueno que el pan; **be ~!** (*morally*) ¡sé bueno!, (*in behaviour*) ¡pórtate bien!, (*at this moment*) ¡estáte formal!

(i) (*at least*) **a ~ 3 hours** 3 horas largas; **a ~ 4 miles** 4 millas largas; **a ~ £10** lo menos 10 libras.

(j) (*practically*) **it's as ~ as new** está como nuevo; **it's as ~ as done** está casi terminado; **it's as ~ as lost** puede darse por perdido; **they're as ~ as beaten** pueden darse por vencidos; **it was as ~ as a holiday** nos ha valido tanto como unas vacaciones; **she as ~ as told me so** casi me lo dijo.

(k) to make ~ *promise* cumplir, *accusation* hacer bueno, probar, *claim* justificar; *loss* compensar, reparar; *damage* reparar; pagar; **to make a chair ~** reparar una silla.

2 ADV **(a)** bien; **a ~ strong stick** un bastón bien sólido; **a ~ long walk** un paseo bien largo; **to come ~*** empezar a dar de sí, dar buenos resultados; justificarse; alcanzar su plenitud; **to look ~** tener buen aspecto; **it's looking ~** promete, parece muy bien; **you're looking ~!** ¡qué guapa estás!; **to feel ~** estar satisfecho, creer haber hecho algo meritorio, (*in health*) estar como un reloj; **to give as ~ as one gets** devolver golpe por golpe; **you never had it so ~** nunca habéis estado mejor; **to hold ~** ser valedero, seguir verdadero (*of* con respecto a); **to make ~** salir bien, tener éxito, demostrar tener capacidad.

(b) ~ and* bien; **~ and hot** bien caliente; **~ and strong** bien fuerte; **they were cheated ~ and proper** fueron timados por las buenas; **they were beaten ~ and proper** fueron vencidos rotundamente.

3 N **(a)** bien *m*, provecho *m*, utilidad *f*; **the ~** (*abstract*) lo bueno, (*people*) los buenos; **~ and evil** el bien y el mal; **there is much ~ in him** tiene buenas cualidades; **there is some ~ in him** no es del todo malo; **for ~** definitivamente, para siempre; **he's gone for ~** se ha ido para no volver; **for the ~ of** en beneficio de; **it's for your own ~** es por su propio bien; **it's no ~** es inútil, no sirve para nada; **it's no ~ complaining** de nada sirve quejarse, no vale la pena de quejarse; **what's the ~ of it?** ¿para qué sirve?; **I'm no ~ at such things** yo no sirvo para tales cosas; **he's no ~** (*morally*) es un perdido; **he's up to no ~** está tramando algo malo; **he'll come to no ~** acabará mal, tendrá mal fin; **we're £2 to the ~** hemos ganado 2 libras; **we're a spoon to the ~** tenemos una cuchara de sobra; **to do ~** hacer bien; **he never did any ~** nunca hizo nada bueno; **it can't do any ~** es imposible que sea útil; **it will do him no ~ at all** no le aprovechará en lo más mínimo; **this medicine will do you ~** esta medicina le sentará bien; **much ~ may it do him!** ¡buen provecho le haga!

▼**(b) ~s** bienes *mpl*, efectos *mpl*; (*Comm*) géneros *mpl*, artículos *mpl*, mercancías *fpl*; **~ and chattels** (*Jur*) bienes *mpl* muebles; (*loosely*) cosas *fpl*, enseres *mpl*; **to deliver the ~s*** cumplir lo prometido.

4 ATTR: **~s siding** apartadero *m* de mercancías; **~s station** estación *f* de mercancías; **~s train** (tren *m*) mercancías *m*; **~s vehicle** vehículo *m* de transporte, camión *m* de mercancías; **~s wagon** vagón *m* de mercancías; **~s yard** estación *f* de mercancías.

goodbye ['gʊd'baɪ] **1** INTERJ ¡adiós!

2 N adiós *m*; **to say ~ to** despedirse de; (*fig*) dar por perdido; **you can say ~ to your wallet** ya no volverás a ver la cartera.

good-for-nothing ['gʊdfə'nʌθɪŋ] **1** ADJ inútil.

2 N perdido *m*, pelafustán *m*.

good-hearted [,gʊd'hɑːtɪd] ADJ de buen corazón.

good-humoured, (*US*) **good-humored** ['gʊd'hjuːməd] ADJ *person* afable, jovial; (*in mood*) de buen humor; *remark etc* jovial; *discussion*
de tono amistoso.

good-humouredly, (*US*) **good-humoredly** [,gʊd'hjuːmədlɪ] ADV afablemente; jovialmente; amistosamente.

GOOD	*see also main entry*

"Bueno shortened to "buen"

• *Bueno* must be shortened to *buen* before a masculine singular noun:

It's a good method
Es un buen método

Position of "bueno"

• *Buen/Buena* etc precedes the noun in general comments. Here, there is no attempt to compare or rank the person or thing involved:

If he set his mind to it, he could be a very good painter
Si se lo propusiera, podría ser muy buen pintor
At the end of the day, it's a good investment
A fin de cuentas es una buena inversión

• *Bueno/Buena* etc follows the noun when there is implied or explicit comparison:

We could make a list of good teachers
Podríamos hacer una lista de profesores buenos
I'm not saying it's a good thing or a bad thing
No digo que sea una cosa buena, ni mala

Ser/Estar bueno

• In general, you should use *ser* with *bueno*:

The idea is a good one
La idea es buena
It's good to be aware of the views of intelligent people
Es bueno conocer los puntos de vista de la gente inteligente

! Don't confuse *ser bueno* and *estar bueno*. If you describe someone using the very informal *estar bueno*, you mean you find them attractive or fanciable. *Estar bueno* is also used to describe good food:

Se fue a Ibiza con una rubia guapísima - él también está muy bueno
He went to Ibiza with a gorgeous blonde - he's pretty hunky too
La paella estaba muy buena
The paella was very good

Estar bien

• Use *estar* with the adverb *bien* to give a general comment on a situation:

You've written a book, which is good as you'll now be able to stop working
Has escrito un libro, lo que está bien porque así podrás dejar de trabajar
For further uses and examples, see main entry.

---

good-looker* [,gʊd'lʊkər] N (*man*) hombre *m* guapo, tío* *m* bueno; (*woman*) mujer *f* guapa, tía* *f* buena; (*horse etc*) caballo *m* etc de buena estampa.

good-looking ['gʊd'lʊkɪŋ] ADJ bien parecido, guapo.

goodly ['gʊdlɪ] ADJ (*fine*) agradable, excelente; (*handsome*) hermoso, bien parecido; *sum etc* importante; *number* crecido.

good-natured ['gʊd'neɪtʃəd] ADJ *person* afable, bonachón; *discussion* de tono amistoso.

goodness ['gʊdnɪs] N (*virtue, kindness*) bondad *f*; (*good quality*) buena calidad *f*; (*essence*) sustancia *f*, lo mejor; **~!, ~ gracious!, ~ me!** ¡Dios mío!; **for ~' sake!** ¡por Dios!; **~ only knows!** ¡quién sabe!; **thank ~!** ¡gracias a Dios!

good-tempered ['gʊd'tempəd] ADJ afable, ecuánime, de natural apacible; *tone* afable, amistoso; *discussion* sereno, sin pasión.

good-time ['gʊd'taɪm] ADJ: **~ girl** chica *f* alegre.

goodwill ['gʊd'wɪl] N **(a)** buena voluntad *f*; **~ mission** misión *f* de buena voluntad. **(b)** (*Comm*) clientela *f*; fondo *m* de comercio.

goody* ['gʊdɪ] (*esp US*) **1** ADJ beatuco*, santurrón.

2 INTERJ (*also* **~ ~**) ¡qué bien!, ¡qué estupendo!*

3 N **(a)** (*Culin*) golosina *f*. **(b)** (*Cine*) bueno *m*; **the goodies** los buenos.

goody bag* ['gʊdɪbæg] N bolsa *f* de regalos, obsequio *m* promocional.

goody-goody* [,gʊdɪ'gʊdɪ] **1** ADJ virtuosillo*, beato.

2 N pequeño santo *m*, pequeña santa *f*, angelito* *m*.

gooey* ['guːɪ] ADJ pegajoso, viscoso; *sweet* empalagoso.

goof: [guːf] **1** N bobo *m*, -a *f*.

2 VI **(a)** (*err*) tirarse una plancha. **(b)** (*US: also* **to ~ off**) gandulear.

◆**goof around*** VI (*US*) hacer el tonto.

goofy: ['guːfɪ] ADJ bobo.

gook: [guːk] N (*US: pej*) asiático *m*, -a *f*.

goolies: ['guːlɪz] NPL cataplines: *mpl*.

goon [guːn] N **(a)** imbécil *mf*, idiota *mf*. **(b)** (*US: Hist*) gorila contratado *para sembrar el terror entre los obreros.* **(c)** *(US)* guardaespaldas *m*, esbirro *m*.

goose [guːs] **1** N, PL **geese** [giːs] *(domestic)* ganso *m*, -a *f*, oca *f*; *(wild)* ánsar *m*; **to cook sb's ~** hacer la santísima a uno; **to kill the ~ that lays the golden eggs** matar la gallina de los huevos de oro.
2 VT (*) *girl* palpar, meter mano a.

gooseberry ['guzbərı] N grosella *f* espinosa; **to play ~** hacer de carabina; **I don't want to play ~** *(Brit)* no quiero estar de más, no quiero llevar la cesta.

gooseberry-bush ['guzbərı,buʃ] N grosellero *m* espinoso.

goosebumps ['guːsbʌmps] NPL *(US)*, **gooseflesh** ['guːsfleʃ] N, **goosepimples** ['guːs,pımplz] NPL carne *f* de gallina.

goose-step ['guːsstep] **1** N paso *m* de ganso, paso *m* de la oca.
2 VI marchar a paso de ganso (*or* de la oca).

GOP N *(US Pol)* ABBR *of* **Grand Old Party** Partido *m* Republicano.

gopher ['gəʊfər] N **(a)** ardillón *m*, ardilla *f* de tierra. **(b)** *(Comput)* gopher *m*.

gorblimey [ˌgɔː'blaımı] EXCL *(Brit)* ¡puñetas!✶

Gordian ['gɔːdıən] ADJ: **to cut the ~ knot** cortar el nudo gordiano.

gore¹ [gɔːr] N sangre *f* (derramada).

gore² [gɔːr] VT cornear.

gorge [gɔːdʒ] **1** N **(a)** *(Geog)* cañón *m*, barranco *m*, garganta *f*. **(b)** *(Anat)* garganta *f*; **my ~ rises at it** me da asco.
2 VT engullir.
3 VI *(also vr:* **to ~ o.s.)** hartarse, atracarse *(on* de).

gorgeous ['gɔːdʒəs] ADJ magnífico, brillante, vistoso; (*) maravilloso; **hullo ~!**✶ ¿qué hay, ricura?✶

gorgon ['gɔːgən] N: **G~** *(Mit)* Gorgona *f*; *(fig: woman)* pécora *f*.

gorilla [gə'rılə] N gorila *m*.

gormandize ['gɔːməndaız] VI glotonear.

gormless✶ ['gɔːmlıs] ADJ *(Brit)* bobo, idiota; torpe.

gorse [gɔːs] N aulaga *f*, tojo *m*.

gory ['gɔːrı] ADJ ensangrentado; *details, story* sangriento.

gosh✶ [gɒʃ] INTERJ ¡cielos!; **~ darn!** *(US)* ¡caramba!

goshawk ['gɒshɔːk] N azor *m*.

gosling ['gɒzlıŋ] N ansarino *m*.

go-slow ['gəʊ'sləʊ] *(Brit)* **1** N huelga *f* de celo.
2 VI hacer huelga de celo, *(strictly)* trabajar con arreglo a las bases.

gospel ['gɒspəl] **1** N evangelio *m*; **the G~ according to St Mark** el Evangelio según San Marcos; **as though it were ~ truth** como si fuese el evangelio.
2 ATTR: **~ music** música *f* de espiritual negro; **~ song** espiritual *m* negro.

gossamer ['gɒsəmər] N hilos *mpl* de telaraña; *(fabric)* gasa *f* sutil; **~ thin** muy delgado.

gossip ['gɒsıp] **1** N **(a)** *(person: great talker)* hablador *m*, -ora *f*; *(pej)* chismoso *m*, -a *f*, murmurador *m*, -ora *f*, comadre *f*, mala lengua *f*. **(b)** *(conversation)* charla *f*; **we had a good old ~** charlamos un buen rato, echamos un buen párrafo. **(c)** *(scandal)* chismes *mpl*, chismorreo *m*, comadreo *m*, habladurías *fpl*, murmuración *f*; **piece of ~** chisme *m*, habililla *f*.
2 VI *(talk)* charlar, echar un párrafo; *(talk scandal)* cotillear, contar chismes.

gossip column ['gɒsıp,kɒləm] N gacetilla *f*, crónica *f* de sociedad.

gossiping ['gɒsıpıŋ] **1** ADJ chismoso.
2 N chismorreo *m*.

gossip writer ['gɒsıp,raıtər] N cronista *mf* de sociedad.

gossipy ['gɒsıpı] ADJ chismoso; *style* familiar, anecdótico.

got [gɒt] PRET AND PTP *of* **get**.

Goth [gɒθ] N godo *m*, -a *f*.

Gothic ['gɒθık] **1** ADJ *race* godo; *(Archit, Typ)* gótico; *novel etc* horripilante, terrorífico.
2 N *(Archit, Ling etc)* gótico *m*.

gotta✶ ['gɒtə] *(esp US)* = **got to**; *V* **get 1 (l)**.

gotten ['gɒtn] *(US)* PTP *of* **get**.

gouache [gʊ'aːʃ] N guache *m*, gouache *f*.

gouge [gaʊdʒ] **1** N gubia *f*.
2 VT excavar con gubia; *(fig)* excavar.
◆**gouge out** VT: **to ~ sb's eyes out** sacar los ojos a uno.

goulash ['guːlæʃ] N puchero *m* húngaro.

gourd [gʊəd] N calabaza *f*.

gourmand ['gʊəmənd] N glotón *m*.

gourmet ['gʊəmeı] N gastrónomo *m*, -a *f*.

gout [gaʊt] N gota *f*.

gouty ['gaʊtı] ADJ gotoso.

Gov. ABBR *of* **Governor** gobernador *m*.

gov✶ [gʌv] N ABBR *of* **governor** **(d)** jefe *m*, patrón *m*; **yes ~!** ¡sí, jefe!

govern ['gʌvən] VT gobernar; dominar; *(guide)* guiar, regir; *(Gram)* regir; **to ~ one's temper** contenerse, dominarse.

governance ['gʌvənəns] N forma *f* de gobierno.

governess ['gʌvənıs] N institutriz *f*, gobernanta *f*.

governing ['gʌvənıŋ] ADJ: **~ board** *(Brit Scol)* consejo *m* directivo de escuela; **~ body** junta *f* directiva; junta *f* de gobierno, consejo *m* rector; **~ principle** principio *m* rector.

government ['gʌvnmənt] **1** N gobierno *m*; administración *f*; Estado *m*; *(Gram etc)* régimen *m*.
2 ATTR estatal, del Estado; gubernamental, del gobierno; oficial; **~ body** ente *m* gubernamental, ente *m* oficial; **~ bonds** títulos *mpl* del Estado; **~ department** ministerio *m*; **~ expenditure** gasto *m* público; **~ grant** subvención *f* gubernamental; **~ house** *(Brit)* palacio *m* del gobernador; **~ issue** propiedad *f* del Estado; **~-owned corporation** empresa *f* pública, empresa *f* del Estado; **~ policy** política *f* del gobierno; **~ securities** deuda *f* pública del Estado; **~ spending** gastos *mpl* gubernamentales; **~ stock** papel *m* de Estado; **~ subsidy** subvención *f* gubernamental.

governmental [ˌgʌvən'mentl] ADJ gubernamental, gubernativo.

governor ['gʌvənər] N **(a)** gobernador *m*, -ora *f*; *(esp Brit: of prison)* director *m*, -ora *f*, alcaide *m*. **(b)** *(Brit Scol)* miembro *mf* del consejo. **(c)** *(Mech)* regulador *m*. **(d)** *(Brit✶)* *(boss)* jefe *m*, patrón *m*; *(father)* viejo✶ *m*; **thanks, ~!** ¡gracias, jefe!

governor-general ['gʌvənə'dʒenərəl] N *(Brit)* gobernador *m*, -ora *f* general.

governorship ['gʌvənəʃıp] N gobierno *m*, cargo *m* de gobernador(a).

Govt ABBR *of* **government** gobierno *m*, gob.ⁿᵒ.

gown [gaʊn] N *(dress)* vestido *m*, traje *m*; *(Jur, Univ)* toga *f*.

GP N ABBR *of* **general practitioner** médico *m*, -a *f* de cabecera; *ver también* [NHS].

GPA N *(US)* ABBR *of* **grade-point average**; *ver también* [GRADE-POINT AVERAGE].

GPMU N *(Brit)* ABBR *of* **Graphical, Paper and Media Union** *sindicato de trabajadores del sector editorial.*

GPO (a) *(Brit)* ABBR *of* **General Post Office** Administración *f* General de Correos.
(b) *(US)* ABBR *of* **Government Printing Office.**

gr. **(a)** ABBR *of* **gross 2** gruesa *f*. **(b)** *(Comm)* ABBR *of* **gross 1 (d)** bruto, bto.

grab [græb] **1** N **(a)** *(snatch)* arrebatiña *f*, agarro *m*; (*) robo *m*; **it's all up for ~s**✶ todo se ofrece a quien lo quiera, está a disposición de cualquiera; **to make a ~ at sth** tratar de arrebatar algo. **(b)** *(esp Brit Mech)* cubeta *f* (draga), cuchara *f* (de dos mandíbulas).
2 VT **(a)** asir, coger, arrebatar; *(fig)* arrebatarse, apropiarse. **(b)** (✶) chiflar✶; **how does that ~ you?** ¿qué te parece?; **that really ~bed me** aquello me entusiasmó de verdad; **it doesn't ~ me** no me va✶.
3 VI: **to ~ at** *(snatch)* tratar de arrebatar; *(in falling)* tratar de asir.

grace [greıs] **1** N **(a)** *(Rel)* gracia *f*, gracia *f* divina. **(b)** *(gracefulness)* finura *f*, elegancia *f*; *(of shape)* armonía *f*; *(of movement)* garbo *m*, donaire *m*; *(of style)* elegancia *f*, amenidad *f*. **(c)** **with a good ~** de buen talante; **with a bad ~** a regañadientes; **he had the ~ to apologize** tuvo la cortesía de pedir perdón. **(d)** **to get into sb's good ~s** congraciarse con uno. **(e)** *(delay)* demora *f*; **days of ~** *(Brit Jur)* días *mpl* de gracia; **3 days' ~** un plazo de 3 días. **(f)** *(blessing)* bendición *f* de la mesa; **to say ~** bendecir la mesa. **(g)** *(in title: dukes)* **His G~ the Duke** su Excelencia; **yes, Your G~** sí, Excelencia. **(h)** *(in title: Eccl)* **His G~ Archbishop X** su Ilustrísima Monseñor X; **yes, your G~** sí, Ilustrísima.
2 ATTR: **~ period** período *m* de gracia.
3 VT adornar *(with* de), embellecer; **he ~d the meeting with his presence** honró a los asistentes con su presencia.

graceful ['greısfʊl] ADJ gracioso, agraciado; *movement* airoso, elegante, garboso; *compliment* elegante; *lines* grácil.

gracefully ['greısfəlı] ADV elegantemente, con garbo.

graceless ['greıslıs] ADJ desgarbado, torpe; *(impolite)* descortés, grosero.

grace-note ['greısnəʊt] N apoyadura *f*.

gracious ['greıʃəs] ADJ *(merciful)* clemente; *(urbane)* cortés, afable; *monarch* gracioso; **~ (me)!** ¡Dios mío!; **~ living** vida *f* elegante; **he was very ~ to me** estuvo muy amable conmigo.

graciously ['greıʃəslı] ADV *wave, smile* graciosamente; *(with good grace)* agree etc de buena gana; *live* indulgentemente; *(frm)* consent, allow graciosamente; *(Rel)* misericordiosamente, con misericordia.

graciousness ['greıʃəsnıs] N *(of person)* amabilidad *f*; *(of action, style)* gracia *f*; *(of house, room, gardens)* elegancia *f*; *(of wave, smile)* bondad *f*; *(of God)* misericordia *f*.

grad✶ [græd] N *(US)* ABBR *of* **graduate**.

gradate [grə'deıt] **1** VT degradar.
2 VI degradarse.

gradation [grə'deıʃən] N gradación *f*.

grade [greıd] **1** N **(a)** *(degree)* grado *m*; *(quality)* clase *f*, calidad *f*; *(in hierarchy, staff etc)* categoría *f*, rango *m*; *(mark)* nota *f*, clase *f*; **to make the ~** alcanzar el nivel deseado, tener éxito, ser satisfactorio; **to be promoted to a higher ~** ser ascendido a una categoría superior. **(b)** *(US Scol)* curso *m*, año *m*; clase *f*; *ver también* [HIGH SCHOOL].

(c) (*US: slope*) pendiente f.
[2] ATTR: ~ **crossing** (*US*) paso m a nivel; ~ **school** (*US*) escuela f primaria.
[3] VT **(a)** clasificar, graduar.
(b) (*Scol, Univ*) calificar, dar nota a.
♦ **grade down** VT degradar de categoría.
♦ **grade up** VT subir de categoría.

┌─ GRADE ─┐

i En Estados Unidos y Canadá, los cursos escolares se denominan **grades**, desde el primer año de primaria **first grade** hasta el último curso de la enseñanza secundaria **twelfth grade**. A los alumnos de los últimos cursos se les suele conocer por un nombre distinto según el curso en el que estén: **freshmen** si están en el **9th grade**, **sophomores** si están en el **10th grade**, **juniors** en el **11th grade** y **seniors** en el **12th grade**.
⇨ Ver también **┌ HIGH SCHOOL ┐**

---
graded ['greɪdɪd] ADJ graduado.

┌─ GRADE-POINT AVERAGE ─┐

i Los **colleges** y las universidades de Estados Unidos usan una media de calificaciones que se denomina **grade-point average** o **GPA** para determinar el rendimiento académico de sus alumnos, que servirá luego como base para la concesión de becas u otras ayudas de estudio. Para calcularla, se asigna un número a cada una de las notas obtenidas, normalmente se le da un 4 a la A, un 3 a la B, un 2 a la C y un 1 a la D, y se calcula la media aritmética. Así, si por ejemplo, durante un semestre un alumno ha tenido cuatro asignaturas y ha recibido dos Aes, una B y una C, se suman los puntos (4+4+3+2=13) y se dividen entre cuatro, dando un **GPA** de 3,25.
⇨ Ver también **┌ COLLEGE ┐**, **┌ DEAN'S LIST ┐**

---
grader ['greɪdəʳ] N (*US Scol*) examinador m, -ora f.
gradient ['greɪdɪənt] N (*Brit*) pendiente f.
grading ['greɪdɪŋ] N (*gen*) graduación f; (*by size*) gradación f; (*Scol etc*) calificación f.
gradual ['grædjʊəl] ADJ gradual; paulatino; progresivo.
gradualism ['grædjʊəlɪzəm] N gradualismo m.
gradually ['grædjʊəlɪ] ADV gradualmente; poco a poco; paulatinamente; progresivamente.
graduate **[1]** ['grædjʊɪt] N licenciado m, -a f, graduado m, -a f, (*in en*); universitario m, -a f; (*US: in high school*) bachiller mf.
[2] ['grædjʊɪt] ATTR: ~ **course** curso m de pos(t)grado; ~ **school** (*esp US*) escuela f de pos(t)graduado; ~ **student** (*US*) pos(t)graduado m, -a f; ver también **┌ COLLEGE ┐**.
[3] ['grædjʊeɪt] VT graduar.
[4] ['grædjʊeɪt] VI (*Univ*) obtener el título (*in en*); **to ~ as** recibirse de.
graduated ['grædjʊeɪtɪd] ADJ tube, flask, tax etc graduado; **in ~ stages** en pasos escalonados; ~ **pension scheme** plan m de pensiones graduado.
graduation [,grædjʊ'eɪʃən] N graduación f; (*US*) entrega f del bachillerato.
graffiti artist [grə'fiːtɪ,ɑːtɪst] N artista mf de graffiti.
graffito [græ'fiːtəʊ] N, PL **graffiti** [grə'fiːtɪ] pintada f, grafiti m.
graft[1] [grɑːft] (*Hort, Med*) **[1]** N injerto m.
[2] VT injertar (*in, into, on to* en).
graft[2]* [grɑːft] **[1]** N corrupción f, chanchullos mpl; **hard ~** (*Brit*) trabajo m muy duro.
[2] VI **(a)** (*work*) currar*. **(b)** (*swindle*) trampear.
grafter* ['grɑːftəʳ] N **(a)** (*swindler etc*) timador m, estafador m. **(b)** (*Brit: hard worker*) fajador m, -ora f.
graham flour ['greɪəm,flaʊəʳ] N (*US*) harina f de trigo sin cerner.
Grail [greɪl] N: **the ~** el Grial.
grain [greɪn] N **(a)** (*single seed*) grano m; (*corn*) granos mpl, cereales mpl; (*US*) trigo m.
(b) (*fig*) **with a ~ of salt** con un grano de sal; **there's not a ~ of truth in it** eso no tiene ni pizca de verdad.
(c) (*in wood*) fibra f, hebra f; (*in stone*) vena f, veta f; (*in leather*) flor f; (*in cloth*) granilla f; **it goes against the ~ with me to** + infin se me hace cuesta arriba + infin; **to saw with the ~** aserrar a hebra.
(d) (*Pharm*) grano m.
grainy ['greɪnɪ] ADJ (*Phot*) granulado, con grano; substance granulado.
gram [græm] N gramo m.
grammar ['græməʳ] **[1]** N gramática f.
[2] ATTR: ~ **school** (*Brit*) (*state*) instituto m, (*private, religious*) colegio m de segunda enseñanza.
grammarian [grə'mɛərɪən] N gramático m, -a f.
grammatical [grə'mætɪkəl] ADJ gramatical; **in ~ English** en inglés correcto; **that's not ~** eso no es correcto.

┌─ GRAMMAR SCHOOL ─┐

i En el Reino Unido, una **grammar school** es un centro estatal de educación secundaria selectiva que proporciona formación especialmente dirigida a los alumnos que vayan a continuar hasta una formación universitaria. Normalmente no son centros mixtos y para entrar en ellos se exige un examen escrito. Debido a la introducción en los años sesenta y setenta de las **comprehensive schools** para las que no hace falta una prueba de acceso, hoy día quedan pocas **grammar schools**, aunque sí que continúa el debate sobre si la calidad de la educación en estos centros es mejor o si sólo sirven para favorecer el elitismo en la enseñanza.
⇨ Ver también **┌ COMPREHENSIVE SCHOOLS ┐**

---
grammaticality [grə,mætɪ'kælətɪ] N gramaticalidad f.
grammatically [grə'mætɪkəlɪ] ADV bien, correctamente.
grammaticalness [grə'mætɪkəlnɪs] N gramaticalidad f.
gram(me) [græm] N gramo m.
Grammy ['græmɪ] N, PL **Grammys** or **Grammies** (*US*) ≃ Premio m Grammy.
gramophone ['græməfəʊn] **[1]** N (*esp Brit*) gramófono m.
[2] ATTR: ~ **needle** aguja f de gramófono; ~ **record** disco m de gramófono.
Grampian ['græmpɪən] N: **the ~ Mountains, the G~s** los Montes Grampianos.
grampus ['græmpəs] N orca f.
gran* [græn] N (*Brit*) = **grandmother**.
Granada [grə'nɑːdə] N Granada f.
granary ['grænərɪ] N granero m, troj f; ~ **loaf** ® pan m con granos enteros.
grand [grænd] **[1]** ADJ **(a)** (*fine, splendid*) magnífico, imponente, grandioso; person distinguido, augusto; style elevado, sublime; staircase etc principal; ~ **jury** (*US*) jurado m de acusación, gran jurado m; ~ **master** (*Chess, Mus etc*) gran maestro m; ~ **opera** ópera f; ~ **piano** piano m de cola; **G~ Prix** grand prix m, gran premio m; ~ **slam** (*Bridge*) bola f; ~ **total** importe m total; **G~ Tour** gran gira f europea; (*fig*) visita f extensa.
(b) (*) magnífico, bárbaro*, estupendo*; **a ~ game** un magnífico partido; **we had a ~ time** lo pasamos estupendamente*.
[2] N **(a)** (*piano*) piano m de cola.
(b) (*Brit‡*) mil libras fpl, (*US‡*) mil dólares mpl.

┌─ GRAND JURY ─┐

i En el sistema legal estadounidense, un **grand jury** es un jurado de consulta que decide si debe acusarse a una persona de un delito y llevárla a juicio. Este jurado está compuesto por un número de miembros que oscila entre doce y veintitrés, y normalmente llevan a cabo sus reuniones en secreto. El **grand jury** tiene autoridad para citar a testigos a prestar declaración.
Además del **grand jury**, existe en la legislación americana otro jurado llamado **trial jury** (jurado de juicio) o **petit jury**, compuesto de doce miembros, cuya función es la de determinar la inocencia o culpabilidad del acusado ante el tribunal.

┌─ GRAND OLE OPRY ─┐

i El **Grand Ole Opry** es un festival de música **country & western** que se celebra a lo largo de todo el año en las proximidades de Nashville, en el estado norteamericano de Tennessee. El nombre se creó a partir de la versión dialectal del término **grand opera** y su popularidad comenzó a aumentar en 1939, año en que el **Grand Ole Opry** se emitió por radio a todo el país, lo que contribuyó decisivamente a la difusión de la música country o **hillbilly**.

---
grandchild ['græntʃaɪld] N, PL **grandchildren** ['græn,tʃɪldrən] nieto m, -a f; **grandchildren** nietos mpl.
grand(d)ad* ['grændæd] N abuelito* m; **yes, ~** sí, abuelo.
grand(d)addy* ['grændædɪ] N (*US*) = **grandfather**.
granddaughter ['græn,dɔːtəʳ] N nieta f.
grandee [,græn'diː] N grande m de España.
grandeur ['grændjəʳ] N magnificencia f, grandiosidad f, sublimidad f.
grandfather ['grænd,fɑːðəʳ] **[1]** N abuelo m.
[2] ATTR: ~ **clock** reloj m de pie, reloj m de caja.
grandiloquence [græn'dɪləkwəns] N altisonancia f, grandilocuencia f.
grandiloquent [græn'dɪləkwənt] ADJ altisonante, grandilocuente.
grandiloquently [græn'dɪləkwəntlɪ] ADV con grandilocuencia.
grandiose ['grændɪəʊz] ADJ grandioso; (*pej*) building etc ostentoso, hecho para impresionar; scheme, plan vasto, ambicioso; style exagerado, pomposo.
grandly ['grændlɪ] ADV **(a)** **to live ~** vivir por todo lo alto; ~ **elegant** maravillosamente elegante; ~ **decorated** suntuosamente decorado.
(b) (*pompously*) speak, say solemnemente; behave con majestad; ~

called 'The Palace' grandiosamente llamado 'The Palace'.

grandma* ['grænmɑ:] N, **grandmama*** ['grænmə,mɑ:] N abuelita* f; **yes, ~** sí, abuela.

grandmother ['græn,mʌðə'] N abuela f.

grandpa* ['grænpɑ:] N, **grandpapa*** ['grænpə,pɑ:] N abuelito* m; **yes, ~** sí, abuelo.

grandparents ['græn,peərənts] NPL abuelos mpl.

grandson ['grænsʌn] N nieto m.

grandstand ['grændstænd] 1 N tribuna f.
2 ATTR: **to have a ~ view of** abarcar todo el panorama de.

grange [greɪndʒ] N (US Agr) cortijo m, alquería f; (Brit) casa f solariega, casa f de señor.

granite ['grænɪt] N granito m.

granny* ['grænɪ] N abuelita* f, nana f; **yes, ~** sí, abuela.

granny flat* ['grænɪ,flæt] N pisito m para la abuela.

granny knot ['grænɪ,nɒt] N nudo m corredizo.

▼ **grant** [grɑ:nt] 1 N (a) (act) otorgamiento m, concesión f; (thing granted) concesión f; (Jur) cesión f; (gift) donación f. (b) (Brit: scholarship) beca f; (subsidy) subvención f.
▼ 2 VT (bestow, concede) otorgar, conceder; (Jur) ceder; (give) donar; proposition asentir a; **~ed, he's rather old** de acuerdo, es bastante viejo; **~ed that ...** dado que ..., supuesto que ...; **~ing this (to) be so** dado que así sea; **to take sth for ~ed** dar algo por sentado, suponer algo; **we may take that for ~ed** eso es indudable; **he takes her for ~ed** no le aprecia a ella como es debido, no le hace caso alguno a ella.

grant-aided ['grɑ:nt,eɪdɪd] ADJ subvencionado.

grantee [grɑ:n'ti:] N cesionario m, -a f.

grant-in-aid ['grɑ:ntɪn'eɪd] N subvención f.

┌─ **GRANT-MAINTAINED SCHOOL** ─────────────────────┐
ⓘ *Un* **grant-maintained school** *es un colegio público británico financiado por el gobierno central. Este sistema de organización escolar fue establecido para dotar a los colegios de una mayor autonomía y para reducir a la vez el poder de intervención que los ayuntamientos tenían anteriormente en la educación. Aunque muchos centros han preferido seguir adscritos a la autoridad local, los que han optado por el sistema de* **grant-maintained school** *son controlados directamente por un equipo directivo con una representación importante del personal del colegio y de los padres de los alumnos. Este comité se encarga de tomar decisiones tales como la contratación de nuevo personal, el reparto del presupuesto, o el mantenimiento del edificio, asuntos de los que antes se ocupaba la autoridad educativa local.*
└───┘

grantor [grɑ:n'tɔ:', 'grɑ:ntə'] N cedente mf.

granular ['grænjʊlə'] ADJ granular.

granulated ['grænjʊleɪtɪd] ADJ granulado.

granule ['grænju:l] N gránulo m.

grape [greɪp] N uva f; **sour ~s!** ¡están verdes!; **it's just sour ~s with him** es un envidioso.

grapefruit ['greɪpfru:t] N toronja f, pomelo m.

grape harvest ['greɪp,hɑ:vɪst] N vendimia f.

grape hyacinth [,greɪp'haɪəsɪnθ] N jacinto m de penacho.

grape-juice ['greɪpdʒu:s] N mosto m; zumo m de uva, jugo m de uva (LAm).

grapeshot ['greɪpʃɒt] N metralla f.

grapevine ['greɪpvaɪn] N vid f; (trained against wall etc) parra f; (*) teléfono m árabe, medio m de comunicación clandestina; **I hear on the ~ that ...** por rumores que corren sé que ..., me ha dicho alguno que ...

graph [grɑ:f] N gráfica f, gráfico m.

grapheme ['græfi:m] N grafema m.

graphic ['græfɪk] ADJ gráfico; **~ artist** grafista mf; **~ arts** artes fpl gráficas; **~ design** diseño m gráfico; **~ designer** (TV) grafista mf.

graphical ['græfɪkəl] ADJ (gen, also Math) gráfico; **~ display unit** unidad f de demostración gráfica.

graphically ['græfɪkəlɪ] ADV gráficamente.

graphical user interface ['græfɪkəl,ju:zə'ɪntəfeɪs] N (Comput) interfaz m gráfico de usuario.

graphics ['græfɪks] N (a) (art of drawing) artes fpl gráficas; (Math etc: use of graphs) gráficas fpl. (b) (Comput) gráficos mpl; **~ environment** entorno m gráfico; **~ pad** tablero m de gráficos. (c) (TV) dibujos mpl.

graphite ['græfaɪt] N grafito m.

graphologist [græ'fɒlədʒɪst] N grafólogo m, -a f.

graphology [græ'fɒlədʒɪ] N grafología f.

graph paper ['grɑ:f,peɪpə'] N papel m cuadriculado.

grapnel ['græpnəl] N rezón m, arpeo m.

grapple ['græpl] 1 VT asir, agarrar; (Naut) aferrar.
2 VI (wrestlers etc) agarrarse; **to ~ with sb** agarrar a uno, luchar a brazo partido con uno; **to ~ with a problem** esforzarse por resolver un problema, tratar de vencer un problema.

grappling iron ['græplɪŋ,aɪən] N arpeo m, garfio m.

grasp [grɑ:sp] 1 N (a) agarro m, asimiento m; (handclasp) apretón m; **to be within sb's ~** estar al alcance de la mano; **he has a strong ~** agarra muy fuerte; **he lost his ~ and fell** no pudo agarrarse más y cayó.
(b) (fig) (power) garras fpl, control m; (range) alcance m; (mental hold) comprensión f, capacidad f intelectual; **it's within everyone's ~** está al alcance de todos; **to have a good ~ of** dominar, conocer a fondo.
2 VT (a) (hold firmly) asir, agarrar; hand estrechar, apretar; weapon etc empuñar; chance asir; power, territory apoderarse de.
(b) (get mental hold of) comprender.
3 VI: **to ~ at** hacer por asir, tratar de asir.

grasping ['grɑ:spɪŋ] ADJ avaro, codicioso.

grass [grɑ:s] 1 N (a) hierba f; (lawn) césped m; (grazing) pasto m; **'keep off the ~'** 'se prohíbe pisar la hierba'; **to let the ~ grow under one's feet** dejar crecer la hierba; **he doesn't let the ~ grow under his feet** no cría moho; **to put a horse out to ~** echar un caballo al pasto.
(b) (‡) hierba* f, marijuana f.
(c) (Brit‡: person) soplón* m.
2 ATTR: **~ court** pista f de césped; **~ cutter** cortacésped m.
3 VT (also **to ~ over**) cubrir de hierba.
4 VI (Brit‡) soplar*, dar el chivatazo‡; **to ~ on** delatar a.

grass-green ['grɑ:s,gri:n] ADJ verde hierba.

grasshopper ['grɑ:s,hɒpə'] N saltamontes m, chapulín m (CAm, Mex).

grassland ['grɑ:slænd] N pradera f, dehesa f; pasto m.

grass-roots ['grɑ:s'ru:ts] 1 N (Pol etc) base f popular.
2 ATTR básico; popular; **~ opinion** opinión f de las bases populares; **~ politics** política f donde se trata de los problemas corrientes de la gente.

grass-snake ['grɑ:ssneɪk] N culebra f nadadora.

grass widow ['grɑ:s'wɪdəʊ] N (Brit) mujer f cuyo marido está ausente.

grass widower ['grɑ:s'wɪdəʊə'] N (Brit) marido m cuya mujer está ausente; ≃ Rodríguez m.

grassy ['grɑ:sɪ] ADJ herboso, cubierto de hierba.

grate¹ [greɪt] N hogar m; (strictly) parrilla f de hogar, emparrillado m.

grate² [greɪt] 1 VT (a) food rallar; **~d cheese** queso m rallado.
(b) teeth hacer rechinar.
2 VI (make a noise) rechinar; (rub on) rozar; **to ~ on** rozar con, (fig) molestar; **to ~ on the ear** herir el oído; **to ~ on one's nerves** destrozar los nervios a uno.

▼ **grateful** ['greɪtfʊl] ADJ agradecido, reconocido; **with ~ thanks** con mis más efusivas gracias; **I am ~ for your letter** agradezco su carta; **I am most ~ to you** te lo agradezco muchísimo; **I should be ~ if ...** agradecería que + subj.

gratefully ['greɪtfəlɪ] ADV agradecidamente, con agradecimiento; **she looked at me ~** me miró agradecida.

grater ['greɪtə'] N rallador m.

gratification [,grætɪfɪ'keɪʃən] N (a) (reward) gratificación f, recompensa f; (tip) propina f.
(b) (pleasure) placer m, satisfacción f; **to my great ~** con gran satisfacción mía.

gratified ['grætɪfaɪd] ADJ contento, satisfecho.

gratify ['grætɪfaɪ] VT person complacer; whim etc satisfacer; **I was gratified to hear that ...** me alegré de saber que ...; **he was much gratified** estuvo muy contento.

gratifying ['grætɪfaɪŋ] ADJ gratificante, satisfactorio, grato; **with ~ speed** con loable prontitud; **it is ~ to know that ...** me es grato saber que ...

grating¹ ['greɪtɪŋ] N reja f, enrejado m, emparrillado m.

grating² ['greɪtɪŋ] ADJ tone etc áspero.

gratis ['grɑ:tɪs] ADV gratis.

▼ **gratitude** ['grætɪtju:d] N agradecimiento m, reconocimiento m, gratitud f.

gratuitous [grə'tju:ɪtəs] ADJ gratuito, innecesario.

gratuitously [grə'tju:ɪtəslɪ] ADV gratuitamente, de manera gratuita.

gratuity [grə'tju:ɪtɪ] N gratificación f, propina f.

gravamen [grə'veɪmen] N, PL **gravamina** [grə'væmɪnə] (Jur) fundamento principal de una acusación.

grave¹ [greɪv] ADJ grave; serio; (anxious) preocupado; solemne.

grave² [greɪv] N sepultura f; (with monument) tumba f, sepulcro m; **common ~** fosa f común.

grave³ [grɑ:v] ADJ: **~ accent** acento m grave.

gravedigger ['greɪv,dɪgə'] N sepulturero m.

gravel ['grævəl] 1 N grava f, cascajo m, recebo m.
2 ATTR: **~ path** camino m de grava.

gravel bed ['grævl,bed] N gravera f.

gravelled, (US) **graveled** ['grævəld] ADJ engravado, cubierto con grava.

gravelly ['grævəlɪ] ADJ (a) arenisco, cascajoso. (b) voice áspero.

gravel pit ['grævl,pɪt] N gravera f.

gravely ['greɪvlɪ] ADJ gravemente; seriamente; **~ wounded** gravemente herido, herido de gravedad; **he is ~ ill** está grave; he

spoke ~ habló en tono preocupado.

graven ['greɪvən] ADJ: ~ **image** ídolo m; **it is** ~ **on my memory** lo tengo grabado en la memoria.

graveness ['greɪvnɪs] N gravedad f.

graveside ['greɪvsaɪd] N: **at the** ~ junto a la tumba.

gravestone ['greɪvstəʊn] N lápida f (sepulcral).

graveyard ['greɪvjɑːd] N cementerio m (also fig), camposanto m.

graveyard shift ['greɪvjɑːd‚ʃɪft] N (esp US) turno m de noche, turno m nocturno.

graving dock ['greɪvɪŋdɒk] N dique m de carena.

gravitas ['grævɪtæs] N (frm) gravitas f, peso m específico; **a certain air of** ~ cierto aire de seriedad.

gravitate ['grævɪteɪt] VI gravitar; **to** ~ **towards** (fig) dejarse atraer por, tender hacia.

gravitation [‚grævɪ'teɪʃən] N gravitación f; (fig) tendencia f (towards hacia).

gravitational [‚grævɪ'teɪʃənl] ADJ gravitatorio, gravitacional.

gravity ['grævɪtɪ] 1 N (a) (Phys) gravedad f.
(b) (seriousness) gravedad f, seriedad f; solemnidad f; **the** ~ **of the situation** lo grave de la situación, los peligros de la situación; **he spoke with the utmost** ~ habló con la mayor solemnidad.
2 ATTR: ~ **feed** alimentación f por gravedad.

gravy ['greɪvɪ] 1 N (a) salsa f. (b) (US‡) ganga f.
2 ATTR: **to get on the** ~ **train‡** coger un chollo‡.

gravy-boat ['greɪvɪ‚bəʊt] N salsera f.

gray [greɪ] etc (esp US) = **grey** etc.

grayness ['greɪnɪs] (US) = **greyness**.

graze¹ [greɪz] (Agr) 1 VT grass pacer; cattle apacentar, pastar.
2 VI pacer, pastar.

graze² [greɪz] 1 N roce m, abrasión f, desolladura f.
2 VT (touch) rozar al pasar; (scrape) raspar, raer.

grazing ['greɪzɪŋ] N (a) (land) pasto m. (b) (act) apacentimiento m, pastoreo m.

GRE N (US: Univ) ABBR of **Graduate Record Examination** examen de acceso a estudios de posgrado.

grease [griːs] 1 N grasa f; (dirt) mugre f; (of candle) sebo m.
2 VT engrasar, lubricar.

grease-gun ['griːsgʌn] N pistola f engrasadora, engrasadora f a presión.

grease monkey ['griːs‚mʌŋkɪ] N (US) mecánico m, -a f, maquinista mf.

grease-nipple ['griːs‚nɪpl] N engrasador m.

greasepaint ['griːspeɪnt] N maquillaje m.

greaseproof ['griːspruːf] ADJ (Brit) a prueba de grasa, impermeable a la grasa; paper apergaminado.

greaser‡ ['griːsəʳ] N (a) (mechanic) mecánico m. (b) (motorcyclist) motociclista m. (c) (pej: ingratiating person) pelota* mf, cepillo mf (LAm), lameculos‡ mf. (d) (US pej: Latin American) sudacaca‡ m.

grease remover ['griːsrɪ‚muːvəʳ] N quitagrasas m.

greasiness ['griːsɪnɪs] N lo grasiento; lo resbaladizo; mugre f.

greasy ['griːsɪ] ADJ (a) (substance, surface grasiento; road etc resbaladizo; hair graso; (grubby) mugriento; ~ **pole** cucaña f, palo m ensebado. (b) person adulón, cobista, zalamero.

▼ **great** [greɪt] 1 ADJ (a) (large) grande, vasto, enorme; sum importante; care etc especial; age avanzado; time largo; **the G~ Barrier Reef** la Gran Barrera de Coral; **G~ Bear** Osa f Mayor; **G~ Dane** (perro m) danés m; **G~ Powers** Grandes Potencias fpl; **G~ Seal** sello m real; **the G~ Wall of China** la Gran Muralla China; **of** ~ **power** de gran potencia; **to my** ~ **surprise** con gran sorpresa mía; **what a** ~ **(big) dog!** ¡qué perro más grande!; **to be** ~ **friends** ser muy amigos; **it was a** ~ **joke** fue divertidísimo; **to have no** ~ **opinion of** no tener mayor concepto de.
(b) (important) grande, importante, principal; **the** ~ **thing is that ...** lo importante es que ...
(c) (outstanding) grande, famoso, destacado; **a** ~ **man** un gran hombre; **he has a** ~ **future** tiene un brillante porvenir.
(d) (clever) **to be** ~ **at, to be** ~ **on** ser fuerte en, ser bueno para, entender mucho de.
(e) (keen) **he's a** ~ **angler** tiene gran afición a la pesca; **he's a** ~ **arguer** tiene la manía de discutir; **he's a** ~ **eater** tiene buen apetito, es muy comilón.
▼ (f) (*) magnífico, estupendo*, bárbaro* (LAm); ~! ¡magnífico!; **it's** ~! ¡es fabuloso!*; **you were** ~! ¡estuviste magnífico!; **he's a** ~ **guy** es un tío (LAm: tipo) estupendo*.
2 ADV (‡): **the lads done** ~ los chicos han jugado fenómeno*.
3 NPL: **the** ~ los grandes; **the** ~ **and the good** (hum) los grandes y los buenos.

great-aunt ['greɪt'ɑːnt] N tía f abuela.

Great Britain ['greɪt'brɪtn] N Gran Bretaña f.

greatcoat ['greɪtkəʊt] N gabán m, (Mil etc) sobretodo m.

greater ['greɪtəʳ] ADJ (COMP of **great**) mayor; **G~ London** gran Londres.

| GREAT, BIG, LARGE | | see also main entries |

"Grande" shortened to "gran"
• *Grande* must be shortened to *gran* before a singular noun of either gender:
Great Britain
(La) Gran Bretaña

Position of "grande"
• Put *gran/grandes* before the noun in the sense of "great":
It's a great step forward in the search for peace
Es un gran paso en la búsqueda de la paz
He is a (very) great actor
Es un gran actor
• In the sense of *big* or *large*, the adjective will precede the noun in the context of a general, subjective comment. However, when there is implicit or explicit comparison with other things or people that are physically bigger or smaller, it will follow the noun:
It's a big problem
Es un gran problema
...the difference in price between big flats and small ones...
...la diferencia de precio entre los pisos grandes y pequeños...
...a certain type of large passenger plane...
...cierto tipo de avión grande para el transporte de pasajeros...
• Compare the following examples:
...un gran hombre...
...a great man...
...un hombre grande...
...a big man...
For further uses and examples, see main entries at great, big and large.

---

greatest ['greɪtɪst] ADJ (SUPERL of **great**) (a) el mayor, la mayor; **with the** ~ **difficulty** con la mayor dificultad; **the** ~ **writer of his age** el mayor escritor de su época; **when the heat is at its** ~ cuando más aprieta el calor; ~ **common factor**, ~ **common divisor** máximo común divisor m.
(b) (*) **it's the** ~! ¡es el colmo!, ¡es el delirio!*; **he's the** ~! ¡es fabuloso!*

great-grandchild ['greɪt'grænʧaɪld] N, PL **great-grandchildren** ['greɪt'græn‚ʧɪldrən] bisnieto m, -a f.

great-granddaughter [‚greɪt'grænd‚dɔːtəʳ] N bisnieta f.

great-grandfather ['greɪt'grænd‚fɑːðəʳ] N bisabuelo m.

great-grandmother ['greɪt'græn‚mʌðəʳ] N bisabuela f.

great-grandparents ['greɪt'græn‚peərənts] NPL bisabuelos mpl.

great-grandson ['greɪt'grændsʌn] N bisnieto m.

great-great-grandfather ['greɪt'greɪt'grænd‚fɑːðəʳ] N tatarabuelo m.

great-great-grandson ['greɪt'greɪt'grænsʌn] N tataranieto m.

great-hearted ['greɪt'hɑːtɪd] ADJ valiente.

Great Lakes ['greɪt'leɪks] NPL Grandes Lagos mpl.

greatly ['greɪtlɪ] ADV grandemente, mucho, muy, sumamente; ~ **superior** muy superior; **we were** ~ **amused** nos divirtió muchísimo; **it is** ~ **to be regretted** es muy de lamentar; **not** ~ **expensive** no muy caro.

great-nephew ['greɪt‚nefjuː] N sobrinonieto m.

greatness ['greɪtnɪs] N grandeza f.

great-niece ['greɪt‚niːs] N sobrinanieta f.

great tit ['greɪttɪt] N (Orn) carbonero m común.

great-uncle ['greɪt‚ʌŋkl] N tío m abuelo.

Great War ['greɪt'wɔːʳ] N Primera Guerra f Mundial (1914-18).

grebe [griːb] N zampullín m, somormujo m.

Grecian ['griːʃən] ADJ griego.

Greece ['griːs] N Grecia f.

greed [griːd] N, **greediness** ['griːdɪnɪs] N codicia f, avaricia f; avidez f (for de); (for food) gula f, glotonería f; (as a sin) avaricia f.

greedily ['griːdɪlɪ] ADV con avidez; eat vorazmente.

greedy ['griːdɪ] ADJ codicioso, avaro; ávido (for de); (for food) goloso, glotón; **don't be so** ~! ¡no seas glotón!

greedy-guts* ['griːdɪ‚gʌts] N (Brit: hum) comilón* m, -ona f.

Greek [griːk] 1 ADJ griego; ~ **Orthodox Church** Iglesia f Ortodoxa griega.
2 N (a) griego m, -a f. (b)(Ling) griego m; **ancient** ~ griego m antiguo; **it's** ~ **to me** para mí es chino, no entiendo ni palabra.

Greek-Cypriot ['griːk'sɪprɪət] 1 ADJ grecochipriota.
2 N grecochipriota mf.

green [griːn] 1 ADJ (a) verde; (fresh) fresco; (unripe, unseasoned) verde; (raw) crudo; complexion pálido; ~ **algae** algas fpl verdes; ~ **beans** judías fpl verdes, ejotes mpl (Mex), chauchas fpl (SC); ~ **belt** (Brit) zona f verde; **the G~ Berets** los boinas verdes mpl; ~ **card** (Brit Aut, US Admin) tarjeta f verde; **G~ Cross Code** (Brit) código m de seguridad vial; ~ **fingers** (Brit), ~ **thumb** (US) habilidad f para la jardinería; ~ **light** luz f verde; **to give the** ~ **light to** dar luz verde a;

G~ Paper (*Brit Pol*) libro *m* verde; **~ peas** guisantes *mpl*; **~ pepper** (*spice*) pimienta *f* verde; (*vegetable*) pimiento *m* verde, pimentón *m* verde; **~ pound** libra *f* verde; **~ revolution** revolución *f* verde; **~ room** camerino *m*; **~ salad** ensalada *f* (a base de lechuga); **~ vegetables** verdura *f*; **~ wellie brigade*** señoritos *mpl* del campo; **she was ~ with envy** quedaba muda de envidia; le comía la envidia; **to grow ~, to look ~** verdear.

(b) (*inexperienced*) nuevo, novato; (*naïve*) crédulo.

(c) (*Pol*) verde; **~ issues** temas *mpl* verdes; **G~ Party** Partido *m* Verde; **~ policies** programas *mpl* verdes; **~ politics** política *f* verde; **the ~ vote** el voto verde.

2 N **(a)** (*colour*) verde *m*.

(b) (*lawn*) césped *m*; (*field*) prado *m*; (*for bowls etc*) pista *f*; (*Golf*) green *m*; (*of village*) césped *m* comunal.

(c) **~s** (*Brit*) verduras *fpl*.

(d) (*Pol*) **the G~s** los verdes; **I'm a G~ now** ahora yo soy Verde.

greenback ['griːnbæk] N (*US*) billete *m* (de banco).

greenery ['griːnərɪ] N verdura *f*.

green-eyed ['griːnaɪd] ADJ de ojos verdes; **the ~ monster** (*fig*) la envidia.

greenfield ['griːnfiːld] N (*also* **~ site**) solar *m* sin edificar, terreno *m* sin edificar.

greenfinch ['griːnfɪntʃ] N verderón *m*.

greenfly ['griːnflaɪ] N pulgón *m*.

greengage ['griːngeɪdʒ] N (*Brit*) (ciruela *f*) claudia *f*.

greengrocer ['griːn,grəʊsər] N (*Brit*) verdulero *m*, -a *f*; **~'s** (**shop**) verdulería *f*, verdurería *f* (*Carib*).

greenhorn ['griːnhɔːn] N bisoño *m*, novato *m*.

greenhouse ['griːnhaʊs] 1 N, PL **greenhouses** ['griːn,haʊzɪz] invernáculo *m*, invernadero *m*.

2 ATTR: **~ effect** efecto *m* invernadero; **~ gas** gas *m* invernadero.

greenish ['griːnɪʃ] ADJ verdoso.

Greenland ['griːnlənd] N Groenlandia *f*.

Greenlander ['griːnləndər] N groenlandés *m*, -esa *f*.

Greenlandic [ˌgriːn'lændɪk] 1 ADJ groenlandés.

2 N (*Ling*) groenlandés *m*.

greenness ['griːnnɪs] N **(a)** verdor *m*, lo verde. **(b)** (*fig*) inexperiencia *f*; credulidad *f*.

greenstuff ['griːnstʌf] N verduras *fpl*, legumbres *fpl*.

greensward ['griːnswɔːd] N césped *m*.

GREEN-WELLIE BRIGADE

ⓘ *En el Reino Unido las botas altas de goma verdes **green wellingtons** se suelen asociar con las clases acomodadas, ya que son las botas que se utilizan normalmente para montar a caballo, ir de caza o de pesca, deportes que han sido tradicionalmente asociados a la clase alta. Por este motivo, el término **green-wellie brigade** (que podría traducirse al español por el de **señoritos del campo**), se utiliza a veces despectivamente para referirse a ciertos aspectos negativos del comportamiento de dicha clase social.*

Greenwich ['grɪnɪdʒ] ATTR: **~ mean time** hora *f* media de Greenwich.

greet [griːt] VT (*in general*) recibir; (*with words etc*) saludar; (*welcome*) dar la bienvenida a; (*meet one's eyes*) presentarse a; **this was ~ed with relief by everybody** todos sintieron un gran alivio al saber la noticia; **the statement was ~ed with laughter** se recibió la declaración con risas.

greeting ['griːtɪŋ] 1 N (*with words etc*) saludo *m*, salutación *f*; (*welcome*) bienvenida *f*; **~s!** ¡bienvenido!; **~s** (*in letter*) recuerdos *mpl*.

2 ATTR: **~(s) card** tarjeta *f* de saludo; tarjeta *f* de felicitación.

Greg [greg] NM *familiar form of* **Gregory**.

gregarious [grɪ'gɛərɪəs] ADJ gregario.

Gregorian [grɪ'gɔːrɪən] ADJ gregoriano; **~ chant** canto *m* gregoriano.

Gregory ['gregərɪ] NM Gregorio.

gremlin* ['gremlɪn] N duendecillo *m*, diablillo *m*.

Grenada [grə'neɪdə] N Granada *f*.

grenade [grɪ'neɪd] N granada *f*; (*hand* **~**) granada *f* de mano.

grenade-launcher [grɪ'neɪd,lɔːntʃər] N lanzagranadas *m*.

Grenadian [grə'neɪdɪən] 1 ADJ granadino.

2 N granadino *m*, -a *f*.

grenadier [ˌgrenə'dɪər] N granadero *m*.

grenadine ['grenədiːn] N granadina *f*.

grew [gruː] PRET *of* **grow**.

grey [greɪ] 1 ADJ gris; *horse etc* rucio; **~ area** zona *f* en penumbra; (*fig*) zona *f* gris; **~ matter** materia *f* gris, seso *m*; **~ mullet** lisa *f* dorada, mújol *m* dorado; **~ squirrel** ardilla *f* gris; **to go ~, turn ~** (*hair*) encanecer.

2 N **(a)** gris *m*. **(b)** (*horse*) rucio *m*.

3 VI (*hair*) encanecer.

greybeard ['greɪbɪəd] N anciano *m*, viejo *m*.

grey-haired ['greɪ'hɛəd] ADJ canoso.

greyhound ['greɪhaʊnd] 1 N galgo *m*, lebrel *m*.

2 ATTR: **~ track** canódromo *m*.

GREYHOUND RACING

ⓘ *Las carreras de galgos son un deporte muy popular en el Reino Unido, sobre todo entre aquellos a quienes les gusta apostar. Los corredores de apuestas (**bookmakers**) tienen mucha clientela con las carreras que llaman **the dogs**. El canódromo puede ser ovalado o redondo y los galgos persiguen una liebre mecánica que corre sobre un carril.*

---

greying ['greɪɪŋ] ADJ *hair* grisáceo, que encanece.

greyish ['greɪɪʃ] ADJ grisáceo; *hair* entrecano.

greyness, (*US*) **grayness** ['greɪnɪs] N lo gris.

grid [grɪd] N (*with bars*) reja *f*; (*Culin*) parrilla *f*; (*Brit Elec*) red *f*; (*Aut*) portaequipajes *m*, portamaletas *m* (sobre el techo) *etc*; (*of cycle*) parrilla *f*; (*on map*) cuadrícula *f*; (*Aut**) cacharro* *m*; (*US Sport*) = **gridiron**; **~ map** mapa *m* cuadriculado.

griddle ['grɪdl] 1 N plancha *f*.

2 VT asar a la plancha.

gridiron ['grɪd,aɪən] N **(a)** (*Culin etc*) parrilla *f*. **(b)** (*US*) campo *m* de fútbol (americano).

gridlock ['grɪdlɒk] N (*US Aut*) atasco *m*, retención *f*, bloqueo *m*.

grief [griːf] N dolor *m*, pesar *m*, aflicción *f*; **good ~!** ¡demonio!; **to come to ~** sufrir un percance; fracasar, fallar.

grief-stricken ['griːf,strɪkən] ADJ apesadumbrado.

grievance ['griːvəns] N queja *f*, motivo *m* de queja; reivindicación *f*; agravio *m*, injusticia *f*; **~ procedure** sistema *m* de trámite de quejas; **to have a ~ against sb** tener queja de (*or* contra) uno.

grieve [griːv] 1 VT dar pena a; **you ~ me** me das pena; **it ~s one to see ...** da pena ver ...

2 VI afligirse, acongojarse (*about, at* de, por); **to ~ for** llorar, llorar la pérdida (*etc*) de.

grieved [griːvd] ADJ *tone etc* lastimoso, apenado.

grievous ['griːvəs] ADJ *loss etc* cruel, doloroso, penoso; *blow* severo; *pain* fuerte; *crime, offence* grave; *error* lamentable, craso; *task* penoso; **~ bodily harm** graves daños *mpl* corporales.

grievously ['griːvəslɪ] ADV *hurt, offend* gravemente; *err, be mistaken* lamentablemente; **~ wounded** gravemente herido.

griffin ['grɪfɪn] N grifo *m*.

griffon ['grɪfən] N (*dog*) grifón *m*.

grifter ['grɪftər] N (*US*) **(a)** propietario *m* de una caseta de feria (*etc*); gariotero *m*. **(b)** (⁂) fullero *m*; estafador *m*, timador *m*.

grill [grɪl] 1 N (*aparatus*) parrilla *f*, grill *m*; (*meat*) asado *m* a la parrilla; *see also* **grille**.

2 VT **(a)** asar a la parrilla. **(b)** (*) interrogar (sin piedad).

grille [grɪl] N rejilla *f*; (*of window*) reja *f*; (*screen*) verja *f*.

grilled [grɪld] ADJ (asado) a la parrilla.

grilling ['grɪlɪŋ] N (*fig*) interrogatorio *m* intenso; **to give sb a ~** interrogar a uno intensamente.

grillroom ['grɪlrʊm] N parrilla *f*, grill *m*.

grilse [grɪls] N salmón *m* joven (que sólo ha estado una vez en el mar).

grim [grɪm] ADJ **(a)** (*stern*) severo; (*frowning*) ceñudo; (*unrelenting*) inexorable, inflexible; *battle* porfiado, muy reñido, encarnizado; *humour* macabro; (*frightful*) horrible; *outlook, situation* grave; **with a ~ smile** sonriendo inexorable; **the ~ truth** la verdad lisa y llana; **the ~ facts** los hechos inexorables.

(b) (*) horrible, malísimo.

grimace [grɪ'meɪs] 1 N mueca *f*, visaje *m*.

2 VI hacer una mueca, hacer muecas.

grime [graɪm] N mugre *f*, suciedad *f*.

grimly ['grɪmlɪ] ADV severamente; inexorablemente; encarnizadamente; **he smiled ~** sonrió inexorable; **to hang on ~** resistir sin cejar.

grimness ['grɪmnɪs] N (*V adj*) severidad *f*; inflexibilidad *f*; lo porfiado, lo encarnizado; lo macabro; gravedad *f*.

grimy ['graɪmɪ] ADJ mugriento, sucio.

grin [grɪn] 1 N sonrisa *f* (abierta, bonachona, burlona *etc*); (*grimace*) mueca *f*.

2 VI sonreír (mostrando los dientes, bonachón, burlón *etc*; *at* a); **to ~ and bear it** sonreír y resignarse, poner al mal tiempo buena cara.

grind [graɪnd] 1 N trabajo *m* pesado; rutina *f*; (*boredom*) lo pesado; **the daily ~** la rutina diaria; **the work was such a ~** el trabajo era tan pesado.

2 VT (*irr*: PRET AND PTP **ground**) *corn etc* moler; *stone* pulverizar; *teeth* hacer rechinar; (*sharpen*) amolar, afilar; (*oppress*) agobiar, oprimir; (*US Culin*) picar; **to ~ into powder** reducir a polvo.

3 VI (*machine etc*) rechinar, funcionar con dificultad; **to ~ against** ludir ruidosamente con; **to ~ to a halt** (*or* **standstill**) pararse con gran estruendo de frenos.

♦**grind away*** VI trabajar como un esclavo; (*Mus*) tocar laboriosamente*; **to ~ away at grammar** empollar la gramática*, machacar la gramática*.

♦**grind down** VT pulverizar, (*wear away*) desgastar; (*oppress*) agobiar, oprimir; **to ~ down to powder** reducir a polvo.

◆**grind on** VI: **the case went ~ing on for months** el pleito se desarrollaba penosamente durante varios meses.

◆**grind out** VT reproducir mecánicamente (or laboriosamente etc).

◆**grind up** VT pulverizar.

grinder ['graɪndəʳ] N (a) (person) molendero m; (Tech) amolador m; esmerilador m.
(b) (machine) amoladora f; esmeriladora f; (for coffee etc) molinillo m; (US: for meat) picadora f de carne.
(c) ~s (Anat) muelas fpl.

grinding ['graɪndɪŋ] ① ADJ: **~ sound** rechinamiento m; **~ poverty** miseria f absoluta, pura miseria f.
② N molienda f; pulverización f; afilado m.

grindingly ['graɪndɪŋlɪ] ADV: **a ~ familiar routine** una rutina tremendamente monótona; **~ poor** pobrísimo.

grindstone ['graɪndstəʊn] N muela f; **to keep one's nose to the ~** batir el yunque.

gringo ['grɪŋgəʊ] N (US) gringo m, -a f.

grip [grɪp] ① N (a) (grasp) agarre m, asimiento m; (handclasp) apretón m; **to come to ~s with** luchar a brazo partido con; **to get to ~s with a problem** enfrentarse con un problema, esforzarse por resolver un problema.
(b) (handle) asidero m, agarradero m; (of weapon) empuñadura f.
(c) (bag) maletín m, saco m de mano (con cremallera), bolsa f.
(d) (fig: power) garras fpl; control m, dominio m; **in the ~ of winter** paralizado por el invierno; **in the ~ of a strike** paralizado por una huelga; **to lose one's ~** perder las fuerzas, decaer; **get a ~ on yourself!** ¡cálmese!, ¡dómínese!
② VT (a) (hold firmly) agarrar, asir; weapon empuñar; hand apretar; **the wheels ~ the road** las ruedas se agarran a la carretera.
(b) (fig) (interest) absorber la atención de, tener suspenso a; (fear) apoderarse de, agarrar.
③ VI (wheel) agarrarse.

gripe [graɪp] ① N (a) (Med: also ~s) retortijón m de tripas. (b) (*) queja f.
② VT dar cólico a.
③ VI (*) quejarse.

griping ['graɪpɪŋ] ① ADJ pain retortijante.
② N (*) quejadumbre f.

gripping ['grɪpɪŋ] ADJ absorbente, muy emocionante.

grisly ['grɪzlɪ] ADJ horripilante, espeluznante; repugnante, asqueroso.

grist [grɪst] N: **it's all ~ to his mill** saca agua de las piedras, saca provecho de todo.

gristle ['grɪsl] N cartílago m, ternilla f.

gristly ['grɪslɪ] ADJ cartilaginoso, ternilloso.

grit [grɪt] ① N (a) arena f, cascajo m; (dust) polvo m.
(b) ~s (US) sémola f.
(c) (fig: courage) valor m; (firmness of character) firmeza f; (endurance) aguante m.
② VT (a) teeth hacer rechinar; **to ~ one's teeth (and bear it)** apretar los dientes.
(b) road cubrir de arena (or grava etc), enarenar.

gritter ['grɪtəʳ] N vehículo que suelta gravilla o arena en las carreteras en tiempo de heladas.

gritty ['grɪtɪ] ADJ arenisco, arenoso.

grizzle ['grɪzl] VI (Brit) gimotear.

grizzled ['grɪzld] ADJ gris, canoso.

grizzly ['grɪzlɪ] ① ADJ gris, canoso; **~ bear = 2.**
② N oso m pardo.

groan [grəʊn] ① N gemido m, quejido m.
② VT decir gimiendo; **'yes', he ~ed** 'sí', dijo gimiendo.
③ VI gemir, quejarse; (creak) crujirse; **to ~ under** sufrir bajo, (weight) crujir bajo.

groats [grəʊts] NPL avena f a medio moler.

grocer ['grəʊsəʳ] N (esp Brit) tendero m (de ultramarinos), mantequero m, abacero m, almacenero m (SC), bodeguero m (CAm, Carib), abarrotero m (esp LAm); ~'s (shop) tienda f de ultramarinos, tienda f de comestibles, mantequería f, abacería f, almacén m (SC), bodega f (CAm, Carib); tienda f de abarrotes (esp LAm).

groceries ['grəʊsərɪz] NPL comestibles mpl, provisiones fpl.

grocery ['grəʊsərɪ] N (esp Brit) tienda f de ultramarinos, tienda f de comestibles, mantequería f, abacería f; V also **grocer**.

grog [grɒg] N (Brit) grog m.

groggy ['grɒgɪ] ADJ (unsteady) inseguro, vacilante; (after blow) aturdido, turulato; (Boxing) groggy, grogui; **I feel a bit ~** no me siento del todo bien.

groin [grɔɪn] N ingle f.

groom [gru:m] ① N groom m, mozo m de caballos; (bridegroom) novio m.
② VT horse almohazar, cuidar; dog cepillar; **to be well ~ed** (person) estar muy acicalado; **she's always well ~ed** siempre está muy elegante; **to ~ sb for a post** preparar a uno para un puesto.

grooming ['gru:mɪŋ] N (a) (gen, also well-groomedness) acicalamiento m. (b) (of horse) almohazamiento m; (of dog) cepillado m.

groove [gru:v] ① N ranura f, estría f, acanaladura f; (of record) surco m; **to be in a ~** estar metido en una rutina; **to be in the ~** estar en forma; estar de moda, ser lo último*.
② VT (put ~ in) estriar, acanalar.

grooved [gru:vd] ADJ estriado, acanalado.

groovy ['gru:vɪ] ADJ (marvellous) estupendo*, guay‡, total*, tope*; (up-to-date) moderno, nuevo.

grope [grəʊp] ① VT (a) **to ~ one's way** ir a tientas; **to ~ one's way towards** (fig) avanzar a tientas hacia. (b) (*) woman sobar.
② VI ir a tientas; **to ~ for** buscar a tientas (also fig).

◆**grope about, grope around** VI andar a tientas; **to ~ about for sth** buscar algo a tientas.

grosgrain ['grəʊgreɪn] N grogrén m, cordellate m.

gross [grəʊs] ① ADJ (a) (large) grueso, enorme; (fat) muy gordo.
(b) (flagrant) abuse grave; injustice grave, intolerable.
(c) error craso; (vulgar) grosero.
(d) (Comm etc) bruto; **~ income** renta f bruta; **~ margin** margen m bruto; **~ national product** producto m nacional bruto; **~ output** producción f bruta; **~ payment** (pago m) íntegro m; **~ profit** ganancia f bruta; **~ sales** ventas fpl brutas; **~ wage** salario m bruto; **~ weight** peso m bruto; **~ yield** rendimiento m bruto.
(e) (US: disgusting) asqueroso.
② ADV: **she earns £50,000 a year ~** gana en total 50,000 libras al año.
③ N gruesa f; **by the ~** en gruesas; **in (the) ~** en grueso.
④ VT: **he ~es £40,000 a year** gana en total 40,000 libras al año.

◆**gross out*** VT (US) asquear, dar asco a.

◆**gross up*** VT (US) salary etc recaudar en bruto.

grossly ['grəʊslɪ] ADV groseramente; **~ exaggerated** enormemente exagerado; **~ fat** tan gordo que da asco.

grossness ['grəʊsnɪs] N gordura f; grosería f.

grot [grɒt] N (Brit) basura f.

grotesque [grəʊ'tesk] ADJ grotesco.

grotesquely [grəʊ'tesklɪ] ADV grotescamente; exaggerated bestialmente; insensitive brutalmente; **it was ~ unfair** fue tremendamente injusto.

grotto ['grɒtəʊ] N gruta f.

grotty* ['grɒtɪ] ADJ (Brit) sucio; asqueroso, horrible; **I feel a bit ~** no me siento bien.

grouch [graʊtʃ] ① VI refunfuñar, quejarse.
② N (a) (person) refunfuñón m, -ona f, cascarrabias mf. (b) (complaint) queja f.

grouchy* ['graʊtʃɪ] ADJ malhumorado.

▼**ground¹** [graʊnd] ① N (a) (soil) suelo m, tierra f; (US Elec; also **~ wire**) tierra f.
(b) (surface) suelo m, tierra f; (terrain) terreno m; **above ~** sobre la tierra, (fig) vivo, con vida; **on the ~** sobre el terreno; **to break new ~** (fig) hacer algo nuevo; **to cover a lot of ~** recorrer una gran distancia, (fig) tocar muchos puntos; **to cut the ~ from under sb's feet** minar el terreno a uno; **to fall to the ~** caer al suelo, (fig) venirse al suelo, caer por su base; **to get off the ~** (Aer) despegar, (fig) realizarse, resultar factible; **to go to ~** (fox) meterse en su madriguera, (person) esconderse, refugiarse; **to prepare the ~ for sth** preparar el terreno para algo; **to raze sth to the ~** arrasar algo; **to run sb to ~** localizar (por fin) a uno, averiguar el paradero de uno; **it suits you down to the ~** (Brit: dress) te sienta perfectamente; **it suits me down to the ~** (fig) me conviene perfectamente, me viene de perilla.
(c) (surface, fig) terreno m; **to be on dangerous ~** pisar un terreno peligroso; **to be on firm** (or sure) **~** hablar con conocimiento de causa; **to be on one's home ~** tratar materia que uno conoce a fondo; **to gain ~** ganar terreno; **to give** (or lose) **~** perder terreno; **to hold** (or stand) **one's ~** mantenerse firme, mantenerse en sus trece; **to shift one's ~** cambiar de postura.
(d) (pitch) terreno m, campo m; **they won on their own ~** ganaron en su propio terreno.
(e) (estate, property) tierras fpl.
(f) ~s (gardens) jardines mpl, parque m.
(g) ~s (sediment) poso m, sedimento m.
(h) (Art) fondo m; primera capa f; **on a blue ~** sobre un fondo azul.
▼(i) (reason) causa f, motivo m, razón f; (basis) fundamento m; **~(s) for complaint** motivo m de queja; **on the ~(s) of** con motivo de, por causa de, debido a; **on the ~(s) that ...** porque, por + infin, (pej) pretextando que; **on good ~s** con razón; **what ~(s) have you for saying so?** ¿en qué se basa para decir eso?
② ATTR: **~ attack** ataque m de tierra; (Aer) ataque m a superficie; **~ bass** bajo m rítmico; **~ floor** (Brit) planta f baja, primer piso m (LAm); **he got in on the ~ floor** (fig) empezó por abajo; **~ floor flat** (Brit) piso m de planta baja (LAm: de primer piso); **~ forces** fuerzas fpl de tierra; **~ frost** helada f, escarcha f; **~ ivy** hiedra f terrestre; **~ level**

nivel *m* del suelo; ~ **pollution** contaminación *f* del suelo; ~ **rent** (*esp Brit*) alquiler *m* del terreno; ~ **rules** reglas *fpl* básicas; **we can't change the ~ rules at this stage** a estas alturas ya no se pueden cambiar las reglas; ~ **wire** (*US*) cable *m* de toma de tierra.
③ VT (**a**) *ship* varar.
(**b**) (*US Elec*) conectar a tierra.
(**c**) (*Aer*) hacer permanecer en tierra; **he ordered the planes to be ~ed** ordenó que permaneciesen los aviones en tierra; **to be ~ed by bad weather** no poder despegar por el mal tiempo.
(**d**) (*teach*) **to ~ sb in maths** enseñar a uno los rudimentos de las matemáticas; **to be well ~ed in** tener un buen conocimiento de, estar versado en.
(**e**) (*US*) *student* encerrar, no dejar salir.
④ VI (*Naut*) varar, encallar; (*lightly*) tocar (*on* en).
ground² [graund] ① PRET AND PTP **of grind.**
② ADJ *glass* deslustrado; *coffee* molido; (*US*) *meat* picado; ~ **beef** (*US*) picadillo *m*.
groundbait ['graund‚beɪt] N cebo *m* de fondo.
groundbreaking ['graund‚breɪkɪŋ] ADJ *research, work, book* revolucionario.
groundcloth ['graundklɒθ] N (*US*) tela *f* impermeable.
ground-colour ['graund‚kʌləʳ] N primera capa *f*; fondo *m*.
ground-control ['graundkən‚trəʊl] N (*Aer*) control *m* de(sde) tierra.
ground-crew ['graundkru:] N personal *m* de tierra.
groundhog ['graundhɒg] N (*US*) marmota *f* de América.

┌─ **GROUNDHOG DAY** ─┐

ⓘ **Groundhog Day**, que literalmente significa **el día de la marmota**, es una simpática tradición estadounidense, según la cual se puede predecir la duración del invierno por la observación del comportamiento de este animal. La marmota, en inglés **groundhog**, también conocida como **ground squirrel** o **woodchuck**, supuestamente despierta de su hibernación y abandona su madriguera el 2 de febrero (**Groundhog Day**). Si hace sol y la marmota ve su propia sombra, el animal se asusta y vuelve a su madriguera para seguir hibernando durante otras seis semanas, lo cual indica que habrá seis semanas más de invierno. El acontecimiento tiene tal importancia que es televisado a todo el país desde la madriguera más famosa de Punxsutawney, en Pensilvania.

grounding ['graundɪŋ] N (**a**) (*Naut*) varada *f*. (**b**) (*in education*) instrucción *f* en los rudimentos (*in* de); **to give sb a ~ in** enseñar a uno los rudimentos de.
groundkeeper ['graund‚ki:pəʳ] N cuidador *m* del terreno de juego, encargado *m* de la pista de deportes.
groundless ['graundlɪs] ADJ infundado.
groundnut ['graundnʌt] N (*Brit*) cacahuete *m*, maní *m* (*LAm*).
② ATTR: ~ **oil** aceite *m* de cacahuete.
groundplan ['graundplæn] N planta *f*, distribución *f*.
groundsel ['graunsl] N hierba *f* cana.
groundsheet ['graundʃi:t] N tela *f* impermeable.
groundskeeper ['graundz‚ki:pəʳ] N (*US*) = **groundkeeper.**
groundsman ['graundzmən] N, PL **groundsmen** ['graundzmən] encargado *m* de campo, cuidador *m* de campo.
groundspeed ['graund‚spi:d] N (*Aer*) velocidad *f* respecto a la tierra.
groundstaff ['graundstɑ:f] N (*Aer*) personal *m* de tierra.
groundswell ['graundswel] N mar *m* de fondo; (*fig*) marejada *f*.
ground-to-air ['graundtʊ'ɛəʳ] ADJ: ~ **missile** misil *m* tierra-aire.
ground-to-ground ['graundtə'graund] ADJ: ~ **missile** misil *m* tierra-tierra.
groundwater ['graundwɔ:təʳ] N agua *f* subterránea.
groundwork ['graundwɜ:k] N trabajo *m* preliminar, trabajo *m* preparatorio; **to do the ~ for** echar las bases de.
group [gru:p] ① N grupo *m*, agrupación *f*; (*Mus*) conjunto *m* musical.
② ATTR colectivo; *discussion* en grupo; *photo* de conjunto; ~ **booking** reserva *f* por grupos; ~ **captain** (*Brit*) jefe *m* de escuadrilla; ~ **dynamics** dinámica *f* de grupo; ~ **practice** práctica *f* colectiva; ~ **sex** cama *f* redonda, sexo *m* en grupo, fornicación *f* colectiva; ~ **therapy** terapia *f* de grupo, terapia *f* grupal.
③ VT (*also* **to ~ together**) agrupar.
grouper ['gru:pəʳ] N (*Fish*) mero *m*.
groupie* ['gru:pɪ] N groupie* *f*, chica *f* que asedia a las figuras de la música pop.
grouping ['gru:pɪŋ] N agrupamiento *m*.
grouse¹ [graus] N: **black ~** gallo *m* lira; **red ~** lagópodo *m* escocés.
grouse²* [graus] ① N queja *f*; motivo *m* de queja.
② VI quejarse.
grout [graut] ① N lechada *f*.
② VT enlechar.
grouting ['grautɪŋ] N lechada *f*.
grove [grəʊv] N arboleda *f*, bosquecillo *m*; ~ **of pines** pineda *f*; ~ **of poplars** alameda *f*.
grovel ['grɒvl] VI arrastrarse; (*fig*) humillarse (*to* ante).

┌─ GROUP ─┐   ┌─ see also main entry ─┐

Agreement
● When *grupo* is followed by *de* + PLURAL NOUN, following verbs can be in the plural or, less commonly, in the singular:
  A group of youths came up to him
  Un grupo de jóvenes se le acercaron o se le acercó
● Otherwise, use the singular form of the verb:
  The group is *or* are well-known for being aggressive
  El grupo es conocido por su agresividad
  For further uses and examples, see main entry.

grovelling, (*US*) **groveling** ['grɒvlɪŋ] ADJ rastrero, servil.
grow [grəʊ] (*irr*: PRET **grew**, PTP **grown**) ① VT (**a**) (*Agr*) cultivar; *beard etc* dejar crecer; **to be ~n over with** estar cubierto de.
(**b**) **the lizard grew a new tail** al lagarto le salió una cola nueva, al lagarto se le reprodujo la cola.
② VI (**a**) crecer; (*be cultivated*) cultivarse; (*increase*) aumentar; (*industry, market*) extenderse, desarrollarse, expandirse; **that plant does not ~ in England** esa planta no se da en Inglaterra; **will it ~ here?** ¿se puede cultivar aquí?
(**b**) **to ~ to** + *infin* (*fig*) llegar a + *infin*.
(**c**) (*with adj: become*) volverse, ponerse; (*often translated by vi or vr*) **to ~ angry** enfadarse; **to ~ cold** (*thing*) enfriarse, (*person*) empezar a tener frío, (*weather*) empezar a hacer frío; **to ~ dark** ponerse oscuro, oscurecerse, (*at dusk*) anochecer; **to ~ old** envejecer(se).
◆**grow apart** VI (*friends*) irse separando, ir perdiendo el contacto.
◆**grow away from** VT irse separando de, ir perdiendo el contacto con.
◆**grow in** VI (*nail*) crecer hacia adentro; (*hair*) crecer de nuevo.
◆**grow into** VT hacerse, llegar a ser; **to ~ into a job** acostumbrarse a un trabajo.
◆**grow on** VT: **the book ~s on one** el libro gusta cada vez más, el libro llega a gustar con el tiempo; **the habit grew on him** la costumbre arraigó en él.
◆**grow out of** VT (**a**) **she grew out of her clothes** se le hizo pequeña la ropa; **to ~ out of a habit** perder una costumbre (con el tiempo).
(**b**) **to ~ out of** (*originate in*) resultar de, originarse de.
◆**grow up** VI (*person*) crecer (mucho), (*become adult*) hacerse hombre hacerse mujer; (*custom etc*) arraigar, imponerse; ~ **up!** ¡no seas niño!; **hatred grew up between them** nació el odio entre ellos; **she grew up into a lovely woman** con el tiempo se transformó en una mujer hermosa.
growbag ['grəʊbæg] N bolsa *f* de cultivo.
grower ['grəʊəʳ] N cultivador *m*, -ora *f*.
growing ['grəʊɪŋ] ADJ (**a**) *crop etc* que crece, que se desarrolla; ~ **season** época *f* de cultivos; época *f* del desarrollo (de las plantas). (**b**) (*increasing*) creciente. (**c**) *child* que está creciendo; ~ **pains** (*fig*) problemas *mpl* inherentes al crecimiento.
growl [graul] ① N gruñido *m*.
② VI gruñir; rezongar; (*thunder*) reverberar.
③ VT: **'yes', he ~ed** 'sí', dijo refunfuñando.
grown [grəʊn] ① PTP *of* **grow.** ② ADJ crecido, adulto.
grown-up ['grəʊn'ʌp] ① ADJ adulto; propio de persona mayor.
② N persona *f* mayor.
growth [grəʊθ] ① N (**a**) crecimiento *m*; aumento *m*; desarrollo *m*, expansión *f*; **to reach full ~** llegar a la madurez, (*fig*) alcanzar su plenitud.
(**b**) (*Bot*) vegetación *f*; **with 3 days' ~ on his face** con barba de 3 días.
(**c**) (*Med*) tumor *m*.
② ATTR: ~ **area** polo *m* de desarrollo; ~ **hormone** hormona *f* del crecimiento; ~ **industry** industria *f* en desarrollo; ~ **point** punto *m* de desarrollo; ~ **potential** potencial *m* de crecimiento; ~ **rate** (*Econ etc*) tasa *f* de crecimiento, tasa *f* de desarrollo; ~ **shares** (*US*), ~ **stock** acciones *fpl* con perspectivas de valorización; ~ **town** ciudad *f* en vías de desarrollo.
groyne [grɔɪn] N (*esp Brit*) rompeolas *m*, espigón *m*.
GRSM N ABBR *of* **Graduate of the Royal Schools of Music.**
GRT N ABBR *of* **gross register tons** toneladas *fpl* de registro bruto, TRB *fpl.*
grub [grʌb] ① N (**a**) (*larva*) gusano *m*.
(**b**) (‡) comida *f*; ~ **up!** ¡la comida está servida!, ¡a comer!
② VI: **to ~ about in the earth for sth** remover la tierra buscando algo.
◆**grub up** VT arrancar, desarraigar; (*discover*) desenterrar.
grubbiness ['grʌbɪnɪs] N suciedad *f*.
grubby ['grʌbɪ] ADJ sucio, mugriento.
Grub Street* ['grʌbstri:t] N (*Brit*: †) el mundillo de los escritores desconocidos.
grudge [grʌdʒ] ① N (motivo *m* de) rencor *m*; **to bear sb a ~, to have a ~ against sb** tener inquina a uno, guardar rencor a uno.

2 VT (**a**) (*give unwillingly*) escatimar, dar de mala gana.
(**b**) (*envy*) envidiar; **I don't ~ you your success** no te envidio tu éxito; **he ~s us our pleasures** mira con malos ojos nuestros placeres.

grudge match* ['grʌdʒ,mætʃ] N (*Sport*) enfrentamiento *m* entre antagonistas inconciliables; (*fig*) enfrentamiento *m* personal.

grudging ['grʌdʒɪŋ] ADJ *praise etc* poco generoso; **with ~ admiration** admirándolo a pesar de sí.

grudgingly ['grʌdʒɪŋlɪ] ADV de mala gana.

gruel [grʊəl] N gachas *fpl*.

gruelling, (*US*) **grueling** ['grʊəlɪŋ] ADJ duro, penoso; *match etc* muy reñido.

gruesome ['gru:səm] ADJ horrible, horripilante.

gruff [grʌf] ADJ *voice* bronco; *manner* brusco, malhumorado.

gruffly ['grʌflɪ] ADV bruscamente.

grumble ['grʌmbl] 1 N queja *f*; (*noise*) ruido *m* sordo, estruendo *m* lejano.
2 VI refunfuñar, quejarse; (*thunder etc*) retumbar a lo lejos; **to ~ about, to ~ at** quejarse de, murmurar de, protestar de.

grumbling ['grʌmblɪŋ] 1 N: **I couldn't stand his constant ~** no podía soportar su constante regruñir.
2 ADJ *person* gruñón, refunfuñón; **~ sound** gruñido *m*; **~ appendix** falsa apendicitis *f*.

grumpily* ['grʌmpɪlɪ] ADV gruñonamente, malhumorado.

grumpiness* ['grʌmpɪnɪs] N mal humor *m*.

grumpy* ['grʌmpɪ] ADJ gruñón, malhumorado.

grungy ['grʌndʒɪ] ADJ (*dirty*) cutre, roñoso; (*Mus*) de grunge.

grunt [grʌnt] 1 N gruñido *m*.
2 VT *reply etc* decir gruñendo.
3 VI gruñir.

gruppetto [gru:'petəʊ] N grupeto *m*.

gr. wt. ABBR *of* **gross weight** peso *m* bruto.

gryphon ['grɪfən] N = **griffin**.

GSA N (*US*) ABBR *of* **General Services Administration**.

GSUSA N (*US*) ABBR *of* **Girl Scouts of the United States of America**.

GT N ABBR *of* **gran turismo** GT.

Gt ABBR *of* **Great** Gran.

GTi N ABBR *of* **Gran Turismo injection** GTi *m*.

GU (*US Post*) ABBR *of* **Guam**.

guacamole [,gwɑ:kə'məʊlɪ] N guacamole *m*.

Guadeloupe [,gwɑ:də'lu:p] N Guadalupe *f*.

Guam [gwɑ:m] N Guam *f*.

guano ['gwɑ:nəʊ] N guano *m*.

guarantee [,gærən'ti:] 1 N garantía *f*; **there is no ~ that ...** no es seguro que + *subj*; **it is under ~** está bajo garantía; **I give you my ~** se lo aseguro.
2 VT garantizar (*against* contra, *for 3 months* por 3 meses); (*ensure*) asegurar; (*make o.s. responsible for*) responder de; **I ~ that ...** les aseguro que ..., les prometo que ...; **I can't ~ good weather** no puedo garantizar el buen tiempo.

guaranteed [,gærən'ti:d] ADJ garantizado; asegurado, seguro; **~ bonus** bonificación *f* garantizada; **~ loan** préstamo *m* garantizado; **~ prices** precios *mpl* garantizados.

guarantor [,gærən'tɔ:ʳ] N garante *mf*, fiador *m*, -ora *f*; **to act** (*or* **stand**) **as ~ for sb** actuar de fiador para uno.

guaranty ['gærəntɪ] N (*Fin*) garantía *f*, caución *f*; (*agreement*) garantía *f*.

guard [gɑ:d] 1 N (**a**) (*Mil duty, Fencing*) guardia *f*; (*safeguard*) resguardo *m*; **to be on ~** estar de guardia; **on ~!** ¡en guardia!; **to be on one's ~** estar alerta, estar sobre aviso, estar prevenido (*against* contra); **to be off one's ~** estar desprevenido; **to catch sb off his ~** coger (*LAm*: agarrar) a uno desprevenido; **to be under ~** estar bajo guardia; **to drop** (*or* **lower**) **one's ~** bajar la guardia, descuidarse; **to keep ~** vigilar; **to mount ~** montar (la) guardia; **to put sb on his ~** poner a uno en guardia, prevenir a uno (*against* contra); **to stand ~ over sth** montar la guardia sobre algo.
(**b**) (*of sword*) guarda *f*, guarnición *f*.
(**c**) (*regiment, squad of men*) guardia *f*; **he's one of the old ~** es uno de los viejos; **to change ~** relevar la guardia.
(**d**) (*person*) (*soldier*) guardia *m*; (*sentry*) centinela *m*; (*escort*) escolta *f*; (*security ~*) guarda *m* jurado; (*Brit Rail*) jefe *m* de tren.
2 ATTR: **~ duty** guardia *f* de turno.
3 VT *place etc* guardar, proteger, defender (*against, from* de); *person* vigilar, (*while travelling*) escoltar.
◆**guard against** VT guardarse de, precaverse de (*or* contra); (*prevent*) impedir, estorbar, evitar; **in order to ~ against this** para evitar esto.

guard dog ['gɑ:d,dɒg] N perro *m* guardián.

guarded ['gɑ:dɪd] ADJ cauteloso, circunspecto.

guardedly ['gɑ:dɪdlɪ] ADV cautelosamente, con circunspección.

guardhouse ['gɑ:dhaʊs] N, PL **guardhouses** ['gɑ:d,haʊzɪz] cuartel *m* de la guardia; cárcel *f* militar.

guardian ['gɑ:dɪən] 1 N (**a**) protector *m*, -ora *f*, guardián *m*, -ana *f*.
(**b**) (*Jur*) tutor *m*, -ora *f*.
2 ATTR: **~ angel** ángel *m* custodio, ángel *m* de la guarda.

┌─ **GUARDIAN ANGELS** ─┐

*i Los **Guardian Angels** son una organización no oficial de patrullas callejeras creada en 1979 para combatir la delincuencia en el metro de Nueva York. Los voluntarios de esta organización, que aunque no van armados, suelen saber defensa personal, han extendido también su protección a los ciudadanos por las calles de la ciudad. Se les reconoce porque llevan unas boinas rojas y llevan escrito **dare to care** (atrévete a mirar por los demás) en las camisetas. La popularidad de estas patrullas les ha conseguido el favor de la policía y ha hecho que se siga la misma iniciativa en otras ciudades estadounidenses, así como en algunos lugares del Reino Unido, sobre todo en Londres.*

guardianship ['gɑ:dɪənʃɪp] N tutela *f*, custodia *f*; **she was placed under her mother's ~** quedó sometida a la tutela de su madre.

guardrail ['gɑ:dreɪl] N pretil *m*.

guardroom ['gɑ:drʊm] N cuarto *m* de guardia.

guardsman ['gɑ:dzmən] N, PL **guardsmen** ['gɑ:dzmən] (*Brit*) soldado *m* de la guardia real; (*US*) guardia *m* (nacional).

guard's-van ['gɑ:dzvæn] N (*Brit*) furgón *m*.

Guatemala [,gwɑ:tɪ'mɑ:lə] N Guatemala *f*.

Guatemalan [,gwɑ:tɪ'mɑ:lən] 1 ADJ guatemalteco.
2 N guatemalteco *m*, -a *f*.

guava ['gwɑ:və] N guayaba *f*.

Guayana [gaɪ'ɑ:nə] N Guayana *f*.

gubbins* ['gʌbɪnz] N (*Brit*) (**a**) (*thing*) chisme *m*, cacharro* *m*. (**b**) (*silly person*) bobo *m*, -a *f*.

gubernatorial [,gu:bənə'tɔ:rɪəl] ADJ (*esp US*) de(l) gobernador; **~ election** elección *f* de gobernador.

gudgeon[1] ['gʌdʒən] N (*Fish*) gobio *m*.

gudgeon[2] ['gʌdʒən] N (*Tech*) gorrón *m*; cuello *m* de eje.

Guernsey ['gɜ:nzɪ] N Guernesey *m*.

guerrilla [gə'rɪlə] 1 N guerrillero *m*, -a *f*.
2 ATTR: **~ band** guerrilla *f*; **~ warfare** guerra *f* de guerrilleros.

guess [ges] 1 N conjetura *f*, suposición *f*; estimación *f* aproximada; **at a ~** a poco más o menos; **my ~ is that ...** yo conjeturo que ..., imagino que ...; **it's anybody's ~ whether** cualquiera sabe si; **your ~ is as good as mine!** ¡vaya Vd a saber!, lo mismo me lo pregunto yo; **have a ~, I'll give you 3 ~es** a ver si lo adivinas.
2 VTI (**a**) adivinar, conjeturar, suponer; **to ~ right** acertar; **~ what!** ¿sabes lo que pasa?; **~ who!** ¡a ver si adivinas quién soy!, ¿me conoces?; **you'll never ~** no lo adivinarás nunca; **you've ~ed it!** has acertado, estás en lo cierto; **I ~ as much as** tú suponía; **I ~ed him to be about 20** le daba unos 20 años; **all that time we never ~ed** en todo el tiempo no lo sospechábamos; **I never ~ed it was so big** no lo suponía nunca tan grande; **to keep sb ~ing** tener a uno en suspenso; **to ~ at** conjeturar, (tratar de) estimar aproximadamente.
(**b**) (*esp US*) creer, imaginar, suponer; **I ~ we'll buy it** me imagino que lo compraremos; **I ~ so** creo que sí; así será sin duda.

guessing game ['gesɪŋ,geɪm] N acertijo *m*, adivinanza *f*.

guesstimate* ['gestɪmɪt] N estimación *f* aproximada.

guesswork ['geswɜ:k] N conjeturas *fpl*; **it's all ~** son meras conjeturas.

guest [gest] 1 N convidado *m*, -a *f*, invitado *m*, -a *f*; (*at hotel etc, lodger*) huésped *m*, -eda *f*; **~ of honour** agasajado *m*, -a *f*; invitado *m*, -a *f* de honor; **be my ~** (*have a drink etc*) invito yo, ¡te invito!; (*please use it*) está a tu disposición; **we were their ~s last summer** pasamos un rato en casa de ellos el verano pasado.
2 ATTR: **~ artist(e) = guest-star**; **~ book** libro *m* de los huéspedes; **~ speaker** orador *m* invitado, oradora *f* invitada.
3 VI (*US*) aparecer como invitado.

guest-house ['gesthaʊs] N, PL **guest-houses** ['gest,haʊzɪz] casa *f* de huéspedes.

guest-room ['gestrʊm] N cuarto *m* de huéspedes.

guest-star ['geststɑ:ʳ] N estrella *f* invitada.

guff* [gʌf] N música *f* celestial.

guffaw [gʌ'fɔ:] 1 N risotada *f*, carcajada *f*.
2 VI reírse a carcajadas.

GUI N (*Comput*) ABBR *of* **graphical user interface** interfaz *m* gráfico de usuario.

Guiana [gaɪ'ɑ:nə] N Guayana *f*.

guidance ['gaɪdəns] N (*control*) dirección *f*, gobierno *m*; (*advice*) consejos *mpl*; orientación *f*; **under the ~ of** bajo la dirección de; **I tell you this for your ~** te lo digo para tu gobierno.

guide [gaɪd] 1 N (**a**) (*person*) guía *mf*; (*girl ~*) exploradora *f*, muchacha-guía *f*. (**b**) (*book, Mech, fig*) guía *f*.
2 VT guiar; orientar; conducir; (*govern*) dirigir, gobernar.

guidebook ['gaɪdbʊk] N guía *f* (del turista *etc*).

guided ['gaɪdɪd] ADJ: **~ missile** misil *m* teledirigido; **~ tour** excursión *f* con guía.

guide-dog ['gaɪd,dɒg] N perro-guía m.

guideline ['gaɪdlaɪn] N línea f directriz, pauta f; (for writing) falsilla f.

guidepost ['gaɪdpəʊst] N poste m indicador.

guiding ['gaɪdɪŋ] ADJ: ~ **principle** principio m director; ~ **star** estrella f de guía.

guild [gɪld] N gremio m, cofradía f, asociación f benéfica.

guilder ['gɪldər] N florín m (holandés).

guildhall ['gɪld,hɔ:l] N ayuntamiento m, casa f consistorial.

guile [gaɪl] N astucia f, maña f.

guileful ['gaɪlfʊl] ADJ astuto, mañoso.

guileless ['gaɪllɪs] ADJ inocente, candoroso.

guillemot ['gɪlɪmɒt] N arao m.

guillotine [,gɪlə'ti:n] **1** N guillotina f.
2 VT guillotinar.

guilt [gɪlt] N culpa f, culpabilidad f; ~ **complex** complejo m de culpabilidad; **to admit one's** ~ confesarse culpable.

guiltily ['gɪltɪlɪ] ADV: **he said** ~ dijo como confesándose culpable; **he looked round** ~ volvió la cabeza como si fuera culpable.

guiltless ['gɪltlɪs] ADJ inocente, libre de culpa (of de).

guilty ['gɪltɪ] ADJ (a) (Jur etc) culpable (of de); **verdict of** ~ sentencia f de culpabilidad; **to find sb** ~ declarar culpable a uno; **to find sb not** ~ declarar inocente a uno; **to plead** ~ confesarse culpable; **to plead not** ~ negar la acusación; **'not** ~', **he replied** 'soy inocente', contestó.
(b) look lleno de confusión; conscience lleno de remordimiento; thought pecaminoso, criminal.

Guinea ['gɪnɪ] N Guinea f.

guinea ['gɪnɪ] N (Brit) guinea f (= 21 chelines).

Guinea-Bissau ['gɪnɪbɪ'saʊ] N Guinea-Bissau f.

guinea-fowl ['gɪnɪfaʊl] N gallina f de Guinea, pintada f.

Guinean ['gɪnɪən] **1** ADJ guineano.
2 N guineano m, -a f.

guinea-pig ['gɪnɪpɪg] N cobayo m, conejillo m de Indias; (fig) cobayo m.

Guinevere ['gwɪnɪvɪər] NF Ginebra.

guise [gaɪz] N: **in that** ~ de esa manera; **under the** ~ **of** bajo el disfraz de; so capa de.

guitar [gɪ'tɑ:r] N guitarra f.

guitarist [gɪ'tɑ:rɪst] N guitarrista mf; (electric ~) guitarrero m, -a f.

Gujarati, Gujerati [,gʊdʒəʳ'rɑ:tɪ] **1** ADJ gujarati.
2 N (a) (person) Gujarati mf. (b) (Ling) gujarati m.

gulch [gʌlʃ] N (US) barranco m.

gulf [gʌlf] **1** N golfo m; (also fig) abismo m, sima f; **the G~** el Golfo (Pérsico); **G~ of Suez** Golfo m de Suez.
2 ATTR: **G~ States** Estados mpl del Golfo (Pérsico); **G~ Stream** Corriente f del Golfo.

gull [gʌl] **1** N gaviota f.
2 VT estafar, timar.

gullet ['gʌlɪt] N esófago m; garganta f, gaznate m.

gulley ['gʌlɪ] = **gully**.

gullibility [,gʌlɪ'bɪlɪtɪ] N credulidad f, simpleza f.

gullible ['gʌlɪbl] ADJ crédulo, simplón.

gully ['gʌlɪ] N barranco m, torrentera f.

gulp [gʌlp] **1** N trago m, sorbo m; **at one** ~ de un trago; **'yes', he said with a** ~ 'sí', dijo tragando saliva.
2 VT (also **to** ~ **down**) tragarse, engullir.
3 VI tragar saliva.

gum¹ [gʌm] N (Anat) encía f.

gum² [gʌm] **1** N (in general) goma f; (Brit: adhesive) goma f, cola f, pegamento m, cemento m (LAm); (chewing) chicle m; ~ **arabic** goma f arábiga.
2 VT engomar, pegar con goma.
◆**gum up** VT (fig) estropear, paralizar, parar, inutilizar; **to** ~ **up the works** paralizar el mecanismo, (fig) estropearlo todo.

gum³ [gʌm] INTERJ: **by** ~! ¡caramba!

gumbo ['gʌmbəʊ] N (US: Culin) sopa o estofado espesado con quingombó.

gumboil ['gʌmbɔɪl] N flemón m.

gumboots ['gʌmbu:ts] NPL (Brit) botas fpl de agua.

gumdrop ['gʌmdrɒp] N pastilla f de goma.

gummed [gʌmd] ADJ engomado; ~ **envelope** sobre m engomado; ~ **label** etiqueta f engomada.

gummy ['gʌmɪ] ADJ gomoso.

gump* [gʌmp] N (a) (sense) sentido m común. (b) (fool) tonto m, imbécil mf.

gumption* ['gʌmpʃən] N (Brit) seso m, sentido m común.

gumshield ['gʌmʃi:ld] N protector m de dientes.

gumshoe ['gʌmʃu:] N (US) (a) zapato m de goma. (b) (*) detective m.

gum-tree ['gʌmtri:] N árbol m gomero; eucalipto m; **to be up a** ~* (Brit) estar en un aprieto.

gun [gʌn] **1** N (gen) arma f de fuego; (artillery piece) cañón m; (shot~) escopeta f; (rifle) fusil m; (pistol) revólver m, pistola f; **a 21 ~**

salute una salva de 21 cañonazos; **the** ~**s** (Mil) la artillería; **big** ~* pez m gordo, espadón m; **to be going great** ~**s** hacer grandes progresos, ir a las mil maravillas; **to jump the** ~ salir antes de tiempo; (fig) obrar con anticipación, madrugar; **to stick to one's** ~**s** mantenerse en sus trece.
(b) (Brit: person) cazador m; escopeta f.
2 VT disparar sobre, atacar.
◆**gun down** VT abatir a tiros, abalear (LAm).
◆**gun for** VT andar a la caza de, perseguir; **it's really the boss they're** ~**ning for** en realidad esto va contra el jefe.

gun-battle ['gʌn,bætl] N tiroteo m.

gunboat ['gʌnbəʊt] **1** N (seagoing) cañonero m; (small) lancha f cañonera.
2 ATTR: ~ **diplomacy** diplomacia f cañonera.

gun-carriage ['gʌn,kærɪdʒ] N cureña f; (at funeral) armón m de artillería.

gun-cotton ['gʌn,kɒtn] N algodón m pólvora.

gun-crew ['gʌnkru:] N dotación f de un cañón.

gun-dog ['gʌn,dɒg] N perro m de caza.

gunfight ['gʌnfaɪt] N tiroteo m.

gunfire ['gʌnfaɪəʳ] N cañoneo m, fuego m; tiros mpl, tiroteo m.

gunge* [gʌndʒ] **1** N porquería f (viscosa).
2 VT: **to** ~ **up** atascar, obstruir.

gung-ho ['gʌŋ'həʊ] ADJ (a) (over-enthusiastic) (tontamente) optimista; (locamente) entusiasta; (ingenuamente) emprendedor. (b) (jingoistic) militarista; patriotero (con exceso); jingoísta.

gunk* [gʌŋk] N = **gunge**.

gun law ['gʌn,lɔ:] N (a) (rule by the gun) ley f del terror, pistolerismo m. (b) (Jur) ley f que rige la tenencia y uso de armas de fuego.

gun licence ['gʌn,laɪsns] N licencia f de armas.

gun-maker ['gʌn,meɪkəʳ] N armero m.

gunman ['gʌnmən] N, PL **gunmen** ['gʌnmən] pistolero m, gángster m.

gunmetal ['gʌn,metl] N bronce m de cañón.

gunner ['gʌnəʳ] N artillero m.

gunnery ['gʌnərɪ] **1** N (a) (art, skill, science) tiro m, puntería f. (b) (guns) artillería f.
2 ATTR: ~ **officer** oficial m de artillería.

gunny ['gʌnɪ] N arpillera f; (also ~ **bag**, ~ **sack**) saco m de yute.

gunpoint ['gʌnpɔɪnt] N: **to hold sb at** ~ tener a uno cautivo a punta de pistola.

gunpowder ['gʌn,paʊdəʳ] **1** N pólvora f.
2 ATTR: **G~ Plot** (Brit) Conspiración f de la Pólvora; ver también GUY FAWKES NIGHT .

gunroom ['gʌn,rʊm] N (in house) sala f de armas; (Brit Naut) sala f de suboficiales.

gunrunner ['gʌn,rʌnəʳ] N contrabandista m de armas, traficante m de armas.

gunrunning ['gʌn,rʌnɪŋ] N contrabando m de armas.

gunship ['gʌnʃɪp] N helicóptero m de combate, helicóptero m artillado.

gunshot ['gʌnʃɒt] N cañonazo m; tiro m, disparo m; escopetazo m; ~ **wound** escopetazo m; **within** ~ a tiro de fusil.

gunslinger* ['gʌnslɪŋəʳ] N pistolero m, -a f.

gunsmith ['gʌnsmɪθ] N armero m.

gun-turret ['gʌn,tʌrɪt] N torreta f.

gunwale ['gʌnl] N borde m, regala f.

guppy ['gʌpɪ] N guppy m.

gurgle ['gɜ:gl] **1** N (of liquid) gorgoteo m, gluglú m; (baby's) gorjeo m.
2 VI gorgotear, hacer gluglú; gorjear.

Gurkha ['gɜ:kə] N gurkha mf, gurja mf.

guru ['gʊru:] N guru m.

Gus [gʌs] NM familiar form of **Angus, Augustus**.

gush [gʌʃ] **1** N (a) (of liquid) chorro m, borbotón m; (of words) torrente m. (b) (fig) efusión f; sentimentalismo m; afectación f.
2 VT blood etc chorrear, derramar a borbollones.
3 VI (a) (liquid) chorrear, borbotar, salir a borbollones (from de). (b) (person) hacer extremos.
◆**gush over** VT hablar con efusión de, extasiarse ante.

gusher ['gʌʃəʳ] N (a) (oilwell) pozo m surtido. (b) **to be a** ~ (person) ser muy efusivo.

gushing ['gʌʃɪŋ] ADJ efusivo.

gusset ['gʌsɪt] N escudete m.

gust [gʌst] **1** N ráfaga f, racha f.
2 VI soplar racheado; **the wind** ~**ed up to 120 k.p.h.** hubo rachas de hasta 120 km/h.

gustatory ['gʌstətɔ:rɪ] ADJ (frm) sense gustativo; delights, pleasures gastronómico, del paladar.

gusto ['gʌstəʊ] N entusiasmo m; **with** ~ con entusiasmo.

gusty ['gʌstɪ] ADJ borrascoso; wind racheado.

gut [gʌt] **1** N (a) (Anat) intestino m, tripa f; (string) cuerda f de tripa; **to bust a** ~: echar los bofes; **I'll have his** ~**s for garters!:** ¡le despachurro las narices!; **I hate his ~s:** no lo puedo ver ni en pintura; **to spill one's ~s:** contar la propia vida y milagros; **to work one's ~s out** echar los bofes.

(b) ~s (*Anat*) tripas *fpl*; (*fig*) (*content*) meollo *m*, sustancia *f*; (*pluck*) valor *m*; (*staying power*) aguante *m*, resistencia *f*; (*moral strength*) carácter *m*; **to have ~s** tener agallas*.

(c) (*Naut*) estrecho *m*.

2 ADJ: ~ **feeling** instinto *m* visceral; ~ **reaction** reacción *f* visceral.

3 VT *animal* destripar; (*of fire etc*) destruir el interior de.

gutless* ['gʌtlɪs] ADJ cobarde; debilucho, sin carácter.

gutsy* ['gʌtsɪ] ADJ valiente; atrevido; vigoroso.

gutta-percha ['gʌtə'pɜːtʃə] N gutapercha *f*.

gutted* ['gʌtɪd] ADJ (*Brit: disappointed*): **I was ~** me quedé hecho polvo.

gutter¹ ['gʌtəʳ] N (*in street*) arroyo *m*, cuneta *f*, desagüe *m* (*CAm*); (*on roof*) canal *m*, canalón *m*, gotera *f*; **the ~** (*fig*) los barrios bajos, (*criminal*) el hampa; **he rose from the ~** (*fig*) salió de la nada.

gutter² ['gʌtəʳ] VI (*candle*) irse consumiendo.

guttering ['gʌtərɪŋ] N canales *mpl*, canalones *mpl*.

gutter press ['gʌtə'pres] N prensa *f* sensacionalista, prensa *f* amarilla; *ver también* |TABLOIDS AND BROADSHEETS|.

guttersnipe ['gʌtəsnaɪp] N golfillo *m*.

guttural ['gʌtərəl] ADJ gutural.

guv [gʌv] N (= **governor**): **thanks, ~!** ¡gracias, jefe!

guv'nor* ['gʌvnəʳ] = **governor**.

Guy [gaɪ] NM Guido; ~ **Fawkes Day**, ~ **Fawkes Night** (*Brit*) 5 de noviembre, aniversario de la Conspiración de la Pólvora.

┌─────────────────────┐
│ **GUY FAWKES NIGHT** │
└─────────────────────┘

ⓘ *La noche del cinco de noviembre, **Guy Fawkes Night** se celebra en el Reino Unido el fracaso de la conspiración de la pólvora (**Gunpowder Plot**), un intento fallido de volar el Parlamento de Jaime I en 1605. Esa noche se lanzan fuegos artificiales y se hacen hogueras en las que se queman unos muñecos de trapo que representan a **Guy Fawkes**, uno de los cabecillas de la revuelta. Días antes, los niños tienen por costumbre pedir a los transeúntes "a penny for the guy", dinero que emplean en comprar cohetes.*

---

guy¹ [gaɪ] 1 N mamarracho *m*; (*esp US*) tío* *m*, individuo *m*, tipo* *m*; **he's a nice ~** es un buen chico; **hey, (you) ~s!** ¡eh, amigos!; **are you ~s ready to go?** ¿están todos listos para salir?

2 VT ridiculizar; (*Theat etc*) parodiar.

guy² [gaɪ] N, **guy-rope** ['gaɪrəup] N viento *m*, cuerda *f*.

Guyana [gaɪ'ænə] N Guayana *f*.

Guyanese [ˌgaɪə'niːz] 1 ADJ guyanés.

2 N guyanés *m*, -esa *f*.

guzzle ['gʌzl] VT tragarse, engullir.

guzzler ['gʌzləʳ] N trágon *m*, -ona *f*, comilón *m*, -ona *f*; V **gas**.

gym* [dʒɪm] N gimnasio *m*.

gymkhana [dʒɪm'kɑːnə] N (*esp Brit*) gincana *f*.

gymnasium [dʒɪm'neɪzɪəm] N, PL **gimnasia** [dʒɪm'neɪzɪə] gimnasio *m*.

gymnast ['dʒɪmnæst] N gimnasta *mf*.

gymnastic [dʒɪm'næstɪk] ADJ gimnástico.

gymnastics [dʒɪm'næstɪks] N SING AND PL gimnasia *f*.

gymshoes ['dʒɪmʃuːz] NPL zapatillas *fpl* deportivas.

gymslip ['dʒɪmslɪp] N (*Brit*) túnica *f* de gimnasia.

gynaecological, (*US*) **gynecological** [ˌgaɪnɪkə'lɒdʒɪkəl] ADJ ginecológico.

gynaecologist, (*US*) **gynecologist** [ˌgaɪnɪ'kɒlədʒɪst] N ginecólogo *m*, -a *f*.

gynaecology, (*US*) **gynecology** [ˌgaɪnɪ'kɒlədʒɪ] N ginecología *f*.

gyp¹: [dʒɪp] (*US*) 1 N (a) estafa *f*, timo *m*. (b) (*person*) estafador *m*, timador *m*.

2 VT estafar, timar.

gyp²: [dʒɪp] N (*Brit*): **to give sb ~** echar un rapapolvo de aúpa a uno; poner a uno como un trapo; **it's giving me ~** me duele una barbaridad.

gypsum ['dʒɪpsəm] N yeso *m*.

gypsy ['dʒɪpsɪ] N (*esp US*) = **gipsy**.

gyrate [dʒaɪ'reɪt] VI girar.

gyration [ˌdʒaɪ'reɪʃən] N giro *m*, vuelta *f*.

gyratory [ˌdʒaɪ'reɪtərɪ] ADJ giratorio.

gyro... ['dʒaɪrəu] PREF giro...

gyrocompass ['dʒaɪrəu'kʌmpəs] N girocompás *m*.

gyroscope ['dʒaɪrəskəup] N giróscopo *m*.

H

H, h [eɪtʃ] N (*letter*) H, h *f*; **H for Harry, H for How** (*US*) H de Historia.
H: [eɪtʃ] N caballo: *m*, heroína *f*.
h. ABBR *of* **hour(s)** hora(s) *f*(PL), h.
h. & c. ABBR *of* **hot and cold water** con agua corriente caliente y fría.
ha [hɑː] INTERJ ¡ah!
habeas corpus ['heɪbɪəs'kɔːpəs] N hábeas corpus *m*.
haberdasher ['hæbədæʃəʳ] N (*Brit*) mercero *m*, -a *f*, (*US*) camisero *m*, -a *f*; **~'s (shop)** mercería *f*, (*US*) camisería *f*.
haberdashery [,hæbə'dæʃərɪ] N (*Brit*) mercería *f*, (*US*) prendas *fpl* de caballero.
habit ['hæbɪt] N (a) (*custom*) costumbre *f*, hábito *m*; **bad ~** vicio *m*, mala costumbre *f*; **from ~, out of sheer ~** por costumbre; **to be in the ~ of** + *ger* acostumbrar + *infin*, soler + *infin*; **to get into the ~ of** + *ger* acostumbrarse a + *infin*; **to get out of the ~ of** + *ger* perder la costumbre de + *infin*; dejar de + *infin*; **to have a ~*** (*drugs*) drogarse habitualmente; **to make a ~ of sth** aficionarse a algo; **let's hope he doesn't make a ~ of it** esperamos que no siga haciéndolo; **to make a ~ of** + *ger* adquirir la costumbre de + *infin*. (b) (*dress*) hábito *m*.
habitability [,hæbɪtə'bɪlɪtɪ] N (*of building, area*) habitabilidad *f*.
habitable ['hæbɪtəbl] ADJ habitable.
habitat ['hæbɪtæt] N hábitat *m*, habitación *f*.
habitation [,hæbɪ'teɪʃən] N habitación *f*.
habit-forming ['hæbɪt,fɔːmɪŋ] ADJ que conduce al hábito morboso.
habitual [hə'bɪtjʊəl] ADJ habitual, acostumbrado, usual; *drunkard, liar etc* inveterado, empedernido.
habitually [hə'bɪtjʊəlɪ] ADV por costumbre; constantemente.
habituate [hə'bɪtjʊeɪt] VT acostumbrar, habituar (*to* a).
habitué(e) [hə'bɪtjʊeɪ] N asiduo *m*, -a *f*, parroquiano *m*, -a *f*.
hacienda [,hæsɪ'endə] N (*US*) hacienda *f*.
hack¹ [hæk] ① N (*blow, cut*) corte *m*, hachazo *m*, tajo *m*; (*kick*) puntapié *m* (en la espinilla); (*dent*) mella *f*.
② VT (a) (*with knife etc*) cortar, acuchillar, tajar; (*dent*) mellar; **to ~ sb on the shin** dar a uno un puntapié en la espinilla; **to ~ sth to pieces** cortar algo en pedazos (violentamente, despiadadamente *etc*); **to ~ an army to pieces** destrozar un ejército; **to ~ one's way through sth** abrirse paso por algo a fuerza de tajos.
(b) **I can't ~ it** (*US*) no puedo hacerlo.
③ VI (a) **to ~ at** tirar tajos a. (b) (*Comput*) **to ~ into a system** piratear un sistema.
◆**hack around*** VI (*US*) gandulear, vaguear.
◆**hack down** VT derribar a hachazos *etc*.
◆**hack into** VT (*Comput*) conseguir entrar en.
hack² [hæk] N (a) (*Brit*) (*hired horse*) caballo *m* de alquiler; (*bad horse*) rocín *m*. (b) (*writer*) escritorzuelo *m*, -a *f*, plumífero *m*, -a *f*; (*journalist*) periodista *mf*, gacetillero *m*, -a *f*. (c) (*US**) taxi *m*.
② ATTR: **to be a ~ reporter** ser un reportero del tres al cuatro; **~ writer** = ① (b).
③ ADJ = **hackneyed**.
④ VI montar (a caballo).
hackberry ['hækberɪ] N almez *m*.
hacker ['hækəʳ] N (*Comput*) (*enthusiast*) computomaníaco *m*, -a *f*; (*pirate*) pirata *m* informático, pirata *f* informática, intruso *m* informático, intrusa *f* informática.
hackery* ['hækərɪ] N (a) = **hackwork**. (b) = **hacking³**.
hackette* [hæ'ket] N periodista *f*.
hacking¹ ['hækɪŋ] ADJ *cough* seco.
hacking² ['hækɪŋ] ADJ: **~ jacket** (*Brit*) chaqueta *f* de montar.
hacking³ ['hækɪŋ] N: **computer ~** piratería *f* informática, intrusión *f* informática.
hackle ['hækl] N: **with his ~s up** encolerizado; dispuesto a luchar; **to make sb's ~s rise** encolerizar a uno, provocar a uno, poner los pelos de punta a uno.

hackney cab ['hæknɪ'kæb] N, **hackney carriage** ['hæknɪ'kærɪdʒ] N coche *m* de alquiler.
hackneyed ['hæknɪd] ADJ trillado, gastado.
hacksaw ['hæksɔː] N sierra *f* para metales.
hackwork ['hækwɜːk] N trabajo *m* de rutina; trabajo *m* de poca originalidad; (*iro*) periodismo *m*.
had [hæd] PRET AND PTP *of* **have**.
haddock ['hædək] N eglefino *m*, merlango *m*.
Hades ['heɪdiːz] N infierno *m*.
hadn't ['hædnt] = **had not**.
Hadrian ['heɪdrɪən] NM Adriano; **~'s Wall** Muralla *f* de Adriano.
haematological, (*US*) **hematological** [,hiːmətə'lɒdʒɪkəl] ADJ hematológico.
haematologist, (*US*) **hematologist** [,hiːmə'tɒlədʒɪst] N hematólogo *m*, -a *f*.
haematology, (*US*) **hematology** [,hiːmə'tɒlədʒɪ] N hematología *f*.
haematoma, (*US*) **hematoma** [,hiːmə'təʊmə] N hematoma *m*.
haemoglobin, (*US*) **hemoglobin** [,hiːməʊ'gləʊbɪn] N hemoglobina *f*.
haemophilia, (*US*) **hemophilia** [,hiːməʊ'fɪlɪə] N hemofilia *f*.
haemophiliac, (*US*) **hemophiliac** [,hiːməʊ'fɪlɪæk] ① ADJ hemofílico.
② N hemofílico *m*, -a *f*.
haemorrhage, (*US*) **hemorrhage** ['hemərɪdʒ] ① N hemorragia *f*.
② VI sangrar.
haemorrhoids, (*US*) **hemorrhoids** ['hemərɔɪdz] NPL hemorroides *fpl*.
hafnium ['hæfnɪəm] N hafnio *m*.
haft [hɑːft] N mango *m*, puño *m*.
hag [hæg] N bruja *f*.
haggard ['hægəd] ADJ ojeroso, trasnochado.
haggis ['hægɪs] N (*Scot*) asaduras de cordero, avena y especias cocidas en las tripas del animal (*plato escocés*).
haggish ['hægɪʃ] ADJ como de bruja, brujeril.
haggle ['hægl] VI (a) (*discuss*) discutir, disputar; **don't ~!** ¡no discutas! (b) (*in selling*) regatear; **to ~ about** (*or* **over**) **the price** regatear, regatear el precio.
haggling ['hæglɪŋ] N (a) (*discussion*) discusión *f*, disputa *f*. (b) (*over price*) regateo *m*.
hagiographer [,hægɪ'ɒgrəfəʳ] N hagiógrafo *m*, -a *f*.
hagiography [,hægɪ'ɒgrəfɪ] N hagiografía *f*.
hag-ridden ['hægrɪdn] ADJ atormentado por una pesadilla; (*) dominado por una mujer.
Hague [heɪg] N: **The ~** La Haya.
hah [hɑː] = **ha**.
ha-ha ['hɑː'hɑː] INTERJ ¡ja, ja!
hail¹ [heɪl] (*Met*) ① N granizo *m*, pedrisco *m*; **a ~ of bullets** una lluvia de balas.
② VI granizar.
◆**hail down** VT (*fig*) llover.
hail² [heɪl] ① N (*shout*) grito *m*; (*greeting*) saludo *m*; **~!** ¡hola!, (*poet*) ¡salve!; **H~ Mary** Ave María *f*; Dios te salve, María; **to be within ~** estar al alcance de la voz.
② VT (a) (*call to*) llamar a, gritar a; (*greet*) saludar; **within ~ing distance** al habla, al alcance de la voz.
(b) (*acknowledge*) aclamar (*as king* rey).
③ VI: **to ~ from** ser natural de, ser de.
hail-fellow-well-met ['heɪl,feləʊ'wel'met] ADJ (demasiado) efusivo, campechano.
hailstone ['heɪlstəʊn] N granizo *m*, piedra *f* (de granizo).
hailstorm ['heɪlstɔːm] N granizada *f*, granizal *m* (*And*).
hair [hɛəʳ] ① N (a) (*one ~*) pelo *m*, cabello *m*; **~'s breadth** (ancho *m* de un) pelo *m*; **to escape by a ~'s breadth** escapar por un pelo; **to**

be within a ~'s breadth of estar a dos dedos de; **to split ~s** pararse en cosas nimias, hilar muy delgado; **he didn't turn a ~** no se inmutó, ni siquiera pestaneó.
(b) (*head of* ~) pelo *m*, cabello *m*, cabellera *f*; (*on legs etc*) vello *m*; **grey ~, white ~** canas *fpl*; **long ~** melena *f*; **to comb one's ~** peinarse; **to do one's ~, to have one's ~ done** arreglarse el pelo; **keep your ~ on!*** (*Brit*) ¡cálmate!; **to let one's ~ down** (*fig*) (*celebrate*) echar una cana al aire, (*talk freely*) sincerarse, entrar en el terreno de las confidencias; **to part one's ~** hacerse la raya; **this will put ~s on your chest!*** ¡esto te hará la mar de bien!*; **it was enough to make your ~ stand on end** era espeluznante; **to tear one's ~** mesarse el pelo, (*fig*) rasgarse las vestiduras.
[2] ATTR: **to have/make a ~ appointment** tener/pedir hora en la peluquería; **~ follicle** folículo *m* capilar; **~ implant** implante *m* capilar; **~ transplant** trasplante *m* capilar.
hairball [ˈhɛəbɔːl] N (*in cats, calves etc*) bola *f* de pelo.
hairband [ˈhɛəbænd] N cinta *f*.
hairbrush [ˈhɛəbrʌʃ] N cepillo *m* para el pelo.
hair-clip [ˈhɛəklɪp] N horquilla *f*, clipe *m*.
hair-clippers [ˈhɛə‚klɪpəz] NPL maquinilla *f* para cortar el pelo.
hair-conditioner [ˈhɛəkən‚dɪʃənəʳ] N suavizante *m* de cabello.
haircream [ˈhɛəkriːm] N brillantina *f*; fijador *m*, laca *f*.
hair-curler [ˈhɛə‚kɜːləʳ] N chicho *m*, rulo *m*, bigudí *m*.
haircut [ˈhɛəkʌt] N corte *m* de pelo; **to get** (*or* **have**) **a ~** hacerse cortar el pelo.
hairdo [ˈhɛəduː] N peinado *m*.
hairdresser [ˈhɛə‚dresəʳ] N peluquero *m*, -a *f*; **~'s** (**shop** *or* **salon**) peluquería *f*.
hairdressing [ˈhɛədresɪŋ] [1] N peluquería *f*.
[2] ATTR: **~ salon** salón *m* de peluquería.
hair-drier, hair-dryer [ˈhɛədraɪəʳ] N secador *m* de pelo.
-haired [hɛəd] ADJ de pelo ..., *eg* **fair~** pelirrubio; **long~** de pelo largo, melenudo.
hair-grip [ˈhɛəgrɪp] N (*Brit*) horquilla *f*, clipe *m*.
hairless [ˈhɛəlɪs] ADJ sin pelo, pelón, calvo; (*beardless*) lampiño.
hairline [ˈhɛəlaɪn] [1] N límite *m* del pelo; (*in writing*) rayita *f*; (*Tech*) estría *f* muy delgada; **with a receding ~** con acusadas entradas capilares.
[2] ATTR: **~ crack, ~ fracture** grieta *f* muy fina, grieta *f* casi imperceptible.
hairnet [ˈhɛənet] N redecilla *f*.
hair-oil [ˈhɛərɔɪl] N brillantina *f*.
hairpiece [ˈhɛəpiːs] N postizo *m*, tupé *m*; trenza *f* postiza.
hairpin [ˈhɛəpɪn] [1] N horquilla *f*.
[2] ATTR: **~ bend** (*Brit*), **~ curve** curva *f* en horquilla.
hair-raising [ˈhɛə‚reɪzɪŋ] ADJ espeluznante.
hair-remover [ˈhɛərɪ‚muːvəʳ] N depilatorio *m*.
hair-restorer [ˈhɛərɪ‚stɔːrəʳ] N regenerador *m* del pelo, loción *f* capilar.
hair shirt [‚hɛəˈʃɜːt] N cilicio *m*.
hair-slide [ˈhɛəslaɪd] N (*Brit*) pasador *m*.
hair specialist [ˈhɛə‚speʃəlɪst] N especialista *mf* capilar.
hair-splitting [ˈhɛə‚splɪtɪŋ] [1] ADJ nimio; *discussion* sobre detalles nimios.
[2] N sofismas *mpl*, sofistería *f*.
hairspray [ˈhɛəspreɪ] N laca *f* (para el pelo).
hairspring [ˈhɛəsprɪŋ] N muelle *m* espiral muy fino (de un reloj).
hair style [ˈhɛəstaɪl] N peinado *m*.
hair stylist [ˈhɛə‚staɪlɪst] N peluquero *m*, -a *f* estilista.
hair trigger [‚hɛəˈtrɪgəʳ] [1] N gatillo que se dispara con un ligero toque.
[2] ADJ (*fig*) explosivo.
hairy [ˈhɛərɪ] ADJ (a) peludo, velloso. (b) (*) *experience* horripilante, espeluznante; *problem* peliagudo.
Haiti [ˈheɪtɪ] N Haití *m*.
Haitian [ˈheɪʃɪən] [1] ADJ haitiano.
[2] N haitiano *m*, -a *f*.
hake [heɪk] N (*Brit*) merluza *f*.
halal [həˈlɑːl] ADJ *de animales sacrificados conforme a los preceptos musulmanes*.
halcyon [ˈhælsɪən] ADJ: **~ days** días *mpl* felices.
hale [heɪl] ADJ sano, robusto; **~ and hearty** sano y fuerte.
half [hɑːf] N, PL **halves** [hɑːvz] [1] N (a) (*quantity*) mitad *f*; (*Brit: ~ pint*) media pinta *f*; **~ and ~** mitad y mitad; **my better ~, my other ~** mi cara mitad, la media naranja; **by ~** (*fig*) con mucho; **better by ~** con mucho el mejor; **to be too clever by ~** pasarse de listo; **it has increased by ~** ha aumentado en la mitad; **to do sth by halves** hacer algo a medias con sb ir a medias con uno; **to cut sth in ~** cortar algo en dos mitades; **they don't know the ~ of it** no saben de la misa la media; **we have a problem and a ~** tenemos un problema mayúsculo, vaya problemazo que tenemos.
(b) (*Sport: person*) medio *m*, -a *f*.
(c) (*Sport: period*) tiempo *m*; **first/second ~** primer/segundo

tiempo *m*.
[2] ADJ medio; **~ an orange** media naranja; **a pound and a ~,** one and a **~ pounds** libra *f* y media; **3 and a ~ hours, 3 hours and a ~** 3 horas y media; **~ past 4** las 4 y media; **come at ~ 3*** ven a las 3 y media; **~ a moment!, ~ a second!** ¡un momento!
[3] ADV (a) medio, a medias, semi ...; casi; **~ asleep** medio dormido, dormido a medias, semidormido; **~ done** a medio hacer; **~ laughing, ~ crying** medio riendo, medio llorando; **I only ~ read it** lo leí sólo a medias; **he ~ got up** se levantó a medias; **it cost only ~ as much** costó la mitad nada más; **there were only ~ as many people as before** había solamente la mitad de los que había antes; **they paid ~ as much again** pagaron la mitad más.
(b) (*Brit: with* not) **it was not ~ as bad as I had thought** no era ni con mucho tan malo como me lo había imaginado; **he didn't ~ run*** corrió muchísimo; **it didn't ~ rain!*** ¡había que ver cómo llovía!; **it wasn't ~ dear*** nos resultó sumamente caro; **not ~!*** ¡y cómo!, ¡ya lo creo!; *see also* AVERAGE.
half-adder [ˈhɑːf‚ædəʳ] N semisumador *m*.
half-a-dollar [‚hɑːfəˈdɒləʳ] N (*value*) medio dólar *m*.
half-a-dozen [‚hɑːfəˈdʌzən] N media docena *f*.
half-and-half [‚hɑːfəndˈhɑːf] ADV mitad y mitad.
half-an-hour [‚hɑːfənˈaʊəʳ] N media hora *f*.
half-assed‡ [ˈhɑːfæst] ADJ (*US: person*) que tiene pocas luces; (*idea*) muy poco brillante.
half-back [ˈhɑːfbæk] N medio *m*, -a *f*.
half-baked [ˈhɑːfˈbeɪkt] ADJ a medio cocer; (*fig*) *plan, idea* a medio cocer, mal concebido, mal pensado; *person* soso.
half-board [‚hɑːfˈbɔːd] N (*in hotel*) media pensión *f*.
half-bred [ˈhɑːfbred] ADJ mestizo.
half-breed [ˈhɑːfbriːd] N mestizo *m*, -a *f*.
half-brother [ˈhɑːf‚brʌðəʳ] N medio hermano *m*, hermanastro *m*.
half-caste [ˈhɑːfkɑːst] [1] ADJ mestizo.
[2] N mestizo *m*, -a *f*.
half-century [hɑːfˈsentjʊrɪ] N (*Cricket*) cincuenta tantos *mpl*.
half-circle [ˈhɑːfˈsɜːkl] N semicírculo *m*.
half-closed [‚hɑːfˈkləʊzd] ADJ entreabierto.
half-cock [ˈhɑːfˈkɒk] N posición *f* de medio amartillado (de la escopeta *etc*); **to go off at ~** (*fig*) obrar precipitadamente, obrar antes del momento propicio; (*of plan*) ponerse en efecto sin la debida preparación, fracasar por falta de preparación, fallar por prematuro.
half-cocked [‚hɑːfˈkɒkt] ADJ *gun* con el seguro echado; *plan, scheme* mal elaborado.
half-crown [ˈhɑːfˈkraʊn] N (††) media corona *f*.
half-cup [ˈhɑːf‚kʌp] ATTR: **~ brassiere** sostén *m* de media copa.
half-day [‚hɑːfˈdeɪ] N medio día *m*, media jornada *f*; **~ holiday** fiesta *f* de media jornada; **~ closing is on Mondays** los lunes se cierra por la tarde.
half-dead [ˈhɑːfˈded] ADJ medio muerto, más muerto que vivo.
half-dozen [ˈhɑːfˈdʌzn] N media docena *f*.
half-dressed [‚hɑːfˈdrest] ADJ a medio vestir.
half-educated [‚hɑːfˈedjʊkeɪtɪd] ADJ: **he is ~** tiene poca cultura.
half-empty [ˈhɑːfˈempti] ADJ medio vacío; *hall etc* semidesierto.
half fare [‚hɑːfˈfɛəʳ] [1] N medio pasaje *m*.
[2] ADV: **to travel ~** viajar pagando medio pasaje.
half-forgotten [‚hɑːfˈfəˈgɒtn] ADJ medio olvidado.
half-frozen [‚hɑːfˈfrəʊzən] ADJ medio helado.
half-full [ˈhɑːfˈfʊl] ADJ a medio llenar, mediado.
half-hearted [ˈhɑːfˈhɑːtɪd] ADJ poco entusiasta, indiferente; *effort* débil.
half-heartedly [ˈhɑːfˈhɑːtɪdlɪ] ADV con poco entusiasmo.
half-heartedness [‚hɑːfˈhɑːtɪdnɪs] N carencia *f* de entusiasmo.
half-holiday [ˈhɑːfˈhɒlɪdɪ] N (*Brit*) (*Scol*) medio asueto *m*, fiesta *f* de media jornada; (*in shop*) descanso *m*.
half-hour [ˈhɑːfˈaʊəʳ] N media hora *f*.
half-hourly [‚hɑːfˈaʊəlɪ] [1] ADV cada media hora.
[2] ADJ: **at ~ intervals** cada media hora.
half-inch [‚hɑːfˈɪntʃ] [1] N media pulgada *f*.
[2] VT (‡) apañar*.
half-length [ˈhɑːfˈleŋθ] ADJ de medio cuerpo.
half-life [ˈhɑːflaɪf] N (*Phys*) media vida *f*.
half-light [ˈhɑːflaɪt] N media luz *f*.
half-marathon [ˈhɑːfˈmærəθən] N medio maratón *m*, media maratón *f*.
half-mast [ˈhɑːfˈmɑːst] N: **at ~** (*Brit*) a media asta.
half-measures [ˈhɑːfˈmeʒəz] NPL medidas *fpl* poco eficaces, medias tintas *fpl*; **we don't want any ~** no queremos paños calientes.
half-monthly [‚hɑːfˈmʌnθlɪ] ADJ quincenal.
half-moon [ˈhɑːfˈmuːn] N media luna *f*.
half-naked [ˈhɑːfˈneɪkɪd] ADJ semidesnudo.
half note [ˈhɑːfˈnəʊt] N (*US Mus*) blanca *f*.
half-open [‚hɑːfˈəʊpən] ADJ medio abierto.

half-panelled, (US) **half-paneled** [ˌhɑːfˈpænəld] ADJ chapado hasta media altura.

half-pay [ˈhɑːfˈpeɪ] ① N media paga f; **to retire on** ~ jubilarse con media paga.
  ② ATTR: **a** ~ **officer** un militar retirado.

halfpenny [ˈheɪpnɪ] N medio penique m.

half-pint [ˌhɑːfˈpaɪnt] N media pinta f; (*) enano m, -a f.

half-price [ˈhɑːfˈpraɪs] ① ADV a mitad de precio.
  ② ADJ ticket etc a mitad de precio.

half-seas over [ˈhɑːfsiːzˈəʊvəʳ] ADV: **to be** ~ estar entre dos velas.

half-serious [ˌhɑːfˈsɪərɪəs] ADJ entre serio y en broma.

half-sister [ˈhɑːfˌsɪstəʳ] N media hermana f, hermanastra f.

half-size [ˈhɑːfˌsaɪz] N (in shoes) media talla f.

half-size(d) [ˌhɑːfˈsaɪz(d)] ADJ medio, de tamaño medio.

half-term [ˈhɑːfˈtɜːm] N (Brit) vacación f a mediados del trimestre.

half-timbered [ˌhɑːfˈtɪmbəd] ADJ con entramado de madera.

half-time [ˈhɑːfˈtaɪm] ① N (Sport) descanso m.
  ② ATTR: ~ **work** trabajo m de media jornada.
  ③ ADV: **to work** ~ trabajar media jornada.

half-tone [ˈhɑːftəʊn] ① ADJ: ~ **illustration** fotograbado m a media tinta.
  ② N (US) semitono m.

half-track [ˈhɑːfˈtræk] N camión m semi-oruga.

half-truth [ˈhɑːfˈtruːθ] N, PL **half-truths** [ˈhɑːfˈtruːðz] verdad f a medias.

half-volley [ˈhɑːfˈvɒlɪ] N media volea f.

halfway [ˈhɑːfˈweɪ] ① ADV a medio camino; **we're** ~ **there** estamos a medio camino; ~ **through the film** hacia la mitad de la película; **to meet sb** ~ partir el camino con uno, (fig) hacer concesiones mutuas.
  ② ADJ intermedio; ~ **house** (fig) punto m intermediario, término m medio.

halfwit [ˈhɑːfwɪt] N bobo m, -a f.

half-witted [ˈhɑːfˈwɪtɪd] ADJ imbécil, bobo.

half-year [ˌhɑːfˈjɪəʳ] N medio año m, semestre m; **results for the** ~ resultados mpl para el semestre, resultados mpl semestrales.

half-yearly [ˈhɑːfˈjɪəlɪ] (esp Brit) ① ADV semestralmente.
  ② ADJ semestral; ~ **results** resultados mpl semestrales.

halibut [ˈhælɪbət] N halibut m, hipogloso m.

halitosis [ˌhælɪˈtəʊsɪs] N halitosis f.

hall [hɔːl] N (entrance-~) vestíbulo m, hall m; (for concerts etc) sala f; (dining-room) comedor m; (Brit Univ: central ~) paraninfo m; (hostel: also ~ **of residence**) residencia f, colegio m mayor; (large house) casa f solariega.

hallelujah [ˌhælɪˈluːjə] N aleluya f.

hallmark [ˈhɔːlmɑːk] N (marca f del) contraste m; (fig) sello m; **the outrage has all the** ~**s of the CLF** el atentado lleva el auténtico sello del CLF.

hallo [hʌˈləʊ] = **hullo.**

halloo [həˈluː] ① INTERJ ¡sus!, ¡hala!
  ② N˙grito m.
  ③ VI gritar.

hallow [ˈhæləʊ] VT santificar.

hallowed [ˈhæləʊd] ADJ ground etc sagrado, santificado.

Hallowe'en [ˈhæləʊˈiːn] N (Scot, US) víspera f de Todos los Santos.

HALLOWE'EN

ⓘ La festividad de **Hallowe'en** se celebra, tanto en el Reino Unido como en EE.UU., la noche del 31 de octubre. Aunque antes la fiesta se asociaba a la creencia de que las almas de los difuntos regresaban a sus hogares en esa fecha, actualmente **Hallowe'en** no es más que un pretexto para la diversión. Los niños se disfrazan de fantasmas y brujas y hacen farolillos con calabazas vacías en cuyo interior colocan una vela. Así vestidos, van de casa en casa por todo el barrio pidiendo caramelos y dinero, una costumbre que se conoce sobre todo en Estados Unidos como **trick or treat** porque los niños amenazan con gastarle una broma al dueño de la casa si no reciben los caramelos. También suelen celebrarse en **Hallowe'en** fiestas de disfraces para niños y para adultos.

---

hall-porter [ˌhɔːlˈpɔːtəʳ] N (Brit) portero m, conserje m.

hallstand [ˈhɔːlstænd] N perchero m.

hallucinate [həˈluːsɪneɪt] VI alucinar, tener aiucinaciones.

hallucination [həˌluːsɪˈneɪʃən] N alucinación f; ilusión f, fantasma m.

hallucinatory [həˈluːsɪnətərɪ] ADJ alucinante.

hallucinogen [həˈluːsɪnəˌdʒen] N alucinógeno m.

hallucinogenic [həˌluːsɪnəʊˈdʒenɪk] ① ADJ alucinógeno.
  ② N alucinógeno m.

hallucinosis [həˌluːsɪˈnəʊsɪs] N alucinosis f.

hallway [ˈhɔːlweɪ] N vestíbulo m, hall m.

halo [ˈheɪləʊ] N halo m, aureola f, nimbo m.

halogen [ˈheɪləʊdʒɪn] N halógeno m; ~ **lamp** lámpara f halógena.

halogenous [həˈlɒdʒɪnəs] ADJ halógeno.

halt [hɔːlt] ① N (a) alto m, parada f; interrupción f; **10 minutes'** ~ parada f de 10 minutos; **to call a** ~ mandar hacer alto, parar; **to call a** ~ **to** parar, atajar; **to come to a** ~ pararse, (process etc) interrumpirse.
  (b) (Brit Rail) apeadero m.
  ② ATTR: ~ **sign** señal f de stop.
  ③ VT parar, detener; interrumpir.
  ④ VI hacer alto; pararse; (process etc) interrumpirse; ~! ¡alto!

halter [ˈhɔːltəʳ] N cabestro m, ronzal m; (noose) dogal m.

halting [ˈhɔːltɪŋ] ADJ vacilante, titubeante.

haltingly [ˈhɔːltɪŋlɪ] ADV vacilantemente, titubeantemente; con vacilación.

halve [hɑːv] ① VT object partir por mitad; quantity reducir en la mitad; **to** ~ **a game** empatar.
  ② VI reducirse en la mitad.

halves [hɑːvz] NPL of half.

halyard [ˈhæljəd] N driza f.

ham [hæm] ① N (a) jamón m; pernil m; ~**s** (Anat) nalgas fpl. (b) (*) maleta* m; (Theat: also ~ **actor**) comicastro m, racionista mf. (c) (Rad*) radioaficionado m, -a f.
  ② VT: **to** ~ **it up** = **3**.
  ③ VI (Theat*) actuar de una manera exagerada (or paródica, melodramática).

Hamburg [ˈhæmbɜːg] N Hamburgo.

hamburger [ˈhæmˌbɜːgəʳ] N hamburguesa f; (US: also ~ **meat**) carne f picada.

ham-fisted [ˈhæmˈfɪstɪd] ADJ, **ham-handed** [ˈhæmˈhændɪd] ADJ torpe, desmañado.

Hamitic [hæˈmɪtɪk] ADJ camítico.

hamlet [ˈhæmlɪt] N aldehuela f, caserío m.

hammer [ˈhæməʳ] ① N martillo m; (Mus) macillo m; (of firearm) percusor m; ~ **and sickle** hoz f y martillo; **to come under the** ~ ser subastado; **to go at it** ~ **and tongs** luchar (etc) a brazo partido.
  ② VT (a) martillar; batir; **to** ~ **a post into the ground** hincar un poste en el suelo a martillazos; **to** ~ **a point home** subrayar repetidas veces un argumento; **to** ~ **some sense into sb** hacer que uno vaya comprendiendo algo a fuerza de repetírselo; **to** ~ **sth into shape** formar algo a martillo.
  (b) (*: Sport etc) cascar*, dar una paliza a.
  (c) (Fin) declarar insolvente.
  ③ VI: **to** ~ **at** (or **on**) **a door** dar golpes en una puerta; **to** ~ **away at** subject insistir con ahinco en, machacar en, work trabajar asiduamente en; **to** ~ **away on the piano** tocar estrepitosamente el piano.

◆**hammer down** VT lid asegurar con clavos.

◆**hammer in** VT: **to** ~ **sth in** clavar algo con martillo.

◆**hammer out** VT dent quitar a martillo, extender bajo el martillo; (fig) settlement etc elaborar trabajosamente.

◆**hammer together** VT pieces of wood etc clavar.

hammerhead [ˈhæməhed] N (shark) pez m martillo.

hammering [ˈhæmərɪŋ] N (a) martilleo m. (b) (*) paliza* f; **to give sb a** ~ dar una paliza a uno; **to get** (or **take**) **a** ~ recibir una paliza.

hammertoe [ˈhæmətəʊ] N dedo m (en) martillo.

hammock [ˈhæmək] N hamaca f, (Naut) coy m.

hammy [ˈhæmɪ] ADJ actor exagerado, melodramático.

hamper¹ [ˈhæmpəʳ] N cesto m, canasta f.

hamper² [ˈhæmpəʳ] VT estorbar, impedir.

hamster [ˈhæmstəʳ] N hámster m.

hamstring [ˈhæmstrɪŋ] ① N tendón m de la corva; ~ **injury** lesión f del tendón de la corva.
  ② VT (irr: V string) desjarretar; (fig) paralizar.

hand [hænd] ① N (a) (gen) mano f; ~**s off!** ¡no tocar!; ¡fuera las manos!; ~**s off Ruritania!** ¡manos fuera de Ruritania!; ~**s up!** ¡arriba las manos!; **to be clever with one's** ~**s** tener mucha destreza manual; **to go on one's** ~**s and knees** ir a gatas.
  (b) (phrases with verb) **A is** ~ **in glove with B** A y B son uña y carne, están conchabados A y B; **his** ~ **was everywhere** se notaba su influencia por todas partes; **to bear a** ~ arrimar el hombro; **to change** ~**s** cambiar de dueño; **to clutch at an offer with both** ~**s** agarrar una oferta con las dos manos; **he never does a** ~**'s turn** no da golpe; **to force sb's** ~ forzar la mano a uno; **to get one's** ~ **in** adquirir práctica, irse acostumbrando; **to give sb a** ~ echarle una mano a uno; **to have a** ~ **in** tomar parte en, intervenir en; **he had no** ~ **in it** no tuvo arte ni parte en ello; **to hold** ~**s** (children) ir cogidos (LAm: tomados) de la mano, (lovers) hacer manitas; **to join** ~**s** darse las manos; **to keep one's** ~ **in** conservar la práctica (at de), mantenerse en forma; **to keep one's** ~**s off sth** no tocar algo; **to lay** ~**s on** echar mano a, (obtain) conseguir, (Eccl) imponer las manos a; **to lend a** ~ arrimar el hombro; **to lend sb a** ~ echarle una mano a uno; **lend a** ~! ¡manos a la obra!; **to make money** ~ **over fist** amasar una fortuna muy rápidamente; **to put one's** ~ **to sth** emprender algo; **to shake** ~**s** estrecharse la mano, darse las manos; **to**

shake **~s with sb** estrechar la mano a uno; **we shook ~s on it** nos dimos las manos para confirmar el acuerdo; **to show one's ~** revelar su intención; **to sit on one's ~s** (*US**) (*audience*) aplaudir con desgana; (*committee etc*) no hacer nada, no dar golpe; **to take a ~** tomar parte, intervenir (*at, in* en); **to throw up one's ~s (in horror)** escandalizarse; **I could do it with one ~ tied behind my back** lo podría hacer con una mano atada a la espalda; **to try one's ~** at sth probar algo, ensayar algo; **to turn one's ~ to** dedicarse a; **he can turn his ~ to anything** vale tanto para un barrido como para un fregado; **to wash one's ~s of** desentenderse de; **to win ~s down** ganar fácilmente.

(**c**) (*phrases with adj*) **to rule with a firm ~** gobernar con firmeza; **they gave him a big ~*** le aplaudieron calurosamente; **let's give X a big ~!*** ¡muchos aplausos para X!; **to give sb a free ~** dar carta blanca a uno; **to have a free ~** tener carta blanca; **to have one's ~s full** estar ocupado; **with a heavy ~** con mano dura; **with a high ~** despóticamente; **to give sb a helping ~** echar una mano a uno; **to get** (*or* **gain**) **the upper ~** empezar a dominar; **to have the upper ~** tener la ventaja; **many ~s make light work** muchas manos facilitan el trabajo.

(**d**) (*phrases with prep before n*) (*at*) **at ~** a mano; **to be near** (*or* **close**) **at ~** estar a la mano; estar cerca; **winter was at ~** se acercaba el invierno; **at first ~** de primera mano, directamente; de buena tinta; **I heard it only at second ~** lo supe sólo de modo indirecto; **to suffer at the ~s of** (*by*) **make a** mano, **raise** *etc* a fuerza de brazos; **'by ~'** (*on envelope*) 'en su mano'; **to send a letter by ~** enviar una carta en mano; **to take sb by the ~** llevar a uno de la mano; (*from*) **to live from ~ to mouth** vivir al día, vivir de la mano a la boca; (*in*) **gun in ~** el revólver en la mano, empuñando el revólver; **to be in sb's ~s** estar en manos de uno; **they were going along ~ in ~** iban cogidos de la mano; **these matters go ~ in ~** estos asuntos están estrechamente relacionados; **to have sth in ~** tener algo entre manos; **to have a matter in ~** estar estudiando un asunto; **the situation is in ~** se ha conseguido dominar la situación; **he has them well in ~** los domina perfectamente; **to put sth in ~** emprender algo; **to take sb in ~** enseñar a uno, entrenar a uno; imponer disciplina a uno; **to take sth in ~** hacerse cargo de algo; **I like to have sth in ~** me gusta tener algo en reserva; **money in ~** dinero *m* disponible; **how much have we in ~?** ¿cuánto tenemos en el haber?, ¿cuánto tenemos en efectivo?; (*into*) **to fall into enemy ~s** caer en manos del enemigo; **to play into sb's ~s** ceder la ventaja a un contrario; **to put sth into a lawyer's ~s** poner un asunto en manos de un abogado; **to take justice into one's own ~s** tomar la justicia por su mano; (*off*) **to get sth off one's ~s** deshacerse de algo; terminar de hacer algo; (*on*) **on the left ~** a la izquierda, **on the right ~** a la derecha; **on every ~**, **on all ~s** por todas partes; **on the one ~** por una parte; **on the other ~** por otra parte; **to be on ~** estar a la mano; **he's on my ~s all day** está conmigo todo el día; **to have work on ~** tener trabajo entre manos; **the goods were left on his ~s** los géneros resultaron ser invendibles; (*out*) **to condemn sb out of ~** condenar a uno sin más; **to shoot sb out of ~** fusilar a uno sin más; **to get out of ~** desmandarse; (*matter*) desorbitarse, salirse de los límites; (*to*) **to come to ~** llegar; aparecer; **your letter of the 3rd is to ~** he recibido su carta del 3.

(**e**) (*of instrument*) aguja *f*; (*of clock*) manecilla *f*.

(**f**) (*measure*) palmo *m*.

(**g**) (*Cards*) mano *f*; **to have a ~ of bridge** echar una partida de bridge.

(**h**) (*writing*) escritura *f*, letra *f*; **in one's own ~** de puño y letra de uno; **he writes a good ~** tiene buena letra; **to put one's ~ to sth** firmar algo.

(**i**) (*in marriage*) **to ask for sb's ~** pedir la mano de una; **she gave him her ~** se casó con él.

(**j**) (*person*) operario *m*, -a *f*; (*Agr etc*) peón *m*; **~s** (*Naut*) tripulación *f*; **all ~s on deck!** ¡todos a la cubierta!; **to be lost with all ~s** desaparecer con toda la tripulación; **to be a good ~ at** tener buena mano para, ser hábil en; **to be an old ~** ser perro viejo.

[2] VT dar, entregar, poner en manos de; alargar; pasar; **you've got to ~ it to him** hay que reconocer que lo hace (*etc*) muy bien.

◆**hand around** VT = **hand round**.
◆**hand back** VT devolver.
◆**hand down** VT bajar, pasar; *heirloom* pasar, dejar en herencia; *tradition* transmitir; (*US*) *judgement* dictar, imponer; *person* ayudar a bajar.
◆**hand in** VT entregar; *resignation* presentar; *person* ayudar a subir.
◆**hand off** VT (*Rugby*) rechazar.
◆**hand on** VT *tradition* transmitir; *news* comunicar; *object* pasar.
◆**hand out** VT repartir, distribuir.
◆**hand over** [1] VT entregar.
　[2] VI: **to ~ over to** ceder su puesto a, entregar sus funciones a.
◆**hand round** VT pasar de mano en mano; (*distribute*) repartir; *chocolates etc* ofrecer.
◆**hand up** VT subir.

handbag ['hændbæg] [1] N bolso *m*, cartera *f* (*LAm*).
　[2] VT (*) poner fuera de combate a golpe de bolso, eliminar a bolsazos.
handball ['hændbɔ:l] [1] N (*Sport*) balonmano *m*; (*offence in football*) mano *f*.
　[2] VT (*) pasar en cadena humana.
handbasin ['hænd,beɪsn] N lavabo *m*.
handbell ['hændbel] N campanilla *f*.
handbill ['hændbɪl] N prospecto *m*, folleto *m*.
handbook ['hændbʊk] N manual *m*; (*guide*) guía *f*.
handbrake ['hændbreɪk] N (*Brit*) freno *m* de mano.
handcart ['hændkɑ:t] N carretilla *f*, carretón *m*.
handclap ['hændklæp] N palmada *f*; **to give a player the slow ~** batir palmas a ritmo lento (para que un jugador se esfuerce más o se dé prisa).
handclasp ['hændklɑ:sp] N apretón *m* de manos.
hand controls ['hændkən,trəʊlz] NPL controles *mpl* manuales.
handcraft ['hændkrɑ:ft] VT (*US*) hacer a mano; **~ed products** productos *mpl* hechos a mano, productos *mpl* artesanales.
handcream ['hændkri:m] N crema *f* para las manos.
handcuff ['hændkʌf] VT poner las esposas a, esposar.
handcuffs ['hændkʌfs] NPL esposas *fpl*.
hand-drier, hand-dryer ['hænd,draɪəʳ] N secamanos *m* automático.
-handed ['hændɪd] ADJ de ... mano(s); de mano(s) ...; **four~ game** juego *m* para cuatro personas.
-hander ['hændəʳ] N *ending in compounds* (*esp Brit: Theat, TV*): **two~** con dos personajes; **three~** con tres personajes; *see also* **left~, right~**.
handful ['hændfʊl] N puñado *m*, manojo *m*; **a ~ of people** un puñado de gente; **he's a real ~** tiene el diablo en el cuerpo.
hand-grenade ['hændgrɪ,neɪd] N granada *f* (de mano).
handgrip ['hændgrɪp] N = **handle**; = **grip**.
handgun ['hændgʌn] N (*esp US*) revólver *m*, pistola *f*.
hand-held ['hændheld] ADJ portátil.
handicap ['hændɪkæp] [1] N desventaja *f*, estorbo *m*, obstáculo *m*; (*Med*) minusvalía *f*, discapacidad *f*; (*Sport*) hándicap *m*.
　[2] VT perjudicar, estorbar; (*Sport*) handicapar; **he has always been ~ped by his accent** su acento siempre ha sido una desventaja para él.
handicapped ['hændɪkæpt] [1] ADJ: **mentally ~** minusválido mental; **physically ~** mutilado, tullido, minusválido, discapacitado.
　[2] N: **the ~** los minusválidos.
handicraft ['hændɪkrɑ:ft] [1] N artesanía *f*; (*skill*) destreza *f* manual.
　[2] ATTR: **~ teacher** profesor *m*, -ora *f* de oficios manuales.
handily ['hændɪlɪ] ADV (**a**) *positioned etc* cómodamente, convenientemente.
(**b**) (*US*) *win etc* fácilmente.
handiness ['hændɪnɪs] N (**a**) (*nearness*) proximidad *f*, lo cercano *f*; **because of the ~ of the library** debido a que la biblioteca está tan cerca, porque resulta tan cómodo ir a la biblioteca.
(**b**) (*convenience*) conveniencia *f*, comodidad *f*; carácter *m* manuable, facilidad *f* en el manejo.
(**c**) (*skill*) habilidad *f*, destreza *f*; **his ~ with a gun** su destreza con un fusil.
hand-in-hand ['hændɪn'hænd] ADV: **to go ~** ir cogidos de la mano; **it goes ~ with** está estrechamente relacionado con; **these plans should go ~** estos proyectos deben realizarse al mismo ritmo.
handiwork ['hændɪwɜ:k] N obra *f*.
handkerchief ['hæŋkətʃɪf] N pañuelo *m*.
hand-knitted [,hænd'nɪtɪd] ADJ tricotado a mano.
handle ['hændl] [1] N (*haft*) mango *m*; puño *m*; (*lever*) palanca *f*; (*crank*) manivela *f*; (*for winding*) manubrio *m*; (*of basket, jug etc*) asa *f*, asidero *m*; (*of door, drawer etc*) tirador *m*, manija *f*, puño *m*; (*fig*) pretexto *m*, asidero *m*; (*) título *m*; **to have a ~ to one's name*** tener título de nobleza; **to fly off the ~*** salirse de sus casillas, perder los estribos.
　[2] VT (**a**) (*touch*) tocar, (*improperly*) manosear; (*Sport*) tocar con la mano; (*delicately*) manejar, manipular; **'~ with care'** 'manéjese con cuidado'; **don't ~ the fruit** no manosees la fruta; **the police ~d him roughly** la policía le trató severamente.
(**b**) (*fig*) *situation, theme, resources etc* manejar; *car* conducir, *ship* gobernar; *unruly element* saber dominar; **I'll ~ this** yo me encargo de esto; **do you ~ tax matters?** ¿tiene Vd que ver con las contribuciones?; **we ~ 2000 travellers a day** por aquí pasan 2000 viajeros cada día; **can the port ~ big ships?** ¿el puerto tiene capacidad para los buques grandes?
(**c**) (*Comm*) *product* tratar en, comerciar en.
　[3] VI (*horse, car*) comportarse.
handlebar ['hændlbɑ:ʳ] [1] N manillar *m*, manubrio *m*.
　[2] ATTR: **~ moustache** bigote *m* Dalí, bigote *m* daliniano.
-handled ['hændld] ADJ *ending in compounds* con mango de ...; **a wooden~ spade** una pala con mango de madera.
handler ['hændləʳ] N (*Comm*) tratante *m*, comerciante *m*; (*Sport*) en-

trenador *m*, -ora *f*; (*of dog*) amo *m*, -a *f*.

handling ['hændlɪŋ] **1** N manejo *m*, manejar *m*; manipulación *f*; manoseo *m*; (*of car*) conducción *f*; (*of ship*) gobierno *m*; (*Aer*) asistencia *f* en tierra; servicio *m* de equipajes; **rough ~** malos tratos *mpl*; **his ~ of the matter** su manejo del asunto, su modo de manejar el asunto.
2 ATTR: **~ charge** gastos *mpl* de tramitación.

hand lotion ['hænd,ləʊʃən] N loción *f* para las manos.

hand-luggage ['hænd,lʌgɪdʒ] N equipaje *m* de mano, bultos *mpl* de mano.

handmade ['hændmeɪd] ADJ hecho a mano; de artesanía; **~ paper** papel *m* de tina, papel *m* de mano.

handmaid(en) ['hændmeɪd(ən)] N (*Hist*) criada *f*; azafata *f*.

hand-me-down* ['hændmɪdaʊn] N (*US*) prenda *f* usada.

handout ['hændaʊt] N (**a**) (*act*) distribución *f*, repartimiento *m*. (**b**) (*charity*) limosna *f*, caridad *f*. (**c**) (*press ~*) nota *f* de prensa; (*leaflet*) folleto *m*; impreso *m*, octavilla *f*; (*at lecture*) jandote *m*.

handover ['hændəʊvər] N entrega *f*.

hand-picked ['hænd'pɪkt] ADJ seleccionado a mano, muy escogido, seleccionado cuidadosamente.

hand print ['hændprɪnt] N manotada *f*.

hand puppet ['hænd,pʌpɪt] N títere *m*.

handrail ['hændreɪl] N pasamano *m*.

handset ['hændset] N (*Telec*) aparato *m*, auricular *m*.

hands-free [,hændz'friː] ADJ: **~ car phone** teléfono *m* (móvil) manos libres.

handshake ['hændʃeɪk] N apretón *m* de manos; (*Comput*) coloquio *m*, (*as data signal*) 'acuse de recibo'.

hand signal ['hænd,sɪgnl] N (*Auto*) señalización *f* con el brazo, señal *f* con la mano; **they had to communicate in ~s** tuvieron que comunicarse por señas.

hands-off [,hændz'ɒf] ADJ *policy etc* de no intervención.

handsome ['hænsəm] ADJ (**a**) (*beautiful*) hermoso, bello; elegante; *man* guapo, bien parecido, distinguido. (**b**) *gesture, salary, treatment etc* generoso; *fortune, profit* considerable; *victory* fácil, agobiador.

handsomely ['hænsəmlɪ] ADV (**a**) elegantemente; generosamente. (**b**) *win* fácilmente.

hands-on [,hændz'ɒn] ADJ práctico; inmediato; personal; **~ experience** experiencia *f* práctica.

handspring ['hændsprɪŋ] N voltereta *f* sobre las manos, salto *m* de paloma.

handstand ['hændstænd] N posición *f* de manos, pino *m*; **to do a ~** hacer el pino.

hand-stitched [,hænd'stɪtʃt] ADJ cosido a mano.

hand-to-hand ['hændtə'hænd] ADV, ADJ cuerpo a cuerpo.

hand-to-mouth ['hændtə'maʊθ] **1** ADJ *existence* precario.
2 ADV: **to live ~** vivir precariamente.

hand towel ['hænd,taʊəl] N toalla *f* de manos.

hand-wash ['hænd'wɔːʃ] VT lavar a mano.

hand-woven [,hænd'wəʊvən] ADJ tejido a mano.

handwriting ['hænd,raɪtɪŋ] N escritura *f*, letra *f*.

handwritten ['hænd'rɪtn] ADJ escrito a mano.

handy ['hændɪ] ADJ (**a**) (*near*) a mano; próximo, cercano; **the shop is ~** la tienda está cerca; **to keep sth ~** tener algo listo para usar.
(**b**) (*convenient*) cómodo, práctico; *machine etc* manuable, fácil de manejar; **a ~ little car** un coche práctico; **it's ~ living here** resulta muy práctico vivir aquí; **it's ~ for the shops** está muy cerca de las tiendas; **to come in ~** venir bien, servir.
(**c**) (*skilful*) hábil, diestro; **to be ~ with one's fists** saber defenderse con los puños; **to be ~ with a gun** saber manejar una pistola; **I'm not at all ~** no soy nada manitas.

handyman ['hændɪmæn] N, PL **handymen** ['hændɪmən] factótum *m*; hombre *m* que tiene dotes prácticas (para hacer trabajos de carpintería en casa *etc*).

hang [hæŋ] (*irr*: PRET AND PTP **hung**, (*Jur*) PRET AND PTP **hanged**) **1** VT (**a**) (*suspend*) colgar, suspender; *wallpaper* pegar; *meat* manir.
(**b**) *head* bajar, inclinar.
(**c**) (*decorate*) ornar, decorar; **to ~ a room with tapestries** entapizar un cuarto, adornar un cuarto con tapicerías; **balconies hung with flags** balcones *mpl* engalanados con banderas; **trees hung with lights** árboles *mpl* llenos de farolillos; **a wall hung with ivy** un muro cubierto de hiedra.
(**d**) *criminal* ahorcar; **~ the fellow!** ¡qué tío!, ¡qué tipo! (*LAm*); **~ it (all)!** ¡por Dios!, ¡demonio!; **~ the expense!** ¡que no se hable de los gastos!; **I'll be ~ed if I know** que me maten si lo sé.
(**e**) (*US**: *turn*) **'~ a right here, buddy'** 'oye, tira a la derecha aquí'.
2 VI colgar, pender, estar suspendido (*from* de, *on* en); (*garment, hair*) caer; **a picture ~ing on the wall** un cuadro colgado en la pared; **the hawk hung motionless in the sky** el halcón se mantenía inmóvil en el cielo; **he'll ~ for it** por este crimen le ahorcarán.
3 VR: **to ~ o.s.** ahorcarse.
4 N (**a**) (*of garment*) caída *f*.

(**b**) **to get the ~ of it** coger el tino; **to get the ~ of sth** lograr entender algo; **I can't get the ~ of this machine** no entiendo el modo de manejar esta máquina.

◆**hang about, hang around 1** VT *place* frecuentar; (*haunt*) rondar, merodear; **to ~ about a woman** andar rondando a una mujer, andar detrás de una mujer; **the clouds hung about the summit** las nubes se pegaban a la cumbre.
2 VI (*idle*) no hacer nada, haraganear; (*wait*) esperar; **to keep sb ~ing about** hacer esperar a uno.

◆**hang back** VI quedarse atrás, resistirse a pasar adelante; (*fig*) vacilar, no resolver.

◆**hang down 1** VT: **her hair ~s down her back** el pelo le cae por la espalda.
2 VI colgar, pender.

◆**hang in*** VI: **~ in there!** (*US*) ¡mantente firme!

◆**hang on 1** VT: **to ~ on sb's words** escuchar atentamente lo que dice uno; **everything ~s on his decision** todo depende de su decisión; **we are all ~ing on his decision** todos estamos pendientes de su decisión; **time ~s heavy on him** se le hacen las horas siglos, para él no corre el tiempo.
2 VI (**a**) (*: *wait*) esperar; **~ on!** ¡espera (un momento)!
(**b**) (*hold out*) resistir; **they're still ~ing on** siguen resistiendo; **to ~ on like grim death** resistir con la mayor tenacidad, aguantarlo sin cejar.
(**c**) **to ~ on to** *object* agarrarse a; *principle* aferrarse a; (*: *keep*) guardar, quedarse con; conservar; **~ on to it till I see you** guárdalo hasta que nos veamos.

◆**hang out 1** VT *washing, banner* tender; *streamer etc* colgar.
2 VI (**a**) (*hang*) colgar (fuera); **to ~ out of the window** asomarse por la ventana.
(**b**) (*) (*live*) vivir; (*spend time*) pasar el rato.
(**c**) (*: *hold out*) resistir, aguantar; **they're ~ing out for more** siguen firmes en pedir más.
(**d**) **to let it all ~ out*** (*US*) contarlo todo, revelarlo todo; abrir su pecho; soltarse el pelo.

◆**hang over** VT (**a**) **to be hung over*** tener resaca*.
(**b**) (*hang*) colgar por el borde; sobresalir; **he hung over the table** se inclinó sobre la mesa.
(**c**) (*fig*) cernerse sobre; **a heavy silence hung over the town** se cernía sobre la ciudad un profundo silencio; **the threat ~ing over us** la amenaza que se cierne sobre nosotros.

◆**hang together** VI (**a**) (*persons*) mantenerse unidos.
(**b**) (*argument etc*) ser consistente, ser lógico.

◆**hang up 1** VT (**a**) colgar, suspender; (*Telec*) colgar.
(**b**) (*delay*) causar un retraso a; **we were hung up in the fog** sufrimos un retraso debido a la niebla; **he's hung up with a visitor** se retrasa por una visita; **we are hung up for a lack of bricks** no podemos ir adelante por falta de ladrillos.
(**c**) (*) **to be hung up** (*tense*) estar acomplejado (*about* por); **to be hung up on sth** estar obsesionado por algo.
2 VI (*Telec*) colgar.

hangar ['hæŋər] N hangar *m*.

hangdog ['hæŋdɒg] ADJ avergonzado; **he had a ~ look** tenía cara de pocos amigos.

hanger ['hæŋər] N (**a**) (*for clothes*) percha *f*, colgadero *m*. (**b**) (*Jur*) partidario *m*, -a *f* del restablecimiento de la pena de muerte.

hanger-on ['hæŋər'ɒn] N parásito *m*, pegote *m*.

hang-glide ['hæŋ,glaɪd] VI hacer vuelo con ala delta.

hang-glider ['hæŋ,glaɪdər] N ala *f* delta, cometa *f* delta.

hang-gliding ['hæŋ,glaɪdɪŋ] N vuelo *m* libre, vuelo *m* con cometa delta.

hanging ['hæŋɪŋ] **1** ADJ pendiente, colgante; *lamp* de techo; *garden* colgante, pensil; **~ basket** macetero *m* colgante; **~ committee** junta *f* seleccionadora (de una exposición); **~ judge** (*Hist*) juez *m* muy severo, juez *m* amigo de la horca; **it's not a ~ matter** no es cosa de vida o de muerte.
2 N (**a**) (*execution*) ahorcadura *f*, ejecución *f* (en la horca). (**b**) (*curtains etc*) **~s** colgaduras *fpl*, tapices *mpl*.

hangman ['hæŋmən] N, PL **hangmen** ['hæŋmən] verdugo *m*.

hangnail ['hæŋneɪl] N padrastro *m*.

hang-out* ['hæŋaʊt] N guarida *f*, nidal *m*.

hangover ['hæŋ,əʊvər] N (**a**) (*after drinking*) resaca *f*, cruda *f* (*LAm*). (**b**) (*left-over*) restos *mpl*, vestigio *m*; asunto *m* sin resolver; **it's a ~ from pre-war days** es de la preguerra.

hang-up* ['hæŋʌp] N (**a**) (*problem*) problema *m*, lío* *m*; (*delay*) retraso *m*. (**b**) (*complex*) complejo *m*; (*obsession*) obsesión *f*.

hank [hæŋk] N madeja *f*.

hanker ['hæŋkər] VI: **to ~ after** añorar; **to ~ for** anhelar, suspirar por.

hankering ['hæŋkərɪŋ] N (*feeling*) añoranza *f*; (*wish*) anhelo *m*; **to have a ~ for** anhelar, suspirar por.

hankie*, hanky* ['hæŋkɪ] N pañuelo *m*.

hanky-panky* ['hæŋkɪ'pæŋkɪ] N trucos *mpl*, trampas *fpl*, supercherías *fpl*; (*sexual*) relaciones *fpl* sospechosas; **there's some ~ going on** esto huele a camelo, aquí hay trampa; **we want no ~ with the girls** aquí nadie se meta en líos con las chicas*.

Hannibal ['hænɪbəl] NM Aníbal.

Hanover ['hænəvəʳ] N Hanovre *m*.

Hanoverian [ˌhænəʊ'vɪərɪən] 1 ADJ hanoveriano.
2 N hanoveriano *m*, -a *f*.

Hansard ['hænsɑːd] N Actas *fpl* oficiales de los debates del parlamento británico.

Hanseatic [ˌhænzɪ'ætɪk] ADJ: **the ~ League** La Liga Hanseática.

hansom ['hænsəm] N cabriolé *m*.

Hants [hænts] N ABBR *of* **Hampshire**.

ha'penny* ['heɪpnɪ] N = **halfpenny**.

haphazard [ˌhæp'hæzəd] 1 ADJ fortuito.
2 ADV de cualquier modo, a la buena de Dios.

haphazardly [ˌhæp'hæzədlɪ] ADV *arrange* de cualquier modo; *select* al azar.

hapless ['hæplɪs] ADJ desventurado.

happen ['hæpən] VI **(a)** (*occur*) pasar, suceder, ocurrir, acontecer, acaecer; producirse; (*take place*) tener lugar, verificarse; **what ~ed?** ¿qué pasó?; **how did it ~?** ¿cómo fue esto?; **an explosion ~ed** se produjo una explosión; **these things ~** son cosas que pasan; **whatever ~s** suceda lo que suceda; **see it doesn't ~ again** y que no vuelva a ocurrir; **as it ~s, it (so) ~s that ...** da la casualidad que ...; lo que pasa es que ...; **as if nothing had ~ed** como si tal cosa; **how does it ~ that ...?** ¿cómo es posible que ... + *subj*?; **a funny thing ~ed to me** me pasó algo raro; **if anything should ~ to him** si le sobreviniera algo malo; **what ~ed to him?** ¿qué fue de él?
(b) (*chance*) **I ~ed to be there** me encontraba allí por casualidad; **if anyone should ~ to see you** si acaso te ven; **do you ~ to know him?** ¿le conoces por ventura?; **I ~ to know that ...** pues me consta que ...; **it ~s to be true** a pesar de todo es verdad, da la casualidad que es verdad.
♦**happen (up)on** VT: **to ~ (up)on sth** tropezar con algo; **to ~ (up)on the solution** dar con la solución.

happening ['hæpnɪŋ] 1 N suceso *m*, acontecimiento *m*; (*Theat etc*) happening *m*, acontecimiento *m*; **there will be a '~' in the park** habrá un 'acontecimiento' en el parque.
2 ATTR (*) que es lo último*, de lo último.

happenstance ['hæpənstæns] N (*US*) azar *m*, casualidad *f*; **by ~** por casualidad.

happily ['hæpɪlɪ] ADV **(a)** (*fortunately*) por fortuna, afortunadamente.
(b) (*merrily*) alegremente; **now they are living ~ in Seville** ahora viven muy contentos en Sevilla; **they lived ~ ever after** vivieron felices. **(c)** (*aptly*) felizmente.

happiness ['hæpɪnɪs] N (*contentment*) felicidad *f*, dicha *f*, contento *m*; (*merriment*) alegría *f*.

▼**happy** ['hæpɪ] ADJ **(a)** (*fortunate*) feliz, dichoso, afortunado; **that ~ age** aquella época tan feliz; **we ~ few** nosotros tan pocos y tan afortunados.
▼**(b)** (*contented*) contento, satisfecho; **~ hour** hora *f* de la felicidad; **~ birthday!** ¡feliz cumpleaños!; **are you ~?** ¿estás contento?; **are you ~ with him?** ¿eres feliz con él?; **we are not entirely ~ about the plan** no estamos del todo contentos con el proyecto, no nos satisface del todo el proyecto; **your success makes us all ~** su éxito nos alegra a todos; **he tried to make her ~** se esforzó por hacerla feliz; **this should keep everyone ~** esto deberá tenerles a todos contentos; **we're very ~ for you** nos alegramos mucho por ti; **we were ~ to hear it** nos alegramos de saberlo; **I am ~ to inform you that ...** tengo mucho gusto en comunicarle que ...
(c) (*merry, cheerful*) alegre; (*) entre dos velas*; *ending of book etc* feliz; **to be as ~ as a lark** (*or* **sand-boy**) estar como unas pascuas.
(d) (*apt*) feliz, oportuno; **~ mean, ~ medium** justo *m* medio, término *m* medio; **it seems to be a ~ solution** parece ser una solución satisfactoria.

happy-go-lucky ['hæpɪgəʊ'lʌkɪ] ADJ despreocupado.

Hapsburg ['hæpsbɜːg] N Habsburgo.

hara-kiri ['hærə'kɪrɪ] N haraquiri *m*.

harangue [hə'ræŋ] 1 N arenga *f*.
2 VT arengar.

harass ['hærəs] VT acosar, hostigar; (*Mil*) hostilizar, picar; *person* (*with worries etc*) atormentar, perseguir; **to be ~ed by doubts** ser atormentado por las dudas.

harassed ['hærəst] ADJ *look* preocupado.

harassment ['hærəsmənt] N acoso *m*, hostigamiento *m*; (*sexual*) importunación *f*, acoso *m*.

harbinger ['hɑːbɪndʒəʳ] N heraldo *m*, nuncio *m*; precursor *m*; presagio *m*; **~ of doom** presagio *m* del desastre; **the swallow is a ~ of spring** la golondrina anuncia la venida de la primavera.

harbour, (*US*) **harbor** ['hɑːbəʳ] 1 N puerto *m*; **outer ~** rada *f*.
2 ATTR portuario; **~ dues, ~ fees** derechos *mpl* portuarios.
3 VT *fear, hope etc* abrigar; (*lodge*) hospedar; (*conceal*) esconder; **that**

corner ~s the dust en ese rincón se amontona el polvo.

harbour master, (*US*) **harbor master** ['hɑːbəˌmɑːstəʳ] N capitán *m* de puerto.

hard [hɑːd] 1 ADJ **(a)** (*unyielding, also fig*) duro; sólido, firme; *mud, snow* endurecido; *muscle* firme; *line, outline* sólido, firme, claro; *court, currency, water* duro; *drink* alcohólico; *liquor* espiritoso; *decision* (*final*) definitivo, irrevocable; *look* fijo; **he's as ~ as nails** tiene muchísima resistencia; **~ ass** (*US*) bestia* *mf*, duro *m*, -a *f* de pelar; **~ cash** dinero *m* contante y sonante; **~ center** (*US*), **~ centre** relleno *m* duro; **~ copy** copia *f* impresa; **~ court** cancha *f* (de tenis) de cemento; **~ currency** moneda *f* dura, divisa *f* dura; **~ disk** disco *m* duro (*or* rígido); **~ drug** droga *f* dura; **~ goods** artículos *mpl* de equipo; **~ hat** (*of construction worker etc*) casco *m*; (*riding hat*) sombrero *m* de montar; (*fig: construction worker*) albañil *m*; (ADJ: *fig*) conservador; **~ landing** aterrizaje *m* duro; **~ liquor** licor *m* espiritoso; **~ news** noticias *fpl* fidedignas, información *f* sólida; **~ palate** paladar *m*; **~ porn*** pornografía *f* dura; (ATTR) porno duro; **~ rock** rock *m* duro; **~ sell** venta *f* (con propaganda) agresiva; publicidad *f* agresiva; venta *f* difícil; **~ sell tactics** (*or* **techniques**) táctica *f* (*or* técnicas *fpl*) de promoción agresiva; **~ shoulder** (*Brit*) arcén *m*; **~ stuff*** (*alcohol*) bebidas *fpl* fuertes; (*drugs*) droga *f* dura; (*Aut*) **~ top** techo *m* duro; **~ top car** coche *m* de techo duro.
(b) (*harsh, tough*) *work* arduo, penoso, agotador; *blow* duro, (*fig*) cruel, rudo; *frost* fuerte; *weather, winter* severo; *climate* áspero; *light* duro; *fight, match* muy reñido; *rule* severo; *decision* injusto; *fact* concreto; sólido; *word* nada amistoso; *luck, times* malo; **~ lines!, ~ luck!** (*Brit*) ¡mala suerte!
(c) (*person*) severo, inflexible; (*Pol*) **the ~ left** la izquierda dura; **you're a ~ man** eres cruel; **to be ~ on sb** ser muy duro con uno; **to be ~ on one's clothes** destrozar la ropa.
(d) (*difficult*) difícil; **to be ~ to beat** ser difícil de vencer; **I find it ~ to believe that ...** se me hace cuesta arriba creer que ...; **to be ~ to please** ser exigente, ser quisquilloso; **he's ~ of hearing** es duro de oído; **we shall have to do it the ~ way** tendremos que hacerlo a pulso.
2 ADV **(a)** (*strenuously*) mucho; de firme; **to pull a rope ~** tirar fuertemente de una cuerda; **he threw it ~ down** lo arrojó violentamente; **to hit sb ~** dar un golpe recio a uno, (*fig*) ser un golpe cruel para uno; **to be ~ at it** trabajar (*etc*) con ahinco; **to work ~** trabajar mucho; **to rain ~** llover mucho; **to beg ~ for sth** pedir algo con insistencia; **to think ~** pensar mucho, meditar profundamente; **to look ~** mirar fijamente; **to drink ~** beber con exceso; **hold ~!** ¡para el carro!; ¡un momento!, ¡despacito!; **to try one's ~est to** + *infin* esforzarse mucho por + *infin*.
(b) to be ~ up* estar a la cuarta pregunta*; **to be ~ up for books*** no tener casi libros, estar muy falto de libros; **I was ~ put to it** estuve en un aprieto; **to be ~ put to it to decide** encontrar difícil decidir; **to be ~ done by** (*Brit*) ser tratado injustamente; **he took it pretty ~** fue un golpe bastante rudo para él.
(c) **~ by** (ADV) muy cerca; (PREP) muy cerca de; **A followed ~ upon B** A siguió de cerca a B.

hard-and-fast ['hɑːdən'fɑːst] ADJ *rule* rígido; *decision* definitivo, irrevocable.

hardback ['hɑːdbæk] 1 ADJ empastado, de tapa dura; **~ book** = 2.
2 N libro *m* empastado, libro *m* de tapa dura.

hard-bitten ['hɑːd'bɪtn] ADJ de carácter duro.

hardboard ['hɑːdbɔːd] N chapa *f* de madera dura.

hard-boiled ['hɑːd'bɔɪld] ADJ *egg* cocido, duro; *person* de carácter duro, severo.

hard-core ['hɑːdkɔːʳ] ADJ: **~ pornography** pornografía *f* dura; **~ resistance** resistencia *f* empedernida, resistencia *f* incondicional.

hard-cover ['hɑːd,kʌvəʳ] ADJ: **~ book** libro *m* encuadernado.

hard-drinking ['hɑːd'drɪŋkɪŋ] ADJ bebedor.

hard-earned ['hɑːd'ɜːnd] ADJ ganado con el sudor de la frente.

hard-edged ['hɑːd'edʒd] ADJ (*fig*) *style, story* contundente, duro.

harden ['hɑːdn] 1 VT endurecer (*also Comm*), solidificar; **to ~ sb to adversity** acostumbrar a uno a la adversidad; **to ~ sb to war** aguerrir a uno; **he ~ed his heart** se mostró más inflexible.
2 VI endurecerse (*also Comm*), solidificarse; **his voice ~ed** adoptó un tono más áspero.

hardened ['hɑːdnd] ADJ *criminal* habitual.

hardening ['hɑːdnɪŋ] N endurecimiento *m* (*also Comm*); **~ of the arteries** endurecimiento *m* de las arterias, arteriosclerosis *f*.

hard-faced ['hɑːdfeɪst] ADJ severo, inflexible.

hard-fought ['hɑːd'fɔːt] ADJ muy reñido.

hard-headed ['hɑːd'hedɪd] ADJ práctico, realista, poco sentimental.

hard-hearted ['hɑːd'hɑːtɪd] ADJ duro de corazón, insensible.

hard-hit ['hɑːd'hɪt] ADJ perjudicado, afectado (negativamente).

hard-hitting ['hɑːd,hɪtɪŋ] ADJ *speech etc* contundente.

hardiness ['hɑːdɪnɪs] N robustez *f*; resistencia *f*.

hard-line ['hɑːd'laɪn] ADJ *communist, conservative* de línea dura, extremista; *approach, policy* radical; **to take a hard line against sb/sth**

adoptar una postura severa contra uno/algo.

hard-liner [ˌhɑːd'laɪnəʳ] N duro *m*, -a *f*; partidario *m*, -a *f*, político *m* (*etc*) de línea dura.

hard-luck ['hɑːdlʌk] ATTR: **he pitched me a ~ story** me contó sus infortunios, me contó su historia tan trágica.

hardly ['hɑːdlɪ] ADV **(a)** (*in a hard manner*) duramente; difícilmente; (*badly*) mal.
(b) (*scarcely*) apenas; **he can ~ read** apenas sabe leer; **that can ~ be true** eso difícilmente puede ser verdad; **~ anyone** casi nadie; **~ ever** casi nunca; **~!** ¡nada de eso!

hardness ['hɑːdnɪs] N dureza *f*; dificultad *f*; rigor *m*; severidad *f*; **~ of hearing** dureza *f* de oído; **~ of heart** insensibilidad *f*.

hard-nosed [ˌhɑːd'nəʊzd] ADJ (*fig*) duro.

hard-on⁑ ['hɑːdɒn] N empalme⁑ *m*, erección *f*.

hard-pressed ['hɑːdprest] ADJ: **to be ~** estar en apuros; **our ~ economy** nuestra economía erizada de problemas.

hardship ['hɑːdʃɪp] [1] N trabajos *mpl*, penas *fpl*; infortunio *m*; prueba *f*; (*economic etc*) apuro *m*, privación *f*; **to suffer ~(s)** pasar apuros; **it is no ~ to him** (**to give up smoking**) no le cuesta nada (dejar de fumar).
[2] ATTR: **~ clause** (*Jur*) cláusula *f* de salvaguarda.

hardtack ['hɑːdtæk] N (*Naut*) galleta *f*.

hardware ['hɑːdwɛəʳ] [1] N ferretería *f*, quincalla *f*; (*Mil*) armas *fpl*, armamento *m*; (*Comput*) hardware *m*, equipos *mpl*, material *m* informático, soporte *m* físico.
[2] ATTR: **~ dealer** ferretero *m*; **~ shop, ~ store** ferretería *f*, quincallería *f*; **~ specialist** (*Comput*) especialista *mf* en hardware.

hard-wearing ['hɑːd'wɛərɪŋ] ADJ resistente, duradero.

hard-won ['hɑːd'wʌn] ADJ ganado a duras penas.

hardwood ['hɑːdwʊd] N madera *f* dura; **~ tree** árbol *m* de hojas caducas.

hard-working ['hɑːd'wɜːkɪŋ] ADJ trabajador.

hardy ['hɑːdɪ] ADJ fuerte, robusto; (*Bot*) resistente.

hare [hɛəʳ] [1] N liebre *f*; **first catch your ~** no hay que empezar por el tejado.
[2] VI (*) correr, ir rápidamente; **he went haring past** pasó como un rayo; **to ~ in, out, through** *etc* (*Brit*) entrar, salir, pasar *etc* a toda pastilla*.

harebell ['hɛəbel] N campánula *f*.

hare-brained ['hɛəbreɪnd] ADJ casquivano.

harelip ['hɛə'lɪp] N labio *m* leporino.

harelipped [ˌhɛə'lɪpt] ADJ de labio leporino, labihendido.

harem [hɑː'riːm] N harén *m*.

haricot ['hærɪkəʊ] N (*Brit: also* **~ bean**) alubia *f*, judía *f*.

hark [hɑːk] VI: **~!** ¡escucha!; **~ at this!** ¡oye!; **~ at him!** ¡qué cosas dice!, ¡quién fue a hablar!; **~ at him singing!** ¡cómo canta el tío!; **to ~ to** escuchar.
◆ **hark back** VI: **to ~ back to** *matter* volver a, *earlier occasion* recordar; **he's always ~ing back to that** siempre está con la misma canción.

harken ['hɑːkən] = **hearken**.

Harlequin ['hɑːlɪkwɪn] NM Arlequín.

Harley Street ['hɑːlɪstriːt] N (*Brit*) *calle de Londres donde tienen su consulta muchos médicos especialistas prestigiosos.*

harlot ['hɑːlət] N ramera *f*.

▼ **harm** [hɑːm] [1] N daño *m*, mal *m*; perjuicio *m*; **to be out of ~'s way** estar a salvo; **to keep out of ~'s way** evitar el peligro, permanecer (*or* mantenerse) lejos del sitio peligroso; **there's no ~ in** + *ger* no hay ningún mal en + *infin*; **I see no ~ in that** no veo nada en contra de eso; **to do sb ~** hacer daño a uno, (*fig*) perjudicar a uno; **it does more ~ than good** es peor el remedio que la enfermedad; **the ~ is done now** el mal ya está hecho; **he means no ~** tiene buenas intenciones.
[2] VT *person* hacer daño a, hacer mal a; *crops etc* dañar, estropear; *interests etc* perjudicar.
[3] VI sufrir daños; **will it ~ in the rain?** ¿lo estropeará la lluvia?; **it won't ~ for that** eso no le hará daño.

harmful ['hɑːmfʊl] ADJ perjudicial (*to* para), dañoso, nocivo; *pest, tobacco etc* dañino.

harmless ['hɑːmlɪs] ADJ inocuo, inofensivo; **to make a bomb ~** desactivar una bomba.

harmlessly ['hɑːmlɪslɪ] ADV inocuamente, inofensivamente; sin causar daños.

harmonic [hɑː'mɒnɪk] ADJ armónico.

harmonica [hɑː'mɒnɪkə] N armónica *f*.

harmonics [hɑː'mɒnɪks] N armonía *f*.

harmonious [hɑː'məʊnɪəs] ADJ armonioso.

harmoniously [hɑː'məʊnɪəslɪ] ADV armoniosamente.

harmonium [hɑː'məʊnɪəm] N armonio *m*.

harmonize ['hɑːmənaɪz] VTI armonizar (*with* con).

harmony ['hɑːmənɪ] N armonía *f*; **close ~** armonía *f* cerrada.

harness ['hɑːnɪs] [1] N guarniciones *fpl*, arreos *mpl*; **~ race** carrera *f* de trotones; **to die in ~** morir con las botas puestas; **to get back in ~**

---

volver al trabajo, volver a su puesto.
[2] VT **(a)** *horse* poner guarniciones a, enjaezar; **to ~ a horse to a cart** enganchar un caballo a un carro.
(b) *resources etc* hacer trabajar, utilizar, aprovechar.

harp [hɑːp] [1] N arpa *f*.
[2] VI: **to ~ on** hablar constantemente de; **stop ~ing on it!** ¡no machaques!

harpist ['hɑːpɪst] N arpista *mf*.

harpoon [hɑː'puːn] [1] N arpón *m*.
[2] VT arponear.

harpsichord ['hɑːpsɪkɔːd] N clavicordio *m*, clavicémbalo *m*.

harpy ['hɑːpɪ] N arpía *f*.

harquebus ['hɑːkwɪbəs] N (*Hist*) arcabuz *m*.

harridan ['hærɪdən] N bruja *f*.

harried ['hærɪd] ADJ *expression etc* preocupado.

harrier ['hærɪəʳ] N **(a)** (*dog*) perro *m* de caza. **(b)** **~s** (*cross-country runners*) corredores *mpl* de cross. **(c)** (*Orn*) aguilucho *m*.

Harris ['hærɪs] ADJ: **~ Tweed** ® tweed *m* producido en la isla de Harris.

harrow ['hærəʊ] [1] N grada *f*.
[2] VT **(a)** (*Agr*) gradar. **(b)** (*fig*) torturar, destrozar.

harrowing ['hærəʊɪŋ] ADJ horrendo, horroroso, angustioso.

Harry ['hærɪ] NM Enrique; **to play old ~ with*** endiablar, estropear.

harry ['hærɪ] VT (*devastate*) asolar; (*Mil*) hostilizar; *person etc* hostigar, acosar.

harsh [hɑːʃ] ADJ *person, decision etc* severo, duro, cruel; *voice, cloth etc* áspero; *contrast* violento; *weather* severo; *colour* chillón; *taste* acerbo; *words* nada amistoso.

harshly ['hɑːʃlɪ] ADV severamente, duramente; ásperamente.

harshness ['hɑːʃnɪs] N severidad *f*, dureza *f*, rigor *m*; aspereza *f*.

hart [hɑːt] N ciervo *m*.

harum-scarum ['hɛərəm'skɛərəm] [1] ADJ tarambana, atolondrado.
[2] N tarambana *mf*.

harvest ['hɑːvɪst] [1] N cosecha *f*, recolección *f*; (*time of year*) siega *f*; (*of grape*) vendimia *f*; (*fig*) cosecha *f*.
[2] ATTR: **~ festival** fiesta *f* de la cosecha.
[3] VT cosechar (*also fig*), recoger, recolectar.
[4] VI cosechar, segar.

harvester ['hɑːvɪstəʳ] N (*person*) segador *m*, -ora *f*; (*machine*) cosechadora *f*, segadora-trilladora *f*.

harvest home [ˌhɑːvɪst'həʊm] N (*festival*) ≃ fiesta *f* de la cosecha; (*season*) cosecha *f*.

harvesting ['hɑːvɪstɪŋ] N cosecha *f*, cosechado *m*.

harvest time ['hɑːvɪst,taɪm] N siega *f*.

has [hæz] V have.

has-been ['hæzbiːn] N celebridad *f* del pasado; persona *f* quemada; vieja gloria *f*.

hash¹ [hæʃ] N picadillo *m*; (*) embrollo *m*, lío* *m*; **to make a ~ of sth** armarse un lío con algo*, estropear algo, hacer algo muy mal; **to settle sb's ~*** cargarse a uno*, acabar con uno.
◆ **hash up** VT: **to ~ sth up** rehacer algo (y presentarlo como nuevo).

hash²⁑ [hæʃ] N hachís *m*, chocolate⁑ *m*.

hash browns ['hæʃ'braʊnz] NPL (*US*) croquetas de patata hervida y cebolla.

hashish ['hæʃɪʃ] N hachís *m*.

hasn't ['hæznt] = **has not**.

hasp [hɑːsp] N pasador *m*, sujetador *m*.

Hassidic [hə'sɪdɪk] ADJ hasídico.

hassle* ['hæsl] [1] N (*squabble*) pelea *f*, riña *f*; (*difficulty*) lío* *m*, problema *m*; (*bustle*) bullicio *m*; **no ~!** ¡no hay problema!; **it's not worth the ~** no vale la pena.
[2] VT molestar, fastidiar, dar la lata a*.

hassock ['hæsək] N (*Eccl*) cojín *m*.

hast [hæst] (††) V have.

haste [heɪst] N prisa *f*, precipitación *f*; **more ~ less speed, make ~ slowly** vísteme despacio que tengo prisa; **to do sth in ~** hacer algo de prisa; hacer algo precipitadamente; **to make ~** darse prisa; **make ~!** ¡date prisa!; **to make ~ to** + *infin* apresurarse a + *infin*.

hasten ['heɪsn] [1] VT acelerar; **to ~ one's steps** apretar el paso.
[2] VI darse prisa, apresurarse; **to ~ to** + *infin* apresurarse a + *infin*.
◆ **hasten away** VI marcharse precipitadamente (*from* de).
◆ **hasten back** VI volver con toda prisa, darse prisa para volver.
◆ **hasten off** VI = **hasten away**.
◆ **hasten on** VI seguir adelante con toda prisa.
◆ **hasten up** VI llegar apresuradamente, acudir rápidamente.

hastily ['heɪstɪlɪ] ADV (*hurriedly*) de prisa, precipitadamente; *speak* sin reflexión, con impaciencia; *judge* a la ligera; **I ~ suggested that ...** me apresuré a sugerir que ...

hasty ['heɪstɪ] ADJ (*hurried*) apresurado, precipitado; (*rash*) irreflexivo, inconsiderado, imprudente; (*quick-tempered*) impaciente, que tiene genio; (*superficial*) ligero; **don't be so ~** hay que tomar las cosas con más calma.

hat [hæt] N sombrero m; **my ~!** ¡caramba!; **that's old ~** eso es de lo más anticuado; eso lo tenemos archisabido; **I'll eat my ~ if ...** que me maten si ...; **to hang one's ~ up** (fig) jubilarse; **keep it under your ~** de esto no digas ni pío; **to pass the ~ round** pasar el platillo; **to raise** (or **take off**) **one's ~** descubrirse; **to take one's ~ off to** (fig) descubrirse ante; saludar con respeto; **~s off to Joe!** ¡muy bien Paco!; **to wear two ~s** (fig) ostentar dos representaciones; **to talk through one's ~** decir tonterías; **now wearing my other ~** (fig) hablando ahora en mi otra calidad de ...

hatband ['hætbænd] N cinta f de sombrero.

hatbox ['hætbɒks] N sombrerera f.

hatch¹ [hætʃ] N (a) (Naut) escotilla f; (Aut) portón m. (b) (Brit) (**service** or **serving**) **~** ventanilla f para servir.

hatch² [hætʃ] 1 VT (a) chick empollar, incubar; sacar del cascarón. (b) (fig: also to **~ up**) idear; plot tramar.
2 VI (bird) salir del huevo; (insect) eclosionar; **the egg ~ed** el pollo rompió el cascarón y salió; **those eggs never ~ed** esos huevos resultaron ser hueros.

hatch³ [hætʃ] VT (Art) sombrear.

hatchback ['hætʃbæk] N (door) puerta f trasera, portón m; (vehicle) coche m con portón trasero.

hat-check ['hæt.tʃek] ATTR: **~ girl** (US) encargada f del guardarropa.

hatchery ['hætʃəri] N criadero m, vivero m.

hatchet ['hætʃit] 1 N hacha f (pequeña), machado m; **to bury the ~** echar pelillos a la mar, envainar la espada.
2 ATTR: **~ job*** golpe m cruel pero eficaz; faena f desagradable pero necesaria; **~ man*** (US) asesino m a sueldo; ejecutor m de faenas desagradables por cuenta de otro.

hatchet-faced ['hætʃit.feist] ADJ de cara de cuchillo.

hatching¹ ['hætʃiŋ] N incubación f; salida f del huevo; eclosión f; (fig) ideación f; preparación f, maquinación f.

hatching² ['hætʃiŋ] N (Art) sombreado m.

hatchway ['hætʃwei] N escotilla f.

▼ **hate** [heit] 1 N (a) odio m; **~ campaign** campaña f de desprestigio; **~ mail** cartas fpl en las que se expresa odio al destinatario.
(b) **one of my pet ~s** uno de mis hinchas, una de las cosas que más detesto.
▼ 2 VT (a) odiar, detestar, aborrecer; **to ~ sb like poison** odiar a uno a muerte.
(b) **I ~ to see that** me da asco ver aquello; **I ~ to say so** lamento tener que decirlo; **I ~ having to do it** me repugna hacerlo; **I ~ to trouble you** siento muchísimo molestarle; **I should ~ to have to sell it** lamentaría tener que venderlo; **he ~s to be corrected** detesta que le corrijan.

hateful ['heitfʊl] ADJ odioso, repugnante.

hath [hæθ] (††) V **have**.

hatless ['hætlis] ADJ sin sombrero, descubierto.

hatpin ['hætpin] N agujón m.

hatrack ['hætræk] N percha f para sombreros.

hatred ['heitrid] N odio m (for a), aborrecimiento m (for de).

hat shop ['hætʃɒp] N sombrerería f.

hatstand ['hætstænd] N percha f para sombreros, sombrerera f (Carib).

hatter ['hætər] N sombrerero m.

hat tree ['hættriː] N (US) percha f para sombreros.

hat-trick ['hættrik] N (fig) tres tantos mpl (or triunfos mpl) en un partido; serie f de tres victorias (etc); **to do the ~, to get** (or **score**) **a ~** marcar tres tantos en un partido.

haughtily ['hɔːtili] ADV arrogantemente.

haughtiness ['hɔːtinis] N altanería f, arrogancia f, altivez f.

haughty ['hɔːti] ADJ altanero, arrogante, altivo.

haul [hɔːl] 1 N (a) (act of pulling) tirón m, estirón m (on de).
(b) (distance) recorrido m, trayecto m; **it's a good** (or **long**) **~** es mucho camino.
(c) (amount of fish) redada f; (financial) ganancia f; (stolen) botín m; (arms ~, drugs ~) alijo m; **the thieves made a good ~** los ladrones obtuvieron un cuantioso botín.
2 VT (drag) tirar, arrastrar; (transport) acarrear, transportar; **he was ~ed before the manager** tuvo que presentarse al gerente.
3 VI: **to ~ on, to ~ at** tirar de; (Naut) halar.

♦ **haul down** VT flag arriar.

♦ **haul in** VT net etc ir recogiendo.

♦ **haul up** VT (a) ir levantando. (b) **he was ~ed up in court** fue llevado ante el tribunal.

haulage ['hɔːlidʒ] N (act) acarreo m, transporte m; (cost) gastos mpl de acarreo; **~ company** compañía f de transportes (por carretera); **~ contractor** contratista m de transportes, transportista m.

hauler ['hɔːlər] (US), **haulier** ['hɔːliər] N contratista m de transportes, transportista m.

haunch [hɔːntʃ] N anca f; (of meat) pierna f; **to sit on one's ~es** sentarse en cuclillas.

haunt [hɔːnt] 1 N (animal's) nidal m, guarida f, querencia f; **I know his ~s** conozco sus sitios favoritos, sé dónde suele estar; **it's a ~ of**

artists es lugar predilecto de los artistas.
2 VT (a) (frequent) frecuentar, rondar; **he ~s the theatres** aparece constantemente en los teatros.
(b) (of ghost) aparecer en, andar por; **the house is ~ed** en la casa andan fantasmas, la casa está embrujada; **~ed house** casa f de fantasmas, casa f encantada.
(c) person perseguir; obsesionar; **he is ~ed by memories** le persiguen sus recuerdos, le atormentan sus recuerdos; **he is ~ed by the thought that ...** le obsesiona el pensamiento de que ...

haunted ['hɔːntid] ADJ look etc obsesionado.

haunting ['hɔːntiŋ] ADJ obsesionante; melody inolvidable.

hauntingly ['hɔːntiŋli] ADV: **a ~ lovely scene** una escena de una belleza inolvidable.

haute couture [otkutyr] N alta costura f.

haute cuisine [otkwizin] N alta cocina f.

hauteur [əʊ'tɜː] N (frm) = **haughtiness**.

Havana [hə'vænə] N La Habana.

▼ **have** [hæv] (irr: 3rd sing present **has**, PRET AND PTP **had**) 1 VT (a) (possess) tener; poseer; **all I ~** todo lo que tengo; **~ you any bananas?** (in shop) ¿hay plátanos?; **I ~ no words to express ...** no encuentro palabras para expresar ...; **I ~ no German** no sé alemán; **I ~ it!** ¡ya!; ... **and what ~ you ...** y qué sé yo qué más; etcétera, etcétera; **the dog had him by the throat** el perro le tenía agarrado por la garganta; **I never guessed he had it in him** no le suponía nunca capaz de eso; **you must give it all you ~, you must put everything you ~ into it** tienes que emplearte a fondo.
(b) (bear, carry) tener, llevar; **the book has no name on it** el libro no lleva el nombre del dueño; **to ~ a hat on** llevar un sombrero (puesto); **do you ~ a pound about you?** ¿llevas encima una libra?
(c) baby parir, dar a luz; **she's going to ~ a baby** va a tener un niño.
(d) (obtain, acquire, hand over) **to ~ a letter from sb** recibir una carta de uno; **I ~ no news** no tengo noticias; **I ~ it on good authority that ...** sé de buena tinta que ...; **it is to be had at the chemist's** se vende en la farmacia; **it's not to be had anywhere** no se consigue en ninguna parte; **I must ~ £5 at once** necesito 5 libras en seguida; **you can ~ it for £2** te lo vendo por 2 libras; **let me ~ your pen** ¿me prestas la pluma?; **he let me ~ some money** me facilitó dinero; **I will let you ~ my reply tomorrow** les daré mi respuesta mañana.
(e) (strike) dar, pegar; **let him ~ it!** ¡dale!; **then they let him ~ it** luego empezaron a pegarle, (fig: scold) luego le dijeron cuatro verdades.
(f) (eat, drink etc) tomar; **I don't ~ anything at night** por la noche no tomo nada; **to ~ tea with sb** tomar el té con uno, merendar con uno; **he's having his dinner** está comiendo; **what did you ~ at the dinner?** ¿qué te dieron de comer en el banquete?; **will you ~ a drink?** ¿quieres tomar algo?; **will you ~ some more?** ¿quieres más?; **to ~ a cigarette** fumar un pitillo.
(g) (N phrases; see also n) **to ~ a game** echar una partida; **to ~ a bath** tomar un baño; **to ~ a lesson** tomar lección; **to ~ measles** tener sarampión; **to ~ a good time** pasarlo bien; **did you ~ any trouble?** ¿tuviste alguna dificultad?; **I had a strange adventure** me pasó algo raro; **I never seem to ~ anything happen to me** parece que no me pasa nunca nada.
(h) (wish) **which will you ~?** ¿cuál quieres?; **what more would you ~?** ¿qué más quieres?; **as ill-luck would ~ it** desgraciadamente, como quiso la suerte; **I would ~ you know that ...** sepa Vd que ...
▼ (i) (permit) permitir, tolerar; **I won't ~ such behaviour** no tolero esta conducta; **I'm not having that** no puedo consentir en que se haga (or diga etc) eso; **we can't ~ that** eso no se puede consentir; **we don't ~ children here** aquí no recibimos a los matrimonios que traigan hijos, aquí no se reciben niños.
(j) (insist, say) **he will ~ it that ...** sostiene que ...; **he will not ~ it that ...** no quiere reconocer que ...; **as rumour has it** según se dice; **as Keats has it** según (dice) Keats.
(k) (*: deceive) **you've been had** te han engañado; **I'm not to be had that way** no se me engaña así; **there you ~ me** de eso no sé nada en absoluto.
▼ (l) (obligation) **to ~ to do sth** tener que hacer algo; **it has to be done this way** ha de hacerse de este modo; **does it ~ to be ironed?** ¿hay que plancharlo?
(m) (causative) **to ~ sth done** hacer hacer algo; **to ~ a suit made** mandar confeccionar un traje; **please ~ it repaired** por favor mándelo componer; **he had his watch stolen** le robaron el reloj; **he had his arm broken** se rompió el brazo; **I won't ~ her insulted** no permito que se le insulte; **to ~ sb do sth** hacer que uno haga algo; **he would ~ me do it** insistió en que yo lo hiciera; **what else would you ~ me do?** ¿qué más queréis que haga?; **there was a general desire to ~ it over with** todos estaban deseando que se concluyese de una vez.
(n) **I ~ letters to write** tengo cartas que escribir; **~n't you anything to do?** ¿no tienes nada que hacer?

(o) (*auxiliary*) haber; **he has gone** ha ido; **he had spoken** había hablado; **it has been raining for 3 days** llueve desde hace 3 días; **I ~n't seen him for 2 years** hace 2 años que no le veo; **never having seen it before, I** ... como no lo había visto antes, yo ...; **'I ~ 2 cars'** ... **'so ~ I'** 'tengo 2 coches' ... 'yo también'; **'it's gone!'** ... **'so it has!'** '¡ha desaparecido!' ... '¡es verdad!'

(p) I had better, sooner *etc*. **I better, sooner** *etc*.

(q) you've had it!* ¡estás listo!*; **we must run or we've had it*** tenemos que correr o estamos listos*; **I've had it*** estoy hasta las narices (*or* el último pelo)*.

(r) (*have sex with*) poseer, dormir con.

   2 N: **the ~s and the ~-nots** los ricos y los pobres.

◆ **have away = have off.**

◆ **have down** VT: **we are having the Smiths down for a few days** hemos invitado a los Smith a pasar unos días con nosotros.

◆ **have in** VT **(a)** *person* hacer entrar; *doctor etc* llamar; **let's ~ him in!** ¡que pase!, ¡que entre!; **to ~ sb in to supper** invitar a uno a cenar; **we're having people in** tenemos invitados.

   (b) to ~ it in for sb* tener manía a uno, tenérsela jurada a uno.

◆ **have off** VT: **to ~ it off**** (*Brit*) echar un polvo**; **to ~ it off with sb**** tirarse con una**.

◆ **have on** VT **(a)** *clothes* llevar, tener puesto; **he had nothing on** estaba desnudo.

   (b) (*Brit: be busy*) **I ~ a lot on this week** tengo muchos compromisos esta semana, esta semana estoy muy ocupado; **do you ~ anything on tonight?** ¿tienes compromiso para esta noche?

   (c) (*Brit*) (*tease*) tomar el pelo a; (*deceive*) embaucar; **they're having you on** te están tomando el pelo.

◆ **have out** VT **(a)** *tooth* hacer sacar.

   (b) to ~ it out with sb resolver un problema hablando con uno; (*unfriendly*) ajustar cuentas con uno; **I'm going to ~ it out with him** voy a poner las cosas en claro con él.

◆ **have up** VT **(a)** *guest* hacer venir, invitar.

   (b) (*: *charge*) **to ~ sb up** llevar a uno ante los tribunales (*for* acusándole de); **he was had up for larceny** le procesaron por ladrón.

┌─ HAVE ─┐   **│ see also main entry │**

● Don't translate the *a* in sentences like *has he got a girlfriend?*, *I haven't got a washing-machine* if the number of such items is not significant since people normally only have one at a time:

     Has he got a girlfriend?
     ¿Tiene novia?
     I haven't got a washing-machine
     No tengo lavadora

● Do translate the *a* if the person or thing is qualified:

     He has a Spanish girlfriend
     Tiene una novia española
     For further uses and examples, see main entry.

---

haven ['heɪvn] N puerto *m*; (*fig*) refugio *m*, asilo *m*.

have-nots ['hævnɒts] NPL: **the ~** los pobres, los desposeídos.

haven't ['hævnt] = **have not.**

haversack ['hævəsæk] N mochila *f*.

havoc ['hævək] N estragos *mpl*, destrucción *f*; **to make ~ of, to play ~ with** hacer estragos en, arruinar, estropear.

haw¹ [hɔː] N baya *f* del espino.

haw² [hɔː] VI: **to hem and ~, to hum and ~** vacilar.

Hawaii [həˈwaɪiː] N (Islas *fpl*) Hawai *m*.

Hawaiian [həˈwaɪjən] **1** ADJ hawaiano.

   2 N hawaiano *m*, -a *f*.

hawfinch ['hɔːfɪntʃ] N picogordo *m*.

hawk¹ [hɔːk] N (*Orn*) halcón *m*, gavilán *m*; (*Pol*) halcón *m*; **he was watching me like a ~** me vigilaba estrechamente, no me quitaba ojo.

hawk² [hɔːk] VT pregonar, vender por las calles.

hawk³ [hɔːk] VI carraspear.

◆ **hawk up** VT arrojar tosiendo.

hawker ['hɔːkər] N vendedor *m* ambulante.

hawk-eyed [ˌhɔːkˈaɪd] ADJ con ojos de lince.

hawkish ['hɔːkɪʃ] ADJ (*Pol etc*) duro.

hawser ['hɔːzər] N guindaleza *f*, calabrote *m*, maroma *f*.

hawthorn ['hɔːθɔːn] N espino *m*, oxiacanta *f*.

hay [heɪ] N heno *m*; **to hit the ~*** acostarse; **to make ~ of*** *enemy* desbaratar; *team* cascar*; *argument* destruir; **to make ~ while the sun shines** hacer su agosto; **that ain't ~** (*US**) no es moco de pavo*, es una pasta gansa*.

haycock ['heɪkɒk] N montón *m* de heno.

hay fever ['heɪˌfiːvər] N fiebre *f* del heno, catarro *m* del heno.

hayfork ['heɪfɔːk] N bieldo *m*.

hayloft ['heɪlɒft] N henil *m*, henal *m*.

haymaker ['heɪmeɪkər] N heneador *m*, -ora *f*, labrador *m*, -ora *f* que

trabaja en la siega (*or* la recolección) del heno.

haymaking ['heɪmeɪkɪŋ] N henificación *f*; época *f* del heno, siega *f* del heno, recolección *f* del heno.

hayseed* ['heɪsiːd] N (*US*) palurdo *m*, paleto* *m*.

haystack ['heɪstæk] N almiar *m*.

haywire* ['heɪwaɪər] ADJ (*confused*) en desorden; descompuesto; (*mad*) loco; **to go ~** (*person*) destornillarse*; (*scheme etc*) embrollarse, embarrullarse; **it's all gone ~** en eso existe la mayor confusión, todo está en desorden.

hazard ['hæzəd] **1** N riesgo *m*.

   2 ATTR: **~ warning lights** señales *fpl* de emergencia.

   3 VT **(a)** arriesgar, poner en peligro. **(b)** *guess, remark* atreverse a hacer, aventurar.

hazardous ['hæzədəs] ADJ arriesgado, peligroso; **~ pay** (*US*) prima *f* por trabajos peligrosos.

haze¹ [heɪz] N calina *f*, neblina *f*; (*fig*) confusión *f*; **a ~ of tobacco smoke filled the room** el cuarto estaba lleno de humo de tabaco.

haze² [heɪz] VT (*US*) gastar novatadas a.

hazel ['heɪzl] **1** N avellano *m*.

   2 ADJ *eyes* garzo.

hazelnut ['heɪzlnʌt] N avellana *f*.

hazelwood ['heɪzl,wʊd] N madera *f* de avellano.

haziness ['heɪzɪnɪs] N **(a)** lo calinoso, lo brumoso. **(b)** (*fig*) confusión *f*, vaguedad *f*.

hazing ['heɪzɪŋ] N (*US*) novatadas *fpl*; *ver también* │ SORORITY/FRATERNITY │.

hazy ['heɪzɪ] ADJ **(a)** calinoso, brumoso. **(b)** (*fig*) confuso, vago; **he's ~ about dates** no recuerda exactamente las fechas; **I'm ~ about maths** tengo solamente una idea vaga de las matemáticas; **he seemed very ~** parecía no tener ninguna idea clara.

H-bomb ['eɪtʃbɒm] N bomba *f* H.

HC, h. & c. ABBR *of* **hot and cold (water)**; *V* **hot 1(a)**.

HCF N ABBR *of* **highest common factor** máximo común divisor *m*.

HDTV N ABBR *of* **high definition television** televisión *f* de alta definición.

HE (a) ABBR *of* **high explosive. (b)** ABBR *of* **His** *or* **Her Excellency** Su Excelencia, S.E. **(c)** (*Eccl*) ABBR *of* **His Eminence** Su Eminencia, S.Emª.

he [hiː] **1** PRON él; **~ who** el que, quien.

   2 N macho *m*, varón *m*; **to play ~** (*children's game*) dar la despedida.

   3 ATTR macho.

head [hed] **1** N **(a)** (*Anat*) cabeza *f*; **~ of hair** cabellera *f*; **~ first, ~ foremost** de cabeza; **to go ~ over heels** caer patas arriba; **to fall ~ over heels in love with sb** enamorarse perdidamente de uno; **from ~ to foot** de pies a cabeza; **we are banging our ~s against a brick wall** estamos machacando en hierro frío; **to bite sb's ~ off** echar un rapapolvo a uno; **to give a horse its ~** dar rienda suelta a un caballo; **to give sb his ~** dar rienda suelta a uno; **she has her ~ in the clouds** está en las nubes; **to hide one's ~ in the sand** meter la cabeza debajo del ala; **now he can hold his ~ up again** ahora ha recuperado la propia estimación; **to keep one's ~ above water** (*fig*) ir tirando; **to laugh one's ~ off*** desternillarse de risa*; **to nod one's ~** asentir con la cabeza, mover la cabeza afirmativamente; **to shake one's ~** negar algo con la cabeza, mover la cabeza negativamente; **he stands ~ and shoulders above the rest** los demás no le llegan a la suela del zapato; **I could do it standing on my ~** lo podría hacer sin mirar; **to talk one's ~ off** hablar por los codos; **to turn one's ~ the other way** (*fig*) hacer la vista gorda; **he is taller than his brother by a ~** le saca la cabeza a su hermano; **to win by a (short) ~** ganar por una cabeza (escasa); **on his own ~ be it** sea bajo su propia responsabilidad; **to put a price on sb's ~** poner precio a la cabeza de uno; **to stand on one's ~** hacer el pino; **to stand an argument on its ~** demostrar la falsedad de un argumento; **to give orders over sb's ~** dar órdenes sin consultar a uno; **they went over my ~ to the mayor** hablaron con el alcalde sin hacer caso de mí; **to sell a house over sb's ~** vender una casa sin decir nada a uno; **the wine goes to my ~** el vino se me sube a la cabeza; **success has gone to his ~** el éxito le ha subido a la cabeza.

(b) (*intellect, mind*) cabeza *f*, inteligencia *f*; talento *m*; **two ~s are better than one** cuatro ojos ven más que dos; **don't bother your ~ about it** no te preocupes, no te canses tratando de explicarlo (*etc*); **it never entered my ~** jamás se me pasó por la cabeza; **to have a bad ~** tener dolor de cabeza; **to have a swelled** (*or* **swollen**) **~** ser vanidoso; **to have a ~ for business** tener talento para los negocios; **to have a ~ for languages** tener aptitud para los idiomas; **to have no ~ for heights** no tener cabeza para las alturas; **he has a good ~ on him** es inteligente, tiene cabeza, tiene talento; **to keep one's ~** no perder la cabeza; **to lose one's ~** perder la cabeza; **so we put our ~s together** así que tratamos los dos de resolverlo; **to turn sb's ~** (*make mad*) trastornar el juicio de uno, (*make vain*) envanecer a uno.

(c) (*phrases with prep*) **it was above their ~s** estaba fuera de su alcance, no eran lo bastante inteligentes para comprenderlo; **to do a sum in one's ~** hacer un cálculo mental; **to be soft** (*or* **weak**) **in the ~** ser un poco tocado, andar mal de la cabeza; **to get sth into**

sb's ~ meter a uno algo en la cabeza; **he has got it into his ~ that ...** cree firmemente que ...; **get it into your ~ that ...** date cuenta de que ...; **I can't get that tune out of my ~** me obsesiona esa melodía; **what put that into your ~?** ¿de dónde sacas eso?; **to take it into one's ~ to +** infin ocurrirse a uno + infin; **to be off one's ~** estar loco; **you must be off your ~!** ¿estás loco?; **this will bring matters to a ~** con esto las cosas llegarán a la crisis, con esto llegamos al momento de la verdad.

(d) (person) (leader) jefe m, cabeza m; (of school) director m, -ora f; **~ of a department** jefe m, -a f de departamento; **~ of state** jefe m, -a f de estado; **crowned ~** testa f coronada; **£5 a ~** 5 libras por persona (or por cabeza).

(e) (on coin) cara f; **to toss ~s or tails** echar a cara o cruz; **~s I win, tails you lose** cara, yo gano, cruz, tu pierdes; **I couldn't make ~ or tail of it** no logré sacar nada en claro, no tiene pies ni cabeza.

(f) **20 ~ of cattle** 20 reses fpl; **20 ~ of sheep** 20 ovejas fpl.

(g) (of objects etc) (of bed) cabecera f; (of table, bridge, nail etc) cabeza f; (of arrow etc) punta f; (of stick) puño m; (of cylinder) culata f; (Comput) cabeza f (grabadora), cabezal m; (Naut) proa f; (Geog) punta f; (of water) altura f de caída; (on beer) espuma f; (Bot) flor f, cabezuela f; (of tree) copa f; (of corn) espigas fpl; **at the ~ of the valley** al final del valle; **to bring sth to a ~** hacer que algo llegue a su punto decisivo; **to come to a ~** (abscess) supurar, (fig) llegar a la crisis.

(h) (heading) título m, encabezamiento m; (section) sección f, apartado m; **under this ~** en este apartado.

(i) (front place) cabeza f; **~ of the family** cabeza mf de la familia; **to be at the ~ of the list** encabezar la lista; **to be at the ~ of the league** ir en cabeza de la liga.

(j) **acid ~**✱ aficionado m, -a f al ácido.

(k) (US✱) cagadero✱ m.

2 ATTR **(a)** principal, primero; **~ boy** (Brit Scol) alumno m principal; **~ buyer** comprador m, -ora f principal; **~ clerk** encargado m, -a f; **~ cook** primer cocinero m, primera cocinera f, jefe m, -a f de cocina; **~ girl** (Brit Scol) alumna f principal; **~ man** (hum) jefe m; **~ office** oficina f central; **~ salesman** vendedor m en jefe; **to have a ~ start** (fig) empezar con gran ventaja (over con respecto a); **~ teacher** director m, -ora f; **~ waiter** jefe m de comedor.

(b) part delantero, de frente.

3 VT **(a)** list etc encabezar, estar a la cabeza de; league ir en cabeza de; poll ganar; rebellion acaudillar; company dirigir; team capitanear.

(b) football cabecear; goal cabecear, rematar con la cabeza.

(c) **he ~ed the boat for the shore** dirigió la barca hacia la costa; **to be ~ed for** ir con rumbo a.

4 VI: **to ~ for, to ~ towards** dirigirse a (or hacia); encaminarse a; **to be ~ing for** ir con rumbo a; **where are you ~ing for?** ¿adónde se dirige?; **we are ~ing for ruin** vamos camino de la ruina.

◆**head off** VT interceptar, atajar; desviar; (fig) distraer, apartar.

◆**head up** VT group, team estar a la cabeza de, dirigir.

headache ['hedeɪk] N dolor m de cabeza; (sick) jaqueca f; (fig) quebradero m de cabeza, dolor m de cabeza; **that's his ~** allá él, eso a él.

headband ['hedbænd] N cinta f (para la cabeza), venda f (para la cabeza).

headboard ['hedbɔːd] N cabecera f.

headcase✱ ['hedkeɪs] N (Brit) locatis✱ mf invar, majara✱ mf.

headcheese ['hedtʃiːz] N (US) carne f en gelatina.

head cold ['hedkəʊld] N resfriado m de cabeza.

headcount ['hedkaʊnt] N recuento m de la asistencia.

head-dress ['heddres] N toca f, tocado m.

headed ['hedɪd] ADJ notepaper membretado, con membrete.

-headed ['hedɪd] ADJ con cabeza ..., de cabeza ..., eg **small~** de cabeza pequeña; **fair~** pelirrubio.

header ['hedəʳ] N (fall) caída f de cabeza; (dive) salto m de cabeza; (Sport) cabezazo m; (Typ, Comput) encabezamiento m.

header-block ['hedə,blɒk] N bloque m de encabezamiento, encabezamiento m.

head-first [,hed'fɜːst] ADV de cabeza.

headgear ['hedɡɪəʳ] N sombrero m; (woman's) tocado m.

headguard ['hedɡɑːd] N casco m protector; protector m facial.

headhunt ['hed,hʌnt] VT cazar; **he was ~ed by a bank** fue cazado por un banco.

headhunter ['hed,hʌntəʳ] N cazador m de cabezas; (fig) cazatalentos mf, cazaejecutivos m, cazador m, -ora f de cabezas.

headhunting ['hed,hʌntɪŋ] **1** N (fig) caza f de cabezas, (fig) caza f de talentos, caza f de cerebros.

2 ATTR: **~ agency** agencia f de caza de talentos.

heading ['hedɪŋ] N (title) encabezamiento m, título m; (letterhead) membrete m; (section) sección f, apartado m; **to come under the ~ of** clasificarse bajo, estar incluido en.

headlamp ['hedlæmp] N (Brit) faro m.

headland ['hedlənd] N promontorio m.

headless ['hedlɪs] ADJ sin cabeza; acéfalo.

headlight ['hedlaɪt] N faro m.

headline ['hedlaɪn] **1** N encabezamiento m, cabeza f; **~s** titulares mpl; **this will hit the ~s** saldrá en primera plana, esto es sensacional.

2 VT anunciar con titulares.

headline news [,hedlaɪn'njuːz] N titulares mpl, noticias fpl de cabecera; **to be ~** ser noticia de cabecera; **to make ~** aparecer en los titulares.

headline rate ['hedlaɪn,reɪt] N: **the ~ of inflation** la tasa de inflación (calculada con variables como el tipo de interés hipotecario).

headlock ['hedlɒk] N: **to get/have sb in a ~** hacerle a uno una llave de cabeza, hacerle a uno una llave de yudo.

headlong ['hedlɒŋ] **1** ADJ fall de cabeza, de bruces; rush etc precipitado.

2 ADV de cabeza, de bruces; precipitadamente.

headman ['hedmæn] N, PL **headmen** ['hedmen] cacique m.

headmaster ['hed'mɑːstəʳ] N (Brit) director m (de colegio etc).

headmistress ['hed'mɪstrɪs] N (Brit) directora f (de colegio etc).

head-on ['hed'ɒn] **1** ADJ collision de frente, frontal.

2 ADV de frente; **he crashed ~ with a truck** colisionó frontalmente con un camión.

headphone(s) ['hedfəʊn(z)] N(PL) auricular(es) m(pl), audífono(s) m(pl).

headquarter ['hedkwɔːtəʳ] VT (US): **the company is ~ed in Reno** la compañía tiene su sede en Reno.

headquarters ['hed'kwɔːtəz] **1** NPL (Mil) cuartel m general; (of party, organization) sede f; (Comm) oficina f central, central f; (of revolt etc) centro m, foco m.

2 ATTR: **~ staff** plantilla f de la oficina central.

headrest ['hedrest] N reposacabezas m, apoyacabezas m.

head restraint ['hedrɪs'treɪnt] N (Aut) apoyacabezas m.

headroom ['hedrʊm] N espacio m para la cabeza; espacio m para estar (derecho) de pie; (under bridge etc) luz f, altura f libre; **'2 m ~'** '2 m. de altura libre'.

headscarf ['hedskɑːf] N, PL **~s** or **headscarves** ['hedskɑːvz] pañuelo m.

headset ['hedset] N auriculares mpl, audífonos mpl.

headship ['hedʃɪp] N jefatura f; dirección f; (of school) puesto m de director(a).

head-shrinker✱ ['hed,ʃrɪŋkəʳ] N psiquíatra mf.

headsman ['hedzmən] N, PL **headsmen** ['hedzmən] verdugo m.

headsquare ['hedskwɛəʳ] N pañuelo m de cabeza.

headstand ['hedstænd] N posición f de cabeza.

headstone ['hedstəʊn] N lápida f (mortuoria).

headstrong ['hedstrɒŋ] ADJ voluntarioso, impetuoso, testarudo.

headwaters ['hed,wɔːtəz] NPL cabecera f (de un río).

headway ['hedweɪ] N progreso m; **to make ~** avanzar, (fig) hacer progresos; **we could make no ~ against the current** no logramos avanzar contra la corriente, la corriente nos impidió avanzar; **I didn't make much ~ with him** no he conseguido hacer carrera con él.

headwind ['hedwɪnd] N viento m contrario, viento m de proa.

headword ['hedwɜːd] N (palabra f que encabeza un) artículo m.

heady ['hedɪ] ADJ wine fuerte, lleno, cabezudo; (fig) embriagador.

heal [hiːl] **1** VT curar, sanar (of de); (fig) curar, remediar.

2 VI (also **to ~ up**) cicatrizarse.

healer ['hiːləʳ] N curador m, -ora f.

healing ['hiːlɪŋ] **1** ADJ curativo, sanativo.

2 N curación f.

health [helθ] **1** N **(a)** (of person) salud f; (public ~) sanidad f, higiene f; (Brit) **Department of/Secretary of State for H~ and Social Security**, (US) **Department/Secretary of H~ and Human Services** Ministerio m de/Secretario m de Estado de Sanidad y Seguridad Social; **Minister/Ministry of H~** (Brit) Ministro m/Ministerio m de Sanidad, Dirección f General de Sanidad (Spain); **to be in good** (or **bad**) **~** estar bien (o mal) de salud; **to restore sb to ~** devolver la salud a uno.

(b) (toast) brindis m; **good ~!** ¡salud!; **here's a ~ to X!** ¡vaya por X!; **to drink (to) sb's ~** beber a la salud de uno, brindar por uno.

2 ATTR: **H~ Authority** (Brit) autoridades fpl sanitarias; **~ benefit** (US) subsidio m de enfermedad; **~ care** asistencia f sanitaria; **~ center** (US), **~ centre** centro m médico, ambulatorio m; **~ club** gimnasio m; **~ education** educación f sanitaria; **~ farm** centro m de salud; **~ foods** alimentos mpl naturales; **~ hazard** riesgo m para la salud; **~ insurance** seguro m de enfermedad; **~ problem** (personal) problema m de salud, (public) problema m sanitario; **~ resort** (watering place) balneario m; (in mountains) sanatorio m; **National H~ Service** Sistema m Nacional de Salud; **H~ Service doctor** médico m de la Seguridad Social; **~ visitor** auxiliar m sanitario, auxiliar f sanitaria.

healthful ['helθfʊl] ADJ, **health-giving** ['helθ,ɡɪvɪŋ] ADJ sano, saludable.

healthily ['helθɪlɪ] ADV live etc sanamente; **~ sceptical about ...** sanamente escéptico acerca de ...

healthy ['helθɪ] ADJ **(a)** (healthful) sano, saludable; place etc salubre. **(b)**

person sano, con buena salud; **to be ~** tener buena salud.

heap [hiːp] **1** N montón *m*, pila *f*, rimero *m*; (*fig**) montón* *m*; **a whole ~ of trouble** un montón de disgustos*; **a whole ~ of people** muchísimas personas; **~s of times** muchísimas veces; **we have ~s** tenemos montones*; **we have ~s of time** nos sobra tiempo, tenemos tiempo de sobra; **the news struck him all of a ~** la noticia le tumbó.
2 VT (*also* **to ~ up**) amontonar, apilar; *plate, spoon etc* colmar (*with* de); **to ~ together** juntar en un montón; **to ~ favours on sb** colmar a uno de favores.
3 ADV (*) **~s muchísimo; ~s better** muchísimo mejor.

hear [hɪəʳ] (*irr*: PRET AND PTP **heard**) **1** VT oír; (*perceive*) sentir; (*listen to*) escuchar; *lecture* asistir a; *piece of news* saber; (*Jur*) *case* ver; **do you ~ me?** ¿me oyes?; **I ~ bad reports of him** me dan malos informes sobre él; **I never ~d such rubbish!** ¡en mi vida he oído tantos disparates!; **I have ~d it said that ...** he oído decir que ...; **to ~ sb speak** oír hablar a uno; **I could hardly make myself ~d** apenas pude hacerme oír; **to ~ that ...** oír decir que ...; **when I ~d that ...** cuando supe que ...
2 VI oír; **~ ~!** ¡muy bien!; **to ~ about, to ~ of** oír hablar de, oír mentar (*LAm*), saber, enterarse de; **when I ~d of it** cuando lo supe; **I've never ~d of him** no le conozco en absoluto; **he won't ~ of it** no lo permite, no quiere autorizarlo; **I won't ~ of it!** ¡ni hablar!; **to ~ from** tener noticias de, recibir carta de; **you'll be ~ing from me** le escribiré; **you will ~ from my solicitor** Vd recibirá una comunicación de mi abogado; **let's ~ from you soon!** ¡no dejes de escribirnos pronto!, ¡mándanos noticias tuyas!
◆**hear out** VT: **to ~ sb out** escuchar a uno hasta el fin; **let us ~ him out** que diga todo lo que quiera.

heard [hɜːd] PRET AND PTP *of* **hear.**

hearer [ˈhɪərəʳ] N oyente *mf*.

hearing [ˈhɪərɪŋ] N **(a)** (*sense of ~*) oído *m*; **~ defect** defecto *m* auditivo; **in my ~** en mi presencia, estando yo delante; **to be out of ~** estar fuera del alcance del oído; **to be within ~** estar al alcance del oído. **(b)** (*act*) audición *f*; (*Jur*) vista *f*; **to condemn sb without a ~** condenar a uno sin escuchar su defensa; **he never got a fair ~** en ningún momento se le permitió explicar su punto de vista; (*Jur*) no se le juzgó imparcialmente.

hearing-aid [ˈhɪərɪŋeɪd] N aparato *m* del oído, audífono *m*.

hearing-assisted [ˈhɪərɪŋəˈsɪstɪd] ADJ (*US*): **~ telephone** teléfono *m* con sonido aumentado.

hearken [ˈhɑːkən] VI: **to ~ to** (††, *liter*) escuchar.

hearsay [ˈhɪəseɪ] **1** N rumores *mpl*, hablillas *fpl*; **it's just ~** son rumores; **by ~** de oídas.
2 ATTR: **~ evidence** testimonio *m* basado en lo que ha dicho otro.

hearse [hɜːs] N coche *m* fúnebre, coche *m* mortuorio.

heart [hɑːt] **1** N **(a)** (*Anat*) corazón *m*; **she spoke with beating ~** le palpitaba el corazón al decirlo; **to clasp sb to one's ~** abrazar a uno estrechamente; **to have a weak ~** ser cardíaco.
(b) (*fig*) (*Cards*) corazones *mpl*; (*in Spanish pack*) copas *fpl*; (*of lettuce*) cogollo *m*; (*of place, earth etc*) corazón *m*, seno *m*, centro *m*; **in the ~ of the country** en lo más retirado del campo; **in the ~ of the wood** en el centro del bosque; **the ~ of the matter** lo esencial, el quid del asunto, el grano.
(c) (*symbol of love*) corazón *m*; **with all one's ~** de todo corazón, con toda el alma; **affair of the ~** aventura *f* sentimental; **to break sb's ~** (*in love*) partir el corazón a uno, (*by behaviour etc*) matar a uno a disgustos; **to break one's ~ over** partirse el corazón por; **to die of a broken ~** morir de pena; **to lose one's ~ to** enamorarse de; **to wear one's ~ on one's sleeve** llevar el corazón en la mano; **to win sb's ~** enamorar a uno.
(d) (*seat of feeling, sympathy etc*) corazón *m*, alma *f*; **he's a man after my own ~** es un hombre como me gustan; **at ~** en el fondo; **to have sb's interests at ~** tener presente el interés de uno; **to be sick at ~** estar muy deprimido, sentirlo en el alma; **from the ~** con toda sinceridad; **his words came from the ~** sus palabras salieron del corazón; **in his ~ of ~s** en lo más íntimo de su corazón; **the plan is dear** (*or* **close**) **to my ~** con este proyecto se asocian mis sentimientos más íntimos; **with a heavy ~** con dolor, sintiéndolo; **his ~ is in the right place** es buena persona, tiene buen corazón; **to cut sb to the ~** herir a uno en lo vivo; **to cry one's ~ out** llorar a mares; **it would have done your ~ good** te habría alegrado el corazón; **to eat one's ~ out** estar muriéndose de pena; sufrir en silencio; **to have no ~** no tener entrañas; **have a ~!** ¡ten un poco de piedad!; **he has a ~ of gold** es buenísima persona, tiene buenísimo corazón; **to open one's ~ to sb** abrir su pecho con uno; **to set sb's ~ at rest** tranquilizar a uno; **to take sth to ~** tomar algo a pecho.
(e) (*seat of desire, intention*) **his ~ was not in it** no tenía fe en lo que estaba haciendo; **to set one's ~ on** poner el corazón en; **to throw o.s. ~ and soul into an enterprise** lanzarse de todo corazón a una empresa; *V* **content** *etc*.
(f) (*symbol of courage*) **to be in good ~** estar lleno de confianza,

(*soil*) estar en buen estado; **I could not find it in my ~ to + infin, I did not have the ~ to + infin** no tuve valor para + infin; **to have one's ~ in one's mouth** tener el alma en un hilo, tener el corazón en un puño; **to lose ~** descorazonarse; **to put new ~ into sb** infundir ánimo a uno; **my ~ sank** se me cayeron las alas del corazón; **to take ~** cobrar ánimo; **we may take ~ from the fact that ...** que nos aliente el hecho de que ...
(g) by ~ de memoria.
2 ATTR: **he's a ~ case, he has a ~ condition** sufre de una condición cardíaca; **~ complaint, ~ disease** enfermedad *f* cardíaca; **~ murmur** soplo *m* del corazón; **~ surgeon** cirujano *m* cardiólogo; **~ surgery** cirugía *f* cardíaca; **~ transplant** trasplante *m* del corazón; **~ trouble** enfermedad *f* cardíaca.

heartache [ˈhɑːteɪk] N angustia *f*, pena *f*.

heart-attack [ˈhɑːtətæk] N ataque *m* cardíaco.

heartbeat [ˈhɑːtbiːt] N latido *m* del corazón.

heartbreak [ˈhɑːtbreɪk] N angustia *f*, congoja *f*.

heartbreaking [ˈhɑːtˌbreɪkɪŋ] ADJ angustioso, desgarrador, que parte el corazón.

heartbroken [ˈhɑːtˌbrəʊkən] ADJ angustiado, acongojado; **she was ~ about it** esto le partió el corazón.

heartburn [ˈhɑːtbɜːn] N acedía *f*.

heartburning [ˈhɑːtˌbɜːnɪŋ] N (*bad feeling*) envidia *f*, rencor *m*; (*regret*) sentimiento *m*.

-hearted [ˈhɑːtɪd] ADJ de corazón ...; **faint~** medroso, pusilánime, apocado.

hearten [ˈhɑːtn] VT animar, alentar, infundir ánimo a.

heartening [ˈhɑːtnɪŋ] ADJ alentador.

heart failure [ˈhɑːtˌfeɪljəʳ] N fallo *m* de corazón, colapso *m* cardíaco.

heartfelt [ˈhɑːtfelt] ADJ cordial, sincero; *sympathy* más sentido; *thanks* más efusivo.

hearth [hɑːθ] N (*lit, fig*) hogar *m*, chimenea *f*.

hearth-rug [ˈhɑːθrʌg] N alfombrilla *f*.

heartily [ˈhɑːtɪlɪ] ADV sinceramente, cordialmente; enérgicamente; fuertemente; *laugh* a carcajadas; *eat* con buen apetito; *thank* con efusión; *sing* con entusiasmo; **to be ~ glad** alegrarse sinceramente; **to be ~ sick of** estar completamente harto de.

heartland [ˈhɑːtlænd] N corazón *m*; zona *f* central, zona *f* interior.

heartless [ˈhɑːtlɪs] ADJ cruel, inhumano.

heartlessly [ˈhɑːtlɪslɪ] ADV cruelmente, despiadadamente.

heartlessness [ˈhɑːtlɪsnɪs] N crueldad *f*, inhumanidad *f*.

heart-lung machine [ˌhɑːtˈlʌŋməˌʃiːn] N máquina *f* de circulación extracorpórea.

heartrending [ˈhɑːtˌrendɪŋ] ADJ angustioso, desgarrador; **it was ~ to see them** se me (*etc*) partía el corazón al verlos.

heart-searching [ˈhɑːtˌsɜːtʃɪŋ] N examen *m* de conciencia.

heart-shaped [ˈhɑːtʃeɪpt] ADJ acorazonado, en forma de corazón.

heartstrings [ˈhɑːtstrɪŋz] NPL fibras *fpl* del corazón; **to pull at** (*or* **touch**) **sb's ~** tocar la fibra sensible de uno.

heart-throb* [ˈhɑːtθrɒb] N persona *f* idolatrada; **Bogart was my mother's ~** mi madre idolatraba a Bogart; **he's the ~ of the teenagers** es el ídolo de las quinceañeras; **we met her latest ~** conocimos a su amiguito del momento.

heart-to-heart [ˈhɑːttəˈhɑːt] **1** ADJ íntimo, franco; **~ talk** = **2.**
2 N conversación *f* íntima.

heart-warming [ˈhɑːtˌwɔːmɪŋ] ADJ reconfortante, grato.

hearty [ˈhɑːtɪ] **1** ADJ *person* campechano, francote; *feelings* sincero, cordial; *effort* enérgico; *kick, slap etc* fuerte; *laugh* sano, franco; *appetite* bueno; *meal* abundante; *thanks* efusivo; **to be a ~ eater** tener buen diente.
2 N (*) tipo *m* campechano*.

heat [hiːt] **1** N **(a)** (*warmth*) calor *m*; (*heating system*) calefacción *f*; **in the ~ of the day** en las horas de más calor.
(b) (*fig*) calor *m*, ardor *m*, vehemencia *f*, pasión *f*; tensión *f*; **in the ~ of the moment** en el calor del momento; **when the ~ is on** cuando se aplican las presiones; **he replied with some ~** contestó bastante indignado; **it'll take the ~ off us** esto nos dará un respiro; **to take the ~ out of a situation** reducir la tensión de una situación; **to turn on the ~** empezar a ejercer presiones, (*Pol*) crear un ambiente de crisis.
(c) (*Sport*) (*prueba f*) eliminatoria *f*, prueba *f* clasificatoria.
(d) (*Zool*) celo *m*; **to be on ~** (*Brit*) estar en celo.
(e) (*US*‡: *police*) bofia‡ *f*.
(f) (*US*‡: *criticism*) **he took a lot of ~ for that mistake** le abuchararon por ese error‡.
2 ATTR: **~ exhaustion** agotamiento *m* por calor, debilidad *f* por calor; **~ loss** pérdida *f* de calor.
3 VT (*also* **to ~ up**) calentar; (*fig*) acalorar.
4 VI (*also* **to ~ up**) calentarse; (*fig*) calentarse, acalorarse.

heated [ˈhiːtɪd] ADJ **(a)** calentado; **~ pool** piscina *f* de agua calentada; **~ rear window** luneta *f* trasera térmica. **(b)** (*fig*) *discussion etc* acalorado; **to become ~** acalorarse.

heatedly ['hi:tɪdlɪ] ADV con vehemencia, con pasión; **he replied ~** contestó indignado.

heater ['hi:təʳ] N calentador *m*.

heath [hi:θ] N (*place*) brezal *m*; (*plant*) brezo *m*; **native ~** patria *f* chica.

heat haze ['hi:theɪz] N neblina *f* de calor.

heathen ['hi:ðən] **1** ADJ pagano.
2 N pagano *m*, -a *f*; (*fig*) bárbaro *m*, -a *f*.

heathenish ['hi:ðənɪʃ] ADJ pagano, gentílico.

heathenism ['hi:ðənɪzəm] N paganismo *m*.

heather ['heðəʳ] N brezo *m*.

heating ['hi:tɪŋ] **1** N calefacción *f*.
2 ATTR: **~ engineer** técnico *m* en calefacciones; **~ plant** = **~ system**; **~ power** poder *m* calorífico; **~ system** sistema *m* de calefacción.

heatproof ['hi:tpru:f] ADJ, **heat-resistant** ['hi:trɪ,zɪstənt] ADJ termorresistente, a prueba de calor; *ovenware* refractario.

heat rash ['hi:træʃ] N sarpullido *m*.

heat-seeking ['hi:tsi:kɪŋ] ADJ: **~ missile** misil *m* buscador del calor.

heat-sensitive ['hi:t'sensɪtɪv] ADJ sensible al calor.

heat-shield ['hi:tʃi:ld] N escudo *m* contra el calor.

heatstroke ['hi:tstrəʊk] N insolación *f*, golpe *m* de calor.

heat treatment ['hi:t,tri:tmənt] N tratamiento *m* de calor.

heatwave ['hi:tweɪv] N ola *f* de calor.

heave [hi:v] **1** N (*lift*) esfuerzo *m* para levantar; (*pull*) tirón *m* (on de); (*push*) empujón *m*; (*throw*) echada *f*, tirada *f*; **with a ~ of his shoulders** con un fuerte movimiento de hombros; **one more ~ and they're out** un empujón más y los echamos fuera a todos.
2 VT (*irr: pret and ptp* **heaved**, (*Naut*) PRET AND PTP **hove**) (*pull*) tirar de; (*push*) empujar; (*lift*) levantar; (*drag*) arrastrar; (*carry*) llevar; (*throw*) tirar, lanzar; *sigh* exhalar.
3 VI (**a**) (*water etc*) subir y bajar, agitarse; (*surface*) palpitar, ondular; (*feel sick*) basquear, tener náuseas; **it makes me ~** me da asco; **to ~ at, to ~ on** tirar de; (*Naut*) jalar. (**b**) **to ~ in(to) sight** aparecer.
◆**heave to** VI ponerse al pairo.
◆**heave up** VT (*vomit*) devolver, arrojar.

heave-ho ['hi:v'həʊ] INTERJ ¡ahora!, (*Naut*) ¡iza!; **to give sb the ~*** dar el pasaporte a uno*.

heaven ['hevn] N (**a**) cielo *m*; **~s** cielos *mpl*; (*good*) **~s!** ¡cielos!; **thank ~!** ¡gracias a Dios!; **~ forbid!** ¡no lo quiera Dios!; **~ forbid that I ...** Dios me libre de + *infin*; **for ~'s sake!** ¡por Dios!; **seventh ~** paraíso *m*; **to be in seventh ~** estar en el séptimo cielo; **an injustice that cries out to ~** una injusticia que clama al cielo; **~ knows why** Dios sabe por qué; **~ knows I tried enough** Dios sabe lo mucho que me esforcé; **what in ~'s name does that mean?** ¿qué demonios quieres decir con eso?; **to move ~ and earth** remover cielo y tierra, remover Roma con Santiago (*to* + *infin* para + *infin*); **to stink to high ~** heder a perro muerto.
(**b**) (*fig*) paraíso *m*; **the trip was ~** el viaje fue una maravilla; **this place is just ~** este lugar es el paraíso; **isn't he ~?** ¡qué hombre más estupendo!

heavenly ['hevnlɪ] ADJ (**a**) celestial; (*Astron*) celeste; **~ body** cuerpo *m* celeste; **H~ Father** Padre *m* celestial. (**b**) (*fig*) maravilloso, estupendo.

heaven-sent ['hevn'sent] ADJ milagroso, como llovido del cielo.

heavenward(s) ['hevnwəd(z)] ADV hacia el cielo.

heavily ['hevɪlɪ] ADV *fall, move, tread* pesadamente; *rain* fuertemente, mucho; *concentrate* densamente; *sigh, sleep* profundamente; *drink* con exceso; **~ underlined** subrayado con línea gruesa; **to be ~ in debt** estar muy endeudado; **your account is ~ overdrawn** su cuenta tiene un grave saldo deudor; **to lean ~ on** apoyarse mucho en; **to lose ~** (*team*) sufrir una grave derrota, (*gambler*) tener pérdidas cuantiosas; **it weighs ~ on him** pesa mucho sobre él; **she's ~ into spiritualism*** (*esp Brit*) está profundamente metida en el espiritismo, se dedica con pasión al espiritismo.

heavily-built ['hevɪlɪ'bɪlt] ADJ corpulento.

heavily-laden [,hevɪlɪ'leɪdən] ADJ muy cargado.

heaviness ['hevɪnɪs] N peso *m*; pesadez *f* (*also fig*); lo fuerte, fuerza *f*; densidad *f*; gravedad *f*; (*drowsiness*) letargo *m*, modorra *f*; **~ of heart** tristeza *f*.

heavy ['hevɪ] **1** ADJ (**a**) pesado; **to be ~** ser pesado, pesar mucho; **is it ~?** ¿pesa mucho?; **how ~ are you?** ¿cuánto pesas?
(**b**) (*fig*) *cruiser, fall, industry, tread* pesado; *cloth, features, line, sea, type* grueso; *emphasis, expense, meal, rain, scent, shower* fuerte; *concentration, population, traffic* denso; (*boring*) pesado; *book, film* pesado; *atmosphere* pesado, opresivo; *blow* fuerte, duro; *build of person* corpulento; *burden* (*fig*) grave, oneroso; *crop* abundante; *defeat* grave; *feeling* aletargado; *fire* (*Mil*) intenso; *food* indigesto; *heart* triste; *humour* laborioso; *liquid* espeso, viscoso; *loss* considerable, cuantioso; *movement* lento, torpe, pesado; *part* (*Theat*) serio, trágico; *responsibility* grave; *sigh, silence, sleep* profundo; *sky* encapotado; *soil* arcilloso; *surface* difícil; *task* duro, penoso; **~ artillery** artillería *f* pesada; **~ breathing** respiración *f* agitada; **~ cream** (*US*) nata *f* enriquecida; **~ goods** géneros *mpl* de

bulto; **~ goods vehicle** vehículo *m* pesado; **~ industry** industria *f* pesada; **~ smoker** gran fumador *m*; **~ type** negrita *f*; **~ user** usuario *m*, -a *f* de gran cantidad; **we are ~ users of paper** usamos mucho papel, somos grandes consumidores de papel; **~ water** agua *f* pesada; **~ wine** vino *m* fuerte; **the mayor's ~ mob*** los forzudos del alcalde, los esbirros del alcalde; **eyes ~ with sleep** ojos de sueño; **the air was ~ with scent** el aire estaba cargado de perfumes; **I've had a ~ day** he tenido un día muy cargado; **to be a ~ drinker** (*etc*) beber (*etc*) mucho, beber (*etc*) con exceso; **to be a ~ sleeper** tener el sueño profundo; **the book has a lot of ~ symbolism** el libro tiene gran densidad de simbolismo, el libro tiene mucho simbolismo concentrado.
2 N (**a**) (*) forzudo *m*, gorila* *m*, matón *m*. (**b**) (*Scot: beer*) cerveza tostada.

heavy-duty [,hevɪ'dju:tɪ] ATTR para cargas pesadas.

heavy-handed [,hevɪ'hændɪd] ADJ (*harsh*) de mano dura; (*clumsy*) torpe, desmañado.

heavy-hearted [,hevɪ'hɑ:tɪd] ADJ afligido, apesadumbrado.

heavy-laden [,hevɪ'leɪdn] ADJ lastrado.

heavy-set ['hevɪ'set] ADJ (*US*) corpulento, fornido.

heavyweight ['hevɪweɪt] **1** ADJ pesado, de mucho peso.
2 N (*Boxing*) peso *m* pesado; (*important person*) pez *m* gordo*.

Hebe‡ ['hi:bɪ] N (*US pej*) judío *m*, -a *f*.

he-bear ['hi:bɛəʳ] N oso *m* macho.

Hebraic [hɪ'breɪɪk] ADJ hebraico.

Hebraist ['hi:breɪɪst] N hebraísta *mf*.

Hebrew ['hi:bru:] **1** ADJ hebreo.
2 N (**a**) hebreo *m*, -a *f*. (**b**) (*Ling*) hebreo *m*.

Hebrides ['hebrɪdi:z] NPL Hébridas *fpl*.

heck [hek] INTERJ (*euph*) = **hell**.

heckle ['hekl] VTI interrumpir, molestar con preguntas.

heckler ['hekləʳ] N el (la) que interrumpe (*or* molesta) a un orador.

heckling ['heklɪŋ] N interrupciones *fpl*, gritos *mpl* de protesta.

hectare ['hektɑ:ʳ] N hectárea *f*.

hectic ['hektɪk] ADJ (*fig*) febril; *speed* loco; **we had 3 ~ days** tuvimos 3 días llenos de frenética actividad, tuvimos 3 días llenos de confusión (or incertidumbre *etc*); **he has a ~ life** tiene una vida muy agitada; **things are pretty ~ here** aquí es la monda; **the journey was pretty ~** el viaje era para volverse loco.

hectogram(me) ['hektəʊgræm] N hectogramo *m*.

hectolitre, (*US*) **hectoliter** ['hektəʊ,li:təʳ] N hectolitro *m*.

Hector ['hektəʳ] NPR Héctor.

hector ['hektəʳ] **1** VT intimidar con bravatas.
2 VI echar bravatas.

hectoring ['hektərɪŋ] ADJ *person* lleno de bravatas; *tone, remark* amedrentador.

he'd [hi:d] = **he would**; **he had.**

hedge [hedʒ] **1** N (**a**) seto *m* vivo. (**b**) (*fig*) defensa *f*, protección *f*; (*Fin*) cobertura *f*; **as a ~ against inflation** para protegerse contra la inflación.
2 VT (**a**) cercar con un seto.
(**b**) (*fig*) **to ~ sth about, to ~ sth in** rodear algo, encerrar algo; **to be ~d about with** estar erizado de.
(**c**) **to ~ a bet** hacer apuestas compensatorias.
3 VI (**a**) contestar con evasivas, no querer comprometerse a nada; **stop ~ing!, don't ~ with me!** ¡dímelo sin sofismas!
(**b**) (*Fin*) **to ~ against inflation** cubrirse contra la inflación.
◆**hedge off** VT separar con un seto.

hedge clippers ['hedʒ,klɪpəz] NPL tijeras *fpl* de podar.

hedgehog ['hedʒhɒg] N erizo *m*.

hedgehop ['hedʒhɒp] VI volar a ras de tierra.

hedgerow ['hedʒrəʊ] N seto *m* vivo.

hedgesparrow ['hedʒ,spærəʊ] N acentor *m* (común).

hedging ['hedʒɪŋ] N (**a**) (*Bot*) seto *m* vivo; **~ plant** planta *f* para seto vivo. (**b**) (*fig: evasions*) evasivas *fpl*; sofismas *mpl*. (**c**) (*Fin etc*) cobertura *f*.

hedonism ['hi:dənɪzəm] N hedonismo *m*.

hedonist ['hi:dənɪst] N hedonista *mf*.

hedonistic [,hi:də'nɪstɪk] ADJ hedonista.

heebie-jeebies* [,hi:bɪ'dʒi:bɪz] NPL: **to have the ~** (*shaking*) tener un tembleque*; (*fright, nerves*) estar hecho un flan*, estar que no se cabe dentro de la camisa*; **it gives me the ~** (*revulsion*) me da asco; (*fright, apprehension*) me da escalofríos.

heed [hi:d] **1** N atención *f*; **to give** (*or* **pay**) **~ to** prestar atención a, hacer caso de; **to take no ~ of sth** no hacer caso de algo, hacer caso omiso de algo, no tener algo en cuenta; **to take ~ to** + *infin* poner atención en + *infin*; **take ~!** ¡ten cuidado!; ¡atención!
2 VT prestar atención a, hacer caso de; tener en cuenta.

heedless ['hi:dlɪs] ADJ desatento, descuidado; **to be ~ of** no hacer caso de.

heedlessly ['hi:dlɪslɪ] ADV sin hacer caso.

heehaw ['hi:hɔ:] **1** N rebuzno *m*.

2 VI rebuznar.

heel¹ [hi:l] **1** N (**a**) (*Anat*) talón *m*, calcañar *m*; (*of shoe*) tacón *m*; **to be at** (*or* **on**) **sb's ~s** pisar los talones a uno; **to be down at ~** ir mal vestido, estar desaseado; **to be under the ~ of** estar bajo los talones de; **to bring sb to ~** sobreponerse a uno, meter a uno en cintura; **to cool one's ~s** hacer antesala, tener que esperar; **to dig one's ~s in** mantenerse en sus trece; **to drag one's ~** arrastrar los pies; **to follow hard on sb's ~s** seguir a uno muy de cerca; **to be hot on sb's ~s**, **to tread hard on sb's ~s** pisar los talones de uno; **to keep to ~** (*dog*) obedecer, seguir de cerca al dueño (*etc*); **to kick one's ~s** no tener nada que hacer; **to show sb a clean pair of ~s**, **to take to one's ~s** poner pies en polvorosa; **to turn on one's ~** dar media vuelta.
(**b**) (*) canalla *m*.
2 VT (**a**) *shoe* poner tacón a; **to be well ~ed*** ser un ricacho.
(**b**) *ball* talonear.

heel² [hi:l] VI: **to ~ over** ladearse, (*Naut*) zozobrar, escorar.

heel bar ['hi:lbɑ:ʳ] N rápido *m*, (tienda *f* de) reparación *f* de calzado al momento.

heft* [heft] **1** N (*US*) peso *m*; (*fig*) influencia *f*; **the ~ of** la mayor parte de.
2 VT levantar; sopesar.

hefty* ['heftɪ] ADJ *object* pesado; *person* fuerte, fornido; *dose etc* grande, mayúsculo; *book, file etc* abultado.

hegemony [hɪ'gemənɪ] N hegemonía *f*.

hegira [he'dʒaɪərə] N hégira *f*.

he-goat ['hi:gəʊt] N macho *m* cabrío.

heifer ['hefəʳ] N novilla *f*, vaquilla *f*.

heigh [heɪ] INTERJ ¡oye!, ¡eh!

heigh-ho ['heɪ'həʊ] INTERJ ¡ay!

height [haɪt] N (**a**) (*altitude*) altura *f*, elevación *f*, altitud *f*; **~ above sea level** altura *f* sobre el nivel del mar; **at a ~ of 2000 m** a una altura de 2000 m; **to be 20 m in ~** medir (*LAm*: tener) 20 m de alto, tener una altura de 20 m; **to gain ~** ganar altura; **to lose ~** perder altura.
(**b**) (*of person*) talla *f*, estatura *f*; **of average ~** de mediana estatura, de talla mediana; **he drew himself up to his full ~** se irguió; **what ~ are you?** ¿cuánto mides de alto?
(**c**) (*hill*) colina *f*, cerro *m*; **the ~s** las cumbres.
(**d**) (*fig*) (*of fever*) crisis *f*; **the ~ of absurdity** el colmo de lo absurdo; **it's the ~ of fashion** está muy de moda; **at the ~ of summer** en los días más calurosos del verano; **at the ~ of the battle** en los momentos más críticos de la batalla; **his performance never reached the ~s** su actuación nunca llegó a las alturas.

heighten ['haɪtn] VT (*raise*) elevar, hacer más alto; (*increase*) aumentar; (*enhance*) realzar, intensificar.

heinous ['heɪnəs] ADJ atroz, nefando.

heir [ɛəʳ] N heredero *m*, -a *f*; **~ apparent**, **~ at law** heredero *m* forzoso, heredera *f* forzosa; **~ to the throne** heredero *m*, -a *f* del trono; **he is ~ to a fortune** ha de heredar una fortuna.

heiress ['ɛəres] N heredera *f*; (*) soltera *f* adinerada.

heirloom ['ɛəlu:m] N reliquia *f* de familia.

heist: [haɪst] (*US*) **1** N robo *m* a mano armada.
2 VT robar a mano armada.

held [held] PRET AND PTP *of* **hold**.

Helen ['helɪn] NF Elena, Helena.

helical ['helɪkəl] ADJ helicoidal.

helicopter ['helɪkɒptəʳ] **1** N helicóptero *m*.
2 ATTR: **~ gunship** helicóptero *m* de combate, helicóptero *m* artillado; **~ pad = helipad**; **~ station** helipuerto *m*.
3 VT: **to ~ troops in** transportar tropas por helicóptero, helitransportar tropas.

heliograph ['hi:lɪəʊgrɑ:f] N heliógrafo *m*.

heliostat ['hi:lɪəʊstæt] N heliostato *m*.

heliotrope ['hi:lɪətrəʊp] N heliotropo *m*.

helipad ['helɪpæd] N plataforma *f* de helicóptero, pista *f* de helicóptero.

heliport ['helɪpɔ:t] N helipuerto *m*.

helium ['hi:lɪəm] N helio *m*.

helix ['hi:lɪks] N, PL **helices** ['helɪsi:z] hélice *f*.

hell [hel] N infierno *m*; **~!, oh ~!** ¡demonio!; **all ~ was let loose** se desencadenó un ruido infernal; fue la monda; **a ~ of a lot** muchísimos, la mar de, una barbaridad de; **a ~ of a noise** un ruido de todos los diablos; **we had a ~ of a time** (*bad*) pasamos un rato malísimo, (*good*) lo pasamos en grande; **they did it just for the ~ of it** lo hicieron sólo por el gusto de hacerlo, lo hicieron porque sí; **who the ~ are you?** ¿quién demonios es Vd?; **what the ~!** ¡qué diantre!; **what the ~ do you want?** ¿qué demonios quieres?; **like ~!** ¡ni hablar!; **to run like ~** correr a todo correr; **to work like ~** trabajar como un demonio; **it was as hot as ~** hacía un calor del infierno; **come ~ or high water** contra viento y marea; **get the ~ out of here!** ¡vete al diablo!; **let's get the ~ out of here!** ¡vámonos!;

to give sb ~ poner a uno como un trapo; **to go ~ for leather** ir como el demonio; **go to ~!** ¡vete al diablo!; **till ~ freezes over** hasta cuando la rana críe pelo; **I hope to ~ that ...!** ¡ojalá ...!; **to make sb's life ~** amargar la vida a uno; **there'll be (all) ~ to pay** esto sí que nos va a costar carísimo; **to raise ~** armar la gorda.

he'll [hi:l] = **he will**; **he shall**.

hellacious* [he'leɪʃəs] ADJ (*US*) infernal.

hellbent ['hel'bent] ADJ (**a**) (*determined*) totalmente resuelto; **to be ~ on doing sth** estar totalmente resuelto a hacer algo. (**b**) (*fast*) rapidísimo, velocísimo.

hellcat ['helkæt] N harpía *f*, bruja *f*.

hellebore ['helɪbɔ:ʳ] N eléboro *m*.

Hellene ['heli:n] N heleno *m*, -a *f*.

Hellenic [he'li:nɪk] ADJ helénico.

Hellespont ['helɪspɒnt] N Helesponto *m*.

hellfire ['helfaɪəʳ] N llamas *fpl* del infierno.

hellhole ['helhəʊl] N infierno *m*.

hellish ['helɪʃ] **1** ADJ infernal, diabólico; (*) horrible.
2 ADV (‡) muy, terriblemente.

hellishly* ['helɪʃlɪ] ADV endemoniadamente.

hello [hʌ'ləʊ] = **hullo**.

hell's angel [,helz'eɪndʒəl] N ángel *m* del infierno.

helluva: ['heləvə] = **hell of a**; V **hell**.

helm [helm] N timón *m*; **to be at the ~** (*fig*) gobernar, estar en el mando.

helmet ['helmɪt] N casco *m*.

helmsman ['helmzmən] N, PL **helmsmen** ['helmzmən] timonel *m*.

▼ **help** [help] **1** N (**a**) ayuda *f*; auxilio *m*, socorro *m*; favor *m*, protección *f*; **~!** ¡socorro!; **by** (*or* **with**) **the ~ of** con la ayuda de; **without ~** sin ayuda de nadie; **to call for ~** pedir socorro; **to come to sb's ~** acudir en auxilio de uno; **there's no ~ for it** no hay más remedio; **to be past ~** estar desahuciado.
(**b**) (*person: servant*) criada *f*, (*in shop etc*) empleado *m*; **daily ~** asistenta *f*; **mother's ~** niñera *f*; **she has no ~ in the house** no tiene criada; **we're short of ~ in the shop** nos falta personal en la tienda; **'~ wanted'** (*US*) 'ofertas *fpl* de trabajo'; **he's a great ~** me ayuda muchísimo; **you're a great ~!** (*iro*) ¡valiente ayuda!

▼ **2** VT (**a**) ayudar; (*esp in distress*) auxiliar, socorrer; *scheme etc* promover; *progress* facilitar; *pain* aliviar; **so ~ me God!** bien lo sabe Dios; (*as oath*) ¡así Dios me salve!; **to ~ sb to do sth** ayudar a uno a hacer algo; **this will ~ to save it** esto contribuirá a salvarlo; **to ~ sb down** ayudar a uno a bajar; **to ~ sb on with a dress** ayudar a uno a ponerse un vestido; **to ~ sb out of a jam** ayudar a uno a salir de un apuro; **to ~ sb up** ayudar a uno a subir.
(**b**) (*at table*) servir; **to ~ sb to soup** servir la sopa a uno.
(**c**) (*avoid*) **he can't ~ coughing** no puede dejar de toser; **I couldn't ~ (doing) it** no pude menos de hacerlo; **he's a chap you couldn't ~ but admire** es un tío que no se puede menos de admirar; **it can't be ~ed** no hay más remedio, no queda otra (*LAm*); **he won't if I can ~** it no lo hará si yo puedo evitarlo; **can I ~ it if it rains?** ¿es que yo puedo impedir que llueva?; **don't spend more than you can ~** no gastes más de lo necesario.

▼ **3** VI ayudar.
4 VR: **to ~ o.s.** ayudarse a sí mismo; (*at table*) servirse; **~ yourself** (*to food*) ¡sírvete!, (*to other things*) está a tu disposición, toma cuanto quieras; **to ~ o.s. to** *food* servirse, (*steal*) alzarse con, llevarse, robar.

◆ **help along** VT *person* ayudar; *scheme etc* promover, fomentar.

◆ **help out 1** VT: **to ~ sb out** ayudar a uno; (*of a vehicle*) ayudar a uno a bajar.
2 VI ayudar.

helper ['helpəʳ] N ayudante *mf*, asistente *mf*; auxiliar *mf*; (*co-worker*) colaborador *m*, -ora *f*.

helpful ['helpfʊl] ADJ útil, provechoso; *attitude, remark* positivo; *person* servicial, atento; **he was very ~ to me** me ayudó mucho; **you have been most ~** Vd ha sido muy amable; **it would be ~ if you could come** sería bueno que pudieras venir; **would it be ~ if ...?** ¿sería conveniente que ...?

helpfully ['helpfəlɪ] ADV amablemente.

helpfulness ['helpfʊlnɪs] N utilidad *f*; (*of person*) amabilidad *f*.

helping ['helpɪŋ] **1** ADJ: **to give sb a ~ hand** echar una mano a uno.
2 N porción *f*, ración *f*; **will you have a second ~?** ¿quieres servirte más?

helpless ['helplɪs] ADJ (*forsaken*) desamparado; (*destitute*) desvalido; (*powerless*) impotente; (*of weak character*) débil, incapaz, inútil; *creature* indefenso; *invalid* imposibilitado; **we were ~ to do anything about it** nos veíamos imposibilitados para remediarlo; **to feel ~** sentirse perplejo, estar indeciso.

helplessly ['helplɪslɪ] ADV *struggle* en vano; **he said ~** dijo indeciso.

helplessness ['helplɪsnɪs] N desamparo *m*; impotencia *f*; incapacidad *f*, inutilidad *f*; irresolución *f*.

helpline ['helplaɪn] N teléfono *m* de la esperanza.

helpmate ['helpmeɪt] N buen compañero *m*, buena compañera *f*;

Helsinki ['helsɪŋkɪ] N Helsinki *m*.
helter-skelter ['heltə'skeltəʳ] ① ADV atropelladamente.
  ② N **(a)** (*rush*) desbandada *f* general. **(b)** (*Brit: at fair*) tobogán *m*.
hem [hem] N dobladillo *m*; (*edge*) orilla *f*.
◆**hem in** VT encerrar, cercar (*also Mil*).
he-man* ['hi:mæn] N, PL **he-men** ['hi:men] machote *m*.
hematology [,hi:mə'tɒlədʒɪ] N (*US*) = **haematology**.
hematoma [,hi:mə'təumə] N (*US*) = **haematoma**.
hemicycle ['hemɪsaɪkl] N hemiciclo *m*.
hemiplegia [hemɪ'pli:dʒɪə] N hemiplejía *f*.
hemiplegic [,hemɪ'pli:dʒɪk] ① ADJ hemiplégico.
  ② N hemiplégico *m*, -a *f*.
hemisphere ['hemɪsfɪəʳ] N hemisferio *m*.
hemispheric ['hemɪsferɪk] ADJ de este hemisferio; **a ~ free trade zone** zona de libre comercio en este hemisferio; **Western ~ nations** naciones del hemisferio occidental.
hemistich ['hemɪstɪk] N hemistiquio *m*.
hemline ['hemlaɪn] N bajo *m* (del vestido).
hemlock ['hemlɒk] N cicuta *f*.
hemo... ['hi:məu] *etc* (*US*) = **haemo...** *etc*.
hemp [hemp] N cáñamo *m*; (*Indian ~*) hachís *m*.
hemstitch ['hemstɪtʃ] N vainica *f*.
hen [hen] ① N gallina *f*; (*female bird*) hembra *f*.
  ② ADJ **(a)** (*Orn*) **the ~ bird** el pájaro hembra. **(b)** de mujeres, para mujeres; femenino; **~ party** reunión *f* de mujeres; **Tuesday is ~ night in this pub** la noche del martes en este bar es para mujeres (solas).
henbane ['henbeɪn] N beleño *m*.
hence [hens] ADV **(a)** (*place*) de aquí, desde aquí; (*poet*) **~!** ¡fuera de aquí! **(b)** (*time*) desde ahora; **5 years ~** de aquí a 5 años.
  (c) (*therefore*) por lo tanto, por eso; **~ my letter** de aquí que le escribiera; **~ the fact that ...** de aquí que ...
henceforth ['hens'fɔ:θ] ADV, **henceforward** ['hens'fɔ:wəd] ADV de hoy en adelante, (*of past time*) en lo sucesivo.
henchman ['hentʃmən] N, PL **henchmen** ['hentʃmən] (*follower*) secuaz *m*, partidario *m*; (*guard*) guardaespaldas *m*.
hen-coop ['hen,ku:p] N gallinero *m*.
hendecasyllabic ['hendekəsɪ'læbɪk] ADJ endecasílabo.
hendecasyllable ['hendekə,sɪləbl] N endecasílabo *m*.
henhouse ['hen'haus] N, PL **henhouses** ['hen,hauzɪz] gallinero *m*.
henna ['henə] N alheña *f*.
hennaed ['henəd] ADJ *hair* alheñado.
henpecked ['henpekt] ADJ dominado por su mujer; **~ husband** calzonazos* *m*.
Henry ['henrɪ] NM Enrique.
hepatitis [,hepə'taɪtɪs] N hepatitis *f*.
heptagon ['heptəgən] N heptágono *m*.
heptagonal [hep'tægənəl] ADJ heptagonal.
heptameter [hep'tæmɪtəʳ] N heptámetro *m*.
heptathlon [hep'tæθlən] N heptatlón *m*.
her [hɜ:ʳ] ① PRON **(a)** (*direct*) la; **I see ~** la veo; **I have never seen HER** a ella no la he visto nunca; **H~ Indoors***, **H~ Inside*** la parienta*.
  (b) (*indirect*) le; **I gave ~ the book** le di el libro; **I'm speaking to ~** le estoy hablando. **(c)** (*after prep*) ella; **he thought of ~** pensó en ella; **without ~** sin ella; **if I were ~** yo que ella; **it's ~** es ella; **younger than ~** más joven (*or* menor) que ella.
  ② POSS ADJ su, sus; **~ book/table** su libro/mesa; **~ friends** sus amigos.
Heracles ['herə,kli:z] NM Heracles.
Heraclitus [,herə'klaɪtəs] NM Heráclito.
herald ['herəld] ① N heraldo *m*; (*fig*) precursor *m*, anunciador *m*.
  ② VT anunciar, proclamar.
heraldic [he'rældɪk] ADJ heráldico.
heraldry ['herəldrɪ] N heráldica *f*.
herb [hɜ:b, *US* ɜ:rb] N hierba *f* (fina); **~ tea** infusión *f* de hierbas.
herbaceous [hɜ:'beɪʃəs] ADJ herbáceo.
herbage ['hɜ:bɪdʒ] N herbaje *m*, vegetación *f*, plantas *fpl*.
herbal ['hɜ:bəl] ADJ herbario; **~ tea** infusión *f* de hierbas.
herbalism ['hɜ:bəlɪzəm] N fitoterapia *f*, uso de plantas medicinales.
herbalist ['hɜ:bəlɪst] N herbolario *m*, -a *f*.
herbarium [hɜ:'beərɪəm] N herbario *m*.
herbert* ['hɜ:bət] N tipo* *m*, tío* *m*; **some ~** algún tío*.
herb-garden ['hɜ:b,gɑ:dn] N jardín *m* de hierbas finas.
herbicide ['hɜ:bɪsaɪd] N herbicida *m*.
herbivore ['hɜ:bɪ,vɔ:ʳ] N herbívoro *m*.
herbivorous [hɜ:'bɪvərəs] ADJ herbívoro.
Herculean [,hɜ:kju'li:ən] ADJ hercúleo; **~ task** obra *f* de romanos.
Hercules ['hɜ:kjuli:z] NM Hércules.
herd [hɜ:d] ① N rebaño *m*, hato *m*, manada *f*; (*of pigs*) piara *f*; (*of people etc*) multitud *f*, tropel *m*; **the common ~** el vulgo; **~ instinct** instinto *m* gregario.

② VT (*tend*) guardar; (*gather*) reunir en manada (*etc*); (*move*) llevar en manada.
◆**herd together** VI reunirse en manada, (*in confusion*) apiñarse unos contra otros; (*people*) reunirse, ir juntos.
herd-book ['hɜ:dbuk] N libro *m* genealógico.
herdsman ['hɜ:dzmən] N, PL **herdsmen** ['hɜ:dzmən] (*of cattle*) vaquero *m*; (*of sheep etc*) pastor *m*.
here [hɪəʳ] ① ADV (*place where*) aquí; (*motion to*) acá; **~!** (*at roll call*) ¡presente!, (*offering sth*) ¡toma!, (INTERJ) ¡oye!, ¡eh!; **~ and now** ahora mismo; **~ and there** aquí y allá; **~, there and everywhere** en todas partes; **~ below** aquí abajo; **in ~, please** por aquí, por favor; **up to ~** hasta aquí; **my mate ~ will do it** este compañero mío lo hará; **and ~ he laughed** y en este punto se rió; **~ is, ~ are** he aquí; **~ it is** aquí lo tienes; **that's neither ~ nor there** eso no viene al caso; **spring is ~** ha llegado la primavera; **he's ~ at last** por fin ha llegado; **~'s to X!** ¡vaya por X!; **come ~!** ¡ven acá!; **~ he comes** ya viene.
  ② N: **the ~ and now** la situación actual; el mundo tal como es; el presente.
hereabouts ['hɪərə,bauts] ADV por aquí (cerca).
hereafter [hɪər'ɑ:ftəʳ] ① ADV en el futuro; **Central Bank, ~ CB** Banco Central, en lo sucesivo BC.
  ② N futuro *m*; **the ~** la otra vida, el más allá.
hereby ['hɪə'baɪ] ADV por este medio; (*with reference to document*) por la presente.
hereditaments [,herɪ'dɪtəmənts] NPL herencia *f*, bienes *mpl* por heredar.
hereditary [hɪ'redɪtərɪ] ADJ hereditario; **~ disease** enfermedad *f* hereditaria.
heredity [hɪ'redɪtɪ] N herencia *f*.
herein [,hɪər'ɪn] ADV (*liter*) en esto; (*in letter*) en ésta.
hereinafter [,hɪərɪn'ɑ:ftəʳ] ADV (*Jur*) más adelante, más abajo, a continuación; (*frm*) de ahora en adelante.
hereof [,hɪər'ɒv] ADV (*liter*) de esto.
heresiarch [he'ri:zɪɑ:k] N heresiarca *mf*.
heresy ['herəsɪ] N herejía *f*.
heretic ['herətɪk] N hereje *mf*.
heretical [hɪ'retɪkəl] ADJ herético.
hereto [,hɪə'tu:] ADV a esto; **the parties ~** las partes abajo firmantes.
heretofore [,hɪətu'fɔ:ʳ] ADV (*liter*) hasta ahora; hasta este momento.
hereupon ['hɪərə'pɒn] ADV en seguida.
herewith ['hɪə'wɪð] ADV junto con esto; **I send you ~ ...** le mando adjunto ...
heritable ['herɪtəbl] ADJ *objects, property etc* heredable, hereditable; *person* que puede heredar.
heritage ['herɪtɪdʒ] N herencia *f*; (*fig*) patrimonio *m*.
hermaphrodite [hɜ:'mæfrədaɪt] ① ADJ hermafrodita.
  ② N hermafrodita *m*.
hermetic [hɜ:'metɪk] ADJ hermético.
hermetically [hɜ:'metɪkəlɪ] ADV herméticamente; **~ sealed** cerrado herméticamente.
hermeticism [hɜ:'metɪsɪzəm] N hermetismo *m*.
hermit ['hɜ:mɪt] N ermitaño *m*; **~ crab** ermitaño *m*.
hermitage ['hɜ:mɪtɪdʒ] N ermita *f*.
hernia ['hɜ:nɪə] N hernia *f*.
hero ['hɪərəu] N, PL **heroes** ['hɪərəuz] héroe *m*; (*Liter etc*) protagonista *m*, personaje *m* principal.
Herod ['herəd] NM Herodes.
heroic [hɪ'rəuɪk] ADJ heroico.
heroically [hɪ'rəuɪkəlɪ] ADV heroicamente.
heroics [hɪ'rəuɪks] N (*slightly pej: language*) lenguaje *m* altisonante; (*deeds*) acciones *fpl* heroicas, acciones *fpl* extravagantes; (*behaviour*) comportamiento *m* atrevido.
heroin ['herəuɪn] ① N heroína *f*.
  ② ATTR: **~ addict** heroinómano *m*, -a *f*; **~ addiction** heroinomanía *f*; **~ user** heroinómano *m*, -a *f*.
heroine ['herəuɪn] N heroína *f*; (*Liter etc*) protagonista *f*, personaje *m* principal.
heroism ['herəuɪzəm] N heroísmo *m*.
heron ['herən] N garza *f* (real).
hero-worship ['hɪərəu,wɜ:ʃɪp] N culto *m* a los héroes; **he was the object of real ~** fue el objeto de un verdadero culto.
herpes ['hɜ:pi:z] N herpes *m or fpl*.
herring ['herɪŋ] N arenque *m*; **V red**.
herringbone ['herɪŋbəun] ATTR: **~ pattern** (*Sew*) muestra *f* espiga; (*of floor*) espinapez *m*; **~ stitch** punto *m* de escapulario.
herring-gull ['herɪŋ,gʌl] N gaviota *f* argéntea.
herring-pond ['herɪŋpɒnd] N: **to cross the ~** (*hum*) cruzar el charco (*el Atlántico*).
hers [hɜ:z] POSS PRON (el/la) suyo/a, (los/las) suyos/as, de ella; **this car is ~** este coche es suyo (*or* de ella); **a friend of ~** un amigo suyo; **is this poem ~?** ¿es de ella este poema?; **the one I like best is ~** el que

más me gusta es el suyo.

herself [hɜː'self] PRON *(reflexive)* se; *(emphatic)* ella misma; *(after prep)* sí (misma); **she washed ~** se lavó; **she said to ~** dijo entre *(or* para*)* sí; **she did it ~** lo hizo ella misma; **she went ~** fue ella misma, fue en persona; **she did it by ~** lo hizo ella sola.

Herts [hɑːts] N ABBR *of* **Hertfordshire.**

hertz [hɜːts] N hercio *m,* hertzio *m,* hertz *m.*

he's [hiːz] = **he is; he has.**

hesitancy ['hezɪtənsɪ] N = **hesitation.**

hesitant ['hezɪtənt] ADJ vacilante, irresoluto, indeciso; **I am somewhat ~ about accepting it** no me resuelvo a aceptarlo.

hesitantly ['hezɪtəntlɪ] ADV irresolutamente, indecisamente; *speak, suggest* con indecisión.

▼ **hesitate** ['hezɪteɪt] VI vacilar, mostrarse indeciso; *(in speech)* titubear; **to ~ about, to ~ over** no tomar una resolución sobre; **he ~d over his reply** tardó en dar su respuesta; **to ~ to +** *infin* vacilar en + *infin*; **I ~ to condemn him outright** no me puedo persuadir a condenarlo del todo, no me decido todavía a condenarlo del todo; **don't ~ to ask me** no vaciles en pedírmelo.

hesitation [ˌhezɪ'teɪʃən] N vacilación *f,* irresolución *f,* indecisión *f;* **without the slightest ~** sin vacilar un momento; **I feel a certain ~ about it** tengo algunas dudas acerca de ello.

hessian ['hesɪən] 1 N arpillera *f.*
2 ATTR *(made of ~)* de arpillera.

het* [het] ADJ: **to get ~ up** acalorarse, emocionarse *(about, over* por*)*; **don't get so ~ up!** ¡tranquilízate!

hetero* ['hetərəʊ] = **heterosexual.**

heterodox ['hetərədɒks] ADJ heterodoxo.

heterodoxy ['hetərədɒksɪ] N heterodoxia *f.*

heterogeneity [ˌhetərəʊdʒə'niːɪtɪ] N heterogeneidad *f.*

heterogeneous [ˌhetərəʊ'dʒiːnɪəs] ADJ heterogéneo.

heterosexual ['hetərəʊ'seksjʊəl] 1 ADJ heterosexual.
2 N heterosexual *mf.*

heterosexuality ['hetərəʊˌseksjʊ'ælɪtɪ] N heterosexualidad *f.*

heuristic [hjʊə'rɪstɪk] ADJ heurístico; **~ search** investigación *f* heurística.

hew [hjuː] VT *(irr:* PRET **hewed,** PTP **hewed** *or* **hewn)** cortar, tajar; *(shape)* labrar, tallar.

◆ **hew down** VT talar.

◆ **hew out** VT excavar; **a figure ~n out of the rock** una figura tallada en la roca; **to ~ out a career** hacerse una carrera, abrirse paso en su profesión.

hewn [hjuːn] PTP *of* **hew.**

hex¹* [heks] *(US)* 1 N **(a)** *(spell)* maleficio *m,* mal *m* de ojo, aojo *m.* **(b)** *(witch)* bruja *f.*
2 VT embrujar.

hex² [heks] ADJ *(Comput)* hexadecimal; **~ code** código *m* hexadecimal.

hexadecimal [ˌheksə'desɪməl] ADJ hexadecimal; **~ notation** notación *f* hexadecimal.

hexagon ['heksəgən] N hexágono *m.*

hexagonal [hek'sægənəl] ADJ hexagonal.

hexagram ['heksəˌgræm] N hexagrama *m.*

hexameter [hek'sæmɪtə'] N hexámetro *m.*

hey [heɪ] INTERJ ¡oye!, ¡eh!

heyday ['heɪdeɪ] N auge *m,* apogeo *m,* buenos tiempos *mpl;* **in the ~ of the theatre** en el apogeo del teatro.

Hezbollah ['hezbəˈlɑ:] N Hezbolá *m,* Hizbulá *m.*

H.F. N ABBR *of* **high frequency** alta frecuencia *f.*

hg ABBR *of* **hectogram(s)** hg.

HGV N ABBR *of* **heavy goods vehicle** camión *m* de gran capacidad.

H.H. (a) ABBR *of* **His** *(or* **Her) Highness** Su Alteza, S.A. **(b)** *(Eccl)* ABBR *of* **His Holiness** Su Santidad, S.S.

HI *(US Post)* ABBR *of* **Hawaii.**

hi [haɪ] INTERJ ¡oye!, ¡eh!; *(hullo)* ¡hola!, ¡buenas!

hiatus [haɪ'eɪtəs] N *(Gram)* hiato *m;* *(fig)* vacío *m,* laguna *f,* interrupción *f;* solución *f* de continuidad.

hibernate ['haɪbəneɪt] VI invernar, hibernar.

hibernation [ˌhaɪbə'neɪʃən] N hibernación *f.*

Hibernia [haɪ'bɜːnɪə] N Hibernia *f.*

hibiscus [hɪ'bɪskəs] N hibisco *m.*

hic [hɪk] INTERJ ¡hip!

hiccough ['hɪkʌp], **hiccup** ['hɪkʌp] 1 N **(a)** hipo *m;* **it gives me ~s** me da hipo, me hace hipar; **to have ~s** tener hipo. **(b) a slight ~ in the proceedings** *(fig)* una pequeña dificultad *(or* interrupción*)* en los actos.
2 VT decir hipando; **'yes', he ~ed** 'sí', dijo hipando.
3 VI hipar.

hick [hɪk] *(US)* 1 ADJ rústico, de aldea.
2 N palurdo *m,* paleto *m.*

hickory ['hɪkərɪ] N nuez *f* dura, nogal *m* americano.

hid [hɪd] PRET *of* **hide.**

hidden ['hɪdn] 1 PTP *of* **hide.**

2 ADJ escondido; *(fig)* oculto, secreto; **~ assets** activo *m* oculto; **~ reserves** reservas *fpl* ocultas.

hide¹ [haɪd] N *(skin)* piel *f,* pellejo *m;* *(tanned)* cuero *m;* *(of person)* pellejo *m.*

hide² [haɪd] 1 N *(Brit Hunting)* paranza *f,* puesto *m,* trepa *f;* *(Orn)* observatorio *m;* escondite *m,* aguardado *m.*
2 VT *(irr:* PRET **hid,** PTP **hidden)** esconder *(from* de*)*; ocultar *(from* a, de*)*; *feeling etc* ocultar, encubrir, disimular; **I have nothing to ~** no tengo nada que ocultar.
3 VI esconderse, ocultarse *(from* de*)*; **he's hiding behind his chief** se está buscando la protección de su jefe.

◆ **hide away** 1 VT esconder, ocultar.
2 VI esconderse.

◆ **hide out, hide up** VI quedar ocultado, ocultarse *(por* mucho tiempo*)*.

hide-and-seek ['haɪdən'siːk] N escondite *m;* **to play ~ with** jugar al escondite con *(also fig)*.

hideaway ['haɪdəweɪ] N escondrijo *m,* escondite *m.*

hidebound ['haɪdbaʊnd] ADJ rígido, aferrado a la tradición.

hideous ['hɪdɪəs] ADJ horrible.

hideously ['hɪdɪəslɪ] ADV horriblemente; **~ ugly** feísimo.

hideout ['haɪdaʊt] N escondrijo *m,* guarida *f.*

hidey-hole* ['haɪdɪhəʊl] N escondite *m,* escondrijo *m.*

hiding¹* ['haɪdɪŋ] N *(beating)* paliza *f;* **to be on a ~ to nothing** tener todas las de perder, no tener posibilidad alguna de ganar.

hiding² ['haɪdɪŋ] N: **to be in ~** estar escondido; **he is in ~ in France** se ha refugiado en Francia; **to go into ~** ocultarse, refugiarse; *(Pol)* pasar a la clandestinidad.

hiding place ['haɪdɪŋpleɪs] N escondrijo *m.*

hie [haɪ] *(arch or hum)* 1 VT apresurar.
2 VI ir, ir volando, correr.
3 VR: **to ~ o.s. home** apresurarse a volver a casa.

hierarchic(al) [ˌhaɪə'rɑːkɪk(əl)] ADJ jerárquico.

hierarchy ['haɪərɑːkɪ] N jerarquía *f.*

hieratic [haɪə'rætɪk] ADJ *(frm)* hierático.

hieroglyph ['haɪərəglɪf] N jeroglífico *m.*

hieroglyphic [ˌhaɪərə'glɪfɪk] 1 ADJ jeroglífico.
2 N jeroglífico *m.*

hifalutin'* [ˌhaɪfə'luːtɪn] = **highfalutin(g).**

hi-fi ['haɪ'faɪ] *(ABBR of* **high fidelity)** 1 ADJ de alta fidelidad; **~ equipment** equipo *m* de alta fidelidad; **~ set** equipo *m* de hi-fi *(or* de alta fidelidad*)*; **~ system** sistema *m* de alta fidelidad.
2 N alta fidelidad *f.*

higgledy-piggledy* ['hɪgldɪ'pɪgldɪ] 1 ADV *be etc* en desorden; *do etc* de cualquier modo, de trochemoche, a la buena de Dios.
2 ADJ revuelto, desordenado.

high [haɪ] 1 ADJ **(a)** alto; **it's 20 m ~** tiene 20 m de alto; **how ~ is that tree?** ¿qué altura tiene ese árbol?, ¿cuánto mide ese árbol de alto?; **I knew him when he was so ~** le conocí tamañito, le conocí de niño; **~ altar** altar *m* mayor; **~ chair** silla *f* alta; **~ heels** tacones *mpl* altos; *(shoes)* zapatos *mpl* de tacón alto; **V tide; ~ wire** cuerda *f* floja.
(b) *(fig) frequency, tension, temperature, treason etc* alto; *number, speed* grande; *price, rent, stake* elevado; *post* importante; *street* mayor; *quality* superior, bueno; *opinion* bueno; *note* agudo; *sea* tempestuoso; *wind* recio, fuerte; *polish* brillante; *(Culin)* pasado, manido; *(rotten)* pasado; **to play for ~ stakes** arriesgarse, jugarse el todo por el todo; **~ and dry** en seco; **to leave sb ~ and dry** dejar a uno plantado, dar plantón a uno *(LAm)*; **~ and mighty** engreído; **~ beam** *(Aut)* luces *fpl* largas, luces *fpl* de carretera; **H~ Church** *sector de la Iglesia Anglicana de tendencia conservadora*; **~ color** *(US)*, **~ colour** color *m* subido; **~ comedy** alta comedia *f;* **~ command** alto mando *m;* **~ commission** alta comisión *f;* **~ commissioner** alto comisario *m;* **~ court** tribunal *m* supremo; **~ finance** altas finanzas *fpl;* **H~ German** alto alemán *m;* **~ hurdles** vallas *fpl* altas; **to have ~ jinks** pasárselo pipa; **~ life** vida *f* de la buena sociedad; **~ living** vida *f* regalada; **~ mass** misa *f* mayor, misa *f* solemne; **V noon; ~ official** alto funcionario *m;* **~ point** *(of show, evening)* clímax *m,* punto *m* climático; *(of visit, holiday)* momento *m* más interesante; **~ priest** sumo sacerdote *m;* **~ priestess** suma sacerdotisa *f;* **~ school** *(Scot, US)* instituto *m;* **~ seas** alta mar *f;* **~ season** temporada *f* alta; **~ season prices** precios *mpl* de temporada alta; **~ society** buena sociedad *f;* **V spirit; ~ spot = ~ point; ~ summer** parte *f* más calurosa del verano, estío *m;* **~ tech(nology)** alta tecnología *f.*
(c) to be ~ *(on drugs)*‡ estar iluminado‡, estar colocado‡.
2 ADV **(a)** *fly etc* a gran altura; **~ above my head** muy por encima de mi cabeza; **it rose ~ in the air** se elevó por los aires; **it sailed ~ over the house** voló por los aires muy por encima de la casa.
(b) to aim ~ picar muy alto; **to blow ~** soplar recio; **the numbers go as ~ as 20** los números llegan hasta 20; **I had to go as ~ as £8 for it** tuve que pagar 8 libras nada menos por él; **the bidding went as ~ as £50** se ofrecieron hasta 50 libras; **it went for as ~ as £60** se vendió por 60 libras nada menos; **to live ~ on the hog** *(US*)* vivir

como un rajá; **to hunt ~ and low for sb** buscar a uno por todas partes; **to run ~** (*sea*) embravecerse, (*river*) estar crecido; (*feelings*) encenderse, exaltarse; **feelings were running ~** la gente estaba muy acalorada.

3 N (*Met*) zona *f* de alta presión; (*Met*: *esp US*) temperatura *f* máxima; (*Fin*) máximo *m*; **on ~** en las alturas, en el cielo; **exports have reached a new ~** las exportaciones han alcanzado cifras nunca conocidas antes; **to be on a ~*** estar a las mil maravillas.

HIGH SCHOOL

*ⓘ En Estados Unidos las **high schools** son los institutos donde los adolescentes de 15 a 18 años realizan la educación secundaria, que dura tres cursos (**grades**), desde el noveno hasta el duodécimo año de la enseñanza; al final del último curso se realiza un libro conmemorativo con fotos de los alumnos y profesores de ese año (**Yearbook**) y los alumnos reciben el diploma de **high school** en una ceremonia formal de graduación. Estos centros suelen ser un tema frecuente en las películas y programas de televisión estadounidenses en los que se resalta mucho el aspecto deportivo - sobre todo el fútbol americano y el baloncesto - además de algunos acontecimientos sociales como el baile de fin de curso, conocido como **Senior Prom**.*

⤷ Ver también [EDUCATION], [PROM], [YEARBOOK]

---

highball ['haɪbɔːl] N (*US*) jáibol *m*, whisky *m* soda.
highborn ['haɪbɔːn] ADJ linajudo, de ilustre cuna.
highboy ['haɪbɔɪ] N (*US*) cómoda *f* alta.
highbrow ['haɪbrau] (*freq pej*) **1** ADJ intelectual, culto, esotérico.
2 N intelectual *mf*, persona *f* culta.
high-class ['haɪ'klɑːs] ADJ de clase superior.
high-definition [,haɪdefɪ'nɪʃən] ADJ *television, video* de alta definición.
high-density [,haɪ'densɪtɪ] ATTR: **~ housing** alta densidad *f* de inquilinos.
high-diving ['haɪ,daɪvɪŋ] N salto *m* de palanca.
high-energy [,haɪ'enədʒɪ] ATTR: **~ particle** partícula *f* de alta energía; **~ physics** física *f* de altas energías.
higher ['haɪəʳ] **1** ADJ *comp of* **high**; más alto; *form, study etc* superior; *price* más elevado; *number, speed* mayor; **~ education** educación *f* (or enseñanza *f*) superior; **~ rate tax** impuesto *m* en la banda superior; **any number ~ than 6** cualquier número superior a 6.
2 ADV *comp of* **high**; **to fly ~ than the clouds** volar encima de las nubes; **to fly ~ still** volar a mayor altura todavía; **~ up the hill** más arriba en la colina; **~ up the road** más hacia el final de la calle.
3 N (*Scot Scol*) = **Higher Grade**; *V* **4.**
4 ATTR: **H~ Grade** (*Scot Scol*) *examen de estado que se realiza a la edad de 16 años;* ≈ (*Sp*) Curso *m* de Orientación Universitaria (COU); **H~ National Certificate** (*Brit*) Certificado *m* Nacional de Estudios Superiores; **H~ National Diploma** (*Brit*) Diploma *m* Nacional de Estudios Superiores; *ver también* [ADVANCED LEVELS], [EDUCATION].
highest ['haɪɪst] ADJ SUPERL *of* **high** el/la más alto/a.
high-explosive ['haɪks'pləusɪv] **1** N explosivo *m* fuerte, explosivo *m* rompedor.
2 ADJ: **~ shell** obús *m* de alto explosivo.
highfalutin(g) ['haɪfə'luːtɪn] ADJ presuntuoso, pomposo.
high-fibre, (*US*) **high-fiber** ['haɪ'faɪbəʳ] ADJ: **~ diet** dieta *f* rica en fibra.
high-fidelity [,haɪfɪ'delɪtɪ] ADJ de alta fidelidad.
high-flier [,haɪ'flaɪəʳ] N (*fig*) persona *f* de mucho talento, persona *f* de grandes dotes; ambicioso *m*, -a *f*.
high-flown ['haɪfləun] ADJ exagerado, altisonante.
high-flying ['haɪ'flaɪɪŋ] ADJ de gran altura; (*fig*) *aim, ambition* de altos vuelos; *person* superdotado.
high-frequency [,haɪ'friːkwənsɪ] ADJ de alta frecuencia.
high-grade ['haɪ'greɪd] ADJ de calidad superior.
high-handed ['haɪ'hændɪd] ADJ arbitrario, despótico.
high-handedly [,haɪ'hændɪdlɪ] ADV arbitrariamente, despóticamente.
high-hat* ['haɪ'hæt] **1** ADJ encopetado, esnob*.
2 N sombrero *m* de copa, cilindro* *m*.
high-heeled ['haɪhiːld] ADJ *shoes* de tacones altos.
high-intensity [,haɪɪn'tensɪtɪ] ADJ: **~ lights** (*Aut*) faros *mpl* halógenos.
highjack ['haɪdʒæk] *etc* = **hijack** *etc*.
high jump ['haɪdʒʌmp] N salto *m* de altura; **he's for the ~*** (*Brit*) (*reprimand*) le van a dar una buena bronca; (*going to be sacked*) le van a despedir.
highland ['haɪlənd] **1** N tierras *fpl* altas, montañas *fpl*; **the H~s** (*Brit*) las Tierras Altas de Escocia.
2 ATTR *people* montañés, de montaña; *region* montañoso; **H~ dress** traje *m* tradicional de las Tierras Altas; **H~ fling** cierto baile escocés; **H~ Games** juegos *mpl* escoceses; *ver también* [KILT].
highlander ['haɪləndəʳ] N montañés *m*, -esa *f*; **H~** (*Brit*) habitante *mf* de las tierras altas de Escocia.
high-level ['haɪ'levl] ADJ de alto nivel; **~ nuclear waste** desechos *mpl* nucleares de alta radiactividad; **~ language** lenguaje *m* de alto nivel.

HIGHLAND GAMES

*ⓘ Los **Highland Games** se celebran anualmente en distintos lugares de Escocia y en ellos se realizan competiciones de deportes tradicionales celtas, junto con bailes típicos y concursos de gaitas. Probablemente, de todos los juegos, el más famoso es el que tiene lugar en Braemar, cerca de Balmoral, en el noreste de Escocia. Entre las competiciones normalmente asociadas con estos juegos están el lanzamiento de troncos (**tossing the caber**) y el lanzamiento de martillo.*

---

highlight ['haɪlaɪt] **1** N (*Art*) claro *m*, realce *m*, toque *m* de luz; (*fig*) aspecto *m* notable, aspecto *m* interesante; momento *m* culminante; **~s** (*in hair*) vetas *fpl*, reflejos *mpl*.
2 VT subrayar, destacar; *hair* vetear, poner reflejos en.
highlighter ['haɪlaɪtəʳ] N (*pen*) marcador *m*.
highly ['haɪlɪ] ADV (a) muy, muy bien, sumamente; **~ amusing** divertidísimo; **~ coloured** (*fig*) exagerado; **~ paid** muy bien pagado, muy bien retribuido; **~ placed official** oficial *m* de categoría, funcionario *m* importante; **~ regarded** muy estimado, muy bien reputado; **~ seasoned** muy picante; **~ strung** (*Brit*) muy excitable, (muy) nervioso, hipertenso.
(b) **to praise sb ~** alabar mucho a uno; **to speak ~ of** decir mil bienes de; **to think ~ of sb** tener en mucho a uno.
highly-charged [,haɪlɪ'tʃɑːdʒd] ADJ *atmosphere, debate* muy tenso, muy crispado.
high-minded ['haɪ'maɪndɪd] ADJ *person* de nobles pensamientos, magnánimo; *act* noble, altruista.
high-mindedness ['haɪ'maɪndɪdnɪs] N nobleza *f* de pensamientos, magnanimidad *f*; altruismo *m*.
high-necked [,haɪ'nekt] ADJ de cuello alto.
highness ['haɪnɪs] N altura *f*; **H~** (*as title*) Alteza *f*; **His** (*or* **Her**) **Royal H~** Su Alteza Real.
high-octane ['haɪ,ɒkteɪn] ATTR: **~ petrol** gasolina *f* de alto octanaje, supercarburante *m*.
high performance [,haɪpə'fɔːməns] ADJ de gran rendimiento.
high-pitched ['haɪ'pɪtʃt] ADJ de tono alto, agudo; *voice* aflautado.
high-powered ['haɪ'pauəd] ADJ de gran potencia; *person* enérgico, dinámico.
high-pressure ['haɪ'preʃəʳ] ADJ de alta presión; (*fig*) enérgico, dinámico, apremiante; **~ salesman** vendedor *m* enérgico; **~ selling** venta *f* (con propaganda) agresiva.
high-priced [,haɪ'praɪst] ADJ muy caro.
high-profile ['haɪ'prəufaɪl] ATTR: **~ activity** actividad *f* que quiere llamar la atención, actividad *f* que trata de darse publicidad.
high-protein [,haɪ'prəutiːn] ADJ rico en proteínas.
high-quality ['haɪ'kwɒlɪtɪ] ADJ de gran calidad, de calidad superior.
high-ranking ['haɪ'ræŋkɪŋ] ADJ de categoría; *official* de alto rango, de alto grado; (*Mil*) de alta graduación.
high-resolution ['haɪ'rezə'luːʃən] ADJ *image, screen* de alta resolución.
high-rise ['haɪraɪz] ATTR: **~ building** edificio *m* elevado, torre *f*.
high-risk [,haɪ'rɪsk] ATTR *investment, policy* de alto riesgo.
highroad ['haɪrəud] N (*esp Brit*) carretera *f*; (*fig*) camino *m* real (*to* de).
high-sounding ['haɪ'saundɪŋ] ADJ altisonante.
high-speed ['haɪ'spiːd] ADJ *vehicle etc* de alta velocidad; *test etc* rápido; **~ train** tren *m* de alta velocidad.
high-spending ['haɪ'spendɪŋ] ADJ que gasta mucho; (*pej*) derrochador, pródigo.
high-spirited ['haɪ'spɪrɪtɪd] ADJ brioso, animoso; *horse* fogoso; (*merry*) alegre.
high street ['haɪstriːt] N (*Brit*) calle *f* mayor; **~ banks** bancos *mpl* de la calle mayor (que aceptan depósitos de clientes individuales).
high-strung ['haɪ,strʌŋ] ADJ (*US*) muy excitable, (muy) nervioso, hipertenso.
hightail* ['haɪteɪl] VT: **to ~ it** (*esp US*) darse el piro*, salir pitando*.
high tea [,haɪ'tiː] N (*Brit*) merienda-cena *f*; *ver también* [TEA].
high-tech* [,haɪ'tek] ATTR al-tec*, de alta tecnología.
high-tension ['haɪ'tenʃən] ADJ de alta tensión.
high-test ['haɪ'test] ADJ: **~ fuel** supercarburante *m*.
high-up* ['haɪ'ʌp] **1** ADJ de categoría, importante.
2 N oficial *m* importante, alto cargo *m*, pez *m* gordo*.
high water ['haɪ'wɔːtəʳ] **1** N pleamar *f*, marea *f* alta.
2 ATTR: **~ mark** línea *f* de pleamar.
highway ['haɪweɪ] **1** N carretera *f*; autopista *f*; **~s department** administración *f* de carreteras.
2 ATTR: **~ code** (*Brit*) código *m* de la circulación; **~ robbery** salteamiento *m*, atraco *m* (en la carretera).
highwayman ['haɪweɪmən] N, PL **highwaymen** ['haɪweɪmən] salteador *m* de caminos.
hijack ['haɪdʒæk] **1** N = **hijacking**.
2 VT piratear, secuestrar (*esp en el aire*).
hijacker ['haɪdʒækəʳ] N pirata *m* (aéreo), secuestrador *m* (aéreo).
hijacking ['haɪdʒækɪŋ] N piratería *f* (aérea), secuestro *m* (aéreo).

hike¹ [haɪk] **1** N caminata *f*, excursión *f* a pie; **to go on a ~** dar una caminata; **take a ~!** ¡lárgate!*
  2 VT: **to ~ it** ir a pie.
  3 VI dar una caminata, ir de excursión (a pie); ir a pie, ir andando.
hike² [haɪk] (*US*) **1** N aumento *m*.
  2 VT aumentar, subir.
◆ **hike up** VT (**a**) *skirt, socks* subirse. (**b**) *prices, amounts* subir de golpe, aumentar.
hiker ['haɪkəʳ] N excursionista *mf* (a pie), caminador *m*, -ora *f*.
hiking ['haɪkɪŋ] N excursionismo *m* (a pie).
hilarious [hɪ'lɛərɪəs] ADJ *scene etc* divertido, regocijante; *laughter* alegre.
hilariously [hɪ'lɛərɪəslɪ] ADV *speak, describe* con mucha gracia; **~ funny** para morirse de risa.
hilarity [hɪ'lærɪtɪ] N regocijo *m*, alegría *f*; **there was some ~ at this** en esto hubo algunas risas; **it caused ~ in the audience** provocó las carcajadas del público.
hill [hɪl] N colina *f*, cerro *m*, otero *m*; (*high*) montaña *f*; (*slope*) cuesta *f*; **to be over the ~** estar en la pendiente vital, ser demasiado viejo; no servir ya; **to chase sb up ~ and down dale** perseguir a uno por todas partes; **to curse sb up ~ and down dale** echar mil pestes de uno; **to take to the ~s** echarse al monte.
hillbilly ['hɪl'bɪlɪ] (*US*) **1** N rústico *m* montañés; (*pej*) palurdo *m*, -a *f*.
  2 ATTR: **~ music** música *f* country; *ver también* GRAND OLE OPRY .
hill climb ['hɪlklaɪm] N (*Sport*) ascensión *f* de montaña.
hill-farmer ['hɪl,fɑːməʳ] N agricultor *m*, -ora *f* de montaña.
hill-farming ['hɪl,fɑːmɪŋ] N agricultura *f* de montaña.
hillfort ['hɪl'fɔːt] N castro *m*.
hilliness ['hɪlɪnɪs] N montañosidad *f*.
hillock ['hɪlək] N montículo *m*, altozano *m*.
hillside ['hɪlsaɪd] N ladera *f*.
hilltop ['hɪltɒp] N cumbre *f*.
hill-walker ['hɪl,wɔːkəʳ] N montañero *m*, -a *f*.
hill-walking ['hɪl,wɔːkɪŋ] N caminatas *fpl* de montaña.
hilly ['hɪlɪ] ADJ montuoso, montañoso, accidentado; *road* de fuertes pendientes.
hilt [hɪlt] N puño *m*, empuñadura *f*; **up to the ~** hasta las cachas; **he's in debt (right) up to the ~** está agobiado de deudas; **to back sb up to the ~** apoyar a uno incondicionalmente; **to prove sth up to the ~** probar algo completamente, demostrar algo hasta la saciedad.
him [hɪm] PRON (**a**) (*direct*) le, lo (*esp LAm*); **I see ~** le (*or* lo) veo; **I have never seen HIM** a él no le (*or* lo) he visto nunca. (**b**) (*indirect*) le; **I gave ~ the book** le di el libro; **I'm speaking to ~** le estoy hablando. (**c**) (*after prep*) él; **she thought of ~** pensó en él; **without ~** sin él; **if I were ~** yo que él; **it's ~** es él; **younger than ~** más joven (*or* menor) que él.
Himalayan [,hɪmə'leɪən] ADJ del Himalaya, himalayo.
Himalayas [,hɪmə'leɪəz] NPL los montes Himalaya, el Himalaya.
himself [hɪm'self] PRON (*reflexive*) se; (*emphatic*) él mismo; (*after prep*) sí (mismo); **he washed ~** se lavó; **he said to ~** dijo entre (*or* para) sí; **he did it ~** lo hizo él mismo; **he went ~** fue él mismo, fue en persona; **he did it by ~** lo hizo él solo.
hind¹ [haɪnd] N cierva *f*.
hind² [haɪnd] ADJ trasero, posterior.
hinder¹ ['hɪndəʳ] VT *person* estorbar, impedir, *progress etc* estorbar, dificultar; *trade, traffic* entorpecer; **to ~ sb from doing sth** impedir a uno hacer algo.
hinder² ['haɪndəʳ] ADJ *part* trasero.
Hindi ['hɪndiː] N hindi *m*.
hindmost ['haɪndməʊst] ADJ postrero, último.
hindquarters ['haɪnd,kwɔːtəz] NPL cuartos *mpl* traseros.
hindrance ['hɪndrəns] N estorbo *m*, obstáculo *m* (to para).
hindsight ['haɪndsaɪt] N percepción *f* retrospectiva, comprensión *f* a posteriori; **with the benefit of ~** como vemos en retrospectiva, con la perspectiva del tiempo transcurrido.
Hindu ['hɪn'duː] **1** ADJ hindú.
  2 N hindú *mf*.
Hinduism ['hɪnduːɪzəm] N hinduismo *m*.
Hindustan [,hɪndʊ'stɑːn] N Indostán *m*.
Hindustani ['hɪndʊ'stɑːnɪ] N (*Ling*) indostánico *m*, indostani *m*.
hinge [hɪndʒ] **1** N gozne *m*, bisagra *f*; charnela *f* (*also Zool*); (*for stamps*) fijasellos *m*; (*fig*) eje *m*.
  2 VT engoznar.
  3 VI moverse sobre goznes; **to ~ on** moverse sobre, girar sobre; (*fig*) depender de.
hinged [hɪndʒd] ADJ con goznes, de bisagra.
hint [hɪnt] **1** N (**a**) (*suggestion*) indirecta *f*, indicación *f*, insinuación *f*; (*advice*) consejo *m*; **broad ~** indicación *f* inconfundible; **~s for purchasers** aviso *m* a los compradores; **~s on maintenance** instrucciones *fpl* para la manutención; **to drop** (*or* **let fall, throw out**) **a ~** soltar una indirecta; **to drop a ~ that ...** insinuar que ...; **take a ~ from me** permite que te dé un consejo; **to take the ~** aprovechar la indicación; darse por aludido.

(**b**) (*trace*) señal *f*, indicio *m*; **without the least ~ of** sin la menor señal de; **with just a ~ of garlic** con un ligerísimo sabor a ajo; **with a ~ of irony** con un dejo de ironía.
  2 VT: **to ~ that ...** insinuar que ...
  3 VI soltar indirectas; **to ~ at** hacer alusión a; **what are you ~ing (at)?** ¿qué pretendes insinuar?
hinterland ['hɪntəlænd] N hinterland *m*, interior *m*, traspaís *m*.
hip¹ [hɪp] **1** N (*Anat*) cadera *f*; **to shoot from the ~** (sacar el revólver y) disparar sin apuntar.
  2 ATTR: **~ replacement (operation)** operación *f* de trasplante de cadera; **~ size** talla *f* de cadera.
hip² [hɪp] N (*Bot*) escaramujo *m*.
hip³ [hɪp] INTERJ: **~ ~ hurray!** ¡viva!
hip⁴* [hɪp] ADJ: **to be ~** (*up-to-date*) estar al día; (*well-informed*) estar al tanto (de lo que pasa), estar enterado.
hip-bath ['hɪpbɑːθ] N, PL **hip-baths** ['hɪpbɑːðz] baño *m* de asiento, polibán *m*.
hipbone ['hɪpbəʊn] N hueso *m* de la cadera.
hip-flask ['hɪpflɑːsk] N frasco *m* de bolsillo.
hip-joint ['hɪp,dʒɔɪnt] N articulación *f* de la cadera.
hipped¹ [hɪpt] ADJ (*Archit*) a cuatro aguas.
hipped²* [hɪpt] ADJ (*US*) triste; enojado, resentido; **~ on** obsesionado por.
hippie* ['hɪpɪ] **1** N hippie* *mf*, hippy* *mf*.
  2 ADJ hippy*, hippie*.
hippo* ['hɪpəʊ] N hipopótamo *m*.
hip-pocket ['hɪp'pɒkɪt] N bolsillo *m* trasero.
Hippocrates [hɪ'pɒkrətiːz] NM Hipócrates.
Hippocratic [,hɪpəʊ'krætɪk] ADJ: **~ oath** juramento *m* hipocrático.
hippodrome ['hɪpədrəʊm] N (*Hist*) hipódromo *m*.
Hippolytus [hɪ'pɒlɪtəs] NM Hipólito.
hippopotamus [,hɪpə'pɒtəməs] N, PL **hippopotamuses** [,hɪpə'pɒtəməsɪz] *or* **hippopotami** [,hɪpə'pɒtəmaɪ] hipopótamo *m*.
hippy* ['hɪpɪ] = **hippie***.
hipster ['hɪpstəʳ] **1** N (**a**) **~s** (*Brit*) pantalón que se lleva a la altura de la cadera. (**b**) (*US**) entusiasta *mf* del jazz.
  2 ATTR: **~ skirt** (*Brit*) falda *f* abrochada en la cadera.
hire ['haɪəʳ] **1** N alquiler *m*; (*of person*) salario *m*, jornal *m*; **'for ~'** 'se alquila'; **to be on ~** estar de alquiler.
  2 ATTR: **~ car** (*Brit*) coche *m* de alquiler; **~ charges** tarifa *f* de alquiler.
  3 VT *thing*, (*Brit*) *car* alquilar; *person* contratar, emplear.
◆ **hire out** VT *car, tools* alquilar.
hired ['haɪəd] ADJ: **~ car** coche *m* alquilado, coche *m* de alquiler; **~ killer** asesino *m* a sueldo.
hireling ['haɪəlɪŋ] N mercenario *m*.
hire purchase ['haɪə'pɜːtʃɪs] **1** N (*Brit*) compra *f* a plazos; **to buy sth on ~** comprar algo a plazos.
  2 ATTR: **~ agreement** acuerdo *m* de compra a plazos; **~ finance company** compañía *f* de crédito comercial.
hirsute ['hɜːsjuːt] ADJ hirsuto.
his [hɪz] **1** POSS ADJ su, sus; **~ book/table** su libro/mesa; **~ friends** sus amigos.
  2 POSS PRON (el/la) suyo/a, (los/las) suyos/as, de él; **this book is ~** este libro es suyo (*or* de él); **a friend of ~** un amigo suyo; **is this painting ~?** ¿es de él este cuadro?; **the one I like best is ~** el que más me gusta es el suyo.
Hispanic [hɪs'pænɪk] **1** ADJ hispánico; (*within US*) hispano.
  2 N (*within US*) hispano *m*, -a *f*.
hispanicism [hɪs'pænɪsɪzəm] N hispanismo *m*.
hispanicize [hɪs'pænɪsaɪz] VT españolizar, hispanizar.
Hispanism ['hɪspænɪzəm] N hispanismo *m*.
hispanist ['hɪspənɪst] N hispanista *mf*.
Hispano... [hɪ'spænəʊ] PREF hispano...
hispanophile [hɪs'pænəʊfaɪl] N hispanófilo *m*, -a *f*.
hispanophobe [hɪs'pænəʊfəʊb] N hispanófobo *m*, -a *f*.
hiss [hɪs] **1** N silbido *m*, siseo *m*; (*of protest*) silbido *m*.
  2 VT silbar; **to ~ an actor off the stage** abuchear a un actor (hasta que abandone la escena).
  3 VI silbar, sisear; (*in protest*) silbar.
histogram ['hɪstəgræm] N histograma *m*.
histologist [hɪs'tɒlədʒɪst] N histólogo *m*, -a *f*.
histology [hɪs'tɒlədʒɪ] N histología *f*.
historian [hɪs'tɔːrɪən] N historiador *m*, -ora *f*.
historic(al) [hɪs'tɒrɪk(əl)] ADJ histórico.
historically [hɪs'tɒrɪkəlɪ] ADV históricamente.
historicism [hɪ'stɒrɪsɪzəm] N historicismo *m*.
historicist [hɪ'stɒrɪsɪst] ADJ historicista.
historiographer [,hɪstɒrɪ'ɒgrəfəʳ] N historiógrafo *m*, -a *f*.
historiography [,hɪstɒrɪ'ɒgrəfɪ] N historiografía *f*.
history ['hɪstərɪ] N historia *f*; **that's ancient ~** ésa es cosa vieja; **to go down in ~** pasar a la historia (*as* como); **to know the inner ~ of an**

affair conocer el secreto de un asunto; **to make ~** hacer época, marcar un hito.

histrionic [ˌhɪstrɪˈɒnɪk] ADJ histriónico.

histrionics [ˌhɪstrɪˈɒnɪks] NPL histrionismo *m*; **I'm tired of his ~** estoy harto de sus payasadas.

hit [hɪt] **1** N **(a)** *(blow)* golpe *m*; *(shot)* tiro *m* certero; *(Baseball)* jit *m*; *(with shell etc)* impacto *m*; *(good guess)* acierto *m*; **direct ~** impacto *m* directo; **we made 3 ~s on the target** dimos 3 veces en el blanco; **that's a ~ at you** lo dijo por ti; **he made a ~ at the government** hizo un ataque contra el gobierno.
(b) *(Mus, Theat etc)* éxito *m*, sensación *f*; *(in pop music)* impacto *m*, hit *m*; **to be a ~** obtener un éxito, ser un triunfo; **the song was a big ~** la canción tuvo un exitazo; **to make a ~ with sb** caer en gracia a uno, chiflar a uno*.
2 ATTR (*) sensacional; **~ show** espectáculo *m* de éxito; **~ song** canción *f* éxito.
3 *(irr: PRET AND PTP hit)* VT **(a)** *(strike)* *person* golpear, pegar; *(wound)* herir; *target* alcanzar, hacer blanco en, acertar, dar en; **to ~ sb a blow** dar un golpe a uno; **to ~ one's head against a wall** dar con la cabeza contra una pared; **the president was ~ by 3 bullets** el presidente fue alcanzado por 3 balas; **the house was ~ by a bomb** la casa fue blanco de una bomba; **I realized my plane had been ~** me di cuenta de que mi avión había sido tocado; **his father used to ~ him** su padre le pegaba; **then it ~ me** *(fig)* aquello fue el flechazo; en seguida me di cuenta; **a lot of what he said ~ home** gran parte de lo que dijo dio en el blanco (*or* hizo mella); **to ~ the road*** ponerse en camino, largarse*.
(b) *(collide with)* chocar con, dar contra.
(c) *(damage)* hacer daño a, afectar; **the crops were ~ by the rain** las lluvias dañaron los cultivos; **the news ~ him hard** la noticia le afectó mucho; **the company has been hard ~** la compañía ha sido afectada de mala manera, la compañía ha sufrido un rudo golpe; **to ~ the bottle*** beber mucho.
(d) *(find, reach)* llegar a, alcanzar; *problem* tropezar con; **when we ~ the main road** cuando lleguemos a la carretera.
(e) (*) **he ~ me for 10 bucks** *(US)* me dio un sablazo de 10 dólares*; **how much can we ~ them for?** ¿qué cantidad podremos sacarles?
4 VI *(collide)* chocar; **to ~ against** chocar con, dar contra; **to ~ at** asestar un golpe a, *(fig)* atacar, apuntar a, satirizar; **to do sth ~ or miss** hacer algo a la buena de Dios; **to ~ and run** atacar y retirarse.
◆**hit back** VI devolver golpe por golpe, defenderse.
◆**hit off** VT **(a)** *(imitate)* imitar, remedar; *resemblance* coger; *(describe)* describir con gran acierto. **(b) to ~ it off with sb** hacer buenas migas con uno; **they don't ~ it off** no se llevan bien.
◆**hit out** VI lanzar un ataque, *(wildly)* repartir golpes; **to ~ out at sb** asestar un golpe a uno, *(fig)* atacar a uno.
◆**hit (up)on** VT dar con, tropezar con; **I ~ (up)on the idea** se me ocurrió la idea.

hit-and-miss [ˌhɪtənˈmɪs] ADJ al azar; **it's all rather ~** todo es a la buena de Dios.

hit-and-run [ˈhɪtənˈrʌn] ADJ: **~ accident** accidente de carretera en el que el conductor se da a la fuga; **~ driver** conductor *m* que atropella y huye; **~ raid** ataque *m* relámpago.

hitch [hɪtʃ] **1** N **(a)** *(tug)* tirón *m*.
(b) *(knot)* cote *m*, vuelta *f* de cabo.
(c) *(fig)* obstáculo *m*, dificultad *f*, interrupción *f*; **without a ~** a pedir de boca; **there was a ~ of 15 minutes** hubo un retraso de 15 minutos; **there's been a ~** ha surgido una dificultad.
2 VT **(a)** *(shift)* mover de un tirón; **he ~ed a chair over** acercó una silla a tirones.
(b) *(fasten)* atar, amarrar *(to* a); **to ~ a horse to a wagon** enganchar un caballo a un carro.
(c) to ~ lifts hacer autostop, hacer dedo *(SC)*, pedir aventón *(Mex)*; **to ~ a lift to Rome** llegar a Roma en autostop.
(d) to get ~ed: casarse.
3 VI (*) = **hitch-hike**.
◆**hitch up** VT alzar.

hitch-hike [ˈhɪtʃhaɪk] VI hacer autostop, hacer dedo *(SC)*, pedir aventón *(Mex)*.

hitch-hiker [ˈhɪtʃhaɪkəʳ] N autostopista *mf*.

hitch-hiking [ˈhɪtʃhaɪkɪŋ] N autostop *m*, autostopismo *m*.

hi-tech* [ˈhaɪˈtek] ATTR al-tec*, de alta tecnología.

hither [ˈhɪðəʳ] ADV *(liter)* acá; **~ and thither** acá y acullá.

hitherto [ˈhɪðəˈtuː] ADV hasta ahora.

Hitlerian [hɪtˈlɪərɪən] ADJ hitleriano.

hitlist [ˈhɪtlɪst] N lista *f* de los 'sentenciados a muerte'.

hitman [ˈhɪtmæn] N, PL **hitmen** [ˈhɪtmen] pistolero *m*, asesino *m* (a sueldo), hombre *m* del gatillo.

hit-or-miss [ˈhɪtɔːˈmɪs] ADJ: **~ shot** disparo *m* hecho sin apuntar; **with his ~ attitude** con su actitud despreocupada; **he operates on a ~ basis** funciona a la buena de Dios.

hit parade [ˈhɪtpəreɪd] N relación *f* de discos más populares, escala *f*

de éxitos.

hit-squad [ˈhɪtskwɒd] N escuadrón *m* de la muerte.

Hittite [ˈhɪtaɪt] **1** ADJ heteo, hitita.
2 N **(a)** heteo *m*, -a *f*, hitita *mf*. **(b)** *(Ling)* hitita *m*.

HIV N ABBR *of* **human immunodeficiency virus** virus *m* de la inmunodeficiencia humana, VIH *m*; **~ negative** VIH negativo; **~ positive** VIH positivo.

hive [haɪv] N colmena *f*; **a ~ of industry** un centro de industria, un lugar donde se trabaja muchísimo.
◆**hive off** VT separar; *(Fin)* vender (por separado); *(privatize)* privatizar.

hives [haɪvz] NPL *(Med)* urticaria *f*.

hiya* [ˈhaɪjə] EXCL ¡hola!

Hizbollah [hɪzbəˈlɑː], **Hizbullah** [ˈhɪzbəˈlɑː] = **Hezbollah**.

HK ABBR *of* **Hong Kong**.

hl ABBR *of* **hectolitre(s)** hectolitro(s), *m*(PL), hl.

HM ABBR *of* **Her** (*or* **His**) **Majesty** Su Majestad, S.M.

HMG N *(Brit)* ABBR *of* **Her** (*or* **His**) **Majesty's Government** el Gobierno de Su Majestad; V **majesty**.

HMI N *(Brit)* ABBR *of* **Her** (*or* **His**) **Majesty's Inspector**.

HMO N *(US)* ABBR *of* **health maintenance organization** seguro *m* médico global.

HMS N *(Brit)* ABBR *of* **Her** (*or* **His**) **Majesty's Ship** buque de guerra británico.

HMSO N *(Brit)* ABBR *of* **Her** (*or* **His**) **Majesty's Stationery Office** imprenta del gobierno.

HNC N *(Brit Scol)* ABBR *of* **Higher National Certificate** Certificado *m* Nacional de Estudios Superiores; V **higher**.

HND N *(Brit Scol)* ABBR *of* **Higher National Diploma** Diploma *m* Nacional de Estudios Superiores; V **higher**.

HO **(a)** *(Comm etc)* ABBR *of* **head office**. **(b)** *(Brit Pol)* ABBR *of* **Home Office**.

hoard [hɔːd] **1** N acumulación *f*; provisión *f*; *(money)* tesoro *m* escondido; *(arms)* alijo *m*.
2 VT *(also* **to ~ up**) acumular, amontonar (en secreto); *money* atesorar; *goods in short supply* retener, acaparar.

hoarder [ˈhɔːdəʳ] N: **to be a ~** ser un acaparador.

hoarding¹ [ˈhɔːdɪŋ] N *(act)* acumulación *f*, retención *f*; acaparamiento *m*.

hoarding² [ˈhɔːdɪŋ] N *(Brit)* *(fence)* valla *f* de construcción; *(for posters)* valla *f* publicitaria, cartelera *f*.

hoarfrost [ˈhɔːˈfrɒst] N escarcha *f*.

hoarse [hɔːs] ADJ ronco; **to be ~** tener la voz ronca; **in a ~ voice** con voz ronca; **to shout o.s. ~** enronquecer a fuerza de gritar.

hoarsely [ˈhɔːslɪ] ADV en voz ronca.

hoarseness [ˈhɔːsnɪs] N *(Med)* ronquera *f*; *(hoarse quality)* ronquedad *f*.

hoary [ˈhɔːrɪ] ADJ cano; *joke etc* viejo.

hoax [həʊks] **1** N trampa *f*, truco *m*, mistificación *f*.
2 VT engañar, burlar, mistificar.

hoaxer [ˈhəʊksəʳ] N trampista *mf*.

hob [hɒb] N quemador *m*.

hobble [ˈhɒbl] **1** N *(lameness)* cojera *f*; *(rope)* maniota *f*; **to walk with a ~** cojear.
2 VT *horse* manear.
3 VI *(also* **to ~ along**) cojear, andar cojeando; **to ~ to the door** ir cojeando a la puerta.

hobbledehoy [ˈhɒbldɪˈhɔɪ] N gamberro *m*.

hobby [ˈhɒbɪ] N hobby *m*, pasatiempo *m*, afición *f*; **it's just a ~** es sólo un pasatiempo; **he began to paint as a ~** empezó a pintar como distracción.

hobby-horse [ˈhɒbɪhɔːs] N caballito *m* (de niño), caballo *m* mecedor; *(fig)* caballo *m* de batalla, tema *f*, manía *f*; **he's riding his ~ again** ha vuelto a la misma canción.

hobbyist [ˈhɒbɪɪst] N persona que practica un hobby.

hobgoblin [hɒbˈgɒblɪn] N duende *m*, trasgo *m*.

hobnail [ˈhɒbneɪl] N clavo *m* (de botas).

hobnailed [ˈhɒbneɪld] ADJ *boots* con clavos.

hobnob [ˈhɒbnɒb] VI tratarse con familiaridad; **to ~ with** codearse con, alternar con.

hobo [ˈhəʊbəʊ] N *(US)* vagabundo *m*; obrero *m* temporero, obrero *m* migratorio.

Hobson's choice [ˈhɒbsənzˈtʃɔɪs] N *(Brit)* opción *f* única; **it's ~** o lo tomas o lo dejas.

hock¹ [hɒk] N *(Anat)* corvejón *m*.

hock² [hɒk] N *(Brit: wine)* vino *m* del Rin.

hock³* [hɒk] **1** VT empeñar.
2 N: **in ~** *person* empeñado, endeudado; *object* empeñado.

hockey [ˈhɒkɪ] **1** N hockey *m*; *(Brit: also US* **field ~**) hockey *m* sobre hierba; *(US: also Brit* **ice ~**) hockey *m* sobre hielo.
2 ATTR: **~ player** jugador *m*, -ora *f* de hockey; **~ stick** palo *m* de hockey.

hocus-pocus [ˈhəʊkəsˈpəʊkəs] N *(jugglery)* abracadabra *m*, pasapasa *m*; *(deception)* trampa *f*, mistificación *f*.

hod [hɒd] N capacho *m*.

hodgepodge ['hɒdʒpɒdʒ] N = **hotchpotch**.

hoe [həʊ] 1 N azada *f*, azadón *m*, sacho *m*.
2 VT *earth* azadonar; *crop* sachar.

hog [hɒg] 1 N (a) (*lit, fig*) cerdo *m*, puerco *m*, chancho *m* (*LAm*); **to go the whole ~** liarse la manta a la cabeza, echar el todo por el todo. (b) (*US**) (*car*) cochazo* *m*, coche *m* grande; (*motorbike*) moto *f* grande.
2 VT *food* devorar; (*take for o.s.*) acaparar, tragarse lo mejor de; **to ~ all the credit** acapararse todo el mérito.

Hogmanay ['hɒgmənei] N (*Scot*) noche *f* vieja.

┌─────────────┐
│ *HOGMANAY* │
└─────────────┘

Hogmanay es el nombre que recibe el día de Fin de Año en Escocia. La gente suele organizar fiestas y, cuando suenan las doce campanadas, cantan **Auld Lang Syne***, una canción típica escocesa, y brindan por el nuevo año. Después es costumbre salir a visitar a los amigos para dar juntos la bienvenida al año que comienza. La costumbre de ser los primeros en hacerlo se denomina* **first footing***. Según la tradición es señal de prosperidad y buena suerte en el nuevo año si la primera persona que llega a la casa después de las doce de la noche es un hombre moreno que lleve algo de comida, bebida y un trozo de carbón.*
⇨ *Ver también* AULD LANG SYNE

hogshead ['hɒgzhed] N *medida de capacidad esp del vino* (= 52,5 *galones* = (*approx*) 225 *litros*), pipa *f*.

hogwash ['hɒgwɒʃ] N (*US*) bazofia *f*; (*fig*) cuentos *mpl*, bazofia *f*.

hoi polloi [,hɔɪpə'lɔɪ] N: **the ~** las masas; la plebe, el vulgo.

hoist [hɔɪst] 1 N (*lift*) montacargas *m*; (*crane*) grúa *f*; **to give sb a ~ (up)** ayudar a uno a subir.
2 VT (*also* **to ~ up**) alzar, levantar; *flag* enarbolar, (*Naut*) izar.

hoity-toity ['hɔɪtɪ'tɔɪtɪ] 1 ADJ presumido, repipi*.
2 INTERJ ¡tate!

hokum* ['həʊkəm] N (*US*) tonterías *fpl* (sentimentales).

hold [həʊld] 1 N (a) (*grasp*) agarro *m*, asimiento *m*; (*Wrestling*) presa *f*; **with no ~s barred** (*fig*) sin restricción, permitiéndose todo; sin cuartel; **to catch** (*or* **get, lay, seize, take**) **~ of** agarrar, asirse de, coger (*Sp*); **catch ~!** ¡toma!; **to get ~ of** (*fig*) (*take over*) adquirir, apoderarse de, (*obtain*) procurarse, conseguir; **where did you get ~ of that?** ¿dónde has adquirido eso?; **we're trying to get ~ of him** tratamos de ponernos en contacto con él; **where did you get ~ of that idea?** ¿de dónde te salió esa idea?; **you get ~ of some odd ideas** te formas unas ideas muy raras; **to have ~ of** estar agarrado a; **to keep ~ of** seguir agarrado a; (*fig*) guardar para sí; **to relax one's ~** desasirse (*on* de).
(b) (*place to grip*) asidero *m*.
(c) (*fig*) influencia *f*, dominio *m* (*over* sobre); arraigo *m*; **this broke the dictator's ~** esto acabó con el dominio del dictador; **to gain a firm ~ over sb** llegar a dominar a uno; **drink has a ~ on him** la bebida está muy arraigada en él; **to have a ~ over** (*person*) dominar a uno, ejercer gran influencia sobre uno.
(d) (*Naut*) bodega *f*; (*Aer*) compartimiento *m* de carga, bodega *f* de carga.
(e) **to put a plan on ~** suspender temporalmente la ejecución de un plan; (*Telec*) **to put sb on ~** poner al comunicante en espera; **to be on ~** estar en espera.
2 (*irr:* PRET AND PTP **held**) VT (a) (*gen*) tener; (*take ~ of*) agarrar, coger (*Sp*); (*bear weight of*) soportar; *attention* mantener; *belief* tener; *note* sostener; *road* agarrarse a; **~ him or he'll fall** sóstenle que va a caer; **he held my arm** me tuvo por el brazo; **~ this for a moment** coge esto un momento; **to ~ sth tight** agarrar algo fuertemente; **to ~ sb tight** abrazar a uno estrechamente; **to ~ sth in place** sujetar algo en un lugar; **to ~ sb to his promise** hacer que uno cumpla su promesa; **he ~s the key to the mystery** él tiene la clave del misterio; **he held us spellbound** nos tuvo embelesados; **can he ~ an audience?** ¿sabe mantener el interés de un público?
(b) (*keep back*) retener, guardar; **I will ~ the money for you** guardaré el dinero para ti; **'~ for arrival'** (*US: on letters*) 'no reexpedir', 'reténgase'; **the police held him for 3 days** le detuvo la policía durante 3 días; **we are ~ing it pending inquiries** lo guardamos mientras se hagan indagaciones.
(c) (*check, restrain*) *enemy, breath* contener; **~ it!** ¡para!, para el carro!; **~ everything!** ¡que se pare todo!; **there was no ~ing him** no había manera de detenerle.
(d) (*possess*) *post, town, lands* ocupar; *shares, title* tener; *reserves* tener en reserva, tener guardado; *record* ostentar, estar en posesión de.
(e) (*contain*) contener, tener capacidad (*or* cabida) para; **this ~s the money** esto contiene el dinero; **this bag won't ~ them all** en este saco no caben todos; **a car that ~s 6** un coche de 6 plazas; **what the future ~s for us** lo que el futuro guarda para nosotros.
(f) *interview, meeting, election* celebrar; *conversation* tener, (*formally*) celebrar; **the meeting will be held on Monday** se celebrará la

reunión el lunes, la reunión tendrá lugar el lunes.
(g) (*consider*) **to ~ that ...** creer que ..., sostener que ...; **I ~ that ...** tengo para mí que ...; **it is held by some that ...** hay quien cree que ...; **to ~ sth to be true** creer que algo es verdad; **to ~ sb guilty** juzgar a uno culpable; **to ~ sb responsible** hacer a uno responsable (*for* de); **to ~ sb in respect** tener respeto a uno; **to ~ sb dear** tener cariño a uno.
3 VI (a) (*stick*) pegarse; (*not give way*) mantenerse firme, resistir; (*weather*) continuar, seguir bueno; **the ceasefire seems to be ~ing** el cese de fuego parece que se mantiene.
(b) (*be true*) valer, ser valedero; **the objection does not ~** la objeción no vale.
4 VR: **to ~ o.s. ready** (*or* **in readiness**) estar listo (*for* para); **to ~ o.s. upright** mantenerse erguido.

◆**hold against** VT: **they held his origins against him** creían que sus orígenes eran deshonrosos para él; **you won't ~ this against me, will you?** ¿verdad que no vas a pensar mal de mí por esto?

◆**hold back** 1 VT (*keep*) guardar, retener; (*stop*) *water etc* retener; *progress* refrenar; *information* ocultar, no revelar; *names etc* no comunicar; *emotion, tears* contener; **are you ~ing sth back from me?** ¿me estás ocultando algo?
2 VI refrenarse; mantenerse a distancia; (*in doubt*) vacilar; **I could hardly ~ back from** + *ger* apenas pude abstenerme de + *infin*.
3 VR: **to ~ o.s. back** contenerse, refrenarse.

◆**hold down** VT (a) *object* sujetar.
(b) (*oppress*) oprimir, subyugar.
(c) **to ~ down a job** (*retain*) mantenerse en su puesto; (*be equal to*) estar a la altura de su cargo.

◆**hold forth** VI hablar largamente (*about, on* de); disertar pomposamente.

◆**hold in** VT *emotion* contener.

◆**hold off** 1 VT *attack, enemy* rechazar; tener a raya; *threat* apartar; *person* defenderse contra.
2 VI (a) mantenerse a distancia; no tomar parte; (*wait*) esperar.
(b) **if the rain ~s off** si no llueve.

◆**hold on** VI (a) (*grip*) agarrarse bien.
(b) (*not give way*) aguantar, resistir; defenderse; **~ on!** ¡ánimo!; **can you ~ on?** ¿te animas a continuar?
(c) (*wait*) esperar, seguir esperando; **~ on!** ¡tente!, ¡espera!, (*Telec*) ¡no cuelgue!

◆**hold on to** VT (a) (*grip*) agarrarse bien a.
(b) (*retain*) guardar, quedarse con; *post* retener.

◆**hold out** 1 VT *hand* tender, alargar; *arm* extender; *object* ofrecer, alargar; *possibility* ofrecer; *hope* dar.
2 VI (a) (*resist*) resistir (*against* a), aguantar; **to ~ out for sth** resistir hasta conseguir algo, insistir en algo.
(b) (*last*) durar.
(c) **to ~ out on sb** no acceder a los deseos de uno; ocultar algo a uno.

◆**hold over** VT aplazar, posponer.

◆**hold to** VT atenerse a.

◆**hold together** 1 VT *persons* mantener unidos; *company, group* mantener la unidad de.
2 VI (a) (*persons*) mantenerse unidos.
(b) (*argument*) ser sólido, ser lógico; (*deal etc*) mantenerse.

◆**hold up** 1 VT (a) (*support*) apoyar, sostener.
(b) (*raise*) *hand* levantar, alzar; *head* mantener erguido; **to ~ sth up to the light** acercar algo a la luz.
(c) (*display*) mostrar, enseñar; **to ~ sth up as a model** presentar algo como modelo.
(d) (*delay*) atrasar; (*stop*) detener, parar; *work* interrumpir; *delivery, payment* suspender; **we were held up for 3 hours** no nos pudimos mover durante 3 horas; **the train was held up** el tren sufrió un retraso; **the train was held up by fog** el tren venía con retraso debido a la niebla; **we are held up for** (*or* **by lack of**) **bricks** la escasez de ladrillos entorpece el trabajo.
(e) (*rob*) atracar, asaltar.
2 VI (a) (*weather*) seguir bueno.
(b) **to ~ up under the strain** soportar bien la presión.
(c) (*remain strong*) durar; mantenerse bien, seguir en pie.

◆**hold with** VT estar de acuerdo con, aprobar.

holdall ['həʊldɔːl] N (*Brit*) funda *f*, neceser *m*, bolsa *f* de viaje.

holder ['həʊldər] N (a) (*person*) tenedor *m*, -ora *f*, poseedor *m*, -ora *f*; (*of bonds*) tenedor *m*, -ora *f*; (*of title, credit card, office, passport*) titular *mf*; (*of record*) poseedor *m*, -ora *f*, detentor *m*, -ora *f*.
(b) (*support*) soporte *m*; (*handle*) asidero *m*; (*haft*) mango *m*; (*vessel*) receptáculo *m*; (*for cigarette*) boquilla *f*; (*in compounds*) porta ..., *eg* **lamp-~** portalámparas *m*.

holding ['həʊldɪŋ] 1 N (a) (*act*) tenencia *f*.
(b) (*thing*) posesión *f*, propiedad *f*.
(c) (*Comm*) participación *f*; **~s** valores *mpl* en cartera.
2 ATTR: **~ company** (compañía *f*) holding *m*, compañía *f* tenedora;

~ operation operación *f* de contención.

holdout ['həʊldaʊt] N (*US*): **Britain has been the ~ in trying to negotiate** Gran Bretaña es el único que se resiste a negociar.

holdup ['həʊldʌp] N (a) (*robbery*) atraco *m*; **~ man** atracador *m*. (b) (*Brit*) (*stoppage*) parada *f*, interrupción *f*, suspensión *f*; (*delay*) retraso *m*; (*of traffic*) embotellamiento *m*, retención *f*.

hole [həʊl] **1** N (a) agujero *m*; (*in ground*) hoyo *m*; (*Golf*) hoyo *m*, cazoleta *f*; (*hollow*) cavidad *f*, hueco *m*; (*in road*) bache *m*; (*in wall*) boquete *m*; (*in defences, dam*) brecha *f*; (*burrow*) madriguera *f*; (*in clothes*) roto *m*; **through a ~ in the clouds** a través de un agujero de las nubes; **to bore** (*or* **make**) **a ~** hacer un agujero en. (b) (*fig: defect*) defecto *m*, fallo *m*; **this will make a ~ in my salary** esto dejará temblando mi sueldo; **his injury leaves a ~ in the team** su lesión deja un vacío en el equipo; **to pick ~s in** encontrar defectos en. (c) (*fig: jam*) apuro *m*, aprieto *m*; **to be in a ~** estar en un aprieto; **to get sb out of a ~** sacar a uno de un aprieto. (d) (*) (*room*) cuchitril *m*; (*house*) casucha *f*; (*town*) poblacho *m*, pueblo *m* muerto.
2 VT (a) (*pierce*) agujerear, perforar; **ship** *etc* abrir una brecha en, causar desperfectos a. (b) *ball* (*Golf*) embocar; (*Snooker*) meter en la tronera.
3 VI: **to ~ in one** hacer un hoyo de un golpe; **to ~ out** embocar; **to ~ out in 7** terminar en 7 golpes.
♦**hole up** VI (*animal*) ocultarse (en la querencia), retirarse (a la madriguera *etc*); (*wanted man*) esconderse, refugiarse.

hole-and-corner ['həʊlən'kɔːnər] ADJ furtivo; **to do sth in a ~ way** hacer algo de tapadillo.

hole-in-the-heart ['həʊlɪnðə'hɑːt] N soplo *m* cardíaco.

hole-in-the-wall* ['həʊlɪnðə'wɔːl] N (*Brit*) cajero *m* automático.

holey* ['həʊlɪ] ADJ lleno de rotos; agujereado.

holiday ['hɒlədɪ] **1** N (*day*) (día *m* de) fiesta *f*, día *m* festivo, (día *m*) feriado *m* (*LAm*); (*period*) vacaciones *fpl*; **~s with pay** vacaciones *fpl* retribuidas; **tomorrow is a ~** mañana es fiesta; **to be on** (*one's*) **~(s)** estar de vacaciones; **to declare a day a ~** declarar un día festivo; **to take a ~** tomarse unas vacaciones; **it was no ~ (I can tell you)** no era ningún lecho de rosas (te lo aseguro).
2 ATTR *town* de veraneo; *mood etc* alegre, festivo; **~ clothes** ropa *f* de veraneo, traje *m* de sport; **~ home** casa *f* (*or* piso *m etc*) para ocupar durante las vacaciones; **~ pay** sueldo *m* de vacaciones; **~ resort** punto *m* de veraneo; centro *m* turístico; **~ season** (*Brit*) temporada *f* de vacaciones; (*US*) Navidades *fpl*; **~ spirit** espíritu *m* festivo; **~ traffic** tráfico *m* de coches que van de vacaciones.
3 VI (*Brit*) pasar las vacaciones, (*esp*) veranear.

holiday-camp ['hɒlədɪkæmp] N (*Brit*) colonia *f* veraniega.

holiday-maker ['hɒlədɪˌmeɪkər] N (*esp Brit*) veraneante *mf*, excursionista *mf*, turista *mf*.

holier-than-thou ['həʊlɪəðən'ðaʊ] ADJ fariseo; **he's always so ~** es un doña perfecta.

holiness ['həʊlɪnɪs] N santidad *f*; **His H~** Su Santidad.

holistic [həʊ'lɪstɪk] ADJ holístico.

Holland ['hɒlənd] N Holanda *f*.

hollandaise [ˌhɒlən'deɪz] ADJ: **~ sauce** salsa *f* holandesa.

holler* ['hɒlər] VTI (*also* **to ~ out**) gritar, vocear.

hollow ['hɒləʊ] **1** ADJ (a) hueco, ahuecado; *cheeks, eyes* hundido. (b) (*fig*) *sound* sordo; *voice* sepulcral, cavernoso; *laughter* irónico; *doctrine etc* vacío, falso; *victory* más aparente que real, pírrico; *promise* sin efecto práctico, falso.
2 ADV (a) **to sound** sonar a hueco; (*fig*) sonar a falso. (b) **to beat sb ~*** cascar a uno*, vencer a uno fácilmente.
3 N hueco *m*; concavidad *f*; (*in ground*) hoyo *m*, depresión *f*; (*small valley*) hondonada *f*; **in the ~ of one's back** en los riñones; **in the ~ of one's hand** en el hueco de la mano.
4 VT (*also* **to ~ out**) ahuecar, excavar, vaciar.

hollow-cheeked [ˌhɒləʊ'tʃiːkt] ADJ de mejillas hundidas.

hollow-eyed ['hɒləʊ'aɪd] ADJ de ojos hundidos; (*with fatigue etc*) ojeroso.

hollowly ['hɒləʊlɪ] ADV: **to laugh ~** reír huecamente.

hollowness ['hɒləʊnɪs] N (a) oquedad *f*, lo hueco. (b) (*fig*) vaciedad *f*; falsedad *f*.

holly ['hɒlɪ] **1** N (*also* **~ tree**) acebo *m*.
2 ATTR: **~ berry** baya *f* de acebo.

hollyhock ['hɒlɪhɒk] N malva *f* loca.

Hollywood ['hɒlɪˌwʊd] N Hollywood *m*.

holmium ['hɒlmɪəm] N holmio *m*.

holm oak ['həʊm'əʊk] N encina *f*.

holocaust ['hɒləkɔːst] N holocausto *m* (*also fig*).

hologram ['hɒləgræm] N holograma *m*.

holograph ['hɒləgrɑːf] **1** ADJ ológrafo.
2 N ológrafo *m*.

holography [hɒ'lɒgrəfɪ] N holografía *f*.

hols* [hɒlz] NPL = **holidays**.

holster ['həʊlstər] N pistolera *f*, funda *f* (de pistola).

holy ['həʊlɪ] **1** ADJ santo; sagrado; **H~ Bible** Santa Biblia *f*; **H~ Communion** Sagrada Comunión *f*; **H~ Family** Sagrada Familia *f*; **the H~ Father** el Santo Padre; **H~ Ghost** Espíritu *m* Santo; **H~ Land** Tierra *f* Santa; **H~ Office** Santo Oficio *m*; **~ orders** órdenes *fpl* sagradas; **to take ~ orders** ordenarse (de sacerdote); **H~ See** Santa Sede *f*; **H~ Spirit** Espíritu *m* Santo; **H~ Trinity** Santa Trinidad *f*; **~ water** agua *f* bendita; **H~ Week** Semana *f* Santa; **H~ Writ** Sagrada Escritura *f*; **by all that's ~** por todo lo más sagrado; **~ cow!***, **~ smoke!*** (*etc*) ¡santo cielo!; **he's a ~ terror*** (*child*) tiene el diablo en el cuerpo; (*master*) es un amo de lo más feroz.
2 N: **the ~ of holies** el sanctum sanctorum.

homage ['hɒmɪdʒ] N homenaje *m*; **~ volume** tomo-homenaje *m*; **to do** (*or* **pay**) **~ to** rendir homenaje a.

homburg ['hɒmbɜːg] N sombrero *m* de fieltro.

home [həʊm] **1** N (a) casa *f*; (*more officially*) domicilio *m*; (*more sentimentally*) hogar *m*; (*town*) ciudad *f* natal, (*region, native land*) patria *f*; (*Bio*) habitat *m*, (*environment*) ambiente *m* natural; (*Sport*) meta *f*; (*in children's games*) la madre; (*for the elderly*) residencia *f*; (*institution*) asilo *m*; **~ for the aged** asilo *m* de ancianos; **we live in Madrid but my ~ is in Jaén** vivimos en Madrid pero nací en Jaén; **for some years he made his ~ in France** durante algunos años vivió en Francia; **refugees who made their ~ in Britain** los refugiados que se establecieron en Gran Bretaña; **Scotland is the ~ of whisky** Escocia es la patria del whisky; **for us it's a ~ from ~** (*Brit*) aquí estamos como en casa; **an Englishman's ~ is his castle** para el inglés su casa es como su castillo; **there's no place like ~** no hay nada como la propia casa; **that remark came near ~** esa observación le hirió en lo vivo; **he comes from a good ~** es de buena familia; **to have a ~ of one's own** tener casa propia; **to give sb a ~** recibir a uno en casa; **he leaves ~ at 8** sale de casa a las 8; **'good ~ wanted for puppy'** 'búscase buen hogar para perrito'; **the puppy went to a good ~** el perrito fue a vivir con una buena familia; **this tool has no ~** esta herramienta no tiene lugar propio. (b) (*Comput*) punto *m* inicial, punto *m* de partida. (c) (*phrases with at*) **at ~** en casa; **at ~ and abroad** dentro y fuera del país; **is Mr Pérez at ~?** ¿está (en casa) el Sr Pérez?; **the duchess is at ~ on Fridays** la duquesa recibe los viernes; **Lady Rebecca is not at ~ to anyone** Lady Rebecca no recibe a nadie; **he's at ~ on any subject** sabe de cualquier materia; **I'm not at ~ in Japanese** apenas me defiendo en japonés, sé muy poco de japonés; **to feel at ~** sentirse como en casa; **make yourself at ~!** ¡estás en tu casa!; **to make sb feel at ~** hacer que se sienta como en casa; **he immediately made himself at ~ in the new job** en seguida se familiarizó con el nuevo trabajo. (d) (*Sport*) **to play at ~** jugar en casa, jugar en el propio terreno, jugar en campo propio; **Villasanta are at ~ to Castroforte** Villasanta recibe en casa a Castroforte; **they lost nine games at ~** perdieron nueve partidos en casa.
2 ATTR (a) casero, de casa, doméstico; **~ address** (*on form etc*) domicilio *m*; **my ~ address** mi dirección particular, las señas de mi casa; **~ banking** banco *m* en casa; **~ brew** cerveza *f* casera; **~ comforts** comodidades *fpl* domésticas; **~ computer** ordenador *m* doméstico; **~ computing** informática *f* doméstica; **~ cooking** cocina *f* doméstica; **~ economics** (*Scol*) ciencia *f* del hogar; **~ fries** (*US*) carne picada frita con patatas y col; **to be on ~ ground** (*or* **territory**) (*fig*) estar en su terreno (*or* lugar); **~ help** (*act*) atención *f* domiciliaria, ayuda *f* a domicilio; (*Brit: person*) asistenta *f*; **~ improvements** reformas *fpl* en casa; **~ journey** viaje *m* a casa, viaje *m* de vuelta; **~ leave** permiso *m* para irse a casa; **~ life** vida *f* doméstica, vida *f* de familia; **~ owners** propietarios *mpl* de viviendas; **~ ownership** propiedad *f* de viviendas; **~ page** (*Comput*) página *f* digital, home page *f*; **~ run** (*of ship, truck*) viaje *m* de vuelta; **~ shopping** venta *f* por correo; (*by TV, telephone*) televenta *f*; **~ truths** verdades *fpl* bien claras; **to tell sb a few ~ truths** decir a uno cuatro verdades; **~ video** vídeo *m* doméstico; **~ visit** visita *f* a domicilio. (b) (*Sport*) **to play at one's ~ ground** jugar en casa; **~ match** partido *m* de casa (*or* en casa); **~ run** (*Baseball*) carrera *f* completa, home run *m*, jonrón *m* (*LAm*); **the ~ side** el equipo de casa, el equipo local; **~ victory** victoria *f* local. (c) (*Racing*) **~ straight**, (*US*) **~ stretch** recta *f* final, recta *f* de llegada; **we're on the ~ stretch** (*fig*) ésta es la última etapa. (d) (*native*) natal; **~ area** región *f* natal; **~ port** puerto *m* de origen; **~ town** ciudad *f* natal. (e) *defence, industry, product, flight* nacional; *population* metropolitano; *news* del país, nacional, doméstico; *policy* doméstico; *trade* interior; **H~ Counties** los condados alrededor de Londres; **~ country** patria *f*, país *m* de origen; **on the ~ front** (*Mil, Pol etc*) en el país; (*hum*: *at home*) en casa; **H~ Guard** (*Brit*) cuerpo *m* de voluntarios para la defensa nacional (*1940-45*); **~ market** mercado *m* nacional, mercado *m* interior; **~ news** (*gen*) noticias *fpl* de casa; (*Pol*) información *f* nacional; **H~ Office** (*Brit*) Ministerio *m* del Interior; **~ rule**

autonomía f, autogobierno m; **~ sales** ventas fpl nacionales; **H~ Secretary** (Brit) Ministro m, -a f del Interior; **~ waters** aguas fpl territoriales.

3 ADV **(a) to be ~** estar en casa; (return) estar de vuelta; **to be ~ and dry** lograr ponerse a salvo, llegar a buen puerto; **to come ~** volver a casa, (from abroad) volver a la patria; **to get ~** llegar a casa; **to go ~, to return ~** ir a casa, (from abroad) volver a la patria; **to see sb ~** acompañar a uno a su casa; **to send sb ~** enviar a uno a su casa; **to stay ~** quedarse en casa; **to write ~** escribir a la familia; **it's nothing to write ~ about*** no tiene nada de particular; **as we say back ~** como dicen en mi tierra; **the first ~ gets the cup** el primero que llegue se lleva la copa; **it's a long journey ~** hay mucho camino para llegar a casa.

(b) (right in etc) **to bring sth ~ to sb** hacer que uno se dé cuenta cabal de algo; **it came ~ to me that ...** me di cuenta cabal de que ...; **to drive a nail ~** hacer que un clavo entre a fondo; **to press an advantage ~** aprovecharse todo lo posible de una ventaja; **to drive a point ~** subrayar un punto; **to strike ~** (shell etc) hacer blanco; (argument etc) herir en lo vivo.

4 VI volver a casa; (animal) buscar la querencia.

◆**home in on** VT: **to ~ in on the target** buscar el blanco; **they ~d in on the pub** fueron derechito a la taberna.

┌─── **HOME COUNTIES** ───┐

i *Los **Home Counties** son los condados que se encuentran en los alrededores de Londres: Berkshire, Buckinghamshire, Essex, Hertfordshire, Kent y Middlesex, un alto porcentaje de cuya población se encuentra en buena posición económica. De ahí que el término **Home Counties** haya adquirido dimensiones culturales y a la gente que vive en ellos se les considere en general personas adineradas de clase media-alta que, además, tienen al hablar un acento muy particular, conocido como **RP**.*
⇨ *Ver también* ENGLISH

home-baked ['həʊm'beɪkt] ADJ bread etc casero.
homebody ['həʊmbɒdɪ] N (US) persona f hogareña.
homebound ['həʊmbaʊnd] ADJ: **the ~ traveller** el viajero que vuelve a (or se dirige a) casa.
homeboy* ['həʊmbɔɪ] N (US) chico m del barrio.
home-brewed ['həʊm'bruːd] ADJ hecho en casa.
home buying ['həʊm,baɪɪŋ] N compra f de vivienda.
homecoming ['həʊmkʌmɪŋ] N regreso m (al hogar).
Homecoming Queen ['həʊmkʌmɪŋ,kwiːn] N (US) reina de la fiesta de antiguos alumnos; ver también YEARBOOK.
homegirl* ['həʊmgɜːl] N (US) chica f del barrio.
home-grown ['həʊm'grəʊn] ADJ de cosecha propia (also fig).
homeland ['həʊmlænd] N **(a)** tierra f natal, patria f. **(b)** (S. Africa) bantustán m, territorio m nativo.
homeless ['həʊmlɪs] **1** ADJ sin hogar, sin techo; **the storm left a hundred ~** la tormenta dejó sin hogar a cien personas.
2 NPL: **the ~** los sin hogar.
homelessness ['həʊmlɪsnɪs] N el estar sin hogar; **the increase in ~** el aumento de la cifra de los que no tienen hogar.
homeliness ['həʊmlɪnɪs] N llaneza f, sencillez f.
home loan ['həʊm'ləʊn] N hipoteca f.
home-lover ['həʊm,lʌvəʳ] N persona f hogareña.
home-loving ['həʊm,lʌvɪŋ] ADJ hogareño, casero, apegado al hogar.
homely ['həʊmlɪ] ADJ **(a)** casero, doméstico, familiar; (unpretentious) llano, sencillo; atmosphere acogedor; **it's very ~ here** aquí se está como en casa. **(b)** (US) feo, poco atractivo.
home-made ['həʊm'meɪd] ADJ casero, de fabricación casera.
home-maker ['həʊm,meɪkəʳ] N (US) ama f de casa.
homeopath ['həʊmɪəʊpæθ] etc (US) = **homoeopath** etc.
Homer ['həʊməʳ] NM Homero.
homer* ['həʊməʳ] N (Brit) trabajo m fuera de hora, chollo♣ m.
Homeric [həʊ'merɪk] ADJ homérico.
homesick ['həʊmsɪk] ADJ nostálgico; **to be ~** sentir nostalgia, tener morriña.
homesickness ['həʊmsɪknɪs] N nostalgia f, morriña f.
homespun ['həʊmspʌn] ADJ tejido en casa, hecho en casa; (fig) llano, llanote.
homestead ['həʊmsted] N (US) casa f, caserío m; (farm) granja f.
homeward ['həʊmwəd] ADJ: **~ journey** viaje m hacia casa, viaje m de regreso.
homeward(s) ['həʊmwəd(z)] ADV hacia casa; (from abroad) hacia la patria; **~ bound** (Naut) con rumbo al puerto de origen.
homework ['həʊmwɜːk] N deberes mpl, tarea(s) f(PL); **to do one's ~** (fig) documentarse, prepararse, hacer el trabajo preparatorio; **~ exercise** deberes mpl.
homeworker ['həʊmwɜːkəʳ] N asalariado m, -a f que trabaja desde casa.
homeworking ['həʊmwɜːkɪŋ] N trabajo m desde casa.
homey* ['həʊmɪ] ADJ (US) íntimo, cómodo.

homicidal [,hɒmɪ'saɪdl] ADJ homicida; **to feel ~** (fig) sentirse capaz de matar, tener ganas de matar.
homicide ['hɒmɪsaɪd] N (act) homicidio m; (person) homicida mf.
homily ['hɒmɪlɪ] N homilía f; (fig) sermón m.
homing ['həʊmɪŋ] ADJ: **~ device** dispositivo m buscador de blancos; **~ instinct** instinto m de buscar la querencia; **~ pigeon** paloma f mensajera, paloma f buscadora de blancos.
hominid ['hɒmɪnɪd] N homínido m.
hominy ['hɒmɪnɪ] N (US) maíz m molido.
homo♣ ['həʊməʊ] N (pej) ABBR of **homosexual** marica♣ m.
homoeopath, (US) **homeopath** ['həʊmɪəʊpæθ] N homeópata mf.
homoeopathic, (US) **homeopathic** [,həʊmɪəʊ'pæθɪk] ADJ homeopático.
homoeopathy, (US) **homeopathy** [,həʊmɪ'ɒpəθɪ] N homeopatía f.
homogeneity ['həʊməʊdʒə'niːɪtɪ] N homogeneidad f.
homogeneous [,həʊmə'dʒiːnɪəs] ADJ homogéneo.
homogenize [hə'mɒdʒənaɪz] VT homogenizar.
homogenous [hə'mɒdʒɪnəs] = **homogeneous**.
homograph ['hɒməʊgrɑːf] N homógrafo m.
homonym ['hɒmənɪm] N homónimo m.
homophobe [,həʊməʊ'fəʊb] N homófobo m, -a f.
homophobia ['hɒməʊ'fəʊbɪə] N homofobia f.
homophobic ['hɒməʊ'fəʊbɪk] ADJ homofóbico.
homophone ['hɒməfəʊn] N homófono m.
homophonic [,hɒmə'fɒnɪk] ADJ homófono.
homosexual ['hɒməʊ'seksjʊəl] **1** ADJ homosexual.
2 N homosexual mf.
homosexuality ['hɒməʊseksjʊ'ælɪtɪ] N homosexualidad f.
Hon. ABBR of **Honorary** or **Honourable** (in titles).
Honduran [hɒn'djʊərən] **1** ADJ hondureño.
2 N hondureño m, -a f.
Honduras [hɒn'djʊərəs] N Honduras f.
hone [həʊn] **1** N piedra f de afilar.
2 VT afilar.
▼ **honest** ['ɒnɪst] ADJ (upright) honrado, recto; (speaking openly) franco, sincero; **by ~ means** por medios legales; **the ~ truth is** la pura verdad es; **what is your ~ opinion?** ¿qué piensas francamente de esto?; **be ~!** ¡di la verdad!; **to be perfectly ~ with you, ...** para decirlo con toda franqueza ...; **you were not entirely ~ with me** no fuiste completamente franco conmigo.
honest broker ['ɒnɪst'brəʊkəʳ] N mediador m, -ora f.
honestly ['ɒnɪstlɪ] ADV honradamente; francamente; **I don't ~ know, ~ I don't know** francamente no lo sé; **~?** ¿de veras?
honest-to-God ['ɒnɪstə'gɒd] ADJ, **honest-to-goodness** ['ɒnɪstə'gʊdnɪs] ADJ cien por cien.
honesty ['ɒnɪstɪ] N honradez f, rectitud f; franqueza f; **in all ~** con toda franqueza; **~ is the best policy** la honradez es el mejor capital.
honesty box ['ɒnɪstɪ,bɒks] N caja donde se deposita el dinero por algo cuando no hay nadie para recogerlo en persona.
honey ['hʌnɪ] N **(a)** miel f. **(b)** (*) **yes, ~** sí, querida; **hullo ~!** ¡oye, guapa!; **she's a ~** es un encanto, ¡qué guapa!, ¡qué linda! (LAm).
honeybee ['hʌnɪbiː] N abeja f (obrera).
honey blonde [,hʌnɪ'blɒnd] **1** ADJ rubio miel.
2 N rubia f miel.
honeybunch* ['hʌnɪbʌntʃ], **honeybun*** ['hʌnɪbʌn] N (esp US) cielito m.
honeycomb ['hʌnɪkəʊm] **1** N panal m.
2 VT: **the building is ~ed with passages** hay un sinfín de pasillos en el edificio; **the hill is ~ed with galleries** una multitud de galerías penetran por la colina.
honeydew melon ['hʌnɪdjuː'melən] N melón m dulce.
honeyed ['hʌnɪd] ADJ meloso, melifluo.
honeyfuggle* ['hʌnɪ,fʌgəl] VT (US) obtener mediante un truco.
honeymoon ['hʌnɪmuːn] **1** N luna f de miel, viaje m de novios.
2 ATTR: **the ~ couple** la pareja de recién casados; **~ period** (Pol etc) período m de gracia, cien días mpl.
3 VI pasar la luna de miel.
honeymooner ['hʌnɪ,muːnəʳ] N persona que está en su luna de miel.
honeypot ['hʌnɪpɒt] N mielera f.
honeysuckle ['hʌnɪ,sʌkl] N madreselva f.
Hong Kong [,hɒŋ'kɒŋ] N Hong Kong m.
honk [hɒŋk] **1** N (Orn) graznido m; (Aut) bocinazo m.
2 VI graznar; tocar la bocina, bocinar.
honky♣ ['hɒŋkɪ] N (US pej) blanco m, blancucho* m.
honky-tonk* ['hɒŋkɪ,tɒŋk] N **(a)** (US: club) garito m. **(b)** (Mus) honky-tonk* m.
Honolulu [,hɒnə'luːluː] N Honolulú m.
honor ['ɒnəʳ] (US) = **honour**.
honorable ['ɒnərəbl] (US) = **honourable**.
honorably ['ɒnərəblɪ] (US) = **honourably**.
honorarium [,ɒnə'reərɪəm] N honorarios mpl.
honorary ['ɒnərərɪ] ADJ honorario; president, member de honor;

(*unpaid*) no remunerado; ~ **degree** doctorado *m* honoris causa; ~ **secretary** secretario *m* honorario, secretaria *f* honoraria.

honorific [ɒnəˈrɪfɪk] ①︎ ADJ honorífico.
②︎ N título *m* honorífico.

honour, (*US*) **honor** [ˈɒnər] ①︎ N **(a)** honor *m*; (*good name*) honra *f*; (*uprightness*) honradez *f*; **in ~ of** en honor de; **on my ~!** ¡palabra de honor!; **it's a great ~ for him** es un gran honor para él; **to be on one's ~ to** + *infin*, **to be (in) ~ bound to** + *infin* estar moralmente obligado a + *infin*; **I consider it an ~ to** + *infin* tengo a mucha honra + *infin*; **I had the ~ to** + *infin* (*or* **of** + *ger*) tuve el honor de + *infin*; **to hold sb in high ~** tener un altísimo concepto de uno.
(b) **Your H~** (*title*) Señor Juez.
(c) (*Brit: medal etc*) condecoración *f*.
(d) **~s** honores *mpl*; **last ~s** honras *fpl* fúnebres; **the ~s are even** se ha logrado un empate; **to bury sb with full military ~s** sepultar a uno con todos los honores militares; **to do the ~s of the house** hacer los honores de la casa.
(e) **to take ~s in chemistry** (*Brit Univ*) licenciarse en química.
(f) (*Bridge*) **~s** honores *mpl*; **3 ~s tricks** 3 bazas *fpl* de honores.
②︎ ATTR: **~s course** (*Brit Univ*) licenciatura *f*; **~s degree** (*Brit Univ*) licenciatura *f*; **H~s List** (*Brit*) lista *f* de condecoraciones; **~roll** (*US Univ*) lista de honor académica; *ver también* DEAN'S LIST , DEGREE .
③︎ VT honrar; *pledge, signature* hacer honor a; *cheque* aceptar, pagar; (*respect*) respetar, reverenciar; **I ~ you for it** te respeto más por esto; **to ~ sb with one's confidence** honrar a uno con su confianza; **I am deeply ~ed** lo tengo a mucha honra; **I should be ~ed if ...** estimaría que + *subj*.

HONOURS LIST

ⓘ *La* **Honours List** *es una lista de personas a las que se considera merecedoras de un reconocimiento especial por su labor, tanto en la vida pública como por servicios prestados a la zona en la que viven. Esta lista es elaborada por el Primer Ministro británico con la aprobación del monarca y se publica dos veces al año, la primera en Año Nuevo - la* **New Year's Honours List** *- y la segunda en junio, el día del cumpleaños de la reina -la* **Queen's Birthday Honours List**. *En la mayoría de los casos a estas personas se les reconoce su mérito con la concesión del título de miembro de la Orden del Imperio Británico,* **Member of the Order of the British Empire** *o* **MBE**, *u oficial de la Orden del Imperio Británico* **Officer of the Order of the British Empire** *u* **OBE**.

honourable, (*US*) **honorable** [ˈɒnərəbl] ADJ (*worthy*) honorable; (*upright*) honrado; *title, deed etc* honroso; *mention* honorífico; **the ~ member for Woodford** el señor diputado de Woodford.

honourably, (*US*) **honorably** [ˈɒnərəblɪ] ADV honradamente.

Hons. (*Univ*) ABBR of **Honours**.

Hon. Sec. ABBR of **Honorary Secretary**.

hooch* [huːtʃ] N (*US*) licor *m* (*esp* ilícito).

hood¹ [hʊd] N (*of cloak, raincoat, Eccl*) capucha *f*; (*Univ*) muceta *f* (con capucha); (*of penitent, hawk*) capirote *m*; (*Brit Aut*) capota *f*, toldo *m* (*Mex*); (*US Aut*) capó *m*.

hood²‡ [hʊd] (*US*) N = **hoodlum**.

hooded [ˈhʊdɪd] ADJ encapuchado; encapirotado.

hoodlum* [ˈhuːdləm] N (*US*) gorila* *m*, matón *m*.

hoodoo [ˈhuːduː] N vudú *m*; gafe *m*, gafancia *f*, mala suerte *f*; **there's a ~ on it** tiene gafe.

hoodwink [ˈhʊdwɪŋk] VT burlar, engañar.

hooey* [ˈhuːɪ] N música *f* celestial*; **~!** ¡tonterías!

hoof [huːf] ①︎ N, PL **hoofs** *or* **hooves** [huːvz] casco *m*, pezuña *f*; (*foot*) pata *f*; **cattle on the ~** ganado *m* en pie; **~ and mouth disease** (*US*) fiebre *f* aftosa, glosopeda *f*.
②︎ VT (*): **to ~ it** (*walk*) ir a pie, (*depart*) liar el petate.

hoofed [huːft] ADJ ungulado.

hoofer [ˈhuːfər]† N (*esp US: dancer*) bailarín *m*, -ina *f*.

hoo-ha* [ˈhuːˌhɑː] N (*fuss*) lío* *m*, follón* *m*; (*noise*) estrépito *m*; (*publicity etc*) bombo* *m*; **there was a great ~ about it** se armó un tremendo follón*.

hook [hʊk] ①︎ N **(a)** gancho *m*; garfio *m*; (*Fishing*) anzuelo *m*; (*hanger*) colgadero *m*; **~s and eyes** corchetes *mpl*; **to swallow sth ~, line and sinker** tragar algo completamente; **by ~ or by crook** como sea, por las buenas o por las malas; **to get sb off the ~** sacar a uno del atolladero; **to let sb off the ~** dejar escapar a uno, permitir que uno se salve; **to sling one's ~‡** (*depart*) largarse*; (*stop work*) suspender el trabajo; **to take the phone off the ~** descolgar el teléfono.
(b) (*Boxing*) gancho *m*, crochet *m*.
(c) (*Golf*) golpe *m* con efecto a la izquierda.
(d) **~s‡** manos *fpl*.
②︎ VT **(a)** (*attach*) enganchar; (*Fishing*) pescar, coger, enganchar; **to ~ sth to a rope** enganchar algo a una cuerda; **to ~ a rope round a nail** atar una cuerda a un clavo; **she finally ~ed him*** ella por fin le pescó; **to ~ it*** largarse*.
(b) (*curve*) encorvar.

(c) (*) **to be ~ed on** estar adicto a, entregarse a; (*pej*) enviciarse con; **to be ~ed on drugs** quedar enganchado a la droga*, quedar colgado*.
③︎ VI **(a)** engancharse (*on to* a).
(b) encorvarse.
(c) (*US**) trabajar como prostituta.
◆ **hook up** VT enganchar, *dress* abrochar.

hookah [ˈhʊkɑː] N narguile *m*.

hooked [hʊkt] ADJ ganchudo.

hooker [ˈhʊkər] N **(a)** (*Sport*) talonador *m*. **(b)** (*US*‡) puta *f*.

hook(e)y [ˈhʊkɪ] N: **to play ~** (*esp US*) hacer novillos.

hook-nosed [ˌhʊkˈnəʊzd] ADJ de nariz ganchuda.

hookup [ˈhʊkʌp] N (*Elec*) acoplamiento *m*; (*Rad*) transmisión *f* en circuito; **a ~ with Eurovision** una emisión conjunta con Eurovisión.

hookworm [ˈhʊkwɜːm] N anquilostoma *m*.

hooligan [ˈhuːlɪgən] N gamberro *m*.

hooliganism [ˈhuːlɪgənɪzəm] N gamberrismo *m*.

hoop [huːp] N aro *m*; (*in croquet*) arco *m*, aro *m*.

hoopoe [ˈhuːpuː] N abubilla *f*.

hooray [hʊˈreɪ] = **hurrah**.

Hooray Henry [ˌhuːreɪˈhenrɪ] N (*Brit pej*) señorito *m*.

hoot [huːt] ①︎ N **(a)** (*of owl*) grito *m*, ululato *m*; (*of horn*) bocinazo *m*; (*of ship, factory*) toque *m* de sirena.
(b) (*laugh*) risotada *f*; **it was a ~!*** (*Brit*) ¡era para morirse de risa!
②︎ VT (*of owl*) silbar, abuchear; **to ~ sb off the stage** abuchear a uno hasta que abandone la escena.
③︎ VI (*owl*) ulular, gritar; (*person*) silbar; (*Aut: person*) tocar la bocina, (*car*) dar un bocinazo; (*ship*) dar un toque de sirena; **to ~ with laughter** morirse de risa.

hooter [ˈhuːtər] N **(a)** (*of ship, factory*) sirena *f*; (*Brit Aut*) bocina *f*, claxon *m*. **(b)** (*Brit*‡) nariz *f*, napias‡ *fpl*.

Hoover [ˈhuːvər] ®︎ ①︎ N aspirador *m*.
②︎ VTI limpiar con aspirador, pasar la aspiradora por.

hooves [huːvz] NPL of **hoof**.

hop¹ [hɒp] N (*Bot: also* **~s**) lúpulo *m*.

hop² [hɒp] ①︎ N **(a)** salto *m*, saltito *m*, brinco *m*; (*Aer*) salto *m*, etapa *f* de un vuelo; **~, skip and jump** triple salto *m*; **in one ~** de un salto, (*Aer*) sin hacer escala; **to catch sb on the ~** coger a uno desprevenido; **the uncertainty should keep them on the ~** la incertidumbre deberá mantenerles en estado de alerta.
(b) (*: *dance*) baile *m*.
②︎ VT cruzar de un salto; **to ~ it*** escabullirse, largarse*; **~ it!** ¡lárgate!*
③︎ VI saltar, brincar; saltar con un pie; saltar a la pata coja; (*limp*) cojear; **to be ~ping mad*** echar chispas*.
◆ **hop along** VI avanzar a saltos.
◆ **hop off** ①︎ VT bajar de.
②︎ VI **(a)** bajar.
(b) (*) largarse; **~ off!** ¡lárgate!
◆ **hop on** ①︎ VT subir a.
②︎ VI subir; **~ on!** ¡sube!
◆ **hop out** VI salir de un salto; **to ~ out of bed** saltar de la cama.

▼ **hope** [həʊp] ①︎ N esperanza *f*; (*trust*) confianza *f*; (*hopefulness*) ilusión *f*; (*chance*) posibilidad *f*; **some ~s!, not a ~!** ¡ni esperanza!, ¡ni peligro!, ¡de eso ni hablar!; **my ~ is that ...** yo espero que ...; **there is no ~ of that** no hay posibilidad alguna de eso; **you are my last ~** tú eres mi única salvación; **he's the bright ~ of the team** es la esperanza dorada del equipo; **to be full of ~** estar lleno de ilusión, estar muy ilusionado; **to build up ~s** hacerse ilusiones; **to conceive the ~ that ...** hacerse la ilusión de + *infin*; **you haven't got a ~ in hell of that** no tienes la más remota posibilidad de lograrlo; **he held out the ~ that ...** ofreció la esperanza de que ...; **to live in ~ of sth** vivir con (*or* en) la esperanza de algo; **to lose ~** perder la esperanza, desesperarse; **to place ~ in sth** poner esperanzas en algo; **to raise sb's ~s** hacer que uno conciba esperanzas.
②︎ ATTR: **~ chest** (*US*) ajuar *m* (de novia).
▼③︎ VT: **to ~ that ...** esperar que + *subj*; **I ~ he comes soon** ojalá venga pronto; **I ~ you don't think I'm going to do it!** ¡no pensarás que lo haga yo!; **I should ~ so!** ¡ya era hora!; **to ~ to** + *infin* esperar + *infin*; **hoping to hear from you** en espera de tus gratas noticias; **what do you ~ to gain from that?** ¿qué pretendes ganar con eso?
④︎ VI esperar; **to ~ for sth** esperar algo; **we'll just have to ~ for the best** tendremos que mantener el optimismo a pesar de todo; **to ~ against ~** esperar desesperando; **to ~ in** confiar en.

hoped-for [ˈhəʊptˌfɔːr] ADJ (tan) esperado.

hopeful [ˈhəʊpfʊl] ①︎ ADJ *person* lleno de esperanzas, optimista, (*falsely*) ilusionado; *prospect etc* esperanzador, prometedor; **he wasn't very ~** no se mostró muy optimista; **I'm not very ~ that ...** no me hago muchas ilusiones de que + *subj*; **it looks ~** promete mucho.
②︎ N aspirante *mf*; candidato *m*, -a *f*; **young ~** joven *m* ilusionado, joven *f* ilusionada.

hopefully [ˈhəʊpfəlɪ] ADV **(a)** con optimismo; con ilusión. **(b)** (*one* hopes) **~!** ¡ojalá!; **~ I shan't need it** en el mejor de los casos no lo voy a necesitar; **~ they won't come** es de esperar que no vengan.

hopeless ['həʊplɪs] ADJ **(a)** *person* (*without hope*) desesperado, sin esperanza.
(b) (*impossible, useless*) *situation* desesperado, irremediable; *task* imposible; (*Med*) *case* desahuciado; *drunkard etc* incurable; **to give sth up as ~** renunciar a algo por imposible; **the boss is ~** el jefe es un caso perdido; **I'm ~ at it** yo soy inútil para eso; **it's ~** todo es inútil, no tiene remedio; **it's ~ trying to** + *infin* es inútil tratar de + *infin*.

hopelessly ['həʊplɪslɪ] ADV *live etc* sin esperanza; **she looked at me ~** me miró desesperada; **I'm ~ confused** estoy totalmente despistado; **it's ~ dear for us** es excesivamente caro para nosotros.

hopelessness ['həʊplɪsnɪs] N desesperación *f*; lo irremediable; imposibilidad *f*.

hop field ['hɒpfiːld] N campo *m* de lúpulo.

hopper ['hɒpər] N (*Agr etc*) tolva *f*; (*Rail*) vagón *m* tolva.

hop-picking ['hɒp,pɪkɪŋ] N recolección *f* del lúpulo.

hopscotch ['hɒpskɒtʃ] N: **to play ~** jugar a la pata coja, jugar a la reina mora.

Horace ['hɒrɪs] NM Horacio.

Horatian [hɒ'reɪʃən] ADJ horaciano.

horde [hɔːd] N horda *f*; (*fig*) multitud *f*, muchedumbre *f*.

horizon [hə'raɪzn] N horizonte *m*; **there are new schemes on the ~** hay nuevos planes en perspectiva; **that's over the ~ now** eso queda ya a la espalda.

horizontal [,hɒrɪ'zɒntl] ADJ horizontal; **~ integration** integración *f* horizontal.

horizontally [,hɒrɪ'zɒntəlɪ] ADV horizontalmente.

hormonal [hɔː'məʊnəl] ADJ hormonal.

hormone ['hɔːməʊn] **1** N hormona *f*.
2 ATTR: **~ treatment** tratamiento *m* de hormonas.

horn [hɔːn] N **(a)** (*of bull etc*) cuerno *m*; (*of deer*) asta *f*; (*of insect*) antena *f*; (*of snail*) tentáculo *m*; (*material*) cuerno *m*; **H~ of Africa** Cuerno *m* de Africa; **~ of plenty** cuerno *m* de la abundancia, cornucopia *f*; **to be on the ~s of a dilemma** estar entre la espada y la pared; **to draw in one's ~s** recoger velas, (*with money*) hacer economías.
(b) (*Mus*) cuerno *m*, trompa *f*; (*Aut*) bocina *f*, claxon *m*; **to blow (or sound) one's ~** tocar la bocina, tocar el claxon.
(c) (*US‡*) teléfono *m*; **to get on the ~ to sb** telefonear a uno.
◆**horn in*** VI (*esp US*) entrometerse (*on* en).

hornbeam ['hɔːnbiːm] N carpe *m*.

hornbill ['hɔːnbɪl] N búcero *m*.

horned [hɔːnd] ADJ con cuernos, enastado; (*in compounds*) de cuernos ...

hornet ['hɔːnɪt] N avispón *m*; **~'s nest** (*fig*) avispero *m*.

hornless ['hɔːnlɪs] ADJ sin cuernos, mocho.

hornpipe ['hɔːnpaɪp] N **(a)** (*Mus*) chirimía *f*. **(b)** (*Naut*) *cierto baile de marineros*.

horn-rimmed ['hɔːnrɪmd] ADJ *spectacles* de concha, de carey (*LAm*).

horny ['hɔːnɪ] ADJ **(a)** *material* córneo; *hand* calloso. **(b)** (*esp US‡*) cachondo, caliente.

horology [hɒ'rɒlədʒɪ] N horología *f*.

horoscope ['hɒrəskəʊp] N horóscopo *m*; **to cast a ~** sacar un horóscopo.

horrendous [hɒ'rendəs] ADJ horrendo; (*hum*) horroroso.

horrible ['hɒrɪbl] ADJ horrible.

horribly ['hɒrɪblɪ] ADV horriblemente; **it's ~ difficult** es terriblemente difícil; **he swore most ~** soltó unos tacos espantosos.

horrid ['hɒrɪd] ADJ horrible, horroroso; (*•*) horrible; *person etc* de lo más antipático, inaguantable; **you ~ thing!** ¡qué ofensivo!, ¡qué antipático!; **to be ~ to sb** tratar a uno muy mal, portarse muy mal con uno; **don't be ~!** ¡no fastidies!

horrific [hɒ'rɪfɪk] ADJ horrendo.

horrifically [hɒ'rɪfɪklɪ] ADV espantosamente, terriblemente; **~ injured** con heridas espantosas.

horrify ['hɒrɪfaɪ] VT horrorizar; (*shock*) escandalizar, pasmar; **they were all horrified** se escandalizaron todos; **I was horrified to discover that ...** me horrorizó descubrir que ...

horrifying ['hɒrɪfaɪɪŋ] ADJ horroroso, horripilante.

horrifyingly ['hɒrɪ,faɪɪŋlɪ] ADV horrorosamente, de manera horripilante.

horror ['hɒrər] **1** N horror *m*; **to have a ~ of** tener horror a; **I found to my ~ that ...** me horroricé al descubrir que ...; **then to my ~ it moved** luego — ¡qué susto! — se movió; **it gives me the ~s** me da horror; **~s!** ¡qué horror!; **you ~!** ¡bestia!
2 ATTR: **~ film** película *f* de miedo.

horror-stricken ['hɒrə,strɪkən] ADJ, **horror-struck** ['hɒrə,strʌk] ADJ horrorizado.

hors de combat ['ɔːdəkɒ̃bɑ] ADJ fuera de combate.

hors d'oeuvres [ɔː'dɜːvr] NPL entremeses *mpl*.

horse [hɔːs] **1** N **(a)** (*Zool*) caballo *m*; (*in gymnastics*) potro *m*; (*Tech*)

caballete *m*; (*cavalry*) caballería *f*; **that's a ~ of a different colour** eso es harina de otro costal; **it's straight from the ~'s mouth** lo sé de buena tinta, me lo dijo el mismo interesado; **to change ~s in midstream** cambiar de política (*or personal etc*) a mitad de camino; **to eat like a ~** comer como una vaca; **to get on one's high ~** darse ínfulas, adoptar una actitud altanera; **hold your ~s!** ¡para el carro!, ¡despacito!
(b) (‡) caballo‡ *m*, heroína *f*.
2 ATTR: **H~ Guards** (*Brit*) Guardia *f* Montada.
◆**horse about***, **horse around*** VI hacer el borde*, hacer el animal*, tontear.

horse-artillery ['hɔːsɑː'tɪlərɪ] N artillería *f* montada.

horseback ['hɔːsbæk] **1** N: **on ~** a caballo.
2 ATTR: **~ riding** (*US*) equitación *f*.

horse-box ['hɔːsbɒks] N remolque *m* para caballerías, (*Rail*) vagón *m* para caballerías.

horse brass ['hɔːsbrɑːs] N jaez *m*.

horse-breaker ['hɔːs,breɪkər] N domador *m*, -ora *f* de caballos.

horse-breeder ['hɔːs,briːdər] N criador *m*, -ora *f* de caballos.

horse chestnut ['hɔːs'tʃesnʌt] N (*fruit*) castaña *f* de Indias; (*tree*) castaño *m* de Indias.

horse-collar ['hɔːs,kɒlər] N collera *f*.

horse-dealer ['hɔːs,diːlər] N chalán *m*.

horse-doctor ['hɔːs,dɒktər] N veterinario *m*, -a *f*.

horse-drawn ['hɔːsdrɔːn] ADJ de tracción de sangre, de tracción animal, traído por caballo(s).

horseflesh ['hɔːsfleʃ] N **(a)** (*meat*) carne *f* de caballo. **(b)** (*horses*) caballos *mpl*.

horsefly ['hɔːsflaɪ] N tábano *m*.

horsehair ['hɔːsheər] N crin *f*.

horsehide ['hɔːshaɪd] N cuero *m* de caballo.

horse-laugh ['hɔːslɑːf] N risotada *f*, carcajada *f*.

horse mackerel ['hɔːs'mækrəl] N jurel *m*.

horseman ['hɔːsmən] N, PL **horsemen** ['hɔːsmən] (*rider*) jinete *m*, charro *m* (*Mex*); (*expert*) caballista *m*.

horsemanship ['hɔːsmənʃɪp] N equitación *f*, manejo *m* (del caballo).

horse-manure ['hɔːsmə,njʊər] N abono *m* de caballo.

horsemeat ['hɔːsmiːt] N (*Culin*) carne *f* de caballo.

horse opera ['hɔːs,ɒpərə] N (*US*) película *f* del Oeste.

horseplay ['hɔːspleɪ] N payasadas *fpl*, pelea *f* amistosa.

horsepower ['hɔːs,paʊər] **1** N caballo *m* (de fuerza), caballaje *m*; potencia *f* en caballos; **what is the ~ of this car?** ¿qué potencia tiene este coche?
2 ATTR: **a 20 ~ engine** un motor de 20 caballos.

horse-race ['hɔːsreɪs] N carrera *f* de caballos.

horse-racing ['hɔːs,reɪsɪŋ] N carreras *fpl* de caballos, hipismo *m*.

horseradish ['hɔːs,rædɪʃ] N rábano *m* picante.

horse-riding ['hɔːs,raɪdɪŋ] N (*Brit*) equitación *f*.

horse-sense ['hɔːssens] N sentido *m* común.

horseshit‡ ['hɔːsʃɪt] N (*lit*) caca‡ *f* de caballo; (*fig*) gilipollada‡ *f*.

horseshoe ['hɔːsʃuː] **1** N herradura *f*.
2 ATTR: **~ arch** arco *m* de herradura.

horse show ['hɔːsʃəʊ] N concurso *m* hípico.

horse-trading ['hɔːs,treɪdɪŋ] N (*Pol etc*) toma y daca *m*, intercambio *m* de favores, chalaneo *m*.

horse trailer ['hɔːs,treɪlər] N (*US*) remolque *m* para caballerías.

horse trials ['hɔːstraɪəlz] NPL concurso *m* hípico.

horsewhip ['hɔːswɪp] **1** N látigo *m*.
2 VT zurriagar.

horsewoman ['hɔːs,wʊmən] N, PL **horsewomen** ['hɔːs,wɪmɪn] amazona *f*, caballista *f*, charra *f* (*Mex*).

hors(e)y ['hɔːsɪ] ADJ (*fond of horses*) aficionado a los caballos; (*fond of racing*) aficionado a las carreras de caballos, carrerista; *appearance* caballuno.

horticultural [,hɔːtɪ'kʌltʃərəl] ADJ hortícola; **~ show** exposición *f* de horticultura.

horticulture ['hɔːtɪkʌltʃər] N horticultura *f*.

horticulturist [,hɔːtɪ'kʌltʃərɪst] N horticultor *m*, -ora *f*.

hose [həʊz] **1** N **(a)** (*stockings*) medias *fpl*; (*socks*) calcetines *mpl*; (††) calzas *fpl*.
(b) (*Brit: hosepipe*) manga *f*, manguera *f*.
2 VT (*also* **~ down**) regar (*or limpiar etc*) con manga.
◆**hose out** VT regar con manguera.

hosepipe ['həʊzpaɪp] N manga *f*, manguera *f*.

hosier ['həʊʒɪər] N calcetero *m*, -a *f*.

hosiery ['həʊʒɪərɪ] N calcetería *f*.

hosp [hɒsp] ABBR *of* **hospital** hospital *m*, Hosp *m*.

hospice ['hɒspɪs] N hospicio *m*.

hospitable [hɒs'pɪtəbl] ADJ hospitalario; *atmosphere etc* acogedor.

hospitably [hɒs'pɪtəblɪ] ADV de modo hospitalario.

hospital ['hɒspɪtl] **1** N hospital *m*.
2 ATTR: **~ administration** administración *f* de hospital; **~ adminis-**

trator (*Brit*) administrador *m*, -ora *f* de hospital; (*US*) director *m*, -ora *f* de hospital; **~ doctor** interno *m*, -a *f*; **~ facilities** instalaciones *fpl* hospitalarias; **~ management** (*act*) gestión *f* hospitalaria, (*persons*) dirección *f* de hospital; **~ nurse** enfermera *f* de hospital; **~ ship** buque *m* hospital; **90% of ~ cases are released within 3 weeks** el 90% de los casos clínicos son dados de alta en tres semanas.

hospitality [ˌhɒspɪ'tælɪtɪ] N hospitalidad *f*; **corporate ~** atenciones de una empresa con sus invitados.

hospitalization [ˌhɒspɪtəlaɪ'zeɪʃən] N hospitalización *f*.

hospitalize ['hɒspɪtəlaɪz] VT hospitalizar.

host¹ [həʊst] N (**a**) (*crowd*) multitud *f*; **I have a ~ of problems** tengo un montón de problemas; **for a whole ~ of reasons** por muchísimas razones; **they came in ~s** acudieron a millares.
(**b**) (††) hueste *f*, ejército *m*.

host² [həʊst] ① N (*to guest*) huésped *m*, -eda *f*; (*Bio*) huésped *m*, hospedador *m*; (*at meal*) anfitrión *m*, -ona *f*; (*of inn*) patrón *m*, mesonero *m*; **I thanked my ~s** di las gracias a los que me habían invitado; **we were ~s for a week to a Spanish boy** recibimos en casa durante una semana a un joven español.
② ATTR: **~ country** (*for conference, games etc*) país *m* anfitrión.
③ VT *congress* organizar; (*TV*) *show* presentar.

host³ [həʊst] N (*Eccl*) hostia *f*.

hostage ['hɒstɪdʒ] N rehén *m*; **to take sb ~** tomar a uno como rehén.

hostel ['hɒstəl] N parador *m*; (*youth ~*) albergue *m* para jóvenes; (*Univ*) residencia *f* (de estudiantes).

hosteller, (*US*) **hosteler** ['hɒstələʳ] N persona que va de albergues para jóvenes.

hostelling, (*US*) **hosteling** ['hɒstəlɪŋ] N vacaciones *fpl* a base de albergues; **~ is very popular among the young** ir de albergues es popular entre la gente joven.

hostelry ['hɒstəlrɪ] N mesón *m*.

hostess ['həʊstes] N huéspeda *f*; anfitriona *f* (V **host²**); (*Aer*) azafata *f*; (*in night club*) cabaretera *f*.

hostile ['hɒstaɪl] ADJ (*enemy*) enemigo, hostil; *manner, voice etc* nada amistoso; *circumstances etc* adverso, desfavorable; **they were ~ to the plan** se opusieron al proyecto.

hostility [hɒs'tɪlɪtɪ] N hostilidad *f* (*to, towards* hacia), enemistad *f*, antagonismo *m*; **hostilities** hostilidades *fpl*; **to start hostilities** romper las hostilidades; **to call for an end to hostilities** abogar por un cese de hostilidades.

hostler ['ɒsləʳ] N (††) mozo *m* de cuadra.

hot [hɒt] ① ADJ (**a**) caliente; *climate* cálido; *day, summer* caluroso, de calor; *sun* abrasador; *spring* termal; **with running ~ and cold** (**water**) con agua corriente caliente y fría; **to be ~** (*person*) tener calor, (*thing*) estar caliente, (*weather*) hacer calor; (*in children's games*) estar caliente; **to be very ~** (*person*) tener mucho calor, (*thing*) estar muy caliente, (*weather*) hacer mucho calor; **to get ~** (*thing*) calentarse, (*weather*) empezar a hacer calor; **it made me go ~ and cold** me dio escalofríos; **it was a very ~ day** fue un día de mucho calor; **it was a ~ and tiring walk** fue una caminata que nos hizo sudar y nos cansó mucho; **to get ~ and bothered** sofocarse.
(**b**) (*fig*) *taste* picante; *contest* muy reñido; *dispute* acalorado; *temper* vivo; *temperament* apasionado, ardiente, vehemente; *situation* caliente, muy difícil, apurado; *pursuit* enérgico; *supporter* acérrimo; (*:* *sexually*) *animal* en celo; *person* cachondo; (*:* *stolen*) robado; **~ air** (*empty talk*) palabras *fpl* huecas, (*nonsense*) música *f* celestial*; **to blow ~ air*** fanfarronear; **~ flush** sofoco *m* de calor; **~ line** teléfono *m* rojo; teléfono *m* de emergencia; **~ money** dinero *m* caliente; **she's a ~ piece:** está muy buena*; **~ potato** (*fig*) carbón *m* ardiente; **~ pursuit** persecución *f* en caliente, persecución *f* armada (a través de una frontera *etc*); **~ seat** (*US: electric chair*) silla *f* eléctrica; **to be in the ~ seat** (*fig*) ser quien sufre las consecuencias, estar en primera fila; **~ spot*** (*for amusement*) lugar *m* de diversión; (*night club*) sala *f* de fiestas; (*Brit: trouble area*) punto *m* (or lugar *m*) caliente; **~ war** guerra *f* a tiros; **that's ~** (*esp US**) qué bueno, qué estupendo; V **stuff 1** (**e**), **temper 1** (**a**).
(**c**) *news* **~ from the press** una noticia que acaba de publicarse en la prensa; **to be ~ on sb's trail** seguir enérgicamente la pista de uno; **he's pretty ~ at maths** una con hacha para las matemáticas, es muy fuerte en matemáticas; **he's a pretty ~ player** es un jugador experto; **to make a place too ~ for sb** hacer que uno abandone un lugar; **to make things ~ for sb** amargar la vida a uno, hacer insoportable la vida a uno.
② ADV: **to blow ~ and cold** ser veleta, mudar a todos los vientos; **to give it to sb ~ and strong** no morderse la lengua con uno; **to go at it ~ and strong** pelearse (*etc*) violentamente.
③ N: **he's got the ~s for her:** ella le pone cachondo.
◆**hot up*** ① VT *food* (re)calentar; *engine* aumentar la potencia de; *pace* forzar, aumentar.
② VI (*dispute*) acalorarse; (*tension*) intensificarse; (*party*) animarse.

hot-air [ˌhɒt'ɛəʳ] ATTR: **~ balloon** globo *m* de aire caliente.

hotbed ['hɒtbed] N (*fig*) semillero *m*.

hot-blooded ['hɒt'blʌdɪd] ADJ apasionado, impetuoso.

hotchpotch ['hɒtʃpɒtʃ] N mezcolanza *f*, baturrillo *m*.

hot cross bun [ˌhɒt,krɒs'bʌn] N bollo a base de especias y pasas marcado con una cruz y que se come en Viernes Santo.

hot dog ['hɒtdɒg] N (*Culin*) perrito *m* caliente.

hotel [həʊ'tel] ① N hotel *m*.
② ATTR: **~ industry** comercio *m* hotelero; **~ manager** director *m*, -ora *f* de hotel; **~ receptionist** recepcionista *mf* de hotel; **~ room** habitación *f* de hotel; **~ staff** plantilla *f* de hotel; **~ work** trabajo *m* de hostelería; **~ workers** trabajadores *mpl*, -oras *fpl* de hostelería.

hotelier [həʊ'teliəʳ] N, **hotelkeeper** [həʊ'tel,ki:pəʳ] N hotelero *m*.

hotfoot ['hɒt'fʊt] ① ADV a toda prisa.
② VT: **to ~ it*** ir volando.

hothead ['hɒthed] N exaltado *m*, -a *f*, fanático *m*, -a *f*, extremista *mf*.

hotheaded ['hɒt'hedɪd] ADJ (*extreme*) exaltado, fanático, extremista; (*rash*) impetuoso.

hothouse ['hɒthaʊs] N, PL **hothouses** ['hɒthaʊzɪz] invernáculo *m*.

hotly ['hɒtlɪ] ADV con pasión, con vehemencia.

hotpants ['hɒtpænts] NPL shorts *mpl*.

hotplate ['hɒtpleɪt] N calentador *m*, placa *f* calentadora *f*, calienta-platos *m*.

hotpot ['hɒtpɒt] N (*esp Brit*) estofado *m*.

hotrod: ['hɒtrɒd] N (*US Aut*) bólido *m*.

hotshot: ['hɒtʃɒt] (*US*) ① ADJ de primera, de aúpa*.
② N personaje *m*, pez *m* gordo*.

hot-tempered [ˌhɒt'tempəd] ADJ irascible.

Hottentot ['hɒtəntɒt] ① ADJ hotentote.
② N (**a**) hotentote *mf*. (**b**) (*Ling*) hotentote *m*.

hot tub ['hɒt'tʌb] N jacuzzi *m*.

hot-water bottle [hɒt'wɔ:tə,bɒtl] N bolsa *f* de agua caliente.

hot-wire* ['hɒtwaɪəʳ] VT hacerle el puente a.

hound [haʊnd] ① N (**a**) perro *m* (de caza), podenco *m*, sabueso *m*. (**b**) (*fig*) canalla *m*.
② VT acosar, perseguir; **they ~ed him for the money** le persiguieron para que pagase el dinero; **I will not be ~ed into a decision** no tolero que me presionen para decidirme.
◆**hound down** VT: **to ~ sb down** perseguir a uno hasta encontrarle.
◆**hound on** VT: **to ~ sb on** incitar a uno (*to* + *infin* a + *infin*).
◆**hound out** VT: **to ~ sb out** hacer que uno abandone su puesto (*etc*) a fuerza de darle guerra.

hour [aʊəʳ] N hora *f*; **30 miles an ~** 30 millas por hora; **after ~s** (*Brit*) fuera de horas; **at all ~s of the day and night** a todas las horas del día y de la noche; **by the ~** por horas; **~ by ~** hora tras hora, cada hora; **on the ~** a la hora en punto; **out of ~s** fuera de horas; **she's out till all ~s** se queda fuera hasta muy tarde, vuelve a casa a las tantas; **to keep late ~s** trasnochar, acostarse a altas horas de la noche; **to strike the ~** dar la hora; **it takes ~s** es cosa de muchas horas; **we waited ~s** esperamos horas y horas; **to work long ~s** trabajar largas horas.

hourglass ['aʊəgla:s] N reloj *m* de arena.

hourhand ['aʊəhænd] N horario *m*.

hourly ['aʊəlɪ] ① ADJ de cada hora; **the ~ rate** el sueldo por hora; **~ wage** sueldo *m* por hora; **there's an ~ bus** hay un autobús cada hora.
② ADV cada hora; **we expected him ~** le esperábamos de un momento a otro.

hourly-paid [ˌaʊəlɪ'peɪd] ADJ pagado por hora.

house [haʊs] N, PL **houses** ['haʊzɪz] ① N casa *f*; (*Comm*) casa *f*, firma *f*; (*Theat: auditorium*) sala *f*, (*audience*) público *m*, (*Parl*) cámara *f*; (*Brit Scol*) subdivisión de un colegio de internado; (*Univ*) colegio *m*, (*part of college or school*) pabellón *m*; (*lineage*) casa *f*, familia *f*; **'~ full'** 'no hay localidades'; **~ and home** hogar *m*; **~ of cards** castillo *m* de naipes; **the H~, the H~ of Commons** La Cámara de los Comunes; **~ of God** templo *m*, iglesia *f*; **H~ of Lords** Cámara *f* de los Lores; **H~s of Parliament** Parlamento *m*, Cámara *f* de los Lores y la de los Comunes; **H~ of Representatives** (*US*) Cámara *f* de Representantes; **training in ~** formación *f* en la empresa; **it's on the ~** la casa invita, es cortesía de la casa, está pagado (por el dueño); **to bring the ~ down** (*Theat*) hacer venirse abajo el teatro, (*speech*) obtener un exitazo, ser muy aplaudido, (*joke*) hacer morir de risa a todos; **to get on like a ~ on fire** (*progress*) avanzar rapidísimamente, (*2 persons*) llevarse la mar de bien, avenirse maravillosamente; **to keep ~** llevar la casa (*for a, para*); **to keep open ~** recibir a todo el mundo, ser muy hospitalario; (*US*) recibir en casa las visitas; **to move ~** mudarse; **to put one's ~ in order** arreglar los asuntos personales; reformar la propia vida; **to set up ~** poner casa, establecerse;
ver también SPEAKER.
② ATTR: **~ contents insurance** seguro *m* del contenido de una casa; **~ dog** perro *m* de casa; **~ guest** invitado *m*, -a *f*; **~ journal, ~ magazine** revista *f* de la empresa (*de circulación interna*); **~ (music)** música *f* acid*; **~ prices** precios *mpl* de la propiedad inmobiliaria; **~ sale** venta *f* de una casa; **~ wine** vino *m* de la casa.

3 [haʊz] VT *person* alojar, hospedar; *population* proveer viviendas para; (*store*) guardar, almacenar; (*Mech*) encajar; **the building will not ~ them all** no cabrán todos en el edificio.

house-agent ['haʊs,eɪdʒənt] N (*Brit*) agente *m* inmobiliario, agente *f* inmobiliaria.

house arrest ['haʊsə,rest] N arresto *m* domiciliario.

houseboat ['haʊsbəʊt] N casa *f* flotante, bote-vivienda *m*.

housebound ['haʊsbaʊnd] ADJ que no puede salir de casa.

houseboy ['haʊsbɔɪ] N muchacho *m* de casa.

housebreaker ['haʊs,breɪkəʳ] N ladrón *m* de casas.

housebreaking ['haʊs,breɪkɪŋ] N robo *m* en una casa.

housebroken ['haʊs,brəʊkən] ADJ (*US*) domesticado.

housecleaning ['haʊs'kliːnɪŋ] N limpieza *f* de la casa.

housecoat ['haʊskəʊt] N bata *f*.

housedress ['haʊsdres] N vestido *m* de casa, vestido *m* sencillo.

housefather ['haʊs,fɑːðəʳ] N hombre *m* encargado de una residencia de niños.

housefly ['haʊsflaɪ] N mosca *f* doméstica.

houseful ['haʊsfʊl] N: **there was a ~ of people** la casa estaba llena de gente.

household ['haʊshəʊld] **1** N casa *f*, familia *f*.

2 ATTR doméstico, de (la) casa; **~ accounts** cuentas *fpl* de la casa; **H~ Cavalry** (*Brit*) Caballería *f* de la Guardia Real; **~ chores** quehaceres *mpl* domésticos; **~ gods** penates *mpl*; **~ goods** enseres *mpl* domésticos; **~ linen** ropa *f* de casa; **~ refuse** basura *f* doméstica; **~ soap** jabón *m* familiar; **~ troops** (*Brit*) guardia *f* real; **he's a ~ name** es una persona conocidísima; **it's a ~ word** es un nombre conocidísimo.

householder ['haʊs,həʊldəʳ] N amo *m*, -a *f* (de casa); cabeza *f* de familia; dueño *m*, -a *f* de una casa, arrendatario *m*, -a *f*, inquilino *m*, -a *f*; (*as electoral qualification*) propietario *m*, -a *f* de vivienda.

house-hunt ['haʊshʌnt] VI (*Brit*) buscar casa.

house-hunting ['haʊs,hʌntɪŋ] N búsqueda *f* de vivienda.

house-husband ['haʊs,hʌzbənd] N marido que trabaja en la casa.

housekeeper ['haʊs,kiːpəʳ] N (*in house*) ama *f* de casa, ama *f* de llaves; (*in hotel*) gobernanta *f*.

housekeeping ['haʊs,kiːpɪŋ] N gobierno *m* de la casa, faenas *fpl* domésticas, (*Comput*) gestión *f* interna; **~ (money)** dinero *m* para gastos domésticos.

houselights ['haʊslaɪts] NPL (*Theat*) luces *fpl* de la sala.

housemaid ['haʊsmeɪd] N criada *f*, mucama *f* (*LAm*); **~'s knee** (*Med*) higroma *m*, hidrartrosis *f*.

houseman ['haʊsmən] N, PL **housemen** ['haʊsmən] (*Brit*: *in hospital*) interno *m*.

house manager ['haʊs'mænɪdʒəʳ] N empresario *m* teatral.

housemartin ['haʊs,mɑːtɪn] N avión *m* común.

housemaster ['haʊs,mɑːstəʳ] N, **housemistress** ['haʊs,mɪstrɪs] N (*Brit Scol*) profesor/profesora a cargo de la subdivisión de un colegio de internado.

housemate ['haʊsmeɪt] N compañero *m*, -a *f* de piso.

housemother ['haʊs,mʌðəʳ] N mujer *f* encargada de una residencia de niños.

house-owner ['haʊs,əʊnəʳ] N propietario *m*, -a *f* de una casa.

house painter ['haʊs,peɪntəʳ] N pintor *m* (de brocha gorda).

house party ['haʊs,pɑːtɪ] N grupo *m* de invitados (que pasan varios días en una casa de campo).

house physician ['haʊsfɪ,zɪʃən] N (*Brit*) médico *m* interno, médica *f* interna.

house plant ['haʊsplɑːnt] N planta *f* de interior.

house-proud ['haʊspraʊd] ADJ: **she's very ~** tiene la casa como una plata.

houseroom ['haʊsrʊm] N capacidad *f* de una casa; **to give sth ~** guardar algo en su casa; **I wouldn't give it ~** no lo admitiría en mi casa.

house-sit ['haʊssɪt] VT (*irr*: *V* **sit**): **I'm ~ting for the Sinclairs** vivo en la casa de los Sinclair para vigilarla en ausencia de los dueños.

house-sparrow ['haʊs,spærəʊ] N gorrión *m* común.

house surgeon ['haʊs,sɜːdʒən] N (*Brit*) cirujano *m* interno, cirujana *f* interna, médico *m* interno, médica *f* interna (en el hospital).

house-to-house ['haʊstə'haʊs] ADJ *and adv* de casa en casa.

housetop ['haʊstɒp] N tejado *m*; **to shout sth from the ~s** pregonar algo a los cuatro vientos.

house-train ['haʊstreɪn] VT (*Brit*) educar, enseñar.

house-trained ['haʊstreɪnd] ADJ (*Brit*) *pet* bien enseñado, limpio, domesticado.

housewares ['haʊswɛəz] NPL (*US*) artículos *mpl* de uso doméstico, utensilios *mpl* domésticos.

house-warming ['haʊs,wɔːmɪŋ] N fiesta *f* de estreno de una casa.

housewife ['haʊswaɪf] N, PL **housewives** ['haʊswaɪvz] ama *f* de casa; madre *f* de familia.

housewifely ['haʊswaɪflɪ] ADJ doméstico.

housewifery ['haʊswɪfərɪ] N gobierno *m* de la casa, faenas *fpl* domésticas.

housework ['haʊswɜːk] N quehaceres *mpl* domésticos.

housing ['haʊzɪŋ] **1** N (a) (*act*) alojamiento *m*; provisión *f* de vivienda.

(b) (*houses*) casas *fpl*, viviendas *fpl*; **there's a lot of new ~** hay muchas casas nuevas.

(c) (*Mech*) caja *f*, cubierta *f*, tapa *f*.

2 ATTR: **~ association** asociación *f* de la vivienda; **~ benefit** subsidio *m* de vivienda; **~ cooperative** cooperativa *f* de la vivienda; **~ development** (*US*), **~ estate** (*Brit*), **~ scheme** (*Brit*) urbanización *f*, reparto

---

HOW   *see also main entry*

In direct and indirect questions

With verb

- You can usually use *cómo* to translate *how* in questions as well as after report verbs and verbs of (un)certainty and doubt (e.g. *no sé*):

    How do you spell it?
    ¿Cómo se escribe?
    Please tell me how to do it
    Por favor, dígame cómo hacerlo
    I wasn't sure how to make soup
    No sabía muy bien cómo preparar una sopa

With adjective

- *How* + ADJECTIVE in questions can often be translated using *cómo es/era de* + ADJECTIVE (agreeing with the noun), but other constructions might be more usual depending on the context:

    How difficult was the exam?
    ¿Cómo fue de difícil el examen?
    How long is this bed?
    ¿Cómo es de larga esta cama? ◊ *¿Cuánto mide (de largo) esta cama?*

With adverb

- Various translations are possible depending on the context. A very common construction is PREPOSITION + *qué* + NOUN:

    How fast can this car go?
    ¿A qué velocidad puede ir este coche?
    How often do you go?
    ¿Con qué frecuencia vas?

In exclamations

- You can often translate *how* + ADJECTIVE/ADVERB using *qué* + ADJECTIVE/ADVERB:

    How pretty!
    ¡Qué bonito!
    How nice!
    ¡Qué bien!
    How quickly the time passed!
    ¡Qué de prisa pasó el tiempo!

- *Cuánto* + VERB is often used to translate *how* + VERB and *how* + ADJECTIVE when there is an implication of quantity:

    How they talk!
    ¡Cuánto hablan!
    How sorry I am!
    ¡Cuánto lo siento!

In statements

With verb

- Translate *how* with verbs other than report ones or verbs of certainty and doubt using *como* (without an accent):

    This is how you do it
    Así es como se hace

With adjective, adverb

- Use *lo* + ADJECTIVE/ADVERB:

    I didn't know how expensive the tickets were
    No sabía lo caras que eran las entradas
    They've been telling me how well you did in your exams
    Ya me han contado lo bien que te salieron los exámenes

! The presence of *lo* does not affect agreement; any adjective must still agree with the noun referred to.

    For further uses and examples, see main entry.

m (*Mex*); **~ market** mercado *m* de la vivienda; **~ policy** política *f* de la vivienda; **~ project** proyecto *m* para la construcción de viviendas; **~ shortage** crisis *f* de la vivienda; **~ stock** total *m* de viviendas; **~ subsidy** subsidio *m* por vivienda.

hove [həʊv] PRET AND PTP *of* **heave** (*Naut*).

hovel ['hɒvəl] N casucha *f*, tugurio *m*.

hover ['hɒvəʳ] VI permanecer inmóvil (en el aire), estar suspendido, flotar (en el aire); (*hawk etc*) cernerse; **to ~ round sb** rondar a uno, girar en torno a uno.

hovercraft ['hɒvəkrɑːft] N hidrodeslizador *m*, aerodeslizador *m*.

hoverport ['hɒvəˌpɔːt] N terminal *f* de hidrodeslizador.

how [haʊ] ADV (a) (*in what way*) **~ did you do it?** ¿cómo lo hiciste?; **I know ~ you did it** yo sé cómo lo hiciste; **~ is it that ...?** ¿cómo resulta que ...?, ¿por qué ...? ¿cómo es posible que ... + *subj*?; **~ can that be?** ¿cómo puede ser eso?; **I see ~ it is** comprendo la situación; **~ was the play?** ¿qué tal la comedia?; **~ do you like your steak?** ¿cómo le gusta que se le sirva el biftec?; **~ do you like the steak?** ¿qué tal te parece el biftec?; **~'s that for cheek?** ¿qué opinas de eso como ejemplo de cara dura?; **to know ~ to do sth** saber hacer algo; **to learn ~ to do sth** aprender a hacer algo, aprender cómo se hace algo, aprender el modo de hacer algo; **and ~!** ¡y cómo!; **I like it, but ~ about you?** a mí me gusta, pero ¿y tú?; *V* **about 2** (c).

(b) (*health*) **~ are you?** ¿cómo está Vd?, ¿qué tal estás?

(c) (*with adj or adv etc*) **~ beautiful!** ¡qué hermoso!; **~ big it is!** ¡qué grande es!; **I know ~ hard it is** yo sé lo difícil que esto es; **~ kind of you!** es Vd muy amable; **~ fast?** ¿a qué velocidad?; **~ big is it?** ¿cómo es de grande?, ¿de qué tamaño es?; **~ wide is this room?** ¿cuánto tiene este cuarto de ancho?; **~ wide shall I make it?** ¿de qué ancho lo hago?; **~ old are you?** ¿cuántos años tienes?; **~ glad I am to see you!** ¡cuánto me alegro de verte!; **~ sorry I am for you!** ¡cuánto te compadezco!; **~ she's changed!** ¡cuánto ha cambiado!; *V* **about, else, much** *etc*.

howdy ['haʊdɪ] EXCL (*US*) ¡hola!

how-d'ye-do ['haʊdjə'duː] N lío *m*; **this is a fine ~!** ¡en buen berenjenal nos hemos metido!, ¡vaya problemazo!

▼ **however** [haʊ'evəʳ] **1** ADV (a) (*with verb*) **~ I do it** como quiera que lo haga; **~ he may want to do it** de cualquier modo que quiera hacerlo; **~ that may be** sea como sea.

▼ (b) (*with adj or adv*) por (muy) ... que + *subj*; **~ rough it is** por (muy) tosco que sea; **~ fast he runs** por rápido que corra; **~ hot it is** por mucho calor que haga; *V* **many, much.**

▼ **2** CONJ sin embargo, no obstante.

> **HOWEVER**
>
> Unlike *however*, *sin embargo* and *no obstante* can never end a sentence; they must always go at the beginning of it or between the clauses:
>
> He has one problem, however
> *Sin embargo, tiene un problema*
> He does not expect to come out of the meeting with anything concrete, however
> *No obstante, no espera salir de la reunión con nada concreto*

howitzer ['haʊitsəʳ] N obús *m*.

howl [haʊl] **1** N aullido *m*, chillido *m*, grito *m*, alarido *m*; berrido *m*; bramido *m*; **with a ~ of rage** dando un alarido de furia; **to set up a ~** (*fig*) poner el grito en el cielo.

2 VI (*animal etc*) aullar, chillar; (*person*) gritar, dar alaridos; (*child*) berrear; (*with laughter*) reírse a carcajadas; (*wind*) bramar; **to ~ with rage** bramar de furia, bramar furioso.

◆ **howl down** VT: **to ~ sb down** hacer callar a uno a gritos.

howler ['haʊləʳ] N plancha *f*, planchazo *m*, falta *f* garrafal.

howling ['haʊlɪŋ] ADJ *success* clamoroso.

howsoever [haʊsəʊ'evəʳ] ADV (*frm*) comoquiera que.

hoy [hɔɪ] INTERJ ¡eh!, ¡hola!

hoyden ['hɔɪdn] N marimacho *f*.

HP N (*Brit*) ABBR *of* **hire purchase** compra *f* a plazos.

h.p. N ABBR *of* **horsepower** caballos *mpl* de vapor, C.V.

HQ N ABBR *of* **headquarters** cuartel *m* general, Estado *m* Mayor, E.M.

HR N (*US*) ABBR *of* **House of Representatives**.

hr(s) ABBR *of* **hour(s)** hora(s) *f*(PL), h.

H.R.H. ABBR *of* **Her** (**His**) **Royal Highness** Su Alteza Real, S.A.R.

HRT N ABBR *of* **hormone replacement therapy**.

H.S. (*US*) ABBR *of* **high school**.

HST N (*US*) ABBR *of* **Hawaiian Standard Time**.

HT N ABBR *of* **high tension** alta tensión *f*.

ht ABBR *of* **height** altura *f*, alt.

hub [hʌb] N cubo *m*; (*fig*) centro *m*, eje.

hubbub ['hʌbʌb] N barahúnda *f*, batahóla *f*; **a ~ of voices** un ruido confuso de voces.

hubby ['hʌbɪ] N marido *m*.

hubcap ['hʌbkæp] N tapacubos *m*.

hubris ['hjuːbrɪs] N orgullo *m* (desmesurado).

huckster ['hʌkstəʳ] N (*US*) vendedor *m* ambulante, mercachifle *m*, buhonero *m*.

HUD N (*US*) ABBR *of* **Department of Housing and Urban Development**.

huddle ['hʌdl] **1** N (*of things*) montón *m*, grupo *m*; (*of persons*) grupo *m*, corrillo *m*; **to go into a ~** ir aparte para conferenciar.

2 VT amontonar, poner muy juntos.

3 VI amontonarse, apretarse (unos contra otros); acurrucarse; **the chairs were ~d in a corner** las sillas estaban amontonadas en un rincón; **we ~d round the fire** nos arrimamos al fuego, nos apiñábamos junto a la lumbre.

◆ **huddle down** VI (*crouch*) agacharse; (*snuggle*) acurrucarse, apretarse.

◆ **huddle together** **1** VT = **huddle 2**.

2 VI amontonarse, apretarse (unos contra unos); acurrucarse; **they were huddling together for warmth** estaban acurrucados para darse calor.

◆ **huddle up** VI amontonarse, apretarse (unos contra unos); acurrucarse.

hue[1] [hjuː] N (*colour*) color *m*; (*shade*) matiz *m*, tono *m*; (*of opinion*) matiz *m*; **people of every political ~** gente *f* de todos los matices políticos.

hue[2] [hjuː] N: **~ and cry** alarma *f*; (*of protest*) clamor *m*, griterío *m*; **they set up a great ~ and cry** protestaron clamorosamente; **there was a ~ and cry after him** se le persiguió enérgicamente.

huff [hʌf] **1** N rabieta *f*; **to go off in a ~** irse amostazado; **to get into a ~** amostazarse, picarse.

2 VI: **to ~ and puff** (*out of breath*) jadear, resollar; **he ~ed and puffed a lot and then said yes** resopló mucho y luego dijo que bueno.

huffed [hʌft] ADJ enojado.

huffily ['hʌfɪlɪ] ADV malhumoradamente; **he said ~** dijo malhumorado.

huffiness ['hʌfɪnɪs] N mal humor *m*.

huffy ['hʌfɪ] ADJ (*of character*) enojadizo; (*in mood*) malhumorado, ofendido; **he was a bit ~ about it** se ofendió un tanto por ello.

hug [hʌg] **1** N abrazo *m*; **give me a ~** dame un abrazo.

2 VT (*lovingly*) abrazar; (*of bear etc*) apretar con los brazos, apretujar; *coast* no apartarse de; *prejudice etc* acariciar; *idea* aferrarse a; *belief* afirmarse en.

3 VR: **to ~ o.s.** felicitarse (*on* por).

huge [hjuːdʒ] ADJ enorme, vasto, inmenso; (*over-large*) descomunal.

hugely ['hjuːdʒlɪ] ADV enormemente; **we enjoyed ourselves ~** nos divertimos una barbaridad; **he laughed ~** se rio una barbaridad.

hugeness ['hjuːdʒnɪs] N inmensidad *f*.

hugger-mugger ['hʌgəˌmʌgəʳ] **1** N confusión *f*; **a ~ of books** un montón de libros en desorden.

2 ADV desordenadamente.

-hugging ['hʌgɪŋ] ADJ *ending in compounds*: **figure~** ajustado, ceñido al cuerpo.

Hugh [hjuː] NM Hugo, Ugo.

Huguenot ['hjuːgənəʊ] **1** ADJ hugonote.

2 N hugonote *m*, -a *f*.

huh [hʌ] EXCL ¡eh!

Hula Hoop ['huːləˌhuːp] ® N Hula Hoop *m*.

hulk [hʌlk] N (*wreck*) barco *m* viejo; (*hull*) casco *m* (arrumbado); (*large, unwieldy vessel*) carcamán *m*; (*mass*) bulto *m*, mole *f*.

huiking ['hʌlkɪŋ] ADJ grueso, pesado; **~ great brute** hombracho *m*, hombretón *m*.

hull [hʌl] **1** N casco *m*.

2 VT *fruit* descascarar.

hullabaloo [ˌhʌləbə'luː] N (*noise*) vocería *f*, tumulto *m*; (*fuss*) lío *m*, bronca *f*; **a great ~ broke out** estalló un ruido espantoso; **that ~ about the money** ese lío que se armó por el dinero*.

hullo [hʌ'ləʊ] INTERJ (*greeting*) ¡hola!; (*surprise*) ¡caramba!; (*Telec: calling*) ¡oiga!, (*answering*) ¡diga!, ¡bueno! (*Mex*), ¡hola! (*SC*), ¡aló! (*And*); **~, what's all this!** ¡vamos a ver!

hum [hʌm] **1** N zumbido *m*; tarareo *m*; (*of voices etc*) ruido *m* confuso, murmullo *m*.

2 VT *tune* tararear, canturrear.

3 VI (a) (*insect, wire etc*) zumbar; (*person*) canturrear, tararear una canción; **to ~ with activity** bullir de actividad; **to make things ~** desplegar gran actividad; avivarlo, estimular la actividad; **then things began to ~** entonces sí empezaron a pasar cosas, hubo luego una actividad frenética.

(b) (*) oler mal.

(c) **to ~ and haw** vacilar, no resolverse.

human ['hjuːmən] **1** ADJ humano; **~ being** ser *m* humano; **~ factor** factor *m* humano; **~ interest** interés *m* humano; **~ interest story** historia *f* de interés humano; **~ nature** naturaleza *f* humana; **it's ~ nature to be jealous** es cosa natural tener celos; **~ race** género *m*

humano; **~ relations** relaciones *fpl* humanas; **~ remains** restos *mpl* humanos; **~ resources** recursos *mpl* humanos; **~ rights** derechos *mpl* humanos; **~ shield** escudo *m* humano.
  2 N humano *m*, -a *f*.

humane [hjuː'meɪn] ADJ **(a)** (*compassionate*) humano, humanitario. **(b)** **~ studies** ciencias *fpl* humanas, humanidades *fpl*.

humanely [hjuː'meɪnlɪ] ADV humanamente.

humaneness [hjuː'meɪnnɪs] N humanidad *f*.

humanism ['hjuːmənɪzəm] N humanismo *m*.

humanist ['hjuːmənɪst] N humanista *mf*.

humanistic [ˌhjuːmə'nɪstɪk] ADJ humanístico.

humanitarian [hjuːˌmænɪ'teərɪən] **1** ADJ humanitario.
  2 N humanitario *m*, -a *f*.

humanitarianism [hjuːˌmænɪ'teərɪənɪzəm] N humanitarismo *m*.

humanity [hjuː'mænɪtɪ] N humanidad *f*; **the humanities** las humanidades.

humanization [ˌhjuːmənaɪ'zeɪʃən] N humanización *f*.

humanize ['hjuːmənaɪz] VT humanizar.

humankind ['hjuːmən'kaɪnd] N género *m* humano.

humanly ['hjuːmənlɪ] ADV humanamente; **all that is ~ possible** todo lo que pueda hacer un hombre, todo lo que cabe dentro de las posibilidades humanas.

humanoid ['hjuːmənɔɪd] **1** ADJ humanoide.
  2 N humanoide *mf*.

humble ['hʌmbl] **1** ADJ humilde.
  2 VT humillar.
  3 VR: **to ~ o.s.** humillarse.

humble-bee ['hʌmblbiː] N abejorro *m*.

humbleness ['hʌmblnɪs] N humildad *f*.

humbly ['hʌmblɪ] ADV humildemente, con humildad.

humbug ['hʌmbʌɡ] N **(a)** (*nonsense*) bola *f*, embustes *mpl*, disparates *mpl*; **~!** ¡bobadas!
  (b) (*Brit: sweet*) caramelo *m* de menta.
  (c) (*person*) farsante *mf*, charlatán *m*, -ana *f*; **he's an old ~** es un farsante.

humdinger* ['hʌmdɪŋəʳ] N: **it's a ~!** ¡es una auténtica maravilla!; **a real ~ of a car** un coche maravilloso.

humdrum ['hʌmdrʌm] ADJ monótono, aburrido; tedioso; vulgar, ordinario; rutinario; mediocre, sin interés.

humerus ['hjuːmərəs] N, PL **humeri** ['hjuːməraɪ] húmero *m*.

humid ['hjuːmɪd] ADJ húmedo.

humidifier [hjuː'mɪdɪfaɪəʳ] N humectador *m*, humedecedor *m*.

humidify [hjuː'mɪdɪfaɪ] VT humedecer.

humidity [hjuː'mɪdɪtɪ] N humedad *f*.

humiliate [hjuː'mɪlɪeɪt] VT humillar.

humiliating [hjuː'mɪlɪeɪtɪŋ] ADJ vergonzoso, humillante.

humiliatingly [hjuː'mɪlɪeɪtɪŋlɪ] ADV vergonzosamente, de manera humillante; **we were ~ defeated** sufrimos una derrota vergonzosa.

humiliation [hjuːmɪlɪ'eɪʃən] N humillación *f*.

humility [hjuː'mɪlɪtɪ] N humildad *f*.

humming ['hʌmɪŋ] N zumbido *m*; tarareo *m*, canturreo *m*.

hummingbird ['hʌmɪŋbɜːd] N colibrí *m*, picaflor *m*.

humming-top ['hʌmɪŋtɒp] N trompa *f*.

hummock ['hʌmək] N montecillo *m*, morón *m*.

hummus, hummous ['huməs] N paté de garbanzos originario del Oriente Medio.

humongous* [hjuː'mɒŋɡəs], **humungous*** [hjuː'mʌŋɡəs] ADJ: **she is such a ~ star** es una superestrella; **we had a ~ row** tuvimos una pelea de órdago*.

humor ['hjuːməʳ] *etc* (*US*) = **humour** *etc*.

humorist ['hjuːmərɪst] N persona *f* chistosa; bromista *mf*; (*writer*) humorista *mf*; **what a ~ you are!** ¡qué gracioso eres!

humorless ['hjuːməlɪs] (*US*) = **humourless**.

humorous ['hjuːmərəs] ADJ *person* gracioso, chistoso, divertido; *writer, genre* festivo, cómico; *joke, event, book* divertido; *tone* festivo.

humorously ['hjuːmərəslɪ] ADV graciosamente, de manera divertida; en tono festivo.

humour, (*US*) **humor** ['hjuːməʳ] **1** N **(a)** (*amusingness*) humorismo *m*; (*sense of* ~) sentido *m* del humor; (*creative talent*) vis *f* cómica; (*of joke, event*) gracia *f*; (*of situation*) comicidad *f*; **he has no ~** no tiene sentido del humor; **I see no ~ in that** eso no me hace gracia alguna; **this is no time for ~** no es tiempo para chistes; **I don't like the ~ in 'Macbeth'** no me gustan las escenas cómicas de 'Macbeth'.
  (b) (*mood*) humor *m*; **to be in good ~** estar de buen humor; **to be in high good ~** estar de excelente humor; **they were in no ~ for fighting** no estaban de humor para pelear; **to be out of ~** estar de mal humor.
  (c) (*whim*) capricho *m*.
  (d) (*Med* ††) humor *m*.
  2 VT complacer, seguir el humor a; (*indulge*) mimar.

-humoured, (*US*) **-humored** ['hjuːməd] ADJ de humor ...

humourless, (*US*) **humorless** ['hjuːməlɪs] ADJ *person* sin sentido del

humor; *joke* sin gracia.

hump [hʌmp] **1** N (*Anat*) joroba *f*, corcova *f*, giba *f*; (*camel's*) giba *f*; (*in ground*) montecillo *m*; **to give sb the ~** (*Brit*) jorobar a uno, fastidiar a uno; **to have the ~** (*Brit*) estar de mal humor; **to be over the ~*** estar en la pendiente vital, ser demasiado viejo; no servir ya; **we're over the ~ now** ya hemos vencido la cuesta.
  2 VT **(a)** **to ~ one's back** encorvarse, corcovarse.
  (b) (*: *carry*) llevar, llevar al hombro.
  (c) (⁑) joder⁑ (*Sp*), coger⁑ (*LAm*).

humpback ['hʌmpbæk] N **(a)** (*person*) jorobado *m*, -a *f*; (*whale*: *also* ~ **whale**) rorcual *m*; **to have a ~** ser jorobado.

humpbacked ['hʌmpbækt] ADJ corcovado, jorobado; (*Brit*) *bridge* de fuerte pendiente.

humph [mmm] INTERJ ¡bah!; ¡veremos!

humpy ['hʌmpɪ] ADJ desigual.

humus ['hjuːməs] N humus *m*.

Hun [hʌn] N (*Hist*) huno *m*; (*pej*) tudesco *m*, alemán *m*; **a ~** un alemán, **the ~** los alemanes.

hunch [hʌntʃ] **1** N **(a)** (*Anat*) V **hump**.
  (b) (*premonition*) corazonada *f*, pálpito *m*; sospecha *f*; **it's only a ~** no es más que una sospecha que tengo; **I have a ~ that ...** me da el pálpito que ...; **the detective had one of his ~es** el detective tuvo uno de sus pálpitos; **~es sometimes pay off** a veces los presentimientos se cumplen.
  2 VT (*also* **to ~ up**) encorvar; **to ~ one's back** encorvarse; **to sit ~ed up** estar sentado con el cuerpo doblado.

hunchback ['hʌntʃbæk] N jorobado *m*, -a *f*, corcovado *m*, -a *f*.

hunchbacked ['hʌntʃbækt] ADJ jorobado, corcovado.

hundred ['hʌndrɪd] **1** ADJ ciento, (*before n*) cien; **a ~ and one** ciento uno; **I've got a ~ and one things to do** tengo la mar de cosas que hacer; **a ~ and ten** ciento diez; **a ~ thousand** cien mil; **a ~ per cent** (*fig*) cien por cien; **H~ Years' War** Guerra *f* de los Cien Años.
  2 N ciento *m*, (*less exactly*) centenar *m*, centena *f*; **~s of people** centenares *mpl* de personas; **in ~s, by the ~** a centenares; **for ~s of thousands of years** durante centenares de miles de años; **I've told you ~s of times** te lo he dicho cientos de veces.

HUNDRED   *see also main entry*

"Ciento" or "cien"?

- Use *cien* before a *noun* (even when it follows *mil*):
  ...a *or* one hundred soldiers...
  ...*cien soldados*...
  ...eleven hundred metres...
  ...*mil cien metros*...

! Don't translate numbers like *eleven hundred* literally. Translate their equivalent in thousands and hundreds instead.

- Use *cien* before *mil* and *millón*:
  ...a *or* one hundred thousand dollars...
  ...*cien mil dólares*...
  ...a *or* one hundred million lira...
  ...*cien millones de liras*...

- But use *ciento* before another *number*:
  ...a *or* one hundred and sixteen stamps...
  ...*ciento dieciséis sellos*...

- When *hundred* follows another number, use the compound forms (*doscientos, -as, trescientos, -as etc*) which must agree with the noun:
  ...two hundred and fifty women...
  ...*doscientas cincuenta mujeres*...
  For further uses and examples, see main entry.

---

hundredfold ['hʌndrɪdfəʊld] **1** ADJ céntuplo.
  2 ADV cien veces.

hundredth ['hʌndrɪdθ] **1** ADJ centésimo.
  2 N centésimo *m*, centésima parte *f*.

hundredweight ['hʌndrɪdweɪt] N (*Brit, Canada*: = 112 *libras* = 50,8 *kilogramos*) approx quintal *m*, (*US*: = 100 *libras* = 45,3 *kilogramos*).

hung [hʌŋ] PRET AND PTP *of* **hang**; **~ jury** jurado *m* cuyos miembros no se pueden poner de acuerdo; **~ parliament** parlamento en el que ningún partido alcanza mayoría absoluta.

Hungarian [hʌŋ'ɡeərɪən] **1** ADJ húngaro.
  2 N **(a)** húngaro *m*, -a *f*. **(b)** (*Ling*) húngaro *m*.

Hungary ['hʌŋɡərɪ] N Hungría *f*.

hunger ['hʌŋɡəʳ] **1** N hambre *f* (*also fig: for* de).
  2 VI tener hambre, estar hambriento; **to ~ after, to ~ for** tener hambre de, ansiar, anhelar.

hunger march ['hʌŋɡəmɑːtʃ] N (*Brit*) marcha *f* del hambre.

hunger strike ['hʌŋɡəstraɪk] N huelga *f* de hambre.

hung-over*, hungover* [hʌŋ'ɡəʊvəʳ] ADJ: **to be ~** tener resaca.

hungrily ['hʌŋɡrɪlɪ] ADV *eat etc* ansiosamente, ávidamente; **to look ~ at sth** mirar algo con ganas de comerlo.

hungry ['hʌŋɡrɪ] ADJ hambriento; *land* pobre, estéril; **to be ~** tener hambre (*for* de); **to be very ~** tener mucha hambre; **to go ~** pasar hambre; **to make sb ~** hambrear a uno, hacer pasar hambre a uno.

hunk [hʌŋk] N **(a)** (*chunk*) pedazo *m* (grande), (buen) trozo *m*. **(b)** (*: man*) tío *m* bueno*, cachas* *m*.

hunker* ['hʌŋkəʳ] VI: **to ~ down** agacharse.

hunky* ['hʌŋkɪ] ADJ **(a)** (*strong*) fornido, fuerte, macizo. **(b)** (*: attractive*) bueno*.

hunky-dory* [,hʌŋkɪ'dɔːrɪ] ADJ (*esp US*) guay*; **it's all ~** es guay del Paraguay*.

hunt [hʌnt] **1** N caza *f*, cacería *f* (*for* de); (*party*) partida *f* de caza; grupo *m* de cazadores; (*search*) busca *f*, búsqueda *f* (*for* de); (*pursuit*) persecución *f*; **the ~ for the murderer** la persecución del asesino; **to be on the ~ for** ir a la caza de; **the ~ is on, the ~ is up** ha comenzado la búsqueda; **we joined in the ~ for the missing key** ayudamos a buscar la llave perdida.

2 VT *animal* cazar; (*search for*) buscar; (*pursue*) perseguir; *hounds etc* emplear en la caza; *country* recorrer de caza, cazar en.

3 VI cazar; dedicarse a la caza; **to ~ for** buscar; **to ~ about for** buscar por todas partes; **he ~ed for it in his pocket** lo buscó en el bolsillo; **to go ~ing** ir de caza.

◆**hunt down** VT *person* perseguir (y encontrar); *thing* buscar hasta dar con.

◆**hunt out, hunt up** VT (*look for*) buscar; (*find*) encontrar.

hunter ['hʌntəʳ] N **(a)** cazador *m*, -ora *f*. **(b)** (*horse*) caballo *m* de caza.

hunter-gatherer ['hʌntə'gæðərəʳ] N cazador-recolector *m*.

hunting ['hʌntɪŋ] **1** N caza *f*, montería *f*.

2 ATTR de caza; **the ~ fraternity** los aficionados a la caza; **~ lodge** pabellón *m* de caza; **~ pink** chaqueta *f* de caza roja; **~ season** época *f* de caza; *ver también* [FOXHUNTING].

hunting-box ['hʌntɪŋbɒks] N pabellón *m* de caza.

hunting-ground ['hʌntɪŋgraʊnd] N cazadero *m*; **a happy ~ for** un buen terreno para.

hunting-horn ['hʌntɪŋ,hɔːn] N cuerno *m* de caza.

huntress ['hʌntrɪs] N cazadora *f*.

Hunts [hʌnts] N ABBR *of* **Huntingdonshire.**

hunt-sabbing* ['hʌnt,sæbɪŋ] = **sabbing.**

huntsman ['hʌntsmən] N, PL **huntsmen** ['hʌntsmən] cazador *m*, montero *m*.

hurdle ['hɜːdl] N zarzo *m*, valla *f*; (*Sport*) valla *f*; (*fig*) obstáculo *m*.

hurdler ['hɜːdləʳ] N vallista *mf*.

hurdle race ['hɜːdlreɪs] N carrera *f* de vallas.

hurdling ['hɜːdlɪŋ] N salto *m* de vallas.

hurdy-gurdy ['hɜːdɪ,gɜːdɪ] N organillo *m*.

hurl [hɜːl] **1** VT lanzar, arrojar; **to ~ back** *enemy* rechazar; **to ~ insults at sb** llenar a uno de improperios.

2 VR: **to ~ o.s. at** (*or* **upon**) **sb** abalanzarse sobre uno; **to ~ o.s. into the fray** lanzarse a la batalla; **to ~ o.s. over a cliff** arrojarse por un precipicio.

hurling ['hɜːlɪŋ], **hurley** ['hɜːlɪ] N *juego irlandés parecido al hockey.*

hurly-burly ['hɜːlɪ'bɜːlɪ] N tumulto *m*; **the ~ of politics** la vida alborotada de la política.

hurrah [hʊ'rɑː], **hurray** [hʊ'reɪ] **1** INTERJ ¡viva!, ¡vítor!; **~ for Brown!** ¡viva Brown!

2 N vítor *m*.

hurricane ['hʌrɪkən] **1** N huracán *m*.

2 ATTR: **~ lamp** lámpara *f* a prueba de viento.

hurried ['hʌrɪd] ADJ apresurado, hecho de prisa; *reading etc* superficial; **he had a ~ meal** comió de prisa.

hurriedly ['hʌrɪdlɪ] ADV con prisa, apresuradamente; *study etc* superficialmente; *write etc* a vuela pluma; **I left ~** me apresuré a salir.

hurry ['hʌrɪ] **1** N prisa *f*, apuro *m* (*LAm*); **to be in a ~** tener prisa, tener apuro (*LAm*) (*to do* por hacer), estar de prisa; **I'm in no ~, I'm not in any ~** no tengo prisa; **they were in no ~ to pay us** no se dieron prisa por pagarnos; **to do sth in a ~** hacer algo de prisa; **are you in a ~ for this?** ¿corre prisa esto?; **is there any ~?** ¿corre prisa?; **what's all the ~?, what's your ~?** ¿por qué tanta prisa?, ¿por qué tanto apuro? (*LAm*); **there's no (great) ~** no hay prisa; **I shan't come back here in a ~** aquí no pongo los pies nunca más; **he won't do that again in a ~** no volverá a hacer eso si puede evitarlo.

2 VT *work etc* (*also* **to ~ along, to ~ on, to ~ up**) apresurar, dar prisa a, apurar, acelerar; **they hurried him to a doctor** le llevaron con toda prisa a un médico; **troops were hurried to the spot** se enviaron tropas al lugar con toda prisa; **this is a plan that cannot be hurried** éste es proyecto que no admite prisa; **to ~ the work along** acelerar el ritmo del trabajo; **to ~ sb away, to ~ sb off** hacer marchar a uno de prisa; **the policeman hurried him away** el policía se le llevó apresuradamente; **to ~ sb out** dar prisa a uno para que salga.

3 VI apresurarse (*to do* a hacer), darse prisa (*to do* para hacer), apurarse (*LAm*) (*to do* para hacer); **~!** ¡dése prisa!; **don't ~!** ¡no hay prisa!; **I must ~** tengo prisa, tengo que correr; **she hurried home** se dio prisa para llegar a casa; **to ~ after sb** correr detrás de uno; **to ~**

along correr, ir de prisa; **to ~ away, to ~ off** marcharse de prisa; **to ~ back** darse prisa para volver, volver de prisa; **to ~ in** entrar de prisa, entrar corriendo; **to ~ out** salir de prisa, salir corriendo; **to ~ over** *place* cruzar rápidamente; *work* concluir aprisa, hacer con precipitación.

◆**hurry up** **1** VT: **to ~ sb up** hacer que uno se dé prisa.

2 VI darse prisa; **~ up!** ¡date prisa!

hurt [hɜːt] **1** N (*wound etc*) herida *f*, lesión *f*; (*harm*) daño *m*, mal *m*, perjuicio *m*.

2 (*irr*: PRET AND PTP **hurt**) VT (*injure, bodily*) herir, hacer mal a, hacer daño a, lastimar; (*cause pain to*) doler; (*damage*) dañar; *business, interests etc* perjudicar, afectar; *feelings* herir, ofender; (*be bad for*) hacer daño a; **he ~ his foot** se lastimó el pie; **where does it ~ you?** ¿dónde le duele?; **to get ~** hacerse daño; **in such affairs sb's bound to get ~** en estos asuntos siempre sale alguno perjudicado; **wine never ~ anybody** el vino no hizo nunca daño a nadie; **she's feeling rather ~ about it** se ha ofendido bastante por ello.

3 VI (*feel pain*) doler; (*take harm*) sufrir daño, estropearse, echarse a perder; **does it ~ much?** ¿duele mucho?; **it won't ~ for being left another week** no se va a estropear si lo dejamos una semana más.

4 VR: **to ~ o.s.** hacerse daño, lastimarse.

5 ADJ *foot etc* lastimado, lisiado; *feelings* ofendido; **with a ~ look** con cara de ofendido; **in a ~ tone** quejoso, ofendido; **~ books** (*US*) libros *mpl* deteriorados (en tienda).

hurtful ['hɜːtfʊl] ADJ dañoso, perjudicial; *remark etc* hiriente.

hurtfully ['hɜːtfʊlɪ] ADV de manera hiriente.

hurtle ['hɜːtl] **1** VT arrojar (violentamente).

2 VI: **to ~ along, to ~ past** (ADV) ir como un rayo; **to ~ down** caer con violencia; **the car ~d past us** el coche cruzó como un rayo delante de nosotros; **the rock ~d over the cliff** la roca cayó estrepitosamente por el precipicio.

husband ['hʌzbənd] **1** N marido *m*; esposo *m*; **now they're ~ and wife** ahora son marido y mujer.

2 VT economizar, ahorrar, manejar prudentemente.

husbandry ['hʌzbəndrɪ] N **(a)** (*Agr*) agricultura *f*, labranza *f*. **(b)** (*fig: also* **good ~**) buen gobierno *m*, manejo *m* prudente.

hush [hʌʃ] **1** N silencio *m*; **a ~ fell** se hizo un silencio.

2 VI hacer callar, acallar, imponer silencio a.

3 VI callar(se); **~!** ¡chitón!; ¡cállate!

◆**hush up** VT *affair* encubrir, echar tierra a; *person* tapar la boca a.

hushed [hʌʃt] ADJ *tone* callado, muy bajo; *silence* profundo; **all were ~** se callaron todos.

hush-hush* ['hʌʃ'hʌʃ] ADJ muy secreto.

hush-money* ['hʌʃ,mʌnɪ] N mamela* *f*, precio *m* del silencio, dinero *m* por callar.

husk [hʌsk] **1** N cáscara *f*, vaina *f*; hollejo *m*, (*of corn*) cascabillo *m*.

2 VT descascarar, desvainar.

huskily ['hʌskɪlɪ] ADV roncamente, en voz ronca.

huskiness ['hʌskɪnɪs] N ronquedad *f*.

husky[1] ['hʌskɪ] ADJ **(a)** *voice, person* ronco. **(b)** (*tough*) fornido.

husky[2] ['hʌskɪ] N perro *m* esquimal.

hussar [hə'zɑːʳ] N húsar *m*.

hussy ['hʌsɪ] N pícara *f*, desvergonzada *f*; **you ~!** ¡lagarta!; **she's a little ~** es una fresca.

hustings ['hʌstɪŋz] NPL (*esp Brit*) elecciones *fpl*; campaña *f* electoral.

hustle ['hʌsl] **1** N **(a)** actividad *f* febril, bullicio *m*; (*pushfulness*) empuje *m*; **~ and bustle** ajetreo *m*, actividad *f* bulliciosa; **to get a ~ on*** darse prisa. **(b)** (*US**) timo *m*, chanchullo* *m*.

2 VT **(a)** (*jostle*) empujar, codear; (*hurry up*) *person* dar prisa a, *thing* acelerar; **I refuse to be ~d** no tolero que me den prisa; **I won't be ~d into anything** yo no resuelvo las cosas de prisa; **they ~d him into a car** le metieron en un coche a empellones, le hicieron entrar sin ceremonia en un coche; **to ~ sb out of a room** echar a uno de un cuarto a empellones.

(b) (*US‡*) solicitar (mediante presiones ilícitas), (*less vigorously*) enrollarse con.

3 VI **(a)** darse prisa, menearse.

(b) (*US*) (*: *work*) currelar‡, currar*; (‡: *prostitute o.s.*) prostituirse.

◆**hustle in** **1** VT: **to ~ sb in** hacer entrar a empellones, hacer entrar sin ceremonia.

2 VI entrar de prisa.

◆**hustle out** **1** VT: **they ~d him out** le echaron a empellones, le hicieron salir sin ceremonia.

2 VI salir de prisa.

hustler ['hʌsləʳ] N (*go-getter*) persona *f* dinámica; (*swindler*) estafador *m*, timador *m*; (*prostitute*) puta *f*, ramera *f*.

hut [hʌt] N casilla *f*; (*shed*) cobertizo *m*; (*hovel*) barraca *f*, cabaña *f*; choza *f*, (*mountain ~*) albergue *m* de montaña.

hutch [hʌtʃ] N conejera *f*.

HV, h.v. N ABBR *of* **high voltage** alto voltaje *m*.

HVT N ABBR *of* **high-velocity train** tren *m* de alta velocidad, TAV *m*.

hyacinth ['haɪəsɪnθ] N (*Bot, Min*) jacinto *m*.

hyaena [haɪ'iːnə] N hiena f.
hybrid ['haɪbrɪd] **1** ADJ híbrido.
  2 N híbrido m, -a f.
hybridism ['haɪbrɪdɪzəm] N hibridismo m.
hybridization [ˌhaɪbrɪdaɪ'zeɪʃən] N hibridación f.
hybridize ['haɪbrɪdaɪz] VTI hibridar.
hydra ['haɪdrə] N hidra f; **H~** (Myth) Hidra f.
hydrangea [haɪ'dreɪndʒə] N hortensia f.
hydrant ['haɪdrənt] N boca f de riego; (fire ~) boca f de incendios.
hydrate ['haɪdreɪt] **1** N hidrato m.
  2 VT hidratar.
hydraulic [haɪ'drɒlɪk] ADJ hidráulico; **~ brake** freno m hidráulico; **~ press** prensa f hidráulica; **~ suspension** suspensión f hidráulica.
hydraulics [haɪ'drɒlɪks] N hidráulica f.
hydro... ['haɪdrəʊ] PREF hidro...
hydro ['haɪdrəʊ] N (Brit) balneario m.
hydrocarbon ['haɪdrəʊ'kɑːbən] N hidrocarburo m.
hydrochloric ['haɪdrə'klɒrɪk] ADJ: **~ acid** ácido m clorhídrico.
hydrocyanic ['haɪdrəsaɪ'ænɪk] ADJ: **~ acid** ácido m cianhídrico.
hydrodynamics ['haɪdrəʊdaɪ'næmɪks] N hidrodinámica f.
hydroelectric ['haɪdrəʊɪ'lektrɪk] ADJ hidroeléctrico; **~ power station**, **~ power plant** central f hidroeléctrica.
hydroelectricity [ˌhaɪdrəʊlek'trɪsɪtɪ] N hidroelectricidad f.
hydrofoil ['haɪdrəʊfɔɪl] N hidroala f.
hydrogen ['haɪdrɪdʒən] **1** N hidrógeno m.
  2 ATTR: **~ bomb** bomba f de hidrógeno; **~ chloride** cloruro m de hidrógeno; **~ peroxide** peróxido m de hidrógeno.
hydrography [haɪ'drɒɡrəfɪ] N hidrografía f.
hydrolysis [haɪ'drɒlɪsɪs] N hidrólisis f.
hydrolyze ['haɪdrəʊlaɪz] **1** VT hidrolizar.
  2 VI hidrolizarse.
hydrometer [haɪ'drɒmɪtəʳ] N aerómetro m.
hydrophobia [ˌhaɪdrə'fəʊbɪə] N hidrofobia f.
hydrophobic [ˌhaɪdrə'fəʊbɪk] ADJ hidrofóbico.
hydroplane ['haɪdrəʊpleɪn] N hidroavión m.
hydroponic [ˌhaɪdrəʊ'pɒnɪk] ADJ hidropónico.
hydroponics [ˌhaɪdrəʊ'pɒnɪks] N SING hidroponia f.
hydropower ['haɪdrəʊˌpaʊəʳ] N hidrofuerza f.
hydrotherapy [ˌhaɪdrəʊ'θerəpɪ] N hidroterapia f.
hydroxide [haɪ'drɒksaɪd] N hidróxido m.
hyena [haɪ'iːnə] N hiena f.
hygiene ['haɪdʒiːn] N higiene f.
hygienic [haɪ'dʒiːnɪk] ADJ higiénico.
hygienist [haɪ'dʒiːnɪst] N: **dental ~** higienista mf dental.
hymen ['haɪmen] N himen m.
hymn [hɪm] N himno m.
hymnal ['hɪmnəl] N, **hymn book** ['hɪmbʊk] N himnario m.
hype* [haɪp] **1** N exageraciones fpl, cuentos mpl; superchería f; propaganda f; (Comm) bombo m publicitario*, promoción f de lanzamiento.
  2 VT (Comm) dar bombo publicitario a*.
◆**hype up*** **1** VT exagerar, dar bombo a*; person excitar; numbers aumentar.
  2 VI pincharse*, picarse*.
hyper... ['haɪpəʳ] PREF hiper...
hyper ['haɪpəʳ] ADJ hiperactivo, histérico.
hyperacidity ['haɪpərə'sɪdɪtɪ] N hiperacidez f.
hyperactive [ˌhaɪpər'æktɪv] ADJ hiperactivo, hipercenético.
hyperactivity [ˌhaɪpəræk'tɪvɪtɪ] N hiperactividad f.
hyperbola [haɪ'pɜːbələ] N hipérbola f.
hyperbole [haɪ'pɜːbəlɪ] N hipérbole f.
hyperbolic(al) [ˌhaɪpə'bɒlɪk(əl)] ADJ hiperbólico.

hypercorrection [ˌhaɪpəkə'rekʃən] N hipercorrección f, ultracorrección f.
hypercritical ['haɪpə'krɪtɪkəl] ADJ hipercrítico.
hyperinflation ['haɪpəɪn'fleɪʃən] N hiperinflación f.
hypermarket ['haɪpəˌmɑːkɪt] N (Brit) hipermercado m.
hypermetropia [ˌhaɪpəmɪ'trəʊpɪə], **hypermetropy** [ˌhaɪpə'metrəpɪ] N hipermetropía f.
hyperopia ['haɪpər'əʊpɪə] N hipermetropía f.
hypersensitive ['haɪpə'sensɪtɪv] ADJ hipersensible.
hypertension ['haɪpə'tenʃən] N hipertensión f.
hypertext ['haɪpəˌtekst] N (Comput) hipertexto m.
hypertrophy [haɪ'pɜːtrəfɪ] N hipertrofía f.
hyperventilate [ˌhaɪpə'ventɪleɪt] VI hiperventilar.
hyphen ['haɪfən] N guión m.
hyphenate ['haɪfəneɪt] VT escribir (or unir, separar) con guión.
hypnosis [hɪp'nəʊsɪs] N hipnosis f.
hypnotherapist [ˌhɪpnəʊ'θerəpɪst] N hipnoterapeuta mf.
hypnotherapy [ˌhɪpnəʊ'θerəpɪ] N hipnoterapia f.
hypnotic [hɪp'nɒtɪk] **1** ADJ hipnótico.
  2 N hipnótico m.
hypnotism ['hɪpnətɪzəm] N hipnotismo m.
hypnotist ['hɪpnətɪst] N hipnotista mf.
hypnotize ['hɪpnətaɪz] VT hipnotizar.
hypo ['haɪpəʊ] N hiposulfito m sódico.
hypoallergenic [ˌhaɪpəʊˌælə'dʒenɪk] ADJ hipoalérgeno.
hypochondria [ˌhaɪpəʊ'kɒndrɪə] N hipocondría f.
hypochondriac [ˌhaɪpəʊ'kɒndrɪæk] **1** ADJ hipocondríaco.
  2 N hipocondríaco m, -a f.
hypocrisy [hɪ'pɒkrɪsɪ] N hipocresía f.
hypocrite ['hɪpəkrɪt] N hipócrita mf.
hypocritical [ˌhɪpə'krɪtɪkəl] ADJ hipócrita.
hypocritically [ˌhɪpə'krɪtɪkəlɪ] ADV hipócritamente.
hypodermic [ˌhaɪpə'dɜːmɪk] N (also ~ **needle**) aguja f hipodérmica.
hypoglycaemia, (US) **hypoglycemia** [ˌhaɪpəʊɡlaɪ'siːmɪə] N hipoglucemia f.
hypoglycaemic, (US) **hypoglycemic** [ˌhaɪpəʊɡlaɪ'siːmɪk] ADJ hipoglucémico.
hyponym ['haɪpənɪm] N hipónimo m.
hyponymy [haɪ'pɒnɪmɪ] N hiponimia f.
hypostasis [haɪ'pɒstəsɪs] N, PL **hypostases** [haɪ'pɒstəsiːz] (Rel) hipóstasis f.
hypostatic [ˌhaɪpəʊ'stætɪk] ADJ (Rel) hipostático.
hypotenuse [haɪ'pɒtɪnjuːz] N hipotenusa f.
hypothalamus [ˌhaɪpə'θæləməs] N, PL **hypothalami** [ˌhaɪpə'θæləmaɪ] hipotálamo m.
hypothermia [ˌhaɪpəʊ'θɜːmɪə] N hipotermia f.
▼ **hypothesis** [haɪ'pɒθɪsɪs] N, PL **hypotheses** [haɪ'pɒθɪsiːz] hipótesis f.
hypothesize [haɪ'pɒθɪsaɪz] VI hipotetizar.
▼ **hypothetic(al)** [ˌhaɪpəʊ'θetɪk(əl)] ADJ hipotético.
hypothetically [ˌhaɪpəʊ'θetɪkəlɪ] ADV hipotéticamente.
hyssop ['hɪsəp] N (Bot) hisopo m.
hysterectomy [ˌhɪstə'rektəmɪ] N histerectomía f.
hysteria [hɪs'tɪərɪə] N histerismo m, histeria f.
hysterical [hɪs'terɪkəl] ADJ histérico; **~ laughter** risa f histérica; **to get ~** ponerse histérico, excitarse locamente.
hysterically [hɪs'terɪkəlɪ] ADV histéricamente; **to weep ~** llorar histéricamente; **to laugh ~** reír histéricamente; '**come here**', she shouted **~** 'ven acá', gritó histérica.
hysterics [hɪs'terɪks] NPL histerismo m, paroxismo m histérico; **to go into ~** ponerse histérico; **we were in ~ about it** casi nos morimos de risa.
Hz (Rad etc) ABBR of **hertz** hertzio m, Hz.

I

I, i [aɪ] N (*letter*) I, i *f*; **I for Isaac, I for Item** (*US*) I de Inés, I de Isabel; **to dot the i's and cross the t's** poner los puntos sobre las íes.
I [aɪ] PRON yo.
I. (*Geog*) ABBR *of* **Island, Isle** isla *f*.
i. ABBR *of* **interest** interés *m*.
IA (*US Post*) ABBR *of* **Iowa**.
IAAF N ABBR *of* **International Amateur Athletic Federation** Federación *f* Internacional de Atletismo Amateur o Aficionado.
IAEA N ABBR *of* **International Atomic Energy Agency** Organización *f* (*or* Organismo *m*) Internacional de Energía Atómica, OIEA *f*.
iambic [aɪˈæmbɪk] **1** ADJ yámbico; **~ pentameter** pentámetro *m* yámbico.
　　2 N yambo *m*, verso *m* yámbico.
IATA [aɪˈɑːtə] N ABBR *of* **International Air Transport Association** Asociación *f* Internacional del Transporte Aéreo, IATA *f*, AITA *f*.
IBA N (*Brit*) ABBR *of* **Independent Broadcasting Authority** *entidad que controla los medios privados de televisión y radio*.
Iberia [aɪˈbɪərɪə] N Iberia *f*.
Iberian [aɪˈbɪərɪən] **1** ADJ ibero, ibérico.
　　2 N ibero *m*, -a *f*.
Iberian Peninsula [aɪˈbɪərɪənpəˈnɪnsjʊlə] N Península *f* Ibérica.
IBEW N (*US*) ABBR *of* **International Brotherhood of Electrical Workers**.
ibex [ˈaɪbeks] N cabra *f* montés, íbice *m*.
ib(id) ADV ABBR *of* **ibidem** ibídem.
ibis [ˈaɪbɪs] N ibis *f*.
IBM N ABBR *of* **International Business Machines**.
IBRD N ABBR *of* **International Bank of Reconstruction and Development** Banco *m* Internacional para la Reconstrucción y el Desarrollo, BIRD *m*.
i/c. ABBR *of* **in charge** (**of**) encargado (de).
ICA N (*Brit*) (a) ABBR *of* **Institute of Contemporary Arts**. (b) ABBR *of* **Institute of Chartered Accountants**.
ICAO N ABBR *of* **International Civil Aviation Organization** Organización *f* de Aviación Civil Internacional, OACI *f*.
ICBM N ABBR *of* **intercontinental ballistic missile** misil *m* balístico intercontinental.
ICC N (a) ABBR *of* **International Chamber of Commerce** Cámara *f* de Comercio Internacional, CCI *f*. (b) (*US*) ABBR *of* **Interstate Commerce Commission**.
ice [aɪs] **1** N (a) hielo *m*; **my feet are like ~** tengo los pies helados; **to break the ~** (*fig*) romper el hielo; **he cuts no ~** ni pincha ni corta, no pinta nada; **it cuts no ~ with me** no me convence; **to keep sth on ~** conservar algo en frigorífico, (*fig*) tener algo en reserva; **to put a plan on ~** posponer un proyecto; **to skate on thin ~** pisar terreno peligroso.
　　(b) (*Brit: ice cream*) helado *m*.
　　2 VT (a) helar; *drink* enfriar, echar cubos de hielo a.
　　(b) *cake* alcorzar, escarchar, garapiñar.
　　3 VI (*also* **to ~ over, to ~ up**) helarse.
ice-age [ˈaɪseɪdʒ] **1** N época *f* glacial.
　　2 ADJ de la época glacial.
ice-axe, (*US*) **ice-ax** [ˈaɪsæks] N piolet *m*, piqueta *f*.
iceberg [ˈaɪsbɜːɡ] N iceberg *m*; **~ lettuce** lechuga *f* repollo.
ice-blue [ˌaɪsˈbluː] ADJ azul claro, azul pálido.
icebound [ˈaɪsbaʊnd] ADJ *road* helado, bloqueado por el hielo; *ship* preso entre los hielos.
icebox [ˈaɪsbɒks] N (a) (*Brit: part of refrigerator*) congelador *m*; **this room is like an ~** este cuarto es como un congelador.
　　(b) (*US: refrigerator*) nevera *f*, frigo *m*, refrigeradora *f* (*LAm*), heladera *f* (*SC*).
icebreaker [ˈaɪsˌbreɪkəʳ] N rompehielos *m*.
ice-bucket [ˈaɪsˌbʌkɪt] N cubito *m* para hielo.
icecap [ˈaɪskæp] N casquete *m* de hielo.

ice-cold [ˈaɪsˈkəʊld] ADJ más frío que el hielo; *drink* helado.
ice-cream [ˈaɪsˈkriːm] N helado *m*.
ice-cream soda [ˈaɪskriːmˌsəʊdə] N soda *f* mezclada con helado.
ice-cube [ˈaɪskjuːb] N cubito *m* de hielo, cubeta *f* de hielo.
iced [aɪst] ADJ *cake* escarchado; *drink* con hielo.
ice dance [ˈaɪsdɑːns] N baile *m* sobre hielo.
icefield [ˈaɪsfiːld] N campo *m* de hielo, banquisa *f*.
icefloe [ˈaɪsfləʊ] N témpano *m* de hielo.
ice-hockey [ˈaɪsˈhɒkɪ] N hockey *m* sobre hielo.
icehouse [ˈaɪshaʊs] N, PL **icehouses** [ˈaɪshaʊzɪz] (a) (*US*) nevera *f*. (b) (*of Eskimo*) iglú *m*.
Iceland [ˈaɪslənd] **1** N Islandia *f*.
　　2 ATTR: **~ spar** espato *m* de Islandia.
Icelander [ˈaɪsləndəʳ] N islandés *m*, -esa *f*.
Icelandic [aɪsˈlændɪk] **1** ADJ islandés.
　　2 N islandés *m*.
ice-lolly [ˌaɪsˈlɒlɪ] N (*Brit*) polo *m*, paleta *f* (*LAm*).
ice maiden* [ˈaɪsˌmeɪdn] N mujer *f* de hielo.
iceman [ˈaɪsmæn] N, PL **icemen** [ˈaɪsmen] (*US*) vendedor *m* de hielo, repartidor *m* de hielo.
icepack [ˈaɪspæk] N compresa *f* de hielo.
ice-pick [ˈaɪspɪk] N piolet *m*, piqueta *f*.
ice-rink [ˈaɪsrɪŋk] N pista *f* de hielo, pista *f* de patinaje.
ice-skate [ˈaɪsskeɪt] **1** N patín *m* de hielo, patín *m* de cuchilla.
　　2 VI patinar sobre hielo.
ice skater [ˈaɪsˌskeɪtəʳ] N patinador *m*, -ora *f* (*artístico/a*), patinador *m*, -ora *f* sobre hielo.
ice-skating [ˈaɪsˌskeɪtɪŋ] N patinaje *m* artístico, patinaje *m* sobre hielo.
ice water, iced water [ˈaɪswɔːtəʳ] N agua *f* helada, agua *f* fría (*de la nevera*).
ichthyology [ˌɪkθɪˈɒlədʒɪ] N ictiología *f*.
icicle [ˈaɪsɪkl] N carámbano *m*.
icily [ˈaɪsɪlɪ] ADV glacialmente (*also fig*).
iciness [ˈaɪsɪnɪs] N (*fig*) lo glacial.
icing [ˈaɪsɪŋ] N formación *f* de hielo; (*on cake*) alcorza *f*, garapiña *f*; (*bonus*) prima *f* imprevista; **this is the ~ on the cake** (*fig*) ésta es la guinda que corona la tarta.
icing-sugar [ˈaɪsɪŋˈʃʊɡəʳ] N (*Brit*) azúcar *m* de alcorza, azúcar *m* glas, azúcar *m* flor (*SC*).
ICJ N ABBR *of* **International Court of Justice** Corte *f* Internacional de Justicia, CJI *f*.
icky‡ [ˈɪkɪ] ADJ (*US*) (*messy*) desordenado; (*fig: horrible*) asqueroso.
icon [ˈaɪkɒn] N icono *m*; (*Comput*) símbolo *m* gráfico.
iconic [aɪˈkɒnɪk] ADJ (a) *image* simbólico; **the singer achieved ~ status with teenagers** el cantante ha sido beatificado por los adolescentes. (b) (*Comput, Math*) icónico.
iconoclasm [aɪˈkɒnəˌklæzəm] N iconoclastia *f*.
iconoclast [aɪˈkɒnəklæst] N iconoclasta *mf*.
iconoclastic [aɪˌkɒnəˈklæstɪk] ADJ iconoclasta.
iconographer [ˌaɪkɒˈnɒɡrəfəʳ] N iconógrafo *m*, -a *f*.
iconographic [aɪˌkɒnəˈɡræfɪk] ADJ iconográfico.
iconography [ˌaɪkɒˈnɒɡrəfɪ] N iconografía *f*.
ICR N (*US*) ABBR *of* **Institute for Cancer Research**.
ICRC N ABBR *of* **International Committee of the Red Cross** Comité *m* Internacional de la Cruz Roja, CICR *m*.
ICU N ABBR *of* **intensive care unit** unidad *f* de vigilancia intensiva, UVI *f*.
icy [ˈaɪsɪ] ADJ helado, glacial; (*fig*) glacial; **it's ~ cold** hace un frío glacial.
ID (a) (*US Post*) ABBR *of* **Idaho**. (b) N ABBR *of* **identification, identity**; V **identification, identity**.
id [ɪd] N id *m*.
I'd [aɪd] = **I would; I had**.

IDA N ABBR *of* **International Development Association** Asociación *f* Internacional de Fomento, AIF *f*.

Ida. (*US*) ABBR *of* **Idaho**.

IDB N ABBR *of* **International Development Bank** BID *m*.

ID card [ˌaɪˈdiːˌkɑːd] N ABBR *of* **identity card** carnet *m* de identidad, C.I. *m*.

IDD N ABBR *of* **international direct dialling** marcado *m* directo internacional.

▼ **idea** [aɪˈdɪə] N idea *f*; concepto *m*; ocurrencia *f*; **good ~!** ¡buena idea!; **what an ~!, the very ~!** ¡ni hablar!, ¡qué cosas dices!; **the ~ is to sell it** nos proponemos venderlo; **whose ~ was it to come this way?** ¿a quién se le ocurrió venir por aquí?; **it would not be a bad ~ to paint it** no le vendría mal una mano de pintura; **that's the ~!** ¡eso es!; **what's the big ~?** ¿qué haces ahí?, ¿qué pretendes con esto?; ¿a santo de qué ...?; **you'll have to buck up your ~s** tendrás que menearte; **to get an ~ of sth** hacerse una idea de algo; **to get an ~ for a novel** encontrar la inspiración para hacer una novela; **you're getting the ~** (*plan etc*) estás empezando a comprender, (*knack*) estás cogiendo el tino; **to get an ~ into one's head** metérsele a uno una idea en la cabeza; **don't go getting ~s** no te hagas ilusiones; no se te ocurra pensar que ...; **where did you get that ~?** ¿de dónde sacas eso?; **he has some ~ of French** tiene algunas nociones de francés; **I've no ~!** ¡ni idea!; **I haven't the foggiest** (*or remotest etc*) **~** no tengo la más remota idea; **I had no ~ that ...** no tenía la menor idea de que ...; **it was awful, you've no ~** fue horrible, te lo aseguro; **he hit on the ~ of** + *ger* se le ocurrió + *infin*; **to put ~s into sb's head** sugerir ideas a uno.

ideal [aɪˈdɪəl] **1** ADJ ideal; perfecto; soñado.
    2 N ideal *m*.

idealism [aɪˈdɪəlɪzəm] N idealismo *m*.

idealist [aɪˈdɪəlɪst] N idealista *mf*.

idealistic [aɪˌdɪəˈlɪstɪk] ADJ idealista.

idealization [aɪˌdɪəlaɪˈzeɪʃən] N idealización *f*.

idealize [aɪˈdɪəlaɪz] VT idealizar.

ideally [aɪˈdɪəlɪ] ADV idealmente; perfectamente; **they are ~ suited to each other** hacen una pareja ideal, están hechos idealmente el uno para la otra; **~, we should all go** en el mejor de los casos, debemos ir todos.

idée fixe [ˈiːdeɪˈfiːks] N idea *f* fija.

ident* [ˈaɪdent] N (*also* **station ~**) (*TV, Radio*) identificativo *m*.

identical [aɪˈdentɪkəl] ADJ idéntico; **~ twins** gemelos *mpl* idénticos, gemelas *fpl* idénticas.

identically [aɪˈdentɪkəlɪ] ADV idénticamente.

identifiable [aɪˌdentɪˈfaɪəbl] ADJ identificable.

identifier [aɪˈdentɪfaɪər] N identificador *m*.

identification [aɪˌdentɪfɪˈkeɪʃən] **1** N identificación *f*.
    2 ATTR: **~ mark** señal *f* de identificación; **~ papers** documentos *mpl* de identidad, papeles *mpl*; **~ parade** (*Brit*) = **identity parade**; **~ tag** (*US*) chapa *f* de identificación.

identify [aɪˈdentɪfaɪ] **1** VT identificar; acertar.
    2 VI: **to ~ with** identificarse con.
    3 VR: **to ~ o.s.** identificarse, establecer su identidad; **to ~ o.s. with** identificarse con.

identikit [aɪˈdentɪkɪt] N: **~ picture** retrato-robot *m*.

identity [aɪˈdentɪtɪ] **1** N identidad *f*; **to withhold sb's ~** silenciar el nombre de uno.
    2 ATTR: **~ card** cédula *f* personal, carnet *m* de identidad; **~ crisis** crisis *f* de identidad; **~ disc** chapa *f* de identidad; **~ papers** documentación *f* personal, carnet *m* de identidad; **~ parade** (*Brit*) careo *m* de sospechosos, rueda *f* de reconocimiento.

ideogram [ˈɪdɪəɡræm] N ideograma *m*.

ideographic [ˌɪdɪəˈɡræfɪk] ADJ ideográfico.

ideological [ˌaɪdɪəˈlɒdʒɪkəl] ADJ ideológico.

ideologically [ˌaɪdɪəˈlɒdʒɪkəlɪ] ADV ideológicamente.

ideologist [ˌaɪdɪˈɒlədʒɪst] N ideólogo *m*, -a *f*.

ideologue [ˈɪdɪəlɒɡ] N ideólogo *m*, -a *f*.

ideology [ˌaɪdɪˈɒlədʒɪ] N ideología *f*.

ides [aɪdz] NPL idus *mpl*.

idiocy [ˈɪdɪəsɪ] N imbecilidad *f*; estupidez *f*.

idiom [ˈɪdɪəm] N (**a**) (*phrase*) idiotismo *m*, modismo *m*, locución *f*. (**b**) (*style of expression*) lenguaje *m*.

idiomatic [ˌɪdɪəˈmætɪk] ADJ idiomático.

idiomatically [ˌɪdɪəˈmætɪkəlɪ] ADV idiomáticamente.

idiosyncrasy [ˌɪdɪəˈsɪŋkrəsɪ] N idiosincrasia *f*.

idiosyncratic [ˌɪdɪəsɪŋˈkrætɪk] ADJ idiosincrásico.

idiot [ˈɪdɪət] N idiota *mf*, imbécil *mf*, tonto *m*, -a *f*; **you ~!** ¡imbécil!; **~ board*** (*TV*) chuleta* *f*, autocue *m*.

idiotic [ˌɪdɪˈɒtɪk] ADJ idiota, imbécil, tonto, estúpido; (*laughter*) tonto; **that was ~ of you** has hecho el tonto.

idiotically [ˌɪdɪˈɒtɪkəlɪ] ADV tontamente, estúpidamente; **to laugh ~** reírse como un tonto.

idiot-proof* [ˈɪdɪətpruːf] ADJ para torpes*, de fácil manejo.

idle [ˈaɪdl] **1** ADJ (**a**) ocioso; (*lazy*) holgazán, flojo (*LAm*); (*work-shy*) vago; *student etc* gandul; (*without work*) desocupado; *moment* de ocio, libre; **the machine is never ~** la máquina no está parada jamás; **the strike made 100 workers ~** la huelga dejó sin trabajo a 100 obreros; **the machine stood ~ for hours** la máquina estaba parada durante horas enteras.
    (**b**) (*Comm*) **~ capacity** capacidad *f* sin utilizar; **~ money** capital *m* improductivo; **~ time** tiempo *m* de paro.
    (**c**) (*vain*) *fear* vano, infundado; ocioso, inútil; *question* ocioso; **~ chatter, ~ talk** charla *f* insustancial.
    2 VI haraganear, gandulear; (*Mech*) marchar en vacío; **we spent a few days idling in Paris** pasamos unos días ociosos en París; **we ~d over our meal** no nos dimos prisa para terminar la comida.
◆ **idle away** VT *time* perder, malgastar.

idleness [ˈaɪdlnɪs] N (*V* ADJ) (**a**) ociosidad *f*; holgazanería *f*; flojera *f* (*LAm*); gandulería *f*; desocupación *f*; **to live in ~** vivir en el ocio. (**b**) inutilidad *f*; frivolidad *f*.

idler [ˈaɪdlər] N ocioso *m*, -a *f*, holgazán *m*, -ana *f*, vago *m*, -a *f*; (*student etc*) gandul *m*.

idling [ˈaɪdlɪŋ] ADJ: **~ speed** velocidad *f* de marcha en vacío.

idly [ˈaɪdlɪ] ADV ociosamente; vanamente, inútilmente; **he glanced ~ out of the window** miró distraído por la ventana.

idol [ˈaɪdl] N ídolo *m*.

idolater [aɪˈdɒlətər] N idólatra *mf*.

idolatrous [aɪˈdɒlətrəs] ADJ idólatra, idolátrico.

idolatry [aɪˈdɒlətrɪ] N idolatría *f*.

idolize [ˈaɪdəlaɪz] VT idolatrar.

IDP N ABBR *of* **integrated data processing** proceso *m* integrado de datos, PID *m*.

idyll [ˈɪdɪl] N idilio *m*.

idyllic [ɪˈdɪlɪk] ADJ idílico.

i.e. ABBR *of* **id est, that is, namely** esto es, a saber.

if [ɪf] **1** CONJ (**a**) si; (*open condition*) **~ he comes I'll go** si él viene yo iré; (*past: habit*) **~ it was fine we went out** si hacía buen tiempo dábamos un paseo; (*past: unfulfilled*) **~ you were to say that you would be wrong** si dijeses eso te equivocarías; **~ you had said that you would have been wrong** si hubieras dicho eso te habrías equivocado; **~ I had known I would have told you** de haberlo sabido te lo habría dicho, si lo sé te lo digo*; **~ I were you** yo en tu lugar, yo que tú; **~ and when she comes** si (en efecto) viene, en el caso de que venga.
    (**b**) (*although*) **I couldn't eat it ~ I tried** no lo podría comer ni que me lo propusiera; **a nice film ~ rather long** una buena película si bien es algo larga.
    (**c**) (*whether*) si; **I don't know ~ he's here** no sé si está aquí.
    (**d**) **~ anything this one is better** hasta creo que éste es mejor; éste es mejor si cabe; **~ not** si no; **~ so** si es así; **~ it isn't old Bludnok!** ¡qué sorpresa ver al amigo Bludnok!
    (**e**) **~ only to see him** aunque sea sólo para verle; **~ only for a few hours** aunque sea sólo por unas pocas horas; **~ only I could!** ¡ojalá pudiera!, ¡si solamente pudiera!; **~ only I had known!** ¡si lo hubiese sabido!; **~ only we had a car!** ¡quién tuviera coche!; *V* **as, even** etc.
    2 N hipótesis *f*; duda *f*; **there are a lot of ~s and buts** hay muchas dudas no resueltas; **it's a big ~** es una duda importante, es sumamente dudoso.

IFAD N ABBR *of* **International Fund for Agricultural Development** Fondo *m* Internacional de Desarrollo Agrícola, FIDA *m*.

IFC N ABBR *of* **International Finance Corporation**.

iffy* [ˈɪfɪ] ADJ dudoso, incierto.

IFTO N ABBR *of* **International Federation of Tour Operators** Federación *f* Internacional de Touroperadores.

IG N (*US*) ABBR *of* **Inspector General**.

igloo [ˈɪɡluː] N iglú *m*.

Ignatius [ɪɡˈneɪʃəs] NM Ignacio, Íñigo.

igneous [ˈɪɡnɪəs] ADJ ígneo.

ignite [ɪɡˈnaɪt] **1** VT encender, incendiar, pegar (*LAm*: prender) fuego a.
    2 VI encenderse, incendiarse.

ignition [ɪɡˈnɪʃən] **1** N ignición *f*; (*Aut*) encendido *m*.
    2 ATTR: (*Aut*) **~ coil** bobina *f* de encendido; **~ key** llave *f* de contacto; **~ switch** interruptor *m* de encendido.

ignoble [ɪɡˈnəʊbl] ADJ innoble, vil.

ignominious [ˌɪɡnəˈmɪnɪəs] ADJ ignominioso, oprobioso; *defeat* vergonzoso.

ignominiously [ˌɪɡnəˈmɪnɪəslɪ] ADV ignominiosamente; **to be ~ defeated** sufrir una derrota vergonzosa.

ignominy [ˈɪɡnəmɪnɪ] N ignominia *f*, oprobio *m*, vergüenza *f*.

ignoramus [ˌɪɡnəˈreɪməs] N ignorante *mf*.

ignorance [ˈɪɡnərəns] N ignorancia *f*; **to be in ~ of sth** ignorar algo, desconocer algo.

ignorant [ˈɪɡnərənt] ADJ ignorante; **to be ~ of** ignorar, no saber, desconocer.

IF *see also main entry*

Indicative/Subjunctive after "si"
Si can be followed by both the *indicative* and the *subjunctive*. The *indicative* describes facts and likely situations; the *subjunctive* describes remote or hypothetical situations.

Indicative
- Use *si* + PRESENT INDICATIVE to translate *if* + PRESENT in English:
  If you go on overeating, you'll get fat
  Si sigues comiendo tanto, vas a engordar
  Don't do it if you don't want to
  No lo hagas si no quieres
  ! Don't use *si* with the PRESENT SUBJUNCTIVE.

Subjunctive
- Use *si* + IMPERFECT SUBJUNCTIVE to translate *if* + PAST for remote or uncertain possibilities and hypotheses:
  If we won the lottery, we would never have to work again
  Si nos tocase or *tocara la lotería, no tendríamos que trabajar nunca más*
  What would you do if I weren't here?
  ¿Qué harías si yo no estuviese or *estuviera aquí?*
- Use *si* + PLUPERFECT SUBJUNCTIVE (= *hubiera* or *hubiese* + PAST PARTICIPLE) to translate *if* + *had* + PAST PARTICIPLE:
  If Paula hadn't lost her ticket, she would have left today
  Si Paula no hubiera or *hubiese perdido el billete, habría salido hoy*
  NOTE: Alternatively, instead of a clause with *si*, you can often use *de (no) haber* + PAST PARTICIPLE:
  If Paula hadn't lost her ticket, she would have left today
  De no haber perdido Paula el billete, habría salido hoy
  For further uses and examples, see main entry.

ignorantly ['ɪgnərəntlɪ] ADV neciamente; **we ~ went to the next house** por ignorancia fuimos a la casa de al lado.
ignore [ɪgˈnɔːʳ] VT **(a)** no hacer caso de, desatender; (*omit*) hacer caso omiso de; pasar por alto; *awkward fact* cerrar los ojos ante; **we can safely ~ that** eso lo podemos dejar a un lado. **(b)** *person* no hacer el menor caso de; **I smiled but she ~d me** le sonreí pero ella hizo como si no me viera; **just ~ him** haz como si no existiera.
iguana [ɪˈgwɑːnə] N iguana *f*.
ikon ['aɪkɒn] N icono *m*.
IL (*US Post*) ABBR of **Illinois**.
ILA N (*US*) ABBR of **International Longshoremen's Association**.
ILEA ['ɪlɪə] (*formerly*) N ABBR of **Inner London Education Authority**.
ileum ['ɪlɪəm] N (*Anat*) íleon *m*.
ilex ['aɪleks] N encina *f*.
ILGWU N (*US*) ABBR of **International Ladies' Garment Workers Union**.
Iliad ['ɪlɪæd] N Ilíada *f*.
ilk [ɪlk] N: **and others of that ~** y otros de ese jaez.
Ill. (*US*) ABBR of **Illinois**.
ill [ɪl] **1** ADJ **(a)** (*Med*) enfermo, malo; **to be ~** estar enfermo; **to fall** (or **take, be taken**) **~** ponerse enfermo, enfermar; **to feel ~** sentirse mal; **it made me quite ~** me hizo sentirme mal.
(b) *fame, temper, turn etc* malo; V **ease 1 (d)**.
2 ADV malo; **we can ~ afford to lose him** mal podemos permitir que se vaya; **to speak ~ of sb** hablar mal de uno, criticar a uno; **he took it very ~** se ofendió bastante; **don't take it ~** no lo tomes a mal.
3 N (*Med*) mal *m*; (*fig*) infortunio *m*, desgracia *f*; **the ~s of the economy** la dolencia de la economía.
I'll [aɪl] = **I will**, **I shall**.
ill-advised ['ɪlad'vaɪzd] ADJ inconsiderado, imprudente; **an ~ plan** un proyecto nada recomendable; **you were very ~** en eso no anduvo muy acertado; **you would be ~ to** + *infin* sería poco aconsejable que + *subj*.
ill-assorted ['ɪlə'sɔːtɪd] ADJ mal avenido.
ill-at-ease ['ɪlət'iːz] ADJ molesto; inquieto, intranquilo.
ill-bred ['ɪl'bred] ADJ mal educado, mal criado.
ill-breeding [,ɪl'briːdɪŋ] N mala educación *f*.
ill-considered ['ɪlkən'sɪdəd] ADJ *plan* nada recomendable; *act* irreflexivo.
ill-disposed ['ɪldɪs'pəʊzd] ADJ malintencionado; **to be ~ towards sb** estar maldispuesto hacia uno; **he is ~ towards the idea** la idea no le hace gracia.
ill-effects ['ɪl'fekts] NPL efectos *mpl* adversos.
illegal [ɪ'liːgəl] ADJ ilegal, ilícito.
illegality [,ɪliː'gælɪtɪ] N ilegalidad *f*.
illegally [ɪ'liːgəlɪ] ADV ilegalmente, ilícitamente.
illegible [ɪ'ledʒəbl] ADJ ilegible.
illegibly [ɪ'ledʒəblɪ] ADV de un modo ilegible.
illegitimacy [,ɪlɪ'dʒɪtɪməsɪ] N ilegitimidad *f*.
illegitimate [,ɪlɪ'dʒɪtɪmɪt] ADJ ilegítimo.
illegitimately [,ɪlɪ'dʒɪtɪmɪtlɪ] ADV ilegítimamente.

ill-equipped ['ɪlɪ'kwɪpt] ADJ *expedition etc* defectuosamente equipado; **he was ~ for the task** no tenía talento para el cometido, no reunía las cualidades para la tarea.
ill-fated ['ɪl'feɪtɪd] ADJ malogrado, malhadado, funesto.
ill-favoured, (*US*) **ill-favored** ['ɪl'feɪvəd] ADJ feo, mal parecido.
ill-feeling ['ɪl'fiːlɪŋ] N hostilidad *f*, rencor *m*.
ill-formed [,ɪl'fɔːmd] ADJ mal formado.
ill-founded ['ɪl'faʊndɪd] ADJ *claim etc* mal fundado, infundado.
ill-gotten ['ɪl'gɒtn] ADJ mal adquirido, malhabido.
ill health ['ɪl'helθ] N mala salud *f*; **to be in ~** no estar bien de salud.
ill humour, (*US*) **ill humor** ['ɪl'hjuːməʳ] N mal humor *m*.
ill-humoured, (*US*) **ill-humored** ['ɪl'hjuːməd] ADJ malhumorado.
illiberal [ɪ'lɪbərəl] ADJ iliberal; intolerante.
illicit [ɪ'lɪsɪt] ADJ ilícito.
illicitly [ɪ'lɪsɪtlɪ] ADV ilícitamente.
illimitable [ɪ'lɪmɪtəbl] ADJ ilimitado, sin límites.
ill-informed ['ɪlɪn'fɔːmd] ADJ mal informado, poco enterado, ignorante.
illiquid [ɪ'lɪkwɪd] ADJ: **~ assets** activos *mpl* no realizables (a corto plazo).
illiteracy [ɪ'lɪtərəsɪ] N analfabetismo *m*.
illiterate [ɪ'lɪtərɪt] **1** ADJ analfabeto; (*fig*) sin instrucción, poco instruido; iletrado; *style etc* inculto.
2 N analfabeto *m*, -a *f*.
ill-judged ['ɪl'dʒʌdʒd] ADJ imprudente.
ill-kempt ['ɪl'kempt] ADJ desaliñado, desaseado.
ill luck ['ɪl'lʌk] N mala suerte *f*; **as ~ would have it** desgraciadamente, como quiso la suerte.
ill-mannered ['ɪl'mænəd] ADJ mal educado, sin educación.
ill-natured ['ɪl'neɪtʃəd] ADJ malévolo, malicioso.
illness ['ɪlnɪs] N enfermedad *f*, mal *m*, dolencia *f*; indisposición *f*.
ill-nourished [,ɪl'nʌrɪʃt] ADJ malnutrido.
illogic [ɪ'lɒdʒɪk] N falta *f* de lógica.
illogical [ɪ'lɒdʒɪkəl] ADJ falto de lógica, ilógico.
illogicality [ɪ,lɒdʒɪ'kælɪtɪ] N falta *f* de lógica, contrasentido.
illogically [ɪ'lɒdʒɪkəlɪ] ADV ilógicamente.
ill-omened ['ɪl'əʊmənd] ADJ de mal agüero; nefasto.
ill-prepared [,ɪlprɪ'peəd] ADJ mal preparado.
ill-starred ['ɪl'stɑːd] ADJ malhadado, malogrado.
ill-suited ['ɪl'suːtɪd] ADJ impropio; mal avenido; **they are ~** no se convienen uno a otro; **he is ~ to the job** no conviene al puesto.
ill-tempered ['ɪl'tempəd] ADJ *person* de mal genio; *remark, tone etc* malhumorado.
ill-timed ['ɪl'taɪmd] ADJ inoportuno, intempestivo.
ill-treat ['ɪl'triːt] VT maltratar, tratar mal.
ill-treatment ['ɪl'triːtmənt] N maltratamiento *m*, maltrato *m*, malos tratos *mpl*.
illuminate [ɪ'luːmɪneɪt] VT iluminar (*also Art*); (*decorate with lights*) poner luminarias en; *subject* aclarar; **the castle is ~d in summer** en el verano el castillo está iluminado.
illuminated [ɪ'luːmɪneɪtɪd] ADJ *sign etc* luminoso; *manuscript* iluminado.
illuminating [ɪ'luːmɪneɪtɪŋ] ADJ aclaratorio; *book, speech etc* instructivo; *remark etc* revelador, significativo.
illumination [ɪ,luːmɪ'neɪʃən] N iluminación *f* (*also Art*), alumbrado *m*; (*Brit: for special effect*) iluminación *f*; **~s** (*festive etc*) luminarias *fpl*, luces *fpl*.
illuminator [ɪ'luːmɪneɪtəʳ] N iluminador *m*, -ora *f*.
illumine [ɪ'luːmɪn] VT = **illuminate**.
ill-use ['ɪl'juːz] VT maltratar, tratar mal.
illusion [ɪ'luːʒən] N apariencia *f*; espejismo *m*; imaginaciones *fpl*; (*optical ~*) ilusión *f* de óptica; **to be under an ~** estar equivocado; **I am under no ~s on that score** sobre eso punto no tengo ilusiones; **he cherishes the ~ that ...** abriga la esperanza de que + *subj*; **it gives an ~ of space** crea una impresión de espacio.
illusionist [ɪ'luːʒənɪst] N prestidigitador *m*, -ora *f*, ilusionista *mf*.
illusive [ɪ'luːsɪv] ADJ, **illusory** [ɪ'luːsərɪ] ADJ ilusorio.
▼ **illustrate** ['ɪləstreɪt] VT **(a)** (*exemplify*) ilustrar; *subject* aclarar; *point* ejemplificar, demostrar; **I can best ~ this in the following way** esto quedará más claro si se explica del modo siguiente. **(b)** *book* ilustrar; **a book ~d by X** un libro con grabados (*etc*) de X.
illustrated ['ɪləstreɪtɪd] ADJ: **~ paper** revista *f* gráfica.
illustration [,ɪləs'treɪʃən] N (*example*) ejemplo *m*; (*explanation*) explicación *f*, aclaración *f*; (*in book*) grabado *m*, lámina *f*, ilustración *f*; **by way of ~** como ejemplo, a modo de ejemplo.
illustrative ['ɪləstrətɪv] ADJ ilustrativo, ilustrador, aclaratorio; **to be ~ of sth** ejemplificar algo.
illustrator ['ɪləstreɪtəʳ] N ilustrador *m*, -ora *f*.
illustrious [ɪ'lʌstrɪəs] ADJ ilustre.
illustriously [ɪ'lʌstrɪəslɪ] ADV ilustremente.
ill-will ['ɪl'wɪl] N mala voluntad *f*; (*spite*) rencor *m*, encono *m*; **I bear you no ~ for that** no le guardo rencor por eso.

ILO N ABBR of **International Labour Organization** Organización *f* Internacional del Trabajo, OIT *f*.

ILS N (*Aer*) ABBR of **Instrument Landing System**.

ILWU N (*US*) ABBR of **International Longshoremen's and Warehousemen's Union**.

I'm [aɪm] = **I am**.

image ['ɪmɪdʒ] N (a) imagen *f* (*also Liter, Eccl*); **~ processing** proceso *m* de imágenes; **to be the very** (*or* **spitting**) **~ of** ser el vivo retrato (*or* la viva imagen) de; **to make sb in one's own ~** hacer a uno a su imagen.
(b) (*public face*) imagen *f*; reputación *f*, opinión *f*; **the company's ~** la reputación de la compañía; **we must improve our ~** tenemos que mejorar nuestra imagen.

imagery ['ɪmɪdʒərɪ] N (*Liter*) imágenes *fpl*, metáforas *fpl*.

imaginable [ɪ'mædʒɪnəbl] ADJ imaginable; **the biggest surprise ~** la mayor sorpresa que se puede imaginar.

imaginary [ɪ'mædʒɪnərɪ] ADJ imaginario.

imagination [ɪ,mædʒɪ'neɪʃən] N imaginación *f*; (*capacity for ~*) imaginativa *f*; (*inventiveness*) inventiva *f*; **it's all ~!** ¡es pura fantasía!, ¡lo has soñado!; **she lets her ~ run away with her** se deja llevar por la imaginación.

imaginative [ɪ'mædʒɪnətɪv] ADJ imaginativo.

imaginatively [ɪ'mædʒɪnətɪvlɪ] ADV imaginativamente.

imaginativeness [ɪ'mædʒɪnətɪvnɪs] N imaginativa *f*.

imagine [ɪ'mædʒɪn] VT imaginar, imaginarse, figurarse; (**just**) **~!** ¡imagínate!, ¡fíjate!; **you can ~ how I felt!** ¡puedes suponer lo que yo sufría!; **don't ~ that ...** no te vayas a pensar que yo + *subj*; **to fondly ~ that ...** hacerse la ilusión de que ..., creer inocentemente que ...

imaginings [ɪ'mædʒɪnɪŋz] N (*liter*) imaginaciones *fpl*, figuraciones *fpl*.

imam [ɪ'mɑːm] N imán *m*.

imbalance [ɪm'bæləns] N desequilibrio *m*, falta *f* de equilibrio.

imbalanced [ɪm'bælənst] ADJ desequilibrado.

imbecile ['ɪmbəsiːl] [1] ADJ imbécil.
[2] N imbécil *mf*; **you ~!** ¡imbécil!

imbecility [,ɪmbɪ'sɪlɪtɪ] N imbecilidad *f*.

imbibe [ɪm'baɪb] [1] VT (*drink*) beber; (*absorb*) embeber; (*fig*) embeberse de (*or* en), empaparse de.
[2] VI beber.

imbroglio [ɪm'brəʊlɪəʊ] N embrollo *m*, lío *m*.

imbue [ɪm'bjuː] VT: **to ~ sth with** imbuir algo de (*or* en), empapar algo de; **to be ~d with** estar empapado de.

IMF N ABBR of **International Monetary Fund** Fondo *m* Monetario Internacional, FMI *m*.

IMHO ABBR of **In My Honest Opinion**.

imitable ['ɪmɪtəbl] ADJ imitable.

imitate ['ɪmɪteɪt] VT imitar; (*pej*) remedar; (*make another copy of*) copiar, reproducir.

imitation [,ɪmɪ'teɪʃən] [1] N imitación *f*; (*pej*) remedo *m*; **in ~ of** a imitación de; **beware of ~s** desconfíe de las imitaciones.
[2] ATTR: **~ gold** oro *m* de imitación; **~ jewels, ~ jewellery** bisutería *f*, joyas *fpl* de imitación; **~ leather** imitación *f* a piel; **~ marble** mármol *m* artificial.

imitative ['ɪmɪtətɪv] ADJ imitativo; imitador; **a style ~ of Joyce's** un estilo que imita el de Joyce.

imitator ['ɪmɪteɪtəʳ] N imitador *m*, -ora *f*.

immaculate [ɪmækjʊlɪt] ADJ (*spotless*) limpísimo, perfectamente limpio, inmaculado; *style etc* perfecto; (*Eccl*) inmaculado, purísimo; **I~ Conception** Inmaculada Concepción *f*.

immaculately [ɪ'mækjʊlɪtlɪ] ADV (*clean*) perfectamente; (*behave*) impecablemente, perfectamente, intachablemente; (*dressed*) impecablemente.

immanent ['ɪmənənt] ADJ inmanente.

Immanuel [ɪ'mænjʊəl] NM Emanuel.

immaterial [,ɪmə'tɪərɪəl] ADJ inmaterial, incorpóreo; **it is ~ whether ... no importa si ...; that is quite ~** eso no hace al caso; **that is ~ to me** eso me es indiferente.

immature [,ɪmə'tjʊəʳ] ADJ inmaturo, no maduro; *specimen* joven; *fruit* verde; *work* juvenil.

immaturity [,ɪmə'tjʊərɪtɪ] N inmadurez *f*, falta *f* de madurez; juventud *f*.

immeasurable [ɪ'meʒərəbl] ADJ inmensurable, inconmensurable.

immeasurably [ɪ'meʒərəblɪ] ADV enormemente.

immediacy [ɪ'miːdɪəsɪ] N inmediatez *f*; urgencia *f*.

immediate [ɪ'miːdɪət] ADJ inmediato; (*pressing*) urgente, apremiante; *danger* inminente; (*prime*) primero, principal; **~ access** entrada *f* inmediata; **the ~ area** las inmediaciones; **for ~ delivery** para entrega inmediata; **my ~ object** mi primer propósito; **we must take ~ action** hay que obrar inmediatamente.

immediately [ɪ'miːdɪətlɪ] [1] ADV (a) (*of time*) inmediatamente, enseguida, en seguida; sin demora; en el acto; **~ following the dinner** inmediatamente después de la cena; **~ following this discussion**

a raíz de esta discusión.
(b) (*of place*) **~ next to the wall** muy junto a la pared.
[2] CONJ (*Brit*) así que, luego que, al instante que; **let me know ~ he comes** avíseme en cuanto venga.

immemorial [,ɪmɪ'mɔːrɪəl] ADJ inmemorial, inmemorable; **from time ~** desde tiempo inmemorial.

immense [ɪ'mens] ADJ inmenso, enorme.

immensely [ɪ'menslɪ] ADV enormemente; **we were ~ cheered** nos alegramos enormemente; **did you enjoy yourselves? yes, ~** ¿qué tal lo pasasteis? estupendamente; **it is ~ difficult** es enormemente difícil.

immensity [ɪ'mensɪtɪ] N inmensidad *f*.

immerse [ɪ'mɜːs] [1] VT sumergir, sumir, hundir; **to be ~d in** (*fig*) estar absorto en.
[2] VR: **to ~ o.s. in** (*fig*) sumergirse en.

immersion [ɪ'mɜːʃən] [1] N inmersión *f*, sumersión *f*.
[2] ATTR: **~ course** curso *m* de inmersión; **~ heater** (*Brit*) calentador *m* de inmersión.

immigrant ['ɪmɪgrənt] [1] ADJ inmigrante; **~ community** comunidad *f* de inmigrantes; **~ worker** trabajador *m*, -ora *f* inmigrante.
[2] N inmigrante *mf*.

immigrate ['ɪmɪgreɪt] VI inmigrar.

immigration [,ɪmɪ'greɪʃən] N inmigración *f*; **~ authorities** autoridades *fpl* de inmigración; **~ control** control *m* de inmigración; **I~ (Department)** (Departamento *m* de) Inmigración *f*; **~ quota** cuota *f* de inmigración.

imminence ['ɪmɪnəns] N inminencia *f*.

imminent ['ɪmɪnənt] ADJ inminente.

immobile [ɪ'məʊbaɪl] ADJ inmóvil, inmoble.

immobiliser [ɪ'məʊbɪlaɪzəʳ] N (*Auto*) inmovilizador *m*.

immobility [,ɪməʊ'bɪlɪtɪ] N inmovilidad *f*.

immobilize [ɪ'məʊbɪlaɪz] VT inmovilizar.

immoderate [ɪ'mɒdərɪt] ADJ excesivo, inmoderado.

immoderately [ɪ'mɒdərɪtlɪ] ADV excesivamente; **to drink ~** beber en exceso.

immodest [ɪ'mɒdɪst] ADJ (*indecent*) deshonesto, impúdico; (*impudent*) descarado.

immodestly [ɪ'mɒdɪstlɪ] ADV impúdicamente; descaradamente.

immodesty [ɪ'mɒdɪstɪ] N deshonestidad *f*, impudicia *f*; descaro *m*.

immolate ['ɪməʊleɪt] VT inmolar.

immoral [ɪ'mɒrəl] ADJ inmoral; *earnings* ilícito.

immorality [,ɪmə'rælɪtɪ] N inmoralidad *f*.

immortal [ɪ'mɔːtl] [1] ADJ inmortal; *fame etc* imperecedero.
[2] N inmortal *mf*.

immortality [,ɪmɔː'tælɪtɪ] N inmortalidad *f*.

immortalize [ɪ'mɔːtəlaɪz] VT inmortalizar.

immovable [ɪ'muːvəbl] [1] ADJ inmoble, inmóvil; que no se puede mover; *feast etc* fijo; (*fig*) inalterable, inconmovible; **he was quite ~** estuvo inflexible.
[2] **~s** NPL inmuebles *mpl*.

immune [ɪ'mjuːn] ADJ inmune (*also Med; from, to* a, contra); **~ system** sistema *m* inmunológico; **to be ~ from taxes** estar exento de impuestos.

immunity [ɪ'mjuːnɪtɪ] N inmunidad *f* (*also Med; from, to* contra); exención *f* (*from* de); **diplomatic ~** inmunidad *f* diplomática.

immunization [,ɪmjʊnaɪ'zeɪʃən] N inmunización *f*.

immunize ['ɪmjʊnaɪz] VT inmunizar.

immunodeficiency [ɪ,mjuːnəʊdɪ'fɪʃənsɪ] N inmunodeficiencia *f*.

immunodepressant [ɪ,mjʊnəʊdɪ'presnt] N, inmunodepresor *m*.

immunoglobulin [,ɪmjʊnəʊ'glɒbjʊlɪn] N inmunoglobulina *f*.

immunological [ɪ,mjuːnə'lɒdʒɪkəl] ADJ inmunológico; **~ defences** defensas *fpl* inmunológicas.

immunologist [ɪmjʊ'nɒlədʒɪst] N inmunólogo *m*, -a *f*.

immunology [,ɪmjʊ'nɒlədʒɪ] N inmunología *f*.

immunosuppressant [ɪ'mjuː:nəʊsə'presənt] [1] ADJ inmunosupresivo.
[2] N inmunosupresivo *m*, inmunosupresor *m*.

immunosuppression [ɪ'mjuː:nəʊsə'preʃən] N inmunosupresión *f*.

immunosuppressive [ɪ'mjuː:nəʊsə'presɪv] ADJ inmunosupresivo, inmunosupresor.

immunotherapy [,ɪmjʊnəʊ'θerəpɪ] N inmunoterapia *f*.

immure [ɪ'mjʊəʳ] VT emparedar; (*fig*) encerrar; **to be ~d in** estar encerrado en.

immutability [ɪ,mjuːtə'bɪlɪtɪ] N inmutabilidad *f*, inalterabilidad *f*.

immutable [ɪ'mjuːtəbl] ADJ inmutable, inalterable.

immutably [ɪ'mjuːtəblɪ] ADV inmutablemente; inalterablemente.

IMO (a) ABBR of **In My Opinion** en mi opinión. **(b)** N ABBR of **International Miners' Organisation** Organización *f* Internacional de Mineros. **(c)** N ABBR of **International Maritime Organisation** Organización *f* Marítima Internacional.

imp [ɪmp] N diablillo *m*; (*fig*) diablillo *m*, pícaro *m*, pillín *m*.

imp. ABBR of *imperial*.

impact ['ɪmpækt] [1] N impacto *m*, choque *m*; (*fig*) impacto *m*, efecto

m, consecuencias *fpl*; **the book had a great ~ on its readers** el libro conmovió profundamente a sus lectores; **the speech made no ~** el discurso no hizo mella.
2 ATTR: **~ printer** impresora *f* de impacto.
3 [im'pækt] VT (*US*) impactar, afectar (a), tener un efecto en (*or* sobre).
♦ **impact on** VT impactar en, tener un impacto sobre.
impacted [im'pæktid] ADJ *tooth* impactado; **~ area** (*US*) zona *f* superpoblada.
impair [im'peə'] VT perjudicar, dañar, deteriorar, debilitar.
impaired [im'peəd] ADJ dañado, deteriorado; **~ capital** capital *m* disminuido.
impairment [im'peəmənt] N *physical, mental* discapacidad *f*; (*deterioration*) deterioro *m*.
impala [im'pɑːlə] N impala *m*.
impale [im'peil] 1 VT (*as punishment*) empalar; (*on sword etc*) espetar, atravesar.
2 VR: **to ~ o.s. on** atravesarse en.
impalpable [im'pælpəbl] ADJ impalpable; (*fig*) intangible, inaprensible.
imparity [im'pæriti] N disparidad *f*.
impart [im'pɑːt] VT comunicar, impartir, hacer saber.
impartial [im'pɑːʃəl] ADJ imparcial.
impartiality [im,pɑːʃi'æliti] N imparcialidad *f*.
impartially [im'pɑːʃəli] ADV imparcialmente.
impassable [im'pɑːsəbl] ADJ intransitable; *river etc* invadeable; *barrier* infranqueable.
impasse [æm'pɑːs] N callejón *m* sin salida; cerrazón *f*; parálisis *f*, situación *f* sin solución; **the ~ lasted 3 months** la parálisis duró 3 meses; **the ~ is complete** la parálisis es total; **negotiations have reached an ~** las negociaciones han llegado a un punto muerto, las negociaciones están en un callejón sin salida.
impassioned [im'pæʃnd] ADJ apasionado, exaltado.
impassive [im'pæsiv] ADJ impasible, imperturbable.
impassively [im'pæsivli] ADV imperturbablemente; **he listened ~** escuchó impasible.
impatience [im'peiʃəns] N impaciencia *f*.
impatiens [im'peiʃi,enz] N impatiens *f*.
impatient [im'peiʃənt] ADJ impaciente; intolerante; **to be ~ to +** *infin* impacientarse por + *infin*; **to be ~ of sth** no sufrir algo con paciencia, no aguantar algo; **to get** (*or* **become, grow**) **~ about sth** impacientarse ante algo, impacientarse por algo; **to get ~ with sb** perder la paciencia con uno; **to make sb ~** impacientar a uno.
impatiently [im'peiʃəntli] ADV con impaciencia, impacientemente.
impeach [im'piːtʃ] VT (a) (*accuse*) acusar (*esp* de alta traición); (*try*) procesar; (*US*) someter a un proceso de incapacitación (presidencial). (b) (*criticize*) censurar; tachar.
impeachable [im'piːtʃəbl] ADJ sujeto a acusación (de alta traición); (*US*) sujeto a proceso de incapacitación (presidencial).
impeachment [im'piːtʃmənt] N denuncia *f*, acusación *f* (*esp* de alta traición); proceso *m*; (*US*) proceso *m* de incapacitación (presidencial).
impeccable [im'pekəbl] ADJ impecable, intachable.
impeccably [im'pekəbli] ADV *clean* impecablemente; *behave* impecablemente; intachablemente; *dress* impecablemente.
impecunious [,impi'kjuːniəs] ADJ inope, indigente, falto de dinero.
impedance [im'piːdəns] N (*Elec*) impedancia *f*.
impede [im'piːd] VT *person* estorbar; (*fig*) dificultar, estorbar, impedir.
impediment [im'pedimənt] N obstáculo *m*, estorbo *m* (**to** para); (*Jur*) impedimento *m*; (*in speech*) defecto *m* del habla, impedimento *m*.
impedimenta [im,pedi'mentə] NPL equipaje *m*; (*Mil*) impedimenta *f*.
impel [im'pel] VT impulsar, mover (**to +** *infin* a + *infin*); **I feel ~led to say ...** me veo obligado a decir ...
impend [im'pend] VI amenazar, ser inminente, cernerse.
impending [im'pendiŋ] ADJ inminente; (*near*) próximo; **his ~ fate** el hado que le amenaza; **his ~ retirement** su jubilación que va a realizarse en breve; **our ~ removal** nuestra mudanza en fecha próxima.
impenetrability [im,peni'trə'biliti] N impenetrabilidad *f*.
impenetrable [im'penitrəbl] ADJ impenetrable (**to** a); *mind etc* insondable, enigmático.
impenitence [im'penitəns] N impenitencia *f*.
impenitent [im'penitənt] ADJ impenitente.
impenitently [im'penitəntli] ADV impenitentemente, incorregiblemente.
imperative [im'perətiv] 1 ADJ (a) *tone* imperioso, perentorio; (*necessary*) esencial, indispensable; (*pressing*) urgente, apremiante; **it is ~ that ...** es imprescindible que + *subj*.
(b) (*Gram*) imperativo; **~ mood** modo *m* imperativo.
2 N imperativo *m* (*also Gram*).
imperatively [im'perətivli] ADV (*speak*) imperiosamente; perentoriamente.

imperceptible [,impə'septəbl] ADJ imperceptible, insensible.
imperceptibly [,impə'septəbli] ADV imperceptiblemente, insensiblemente.
imperfect [im'pɜːfikt] 1 ADJ imperfecto (*also Gram*), defectuoso; **~ competition** competición *f* imperfecta.
2 N imperfecto *m*.
imperfection [,impə'fekʃən] N (*state*) imperfección *f*; (*blemish*) desperfecto *m*, tacha *f*.
imperfectly [im'pɜːfiktli] ADV defectuosamente.
imperial [im'piəriəl] ADJ imperial; **~ gallon** (*Brit*) galón *m* inglés; **~ system** sistema *m* británico de pesos y medidas.

IMPERIAL SYSTEM
---

*i Aunque el sistema métrico decimal se implantó oficialmente en 1971 en el Reino Unido para medidas y pesos y es el que se enseña en los colegios, en el lenguaje cotidiano aún se sigue usando en muchos casos el llamado imperial system. Por ejemplo, en las tiendas se sigue pesando en libras (**pounds**) y la gente suele decir su peso en **stones** y **pounds**. La cerveza se mide en pintas (**pints**), las distancias en millas (**miles**) y la longitud, la altura o la profundidad en pies (**feet**) y pulgadas (**inches**).*
*En Estados Unidos el sistema imperial también se usa para todas las medidas y pesos, aunque la capacidad de la onza (**ounce**), del galón (**gallon**) y de la pinta (**pint**) es ligeramente inferior a la del Reino Unido. Por otro lado, en EE.UU. la gente mide su peso sólo en libras (**pounds**) y no en stones.*

imperialism [im'piəriəlizəm] N imperialismo *m*.
imperialist [im'piəriəlist] N imperialista *mf*.
imperialistic [im,piəriə'listik] ADJ imperialista.
imperil [im'peril] VT poner en peligro, arriesgar.
imperious [im'piəriəs] ADJ imperioso, arrogante; *need* apremiante.
imperiously [im'piəriəsli] ADV imperiosamente.
imperishable [im'periʃəbl] ADJ imperecedero.
impermanence [im'pɜːmənəns] N impermanencia *f*.
impermanent [im'pɜːmənənt] ADJ impermanente.
impermeable [im'pɜːmiəbl] ADJ impermeable (**to** a).
impersonal [im'pɜːsnl] ADJ impersonal.
impersonality [im,pɜːsə'næliti] N impersonalidad *f*.
impersonally [im'pɜːsnəli] ADV impersonalmente.
impersonate [im'pɜːsəneit] VT hacerse pasar por; (*Theat*) imitar, personificar.
impersonation [im,pɜːsə'neiʃən] N (*Theat*) imitación *f*.
impersonator [im'pɜːsəneitə'] N (*Theat*) imitador *m*, -ora *f*.
impertinence [im'pɜːtinəns] N impertinencia *f*, insolencia *f*, descaro *m*; **an ~, a piece of ~** una impertinencia; **it would be an ~ to +** *infin* sería improcedente + *infin*; **what ~!, the ~ of it!** ¡qué frescura!
impertinent [im'pɜːtinənt] ADJ impertinente, insolente, descarado; **to be ~ to sb** decir impertinencias a uno; **don't be ~!** ¡no seas fresco!
impertinently [im'pɜːtinəntli] ADV impertinentemente, descaradamente.
imperturbable [,impə'tɜːbəbl] ADJ imperturbable.
impervious [im'pɜːviəs] ADJ impermeable, impenetrable (**to** a); (*fig*) insensible (**to** a).
impetigo [,impi'taigəu] N impétigo *m*.
impetuosity [im,petju'ositi] N impetuosidad *f*, irreflexión *f*.
impetuous [im'petjuəs] ADJ impetuoso, irreflexivo.
impetuously [im'petjuəsli] ADV impetuosamente, irreflexivamente.
impetus ['impitəs] N ímpetu *m*; (*fig*) impulso *m*, incentivo *m*; **to give an ~ to sales** impulsar las ventas, incentivar las ventas.
impiety [im'paiəti] N impiedad *f*.
impinge [im'pindʒ] VI: **to ~ on** afectar a.
impingement [im'pindʒmənt] N intrusión *f*, usurpación *f*.
impious ['impiəs] ADJ impío.
impiously ['impiəsli] ADV impíamente.
impish ['impiʃ] ADJ travieso, endiablado.
implacable [im'plækəbl] ADJ implacable.
implacably [im'plækəbli] ADV implacablemente.
implant 1 ['implɑːnt] N implante *m*.
2 [im'plɑːnt] VT implantar.
implausible [im'plɔːzəbl] ADJ inverosímil; poco convincente.
implausibly [im'plɔːzəbli] ADV inverosímilmente, poco convincentemente.
implement 1 ['implimənt] N herramienta *f*, instrumento *m*; (*Agr*) apero *m*; **~s** aperos *mpl*, implementos *mpl*.
2 ['impliment] VT poner por obra, llevar a cabo, hacer efectivo; realizar, ejecutar.
implementation [,implimen'teiʃən] N realización *f*, ejecución *f*.
implicate ['implikeit] VT comprometer, implicar, involucrar; enredar; **he ~d 3 others** acusó a 3 más (de haber tomado parte en el delito); delató a 3 cómplices suyos; **with 2 others ~d in the crime** con otros 2 implicados en el delito; **are you ~d in this?** ¿andas metido en esto?

implication [ˌɪmplɪˈkeɪʃən] N (a) (act) comprometimiento m.
(b) (in crime) complicidad f, implicación f.
(c) (consequence etc) consecuencia f, inferencia f; implicación f; ~s consecuencias fpl, trascendencia f; by ~, then ... de ahí se deduce, pues, ...; he did not realize the full ~s of his words no se dio cuenta de la trascendencia de sus palabras; we shall have to study all the ~s tendremos que estudiar todas las consecuencias.

implicit [ɪmˈplɪsɪt] ADJ implícito; faith etc incondicional, absoluto.

implicitly [ɪmˈplɪsɪtlɪ] ADV implícitamente; sin reservas, incondicionalmente.

implied [ɪmˈplaɪd] ADJ implícito, tácito; ~ contract contrato m tácito; ~ warranty garantía f implícita; it is not stated but it is ~ no se declara abiertamente pero se sobreentiende.

implode [ɪmˈpləʊd] ① VT (a) implosionar. (b) (Phon) pronunciar implosivamente.
② VI implosionar.

implore [ɪmˈplɔːr] VT thing implorar, suplicar; person suplicar; I ~ you! ¡se lo suplico!; to ~ sb to do sth suplicar a uno hacer algo.

imploring [ɪmˈplɔːrɪŋ] ADJ suplicante; look etc lleno de suplicación.

imploringly [ɪmˈplɔːrɪŋlɪ] ADV de modo suplicante.

implosion [ɪmˈpləʊʒən] N implosión f (also Phon).

imply [ɪmˈplaɪ] VT (involve) implicar, suponer, presuponer; (mean) querer decir, significar; (state indirectly) dar a entender; (hint) insinuar; that implies some intelligence eso supone cierta inteligencia; are you ~ing that ...? ¿quieres decir que ...?; what do you ~ by that? ¿qué quieres insinuar con eso?; he implied he would do it dio a entender que lo haría; it implies a lot of work for him supone mucho trabajo para él, representa mucho trabajo para él.

impolite [ˌɪmpəˈlaɪt] ADJ descortés, mal educado.

impolitely [ˌɪmpəˈlaɪtlɪ] ADV con descortesía.

impoliteness [ˌɪmpəˈlaɪtnɪs] N mala educación f, descortesía f.

impolitic [ɪmˈpɒlɪtɪk] ADJ impolítico.

imponderable [ɪmˈpɒndərəbl] ① ADJ imponderable.
② ~s NPL (elementos mpl) imponderables mpl.

import ① [ˈɪmpɔːt] N (a) (Comm) importación f, artículo m importado.
(b) (meaning) significado m, sentido m; importancia f; of general ~ de significado general.
② [ˈɪmpɔːt] ATTR: ~ duty derechos mpl de entrada; ~ levy impuesto m sobre importaciones; ~ licence, ~ license (US), ~ permit permiso m de importación; ~ quota cupo m de importación; ~ surcharge sobrecarga f de importación; ~ trade comercio m importador.
③ [ɪmˈpɔːt] VT (a) (Comm) importar (from de, into en).
(b) (mean) significar, querer decir.

▼ **importance** [ɪmˈpɔːtəns] N importancia f; of some ~ de cierta importancia, importante; a fact of the first ~ un hecho primordial; to attach great ~ to sth conceder mucha importancia a algo; to be of ~ tener importancia; that's of no ~ eso no importa; to be full of one's own ~ darse ínfulas.

▼ **important** [ɪmˈpɔːtənt] ADJ importante; de categoría; news etc destacado, trascendente; personage destacado; it's not ~ no importa, no tiene importancia; to become ~ cobrar importancia; to try to look ~ tratar de hacer figura.

importantly [ɪmˈpɔːtəntlɪ] ADV say etc en tono rimbombante.

importation [ˌɪmpɔːˈteɪʃən] N importación f.

imported [ɪmˈpɔːtɪd] ADJ article de importación.

importer [ɪmˈpɔːtər] N importador m, -ora f.

import-export trade [ˌɪmpɔːtˈekspɔːt,treɪd] N comercio m de importación y exportación.

importing [ɪmˈpɔːtɪŋ] ADJ: ~ company empresa f importadora, empresa f de importación; ~ country país m importador.

importunate [ɪmˈpɔːtjʊnɪt] ADJ demand etc importuno; person molesto, pesado.

importune [ˌɪmpɔːˈtjuːn] VT importunar, perseguir, fastidiar; (prostitute) abordar con fines inmorales.

importunity [ˌɪmpɔːˈtjuːnɪtɪ] N importunidad f; pesadez f.

impose [ɪmˈpəʊz] ① VT imponer (on a); (palm off) hacer aceptar (on a).
② VI: to ~ upon (deceive) embaucar; (take advantage of) kindness etc abusar de, person abusar de la amabilidad de; I don't wish to ~ upon you no quiero abusar, no quiero molestarle.

imposing [ɪmˈpəʊzɪŋ] ADJ imponente, impresionante; majestuoso.

imposition [ˌɪmpəˈzɪʃən] N (act) imposición f; (burden) carga f, molestia f; abuso m; (tax) impuesto m; it's a bit of an ~ me resulta algo molesto; I fear it's rather an ~ for you me temo que le vaya a molestar bastante.

impossibility [ɪm,pɒsəˈbɪlɪtɪ] N imposibilidad f.

▼ **impossible** [ɪmˈpɒsəbl] ① ADJ imposible; person inaguantable, insufrible; you're ~! ¡eres imposible!, ¡no puedo contigo!; to make it ~ for sb to do sth quitar a uno la posibilidad de hacer algo, imposibilitar algo a uno.
② N: to do the ~ hacer lo imposible;

ver también EASY, DIFFICULT, IMPOSSIBLE .

impossibly [ɪmˈpɒsəblɪ] ADV imposiblemente; ~ difficult de lo más difícil, tan difícil que resulta imposible.

impost [ˈɪmpəʊst] N impuesto m.

impostor [ɪmˈpɒstər] N impostor m, -ora f, embustero m, -a f.

imposture [ɪmˈpɒstʃər] N impostura f, engaño m, fraude m.

impotence [ˈɪmpətəns] N impotencia f.

impotent [ˈɪmpətənt] ADJ impotente.

impound [ɪmˈpaʊnd] VT goods embargar, confiscar.

impoundment [ɪmˈpaʊndmənt] N (US: Fin) aprehensión f.

impoverish [ɪmˈpɒvərɪʃ] VT empobrecer, reducir a la miseria; land agotar.

impoverished [ɪmˈpɒvərɪʃt] ADJ empobrecido, necesitado, indigente; land agotado.

impoverishment [ɪmˈpɒvərɪʃmənt] N empobrecimiento m; agotamiento m.

impracticability [ɪm,præktɪkəˈbɪlɪtɪ] N impracticabilidad f, imposibilidad f.

impracticable [ɪmˈpræktɪkəbl] ADJ impracticable, no factible, imposible de realizar.

impractical [ɪmˈpræktɪkəl] ADJ falto de sentido práctico, poco práctico; (awkward) desmañado.

impracticality [ɪm,præktɪˈkælɪtɪ] N falta f de sentido práctico.

imprecation [ˌɪmprɪˈkeɪʃən] N imprecación f.

imprecise [ˌɪmprɪˈsaɪs] ADJ impreciso.

imprecision [ˌɪmprɪˈsɪʒən] N imprecisión f.

impregnable [ɪmˈpregnəbl] ADJ inexpugnable.

impregnate [ˈɪmpregneɪt] VT impregnar, empapar (with de); (Bio) fecundar; to become ~d with impregnarse de.

impregnation [ˌɪmpregˈneɪʃən] N impregnación f; (Bio) fecundación f.

impresario [ˌɪmpreˈsɑːrɪəʊ] N empresario m.

impress ① [ˈɪmpres] N impresión f, señal f; (fig) sello m, huella f.
② [ɪmˈpres] VT (a) (mark, stamp) estampar; (fig) grabar, inculcar; I must ~ upon you that ... tengo que subrayar que ...; it ~ed itself upon my mind quedó grabado en mi memoria; I tried to ~ the importance of the job on him traté de convencerle de la importancia del puesto.
(b) (affect) impresionar; he does it just to ~ people lo hace sólo para impresionar a la gente; he is not easily ~ed no se deja impresionar fácilmente; I was not ~ed no me hizo buena impresión; he ~ed me quite favourably me hizo una impresión bastante buena; how did it ~ you? ¿qué impresión te produjo?; the play deeply ~ed everyone la obra causó honda impresión en todos.
③ [ɪmˈpres] VI hacer buena impresión.

▼ **impression** [ɪmˈpreʃən] N (a) (effect) impresión f; to make an ~ impresionar; she's out to make an ~ se dedica a impresionar, quiere causar una sensación; to make an ~ on sb impresionar a uno; what ~ did it make on you? ¿qué impresión le produjo?; all our arguments seemed to make no ~ on him todos nuestros argumentos al parecer no tuvieron efecto alguno en él; he could make no ~ on his opponent's majority no logró rebajar la mayoría de su rival.
▼ (b) (vague idea) impresión f; to be under the ~ that ..., to have the ~ that ... tener la impresión de que ...; my ~s of Ruritania mis impresiones de Ruritania.
(c) (imprint) impresión f; huella f, señal f.
(d) (esp Brit Typ) edición f, tirada f.
(e) (Theat) imitación f.

impressionable [ɪmˈpreʃnəbl] ADJ impresionable; influenciable; sensible; at an ~ age en una edad impresionable.

impressionism [ɪmˈpreʃənɪzəm] N impresionismo m.

impressionist [ɪmˈpreʃənɪst] ① ADJ impresionista.
② N (a) (Art) impresionista mf. (b) (Theat) imitador m, -ora f.

impressionistic [ɪm,preʃəˈnɪstɪk] ADJ impresionista.

impressive [ɪmˈpresɪv] ADJ impresionante.

impressively [ɪmˈpresɪvlɪ] ADV de modo impresionante.

imprest [ɪmˈprest] ATTR: ~ system sistema m de fondo fijo.

imprimatur [ˌɪmprɪˈmeɪtər] N imprimátur m.

imprint ① [ˈɪmprɪnt] N impresión f, huella f, señal f; (Typ) pie m de imprenta; under the HarperCollins ~ publicado por HarperCollins.
② [ɪmˈprɪnt] VT imprimir, estampar (on en); (fig) grabar (on the mind en la memoria); (Bio, Psych) imprimir (on a).

imprinting [ɪmˈprɪntɪŋ] N (Bio, Psych) impresión f.

imprison [ɪmˈprɪzn] VT encarcelar, poner en la cárcel; the judge ~ed him for 10 years el juez le condenó a 10 años de prisión.

imprisonment [ɪmˈprɪznmənt] N encarcelamiento m, detención f, prisión f; ~ without trial detención f sin procesamiento; the judge sentenced him to 10 years' ~ el juez le condenó a 10 años de prisión; to escape from ~ escapar de la cárcel.

improbability [ɪm,prɒbəˈbɪlɪtɪ] N improbabilidad f; inverosimilitud f.

improbable [ɪmˈprɒbəbl] ADJ improbable; inverosímil; it is ~ that it will happen no es probable que ocurra, es poco probable que

---

ocurra.

improbably [ɪmˈprɒbəblɪ] ADV sorprendentemente; **this area is, ~, one of the best in town** en contra de lo que cabría esperar, este barrio es uno de los mejores de la ciudad.

impromptu [ɪmˈprɒmptjuː] ① ADJ *performance* improvisado, no preparado de antemano; *utterance* espontáneo, impremeditado.
② ADV *perform* de improviso, sin preparación; *say etc* de repente.
③ N improvisación *f*.

improper [ɪmˈprɒpəʳ] ADJ impropio, incorrecto, indebido; (*Comput*) incorrecto; (*unseemly*) indecoroso; (*indecent*) indecente, deshonesto.

improperly [ɪmˈprɒpəlɪ] ADV impropiamente, incorrectamente, indebidamente; indecorosamente; indecentemente, deshonestamente.

impropriety [ˌɪmprəˈpraɪətɪ] N inconveniencia *f*; incorrección *f*; falta *f* de decoro; indecencia *f*, deshonestidad *f*; (*of language*) impropiedad *f*.

improve [ɪmˈpruːv] ① VT mejorar; perfeccionar; reformar; (*beautify*) embellecer; *land* abonar, bonificar; *property* aumentar el valor de; *production, yield* aumentar; *mind* ilustrar, edificar; *opportunity* aprovechar.
② VI mejorar(se); perfeccionarse; (*production, yield*) aumentar(se); (*price*) subir; (*weather*) mejorar, componerse; (*in skill, studies etc*) hacer progresos; **the patient is improving** el enfermo está mejor; **he is in ~d health** está mejor de salud; **in these ~d circumstances** en mejores circunstancias.
③ VR: **to ~ o.s.** (*in mind*) instruirse; (*in wealth etc*) mejorar su situación.
◆ **improve on** VT mejorar, perfeccionar; **to ~ on sb's offer** ofrecer más que otro; **it cannot be ~d on** es inmejorable.

improvement [ɪmˈpruːvmənt] ① N mejora *f*, mejoramiento *m*; perfeccionamiento *m*; reforma *f*; embellecimiento *m*; aumento *m*, subida *f* (*in* de); progreso *m*, adelantamiento *m*; (*Med*) mejoría *f*; enmienda *f*; **there has been some ~ in the patient's condition** el enfermo está algo mejor; **it's an ~ on the old one** es mejor que el antiguo; **to make ~s in a text** enmendar un texto; **to make ~s to a property** hacer reformas en un inmueble.
② ATTR: **~ grant** subvención *f* para modernizar (una casa *etc*).

improvidence [ɪmˈprɒvɪdəns] N imprevisión *f*.

improvident [ɪmˈprɒvɪdənt] ADJ impróvido, imprevisor.

improvidently [ɪmˈprɒvɪdəntlɪ] ADV impróvidamente.

improving [ɪmˈpruːvɪŋ] ADJ edificante, instructivo.

improvisation [ˌɪmprəvaɪˈzeɪʃən] N improvisación *f*.

improvise [ˈɪmprəvaɪz] VTI improvisar, repentizar.

imprudence [ɪmˈpruːdəns] N imprudencia *f*.

imprudent [ɪmˈpruːdənt] ADJ imprudente.

imprudently [ɪmˈpruːdəntlɪ] ADV imprudentemente.

impudence [ˈɪmpjʊdəns] N descaro *m*, insolencia *f*, atrevimiento *m*; **what ~!** ¡qué frescura!; **he had the ~ to say that ...** tuvo la cara (dura) de decir que ...

impudent [ˈɪmpjʊdənt] ADJ descarado, insolente, atrevido.

impudently [ˈɪmpjʊdəntlɪ] ADV descaradamente, insolentemente.

impugn [ɪmˈpjuːn] VT impugnar.

impulse [ˈɪmpʌls] ① N (*Mech etc*) impulso *m*; (*fig*) impulso *m*, impulsión *f*, estímulo *m*; incitación *f*; **to act on ~** obrar por capricho, obrar sin reflexión; **my first ~ was to** + *infin* mi primer impulso fue de + *infin*, primero intenté + *infin*; **to yield to a sudden ~** dejarse llevar por un impulso.
② ATTR: **~ buy(ing), ~ purchase** compra *f* impulsiva; **~ goods** mercancías *fpl* expuestas para la compra impulsiva; **~ sales** ventas *fpl* impulsivas.

impulsion [ɪmˈpʌlʃən] N impulsión *f*.

impulsive [ɪmˈpʌlsɪv] ADJ *person* irreflexivo, que no reflexiona, impulsivo; *act* irreflexivo.

impulsively [ɪmˈpʌlsɪvlɪ] ADV por impulso; sin reflexión, sin pensar.

impulsiveness [ɪmˈpʌlsɪvnɪs] N, **impulsivity** [ɪmpʌlˈsɪvɪtɪ] N (*US*) irreflexión *f*; carácter *m* impulsivo.

impunity [ɪmˈpjuːnɪtɪ] N impunidad *f*; **with ~** impunemente.

impure [ɪmˈpjʊəʳ] ADJ impuro; adulterado, mezclado; (*morally*) deshonesto.

impurity [ɪmˈpjʊərɪtɪ] N impureza *f*; deshonestidad *f*.

imputation [ˌɪmpjʊˈteɪʃən] N imputación *f*; acusación *f*.

impute [ɪmˈpjuːt] VT imputar, achacar, atribuir (*to* a); acusar.

IN (*US Post*) ABBR of **Indiana**.

in [ɪn] ① ADV (**a**) dentro, adentro; **~ here** aquí dentro; **~ there** allí dentro; **day ~, day out** día tras día; **£200 a week all ~** 200 libras por semana todo incluido.
(**b**) **to be ~** (*person*) estar, estar en casa, estar en la oficina (*etc*); **is Mr Eccles ~?** ¿está el Sr Eccles?; **the train is ~** ha llegado el tren; **when the Tories were ~** cuando los conservadores estaban en el poder; **when the sun is ~** cuando el sol está escondido; **the harvest is ~** ha terminado la recolección; **strawberries are ~** es la temporada de las fresas, las fresas están en sazón; **short skirts were ~** la falda corta estaba de moda.

(**c**) **to be ~ for a post** ser candidato a un puesto, solicitar un puesto; **to be ~ for a competition** concurrir a un certamen, tomar parte en un concurso; **to be ~ for an exam** presentarse a un examen; **we're ~ for it now** aquí se va a armar la gorda; **you don't know what you're ~ for** no sabes lo que te pescas; **we're ~ for a hard time** vamos a pasar un mal rato; **he's ~ for a surprise** le espera una sorpresa.
(**d**) **to be ~ on the secret** estar en el secreto; **to be ~ on a plan** estar enterado de un proyecto.
(**e**) **to be well ~ with sb** estar muy metido con uno, tener mucha confianza con uno.
(**f**) **to be all ~, to feel all ~** estar rendido, no poder más.
(**g**) (*: in prison*) **he's ~ for larceny** está preso por ladrón; **he's ~ for 5 years** cumple una condena de 5 años; **what's he ~ for?** ¿de qué delito se le acusa?

② PREP (**a**) (*place*) en; dentro de; **~ the house** en la casa; **~ one's hand** en la mano; **~ Rome** en Roma; **~ Italy** en Italia; **~ prison** en la cárcel; **~ school** en la escuela; **~ the distance** a lo lejos; **~ everybody's eyes** a los ojos de todos; **it is not ~ him to do that** no es capaz de hacer eso, no cabe en él hacer eso; **he has it ~ him to succeed** es capaz de triunfar; **our colleagues ~ Madrid** nuestros colegas de Madrid; **we find it ~ Galdós** lo encontramos en Galdós; **~ him we have a great leader** en él tenemos un gran caudillo.
(**b**) (*in respect of*) **better ~ health** mejor de salud; **strong ~ maths** fuerte en matemáticas; **a change ~ policy** un cambio de política; **a rise ~ prices** una subida de los precios; **3 metres ~ length** 3 metros de largo; **long ~ the leg** de piernas largas; **diseased ~ mind** de mentalidad anormal; **deaf ~ one ear** sordo de un oído.
(**c**) (*ratio*) **1 ~ 7** 1 sobre 7, 1 de cada 7; **15 pence ~ the pound** 15 peniques de cada libra.
(**d**) (*time*) **~ 1972** en 1972; **~ the 20th century** en el siglo XX; **~ May** en mayo; **~ summer** en el verano; **~ the past** en el pasado; **~ these times** en estos tiempos; **~ the reign of** bajo el reinado de; **it was built ~ a week** fue construido en una semana; **I'll bring it back ~ a week** lo devolveré dentro de una semana, lo devolveré de aquí a ocho días; **~ a week he was back** al cabo de una semana volvió; **~ the morning** por la mañana; **at 8 ~ the morning** a las 8 de la mañana; **~ the daytime** de día, durante el día; **I haven't seen him ~ years** hace años que no le veo.
(**e**) (*state, fig*) **~ tears** llorando; **~ despair** desesperado; **~ good health** en buen estado de salud; **~ ruins** en ruinas; **any man ~ his senses** cualquier hombre sensato.
(**f**) (*clothed in*) **the girl ~ green** la chica vestida de verde; **he went out ~ his new raincoat** al salir se puso el impermeable nuevo; **she looks nice ~ that hat** con ese sombrero está guapísima.
(**g**) (*weather*) **~ the rain** bajo la lluvia; **~ the July sun** bajo el sol de julio.
(**h**) (*concerned with*) **he's ~ the tyre business** se dedica al comercio de neumáticos, tiene un negocio de neumáticos; **those ~ teaching** los profesores, los que se dedican a enseñar; **he travels ~ soap** es viajante en jabones; **she has shares ~ oil** tiene acciones de compañías de petróleo; **he's something ~ advertising** tiene un puesto (importante) en la publicidad; **the latest thing ~ hats** lo más nuevo en sombreros.
(**i**) (*manner*) **~ this way** de este modo; **~ the American fashion** a la americana; **~ alphabetical order** por orden alfabético; **cut ~ half** cortado por el medio; **~ French** en francés; **written ~ pencil** escrito con (*or* a) lápiz; **painted ~ black** pintado de negro; **packed ~ dozens** envasados por docenas; **~ hundreds** a cientos, a centenares; **~ cash** en metálico; **~ mourning** de luto; **~ his shirt** en camisa; **~ writing** por escrito; **~ anger** con enojo.
(**j**) (*after superlative*) **the best pupil ~ the class** el mejor alumno de la clase; **the biggest ~ Europe** el mayor de Europa.
(**k**) (*with verb*) **saying this** al decir esto; **~ making a fortune he lost his wife** mientras se ganaba una fortuna, perdió a su mujer.
③ N: **~s and outs** recovecos *mpl*; (*fig*) detalles *mpl* nimios; interioridades *fpl*.
④ ADJ (*) **an ~ joke** un chiste para iniciados; **it's the ~ thing** está de moda; **it's the ~ place to eat** es el restaurante que está de moda; **she wore a very ~ dress** llevaba un vestido de lo más 'in'*.

in. ABBR *of* **inch** pulgada *f*.

in... [ɪn] PREF in...

-in [ɪn] N *ending in compounds*: *eg* **love~** reunión *f* de fraternidad colectiva; **sit~** sentada *f*; **teach~** reunión *f* de autoenseñanza colectiva.

inability [ˌɪnəˈbɪlɪtɪ] N incapacidad *f*, falta *f* de aptitud; **my ~ to come** el que yo no pueda venir.

in absentia [ˈɪnæbˈsentɪə] ADV in absentia.

inaccessibility [ˈɪnækˌsesəˈbɪlɪtɪ] N inaccesibilidad *f*.

inaccessible [ˌɪnækˈsesəbl] ADJ inaccesible.

inaccuracy [ɪnˈækjʊrəsɪ] N inexactitud *f*, incorrección *f*.

inaccurate [ɪnˈækjʊrɪt] ADJ inexacto, incorrecto, erróneo.

inaccurately [ɪnˈækjʊrɪtlɪ] ADV erróneamente.
inaction [ɪnˈækʃən] N inacción f.
inactive [ɪnˈæktɪv] ADJ inactivo.
inactivity [ˌɪnækˈtɪvɪtɪ] N inactividad f.
inadequacy [ɪnˈædɪkwəsɪ] N insuficiencia f; (of person) incapacidad f.
inadequate [ɪnˈædɪkwɪt] ADJ insuficiente, inadecuado; defectuoso; *person* incapaz.
inadequately [ɪnˈædɪkwɪtlɪ] ADV de modo inadecuado.
inadmissible [ˌɪnədˈmɪsəbl] ADJ inadmisible.
inadvertence [ˌɪnədˈvɜːtəns] N inadvertencia f; **by ~** por inadvertencia, por equivocación, por descuido.
inadvertent [ˌɪnədˈvɜːtənt] ADJ inadvertido; accidental.
inadvertently [ˌɪnədˈvɜːtəntlɪ] ADV por equivocación, por descuido.
inadvisability [ˈɪnədˌvaɪzəˈbɪlɪtɪ] N imprudencia f, inconveniencia f.
▼ **inadvisable** [ˌɪnədˈvaɪzəbl] ADJ no aconsejable, desaconsejable, imprudente, inconveniente.
inalienable [ɪnˈeɪlɪənəbl] ADJ inalienable.
inamorata [ɪnˌæməˈrɑːtə] N amada f, querida f.
inane [ɪˈneɪn] ADJ necio, fatuo, sonso (*LAm*).
inanimate [ɪnˈænɪmɪt] ADJ inanimado.
inanition [ˌɪnəˈnɪʃən] N inanición f.
inanity [ɪˈnænɪtɪ] N necedad f, fatuidad f, inutilidad f; **inanities** estupideces fpl, necedades fpl.
inapplicable [ɪnˈæplɪkəbl] ADJ inaplicable.
inappropriate [ˌɪnəˈprəʊprɪɪt] ADJ inoportuno, inconveniente, impropio, poco apropiado.
inappropriately [ˌɪnəˈprəʊprɪɪtlɪ] ADV inoportunamente.
inappropriateness [ˌɪnəˈprəʊprɪɪtnɪs] N impropiedad f.
inapt [ɪnˈæpt] ADJ impropio; (*lacking skill*) inhábil.
inaptitude [ɪnˈæptɪtjuːd] N impropiedad f; inhabilidad f.
inarticulate [ˌɪnɑːˈtɪkjʊlɪt] ADJ (of character) incapaz de expresarse, que habla poco y mal; **an ~ speech** un discurso mal pronunciado; **he was ~ with rage** la rabia le embargó la voz.
inarticulately [ˌɪnɑːˈtɪkjʊlɪtlɪ] ADV: **he speaks ~** habla poco y mal; **he was mumbling ~** hablaba entre dientes y apenas se le entendía.
inartistic [ˌɪnɑːˈtɪstɪk] ADJ *work* poco artístico, antiestético, burdo, mal hecho; *person* falto de talento artístico.
inasmuch [ˌɪnəzˈmʌtʃ]: **~ as** CONJ puesto que, ya que, por cuanto que.
inattention [ˌɪnəˈtenʃən] N inatención f, desatención f, distracción f.
inattentive [ˌɪnəˈtentɪv] ADJ desatento, distraído.
inattentively [ˌɪnəˈtentɪvlɪ] ADV distraídamente.
inaudible [ɪnˈɔːdəbl] ADJ inaudible, que no se puede oír; **he was almost ~** apenas se le podía oír.
inaudibly [ɪnˈɔːdəblɪ] ADV de modo inaudible; **he spoke almost ~** habló tan bajo que apenas se le podía oír.
inaugural [ɪˈnɔːgjʊrəl] ADJ inaugural; *speech* de apertura.
inaugurate [ɪˈnɔːgjʊreɪt] VT inaugurar.
inauguration [ɪˌnɔːgjʊˈreɪʃən] N inauguración f; ceremonia f de apertura; (*US Pol*) toma f de posesión (*de su cargo por el presidente*).
inauspicious [ˌɪnɔːsˈpɪʃəs] ADJ poco propicio, desfavorable.
inauspiciously [ˌɪnɔːsˈpɪʃəslɪ] ADV de modo poco propicio, en condiciones desfavorables.
in-between [ˈɪnbɪˈtwiːn] ADJ intermedio; de en medio; **it's rather ~** ocupa una posición más bien intermedia, no es ni lo uno ni lo otro.
inboard [ˈɪnbɔːd] ADJ *engine* interior.
inborn [ˈɪnˈbɔːn] ADJ innato, ingénito; instintivo.
inbound [ˈɪnˌbaʊnd] (*US*) [1] ADV hacia el interior.
[2] ADJ que va hacia el interior; *flight* entrante.
inbred [ˈɪnˈbred] ADJ *tendency etc* innato, ingénito; instintivo; (*of race*) engendrado por endogamia; **people there are very ~** allí la endogamia ha debilitado a la gente.
inbreeding [ˈɪnˈbriːdɪŋ] N endogamia f.
inbuilt [ˈɪnˈbɪlt] ADJ *feeling etc* innato, inherente.
Inc. (*US*) ABBR of **Incorporated** sociedad f anónima, S.A.
inc. ABBR of **including, inclusive**.
Inca [ˈɪŋkə] [1] N inca mf.
[2] ATTR incaico, incásico.
incalculable [ɪnˈkælkjʊləbl] ADJ incalculable; *person etc* voluble, veleidoso.
Incan [ˈɪŋkən] ADJ inca, incaico, de los incas.
incandescence [ˌɪnkænˈdesns] N incandescencia f.
incandescent [ˌɪnkænˈdesnt] ADJ incandescente; **she was ~ (with rage)** estaba que trinaba.
incantation [ˌɪnkænˈteɪʃən] N conjuro m, ensalmo m.
incapability [ɪnˌkeɪpəˈbɪlɪtɪ] N incapacidad f.
▼ **incapable** [ɪnˈkeɪpəbl] ADJ incapaz (of de); incompetente; (*physically*) imposibilitado; **to be ~ of speech** no poder hablar; **she is ~ of shame** no tiene vergüenza; **he was drunk and ~** estaba totalmente borracho.
incapacitate [ˌɪnkəˈpæsɪteɪt] VT incapacitar, inhabilitar; descalificar; (*physically*) imposibilitar.
incapacity [ˌɪnkəˈpæsɪtɪ] N incapacidad f; insuficiencia f.

incarcerate [ɪnˈkɑːsəreɪt] VT encarcelar.
incarceration [ɪnˌkɑːsəˈreɪʃən] N encarcelamiento m, encarcelación f.
in-car entertainment [ˈɪnˌkɑːrˌentəˈteɪnmənt] N radio-cassette f de coche.
incarnate [1] [ɪnˈkɑːnɪt] ADJ: **the devil ~** el mismo diablo, el diablo en persona; **to become ~** encarnar.
[2] [ˈɪnkɑːneɪt] VT encarnar.
incarnation [ˌɪnkɑːˈneɪʃən] N encarnación f; **to be the ~ of vice** ser el mismo vicio.
incautious [ɪnˈkɔːʃəs] ADJ incauto, imprudente.
incautiously [ɪnˈkɔːʃəslɪ] ADV incautamente.
incendiary [ɪnˈsendɪərɪ] [1] ADJ incendiario; **~ bomb** bomba f incendiaria.
[2] N (a) (*person*) incendiario m, pirómano m, -a f. (b) (*bomb*) bomba f incendiaria.
incense¹ [ˈɪnsens] N incienso m.
incense² [ɪnˈsens] VT indignar, encolerizar.
incensed [ɪnˈsenst] ADJ furioso, encolerizado.
incentive [ɪnˈsentɪv] [1] N incentivo m, estímulo m; **an ~ to harder work** un incentivo para que se trabaje más.
[2] ATTR: **~ bonus** prima f de incentiva; **~ scheme** sistema m de primas de incentiva, plan m de incentivos; **~ wage** salario m incentivo.
inception [ɪnˈsepʃən] N comienzo m, principio m; **from its ~** desde los comienzos.
incertitude [ɪnˈsɜːtɪtjuːd] N incertidumbre f.
incessant [ɪnˈsesnt] ADJ incesante, constante, continuo.
incessantly [ɪnˈsesntlɪ] ADV constantemente, sin cesar.
incest [ˈɪnsest] N incesto m.
incestuous [ɪnˈsestjʊəs] ADJ incestuoso.
inch [ɪntʃ] [1] N pulgada f (= 2,54 cm); **~es** (of person: height) estatura f, (of waist) cintura f; **not an ~ from my face** a dos centímetros de mi cara; **~ by ~, by ~es** palmo a palmo; **not an ~ of territory** ni un palmo de territorio; **we searched every ~ of the room** registramos minuciosamente el cuarto; **every ~ of soil is used** se aprovecha la tierra hasta el último centímetro; **he's every ~ a man** es todo un hombre; **he's every ~ a soldier** es lo que se llama un soldado; **to be within an ~ of** estar a dos dedos de; **he didn't give an ~** no nos ofreció la menor concesión; **give him an ~ and he'll take a yard** dale un dedo y se toma hasta el codo; *ver también* IMPERIAL SYSTEM .
[2] VT: **to ~ forward** mover poco a poco hacia adelante.
[3] VI: **to ~ (one's way) forward** avanzar palmo a palmo; **prices are ~ing up** los precios suben paulatinamente.
◆ **inch out** [1] VT derrotar por la mínima.
[2] VI avanzar muy despacio.
inchoate [ˈɪnkəʊeɪt] ADJ rudimentario, incompleto, todavía no formado.
inchoative [ɪnˈkəʊətɪv] ADJ *aspect, verb* incoativo.
inch tape [ˈɪntʃteɪp] N cinta f en pulgadas para medir.
incidence [ˈɪnsɪdəns] N frecuencia f; extensión f; intensidad f; distribución f; **the ~ of measles in children** la frecuencia del sarampión en los niños; **the ~ of taxation** el peso de las contribuciones.
incident [ˈɪnsɪdənt] N incidente m, episodio m, suceso m; **~ room** centro m de coordinación; **the Agadir ~** el episodio de Agadir; **to provoke a diplomatic ~** provocar un incidente diplomático; **a life full of ~** una vida azarosa, una vida llena de acontecimientos; **to arrive without ~** llegar sin novedad.
incidental [ˌɪnsɪˈdentl] [1] ADJ incidental, (casual) fortuito; (inessential) no esencial, accesorio, de importancia secundaria; **~ expenses** (gastos mpl) imprevistos mpl, gastos mpl accesorios; **~ music** música f de fondo; **the troubles ~ to any journey** las dificultades que acarrea cualquier viaje; **but that is ~ to my purpose** pero eso queda al margen de mi propósito.
[2] N (a) (event etc) cosa f fortuita; cosa f accesoria, cosa f sin importancia.
(b) **~s** (Comm etc) imprevistos mpl.
incidentally [ˌɪnsɪˈdentəlɪ] ADV por cierto; de paso, de pasada; incidentemente; **and ~ ...** y a propósito ...; **it was interesting only ~** tenía un interés solamente incidental.
incinerate [ɪnˈsɪnəreɪt] VT incinerar, quemar.
incineration [ɪnˌsɪnəˈreɪʃən] N incineración f.
incinerator [ɪnˈsɪnəreɪtər] N incinerador m.
incipient [ɪnˈsɪpɪənt] ADJ incipiente, naciente.
incise [ɪnˈsaɪz] VT cortar; (Art) grabar, tallar; (Med) incidir, hacer una incisión en.
incision [ɪnˈsɪʒən] N incisión f, corte m.
incisive [ɪnˈsaɪsɪv] ADJ *mind* penetrante; *tone* mordaz; *words, criticism, speech* tajante, incisivo.
incisively [ɪnˈsaɪsɪvlɪ] ADV con penetración; mordazmente; de modo tajante.
incisiveness [ɪnˈsaɪsɪvnɪs] N penetración f; mordacidad f; lo tajante.

incisor [ɪn'saɪzəʳ] N incisivo m.

incite [ɪn'saɪt] VT incitar, estimular, provocar; **to ~ sb to do sth** incitar a uno a hacer algo.

incitement [ɪn'saɪtmənt] N incitación f, instigación f (*to* de).

incivility [ˌɪnsɪ'vɪlɪtɪ] N descortesía f, incivilidad f.

incl. ABBR *of* **included, including, inclusive (of).**

inclemency [ɪn'klemənsɪ] N inclemencia f; (*of weather*) intemperie f.

inclement [ɪn'klemənt] ADJ inclemente, riguroso; *weather* malo, feo.

inclination [ˌɪnklɪ'neɪʃən] N (a) (*slope*) inclinación f.
(b) (*tendency*) inclinación f, propensión f; **my ~ is to** + *infin* yo prefiero la idea de + *infin*; **what are his natural ~s?** ¿cuáles son sus propensiones naturales?; **to have an ~ to meanness** tener tendencia a ser tacaño; **I have no ~ to help him** no estoy dispuesto a ayudarle, tengo pocas ganas de ayudarle; **to follow one's ~** seguir su capricho, hacer lo que le dé la gana.

incline [1] ['ɪnklaɪn] N cuesta f, pendiente f.
[2] [ɪn'klaɪn] VT (a) (*slope*) inclinar, ladear, poner oblicuamente; **he ~d his head** inclinó la cabeza, bajó la cabeza.
(b) (*fig*) **to ~ sb to adopt a plan** inducir a uno a adoptar un plan.
(c) **to be ~d to** + *infin* (*tendency*) inclinarse a + *infin*, tener tendencia a + *infin*, ser propenso a + *infin*; (*person's volition*) estar dispuesto a + *infin*, estar por + *infin*; **it's ~d to break** tiende a romperse; **I'm ~d to believe you** estoy dispuesto a creerte; **the child is ~d to be left-handed** el niño tiene tendencias de zurdo; **he's that way ~d** él es así; **if you feel so ~d** si quieres.
[3] [ɪn'klaɪn] VI (a) (*slope, act*) inclinarse, ladearse, (*state*) estar inclinado, estar ladeado.
(b) (*fig*) **I ~ to the belief that ...** yo prefiero creer que ..., yo creo más lógica la opinión de que ...; **yellow inclining to red** amarillo que tira a rojo.

inclined [ɪn'klaɪnd] ADJ *plane* inclinado.

inclose [ɪn'kləʊz] VT = **enclose.**

include [ɪn'kluːd] VT incluir; comprender, contener, encerrar; (*with letter*) adjuntar, enviar adjunto; **your name is not ~d in the list** su nombre no figura en la lista; **does that remark ~ me?** ¿se refiere esa observación también a mí?; **he is not ~d in the team** no forma parte del equipo; **he sold the lot, books ~d** lo vendió todo, incluso los libros; **everything ~d** (*hotel etc*) todo incluido; **all the team members, myself ~d** todos los miembros del equipo, yo entre ellos.
♦**include out** VT (*hum*) excluir, dejar fuera; **~ me out** no contéis conmigo.

including [ɪn'kluːdɪŋ] *as* PREP incluso, inclusive, con inclusión de; **seven ~ this one** siete con (inclusión de) éste; **everyone came, ~ the priest** vinieron todos, incluso (*or* hasta) el cura; **terms £80, not ~ service** precio 80 libras, servicio no incluido; **up to and ~ Chapter 7** hasta el capítulo 7 inclusive; **$20 ~ post and packing** $20 incluido gastos de envío.

inclusion [ɪn'kluːʒən] N inclusión f.

inclusive [ɪn'kluːsɪv] [1] ADJ inclusivo, completo; **~ terms** todo incluido; **to be ~ of** incluir.
[2] ADV inclusive; **from the 10th to the 15th ~** del 10 al 15 ambos inclusive.

inclusively [ɪn'kluːsɪvlɪ] ADV = **inclusive 2.**

incognito [ɪn'kɒgnɪtəʊ] [1] ADV *travel etc* de incógnito.
[2] N incógnito m.

incoherence [ˌɪnkəʊ'hɪərəns] N incoherencia f; ininteligibilidad f.

incoherent [ˌɪnkəʊ'hɪərənt] ADJ incoherente, inconexo; ininteligible; *argument etc* sin pies ni cabeza; **his speech became ~** empezó a hablar de modo ininteligible; **he was ~ with rage** no podía hablar de rabia.

incoherently [ˌɪnkəʊ'hɪərəntlɪ] ADV de modo incoherente; de modo ininteligible.

incohesive [ˌɪnkəʊ'hiːsɪv] ADJ sin cohesión.

incombustible [ˌɪnkəm'bʌstəbl] ADJ incombustible.

income ['ɪnkʌm] [1] N ingresos *mpl*, renta f, entrada f; (*profit*) rédito m (*from* de); **to live up to one's ~** gastarse toda la renta; **to live beyond one's ~** gastar más de lo que se gana; **to live within one's ~** vivir con arreglo a los ingresos; **I can't live on my ~** no puedo vivir con lo que gano.
[2] ATTR: **~ and expenditure account** cuenta f de gastos e ingresos; **~ band, ~ bracket, ~ group** categoría f económica; **the lower ~ groups** los económicamente débiles; **~s policy** política f de rentas; **~ support** (*Brit*) ayuda f compensatoria.

incomer ['ɪn,kʌməʳ] N recién llegado m, recién llegada f; persona f nueva (en una sociedad *etc*); inmigrante *mf*.

income-tax ['ɪnkʌmtæks] [1] N impuesto m sobre la renta.
[2] ATTR: **~ inspector** recaudador m, -ora f de impuestos; **~ return** declaración f de ingresos.

incoming ['ɪn,kʌmɪŋ] ADJ entrante, nuevo; *tide* ascendente; **~ call** llamada f que se recibe; **~ flight** vuelo m entrante; **~ mail** correo m entrante.

incomings ['ɪn,kʌmɪŋz] NPL ingresos *mpl*.

incommensurable [ˌɪnkə'menʃərəbl] ADJ inconmensurable.

incommensurate [ˌɪnkə'menʃərɪt] ADJ desproporcionado; **to be ~ with** no guardar relación con.

incommode [ˌɪnkə'məʊd] VT incomodar, molestar.

incommodious [ˌɪnkə'məʊdɪəs] ADJ estrecho, nada espacioso; incómodo.

incommunicado [ˌɪnkəmjʊnɪ'kɑːdəʊ] ADJ incomunicado.

in-company ['ɪnkʌmpənɪ] ADJ: **~ training** formación f en la empresa.

incomparable [ɪn'kɒmpərəbl] ADJ incomparable, sin par.

incomparably [ɪn'kɒmpərəblɪ] ADV incomparablemente; **this one is ~ better** éste es mejor sin ningún género de dudas.

incompatibility ['ɪnkəm,pætə'bɪlɪtɪ] N incompatibilidad f.

incompatible [ɪn'kəm'pætəbl] ADJ incompatible (*with* con).

incompetence [ɪn'kɒmpɪtəns] N incompetencia f, inhabilidad f, incapacidad f.

incompetent [ɪn'kɒmpɪtənt] ADJ incompetente, inhábil, incapaz.

incomplete [ˌɪnkəm'pliːt] ADJ incompleto, defectuoso; (*unfinished*) sin terminar, inacabado.

incompletely [ˌɪnkəm'pliːtlɪ] ADV incompletamente.

incompleteness [ˌɪnkəm'pliːtnɪs] N lo incompleto, estado m incompleto; **because of its ~** debido a que no está terminado.

incomprehensible [ɪn,kɒmprɪ'hensəbl] ADJ incomprensible.

incomprehensibly [ɪn,kɒmprɪ'hensəblɪ] ADV de modo incomprensible.

incomprehension [ˌɪnkɒmprɪ'henʃən] N incomprensión f.

inconceivable [ˌɪnkən'siːvəbl] ADJ inconcebible.

inconceivably [ˌɪnkən'siːvəblɪ] ADJ inconcebiblemente.

inconclusive [ˌɪnkən'kluːsɪv] ADJ *reasoning etc* poco concluyente, poco convincente, cuestionable; *interview, investigation* que no da resultados definitivos.

inconclusively [ˌɪnkən'kluːsɪvlɪ] ADV de modo inconcluyente, de modo poco convincente; **it ended ~** terminó sin resultados definitivos.

incongruity [ˌɪnkɒŋ'gruːɪtɪ] N incongruencia f; desacuerdo m, falta f de lógica; lo absurdo.

incongruous [ɪn'kɒŋgrʊəs] ADJ incongruo; disonante, que no concuerda, nada lógico; *appearance etc* estrafalario, absurdo; **it seems ~ that** parece extraño que.

inconsequent [ɪn'kɒnsɪkwənt] ADJ inconsecuente.

inconsequential [ɪn,kɒnsɪ'kwenʃəl] ADJ inconsecuente; (*unimportant*) sin trascendencia.

inconsequentially [ˌɪnkɒnsɪ'kwenʃəlɪ] ADV *talk etc* sin sustancia, sin propósito serio.

inconsiderable [ˌɪnkən'sɪdərəbl] ADJ insignificante.

inconsiderate [ˌɪnkən'sɪdərɪt] ADJ desconsiderado; **it was most ~ of you** has obrado con poca formalidad.

inconsistency [ˌɪnkən'sɪstənsɪ] N inconsecuencia f; incongruencia f; anomalía f; **I see an ~ here** aquí veo una contradicción.

inconsistent [ˌɪnkən'sɪstənt] ADJ inconsecuente; incongruo; anómalo; **this is ~ with what you told me** esto no concuerda con lo que me dijiste.

inconsolable [ˌɪnkən'səʊləbl] ADJ inconsolable.

inconsolably [ˌɪnkən'səʊləblɪ] ADV inconsolablemente.

inconspicuous [ˌɪnkən'spɪkjʊəs] ADJ apenas visible, discreto, que no llama la atención; (*fig*) poco llamativo, modesto; **try to be as ~ as possible** procure no llamar la atención.

inconspicuously [ˌɪnkən'spɪkjʊəslɪ] ADV de modo apenas visible, discretamente, sin llamar la atención; de modo poco llamativo, modestamente.

inconstancy [ɪn'kɒnstənsɪ] N inconstancia f, veleidad f.

inconstant [ɪn'kɒnstənt] ADJ inconstante, mudable, veleidoso.

incontestable [ˌɪnkən'testəbl] ADJ incontestable.

incontinence [ɪn'kɒntɪnəns] N incontinencia f (*also Med*).

incontinent [ɪn'kɒntɪnənt] ADJ incontinente.

incontrovertible [ɪn,kɒntrə'vɜːtəbl] ADJ incontrovertible.

incontrovertibly [ɪn,kɒntrə'vɜːtɪblɪ] ADV de manera incontrovertible; **this is ~ true** ésta es una verdad incontrovertible.

▼**inconvenience** [ˌɪnkən'viːnɪəns] [1] N incomodidad f, molestia f, inconvenientes *mpl*; **the ~ of living at a distance** los inconvenientes de vivir lejos; **you caused a lot of ~** nos creó muchas dificultades; **to put sb to ~** molestar a uno.
[2] VT incomodar, molestar, causar inconvenientes a.

inconvenient [ˌɪnkən'viːnɪənt] ADJ *house, journey etc* incómodo, poco práctico, molesto; *time* malo, inoportuno; **it is ~ for me to have no car** me es incómodo no tener coche; **it's all very ~** es muy difícil.

inconveniently [ˌɪnkən'viːnɪəntlɪ] ADV incómodamente, de modo poco práctico; a deshora, inoportunamente, en un momento inoportuno; **to come ~ early** venir tan temprano que crea dificultades.

inconvertibility ['ɪnkən,vɜːtɪ'bɪlɪtɪ] N inconvertibilidad f.

inconvertible [ˌɪnkən'vɜːtəbl] ADJ inconvertible.

incorporate [ɪn'kɔːpəreɪt] VT incorporar (*in, into* a); incluir; comprender, contener; (*add*) agregar, añadir; **a product incorporating vitamin Q** un producto que contiene vitamina Q; **to ~ a company** constituir una compañía en sociedad (anónima).

incorporated [ɪnˈkɔːpəreɪtɪd] ADJ (*US Comm*): **Jones & Lloyd I~** Jones y Lloyd Sociedad Anónima (ABBR S.A.).

incorporation [ɪn,kɔːpəˈreɪʃən] N incorporación *f*; inclusión *f*, adición *f*; (*Comm*) constitución *f* en sociedad anónima.

incorporeal [,ɪnkɔːˈpɔːrɪəl] ADJ (*liter*) incorpóreo.

incorrect [,ɪnkəˈrekt] ADJ incorrecto, erróneo, inexacto.

incorrectly [,ɪnkəˈrektlɪ] ADV incorrectamente, erróneamente; **a letter ~ addressed** una carta con las señas mal puestas.

incorrigible [ɪnˈkɒrɪdʒəbl] ADJ incorregible; **an ~ smoker** un fumador impenitente; **you're ~!** ¡eres un perdido!

incorrigibly [ɪnˈkɒrɪdʒəblɪ] ADV de manera incorregible.

incorruptible [,ɪnkəˈrʌptəbl] ADJ incorruptible; (*not open to bribery*) insobornable.

increase ☐ [ˈɪnkriːs] N aumento *m*, incremento *m* (*in* de); crecimiento *m*; (*in price*) subida *f*, alza *f*; **an ~ in pay** un aumento de sueldo; **to be on the ~** ir en aumento.
② [ɪnˈkriːs] VT aumentar, acrecentar, incrementar.
③ [ɪnˈkriːs] VI aumentar(se), acrecentarse, tomar incremento; crecer, ir creciendo; (*price*) subir; **to ~ from 8% to 10%** pasar de 8 a 10 por cien.

increasing [ɪnˈkriːsɪŋ] ADJ creciente.

increasingly [ɪnˈkriːsɪŋlɪ] ADV cada vez más, más y más, de más en más; crecientemente; **it becomes ~ difficult** se hace más y más difícil; **our ~ difficult task** nuestra labor cada vez más difícil.

incredible [ɪnˈkredəbl] ADJ increíble.

incredibly [ɪnˈkredəblɪ] ADV increíblemente.

incredulity [,ɪnkrɪˈdjuːlɪtɪ] N incredulidad *f*.

incredulous [ɪnˈkredjʊləs] ADJ incrédulo.

incredulously [ɪnˈkredjʊləslɪ] ADV con incredulidad.

increment [ˈɪnkrɪmənt] N aumento *m*, incremento *m* (*in* de); **an ~ in salary** un aumento de sueldo.

incremental [ɪnkrɪˈmentəl] ADJ incremental; **~ compiler** compilador *m* incremental.

incriminate [ɪnˈkrɪmɪneɪt] VT acriminar, incriminar.

incriminating [ɪnˈkrɪmɪneɪtɪŋ] ADJ, **incriminatory** [ɪnˈkrɪmɪnətərɪ] ADJ acriminador, incriminatorio.

incrimination [ɪn,krɪmɪˈneɪʃən] N acriminación *f*, incriminación *f*.

incrust [ɪnˈkrʌst] VT incrustar (*with* de).

incrustation [,ɪnkrʌsˈteɪʃən] N incrustación *f*; costra *f*.

incubate [ˈɪnkjʊbeɪt] ① VT *egg* empollar, incubar; (*Med*) incubar.
② VI incubarse.

incubation [,ɪnkjʊˈbeɪʃən] N incubación *f*; **~ period** período *m* de incubación.

incubator [ˈɪnkjʊbeɪtəʳ] N incubadora *f*.

incubus [ˈɪnkjʊbəs] N íncubo *m*.

inculcate [ˈɪnkʌlkeɪt] VT inculcar (*in* en).

inculcation [ɪnkʌlˈkeɪʃən] N inculcación *f*.

incumbency [ɪnˈkʌmbənsɪ] N incumbencia *f*.

incumbent [ɪnˈkʌmbənt] ① ADJ: **to be ~ on sb** incumbir a uno (*to do* hacer).
② N titular *mf*, poseedor *m*, -ora *f* (de un cargo o dignidad); (*Eccl*) beneficiado *m*.

incunabula [,ɪnkjʊˈnæbjʊlə] NPL incunables *mpl*.

incur [ɪnˈkɜːʳ] VT incurrir en; *debt, obligation* contraer; *expenditure* hacer; *loss* sufrir; *expenses, charges* incurrir en.

incurable [ɪnˈkjʊərəbl] ① ADJ incurable; (*fig*) irremediable.
② N incurable *mf*.

incurably [ɪnˈkjʊərəblɪ] ADV (*fig*) irremediablemente; **to be ~ optimistic** tener un optimismo indestructible.

incurious [ɪnˈkjʊərɪəs] ADJ poco curioso.

incuriously [ɪnˈkjʊərɪəslɪ] ADV *look etc* sin curiosidad, sin interés.

incursion [ɪnˈkɜːʃən] N incursión *f*, invasión *f*.

Ind. (*US*) ABBR of **Indiana**.

indebted [ɪnˈdetɪd] ADJ endeudado; (*fig*): **to be ~ to sb** estar en deuda con uno; **I am ~ to you for your help** agradezco su ayuda.

indebtedness [ɪnˈdetɪdnɪs] N (a) (*Fin*) endeudamiento *m*, deuda *f*. (b) (*fig*) deuda *f* (*to* con); agradecimiento *m*.

indecency [ɪnˈdiːsnsɪ] N indecencia *f*.

indecent [ɪnˈdiːsnt] ADJ indecente; *haste* nada decoroso; **~ assault** atentado *m* contra el pudor; **~ exposure** exhibicionismo *m* (sexual).

indecently [ɪnˈdiːsntlɪ] ADV indecentemente.

indecipherable [,ɪndɪˈsaɪfərəbl] ADJ indescifrable.

indecision [,ɪndɪˈsɪʒən] N irresolución *f*, indecisión *f*.

indecisive [,ɪndɪˈsaɪsɪv] ADJ (a) *person* irresoluto, indeciso, vacilante. (b) *result etc* poco decisivo, que no resuelve nada.

indecisively [,ɪndɪˈsaɪsɪvlɪ] ADV (a) con irresolución, indecisamente, de modo vacilante. (b) **it ended ~** terminó sin resultados definitivos.

indecisiveness [,ɪndɪˈsaɪsɪvnɪs] N (a) irresolución *f*, indecisión *f*. (b) lo poco decisivo.

indeclinable [,ɪndɪˈklaɪnəbl] ADJ indeclinable.

indecorous [ɪnˈdekərəs] ADJ indecoroso.

indecorously [ɪnˈdekərəslɪ] ADV indecorosamente.

indecorum [,ɪndɪˈkɔːrəm] N indecoro *m*, falta *f* de decoro.

indeed [ɪnˈdiːd] ADV (a) (*really, in fact*) en efecto; **and ~ he did** y en efecto lo hizo; **it is ~ true that ...** es en efecto verdad que ...; **~ you may** claro que puedes; **it is ~ difficult** es verdaderamente difícil, es difícil de verdad; **it is ~ a big house** es en efecto una casa grande, es una casa realmente grande; **I may ~ be wrong** es posible en efecto que me equivoque.
(b) (*intensifies*) **~!, ~ yes!, yes ~!** ¡claro que sí!, ¡ya lo creo!; **that is praise ~** eso sí es una alabanza; **I'm very glad ~** me alegro muchísimo; **they're very bad ~** son malísimos; **onions ~!** ¡ nada de cebollas!, ¡cebollas, ni hablar!
(c) (*showing interest etc*) **~?, is it ~?, did you ~?** ¿de veras?

indefatigable [,ɪndɪˈfætɪgəbl] ADJ incansable.

indefatigably [,ɪndɪˈfætɪgəblɪ] ADV incansablemente.

indefensible [,ɪndɪˈfensəbl] ADJ indefendible; *theory etc* insostenible; **your conduct has been ~** su conducta no tiene excusa, su conducta no admite disculpa.

indefensibly [,ɪndɪˈfensəblɪ] ADV indefendiblemente.

indefinable [,ɪndɪˈfaɪnəbl] ADJ indefinible.

indefinably [,ɪndɪˈfaɪnəblɪ] ADV indefiniblemente.

indefinite [ɪnˈdefɪnɪt] ADJ (a) impreciso, indefinido; incierto, poco seguro; **he was very ~ about it all** mostró no tener ninguna idea clara sobre el asunto; **our plans are somewhat ~ as yet** todavía no tenemos plan concreto; **to be on ~ leave** estar de permiso indefinido. (b) (*Gram*) indefinido; **~ article** artículo *m* indefinido.

indefinitely [ɪnˈdefɪnɪtlɪ] ADV (a) indefinidamente; **it extends ~ into space** se prolonga indefinidamente en el espacio.
(b) **we can carry on ~** podemos continuar hasta cuándo sea (*or* por tiempo indefinido).

indelible [ɪnˈdeləbl] ADJ indeleble, imborrable (*also fig*); **~ pencil** lápiz *m* tinta.

indelibly [ɪnˈdeləblɪ] ADV indeleblemente, imborrablemente.

indelicacy [ɪnˈdelɪkəsɪ] N indecoro *m*, falta *f* de decoro; inoportunidad *f*.

indelicate [ɪnˈdelɪkɪt] ADJ indecoroso, inoportuno.

indemnification [ɪn,demnɪfɪˈkeɪʃən] N indemnización *f*.

indemnify [ɪnˈdemnɪfaɪ] VT indemnizar, resarcir (*against, for* de).

indemnity [ɪnˈdemnɪtɪ] N (*security*) indemnidad *f*; (*compensation*) indemnización *f*, reparación *f*.

indent ① [ˈɪndent] N (*Brit Comm*) pedido *m*; (*Mil etc*) requisición *f*.
② [ɪnˈdent] VT (*cut into*) endentar, mellar; (*Typ, Comput*) sangrar.
③ [ɪnˈdent] VI: **to ~ for** pedir, requisar; **to ~ on sb for sth** (*Brit*) pedir algo a uno, requisar algo a uno.

indentation [,ɪndenˈteɪʃən] N mella *f*, muesca *f*; (*Typ*) sangría *f*.

indented [ɪnˈdentɪd] ADJ *type* sangrado; *surface* abollado.

indenture [ɪnˈdentʃəʳ] N (*Comm*) escritura *f*, instrumento *m*; carta *f* partida (por ABC); (*freq* PL) contrato *m* de aprendizaje.

independence [,ɪndɪˈpendəns] ① N independencia *f*.
② ATTR: **~ day** día *m* de la independencia; **I~ Day** (*US*) Día *m* de la Independencia (*4 julio*); *ver también* FOURTH OF JULY.

independent [,ɪndɪˈpendənt] ① ADJ independiente (*of* de); **~ school** (*Brit*) escuela *f* privada; **of ~ means** acomodado; **to become ~** independizarse (*of* de).
② N (*Pol*) diputado *m* independiente, diputada *f* independiente.

┌─ **INDEPENDENT COUNSEL** ─┐

ⓘ   *Según las leyes de Estados Unidos, el **independent counsel** es un funcionario del Estado que se encarga de investigar a los altos cargos del gobierno acusados de algún delito. Se nombra a petición del Ministro de Justicia y su independencia evita el posible conflicto de intereses que se podría crear si la Administración pública investigara directamente a sus altos cargos. Este puesto se creó en 1970 de acuerdo con la Ley de Ética Gubernamental, **Ethics in Government Act**, después de la investigación que se le realizó al presidente Nixon durante el escándalo **Watergate**.*

independently [,ɪndɪˈpendəntlɪ] ADV independientemente; **~ of what he may decide** sin tomar en cuenta lo que él decida.

in-depth [ˈɪn,depθ] ADJ *study etc* a fondo, exhaustivo; **~ investigation** investigación *f* en profundidad.

indescribable [,ɪndɪsˈkraɪbəbl] ADJ indescriptible; (*pej*) indecible, incalificable.

indescribably [,ɪndɪsˈkraɪbəblɪ] ADV indescriptiblemente; (*pej*) indeciblemente, de modo incalificable; **~ bad** tan malo que resulta incalificable.

indestructibility [,ɪndɪstrʌktəˈbɪlɪtɪ] N indestructibilidad *f*.

indestructible [,ɪndɪsˈtrʌktəbl] ADJ indestructible.

indeterminable [,ɪndɪˈtɜːmɪnəbl] ADJ indeterminable.

indeterminacy [,ɪndɪˈtɜːmɪnəsɪ] N carácter *m* indeterminado.

indeterminate [,ɪndɪˈtɜːmɪnɪt] ADJ indeterminado.

indeterminately [ˌɪndɪ'tɜːmɪntlɪ] ADV de modo indeterminado.

index ['ɪndeks] **1** N, PL **indexes** or **indices** ['ɪndɪsiːz] (finger, of book, Econ) índice m; (Math) exponente m; (fig) indicación f (to de); (Eccl) I~ índice m expurgatorio.

2 ATTR: ~ **card** ficha f; ~ **finger** (dedo m) índice m; ~ **number** índice m, indicador m.

3 VT book poner índice a; book (for catalogue) indizar; entry poner en un índice; **it is ~ed under Smith** está clasificado bajo Smith, está clasificado en el artículo Smith.

indexation [ˌɪndek'seɪʃən] N, **indexing** ['ɪndeksɪŋ] N indexación f, indización f, indiciación f.

indexed ['ɪndekst] ADJ, **index-linked** [ɪndeks'lɪŋkt] ADJ indexado, indiciado.

index-linking [ˌɪndeks'lɪŋkɪŋ] N indexación f, indiciación f.

India ['ɪndɪə] **1** N la India.

2 ATTR: ~ **paper** papel m de China, papel m biblia.

Indian ['ɪndɪən] **1** ADJ indio; (American Indian) indio, indígena; ~ **club** maza f de gimnasia; ~ **elephant** elefante m asiático; ~ **file** fila f india; ~ **hemp** cáñamo m índico; ~ **ink** tinta f china; ~ **summer** veranillo m de San Martín; ~ **tea** té m indio; ~ **tonic (water)** agua f tónica.

2 N indio m, -a f; (American Indian) indio m, -a f, indígena mf.

Indian Ocean ['ɪndɪən'əʊʃən] N Océano m Índico.

indiarubber ['ɪndɪə'rʌbəʳ] N caucho m; (eraser) goma f de borrar.

indicate ['ɪndɪkeɪt] VT indicar.

▼ **indication** [ˌɪndɪ'keɪʃən] N indicación f, indicio m, señal f.

indicative [ɪn'dɪkətɪv] **1** ADJ indicativo (also Gram); **to be ~ of** indicar.

2 N indicativo m.

indicator ['ɪndɪkeɪtəʳ] N indicador m (also Econ etc); (Brit Aut) indicador m de dirección, (light) intermitente m.

indices ['ɪndɪsiːz] NPL of **index**.

indict [ɪn'daɪt] VT (a) acusar (for, on a charge of de), encausar, procesar. (b) (fig) condenar, criticar severamente, enjuiciar duramente.

indictable [ɪn'daɪtəbl] ADJ procesable, denunciable.

indictment [ɪn'daɪtmənt] N (a) (charge) acusación f, sumaria f; (act) procesamiento m. (b) (fig) condenación f, crítica f severa, enjuiciamiento m duro; **the report is an ~ of our whole system** el informe critica duramente todo nuestro sistema.

indie* ['ɪndɪ] ADJ ABBR of **independent** (Brit) music, band independiente.

Indies ['ɪndɪz] NPL las Indias; V **East** ~ etc.

indifference [ɪn'dɪfrəns] N indiferencia f (to ante); ~ **analysis** análisis m de indiferencia; ~ **curve** curva f de indiferencia; **it is a matter of supreme ~ to me** no me importa en lo más mínimo.

indifferent [ɪn'dɪfrənt] ADJ (a) indiferente; desinteresado, imparcial; **it is ~ to me** me es igual, me es indiferente. (b) (mediocre) ordinario, regular.

indifferently [ɪn'dɪfrəntlɪ] ADV (a) indiferentemente; **they go ~ to one or the other** van sin distinción al uno o al otro. (b) (pej) regularmente; **she performed ~** su actuación fue regular nada más.

indigence ['ɪndɪdʒəns] N indigencia f.

indigenous [ɪn'dɪdʒɪnəs] ADJ indígena (to de).

indigent ['ɪndɪdʒənt] ADJ indigente.

indigestible [ˌɪndɪ'dʒestəbl] ADJ indigesto; indigerible, indigestible.

indigestion [ˌɪndɪ'dʒestʃən] N indigestión f, empacho m.

indignant [ɪn'dɪgnənt] ADJ indignado; **to be ~ about sth** indignarse por algo; **to get ~ with sb** indignarse con uno; **it's no good getting ~** de nada sirve perder la paciencia; **to make sb ~** indignar a uno.

indignantly [ɪn'dɪgnəntlɪ] ADV con indignación, indignado.

indignation [ˌɪndɪg'neɪʃən] N indignación f; ~ **meeting** mitin m de protesta.

indignity [ɪn'dɪgnɪtɪ] N indignidad f; ultraje m, afrenta f; **to suffer the ~ of** + ger sufrir la indignidad de + infin.

indigo ['ɪndɪgəʊ] **1** N añil m.

2 ADJ añil (invar), color de añil.

indirect [ˌɪndɪ'rekt] ADJ indirecto; ~ **exporting** exportación f indirecta; ~ **free kick** golpe m libre indirecto; ~ **labour** (workers) mano f de obra indirecta, (work) trabajo m indirecto; ~ **speech** oración f indirecta; ~ **tax** contribución f indirecta.

indirectly [ˌɪndɪ'rektlɪ] ADV indirectamente.

indirectness [ˌɪndɪ'rektnɪs] N oblicuidad f, tortuosidad f.

indiscernible [ˌɪndɪ's3ːnəbl] ADJ imperceptible.

indiscipline [ɪn'dɪsɪplɪn] N indisciplina f.

indiscreet [ˌɪndɪs'kriːt] ADJ indiscreto, imprudente.

indiscreetly [ˌɪndɪs'kriːtlɪ] ADV indiscretamente.

indiscretion [ˌɪndɪs'kreʃən] N indiscreción f, imprudencia f.

indiscriminate [ˌɪndɪs'krɪmɪnət] ADJ indistinto, sin distinción; bombing, terrorism indiscriminado; person falto de discernimiento; admirer ciego.

indiscriminately [ˌɪndɪs'krɪmɪnɪtlɪ] ADV indistintamente, sin distinción; indiscriminadamente; admire ciegamente.

indispensable [ˌɪndɪs'pensəbl] ADJ indispensable, imprescindible.

indisposed [ˌɪndɪs'pəʊzd] ADJ: **to be ~** estar indispuesto.

indisposition [ˌɪndɪspə'zɪʃən] N indisposición f, enfermedad f.

indisputable [ˌɪndɪs'pjuːtəbl] ADJ incontestable, incuestionable, indiscutible.

indisputably [ˌɪndɪs'pjuːtəblɪ] ADV incontestablemente; **it is ~ the best** es el mejor sin ningún género de dudas; **oh, ~** claro que sí.

indissoluble [ˌɪndɪ'sɒljʊbl] ADJ indisoluble; link irrompible.

indissolubly [ˌɪndɪ'sɒljʊblɪ] ADV indisolublemente; **to be ~ linked** tener vínculos irrompibles.

indistinct [ˌɪndɪs'tɪŋkt] ADJ indistinto; confuso.

indistinctly [ˌɪndɪs'tɪŋktlɪ] ADV indistintamente; confusamente.

indistinguishable [ˌɪndɪs'tɪŋgwɪʃəbl] ADV indistinguible (from de).

indite [ɪn'daɪt] VT (liter) letter endilgar.

individual [ˌɪndɪ'vɪdjʊəl] **1** ADJ individual; personal; (for one person alone) particular, propio; ~ **bargaining** negociación f individual; **we do not sell the ~ volumes** no vendemos los tomos sueltos; **he has a very ~ style** tiene un estilo muy personal (or muy suyo).

2 N individuo m.

individualism [ˌɪndɪ'vɪdjʊəlɪzəm] N individualismo m.

individualist [ˌɪndɪ'vɪdjʊəlɪst] N individualista mf.

individualistic ['ɪndɪˌvɪdjʊə'lɪstɪk] ADJ individualista.

individuality [ˌɪndɪˌvɪdjʊ'ælɪtɪ] N individualidad f, personalidad f.

individualize [ˌɪndɪ'vɪdjʊəlaɪz] VT individuar, individualizar.

individually [ˌɪndɪ'vɪdjʊəlɪ] ADV individualmente; particularmente; **they're all right ~** cada uno de por sí es buena persona.

indivisibility [ˌɪndɪˌvɪzə'bɪlɪtɪ] N indivisibilidad f.

indivisible [ˌɪndɪ'vɪzəbl] ADJ indivisible.

indivisibly [ˌɪndɪ'vɪzəblɪ] ADV indivisiblemente; **to be ~ linked to sth** estar indisolublemente ligado a algo.

Indo... ['ɪndəʊ] PREF indo...

Indo-China ['ɪndəʊ'tʃaɪnə] N la Indochina.

indoctrinate [ɪn'dɒktrɪneɪt] VT adoctrinar (with en).

indoctrination [ɪnˌdɒktrɪ'neɪʃən] N adoctrinamiento m, adoctrinación f.

Indo-European ['ɪndəʊˌjʊərə'piːən] **1** ADJ indoeuropeo.

2 N (a) indoeuropeo m, -a f. (b) (Ling) indoeuropeo m.

indolence ['ɪndələns] N indolencia f, pereza f.

indolent ['ɪndələnt] ADJ indolente, perezoso.

indolently ['ɪndələntlɪ] ADV perezosamente.

indomitable [ɪn'dɒmɪtəbl] ADJ indómito, indomable.

indomitably [ɪn'dɒmɪtəblɪ] ADV indómitamente, indomablemente.

Indonesia [ˌɪndəʊ'niːzɪə] N Indonesia f.

Indonesian [ˌɪndəʊ'niːzɪən] **1** ADJ indonesio.

2 N indonesio m, -a f.

indoor ['ɪndɔːʳ] ADJ interior; de casa; de puertas adentro; ~ **aerial** antena f interior; ~ **athletics** atletismo m en sala, atletismo m en pista cubierta; ~ **football** fútbol m (en) sala; ~ **games** juegos mpl de salón; ~ **plant** planta f de interior; ~ **pool** piscina f cubierta.

indoors [ɪn'dɔːz] ADV en casa; dentro; bajo techado; **Her I~*** (hum) la parienta*; **to go ~** entrar (en la casa); **he had to spend a week ~** tuvo que estar una semana en casa; **I like the outside but what's it like ~?** me gusta lo de fuera, pero ¿qué tal está por dentro?

indrawn [ˌɪn'drɔːn] ADJ: **we watched with ~ breath** mirábamos casi sin respirar.

indubitable [ɪn'djuːbɪtəbl] ADJ indudable.

indubitably [ɪn'djuːbɪtəblɪ] ADV indudablemente, sin duda.

induce [ɪn'djuːs] VT inducir; producir, ocasionar; sleep etc provocar; (Elec) inducir; **to ~ sb to do sth** inducir a uno a hacer algo, persuadir a uno a hacer algo; **nothing would ~ me to go** nada me persuadiría a ir.

inducement [ɪn'djuːsmənt] N incentivo m, aliciente m, estímulo m; **to hold out sth to sb as an ~** ofrecer algo a uno como aliciente; **it offers no ~ to harder work** no ofrece estímulo para trabajar más; **as an added ~ it has ...** tiene además el atractivo de ...

induct [ɪn'dʌkt] VT (Eccl) instalar; new member etc iniciar (into en); (US Mil) quintar.

induction [ɪn'dʌkʃən] **1** N (Eccl) instalación f; (of member) iniciación f; (US Mil) quinta f; (Elec, Philos) inducción f.

2 ATTR: ~ **coil** carrete m de inducción; ~ **course** curso m (or cursillo m) introductorio.

inductive [ɪn'dʌktɪv] ADJ inductivo.

indulge [ɪn'dʌldʒ] **1** VT desire etc satisfacer, dar rienda suelta a; whim condescender con; person complacer, dar gusto a; child etc consentir, mimar.

2 VI (*: drink) beber (con exceso); **to ~ in** darse el lujo de, permitirse; (viciously) darse a, abandonarse a.

3 VR: **to ~ o.s.** darse gusto, permitirse un lujo.

indulgence [ɪn'dʌldʒəns] N (a) (of desire etc) satisfacción f, gratificación f; (vicious) abandono m (in a), desenfreno m; (tolerance) tolerancia f, complacencia f. (b) (Eccl) indulgencia f.

indulgent [ɪn'dʌldʒənt] ADJ indulgente (towards con).

► LANGUAGE IN USE: **indication → 15.2**

indulgently [ɪn'dʌldʒəntlɪ] ADV indulgentemente.

Indus ['ɪndəs] N Indo *m*.

industrial [ɪn'dʌstrɪəl] **1** ADJ industrial; laboral, de trabajo; **~ accident** accidente *m* laboral, accidente *m* de trabajo; **~ action** huelga *f*; **~ archaeology** arqueología *f* industrial; **~ belt**, **~ estate** (*Brit*), **~ park**, **~ zone** (*US*) zona *f* industrial; **~ correspondent** (*Brit*) corresponsal *mf* de información laboral; **~ court** = **~ tribunal**; **~ design** diseño *m* industrial; **~ diamond** diamante *m* natural, diamante *m* industrial; **~ dispute** (*Brit*) conflicto *m* laboral; **~ espionage** espionaje *m* industrial; **~ goods** bienes *mpl* de producción; **~ hygiene** higiene *f* industrial; **~ injury** accidente *m* laboral, accidente *m* de trabajo; **~ injury benefit** subsidio *m* por accidente laboral; **~ potential** potencial *m* industrial; **~ relations** relaciones *fpl* empresariales; **I~ Revolution** Revolución *f* Industrial; **~ safety** seguridad *f* industrial; **~ tribunal** magistratura *f* del trabajo, tribunal *m* laboral; **~ union** sindicato *m* industrial; **~ unrest** conflictividad *f* laboral; **~ waste** (*Brit*) residuos *mpl* (*or* vertidos *mpl*) industriales.
2 **~s** NPL acciones *fpl* industriales.

industrialism [ɪn'dʌstrɪəlɪzəm] N industrialismo *m*.

industrialist [ɪn'dʌstrɪəlɪst] N industrial *m*.

industrialization [ɪn,dʌstrɪəlaɪ'zeɪʃən] N industrialización *f*.

industrialize [ɪn'dʌstrɪəlaɪz] VT industrializar.

industrial-strength [ɪn'dʌstrɪəl'streŋθ] ADJ *product* muy resistente; (*: hum*) *wine* peleón.

industrious [ɪn'dʌstrɪəs] ADJ trabajador, laborioso; *student* aplicado, diligente.

industriously [ɪn'dʌstrɪəslɪ] ADV laboriosamente; con aplicación, diligentemente.

industriousness [ɪn'dʌstrɪəsnɪs] N laboriosidad *f*; aplicación *f*, diligencia *f*.

industry ['ɪndəstrɪ] N **(a)** (*Tech*) industria *f*; **the hotel ~** el comercio hotelero; **the tourist ~** el turismo.
(b) (*industriousness*) laboriosidad *f*, aplicación *f*, diligencia *f*.

inebriate **1** [ɪ'niːbrɪɪt] N borracho *m*, -a *f*.
2 [ɪ'niːbrɪeɪt] VT embriagar, emborrachar.

inebriated [ɪ'niːbrɪeɪtɪd] ADJ ebrio, borracho.

inebriation [ɪ,niːbrɪ'eɪʃən] N embriaguez *f*.

inedible [ɪn'edɪbl] ADJ incomible, no comestible.

ineducable [ɪn'edjʊkəbl] ADJ ineducable.

ineffable [ɪn'efəbl] ADJ inefable.

ineffaceable [,ɪnɪ'feɪsəbl] ADJ imborrable.

ineffective [,ɪnɪ'fektɪv] ADJ, **ineffectual** [,ɪnɪ'fektjʊəl] *remedy etc* ineficaz, inútil; *person* incapaz, inútil; **he's wholly ~** es un cero a la izquierda; **the plan proved ~** el proyecto no surtió efecto.

ineffectively [,ɪnɪ'fektɪvlɪ] ADV ineficazmente, inútilmente.

ineffectual [,ɪnɪ'fektjʊəl] ADJ ineficaz, inútil.

ineffectually [,ɪnɪ'fektjʊəlɪ] ADV ineficazmente, inútilmente.

inefficacious [,ɪnefɪ'keɪʃəs] ADJ ineficaz.

inefficacy [ɪn'efɪkəsɪ] N ineficacia *f*.

inefficiency [,ɪnɪ'fɪʃənsɪ] N ineficacia *f*; incapacidad *f*, incompetencia *f*.

inefficient [,ɪnɪ'fɪʃənt] ADJ ineficaz, ineficiente; *person* incapaz, incompetente.

inefficiently [,ɪnɪ'fɪʃəntlɪ] ADV ineficazmente; de modo incompetente.

inelastic [,ɪnɪ'læstɪk] ADJ inelástico; (*fig*) rígido, poco flexible; **~ demand** demanda *f* inelástica; **~ supply** suministro *m* inelástico.

inelegant [ɪn'elɪgənt] ADJ inelegante, poco elegante.

inelegantly [ɪn'elɪgəntlɪ] ADV inelegantemente.

ineligible [ɪn'elɪdʒəbl] ADJ inelegible; **to be ~ to vote** no tener derecho a votar.

ineluctable [,ɪnɪ'lʌktəbl] ADJ ineludible.

inept [ɪ'nept] ADJ inepto; *person* incompetente, incapaz.

ineptitude [ɪ'neptɪtjuːd] N, **ineptness** [ɪ'neptnɪs] N inepcia *f*, ineptitud *f*; incompetencia *f*, incapacidad *f*.

inequality [,ɪnɪ'kwɒlɪtɪ] N desigualdad *f*.

inequitable [ɪn'ekwɪtəbl] ADJ injusto.

inequity [ɪn'ekwɪtɪ] N injusticia *f*.

ineradicable [,ɪnɪ'rædɪkəbl] ADJ inextirpable.

inert [ɪ'nɜːt] ADJ inerte, inactivo; (*motionless*) inmóvil; **he lay ~ on the floor** estuvo tumbado sin moverse en el suelo.

inertia [ɪ'nɜːʃə] N inercia *f* (*also Phys*), inacción *f*; pereza *f*; **~ selling** venta *f* por inercia.

inertia-reel [ɪ'nɜːʃə,riːl] ATTR: **~ seat-belt** cinturón *m* de seguridad retráctil.

inescapable [,ɪnɪs'keɪpəbl] ADJ ineludible.

inessential ['ɪnɪ'senʃəl] **1** ADJ no esencial.
2 N cosa *f* no esencial.

inestimable [ɪn'estɪməbl] ADJ inapreciable, inestimable.

inevitability [ɪn,evɪtə'bɪlɪtɪ] N inevitabilidad *f*.

inevitable [ɪn'evɪtəbl] ADJ inevitable, ineludible; forzoso; **it was ~ it should happen** tuvo forzosamente (*or* fatalmente) que ocurrir.

inevitably [ɪn'evɪtəblɪ] ADV inevitablemente, forzosamente.

inexact [,ɪnɪg'zækt] ADJ inexacto.

inexactitude [,ɪnɪg'zæktɪtjuːd] N inexactitud *f*.

inexactly [,ɪnɪg'zæktlɪ] ADV de modo inexacto.

inexcusable [,ɪnɪks'kjuːzəbl] ADJ imperdonable.

inexcusably [,ɪnɪks'kjuːzəblɪ] ADV imperdonablemente.

inexhaustible [,ɪnɪg'zɔːstəbl] ADJ inagotable.

inexorable [ɪn'eksərəbl] ADJ inexorable, implacable.

inexorably [ɪn'eksərəblɪ] ADV inexorablemente, implacablemente.

inexpedient [,ɪnɪks'piːdɪənt] ADJ inoportuno, inconveniente, imprudente.

inexpensive [,ɪnɪks'pensɪv] ADJ económico, barato.

inexpensively [,ɪnɪks'pensɪvlɪ] ADV económicamente.

inexperience [,ɪnɪks'pɪərɪəns] N inexperiencia *f*, falta *f* de experiencia.

inexperienced [,ɪnɪks'pɪərɪənst] ADJ inexperto, falto de experiencia.

inexpert [ɪn'ekspɜːt] ADJ imperito, inexperto, inhábil.

inexpertly [ɪn'ekspɜːtlɪ] ADV sin habilidad, desmañadamente.

inexplicable [,ɪnɪks'plɪkəbl] ADJ inexplicable.

inexplicably [,ɪnɪks'plɪkəblɪ] ADV inexplicablemente, misteriosamente.

inexpressible [,ɪnɪks'presəbl] ADJ inefable.

inexpressive [,ɪnɪks'presɪv] ADJ *style etc* inexpresivo; *person* reservado, callado.

inextinguishable [,ɪnɪks'tɪŋgwɪʃəbl] ADJ inextinguible, inapagable.

in extremis [ɪnɪks'triːmɪs] ADV (*frm*) in extremis.

inextricable [,ɪnɪks'trɪkəbl] ADJ inextricable, inseparable, imposible de desenredar (*etc*).

inextricably [,ɪnɪks'trɪkəblɪ] ADV: **~ entwined** entrelazados de modo inextricable.

infallibility [ɪn,fælə'bɪlɪtɪ] N infalibilidad *f*.

infallible [ɪn'fæləbl] ADJ infalible; indefectible.

infallibly [ɪn'fæləblɪ] ADV infaliblemente; indefectiblemente.

infamous ['ɪnfəməs] ADJ infame.

infamy ['ɪnfəmɪ] N infamia *f*.

infancy ['ɪnfənsɪ] N infancia *f*; (*Jur*) menor edad *f*; **from ~** desde niño; **it is still in its ~** está todavía en mantillas.

infant ['ɪnfənt] **1** ADJ *mortality etc* infantil; *class, school* de párvulos; *industry etc* naciente; **~ mortality** mortandad *f* infantil, mortalidad *f* infantil; **~ school** centro *m* de educación primaria (*primer ciclo*); **~ welfare clinic** clínica *f* pediátrica; *ver también* EDUCATION.
2 N criatura *f*, niño *m*, -a *f*; (*Jur*) menor *mf*; **the ~ Jesus** el niño Jesús.

infanta [ɪn'fæntə] N infanta *f*.

infante [ɪn'fæntɪ] N infante *m*.

infanticide [ɪn'fæntɪsaɪd] N **(a)** (*act*) infanticidio *m*. **(b)** (*person*) infanticida *mf*.

infantile ['ɪnfəntaɪl] ADJ infantil (*also Med*); **~ paralysis** parálisis *f* infantil; **don't be so ~!** ¡no seas niño!

infantilism [ɪn'fæntɪ,lɪzəm] N infantilismo *m*.

infantilize [ɪn'fæntɪlaɪz] VT infantilizar.

infantry ['ɪnfəntrɪ] N infantería *f*.

infantryman ['ɪnfəntrɪmən] N, PL **infantrymen** ['ɪnfəntrɪmən] soldado *m* de infantería; (*Hist*) infante *m*, peón *m*.

infatuated [ɪn'fætjʊeɪtɪd] ADJ: **to be ~ with** *idea etc* encapricharse por; *person* estar chiflado por.

infatuation [ɪn,fætjʊ'eɪʃən] N encaprichamiento *m*; chifladura *f*.

infect [ɪn'fekt] VT *air, well, wound etc* infectar, inficionar; *person* contagiar (*with* con); (*fig*) contagiar, comunicar; (*pej*) corromper, inficionar; **to be ~ed with** (*act*) contagiarse de, (*state*) estar contagiado de; **he ~s everybody with his enthusiasm** contagia a todos con su entusiasmo.

infected [ɪn'fektɪd] ADJ infectado.

infection [ɪn'fekʃən] N (*Med*) infección *f*, contagio *m*; (*fig*) contagio *m*; **she has a slight ~** está ligeramente indispuesta.

infectious [ɪn'fekʃəs] ADJ contagioso (*also fig*), infeccioso.

infectiousness [ɪn'fekʃəsnɪs] N contagiosidad *f*.

infective [ɪn'fektɪv] ADJ *disease, agent* infeccioso.

infelicitous [,ɪnfɪ'lɪsɪtəs] ADJ poco feliz, inoportuno, impropio.

infelicity [,ɪnfɪ'lɪsɪtɪ] N inoportunidad *f*, impropiedad *f*.

infer [ɪn'fɜːʳ] VT deducir, colegir, inferir (*from* de).

inference ['ɪnfərəns] N deducción *f*, inferencia *f*, conclusión *f*.

inferential [,ɪnfə'renʃəl] ADJ ilativo, deductivo.

inferentially [,ɪnfə'renʃəlɪ] ADV por inferencia, por deducción.

inferior [ɪn'fɪərɪəʳ] **1** ADJ inferior (*to* a).
2 N inferior *mf*.

inferiority [ɪn,fɪərɪ'ɒrɪtɪ] **1** N inferioridad *f*.
2 ATTR: **~ complex** complejo *m* de inferioridad.

infernal [ɪn'fɜːnl] ADJ infernal; (*fig*) maldito, infernal.

infernally [ɪn'fɜːnəlɪ] ADV: **it's ~ awkward** es terriblemente difícil.

inferno [ɪn'fɜːnəʊ] N infierno *m*; **it's like an ~ in there** allí dentro hace un calor insufrible; **in a few minutes the house was a blazing ~** en pocos minutos la casa estaba hecha una hoguera.

infertile [ɪn'fɜːtaɪl] ADJ estéril, infecundo.

infertility [ˌɪnfɜːˈtɪlɪtɪ] ADJ esterilidad *f*, infecundidad *f*.
infest [ɪnˈfest] VT infestar; **to be ~ed with** estar plagado de.
infestation [ˌɪnfesˈteɪʃən] N infestación *f*, plaga *f*.
infidel [ˈɪnfɪdəl] **1** ADJ infiel, pagano, descreído.
  2 N infiel *mf*, pagano *m*, -a *f*, descreído *m*, -a *f*; **the I~** los descreídos, la gente descreída.
infidelity [ˌɪnfɪˈdelɪtɪ] N infidelidad *f* (**to** para con); **marital ~** infidelidad *f* conyugal.
in-fighting [ˈɪnfaɪtɪŋ] N lucha *f* cuerpo a cuerpo, (*fig*) riñas *fpl*, disputas *fpl*; dimes *mpl* y diretes; **political ~** riñas *fpl* políticas.
infill [ˈɪnfɪl] N (*Constr, Geol*) relleno *m*.
infiltrate [ˈɪnfɪltreɪt] **1** VT infiltrarse en.
  2 VI infiltrarse.
infiltration [ˌɪnfɪlˈtreɪʃən] N infiltración *f*.
infiltrator [ˈɪnfɪltreɪtəʳ] N agente *mf*; persona *f* que se infiltra en una organización (*or* a través de una frontera *etc*).
infinite [ˈɪnfɪnɪt] **1** ADJ infinito, (*fig*) infinito, inmenso, enorme; **we had ~ trouble finding it** nos costó la mar de trabajo encontrarlo; **he took ~ pains over it** lo hizo con el mayor esmero.
  2 N: **the ~** el infinito.
infinitely [ˈɪnfɪnɪtlɪ] ADV infinitamente; **this is ~ harder** esto es muchísimo más difícil, esto es mil veces más difícil.
infiniteness [ˈɪnfɪnɪtnɪs] N infinidad *f*.
infinitesimal [ˌɪnfɪnɪˈtesɪməl] ADJ infinitesimal.
infinitive [ɪnˈfɪnɪtɪv] **1** ADJ infinitivo.
  2 N infinitivo *m*.
infinitude [ɪnˈfɪnɪtjuːd] N infinitud *f*.
infinity [ɪnˈfɪnɪtɪ] N (*Math*) infinito *m*; (*fig*) infinidad *f*; **an ~ of** infinidad de, un sinfín de.
infirm [ɪnˈfɜːm] ADJ enfermizo, achacoso, débil; **~ of purpose** irresoluto; **the old and ~** los ancianos y enfermos.
infirmary [ɪnˈfɜːmərɪ] N hospital *m*; (*at bullring etc*) enfermería *f*.
infirmity [ɪnˈfɜːmɪtɪ] N (*state*) debilidad *f*; (*illness*) enfermedad *f*, achaque *m*, dolencia *f*; (*moral*) flaqueza *f*.
infix [ˈɪnfɪks] N infijo *m*.
in flagrante delicto [ɪnfləˈɡræntɪdɪˈlɪktəʊ] ADV en flagrante.
inflame [ɪnˈfleɪm] VT inflamar (*also Med*); **to be ~d with** arder de, inflamarse de.
inflammable [ɪnˈflæməbl] ADJ inflamable; (*situation etc*) explosivo, de gran tirantez.
inflammation [ˌɪnfləˈmeɪʃən] N inflamación *f*.
inflammatory [ɪnˈflæmətərɪ] ADJ inflamatorio; *propaganda, speech* incendiario.
inflatable [ɪnˈfleɪtəbl] ADJ inflable, hinchable.
inflate [ɪnˈfleɪt] VT hinchar, inflar (**with** de); (*fig*) hinchar (**with** de); *report etc* exagerar; *price* inflar, aumentar de modo excesivo; *currency* provocar la inflación de.
inflated [ɪnˈfleɪtɪd] ADJ *report* exagerado; *price* excesivo.
inflation [ɪnˈfleɪʃən] N inflación *f* (*also Fin*); **~ accounting** contabilidad *f* de inflación.
inflationary [ɪnˈfleɪʃnərɪ] ADJ inflacionista, inflacionario; **~ gap** desequilibrio *m* inflacionario.
inflationism [ɪnˈfleɪʃənɪzəm] N inflacionismo *m*.
inflationist [ɪnˈfleɪʃənɪst] **1** ADJ inflacionista, inflacionario.
  2 N partidario *m*, -a *f* de la inflación.
inflation-proof [ɪnˈfleɪʃənˌpruːf] ADJ resistente a la inflación.
inflect [ɪnˈflekt] VT (a) torcer, doblar; *voice* modular. (b) (*Gram*) *noun etc* declinar; *verb* conjugar.
inflected [ɪnˈflektɪd] ADJ *language* flexional.
inflection [ɪnˈflekʃən] N inflexión *f*.
inflectional [ɪnˈflekʃnl] ADJ con inflexión.
inflexibility [ɪnˌfleksɪˈbɪlɪtɪ] N inflexibilidad *f*; (*fig*) rigidez *f*.
inflexible [ɪnˈfleksəbl] ADJ inflexible.
inflexion [ɪnˈflekʃən] N inflexión *f*.
inflict [ɪnˈflɪkt] **1** VT *wound etc* infligir, inferir (**on** a); *penalty, tax etc* imponer (**on** a); *grief, damage etc* causar (**on** a).
  2 VR: **to ~ o.s. on sb** molestar a uno acompañándole (*or* visitándole *etc*).
infliction [ɪnˈflɪkʃən] N (*act*) imposición *f*; (*penalty etc*) pena *f*, castigo *m*.
in-flight [ˈɪnflaɪt] ATTR: **~ meal** comida *f* servida durante el vuelo; **~ movie** película *f* proyectada durante el vuelo; **~ services** servicios *mpl* de a bordo.
inflow [ˈɪnfləʊ] **1** N afluencia *f*.
  2 ATTR: **~ pipe** tubo *m* de entrada.
influence [ˈɪnfluəns] **1** N influencia *f*, influjo *m* (**on** sobre); ascendiente *m* (**over** sobre); valimiento *m* (**with** cerca de); **a man of ~** un hombre influyente; **to be under the ~ (of drink)** estar borracho; **to be under the ~ of drugs** estar bajo los efectos de las drogas; **to drive under the ~** conducir en estado de embriaguez; **to bring every ~ to bear on sb** ejercer todas las presiones posibles sobre uno; **to have ~ (person)** tener el padre alcalde, tener buenas aldabas;

you've got to have ~ to get a job para conseguir un puesto hay que tener un buen enchufe; **to have ~ over sb** tener ascendiente sobre uno.
  2 VT *person etc* influir en, influenciar; sugestionar; *decision etc* influir en, afectar; **the novelist has been ~d by Torrente** el novelista ha sufrido la influencia de Torrente, el novelista está influido por Torrente; **what factors ~d your decision?** ¿qué factores influyeron en tu decisión?; **don't let him ~ you** no te dejes convencer por él; **to be easily ~d** ser sugestionable.
influential [ˌɪnfluˈenʃəl] ADJ influyente, prestigioso.
influenza [ˌɪnfluˈenzə] N gripe *f*.
influx [ˈɪnflʌks] N afluencia *f*; (*Mech etc*) aflujo *m*, entrada *f*.
info* [ˈɪnfəʊ] N = **information**.
infobahn [ˈɪnfəʊbɑːn] N: **the ~** = **information superhighway**.
infomercial [ˈɪnfəʊmɜːʃl] N publirreportaje *m*.
▼ **inform** [ɪnˈfɔːm] **1** VT informar (**about** sobre, **of** de); avisar; comunicar, participar; **I am happy to ~ you that ...** tengo el gusto de comunicarle que ...; **well ~ed** enterado, instruido; **to be ~ed about sth** estar enterado de algo, estar al corriente de algo; **why was I not ~ed?** ¿por qué no me avisaron?; **I should like to be ~ed as soon as he comes** que me avisen en cuanto llegue; **to keep sb ~ed about sth** tener a uno al corriente de algo.
  2 VI soplar; **to ~ against** (*or* **on**) **sb** delatar a uno, denunciar a uno.
  3 VR: **to ~ o.s. about sth** informarse sobre algo.
informal [ɪnˈfɔːml] ADJ *person* desenvuelto, afable, poco ceremonioso; *occasion* informal, sin ceremonia, sin protocolo; *dance* sin etiqueta; *visit, gathering* de confianza, íntimo; *tone, manner* familiar; llano, sencillo; (*unofficial*) extraoficial, oficioso.
informality [ˌɪnfɔːˈmælɪtɪ] N afabilidad *f*; informalidad *f*; falta *f* de ceremonia; intimidad *f*; familiaridad *f*; llaneza *f*, sencillez *f*; **we liked the ~ of the occasion** nos gustó la función por su ausencia de ceremonia.
informally [ɪnˈfɔːməlɪ] ADV: **it was organized very ~** se organizó sin ceremonia; **the president spoke ~ to the journalists** el presidente habló en tono de confianza con los periodistas; **I have been told ~ that ...** me han dicho de modo extraoficial que ..., me han dicho oficiosamente que ...
informant [ɪnˈfɔːmənt] N informante *mf*; **my ~** el que me lo dijo; **who was your ~?** ¿quién te lo dijo?.
informatics [ˌɪnfɔːˈmætɪks] N informática *f*.
▼ **information** [ˌɪnfəˈmeɪʃən] **1** N (a) (*gen*) información *f*, informes *mpl*, datos *mpl*; (*news*) noticias *fpl*; **a piece of ~** una información, un dato, una noticia; **'~'** 'informaciones'; **to ask for ~** pedir informes; **to gather ~ about sth** tomar informes sobre algo, informarse sobre algo, reunir datos acerca de algo; **we have no ~ on that point** no tenemos información sobre ese particular.
  (b) (*knowledge*) conocimientos *mpl*; **he writes well but is short of ~** escribe bien pero tiene escasos conocimientos; **for your ~** para su gobierno; para sacarle de duda.
  (c) (*Jur*) denuncia *f*, delatación *f*; **to lay ~ about a crime** denunciar un crimen; **to lay ~ against sb** delatar a uno.
  2 ATTR: **~ bureau, ~ office** centro *m* (*or* oficina *f*) de informaciones; **~ line** línea *f* de información; **~ network** red *f* informativa; **~ processing** proceso *m* de información; **~ retrieval** recuperación *f* de informaciones (*or* de la información); **~ room** centro *m* de información; **~ service** servicio *m* de información; **the ~ superhighway** la autopista de la información; **~ technology** informática *f*; **~ theory** teoría *f* de la información.
informational [ˌɪnfəˈmeɪʃənl] ADJ *needs, requirements* de información; *video* informativo, didáctico.
informative [ɪnˈfɔːmətɪv] ADJ informativo.
informativity [ɪnˌfɔːməˈtɪvɪtɪ] N informatividad *f*.
informed [ɪnˈfɔːmd] ADJ informado.
informer [ɪnˈfɔːməʳ] N (*Jur*) denunciante *mf*, delator *m*, -ora *f*; (*police* ~) informador *m*, -ora *f*, soplón *m*, -ona* *f*, oreja* *mf* (*LAm*).
infra... [ˈɪnfrə] PREF infra...
infraction [ɪnˈfrækʃən] N infracción *f*, violación *f*.
infra dig* [ˈɪnfrəˈdɪɡ] ADJ deshonroso, indecoroso; **he thinks it ~ to explain** considera el explicarse un menoscabo de su dignidad.
infra-red [ˈɪnfrəˈred] ADJ infrarrojo.
infrasonic [ˈɪnfrəˌsɒnɪk] ADJ infrasónico.
infrasound [ˈɪnfrəˌsaʊnd] N infrasonido *m*.
infrastructure [ˈɪnfrəˌstrʌktʃəʳ] N infraestructura *f*.
infrequency [ɪnˈfriːkwənsɪ] N infrecuencia *f*, rareza *f*.
infrequent [ɪnˈfriːkwənt] ADJ poco frecuente, infrecuente, raro.
infrequently [ɪnˈfriːkwəntlɪ] ADV rara vez, pocas veces.
infringe [ɪnˈfrɪndʒ] **1** VT infringir, vulnerar, violar.
  2 VI: **to ~ on** invadir, usurpar.
infringement [ɪnˈfrɪndʒmənt] N infracción *f*, vulneración *f*, violación *f*; (*of rights etc*) invasión *f*, abuso *m*; (*Sport*) falta *f*.
infuriate [ɪnˈfjʊərɪeɪt] VT enfurecer, poner rabioso; **to be ~d** estar furioso; **this kind of thing ~s me** estas cosas me hacen rabiar; **at**

➤ LANGUAGE IN USE: **inform: 1** → 21.1   **information: 1a** → 20.2, 21.1, 21.2

times you ~ **me** hay veces que me sacas de quicio.

infuriating [ɪnˈfjʊərɪeɪtɪŋ] ADJ enloquecedor; **it's simply** ~ es para volverse loco.

infuriatingly [ɪnˈfjʊərɪeɪtɪŋlɪ] ADV enloquecedoramente.

infuse [ɪnˈfjuːz] VT **(a)** infundir (*into* a); **to ~ courage into sb** infundir ánimo a uno; **they were ~d with a new hope** se les infundió una nueva esperanza. **(b)** *tea etc* preparar, hacer una infusión de.

infusion [ɪnˈfjuːʒən] N infusión *f*; ~ **of tea** infusión *f* de té.

ingenious [ɪnˈdʒiːnɪəs] ADJ ingenioso, inventivo, hábil; *machine etc* ingenioso; *scheme etc* genial.

ingeniously [ɪnˈdʒiːnɪəslɪ] ADV ingeniosamente, hábilmente; con genialidad.

ingénue [ˌɛnʒeɪˈnjuː] N ingenua *f*, muchacha *f* candorosa.

ingenuity [ˌɪndʒɪˈnjuːɪtɪ] N ingeniosidad *f*, inventiva *f*, habilidad *f*; genialidad *f*.

ingenuous [ɪnˈdʒenjʊəs] ADJ ingenuo, candoroso.

ingenuously [ɪnˈdʒenjʊəslɪ] ADV ingenuamente, cándidamente.

ingenuousness [ɪnˈdʒenjʊəsnɪs] N ingenuidad *f*, candidez *f*.

ingest [ɪnˈdʒest] VT ingerir.

ingestion [ɪnˈdʒestʃən] N ingestión *f*.

inglenook [ˈɪŋɡlnʊk] N rincón *m* de la chimenea.

inglorious [ɪnˈɡlɔːrɪəs] ADJ ignominioso, vergonzoso.

in-going [ˈɪnɡəʊɪŋ] ADJ entrante.

ingot [ˈɪŋɡət] N lingote *m*, barra *f*; ~ **steel** acero *m* en lingotes.

ingrained [ˈɪnˈɡreɪnd] ADJ (profundamente) arraigado.

ingrate [ˈɪŋɡreɪt] N ingrato *m*, -a *f*.

ingratiate [ɪnˈɡreɪʃɪeɪt] VR: **to ~ o.s. with sb** congraciarse con uno, hacerse simpático a uno, insinuarse en el favor de uno.

ingratiating [ɪnˈɡreɪʃɪeɪtɪŋ] ADJ *smile etc* insinuante, lleno de insinuación; *person* congraciador, zalamero.

ingratitude [ɪnˈɡrætɪtjuːd] N ingratitud *f*, desagradecimiento *m*.

ingredient [ɪnˈɡriːdɪənt] N ingrediente *m*, componente *m*.

ingress [ˈɪnɡres] N ingreso *m*, entrada *f*.

in-group [ˈɪnˌɡruːp] N grupo *m* exclusivista (*or* excluyente).

ingrowing [ˈɪnˌɡrəʊɪŋ] ADJ: ~ **(toe)nail** uñero *m*, uña *f* encarnada.

inguinal [ˈɪŋɡwɪnl] ADJ inguinal.

inhabit [ɪnˈhæbɪt] VT habitar; vivir en; ocupar.

inhabitable [ɪnˈhæbɪtəbl] ADJ habitable.

inhabitant [ɪnˈhæbɪtənt] N habitante *m*.

inhabited [ɪnˈhæbɪtɪd] ADJ habitado, poblado.

inhalant [ɪnˈheɪlənt] N inhalante *m*.

inhalation [ˌɪnhəˈleɪʃən] N aspiración *f*; (*Med*) inhalación *f*.

inhalator [ˈɪnhəleɪtə^r] N inhalador *m*.

inhale [ɪnˈheɪl] **1** VT aspirar; (*Med*) inhalar.
  2 VI (*smoker*) aspirar el humo.

inhaler [ɪnˈheɪlə^r] N inhalador *m*.

inharmonious [ˌɪnhɑːˈməʊnɪəs] ADJ inarmónico, disonante; (*fig*) discorde, poco armonioso.

inhere [ɪnˈhɪə^r] VI ser inherente (*in* a).

inherent [ɪnˈhɪərənt] ADJ inherente, innato, inmanente, intrínseco; ~ **vice** vicio *m* inherente; ~ **in** inherente a; **with all the ~ difficulties** con todas las dificultades inevitables.

inherently [ɪnˈhɪərəntlɪ] ADV intrínsecamente.

inherit [ɪnˈherɪt] VT heredar.

inheritance [ɪnˈherɪtəns] N herencia *f*; (*fig*) patrimonio *m*, legado *m*; ~ **law** ley *f* de herencia; ~ **tax** impuesto *m* de sucesión; **our national** ~ nuestro patrimonio nacional; **it's an ~ from the last government** es un legado del gobierno anterior.

inheritor [ɪnˈherɪtə^r] N heredero *m*, -a *f*.

inhibit [ɪnˈhɪbɪt] VT inhibir, impedir, imposibilitar; **to ~ sb from doing sth** impedir a uno hacer algo; **don't let my presence ~ the discussion** no quiero que mi presencia impida la discusión; **we cannot ~ change** no podemos detener los cambios.

inhibited [ɪnˈhɪbɪtɪd] ADJ cohibido; **to feel rather ~** sentirse algo cohibido.

inhibition [ˌɪnhɪˈbɪʃən] N inhibición *f*.

inhibitory [ɪnˈhɪbɪtərɪ] ADJ inhibitorio.

inhospitable [ˌɪnhɒsˈpɪtəbl] ADJ inhospitalario; *place, country* inhóspito; *attitude, remark* poco amistoso.

inhospitably [ˌɪnhɒsˈpɪtəblɪ] ADV de modo inhospitalario.

inhospitality [ˈɪnˌhɒspɪˈtælɪtɪ] N inhospitalidad *f*.

in-house [ˈɪnˈhaʊs] **1** ADV dentro de la empresa.
  2 ADJ interno, en casa; ~ **training** formación *f* en la empresa.

inhuman [ɪnˈhjuːmən] ADJ inhumano.

inhumane [ˌɪnhjuː(ː)ˈmeɪn] ADJ inhumano.

inhumanity [ˌɪnhjuːˈmænɪtɪ] N inhumanidad *f*.

inhumation [ˌɪnhjuːˈmeɪʃən] N inhumación *f*.

inimical [ɪˈnɪmɪkəl] ADJ: ~ **to** opuesto a, contrario a, perjudicial para.

inimitable [ɪˈnɪmɪtəbl] ADJ inimitable.

inimitably [ɪˈnɪmɪtəblɪ] ADV inimitablemente.

iniquitous [ɪˈnɪkwɪtəs] ADJ inicuo; enorme; monstruoso; diabólico.

iniquitously [ɪˈnɪkwɪtəslɪ] ADV inicuamente; enormemente; mons-

truosamente; diabólicamente.

iniquity [ɪˈnɪkwɪtɪ] N iniquidad *f*; perversidad *f*; injusticia *f*; enormidad *f*; **iniquities** (*of system*) injusticias *fpl*, (*of person*) excesos *mpl*, desmanes *mpl*.

initial [ɪˈnɪʃəl] **1** ADJ inicial; primero; ~ **expenses** gastos *mpl* iniciales; **in the ~ stages** al principio, en las primeras etapas; **my ~ reaction was to ...** mi primera reacción era de ...
  2 N inicial *f*, letra *f* inicial (*also* ~ **letter**); ~**s** (*of person etc*) iniciales *fpl*, (*used as abbreviation*) sigla *f*.
  3 VT marcar (*or* firmar *etc*) con sus iniciales.

initialize [ɪˈnɪʃəlaɪz] VT inicializar.

initially [ɪˈnɪʃəlɪ] ADV al principio, en un principio.

initiate **1** [ɪˈnɪʃɪt] N iniciado *m*, -a *f*.
  2 [ɪˈnɪʃɪeɪt] VT **(a)** (*begin*) iniciar, empezar, dar comienzo a, dar origen a; *reform etc* promover; *fashion* introducir; (*Jur*) *proceedings* entablar.
  (b) **to ~ sb into a secret** iniciar a uno en un secreto; **to ~ sb into a society** admitir a uno a una sociedad.

initiation [ɪˌnɪʃɪˈeɪʃən] N iniciación *f*; principio *m*, comienzo *m*; admisión *f*; ~ **rite** ceremonia *f* de iniciación.

initiative [ɪˈnɪʃətɪv] N iniciativa *f*; **on one's own ~** por iniciativa propia, motu proprio; **to take the ~** tomar la iniciativa; **to use one's own ~** obrar por cuenta propia.

initiator [ɪˈnɪʃɪeɪtə^r] N iniciador *m*, -ora *f*.

inject [ɪnˈdʒekt] VT (*Med etc*) inyectar (*into* en); (*fig*) injertar, introducir (*into* en), infundir (*into* a); **to ~ sb with sth** inyectar algo en uno; **to ~ new life into a club** infundir un espíritu nuevo a un club.

injection [ɪnˈdʒekʃən] N inyección *f*.

injudicious [ˌɪndʒʊˈdɪʃəs] ADJ imprudente, indiscreto.

injudiciously [ˌɪndʒʊˈdɪʃəslɪ] ADV imprudentemente, indiscretamente.

injunction [ɪnˈdʒʌŋkʃən] N mandato *m*; (*Jur*) entredicho *m*; interdicto *m*.

injure [ˈɪndʒə^r] **1** VT **(a)** (*physically*) herir, hacer daño a, lastimar, lesionar, (*permanently*) lisiar; **he ~d his arm** se lesionó el brazo.
  (b) *chances, reputation, trade etc* perjudicar; (*offend*) ofender, agraviar; *feelings* herir.
  2 VR: **to ~ o.s.** hacerse daño, lesionarse.

injured [ˈɪndʒəd] **1** ADJ *person* herido; lesionado; **with an ~ arm** con un brazo lesionado; **an ~ player** un jugador lesionado; **there were 4 ~** hubo 4 heridos; **in an ~ tone** en tono ofendido; **the ~ party** la persona ofendida, la persona perjudicada.
  2 NPL: **the ~** los heridos.

injurious [ɪnˈdʒʊərɪəs] ADJ (*harmful*) nocivo, dañoso, perjudicial (*to* para); (*insulting*) injurioso, ofensivo; ~ **to health** perjudicial para la salud.

injury [ˈɪndʒərɪ] N **(a)** (*physical*) herida *f*, lesión *f*; ~ **benefit** subsidio *m* por daño; ~ **time** tiempo *m* de descuento; **3 players have injuries** 3 jugadores están lesionados; **to do sb an ~** herir a uno; **to do o.s. an ~** hacerse daño, lesionarse.
  (b) (*fig*) perjuicio *m*, daño *m*; **our reputation has suffered ~** nuestra reputación ha sido perjudicada.

injustice [ɪnˈdʒʌstɪs] N injusticia *f*; **you do me an ~** me juzgas mal, eres injusto conmigo.

ink [ɪŋk] **1** N tinta *f*; **in ~** con tinta.
  2 VT **(a)** (*Typ*) entintar. **(b)** (*US**) firmar.
 ◆ **ink in** VT entintar.
 ◆ **ink out** VT tachar con tinta.
 ◆ **ink over** VT volver a escribir con tinta.

ink blot [ˈɪŋkblɒt] N borrón *m* de tinta.

ink-jet printer [ˈɪŋkdʒetˈprɪntə^r] N impresora *f* de chorro de tinta.

inkling [ˈɪŋklɪŋ] N (*hint*) indicio *m*; (*suspicion*) sospecha *f*; (*vague idea*) atisbo *m*; idea *f* vaga; **I had no ~ that ...** no se me ocurrió que ..., no tuve la menor idea de que ...; **we had some ~ of it** nos habíamos formado alguna idea de ello; **there was no ~ of the disaster to come** no había indicio alguno del desastre que había de sobrevenir.

inkpad [ˈɪŋkpæd] N almohadilla *f*, tampón *m* (de entintar).

inkpot [ˈɪŋkpɒt] N tintero *m*.

inkstain [ˈɪŋksteɪn] N mancha *f* de tinta.

inkstand [ˈɪŋkstænd] N escribanía *f*.

inkwell [ˈɪŋkwel] N tintero *m*.

inky [ˈɪŋkɪ] ADJ (*stained*) manchado de tinta; (*black*) negro como la tinta.

INLA [ˈɪnlə] N (*Brit*) ABBR of **Irish National Liberation Army**.

inlaid [ˈɪnˈleɪd] **1** PRET AND PTP of **inlay**. **2** ADJ: ~ **floor** entarimado *m*; ~ **work** taracea *f*.

inland **1** [ˈɪnlənd] ADJ interior; del interior; **I~ Revenue** Hacienda *f*, Fisco *m*; ~ **revenue stamp** timbre *m* fiscal; ~ **sea** mar *m* interior; ~ **town** ciudad *f* del interior; ~ **waterway** canal *m*.
  2 [ˈɪnˌlænd] ADV tierra adentro, hacia el interior.
  3 [ˈɪnˌlænd] N interior *m* (del país).

in-laws [ˈɪnˌlɔːz] NPL parientes *mpl* políticos, suegros *mpl*.

inlay [1] ['ɪnleɪ] N taracea f; incrustación f.
[2] ['ɪn'leɪ] VT (irr: V **lay**) taracear, embutir, incrustar; **a sword inlaid with jewels** una espada incrustada de joyas.
inlet ['ɪnlet] [1] N **(a)** (Geog) ensenada f, cala f, entrante m. **(b)** (Mech) admisión f, entrada f.
[2] ATTR (Mech): **~ pipe** tubo m de entrada; **~ valve** válvula f de entrada, válvula f de admisión.
inmate ['ɪnmeɪt] N habitante mf, ocupante mf, residente mf; inquilino m, -a f; (of hospital) enfermo m, -a f, (of asylum) internado m, -a f; (of prison) preso m, -a f, presidiario m, -a f.
inmost ['ɪnməʊst] ADJ = **innermost**.
inn [ɪn] [1] N posada f, hostería f, mesón m; (poor, wayside) venta f; (large, wayside) fonda f; (pub) taberna f; **I~s of Court** (London) Colegio m de Abogados.
[2] ATTR: **~ sign** letrero m de mesón.
innards* ['ɪnədz] NPL tripas fpl.
innate [ɪ'neɪt] ADJ innato.
innately [ɪ'neɪtlɪ] ADV de manera innata; **it is not ~ evil** no es malo de por sí.
inner ['ɪnəʳ] ADJ interior, interno; thoughts etc íntimo, secreto; **~ cabinet** consejillo m; **~ city** barrios mpl céntricos de la ciudad; **~ city problems** problemas mpl de los barrios céntricos; **~ ear** oído m interno; **the ~ life** la vida interior; **the ~ man** el estómago; **~ ring-road** carretera f de circunvalación interior; **~ rooms** habitaciones fpl interiores; **~ tube** cámara f de aire, llanta f (LAm).
innermost ['ɪnəməʊst] ADJ (más) interior, más central; thoughts etc más íntimo, más secreto.
innerspring ['ɪnə,sprɪŋ] ATTR: **~ mattress** (US) colchón m de muelles interiores.
inning ['ɪnɪŋ] N (US: Baseball) inning m; **~s** sing and pl (Cricket) turno m, entrada f; (fig) turno m, oportunidad f; **he's had a good ~s** ha tenido una vida (or carrera etc) larga.
innkeeper ['ɪnki:pəʳ] N posadero m, -a f, mesonero m -a f; ventero m, -a f; fondista mf; tabernero m, -a f (V **inn**).
innocence ['ɪnəsns] N inocencia f; **in all ~** inocentemente; sin segunda intención, sin malicia.
Innocent ['ɪnəsnt] NM (pope) Inocencio.
innocent ['ɪnəsnt] [1] ADJ inocente (of de); amusement etc honesto.
[2] N inocente mf.
innocently ['ɪnəsntlɪ] ADV inocentemente.
innocuous [ɪ'nɒkjʊəs] ADJ innocuo, inofensivo.
innovate ['ɪnəʊveɪt] VI introducir novedades.
innovation [,ɪnəʊ'veɪʃən] N innovación f, novedad f.
innovative ['ɪnəʊ,veɪtɪv] ADJ innovativo.
innovator ['ɪnəʊveɪtəʳ] N innovador m, -ora f.
innovatory ['ɪnəʊ,veɪtərɪ] ADJ innovador.
innuendo [,ɪnjʊ'endəʊ] N, PL **~es** indirecta f, insinuación f.
Innuit ['ɪnjuːɪt] = **Inuit**.
innumerable [ɪ'njuːmərəbl] ADJ innumerable; **there are ~ reasons** hay infinidad de razones; **I've told you ~ times** te lo he dicho mil veces.
innumeracy [ɪ'njuːmərəsɪ] N incompetencia f en el cálculo, incompetencia f en matemáticas.
innumerate [ɪ'njuːmərɪt] ADJ incompetente en el cálculo, incompetente en matemáticas.
inoculate [ɪ'nɒkjʊleɪt] VT inocular (against contra, with de).
inoculation [ɪ,nɒkjʊ'leɪʃən] N inoculación f.
inoffensive [,ɪnə'fensɪv] ADJ inofensivo.
inoperable [ɪn'ɒpərəbl] ADJ inoperable.
inoperative [ɪn'ɒpərətɪv] ADJ inoperante.
inopportune [ɪn'ɒpətjuːn] ADJ inoportuno.
inopportunely [ɪn'ɒpətjuːnlɪ] ADV inoportunamente, a deshora.
inordinate [ɪ'nɔːdɪnɪt] ADJ desmesurado, excesivo, desmedido.
inordinately [ɪ'nɔːdɪnɪtlɪ] ADV desmesurada, excesivamente.
inorganic [,ɪnɔː'gænɪk] ADJ inorgánico; **~ chemistry** química f inorgánica.
in-patient ['ɪn,peɪʃənt] N paciente m interno, paciente f interna.
input ['ɪnpʊt] [1] N (contribution) contribución f, aportación f; (of effort, time) inversión f; (Elec, Mech) entrada f, potencia f de entrada; (Fin) dinero m invertido, inversión f; (Comput) entrada f, introducción f, input m.
[2] VT introducir, entrar.
input-output device [,ɪnpʊt'aʊtpʊtdɪ'vaɪs] N dispositivo m de entrada y salida.
inquest ['ɪnkwest] N **(a)** (Jur) investigación f, pesquisa f judicial; (coroner's) **~** encuesta f judicial, encuesta f post-mortem.
(b) (fig) indagación f, encuesta f; **an ~ was held on the defeat** la derrota fue objeto de amplio análisis; **he likes to hold an ~ on every game** le gusta discutir cada partido hasta la saciedad.
▼**inquire** [ɪn'kwaɪəʳ] [1] VT preguntar; informarse de, pedir informes sobre; **to ~ sth of sb** preguntar algo a uno; **he ~d the price** preguntó cuánto costaba.

▼[2] VI preguntar; **to ~ about, to ~ after, to ~ for** preguntar por, pedir informes sobre; **to ~ into** investigar, examinar, indagar; **to ~ into the truth of sth** averiguar la verdad de un suceso; **to ~ of sb** preguntar a uno; **'~ at No. 14'** 'razón: núm. 14'; **'~ within'** 'se dan informaciones'; **I was only inquiring** era una simple pregunta.
inquirer [ɪn'kwaɪərəʳ] N (asker) el (or la etc) que pregunta; (researcher) investigador m, -ora f (into de).
inquiring [ɪn'kwaɪərɪŋ] ADJ mind activo, penetrante, curioso; look etc interrogativo, de interrogación.
inquiringly [ɪn'kwaɪərɪŋlɪ] ADV look etc interrogativamente.
▼**inquiry** [ɪn'kwaɪərɪ] [1] N **(a)** (question) pregunta f; petición f de informes; (Comput) interrogación f; **'Inquiries'** (sign etc) 'Informaciones'; **'inquiries at No. 14'** 'razón: núm. 14'; **'all inquiries to the secretary'** 'dirigirse al secretario'; **on ~** al preguntar; **have you an ~?** ¿quiere Vd preguntar algo?; **to make inquiries** pedir informes, tomar informes (about, on sobre; of a).
(b) **a look of ~** una mirada interrogativa.
(c) (Jur etc) investigación f, pesquisa f, indagación f, examen m, encuesta f; **there will have to be an ~** esto tendrá que ser investigado; **to hold an ~ into sth** investigar algo, examinar algo; **the police are making inquiries** la policía está investigando el asunto.
(d) (commission etc) comisión f de investigación, comisión f investigadora; **to set up an ~ into the disaster** nombrar una comisión para investigar el desastre.
[2] ATTR: **~ agent** investigador m privado, investigadora f privada; **~ desk** mesa f de informaciones; **~ office** oficina f de informaciones.
inquisition [,ɪnkwɪ'zɪʃən] N investigación f, inquisición f; **the I~** la Inquisición, el Santo Oficio.
inquisitive [ɪn'kwɪzɪtɪv] ADJ mind etc inquiridor, activo, curioso; (pej) preguntón, fisgón, curioso.
inquisitively [ɪn'kwɪzɪtɪvlɪ] ADV con curiosidad f.
inquisitiveness [ɪn'kwɪzɪtɪvnɪs] N curiosidad f.
inquisitor [ɪn'kwɪzɪtəʳ] N inquisidor m.
inquisitorial [ɪn,kwɪzɪ'tɔːrɪəl] ADJ inquisitorial.
inroad ['ɪnrəʊd] N incursión f, irrupción f (into en); (fig) invasión f, usurpación f (into de); **to make ~s into one's savings** mermar los ahorros de uno.
inrush ['ɪnrʌʃ] N irrupción f; (of tourists etc) afluencia f.
INS N (US) ABBR of **Immigration and Naturalization Service**.
ins. **(a)** ABBR of **insurance** seguro m. **(b)** ABBR of **inches** pulgadas fpl.
insalubrious [,ɪnsə'luːbrɪəs] ADJ insalubre, malsano.
insane [ɪn'seɪn] ADJ person loco, demente; act etc insensato; **you must be ~!** ¿estás loco?; **to become ~** volverse loco; **to drive sb ~** volver loco a uno.
insanely [ɪn'seɪnlɪ] ADV: **to laugh ~** reírse como un loco; **to be ~ jealous** ser terriblemente celoso.
insanitary [ɪn'sænɪtərɪ] ADJ insalubre, antihigiénico.
insanity [ɪn'sænɪtɪ] N locura f, demencia f; (of act etc) insensatez f; **to drive sb to ~** volver loco a uno.
insatiable [ɪn'seɪʃəbl] ADJ insaciable.
insatiably [ɪn'seɪʃəblɪ] ADV eat con un hambre insaciable; kiss con una pasión insaciable; **to be ~ hungry/curious/greedy** tener un hambre/una curiosidad/una avaricia insaciable.
inscribe [ɪn'skraɪb] VT inscribir; book dedicar; **~d stock** acciones fpl registradas.
inscription [ɪn'skrɪpʃən] N inscripción f; (in book) dedicatoria f; (label) rótulo m, letrero m.
inscrutability [ɪn,skruːtə'bɪlɪtɪ] N inescrutabilidad f.
inscrutable [ɪn'skruːtəbl] ADJ inescrutable, enigmático, insondable.
inseam ['ɪnsiːm] ATTR (US): **~ measurement** medida f de pernera.
insect ['ɪnsekt] [1] N insecto m.
[2] ATTR: **~ bite** picadura f de insecto; **~ powder** insecticida m en polvo; **~ repellent** repelente m de insectos; **~ spray** insecticida m en aerosol.
insecticide [ɪn'sektɪsaɪd] N insecticida m.
insectivorous [,ɪnsek'tɪvərəs] ADJ insectívoro.
insecure [,ɪnsɪ'kjʊʳ] ADJ inseguro.
insecurity [,ɪnsɪ'kjʊərɪtɪ] N inseguridad f.
inseminate [ɪn'semɪneɪt] VT inseminar.
insemination [ɪn,semɪ'neɪʃən] N inseminación f, fecundación f.
insensate [ɪn'senseɪt] ADJ insensato.
insensibility [ɪn,sensə'bɪlɪtɪ] N **(a)** insensibilidad f (to a), impasibilidad f; inconsciencia f (of de).
(b) (Med) estupor m, desmayo m, pérdida f de conocimiento.
insensible [ɪn'sensəbl] ADJ **(a)** (insensitive) insensible (to a), impasible, inconmovible; (unaware) inconsciente (of de).
(b) (Med) sin conocimiento; **he fell down ~** cayó sin conocimiento; **the blow knocked him ~** el golpe le hizo perder el conocimiento; **to drink o.s. ~** beber hasta perder el conocimiento.
insensibly [ɪn'sensɪblɪ] ADV change insensiblemente, imperceptiblemente.

➤ LANGUAGE IN USE: **inquire: 2** → 20.2, 21.1   **inquiry: 1a** → 20.2

insensitive [ɪnˈsensɪtɪv] ADJ insensible (*to* a).
insensitivity [ɪnˌsensɪˈtɪvɪtɪ] N insensibilidad *f.*
inseparable [ɪnˈsepərəbl] ADJ inseparable, indisoluble; **the two questions are ~** los dos asuntos no se pueden considerar por separado.
inseparably [ɪnˈsepərəblɪ] ADV inseparablemente, indisolublemente.
insert ① [ˈɪnsɜːt] N cosa *f* insertada; (*page*) hoja *f* suelta; (*section*) sección *f* añadida, materia *f* adicional.
② [ɪnˈsɜːt] VT insertar, intercalar; *object, finger etc* introducir, meter dentro; (*in newspaper*) publicar; *advert* poner; (*Comput*) insertar.
insertion [ɪnˈsɜːʃən] N inserción *f*; introducción *f*; publicación *f*; (*new section*) sección *f* añadida, materia *f* adicional.
in-service [ˈɪnˈsɜːvɪs] ADJ: **~ benefits** beneficios *mpl* en funcionamiento; **~ course** cursillo *m* en funcionamiento; **~ training** formación *f* en funcionamiento.
inset [ˈɪnset] ① N (*Typ*) grabado *m* (*or* mapa, dibujo *etc*) que se imprime en un ángulo de otro mayor; recuadro *m*, encarte *m.*
② VT (*irr: V* set) insertar; (*Typ*) imprimir como recuadro (*or* encarte); (*indent*) sangrar.
inshore [ˈɪnˈʃɔːr] ① ADV *be, fish* cerca de la orilla; *blow, flow, go* hacia la orilla.
② ADJ costero, cercano a la orilla; **~ fishing** pesca *f* de bajura.
inside [ˈɪnˈsaɪd] ① ADV (**a**) dentro; hacia dentro; por dentro; (*on bus*) en el piso inferior, abajo; **he wouldn't come ~** no quiso entrar; **please step ~** pase Vd; **to pass the ball ~** pasar el balón hacia dentro.
(**b**) (‡) **to be ~** estar a la sombra‡; **he's gone ~ for 5 years** le han metido a la sombra por 5 años‡; **they put him ~** le metieron a la sombra‡.
② PREP (*also* **~ of**) (**a**) (*place*) dentro de; en el interior de.
(**b**) (*time*) **~ 4 hours** en menos de 4 horas; **~ the record** en tiempo inferior a la marca; **his time was 5 seconds ~ the record** superó el récord en 5 segundos.
③ ADJ (**a**) interior; interno.
(**b**) (*Brit Aut*) **~ lane** carril *m* de la izquierda, (*most countries*) carril *m* de la derecha.
(**c**) *information* secreto, confidencial; **the ~ story** la historia (hasta ahora) secreta; **it must be an ~ job*** tiene que ser obra de un empleado de la casa.
④ N (**a**) interior *m*, parte *f* interior; (*lining*) forro *m*; **to know the ~ of an affair** conocer el secreto de un asunto; **to see a firm from the ~** estudiar una empresa por dentro; **on the ~** por dentro; **ladies walk on the ~ of the pavement** las señoras van en la parte de la acera más alejada de la calzada; **to overtake on the ~** (*Brit*) adelantar por la izquierda, (*most countries*) adelantar por la derecha.
(**b**) **to be ~ out** estar al revés; **to put a dress on ~ out** ponerse un vestido al revés; **to turn sth ~ out** volver algo al revés; **they turned the whole place ~ out** lo revolvieron todo, lo registraron todo de arriba abajo; **to know a subject ~ out** conocer un tema de cabo a rabo.
(**c**) (*Anat*: also* **~s**) estómago *m*, tripas *fpl*; **I have a pain in my ~** me duele el estómago.
inside-forward [ˈɪnsaɪdˈfɔːwəd] N delantero *m*, -a *f* interior.
inside-left [ˈɪnsaɪdˈleft] N interior *m* izquierdo, interior *f* izquierda.
inside-leg [ˈɪnsaɪdˈleg] N (*also* **~ measurement**) medida *f* de pernera.
insider [ɪnˈsaɪdər] ADJ N persona *f* enterada; persona *f* que es de la casa (*etc*), empleado *m*, -a *f* de la casa; **~ dealing**, **~ trading** operaciones *fpl* de iniciados, abuso *m* de información privilegiada.
inside-right [ˈɪnsaɪdˈraɪt] N interior *m* derecho, interior *f* derecha.
insidious [ɪnˈsɪdɪəs] ADJ insidioso; pernicioso; maligno; *agitation etc* clandestino, subversivo.
insidiously [ɪnˈsɪdɪəslɪ] ADV insidiosamente; perniciosamente; clandestinamente.
insight [ˈɪnsaɪt] N penetración *f* (psicológica), perspicacia *f*, intuición *f*; nueva percepción *f*, revelación *f*; **the visit gave us an ~ into their way of life** la visita fue para nosotros una revelación de su manera de vivir; **to gain (*or* get *etc*) an ~ into sth** adquirir una nueva percepción de algo, comprender algo mejor.
insightful [ˈɪnˌsaɪtful] ADJ (*US*) penetrante.
insignia [ɪnˈsɪgnɪə] NPL insignias *fpl.*
insignificance [ˌɪnsɪgˈnɪfɪkəns] N insignificancia *f*; **A pales into ~ beside B** A pierde toda su importancia al compararse con B.
insignificant [ˌɪnsɪgˈnɪfɪkənt] ADJ insignificante.
insincere [ˌɪnsɪnˈsɪər] ADJ poco sincero, insincero, nada franco, doble.
insincerity [ˌɪnsɪnˈserɪtɪ] N falta *f* de sinceridad, insinceridad *f*, doblez *f.*
insinuate [ɪnˈsɪnjʊeɪt] ① VT (**a**) *object* insinuar, introducir (*into* en).
(**b**) (*hint*) insinuar; **what are you insinuating?** ¿qué quieres insinuar?; **to ~ that ...** insinuar que ..., dar a entender que ...
② VR: **to ~ o.s. into** insinuarse en, introducirse en.
insinuating [ɪnˈsɪnjʊeɪtɪŋ] ADJ insinuador; *remark* malintencionado, con segunda intención.
insinuation [ɪnˌsɪnjʊˈeɪʃən] N (**a**) (*act*) insinuación *f*, introducción *f.*

(**b**) (*hint*) insinuación *f*, indirecta *f*, sugestión *f*; **it carries the ~ that ...** lleva implícita la noción de que ...; **he made certain ~s** soltó ciertas indirectas.
insipid [ɪnˈsɪpɪd] ADJ insípido, soso, insulso.
insipidity [ˌɪnsɪˈpɪdɪtɪ] N insipidez *f*, sosería *f*, insulsez *f.*
insist [ɪnˈsɪst] ① VT: **to ~ that sth is so** insistir en que algo es así; **to ~ that sth be done** insistir en que algo se haga.
② VI insistir; (*obstinately*) porfiar, empeñarse, persistir; **if you ~** si Vd insiste; **to ~ on sth** insistir en algo, exigir algo; **to ~ on doing sth** insistir en hacer algo, empeñarse en hacer algo, obstinarse en hacer algo.
insistence [ɪnˈsɪstəns] N insistencia *f* (*on* en); empeño *m* (*on* en); porfía *f*; **I did it at his ~** lo hice ante su insistencia, lo hice cediendo a sus ruegos.
insistent [ɪnˈsɪstənt] ADJ insistente; porfiado, persistente; urgente; **he was most ~ about it** se empeñó mucho en ello; **he said in ~ tones** dijo en tono apremiante.
insistently [ɪnˈsɪstəntlɪ] ADV con insistencia; porfiadamente; urgentemente.
in situ [ɪnˈsɪtjuː] ADV in situ, en el sitio.
insofar [ɪnsəˈfɑːr] CONJ: **~ as** en tanto que + *subj.*
insole [ˈɪnsəʊl] N plantilla *f.*
insolence [ˈɪnsələns] N insolencia *f*, descaro *m*, atrevimiento *m.*
insolent [ˈɪnsələnt] ADJ insolente, descarado, atrevido; **don't be ~!** ¡qué frescura!
insolently [ˈɪnsələntlɪ] ADV insolentemente, descaradamente.
insolubility [ɪnˌsɒljʊˈbɪlɪtɪ] N insolubilidad *f.*
insoluble [ɪnˈsɒljʊbl] ADJ insoluble.
insolvable [ɪnˈsɒlvəbl] ADJ irresoluble.
insolvency [ɪnˈsɒlvənsɪ] N insolvencia *f.*
insolvent [ɪnˈsɒlvənt] ADJ insolvente; **to declare sb ~** declarar a uno insolvente.
insomnia [ɪnˈsɒmnɪə] N insomnio *m.*
insomniac [ɪnˈsɒmnɪæk] ① ADJ insomne.
② N insomne *mf.*
insomuch [ˌɪnsəʊˈmʌtʃ] ADV: **~ as** puesto que, ya que, por cuanto que; **~ that ...** hasta tal punto que ...
insouciance [ɪnˈsuːsɪəns] N despreocupación *f.*
insouciant [ɪnˈsuːsɪənt] ADJ despreocupado.
Insp. ABBR *of* **inspector.**
inspect [ɪnˈspekt] VT inspeccionar, examinar; (*officially*) registrar, reconocer; *troops* pasar revista a; (*Brit: ticket*) revisar.
inspection [ɪnˈspekʃən] ① N inspección *f*, examen *m*; registro *m*, reconocimiento *m*; (*Mil*) revista *f.*
② ATTR: **~ pit** (*Aut*) foso *m* de reconocimiento.
inspector [ɪnˈspektər] N inspector *m*, -ora *f*; (*Brit Rail, on bus etc*) revisor *m*, -ora *f*, controlador *m*, -ora *f* (*LAm*); **~ of schools** (*Brit*) inspector *m*, -ora *f* de enseñanza; **~ of taxes** inspector *m*, -ora *f* de Hacienda.
inspectorate [ɪnˈspektərɪt] N inspectorado *m.*
inspiration [ˌɪnspəˈreɪʃən] N inspiración *f*; **to find ~ in** inspirarse en; **you have been an ~ to us all** nos ha inspirado a todos.
inspirational [ˌɪnspɪˈreɪʃənl] ADJ inspirador.
inspire [ɪnˈspaɪər] VT inspirar; **to ~ sth in sb, to ~ sb with sth** inspirar algo a uno, infundir algo a uno, llenar a uno de algo; **to ~ sb to do sth** mover a uno a hacer algo.
inspired [ɪnˈspaɪəd] ADJ *move, work etc* genial; **in an ~ moment** en un momento de inspiración.
inspiring [ɪnˈspaɪərɪŋ] ADJ inspirador.
Inst. ABBR *of* **Institute** Instituto *m.*
inst. ABBR *of* **instant, of the present month** corriente, de los corrientes, cte.
instability [ˌɪnstəˈbɪlɪtɪ] N inestabilidad *f.*
instal(l) [ɪnˈstɔːl] ① VT instalar; **to be ~ed in office** tomar posesión de su cargo.
② VR: **to ~ o.s.** instalarse.
installation [ˌɪnstəˈleɪʃən] N instalación *f.*
instalment, (*US*) **installment** [ɪnˈstɔːlmənt] ① N (*of story etc*) entrega *f*; (*Comm*) plazo *m*; **payment by ~s** pago *m* a plazos; **to pay in ~s** pagar a plazos.
② ATTR: **~ plan** (*US*) pago *m* a plazos, compra *f* a plazos.
instance [ˈɪnstəns] ① N (**a**) (*example*) ejemplo *m*; caso *m*; **for ~** por ejemplo; **in that ~** en ese caso; **in many ~s** en muchos casos; **in the present ~** en el caso presente; **in the first ~** primero, en primer lugar; **let's take an actual ~** tomemos un caso concreto.
(**b**) **at the ~ of** (*Jur*) a instancia de, a petición de.
② VT poner por caso, citar como ejemplo.
instant [ˈɪnstənt] ① ADJ inmediato, instantáneo; **~ coffee** café *m* instantáneo; **~ replay** repetición *f* de jugada; **the 3rd ~** el 3 del (mes) corriente.
② N instante *m*, momento *m*; **in an ~, on the ~, this ~** al instante, en seguida.

3 *as* CONJ: **tell me the ~ he comes** avíseme en cuanto venga, avíseme en seguida que venga; **the ~ I heard it** en el momento en que lo supe.

instantaneous [ˌɪnstən'teɪnɪəs] ADJ instantáneo.

instantaneously [ˌɪnstən'teɪnɪəslɪ] ADV instantáneamente.

instantly ['ɪnstəntlɪ] ADV al instante, inmediatamente, en seguida.

instead [ɪn'sted] ADV en cambio, en lugar de eso; **~ of** en lugar de, en vez de; **he went ~ of me** fue en mi lugar; **this is ~ of a Christmas present** esto hace las veces de un regalo de Reyes.

instep ['ɪnstep] N empeine *m*.

instigate ['ɪnstɪgeɪt] VT instigar.

instigation [ˌɪnstɪ'geɪʃən] N instigación *f*; **at the ~ of** a instigación de.

instigator ['ɪnstɪgeɪtə'] N instigador *m*, -ora *f*.

instil, (*US*) **instill** [ɪn'stɪl] VT infundir, inculcar; **to ~ sth into sb** infundir algo a uno, inculcar algo en uno.

instinct **1** [ɪn'stɪŋkt] ADJ: **~ with** lleno de, imbuido de.

2 ['ɪnstɪŋkt] N instinto *m*; **by ~** por instinto.

instinctive [ɪn'stɪŋktɪv] ADJ instintivo.

instinctively [ɪn'stɪŋktɪvlɪ] ADV instintivamente, por instinto.

instinctual [ɪn'stɪŋktjuəl] ADJ instintivo.

institute ['ɪnstɪtjuːt] **1** N instituto *m*; (*for professional training*) escuela *f*; (*of professional body*) colegio *m*, asociación *f*; (*US: course*) curso *m*, cursillo *m*.

2 VT (*found*) instituir, establecer, fundar; *inquiry etc* iniciar, empezar; *proceedings* entablar.

institution [ˌɪnstɪ'tjuːʃən] N **(a)** (*act*) institución *f*, establecimiento *m*, fundación *f*; iniciación *f*; entablación *f*.

(b) (*organization*) instituto *m*, asociación *f*.

(c) (*workhouse etc*) asilo *m*; (*madhouse*) manicomio *m*; (*Med*) hospital *m*.

(d) (*custom etc*) institución *f*, costumbre *f*, tradición *f*; (*person etc*) persona *f* conocidísima; **it is too much of an ~ to abolish** es una costumbre demasiado arraigada para poder suprimirla; **tea is a British ~** el té es una institución en Gran Bretaña.

institutional [ˌɪnstɪ'tjuːʃənl] ADJ institucional; **~ investor** inversionista *mf* institucional.

institutionalize [ˌɪnstɪ'tjuːʃnəlaɪz] VT **(a)** reglamentar; institucionalizar. **(b)** *person* meter en un asilo.

institutionalized [ˌɪnstɪ'tjuːʃənəˌlaɪzd] ADJ institucionalizado.

in-store ['ɪn,stɔːr] ADJ en el establecimiento.

instruct [ɪn'strʌkt] VT **(a)** (*teach*) instruir (*about, in* de, en, sobre); **to ~ sb in maths** enseñar matemáticas a uno.

(b) (*order*) **to ~ sb to do sth** mandar a uno hacer algo.

(c) (*Brit*) *solicitor* dar instrucciones a, instruir; *barrister* constituir.

instruction [ɪn'strʌkʃən] **1** N **(a)** (*teaching*) instrucción *f*, enseñanza *f*; **to give sb ~ in fencing** enseñar esgrima a uno.

(b) (*order*) orden *f*, mandato *m*; (*Comput*) instrucción *f*; **~s** instrucciones *fpl*; órdenes *fpl*; **'~s for use'** (*on packet etc*) 'modo de empleo' *m*; **operating ~s** (*of pilot etc*) órdenes *fpl*, consigna *f*; **on the ~s of** por orden de; **we have given ~s for the transfer of ...** hemos cursado órdenes para la transferencia de ...

2 ATTR: **~ book** manual *m* de instrucciones; **~ cycle** ciclo *m* de instrucción.

instructive [ɪn'strʌktɪv] ADJ instructivo, informativo, aleccionador.

instructor [ɪn'strʌktə'] N instructor *m*, -ora *f*, profesor *m*, -ora *f*; (*US Univ*) profesor *m* -ora *f* auxiliar; (*ski ~*) monitor *m*, -ora *f*.

instructress [ɪn'strʌktrɪs] N instructora *f*; profesora *f*.

instrument ['ɪnstrumənt] **1** N (*all senses*) instrumento *m*.

2 ATTR: **~ board** (*Aut, Aer*) tablero *m* (*or* cuadro *m*) de instrumentos (*or* de mandos); **~ panel** (*US Aut*) salpicadero *m*; (*Aer*) tablero *m* de instrumentos; **set of ~s** instrumental *m*; **to fly on ~s** volar por instrumentos.

instrumental [ˌɪnstru'mentl] ADJ **(a)** (*Mus*) instrumental; **~ music** músic *f* instrumental; **~ performer** instrumentista *mf*. **(b) to be ~ in** + *ger* contribuir materialmente a + *infin*, ser instrumento eficaz para + *infin*.

instrumentalist [ˌɪnstru'mentəlɪst] N instrumentista *mf*.

instrumentality [ˌɪnstrumen'tælɪtɪ] N mediación *f*, agencia *f*; **by** (*or* **through**) **the ~ of** por medio de, gracias a.

instrumentation [ˌɪnstrumen'teɪʃən] N instrumentación *f*.

insubordinate [ˌɪnsə'bɔːdənɪt] ADJ insubordinado, desobediente, rebelde.

insubordination ['ɪnsə,bɔːdɪ'neɪʃən] N insubordinación *f*, desobediencia *f*, rebeldía *f*.

insubstantial [ˌɪnsəb'stænʃəl] ADJ insustancial.

insufferable [ɪn'sʌfərəbl] ADJ insufrible, inaguantable.

insufferably [ɪn'sʌfərəblɪ] ADV de modo insufrible; **~ rude** de lo más grosero.

insufficiency [ˌɪnsə'fɪʃənsɪ] N insuficiencia *f*.

insufficient [ˌɪnsə'fɪʃənt] ADJ insuficiente.

insufficiently [ˌɪnsə'fɪʃəntlɪ] ADV insuficientemente.

insular ['ɪnsjələr] ADJ insular; (*fig*) de miras estrechas.

insularity [ˌɪnsju'lærɪtɪ] N insularidad *f*; (*fig*) estrechez *f* de miras.

insulate ['ɪnsjuleɪt] VT aislar (*from* de).

insulating tape ['ɪnsjuleɪtɪŋˌteɪp] N (*Brit*) cinta *f* aislante, cinta *f* aisladora.

insulation [ˌɪnsju'leɪʃən] **1** N aislamiento *m*.

2 ATTR: **~ material** material *m* aislante.

insulator ['ɪnsjuleɪtər] N aislante *m*, aislador *m*.

insulin ['ɪnsjulɪn] N insulina *f*.

insult **1** ['ɪnsʌlt] N insulto *m*, injuria *f*, ultraje *m*, ofensa *f*; **they are an ~ to the profession** son un insulto para la profesión; **and to add ~ to injury ...** y por si esto fuera poco ..., para más inri, y encima ...

2 [ɪn'sʌlt] VT insultar, injuriar; ofender; **he felt ~ed by this offer** creyó que tal oferta era deshonrosa para él; **now don't feel ~ed** pues no te vayas a ofender.

insulting [ɪn'sʌltɪŋ] ADJ insultante, injurioso; ofensivo; deshonroso.

insultingly [ɪn'sʌltɪŋlɪ] ADV injuriosamente, ofensivamente.

insuperable [ɪn'suːpərəbl] ADJ insuperable.

insuperably [ɪn'suːpərəblɪ] ADV: **~ difficult** dificilísimo; **A is ~ better than B** A es con mucho mejor que B.

insupportable [ˌɪnsə'pɔːtəbl] ADJ insoportable.

insurable [ɪn'ʃuərəbl] ADJ asegurable.

insurance [ɪn'ʃuərəns] **1** N (*Comm*) seguro *m*.

2 ATTR: **~ agent** agente *mf* de seguros; **~ broker** corredor *m*, -ora *f* de seguros, agente *mf* de seguros; **~ certificate** certificado *m* de seguro; **~ claim** demanda *f* de seguro; **~ company** compañía *f* de seguros; **~ office** oficina *f* aseguradora, oficina *f* de seguros; **~ policy** póliza *f* (de seguros); **~ premium** prima *f* de seguros; **~ rates** tipo *m* de seguro; **~ scheme** plan *m* de seguro; **~ stamp** sello *m* de pago de la Seguridad Social; **~ surveyor** tasador *m*, -ora *f* de seguros.

insure [ɪn'ʃuə'] **1** VT asegurar (*against* contra).

2 VI asegurarse (*against* contra).

insured [ɪn'ʃuəd] N: **the ~** el asegurado, la asegurada.

insurer [ɪn'ʃuərə'] N asegurador *m*, -ora *f*.

insurgency [ɪn'sɜːdʒənsɪ] N insurrección *f*.

insurgent [ɪn'sɜːdʒənt] **1** ADJ insurrecto, insurgente.

2 N insurrecto *m*, -a *f*, insurgente *mf*.

insurmountable [ˌɪnsə'maʊntəbl] ADJ insuperable.

insurrection [ˌɪnsə'rekʃən] N sublevación *f*, insurrección *f*.

insurrectionary [ˌɪnsə'rekʃnərɪ] ADJ rebelde, insurreccional.

insurrectionist [ˌɪnsə'rekʃənɪst] N insurgente *mf*, insurrecto *m*, -a *f*.

Int. ABBR *of* **International** Internacional.

int. ABBR *of* **interest** interés *m*.

intact [ɪn'tækt] ADJ intacto; íntegro; ileso, entero, sano; **not a window was left ~** no quedaba cristal sano (*or* sin romper).

intake ['ɪnteɪk] N **(a)** (*Mech*) admisión *f*, toma *f*, entrada *f*; tubo *m* de admisión, válvula *f* de admisión.

(b) (*quantity*) cantidad *f* admitida, número *m* admitido; **what is your student ~?** ¿cuántos alumnos se matriculan (cada año)?

(c) (*of food*) consumo *m*.

2 ATTR: **~ valve** válvula *f* de admisión.

intangible [ɪn'tændʒəbl] ADJ intangible; **~ assets** activo *m* intangible.

integer ['ɪntɪdʒər] N (número *m*) entero *m*.

integral ['ɪntɪgrəl] **1** ADJ (*whole*) íntegro; *part, component* integrante; (*Math*) integral; **it is an ~ part of the plan** es parte integrante (*or* esencial) del proyecto.

2 N (*Math*) integral *f*.

integrate ['ɪntɪgreɪt] **1** VT integrar (*also Math*); combinar en un todo, formar un conjunto como.

2 VI integrarse (*into* en).

integrated ['ɪntɪgreɪtɪd] ADJ *plan* de conjunto, que forma un conjunto; *personality* armonioso, estable, sano; *population, school* integrado, sin separación racial; **~ circuit** circuito *m* integrado.

integration [ˌɪntɪ'greɪʃən] N integración *f*.

integrator ['ɪntɪgreɪtər] N integrador *m*.

integrity [ɪn'tegrɪtɪ] N integridad *f*, honradez *f*, rectitud *f*; (*Comput*) integridad *f*.

integument [ɪn'tegjumənt] N integumento *m*.

intellect ['ɪntɪlekt] N intelecto *m*.

intellectual [ˌɪntɪ'lektjuəl] **1** ADJ intelectual.

2 N intelectual *mf*.

intellectualize [ˌɪntɪ'lektjuəlaɪz] **1** VT intelectualizar, racionalizar.

2 VI dar razones.

intellectually [ˌɪntɪ'lektjuəlɪ] ADV intelectualmente.

intelligence [ɪn'telɪdʒəns] **1** N **(a)** (*understanding*) inteligencia *f*.

(b) (*information*) información *f*, informes *mpl*, noticias *fpl*; **shipping ~** noticias *fpl* navieras; **according to our latest ~** según las últimas noticias.

2 ATTR: **~ agent** agente *mf* de inteligencia, agente *m* secreto; **I~ Corps** (*Brit*) Cuerpo *m* de Informaciones; **~ officer** oficial *m* de informaciones; **~ quotient** cociente *m* intelectual; **~ service** servicio *m* de información; **~ test** test *m* de inteligencia; **I~ work** trabajo *m* de inteligencia.

intelligent [ɪnˈtelɪdʒənt] ADJ inteligente.

intelligently [ɪnˈtelɪdʒəntlɪ] ADV inteligentemente.

intelligentsia [ɪnˌtelɪˈdʒentsɪə] N intelectualidad *f*.

intelligibility [ɪnˌtelɪdʒəˈbɪlɪtɪ] N inteligibilidad *f*.

intelligible [ɪnˈtelɪdʒəbl] ADJ inteligible, comprensible; **it is scarcely ~ that ...** apenas es creíble que ...

intelligibly [ɪnˈtelɪdʒəblɪ] ADV inteligiblemente, de modo inteligible.

INTELSAT [ˈɪntelˌsæt] N ABBR *of* **International Telecommunications Satellite Organization** Organización *f* Internacional de Telecomunicaciones por Satélite.

intemperance [ɪnˈtempərəns] N intemperancia *f*, inmoderación *f*; (*drunkenness*) exceso *m* en la bebida.

intemperate [ɪnˈtempərɪt] ADJ intemperante, inmoderado; (*drunken*) dado a la bebida, que bebe con exceso.

▼ **intend** [ɪnˈtend] VT **(a)** (N *object*) **what does he ~ by that?** ¿qué quiere decir con eso?; **I ~ it as a present** pienso darlo como regalo; **it is ~ed for John** está destinado a Juan, es para Juan; **no offence was ~ed, he ~ed no offence** no tenía la intención de ofender a nadie; **I ~ no disrespect** no quiero faltarle al respeto; **that remark was ~ed for you** esa observación iba dirigida a ti, eso lo dijo por ti.

▼ **(b)** (*with verb*) **to ~ to** + *infin*, **to ~** + *ger* pensar + *infin*, proponerse + *infin*; **what do you ~ to do about it?** ¿qué piensas hacer?; **this scheme is ~ed to help** este proyecto tiene la finalidad de ayudar; **I ~ that he should see it** pretendo que él lo vea, quiero que él lo vea; **I fully ~ to punish him** tengo la firme intención de castigarle.

intended [ɪnˈtendɪd] **1** ADJ deseado.

2 N († *or hum*) prometido *m*, -a *f*.

intense [ɪnˈtens] ADJ intenso; *interest etc* muy grande, sumo, enorme; *person* exagerado, nervioso; *look* penetrante; ardiente.

intensely [ɪnˈtenslɪ] ADV intensamente; **~ difficult** sumamente difícil, terriblemente difícil, dificilísimo; **she speaks so ~** habla en tono tan exagerado.

intensification [ɪnˌtensɪfɪˈkeɪʃən] N intensificación *f*.

intensifier [ɪnˈtensɪˌfaɪəʳ] N intensificador *m*.

intensify [ɪnˈtensɪfaɪ] **1** VT intensificar; aumentar, reforzar.

2 VI intensificarse; aumentar(se), reforzarse.

intensity [ɪnˈtensɪtɪ] N intensidad *f*; (*of interest etc*) fuerza *f*; (*of person*) exageración *f*, nerviosismo *m*, hipertensión *f*.

intensive [ɪnˈtensɪv] ADJ intensivo; *course* intensivo, concentrado; *study* profundo, detenido; **~ care** asistencia *f* intensiva, vigilancia *f* intensiva; **~ care unit** unidad *f* de vigilancia intensiva.

intensively [ɪnˈtensɪvlɪ] ADV intensivamente; profundamente, detenidamente.

intent [ɪnˈtent] **1** ADJ (*absorbed*) absorto (*on* en), atento; **to be ~ on doing sth** estar resuelto a hacer algo.

2 N intento *m*, propósito *m*; **with ~ to** + *infin* con el propósito de + *infin*; **to all ~s and purposes** prácticamente, en realidad, en efecto.

▼ **intention** [ɪnˈtenʃən] N intención *f*; intento *m*, propósito *m*; proyecto *m*; **my ~ is to** + *infin* me propongo + *infin*, intento + *infin*; **it is no ~ of** + *ger* no es mi propósito + *infin*; **with the best ~s** con buena voluntad; **what are your ~s?** ¿qué piensas hacer?, ¿qué proyectos tienes?; **his ~s towards the girl were strictly honourable** pensaba casarse honradamente con la joven.

intentional [ɪnˈtenʃənl] ADJ intencional, deliberado.

intentionally [ɪnˈtenʃnəlɪ] ADV intencionalmente, de propósito, adrede.

intently [ɪnˈtentlɪ] ADV atentamente, fijamente.

intentness [ɪnˈtentnɪs] N (*concentration*) atención *f*; (*of gaze*) intensidad *f*; **~ of purpose** resolución *f*.

inter [ɪnˈtɜːʳ] VT enterrar, sepultar.

inter... [ˈɪntəʳ] PREF inter..., entre...

interact [ˌɪntərˈækt] VI obrar recíprocamente (*on* en); (*Comput*) interactuar, interaccionar (*with* con).

interaction [ˌɪntərˈækʃən] N interacción *f*, acción *f* recíproca, influencia *f* mutua; (*Comput*) interactuación *f*, interacción *f*.

interactive [ˌɪntərˈæktɪv] ADJ interactivo; **~ computing** computación *f* interactiva; **~ processing** procesamiento *m* interactivo; **~ video** vídeo *m* interactivo.

interactively [ˌɪntərˈæktɪvlɪ] ADV interactivamente.

inter alia [ˌɪntərˈælɪə] ADV entre otros.

inter-bank [ˈɪntəˌbæŋk] ADJ interbancario; **~ loan** préstamo *m* entre bancos; **~ rate** tasa *f* de descuento entre bancos.

interbreed [ˈɪntəˈbriːd] (*irr: V* **breed**) **1** VT cruzar.

2 VI cruzarse.

intercalate [ɪnˈtɜːkəleɪt] VT intercalar.

intercalation [ɪnˌtɜːkəˈleɪʃən] N intercalación *f*.

intercede [ˌɪntəˈsiːd] VI interceder (*for* por, *with* con).

intercept [ˌɪntəˈsept] VT interceptar; detener; (*Math*) cortar; (*cut off*) atajar.

interception [ˌɪntəˈsepʃən] N interceptación *f*, detención *f*; atajo *m*.

interceptor [ˌɪntəˈseptəʳ] N interceptor *m*.

intercession [ˌɪntəˈseʃən] N intercesión *f*, mediación *f*.

interchange **1** [ˈɪntəˈtʃeɪndʒ] N **(a)** intercambio *m*, cambio *m*; canje *m*; alternación *f*.

(b) (*Aut*) cruce *m*.

2 [ˌɪntəˈtʃeɪndʒ] VT intercambiar, cambiar; *prisoners, publications etc* canjear; (*alternate*) alternar.

interchangeable [ˌɪntəˈtʃeɪndʒəbl] ADJ intercambiable.

interchangeably [ˌɪntəˈtʃeɪndʒəblɪ] ADV de manera intercambiable, intercambiando los dos (*etc*).

inter-city [ˈɪntəˈsɪtɪ] **1** N (*Brit Rail: also* **~ train**) tren *m* de largo recorrido, tren *m* intercity.

2 ADJ de largo recorrido, intercity.

intercollegiate [ˈɪntəkəˈliːdʒɪɪt] ADJ interuniversitario.

intercom* [ˈɪntəkɒm] N intercomunicador *m*, interfono *m*.

intercommunicate [ˌɪntəkəˈmjuːnɪkeɪt] VI comunicarse.

intercommunication [ˈɪntəkəˌmjuːnɪˈkeɪʃən] N intercomunicación *f*.

intercommunion [ˌɪntəkəˈmjuːnɪən] N intercomunión *f*.

inter-company [ˌɪntəˈkʌmpənɪ] ADJ: **~ relations** relaciones *fpl* entre compañías.

interconnect [ˌɪntəkəˈnekt] VT interconectar.

interconnecting [ˌɪntəkəˈnektɪŋ] ADJ *rooms* comunicados; *trains* con correspondencia.

interconnection [ˌɪntəkəˈnekʃən] N interconexión *f*.

intercontinental [ˈɪntəˌkɒntɪˈnentl] ADJ intercontinental.

intercostal [ˌɪntəˈkɒstl] ADJ intercostal.

intercourse [ˈɪntəkɔːs] N **(a)** (*social*) trato *m*, relaciones *fpl*, comercio *m*. **(b)** (*sexual*) comercio *m* sexual, trato *m* sexual, coito *m*; **to have (sexual) ~ with** tener comercio sexual con.

intercut [ˌɪntəˈkʌt] VT: **to be ~ with** (*Cine*) alternarse con.

interdenominational [ˈɪntədɪˌnɒmɪˈneɪʃənl] ADJ interconfesional.

interdepartmental [ˈɪntəˌdiːpɑːtˈmentl] ADJ interdepartamental.

interdependence [ˌɪntədɪˈpendəns] N interdependencia *f*.

interdependent [ˌɪntədɪˈpendənt] ADJ interdependiente.

interdict [ˈɪntədɪkt] N entredicho *m*, interdicto *m*.

interdiction [ˌɪntəˈdɪkʃən] N interdicción *f*.

interdisciplinary [ˌɪntəˈdɪsɪplɪnərɪ] ADJ interdisciplinario.

interest [ˈɪntrɪst] **1** N **(a)** (*curiosity*) interés *m*; **of great ~** de gran interés; **questions of public ~** asuntos *mpl* de interés público; **to be of ~** interesar; **it is of no ~ to us** no nos interesa; **what are your ~s?** ¿qué cosas te interesan?; ¿qué pasatiempos tienes?; **to do sth just for ~** hacer algo como pasatiempo nada más; **to have an ~ in** estar interesado en, interesarse en (*or* por); **to show ~** mostrar interés (*in* en, por); **to take an ~ in sth** interesarse en (*or* por) algo; **to take no further ~ in sth** dejar de interesarse en algo; no participar más en algo.

(b) (*profit, advantage*) ventaja *f*, provecho *m*, beneficio *m*; **in one's own ~(s)** en beneficio propio; **it is in your own ~ to confess** hay que confesarlo en beneficio propio; **in the ~s of hygiene** en interés de la higiene; **to act in sb's ~s** obrar en beneficio de uno; **to declare an ~** declarar su interés (*in* en); **to promote sb's ~s** fomentar los intereses de uno; **it is not in Ruritania's ~ to leave the base** le perjudicará a Ruritania abandonar la base.

(c) (*Comm: share, stake*) participación *f*, interés *m*; **~s** intereses *mpl*; **the coal ~** la industria hullera, los propietarios de las minas de carbón; **the conservative ~** los conservadores, el partido conservador; **the landed ~** los terratenientes; **business ~s** los negocios, el mundo de los negocios, los empresarios; **Switzerland is looking after British ~s** Suiza se encarga de los intereses británicos; **to have a financial ~ in a company** tener acciones en una compañía, ser accionista de una compañía.

(d) (*Comm: on loan, shares etc*) interés *m*; rédito *m*; **at an ~ of 5%** con interés de 5 por ciento; **to bear ~** devengar intereses; **to bear ~ at 5%** producir un 5 por ciento de interés; **to lend at ~** dar a interés; **to put out at ~** poner a interés; **to repay with ~** (*iro*) devolver con creces; **shares that yield a high ~** acciones *fpl* que rinden bien.

2 ATTR: **~ group** grupo *m* de intereses; **~ rate** tipo *m* de interés; **~ warrant** cupón *m* de interés.

3 VT interesar; **to be ~ed in** (*financially*) estar interesado en, (*from curiosity*) interesarse en (*or* por); **the company is ~ed in acquiring 200** la compañía está interesada en adquirir 200; **I'm not ~ed in football** no me interesa el fútbol.

4 VR: **to ~ o.s. in** interesarse en (*or* por).

interest-bearing [ˈɪntrɪstˌbeərɪŋ] ADJ con interés.

interested [ˈɪntrɪstɪd] ADJ: **~ party, ~ person** interesado *m*, -a *f*.

interest-free [ˌɪntrɪstˈfriː] ADJ sin intereses.

interesting [ˈɪntrɪstɪŋ] ADJ interesante.

interestingly [ˈɪntrɪstɪŋlɪ] ADV interesantemente.

interface [ˈɪntəfeɪs] **1** N interfaz *f*, interface *m* (*also Comput*).

2 VI: **to ~ with** conectar con.

interfacing [ˈɪntəfeɪsɪŋ] N acoplamiento *m*.

interfere [ˌɪntəˈfɪəʳ] VI intervenir, entrometerse, mezclarse (*in* en); **to ~ with** (*hinder*) estorbar, dificultar, impedir; (*damage*) manosear, estropear; (*Rad etc*) interferir; **who told you to ~?** ¿quién te mete a ti en esto?

interference [ˌɪntəˈfɪərəns] N intervención *f*, intromisión *f*, entrometimiento *m*; interposición *f*; (*Rad etc*) interferencia *f*.

interfering [ˌɪntəˈfɪərɪŋ] ADJ entrometido.

interferon [ˌɪntəˈfɪərɒn] N interferón *m*.

intergalactic [ˌɪntəgəˈlæktɪk] ADJ intergaláctico.

intergovernmental ADJ [ˌɪntəˌgʌvnˈmentl] *adj* intergubernamental.

interim [ˈɪntərɪm] **1** N ínterin *m*, intermedio *m*; **in the ~** entretanto, en el ínterin, interinamente.
2 ATTR interino, provisional; **~ dividend** dividendo *m* a cuenta, dividendo *m* parcial.

interior [ɪnˈtɪərɪəʳ] **1** ADJ interior, interno; **~ decorating** decoración *f* del hogar; **decoración** *f* **de interiores**; **~ decorator**, **~ designer** decorador *m*, -ora *f* de interiores, diseñador *m*, -ora *f* de interiores; **~ sprung mattress** colchón *m* de muelles.
2 N interior *m*; **Ministry** (or **Department** *etc*) **of the I~** Ministerio *m* del Interior.

interject [ˌɪntəˈdʒekt] VT interponer.

interjection [ˌɪntəˈdʒekʃən] N interposición *f*; (*word*) interjección *f*, exclamación *f*.

interlace [ˌɪntəˈleɪs] **1** VT entrelazar.
2 VI entrelazarse.

interlard [ˌɪntəˈlɑːd] VT: **to ~ with** salpicar de, entreverar de.

interleave [ˌɪntəˈliːv] VT interfoliar; (*Comput*) intercalar.

interleaving [ˌɪntəˈliːvɪŋ] N interfoliación *f*; (*Comput*) intercalación *f*.

inter-library [ˌɪntəˈlaɪbrərɪ] ATTR: **~ loan** préstamo *m* interbibliotecario.

interline [ˌɪntəˈlaɪn] VT (a) (*Typ*) interlinear. (b) (*Sew*) entretelar.

interlinear [ˌɪntəˈlɪnɪəʳ] ADJ interlineal.

interlink [ˌɪntəˈlɪŋk] VT vincular, enlazar.

interlinked [ˌɪntəˈlɪŋkt] ADJ vinculados (entre sí).

interlock [ˌɪntəˈlɒk] **1** VT trabar, unir, entrelazar; **wheels** endentar, engranar.
2 VI trabarse, unirse, entrelazarse; (*wheels etc*) endentarse, engranar; **the parts of the plan ~** las partes del plan tienen una fuerte trabazón.

interlocutor [ˌɪntəˈlɒkjʊtəʳ] N interlocutor *m*, -ora *f*.

interloper [ˈɪntələʊpəʳ] N intruso *m*, -a *f*; (*Comm*) intérlope *m*, comerciante *m* (*etc*) no autorizado.

interlude [ˈɪntəluːd] N intervalo *m*, intermedio *m*; (*rest*) descanso *m*; (*Theat: playlet, interval*) intermedio *m*; (*Mus*) interludio *m*.

intermarriage [ˌɪntəˈmærɪdʒ] N matrimonio *m* mixto; matrimonio *m* entre parientes.

intermarry [ˈɪntəˈmærɪ] VI casarse (parientes *or* personas de distintas razas, religiones *etc*); **in this village they have intermarried for centuries** en este pueblo se vienen casando los parientes desde hace siglos.

intermediary [ˌɪntəˈmiːdɪərɪ] **1** ADJ intermediario.
2 N intermediario *m*, -a *f*.

intermediate [ˌɪntəˈmiːdɪət] **1** ADJ intermedio, medio; intermediario; **~ goods** productos *mpl* intermedios; **~ range ballistic missile** misil *m* balístico de alcance medio; **~ range weapon** arma *f* de medio alcance; **~ stop** escala *f*.
2 N (*US*) (*person*) intermediario *m*, -a *f*; (*Aut*) coche *m* de tamaño mediano.

interment [ɪnˈtɜːmənt] N entierro *m*.

intermezzo [ˌɪntəˈmetsəʊ] N intermezzo *m*.

interminable [ɪnˈtɜːmɪnəbl] ADJ inacabable, interminable.

interminably [ɪnˈtɜːmɪnəblɪ] ADV: **he spoke ~** habló como si nunca fuera a acabar.

intermingle [ˌɪntəˈmɪŋgl] **1** VT entremezclar.
2 VI entremezclarse.

intermission [ˌɪntəˈmɪʃən] N intermisión *f*, interrupción *f*, intervalo *m*; (*Theat*) descanso *m*; **it went on without ~** continuó sin interrupción.

intermittent [ˌɪntəˈmɪtənt] ADJ intermitente.

intermittently [ˌɪntəˈmɪtəntlɪ] ADV a intervalos, a ratos.

intern **1** [ɪnˈtɜːn] VT internar, recluir, encerrar.
2 [ˈɪntɜːn] N (*US Med*) interno *m*, -a *f* de hospital.

internal [ɪnˈtɜːnl] ADJ interno, interior; **~ audit** auditoría *f* interna; **~ combustion engine** motor *m* de explosión; **I~ Revenue Service** (*US*) Hacienda *f*, Fisco *m*; **as we know from ~ evidence** como sabemos por indicios internos; *ver también* TREASURY.

internalization [ɪnˌtɜːnəlaɪˈzeɪʃən] N interiorización *f*.

internalize [ɪnˈtɜːnəlaɪz] VT interiorizar.

internally [ɪnˈtɜːnəlɪ] ADV interiormente; **not to be taken ~** (*Med*) sólo para uso externo.

internal market [ɪnˈtɜːnlˈmɑːkɪt] N mercado *m* interno, mercado *m* interior.

international [ˌɪntəˈnæʃnəl] **1** ADJ internacional; **I~ Atomic Energy Authority** Organización *f* Internacional de Energía Atómica; **I~ Brigade** (*1936*) Brigadas *fpl* Internacionales; **I~ Chamber of Commerce** Cámara *f* de Comercio Internacional; **I~ Court of Justice** Corte *f* Internacional de Justicia; **~ date line** línea *f* de cambio de fecha; **I~ Labour Organization** Organización *f* Internacional del Trabajo; **~ law** derecho *m* internacional, derecho *m* de gentes; **I~ Monetary Fund** Fondo *m* Monetario Internacional; **~ money order** giro *m* postal internacional; **I~ Standards Organization** Organización *f* Internacional de Normalización.
2 N (a) (*Sport: game*) partido *m* internacional, (*player*) jugador *m*, -ora *f* internacional. (b) **I~** (*Pol*) Internacional *f*.

Internationale [ˌɪntəˌnæʃəˈnɑːl] N Internacional *f*.

internationalism [ɪntəˈnæʃnəlɪzəm] N internacionalismo *m*.

internationalist [ˌɪntəˈnæʃnəlɪst] **1** ADJ internacionalista.
2 N internacionalista *mf*.

internationalize [ˌɪntəˈnæʃnəlaɪz] VT internacionalizar.

internationally [ɪntəˈnæʃnəlɪ] ADV internacionalmente.

internecine [ˌɪntəˈniːsaɪn] ADJ: **~ war** guerra *f* de aniquilación mutua.

internee [ˌɪntɜːˈniː] N internado *m*, -a *f*.

Internet [ˈɪntənet] N: **the ~** (el *or* la) Internet; **to surf the ~** navegar por Internet.

internment [ɪnˈtɜːnmənt] **1** N internamiento *m*; internación *f*.
2 ATTR: **~ camp** campo *m* de internamiento.

interoperability [ˌɪntərɒpərəˈbɪlɪtɪ] N (*Comput*) interoperabilidad *f*.

interpersonal [ˌɪntəˈpɜːsənl] ADJ entre personas, interpersonal.

interphone [ˈɪntəˌfəʊn] N interfono *m*.

interplanetary [ˌɪntəˈplænɪtərɪ] ADJ interplanetario.

interplay [ˈɪntəpleɪ] N interacción *f*.

Interpol [ˈɪntəˌpɒl] N ABBR *of* **International Criminal Police Organization** Interpol *f*.

interpolate [ɪnˈtɜːpəleɪt] VT interpolar.

interpolation [ɪnˌtɜːpəˈleɪʃən] N interpolación *f*.

interpose [ˌɪntəˈpəʊz] VT interponer; *remark* introducir, hacer de paso; **'never!', ~d John** '¡jamás!', cortó Juan.

▼ **interpret** [ɪnˈtɜːprɪt] **1** VT interpretar; (*translate*) interpretar, traducir; (*understand*) entender, explicar; **how are we to ~ that remark?** ¿cómo hemos de entender esa observación?; **if I ~ your wishes correctly** si entiendo bien sus deseos; **that is not how I ~ it** yo lo entiendo de otro modo.
2 VI interpretar; servir de intérprete (*for* para).

interpretation [ɪnˌtɜːprɪˈteɪʃən] N interpretación *f*; traducción *f*; (*meaning*) significado *m*; **what ~ am I to place on your conduct?** ¿cómo he de entender tu conducta?; **the words bear another ~** las palabras tienen otro significado, las palabras pueden entenderse de otro modo.

interpretative [ɪnˈtɜːprɪtətɪv] ADJ interpretativo, aclaratorio, explicativo.

interpreter [ɪnˈtɜːprɪtəʳ] N intérprete *mf*.

interpreting [ɪnˈtɜːprɪtɪŋ] N interpretación *f*.

interregnum [ˌɪntəˈregnəm] N interregno *m*.

interrelate [ˌɪntərɪˈleɪt] VT interrelacionar.

interrelated [ˌɪntərɪˈleɪtɪd] ADJ interrelacionado.

interrelation [ˌɪntərɪˈleɪʃən] N interrelación *f*.

interrelationship [ˌɪntərɪˈleɪʃənʃɪp] N interrelación *f*.

interrogate [ɪnˈterəgeɪt] VT interrogar (*also Comput*).

interrogation [ɪnˌterəˈgeɪʃən] **1** N interrogación *f*.
2 ATTR: **~ mark**, **~ point** signo *m* (*or* punto *m*) de interrogación.

interrogative [ˌɪntəˈrɒgətɪv] **1** ADJ interrogativo.
2 N interrogativo *m*.

interrogatively [ˌɪntəˌrɒgətɪvlɪ] ADV interrogativamente.

interrogator [ɪnˈterəgeɪtəʳ] N interrogador *m*, -ora *f*.

interrogatory [ˌɪntəˈrɒgətərɪ] ADJ interrogante.

interrupt [ˌɪntəˈrʌpt] VTI interrumpir.

interruption [ɪntəˈrʌpʃən] N interrupción *f*.

intersect [ˌɪntəˈsekt] **1** VT cruzar, cortar.
2 VI (*Geom*) intersecarse; (*roads etc*) cruzarse.

intersection [ˌɪntəˈsekʃən] N intersección *f*; cruce *m*.

intersperse [ˌɪntəˈspɜːs] VT esparcir, entremezclar; **dashes ~d with dots** rayas con puntos a intervalos (*or* a ratos); **a speech ~d with jokes** un discurso salpicado de chistes.

interstate [ˌɪntəˈsteɪt] ADJ (*esp US*) interestatal; **~ highway** autopista *f*.

interstellar [ˌɪntəˈsteləʳ] ADJ interestelar.

interstice [ɪnˈtɜːstɪs] N intersticio *m*.

intertextuality [ˌɪntətekstjuˈælɪtɪ] N intertextualidad *f*.

intertwine [ˌɪntəˈtwaɪn] **1** VT entrelazar, entretejer.
2 VI entrelazarse, entretejerse.

interurban [ˌɪntɜːrˈɜːbən] ADJ interurbano.

interval [ˈɪntəvəl] N intervalo *m*; (*Theat*) descanso *m*, intermedio *m*; (*more formally*) entreacto *m*; (*TV*) intermedio *m*; (*Sport etc*) descanso *m*; **at ~s** de vez en cuando, de trecho a trecho, a ratos, a intervalos; **at rare ~s** muy de tarde en tarde; **at regular ~s** con regularidad; **the**

work went on without an ~ el trabajo continuó sin interrupción; **there was an ~ for meditation** se hizo una pausa para la meditación.

intervene [ˌɪntəˈviːn] VI **(a)** (*person*) intervenir (*in* en); tomar parte, participar (*in* en). **(b)** (*occur*) surgir, interponerse, sobrevenir; **if nothing ~s to prevent it** si no surge nada que lo impida.

intervening [ˌɪntəˈviːnɪŋ] ADJ intermedio.

intervention [ˌɪntəˈvenʃən] [1] N intervención *f*.
  [2] ATTR: **~ price** precio *m* de intervención.

interventionism [ˌɪntəˈvenʃənɪzəm] N dirigismo *m*.

interventionist [ˌɪntəˈvenʃənɪst] [1] ADJ dirigista.
  [2] N dirigista *mf*.

▼ **interview** [ˈɪntəvjuː] [1] N entrevista *f*, (*for press, TV etc*) interviú *f*; **to have an ~ with sb** entrevistarse con uno.
  [2] VT entrevistarse con, (*for press, TV etc*) hacer una interviú a, interviuvar; **3% of those ~ed did not know that ...** un 3 por cien de los entrevistados ignoraban que ...

interviewee [ˌɪntəˌvjuːˈiː] N persona *f* entrevistada.

interviewer [ˈɪntəvjuːəʳ] N interviuvador *m*, -ora *f*; (*Press*) reportero *m*, periodista *mf*.

inter vivos [ˈɪntəˈviːvɒs] ADJ (*Jur*): **~ gift** donación *f* inter vivos.

inter-war [ˌɪntəˈwɔːʳ] ADJ: **the ~ years** el período de entreguerras, los años entre las guerras.

interweave [ˌɪntəˈwiːv] (*irr. V* **weave**) VT entretejer.

intestate [ɪnˈtestɪt] ADJ intestado.

intestinal [ˌɪntesˈtaɪnl] ADJ intestinal.

intestine [ɪnˈtestɪn] N intestino *m*; **large ~** intestino *m* grueso; **small ~** intestino *m* delgado.

intifada [ˌɪntɪˈfaːdə] N intifada *f*.

intimacy [ˈɪntɪməsɪ] N intimidad *f*; (*euph*) relaciones *fpl* íntimas; **intimacies** familiaridades *fpl*.

intimate [1] [ˈɪntɪmeɪt] VT dar a entender, indicar, intimar.
  [2] [ˈɪntɪmɪt] ADJ íntimo; *friendship etc* estrecho; *knowledge* profundo, detallado; *detail etc* personal, privado; **they are ~ friends** son íntimos amigos; **they are very ~** son muy amigos; **he was ~ with her** (*euph*) tuvo relaciones íntimas con ella; **they became ~** se intimaron; **A became ~ with B** A se intimó con B.
  [3] [ˈɪntɪmɪt] N amigo *m*, -a *f* de confianza; (*pej*) compinche *m*.

intimately [ˈɪntɪmɪtlɪ] ADV íntimamente; a fondo, profundamente.

intimation [ˌɪntɪˈmeɪʃən] N (*news*) indicación *f*, intimación *f*; (*hint*) insinuación *f*, indirecta *f*; **it was the first ~ we had had of it** fue la primera indicación que habíamos tenido de ello.

intimidate [ɪnˈtɪmɪdeɪt] VT intimidar, acobardar, amedrentar.

intimidating [ɪnˈtɪmɪdeɪtɪŋ] ADJ amedrentador.

intimidation [ɪnˌtɪmɪˈdeɪʃən] N intimidación *f*.

intimidatory [ɪnˈtɪmɪˌdeɪtərɪ] ADJ intimidatorio.

into [ˈɪntʊ] PREP en; a; dentro de; hacia el interior de; **to put sth ~ a box** poner algo en una caja; **to go ~ the wood** penetrar en el bosque; **to go off ~ the desert** ir hacia el interior del desierto; **to go ~ town** ir a la ciudad; **it got ~ the cage** entró en la jaula; **they got ~ the plane** subieron al avión; **it fell ~ the lake** cayó al lago, cayó en el lago; **to change sth ~ sth else** convertir algo en otra cosa; **to translate a text ~ Latin** traducir un texto al latín; **to grow ~ a man** hacerse hombre; **she's ~ spiritualism*** se le ha dado la manía del espiritismo, le ha dado por el espiritismo; **what are you ~ now?*** ¿a qué te dedicas ahora?

▼ **intolerable** [ɪnˈtɒlərəbl] ADJ intolerable, inaguantable, insufrible; **it is ~ that ...** no se puede consentir que + *subj*.

intolerably [ɪnˈtɒlərəblɪ] ADJ insufriblemente; **he is ~ vain** es tremendamente vanidoso.

intolerance [ɪnˈtɒlərəns] N intolerancia *f*, intransigencia *f*.

intolerant [ɪnˈtɒlərənt] ADJ intolerante (*of* con, para), intransigente.

intonation [ˌɪntəʊˈneɪʃən] N entonación *f*.

intone [ɪnˈtəʊn] VT entonar; (*Eccl etc*) salmodiar.

in toto [ɪnˈtəʊtəʊ] ADV en total, en conjunto.

intoxicant [ɪnˈtɒksɪkənt] [1] ADJ embriagador.
  [2] N bebida *f* alcohólica.

intoxicate [ɪnˈtɒksɪkeɪt] VT embriagar (*also fig*); (*Med*) intoxicar.

intoxicated [ɪnˈtɒksɪkeɪtɪd] ADJ ebrio, borracho; **to be ~ with** (*fig*) estar ebrio de.

intoxicating [ɪnˈtɒksɪkeɪtɪŋ] ADJ embriagador; **~ drink** bebida *f* alcohólica.

intoxication [ɪnˌtɒksɪˈkeɪʃən] N embriaguez *f* (*also fig*); (*Med*) intoxicación *f*.

intra... [ˈɪntrə] PREF intra...

intractability [ɪnˌtræktəˈbɪlɪtɪ] N (*of person*) indocilidad *f*, intratabilidad *f*; (*problem*) insolubilidad *f*; (*situation*) dificultad *f*; (*Med, disease*) incurabilidad *f*.

intractable [ɪnˈtræktəbl] ADJ *person* intratable; *material* difícil de trabajar; *problem* insoluble, espinoso.

intramural [ˌɪntrəˈmjʊərəl] ADJ entre muros.

intramuscular [ˌɪntrəˈmʌskjʊləʳ] ADJ intramuscular.

intransigence [ɪnˈtrænsɪdʒəns] N intransigencia *f*.

intransigent [ɪnˈtrænsɪdʒənt] ADJ intransigente.

intransitive [ɪnˈtrænsɪtɪv] ADJ intransitivo, neutro.

intransitivity [ɪnˌtrænsɪˈtɪvɪtɪ] N intransitividad *f*.

intrauterine [ˌɪntrəˈjuːtəraɪn] ADJ intrauterino; **~ coil, ~ device** dispositivo *m* intrauterino, espiral *f*.

intravenous [ˌɪntrəˈviːnəs] ADJ intravenoso.

intravenously [ˌɪntrəˈviːnəslɪ] ADV por vía intravenosa.

in-tray [ˈɪnˌtreɪ] N bandeja *f* de entrada.

intrepid [ɪnˈtrepɪd] ADJ intrépido.

intrepidity [ˌɪntrɪˈpɪdɪtɪ] N intrepidez *f*.

intrepidly [ɪnˈtrepɪdlɪ] ADV intrépidamente.

intricacy [ˈɪntrɪkəsɪ] N lo intrincado; complejidad *f*.

intricate [ˈɪntrɪkɪt] ADJ intrincado; complejo.

intricately [ˈɪntrɪkɪtlɪ] ADV intrincadamente, de modo intrincado.

intrigue [ɪnˈtriːg] [1] N intriga *f*; (*amorous*) amoríos *mpl*, lío *m*.
  [2] VT intrigar, interesar, fascinar, despertar la curiosidad de; **she ~s me** ella me fascina; **I am ~d to know whether** me interesa saber si; **I am much ~d by your news** me interesa muchísimo esa noticia; **we were ~d by a sign** nos llamó la atención un letrero, un letrero despertó nuestra curiosidad.
  [3] VI intrigar, andar en intrigas, meterse en líos.

intriguer [ɪnˈtriːgəʳ] N intrigante *mf*.

intriguing [ɪnˈtriːgɪŋ] ADJ **(a)** (*scheming*) enredador.
  (b) (*fascinating*) intrigante, fascinador, curioso, interesante; seductor; misterioso; **a most ~ problem** un problema interesantísimo; **an ~ gadget** un chisme de los más curiosos; **how very ~!** ¡qué raro!, ¡muy interesante!

intrinsic [ɪnˈtrɪnsɪk] ADJ intrínseco; **~ value** valor *m* intrínseco.

intrinsically [ɪnˈtrɪnsɪklɪ] ADV intrínsecamente.

intro... [ˈɪntrəʊ, ˈɪntrə] PREFIX intro...

introduce [ˌɪntrəˈdjuːs] VT **(a)** (*insert*) introducir, meter, insertar (*into* en).
  (b) (*put forward*) *new thing, reform etc* introducir; *new fashion* introducir, poner de moda, lanzar; *new product, bill* presentar; *newcomer* presentar, dar a conocer; *book* (PREF*ace*) prologar; *subject into conversation* mencionar, sacar a colación; **be careful how you ~ the subject** hay que abordar el tema con mucho cuidado; **I was ~d into a dark room** me hicieron entrar en un cuarto oscuro; **I was ~d into his presence** me llevaron ante él; **I was ~d to chess at 8** empecé a jugar al ajedrez a los 8 años; **I was ~d to Milton too young** me hicieron leer a Milton demasiado temprano.
  (c) *person* presentar; **may I ~ Mr X?** permítame presentarle al Sr X; **I don't think we've been ~d** creo que no nos han presentado.

introduction [ˌɪntrəˈdʌkʃən] N introducción *f*, inserción *f*; (*of persons*) presentación *f*; (*to book*) prólogo *m*, introducción *f*; **my ~ to life in Cadiz** mi primera experiencia de la vida en Cádiz; **to give sb an ~ to a person** dar a uno una carta de recomendación para una persona; **will you make the ~s?** ¿quieres presentarnos?

introductory [ˌɪntrəˈdʌktərɪ] ADJ preliminar; **~ offer** oferta *f* preliminar.

introit [ˈɪntrɔɪt] N introito *m*.

introspection [ˌɪntrəʊˈspekʃən] N introspección *f*.

introspective [ˌɪntrəʊˈspektɪv] ADJ introspectivo.

introspectiveness [ˌɪntrəʊˈspektɪvnɪs] N introspección *f*.

introversion [ˌɪntrəʊˈvɜːʃən] N introversión *f*.

introvert [ˈɪntrəʊvɜːt] [1] ADJ introvertido.
  [2] N introvertido *m*, -a *f*.

introverted [ˌɪntrəʊˈvɜːtɪd] ADJ introvertido.

intrude [ɪnˈtruːd] [1] VT introducir (sin derecho), meter (*in* en); imponer (*upon* a).
  [2] VI entrometerse, encajarse (*upon* en); estorbar, molestar; **am I intruding?** ¿te molesto?, (*esp LAm*) ¿te estorbo?; **to ~ on sb's privacy** molestar a uno cuando quiere estar a solas;; **sometimes sentimentality ~s** a veces se asoma el sentimentalismo; **he lets no feelings of pity ~** no deja lugar a la compasión.

intruder [ɪnˈtruːdəʳ] N intruso *m*, -a *f*.

intrusion [ɪnˈtruːʒən] N intrusión *f*; invasión *f*; **the ~ of sentimentality** la aparición del sentimentalismo; **please pardon the ~** siento tener que molestarle.

intrusive [ɪnˈtruːsɪv] ADJ intruso.

intuit [ɪnˈtjuːɪt] VT (*esp US*) intuir.

intuition [ˌɪntjuːˈɪʃən] N intuición *f*.

intuitive [ɪnˈtjuːɪtɪv] ADJ intuitivo.

intuitively [ɪnˈtjuːɪtɪvlɪ] ADV intuitivamente, por intuición.

Inuit [ˈɪnjuːɪt], PL **Inuit** or **Inuits** [1] ADJ Inuit.
  [2] N: **the ~s** los Inuit.

inundate [ˈɪnʌndeɪt] VT inundar (*also fig*).

inundation [ˌɪnʌnˈdeɪʃən] N inundación *f*.

inure [ɪnˈjʊəʳ] VT acostumbrar, habituar (*to* a), endurecer; **to be ~d to** estar habituado a.

inv. ABBR *of* **invoice**.

invade [ɪn'veɪd] VT invadir.

invader [ɪn'veɪdəʳ] N invasor *m*, -ora *f*.

invading [ɪn'veɪdɪŋ] ADJ invasor.

invalid¹ [ɪn'vælɪd] ADJ inválido, nulo; **to become ~** caducar.

invalid² ['ɪnvəlɪd] **1** ADJ inválido, enfermo, minusválido.
　2 N inválido *m*, -a *f*, minusválido *m*, -a *f*.
　3 ATTR: **~ car, ~ carriage** (*Brit*) coche *m* de inválido.
　4 VT: **to ~ sb out of the army** (*esp Brit*) licenciar a uno por invalidez.

invalidate [ɪn'vælɪdeɪt] VT invalidar, anular, quitar valor a; *argument* destruir.

invalidity [ˌɪnvə'lɪdɪtɪ] N invalidez *f*; nulidad *f*.

invaluable [ɪn'væljʊəbl] ADJ inestimable, inapreciable.

invariable [ɪn'veərɪəbl] ADJ invariable, inalterable.

invariably [ɪn'veərɪəblɪ] ADV invariablemente; **it ~ happens that ...** ocurre siempre que ...; **he is ~ late** siempre llega tarde.

invasion [ɪn'veɪʒən] N invasión *f*.

invasive [ɪn'veɪsɪv] ADJ invasor.

invective [ɪn'vektɪv] N invectiva *f*; palabras *fpl* fuertes, improperios *mpl*.

inveigh [ɪn'veɪ] VI: **to ~ against** vituperar, hablar en contra de, condenar.

inveigle [ɪn'viːgl] VT: **she ~d him up to her room** le indujo mañosamente a subir a su habitación; **he was ~d into the duke's service** fue persuadido a entrar a servir al duque; **to ~ sb into sth** inducir (engañosamente) a uno a algo; **to ~ sb into doing sth** persuadir (mañosamente) a uno a hacer algo; **he let himself be ~d into it** se dejó engatusar para que lo hiciera.

invent [ɪn'vent] VT inventar; idear.

invention [ɪn'venʃən] N (a) (*gadget etc*) invención *f*, invento *m*. (b) (*inventiveness*) inventiva *f*. (c) (*falsehood*) ficción *f*, mentira *f*; **it's sheer ~ on her part** son cosas que ella ha soñado, son cosas de ella; **it's ~ from start to finish** es mentira desde el principio hasta el fin.

inventive [ɪn'ventɪv] ADJ inventivo, ingenioso.

inventiveness [ɪn'ventɪvnɪs] N inventiva *f*, ingenio *m*.

inventor [ɪn'ventəʳ] N inventor *m*, -ora *f*.

inventory ['ɪnvəntrɪ] **1** N inventario *m*.
　2 ATTR: **~ control** control *m* de existencias (*or* del inventario).
　3 VT inventariar.

inverse ['ɪn'vɜːs] **1** ADJ inverso.
　2 N: **the ~** lo inverso, lo contrario.

inversely [ɪn'vɜːslɪ] ADV a la inversa.

inversion [ɪn'vɜːʃən] N inversión *f*.

invert [ɪn'vɜːt] VT invertir, volver al revés, trastrocar.

invertebrate [ɪn'vɜːtɪbrɪt] **1** ADJ invertebrado.
　2 N invertebrado *m*.

inverted [ɪn'vɜːtɪd] ADJ: **~ commas** (*Brit*) comillas *fpl*; **in ~ commas** entre comillas; **~ snob** esnob *mf* a la inversa; **~ snobbery** esnobismo *m* a la inversa.

invert sugar ['ɪnvɜːt'ʃʊgəʳ] N azúcar *m* invertido.

invest [ɪn'vest] **1** VT (a) *money* invertir (*in* en); **~ed capital** capital *m* invertido.
　(b) (*Mil*) sitiar, cercar.
　(c) **to ~ sb with sth** investir a uno de (*or* con) algo; **to be ~ed with a dignity** revestirse con una dignidad; **he ~ed it with a certain mystery** lo revistió con cierto misterio; **he seems to ~ it with some importance** parece que da cierta importancia a la cosa.
　2 VI: **to ~ in** *company etc* invertir dinero en; (*buy*) comprar, adquirir; (*support*) apoyar, demostrar tener confianza en; **to ~ with** invertir dinero en.

investigate [ɪn'vestɪgeɪt] VT investigar; examinar, estudiar.

investigation [ɪnˌvestɪ'geɪʃən] N investigación *f*; pesquisa *f*; examen *m*, estudio *m* (*into* de).

investigative [ɪn'vestɪˌgeɪtɪv] ADJ investigador; **~ journalism** periodismo *m* de investigación.

investigator [ɪn'vestɪgeɪtəʳ] N investigador *m*, -ora *f*.

investigatory [ɪn'vestɪˌgeɪtərɪ] ADJ: **~ group/panel** grupo investigador/comisión investigadora.

investiture [ɪn'vestɪtʃəʳ] N investidura *f*.

investment [ɪn'vestmənt] **1** N (a) (*Comm*) inversión *f*; **~s** inversiones *fpl*, fondos *mpl* invertidos, (*shares*) valores *mpl* en cartera.
　(b) (*Mil*) sitio *m*, cerco *m*.
　(c) (*investiture*) investidura *f*.
　2 ATTR: **~ analyst** analista *mf* financiero; **~ bank** (*US*) banco *m* de inversión; **~ company** compañía *f* de inversiones; **~ goods** bienes *mpl* de inversión; **~ grant** subvención *f* para la inversión; **~ income** ingresos *mpl* procedentes de inversiones; **~ policy** política *f* inversionista; **~ portfolio** cartera *f* de inversiones; **~ trust** compañía *f* inversionista, sociedad *f* de cartera.

investor [ɪn'vestəʳ] N inversionista *mf*.

inveterate [ɪn'vetərɪt] ADJ inveterado, empedernido, habitual, incu-

rable.

invidious [ɪn'vɪdɪəs] ADJ odioso, injusto.

invigilate [ɪn'vɪdʒɪleɪt] (*Brit*) **1** VT *examination* vigilar.
　2 VI vigilar (durante los exámenes).

invigilator [ɪn'vɪdʒɪleɪtəʳ] N (*Brit*) celador *m*, -ora *f*.

invigorate [ɪn'vɪgəreɪt] VT vigorizar; *campaign etc* avivar, estimular.

invigorating [ɪn'vɪgəreɪtɪŋ] ADJ vigorizante, vigorizador.

invincibility [ɪnˌvɪnsɪ'bɪlɪtɪ] N invencibilidad *f*.

invincible [ɪn'vɪnsəbl] ADJ invencible.

invincibly [ɪn'vɪnsəblɪ] ADV de manera invencible; **~ ignorant** irremediablemente ignorante; **~ right** irrebatiblemente correcto.

inviolability [ɪnˌvaɪələ'bɪlɪtɪ] N inviolabilidad *f*.

inviolable [ɪn'vaɪələbl] ADJ inviolable.

inviolate [ɪn'vaɪəlɪt] ADJ inviolado.

invisibility [ɪnˌvɪzə'bɪlɪtɪ] N invisibilidad *f*.

invisible [ɪn'vɪzəbl] **1** ADJ invisible; **~ assets** activo *m* invisible; **~ balance** balance *m* invisible; **~ earnings** ingresos *mpl* invisibles; **~ exports** exportaciones *fpl* invisibles; **~ imports** importaciones *fpl* invisibles; **~ ink** tinta *f* simpática; **~ mending** puntada *f* invisible.
　2 ~s NPL (*Comm*) ingresos *mpl* invisibles.

invisibly [ɪn'vɪzɪblɪ] ADV invisiblemente.

▼ **invitation** [ˌɪnvɪ'teɪʃən] **1** N invitación *f*; convite *m*.
　2 ATTR: **~ card** tarjeta *f* de invitación.

invitational [ˌɪnvɪ'teɪʃənl] ADJ (*Sport*) *event, tournament* invitacional, *en el que sólo participan deportistas invitados*.

▼ **invite 1** [ɪn'vaɪt] VT (a) (*gen*) invitar, (*esp to food and drink*) convidar; **to ~ sb to supper** invitar a uno a cenar; **to ~ sb to do sth** invitar a uno a hacer algo; **to ~ sb to have a drink** convidar a uno a tomar algo.
　(b) (*request*) pedir, rogar; **he ~s our opinions** pide nuestras opiniones.
　(c) *trouble etc* correr a, buscarse; **it's just inviting trouble** esto es crear dificultades para sí; **to do so is to ~ defeat** hacer esto es procurar la propia derrota.
　(d) (*induce*) inducir a, sugerir; **A ~s comparison with B** A nos induce a compararlo con B, se impone la comparación de A con B; **she seems to ~ stares** según parece le gusta que la mire la gente.
　2 ['ɪnvaɪt] N (*) invitación *f*.
　◆ **invite in** VT invitar a entrar.
　◆ **invite out** VT invitar, convidar (*a un restaurante, al cine etc*).
　◆ **invite over** VT convidar, invitar (*a casa*).

inviting [ɪn'vaɪtɪŋ] ADJ atractivo, atrayente, tentador; *look* incitante, provocativo; *food* apetitoso.

invitingly [ɪn'vaɪtɪŋlɪ] ADV de modo atractivo (*etc*); de modo incitante; apetitosamente.

in vitro [ɪn'viːtrəʊ] ADJ, ADV in vitro; **~ fertilization** fecundación *f* in vitro.

invocation [ˌɪnvəʊ'keɪʃən] N invocación *f*.

▼ **invoice** ['ɪnvɔɪs] **1** N factura *f*; **as per ~** según factura; **to send an ~** pasar factura, presentar factura.
　2 ATTR: **~ clerk** facturador *m*, -ora *f*.
　3 VT facturar; **~d value** valor *m* según facturación.

invoicing ['ɪnvɔɪsɪŋ] N facturación *f*.

invoke [ɪn'vəʊk] VT invocar; *aid* suplicar, implorar; *law* recurrir a, acogerse a; *spirit* conjurar.

involuntarily [ɪn'vɒləntərɪlɪ] ADV involuntariamente, sin querer.

involuntary [ɪn'vɒləntərɪ] ADJ involuntario.

involuted [ˌɪnvə'luːtɪd] ADJ *design, system* intrincado.

▼ **involve** [ɪn'vɒlv] **1** VT (a) (*physically*) enredar, enmarañar; *matter* complicar, enentebrecer.
　(b) (*implicate etc*) implicar, involucrar, comprometer; **to ~ sb in a quarrel** mezclar a uno en una disputa; **the persons ~d** los interesados; **the forces ~d** las fuerzas en juego; **a question of principle is ~d** aquí está en juego un principio; **to be ~d in** estar implicado en, estar metido en, andar envuelto en; **to be ~d in a plot** estar implicado en un complot; **was he ~d in it?** ¿anduvo él metido en ello?, ¿tuvo él que ver con el asunto?; **how did you come to be ~d?** ¿cómo llegaste a estar envuelto en esto?; **to get** (*or* **become**) **~d in** meterse en, enredarse en, embrollarse en; **he got ~d with a girl** tuvo un lío con una joven; **I don't want to get ~d** no quiero dejarme ir demasiado lejos, allí no entro yo.
　▼ (c) (*imply*) suponer, implicar, traer consigo, acarrear, ocasionar; **it ~s moving house** ello supone que tendremos que mudar de casa; **it ~d a lot of expense** nos acarreó muchos gastos; **does it ~ much trouble?** ¿esto supone mucho trabajo para Vd?
　2 VR: **to ~ o.s. in** interesarse en; tomar parte en, participar en; (*pej*) involucrarse en.

involved [ɪn'vɒlvd] ADJ complicado; *style* enrevesado, laberíntico; **to become ~, to get ~** complicarse.

involvement [ɪn'vɒlvmənt] N enredo *m*; compromiso *m*; (*difficulty*) apuro *m*, dificultad *f*; **we don't know the extent of his ~** no sabemos hasta qué punto se había comprometido; **his ~ in the plot**

➤ LANGUAGE IN USE:　**invitation:** 1 → 25.1, 25.2, 25.3　**invite:** 1a → 25.3　**invoice:** 1 → 20.6, 20.7　**involve:** 1c → 26.3

su participación en el complot; **we must keep out of ~s** hay que evitar los compromisos.

invulnerability [ɪn,vʌlnərə'bɪlɪtɪ] N invulnerabilidad *f*.

invulnerable [ɪn'vʌlnərəbl] ADJ invulnerable.

inward ['ɪnwəd] ADJ interior, interno; íntimo; espiritual.

inward-looking ['ɪnwəd,lʊkɪŋ] ADJ introvertido.

inwardly ['ɪnwədlɪ] ADV interiormente; *laugh etc* para sí, entre sí, para sus adentros.

inward(s)¹ ['ɪnwəd(z)] ADV hacia dentro, para dentro.

inwards² ['ɪnədz] NPL tripas *fpl*.

in-your-face:, in-yer-face: [,ɪnjə'feɪs] ADJ *attitude, music, theatre* agresivo y descarado.

I/O N (*Comput*) ABBR *of* **input/output** entrada/salida, E/S; **~ error** error *m* de E/S.

IOC N ABBR *of* **International Olympic Committee** Comité *m* Olímpico Internacional, COI *m*.

iodide ['aɪədaɪd] N yoduro *m*.

iodine ['aɪədiːn] N yodo *m*.

iodoform [aɪ'ɒdəfɔːm] N yodoformo *m*.

IOM (*Brit*) ABBR *of* **Isle of Man**.

ion ['aɪən] N ion *m*.

Ionian [aɪ'əʊnɪən] ADJ jonio, jónico.

Ionian Sea [aɪ,əʊnɪən'siː] N Mar *m* Jónico.

Ionic [aɪ'ɒnɪk] ADJ jónico.

ionic [aɪ'ɒnɪk] ADJ (*Chem*) iónico.

ioniser ['aɪənaɪzəʳ] = **ionizer**.

ionize ['aɪənaɪz] VT ionizar.

ionizer ['aɪənaɪzəʳ] N ionizador *m*.

ionosphere [aɪ'ɒnəsfɪəʳ] N ionosfera *f*.

iota [aɪ'əʊtə] N (*letter*) iota *f*; (*fig*) jota *f*, ápice *m*; **there's not one ~ of truth in it** eso no tiene ni pizca de verdad; **if he had an ~ of sense** si tuviera un poquito de inteligencia.

IOU N ABBR *of* **I owe you** pagaré *m*.

IOW (*Brit*) ABBR *of* **Isle of Wight**.

IPA N ABBR *of* **International Phonetic Alphabet**.

ipecacuanha [,ɪpɪkækjʊ'ænə] N ipecacuana *f*.

IQ N ABBR *of* **intelligence quotient** cociente *m* intelectual, C.I. *m*.

IR ABBR *of* **Inland Revenue**.

IRA N (a) (*Pol*) ABBR *of* **Irish Republican Army** IRA *m*. (b) (*US*) ABBR *of* **individual retirement account** cuenta *f* individual para la jubilación.

Irak [ɪ'rɑːk] N Irak *m*, Iraq *m*.

Iraki [ɪ'rɑːkɪ] [1] ADJ iraquí.
[2] N iraquí *mf*.

Iran [ɪ'rɑːn] N Irán *m*.

Iranian [ɪ'reɪnɪən] [1] ADJ iranio, iraní.
[2] N (*ancient*) iranio *m*, -a *f*, (*modern*) iraní *mf*.

Iraq [ɪ'rɑːk] N Irak *m*, Iraq *m*.

Iraqi [ɪ'rɑːkɪ] [1] ADJ iraquí.
[2] N iraquí *mf*.

irascibility [ɪ,ræsɪ'bɪlɪtɪ] N irascibilidad *f*.

irascible [ɪ'ræsɪbl] ADJ irascible, de prontos enojos.

irascibly [ɪ'ræsɪblɪ] ADV: **he said ~** dijo colérico.

irate [aɪ'reɪt] ADJ colérico, enojado, indignado; **he got very ~** se encolerizó mucho.

IRBM N ABBR *of* **intermediate range ballistic missile** misil *m* balístico de alcance medio.

ire [aɪəʳ] N (*liter*) ira *f*, cólera *f*, iracundia *f*; **to rouse sb's ~** provocar la ira de uno; **that always rouses his ~** eso siempre le saca de quicio.

Ireland ['aɪələnd] N Irlanda *f*; **Northern ~** Irlanda *f* del Norte; **Republic of ~** República *f* de Irlanda.

iridescence [,ɪrɪ'desns] N irisación *f*.

iridescent [,ɪrɪ'desnt] ADJ iridiscente, irisado, tornasolado.

iridium [ɪ'rɪdɪəm] N iridio *m*.

iris ['aɪərɪs] N (*Anat*) iris *m*; (*Bot*) lirio *m*.

Irish ['aɪərɪʃ] [1] ADJ irlandés; **~ coffee** café *m* irlandés; **~ stew** estofado *m* irlandés.
[2] N (a) **the ~** los irlandeses. (b) (*Ling*) irlandés *m*.

Irish Free State ['aɪərɪʃfriː'steɪt] N Estado *m* Libre de Irlanda.

Irishman ['aɪərɪʃmən] N, PL **Irishmen** ['aɪərɪʃmən] irlandés *m*.

Irish Sea ['aɪərɪʃ'siː] N Mar *m* de Irlanda.

Irishwoman ['aɪərɪʃ,wʊmən] N, PL **Irishwomen** ['aɪrɪʃ,wɪmɪn] irlandesa *f*.

irk [ɜːk] VT fastidiar, molestar.

irksome ['ɜːksəm] ADJ molesto, pesado, fastidioso.

IRN N (*Brit*) ABBR *of* **Independent Radio News** servicio de noticias en las cadenas de radio privadas.

IRO N (a) (*Brit*) ABBR *of* **inland Revenue Office**. (b) (*US*) ABBR *of* **International Refugee Organization**.

iron ['aɪən] [1] N (a) (*Min*) hierro *m*, fierro *m* (*Méx*); (*fig*) hierro *m*, acero *m*; **man of ~** hombre *m* de acero; **old ~** chatarra *f*, hierro *m* viejo; **to strike while the ~ is hot** a hierro candente batir de repente.
(b) **~s** (*fetters*) hierros *mpl*, grillos *mpl*; (*) (*at table*) cuchillo *m* y tenedor *m*; (*guns*) pistolas *fpl*; **to have too many ~s in the fire** tener demasiados asuntos entre manos; **to put sb in ~s** aherrojar a uno, echar grillos a uno.
(c) (*Golf*) hierro *m*.
(d) (*flat ~*) plancha *f*, planchador *m*.
[2] ATTR de hierro; **I~ Age** Edad *f* de(l) Hierro; **~ constitution** constitución *f* de hierro; **I~ Curtain** telón *m* de acero; **I~ Curtain Countries** (*Hist*) países *mpl* más allá del telón de acero; **the I~ Duke** el Duque de Wellington; **with an ~ hand** (*or* **fist**) con mano de hierro; **the ~ fist in the velvet glove** la mano de hierro en guante de terciopelo; (*Brit Pol*) **the I~ Lady** la Dama de hierro; **~ lung** pulmón *m* de acero, pulmotor *m*; **~ oxide** óxido *m* de hierro; **~ pyrites** pirita *f* ferruginosa; **~ rations** ración *f* de reserva, víveres *mpl* de reserva; **~ and steel industry** (industria *f*) siderúrgica *f*; **~ will** voluntad *f* férrea.
[3] VT *clothes* planchar.
◆ **iron out** VT *unevenness* allanar; *crease* quitar; *difficulties* allanar, suprimir; *problems* suavizar; *differences* nivelar.

ironclad ['aɪənklæd] [1] ADJ acorazado; (*fig*) *guarantee* firme, a toda prueba.
[2] N acorazado *m*.

iron-foundry ['aɪən,faʊndrɪ] N fundición *f* de hierro, fundidora *f* (*LAm*).

ironic(al) [aɪ'rɒnɪk(əl)] ADJ irónico.

ironically [aɪ'rɒnɪkəlɪ] ADV irónicamente; *say etc* con ironía; **~ enough** paradójicamente, como quiso la suerte.

ironing ['aɪənɪŋ] N (*act*) planchado *m*; (*clothes*) ropa *f* por planchar, ropa *f* planchada; **to give a dress an ~** planchar un vestido.

ironing-board ['aɪənɪŋbɔːd] N tabla *f* de planchar.

ironist ['aɪərənɪst] N ironista *mf*; **the master ~** el maestro de la ironía.

ironmonger ['aɪən,mʌŋgəʳ] N (*Brit*) ferretero *m*, quincallero *m*; **~'s (shop)** ferretería *f*, quincallería *f*.

ironmongery ['aɪən,mʌŋgərɪ] N (*Brit*) quincalla *f*, ferretería *f* (*also fig*).

iron ore ['aɪənɔːʳ] N mineral *m* de hierro.

ironstone ['aɪən,stəʊn] N (*china*) porcelana *f* resistente.

ironwork ['aɪənwɜːk] N herraje *m*; obra *f* de hierro.

ironworks ['aɪənwɜːks] N SING AND PL herrería *f*, fundición *f*, fábrica *f* de hierro.

irony ['aɪərənɪ] N ironía *f*; **the ~ of fate** lo irónico del destino; **the ~ of it is that ...** lo irónico es que ...

Iroquois ['ɪrəkwɔɪ] [1] ADJ iroqués.
[2] N (a) iroqués *m*, -esa *f*. (b) (*Ling*) iroqués *m*.

irradiate [ɪ'reɪdɪeɪt] VT irradiar.

irradiation [ɪ,reɪdɪ'eɪʃən] N irradiación *f*.

irrational [ɪ'ræʃənl] ADJ irracional.

irrationality [ɪ,ræʃə'nælɪtɪ] N irracionalidad *f*.

irrationally [ɪ'ræʃnəlɪ] ADV irracionalmente.

irreconcilable [ɪ,rekən'saɪləbl] ADJ irreconciliable, inconciliable.

irrecoverable [,ɪrɪ'kʌvərəbl] ADJ irrecuperable, incobrable.

irredeemable [,ɪrɪ'diːməbl] ADJ irredimible; (*Comm*) perpetuo, no amortizable.

irredeemably [,ɪrɪ'diːməblɪ] ADV: **~ lost/ruined** perdido/arruinado sin remedio.

irreducible [,ɪrɪ'djuːsəbl] ADJ irreducible.

irrefutable [,ɪrɪ'fjuːtəbl] ADJ irrefutable, irrebatible.

irregardless [ɪrɪ'gɑːdlɪs] ADV (*US*) de cualquier modo; a pesar de todo.

irregular [ɪ'regjʊləʳ] [1] ADJ irregular; anormal; *surface* desigual; (*unlawful*) ilegal, no conforme con la ley; **this is really most ~** realmente esto no se debiera permitir.
[2] N guerrillero *m*.

irregularity [ɪ,regjʊ'lærɪtɪ] N irregularidad *f*; anormalidad *f*; desigualdad *f*.

irregularly [ɪ'regjʊləlɪ] ADV de manera irregular.

irrelevance [ɪ'reləvəns] N impertinencia *f*, inoportunidad *f*, inaplicabilidad *f*.

irrelevant [ɪ'reləvənt] ADJ impertinente, inoportuno, inaplicable, fuera de propósito; **that's ~** eso no hace al caso.

irrelevantly [ɪ'reləvəntlɪ] ADV impertinentemente, inoportunamente.

irreligious [,ɪrɪ'lɪdʒəs] ADJ irreligioso.

irremediable [,ɪrɪ'miːdɪəbl] ADJ irremediable.

irremediably [,ɪrɪ'miːdɪəblɪ] ADV irremediablemente.

irremovable [,ɪrɪ'muːvəbl] ADJ inamovible.

irreparable [ɪ'repərəbl] ADJ irreparable.

irreparably [ɪ'repərəblɪ] ADV irreparablemente.

irreplaceable [,ɪrɪ'pleɪsəbl] ADJ insustituible, irreemplazable.

irrepressible [,ɪrɪ'presəbl] ADJ incontrolable, irrefrenable.

irreproachable [,ɪrɪ'prəʊtʃəbl] ADJ irreprochable, intachable.

irresistible [,ɪrɪ'zɪstəbl] ADJ irresistible.

irresistibly [,ɪrɪ'zɪstəblɪ] ADV irresistiblemente.

irresolute [ɪ'rezəluːt] ADJ irresoluto, indeciso.

irresolutely [ɪ'rezəluːtlɪ] ADV irresolutamente, indecisamente.

irresoluteness [ɪ'rezəluːtnɪs] N irresolución *f*, indecisión *f*.

irrespective [ˌɪrɪ'spektɪv]: **~ of** PREP aparte de, sin consideración a, con independencia de.

irresponsibility [ˈɪrɪsˌpɒnsə'bɪlɪtɪ] N irresponsabilidad *f*, falta *f* de seriedad.

irresponsible [ˌɪrɪs'pɒnsəbl] ADJ irresponsable, poco serio.

irresponsibly [ˌɪrɪs'pɒnsəblɪ] ADV irresponsablemente, poco seriamente.

irretrievable [ˌɪrɪ'triːvəbl] ADJ irrecuperable; *error* irreparable.

irretrievably [ˌɪrɪ'triːvəblɪ] ADV: **~ lost** totalmente perdido, perdido sin remedio.

irreverence [ɪ'revərəns] N irreverencia *f*; falta *f* de respeto.

irreverent [ɪ'revərənt] ADJ irreverente, irrespetuoso.

irreverently [ɪ'revərəntlɪ] ADV de modo irreverente, irrespetuosamente.

irreversible [ˌɪrɪ'vɜːsəbl] ADJ *process* irreversible; *decision* irrevocable.

irrevocable [ɪ'revəkəbl] ADJ irrevocable.

irrevocably [ɪ'revəkəblɪ] ADV irrevocablemente.

irrigable ['ɪrɪgəbl] ADJ regable.

irrigate ['ɪrɪgeɪt] VT (*Agr*) regar; (*Med*) irrigar.

irrigated ['ɪrɪgeɪtɪd] ADJ regado; **~ land** tierra *f* de regadío.

irrigation [ˌɪrɪ'geɪʃən] [1] N (*Agr*) riego *m*; (*Med*) irrigación *f*.
[2] ATTR: **~ channel** canal *m* de riego, acequia *f*.

irritability [ˌɪrɪtə'bɪlɪtɪ] N irritabilidad *f*.

irritable ['ɪrɪtəbl] ADJ (*temperament*) irritable, de prontos enojos; (*mood*) de mal humor; **to get ~** ponerse nervioso.

irritably ['ɪrɪtəblɪ] ADV: **he said ~** dijo malhumorado.

irritant ['ɪrɪtənt] N irritante *m*.

irritate ['ɪrɪteɪt] VT (a) irritar, sacar de quicio, impacientar, molestar; **to get ~d** irritarse, enfadarse. (b) (*Med*) irritar.

irritating ['ɪrɪteɪtɪŋ] ADJ *person etc* molesto, pesado, enojoso; *thing* molesto, fastidioso; **it's really most ~** es para sacar a uno de quicio.

irritatingly ['ɪrɪteɪtɪŋlɪ] ADV pesadamente, enojosamente; fastidiosamente.

irritation [ˌɪrɪ'teɪʃən] N (a) irritación *f*, enojo *m*. (b) (*Med*) picazón *f*, picor *m*.

irruption [ɪ'rʌpʃən] N irrupción *f*.

IRS N (*US*) ABBR of **Internal Revenue Service**; *ver también* TREASURY .

is [ɪz] V **be**.

Is. ABBR of **Isle(s)**, **Island(s)** Isla(s) *f(pl)*.

Isaac ['aɪzək] NM Isaac.

Isabel ['ɪzəbel] NF Isabel.

Isaiah [aɪ'zaɪə] NM Isaías.

ISBN N ABBR of **International Standard Book Number** Numeración *f* Internacional Normalizada de Libros, ISBN *f*.

ISDN N ABBR of **Integrated Services Digital Network** Red *f* Digital de Servicios Integrados, RDSI *f*.

-ish [ɪʃ] SUFFIX (a) black**~** negruzco; dear**~** algo caro; small**~** más bien pequeño; cold**~** un poco frío. (b) at four**~** a eso de las 4; **she must be forty~** tendrá alrededor de 40 años.

isinglass ['aɪzɪŋglɑːs] N cola *f* de pescado.

Islam ['ɪzlɑːm] N Islam *m*.

Islamic [ɪz'læmɪk] ADJ islámico; **~ law** derecho *m* islámico; **~ revolution** revolución *f* islámica.

Islamicist [ɪz'læmɪsɪst] N islamista *mf*.

island ['aɪlənd] [1] N isla *f*; (*in street*) refugio *m*.
[2] ATTR isleño.

islander ['aɪləndər] N isleño *m*, -a *f*.

isle [aɪl] N isla *f*.

islet ['aɪlɪt] N isleta *f*, islote *m*.

ism ['ɪzəm] N (*pej*) ismo *m*.

isn't ['ɪznt] = **is not**.

ISO N ABBR of **International Standards Organization** Organización *f* Internacional de Normalización, OIN *f*.

iso... ['aɪsəʊ] PREF iso...

isobar ['aɪsəʊbɑːr] N isobara *f*.

isolate ['aɪsəʊleɪt] VT aislar.

isolated ['aɪsəʊleɪtɪd] ADJ *place etc* aislado, apartado; *case* único; **to feel ~** sentirse aislado.

isolation [ˌaɪsəʊ'leɪʃən] [1] N aislamiento *m*; **we cannot discuss this in ~** no podemos discutir esto como tema independiente; **things like this don't happen in ~** estas cosas no ocurren aisladas; **she's being kept in ~** (*Med*) está en una sala de aislamiento.
[2] ATTR: **~ hospital** hospital *m* de contagiosos; **~ ward** sala *f* de aislamiento.

isolationism [ˌaɪsəʊ'leɪʃənɪzəm] N aislacionismo *m*.

isolationist [aɪsəʊ'leɪʃənɪst] [1] ADJ aislacionista.
[2] N aislacionista *mf*.

Isolde [ɪ'zɒldə] NF Iseo, Isolda.

isomer ['aɪsəmər] N isómero *m*.

isometric [ˌaɪsəʊ'metrɪk] [1] ADJ isométrico; **~ exercises** ejercicios *mpl* isométricos.
[2] **~s** NPL isométrica *f*.

isomorphic [ˌaɪsəʊ'mɔːfɪk] ADJ isomorfo.

isosceles [aɪ'sɒsɪliːz] ADJ: **~ triangle** triángulo *m* isósceles.

isotherm ['aɪsəʊθɜːm] N isoterma *f*.

isothermal [ˌaɪsəʊ'θɜːməl] ADJ isotérmico.

isotonic [ˌaɪsəʊ'tɒnɪk] ADJ isotónico.

isotope ['aɪsəʊtəʊp] N isótopo *m*.

I-spy ['aɪ'spaɪ] N (*Brit*) veo-veo *m*.

Israel ['ɪzreɪl] N Israel *m*.

Israeli [ɪz'reɪlɪ] [1] ADJ israelí.
[2] N israelí *mf*.

Israelite ['ɪzrɪəlaɪt] [1] ADJ israelita.
[2] N israelita *mf*.

iss. ABBR of **issue**.

▼ **issue** ['ɪʃuː] [1] N (a) (*outcome*) resultado *m*, consecuencia *f*; **in the ~** en fin; **until the ~ is decided** hasta que se sepa el resultado; **to await the ~** esperar el resultado.

▼ (b) (*matter*) cuestión *f*, asunto *m*, problema *m*, punto *m*; **an ~ of fact** una cuestión de hechos; **side ~** cuestión *f* secundaria; **the point at ~** el punto en cuestión, el asunto en litigio; **the ~ is whether ...** se trata de decidir si ...; **it's not a political ~** no es una cuestión política; **to cloud** (or **confuse**) **the ~** entenebrecer el asunto; **to evade the ~** evadir el tema, esquivar la pregunta; soslayar el problema; **to face the ~** afrontar la situación; **to force the ~** forzar una decisión; **to join** (or **take**) **~ with sb** llevar la contraria a uno, oponerse a uno; **I think we should make an ~ of this** creo que éste es un punto clave, creo que esto vale como tema de discusión (or protesta *etc*); **do you want to make an ~ of it?** ¿quieres que esto llegue a ser un asunto conflictivo?; **I feel I must take ~ with you over that** permítaseme disentir de esa opinión.

(c) (*of shares, stamps etc*) emisión *f*; (*of rations*) distribución *f*, repartimiento *m*.

(d) (*of book: size of ~*) edición *f*, tirada *f*; (*copy*) número *m*.

(e) (*offspring*) sucesión *f*, descendencia *f*; **to die without ~** morir sin dejar descendencia.

(f) (*Med*) flujo *m*.

[2] ATTR (*Mil etc*) reglamentario; (*Fin*) **~ price** precio *m* de emisión.

[3] VT *shares, stamps etc* emitir; poner en circulación; *rations etc* distribuir, repartir; *book* publicar; *book* (*in library*) servir; *order* dar; *decree* promulgar; *certificate, passport etc* expedir; *cheque* extender; *licence* facilitar; **'when ~d'** (*St Ex*) 'cuando se emita'; **a warrant has been ~d for the arrest of X** se ha ordenado la detención de X; **to ~ a rifle to each man, to ~ each man with a rifle** dar un fusil a cada hombre; **we were ~d with 10 rounds each** nos dieron a cada uno 10 cartuchos.

[4] VI salir (*from* de); **to ~ from** (*fig*) provenir de; **to ~ in** dar por resultado.

issued ['ɪʃuːd] ADJ: **~ capital** capital *m* emitido.

issuer ['ɪʃuər] N (*Fin: St Ex*) emisor *m*, sociedad *f* emisora.

Istanbul ['ɪstæn'buːl] N Estambul *m*.

isthmus ['ɪsməs] N istmo *m*.

IT N (a) (*Comput*) ABBR of **information technology** informática *f*. (b) (*Fin*) ABBR of **income-tax** impuesto *m* sobre la renta.

it¹ [ɪt] PRON (a) (*nom*) el, ella, ello; (*acc*) lo, la; (*dat*) le; (*after prep*) él, ella, ello.

(b) (NOM PRON *referring to a specific noun, freq not translated*) **~'s on the table** está en la mesa; **where is ~?** ¿dónde está?

(c) (PRON *referring to 'this affair', 'that whole business'*) ello, eso, *eg* **~ is difficult** es difícil, ello es difícil; **I have no money for ~** no tengo dinero para ello; **he won't agree to ~** no quiere consentir en eso; **he's dropped us in ~*** nos la ha hecho buena*.

(d) (*never translated in such cases as*) **~ is true that ...** es verdad que ...; **~ was raining** llovía; **~ is 4 o'clock** son las 4; **~ is not in him to do it** no es capaz de hacer eso; **~ is said that ...** se dice que ...; **I have heard ~ said that ...** he oído decir que ...; **I do not think ~ (is) wise to go** creo que es más prudente no ir; **~ is I, ~'s me** soy yo; **~'s Jack** soy Juanito; **~ was he who brought them** fue él quien los trajo.

(e) (*special uses with to be*) **this is ~** ya llegó la hora; ahí viene; (*before action*) ¡vamos!, ¡a ello!; **that's ~** (*agreeing*) eso es; (*adjusting machine etc*) ya está, está bien; (*on finishing sth*) eso es todo, hemos terminado, está hecho, nada más; **that's ~ then!** ¡muy bien!; **that's just ~!** ¡ahí está la dificultad!; **the worst of ~ is that ...** lo peor del caso es que ...; **how is ~ that ...?** ¿cómo resulta que ...? (*and V* how (a)).

(f) (*predicative*) **you're ~!** (*children's games*) ¡tú te quedas!; **she thinks she's just ~*** se da mucho tono, se cree la mar de elegante*.

(g) (*) (*sexual attraction*) aquél* *m*, atracción *f* sexual; **she's got ~** tiene aquél*, tiene tilín*; **he's got ~** (*talent*) tiene talento, reúne las cualidades necesarias; **he hasn't quite got ~** no alcanza el nivel deseado; queda algo corto.

it²* [ɪt] N vermú *m* italiano.

ITA N (*Brit*) ABBR of **initial teaching alphabet** alfabeto *parcialmente* fonético, para enseñar lectura.

Italian [ɪˈtælɪən] **1** ADJ italiano.
2 N **(a)** italiano *m*, -a *f*. **(b)** (*Ling*) italiano *m*.

Italianate [ɪˈtæljəneɪt] ADJ de estilo italiano, italianizante.

italic [ɪˈtælɪk] ADJ (*Typ*) en bastardilla; (*of Italy*) itálico.

italicize [ɪˈtælɪsaɪz] VT poner en bastardilla, subrayar.

italics [ɪˈtælɪks] NPL (letra) bastardilla *f*, cursiva *f*; **in ~** en bastardilla, en cursiva; **my ~** lo subrayado es mío.

Italy [ˈɪtəlɪ] N Italia *f*.

ITC N (*Brit*) ABBR *of* **Independent Television Commission.**

itch [ɪtʃ] **1** N **(a)** (*Med*) (*an ~*) picazón *f*, comezón *f*; (*the ~*) sarna *f*. **(b)** (*fig*) prurito *m*, deseo *m* vehemente; **to have the ~ to do sth** tener el prurito de hacer algo, rabiar por hacer algo.
2 VI **(a)** picar, sentir comezón; **my leg ~es** me pica la pierna, siento co- mezón en la pierna.
(b) to ~ to do sth tener el prurito de hacer algo, rabiar por hacer algo.

itching [ˈɪtʃɪŋ] N picazón *f*, comezón *f*.

itching powder [ˈɪtʃɪŋˌpaʊdəʳ] N polvos *mpl* de pica-pica.

itchy [ˈɪtʃɪ] ADJ: **to feel ~** sentir comezón; **to have ~ feet** (*fig*) tener mal asiento, no querer estar quieto; **to have an ~ leg** sentir comezón en la pierna.

it'd [ˈɪtd] = **it would; it had.**

▼ **item** [ˈaɪtəm] N artículo *m*; (*detail*) detalle *m*; (*Comm*) partida *f*; (*in programme*) número *m*; (*on agenda*) asunto *m* a tratar; (*in newspaper*) noticia *f*, información *f*, suelto *m*; **~ of clothing** prenda *f* (de vestir); **what's the next ~?** ¿qué viene después?; **it's an important ~ in our policy** es un punto importante de nuestra política; **they're something of an ~** son una pareja inseparable.

itemize [ˈaɪtəmaɪz] VT detallar, particularizar, especificar; **~d bill** (*of customer*) cuenta *f* detallada, (*Comm*) factura *f* detallada.

iterative [ˈɪtərətɪv] ADJ iterativo; **~ statement** (*Comput*) sentencia *f* iterativa.

itinerant [ɪˈtɪnərənt] ADJ ambulante.

itinerary [aɪˈtɪnərərɪ] N ruta *f*, itinerario *m*; (*book, map*) guía *f*.

it'll [ˈɪtl] = **it will; it shall.**

ITN N (*Brit*) ABBR *of* **Independent Television News** servicio de noticias en las cadenas privadas de televisión; *ver también* ITV .

ITO N ABBR *of* **International Trade Organization** Organización *f* Internacional de Comercio, OIC *f*.

its [ɪts] **1** POSS ADJ su(s).
2 POSS PRON (el) suyo, (la) suya *etc*.

it's [ɪts] = **it is, it has.**

itself [ɪtˈself] PRON (*nom*) él mismo, ella misma, ello mismo; (*acc,* *dat*) se; (*after* PREP) sí mismo, sí misma; **he is always politeness ~** siempre es la misma cortesía, siempre es la cortesía en persona; **that was an achievement in ~** eso fue un triunfo de por sí; **V oneself.**

ITU N ABBR *of* **International Telecommunications Union** Unión *f* Internacional para las Telecomunicaciones, UIT *f*.

ITV N (*Brit*) ABBR *of* **Independent Television** cadenas privadas de televisión.

┌─ ITV ─┐

ⓘ *La* **ITV** *o* **Independent Television** *es la tercera cadena de televisión británica compuesta por quince compañías regionales con licencia para emitir programas en su región. A diferencia de la* **BBC**, *las compañías no reciben ninguna subvención estatal, sino que se financian a través de la publicidad. Los programas que se emiten varían según las regiones, aunque comparten los mismos servicios informativos, que son realizados por la* **ITN** *o* **Independent Television News**. *Su programación dura las 24 horas del día, de las cuales un tercio se dedica a programas informativos y el resto a programas dirigidos a una amplia audiencia.*
⇨ *Ver también* BBC

IUD N ABBR *of* **intrauterine device** dispositivo *m* intrauterino, DIU *m*.

I.V. N (*US*) gota a gota *m*.

i.v. ABBR *of* **invoice value** valor *m* total de factura.

I've [aɪv] = **I have.**

IVF N ABBR *of* **in vitro fertilization.**

ivory [ˈaɪvərɪ] **1** N marfil *m*; **ivories*** (*teeth*) dientes *mpl*, (*Mus*) teclas *fpl*, (*Billiards*) bolas *fpl*; **to tickle the ivories*** tocar el piano.
2 ATTR de marfil; **~ tower** torre *f* de marfil.

Ivory Coast [ˈaɪvərɪˈkəʊst] N Costa *f* de Marfil.

ivy [ˈaɪvɪ] **1** N hiedra *f*.
2 ATTR: **I~ League** (*US*) grupo de ocho universidades privadas de Nueva Inglaterra (*de gran prestigio*).

┌─ IVY LEAGUE ─┐

ⓘ *En el noreste de los Estados Unidos, la* **Ivy League** *está formada por ocho universidades de gran prestigio tanto académico como social. El término procede de los tiempos en los que estas ocho universidades,* **Harvard, Yale, Pennsylvania, Princeton, Columbia, Brown, Dartmouth** *y* **Cornell** *formaron una liga para impulsar las competiciones deportivas entre ellas y tiene su origen en la hiedra* **ivy** *que cubre los muros de las facultades y colegios universitarios. A los estudiantes de estas universidades se les denomina* **Ivy Leaguers**.

J

J, j [dʒeɪ] N (*letter*) J, j *f*; **J for Jack, J for Jig** (*US*) J de José.
JA N ABBR *of* **judge advocate**.
J/A ABBR *of* **joint account** cuenta *f* conjunta.
jab [dʒæb] **1** N (*poke*) pinchazo *m*; (*with elbow*) codazo *m*; (*blow*) golpe *m*; (*Boxing*) gancho *m*; (*prick*) pinchazo *m*; (*Med**) inyección *f*; (‡: *of drug*) chut‡ *m*.
2 VT hurgonear; dar un codazo a; golpear, dar un golpe rápido a; pinchar; **he ~bed a gun in my back** me puso un revólver en los riñones; **I ~bed the knife in my arm** me pinché el brazo con el cuchillo; **he ~bed the knife into the table** clavó el cuchillo en la mesa; **he ~bed a finger at the map** dio con el dedo en el mapa.
3 VI: **to ~ at sb with a knife** tratar de acuchillar a uno; **he ~bed at the map with a finger** dio con el dedo en el mapa.
jabber ['dʒæbəʳ] **1** N (*also* **jabbering** ['dʒæbərɪŋ]) torrente *m* de palabras ininteligibles; farfulla *f*; (*of monkeys*) chillidos *mpl*; **a ~ of French** un torrente de francés; **a ~ of voices** un ruido confuso de voces.
2 VT decir atropelladamente.
3 VI hablar atropelladamente, hablar de modo ininteligible; farfullar; (*monkeys*) chillar; **they were ~ing away in Russian** hablaban atropelladamente en ruso.
jabbering ['dʒæbərɪŋ] = **jabber 1**.
jacaranda [,dʒækə'rændə] N jacarandá *m*.
jack [dʒæk] N (*Mech*) gato *m*, gata *f* (*And*, *SC*); (*boot~*) sacabotas *m*; (*Bowls*) boliche *m*; (*Cards*) valet *m*, criado *m*, (*in Spanish pack*) sota *f*; (*Naut*) marinero *m*; (*Fish*) lucio *m* joven.
◆**jack in** VT dejar, abandonar.
◆**jack off**‡ VI (*US*) masturbar, hacerse una paja‡.
◆**jack up** VT (*Mech*) alzar con gato; *price, production etc* aumentar.
Jack [dʒæk] NM *familiar form of* **John** (Juanito); **I'm all right, ~!** ¡a mí nada!; **~ Frost** personificación del hielo; **~ Ketch** el verdugo; **before you can say ~ Robinson** en un decir Jesús; **~ Tar** el marinero.
jackal ['dʒækɔ:l] N chacal *m*; (*fig*) paniaguado *m*, secuaz *m*.
jackanapes ['dʒækəneɪps] N mequetrefe *m*.
jackass ['dʒækæs] N burro *m* (*also fig*).
jackboot ['dʒækbu:t] N bota *f* de montar, bota *f* militar; **under the ~ of the Nazis** bajo el azote de los nazis.
jackdaw ['dʒækdɔ:] N grajilla *f*, grajo *m*.
jacket ['dʒækɪt] **1** N chaqueta *f*, americana *f*, saco *m* (*LAm*); (*of boiler etc*) camisa *f*, envoltura *f*; (*of book*) sobrecubierta *f*, camisa *f*; (*US: of record*) funda *f*.
2 ATTR: **~ potatoes, potatoes baked in their ~s** (*Brit*) patatas *fpl* enteras, patatas *fpl* con su piel.
jackhammer ['dʒæk,hæməʳ] N (*esp US*) taladradora *f*, martillo *m* picador.
jack-in-the-box ['dʒækɪnðəbɒks] N caja *f* sorpresa, caja *f* de resorte.
jack-knife ['dʒæknaɪf] **1** N, PL **jack-knives** ['dʒæknaɪvz] navaja *f*.
2 ATTR: **~ dive** salto *m* de carpa.
3 VI: **the lorry ~d** el remolque del camión quedó atravesado.
jack-of-all-trades ['dʒækəv'ɔ:ltreɪdz] N factótum *m*, chico *m* para todo, manitas *m*; aprendiz *m* de todo, maestro de nada.
jack-o'-lantern ['dʒækəʊ'læntən] N fuego *m* fatuo; (*US*) linterna *f* hecha con una calabaza vaciada.
jack plane ['dʒækpleɪn] N garlopa *f*.
jack plug ['dʒækplʌg] N enchufe *m* de clavija.
jackpot ['dʒækpɒt] N bote *m*; (*fig*) premio *m* gordo; **he hit the ~** sacó el premio gordo (*LAm*: la gorda), (*fig*) acertó, se puso las botas, dio en el blanco.
jack rabbit ['dʒæk,ræbɪt] N (*US*) liebre *f* grande.
jacks [dʒæks] N SING (*game*) cantillos *mpl*.
jackstraw ['dʒækstrɔ:] N (*US*) pajita *f*.
Jacob ['dʒeɪkəb] NM Jacob.
Jacobean [,dʒækə'bi:ən] ADJ de la época de Jacobo I (de Inglaterra).

Jacobin ['dʒækəbɪn] **1** ADJ jacobino.
2 N jacobino *m*, -a *f*.
Jacobite ['dʒækəbaɪt] **1** ADJ jacobita.
2 N jacobita *mf*.
Jacuzzi [dʒə'ku:zɪ] ® N jacuzzi ® *m*, baño *m* de burbujas, hidromasaje *m*.
jade¹ [dʒeɪd] N (*horse*) rocín *m*; (†: *woman*) mujerzuela *f*; **you ~!** ¡picarona!, ¡lagarta!
jade² [dʒeɪd] **1** N (*Min*) jade *m*.
2 ADJ verde jade (*invar*).
jaded ['dʒeɪdɪd] ADJ cansado, (*fed up*) hastiado; **to feel ~** estar cansado; **to get ~** cansarse, perder el entusiasmo.
jade-green ['dʒeɪd'gri:n] ADJ verde jade (*invar*).
jag¹ [dʒæg] N punta *f*, púa *f*.
jag²* [dʒæg] N: **to go on a ~** ir de juerga.
jagged ['dʒægɪd] ADJ dentado, mellado, desigual.
jaguar ['dʒægjʊəʳ] N jaguar *m*.
jail [dʒeɪl] **1** N cárcel *f*; **2 years' ~** 2 años de prisión, condena *f* de 2 años.
2 VT encarcelar.
jailbait* ['dʒeɪlbeɪt] N *menor con la que el mantener relaciones sexuales está penado*.
jailbird ['dʒeɪlbɜ:d] N presidiario *m*.
jailbreak ['dʒeɪlbreɪk] N fuga *f* (de la cárcel).
jailbreaker ['dʒeɪl,breɪkəʳ] N evadido *m*, -a *f*, fugado *m*, -a *f*.
jailer ['dʒeɪləʳ] N carcelero *m*.
jailhouse ['dʒeɪlhɒus] N (*esp US*) cárcel *f*, prisión *f*.
jakes‡ [dʒeɪks] NM meadero *m*.
jalop(p)y [dʒə'lɒpɪ] N cacharro *m*, armatoste *m*.
jalousie ['ʒælu(:)zi:] N celosía *f*.
jam¹ [dʒæm] **1** N (a) (*food*) mermelada *f*.
(b) (*: *the best*) lo mejor, la parte más rica; **you want ~ on it!** (*Brit*) ¡y un jamón con chorreras!*; **the ~ is spread very thin** hay cosas buenas pero forman una capa muy delgada. (c) (‡: *luck*) chorra‡; **look at that for ~!** ¡qué chorra tiene el tío!‡
2 VT hacer mermelada de.
jam² [dʒæm] **1** N (a) (*blockage*) atasco *m*, obstrucción *f*; (*of people*) agolpamiento *m*; (*Aut*) embotellamiento *m*, aglomeración *f*; colapso *m*; caravana *f*, tapón *m* (*Carib*); **there's a ~ in the pipe** se ha atascado el tubo, está atascado el tubo; **there was a ~ in the doorway** se había agolpado la gente en la puerta; **you never saw such a ~!** ¡había que ver cómo se agolpaba la gente!; **a 5-km ~ of cars** una cola de coches que se extiende hasta 5 km; **there are always ~s here** aquí siempre se embotella el tráfico.
(b) (*: *difficulty*) apuro *m*, aprieto *m*; **to be in a ~** estar en un aprieto; **to get into a ~** meterse en un apuro; **to get into a ~ with a problem** armarse un lío con un problema; **to get sb out of a ~** ayudar a uno a salir del paso.
2 VT *pipe etc* atascar, obstruir; *wheel* trabar; *exit, road* cerrar, obstruir; colapsar; (*Rad*) interferir, embrollar; **it's got ~med** se ha atascado, no se puede mover (*or* quitar, retirar *etc*); **people ~med all the exits** la gente se agolpaba en todas las salidas; **the room was ~med with people** el cuarto estaba atestado de gente; **to ~ one's fingers in the door** cogerse los dedos en la puerta; **to ~ sth into a box** meter algo apretadamente en una caja.
3 VI (a) (*pipe etc*) atascarse, obstruirse; (*nut, part, wheel etc*) trabarse; (*gun*) encasquillarse; **this part has ~med** no se puede mover esta pieza.
(b) (*Mus**) improvisar.
◆**jam in** VT: **if we can ~ 2 more books in** si podemos introducir a la fuerza 2 libros más; **there were 15 people ~med in one room** había 15 personas apretadas unas contra otras en un cuarto.
◆**jam on** VT (a) **to ~ a hat on one's head** encasquetarse un sombrero;

with his hat ~med on his head con la cabeza encasquetada en un sombrero. (b) to ~ one's brakes on echar los frenos con violencia, frenar de repente.

Jamaica [dʒə'meɪkə] N Jamaica f.

Jamaican [dʒə'meɪkən] [1] ADJ jamaiquino.
[2] N jamaiquino m, -a f.

jamb [dʒæm] N jamba f.

jamboree [ˌdʒæmbə'riː] N (of Scouts) congreso m de exploradores; (*) francachela f, juerga f.

James [dʒeɪmz] NM Jaime, Diego; (Saint) Santiago; (British kings) Jacobo.

jam-full ['dʒæm'fʊl] ADV de bote en bote.

jamjar ['dʒæmdʒɑːr] N pote m para (or de) mermelada.

jamming ['dʒæmɪŋ] N (Rad) interferencia f.

jammy: ['dʒæmɪ] ADJ chorrero:.

jam-packed ['dʒæm'pækt] ADJ atestado, lleno a rebosar.

jam-pot ['dʒæmpɒt] N pote m para (or de) mermelada.

jam roll [ˌdʒæm'rəʊl] N brazo m de gitano con mermelada.

jam session* ['dʒæm,seʃən] N sesión f de improvisación de jazz (or de rock).

Jan. ABBR of **January** enero m, ene, en.º.

Jane [dʒeɪn] NF Juana.

jangle ['dʒæŋgl] [1] N sonido m discordante (metálico), cencerreo m.
[2] VT chocar, hacer sonar de manera discordante.
[3] VI sonar de manera discordante, cencerrear.

jangling ['dʒæŋglɪŋ] [1] ADJ discordante, desapacible, ruidoso.
[2] N cencerreo m.

janitor ['dʒænɪtər] N portero m, conserje m; (Scol) bedel m.

January ['dʒænjʊərɪ] N enero m.

Janus ['dʒeɪnəs] NM Jano.

Jap* [dʒæp] (US:) = **Japanese**.

Japan [dʒə'pæn] N el Japón.

japan [dʒə'pæn] [1] N laca f japonesa.
[2] VT charolar con laca japonesa.

Japanese [ˌdʒæpə'niːz] [1] ADJ japonés.
[2] N (a) japonés m, -esa f; the ~ (PL) los japoneses. (b) (Ling) japonés m.

jape [dʒeɪp] N burla f, broma f.

japonica [dʒə'pɒnɪkə] N rosal m de China, rosal m japonés.

jar¹ [dʒɑːr] N (small) tarro m, pote m; frasco m; (with handles) jarra f; (large) tinaja f; **to have a ~*** tomar un trago.

jar² [dʒɑːr] [1] N (a) (jolt) sacudida f, choque m; vibración f. (b) (fig) sacudida f, sorpresa f desagradable; **it gave me a bit of a ~** me chocó bastante.
[2] VT (jog) tocar; mover; (shake) sacudir, hacer vibrar; **he must have ~red the camera** ha debido mover ligeramente la máquina; **sb ~red my elbow** alguien me hizo mover el codo.
[3] VI (grate) chirriar; (shake) vibrar; (sounds) ser discorde, sonar mal; (colours) chillar; **to ~ on sb** poner a uno los nervios de punta, crispar los nervios a uno.

jar³ [dʒɑːr] N: **on the ~** V ajar.

jargon ['dʒɑːgən] N (incomprehensible) jerigonza f; (specialist) jerga f.

jarring ['dʒɑːrɪŋ] ADJ sound discorde, desapacible; colour chillón; (fig) opuesto, adverso, discorde.

Jas. ABBR of **James**.

jasmin(e) ['dʒæzmɪn] N jazmín m.

jasper ['dʒæspər] N jaspe m.

jaundice ['dʒɔːndɪs] N ictericia f.

jaundiced ['dʒɔːndɪst] ADJ (fig: envious, sour) envidioso, avinagrado, agrio; (disillusioned) desilusionado, decepcionado.

jaunt [dʒɔːnt] N excursión f (corta) (also fig); viajecito m.

jauntily ['dʒɔːntɪlɪ] ADV con garbo, airosamente; con confianza; **he replied ~** contestó satisfecho.

jauntiness ['dʒɔːntɪnɪs] N garbo m; confianza f, satisfacción f.

jaunting car ['dʒɔːntɪŋ,kɑːr] N tílburi m (irlandés).

jaunty ['dʒɔːntɪ] ADJ garboso, airoso; alegre; desenvuelto; confiado, satisfecho.

Java ['dʒɑːvə] N Java f.

Javanese [ˌdʒɑːvə'niːz] [1] ADJ javanés.
[2] N javanés m, -esa f.

javelin ['dʒævlɪn] [1] N jabalina f; **to throw the ~** lanzar la jabalina.
[2] ATTR: **~ thrower** lanzador m, -ora f de jabalina; **~ throwing** lanzamiento m de jabalina.

jaw [dʒɔː] [1] N (a) (Anat) mandíbula f; (of horse etc) quijada f; (Mech) mordaza f, mandíbula f.
(b) **~s** (Anat) boca f; (fig: swallowing) boca f, fauces fpl; (holding) garras fpl; **they rode into the very ~s of death** entraron en la misma boca del infierno.
(c) (*) cháchara f; palabrería f; **we had a good old ~** charlamos largo rato; **it's just a lot of ~** mucho ruido y pocas nueces; **hold your ~!** ¡cállate la boca!
[2] VT (:) soltar el rollo a*.
[3] VI (*) charlar; hablar por los codos, hablar interminablemente.

jawbone ['dʒɔːbəʊn] [1] N mandíbula f, maxilar m.
[2] VT (US*) presionar, ejercer presión sobre.

jawbreaker* ['dʒɔː,breɪkər] N (US) trabalenguas m, palabra f kilométrica, terminacho m.

jawline ['dʒɔːlaɪn] N mandíbula f.

jay [dʒeɪ] N arrendajo m.

jaywalk ['dʒeɪwɔːk] VI cruzar la calle descuidadamente; ir a pie por la calzada.

jaywalker ['dʒeɪ,wɔːkər] N peatón m imprudente.

jaywalking ['dʒeɪ,wɔːkɪŋ] N imprudencia f al cruzar la calle.

jazz [dʒæz] [1] N (a) jazz m. (b) (*) palabrería f, disparates mpl; rollo* m; **and all that ~** y todo el rollo ése*; **don't give me that ~!** ¡no me vengas con cuentos!
[2] ATTR de jazz.
[3] VT (a) (also to ~ up) sincopar; (fig) animar, avivar. (b) (US*) exagerar.

jazz ballet ['dʒæz'bæleɪ] N jazz-ballet m.

jazz band ['dʒæzbænd] N orquesta f de jazz.

jazzy ['dʒæzɪ] ADJ (Mus) sincopado; dress etc de colores llamativos, de colores chillones.

JC N ABBR of **Jesus Christ** Jesucristo m, JC m.

JCB ['dʒeɪ'siː'biː] ® N excavadora f.

JCC N (US) ABBR of **Junior Chamber of Commerce**.

JCS N (US) ABBR of **Joint Chiefs of Staff**.

jct. (Rail) ABBR of **junction**.

J.D. N (US) (a) ABBR of **Doctor of Laws** título universitario. (b) ABBR of **Justice Department**.

jealous ['dʒeləs] ADJ celoso; envidioso; **~ husband** marido m celoso; **with ~ care** con el mayor celo; **to be ~** tener celos (of sb de uno); **to make sb ~** dar celos a uno.

jealously ['dʒeləslɪ] ADV celosamente; envidiosamente.

jealousy ['dʒeləsɪ] N celos mpl; envidia f.

jeans [dʒiːnz] NPL (pantalones mpl) vaqueros mpl, tejanos mpl.

jeep [dʒiːp] N jeep m, yip m.

jeer [dʒɪər] [1] N (shout) mofa f, befa f, grito m de sarcasmo, grito m de protesta; (insult) insulto m, dicterio m; (boo) abucheo m.
[2] VT mofarse de; llenar de insultos; abuchear.
[3] VI mofarse (at de), befar; gritar con sarcasmo (etc; at a), prorrumpir en befas (or gritos sarcásticos etc).

jeering ['dʒɪərɪŋ] [1] ADJ mofador, sarcástico; **he was led through a ~ crowd** le hicieron pasar por una multitud que le llenó de insultos.
[2] N mofas fpl, befas fpl, gritos mpl de sarcasmo, protestas fpl; insultos mpl; abucheo m.

Jeez: [dʒiːz] INTERJ ¡Santo Dios!

jehad [dʒɪ'hæd] N yihad m.

Jehovah [dʒɪ'həʊvə] NM Jehová; **~'s Witnesses** Testigos mpl de Jehová.

jejune [dʒɪ'dʒuːn] ADJ árido; insípido, sin sustancia.

jell [dʒel] VI convertirse en jalea, cuajar; (fig) cuajar.

jellabah ['dʒeləbə] N chilaba f.

jellied ['dʒelɪd] ADJ eels, meat etc en gelatina.

jello ['dʒeləʊ] N (US) = **jelly¹**.

jelly¹ ['dʒelɪ] N jalea f, gelatina f; **my legs turned to ~** las piernas no me sostenían.

jelly²: ['dʒelɪ] N = **gelignite**.

jelly baby [ˌdʒelɪ'beɪbɪ] N caramelo m de goma (en forma de niño).

jelly bean [ˌdʒelɪ'biːn] N caramelo m de goma (en forma de judía).

jellyfish ['dʒelɪfɪʃ] N medusa f, aguamala f.

jemmy ['dʒemɪ] N (Brit) pie m de cabra, palanqueta f.

Jenny, Jennie ['dʒenɪ] NF familiar form of **Jennifer**.

jeopardize ['dʒepədaɪz] VT arriesgar, poner en peligro, comprometer.

jeopardy ['dʒepədɪ] N: **to be in ~** estar en peligro, correr riesgo; **to put sth in ~** poner algo en peligro, hacer peligrar algo.

jeremiad [ˌdʒerɪ'maɪəd] N jeremiada f.

Jeremiah [ˌdʒerɪ'maɪə] NM, **Jeremy** ['dʒerəmɪ] NM Jeremías.

Jericho ['dʒerɪkəʊ] N Jericó m.

jerk [dʒɜːk] [1] N (a) (push, pull, twist etc) tirón m, sacudida f; (Med) espasmo m muscular; **physical ~s** (Brit) ejercicios mpl físicos, gimnasia f; **by ~s** a sacudidas; **he sat up with a ~** se incorporó de repente, se incorporó con un movimiento brusco; **to put a ~ in it*** menearse.
(b) (:) pelmazo* m, memo m; **what a ~!:** ¡qué pesado!
[2] VT (shake etc) sacudir, dar una sacudida a; (pull) tirar bruscamente de; (throw) arrojar con un movimiento rápido; meat (US) atasajar; **to ~ sth along** mover algo a tirones; **to ~ sth away from sb** quitar algo a uno de un tirón.
[3] VI sacudirse, dar una sacudida; **to ~ along** moverse a sacudidas, avanzar a tirones.
[4] VR: **to ~ o.s. free** librarse con un movimiento brusco; **to ~ o.s. along** moverse a sacudidas, avanzar a tirones.

◆**jerk off:** VI hacerse una paja:.

◆**jerk out** VT words decir con voz entrecortada.

jerkily ['dʒɜːkɪlɪ] ADV *move etc* a tirones, a sacudidas; *play, write etc* de modo desigual, nerviosamente.

jerkin ['dʒɜːkɪn] N justillo *m*.

jerkwater* ['dʒɜːkˌwɔːtəʳ] ADJ (*US*) de poca monta; **a ~ town** un pueblucho*.

jerky ['dʒɜːkɪ] ADJ *movement* espasmódico, nervioso; (*uneven*) desigual, nervioso.

Jeroboam [ˌdʒerəˈbəʊəm] NM Jeroboam.

Jerome [dʒəˈrəʊm] NM Jerónimo.

Jerry¹ ['dʒerɪ] NM *familiar form of* Gerald, Gerard.

Jerry²* ['dʒerɪ] N (*Brit Mil*): **a ~** un alemán; **~** los alemanes.

jerry* ['dʒerɪ] N (*Brit*) orinal *m*.

jerry-builder ['dʒerɪˌbɪldəʳ] N mal constructor *m*, tapagujeros *m*.

jerry-building ['dʒerɪˌbɪldɪŋ] N mala construcción *f*, construcción *f* defectuosa.

jerry-built ['dʒerɪbɪlt] ADJ mal construido, de pacotilla, chapucero.

jerry-can ['dʒerɪkæn] N bidón *m*.

Jersey ['dʒɜːzɪ] N (a) (*Geog*) (Isla *f* de) Jersey *m*. (b) (*Zool*) vaca *f* de Jersey.

jersey ['dʒɜːzɪ] N jersey *m*.

Jerusalem [dʒəˈruːsələm] ☐ N Jerusalén *m*.
   ☐ ATTR: **~ artichoke** aguaturma *f*, pataca *f*, tupinambo *m*.

jessamine ['dʒesəmɪn] N jazmín *m*.

jest [dʒest] ☐ N chanza *f*, broma *f*; (*verbal*) chiste *m*; **in ~** en broma, de guasa.
   ☐ VI bromear, chancearse; **he was only ~ing** lo dijo en broma nada más.

jester ['dʒestəʳ] N bufón *m*.

jesting ['dʒestɪŋ] ☐ ADJ *person* chistoso, guasón; *tone* guasón; *reference* burlón, en broma.
   ☐ N chanzas *fpl*, bromas *fpl*; chistes *mpl*.

Jesuit ['dʒezjʊɪt] ☐ ADJ jesuita.
   ☐ N jesuita *m*.

Jesuitical [ˌdʒezjʊˈɪtɪkəl] ADJ jesuítico.

Jesus ['dʒiːzəs] ☐ NM Jesús; **~ Christ** Jesucristo; **~ Christ!*** ¡Santo Dios!
   ☐ ATTR: **~ freak*** sectario *m* fanático de Jesús; **~ sandals** (*Brit*) sandalias *fpl* nazarenas.

jet¹ [dʒet] N (*Min*) azabache *m*.

jet² [dʒet] ☐ N (a) (*of liquid*) chorro *m*, surtidor *m*; (*gas burner*) mechero *m*; **a ~ of flame** una llama.
   (b) (*Aer*) jet *m*, avión *m* a reacción.
   ☐ ATTR (*Aer*) a reacción, a chorro; **the ~ age** la época de los jet; **~ engine** motor *m* a reacción, reactor *m*; **~ fighter** avión *m* de caza a reacción, caza *m* a reacción; **~ plane = 1** (b); **~ propulsion** propulsión *f* por reacción, propulsión *f* a chorro.
   ☐ VT lanzar en chorro, echar en chorro.
   ☐ VI chorrear, salir a chorro.
◆**jet off*** VI salir de viaje (*en avión*).

jet-black ['dʒet'blæk] ADJ de azabache, negro como el azabache.

jet-lag ['dʒet,læg] ☐ N jet-lag *m*, desfase *m* horario, desfase *m* debido a un largo viaje en avión.
   ☐ VT: **to be ~ged** tener jet-lag, estar desfasado por el viaje (en avión).

jetliner ['dʒet,laɪnəʳ] N (*US*) avión *m* de pasajeros.

jet-powered ['dʒet'paʊəd] ADJ, **jet-propelled** ['dʒetprə'peld] ADJ a reacción, a chorro.

jetsam ['dʒetsəm] N echazón *f*, cosas *fpl* desechadas.

jet-set ['dʒetset] N alta sociedad *f* internacional, jet-set *f*, jet *f*.

jet-setter ['dʒet,setəʳ] N miembro *mf* de la jet-set.

jet-setting ['dʒetsetɪŋ] ADJ de la jet set.

jet ski ['dʒetskiː] N moto *f* acuática, jet ski *m*.

jet-stream ['dʒetstriːm] N corriente *f* en chorro.

jettison ['dʒetɪsn] VT (*Naut etc*) echar al mar, echar por la borda; (*Aer*) vaciar; (*fig*) desechar, abandonar, librarse de; **we can safely ~ that** bien podemos prescindir de eso.

jetty ['dʒetɪ] N malecón *m*, muelle *m*, embarcadero *m*.

Jew [dʒuː] N judío *m*, -a *f*.

jewel ['dʒuːəl] N joya *f* (*also fig*), alhaja *f*; (*of watch*) rubí *m*.

jewel-case ['dʒuːəlkeɪs] N joyero *m*, estuche *m* de joyas, guardajoyas *m*.

jewelled, (*esp US*) **jeweled** ['dʒuːəld] ADJ adornado con piedras preciosas, enjoyado; *watch* con rubíes.

jeweller, (*esp US*) **jeweler** ['dʒuːələʳ] N joyero *m*; **~'s (shop)** joyería *f*.

jewellery, (*esp US*) **jewelry** ['dʒuːəlrɪ] N joyas *fpl*, alhajas *fpl*; **~ box** = **jewel-case**; **jewelry store** (*US*) joyería *f*.

Jewess ['dʒuːɪs] N judía *f*.

Jewish ['dʒuːɪʃ] ADJ judío.

Jewishness ['dʒuːɪʃnɪs] N carácter *m* judaico.

Jewry ['dʒʊərɪ] N judería *f*, los judíos.

Jew's-harp ['dʒuːz'hɑːp] N birimbao *m*.

Jezebel ['dʒezəbel] NF Jezabel.

JFK N (*US*) ABBR *of* **John Fitzgerald Kennedy International Airport.**

jib¹ [dʒɪb] ☐ N (*Naut*) foque *m*; (*Mech*) aguilón *m*, brazo *m*.
   ☐ ATTR: **~ boom** botalón *m* de foque.

jib² [dʒɪb] VI (*horse*) plantarse, rehusar; (*person*) rehusar; **I ~ at that** no puedo consentir en eso; **he ~bed at it** se negó a aprobarlo (*etc*), no quiso permitirlo, se opuso a ello.

jibe [dʒaɪb] ☐ N pulla *f*, dicterio *m*.
   ☐ VI mofarse (*at de*).

jiffy* ['dʒɪfɪ] N instante *m*, momento *m*; **I'll be with you in a ~** un momento y estoy con vosotros; **to do sth in a ~** hacer algo en un decir Jesús, hacer algo en un santiamén.

jig¹ [dʒɪg] ☐ N (*dance*) giga *f*.
   ☐ VI (*dance*) bailar (la giga); **to ~ along, to ~ up and down** vibrarse, sacudirse, (*person*) moverse a saltitos; **to keep ~ging up and down** no poder estarse quieto.

jig² [dʒɪg] N (*Mech*) plantilla *f* (de guía); (*Rail*) gálibo *m*.

jigger¹ ['dʒɪgəʳ] N (*Min*) criba *f*; (*Mech*) aparato *m* vibratorio.

jigger²* ['dʒɪgəʳ] N (*US*) medida *f* (de whisky *etc*); (*thingummy*) chisme *m*.

jiggered* ['dʒɪgəd] ADJ (*Brit*): **well I'm ~!** ¡caramba!; **I'm ~ if I will** que me cuelguen si lo hago.

jiggery-pokery* ['dʒɪgərɪ'pəʊkərɪ] N (*Brit*) trampas *fpl*, embustes *mpl*, maniobras *fpl* poco limpias; **there's some ~ going on** hay trampa; están maquinando algo.

jiggle ['dʒɪgl] ☐ N zangoloteo *m*.
   ☐ VT zangolotear.
   ☐ VI zangolotearse.

jigsaw ['dʒɪgsɔː] N (a) sierra *f* de vaivén. (b) (*also ~ puzzle*) rompecabezas *m*, puzzle *m*.

jihad [dʒɪ'hæd] N (*Rel*) jihad *f*, guerra santa musulmana.

jilt [dʒɪlt] VT dar calabazas a, dejar plantado a; **her ~ed lover** su amante abandonado.

Jim [dʒɪm] NM *familiar form of* **James.**

jimdandy* ['dʒɪm'dændɪ] ADJ (*US*) estupendo*, fenomenal*.

jimjams: ['dʒɪmdʒæmz] NPL delírium *m* tremens; **it gives me the ~** me horripila, me da grima.

Jimmy ['dʒɪmɪ] NM *familiar form of* **James**; **to have a ~ (Riddle):** mear:.

jimmy ['dʒɪmɪ] N (*US*) = **jemmy**.

jingle ['dʒɪŋgl] ☐ N (a) (*sound*) tintineo *m*, retintín *m*, ruido *m* (de campanita, monedas *etc*); cascabeleo *m*. (b) (*Liter*) verso *m*, poemita *m* popular, rima *f* infantil; (*TV etc*) anuncio *m* cantado, anuncio *m* rimado; (*Pol: slogan*) pareado *m*.
   ☐ VT hacer sonar.
   ☐ VI tintinear, retiñir, cascabelear.

jingo ['dʒɪŋgəʊ] N patriotero *m*, -a *f*, jingoísta *mf*; **by ~!** ¡caramba!

jingoism ['dʒɪŋgəʊɪzəm] N patriotería *f*, jingoísmo *m*.

jingoist(ic) [ˌdʒɪŋgəʊ'ɪst(ɪk)] ADJ patriotero, jingoísta.

jink* [dʒɪŋk] VI (*zigzag*) dar un bandazo; **he ~ed out of the way** se salió del camino dando un bandazo.

jinks [dʒɪŋks] NPL: **high ~** jolgorio *m*; fiesta *f* animadísima; **we had high ~ last night** anoche nos lo pasamos pipa.

jinx* [dʒɪŋks] ☐ N cenizo* *m*, gafe* *m*; (*gremlin*) duendecillo *m*; **there's a ~ on it** esto está como encantado, esto está que da rabia.
   ☐ VT traer mala suerte a; gafar*.

jitney* ['dʒɪtnɪ] N (*US*) (a) autobús *m* pequeño, colectivo *m* (*LAm*). (b) *moneda* de 5 centavos.

jitterbug ['dʒɪtəbʌg] ☐ N (*dance*) baile acrobático al ritmo de jazz o bugui-bugie; (*person*) persona *f* aficionada a bailar el jitterbug.
   ☐ VI bailar (el jazz).

jitters* ['dʒɪtəz] NPL inquietud *f*, nerviosismo *m*; mieditis* *f*; **to get the ~** ponerse nervioso; **to have the ~** estar nervioso; **to give sb the ~** poner nervioso a uno.

jittery* ['dʒɪtərɪ] ADJ muy inquieto, nervioso; **to get ~** inquietarse, ponerse nervioso.

jiujitsu [dʒuː'dʒɪtsuː] N jiu-jitsu *m*.

jive [dʒaɪv] ☐ N (a) (*music, dancing*) swing *m*, jazz *m*.
   (b) (*US:*) (*big talk*) alardes *mpl*, jactancias *fpl*; (*nonsense*) chorradas: *fpl*; (*of blacks etc; also ~ talk*) jerga *f*; **don't give me all that ~** deja de decir chorradas:.
   ☐ VI (a) (*dance*) bailar el swing, bailar el jazz.
   (b) (:: *be kidding*) bromear.

Jly ABBR *of* **July** julio, jul.

Jnr (*US*) ABBR *of* **junior** junior, jr.

Jo [dʒəʊ] NF *familiar form of* **Josephine.**

Joan [dʒəʊn] NF Juana; **~ of Arc** Juana de Arco.

▼**job** [dʒɒb] ☐ N (a) (*piece of work*) trabajo *m*, tarea *f*; (*Comput*) trabajo *m*; **the man for the ~** el más apropiado, el hombre ideal; **the ~ in hand** el trabajo que tenemos entre manos; **to be on the ~** estar trabajando; **she's doing a good ~** trabaja bien; **he has done a good ~ with the book** el libro le ha salido bien; **he never did a ~ in his life** no ha trabajado nunca; **to fall down on the ~** fracasar, demostrar no tener capacidad; **she had a nose ~ done*** tuvo cirugía estética para mejorar la nariz; **he knows his ~** sabe su oficio; **to**

make a good ~ of sth hacer algo bien; *V* **odd**.
(b) (*: *crime*) golpe* *m*, robo *m*; **that warehouse ~** ese robo en el almacén.
(c) (*piecework*) destajo *m*; **by the ~** a destajo.
(d) (*duty*) deber *m*, cometido *m*; **my ~ is to sell them** mi deber es venderlos, yo estoy encargado de venderlos; **that's not his ~** eso no le incumbe a él; **he does his ~** cumple con su deber; **I had the ~ of telling him** a mí me tocó decírselo.
▼**(e)** (*post, employment*) empleo *m*, puesto *m*, trabajo *m*; **we shall create 1000 new ~s** vamos a crear 1000 puestos de trabajo más; **~s for the boys*** amiguismo* *m*, enchufismo* *m*; **to be in a ~** tener trabajo; **to be out of a ~** estar sin trabajo, estar desocupado; **to lie down on the ~** echarse en el surco; **to look for a ~** buscar un empleo; **to lose one's ~** perder su empleo, ser despedido; **automation has put them out of a ~** la automatización les ha quitado el trabajo, han sido despedidos debido a la automatización.
(f) (*state of affairs*) **it's a bad ~** es una situación difícil; es lamentable, es terrible; **she gave him up as a bad ~** por imposible rompió con él; **to make the best of a bad ~** poner a mal tiempo buena cara; sacar el máximo partido de una situación (adversa); **that's a good ~!**, **and a good ~ too!** ¡menos mal!; **it's a good ~ that ...** menos mal que ...
(g) (*difficulty*) **we had quite a ~ getting here** nos costó trabajo venir aquí; **he has a ~ to express himself** le cuesta expresarse.
(h) (*) **it's just the ~!** ¡estupendo!*; **a holiday in Majorca would be just the ~** sería estupendo pasar unas vacaciones en Mallorca*; **this machine is just the ~** esta máquina nos viene perfecto.
2 ATTR **(a)** **~ analysis** análisis *m* del trabajo, análisis *m* ocupacional; **~ centre** (*Brit*) oficina *f* de empleo; **~ classification** clasificación *f* de trabajos; **~ club** grupo *m* de asesoramiento para desempleados; **~ control language** lenguaje *m* de control de trabajo; **~ creation** creación *f* de empleo; **~ creation scheme** plan *m* de creación de nuevos empleos; **~ description** descripción *f* del trabajo; **~ evaluation**, **~ grading** evaluación *f* de empleos; **~ hunting** búsqueda *f* de trabajo; **500 ~ losses** pérdida *f* de 500 puestos de trabajo; **~ number** número *m* del trabajo; **~ opportunity** oportunidad *f* de trabajo; **~ queue** (*Comput*) cola *f* de trabajos; (*persons*) cola *f* de los que buscan trabajo; **~ satisfaction** satisfacción *f* profesional, satisfacción *f* laboral; **~ security** seguridad *f* en el trabajo, garantía *f* de trabajo; **~ seeker** persona *f* que busca trabajo; **~ seeker's allowance** (*Brit*) ≃ prestación *f* por desempleo; **~ share** (*or* **sharing**) **scheme** plan *m* para compartir empleos; **~ specification** especificación *f* del trabajo, profesinagrama *m*; **~ study** estudio *m* del trabajo.
(b) **~ lot** lote *m* suelto de mercancías, saldo *m*.
-job* [-dʒɒb] N *ending in compounds*: **to have a chin~*** hacerse la cirugía plástica en la barbilla; **to have an eye~*** hacerse la cirugía plástica en los ojos.
Job [dʒəʊb] NM Job; **~'s comforter** *el que, bajo pretexto de animar a otro, le desconsuela todavía más*.
jobber ['dʒɒbəʳ] N (*Brit St Ex*) agiotista *mf*; (*agent*) corredor *m*, -ora *f*; (*middleman*) intermediario *m*, -a *f*.
jobbery ['dʒɒbərɪ] N (*Brit*) intrigas *fpl*, chanchullos *mpl*; **piece of ~** intriga *f*, chanchullo *m*; **by a piece of ~** por enchufe.
jobbing ['dʒɒbɪŋ] **1** ADJ que trabaja a destajo; **~ printer** impresor *m* de circulares, folletos *etc*.
2 N agiotaje *m*; comercio *m* de intermediario.
jobholder ['dʒɒb,həʊldəʳ] N empleado *m*, -a *f*.
jobless ['dʒɒblɪs] **1** ADJ sin trabajo.
2 NPL: **the ~** los desocupados, los parados; **the ~ figures** las cifras de personas sin trabajo.
joblessness ['dʒɒblɪsnɪs] N carencia *f* de trabajo.
job seeker ['dʒɒb,siːkəʳ] N demandante *mf* de empleo; **~'s allowance** prestación *f* por desempleo.
jock* [dʒɒk] NM *el escocés típico*; **the ~s** los escoceses.
jock [dʒɒk] N **(a)** = **jockstrap**. **(b)** (*US*) deportista *m*.
jockey ['dʒɒkɪ] **1** N jockey *m*, yoquei *m*; **~ shorts** calzoncillos *mpl* de jockey.
2 VT: **to ~ sb into doing sth** persuadir mañosamente a uno a hacer algo; **to ~ sb out of doing sth** disuadir mañosamente a uno de hacer algo; **to ~ sb out of a post** lograr mañosamente que uno renuncie a un puesto.
3 VI: **to ~ for a position** maniobrar para conseguir una posición.
jockstrap ['dʒɒkstræp] N suspensorio *m*.
jocose [dʒə'kəʊs] ADJ, **jocular** ['dʒɒkjʊləʳ] ADJ (*merry*) alegre, de buen humor; (*humorous*) guasón, zumbón, jocoso.
jocularity [,dʒɒkjʊ'lærətɪ] N jocosidad *f*.
jodhpurs ['dʒɒdpɜːz] NPL pantalones *mpl* de montar.
Joe [dʒəʊ] NM *familiar form of* **Joseph** (Pepe); (*US*) tipo* *m*, tío* *m*; **the average ~** el hombre de la calle; **a good ~** un buen chico; **~ Bloggs***, **~ Public*** (*Brit*) ciudadano de a pie británico; **~ College** (*US*) *típico estudiante norteamericano*; **~ Soap*** fulano *m*.
jog [dʒɒg] **1** N **(a)** (*push etc*) empujoncito *m*, sacudida *f* (ligera),

codazo *m*; (*encouragement*) estímulo *m*; **to give sb's memory a ~** refrescar la memoria de uno.
(b) (*pace*) trote *m* corto; **to go at a steady ~** andar a trote corto.
(c) **to go for a ~** hacer footing.
2 VT (*push etc*) empujar (ligeramente), sacudir (levemente); (*encourage*) estimular; *memory* refrescar; **he ~ged my arm** me dio ligeramente con el codo; **to ~ sb's memory** refrescar la memoria de uno.
3 VI **(a)** (*also* **to ~ along**) andar a trote corto, avanzar despacio; (*fig*) hacer algunos progresos, avanzar pero sin prisa; **we keep ~ging along** vamos tirando.
(b) (*Sport*) hacer footing.
jogger ['dʒɒgəʳ] N persona *f* que hace footing.
jogging ['dʒɒgɪŋ] **1** N footing *m*, futing *m*, jogging *m*.
2 ATTR: **~ shoes** zapatillas *fpl* de jogging; **~ suit** chandal *m*.
joggle ['dʒɒgl] **1** N traqueo *m*.
2 VT traquetear.
3 VI traquetear.
jog-trot ['dʒɒg'trɒt] N: **at a ~** a trote corto.
John [dʒɒn] NM Juan; **~ the Baptist** San Juan Bautista; **~ Bull** *personificación del pueblo inglés*; **~ Doe** (*US*) fulano *m*; *el norteamericano medio*; **~ Dory** ceo *m*; **~ Hancock***, **~ Henry*** firma *f*, rúbrica *f*; **~ Q Public*** (*US*) *el hombre de la calle, el público*; **St ~ the Evangelist** San Juan Evangelista; **St ~ of the Cross** San Juan de la Cruz; **Pope ~ Paul II** el Papa Juan Pablo II.
john¹* [dʒɒn] N (*US*) wáter *m*; *ver también* ⟨TOILET⟩ .
john²; [dʒɒn] N (*US*) cliente *m* de prostituta.
Johnny ['dʒɒnɪ] NM Juanito.
johnny* ['dʒɒnɪ] N tío* *m*, sujeto *m*.
joie de vivre ['ʒwɑːdə'viːvr] N goce *m* del vivir, alegría *f* vital.
join [dʒɔɪn] **1** N juntura *f*; (*Sew*) costura *f*.
2 VT **(a)** *two things* unir, juntar, poner juntos; (*Tech*) unir, acoplar, ensamblar; **everybody ~ed hands** se cogieron (*LAm*: se tomaron) todos de la mano; **to his genius he ~s humanity** a su genialidad une la humanidad.
(b) *society* ingresar en; *club* hacerse socio de; *party* afiliarse a, hacerse miembro de; *company* entrar en, tomar un puesto en; llegar a formar parte de; (*Mil*) alistarse en; **to ~ one's regiment** incorporarse a su regimiento; **to ~ one's ship** volver a su buque; **where the track ~s the road** donde el camino empalma con la carretera.
(c) *person* reunirse con, unirse a, juntarse con; **may I ~ you?** ¿se permite?; **will you ~ me in a drink?** ¿quieres tomar algo conmigo?; **they ~ed us last Friday** vinieron a estar con nosotros el viernes pasado; **they will ~ us for the holidays** vendrán a pasar las vacaciones con nosotros; **to ~ sb in doing sth** acompañar a uno en hacer algo, hacer juntamente con uno; **they ~ed us in protesting** se hicieron eco de nuestras protestas.
(d) (*river*) desembocar en, confluir con; (*road*) empalmar con, unirse a.
3 VI **(a)** unirse, juntarse; (*lines*) empalmar; (*rivers*) confluir; **where the paths ~** donde empalman los caminos.
(b) **to ~ with sb in sth** acompañar a uno en algo, participar juntamente con uno en algo; **we ~ with you in that feeling** compartimos esa opinión, nos hacemos eco de eso; **we ~ with you in hoping that ...** lo mismo que Vds esperamos que ...
(c) (*Pol etc*) hacerse miembro.
◆**join in** **1** VT: **she ~ed in the discussion** intervino en el debate.
2 VI tomar parte (en), participar (en); **he doesn't ~ in much** apenas participa en nuestras actividades; **they all ~ed in singing the last song** todos cantaron la última canción.
◆**join on** **1** VT unir; añadir.
2 VI: **he ~ed on to the queue** se unió a la cola; **it ~s on here** se coloca aquí.
◆**join together** **1** VT unir.
2 VI unirse (*to* + *infin* para + *infin*).
◆**join up** **1** VT **(a)** unir; **~ed up writing** escritura *f* cursiva. **(b)** = **join 2 (a)**.
2 VI **(a)** unirse; **to ~ up with sb** reunirse con uno. **(b)** (*Mil*) alistarse.
joiner ['dʒɔɪnəʳ] N (*Brit*) carpintero *m* (de blanco), ensamblador *m*.
joinery ['dʒɔɪnərɪ] N (*Brit*) carpintería *f*.
joint [dʒɔɪnt] **1** ADJ (en) común; combinado; *action, effort, product etc* conjunto, colectivo; *agreement* mutuo; *declaration etc* conjunto; *responsibility* solidario, que comparten todos; *committee etc* mixto; (*in compounds*) co ...; **~ account** cuenta *f* indistinta, cuenta *f* conjunta; **~ author** coautor *m*, -ora *f*; **~ communiqué** comunicado *m* conjunto; **~ consultations** consultas *fpl* bilaterales; **~ heir** coheredero *m*, -a *f*; **~ interest** (*Comm*) coparticipación *f*; **~ liability** responsabilidad *f* solidaria; obligación *f* mancomunada; **~ owners** copropietarios *mpl*; **~ ownership** copropiedad *f*; **~ partner** copartícipe *mf*; **~ stock** fondo *m* social; **~-stock bank** banco *m* por acciones; **~ stock company** sociedad *f* anónima; **~ venture** (*Fin*) empresa *f* (*or* sociedad *f*) conjunta; acuerdo *m* de riesgos compartidos.

2 N **(a)** (*Tech: metal*) junta *f*, juntura *f*, unión *f*; (*wood*) ensambladura *f*; (*hinge*) bisagra *f*; (*Anat*) articulación *f*, coyuntura *f*; (*knuckle*) nudillo *m*; (*Bot*) nudo *m*; (*Brit: of meat*) cuarto *m*; **to be out of ~** (*bone*) estar descoyuntado, estar dislocado; (*fig*) estar fuera de quicio; **to put a bone out of ~** dislocarse un hueso; **to put sb's nose out of ~** desconcertar a uno (adelantándose a él); **to throw sb's plans out of ~** estropear los planes de uno.
(b) (‡: *place*) antro *m*, tugurio *m*, garito *m*.
(c) (‡: *drugs*) porro‡ *m*, cigarrillo *m* de marijuana.
3 VT articular; *parts* juntar, unir; *wood etc* ensamblar; (*Brit Culin*) cortar.

jointed ['dʒɔɪntɪd] ADJ articulado; (*folding*) plegadizo, plegable.
jointly ['dʒɔɪntlɪ] ADV en común; colectivamente; mutuamente; conjuntamente.
joist [dʒɔɪst] N viga *f*, vigueta *f*.
jojoba [həʊ'həʊbə] **1** N jojoba *f*.
2 ATTR de jojoba.
▼ **joke** [dʒəʊk] **1** N (*hoax etc*) broma *f*, burla *f*; (*witticism, story*) chiste *m*; (*person*) hazmerreír *m*; **he's a standing ~** es un pobre hombre, es un hombre que da risa; **it's a standing ~ here** aquí eso siempre provoca a risa; **it's no ~** no es cosa de risa, no es para reírse; **it's no ~ having to** + *infin* no tiene nada de divertido + *infin*; **the ~ is that** lo gracioso es que; **the ~ is on you** tu eres el aludido, eso lo dicen por ti; **it's beyond a ~** esto es el colmo, esto pasa de castaño oscuro; **what sort of a ~ is this?** ¿qué broma es ésta?; **is that your idea of a ~?** ¿es que eso tiene gracia?; **to crack** (*or* **make**) **a ~** hacer un chiste; **to crack ~s with sb** contar chistes con uno; **they spent an evening cracking ~s together** pasaron una tarde contándose chistes; **he will have his little ~** siempre está con sus bromas, le gusta tomar el pelo; **he made a ~ of the disaster** tomó el desastre en chunga; **to play a ~ on sb** gastar una broma a uno; **I can take a ~** tengo mucho aguante; **he can't take a ~** no le gusta que se le tome el pelo; **to tell a ~** contar un chiste; **why do you have to turn everything into a ~?** ¿eres incapaz de tomar nada en serio?
▼ **2** VI bromear, chancearse, chunguearse; hablar en broma; (*tell ~s*) contar chistes; **I was only joking** lo dije en broma; **I'm not joking** esto lo digo en serio; **you must be joking!** pero ¿lo dices en serio?; **to ~ about sth** tomar algo en chunga.
jokebook ['dʒəʊk,bʊk] N libro *m* de chistes.
joker ['dʒəʊkə'] N **(a)** (*wit*) chistoso *m*, -a *f*, guasón *m*, -ona *f*; (*practical ~*) bromista *mf*. **(b)** (*Cards*) comodín *m*; **he's the ~ in the pack** (*fig*) es el elemento desconocido. **(c)** (*) **some ~** algún gracioso.
jokester ['dʒəʊkstə'] N bromista *mf*.
jokey ['dʒəʊkɪ] ADJ *person* chistoso, guasón; *reference etc* humorístico; *mood, tone* guasón.
joking ['dʒəʊkɪŋ] **1** ADJ *reference etc* humorístico; *tone* guasón; **I'm not in a ~ mood** no estoy para bromas.
2 N bromas *fpl*; chistes *mpl*; **but ~ apart, ...** pero bromas aparte, ...
jokingly ['dʒəʊkɪŋlɪ] ADV humorísticamente; **he said ~** dijo en broma, dijo guasón.
jollification [,dʒɒlɪfɪ'keɪʃən] N (*merriment*) regocijo *m*, festividades *fpl*; (*party*) fiesta *f*, guateque *m*.
jolliness ['dʒɒlɪnɪs] N jovialidad *f*.
jollity ['dʒɒlɪtɪ] N alegría *f*, regocijo *m*.
jolly ['dʒɒlɪ] **1** ADJ alegre; divertido; *character* alegre, jovial; **J~ Roger** pabellón *m* negro (de los piratas); **it was all very ~** todo ha sido muy agradable; **to get ~*** achisparse*; **we had a ~ time** lo pasamos muy bien, nos divertimos mucho; **it wasn't very ~ for the rest of us** los demás no nos divertimos nada.
2 (*Brit**) ADV muy, terriblemente; **it's ~ hard** es terriblemente difícil; **we were ~ glad** nos alegramos muchísimo; **you did ~ well** lo hiciste la mar de bien*; **you've ~ well got to** no tienes más remedio en absoluto; **~ good!** ¡estupendo!*
3 VT: **to ~ sb along** engatusar a uno, seguir el humor a uno; **to ~ sb into doing sth** engatusar a uno para que haga algo.
jollyboat ['dʒɒlɪbəʊt] N esquife *m*.
jolt [dʒəʊlt] **1** N sacudida *f*, choque *m*; **to give sb a ~** (*fig*) dar una sacudida a uno; **it gave me a bit of a ~** me dio un susto, con eso me pegué un susto.
2 VT sacudir; *elbow etc* empujar (ligeramente), sacudir (levemente); **to ~ sb into doing sth** dar una sacudida a uno para animarle a hacer algo; **to ~ sb out of his complacency** hacer que uno se dé cuenta de la necesidad de hacer algo, destruir el optimismo de uno.
3 VI (*vehicle*) traquetear, dar saltos.
jolting ['dʒəʊltɪŋ] N (*of vehicle*) traqueteo *m*.
jolty ['dʒəʊltɪ] ADJ *vehicle* que traquetea, que da saltos.
Jonah ['dʒəʊnə] NM Jonás.
Jonathan ['dʒɒnəθən] NM Jonatás.
jonquil ['dʒɒŋkwɪl] N junquillo *m*.
Jordan ['dʒɔːdn] N **(a)** (*river*) Jordán *m*. **(b)** (*country*) Jordania *f*.
Jordanian [dʒɔː'deɪnɪən] **1** ADJ jordano.
2 N jordano *m*, -a *f*.

Joseph ['dʒəʊzɪf] NM José.
Josephine ['dʒəʊzɪfiːn] NF Josefina.
josh‡ [dʒɒʃ] VT (*US*) tomar el pelo a.
Joshua ['dʒɒʃwə] NM Josué.
josser‡ ['dʒɒsə'] N tío *m*, individuo *m*.
joss-stick ['dʒɒsstɪk] N pebete *m*.
jostle ['dʒɒsl] **1** N empujón *m*, empellón *m*, codazo *m*.
2 VT empujar, zarandear.
3 VI empujar(se), dar(se) empellones, codear(se); **they were all jostling for a place** todos se estaban empujando para asegurarse un sitio.
jot [dʒɒt] **1** N jota *f*, pizca *f*; **there's not a ~ of truth in it** eso no tiene ni pizca de verdad; V **care**.
2 VT: **to ~ down** apuntar.
jotter ['dʒɒtə'] N (*Brit*) cuaderno *m*, bloc *m*, taco *m* para notas.
jottings ['dʒɒtɪŋz] NPL apuntes *mpl*.
joule [dʒuːl] N julio *m*, joule *m*.
journal ['dʒɜːnl] N **(a)** (*newspaper*) periódico *m*; (*review, magazine*) revista *f*; (*diary*) diario *m*; (*Naut*) diario *m* de navegación. **(b)** (*Mech*) gorrón *m*, muñón *m*.
journal bearing ['dʒɜːnl'beərɪŋ] N cojinete *m*.
journalese [,dʒɜːnə'liːz] N lenguaje *m* (*or* estilo *m*) periodístico.
journalism ['dʒɜːnəlɪzəm] N periodismo *m*.
journalist ['dʒɜːnəlɪst] N periodista *mf*.
journalistic [,dʒɜːnə'lɪstɪk] ADJ periodístico.
journey ['dʒɜːnɪ] **1** N viaje *m*; trayecto *m*; camino *m*; **Scott's ~ to the Pole** la expedición de Scott al Polo; **the capsule's ~ through space** el trayecto de la cápsula por el espacio; **pleasant ~!** ¡buen viaje!; **at ~'s end** al fin del viaje; **to be on a ~** estar de viaje; **have you much ~ left?** ¿le queda mucho camino?
2 VI viajar.
journeyman ['dʒɜːnɪmən] N, PL **journeymen** ['dʒɜːnɪmən] oficial *m*.
journo* ['dʒɜːnəʊ] N (*Brit*) periodista *mf*.
joust [dʒaʊst] **1** N justa *f*, torneo *m*.
2 VI justar.
Jove [dʒəʊv] NM Júpiter; **by ~!** ¡caramba!, ¡por Dios!
jovial ['dʒəʊvɪəl] ADJ jovial.
joviality [,dʒəʊvɪ'ælɪtɪ] N jovialidad *f*.
jovially ['dʒəʊvɪəlɪ] ADV *say* jovialmente.
jowl [dʒaʊl] N (*Anat: jaw*) quijada *f*; (*chin*) barba *f*; (*cheek*) carrillo *m*; (*Zool*) papada *f*.
-jowled ['dʒaʊld] ADJ *ending in compounds*: **square~** de mandíbulas cuadradas.
jowly ['dʒaʊlɪ] ADJ de mejillas caídas.
joy [dʒɔɪ] N (*gladness*) alegría *f*, júbilo *m*, regocijo *m*, gozo *m*; (*pleasant quality*) deleite *m*, encanto *m*; **the ~s of opera** los encantos de la ópera; **it's a ~ to hear him** da gozo escucharle; **to be a ~ to the eye** ser un gozo para los ojos; **to be beside o.s. with ~** no caber en sí de gozo; **to jump for ~** saltar de alegría; **I wish you ~!** ¡enhorabuena! (*also iro*); **no ~!*** ¡nada!; **we got no ~ out of it** no logramos nada, no nos sirvió de nada, no nos dio resultado alguno.
joyful ['dʒɔɪfʊl] ADJ alegre; jubiloso, regocijado; **to be ~ about** alegrarse de.
joyfully ['dʒɔɪfəlɪ] ADV alegremente; con júbilo, regocijadamente.
joyfulness ['dʒɔɪfʊlnɪs] N alegría *f*; júbilo *m*, regocijo *m*.
joyless ['dʒɔɪlɪs] ADJ sin alegría, triste.
joyous ['dʒɔɪəs] ADJ alegre.
joyride ['dʒɔɪraɪd] **1** N paseo *m* en coche (*etc*) (sin permiso del dueño), excursión *f* en coche (*etc*).
2 VI pasearse en coche (*etc*) (sin permiso del dueño).
joystick ['dʒɔɪstɪk] N (*Aer*) palanca *f* de mando; (*Comput*) palanca *f* de control, bastoncillo *m* de mando.
JP N (*Brit*) ABBR *of* **Justice of the Peace** juez *m* de paz; *ver también* MAGISTRATE .
Jr ABBR *of* **junior** junior, jr.
JTPA N (*US*) ABBR *of* **Job Training Partnership Act** programa *m* gubernamental de formación profesional.
jubilant ['dʒuːbɪlənt] ADJ jubiloso.
jubilation [,dʒuːbɪ'leɪʃən] N júbilo *m*.
jubilee ['dʒuːbɪliː] N (*Hist, Eccl*) jubileo *m*; (*anniversary: strictly*) quincuagésimo aniversario *m*; V **silver** *etc*.
Judaea [dʒuː'dɪə] N Judea *f*.
Judaeo-Christian, (*US*) **Judeo-Christian** [dʒuː:,deɪəʊ'krɪstɪən] ADJ judeo-cristiano.
Judah ['dʒuːdə] N Judá *m*.
Judaic [dʒuː'deɪk] ADJ judaico.
Judaism ['dʒuːdeɪɪzəm] N judaísmo *m*.
Judaize ['dʒuːdeʌaɪz] VI judaizar.
Judaizer ['dʒuːdeɪˌaɪzə'] N judaizante *mf*.
Judas ['dʒuːdəs] NM Judas.
judder ['dʒʌdə'] (*Brit*) **1** N vibración *f*.
2 VI vibrar.

Judeo-Spanish ['dʒu:deɪəʊ'spænɪʃ] [1] ADJ judeoespañol, sefardí.
   [2] N (*Ling*) judeoespañol *m*, ladino *m*.

▼ **judge** [dʒʌdʒ] [1] N (*Jur*) juez *mf* (*also* -a *f*); (*Sport*) árbitro *m*, (*in races*) juez *m*; (*connoisseur*) conocedor *m*, -ora *f* (*of* de), (*expert*) perito *m* (*of* en); **Book of J~s** (Libro *m* de los) Jueces *mpl*; **~ of appeal** juez *m* de alzadas, juez *m* de apelaciones; **the ~'s rules** (*Brit*) los derechos del detenido; **he's a fine ~ of horses** es un excelente conocedor de caballos; **I'm no ~ of wines** yo no entiendo de vinos; **I'll be the ~ of that** yo decidiré aquello, lo juzgaré yo mismo.
   [2] VT *person, case* juzgar; *question* decidir, resolver; (*Sport*) arbitrar; (*consider*) juzgar, considerar; **I ~ it to be right** lo considero acertado; **I ~ him a fool** considero que es tonto; **as far as can be ~d** a mi modo de ver, según mi juicio; **one has to ~ the distance** hay que calcular la distancia; **he ~d the moment well** acertó escogiendo tal momento; **who can ~ this question?** ¿quién puede resolver esta cuestión?
   ▼ [3] VI juzgar; opinar, expresar una opinión; **to ~ by, judging by** a juzgar por; **to ~ of** juzgar de, opinar sobre; **who am I to ~?** ¿es que yo soy capaz de juzgar? **only an expert can ~** sólo lo puede decidir un experto; **to ~ for o.s.** formar su propia opinión.

judge-advocate ['dʒʌdʒ'ædvəkɪt] N (*Mil*) auditor *m* de guerra.

judg(e)ment ['dʒʌdʒmənt] N (a) (*Jur*) juicio *m*; sentencia *f*, fallo *m*; **Last J~** Juicio *m* Final; **J~ Day** día *m* del Juicio Final; **~ seat** tribunal *m*; **it's a ~ on you for lying** es un castigo por haber mentido; **to pass** (*or* **pronounce**) **~** (*Jur*) pronunciar sentencia (*on* en, sobre), (*fig*) emitir un juicio crítico sobre, dictaminar sobre.
   (b) (*opinion*) opinión *f*, parecer *m*; juicio *m*; **a critical ~ of Auden** un juicio crítico de Auden.
   (c) (*understanding*) juicio *m*; criterio *m*; entendimiento *m*, discernimiento *m*; buen sentido *m*; **against my better ~** en contra de lo que me aconsejaba mi juicio; **in my ~** en mi opinión; **to the best of my ~** según mi leal saber y entender; **to have good** (*or* **sound**) **~** tener buen juicio, tener buen criterio.

judg(e)mental [dʒʌdʒ'mentl] ADJ crítico.

judg(e)ment call ['dʒʌdʒmənt,kɔːl] N (*esp US*) decisión que depende de la conciencia de cada uno.

judicature ['dʒu:dɪkətʃəʳ] N judicatura *f*.

judicial [dʒu:'dɪʃəl] ADJ judicial; imparcial; *murder, separation etc* legal; **~ inquiry** investigación *f* judicial.

judicially [dʒu:'dɪʃəlɪ] ADV judicialmente; legalmente.

judiciary [dʒu:'dɪʃərɪ] [1] ADJ judicial.
   [2] N judicatura *f*.

judicious [dʒu:'dɪʃəs] ADJ juicioso; prudente, sensato, acertado.

judiciously [dʒu:'dɪʃəslɪ] ADV juiciosamente; prudentemente, acertadamente.

Judith ['dʒu:dɪθ] NF Judit.

judo ['dʒu:dəʊ] N judo *m*, yudo *m*.

judoka ['dʒu:dəʊ,kɑ:] N judoka *mf*.

Judy ['dʒu:dɪ] NF *familiar form of* **Judith.**

jug [dʒʌg] [1] N (a) jarro *m*. (b) (‡: *jail*) chirona‡ *f*. (c) **~s** (US‡) tetas* *fpl*.
   [2] VT (a) **~ged hare** liebre *f* en estofado. (b) (‡) meter a la sombra‡.

juggernaut ['dʒʌgənɔːt] N monstruo *m* destructor de los hombres; (*Aut*) camión *m* grande, camionazo *m*.

juggins‡ ['dʒʌgɪnz] N bobo *m*, -a *f*.

juggle ['dʒʌgl] [1] VI hacer juegos malabares, hacer juegos de manos (*with* con); **to ~ with** (*fig*) = 2.
   [2] VT arreglar de otro modo; (*pej*) falsear, falsificar, hacer trampa con.

juggler ['dʒʌgləʳ] N malabarista *mf*.

jugglery ['dʒʌglərɪ] N, **juggling** ['dʒʌglɪŋ] N juegos *mpl* malabares, malabarismo *m*, juegos *mpl* de manos; (*pej*) trampas *fpl*, fraude *m*.

juggling act ['dʒʌglɪŋ,ækt] N (*fig*) malabarismos *mpl*; **balancing the budget is a complex ~** hay que hacer malabarismos para nivelar el presupuesto.

Jugoslav ['ju:gəʊ'slɑ:v] [1] ADJ yugoslavo.
   [2] N yugoslavo *m*, -a *f*.

Jugoslavia ['ju:gəʊ'slɑ:vɪə] N Yugoslavia *f*.

jugular ['dʒʌgjʊləʳ] [1] ADJ: **~ vein** vena *f* yugular.
   [2] N vena *f* yugular.

juice [dʒu:s] N (a) (*fruit ~*) jugo *m*, zumo *m*. (b) (*Brit Aut*) gasolina *f*. (c) (*Elec*) fluido *m*, fuerza *f*, corriente *f*.

juicer ['dʒu:səʳ] N (*US*) licuadora *f*.

juiciness ['dʒu:sɪnɪs] N (a) jugosidad *f*. (b) (*) lo picante, lo sabroso.

juicy ['dʒu:sɪ] ADJ (a) jugoso, zumoso. (b) (*) *story etc* picante, sabroso; *contract etc* sustancioso, ganancioso.

jujube ['dʒu:dʒu:b] N pastilla *f*.

jujutsu [dʒu:'dʒɪtsʊ] N jiu-jitsu *m*.

jukebox ['dʒu:kbɒks] N tocadiscos *m* automático, tocadiscos *m* tragaperras, gramola *f*.

Jul. ABBR *of* **July** julio *m*, jul.

julep ['dʒu:lep] N julepe *m*.

Julian ['dʒu:lɪən] NM Juliano, Julián.
Juliet ['dʒu:lɪet] NF Julieta.
Julius ['dʒu:lɪəs] NM Julio; **~ Caesar** Julio César.
July [dʒu:'laɪ] N julio *m*.

jumble ['dʒʌmbl] [1] N (a) revoltijo *m*, confusión *f*; **a ~ of furniture** un montón de muebles revueltos; **a ~ of sounds** unos ruidos confusos. (b) (*at sale*) objetos *mpl* usados, (*esp*) ropa *f* usada.
   [2] VT (*also* **to ~ together, to ~ up**) mezclar, emburujar; **papers ~d up together** papeles *mpl* revueltos; **they were just ~d together anyhow** estaban amontonados sin orden.

jumble sale ['dʒʌmblseɪl] N (*Brit*) venta *f* de objetos usados (con fines benéficos), bazar *m* benéfico, rastrillo* *m* (benéfico).

┌─ *JUMBLE SALE/RUMMAGE SALE* ─┐

ⓘ *Se conoce como* **jumble sale** *en el Reino Unido o como* **rummage sale** *en Estados Unidos el mercadillo que se organiza con fines benéficos en los locales de un colegio, iglesia, ayuntamiento u otro centro público. En él se venden artículos baratos de segunda mano como por ejemplo libros, juguetes, joyas o ropa y también se suelen colocar puestos de té o café.*

jumbo ['dʒʌmbəʊ] [1] N (a) elefante *m*.
   (b) (*Aer: also* **~ jet**) jumbo *m*.
   [2] ADJ colosal, enorme; (*Comm: also* **~ sized**) de tamaño extra.

jump [dʒʌmp] [1] N salto *m*, brinco *m*; (*Sport*) salto *m*; (*Comput*) salto *m*; (*fig*) ascenso *m*, aumento *m*; **to give a ~** dar un saltito; **to give sb a ~** dar un susto a uno; **you gave me quite a ~!** ¡ay qué susto me diste!; **to have the ~ on sb*** llevar ventaja a uno; **the temperature took a ~** subió rápidamente la temperatura; **there has been a big ~ in the reserves** las reservas han subido de golpe; **to keep one ~ ahead** mantener la delantera (*of sb* con respecto a uno); **in one ~ he went from novice to master** en limpio salto pasó de novicio a maestro.
   [2] VT (a) *ditch etc* saltar, saltar por encima de, salvar; **to ~ the lights*** (*Aut*) saltarse un semáforo en rojo; *V* **gun, rail** *etc*.
   (b) *horse* hacer saltar; presentar en un concurso hípico.
   (c) (*omit*) pasar por alto, omitir.
   [3] VI (a) (*leap*) saltar, brincar, dar saltos; (*Sport*) saltar; (*Aer*) lanzarse (en paracaídas); (*Comput*) saltar.
   (b) (*fig: start*) asustarse, sobresaltarse, pegar un bote; **to make sb ~** dar un susto a uno; **you did make me ~!** ¡ay qué susto me diste!
   (c) (*fig: emotion*) **to ~ for joy** saltar de alegría, no caber en sí de gozo; **everyone was ~ing up and down** (*angry*) todos estaban que brincaban, (*excited*) todos brincaban de emoción.

◆**jump about, jump around** VI dar saltos, brincar; moverse de un lado para otro.

◆**jump across** VT: **to ~ across a stream** cruzar un arroyo de un salto, saltar por encima de un arroyo.

◆**jump at** VT: **to ~ at a chance** apresurarse a aprovechar una oportunidad; **to ~ at an offer** aceptar una oferta con entusiasmo, agarrarse a una oferta.

◆**jump down** VI bajar de un salto, saltar a tierra.

◆**jump in** VI: **~ in!** ¡sube!, ¡vamos!; **to ~ into a car** entrar de prisa en un coche.

◆**jump off** VI (*Showjumping*) participar en un desempate.

◆**jump on** VT (a) **to ~ on** (**to**) **a chair** ponerse encima de una silla de un salto; **we ~ed on** (**to**) **the train** subimos de prisa al tren.
   (b) (*) **to ~ on sb** poner verde a uno*; **we must ~ on this abuse** tenemos que acabar con este abuso.

◆**jump out** VI: **to ~ out of bed** saltar de la cama; **I nearly ~ed out of my skin!** ¡vaya susto que me pegué!; **he ~ed out from behind a tree** salió de repente de detrás de un árbol; **it ~s out at you** (*fig*) salta a la vista.

◆**jump over** VT saltar, saltar por (encima de), salvar.

◆**jump to** VT: **~ to it!** ¡apúrate!, ¡volando!

◆**jump up** VI ponerse de pie de un salto.

jumped-up ['dʒʌmpt'ʌp] ADJ arribista, presuntuoso.

jumper ['dʒʌmpəʳ] N (a) (*person*) N saltador *m*, -ora *f*. (b) (*Brit: pullover*) suéter *m*, jersey *m*; (*US: pinafore dress*) mandil *m*.

jumper cables ['dʒʌmpəʳ,keɪbəlz] NPL (*US*) = **jump leads.**

jumping ['dʒʌmpɪŋ] N (*Sport*) pruebas *fpl* de salto.

jumping bean ['dʒʌmpɪŋ,bi:n] N judía *f* saltadora, fríjol *m* saltador.

jumping-off ['dʒʌmpɪŋ'ɒf] ATTR: **~ place** punto *m* de partida; base *f* avanzada.

jump-jet ['dʒʌmpdʒet] N avión *m* (a chorro) de despegue vertical.

jump leads ['dʒʌmp,li:dz] NPL (*Brit Aut*) cables *mpl* puente de batería, cables *mpl* de emergencia.

jump-off ['dʒʌmpɒf] N (*Showjumping*) prueba *f* (*or* saltos *mpl*) de desempate.

jump-rope ['dʒʌmprəʊp] N (*US*) comba *f*, cuerda *f* de saltar.

jump-seat ['dʒʌmpsi:t] N asiento *m* plegable.

jump-start ['dʒʌmpstɑ:t] [1] N arranque *m* en segunda.
   [2] VT arrancar en segunda.

jumpsuit ['dʒʌmpsuːt] N (US) mono m.
jumpy ['dʒʌmpɪ] ADJ nervioso, asustadizo.
Jun. ABBR of **June** junio, jun.
junction ['dʒʌŋkʃən] N juntura f, unión f; (Brit: of roads) cruce m, entronque m (Méx), crucero m (LAm); (Brit Rail) empalme m; (Brit: of rivers) confluencia f.
junction box ['dʒʌŋkʃənbɒks] N caja f de empalmes.
juncture ['dʒʌŋktʃər] N coyuntura f; **at this ~** en este momento, en esta coyuntura; a estas alturas.
June [dʒuːn] N junio m.
Jungian [jʊŋɪən] ① ADJ jungiano.
  ② N jungiano m, -a f.
jungle ['dʒʌŋgl] ① N selva f, jungla f; (fig) maraña f, selva f.
  ② ATTR: **~ bunny** (US‡) negrito* m, -a* f; **~ warfare** guerra f de la selva.
junior ['dʒuːnɪər] ① ADJ (in age) menor, más joven; (on a staff) más nuevo; position, rank subalterno; section (in competition etc) juvenil, para menores; **Roy Smith, J~** Roy Smith, hijo; **~ college** (US) centro universitario donde se imparten cursos de dos años; **~ executive** joven ejecutivo m, -a f, ejecutivo m subalterno, ejecutiva f subalterna; **~ high school** (US) centro de enseñanza secundaria; **~ minister** subsecretario m, -a f; **~ partner** socio mf menos antiguo; **~ school** (Brit) escuela f primaria; ver también EDUCATION .
  ② N menor mf, joven mf; (US*) hijo m, niño m; (Brit Scol) alumno m (or alumna f) de 8 a 11 años; (US Univ) estudiante mf del penúltimo año; (office ~) recadero m; **he is my ~ by 3 years, he is 3 years my ~** tiene 3 años menos que yo, le llevo 3 años; ver también GRADE .
juniper ['dʒuːnɪpər] N enebro m.
junk¹ [dʒʌŋk] N (Naut) junco m.
junk² [dʒʌŋk] ① N (lumber) trastos mpl viejos; (rubbish) basura f, desperdicios mpl; (iron) chatarra f, hierro m viejo; (cheap goods) baratijas fpl; **the play is a lot of ~** la obra es una porquería; **he talks a lot of ~** no habla más que tonterías.
  ② VT (esp US) echar a la basura, tirar, desechar.
junk-bonds ['dʒʌŋkbɒndz] NPL obligaciones fpl basura.
junk dealer ['dʒʌŋk,diːlər] N vendedor m, -ora f de objetos usados.
junket ['dʒʌŋkɪt] ① N (a) dulce m de leche cuajada. (b) (*) fiesta f, juerga* f, jira f, excursión f.
  ② VI ir de juerga*, estar de fiesta; ir de jira.
junketing ['dʒʌŋkɪtɪŋ] N (also ~s) festividades fpl, fiestas fpl.
junk-food ['dʒʌŋkfuːd] N comida f basura.
junkheap ['dʒʌŋkhiːp] N: **to end up on the ~** terminar en el cubo de la basura.
junkie‡ ['dʒʌŋkɪ] N drogadicto m, -a f, yonqui‡ mf; **chocolate ~** adicto m, -a f al chocolate.
junkmail ['dʒʌŋkmeɪl] N propaganda f de buzón, materiales mpl publicitarios enviados por correo.
junkman ['dʒʌŋkmæn] N, PL **junkmen** ['dʒʌŋkmen] chatarrero m.
junk room ['dʒʌŋkruːm] N trastero m.
junkshop ['dʒʌŋkʃɒp] N tienda f de trastos viejos.
junkyard ['dʒʌŋkjɑːd] N depósito m de chatarra, chatarrería f.
Juno ['dʒuːnəʊ] NF Juno.
Junoesque [,dʒuːnəʊ'esk] ADJ figure imponente, majestuoso; woman de belleza majestuosa.
Jun(r). ABBR of **junior** junior, jr.
junta ['dʒʌntə] N junta f.
Jupiter ['dʒuːpɪtər] NM Júpiter.
Jurassic [dʒʊ'ræsɪk] ADJ jurásico.
juridical [dʒʊə'rɪdɪkəl] ADJ jurídico.
jurisdiction [,dʒʊərɪs'dɪkʃən] N jurisdicción f; competencia f; **to come within sb's ~** ser de la competencia de uno.
jurisdictional [,dʒʊərɪs'dɪkʃənl] ADJ (US) dispute, rights jurisdiccional.
jurisprudence [,dʒʊərɪs'pruːdəns] N jurisprudencia f; **medical ~** medicina f legal.
jurist ['dʒʊərɪst] N jurista m.
juror ['dʒʊərər] N jurado m (persona).
jury ['dʒʊərɪ] N jurado m (conjunto de jurados); **to be on the ~** ser miembro del jurado; ver también GRAND JURY .
jury-box ['dʒʊərɪbɒks] N tribuna f del jurado.
jury duty ['dʒʊərɪ,djuːtɪ] N: **to do ~** actuar como jurado.
juryman ['dʒʊərɪmən] N, PL **jurymen** ['dʒʊərɪmən] (miembro m del) jurado m.
jury-mast ['dʒʊərɪmɑːst] N bandola f.
jury-rig ['dʒʊərɪrɪg] N aparejo m provisional.
jury-rigging ['dʒʊərɪ,rɪgɪŋ] N amaño m de un jurado.
jurywoman ['dʒuːrɪwʊmən] N, PL **jurywomen** ['dʒuːrɪwɪmɪn] (miembro f (femenino) del jurado.
just¹ [dʒʌst] ADJ (upright) justo, recto, imparcial; (accurate) exacto, correcto; (deserved) merecido, apropiado; (well grounded) justificado, lógico; **as is only ~** como es justo, como es de razón; **the ~** los justos.

just² ADV (a) (exactly) exactamente, precisamente; justo, justamente; **~ at that moment** en aquel mismo momento; **~ here** aquí mismo; **~ by the church** al lado mismo de la iglesia, justo al lado de la iglesia, muy cerca de la iglesia; **~ beyond the pub** justo después de la tasca, un poco más allá de la tasca; **it's ~ (on) 4 o'clock** son las 4 en punto; **~ so!** ¡eso es!, ¡perfectamente!, ¡precisamente!; **that's ~ it!** ¡ahí está la dificultad!; **it's ~ the same** es exactamente igual; **~ like that** así nada más; **it's ~ what I needed** es precisamente lo que necesitaba, es justamente lo que me hacía falta; **they were ~ like two brothers** eran (en todo) como dos hermanos; **we were ~ talking about it** precisamente estábamos hablando de eso; **~ when he started to sing** precisamente cuando empezaba a cantar; **I was ~ going** estaba a punto de marcharme; **now ~ what did he say?** ¿qué es lo que dijo, en concreto?; **~ how many we don't know** no sabemos exactamente cuántos; **a policeman? that's ~ what I am** ¿un policía? justamente yo lo soy.
(b) (with as) **you sing ~ as well as I do** cantas tan bien como yo; **~ as you wish** como quieras; **~ as it started to rain** justo cuando empezó a llover, en el momento en que empezó a llover; **we left everything ~ as it was** lo dejamos todo exactamente como estaba; **it's ~ as well it's insured** menos mal que está asegurado; **it would be ~ as well if he went** más vale que se vaya él.
(c) (only) solamente, sólo, tan sólo; **~ as a joke** en broma nada más; **~ for a laugh** sólo para hacer reír; **~ once** una vez nada más, solamente una vez, una vez solamente; **~ the two of us** nosotros dos solamente; **we're ~ good friends** somos amigos nada más; **~ a little bit** un poquito; **~ a few** unos pocos; **he's ~ a lad** no es más que un chico; **~ let me get at him!** ¡que me dejen llegar a él!
(d) (merely) **I ~ told him to go away** le dije que se fuera, nada más; **it's ~ that I don't like it** es que no me gusta; **we're ~ amateurs** somos simples aficionados; **~ wait a moment!** ¡espere un momento!; **~ imagine!** ¡imagínese!; **~ listen!** ¡escucha un poco!; **~ look!** ¡mira!, ¡fíjate!; **~ a tick!** ¡un momentito!
(e) (positively) **it's ~ fine!** ¡es francamente maravilloso!, ¡es sencillamente maravilloso!; **it's ~ perfect!** ¡qué maravilla!
(f) (barely) **I ~ managed to catch it** por poco lo perdí; **he was only ~ saved from drowning** poco faltó para que muriese ahogado; **you're ~ in time** llegas justamente con tiempo; **~ before it rained** momentos antes de que lloviese.
(g) (with have etc) **I have ~ seen him** acabo de verle; **I had ~ seen him** acababa de verle; **the book is ~ out** el libro acaba de publicarse; **~ appointed** recién nombrado; **~ received** acabado de recibir; **~ cooked** recién hecho, recién salido del horno.
(h) (emphatic) **don't I ~!* ¡ya lo creo!, ¡y cómo!; V now, yet etc.
justice ['dʒʌstɪs] N (a) justicia f; **to bring sb to ~** llevar a uno ante el tribunal, hacer que uno sea procesado; **to do sb ~** hacer justicia a uno, tratar debidamente a uno; **to do o.s. ~** quedar bien; **to do a meal ~** hacer los debidos honores a una comida; **this work does not do your talents ~** este ensayo no está a la altura de su talento.
(b) (Brit: person) juez m, juez m municipal; **~ of the peace** (approx) juez m de paz; **(Lord) Chief J~** Presidente m del Tribunal Supremo; ver también MAGISTRATE .
justifiable ['dʒʌstɪfaɪəbl] ADJ justificable; justificado.
justifiably ['dʒʌstɪfaɪəblɪ] ADV justificadamente; **and ~ so** y con razón; **~ proud** orgulloso y con razón.
▼ **justification** [,dʒʌstɪfɪ'keɪʃən] N justificación f.
justified ['dʒʌstɪfaɪd] ADJ (a) justificado; **~ homicide** homicidio m justificado. (b) (Typ) margin justificado; **right ~** justificado a la derecha.
▼ **justify** ['dʒʌstɪfaɪ] VT (a) justificar, vindicar; dar motivo para; (excuse) disculpar; **the future does not ~ the slightest optimism** el futuro no autoriza el más leve optimismo; **to be justified in** + ger tener motivo para + infin, tener plenamente razón al + infin; **you were not justified in that** en eso no tuviste razón; **am I justified in thinking that ...?** ¿hay motivo para creer que ...? (b) (Typ, Comput) alinear, justificar.
justly ['dʒʌstlɪ] ADV justamente, con justicia; con derecho; debidamente; con razón; **it has been ~ said that ...** con razón se ha dicho que ...
justness ['dʒʌstnɪs] N justicia f; rectitud f.
jut [dʒʌt] VI (also **to ~ out**) sobresalir.
Jute [dʒuːt] N juto m, -a f.
jute [dʒuːt] N yute m.
juvenile ['dʒuːvənaɪl] ① ADJ juvenil; de (or para) menores; (pej) infantil; **~ court** tribunal m tutelar de menores; **~ delinquency** delincuencia f juvenil; **~ delinquent** delincuente mf juvenil.
  ② N joven mf.
juvenilia [,dʒuːvɪ'nɪlɪə] NPL obras fpl de juventud.
juxtapose ['dʒʌkstəpəʊz] VT yuxtaponer.
juxtaposition [,dʒʌkstəpə'zɪʃən] N yuxtaposición f.

K

K, k [keɪ] N (*letter*) K, k *f*; **K for King** K de Kilo.
K (a) ABBR of **kilo-** kilo-.
  (b) N ABBR of **a thousand**; **£100K** 100.000 libras.
  (c) (*Brit*) ABBR of **Knight** caballero de una orden.
  (d) N (*Comput*) ABBR of **kilobyte**.
Kabala [kə'bɑːlə] N Cábala *f*, Kábala *f*.
Kaffir ['kæfəʳ] N cafre *mf*.
Kafkaesque [ˌkæfkɑ'esk] ADJ kafkiano.
kaftan ['kæftæn] N caftán *m*.
Kaiser ['kaɪzəʳ] N emperador *m*.
Kalahari Desert [ˌkælə'hɑːrɪ'dezət] N desierto *m* de Kalahari.
kale [keɪl] N (a) (*cabbage*) col *f* rizada. (b) (*US**) pasta* *f*.
kaleidoscope [kə'laɪdəskəʊp] N calidoscopio *m*.
kaleidoscopic [kəˌlaɪdə'skɒpɪk] ADJ calidoscópico.
Kamasutra [ˌkɑːmə'suːtrə] N Kamasutra *m*.
kamikaze [ˌkæmɪ'kɑːzɪ] N kamikaze *m*.
Kampala [kæm'pɑːlə] N Kampala *f*.
Kampuchea [ˌkæmpʊ'tʃɪə] N Kampuchea *f*.
Kampuchean [ˌkæmpʊ'tʃɪən] ① ADJ kampucheano.
  ② N kampucheano *m*, -a *f*.
Kan. (*US*) ABBR of **Kansas**.
kanga* ['kæŋgə] N boca* *m*.
kangaroo [ˌkæŋgə'ruː] ① N canguro *m*.
  ② ATTR: ~ **court** tribunal *m* desautorizado.
Kans. (*US*) ABBR of **Kansas**.
Kantian ['kæntɪən] ① ADJ kantiano. ② N kantiano *m*, -a *f*.
kaolin ['keɪəlɪn] N caolín *m*.
kapok ['keɪpɒk] N capoc *m*.
kaput* [kə'pʊt] ADJ: **it's ~** está kaput*, está roto, está estropeado; se acabó; **it went ~** hizo kaput*, se rompió, se estropeó.
karaoke [kɑːrə'əʊkɪ] N karaoke *m*.
karat ['kærət] N = **carat**.
karate [kə'rɑːtɪ] N karate *m*.
karma ['kɑːmə] N (*Rel*) karma *m*.
kart [kɑːt] ① N kart *m*.
  ② VI conducir un kart.
karting ['kɑːtɪŋ] N carrera *f* de karts, kárting *m*.
kasbah ['kæzbɑː] N casba(h) *f*.
Kashmir [kæʃ'mɪəʳ] N Cachemira *f*.
Kate [keɪt] NF familiar form of **Catherine** etc.
Katharine, Katherine ['kæθərɪn] NF, **Kathleen** ['kæθliːn] NF Catalina.
kayak ['kaɪæk] N cayac *m*.
Kazak(h) [kə'zɑːk] ① ADJ kazajo. ② N kazajo *m*, -a *f*.
Kazakhstan [ˌkæzək'stɑːn] N Kazajistán *m*, Kazajstán *m*.
kazoo [kə'zuː] N kazoo *m*, chiflato *m*.
KB N ABBR of **kilobyte**.
KBE N ABBR of **Knight of the British Empire** un título ceremonial.
KC N (*Brit*) ABBR of **King's Counsel** abogado *mf* (de categoría superior); ver también QC/KC.
kd (*US*) ABBR of **knocked down** desmontado.
kebab [kə'bæb] N kebab *m*, pincho *m* (moruno), broqueta *f* (*LAm*), brocheta *f* (*LAm*).
kedge [kedʒ] N anclote *m*.
kedgeree [ˌkedʒə'riː] N (*Brit*) plato de pescado desmenuzado, huevos y arroz.
keel [kiːl] ① N quilla *f*; **on an even ~** (*Naut*) en iguales calados, (*fig*) en equilibrio, equilibrado; **to keep sth on an even ~** mantener el equilibrio de algo.
  ② VI: **to ~ over** (*Naut*) zozobrar, dar de quilla, (*fig*) volcar(se), (*person*) desplomarse.
keelhaul ['kiːlhɔːl] VT pasar por debajo de la quilla (*como castigo*).
▼ **keen¹** [kiːn] ADJ (a) *edge* afilado; *wind* penetrante, glacial; *eyesight, hearing* agudo; *mind* agudo, penetrante, perspicaz; *look* fijo, penetrante; (*Brit*) *price* bajo, competitivo, económico; *competition* intenso; *interest* grande; *emotion* intenso, vivo, hondo; *appetite* bueno; **to have a ~ sense of history** tener un profundo sentido de la historia.
  ▼ **(b)** (*Brit: of person*) entusiasta; celoso; **he's a ~ footballer** es muy aficionado a jugar al fútbol; **he's a ~ socialist** es un socialista acérrimo; **try not to seem too ~** procura no mostrar demasiado entusiasmo; **to be as ~ as mustard** ser extraordinariamente entusiasta; **I'm terribly ~ about the new play** la nueva obra me hace muchísima ilusión; **he's very ~ about the programme** tiene mucho entusiasmo por el programa; **to be ~ on sth** ser aficionado a

algo; **are you ~ on opera?** ¿te gusta la ópera?; **I'm not all that ~ on grapes** no me gustan mucho las uvas; **I'm not ~ on the idea** no me hace gracia la idea; **he's ~ on her** ella le interesa bastante; **I'm not very ~ on him** no le es santo de mi devoción; **to be ~ to** + *infin* tener vivo deseo de + *infin*, tener muchas ganas de + *infin*, ansiar + *infin*; **I'm not ~ to do it** no tengo ganas de hacerlo.
keen² [kiːn] N (*Ir Mus*) lamento *m* fúnebre por la muerte de una persona.
keenly ['kiːnlɪ] ADV (a) de modo penetrante; agudamente; (*intensely*) intensamente, (*acutely*) vivamente; **he felt her death ~** su muerte le afectó profundamente; **he looked at me ~** me miró fijamente.
  (b) *work etc* con entusiasmo.
keenness ['kiːnnɪs] N (a) (*of edge, wind, hearing etc*) penetración *f*; agudeza *f*; intensidad *f*, viveza *f*.
  (b) (*of person*) entusiasmo *m*, ilusión *f*; interés *m*, afición *f*.
keep [kiːp] (*irr: PRET AND PTP kept*) ① VT (a) (*observe, fulfil*) *promise* cumplir; *rule* observar, atenerse a; *appointment* acudir a; *festivity* observar, celebrar.
  (b) (*impose*) *order* mantener, imponer.
  (c) (*possess etc*) *dog, servant* tener; *chicken, sheep etc* criar, dedicarse a criar, ocuparse en la cría de; *family* mantener; *shop* tener; *business, hotel etc* ser propietario de, dirigir; *diary* escribir; *account, record, house* llevar; **he ~s a good cellar** mantiene una buena bodega; **he doesn't ~ his garden neat** no mantiene en buen estado su jardín; **he ~s his 3 daughters in clothes** les paga los vestidos a sus 3 hijas; **he has his parents to ~** tiene que mantener a sus padres.
  (d) (*detain*) detener; (*in conversation etc*) entretener; **they kept him in prison for 6 months** le tuvieron 6 meses en la cárcel; **illness kept her at home** se quedó en casa debido a la enfermedad, la enfermedad no le permitió salir de casa; **what kept you?** ¿por qué vienes tarde?, ¿a qué se debe este retraso?; **I musn't ~ you** no te entretengo más.
  (e) (*prevent*) **to ~ sb from doing sth** impedir a uno hacer algo, no dejar a uno hacer algo.
  (f) (*save*) poner aparte, tener guardado, reservar; **I was ~ing it for you** lo guardaba para ti.
  (g) (*retain*) guardar, retener; reservar; *secret, figure etc* guardar; *job* retener, mantenerse en; (*not give back*) quedarse con; (*in museum etc*) conservar, custodiar; **~ the change** quédese con la vuelta; **to ~ one's seat** permanecer sentado, (*Parl*) retener su escaño; **to ~ money by one** guardar algún dinero para un apuro.
  (h) (*with adj, verb etc*) **to ~ sth clean** conservar algo limpio; **'K~ Spain Clean'** 'Mantenga limpia España'; **she always ~s the house very clean** tiene la casa siempre muy limpia; **to ~ sth safe** tener algo seguro; **to ~ sth warm** tener algo caliente, mantener el calor de algo; **to ~ sb talking** entretener a uno en conversación; **to ~ sb waiting** hacer que uno espere, hacer esperar a uno; **to ~ one's eyes fixed on sth** tener los ojos puestos en algo; **to ~ sb at it** obligar a uno a seguir trabajando (*etc*).
  ② VI (a) (*remain*) quedar(se), permanecer; seguir, continuar; **to ~ quiet** no hacer ruido; no decir nada, quedar callado, callarse; **~ still!** ¡estáte quieto!; **to ~ clear of** evitar cualquier contacto con; seguir libre de; **how are you ~ing?** ¿cómo sigue Vd?; **to ~ well** estar bien de salud.
  (b) (*with ger*) **to ~ + ger** seguir + *ger*, continuar + *ger*; no dejar de + *infin*; **she ~s talking** no deja de hablar; **he ~s asking me for it** me lo está pidiendo constantemente; **to ~ smiling** seguir con la sonrisa en los labios; **to ~ standing** seguir en pie; **to ~ going** seguir adelante, no cejar; **we ~ going somehow** vamos tirando; nos arreglamos para continuar; **I can ~ going in French** me defiendo en francés.
  (c) (*continue*) seguir, continuar; **to ~ at work** seguir trabajando, mantenerse en su puesto; **~ straight on for Madrid** para ir a Madrid vaya Vd todo seguido; **to ~ to the left** circular por la izquierda.
  (d) (*of food*) conservarse fresco, conservarse en buen estado; **an apple that ~s** una manzana que dura; **the news will ~ till I see you** no pierdes nada si me guardo la noticia hasta que nos veamos.
  ③ VR: **he ~s himself now** ahora se mantiene a sí mismo; **to ~ o.s. clean** mantenerse limpio, cuidar su limpieza personal; **they ~ themselves to themselves** evitan tener contacto con otros, permanecen aislados.
  ④ N (a) comida *f*, subsistencia *f*; **to earn one's ~** trabajar por la comida, pagar la comida trabajando; (*fig*) producir (*etc*) bastante; **I pay £50 a week for my ~** la pensión me cuesta 50 libras a la

semana; **he isn't worth his ~** no trabaja como debe, no merece que sigamos empleándole.

(b) (*Hist*) torreón *m*, torre *f* del homenaje.

(c) for ~s* para siempre jamás, permanentemente, para guardar.

◆ **keep at** VT: **to ~ at sth** trabajar sin descansar en algo, no cejar en algo, perseverar en algo; **~ at it!** ¡dale!

◆ **keep away** VT: **to ~ sb away** mantener a uno a distancia, alejar a uno (*from* de), no dejar a uno acercarse (*from* a); **they kept him away from school** no le dejaron ir a la escuela; **it ~s rats away** aleja las ratas; **one should ~ guns away from children** hay que guardar las armas de fuego fuera del alcance de los niños.

2 VI mantener alejado (*from* de), mantenerse a distancia; (*not attend*) no venir, no acudir; no dejarse ver; **to ~ away from sb** evitar a uno, evitar cualquier contacto con uno; no meterse en líos con uno; **you ~ away from my daughter!** ¡no venga más a ver a mi hija!; **he can't ~ away from the subject** siempre vuelve al mismo tema.

◆ **keep back** 1 VT **(a)** (*retain*) guardar, retener.

(b) (*conceal*) *information* ocultar, guardar secreto; *emotion* contener, reprimir; *names of victims* no comunicar.

(c) *enemy* no dejar avanzar, tener a raya; *progress* estorbar, cortar el paso a.

2 VI mantenerse atrás; no acercarse; hacerse a un lado; **~ back, please!** ¡más atrás, por favor!

◆ **keep down** 1 VT **(a)** (*hold down*) sujetar; no dejar subir.

(b) *price, temperature* mantener bajo; *growth, spending* restringir, limitar.

(c) (*oppress*) oprimir; dominar; **you can't ~ a good man down** a la larga los realmente buenos salen a flote.

(d) she can't ~ any food down vomita toda la comida.

2 VI seguir acurrucado (*or* tumbado *etc*); no levantar la cabeza; **~ down!** ¡abajo!

◆ **keep from** 1 VT **(a) to ~ sth from sb** ocultar algo a uno, no decir algo a uno.

(b) to ~ from + *gen* abstenerse de + *infin*, guardarse de + *infin*; **I can't ~ from wishing that ...** no puedo dejar de desear que ...

2 VR: **to ~ o.s. from** + *ger* = **1 (b)**.

◆ **keep in** 1 VT **(a)** *fire* mantener encendido.

(b) *feelings* contener.

(c) *person, pet* no dejar salir, tener encerrado; (*in school*) hacer quedar en la escuela (como castigo).

2 VI: **to ~ in with sb** mantener buenas relaciones con uno, cultivar la amistad de uno; (*pej*) asegurarse de la protección de uno.

◆ **keep off** 1 VT **(a)** tener a raya, cerrar el paso a; no dejar entrar; alejar; **~ the dog off!** ¡que no se acerque más el perro!; **to ~ off the grass** no pisar la hierba.

(b) to ~ sb off a subject procurar que uno no toque un tema, convencer a uno para que no discuta un asunto; **to ~ off a subject** no tocar un tema.

2 VI mantenerse a distancia; **'~ off'** 'no acercarse', 'prohibida la entrada'; **if the rain ~s off** si no llueve.

◆ **keep on** 1 VT **(a) to ~ one's hat on** no quitarse el sombrero, seguir con el sombrero puesto.

(b) to ~ the light on tener la luz puesta (*LAm*: prendida).

(c) to ~ sb on in a job mantener a uno en un puesto; **they kept him on for years** siguieron empleándole durante muchos años.

2 VI **(a)** continuar; seguir avanzando, ir adelante; **to ~ on with sth** continuar con algo; **to ~ on** + *ger* seguir + *ger*, continuar + *ger*; **he ~s on hoping** no renuncia a esperar, no pierde la esperanza.

(b) she does ~ on machaca mucho, es muy machacona; **don't ~ on (so)!** (*Brit*) ¡no machaques!; **to ~ on at sb about sth** (*Brit*) insistir en algo con uno.

◆ **keep out** 1 VT no dejar entrar, excluir.

2 VI permanecer fuera; **'~ out'** 'no acercarse', 'prohibida la entrada'; **to ~ out of** *place, organization* no entrar en, *affair* no meterse en, *trouble* evitar; **you ~ out of this!** ¡no te metas en esto!

◆ **keep to** VT **(a) to ~ sth to o.s.** guardar algo para sí; guardar algo en secreto; **but he kept the news to himself** pero no comunicó la noticia a nadie.

(b) to ~ sb to his promise obligar a uno a cumplir su promesa.

◆ **keep together** 1 VT mantener unido(s); no separar, no dispersar.

2 VI mantenerse unidos; no separarse, no dispersarse.

◆ **keep under** VT: **to ~ sb under** tener a uno subyugado.

◆ **keep up** 1 VT **(a)** (*maintain*) mantener; conservar; *correspondence, study etc* continuar; *custom* mantener.

(b) (*hold up*) sostener.

(c) to ~ sb up at night hacer trasnochar a uno, tener a uno en vela; **I don't want to ~ you up** no quiero entretenerte más.

(d) to ~ it up mantener el nivel, seguir como antes; no cejar; **~ it up!** ¡ánimo!, ¡dale!

2 VI no rezagarse; **to ~ up with** (*in pace*) ir al paso de, *friends* mantener contacto con, seguir en contacto con, *rival* emular,

mantenerse a la altura de; **to ~ up with the Joneses** procurar no quedar en menos con respecto a los vecinos; **to ~ up with one's work** hacer su trabajo al ritmo apropiado, mantenerse al día en su trabajo; **to ~ up with the times** ir con los tiempos, mantenerse al día.

keeper ['kiːpər] N (*game~*) guardabosque *m*; (*in art gallery, museum, library: expert*) conservador *m*, -ora *f*; (*attendant*) vigilante *mf*, cuidadero *m*, -a *f*; (*in record office*) archivero *m*, -a *f*; (*in zoo*) guardián *m*; (*in park*) guarda *m*; **am I my brother's ~?** ¿soy yo guarda de mi hermano?

keep-fit [ˌkiːpˈfɪt] 1 N ejercicios *mpl* para mantenerse en forma (*or* de mantenimiento).

2 ATTR: **~ classes** clases *fpl* de mantenimiento (*or* para mantenerse en forma).

keeping ['kiːpɪŋ] N **(a) to be in ~ with** estar de acuerdo con, estar en armonía con; **to be out of ~ with** estar en desacuerdo con.

(b) to be in the ~ of X estar en manos de X, estar bajo la custodia de X; **to be in safe ~** estar en un lugar seguro, estar en buenas manos; **to give sth to sb for safe ~** dar algo a uno para mayor seguridad.

keepsake ['kiːpseɪk] N recuerdo *m*.

keester* ['kiːstər] N (*US*) trasero* *m*.

keg [keg] 1 N barrilete *m*, cuñete *m*.

2 ATTR: **~ beer** cerveza *f* de barril.

keks‡ [keks] NPL (*Brit*) pantalones *mpl*.

kelp [kelp] N quelpo *m* (de Patagonia).

Kelper* ['kelpər] N nativo *m*, -a *f* (*or* habitante *mf*) de las Malvinas.

Ken [ken] NM *familiar form of* **Kenneth**.

Ken. (*US*) ABBR *of* **Kentucky**.

ken [ken] 1 N: **to be beyond sb's ~** ser incomprensible para uno; **to be within sb's ~** ser comprensible para uno.

2 VT (*Scot*) *person etc* conocer, *fact* saber; (*recognize*) reconocer.

kennel ['kenl] 1 N (*doghouse*) perrera *f*, caseta *f* de perro; (*pack*) jauría *f*; **~s** (*dogs' home*) residencia *f* canina.

2 ATTR: **~ maid** chica *f* que trabaja en una residencia canina.

Kenya ['kenjə] N Kenia *f*.

Kenyan ['kenjən] 1 ADJ keniano.

2 N keniano *m*, -a *f*.

kepi ['keɪpɪ] N quepis *m*.

kept [kept] 1 PRET AND PTP *of* **keep**.

2 ADJ: **~ woman** querida *f*, amante *f*.

kerb [kɜːb] N, **kerbstone** ['kɜːbstəʊn] N (*Brit*) bordillo *m*, encintado *m*, cordón *m* (*SC*), cuneta *f* (*CAm*); **~ broker** corredor *m*, -ora *f* que no es miembro de la Bolsa; **~ market** mercado *m* no oficial (que funciona después del cierre de la Bolsa).

kerb-crawler ['kɜːbˌkrɔːlər] N conductor *m* que busca prostitutas desde su coche.

kerb-crawling ['kɜːbˌkrɔːlɪŋ] N busca *f* de prostitutas desde el coche.

kerb drill ['kɜːbdrɪl] N enseñanza *f* (a niños) de la disciplina del peatón; prácticas *fpl* de cruce.

kerchief ['kɜːtʃɪf] N pañuelo *m*, pañoleta *f*.

kerfuffle* [kəˈfʌfl] N (*Brit*) lío* *m*, follón* *m*.

kernel ['kɜːnl] N almendra *f*; (*fig*) núcleo *m*, meollo *m*; **a ~ of truth** un grano de verdad.

kerosene ['kerəsiːn] N keroseno *m*, queroseno *m*, querosén *m* (*LAm*); **~ lamp** lámpara *f* de petróleo.

kestrel ['kestrəl] N cernícalo *m* (vulgar).

ketch [ketʃ] N queche *m*.

ketchup ['ketʃəp] N salsa *f* de tomate, catsup *m*.

kettle ['ketl] N (*approx*) hervidor *m*, olla *f* en forma de cafetera (*or* tetera), pava *f*; **this is a pretty ~ of fish!** ¡en buen berenjenal nos hemos metido!; **that's another** (*or* **a different**) **~ of fish** eso es harina de otro costal.

kettledrum ['ketldrʌm] N timbal *m*.

key [kiː] 1 N **(a)** (*door~ etc*) llave *f*; (*Comput, of typewriter, piano etc*) tecla *f*; (*of wind instrument*) llave *f*, pistón *m*; (*Telec*) manipulador *m*; (*Tech*) chaveta *f*, cuña *f*; (*Elec*) llave *f*, interruptor *m*; (*Archit*) clave *f*.

(b) (*Mus*) tono *m*; **major ~** tono *m* mayor; **minor ~** tono *m* menor; **change of ~** cambio *m* de tonalidad; **to be in ~** estar a tono, estar templado; **to play off ~** desafinar, tocar desafinadamente; **to make a speech in a low ~** pronunciar un discurso en un tono bajo.

(c) (*fig: to problem, also Bio, Chess*) clave *f* (*to* de); **the ~ to the mystery** la clave del misterio.

2 ATTR clave; **~ industry** industria *f* clave; **~ man** hombre *m* clave; **~ move** movida *f* clave; **~ question** cuestión *f* principal, cuestión *f* madre; **~ signature** (*Mus*) armadura *f*.

3 VT (*Tech*) enchavetar, acuñar; (*Mus*) templar, afinar; (*Comput, Typ*) teclear, meter.

◆ **key in** VT (*Comput, Typ*) picar, teclear.

◆ **key up** VT **(a)** emocionar; **to be all ~ed up** estar emocionadísimo, tener los nervios en punta. **(b)** (*Comput*) teclear, meter (en el ordenador).

keyboard ['kiːbɔːd] ☐1 N teclado *m*; ~**s** (*Mus*) teclados *mpl*.
  ☐2 ATTR: ~ **instruments** instrumentos *mpl* de teclado; ~ **player** teclista *mf*.
  ☐3 VT (*Comput*) *text* teclear.
keyboarder ['kiːˌbɔːdəʳ] N, **keyboard operator** ['kiːbɔːd,ɒpəreɪtəʳ] N teclista *mf*.
keyboardist ['kiːbɔːdɪst] N (*Mus*) teclista *mf*.
key card ['kiːkɑːd] N tarjeta *f* de acceso.
keyhole ['kiːhəʊl] N ojo *m* de la cerradura.
keying ['kiːɪŋ] N (*Comput*) introducción *f* de datos.
key-money ['kiːˌmʌnɪ] N entrada *f*.
Keynesian ['kiːnzɪən] ☐1 ADJ keynesiano.
  ☐2 N keynesiano *m*, -a *f*.
keynote ['kiːnəʊt] N tónica *f*; (*fig*) tónica *f*, piedra *f* clave, idea *f* fundamental; ~ **speech** discurso *m* de apertura, discurso *m* en que se sientan las bases de una política (*or* programa).
keypad ['kiːpæd] N teclado *m* numérico.
key-puncher ['kiːˌpʌnʃəʳ] N teclista *mf*.
key-ring ['kiːrɪŋ] N llavero *m*.
keystone ['kiːstəʊn] N piedra *f* clave; (*fig*) piedra *f* angular.
keystroke ['kiːstrəʊk] N pulsación *f* (de una tecla).
keyword ['kiːwɜːd] N palabra *f* clave.
kg ABBR *of* **kilogram(me)** (**s**) kilogramo(s) *mpl*, kg.
KGB N KGB *f*.
khaki ['kɑːkɪ] ☐1 N caqui *m*.
  ☐2 ADJ caqui.
kharja ['χɑːʒə] N jarcha *f*.
Khartoum [kɑːˈtuːm] N Jartum *m*.
Khmer [kmeəʳ] ☐1 N jemer *mf*; **the ~ Rouge** los jemeres rojos.
  ☐2 ADJ jemer.
Khyber Pass [ˌkaɪbəˈpɑːs] N pasaje *m* de Kyber.
KHz ABBR *of* **kilohertz**.
kibbutz [kɪˈbʊts] N, PL **kibbutzim** [kɪˈbʊtsɪm] kibbutz *m*.
kibitzer ['kɪbɪtsəʳ] N (*US*) mirón *m*, -ona *f*.
kibosh: ['kaɪbɒʃ] N: **to put the ~ on sth** desbaratar algo, acabar con algo definitivamente.
kick [kɪk] ☐1 N (**a**) patada *f*, puntapié *m*; (*Sport*) puntapié *m*, golpe *m*, tiro *m*; (*of animal*) coz *f*; **a ~ at goal** un tiro a gol; **I got a ~ on the leg** recibí un golpe en la pierna; **I gave him a ~ in the pants*** le di una patada en el trasero*; **what he needs is a good ~ in the pants*** hay que empujarle a patadas; **it was like a ~ in the teeth*** me sentó como una patada en la barriga*; **to take a ~ at** dirigir un puntapié a.
  (**b**) (*of firearm*) culatazo *m*.
  (**c**) (*: of drink etc*) fuerza *f*; **a drink with a ~ to it** una bebida muy fuerte.
  (**d**) (*: thrill*) **to do sth for ~s** hacer algo sólo para disfrutar de la emoción que ello produce, hacer algo sólo para divertirse; **I get a ~ out of it** me entusiasma, encuentro placer en esto, lo hago porque me gusta.
  (**e**) **he's on a fishing ~ now** (*) ahora le ha dado por la pesca; **she's on this liberation ~** está metida en el tinglado de la liberación.
  ☐2 VT (**a**) *ball etc* dar un puntapié a; golpear (con el pie); *goal* marcar; *person* dar una patada a; (*animal*) dar de coces a; **to ~ sb's bottom** dar a uno una patada en el trasero; **to ~ a man when he's down** dar a moro muerto gran lanzada; **to ~ sb downstairs** echar a uno escaleras abajo a patadas; **to ~ sb upstairs*** deshacerse de uno ascendiéndole; (*Brit Parl*) hacer que un miembro de los Comunes pase a serlo de los Lores; **to ~ a door shut** cerrar una puerta violentamente con el pie; **to ~ one's legs in the air** agitar las piernas.
  (**b**) (*) **to ~ it** dejarlo, abandonarlo; **to ~ a habit** deshacerse de un vicio; **I've ~ed smoking** ya no fumo.
  ☐3 VI (**a**) dar coces, cocear; dar patadas.
  (**b**) (*gun*) dar un culetazo, recular.
  (**c**) (*) protestar, quejarse; respingar, reaccionar.
  ☐4 VR: **I could have ~ed myself** me mordía las manos, me dio rabia por tonto yo.
◆**kick about** ☐1 VT (**a**) **to ~ a ball about** divertirse con un balón; **he's been ~ed about a lot** ha sufrido muchos malos tratos, le han maltratado mucho.
  (**b**) (*) **he's ~ed about the world** ha viajado mucho, ha visto mucho mundo.
  ☐2 VI (*) **it's ~ing about here somewhere** andará por ahí; **I ~ed about in London for two years** durante 2 años viví a la buena de Dios en Londres.
◆**kick against** VT protestar contra; reaccionar contra.
◆**kick around** ☐1 VT: **to ~ an idea around** dar vueltas a una idea; **to ~ sb around** (*fig*) tratar a uno a patadas.
  ☐2 VI: **they just ~ around all day** se pasan el día sin hacer nada (*or* sin dar golpe).
◆**kick away** VT apartar con el pie.

◆**kick back** VI (*gun*) dar un culetazo, recular.
◆**kick down** VT derribar.
◆**kick in** VT (**a**) romper a patadas. (**b**) (*US:*) sacudir*, apoquinar.
◆**kick off** VI (*Sport*) hacer el saque inicial; (*loosely*) comenzar; (*fig*) comenzar, empezar.
◆**kick out** ☐1 VT: **to ~ sb out** echar a uno a puntapiés, (*fig*) poner a uno de patitas en la calle, expulsar a uno.
  ☐2 VI repartir coces; ~ **out against** V ~ **against**.
◆**kick up*** VT *fuss, row etc* armar.
kickback ['kɪkbæk] N (**a**) (*Mil*) culatazo *m*. (**b**) (*fig*) reacción *f*, resaca *f*, contragolpe *m*. (**c**) (*) soborno *m*, bocado* *m*, mordida* *f*.
kicker ['kɪkəʳ] N (*Rugby*) pateador *m*.
kick-off ['kɪkɒf] N saque *m* inicial.
kick-start ['kɪkˈstɑːt] ☐1 N arranque *m* por pedal.
  ☐2 VT arrancar con el pedal.
kick-starter ['kɪkˌstɑːtəʳ] N pedal *m* de arranque.
kick turn ['kɪkˌtɜːn] N (*Ski*) cambio *m* brusco de marcha.
kid [kɪd] ☐1 N (**a**) (*Zool*) cabrito *m*, -a *f*, chivo *m*, -a *f*; (*meat*) carne *f* de cabrito; (*skin*) cabritilla *f*.
  (**b**) (*) *child*) chiquillo *m*, -a *f*, chaval* *m*, -ala *f*, pibe* *m*, -a *f* (*And, SC*), escuincle* *mf* (*Mex*); (*US: form of address*) chico *m*, -a *f*; **when I was a ~** cuando yo era chaval*; **that's ~'s stuff** eso es para chicos, son chiquilladas.
  ☐2 ATTR: ~ **brother*** hermano *m* menor; ~ **gloves** guantes *mpl* de cabritilla; (*fig*) trato *m* de guante blanco.
  ☐3 VT (*) tomar el pelo a*; **you can't ~ me** no se me engaña así; **I ~ you not** no bromeo, sin bromas.
  ☐4 VI (*) bromearse, chunguearse*; **I was only ~ding** lo decía en broma; **no ~ding!** ¡en serio!; **are you ~ding?** ¿lo dices en serio?; **are you ~ding!** ¡ni hablar!; **you must be ~ding!** ¡me estás tomando el pelo!*, ¡no es posible!
  ☐5 VR (*) **to ~ o.s.** engañarse a sí mismo, hacerse ilusiones; **he ~s himself that ...** se hace creer que ...; **it's time we stopped ~ding ourselves** es hora ya de desengañarnos, es hora ya de despertar a la realidad.
◆**kid on*** ☐1 VT: **he's ~ding you on*** te está tomando el pelo*.
  ☐2 VI bromear.
kiddy* ['kɪdɪ] N chiquillo *m*, -a *f*.
kidnap ['kɪdnæp] VT secuestrar, raptar.
kidnapper, (*US*) **kidnaper** ['kɪdnæpəʳ] N secuestrador *m*, -ora *f*, raptor *m*, -ora *f*.
kidnapping, (*US*) **kidnaping** ['kɪdnæpɪŋ] N secuestro *m*, rapto *m*.
kidney ['kɪdnɪ] ☐1 N riñón *m*; (*fig*) índole *f*, especie *f*.
  ☐2 ATTR: ~ **disease** enfermedad *f* renal; ~ **failure** fracaso *m* renal; ~ **machine** riñón *m* artificial; ~ **stone** cálculo *m* renal; ~ **transplant** trasplante *m* de riñón (*or* renal).
kidney bean ['kɪdnɪˌbiːn] N judía *f* enana, frijol *m*, poroto *m* (*SC*).
kidney dish ['kɪdnɪˌdɪʃ] N batea *f*.
kidney-shaped ['kɪdnɪˌʃeɪpt] ADJ ariñonado, con forma de riñón.
kidology* [kɪˈdɒlədʒɪ] N (*Brit*) guasa *f*
kike: [kaɪk] N (*US*) judío *m*, -a *f*
Kilimanjaro [ˌkɪlɪmænˈdʒɑːrəʊ] N Kilimanjaro *m*.
kill [kɪl] ☐1 VT (**a**) matar; dar muerte a; asesinar; destruir; **he was ~ed by savages** le mataron los salvajes, fue muerto por los salvajes; **I'll ~ you for this!** (*hum*) ¡te voy a matar!; **thou shalt not ~** no matarás.
  (**b**) (*fig*) *rumour, threat* acabar con; *feeling, hope etc* destruir; *flavour, taste* quitar; *lights* apagar; (*Parl*) *bill* ahogar; (*) hacer morir de risa; (*) hacer una impresión irresistible en; **this heat is ~ing me** este calor acabará conmigo; **I'll do it if it ~s me** lo haré aunque me vaya en ello la vida; **the pace is ~ing him** se está matando trabajando (*etc*) a tal ritmo; **my feet are ~ing me!*** ¡los pies me están matando!*; **this will ~ you*** vas a morir de risa*; **to be dressed to ~** ir pero muy acicalada, estar de punto en blanco.
  ☐2 VR: **to ~ o.s.** matarse; suicidarse; **to ~ o.s. with work** matarse trabajando; **to ~ o.s. laughing*** morir de risa*.
  ☐3 N (**a**) (*Hunting*) pieza *f*, animal *m* matado, (*collectively*) piezas *fpl*, animales *mpl* matados.
  (**b**) (*act of ~ing*) matanza *f*; **to go in for the ~** entrar a matar.
◆**kill off** VT exterminar; acabar de matar, rematar.
killer ['kɪləʳ] ☐1 N (**a**) matador *m*, -ora *f*; (*murderer*) asesino *m*, -a *f*; **diphtheria used to be a ~** antes la difteria mataba a sus víctimas.
  (**b**) (*fig*) **it's a ~** (*joke*) es de morirse de risa; (*task*) es agotador; (*question*) es muy difícil; (*very impressive*) es muy impresionante.
  ☐2 ATTR: ~ **disease** enfermedad *f* mortal; **the ~ instinct** el instinto de matar; ~ **punch** puñetazo *m* mortal.
killer bee ['kɪləbiː] N abeja *f* asesina.
killer whale ['kɪləweɪl] N orca *f*.
killing ['kɪlɪŋ] ☐1 ADJ (**a**) *disease etc* que mata, mortal.
  (**b**) (*fig*) *journey, work* agotador, durísimo; *burden* abrumador.
  (**c**) (*ravishing*) irresistible; (*funny*) divertidísimo, muy cómico; **it was ~** fue para morirse de risa.
  ☐2 N (**a**) matanza *f*; (*murder*) asesinato *m*.

(b) (*Fin*) éxito *m* financiero; **to make a ~** tener un gran éxito financiero, hacer su agosto.

killingly [ˈkɪlɪŋlɪ] ADV: **~ funny** divertidísimo; **it was ~ funny** fue para morirse de risa.

killjoy [ˈkɪldʒɔɪ] N aguafiestas *mf*; **don't be such a ~!** ¡no vayas a aguar la fiesta!

kiln [kɪln] N horno *m*.

kilo [ˈkiːləʊ] N kilo *m*.

kilobyte [ˈkɪləʊˌbaɪt] N kilobyte *m*, kiloocteto *m*.

kilocycle [ˈkɪləʊˌsaɪkl] N kilociclo *m*.

kilogram(me) [ˈkɪləʊɡræm] N kilo(gramo) *m*.

kilohertz [ˈkɪləʊˌhɜːts] N kilohercio *m*.

kilolitre, (*US*) **kiloliter** [ˈkɪləʊˌliːtər] N kilolitro *m*.

kilometre, (*US*) **kilometer** [ˈkɪləʊmiːtər] N kilómetro *m*.

kilometric [ˌkɪləʊˈmetrɪk] ADJ kilométrico.

kiloton [ˈkɪləʊˌtʌn] N kilotón *m*.

kilowatt [ˈkɪləʊwɒt] N kilovatio *m*.

kilowatt-hour [ˈkɪləʊwɒtˌaʊə] N kilovatio-hora *m*; **200 ~s** 200 kilovatios-hora.

kilt [kɪlt] N falda *f* escocesa.

┌─ *KILT* ─

ⓘ *Las faldas escocesas tradicionales no son **skirts**, sino **kilts**. Son faldas hechas de la famosa tela **tartan**, que van cruzadas, plisadas en la parte de atrás y lisas por delante y sujetas con un imperdible grueso llamado **kilt pin**. Se usan normalmente como vestimenta de gala, por ejemplo para una boda, o como símbolo de identidad. Los hombres suelen llevar una bolsa que pende de la cintura, denominada **sporran**, para mantener la falda en su sitio y para que no se levante con el viento. El traje tradicional de las Tierras Altas de Escocia, **highland dress**, también incluye un manto que se lleva sobre el hombro, llamado **plaid**.*

Según la tradición, los hombres no llevan ropa interior bajo la falda, lo cual ha dado lugar a muchos chistes y bromas. Es fácil encontrar postales picantes donde las faldas se levantan a merced del viento.

---

kilted [ˈkɪltɪd] ADJ *man* vestido con falda escocesa; **~ skirt** falda *f* escocesa.

kilter [ˈkɪltər] N: **to be out of ~** (*esp US*) estar descentrado; estar desfasado; quedar desbaratado.

kimono [kɪˈməʊnəʊ] N quimono *m*, kimono *m*.

kin [kɪn] N familia *f*, parientes *mpl*, parentela *f*; **next of ~** pariente *m* más próximo, parientes *mpl* más proximos.

▼ **kind** [kaɪnd] **1** ADJ **(a)** *person* bondadoso, amable, bueno; **you're very ~, you're too ~** eres muy amable; **to be ~ to sb** ser amable con uno; **please be so ~ as to** + *infin* tenga la bondad de + *infin*; **would you be so ~ as to** + *infin*? ¿me hace el favor de + *infin*?; **he was ~ enough to** + *infin* tuvo la amabilidad de + *infin*; **they were not ~ to the play in New York** trataron la obra algo duramente en Nueva York; **we must be ~ to animals** hay que tratar bien a los animales.

▼**(b)** *act* bueno; *climate* bueno, benigno; *criticism, remark, word* elogioso, comprensivo, favorable; *tone of voice* cariñoso, tierno; *treatment* bueno, blando; **it's very ~ of you** es muy amable; **that wasn't very ~ of you** eso me ha parecido algo injusto, en eso fuiste demasiado duro.

2 N **(a)** clase *f*, género *m*, especie *f*; **but not that ~** pero no de ese tipo, pero no como eso; **he's the ~ who'll cheat you** es de los que te engañarán; **to pay in ~** pagar en especie, (*fig*) pagar en la misma moneda.

(b) (*a ~ of*) **a ~ of** uno a modo de; **he's a ~ of agent** es algo así como un agente; **I'm not that ~ of girl** yo no soy de ésas; **he's not that ~ of person** no es capaz de hacer eso, no es de los que hacen tales cosas; **I felt a ~ of pity** sentí algo parecido a la compasión, en cierto modo sentí compasión; **and all that ~ of thing** y otras cosas por el estilo; **it's not my ~ of thing** es una cosa que no me gusta; yo no sé nada de eso; **that's the ~ of thing I mean** eso es precisamente lo que quiero decir; **I don't like that ~ of talk** no me gusta ese modo de hablar; **what ~ of book?** ¿qué clase de libro?; **what ~ of man is he?** ¿qué clase de hombre es?; **it takes all ~s (of people)** cada loco con su tema.

(c) (*of a ~*) **three of a ~** tres de la misma especie; (*pej*) tres del mismo jaez; **one of a ~** modelo *m* exclusivo, modelo *m* único; **he's one of a ~** es un fuera de serie; **books of all ~s** toda clase de libros, libros de toda clase; **it's tea of a ~** es té pero apenas, es lo que apenas se puede llamar té; **perfect of its ~** perfecto en su línea; **sth of the ~** algo por el estilo; **nothing of the ~!** ¡nada de eso!, ¡ni hablar!

3 ADV (*****: *~ of*) **it's ~ of awkward** es bastante difícil; **it's ~ of blue** es más bien azul; **it's ~ of hot in here** hace bastante calor aquí; **it's ~ of finished** está más o menos terminado; **aren't you pleased? ~ of** ¿no te alegras? en cierto modo.

kinda* [ˈkaɪndə] = **kind of**; V **kind**.

kindergarten [ˈkɪndəˌɡɑːtn] N jardín *m* de infancia, kindergarten *m*,

kinder* *m*.

kind-hearted [ˈkaɪndˈhɑːtɪd] ADJ bondadoso, de buen corazón.

kind-heartedness [ˈkaɪndˈhɑːtɪdnɪs] N bondad *f*.

kindle [ˈkɪndl] **1** VT encender (*also fig*).

2 VI encenderse (*also fig*).

kindliness [ˈkaɪndlɪnɪs] N bondad *f*, benevolencia *f*.

kindling [ˈkɪndlɪŋ] N leña *f* menuda, astillas *fpl*.

kindly [ˈkaɪndlɪ] **1** ADJ bondadoso, benévolo; *climate etc* bueno, benigno; *remark etc* elogioso, comprensivo, favorable; *tone of voice* cariñoso, tierno; *treatment* bueno, blando.

2 ADV **(a)** bondadosamente, amablement .; **he very ~ helped me** muy amablemente me ayudó; **to take ~ to sth** aceptar algo de buen grado; **to think ~ of sb** tener un buen concepto de uno; **he would take it ~ if you did so** te agradecería que lo hicieses.

(b) **~ pass the salt** ¿me haces el favor de pasar la sal?; **~ wait a moment** haga el favor de esperar un momento; **'~ pay here'** 'se ruega pagar aquí'.

kindness [ˈkaɪndnɪs] N **(a)** bondad *f*, amabilidad *f*, benevolencia *f*; atención *f*, consideración *f*; **they treated him with every ~** le trataron con todo género de consideraciones; **to show ~ to sb** mostrarse bondadoso con uno.

(b) (*a ~*) favor *m*; **to do sb a ~** hacer un favor a uno; **it would be a ~ to tell him** decírselo sería un favor.

kindred [ˈkɪndrɪd] **1** ADJ (*related by blood*) emparentado; (*fig*) afín, semejante, análogo; **~ spirits** espíritus *mpl* afines.

2 N (*relationship*) parentesco *m*; (*relations*) familia *f*, parientes *mpl*.

kinescope [ˈkɪnəskəʊp] N (*US*) tubo *m* de rayos catódicos, cinescopio *m*.

kinesiology [kɪˌniːsɪˈɒlədʒɪ] N kinesiología *f*.

kinetic [kɪˈnetɪk] ADJ cinético; **~ energy** energía *f* cinética.

kinetics [kɪˈnetɪks] NPL cinética *f*.

king [kɪŋ] **1** N **(a)** rey *m*; (*fig, Chess, Cards*) rey *m*; (*Draughts*) dama *f*; **an oil ~** un magnate del petróleo; **the ~ and queen** los reyes; **the Three K~s** los Reyes, los Reyes Magos; **to live like a ~** vivir a cuerpo de rey.

(b) (*Brit Jur*) **K~'s Bench** departamento *m* del Tribunal Supremo; **K~'s Counsel** abogado *mf* (*de categoría superior*); **to turn K~'s evidence** delatar a los cómplices; *ver también* QC/KC.

2 ATTR: **~ penguin** pingüino *m* real.

kingcup [ˈkɪŋkʌp] N botón *m* de oro.

kingdom [ˈkɪŋdəm] N reino *m*; **till K~ come*** hasta el día del Juicio.

kingfisher [ˈkɪŋfɪʃər] N martín *m* pescador.

kingly [ˈkɪŋlɪ] ADJ real, regio; digno de un rey.

kingmaker [ˈkɪŋˌmeɪkər] N persona *f* muy influyente.

kingpin [ˈkɪŋpɪn] N (*Tech*) perno *m* real, perno *m* pinzote; (*fig*) piedra *f* angular, cosa *f* fundamental, persona *f* principal.

kingship [ˈkɪŋʃɪp] N dignidad *f* real, monarquía *f*; **they offered him the ~** le ofrecieron el trono (*o* la corona).

king-size(d) [ˈkɪŋsaɪz(d)] ADJ de tamaño extra, extra largo; **~ bed** cama *f* de gran tamaño.

kink [kɪŋk] **1** N **(a)** (*in rope etc*) coca *f*, enroscadura *f*; (*in hair*) rizo *m*; (*in paper etc*) arruga *f*, pliegue *m*. **(b)** (*fig*) peculiaridad *f*, manía *f*, (*sexual*) perversión *f*.

2 VI formar cocas (*etc*).

kinky [ˈkɪŋkɪ] ADJ **(a)** enroscado; rizado, ensortijado; arrugado. **(b)** (*fig*) peculiar; torcido, (*esp*) de gustos sexuales pervertidos; *dress etc* excéntrico.

kinsfolk [ˈkɪnzfəʊk] NPL familia *f*, parientes *mpl*.

kinship [ˈkɪnʃɪp] N (*of family*) parentesco *m*; (*fig*) afinidad *f*, relación *f*.

kinsman [ˈkɪnzmən] N, PL **kinsmen** [ˈkɪnzmən] pariente *m*.

kinswoman [ˈkɪnzˌwʊmən] N, PL **kinswomen** [ˈkɪnzˌwɪmɪn] parienta *f*.

kiosk [ˈkiːɒsk] N (*Brit*) quiosco *m*, kiosco *m*; (*Brit Telec*) cabina *f*.

kip‡ [kɪp] (*Brit*) **1** N (*lodging*) alojamiento *m*; (*bed*) pulguero‡ *m*; (*sleep*) sueño *m*; **to have a ~** dormir un rato.

2 VI dormir; **to ~ down** echarse a dormir.

kipper [ˈkɪpər] N (*Brit*) arenque *m* ahumado.

kirby grip [ˈkɜːbɪˌɡrɪp] N horquilla *f*.

kirk [kɜːk] N (*Scot*) iglesia *f*; **the K~** la Iglesia (Presbiteriana) de Escocia.

kirsch [kɪəʃ] N kirsch *m*.

kiss [kɪs] **1** N beso *m*; (*light touch*) roce *m*; **~ of death** beso *m* de la muerte; **~ of life** beso *m* de la vida, respiración *f* boca a boca; **to blow sb a ~** tirar un beso a uno, dar un beso volado a uno.

2 VT besar; **to ~ sb good-bye** besar a uno y decirle adios; **he ~ed her goodnight** le dio un beso de despedida.

3 VI: **they ~ed** se besaron, se dieron un beso; **to ~ and be friends** hacer las paces; **to ~ and tell** (*fig*) dar un beso y confesarlo todo (vendiendo una historia escandalosa a un periódico).

◆ **kiss away** VT curar con un beso.

kiss-curl [ˈkɪskɜːl] N (*Brit*) caracol *m*.

kisser‡ [ˈkɪsər] N (*face*) jeta‡ *f*; (*mouth*) morrera‡ *f*.

► LANGUAGE IN USE: **kind: 1a → 4 1b → 22**

kiss-off* ['kɪsɒf] N (US): **to give sth the ~** tirar algo, despedirse de algo; **to give sb the ~** (employee) poner a uno de patitas en la calle*, despedir a uno; (boyfriend) plantar a uno*, dejar a uno.

kissogram ['kɪsə,græm] N besograma m.

kissproof ['kɪspruːf] ADJ indeleble.

Kit [kɪt] NMF familiar form of **Catherine etc, Christopher.**

kit [kɪt] N (gear in general) avíos mpl; (baggage) equipaje m; (tools) herramientas fpl, herramental m; (first-aid) botiquín m; (Mil) equipo m; **the whole ~ and caboodle** toda la pesca.
♦ **kit out, kit up** VT: **to ~ sb out** (or **up**) equipar a uno (with de).

kitbag ['kɪtbæg] N saco m de viaje; (Mil) mochila f.

kitchen ['kɪtʃɪn] [1] N cocina f.
[2] ATTR: **~ cabinet** (Pol) grupo m de asesores personales; **~ garden** huerto m; **~ knife** cuchillo m de cocina; **~ paper** toallitas fpl de papel; **~ range** cocina f económica; **~ roll** rollo m de cocina; **~ salt** sal f de cocina; **~ sink** fregadero m; **they had everything with them except the ~ sink** lo tenían todo consigo menos la abuela; **~ sink play** obra f ultrarrealista, obra f que tiene por tema la vida doméstica cruda; **~ unit** módulo m de cocina; ver también CABINET .

kitchenette [,kɪtʃɪ'net] N cocina f pequeña.

kitchenmaid ['kɪtʃɪn,meɪd] N ayudanta f de cocina.

kitchenware ['kɪtʃɪnweə'] N batería f de cocina.

kite [kaɪt] [1] N (a) (Orn) milano m real. (b) (toy) cometa f; **~ mark** señal f de aprobación (de la BSI); **to fly a ~** (fig) lanzar una idea para sondear la opinión, (pej) soltar una especie; **go fly a ~!*** (US) ¡vete al cuerno!* (c) (Fin:) cheque m sin valor.
[2] VI (:) estafar un banco.

kith [kɪθ] N: **~ and kin** parientes mpl y amigos.

kitsch [kɪtʃ] [1] ADJ kitsch; cursi.
[2] N kitsch m; cursilería f.

kitten ['kɪtn] N gatito m, -a f, minino m, -a f; **I was having ~s*** (Brit), **I nearly had ~s*** (Brit) me llevé un tremendo susto*.

kittenish ['kɪtənɪʃ] ADJ (fig) picaruelo, coquetón, retozón.

kittiwake ['kɪtɪweɪk] N gaviota f tridáctila, gavina f.

Kitty ['kɪtɪ] NF familiar form of **Catherine etc.**

kitty ['kɪtɪ] N (collection) colecta f, fondo m; (Cards) puesta f, bote m, polla f; **how much have we in the ~?** ¿cuánto tenemos en el bote?

kiwi ['kiːwiː] N (Orn) kiwi m; (*: New Zealander) neozelandés m, -esa f; **~ fruit** kiwi m.

KKK N (US) ABBR of **Ku Klux Klan.**

Klansman ['klænzmən] N, PL **Klansmen** ['klænzmen] (US) miembro m del Ku Klux Klan.

klaxon ['klæksn] N claxon m.

Kleenex ['kliːneks] ® N, PL **Kleenex** or **Kleenexes** (US) Kleenex m ®.

kleptomania [,kleptəʊ'meɪnɪə] N cleptomanía f.

kleptomaniac [,kleptəʊ'meɪnɪæk] N cleptómano m, -a f.

klutz: [klʌts] N (US) gilipollas: mf, persona f torpe, persona f atontada.

km ABBR of **kilometre(s)** kilómetro(s) m(pl), km.

km/h ABBR of **kilometre(s) per hour** kilómetros mpl por hora, km/h.

knack [næk] N tino m; maña f, destreza f, tranquillo m, truco m; **it's just a ~** es un truco que se aprende; **to get the ~ of doing sth** aprender el modo de hacer algo; **to have the ~ of doing sth** tener el don de hacer algo; **he has a happy ~ of saying the right thing** siempre acierta al escoger la palabra exacta.

knacker ['nækə'] (Brit) [1] N matarife m de caballos.
[2] VT (*) agotar, reventar; **I'm ~ed** estoy agotado, no puedo más.

knapsack ['næpsæk] N mochila f.

knave [neɪv] N bellaco m, bribón m; (Cards) valet m, (in Spanish pack) sota f.

knavery ['neɪvərɪ] N bellaquería f.

knavish ['neɪvɪʃ] ADJ bellaco, bribón, vil.

knead [niːd] VT amasar, sobar; (fig) formar.

knee [niː] [1] N rodilla f; **on bended ~, on one's ~s** de rodillas; **to bow the ~ to** humillarse ante, someterse a; **to bring sb to his ~s** someter a uno, humillar a uno; **to fall on one's ~s, to go down on one's ~s** arrodillarse, caer de rodillas; **to go down on one's ~s to sb** implorar a uno de rodillas.
[2] VT dar un rodillazo a.

kneebend ['niːbend] N flexión f de piernas.

knee-breeches ['niːbrɪtʃɪz] NPL calzón m corto.

kneecap ['niːkæp] [1] N rótula f, choquezuela f.
[2] VT: **to ~ sb** destrozar a tiros la rótula de uno.

kneecapping ['niːkæpɪŋ] N destrozo m a tiros de la rótula de uno.

knee-deep ['niː'diːp] ADV: **to be ~ in** estar metido hasta las rodillas en; **the place was ~ in paper** había montones de papeles por todos lados; **to go into the water ~** avanzar hasta que el agua llegue a las rodillas.

knee-high ['niː'haɪ] [1] ADV hasta las rodillas; al nivel de las rodillas.
[2] ADJ: **~ grass** hierba f que crece hasta la altura de las rodillas.

knee-jerk ['niːdʒɜːk] N reflejo m rotular; (fig) reacción f instintiva, reacción f automática; **he's a ~ conservative** es de derechas hasta la

médula.

knee-joint ['niːdʒɔɪnt] N articulación f de la rodilla.

kneel [niːl] (irr: PRET AND PTP **knelt**) VI (also **to ~ down**) (act) arrodillarse, ponerse de rodillas, hincarse de rodillas; (state) estar de rodillas; **to ~ to** (fig) hincar la rodilla ante.

knee-length ['niːleŋθ] ATTR: **~ sock** calcetín m de media.

knee-level ['niːlevl] N altura f de la rodilla.

kneeling ['niːlɪŋ] ADJ figure arrodillado, de rodillas.

kneepad ['niːpæd] N rodillera f.

kneeroom ['niːrʊm] N espacio m para las piernas.

knees-up* ['niːzʌp] N (Brit hum) baile m.

knell [nel] N toque m de difuntos, doble m; V **deathknell.**

knelt [nelt] PRET AND PTP of **kneel.**

knew [njuː] PRET of **know.**

knickerbockers ['nɪkəbɒkəz] NPL pantalones mpl cortos; (US) pantalones mpl de golf, pantalones mpl holgados.

knickers ['nɪkəz] NPL (a) (Brit) bragas fpl; (old-fashioned) pantalones mpl de señora; **~!:** ¡narices!:; **to get one's ~ in a twist*** armarse un lío*. (b) (††) = **knickerbockers.**

knick-knack ['nɪknæk] N chuchería f, bujería f, baratija f.

knife [naɪf] [1] N, PL **knives** [naɪvz] cuchillo m; (folding) navaja f; (Mech) cuchilla f; **~ and fork** (at table) cubierto m; **war to the ~** guerra f a muerte; **to have one's ~ into sb** tener inquina a uno; **before you can say ~** en un decir Jesús; **to turn the ~ in the wound** remover el cuchillo en la llaga.
[2] VT acuchillar.

knifebox ['naɪfbɒks] N portacubiertos m.

knife-edge ['naɪfedʒ] N filo m (de cuchillo); **to be balanced on a ~** (fig) estar pendiente de un hilo.

knife-grinder ['naɪf,graɪndə'] N amolador m, afilador m.

knife-point ['naɪfpɔɪnt] N: **at ~** a punta de navaja.

knifing ['naɪfɪŋ] N cuchillazo m, navajazo m; herida f (or muerte f) con cuchillo.

knight [naɪt] [1] N caballero m; (Chess) caballo m; **~ in shining armour** príncipe m azul; **K~ (of the Order) of the Garter** (Brit) caballero m de la orden de la Jarretera.
[2] VT (Hist) armar caballero; (modern British) dar el título de Sir a.

knight-errant ['naɪt'erənt] N caballero m andante.

knight-errantry ['naɪt'erəntrɪ] N caballería f andante.

knighthood ['naɪthʊd] N (a) (order) caballería f. (b) (title) título m de caballero; (modern British) título m de Sir.

knightly ['naɪtlɪ] ADJ caballeroso, caballeresco.

Knight Templar ['naɪt'templə'] N caballero m templario, templario m.

knit [nɪt] [1] VT dress hacer a punto de aguja, tricotar, tejer (LAm); brows fruncir.
[2] VI hacer calceta, hacer media, hacer punto, tricotar, tejer (LAm); (bone) soldarse; (fig) unirse.
♦ **knit together** VT (fig) juntar, unir.
♦ **knit up** [1] VT montar.
[2] VI (wound) cerrarse, curarse.

knit stitch ['nɪt,stɪtʃ] N punto m de media.

knitted ['nɪtɪd] ADJ de punto; **~ goods** géneros mpl de punto.

knitting ['nɪtɪŋ] N labor f de punto; **she was doing her ~** estaba haciendo calceta.

knitting-machine ['nɪtɪŋmə,ʃiːn] N máquina f de tricotar, tricotosa f, tejedora f.

knitting-needle ['nɪtɪŋ,niːdl] N, **knitting-pin** ['nɪtɪŋ,pɪn] N aguja f de hacer calceta (or punto).

knitting pattern ['nɪtɪŋ,pætən] N instrucciones fpl para hacer punto.

knitting-wool ['nɪtɪŋ,wʊl] N lana f para labores.

knitwear ['nɪtweə'] N géneros mpl de punto.

knives [naɪvz] NPL of **knife.**

knob [nɒb] N (natural) protuberancia f, bulto m; (Mech etc) botón m; (of door) tirador m; (of stick) puño m; **~ of sugar** terrón m de azúcar.

knobbly ['nɒblɪ] ADJ, **knobby** ['nɒbɪ] ADJ nudoso.

knock [nɒk] [1] N (a) (blow) golpe m; (in collision) choque m; (on door) llamada f; (Aut) golpeteo m; **there was a ~ on the door** se llamó a la puerta; **he got a ~ on the head** recibió un golpe en la cabeza; **to get the ~:** mosquearse, ofenderse; ponerse negro*.
(b) (fig) golpe m; **the team took a hard ~ yesterday** ayer el equipo recibió un rudo golpe; **he can take plenty of hard ~s** sabe aguantar todos los reveses.
[2] VT (a) (strike) golpear; (collide with) chocar contra; **to ~ a hole in sth** abrir a la fuerza un agujero en algo; **to ~ the bottom out of a box** desfondar una caja; **to ~ the smile off sb's face** hacer que uno deje de sonreír a fuerza de golpes; **to ~ sb on the head** golpear a uno en la cabeza; **to ~ one's head on a beam** dar con la cabeza contra una viga; **to ~ sth to the floor** dar con algo en el suelo.
(b) (*: criticize) criticar, denigrar, hablar mal de; (Comm) hacer publicidad en contra de.
[3] VI golpear; (at door) llamar a la puerta; (Aut) golpear, martillear.

◆**knock about** [1] VT *person* pegar, maltratar, (*beat up*) aporrear; **the place was badly ~ed about** el lugar sufrió grandes estragos; **the car was rather ~ed about** el coche sufrió algunos desperfectos.
[2] VI vagabundear, andar vagando, rodar; **I've ~ed about a bit** he visto mucho mundo; **he's ~ing about somewhere** andará por ahí, estará rodando por ahí; **he ~s about with some strange friends** anda con unas amistades rarísimas.

◆**knock against** VT chocar contra, dar contra.

◆**knock around** [1] VT: **to ~ an idea around** dar vueltas a una idea.
[2] VI holgazanear, no hacer nada; *V ~* **about**.

◆**knock back*** VT **(a)** *drink* beberse (de un trago); **he can certainly ~ them back** él sí sabe beber.
(b) **it ~ed us back £500** nos costó 500 libras.
(c) (*shock*) asombrar, pasmar; **the smell ~s you back** el olor le echa a uno para atrás*.

◆**knock down** VT **(a)** (*demolish*) *building* derribar, demoler, echar por tierra; *person* derribar; *pedestrian* atropellar; *argument etc* destruir.
(b) *price* rebajar.
(c) (*at auction*) **to ~ sth down to sb for £50** rematar algo a uno en 50 libras; **it was ~ed down to X** se adjudicó a X.
(d) **completely ~ed down** sin montar, a montar por el comprador (y a su coste).

◆**knock in** VT hacer entrar a golpes; *nail* clavar; *container* abrir a golpes.

◆**knock into** VT chocar contra, dar con; (*) *person* topar.

◆**knock off** [1] VT **(a)** (*remove*) quitar (de un golpe); (*make fall*) hacer caer.
(b) (*Brit*‡: *steal*) birlar*, limpiar‡.
(c) (‡) (*arrest*) detener; (*kill*) despenar‡, cargarse*.
(d) (‡) *woman* tirarse a‡.
(e) (*: *finish*) *task* ejecutar prontamente, despachar; *work* terminar, suspender; **to ~ off smoking** dejar de fumar; **so we had to ~ it off** así que tuvimos que dejarlo; **~ it off, will you?** ¡déjalo, por Dios!
(f) (*discount*) **to ~ £20 off the price** rebajar el precio en 20 libras, descontar 20 libras del precio; **to ~ 3 seconds off the record** mejorar la marca en 3 segundos.
[2] VI (*) suspender el trabajo, terminar; salir del trabajo; **he ~s off at 5** sale del trabajo a las 5.

◆**knock on** VI: **he's ~ing on** es bastante viejo; **he's ~ing on 60** va para los 60.

◆**knock out** VT **(a)** (*stun*) dejar sin sentido, hacer perder el conocimiento; (*Boxing*) poner fuera de combate, dejar K.O.
(b) (*remove*) *teeth* romper; *passage in text* suprimir, quitar; (*from competition*) eliminar.
(c) *product* producir, fabricar; hacer.
(d) (*shock*) pasmar, aturdir; (*exhaust*) agotar, dejar para el arrastre.
(e) (*stop*) estropear, dejar fuera de servicio.

◆**knock over** VT volcar; *pedestrian* atropellar.

◆**knock together** [1] VT construir (*or* componer *etc*) de prisa.
[2] VI (*knees*) entrechocarse.

◆**knock up** [1] VT **(a)** (*build*) construir de prisa; construir toscamente; *meal* preparar de prisa.
(b) (*Brit*: *wake*) despertar, llamar.
(c) (*Brit*) (*tire*) agotar; (*make ill*) dejar enfermo; **he was ~ed up for a month** el agotamiento le duró un mes.
(d) (‡: *make pregnant*) dejar encinta.
[2] VI (*Tennis etc*) pelotear.

◆**knock up against** VT *difficulties, people* tropezarse con.

knockabout ['nɒkəbaut] ADJ bullicioso, tumultuoso, confuso; **~ comedy** farsa *f* bulliciosa, (*fig*) payasadas *fpl*.

knock-back* ['nɒkbæk] N rechazo *m*, feo *m*; **to get the ~** sufrir un feo.

knockdown ['nɒkdaun] ADJ: **~ price** (*Brit*) precio *m* obsequio, precio *m* de saldo.

knocker ['nɒkər] N **(a)** (*on door*) aldaba *f*. **(b)** (*: *critic*) detractor *m*, -ora *f*, crítico *m*, -a *f*. **(c)** **~s‡** tetas *fpl*.

knocker-up ['nɒkə'rʌp] N (*Brit*) despertador *m*.

knock-for-knock ['nɒkfə'nɒk] ATTR: **~ agreement** acuerdo *m* de pago respectivo.

knocking ['nɒkɪŋ] [1] ADJ: **~ copy** anuncio *m* destinado a denigrar el producto de otro, contrapublicidad *f*.
[2] N golpes *mpl*, golpeo *m*; (*at door*) llamada *f*; (*Aut*) golpeteo *m*.

knocking-off time* [ˌnɒkɪŋ'ɒf,taim] N hora *f* de salir del trabajo.

knocking-shop‡ ['nɒkɪŋʃɒp] N casa *f* de putas.

knock-kneed ['nɒk'ni:d] ADJ patizambo; (*fig*) débil, irresoluto.

knock-on ['nɒk'ɒn] [1] ATTR: **~ effect** repercusiones *fpl*, consecuencias *fpl*, reacción *f* en cadena.
[2] N (*Rugby*) autopase *m*.

knockout ['nɒkaut] [1] ADJ: **~ agreement** acuerdo *m* secreto para no hacerse competencia; **~ blow** golpe *m* aplastante, (*Boxing*) K.O. *m*, queo *m*; **~ competition** concurso *m* eliminatorio, eliminatoria *f*.
[2] N **(a)** (*Boxing*) knock-out *m*, K.O. *m*, queo *m*. **(b)** (*competition*) concurso *m* eliminatorio, eliminatoria *f*. **(c)** (*) **he's a ~!** ¡es la

monda!*; **she's a ~** es una chica estupenda; **it was a real ~** fue una noticia (*etc*) sorprendente, la noticia nos pasmó.

knock-up ['nɒkʌp] N (*Tennis*) peloteo *m*.

knoll [nəul] N otero *m*, montículo *m*.

knot [nɒt] [1] N nudo *m* (*also Naut, in wood*); (*bow*) lazo *m*; (*of people*) grupo *m*, corrillo *m*; **to tie the ~** (*fig*) prometerse, casarse; **to get tied up in ~s** anudarse, enmarañarse, (*fig*) armarse un lío, crearse confusiones; **to tie a ~** hacer un nudo.
[2] VT anudar, atar; **get ~ted!‡** ¡fastídiate!*
[3] VI anudarse.

◆**knot together** VT atar, anudar.

knot-hole ['nɒthəul] N agujero *m* (que deja un nudo en la madera).

knotted ['nɒtid] ADJ *rope etc* anudado, con nudos.

knotty ['nɒti] ADJ nudoso; (*fig*) difícil, complicado, espinoso.

knout [naut] N knut *m*.

▼**know** [nəu] (*irr*: PRET **knew**, PTP **known**) [1] VT **(a)** (*gen*) *fact etc* saber; **to ~ Japanese** saber japonés; **what do you ~?*** ¿qué hay de nuevo?; **well, what do you ~!** ¡caramba!, ¡qué cosa más rara!; **don't I ~ it!** ¡y tú que me lo dices!, ¡si lo sabré yo!; **not if I ~ it** no será, si puedo evitarlo; **you ~ what you can do with it!‡** ¡métetelo por donde te quepa!‡; **to ~ what's what** saber cuántas son cinco; **it was big, (you) ~ what I mean?** era grande, ¿sabes?; **you don't ~ how glad I am to see you** no sabes cuánto me alegro de verte; **to get to ~ sth** (llegar a) saber algo, enterarse de algo.
(b) (*be acquainted with*) *person, book, subject etc* conocer; **do you ~ him?** ¿le conoces?; **if I ~ him he'll say no** estoy seguro que dirá que no; **do you ~ Spain?** ¿conoces España?; **to come to ~ sb, to get to ~ sb** (llegar a) conocer a uno.
(c) (*recognize*) conocer, reconocer; **to ~ sb by sight** conocer a uno de vista; **to ~ sb by** (*or* from) **his walk** conocer a uno por su modo de andar; **I knew him at once** le reconocí en seguida.
[2] VI **(a)** (*gen*) saber **I ~!** ¡ya sé!; **who ~s?** ¿quién sabe?; **one never ~s, you never ~** nunca se sabe; **I don't ~, I wouldn't ~** no sé; **how should I ~?** ¿yo qué sé?; **it's not easy, you ~** mire, esto no es fácil; **it was big, you ~** era grande, sabes; **we'll let you ~** le avisaremos; **why didn't you let me ~?** ¿por qué no me has avisado?; **afterwards they just don't want to ~** después 'si te vi no me acuerdo'; **it's been there for as long as I've ~n** está allí desde siempre.
(b) **to ~ about, to ~ of** saber de, tener conocimiento de, estar enterado de; **I don't ~ about you, but I ...** por ti no sé, pero yo ...; **I didn't ~ about that** no sabía nada de eso, lo ignoraba; **oh, I don't ~ about that** pues eso no es cierto; ¡hombre, no tanto!; **she ~s about cats** ella entiende de gatos; **did you ~ about John?** ¿has oído lo de Juan?; **I don't ~ about you!** (*despairing*) ¿qué le vamos a hacer?; **not that I ~ of** que yo sepa, no.
▼**(c)** **to ~ how to** + *infin* saber + *infin*.
[3] N **(a)** **to be in the ~** estar enterado, estar en el ajo; **those not in the ~** los no avisados.
(b) **there were 7% don't ~s** hubo un 7 por ciento que 'no sabe, no contesta'.

knowable ['nəuəbl] ADJ conocible.

know-all ['nəuɔ:l] N sabelotodo *mf*.

know-how ['nəuhau] N saber hacer *m*, know-how *m*; habilidad *f*, destreza *f*; experiencia *f*; (*expertise*) pericia *f*; **a certain amount of technical ~** algunos conocimientos *mpl* técnicos.

knowing ['nəuiŋ] [1] ADJ (*sharp*) astuto, avispado; *look etc* de complicidad, malicioso; **worth ~** digno de saberse.
[2] N: **there's no ~** no hay modo de saberlo; **there's no ~ what he'll do** es imposible adivinar lo que hará.

knowingly ['nəuiŋli] ADV **(a)** (*intentionally*) a sabiendas, adrede. **(b)** *look etc* maliciosamente, con malicia.

know-it-all ['nəuitɔ:l] N (*US*) sabelotodo *mf*.

▼**knowledge** ['nɒlidʒ] N (*knowing*) conocimiento *m*; (*person's range of information*) conocimientos *mpl*, saber *m*; (*learning*) erudición *f*, ciencia *f*; **the advance of ~** el progreso de la ciencia; **his ~ will die with him** morirá su erudición con él; **to my ~, to the best of my ~** según mi leal entender y saber, que yo sepa; **not to my ~** que yo sepa; **without my ~** sin saberlo yo; **that is common ~** eso lo sabe todo el mundo; **his failure is common ~** su fracaso es ya del dominio público; **it is common ~ that ...** se sabe perfectamente que ..., es notorio que ...; **it has come to my ~ that** he llegado a saber que; **to have a ~ of Welsh** saber algo de galés; **to have a working ~ of** dominar los principios esenciales de; **to have a thorough ~ of** conocer a fondo.

knowledgeable ['nɒlidʒəbl] ADJ *person* entendido, erudito (*about* en); *remark* informado.

knowledgeably ['nɒlidʒəbli] ADV de manera erudita, con conocimiento de causa.

known [nəun] [1] PTP of **know**; **X, ~ as Y** X, conocido por el nombre de Y; **a product ~ everywhere** un producto conocido en todas partes; **he is ~ everywhere** se le conoce en todas partes; **to become ~** (*fact*) llegar a saberse, (*person*) llegar a ser conocido; **it became ~**

that ... se supo que ...; **he let it be ~ that** ... dio a entender que ..., informó que ...; **to make o.s. ~** darse a conocer (*to* a); **to make sth ~ to sb** anunciar algo a uno, hacer que uno se entere de algo; **to make one's wishes ~** hacer que se sepa lo que uno desea.

2 ADJ: **a ~ thief** un ladrón conocido; **a ~ expert** un experto reconocido como tal; **he is a ~ quantity** es alguien que por lo menos conocemos, es de sobra conocido; **the ~ facts** los hechos establecidos, los hechos ciertos.

knuckle ['nʌkl] N nudillo *m*; **it was a bit near the ~** rayaba en la indecencia; **to rap sb's ~s, to rap sb over the ~s** echar un rapapolvo a uno.

◆**knuckle down** VI: **to ~ down to sth** ponerse a hacer algo con ahinco, dedicarse a algo en serio.

◆**knuckle under** VI darse por vencido, someterse; **to ~ under to threats** someterse ante las amenazas.

knucklebone ['nʌkl,bəʊn] N nudillo *m*.

knuckleduster ['nʌkl,dʌstər] N puño *m* de hierro.

knucklehead: ['nʌkl,hed] N cabezahueca *m*.

knurl [nɜːl] **1** N nudo *m*, protuberancia *f*; (*of coin*) cordón *m*. **2** VT *coin* acordonar.

knurled [nɜːld] ADJ nudoso; *coin* moleteado.

K.O. ABBR *of* **knockout.**

koala [kəʊ'ɑːlə] N coala *f*.

kohlrabi [kəʊl'rɑːbɪ] N colinabo *m*.

kook* [kuːk] N (*US*) majareta* *mf*, excéntrico *m*, -a *f*.

kookie:, kooky: ['kuːkɪ] ADJ (*US*) loco, chiflado*.

Koran [kɒ'rɑːn] N Corán *m*, Alcorán *m*.

Koranic [kɒ'rænɪk] ADJ coránico, alcoránico.

Korea [kə'rɪə] N Corea *f*; **North ~** Corea *f* del Norte; **South ~** Corea *f* del Sur.

Korean [kə'rɪən] **1** ADJ coreano. **2** N coreano *m*, -a *f*.

kosher ['kəʊʃər] ADJ autorizado por la ley judía, kosher, cosher.

kowtow ['kaʊ'taʊ] VI (*bow*) saludar humildemente; **to ~ to sb** humillarse ante uno, doblegarse servilmente ante uno.

kph ABBR *of* **kilometres per hour** kilómetros *mpl* por hora, kph.

Kraut: [kraʊt] **1** ADJ alemán. **2** N alemán *m*, -ana *f*.

Kremlin ['kremlɪn] N: **the ~** el Kremlin.

Kremlinologist [,kremlɪ'nɒlədʒɪst] N kremlinólogo *m*, -a *f*.

Kremlinology [,kremlɪ'nɒlədʒɪ] N kremlinología *f*.

krill [krɪl] N, PL **krill** camarón *m* antártico.

krugerrand ['kruːgə,rænd] N krugerrand *m*.

krum(m)horn ['krʌmhɔːn] N cuerno *m*.

Kruschev [kruːs'tʃɒf] NM Jruschov.

krypton [krɪptɒn] N criptón *m*.

KS (*US Post*) ABBR *of* **Kansas.**

Kt (*Brit*) ABBR *of* **Knight** *caballero de una orden.*

Kuala Lumpur ['kwɑːlə'lʊmpʊər] N Kuala Lumpur *m*.

kudos* ['kjuːdɒs] N prestigio *m*, gloria *f*.

Ku Klux Klan ['kuː'klʌks'klæn] N: **the ~** el Ku Klux Klan.

kummel ['kʊməl] N cúmel *m*, kummel *m*.

kumquat ['kʌmkwɒt] N naranja *f* china.

kung fu ['kʌŋ'fuː] N kung fu *m*.

Kurd [kɜːd] N kurdo *m*, -a *f*.

Kurdish ['kɜːdɪʃ] **1** ADJ kurdo. **2** N (*Ling*) kurdo *m*.

Kurdistan [,kɜːdɪ'stæn] N Kurdistán *m*.

Kuwait [kʊ'weɪt] N Kuwait *m*, Koweit *m*, Koveit *m*.

Kuwaiti [kʊ'weɪtɪ] ADJ, N kuwaití *mf*, koweití *mf*, koveití *mf*.

kW. ABBR *of* **kilowatt(s)** kilovatio(s) *mpl*, kv.

kW/h. ABBR *of* **kilowatt-hours** kilovatios-hora *mpl*, kv/h.

KY (*US Post*) ABBR *of* **Kentucky.**

Kyrgyzstan [,kɜːgɪs'tɑːn] N Kirguizistán *f*, Kirguizstán *f*, Kirguizia *f*.

L

L, l [el] N (*letter*) L, l *f*; **L for Lucy, L for Love** '*US*) L de Lorenzo.
L (a) (*maps etc*) ABBR of **lake.**
  (b) (*Aut*) ABBR of **learner; L-plate** (*Brit*) placa *f* de la L (*de conductor en prácticas*); *ver también* DRIVING LICENCE/DRIVER'S LICENSE .
  (c) (*garment size*) ABBR of **large.**
  (d) ABBR of **left** izquierda, izq.
l. (a) ABBR of **left** izquierdo, izq. **(b)** ABBR of **litre**(s) litro(s) *m*(*pl*), l.
LA (a) (*US Post*) ABBR of **Louisiana. (b)** ABBR of **Los Angeles.**
La. (*US*) ABBR of **Louisiana.**
lab [læb] N = **laboratory.**
Lab. (a) [læb] N ABBR of **Labour** laborista *mf*; *also* ADJ. **(b)** (*Canada*) ABBR of **Labrador.**
label ['leɪbl] [1] N etiqueta *f*, rótulo *m*, marbete *m*; (*on specimen etc*) letrero *m*; (*on spine of book*) tejuelo *m*; (*fig*) calificación *f*, designación *f*, descripción *f*, clasificación *f*; **a record on the CCS ~** un disco de la marca CCS.
  [2] VT **(a)** etiquetar, poner etiqueta a; rotular, poner un letrero a; **it is not clearly ~led** la etiqueta no es legible; no hay etiqueta (*etc*) que lo describa claramente; **every case must be ~led** cada maleta ha de llevar una etiqueta.
  (b) (*fig*) calificar (*as* de), designar (*as* como), describir (*as* como); apodar; **to ~ sb as** (*fig*) tachar a uno de; **to be ~led as** estar encasillado como; **he got himself ~led a troublemaker** se hizo una reputación de turbulento.
labelling ['leɪbəlɪŋ] N etiquetado *m*, etiquetaje *m*.
labia ['leɪbɪə] NPL of **labium.**
labial ['leɪbɪəl] [1] ADJ labial.
  [2] N labial *f*.
labiodental [,leɪbɪəʊ'dentəl] [1] ADJ labiodental.
  [2] N labiodental *f*.
labiovelar [,leɪbɪəʊ'viːləʳ] ADJ, N labiovelar *f*.
labium ['leɪbɪəm] N, PL **labia** ['leɪbɪə] labio *m*.
labor ['leɪbəʳ] (*US*) = **labour.**

LABOR DAY

ⓘ *El **Labor Day** (Día del Trabajo) es una festividad nacional en honor al trabajo, que se celebra en Estados Unidos y en Canadá el primer lunes de septiembre. Fue instaurada en 1894 por el Congreso de los Estados Unidos, después de que los trabajadores la solicitaran durante más de doce años. En la actualidad, ya sin las connotaciones políticas de sus orígenes y coincidiendo con el final del verano y con el principio del curso escolar, se celebran desfiles, mítines y comidas campestres.*

---

laboratory [lə'bɒrətərɪ, US 'læbrə,tɔːrɪ] N laboratorio *m*; **~ assistant** ayudante *mf* de laboratorio; **~ coat** bata *f* de laboratorio; **~ test** prueba *f* de laboratorio.
laborious [lə'bɔːrɪəs] ADJ penoso; difícil, pesado.
laboriously [lə'bɔːrɪəslɪ] ADV penosamente, con dificultad.
labour, (*US*) **labor** ['leɪbəʳ] [1] N **(a)** (*work in general*) trabajo *m*; **Ministry of L~** Ministerio *m* de Trabajo.
  (b) (*task*) trabajo *m*, labor *f*, faena *f*, tarea *f*; **a ~ of love** una tarea muy grata, un trabajo agradable; **~s of Hercules** trabajos *mpl* de Hércules.
  (c) (*toil*) pena *f*, fatiga *f*, esfuerzo *m*; **after much ~** tras grandes esfuerzos.
  (d) (*Jur*) **hard ~** trabajos *mpl* forzados; **5 years' hard ~** 5 años de trabajos forzados.
  (e) (*persons*) obreros *mpl*, mano *f* de obra; (*as class*) clase *f* obrera; **we are short of ~** nos falta mano de obra; **capital and ~** la empresa y los obreros.
  (f) (*Brit Pol*) **L~** laborismo *m*, Partido *m* Laborista; **to vote ~** votar por un candidato laborista.
  (g) (*Med*) parto *m*; (*also* **~ pains**) dolores *mpl* del parto; **to be in ~**

estar de parto.
  [2] ATTR de trabajo; laboral; **~ camp** campamento *m* de trabajo; **~ cost** costo *m* de la mano de obra; **L~ Day** Día *m* del Trabajo (*en Reino Unido 1 mayo; en US, Canada, primer lunes de setiembre*); **~ dispute** conflicto *m* laboral; **~ exchange** (*Brit*†) bolsa *f* de trabajo; **~ force** mano *f* de obra, fuerza *f* laboral; **~ law** (*as study*) derecho *m* del trabajo, derecho *m* laboral; **~ lawyer** abogado *mf* laboralista; **~ market** mercado *m* del trabajo (*or* laboral); **~ movement** movimiento *m* obrero; **L~ Party** Partido *m* Laborista; **~ relations** relaciones *fpl* laborales; **~ shortage** escasez *f* de mano de obra; **~ supply** oferta *f* de mano de obra; **~ union** (*US*) sindicato *m*; **~ ward** (*Med*) sala *f* de partos.
  [3] VT *point etc* insistir en, machacar en, desarrollar con nimiedad; **I won't ~ the point** me abstengo de subrayar esto, no hace falta insistir en esto.
  [4] VI **(a)** (*work*) trabajar (*at* en); **to ~ in vain** trabajar en balde; **to ~ to do sth** afanarse por hacer algo; **to ~ under a delusion** estar equivocado.
  (b) (*move etc*) moverse penosamente, avanzar con dificultad; **to ~ up a hill** subir penosamente una cuesta; **the engine is ~ing** el motor no funciona bien.
laboured, (*US*) **labored** ['leɪbəd] ADJ *breathing* fatigoso; *movement* torpe, lento, penoso; *style* pesado, premioso.
labourer, (*US*) **laborer** ['leɪbərəʳ] N (*on roads etc*) peón *m*; (*farm ~*) labriego *m*, bracero *m*, peón *m*, afanador *m* (*Mex*); (*day ~*) jornalero *m*; **bricklayer's ~** peón *m* de albañil.
labouring, (*US*) **laboring** ['leɪbərɪŋ] ADJ *class* obrero.
labour-intensive, (*US*) **labor-intensive** ['leɪbərɪn'tensɪv] ADJ: **~ industry** industria *f* en que se emplea mucha mano de obra.
labourite, (*US*) **laborite** ['leɪbəraɪt] N (*pej*) laborista *mf*.
labour-saving, (*US*) **labor-saving** ['leɪbə,seɪvɪŋ] ADJ que ahorra trabajo; **~ device** máquina *f* que ahorra trabajo.
labrador ['læbrədɔːr] N labrador *m*.
laburnum [lə'bɜːnəm] N lluvia *f* de oro, codeso *m*.
labyrinth ['læbərɪnθ] N laberinto *m*.
labyrinthine [,læbə'rɪnθaɪn] ADJ laberíntico.
lac [læk] N laca *f*.
lace [leɪs] [1] N **(a)** (*open fabric*) encaje *m*, (*as trimming*) puntilla *f*; (*of gold, silver*) galón *m*. **(b)** (*of shoe etc*) cordón *m*, agujeta *f* (*Mex*).
  [2] VT **(a)** (*Sew*) guarnecer con encajes (*etc*). **(b)** (*also* **to ~ up**) *shoe etc* atar, atar el cordón de. **(c)** *drink* echar licor a; **a drink ~d with brandy** una bebida reforzada con coñac.
◆**lace into**: VT: **to ~ into sb** dar una paliza a uno.
lace-maker ['leɪs,meɪkəʳ] N encajero *m*, -a *f*.
lacemaking ['leɪs,meɪkɪŋ] N labor *f* de encaje.
lacerate ['læsəreɪt] VT lacerar; *feelings etc* herir.
laceration [,læsə'reɪʃən] N laceración *f*.
lace-ups ['leɪsʌps] NPL (*also* **lace-up shoes**) zapatos *mpl* con cordones.
lachrymal ['lækrɪməl] ADJ lagrimal.
lachrymose ['lækrɪməʊs] ADJ lacrimoso, lloroso.
lack [læk] [1] N falta *f*, ausencia *f*, carencia *f*; escasez *f*; **for ~ of, through ~ of** por falta de; **there is a grave ~ of water** nos hace muchísima falta el agua; **there is no ~ of money** no es que falte dinero.
  [2] VT no tener; carecer de, necesitar; **we ~ time to do it** nos falta tiempo para hacerlo; **we're ~ing 3 players to make up a team** nos hacen falta 3 jugadores para completar el equipo; **he does not ~ talent** no carece de talento, es cierto que tiene talento; **what is it that you ~?** ¿qué es lo que te hace falta?; **he ~s confidence** no tiene confianza en sí mismo; **~ing men, what can we do?** a falta de hombres, ¿qué podemos hacer?
  [3] VI **(a)** (*thing*) **to be ~ing** faltar, estar ausente, no haber; **but money is ~ing** pero no hay dinero, pero falta el dinero; **nothing was**

~ing to make the play succeed no faltaba nada para que la obra obtuviera un éxito; where decency is ~ing donde falta la decencia.
(b) (person) he is ~ing in confidence no tiene confianza en sí mismo, le falta confianza en sí mismo, carece de confianza en sí mismo; it's not that he's ~ing in good qualities no es que le falten buenas cualidades.

lackadaisical [,lækə'deɪzɪkəl] ADJ lánguido, indiferente; (dreamy) ensimismado, despistado, distraído; (slow) perezoso, tardo; (careless) descuidado, informal.

lackey ['lækɪ] N lacayo m (also fig).

lacklustre, (US) lackluster ['læk,lʌstəʳ] ADJ surface deslustrado, deslucido; style etc inexpresivo; eyes apagado; person pesado, soso.

laconic [lə'kɒnɪk] ADJ lacónico.

laconically [lə'kɒnɪkəlɪ] ADV lacónicamente.

lacquer ['lækəʳ] ① N laca f, maque m, pintura f al duco.
② VT laquear, maquear, pintar al duco.

lacquered ['lækəd] ADJ barnizado con laca, laqueado, pintado al duco.

lacrosse [lə'krɒs] N lacrosse f.

lactate ['lækteɪt] VI lactar.

lactation [læk'teɪʃən] N lactancia f.

lacteal ['læktɪəl] ADJ lácteo.

lactic ['læktɪk] ADJ láctico.

lacto-ovo-vegetarian [,læktəʊ,əʊvəʊ,vedʒɪ'teərɪən] N lacto-ovo-vegetariano m, -a f.

lactose ['læktəʊs] N lactosa f.

lacto-vegetarian [,læktəʊ,vedʒɪ'teərɪən] N lacto-vegetariano m, -a f.

lacuna [lə'kjuːnə] N, PL **lacunae** [lə'kjuːniː] laguna f.

lacustrine [lə'kʌstraɪn] ADJ lacustre.

lacy ['leɪsɪ] ADJ (of lace) de encaje; (like lace) parecido a encaje; (fig) transparente, diáfano.

lad [læd] N muchacho m, chico m, pibe m (And, SC), chavo m (Mex); (country ~) mozo m, zagal m; (in stable etc) mozo m; young ~ muchacho m, mozalbete m; when I was a ~ cuando yo era chaval; he's only a ~ es muy joven; don't do that, ~! ¡no hagas eso, joven!; come on, ~s! ¡vamos, muchachos!; all together, ~s! ¡todos juntos, muchachos!; he's a bit of a ~ es un chico poco formal; es un tipo muy divertido; he's a bit of a ~ with the girls les da guerra a las chicas, se bromea mucho con las chicas.

ladder ['lædəʳ] ① N (a) escalera f (de mano), escala f; (Brit: in stocking) carrera f.
(b) (fig) camino m, escalón m (to de); social ~ escala f social; it's a first step up the ~ es el primer peldaño; to be at the top of the ~ estar en la cumbre de su profesión (etc), ocupar el rango más alto.
② ATTR: ~ truck (US) coche-escala m.
③ VT (Brit) stocking hacer una carrera en.
④ VI (Brit: stocking) hacerse una carrera, desmallarse.

ladderproof ['lædəpruːf] ADJ (Brit) stocking indesmallable.

laddie* ['lædɪ] N (esp Scot) = lad.

lade [leɪd] (irr: PRET **laded**, PTP **laden**) ① VT cargar (with de).
② VI tomar cargamento.

laden ['leɪdn] PTP of lade; ~ with cargado de.

la-di-da* ['lɑːdɪ'dɑː] ① ADJ afectado, repipi*.
② ADV talk etc de manera afectada, con afectación.

lading ['leɪdɪŋ] N cargamento m, flete m.

ladle ['leɪdl] ① N (at table) cucharón m, cacillo m; (in kitchen) cazo m.
② VT (also to ~ out) servir (or sacar etc) con cucharón; (fig) repartir generosamente, distribuir a manos llenas.

lady ['leɪdɪ] ① N señora f; (aged, distinguished, noble) dama f; (Brit title) L~ (Gladys) Crumm Lady (Gladys) Crumm; 'Ladies' (lavatory) 'Señoras'; 'Ladies Only' 'Sólo Damas'; ladies and gentlemen! ¡señoras y señores!; ~ of the house señora f de la casa; the minister and his ~ el ministro y su esposa; your good ~ su esposa; Our L~ Nuestra Señora f; young ~ señorita f, joven f; his young ~ su novia; she's no ~ esa mujer no es lo que aparenta, es una mujer que tiene historia; shall we join the ladies? ¿pasamos a estar con las señoras?; ~'s cycle bicicleta f de señora; ladies' final final f femenina; ladies' man hombre m de salón, Perico m entre ellas; ladies' room lavabo m de señoras; ver también TOILET.
② ATTR (a) ~ doctor médica f; ~ friend amiga f; ~ guest invitada f; ~ mayoress (Brit) alcaldesa f; ~ member socio f, señora f socio.
(b) (Rel) L~ Chapel capilla f de la Virgen; L~ Day (Brit) día m de la Anunciación (25 marzo).

ladybird ['leɪdɪbɜːd] (Brit) N, (US) **ladybug** ['leɪdɪbʌg] N mariquita f, vaca f de San Antón.

lady-in-waiting ['leɪdɪn'weɪtɪŋ] N dama f de honor.

ladykiller ['leɪdɪ,kɪləʳ] N tenorio m, ladrón m de corazones.

ladylike ['leɪdɪlaɪk] ADJ elegante, fino, distinguido, bien educado; (pej) afeminado.

lady-love ['leɪdɪlʌv] N amada f.

lady's finger ['leɪdɪz,fɪŋgəʳ] N (Bot) quimbombó m.

ladyship ['leɪdɪʃɪp] N: Her L~, Your L~ Su Señoría.

lady's maid ['leɪdɪz,meɪd] N doncella f.

LAFTA ['læftə] N ABBR of **Latin-American Free Trade Association** Asociación f Latinoamericana de Libre Comercio, ALALC f.

lag¹ [læg] ① N retraso m.
② VI retrasarse; (in pace) rezagarse, quedarse atrás.
◆ **lag behind** ① VI retrasarse; (in pace) rezagarse, quedarse atrás; we ~ behind in space exploration nos hemos retrasado en la exploración espacial.
② VT: Ruritania ~s behind Slobodia Ruritania anda a rastras detrás de Eslobodia, Ruritania no ha hecho tantos progresos como Eslobodia.

lag² [læg] VT (Tech) revestir, recubrir, forrar (with de); boiler calorifugar.

lag³‡ [læg] ① N (esp Brit: also old ~) presidiario m.
② VT meter a la sombra‡.

lager ['lɑːgəʳ] N cerveza f ligera dorada; ~ lout (Brit*) gamberro m de litrona; ver también BEER.

laggard ['lægəd] N (having fallen behind) rezagado m, -a f; (idler) holgazán m, -ana f.

lagging ['lægɪŋ] N (Tech) revestimiento m, forro m.

lagoon [lə'guːn] N laguna f.

Lagos ['leɪgɒs] N Lagos m.

lah [lɑː] N (Mus) la m.

lah-di-dah [,lɑːdɪ'dɑː] = **la-di-da**.

laicize ['leɪɪsaɪz] VT laicizar.

laid [leɪd] PRET AND PTP of lay; to be ~ up (Med) estar enfermo, tener que guardar cama (with a causa de); (car etc) estar fuera de circulación, estar en garaje.

laid-back* [,leɪd'bæk] ADJ (esp US) person relajado, ecuánime; party tranquilo, pacífico.

lain [leɪn] PTP of lie².

lair [lɛəʳ] N cubil m, guarida f.

laird [lɛəd] N (Scot) señor m; terrateniente m, propietario m.

laissez-faire ['leɪseɪ'fɛəʳ] N laissez-faire m.

laity ['leɪɪtɪ] N laicado m, legos mpl; (fig) legos mpl.

lake¹ [leɪk] N (colour) laca f.

lake² [leɪk] N (Geog) lago m; the L~s (England) los Lagos; ~ Michigan el Lago Michigan.

Lake District ['leɪk,dɪstrɪkt] N País m de los Lagos.

lake-dweller ['leɪk,dweləʳ] N (Hist) persona f que vive en una habitación f lacustre.

lake-dwelling ['leɪk,dwelɪŋ] N habitación f lacustre.

lakeside ['leɪksaɪd] N ribera f de(l) lago, orilla f de(l) lago.

Lallans ['lælənz] N dialecto y lengua literaria de las Tierras Bajas (Lowlands) de Escocia.

lam¹‡ [læm] ① VT pegar, dar una paliza a.
② VI: to ~ into sb dar una paliza a uno.

lam²‡ [læm] N: to be on the ~ (US) ser fugitivo de la justicia.

lama ['lɑːmə] N lama m.

lamb [læm] ① N cordero m, -a f; (older) borrego m, -a f; (meat) (carne f de) cordero m; the L~ of God el Cordero de Dios; my poor ~! ¡pobrecito!; he took it like a ~ recibió la noticia con la mayor tranquilidad, no se ofendió en lo más mínimo; to go like a ~ to the slaughter ir como borrego al matadero.
② ATTR: ~ chop chuleta f de cordero.
③ VI parir (la oveja).

lambada [,læm'bɑːdə] N lambada f.

lambast(e) [læm'beɪst] VT dar una paliza a; (fig) poner como un trapo.

lambing ['læmɪŋ] N (época f del) parto m de las ovejas.

lamb-like ['læmlaɪk] ADJ manso como un cordero.

lambskin ['læmskɪn] N (piel f de) cordero m.

lamb's lettuce ['læmz'letɪs] N valeriana f.

lamb's wool, lambswool ['læmzwʊl] N lana f de cordero, añinos mpl.

lame [leɪm] ① ADJ (a) animal, person cojo, lisiado; ~ duck (St Ex) especulador m, -ora f insolvente; (fig) persona f quemada; persona f completamente incapaz; ~ duck industry industria f insolvente; industria f en declive; ~ duck president (etc) presidente m (etc) no reelegido en los últimos meses de su mandato; to be ~ (permanently) ser cojo, (temporarily) estar cojo; to be ~ in one foot ser cojo de un pie, cojear de un pie; to go ~ estropearse un pie, lisiarse un pie, empezar a cojear.
(b) (fig) excuse débil, poco convincente; argument flojo; (Liter) metre defectuoso, que cojea.
② VT lisiar, dejar cojo; incapacitar.

lamé ['lɑːmeɪ] N lamé m, lama f.

lamely ['leɪmlɪ] ADV walk etc cojeando; argue, say etc sin convicción.

lameness ['leɪmnɪs] N cojera f; incapacidad f; (fig) falta f de convicción; flojedad f.

lament [lə'ment] ① N lamento m; queja f; (Liter etc) elegía f (for por).
② VT lamentar, lamentarse de; to ~ sb llorar a uno, llorar la pérdida de uno; it is much to be ~ed that ... es de lamentar que + subj.

3 VI lamentarse (*for, over* de).
lamentable ['læməntəbl] ADJ lamentable.
lamentably ['læməntəblɪ] ADV lamentablemente.
lamentation [ˌlæmən'teɪʃən] N lamentación *f*.
laminate 1 ['læmɪneɪt] VT laminar.
2 ['læmɪnɪt] N laminado *m*.
laminated ['læmɪneɪtɪd] ADJ laminado; *document* plastificado; *glass* inastillable; ~ **wood** contrachapado *m*.
lamp [læmp] N lámpara *f*; linterna *f*; (*in street*) farol *m*; (*Aut, Rail etc*) faro *m*; (*bulb*) bombilla *f*; (*fig*) antorcha *f*.
lampblack ['læmpblæk] N negro *m* de humo.
lamp-bracket ['læmp,brækɪt] N brazo *m* de lámpara.
lamp-chimney ['læmp,tʃɪmnɪ] N, **lampglass** ['læmpglɑːs] N tubo *m* de lámpara.
lampholder ['læmp,həʊldəʳ] N portalámpara *m*.
lamplight ['læmplaɪt] N luz *f* de (la) lámpara; **by ~, in the ~** a la luz de la lámpara.
lamplighter ['læmp,laɪtəʳ] N farolero *m*.
lampoon [læm'puːn] 1 N pasquín *m*, sátira *f*.
2 VT pasquinar, satirizar.
lamppost ['læmppəʊst] N (*Brit*) (poste *m* de) farol *m*, farola *f*.
lamprey ['læmprɪ] N lamprea *f*.
lampshade ['læmpʃeɪd] N pantalla *f* (de lámpara).
lamp-standard ['læmp,stændəd] N poste *m* de farola.
LAN [læn] N ABBR *of* **local area network** red *f* de área local, RAL *f*.
Lancastrian [læŋ'kæstrɪən] 1 ADJ de Lancashire.
2 N nativo *m*, -a *f* (*or* habitante *mf*) de Lancashire.
lance [lɑːns] 1 N lanza *f*.
2 VT alancear, herir con lanza; (*Med*) abrir con lanceta.
lance-corporal ['lɑːns'kɔːpərəl] N (*Brit*) soldado *m* de primera, cabo *m* interino.
Lancelot ['lɑːnslət] NM Lanzarote.
lancer ['lɑːnsəʳ] N lancero *m*; **~s** (*dance*) lanceros *mpl*.
lancet ['lɑːnsɪt] N lanceta *f*; ~ **arch** ojiva *f* aguda; ~ **window** ventana *f* ojival.
Lancs. [læŋks] N ABBR *of* **Lancashire**.
land [lænd] N (*in most senses*) tierra *f*; (*nation*) país *m*; (*region*) tierra *f*, región *f*; (*soil*) tierra *f*, suelo *m*; (*as property*) tierras *fpl*, finca *f*; (*tract of* ~) terreno *m*; (*Agr, fig*) campo *m*, agricultura *f*, *eg* **the drift from the ~** la despoblación del campo, el éxodo rural; **he went on the ~** se dedicó a la agricultura; ~ **of milk and honey** paraíso *m* terrenal, jauja *f*; ~ **of promise, promised** ~ tierra *f* de promisión; **back to the ~!** ¡a cultivar la tierra! (*campaña de tiempos de guerra*); **by** ~ por tierra, por vía terrestre; **on** ~ en tierra; **to live off the** ~ (*army etc*) vivir sobre el país; **to see how the** ~ **lies** tantear el terreno, hacer un reconocimiento.
2 ATTR *breeze etc* de tierra; *defences, forces, route* terrestre; *law, question* agrario; ~ **agent** administrador *m*, -ora *f* (de una finca); ~ **forces** fuerzas *fpl* terrestres; ~ **office business** (*US**) negocio *m* próspero; ~ **reform** reforma *f* agraria; ~ **register,** ~ **registry** catastro *m*, registro *m* catastral, registro *m* de la propiedad inmobiliaria.
3 VT (a) *person, goods, fish at port etc* desembarcar.
(b) *fish* (*on hook*) pescar, coger, sacar del agua, traer a la orilla; (*fig: obtain*) conseguir, lograr; *prize* obtener, ganar, sacar; *job* conseguir.
(c) *plane* poner en tierra.
(d) *blow* dar, asestar (*on* en).
(e) (*Brit: place*) **it ~ed him in debt** le hizo contraer deudas; **it ~ed him in jail** por ello acabó en la cárcel; **it ~ed me in a mess** me puso en un apuro, me creó un lío; **I got ~ed with the job** tuve que cargar con el cometido; **I got ~ed with him for 2 hours** tuve que cargar con él durante 2 horas.
4 VI (a) (*from ship*) desembarcar (*at* en).
(b) (*Aer*) aterrizar, tomar tierra; (*on sea*) amerizar, amarar; (*on moon*) alunizar; (*bird, insect*) posar(se).
(c) (*hit, strike*) dar en, hacer blanco en; **the hat ~ed in my lap** el sombrero cayó sobre mis rodillas; **it ~ed square on the target** dio de lleno en el blanco; **the bomb ~ed on the building** la bomba hizo blanco en el edificio; **the blow ~ed on his cheek** el golpe le dio en la mejilla; **to ~ on one's feet** caer de pies; **to ~ on one's head** caer de cabeza; **where did it ~?** ¿dónde fue a caer?
(d) (*fig*) llegar; terminar; **to ~ up at Wigan** ir a parar a Wigan; **to ~ up in a dreadful mess** terminar haciéndose un tremendo lío.

⌐| LAND OF HOPE AND GLORY |

ⓘ **Land of Hope and Glory** *es el título de una canción patriótica británica. Para muchos ciudadanos, sobre todo en Inglaterra, es un símbolo más del país, casi como el himno o la bandera nacional. Se suele entonar al final del congreso anual del Partido Conservador y en la última noche de los Proms, junto con otras conocidas canciones patrióticas.*
⇨ *Ver también* PROM

landau ['lændɔː] N landó *m*.

landed ['lændɪd] ADJ (a) *person* hacendado, que posee tierras; *property* que consiste en tierras; ~ **gentry** terratenientes *mpl*, pequeña aristocracia *f* rural; ~ **property** bienes *mpl* raíces. (b) (*Comm*) ~ **cost** precio *m* más otros costes incluyendo derechos de importación.
landfall ['lændfɔːl] N (*Naut*) recalada *f*; aterrada *f*.
landfill ['lændfɪl] 1 N vertedero *m* de basuras.
2 ATTR: ~ **site** vertedero *m* de basuras.
landholder ['lænd,həʊldəʳ] N terrateniente *mf*.
landing ['lændɪŋ] N (a) (*Naut*) desembarco *m*, desembarque *m*.
(b) (*Aer*) aterrizaje *m*; (*on sea*) amaraje *m*, amerizaje *m*; (*on moon*) alunizaje *m*; (*descent*) descenso *m*.
(c) (*of stairs*) descanso *m*, rellano *m*.
landing-card ['lændɪŋ,kɑːd] N tarjeta *f* de desembarque.
landing-craft ['lændɪŋkrɑːft] N barcaza *f* (*or* lancha *f*) de desembarco.
landing-field ['lændɪŋfiːld] N campo *m* de aterrizaje.
landing-gear ['lændɪŋgəʳ] N tren *m* de aterrizaje.
landing-ground ['lændɪŋgraʊnd] N campo *m* de aterrizaje.
landing-lights ['lændɪŋlaɪts] NPL luces *fpl* de aterrizaje.
landing-net ['lændɪŋnet] N salabardo *m*, manga *f*, cuchara *f*.
landing-party ['lændɪŋpɑːtɪ] N destacamento *m* de desembarco.
landing-run ['lændɪŋrʌn] N recorrido *m* de aterrizaje.
landing-stage ['lændɪŋsteɪdʒ] N (*Brit*) desembarcadero *m*.
landing-strip ['lændɪŋstrɪp] N pista *f* de aterrizaje.
landing-wheels ['lændɪŋwiːlz] NPL ruedas *fpl* de aterrizaje.
landlady ['lænd,leɪdɪ] N (*owner*) dueña *f*; (*of boarding house*) patrona *f*; (*of flat*) propietaria *f*.
landless ['lændlɪs] 1 ADJ *peasant etc* sin tierras, que no posee tierras.
2 NPL: **the ~** los (campesinos *etc*) sin tierra, los desposeídos, los de abajo.
landlessness ['lændlɪsnɪs] N situación *f* de los desposeídos (de tierra).
landlocked ['lændlɒkt] ADJ cercado de tierra, mediterráneo, sin acceso al mar.
landlord ['lændlɔːd] N (*of property, land*) propietario *m*, dueño *m*; (*Brit: of boarding house*) patrón *m*; (*of flat*) casero *m*; (*of inn*) posadero *m*, mesonero *m*; (*Brit: of pub*) patrón *m*.
landlubber ['lænd,lʌbəʳ] N contramaestre *m* de muralla.
landmark ['lænd,mɑːk] N (a) (*Naut*) marca *f*, señal *f* fija; (*boundary mark*) mojón *m*; (*high place*) punto *m* destacado, punto *m* (*or* edificio *etc*) prominente; (*well-known thing*) lugar *m* muy conocido.
(b) **to be a ~** (*fig*) hacer época, formar época, marcar un hito histórico.
landmass ['lænd,mæs] N masa *f* continental.
landmine ['lændmaɪn] N mina *f* terrestre.
landowner ['lænd,əʊnəʳ] N terrateniente *mf*, hacendado *m*, -a *f*.
landowning ['lændəʊnɪŋ] ADJ terrateniente.
Land Rover ['lænd,rəʊvəʳ]® N (*Aut*) (vehículo *m*) todo terreno *m*.
landscape ['lænskeɪp] 1 N paisaje *m*.
2 ATTR: ~ **gardener** jardinero *m*, -a *f* paisajista, arquitecto *m*, -a *f* de jardines; ~ **gardening** arquitectura *f* de jardines, paisajismo *m*; ~ **orientation** (*Inform*) formato *m* horizontal; ~ **painter** paisajista *mf*.
3 VT *park etc* reformar artísticamente, *terrain* ajardinar, convertir en parque.
landscaping ['lænskeɪpɪŋ] N arquitectura *f* paisajista.
landslide ['lændslaɪd] 1 N corrimiento *m* de tierras, desprendimiento *m* de tierras; (*Pol*) victoria *f* electoral arrolladora; **the Liberal ~ of 1906** la victoria arrolladora de los liberales en 1906.
2 ATTR: ~ **majority** mayoría *f* abrumadora (*or* aplastante); **to win a ~ majority** barrer (*or* ganar) por mayoría abrumadora; ~ **victory** victoria *f* abrumadora (*or* aplastante).
landslip ['lændslɪp] V **landslide**.
land tax ['lændtæks] N contribución *f* territorial.
landward ['lændwəd] ADJ de hacia tierra, de la parte de la tierra; **on the ~ side** en el lado de la tierra.
landward(s) ['lændwəd(z)] ADV hacia tierra; **to ~** en la dirección de la tierra.
lane [leɪn] 1 N (*in country*) camino *m* vecinal, vereda *f*; (*in town*) callejón *m*; (*between plantations*) vereda *f*; (*Sport*) calle *f*, banda *f*; (*Aut*) carril *m*; (*Aer*) vía *f* aérea, pasillo *m* aéreo; (*Naut*) ruta *f* marítima.
2 ATTR: ~ **closure** cierre *m* de carril; ~ **markings** líneas *fpl* divisorias.
langlauf ['lɑːn,laʊf] N esquí *m* nórdico.
language ['læŋgwɪdʒ] 1 N (*faculty of speech, mode of speech*) lenguaje *m*; (*national tongue*) lengua *f*, idioma *m*; (*style*) lengua *f*, estilo *m*; redacción *f*; (*Comput*) lenguaje *m*; **bad ~** lenguaje *m* indecente; palabrotas *fpl*, tacos *mpl*; **to use bad ~** (*habitually*) ser mal hablado; **modern ~s** lenguas *fpl* modernas; **strong ~** palabras *fpl* mayores; **that's no ~ to use to your mother!** ¡así no se habla a tu madre!; **we don't talk the same ~** (*fig*) no hablamos la misma lengua.
2 ATTR: ~ **barrier** barrera *f* lingüística; ~ **laboratory** laboratorio *m* de idiomas.
languid ['læŋgwɪd] ADJ lánguido.
languidly ['læŋgwɪdlɪ] ADV lánguidamente.
languidness ['læŋgwɪdnɪs] N languidez *f*.

languish ['læŋgwɪʃ] VI languidecer; (*in prison*) pudrirse; (*pine*) consumirse (*for* por); (*amorously*) ponerse sentimental.

languishing ['læŋgwɪʃɪŋ] ADJ lánguido; *look, tone etc* amoroso, sentimental.

languor ['læŋgəʳ] N languidez *f*.

languorous ['læŋgərəs] ADJ lánguido.

lank [læŋk] ADJ *person* alto y flaco; *hair* lacio; *grass* largo.

lanky ['læŋkɪ] ADJ larguirucho, desmadejado.

lanolin(e) ['lænəʊlɪn] N lanolina *f*.

lantern ['læntən] N linterna *f* (*also Archit*); (*Naut*) faro *m*, farol *m*; (*of lighthouse*) fanal *m*.

lantern-jawed ['læntən'dʒɔːd] ADJ chupado de cara.

lantern lecture ['læntən,lektʃəʳ] N conferencia *f* con proyecciones.

lantern slide ['læntənslaɪd] N diapositiva *f*.

lanyard ['lænjəd] N acollador *m*.

Laos [laʊs] N Laos *m*.

Laotian ['laʊʃɪən] 1 ADJ laosiano.
　2 N laosiano *m*, -a *f*.

lap¹ [læp] 1 N (*Anat*) regazo *m*; (*knees*) rodillas *fpl*; (*skirt*) falda *f*; (*fig*) seno *m*; (*overlap*) traslapo *m*, solapa *f*; **to sit on sb's ~** (*woman's*) estar sentado en el regazo (*or* en el halda) de una, (*man's*) estar sentado en las rodillas de uno; **it's in the ~ of the gods** está en manos de los dioses; **to live in the ~ of luxury** nadar en la abundancia.
　2 VT (*overlap*) traslapar; (*wrap*) envolver (*in* en; *also fig*); **to ~ sth about with** cercar algo de, (*fig*) envolver algo en.
　3 VI (*overlap*) traslaparse.

lap² [læp] (*Sport*) 1 N (*round*) vuelta *f*; (*stage*) etapa *f*, fase *f*; **~ of honour** vuelta *f* de honor; **we're on the last ~ now** (*fig*) ésta es la última etapa, hemos vencido la cuesta ya.
　2 VT: **to ~ sb** doblar a uno, aventajar a uno en una vuelta entera.
　3 VI: **to ~ at 190 k.p.h.** hacer una vuelta a 190 k.p.h.

lap³ [læp] 1 N (*lick*) lamedura *f*, lametada *f*, lengüetada *f*; (*of waves*) chapaleteo *m*.
　2 VT (a) (*lick*) lamer.
　(b) (*of water*) estar al nivel de, correr tan alto como.
　3 VI (*waves*) chapalear; **to ~ against** besar, tocar, lamer.
◆ **lap over** VT desbordarse, irse, salir fuera.
◆ **lap up** VT beber con la lengua, tomar a lengüetadas; (*fig*) aceptar con entusiasmo, absorber, aprender con facilidad.

laparoscopy [,læpə'rɒskəpɪ] N laparoscopia *f*.

laparotomy [,læpə'rɒtəmɪ] N laparotomía *f*.

La Paz [lae'pæz] N La Paz.

LAPD (*US*) ABBR **of Los Angeles Police Department**.

lapdog ['læpdɒg] N perro *m* faldero.

lapel [lə'pel] N solapa *f*.

lapidary ['læpɪdərɪ] 1 ADJ lapidario.
　2 N lapidario *m*, -a *f*.

lapis lazuli ['læpɪs'læzjʊlaɪ] N lapislázuli *m*.

Lapland ['læplænd] N Laponia *f*.

Laplander ['læplændəʳ] N lapón *m*, -ona *f*.

Lapp [læp] N (a) lapón *m*, -a *f*. (b) (*Ling*) lapón *m*.

lapping ['læpɪŋ] N (*of water*) chapaleteo *m*.

Lappish ['læpɪʃ] N (*Ling*) lapón *m*.

lapse [læps] 1 N (a) (*error*) error *m*, equivocación *f*; (*moral*) desliz *m*, falta *f*; lapso *m*; (*relapse*) recaída *f* (*into* en).
　(b) (*of time*) intervalo *m*, período *m*, lapso *m*; **after a ~ of 4 months** después de un período de 4 meses, al cabo de 4 meses.
　2 VI (a) (*err*) caer en el error, equivocarse; (*morally*) cometer un desliz; (*relapse*) recaer, reincidir (*into* en); **to ~ from duty** faltar a su deber; **to ~ into one's old ways** volver a las andadas, volver a las malas costumbres; **he ~d into the vernacular** recurrió a la lengua vernácula; **he ~d into silence** se calló, quedó callado, no dijo más.
　(b) (*expire*) caducar; (*cease to exist*) dejar de existir, desaparecer.
　(c) (*time*) pasar, transcurrir.

lapsed [læpst] ADJ (*Rel*) que no practica.

laptop ['læptɒp] N (*also ~ computer*) ordenador *m* portátil plegable.

lapwing ['læpwɪŋ] N avefría *f*.

larboard ['laːbəd] 1 ADJ de babor.
　2 N babor *m*.

larceny ['laːsənɪ] N hurto *m*, ratería *f*, latrocinio *m*; **grand ~** (*US*) robo *m* de cantidad importante; **petty ~** robo *m* de menor cuantía *f*.

larch [laːtʃ] N (*also ~ tree*) alerce *m*.

lard [laːd] 1 N manteca *f* de cerdo.
　2 VT lardear, mechar; (*fig*) **to ~ sth with** adornar algo de, salpicar algo de, sembrar algo de.

larder ['laːdəʳ] N despensa *f*.

lardy ['laːdɪ] ADJ mantecoso.

large [laːdʒ] 1 ADJ grande; *packet etc* abultado, voluminoso; *interests* extenso; *powers* amplio, extenso; *sum* importante; *family* numeroso; (*main, chief*) principal; **as ~ as life** así como es; en persona; **there he was as ~ as life** ahí estaba en persona; **there it was as ~ as life** allí

se nos apareció de modo inconfundible; **it looked ~r than life** parecía más grande de lo que era en realidad.
　2 N: **ambassador at ~** embajador *m* itinerante (que no está acreditado permanentemente en ningún país); **people at ~** la gente en general; **the world at ~** el mundo en general; **the prisoner is still at ~** el preso está todavía en libertad; **the virus is still at ~** el virus constituye todavía un peligro, el virus todavía no ha sido controlado.
　3 ADV V **by**.

largely ['laːdʒlɪ] ADV en su mayor parte, en gran parte.

largeness ['laːdʒnɪs] N gran tamaño *m*; lo abultado (*etc*); extensión *f*; importancia *f*; lo numeroso.

larger ['laːdʒəʳ] ADJ comp of **large**; más grande, mayor; **to grow ~** crecer; aumentar(se); **to make ~** hacer más grande; aumentar; *premises etc* ampliar, ensanchar.

large-scale ['laːdʒ'skeɪl] ADJ en gran escala, de gran envergadura; **very ~ integration** integración *f* a muy gran escala.

large-size(d) ['laːdʒ'saɪz(d)] ADJ de gran tamaño, de tamaño extra.

largesse [laː'ʒes] N generosidad *f*, liberalidad *f*; (*gift*) dádiva *f* espléndida.

largish ['laːdʒɪʃ] ADJ bastante grande, más bien grande.

largo ['laːgəʊ] N (*Mus*) largo *m*.

lariat ['lærɪət] N lazo *m*.

lark¹ [laːk] N (*Orn*) alondra *f*; **to get up with the ~** levantarse con las gallinas, madrugar; V **happy**.

lark² [laːk] 1 N (a) (*joke etc*) broma *f*, travesura *f*; **that's a ~!, what a ~!** ¡qué bien!, ¡qué risa!; **that was a ~!** ¡cómo nos reímos con aquello!; **isn't he a ~?** ¿es célebre, no?; **to do sth for a ~** hacer algo para divertirse, divertirse haciendo algo; **to hell with this for a ~!** ¡vaya lío*!, ¡qué follón!*; **to have a ~ with sb** gastar una broma a uno, tomar el pelo a uno*.
　(b) (*business, affair*) **that ice-cream ~** ese asunto de los helados; **the Suez ~** la fiestecita de Suez; **this dinner-jacket ~** esta faena de ponerse smoking*.
　2 VI (*be on a spree*) andar de jarana; (*amuse o.s.*) divertirse.
◆ **lark about, lark around** VI hacer travesuras, gastarse bromas, divertirse tontamente; **stop ~ing about!** ¡basta de bromas!; **to ~ about with sth** (*play*) divertirse con algo, jugar con algo, (*damage*) estropear algo, manosear algo.

larkspur ['laːkspɜːʳ] N espuela *f* de caballero.

larky* ['laːkɪ] ADJ guasón, bromista.

Larry ['lærɪ] NM familiar form of **Laurence, Lawrence**.

larva ['laːvə] N, PL **larvae** ['laːviː] larva *f*.

laryngitis [,lærɪn'dʒaɪtɪs] N laringitis *f*.

larynx ['lærɪŋks] N laringe *f*.

lasagna, lasagne [lə'zænjə] N lasaña *f*.

lascivious [lə'sɪvɪəs] ADJ lascivo, lujurioso.

lasciviously [lə'sɪvɪəslɪ] ADV lascivamente.

lasciviousness [lə'sɪvɪəsnɪs] N lascivia *f*, lujuria *f*.

laser ['leɪzəʳ] 1 N láser *m*.
　2 ATTR: **~ beam** rayo *m* láser; **~ printer** impresora *f* (por) láser; **~ rangefinder** telémetro *m* lasérico; **~ surgery** cirugía *f* (con) láser.

lash [læʃ] 1 N (a) (*whip*) látigo *m*, (*used for punishment*) azote *m*; (*thong*) tralla *f*.
　(b) (*stroke*) latigazo *m*, (*as punishment*) azote *m*; (*of tail*) coletazo *m*; **the ~ of the rain** el azote de la lluvia; **under the ~ of the Nazis** bajo el azote de los nazis.
　(c) (*Anat*) pestaña *f*.
　2 VT (a) (*beat etc*) azotar, dar latigazos a, fustigar; (*of hail, rain, waves*) azotar; (*fig: criticize*) fustigar, dar una paliza a, increpar; **the lion was ~ing its tail** el león daba coletazos; **he was ~ing the horse along** le daba duramente al caballo con el látigo; **the wind ~ed the trees** el viento azotaba los árboles; **the wind ~ed the sea into a fury** el viento levantaba enormes olas; **to ~ sb with one's tongue** increpar duramente a uno; **to ~ sb into a fury** provocar a uno hasta la furia.
　(b) (*tie*) atar, (*Naut*) trincar, amarrar (*to* a).
　3 VR: **to ~ o.s. into a fury** montar en cólera.
◆ **lash about** VI gesticular violentamente.
◆ **lash down** VT sujetar, atar firmemente.
◆ **lash out** 1 VT (*) **he had to ~ out £50** tuvo que desembolsar 50 libras; **he was ~ing out the money** gastaba pródigamente; **they were ~ing out the drink** estaban sirviendo las bebidas en grandes cantidades.
　2 VI (a) (*) desdinerarse, pagar; repartir dinero generosamente; **now we can really ~ out** ahora sí podemos gastar; **he ~ed out and bought himself a Rolls** dejó de economizar y se compró un Rolls.
　(b) (*with fists*) repartir golpes a diestro y siniestro, dar golpes furiosos sin mirar a quien; (*with feet*) tirar coces; **to ~ out at** (*or* **against**) arremeter contra.

lashing ['læʃɪŋ] N (a) (*beating*) azotamiento *m*, azotes *mpl*; **to give sb a ~** azotar a uno, (*fig*) dar una paliza a uno. (b) (*tie*) atadura *f*, (*Naut*) trinca *f*, amarradura *f*. (c) **~s*** (*esp Brit*) montones* *mpl*.

lash-up* ['læʃʌp] N reparación *f* improvisada; arreglo *m* provisional, improvisación *f*.

lass [læs] N (*esp Scot*) muchacha *f*, chica *f*, joven *f*, piba *f* (*And, SC*), chava *f* (*Mex*); (*country ~*) moza *f*, zagala *f*.

lassie* ['læsɪ] N (*esp Scot*) = **lass**.

lassitude ['læsɪtjuːd] N lasitud *f*.

lasso [læ'suː] ① N lazo *m*.
② VT lazar, coger con el lazo.

last¹ [lɑːst] ① ADJ último; final; extremo; *week, month etc* pasado; **the L~ Supper** la Última Cena; **~ Monday, on Monday ~** el lunes pasado; **~ night** anoche; **the night before ~** anteanoche; **the year before ~** el año antepasado; **the ~ trick but one** la penúltima baza; **the ~ day but two of the trial** el antepenúltimo día del proceso; **the ~ trick but 3** la tercera baza antes de la última; **during the ~ 20 years** en los últimos 20 años; **he has not been seen these ~ 3 years** hace 3 años que no se le ve; **to be the ~ (one) to do sth** ser el último en hacer algo; **to be ~ but not least** ser el último pero no el menos importante; **and ~ but not least came John** y como fin de fiesta se presentó Juan; **you must pick up every ~ one** hay que recoger absolutamente todos; **that's the ~ thing to worry about** eso es lo de menos; **that was the ~ thing I expected** eso era lo que menos yo esperaba; **I'll drink it if it's the ~ thing I do** lo beberé y ¡arda Troya! (*V also* **thing (c)**); **they left me till ~** me atendieron (*etc*) el último, me dejaron hasta el fin; **you're the ~ person to be entrusted with it** tú eres el menos indicado para hacerse cargo de ello. ② N último *m*, -a *f*, última cosa *f*, lo último; (*end*) fin *m*; **each one better than the ~** cada uno mejor que el anterior (*or* precedente); **my ~** mi última carta; **at ~** por fin; **at long ~** por fin, después de tanto tiempo (*or* esperar *etc*); **to the ~** hasta el fin; **this is the ~ of it** éste es el último de la serie (*etc*), con éste terminamos, después de éste no quedan más; **that was the ~ we saw of him** no le volvimos a ver; **I shall be glad to see the ~ of this** estoy deseando que termine esto; **to breathe one's ~** exhalar el último suspiro; **we shall never hear the ~ of it** no nos dejarán olvidarlo nunca; **you haven't heard the ~ of this** este asunto no se puede dar por concluido; **the ~ we heard of him he was in Río** según las últimas noticias estaba en Río; **to look one's ~ on sth** ver algo por última vez, despedirse de algo (antes de su desaparición). ③ ADV por último; en último lugar; por última vez; finalmente; **to arrive ~** llegar el último; **the horse came in ~** el caballo llegó el último, el caballo ocupó el último puesto en la clasificación; **when I ~ saw him** cuando le vi por última vez.

last² [lɑːst] ① VT durar; **it ~ed me a lifetime** me duró toda la vida; **the car has ~ed me 8 years** el coche me ha durado 8 años. ② VI durar; perdurar; permanecer, resistir; sostenerse, mantenerse; (*continue*) continuar, seguir; (*cloth etc*) ser duro, ser resistente; **it ~s 2 hours** dura 2 horas; **it can't ~** no puede seguir así; **things are too good to ~** las cosas van demasiado bien para que duren; **will this material ~?** ¿es resistente este paño?; **he won't ~ long in this job** no durará mucho tiempo en este puesto; **the previous boss ~ed only a week** el jefe anterior permaneció solamente una semana en el puesto.

◆**last out** ① VT: **I can ~ you out any time** de todos modos yo resisto mejor que tú; **he ~ed all his colleagues out** sobrevivió a todos sus colegas; **my money doesn't ~ out the month** el dinero no me llega para un mes entero; **can you ~ out another mile?** ¿aguantas una milla más? ② VI resistir, continuar; (*money, resources*) durar, llegar, alcanzar; **I can't ~ out** no puedo más, no resisto más.

last³ [lɑːst] N horma *f*; **stick to your ~!** ¡zapatero, a tus zapatos!

last-ditch ['lɑːst'dɪtʃ] ADJ *defence, stand* de lo más terco, de último recurso, que continúa hasta quemar el último cartucho; **a ~ effort** un último esfuerzo.

last-gasp ['lɑːst'gɑːsp] ADJ de última hora.

lasting ['lɑːstɪŋ] ADJ duradero, perdurable, permanente, constante; *shame etc* eterno; *colour* sólido.

▼**lastly** ['lɑːstlɪ] ADV por último, finalmente.

last-minute ['lɑːst'mɪnɪt] ADJ *decision etc* de última hora.

lat. ABBR *of* **latitude** latitud *f*.

latch [lætʃ] ① N picaporte *m*, pestillo *m*; **to be on the ~** estar cerrado con picaporte; **to drop the ~** echar el pestillo. ② VT cerrar con picaporte; (*fig*) sujetar, asegurar.

◆**latch on*** VI (*understand*) comprender.

◆**latch on to** VT adherirse a; **to ~ on to sth** fijarse en algo; **to ~ on to sb** pegarse a uno.

latchkey ['lætʃkiː] ① N llavín *m*. ② ATTR: **~ child** niño *m*, -a *f* cuya madre trabaja.

late [leɪt] ① ADJ (a) (*person*) **to be ~ for sth** llegar tarde para algo; **I was too ~ for it** llegué tarde para ello; **I was ~ in getting up** tardé en levantarme; **I don't want to make you ~** no quiero entretenerle. (b) (*impersonal*) **it's ~** es tarde; **it's ~ in the day to change your mind** es tarde para mudar de opinión; **it's getting ~** se está

haciendo tarde. (c) (*far on in day, season etc*) tardío; *hour* avanzado; *delivery* atrasado; *entry* tardío; **~ frost** helada *f* tardía; **~ potato** patata *f* tardía; **at a ~ hour** a una hora avanzada, a última hora; **we had a ~ night last night** anoche no volvimos a casa hasta muy tarde; anoche continuó la fiesta (*etc*) hasta muy tarde; **in the ~ eighties** en los últimos años ochenta; **in the ~ spring** hacia fines de la primavera; **in the ~ morning** en la última parte de la mañana; **a ~ 18th century building** un edificio de fines del siglo XVIII; **L~ Stone Age** período *m* neolítico; **L~ Latin** latín *m* tardío; **Easter is ~ this year** la Semana Santa cae tarde este año. (d) (*deceased*) fallecido, difunto, finado; **the ~ king** el finado rey. (e) (*former*) antiguo, ex; **~ prime minister** antiguo primer ministro *m*, ex primer ministro *m*. ② ADV (a) (*not on time*) tarde; **to come ~** llegar tarde; **to arrive too ~** llegar tarde (*for para*); **the train arrived 8 minutes ~** el tren llegó con 8 minutos de retraso; **better ~ than never** más vale tarde que nunca; **to sit up ~, to stay up ~** velar, no acostarse hasta las altas horas, trasnochar; **you've left it a bit ~** lo has dejado un poco tarde; **~ in the day** a última hora del día; **it's a bit ~ in the day to change your mind** es algo tarde para cambiar de idea; **~ at night, ~ in the night** ya muy entrada la noche; **~ into the night** hasta muy entrada la noche; **~ in the afternoon** a última hora de la tarde; **~ in the year** hacia fines del año; **~ in life** a una edad avanzada; **~ last century** hacia fines del siglo pasado; **of ~** últimamente, recientemente; **as ~ as 1900** todavía en 1900. (b) **~ of No. 13** que vivió hasta hace poco en el núm. 13; **~ of the Diplomatic Service** hasta hace poco miembro del Cuerpo Diplomático, ex miembro del Cuerpo Diplomático.

latecomer ['leɪtkʌmər] N recién llegado *m*, -a *f*; el (*etc*) que llega tarde; **the firm is a ~ to the industry** la compañía es nueva en la industria, la compañía acaba de establecerse en la industria.

lateen [lə'tiːn] N vela *f* latina.

late-lamented ['leɪtlə'mentɪd] ADJ malogrado, fallecido.

lately ['leɪtlɪ] ADV últimamente, recientemente; hace poco; **till ~** hasta hace poco.

latency ['leɪtənsɪ] N estado *m* latente.

lateness ['leɪtnɪs] N lo tarde; lo tardío; lo reciente; (*of hour*) lo avanzado; (*delay*) retraso *m*; **he was fined for persistent ~** le impusieron una multa por venir constantemente tarde.

late-night ['leɪt'naɪt] ADJ: **~ show, ~ performance** sesión *f* de noche; **~ opening** (*or* **shopping**) **is on Thursdays** se abre tarde los jueves; **is there a ~ bus?** ¿hay autobús a última hora de la noche?

latent ['leɪtənt] ADJ latente; **~ defect** defecto *m* latente.

later ['leɪtər] ① ADJ *comp of* **late**; más tardío; (*in newness*) más reciente; (*in series*) posterior, ulterior; *hour* más avanzada; **his ~ symphonies** sus sinfonías más recientes, sus sinfonías posteriores; **this version is ~ than that one** esta versión es posterior a ésa; **at a ~ meeting** en una reunión celebrada después; **in his ~ years** en sus últimos años. ② ADV *comp of* **late**; más tarde; (*afterwards*) luego, después; posteriormente; **a moment ~** un momento después; **a few years ~** a los pocos años; varios años después; **yes dear, ~** (*on being interrupted*) sí querida, luego; **see you ~!** ¡hasta pronto!; **no ~ than yesterday** no más lejos que ayer, ayer sin ir más lejos; **not ~ than 1980** antes de 1980; **~ on** más tarde, después.

lateral ['lætərəl] ADJ lateral; **~ thinking** pensamiento *m* lateral.

laterally ['lætərəlɪ] ADV lateralmente.

latest ['leɪtɪst] ① ADJ *superl of* **late**; último; más reciente; *fashion, news etc* último; **his ~ painting** su última cuadro, su cuadro más reciente; **to be the ~ to do sth** ser el último en hacer algo; **what is the ~ date you can come?** ¿hasta qué fecha estás libre para venir? ② ADV *superl of* **late**; **he came ~** él vino el último. ③ N (a) **what's the ~ on ...?** ¿qué noticias hay sobre ...?; **it's the ~ in computers** es lo último en ordenadores; **have you seen John's ~?*** (*girl*) ¿has visto a la amiguita actual de Juan?; **have you heard John's ~?** (*joke*) ¿has oído el último chiste de Juan?; **did you hear about John's ~?** (*exploit*) ¿te han contado la última de Juan?, ¿has oído lo de Juan? (b) **at the ~** a lo más tarde, a más tardar, como límite.

latex ['leɪteks] N látex *m*.

lath [læθ] N, PL **laths** [lɑːðz] listón *m*.

lathe [leɪð] N torno *m*.

lather ['lɑːðər] ① N espuma *f* (de jabón), jabonaduras *fpl*; (*of sweat*) espuma *f*; **the horse was in a ~** el caballo estaba cubierto de espuma; **he arrived in a ~** llegó todo sudado. ② VT enjabonar; (*) zurrar. ③ VI hacer espuma.

latifundia [ˌlætɪ'fʊndɪə] NPL latifundios *mpl*.

Latin ['lætɪn] ① ADJ latino; **~ lover** galán *m* latino; **~ quarter** barrio *m* latino. ② N (a) (*person*) latino *m*, -a *f*; **the ~s** los latinos. (b) (*Ling*) latín *m*.

Latin America [ˈlætɪnəˈmerɪkə] N América *f* Latina, Latinoamérica *f*, Hispanoamérica *f*.
Latin-American [ˈlætɪnəˈmerɪkən] ① ADJ latinoamericano. ② N latinoamericano *m*, -a *f*.
latinism [ˈlætɪnɪzəm] N latinismo *m*.
latinist [ˈlætɪnɪst] N latinista *mf*.
latinity [ləˈtɪnɪtɪ] N latinidad *f*.
latinization [ˌlætɪnarˈzeɪʃən] N latinización *f*.
latinize [ˈlætɪnaɪz] VTI latinizar.
latish [ˈleɪtɪʃ] ① ADV algo tarde. ② ADJ algo tardío.
latitude [ˈlætɪtjuːd] N latitud *f*; (*fig*) libertad *f*.
latitudinal [ˌlætɪˈtjuːdɪnl] ADJ latitudinal.
Latium [ˈleɪʃɪəm] N Lacio *m*.
latrine [ləˈtriːn] N letrina *f*.
▼ **latter** [ˈlætər] ADJ (a) (*later*) más reciente; posterior; último; (*of two*) segundo; **the ~ part of the story** la segunda mitad del cuento; **in the ~ part of the century** hacia fines del siglo; **the ~ opinion** esta (última) opinión; **his ~ end** el final de su vida, su muerte.
▼ (b) **the former ... the ~** aquél ... éste.
latter-day [ˈlætəˈdeɪ] ADJ moderno, reciente; **L~ Saints** los Mormones.
latterly [ˈlætəlɪ] ADJ últimamente, recientemente.
lattice [ˈlætɪs] ① N enrejado *m*; (*on window*) reja *f*, celosía *f*. ② ATTR: **~ window** ventana *f* de celosía; **~ work** enrejado *m*, celosía *f*.
latticed [ˈlætɪst] ADJ *window* con reja.
Latvia [ˈlætvɪə] N Letonia *f*, Latvia *f*.
Latvian [ˈlætvɪən] ① ADJ letón, latvio. ② N letón *m*, -ona *f*, latvio *m*, -a *f*.
laud [lɔːd] VT (*liter*) alabar, elogiar.
laudable [ˈlɔːdəbl] ADJ loable; plausible.
laudably [ˈlɔːdəblɪ] ADV de modo loable, loablemente.
laudanum [ˈlɔːdnəm] N láudano *m*.
laudatory [ˈlɔːdətərɪ] ADJ laudatorio.
laugh [lɑːf] ① N risa *f*; (*loud*) carcajada *f*, risotada *f*; **what a ~!** ¡qué risa!, ¡qué bien!; **just for a ~** sólo para hacer reír; **it's a (bit of a) ~** es cosa de risa; **he's a (bit of a) ~** es un tío tonto; **he got a ~** hizo reír a la gente; **to have a good ~ over sth** reírse mucho con algo; **to have the ~ over sb** llevar ventaja a uno, quedar por encima de uno; **to have the last ~** reírse el último; **to play sth for ~s** representar algo con el propósito de hacer reír al público; **the joke didn't raise a ~** el chiste no hizo reír a nadie. ② VI reír, reírse; (*loud*) reírse a carcajadas, carcajearse; **to ~ about sth, to ~ over sth** reírse con algo; **it's nothing to ~ about** no es cosa de risa (*or* reírse (*LAm*)); **to ~ at sb** reírse de uno, burlarse de uno; **we must be able to ~ at ourselves** hay que ver los aspectos ridículos de nosotros mismos; **to ~ out loud** soltar la carcajada, reírse abiertamente; **he who ~s last ~s longest** el último que ríe ríe más fuerte, al freír será el reír; **to ~ like a hyena** reírse como un loco; **don't make me ~!** (*iro*) ¡me haces reír!; **they'll be ~ing all the way to the bank** irán contentísimos al banco; **it's all right for him, he's ~ing** para él no hay problema.
◆ **laugh down** VT ridiculizar.
◆ **laugh off** VT: **to ~ sth off** tomar algo a risa; **he ~s everything off** no toma nada en serio; *V* **scorn**.
laughable [ˈlɑːfəbl] ADJ ridículo, absurdo; cómico, divertido; **it's ~ that ...** es absurdo que + *subj*.
laughing [ˈlɑːfɪŋ] ① ADJ risueño, alegre; **it's no ~ matter** no es cosa de risa. ② N risa *f*.
laughing-gas [ˈlɑːfɪŋˈɡæs] N gas *m* hilarante.
laughingly [ˈlɑːfɪŋlɪ] ADV: **he said ~** dijo riendo; **what is ~ called progress** lo que se llama irónicamente el progreso.
laughing-stock [ˈlɑːfɪŋstɒk] N hazmerreír *m*.
laughter [ˈlɑːftər] ① N risa *f*, risas *fpl*; **amid the ~ of those present** entre las risas de los asistentes; **at this there was ~** en esto hubo risas; **to burst into ~** soltar la carcajada. ② ATTR: **~ line** (*Brit*) arruga *f* producida al reír.
Launcelot [ˈlɑːnslət] NM Lanzarote.
launch [lɔːntʃ] ① N (a) (*act: Naut*) botadura *f*; (*Aer etc*) lanzamiento *m*; (*Comm etc*) lanzamiento *m*, presentación *f*. (b) (*vessel*) lancha *f*, falúa *f*. ② ATTR: **~ pad** rampa *f* de lanzamiento; **~ vehicle** (*Space*) lanzadera *f*. ③ VT (*throw*) lanzar; *rocket etc* lanzar; *new vessel* botar; *lifeboat* echar al agua, largar; *offensive* emprender, comenzar; *company* crear, fundar, lanzar; *new product* lanzar, presentar, introducir en el mercado; *film, play* estrenar; *idea* lanzar; *plan* poner en operación; *share issue etc* emitir; **to ~ sb on his way** ayudar a uno a emprender su carrera, poner a uno en camino; **once he is ~ed on this subject we shall never stop him** en cuanto se ponga a hablar de este tema no le haremos nunca callar.

◆ **launch forth** VI lanzarse, ponerse en marcha.
◆ **launch into** *V* ~ **out into**.
◆ **launch out** VI lanzarse, ponerse en marcha; **now we can afford to ~ out a bit** ahora nos podemos permitir algunas cosas de lujo, ahora podemos extender nuestras actividades (*etc*); **to ~ out into** lanzarse a; **to ~ out into business** engolfarse en los negocios; **to ~ out into a career** emprender una carrera; **he ~ed out into a violent speech** pasó a pronunciar un discurso violento.
launcher [ˈlɔːntʃər] N (*for rocket*) lanzacohetes *m*.
launching [ˈlɔːntʃɪŋ] ① N botadura *f*; lanzamiento *m*; inauguración *f*, iniciación *f*; estreno *m*; emisión *f*. ② ATTR: **~ ceremony** ceremonia *f* de botadura.
launching-pad [ˈlɔːntʃɪŋpæd] N rampa *f* de lanzamiento.
launching-site [ˈlɔːntʃɪŋsaɪt] N rampa *f* de lanzamiento.
launder [ˈlɔːndər] ① VT (a) lavar (y planchar). (b) (*) *money* lavar*, blanquear*. ② VI resistir el lavado (bien, mal *etc*).
launderette [ˌlɔːndəˈret] N (*Brit*) lavandería *f* automática.
laundering [ˈlɔːndərɪŋ] N (a) colada *f*. (b) (*: of money*) lavado* *m*, blanqueo* *m*.
laundress [ˈlɔːndrɪs] N lavandera *f*.
Laundromat [ˈlɔːndrəˌmæt] ® N (*US*) lavandería *f* automática.
laundry [ˈlɔːndrɪ] ① N (a) (*establishment*) lavadero *m*, lavandería *f*. (b) (*clothes: dirty*) ropa *f* sucia, ropa *f* por lavar, (*washed*) ropa *f* lavada, colada *f*. ② ATTR: **~ basket** cesto *m* de la ropa sucia; **~ list** lista *f* de ropa para lavar; **~ mark** marca *f* de lavandería.
laureate [ˈlɔːrɪɪt] N laureado *m*; **Poet L~** (*Brit*) Poeta *m* Laureado.
laurel [ˈlɒrəl] N laurel *m* (*cerezo*); **to look to one's ~s** no dormirse sobre sus laureles; **to rest on one's ~s** dormirse sobre sus laureles; **to win one's ~s** cargarse de laureles, laurearse.
laurel wreath [ˈlɒrəlˌriːθ] N corona *f* de laurel, laureles *mpl*.
Laurence [ˈlɒrəns] NM Lorenzo.
Lausanne [ləʊˈzæn] N Lausana *f*.
lav* [læv] N = **lavatory**; *ver también* TOILET .
lava [ˈlɑːvə] ① N lava *f*. ② ATTR: **~ flow** torrente *m* de lava.
lavatorial [ˌlævəˈtɔːrɪəl] ADJ *humour* cloacal, escatológico.
lavatory [ˈlævətrɪ] ① N (*Brit*) wáter *m*, excusado *m*, inodoro *m*; (*room*) lavabo *m*, aseos *mpl*; **public ~** urinarios *mpl*; *ver también* TOILET . ② ATTR: **~ bowl, ~ pan** taza *f* de lavabo; **~ paper** papel *m* higiénico; **~ seat** asiento *m* de retrete.
lavender [ˈlævɪndər] ① N espliego *m*, lavanda *f*, lavándula *f*. ② ATTR: **~ blue** ADJ azul lavanda.
lavender water [ˈlævɪndəˌwɔːtər] N lavanda *f*.
lavish [ˈlævɪʃ] ① ADJ (a) (*abundant*) profuso, abundante; (*luxurious*) lujoso. (b) (*of person, prodigal*) pródigo; *expenditure* pródigo, liberal; **to be ~ of** ser pródigo de, prodigar, no escatimar; **to be ~ with one's money** gastar libremente su dinero, derrochar su dinero. ② VT: **to ~ care on sth** poner la máxima atención en algo; **to ~ attentions on sb** colmar a uno de atenciones.
lavishly [ˈlævɪʃlɪ] ADV profusamente, en profusión, abundantemente; lujosamente; pródigamente; **the house is ~ furnished** la casa está lujosamente amueblada; **he spends money ~** derrocha su dinero.
lavishness [ˈlævɪʃnɪs] N (a) (*abundance*) profusión *f*, abundancia *f*; lujo *m*. (b) (*of person*) prodigalidad *f*.
law [lɔː] ① N (a ~, the ~) ley *f*; (*study, body of ~s*) derecho *m*, jurisprudencia *f*; (*Sport, games*) regla *f*; **the L~** (*Jewish*) la ley de Moisés, (*) la policía; **~ and order** orden *m* público; **~ and order in tourist areas** la seguridad ciudadana en las zonas turísticas; **the forces of ~ and order** las fuerzas del orden; **by the ~ of averages** por la estadística, estadísticamente; **~ of gravity** ley *f* de la gravedad; **~ of nature** ley *f* natural; **~ of supply and demand** ley *f* de la oferta y demanda; **according to ~, in ~** según derecho; **by ~** según la ley, de acuerdo con la ley; **in-~** político, *eg* **brother-in-~** hermano *m* político, cuñado *m*; **it's the ~** es la ley; **his word is ~** su palabra es ley; **is there a ~ against it?** ¿hay una ley que lo prohíba?; **he is above the ~** está por encima de la ley; **he is outside the ~** está fuera de la ley; **to be a ~ unto o.s.** obrar por cuenta propia, no hacer caso alguno de los demás; **to go to ~** pleitear, poner pleito (*about* sobre), recurrir a la ley; **to have the ~ on sb** denunciar a uno a la policía, llevar a uno ante el tribunal; **to keep within the ~** obrar legalmente; **to lay down the ~** hablar autoritariamente; **to practise ~** ejercer de abogado, ejercer la abogacía; **to take the ~ into one's own hands** tomarse la justicia por su mano; **to take a case to ~** recurrir a la vía judicial. ② ATTR: **~ enforcement officer** policía *m*; **~ faculty** facultad *f* de Derecho; **L~ Lords** (*Brit Parl*) jueces *mpl* que son miembros de la Cámara de los Lores; **~ partner** compañero *m*, -a *f* de bufete; **~ reports** actas *fpl* de procesos; **~ school** (*US*) facultad *f* de Derecho; **~ student** estudiante *mf* de Derecho.

► LANGUAGE IN USE: **latter: b** → 26.2

law-abiding ['lɔːə,baɪdɪŋ] ADJ observante de la ley, que vive conforme a la ley; decente.

lawbreaker ['lɔː,breɪkəʳ] N transgresor *m*, -ora *f*, infractor *m*, -ora *f* de la ley.

law-breaking ['lɔː,breɪkɪŋ] [1] ADJ infractor de la ley, transgresor de la ley.
[2] N infracción *f* de la ley, transgresión *f* de la ley.

lawcourt ['lɔːkɔːt] N tribunal *m* (de justicia).

lawful ['lɔːfʊl] ADJ legítimo, lícito, legal; **~ money** moneda *f* legal.

lawfully ['lɔːfəlɪ] ADV legítimamente, lícitamente.

lawgiver ['lɔː,gɪvəʳ] N (*Brit*) legislador *m*, -ora *f*.

lawless ['lɔːlɪs] ADJ *act* ilegal; *person* rebelde, violento, criminal; *country* sin leyes, ingobernable, anárquico.

lawlessness ['lɔːlɪsnɪs] N desorden *m*; violencia *f*; anarquía *f*; criminalidad *f*.

lawmaker ['lɔː,meɪkəʳ] N legislador *m*, -ora *f*.

lawn¹ [lɔːn] N (*grass*) césped *m*.

lawn² [lɔːn] N (*cloth*) linón *m*.

lawnmower ['lɔːn,məʊəʳ] N cortacésped *m*, segadora *f* (*LAm*).

lawn tennis ['lɔːn'tenɪs] N tenis *m*.

Lawrence ['lɒrəns] NM Lorenzo.

lawrencium [lɒ'rensɪəm] N laurencio *m*.

lawsuit ['lɔːsuːt] N pleito *m*, litigio *m*, proceso *m*; **to bring a ~ against sb** entablar demanda judicial contra uno.

lawyer ['lɔːjəʳ] N abogado *mf* (*also* -a *f*).

┌─ LAWYERS ──────────────────────────────┐

(i) *En el Reino Unido existen dos tipos diferentes de abogados:* **solicitors** *y* **barristers** *(estos últimos reciben el nombre de* **advocates** *en Escocia). Los* **solicitors** *defienden a sus clientes ante tribunales de menor importancia y se encargan de asuntos civiles tales como la compra o venta de propiedades, testamentos, divorcios o el cobro de deudas, aunque pueden ser contratados directamente por el cliente para que los representen en casos tanto civiles como penales. Por su parte, los* **barristers** *o* **advocates** *no tratan directamente con sus clientes sino que, en los asuntos legales particulares, asesoran solamente en aquellos casos que les son remitidos por los* **solicitors**, *ya que su formación va más bien dirigida para actuar ante el Tribunal Supremo.*
⇨ *Ver también* [ATTORNEY]

lax [læks] ADJ flojo; negligente, descuidado, poco exigente; indisciplinado; (*morally*) laxo; **to be ~ in + *ger*** ser negligente en + *infin*; **things are very ~ at the school** en la escuela hay poca disciplina; **he is ~ in his approach** su actitud es poco seria.

laxative ['læksətɪv] [1] ADJ laxante.
[2] N laxante *m*.

laxity ['læksɪtɪ] N, **laxness** ['læksnɪs] N flojedad *f*; negligencia *f*, descuido *m*; falta *f* de disciplina; (*moral*) laxitud *f*, relajamiento *m*.

lay¹ [leɪ] N (*Mus, Liter*) trova *f*, canción *f*.

lay² [leɪ] ADJ (*not in orders*) laico, lego, seglar; (*not expert*) profano, no experto; **~ person** (*Rel*) lego *m*, -a *f*; (*non-specialist*) profano *m*, -a *f*.

lay³ [leɪ] PRET de **lie²**.

lay⁴ [leɪ] [1] N (a) (*of countryside, district etc*) disposición *f*, situación *f*; **the ~ of the land** la configuración del terreno, (*fig*) la situación actual, el estado actual de las cosas.
(b) **hen in ~** gallina *f* ponedora; **to come into ~** empezar a poner huevos; **to go out of ~** dejar de poner huevos.
(c) (‡) **she's an easy ~** es un coño caliente‡, es una tía fácil*; **she's a good ~** es una tía buena*.
(d) (*‡: act*) polvo‡ *m*.
[2] (*irr*: PRET, PTP **laid**) VT (a) (*prostrate, etc*) *corn* abatir, encamar; *dust* matar; *fears* aquietar, acallar; *ghost* conjurar, exorcizar; **to ~ sth flat** derribar algo, tirar algo al suelo; extender algo (sobre la mesa *etc*); **to ~ a town flat** arrasar (*or* destruir) una ciudad.
(b) (*place, put*) poner, colocar; dejar; *blame* echar (*on* a); *bricks* poner, colocar; *cable, mains, track* tender; *cloth, meal* poner; *carpet, lino* extender; *fire* preparar; *foundations* echar; *foundation stone* colocar; *gun* apuntar; *hand etc* poner (*on* en); *bomb, explosives* colocar; *mines* sembrar; *pipes etc* (*in building*) instalar; *plans* hacer, formar, preparar; *responsibility* atribuir (*on* a); *scene* poner, situar; *tax* imponer (*on* a); **to ~ the table** (*Brit*) poner la mesa; **to ~ a plan before sb** exponer un proyecto ante uno; **to ~ a claim before sb** presentar una reivindicación a uno.
(c) *egg* poner; **to ~ eggs** (*hen*) poner huevos, (*fish, insect etc*) desovar.
(d) *bet* hacer; *money* apostar (*on* a); **to ~ that ...** apostar a que ...; **I ~ you a fiver on it!** ¡te apuesto 5 libras a que es así!
(e) *accusation, charge* hacer; *complaint* formular, presentar; *information* dar.
(f) (‡) tirarse a‡‡, follar‡‡.
[3] VI (*hen*) poner, poner huevos.
[4] VR: **to ~ o.s. open to attack** exponerse al ataque, dejarse

expuesto al ataque; *see also* **charge 1(c), open 1(d)**.

◆**lay about** VI: **to ~ about one** dar palos de ciego, repartir golpes a diestro y siniestro.

◆**lay aside** VT (a) (*save*) ahorrar, guardar.
(b) (*put away*) poner aparte, poner a un lado; *book, pen etc* dejar; *work* dejar, suspender.
(c) (*abandon*) desechar; *plan etc* arrinconar, dar carpetazo a.

◆**lay away** VT (*US*) = **lay aside (a)**.

◆**lay by** VT = **lay aside (a) (b)**.

◆**lay down** [1] VT (a) (*put down*) *book, pen etc* dejar, poner a un lado; (*lay flat*) acostar, poner en tierra, extender; *burden* posar, depositar en tierra; *cards* extender sobre el tapete.
(b) *ship* colocar la quilla de.
(c) *wine* poner en bodega, guardar en cava.
(d) (*give up*) *arms* deponer, rendir, dejar; *life* dar, sacrificar.
(e) (*establish*) *condition* asentar, trazar, marcar; *policy* asentar, trazar, marcar; *precedent* sentar, establecer; *principle* afirmar; *ruling* dictar; **to ~ it down that ...** asentar que ..., dictaminar que ...
[2] VI (*Cards*) poner sus cartas sobre el tapete; (*Bridge*: *as dummy*) tumbarse.
[3] VR: **to ~ o.s. down** tumbarse, echarse.

◆**lay in** VT *supplies* proveerse de; (*amass*) acumular; (*buy*) comprar.

◆**lay into*** VT (*attack, criticize*) dar una paliza a; *food etc* lanzarse sobre, asaltar.

◆**lay off** [1] VT (a) *workers* despedir (temporalmente, por falta de trabajo), suspender. (b) (*) **to ~ off sb** dejar a uno en paz; dejar de acosar a uno; **to ~ off cigarettes** dejar de fumar (cigarrillos).
[2] VI (a) (*Naut*) virar de bordo.
(b) (*) **~ off, will you?** ¡déjalo!, por Dios!; **to ~ off + *ger*** dejar de + *infin*.

◆**lay on** [1] VT (a) (*Brit*: *install*) instalar; conectar; **a house with water laid on** una casa con agua corriente.
(b) *paint etc* poner, pintar; **to ~ it on (thick)*** (*flatter*) elogiar más de la cuenta, (*exaggerate*) recargar las tintas.
(c) *tax etc, duty* imponer (a).
(d) *blows* descargar (sobre); **to ~ it on sb** dar una paliza a uno.
[2] VI arremeter, empezar a luchar, darse golpes.

◆**lay out** [1] VT (a) (*dispose*) tender, extender; disponer, arreglar; *garden, town* trazar, hacer el trazado de; *ideas* exponer, explicar; **the house is well laid out** la casa está bien distribuida; **the town is well laid out** la ciudad tiene un trazado elegante.
(b) *corpse* amortajar.
(c) *money* (*spend*) gastar; (*invest*) invertir, emplear (*on* en).
(d) (*) (*knock out*) derribar; poner fuera de combate; (*Boxing*) dejar K.O.; (*with drink*) hacer perder el conocimiento a; (*illness*) debilitar gravemente.
[2] VR: **to ~ o.s. out** hacer un gran esfuerzo (*to* + *infin* por + *infin*); **to ~ o.s. out for sb** hacer lo posible por ayudar (*or* complacer *etc*) a uno; **to ~ o.s. out to please** volcarse por complacer a uno.

◆**lay over** VI (*US*) pasar la noche, descansar.

◆**lay up** [1] VT (a) (*store*) guardar; almacenar; (*amass*) acumular; (*save*) ahorrar, atesorar; *trouble* crear para sí.
(b) (*put into reserve*) *ship* desarmar; *boat* amarrar; *car etc* encerrar en el garaje, dejar de usar temporalmente.
(c) (*Med*) obligar a guardar cama; **she was laid up for weeks** tuvo que guardar cama durante varias semanas.
[2] VR: **to ~ o.s. up** agotarse, enfermar.

layabout ['leɪəbaʊt] N (*Brit*) gandul *m*, vago *m*, -a *f*.

lay brother ['leɪ'brʌðəʳ] N donado *m*, lego *m*, hermano *m* lego.

layby ['leɪbaɪ] N (*Brit Aut*) apartadero *m*.

lay days ['leɪdeɪz] NPL (*Comm*) días *mpl* de detención (*or* inactividad).

layer ['leɪəʳ] [1] N (a) (*gen*) capa *f*; (*Geol*) estrato *m*. (b) (*Agr*) acodo *m*. (c) (*hen*) gallina *f* ponedora; **the best ~** la más ponedora.
[2] VT (*Agr*) acodar.

layette [leɪ'et] N canastilla *f*, ajuar *m* (de niño).

lay figure ['leɪ'fɪgəʳ] N maniquí *m*.

laying ['leɪɪŋ] N (*placing*) colocación *f*; (*of cable, track etc*) tendido *m*; (*of eggs*) puesta *f*, postura *f*; **~ on of hands** imposición *f* de manos.

layman ['leɪmən] N, PL **laymen** ['leɪmən] (*Eccl*) seglar *m*, lego *m*; (*fig*) profano *m*, persona *f* no experta, lego *m*.

lay-off ['leɪɒf] N paro *m* involuntario, despido *m* (temporal).

layout ['leɪaʊt] N plan *m*, distribución *f*, trazado *m*; disposición *f*; (*Typ etc*) composición *f*.

layover ['leɪəʊvəʳ] N (*US*) parada *f* intermedia; (*Aer*) escala *f*.

layperson ['leɪpɜːsn] N (*Eccl*) seglar *mf*, lego *m*, -a *f*; (*fig*) profano *m*, -a *f*, lego *m*, -a *f*.

lay sister ['leɪ'sɪstəʳ] N donada *f*, lega *f*.

Lazarus ['læzərəs] NM Lázaro.

laze [leɪz] [1] N: **to have a ~*** descansar.
[2] VI (*also* **to ~ about**) no hacer nada, darse al ocio; (*pej*) holgazanear, gandulear; **we ~d in the sun for a week** durante una semana tomamos el sol y nada más.

lazily ['leɪzɪlɪ] ADV perezosamente; lentamente.

laziness ['leɪzɪnɪs] N pereza f, holgazanería f, vaguedad f, indolencia f.

lazy ['leɪzɪ] ADJ perezoso, holgazán, vago; *movement etc* lento; *excuse etc* poco convincente; **we had a ~ holiday** pasamos unas vacaciones descansadas; **to have a ~ eye** tener un ojo vago.

lazybones ['leɪzɪˌbəʊnz] N gandul m, vago m, -a f.

lazy Susan [ˌleɪzɪ'suːzn] N (*dish*) bandeja f giratoria para servir la comida en la mesa.

LB (*Canada*) ABBR *of* **Labrador**.

lb. ABBR *of* **libra, pound** libra f.

LBO N ABBR *of* **leveraged buy-out**.

l.b.w. (*Cricket*) ABBR *of* **leg before wicket**.

L/C (*Comm*) ABBR *of* **letter of credit** letra f de crédito.

L.C. N (*US*) ABBR *of* **Library of Congress** Biblioteca f del Congreso.

l.c. (*Typ*) ABBR *of* **lower case** minúscula f, mín.

LCD N ABBR *of* **liquid crystal display** visualizador m cristal líquido, VCL m.

L-Cpl ABBR *of* **lance-corporal**.

Ld ABBR *of* **Lord**.

LDS N (a) ABBR *of* **Licentiate in Dental Surgery**. (b) ABBR *of* **Latter-day Saints** Iglesia f de Jesucristo de los Santos de los últimos días.

LEA N (*Brit*) ABBR *of* **Local Education Authority**.

lea [liː] N (*poet*) prado m.

leach [liːtʃ] **1** VT lixiviar.
2 VI lixiviarse.

lead¹ [led] **1** N (*metal*) plomo m; (*Naut*) sonda f, escandallo m; (*Typ*) regleta f, interlínea f; (*in pencil*) mina f; **they filled him full of ~*** le acribillaron a balazos; **to swing the ~*** fingirse enfermo, racanear*, hacer el rácano*.
2 ATTR: **~ acetate** acetato m de plomo; **~ oxide** óxido m de plomo; **~ paint** pintura f a base de plomo; **~ pencil** lápiz m; **~ pipe** tubería f de plomo; **~ poisoning** saturnismo m, plumbismo m, intoxicación f por el plomo; **~ seal** sello m de plomo; **~ shot** perdigonada f.

lead² [liːd] **1** N (a) (*front position*) delantera f, cabeza f; (*leading position*, *Sport*) liderato m; (*distance, time ahead*) ventaja f; **to be in the ~** ir en cabeza, ir primero; (*in league etc*) ocupar el primer puesto; **to take the ~** tomar la delantera, tomar el mando; (*Sport*) tomar la delantera, tomar la cabeza; **to have 2 minutes' ~ over sb** llevar a uno una ventaja de 2 minutos; **to have a ~ of half a length** tener medio cuerpo de ventaja.
(b) (*example*) ejemplo m; iniciativa f; **to follow sb's ~** seguir el ejemplo de uno; **to give sb a ~** guiar a uno, dar el ejemplo a uno, mostrar el camino a uno; **to take the ~** tomar la iniciativa (*in* en, *in doing* en hacer).
(c) (*clue*) pista f, indicación f; **the police have a ~** la policía tiene una pista; **it gave the police a ~ to the criminal** puso a la policía sobre la pista del criminal; **give me a ~** (*in guessing*) ¿me puedes dar alguna indicación?
(d) (*Cards*) **it's my ~** soy mano, salgo yo; **whose ~ is it?** ¿quién sale?; **if the ~ is in hearts** si la salida es a corazones.
(e) (*Theat*) papel m principal; (*in opera*) voz f cantante; (*person*) primer actor m, primera actriz f; **with Garbo in the ~** con la Garbo en el primer papel; **~ singer** cantante mf; **to play the ~** tener el papel principal; **to sing the ~** llevar la voz cantante.
(f) (*leash*) traílla f, cuerda f, correa f (*LAm*).
(g) (*Elec*) conductor m, cable m (eléctrico).
(h) (*Press*) primer párrafo m, entrada f.
2 ATTR: **~ story** reportaje m principal, noticia f más sobresaliente; **~ time** margen m de tiempo; tiempo m desde el pedido hasta la entrega.
3 (*irr: PRET AND PTP* **led**) VT (a) (*conduct*) conducir; llevar; guiar; **to ~ sb to a table** conducir a uno a una mesa; **kindly ~ me to him** haga el favor de conducirme a su presencia (*or* de llevarme donde está); **each reference led me to another** cada referencia me llevó a otra; **one thing led to another** una cosa nos (*etc*) llevó a otra; **this ~s me to an important point** esto me lleva a un punto importante; **what led you to Venice?** ¿qué te llevó a Venecia?, ¿con qué motivo fuiste a Venecia?; **to ~ the way** ir primero, (*fig*) dar el ejemplo, mostrar el camino; **he is easily led** es muy sugestionable; **they led him into the king's presence** le condujeron ante el rey; **to ~ sb into error** inducir a uno a error.
(b) (*be the leader of, govern*) *government* dirigir, encabezar; *party* encabezar, ser el jefe de; *expedition, regiment* mandar; *team* capitanear; *movement, revolution* encabezar, acaudillar; *orchestra* (*Brit*) ser primer violín de, (*US*) dirigir; *league, procession* ir a la cabeza de, encabezar.
(c) (*be first in*) ser el primero en, sobresalir en, ocupar el primer puesto en; **to ~ the field** ir el primero de todos, estar a la cabeza, ganar; **they led us by 30 seconds** nos llevaban una ventaja de 30 segundos; **A ~s B by 4 games to 1** A aventaja a B por 4 juegos a 1; **Britain led the world in textiles** en la industria textil Inglaterra superaba a los demás, en los textiles Inglaterra ocupaba el primer puesto.

(d) *card* salir con, salir de.
(e) *life* llevar; **to ~ a strange life** llevar una vida muy rara; **to ~ sb a wretched life** amargar la vida a uno, tratar a uno como una basura; *see also* **dance, life**.
(f) (*induce*) **to ~ sb to do sth** inducir (*or* llevar, inclinar, persuadir, mover) a uno a hacer algo; **to ~ sb to believe that ...** hacer creer a uno que ...; **I am led to the conclusion that ...** llego a la conclusión de que ...
4 VI (a) (*go in front*) llevar la delantera, ir primero; **~ on!** ¡adelante!; **to ~ by 10 metres** tener una ventaja de 10 metros; **he easily ~s** sobresale, supera fácilmente a los demás.
(b) (*be in command*) tener el mando, ser el jefe.
(c) (*Cards*) ser mano, salir; **who ~s?** ¿quién sale?; **South ~s** Sur sale.
(d) (*of street etc*) **to ~ to** conducir a, llevar a, salir a, desembocar en; **this street ~s to the station** esta calle conduce a la estación, por esta calle se va a la estación; **where does this corridor ~?** ¿adónde conduce este pasillo?; **it ~s into that room** comunica con ese cuarto.
(e) (*result in*) dar, producir; **it led to a result** dio un resultado; **it led to a change** produjo un cambio; **it led to nothing** no dio resultado, no surtió efecto, no condujo a nada; **it led to his arrest** dio lugar a su detención; **it led to war** causó la guerra.

◆**lead along** VT llevar (por la mano *etc*).

◆**lead away** VT conducir a otra parte, llevar fuera; **he was led away by the police** se lo llevó la policía; **we must not be led away from the main issue** no nos apartemos del asunto principal.

◆**lead back** **1** VT: **to ~ sb back** hacer volver a uno, conducir a uno a donde estaba; **this road ~s you back to Jaca** por este camino se vuelve a Jaca.
2 VI: **this road ~s back to Burgos** por este camino se vuelve a Burgos; **it all ~s back to the butler** todo nos lleva de nuevo al mayordomo (como sospechoso).

◆**lead in** **1** VT hacer entrar a.
2 VI: **this is a way of ~ing in** ésta es una manera de introducir el argumento (*etc*).

◆**lead off** **1** VT (a) = **lead away**.
(b) **the streets that ~ off (from) the square** las calles que salen de la plaza; **a room ~ing off (from) another** un cuarto que comunica con otro.
2 VI (*begin*) empezar; (*Sport*) comenzar, abrir el juego; (*Cards*) salir (*with* con).

◆**lead on** **1** VT (*persuade*) engatusar, halagar; (*amorously*) coquetear con, ir dando esperanzas a; (*morally*) seducir; (*make talk*) hacer hablar a, tirar de la lengua a; **this led him on to say that ...** esto hizo que dijera a continuación que ...
2 VI ir primero, ir a la cabeza; **you ~ on** tú primero; **~ on!** ¡vamos!

◆**lead out** VT conducir fuera, llevar fuera; **to ~ a girl out to dance** sacar a una chica a bailar.

◆**lead up** VI (a) **to ~ up to** conducir a; preparar el terreno para; **events that led up to the war** los sucesos que condujeron a la guerra; **what's all this ~ing up to?** ¿qué propósito tiene todo esto?, ¿adónde conduce todo esto?; **he led carefully up to the proposal** preparó el terreno con cuidado antes de formular la propuesta.
(b) **the years that led up to the war** los años que precedieron a la guerra.

leaded ['ledɪd] ADJ (a) **~ lights** cristales mpl emplomados. (b) (*also* N) **~ petrol** gasolina f con plomo.

leaden ['ledn] ADJ (*of lead*) de plomo, plúmbeo; (*in colour*) plomizo; (*fig*) pesado, triste.

leaden-eyed [ˌledn'aɪd] ADJ: **to be ~** tener los párpados pesados.

leader ['liːdər] N (a) (*person: gen*) jefe mf, líder mf; (*Pol*) líder mf; jefe mf, dirigente mf; (*esp military*) caudillo m; (*of gang*) cuadrillero m; (*of rebels*) cabecilla mf; (*guide*) guía mf, conductor m, -ora f; (*Brit Mus: of orchestra*) primer violín m, (*of band*) director m, -ora f; (*US Mus: of orchestra*) director m, -ora f; **L~ of the House** (*of Commons*) Presidente mf de la Cámara de los Comunes; (*of Lords*) Presidente mf de la Cámara de los Lores; **~ of the opposition** jefe mf de la oposición; **~ of the party** jefe mf del partido; **a ~ of the masses** un conductor de masas; **our political ~s** nuestros dirigentes políticos.
(b) (*Sport*) (*person*) primero m, -a f; (*in league*) líder m; (*horse etc*) caballo m (*etc*) delantero, caballo m (*etc*) que va en primer lugar.
(c) (*Brit Press*) artículo m de fondo, editorial m.
(d) (*Comm: company, product*) líder m; (*share*) acción f líder; (*indicator*) índice m, indicador m (económico).

leaderene [ˌliːdə'riːn] N (*hum*) líder f.

┌─ *LEADER OF THE HOUSE* ─┐

i **Leader of the House** es el término que, en el Reino Unido, hace referencia tanto al presidente de la Cámara de los Comunes como al presidente de la Cámara de los Lores. Ambos pertenecen al gobierno británico y son los encargados de organizar y hacer público el horario semanal de debates y otros asuntos en sus respectivas cámaras, previa

*consulta con su homólogo de la oposición (**Shadow Leader of the House**) y
con los **Whips de cada partido.**
⇨ Ver también* WHIP , SPEAKER

leadership ['li:dəʃɪp] N (a) *(persons, office)* jefatura *f*, dirección *f*; mando *m*; liderato *m*, liderazgo *m*; protagonismo *m*; caudillaje *m*; **under the ~ of** bajo la jefatura de; **a crisis in the ~** una crisis de dirección, una crisis en la dirigencia; **to resign the ~** dimitir la jefatura; **to take over the ~** asumir la dirección, tomar el mando.
(b) *(quality)* iniciativa *f*; *(powers of ~)* dotes *fpl* de mando.
leader-writer ['li:də,raɪtəʳ] N *(Brit)* editorialista *mf*.
lead-free [,led'fri:] ADJ sin plomo.
lead-in ['li:d'ɪn] N introducción *f*; entrada *f*; **a useful ~ to a discussion** una manera útil de introducir una discusión.
leading ['li:dɪŋ] ADJ (a) *(front)* delantero; *wheel* delantero, conductor; **~ edge** *(Aer)* borde *m* de ataque; **~ edge technology** tecnología *f* punta; **to be at (or on) the ~ edge of technology** estar a la vanguardia de la tecnología.
(b) *part, person, idea etc* principal, importante; *(outstanding)* sobresaliente, destacado; *(in race)* primero, delantero; **~ article** *(Brit)* artículo *m* de fondo, editorial *m*; **~ brand** marca *f* líder; **~ lady** primera actriz *f*; **~ light** figura *f* principal; **~ man** primer galán *m*; **~ note** sensible *f*; **~ product** producto *m* líder; **~ role** papel *m* principal; **~ supplier** proveedor *m* líder.
(c) **~ question** *(Jur)* pregunta *f* inductiva; **~ strings** andadores *mpl*.
lead-up ['li:d'ʌp] N período *m* preparatorio *(to* de); **during the ~ to the election...** durante la precampaña electoral...; **the ~ to the wedding** los meses antes de la boda.
leaf [li:f] **1** N, PL **leaves** [li:vz] hoja *f*; **~ tobacco** tabaco *m* en rama; **to come into ~** echar hojas, cubrirse de hojas; **to take a ~ out of sb's book** seguir el ejemplo de uno; **to turn over a new ~** reformarse, cambiar de modo de ser, hacer vida nueva.
2 VI *(Bot)* echar hojas.
◆**leaf through** VT: **to ~ through a book** hojear un libro, trashojar un libro.
leaf bud ['li:fbʌd] N yema *f*.
leafless ['li:flɪs] ADJ sin hojas, deshojado.
leaflet ['li:flɪt] **1** N folleto *m*, hoja *f* volante; prospecto *m*.
2 VT: **to ~ a constituency** *(Pol)* repartir folletos en un distrito.
leaf mould, *(US)* **leaf mold** ['li:fməʊld] N mantillo *m* (de hojas), abono *m* verde.
leafy ['li:fɪ] ADJ frondoso.
league¹ [li:g] N *(measure)* legua *f*.
league² [li:g] **1** N liga *f* *(also Sport)*; sociedad *f*, asociación *f*, comunidad *f*; **L~ of Nations** Sociedad *f* de las Naciones; **he's not in the same ~** *(fig)* pertenece a otra clase; **to be in ~ with sb** estar de manga con uno, haberse confabulado con uno.
2 ATTR: **~ champions** campeón *m* de liga; **~ leader** líder *m* de la liga; **~ table** clasificación *f*.
leak [li:k] **1** N *(hole)* agujero *m*; *(Naut)* vía *f* de agua; *(of blood)* derrame *m*; *(in roof etc)* gotera *f*; *(of gas, liquid)* escape *m*, fuga *f*, pérdida *f*, salida *f*; *(of information, money)* filtración *f*; **to spring a ~** abrirse una vía de agua; **to take a ~⁑** hacer aguas⁑.
2 VT (a) rezumar, dejar perderse, derramar; **it's ~ing acid all over the place** se está derramando el ácido por todas partes.
(b) *information* filtrar *(to* a).
3 VI (a) *(ship)* hacer agua; *(receptacle)* rezumarse, tener agujeros, estar agujereado; *(pipe)* tener fugas, dejar fugarse el gas *(etc)*; *(pen)* derramar tinta, derramarse.
(b) *(gas, liquid etc)* escaparse, fugarse, salirse, irse; *(ooze out)* rezumarse; *(drop by drop)* gotear; *(information, money)* filtrarse.
◆**leak away** VI irse, agotarse debido a una fuga.
◆**leak in** VI filtrarse, gotear.
◆**leak out** VI (a) = **leak away**. (b) *(news)* filtrarse, divulgarse (sin autorización), llegar a saberse, trascender; **finally it ~ed out that ...** por fin se supo que ...
leakage ['li:kɪdʒ] N = **leak**.
leakproof ['li:kpru:f] ADJ estanco, hermético.
leaky ['li:kɪ] ADJ *boat* que hace agua, que tiene vías de agua; *roof* que tiene goteras; *receptacle* agujereado, defectuoso; *organization* muy sujeto a filtraciones.
lean¹ [li:n] **1** ADJ *(thin)* flaco; magro; *face* enjuto; *meat* magro; *year* difícil, de carestía; **a ~er and fitter economy** una economía más enjuta y más dinámica; **the ~ years** los años de las vacas flacas; **to grow ~** enflaquecer.
2 N carne *f* magra.
lean² [li:n] **1** N inclinación *f*.
2 *(irr: PRET AND PTP* **leaned** *or* **leant)** VT ladear, inclinar, poner oblicuamente; **to ~ a ladder against a wall** poner *(or* apoyar) una escala contra una pared; **to ~ one's head on sb's shoulder** apoyar la cabeza en el hombro de uno.
3 VI ladearse, inclinarse, estar ladeado, estar inclinado; **to ~ against**

sth apoyarse en algo; **to ~ on sth** apoyarse en algo *(also fig)*; **to ~ on sb for support** contar con el apoyo de uno; **to ~ on sb*** ejercer presión sobre uno, intimidar a uno, amenazar a uno; **to ~ to the Left** inclinarse a la izquierda; **to ~ towards sb's opinion** inclinarse hacia la opinión de uno.
◆**lean back** VI reclinarse, echar el cuerpo atrás.
◆**lean forward** VI inclinarse.
◆**lean out** VI asomarse *(of* a).
◆**lean over** **1** VT: **to ~ over sb** inclinarse sobre uno.
2 VI inclinarse; **to ~ over backwards to help sb** volcarse por ayudar a uno, desvivirse por ayudar a uno; **we have ~ed over backwards to get agreement** hemos hecho todas las concesiones posibles para llegar a un acuerdo.
Leander [li:'ændəʳ] NM Leandro.
leaning ['li:nɪŋ] **1** ADJ inclinado; **the L~ Tower of Pisa** la Torre Inclinada de Pisa.
2 N inclinación *f* *(to, towards* hacia); tendencia *f*, propensión *f* *(to* a); predilección *f* *(to, towards* por); **what are his ~s?** ¿cuál es su predilección?; **he has artistic ~s** se siente atraído por una carrera artística.
leanness ['li:nnɪs] N flaqueza *f*; magrez *f*; carestía *f*, pobreza *f*.
leant [lent] PRET AND PTP of **lean²**.
lean-to ['li:ntu:] N colgadizo *m*, alpende *m*.
leap [li:p] **1** N salto *m*, brinco *m*; *(fig)* salto *m*; **~ of faith** acto *m* de fe; **the great ~ forward** *(China)* el gran salto hacia adelante; **~ in the dark** salto *m* en el vacío; **by ~s and bounds** a pasos agigantados; **in one ~** de un salto.
2 *(irr: PRET AND PTP* **leaped** *or* **leapt)** VT saltar, saltar por encima de.
3 VI saltar, brincar, dar un salto; *(of fish)* saltar, bañarse; **my heart ~ed** mi corazón dio un vuelco; **to ~ at a chance** agarrar (con ambas manos) una oportunidad; **to ~ at an offer** apresurarse a aceptar una oferta; **to ~ down** bajar de un salto, saltar en tierra; **to ~ for joy** saltar de alegría; **to ~ out of a car** saltar de un coche; **the answer ~t out at me** *(or off the page)* la solución se ofreció de golpe; **to ~ over** saltar, saltar por (encima de), salvar; **to ~ to one's feet** ponerse de pie de un salto.
◆**leap about** VI dar saltos, brincar.
◆**leap up** VI *(person)* ponerse de pie de un salto, *(flame)* subir de repente, brotar, *(figure etc)* subir de punto.
leapfrog ['li:pfrɒg] **1** N pídola *f*, fil *m* derecho, saltacabrilla *f*; **to play ~** jugar a la pídola.
2 VT saltar por encima de *(also fig)*.
3 VI jugar a la pídola, saltar.
leapt [lept] PRET AND PTP of **leap**.
leap year ['li:pjɪəʳ] N año *m* bisiesto.
learn [lɜ:n] *(irr: PRET AND PTP* **learned** *or* **learnt)** VTI (a) *(in general)* aprender; *news, facts etc* saber, enterarse de; *(discover, find out)* descubrir, averiguar; **he'll ~!** ¡un día aprenderá!; **to ~ to do sth** aprender a hacer algo; **to ~ how to do sth** aprender a hacer algo, aprender cómo se hace algo, aprender el modo de hacer algo; **he's ~ing the hard way** aprende por el método duro; **to ~ about sth** *(hear of)* saber algo, *(instruct o.s.)* informarse sobre algo, instruirse en algo; **to ~ from experience** aprender por experiencia; **to ~ from others' mistakes** escarmentar en cabeza ajena; **to ~ of** saber, tener noticia de.
(b) *(⁑)* enseñar; **I'll ~ you!** ¡yo te enseñaré!
◆**learn off** VT aprender de memoria.
◆**learn up** VT esforzarse por aprender, repasar, empollar.
learned ['lɜ:nɪd] ADJ *person* docto, sabio, erudito; *remark, speech* erudito; *profession* liberal; **~ body** academia *f*; **~ society** sociedad *f* científica; **to be ~** in ser erudito en, ser muy entendido en.
learnedly ['lɜ:nɪdlɪ] ADV eruditamente.
learner ['lɜ:nəʳ] N principiante *mf*, aprendiz *m*, -iza *f* *(also Brit Aut)*; *(student)* estudiante *mf*, estudioso *m*, -a *f*.
learner-centred, *(US)* **learner-centered** ['lɜ:nə,sentəd] ADJ centrado en el alumno.
learner-driver ['lɜ:nə'draɪvəʳ] N *(Brit)* aprendiz *m* de conductor, aprendiza *f* de conductora.
learning ['lɜ:nɪŋ] N (a) *(act)* el aprender, aprendizaje *m*, estudio *m*; **~ curve** curva *f* de aprendizaje; **it's a ~ curve** hay que ir aprendiendo poco a poco; **it's been a steep ~ curve** nos ha costado ir aprendiendo; **~ difficulties** dificultades *fpl* de aprendizaje. (b) *(fund of ~)* saber *m*, conocimientos *mpl*; *(erudition)* saber *m*, erudición *f*; **man of ~** sabio *m*, erudito *m*; **seat of ~** centro *m* de estudios.
learnt [lɜ:nt] PRET AND PTP of **learn**.
lease [li:s] **1** N arriendo *m*, contrato *m* de arrendamiento; **to take a house on a 99-year ~** tomar una casa con un contrato de arriendo de 99 años; **to let sth out on ~** dar algo en arriendo; **to give sb a new ~ of life** *(Brit)* devolver la vitalidad a uno, servir de tónico a uno; sacar a uno a flote; **to take on a new ~ of life** *(person)* recobrar su vigor, *(thing)* renovarse.
2 VT *(take)* arrendar *(from* de), tomar en arriendo; *(give: also* **to ~**

out) arrendar, dar en arriendo.

◆**lease back** VT subarrendar.

leaseback ['liːsbæk] N rearrendamiento *m* al vendedor, subarriendo *m*.

leasehold ['liːshəʊld] ⊡ N (*contract*) arrendamiento *m*; (*property*) inmueble *m* arrendado.

⊡ ATTR arrendado, alquilado; ~ **reform** reforma *f* del sistema de arriendos.

leaseholder ['liːshəʊldəʳ] N arrendatario *m*, -a *f*.

leash [liːʃ] N traílla *f*, cuerda *f*.

leasing ['liːsɪŋ] N (*option to buy*) alquiler *m* con opción a compra, leasing *m*; (*renting*) arrendamiento *m*, alquiler *m*; (*Fin*) arrendamiento *m* financiero.

▼ **least** [liːst] ⊡ ADJ menor; más pequeño; mínimo; menos importante, menos considerable; **the ~ of them** el menor de ellos; **with the ~ possible expenditure** gastándose lo menos posible; **that's the ~ of my worries** eso es lo de menos; **not the ~ of her qualities was ...** no era la menos importante de sus cualidades ...

⊡ ADV menos; **the ~ expensive car** el coche menos costoso; **he deserves it ~ of all** se lo merece menos que todos los demás; **she is ~ able to afford it** ella es quien menos puede permitírselo; **of all would I wish to offend him** ante todo no quiero ofenderle; **nobody knew, ~ of all Jennie** nadie lo sabía, y Jennie menos que todos; **in all countries, not ~ in the USA** en todos los países, y más en EE.UU.

⊡ N lo menos; **it's the ~ one can ask** es lo menos que se puede pedir; **you gave yourself the ~** te has servido la ración más pequeña; **at ~** a lo menos, al menos, por lo menos, cuando menos; **at ~ it's true** dejando eso de lado, consideremos ...; **there were 8 at ~** había a lo menos 8; **we can at ~ try** al menos podemos probarlo; **at the very ~** lo menos; **I'm not the ~ bit hungry** no tengo el más mínimo apetito; **not in the ~!** ¡en absoluto!, ¡de ninguna manera!;

▼ **he was not in the ~ upset** no se alteró en lo más mínimo; **to say the ~** para no decir más.

leastways* ['liːstweɪz] ADV de todos modos.

leastwise ['liːstwaɪz] ADV por lo menos.

least-worst ['liːstwɜːst] ADJ menos malo; **the ~ scenario** el panorama menos malo (de todos).

leather ['leðəʳ] ⊡ N cuero *m*; piel *f*; (*wash ~*) gamuza *f*.

⊡ ATTR: ~ **goods** artículos *mpl* de cuero; ~ **jacket** cazadora *f* de piel (*or* de cuero), chupa‡ *f* de cuero.

⊡ VT (*) zurrar*.

leather-bound ['leðəˌbaʊnd] ADJ encuadernado en cuero.

leatherette [ˌleðə'ret] N piel *f* sintética, polipiel *f*.

leathering* ['leðərɪŋ] N: **to give sb a ~** dar una paliza a uno.

leathern ['leðə(ː)n] ADJ de cuero.

leatherneck* ['leðənek] N (*US*) infante *m* de marina.

leathery ['leðərɪ] ADJ correoso; *skin* curtido.

leave [liːv] ⊡ N (a) (*permission*) permiso *m*; **by your ~** con permiso de Vd; **without so much as a 'by your ~'** sin pedir permiso a nadie; **to ask ~ to do sth** pedir permiso para hacer algo; **I take ~ to doubt it** me permito dudarlo.

(b) (*permission to be absent*) permiso *m*; (*Mil, brief*) permiso *m*, (*lengthy, compassionate etc*) licencia *f*; ~ **of absence** permiso *m* para estar ausente, excedencia *f*; **to be on ~** estar de permiso, estar de licencia.

(c) (*departure*) **to take one's ~** despedirse (*of* de); **I must take my ~** tengo que marcharme; **to take ~ of one's senses** perder el juicio; **have you taken ~ of your senses?** ¿se te ha vuelto el juicio?

⊡ (*irr*: PRET AND PTP **left**) VT (a) (*allow to remain*) dejar; **to ~ 2 pages blank** dejar 2 páginas en blanco; **let's ~ it at that** dejemos las cosas así; **to ~ sth with sb** dejar algo en manos de uno; entregar algo a uno; **to ~ things lying about** dejar las cosas de cualquier modo; **to ~ one's supper** dejar la cena sin comer; **to ~ one's greens** no comer las verduras; **to ~ a good impression on sb** producir a uno una buena impresión; **it ~s much to be desired** deja mucho que desear; **take it or ~ it** lo tomas o lo dejas, una de dos, o esto o lo otro, como quieras.

(b) (*forget*) dejar, olvidar.

(c) (*person*) **I'll ~ you at the station** te dejo en la estación; **to ~ a wife and 2 children** dejar una viuda y 2 hijos; **he has left his wife** ha abandonado a su mujer; **I must ~ you** tengo que despedirme de vosotros, con permiso de vosotros me voy; **you may ~ us** Vd puede retirarse; **to ~ sb free for the afternoon** dejar a uno la tarde libre.

(d) (*bequeath*) dejar, legar.

(e) (*Math*) **3 from 10 ~s 7** de 3 a 10 van 7, 10 menos 3 son 7.

(f) (*remain, be over, be left*) quedar; sobrar; **all the money I have left** todo el dinero que me queda; **how many are there left?** ¿cuántos quedan?; **we were left with 4** quedamos con 4, nos quedaron 4; **nothing was left for me but to sell it** no tuve más remedio que venderlo; **there are 3 left over** sobran 3.

(g) (*entrust*) **I ~ it to you** le toca a Vd decidir, que lo decida Vd;

~ **it to me** yo me encargo de eso; **I ~ it to you to do** lo dejo en sus manos; que lo haga Vd; **I ~ it to you to judge** júzguelo Vd.

(h) (*depart from, quit*) salir de, abandonar; dejar; **to ~ a place** salir de un lugar, abandonar un lugar; **when the king left Rome** cuando el rey abandonó Roma; **to ~ home** salir de su casa; **to ~ prison** salir de la cárcel; **to ~ school** salir del colegio; **to ~ the table** levantarse de la mesa; **to ~ one's post** dejar su puesto, dimitir su cargo, (*improperly*) abandonar su puesto; **to ~ the road** salir fuera de la carretera; **to ~ the rails** descarrilar.

⊡ VI irse, marcharse; salir (*for* para); (*of train etc*) salir.

⊡ VR: **he left himself with two problems** se quedó con dos problemas.

◆**leave about, leave around** VT dejar tirado.

◆**leave aside** VT dejar de lado, omitir; prescindir de; **leaving that aside, let's consider ...** dejando eso de lado, consideremos ...

◆**leave behind** VT (a) (*not take*) *person* dejar, no llevar consigo; **we have left all that behind us** todo eso ha quedado a la espalda; **he left the children behind** no llevó consigo a los niños, dejó allí a los niños.

(b) (*forget*) olvidar, dejar.

(c) (*outdistance*) dejar atrás.

◆**leave in** VT *passage, words* dejar tal como está, conservar; *plug etc* dejar puesto.

◆**leave off** ⊡ VT (a) (*stop*) *habit* renunciar a, dejar; *work* terminar, suspender; **to ~ off smoking** dejar de fumar; **to ~ off working** dejar de trabajar; terminar de trabajar; **when it ~s off raining** cuando deje de llover.

(b) (*lid*) no poner, dejar sin poner; *clothes* quitarse, no ponerse.

(c) (*gas etc*) no poner, no encender.

⊡ VI terminar, cesar; suspender el trabajo (*etc*); **when the rain ~s off** cuando deje de llover; ~ **off, will you?** ¡déjalo!

◆**leave on** VT (a) (*lid etc*) dejar puesto; **to ~ one's hat on** seguir con el sombrero puesto, no quitarse el sombrero.

(b) (*gas, light*) dejar puesto, dejar encendido, dejar prendido (*LAm*).

◆**leave out** VT (a) (*omit*) omitir, suprimir; prescindir de; *person* dejar fuera; **poor Jane felt left out** la pobre de Jane se sentía excluida; **nobody wanted to be left out** nadie quería quedar fuera.

(b) (*not put back*) dejar fuera; no devolver a su lugar; **it got left out in the rain** quedó fuera bajo la lluvia; **the cat was left out all night** el gato pasó toda la noche fuera.

◆**leave over** VT (a) (*remain*) quedar; **there's nothing left over** no queda nada.

(b) (*postpone*) dejar, posponer.

leaven ['levn] ⊡ N levadura *f*; (*fig*) mezcla *f*; estímulo *m*.

⊡ VT leudar; (*fig*) penetrar e influenciar, servir de estímulo a, ayudar a transformar.

leavening ['levnɪŋ] N levadura *f*; (*fig*) mezcla *f*, estímulo *m*.

leaves [liːvz] NPL of **leaf**.

leave-taking ['liːvˌteɪkɪŋ] N despedida *f*.

leaving ['liːvɪŋ] ⊡ ADJ *ceremony, present* de despedida.

⊡ N (*departure*) salida *f*.

leavings ['liːvɪŋz] NPL sobras *fpl*, restos *mpl*.

Lebanese [ˌlebə'niːz] ⊡ ADJ libanés.

⊡ N libanés *m*, -esa *f*.

Lebanon ['lebənən] N Líbano *m*.

lech* [letʃ] ⊡ N sátiro* *m*.

⊡ VI: **to ~ after sb: he's ~ing after his secretary** se le van los ojos detrás de su secretaria*, se le alegran las pajarillas cuando ve a su secretaria *hum*.

lecher ['letʃəʳ] N libertino *m*.

lecherous ['letʃərəs] ADJ lascivo, lujurioso.

lecherously ['letʃərəslɪ] ADV lascivamente.

lechery ['letʃərɪ] N lascivia *f*, lujuria *f*.

lectern ['lektə(ː)n] N atril *m*; (*Eccl*) facistol *m*.

lector ['lektɔːʳ] N (*Univ*) lector *m*, -ora *f*.

lecture ['lektʃəʳ] ⊡ N (*formal, by visitor etc*) conferencia *f*; (*Univ class*) clase *f*; explicación *f*; (*fig*) sermoneo *m*; **to attend ~s on** seguir un curso sobre (*or* de); **to give a ~** dar una conferencia; **to read sb a ~** sermonear a uno.

⊡ ATTR: ~ **course** ciclo *m* de conferencias; ~ **notes** apuntes *mpl* de clase.

⊡ VT (*scold*) sermonear; **he ~s us in French** nos da clases de francés.

⊡ VI dar una conferencia, dar una clase; **he ~s in Law** da clases de derecho; **to ~ on** (*Univ*) dar un curso sobre, explicar; **he ~s at 9 o'clock** da su clase a las 9; **he ~s at Princeton** es profesor en Princeton; **he's lecturing at the moment** ahora está en clase; **he ~s well** habla muy bien.

lecture-hall ['lektʃəˌhɔːl] N = **lecture-room**.

lecturer ['lektʃərəʳ] N (*visitor*) conferenciante *mf*, conferencista *mf*; (*Brit Univ*) profesor *m*, -ora *f*.

lecture-room ['lektʃəˌrʊm] N, **lecture-theater** ['lektʃəˌθɪətəʳ] N (*US*)

sala *f* de conferencias; (*Univ*) aula *f*.
lectureship ['lektʃəʃɪp] N cargo *m* (*or* puesto *m*) de profesor (adjunto).
LED N ABBR *of* **light-emitting diode** diodo *m* emisor de luz.
led [led] PRET AND PTP *of* **lead**.
ledge [ledʒ] N repisa *f*, reborde *m*; (*along wall*) retallo *m*; (*of window*) antepecho *m*, alféizar *m*; (*shelf*) anaquel *m*; (*on mountain*) plataforma *f*, saliente *m*, cama *f* de roca.
ledger ['ledʒər] N libro *m* mayor.
ledger line ['ledʒə,laɪn] N línea *f* suplementaria.
lee [liː] 1 ADJ a sotavento, de sotavento.
2 N sotavento *m*; (*shelter*) socaire *m*; **in the ~ of** al socaire de, al abrigo de.
leech [liːtʃ] N sanguijuela *f* (*also fig*).
leek [liːk] N puerro *m*.
leer [lɪər] 1 N mirada *f* impúdica, mirada *f* maliciosa; sonrisa *f* impúdica; **he said with a ~** dijo sonriendo impúdico.
2 VI mirar impúdico, mirar malicioso (*at sb* a uno); sonreír impúdico (*at sb* a uno).
leery ['lɪərɪ] ADJ (*US*) cauteloso; sospechoso; **to be ~ of** recelar de.
lees [liːz] NPL heces *fpl*, poso *m*.
leeward ['liːwəd] 1 ADJ a sotavento, de sotavento.
2 ADV a sotavento.
3 N sotavento *m*; **to ~** a sotavento (*of* de).
Leeward Isles ['liːwəd,aɪlz] NPL Islas *fpl* de Sotavento.
leeway ['liːweɪ] N (*Naut*) deriva *f*; (*fig: scope*) libertad *f* de acción; (*fig: backlog etc*) atraso *m*, tiempo *m* (*etc*) perdido; **to make up ~** salir del atraso, recuperar el tiempo perdido.
left¹ [left] PRET AND PTP *of* **leave**.
left² [left] 1 ADJ a) izquierdo; **~ back** defensa *m* izquierdo, defensa *f* izquierda; **~ half** medio *m* izquierda, medio *m* volante izquierda; **~ wing** (*Mil, Sport*) ala *f* izquierda.
(b) (*Pol*) izquierdista.
2 ADV a la izquierda, hacia la izquierda; **we are a ~ of centre party** somos un partido del centro izquierdo; **they were coming at us ~, right, and centre** nos atacaban desde todas partes.
3 N (a) izquierda *f*; **on the ~, to the ~** a la izquierda; **to keep to the ~** (*Aut*) circular por la izquierda.
(b) (*Pol*) izquierda *f*, izquierdas *fpl*; **he has always been on the ~** siempre ha sido de izquierdas; **he's further to the ~ than I am** es más izquierdista que yo.
(c) (*Boxing*) izquierdazo *m*.
left field [left'fiːld] N (*Baseball: area*) jardín *m* izquierdo; (*position*) jardinero *m* izquierdo, jardinera *f* izquierda; **to come out of ~** (*esp US: fig*) *action, remark, etc* no venir a cuento.
left-hand ['lefthænd] ADJ: **~ drive** conducción *f* por la izquierda; **~ page** página *f* izquierda; **~ side** izquierda *f*; **~ turn** vuelta *f* a la izquierda.
left-handed ['left'hændɪd] ADJ zurdo; (*fig*) *person* torpe, desmañado; *compliment* ambiguo, de doble filo; *marriage* de la mano izquierda, morganático; *tool* para zurdo.
left-hander [,left'hændər] N zurdo *m*, -a *f*.
leftism ['leftɪzəm] N izquierdismo *m*.
leftist ['leftɪst] 1 ADJ izquierdista.
2 N izquierdista *mf*.
left-luggage ['left'lʌgɪdʒ] 1 N (*also ~ office*) (*Brit*) consigna *f*.
2 ATTR: **~ locker** (*Brit*) consigna *f* automática.
left-over ['leftəʊvər] 1 ADJ sobrante, restante.
2 N (a) (*survivor*) superviviente *mf*; **a ~ from another age** una reliquia de otra edad. (b) **~s** sobras *fpl*, restos *mpl*.
leftward ['leftwəd] ADJ *movement etc* a (*or* hacia) la izquierda.
leftward(s) ['leftwəd(z)] ADV *move etc* a (*or* hacia) la izquierda.
left-wing ['left,wɪŋ] ADJ izquierdista.
left-winger ['left'wɪŋər] N izquierdista *mf*.
lefty* ['leftɪ] N (*Pol*) izquierdista *mf*, rojillo *m*, -a *f*.
leg [leg] 1 N (a) (*Anat*) pierna *f*; (*of animal, bird, furniture*) pata *f*; (*support*) pie *m*; (*of trousers*) pernera *f*; (*of stocking*) caña *f*; (*of pork*) pernil *m*; (*of lamb, veal, boot*) pierna *f*; **I've been on my ~s all day** he estado trajinando todo el santo día; **to be on one's last ~s** estar en las últimas; **to give sb a ~ up** ayudar a uno a subir (*also fig*); **he hasn't a ~ to stand on** no tiene razón alguna, no hay nada que hable a su favor; **to pull sb's ~*** tomar el pelo a uno*; **to shake a ~*** bailar; **to show a ~*** despertar, levantarse; **show a ~!*** ¡a levantarse!; **to stand on one's own two ~s** (*fig*) ser independiente; **to stretch one's ~s** estirar las piernas, (*after stiffness*) desentumecerse las piernas, (*fig*) dar un paseíto; **to take to one's ~s** poner pies en polvorosa, echar a correr; **to walk sb off his ~s** dejar a uno rendido tras una larguísima caminata.
(b) (*of competition*) etapa *f*, fase *f*; vuelta *f*; **first ~** primera vuelta *f*.
2 VT: **to ~ it** ir andando, ir a pie.
legacy ['legəsɪ] N legado *m*; (*fig*) herencia *f*, patrimonio *m*.
legal ['liːgəl] ADJ (a) (*lawful*) lícito, legítimo. (b) (*relating to the law*) legal; *department, entity, inquiry* jurídico; *matter* de derecho; **~ action**

demanda *f* judicial; **to take ~ action against sb** entablar una demanda judicial contra uno; **~ advice** asesoría *f* jurídica; **~ aid** asistencia *f* letrada; **~ costs** costas *fpl*; **~ holiday** (*US*) fiesta *f* oficial; **~ owner** propietario *m*, -a *f* en derecho; **~ profession** abogacía *f*; **~ tender** moneda *f* de curso legal.
legalese [,liːgə'liːz] N jerga *f* legal.
legalistic [,liːgə'lɪstɪk] ADJ legalista.
legality [lɪ'gælɪtɪ] N legalidad *f*.
legalization [,liːgəlaɪ'zeɪʃən] N legalización *f*.
legalize ['liːgəlaɪz] VT legalizar; autorizar, legitimar.
legally ['liːgəlɪ] ADV según la ley, según el derecho; legalmente; **~ enforceable** legalmente ejecutable; **to be ~ responsible for sth** tener responsabilidad legal por algo; V **binding**.
legate ['legɪt] N legado *m*.
legatee [,legə'tiː] N legatario *m*, -a *f*.
legation [lɪ'geɪʃən] N legación *f*.
legato [lɪ'gɑːtəʊ] (*Mus*) 1 ADJ ligado.
2 ADV ligado.
3 N ligadura *f*.
leg-bone ['legbəʊn] N tibia *f*.
legend ['ledʒənd] N leyenda *f*.
legendary ['ledʒəndərɪ] ADJ legendario.
legerdemain ['ledʒədə'meɪn] N juego *m* de manos, prestidigitación *f*; (*fig*) trapacería *f*.
-legged ['legɪd] ADJ de piernas ..., *eg* **long~** de piernas largas, zancudo; **three~** de tres piernas, *stool* de tres patas.
leggings ['legɪŋz] NPL polainas *fpl*; (*baby's*) pantalones *mpl* polainas.
leggo* ['le'gəʊ] EXCL = **let go**; V **go 1(u)**.
leggy ['legɪ] ADJ zanquilargo, zancudo, patilargo; *girl* de piernas largas; de piernas atractivas.
Leghorn ['leg'hɔːn] N Livorno *m*, (*Hist*) Liorna *f*.
legibility [,ledʒɪ'bɪlɪtɪ] N legibilidad *f*.
legible ['ledʒəbl] ADJ legible.
legibly ['ledʒəblɪ] ADV legiblemente.
legion ['liːdʒən] N legión *f* (*also fig*); **they are ~** son legión, son muchos.

legionary ['liːdʒənərɪ] 1 ADJ legionario.
2 N legionario *m*.
legionnaire [,liːdʒə'neər] N legionario *m*; **~'s disease** enfermedad *f* del legionario, legionella *f*.
leg-iron ['leg,aɪən] N aparato *m* ortopédico.
legislate ['ledʒɪsleɪt] 1 VT: **to ~ sth out of existence** matar algo con legislación.
2 VI legislar; **one cannot ~ for every case** es imposible legislar para todo.
legislation [,ledʒɪs'leɪʃən] N legislación *f*.
legislative ['ledʒɪslətɪv] ADJ legislativo; **~ action** tramitación *f* legislativa; **~ body** cuerpo *m* legislativo.
legislator ['ledʒɪsleɪtər] N legislador *m*, -ora *f*.
legislature ['ledʒɪslətʃər] N cuerpo *m* legislativo, asamblea *f* legislativa.
legist ['liːdʒɪst] N legista *m*.
legit* [lə'dʒɪt] ADJ = **legitimate**.
legitimacy [lɪ'dʒɪtɪməsɪ] N legitimidad *f*.
legitimate 1 [lɪ'dʒɪtɪmɪt] ADJ legítimo; (*proper*) admisible, justo; **the ~ theatre** el teatro teatro, el teatro propiamente dicho, el teatro verdadero.
2 [lɪ'dʒɪtɪmeɪt] VT legitimar.
legitimately [lɪ'dʒɪtɪmɪtlɪ] ADV legítimamente; admisiblemente, justamente.
legitimation [lɪ,dʒɪtɪ'meɪʃən] N legitimación *f*.
legitimize [lɪ'dʒɪtɪmaɪz] VT = **legitimate 2**.
legless ['leglɪs] ADJ sin piernas; sin patas; (*) borracho.
legman ['legmæn] N, PL **legmen** ['legmen] (reportero) *m*, -a *f*.
leg-pull* ['legpʊl] N broma *f*, tomadura *f* de pelo*.
leg-puller* ['legpʊlər] N bromista *mf*.
leg-pulling* ['leg,pʊlɪŋ] N tomadura *f* de pelo*.
legroom ['legrʊm] N espacio *m* para las piernas.

leg-show ['legʃəʊ] N exhibición f de piernas, varietés mpl.
legume ['legjuːm] N (species) legumbre f; (pod) vaina f.
leguminous [le'gjuːmɪnəs] ADJ leguminoso.
legwarmers ['leg,wɔːməz] NPL calientapiernas mpl, calentadores mpl de piernas.
legwork ['legwɜːk] N trabajo m callejero; **to do the ~** hacer los preparativos.
Leics. ABBR of **Leicestershire**.
leisure ['leʒəʳ] ① N ocio m, tiempo m libre; **people of ~** gente f acomodada, gente f con tiempo libre; **a life of ~** una vida regalada; **to be at ~** estar desocupado, no tener nada que hacer; **do it at your ~** hágalo en sus ratos libres, hágalo cuando tenga tiempo; **to have the ~ to do sth** disponer de bastante tiempo para hacer algo.
  ② ATTR: **~ centre** polideportivo m; **~ industry** industria f que produce lo que pide la gente para ocupar su tiempo libre; **~ occupation** pasatiempo m, modo m de ocuparse durante los ratos libres; **in one's ~ time** en sus ratos libres, en los momentos de ocio; **~ suit** conjunto m tipo chandal; **~ wear** ropa f de sport.
leisured ['leʒəd] ADJ pace pausado; class acomodado.
leisurely ['leʒəlɪ] ① ADJ pausado, lento.
  ② ADV pausadamente, despacio, con calma.
leitmotiv ['laɪtməʊ,tiːf] N leitmotiv m.
lemma ['lemə] N, PL **~s** or **lemmata** ['lemətə] lema m.
lemmatization [,lemətaɪ'zeɪʃən] N lematización f.
lemmatize ['lemətaɪz] VT lematizar.
lemmatizer ['lemətaɪzəʳ] N lematizador m.
lemming ['lemɪŋ] N lem(m)ing m.
lemon ['lemən] ① N (a) (fruit) limón m; (tree) limonero m. (b) (drink) limonada f. (c) (*) bobo m, -a f; **I felt a bit of a ~** aparecía como bastante tonto; **you ~!** ¡bobo!
  ② ATTR de limón; limonero; (colour) limonado, (de) color limón, alimonado.
  ③ ADJ = **2**.
lemonade [,lemə'neɪd] N limonada f.
lemon cheese [,lemən'tʃiːz] N, **lemon curd** [,lemən'kɜːd] N (Brit) cuajado m de limón.
lemon-grove ['leməngrəʊv] N limonar m.
lemon-juice ['leməndʒuːs] N zumo m de limón.
lemon sole [,lemən'səʊl] N (Brit) platija f.
lemon-squash ['lemən'skwɒʃ] N bebida f de limón, zumo m de limón.
lemon-squeezer ['lemən,skwiːzəʳ] N exprimelimones m, exprimidor m, prensalimones m.
lemon tea [,lemən'tiː] N té m con limón.
lemur ['liːməʳ] N lémur m.
Len [len] NM familiar form of **Leonard**.
lend [lend] (irr: PRET AND PTP **lent**) ① VT prestar; dejar; (fig) prestar, dar, añadir.
  ② VI: **to ~ at 10%** prestar dinero a 10 por ciento.
  ③ VR: **to ~ o.s. to** prestarse a; **it does not ~ itself to being filmed** no es apto para ser transformado en película.
♦**lend out** VT prestar.
lender ['lendəʳ] N prestador m, -ora f; (professional) prestamista mf.
lending ['lendɪŋ] ADJ: **~ library** biblioteca f de préstamo; **~ limit** límite m de préstamo; **~ policy** política f de préstamos; **~ rate** tipo m de interés.
length [leŋθ] N (a) (gen) largo m, longitud f; (Naut) eslora f; **along the whole ~ of the river** a lo largo de todo el río; **over the ~ and breadth of England** por toda Inglaterra, en toda la extensión de Inglaterra; **the ~ of skirts** el largo de las faldas; **the ~ of this letter** la extensión de esta carta; **to be 4 metres in ~, to have a ~ of 4 metres** tener 4 metros de largo; **what ~ is it?** ¿cuánto tiene de largo?; **what ~ do you want?** ¿cuánto quiere?; **to measure one's ~ (on the floor)** medir el suelo; **to go to any ~(s)** no pararse en barras; ser capaz de hacer cualquier cosa; **to go to any ~(s) to +** infin hacer todo lo posible para + infin; **to go to great ~s in** extremarse en; **to go to the ~ of +** ger llegar al extremo de + infin.
  (b) (Sport: in race) cuerpo m; **to win by half a ~** ganar por medio cuerpo; **to win by 4 ~s** ganar por 4 cuerpos.
  (c) (Sport: of pool) larga f; **to swim 40 ~s** nadar 40 largas.
  (d) (section: of cloth) corte m; (of road, track etc) tramo m.
  (e) (of time) espacio m, extensión f, duración f; **~ of life** duración f de la vida; **~ of service** duración f del servicio; **~ of a syllable** cantidad f de una sílaba; **for what ~ of time?** ¿durante cuánto tiempo?; **at ~** (finally) por fin, finalmente; **to speak at ~** hablar largamente; **to discuss sth at ~** discutir algo detenidamente; **to explain sth at ~** explicar algo por extenso.
lengthen ['leŋθən] ① VT alargar, prolongar, extender.
  ② VI alargarse, prolongarse, extenderse; (days) crecer.
lengthily ['leŋθɪlɪ] ADV largamente, extensamente.
length mark ['leŋθ,mɑːk] N (Phon) signo m de vocal larga.
lengthways ['leŋθweɪz], **lengthwise** ['leŋθwaɪz] ① ADJ longitudinal,

de largo.
  ② ADV longitudinalmente; a lo largo; **to measure sth ~** medir el largo de algo.
lengthy ['leŋθɪ] ADJ largo, extenso; (pej) larguísimo; illness etc de larga duración; meeting prolongado.
lenience ['liːnɪəns] N, **leniency** ['liːnɪənsɪ] N lenidad f, poca severidad f; indulgencia f.
lenient ['liːnɪənt] ADJ poco severo, más bien blando; indulgente.
leniently ['liːnɪəntlɪ] ADV con poca severidad, con indulgencia.
Leningrad ['lenɪngræd] N Leningrado m.
Leninism ['lenɪnɪzəm] N leninismo m.
Leninist ['lenɪnɪst] ① ADJ leninista.
  ② N leninista mf.
lenitive ['lenɪtɪv] ADJ lenitivo.
lens [lenz] N (Opt, Phot) lente f; (of camera) objetivo m; (hand~, for stamps etc) lupa f; (Anat) cristalino m.
lens cap ['lenzkæp] N tapa f de objetivo.
lens hood ['lenshʊd] N parasol m de objetivo.
Lent [lent] N cuaresma f.
lent [lent] PRET AND PTP of **lend**.
Lenten ['lentən] ADJ cuaresmal.
lentil ['lentl] ① N lenteja f.
  ② ATTR: **~ soup** sopa f de lentejas.
Leo ['liːəʊ] N (Zodiac) Leo m.
Leon ['liːɒn] N León m.
Leonese [liːə'niːz] ① ADJ leonés.
  ② N (a) leonés m, -esa f. (b) (Ling) leonés m.
leonine ['liːənaɪn] ADJ leonino.
leopard ['lepəd] N leopardo m; **the ~ cannot change its spots** genio y figura hasta la sepultura.
leopardess ['lepədes] N leopardo m hembra.
leopardskin ['lepədskɪn] N piel f de leopardo.
leotard ['liːətɑːd] N leotardo m.
leper ['lepəʳ] ① N leproso m, -a f (also fig).
  ② ATTR: **~ colony** leprosería f, colonia f de leprosos.
lepidoptera [,lepɪ'dɒptərə] NPL lepidópteros mpl.
lepidopterist [,lepɪ'dɒptərɪst] N lepidopterólogo m, -a f.
leprechaun ['leprəkɔːn] N (Ir) duende m.
leprosy ['leprəsɪ] N lepra f.
leprous ['leprəs] ADJ leproso.
lesbian ['lezbɪən] ① ADJ lesbio.
  ② N lesbiana f.
lesbianism ['lezbɪənɪzəm] N lesbianismo m.
lèse-majesté, lese-majesty [leɪz'mæʒəstɪ] N lesa majestad f.
lesion ['liːʒən] N lesión f.
Lesotho [lɪ'suːtuː] N Lesoto m.
▼**less** [les] ① ADJ (a) (in size, degree etc) menor, inferior; **a sum ~ than £1** una cantidad inferior a 1 libra; **A or B, whichever is the ~** la menor de las dos cantidades A o B; **it's nothing ~ than a disaster** es nada menos que un desastre; **it's nothing ~ than disgraceful** es francamente vergonzoso; **St James the L~** Santiago el Menor; **no ~ a person than the bishop** no otro que el obispo, el obispo y no otro, el mismísimo obispo; **that was told me by the minister no ~** eso me lo dijo el mismo ministro.
  (b) (in quantity) menos; **now we eat ~ bread** ahora comemos menos pan; **of ~ importance** de menos importancia; **~ noise please!** ¡menos ruido por favor!; **~ of it!** ¡basta ya!; **to grow ~** menguar, decrecer, disminuir.
▼② ADV menos; **~ and ~** cada vez menos; **~ than 6** menos de 6; **in ~ than an hour** en menos de una hora; **he works ~ than I (do)** él trabaja menos que yo; **it's ~ than you think** es menos de lo que piensas; **he is ~ well known** es menos conocido; **the ~ he works the ~ he earns** cuando menos trabaja menos gana; **even ~** menos aun; **still ~** menos todavía; **none the ~** sin embargo, a pesar de todo, con todo; **there will be so much the ~ to pay** tanto menos habrá que pagar; **can't you let me have it for ~?** ¿no me lo puedes dejar en menos?; **the problem is ~ one of capital than of personnel** el problema más que de capitales es de personal.
  ③ PREP menos; **the price ~ 10%** el precio menos 10 por ciento; **the price ~ VAT** el precio excluyendo el IVA; **a year ~ 4 days** un año menos 4 días.
-less [lɪs] SUFFIX sin, eg hat~ sin sombrero, sun~ sin sol.
lessee [le'siː] N arrendatario m, -a f, inquilino m, -a f.
lessen ['lesn] ① VT disminuir, reducir, aminorar; cost, stature etc rebajar.
  ② VT disminuir(se), reducirse, menguar.
lessening ['lesnɪŋ] N disminución f, reducción f.
lesser ['lesəʳ] ADJ comp of **less**; menor, más pequeño; inferior; **to a ~ extent** en menor grado; V evil.
lesson ['lesn] N lección f; clase f; **~s** clases fpl; **a French ~** una clase de francés; **to give a ~** dar clase; **to have a ~** tomar lección; **to learn one's ~** (fig) escarmentar; **let that be a ~ to you!** ¡que te sirva

de lección!, ¡para que aprendas!; **to teach sb a ~** (*fig*) hacer que uno vaya aprendiendo.

lessor [le'sɔːʳ] N arrendador *m*, -ora *f*.

| LESS THAN, FEWER THAN | | see also main entries |

"Menos ... que" or "menos ... de"?

- Use *menos* with *que* before nouns and pronouns (provided they are not followed by clauses) as well as before adverbs and prepositions:

  He has less money than his sister
  Tiene menos dinero que su hermana
  He sells less/fewer than I do *or* than me
  Vende menos que yo
  These days I'm much less shy than before
  Hoy en día soy mucho menos tímida que antes

- Use *menos ... de lo que/del que/de la que/de los que/de las que* with following clauses:

  He earns less than I thought
  Gana menos de lo que yo creía
  They have 16 seats - five fewer than they had before these elections
  Tienen 16 escaños - cinco menos de los que tenían antes de estas elecciones
  It provides the body with fewer calories than it needs
  Proporciona al organismo menos calorías de las que necesita

- Use *menos* with *de* before *lo* + ADJECTIVE/PAST PARTICIPLE:
  The price of wheat went up less than expected
  El precio del trigo subió menos de lo previsto

- Use *menos* with *de* in comparisons involving numbers or quantity:
  ...in less than 8 seconds...
  ...en menos de 8 segundos...
  You won't get it for less than a million pesetas
  No lo conseguirás por menos de un millón de pesetas

! But use *que* instead in emphatic expressions like *nada menos que* and *ni más ni menos que* even when followed by numbers:
  They offered him no less than 30 million pesetas a year!
  ¡Le ofrecieron nada menos que or ni más ni menos que 30 millones de pesetas al año!

A lot less, far fewer

- When translating *a lot less, far fewer* etc remember to make the *mucho* in *mucho menos* agree with any noun it describes or refers to:

  These bulbs use much less electricity than conventional ones
  Estas bombillas gastan mucha menos electricidad que las normales
  They have had far fewer opportunities than wealthy people
  Han gozado de muchas menos oportunidades que la gente rica
  For further uses and examples, see main entries at *fewer* and *less*.

---

lest [lest] CONJ para que no + *subj*, de miedo que + *subj*; **~ we forget** para que no olvidemos; **~ he catch me unprepared** para que no me coja (*LAm*: agarre) desprevenido; **I feared ~ he should fall** temía que fuera a caer; **I didn't do it ~ sb should object** no lo hice por miedo de que alguien pusiera peros.

let¹ [let] N (a) (*Tennis*) dejada *f*, let *m*. (b) (*Jur*) **without ~ or hindrance** sin estorbo ni obstáculo.

▼**let²** [let] (*irr*: PRET AND PTP **let**) ① VT (a) (*allow*) dejar, permitir; **to ~ sb do sth** dejar a uno hacer algo, permitir a uno hacer algo, permitir que uno haga algo; **~ me help you** déjeme ayudarle.
(b) *blood* (*surgically*) sacar.
(c) (*hire out*) alquilar; **'to ~'** 'se alquila'; **we can't find a house to ~** no encontramos una casa que alquilar.
(d) (*v aux, gen translated by subj*) **~ us pray** oremos; **~'s go!** ¡vamos!; **~'s get out here** (*bus, train*) bajémonos aquí; **~ there be light** haya luz; **~ there be no mistake about it** entiéndase bien que ...; **~ them all come!** ¡que vengan todos!; **~ their need be never so great** por muy grande que sea su necesidad; **~ X be 6** supongamos que X equivale a 6.
② VI (*be hired*) alquilarse (*at, for* en).
③ VR: **to ~ o.s. be seen** dejarse ver.
◆**let away** VT: **to ~ sb away with sth** dejar a uno salirse con la suya.
◆**let by** VT dejar pasar.
◆**let down** ① VT (a) (*lower*) *window etc* bajar; (*on rope*) bajar (*to* a); *hair* soltar, dejar suelto; *dress* alargar; **to ~ sb down on a rope** descolgar a uno con una cuerda.
(b) (*disappoint, defraud*) **to ~ sb down** faltar a uno; desilusionar a uno; defraudar la confianza (*or* las esperanzas *etc*) de uno; dejar a uno plantado; **it has never ~ us down yet** no nos ha fallado nunca; **the weather ~ us down** el tiempo nos defraudó; **we all felt ~ down** todos nos sentimos defraudados; **I was badly ~ down** me llevé un gran chasco.

(c) **to ~ sb down gently** ser indulgente con uno, castigar a uno con poca severidad.
(d) *tyre* desinflar, deshinchar.
② VR: **to ~ o.s. down** no estar a la altura de su fama.
◆**let in** ① VT (a) (*allow to enter*) dejar entrar; *visitor* hacer pasar; **shoes that ~ in water** zapatos que dejan entrar el agua.
(b) (*commit*) **I got ~ in for £50** tuve que pagar (*or* contribuir *etc*) 50 libras; **it ~ us in for a lot of trouble** nos causó muchas molestias, nos planteó muchos problemas.
(c) **to ~ sb in on a secret** revelar un secreto a uno; **to ~ sb in on a deal** dejar que uno participe en un trato.
② VR: **you don't know what you're ~ting yourself in for** no sabes lo que te pescas.
◆**let into** VT (a) **to ~ sb into a house** dejar a uno entrar en una casa.
(b) **a plaque ~ into a wall** una lápida empotrada en una pared.
◆**let off** VT (a) (*fire*) *arrow, gun* disparar; *firework* hacer estallar; *steam* dejar escapar.
(b) (*pardon*) perdonar, dejar libre, absolver; **to ~ sb off a duty** perdonar una obligación a uno; **they ~ him off with a warning** le dejaron salir con una amonestación; **he was ~ off with a fine** escapó con una multa.
(c) (*allow to leave*) dejar salir.
(d) (*hire*) alquilar.
◆**let on*** VI revelar el secreto, cantar*; **to ~ on about sth to sb** revelar algo a uno; **he's not ~ting on** no dice nada; **don't go and ~ on about this** de esto no digas ni pío; **he ~ on that ...** reveló que ...
◆**let out** VT (a) (*allow out*) *person* dejar salir; *prisoner* poner en libertad; *cattle etc* soltar, echar al pasto; **I'll ~ you out** te acompaño a la puerta; **the watchman ~ me out** el sereno me abrió la puerta; **the dog is ~ out at 8** se le deja salir al perro a las 8.
(b) *secret* revelar, decir.
(c) *fire* dejar que se apague.
(d) *dress* ensanchar; *belt* desabrochar.
(e) (*hire*) alquilar.
(f) (*exonerate*) **that ~s me out** eso me deja libre; **that fact ~s him out** ese hecho le disculpa.
(g) (*utter*) yell dar.
◆**let past** VT = **let by**.
◆**let through** VT = **let by**.
◆**let up** VI (a) (*cease*) terminar, cesar; **when the rain ~s up** cuando deje de llover tanto.
(b) (*cease to press*) dejar de presionar, moderarse (*on* en el uso de, en el consumo de); trabajar (*etc*) con menos intensidad; **to ~ up on sb** tratar a uno con menos rigor.

letch* [letʃ] = **lech**.

let-down ['letdaʊn] N decepción *f*, chasco *m*, desilusión *f*.

lethal ['liːθəl] ADJ (a) mortífero; *wound etc, dose* mortal, letal; *weapon* mortífero. (b) (*) fatal, atroz.

lethargic [le'θɑːdʒɪk] ADJ aletargado, letárgico.

lethargy ['leθədʒɪ] N letargo *m*.

Lethe ['liːθiː] N Lete(o) *m*.

let-out ['letaʊt] N (*Brit*) escapatoria *f*; **~ clause** cláusula *f* que incluye una escapatoria.

Lett [let] = **Latvian**.

▼**letter** ['letəʳ] ① N (a) (*of alphabet*) letra *f*; **the ~ of the law** la ley escrita; **to the ~** a la letra, al pie de la letra.
▼(b) (*missive*) carta *f*; **~ of acknowledgement** carta *f* de acuse de recibo; **~ of advice** carta *f* de aviso; **~ of allotment** carta *f* de asignación; **~ of application** carta *f* de solicitud; **~ of appointment** carta *f* de confirmación de un puesto de trabajo; **~ of attorney** poder *m*; **~s of credence** cartas *fpl* credenciales; **~ of credit** carta *f* de crédito; **documentary ~ of credit** carta *f* de crédito documentaria; **irrevocable ~ of credit** carta *f* de crédito irrevocable; **~ of intent** carta *f* de intenciones; **~ of introduction** carta *f* de recomendación (*to* para); **~ of lien** carta *f* de gravamen; **~ of reference** carta *f* de recomendación; **~s of Galdós** (*as published*) epistolario *m* de Galdós; **~s patent** patente *m* de privilegio, letra *f* de patente; **by ~** por carta, por escrito.
(c) **~s** (*learning*) letras *fpl*; **man of ~s** hombre *m* de letras, literato *m*.
② ATTR: **~ quality printer** impresora *f* calidad carta.
③ VT rotular, inscribir, estampar con letras.

letter-bomb ['letəbɒm] N carta-bomba *f*.

letterbox ['letəbɒks] N (*esp Brit*) buzón *m*.

letter-card ['letəkɑːd] N (*Brit*) carta-tarjeta *f*.

lettered ['letəd] ADJ *person* culto; *object* rotulado, marcado con letras; **~ in gold** marcado con letras doradas.

letterfile ['letəfaɪl] N carpeta *f*, guardacartas *m*.

letterhead ['letəhed] N membrete *m*, encabezamiento *m*.

lettering ['letərɪŋ] N letras *fpl*, inscripción *f*, rótulo *m*.

letter-opener ['letər‚əʊpnəʳ] N abrecartas *m*.

letterpress ['letəpres] N (*Typ*) texto *m* impreso, impresión *f* tipográfica; (*method*) prensa *f* de copiar.

► LANGUAGE IN USE: **let²: 1a** → 3, 9.1, 9.3 **letter: 1b** → 20.2, 21.1

letter-writer [ˈletəˌraɪtəʳ] N escritor m, -ora f de cartas (or de la carta etc); **I'm not much of a ~** yo apenas escribo cartas.
letting [ˈletɪŋ] N arrendamiento m.
lettuce [ˈletɪs] N lechuga f.
let-up* [ˈletʌp] N (break) calma f, respiro m, tregua f, descanso m; (reduction) reducción f, disminución f (in de); **we worked 5 hours without a ~** trabajamos 5 horas sin interrupción; **there was no ~** no hubo ningún intervalo de calma; **if there is a ~ in the rain** si deja un momento de llover.
leucocyte [ˈluːkəˌsaɪt] N leucocito m.
leukaemia, (esp US) **leukemia** [luːˈkiːmɪə] N leucemia f.
Levant [lɪˈvænt] N Oriente m Medio.
Levantine [ˈlevəntaɪn] ① ADJ levantino.
  ② N levantino m, -a f.
levee[1] [ˈlevɪ] N (reception) besamanos m, recepción f.
levee[2] [ˈlevɪ] N (bank) ribero m, dique m.
level [ˈlevl] ① ADJ llano, plano, raso; a nivel, nivelado; igual, uniforme; spoonful rasado; gaze, tone ecuánime; judgement, mind juicioso; **to be ~ with** estar a nivel con; **to be ~ with the ground** estar a ras de tierra; **to be ~ with the water** estar a flor del agua; **I'll do my ~ best** haré todo lo que pueda.
  ② ADV (with ground; horizontally) a nivel; ras con ras; **to draw ~ with sb** llegar a la altura de uno, alcanzar a uno, (in league etc) llegar a empatar con uno, colocarse en igual posición que uno.
  ③ N (a) (instrument) nivel m.
  (b) (altitude, degree) nivel m; **at eye ~** a la altura del ojo; **at roof ~** a la altura de los tejados; **speed on the ~** velocidad f sobre superficie llana; **on the international ~** a nivel internacional; **it's on the ~*** es un negocio serio; es un negocio limpio; **is he on the ~?*** ¿es de fiar?, ¿es una persona honrada?; **are you telling me this on the ~?*** ¿me lo dices en serio?; **to be on a ~ with** estar al nivel de; **to be on a ~ with the ground** estar a ras de la tierra; **to be on a ~ with** (fig) estar al nivel de; ser parangonable con; **that trick is on a ~ with the other** esa jugada es tan vil como la otra; **to come down to sb's ~** bajar al nivel en que está uno.
  (c) (flat place) llano m.
  ④ VT (a) ground etc nivelar, allanar; building derribar; site desmontar, despejar; quantities igualar, nivelar; **to ~ sth to (or with) the ground** arrasar algo.
  (b) blow asestar (at a); weapon apuntar (at a); accusation dirigir (against, at a), hacer (against, at contra).
  ⑤ VI (US*): **I'll ~ with you** te lo voy a decir con franqueza; **you didn't ~ with me** no has sido franco conmigo.
◆**level down** VT nivelar por abajo, rebajar al mismo nivel.
◆**level off, level out** VI nivelarse; (of prices etc) estabilizarse; (Aer) enderezarse.
◆**level up** VT elevar al mismo nivel.
level-crossing [ˈlevlˈkrɒsɪŋ] N (Brit) paso m a nivel.
leveler [ˈlevələʳ] N (US) = **leveller**.
level-headed [ˈlevlˈhedɪd] ADJ juicioso, sensato.

leveller, (US) **leveler** [ˈlevələʳ] N persona en pro de la igualdad de derechos.
levelling, (US) **leveling** [ˈlevlɪŋ] ① N nivelación f; aplanamiento m.
  ② ADJ: **~ process** proceso m de nivelación.
levelling-off [ˌlevəlɪŋˈɒf] N nivelación f.
levelly [ˈlevlɪ] ADV gaze etc con compostura, con ecuanimidad, sin emocionarse.
level-peg [ˌlevlˈpeg] VI: **they were ~ging** iban empatados.
level-pegging [ˌlevlˈpegɪŋ] N igualdad f, situación f de empate; **it's ~ now** van muy iguales, están empatados.
lever [ˈliːvəʳ] ① N palanca f (also fig).
  ② VT apalancar.
◆**lever up** VT: **to ~ sth up** alzar algo con palanca.
leverage [ˈliːvərɪdʒ] ① N apalancamiento m; (fig) influencia f; fuerza f; ventaja f.
  ② as VT: **~d buy-out** compra de todas las acciones de una compañía pagándolas con dinero prestado a cambio de asegurar que las acciones serán compradas.
leveret [ˈlevərɪt] N lebrato m.
leviathan [lɪˈvaɪəθən] N leviatán m; (fig) buque m (etc) enorme.
Levi's [ˈliːvaɪz] ® NPL vaqueros mpl, levis mpl.
levitate [ˈlevɪteɪt] ① VT elevar por levitación.
  ② VI elevarse por levitación.
levitation [ˌlevɪˈteɪʃən] N levitación f.
Levite [ˈliːvaɪt] N levita m.
Leviticus [lɪˈvɪtɪkəs] N Levítico m.
levity [ˈlevɪtɪ] N frivolidad f, ligereza f, informalidad f; (mirth) risas fpl.
levy [ˈlevɪ] ① N (a) (act) exacción f (de tributos); (tax) impuesto m; (surcharge) sobrecarga f, sobretasa f. (b) (Mil) leva f.
  ② VT (a) tax exigir (on a), recaudar; fine imponer (on a). (b) (Mil) reclutar.
lewd [luːd] ADJ impúdico, obsceno; song, story etc verde, colorado (LAm).
lewdly [ˈluːdlɪ] ADV impúdicamente, obscenamente.
lewdness [ˈluːdnɪs] N impudicia f, obscenidad f; lo verde.
lexeme [ˈleksiːm] N lexema m.
lexical [ˈleksɪkəl] ADJ léxico.
lexicalize [ˈleksɪkəlaɪz] VT lexicalizar.
lexicographer [ˌleksɪˈkɒgrəfəʳ] N lexicógrafo m, -a f.
lexicographical [ˌleksɪkəʊˈgræfɪkəl] ADJ lexicográfico.
lexicography [ˌleksɪˈkɒgrəfɪ] N lexicografía f.
lexicologist [ˌleksɪˈkɒlədʒɪst] N lexicólogo m, -a f.
lexicology [ˌleksɪˈkɒlədʒɪ] N lexicología f.
lexicon [ˈleksɪkən] N léxico m.
lexis [ˈleksɪs] N vocabulario m.
Leyden [ˈlaɪdn] ① N Leiden.
  ② ATTR: **~ jar** botella f de Leiden.
LGV N ABBR of **Large Goods Vehicle** vehículo pesado.
l.h. ABBR of **left hand** izquierda f, izq.
LI (US Post) ABBR of **Long Island.**

┌ LET ┐   ┌ see also main entry ┐

Meaning "allow"

• Translate using either *dejar*, especially in informal contexts, or *permitir*, especially in more formal contexts. Both verbs can be followed either by an infinitive or by *que* + SUBJUNCTIVE:

  Let me do it
  Déjame hacerlo ◊ Déjame que lo haga
  Let her have a look
  Deja que ella lo vea ◊ Déjale verlo
  We must not let the children see this
  No debemos permitir que los niños vean esto or permitir a los niños ver esto

Imperative

First person plural

• Translate *let's* and *let us* + VERB using either *vamos a* + INFINITIVE or using the present subjunctive of the main verb. The second construction is used particularly in formal language and when translating *let's not*:

  Let's go for a walk!
  Vamos a dar un paseo
  Let's consider the implications of the Government's decision
  Consideremos las implicaciones de la decisión del Gobierno
  Let's not waste any more time
  No perdamos más tiempo

  NOTE: To translate *let's go*, use *vamos* or *vámonos* on its own without a following infinitive:

  Let's go to the theatre
  ¡Vamos al teatro!

• When *let's* is used on its own to reply to a suggestion, translate using *vamos* or *vámonos* if the verb in the suggestion was *ir*. Use *vale* or *venga* if not:
  "Shall we go?" - "Yes, let's"
  "¿Nos vamos?" - "¡Sí, vamos!" or "¡Sí, vámonos!"
  "Shall we watch the match?" - "Yes, let's"
  "¿Vemos el partido?" - "Sí, vale" or "Sí, venga"

Third person

• When *let* introduces a command, suggestion or wish in the third person, translate using *que* + SUBJUNCTIVE:
  Let him come up!
  ¡Que suba!
  Let there be no misunderstanding about this
  ¡Que no haya ningún malentendido sobre esto!
  Let them do as they like
  ¡Que hagan lo que quieran!

• Be careful to distinguish between the "permission" sense of *let sb do something* and the "command" sense:
  Please let them stay here (i.e. Please allow them to stay)
  Déjalos que se queden aquí or Déjalos quedarse aquí, por favor
  Let them stay here! (i.e. expressing a decision or an order)
  ¡Que se queden aquí!

  NOTE: When *que* is used in this sense, it never takes an accent.
  For further uses and examples, see main entry.

liability [ˌlaɪəˈbɪlɪtɪ] N (a) (*responsibility*) responsabilidad *f*; riesgo *m*; (*burden*) carga *f* onerosa, lastre *m*; desventaja *f*; ~ **insurance** seguro *m* contra responsabilidades, seguro *m* contra terceros; **one's ~ for tax** la cantidad que uno puede ser llamado a pagar en impuestos; **he's a real ~** es un estorbo, es un cero a la izquierda.
(b) **liabilities** obligaciones *fpl*, compromisos *mpl*; (*Comm*) pasivo *m*, deudas *fpl*; **to meet one's liabilities** satisfacer sus deudas.

liable [ˈlaɪəbl] ADJ (a) (*subject*) **to be ~** ser el responsable; **to be ~ for** ser responsable de, responder de; **to be ~ for taxes** (*thing*) estar sujeto a impuestos, (*person*) tener que pagar impuestos; **the plan is ~ to changes** el plan bien puede sufrir cambios. (b) (*likely*) **to be ~ to + infin** tener tendencia a + infin, ser propenso a + infin; estar predispuesto a + infin; **he is ~ not to come** es capaz de no venir, tiene tendencia a no venir; es fácil que no venga; **the pond is ~ to freeze** el estanque tiene tendencia a helarse, el estanque bien puede helarse; **we are ~ to get shot at here** aquí corremos el riesgo de que disparen sobre nosotros, aquí estamos expuestos a los tiros.

liaise [lɪˈeɪz] VI: **to ~ with** (*Brit*) enlazar con.

liaison [liˈeɪzɒn] **1** N (a) (*coordination*) enlace *m*, conexión *f*, coordinación *f*; (*Mil*) enlace *m*. (b) (*affair*) lío *m*, relaciones *fpl* (amorosas).
2 ATTR: ~ **committee** comité *m* coordinador; ~ **officer** oficial *m* de enlace.

liana [lɪˈɑːnə] N bejuco *m*, liana *f*.

liar [ˈlaɪəʳ] N mentiroso *m*, -a *f*, embustero *m*, -a *f*; ~**!** ¡mentira!

Lib. [lɪb] (*Pol*) (a) N ABBR of **Liberal** liberal *mf*; *also* ADJ. (b) N ABBR of **Liberation: Women's Lib.** = **Women's Liberation Movement** Movimiento *m* de Liberación de la Mujer.

libation [laɪˈbeɪʃən] N libación *f*.

libber* [ˈlɪbəʳ] N liberacionista *f*, feminista *f*.

libel [ˈlaɪbəl] **1** N difamación *f*, calumnia *f* (*on* de); (*written*) libelo *m*; **it's a ~!** (*hum*) ¡es mentira!; **it's a ~ on all of us!** ¡esto nos calumnia a todos!
2 ATTR: ~ **laws** leyes *fpl* contra la difamación; ~ **suit** pleito *m* por difamación.
3 VT difamar, calumniar.

libellous, (*US*) **libelous** [ˈlaɪbələs] ADJ difamatorio, calumnioso.

liberal [ˈlɪbərəl] **1** ADJ liberal (*also Pol*); *offer etc* generoso; *supply* abundante; (*in views*) tolerante; ~ **arts** artes *fpl* liberales; **L~ Democratic Party, L~ Democrats** (*Brit Pol*) partido *m* democrático liberal.
2 N liberal *mf*.

liberalism [ˈlɪbərəlɪzəm] N liberalismo *m*.

liberality [ˌlɪbəˈrælɪtɪ] N generosidad *f*, liberalidad *f*.

liberalization [ˌlɪbərəlaɪˈzeɪʃən] N liberalización *f*.

liberalize [ˈlɪbərəlaɪz] VT liberalizar.

liberally [ˈlɪbərəlɪ] ADV liberalmente; generosamente; abundantemente; con tolerancia.

liberal-minded [ˈlɪbərəlˈmaɪndɪd] ADJ tolerante, de amplias miras.

liberal-mindedness [ˈlɪbərəlˈmaɪndɪdnɪs] N tolerancia *f*, amplitud *f* de miras.

liberate [ˈlɪbəreɪt] VT (*free*) libertar, librar (*from* de); *prisoner* poner en libertad; *gas etc* dejar escapar.

liberated [ˈlɪbəreɪtɪd] ADJ liberado.

liberation [ˌlɪbəˈreɪʃən] N liberación *f*; ~ **theology** teología *f* de la liberación; *see also* **Lib.**

liberator [ˈlɪbəreɪtəʳ] N libertador *m*, -ora *f*.

Liberia [laɪˈbɪərɪə] N Liberia *f*.

Liberian [laɪˈbɪərɪən] **1** ADJ liberiano.
2 N liberiano *m*, -a *f*.

libertarian [ˌlɪbəˈtɛərɪən] **1** ADJ libertario.
2 N libertario *m*, -a *f*.

libertarianism [ˌlɪbəˈtɛərɪənɪzəm] N (*philosophy*) libertarismo *m*, doctrina *f* libertaria; (*personal philosophy*) ideas *fpl* libertarias.

libertinage [ˈlɪbətɪnɪdʒ] N libertinaje *m*.

libertine [ˈlɪbətiːn] N libertino *m*.

liberty [ˈlɪbətɪ] **1** N libertad *f*; ~ **of conscience** libertad *f* de conciencia; ~ **of the press** libertad *f* de prensa; **it's a (dead) ~!*** ¡no hay derecho!; **taking the car without permission was a bit of a ~** tomarse el coche sin permiso era un poco fuerte; **to be at ~** estar en libertad, (*at leisure*) estar desocupado; **to be at ~ to + infin** tener permiso para + infin, tener el derecho de + infin, estar autorizado para + infin; **is he at ~ to come?** ¿está libre para venir?; **when you are at ~ to study it** cuando tengas tiempo para estudiarlo; **to restore sb to ~** devolver la libertad a uno; **to set sb at ~** poner a uno en libertad; **I have taken the ~ of giving your name** me he tomado la libertad de darles su nombre; **to take liberties with a text** tomarse libertades con un texto; **to take liberties with sb** tratar a uno con demasiada familiaridad, (*sexually*) propasarse con una.
2 ATTR: **it's ~ hall here** aquí hay un régimen de libertad total.

libidinous [lɪˈbɪdɪnəs] ADJ libidinoso.

libido [lɪˈbiːdəʊ] N libido *f*.

Libor N ABBR of **London inter-bank offered rate**.

Libra [ˈliːbrə] N (*Zodiac*) Libra *f*.

librarian [laɪˈbrɛərɪən] N bibliotecario *m*, -a *f*.

librarianship [laɪˈbrɛərɪənʃɪp] N (a) (*post*) puesto *m* de bibliotecario. (b) (*esp Brit: science*) biblioteconomía *f*, bibliotecnia *f*, bibliotecología *f*.

library [ˈlaɪbrərɪ] **1** N biblioteca *f*; (*esp private*) librería *f*; (*Comput*) biblioteca *f*.
2 ATTR: ~ **book** libro *m* de biblioteca; ~ **card**, ~ **ticket** carnet *m* (de biblioteca); ~ **pictures** (*TV*) imágenes *fpl* de archivo; ~ **science** = **librarianship** (b); ~ **software** programa *m* de biblioteca.

> ┌─────────────────────────┐
> │ **LIBRARY OF CONGRESS** │
> └─────────────────────────┘
>
> *ⓘ La Biblioteca del Congreso es la biblioteca nacional de EE.UU. y tiene su sede en Washington D.C. Se fundó en 1800 como fuente de referencia para los miembros del Congreso y actualmente registra también los derechos de autor de todos los libros publicados en Estados Unidos, por lo que recibe dos ejemplares de cada publicación. Posee un fondo inmenso de libros y manuscritos históricos, así como partituras, mapas, películas, grabaciones sonoras y microfilmes.*

librettist [lɪˈbretɪst] N libretista *mf*.

libretto [lɪˈbretəʊ] N libreto *m*.

Libya [ˈlɪbɪə] N Libia *f*.

Libyan [ˈlɪbɪən] **1** ADJ libio.
2 N libio *m*, -a *f*.

lice [laɪs] NPL of **louse**.

licence, (*US*) **license¹** [ˈlaɪsəns] N (a) (*permit*) licencia *f*, permiso *m*; autorización *f*; (*Aut etc*) carnet *m*, permiso *m*; **to manufacture sth under ~** fabricar algo bajo licencia.
(b) (*excess*) libertinaje *m*, desenfreno *m*; (*freedom*) libertad *f*; **you can allow some ~ in translation** puedes permitirte cierta libertad al traducirlo.

licence number [ˈlaɪsəns,nʌmbəʳ] N (*Aut*) número *m* de matrícula.

license² [ˈlaɪsəns] **1** VT licenciar, autorizar, dar permiso a; *car* sacar la patente (*LAm*: la matrícula) de; **to be ~d to + infin** tener permiso para + infin, estar autorizado para + infin.
2 N (*US*) = **licence**.

licensed [ˈlaɪsənsd] ADJ *car* con matrícula; *dog, gun* con licencia, que tiene licencia; *dealer, restaurant* autorizado; ~ **premises** (*Brit*) establecimiento *m* autorizado para la venta de bebidas alcohólicas; ~ **trade** comercio *m* autorizado, negocio *m* autorizado; ~ **victualler** vendedor *m*, -ora *f* de bebidas alcohólicas.

licensee [ˌlaɪsənˈsiː] N concesionario *m*, -a *f*, licenciatario *m*, -a *f*; (*Brit: of bar*) patrón *m*, -ona *f*.

license plate [ˈlaɪsəns,pleɪt] N (*US Aut*) placa *f* de matrícula, patente *f* (*SC*).

licensing [ˈlaɪsənsɪŋ] **1** N licenciación *f*; autorización *f*; (*Aut*) matrícula *f*.
2 ATTR: ~ **hours** horas *fpl* durante las cuales se permite la venta y consumo de alcohol (*en un bar etc*); ~ **laws** (*Brit*) leyes *fpl* reguladoras de la venta y consumo de alcohol.

licentiate [laɪˈsenʃɪt] N (*person*) licenciado *m*, -a *f*; (*title*) licencia *f*, licenciatura *f*.

licentious [laɪˈsenʃəs] ADJ licencioso.

lichee [ˌlaɪˈtʃiː] = **lychee**.

lichen [ˈlaɪkən] N liquen *m*.

lichgate [ˈlɪtʃɡeɪt] N entrada *f* de cementerio.

licit [ˈlɪsɪt] ADJ lícito.

lick [lɪk] **1** N (a) lamedura *f*, lengüetada *f*; **a ~ of paint** una mano de pintura; **a ~ of polish** un poquito de cera. (b) (*) **to go at a good ~** ir a buen tren, correr rápidamente.
2 VT (a) (*with tongue, of flames*) lamer; (*of waves*) besar. (b) (*: *tan, defeat*) dar una paliza a.
♦**lick off** VT quitar de un lametazo.
♦**lick up** VT beber a lengüetadas.

licking [ˈlɪkɪŋ] N (a) lamedura *f*. (b) (*) paliza *f*; **to give sb a ~** dar una paliza a uno.

lickspittle* [ˈlɪkspɪtl] N cobista* *mf*, pelotillero* *m*, -a *f*.

licorice [ˈlɪkərɪs] N (*US*) regaliz *m*, orozuz *m*.

lid [lɪd] N (a) (*of box, case, pot etc*) tapa *f*; (*of pan etc*) cobertera *f*; (*: *hat*) techo* *m*; **he's flipped his ~‡** ha perdido la chaveta*; **that puts the ~ on it** se acabó, eso es el fin; **to take the ~ off a scandal** tirar de la manta para revelar un escándalo. (b) (*Anat*) párpado *m*.

lidded [ˈlɪdɪd] ADJ (a) *pot etc* con tapa, con cobertera. (b) **heavily ~ eyes** ojos *mpl* con párpados gruesos.

lido [ˈliːdəʊ] N (*bathing*) establecimiento *m* de baños; (*Brit: swimming*) centro *m* de natación, piscina *f*, alberca *f* (*LAm*); (*boating*) centro *m* de balandrismo.

lie¹ [laɪ] **1** N mentira *f*; **it's a ~!** ¡es mentira!; **to give the ~ to** *person* dar el mentís a, *report* desmentir; **to tell a ~** mentir.
2 VT: **to ~ one's way out of it** salir del apuro mintiendo.
3 VI mentir.

lie² [laɪ] (irr: PRET **lay**, PTP **lain**) 1 VI **(a)** (person etc: act) echarse, acostarse, tenderse; (state) estar echado, estar tumbado, estar acostado, estar tendido; (in grave) yacer, estar enterrado; **here ~s aquí** aquí yace; **he lay where he had fallen** quedaba donde había caído; **to let things ~** dejar estar las cosas como están; **don't ~ on the grass** no te eches sobre el césped; **to ~ asleep** estar dormido; **to ~ dead** yacer muerto; **to ~ in bed** estar en la cama, (lazily) seguir en la cama; **to ~ helpless** estar tumbado sin poder ayudarse; **to ~ resting** estar descansando; **to ~ still** quedarse inmóvil.

(b) (objects etc) estar; (be situated) estar, estar situado, encontrarse; (stretch) extenderse; **Slobodia ~s in third place** Eslobodia está en tercer lugar, Eslobodia ocupa la tercera posición; **the book lay on the table** el libro estaba en la mesa; **the book lay unopened** el libro quedaba sin abrir; **the snow lay half a metre deep** había medio metro de nieve; **the snow did not ~** la nieve se derritió; **the money is lying in the bank** el dinero sigue en el banco; **it ~s further on** cae más adelante; **our road lay along the river** nuestro camino seguía a lo largo del río; **the road ~s over the hills** el camino cruza las colinas; **the factory lay idle** la fábrica estaba parada; **obstacles ~ in the way** hay obstáculos por delante; **the plain lay before us** la llanura se extendía delante de nosotros; **how does the land ~?** ¿cuál es el estado actual de las cosas?; **where does the difficulty ~?** ¿en qué consiste la dificultad?; **the fault ~s with you** la falta es tuya, tú eres el culpable; **it ~s with you to reform it** te corresponde a ti reformarlo; **it does not ~ with me** no depende de mí, no me toca a mí.

(c) (evidence etc) ser admisible.

2 N (of ball etc) posición f; **~ of the land** configuración f del terreno, (fig) estado m actual de las cosas.

◆ **lie about, lie around** VI (objects) estar esparcidos; estar en desorden; (person) pasar el tiempo sin hacer nada; **we lay about on our beds** quedamos tumbados en las camas; **it must be lying about somewhere** estará por aquí, debe de andar por aquí.

◆ **lie back** VI recostarse (against, on sobre); **~ back and think of England!** ¡tranquilízate y piensa en la patria!

◆ **lie behind** VT (fig) subyacer a; estar detrás de; ser la razón fundamental de; **what ~s behind his attitude?** ¿cuál es la verdadera razón de su actitud?

◆ **lie down** VI **(a)** (act) echarse, acostarse; tumbarse; (state) estar echado, estar tumbado; estar tendido; **~ down!** (to dog) ¡échate!; **to ~ down on the job** gandulear.

(b) (fig) **to ~ down under it, to take it lying down** aceptarlo sin protestar, soportarlo sin chistar, tragarlo; **he's not one to take things lying down** no es de los que aceptan mansamente las injusticias.

◆ **lie in** VI seguir en la cama, no levantarse.

◆ **lie over** VI quedar aplazado, quedar en suspenso.

◆ **lie to** VI (Naut: act) ponerse a la capa, (state) estar a la capa.

◆ **lie up** VI (hide) esconderse; (rest) descansar; (Naut) estar amarrado.

lie-abed ['laɪəbed] N dormilón m, -ona f.

Liechtenstein ['lɪktənstaɪn] N Liechtenstein m.

lied [liːd], PL **lieder** ['liːdəʳ] N lied m.

lie-detector ['laɪdɪˌtektəʳ] 1 N detector m de mentiras.

2 ATTR: **~ test** prueba f con el detector de mentiras.

lie-down* [ˌlaɪ'daʊn] N (Brit) breve descanso m, siestecita f.

lief [liːf] ADV: **I'd as ~ not go** igual me da no ir, de igual gana no voy.

Liège [lɪ'eɪʒ] N Lieja f.

liege [liːdʒ] N (lord) señor m feudal; (vassal) vasallo m; **my ~** señor.

liege lord ['liːdʒˌlɔːd] N señor m feudal.

liegeman ['liːdʒmæn] N, PL **liegemen** ['liːdʒmen] vasallo m.

lie-in [ˌlaɪ'ɪn] N: **to have a ~** (Brit) seguir en la cama.

lien [lɪən] N derecho m de retención (on de); **banker's ~** gravamen m bancario; **general ~** gravamen m general; **vendor's ~** gravamen m del vendedor.

lieu [luː] N: **in ~ of** en lugar de, en vez de.

Lieut. ABBR of **Lieutenant**.

lieutenant [lef'tenənt] N lugarteniente m; (Brit Mil) teniente m; (Brit, US Naut) teniente m de navío.

lieutenant-colonel [lef'tenənt'kɜːnl] N (Brit, US Mil) teniente m coronel.

lieutenant-commander [lef'tenəntkə'mɑːndəʳ] N capitán m de corbeta.

lieutenant-general [lef'tenənt'dʒenərəl] N (Brit, US Mil) teniente m general.

life [laɪf] N, PL **lives** [laɪvz] 1 **(a)** (gen) vida f; ser m, existencia f; modo m de vivir; (of licence etc) vigencia f, validez f; (of battery) vida f, duración f; **bird ~** los pájaros; **plant ~** vida f vegetal, las plantas; **there is not much insect ~ here** aquí hay pocos insectos.

(b) (with adj) **early ~** juventud f, años mpl juveniles; **in her early ~** en su juventud; **in later ~** más tarde, en los años posteriores; **the good ~** una vida agradable, (Rel) la vida santa; **it's a good ~** es una vida agradable; **low ~** hampa f; **private ~** vida f privada; **the private**

~ of Henry VIII la vida íntima de Enrique VIII; **Woodhouse, known in private ~ as Plum** Woodhouse, conocido en la intimidad como Plum; **in real ~** en la vida real; **my ~!*** ¡Dios mío!; **what a ~!** (bad) ¡qué vida ésta!, (good) ¡vaya vida!, ¡vaya vidorra!

(c) (with to be) **is there ~ after death?** ¿hay vida después de la muerte?; **to be a matter of ~ and death** ser cosa de vida o de muerte; **to be the ~ and soul of the party** ser el alma de la fiesta; **such is ~!**, **that's ~!** ¡así es la vida!; **how's ~?** ¿qué tal?, ¿cómo van tus cosas?; **this is the ~!** ¡qué vida nos chupamos!, ¡esto es jauja!; **it's more than my ~'s worth** sería jugarme la vida.

(d) (with prep) **at my time of ~** a mi edad, con los años que yo tengo; **for ~** de por vida; **to be on trial for one's ~** ser acusado de un crimen capital; **for one's ~**, **for dear ~** para salvarse la vida, desesperadamente, (all out) a más no poder; **run for your lives!** ¡sálvese el que pueda!; **for the ~ of me I can't see why** que me maten si comprendo por qué; **from ~** del natural; **never in my ~** en mi vida; **not on your ~!** ¡ni hablar!; **to the ~** al vivo; **true to ~** conforme con la realidad, verdadero; **she brought the party to ~** animó la fiesta; **his acting brought the character to ~** su actuación dio vida al personaje; **to come to ~** resucitar(se), (fig) empezar a animarse.

(e) (with verb other than to be) **to bear a charmed ~** salir milagrosamente ileso de todos los peligros; **she began ~ as a teacher** primero se dedicó a la enseñanza; **~ begins at 40** la vida comienza a los 40; **to depart this ~** partir de esta vida; **you gave me the fright of my ~** ¡qué susto me diste!; **to lay down one's ~** dar su vida, entregar su vida; **to lead a quiet ~** llevar una vida tranquila; **to lead a strange ~** llevar una vida muy rara; **to live the ~ of Riley** darse buena vida; **to live one's own ~** ser dueño de su propia vida; **how many lives were lost?** ¿cuántas víctimas hubo?; **no lives were lost** no hubo víctimas; **to make a new ~ for oneself, to start a new ~** comenzar una vida nueva; **to paint from ~** pintar del natural; **to put new ~ into sb** reanimar a uno, infundir nueva vida a uno; **to risk ~ and limb** jugarse la vida; **he can't spell to save his ~** no sabe escribir correctamente aun si le va la vida en ello; **to see ~** ver mundo; **to sell one's ~ dearly** vender muy cara la vida; **to take one's ~ in one's hands** jugarse la vida; **to take sb's ~** quitar la vida a uno; **to take one's own ~** suicidarse.

(f) (*) = **~ imprisonment**; **to do ~** cumplir una condena de reclusión perpetua; **to get ~** ser condenado a reclusión perpetua.

(g) (liveliness) vida f, vivacidad f, vitalidad f; animación f.

(h) (Liter) vida f, biografía f.

2 ATTR: **~ and death struggle** lucha f a muerte; **~ annuity** pensión f (or anualidad f) vitalicia; **~ assurance** (esp Brit) seguro m sobre la vida; **~ class** clase f de dibujo al natural; **~ expectancy** esperanza f de vida; **~ force** fuerza f vital; **~ form** forma f de vida; **~ imprisonment** prisión f a perpetuidad, condena f perpetua; **~ insurance** seguro m sobre la vida; **~ interest** usufructo m vitalicio; **to take out a ~ membership** inscribirse como miembro por vida; **~ peer** (Brit Parl) miembro de la Cámara de los Lores de carácter no hereditario; **~ president** presidente mf de por vida; **~ sciences** ciencias fpl de la vida; **~ sentence** condena f a perpetuidad; **~ span** vida f; (of product) vida f útil; **~ story** biografía f; historia f de la vida (de uno); **it was her ~'s work** fue el trabajo de toda su vida.

life-and-death ['laɪfəndeθ] ADJ: **~ struggle** lucha f encarnizada, lucha f a vida o muerte.

lifebelt ['laɪfbelt] N cinturón m salvavidas.

lifeblood ['laɪfblʌd] N sangre f vital; (fig) alma f, nervio m, sustento m.

lifeboat ['laɪfbəʊt] 1 N (from shore) lancha f de socorro; (from ship) bote m salvavidas.

2 ATTR: **~ station** estación f de lancha de socorro.

lifeboatman ['laɪfbəʊtmən] N, PL **lifeboatmen** ['laɪfbəʊtmən] tripulante m de una lancha de socorro.

lifebuoy ['laɪfbɔɪ] N boya f salvavidas, guindola f.

life-cycle ['laɪfˌsaɪkl] N ciclo m vital.

life-enhancing ['laɪfɪn'hɑːnsɪŋ] ADJ experience etc edificante; drugs que alargan la vida.

life-giving ['laɪfɡɪvɪŋ] ADJ que da vida, vivificante.

lifeguard ['laɪfɡɑːd] N (on beach) vigilante m, salvavidas m; (Mil) guardia m de corps.

Life Guards ['laɪfˌɡɑːdz] NPL (Brit Mil) regimiento de caballería.

life-jacket ['laɪfˌdʒækɪt] N chaleco m salvavidas.

lifeless ['laɪflɪs] ADJ sin vida, muerto, exánime; (fig) soso, flojo.

lifelessness ['laɪflɪsnɪs] N (fig) falta f de vida, sosería f, flojedad f.

lifelike ['laɪflaɪk] ADJ natural, vivo.

lifeline ['laɪflaɪn] N cuerda f salvavidas; (fig) alma f, sustento m.

lifelong ['laɪflɒŋ] ADJ de toda la vida.

life preserver ['laɪfprɪˌzɜːvəʳ] N **(a)** (Brit) cachiporra f. **(b)** (US) chaleco m salvavidas.

lifer* ['laɪfəʳ] N presidiario m de por vida, persona f condenada a reclusión perpetua.

life-raft ['laɪfrɑːft] N balsa f salvavidas.

life-saver ['laɪf,seɪvər] N salvador m, -ora f, socorrista mf.
life-saving ['laɪfseɪvɪŋ] **1** N salvamento m; (*training for* ~) socorrismo m.
  2 ATTR de salvamento, salvavidas; ~ **raft** balsa f salvavidas.
life-size(d) ['laɪf'saɪz(d)] ADJ de tamaño natural.
life-style ['laɪfstaɪl] N estilo m de vida.
life-support ['laɪfsə,pɔːt] ATTR: ~ **system** sistema m de respiración artificial (*pulmón artificial etc*).
lifetime ['laɪftaɪm] N (a) vida f; **the ~ of a horse** el término medio de vida de un caballo; **once in a ~** una vez en la vida; **in my ~** durante mi vida; **in the ~ of this parliament** en la vida de este parlamento; **she gave half away in her ~** cedió la mitad en vida; **the chance of a ~** una oportunidad única en la vida; **the work of a ~** el trabajo de una vida entera.
  (b) (*fig*) eternidad f, mucho tiempo m; **it seemed a ~** parecía una eternidad.
lifework ['laɪf'wɜːk] N trabajo m de toda la vida.
LIFO ['laɪfəʊ] ABBR *of* **last in, first out** último en entrar, primero en salir, UEPS.
lift [lɪft] **1** N (a) (*act of ~ing*) alzamiento m, levantamiento m, elevación f; (*effort*) esfuerzo m para levantar; (*upward push*) empuje m para arriba; (*help*) ayuda f (para levantar); (*Aer*) sustentación f, fuerza f de sustentación; (*Mech, of valve etc*) carrera f, juego m; **give me a ~ with this trunk** ¿me ayudas a levantar este baúl?
  (b) (*Brit: in car etc*) viaje m gratuito, viaje m en coche (*etc*) ajeno, aventón m (*LAm*), raid m (*LAm*); **to give sb a ~** llevar a uno (gratis) en su coche, dar aventón (*or* raid) a uno (*LAm*); **I can give you a ~ to Burgos** le puedo llevar a Burgos; **can I give you a ~?** ¿quiere que le lleve?
  (c) (*Brit: elevator*) ascensor m, elevador m (*LAm*); (*for goods*) montacargas m.
  (d) (*boost*) estímulo m; **it gave us a ~** nos alentó, nos animó.
  2 VT (a) (*raise*) alzar, levantar, elevar; (*pick up*) coger (*Sp*), agarrar (*LAm*), recoger; *potatoes etc* recoger; *child etc* levantar en brazos; *hat* quitarse; (*by air*) transportar en avión, transportar por puente aéreo.
  (b) (*fig*) *restrictions etc* levantar, suprimir.
  (c) (*) birlar*, ratear*; (*Liter etc*) copiar, plagiar (*from* de).
  (d) (*boost*) alentar, animar.
  3 VI levantarse, alzarse; (*clouds*) disiparse.
◆**lift down** VT: **to ~ sb down** bajar a uno en brazos; **to ~ sth down carefully** bajar algo con cuidado.
◆**lift off** VI (*rocket*) despegar.
◆**lift out** VT sacar.
◆**lift up** VT alzar, levantar, elevar.
lift-attendant ['lɪftə,tendənt] (*Brit*) N, **lift-boy** ['lɪftbɔɪ] (*Brit*) N, **lift-man** ['lɪftmæn] N, PL **liftmen** ['lɪftmen] ascensorista m.
lift-cage ['lɪftkeɪdʒ] N (*Brit*) caja f de ascensor.
lift-off ['lɪftɒf] N despegue m.
lift-shaft ['lɪftʃɑːft] N (*Brit*) hueco m del ascensor.
ligament ['lɪgəmənt] N ligamento m.
ligature ['lɪgətʃər] N (*Med, Mus*) ligadura f; (*Typ*) ligado m.
light¹ [laɪt] **1** N (a) (*gen*) luz f; lumbre f; ~ **and shade** luz f y sombra; **the ~ of day** la luz del día; **this report will never see the ~ of day** este informe no verá nunca la luz pública; **in the cold ~ of day** a la luz del día; **against the ~** a trasluz; **at first ~** al rayar el día; **by the ~ of a candle** a la luz de una vela; **in the ~ of** a la luz de; **you're in my ~** me estás quitando la luz; **in the ~ of what you say** por lo que dices; **it is ~ now** ahora es de día; **there is ~ at the end of the tunnel** se empieza a ver un rayo de esperanza; **hay luz al final del túnel; to bring to ~** sacar a luz, descubrir; **to come to ~** salir a luz, descubrirse; **to cast** (*or* **shed, throw**) ~ **on** aclarar, arrojar luz sobre; **it revealed him in a strange ~** le reveló bajo una luz extraña; **to see the ~** (*be born*) nacer; (*understand*) comprender, caer en la cuenta; (*Rel*) convertirse, darse cuenta de su error; **I don't see things in that ~** yo no veo las cosas así; **to see things in a new ~** ver las cosas bajo otro aspecto, ver las cosas desde otro punto de vista; **to stand in sb's ~** quitar la luz a uno.
  (b) (*lamp*) luz f, lámpara f; (*Aut, Naut*) faro m; ~**s out** hora f de apagar las luces; toque m de silencio; **what time is ~s out?** ¿a qué hora se apagan las luces?; **I went out like a ~*** me quedé dormido en seguida; **to hide one's ~ under a bushel** ocultar las cualidades propias, darse de menos, retirarse modestamente; **to show sb a ~** alumbrar a uno.
  (c) (*signal*) **the ~s** (*Aut*) el semáforo, las luces de tráfico; **green ~** (*also fig*) luz f verde; **to get the green ~ from sb** recibir luz verde de uno; **to give sb the green ~** dar luz verde a uno; **red ~** luz f roja (*also fig*).
  (d) (*flame*) fuego m, lumbre f; **have you a ~?** ¿tienes fuego?; **to put a ~ to sth, to set ~ to sth** pegar fuego a algo, encender algo.
  (e) (*Art*) toque m de luz; ~ **and shade** claroscuro m.
  (f) (*Archit*) cristal m, vidrio m.
  (g) (*person*) **leading** ~ figura f principal, figura f más destacada (*in*

de); **shining** ~ lumbrera f, figura f genial.
  (h) ~**s** (*intelligence*) luces fpl, conocimientos mpl; **according to his ~s** según Dios le da a entender.
  2 ADJ (a) (*bright*) claro; (*illuminated*) bañado de luz, con mucha luz; **to grow** ~ clarear, hacerse de día.
  (b) *colour* claro; *hair* rubio; *skin* blanco; **a ~ green dress** un vestido verde claro.
  3 (*irr:* PRET AND PTP **lit** *or* **lighted**) VT (a) (*illuminate*) alumbrar, iluminar; **she appeared at a ~ed window** se asomó a una ventana iluminada; **to ~ the way for sb** alumbrar a uno.
  (b) *cigarette, fire etc* encender; **with a ~ed candle** con una vela encendida.
  4 VI (a) (*begin to shine*) alumbrarse, iluminarse.
  (b) (*ignite, switch on*) encenderse.
  (c) **to ~ into sb‡** embestir a uno, empezar a pegar a uno.
◆**light out** VI largarse* (*for* para).
◆**light up** **1** VT (*illuminate*) alumbrar, iluminar; **a smile lit up her face** una sonrisa le iluminó la cara.
  2 VI (a) (*begin to shine*) alumbrarse, iluminarse; **her face lit up** se iluminó su cara. (b) (*smoke*) encender un cigarrillo (*etc*), empezar a fumar.
light² [laɪt] (*irr:* PRET AND PTP **lit** *or* **lighted**) VI: **to ~ on** dar con, tropezar con, encontrar.
light³ [laɪt] **1** ADJ (a) (*in weight*) ligero; *food, gun, meal, sleep, troops, wine, work* ligero; *soil* poco denso; (*Naut*) sin lastre; *lorry, train* vacío, sin carga; *breeze, punishment, tax, wound etc* leve; *task* fácil; *comedy, reading* ameno, de puro entretenimiento; (*morally*) ligero, liviano; (*cheerful*) alegre; ~ **flyweight** peso m mosca ligero; ~ **industry** industria f ligera; ~ **opera** opereta f, ≈ (*Sp*) zarzuela f; ~ **verse** poesías fpl festivas; **as ~ as air, as ~ as a feather** tan ligero como la pluma; **to be ~ on one's feet** ser ligero de pies, moverse con agilidad; **it was no ~ matter** era un asunto bastante grave, no era ninguna bagatela; **to make ~ of** no dar importancia a, restar importancia a.
  2 ADV: **to sleep ~** tener el sueño ligero; **to travel ~** viajar con poco equipaje.
  3 N: ~**s** (*Anat*) bofes mpl.
light bulb ['laɪtbʌlb] N bombilla f, foco m (*LAm*).
light-coloured ['laɪt'kʌləd] ADJ claro, de color claro.
light-emitting ['laɪtɪ,mɪtɪŋ] ADJ: ~ **diode** diodo m luminoso.
lighten¹ ['laɪtn] **1** VT (a) (*light*) iluminar. (b) *color* hacer más claro.
  2 VI (a) (*sky etc*) clarear. (b) (*Met*) relampaguear.
lighten² ['laɪtn] **1** VT *load* aligerar, hacer menos pesado; *cares* aliviar; *heart* alegrar.
  2 VI (*load*) aligerarse, hacerse menos pesado; (*heart*) alegrarse.
lighter¹ ['laɪtər] **1** N encendedor m, mechero m.
  2 ATTR: ~ **flint** piedra f de mechero; ~ **fuel** gas m de encendedor.
lighter² ['laɪtər] N (*Naut*) gabarra f, barcaza f.
light-fingered ['laɪt'fɪŋgəd] ADJ largo de uñas.
light fitting ['laɪt,fɪtɪŋ] N guarnición f del alumbrado.
light-footed ['laɪt'futɪd] ADJ ligero (de pies).
light-haired ['laɪt'heəd] ADJ rubio.
light-headed ['laɪt'hedɪd] ADJ (*by temperament*) ligero de cascos, casquivano; (*dizzy*) mareado; (*with fever*) delirante; (*with excitement*) exaltado; **wine makes me ~** el vino me sube a la cabeza.
light-hearted ['laɪt'hɑːtɪd] ADJ alegre; *remark etc* poco serio, dicho en tono festivo.
light-heartedly ['laɪt'hɑːtɪdlɪ] ADV alegremente.
lighthouse ['laɪthaʊs] N, PL **lighthouses** ['laɪthaʊzɪz] faro m.
lighthouse-keeper ['laɪthaʊs,kiːpər] N torrero m.
lighting ['laɪtɪŋ] **1** N (*act*) iluminación f; encendimiento m; (*system*) alumbrado m; (*at pop show*) equipo m luminoso.
  2 ATTR: ~ **effects** efectos mpl luminosos; ~ **engineer** luminotécnico m; ~ **engineering** luminotecnia f; ~ **fixtures** guarniciones fpl de alumbrado; ~ **man** (*TV*) iluminista m.
lighting-up ['laɪtɪŋ'ʌp] N: ~ **time** (*Brit*) hora f de encender las luces.
lightly ['laɪtlɪ] ADV ligeramente; levemente; ágilmente; alegremente; *act etc* sin pensarlo bien, a la ligera; ~ **clad** vistiendo ropa ligera, con muy poca ropa; ~ **wounded** levemente herido; **to get off ~** escapar casi indemne; ser castigado con poca severidad; **this is not a charge to be made ~** este tipo de acusación no se hace a la ligera; **to speak ~ of sb** hablar de uno en términos despreciativos; **to speak ~ of dangers** despreciar los peligros; **to touch ~ on a matter** mencionar un asunto de paso.
light meter ['laɪt,miːtər] N fotómetro m, exposímetro m.
lightness¹ ['laɪtnɪs] N (*brightness*) claridad f, luminosidad f; (*of colour*) claridad f.
lightness² ['laɪtnɪs] N (*in weight etc*) ligereza f, poco peso m; levedad f; agilidad f; alegría f.
lightning ['laɪtnɪŋ] **1** N relámpago m, (*doing damage*) rayo m; **as quick as ~, like** (**greased**) ~ como un relámpago; **where the ~ struck** donde dio el rayo.
  2 ATTR relámpago; ~ **attack** ataque m relámpago; ~ **strike** huelga f

relámpago; **~ visit** visita *f* relámpago.

lightning conductor [ˈlaɪtnɪŋkənˌdʌktər] N, *(US)* **lightning rod** [rɒd] N pararrayos *m*.

light pen [ˈlaɪtpen] N, **light pencil** [ˈlaɪtˌpensl] N lápiz *m* óptico, fotoestilo *m*.

lightship [ˈlaɪtʃɪp] N buque-faro *m*.

light show [ˈlaɪtʃəʊ] N óptico-cinético *m*, psicodélico *m*, juego *m* de luces.

light-skinned [ˌlaɪtˈskɪnd] ADJ de piel blanca.

light wave [ˈlaɪtweɪv] N onda *f* luminosa.

lightweight [ˈlaɪtweɪt] **1** ADJ ligero, de poco peso.
2 N persona *f* de poco peso; *(Boxing)* peso *m* ligero; *(fig)* persona *f* de poca importancia.

light-year [ˈlaɪtjɪər] N año *m* luz; **3000 ~s away** a una distancia de 3000 años-luz.

ligneous [ˈlɪɡnɪəs] ADJ leñoso.

lignite [ˈlɪɡnaɪt] N lignito *m*.

lignum vitae [ˈlɪɡnəmˈviːtaɪ] N palo *m* santo; *(tree)* guayaco *m*.

Ligures [ˈlɪɡjʊəz] NPL ligures *mpl*.

Ligurian [lɪˈɡjʊərɪən] **1** ADJ ligur.
2 N ligur *mf*.

likable [ˈlaɪkəbl] = **likeable**.

▼**like** [laɪk] **1** ADJ parecido, semejante; igual; mismo; **in ~ cases** en casos parecidos; **on this and ~ subjects** sobre este tema y otros parecidos; **two birds of ~ genus** dos pájaros del mismo género; **the 3 divided the work into a ~ number of parts** los 3 se dividieron el trabajo en otras tantas porciones; **~ father ~ son** de tal palo tal astilla; **they are as ~ as two peas** se parecen como dos gotas de agua.

▼**2** PREP **(a)** *(similar to)* **to be ~ sb** parecerse a uno; **they are very ~ each other** se parecen mucho; **a house ~ mine** una casa parecida a la mía, una casa como la mía; **eyes ~ stars** ojos como estrellas; **I found one ~ it** encontré otro parecido *(or* igual*)*; **people ~ that** las personas de esa clase; **the Russians are ~ that** los rusos son así; **he is rather ~ you** tiene bastante parecido contigo; **who(m) is he ~?** ¿a quién se parece?; **what's he ~?** ¿cómo es?, ¿qué tal es?; **what's the coat ~?** ¿cómo es el abrigo?; **she was ~ a sister to me** fue (como) una hermana para mí; **the portrait is not ~ him** el retrato no le representa bien; **the figure is more ~ 300** la cifra se acerca más bien a 300.
(b) *(idioms)* **it's not ~ him** no es propio de él *(to come late* venir tarde*)*, no es característico de él; **I never saw anything ~ it** no he visto nunca nada igual; **isn't it ~ him?** ¡son cosas de él!; **that's just ~ a woman!** ¡eso es muy de mujeres!; **that's more ~ it!** ¡eso es mucho mejor!; **that hat's nothing ~ as nice as this one** ese sombrero es muy inferior a éste; **that's sth ~ a fish!** ¡eso es mucho pez!; **I was thinking of sth ~ a doll** pensaba en algo así como una muñeca, pensaba en una muñeca o algo por el estilo; *V* **feel, look** *etc.*
(c) *(in a similar way)* como; del mismo modo que, igual que; tal como; **~ a man** como un hombre; **~ mad** como un loco *(see also* **mad**); **~ that** así; **he thinks ~ us** opina lo mismo que nosotros; **just ~ anybody else** igual que cualquier otro; **A, ~ B, thinks that ...** A, al igual que B, considera que ...

3 ADV: **it's nothing ~** no tiene parecido alguno, no se parece ni con mucho; **very ~, ~ enough, as ~ as not** a lo mejor; **I found this money, ~*** *(Brit)* me encontré este dinero, sabes.

▼**4** CONJ **(*:** *as)* como, del mismo modo que; **~ we used to (do)** como hacíamos antes; **do it ~ I do** hazlo como yo; **it's just ~ I say** es como yo lo digo; **you look ~ you'd seen a ghost** parece que acabas de ver un fantasma; **he felt ~ he'd won the pools** estaba como si hubiera ganado el premio gordo.

5 N **(a)** *(equal etc)* semejante *mf*; **we shall not see his ~ again** otro como él no le veremos nunca; **did you ever see the ~?** ¿se vio jamás tal cosa?; **and the ~, and such ~** y otros por el estilo, y otros de ese jaez; **I've no time for the ~s of him*** los hombres así no los puedo ver.
(b) *(taste)* **~s** gustos *mpl*, simpatías *fpl*; **~s and dislikes** predilecciones *fpl* y aversiones, simpatías *fpl* y antipatías.

▼**6** VT **(a)** *person* **I ~ him** me cae bien, me resulta simpático; **I don't ~ him at all** me resulta totalmente antipático; **don't you ~ me a little bit?** ¿no me quieres un poquitín?; **how do you ~ him?** ¿qué tal te parece?; **he is well ~d** aquí se le quiere mucho.
▼**(b)** *(find pleasure in)* gustar, *eg* **I ~ black shoes** me gustan los zapatos negros; **I ~ football** me gusta el fútbol; **I ~ dancing** me gusta bailar; **we ~ it here** nos gusta aquí; **your father won't ~ it** esto no le va a gustar a tu padre; **I ~ your nerve!** ¡qué frescura!; **well, I ~ that!** *(iro)* ¡habráse visto!; **how do you ~ Cádiz?** ¿qué te parece Cádiz?; **how do you ~ it here?** ¿estás contento aquí?; **how would you ~ a walk?** ¿te apetece *(LAm:* se te antoja*)* dar un paseo?
▼**(c)** *(wish, wish for)* querer; **I should ~ more time** quisiera tener más tiempo; **I should ~ to know why** quisiera saber por qué; **I should ~ you to do it** quiero que lo hagas; **I ~ to be obeyed** me gusta que me obedezcan; **whether he ~s it or not** quiera o no quiera, de buen o mal grado; **~ it or not, Lord Lucan lives** quieras o no, vive Lord Lucan; **he is free to act as he ~s** está libre para hacer lo que le dé la gana; **as you ~** como quieras; **if you ~** si quieres; **a cat or, if you ~, a feline** un gato, o si se prefiere, un felino; **when you ~** cuando quieras; **would you ~ a drink?** ¿quieres tomar algo?; **would you ~ to go to Seville?** ¿te gustaría ir a Sevilla?

-like [laɪk] *ending in compounds* parecido a, semejante a, como; **bird~** como un pájaro; **with queen~ dignity** con dignidad de reina; *V* **cat~** *etc.*

likeable [ˈlaɪkəbl] ADJ simpático.

likeableness [ˈlaɪkəblnɪs] N simpatía *f*.

likelihood [ˈlaɪklɪhʊd] N probabilidad *f*; **in all ~** según todas las probabilidades; **there is no ~ of that** eso no es probable; **there is little ~ that ...** es poco probable que + *subj*.

▼**likely** [ˈlaɪklɪ] **1** ADJ **(a)** *(probable)* probable; verosímil; **a ~ explanation** una razón verosímil, una explicación razonable; **a ~ story!** ¡puro cuento!, ¡qué cuento más inverosímil!; **the ~ outcome** el resultado más probable; **the plan most ~ to succeed** el plan con mejores probabilidades de éxito; **an incident ~ to cause trouble** un incidente que bien pudiera dar lugar a disturbios; **he is not ~ to**

┌─ **LIKE** ───

Verb

"Gustar" better avoided

- While *gustar* is one of the main ways of translating *like*, its use is not always appropriate. Used to refer to people, it may imply sexual attraction. Instead, use expressions like *caer bien* or *parecer/resultar simpático/agradable*. These expressions work like *gustar* and need an indirect object:

  I like Francis very much
  Francis me cae muy bien or *me parece muy simpático* or *agradable*
  She likes me, but that's all
  (A ella) le caigo bien, pero nada más

Like + verb

- Translate *to like doing sth* and *to like to do sth* using *gustar* + INFINITIVE:

  Doctors don't like having to go out to visit patients at night
  A los médicos no les gusta tener que salir a visitar pacientes por la noche
  My brother likes to rest after lunch
  A mi hermano le gusta descansar después de comer

- Translate *to like sb doing sth* and *to like sb to do sth* using *gustar* + *que* + SUBJUNCTIVE:

  My wife likes me to do the shopping
  A mi mujer le gusta que haga la compra
  I don't like Irene living so far away
  No me gusta que Irene viva tan lejos

"How do you like...?"

- Use *qué* + *parecer* to translate *how do/did you like* when asking someone's opinion:

  How do you like this coat?
  ¿Qué te parece este abrigo?
  How did you like the concert?
  ¿Qué te ha parecido el concierto?

- But use *cómo* + *gustar* when using *how do you like* more literally:

  How do you like your steak?
  ¿Cómo le gusta la carne?

Would like

- When translating *would like*, use *querer* with requests and offers and *gustar* to talk about preferences and wishes:

  Would you like a glass of water?
  ¿Quiere un vaso de agua?
  What would you like me to do about the tickets?
  ¿Qué quieres que haga respecto a los billetes?
  I'd very much like to go to Spain this summer
  Me gustaría mucho ir a España este verano

  NOTE: Literal translations of *I'd like* are better avoided when making requests in shops and restaurants. Use expressions like the following:

  I'd like steak and chips
  ¿Me pone un filete con patatas fritas? ◊ *(Yo) quiero un filete con patatas fritas*
  For further uses and examples, see main entry.

see also main entry
└───

come no es probable que venga, es difícil que venga; **is it ~ that I did?** ¿es probable que lo hiciera yo?
(b) (*suitable*) apropiado; **I asked 6 ~ people** se lo pregunté a 6 personas apropiadas.
(c) (*promising*) prometedor; **a ~ youth** un joven prometedor, un joven que promete.
2 ADV probablemente; **as ~ as not** a lo mejor; **very ~ they've lost it** a lo mejor lo han perdido; **not ~!** ¡ni hablar!
like-minded ['laɪk'maɪndɪd] ADJ animado por los mismos sentimientos; **they looked for others ~** buscaron otros de igual parecer.
liken ['laɪkən] VT comparar (*to* con), asemejar (*to* a).
likeness ['laɪknɪs] N **(a)** (*resemblance*) parecido *m*, semejanza *f*; **family ~** aire *m* de familia.
(b) (*appearance*) aspecto *m*; forma *f*; **in the ~ of** bajo el aspecto de; **to assume the ~ of** tomar la forma de, adoptar la apariencia de.
(c) (*portrait*) retrato *m*; **speaking ~** retrato *m* vivo.
likewise ['laɪkwaɪz] ADV asimismo, igualmente; además; lo mismo; **~ it is true that ...** asimismo es verdad que ...; **he did ~** él hizo lo mismo.
liking ['laɪkɪŋ] N **(a)** (*for person*) simpatía *f* (*for* a), cariño *m* (*for* a); afición *f* (*for* a); **to have a ~ for sb** tener simpatía a uno, tener cariño a uno; **to take a ~ to sb** tomar cariño a uno, coger simpatía a uno.
(b) (*for thing*) gusto *m* (*for* por), afición *f* (*for* a); **it's too strong for my ~** para mí es demasiado fuerte, es fuerte para mi gusto; **to be to sb's ~** ser del gusto de uno; **to have a ~ for sth** ser aficionado a algo; **to take a ~ to sth** tomar gusto a algo, cobrar afición a algo.
lilac ['laɪlək] **1** N lila *f*. **2** ADJ color de lila.
Lille [liːl] N Lila *f*.
Lilliputian [,lɪlɪ'pjuːʃən] **1** ADJ liliputiense.
    2 N liliputiense *mf*.
Lilo ['laɪləʊ] ® N colchón *m* inflable.
lilt [lɪlt] N (*sound*) ritmo *m* marcado, compases *mpl*, armonía *f*; (*song*) canción *f*; **a song with a ~ to it** una canción de agradable ritmo.
lilting ['lɪltɪŋ] ADJ *voice* armonioso, melodioso.
lily ['lɪlɪ] N lirio *m*, azucena *f*; **~ of the valley** muguete *m*, lirio *m* de los valles.
lily-livered ['lɪlɪ'lɪvəd] ADJ cobarde, pusilánime.
lily pad ['lɪlɪpæd] N hoja *f* de nenúfar.
lily-white ['lɪlɪwaɪt] ADJ blanco como la azucena.
Lima ['liːmə] N Lima *f*.
lima bean ['liːmə,biːn] N (*US*) fríjol *m* de media luna, judía *f* de la peladilla.
limb [lɪm] N (*Anat*) miembro *m*; (*Bot*) rama *f*; **to be** (*or* **go**) **out on a ~** estar aislado; estar (*or* quedar) en (una) situación peligrosa (*or* desventajosa); **to tear sb ~ from ~** despedazar a uno, desmembrar a uno.
-limbed [lɪmd] ADJ *ending in compounds*: V **long-limbed.**
limber¹ ['lɪmbər] **1** ADJ ágil; flexible. **2** VT hacer flexible.
◆**limber up** VI agilitarse; (*Sport*) entrar en calor, hacer ejercicios preparatorios; (*fig*) entrenarse, prepararse.
limber² ['lɪmbər] N (*Mil*) armón *m* (de artillería).
limbless ['lɪmlɪs] ADJ (que está) falto de un brazo (*or* pierna).
limbo¹ ['lɪmbəʊ] N limbo *m*; **to be in ~** (*fig*) estar olvidado; quedar en un estado indeterminado, quedar sin resolver.
limbo² ['lɪmbəʊ] N (*dance*) limbo *m*.
lime¹ [laɪm] N (*Geol*) **1** N cal *f*; (*bird~*) liga *f*.
    2 VT (*Agr*) abonar con cal.
lime² [laɪm] N (*Bot: linden*) tilo *m*.
lime³ [laɪm] N (*Bot: citrus fruit*) lima *f*; (*tree*) limero *m*.
lime-green [,laɪm'griːn] ADJ verde lima.
lime-juice ['laɪmdʒuːs] N jugo *m* de lima.
limekiln ['laɪmkɪln] N horno *m* de cal.
limelight ['laɪmlaɪt] N luz *f* de calcio; **to be in the ~** estar a la vista del público, ser el centro de atención, estar en el candelero; **he had long experience of the ~** tuvo una larga experiencia de estar a la luz de la publicidad; **to hog the ~** chupar cámara; **he never sought the ~** no trató nunca de llamar hacia sí la atención.
limerick ['lɪmərɪk] N *especie de quintilla jocosa*.

limestone ['laɪmstəʊn] N piedra *f* caliza.
lime-tree ['laɪmtriː] N (*linden*) tilo *m*.
limey* ['laɪmɪ] N (*US, Canada: pej*) inglés *m*, -esa *f*.

limit ['lɪmɪt] **1** N límite *m*; **it's the (very) ~!** ¡es el colmo!, ¡no faltaba más!; **he's the ~!, isn't he the ~?** ¿qué le vamos a hacer?, ¡qué tío!; **to be at the ~ of one's endurance** ya no poder más, estar completamente agotado; **I am at the ~ of my patience** ya no tengo más paciencia; **to be off ~s** (*US*) estar fuera de los límites; **he was 3 times over the ~** (*Aut*) había ingerido 3 veces más de la cantidad de alcohol permitida; **there is a ~ to what one can do** no es infinita la fuerza que tiene uno; **it is true within ~s** es verdad dentro de ciertos límites; **to go to the ~ to help sb** hacer todo lo posible para ayudar a uno, volcarse por ayudar a uno; **to know no ~s** ser infinito, no tener límites.
2 VT limitar, restringir (*to* a); **that plant is ~ed to Spain** esa planta se encuentra únicamente en España; **are you ~ed as to time?** ¿hay restricción de tiempo?
3 VR: **to ~ o.s. to a few remarks** limitarse a unas pocas observaciones; **I ~ myself to 10 cigarettes a day** me permito tan sólo 10 cigarrillos al día.
limitation [,lɪmɪ'teɪʃən] N limitación *f*, restricción *f*; (*Jur*) prescripción *f*; **he has his ~s** tiene su puntos flacos; **there is no ~ on exports** no hay restricción de artículos exportados.
limited ['lɪmɪtɪd] ADJ limitado, restringido; *edition* limitado; *intelligence* más bien mediocre; *means* escaso, reducido; *person* de cortos alcances, de miras estrechas; **L~** (*Brit: Comm, Jur*) sociedad *f* anónima; **~ (liability) company** sociedad *f* anónima; **~ partner** socio *mf* con responsabilidad equivalente a la cantidad invertida en la sociedad; **~ partnership** sociedad *f* en comandita, sociedad *f* limitada; **to a ~ extent** hasta cierto punto.
limiting ['lɪmɪtɪŋ] ADJ restrictivo.
limitless ['lɪmɪtlɪs] ADJ ilimitado, sin límites.
limo* ['lɪməʊ] N (*US*) = **limousine.**
limousine ['lɪməziːn] N limusina *f*, limosina *f*.
limp¹ [lɪmp] **1** N cojera *f*; **to walk with a ~** cojear.
    2 VI cojear; **he ~ed off** se marchó cojeando; **he ~ed to the door** se fue cojeando a la puerta; **the ship managed to ~ to port** el buque llegó con dificultad al puerto.
limp² [lɪmp] ADJ flojo, lacio; fláccido; *cover etc* flexible; *movement etc* lánguido; **I feel ~ today** hoy me siento sin fuerzas; **she felt ~ all over** tenía un desmayo en todo el cuerpo; **he said in a ~ voice** dijo en tono desmayado; **let your body go ~** deja que el cuerpo pierda su rigidez.
limpet ['lɪmpɪt] **1** N lapa *f*; (*fig*) persona *f* tenaz.
    2 ATTR: **~ mine** mina-ventosa *f*.
limpid ['lɪmpɪd] ADJ *liquid* límpido, cristalino, transparente; *air* diáfano, puro; *eyes* claro.
limply ['lɪmplɪ] ADV flojamente; lánguidamente; **he said ~** dijo en tono desmayado.
limpness ['lɪmpnɪs] N flojedad *f*; languidez *f*.
limp-wristed* ['lɪmp'rɪstɪd] ADJ inútil; (*pej, gay*) de la acera de enfrente, sarasa⁑.
limy ['laɪmɪ] ADJ calizo.
linage ['laɪnɪdʒ] N (*US: Press*) (*also* **advertising ~**) espacio *m* destinado a publicidad.
linchpin ['lɪntʃpɪn] N pezonera *f*; (*fig*) pivote *m*, eje *m*.
Lincs [lɪŋks] ABBR *of* **Lincolnshire.**
linctus ['lɪŋktəs] N jarabe *m* para la tos.
linden ['lɪndən] N (*also* **~ tree**) tilo *m*.
line¹ [laɪn] **1** N **(a)** (*rope etc*) cuerda *f*; (*washing ~*) cuerda *f* de tender la ropa; (*fishing ~*) sedal *m*.
(b) (*Geom etc*) línea *f*; (*on tennis court etc*) raya *f*; (*on face, palm*) arruga *f*, (*in palmistry*) raya *f*, línea *f*; (*Mil: front*) frente *m*; **the L~** (*Geog*) el ecuador; **~ of command** cadena *f* de mando; **~ of fire** línea *f* de tiro; **~ of life** línea *f* de la vida; **~ of sight, ~ of vision** visual *f*; **the ~s of a ship** las formas de un buque; **all along the ~** en toda la línea, (*fig*) completamente, cien por cien; **I draw the ~ at that** yo de ahí no paso; **I draw the ~ at blasphemy** no tolero la blasfemia; **one must draw the ~ somewhere** hay que fijar ciertos límites; **to know where to draw the ~** tener sentido de la moderación, saber dónde conviene detenerse; **his job is on the ~** su

puesto está en peligro, se expone a perder su puesto; **to lay it on the** ~ decirlo claramente, hablar con franqueza; **to lay one's reputation on the** ~ arriesgar su reputación; **to shoot a** ~* darse bombo*, tirarse un farol*.

(c) (*row*) fila *f*, hilera *f*, línea *f*; (*Sport*) línea *f*; (*of waiting cars etc*) cola *f*, (*of parked cars*) fila *f*; (*US: queue*) cola *f*; **ship of the** ~ navío *m* de línea; ~ **of battle** línea *f* de batalla; ~ **of traffic** cola *f* de coches; **to fall** (*or* **get**) **into** ~ (*abreast*) meterse en fila, (*behind one another*) formar hilera, hacer cola; **to stand in** ~ (*US*) hacer cola.

(d) (*in factory*) línea *f*.

(e) (*Elec*) línea *f*; **to be on** ~ estar en (pleno) funcionamiento; **to come on** ~ entrar en (pleno) funcionamiento.

(f) (*of aircraft, liners*) línea *f*.

(g) (*of descent*) línea *f*, linaje *m*; **in an unbroken** ~ en línea directa; **in the male** ~ por el lado de los varones; **descent in the male** ~ varonía *f*.

(h) (*Rail: gen*) línea *f*; (*track*) vía *f*; **down** ~ vía *f* descendente; **up** ~ vía *f* ascendente; **to cross the** ~(s) cruzar la vía; **to leave the** ~(s) descarrilar; **the** ~ **to Palencia** el ferrocarril de Palencia, la línea de Palencia.

(i) (*Telec*) línea *f*; (*flex*) hilo *m*; **on** ~ (*Comput*) en línea; **to be on the** ~ **to sb** estar al habla con uno; **hold the** ~! ¡no cuelgue Vd!, ¡espere un momento!; **can you get me a** ~ **to Chicago?** ¿me puede poner con Chicago?

(j) (*of print*) renglón *m*, línea *f*; (*Poet*) verso *m*; ~**s** (*Theat*) papel *m*; **below the** ~ **expenditure** gastos *mpl* por debajo de los costos; **in the very next** ~ a renglón seguido; **to drop sb a** ~ poner unas líneas a uno; **to read between the** ~**s** leer entre líneas.

(k) (*fig: course*) ~ **of argument** argumento *m*; ~ **of conduct** línea *f* de conducta; ~ **of inquiry** línea *f* de investigación; pista *f*; ~ **of thought** hilo *m* del pensamiento; **to be on the right** ~**s** ir bien, ir por buen camino; **he takes the** ~ **that ...** razona que ..., arguye que ...; **to take a hard** ~ seguir una política de mano dura; **hard** ~**s!** ¡mala suerte!; **it's hard** ~**s on Joe** es mala suerte para Pepe; **what** ~ **is the government taking?** ¿cuál es la actitud del gobierno?; **this is the official** ~ ésta es la versión oficial; **somewhere along the** ~ **we went wrong** en algún punto nos hemos equivocado; **to take a strong** ~ **with sb** adoptar una actitud firme con uno.

(l) (*fig: clue*) pista *f*; indicación *f*; **to give sb a** ~ **on sth** poner a uno sobre la pista de algo; **can you give me a** ~ **on it?** ¿me puedes dar algunas indicaciones acerca de ello?; **the police have a** ~ **on the criminal** la policía tiene una información sobre el delincuente.

(m) (*fig: notions of conformity*) **along the** ~**s of, on the** ~**s of** de acuerdo con, conforme a, a tenor de; **sth along these** ~**s** algo por el estilo, algo en este sentido; **it's all in the** ~ **of duty** es una parte normal del deber; **he did it in the** ~ **of duty** lo hizo cumpliendo su deber; **he's in** ~ **for promotion** tiene posibilidades para el ascenso; **to be in** ~ **with** estar de acuerdo con, ser conforme a; **to be out of** ~ **with** no ser conforme con; **to bring sth into** ~ **with** alinear algo con; **to fall into** ~ **with** conformarse con; **to get out of** ~ salir de la fila; **to keep the party in** ~ mantener la disciplina del partido; **to keep people in** ~ mantener a la gente a raya; **to step out of** ~ salir de la fila; **to toe the** ~ conformarse, someterse, acatar lo dispuesto.

(n) (*fig: métier, speciality*) especialidad *f*, rama *f*; profesión *f*; **the best in its** ~ el mejor en su línea; **what** ~ **are you in?** ¿a qué se dedica?; **that's not in my** ~ eso no es de mi especialidad; **fishing's more in my** ~ me interesa más la pesca, de pesca sí sé algo; **we have a good** ~ **in spring hats** tenemos un buen surtido de sombreros para primavera; **that** ~ **did not sell at all** ese género resultó ser invendible.

2 ATTR: ~ **drawing** dibujo *m* de líneas.

3 VT **(a)** (*cross with* ~s) rayar; *field etc* surcar; *face etc* arrugar.

(b) to ~ **the streets** ocupar las aceras; **to** ~ **the route** alinearse a lo largo de la ruta; **the streets were** ~**d with cheering crowds** en las calles había a cada lado multitudes que gritaban entusiastas; **portraits** ~**d the walls** las paredes estaban llenas de retratos.

◆**line up** 1 VT *people, objects* alinear, poner en fila; *support* alinear, organizar.

2 VI (*along street etc*) alinearse, (*in queue*) hacer cola, ponerse en fila, (*Mil: abreast*) meterse en fila, (*behind one another*) formar fila; **they** ~**d up in opposition to** (*or* **against**) **the chairman** se alinearon para oponerse al presidente; **they** ~**d up behind** (*or* **with**) **the head** se alinearon para apoyar al director; **the teams** ~**d up like this ...** los equipos formaron así ...

line² [laɪn] VT *clothes etc* forrar (*with* de); (*Tech*) revestir (*with* de); *brakes* guarnecer.

lineage ['lɪnɪɪdʒ] N linaje *m*.

lineal ['lɪnɪəl] ADJ lineal, en línea recta; *descent* en línea directa.

lineament ['lɪnɪəmənt] N lineamento *m*.

linear ['lɪnɪəʳ] ADJ lineal; *measure* de longitud.

linebacker ['laɪnbækəʳ] N (*US: Sport*) defensa *mf* (*en fútbol americano*).

lined [laɪnd] ADJ *face etc* arrugado; *paper* reglado; *coat* forrado, con forro; (*Tech*) revestido; **to become** ~ arrugarse.

line editing ['laɪn'edɪtɪŋ] N corrección *f* por líneas.

line feed ['laɪn'fiːd] N avance *m* de línea.

line fishing ['laɪn,fɪʃɪŋ] N pesca *f* con caña.

line judge ['laɪn,dʒʌdʒ] N juez *mf* de fondo.

linen ['lɪnɪn] 1 N **(a)** lino *m*, hilo *m*; lienzo *m*. **(b)** (*household* ~) ropa *f* de casa; (*bed* ~) ropa *f* de cama; (*table* ~) mantelería *f*; (*personal*) ropa *f* blanca; **clean** ~ ropa *f* limpia; **dirty** ~ ropa *f* sucia, ropa *f* para lavar; **to wash one's dirty** ~ **in public** lavar los trapos sucios en público.

2 ADJ de lino.

linen-basket ['lɪnɪn,bɑːskɪt] N canasta *f* (*or* cesto *m*) de la ropa.

linen-closet ['lɪnɪn,klɒzɪt] N, **linen-cupboard** ['lɪnɪn,kʌbəd] N armario *m* para ropa blanca.

line-out ['laɪnaʊt] N saque *m* de banda.

line-printer ['laɪn,prɪntəʳ] N impresora *f* de línea.

liner¹ ['laɪnəʳ] N (*Naut*) transatlántico *m*, vapor *m* de línea.

liner² ['laɪnəʳ] N (*bin* ~) bolsa *f* (de la basura).

linesman ['laɪnzmən] N, PL **linesmen** ['laɪnzmən] (*Sport*) juez *m* de línea, linier *m*, rayador *m* (*SC*); (*Rail*) guardavía *m*; (*Elec*) celador *m*, recorredor *m* de la línea.

line-up ['laɪnʌp] N (*Sport etc*) alineación *f*, formación *f*; (*US: suspects*) desfile *m* de sospechosos, rueda *f* de presos; (*queue*) cola *f*.

ling¹ [lɪŋ] N (*Fish*) especie *f* de abadejo *m*.

ling² [lɪŋ] N (*Bot*) brezo *m*.

linger ['lɪŋgəʳ] VI **(a)** (*also to* ~ **on**; *be unwilling to go*) tardar en marcharse, permanecer por indecisión; (*in dying*) tardar en morirse; (*pain*) persistir, durar; (*of doubts etc*) persistir, quedar; **won't you** ~ **here a while?** ¿no puedes quedarte aquí un rato?

(b) (*take one's time: on journey etc*) quedarse atrás, retardarse; **to** ~ **on a subject** dilatarse en un tema; **I let my eye** ~ **on the scene** seguía sin apartar los ojos de la escena; **to** ~ **over a meal** comer despacio, no darse prisa por terminar de comer; **to** ~ **over a task** hacer un trabajo despacio.

lingerie ['lænʒariː] N ropa *f* blanca, ropa *f* interior (de mujer), ropa *f* íntima (*LAm*).

lingering ['lɪŋgərɪŋ] ADJ lento, prolongado; *death* lento; *doubt* persistente, que no se desvanece; *look* fijo.

lingo* ['lɪŋgəʊ] N (*language*) lengua *f*, idioma *m*; (*specialist jargon*) jerga *f*.

lingua franca ['lɪŋgwə'fræŋkə] N lengua *f* franca.

linguist ['lɪŋgwɪst] N **(a)** (*speaker of languages*) polígloto *m*, -a *f*, políglota *mf*; (*Univ etc*) estudiante *mf* de idiomas; **he's a good** ~ domina varios idiomas, aprende los idiomas con facilidad; **I'm no** ~ no puedo con los idiomas; **the company needs more** ~**s** la compañía necesita más gente que sepa idiomas.

(b) (*specialist in linguistics*) lingüista *mf*.

linguistic [lɪŋ'gwɪstɪk] ADJ lingüístico.

linguistically [lɪŋ'gwɪstɪkəlɪ] ADV lingüísticamente; **she's very gifted** ~ se le dan muy bien los idiomas.

linguistician [,lɪŋgwɪs'tɪʃən] N lingüista *mf*, especialista *mf* en lingüística.

linguistics [lɪŋ'gwɪstɪks] N lingüística *f*.

liniment ['lɪnɪmənt] N linimento *m*.

lining ['laɪnɪŋ] N (*of clothes etc*) forro *m*; (*Anat, Tech*) revestimiento *m*; (*of brake*) guarnición *f*.

link [lɪŋk] 1 N (*of chain*) eslabón *m*; (*fig: connection*) enlace *m*, conexión *f*; (*bond*) lazo *m*, vínculo *m*; **a new rail** ~ **for El Toboso** nuevo enlace *m* ferroviario para El Toboso; **cultural** ~**s** relaciones *fpl* culturales; **the** ~**s of friendship** los lazos de la amistad.

2 VT eslabonar; *spaceships* acoplar; (*fig*) enlazar, unir, vincular; **to** ~ **arms** cogerse del brazo; **we are** ~**ed by telephone to ...** tenemos conexión telefónica con ...; **we are** ~**ed in friendship** nos vincula la amistad; **the two companies are now** ~**ed** ahora están unidas las dos compañías.

◆**link together** 1 VT = **link**.

2 VI (*parts*) eslabonarse.

◆**link up** 1 VT = **link**.

2 VI (*persons*) reunirse (*with* con); (*companies etc*) unirse; (*spaceships etc*) acoplarse; (*railway lines*) empalmar.

linkage ['lɪŋkɪdʒ] N **(a)** unión *f*, conexión *f*, enlace *m*. **(b)** (*Tech*) articulación *f*; acoplamiento *m*; (*Comput*) enlace *m*.

linked [lɪŋkt] ADJ *problems etc* relacionado, vinculado.

linking verb ['lɪŋkɪŋ,vɜːb] N verbo *m* copulativo.

linkman ['lɪŋkmæn] N, PL **linkmen** ['lɪŋkmen] (*Rad, TV*) locutor *m*, -ora *f* de continuidad.

links [lɪŋks] NPL campo *m* de golf, cancha *f* de golf (*LAm*).

link-up ['lɪŋkʌp] N unión *f*; enlace *m*, vinculación *f*; (*of spaceships*) acoplamiento *m*, atraque *m*.

linnet ['lɪnɪt] N pardillo *m* (común).

lino ['laɪnəʊ] (*Brit*) N, **linoleum** [lɪ'nəʊlɪəm] N linóleo *m*.

Linotype ['laɪnəʊtaɪp] ® N linotipia f.
linseed ['lɪnsi:d] 1 N linaza f.
 2 ATTR: **~ oil** aceite m de linaza.
lint [lɪnt] N hilas fpl.
lintel ['lɪntl] N dintel m.
lion ['laɪən] N león m; (fig) celebridad f; **~'s share** parte f del león; **to beard the ~ in his den** entrar en el cubil de la fiera; **to put one's head in the ~'s mouth** meterse en la boca del lobo.
lion cub ['laɪən,kʌb] N cachorro m de léon.
lioness ['laɪənɪs] N leona f.
lion-hearted [,laɪən'hɑ:tɪd] ADJ valiente.
lionize ['laɪənaɪz] VT: **to ~ sb** tratar a uno como una celebridad.
lion-tamer ['laɪən,teɪmər] N domador m, -ora f de leones.
lip [lɪp] N (a) (Anat and fig) labio m; (of jug) pico m; (of cup, crater) borde m; **my ~s are sealed** soy como una esfinge; **to bite one's ~** (fig) morderse el labio; **to hang on sb's ~s** estar pendiente de las palabras de uno; **to keep a stiff upper ~** no inmutarse, aguantarlo todo sin chistar; poner a mal tiempo buena cara; **to lick** (or **smack**) **one's ~s** relamerse, chuparse los labios; **to read sb's ~s** leer en los labios de uno.
 (b) (‡: abuse) injurias fpl; (backchat) insolencia f; **none of your ~!** ¡cállate la boca!
lip-gloss ['lɪpglɒs] N brillo m de labios.
lipid ['laɪpɪd] N lípido m.
liposuction ['lɪpəʊ,sʌkʃən] N liposucción f.
lippy* ['lɪpɪ] ADJ (Brit) contestón*, descarado.
lipread ['lɪpri:d] (irr: V **read**) 1 VT leer los labios a.
 2 VI leer en los labios.
lip-reading ['lɪp,ri:dɪŋ] N labiolectura f, lectura f labial.
lip-salve ['lɪpsælv] N (Brit) manteca f de cacao, crema f protectora para labios.
lip-service ['lɪp,sɜ:vɪs] N jarabe m de pico; **to pay ~ to an ideal** alabar un ideal pero por cumplir; **that was only ~** eso fue solamente de dientes para fuera.
lipstick ['lɪpstɪk] N lápiz m labial, rojo m de labios, barra f de labios.
liquefaction [,lɪkwɪ'fækʃən] N licuefacción f.
liquefy ['lɪkwɪfaɪ] 1 VT licuar, liquidar.
 2 VI licuarse, liquidarse.
liqueur [lɪ'kjʊər] 1 N licor m.
 2 ATTR: **~ glass** copa f de licores.
liquid ['lɪkwɪd] 1 ADJ (a) líquido; measure para líquidos; **~ crystal display** visualizador m de cristal líquido; **~ waste** vertidos mpl líquidos. (b) (fig) sound claro, puro, (in Phonetics) líquido; air diáfano; **~ assets** activo m circulante, activo m líquido.
 2 N líquido m; (Phonetics) líquida f.
liquidate ['lɪkwɪdeɪt] VT (all senses) liquidar.
liquidation [,lɪkwɪ'deɪʃən] N liquidación f; **to go into ~** entrar en liquidación.
liquidator ['lɪkwɪdeɪtər] N liquidador m, -ora f.
liquidity [lɪ'kwɪdɪtɪ] N liquidez f; **~ ratio** relación f de liquidez.
liquidize ['lɪkwɪdaɪz] 1 VT licuar, liquidar.
 2 VI licuarse, liquidarse.
liquidizer ['lɪkwɪdaɪzər] N licuadora f.
Liquid Paper ['lɪkwɪd'peɪpər] ® N Tipp-Ex ® m.
liquor ['lɪkər] 1 N bebidas fpl fuertes; **hard ~** licor m espiritoso; **to be in ~** estar borracho; **to be the worse for ~** haber bebido más de la cuenta, estar algo borracho.
 2 ATTR: **~ cabinet** (US) mueble-bar m; **~ store** (US) bodega f, tienda f de bebidas alcohólicas, licorería f (LAm).
liquorice ['lɪkərɪs] N (Brit) regaliz m, orozuz m.
lira ['lɪərə] N lira f.
Lisbon ['lɪzbən] N Lisboa f.
lisle [laɪl] N hilo m de Escocia.
lisp [lɪsp] 1 N ceceo m; (of child) balbuceo m; **to speak with a ~** cecear.
 2 VT decir ceceando; decir balbuceando.
 3 VI cecear; balbucear.
lissom ['lɪsəm] ADJ ágil, ligero.
lissome ['lɪsəm] ADJ flexible, ágil.
list¹ [lɪst] 1 N lista f; listado m; relación f; catálogo m; (of officials) escalafón m; (Mil etc) anuario m; **to be on the active ~** estar en activo.
 2 ATTR: **~ price** precio m de lista, precio m de catálogo.
 3 VT poner en una lista; registrar, inscribir; hacer una lista de; catalogar; (Fin) cotizar (at a); (Comput) listar; **he began to ~ all he had been doing** empezó a enumerar todas las cosas que había hecho; **my ~ed** no consta (en la lista).
list² [lɪst] (Naut) 1 N escora f, inclinación f; **to have a bad ~** escorar de modo peligroso; **to have a ~ of 20°** escorar a un ángulo de 20°.
 2 VI escorar (to port a babor), inclinarse; **to ~ badly** escorar de modo peligroso.
listed ['lɪstɪd] ADJ: **~ building** (Brit) monumento m histórico, edificio

m declarado de interés histórico-artístico; **~ company** compañía f cotizable; **~ securities** valores mpl registrados en bolsa.
listen ['lɪsn] VI (hear) escuchar, oír (to sth algo, to sb a uno); (heed) escuchar, prestar atención, dar oídos, atender (to a); **~!** ¡escucha!; **~ to me!** ¡escúchame!; **he wouldn't ~** no quiso escuchar.
◆**listen in** VI escuchar (also Rad); **to ~ in to** conversation, programme escuchar.
◆**listen out for** VT estar a la escucha de.
listener ['lɪsnər] N oyente mf; (Rad) radioescucha mf, radioyente mf; **dear ~s!** (Rad) ¡queridos oyentes!; **to be a good ~** tener mucha paciencia, saber escuchar.
listening ['lɪsnɪŋ] 1 N: **good ~!** ¡que gocen!; **we don't do much ~ now** ahora escuchamos muy poco la radio.
 2 ATTR: **~ comprehension test** ejercicio m de comprensión auditiva; **~ device** aparato m auditivo, aparato m de escucha.
listening-post ['lɪsnɪŋpəʊst] N puesto m de escucha.
listeria [lɪs'tɪərɪə] N listeria f.
listeriosis [lɪs,tɪərɪ'əʊsɪs] N listeriosis f.
listing ['lɪstɪŋ] N (a) (gen, Comput) listado m. (b) (St Ex) **they have a ~ on the Stock Exchange** cotizan en la Bolsa. (c) **~s** NPL cartelera f, guía f del espectáculo.
listless ['lɪstlɪs] ADJ lánguido, desmayado, apático, indiferente.
listlessly ['lɪstlɪslɪ] ADV lánguidamente, con apatía, con indiferencia.
listlessness ['lɪstlɪsnɪs] N languidez f, desmayo m, apatía f, indiferencia f.
lists [lɪsts] NPL (Hist) liza f; **to enter the ~** (fig) salir a la palestra.
lit [lɪt] PRET AND PTP of **light**; **to be ~ up*** estar achispado*.
Lit. [lɪt] N ABBR of **literature**.
litany ['lɪtənɪ] N letanía f.
liter ['li:tər] N (US) = **litre**.
literacy ['lɪtərəsɪ] 1 N alfabetismo m, capacidad f de leer y escribir; **~ is low in Slobodia** en Eslobodia son pocos los que saben leer y escribir.
 2 ATTR: **~ campaign** campaña f de alfabetización; **~ test** prueba f de saber leer y escribir.
literal ['lɪtərəl] 1 ADJ (a) literal. (b) (fig) material.
 2 NM (Typ) errata f.
literally ['lɪtərəlɪ] ADV (a) (in a literal way) literalmente. (b) (fig) materialmente, eg **it was ~ impossible to work there** era materialmente imposible trabajar allí; **it had ~ ceased to exist** había dejado materialmente de existir.
literal-minded ['lɪtərəl'maɪndɪd] ADJ sin imaginación, poco imaginativo.
literary ['lɪtərərɪ] ADJ literario; **~ agent** agente m literario, agente f literaria; **~ remains** obras fpl póstumas.
literate ['lɪtərɪt] ADJ alfabetizado, que sabe leer y escribir; **highly ~** (fig) muy culto; **not very ~** (fig) poco culto, que tiene poca cultura.
literati [,lɪtə'rɑ:ti:] NPL literatos mpl.
literature ['lɪtərɪtʃər] N (a) literatura f. (b) (brochures etc) impresos mpl, folletos mpl; información f impresa; (learned studies of subject) estudios mpl impresos, bibliografía f.
lithe [laɪð] ADJ ágil, ligero.
lithium ['lɪθɪəm] N litio m.
lithograph ['lɪθəʊgrɑ:f] 1 N (also **litho**) litografía f.
 2 VT litografiar.
lithographer [lɪ'θɒgrəfər] N litógrafo m.
lithographic [lɪθəʊ'græfɪk] ADJ litográfico.
lithography [lɪ'θɒgrəfɪ] N litografía f.
Lithuania [,lɪθjʊ'eɪnɪə] N Lituania f.
Lithuanian [,lɪθjʊ'eɪnɪən] 1 ADJ lituano.
 2 N (a) lituano m, -a f. (b) (Ling) lituano m.
litigant ['lɪtɪgənt] N litigante mf.
litigate ['lɪtɪgeɪt] VI litigar, pleitear.
litigation [,lɪtɪ'geɪʃən] N litigio m, litigación f, pleitos mpl.
litigator ['lɪtɪgeɪtər] N litigante mf.
litigious [lɪ'tɪdʒəs] ADJ litigioso.
litmus ['lɪtməs] N tornasol m; **~ paper** papel m de tornasol; **~ test** prueba f de tornasol, (fig) prueba f de fuego.
litre, (US) **liter** ['li:tər] N litro m.
litter ['lɪtər] 1 N (a) (vehicle) litera f; (Med) camilla f.
 (b) (bedding) lecho m, cama f de paja.
 (c) (Zool) camada f, cría f, críos mpl.
 (d) (rubbish) basura f, desperdicios mpl; (papers) papeles mpl (viejos); (wrappings) envases mpl; **'No ~'**, **'Take your ~ home'** 'No tirar basura'.
 (e) (general untidiness) desorden m, confusión f; **in a ~** en desorden; **a ~ of books** un montón de libros en desorden, un revoltijo de libros.
 2 VT (a) animal dar cama de paja a.
 (b) (give birth to) parir.
 (c) **to ~ papers about a room, to ~ a room with papers** esparcir papeles por un cuarto, dejar los papeles esparcidos por un cuarto; **a**

page ~ed with mistakes una página plagada de errores; **a street ~ed with paper** una calle llena de papeles.

3 VI *(cat)* parir.

litter-basket ['lɪtəbɑːskɪt] N, **litter-bin** ['lɪtəbɪn] N papelera *f*.

litterbug ['lɪtəbʌg] N, **litter-lout** ['lɪtəlaʊt] N persona *f* que esparce papeles usados *(or envases etc)* por las calles *(or en el campo)*.

little ['lɪtl] 1 ADJ **(a)** pequeño, chico; poco; escaso; **a ~ book** un libro pequeño; **a ~ wine** un poco de vino; **her ~ brother** su hermano menor, su hermanito; **with no ~ trouble** con bastante dificultad, con no poca dificultad.
(b) *(~ with noun, often translated by suffix, eg)* **a ~ house** una casita; **just a ~ gift** *(as charity)* una limosnita; **a very ~ fish** un pececillo; **a ~ sip** un sorbito.
2 ADV poco; **he reads ~** lee poco; **a ~ read book** un libro poco leído, un libro que se lee poco; **a ~ better** un poco mejor; **~ more than a month ago** hace poco más de un mes; **we were not a ~ worried** nos inquietamos bastante, quedamos muy inquietos; **does he know that ...** no tiene la menor idea de que ...; **I walk as ~ as possible** voy a pie lo menos posible.
3 N poco *m*; **he knows ~** sabe poco; **to spend ~ or nothing** gastar poco o nada; **he had ~ to say** poco fue lo que tenía que decir, apenas tenía nada que decir; **there was (but) ~ we could do** apenas había nada que hacer; **give me a ~** dame un poco; **~ by ~** poco a poco; **for a ~** un rato, por un rato, durante un rato; **in ~** en pequeño; **to make ~ of sth** sacar poco en claro de algo.

little-known [,lɪtl'nəʊn] ADJ poco conocido.

littleness ['lɪtlnɪs] N pequeñez *f*; poquedad *f*; *(fig)* mezquindad *f*.

littoral ['lɪtərəl] 1 ADJ litoral.
2 N litoral *m*.

liturgical [lɪ'tɜːdʒɪkəl] ADJ litúrgico.

liturgy ['lɪtədʒɪ] N liturgia *f*.

livable ['lɪvəbl] ADJ llevadero, soportable.

livable-in ['lɪvəbl,ɪn] ADJ habitable.

livable-with ['lɪvəbl,wɪð] ADJ tratable, simpático.

live¹ [lɪv] 1 VT *life* llevar, tener, pasar; *experience* vivir; **to ~ a happy life** tener *(or* llevar*)* una vida feliz; **to ~ a part** encarnar brillantemente un papel, *(pej)* vivir como un personaje de teatro.
2 VI vivir; **long ~ the Queen!** ¡viva la reina!; **to ~ and learn** vivir para ver; **one ~s and learns** todos los días se aprende algo; **to ~ and let ~** vivir y dejar vivir, ser tolerante con todos; **to ~ from hand to mouth** vivir al día; **to ~ high, to ~ well** darse buena vida, nadar en la abundancia; **to ~ like a king** *(or* lord*)* vivir a cuerpo de rey; **as long as I ~** mientras viva; **he hasn't long to ~** no le queda mucho de vida; **to ~ again** volver a vivir; **he ~d by certain ideals** vivió con arreglo a ciertos ideales; **to ~ by one's pen** vivir de su pluma; **I ~ for the day (when) I retire** que venga pronto el día en que me jubile; **a night that will ~ in the nation's history** una noche que vivirá en la historia nacional; **her voice will ~ with me until I die** su voz vivirá siempre en mi memoria; **if you haven't been to Río you haven't ~d** si no has estado en Río no sabes qué es vivir; **they all ~d happily ever after** todos comieron perdices y fueron felices.

◆**live down** VT lograr borrar.

◆**live in** 1 VT *house etc* vivir en, habitar, ocupar; **a house not fit to be ~d in** una casa no habitable.
2 VI *(servant etc)* estar de interno, ser interno.

◆**live off** VT **(a)** vivir de; **to ~ off one's estate** vivir de las rentas de su finca; **he ~s off his uncle** vive a costa de su tío; V **land**.
(b) *food* alimentarse de, comer (únicamente).

◆**live on** 1 VT *(a)* V **live off (b)**.
(b) to ~ on a private income vivir de unas rentas particulares; **what does he ~ on?** ¿de qué vive?; **she doesn't earn enough to ~ on** no gana bastante para vivir; **to ~ on hope** nutrirse de esperanzas.
(c) he ~s on his uncle vive a costa de su tío.
2 VI *(go on living)* vivir, seguir viviendo; *(memory)* seguir vivo.

◆**live out** 1 VT *period, reign* vivir hasta el fin de, sobrevivir a; **to ~ out one's life** pasar el resto de la vida.
2 VI *(servant)* vivir fuera.

◆**live through** VT: **to ~ through an experience** vivir una experiencia.

◆**live together** VI *(in amity)* convivir; *(as lovers)* vivir juntos, vivir liados.

◆**live up** 1 VT *(*)* **to ~ it up** correr las grandes juergas*; **let's go and ~ it up** vamos a echar una cana al aire; **he was living it up with a Swede** lo pasaba en grande con una sueca*.
2 VI: **to ~ up to a standard** vivir con arreglo a *(or* en conformidad con*)* una norma; **to ~ up to a promise** cumplir una promesa; **to ~ up to one's reputation** estar a la altura de su fama; **it ~d up to our hopes** correspondía a nuestras esperanzas; **this will give him sth to ~ up to** esto le dará una meta que seguir.

◆**live with** VT *person* vivir con; **to ~ with the knowledge that ...** vivir sabiendo que ...; **it's a fact one has to ~ with** es un hecho que uno tiene que aceptar; **you'll learn to ~ with it** aprenderás a aguantarlo.

live² [laɪv] 1 ADJ **(a)** *person* vivo; **a real ~ duke** un duque en persona, un duque de carne y hueso.
(b) *(fig) issue etc* candente, de actualidad.
(c) *(lively)* vivo, dinámico, lleno de vida; **a very ~ class** una clase de mucha animación.
(d) ~ broadcast transmisión *f* en directo, transmisión *f* en vivo; **~ performance**, **~ show** actuación *f* en vivo.
(e) *weight* en vivo; *cartridge* con bala; **~ coal** ascua *f*, brasa *f*; **~ export** exportación *f* en pie; **~ rail** raíl *m* electrizado; **~ shell** obús *m* con carga explosiva; **~ wire** alambre *m* con corriente, alambre *m* conectado, *(fig)* persona *f* dinámica, persona *f* emprendedora.
2 ADV: **to broadcast ~** transmitir en directo, transmitir en vivo.

lived-in ['lɪvd,ɪn] ADJ acogedor, familiar; reconfortante.

live-in ['lɪv,ɪn] ATTR: **~ lover** compañero *m*, -a *f*; **~ maid** criada *f* interna, criada *f* que duerme en la casa donde sirve.

livelihood ['laɪvlɪhʊd] N vida *f*; sustento *m*; **rice is their ~** el arroz es su único sustento; **to earn a ~** ganarse la vida.

liveliness ['laɪvlɪnɪs] N vida *f*, vivacidad *f*, viveza *f*; energía *f*; animación *f*; alegría *f*.

livelong ['lɪvlɒŋ] ADJ: **all the ~ day** todo el santo día.

lively ['laɪvlɪ] ADJ *person, imagination, account etc* vivo; *campaign, effort, speech* enérgico; *conversation* animado; *interest* grande; *horse* brioso; *pace* rápido; *party, scene etc* bullicioso, alegre; *tune* alegre; **things are getting ~** se está animando la fiesta; **esto se está complicando; to have a ~ time of it** pasar un rato lleno de incidentes; **to look ~** estar espabilado.

liven ['laɪvn] 1 VT: **to ~ up** animar, estimular; alegrar.
2 VI: **to ~ up** animarse; alegrarse.

liver¹ ['lɪvə¹] N: **fast ~** calavera *m*; **good ~** gastrónomo *m*; persona *f* que se da buena vida.

liver² ['lɪvə¹] 1 N *(Anat)* hígado *m*.
2 ATTR: **~ complaint** mal *m* de hígado, afección *f* hepática.

liveried ['lɪvərɪd] ADJ en librea.

liverish ['lɪvərɪʃ] ADJ: **to be ~, to feel ~** sentirse mal del hígado.

liver pâté [,lɪvə'pæteɪ] N foie gras *m*, paté *m* de hígado.

Liverpudlian [,lɪvə'pʌdlɪən] 1 ADJ de Liverpool.
2 N habitante *mf* *(or* nativo *m*, -a *f)* de Liverpool.

liver sausage ['lɪvə,sɒsɪdʒ] N salchicha *f* de hígado.

liverwort ['lɪvə,wɜːt] N hepática *f*.

liverwurst ['lɪvəwɜːst] N *(esp US)* embutido *m* de hígado.

livery ['lɪvərɪ] 1 N librea *f*; *(liter)* ropaje *m*.
2 ATTR: **~ company** *(Brit)* gremio *m* *(antiguo, de la Ciudad de Londres)*; **~ stable** caballeriza *f* de alquiler.

lives [laɪvz] NPL *of* life.

livestock ['laɪvstɒk] N ganado *m*, ganadería *f*, hacienda *f* *(SC)*.

livid ['lɪvɪd] ADJ **(a)** *(in colour)* lívido. **(b)** *(furious)* **he was ~** estaba furioso; **he got ~** se puso negro.

living ['lɪvɪŋ] 1 ADJ vivo, viviente; *image, language* vivo; **~ or dead** vivo o muerto; **'The L~ Desert'** 'El desierto viviente'; **a ~ death** una vida peor que la muerte; **a ~ skeleton** un esqueleto ambulante; **the biggest flood in ~ memory** la mayor inundación de que hay memoria *(or* que se recuerda*)*; **the greatest ~ pianist** el *(or* la*)* mejor pianista que vive hoy *(or* de los que viven hoy*)*.
2 N **(a)** vida *f*; **to earn** *(or* make*)* **a ~** ganarse la vida; **to make a bare ~** ganar lo justo para vivir; **he thinks the world owes him a ~** se cree con derecho a todo; **the quality of urban ~** la calidad de la vida urbana; **to work for one's ~** ganarse la vida trabajando.
(b) *(Brit Eccl)* beneficio *m*.
(c) **the ~** *(PL: people)* los vivos.
3 ATTR de vida; **~ conditions** condiciones *fpl* de vida; **~ expenses** gastos *mpl* de mantenimiento; **~ quarters** alojamiento *m*, residencia *f*; **~ standards** nivel *m* de vida; **~ wage** jornal *m* suficiente para vivir.

living-room ['lɪvɪŋrʊm] N cuarto *m* de estar, living *m*, estancia *f* *(LAm)*.

living-space ['lɪvɪŋspeɪs] N espacio *m* vital *(also fig)*.

Livy ['lɪvɪ] NM Tito Livio.

Liz [lɪz] NF familiar form of **Elizabeth.**

lizard ['lɪzəd] N lagarto *m*, *(small)* lagartija *f*.

ll. ABBR *of* lines líneas *fpl*.

llama ['lɑːmə] N llama *f*.

LL.B. N ABBR *of* **Bachelor of Laws** licenciado *m*, -a *f* en Derecho, Ldo, -a en Dcho.

LL.D. N ABBR *of* **Doctor of Laws** Doctor *m*, -ora *f* en Derecho, Dr. (Dra.) en Dcho.

LMS N ABBR *of* **local management of schools**.

LMT N *(US)* ABBR *of* **Local Mean Time**.

LNG N ABBR *of* **liquefied natural gas** gas *m* natural licuado.

lo [ləʊ] INTERJ: **~ and behold the result!** ¡he aquí el resultado!, ¡ved aquí el resultado!; **and ~ and behold there it was** y por milagro ahí estaba.

loach [ləʊtʃ] N locha *f*.

load [ləʊd] **1** N **(a)** (thing carried) carga f (also fig); (weight) peso m; (quantity: of mail, washing etc) cantidad f; (Agr etc: as measure) carretada f; **under full ~** en plena carga.
(b) (Elec, Tech) carga f; **to spread the ~** repartir la carga, (fig) repartir el trabajo, repartir la responsabilidad (etc).
(c) **~s of, a ~ of** gran cantidad de, montones de; **thanks, we have ~s** gracias, tenemos bastante; **it's a ~ of old rubbish*** es una basura, no vale para nada; **that's a ~ off my mind** ¡qué alivio!, ¡se me quita un peso de encima!; **get a ~ of this!*** ¡mírame esto!, ¡escucha esto un poco!
2 VT (gen, Comput, Elec) cargar (with con, de); (burden, weigh down) agobiar (with de); **to ~ sb with honours** llenar a uno de honores, colmar a uno de honores; **the branch was ~ed with pears** la rama estaba cargada de peras; **the whole thing is ~ed with problems** el asunto está erizado de dificultades; **we're ~ed with debts** estamos llenos de deudas.
3 VI **(a)** (lorry etc) cargar, tomar carga; **'~ing and unloading'** (street sign) 'permitido carga y descarga'.
(b) (Mil) cargar; **~!** ¡carguen armas!; **how does this gun ~?** ¿cómo se carga esta escopeta?; **to ~ again** volver a cargar.
4 VR: **to ~ o.s. with** cargarse de.
◆**load down** VT cargar, sobrecargar (with de); **he was ~ed down with debt** estaba cargado de deudas; **we're ~ed down with work** tenemos trabajo hasta encima de las cejas.
◆**load up** VT cargar (with de).
load-bearing ['ləʊd,beərɪŋ] ADJ beam etc maestro.
loaded ['ləʊdɪd] ADJ **(a)** cargado; dice cargado, lastrado; gun cargado.
(b) question intencionado, que sugiere una contestación. **(c) to be ~‡** (drunk) estar trompa‡; (rich) estar podrido de dinero*, (carry much money) llevar encima mucho dinero.
loader ['ləʊdə^r] N cargador m.
loading ['ləʊdɪŋ] N (Comm: Insurance) sobreprima f.
loading-bay ['ləʊdɪŋ,beɪ] N, **loading-dock** ['ləʊdɪŋ,dɒk] N área f de carga y descarga.
loadline ['ləʊdlaɪn] N línea f de flotación (con carga), línea f de carga.
loadstone ['ləʊdstəʊn] N piedra f imán.
loaf¹ [ləʊf] N, PL **loaves** [ləʊvz] pan m; (large, cottage) hogaza f; (small, French) barra f; (of sugar) pan m, pilón m; **half a ~ is better than no bread** menos da una piedra, peor es nada; **use your ~!‡** (Brit) ¡despabílate!; ver también RHYMING SLANG .
loaf² [ləʊf] VI haraganear, gandulear.
loafer ['ləʊfə^r] N vago m, gandul m; (in street) azotacalles m.
loaf sugar ['ləʊfˌʃʊɡə^r] N pan m de azúcar.
loaf tin ['ləʊftɪn] N bandeja f de horno.
loam [ləʊm] N marga f.
loamy ['ləʊmɪ] ADJ margoso.
loan [ləʊn] **1** N (thing lent between persons) préstamo m; (Comm, public) empréstito m; **it's on ~** está prestado; **I asked for the ~ of the book** le pedí prestado el libro; **I had it on ~ from the company** me lo prestó la compañía; **she is on ~ to another department** presta sus servicios en otra sección; **to raise a ~** (public) procurar un empréstito, lanzar un empréstito; **to subscribe a ~** suscribir un préstamo.
2 ATTR: **~ account** cuenta f de crédito; **~ agreement** acuerdo m de préstamo; **~ capital** empréstito m; **~ fund** fondo m de empréstitos; **~ shark** tiburón m, usurero m extorsionador.
3 VT (US, also Brit*) prestar.
loan-translation [,ləʊntrænz'leɪʃən] N calco m lingüístico.
loanword ['ləʊnwɜːd] N préstamo m.
loath [ləʊθ] ADJ: **nothing ~** de buena gana; **to be ~ to do sth** estar poco dispuesto a hacer algo; **to be ~ for sb to do sth** no querer en absoluto que uno haga algo.
loathe [ləʊð] VT thing abominar, detestar, aborrecer; person odiar; **I ~ doing it** me repugna hacerlo; **he ~s being corrected** abomina que se le corrija.
loathing ['ləʊðɪŋ] N aversión f (of hacia, por); aborrecimiento m (of de); odio m (of hacia, por); **it fills me with ~** me da asco; **the ~ which I felt for him** el odio que sentía hacia él.
loathsome ['ləʊðsəm] ADJ thing asqueroso, repugnante; person odioso.
loathsomeness ['ləʊðsəmnɪs] N lo asqueroso; lo odioso.
loaves [ləʊvz] NPL of **loaf**.
lob [lɒb] **1** N voleo m alto, lob m, globo m.
2 VT ball volear por alto; **to ~ sth over to sb** tirar algo a uno.
3 VI volear por alto.
lobby ['lɒbɪ] **1** N **(a)** (entrance hall) vestíbulo m; (corridor) pasillo m; (anteroom) antecámara f; (waiting-room) sala f de espera.
(b) (Brit Parl etc) lobby m, cabildo m; **the environmentalist ~** el lobby ambientista.
2 ATTR: **~ correspondent** (Brit) periodista m parlamentario, periodista f parlamentaria.
3 VT: **to ~ one's member of parliament** presionar para convencer a su diputado, ejercer presión sobre su diputado.

4 VI cabildear, ejercer presión, presionar, capitular (And, SC); **to ~ for a reform** hacer lobby a favor de una reforma, presionar en pro de una reforma.
lobbyer ['lɒbɪə^r] (US) = **lobbyist**.
lobbying ['lɒbɪɪŋ] N cabildeo m.
lobbyist ['lɒbɪɪst] N cabildero m, -a f.
lobe [ləʊb] N lóbulo m.
lobelia [ləʊ'biːlɪə] N lobelia f.
lobotomy [ləʊ'bɒtəmɪ] N lobotomía f.
lobster ['lɒbstə^r] N langosta f; (large) bogavante m.
lobster-pot ['lɒbstəpɒt] N langostera f, nasa f.
local ['ləʊkəl] **1** ADJ local; government, colour, anaesthetic, (Telec) call local; radio station comarcal, regional; train de cercanías; road vecinal; usage, word local, regional, restringido; (in distribution, frequency) poco común, localizado, que no se encuentra en todos los sitios, de distribución restringida; **he's a ~ man** es de aquí; **~ area network** red f de área local; **~ authority** autoridad f local; **the ~ doctor** el médico del pueblo, el médico del barrio; **~ time** hora f local; **to drink the ~ wine** beber el vino del país.
2 VT (*) **(a) the ~** (Brit) la taberna.
(b) the ~s los vecinos, el vecindario, los de aquí; **he's one of the ~s** es de aquí.
locale [ləʊ'kɑːl] N lugar m, escenario m.
locality [ləʊ'kælɪtɪ] N localidad f.
localize ['ləʊkəlaɪz] VT localizar.
localized ['ləʊkəlaɪzd] ADJ localizado, local.
locally ['ləʊkəlɪ] ADV: **houses are dear ~** por aquí las casas cuestan bastante; **we deliver free ~** en la ciudad y sus inmediaciones la entrega a domicilio es gratuita; **the plant is common ~** la planta es común en ciertas localidades.
locate [ləʊ'keɪt] VT **(a)** (place) colocar, establecer, ubicar (esp LAm); **to be ~d at** estar situado en, estar ubicado en, radicar en.
(b) (find) encontrar, localizar; **we ~d it eventually** por fin lo encontramos; por fin averiguamos su paradero.
location [ləʊ'keɪʃən] N **(a)** (place) situación f, posición f; ubicación f; (placing) colocación f.
(b) (finding) localización f.
(c) (Cine) rodaje m fuera del estudio; terreno m para rodaje de exteriores; **to be on ~ in Mexico** estar rodando en Méjico; **to film on ~** filmar en exteriores.
locative ['lɒkətɪv] N (also **~ case**) locativo m.
loch [lɒx] N (Scot) lago m; (sea ~) ría f, brazo m de mar.
loci ['ləʊsaɪ] NPL of **locus**.
lock¹ [lɒk] N (of hair) mechón m, guedeja f; (ringlet) bucle m; **~s** cabellos mpl.
lock² [lɒk] **1** N **(a)** (on door, box etc) cerradura f; (Mech) retén m, tope m; (of gun; also Wrestling) llave f; **~, stock and barrel** por completo, del todo; **to put sth under ~ and key** encerrar algo bajo llave.
(b) (on canal) esclusa f; (pressure chamber) cámara f intermedia.
2 VT door cerrar con llave; (Mech) trabar; steering-wheel bloquear; (Comput) screen desactivar; **the armies were ~ed in combat** los ejércitos estaban luchando encarnizadamente; **they were ~ed in each other's arms** quedaban estrechamente abrazados.
3 VI cerrarse con llave; (Mech) trabarse.
◆**lock away** VT: **to ~ sth away** guardar algo bajo llave.
◆**lock in** VT encerrar; **to ~ sb in a room** encerrar a uno en un cuarto.
◆**lock on** VI seguir, perseguir; **to ~ on to** (Mech) acoplarse a, unirse a.
◆**lock out** VT: **to ~ sb out** cerrar la puerta a uno, dejar a uno en la calle; **the workers were ~ed out** los obreros quedaron sin trabajo por lock-out; **to find o.s. ~ed out** estar fuera sin llave para abrir la puerta.
◆**lock up** **1** VT encerrar; (in prison) encarcelar; capital inmovilizar; **you ought to be ~ed up!** ¡irás a parar a la cárcel!
2 VI echar la llave.
locker ['lɒkə^r] N armario m (particular); cajón m con llave; (Rail etc) casillero m (de consigna), consigna f automática; (US) cámara f de frío; (of gymnasium) cabina f.
locker-room ['lɒkə,rʊm] N vestuario m.
locket ['lɒkɪt] N medallón m, guardapelo m.
lockgate ['lɒkɡeɪt] N puerta f de esclusa.
locking ['lɒkɪŋ] ADJ door, container, cupboard que se cierra con llave; **~ petrol cap** (Aut) tapón m de gasolina con llave; see also **central**.
lockjaw ['lɒkdʒɔː] N trismo m.
lock-keeper ['lɒk,kiːpə^r] N esclusero m.
locknut ['lɒknʌt] N contratuerca f.
lockout ['lɒkaʊt] N lock-out m, cierre m patronal.
lock-picker ['lɒk,pɪkə^r] N espadista m.
locksmith ['lɒksmɪθ] N cerrajero m.
lock-up ['lɒkʌp] **1** N (prison) cárcel f, jaula f; (Brit: shop) tienda f sin trastienda.
2 ATTR con cerradura; **~ (garage)** (Brit) garaje m, (inside large garage) jaula f; **~ stall** (US) jaula f, cochera f.

loco¹* [ˈləʊkəʊ] N = **locomotive.**

loco² [ˈləʊkəʊ] (*Comm*) **1** ATTR: **~ price** *precio cotizado en un lugar (aceptando el comprador todos los costos y riesgos al trasladar la mercancía a otro lugar).*
2 ADV: **~ Southampton** *lo mismo que* 1, *más: la mercancía se halla en Southampton como lugar de origen.*

locomotion [ˌləʊkəˈməʊʃən] N locomoción *f*.

locomotive [ˌləʊkəˈməʊtɪv] **1** ADJ locomotor.
2 N locomotora *f*, máquina *f*.

locum (tenens *Brit frm*) [ˈləʊkəm(ˈtenenz)] N interino *m*, -a *f*.

locus [ˈlɒkəs] N, PL **loci** [ˈlɒkiː] punto *m*, sitio *m*; (*Math*) lugar *m* (geométrico).

locust [ˈləʊkəst] N (a) (*Zool*) langosta *f*, acridio *m* (*Mex, SC*). (b) (*Bot*) algarroba *f*.

locust tree [ˈləʊkəst,triː] N acacia *f* falsa; algarrobo *m*.

locution [ləˈkjuːʃən] N locución *f*.

locutory [ˈlɒkjʊtərɪ] N locutorio *m*.

lode [ləʊd] N filón *m*, veta *f*.

lodestar [ˈləʊdstɑːʳ] N estrella *f* polar; (*fig*) norte *m*.

lodestone [ˈləʊdstəʊn] N piedra *f* imán.

lodge [lɒdʒ] **1** N (*in park*) casa *f* del guarda; (*porter's*) portería *f*; (*Univ, master's*) rectoría *f*; (*masonic*) logia *f*.
2 VT *person* alojar, hospedar; *object* (*place*) colocar, (*insert*) meter, introducir; *complaint* presentar (*with a*); **to ~ sth with sb** dejar algo en manos de uno, entregar algo a uno; **the bullet is ~d in the lung** la bala se ha alojado en el pulmón.
3 VI alojarse, hospedarse (*at, in* en; *with* con, en casa de); (*of object: end up*) ir a parar; (*remain*) quedarse, fijarse, quedar empotrado (*in* en); introducirse, penetrar (*in* en); **where do you ~?** ¿dónde tienes tu pensión?, ¿en qué pensión vives?; **the bullet ~d in the lung** la bala se alojó en el pulmón; **a bomb ~d in the engine-room** una bomba se incrustó en la sala de máquinas.

lodger [ˈlɒdʒəʳ] N (*Brit*) huésped *m*, -eda *f*; **I was a ~ there once** hace tiempo me hospedé allí; **she takes ~s** tiene una pensión.

lodging [ˈlɒdʒɪŋ] N alojamiento *m*, hospedaje *m*; **~s** (*in general*) alojamiento *m*, pensión *f*; (*room*) habitación *f*; **they gave me a night's ~** me recibieron en su casa esa noche; **to look for ~s** buscar alojamiento, buscar una pensión; **we took ~s with Mrs P** nos hospedamos en casa de la Sra de P; **are they good ~s?** ¿es buena la pensión?

lodging-house [ˈlɒdʒɪŋhaʊs] N, PL **lodging-houses** [ˈlɒdʒɪŋ,haʊzɪz] casa *f* de huéspedes, pensión *f*.

loess [ˈləʊɪs] N loess *m*.

loft [lɒft] **1** N (*of house*) desván *m*; (*straw~*) pajar *m*; (*Eccl*) galería *f*.
2 VT *pelota* liftar.

loftily [ˈlɒftɪlɪ] ADV en alto, hacia lo alto; *say etc* orgullosamente, arrogantemente.

loftiness [ˈlɒftɪnɪs] N altura *f*; grandiosidad *f*; sublimidad *f*; altanería *f*, orgullo *m*.

lofty [ˈlɒftɪ] ADJ (*high*) alto, elevado, encumbrado; (*grandiose*) grandioso; (*noble*) noble, sublime; (*haughty*) altanero, orgulloso.

log¹ [lɒg] **1** N (a) leño *m*, tronco *m*. (b) (*Naut: apparatus*) corredera *f*; V **logbook.**
2 ATTR: **~ cabin** cabina *f* de troncos; **~ fire** fuego *m* de madera.
3 VT apuntar, anotar, registrar; **we ~ged 50 kilometres that day** ese día recorrimos (*o* cubrimos) 50 kilómetros.
4 VI cortar (y transportar) troncos.
◆**log in** **1** VT meter en el sistema.
2 VI entrar al sistema, acceder, iniciar la sesión, tomar contacto.
◆**log off** **1** VT sacar del sistema.
2 VI salir del sistema, terminar de operar, finalizar la sesión.
◆**log on** VT, VI = **log in.**
◆**log out** VT, VI = **log off.**
◆**log up** VT registrar.

log² [lɒg] **1** N ABBR *of* **logarithm** logaritmo *m*, log.
2 ATTR: **~ tables** tablas *fpl* de logaritmos.

loganberry [ˈləʊgənbərɪ] N (*fruit*) frambuesa *f* norteamericana; (*bush*) frambueso *m* norteamericano.

logarithm [ˈlɒgərɪθəm] N logaritmo *m*.

logbook [ˈlɒgbʊk] N (*Naut*) cuaderno *m* de bitácora, diario *m* de navegación, diario *m* de a bordo; (*Aer*) libro *m* de vuelo; (*Tech*) cuaderno *m* de trabajo.

logger [ˈlɒgəʳ] N (*dealer*) maderero *m*, negociante *m* en maderas; (*woodcutter*) leñador *m*.

loggerheads [ˈlɒgəhedz] NPL: **to be at ~** estar de pique (*with* con).

loggia [ˈlɒdʒə] N logia *f*.

logging [ˈlɒgɪŋ] N explotación *f* forestal; transporte *m* de troncos.

logic [ˈlɒdʒɪk] N lógica *f*; **in ~** lógicamente.

logical [ˈlɒdʒɪkəl] ADJ lógico; **~ circuit** circuito *m* lógico; **~ record** registro *m* lógico.

logically [ˈlɒdʒɪkəlɪ] ADV lógicamente.

logician [lɒˈdʒɪʃən] N lógico *mf*.

logistic [lɒˈdʒɪstɪk] ADJ logístico.

logistically [lɒˈdʒɪstɪkəlɪ] ADV logísticamente, desde el punto de vista logístico.

logistics [lɒˈdʒɪstɪks] N logística *f*.

logjam [ˈlɒgdʒæm] N (*fig*) atolladero *m*; bloqueo *m*; **to clear the ~** desbloquear el camino, quitar los obstáculos.

logo [ˈləʊgəʊ] N logo *m*, logotipo *m*.

log-off [ˈlɒgˈɒf] N salida *f* del sistema.

log-on [ˈlɒgˈɒn] N entrada *f* al sistema.

log-rolling [ˈlɒg,rəʊlɪŋ] N intercambio *m* de favores políticos, sistema *m* de concesiones mutuas.

logy [ˈləʊgɪ] ADJ (*US*) torpe, lerdo.

loin [lɔɪn] N ijada *f*; (*of meat*) lomo *m*; **~s** lomos *mpl*; **to gird up one's ~s** aprestarse para la lucha.

loin chop [ˌlɔɪnˈtʃɒp] N chuleta *f*.

loincloth [ˈlɔɪnklɒθ] N, PL **loincloths** [ˈlɔɪnklɒðz] taparrabo *m*.

Loire [lwɑːʳ] N Loira *m*.

loiter [ˈlɔɪtəʳ] VI (*waste time*) perder el tiempo; (*idle*) gandulear, holgazanear; (*fall behind*) rezagarse; (*on the way*) entretenerse; **don't ~ on the way!** ¡no te entretengas!; **to ~ with intent** rondar un edificio (*etc*) con fines criminales, merodear con fines criminales.
◆**loiter away** VT: **to ~ away the time** perder el tiempo.

loll [lɒl] VI (*head*) colgar, caer; **to ~ against** recostarse con indolencia contra.
◆**loll about, loll around** VI repantigarse.
◆**loll back** VI: **to ~ back on** = **loll against**; **to ~ back in a chair** repanchigarse en un asiento, estar repanchigado en un asiento.
◆**loll out** VI: **the dog's tongue was ~ing out** la lengua del perro colgaba hacia fuera.

lollipop [ˈlɒlɪpɒp] **1** N pirulí *m*; (*round*) chupachupa *f*, (*flat*) piruleta *f*; (*iced ~*) polo *m*.
2 ATTR: **~ lady***, **~ man*** (*Brit*) vigilante *mf* de paso de peatones (*que vigila a los niños cerca de las escuelas*).

LOLLIPOP LADY/MAN

① *Se llama* **lollipop man** *o* **lollipop lady** *a la persona encargada de parar el tráfico en las calles cercanas a los colegios en el Reino Unido, para que los niños las crucen sin peligro. Suelen ser personas ya jubiladas, que van vestidas con una gabardina fosforescente y que llevan una señal de stop en un poste portátil, lo que recuerda por su forma a una piruleta, y de ahí su nombre.*

lollop [ˈlɒləp] VI (*esp Brit*) moverse desgarbadamente; **to ~ along** moverse torpemente, arrastrar los pies.

lolly [ˈlɒlɪ] N (a) (‡: *money*) parné‡ *m*. (b) (*) = **lollipop.**

Lombard [ˈlɒmbɑːd] **1** ADJ lombardo.
2 N lombardo *m* -a *f*.

Lombardy [ˈlɒmbədɪ] **1** N Lombardía *f*.
2 ATTR: **~ poplar** chopo *m* lombardo.

London [ˈlʌndən] **1** N Londres *m*.
2 ATTR londinense.

Londoner [ˈlʌndənəʳ] N londinense *mf*.

London pride [ˌlʌndənˈpraɪd] N (*Bot*) corona *f* de rey.

lone [ləʊn] ADJ solitario, único, aislado; **~ ranger** llanero *m* solitario; **to play a ~ hand** actuar solo; **to be a ~ wolf** ser un solitario; V **lonely.**

loneliness [ˈləʊnlɪnɪs] N soledad *f*; aislamiento *m*.

lonely [ˈləʊnlɪ] ADJ solitario, solo; *place etc* aislado, remoto; (*deserted*) desierto; **~ hearts column** sección *f* del corazón solitario; **to feel ~** sentirse muy solo; **it's a ~ life** es una vida solitaria; **it's terribly ~ out here** aquí se siente uno terriblemente solo.

lone parent family [ˈləʊn,pɛərəntˈfæmɪlɪ] N familia *f* monoparental.

loner [ˈləʊnəʳ] N individualista *mf*, solitario *m*, -a *f*.

lonesome [ˈləʊnsəm] ADJ solitario, aislado.

long¹ [lɒŋ] **1** ADJ (a) (*of size*) largo; *mirror* de cuerpo entero; *division, drink, memory* largo; (*Cards*) *suit* fuerte; *person** alto; **it is 6 metres ~** tiene 6 metros de largo; **how ~ is it?** ¿cuánto tiene de largo?; **the ~ arm of the law** el brazo de la ley; el alcance de la ley; **a list as ~ as your arm** una lista larguísima; **~ drink** refresco *m*, bebida *f* no alcohólica; **not by a ~ chalk, not by a ~ shot** ni con mucho; **to pull a ~ face** hacer una mueca; **to be ~ in the leg** tener piernas largas; **~ sight** presbicia *f*, hipermetropía *f*; **to have ~ sight** ser présbita; **he's a bit ~ in the tooth*** es bastante viejo ya; **the speech was ~ on rhetoric and short on details** el discurso tenía mucho retoricismo y pocos detalles.
(b) (*of time*) largo; prolongado; *job* de muchas horas, de muchos años (*etc*); **to be ~ in** + *ger* tardar en + *infin*; **how ~ is the lesson?** ¿cuánto tiempo dura la clase?; **the days are getting ~er** los días se están alargando; **the course is 6 months ~** el curso es de 6 meses, el curso dura 6 meses; V **time** *etc*.
2 ADV (a) (*a long time*) largo tiempo, mucho tiempo; largamente; **don't be ~!** ¡vuelve pronto!; **I shan't be ~** (*in finishing*) termino

pronto, en seguida concluyo; no voy a tardar; (*in returning*) vuelvo pronto; **will you be ~?** ¿vas a tardar mucho?; **how ~ is it since you saw him?** ¿cuánto tiempo hace que no le ves?; **how ~ have you been learning Spanish?** ¿desde cuándo aprendes español?; **it didn't last ~** fue cosa de unos pocos minutos (*or* días *etc*); **we didn't stay ~** no nos quedamos mucho tiempo; **he talked ~ about politics** habló largamente de política; **it has ~ been useless** desde hace tiempo no sirve; **I have ~ wanted to say that ...** desde hace mucho estoy deseando decir que ...; **to live ~** ser longevo; **women live ~er than men** las mujeres son más longevas que los hombres; **~ before** (ADV) mucho antes, mucho tiempo antes; **you should have done it ~ before now** debiste hacerlo hace mucho tiempo ya; **~ before** (CONJ) mucho antes de que + *subj*; **not ~ before** (ADV) poco tiempo antes; **all night ~** toda la noche.

(b) **~er** más tiempo; **we stayed ~er than you** quedamos más tiempo que vosotros; **how much ~er can you stay?** ¿hasta cuándo podéis quedaros?; **wait a little ~** espera un poco más; **how much ~er do we have to wait?** ¿hasta cuándo tenemos que esperar?; **he no ~er comes** ya no viene.

(c) (*in comparisons*) **as ~ as** mientras; **as ~ as the war lasted** mientras duró la guerra; **as ~ as the war lasts** mientras dure la guerra; **stay ~ as you like** quédate hasta cuando quieras, quédate el tiempo que quieras; **as ~ as, so ~ as** (*provided that*) con tal que + *subj*.

(d) **so ~!** ¡hasta luego!; *V* **ago**.

3 N (a) **the ~ and the short of it is that ...** en resumidas cuentas ...; **before ~** en breve, dentro de poco, (*in past contexts*) poco tiempo después; **are you going for ~?** ¿vas a estar mucho tiempo?; **to take ~ to** + *infin* tardar en + *infin*.

(b) (*Fin*) **~s** PL valores *mpl* a largo plazo.

long² [lɒŋ] VI: **to ~ for sth** anhelar algo, suspirar por algo; **to ~ for sb** sentir la ausencia de uno, suspirar por uno; **to ~ to do sth** anhelar hacer algo.

long. ABBR *of* **longitude** longitud *f*.

-long [lɒŋ] ADJ: *eg* **month~** que dura un mes (entero); *V* **day~** *etc*.

long-armed ['lɒŋ'ɑːmd] ADJ de brazos largos.

long-awaited ['lɒŋə'weɪtɪd] ADJ anhelado, esperado.

longboat ['lɒŋbəʊt] N lancha *f*.

longbow ['lɒŋbəʊ] N arco *m*.

long-dated ['lɒŋ'deɪtɪd] ADJ a largo plazo.

long-distance ['lɒŋ'dɪstəns] **1** ADJ *bus* para servicio interurbano; *race* de fondo, de larga distancia, de resistencia; *train* de largo recorrido; **~ call** conferencia *f* (interurbana); **~ flight** vuelo *m* de larga distancia.

2 ADV: **to call sb ~** llamar a uno por conferencia interurbana.

long-drawn-out ['lɒŋdrɔːn'aʊt] ADJ muy prolongado, larguísimo, interminable.

long-eared ['lɒŋ'ɪəd] ADJ orejudo, de orejas largas.

long-grain ['lɒŋgreɪn] ADJ *rice* de grano largo.

longed-for ['lɒŋdfɔːr] ADJ ansiado, apetecido.

longevity [lɒn'dʒevɪtɪ] N longevidad *f*.

long-forgotten ['lɒŋfə'gɒtn] ADJ olvidado hace mucho tiempo.

long-haired ['lɒŋ'heəd] ADJ *person* de pelo largo, pelilargo, melenudo; *dog etc* de pelo largo.

longhand ['lɒŋhænd] **1** ADJ escrito a mano.

2 N escritura *f* normal; **in ~** en escritura normal.

long-haul ['lɒŋ,hɔːl] ADJ *transport* de larga distancia.

longing ['lɒŋɪŋ] **1** ADJ anhelante.

2 N anhelo *m*, ansia *f*, deseo *m* vehemente (**for** de); nostalgia *f* (**for** de); (*sexual*) hambre *f* sexual, instinto *m* sexual.

longingly ['lɒŋɪŋlɪ] ADV con anhelo, con ansia.

longish ['lɒŋɪʃ] ADJ bastante largo.

longitude ['lɒŋgɪtjuːd] N longitud *f*.

longitudinal [,lɒŋgɪ'tjuːdɪnl] ADJ longitudinal.

longitudinally [,lɒŋgɪ'tjuːdɪnəlɪ] ADV longitudinalmente.

longjohns* ['lɒŋdʒɒnz] NPL calzoncillos *mpl* largos.

long-jump ['lɒŋdʒʌmp] N (*Brit*) salto *m* de longitud.

long-jumper ['lɒŋˌdʒʌmpər] N saltador *m*, -ora *f* de longitud.

long-lasting ['lɒŋ'lɑːstɪŋ] ADJ largo; duro; *material, memory etc* duradero.

long-legged ['lɒŋ'legɪd] ADJ de piernas largas, zancudo.

long-life ['lɒŋ'laɪf] ADJ de larga duración.

long-limbed ['lɒŋ'lɪmd] ADJ patilargo.

long-lived ['lɒŋ'lɪvd] ADJ longevo, de larga vida, que vive hasta una edad avanzada; *rumour etc* duradero, persistente; **women are more ~ than men** las mujeres son más longevas que los hombres.

long-lost ['lɒŋ'lɒst] ADJ perdido hace mucho tiempo, desaparecido hace mucho tiempo.

long-playing ['lɒŋ'pleɪɪŋ] ADJ: **~ record** elepé *m*.

long-range ['lɒŋ'reɪndʒ] ADJ *gun* de gran alcance; *aircraft* de gran autonomía, de largo radio de acción; *plan* a largo plazo; **~ weather forecast** predicción *f* meteorológica a largo plazo.

long-run ['lɒŋrʌn] ADJ largo, de alcance largo.

long-running ['lɒŋ'rʌnɪŋ] ADJ *dispute etc* largo; *play* taquillero, que se mantiene mucho tiempo en la cartelera; *programme* de alcance largo.

longship ['lɒŋʃɪp] N (*Viking*) barco *m* vikingo.

longshoreman ['lɒŋʃɔː'mən] N, PL **longshoremen** ['lɒŋʃɔː'mən] (*esp US*) estibador *m*, obrero *m* portuario.

long-sighted ['lɒŋ'saɪtɪd] ADJ (*Brit Med*) présbita; (*fig*) previsor, clarividente.

long-sightedness ['lɒŋ'saɪtɪdnɪs] N (*Med*) presbicia *f*, hipermetropía *f*; (*fig*) previsión *f*, clarividencia *f*.

long-sleeved ['lɒŋsliːvd] ADJ de manga larga.

long-standing ['lɒŋ'stændɪŋ] ADJ de mucho tiempo, existente desde hace mucho tiempo, viejo.

long-stay ['lɒŋsteɪ] ADJ *hospital* para enfermos de larga duración; *patient* de larga duración; *car park* de tiempo ilimitado.

long-suffering ['lɒŋ'sʌfərɪŋ] ADJ sufrido, resignado.

long-term ['lɒŋ'tɜːm] ADJ a largo plazo (*also fig*); **~ unemployment** desempleo *m* de larga duración.

long-time ['lɒŋ'taɪm] ADJ = **long-standing**.

long-wave ['lɒŋ'weɪv] ADJ de onda larga.

longways ['lɒŋweɪz] ADV longitudinalmente, a lo largo.

long-winded ['lɒŋ'wɪndɪd] ADJ prolijo; interminable.

long-windedly ['lɒŋ'wɪndɪdlɪ] ADV prolijamente.

loo* [luː] N (*Brit*) wáter *m*; *ver también* TOILET .

loofah ['luːfər] N (*Brit*) esponja *f* de lufa.

▼ **look** [lʊk] **1** N (a) (*glance*) mirada *f*; vistazo *m*, ojeada *f*; **he gave me a furious ~** me miró furioso, me lanzó una mirada furiosa; **she gave me a dirty ~** me miró recelosa, me lanzó una mirada llena de recelo; **we got some very odd ~s** la gente nos miró extrañada; **to have** (*or* **take**) **a ~ at sth** echar un vistazo a algo; **have a ~ at this!** mírame esto!; ¡vean esto!; **let's have a ~** déjame verlo, a ver; **do you want a ~?** ¿quieres verlo?; **to take a good ~ at sth** mirar algo con cuidado, examinar algo detenidamente; **take a long hard ~ before deciding** antes de decidir conviene pensar muchísimo; **to have a ~ round a house** inspeccionar una casa; **shall we have a ~ round the town?** ¿visitamos la ciudad?

(b) (*search*) **to have a ~ for sth** buscar algo; **have another ~!** ¡vuelve a buscar!; **I've had a good ~ for it already** lo he buscado ya en todas partes.

(c) (*air, appearance*) aspecto *m*, apariencia *f*; aire *m*; traza *f*; **good ~s** buen parecer *m*; **by the ~ of things** según parece; **by the ~ of him** a juzgar por su aspecto; **you can't go by ~s alone** es arriesgado juzgar por las apariencias nada más; **he had the ~ of a sailor** tenía aire de marinero; **he had a sad ~** tenía un aire triste; **I don't like the ~ of him** no me hace buena impresión; **I don't like the ~ of it at all** esto tiene traza de ser peligroso (*etc*), no me fío de esto; **she has kept her ~s** sigue tan guapa como siempre; **she's losing her ~s** no es tan guapa como antes; **~s aren't everything** la belleza no lo es todo.

(d) (*fashion*) moda *f*, estilo *m*; **the 1999 ~** la moda de 1999; **the new ~** la nueva moda.

2 VT (a) *emotion* expresar con los ojos, expresar con la mirada.

(b) **to ~ sb** (**straight**) **in the eye** mirar directamente a los ojos de uno; **I would never be able to ~ him in the eye** (*or* **face**) **again** no podría resistir su mirada, siempre me avergonzaría al verle; **he ~ed me up and down** me miró de arriba abajo.

(c) (*heed*) **~ where you're going!** ¡cuidado!, ¡atención!; **~ what you've done now!** ¡mira lo que has hecho!

(d) *age* representar; **she's 70 but doesn't ~ it** tiene 70 años pero no los representa.

3 VI (a) (*see, glance*) mirar; **~ here!** ¡oye!; **just ~!** ¡mira!, ¡fíjate!; **~ before you leap** antes de que te cases mira lo que haces.

(b) (*search*) mirar, buscar; **~ again!** ¡vuelve a buscar!; **you can't have ~ed far** no has mirado mucho.

(c) **it ~s south** (*house etc*) mira hacia el sur, está orientada hacia el sur, tiene orientación sur.

▼ (d) (*seem*) parecer; tener aire de, tener traza de; mostrarse; **he ~s happy** parece contento; **it ~s all right to me** me parece que está bien; **how does it ~ to you?** ¿qué te parece?; **she was not ~ing herself** parecía otra, no parecía la misma; **he ~ed surprised** hizo un gesto de extrañeza; **she ~ed prettier than ever** estaba más guapa que nunca; **how pretty you ~!** ¡qué guapa estás!; **to ~ well** (*person*) tener buena cara; **it ~s well** parece muy bien, tiene buena apariencia; **it ~s well on you** te sienta bien, te cae bien.

(e) **to ~ like** parecerse a; **he ~s like his brother** se parece a su hermano; **the picture doesn't ~ like him** el retrato no se le parece, el retrato no le representa bien; **it ~s like rain** parece que va a llover; **it ~s like cheese to me** me parece que es queso; **the festival ~s like being lively** el festival se anuncia animado.

◆ **look about, look around 1** VT: **to ~ around one** mirar a su alrededor.

2 VI mirar alrededor; **to ~ about for sth** andar buscando algo.

◆ **look after 1** VT (*attend to*) ocuparse de, encargarse de; (*watch over*) vigilar; *person* cuidar de.

$\boxed{2}$ VR: **he can ~ after himself** sabe valerse por sí mismo; **she can't ~ after herself any more** ya no puede cuidarse de sí misma.

◆**look at** VT **(a)** (*observe*) mirar.

(b) (*consider*) considerar, examinar; *problem* enfocar; estudiar; **it depends how you ~ at it** depende de cómo se enfoca la cuestión, depende del punto de vista de uno; **whichever way you ~ at it** se mire por donde se mire.

(c) (*check*) examinar, escudriñar; revisar; **will you ~ at the engine?** ¿quiere revisar el motor?; **I'll ~ at it tomorrow** lo veré mañana.

(d) (*accept*) **I wouldn't even ~ at the job** no aceptaría el puesto por nada del mundo; **the landlady won't ~ at Ruritanians** la patrona no aguanta los ruritanianos.

◆**look away** VI desviar los ojos, apartar la mirada (*from* de).

◆**look back** VI **(a)** (*look behind*) mirar hacia atrás, volver la cabeza. **(b)** (*in memory*) considerar el pasado, volverse atrás; **to ~ back on** recordar, evocar.

◆**look down** VI **(a)** (*lower eyes*) bajar los ojos; (*look downward*) mirar hacia abajo.

(b) **the castle ~s down on the town** el castillo domina la ciudad.

(c) **to ~ down on** (*fig*) despreciar, mirar por encima del hombro.

◆**look for** VT **(a)** (*seek*) buscar.

(b) (*expect*) esperar.

▼◆**look forward** VI **(a)** considerar el futuro; mirar hacia el futuro.

▼**(b)** **to ~ forward to** alegrarse de antemano de, pensar con mucha ilusión en, prometerse; **I'm so ~ing forward to the trip** el viaje me hace mucha ilusión; **we had been ~ing forward to it for weeks** durante semanas enteras veníamos pensando en eso con mucha ilusión; **I'm not ~ing forward to it at all** no me prometo nada bueno con respecto a eso; **to ~ forward to** + *ger* tener ganas de + *infin*.

◆**look in** VI **(a)** (*see in*) mirar hacia dentro.

(b) (*visit*) hacer una breve visita (*on* a), pasar por casa, entrar por un instante, caer por casa (*LAm*); **I'll ~ in on Monday** pasaré por casa el lunes.

(c) (*TV*) mirar la televisión.

◆**look into** VT investigar.

◆**look on** $\boxed{1}$ VT (*consider*) considerar; **I ~ on him as a friend** le considero como amigo; **we do not ~ on it with favour** no lo enjuiciamos favorablemente.

$\boxed{2}$ VI **(a)** (*watch*) mirar; (*pej*) estar de mirón.

(b) **it ~s on to the garden** da al jardín.

◆**look out** $\boxed{1}$ VT (*Brit*) (*search for*) buscar; (*choose*) escoger.

$\boxed{2}$ VI **(a)** (*look outside*) mirar hacia fuera; **to ~ out of the window** mirar por la ventana; **it ~s out on to the garden** da al jardín.

(b) (*take care*) tener cuidado, tener ojo; **~ out!** ¡ojo!; ¡atención!; **to ~ out for o.s.** valerse por sí mismo; **he's only ~ing out for himself** (*pej*) sólo considera sus propios intereses; **do ~ out for pickpockets** ten ojo con los carteristas.

(c) **to ~ out for** (*seek*) buscar; estar a la mira de; (*expect*) estar a la expectativa de; (*await*) esperar.

◆**look over** VT examinar; revisar; **to ~ a place over** dar un vistazo a un sitio; **he was ~ing me over** me miraba de arriba abajo.

◆**look round** VI **(a)** (*look about one*) mirar a su alrededor; **to ~ round for sb** buscar a uno.

(b) (*look back*) volver la cabeza; mirar hacia atrás.

(c) (*visit*) inspeccionar, visitar; **we're just ~ing round** lo estamos viendo nada más; **do you mind if we ~ round?** ¿le importa que entremos a verlo?

◆**look through** VT **(a)** *window* mirar por. **(b)** *papers etc* hojear, registrar; *belongings* registrar. **(c)** **he ~ed through me** me miró sin verme, me miró como si fuera transparente.

◆**look to** VT **(a)** (*attend to*) ocuparse de, mirar por; **we must ~ to the future** tenemos que fijar la mira en el futuro.

(b) (*look after*) cuidar de, ocuparse de.

(c) (*rely on*) contar con; acudir a; tener puestas las esperanzas en; **it's no good ~ing to me for help** es inútil acudir a mí buscando ayuda; **to ~ to sb to** + *infin* esperar que uno + *subj*, contar con uno para + *infin*.

◆**look up** $\boxed{1}$ VT **(a)** (*visit*) ir a ver, visitar.

(b) (*seek out*) buscar; averiguar.

$\boxed{2}$ VI **(a)** (*raise eyes*) levantar los ojos; (*look upward*) mirar para arriba.

(b) (*improve*) mejorar, ir mejor; **things are ~ing up** las cosas van mejor.

(c) **to ~ up to sb** respetar a uno, admirar a uno.

◆**look upon** = **look on 1**.

look-alike ['lʊkə,laɪk] N parecido *m*, -a *f*.

looked-for ['lʊktfɔːʳ] ADJ esperado, deseado.

looker⁎ ['lʊkəʳ] N (*US*) guapa *f*.

looker-on ['lʊkər'ɒn] N espectador *m*, -ora *f*; (*pej*) mirón *m*, -ona *f*.

look-in⁎ ['lʊkɪn] N oportunidad *f* para tomar parte; **we never got (or had) a ~** no nos dejaron participar, (*of losers*) nunca tuvimos

posibilidades de ganar.

-looking ['lʊkɪŋ] ADJ *ending in compounds*: **strange~** de aspecto raro; **mad~** que parece loco.

looking-glass ['lʊkɪŋglɑːs] N espejo *m*.

look-out ['lʊkaʊt] $\boxed{1}$ N **(a)** (*tower etc*) atalaya *f*, puesto *m* de observación; (*viewpoint*) miradero *m*.

(b) (*person*) vigía *m*.

(c) (*act*) observación *f*, vigilancia *f*; **to be on the ~ for, to keep a ~ for** estar a la mira de; **to keep a sharp ~** estar ojo avizor.

(d) (*esp Brit*⁎: *prospect*) perspectiva *f*; **it's a poor ~ for cotton** el algodón tiene un porvenir dudoso; **it's a grim ~ for us** es una perspectiva negra para nosotros, esto no nos promete nada bueno; **that's his ~!** ¡allá él!

$\boxed{2}$ ATTR: **~ post** puesto *m* de observación.

| **LOOK FOR** | *see also main entry* |

Omission of article

● Don't translate the article *a* in sentences like *I'm looking for a flat*, when the number of such things is not significant since people normally only look for one at a time:

I'm looking for a flat
Estoy buscando piso
He's looking for a secretary
Busca secretaria

NOTE: The Spanish personal *a* is not used before people when the article is omitted as above.

● Do translate the article when the thing or person is qualified:

He's looking for a little flat
Busca un piso pequeño

! When translating examples like *I'm looking for someone to...* translate the English to-infinitive using *que* + SUBJUNCTIVE:

I'm looking for someone to help with the children
Busco a alguien que me ayude con los niños
I'm looking for a mechanic to repair my car
Busco a un mecánico que me arregle el coche

For further uses and examples, see main entry.

---

look-see⁎ ['lʊksiː] N vistazo *m*.

look-up ['lʊkʌp] N consulta *f*; **~ table** tabla *f* de consulta.

LOOM N (*US*) ABBR *of* **Loyal Order of Moose** asociación benéfica.

loom¹ [luːm] N telar *m*.

loom² [luːm] VI (*also to ~ up*) surgir, aparecer, asomarse; (*threaten*) amenazar; **dangers ~ ahead** se vislumbran los peligros que hay por delante; **the ship ~ed up out of the mist** el buque surgió de la niebla; **to ~ large** ser de gran importancia, presentarse muy importante.

looming ['luːmɪŋ] ADJ *danger etc* que amenaza, inminente.

loon [luːn] N bobo *m*, -a *f*.

loony⁎ ['luːnɪ] $\boxed{1}$ ADJ loco; **the ~ left** la izquierda tonta; **to drive sb ~** volver loco a uno; **to go ~** volverse loco.

$\boxed{2}$ N loco *m*, -a *f*.

loony bin⁎ ['luːnɪbɪn] N manicomio *m*.

loop [luːp] $\boxed{1}$ N (*knot*) lazo *m*, (*Naut*) gaza *f*; (*bend*) curva *f*, vuelta *f*, recodo *m*; (*Elec*) circuito *m* cerrado; (*Comput*) bucle *m*; (*Sew*) presilla *f*; (*Aer*) rizo *m*; **to knock sb for a ~⁎** (*US*) dejar a uno pasmado; **to loop the ~** hacer el rizo, rizar el rizo.

$\boxed{2}$ VT *rope etc* hacer gaza con; (*fasten*) asegurar con gaza (*or* presilla); **to ~ a rope round a post** pasar una cuerda alrededor de un poste.

$\boxed{3}$ VI (*rope etc*) formar lazo; (*line, road etc*) serpentear.

loophole ['luːphəʊl] N (*Mil*) aspillera *f*, tronera *f*; (*fig*) escapatoria *f*; pretexto *m*; (*in law*) rendija *f*; **every law has a ~** hecha la ley hecha la trampa.

loop-line ['luːplaɪn] N (*Rail*) desviación *f*.

loopy⁎ ['luːpɪ] ADJ chiflado⁎.

loose [luːs] $\boxed{1}$ ADJ **(a)** (*not attached, not firm*) suelto; *change, end* suelto; (*untied*) suelto, desatado; (*not tight*) flojo; (*movable*) movible, movedizo; *earth* poco firme; *bandage, button, knot, screw* flojo; *tooth* inseguro; *dress* holgado, ancho; *pulley, wheel* (*Mech*) loco, flotante; *connection* desconectado; **these trousers are too ~ round the waist** estos pantalones son demasiado holgados por la cintura; **'~ chippings'** 'gravilla suelta'; **~ cover** funda *f* que se puede quitar; **~ end** cabo *m* suelto; **to tie up ~ ends** atar cabos; **~ scrum** melé *f* abierta; **~ talk** (*careless*) palabras *fpl* pronunciadas sin pensar; (*indecent*) palabras *fpl* indecentes; **to have a ~ tongue** (*talkative*) ser muy hablador, (*gossipy*) ser chismoso, ser una mala lengua, (*telling secrets*) no saber guardar un secreto; **to become** (*or* **come, get, work**) **~** (*part*) soltarse, desprenderse, (*knot*) aflojarse, desatarse; **to break ~** desatarse, escaparse, (*fig*) desencadenarse; **to cast** (*or* **let, set, turn**) **~** soltar; **to cut ~** separarse, independizarse (*from* de); **to hang ~** caer suelto; (*US*⁎) relajarse, tomar las cosas con calma; **to tear sth ~** arrancar algo, quitar algo violentamente; **to tear o.s. ~** soltarse;

quitarse violentamente las trabas.

(b) (*unpacked*) sin envase, a granel, suelto.

(c) (*not exact*) *translation* libre, aproximado, (*pej*) poco exacto; *thinking* ilógico; *style* impreciso, vago; **there is a ~ connection between them** entre ellos existe una relación no muy estrecha.

(d) (*morally*) relajado; *conduct, life* inmoral, disoluto; *woman* fácil.

2 N (*) **to be on the ~** (*free*) estar en libertad; **to be** (*or* **go**) **on the ~** ir de juerga*, echar una cana al aire.

3 VT (*free*) soltar; (*untie*) desatar; (*slacken*) aflojar; *storm, abuse etc* desencadenar.

◆**loose off** VT *gun* disparar (*at* sobre).

◆**loose off at** VT (*fire*) disparar sobre; (*verbally*) empezar a soltar injurias contra.

loose box ['luːsˌbɒks] N (*Brit: for horses*) establo *m* móvil.

loose cannon* ['luːs'kænən] N bomba *f* de relojería.

loose-fitting ['luːs'fɪtɪŋ] ADJ suelto.

loose-leaf ['luːs'liːf] ADJ *book* de hojas sueltas, de hojas cambiables; **~ binder, ~ folder** carpeta *f* de anillas.

loose-limbed ['luːs'lɪmd] ADJ de movimientos sueltos, ágil.

loose-living ['luːs'lɪvɪŋ] ADJ de vida airada, de vida inmoral.

loosely ['luːslɪ] ADV sueltamente; flojamente; holgadamente; libremente, aproximadamente; con poca exactitud; ilógicamente; imprecisamente; disolutamente; **it is ~ translated as** se traduce aproximadamente por; **~ dressed** con vestidos holgados.

loosen ['luːsn] **1** VT (*free*) soltar; (*untie*) desatar; (*slacken*) aflojar; *restrictions* aflojar, liberalizar; V **tongue** *etc*.

2 VI soltarse; desatarse; aflojarse.

◆**loosen up 1** VT *muscles* desentumecer.

2 VI (*before game*) desentumecer los músculos, entrar en calor; **to ~ up on sb** tratar a uno con menos rigor.

looseness ['luːsnɪs] N **(a)** soltura *f*; flojedad *f*; holgura *f*; libertad *f*. **(b)** imprecisión *f*. **(c)** disolución *f*; relajación *f*. **(d)** (*Med*) diarrea *f*.

loot [luːt] **1** N botín *m*, presa *f*; (*) ganancias *fpl*, botín *m*, (*money*) pasta* *f* (*Sp*), plata *f*.

2 VT saquear.

looter ['luːtər] N saqueador *m*, -ora *f*.

looting ['luːtɪŋ] N saqueo *m*.

lop [lɒp] VT *tree* mochar, desmochar; *branches* podar; (*esp fig*) cercenar.

◆**lop away, lop off** VT cortar.

lope [ləʊp] VI (*also* **to ~ along**) correr a paso largo; **to ~ off** alejarse a paso largo.

lop-eared ['lɒpˌɪəd] ADJ de orejas caídas.

lop-sided ['lɒp'saɪdɪd] ADJ desproporcionado; desequilibrado; ladeado, sesgado; (*fig*) desequilibrado, falso.

loquacious [lə'kweɪʃəs] ADJ locuaz.

loquacity [lə'kwæsɪtɪ] N locuacidad *f*.

lord [lɔːd] **1** N **(a)** señor *m*; (*Brit title*) lord *m*; **L~** (**John**) **Smith** (*Brit*) Lord (John) Smith; **the L~s** (*Parl*) la Cámara de los Lores; **the ~s of England** (*peers*) los nobles de Inglaterra; **my ~** (*to bishop*) Ilustrísima, (*to noble*) señor, (*to judge*) señor juez; **~ of the manor** señor *m* feudal; **~ and master** dueño *m*.

(b) (*Rel*) **the L~** el Señor; **Our L~** Nuestro Señor; **L~'s Prayer** padrenuestro *m*; **good L~!** ¡Dios mío!; **L~ knows where ...!*;** ¡Dios sabe dónde ...!

2 ATTR: **my ~ bishop of Tooting** su Ilustrísima el obispo de Tooting; **L~ Lieutenant** *representante de la Corona en un condado*; **L~ Mayor, L~ Provost** (*Scot*) alcalde *m*.

3 VT: **to ~ it** hacer el señor, mandar despóticamente; **to ~ it over sb** dominar a uno despóticamente, mandar a uno como señor.

┌─ *LORD* ─

ⓘ *El título de* **Lord** *se les da a los miembros masculinos de la nobleza británica, especialmente a los marqueses, condes, vizcondes y barones, personas que ocupan un escaño en la Cámara de los Lores. El término forma parte también del nombre de algunos cargos oficiales: el* **Lord Chancellor** *es la máxima autoridad judicial en Inglaterra y Gales, el* **Lord Chief Justice** *es el cargo inmediatamente inferior, mientras que en Escocia el encargado del sistema judicial es el* **Lord Advocate**. *Por su parte, el* **Lord Chamberlain** *es el encargado del mantenimiento de las residencias oficiales de la realeza británica.*

lordliness ['lɔːdlɪnɪs] N lo señorial, carácter *m* señorial; (*pej*) altivez *f*, arrogancia *f*.

lordly ['lɔːdlɪ] ADJ *house, vehicle etc* señorial, señoril; *manner* altivo, arrogante; *command* imperioso.

lords-and-ladies ['lɔːdzənd'leɪdɪz] N (*Bot*) aro *m*.

lordship ['lɔːdʃɪp] N (*title*) señoría *f*; (*rule*) señorío *m*; **his ~** su señoría; **your L~** Señoría.

lore [lɔːr] N saber *m* popular; ciencia *f*, tradiciones *fpl*; **in local ~** según la tradición local; **he knows a lot about plant ~** sabe mucho de las plantas, es muy erudito en botánica.

lorgnette [lɔː'njet] N impertinentes *mpl*.

Lorraine [lɒ'reɪn] N Lorena *f*.

lorry ['lɒrɪ] N (*Brit*) camión *m*; **it fell off the back of a ~*** es de trapicheo*, es de segunda mano.

lorry-driver ['lɒrɪˌdraɪvər] N camionero *m*, camionista *m*, conductor *m* de camión.

lorry-load ['lɒrɪˌləʊd] N carga *f* (de un camión).

lose [luːz] (*irr:* PRET AND PTP **lost**) **1** VT **(a)** (*gen*) perder; quedarse sin; *patient* no lograr salvar la vida de.

(b) (*passive with* lost) **to be lost** perderse, quedar perdido; **to be lost at sea** (*person*) perecer en el mar, morir ahogado; **the ship was lost with all hands** el buque se hundió con toda la tripulación; **all is lost!** ¡todo está perdido!, ¡se acabó todo!; **to get lost** perderse, extraviarse, errar el camino; **get lost!*;** ¡vete a la porra!*;*; **to be lost in thought** estar absorto en meditación; **to be lost in wonder** quedar asombrado; **after his death I felt lost** después de su muerte me sentía perdido; **I'm lost without my secretary** sin mi secretaria no valgo para nada, no puedo hacer nada sin mi secretaria; **to give sb up for lost** dar a uno por perdido; **the motion was lost** se rechazó la moción; **he was lost to science** se perdió para la ciencia; **he is lost to all finer feelings** es insensible a todos los sentimientos nobles; **the joke was lost on her** no comprendió el chiste; **the remark was lost on him** la observación pasó inadvertida por él; **this modern music is lost on me** no entiendo esta música moderna.

(c) (*outstrip etc*) dejar atrás, adelantarse a; *pursuers* zafarse de; *unwanted companion* deshacerse de.

(d) (*cause loss of*) hacer perder; **it lost him the job** le costó el puesto; **that lost us the war** eso nos hizo perder la guerra; **that lost us the game** eso nos costó la victoria.

2 VI **(a)** perder; ser vencido; **you can't ~** no tienes pérdida, tienes forzosamente que salir ganando; **the story did not ~ in the telling** el cuento no perdió en la narración.

(b) **the clock is losing** el reloj atrasa.

3 VR: **to ~ o.s.** perderse, extraviarse, errar el camino; (*in speech*) padecer una confusión, perder el hilo; **to ~ o.s. in thought** ensimismarse.

◆**lose out** VI perder, salir perdiendo.

loser ['luːzər] N (*person*) perdedor *m*, -ora *f*; fracasado *m*, -a *f*, desgraciado *m*, -a *f* (*Sport etc*) el que pierde, el vencido, el equipo derrotado; (*card*) carta *f* perdedora; **to be a bad ~** no saber perder, tener mal perder; **to be a good ~** saber perder, tener buen perder; **to come off the ~** salir perdiendo.

losing ['luːzɪŋ] **1** ADJ *team* vencido, derrotado; *trick etc* perdedor.

2 NPL **~s** pérdidas *fpl*.

loss [lɒs] N **(a)** (*gen*) pérdida *f*; **~ of appetite** inapetencia *f*; **~ of earnings** pérdida *f* de sueldo; **~ of memory** amnesia *f*; **without ~ of time** sin pérdida de tiempo, sin demora; **since the ~ of his wife** desde que perdió a su mujer, desde que se murió su mujer; **there was a heavy ~ of life** hubo muchas víctimas, perecieron muchos; **the army suffered heavy ~es** el ejército sufrió pérdidas cuantiosas; **to cut one's ~es** cortar por lo sano; **the company makes a ~ on this product** la empresa pierde dinero con este producto; **the company made a ~ in 1999** la empresa tuvo un balance adverso en 1999, la compañía salió con déficit en 1999.

(b) **it's your ~** Vd es el que pierde; **he's no ~** no vamos a sentir su ausencia; **he's a dead ~** es una calamidad; **the book is a dead ~** el libro es absolutamente inútil, el libro no vale para nada en absoluto; **the ship is a total ~** el buque puede considerarse como totalmente perdido.

(c) **to be at a ~** estar perplejo, no saber qué hacer; **to be at a ~ to explain sth** no saber cómo explicarse algo; **we are at a ~ to know why** no sabemos en absoluto por qué; **to be at a ~ for words** no encontrar palabras con que expresarse; **he's never at a ~ (for words)** tiene mucha facilidad de palabra, tiene la palabra facilísima; **to sell sth at a ~** vender algo con pérdida.

loss-leader ['lɒsˌliːdər] N artículo *m* de lanzamiento.

loss-maker ['lɒsˌmeɪkər] N (*business*) negocio *m* no rentable, negocio *m* deficitario; (*product*) producto *m* no rentable.

loss-making ['lɒsˌmeɪkɪŋ] ADJ *enterprise* deficitario, no rentable.

lost [lɒst] **1** PRET AND PTP *of* **lose**.

2 ADJ perdido; **~ days** (*at work*) días *mpl* no trabajados; **'~ property'** (*notice*) 'objetos perdidos'; **~ time** tiempo *m* perdido.

lost-and-found department ['lɒstən'faʊndɪˌpɑːtmənt] N (*US*), **lost property office** ['lɒst'prɒpətɪˌɒfɪs] N oficina *f* de objetos perdidos.

lot [lɒt] N **(a)** (*random selection*) **by ~** echando suertes; mediante sorteo; **to cast ~s, to draw ~s** echar suertes (*for sth* para decidir quién tendrá algo, *to decide sth* para decidir algo); **the ~ fell on him** él resultó elegido, la suerte le tocó a él; **to throw in one's ~ with sb** unirse a la suerte de uno.

(b) (*share*) porción *f*, parte *f*; (*destiny*) suerte *f*; **his ~ was different** su suerte fue otra; **it fell to my ~** me cayó en suerte, me cupo en suerte; **it falls to my ~ to** + *infin* me incumbe + *infin.*

(c) (*plot*) solar *m*, terreno *m*; (*Cine*) solar *m.*

(d) (*at auction*) lote *m*; **he's a bad ~** es un mal sujeto; **I'll send it in 3 ~s** (*Comm*) se lo mando en 3 paquetes (*or* tandas).

(e) (*quantity*) cantidad *f*; grupo *m*, colección *f*; **a fine ~ of students** un buen grupo de estudiantes; **a ~ of money** mucho dinero; **a ~ of books, ~s of books** muchos libros; **quite a ~ of books** bastantes libros; **such a ~ of books** tantos libros; **an awful ~ of things to do** la mar de cosas que hacer; **we have ~s of flowers (that we don't want)** nos sobran flores, tenemos flores de sobra; **that's the ~** eso es todo; **the whole ~ of them** ellos todos, todos ellos sin excepción; **he collared the ~** se los llevó todos; **big ones, little ones, the ~!** ¡los grandes, los pequeños, todos!

(f) (*as adv*) **I read a ~** leo bastante; **we don't go out a ~** no salimos mucho; **things have changed a ~** las cosas han cambiado mucho; **there wasn't a ~ we could do** apenas había nada que pudiéramos hacer; **he drinks an awful ~** bebe una barbaridad; **I'd give a ~ to know** me gustaría muchísimo saberlo; **I feel ~s better** me encuentro mucho mejor; **thanks a ~!** ¡muchas gracias!

loth [ləʊθ] ADJ = **loath.**

lotion ['ləʊʃən] N loción *f.*

lottery ['lɒtərɪ] N lotería *f.*

lotto ['lɒtəʊ] N (*game*) lotería *f.*

lotus ['ləʊtəs] N loto *m*; **~ position** postura *f* del loto.

louche [luːʃ] ADJ *person* crápula; *place* siniestro.

loud [laʊd] **1** ADJ **(a)** *voice, tone etc* alto; *shout etc* fuerte, recio; (*noisy*) ruidoso, estrepitoso; *applause* fuerte, estrepitoso; *behaviour* ruidoso, turbulento, maleducado; (*~-mouthed*) gritón.

(b) *colour* chillón; (*in bad taste*) charro, cursi.

2 ADV V **loudly; to say sth out ~** decir algo en voz alta.

loudhailer ['laʊd'heɪləʳ] N (*Brit*) megáfono *m*, bocina *f.*

loudly ['laʊdlɪ] ADV en voz alta; fuertemente; ruidosamente, estrepitosamente.

loud-mouth ['laʊdmaʊθ] N bocazas* *m.*

loud-mouthed ['laʊd'maʊðd] ADJ gritón.

loudness ['laʊdnɪs] N lo alto; fuerza *f*; ruido *m*; lo chillón; vulgaridad *f.*

loudspeaker ['laʊd'spiːkəʳ] N altavoz *m*, altoparlante *m.*

Louis ['luːɪ] NM Luis.

Louisiana [lʊ,iːzɪ'ænə] N Luisiana *f.*

lounge [laʊndʒ] **1** N (*esp Brit: in house*) salón *m*, cuarto *m* de estar, living *m*, estancia *f* (*LAm*); (*Aer*) sala *f*; (*on liner etc*) salón *m.*

2 ATTR: **~ bar** salón-bar *m*; **~ suit** (*Brit*) traje *m* de calle.

3 VI (*saunter*) pasearse despacito; (*idle*) gandulear, pasar un rato sin hacer nada; **to ~ against a wall** apoyarse distraídamente en una pared; **to ~ back in a chair** repanchigarse en un asiento; **we spent a week lounging in Naples** pasamos una semana en Nápoles sin hacer nada.

◆ lounge about, lounge around VI holgazanear, gandulear, tirarse a la bartola.

lounger ['laʊndʒəʳ] N gandul *m*, haragán *m*, -ana *f*; azotacalles *mf.*

louse [laʊs] N, PL **lice** [laɪs] **(a)** (*insect*) piojo *m.* **(b)** (‡) canalla *m*, mierda‡ *m.*

◆ louse up‡ VT: **to ~ sth up** joder algo‡.

lousy ['laʊzɪ] ADJ **(a)** piojoso. **(b)** (‡) malísimo, horrible; *trick etc* vil, asqueroso; **I'm a ~ player** yo juego fatal*; **all for a few ~ quid** todo por unas jodidas libras‡; **we had a ~ time** lo pasamos fatal*. **(c)** (‡) **to be ~ with money** estar podrido de dinero*.

lout [laʊt] N gamberro *m*; patán *m.*

loutish ['laʊtɪʃ] ADJ grosero, maleducado.

Louvain ['luːveɪn] N Lovaina *f.*

louver, louvre ['luːvəʳ] N (*Archit*) lumbrera *f*; (*blind*) persiana *f.*

louvred, (*US*) **louvered** ['luːvəd] ADJ *shutters, windows* de láminas, de listones.

lovable ['lʌvəbl] ADJ amable, simpático.

▼ love [lʌv] **1** N **(a)** amor *m* (*for, of, towards* a, de); cariño *m*; (*for hobby etc*) afición *f* (*for, of* a); **first ~** primer amor *m*; **~ in a cottage** contigo pan y cebolla; **~ at first sight** amor *m* a primera vista, flechazo *m*; **for ~** por amor, (*free*) gratis, (*without stakes*) sin jugarse dinero, sin apuestas; **not for ~ nor money** por nada del mundo; **for the ~ of** por el amor de; **the ~ of God** (*for man*) el amor de Dios; **the ~ of (man for) God** el amor a Dios; **for the ~ of God!** ¡por Dios!; **to marry for ~** casarse por amor; **he studies history for the ~ of it** estudia la historia por pura afición al tema; **to be in ~** estar enamorado (*with* de); **to fall in ~** enamorarse (*with* de); **to make ~** hacer el amor, (*court*) pretender a una, (*sexually*) hacer el amor a una, (*fig: butter up, work on*) hacer la pelotilla a uno; **there is no ~ lost between them** existe entre ellos una fuerte antipatía, no se pueden ver.

(b) (*greetings, in letters etc*) '(**with my**) ~', '~ **from** ...' 'besos'; **give him my ~** mándale recuerdos míos; **to send one's ~ to sb** mandar cariñosos saludos a uno.

(c) (*person*) amado *m*, -a *f*; **yes, ~** sí, querida; sí, cariño; **my ~** mi amor, mi vida, mi cielo; **the child's a little ~** el niño es una monada.

(d) (*Tennis*) **~ all** cero-cero; **15 ~** 15 a cero.

2 ATTR: **~ game** (*Tennis*) juego en el cual el que recibe no ha marcado ningún punto.

▼ 3 VT *person etc* querer, amar; (*be fond of*) tener cariño a; *hobby etc* ser muy aficionado a; **she ~s me, she ~s me not** me quiere, no me quiere; **I ~ Madrid** me encanta Madrid, me gusta muchísimo Madrid; **I ~ this record** me encanta este disco; **he ~s swimming, he ~s to swim** le gusta muchísimo nadar, le entusiasma la natación; **I should ~ to come** me gustaría mucho venir, me encantaría venir; **I'd ~ to!** ¡con mucho gusto!, ¡yo, encantado!; **~ me ~ my dog** quien quiere a Beltrán quiere a su can.

LOVE   *see also main entry*

Love can usually be translated by *querer.*

- With people, pets and native lands, *querer* is the most typical translation:

  I love you
  Te quiero
  Timmy loves his mother more than his father
  Timmy quiere más a su madre que a su padre
  When he lived abroad he realized how much he loved his country
  Cuando vivía en el extranjero, se dio cuenta de lo mucho que quería a su país

- *Querer* is commonly used with *mucho* in statements like the following:

  I love my parents
  Quiero mucho a mis padres
  He loved his cat and was very depressed when it died
  Quería mucho a su gato y tuvo una gran depresión cuando murió

- Use *amar*, especially in formal language, to talk about spiritual or elevated forms of love:

  To love God above everything else
  Amar a Dios sobre todas las cosas
  Their duty was to love and respect their parents
  Su deber era amar y respetar a sus padres

- Use the impersonal *encantarle a uno* to talk about things and people that you like very much:

  He loved playing tennis
  Le encantaba jugar al tenis
  I love children
  (A mí) me encantan los niños

For further uses and examples, see main entry.

---

love-affair ['lʌvə,fɛəʳ] N amores *mpl*; aventura *f* sentimental; (*pej*) amoríos *mpl.*

lovebird ['lʌvbɜːd] N periquito *m*; **~s** (*fig*) palomitos *mpl*, tórtolos *mpl.*

love-bite ['lʌv,baɪt] N mordisco *m* amoroso.

love-child ['lʌvtʃaɪld] N, PL **love-children** ['lʌv,tʃɪldrən] hijo *m*, -a *f* de ganancia, hijo *m*, -a *f* natural.

-loved [lʌvd] ADJ *ending in compounds*: **much~** muy querido; **best~** más querido.

love handles‡ ['lʌvhændlz] NPL agarraderas* *fpl*, michelines* *mpl.*

love-hate ['lʌvheɪt] ATTR: **~ relationship** relación *f* de amor-odio.

loveless ['lʌvlɪs] ADJ sin amor.

love-letter ['lʌv,letəʳ] N carta *f* amorosa, carta *f* de amor.

love-life ['lʌvlaɪf] N vida *f* sentimental; vida *f* sexual.

loveliness ['lʌvlɪnɪs] N hermosura *f*, belleza *f*; encanto *m.*

lovelorn ['lʌvlɔːn] ADJ suspirando de amor, herido de amor; abandonado por su amante.

lovely ['lʌvlɪ] **1** ADJ (*beautiful*) hermoso; bello; (*delightful*) encantador, precioso, delicioso; (*pleasing, of objects etc*) mono, precioso, rico; *person* (*charming*) simpático; **isn't it ~?** ¿verdad que es precioso?; ¡qué rico!, ¡qué monada!; **we had a ~ time** lo pasamos la mar de bien; **I hope you have a ~ time!** ¡que os divirtáis!; **it's been ~ to see you** ha sido una visita encantadora; **he was a ~ man** era una bella persona.

2 N (*) belleza *f*, guapa *f.*

love-making ['lʌv,meɪkɪŋ] N (*courtship*) galanteo *m*; (*sexual*) trato *m* sexual, relaciones *fpl* sexuales.

love-match ['lʌvmætʃ] N matrimonio *m* por amor.

love-nest ['lʌvnest] N nido *m* de amor.

love-potion ['lʌv,pəʊʃən] N filtro *m.*

lover ['lʌvəʳ] N **(a)** amante *mf*; (*pej*) amante *mf*, querido *m*, -a *f*; **he became her ~** se hizo amante de ella; **we were ~s for 2 years** durante 2 años fuimos amantes; **so she took a ~** así que tomó un amante; **the ~s** los amantes, los novios.

(b) **a ~ of** (*hobby, wine etc*) un amigo de, una amiga de, un aficionado a, una aficionada a; **he is a great ~ of the violin** tiene muchísima afición al violín.

(c) (*in compounds*) *eg* **music-~** persona *f* aficionada a la música, melómano *m*, -a *f*; **football-~s everywhere** los aficionados al fútbol de todas partes.
lover-boy ['lʌvə,bɔɪ] N (*hum, iro*) macho *m*, macarra *m*.
loveseat ['lʌv,siːt] N (*US*) canapé *m*, confidente *m*.
lovesick ['lʌvsɪk] ADJ enfermo de amor, amartelado.
lovesong ['lʌvsɒŋ] N canción *f* de amor.
love-story ['lʌv,stɔːrɪ] N historia *f* de amor.
love-token ['lʌv,təʊkən] N prenda *f* (*or* prueba *f*) de amor.
love triangle ['lʌv,traɪæŋgl] N triángulo *m* amoroso.
lovey-dovey* [,lʌvɪ'dʌvɪ] ADJ tierno, sentimental.
loving ['lʌvɪŋ] ADJ amoroso; cariñoso, tierno.
-loving ['lʌvɪŋ] ADJ *ending in compounds*: **money~** amante del dinero, aficionado al dinero.
loving-cup ['lʌvɪŋkʌp] N copa *f* de la amistad (que circula en una cena *etc*, en que beben todos).
lovingly ['lʌvɪŋlɪ] ADV amorosamente; cariñosamente, tiernamente.
low¹ [ləʊ] 1 ADJ bajo; *light, number, rate, speed, temperature, voice* bajo; *bow* profundo; *blow* sucio; *dress* escotado; *card* pequeño; *gear* primero; *price* bajo; *reducido, módico; stock* escaso; *diet* deficiente; *note, tone* grave; *health* débil, malo; *birth, rank* humilde; *manners* grosero; *character* vil; *opinion* malo; *joke, song* verde; *trick* sucio, malo; *comedian* chabacano; **~ beam headlights** (*US*) luces *fpl* de cruce; **L~ Church** sector *m* de la Iglesia Anglicana de tendencia más protestante; **~ comedy** farsa *f*; **L~ Latin** bajo latín *m*; **~ mass** misa *f* rezada; **~ point** punto *m* (más) bajo; **~ salt** sal *f* dietética; **~ season** temporada *f* baja; **L~ Sunday** Domingo *m* de Cuasimodo; **~ vowel** vocal *f* grave; **5 at the ~est** 5 como mínimo; **activity is at its ~est** las actividades están en su punto más bajo; **the battery is ~** la batería se está acabando; **the temperature is in the ~ 40s** la temperatura es de 40 grados y alguno más; **to feel ~** estar por el suelo*; **stocks are getting ~** las existencias van escaseando; **to cook on a ~ heat** (*or oven, stove*) cocer a fuego lento; **we are getting ~ on fuel** tenemos poco combustible, se nos está agotando el combustible; *V* **tide**.
2 ADV *swing etc* bajo, cerca de la tierra (*etc*); *say, sing* bajo, en voz baja; **to bow ~** hacer una profunda reverencia; **a dress cut ~ in the back** un vestido muy escotado de espalda; **to fall ~** (*morally*) envilecerse, caer muy bajo; **England never fell so ~** Inglaterra nunca cayó tan bajo; **to lay sb ~** derribar a uno, abatir a uno, poner a uno fuera de combate; **to be laid ~ with 'flu** ser postrado por la gripe; **to lie ~** estar escondido, no asomar la cabeza; **to play ~** (*Cards*) poner pequeño; **to run ~** escasear, casi agotarse; **to sink ~** = **to fall ~**.
3 N **(a)** (*Met*) área *f* de baja presión, depresión *f*; (*US*) temperatura *f* mínima.
(b) (*Aut*) primera (marcha) *f*.
(c) (*fig*) punto *m* más bajo; **to reach a new ~** caer a su punto más bajo; **this represents a new ~ in deceit** ésta es la peor forma de vileza; no se ha visto cosa más vil; *V* **all-time**.
low² [ləʊ] 1 N mugido *m*.
2 VI mugir.
low-alcohol ['ləʊ'ælkəhɒl] ADJ con baja graduación.
lowborn ['ləʊ'bɔːn] ADJ de humilde cuna.
lowbrow ['ləʊbraʊ] 1 ADJ nada intelectual, poco culto.
2 N persona *f* nada intelectual, persona *f* de poca cultura.
low-budget [,ləʊ'bʌdʒɪt] ADJ de bajo presupuesto; **~ film** película *f* de presupuesto modesto.
low-cal* [,ləʊ'kæl] ADJ light.
low-calorie [,ləʊ'kælərɪ] ADJ bajo en calorías, acalórico.
low-class ['ləʊ,klɑːs] ADJ de clase baja.
low-cost ['ləʊ'kɒst] ADJ económico.
Low Countries ['ləʊ,kʌntrɪz] NPL Países *mpl* Bajos.
low-cut ['ləʊ'kʌt] ADJ *dress* escotado.
low-density [,ləʊ'densɪtɪ] ATTR de baja densidad.
low-down ['ləʊdaʊn] 1 ADJ bajo, vil.
2 N (*) verdad *f*; informes *mpl* confidenciales; **he gave me the ~ on it** me contó la verdad del caso; **come on, give us the ~** ven, dinos la verdad.
lower¹ ['ləʊər] 1 ADJ *comp of* **low**; más bajo, menos alto; inferior; **~ classes** clase *f* baja; **~ middle class** clase *f* media-baja; **L~ House** (*Brit Parl*) Cámara *f* baja; **the ~ income groups** los grupos de renta baja.
2 ADV *comp of* **low**; más bajo.
3 VT bajar; *boat* lanzar; *flag, sail* arriar; (*reduce*) reducir, disminuir; *price* rebajar; *morale, resistance* debilitar; *guard* aflojar; (*in dignity*) humillar; **to ~ one's headlights** (*US*) poner luces de cruce.
4 VR: **to ~ o.s.** descolgarse (*by, on, with* con); (*fig*) envilecerse; **to ~ o.s. to do sth** rebajarse a hacer algo.
lower² ['laʊər] VI (*person*) fruncir el entrecejo, mirar con ceño; (*sky*) encapotarse.
lower-case ['ləʊə,keɪs] ATTR minúsculo, de letra minúscula; **~ letter** minúscula *f*.
lower-class ['ləʊə,klɑːs] ADJ de la clase baja.

lowering ['laʊərɪŋ] ADJ ceñudo; amenazador; *sky* encapotado.
low-fat ['ləʊ'fæt] ATTR: **~ foods** alimentos *mpl* bajos en grasas; **~ milk** leche *f* desnatada.
low-flying ['ləʊ,flaɪɪŋ] ADJ de baja cota.
low-grade ['ləʊ'greɪd] ADJ de baja calidad.
low-heeled ['ləʊ'hiːld] ADJ *shoes* de tacones bajos.
lowing ['ləʊɪŋ] N mugidos *mpl*.
low-key [,ləʊ'kiː] ADJ *speech* moderado, en un tono bajo.
lowland ['ləʊlənd] 1 N tierra *f* baja; **the L~s** las tierras bajas de Escocia.
2 ADJ de tierra baja.
lowlander ['ləʊləndər] N habitante *mf* de tierra baja.
low-level ['ləʊ'levl] ADJ de bajo nivel; **~ language** lenguaje *m* de bajo nivel.
lowlights ['ləʊlaɪts] NPL **(a)** (*Hairdressing*) reflejos *mpl* oscuros, mechas *fpl* oscuras. **(b)** (*gen hum*: *of TV programme, football match etc*) momentos *mpl* más aburridos.
lowliness ['ləʊlɪnɪs] N humildad *f*.
low-loader [,ləʊ'ləʊdər] N (*Aut*) camión de plataforma baja para el transporte de maquinaria pesada.
lowly ['ləʊlɪ] ADJ humilde.
low-lying ['ləʊ,laɪɪŋ] ADJ bajo.
low-minded ['ləʊ'maɪndɪd] ADJ vulgar, vil, mezquino.
low-necked ['ləʊ'nekt] ADJ escotado.
lowness ['ləʊnɪs] N bajeza *f*, lo bajo; escasez *f*; gravedad *f*; humildad *f*; vileza *f*; lo verde; (*of spirits*) abatimiento *m*.
low-paid [,ləʊ'peɪd] 1 ADJ mal pagado.
2 NPL: **the ~** los mal pagados.
low-pitched ['ləʊpɪtʃt] ADJ *note, voice* bajo; *campaign, speech* en tono menor.
low-powered ['ləʊpaʊəd] ADJ de baja potencia.
low-pressure ['ləʊ'preʃər] ADJ de baja presión.
low-priced [,ləʊ'praɪst] ADJ barato, económico.
low-profile ['ləʊ'prəʊfaɪl] ATTR: **~ activity** actividad *f* discreta, actividad *f* que evita llamar la atención.
low-ranking [,ləʊ'ræŋkɪŋ] ADJ (*Mil*) official de baja graduación.
low-rise ['ləʊraɪz] ADJ de baja altura.
low-risk [,ləʊ'rɪsk] ATTR de bajo riesgo.
low-slung ['ləʊslʌŋ] ADJ *chair* con el asiento bajo; *sports car* con el suelo bajo.
low-spirited ['ləʊ'spɪrɪtɪd] ADJ deprimido, abatido.
low-tech ['ləʊtek] ADJ de tecnología poco avanzada.
low-tension ['ləʊ'tenʃən] ADJ de baja tensión.
low water ['ləʊ'wɔːtər] 1 N bajamar *f*, marea *f* baja.
2 ATTR: **~ mark** línea *f* de bajamar.
loyal ['lɔɪəl] ADJ leal, fiel (*to* a).
loyalist ['lɔɪəlɪst] N legitimista *mf*, gubernamental *mf*; (*Spain, 1936*) republicano *m*, -a *f*; (*eg Ulster*) lealista *mf*.
loyally ['lɔɪəlɪ] ADV lealmente.
loyalty ['lɔɪəltɪ] N lealtad *f*, fidelidad *f* (*to* a); **one's loyalties** la lealtad de uno.
lozenge ['lɒzɪndʒ] N **(a)** (*Med*) pastilla *f*. **(b)** (*Math*) rombo *m*; (*Her*) losange *m*.
LP N **(a)** (*Pol*) ABBR *of* **Labour Party** Partido *m* Laborista. **(b)** (*Mus*) ABBR *of* **long-playing record** elepé *m*.
L-plate ['elpleɪt] N placa *f* de la L (*de conductor en prácticas*); *ver también* DRIVING LICENCE/DRIVER'S LICENSE .
LPN N (*US*) ABBR *of* **Licensed Practical Nurse** enfermera practicante.
LPU N ABBR *of* **least publishable unit** cuanto *m* de publicación.
LRAM N (*Brit*) ABBR *of* **Licentiate of the Royal Academy of Music** Licenciado *m*, -a *f* de la Real Academia de Música.
LRCP N (*Brit*) ABBR *of* **Licentiate of the Royal College of Physicians** ≃ médico *m* colegiado, médica *f* colegiada.
LRCS N (*Brit*) ABBR *of* **Licentiate of the Royal College of Surgeons** ≃ cirujano *m* colegiado, cirujana *f* colegiada.
LSAT N (*US*) ABBR *of* **Law School Admission Test**.
LSD N ABBR *of* **lysergic acid diethylamide** dimetilamida *f* del ácido lisérgico, LSD *f*.
L.S.D. N (*Brit* ††) ABBR *of* **librae, solidi, denarii** = **pounds, shillings and pence** antigua moneda británica; (*) pasta* *f*.
LSE N (*Brit*) ABBR *of* **London School of Economics**.
LSI N ABBR *of* **large-scale integration** integración *f* a gran escala.
LST N (*US*) ABBR *of* **Local Standard Time**.
LT N (*Elec*) ABBR *of* **low tension** baja tensión *f*.
Lt ABBR *of* **lieutenant** teniente *m*, ten.ᵗᵉ
Lt.-Col. ABBR *of* **lieutenant-colonel** teniente *m* coronel.
Ltd ABBR *of* **limited** Sociedad *f* Anónima, S.A.
Lt.-Gen. ABBR *of* **lieutenant-general** teniente *m* general.
lubricant ['luːbrɪkənt] 1 ADJ lubricante.
2 N lubricante *m*.
lubricate ['luːbrɪkeɪt] VT lubricar, engrasar.
lubricating ['luːbrɪkeɪtɪŋ] ADJ lubricante; **~ oil** aceite *m* lubricante.

lubrication [ˌluːbrɪˈkeɪʃən] N lubricación f, engrase m.
lubricator [ˈluːbrɪkeɪtəʳ] N lubricador m.
lubricious [luːˈbrɪʃəs] ADJ verde, salaz, lascivo.
lubricity [luːˈbrɪsɪtɪ] N lubricidad f.
Lucan [ˈluːkən] NM Lucano.
lucerne [luːˈsɜːn] N (esp Brit) alfalfa f.
lucid [ˈluːsɪd] ADJ claro, lúcido; **~ interval** intervalo m lúcido.
lucidity [luːˈsɪdɪtɪ] N lucidez f.
lucidly [ˈluːsɪdlɪ] ADV claramente, con claridad.
Lucifer [ˈluːsɪfəʳ] NM Lucifer.
▼ **luck** [lʌk] N suerte f, fortuna f; azar m; **bad ~, hard ~** mala suerte f; **bad ~!** ¡mala suerte!; **good ~** suerte f; **best of ~!, good ~!** ¡que tengas suerte!; **beginner's ~** suerte f del principiante; **any ~?** ¿y qué?; **here's ~!** (toast) ¡salud!; **no such ~!** ¡ojalá!; **with any ~** a lo mejor; **worse ~!** ¡desgraciadamente!; **better ~ next time!** ¡a la tercera va la vencida!; **and the best of ~!** (iro) ¡Dios te la depare buena!; **to be in ~** estar de suerte, tener suerte; **to be out of ~, to be down on one's ~** estar de malas; **to bring sb bad ~** traer mala suerte a uno; **as ~ would have it** quiso la suerte que ...; **to have the devil's own ~, to have the ~ of the devil** tener buena chorra, tener buena pata; **to have the ~ to** + infin tener la suerte de + infin; **to keep sth for ~** guardar algo por si trae suerte; **take this for ~** toma esto por si trae suerte; **to do sth trusting to ~** hacer algo a la buena de Dios; **to try one's ~** probar fortuna.
luckily [ˈlʌkɪlɪ] ADV afortunadamente, por fortuna.
luckless [ˈlʌklɪs] ADJ desdichado, desafortunado.
lucky [ˈlʌkɪ] ADJ person afortunado, feliz, que tiene suerte; day de buen agüero; move, shot etc afortunado; charm que trae suerte; **~ dip** (Brit) caja f de las sorpresas; **~ number** número m afortunado; **this is my ~ day** éste es mi día de suerte; **third time ~!** ¡a la tercera va la vencida!; **~ you!** ¡qué suerte!; **to be ~** (person) tener suerte; (charm etc) traer suerte; **you'll be ~!** (*: iro) ¡sería milagro!; **I should be so ~!** ¡ojalá!; **you'll be ~ to get £50 for that old banger** sería un milagro si te dieran 50 libras por el cacharro ese*; **to be a ~ sort** tener buena sombra; **to be born ~** nacer de pie; **to be ~ in that ...** tener la suerte de que ...; **that was very ~ for you** en eso tuviste mucha suerte; **to believe in one's ~ star** creer en su buena estrella; **to strike (it) ~** tener suerte, estar de suerte; **you can think yourself ~ that ...** puedes considerarte afortunado que ...
lucrative [ˈluːkrətɪv] ADJ lucrativo, provechoso.
lucre [ˈluːkəʳ] N: **filthy ~** el vil metal.
Lucretia [luːˈkriːʃə] NF Lucrecia.
Lucretius [luːˈkriːʃəs] NM Lucrecio.
lucubration [ˌluːkjʊˈbreɪʃən] N lucubración f.
Lucy [ˈluːsɪ] NF Lucía.
Luddite [ˈlʌdaɪt] **1** ADJ ludista.
  2 N ludista mf.
ludic [ˈluːdɪk] ADJ lúdico.
ludicrous [ˈluːdɪkrəs] ADJ absurdo, ridículo.
ludicrously [ˈluːdɪkrəslɪ] ADV absurdamente, ridículamente.
ludo [ˈluːdəʊ] N (Brit) ludo m.
luff [lʌf] **1** N orza f.
  2 VI orzar.
luffa [ˈlʌfə] N (US) esponja f de lufa.
lug [lʌg] **1** N (a) oreja f; agarradera f; (Tech) orejeta f; (:) oreja f.
  (b) (tug) tirón m.
  2 VT (drag) arrastrar; llevar con dificultad; (pull) tirar de; **to ~ sth about (or around) with one** llevar algo consigo (con dificultad); **to ~ sth along** arrastrar algo; **to ~ sth in** llevar algo dentro arrastrándolo, subject sacar a colación; **they ~ged him off to the theatre** le llevaron contra su voluntad al teatro.
luggage [ˈlʌgɪdʒ] N equipaje m.
luggage-boot [ˈlʌgɪdʒˌbuːt] N (Brit Aut) maletero m, portaequipajes m.
luggage car [ˈlʌgɪdʒˌkɑːr] N (US) furgón m de equipaje.
luggage-carrier [ˈlʌgɪdʒˌkærɪəʳ] N, **luggage-grid** [ˈlʌgɪdʒˌgrɪd] N portaequipajes m, baca f.
luggage checkroom [ˈlʌgɪdʒˌtʃekrʊm] N (US) consigna f.
luggage-handler [ˈlʌgɪdʒˌhændləʳ] N despachador m de equipaje.
luggage-label [ˈlʌgɪdʒˌleɪbl] N etiqueta f de equipaje.
luggage-locker [ˈlʌgɪdʒˌlɒkəʳ] N consigna f automática.
luggage-rack [ˈlʌgɪdʒˌræk] N (Rail etc) rejilla f, redecilla f; (Aut) portaequipajes m, baca f.
luggage-van [ˈlʌgɪdʒˌvæn] N (Brit) furgón m (de equipajes).
lugger [ˈlʌgəʳ] N lugre m.
lughole: [ˈlʌgəʊl] N oreja f; oído m.
lugsail [ˈlʌgsl] N vela f al tercio.
lugubrious [luːˈguːbrɪəs] ADJ lúgubre, triste.
lugubriously [luːˈguːbrɪəslɪ] ADV lúgubremente, tristemente.
lugworm [ˈlʌgˌwɜːm] N lombriz f de mar.
Luke [luːk] NM Lucas.
lukewarm [ˈluːkwɔːm] ADJ tibio, templado; (fig) tibio, indiferente,

poco entusiasta.
lull [lʌl] **1** N tregua f, respiro m, intervalo m de calma; (in storm, wind) recalmón m.
  2 VT person calmar, (to sleep) adormecer, arrullar; fears etc calmar, aquietar, sosegar.
lullaby [ˈlʌləbaɪ] N nana f, canción f de cuna.
lumbago [lʌmˈbeɪgəʊ] N lumbago m.
lumbar [ˈlʌmbəʳ] ADJ lumbar.
lumber¹ [ˈlʌmbəʳ] **1** N (a) (timber) maderos mpl, maderas fpl (de sierra).
  (b) (junk) trastos mpl viejos.
  2 VT (a) space, room obstruir (with de); **to ~ things together** amontonar cosas; (fig) juntar cosas sin orden.
  (b) (Brit*) **to ~ sb with sth** hacer que uno cargue con algo; **he got ~ed with the job** tuvo que cargar con el trabajo; **I got ~ed with the girl for the evening** tuve que pasar toda la tarde con la chica.
  3 VI cortar y aserrar árboles, explotar los bosques.
lumber² [ˈlʌmbəʳ] VI: **to ~ about, to ~ along** moverse pesadamente, avanzar con ruido sordo.
lumbering¹ [ˈlʌmbərɪŋ] N (US) explotación f forestal.
lumbering² [ˈlʌmbərɪŋ] ADJ pesado, torpe.
lumberjack [ˈlʌmbədʒæk] N, **lumberman** [ˈlʌmbəmən] N, PL **lumbermen** [ˈlʌmbəmən] maderero m, hachero m, leñador m; trabajador m forestal.
lumber jacket [ˈlʌmbəˌdʒækɪt] N chaqueta f de leñador.
lumber mill [ˈlʌmbəˌmɪl] N aserradero m.
lumber room [ˈlʌmbərʊm] N trastera f.
lumberyard [ˈlʌmbəjɑːd] N (US) almacén m de madera.
luminary [ˈluːmɪnərɪ] N lumbrera f.
luminescence [ˌluːmɪˈnesns] N luminescencia f.
luminosity [ˌluːmɪˈnɒsɪtɪ] N luminosidad f.
luminous [ˈluːmɪnəs] ADJ luminoso.
lumme: [ˈlʌmɪ] INTERJ (Brit) = **lummy.**
lummox* [ˈlʌməks] N (US) bobo m.
lummy: [ˈlʌmɪ] INTERJ (Brit) ¡caray!*
lump [lʌmp] **1** N (a) (of earth, sugar etc) terrón m; (mass) masa f informe; (fragment) trozo m, pedazo m; (swelling) bulto m, hinchazón f; (on surface) protuberancia f; (in throat) nudo m; (person) zoquete m, paquete m (LAm); **with a ~ in one's throat** con un nudo en la garganta; **I get a ~ in my throat** se me anuda la garganta.
  (b) (*: person) zoquete m, paquete m (LAm); **ugly ~** foca* f.
  2 ATTR: **~ sugar** azúcar m en terrones, azúcar m de cortadillo; **~ sum** suma f global.
  3 VT: (Brit*) **to ~ it** (go) largarse*; (bear it) aguantarlo; **you'll have to ~ it** tendrás que aguantarlo; **if he doesn't like it he can ~ it** si no le gusta que se fastidie*.
◆ **lump together** VT objects amontonar; persons, subjects poner juntos, agrupar, mezclar.
lumpish [ˈlʌmpɪʃ] ADJ torpe, pesado.
lumpy [ˈlʌmpɪ] ADJ soil aterronado; liquid etc lleno de grumos, con muchos grumos; bed etc desigual, nada cómodo.
lunacy [ˈluːnəsɪ] N locura f; **it's sheer ~!** ¡es una locura!
lunar [ˈluːnəʳ] ADJ lunar; **~ eclipse** eclipse m lunar; **~ module** módulo m lunar; **~ month** mes m lunar.
lunatic [ˈluːnətɪk] **1** ADJ lunático, loco, demente; **~ asylum** manicomio m; **~ fringe** franja f lunática.
  2 N loco m, -a f.
lunch [lʌntʃ] **1** N (also more formally **luncheon** [ˈlʌntʃən]) almuerzo m, comida f; (snack) bocadillo m; **he's out to ~*** (US) está en la luna; **to have ~, to take ~** almorzar, comer.
  2 VI almorzar, comer (on fish pescado); tomar un bocadillo.
lunchbox [ˈlʌntʃbɒks] N (a) fiambrera f, tartera f. (b) (*: hum) paquete: m.
lunch-break [ˈlʌntʃˌbreɪk] N descanso m de comer.
lunch counter [ˈlʌntʃˌkaʊntəʳ] (US) N (café) cafetería donde se sirven comidas; (counter) mostrador o barra donde se come.
luncheonette [ˌlʌntʃəˈnet] N bar m para almuerzos.
luncheon meat [ˈlʌntʃənˌmiːt] N carne f en conserva, carne f en lata.
luncheon voucher [ˈlʌntʃənˌvaʊtʃəʳ] N (Brit) vale m de comida.
lunch-hour [ˈlʌntʃaʊəʳ] N hora f de comer.
lunchtime [ˈlʌntʃtaɪm] N hora f de comer.
lung [lʌŋ] **1** N pulmón m.
  2 ATTR: **~ cancer** cáncer m de pulmón.
lunge [lʌndʒ] **1** N arremetida f, embestida f; (Fencing) estocada f.
  2 VI arremeter (at contra, with con), embestir; dar una estocada; **to ~ at sb** abalanzarse sobre uno; **he ~d with his right** le asestó un derechazo.
lupin [ˈluːpɪn] N altramuz m, lupino m.
lurch¹ [lɜːtʃ] N: **to leave sb in the ~** dejar a uno en la estacada, dejar a uno plantado.
lurch² [lɜːtʃ] **1** N sacudida f, tumbo m, movimiento m repentino; (Naut) bandazo m; **to give a ~** dar un tumbo (etc).

► LANGUAGE IN USE: luck → 23.5

2 VI (*vehicle etc*) dar sacudidas, dar tumbos, dar un tumbo; (*Naut*) dar un bandazo; (*person*) tambalearse.

◆**lurch along** VI (*vehicle*) ir dando tumbos; (*person*) avanzar tambaleándose.

◆**lurch in** VI entrar tambaleándose.

◆**lurch out** VI salir tambaleándose.

lure [ljʊəʳ] 1 N (a) (*bait*) cebo *m*; (*decoy*) señuelo *m*.
(b) (*fig*) aliciente *m*, atractivo *m*; encanto *m*; (*deceitful*) señuelo *m*.
2 VT atraer (con señuelo); *person* atraer, tentar; seducir; **to ~ sb into a trap** hacer que uno caiga en una trampa; **to ~ sb into a house** persuadir mañosamente a uno a entrar en una casa.

◆**lure away** VT: **to ~ sb away from** apartar a uno de.

◆**lure on** VT: **to ~ sb on to destruction** hacer que uno avance ciegamente hacia su ruina.

◆**lure out** VT: **to ~ sb out** persuadir mañosamente a uno a salir.

lurex ['lʊəreks] N lúrex *m*.

lurgy: ['lɜːgɪ] N (*Brit: hum*): **to have the ~** (*flu, cold*) tener la gripe.

lurid ['ljʊərɪd] ADJ *light* misterioso, fantástico; *colour of skin* lívido, cárdeno; *dress etc* chillón; *language* fuerte, pintoresco; *account* sensacional; *detail* horripilante, espeluznante.

lurk [lɜːk] VI estar escondido; estar en acecho.

lurking ['lɜːkɪŋ] ADJ *fear etc* vago, indefinible.

luscious ['lʌʃəs] ADJ delicioso, suculento, riquísimo, exquisito; *style* empalagoso; *girl* delicioso, apetitoso.

lusciousness ['lʌʃəsnɪs] N suculencia *f*, riqueza *f*; exquisitez *f*; lo empalagoso.

lush [lʌʃ] 1 ADJ (a) *growth, vegetation* lozano, exuberante; *pasture* rico.
(b) *fruit etc* V **luscious**. (c) (*opulent*) opulento, lujoso.
2 N (‡) alcohólico *m*, -a *f*.

lushness ['lʌʃnɪs] N (a) lozanía *f*, exuberancia *f*. (b) V **lusciousness**. (c) opulencia *f*, lujo *m*.

lust [lʌst] 1 N (*sexual*) lujuria *f*, lascivia *f*; sensualidad *f*; (*greed*) codicia *f*, deseo *m* vehemente (*for* de).
2 VI lujuriar.

◆**lust after, lust for** VT (*sexually*) apetecer contacto carnal con; *object* codiciar.

luster ['lʌstəʳ] N (*US*) = **lustre**.

lustful ['lʌstfʊl] ADJ lujurioso, libidinoso; *look etc* lascivo.

lustfully ['lʌstfəlɪ] ADV lujuriosamente, libidinosamente; lascivamente.

lustfulness ['lʌstfʊlnɪs] N lujuria *f*, lascivia *f*; sensualidad *f*.

lustre, (*US*) **luster** ['lʌstəʳ] N lustre *m*, brillo *m*.

lustreless, (*US*) **lusterless** ['lʌstəlɪs] ADJ deslustrado; *eyes* apagado.

lustrous ['lʌstrəs] ADJ lustroso, brillante.

lusty ['lʌstɪ] ADJ *person* vigoroso, fuerte, robusto; *plant* lozano; *cry* fuerte; *effort etc* grande.

lute [luːt] N laúd *m*.

lutetium [lʊ'tiːʃɪəm] N lutecio *m*.

Luther ['luːθəʳ] NM Lutero.

Lutheran ['luːθərən] 1 ADJ luterano.
2 N luterano *m*, -a *f*.

Lutheranism ['luːθərənɪzəm] N luteranismo *m*.

luv* [lʌv] N (= **love**): **yes, ~** sí, cariño.

luvvies* ['lʌvɪz] NPL (*Brit: pej: actors*) gente *f* de la farándula.

Luxembourg ['lʌksəmbɜːg] N Luxemburgo *m*.

Luxembourger ['lʌksəmbɜːgəʳ] N luxemburgués *m*, -ésa *f*.

luxuriance [lʌg'zjʊərɪəns] N lozanía *f*, exuberancia *f*.

luxuriant [lʌg'zjʊərɪənt] ADJ lozano, exuberante.

luxuriantly [lʌg'zjʊərɪəntlɪ] ADV con lozanía, de manera exuberante.

luxuriate [lʌg'zjʊərɪeɪt] VI (*plant*) crecer con exuberancia; (*person*) disfrutar; **to ~ in** disfrutar de, deleitarse con, entregarse al lujo de.

luxurious [lʌg'zjʊərɪəs] ADJ lujoso.

luxuriously [lʌg'zjʊərɪəslɪ] ADV lujosamente.

luxury ['lʌkʃərɪ] 1 N (*gen*) lujo *m*; (*article*) artículo *m* de lujo; **to live in ~** vivir en el lujo.
2 ATTR de lujo; **~ tax** impuesto *m* de lujo.

LV ABBR of **luncheon voucher**.

LW N (*Rad*) ABBR of **long wave** onda *f* larga, OL *f*.

lyceum [laɪ'siːəm] N liceo *m*.

lychee [ˌlaɪ'tʃiː] N lychee *m*, lichi *m*.

lychgate ['lɪtʃgeɪt] N entrada *f* de cementerio.

Lycra ['laɪkrə] ® N licra *f*.

lye [laɪ] N lejía *f*.

lying¹ ['laɪɪŋ] 1 ADJ mentiroso, falso.
2 N mentiras *fpl*.

lying² ['laɪɪŋ] V **lie²**.

lying-in ['laɪɪŋ'ɪn] 1 N (*Med*) parto *m*.
2 ATTR: **~ ward** sala *f* de maternidad.

lymph [lɪmf] 1 N linfa *f*.
2 ATTR: **~ gland** ganglio *m* linfático.

lymphatic [lɪm'fætɪk] 1 ADJ linfático.
2 N vaso *m* linfático.

lymphocyte ['lɪmfəʊˌsaɪt] N linfocito *m*.

lynch [lɪntʃ] VT linchar.

lynching ['lɪntʃɪŋ] N linchamiento *m*.

lynch law ['lɪntʃlɔː] N ley *f* del linchamiento.

lynch mob ['lɪntʃˌmɒb] N panda *f* de linchadores.

lynchpin ['lɪntʃpɪn] = **linchpin**.

lynx [lɪŋks] N lince *m*.

lynx-eyed ['lɪŋksaɪd] ADJ de ojos de lince.

Lyons ['laɪənz] N Lyón *m*.

lyre ['laɪəʳ] N lira *f*.

lyrebird ['laɪəbɜːd] N ave *f* lira.

lyric ['lɪrɪk] 1 ADJ lírico.
2 N (*poem*) poema *m* lírico, poesía *f* lírica; (*genre*) lírica *f*; (*words of song*) letra *f* de una canción.

lyrical ['lɪrɪkəl] ADJ lírico; (*fig*) elocuente, entusiasta; **to grow** (*or* **wax**) **~ about sth** entusiasmarse por algo, extasiarse ante algo.

lyricism ['lɪrɪsɪzem] N lirismo *m*.

lyricist ['lɪrɪsɪst] N letrista *mf*.

lysergic [lɪ'sɜːdʒɪk] ADJ: **~ acid** ácido *m* lisérgico.

Lysol ['laɪsɒl] ® N lisol ® *m*.

M

M, m [em] N (*letter*) M, m *f*; **M for Mary, M for Mike** (*US*) M de Madrid.

M (**a**) ABBR *of* **million(s)**. (**b**) (*garment size*) ABBR *of* **medium**.

m (**a**) ABBR *of* **married** se casó con. (**b**) ABBR *of* **metre(s)** metro(s) *m(pl)*, m. (**c**) ABBR *of* **mile(s)** milla(s) *f(pl)*. (**d**) ABBR *of* **male** macho *m*. (**e**) ABBR *of* **minute(s)** minuto(s) *m(pl)*, m.

MA (**a**) N (*Univ*) ABBR *of* **Master of Arts**; *ver también* ⎡DEGREE⎤ . (**b**) (*US Post*) ABBR *of* **Massachusetts**.

M.A. (*US*) ABBR *of* **Military Academy**.

ma* [mɑː] N mamá* *f*.

ma'am [mæm] N = **madam**.

mac [mæk] N (**a**) (*Brit*) impermeable *m*. (**b**) **this way, M~!*** ¡por aquí, amigo!

macabre [məˈkɑːbr] ADJ macabro.

macadam [məˈkædəm] N macadán *m*.

macadamize [məˈkædəmaɪz] VT macadamizar.

macaroni [ˌmækəˈrəʊnɪ] N macarrones *mpl*.

macaronic [ˌmækəˈrɒnɪk] ADJ macarrónico.

macaroon [ˌmækəˈruːn] N macarrón *m* (de almendras), mostachón *m*.

macaw [məˈkɔː] N guacamayo *m*, avacanza *m*.

mace¹ [meɪs] N (*Bot*) macis *f*.

mace² [meɪs] N maza *f*.

macebearer [ˈmeɪsˌbeərəʳ] N macero *m*.

Macedonia [ˌmæsɪˈdəʊnɪə] N Macedonia *f*.

Macedonian [ˌmæsɪˈdəʊnɪən] ⎡1⎤ ADJ, N macedonio *m*, -a *f*.
⎡2⎤ N (*Ling*) macedonio *m*.

macerate [ˈmæsəreɪt] ⎡1⎤ VT macerar.
⎡2⎤ VI macerar(se).

Mach [mæk] N mach *m*.

machete [məˈtʃeɪtɪ] N machete *m*.

Machiavelli [ˌmækɪəˈvelɪ] NM Maquiavelo.

Machiavellian [ˌmækɪəˈvelɪən] ADJ maquiavélico.

machination [ˌmækɪˈneɪʃən] N maquinación *f*.

machine [məˈʃiːn] ⎡1⎤ N (**a**) máquina *f* (*also fig*); aparato *m*; (*Aut*) coche *m*; (*cycle*) bicicleta *f*; (*Aer*) aparato *m*, avión *m*.
(**b**) (*Pol etc*) organización *f*, aparato *m*.
⎡2⎤ ATTR mecánico, (hecho) a máquina; **~ age** época *f* de la máquina; **~ code** código *m* máquina; **~ error** error *m* de la máquina; **~ intelligence** inteligencia *f* máquina; **~ language** lenguaje *m* máquina; **~ operator** maquinista *mf*; **~ time** tiempo *m* máquina; **~ translation** traducción *f* automática, traducción *f* automatizada.
⎡3⎤ VT (*Tech*) trabajar a máquina, acabar a máquina; (*Sew*) coser a máquina.

machine-gun [məˈʃiːngʌn] ⎡1⎤ N ametralladora *f*.
⎡2⎤ VT ametrallar.

machine-gunner [məˈʃiːngʌnəʳ] N ametrallador *m*.

machine-made [məˈʃiːnmeɪd] ADJ hecho a máquina.

machine-readable [məˈʃiːnˈriːdəbl] ADJ legible por máquina; **in ~ form** en forma legible por máquina; **~ code** código *m* legible por máquina.

machinery [məˈʃiːnərɪ] N (**a**) (*machines*) maquinaria *f*; (*mechanism*) mecanismo *m*. (**b**) (*fig*) mecanismo *m*, organización *f*, sistema *m*.

machine-shop [məˈʃiːnʃɒp] N taller *m* de máquinas.

machine-stitch [məˈʃiːnˌstɪtʃ] VT coser a máquina.

machine-tool [məˈʃiːntuːl] N máquina *f* herramienta.

machine-wash [məˈʃiːnwɒʃ] VT lavar a máquina.

machine-washable [məˈʃiːnwɒʃəbl] ADJ lavable en la lavadora.

machinist [məˈʃiːnɪst] N (*Tech*) maquinista *mf*; operario *m* de máquina, mecánico *m*; (*Sew*) costurera *f* a máquina.

machismo [məˈtʃɪzməʊ] N machismo *m*.

macho [ˈmætʃəʊ] ⎡1⎤ ADJ macho, masculino.
⎡2⎤ N macho *m*, machista *m*, machote *m*.

mackerel [ˈmækrəl] ⎡1⎤ N caballa *f*, berdel *m*, escombro *m*.

⎡2⎤ ATTR: **~ sky** cielo *m* aborregado.

mackintosh [ˈmækɪntɒʃ] N impermeable *m*.

macramé [məˈkrɑːmɪ] N macramé *m*.

macro... [ˈmækrəʊ] PREF macro...

macro [ˈmækrəʊ] N (*Comput*) ABBR *of* **macro-instruction** macro-instrucción *f*, macro *m*.

macrobiotic [ˌmækrəʊbaɪˈɒtɪk] ADJ macrobiótico.

macrobiotics [ˌmækrəʊbaɪˈɒtɪks] N macrobiótica *f*.

macrocosm [ˈmækrəʊkɒzm] N macrocosmo *m*.

macroeconomic [ˌmækrəʊˌiːkəˈnɒmɪk] ADJ macroeconómico.

macroeconomics [ˌmækrəʊˌiːkəˈnɒmɪks] N macroeconomía *f*.

macroeconomy [ˌmækrəʊˈkɒnəmɪ] N macroeconomía *f*.

macroscopic [ˌmækrəˈskɒpɪk] ADJ macroscópico.

⎡ **MACY'S THANKSGIVING PARADE** ⎤

ⓘ **Macy's Thanksgiving Parade** *es una cabalgata anual que tiene lugar en Nueva York el Día de Acción de Gracias, el cuarto jueves de noviembre. Patrocinado por los grandes almacenes* **Macy's**, *este desfile de globos con personajes de dibujos animados, bandas de música y grupos de personas que vienen de todas las partes de EE.UU. recorre las calles de Broadway a la vez que se televisa a todo el país. En el desfile son típicas unas carrozas profusamente adornadas llamados* **floats**, *en las que van montados cantantes famosos y estrellas de Broadway. A pesar de que se celebra el Día de Acción de Gracias, el tema del desfile es la Navidad y Santa Claus siempre va en la última carroza.*
⇨ *Ver también* ⎡THANKSGIVING⎤

mad [mæd] ⎡1⎤ ADJ (**a**) (*deranged*) loco; demente; *dog* rabioso; *idea* loco, insensato, disparatado; *gallop, rush etc* loco, precipitado; **~ cow disease** encefalopatía *f* espongiforme bovina; **~ as a hatter**, **~ as a March hare** más loco que una cabra; **raving ~**, **stark (staring) ~** loco de atar; **a ~ thing (to do)** una locura; **are you ~?** ¿estás loco?; **you must be ~!** ¡qué locura!; **to be ~ with joy** estar loco de alegría; **to drive sb ~** volver loco a uno; **to go ~** volverse loco, enloquecer; **this is patriotism gone ~** esto es el patriotismo en grado ridículo; **to play** (*etc*) **like ~** tocar (*etc*) como un loco; **to rain like ~** llover muchísimo; **the plant grows like ~** la planta crece con una rapidez asombrosa.
(**b**) (*: *angry*) furioso; **to be ~ about sth** estar furioso por algo; **to be ~ about** (*or* **at**) **sb** estar furioso contra uno; **to get ~** enfadarse, ponerse furioso (**with** con); **it's no good getting ~ with me** de nada sirve ponerte furioso conmigo; **it makes me ~** me saca de quicio, me da rabia; **~ as a hornet** (*US*) cabreadísimo*.
(**c**) (*: *enthusiastic*) loco; **to be ~ about** (*or* **on**) estar loco por, ser muy aficionado a, entusiasmarse por; **he's ~ about her** está locamente enamorado de ella; **I'm just ~ about you** ando loco por ti; **I can't say I'm ~ about the idea** la idea no me apasiona que digamos.
⎡2⎤ (*) ADV: **to be ~ keen on sth** entusiasmarse como un loco por algo; **to be ~ keen to do sth** desear con vehemencia hacer algo.

-mad [mæd] ADJ *ending in compounds eg* **pony~** teenagers quinceañeras *fpl* locas por los caballitos; **soccer~ boys** chicos *mpl* con la manía del fútbol.

Madagascar [ˌmædəˈgæskəʳ] N Madagascar *m*.

madam [ˈmædəm] N señora *f*; **yes ~** sí señora; **little ~** niña *f* precoz, niña *f* repipi; *V* **dear**.

madame [ˈmædəm] N, PL **mesdames** [ˈmeɪdæm] (**a**) madama *f*, señora *f*; **M~ Dupont** la señora de Dupont. (**b**) (*of brothel*) ama *f*, dueña *f*.

madcap [ˈmædkæp] ⎡1⎤ ADJ atolondrado.
⎡2⎤ N locuelo *m*, -a *f*, tarambana *mf*.

madden [ˈmædn] VT volver loco; (*fig*) volver loco, enfurecer, sacar de quicio; **a ~ed bull** un toro enloquecido; **it ~s me** me saca de quicio, me da rabia.

maddening ['mædnɪŋ] ADJ *delay etc* desesperante, exasperante; **he can be ~ at times** hay veces cuando saca a todos de quicio; **isn't it ~?** ¡es para volverse loco!

maddeningly ['mædnɪŋlɪ] ADV de modo desesperante; **~ slow** terriblemente lento.

made [meɪd] PRET AND PTP *of* **make**.

Madeira [mə'dɪərə] N Madera *f*; (*wine*) vino *m* de Madera.

made-to-measure [,meɪdtə'meʒəʳ] ADJ (*Brit*) hecho a la medida.

made-to-order [,meɪdtə'ɔ:dəʳ] ADJ (*Brit*) hecho de encargo, (*US*) hecho a la medida.

made-up ['meɪdʌp] ADJ hecho; compuesto, artificial; *dress* confeccionado; *story* ficticio; *face* pintado, maquillado.

Madge [mædʒ] NF *familiar form of* **Margaret**.

madhouse ['mædhaʊs] N, PL **madhouses** ['mæd,haʊzɪz] manicomio *m*, casa *f* de locos; **this is a ~!** ¡esto es un guirigay!

madly ['mædlɪ] ADV locamente; furiosamente, como un loco; con rabia; **it was ~ exciting** fue divertidísimo, nos divertimos una barbaridad; **to be ~ in love with sb** estar enamorado perdidamente de uno.

madman ['mædmən] N, PL **madmen** ['mædmən] loco *m*.

▼ **madness** ['mædnɪs] N locura *f*; demencia *f*; furia *f*; rabia *f*; **it's sheer ~!** ¡es una locura!; **what ~!** ¡qué locura!

Madonna [mə'dɒnə] N Virgen *f*.

Madrid [mə'drɪd] ①̄ N Madrid *m*.
②̄ ATTR madrileño, matritense.

madrigal ['mædrɪɡəl] N madrigal *m*.

madwoman ['mædwʊmən] N, PL **madwomen** ['mæd,wɪmɪn] loca *f*.

maelstrom ['meɪlstrəʊm] N maelstrom *m*; (*fig*) vórtice *m*, remolino *m*.

maestro [mɑː'estrəʊ] N maestro *m*.

Mae West ['meɪ'west] N (*Aer: hum*) chaleco *m* salvavidas.

MAFF N (*Brit*) ABBR *of* **Ministry of Agriculture, Fisheries and Food**.

mafia ['mæfɪə] N mafia *f*.

mafioso [,mæfɪ'əʊsəʊ] N, PL **mafiosi** [,mæfɪ'əʊsɪ] mafioso *m*.

mag* [mæɡ] N revista *f*.

magazine [,mæɡə'zi:n] N (a) (*journal*) revista *f*. (b) (*in rifle*) depósito *m* de cartuchos, recámara *f*; (*Typ*) almacén *m* de matrices; (*Rad etc*) depósito *m*; (*Mil: store*) almacén *m*, (*for powder*) polvorín *m*, (*Naut*) santabárbara *f*. (c) (*programme*) magazine *m*, programa *m* magazine.

Magdalen ['mæɡdəlɪn] NF Magdalena.

Magellan [mə'ɡelən] ①̄ NM Magallanes.
②̄ ATTR: **~ Straits** Estrecho *m* de Magallanes.

magenta [mə'dʒentə] ①̄ N magenta *f*.
②̄ ADJ color magenta.

Maggie ['mæɡɪ] NF *familiar form of* **Margaret**.

maggot ['mæɡət] N cresa *f*, gusano *m*.

maggoty ['mæɡətɪ] ADJ agusanado, lleno de gusanos.

Maghrib ['mʌɡrəb] N Magreb *m*.

Magi ['meɪdʒaɪ] NPL: **the ~** los Reyes Magos.

magic ['mædʒɪk] ①̄ ADJ (a) mágico; **~ carpet** alfombra *f* encantada; **~ lantern** linterna *f* mágica; **to say the ~ word** dar la fórmula mágica. (b) (*) fabuloso*, estupendo*.
②̄ N magia *f*; **by ~** por arte de magia; **as if by ~** como por ensalmo, como por encanto; **the ~ of that moment** la magia de ese momento; **her dance was utter ~** su baile era la más pura poesía; **Matthews is ~*** Matthews es fabuloso*.

◆ **magic away** VT hacer desaparecer como por arte de magia.

◆ **magic up** VT hacer aparecer como por arte de magia.

magical ['mædʒɪkəl] ADJ mágico.

magically ['mædʒɪkəlɪ] ADV por arte de magia; (*fig*) como por ensalmo.

magician [mə'dʒɪʃən] N mago *m*, mágico *m*, brujo *m*; (*conjuror*) mago *m*, prestidigitador *m*.

magisterial [,mædʒɪs'tɪərɪəl] ADJ magistral.

magistracy ['mædʒɪstrəsɪ] N magistratura *f*.

magistrate ['mædʒɪstreɪt] N juez *mf* (municipal); **~s' court** juzgado *m* de paz, juzgado *m* correccional; *ver también* ⃞COURTS⃞.

⎡ ⃞MAGISTRATE⃞

🅘 *En el Reino Unido los tribunales llamados magistrates' courts están presididos por jueces de paz, conocidos como magistrates, justices of the peace o JPs, que juzgan allí los delitos menores. Aunque en los juzgados con mayor volumen de trabajo los jueces (stipendiary magistrates) sí son profesionales y cobran por su trabajo, la mayoría de estos juzgados suelen estar presididos por legos (lay magistrates), que son elegidos por ser personas conocidas y respetadas en su zona y no reciben retribución alguna por su trabajo. Al no ser licenciadas en Derecho, estas personas son asesoradas por un funcionario con conocimientos legales.*

En los Estados Unidos, magistrate es un cargo de menor responsabilidad, ya que suelen ser jueces de paz con una jurisdicción muy pequeña, aunque también se les da el nombre de magistrate a funcionarios encargados del

cumplimiento de la ley. A veces se utiliza el término **chief magistrate** para referirse al Presidente de los Estados Unidos.
⇨ *Ver también* ⃞COURTS⃞

magma ['mæɡmə] N magma *m*.

Magna C(h)arta ['mæɡnə'kɑ:tə] N (*Brit*) Carta *f* Magna.

magnanimity [,mæɡnə'nɪmɪtɪ] N magnanimidad *f*.

magnanimous [mæɡ'nænɪməs] ADJ magnánimo.

magnanimously [mæɡ'nænɪməslɪ] ADV magnánimamente.

magnate ['mæɡneɪt] N magnate *m*, potentado *m*.

magnesia [mæɡ'ni:ʃə] N magnesia *f*.

magnesium [mæɡ'ni:zɪəm] N magnesio *m*; **~ sulphate** sulfato *m* magnésico.

magnet ['mæɡnɪt] N imán *m* (*also fig*).

magnetic [mæɡ'netɪk] ADJ magnético; (*fig*) magnético, atractivo; **~ card reader** lector *m* de tarjeta magnética; **~ disk** disco *m* magnético; **~ field** campo *m* magnético; **~ mine** mina *f* magnética; **~ needle** aguja *f* magnética; **~ north** polo *m* magnético; **~ stripe** raya *f* magnética; **~ tape** cinta *f* magnética.

magnetically [mæɡ'netɪkəlɪ] ADV magnéticamente.

magnetism ['mæɡnɪtɪzəm] N magnetismo *m*; (*fig*) magnetismo *m* personal.

magnetizable [,mæɡnɪ'taɪzəbl] ADJ magnetizable.

magnetize ['mæɡnɪtaɪz] VT magnetizar (*also fig*), iman(t)ar.

magneto [mæɡ'ni:təʊ] N magneto *f*.

magnetometer [,mæɡnɪ'tɒmɪtəʳ] N magnetómetro *m*.

magnetosphere [mæɡ'ni:təʊ,sfɪəʳ] N magnetosfera *f*.

magnificat [mæɡ'nɪfɪkæt] N magníficat *m*.

magnification [,mæɡnɪfɪ'keɪʃən] N (a) (*Opt*) aumento *m*, ampliación *f*; **high ~** gran aumento *m*, **low ~** pequeño aumento *m*. (b) (*fig*) exageración *f*.

magnificence [mæɡ'nɪfɪsəns] N magnificencia *f*.

magnificent [mæɡ'nɪfɪsənt] ADJ magnífico; suntuoso; **~!** ¡magnífico!

magnificently [mæɡ'nɪfɪsəntlɪ] ADV magníficamente; **you did ~** lo hiciste estupendamente bien.

magnify ['mæɡnɪfaɪ] VT (a) (*Opt*) aumentar; **to ~ sth 7 times** aumentar algo 7 veces; **~ing glass** lente *f* de aumento, lupa *f*; **~ing power** aumento *m*. (b) (*fig*) agrandar, exagerar; (*praise*) magnificar.

magnitude ['mæɡnɪtju:d] N magnitud *f*; (*fig*) magnitud *f*, envergadura *f*; **a star of the first ~** una estrella de primera magnitud; **in operations of this ~** en operaciones de esta envergadura.

magnolia [mæɡ'nəʊlɪə] N magnolia *f*.

magnox reactor ['mæɡnɒksrɪ'æktəʳ] N reactor *m* magnox.

magnum ['mæɡnəm] ①̄ N botella *f* doble, botella *f* de litro y medio.
②̄ ADJ: **~ opus** obra *f* maestra.

magpie ['mæɡpaɪ] N urraca *f*, marica *f*.

Magyar ['mæɡjɑːʳ] ①̄ ADJ magiar. ②̄ N magiar *mf*.

maharajah [,mɑːhə'rɑːdʒə] N maharajá *m*.

maharani [,mɑːhə'rɑːniː] N maharaní *f*.

Mahdi ['mɑːdɪ] N mahdi *m*.

mahjong(g) [,mɑː'dʒɒŋ] N dominó *m* chino.

mahogany [mə'hɒɡənɪ] N caoba *f*.

Mahomet [mə'hɒmɪt] NM Mahoma.

Mahometan [mə'hɒmɪtən] ①̄ ADJ mahometano.
②̄ N mahometano *m*, -a *f*.

maid [meɪd] N (a) (*servant*) criada *f*, doncella *f*, sirvienta *f* (*esp LAm*); (*in hotel etc*) camarera *f*; **lady's ~** doncella *f*; **~ of honour** dama *f* de honor. (b) (††, *liter*) doncella *f*; (*young girl*) muchacha *f*; **old ~** solterona *f*; **she'll be an old ~** quedará para vestir santos.

maiden ['meɪdn] ①̄ N doncella *f*.
②̄ ADJ virginal, intacto; soltera; *flight, voyage etc* de estreno, inaugural; *speech* primero, inaugural.
③̄ ATTR: **~ aunt** tía *f* solterona; **~ lady** soltera *f*; **~ name** apellido *m* de soltera.

maidenhair ['meɪdnhɛəʳ] N (*also* **~ fern**) cabello *m* de Venus, culantrillo *m*.

maidenhead ['meɪdnhed] N virginidad *f*, himen *m*.

maidenhood ['meɪdnhʊd] N doncellez *f*.

maidenly ['meɪdnlɪ] ADJ virginal; recatado, modesto.

maid-of-all-work [,meɪdəv'ɔːl,wɜːk] N chica *f* para todo.

maidservant ['meɪd,sɜːvənt] N criada *f*, sirvienta *f*.

mail¹ [meɪl] ①̄ N (*Mil*) malla *f*, cota *f* de malla.
②̄ VT: **the ~ed fist** (*fig*) la mano dura.

mail² [meɪl] ①̄ N (*in general*) correo *m*; (*letters*) cartas *fpl*, correspondencia *f*; **is there any ~ for me?** ¿hay cartas para mí?
②̄ VT (*esp US*) (*post off*) echar al correo; (*send by ~*) enviar por correo.

mailbag ['meɪlbæɡ] N saca *f* de correos.

mailboat ['meɪlbəʊt] N vapor *m* correo.

mailbomb ['meɪlbɒm] N (*US*) paquete-bomba *m*.

mailbox ['meɪlbɒks] N (*US: in street*) buzón *m*; (*in office etc*) casilla *f*; (*Comput*) buzón *m*.

mailcar ['meɪlkɑːʳ] N (US Rail) furgón m postal, vagón-correo m.

mailcarrier ['meɪlkærɪəʳ] N (US) cartero m, -a f.

mailcoach ['meɪlkəʊtʃ] N (Hist) diligencia f, coche m correo; (Rail) furgón m postal, vagón-correo m.

maildrop ['meɪldrɒp] N (act) entrega f de correo; (address) dirección f para correo.

mailing ['meɪlɪŋ] ① N envío m.
② ATTR: ~ **list** lista f de envío.

mailman ['meɪlmæn] N, PL **mailmen** [meɪlmen] (US) cartero m.

mail-merge ['meɪlmɜːdʒ] N fusión f del correo electrónico.

mail-order ['meɪlˌɔːdəʳ] N pedido m postal; ~ **catalog** (US), ~ **catalogue** catálogo m de ventas por correo; ~ **firm,** ~ **house** casa f de ventas por correo.

mailroom ['meɪlrʊm] N sala f de correo, departamento m de registro (de entradas y salidas).

mailshot ['meɪlʃɒt] N circular f, mailing m.

mailtrain ['meɪltreɪn] N tren-correo m, tren m postal.

mailvan ['meɪlvæn] N (Brit Rail) furgón m postal, vagón-correo m.

maim [meɪm] VT mutilar, lisiar, estropear; **to be ~ed for life** quedar lisiado de por vida.

main [meɪn] ① ADJ principal, más importante; mayor; beam, pipe etc maestro; floor primero, bajo; office central; **the ~ objective is ...** el objetivo principal es ...; **the ~ thing is to** + infin lo más importante es + infin; ~ **clause** oración f principal; ~ **course** plato m principal; ~ **line** (Rail) línea f principal, línea f troncal, (of argument) argumento m central; ~ **memory** memoria f principal, memoria f central; ~ **road** carretera f, ruta f principal; ~ **street** calle f mayor.
② N (a) (pipe) cañería f maestra, tubería f matriz, conducción f; (Elec: also ~s) red f eléctrica; ~s **supply** suministro m de la red; **it runs off the ~s** funciona con electricidad de la red.
(b) **the ~** (poet) el océano, la alta mar; **Spanish M~** Mar m de las Antillas, Mar m Caribe.
(c) **in the ~** en general, en su mayoría, en su mayor parte.

mainbrace ['meɪnbreɪs] N braza f de mayor.

mainframe ['meɪnfreɪm] N (also ~ **computer**) computadora f (or ordenador m) central.

mainland ['meɪnlənd] N tierra f firme, continente m.

mainline: ['meɪnlaɪn] VTI chutarse‡, inyectarse.

mainly ['meɪnlɪ] ADV principalmente; en su mayoría, en su mayor parte.

mainmast ['meɪnmɑːst] N palo m mayor.

mainsail ['meɪnsl] N vela f mayor.

mainspring ['meɪnsprɪŋ] N (of watch) muelle m real; (fig) motivo m principal, origen m.

mainstay ['meɪnsteɪ] N estay m mayor; (fig) sostén m principal, pilar m.

mainstream ['meɪnstriːm] (fig) ① N corriente f principal, línea f central (de evolución etc); **to be in the ~ of modern philosophy** estar en la línea central de la evolución de la filosofía moderna.
② ATTR de la corriente principal, en la línea central.

▼ **maintain** [meɪn'teɪn] VT (a) (continue) attitude, correspondence, order, progress, speed etc mantener; advantage, silence guardar; war continuar, sostener; rights mantener, sostener, afirmar; opposition afirmar (to a); **if the improvement is ~ed** si se mantiene la mejora.
(b) (support) family mantener, sustentar; student pagar los estudios de.
(c) road etc conservar en buen estado; (Mech) entretener, mantener.
▼ (d) (assert) sostener, afirmar; **to ~ that ...** sostener que ...

maintenance ['meɪntɪnəns] ① N mantenimiento m; conservación f; (Mech) entretenimiento m; manutención f.
② ATTR: ~ **agreement,** ~ **contract** contrato m de mantenimiento; ~ **allowance** pensión f alimenticia; ~ **charges,** ~ **costs** gastos mpl de conservación; ~ **crew** personal m de servicios; ~ **grant** pensión f alimenticia, (of student) beca f; ~ **man** reparador m; ~ **order** obligación f alimenticia; ~ **staff** personal m de servicios.

Mainz [maɪnts] N Maguncia f.

maisonette [ˌmeɪzə'net] N (esp Brit) casita f, dúplex m.

maître d'hôtel [ˌmetrədəʊ'tel] N (US also **maître d'** ['metrəˌdiː]) jefe m de comedor, maître m.

maize [meɪz] N (Brit) maíz m, milpa f (Mex), choclo m (LAm).

maize-field ['meɪzfiːld] N maizal m.

Maj. ABBR of **Major** comandante m.

majestic [mə'dʒestɪk] ADJ majestuoso.

majestically [mə'dʒestɪkəlɪ] ADV majestuosamente.

majesty ['mædʒɪstɪ] N majestad f; **Her M~, His M~** Su Majestad; **Your M~** (Vuestra) Majestad.

Maj.-Gen. ABBR of **Major-General** general m de división.

major ['meɪdʒəʳ] ① ADJ mayor (also Mus), principal; **of ~ interest** de máximo interés; **of ~ importance** de la mayor importancia; ~ **league** (US) liga f principal; ~ **part,** ~ **portion** mayor parte f; **Smith M~** (Brit Scol) Smith el mayor; ~ **suit** (Cards) palo m mayor.
② N (a) (Jur) mayor mf de edad. (b) (Mil) comandante m. (c) (US Univ: course) asignatura f principal, especialidad f. (d) (US Univ) **he's a**

Spanish ~ estudia el español como asignatura principal.
③ VI (US Univ): **to ~ in French** estudiar el francés como asignatura principal, especializarse en francés.

Majorca [mə'jɔːkə] N Mallorca f.

Majorcan [mə'jɔːkən] ① ADJ mallorquín.
② N (a) mallorquín m, -ina f. (b) (Ling) mallorquín m.

majordomo ['meɪdʒə'dəʊməʊ] N mayordomo m.

majorette [ˌmeɪdʒə'ret] N batonista f.

major-general ['meɪdʒə'dʒənərəl] N general m de división.

majority [mə'dʒɒrɪtɪ] ① N mayoría f; **a two-thirds ~** una mayoría de las dos terceras partes; **the great ~ of lecturers** la mayor parte de los conferenciantes; **the vast ~** la inmensa mayoría; **to attain one's ~** llegar a mayoría de edad; **such people are in a ~** tales personas son las más, predominan tales personas; **to be in a ~ of 3** formar parte de una mayoría de 3.
② ATTR mayoritario; **by a ~ decision** por decisión de la mayoría; ~ **interest** interés m mayoritario; ~ **rule** gobierno m mayoritario, gobierno m de la mayoría; ~ **(share)holding** accionado m mayoritario; **by a ~ verdict** por fallo mayoritario; **by a ~ vote** por la mayoría de los votos.

┌─ MAJORITY, MOST ───────────── see also main entries ─┐

Singular or plural verb?

When *mayoría* is the subject of a verb, the verb can be in the singular or the plural, depending on the context.

• When translating *majority* rather than *most*, put the verb in the singular if *majority* is seen as a unit rather than a collection of individuals:

  The socialist majority voted against the four amendments
  La mayoría socialista votó en contra de las cuatro enmiendas

• If *la mayoría* is seen as a collection of individuals, particularly when it is followed by *de* + PLURAL NOUN, the plural form of the verb is more common than the singular, though both are possible:

  The majority still wear this uniform
  La mayoría siguen vistiendo or *sigue vistiendo este uniforme*
  Most scientists believe it is a mistake
  La mayoría de los científicos creen or *cree que se trata de un error*

• The plural form must be used when *la mayoría* or *la mayoría de* + PLURAL NOUN is followed by *ser* or *estar* + PLURAL COMPLEMENT:

  Most of them are men
  La mayoría son hombres
  Most of the dead were students
  La mayoría de los muertos eran estudiantes
  Most of the children were black
  La mayoría de los niños eran negros

For further uses and examples, see main entries at *majority* and *most*.

└──┘

make [meɪk] (irr: PRET and PTP **made**) ① VT (a) (gen) hacer; (manufacture) fabricar; (build) construir; (confect) elaborar; (form) formar; (create) crear; (put together) componer; bed, effort, fire, noise, peace, remark, tea, war, will hacer; dress confeccionar; meal preparar; speech pronunciar; error cometer; payment efectuar; cards barajar; face poner; sense tener; **to ~ sb a judge** constituir a uno juez, nombrar a uno juez; **to ~ sb king** elevar a uno al trono; **they've made Eccles secretary** han nombrado secretario a Eccles; **to ~ a friend of sb** trabar amistad con uno; **he's as cunning as they ~ 'em** es de lo más astuto que hay; **to ~ A into B** convertir A en B, transformar A en B; **I'm not made for running** yo no estoy hecho para correr; **to be made of** estar hecho de, estar compuesto de, consistir en, constar de; **it's made of gold** es de oro, está hecho de oro; **to show what one is made of** demostrar las cualidades que tiene uno; **what do you ~ of this?** ¿qué te parece esto?; **what did you ~ of the film?** ¿qué impresión te produjo la película?; **what do you ~ of him?** ¿qué piensas de él?, ¿qué impresión te has formado de él?; **I can ~ nothing of it** no lo entiendo, no saco nada en claro; **I don't know what to ~ of it** no me lo explico; **they don't ~ songs** (etc) **like that any more** ya no hay canciones (etc) como las de antes.
(b) (complete, constitute) circuit cerrar; trick ganar, hacer; **2 and 2 ~ 4** 2 y 2 son 4; **that ~s 20** eso hace 20, con ése son 20; **it still doesn't ~ a set** todavía no completa un juego entero; **it doesn't ~ a full course** no equivale a una asignatura completa; **to ~ a contract** (Cards) cumplir un contrato; **South leads and ~s 5 tricks** Sur sale y efectúa 5 bazas; **it made a nice surprise** fue una sorpresa agradable; **partridges ~ good eating** las perdices son buenas para comer; **it ~s pleasant reading** da gusto leerlo; **he made a good husband** resultó ser un buen marido; **he'll ~ a good footballer** será buen futbolista, tiene madera de futbolista; **I made one of the party** yo era (uno) del grupo; V **night** etc.
(c) (earn etc) ganar; **he ~s £300 a week** gana 300 libras a la semana; **how much do you ~?** ¿cuánto ganas?, ¿qué sueldo cobras?; **to ~ a**

───
➤ LANGUAGE IN USE: **maintain: d → 26.1, 26.2**

fortune enriquecerse, hacer su pacotilla*; **what will you ~ by it?** ¿cuánto vas a ganar en esto?; **how much do you stand to ~?** ¿cuánto esperas ganar?

(d) (*assure future of*) hacer la fortuna de; asegurar el triunfo de; **it made my day** me dio un día feliz, hizo un buen día para mí; **he's got it made*** lo tiene asegurado, se lo tiene apañado*; **this film made her** esta película fue el principio de su éxito; **he was made for life** se aseguró un porvenir brillante; **to ~ or break sb** hacer la fortuna o ser la ruina de uno; **to ~ or mar sth** decidir de una vez la suerte de algo.

(e) (*with pred adj*) hacer; **to ~ sb happy** hacer a uno feliz; **to ~ sb angry** irritar a uno, provocar a uno, sacar a uno de quicio; **to ~ sb ashamed** dar vergüenza a uno; **to ~ sb sleepy** dar sueño a uno; **to ~ sb rich** enriquecer a uno; **to ~ sb ill** sentar a uno mal; **to ~ sth ready** preparar algo; **to ~ iron hot** calentar un trozo de hierro; **to ~ one's voice heard** hacer que se le escuche a uno.

(f) (*say, agree*) **let's ~ it 9 o'clock** citémonos para las 9, pongamos las 9.

(g) (*judge*) creer; representar, pintar; **the situation is not so bad as you ~ it** la situación es menos grave de lo que crees, la situación no es tan grave como la pintas.

(h) (*calculate*) calcular; **what do you ~ the time?** ¿qué hora tienes?; **I ~ it 7.30** yo tengo las 7 y media; **how many do you ~ it?** ¿cuántos dices tú?, ¿cuántos tienes en total?; **I ~ the distance 98 km** calculo que la distancia es de 98 km; **I ~ the total 17** calculo que hay 17 en total.

(i) (*force*) **to ~ sb do sth** forzar (*or* obligar, compeler) a uno a hacer algo; (*persuade*) inclinar (*or* inducir) a uno a hacer algo; **you can't ~ me** no puedes forzarme a hacerlo; **what ~s you do it?** ¿por qué te ves obligado a hacerlo?; **what made you say that?** ¿por qué dijiste eso?; **to ~ sb laugh** darle risa a uno, hacerle reír a uno.

(j) (*reach, attain*) **we made 15 knots** alcanzamos una velocidad de 15 nudos; **we shall never ~ the shore** no llegamos nunca a la playa, será imposible alcanzar la playa; **to ~ it** (*arrive*) llegar; (*achieve sth*) conseguir lo que se deseaba; (*succeed*) tener éxito, triunfar; **eventually we made it** por fin llegamos; **we just made it in time** llegamos justo a tiempo; **can you ~ it by 10?** ¿puedes llegar para las 10?; **to ~ it with sb:** darse el lote con una:.

2 VI **(a)** (*tide*) crecer, subir.

(b) **he made as if to +** *infin* hizo como si quisiese **+** *infin*, fingió que iba a **+** *infin*, hizo además de **+** *infin*; **he was making like he didn't have any money*** (*US*) hacía como que no tenía dinero.

(c) **it's ~ or break week** es la semana del triunfo o del fracaso.

3 VR **(a)** (*become*) **to ~ o.s. an expert in** llegar a ser experto en; **to ~ o.s. dictator** hacerse dictador, constituirse en dictador.

(b) (*with pred adj*) **to ~ o.s. comfortable** acomodarse a su gusto; **to ~ o.s. ill with work** enfermar por exceso de trabajo; **to ~ o.s. ridiculous** ponerse en ridículo; *V* **hear** *etc*.

(c) (*force*) **to ~ o.s. do sth** obligarse a hacer algo; **I have to ~ myself (do it)** tengo que hacer un esfuerzo (por hacerlo).

4 N **(a)** (*brand*) marca *f*; (*type etc*) tipo *m*, modelo *m*; **it's a good ~** es buena marca; **what ~ of car was it?** ¿qué marca de coche fue?; **these are my own ~** estos son según mi propia receta; **they have rifles of Belgian ~** tienen fusiles de fabricación belga.

(b) (*) **to be on the ~** barrer hacia dentro*; **the town is full of dealers on the ~** la ciudad está llena de comerciantes que no pierden ripio.

◆**make after** VT seguir a, perseguir a.

◆**make away** VI = make off.

◆**make away with** VT (*murder*): **to ~ away with sb** eliminar a uno; **to ~ away with o.s.** quitarse la vida, suicidarse.

◆**make for** VI **(a)** (*place*) dirigirse a, encaminarse a; **where are you making for?** ¿adónde se dirige Vd?

(b) **to ~ for sb** atacar a uno, abalanzarse sobre uno.

(c) *result* contribuir a, conducir a; **it ~s for optimism** ayuda a crear el optimismo, fomenta el optimismo; **it ~s for difficulties** tiende a crear dificultades.

◆**make off** VI largarse; huir, escaparse; **to ~ off with** llevarse, alzarse con; escaparse con.

◆**make out** **1** VT **(a)** (*draw up*) *cheque, document, receipt* extender; *list* hacer, redactar; *form* llenar; *case* exponer, explicar; justificar; **the cheque should be made out to Pérez** el cheque será nominativo a favor de Pérez, el cheque se debe girar a favor de Pérez (*LAm*).

(b) (*see, distinguish*) distinguir, vislumbrar, divisar; *writing* (*lograr*) leer, descifrar; (*understand*) entender; **I can't ~ it out at all** no me lo explico, no lo entiendo; **I can't properly ~ him out** no le acabo de entender.

(c) (*claim*) representar; **you ~ him out to be better than he is** haces creer que es mejor de lo que es en realidad; **he's not as rich as people ~ out** es menos rico de lo que dice la gente; **how do you ~ that out?** ¿cómo deduces eso?, ¿cómo llegas a esa conclusión?; **he ~s out that ...** da a entender que ..., da la impresión de que ...; **nos hace**

creer que ...; **all the time he made out he was working** todo el tiempo hacía creer que estaba trabajando; **the play ~s him out to be a fool** la obra le representa como tonto.

2 VI arreglárselas, salir bien; **we're making out** vamos tirando; **we made out eventually** por fin nos las arreglamos; **how are you making out?** ¿cómo te va esto?; **how did you ~ out?** ¿qué tal te fue?; **to ~ out with a girl:** (*US*) darse el lote con una chica:.

◆**make over** VT ceder, traspasar (*to* a).

◆**make up** **1** VT **(a)** (*invent*) inventar; **you're making it up!** ¡puro cuento!

(b) (*put together*) hacer; fabricar; confeccionar; *medicine* preparar; *bed* hacer; *collection* formar, reunir; *parcel* empaquetar; *list* hacer, redactar; (*Typ*) componer.

(c) (*counterbalance, replace*) *loss* reponer, compensar; *deficit* cubrir; **to ~ up (lost) time** recuperar el tiempo perdido; **to ~ it up to sb** compensar a uno por sus pérdidas.

(d) (*settle*) *dispute* componer, arreglar; **to ~ up a quarrel with sb, to ~ it up with sb** hacer las paces con uno.

(e) *face* pintarse, maquillarse; **to ~ up an actor** maquillar a un actor.

(f) (*constitute*) componer, integrar; formar, constituir; **the parts which ~ it up** las partes que lo integran; **the group was made up of 8 bishops** el grupo lo integraban 8 obispos.

(g) (*complete*) completar, hacer.

(h) *fire* echar carbón (*etc*) a.

2 VI **(a)** (*become friends*) hacer las paces.

(b) (*apply cosmetics*) pintarse, maquillarse.

◆**make up for** VT: **to ~ up for sb's losses** compensar a uno por sus pérdidas, indemnizar a uno de sus pérdidas; **to ~ up for a lack of** suplir una falta de; **to ~ up for lost time** recuperar el tiempo perdido.

◆**make up on** VT alcanzar, coger.

◆**make up to*** VT: **to ~ up to sb** (*procurar*) congraciarse con uno, (*procurar*) ganarse la amistad de uno; halagar a uno, hacer zalamerías a uno.

make-believe ['meɪkbɪ,liːv] **1** ADJ fingido, simulado; *world etc* de ensueño, soñado.

2 N ficción *f*, invención *f*; imaginación *f*; **a world of ~** un mundo de ensueño; **don't worry, it's just ~** no te apures, es de mentirijillas.

3 VI fingir.

maker ['meɪkəʳ] N hacedor *m*, -ora *f*, creador *m*, -ora *f*; artífice *mf*; (*builder*) constructor *m*, -ora *f*; (*manufacturer*) fabricante *m*; **the M~** el Hacedor; **to go to meet one's M~** pasar a mejor vida.

makeshift ['meɪkʃɪft] **1** ADJ improvisado; provisional, temporal.

2 N improvisación *f*; expediente *m*; arreglo *m* provisional.

make-up ['meɪkʌp] **1** N **(a)** (*composition*) composición *f*; estructura *f*; (*of person etc*) carácter *m*, modo *m* de ser, naturaleza *f*; (*of clothes*) confección *f*; (*Typ*) ajuste *m*.

(b) (*for face*) maquillaje *m*, cosméticos *mpl*; (*Theat: for a role*) caracterización *f*.

2 ATTR: **~ artist** maquillador *m*, -ora *f*; **~ bag** bolsa *f* del maquillaje; **~ girl** maquilladora *f*; **~ man** maquillador *m*; **~ remover** desmaquillador *m*.

makeweight ['meɪkweɪt] N contrapeso *m*; (*fig*) suplente *m*, sustituto *m*; (*pej*) tapa(a)gujeros *m*.

making ['meɪkɪŋ] N **(a)** fabricación *f*; construcción *f*; elaboración *f*; formación *f*; creación *f*; confección *f*; preparación *f*; **in the ~** en vías de formarse (*or* hacerse *etc*); **it's still in the ~** está todavía en construcción, está todavía sin acabar; **while it was still in the ~** mientras se estaba haciendo; **it's a civil war in the ~** es una guerra civil en potencia; **it's history in the ~** es la historia como proceso actual, es la historia que actualmente se está escribiendo; **the mistake was not of my ~** no soy yo el responsable del error; **it was the ~ of him** fue la causa de su éxito, (*morally*) fue el motivo de su reforma moral.

(b) **~s** elementos *mpl* (*necesarios*); ingredientes *mpl*; **he has the ~s of an actor** tiene talento para ser actor, tiene madera de actor.

Malachi ['mælə,kaɪ] NM Malaquías *m*.

malachite ['mælə,kaɪt] N malaquita *f*.

maladjusted ['mælə'dʒʌstɪd] ADJ inadaptado.

maladjustment ['mælə'dʒʌstmənt] N inadaptación *f*, desajuste *m*.

maladministration ['mæləd,mɪnɪs'treɪʃən] N mala administración *f*.

maladroit ['mælə'drɔɪt] ADJ torpe.

maladroitly ['mælə'drɔɪtlɪ] ADV torpemente.

maladroitness ['mælə'drɔɪtnɪs] N torpeza *f*.

malady ['mælədɪ] N mal *m*, enfermedad *f*.

Malagasy ['mæləgɑːzɪ] **1** ADJ madagascarí.

2 N madagascarí *mf*.

malaise [mæ'leɪz] N malestar *m*.

malapropism ['mæləprɒpɪzəm] N despropósito *m* lingüístico, equivocación *f* de palabras.

malaria [mə'lɛərɪə] **1** N paludismo *m*, malaria *f*.

[2] ATTR: **~ control** lucha *f* antimalaria.
malarial [mə'lɛərɪəl] ADJ palúdico.
Malawi [mə'lɑːwɪ] N Malawi *m*, Malaui *m*.
Malawian [mə'lɑːwɪən] [1] ADJ malawiano, malauiano.
  [2] N malawiano *m*, -a *f*, malauiano *m*, -a *f*.
Malay [mə'leɪ] [1] ADJ malayo.
  [2] N **(a)** malayo *m*, -a *f*. **(b)** (*Ling*) malayo *m*.
Malaya [mə'leɪə] N Malaya *f*, Malaca *f*.
Malayan [mə'leɪən] [1] ADJ malayo.
  [2] N malayo *m*, -a *f*.
Malaysia [mə'leɪzɪə] N Malasia *f*.
Malaysian [mə'leɪzɪən] [1] ADJ malasio.
  [2] N malasio *m*, -a *f*.
malcontent ['mælkən'tent] [1] ADJ malcontento, desafecto, revoltoso.
  [2] N malcontento *m*, -a *f*, desafecto *m*, -a *f*, revoltoso *m*, -a *f*.
Maldives ['mɔːldaɪvz] NPL Maldivas *fpl*.
male [meɪl] [1] ADJ (*Bio, Mech*) macho; (*manly*) viril, masculino; *attire etc* de hombres, para hombre; **~ chauvinist pig** V *chauvinist*; **~ child** hijo *m* varón; **~ menopause** (*hum*) menopausia *f* masculina; **~ nurse** enfermero *m*; **~ prostitute** prostituto *m*; **~ sex** sexo *m* masculino; **~ voice choir** coro *m* de hombres.
  [2] N macho *m* (*also Bio*); varón *m*.
malediction [,mælɪ'dɪkʃən] N maldición *f*.
male-dominated ['meɪl'dɒmɪneɪtɪd] ADJ dominado por los hombres.
malefactor ['mælɪfæktər] N malhechor *m*, -ora *f*.
maleness ['meɪlnɪs] N masculinidad *f*, virilidad *f*.
malevolence [mə'levələns] N malevolencia *f*.
malevolent [mə'levələnt] ADJ malévolo.
malevolently [mə'levələntlɪ] ADV con malevolencia.
malformation ['mælfɔː'meɪʃən] N malformación *f*, deformidad *f*.
malformed [,mæl'fɔːmd] ADJ malformado, deforme.
malfunction [mæl'fʌŋkʃən] [1] N funcionamiento *m* defectuoso.
  [2] VI funcionar mal.
Malgache [mæl'gætʃɪ] N Malgache *m*.
malice ['mælɪs] N malevolencia *f*, mala voluntad *f*; (*Jur*) intención *f* delictuosa; **out of ~** por malevolencia; **with ~ toward none** sin malevolencia para nadie; **to bear sb ~** guardar rencor a uno; **I bear him no ~** no le guardo rencor.
malicious [mə'lɪʃəs] ADJ malévolo, maligno; rencoroso; **~ damage** daños *mpl* intencionados; **~ slander** calumnia *f* intencionada.
maliciously [mə'lɪʃəslɪ] ADV con malevolencia, con malignidad; rencorosamente.
malign [mə'laɪn] [1] ADJ maligno, enconoso.
  [2] VT calumniar, difamar; tratar injustamente, ser injusto con; **you ~ me** eso no es justo, ésa no era mi intención.
malignancy [mə'lɪgnənsɪ] N malignidad *f*.
malignant [mə'lɪgnənt] ADJ maligno (*also Med*).
malignity [mə'lɪgnɪtɪ] N malignidad *f*.
malinger [mə'lɪŋgər] VI fingirse enfermo, hacer la encorvada*.
malingerer [mə'lɪŋgərər] N enfermo *m* fingido, enferma *f* fingida, calandria* *mf*.
mall [mɔːl] N **(a)** alameda *f*, paseo *m*; (*US: pedestrian street*) calle *f* peatonal. **(b)** (*esp US: also* **shopping ~**) centro *m* comercial.
mallard ['mæləd] N pato *m* real, ánade *m* real.
malleability [,mælɪə'bɪlɪtɪ] N maleabilidad *f*.
malleable ['mælɪəbl] ADJ maleable.
mallet ['mælɪt] N mazo *m*.
mallow ['mæləʊ] N malva *f*.
malnourished [,mæl'nʌrɪʃt] ADJ desnutrido.
malnutrition ['mælnjʊ'trɪʃən] N desnutrición *f*.
malodorous [mæ'ləʊdərəs] ADJ maloliente, hediondo.
malpractice ['mæl'præktɪs] N procedimientos *mpl* ilegales (*or* inmorales); práctica *f* abusiva; abuso *m* de autoridad; mala conducta *f*; (*Med*) negligencia *f*.
malt [mɔːlt] [1] N malta *f*.
  [2] ATTR: **~ extract** extracto *m* de malta; **~ liquor** (*US*) cerveza *f*; **~ whisky** (*Brit*) whisky *m* de malta.
  [3] VT *barley* hacer germinar; *drink etc* preparar con malta; **~ed milk** leche *f* malteada; **~ing barley** cebada *f* cervecera.
Malta ['mɔːltə] N Malta *f*.
Maltese ['mɔːl'tiːz] [1] ADJ maltés; **~ Cross** cruz *f* de Malta.
  [2] N **(a)** maltés *m*, -esa *f*. **(b)** (*Ling*) maltés *m*.
malthusianism [mæl'θjuːzɪə,nɪzəm] N malt(h)usianismo *m*.
maltreat [mæl'triːt] VT maltratar, tratar mal.
maltreatment [mæl'triːtmənt] N maltrato *m*, maltratamiento *m*, malos tratos *mpl*.
Malvinas [mæl'viːnɑːs] N: **the ~** las Malvinas.
mam [mæm] N (*Brit*) mamá *f*.
mamba ['mæmbə] N mamba *f*.
mam(m)a ['məˈmɑː] N mamá *f*.
mammal ['mæməl] N mamífero *m*.
mammalian [mæ'meɪlɪən] ADJ mamífero.

mammary ['mæmərɪ] [1] ADJ mamario; **~ gland** mama *f*, teta *f*.
  [2] N: **mammaries** (*hum*) pechos *mpl*.
mammogram ['mæməgræm] N mamografía *f*.
mammography [mæ'mɒgrəfɪ] N mamografía *f*.
Mammon ['mæmən] NM Mammón.
mammoth ['mæməθ] [1] N mamut *m*.
  [2] ADJ gigantesco, colosal; (*Comm*) de tamaño extra.
mammy ['mæmɪ] N **(a)** (*) mamaíta* *f*. **(b)** (*US*) nodriza *f* negra.
man [mæn] [1] N, PL **men** [men] **(a)** (*gen*) hombre *m*; varón *m*; (*humanity in general*) el hombre, los hombres, el género humano; (*servant*) criado *m*; (*workman*) obrero *m*; (*Mil*) soldado *m*; (*Naut*) marinero *m*; **men's doubles** *mpl* masculinos; **men's final** final *f* masculina; **men's room** (*esp US*) lavabo *m* de caballeros; *ver también* TOILET.
  (b) (*with adj*) **best ~** padrino *m* de boda, testigo *m* del novio; **~ Friday** criado *m* fiel; **all good men and true** todos los que merecen llamarse hombres; **her ~** su marido; **our ~ in Slobodia** (*agent*) nuestro agente en Eslobodia, (*representative*) nuestro representante en Eslobodia, (*ambassador*) nuestro embajador en Eslobodia; **old ~** viejo *m*, anciano *m*; **my old ~*** el viejo*, el pariente*; **the grand old ~ of the party** el líder veterano del partido; **the strong ~ of the government** el hombre fuerte del gobierno; **young ~** joven *m*; **her young ~** su novio.
  (c) (*with qualifying phrase*) **~ about town** hombre *m* mundano, joven *m* amigo de los placeres, señorito *m*; **~ and boy** desde pequeño; **~ and wife** marido y mujer; **~ in the moon** mujer *f* de la luna; **~ in the street** hombre *m* de la calle, hombre *m* medio; **~ of letters** literato *m*; **~ of means, ~ of property** hombre *m* acaudalado; **~ of parts** hombre *m* de talento; **~ of the world** hombre *m* de mundo.
  (d) (*used as pron etc*) **men say that ...** se dice que ...; **when a ~ needs a wash** cuando uno necesita lavarse; **what else could a ~ do?** ¿es que se podía hacer otra cosa?; **one ~ one vote** un voto para cada uno; **any ~** cualquiera, cualquier hombre; **no ~** nadie; **that ~ Jones** ese Jones; **as one ~** unánimemente; como un sólo hombre, todos a uno; **~ to ~** de hombre a hombre; **they're communists to a ~** todos sin excepción son comunistas.
  (e) (*sort, type*) **I'm not a drinking ~** no bebo; **I'm not a football ~** no soy aficionado al fútbol, no me gusta el fútbol; **he's a 4-pint ~** es de los que se beben 4 pintas; **I'm a whisky ~ myself** yo prefiero el whisky; **he's a Celtic ~** es del Celtic; **he's his own ~** es un hombre muy fiel a sí mismo; **he's a ~'s ~** es un hombre estimado entre otros hombres; **are you ~ enough to do it?** ¿tienes bastante valor para hacerlo?; **it's got to be a local ~** tiene que ser uno de aquí; **then I'm your ~** entonces yo soy el que busca Vd; **to feel (like) a new ~** sentirse como nuevo.
  (f) (*in direct address*) **you can't do that, ~** hombre, no puedes hacer eso; **~, was I startled!** ¡vaya susto que me llevé!; **hey ~!*** ¡oye, tronco!*; **my good ~** buen hombre; **good ~!** ¡bravo!, ¡muy bien!; **look here, old ~** mira, amigo.
  (g) (*verb phrases*) **he's not the ~ to do it** no es capaz de hacerlo; **he's not the ~ for the job** no es persona adecuada para el puesto; **to make a ~ of sb** hacer un hombre de uno; **~ proposes, God disposes** el hombre propone y Dios dispone; **to reach ~'s estate** llegar a la edad viril; **this will separate** (*or sort*) **the men from the boys** con esto se verá quiénes son hombres y quiénes no.
  (h) (*Chess etc*) pieza *f*, ficha *f*, trebejo *m*.
  (i) **the M~**: (*US*) (*boss*) el jefe; (*police*) el policía; (*white man*) el blanco.
  [2] VT *ship* tripular; *fortress, watchtower* guarnecer; *guns* servir; *pumps* acudir a, hacer funcionar; **a fully ~ned ship** un buque con toda su tripulación; **the telephone is ~ned all day** el telefonista está de servicio todo el día; **~ning levels** niveles *mpl* de personal; *see also* **manned**.
manacle ['mænəkl] [1] N manilla *f*; **~s** esposas *fpl*, grillos *mpl*.
  [2] VT poner esposas a; **they were ~d together** iban esposados juntos; **his hands were ~d** llevaba esposas en las muñecas.
manage ['mænɪdʒ] [1] VT **(a)** *tool etc* manejar; manipular; *car* conducir; *ship* gobernar.
  (b) *company* dirigir; *organization* regir, administrar; (*Comput*) *system, network* gestionar; *property* administrar; *affair* manejar; *election* (*pej*) falsificar; **~d currency** moneda *f* dirigida, moneda *f* planificada; **~d fund** fondo *m* dirigido.
  (c) *person, child, animal* manejar; **she can't ~ children** no puede con los niños; **I can ~ him** yo sé llevarle.
  (d) (*contrive, offer, take*) **£5 is the most I can ~** 5 libras es todo lo que puedo darte (*or pagar etc*); **I shall ~ it** yo sabré hacerlo; **you'll ~ it next time** lo harás la próxima vez; **can you ~ the cases?** ¿puedes llevar las maletas?; **thanks, I can ~ them** gracias, yo puedo con ellas; **can you ~ two more in the car?** ¿puedes llevar dos más en el coche?; **can you ~ 8 o'clock?** ¿puedes venir para las 8?; **can you ~ another cup?** ¿quieres otra taza?; **I can ~ another cake** me atrevo con otra pasta; **I couldn't ~ another mouthful** no podría comer ni

un bocado más.

(e) (*with verb*) **to ~ to do sth** lograr hacer algo; arreglárselas para hacer algo, ingeniarse para hacer algo; **how did you ~ to get it?** ¿cómo lo conseguiste?; **he ~d not to get his feet wet** logró no mojarse los pies.

[2] VI arreglárselas, ir tirando; **can you ~?** ¿tú puedes con eso?; **thanks, I can ~** gracias, yo puedo; **she ~s well enough** se las arregla bastante bien; **how do you ~?** ¿cómo te las arreglas?; **to ~ without sth** saber pasarse sin algo; **to ~ without sb** saber prescindir de uno.

manageable ['mænɪdʒəbl] ADJ manejable; *person, animal* dócil; **of ~ size** de tamaño razonable.

management ['mænɪdʒmənt] [1] N **(a)** (*act*) manejo *m*; gobierno *m*; dirección *f*; gerencia *f*, gerenciación *f*, administración *f*.
(b) (*persons*) dirección *f*; junta *f* de directores; (*as a class*) empresariado *m*, empresa *f*, clase *f* patronal; (*Theat*) empresa *f*; **~ and labour** dirección *f* y obreros; **'under new ~'** 'nueva dirección'; **almost always ~ is at fault** las más veces la empresa tiene la culpa.
[2] ATTR: **~ accounting** contabilidad *f* de gestión; **~ audit** auditoría *f* administrativa; **~ chart** gestionigrama *m*; **~ committee** consejo *m* de administración, comité *m* directivo; **~ consultancy** consultoría *f* gerencial; **~ consultant** consultor *m*, -ora *f* en dirección de empresas; **~ fee** honorarios *mpl* de dirección; **~ review** revisión *f* de gestión (de la gerencia); **~ services** servicios *mpl* de administración; **~ trainee** aspirante *mf* a un puesto directivo.

manager ['mænɪdʒəʳ] N (*Comm etc*) director *m*, -ora *f*; gerente *mf*; (*of estate etc*) administrador *m*, -ora *f*; (*Sport*) mánager *m*; (*Theat*) empresario *m*; (*of farm*) mayoral *m*; **she's a good ~** es buena administradora, es muy económica.

manageress ['mænɪdʒə'res] N directora *f*; administradora *f*.

managerial [,mænə'dʒɪərɪəl] ADJ directivo, directorial; gerencial; administrativo; **the ~ class** la clase patronal; **at ~ level** a nivel directivo; **~ responsibilities** obligaciones *fpl* directivas; responsabilidades *fpl* de administración; **the ~ society** la sociedad patronal; **~ staff** personal *m* dirigente; **~ structure** estructura *f* administrativa; **~ style** estilo *m* administrativo.

managing ['mænɪdʒɪŋ] ADJ **(a)** (*Brit pej*) mandón. **(b)** **~ director** (*Brit*) director *m*, -ora *f* general; **~ partner** socio *mf* gerente.

man-at-arms ['mænət'ɑ:mz] N, PL **men-at-arms** ['menət'ɑ:mz] hombre *m* de armas.

manatee [,mænə'ti:] N manatí *m*.

Manchuria [mæn'tʃʊərɪə] N Manchuria *f*.

Manchurian [mæn'tʃʊərɪən] [1] ADJ manchuriano.
[2] N manchuriano *m*, -a *f*.

Mancunian [mæn'kju:nɪən] [1] ADJ de Manchester.
[2] N habitante *mf* (or nativo *m*, -a *f*) de Manchester.

mandarin ['mændərɪn] N **(a)** (*person*) mandarín *m* (*also fig*). **(b)** (*Ling*) **M~** mandarina *f*. **(c)** (*also* **~ orange**) mandarina *f*.

mandate ['mændeɪt] [1] N mandato *m*; (*country*) territorio *m* bajo mandato.
[2] VT **(a)** asignar como mandato (*to* a). **(b)** *delegate* encargar.

mandated ['mændeɪtɪd] ADJ **(a)** *territory* bajo mandato. **(b)** *delegate* encargado.

mandatory ['mændətərɪ] ADJ obligatorio; preceptivo; **to be ~ upon sb to do sth** incumbir a uno como obligación hacer algo.

man-day ['mæn'deɪ] N, PL **man-days** ['mæn'deɪz] día-hombre *m*.

Mandelbrot set ['mændəl,brɒt,set] N (*Maths*) conjunto *m* de Mandelbrot.

mandible ['mændɪbl] N mandíbula *f*.

mandolin(e) ['mændəlɪn] N mandolina *f*, bandolina *f* (*LAm*).

mandrake ['mændreɪk] N mandrágora *f*.

mandrill ['mændrɪl] N mandril *m*.

mane [meɪn] N (*of lion, person*) melena *f*; (*of horse*) crin *f*, crines *fpl*.

man-eater ['mæn,i:təʳ] N tigre *m* (*etc*) cebado, tigre *m* (*etc*) devorador de hombres; (**: woman*) devoradora *f* de hombres.

man-eating ['mæn,i:tɪŋ] ADJ antropófago.

maneuver [mə'nu:vəʳ] *etc* (*US*) = **manoeuvre** etc.

manful ['mænfʊl] ADJ valiente, resuelto.

manfully ['mænfəlɪ] ADV valientemente, resueltamente.

manganese [,mæŋgə'ni:z] [1] N manganeso *m*.
[2] ATTR: **~ oxide** óxido *m* de manganeso; **~ steel** acero *m* manganésico.

mange [meɪndʒ] N roña *f*, sarna *f*.

mangel(-wurzel) ['mæŋgl('wɜ:zl)] N remolacha *f* forrajera.

manger ['meɪndʒəʳ] N pesebre *m*.

mangetout ['mɒnʒ'tu:] N (*also* **~ pea**) guisante *m*, arveja *f* (*LAm*) (*con vaina comestible*).

mangle¹ ['mæŋgl] [1] N exprimidor *m*.
[2] VT pasar por el exprimidor.

mangle² ['mæŋgl] VT destrozar, mutilar, magullar; *text etc* mutilar, estropear.

mango ['mæŋgəʊ] N, PL **mangoes** or **mangos** ['mæŋgəʊz] (*fruit and tree*) mango *m*.

mangold(-wurzel) ['mæŋgəld('wɜ:zl)] N remolacha *f* forrajera.

mangrove ['mæŋgrəʊv] [1] N mangle *m*.
[2] ATTR: **~ swamp** manglar *m*.

mangy ['meɪndʒɪ] ADJ roñoso, sarnoso.

manhandle ['mæn,hændl] VT (*esp Brit*) mover a brazo; (*fig*) maltratar.

manhole ['mænhəʊl] [1] N agujero *m* de hombre, registro *m* de inspección, pozo *m* de visita.
[2] ATTR: **~ cover** tapa *f* de registro, tapadera *f* de cloaca.

manhood ['mænhʊd] N **(a)** (*state*) virilidad *f*; (*age*) edad *f* viril; **to reach ~** llegar a la edad viril.
(b) (*manliness*) hombradía *f*, masculinidad *f*.
(c) (*men collectively*) **English ~, England's ~** todos los ingleses, todos los hombres de Inglaterra.

man-hour ['mæn'aʊəʳ] N, PL **man-hours** ['mæn'aʊəz] hora-hombre *f*.

manhunt ['mænhʌnt] N persecución *f* (de un criminal), caza *f* (de hombre).

mania ['meɪnɪə] N manía *f*; **to have a ~ for sth** tener la manía de algo; **to have a ~ for doing sth** tener la manía de hacer algo; **speed ~** manía *f* de la velocidad.

maniac ['meɪnɪæk] [1] ADJ maníaco.
[2] N maníaco *m*, -a *f*; (*fig*) maniático *m*, -a *f*; **these sports ~s** estos fanáticos del deporte; **he drives like a ~** conduce como un loco.

maniacal [mə'naɪəkəl] ADJ maníaco.

maniacally [mə'naɪəkəlɪ] ADV *laugh etc* como un maníaco.

manic ['mænɪk] ADJ maníaco.

manic-depressive ['mænɪkdɪ'presɪv] [1] ADJ maníacodepresivo.
[2] N maníacodepresivo *m*, -a *f*.

Manichean [,mænɪ'ki:ən] [1] ADJ maniqueo.
[2] N maniqueo *m*, -a *f*.

Manicheanism [,mænɪ'ki:ənɪzəm] N maniqueísmo *m*.

manicure ['mænɪkjʊəʳ] [1] N manicura *f*.
[2] ATTR: **~ case, ~ set** estuche *m* de manicura.
[3] VT *person* hacer manicura a; *nails* limpiar, arreglar.

manicured ['mænɪkjʊəd] ADJ **(a)** *lawn, garden* muy cuidado. **(b)** *nails, hands* muy cuidado.

manicurist ['mænɪkjʊərɪst] N manicuro *m*, -a *f*.

manifest ['mænɪfest] [1] ADJ manifiesto, evidente, patente; **to make sth ~** poner algo de manifiesto.
[2] N (*Naut, Comm*) manifiesto *m*.
[3] VT mostrar, revelar, patentizar.

manifestation [,mænɪfes'teɪʃən] N manifestación *f*.

manifestly ['mænɪfestlɪ] ADV evidentemente.

manifesto [,mænɪ'festəʊ] N, PL **manifestoes** or **manifestos** [,mænɪ'festəʊz] proclama *f*, manifiesto *m*.

manifold ['mænɪfəʊld] [1] ADJ múltiple.
[2] N (*Aut*) colector *m*.

manikin ['mænɪkɪn] N **(a)** (*dwarf*) enano *m*. **(b)** (*Art*) maniquí *m*; (*fashion model*) maniquí *f*, modelo *f*.

Manila [mə'nɪlə] N Manila *f*.

manil(l)a [mə'nɪlə] ADJ *paper, envelope* manila.

manioc ['mænɪɒk] N mandioca *f*, yuca *f*.

manipulate [mə'nɪpjʊleɪt] VT manipular, manejar.

manipulation [mə,nɪpjʊ'leɪʃən] N manipulación *f*, manipuleo *m*.

manipulative [mə'nɪpjʊlətɪv] ADJ manipulativo.

manipulator [mə'nɪpjʊ,leɪtəʳ] N manipulador *m*, -ora *f*.

mankind [mæn'kaɪnd] N humanidad *f*, género *m* humano, los hombres.

manlike ['mænlaɪk] ADJ **(a)** (*manly*) varonil. **(b)** (*like man*) parecido al hombre.

manliness ['mænlɪnɪs] N virilidad *f*, masculinidad *f*, hombría *f*.

manly ['mænlɪ] ADJ varonil, viril, masculino; (*courageous*) valiente; (*strong*) fuerte; **to be very ~** ser muy hombre, ser todo un hombre.

man-made ['mæn'meɪd] ADJ artificial, sintético.

manna ['mænə] N maná *m*; **~ from heaven** maná *m* caído del cielo.

manned [mænd] ADJ tripulado; *satellite etc* pilotado.

mannequin ['mænɪkɪn] [1] N (*Art*) maniquí *m*; (*fashion ~*) modelo *f*.
[2] ATTR: **~ parade** desfile *m* de modelos.

manner ['mænəʳ] N **(a)** (*mode*) manera *f*, modo *m*; **~ of payment** modo *m* de pago, forma *f* de pago; **after this ~, in this ~** de esta manera; **after** (*or* **in**) **the ~ of X** a la manera de X, en el estilo de X; **in like ~** de la misma manera; **in such a ~ that ...** de tal manera que ...; **a painter in the grand ~** un pintor de cuadros grandiosos; **in a ~ of speaking** (*so to speak*) por así decirlo, como si dijéramos, (*up to a point*) hasta cierto punto, en cierto modo; **it's a ~ of speaking** es un modo de decir; **as** (*if*) **to the ~ born** como si estuviese acostumbrado desde la cuna.
(b) **~s** (*of society*) costumbres *fpl*; **a novel of ~s** una novela de costumbres; **~s maketh man** la conducta forma al hombre.
(c) (*behaviour etc*) conducta *f*; aire *m*, ademán *m*, porte *m*; manera *f* de ser; **his ~ to his parents** su modo de comportarse con sus padres; **I don't like his ~** no me gusta su actitud; **he had the ~ of an old man** tenía aire de viejo; **there's sth odd about his ~** tiene un aire

algo raro.

(d) ~s (*good, bad etc*) modales *mpl*; educación *f*, crianza *f*; **bad ~s** mala educación *f*; **good ~s** educación *f*; **road ~s** educación *f* en la carretera, comportamiento *m* en la carretera; **it's bad ~s to yawn** es de mala educación bostezar; **good ~s demand that ...** la educación exige que ...; **to have bad ~s** ser mal criado, ser mal educado; **he has no ~s** no tiene crianza, es un mal criado; **to forget one's ~s** descomedirse; **to teach sb ~s** enseñarle a uno a portarse bien.

(e) (*class, type*) clase *f*, especie *f*; **all ~ of birds** toda clase de aves, aves de toda clase; **no ~ of doubt** sin ningún género de duda; **by no ~ of means** de ningún modo; **what ~ of man is he?** ¿qué tipo de hombre es?

mannered ['mænəd] ADJ *style* amanerado; (*in compounds*) de modales ...; V **bad-~** *etc*.

mannerism ['mænərɪzəm] N **(a)** (*Art, Liter*) manierismo *m*, (*pej*) amaneramiento *m*. **(b)** (*trick of speech, gesture*) movimiento *m* típico, peculiaridad *f*.

mannerist ['mænərɪst] [1] ADJ manierista.
  [2] N manierista *mf*.

mannerliness ['mænəlɪnɪs] N (buena) educación *f*, crianza *f*, cortesía *f*.

mannerly ['mænəlɪ] ADJ (bien) educado, bien criado, cortés.

mannikin ['mænɪkɪn] N = **manikin**.

mannish ['mænɪʃ] ADJ hombruno.

manoeuvrability, (*US*) **maneuverability** [mə,nuːvrə'bɪlɪtɪ] N maniobrabilidad *f*.

manoeuvrable, (*US*) **maneuverable** [mə'nuːvrəbl] ADJ maniobrable, manejable.

manoeuvre, (*US*) **maneuver** [mə'nuːvəʳ] [1] N maniobra *f*; **this leaves us little room for ~** esto apenas nos deja espacio en que hacer cambios de posición, con esto nos quedan pocas posibilidades de hacer ajustes.
  [2] VT hacer maniobrar; manipular, manejar; **to ~ a gun into position** mover un cañón a su posición; **I was ~d into it** me embaucaron para que lo hiciera; **to ~ sb into doing sth** lograr mañosamente que uno haga algo.
  [3] VI maniobrar (*also fig*).

manoeuvring, (*US*) **maneuvering** [mə'nuːvrɪŋ] N el maniobrar; **political ~s** maniobras *fpl* políticas.

man-of-war ['mænəv'wɔːʳ] N, PL **men-of-war** ['menəv'wɔːʳ] N buque *m* de guerra.

manometer [mə'nɒmɪtəʳ] N manómetro *m*.

manor ['mænəʳ] N **(a)** (*feudal*) feudo *m*; señorío *m*; (*modern*) finca *f*. **(b)** (*Brit**) distrito *m*, barrio *m*; V **manor house**.

manor house ['mænəhaʊs] N, PL **manor houses** ['mænə,haʊzɪz] casa *f* señorial, casa *f* solariega.

manorial [mə'nɔːrɪəl] ADJ señorial.

manpower ['mænpaʊəʳ] N mano *f* de obra; personal *m*; recursos *mpl* humanos, potencial *m* humano; **~ planning** planificación *f* de personal.

manqué ['mɔːŋkeɪ] ADJ: **a novelist ~** uno que hubiera podido ser novelista.

manse [mæns] N (*esp Scot*) casa *f* del pastor (protestante).

manservant ['mæn,sɜːvənt] N, PL **menservants** ['men,sɜːvənts] criado *m*.

mansion ['mænʃən] N palacio *m*, hotel *m*; casa *f* grande; (*of ancient family*) casa *f* solariega; **M~ House** residencia del alcalde de Londres.

man-sized ['mænsaɪzd] ADJ de tamaño de hombre; (*fig*) bien grande, grandote.

manslaughter ['mæn,slɔːtəʳ] N homicidio *m* sin premeditación.

mantelpiece ['mæntlpiːs] N, **mantelshelf** ['mæntlʃelf] N, PL **mantelshelves** ['mæntlʃelvz] manto *m* (de chimenea), repisa *f* de chimenea.

mantilla [mæn'tɪlə] N mantilla *f*, velo *m*.

mantis ['mæntɪs] N: **praying ~** mantis *f* religiosa.

mantle ['mæntl] [1] N **(a)** (*cloak: also fig, Zool*) manto *m*, capa *f*. **(b)** (*gas ~*) manguito *m* incandescente, camisa *f* incandescente.
  [2] VT cubrir, ocultar; envolver (*in en*).

man-to-man ['mæntə'mæn] ADJ, ADV de hombre a hombre.

mantra ['mæntrə] N mantra *m*.

mantrap ['mæntræp] N cepo *m*.

manual ['mænjʊəl] [1] ADJ manual; **~ training** enseñanza *f* de artes y oficios; **~ worker** trabajador *m*, -ora *f* manual.
  [2] N **(a)** (*book*) manual *m*. **(b)** (*Mus*) teclado *m*.

manually ['mænjʊəlɪ] ADV manualmente, a mano.

manufacture [,mænjʊ'fæktʃəʳ] [1] N **(a)** (*act*) fabricación *f*. **(b)** (*product*) manufactura *f*, producto *m*.
  [2] VT fabricar (*also fig*), manufacturar; **~d goods** artículos *mpl* manufacturados.

manufacturer [,mænjʊ'fæktʃərəʳ] N fabricante *mf*, manufactero *m*, industrial *mf*.

manufacturing [,mænjʊ'fæktʃərɪŋ] [1] ADJ manufacturero, fabril; ~

capacity capacidad *f* de fabricación; **~ costs** costos *mpl* de fabricación; **~ industries** industrias *fpl* manufactureras.
  [2] N fabricación *f*.

manure [mə'njʊəʳ] [1] N estiércol *m*, abono *m*.
  [2] ATTR: **~ heap** estercolero *m*.
  [3] VT estercolar, abonar.

manuscript ['mænjuskrɪpt] [1] ADJ manuscrito.
  [2] N manuscrito *m*; (*original of book, article*) original *m*.

Manx [mæŋks] [1] ADJ de la Isla de Man.
  [2] N **(a)** **the ~** los habitantes de la Isla de Man. **(b)** (*Ling*) lengua *f* (*celta*) de la Isla de Man.

Manxman ['mæŋksmən] N, PL **Manxmen** ['mæŋksmən] habitante *m* de la Isla de Man.

many ['menɪ] [1] ADJ muchos, muchas; **~ people** muchas personas, mucha gente, muchos; **in ~ cases** en muchos casos; **~ of them** muchos de ellos; **~ a time I have seen him act**, **~'s the time I have seen him act** muchas veces le he visto representar; **he has as ~ as I have** tiene tantos como yo; **he has 3 times as ~ as I have** tiene 3 veces más que yo; **there were as ~ as 20** había hasta 20; **and as ~ more** y otros tantos; **how ~ were there?** ¿cuántos había?; **however ~ you have** por muchos que tengas; **so ~ flies** tantas moscas; **ever so ~ people** la mar de gente, tantísimas personas; **a good ~ houses**, **a great ~ houses** muchísimas casas, (un) buen número de casas; **too ~ difficulties** demasiadas dificultades; **there's one too ~** hay uno de más, hay uno que sobra, sobra uno.
  [2] N muchos *mpl*, muchas *fpl*; gran número *m*; **the ~** la mayoría, las masas.

many-coloured, (*US*) **many-colored** ['menɪ'kʌləd] ADJ multicolor.

many-sided ['menɪ'saɪdɪd] ADJ *figure* multilátero; *talent, personality* multifacético, polifacético; *problem* complicado.

Maoism ['maʊɪzəm] N maoísmo *m*.

Maoist ['maʊɪst] [1] ADJ maoísta.
  [2] N maoísta *mf*.

Maori ['maʊrɪ] [1] ADJ maorí.
  [2] N maorí *mf*.

Mao Tse-tung ['maʊtseɪ'tʊŋ] NM Mao Zedong.

map [mæp] [1] N mapa *m*; (*of streets, town*) plano *m*; (*chart*) carta *f*; **it's right off the ~** está muy aislado, está en el quinto infierno; **this will put Cheam on the ~** esto dará Cheam a conocer, ahora sí que se hablará de Cheam.
  [2] VT trazar el mapa (*or* plano) de, levantar el plano de.
  ♦ **map out** VT proyectar; ordenar, organizar.

maple ['meɪpl] [1] N (*also ~ tree*) arce *m*, maple *m* (*LAm*).
  [2] ATTR: **~ leaf** hoja *f* de arce; **~ sugar** azúcar *m* de arce; **~ syrup** jarabe *m* de arce.

mapmaker ['mæp,meɪkəʳ] N cartógrafo *m*, -a *f*.

mapmaking ['mæp,meɪkɪŋ] N, **mapping** ['mæpɪŋ] N cartografía *f*; trazado *m* de mapas, levantamiento *m* de planos.

mar [mɑːʳ] VT estropear; desfigurar; echar a perder; *happiness etc* afectar; *enjoyment* aguar.

Mar. ABBR of **March** marzo *m*, mar.

maracas [mər'ækəs] NPL maracas *fpl*.

maraschino [,mærəs'kiːnəʊ] N marrasquino *m*; **~ cherries** guindas *fpl* en conserva de marrasquino.

marathon ['mærəθən] [1] N (*also ~ race*) maratón *m* (*sometimes f*).
  [2] ATTR (*fig*) larguísimo, interminable, maratón, maratoniano.

maraud [mə'rɔːd] VI merodear.

marauder [mə'rɔːdəʳ] N merodeador *m*; intruso *m*.

marauding [mə'rɔːdɪŋ] [1] ADJ merodeador; intruso, indeseable.
  [2] N merodeo *m*.

marble ['mɑːbl] [1] N **(a)** (*material*) mármol *m*. **(b)** (*glass ball*) canica *f*, bola *f*; **to lose one's ~s:** perder la chaveta*; **to play ~s** jugar a las bolas.
  [2] ADJ marmóreo (*also fig*), de mármol; **~ quarry** cantera *f* de mármol; **~ staircase** escalera *f* de mármol.

marbled ['mɑːbld] ADJ *surface* jaspeado.

March [mɑːtʃ] N marzo *m*.

march¹ [mɑːtʃ] [1] N marcha *f* (*also Mus, fig*); (*fig: long walk*) caminata *f*; **an army on the ~** un ejército en marcha; **we were on the ~ to the capital** marchábamos sobre la capital; **it's a day's ~ from here** está a un día de marcha desde aquí; (*fig*) eso queda lejísimos; **to steal a ~ on sb** madrugar, ganar por la mano a uno, sacar la delantera a uno.
  [2] VT **(a)** *soldiers* hacer marchar, llevar.
  (b) *distance* recorrer (marchando); (*fig*) llevar andado.
  [3] VI marchar; (*fig*) andar, ir a pie; (*stalk*) ir resueltamente, caminar con resolución; **forward ~!**, **quick ~!** de frente ¡mar!; **to ~ into a room** entrar resueltamente en un cuarto; **to ~ past** desfilar; **to ~ past sb** desfilar ante uno.
  ♦ **march in** VI entrar (resueltamente *etc*).
  ♦ **march off** [1] VT: **they ~ed him off** se lo llevaron sin ceremonia.
  [2] VI irse (resueltamente *etc*).

◆**march on** [1] VT marchar sobre.
[2] VI seguir marchando.
◆**march out** VI salir (airado, resueltamente *etc*).
◆**march up to** VT: **to ~ up to sb** acercarse resueltamente a uno; abordar a uno tan fresco.
march² [mɑːtʃ] N (*Hist*) marca *f*; **the Spanish M~** la Marca Hispánica; **the Welsh ~es** la marca galesa.
marcher ['mɑːtʃər] N (*on demonstration*) marchista *mf*, manifestante *mf*.
marching ['mɑːtʃɪŋ] ADJ *song etc* de marcha; **to get one's ~ orders*** ser despedido; **to give sb his ~ orders*** despedir a uno.
marchioness ['mɑːʃənɪs] N marquesa *f*.
march-past ['mɑːtʃˌpɑːst] N desfile *m*.
mare [mɛər] N yegua *f*.
mare's-nest ['mɛəznest] N parto *m* de los montes, hallazgo *m* ilusorio.
marg* [mɑːdʒ] N (*Brit*) ABBR of margarine.
Margaret ['mɑːgərɪt] NF Margarita.
margarine [ˌmɑːdʒəˈriːn] N, **marge*** [mɑːdʒ] (*Brit*) N margarina *f*.
Marge [mɑːdʒ] NF *familiar form of* **Margaret, Marjory.**
marge* [mɑːdʒ] N = **marg*.**
margin ['mɑːdʒɪn] N margen *m* (*also Fin, Typ*); (*fig*) margen *m*; reserva *f*; excedente *m*, sobrante *m*; **~ of error** margen *m* de error; **~ of profit** margen *m* de beneficios; **~ of safety** margen *m* de seguridad; **to write sth in the ~** escribir algo al margen; **they live on the ~ of society** viven en el margen de la sociedad.
marginal ['mɑːdʒɪnl] ADJ *note, profit etc* marginal; *case etc* dudoso, incierto; *interest, matter* periférico; **of ~ importance** de dudosa importancia; **~ land** tierras *fpl* marginales; **~ seat** (*Pol*) *escaño que se gana por escasa mayoría.*

┌─ **MARGINAL SEAT** ─┐

*ⓘ En el Reino Unido se llama **marginal seat** o **marginal constituency** al escaño (y al distrito electoral correspondiente) que se gana por escaso margen, con lo cual en las siguientes elecciones hay muchas posibilidades de que pueda ganarlo a su vez la oposición. Debido a esto, si dicho escaño queda vacante por fallecimiento o dimisión de un parlamentario y se convocan elecciones con carácter excepcional para cubrirlo **by-election**, el resultado de las mismas será tomado por los medios de comunicación como un indicador de la popularidad del gobierno. Por el contrario, el escaño que un partido suele ganar por amplia mayoría, debido a la homogeneidad en la tendencia política de los electores, se conoce como **safe seat**.*
⇨ Ver también ⌐BY-ELECTION⌐ , ⌐CONSTITUENCY⌐

marginalize ['mɑːdʒɪnəlaɪz] VT marginar.
marginally ['mɑːdʒɪnəlɪ] ADV ligeramente.
marguerita [ˌmɑːgəˈriːtə] N margarita *f*.
marguerite [ˌmɑːgəˈriːt] N margarita *f*.
Maria [məˈriːə] NF María.
Marian ['mɛərɪən] ADJ mariano.
Marie Antoinette [məˈriːæntwaˈnet] NF María Antonieta.
marigold ['mærɪgəʊld] N caléndula *f*, maravilla *f*.
marihuana, marijuana [ˌmærɪˈhwɑːnə] N marijuana *f*.
marimba [məˈrɪmbə] N marimba *f*.
marina [məˈriːnə] N centro *m* de deportes acuáticos, puerto *m* deportivo.
marinade [ˌmærɪˈneɪd] [1] N escabeche *m*.
[2] VT (*also* **marinate** ['mærɪneɪt]) escabechar, marinar.
marine [məˈriːn] [1] ADJ marino; marítimo; **M~ Corps** (*US*) Infantería *f* de Marina; **~ engineer** ingeniero *m* naval; **~ engineering** ingeniería *f* naval; **~ insurance** seguro *m* marítimo; **~ life** vida *f* marina.
[2] N (a) (*fleet*) marina *f*.
(b) (*person*) infante *m* de marina; **~s** (*Brit*) infantería *f* de marina; **tell that to the ~s!** ¡a otro perro con ese hueso!, ¡cuéntaselo a tu abuela!
mariner ['mærɪnər] N marinero *m*, marino *m*.
mariolatry [ˌmɛərɪˈɒlətrɪ] N mariolatría *f*.
Mariology [ˌmɛərɪˈɒlədʒɪ] N mariología *f*.
marionette [ˌmærɪəˈnet] N marioneta *f*, títere *m*.
marital ['mærɪtl] ADJ marital; matrimonial; **~ counselling** orientación *f* sobre problemas matrimoniales; **~ problems** problemas *mpl* matrimoniales, problemas *mpl* conyugales; **~ status** estado *m* civil.
maritime ['mærɪtaɪm] ADJ marítimo; **~ law** código *m* marítimo, derecho *m* marítimo.
marjoram ['mɑːdʒərəm] N mejorana *f*, orégano *m*.
Mark [mɑːk] NM Marcos; **~ Antony** Marco Antonio.
mark¹ [mɑːk] N (*coin*) marco *m*.
mark² [mɑːk] [1] N (a) (*written symbol on paper etc*) señal *f*, marca *f*; llamada *f*; (*sign, indication*) señal *f*, indicio *m*; (*as signature*) cruz *f*; (*trade~*) marca *f*; (*stain*) mancha *f*; (*imprint, trace*) huella *f*; **gas ~ 1** número 1 del gas; **the ~s of violence** las señales de la violencia; **he had the ~s of old age** tenía los indicios de la vejez; **he left the ring**

without a **~ on his body** salió del cuadrilátero sin llevar señal alguna en el cuerpo; **it's the ~ of a gentleman** así se distinguen los caballeros, es señal de caballerosidad; **as a ~ of my disapproval** en señal de mi desaprobación; **as a ~ of our gratitude** en señal de nuestro agradecimiento; **it bears the ~ of genius** tiene el sello de la genialidad; **to leave one's ~** dejar memoria de sí; **to leave one's ~ on sth** dejar sus huellas en algo; **to make one's ~** firmar con una cruz, (*fig*) señalarse, distinguirse, destacar.
(b) (*Sport*) raya *f*; **on your ~s, get set, go!** ¡preparados, listos, ya!; **to be quick off the ~** ser muy listo; adelantarse a los demás; **to be slow off the ~** ser lerdo; dejar que otros cojan la delantera a uno; **to be up to the ~** ser satisfactorio, estar a la altura de las circunstancias; **to come up to the ~** alcanzar el nivel que era de esperar; **to overstep the ~** propasarse.
(c) (*label*) etiqueta *f*.
(d) **of ~** de categoría, de cierta distinción.
(e) (*target*) blanco *m*; **to be wide of the ~** errar, no dar en el blanco, (*fig*) no acertar, ser erróneo, alejarse de la verdad; **he's on the ~** (*fig*) ha dado en el blanco, está en lo cierto; **he's way off the ~** (*fig*) no acierta ni con mucho; se aleja mucho de la verdad; **to hit the ~** dar en el blanco, (*fig*) acertar, dar en el clavo; **to reach the £1000 ~** alcanzar el total de 1000 libras.
(f) (*in exam; also* **~s**) puntuación *f*; calificación *f*, nota *f*; **52 ~s** 52 puntos, 52 por cien; **to get high ~s in French** sacar buena nota en francés; **you get no ~s at all as a cook** como cocinera no vales para nada; **there are no ~s for guessing** las simples conjeturas no merecen punto alguno.
(g) (*model, type*) serie *f*; **a Spitfire M~ 1** un Spitfire (de) primera serie.
[2] VT (a) (*make a ~ on*) señalar, marcar, poner una señal en; (*stain*) manchar; desfigurar; **~ it with an asterisk** ponga un asterisco allí; **he was not ~ed at all** no mostraba señal alguna de golpe; **a bird ~ed with red** un pájaro manchado de rojo, un pájaro con manchas rojas.
(b) (*label*) rotular, poner un rótulo a; (*Comm*) poner una etiqueta a, indicar el precio de; **this exhibit is not ~ed** este objeto no lleva rótulo; **the chair is ~ed at £20** se indica el precio de la silla como de 20 libras.
(c) (*indicate*) señalar, marcar, indicar; (*characterize*) señalar, distinguir; *anniversary etc* señalar, celebrar; *birthday* festejar; *rhythm, time* (*Mus*) marcar; **stones ~ the path** unas piedras señalan el camino; **this ~s the frontier** esto marca la frontera; **it ~s a change of policy** ello indica un cambio de política; **this ~s him as a future star** esto le señala como un as futuro; **it's not ~ed on the map** no está indicado en el mapa, no consta en el mapa.
(d) (*note down*) apuntar; (*notice*) advertir, observar; (*heed*) prestar atención a; **did you ~ where it fell?** ¿has notado dónde cayó?; **~ you, ~ my words** entiéndase bien que ...; **~ you, he may have been right** fíjate que puede haber tenido razón; **~ what I say** escucha lo que te digo.
(e) *exam* puntuar, calificar; *candidate* dar nota a; **we ~ed him (as) first class** le dimos nota de sobresaliente.
(f) (*Sport*) marcar, doblar.
◆**mark down** VT (a) (*note*) apuntar. (b) (*select*) escoger. (c) (*Comm*) rebajar (*to* a); *student* dar nota mala a; reducir la puntuación de.
◆**mark off** VT (a) señalar; distinguir, separar (*from* de); (*by stages etc*) jalonar. (b) *list* marcar; *names* poner una señal a; (*cross out*) tachar.
◆**mark out** VT (a) *road etc* trazar, marcar; jalonar; **the track is ~ed out by flags** el camino está jalonado de banderas. (b) (*select*) escoger; señalar; (*distinguish*) distinguir, señalar; **he is ~ed out for promotion** se le ha señalado para un ascenso.
◆**mark up** VT (a) (*on board etc*) apuntar. (b) (*Comm*) aumentar, aumentar el precio de.
mark-down ['mɑːkdaʊn] N (*Comm*) reducción *f*.
marked [mɑːkt] ADJ *contrast, accent etc* acusado, fuerte; marcado; *improvement etc* notable, grande; **~ man** hombre *m* que ha llamado la atención; hombre *m* que se ha señalado como futura víctima; **~ price** precio *m* corriente; **it is becoming more ~** se acusa cada vez más.
markedly ['mɑːkɪdlɪ] ADV marcadamente; fuertemente; notablemente; **it is ~ better than the other** es netamente superior al otro; **they are not ~ different** no son obviamente distintos.
marker ['mɑːkər] N (a) (*Billiards etc*) marcador *m*, (*in other games*) ficha *f*. (b) (*in book*) registro *m*. (c) (*signal*) señal *f*; (*signpost*) poste *m* indicador; **to put down a ~** (*fig*) dejar una señal, marcar un lugar. (d) (*also* **~ pen**) rotulador *m*, marcador *m*. (e) (*Comput*) bandera *f*.
market ['mɑːkɪt] [1] N mercado *m*; (*stock exchange*) bolsa *f*; **there's no ~ for pink socks** los calcetines rosados no encuentran salida; **to be in the ~ for sth** estar dispuesto a comprar algo; **to be on the ~** estar de venta; **it's the dearest shirt on the ~** es la camisa más cara del mercado; **to bring (or put) a product on to the ~** lanzar un producto al mercado; **to come on to the ~** (empezar a) venderse,

ponerse en venta, ofrecerse; **to corner the ~ in maize** acaparar el maíz; **to find a ready ~** venderse fácilmente, tener fácil salida; **to flood the ~ with sth** inundar el mercado de algo; **strawberries are flooding the ~** las fresas inundan el mercado; **to play the ~** jugar a la bolsa; **to rig the ~** manipular la lonja.

2 ATTR: **~ analysis** análisis *m* de mercado(s); **~ day** día *m* de mercado; **~ demand** demanda *f* de mercado; **~ economy** economía *f* de mercado; **~ forces** fuerzas *fpl* del mercado; factores *mpl* comerciales; **~ garden** (*Brit*) huerto *m*, (*large*) huerta *f*; **~ gardener** (*Brit*) hortelano *m*; **~ gardening** (*Brit*) horticultura *f*; **~ intelligence** información *f* del mercado; **~ leader** líder *m* del mercado; **~ opportunity** oportunidad *f* comercial; **~ penetration** penetración *f* del mercado; **~ place** mercado *m*, plaza *f* del mercado; **~ potential** potencial *m* comercial; **~ price** precio *m* de mercado, precio *m* corriente; **~ rates** precios *mpl* del mercado, (*Fin*) cotizaciones *fpl*; **~ research** prospección *f* de mercados, análisis *m* de mercados; **~ researcher** prospector *m*, -ora *f* de mercados; **~ share** cuota *f* de mercado, participación *f* en el mercado; **~ square** plaza *f* del mercado; **~ study**, **~ survey** estudio *m* del mercado; **~ town** mercado *m*; **~ trends** tendencias *fpl* de mercado; **~ value** valor *m* en el mercado, valor *m* comercial.

3 VT vender, poner a la venta; *new product etc* llevar al mercado, mercadear, comercializar.

4 VI (*esp US*) ir de compras; hacer las compras.

marketability [ˌmɑːkɪtəˈbɪlɪtɪ] N comerciabilidad *f*, vendibilidad *f*.

marketable [ˈmɑːkɪtəbl] ADJ vendible, comerciable, comercializable; negociable; de valor comercial; **~ securities** valores *mpl* comerciables, valores *mpl* realizables.

marketeer [ˌmɑːkɪˈtɪəʳ] N (*Brit Pol*) partidario *m*, -a *f* del Mercado Común.

marketing [ˈmɑːkɪtɪŋ] 1 N márketing *m*, márquetin *m*, mercadeo *m*; mercadotecnia *f*.

2 ATTR: **~ agreement** acuerdo *m* mercantil; **~ department** sección *f* mercantil, sección *f* de márketing; **~ manager** director *m*, -ora *f* comercial, director *m*, -ora *f* de márketing; **~ plan** plan *m* de distribución de mercancías; **~ strategy** estrategia *f* mercadológica.

market-led [ˈmɑːkɪtˈled] ADJ generado (*or* condicionado) por el mercado.

marking [ˈmɑːkɪŋ] 1 N (*mark*) señal *f*, marca *f*; (*on animal*) mancha *f*, pinta *f*; (*coloration*) coloración *f*; (*of exams*) puntuación *f*, calificación *f*.

2 ATTR: **~ ink** tinta *f* de marcar, tinta *f* indeleble; **~ pen** rotulador *m*, marcador *m*.

mark-reader [ˈmɑːkˌriːdəʳ] N, **mark-scanner** [ˈmɑːkˌskænəʳ] N lector *m* de marcas.

mark-reading [ˈmɑːkˌriːdɪŋ] N, **mark-scanning** [ˈmɑːkˌskænɪŋ] N lectura *f* de marcas.

marksman [ˈmɑːksmən] N, PL **marksmen** [ˈmɑːksmən] tirador *m*.

marksmanship [ˈmɑːksmənʃɪp] N puntería *f*.

mark-up [ˈmɑːkʌp] N margen *m* (de beneficio); valor *m* añadido; aumento *m* de precio.

marl [mɑːl] N marga *f*.

marlin [ˈmɑːlɪn] N (*Fish*) aguja *f*.

marlin(e) [ˈmɑːlɪn] N (*Naut*) merlín *m*, empalmadura *f*, trincafía *f*.

marlinespike [ˈmɑːlɪnspaɪk] N pasador *m*.

marly [ˈmɑːlɪ] ADJ margoso.

marmalade [ˈmɑːməleɪd] 1 N mermelada *f* (de naranjas amargas).

2 ATTR: **~ orange** naranja *f* amarga.

marmoreal [mɑːˈmɔːrɪəl] ADJ marmóreo.

marmoset [ˈmɑːməzet] N tití *m*.

marmot [ˈmɑːmət] N marmota *f*.

maroon[1] [məˈruːn] 1 ADJ granate, corinto, rojo oscuro.

2 N (*colour*) marrón *m*.

maroon[2] [məˈruːn] VT abandonar (en una isla desierta); (*fig*) aislar, dejar aislado; dejar en un sitio peligroso; **we were ~ed by floods** quedamos aislados por las inundaciones.

maroon[3] [məˈruːn] N (*firework*) petardo *m*.

marque [mɑːk] N marca *f*.

marquee [mɑːˈkiː] N (*esp Brit*) tienda *f* grande, entoldado *m*; (*US*) marquesina *f*.

marquess, marquis [ˈmɑːkwɪs] N marqués *m*.

marquetry [ˈmɑːkɪtrɪ] N marquetería *f*.

Marrakesh [ˌmærəˈkeʃ] N Marakech *m*.

▼ **marriage** [ˈmærɪdʒ] 1 N (*as institution*) matrimonio *m*; (*wedding*) boda *f*, bodas *fpl*; casamiento *m*; (*fig*) unión *f*; **~ of convenience** matrimonio *m* de conveniencia; **aunt by ~** tía *f* política; **to be related by ~** estar emparentado; **to become related by ~ to sb** emparentar con uno; **to give sb in ~ to** casar a una con, dar a una en matrimonio a.

2 ATTR: **~ bed** lecho *m* nupcial, tálamo *m*; **~ broker** casamentero *m*, -a *f*; **~ bureau** agencia *f* matrimonial; **~ ceremony** matrimonio *m*; **~ certificate** partida *f* de matrimonio; **~ counseling** (*US*), **~ guidance**

orientación *f* matrimonial; **~ (guidance) counsel(l)or** consejero *m*, -a *f* de orientación matrimonial; **~ licence** licencia *f* de matrimonio (*or* matrimonial); **~ lines** (*Brit*) partida *f* de matrimonio; **~ partner** cónyuge *mf*, consorte *mf*; **~ rate** (índice *m*) de nupcialidad *f*; **~ settlement** contrato *m* matrimonial; capitulaciones *fpl* matrimoniales; **~ vows** votos *mpl* matrimoniales.

marriageable [ˈmærɪdʒəbl] ADJ casadero.

married [ˈmærɪd] ADJ *person* casado; *life, love, state etc* conyugal; **~ couple** matrimonio *m*; **~ man** casado *m*, **~ woman** casada *f*; **the ~ state** el estado matrimonial; **her ~ name** su apellido de casada; **~ quarters** alojamiento *m* para matrimonio.

marrow [ˈmærəʊ] N (a) (*Anat*) médula *f*, tuétano *m*, meollo *m*; (*fig*) meollo *m*; (*as food*) tuétano *m* de hueso; **a Spaniard to the ~** español hasta los tuétanos; **to be frozen to the ~** estar completamente helado.

(b) (*Brit Bot: also* **vegetable ~**) calabacín *m*.

marrowbone [ˈmærəʊbəʊn] N hueso *m* con tuétano; **~s*** (*hum*) rodillas *fpl*.

▼ **marry** [ˈmærɪ] 1 VT (*give or join in marriage*) casar (*to* con); (*take in marriage*) casarse con, casar con; (*fig*) conjugar, unir; **he has 3 daughters to ~ (off)** tiene 3 hijas por casar; **he's married to his job** está casado con su trabajo; **to ~ money** casarse con uno (*or* una) que tiene una fortuna.

▼ 2 VI (*also* **to get married**) casarse; **to ~ again** volver a casarse, casarse en segundas nupcias; **to ~ beneath o.s.** casarse con uno (*or* una) de rango inferior; **to ~ into a family** emparentar con una familia; **to ~ into the peerage** casarse con un título.

◆ **marry up** VT conjugar.

Mars [mɑːz] NM Marte.

Marseillaise [ˌmɑːsəˈleɪz] N: **the ~** la Marsellesa.

Marseilles [mɑːˈseɪlz] N Marsella *f*.

marsh [mɑːʃ] 1 N pantano *m*, ciénaga *f*; (*salt-~*) marisma *f*.

2 ATTR: **~ fever** paludismo *m*; **~ gas** gas *m* de los pantanos, metano *m*; **~ marigold** botón *m* de oro; **~ warbler** papamoscas *m*.

marshal [ˈmɑːʃəl] 1 N (*Mil*) mariscal *m*; (*at ceremony*) maestro *m* de ceremonias; (*Brit: at sports meeting etc*) oficial *m*; (*US*) alguacil *m*, oficial *m* de justicia.

2 VT *facts, ideas etc* ordenar, arreglar; *evidence* presentar; *soldiers, procession* formar.

marshalling yard [ˈmɑːʃəlɪŋˌjɑːd] N (*Rail*) playa *f* de clasificación, estación *f* clasificadora, zona *f* de enganche.

marshland [ˈmɑːʃlænd] N pantanal *m*.

marshmallow [ˈmɑːʃˈmæləʊ] N (*Bot*) malvavisco *m*; (*sweet*) 'esponjas' *fpl*.

marshy [ˈmɑːʃɪ] ADJ pantanoso.

marsupial [mɑːˈsuːpɪəl] 1 ADJ marsupial.

2 N marsupial *m*.

mart [mɑːt] N (*trade centre*) emporio *m*; (*market*) mercado *m*; (*auction-room*) martillo *m*; (*property ~*) (*in newspaper*) bolsa *f* de la propiedad.

marten [ˈmɑːtɪn] N marta *f*.

Martial [ˈmɑːʃəl] NM Marcial.

martial [ˈmɑːʃəl] ADJ marcial; castrense; **~ arts** artes *fpl* marciales; **~ bearing** porte *m* militar; **~ law** ley *f* marcial, gobierno *m* militar.

Martian [ˈmɑːʃən] 1 ADJ marciano.

2 N marciano *m*, -a *f*.

Martin [ˈmɑːtɪn] NM Martín.

martin [ˈmɑːtɪn] N avión *m*.

martinet [ˌmɑːtɪˈnet] N ordenancista *mf*, rigorista *mf*.

Martini [mɑːˈtiːnɪ] ® N vermú *m*; (*US: cocktail*) martini *m* americano (*vermú seco con ginebra*).

Martinique [ˌmɑːtɪˈniːk] N Martinica *f*.

Martinmas [ˈmɑːtɪnməs] N día *m* de San Martín (*11 noviembre*).

martyr [ˈmɑːtəʳ] 1 N mártir *mf*; **to be a ~ to arthritis** ser martirizado por la artritis, ser víctima de la artritis.

2 VT martirizar.

martyrdom [ˈmɑːtədəm] N martirio *m*.

martyrize [ˈmɑːtɪraɪz] VT martirizar.

marvel [ˈmɑːvəl] 1 N maravilla *f*; prodigio *m*; **if he gets there it will be a ~** si llega será milagro; **it's a ~ to me how he does it** no llego a comprender cómo lo hace, me asombra el que lo pueda hacer.

2 VI maravillarse (*at* de, con).

marvellous, (*US*) **marvelous** [ˈmɑːvələs] ADJ maravilloso; **~!** ¡magnífico!; **isn't it ~?** ¡qué bien! (*also iro*).

marvellously, (*US*) **marvelously** [ˈmɑːvələslɪ] ADV maravillosamente; a maravilla.

Marxism [ˈmɑːksɪzəm] N marxismo *m*.

Marxist [ˈmɑːksɪst] 1 ADJ marxista.

2 N marxista *mf*.

Mary [ˈmɛərɪ] NF María *f*; **~ Magdalen** la Magdalena; **~ Queen of Scots**, **~ Stuart** María Estuardo.

marzipan [ˌmɑːzɪˈpæn] N mazapán *m*.

masc. ABBR *of* **masculine** masculino.

► LANGUAGE IN USE: **marriage: 1 → 24.4, 25.1**   **marry: 2 → 24.4**

mascara [mæs'kɑːrə] N rímel m, máscara f.
mascaraed [mæs'kɑːrə] ADJ pintado con rímel.
mascot ['mæskət] N mascota f.
masculine ['mæskjʊlɪn] [1] ADJ masculino; varonil; *woman* hombruno. [2] N masculino m.
masculinist ['mæskjʊlɪnɪst] ADJ masculino.
masculinity [,mæskjʊ'lɪnɪti] N masculinidad f.
masculinize ['mæskjʊlɪnaɪz] VT masculinizar.
MASH [mæʃ] N (*US*) ABBR of **mobile army surgical unit** unidad f quirúrgica móvil del ejército.
mash [mæʃ] [1] N (*mixture*) mezcla f; (*pulp*) pasta f, amasijo m; (*Brit: potatoes*) puré m de patatas; (*in brewing*) malta f remojada; (*bran*) afrecho m remojado.
 [2] VT mezclar; amasar, despachurrar; *potatoes* hacer un puré de.
mashed [mæʃt] ADJ: **~ potatoes** puré m de patatas, puré m de papas (*LAm*).
mashie ['mæʃi] N hierro m número 5.
mask [mɑːsk] [1] N máscara f (*also fig*); (*disguise*) disfraz m; (*protective*) antifaz m; (*Comput, Elec*) máscara f; (*gas ~ etc*) careta f; (*surgeon's, death ~*) mascarilla f; V **masque**.
 [2] VT enmascarar (*also Comput*); (*fig*) encubrir, ocultar, enmascarar; *effect of drug* enmascarar.
masked [mɑːskt] ADJ enmascarado; (*terrorist etc*) encapuchado; **~ ball** baile m de máscaras.
masking tape ['mɑːskɪŋ,teɪp] N cinta f adhesiva protectora (*del margen del área a pintar*).
masochism ['mæzəʊkɪzəm] N masoquismo m.
masochist ['mæzəʊkɪst] N masoquista mf.
masochistic [,mæzəʊ'kɪstɪk] ADJ masoquista.
mason ['meɪsn] N (a) (*builder*) albañil m; (*in quarry*) cantero m; (*of tombs*) escultor m. (b) (*free~*: *also* M~) masón m, francmasón m.

┌─── **MASON-DIXON LINE** ────────────┐

(i) La línea **Mason-Dixon** o **Mason and Dixon** es la línea simbólica que divide el norte y el sur de Estados Unidos y que, hasta el final de la Guerra Civil, marcaba la separación entre aquellos estados en donde existía la esclavitud y aquéllos en los que no. Esta línea de demarcación, que se extiende a lo largo de 377 kilómetros, fue establecida por Charles Mason y Jeremiah Dixon en el siglo XVIII con el fin de solucionar un conflicto que ya duraba 80 años sobre la frontera entre Maryland y Pensilvania. En 1779 la línea se extendió para demarcar la frontera entre Pensilvania y Virginia (hoy Virginia del Oeste); en la actualidad aún sirve como referencia del sur en general y en las canciones de **country & western** los cantantes hablan con nostalgia de "cruzar la línea" para volver a sus tierras sureñas.

└────────────────────────────────────┘

masonic [mə'sɒnɪk] ADJ (*also* M~) masónico.
masonry ['meɪsnri] N (a) albañilería f; mampostería f. (b) (*free~*) masonería f, francmasonería f.
masque [mɑːsk] N mascarada f.
masquerade [,mæskə'reɪd] [1] N baile m de máscaras, mascarada f; (*fig*) farsa f.
 [2] VI: **to ~ as** disfrazarse de, hacerse pasar por.
mass¹ [mæs] N (*Eccl, Mus*: *also* M~) misa f; **to go to ~** ir a misa, oír misa; **to hear ~** oír misa; **to say ~** decir misa.
mass² [mæs] [1] N (a) masa f (*also Phys*); (*vague shape*) bulto m; (*of mountains*) macizo m.
 (b) (*great quantity*) montón m, gran cantidad f; (*of people*) muchedumbre f; **the ~es** las masas; **a great ~ of people** una gran muchedumbre; **the ~ of** la mayoría de; **the great ~ of** la inmensa mayoría de; **in the ~** en conjunto; **to gather in ~es** acudir en masa, reunirse en tropel; **we have ~es** tenemos montones; **he's a ~ of bruises** está cubierto de cardenales; **the garden is a ~ of yellow** el jardín es todo flores amarillas; **he's a ~ of nerves** es una madeja de nervios, tiene una tremenda tensión nerviosa.
 [2] ATTR masivo; en masa; **~ grave** fosa f común; **~ hysteria** histerismo m colectivo; **~ killing(s)** asesinato(s) m(pl) en masa; **~ market** mercado m popular; **~ media** medios mpl de comunicación; **~ meeting** mitín m (*or* reunión f) popular, manifestación f; **~ murder** matanza f; **~ noun** sustantivo m no contable; **~ production** fabricación f en serie; **~ protest** protesta f masiva; **~ psychology** psicología f de masas; **~ resignation(s)** dimisión f en masa; **~ unemployment** paro m masivo.
 [3] VT juntar en masa, reunir; *troops etc* concentrar.
 [4] VI juntarse en masa, reunirse; (*Mil*) concentrarse.
Mass. (*US*) ABBR of **Massachusetts**.
massacre ['mæsəkər] [1] N matanza f, carnicería f, degollina f, masacre f (*also m*); (*fig*) masacre f (*also m*).
 [2] VT hacer una carnicería de, matar despiadadamente, masacrar; (*fig*) masacrar.
massage ['mæsɑːʒ] [1] N masaje m; '**M~**' (*euph*) 'Relax'.
 [2] ATTR: **~ parlor** (*US*), **~ parlour** sala f de masaje; (*euph*) sala f de

relax.
 [3] VT masajear, dar masaje a; (*) *figures* maquillar*.
masseur [mæ'sɜːr] N masajista m.
masseuse [mæ'sɜːz] N masajista f.
massif [mæ'siːf] N macizo m.
massive ['mæsɪv] ADJ (*solid*) macizo, sólido; *head etc* grande, abultado; (*imposing*) imponente, impresionante; *contribution, support, intervention* enérgico, fuerte, masivo, en gran escala.
massively ['mæsɪvlɪ] ADV macizamente, sólidamente; de modo imponente; enérgicamente, fuertemente, masivamente.
massiveness ['mæsɪvnɪs] N macicez f, solidez f; lo grande, lo abultado; energía f, fuerza f.
mass-produce ['mæsprə'djuːs] VT fabricar en serie.
mast¹ [mɑːst] N (*Naut*) mástil m, palo m; (*Rad etc*) torre f, mástil m; **10 years before the ~** 10 años de servicio como marinero.
mast² [mɑːst] N (*Bot: of oak*) bellota f, (*of beech*) hayuco m.
-masted ['mɑːstɪd] ADJ *ending in compounds* de ... palos; **three~** de tres palos.
master ['mɑːstər] [1] N (*of the house etc*) señor m, amo m; (*owner*) dueño m; (*Naut: of ship*) capitán m, (*of boat*) patrón m; (*expert, musician, painter etc*) maestro m; (*of Mil order*) maestre m; (*teacher*) maestro m, (*in secondary school*) profesor m; (*Brit: of college*) director m, rector m; **old ~** (*man*) pintor m clásico, (*work*) obra f clásica, cuadro m de uno de los pintores clásicos; **the young ~** el señorito; **M~ of Arts** licenciado m, -a f (superior) en Filosofía y Letras, (*Hist*) maestro m en artes; **she's working for her M~'s (degree)** estudia para su licenciatura superior; **~ of ceremonies** maestro m de ceremonias; (*of show*) presentador m, animador m; **~ of foxhounds** cazador m mayor; **M~ of the Rolls** (*Brit*) juez mf del tribunal de apelación; **to be a past ~ at politics** ser un político consumado; **to be ~ of** poseer; **to be ~ of the situation** ser dueño de la situación, dueño del baile; **the ~ is not at home** el señor no está; **I am the ~ now** ahora mando yo; **to be ~ in one's own house** mandar en su propia casa; **to be one's own ~** ser independiente; trabajar por cuenta propia; **to be the ~ of one's fate** decidir su propio destino; **to make o.s. ~ of** apoderarse de; **to meet one's ~** ser derrotado por fin, tener que sucumbir por fin; *ver también* [DEGREE], [FOXHUNTING].
 [2] ATTR maestro; **~ baker** maestro m panadero; **~ bedroom** dormitorio m principal; **~ builder** contratista m de construcciones; **~ card** carta f maestra; **~ class** clase f magistral; **~ copy** original m; **~ disk** disco m maestro; **~ file** fichero m maestro; **~ key** llave f maestra; **~ mariner** capitán m; **~ mason** albañil m maestro; **~ plan** plan m maestro, plan m rector; **~ sergeant** (*US*) sargento m mayor; **~ spy** jefe mf de espías, controlador m, -ora f de espías; **~ stroke** toque m magistral; golpe m maestro; **~ switch** interruptor m principal; **~ tape** máster m, cinta f máster, cinta f original.
 [3] VT (*defeat*) vencer, derrotar; *difficulty etc* vencer; *situation* dominar; *one's defects* sobreponerse a; *subject* dominar; *craft* llegar a ser maestro en.
masterful ['mɑːstəfʊl] ADJ imperioso, autoritario; *personality etc* dominante.
masterfully ['mɑːstəfəlɪ] ADV magistralmente.
masterly ['mɑːstəlɪ] ADJ magistral, genial.
mastermind ['mɑːstəmaɪnd] [1] N inteligencia f genial, cerebro m; (*in crime etc*) mente f directora, figura f principal.
 [2] VT *operation etc* dirigir, planear.
masterpiece ['mɑːstəpiːs] N obra f maestra.
Mastersingers ['mɑːstə,sɪŋəz] NPL: '**The ~**' 'Los maestros cantores'.
masterwork ['mɑːstəwɜːk] N obra f maestra.
mastery ['mɑːstərɪ] N (*sway*) dominio m; autoridad f; (*skill*) maestría f; (*over competitors etc*) dominio m, superioridad f; **to gain the ~ of** (*take over*) hacerse el señor de, (*dominate*) llegar a dominar.
masthead ['mɑːsthed] N (a) (*Naut*) tope m. (b) (*of newspaper*) mancheta f.
mastic ['mæstɪk] N masilla f.
masticate ['mæstɪkeɪt] VTI masticar.
mastiff ['mæstɪf] N mastín m, alano m.
mastitis [mæs'taɪtɪs] N mastitis f.
mastodon ['mæstədɒn] N mastodonte m.
mastoid ['mæstɔɪd] [1] ADJ mastoides.
 [2] N mastoides f.
masturbate ['mæstəbeɪt] VI masturbarse.
masturbation [,mæstə'beɪʃən] N masturbación f.
masturbatory ['mæstə'beɪtərɪ] ADJ masturbatorio.
mat¹ [mæt] [1] N estera f, (*small*) esterilla f; (*round*) ruedo m; (*at door*) felpudo m; (*on table*) salvamanteles m; (*of lace etc*) tapetito m; (*of hair*) greña f.
 [2] VT enmarañar, entretejer.
 [3] VI enmarañarse, entretejerse.
mat² [mæt] ADJ mate.
matador ['mætədɔːr] N matador m, diestro m.

match¹ [mætʃ] N cerilla *f*, fósforo *m*; (*fuse*) mecha *f*.

match² [mætʃ] **1** N **(a)** (*person etc*) igual *mf*; **the two of them make a good ~** hacen una buena pareja; **the skirt is a good ~ for the jumper** la falda hace juego con el jersey; **to be a ~ for sb** poder competir (*etc*) con uno en pie de igualdad; **he's a ~ for anybody** puede dar ciento y raya al más pintado; **A is no ~ for B** A no puede con B; **A was more than a ~ for B** A venció fácilmente a B; **to meet one's match** encontrar la horma de su zapato.
(b) (*marriage*) casamiento *m*, matrimonio *m*; **who thought up this ~?** ¿quién ideó este matrimonio?; **she made a good ~** se casó bien; **he's a good ~** es buen partido.
(c) (*Sport*) partido *m*, encuentro *m*; (*race*) carrera *f*; (*Boxing*) lucha *f*; (*Fencing*) asalto *m*; (*quiz etc*) concurso *m*; **they never tried to make a ~ of it** no se esforzaron en ningún momento por vencer; **let's make a ~ of it** juguemos con la intención de ganar.
2 ATTR (*Tennis*) **~ ball** bola *f* de partido; **~ play** partido *m* serio; **~ point** punto *m* de match.
3 VT **(a)** (*pair off*) emparejar, parear; equiparar; **to ~ A against B** hacer que A compita con B; **they're well ~ed** hacen una buena pareja; **the teams are well ~ed** los equipos son muy iguales.
(b) (*equal*) igualar, ser igual a, valer lo que; **A doesn't quite ~ B in originality** en cuanto a originalidad A no vale lo que B; **the results did not ~ our hopes** los resultados no estaban a la altura de nuestras esperanzas.
(c) (*clothes, colours*) hacer juego con; **his tie ~es his socks** su corbata hace juego con los calcetines; **can you ~ this silk?** ¿tiene una seda igual que ésta?
4 VI hacer juego, armonizar, ser a tono; **with a skirt to ~** con una falda acompañada, con una falda a tono.
◆ **match up** VT *two objects* emparejar; *more than two* agrupar.
◆ **match up to** VT estar a la altura de; **he didn't ~ up to the situation** no estaba a la altura de las circunstancias.

matchbox ['mætʃbɒks] N cajita *f* de cerillas.
matching ['mætʃɪŋ] ADJ acompañado, a tono, que hace juego con; **~ funds** (*US*) fondos *mpl* compensatorios.
matchless ['mætʃlɪs] ADJ sin par, incomparable.
matchmaker ['mætʃ,meɪkəʳ] N casamentero *m*, -a *f*.
matchmaking ['mætʃ,meɪkɪŋ] **1** N actividades *fpl* de casamentero. **2** ADJ casamentero.
matchstick ['mætʃstɪk] N fósforo *m*.
matchwood ['mætʃwʊd] N astillas *fpl*; **to smash sth to ~** hacer algo añicos; **to be smashed to ~** ser convertido en un montón de astillas.
maté ['mɑːteɪ] N mate *m* (cocido), yerba *f* mate; **~ kettle** pava *f*.
mate¹ [meɪt] **1** N mate *m*. **2** VTI dar jaque mate a, matar; **white plays and ~s in 2** blanco juega y mata en 2.
mate² [meɪt] **1** N (*companion*) compañero *m*, camarada *m*, compinche *m* (*LAm*); (*married*) compañero *m*, -a *f*; cónyuge *mf*; (*Zool*) macho *m*, hembra *f*; (*assistant*) ayudante *m*, peón *m*; (*Brit Naut*) primer oficial *m*, piloto *m*, segundo *m* de a bordo; (*US Naut*) segundo *m* de a bordo; **John and his ~s** Juan y sus compañeros; **plumber's ~** ayudante *m* de fontanero, aprendiz *m* de fontanero; **look here ~*** mire, amigo; mire, compadre; **yes ~*** sí, hombre.
2 VT (*Zool*) parear, acoplar; (*fig*) unir; **they are well ~d** hacen una buena pareja.
3 VI (*Zool*) parearse, acoplarse; **age should not ~ with youth** no debe casarse el viejo con la joven.
material [məˈtɪərɪəl] **1** ADJ material; importante, esencial; *well-being etc* físico; *loss, damage* importante, considerable; (*Jur*) *fact etc* fundamental, pertinente.
2 N (*ingredient, equipment, also fig*) material *m*; (*substance*) materia *f*; (*data*) datos *mpl*, material *m*; (*cloth*) tejido *m*, tela *f*; **~s material** *m*, materiales *mpl*; **~s science** ciencias *fpl* de los materiales.
materialism [məˈtɪərɪəlɪzəm] N materialismo *m*.
materialist [məˈtɪərɪəlɪst] **1** ADJ materialista. **2** N materialista *mf*.
materialistic [məˌtɪərɪəˈlɪstɪk] ADJ materialista.
materialize [məˈtɪərɪəlaɪz] **1** VT materializar. **2** VI (*spirit*) tomar forma visible; (*idea etc*) materializarse, realizarse, convertirse en hecho.
materially [məˈtɪərɪəlɪ] ADV materialmente; **that does not ~ alter things** eso no afecta la cosa de modo sensible; **they are not ~ different** no difieren en su esencia.
materiel [məˌtɪərɪˈel] N (*US*) material *m* bélico.
maternal [məˈtɜːnl] ADJ *grandfather etc* materno; *affection etc* maternal.
maternity [məˈtɜːnɪtɪ] **1** N maternidad *f*. **2** ATTR: **~ allowance** (*Brit*) subsidio *m* de natalidad; **~ dress** vestido *m* premamá; **~ home, ~ hospital** casa *f* de maternidad; **~ leave** licencia *f* de maternidad, permiso *m* para parto; **~ ward** sala *f* de partos.
mateship ['meɪtʃɪp] N (*esp Australia*) compañerismo *m*, compadreo *m*.

matey* ['meɪtɪ] **1** ADJ (*Brit*) *person* afable, simpático; bonachón; *atmosphere* acogedor; *gathering* sin ceremonias, familiar, de ambiente acogedor.
2 NM (*Brit: in direct address*) chico, hijo.
math [mæθ] N (*US**) = **mathematics** mates* *fpl*.
mathematical [ˌmæθəˈmætɪkəl] ADJ matemático; **he's a ~ genius** tiene un genio para las matemáticas, es un matemático genial; **I'm not very ~** no tengo instinto para las matemáticas, entiendo poco de matemáticas.
mathematically [ˌmæθəˈmætɪkəlɪ] ADV matemáticamente.
mathematician [ˌmæθəməˈtɪʃən] N matemático *m*, -a *f*.
mathematics [ˌmæθəˈmætɪks] N matemáticas *fpl*.
Mat(h)ilda [məˈtɪldə] NF Matilde.
maths* [mæθs], (*US*) **math*** [mæθ] N = **mathematics** mates* *fpl*.
matinée ['mætɪneɪ] **1** N función *f* de tarde. **2** ATTR: **~ idol** ídolo *m* del público.
matinee coat ['mætɪneɪ,kəʊt] N (*Brit*) abriguito *m* de lana.
matiness* ['meɪtɪnɪs] N afabilidad *f*, simpatía *f*; lo bonachón; carácter *m* familiar; ambiente *m* acogedor.
mating ['meɪtɪŋ] **1** N (*Zool*) apareamiento *m*, acoplamiento *m*; (*fig*) unión *f*. **2** ATTR: **~ call** grito *m* del macho; **~ season** época *f* del celo.
matins ['mætɪnz] N SING *or* PL maitines *mpl*.
matriarch ['meɪtrɪɑːk] N matriarca *f*.
matriarchal [ˌmeɪtrɪˈɑːkl] ADJ matriarcal.
matriarchy ['meɪtrɪɑːkɪ] N matriarcado *m*.
matric* [məˈtrɪk] N (*Brit*) = **matriculation.**
matricide ['meɪtrɪsaɪd] N **(a)** (*act*) matricidio *m*. **(b)** (*person*) matricida *mf*.
matriculate [məˈtrɪkjʊleɪt] **1** VT matricular. **2** VI matricularse.
matriculation [məˌtrɪkjʊˈleɪʃən] N matriculación *f*; (*Brit Univ*) examen *m* de ingreso.
matrimonial [ˌmætrɪˈməʊnɪəl] ADJ matrimonial; conyugal.
matrimony ['mætrɪmənɪ] N matrimonio *m*; vida *f* conyugal.
matrix ['meɪtrɪks] N, PL **matrixes** *or* **matrices** ['meɪtrɪsiːz] matriz *f*; molde *m*.
matron ['meɪtrən] N (*married woman*) matrona *f*; (*in hospital*) supervisora *f*, enfermera *f* jefe (*or* jefa); (*in school*) ama *f* de llaves, ecónoma *f*; (*in hotel*) gobernanta *f*.
matronly ['meɪtrənlɪ] ADJ matronal, de matrona; *figure etc* maduro y algo corpulento.
matron-of-honour, (*US*) **matron-of-honor** ['meɪtrənəvˈɒnəʳ] N, PL **matrons-of-hono(u)r** ['meɪtrənzəvˈɒnəʳ] dama *f* de honor (casada).
matt [mæt] ADJ mate.
matted ['mætɪd] ADJ enmarañado, entretejido; espeso; **~ hair** greña *f*.
▼ **matter** ['mætəʳ] **1** N **(a)** (*substance*) materia *f*; sustancia *f*; (*Typ*) material *m*.
(b) (*Med*) pus *m*, materia *f*.
(c) (*Liter etc*) materia *f*, tema *m*; **form and ~** la forma y el contenido, la forma y la materia.
(d) (*question, affair*) asunto *m*, cuestión *f*, cosa *f*; **for that ~, for the ~ of that** si vamos a eso, en cuanto a eso; **in this ~** en este asunto; **in the ~ of** en materia de, en asuntos de; **there's the ~ of my expenses** hay aquello de mis gastos; **it will be a ~ of a few weeks** será cosa de varias semanas; **it's a ~ of a couple of hours** es cosa de dos horas; **in a ~ of 10 minutes** en cosa de 10 minutos; **it is no great ~** es poca cosa, no importa; **that's quite another ~, that's another ~ altogether,** **that's a very different ~** eso es totalmente distinto, eso es harina de otro costal; **it's an easy ~ to + infin** es fácil + infin; **it will be no easy ~** no será fácil; **it's a serious ~** es cosa seria; **it's no laughing ~** no es cosa de risa; **business ~s** negocios *mpl*; **money ~s** asuntos *mpl* financieros; **the ~ in hand** el asunto de que se trata; **as ~s stand** tal como están las cosas; **the ~ is closed** el asunto está concluido; **to make ~s worse** para colmo de desgracias; **he doesn't mince ~s** no tiene pelos en la lengua; **well, not to mince ~s** bueno, para decirlo como es; **as a ~ of course** por rutina; **it's a ~ of course with us** con nosotros es cosa de cajón (*see also* course 1 (b)); **as a ~ of fact ...** en realidad ..., el caso es que ...; a decir verdad; **as a ~ of fact we were just talking about you** precisamente estábamos hablando de ti; **it's a ~ of form** es pura formalidad; **it's a ~ of taste** es cuestión de gusto.
(e) (*importance*) **no ~, it makes no ~** no importa; **what ~?** ¿qué importa?; **no ~ how you do it** no importa cómo lo hagas; **no ~ what he says** diga lo que diga; **no ~ how big it is** por grande que sea; **no ~ how hot it is** por mucho calor que haga; **no ~ when** no importa cuándo; **no ~ who goes** quienquiera que vaya; **get one, no ~ how** procura uno, del modo que sea.
(f) (*difficulty, problem*) **what's the ~?** ¿qué hay?, ¿qué pasa?; **what's the ~ with you?** ¿te pasa algo?, ¿qué tienes?; **what's the ~ with John?** ¿qué le pasa a Juan?; **what's the ~ with my hat?** ¿qué tiene

mi sombrero?; ¿qué le pasa a mi sombrero?; **what's the ~ with singing?** ¿es que está prohibido cantar?; **sth's the ~ with the lights** algo les pasa a las luces; **nothing's the ~** no pasa nada; **as if nothing was the ~** como si no hubiese pasado nada, como si tal cosa.

▼ ② **VI** importar; **it doesn't ~** no importa, lo mismo da, es igual; **what does it ~?** ¿qué importa?; **does it ~ to you if I go?** ¿te importa que yo vaya?; **why should it ~ to me?** y a mí ¿qué?; **some things ~ more than others** algunas cosas son más importantes que otras.

matter-of-fact ['mætərə'fækt] ADJ natural, normal; flemático.

Matthew ['mæθju:] NM Mateo.

matting ['mætɪŋ] N estera *f*.

mattins ['mætɪnz] N SING *or* PL = **matins**.

mattock ['mætək] N azadón *m*.

mattress ['mætrɪs] N colchón *m*.

maturation [mætjʊə'reɪʃən] N (*frm*) maduración *f*.

mature [mə'tjʊə^r] ① ADJ maduro; *cheese, man, wine etc* hecho; (*Comm*) vencido; **~ student** estudiante *mf* de edad superior a la normal (*p.ej.*, de 26 años o más); **of ~ years** de edad madura; **to become ~** (*Comm*) vencer.
② VTI madurar; (*Comm*) vencer.

maturity [mə'tjʊərɪtɪ] N madurez *f*; (*Comm*) vencimiento *m*.

maudlin ['mɔːdlɪn] ADJ (*sentimental*) sensiblero; (*weepy*) llorón, al punto de deshacerse en lágrimas.

maul [mɔːl] VT destrozar, magullar, herir; *writer, play etc* maltratar; *text* estropear; **he got badly ~ed in the press** la prensa le puso como un trapo.

maunder ['mɔːndə^r] VI divagar.

Maundy ['mɔːndɪ] ATTR: **~ money** (*Brit*) dinero que reparte el monarca a los pobres el Jueves Santo; **~ Thursday** Jueves *m* Santo.

Maurice ['mɒrɪs] NM Mauricio.

Mauritania [ˌmɔːrɪ'teɪnɪə] N Mauritania *f*.

Mauritanian [ˌmɔːrɪ'teɪnɪən] ① ADJ mauritano.
② N mauritano *m*, -a *f*.

Mauritian [mə'rɪʃən] ① ADJ mauriciano.
② N mauriciano *m*, -a *f*.

Mauritius [mə'rɪʃəs] N Mauricio *m*.

mausoleum [ˌmɔːsə'liːəm] N mausoleo *m*.

mauve [məʊv] ① ADJ (de) color de malva.
② N color *m* de malva.

maverick ['mævərɪk] ① N (*US Agr*) res *f* sin marcar; (*Pol etc*) disidente *mf*, inconformista *mf*, persona *f* independiente.
② ADJ disidente, inconformista.

maw [mɔː] N (*Anat*) estómago *m*; (*of cow etc*) cuajar *m*; (*of bird*) molleja *f*, buche *m*; (*fig*) fauces *fpl*.

mawkish ['mɔːkɪʃ] ADJ empalagoso, sensiblero, insulso.

mawkishness ['mɔːkɪʃnɪs] N sensiblería *f*, insulsez *f*.

max. ADJ, N ABBR *of* **maximum**.

maxi* ['mæksɪ] N (*skirt*) maxifalda *f*, maxi* *f*; (*coat*) maxi* *f*.

maxi... ['mæksɪ] PREF maxi...

maxilla [mæk'sɪlə] N maxilar *m* superior.

maxillary [mæk'sɪlərɪ] ADJ (*Anat*) maxilar.

maxim ['mæksɪm] N máxima *f*.

maximization [ˌmæksɪmaɪ'zeɪʃən] N maximización *f*; potenciación *f*.

maximize ['mæksɪmaɪz] VT maximizar, llevar al máximo; potenciar.

maximum ['mæksɪməm] ① ADJ máximo; **~ efficiency** eficacia *f* máxima; **~ effort** esfuerzo *m* supremo; **~ expenditure** gasto *m* máximo; **~ load** carga *f* máxima; **~ price** precio *m* máximo; **~ speed** velocidad *f* máxima.
② N, PL **maximums** *or* **maxima** ['mæksɪmə] máximo *m*, máximum *m*; tope *m*; **at the ~** como máximo, a lo sumo; **(up) to the ~** al máximo; **up to a ~ of £8** hasta 8 libras como máximo.

maxisingle ['mæksɪsɪŋɡəl] N maxisingle *m*.

May [meɪ] ① N mayo *m*.
② ATTR: **~ Day** primero *m* de mayo; **~ Queen** reina *f* de mayo.

may¹ [meɪ] N (*Bot*) flor *f* del espino; (*Brit*; *tree*) espino *m*.

▼ **may²** [meɪ] (*irr*: PRET **might**) VI (a) (*of possibility*) poder, ser posible; **it ~ rain** es posible que llueva, puede llover, puede que llueva; **it ~ be that ...** puede ser que + *subj*, quizá + *subj*; **he ~ not be hungry** puede no tener hambre; **I ~ have said so** es posible que lo haya dicho, puedo haberlo dicho; **I might have said so** pudiera haberlo dicho; **yes, I ~** sí, es posible; **be that as it ~** sea como fuere; **that's as ~ be** eso puede ser; **as soon as ~ be** lo más pronto posible.

▼ (b) (*of permission*) poder, tener permiso para; **yes, you ~** sí, puedes; **if I ~** si me lo permites; **~ I?** ¿me permite?, con permiso; **~ I see it?** ¿me permites verlo?; **~ I come in?** ¿se puede?; **~ I go now?** ¿puedo irme ya?; **you ~ smoke** se permite fumar; **you ~ not smoke** se prohíbe fumar; **if I ~ advise you** si permites que te dé un consejo.

(c) (*auxiliary*) **I hope he ~ succeed** espero que lo logre; **I hoped he might succeed this time** esperaba que lo lograra esta vez; **such a policy as might bring peace** una política que pudiera traernos la paz; **we ~ as well go** más vale irnos, bien podemos irnos; **might I**

suggest that ...? me permito sugerir que ...; **mightn't it be better to +** *infin*? ¿no sería aconsejable + *infin*?; **he might have offered to help** bien pudiera habernos ofrecido su ayuda; **you might shut the door!** ¡podrías (*or* podías) cerrar la puerta!; **you might have told me!** ¡habérmelo dicho!; **you might try Smith's** quizá valga la pena de buscarlo en la tienda de Smith; **as you might expect** como era de esperar, según cabía esperar; **run as he might** por mucho que corriese.

(d) (*of wishing*) **~ you be lucky!** ¡que tengas suerte!; **~ you be forgiven!** ¡que Dios le perdone!; **long ~ he reign!** ¡que reine muchos años!; **or ~ I never eat prawns again** o que no vuelva nunca a comer gambas.

(e) (*in questions*) **who might you be?** ¿quién es Vd?; **how old might you be?** ¿cuántos años tendrá Vd?

Maya ['maɪjə], **Mayan** ['maɪjən] ① ADJ maya.
② N maya *mf*.

▼ **maybe** ['meɪbiː] ① ADV quizá, tal vez.
▼ ② CONJ: **~ he'll come** quizá venga.

mayday ['meɪdeɪ] N señal *f* de socorro, s.o.s. *m*.

mayfly ['meɪflaɪ] N cachipolla *f*, efímera *f*.

mayhem ['meɪhem] N (a) alboroto *m*; violencia *f* (personal). (b) (*US Jur*) mutilación *f* criminal.

mayn't [meɪnt] = **may not**.

mayo* ['meɪəʊ] N (*US*) mayonesa *f*.

mayonnaise [meɪə'neɪz] N mayonesa *f*.

mayor [mɛə^r] N alcalde *m*, alcadesa *f*, intendente *m* (*LAm*); **Mr M~** Señor Alcalde; **Madam M~** Señora Alcaldesa.

mayoral ['mɛərəl] ADJ *candidate, election* para alcalde, para la alcaldía.

mayoralty ['mɛərəltɪ] N alcaldía *f*.

mayoress ['mɛəres] N alcaldesa *f*.

maypole ['meɪpəʊl] N mayo *m*.

maze [meɪz] N laberinto *m*; **to be in a ~** (*fig*) estar perplejo.

MB (a) N ABBR *of* **Bachelor of Medicine**. (b) N ABBR *of* **megabyte**. (c) (*Canada*) ABBR *of* **Manitoba**.

MBA N (*US*) ABBR *of* **Master of Business Administration** título universitario; *ver también* ⟨DEGREE⟩ .

MBBS, MChB N ABBRS *of* **Bachelor of Medicine and Surgery** título universitario.

MBE N (*Brit*) ABBR *of* **Member of the Order of the British Empire**; *ver también* ⟨HONOURS LIST⟩ .

MC N (a) ABBR *of* **Master of Ceremonies** (V **master** 1). (b) (*US*) ABBR *of* **Member of Congress** diputado del Congreso de EE.UU.

MCAT N (*US*) ABBR *of* **Medical College Admissions Test**.

McCarthyism [mə'kɑːθɪɪzəm] N (*US: Pol*) macartismo *m*.

MCP N ABBR *of* **male chauvinist pig** (V **chauvinist**).

m/cycle N ABBR *of* **motorcycle** motocicleta *f*.

MD (a) N ABBR *of* **Doctor of Medicine**.
(b) N ABBR *of* **managing director** director *m*, -ora *f* gerente.
(c) ABBR *of* **mentally deficient** de inteligencia inferior a la normal.
(d) (*US Post*) ABBR *of* **Maryland**.

MDT N (*US*) ABBR *of* **Mountain Daylight Time**.

ME (a) N ABBR *of* **myalgic encephalomyelitis**. (b) N (*US*) ABBR *of* **medical examiner**. (c) (*US Post*) ABBR *of* **Maine**.

me¹ [miː] PRON me; (*after prep*) mí; **like ~** como yo; **what, ~?** ¿cómo, yo?; **with ~** conmigo; **dear ~!** ¡vaya!; **it's ~** soy yo; **it's ~, Paul** (*identifying self*) soy Pablo.

me² [miː] N (*Mus*) mi *m*.

mead [miːd] N aguamiel *f*, hidromiel *m*.

meadow ['medəʊ] N prado *m*, pradera *f*; (*esp water ~*) vega *f*.

meadowsweet ['medəʊswiːt] N reina *f* de los prados.

meagre, (US) meager ['miːɡə^r] ADJ escaso, exiguo, pobre.

meal¹ [miːl] N (*flour*) harina *f*.

meal² [miːl] ① N comida *f*; **~s on wheels** servicio *m* de comidas a domicilio (para ancianos); **I don't eat between ~s** no como entre horas; **to have a ~** comer; **to have a good ~** comer bien; **to make a ~ of sth** comer algo, contentarse con comer algo; (*fig*) exagerar un asunto, sacar todo el jugo posible de un asunto.
② ATTR: **~ ticket** vale *m* de comida.

mealie meal ['miːlɪmiːl] N harina *f* de maíz, maicena *f*, Maizena *f*®.

mealtime ['miːltaɪm] N hora *f* de comer.

mealy ['miːlɪ] ADJ harinoso.

mealy-mouthed ['miːlɪ'maʊðd] ADJ excesivamente circunspecto; **let us not be ~ about it** hablemos claro sobre esto.

mean¹ [miːn] ADJ (a) (*Brit: stingy*) tacaño, agarrado.
(b) (*unpleasant, unkind*) mezquino; **a ~ trick** una mala pasada; **don't be ~!** ¡no seas malo!; **you ~ thing!** ¡qué malo eres!; **you were ~ to me** me has tratado mal; **it made me feel ~** me hizo sentir vergüenza; **that was pretty ~ of them** se han portado bastante mal.
(c) (*inferior*) inferior; *birth* humilde, pobre; (*shabby*) humilde, vil; **the ~est citizen** el menor ciudadano; **obvious to the ~est intelligence** obvio para quien tiene un poco de sentido común; **he is no ~ play-**

er es un jugador nada despreciable.

(d) (*US*) formidable, de primera; **he plays a ~ game** juega estupendamente.

mean² [miːn] **1** ADJ medio; **~ life** (*Phys*) vida *f* media.

2 N **(a)** (*middle term*) medio *m*, promedio *m*, término *m* medio; (*Math*) media *f*.

(b) **~s** (*method*) medio *m*, manera *f*, método *m*; **~s to an end** medio *m* de conseguir un fin; **there is no ~s of doing it** no hay modo de hacerlo; **he was the ~s of sending it** fue el quien nos proporcionó un medio de enviarlo; **by all ~s** por todos los medios, (*fig*) por cierto; **by all ~s!** ¡naturalmente!, ¡claro que sí!; **by all ~s take one** por favor toma uno; **by any ~s** de cualquier modo, del modo que sea; **by no ~s, not by any ~s** de ningún modo; **by no ~s!** ¡de ningún modo!; **it is by no ~s difficult** no es nada difícil; **by ~s of** por medio de, mediante; **by this ~s** por este medio, de este modo; **by fair ~s** por medios rectos; **by fair ~s or foul** por las buenas o por las malas.

(c) (*Fin*) **~s** recursos *mpl*, medios *mpl*, fondos *mpl*, dinero *m*; **a man of ~s** un hombre acaudalado; **we have no ~s to do it** nos faltan recursos para hacerlo; **to have private ~s** tener ingresos privados; **to live beyond one's ~s** vivir por encima de sus posibilidades, gastar más de lo que se gana; **to live within one's ~s** vivir con arreglo a los ingresos, vivir dentro de los medios.

3 ATTR: **~s test** averiguación *f* de los recursos económicos (*del que pide asistencia pública etc*).

▼ **mean³** [miːn] (*irr*: PRET AND PTP **meant**) VT **(a)** (*intend*: *with noun etc*) pretender, intentar; **he ~s well** tiene buenas intenciones; **I ~ it** lo digo en serio; **do you ~ it?** ¿lo dices en serio?; **you can't ~ it!** ¡vaya!; **I ~t it as a joke** lo dije en broma; **I ~ what I say** lo digo muy en serio, lo digo con la mayor seriedad; **he ~s no harm** tiene buenas intenciones; **I ~t no harm by what I said** no lo dije con mala idea; **he ~t no offence** no tenía la intención de ofender a nadie; **8, I ~ 9** 8, quiero decir 9; 8, mejor dicho 9, digo 9.

▼ **(b)** (*intend*: *with verb*) **to ~ to** + *infin* pensar + *infin*, proponerse + *infin*, pretender + *infin*; **what do you ~ to do?** ¿qué piensas hacer?; **I ~t to help** tenía la intención de ayudar; **he didn't ~ to do it** lo hizo sin querer; **this picture is ~t to tell a story** este cuadro se propone contar una historia; **this photo is ~t to be Anne** esta foto quiere ser Ana; **she wasn't ~t to be prime minister** no había intención de que ella llegara a ser primera ministra; **I ~ to be obeyed** insisto en que se me obedezca; **I ~ to have it** quiero tenerlo, me propongo obtenerlo; **if he ~s to be awkward** si quiere ser difícil; **we were ~t to arrive at 8** debíamos llegar a las 8.

(c) (*destine*) destinar (*for* a, para); **this present was ~t for you** este regalo era para ti; **do you ~ me?** ¿es a mí?; **was that remark ~t for me?** ¿esa observación iba dirigida contra mí?; **he ~t that for you** lo dijo por ti.

(d) (*suppose*) suponer; **it's ~t to be a good car** este coche se supone que es bueno; **parents are ~t to love their children** se supone que los padres quieren a sus hijos; **you're not ~t to drink it!** ¡no te lo dan para que lo bebas!

▼ **(e)** (*signify*: *person, statement etc*) querer decir (*by* con); (*word*) significar (*to* para); **what does 'ohm' ~?** ¿qué quiere decir 'ohmio'?; **what do you ~ by that?** ¿qué quieres decir con eso?; **'vest' ~s sth different in America** en América 'vest' tiene otro significado, en América 'vest' significa otra cosa; **the name ~s nothing to me** el nombre no me suena; **it ~s a lot of expense for us** nos supone unos grandes gastos; **this ~s our ruin** esto es nuestra ruina, esto significa nuestra ruina; **a pound ~s a lot to her** para ella una libra es mucho dinero; **the play didn't ~ a thing to me** poca cosa saqué en claro de la obra; **your friendship ~s much to me** tu amistad es muy importante para mí; **it ~s a lot to have you with us** nos importa mucho tenerte con nosotros; **you know what it ~s to hit a policeman?** ¿Vd sabe qué consecuencias trae el golpear a un policía?; **don't I ~ anything to you?** ¿no significo yo nada para ti?, ¿no tengo yo siquiera un poquito de importancia para ti?; V **know 2 (a)**.

meander [mɪˈændəʳ] **1** N meandro *m*; **~s** (*fig*) meandros *mpl*.

2 VI (*river*) serpentear; (*person etc*) andar sin propósito fijo, vagar; (*in speech*) divagar.

meandering [mɪˈændərɪŋ] ADJ *river* con meandros; *road* serpenteante; *account, speech etc* largo y confuso, prolijo y poco lógico.

meanderings [mɪˈændərɪŋz] NPL (*fig*) divagaciones *fpl*.

meanie* [ˈmiːnɪ] N: **he's an old ~** es un tío agarrado*.

meaning [ˈmiːnɪŋ] **1** ADJ *look etc* significativo, lleno de intención.

2 N **(a)** (*intention*) intención *f*, propósito *m*; **a look full of ~** una mirada llena de intención; **to mistake sb's ~** interpretar mal la intención de uno.

(b) (*sense of words etc*) sentido *m*, significado *m*; (*particular sense of word*) acepción *f*; (*general impact*) significación *f*; **I don't get your ~** no comprendo lo que quieres decir; **if you get my ~** ¿me entiendes?; **what's the ~ of 'hick'?** ¿qué significa 'hick'?, ¿qué

quiere decir 'hick'?; **what's the ~ of this?** (*as reprimand*) y esto ¿qué quiere decir?; **life has no ~ for her now** ahora para ella la vida no tiene sentido; **honesty? she doesn't understand the ~ of the word** ¿la honradez? ni sabe lo que eso quiere decir.

meaningful [ˈmiːnɪŋfʊl] ADJ significativo, que tiene sentido; válido, justificado; útil; *relationship* serio.

meaningless [ˈmiːnɪŋlɪs] ADJ sin sentido; (*rash, mad*) insensato; **in this situation it is ~** en esta situación no tiene sentido; **to write 'xybj' is ~** escribir 'xybj' carece de sentido.

meanly [ˈmiːnlɪ] ADV **(a)** (*stingily*) de manera tacaña, con tacañería. **(b)** (*unkindly*) de manera mezquina, con mezquindad.

meanness [ˈmiːnnɪs] N humildad *f*; vileza *f*, bajeza *f*; tacañería *f*; mezquindad *f*; maldad *f*.

means-test [ˈmiːnztest] VT *person* averiguar los recursos económicos de; **this benefit is ~ed** este subsidio se otorga después de averiguar los recursos económicos (del que lo pide).

meant [ment] PRET AND PTP *of* **mean³**.

meantime [ˈmiːnˈtaɪm] ADV, **meanwhile** [ˈmiːnˈwaɪl] ADV entretanto, mientras tanto; **in the ~** mientras tanto, en el ínterin.

measles [ˈmiːzlz] N sarampión *m*.

measly* [ˈmiːzlɪ] ADJ miserable, cochino, mezquino.

measurable [ˈmeʒərəbl] ADJ mensurable, que se puede medir; (*perceptible*) apreciable, perceptible.

measure [ˈmeʒəʳ] **1** N **(a)** (*system of ~*) medida *f*; **~ of capacity** medida *f* de capacidad; **I think we have his ~ now** creo que le tenemos calado ya; **to take sb's ~** (*fig*) tomar las medidas a uno.

(b) (*rule etc*) regla *f*; (*glass*: *Chem*) probeta *f* graduada.

(c) (*limit*) **beyond ~** hasta no más; excesivamente; **better beyond ~** incomparablemente mejor; **in full ~** abundantemente; **for good ~** por añadidura; **in great ~, in large ~** en gran parte; **in some ~** hasta cierto punto; **this is due in no small ~ to X** esto se debe en no pequeña medida a X; **we had some ~ of success** hasta cierto punto tuvimos éxito; **it gives a ~ of protection** da cierta protección.

(d) (*step*) medida *f*; (*Parl*) (*bill*) proyecto *m* de ley; (*act*) ley *f*; **to take ~s** tomar medidas (*to* + *infin* para + *infin*); **to take extreme ~s** tomar medidas extremas.

(e) (*Geol*) **coal ~s** depósitos *mpl* de carbón.

(f) (*Mus*) compás *m*.

(g) (*of spirits etc*) ración *f*.

2 VT **(a)** medir; *person* (*for height*) tallar, (*for clothes*) tomar las medidas a; *words etc* pesar, pensar bien; V **length**. **(b)** (*fig*) medir; **how shall we ~ success?** ¿cómo vamos a medir el éxito?; **in this exercise we ~ performance** en este ejercicio evaluamos la actuación; **can we ~ him against his colleagues?** ¿podemos compararle con sus colegas?

3 VI medir; **it ~s 3 metres by 2 metres** mide 3 metros por 2 metros; **what does it ~?** ¿cuánto mide?

◆ **measure off** VT medir.

◆ **measure out** VT medir; (*issue*) repartir, distribuir.

◆ **measure up** VT *person* valorar, juzgar.

◆ **measure up to** VT: **to ~ up to sth** estar a la altura de algo.

measured [ˈmeʒəd] ADJ *tread etc* deliberado, rítmico, acompasado; *tone* mesurado; *statement etc* moderado, circunspecto, prudente.

measureless [ˈmeʒəlɪs] ADJ inmensurable, inmenso.

measurement [ˈmeʒəmənt] N **(a)** (*system*) medición *f*. **(b)** (*measure*) medida *f*; dimensión *f*; **to take sb's ~s** tomar las medidas a uno.

measuring [ˈmeʒərɪŋ] **1** N medición *f*; **to take ~s of** hacer mediciones de.

2 ATTR: **~ chain** cadena *f* de agrimensor; **~ glass, ~ jug** mesura *f*; **~ rod** vara *f* de medir; **~ spoon** cuchara *f* medidora; **~ tape** cinta *f* métrica.

meat [miːt] **1** N carne *f*; (*fig*) sustancia *f*, meollo *m*, jugo *m*; **cold ~** fiambre *m*, carne *f* fiambre; **a book with some ~ in it** un libro sólido, un libro jugoso; **one man's ~ is another man's poison** lo que a uno cura a otro mata; **it's ~ and drink to me** no puedo vivir sin él.

2 ATTR: de carne; *industry etc, product* cárnico; **~ extract** extracto *m* de carne; **~ grinder** (*US*) máquina *f* de picar carne; **~ hook** gancho *m* carnicero; **~ loaf** rollo *m* de carne picada cocida; **~ pie** pastel *m* de carne, empanada *f*; **~ safe** (*Brit*) fresquera *f*.

meatball [ˈmiːtbɔːl] N albóndiga *f*.

meat-eater [ˈmiːtˌiːtəʳ] N persona *f* que come carne; (*Zool*) carnívoro *m*, -a *f*; **we're not ~s** no comemos carne.

meat-eating [ˈmiːtˌiːtɪŋ] ADJ carnívoro.

meatfly [ˈmiːtflaɪ] N mosca *f* de la carne.

meathead‡ [ˈmiːthed] N (*US*) idiota *mf*, gilipollas‡ *mf*.

meatless [ˈmiːtlɪs] ADJ: **~ day** día *m* de vigilia; **~ diet** dieta *f* sin carne.

meaty [ˈmiːtɪ] ADJ carnoso; (*fig*) sustancioso, jugoso, sólido.

Mecca [ˈmekə] N La Meca; **a ~ for tourists** un lugar (*etc*) de grandes atracciones para el turista.

Meccano [mɪˈkɑːnəʊ] ® N (*Brit*) mecano *m*.
mechanic [mɪˈkænɪk] N mecánico *mf*.
mechanical [mɪˈkænɪkəl] ADJ mecánico; (*fig*) maquinal; **~ drawing** dibujo *m* mecánico; **~ engineer** ingeniero *m* mecánico, ingeniera *f* mecánica; **~ engineering** ingeniería *f* mecánica, mecánica *f* industrial; **~ pencil** (*US*) lapicero *m*.
mechanically [mɪˈkænɪkəlɪ] ADV mecánicamente; (*fig*) maquinalmente.
mechanics [mɪˈkænɪks] N mecánica *f*; mecanismo *m*, técnica *f*.
mechanism [ˈmekənɪzəm] N (*most senses*) mecanismo *m*; (*Philos*) mecanicismo *m*.
mechanistic [ˌmekəˈnɪstɪk] ADJ mecánico, maquinal; (*Philos*) mecanístico.
mechanization [ˌmekənaɪˈzeɪʃən] N mecanización *f*.
mechanize [ˈmekənaɪz] VT mecanizar; motorizar.
mechanized [ˈmekənaɪzd] ADJ *process etc* mecanizado; *troops, unit* motorizado.
Med* [med] N: **the ~** el Mediterráneo.
M.Ed. N ABBR *of* **Master of Education** *título universitario*.
medal [ˈmedl] N medalla *f*; **he deserves a ~ for it** merece un galardón; **to have a ~ showing*** tener la farmacia abierta*.
medallion [mɪˈdælɪən] N medallón *m*.
medallist, (*US*) **medalist** [ˈmedəlɪst] N (*Sport*) medallero *m*, -a *f*; V **gold** *etc*.
meddle [ˈmedl] VI entrometerse (*in* en); **to ~ with sth** manosear algo, tocar algo, (*and damage*) estropear algo; **who asked you to ~?** ¿quién le mete a Vd en esto?; **he's always meddling** es un entrometido.
meddler [ˈmedlə^r] N entrometido *m*, -a *f*.
meddlesome [ˈmedlsəm] ADJ, **meddling**[1] [ˈmedlɪŋ] ADJ entrometido.
meddlesomeness [ˈmedlsəmnɪs] N entrometimiento *m*.
meddling[2] [ˈmedlɪŋ] N intromisión *f*.
Mede [miːd] N medo *m*; **the ~s and the Persians** los medos y los persas.
media [ˈmiːdɪə] [1] NPL medios *mpl* de comunicación, medios *mpl* de difusión.
[2] ATTR: **~ analysis** análisis *m* de los medios; **~ coverage** cobertura *f* periodística; **~ event** acontecimiento *m* periodístico; **~ man** periodista *m*; agente *m* de publicidad; **~ person** personaje *m* de los medios de comunicación; **~ research** investigación *f* de los medios de publicidad; **~ studies** (*Univ*) periodismo *m*.
mediaeval [ˌmedɪˈiːvəl] (*etc*) V **medieval** (*etc*).
medial [ˈmiːdɪəl] ADJ medial.
median [ˈmiːdɪən] [1] ADJ mediano.
[2] N (a) (*US*: *also* **~ divider**, **~ strip**) mediana *f*, franja *f* central, faja *f* intermedia. (b) (*Math*) número *m* medio; punto *m* medio.
mediate [ˈmiːdɪeɪt] VI mediar (*between* entre, *in* en).
mediating [ˈmiːdɪeɪtɪŋ] ADJ *role, efforts* mediador; **to play a ~ role** actuar como mediador, tener un papel de mediador.
mediation [ˌmiːdɪˈeɪʃən] N mediación *f*.
mediator [ˈmiːdɪeɪtə^r] N mediador *m*, -ora *f*, árbitro *mf*.
medic* [ˈmedɪk] N médico *mf*; (*Univ*) estudiante *mf* de medicina.
Medicaid [ˈmedɪˌkeɪd] N (*US*) seguro *m* de enfermedad.

medical [ˈmedɪkəl] [1] ADJ médico; **~ bulletin** boletín *m* facultativo; **~ care** atención *f* médica; **~ certificate** certificado *m* médico; **~ corps** cuerpo *m* de sanidad; **~ examination** reconocimiento *m* médico; **~ examiner** (*US*) médico *mf* forense; **~ inspection** visita *f* del médico; **~ jurisprudence** medicina *f* legal; **~ kit** botiquín *m*; **~ man** médico *m*; **~ officer** médico *mf*, (*Mil*) oficial *m* médico, (*of town*) jefe *mf* de sanidad municipal; **~ practitioner** médico *mf*; **the ~ profession** la profesión médica; **~ record** historia *f* clínica; **~ school** facultad *f* de medicina; **~ service** servicio *m* médico; **~ student** estudiante *mf* de medicina; **~ treatment** tratamiento *m* médico, asistencia *f* médica.
[2] N (*) reconocimiento *m* médico.
medically [ˈmedɪkəlɪ] ADV médicamente; **~ speaking** desde el punto de vista médico; **to be ~ examined** tener un reconocimiento médico.
medicament [meˈdɪkəmənt] N medicamento *m*.
Medicare [ˈmedɪkeə^r] N (*US*) seguro *m* de enfermedad.

medicate [ˈmedɪkeɪt] VT medicar; impregnar (*with* de); **~d shampoo** champú *m* médico.
medication [ˌmedɪˈkeɪʃən] N medicación *f*.
medicinal [meˈdɪsɪnl] ADJ medicinal.
medicinally [meˈdɪsɪnəlɪ] ADV *use* con fines médicos.
medicine [ˈmedsɪn, ˈmedɪsɪn] [1] N medicina *f*; medicamento *m*; **to take one's ~** (*fig*) sufrir las consecuencias.
[2] ATTR: **~ box**, **~ cabinet**, **~ chest** botiquín *m*.
medicine ball [ˈmedsɪnˌbɔːl] N (*Sport*) pelota *f* medicinal.
medicine man [ˈmedsɪnmæn] N, PL **medicine men** [ˈmedsɪnmen] hechizador *m*.
medico* [ˈmedɪkəʊ] N médico *mf*.
medieval [ˌmedɪˈiːvəl] ADJ medieval.
medievalism [ˌmedɪˈiːvəlɪzəm] N medievalismo *m*.
medievalist [ˌmedɪˈiːvəlɪst] N medievalista *mf*.
mediocre [ˌmiːdɪˈəʊkə^r] ADJ mediocre, mediano.
mediocrity [ˌmiːdɪˈɒkrɪtɪ] N mediocridad *f*, medianía *f* (*also person*).
meditate [ˈmedɪteɪt] [1] VT meditar.
[2] VI meditar (*on sth* algo), reflexionar (*on* en, sobre).
meditation [ˌmedɪˈteɪʃən] N meditación *f*.
meditative [ˈmedɪtətɪv] ADJ meditabundo.
Mediterranean [ˌmedɪtəˈreɪnɪən] [1] ADJ mediterráneo; **~ Sea** Mar *m* Mediterráneo. [2] N Mediterráneo *m*.
medium [ˈmiːdɪəm] [1] ADJ *quality etc* mediano, regular; *size* mediano, intermedio; *wave* medio; **of ~ height** de estatura regular; **of ~ difficulty** de mediana dificultad; **~ frequency** media frecuencia *f*; **~ range missile** misil *m* de alcance medio; **~ rare** medio hecho, sonrosado.
[2] N (a) (PL *in some senses* **media** [ˈmiːdɪə]) medio *m*; **through the ~ of** por medio de. (b) (*spiritualist*) médium *mf*; *see also* **media**.
medium-dry [ˌmiːdɪəmˈdraɪ] ADJ semi-seco, semi.
medium-fine [ˈmiːdɪəmˈfaɪn] ADJ entrefino.
medium-priced [ˌmiːdɪəmˈpraɪst] ADJ de precio medio.
medium-sized [ˈmiːdɪəmˈsaɪzd] ADJ mediano, de tamaño mediano; **~ business** empresa *f* mediana.
medlar [ˈmedlə^r] N (*fruit*) níspola *f*; (*tree*) níspero *m*.
medley [ˈmedlɪ] N mezcla *f*, mezcolanza *f*; miscelánea *f*; (*Mus*) popurrí *m*.
medulla [meˈdʌlə] N medula *f*.
meek [miːk] ADJ manso, dócil, sumiso; **to be very ~ and mild** (*person*) ser como una malva.
meekly [ˈmiːklɪ] ADV mansamente, dócilmente, sumisamente.
meekness [ˈmiːknɪs] N mansedumbre *f*, docilidad *f*.
meerschaum [ˈmɪəʃəm] N espuma *f* de mar; (*pipe*) pipa *f* de espuma de mar.
meet[1] [miːt] ADJ (*liter*) conveniente, apropiado; **it is ~ that ...** conviene que + *subj*; **to be ~ for** ser apto para.
meet[2] [miːt] (*irr*: PRET AND PTP **met**) [1] VT (a) *person etc* (*encounter*) encontrar; (*accidentally*) encontrarse con; (*by arrangement*) reunirse con, (*formally*) entrevistarse con; **to arrange to ~ sb** citarse con uno, dar una cita a uno.
(b) *difficulty* encontrar, tropezar con; hacer frente a; *death* hallar, encontrar; *opponent, opposing team* enfrentarse con, (*in duel*) batirse con; **he met his death in 1800** halló la muerte en 1800; **to ~ death calmly** enfrentar tranquilamente con la muerte; **to ~ death courageously** ir resueltamente a su muerte.
(c) (*go to ~*) ir a recibir, ir a buscar, esperar, ir al encuentro de; **I'll ~ you at the garage** te espero en el garaje; **we met her at the station** fuimos a recibirla en la estación; **don't bother to ~ me** no os molestéis viniendo a buscarme; **the car will ~ the train** el coche esperará la llegada del tren; **the bus ~s the aircraft** hay correspondencia entre el autobús y el avión.
(d) (*get to know*) conocer; **I never met him** no le conocí nunca, no le llegué a conocer; **I met my wife in 1960** conocí a mi mujer en 1960; **~ Mr Jones** quiero presentarle al Sr Jones; **I am very pleased to ~ you** tengo mucho gusto en conocerle; **pleased to ~ you!** ¡tanto gusto!
(e) **what a scene met my eyes!** ¡qué cosas se presentaron a mis ojos!; **I could not ~ his eye** no podía mirarle a los ojos.

(f) *charge* refutar; *debt* pagar, honrar, satisfacer; *deficit* cubrir; *expense* sostener, correr con, hacer frente a; *liabilities* honrar; *need* satisfacer, cubrir; (*Comm*) *demand* atender, satisfacer; *objection* responder a; *obligation* atender, cumplir; *requirement* satisfacer; *wish* conformarse con, condescender con, satisfacer; *scorn* tener que aguantar.

2 VI **(a)** (*encounter each other*) encontrarse, verse; (*by arrangement*) reunirse, verse; (*meeting, society*) reunirse; **the society ~s at 8 la sociedad se reúne a las 8, la sesión de la sociedad comienza a las 8; let's ~ at 8** citémonos para las 8; **until we ~ again!** ¡hasta la vista!; **keep it until we ~ again** guárdalo hasta que nos veamos.

(b) (*get to know*) conocerse; **we met in Seville** nos conocimos en Sevilla; **we have met before** nos conocemos ya; **have we met?** ¿nos conocimos antes?

(c) (*fight*) batirse; **Bilbao and Valencia will ~ in the final** el Bilbao se enfrentará con el Valencia en la final, Bilbao y Valencia se disputarán la final.

(d) (*join*) encontrarse; **our eyes met** cruzamos una mirada, nos miramos el uno al otro; **where the rivers ~** donde confluyen los ríos; **the roads ~ at Toledo** las carreteras empalman en Toledo; **these qualities ~ in her** estas cualidades se dan cita en ella.

3 N (*US Sport*) encuentro *m*, reunión *f*; (*Hunting*) cacería *f*.

◆**meet up** VI: **to ~ up with sb** reunirse con uno; **this road ~s up with the motorway** esta carretera empalma con la autopista.

◆**meet with** VT (*esp US*) *person* juntarse con, reunirse con; *kindness etc* encontrar; *accident* tener; sufrir; *loss* sufrir; *shock* experimentar; *reaction* suscitar, provocar; *success* tener; *difficulty* tropezar con.

meeting ['miːtɪŋ] N **(a)** (*between 2 persons: accidental*) encuentro *m*, (*arranged*) cita *f*, compromiso *m* (*LAm*), (*formal*) entrevista *f*; **~ of minds** encuentro *m* de inteligencias; **the minister had a ~ with the ambassador** el ministro se entrevistó con el embajador.

(b) (*assembly*) reunión *f*; (*esp of legislative body*) sesión *f*; (*popular gathering*) mitin *m*; **~ of creditors** concurso *m* de acreedores; **~ of minds** acuerdo *m*; **to address the ~** tomar la palabra en la reunión, dirigirse a los asistentes; **to call a ~ of shareholders** convocar una junta de accionistas; **to adjourn** (*or close*) **the ~** levantar la sesión; **to hold a ~** celebrar una junta, (*Parl*) celebrar sesión; **to open the ~** abrir la sesión.

(c) (*Sport: eg athletic*) concurso *m*; (*horse races*) reunión *f*; (*clash between teams*) encuentro *m*.

(d) (*of rivers*) confluencia *f*.

meeting-house ['miːtɪŋˌhaʊs] N, PL **meeting-houses** ['miːtɪŋˌhaʊzɪz] templo *m* (de los cuáqueros).

meeting-place ['miːtɪŋpleɪs] N (*of 2 persons*) lugar *m* de cita, (*of many*) punto *m* de reunión; **this bar was their usual ~** solían citarse en este bar, acostumbraban reunirse en este bar.

Meg [meg] NF *familiar form of* **Margaret**.

mega‡ ['megə] ADJ súper*.

mega... ['megə] PREF mega...

megabuck* ['megəˌbʌk] N: **now he's making ~s** (*US*) ahora está ganando una pasta gansa‡, ahora se está forrando de dinero*; **we're talking ~s** hablamos de muchísimos dólares.

megabyte ['megəˌbaɪt] N megabyte *m*, megaocteto *m*.

megacycle ['megəˌsaɪkl] N megaciclo *m*.

megadeath ['megəˌdeθ] N muerte *f* de un millón de personas.

megahertz ['megəˌhɜːts] N megahercio *m*.

megalith ['megəlɪθ] N megalito *m*.

megalithic [ˌmegə'lɪθɪk] ADJ megalítico.

megalomania ['megələʊ'meɪnɪə] N megalomanía *f*.

megalomaniac [ˌmegələʊ'meɪnɪæk] N megalómano *m*, -a *f*.

megalopolis [ˌmegə'lɒpəlɪs] N megalópolis *f*.

megaphone ['megəfəʊn] N megáfono *m*; **~ diplomacy** diplomacia *f* megafónica.

megaton ['megətʌn] N megatón *m*.

megavolt ['megəvəʊlt] N megavoltio *m*.

megawatt ['megəwɒt] N megavatio *m*.

melamine ['meləmiːn] N melamina *f*.

melancholia [ˌmelən'kəʊlɪə] N melancolía *f*.

melancholic [ˌmelən'kɒlɪk] ADJ melancólico.

melancholically [ˌmelən'kɒlɪklɪ] ADV melancólicamente.

melancholy ['melənkəlɪ] **1** ADJ melancólico; *duty, sight etc* triste.
2 N melancolía *f*.

melange, mélange [me'lɑːnʒ] N mezcolanza *f*, popurrí *m*.

melanin ['melənɪn] N melanina *f*.

melanism ['melənɪzəm] N melanismo *m*.

melanoma [ˌmelə'nəʊmə] N melanoma *m*.

Melba toast ['melbə'təʊst] N tostada *f* delgada.

melée ['meleɪ] N pelea *f* confusa, refriega *f*; tumulto *m*; **there was such a ~ at the booking office** se apiñaba la gente delante de la taquilla; **it got lost in the ~** se perdió en el tumulto.

mellifluous [me'lɪflʊəs] ADJ melifluo.

Mellotron ['melətrɒn] ® N Mellotron *m* ®.

mellow ['meləʊ] **1** ADJ *fruit etc* maduro, dulce; *wine* añejo; *colour,*

---

sound dulce; *light* suave; *voice* suave, meloso; *instrument* melodioso; *character* maduro y tranquilo; **in ~ old age** en la vejez tranquila; **to be ~*** estar entre dos luces*; **to get ~*** achisparse*.

2 VT madurar; suavizar, ablandar.

3 VI madurarse; suavizarse, ablandarse.

mellowing ['meləʊɪŋ] N maduración *f*.

mellowness ['meləʊnɪs] N madurez *f*; dulzura *f*, suavidad *f*; lo melodioso.

melodic [mɪ'lɒdɪk] ADJ melódico.

melodious [mɪ'ləʊdɪəs] ADJ melodioso.

melodiously [mɪ'ləʊdɪəslɪ] ADV melodiosamente.

melodrama ['meləʊˌdrɑːmə] N melodrama *m*.

melodramatic [ˌmeləʊdrə'mætɪk] ADJ melodramático.

melodramatically [ˌmeləʊdrə'mætɪklɪ] ADV melodramáticamente.

melody ['melədɪ] N melodía *f*.

melon ['melən] N melón *m*.

melt [melt] **1** VT *metal* fundir; *snow* derretir; *chemical* disolver; (*fig*) *heart etc* ablandar.
2 VI fundirse; derretirse; disolverse; ablandarse, enternecerse; **it ~s in the mouth** se derrite en la boca; **to ~ into tears** deshacerse en lágrimas; **the gunman ~ed into the crowd** el pistolero desapareció en la multitud.

◆**melt away** VI (*money, confidence etc*) esfumarse, desvanecerse, desaparecer misteriosamente; (*crowd etc*) dispersarse; (*person*) desaparecer silenciosamente, escurrirse.

◆**melt down** VT fundir.

meltdown ['meltdaʊn] N fusión *f* de un reactor, fundido *m*.

melting ['meltɪŋ] **1** ADJ *look etc* tierno, dulce.
2 N fundición *f*; derretimiento *m*; disolución *f*.

melting-point ['meltɪŋpɔɪnt] N punto *m* de fusión.

melting-pot ['meltɪŋpɒt] N crisol *m* (*also fig*); **the plan is in the ~** el plan está sujeto a una revisión completa; **it is a nation in the ~** es una nación en formación.

meltwater ['meltwɔːtəʳ] N agua *f* de fusión de la nieve.

member ['membəʳ] N **(a)** (*person*) miembro *m*; (*of company, society*) miembro *mf*, socio *m*; (*of party*) miembro *mf*, militante *mf*, afiliado *m*, -a *f*; (*Parl*) miembro *mf*, diputado *m*, -a *f*; **'~s only'** 'reservado a los socios', 'sólo para socios'; **~ of Congress** (*US*) miembro *mf* del Congreso; **~ of the family** miembro *m* de la familia; **~ of parliament** (*Brit*) diputado *m*, -a *f*, miembro *mf* del parlamento, parlamentario *m*, -a *f*; **~ of the crew** tripulante *mf*; **if any ~ of the audience ...** si cualquiera de los asistentes ...; **the ~ for Woodford** el diputado por Woodford; **full ~** miembro *mf* de número; **the ~ countries** los países miembros (*of de*); **~ state** estado *m* miembro; **the 15 ~ states** (*EU*) los Quince; *ver también* BY-ELECTION , CONSTITUENCY .

(b) (*Anat*) miembro *m*; (*male ~*) miembro *m* viril.

membership ['membəʃɪp] **1** N **(a)** (*state*) calidad *f* de miembro (*or* socio); (*Pol: members*) militancia *f*; **Britain's ~ of** (*US: in*) **the Common Market** (*act*) el ingreso de Gran Bretaña en el Mercado Común; (*state*) la pertenencia de Gran Bretaña al Mercado Común; **when I applied for ~ of** (*US: in*) **the club** cuando solicité el ingreso en el club, cuando quise hacerme socio del club; **~ carries certain rights** el ser miembro da ciertos derechos.

(b) (*numerical*) número *m* de miembros (*or* socios); **what is your ~?** ¿cuántos miembros tienes?

2 ATTR: **~ card** tarjeta *f* de afiliación; **~ fee** cuota *f* de socio; **~ list** relación *f* de socios.

membrane ['membreɪn] N membrana *f*.

membranous [mem'breɪnəs] ADJ membranoso.

memento [mə'mentəʊ] N recuerdo *m*.

memo* ['meməʊ] N ABBR *of* **memorandum** memorándum *m*, memo *m*; **~ pad** bloc *m* de notas.

memoir ['memwɑːʳ] N memoria *f*; biografía *f*, autobiografía *f*; nota *f* biográfica; **~s** memorias *fpl*.

memorabilia [ˌmemərə'bɪlɪə] NPL (*objects*) cosas *fpl* memorables, recuerdos *mpl*; (*events*) acontecimientos *mpl* notables.

memorable ['memərəbl] ADJ memorable.

memorably ['memərəblɪ] ADV memorablemente.

memorandum [ˌmemə'rændəm] N, PL **memoranda** [ˌmemə'rændə] memorándum *m*, memorando *m*; apunte *m*, nota *f*, memoria *f*.

memorial [mɪ'mɔːrɪəl] **1** ADJ conmemorativo; **~ park** (*US*) cementerio *m*.
2 N **(a)** monumento *m* (conmemorativo). **(b)** (*document*) memorial *m*.

memorialize [mɪ'mɔːrɪəlaɪz] VT conmemorar.

memorize ['meməraɪz] VT aprender de memoria.

memory ['memərɪ] **1** N **(a)** (*faculty*) memoria *f*; (*capacity for ~*) retentiva *f*; (*Comput*) memoria *f*; **to speak from ~** hablar fiándose de su memoria; **to the best of my ~** que yo recuerde; **to commit sth to ~** aprender algo de memoria; encomendar algo a la memoria; **I have a bad ~ for faces** soy mal fisonomista, no recuerdo las caras de las personas; **to have a ~ like a sieve** tener malísima memoria;

to lose one's ~ perder la memoria; **if my ~ serves me** si mi memoria no me falla, si mal no recuerdo; **I speak from ~** hablo de memoria.
(b) (*recollection*) recuerdo *m*; **in ~ of** en memoria de, en conmemoración de; **of blessed ~** de feliz recuerdo, de grata memoria; **'Memories of life in Barataria'** 'Recuerdos *mpl* de la vida en Barataria'; **to have happy memories of** tener agradables recuerdos de; **to keep sb's ~ alive** guardar el recuerdo de uno, mantener vivo el recuerdo de uno.
2 ATTR: **~ bank** banco *m* de memoria; **~ bus** bus *m* de memoria; **~ chip** chip *m* de memoria; **~ lane** mundo *m* de los recuerdos (sentimentales); **to go down ~ lane** adentrarse en el mundo de los recuerdos; **~ management** gestión *f* de la memoria.
memsahib ['mem,sɑːhɪb] N (*India*) mujer *f* casada.
men [men] NPL *of* **man**.
menace ['menɪs] **1** N amenaza *f*; **he's a ~** es peligroso.
2 VT amenazar.
menacing ['menɪsɪŋ] ADJ amenazador.
menacingly ['menɪsɪŋli] ADV de modo amenazador.
ménage [meˈnɑːʒ] N casa *f*, hogar *m*, menaje *m*; **~ à trois** menaje *m* de tres.
menagerie [mɪˈnædʒərɪ] N casa *f* de fieras, colección *f* de fieras.
mend [mend] **1** N (**a**) (*patch*) remiendo *m*; (*darn*) zurcido *m*.
(b) to be on the ~ ir mejorando.
2 VT (*repair*) reparar, componer; (*darn*) zurcir; (*improve*) reformar, mejorar; (*rectify*) remediar.
3 VI mejorar, reponerse.
mendacious [menˈdeɪʃəs] ADJ mendaz.
mendacity [menˈdæsɪtɪ] N mendacidad *f*.
mendelevium [,mendɪˈliːvɪəm] N mendelevio *m*.
Mendelian [menˈdiːlɪən] ADJ mendeliano.
Mendelianism [menˈdiːlɪənɪzəm] N, **Mendelism** ['mendəlɪzəm] N mendelismo *m*.
mendicancy ['mendɪkənsɪ] N mendicidad *f*.
mendicant ['mendɪkənt] **1** ADJ mendicante.
2 N mendicante *mf*.
mendicity [menˈdɪsɪtɪ] N mendicidad *f*.
mending ['mendɪŋ] N (**a**) (*act*) reparación *f*, compostura *f*; zurcidura *f*. (**b**) (*clothes*) ropa *f* de repaso, ropa *f* por zurcir.
Menelaus [,menɪˈleəs] NM Menelao.
menfolk ['menfəʊk] NPL hombres *mpl*.
menhir ['menhɪəʳ] N menhir *m*.
menial ['miːnɪəl] **1** ADJ doméstico; servil; (*pej*) bajo; **~ work** trabajo *m* de baja categoría.
2 N criado *m*, -a *f*.
meningitis [,menɪnˈdʒaɪtɪs] N meningitis *f*.
meniscus [məˈnɪskəs] N menisco *m*.
menopausal [,menəʊˈpɔːzəl] ADJ menopáusico.
menopause ['menəʊpɔːz] N menopausia *f*.
menorrhagia [,menɔːˈreɪdʒɪə] N menorragia *f*.
menses ['mensiːz] NPL menstruo *m*.
menstrual ['menstrʊəl] ADJ menstrual; **~ cycle** ciclo *m* menstrual.
menstruate ['menstrʊeɪt] VI menstruar.
menstruation [,menstrʊˈeɪʃən] N menstruación *f*.
mensuration [,mensjʊəˈreɪʃən] N medición *f*, medida *f*, mensuración *f*.
menswear ['menzweəʳ] N ropa *f* de caballero.
mental ['mentl] ADJ (**a**) mental; **~ age** edad *f* mental; **~ arithmetic** cálculo *m* mental; **~ defective** deficiente *mf* mental; **~ home**, **~ hospital** manicomio *m*, hospital *m* psiquiátrico; **I made a ~ note of it** tomé nota de ello. (**b**) (*Brit**) anormal, tocado; **he must be ~** debe estar ido*.
mentality [menˈtælɪtɪ] N mentalidad *f*.
mentally ['mentəlɪ] ADV mentalmente; **~ defective**, **~ deficient** deficiente mental; **~ disturbed** trastornado; **~ handicapped** minusválido mental; **~ retarded** retardado mental.
menthol ['menθɒl] N mentol *m*.
mentholated ['menθəleɪtɪd] ADJ mentolado.
mention ['menʃən] **1** N (**a**) mención *f*, alusión *f*.
(b) (*Mil*) citación *f*.
2 VT mencionar, aludir a; hablar de; **to ~** (**in dispatches**) citar, nombrar (en el parte); **not to ~** ... sin contar ..., además de ..., amén de ...; **too numerous to ~** demasiado numerosos para mencionar; **don't ~ it!** ¡no hay de qué!, ¡de nada!; **if I may ~ it** si se me permite aludir a ello; **I need hardly ~ that ...** huelga decir que ..., excusado es decir que ...; **I will ~ it to him** se lo diré; **he ~ed no names** no dijo los nombres; **to ~ sb in one's will** mencionar a uno en su testamento, legar algo a uno.
mentor ['mentɔːʳ] N mentor *m*.
menu ['menjuː] N (**a**) carta *f*, lista *f* (de platos), menú *m*. (**b**) (*Comput*) menú *m*; **~-driven** guiado por menú.
meow [mɪˈaʊ] **1** N maullido *m*, miau *m*.

2 VI maullar.
MEP N (*Brit*) ABBR *of* **Member of the European Parliament** eurodiputado *m*, -a *f*.
Mephistopheles [,mefɪsˈtɒfɪliːz] NM Mefistófeles.
Mephistophelian [,mefɪstəˈfiːlɪən] ADJ mefistofélico.
mercantile ['mɜːkəntaɪl] ADJ mercantil; **~ agency** agencia *f* mercantil; **~ marine** marina *f* mercante.
mercantilism ['mɜːkəntɪlɪzəm] N mercantilismo *m*.
mercenary ['mɜːsɪnərɪ] **1** ADJ mercenario.
2 N mercenario *m*.
▼ **merchandise** ['mɜːtʃəndaɪz] N mercancías *fpl*, géneros *mpl*.
merchandize ['mɜːtʃəndaɪz] VT comerciar.
merchandizer ['mɜːtʃəndaɪzəʳ] N comerciante *m*, tratante *m*.
merchandizing ['mɜːtʃəndaɪzɪŋ] N comercialización *f*.
merchant ['mɜːtʃənt] **1** N (**a**) comerciante *m*, negociante *m*; **a diamond ~** un comerciante en diamantes; **'The M~ of Venice'** 'El Mercader de Venecia'.
(b) (*) tío* *m*, sujeto *m*.
2 ATTR: **~ bank** (*Brit*) banco *m* mercantil; **~ marine** (*US*), **~ navy** (*Brit*) marina *f* mercante; **~ seaman** marinero *m* de la marina mercante; **~ ship** mercante *m*; **~ shipping** marina *f* mercante; mercantes *mpl*.
merchantable ['mɜːtʃəntəbl] ADJ comercializable; **of ~ quality** de calidad comerciable.
merchantman ['mɜːtʃəntmən] N, PL **merchantmen** ['mɜːtʃəntmən] buque *m* mercante.
merciful ['mɜːsɪfʊl] ADJ *person* misericordioso, compasivo, clemente; *release etc* afortunado, feliz.
mercifully ['mɜːsɪfəlɪ] ADV *act etc* misericordiosamente, con compasión; **~ it was short** gracias a Dios fue breve.
merciless ['mɜːsɪlɪs] ADJ despiadado.
mercilessly ['mɜːsɪlɪslɪ] ADV despiadadamente, sin piedad.
mercurial [mɜːˈkjʊərɪəl] ADJ (**a**) (*Chem*) mercurial. (**b**) (*lively*) vivo; (*changeable*) veleidoso, voluble.
Mercury ['mɜːkjʊrɪ] NM Mercurio.
mercury ['mɜːkjʊrɪ] N mercurio *m*.
mercy ['mɜːsɪ] **1** N misericordia *f*, compasión *f*, clemencia *f*; **to find sb guilty but with a recommendation to ~** declarar culpable a uno pero recomendar la clemencia; **to be at the ~ of sb** estar a la merced de uno; **it is a ~ that ...** gracias a Dios que ..., menos mal que ...; **to beg for ~** pedir clemencia; **we should be grateful** (*or* **thankful**) **for small mercies** debemos dar las gracias por los pequeños favores; **to have ~ on sb** tener compasión de uno, apiadarse de uno; **have ~!** ¡por piedad!; **to be left to the tender mercies of sb** verse abandonado en las manos nada piadosas de uno; **to show sb no ~** tratar a uno con el mayor rigor; **no ~ was shown to the rioters** no hubo clemencia para los revoltosos; **to throw o.s. on sb's ~** abandonarse a la merced de uno.
2 ATTR: **~ flight** vuelo *m* de emergencia (para rescatar una persona en peligro *etc*); **'~ dash to Palace corgi'** 'fue volando a Palacio para salvar la vida al perro galés'.
mercy-killing ['mɜːsɪ,kɪlɪŋ] N eutanasia *f*.
mere¹ [mɪəʳ] N lago *m*.
mere² [mɪəʳ] ADJ mero, simple; solo, no más que; **he's a ~ clerk** es un simple empleado, no es más que un empleado; **it's ~ nonsense, it's the ~st nonsense** es puro disparate; **it's ~ talk** son palabras al aire, es pura palabrería; **they quarrelled over a ~ nothing** riñeron por una friolera; **it's a ~ formality** es pura fórmula.
merely ['mɪəlɪ] ADV meramente, simplemente; sólo; **I ~ said that ...** sólo dije que ..., lo único que dije era que ...; **she's ~ a secretary** es una simple secretaria, no es más que una secretaria; **it's not ~ broken, it's ruined** no sólo está roto, sino que se ha estropeado del todo.
meretricious [,merɪˈtrɪʃəs] ADJ de oropel, charro, postizo; *style, writing* rimbombante.
merge [mɜːdʒ] **1** VT unir, combinar (*with* con); mezclar; fundir; (*Comm, Comput*) fusionar.
2 VI unirse, combinarse; fundirse; converger; (*Comm*) fusionarse; (*roads*) empalmar; **to ~ into** ir convirtiéndose en; **the bird ~d into its background of leaves** el pájaro se hacía casi invisible contra el fondo de hojas; **this question ~s into that bigger one** esta cuestión se pierde en aquélla mayor.
3 N (*Comput*) fusión *f*.
merger ['mɜːdʒəʳ] N (*Comm*) fusión *f*, concentración *f* (*Mex*).
meridian [məˈrɪdɪən] N (*Astron, Geog*) meridiano *m*; (*fig*) cenit *m*, auge *m*.
meridional [məˈrɪdɪənl] ADJ meridional.
meringue [məˈræŋ] N merengue *m*.
merino [məˈriːnəʊ] **1** ADJ merino.
2 N merino *m*.
merit ['merɪt] **1** N mérito *m*; ventaja *f*, bondad *f*; virtud *f*; **it has the ~ of being clear** tiene el mérito de ser claro; **to treat a case on its**

~s considerar un caso según sus méritos; **~ increase** aumento *m* por méritos; **~ pay** (*US*) plus *m* por méritos.
[2] VT merecer, ser digno de.

meritocracy [ˌmerɪˈtɒkrəsɪ] N meritocracia *f*.
meritocrat [ˈmerɪtəʊkræt] N meritócrata *mf*.
meritorious [ˌmerɪˈtɔːrɪəs] ADJ meritorio.
meritoriously [ˌmerɪˈtɔːrɪəslɪ] ADV merecidamente.
merlin [ˈmɜːlɪn] N esmerejón *m*.
mermaid [ˈmɜːmeɪd] N sirena *f*.
merman [ˈmɜːmæn] N, PL **mermen** [ˈmɜːmen] tritón *m*.
Merovingian [ˌmerəʊˈvɪndʒɪən] [1] ADJ merovingio.
[2] N merovingio *m*, -a *f*.
merrily [ˈmerɪlɪ] ADV alegremente; regocijadamente, con alborozo.
merriment [ˈmerɪmənt] N alegría *f*; regocijo *m*, alborozo *m*; (*laughter*) risas *fpl*; **at this there was much ~** en esto hubo muchas risas.
▼ **merry** [ˈmerɪ] ADJ alegre; regocijado; alborozado; (*joke etc*) divertido; **to be as ~ as a lark** (*or* **cricket**) estar como unas pascuas; **to get ~*** achisparse*; **to make ~** divertirse, estar de juerga; **M~ Christmas!** ¡Felices Pascuas!; **M~ England** la Inglaterra de los buenos tiempos pasados; **Robin Hood and his ~ men** Robin Hood y sus valientes compañeros.
merry-go-round [ˈmerɪɡəʊˌraʊnd] N tiovivo *m*, caballitos *mpl*.
merrymaker [ˈmerɪˌmeɪkəʳ] N juerguista *mf*, parrandero *m*, -a *f*.
merrymaking [ˈmerɪˌmeɪkɪŋ] N festividades *fpl*.
mesa [ˈmeɪsə] N (*US*) colina *f* baja, duna *f*.
mescal [ˈmeskæl] N mezcal *m*.
mescaline [ˈmeskəlɪn] N mescalina *f*.
mesentery [ˈmeːzəntrɪ] N mesenterio *m*.
meseta [məˈseɪtə] N meseta *f*.
mesh [meʃ] [1] N malla *f*; (*Mech*) engrane *m*, engranaje *m*; **~es** (*fig*) red *f*, trampa *f*; **to be in ~** (*Mech*) engranar, estar engranado.
[2] VT: **to get ~ed** enredarse (*in* en).
[3] VI (*Tech*) engranar (*with* con).
mesmeric [mezˈmerɪk] ADJ mesmeriano.
mesmerism [ˈmezmərɪzəm] N mesmerismo *m*.
mesmerize [ˈmezməraɪz] VT mesmerizar, hipnotizar; **to ~ sb into doing sth** inducir a uno a hacer algo hipnotizándole.
mesolith [ˈmesəʊlɪθ] N mesolito *m*.
mesolithic [mesəʊˈlɪθɪk] [1] ADJ mesolítico.
[2] N: **the M~** el Mesolítico.
mesomorph [ˈmesəʊˌmɔːf] N mesomorfo *m*.
meson [ˈmiːzɒn] N mesón *m*.
Mesopotamia [ˌmesəpəˈteɪmɪə] N Mesopotamia *f*.
Mesozoic [ˌmesəʊˈzəʊɪk] [1] ADJ mesozoico.
[2] N mesozoico *m*, -a *f*.
mess [mes] [1] N (a) (*confusion*) confusión *f*; (*of objects*) revoltijo *m*; (*dirt*) suciedad *f*; (*bungled affair*) lío* *m*; **what a ~!** ¡qué sucio está todo!; ¡qué asco!; ¡qué lío!*; **to be in a ~** (*things*) estar revuelto, (*house etc*) estar desarreglado, (*person*) estar en un aprieto; **his life is in a ~** su vida es un fracaso; **she's a ~*** es un desastre; **to get into a ~** (*person*) meterse en un lío*, (*things*) desarreglarse, (*accounts etc*) enredarse; **to leave things in a ~** dejar las cosas en confusión; **to leave a room in a ~** dejar un cuarto revuelto; **to make a ~ of** *objects* desordenar, *job* fracasar en, hacer muy mal, *sb else's life* llenar de confusión, arruinar, *one's life* fracasar en, (*dirty*) ensuciar.
(b) **~ of pottage** plato *m* de lentejas.
(c) (*Mil etc*) (*food*) rancho *m*, comida *f*; (*room*) sala *f* de rancho; **officers' ~** comedor *m* de oficiales.
[2] VI (a) (*feed*) hacer rancho, comer (juntos). (b) (*) **no ~ing!** ¡sin bromas!; **no ~ing?** ¿en serio?, ¿sin bromas?
◆ **mess about, mess around** [1] VT: **to ~ sb about** (*Brit*) fastidiar a uno, desorientar a uno (cambiando una cita *etc* con él).
[2] VI perder el tiempo, ocuparse en fruslerías, trabajar (*etc*) con poca seriedad; **he enjoys ~ing about in boats** le gusta entretenerse con botes; **we ~ed about in Paris for two days** pasamos dos días en París haciendo esto y lo otro; **they kept us ~ing about for an hour** nos hicieron esperar una hora sin decirnos nada; **stop ~ing about!** ¡déjate de tonterías!
◆ **mess about with** VT: **to ~ about with sth** (*handle*) manosear algo, tocar algo, (*amuse o.s.*) divertirse con algo, (*break*) romper algo, estropear algo; **to ~ about with a girl** andar en líos con una chica.
◆ **mess up** VT (*disarrange*) desarreglar, desordenar; (*dirty*) ensuciar; (*ruin*) arruinar, estropear, echar a perder; *affair, deal* fracasar en, (*deliberately*) chafar; (*Psych: disturb*) perturbar, traumatizar; (*US: beat up*) zurrar, dar una paliza a.
◆ **mess with*** VT perder el tiempo con; andar en líos con*.
message [ˈmesɪdʒ] [1] N mensaje *m*, recado *m*; aviso *m*, nota *f*; (*diplomatic etc*) comunicación *f*; (*Comput*) mensaje *m*; (*of telex etc*) texto *m*; (*of speech, book etc*) mensaje *m*, lección *f*, sentido *m*; **to get the ~*** comprender, caer en la cuenta; **do you think he got the ~?*** ¿crees que comprendió?; **to leave a ~** dejar un recado.
[2] ATTR: **~ switching** conmutación *f* de mensajes.

messaging [ˈmesɪdʒɪŋ] N mensajería *f*.
mess-deck [ˈmesdek] N sollado *m*, cubierta *f* de rancho de marineros.
messenger [ˈmesɪndʒəʳ] [1] N mensajero *m*, -a *f*, mandadero *m*, -a *f*.
[2] ATTR: **~ boy** mensajero *m*.
Messiah [mɪˈsaɪə] N Mesías *m*.
messianic [ˌmesɪˈænɪk] ADJ mesiánico.
Messieurs [ˈmesəz] NPL (*Brit*) señores *mpl*.
messmate [ˈmesmeɪt] N compañero *m* de rancho, comensal *m*, (*loosely*) amigo *m*.
Messrs [ˈmesəz] NPL (*Brit*: PL of **Mr**) ABBR *of* **Messieurs** señores *mpl*, Sres.
messtin [ˈmestɪn] N plato *m* de campaña.
mess-up* [ˈmesʌp] N (*Brit*) fracaso *m*; enredo *m*, follón* *m*, lío* *m*; **we had a ~ with the trains** nos hicimos un lío con los trenes*; **what a ~!** ¡qué lío*!
messy [ˈmesɪ] ADJ (*dirty*) sucio; (*untidy*) desaseado, desaliñado, *room etc* en desorden; (*confused*) confuso, nada claro; *divorce* lleno de problemas, lleno de rencores.
mestizo [mɪsˈtiːzəʊ] N, PL **mestizos** *or* **mestizoes** (*US*) mestizo *m*, -a *f*.
met [met] PRET AND PTP *of* **meet²**.
Met. [met] (a) ADJ (*Brit*) ABBR *of* **meteorological**; **the ~ Office** la estación meteorológica estatal. (b) N (*US*) ABBR *of* **Metropolitan Opera**. (c) N (*Brit*) ABBR *of* **Metropolitan Police** policía de Londres.
meta... [ˈmetə] PREF meta...
metabolic [ˌmetəˈbɒlɪk] ADJ metabólico.
metabolism [meˈtæbəlɪzəm] N metabolismo *m*.
metabolize [meˈtæbəlaɪz] VT metabolizar.
metacarpal [ˌmetəˈkɑːpl] N metacarpiano *m*.
metacarpus [ˌmetəˈkɑːpəs] N metacarpo *m*.
metal [ˈmetl] [1] N (a) metal *m*. (b) (*Brit*: *on road*) grava *f*. (c) (*fig*) temple *m*, ánimo *m*. (d) **~s** (*Brit Rail*) rieles *mpl*.
[2] ADJ metálico, de metal; **~ detector** detector *m* de metales; **~ fatigue** fatiga *f* del metal; **~ polish** lustre *m* para metales.
[3] VT (*Brit*) *road* engravar.
metalanguage [ˈmetəˌlæŋɡwɪdʒ] N metalenguaje *m*.
metalinguistic [ˌmetəlɪŋˈɡwɪstɪk] ADJ metalingüístico.
metalinguistics [ˌmetəlɪŋˈɡwɪstɪks] N metalingüística *f*.
metallic [mɪˈtælɪk] ADJ metálico.
metallurgic(al) [ˌmetəˈlɜːdʒɪk(əl)] ADJ metalúrgico.
metallurgist [meˈtælədʒɪst] N metalúrgico *m*, -a *f*.
metallurgy [meˈtælədʒɪ] N metalurgia *f*.
metalwork [ˈmetlwɜːk] N metalistería *f*.
metamorphic [ˌmetəˈmɔːfɪk] ADJ metamórfico.
metamorphose [ˌmetəˈmɔːfəʊz] [1] VT metamorfosear (*into* en).
[2] VI metamorfosearse.
metamorphosis [ˌmetəˈmɔːfəsɪs] N, PL **metamorphoses** [ˌmetəˈmɔːfəsiːz] metamorfosis *f*.
metaphor [ˈmetəfɔːʳ] N metáfora *f*.
metaphorical [ˌmetəˈfɒrɪkəl] ADJ metafórico.
metaphorically [ˌmetəˈfɒrɪklɪ] ADV metafóricamente.
metaphysical [ˌmetəˈfɪzɪkəl] ADJ metafísico.
metaphysics [ˌmetəˈfɪzɪks] N metafísica *f*.
metastasis [mɪˈtæstəsɪs] N metástasis *f*.
metatarsal [ˌmetəˈtɑːsl] N metatarsiano *m*.
metatarsus [ˌmetəˈtɑːsəs] N, PL **metatarsi** [ˌmetəˈtɑːsaɪ] metatarso *m*.
metathesis [meˈtæθəsɪs] N metátesis *f*.
mete [miːt] VT: **to ~ out** repartir; *punishment etc* dar, imponer.
metempsychosis [ˌmetəmsaɪˈkəʊsɪs] N metempsicosis *f*.
meteor [ˈmiːtɪəʳ] N meteoro *m*, bólido *m*; (*esp fig*) meteoro *m*.
[2] ATTR: **~ shower** lluvia *f* de meteoritos.
meteoric [ˌmiːtɪˈɒrɪk] ADJ meteórico (*also fig*).
meteorite [ˈmiːtɪəraɪt] N meteorito *m*, bólido *m*.
meteoroid [ˈmiːtɪərɔɪd] N meteoroide *m*.
meteorological [ˌmiːtɪərəˈlɒdʒɪkəl] ADJ meteorológico.
meteorologically [ˌmiːtɪərəˈlɒdʒɪklɪ] ADV meteorológicamente, en lo que se refiere a la meteorología.
meteorologist [ˌmiːtɪəˈrɒlədʒɪst] N meteorólogo *m*, -a *f*.
meteorology [ˌmiːtɪəˈrɒlədʒɪ] N meteorología *f*.
meter [ˈmiːtəʳ] [1] N contador *m*, medidor *m* (*LAm*); (*US*) = **metre**. [2] VT medir (con contador); (*US*) *mail* franquear.
meterage [ˈmiːtərɪdʒ] N metraje *m*.
metermaid [ˈmiːtəˌmeɪd] N (*US*) controladora *f* de estacionamiento.
methadone [ˈmeθəˌdəʊn] N metadona *f*.
methamphetamine [ˌmeθæmˈfetəmiːn] N metanfetamina *f*.
methane [ˈmiːθeɪn] N metano *m*.
methanol [ˈmeθənɒl] N metanol *m*.
methinks [mɪˈθɪŋks] ADV (††) a mi parecer, a mi entender.
method [ˈmeθəd] [1] N método *m*; sistema *m*, procedimiento *m*; **~ of payment** forma *f* de pago; **there's ~ in his madness** no es tan loco como parece.
[2] ATTR: **~ actor/actress** actor *m* adepto/actriz *f* adepta del método Stanislavski.

methodical [mɪˈθɒdɪkəl] ADJ metódico.
methodically [mɪˈθɒdɪkəlɪ] ADV metódicamente.
Methodism ['meθədɪzəm] N metodismo m.
Methodist ['meθədɪst] [1] ADJ metodista.
　[2] N metodista mf.
methodological [ˌmeθədəˈlɒdʒɪkəl] ADJ metodológico.
methodologically [ˌmeθədəˈlɒdʒɪkəlɪ] ADV metodológicamente, desde el punto de vista metodológico.
methodology [ˌmeθəˈdɒlədʒɪ] N metodología f.
meths* [meθs] (Brit) [1] N ABBR of **methylated spirit(s)**.
　[2] ATTR: ~ **drinker** bebedor m, -ora f de alcohol metilado.
Methuselah [mɪˈθjuːzələ] NM Matusalén.
methylated ['meθɪleɪtɪd] ADJ: ~ **spirit(s)** (Brit) alcohol m metilado, alcohol m desnaturalizado.
meticulous [mɪˈtɪkjʊləs] ADJ meticuloso; minucioso.
meticulously [mɪˈtɪkjʊləslɪ] ADV meticulosamente.
meticulousness [mɪˈtɪkjʊləsnɪs] N meticulosidad f.
métier ['meɪtɪeɪ] N (trade) oficio m; (strong point) fuerte m; (speciality) especialidad f; **it's not my ~** no es de mi especialidad.
met-man* ['metmæn] N, PL **met-men** ['metmen] meteorólogo m.
metre, (US) **meter** ['miːtəʳ] N (all senses) metro m.
metric(al) ['metrɪk(əl)] ADJ métrico; ~ **system** sistema m métrico; ~ **ton** tonelada f métrica; **to go ~*** adoptar el sistema métrico, cambiar al sistema métrico.
metrication [ˌmetrɪˈkeɪʃən] N paso m (or cambio m) al sistema métrico.
metrics ['metrɪks] N métrica f.
metro ['metrəʊ] N metro m.
metrological [ˌmetrəˈlɒdʒɪkəl] ADJ metrológico.
metronome ['metrənəʊm] N metrónomo m.
metronomic [ˌmetrəˈnɒmɪk] ADJ metronómico.
metropolis [mɪˈtrɒpəlɪs] N metrópoli f.
metropolitan [ˌmetrəˈpɒlɪtən] [1] ADJ metropolitano; **M~ Police** la policía de Londres.
　[2] N (Eccl) metropolitano m.
mettle ['metl] N temple m; ánimo m, brío m; valor m; **to be on one's ~** estar dispuesto a mostrar todo lo que uno vale; **to put sb on his ~** picar a uno en el amor propio; **to show one's ~** mostrar lo que uno vale.
mettlesome ['metlsəm] ADJ animoso, brioso, esforzado.
Meuse [mɜːz] N Mosa m.
mew [mjuː] [1] N maullido m.
　[2] VI maullar.
mewl [mjuːl] VI (cat) maullar; (baby) lloriquear.
mews [mjuːz] N (Brit) caballeriza f; calle f de casas pequeñas (antes caballerizas).
Mexican ['meksɪkən] [1] ADJ mejicano, (in Mexico) mexicano; **the ~ wave** la ola.
　[2] N mejicano m, -a f, (in Mexico) mexicano m, -a f.
Mexico ['meksɪkəʊ] N Méjico m, (in Mexico) México m; ~ **City** (Ciudad f de) México.
mezzanine ['mezəniːn] N entresuelo m.
mezzo-soprano ['metsəʊsəˈprɑːnəʊ] N mezzosoprano f.
mezzotint ['metzəʊtɪnt] N grabado m mezzotinto.
MF N ABBR of **medium frequency**.
M.F.A. N (US) ABBR of **Master of Fine Arts** título universitario.
MFH N (Brit) ABBR of **Master of Foxhounds** capataz de caza de zorros.
MFN N (US) ABBR of **most favored nation** nación f más favorecida; ~ **treatment** trato m de nación más favorecida.
mfr(s) ABBR of **manufacturer(s)** fabricante m, fab.
mg ABBR of **miligramme(s)**.
Mgr (a) (Eccl) ABBR of **Monsignor** monseñor m, Mons. (b) (Comm etc) ABBR of **manager**.
MHR N (US) ABBR of **Member of the House of Representatives** diputado del Congreso de EE.UU.
MHz (Rad) ABBR of **megahertz** megahercio m, MHz.
MI (a) N ABBR of **machine intelligence**. (b) (US Post) ABBR of **Michigan**.
mi [miː] (Mus) mi m.
MI5 N (Brit) ABBR of **Military Intelligence 5** servicio de inteligencia contraespionaje.
MI6 N (Brit) ABBR of **Military Intelligence 6** servicio de inteligencia.
MIA ADJ (Mil) ABBR of **missing in action** desaparecido.
miaow [miːˈaʊ] [1] N miau m.
　[2] VI maullar.
miasma [mɪˈæzmə] N, PL **miasmas** or **miasmata** [mɪˈæzmətə] miasma m.
miasmic [mɪˈæzmɪk] ADJ miasmático.
mica ['maɪkə] N mica f.
mice [maɪs] NPL of **mouse**.
Mich. (US) ABBR of **Michigan**.
Michael ['maɪkl] NM Miguel.
Michaelmas ['mɪklməs] [1] N fiesta f de San Miguel (29 setiembre).

[2] ATTR: ~ **daisy** margarita f de otoño; ~ **term** (Brit) trimestre m de otoño, primer trimestre m.
Michelangelo [ˌmaɪkælˈændʒɪləʊ] NM Miguel Ángel.
Mick [mɪk] NM familiar form of **Michael**.
Mickey ['mɪkɪ] NM familiar form of **Michael**; ~ **Finn** bebida f drogada; ~ **Mouse** el ratoncito Mickey; ~ **Mouse money** dinero m de jugar; **it's a ~ Mouse set-up** es un montaje poco serio.
mickey* ['mɪkɪ] N: **to take the ~ out of sb** (Brit) tomar el pelo a uno*.
micro ['maɪkrəʊ] N (a) (Comput) micro m, microordenador m. (b) (*) microondas m.
micro... ['maɪkrəʊ] PREF micro...
microbe ['maɪkrəʊb] N microbio m.
microbial [maɪˈkrəʊbɪəl] ADJ microbiano.
microbiological [ˌmaɪkrəʊbaɪəˈlɒdʒɪkəl] ADJ microbiológico.
microbiologist [ˌmaɪkrəʊbaɪˈɒlədʒɪst] N microbiólogo m, -a f.
microbiology [ˌmaɪkrəʊbaɪˈɒlədʒɪ] N microbiología f.
microbus ['maɪkrəʊbʌs] N (Aut) microbús m.
microchip ['maɪkrəʊtʃɪp] N microchip m, pastilla f.
microcircuit ['maɪkrəʊsɜːkɪt] N microcircuito m.
microcircuitry ['maɪkrəʊsɜːkɪtrɪ] N microcircuitería f.
microclimate ['maɪkrəʊklaɪmɪt] N microclima m.
microcomputer [ˌmaɪkrəʊkəmˈpjuːtəʳ] N microordenador m, microcomputadora f.
microcomputing ['maɪkrəʊkəmˈpjuːtɪŋ] N microcomputación f.
microcosm ['maɪkrəʊkɒzəm] N microcosmo m.
microdot ['maɪkrəʊdɒt] N micropunto m.
microeconomic [ˌmaɪkrəʊ,iːkəˈnɒmɪk] ADJ microeconómico.
microeconomics ['maɪkrəʊ,iːkəˈnɒmɪks] N microeconomía f.
microelectronic ['maɪkrəʊ,iːlekˈtrɒnɪk] ADJ microelectrónico.
microelectronics ['maɪkrəʊ,iːlekˈtrɒnɪks] N SING microelectrónica f.
microfiche ['maɪkrəʊfiːʃ] N microfiche m, microficha f.
microfilm ['maɪkrəʊfɪlm] [1] N microfilm m, microfilme m.
　[2] ATTR: ~ **reader** lector m de microfilm.
　[3] VT microfilmar.
microform ['maɪkrəʊfɔːm] N microforma f.
microgravity [ˌmaɪkrəʊˈgrævɪtɪ] N microgravedad f.
microgroove ['maɪkrəʊgruːv] N microsurco m.
microlight, microlite ['maɪkrəʊlaɪt] N (also ~ **aircraft**) (avión m) ultraligero m, aeroligero m.
micromesh ['maɪkrəʊmeʃ] ATTR: ~ **stockings** medias fpl de malla fina.
micrometer [maɪˈkrɒmɪtəʳ] N micrómetro m.
microorganism ['maɪkrəʊ'ɔːgənɪzəm] N microorganismo m.
microphone ['maɪkrəfəʊn] N micrófono m.
microprocessor [ˌmaɪkrəʊˈprəʊsesəʳ] N microprocesador m.
microprogramming, (US, also freq Comput) **microprograming** [ˌmaɪkrəʊˈprəʊgræmɪŋ] N microprogramación f.
microscope ['maɪkrəskəʊp] N microscopio m.
microscopic(al) [ˌmaɪkrəˈskɒpɪk(əl)] ADJ microscópico.
microscopically [ˌmaɪkrəʊˈskɒpɪklɪ] ADV microscópicamente; ~ **small** microscópico; **to examine sth ~** examinar algo al microscopio.
microscopy [maɪˈkrɒskəpɪ] N microscopía f.
microsecond ['maɪkrəʊ,sekənd] N microsegundo m.
microspacing [ˌmaɪkrəʊˈspeɪsɪŋ] N microespaciado m.
microstructural [ˌmaɪkrəʊˈstrʌktʃərəl] ADJ microestructural.
microstructure ['maɪkrəʊ,strʌktʃəʳ] N microestructura f.
microsurgery [ˌmaɪkrəʊˈsɜːdʒərɪ] N microcirugía f.
microsurgical [ˌmaɪkrəʊˈsɜːdʒɪkəl] ADJ microquirúrgico.
microtechnology [ˌmaɪkrəʊtekˈnɒlədʒɪ] N microtecnología f.
microtransmitter ['maɪkrəʊtrænzˈmɪtəʳ] N microtransmisor m.
microwave ['maɪkrəʊ,weɪv] [1] N microonda f; (~ **oven**) = **2**.
　[2] ATTR: ~ **oven** horno m de microonda, microondas m.
　[3] VT poner en el microondas, cocinar al microondas.
micturate ['mɪktjʊəreɪt] VI orinar.
micturition [ˌmɪktjʊˈrɪʃən] N micción f.
mid [mɪd] [1] ADJ medio, eg **in ~ journey** a medio camino; **in ~ June** a mediados de junio; **in ~ afternoon** a media tarde; **in ~ course** a media carrera; **in ~ channel** en medio del canal.
　[2] PREP (liter, poet) V **amid**.
mid-air ['mɪdeəʳ] [1] ATTR: ~ **collision** colisión f en el aire.
　[2] N: **in ~** entre cielo y tierra; **to leave sth in ~** dejar algo en el aire; **to refuel in ~** repostar combustible en pleno vuelo.
Midas ['maɪdəs] NM Midas.
mid-Atlantic [mɪdətˈlæntɪk] ATTR: accent etc de mitad del Atlántico.
midbrain ['mɪdbreɪn] N mesencéfalo m, cerebro m medio.
midday ['mɪd'deɪ] [1] N mediodía m; **at ~** a mediodía.
　[2] ADJ de mediodía.
midden ['mɪdn] N muladar m.
middle ['mɪdl] [1] ADJ (of place) medio, central; de en medio; intermedio; (in quality, size etc) mediano; ~ **age** mediana edad f; **M~ Ages** Edad f Media; **M~ America** Centroamérica f, (fig) el ciudadano norteamericano medio; ~ **C** (Mus) do m mayor; ~ **class** clase f media; **my ~ daughter** mi segunda hija (de las tres que tengo), la

hija de en medio; **in the ~ distance** (*Art*) a medio fondo; **~ ear** oído *m* medio; **M~ East** Oriente *m* Medio; **M~ English** inglés *m* medio; **~ finger** dedo *m* del corazón; **~ ground** terreno *m* neutral; **M~ High German** alto alemán *m* medio; **~ management** gerencia *f* intermedia; **my ~ name is Albert** mi segundo nombre de pila es Alberto; **his ~ name is 'lover'** le han apodado 'Tenorio'; **~ school** primeros años *mpl* de la enseñanza media; **~ voice** voz *f* media.

2 N **(a)** medio *m*, centro *m*, mitad *f*; **it divides down the ~** se divide por el medio; **in the ~ of the table** en el centro de la mesa; **in the ~ of the field** en medio del campo; **right in the ~ of the room** en el mismo centro del cuarto; **in the ~ of nowhere** donde Cristo dio las tres voces; **in the ~ of summer** en pleno verano; **in** (*or* **about, towards**) **the ~ of May** a mediados de mayo; **in the ~ of the century** a mediados del siglo; **in the ~ of the morning** a media mañana; **I'm in the ~ of reading it** voy a mitad de su lectura.

(b) (*: waist*) cintura *f*.

middle-aged ['mɪdl'eɪdʒd] ADJ de mediana edad, de edad madura; cuarentón, cincuentón.

middlebrow ['mɪdlbraʊ] **1** ADJ de (*or* para) gusto medianamente culto, de gusto entre intelectual y plebeyo.

2 N persona *f* de gusto medianamente culto, persona *f* de cultura mediana.

middle-class ['mɪdl'klɑːs] ADJ de la clase media.

middle-distance [,mɪdl'dɪstəns] ADJ: **~ race** carrera *f* de medio fondo; **~ runner** mediofondista *mf*.

Middle-Eastern [,mɪdl'iːstən] ADJ medio-oriental.

middleman ['mɪdlmæn] N, PL **middlemen** ['mɪdlmen] intermediario *m*.

middle-of-the-road ['mɪdləvðə'rəʊd] ADJ moderado, de posición intermedia.

middle-ranking ['mɪdl'ræŋkɪŋ] ADJ *official etc* medio.

middle-sized ['mɪdl,saɪzd] ADJ de tamaño mediano; *person* de estatura mediana.

middleweight ['mɪdlweɪt] N peso *m* medio; **light ~** peso *m* medio ligero.

Middle West ['mɪdl'west] N (*US*) mediooeste *m* (*llanura central de EE.UU.*).

middling ['mɪdlɪŋ] **1** ADJ mediano, regular.

2 ADV **(a)** regular; **how are you? ... ~** ¿qué tal estás? ... regular. **(b)** (*) **~ good** medianamente bueno, regular.

Middx N (*Brit*) ABBR *of* **Middlesex**.

middy* ['mɪdɪ] N = **midshipman**.

midfield ['mɪdfiːld] **1** N centrocampo *m*, centro *m* del campo.

2 ATTR: **~ player** centrocampista *mf*.

midge [mɪdʒ] N mosca *f*, mosquito *m*.

midget ['mɪdʒɪt] **1** N enano *m*, -a *f*.

2 ADJ en miniatura, en pequeña escala; *submarine etc* de bolsillo.

midi ['mɪdɪ] ADJ: **~ hi-fi, ~ system** cadena *f* musical compacta.

midiskirt ['mɪdɪskɜːt] N midi *m*, midifalda *f*.

midland ['mɪdlənd] **1** ADJ del interior, del centro.

2 N: **the M~s** (*Brit*) la región central de Inglaterra.

Midlander ['mɪdləndər] N nativo *m*, -a *f* (*or* habitante *mf*) de la región central de Inglaterra.

mid-life ['mɪd,laɪf] ATTR: **~ crisis** crisis *f* de los cuarenta.

mid-morning ['mɪd'mɔːnɪŋ] ADJ: **~ coffee** café *m* de media mañana, café *m* de las once.

midnight ['mɪdnaɪt] **1** N medianoche *f*.

2 ATTR de medianoche; **~ mass** misa *f* del gallo; **to burn the ~ oil** quemarse las cejas.

midpoint ['mɪd,pɔɪnt] N punto *m* medio.

midriff ['mɪdrɪf] N diafragma *m*.

midsection ['mɪdsekʃən] N sección *f* de en medio.

midshipman ['mɪdʃɪpmən] N, PL **midshipmen** ['mɪdʃɪpmən] guardia *m* marina.

midships ['mɪdʃɪps] ADV en medio del navío.

midsize(d) ['mɪdsaɪz(d)] ADJ mediano.

midst [mɪdst] **1** N: **in the ~ of** entre, en medio de; **in our ~** entre nosotros; **in the ~ of plenty** en medio de la abundancia.

2 PREP (*liter*) = **amid(st)**.

midstream ['mɪd'striːm] N: **in ~** en medio de la corriente, en medio del río.

midsummer ['mɪd'sʌmər] **1** N pleno verano *m*, (*strictly*) solsticio *m* estival; **M~ (Day)** fiesta *f* de San Juan (*24 junio*); **'M~ Night's Dream'** 'El sueño de una noche de verano'; **at ~** el día del solsticio de verano; **in ~** en pleno verano.

2 ATTR de pleno verano, estival; **~ madness** locura *f* temporal.

mid-term ['mɪd'tɜːm] ATTR: **~ exam** examen *m* de mitad del trimestre; **~ elections** (*US*) elecciones *fpl* de medio mandato (presidencial).

midtown ['mɪd,taʊn] **1** N centro *m* de la ciudad.

2 ATTR: *e.g.* **~ shops** tiendas *fpl* del centro de la ciudad.

midway ['mɪd'weɪ] **1** ADV a mitad del camino; **~ between X and Y** a mitad del camino (*or* a medio camino) entre X e Y; **we are now ~**

ahora estamos a medio camino.

2 ADJ situado a medio camino; **a ~ point** un punto intermedio, un punto equidistante de los dos extremos.

3 N (*US*) avenida *f* central, paseo *m* central.

midweek ['mɪd'wiːk] **1** ADV entre semana.

2 ADJ *flight etc* de entre semana.

Midwest ['mɪd'west] N (*US*) mediooeste *m* (*llanura central de EE.UU.*).

Midwestern [mɪd,westən] ADJ (*US*) del mediooeste (*de EE.UU.*).

Midwesterner [mɪd'westənər] N (*US*) habitante o nativo del Midwest.

midwife ['mɪdwaɪf] N, PL **midwives** ['mɪdwaɪvz] comadrona *f*, partera *f*.

midwifery ['mɪd,wɪfərɪ] N partería *f*.

midwinter ['mɪd'wɪntər] **1** N pleno invierno *m*, (*strictly*) solsticio *m* de invierno; **at ~** el día del solsticio de invierno; **in ~** en pleno invierno.

2 ATTR de pleno invierno.

mien [miːn] N (*liter*) aire *m*, porte *m*, semblante *m*.

miff* [mɪf] **1** N disgusto *m*.

2 VT disgustar, ofender; **he was pretty ~ed about it** se ofendió bastante por eso.

might¹ [maɪt] V may.

might² [maɪt] N fuerza *f*, poder *m*, poderío *m*; **~ is right** es la ley del más fuerte; **with ~ and main** a más no poder, esforzándose muchísimo; **with all one's ~** con todas sus fuerzas, empleándose a fondo.

might-have-been ['maɪtəv,biːn] N esperanza *f* no cumplida.

mightily ['maɪtɪlɪ] ADV fuertemente; poderosamente; **I was ~ surprised** me sorprendí enormemente.

mightiness ['maɪtɪnɪs] N fuerza *f*; poder *m*, poderío *m*.

mightn't ['maɪtnt] = **might not**.

mighty ['maɪtɪ] **1** ADJ **(a)** fuerte; potente, poderoso.

(b) (*) enorme, inmenso.

2 ADV (*) muy, terriblemente; **it's ~ awkward** es terriblemente difícil; **I was ~ surprised** me sorprendí enormemente.

mignonette [,mɪnjə'net] N reseda *f*.

migraine ['miːgreɪn] N jaqueca *f*.

migrant ['maɪgrənt] **1** ADJ migratorio.

2 N peregrino *m*, -a *f*, nómada *mf*; (*Australia*) inmigrante *mf*; (*bird*) ave *f* migratoria, ave *f* de paso; (*insect*) insecto *m* migratorio.

migrate [maɪ'greɪt] VI emigrar, migrar; (*flocks*) trashumar.

migration [maɪ'greɪʃən] N migración *f*; trashumancia *f*.

migratory [maɪ'greɪtərɪ] ADJ migratorio; trashumante.

Mike [maɪk] NM *familiar form of* **Michael**; **for the love of ~!** ¡por Dios!

mike¹ [maɪk] N: **to have a good ~:** no hacer nada, tirarse a la bartola; gandulear, racanear*.

mike²* [maɪk] N (*Rad*) micro *m**.

milady [mɪ'leɪdɪ] N miladi *f*.

Milan [mɪ'læn] N Milán *m*.

milch [mɪltʃ] ATTR: **~ cow** vaca *f* lechera.

mild [maɪld] **1** ADJ (*of character*) apacible, pacífico; manso; *rule etc* blando; *protest* moderado; *climate* templado; *day* blando; *medicine, effect, taste etc* suave, dulce; (*slight*) leve, ligero; (*Med*) benigno.

2 N tipo de cerveza; *ver también* BEER .

mildew ['mɪldjuː] N moho *m*; (*on wheat*) añublo *m*; (*on vine*) mildiu *m*.

mildewed ['mɪldjuːd] ADJ mohoso; añublado; con mildiu.

mildly ['maɪldlɪ] ADV (*V ADJ*) apaciblemente, pacíficamente; blandamente; suavemente, dulcemente; levemente, ligeramente; **to put it ~, and that's putting it ~** para no decir más.

mild-mannered ['maɪld'mænəd] ADJ apacible.

mildness ['maɪldnɪs] N (*V ADJ*) apacibilidad *f*; blandura *f*; suavidad *f*, dulzura *f*; levedad *f*.

mile [maɪl] N (**a**) milla *f* (= 1609,33 m); **~s per gallon** *equivalent to* litros por 100 kilómetros; **not a hundred ~s from here** (*fig*) no muy lejos de aquí; **sorry, I was ~s away** lo siento, se me fue el santo al cielo; **we walked ~s!** ¡hemos andado kilómetros y kilómetros!; **they live ~s away** viven lejísimos de aquí; **you were ~s off the target** no te acercaste ni con mucho al objetivo; **you can tell it a ~ off** eso se ve a la legua; **it smelled for ~s around** olía a muchas leguas a la redonda; **she'll run a ~ from a spider** vuela a la vista de una araña; **it stands out a ~** salta a los ojos, se ve a la legua.

(b) M~ High City *Denver; ver también* CITY NICKNAMES , IMPERIAL SYSTEM .

mileage ['maɪlɪdʒ] N (**a**) (*distance covered*) número *m* de millas, distancia *f* recorrida en millas; (*Aut*) kilometraje *m*; **~ per gallon** ≈ litros por 100 kilómetros; **what ~ has this car done?** ¿qué kilómetros tiene este coche?

(b) (*fig*) **there's no ~ in this story** esta historia sólo tiene un interés pasajero; **he got a lot of ~ out of the affair** explotó el asunto al máximo; **he got a lot of ~ out of it** (*fig*) le sacó mucho partido.

2 ATTR: **~ allowance** gastos *mpl* de viaje por milla recorrida, asignación *f* por kilometraje; **~ indicator** cuentakilómetros *m*; **~ rate** tarifa *f* por distancia; **~ ticket** billete *m* kilométrico.

mileometer ['maɪ'lɒmɪtər] N = **milometer**.

milepost ['maɪlpəʊst] N (*Hist*) poste *m* miliar, mojón *m*.

miler ['maɪlə^r] N corredor *m*, -ora *f* (*etc*) que se especializa en las pruebas de una milla.

milestone ['maɪlstəʊn] N (*Hist*) piedra *f* miliaria; (*in Spain etc*) mojón *m* (kilométrico), hito *m* (kilométrico); (*fig*) hito *m*; **these events are ~s in our history** estos acontecimientos hacen época (*or* son hitos) en nuestra historia.

milieu ['miːljɜː] N, PL **milieus** *or* **milieux** ['miːljɜː] medio *m*, ambiente *m*, medio *m* ambiente.

militancy ['mɪlɪtənsɪ] N militancia *f*; actitud *f* belicosa; activismo *m*.

militant ['mɪlɪtənt] **1** ADJ militante; belicoso, agresivo.
2 N militante *mf*; activista *mf*.

militarily ['mɪlɪ'tɛːrɪlɪ] ADV militarmente.

militarism ['mɪlɪtərɪzəm] N militarismo *m*.

militarist ['mɪlɪtərɪst] **1** ADJ militarista.
2 N militarista *mf*.

militaristic [,mɪlɪtə'rɪstɪk] ADJ militarista.

militarize ['mɪlɪtəraɪz] VT militarizar.

military ['mɪlɪtərɪ] **1** ADJ militar; **~ academy** (*US*) escuela *f* militar; **~ attaché** agregado *m* militar; **~ coup** golpe *m* militar; **~-industrial complex** (*esp US*) complejo *m* militar-industrial; **~ operations** operaciones *fpl* militares; **~ police** policía *f* militar; **~ policeman** policía *m* militar; **~ service** servicio *m* militar; **~ training** instrucción *f* militar, (*loosely*) servicio *m*.
2 N: **the ~** los militares.

militate ['mɪlɪteɪt] VI: **to ~ against** militar contra.

militia [mɪ'lɪʃə] **1** N milicia(s) *f(pl)*.
2 ATTR: **the ~ reserves** (*US*) las reservas (territoriales).

militiaman [mɪ'lɪʃəmən] N, PL **militiamen** [mɪ'lɪʃəmən] miliciano *m*.

milk [mɪlk] **1** N leche *f*; **~ of magnesia** leche *f* de magnesia; **the ~ of human kindness** la compasión (personificada); **it's no good crying over spilt ~** a lo hecho pecho, agua pasada no mueve molino.
2 ATTR *milk diet, milk product etc* lácteo; **~ chocolate** chocolate *m* con leche; **~ products** productos *mpl* lácteos; **~ pudding** arroz *m* con leche; **~ round** recorrido *m* del lechero; (*Comm, Univ*) recorrido anual de las principales empresas por las universidades para entrevistar a estudiantes del último curso con vistas a una posible contratación; **~ teeth** dentición *f* de leche.
3 VT ordeñar; (*fig*) chupar; **they're ~ing the company for all they can get** chupan todo lo que pueden de la compañía.
4 VI dar leche.

milk-and-water ['mɪlkən'wɔːtə^r] ADJ (*fig*) débil, flojo.

milk-bar ['mɪlkbɑː^r] N cafetería *f*.

milk-churn ['mɪlktʃɜːn] N lechera *f*.

milk-float ['mɪlkfləʊt] N (*Brit*) carro *m* de la leche.

milking ['mɪlkɪŋ] **1** ADJ lechero, de ordeño.
2 N ordeño *m*.

milking-machine ['mɪlkɪŋmə,ʃiːn] N ordeñadora *f* mecánica.

milkmaid ['mɪlkmeɪd] N lechera *f*.

milkman ['mɪlkmən] N, PL **milkmen** ['mɪlkmən] lechero *m*, repartidor *m* de leche.

milk run ['mɪlk,rʌn] N (*Aer*) vuelo *m* rutinario.

milkshake ['mɪlk'ʃeɪk] N batido *m* de leche, malteada *f* (*LAm*).

milksop ['mɪlksɒp] N marica *m*.

milk tooth ['mɪlktuːθ] N, PL **milk teeth** ['mɪlktiːθ] diente *m* de leche.

milk truck ['mɪlktrʌk] N (*US*) carro *m* de la leche.

milkweed ['mɪlkwiːd] N algodoncillo *m*.

milk-white ['mɪlk'waɪt] ADJ blanco como la leche.

milky ['mɪlkɪ] ADJ lechoso; **~ coffee** café *m* lechoso; **~ drink** bebida *f* con leche.

Milky Way ['mɪlkɪ'weɪ] N Vía *f* Láctea.

mill [mɪl] **1** N (a) (*wind~*) molino *m*; (*small, for coffee etc*) molinillo *m*; **to go through the ~** pasarlas moradas, sufrir mucho; aprender por experiencia práctica; **to put sb through the ~** someter a uno a un entrenamiento riguroso; hacer que uno aprenda por experiencia práctica; pasar a uno por la piedra.
(b) (*factory*) fábrica *f*; (*spinning ~*) hilandería *f*; (*weaving ~*) tejeduría *f*, fábrica *f* de tejidos; (*steel ~*) acería *f*, fábrica *f* de acero; (*workshop*) taller *m*.
2 VT (a) (*grind*) moler; *cloth* abatanar; *chocolate* batir.
(b) (*Mech*) fresar; *coin* acordonar.
◆ **mill about, mill around** VI circular en masa, moverse por todas partes; **people were ~ing around the booking office** la gente se apiñaba impaciente delante de la taquilla; **stop ~ing around!** ¡quietos!

milled [mɪld] ADJ (a) *grain* molido. (b) *coin* acordonado; **~ edge** cordoncillo *m*.

millenarian [,mɪlə'nɛːrɪən] ADJ milenario.

millenarianism [,mɪlə'nɛːrɪənɪzəm] N milenarismo *m*.

millenary [mɪ'lɛːnərɪ] **1** ADJ milenario.
2 N milenario *m*.

millennial [mɪ'lɛːnɪəl] ADJ milenario.

millennium [mɪ'lɛːnɪəm] N, PL **millennia** [mɪ'lɛːnɪə] milenio *m*, milenario *m*.

Millennium Fund [mɪ'lɛːnɪəm,fʌnd] N (*Brit*) fondo de financiación y desarrollo para el nuevo milenio.

miller ['mɪlə^r] N molinero *m*.

millet ['mɪlɪt] N mijo *m*.

millhand ['mɪlhænd] N obrero *m*, -a *f*, operario *m*, -a *f*.

milli... ['mɪlɪ] PREF mili....

milliard ['mɪlɪɑːd] N (*Brit*) mil millones *mpl*; **a ~ marks** mil millones de marcos.

millibar ['mɪlɪbɑː^r] N milibar *m*.

milligram(me) ['mɪlɪɡræm] N miligramo *m*.

millilitre, (*US*) **milliliter** ['mɪlɪ,liːtə^r] N mililitro *m*.

millimetre, (*US*) **millimeter** ['mɪlɪ,miːtə^r] N milímetro *m*.

milliner ['mɪlɪnə^r] N sombrerera *f*, modista *f* (de sombreros); **~'s (shop)** sombrerería *f*, tienda *f* de sombreros (de señora).

millinery ['mɪlɪnərɪ] N sombrerería *f*, sombreros *mpl* de señora.

milling ['mɪlɪŋ] N (a) (*grinding*) molienda *f*. (b) (*on coin*) cordoncillo *m*.

milling machine ['mɪlɪŋmə,ʃiːn] N fresadora *f*.

million ['mɪljən] N millón *m*; **one ~ fleas** un millón de pulgas; **4 ~ dogs** 4 millones de perros; **she's one in a ~** es una verdadera joya, es un mirlo blanco; **to feel like a ~ dollars** (*US*) sentirse a las mil maravillas; **I've told you ~s of times** te lo he dicho infinidad de veces.

millionaire [,mɪljə'nɛə^r] N millonario *m*, -a *f*.

millionairess [mɪljə'nɛəres] N millonaria *f*.

millionth ['mɪljənθ] **1** ADJ millonésimo.
2 N millonésimo *m*.

millipede ['mɪlɪpiːd] N miriópodo *m*, milpiés *m*.

millisecond ['mɪlɪ,sekənd] N milisegundo *m*.

millpond ['mɪlpɒnd] N represa *f* de molino.

millrace ['mɪlreɪs] N caz *m*.

millstone ['mɪlstəʊn] N piedra *f* de molino, muela *f*; (*fig*) carga *f* pesada; lastre *m*; **it's a ~ round his neck** es una losa que lleva encima.

millstream ['mɪlstriːm] N corriente *f* de agua que mueve un molino.

millwheel ['mɪlwiːl] N rueda *f* de molino.

milometer [maɪ'lɒmɪtə^r] N (*Brit*) cuentakilómetros *m*.

milord [mɪ'lɔːd] N milord *m*.

milt [mɪlt] N lecha *f*.

mime [maɪm] **1** N (a) (*action*) pantomima *f*, mímica *f*; (*ancient play*) mímica *f*, teatro *m* de mímica.
(b) (*actor*) mimo *m*.
2 VT hacer en pantomima, remedar; representar con gestos.
3 VI actuar de mimo.

Mimeograph ['mɪmɪəɡrɑːf] ® **1** N mimeógrafo ® *m*.
2 VT mimeografiar.

mimetic [mɪ'metɪk] ADJ (*frm*) *dance* mimético; *theatre* de mimo; *re-enactment* mímico.

mimic ['mɪmɪk] **1** ADJ mímico; (*pretended*) fingido, simulado.
2 N remedador *m*, -ora *f*, imitador *m*, -ora *f*.
3 VT remedar, imitar.

mimicry ['mɪmɪkrɪ] N imitación *f*, remedo *m*; (*Bio*) mimetismo *m*.

mimosa [mɪ'məʊzə] N mimosa *f*.

Min. (*Brit*) ABBR *of* **Ministry** Ministerio *m*, Min.

min. (a) ABBR *of* **minute(s)** minuto(s) *m(pl)*, m. (b) ABBR *of* **minimum**.

minaret [mɪnə'ret] N alminar *m*.

minatory ['mɪnətərɪ] ADJ (*liter*) amenazador.

mince [mɪns] **1** N (*Brit*) carne *f* picada.
2 VT (*Brit*) desmenuzar; *meat* picar; **she doesn't ~ her words** no tiene pelos en la lengua; **well, not to ~ matters** bueno, para decirlo francamente.
3 VI (*in walking*) andar con pasos menuditos; (*in talking*) hablar remilgadamente.

mincemeat ['mɪnsmiːt] N conserva *f* de picadillo de fruta; (*US*) carne *f* picada; **to make ~ of one's opponent** hacer trizas a su contrario, hacer picadillo a su contrario.

mince pie ['mɪns'paɪ] N pastel *m* de picadillo de fruta.

mincer ['mɪnsə^r] N máquina *f* de picar carne, picadora *f* de carne.

mincing ['mɪnsɪŋ] ADJ remilgado, afectado; *step* menudito.

mincing-machine ['mɪnsɪŋmə,ʃiːn] N máquina *f* de picar carne.

▼ **mind** [maɪnd] **1** N (a) **mente** *f*; (*intellect*) inteligencia *f*, entendimiento *m*; (*memory*) memoria *f*; (*contrasted with matter*) espíritu *m*; (*cast of ~*) mentalidad *f*; (*sanity, judgement*) juicio *m*; (*intention*) intención *f*, voluntad *f*; (*opinion*) opinión *f*, parecer *m*; (*leaning*) inclinación *f*; **~'s eye** imaginación *f*; **state of ~** estado *m* de ánimo; **of unsound ~** mentalmente incapacitado; **time out of ~** tiempo *m* inmemorial; **a triumph of ~ over matter** un triunfo de la inteligencia sobre la materia inerte; **to my ~** en mi opinión; **with one ~** unánimemente; **with an open ~** con espíritu amplio, sin prejuicios, sin ideas preconcebidas; **great ~s think alike** (*hum or iro*) los sabios siempre pensamos igual; **at the back of my ~ I had the feeling that ... tenía** la remota sensación de que ...; **it's all in the ~** son imaginaciones tuyas; **to be in one's right ~** estar en su cabal juicio; **nobody in his right ~ would do it** nadie en su cabal juicio lo haría; **she wrote it with publication in ~** lo escribió con la intención de publicarlo; **to be in two ~s** estar en la duda, no saber a qué carta quedarse (*about* en el asunto de); **I am not clear in my ~ about the incident** no recuerdo el incidente con entera claridad; **I am not clear in my ~ about the plan** no entiendo del todo el proyecto; **to be uneasy in one's ~** estar algo inquieto; **to be of one ~** ser unánimes, estar de acuerdo; **I was of the same ~ as my brother** yo compartía el criterio de mi hermano, mi hermano y yo éramos de la misma opinión; **what's on your ~?** ¿qué es lo que te preocupa?; **the child's death was much on his ~** le angustiaba muchísimo la muerte del niño; **to be out of one's ~** estar fuera de juicio, estar (como) loco; **you must be out of your ~!** ¿se te ha vuelto el juicio?

(b) (*verbal phrases*) **to bear sth in ~** tener algo presente; **I'll bear you in ~** me acordaré de ti, no te olvidaré; **we must bear (it) in ~ that ...** tenemos que recordar que ...; **we were bored out of our ~s** nos aburrimos horriblemente; **to bring** (*or* **call**) **sth to ~** recordar algo; **that calls sth else to ~** eso me trae otra cosa a la memoria; **to change one's ~** cambiar de opinión, mudar de parecer; **to change sb else's ~** hacer que otro cambie de opinión; **it came to my ~ that ...** se me ocurrió que ...; **it crossed my ~** se me ocurrió (*that* que); **yes, it had crossed my ~** sí, eso se me había ocurrido; **it never crossed** (*or* **entered**) **my ~** jamás se me pasó por la cabeza; **does it ever cross your ~ that ...?** ¿piensas alguna vez que ...?; **I can't get it out of my ~** eso no lo puedo quitar de la cabeza; **to give one's ~ to sth** aplicarse a algo; **to go out of one's ~** volverse loco; **to go over sth in one's ~** repasar algo mentalmente; **I have a good ~ to do it, I have half a ~ to do it** casi estoy por hacerlo, tengo ganas de hacerlo, por poco lo hago; **to have a closed ~** tener una mente cerrada; **to have sth in ~** pensar en algo, tener algo pensado; **to have one's ~ on a matter** tener su atención puesta en un asunto; **to have a ~ to** +*infin*, **to have it in ~ to** + *infin* pensar + *infin*, proponerse + *infin*; **whom have you in ~ for the job?** ¿a quién piensas dar el puesto?; **to have sth on one's ~** estar preocupado por algo; **to improve one's ~** edificar su espíritu, educarse, instruirse; **to keep sth in ~** V **to bear sth in ~**; **to keep an open ~ on a subject** evitar tener prejuicios acerca de un asunto; no opinar definitivamente, estar todavía sin decidirse acerca de un asunto; **to know one's own ~** saber lo que uno quiere; **to let one's ~ run on sth** dejar que la mente se distraiga en algo; **to lose one's ~** volverse loco; **to make up one's ~** resolverse, decidirse (*to* + *infin* a + *infin*); tomar partido; **we can't make up our ~s about the house** no nos decidimos a vender (*etc*) la casa; **I can't make up my ~ about him** todavía tengo ciertas dudas con respecto a él; **to pass out of ~** caer en el olvido; **he puts me in ~ of his father** recuerda a su padre, me hace pensar en su padre; **you can put that right out of your ~** conviene no pensar más en eso; **if you put your ~ to it** si te concentras en ello; **to read sb's ~** adivinar el pensamiento de uno; **to set one's ~ on sth** desear algo con vehemencia, estar resuelto a conseguir (*or* hacer *etc*) algo; **it slipped my ~** se me fue el santo al cielo, se me olvidó; **to speak one's ~** hablar con franqueza, hablar claro; **the thought that springs to ~ is ...** el pensamiento que se le ocurre a uno es ...; **she stuck in my ~** quedó grabada en mi recuerdo; **this will take your ~ off it** esto servirá para distraerte.

2 VT (a) (*pay attention to*) hacer caso de; fijarse en; preocuparse de; *rules etc* obedecer, guiarse por; *person etc* (*US**) obedecer; **never ~ him!** no le hagas caso!; **never ~ that!** no te preocupes por eso!; ¡deja eso ya!; **buy it and never ~ the expense** cómpralo sin hacer caso del coste; **I don't ~ the cold** el frío me trae sin cuidado, no me molesta el frío; **~ what you're doing!** ¡cuidado lo que haces!; **don't ~ me!** ¡no te ocupes de mí!; (*iro*) ¿y yo que estoy delante?; **~ what I say!** ¡escucha lo que te digo!; **~ you, I advierto que ~ you, it was raining at the time** hay que tener en cuenta que en ese momento llovía; **it was a big one, ~ you** era grande, eso sí.

▼(b) (*be put out by*) sentirse molesto por, tener inconveniente en; **do you ~ the noise?** ¿te molesta el ruido?; **I don't ~ 4, but 6 is too many** con 4 estoy bien, pero 6 son muchos; **I shouldn't ~ a cup of tea** no vendría mal una taza de té; **do you ~ coming with me?** ¿me hace el favor de acompañarme?; **would you ~ opening the door?** ¿me haces el favor de abrir la puerta?; **if you don't ~ my** (*or* **me**) **saying so, I think you're wrong** si me lo permites, creo que te equivocas; **I don't ~ having to wait** no tengo inconveniente en esperar, no me importa esperar.

(c) (*beware of*) tener cuidado con (*or* de); **~ the stairs!** ¡cuidado con la escalera!; **~ your language!** ¡cuida tu lengua!, ¡cuidado con lo que dices!

(d) (*oversee*) cuidar, vigilar, estar al cuidado de; *children etc* cuidar; *shop* ocuparse de, encargarse de; *machine* atender.

(e) (††, *: remember*) acordarse de, recordar; **I ~ the time when ...** me acuerdo de cuando ...

3 VI (a) (*worry, be concerned*) preocuparse; **never ~!** (*don't worry*) ¡no se preocupe!; (*pay no attention*) ¡no hagas caso!; (*it makes no odds*) ¡es igual!, ¡no importa!, ¡qué más da!; **'who's writing to you?' — 'never you ~'** '¿quién te escribe?' — 'es cosa mía'; **I can't walk, never ~ run** no puedo andar, ni menos correr; **he didn't do it, ~** pero en realidad no lo hizo, la verdad es que no lo hizo.

▼(b) (*be put out*) tener inconveniente; **I don't ~** me es igual, no tengo inconveniente; **do you ~?** ¿se puede?; **do you ~!** (*iro*) ¡por favor!; **a cigarette? - I don't ~** (*if I do*) ¿un cigarrillo? - pues muchas gracias (*or* bueno, no digo que no); **close the door, if you don't ~** haz el favor de cerrar la puerta; **do you ~ if I come?** ¿te importa que yo venga?; **do you ~ if I open the window?** ¿te molesta que abra la ventana?; **if you don't ~, I won't come** si no te importa, yo no vengo.

(c) (*be careful*) tener cuidado; **~!** ¡cuidado!; **~ you don't get wet!** ¡cuidado con mojarte!, ¡ten cuidado de no mojarte!; **~ you do it!** ¡hazlo sin falta!, ¡no dejes de hacerlo!; **~ how you go!** (*as farewell*) ¡cuídate!

◆ **mind out*** VI: **~ out!** ¡cuidado!, ¡atención!; **~ out or you'll break it!** ¡cuidado o lo rompes!

mind-bender* ['maɪndˌbendəʳ] N (*US*) (a) (*drug*) alucinógeno *m*, droga *f* alucinogénica. (b) (*revelation*) noticia *f* (*or* escena *etc*) alucinante*.

mind-bending* ['maɪndˌbendɪŋ] ADJ, **mind-blowing*** ['maɪndˌbləʊɪŋ] ADJ, **mind-boggling*** ['maɪndˌbɒɡlɪŋ] ADJ increíble; detonante*, alucinante*.

minded ['maɪndɪd] ADJ: **if you are so ~** si estás dispuesto a hacerlo, si quieres hacerlo.

-minded ['maɪndɪd] ADJ *ending in compounds* de mente ..., de mentalidad ... inclinado a ..., interesado en ..., consciente de ...; **fair~** imparcial; **an industrially~ nation** una nación consciente de sus industrias, una nación que se dedica a la industria; **a romantically~ girl** una joven de pensamientos románticos, una joven con ideas románticas.

minder* ['maɪndəʳ] N guardaespaldas *m*; acompañante *m*; escolta *m*.

mind-expanding ['maɪndɪksˌpændɪŋ] ADJ *drug* visionario.

mindful ['maɪndfʊl] ADJ: **~ of** consciente de, atento a; **we must be ~ of the risks** hay que tener presentes los riesgos, acordémonos de los riesgos.

mind game ['maɪndɡeɪm] N juego *m* psicológico.

mindless ['maɪndlɪs] ADJ (a) (*stupid*) estúpido, fútil; **the ~ masses** las masas que no piensan; **~ violence** violencia *f* inmotivada. (b) **~ of** indiferente a, inconsciente de.

mind-reader ['maɪndˌriːdəʳ] N adivinador *m*, -ora *f* de pensamientos.

mind-reading ['maɪndˌriːdɪŋ] N adivinación *f* de pensamientos.

mindset ['maɪndset] N actitud *f*, disposición *f*.

mine¹ [maɪn] POSS PRON (el) mío, (la) mía *etc*; **~ and thine** lo mío y lo tuyo; **this car is ~** este coche es mío, éste es mi coche; **is this ~?** ¿es mío esto?; **his friends and ~** sus amigos y los míos; **I have what is ~** tengo lo que es mío; **a friend of ~** un amigo mío, uno de mis amigos; **it's no business of ~** no tiene que ver conmigo; **be ~!** († *or hum*) ¡cásate conmigo!; **I want to make her ~** quiero que sea mi mujer.

mine² [maɪn] **1** N (a) (*Min*) mina *f*; **to work a ~** explotar una mina. (b) (*Mil, Naut etc*) mina *f*; **to lay ~s** sembrar minas; **to sweep ~s** dragar minas, barrer minas. (c) (*fig*) tesoro *m*, pozo *m*; **the book is a ~ of information** el libro es un tesoro de datos útiles.

2 VT (a) *coal, metal* extraer, explotar. (b) (*Mil, Naut*) *channel, road* sembrar minas en; proteger con minas; *ship* hundir con (*or* por medio de) una mina.

3 VI extraer minerales; dedicarse a la minería; **to ~ for tin** buscar estaño abriendo una mina; explotar los yacimientos de estaño.

mine-detector ['maɪndɪˌtektəʳ] N detector *m* de minas.

minefield ['maɪnfiːld] N campo *m* de minas, terreno *m* minado (*also fig*).

minelayer ['maɪnˌleɪəʳ] N minador *m*.

miner ['maɪnəʳ] N minero *m*.

mineral ['mɪnərəl] **1** ADJ mineral; **~ rights** derechos *mpl* al subsuelo; **~ water** agua *f* mineral, (*Brit: loosely*) gaseosa *f*. **2** N mineral *m*.

mineralogist [ˌmɪnəˈrælədʒɪst] N mineralogista *mf*.

mineralogy [ˌmɪnəˈrælədʒɪ] N mineralogía *f*.

Minerva [mɪˈnɜːvə] NF Minerva.

mineshaft ['maɪnʃɑːft] N pozo *m* de mina.

minestrone [ˌmɪnɪˈstrəʊnɪ] N minestrone *f*.

minesweeper ['maɪnˌswiːpəʳ] N dragaminas *m*, barreminas *m*.

mingle ['mɪŋɡl] **1** VT mezclar (*with* con).

2 VI mezclarse; (*become indistinguishable*) confundirse (*in, with* con); **he ~d with people of all classes** se asociaba con personas de todas las clases, vivía con personas de todas las clases.

mingy* ['mɪndʒɪ] ADJ *person* tacaño; *amount, size* escaso, insuficiente, pobre.
Mini ['mɪnɪ] N (*Aut*) Mini *m*.
mini ['mɪnɪ] N (*skirt*) minifalda *f*, mini *f*.
mini... ['mɪnɪ] PREF mini..., micro...
miniature ['mɪnɪtʃəʳ] [1] N miniatura *f*; modelo *m* pequeño; **in ~** en miniatura, en pequeña escala.
[2] ADJ (en) miniatura; **~ golf** golf *m* miniatura; **~ poodle** perro *m* de lanas miniatura; **~ railway** ferrocarril *m* miniatura; **~ submarine** submarino *m* de bolsillo; **~ watches** relojes *mpl* miniatura.
miniaturization [ˌmɪnɪtʃəraɪˈzeɪʃən] N miniaturización *f*.
miniaturize ['mɪnɪtʃəraɪz] VT miniaturizar.
minibar ['mɪnɪbɑːʳ] N minibar *m*.
minibudget ['mɪnɪˌbʌdʒɪt] N presupuesto *m* interino.
minibus ['mɪnɪbʌs] N microbús *m*.
minicab ['mɪnɪkæb] N (*Brit*) (micro)taxi *m*.
minicomputer [ˌmɪnɪkəmˈpjuːtəʳ] N miniordenador *m*, minicomputadora *f*.
minicourse ['mɪnɪˌkɔːs] N (*US*) cursillo *m*.
minidress ['mɪnɪdres] N minivestido *m*.
minim ['mɪnɪm] N blanca *f*.
minimal ['mɪnɪml] ADJ mínimo.
minimalism ['mɪnɪməlɪzəm] N minimalismo *m*.
minimalist ['mɪnɪməlɪst] [1] ADJ minimalista.
[2] N minimalista *mf*.
minimally ['mɪnɪməlɪ] ADV mínimamente; **he was paid, but only ~** le pagaron, pero sólo lo mínimo; **I was ~ successful** tuve un éxito mínimo, apenas tuve éxito.
minimarket ['mɪnɪˌmɑːkɪt] N, **minimart** ['mɪnɪmɑːt] N autoservicio *m*.
minimize ['mɪnɪmaɪz] VT minimizar; aminorar, minorizar, empequeñecer.
minimum ['mɪnɪməm] [1] ADJ mínimo; **~ lending rate** tipo *m* de interés mínimo; **~ wage** salario *m* mínimo.
[2] N, PL **minima** ['mɪnɪmə] mínimo *m*, mínimum *m*; **at the ~** como mínimo; **(down) to the ~** al mínimo; **down to a ~ of 5 degrees** hasta 5 grados como mínimum; **to keep costs down to a (*or* the) ~** mantener los costos en el nivel más bajo posible.
mining ['maɪnɪŋ] [1] N **(a)** (*Min*) minería *f*; explotación *f*, extracción *f*. **(b)** (*Mil*) minado *m*.
[2] ATTR *area, industry, town* minero; *engineer* de minas.
minion ['mɪnjən] N (*favourite*) favorito *m*, -a *f*; (*royal favourite*) privado *m*, valido *m*; (*follower*) secuaz *m*; (*servant*) paniaguado *m*.
minipill ['mɪnɪˌpɪl] N minipíldora *f*.
miniscule ['mɪnɪsˌkjuːl] = **minuscule**.
miniseries ['mɪnɪˌsɪərɪz] N, PL **miniseries** (*TV*) miniserie *f*.
miniskirt ['mɪnɪskɜːt] N minifalda *f*.
minister ['mɪnɪstəʳ] [1] N **(a)** (*Brit Pol etc*) ministro *m*, -a *f* (*for, of* de). **(b)** (*Eccl*) pastor *m*; *ver también* CHURCH OF ENGLAND, CHURCH OF SCOTLAND .
[2] VI: **to ~ to sb** atender a uno; **to ~ to sb's needs** ayudar a uno dándole lo que necesita, satisfacer las necesidades de uno; **to ~ to a result** contribuir a un resultado.
ministerial [ˌmɪnɪsˈtɪərɪəl] ADJ ministerial, de ministro; **~ crisis** crisis *f* de gobierno.
ministration [ˌmɪnɪsˈtreɪʃən] N ayuda *f*, agencia *f*, servicio *m*; (*Eccl*) ministerio *m*.
ministry ['mɪnɪstrɪ] N **(a)** (*Pol*) ministerio *m* (*for, of* de), secretaría *f* (*LAm*). **(b)** (*Eccl*) sacerdocio *m*; **to enter the ~** hacerse sacerdote, (*Protestant*) hacerse pastor.
minium ['mɪnɪəm] N minio *m*.
mink [mɪŋk] [1] N (*Zool*) visón *m*; (*fur*) piel *f* de visón.
[2] ATTR: **~ cape** estola *f* de visón; **~ coat** abrigo *m* de visón.
Minn. (*US*) ABBR of **Minnesota**.
minnow ['mɪnəʊ] N pececillo *m* (*de agua dulce*).
minor ['maɪnəʳ] [1] ADJ menor (*also Eccl, Mus etc*); (*under age*) menor de edad; *writer etc* de segundo orden, secundario; *operation* pequeño, sin trascendencia; *detail* sin importancia; *role, position* secundario, de categoría inferior; **Smith ~** (*Brit Scol*) Smith el joven; **G ~** sol *m* menor; **~ third** tercera *f* menor; **~ ailment** enfermedad *f* benigna; **~ offence, ~ offense** (*US*) delito *m* de menor cuantía.
[2] N **(a)** (*Jur*) menor *mf* de edad. **(b)** (*US Univ*) asignatura *f* secundaria.
[3] VI: **to ~ in Spanish** (*US Univ*) estudiar el español como asignatura secundaria.
Minorca [mɪˈnɔːkə] N Menorca *f*.
minority [maɪˈnɒrɪtɪ] [1] N minoría *f*; (*age*) minoridad *f*, menor edad *f*; **to be in a ~** estar en la minoría; **you are in a ~ of one** Vd es el único que piensa así.
[2] ATTR: **~ government** gobierno *m* minoritario; **~ interest** participación *f* minoritaria; **~ language** lengua *f* minoritaria; **~ shareholding** accionado *m* minoritario.

MINORITY	*see also main entry*

Singular or plural verb?
When *minoría* is the subject of a verb, the verb can be in the singular or the plural, depending on the context:
● Put the verb in the singular if *minority* is seen as a unit rather than a collection of individuals:
A minority should always be respected, however small it may be
Una minoría, aunque sea pequeña, debe ser respetada siempre
● If *la minoría* is seen as a collection of individuals, particularly when it is followed by *de* + PLURAL NOUN, the plural form of the verb is more common than the singular, though both are possible:
A minority of agitators want to introduce anarchy
Una minoría de agitadores quieren or *quiere traer la anarquía*
● The plural form must be used when *la minoría* or *la minoría de* + PLURAL NOUN is followed by *ser* or *estar* + PLURAL COMPLEMENT:
Only a minority of the demonstrators were students
Sólo una minoría de los manifestantes eran estudiantes
For further uses and examples, see main entry.

Minotaur ['maɪnətɔːʳ] N Minotauro *m*.
minster ['mɪnstəʳ] N catedral *f*; iglesia *f* de un monasterio.
minstrel ['mɪnstrəl] N juglar *m*; cantor *m*.
minstrelsy ['mɪnstrəlsɪ] N (*music*) música *f*; (*song*) canto *m*; (*art of epic minstrel*) juglaría *f*; (*art of lyric minstrel*) gaya ciencia *f*.
mint[1] [mɪnt] [1] N casa *f* de moneda; ceca *f*; **Royal M~** (*Brit*) Real Casa *f* de la Moneda; **to be worth a ~** (*of money*) valer un potosí.
[2] ADJ *stamp etc* nuevo, en nuevo, sin usar; **in ~ condition** en perfecto estado, sin estrenar.
[3] VT *coin* acuñar; *phrase etc* idear, inventar.
mint[2] [mɪnt] [1] N (*Bot*) hierbabuena *f*, menta *f*; (*sweet*) pastilla *f* de menta.
[2] ATTR: **~ julep** (*US*) julepe *m* de menta, (bebida *f* de) whisky *m* con menta; **~ sauce** salsa *f* de menta; **~ tea** té *m* a la menta.
minuet [ˌmɪnjʊˈet] N minué *m*.
minus ['maɪnəs] [1] PREP **(a)** menos; **9 ~ 6** 9 menos 6.
(b) (*without, deprived of*) sin, desprovisto de, falto de; **he appeared ~ his trousers** apareció sin pantalón.
[2] ADJ menos; negativo; **~ sign** signo *m* menos.
[3] N (*sign*) signo *m* menos; (*amount*) cantidad *f* negativa.
minuscule ['mɪnəskjuːl] ADJ minúsculo.
minute[1] ['mɪnɪt] [1] N **(a)** (*of degree, time*) minuto *m*; (*fig*) momento *m*, instante *m*; **at the last ~** a última hora; **at 6 o'clock to the ~** a las 6 en punto; **I'll come in a ~** vengo al momento, vengo dentro de un momento; **it was all over in a ~** todo esto ocurrió en un instante; **this very ~** ahora mismo; **they were on the scene within ~s** llegaron a la escena dentro de pocos minutos; **every ~ counts** no hay tiempo que perder; **to leave things until the last ~** dejar las cosas hasta última hora; **up to the ~ news** noticias *fpl* de última hora; **tell me the ~ he comes** avíseme en cuanto venga; **I shan't be a ~** vuelvo (*or* termino *etc*) muy pronto; **we expect him any ~** le esperamos de un momento a otro; **it won't take 5 ~s** es cosa de pocos minutos; **wait a ~!** ¡un momento!
(b) (*draft*) borrador *m*, proyecto *m*, minuta *f*; (*note*) nota *f*, apuntación *f*; **~s** (*of meeting*) acta *f*, actas *fpl*; **to write up the ~s of a meeting** levantar acta de una reunión.
[2] ATTR: **~ hand** minutero *m*; **~ steak** biftec *m* pequeño (que se cuece rápidamente).
[3] VT *meeting* levantar acta de; *remarks* registrar, hacer constar; (*draft*) hacer el borrador de, minutar; **I would like to have that ~d** quiero que eso conste en acta.
minute[2] [maɪˈnjuːt] ADJ (*small*) diminuto, menudo, pequeño; *detail etc* insignificante; (*accurate, searching*) minucioso.
minute book ['mɪnɪtbʊk] N libro *m* de actas.
minutely [maɪˈnjuːtlɪ] ADV minuciosamente, con minuciosidad; **a ~ detailed account** un relato completo hasta en los más pequeños detalles; **anything ~ resembling a fish** cualquier cosa que tuviera el más ligero parecido con un pez.
minutiae [mɪˈnjuːʃiiː] NPL detalles *mpl* minuciosos.
minx [mɪŋks] N picaruela *f*, mujer *f* descarada; **you ~!** ¡lagarta!
Miocene ['maɪəsiːn] [1] ADJ mioceno. [2] N mioceno *m*.
MIPS [mɪps] NPL ABBR of **millions of instructions per second** millones *mpl* de instrucciones por segundo, MIPS *mpl*.
miracle ['mɪrəkl] [1] N milagro *m*; **by a ~, by some ~** por milagro; **it will be a ~ if ...** será un milagro si ...
[2] ATTR: **~ cure** remedio *m* milagro; **~ drug** droga *f* milagro; **~ play** milagro *m*, auto *m*; **I'm not some ~ worker, you know** yo no puedo hacer milagros.
miraculous [mɪˈrækjʊləs] ADJ milagroso.
miraculously [mɪˈrækjʊləslɪ] ADV milagrosamente, por milagro.
mirage ['mɪrɑːʒ] N espejismo *m* (*also fig*).

MIRAS ['maɪræs] N (*Brit*) ABBR *of* **mortgage interest relief at source**.
mire [maɪəʳ] **1** N fango *m*, lodo *m*.
    2 VT (*US*): **to get ~d in** quedar atascado en, quedar preso en.
mirror ['mɪrəʳ] **1** N espejo *m*; (*Aut*) retrovisor *m*; **to look at o.s. in the ~** mirarse en el (*or* al) espejo.
    2 ATTR: **~ image** reflejo *m* exacto, contraimagen *f*; **~ writing** escritura *f* invertida. **3** VT reflejar.
mirth [mɜ:θ] N alegría *f*, regocijo *m*; (*laughter*) risa *f*, risas *fpl*; **at this there was ~** en esto hubo risas; **there was some unseemly ~** se rieron algunos descaradamente.
mirthful ['mɜ:θfʊl] ADJ alegre.
mirthless ['mɜ:θlɪs] ADJ triste, sin alegría.
miry ['maɪrɪ] ADJ fangoso, lodoso; **~ place** lodazal *m*.
MIS N ABBR *of* **management information system** sistema *m* informativo de dirección.
misadventure [,mɪsəd'ventʃəʳ] N desgracia *f*, percance *m*, accidente *m*; **death by ~** muerte *f* accidental.
misalliance [,mɪsə'laɪəns] N casamiento *m* inconveniente, casamiento *m* desigual.
misanthrope ['mɪzənθrəʊp] N misántropo *m*.
misanthropic [,mɪzən'θrɒpɪk] ADJ misantrópico.
misanthropist [mɪ'zænθrəpɪst] N misántropo *m*.
misanthropy [mɪ'zænθrəpɪ] N misantropía *f*.
misapplication ['mɪs,æplɪ'keɪʃn] N mala aplicación *f*, aplicación *f* errónea; abuso *m*.
misapply ['mɪsə'plaɪ] VT aplicar mal; abusar de.
misapprehend ['mɪs,æprɪ'hend] VT comprender mal.
misapprehension ['mɪs,æprɪ'henʃən] N equivocación *f*, error *m*, concepto *m* erróneo; **to be under a ~** estar equivocado; **there seems to be some ~** parece haber algún malentendido.
misappropriate ['mɪsə'prəʊprɪeɪt] VT malversar.
misappropriation ['mɪsə,prəʊprɪ'eɪʃn] N malversación *f*, distracción *f* de fondos.
misbegotten ['mɪsbɪ'gɒtn] ADJ bastardo, ilegítimo; *plan etc* descabellado, llamado a fracasar.
misbehave ['mɪsbɪ'heɪv] VI portarse mal; (*child*) ser malo.
misbehaviour, (*US*) **misbehavior** ['mɪsbɪ'heɪvjəʳ] N mala conducta *f*.
misc. ABBR *of* **miscellaneous**.
miscalculate ['mɪs'kælkjʊleɪt] VTI calcular mal.
miscalculation ['mɪs,kælkjʊ'leɪʃən] N cálculo *m* erróneo; (*fig*) error *m*, desacierto *m*.
miscall ['mɪs'kɔ:l] VT llamar equivocadamente.
miscarriage ['mɪs,kærɪdʒ] N (**a**) (*Med*) aborto *m* espontáneo, malparto *m*. (**b**) (*failure*) fracaso *m*, malogro *m*; (*of letter, goods*) extravío *m*; **~ of justice** error *m* judicial, injusticia *f*.
miscarry [mɪs'kærɪ] VI (**a**) (*Med*) malparir, abortar. (**b**) (*fail*) fracasar, salir mal, frustrarse; (*letter, goods*) extraviarse.
miscast [,mɪs'kɑːst] VT (*irr*: *V* **cast**) *actor* dar un papel poco apropiado a; *play* distribuir mal los papeles de; **he was ~ as Othello** como Otelo tuvo un papel que no le convenía.
miscegenation [,mɪsɪdʒɪ'neɪʃən] N mestizaje *m*, cruce *m* de razas.
miscellaneous [,mɪsɪ'leɪnɪəs] ADJ vario, diverso; **~ expenses** gastos *mpl* diversos.
miscellany [mɪ'selənɪ] N miscelánea *f*.
mischance [mɪs'tʃɑːns] N mala suerte *f*; infortunio *m*, desgracia *f*; **by some ~** por desgracia.
mischief ['mɪstʃɪf] N (**a**) (*naughtiness*) travesura *f*, diablura *f*; (*roguishness*) malicia *f*; **he's up to some ~** está haciendo alguna travesura; **there's some ~ going on** están tramando algo mal; **there's no ~ in him** no es capaz de ninguna maldad; **he's always getting into ~** anda siempre metido en alguna travesura; **to keep sb out of ~** impedir a uno hacer travesuras; **to make ~** armar líos; **to make ~ for sb** crear dificultades para uno, amargar la vida a uno.
(**b**) (*person*) diablillo *m*.
(**c**) (*harm*) mal *m*, daño *m*; **to do sb a ~** hacer mal a uno; **to do o.s. a ~** hacerse daño.
mischief-maker ['mɪstʃɪf,meɪkəʳ] N revoltoso *m*, -a *f*, persona *f* turbulenta, persona *f* que anda metida en líos; chismoso *m*, -a *f*.
mischievous ['mɪstʃɪvəs] ADJ *person* malo, dañoso; (*playful*) malicioso, juguetón; *child* travieso; *attack etc* perjudicial; *glance etc* malicioso, lleno de malicia.
mischievously ['mɪstʃɪvəslɪ] ADV maliciosamente, con malicia; por travesura.
mischievousness ['mɪstʃɪvəsnɪs] N travesuras *fpl*.
misconceive ['mɪskən'siːv] VT entender mal, juzgar mal; **a ~d plan** un proyecto descabellado.
misconception ['mɪskən'sepʃən] N concepto *m* erróneo, idea *f* falsa, equivocación *f*; **but this is a ~** pero esta idea es errónea.
misconduct [mɪs'kɒndʌkt] **1** N mala conducta *f*; extravío *m*; (*sexual*) adulterio *m*.
    2 [,mɪskən'dʌkt] VT manejar mal, dirigir mal.

    3 [,mɪskən'dʌkt] VR: **to ~ o.s.** portarse mal.
misconstruction ['mɪskəns'trʌkʃən] N mala interpretación *f*; mala traducción *f*; (*deliberate*) tergiversación *f*.
misconstrue ['mɪskən'struː] VT interpretar mal; traducir mal; (*deliberately*) tergiversar.
miscount ['mɪs'kaʊnt] **1** VT contar mal, equivocarse en la cuenta de.
    2 VI contar mal.
miscreant ['mɪskrɪənt] N sinvergüenza *mf*, bellaco *m*, -a *f*.
misdeal ['mɪs'diːl] **1** N reparto *m* erróneo.
    2 (*irr*: *V* **deal**) VT *cards* dar mal, repartir mal.
misdeed ['mɪs'diːd] N delito *m*, crimen *m*, fechoría *f*.
misdemeanour, (*US*) **misdemeanor** [,mɪsdɪ'miːnəʳ] N ofensa *f*, delito *m*; (*Brit Jur*) delito *m* de menor cuantía, falta *f*.
misdirect ['mɪsdɪ'rekt] VT *operation etc* manejar mal, dirigir mal; *letter etc* poner unas señas incorrectas a; *person* informar mal (acerca del camino a tomar), hacer perder el camino; *jury* instruir mal.
misdirection ['mɪsdɪ'rekʃən] N mal manejo *m*, mala dirección *f*; instrucciones *fpl* erróneas, información *f* errónea.
miser ['maɪzəʳ] N avaro *m*, -a *f*, avariento *m*, -a *f*, tacaño *m*, -a *f*.
miserable ['mɪzərəbl] ADJ (**a**) (*filthy, wretched*) indecente, vil; (*contemptible*) vil, despreciable; (*valueless*) sin valor; *show, spectacle* de pena; *weather* muy feo, de perros; *wage* raquítico; **it was a ~ failure** fue un rotundo fracaso.
(**b**) (*unhappy*) triste, desdichado, desgraciado; abatido; **what are you so ~ about?** ¿por qué estás tan triste?; **I feel ~ today** hoy me siento abatido; hoy me siento sin fuerzas para nada; **to make sb ~** entristecer a uno, abatir a uno; **to make sb's life ~** amargar la vida a uno.
miserably ['mɪzərəblɪ] ADV *say etc* tristemente; **~ small** lamentablemente pequeño; **~ paid** muy mal pagado; **it failed ~** fracasó rotundamente; **they played ~** jugaron terriblemente mal.
misère [mɪ'zeəʳ] N (*Cards*) nulos *mpl*; **to go ~** jugar a nulos.
miserliness ['maɪzəlɪnɪs] N avaricia *f*, tacañería *f*.
miserly ['maɪzəlɪ] ADJ *person* avariento, tacaño; *amount* muy pequeño, pobre.
misery ['mɪzərɪ] N (**a**) (*suffering*) sufrimiento *m*; (*sadness*) pena *f*, tristeza *f*; (*wretchedness*) aflicción *f*, desdicha *f*; (*squalor*) miseria *f*, sordidez *f*; **a life of ~** una vida desgraciada; **to make sb's life a ~** amargar la vida a uno; **to live in ~** vivir en la miseria; **to put an animal out of its ~** acortar la agonía a un animal, rematar un animal; **to put sb out of his ~** (*fig*) satisfacer por fin a uno (contándole una noticia *or* revelándole un secreto *etc*).
(**b**) (**: person*) aguafiestas *mf*, quejicoso* *m*, -a *f*.
misfile [,mɪs'faɪl] VT *papers* clasificar incorrectamente.
misfire ['mɪs'faɪəʳ] VI fallar.
misfit ['mɪsfɪt] N (**a**) cosa *f* mal ajustada; (*dress*) traje *m* que no cae bien.
(**b**) (*person*) inadaptado *m*, -a *f*, desplazado *m*, -a *f*, persona *f* reñida con su ambiente; **he's always been a ~ here** no se ha adaptado nunca a las condiciones de aquí, en ningún momento ha estado realmente contento aquí.
misfortune [mɪs'fɔːtʃən] N desgracia *f*, infortunio *m*, desventura *f*; **companion in ~** compañero *m*, -a *f* en la desgracia, compañero *m*, -a *f* de infortunio; **it is his ~ that he is lame** tiene la mala suerte de ser cojo; **I had the ~ to meet him** tuve la mala suerte de encontrarme con él.
misgiving [mɪs'gɪvɪŋ] N (*mistrust*) recelo *m*, duda *f*, temor *m*; (*apprehension*) presentimiento *m*; **not without some ~** no sin cierto recelo; **I had ~s about the scheme** tuve mis dudas acerca del proyecto.
misgovern ['mɪs'gʌvən] VTI gobernar mal; administrar mal.
misgovernment ['mɪs'gʌvənmənt] N desgobierno *m*, mal gobierno *m*; mala administración *f*.
misguided ['mɪs'gaɪdɪd] ADJ mal aconsejado, equivocado.
misguidedly ['mɪs'gaɪdɪdlɪ] ADV equivocadamente.
mishandle ['mɪs'hændl] VT manejar mal, administrar mal.
mishandling [,mɪs'hændlɪŋ] N mal manejo *m*, mala administración *f*.
mishap ['mɪshæp] N desgracia *f*, contratiempo *m*, accidente *m*; **without ~** sin novedad; **to have a ~** tener un accidente.
mishear ['mɪs'hɪəʳ] (*irr*: *V* **hear**) VTI oír mal.
mishit **1** ['mɪs,hɪt] N golpe *m* defectuoso. **2** [,mɪs'hɪt] VT golpear mal.
mishmash ['mɪʃmæʃ] N masa *f* informe, masa *f* confusa; baturrillo *m*, ensaladilla *f*.
misinform ['mɪsɪn'fɔːm] VT informar mal, malinformar, dar informes erróneos a.
misinformation [,mɪsɪnfə'meɪʃən] N desinformación *f*; mala información *f*.
misinterpret ['mɪsɪn'tɜːprɪt] VT interpretar mal, malinterpretar; traducir mal; (*deliberately*) tergiversar.
misinterpretation ['mɪsɪn,tɜːprɪ'teɪʃən] N mala interpretación *f*; mala traducción *f*; tergiversación *f*.
misjudge ['mɪs'dʒʌdʒ] VT juzgar mal, equivocarse sobre.

misjudgement [ˌmɪsˈdʒʌdʒmənt] N juicio *m* erróneo.

mislay [mɪsˈleɪ] (*irr. V* **lay⁴**) VT extraviar, perder.

mislead [mɪsˈliːd] (*irr. V* **lead²**) VT llevar a conclusiones erróneas, despistar; (*deliberately*) engañar; (*morally*) corromper, llevar por mal camino; **I fear you have been misled** me temo que se lo hayan dicho mal.

misleading [mɪsˈliːdɪŋ] ADJ erróneo; (*deliberately*) de apariencia engañosa, engañoso.

mismanage [ˈmɪsˈmænɪdʒ] VT manejar mal, administrar mal, gobernar mal.

mismanagement [ˈmɪsˈmænɪdʒmənt] N mal manejo *m*, mala administración *f*, desgobierno *m*; incuria *f*.

mismatch [ˈmɪsˈmætʃ] VT emparejar mal, hermanar mal.

misname [ˈmɪsˈneɪm] VT llamar equivocadamente; **this grotesquely ~d society** esta sociedad con su nombre grotescamente inapropiado.

misnomer [ˈmɪsˈnəʊməʳ] N nombre *m* equivocado, nombre *m* inapropiado; denominación *f* errónea; **that is a ~** ese nombre es impropio.

misogamist [mɪˈsɒɡəmɪst] N misógamo *m*, -a *f*.

misogamy [mɪˈsɒɡəmɪ] N misogamia *f*.

misogynist [mɪˈsɒdʒɪnɪst] N misógino *m*.

misogyny [mɪˈsɒdʒɪnɪ] N misoginia *f*.

misplace [ˈmɪsˈpleɪs] VT (a) colocar mal; poner fuera de su lugar. (b) (*lose*) extraviar, perder.

misplaced [ˈmɪsˈpleɪst] ADJ equivocado; inoportuno; inmerecido; descolocado.

misprint [ˈmɪsprɪnt] ① N errata *f*, error *m* de imprenta.
② [mɪsˈprɪnt] VT imprimir mal.

mispronounce [ˈmɪsprəˈnaʊns] VT pronunciar mal.

mispronunciation [ˈmɪsprəˌnʌnsɪˈeɪʃən] N mala pronunciación *f*.

misquotation [ˈmɪskwəʊˈteɪʃən] N cita *f* equivocada.

misquote [ˈmɪsˈkwəʊt] VT citar mal; **he was ~d in the press** le citaron mal en la prensa.

misread [ˈmɪsˈriːd] (*irr. V* **read**) VT leer mal; interpretar mal.

misrepresent [ˈmɪsˌreprɪˈzent] VT desfigurar, falsificar; describir engañosamente; tergiversar; **he was ~ed in the papers** los informes de los periódicos falsificaron lo que había dicho.

misrepresentation [ˈmɪsˌreprɪzenˈteɪʃən] N desfiguración *f*; falsificación *f*; descripción *f* engañosa; tergiversación *f*; (*Jur*) falsa declaración *f*; **this report is a ~ of what I said** este informe falsifica lo que yo dije.

misrule [ˈmɪsˈruːl] ① N desgobierno *m*, mal gobierno *m*.
② VT desgobernar, gobernar mal.

miss¹ [mɪs] ① N (*shot*) tiro *m* errado, tiro *m* perdido; (*mistake*) error *m*, desacierto *m*; (*failure*) fracaso *m*; **a ~ is as good as a mile** lo mismo da librarse por poco que por mucho; **near ~** (*Aer*) incidente *m* aéreo, air-miss *m*, aproximación *f* peligrosa entre dos aviones; **it was a near ~** (el tiro) anduvo muy cerca; **it was a near ~ with that car** faltó poco para que ese coche chocara con nosotros; **to give sth a ~** (*not go*) dejar de asistir a algo, no asistir a algo, (*not visit*) dejar de visitar algo; **we're giving it a ~ this year** este año no vamos.
② VT (a) (*fail to hit*) *aim, target* errar; **the shot just ~ed me** por poco la bala me alcanzó, el tiro me pasó rozando; **the plane just ~ed the tower** faltó poco para que el avión chocara con la torre; **he narrowly ~ed being run over** por poco le atropellan, faltó poco para que se le atropellara.
(b) (*fail to find, catch, use etc*) *vocation* errar, equivocarse en la elección de; *solution* no acertar; *thing sought* no encontrar; *bus, train, chance, footing etc* perder; *one's way* equivocarse de; *class, lecture* perder; *appointment* no acudir a; *meeting etc* no asistir a, no poder asistir a; **you haven't ~ed much!** ¡no has perdido nada!; **we ~ed the tide** perdimos la pleamar; **we're afraid of ~ing the market** tememos perder el momento más propicio para la venta; **she ~ed her holiday last year** el año pasado no pudo tomarse las vacaciones; **I ~ed you at the station** no te vi en la estación; **they ~ed each other in the crowd** no lograron encontrarse entre tanta gente; **you mustn't ~ this film** no debes perderte esta película, no dejes de ver esta película; **don't ~ the Prado** no dejes de visitar el Prado; **you can't ~ the house** es imposible equivocarse al venir a la casa.
(c) (*fail to hear*) **I ~ed what you said** se me escapó lo que dijiste; **I ~ed that** eso no lo entendí; **you're ~ing the point** no comprendes el punto principal.
(d) (*omit*) omitir; (*overlook*) pasar por alto; **let's ~ the next dance** no bailemos la próxima vez.
(e) (*notice absence of, regret absence of*) echar de menos; notar la falta de; **I ~ the old trams** echo de menos los viejos tranvías; **I ~ you so** te echo mucho de menos, te extraño mucho (*esp LAm*); **he is much ~ed** se le echa mucho de menos; **then I ~ed my wallet** luego me di cuenta de que no tenía ya cartera; **he won't be ~ed** bien podemos prescindir de él; **we're ~ing 8 dollars** nos faltan 8 dólares; **do take it, I shan't ~ it** tómalo, no me hace falta.
③ VI (*shot, person*) errar el blanco, errar el tiro, fallar; (*motor*) fallar;

he ~ed erró el tiro; **he never ~es** siempre acierta; **you can't ~!** ¡es imposible fallar!; **I've not ~ed once in 10 years** en 10 años no he faltado ni una sola vez.
◆**miss out** VT: **he ~ed out a word** omitió una palabra; **he was ~ed out in the promotions** en los ascensos le pasaron por encima.
◆**miss out on** VT perder, dejar pasar, no aprovechar; perder la oportunidad de (*or para*).

miss² [mɪs] N señorita *f*; (*) niña *f* precoz, niña *f* repipi; **a modern ~** una señorita moderna; **M~ Jennie Smith** (la) Señorita Jennie Smith; **yes, M~ Smith** sí, señorita; **M~ Spain 1999** Miss España 1999. *See also* MR, MRS, MISS .

Miss. (*US*) ABBR *of* **Mississippi**.

missal [ˈmɪsəl] N misal *m*.

misshapen [ˈmɪsˈʃeɪpən] ADJ deforme.

missile [ˈmɪsaɪl] N proyectil *m*; (*javelin etc*) arma *f* arrojadiza; (*modern weapon*) misil *m*.

missile base [ˈmɪsaɪlˌbeɪs] N base *f* de misiles.

missile-launcher [ˈmɪsaɪlˌlɔːntʃəʳ] N lanzamisiles *m*, lanzadera *f* de misiles.

missing [ˈmɪsɪŋ] ADJ (a) *person* ausente, (*Mil etc*) desaparecido; *thing* perdido, extraviado, que falta; **~ in action** desaparecido en combate; **~ link** eslabón *m* perdido, eslabón *m* hipotético; **~ person** desaparecido *m*, -a *f*; **supply the ~ letters** poner las letras que faltan; **the three ~ students are safe** los tres estudiantes desaparecidos están a salvo.
(b) **to be ~** faltar; haber desaparecido; **there are 9 books ~, 9 books are ~** faltan 9 libros; **how many are ~?** ¿cuántos faltan?; **two members of the crew are still ~** dos miembros de la tripulación siguen desaparecidos; **one of our aircraft is ~** uno de nuestros aviones no ha vuelto.

mission [ˈmɪʃən] ① N misión *f*; **to send sb on a secret ~** enviar a uno en misión secreta.
② ATTR: **~ control** centro *m* de control; **~ controller** controlador *m*, -ora *f* de (la) misión; **~ statement** declaración *f* de objetivos, declaración *f* de fines.

missionary [ˈmɪʃənrɪ] ① ADJ *zeal etc* misional, misionero; **~ position** (*hum*) postura *f* del misionero; **~ society** sociedad *f* misionera.
② N misionero *m*, -a *f*.

missis* [ˈmɪsɪz] N: **my ~, the ~** la parienta*; **John and his ~** Juan y su costilla; **yes, ~** sí, señora; **is the ~ in?** ¿está la señora?

Mississippi [ˌmɪsɪˈsɪpɪ] N Misisipí *m*.

missive [ˈmɪsɪv] N misiva *f*.

Missouri [mɪˈzʊərɪ] N Misuri *m*.

misspell [ˈmɪsˈspel] (*irr. V* **spell**) VT escribir mal.

misspelling [ˈmɪsˈspelɪŋ] N error *m* de ortografía.

misspend [ˈmɪsˈspend] (*irr. V* **spend**) VT malgastar, desperdiciar, perder; **a misspent youth** una juventud mal empleada, una juventud pasada en la disipación.

misstate [ˈmɪsˈsteɪt] VT declarar erróneamente; (*deliberately*) declarar falsamente.

misstatement [ˈmɪsˈsteɪtmənt] N declaración *f* errónea; declaración *f* falsa.

missus* [ˈmɪsɪz] N = **missis**.

missy* [ˈmɪsɪ] N (*hum or pej*) = **miss²**.

mist [mɪst] ① N (*fog*) niebla *f*; (*slight*) neblina *f*; (*summery; at sea*) bruma *f*; (*on window*) paño *m*, vaho *m*, velo *m*; (*fig*) nube *f*, velo *m*; **through a ~ of tears** por ojos llenos de lágrimas.
② VT (*fig*) empañar, velar.
③ VI (*also to ~ over, to ~ up*) empañarse, velarse; (*eyes*) llenarse de lágrimas.

mistakable [mɪsˈteɪkəbl] ADJ confundible.

▼ **mistake** [mɪsˈteɪk] ① N equivocación *f*, error *m*, falta *f*; **by ~** por equivocación, (*carelessly*) por descuido, (*involuntarily*) sin querer; **it's finished and no ~!** ¡ya lo creo que está terminado!; **he took my hat in ~ for his** confundió mi sombrero con el suyo; **to acknowledge one's ~** confesar su error; **the ~ is mine** la culpa es mía, la culpa la tengo yo; **there must be some ~** ha de haber algún error; **there's no ~ about it** está muy claro, no hay que darle vueltas; **let there be no ~ about it** entiéndase bien que ...; quede perfectamente claro que ...; **to make a ~** equivocarse; **you're making a big ~** te equivocas gravemente, es una decisión totalmente errónea; **make no ~ (about it)** no te hagas ilusiones, y que no queden dudas sobre esto; **to make the ~ of asking too much** cometer el error de pedir demasiado.
② (*irr. V* **take**) VT (a) *meaning* entender mal, equivocarse sobre; *road etc* equivocar, equivocarse de; **there was no mistaking his intention** su intención era clarísima; **you couldn't ~ her walk** no se podía confundir su manera de andar con la de otras.
(b) **to ~ A for B** equivocar A con B, confundir A con B.
(c) **to be ~n** equivocarse, estar equivocado, engañarse; **if I am not ~n** si no me equivoco; **he is often ~n for Peter** se le confunde muchas veces con Pedro; **it cannot possibly be ~n for anything else** es

imposible confundirlo con otra cosa.

mistaken [mɪsˈteɪkən] [1] PTP of **mistake**. [2] ADJ equivocado, erróneo; incorrecto; ~ **identity** identificación f errónea.

mistakenly [mɪsˈteɪkənlɪ] ADV equivocadamente, erróneamente.

mister [ˈmɪstəʳ] N (a) (gen abbr **Mr**) señor m (gen abbr **Sr**). (b) (*: in direct address) hey ~! ¡oiga, usted!; **got a light ~?** ¿tiene fuego, caballero?

mistime [ˈmɪsˈtaɪm] VT act etc hacer (or decir etc) a deshora, hacer en momento poco oportuno; race etc cronometrar mal.

mistle thrush [ˈmɪslθrʌʃ] N zorzal m charlo, tordo m mayor.

mistletoe [ˈmɪsltəʊ] N muérdago m.

mistook [mɪsˈtʊk] PRET of **mistake**.

mistral [mɪˈstrɑːl] N mistral m.

mistranslate [ˈmɪstrænsˈleɪt] VT traducir mal.

mistranslation [ˈmɪstrænsˈleɪʃən] N mala traducción f.

mistreat [mɪsˈtriːt] VT maltratar, tratar mal.

mistreatment [mɪsˈtriːtmənt] N maltrato m, maltratamiento m, malos tratos mpl.

mistress [ˈmɪstrɪs] N (a) (of house etc) señora f, ama f de casa; **to be ~ of the situation** ser dueña de la situación; **to be one's own ~** ser independiente; trabajar por cuenta propia. (b) (lover) querida f, amante f. (c) (Brit: teacher, primary) maestra f, (secondary) profesora f. (d) (abbr **Mrs** [ˈmɪsɪz]) señora f de ...

mistrial [ˌmɪsˈtraɪəl] N (US, Brit) juicio m viciado de nulidad, (US) juicio m nulo por desacuerdo del jurado.

mistrust [ˈmɪsˈtrʌst] [1] N desconfianza f, recelo m. [2] VT desconfiar de, dudar de.

mistrustful [mɪsˈtrʌstfʊl] ADJ desconfiado, receloso; **to be ~ of** recelarse de.

misty [ˈmɪstɪ] ADJ nebuloso, brumoso; day de niebla; (fig) nebuloso, vaporoso; glasses, window empañado; **it's getting ~** se está aneblando, está bajando la niebla; **the window is getting ~** la ventana se está empañando.

misty-eyed [ˈmɪstɪˌaɪd] ADJ sentimental.

misunderstand [ˈmɪsʌndəˈstænd] (irr: V **stand**) VTI entender mal, comprender mal; tomar en sentido erróneo; malinterpretar, interpretar mal; **you ~ me** no me entiendes, no entiendes lo que digo; **don't ~ me** entiéndame, no me malinterprete.

misunderstanding [ˈmɪsʌndəˈstændɪŋ] N equivocación f, error m; concepto m erróneo; (disagreement) desavenencia f; malentendido m; **there must be some ~** debe de haber alguna equivocación.

misunderstood [ˈmɪsʌndəˈstʊd] ADJ incomprendido; insuficientemente estimado.

misuse [ˈmɪsˈjuːs] [1] N abuso m, mal uso m; (of word) empleo m erróneo; (of funds) malversación f; (of person) maltrato m. [2] [ˈmɪsˈjuːz] VT abusar de; word emplear mal; funds malversar; person etc maltratar.

MIT N (US) ABBR of **Massachusetts Institute of Technology**.

mite¹ [maɪt] N (Zool) ácaro m.

mite² [maɪt] N (a) (coin) ardite m, (as contribution) óbolo m. (b) (small quantity) pizca f, poquitín m; **a ~ of consolation** una pizca de consuelo; **there's not a ~ left** no queda ni una sola gota; **well, just a ~ then** bueno, un poquitín; **we were a ~ surprised** quedamos un tanto atónitos, nos sorprendimos un poquito. (c) (child) niño m pequeño, niña f pequeña, nene m, -a f; **poor little ~!** ¡pobrecito!

miter [ˈmaɪtəʳ] N (US) = **mitre**.

Mithraic [mɪθˈreɪɪk] ADJ mitraico.

Mithraism [ˈmɪθreɪɪzəm] N mitraísmo m.

Mithras [ˈmɪθræs] NM Mitra.

mitigate [ˈmɪtɪgeɪt] VT mitigar.

mitigating [ˈmɪtɪgeɪtɪŋ] ADJ atenuante; ~ **circumstances** circunstancias fpl atenuantes.

mitigation [ˌmɪtɪˈgeɪʃən] N mitigación f; **to say a word in ~** decir algo para mitigar la ofensa (etc).

mitre, (US) **miter** [ˈmaɪtəʳ] [1] N (Eccl) mitra f; (Tech) inglete m. [2] ATTR: ~ **box** caja f de ingletes; ~ **joint** ensambladura f de inglete. [3] VT (Tech) ingletear.

mitt [mɪt] N (US: Baseball) guante m; = **mitten**; (*) mano f, aleta‡ f.

mitten [ˈmɪtn] N mitón m, guante m con solo el pulgar separado; **~s** guantes mpl de boxeo; **to get the ~**‡ recibir calabazas*; **to give sb the ~**‡ dar calabazas a uno*.

mix [mɪks] [1] N mezcla f; ingredientes mpl, proporciones fpl. [2] VT mezclar; combinar, unir; confundir; concrete, flour, plaster etc amasar; drinks preparar, mezclar; salad aderezar; **to ~ sugar into sth** añadir azúcar a algo; **to ~ it*** (Brit) venir a las manos, arreglar las cosas a puños. [3] VI mezclarse, poder mezclarse; (ingredients etc) ir bien juntos; (persons: get on well) llevarse bien, congeniar; **to ~ with others** asociarse con otros, ir con otros, alternar con otros, frecuentar la compañía de otros; **you should ~ more with people** hay que mezclarse más con la gente; **he's not keen to ~** tiene pocas ganas de alternar; **to ~**

in high society frecuentar la alta sociedad.

♦**mix in** [1] VT: **to ~ sth in** añadir algo, echar algo. [2] VI: **to ~ in with others** asociarse con otros, ir con otros, alternar con otros, frecuentar la compañía de otros; **he's not keen to ~ in** tiene pocas ganas de alternar.

♦**mix up** VT (a) (confuse) mezclar, confundir; **don't ~ me up** no me confundas; **I've ~ed you up with Michael** le he confundido (or equivocado) con Miguel. (b) (involve) **to be ~ed up in an affair** estar metido en un asunto; **to get ~ed up in an affair** meterse en un asunto, mojar en un asunto; **he got ~ed up with some strange people** formó amistades con gente muy rara; **are you ~ed up in this?** ¿tú andas metido en esto? ¿tú tienes que ver con esto?; **to ~ it up*** (US) zurrarse*, vapulearse.

mixed [mɪkst] ADJ mixto; mezclado; (assorted) variado, surtido; bathing, choir, school etc mixto; **a ~ set of people** un grupo de personas variadas; **I wouldn't say it in ~ company** no lo diría estando mujeres delante, no lo diría ante personas del otro sexo; **with ~ results** con resultados diversos, (pej) con resultados más bien mediocres; **we had ~ weather** el tiempo ha sido variable; ~ **ability class** clase f de distinto coeficiente intelectual; ~ **doubles** dobles mpl mixtos; ~ **economy** economía f mixta; ~ **farming** agricultura f mixta; ~ **feelings** sentimientos mpl encontrados; ~ **grill** (Brit) parrillada f mixta, plato m combinado de fritos; ~ **marriage** matrimonio m mixto (de esposos de diversa religión o raza); ~ **metaphor** metáfora f disparada; **it got a very ~ reception** suscitó reacciones muy diversas.

mixed-up [ˈmɪkstˈʌp] ADJ (a) things mezclados; (disordered) revueltos, confusos. (b) person confuso; **I'm all ~** estoy totalmente confuso; **a badly ~ youth** un joven de mentalidad gravemente confusa, un joven lleno de incertidumbre.

mixer [ˈmɪksəʳ] N (a) (Culin: machine) batidora f, mezcladora f; licuadora f. (b) (Rad) mezclador m. (c) (drink) tónica f. (d) (person) persona f sociable; **to be a good ~** tener don de gentes; **he's not much of a ~** tiene pocas ganas de alternar, no tiene don de gentes. (e) (US Univ) fiesta f de bienvenida para nuevos estudiantes.

mixer tap [ˈmɪksəˌtæp] N (Brit) grifo m único de agua fría y caliente.

mixing-bowl [ˈmɪksɪŋbəʊl] N cuenco m (de remover).

mixture [ˈmɪkstʃəʳ] N mezcla f; (Med) medicina f; **the ~ as before** la misma receta que antes, (fig) lo de siempre; **the family is an odd ~** la familia es una extraña mezcla; **he's an odd ~ of poet and plumber** se reúnen en él de modo bastante raro el poeta y el fontanero.

mix-up [ˈmɪksˈʌp] N confusión f, lío m; **there was a dreadful ~** hubo un tremendo lío; **we got in a ~ with the trains** nos hicimos un lío con los trenes.

mizzen [ˈmɪzn] N mesana f.

mizzenmast [ˈmɪznmɑːst] N palo m de mesana.

mizzle [ˈmɪzl] (* or dial) VI lloviznar.

Mk ABBR of **mark** Mk.

mkt ABBR of **market**.

ml ABBR of **millilitre(s)**.

M.Litt. N ABBR of **Master of Literature, Master of Letters** título universitario.

MLR N ABBR of **minimum lending rate** índice m base de préstamos.

MLS (a) (St Ex) N ABBR of **multiple listing system**. (b) (US: Univ) N ABBR of **Master of Library Science** título de bibliotecario.

MM ABBR of **Messieurs** Señores mpl, Sres.

mm ABBR of **millimetre(s)** milímetro(s) m(pl), mm.

mm ... [mm] INTERJ esto ..., pues ..., vamos a ver ...

MMC N (Brit) ABBR of **Monopolies and Mergers Commission**.

MN (a) N (Brit) ABBR of **Merchant Navy**. (b) (US Post) ABBR of **Minnesota**.

mnemonic [nɪˈmɒnɪk] [1] ADJ (m)nemotécnico. [2] N figura f (or frase f etc) (m)nemotécnica.

mnemonics [nɪˈmɒnɪks] N (m)nemotécnica f.

MO (a) N ABBR of **medical officer** médico mf. (b) (US Post) ABBR of **Missouri**. (c) (*: esp US) ABBR of **modus operandi** manera de actuar.

mo¹* [məʊ] N = **moment**.

mo² ABBR of **month** m.

m.o. ABBR of **money order** giro m, g/.

moan [məʊn] [1] N (groan) gemido m, quejido m; (complaint) queja f, protesta f. [2] VT decir gimiendo, decir con un gemido. [3] VI gemir; quejarse, protestar; **they're ~ing about the food again** han vuelto a quejarse de la comida.

moaner* [ˈməʊnəʳ] N protestón* m, -ona f.

moaning [ˈməʊnɪŋ] N gemidos mpl; quejas fpl, protestas fpl.

moat [məʊt] N foso m.

moated [ˈməʊtɪd] ADJ con foso, rodeado de un foso.

mob [mɒb] [1] N (a) multitud f, muchedumbre f, gentío m; (pej) turba f; **the ~** el populacho; **houses were burnt by the ~s** unas casas fueron incendiadas por las turbas; **they went in a ~ to the town hall** fueron en tropel al ayuntamiento; **to join the ~** echarse a las calles; **the army has become a** ~ el ejército se ha transformado en una turba.

(b) (*) grupo *m*, pandilla *f*, peña *f*; **the M~** (*US*) la Mafia; **Joe and his** ~ Pepe y su peña, Pepe y sus amigotes*; **I had nothing to do with that** ~ no tuve nada que ver con aquéllos; **which** ~ **were you in?** (*Mil*) ¿en qué regimiento (*etc*) estuviste?; **they're a hard-drinking** ~ son unos borrachos.

[2] ATTR: ~ **oratory** demagogia *f*, oratoria *f* populachera; ~ **rule** ley *f* del pueblo, ley *f* de la calle.

[3] VT (*molest*) acosar, atropellar; (*attack*) atacar en masa; *actor etc* festejar tumultuosamente, apiñarse entusiastas en torno de; **the minister was ~bed by journalists** los periodistas se apiñaban en torno del ministro; **he was ~bed whenever he went out** al salir siempre se veía acosado por la gente.

mobcap ['mɒbkæp] N cofia *f*.

mobile ['məubaɪl] [1] ADJ móvil, movible; *canteen etc* ambulante; **now that we're ~*** ahora que tenemos coche; ~ **home** caravana *f*, remolque *m*; ~ **library** biblioteca *f* móvil, bibliobús *m*; ~ **shop** tienda *f* ambulante; ~ **unit** (*TV*) unidad *f* móvil.

[2] N (**a**) (*also:* ~ **phone**) teléfono *m* móvil. (**b**) (*Art*) móvil *m*.

mobility [məu'bɪlɪtɪ] N movilidad *f*; ~ **allowance** subsidio *m* de movilidad; ~ **of labour** movilidad *f* de la mano de obra.

mobilization [ˌməubɪlaɪ'zeɪʃən] N movilización *f*.

mobilize ['məubɪlaɪz] [1] VT movilizar.

[2] VI movilizarse.

mobster* ['mɒbstər] N (*US*) gángster *m*, pandillero *m*.

moccasin ['mɒkəsɪn] N mocasín *m*.

mocha ['mɒkə] N moca *m*.

mock [mɒk] [1] N (**a**) **to make a ~ of sth** poner algo en ridículo. (**b**) (*Scol*) ~**s** exámenes *mpl* de prueba.

[2] ADJ (*sham*) fingido, simulado; (*imitated*) imitado; (*parodied*) burlesco; **in ~ anger** con ira simulada; **a ~ battle** un simulacro de combate; ~ **exam** examen *m* de prueba.

[3] VT (*ridicule*) ridiculizar; (*defy*) burlarse de; (*scoff at*) burlarse de, mofarse de; (*mimic*) remedar, imitar; *efforts, plans etc* frustrar, desbaratar.

[4] VI mofarse (*at* de).

mocker ['mɒkər] N (**a**) mofador *m*, -ora *f*. (**b**) **to put the ~s on sb:** hacer que uno fracase, joder a uno:.

mockery ['mɒkərɪ] N (*derision*) mofas *fpl*, burlas *fpl*; (*object*) parodia *f*, mal remedo *m*; **this is a ~ of justice** esto es una negación de la justicia; **it was a ~ of a trial** fue una parodia de un proceso; **what a ~ this is!** ¡esto es absurdo!, ¡qué tontería!; **he had to put up with a lot of ~** tuvo que aguantar muchas burlas; **to make a ~ of sth** hacer algo ridículo.

mock-heroic ['mɒkhɪ'rəuɪk] ADJ heroicoburlesco.

mocking ['mɒkɪŋ] [1] ADJ *tone etc* burlón.

[2] N burlas *fpl*.

mockingbird ['mɒkɪŋbɜːd] N sinsonte *m*, zenzontle *m* (*LAm*).

mockingly ['mɒkɪŋlɪ] ADV en tono burlón, con sorna.

mock-orange ['mɒk'ɒrɪndʒ] N jeringuilla *f*, celinda *f*.

mock-up ['mɒkʌp] N maqueta *f*.

MOD N (*Brit*) ABBR *of* **Ministry of Defence** Ministerio *m* de Defensa, Min. de D.

modal ['məudl] ADJ modal.

modality [məu'dælɪtɪ] N modalidad *f*.

mod cons [ˌmɒd'kɒnz] NPL ABBR *of* **modern conveniences**.

mode [məud] N (**a**) modo *m* (*also Gram, Mus, Philos*), manera *f*; (*fashion*) moda *f*. (**b**) (*Comput*) modo *m*, modalidad *f*.

model ['mɒdl] [1] N (**a**) (*small-scale representation*) modelo *m*; paradigma *m*, patrón *m*, pauta *f*; (*architect's, town planner's etc*) maqueta *f*; **it is made on the ~ of X** está hecho a imitación de X.

(**b**) (*person*) modelo *mf*; **he is a ~ of good behaviour** es un modelo de buenas costumbres; **to hold sb out** (*or* **up**) **as a ~** presentar a uno como modelo.

(**c**) (*dress, car etc*) modelo *m*.

[2] ADJ (**a**) (*ideal, experimental*) modelo; modélico; ~ **apartment** (*US*) piso *m* modelo; ~ **home** casa *f* piloto; ~ **prison** cárcel *f* modelo; ~ **prisoner** preso *m* modélico; ~ **town** ciudad *f* modelo.

(**b**) (*small-scale*) miniatura *f*; ~ **aeroplane** aeromodelo *m*; ~ **car** coche *m* de juguete; ~ **railway** ferrocarril *m* de juguete, ferrocarril *m* miniatura.

[3] VT (**a**) (*make a* ~) modelar; (*fig*) modelar, formar, planear; **to ~ sth on sth else** modelar algo sobre otra cosa, construir algo a imitación de otra cosa, planear algo según otra cosa.

(**b**) *dress etc* llevar, presentar.

[4] VI servir de modelo (*for a, para*); ejercer la profesión de modelo, ser modelo.

[5] VR: **to ~ o.s. on** modelarse sobre.

modeller, (*US*) **modeler** ['mɒdlər] N modelador *m*, -ora *f*.

modelling, (*US*) **modeling** ['mɒdlɪŋ] [1] N (*V* **model 1a, b**) (**a**) modelado *m*; modelismo *m*. (**b**) profesión *f* de modelo.

[2] ATTR: ~ **clay** plastilina ® *f*.

modem ['məudem] N módem *m*.

moderate [1] ['mɒdərɪt] ADJ moderado (*also Pol*); (*fair, medium*) regular, mediano, mediocre; *increase, price* módico.

[2] ['mɒdərɪt] N (*Pol*) moderado *m*, -a *f*.

[3] ['mɒdəreɪt] VT (**a**) (*lessen*) moderar; mitigar; *wind etc* calmar. (**b**) *exam etc* asesorar.

[4] ['mɒdəreɪt] VI (**a**) moderarse; mitigarse; (*wind etc*) calmarse, amainar.

(**b**) (*act as moderator*) arbitrar, servir de asesor.

moderately ['mɒdərɪtlɪ] ADV moderadamente; medianamente, mediocremente; módicamente; **a ~ expensive suit** un traje medianamente caro; **he was ~ successful** tuvo un razonable éxito.

moderation [ˌmɒdə'reɪʃən] N moderación *f*; temperancia *f*; **in ~** con moderación.

moderator ['mɒdəreɪtər] N (*Brit Univ*) árbitro *m*, asesor *m*, -ora *f*; **M~** (*Eccl*) presidente de la asamblea de la Iglesia Presbiteriana Escocesa y de otras iglesias protestantes; ver también [CHURCH OF ENGLAND].

modern ['mɒdən] [1] ADJ moderno.

[2] N moderno *m*, -a *f*.

modernism ['mɒdənɪzəm] N modernismo *m*.

modernist ['mɒdənɪst] [1] ADJ modernista.

[2] N modernista *mf*.

modernistic [ˌmɒdə'nɪstɪk] ADJ modernista.

modernity [mɒ'dɜːnɪtɪ] N modernidad *f*.

modernization [ˌmɒdənaɪ'zeɪʃən] N modernización *f*; actualización *f*.

modernize ['mɒdənaɪz] [1] VT modernizar; actualizar.

[2] VI modernizarse; actualizarse.

modest ['mɒdɪst] ADJ (**a**) (*not boastful*) modesto; moderado; (*not grand*) modesto; **to be ~ about one's successes** hablar en términos modestos de sus triunfos; **to be ~ in one's demands** ser moderado en sus reclamaciones. (**b**) (††: *chaste etc*) pudoroso, púdico.

modestly ['mɒdɪstlɪ] ADV modestamente; con moderación; pudorosamente.

modesty ['mɒdɪstɪ] N (**a**) (*gen*) modestia *f*; moderación *f*. (**b**) (††: *chasteness*) pudor *m*.

modicum ['mɒdɪkəm] N: **with a ~ of** con una cantidad mínima de, con un poquito de.

modification [ˌmɒdɪfɪ'keɪʃən] N modificación *f*.

modifier ['mɒdɪfaɪər] N modificante *m*.

modify ['mɒdɪfaɪ] VT modificar.

modifying ['mɒdɪfaɪɪŋ] [1] ADJ *note, term, factor* modificador, modificante.

[2] N modificación *f*.

modish ['məudɪʃ] ADJ muy de moda, sumamente elegante.

modishly ['məudɪʃlɪ] ADV elegantemente; **to be ~ dressed** ir vestido con suma elegancia.

modiste [mɒ'diːst] N modista *f*.

Mods [mɒdz] N (*Brit*) ABBR *of* (**Honour**) **Moderations** examen de la licenciatura de la universidad de Oxford.

modular ['mɒdjulər] ADJ modular; ~ **program(m)ing** programación *f* modular.

modularity [ˌmɒdju'lærɪtɪ] N modularidad *f*.

modulate ['mɒdjuleɪt] VTI modular.

modulated ['mɒdjuleɪtɪd] ADJ modulado.

modulation [ˌmɒdju'leɪʃən] N modulación *f*.

module ['mɒdjuːl] N módulo *m*.

modus operandi ['məudəsˌɒpə'rændiː] N modus *m* operandi, modo *m* de proceder.

modus vivendi ['məudəsvɪ'vendiː] N modus *m* vivendi; manera *f* de convivir.

Mogadishu [ˌmɒgə'diʃuː] N Mogadisio *m*.

moggy* ['mɒgɪ] N (*Brit*) gatito *m*, -a *f*, michino* *m*, -a *f*.

mogul ['məugəl] N magnate *m*; **film ~** magnate *m* de la cinematografía; **the Great M~** el Gran Mogol.

MOH N ABBR *of* **Medical Officer of Health**.

mohair ['məuheər] N mohair *m*.

Mohammed [məu'hæmed] NM Mahoma.

Mohammedan [məu'hæmɪdən] [1] ADJ mahometano.

[2] N mahometano *m*, -a *f*.

Mohammedanism [məu'hæmɪdənɪzəm] N mahometanismo *m*.

Mohican [məu'hiːkən] N (**a**) (*Native American*) mohicano *m*, -a *f*. (**b**) (*hairstyle*) cresta *f* mohicana.

moiré ['mwɑːreɪ] N muaré *m*.

moist [mɔɪst] ADJ húmedo; mojado.

moisten ['mɔɪsn] [1] VT humedecer, mojar.

[2] VI humedecerse, mojarse.

moistness ['mɔɪstnɪs] N, **moisture** ['mɔɪstʃər] N humedad *f*.

moisturize ['mɔɪstʃəraɪz] VT humedecer, mojar; *skin etc* hidratar.

moisturizer ['mɔɪstʃəraɪzər] N crema *f* hidratante.

moisturizing cream ['mɔɪstʃəraɪzɪŋ,kriːm] N crema f hidratante.

moke* [məʊk] N (Brit) burro m.

molar ['məʊləʳ] N muela f.

molasses [mə'læsɪz] N SING AND PL melaza f, melazas fpl.

mold [məʊld] N etc (US) = **mould** etc.

Moldavia [mɒl'deɪvɪə] N, **Moldova** [mɒl'dəʊvə] N Moldavia f, Moldova f.

Moldavian [mɒl'deɪvɪən] ADJ, N, **Moldovan** [mɒl'dəʊvən] ADJ, N moldavo m, -a f.

mole¹ [məʊl] N (Anat) lunar m.

mole² [məʊl] N (Zool and fig) topo m.

mole³ [məʊl] N (Naut) malecón m, muelle m.

molecular [mə'lekjʊləʳ] ADJ molecular; **~ biology** biología f molecular.

molecule ['mɒlɪkjuːl] N molécula f.

molehill ['məʊlhɪl] N topera f.

moleskin ['məʊlskɪn] N piel f de topo.

molest [məʊ'lest] VT faltar al respeto a, meterse con, importunar, molestar; (euph) abordar con propósitos deshonestos.

molestation [,məʊles'teɪʃən] N importunidad f, vejación f; (sexual) acoso m, importunación f.

molester [mə'lestəʳ] N (also **child ~**) maníaco m sexual que persigue a niños.

moll* [mɒl] N compañera f (de gángster).

mollify ['mɒlɪfaɪ] VT apaciguar, calmar; **he was somewhat mollified by this** con esto se calmó un poco.

mollusc, (US) mollusk ['mɒləsk] N molusco m.

mollycoddle ['mɒlɪkɒdl] [1] N marica m, niño m mimado.
[2] VT mimar.

mollycoddling ['mɒlɪ,kɒdlɪŋ] N mimo m.

Molotov ['mɒlətɒf] ATTR: **~ cocktail** N cóctel m Molotov.

molt [məʊlt] N etc (US) = **moult** etc.

molten ['məʊltən] ADJ fundido, derretido; lava etc líquido.

molybdenum [mɒ'lɪbdɪnəm] N molibdeno m.

mom* [mɒm] [1] N (US) mamá* f.
[2] ATTR: **~ and pop store** tienda f de la esquina, pequeño negocio m.

moment ['məʊmənt] N (a) (instant) momento m, instante m; (juncture) momento m, coyuntura f; **~ of truth** momento m de la verdad; **man of the ~** hombre m del momento; **odd ~s** momentos mpl de ocio; **at odd ~s** a ratos perdidos; hay veces cuando ...; **at any ~** de un momento a otro; **at the ~** de momento, por ahora; **at the last ~** a última hora; **at this ~** en este momento, ahora mismo; **for the ~** por el momento; **not for a ~** ¡ni pensarlo!, ¡ni soñarlo!; **I'm not saying for a ~ you're wrong** no digo que no tengas razón ni mucho menos; **not for a ~ did I think that ...** en ningún momento pensaba que ...; **from that ~ on** desde entonces, a partir de entonces; **in a ~** en un momento; **yes, in a ~!** ¡sí, en seguida!; **I'll come in a ~** voy en seguida; **it was all over in a ~** todo esto ocurrió en un instante; **to leave things until the last ~** dejar las cosas hasta última hora; **one ~!, half a ~!, wait a ~!** ¡un momento!; **I shan't be a ~** vuelvo muy pronto; termino muy pronto; ahora mismo; **do it this very ~!** ¡hazlo al instante!; **the play has its ~s** la obra tiene sus momentos; **I have just this ~ heard of it** acabo de saberlo; **it won't take a ~** es cosa de unos pocos momentos; **tell me the ~ he comes** avíseme en cuanto venga; **the next ~ he collapsed** al instante sufrió un colapso.
(b) (Mech) momento m; **~ of inertia** momento m de inercia.
(c) (importance) importancia f, momento m; **of little ~** de poca importancia, de poco momento; **matters of ~** asuntos mpl de importancia. See also AS SOON AS.

momentarily ['məʊməntərɪlɪ] ADV (a) momentáneamente; expect etc de un momento a otro. (b) (US: now) en este momento; (soon) dentro de poco, muy pronto.

momentary ['məʊməntərɪ] ADJ momentáneo.

momentous [məʊ'mentəs] ADJ trascendental, muy crítico, de suma importancia, decisivo.

momentousness [məʊ'mentəsnɪs] N trascendencia f, suma importancia f, lo decisivo.

momentum [məʊ'mentəm] N momento m; (fig) impulso m, ímpetu m; **to gather ~** cobrar velocidad.

momma* ['mɒmə] N (US), **mommy*** ['mɒmɪ] N (US) mamá* f.

Mon. ABBR of **Monday** lunes m.

Monaco ['mɒnəkəʊ] N Mónaco m.

monad ['mɒnæd] N mónada f.

Mona Lisa ['məʊnə'liːzə] NF la Gioconda.

monarch ['mɒnək] N monarca m.

monarchic(al) [mɒ'nɑːkɪk(əl)] ADJ monárquico.

monarchism ['mɒnəkɪzəm] N monarquismo m.

monarchist ['mɒnəkɪst] [1] ADJ monárquico.
[2] N monárquico m, -a f.

monarchy ['mɒnəkɪ] N monarquía f.

┌─ **MONARCHY** ─────────────────────────────

ⓘ *La única interrupción de la monarquía en la historia de Gran Bretaña tuvo lugar entre 1649 y 1660, período en que se instauró una república. El monarca es el jefe de los poderes ejecutivo y judicial, de la Iglesia de Inglaterra (**Church of England**), de la **Commonwealth** y de las Fuerzas Armadas y también ocupa un lugar importante en la asamblea legislativa. Como jefe del estado, recibe una asignación anual de varios millones de libras esterlinas llamada **Civil List** por llevar a cabo sus deberes para con la nación.*

⇒ Ver también CHURCH OF ENGLAND , COMMONWEALTH
└──

monastery ['mɒnəstrɪ] N monasterio m, cenobio m.

monastic [mə'næstɪk] ADJ monástico; **~ order** order f monástica; **~ vows** votos mpl monásticos.

monasticism [mə'næstɪsɪzəm] N monacato m, vida f monástica.

Monday ['mʌndɪ] N lunes m.

Monegasque [mɒnə'gæsk] [1] ADJ monegasco.
[2] N monegasco m, -a f.

monetarism ['mʌnɪtərɪzəm] N monetarismo m.

monetarist ['mʌnɪtərɪst] [1] ADJ monetarista.
[2] N monetarista mf.

monetary ['mʌnɪtərɪ] ADJ monetario; **~ policy** política f monetaria; **~ reserves** reservas fpl monetarias; **~ system** sistema m monetario; **~ unit** unidad f monetaria.

money ['mʌnɪ] [1] N dinero m; **your ~ or your life!** ¡la bolsa o la vida!; **'~ back if not satisfied'** 'si no queda satisfecho le devolveremos el dinero'; **~ back guarantee** garantía f de devolver (or reembolsar) el dinero, dinero m reembolsable garantizado; **~ talks** poderoso caballero es don Dinero; **~ makes ~** dinero llama dinero; **there's ~ in it** es un buen negocio; **it's a bargain for the ~** a ese precio es una verdadera ganga; **that's the team for my ~!** ¡ése sí es un equipo!, ¡ése es lo que se llama un equipo!; **for my ~ it's not worthwhile** en cuanto a mí no vale la pena; **it's ~ for jam, it's ~ for old rope** (Brit) es dinero que se gana sin el menor esfuerzo; **my ~ is on Fred** yo apuesto a Fred; **my ~ is on Fred not coming** yo apuesto a que Fred no vendrá; **he must be coining ~** está forrándose de dinero; **to come into ~** heredar dinero; **bad ~ drives out good** el dinero malo echa fuera al bueno; **to earn good ~** tener un buen sueldo; **he gets his ~ on Fridays** cobra los viernes; **when do I get my ~?** ¿cuándo cobro?, ¿cuándo me vas a pagar?; **~ doesn't grow on trees** el dinero no nace en macetas; **to have ~ to burn** estar cargado de dinero; **after that he was in the ~** con eso se estaba forrando, con eso estaba acuñando dinero; **to keep sb in ~** proveer a uno de dinero; **he's made of ~** es de oro; **do you think I'm made of ~?** ¿crees que soy millonario?; **to make ~** (person) ganar dinero, (business) dar dinero, rendir bien; **to make ~ hand over fist** amasar una fortuna; **to put one's ~ where one's mouth is** predicar con el ejemplo; **to be rolling in ~** nadar en dinero; **to throw good ~ after bad** echar la soga tras el caldero.
[2] ATTR: **~ economy** economía f monetaria; **~ market** mercado m de dinero; **~ matters** asuntos mpl financieros; **~ order** giro m postal; **~ payment** pago m en metálico; **~ prize** premio m en metálico; **~ spider** araña f de la suerte; **~ supply** oferta f monetaria, medio m circulante, volumen m monetario; **~ wage** salario m en metálico.

moneybag ['mʌnɪbæg] N gato m, talega f; **~s** (fig) talegas fpl, riqueza f.

money belt ['mʌnɪbelt] N riñonera f.

moneybox ['mʌnɪbɒks] N hucha f.

moneychanger ['mʌnɪ,tʃeɪndʒəʳ] N cambista mf.

moneyed ['mʌnɪd] ADJ adinerado.

moneygrubber ['mʌnɪ,grʌbəʳ] N avaro m, -a f.

moneygrubbing ['mʌnɪ,grʌbɪŋ] [1] ADJ avaro, avariento.
[2] N esfuerzo m por enriquecerse, afán m de dinero.

moneylender ['mʌnɪ,lendəʳ] N prestamista mf.

moneylending ['mʌnɪ,lendɪŋ] N préstamo m.

moneymaker ['mʌnɪ,meɪkəʳ] N artículo m (or producto m, proyecto m, inversión f) que rinde grandes beneficios, fuente f de dinero.

moneymaking ['mʌnɪ,meɪkɪŋ] [1] ADJ provechoso, rentable, lucrativo.
[2] N ganancia f, lucro m.

money-spinner ['mʌnɪ,spɪnəʳ] N (Brit) = **moneymaker**.

money's-worth ['mʌnɪzwɜːθ] N: **to get one's ~** sacar jugo del dinero, estar contento con lo que uno ha adquirido (etc); **to get one's ~ out of an investment** salir bien recompensado de una inversión.

-monger ['mʌŋgəʳ] N ending in compounds traficante m en ..., tratante m en ...; V **fish~** etc.

Mongol ['mɒŋgəl] [1] ADJ mongol; (Med) mongólico.
[2] N (a) mongol m, -ola f; (Med) mongólico m, -a f. (b) (Ling) mongol m.

Mongolia [mɒŋ'gəʊlɪə] N Mongolia f.

Mongolian [mɒŋˈgəʊlɪən] = **Mongol**.

mongolism [ˈmɒŋgəlɪzəm] N mongolismo *m*.

mongoloid [ˈmɒŋgəlɔɪd] ADJ (*Med: dated*) mongoloide, mongólico.

mongoose [ˈmɒŋguːs] N, PL **mongooses** [ˈmɒŋguːsɪz] mangosta *f*.

mongrel [ˈmʌŋgrəl] ①︎ ADJ mestizo; *dog* mestizo, cruzado, (*pej*) callejero.

②︎ N (*person: pej*) mestizo *m*, -a *f*; (*dog*) perro *m* mestizo, (*pej*) perro *m* callejero.

monicker [ˈmɒnɪkəʳ] N (*name*) nombre *m*; (*nickname*) apodo *m*; (*signature*) firma *f*; (*initials*) iniciales *fpl*.

monied [ˈmʌnɪd] = **moneyed**.

monitor [ˈmɒnɪtəʳ] ①︎ N (a) (*Scol*) alumno *m* encargado de la disciplina. (b) (*Rad: person*) escucha *mf*, monitor *m*; (*TV, Comput*) monitor *m*.

②︎ VT *foreign station* escuchar; *TV programme* controlar; *progress* observar, monitorizar, seguir la marcha de, controlar.

monitoring [ˈmɒnɪtərɪŋ] ①︎ N supervisión *f*; control *m*; observación *f*; monitorización *f*, monitoreado *m*.

②︎ ATTR *body, responsibility* de observación, de verificación.

monk [mʌŋk] N monje *m*.

monkey [ˈmʌŋkɪ] ①︎ N mono *m*, -a *f*, mico *m*, -a *f*; (*fig: child*) diablillo *m*, golfillo *m*; **I don't care** (*or* **give**) **a ~'s**‡ me importa un rábano; **to have a ~ on one's back**‡ (*US*) quedar colgado*; **to make a ~ out of sb** poner a uno en ridículo.

②︎ ATTR: **~ business*** trampas *fpl*; trapisondas *fpl*, tejemanejes *mpl*; **~ tricks*** travesuras *fpl*, diabluras *fpl*.

◆**monkey about***, **monkey around*** VI hacer travesuras, juguetear, hacer diabluras; **to ~ about with sth** manosear algo, (*and damage*) estropear algo.

monkeynut [ˈmʌŋkɪnʌt] N (*Brit*) cacahuete *m*, maní *m* (*LAm*).

monkey-puzzle [ˈmʌŋkɪˌpʌzl] N (*Bot*) araucaria *f*.

monkey-wrench [ˈmʌŋkɪˌrentʃ] N llave *f* inglesa; **to throw a ~ into the works*** (*US*) meter un palo en la rueda.

monkfish [ˈmʌŋkfɪʃ] N pejesapo *m*.

monkish [ˈmʌŋkɪʃ] ADJ monacal, de monje; monástico; (*pej*) fraileluno.

monkshood [ˈmʌŋkshʊd] N acónito *m*.

mono [ˈmɒnəʊ] ADJ (= **monophonic**): **~ system** sistema *m* monofónico.

mono... [ˈmɒnəʊ] PREF mono...

monochrome [ˈmɒnəkrəʊm] ①︎ ADJ monocromo.

②︎ N monocromo *m*.

monocle [ˈmɒnəkl] N monóculo *m*.

monoculture [ˈmɒnəʊˌkʌltʃəʳ] N monocultivo *m*.

monogamist [mɒˈnɒgəmɪst] N monógamo *m*, -a *f*.

monogamous [məˈnɒgəməs] ADJ monógamo.

monogamy [məˈnɒgəmɪ] N monogamia *f*.

monogenetic [ˌmɒnəʊdʒɪˈnetɪk] ADJ monogenético.

monoglot [ˈmɒnəʊglɒt] ①︎ ADJ monolingüe.

②︎ N monolingüe *mf*.

monogram [ˈmɒnəgræm] N monograma *m*.

monogrammed [ˈmɒnəgræmd] ADJ con monograma.

monograph [ˈmɒnəgræf] N monografía *f*.

monohull [ˈmɒnəʊˌhʌl] N monocasco *m*.

monokini [ˌmɒnəʊˈkiːniː] N monokini *m*.

monolingual [ˌmɒnəʊˈlɪŋgwəl] ADJ monolingüe.

monolingualism [ˌmɒnəʊˈlɪŋgwəlɪzəm] N monolingüismo *m*.

monolith [ˈmɒnəʊlɪθ] N monolito *m*.

monolithic [ˌmɒnəʊˈlɪθɪk] ADJ monolítico.

monolog(ue) [ˈmɒnəlɒg] N monólogo *m*.

monomania [ˌmɒnəʊˈmeɪnɪə] N monomanía *f*.

monomaniac [ˌmɒnəʊˈmeɪnɪæk] ①︎ ADJ monomaníaco.

②︎ N monomaníaco *m*, -a *f*.

mononucleosis [ˌmɒnəʊˌnjuːklɪˈəʊsɪs] N (*US*) (*also* **infectious ~**) mononucleosis *f* infecciosa.

monophonic [ˌmɒnəʊˈfɒnɪk] ADJ monofónico.

monoplane [ˈmɒnəpleɪn] N monoplano *m*.

monopolist [məˈnɒpəlɪst] N monopolista *m*.

monopolistic [məˌnɒpəˈlɪstɪk] ADJ monopolístico.

monopolization [məˌnɒpəlaɪˈzeɪʃən] N monopolización *f*.

monopolize [məˈnɒpəlaɪz] VT monopolizar (*also fig*), acaparar.

monopoly [məˈnɒpəlɪ] ①︎ N monopolio *m*.

②︎ ATTR: **Monopolies and Mergers Commission** (*Brit*) Comisión de monopolios y fusiones.

monopsony [məˈnɒpsənɪ] N monopsonio *m*.

monorail [ˈmɒnəʊreɪl] N monorail *m*, monocarril *m*.

monoski [ˈmɒnəʊˌskiː] N monoesquí *m*.

monoskier [ˈmɒnəʊˌskiːəʳ] N monoesquiador *m*, -ora *f*.

monoskiing [ˈmɒnəʊˌskiːɪŋ] N monoesquí *m*.

monosodium glutamate [ˌmɒnəʊˌsəʊdɪəmˈgluːtəmeɪt] N glutamato *m* monosódico.

monosyllabic [ˌmɒnəʊsɪˈlæbɪk] ADJ *word* monosílabo; *language, utterance* monosilábico.

monosyllable [ˈmɒnəˌsɪləbl] N monosílabo *m*.

monotheism [ˈmɒnəʊˌθiːɪzəm] N monoteísmo *m*.

monotheist [ˈmɒnəʊˌθiːɪst] N monoteísta *mf*.

monotheistic [ˌmɒnəʊθiːˈɪstɪk] ADJ monoteísta.

monotone [ˈmɒnətəʊn] N monotonía *f*; **to speak in a ~** hablar en un solo tono.

monotonous [məˈnɒtənəs] ADJ monótono.

monotonously [məˈnɒtənəslɪ] ADV de manera monótona, de manera tediosa; **~ reliable/punctual** tediosamente fiable/puntual.

monotony [məˈnɒtənɪ] N monotonía *f*.

Monotype [ˈmɒnəʊtaɪp] ®︎ ①︎ N monotipia ®︎ *f*.

②︎ ATTR: **~ machine** (máquina *f*) monotipo ®︎ *m*.

monoxide [mɒˈnɒksaɪd] N monóxido *m*.

monseigneur [ˌmɒnsenˈjɜːʳ] N monseñor *m*.

monsignor [mɒnˈsiːnjəʳ] N monseñor *m*.

monsoon [mɒnˈsuːn] N monzón *m or f*; **the ~ rains** las lluvias monzónicas; **~ season** época *f* monzónica.

monster [ˈmɒnstəʳ] ①︎ ADJ enorme, monstruoso; (*hum*) grandísimo.

②︎ N monstruo *m*; **a real ~ of a fish** un pez verdaderamente enorme; **a ~ of greed** un monstruo de la avaricia.

monstrance [ˈmɒnstrəns] N custodia *f*, ostensorio *m*.

monstrosity [mɒnsˈtrɒsɪtɪ] N monstruosidad *f*.

monstrous [ˈmɒnstrəs] ADJ (a) (*huge*) monstruoso, enorme. (b) (*unfair*) injusto, escandaloso.

monstrously [ˈmɒnstrəslɪ] ADV enormemente; **~ unfair** terriblemente injusto.

Mont. (*US*) ABBR *of* **Montana**.

montage [mɒnˈtɑːʒ] N montaje *m*.

Mont Blanc [ˌmɔ̃ːmˈblɑ̃ːŋ] N el Monte Blanco.

Montenegran, Montenegrin [mɒntɪˈniːgrən] ①︎ ADJ montenegrino.

②︎ N montenegrino *m*, -a *f*.

Montenegro [mɒntɪˈniːgrəʊ] N Montenegro *m*.

month [mʌnθ] N mes *m*; **30 dollars a ~** 30 dólares al mes, 30 dólares mensuales; **not in a ~ of Sundays** nunca jamás amén; **it went on for ~s** duró meses y meses.

monthly [ˈmʌnθlɪ] ①︎ ADJ mensual; **~ instalment, ~ installment** (*US*), **~ payment** mensualidad *f*; **~ statement** (*Fin*) estado *m* de cuenta mensual.

②︎ ADV cada mes, mensualmente; **40 dollars ~** 40 dólares al mes, 40 dólares mensuales.

③︎ N (a) (*magazine*) revista *f* mensual. (b) **monthlies** (*Med*) regla *f*.

monument [ˈmɒnjʊmənt] N monumento *m* (*to* de, a, que conmemora); **~ to Bolívar** monumento *m* de Bolívar; **~ to the dead** monumento *m* a los muertos.

monumental [ˌmɒnjʊˈmentl] ADJ (a) monumental; **~ mason** escultor *m* de monumentos funerarios, marmolista *m*. (b) *ignorance etc* enorme, colosal, monumental; *error* garrafal.

monumentally [ˌmɒnjʊˈmentlɪ] ADV *dull, popular etc* enormemente; **~ important** enormemente importante.

moo [muː] ①︎ N mugido *m*.

②︎ VI mugir, hacer mu.

mooch [muːtʃ] ①︎ VT (*) (a) (*cadge*) sacar de gorra*. (b) (*esp US: steal*) birlar*.

②︎ VI: **to ~ along** andar arrastrando los pies.

◆**mooch about***, **mooch around*** VI no saber qué hacer, no tener nada que hacer, haraganear.

moo-cow* [ˈmuːkaʊ] N (*child's language*) vaca *f*.

mood[1] [muːd] N (*Gram*) modo *m*.

mood[2] [muːd] ①︎ N humor *m*; disposición *f* (de ánimo); capricho *m*; **to be in a bad ~** estar de mal humor; **to be in a good ~** estar de buen humor; **he's in a bit of a ~** está de mal humor; **to be in a generous ~** sentirse generoso; **to be in an ugly ~** (*person*) estar de muy mal humor, (*crowd*) amenazar violencia; **to be in a forgiving ~** estar dispuesto a perdonar; **to be in no laughing ~, to be in no ~ for laughing** no tener ganas de reír; **are you in a ~ for chess?** ¿te apetece una partida de ajedrez?, ¿quieres jugar al ajedrez?; **to be in the ~ (for love)** sentirse amoroso; **I'm not in the ~** no quiero; **I'm not in the ~ for games** no estoy para juegos; **he plays well when he's in the ~** toca bien cuando está de vena; **he's in one of his ~s** está en uno de sus momentos de mal humor; **that depends on his ~** eso es según el humor que tenga; **he has ~s** (*of anger*) tiene arranques de cólera, (*of gloom*) tiene sus rachas de melancolía.

②︎ ATTR: **~ music** música *f* de fondo (*or* de ambiente).

moodily [ˈmuːdɪlɪ] ADV *answer etc* malhumoradamente; melancólicamente.

moodiness [ˈmuːdɪnɪs] N mal humor *m*; melancolía *f*; humor *m* cambiadizo, propensión *f* a cambiar bruscamente de humor.

moody [ˈmuːdɪ] ADJ: **to be ~** (*angry*) tener arranques de cólera; (*gloomy*) tener rachas de melancolía; (*variable*) ser caprichoso.

moola(h)‡ [ˈmuːlɑː] N (*US*) pasta* *f*, parné‡ *m*.

moon [muːn] ①︎ N luna *f*; (*poet*) mes *m*; **full ~** luna *f* llena, plenilunio

m; **new ~** luna *f* nueva; **once in a blue ~** de higos a brevas, de Pascuas a Ramos; **to ask** (*or* **cry**) **for the ~** pedir la luna; **to be over the ~** estar loco de contento; **to promise the ~** prometer el oro y el moro, prometer la luna.
　2 VI (*) enseñar el culo.

◆**moon about, moon around** VI mirar a las musarañas, pasar el tiempo sin hacer nada; soñar despierto.

◆**moon away** VT: **to ~ away a couple of hours** pasar un par de horas sin hacer nada, pasar un par de horas soñando.

◆**moon over** VT: **she was ~ing over the photo** miraba amorosamente la foto, contemplaba extasiada la foto.

moonbeam ['mu:nbi:m] N rayo *m* de luna.

moonboots ['mu:nbu:ts] NPL botas *fpl* altas acolchadas.

moon buggy ['mu:n,bʌgɪ] N vehículo *m* lunar.

Moonie ['mu:nɪ] N miembro *mf* de la Iglesia de la Unificación.

moon-landing ['mu:n,lændɪŋ] N alunizaje *m.*

moonless ['mu:nlɪs] ADJ sin luna.

moonlight ['mu:nlaɪt] **1** N luz *f* de la luna; **by ~, in the ~** a la luz de la luna; **it was ~** había luna.
　2 ATTR: **~ flit** (*Brit*) mudanza *f* a la chita callando.
　3 VI (*) tener un empleo secundario además del principal, estar pluriempleado, tener un pluriempleo.

moonlighter ['mu:n,laɪtəʳ] N pluriempleado *m,* -a *f.*

moonlighting ['mu:n,laɪtɪŋ] N pluriempleo *m.*

moonlit ['mu:nlɪt] ADJ *object* iluminado por la luna; *night* de luna.

moonrise ['mu:nraɪz] N salida *f* de la luna.

moonscape ['mu:n,skeɪp] N paisaje *m* lunar.

moonshine ['mu:nʃaɪn] N (**a**) luz *f* de la luna. (**b**) (*: *nonsense*) pamplinas *fpl*, música *f* celestial. (**c**) (*US*: *illegal spirits*) licor *m* destilado ilegalmente.

moonshiner ['mu:nʃaɪnəʳ] N (*US*) (**a**) (*distiller*) fabricante *m* de licor ilegal. (**b**) (*smuggler*) contrabandista *mf.*

moonshot ['mu:nʃɒt] N (lanzamiento *m* de una) nave *f* espacial con destino a la luna.

moonstone ['mu:nstəʊn] N feldespato *m,* labradorita *f.*

moonstruck ['mu:nstrʌk] ADJ tocado, trastornado, lunático.

moony ['mu:nɪ] ADJ: **to be ~** estar distraído, estar soñando despierto.

Moor [mʊəʳ] N moro *m,* -a *f.*

moor¹ [mʊəʳ] N páramo *m,* brezal *m;* (*for game*) coto *m.*

moor² [mʊəʳ] **1** VT amarrar, atracar.
　2 VI echar las amarras.

moorhen ['mʊəhen] N polla *f* de agua.

moorings ['mʊərɪŋz] NPL (*ropes*) amarras *fpl;* (*place*) amarradero *m,* punto *m* de atraque.

Moorish ['mʊərɪʃ] ADJ moro; morisco; (*Archit etc*) árabe; **~ arch** arco *m* de herradura.

moorland ['mʊələnd] N páramo *m,* brezal *m.*

moose [mu:s] N alce *m* de América.

moot [mu:t] **1** N (*Hist*) junta *f,* asamblea *f.*
　2 ADJ *point, question* discutible, dudoso.
　3 VT proponer para la discusión; **it has been ~ed whether ...** se ha discutido si ...; **when the question was first ~ed** cuando se discutió la cuestión por primera vez.

mop [mɒp] **1** N (**a**) (*implement*) fregasuelos *m,* lampazo *m,* trapeador *m* (*LAm*).
　(**b**) (*hair*) mata *f,* greña *f;* **~ of hair** pelambrera *f.*
　2 VT fregar, limpiar; *brow* enjugar.

◆**mop up** VT (**a**) *floor, liquid* limpiar, enjugar; (*absorb*) absorber; (*dry up*) secar.
　(**b**) (*Mil*) *terrain* limpiar, *remnants* acabar con.
　(**c**) (*) *drink* beberse.

mope [məʊp] VI estar deprimido, estar abatido; **to ~ for sb** resentirse de la ausencia de uno, estar triste por la pérdida de uno.

◆**mope about, mope around** VI andar alicaído.

moped ['məʊped] N (*Brit*) ciclomotor *m.*

mopping-up ['mɒpɪŋ,ʌp] **1** N limpieza *f.*
　2 ATTR: **~ operation** (*Mil*) operación *f* de limpieza, barrida *f;* (*after flood, storm*) operaciones *fpl* de limpieza y reconstrucción.

moquette [mɒ'ket] N moqueta *f.*

MOR ADJ (*Mus*) ABBR *of* **middle-of-the-road** para el gran público.

moraine [mɒ'reɪn] N morena *f.*

moral ['mɒrəl] **1** ADJ moral; *philosophy, support, victory* moral; (*chaste*) virtuoso; (*honourable*) honrado; **the ~ majority** la mayoría moral.
　2 N (**a**) (*of story*) moraleja *f;* sentido *m* moral; **to draw a ~ from** sacar una moraleja de; **to point the ~** hacer resaltar la moraleja.
　(**b**) **~s** moral *f,* ética *f;* moralidad *f;* (*conduct*) costumbres *fpl;* **the ~s of actors** la moralidad de los actores; **she has no ~s** no tiene sentido moral, carece de toda noción de la moralidad.

morale [mɒ'rɑ:l] N moral *f.*

morale-booster [mɒ'rɑ:lbu:stəʳ] N inyección *f* de ánimo; **his recent win was a great ~** su reciente victoria le levantó mucho la moral.

moralist ['mɒrəlɪst] N moralizador *m,* -ora *f;* (*philosopher, teacher*)

moralista *mf.*

moralistic [,mɒrə'lɪstɪk] ADJ moralizador.

morality [mə'rælɪtɪ] **1** N moralidad *f.*
　2 ATTR: **~ play** moralidad *f.*

moralize ['mɒrəlaɪz] VTI moralizar.

moralizing ['mɒrəlaɪzɪŋ] **1** ADJ moralizador.
　2 N instrucción *f* moral, predicación *f* sobre la moralidad.

morally ['mɒrəlɪ] ADV moralmente.

morass [mə'ræs] N cenagal *m,* pantano *m;* **a ~ of problems** un laberinto de problemas; **a ~ of figures** un mar de cifras.

moratorium [,mɒrə'tɔ:rɪəm] N, PL **moratoriums** *or* **moratoria** [,mɒrə'tɔ:rɪə] moratoria *f.*

Moravia [mə'reɪvɪə] N Moravia *f.*

moray ['mɒreɪ] N (*Fish*) morena *f.*

morbid ['mɔ:bɪd] ADJ insano, malsano; *mind* enfermizo; morboso, patológico; (*Med*) mórbido; (*depressed*) pesimista, melancólico; **don't be so ~!** ¡no digas esas cosas tan feas!

morbidity [mɔ:'bɪdɪtɪ] N, **morbidness** ['mɔ:bɪdnɪs] N lo insano, lo malsano; lo enfermizo; (*Med*) morbosidad *f;* pesimismo *m.*

morbidly ['mɔ:bɪdlɪ] ADV *talk etc* en tono pesimista; *think etc* con pesimismo.

mordacity [mɔ:dæsɪtɪ] N mordacidad *f.*

mordant ['mɔ:dənt] ADJ mordaz.

mordent ['mɔ:dənt] N mordente *m.*

▼**more** [mɔ:ʳ] **1** ADJ (**a**) más; **you have ~ money than I** tienes más dinero que yo; **~ light, please!** ¡más luz, por favor!; **a few ~ weeks** algunas semanas más; **do you want some ~ tea?** ¿quieres más té?; **is there any ~ wine in the bottle?** ¿queda vino en la botella?; **many ~ people** muchas más personas; **much ~ butter** mucha más mantequilla.
　(**b**) (*numerals*) **~ than half** más de la mitad; **~ than one** más de uno; **~ than 15** más de 15; **not ~ than one** no más de uno; **not ~ than 15** no más de quince.
　2 N AND PRON más; **we can't afford ~** no podemos pagar más; **this house cost ~ than ours** esta casa costó más que la nuestra; **it cost ~ than we had expected** costó más de lo que esperábamos; **I shall have ~ to say about this** volveré a hablar de esto; **and what's ~ ...** y además ...; **there's ~ where that came from!** ¡esto no es más que el principio!
　▼**3** ADV más; **~ easily** más fácilmente, con mayor facilidad (*than* que); **~ and ~** más y más, cada vez más; **~ or less** más o menos; **neither ~ nor less** ni más ni menos; **once ~** otra vez, una vez más; **never ~** nunca más; **if he comes here any ~** si vuelve por aquí; **if he says that any ~** si vuelve a decir eso, si dice eso otra vez; **the house is ~ than half built** la casa está más que medio construida; **I had ~ than carried out my obligation** había cumplido con creces mi obligación; **it will ~ than meet the demand** satisfará ampliamente la demanda; **he was ~ surprised than angry** más que enfadarse se sorprendió; **it's ~ a short story than a novel** más que novela es un cuento.
　▼**4** (*the ~*) **the ~ you give him the ~ he wants** cuanto más se le da tanto más quiere; **the ~ he drank the thirstier he got** cuanto más bebía más sed tenía; **it makes me (all) the ~ ashamed** tanto más vergüenza me da; **all the ~ so because** (*or* **as, since**) ... tanto más cuanto que ...; **the ~ the better, the ~ the merrier** cuantos más mejor.
　5 (*no ~ etc*) **I have no ~ pennies** no tengo más peniques; **no ~ singing, I can't bear it!** ¡que no se cante más, no lo aguanto!; **let's say no ~ about it** no se hable más de esto; **he doesn't live here any ~** ya no vive aquí; **Queen Anne is no ~** la reina Ana ya no existe; **we shall see her no ~** no la volveremos a ver; **'I don't understand it' ... 'no ~ do I'** 'no lo comprendo' ... 'ni yo tampoco'; **no ~ than is proper** lo justo y nada más; **not much ~ than £5** poco más de 5 libras; **she's no ~ a duchess than I am** tan duquesa es como mi padre; **he no ~ thought of paying me than of flying to the moon** antes iría volando a la luna que pensar pagarme a mí.

moreish ['mɔ:rɪʃ] ADJ apetitoso.

▼**moreover** [mɔ:'rəʊvəʳ] ADV además, por otra parte; es más ...

mores ['mɔ:reɪz] NPL costumbres *fpl,* tradiciones *fpl;* moralidad *f.*

morganatic [,mɔ:gə'nætɪk] ADJ morganático.

morganatically [,mɔ:gə'nætɪkəlɪ] ADV: **he married her ~** se casó con ella en casamiento morganático.

morgue [mɔ:g] N depósito *m* de cadáveres; (*US*·) archivo *m.*

MORI ['mɔ:rɪ] N ABBR *of* **Market & Opinion Research Institute** compañía especializada en encuestas.

moribund ['mɒrɪbʌnd] ADJ moribundo (*also fig*).

Mormon ['mɔ:mən] **1** ADJ mormónico.
　2 N mormón *m,* -ona *f.*

Mormonism ['mɔ:mənɪzəm] N mormonismo *m.*

morn [mɔ:n] N (*poet*) = **morning**; (*dawn*) alborada *f.*

morning ['mɔ:nɪŋ] **1** N mañana *f;* (*before dawn*) madrugada *f;* **good ~!** ¡buenos días!; **the ~ after** (*hum*) la mañana después de la juerga;

the next ~ la mañana siguiente, a la mañana; **early in the** ~ muy de mañana; **in the** ~ por la mañana; (*following day*) a la mañana (siguiente); **at 7 o'clock in the** ~ a las 7 de la mañana; **at 3 in the** ~ a las 3 de la madrugada; **tomorrow** ~ mañana por la mañana; **yesterday** ~ ayer por la mañana; **he's generally out** ~s por las mañanas en general no está.

2 ATTR de (la) mañana; mañanero; ~ **coat** chaqué *m*; ~ **dress** chaqué *m*; ~ **mist** bruma *f* del alba; ~ **paper** diario *m*; ~ **prayers** oraciones *fpl* de la mañana; ~ **sickness** náuseas *fpl* matutinas; ~ **star** lucero *m* del alba; ~ **tea** té *m* mañanero.

| MORE THAN | see also main entry |

"Más ... que" or "más ... de"?

- Use *más* with *que* before nouns and pronouns (provided they are not followed by clauses) as well as before adverbs and prepositions:
  - It was much more than a book
  - *Era mucho más que un libro*
  - She knows more than I do about such things
  - *Ella sabe más que yo de esas cosas*
  - Spain won more medals than ever before
  - *España logró más medallas que nunca*
- Use *más ... de lo que/del que/de la que/de los que/de las que* with following clauses:
  - It's much more complicated than you think
  - *Es mucho más complicado de lo que te imaginas*
  - There's much more violence now than there was in the seventies
  - *Hay mucha más violencia ahora de la que había en los setenta*
- Use *más* with *de* before *lo* + ADJECTIVE/PAST PARTICIPLE:
  - You'll have to work harder than usual
  - *Tendrás que trabajar más de lo normal*
  - It was more difficult than expected
  - *Fue más difícil de lo previsto*
- Use *más* with *de* in comparisons involving numbers or quantity:
  - There were more than twenty people there
  - *Había más de veinte personas allí*
  - More than half are women
  - *Más de la mitad son mujeres*
  - They hadn't seen each other for more than a year
  - *No se veían desde hacía más de un año*
- But *más ... que* can be used with numbers in more figurative comparisons:
  - A picture is worth more than a thousand words
  - *Una imagen vale más que mil palabras*
- NOTE: *Más ... que* is used before numbers in the construction *no ... más que*, meaning "only". Compare the following:
  - *No gana más que 100.000 ptas al mes*
  - He only earns 100,000 pesetas a month
  - *No gana más de 100.000 ptas al mes*
  - He doesn't earn more than 100,000 pesetas a month

A lot more

- When translating *a lot more, far more* etc remember to make the *mucho* in *mucho más* agree with any noun it describes or refers to:
  - We eat much more junk food than we used to
  - *Tomamos mucha más comida basura que antes*
  - It's only one sign. There are a lot or many more
  - *Sólo es una señal. Hay muchas más*
  - A lot more research will be needed
  - *Harán falta muchos más estudios*
  - For further uses and examples, see main entry at *more*.

---

morning-after ['mɔːnɪŋ'ɑːftər] ATTR: ~ **pill** píldora *f* del día siguiente.
morning-glory ['mɔːnɪŋ'glɔːrɪ] N dondiego *m* de día, ipomea *f*.
Moroccan [mə'rɒkən] **1** ADJ marroquí.
  2 N marroquí *mf*.
Morocco [mə'rɒkəʊ] N Marruecos *m*.
morocco [mə'rɒkəʊ] N (*also* ~ **leather**) marroquí *m*, tafilete *m*.
moron ['mɔːrɒn] N imbécil *mf*.
moronic [mə'rɒnɪk] ADJ imbécil.
morose [mə'rəʊs] ADJ malhumorado, hosco, taciturno.
morosely [mə'rəʊslɪ] ADV malhumoradamente, hoscamente, taciturnamente.
morph [mɔːf] N morfo *m*.
morpheme ['mɔːfiːm] N morfema *m*.
morphemic [mɔː'fiːmɪk] ADJ morfímico.
morphia ['mɔːfɪə] N, **morphine** ['mɔːfiːn] N morfina *f*.
morphing ['mɔːfɪŋ] N (*Cine*) morphing *m*, mutación *f* con efectos especiales.
morphological [ˌmɔːfə'lɒdʒɪkəl] ADJ morfológico.
morphologically [ˌmɔːfə'lɒdʒɪkəlɪ] ADV morfológicamente.

---

morphologist [mɔː'fɒlədʒɪst] N morfólogo *m*, -a *f*.
morphology [mɔː'fɒlədʒɪ] N morfología *f*.
morphosyntax [ˌmɔːfəʊ'sɪntæks] N morfosintaxis *f*.
morris ['mɒrɪs] N *baile tradicional inglés de hombres en el que éstos llevan cascabeles en la ropa.*
morrow ['mɒrəʊ] N: **on the** ~ (*liter*) al día siguiente.
Morse [mɔːs] **1** N morse *m*.
  2 ATTR: ~ **code** alfabeto *m* morse.
morsel ['mɔːsl] N (*small piece*) pedazo *m*, fragmento *m*; (*of food*) bocado *m*.
mort. ABBR *of* **mortgage**.
mortadella [ˌmɔːtə'delə] N mortadela *f*.
mortal ['mɔːtl] **1** ADJ mortal; ~ **combat** combate *m* mortal; ~ **remains** restos *mpl* mortales; ~ **sin** pecado *m* mortal.
  2 N mortal *mf*.
mortality [mɔː'tælɪtɪ] **1** N mortalidad *f*; (*number killed in war, accident*) número *m* de víctimas; **there was heavy** ~ hubo numerosas víctimas, murieron muchos, hubo gran mortandad.
  2 ATTR: ~ **rate** tasa *f* de mortalidad; ~ **table** tabla *f* de mortalidad.
mortally ['mɔːtəlɪ] ADV mortalmente; ~ **wounded** herido de muerte; ~ **offended** mortalmente ofendido.
mortar ['mɔːtər] **1** N (*Tech, Mil*) mortero *m*.
  2 VT bombardear con morteros.
mortarboard ['mɔːtəbɔːd] N (*Univ*) birrete *m*.
mortgage ['mɔːgɪdʒ] **1** N hipoteca *f*; **to pay off a** ~ redimir una hipoteca; **to raise a** ~, **to take out a** ~ obtener una hipoteca (*on* sobre).
  2 ATTR: ~ **broker** especialista *mf* en hipotecas; ~ **company** (*US*) ≃ banco *m* hipotecario; ~ **loan** préstamo *m* hipotecario; ~ **rate** tipo *m* de interés hipotecario.
  3 VT hipotecar; (*fig*) vender, poner en manos ajenas.
mortgageable ['mɔːgədʒəbl] ADJ hipotecable.
mortgagee [ˌmɔːgə'dʒiː] N acreedor *m* hipotecario, acreedora *f* hipotecaria.
mortgager, mortgagor ['mɔːgədʒər] N hipotecante *mf*, deudor *m* hipotecario, deudora *f* hipotecaria.
mortice ['mɔːtɪs] N = **mortise**.
mortician [mɔː'tɪʃən] N (*US*) director *m*, -ora *f* de pompas fúnebres.
mortification [ˌmɔːtɪfɪ'keɪʃən] N mortificación *f*; humillación *f*; (*Med*) gangrena *f*.
mortify ['mɔːtɪfaɪ] **1** VT mortificar; humillar; **I was mortified to find that** ... me avergoncé al descubrir que ...
  2 VI (*Med*) gangrenarse.
mortifying ['mɔːtɪfaɪɪŋ] ADJ humillante.
mortise, mortice ['mɔːtɪs] N muesca *f*, mortaja *f*; ~ **lock** cerradura *f* embutida.
mortuary ['mɔːtjʊərɪ] **1** ADJ mortuorio.
  2 N (*Brit*) depósito *m* de cadáveres; (*US*) funeraria *f*.
Mosaic [məʊ'zeɪɪk] ADJ mosaico.
mosaic [məʊ'zeɪɪk] N mosaico *m*.
Moscow ['mɒskəʊ] N Moscú *m*.
Moselle [məʊ'zel] N Mosela *m*.
Moses ['məʊzɪs] **1** NM Moisés.
  2 ATTR: ~ **basket** moisés *m*.
mosey* ['məʊzɪ] VI: **to** ~ **along** pasearse, deambular; **to** ~ **down to the shops** ir (sin prisa) a las tiendas.
Moslem ['mɒzlem] **1** ADJ musulmán.
  2 N musulmán *m*, -ana *f*.
mosque [mɒsk] N mezquita *f*.
mosquito [mɒs'kiːtəʊ] **1** N, PL **mosquitoes** [mɒs'kiːtəʊz] mosquito *m*.
  2 ATTR: ~ **bite** picadura *f* de mosquito; ~ **net** mosquitero *m*.
moss [mɒs] **1** N (a) (*Bot*) musgo *m*. (b) (*Geog*) pantano *m*, marjal *m*.
  2 ATTR: ~ **stitch** punto *m* de musgo.
mossy ['mɒsɪ] ADJ musgoso, cubierto de musgo.
most [məʊst] **1** ADJ SUPERL (a) (*with sing*) más; **who has** ~ **money?** ¿quién tiene más dinero?
  (b) (*with pl*) ~ **men** la mayor parte de los hombres, la mayoría de los hombres, los más hombres, casi todos los hombres.
  2 N AND PRON: **do the** ~ **you can** haga todo lo que pueda; ~ **of them** casi todos ellos; ~ **of those present** la mayor parte de los asistentes; ~ **of the time** la mayor parte del tiempo; **at** ~, **at the** ~, **at the very** ~ a lo más, a lo sumo, cuando más; **20 minutes at the** ~ 20 minutos como máximo; **it's the** ~!* ¡es fenomenal!*; **this group is the** ~!* ¡este conjunto es fabuloso!*; **the girl with the** ~* la chica más atractiva; **to get the** ~ **out of a situation** sacar el máximo partido de una situación; **to make the** ~ **of an affair** sacar todo el provecho posible de un asunto; **to make the** ~ **of one's advantages** aprovechar bien sus ventajas; **he made the** ~ **of the story** explotó todas las posibilidades del cuento, exageró los detalles del cuento.
  3 ADV (a) SUPERL **he spent** ~ él gastó más; **the** ~ **attractive girl there**

la chica más atractiva allí; **the ~ difficult of our problems** el más difícil de nuestros problemas; **which one did it ~ easily?** ¿quién lo hizo con la mayor facilidad?; **~ favoured nation clause** cláusula *f* de la nación más favorecida.

(b) (*intensive*) muy, sumamente; **~ likely** muy probable; **a ~ expensive toy** un juguete de los más caros, un juguete carísimo; **a ~ interesting book** un libro de lo más interesante, un libro interesantísimo; **you have been ~ kind** ha sido muy amable; **it's ~ holy** santísimo; **~ reverend** reverendísimo; *V* **all** *etc.*

(c) (*US**) **~ everybody** casi todos; **~ always** casi siempre. *See also* MAJORITY, MOST .

-most [məʊst] SUF más; **centre~** más central, **further~** más lejano.

mostly ['məʊstlɪ] ADV en su mayor parte; principalmente; en su mayoría; en general; **they are ~ women** en su mayoría son mujeres, casi todas son mujeres; **~ because ...** principalmente porque ...; **we ~ sell retail** en general vendemos al detalle, principalmente vendemos al por menor; **it's ~ finished** está casi terminado.

MOT N (*Brit*) **(a)** ABBR *of* **Ministry of Transport** ≃ Ministerio *m* de Transportes. **(b)** (*Aut: also* **~ test**) ABBR *of* **Ministry of Transport test** *examen anual de coches obligatorio*; **~** (**test**) **certificate** ≃ Inspección *f* Técnica de Vehículos, ITV *f*.

mote [məʊt] N átomo *m*, mota *f*; **to see the ~ in our neighbour's eye and not the beam in our own** ver la paja en el ojo ajeno y no la viga en el propio.

motel [məʊ'tel] N motel *m*, hotel-garaje *m* (*LAm*).

motet [məʊ'tet] N motete *m*.

moth [mɒθ] N mariposa *f* (nocturna); (*clothes* **~**) polilla *f*.

mothball ['mɒθbɔːl] [1] N bola *f* de naftalina, bola *f* de la polilla; **in ~s** (*Naut etc*) en la reserva.

[2] VT *ship etc* poner en la reserva.

moth-eaten ['mɒθ,iːtn] ADJ apolillado, comido de la polilla.

mother ['mʌðəʳ] [1] N madre *f*; (*US**) = **motherfucker***; **M~ of God** Madre *f* de Dios; **M~ Superior** superiora *f*, madre *f* superiora; **to be a ~ to sb** ser como una madre para uno.

[2] ATTR: **~ church** iglesia *f* metropolitana; **M~ Church** Santa Madre Iglesia *f*; **~ country** patria *f*; **M~s' Day** fiesta *f* de la Madre; **M~ Earth** la madre tierra; **~ figure** figura *f* maternal; **M~ Goose** la Oca; **~ hen** gallina *f* madre; **~ love** amor *m* maternal; **M~ Nature** Dama *f* Naturaleza; **~ ship** buque *m* nodriza; **~ tongue** lengua *f* materna; **~ wit** sentido *m* común.

[3] VT (*give birth to*) parir, dar a luz; (*act as ~ to*) servir de madre a; (*spoil*) mimar; *young animal* prohijar.

motherboard ['mʌðə,bɔːd] N placa *f* madre.

mothercraft ['mʌðəkrɑːft] N arte *m* de cuidar a los niños pequeños, arte *m* de ser madre.

motherfucker* ['mʌðə,fʌkəʳ] N (*US*) hijoputa* *m*, cabronazo* *m*.

motherfucking* ['mʌðə,fʌkɪŋ] ADJ (*US*) pijotero*, condenado*.

motherhood ['mʌðəhʊd] N maternidad *f*; **to prepare for ~** prepararse para ser madre.

mothering ['mʌðərɪŋ] [1] N cuidados *mpl* maternales.

[2] ATTR: **M~ Sunday** (*Brit*) fiesta *f* de la Madre.

mother-in-law ['mʌðərɪnlɔː] N, PL **mothers-in-law** suegra *f*.

motherland ['mʌðəlænd] N patria *f*, (*more sentimentally*) madre patria *f*.

motherless ['mʌðəlɪs] ADJ huérfano de madre, sin madre.

motherly ['mʌðəlɪ] ADJ maternal.

mother-of-pearl ['mʌðərəv'pɜːl] [1] N nácar *m*.

[2] ADJ nacarado.

mother-to-be ['mʌðətə'biː] N, PL **mothers-to-be** futura madre *f*.

moth-hole ['mɒθhəʊl] N apolilladura *f*.

mothproof ['mɒθpruːf] ADJ a prueba de polillas.

motif [məʊ'tiːf] N (*Art, Mus*) motivo *m*; (*of speech etc*) tema *m*; (*Sew*) adorno *m*.

motion ['məʊʃən] [1] N **(a)** (*movement*) movimiento *m*; (*of parts of machine*) marcha *f*, operación *f*, funcionamiento *m*; **to be in ~** estar en movimiento; **to go through the ~s** hacer algo en la debida forma, obrar de acuerdo con las reglas (pero sin creer que se vaya a conseguir nada); obrar por pura fórmula; **to set sth in ~** poner algo en marcha.

(b) (*sign*) ademán *m*, señal *f*; **he made a ~ with his hand** hizo una señal con la mano.

(c) (*Parl etc*) moción *f*, proposición *f*; **to bring forward** (*or* **propose, US make**) **a ~** presentar una moción; **to carry a ~** (*person*) hacer adoptar una moción, (*meeting*) adoptar una moción, aprobar una moción; **to vote on a ~** votar una moción; **the ~ is carried** se ha aprobado la moción; **the ~ is lost** se ha rechazado la moción.

(d) (*Mech, moving part*) mecanismo *m*.

(e) (*Med*) evacuación *f* del vientre.

[2] ATTR: **~ sickness** mareo *m*.

[3] VT: **to ~ sb to do sth** hacer señas a uno para que haga algo, indicar a uno con la mano (*etc*) que haga algo; **he ~ed me to a chair** indicó con la mano que me sentara.

[4] VI: **to ~ to sb to do sth** hacer señas a uno para que haga algo, indicar a uno con la mano (*etc*) que haga algo.

motionless ['məʊʃənlɪs] ADJ inmóvil.

motion picture ['məʊʃən,pɪktʃəʳ] (*US*) [1] N película *f*.

[2] ATTR cinematográfico; **~ camera** cámara *f* cinematográfica; **~ industry** industria *f* del cine; **~ theater** (*US*), **~ theatre** cine *m*.

motivate ['məʊtɪveɪt] VT motivar; **to be ~d to do sth** tener motivo(s) para hacer algo; **he is highly ~d** tiene una fuerte motivación; **the campaign is politically ~d** la campaña tiene una motivación política.

motivation [,məʊtɪ'veɪʃən] N motivación *f*.

motivational [,məʊtɪ'veɪʃənl] ADJ motivacional; **~ research** estudios *mpl* motivacionales.

motive ['məʊtɪv] [1] ADJ motor (*f*: motora, motriz); **~ power** fuerza *f* motriz.

[2] N motivo *m* (*for* de); móvil *m*; **what can his ~ have been?** ¿cuál habrá sido su motivo?, ¿qué motivo habrá tenido?; **my ~s were of the purest** lo hice con la mejor intención.

motiveless ['məʊtɪvlɪs] ADV sin motivo, inmotivado.

motley ['mɒtlɪ] [1] ADJ (*many-coloured*) abigarrado, multicolor; (*diversified*) vario, compuesto de elementos muy diversos.

[2] N botarga *f*, traje *m* de colores; **on with the ~** vistámonos de payaso.

motocross ['məʊtəkrɒs] N motocross *m*.

motor ['məʊtəʳ] [1] ADJ (*giving motion*) motor; (*motorized*) automóvil.

[2] N **(a)** (*engine*) motor *m*. **(b)** (*Brit: car*) coche *m*, automóvil *m*, carro *m* (*LAm*).

[3] ATTR: **~ accident** accidente *m* de circulación; **~ insurance** seguro *m* de automóvil; **~ launch** lancha *f* motora; **~ mechanic** mecánico *m* de automóviles; **~ road** vía *f* pública, pista *f*, carretera *f*; **~ scooter** motosilla *f*, escúter *m*; **~ ship** motonave *f*; **~ show** exposición *f* de automóviles; **the Paris ~ show** el salón del automóvil de París; **~ spirit** gasolina *f*; **~ torpedo-boat** torpedero *m*; **~ trader** comerciante *mf* en automóviles; **~ transport** transporte *m* motorizado; **~ vehicle** automóvil *m*; **~ vessel** motonave *f*.

[4] VI ir en coche, viajar en automóvil; **we ~ed down to Ascot** fuimos en coche a Ascot; **we ~ed over to see them** fuimos a visitarles (en coche).

motorail ['məʊtəreɪl] N motorail *m*.

motorbike* ['məʊtəbaɪk] N moto* *f*.

motorboat ['məʊtəbəʊt] N motora *f*, motorbote *m*, lancha *f* rápida, lancha *f* motora.

motorcade ['məʊtəkeɪd] N (*US*) desfile *m* de automóviles.

motorcar ['məʊtəkɑːʳ] N (*Brit*) coche *m*, automóvil *m*, carro *m* (*LAm*).

motor-coach ['məʊtəkəʊtʃ] N autocar *m*, autobús *m*, camión *m* (*LAm*).

motorcycle ['məʊtə,saɪkl] N motocicleta *f*; **~ combination** motocicleta *f* con sidecar.

motorcycling ['məʊtə,saɪklɪŋ] N motociclismo *m*, motorismo *m*.

motorcyclist ['məʊtə,saɪklɪst] N motociclista *mf*; motorista *mf*.

motor-driven ['məʊtə,drɪvn] ADJ automóvil, propulsado por motor.

-motored ['məʊtəd] ADJ *ending in compounds*: **four~** cuatrimotor, tetramotor; **petrol~** propulsado por gasolina.

motoring ['məʊtərɪŋ] [1] ADJ *accident etc* de automóvil, de tránsito ·(*LAm*), automovilístico, de carretera; **~ holiday** vacaciones *fpl* en coche; **the ~ public** los que viajan en coche; el público aficionado al automovilismo.

[2] N automovilismo *m*; **school of ~** autoescuela *f*, escuela *f* automovilista.

motorist ['məʊtərɪst] N (*Brit*) automovilista *mf*; conductor *m*, -ora *f* (de coche), chófer *m*.

motorization [,məʊtəraɪ'zeɪʃən] N motorización *f*.

motorize ['məʊtəraɪz] VT motorizar; **to get ~d*** adquirir un coche; **now that we're ~d*** ahora que tenemos coche.

motorized ['məʊtəraɪzd] ADJ motorizado.

motorman ['məʊtəmən] N, PL **motormen** ['məʊtəmən] N conductor *m* (de locomotora eléctrica *etc*), maquinista *m*.

motormouth* ['məʊtəmaʊθ] N cotorra* *f*.

motor-mower ['məʊtə,məʊəʳ] N cortacésped *m* a motor.

motor-oil ['məʊtər,ɔɪl] N aceite *m* para motores.

motor-racing ['məʊtə,reɪsɪŋ] [1] N automovilismo *m* deportivo, carreras *fpl* de coches.

[2] ATTR: **~ track** pista *f* de automovilismo.

motorway ['məʊtəweɪ] N (*Brit*) autopista *f*; **~ madness** locura *f* en la autopista; **~ service area** área *f* de servicios de autopista; **~ services** servicios *mpl* en autopista.

mottled ['mɒtld] ADJ abigarrado, multicolor; *marble etc* jaspeado; *complexion* con manchas; *animal, bird* con manchas, moteado; **~ with** manchado de, pintado de.

motto ['mɒtəʊ] N, PL **mottoes** *or* **mottos** ['mɒtəʊz] lema *m*; (*Heraldry*) divisa *f*; (*watchword*) consigna *f*; (*in cracker: verse*) versos *mpl*; (*joke*) chiste *m*.

mould¹, (US) **mold** [məʊld] N (soil) mantillo m.

mould², (US) **mold** [məʊld] **1** N (hollow form) molde m; (~ed object) cosa f moldeada; (fig) carácter m, índole f, temple m; **cast in a heroic ~** de carácter heroico.
2 VT (fashion) moldear; (cast) vaciar; (Carp) moldurar; (fig) amoldar (on a), formar; **~ed plastics** plásticos mpl moldeados; **it is ~ed on ...** está hecho según ...
3 VR: **to ~ o.s. on sb** amoldarse como uno, modelarse sobre uno, tomar a uno como ejemplo.

mould³, (US) **mold** [məʊld] N (fungus) moho m; (iron ~) mancha f de orín.

moulder¹, (US) **molder** ['məʊldər] N (Tech) moldeador m, -ora f.

moulder², (US) **molder** ['məʊldər] VI (also **to ~ away**) desmoronarse, convertirse en polvo; (fig) desmoronarse, decaer.

mouldering ['məʊldərɪŋ] ADJ podrido; carcomido.

mouldiness, (US) **moldiness** ['məʊldɪnɪs] N moho m, lo mohoso, enmohecimiento m.

moulding, (US) **molding** ['məʊldɪŋ] N (act) amoldamiento m; (cast) vaciado m; (Archit) moldura f; (fig) amoldamiento m, formación f.

mouldy, (US) **moldy** ['məʊldɪ] ADJ **(a)** mohoso, enmohecido. **(b)** (*: fig) horrible, malísimo; miserable, cochino; **the play was ~** la obra fue horrible; **all he gave me was a ~ old penny** lo único que me dio fue un cochino penique.

moult, (US) **molt** [məʊlt] **1** N muda f.
2 VT mudar.
3 VI (snake etc) mudar la piel, (bird) mudar la pluma.

mound [maʊnd] N (pile) montón m; (earthwork) terraplén m; (burial ~) túmulo m; (hillock) montículo m.

mount [maʊnt] **1** N **(a)** (Geog: ††, except with names) monte m, montaña f; **M~ Everest** (monte m) Everest m.
(b) (horse etc) montura f, caballería f.
(c) (of machine etc) base f, soporte m; (of jewel) engaste m; (of photo etc) borde m, marco m; (stamp ~) fijasello m.
2 VT **(a)** horse montar, subir a; (in mating) cubrir; platform etc subir a, subir en; ladder subir; throne subir a.
(b) machine etc montar, armar; play poner en escena; exhibition organizar; attack lanzar, hacer.
(c) picture poner un borde a, poner un marco a; stamp pegar, fijar; jewel engastar.
(d) guard montar.
(e) (provide with horse) proveer de caballo.
3 VI **(a)** (climb) subir; (get on horse) montar. **(b)** (also **to ~ up**; of quantity, price etc) subir, aumentar.

mountain ['maʊntɪn] **1** N montaña f; (pile) montón m; **to make a ~ out of a molehill** exagerar ridículamente una dificultad, hacer de una pulga un elefante.
2 ATTR montañés, de montaña; montañero, serrano; **~ ash** serbal m; **~ bike** bicicleta f de montaña; **~ chain, ~ range** sierra f; **~ hut, ~ refuge** albergue m de montaña; **~ lion** (US) puma f; **~ rescue** servicio m de rescate de montañas; **~ sickness** puna f (LAm), soroche m (LAm).

mountaineer [,maʊntɪ'nɪər] **1** N montañero m, -a f, alpinista mf, andinista mf (LAm).
2 VI dedicarse al montañismo, hacer alpinismo.

mountaineering [,maʊntɪ'nɪərɪŋ] **1** N montañismo m, alpinismo m, andinismo m (LAm).
2 ATTR montañero, alpinista.

mountainous ['maʊntɪnəs] ADJ montañoso; (fig) enorme, colosal.

mountainside ['maʊntɪn,saɪd] N ladera f de montaña, falda f de montaña.

mountaintop ['maʊntɪntɒp] N cima f de una montaña, cumbre f de una montaña.

mountebank ['maʊntɪbæŋk] N saltabanco m, saltimbanqui m.

mounted ['maʊntɪd] ADJ montado; **~ police** policía f montada.

Mountie* ['maʊntɪ] N (Canada) miembro m de la policía montada canadiense; **the ~s** la policía montada canadiense.

mounting ['maʊntɪŋ] N (of machine: act) montaje m; (frame, base) armadura f, base f, soporte m; (of jewel) engaste m; (of photo etc) marco m.

mourn [mɔːn] **1** VT llorar, llorar la muerte de, lamentar; (wear ~ing for) llevar luto por.
2 VI afligirse, lamentarse; (wear ~ing) estar de luto; **to ~ for sb** llorar la muerte de uno; **to ~ for sth** llorar la pérdida (or desaparición etc) de algo; **it's no good ~ing over it** de nada sirve afligirse por eso.

mourner ['mɔːnər] N doliente mf; (hired) plañidero m, -a f; **the ~s** los que acompañan el féretro, los acompañantes.

mournful ['mɔːnfʊl] ADJ person triste, afligido; tone, sound triste, lúgubre, lastimero; occasion triste, melancólico.

mournfully ['mɔːnfəlɪ] ADV tristemente.

mournfulness ['mɔːnfʊlnɪs] N tristeza f; aflicción f; melancolía f.

mourning ['mɔːnɪŋ] **1** N (act) lamentación f; (period etc) luto m, duelo m; (dress) luto m; **to be in ~** estar de luto; **to be in ~ for** llevar luto por; **to come out of ~** dejar el luto; **to go into ~** ponerse de luto; **to plunge a town into ~** enlutar una ciudad.
2 ATTR de luto.

mouse [maʊs] **1** N, PL **mice** [maɪs] **(a)** ratón m. **(b)** (Comput) ratón m.
2 VI cazar ratones.

mousehole ['maʊshəʊl] N ratonera f.

mouser ['maʊsər] N cazador m de ratones.

mousetrap ['maʊstræp] **1** N ratonera f.
2 ATTR: **~ cheese*** queso m corriente.

moussaka [mʊ'sɑːkə] N musaca f.

mousse [muːs] N mousse f, crema f batida; **chocolate ~** crema f batida de chocolate.

moustache [məs'tɑːʃ], (US) **mustache** ['mʌstæʃ] N bigote m, bigotes mpl, mostacho m; **to wear a ~** tener bigote.

moustachioed [mə'stɑːʃiəʊd], (US) **mustachioed** [mʌstæʃiəʊd] ADJ bigotudo.

mousy ['maʊsɪ] ADJ person tímido, de personalidad poco fuerte; colour pardusco.

mouth [maʊθ] **1** N, PL **mouths** [maʊðz] boca f; (fig, of bottle, cave etc) boca f; (of river) desembocadura f; (of channel) embocadero m; (of wind instrument) boquilla f; **to be down in the ~** estar deprimido, andar alicaído; **to foam** (or froth) **at the ~** espumajear; **to keep one's ~ shut** (fig) tener la boca cerrada, guardar un secreto; **he never opened his ~ at the meeting** en la reunión no abrió la boca; **she didn't dare to open her ~** no se atrevió a decir ni pío; **to put words into sb's ~** poner palabras en boca de uno; **to shoot off one's ~*** hablar inoportunamente, hablar más de la cuenta; **shut your ~!*** ¡cállate ya!; **to stop sb's ~** hacer callar a uno.
2 [maʊð] VT (affectedly) pronunciar con afectación, articular con rimbombancia; (soundlessly) formar con los labios.
3 [maʊð] VI hablar exagerando los movimientos de la boca.

mouthed [maʊðd] ADJ ending in compounds de boca ..., que tiene la boca ...; **big-~** de boca grande.

mouthful ['maʊθfʊl] N bocado m; (of smoke, air) bocanada f; **the name is a proper ~** es un nombre kilométrico; **you said a ~*** (US) ¡y que lo digas!, ¡tú lo has dicho!

mouthorgan ['maʊθ,ɔːgən] N armónica f.

mouthpiece ['maʊθpiːs] N (Mus) boquilla f; (of bridle) embocadura f; (Telec) micrófono m; (fig, person) portavoz m.

mouth-to-mouth ['maʊθtə'maʊθ] ATTR: **~ resuscitation** resucitación f boca a boca.

mouthwash ['maʊθwɒʃ] N enjuague m (bucal).

mouth-watering ['maʊθ'wɔːtərɪŋ] ADJ sumamente apetitoso.

movable ['muːvəbl] **1** ADJ movible; **~ feast** fiesta f movible; **not easily ~** nada fácil de mover.
2 N: **~s** muebles mpl, mobiliario m; (Jur) bienes mpl muebles.

move [muːv] **1** N **(a)** (movement) movimiento m; **Spain is a country on the ~** España es país en marcha; **to be always on the ~** estar siempre en movimiento, (travelling) estar siempre de viaje, (of animal, child) no saber estar quieto; **you can phone while on the ~** puede telefonear en pleno desplazamiento; **to get a ~ on** (person) menearse, darse prisa; **get a ~ on!** ¡menearse!, ¡espabílate!; **they're getting a ~ on with the bridge now** ahora la construcción del puente avanza rápidamente; **to make a ~** (to go) ponerse en marcha; **it's time we made a ~** es hora de irnos; **it was midnight and no-one had made a ~** era medianoche pero nadie daba señales de irse.
(b) (in game) jugada f; (at chess) jugada f, movimiento m, movida f; **it's my ~** yo juego; **it's your ~** te toca a ti; **whose ~ is it?** ¿a quién le toca jugar?; **he's up to every ~ in the game** se las sabe todas; **to have first ~** empezar, salir, jugar primero; **to make a ~** hacer una jugada, jugar.
(c) (step) paso m, acción f; gestión f; maniobra f; **the government's first ~** la primera gestión del gobierno; **what's the next ~?** ¿qué hacemos ahora?, ¿y ahora qué?; **to make a ~** dar un paso; tomar medidas; **it's up to him to make the first ~** le toca a él dar el primer paso; **without making the least ~ to** + infin sin hacer la menor intención de + infin; **to watch sb's every ~** observar a uno sin perder detalle, acecharle a uno cada movimiento.
(d) (of house) mudanza f; (of person to job) traslado m; **it's our third ~ in two years** ésta es la tercera vez en dos años que nos mudamos; **then he made a ~ to Buenos Aires** luego se trasladó a Buenos Aires.
2 VT **(a)** (change place of) mover; cambiar de sitio, trasladar; (transport) transportar; (propel) propulsar, impeler; date, event cambiar (la fecha or el lugar etc de); trasladar (a otro sitio); **he was ~d to Quito** le trasladaron a Quito; **if we can ~ the table a few inches** si podemos mover la mesa unos centímetros; **to ~ a piece** (Chess) jugar una pieza, mover una pieza; **'we shall not be ~d'** 'no nos moverán'.
(b) **to ~ house** (Brit) mudarse, cambiarse (Mex); **to ~ one's job** cambiar de empleo.

(c) (*cause to ~*) remover, agitar, sacudir, menear; **the breeze ~d the leaves gently** la brisa agitaba dulcemente las hojas; **to ~ the bowels** desocupar el vientre.

(d) (*person, from opinion*) mover, hacer cambiar de opinión; **he will not be easily ~d** no será fácil moverle.

(e) (*emotionally*) conmover, enternecer; impresionar; **to be easily ~d** ser impresionable, ser sensible; **to ~ sb to do sth** mover a uno a hacer algo; **when I feel so ~d** cuando estoy con el ánimo para eso; **to ~ sb to anger** encolerizar a uno; **to ~ sb to tears** hacer llorar a uno.

(f) (*Parl*) **to ~ a resolution** proponer una resolución, hacer una moción; **to ~ that ...** proponer que + *subj*.

(g) (*Comm*) merchandise colocar, vender.

3 VI **(a)** (*gen*) moverse; (*to a place*) trasladarse (*to* a); (*shake*) moverse, agitarse, temblar; **~!** ¡menearse!; **she ~d to the next room** pasó a la habitación inmediata; **let's ~ into the garden** vamos al jardín; **she ~s beautifully** anda con garbo; **I'll not ~ from here** no me muevo de aquí; **to ~ freely** (*part, Mech*) moverse libremente, (*person, traffic*) circular libremente; **to keep the traffic moving** mantener fluida la circulación; **keep moving!** ¡circulen!, ¡vayan pasando por delante!; **to ~ in high society** frecuentar la buena sociedad, alternar con personas de la buena sociedad.

(b) (*depart*) irse, marcharse; **it's time we were moving** es hora de irnos.

(c) (*travel*) ir; estar en movimiento; **the car was not moving** el coche no estaba en marcha; **the bus was moving at 50 kph** el autobús iba a 50 k/h; **the capsule is moving at 18,000 mph** la cápsula se desplaza a 18.000 m/h; **he was certainly moving!** ¡iba como el demonio!

(d) (*progress*) ir adelante, avanzar, hacer progresos; (*of plants*) crecer; **things are moving at last** por fin se están haciendo progresos.

(e) (*~ house*) mudarse, mudar de casa; **the family ~d to a new house** la familia se mudó a una casa nueva.

(f) (*in games*) jugar, hacer una jugada; **who ~s next?** ¿a quién le toca jugar?; **white ~s** (*Chess*) blanco juega.

(g) (*take steps*) dar un paso, hacer una gestión, tomar medidas; **the government must ~ first** el gobierno ha de dar el primer paso; **the council ~d to stop the abuse** el consejo hizo gestiones para corregir el abuso.

◆**move about, move around** **1** VT cambiar (mucho) de lugar, trasladar (a menudo) a otro sitio; mover de acá para allá.

2 VI ir y venir, ir de acá para allá; desplazarse (a menudo); cambiar (mucho) de lugar; **to ~ about freely** circular libremente.

◆**move along** **1** VT *crowd* hacer circular; *passengers* hacer pasar hacia adelante.

2 VI avanzar; (*on bench etc*) correrse.

◆**move aside** **1** VT apartar.

2 VI apartarse; ponerse a un lado, quitarse de en medio.

◆**move away** **1** VT alejar, apartar; quitar de en medio.

2 VI **(a)** alejarse, apartarse (*from* de); (*depart*) marcharse. **(b)** (*move house*) mudar de casa.

◆**move back** **1** VT **(a)** *crowd etc* mover hacia atrás, hacer retroceder. **(b)** (*to original place*) devolver a su lugar. **(c)** (*postpone*) aplazar.

2 VI **(a)** (*withdraw*) retroceder; retirarse. **(b)** (*to original place*) volver a su lugar. **(c)** **they ~d back to Burgos again** (*move house*) volvieron a Burgos.

◆**move down** **1** VT *object etc* bajar.

2 VI **(a)** (*person etc*) bajar, descender. **(b)** (*in league*) descender (a la división inferior *etc*).

◆**move forward** **1** VT **(a)** mover hacia adelante. **(b)** (*help progress*) avanzar, adelantar, promover. **(c)** *meeting etc* adelantar la fecha de.

2 VI avanzar.

◆**move in** **1** VT hacer entrar; llevar dentro, instalar.

2 VI **(a)** (*police etc*) avanzar; intervenir, llegar. **(b)** (*to house*) tomar posesión, instalarse.

◆**move in on** VT (*police etc*) avanzar hacia; **to ~ in on sb** invadir a uno.

◆**move off** VI alejarse; (*depart*) marcharse; ponerse en marcha, ponerse en camino.

◆**move on** **1** VT *crowd etc* hacer circular.

2 VI (*go on*) seguir, seguir andando; reanudar su viaje; (*go forward*) avanzar; (*time*) pasar; **let us ~ on to the next item** pasemos al próximo asunto; **things have ~d on since your visit** las cosas han cambiado después de tu visita.

◆**move out** **1** VT desalojar, trasladar a otra parte.

2 VI salir; irse; abandonar la casa (*etc*).

◆**move over** **1** VT apartar, mover a un lado.

2 VI apartarse, moverse a un lado; correrse hacia un lado; **we should ~ over to a different system** nos conviene cambiar a otro sistema; **she ~d over to give others a chance** cambió de puesto para dar más oportunidades a otros.

◆**move up** **1** VT **(a)** *object* subir; *troops* mover hacia el frente. **(b)**

(*promote*) ascender; (*in class*) trasladar a una clase superior.

2 VI **(a)** (*make room*) hacer sitio, correrse hacia un lado. **(b)** (*rise*) subir. **(c)** (*be promoted*) ser ascendido.

moveable ['muːvəbl] = **movable**.

movement ['muːvmənt] N **(a)** (*act*) movimiento *m* (*also Mil*); (*of part*) juego *m*, movimiento *m*; (*of traffic etc*) circulación *f*; (*on stock exchange*) actividad *f*, (*change of price*) cambio *m* de precio; **~ of capital** movimiento *m* de capitales; **to be in ~** estar en movimiento; **there was a ~ towards the door** se dirigieron algunos hacia la puerta. **(b)** (*Pol*) movimiento *m*. **(c)** (*Mus*) tiempo *m*, movimiento *m*. **(d)** (*Mech, part*) mecanismo *m*. **(e)** (*Med*) evacuación *f*.

mover ['muːvəʳ] N **(a)** (*of motion*) autor *m*, -ora *f*, proponente *mf*. **(b)** (*US*) agente *m* de mudanzas. **(c)** **he's a lovely ~** se mueve con mucho garbo, anda con mucha elegancia.

movie ['muːvɪ] **1** N (*US*) película *f*; **the ~s** el cine; **to go to the ~s** ir al cine.

2 ATTR: **~ camera** cámara *f* cinematográfica; **~ house, ~ theater** (*US*) cine *m*; **~ industry** industria *f* cinematográfica; **~ star** estrella *f* cinematográfica (*or* de cine).

moviegoer ['muːvɪɡəʊəʳ] N (*US*) aficionado *m*, -a *f* al cine.

movieland ['muːvɪlænd] N (*US*) (*dreamworld*) mundo *m* de ensueño creado por el cine; (*eg Hollywood*) centro *m* de la industria cinematográfica.

moving ['muːvɪŋ] ADJ **(a)** (*that moves*) movedor; movedizo; (*motive*) motor; **~ average** promedio *m* móvil; **~ part** pieza *f* móvil; **~ staircase** escalera *f* móvil, escalera *f* mecánica; **~ van** (*US*) camión *m* de mudanzas; **they fired from a ~ vehicle** dispararon desde un vehículo en marcha (*or* movimiento); **a ~ target is hard to hit** es difícil dar en el blanco si éste se mueve. **(b)** (*fig*) conmovedor; emocionante.

movingly ['muːvɪŋlɪ] ADV de modo conmovedor; **he spoke most ~** conmovió profundamente a los que le escuchaban.

mow [məʊ] (*irr*: PRET **mowed**, PTP **mown** *or* **mowed**) VT *corn etc* segar; *grass* cortar; **to ~ down** segar.

mower ['məʊəʳ] N segador *m*, -ora *f*; (*lawn ~*) cortacésped *m*.

mowing ['məʊɪŋ] N siega *f*.

mowing-machine ['məʊɪŋməʃiːn] N segadora *f* (mecánica).

mown [məʊn] PTP *of* **mow**.

moxie;, moxy; ['mɒksɪ] N (*US*) (*courage*) valor *m*; (*nerve*) sangre fría *f*; (*vigor*) vigor *m*, dinamismo *m*.

Mozambican [ˌməʊzæmˈbiːkən] **1** ADJ mozambiqueño.

2 N mozambiqueño *m*, -a *f*.

Mozambique [ˌməʊzəmˈbiːk] N Mozambique *m*.

Mozarab [mɒzˈærəb] N mozárabe *mf*.

┌─ **MR, MRS, MISS** ────────────── *see also main entries* ─┐

Use of article

● Use the article with *Sr./señor, Sra./señora, Srta./señorita* when you are talking *about* someone rather than *to* them:
    Mr Smith is not at home
    El Sr. Smith no está en casa
    Mr and Mrs Crespo are on holiday
    Los Sres. (de) Crespo están de vacaciones
    Have you seen Miss Barrios this morning?
    ¿Ha visto a la Srta. Barrios esta mañana?
    NOTE: The abbreviated form is more common than the full form in writing.

● Don't use the article before *Sr./señor, Sra./señora, Srta./señorita* when addressing someone directly:
    Good morning, Mrs Ramírez
    Buenos días, Sra. Ramírez
    Mr López, there's a telephone call for you
    Sr. López, le llaman por teléfono

Capitalization

● Write the *full forms señor, señora* and *señorita* with a small "s", even when using them as titles:
    El señor Smith no está en casa
    Estaba hablando con la señora (de) Williams

Addressing correspondence

● Use *Sr. Don/Sra. Doña (Sr. D./Sra. Dña.)* rather than *Sr./Sra.* when giving both forename and surname. Don't use the article:
    Mr Bernardo García
    Sr. Don or *Sr. D. Bernardo García*
    Mrs Teresa Álvarez Serrano
    Sra. Doña or *Sra. Dña. Teresa Álvarez Serrano*
    For further uses and examples, see main entries at miss[2], mister and Mrs.

⇨ See also APELLIDO , DON

└──────────────────────────────────┘

Mozarabic [mɒzˈærəbɪk] **1** ADJ mozárabe.
2 N mozárabe m.
mozzarella [ˌmɒtsəˈrelə] N mozzarella f.
MP N **(a)** (Brit Parl) ABBR of **member of parliament** diputado m, -a f, parlamentario m, -a f. **(b)** (Mil) ABBR of **military police** policía f militar, P.M. f. **(c)** (Canada) ABBR of **mounted police** policía f montada.
mpg N (Aut) ABBR of **miles per gallon** millas fpl por galón.
mph N ABBR of **miles per hour** millas fpl por hora, m/h.
M.Phil. N ABBR of **Master of Philosophy** título universitario.
MPS N (Brit) ABBR of **Member of the Pharmaceutical Society.**
Mr [ˈmɪstəʳ] N ABBR of **Mister** señor m, Sr.
MRC N (Brit) ABBR of **Medical Research Council** departamento estatal que controla la investigación médica.
MRCP N (Brit) ABBR of **Member of the Royal College of Physicians.**
MRCS N (Brit) ABBR of **Member of the Royal College of Surgeons.**
MRCVS N (Brit) ABBR of **Member of the Royal College of Veterinary Surgeons.**
MRD N ABBR of **machine-readable dictionary.**
MRP N ABBR of **manufacturer's recommended price** precio m recomendado por el fabricante.
Mrs [ˈmɪsɪz] N ABBR of **Mistress** señora f, Sra.; ~ **Brown** la señora de Brown.
MRSA N ABBR of **methicillin-resistant Staphylococcus aureus** estafilococo m dorado resistente a meticilina, virus asesino sin tratamiento conocido.
MS (a) N ABBR of **multiple sclerosis** esclerosis f múltiple. **(b)** N (US) ABBR of **Master of Science** título universitario. **(c)** (US Post) ABBR of **Mississippi.**
Ms [mɪz, məz] prefijo de nombre de mujer que evita expresar su estado civil.

┌─── **Ms** ───┐
ⓘ La fórmula de tratamiento Ms es el equivalente femenino de Mr y se utiliza frecuentemente en la actualidad para evitar la distinción que los términos tradicionales establecían entre mujer casada (**Mrs**) y soltera (**Miss**). Las formas Ms y Miss nunca llevan punto, pero Mr y Mrs a veces sí.

M.S.A. N (US) ABBR of **Master of Science in Agriculture** título universitario.
MSc N (Brit) ABBR of **Master of Science** título universitario; ver también ⟨DEGREE⟩.
MS-DOS [ˌemˈesdɒs] N ABBR of **Microsoft Disk Operating System.**
MSF N (Brit) ABBR of **Manufacturing, Science, Finance.**
MSG N (esp US) ABBR of **monosodium glutamate.**
Msgr ABBR of **Monsignor** monseñor m, Mons.
MSI N ABBR of **medium-scale integration** integración f a mediana escala.
MS(S) ABBR of **manuscript(s)** manuscrito(s) m(pl).
MST N (US) ABBR of **Mountain Standard Time.**
M.S.W. N (US) ABBR of **Master of Social Work** título universitario.
MT (a) N ABBR of **machine translation. (b)** (US Post) ABBR of **Montana.**
Mt (Geog) ABBR of **Mount, Mountain** monte m, m.
MTB N ABBR of **motor torpedo boat.**
mth ABBR of **month** mes m, m.
much [mʌtʃ] **1** ADJ mucho; ~ **money** mucho dinero; **how ~ money?** ¿cuánto dinero?; **it's too ~!*** (fantastic) ¡esto es demasiado!*, ¡qué demasia(d)o!*, ¡esto es estupendo!*; (excessive) esto pasa de la raya, esto pasa de castaño oscuro.
2 ADV **(a)** mucho; (before ptp) muy; ~ **better** mucho mejor; ~ **pleased** muy satisfecho; **it doesn't ~ matter** no importa mucho; **he's ~ richer than I (am)** es mucho más rico que yo; **ever so ~** muchísimo; **not ~** no mucho, poco; ~ **to my astonishment** con gran sorpresa mía; **that's a bit ~!*** ¡eso es un poco fuerte!
(b) (by far) con mucho; ~ **the biggest** con mucho el más grande; **I would ~ rather stay** prefiero con mucho quedarme.
(c) (almost) casi, más o menos; **they are ~ of an age** tienen casi la misma edad; **they're ~ the same size** tienen más o menos el mismo tamaño.
(d) how ~ is it? ¿cuánto es?, ¿cuánto vale?; **how ~ is it a kilo?** ¿cuánto vale el kilo?
(e) however ~ he tries por mucho que se esfuerce.
3 N: **but ~ remains** pero queda mucho; ~ **of this is true** gran parte de esto es verdad; **we don't see ~ of each other** no nos vemos mucho; **we haven't heard ~ of him lately** hace tiempo apenas sabemos nada de él; **there's not ~ to do** no hay mucho que hacer; **it's not up to ~** no vale gran cosa; **I'm not ~ of a musician** sé muy poco de música, entiendo poco de música, como músico no sirvo para nada; **he's not ~ of a player** como jugador no vale mucho; **that wasn't ~ of a dinner** eso apenas se podía llamar cena; **to make ~ of sb** mimar a uno, hacer fiestas a uno; agasajar a uno; **to make ~ of sth** dar mucha importancia a algo; subrayar la importancia de algo.

4 (with as, so, too) **(a)** ~ **as I should like to** por más que yo quisiera; ~ **as I would like to go** por mucho que me gustara ir; ~ **as I like him** por mucho que le quiera.
(b) (as ~) **as ~ again** otro tanto; **three times as ~ tea** tres veces la cantidad de té; **I thought as ~** ya me lo figuraba, lo había previsto ya.
(c) (as ~ as, so ~ as) **as ~ as possible** todo lo posible; **he has as ~ money as you** tiene tanto dinero como tú; **he spends as ~ as he earns** gasta tanto como gana; **I have three times as ~ as I can eat** tengo tres veces más de lo que puedo comer; **it's as ~ as I can do to stand up** apenas puedo ponerme de pie (or pararme: LAm); **as ~ as to say ...** como si dijera ...; **the problem is not so ~ one of modernization as of investment** el problema más que de modernización es de inversión; **he went without saying so ~ as a single word** se fue sin decir una palabra siquiera; **I haven't so ~ as a penny** no tengo ni un solo penique.
(d) (so ~) **so ~ bad weather** tanto mal tiempo; **it has been so ~ exaggerated** se ha exagerado tanto; **we don't go out so ~ now** ahora no salimos tanto; **without so ~ as a phone-call** sin una llamada siquiera; **so ~ the better** tanto mejor; **so ~ for that!** ¡allá eso!; ¡ya se acabó aquello!; **that's so ~ the less to pay** tanto menos habrá que pagar; **at so ~ a pound** a tantas pesetas (etc) la libra; **so ~ so that ...** tanto que ...
(e) too ~ demasiado; **he talks too ~** habla demasiado; **too ~ jam** demasiada mermelada f, exceso m de mermelada; **you gave me a dollar too ~** me dio un dólar de más; **that's too ~ by half** de eso sobra la mitad; **don't make too ~ of it** no exageres la importancia de esto; **it was all too ~ for her** (emotion) quedaba postrada con tanta emoción, (work) quedaba agobiada por tanto trabajo; **it's too ~ for me to cope with** yo no puedo con tanto trabajo (etc); **his rudeness is too ~** su descortesía es intolerable.
muchness [ˈmʌtʃnɪs] N: **they're much of a ~** son poco más o menos lo mismo.
mucilage [ˈmjuːsɪlɪdʒ] N mucílago m.
mucilaginous [ˌmjuːsɪˈlædʒɪnəs] ADJ mucilaginoso.
muck [mʌk] N **(a)** (dung) estiércol m; (dirt) suciedad f, inmundicias fpl, mierda f; **to be in a ~** estar sucio; **she thinks she's Lady M~!*** ¡se cree toda una duquesa!
(b) (fig) porquería f; **the article is just ~** el artículo es una porquería.
◆**muck about, muck around** (Brit) **1** VT: **to ~ sb about** fastidiar a uno, desorientar a uno (cambiando una cita etc) con él.
2 VI perder el tiempo, ocuparse en fruslerías, trabajar (etc) con poca seriedad; **he enjoys ~ing about in boats** le gusta entretener sus ocios navegando (etc) en bote; **stop ~ing about!** ¡déjate de tonterías!; **to ~ about with sth** (handle) manosear algo, (break) romper algo, estropear algo.
◆**muck in*** VI ayudar.
◆**muck out** VT: **to ~ out a stable** limpiar una cuadra.
◆**muck up*** VT (Brit) **(a)** (disarrange) desarreglar, desordenar; (ruin) arruinar, estropear, echar a perder; affair, deal fracasar en, (deliberately) chafar.
(b) (dirty) ensuciar.
mucker‡ [ˈmʌkəʳ] N compinche m.
muckheap [ˈmʌkˌhiːp] N estercolero m.
muckiness [ˈmʌkɪnɪs] N suciedad f.
muckrake [ˈmʌkreɪk] VI remover el pasado; buscar y revelar cosas vergonzosas en la vida de otros, escarbar vidas ajenas.
muckraker [ˈmʌkˌreɪkəʳ] N escarbador m, -ora f de vidas ajenas.
muckraking [ˈmʌkˌreɪkɪŋ] N remoción f del pasado; revelación f de cosas escandalosas (en la vida de otros).
muck-up* [ˈmʌkʌp] N lío m grande; fracaso m total; **what a ~!** ¡qué faena!*; **that ~ with the timetable** ese lío que nos armamos con el horario.
mucky [ˈmʌkɪ] ADJ sucio; puerco; asqueroso; **to get o.s. all ~** ensuciarse; **to get one's dress all ~** ensuciar el vestido.
mucous [ˈmjuːkəs] ADJ mucoso; ~ **membrane** mucosa f.
mucus [ˈmjuːkəs] N moco m, mocosidad f.
mud [mʌd] **1** N lodo m, barro m, fango m; (fig) fango m; **to stick in the ~** (cart) atascarse, atollarse, (ship) embarrancarse; ~ **in your eye!*** ¡salud y pesetas!; **his name is ~** tiene una reputación malísima, no se le estima en nada; **if people hear this my name will be ~** si esto llega a saberse estoy perdido; **to drag sb's name through the ~** llenar a uno de fango; **to sling** (or throw) ~ **at sb** vilipendiar a uno.
2 ATTR: ~ **flap** cortina f; ~ **hut** choza f de barro; ~ **wall** tapia f.
mudbank [ˈmʌdbæŋk] N banco m de arena.
mudbath [ˈmʌdbɑːθ] N, PL **mudbaths** [ˈmʌdbɑːðz] baño m de lodo, lodos mpl.
muddle [ˈmʌdl] **1** N **(a)** (disorder) desorden m, confusión f; **you should have seen what a ~ there was in the room!** ¡había que ver el desorden que había en el cuarto!; **what a ~!** ¡qué confusión!; **how did things get into such a ~?** ¿cómo se produjo tanta confusión?

(b) *(perplexity)* perplejidad *f*, confusión *f*; **now I'm all in a ~** ahora estoy totalmente confuso.

(c) *(mix-up)* embrollo *m*, lío *m*; **there was a ~ over the seats** hubo un lío con las entradas; **to get into a ~** embrollarse; **to get into a ~ with one's accounts** armarse un lío con las cuentas; **what a ~!** ¡qué lío!, ¡qué faena!

2 VT **(a)** *things* embrollar, confundir; introducir el desorden en.

(b) *person* aturdir, dejar perplejo, confundir; **I was properly ~d** estaba totalmente confuso; **to get ~d** aturdirse; armarse un lío.

♦ **muddle along** VI salir del paso sin saber cómo.

♦ **muddle on** VI hacer las cosas al tuntún.

♦ **muddle through** VI salir del paso sin saber cómo; **I expect we shall ~ through** espero que lo logremos de algún modo u otro.

♦ **muddle up** VT *things* embrollar, confundir; introducir el desorden en; **you've ~d up A and B** has confundido A con B.

muddle-headed ['mʌdl,hedɪd] ADJ *person* atontado, atolondrado; *ideas* confuso.

muddler ['mʌdlər] N persona *f* atolondrada, persona *f* atontada.

muddy ['mʌdɪ] 1 ADJ *place* lodoso, fangoso; *hands, dress etc* cubierto de lodo; *liquid* turbio; *complexion* terroso.

2 VT enlodar; cubrir de lodo; *hands, dress etc* manchar de lodo; *liquid* enturbiar.

mudflats ['mʌdflæts] NPL marisma *f*.

mudguard ['mʌdgɑːd] N *(Brit)* guardabarros *m*, guardalodos *m*, tapabarro *m* *(And)*.

mudlark ['mʌdlɑːk] N galopín *m*.

mudpack ['mʌdpæk] N mascarilla *f* facial de barro.

mud pie [,mʌd'paɪ] N bola *f* de barro.

mudslide ['mʌdslaɪd] N alud *m* de lodo, desprendimiento *m* de tierra.

mud-slinging ['mʌd,slɪŋɪŋ] N injurias *fpl*, vilipendio *m*.

mud wrestling ['mʌdreslɪŋ] N *espectáculo m de lucha sobre un ring de barro*.

muesli ['mjuːzlɪ] N muesli *m*.

muezzin [muː'ezɪn] N almuecín *m*, almuédano *m*.

muff¹ [mʌf] N manguito *m* *(also Tech)*.

muff² [mʌf] VT *ball* dejar escapar; *catch, stop* no lograr por torpeza; *shot* errar; *chance* perder, desperdiciar; *(Theat) entrance, lines* estropear; **to ~ it** fracasar, hacerlo malísimamente, no lograrlo por torpeza.

muffin ['mʌfɪn] N *(Brit)* ≃ mollete *m*; *(US) una especie de pan dulce*, ≃ bollo *m*.

muffle ['mʌfl] VT **(a)** envolver; *person etc* embozar, tapar *(with* de). **(b)** *noise* amortiguar, apagar; *noisy thing* amortiguar el ruido de; *bells, oars* envolver con tela; *drum* enfundar.

♦ **muffle up** 1 VT envolver; *person etc* embozar, tapar *(with* de); **~d up in** embozado de.

2 VR: **to ~ o.s. up** embozarse, taparse.

muffled ['mʌfld] ADJ *sound* sordo, apagado.

muffler ['mʌflər] N *(scarf)* bufanda *f*; *(Mus)* sordina *f*; *(US Mech)* silenciador *m*, *(on motorbike)* mofle *m*.

mufti ['mʌftɪ] N *(Brit)* traje *m* de paisano; **in ~** vestido de paisano.

mug [mʌg] 1 N **(a)** *(cup)* taza *f* (alta, sin platillo); *(for beer)* jarro *m*, jarra *f*.

(b) *(Brit‡: person)* bobo *m*, primo *m*; **what a ~ I've been!** ¡he sido un tonto!; **it's a ~'s game** esto es solamente para tontos.

(c) *(‡: face)* jeta* *f*, hocico* *m*; **what a ~ she's got!** ¡qué jeta tiene!*; **he hit him in the ~** le pegó un tortazo en el hocico*.

2 VT *(*)* asaltar, pegar, aporrear.

♦ **mug up*** VT **(a)** *(Brit)* empollar*, embotellar*, amarrar*.

(b) **to ~ it up** *(US: grimace)* gesticular, hacer muecas; *(Theat)* actuar exagerando.

mugger* ['mʌgər] N asaltador *m*.

mugging* ['mʌgɪŋ] N asalto *m*, vapuleo *m*.

muggins‡ ['mʌgɪnz] N *(Brit)* tonto *m*, primo *m*; **~ will pay for it** este pobre hombre lo pagará; **~ will do it** lo hará este cura*.

muggy ['mʌgɪ] ADJ bochornoso.

mug-shot* ['mʌgʃɒt] N fotografía *f* para las fichas.

mugwump ['mʌgwʌmp] N *(US)* votante *mf* independiente.

Muhammad [mʊ'hæməd] NM Mahoma.

mujaheddin [,muːdʒəhə'diːn] NPL mujaidín *mpl*.

mulatto [mjuː'lætəʊ] 1 ADJ mulato.

2 N, PL **mulattoes** [mjuː'lætəʊz] mulato *m*, -a *f*.

mulberry ['mʌlbərɪ] N *(fruit)* mora *f*; *(tree)* morera *f*, moral *m*.

mulch [mʌltʃ] 1 N capote *m*, mantillo *m*.

2 VT cubrir con capote, cubrir con mantillo.

mulct [mʌlkt] VT **(a)** multar. **(b)** **to ~ sb of sth** quitar algo a uno, privar a uno de algo.

mule¹ [mjuːl] N **(a)** mulo *m*, -a *f*; *(person)* testarudo *m*, -a *f*. **(b)** *(Tech)* máquina *f* de hilar intermitente, selfactina *f*.

mule² [mjuːl] N *(slipper)* babucha *f*.

muleteer [,mjuːlɪ'tɪər] N mulatero *m*, muletero *m*, arriero *m*.

mule-track ['mjuːltræk] N camino *m* de herradura.

mulish ['mjuːlɪʃ] ADJ terco, testarudo.

mulishness ['mjuːlɪʃnɪs] N terquedad *f*, testarudez *f*.

mull [mʌl] VT *wine* calentar con especias.

♦ **mull over** VT: **to ~ sth over** meditar algo, reflexionar sobre algo.

mullah ['mʌlə] N mullah *m*.

mullet ['mʌlɪt] N: **grey ~** mújol *m*; **red ~** salmonete *m*.

mulligatawny [,mʌlɪgə'tɔːnɪ] N sopa *f* de curry angloindia.

mullion ['mʌlɪən] N parteluz *m*.

mullioned ['mʌlɪənd] ADJ *window* dividido con parteluz.

multi... ['mʌltɪ] PREF multi...

multi-access [,mʌltɪ'ækses] 1 N acceso *m* múltiple.

2 ADJ multiacceso, de acceso múltiple.

multicellular [,mʌltɪ'seljʊlər] ADJ multicelular.

multichannel ['mʌltɪ'tʃænl] ADJ *(TV)* multicanal.

multicoloured, *(US)* **multicolored** ['mʌltɪ'kʌləd] ADJ multicolor.

multicultural [,mʌltɪ'kʌltʃərəl] ADJ multicultural.

multidimensional [,mʌltɪdɪ'menʃənl] ADJ multidimensional.

multidirectional [,mʌltɪdɪ'rekʃənl] ADJ multidireccional.

multidisciplinary [,mʌltɪ'dɪsɪplɪnərɪ] ADJ multidisciplinario.

multifaceted [,mʌltɪ'fæsɪtɪd] ADJ multifacético.

multifarious [,mʌltɪ'feərɪəs] ADJ múltiple(s), diversísimo(s), variadísimo(s).

multiform ['mʌltɪfɔːm] ADJ multiforme.

multifunctional ['mʌltɪ'fʌŋkʃənl] ADJ multifuncional.

multigym ['mʌltɪdʒɪm] N gimnasio *m* múltiple.

multihull ['mʌltɪhʌl] N multicasco *m*.

multilateral ['mʌltɪ'lætərəl] ADJ multilátero, multilateral.

multilayer(ed) [,mʌltɪ'leɪə(d)] ADJ multicapa.

multilevel [,mʌltɪ'levl] ADJ *(US)* de muchos pisos.

multilingual [,mʌltɪ'lɪŋgwəl] ADJ plurilingüe.

multilingualism [,mʌltɪ'lɪŋgwəlɪzəm] N plurilingüismo *m*, multilingüismo *m*.

multimedia ['mʌltɪ'miːdɪə] ADJ *aids, presentation (also Comput)* multimedia.

multimillion ['mʌltɪ'mɪljən] ADJ multimillonario.

multimillionaire ['mʌltɪmɪljə'neər] N multimillonario *m*, -a *f*.

multi-million-pound [,mʌltɪ'mɪljən,paʊnd] ADJ *deal, fraud etc* de (varios) millones de libras, multimillonario.

multi-nation ['mʌltɪ'neɪʃən] ADJ *treaty, agreement* multinacional.

multinational [,mʌltɪ'næʃənl] 1 ADJ multinacional.

2 N multinacional *f*.

multi-pack ['mʌltɪpæk] N multipack *m*.

multi-party [,mʌltɪ'pɑːtɪ] ADJ *(Pol) system, democracy* multipartidista, multipartidario; **~ talks** conversaciones *fpl* entre partidos.

multiple ['mʌltɪpl] 1 ADJ *(of many parts)* múltiplo; *(in PL, many and various)* múltiple; *firm* con muchas sucursales; **~ accident** *(Aut)* colisión *f* múltiple, colisión *f* en cadena; **~ birth** parto *m* múltiple; **~ choice questions** preguntas *fpl* de tipo elección múltiple; **~ choice test** ejercicio *m* de tipo elección múltiple; **~ ownership** propiedad *f* múltiple; **~ sclerosis** esclerosis *f* múltiple; **~ stores** *(Brit)* cadena *f* de almacenes.

2 N múltiplo *m*; *(shop: also ~ store)* (cadena *f* de) grandes almacenes *mpl*; **lowest common ~** mínimo común múltiplo *m*.

multiplex ['mʌltɪ,pleks] N *(also ~ cinema)* multicines *m*.

multiplexor ['mʌltɪ,pleksər] N multiplexor *m*.

multiplicand [,mʌltɪplɪ'kænd] N multiplicando *m*.

multiplication [,mʌltɪplɪ'keɪʃən] 1 N multiplicación *f*.

2 ATTR: **~ table** tabla *f* de multiplicar.

multiplicity [,mʌltɪ'plɪsɪtɪ] N multiplicidad *f*; **for a ~ of reasons** por múltiples razones; **a ~ of solutions** una gran diversidad de soluciones.

multiply ['mʌltɪplaɪ] 1 VT multiplicar; **to ~ 8 by 7** multiplicar 8 por 7.

2 VI multiplicarse.

multiprocessing [,mʌltɪ'prəʊsesɪŋ] N multiprocesamiento *m*.

multiprocessor [,mʌltɪ'prəʊsesər] N multiprocesador *m*.

multi-programming, *(US, also freq Comput)* **multi-programing** [,mʌltɪ'prəʊgræmɪŋ] N multiprogramación *f*.

multipurpose [,mʌltɪ'pɜːpəs] ADJ de fines múltiples, multiuso.

multiracial [,mʌltɪ'reɪʃəl] ADJ multirracial.

multirisk ['mʌltɪrɪsk] ATTR: **~ insurance** seguro *m* multirriesgo.

multistorey [,mʌltɪ'stɔːrɪ] ADJ de muchos pisos.

multistrike ['mʌltɪ,straɪk] ATTR: **~ ribbon** cinta *f* de múltiples impactos.

multitask(ing) ['mʌltɪ'tɑːsk(ɪŋ)] N multitarea *f*.

multitrack ['mʌltɪ,træk] ATTR: **~ recording** grabación *f* en bandas múltiples.

multitude ['mʌltɪtjuːd] N multitud *f*; **the ~** *(pej)* las masas, la plebe; **for a ~ of reasons** por múltiples razones; **they came in ~s** acudieron en tropel.

multitudinous [,mʌltɪ'tjuːdɪnəs] ADJ multitudinario; muy numeroso, numerosísimo.

multiuser [,mʌltɪ'juːzər] ADJ multiusuario; **~ system** sistema *m* multiusuario.

mum¹ [mʌm] ADJ: ~'s the word! ¡punto en boca!; to keep ~ callarse; see that you keep ~ about it de esto no digas ni pío; everybody is keeping very ~ about it esto lo tienen todos muy secreto.

mum²* [mʌm] N (*Brit*) mamá *f*.

mumble ['mʌmbl] [1] N: he said in a ~ dijo entre dientes. [2] VT decir entre dientes. [3] VI musitar, hablar entre dientes.

mumbo-jumbo ['mʌmbəʊ'dʒʌmbəʊ] N (*cult*) fetiche *m*; (*spell*) conjuro *m*; (*empty ritual*) mistificación *f*, mixtificación *f*, farsa *f*.

mummer ['mʌmər] N máscara *mf*.

mummery ['mʌməri] N (*fig*) mistificación *f*; ceremonia *f* ridícula, farsa *f*.

mummification [,mʌmɪfɪ'keɪʃən] N momificación *f*.

mummify ['mʌmɪfaɪ] [1] VT momificar. [2] VI momificarse.

mummy¹ ['mʌmɪ] N (*Hist*) momia *f*.

mummy²* ['mʌmɪ] N (*Brit*) mamá* *f*.

mumps [mʌmps] N paperas *fpl*, parótidas *fpl*.

mumsy* ['mʌmzɪ] ADJ *appearance, hair* de señora; she's much more ~ now se la ve más maternal ahora.

munch [mʌntʃ] VT mascar, ronzar.

Munchhausen's Syndrome ['mʌntʃaʊzənz'sɪndrəʊm] N síndrome *m* de Munchhausen.

munchie* [mʌnʃi] N (*US*) piscolabis *m*, algo para picar; to have the ~s tener ganas de picar de aquí y de allá.

mundane ['mʌn'deɪn] ADJ mundano; (*humdrum*) vulgar, trivial.

municipal [mju:'nɪsɪpəl] ADJ municipal.

municipality [mju:,nɪsɪ'pælɪtɪ] N municipio *m*.

munificence [mju:'nɪfɪsns] N munificencia *f*.

munificent [mju:'nɪfɪsnt] ADJ munífico, munificente.

muniments ['mju:nɪmənts] NPL documentos *mpl* (probatorios); (*also ~ room*) archivos *mpl*.

munitions [mju:'nɪʃənz] [1] NPL municiones *fpl*; pertrechos *mpl*. [2] ATTR: ~ dump depósito *m* de municiones; ~ factory fábrica *f* de municiones.

mural ['mjʊərəl] [1] ADJ mural. [2] N pintura *f* mural, mural *m*.

murder ['mɜːdər] [1] N (a) asesinato *m*; (*as Jur term*) homicidio *m*; accused of ~ acusado de homicidio; ~ in the first degree homicidio *m* premeditado; ~ will out todo termina por saberse.

(b) (*) it was ~! ¡un horror!; this job is ~ este trabajo es la monda*; to shout blue ~ protestar enérgicamente, poner el grito en el cielo; she gets away with ~ hace lo que quiere y siempre sale impune. [2] ATTR: ~ case caso *m* de homicidio; ~ inquiry investigación *f* de un homicidio; M~ Squad grupo *m* de homicidios; ~ trial juicio *m* por asesinato; the ~ weapon el arma que se empleó en el homicidio. [3] VT asesinar; matar, dar muerte a; *song etc* arruinar, estropear; *play* degollar; (*) *opponent* derrotar.

murderer ['mɜːdərər] N asesino *m*, (*as Jur term*) homicida *m*.

murderess ['mɜːdərɪs] N asesina *f*, (*as Jur term*) homicida *f*.

murderous ['mɜːdərəs] ADJ homicida, (*fig*) cruel, feroz, sanguinario; *look* homicida, asesino; this heat is ~ este calor es cruel; I felt ~ me vinieron pensamientos homicidas.

murk [mɜːk] N oscuridad *f*, tinieblas *fpl*.

murkiness ['mɜːkɪnɪs] N oscuridad *f*, lobreguez *f*; (*fig*) lo tenebroso, lo turbio.

murky ['mɜːkɪ] ADJ oscuro, lóbrego; (*fig*) tenebroso, turbio.

murmur ['mɜːmər] [1] N (*soft speech*) murmullo *m*; (*of water*) murmullo *m*, murmurio *m*; (*of leaves etc*) susurro *m*; (*of distant traffic etc*) rumor *m*; (*complaint*) queja *f*, murmurio *m*; there were ~s of disagreement hubo murmurios de disconformidad. [2] VT murmurar, decir en voz baja. [3] VI murmullar, murmurar; susurrar; quejarse; to ~ about, to ~ against murmurar de, quejarse de.

Murphy ['mɜːfɪ] N: ~'s law* ley *f* de la indefectible mala voluntad de los objetos inanimados.

Mus.B., Mus. Bac. N ABBR of **Bachelor of Music** *título universitario*.

muscatel [,mʌskə'tel] [1] ADJ moscatel. [2] N moscatel *m*.

muscle ['mʌsl] N (a) músculo *m*; he never moved a ~ se mantuvo inmóvil, no se inmutó en absoluto; to flex one's ~s tensar los músculos.

(b) (*fig*) fuerza *f* muscular, musculatura *f*; political ~ musculatura *f* política.

◆**muscle in*** VI (*Brit*) introducirse por fuerza (*on a deal* en un negocio).

musclebound ['mʌslbaʊnd] ADJ envarado por exceso de ejercicio.

muscleman* ['mʌslmæn] N, PL **musclemen** ['mʌslmen] forzudo *m*.

Muscovite ['mʌskəvaɪt] [1] ADJ moscovita. [2] N moscovita *mf*.

muscular ['mʌskjʊlər] ADJ *tissue etc* muscular; (*having muscles*) musculoso; (*brawny*) fornido, membrudo; ~ dystrophy distrofia *f* muscular.

musculature ['mʌskjʊlətjʊər] N musculatura *f*.

Mus.D., Mus. Doc. N ABBR of **Doctor of Music** *título universitario*.

Muse [mju:z] N musa *f*; the ~s las Musas.

muse [mju:z] [1] VT: 'should we?' he ~d '¿debemos hacerlo?', dijo pensativo. [2] VI meditar, reflexionar, rumiar; to ~ about sth, to ~ on sth meditar algo, reflexionar sobre algo; to ~ on a scene contemplar distraído una escena.

museum [mju:'zɪəm] N museo *m*.

museum piece [mju:'zɪəm,pi:s] N (*fig*) cosa *f* anticuada, antigualla *f*; the car is a real ~ el coche realmente es digno de estar en un museo.

mush¹ [mʌʃ] N (a) (*Culin*) gachas *fpl*; masa *f* blanda y espesa. (b) (*fig*) sensiblería *f*, sentimentalismo *m*.

mush²* [mʌʃ] N jeta* *f*.

mush³* [mʌʃ] N (*in direct address*) tronco* *m*.

mushroom ['mʌʃrʊm] [1] N seta *f*, hongo *m*; (*as food*) champiñón *m*; a great ~ of smoke un enorme hongo de humo; to grow like ~s surgir como hongos, crecer de la noche a la mañana. [2] ATTR: ~ cloud nube *f* en forma de hongo; ~ growth crecimiento *m* rapidísimo; ~ town ciudad *f* que crece rapidísimamente. [3] VI (*town etc*) surgir como hongos, crecer de la noche a la mañana, crecer rapidísimamente; the cloud of smoke went ~ing up subió el humo en forma de hongo; to ~ into convertirse rapidísimamente en.

mushy ['mʌʃɪ] ADJ (a) pulposo, mollar, como gachas. (b) (*fig*) sensiblero, muy sentimental.

music ['mju:zɪk] [1] N música *f*; ~ of the spheres música *f* mundana, armonía *f* celestial; it was ~ to my ears daba gusto escucharlo, eran palabras (*etc*) deliciosas para mí; to face the ~ afrontar las consecuencias; to set a work to ~ poner música a una obra. [2] ATTR: ~ centre (*shop*) tienda *f* de aparatos de sonido de alta fidelidad; ~ critic crítico *mf* de la música; ~ festival festival *m* de música; ~ lesson (*instrumental*) clase *f* de música, (*vocal*) clase *f* de solfeo.

musical ['mju:zɪkəl] [1] ADJ (a) musical; *composition etc* músico; *sound, voice* armonioso, melodioso; ~ box caja *f* de música; ~ chairs juego *m* de las sillas; the politicians are merely playing ~ chairs estos políticos son los mismos perros con distintos collares; ~ comedy comedia *f* musical, (*Sp*) zarzuela *f*; ~ instrument instrumento *m* músico.

(b) dotado para la música; he's very ~ tiene mucho talento para la música; he comes from a ~ family es de familia de músicos. [2] N comedia *f* musical.

musicale [,mju:zɪ'ka:l] N velada *f* musical.

musically ['mju:zɪkəlɪ] ADV armoniosamente, melodiosamente.

music-centre [mju:zɪk,sentər] N equipo *m* estereofónico.

music-hall ['mju:zɪkhɔ:l] N (*Brit*) teatro *m* de variedades.

musician [mju:'zɪʃən] N músico *m*, -a *f*.

musicianship [mju:'zɪʃənʃɪp] N maestría *f* musical.

music-lover ['mju:zɪk,lʌvər] N persona *f* aficionada a la música, melómano *m*, -a *f*.

musicologist [,mju:zɪ'kɒlədʒɪst] N musicólogo *m*, -a *f*.

musicology [,mju:zɪ'kɒlədʒɪ] N musicología *f*.

music paper ['mju:zɪk,peɪpər] N papel *m* de música, papel *m* pautado.

music stand ['mju:zɪkstænd] N atril *m*.

musingly ['mju:zɪŋlɪ] ADV *say etc* con aire distraído, pensativamente.

musings ['mju:zɪŋz] NPL meditaciones *fpl*.

musk [mʌsk] N (*substance*) almizcle *m*; (*scent*) perfume *m* de almizcle; (*smell*) olor *m* a almizcle; (*Bot*) almizcleña *f*.

musket ['mʌskɪt] N mosquete *m*.

musketeer [,mʌskɪ'tɪər] N mosquetero *m*.

musketry ['mʌskɪtrɪ] N (*muskets*) mosquetes *mpl*; (*firing*) fuego *m* de mosquetes, tiros *mpl*.

musk-ox ['mʌskɒks] N, PL **musk-oxen** ['mʌskɒksən] buey *m* almizclado.

muskrat ['mʌskræt] N rata *f* almizclera.

musk-rose ['mʌskrəʊz] N rosa *f* almizcleña.

musky ['mʌskɪ] ADJ almizcleño, almizclado; *smell* a almizcle.

Muslim ['mʊslɪm] = **Moslem**.

muslin ['mʌzlɪn] [1] N muselina *f*. [2] ATTR de muselina.

musquash ['mʌskwɒʃ] N ratón *m* almizclero; (*fur*) piel *f* de rata almizclera.

muss [mʌs] VT (*also to ~ up*) *hair* desarreglar, despeinar; *dress* ajar, chafar.

mussel ['mʌsl] N mejillón *m*.

mussel-bed ['mʌslbed] N criadero *m* de mejillones.

must¹ [mʌst] N (*of wine*) mosto *m*.

must² [mʌst] N = **mustiness**.

▼ **must³** [mʌst] V AUX (*present tense only*) ① (a) (*obligation*) **I ~ do it** debo hacerlo, tengo que hacerlo, he de hacerlo; **one ~ be careful** hay que tener cuidado; **one ~ not be too hopeful** no hay que ser demasiado optimista; **the patient ~ have complete quiet** el enfermo requiere silencio absoluto; **but you ~ come** pero es imprescindible que vengas; **I'll do it if I ~** si me obligan, lo haré; lo haré si es necesario; **do it if you ~** hazlo si es necesario, hazlo si no hay más remedio; **if you ~ know, I'm Ruritanian** si es esencial que lo sepa, soy ruritanio; **there ~ be a reason** debe haber una razón, ha de haber una razón.

▼ (b) (*probability*) **he ~ be there by now** ya debe de estar allí, ya estará allí; **it ~ be cold up there** hará frío allá arriba; **it ~ be about 3 o'clock** serán las 3; **it ~ have been about 5** serían alrededor de las 5; **but you ~ have seen him!** ¡pero debes haberle visto!; **he ~ be a Mexican** debe de ser mejicano.

② N (*) **this programme is a ~ for everybody** este programa no lo ha de perder nadie, es imprescindible que todos escuchen este programa.

must-* [mʌst-] PREF: **a ~see movie** una película que hay que ver, una película que no puede perderse; **leather jeans are the ~have fashion item of the season** los vaqueros de cuero son la prenda de moda imprescindible de la temporada; **a ~read** un libro obligado; **it's a ~visit** es una visita obligada.

mustache ['mʌstæʃ] N (*US*) = **moustache**.

mustang ['mʌstæŋ] N potro *m* mesteño, mustang(o) *m*.

mustard ['mʌstəd] ① N mostaza *f*.
② ADJ: **a ~ (yellow) dress** un vestido mostaza.

mustard-gas ['mʌstədgæs] N gas *m* mostaza.

mustard-plaster ['mʌstedˈplɑːstər] N sinapismo *m*, cataplasma *f* de mostaza.

mustard-pot ['mʌstədpɒt] N mostacera *f*.

muster ['mʌstər] ① N (*gathering*) asamblea *f* (*also Mil*), reunión *f*; (*review*) revista *f*; (*list*) lista *f*, matrícula *f*, (*Naut*) rol *m*; **to pass ~** pasar revista, (*fig*) ser aceptable, ser satisfactorio.
② VT (*call together for inspection*) llamar a asamblea, juntar para pasar revista; (*collect*) juntar, reunir; (*also* **to ~ up**) *courage, strength* cobrar; **the club can ~ 20 members** el club cuenta con 20 miembros, el club consiste en 20 miembros.
③ VI juntarse, reunirse.

mustiness ['mʌstɪnɪs] N moho *m*; ranciedad *f*; (*of room etc*) olor *m* a humedad, olor *m* a cerrado.

mustn't ['mʌsnt] = **must not**.

musty ['mʌstɪ] ADJ mohoso; rancio; *room etc* que huele a humedad, que huele a cerrado; *joke etc* viejo, gastado.

mutability [ˌmjuːtəˈbɪlɪtɪ] N mutabilidad *f*.

mutable ['mjuːtəbl] ADJ mudable.

mutagen ['mjuːtədʒən] N mutagene *m*.

mutant ['mjuːtənt] ① ADJ mutante.
② N mutante *m*.

mutate [mjuːˈteɪt] ① VT mudar.
② VI sufrir mutación.

mutation [mjuːˈteɪʃən] N mutación *f*.

mute [mjuːt] ① ADJ mudo, silencioso; **with H ~** con hache muda; **to become ~** enmudecer.
② N (a) (*person*) mudo *m*, -a *f*. (b) (*Mus*) sordina *f*. (c) (*Gram*) letra *f* muda.
③ VT (*Mus*) poner sordina a; *noise* amortiguar, apagar.

muted ['mjuːtɪd] ADJ *noise* sordo, apagado; *criticism* callado.

mutilate ['mjuːtɪleɪt] VT mutilar.

mutilation [ˌmjuːtɪˈleɪʃən] N mutilación *f*.

mutineer [ˌmjuːtɪˈnɪər] N amotinado *m*, amotinador *m*.

mutinous ['mjuːtɪnəs] ADJ amotinado; (*fig*) turbulento, rebelde; **we were feeling pretty ~** estábamos hartos ya, estábamos dispuestos a rebelarnos.

mutiny ['mjuːtɪnɪ] ① N motín *m*, sublevación *f*.
② VI amotinarse, sublevarse.

mutt* [mʌt] N (a) bobo *m*. (b) (*US*) chucho *m*; perro *m* callejero.

mutter ['mʌtər] ① N murmullo *m*; **a ~ of voices** un rumor de voces.
② VT murmurar, decir entre dientes; **'yes', he ~ed** 'sí', refunfuñó.
③ VI murmurar; (*guns, thunder*) retumbar a lo lejos.

mutton ['mʌtn] N (carne *f* de) cordero *m*; **she's ~ dressed up as lamb*** ella es una carantoña*.

mutton chop ['mʌtnˈtʃɒp] N chuleta *f* de cordero.

mutual ['mjuːtjʊəl] ADJ mutuo; (*loosely*) común; **the feeling is ~** yo comparto esa opinión, lo mismo digo yo; **our ~ friend** nuestro común amigo; **their ~ friend** el amigo de los dos, el amigo que tienen en común; **~ benefit society** mutualidad *f*; **~ fund** fondo *m* mutualista; **~ insurance** seguro *m* mutuo; **~ interest** interés *m* mutuo; **~ savings bank** caja *f* mutua de ahorros; **~ understanding** comprensión *f* mutua; acuerdo *m* mutuo.

mutuality [ˌmjuːtjʊˈælɪtɪ] N mutualidad *f*.

mutually ['mjuːtjʊəlɪ] ADV mutuamente.

Muzak ['mjuːzæk] ® N hilo *m* musical.

muzzle ['mʌzl] ① N (*snout*) hocico *m*; (*for dog*) bozal *m*; (*of gun*) boca *f*.
② VT *dog* abozalar; *criticism etc* estorbar; *critic* amordazar, imponer silencio a.

muzzle-loader ['mʌzlˌləʊdər] N arma *f* que se carga por la boca.

muzzle velocity ['mʌzlvɪˌlɒsɪtɪ] N velocidad *f* inicial.

muzzy ['mʌzɪ] ADJ (*from drinking*) confuso, atontado; *outline* borroso.

MVP N (*US*) ABBR of **most valuable player**.

MW N (*Rad*) ABBR of **medium wave** onda *f* media, OM *f*.

my [maɪ, mɪ] ① POSS ADJ mi.
② INTERJ ¡caramba!

myalgia [maɪˈældʒɪə] N mialgia *f*.

myalgic [maɪˈældʒɪk] ADJ: **~ encephalomyelitis** encefalomielitis *f* miálgica.

Myanmar ['maɪænmɑː] N Myanmar *f*.

mycology [maɪˈkɒlədʒɪ] N micología *f*.

myopia [maɪˈəʊpɪə] N miopía *f*.

myopic [maɪˈɒpɪk] ADJ miope.

myriad ['mɪrɪəd] (*liter*) ① N miríada *f*.
② ADJ: **a ~ flies** una miríada de moscas.

myrmidon ['mɜːmɪdən] N secuaz *m* fiel, satélite *m*, esbirro *m*.

myrrh [mɜːr] N mirra *f*.

myrtle ['mɜːtl] N arrayán *m*, mirto *m*.

myself [maɪˈself] PRON (*subject*) yo mismo, yo misma; (*acc, dat*) me; (*after prep*) mí (mismo, misma); V **oneself**.

mysterious [mɪsˈtɪərɪəs] ADJ misterioso.

mysteriously [mɪsˈtɪərɪəslɪ] ADV misteriosamente.

mystery ['mɪstərɪ] ① N (a) (*gen*) misterio *m*; **there's no ~ about it** aquí no hay misterio; **it's a ~ to me where it can have gone** no tengo la menor idea de dónde se habrá metido; **to make a great ~ out of a matter** envolver un asunto en un ambiente de misterio.
(b) (*Theat: also* **~ play**) auto *m*, misterio *m*.
(c) (*Liter: also* **~ story**) novela *f* de misterio.
② ATTR: **~ man** hombre *m* misterioso; **~ ship** buque *m* misterioso; **~ tour** viaje *m* sorpresa.

mystic ['mɪstɪk] ① ADJ místico.
② N místico *m*, -a *f*.

mystical ['mɪstɪkəl] ADJ místico.

mysticism ['mɪstɪsɪzəm] N misticismo *m*; (*doctrine, literary genre*) mística *f*.

mystification [ˌmɪstɪfɪˈkeɪʃən] N misterio *m*; confusión *f*, perplejidad *f*; **why all the ~?** ¿por qué tanto misterio?; **my ~ increased** creció mi perplejidad.

mystify ['mɪstɪfaɪ] VT dejar perplejo, desorientar, desconcertar; **I am mystified** estoy perplejo; **it completely mystified him** le desorientó por completo, le despistó por completo.

mystifying ['mɪstɪˌfaɪɪŋ] ADJ inexplicable; desconcertante; hecho para desorientar (*or* despistar).

mystique [mɪsˈtiːk] N misterio *m* (profesional *etc*), técnica *f* (al parecer) misteriosa, pericia *f* impresionante.

myth [mɪθ] N mito *m*.

mythic(al) ['mɪθɪk(əl)] ADJ mítico.

mythological [ˌmɪθəˈlɒdʒɪkəl] ADJ mitológico.

mythology [mɪˈθɒlədʒɪ] N mitología *f*.

myxomatosis ['mɪksəʊməˈtəʊsɪs] N mixomatosis *f*.

N

N, n [en] N (*letter*) N, n *f*; **N for Nellie** *or* (*US*) **Nan** N de Navarra; **nth** enésimo; **to the nth degree***, **to the nth (power)** a la enésima; **for the nth time** por enésima vez; **there are ~ ways of doing it** hay X maneras de hacerlo.

N ABBR *of* **north** N. norte *m* (*also adj*).

'n'; [ən] CONJ = **and**.

n/a (a) ABBR *of* **not applicable** no interesa. **(b)** (*Fin*) ABBR *of* **no account**. **(c)** (*Comm*) ABBR *of* **not available**.

NA N (*US*) **(a)** ABBR *of* **Narcotics Anonymous**. **(b)** ABBR *of* **National Academy**.

NAACP N (*US*) ABBR *of* **National Association for the Advancement of Colored People**.

> **[i]** **[NAACP]**
>
> **La NAACP**, siglas que corresponden a **National Association for the Advancement of Colored People** (*Asociación Nacional para el Progreso de la Gente de Color*), es una organización voluntaria estadounidense fundada en 1910 que se opone a la discriminación racial y que lucha por conseguir leyes que protejan los derechos de los ciudadanos de color. En 1953, la **NAACP** anunció que la integración en las escuelas era su objetivo prioritario, y éste se vio cumplido cuando al año siguiente el Tribunal Supremo de los Estados Unidos prohibió las escuelas segregadas conocidas como **separate but equal**. Esta asociación siempre ha propugnado la no violencia y rechazó el **black power movement** de los años sesenta. El movimiento cuenta con el apoyo de cientos de miles de estadounidenses, muchos de ellos de raza blanca.

NAAFI ['næfɪ] N (*Brit*) ABBR *of* **Navy, Army and Air Force Institute** servicio de cantinas etc para las fuerzas armadas.

nab* [næb] VT coger, echar el guante a; (*arrest*) prender.

nabob ['neɪbɒb] N nabab *m*.

nacelle [næ'sel] N barquilla *f*, góndola *f*.

nacho ['nɑːtʃəu] N nacho *m*.

nacre ['neɪkəʳ] N nácar *m*.

nacreous ['neɪkrɪəs] ADJ nacarino, nacarado, de nácar.

NACU N (*US*) ABBR *of* **National Association of Colleges and Universities**.

nadir ['neɪdɪəʳ] N (*Astron*) nadir *m*; (*fig*) punto *m* más bajo, nadir *m*.

naevus, (*US*) **nevus** ['niːvəs] N, PL **naevi**, (*US*) **nevi** ['niːvaɪ] nevo *m*.

naff; [næf] ADJ inferior, inútil; hortera, ordinario, de mal gusto.

♦ **naff off**; VI: ~ **off** vete a paseo*, vete al cuerno*.

NAFTA ['næftə] N ABBR *of* **North American Free Trade Agreement** Tratado *m* de Libre Comercio, TLC *m*.

nag¹ [næg] N jaca *f*; (*pej*) rocín *m*.

nag² [næg] **[1]** VT (*scold*) regañar; (*annoy*) importunar, fastidiar, dar la lata a*; criticar; **don't ~ me so!** ¡no machaques!; **his conscience ~ged him** le remordía la conciencia; **he was ~ged by doubts** estaba acosado por las dudas; **she ~s him all day long** ella le importuna con sus quejas todo el día.

[2] VI ser regañón, ser importuno, dar la lata*; criticar; **to ~ at sb** importunar a uno, criticar a uno; **don't ~, woman!** ¡no machaques, mujer!

nagger ['nægəʳ] N regañón *m*, -ona *f*, criticón *m*, -ona *f*.

nagging ['nægɪŋ] **[1]** ADJ *person* regañón, criticón, marimandón; *pain* continuo; *conscience* nada tranquilo; *doubt, fear etc* persistente, que no se desvanece.

[2] N importunar *m*; críticas *fpl*; quejas *fpl*.

NAHT N (*Brit*) ABBR *of* **National Association of Head Teachers** sindicato de profesores.

naiad ['naɪæd] N náyade *f*.

nail [neɪl] **[1]** N **(a)** (*Anat*) uña *f*; (*of animal*) garra *f*; **to bite one's ~s** comerse las uñas.

(b) (*metal*) clavo *m*; **~ bomb** bomba *f* de metralla; **this is another ~**

in his coffin éste es otro paso hacia su destrucción; **to hit the ~ on the head** dar en el clavo, acertar; **to pay on the ~** pagar a tocateja.

[2] VT **(a)** (*fix with ~s*) clavar, enclavar; adornar con clavos, clavetear; **to ~ two things together** fijar (*or* unir) dos cosas con clavos.

(b) (*fig*) (*catch, get hold of*) coger (*Sp*), agarrar (*LAm*); *lie* acabar con; *rumour etc* desmentir, demostrar la falsedad de; (*locate*) localizar; (*define*) definir, precisar.

♦ **nail down** VT **(a) to ~ sth down** clavar algo, sujetar algo con clavos. **(b)** *date, price* fijar; *policy etc* concretar, establecer; **to ~ sb down** poner a uno entre la espada y la pared; **we ~ed him down to a date** le forzamos a fijar una fecha; **we ~ed him down to come tomorrow** le comprometimos a que viniera mañana; **you can't ~ him down** es imposible hacerle concretar.

♦ **nail up** VT: **to ~ sth up** cerrar algo con clavos.

nail-biting ['neɪl,baɪtɪŋ] **[1]** ADJ tenso, tirante.

[2] N mala costumbre *f* de comerse las uñas.

nailbrush ['neɪlbrʌʃ] N cepillo *m* para las uñas.

nail-clippers ['neɪl,klɪpəz] NPL cortauñas *m*.

nailfile ['neɪlfaɪl] N lima *f* para las uñas.

nail-polish ['neɪl,pɒlɪʃ] N esmalte *m* para las uñas, laca *f* para las uñas; **~ remover** quitaesmalte *m*.

nail-scissors ['neɪlsɪzəz] NPL tijeras *fpl* para las uñas.

nail-varnish ['neɪl,vɑːnɪʃ] N (*Brit*) = **nail-polish**.

Nairobi [naɪ'rəubɪ] N Nairobi *m*.

▼ **naive**, **naïve** [naɪ'iːv] ADJ ingenuo, cándido, sencillo.

naivety, **naïvely** [naɪ'iːvlɪ] ADV ingenuamente.

naïveté, **naivety**, **naïvety** [naɪ'iːvtɪ] N ingenuidad *f*, candor *m*, sencillez *f*.

naked ['neɪkɪd] ADJ desnudo; (*fig*) desabrigado, indefenso; *flame* expuesto al aire; *lamp* sin pantalla; *sword* desenvainado; *attempt* abierto, manifiesto; *emotion* franco, abierto; **the ~ truth** la verdad lisa y llana, la pura verdad; **stark ~** en cueros, en pelota, como le parió su madre; **to go ~** ir desnudo; **to strip sb ~** desnudar a uno completamente, dejar a uno en cueros.

nakedness ['neɪkɪdnɪs] N desnudez *f*.

NALGO ['nælgəu] N (*Brit*) ABBR *of* **National and Local Government Officers' Association** sindicato de funcionarios.

NAM N (*US*) ABBR *of* **National Association of Manufacturers**.

namby-pamby ['næmbɪ'pæmbɪ] **[1]** ADJ soso, ñoño.

[2] N persona *f* sosa, ñoño *m*, -a *f*.

name [neɪm] **[1]** N **(a)** nombre *m*; designación *f*; (*surname*) apellido *m*; (*nickname*) apodo *m*; (*of book etc*) título *m*; **by ~** de nombre; **Pérez by ~** de nombre Pérez, llamado Pérez; **a lady by the ~ of Dulcinea** una señora llamada Dulcinea; **that's the ~ of the game*** así es la cosa; **no ~s no packdrill** es mejor callar los nombres; **I know him by ~ only** le conozco solamente de nombre; **we know it by** (*or* **under**) **another ~** lo conocemos bajo otro nombre; **to go by** (*or* **under**) **the ~ of** ser conocido por el nombre de, vivir bajo el nombre de; **in ~ only** era rey tan sólo de nombre, rey no tenía más que el nombre; **it exists in ~ only** no existe sino de nombre; **he signed on in the ~ of Smith** firmó con el apellido Smith; **at least in ~** al menos nominalmente; **she's the boss in all but ~** para jefa sólo le falta el nombre; **in the ~ of peace** en nombre de la paz; **I thank you in the ~ of all those present** le doy las gracias en nombre de todos los asistentes; **open up, in the ~ of the law!** ¡abran a la justicia!, ¡abran en nombre de la ley!; **what's in a ~?** ¿qué importa un nombre?; **he hasn't a penny to his ~** no tiene donde caerse muerto; **what's your ~?** ¿cómo se llama?; **my ~ is Peter** me llamo Pedro; **I'll do it, or my ~'s not Bloggs!** ¡como me llamo Bloggs, que lo haré!; **to call sb ~s** insultar a uno, poner motes a uno, llenar a uno de injurias; **what ~ are they giving the child?** ¿qué nombre le van a poner al niño?; **they married to give the child a ~** se casaron para darle nombre al niño, se casaron para legitimar al niño; **to lend one's ~ to** prestar su nombre a; **to mention no ~s** no mencionar nombres; **to put one's ~ down for a car** apuntarse para un coche; **what ~ shall I say?** (*Telec*) ¿de parte de quién?; (*announcing arrival*) ¿qué nombre quiere que diga?; **to send in one's ~** presentarse; **to take sb's ~ and address** apuntar las señas de uno; **he had his ~ taken** (*Sport*) el árbitro apuntó su nombre.

(b) (*reputation*) nombre *m*; reputación *f*, fama *f*; **the firm has a good ~** la casa tiene buena reputación; **he has a ~ for carelessness** tiene fama de descuidado, ya se sabe que es poco cuidadoso; **his middle ~ is 'lover'** le han apodado 'el amante'; **to get (o.s.) a bad ~** crearse una mala reputación; **he's giving the place a bad ~** le está dando mala fama al lugar; **to make a ~ for o.s.** darse a conocer, empezar a ser conocido (*as como*); **to make one's ~** llegar a ser famoso.

(c) (*person*) **big ~** (gran) figura *f*, personaje *m* de relieve; **he's a big ~** es todo un personaje; **he's one of the big ~s in the business** es uno de los personajes importantes en ese campo; **this show has no big ~s** este show no tiene figuras.

2 VT (*call*) *thing* llamar; nombrar; designar, denominar; *person* llamar; (*at birth*) bautizar, poner de nombre a; (*surname*) apellidar; (*mention*) mencionar, mentar; (*nominate*) nombrar; *date, price etc* fijar, señalar; **a man ~d Jack** un hombre llamado Juanito; **they ~d the child Mary** a la niña le pusieron María; **you ~ it, we have it** cualquier cosa que pidas la tenemos; **he is not ~d in this list** no figura en esta lista; **you were not ~d in the speech** no se le mencionó en el discurso; **~ the third president of the USA** diga el nombre del tercer presidente de EE.UU.; **to ~ a boy after** *or* (*US*) **for his grandfather** ponerle a un niño un nombre por su abuelo; **they ~d him Winston after Churchill** le pusieron Winston por Churchill; **he was ~d ambassador to Warsaw** le nombraron embajador en Varsovia.

name-calling ['neɪmkɔːlɪŋ] N insultos *mpl*, ofensas *fpl*.

-named [neɪmd] ADJ *ending in compounds*: **first~** primero; **last~** último.

name-day ['neɪmdeɪ] N (*Rel*) día *m* del santo de uno; fiesta *f* onomástica; (*Fin*) día *m* de ajuste de cuentas.

name-dropper ['neɪm,drɒpəˢ] N *persona dada al 'name-dropping'.*

name-dropping ['neɪm'drɒpɪŋ] N *vicio de procurar impresionar mencionando las personas importantes que uno conoce* (*o finge haber conocido*).

nameless ['neɪmlɪs] ADJ anónimo, sin nombre, innominado; *vice* nefando; *dread etc* vago, indecible; **to remain ~** permanecer en el anonimato; **a person who shall be ~** una persona cuyo nombre callo.

namely ['neɪmlɪ] ADV a saber; esto es, es decir.

nameplate ['neɪmpleɪt] N letrero *m* (*or* placa *f*) con nombre (del dueño *etc*); placa *f* del fabricante.

namesake ['neɪmseɪk] N tocayo *m*, -a *f*, homónimo *m*, -a *f*.

name-tag ['neɪmtæg] N placa *f* de identificación.

nametape ['neɪmteɪp] N tirita *f* con el nombre.

Namibia [nɑːˈmɪbɪə] N Namibia *f*.

Namibian [nɑːˈmɪbɪən] **1** ADJ namibio.
2 N namibio *m*, -a *f*.

nan* [næn] N, **nana*** ['nænə] N (*grandmother*) yaya* *f*.

nan bread ['nɑːnbred] N *pan indio sin apenas levadura.*

nance‡ [næns] N, **nancy(-boy)‡** ['nænsɪbɔɪ] N (*Brit*) maricón‡ *m*.

nanny ['nænɪ] N (*Brit*) niñera *f* (*also fig*), chacha* *f*; **~ state** papá-estado *m*.

nanny-goat ['nænɪgəʊt] N cabra *f*.

nannying ['nænɪɪŋ] N **(a)** (*job*) profesión *f* de niñera. **(b)** (*pej: mollycoddling*) protección *f* excesiva.

nano... ['nænəʊ] PREF nano....

nanometre ['nænəʊ,miːtəˢ] N nanómetro *m*.

nanotechnology [,nænəʊtek'nɒlədʒɪ] N nanotecnología *f*.

Naomi ['neɪəmɪ] NF Naomi.

nap¹ [næp] **1** N sueñecito *m*, dormirela *f*; (*in afternoon*) siesta *f*; **to have a ~**, **to take a ~** descabezar un sueño, echar una siesta, dormir la siesta.
2 VI dormitar; dormir la siesta; **to catch sb ~ping** coger a uno desprevenido; **to be caught ~ping** estar desprevenido.

nap² [næp] N (*on cloth*) lanilla *f*.

nap³ [næp] N (*Cards: game*) napolitana *f*; **to go ~** jugarse el todo (*on a*).

NAPA N (*US*) ABBR *of* **National Association of Performing Artists** *sindicato de trabajadores del espectáculo.*

napalm ['neɪpɑːm] N napalm *m*.

nape [neɪp] N (*also ~ of the neck*) nuca *f*, cogote *m*.

naphtha ['næfθə] N nafta *f*.

naphthalene ['næfθəliːn] N naftalina *f*.

napkin ['næpkɪn] N (*table ~*) servilleta *f*; (*Brit: baby's*) pañal *m*; (*woman's*) compresa *f* higiénica.

napkin-ring ['næpkɪnrɪŋ] N servilletero *m*.

Naples ['neɪplz] N Nápoles *m*.

Napoleon [nəˈpəʊlɪən] NM Napoleón.

Napoleonic [nə,pəʊlɪˈɒnɪk] ADJ napoleónico.

napper* ['næpəˢ] N (*head*) coca* *f*.

nappy ['næpɪ] **1** N (*Brit*) pañal *m*.
2 ATTR: **~ liner** pañal *m* interior; **~ rash** escaldamiento *m* por pañales húmedos; **to have ~ rash** tener el culito escaldado.

Narbonne [nɑːˈbɒn] N Narbona *f*.

narc‡ [nɑːk] N (*US*) camello* *m*, traficante *mf* de drogas.

narcissi [nɑːˈsɪsaɪ] NPL *of* **narcissus.**

narcissism [nɑːˈsɪsɪzəm] N narcisismo *m*.

narcissist ['nɑːsɪˌsɪst] N narcisista *mf*.

narcissistic [,nɑːsɪˈsɪstɪk] ADJ narcisista.

Narcissus [nɑːˈsɪsəs] NM Narciso.

narcissus [nɑːˈsɪsəs] N, PL **narcissi** [nɑːˈsɪsaɪ] narciso *m*.

narcolepsy [ˈnɑːkəʊlepsɪ] N narcolepsia *f*.

narcoleptic [,nɑːkəʊˈleptɪk] **1** ADJ narcoléptico.
2 N narcoléptico *m*, -a *f*.

narcosis [nɑːˈkəʊsɪs] N narcosis *f*, narcotismo *m*.

narco-terrorism [,nɑːkəʊˈterərɪzəm] N narcoterrorismo *m*.

narcotic [nɑːˈkɒtɪk] **1** ADJ narcótico.
2 N narcótico *m*.
3 ATTR: **~s agent** agente *mf* de narcóticos; **to be on a ~s charge** estar acusado de traficar con drogas.

narcotism ['nɑːkə,tɪzəm] N narcotismo *m*.

narcotize ['nɑːkətaɪz] VT narcotizar.

narco-trafficker [,nɑːkəʊˈtræfɪkəˢ] N narcotraficante *mf*.

narco-trafficking [,nɑːkəʊˈtræfɪkɪŋ] N narcotráfico *m*.

nard [nɑːd] N nardo *m*.

nark‡ [nɑːk] (*Brit*) **1** N soplón* *m*.
2 VT **(a)** **it ~s me** me fastidia terriblemente; **he got properly ~ed** se puso negro*. **(b)** **~ it!** (*stop it*) ¡déjalo!, (*go away*) ¡lárgate!*.

narked* [nɑːkt] ADJ (*Brit*) cabreado*, encabritado*; **to get ~** cabrearse*, encabritarse*.

narky‡ ['nɑːkɪ] ADJ: **to get ~** (*Brit*) ponerse negro*.

narrate [nəˈreɪt] VT narrar, referir, contar.

narration [nəˈreɪʃən] N narración *f*, relato *m*.

narrative ['nærətɪv] **1** ADJ narrativo.
2 N narrativa *f*, narración *f*.

narrator [nəˈreɪtəˢ] N narrador *m*, -ora *f*.

narrow ['nærəʊ] **1** ADJ estrecho, angosto; *trousers etc* estrecho; *advantage, majority* pequeño; (*restricted*) reducido, corto, restringido; *escape* de milagro, por los pelos; *person* de miras estrechas, intolerante; **~ boat** barcaza *f*; **in the ~ sense of the word** en el sentido estricto de la palabra; **on ~ resources** con escasos recursos.
2 NPL: **~s** (*Naut*) estrecho *m*.
3 VT (*also to ~ down*) estrechar, angostar; reducir; **we have ~ed it down to 3 possibilities** lo hemos reducido a 3 posibilidades; **the police have ~ed the search down to Bristol** la policía ha podido limitar sus pesquisas a Bristol.
4 VI (*also to ~ down*) estrecharse, angostarse, hacerse más angosto; reducirse; **the passage ~s at the end** el pasillo se hace más estrecho hacia el final; **the search has now ~ed to Soho** la búsqueda ha quedado restringida a Soho.
♦**narrow down 1** VT = narrow 3.
2 VI: **so the question ~s down to this ...** así que la cuestión se reduce a esto ...

narrow-gauge ['nærəʊgeɪdʒ] ADJ de vía estrecha.

narrowing ['nærəʊɪŋ] N (*V ADJ*) estrechamiento *m*; reducción *f*, restricción *f*.

narrowly ['nærəʊlɪ] ADV estrechamente; por poco; **the slate ~ missed him** por poco la pizarra le alcanza, faltó poco para que la pizarra le diese; **he ~ missed being elected** no fue elegido por unos pocos votos; **if we define it ~** si lo definimos estrictamente; **they watched me ~** me vigilaban sin quitarme ojo.

narrow-minded ['nærəʊ'maɪndɪd] ADJ de miras estrechas, intolerante.

narrow-mindedness ['nærəʊ'maɪndɪdnɪs] N estrechez *f* de miras, intolerancia *f*.

narrowness ['nærəʊnɪs] N estrechez *f*.

narwhal ['nɑːwəl] N narval *m*.

NAS N (*US*) ABBR *of* **National Academy of Sciences.**

NASA ['næsə] N (*US*) ABBR *of* **National Aeronautics and Space Administration** NASA *f*.

nasal ['neɪzəl] **1** ADJ nasal; (*twanging*) gangoso.
2 N nasal *f*.

nasality [neɪˈzælɪtɪ] N nasalidad *f*.

nasalization [,neɪzəlaɪˈzeɪʃən] N nasalización *f*.

nasalize ['neɪzəlaɪz] VT nasalizar; (*twangingly*) pronunciar con timbre gangoso.

nasally ['neɪzəlɪ] ADV nasalmente; con timbre nasal; **to speak ~** hablar por las narices, ganguear.

nascent ['næsnt] ADJ naciente.

Nassau ['næsɔː] N Nassau *m*.

nastily ['nɑːstɪlɪ] ADV (*V ADJ*) suciamente; horriblemente; groseramente;

gravemente; peligrosamente; **he said** ~ dijo groseramente; **it was raining quite** ~ llovía de muy mala manera.

nastiness ['nɑːstɪnɪs] N suciedad *f*; cosas *fpl* horribles; indecencia *f*; lo asqueroso, lo horrible; lo malo; gravedad *f*; lo peligroso; grosería *f*; rencor *m*.

nasturtium [nəs'tɜːʃəm] N capuchina *f*.

nasty ['nɑːstɪ] ADJ **(a)** (*dirty*) sucio, puerco; (*obscene*) sucio, indecente, obsceno; (*disagreeable*) asqueroso, horrible, repugnante; *smell, taste* horrible; *remark* feo, horrible; (*rude*) grosero; *weather* feo, malo; *accident* grave; *wound etc* peligroso, de gravedad; *corner, turn etc* peligroso; *temper* vivo; *trick* malo; *habit* feo; **a very** ~ **film** una película asquerosa, un film de lo más horrible; **a** ~ **mess** un lío imponente; **what a** ~ **mind you have!** ¡qué mal pensado eres!; **to smell** ~ oler mal, tener un olor desagradable; **to taste** ~ saber mal, tener un sabor desagradable; **to turn** ~ *situation* ponerse difícil, *weather* volverse malo.

(b) *person* antipático; poco afable; (*rude*) grosero; (*malicious*) rencoroso, malévolo; **what a** ~ **man!** ¡qué hombre más horrible!; **to be** ~ **to sb** tratar muy mal a uno, portarse mal con uno; **they were** ~ **to her in the shop** se portaron groseramente con ella en la tienda; **don't be** ~! ¡no digas esas cosas horribles!; ¡no seas mal pensado!; **to turn** ~ ponerse negro*, (*weather*) ponerse feo.

NAS/UWT N (*Brit*) ABBR *of* **National Association of Schoolmasters/ Union of Women Teachers** *sindicato de profesores.*

Natal [nə'tæl] N Natal *m*.

natal ['neɪtl] ADJ natal.

natality [nə'tælɪtɪ] N natalidad *f*.

natatorium [,neɪtə'tɔːrɪəm] N, PL **natatoria** [,neɪtə'tɔːrɪə] (*US*) piscina *f*.

natch‡ [nætʃ] EXCL naturalmente, naturaca‡.

NATFHE N (*Brit*) ABBR *of* **National Association of Teachers in Further and Higher Education** *sindicato de la enseñanza superior.*

nation ['neɪʃən] N nación *f*; **N~ of Islam** (*US*) Nación *f* del Islam.

┌─── **NATION OF ISLAM** ───┐

La **Nation of Islam** (*también conocida como* **Black Muslims** *y rebautizada de forma oficial con el nombre de* **American Muslim Mission**) *es un movimiento religioso y cultural de Estados Unidos que aboga por el separatismo y la ayuda mutua entre la gente de color, como respuesta a la discriminación racial, la pobreza y la delincuencia que padecen. El movimiento, surgido en 1930, estuvo liderado en los años sesenta por* **Malcolm X** *y entre sus miembros más famosos está el boxeador* **Muhammad Ali**. *Cuenta con varios programas educativos y religiosos y con una red de mezquitas establecidas por todo Estados Unidos, y con algunas en el Reino Unido. A los miembros masculinos se les reconoce fácilmente por su traje negro con camisa blanca y pajarita.*

Uno de los grupos que se originó a partir de este movimiento es el **Lost-Found Nation of Islam** *cuyo líder es el controvertido Louis Farrakhan.*

national ['næʃənl] **1** ADJ nacional; ~ **anthem** himno *m* nacional; ~ **costume**, ~ **dress** vestido *m* nacional; **N~ Curriculum** (*Brit*) plan de estudios para las escuelas de Inglaterra y Gales; **N~ Debt** deuda *f* pública; **N~ Enterprise Board** (*Brit*) ≈ Instituto *m* Nacional de Industria (*Sp*); ~ **grid** (*Brit*) red *f* eléctrica nacional; **N~ Guard** (*US*) Guardia *f* Nacional; **N~ Health Service** (*Brit*) servicio *m* nacional de salud; ~ **holiday** fiesta *f* nacional; ~ **income** renta *f* nacional; **N~ Insurance** (*Brit*) seguro *m* social; ~ **park** parque *m* nacional; ~ **press** prensa *f* nacional; ~ **product** producto *m* nacional; **N~ Savings** (*Brit*) ≈ caja *f* nacional de ahorros; **N~ Savings Bank** (*Brit*) ≈ Caja *f* Postal de Ahorros; **N~ Savings Certificate** ≈ bono *m* del Tesoro; ~ **service** (*Brit*) servicio *m* nacional, conscripción *f*; ~ **serviceman** conscripto *m*, recluta *m*; ~ **socialism** nacionalsocialismo *m*; **N~ Trust** (*Brit*) *instituto encargado del patrimonio histórico-artístico nacional y de parajes de interés ambiental*; **N~ Weather Service** (*US*) estación meteorológica estatal. **2** N nacional *mf*, súbdito *m*, -a *f*; *ver también* CURRICULUM - NATIONAL CURRICULUM .

┌─── **NATIONAL GUARD** ───┐

La **National Guard** (*Guardia Nacional*) *es una organización estadounidense que recluta voluntarios no profesionales a los que se prepara para colaborar con el ejército profesional y las fuerzas aéreas en tiempos de crisis. Los requisitos para alistarse son los mismos que para el ejército normal y, aunque su preparación la dirige el gobierno federal, sus miembros pueden ser movilizados para ayudar en situaciones de emergencia, catástrofes naturales y el control de situaciones excepcionales de violencia civil. Los miembros de la* **National Guard** *tienen que prestar juramento de fidelidad a los EE.UU. y al estado al que pertenecen.*

┌─── **NATIONAL TRUST** ───┐

El **National Trust** *es una organización benéfica que se dedica a la conservación de lugares del patrimonio histórico-artístico o de parajes naturales. Se financia a través de donaciones, aportaciones de los socios, y*

dinero procedente de la venta de entradas, souvenirs y de las cafeterías o restaurantes que suele haber en muchos de estos lugares.

national heritage ['næʃnl'herɪtɪdʒ] N patrimonio *m* nacional.

nationalism ['næʃnəlɪzəm] N nacionalismo *m*.

nationalist ['næʃnəlɪst] **1** ADJ nacionalista. **2** N nacionalista *mf*.

nationalistic [,næʃnə'lɪstɪk] ADJ nacionalista.

nationality [,næʃə'nælɪtɪ] N nacionalidad *f*.

nationalization [,næʃnəlaɪ'zeɪʃən] N nacionalización *f*.

nationalize ['næʃnəlaɪz] VT nacionalizar.

nationalized ['næʃnəlaɪzd] ADJ: ~ **industry** industria *f* nacionalizada.

National Lottery ['næʃənl'lɒtərɪ] N (*Brit*) ≈ lotería *f* primitiva.

nationally ['næʃnəlɪ] ADV a escala nacional; por toda la nación; nacionalmente, como nación; desde el punto de vista nacional.

nationhood ['neɪʃənhʊd] N carácter *m* de nación; **to achieve** ~ llegar a constituir una nación, llegar a tener categoría de nación.

nation-state ['neɪʃən'steɪt] N estado-nación *m*.

nationwide ['neɪʃənwaɪd] **1** ADJ por toda la nación, a escala nacional; de toda la nación. **2** ADV por todo el país, a escala nacional.

native ['neɪtɪv] **1** ADJ **(a)** (*innate*) natural, innato; ~ **wit** sentido *m* común.

(b) (*artless*) sencillo, natural.

(c) (*of one's birth*) natal; *town* natal; *language* materno, nativo; ~ **land** patria *f*; **she is not a** ~ **Dutch speaker** el holandés no es su lengua materna.

(d) (*Min*) nativo.

(e) (*indigenous*) indígena; autóctono; *product, resources etc* natural, nacional, del país; **the animal is** ~ **to Africa** el animal es indígena de África, el animal es originario de África.

(f) (*of natives*) indígena, nativo; **the** ~ **customs** las costumbres de los indígenas; **Minister for N~ Affairs** Ministro *m* de Asuntos Indígenas; **to learn the** ~ **language** aprender el idioma vernáculo; **to go** ~ vivir como los indígenas.

2 N **(a)** (*with reference to birth or nationality*) natural *mf*; nacional *mf*; **he was a** ~ **of Seville** nació en Sevilla, era natural de Sevilla, era sevillano; **the plant is a** ~ **of China** la planta es originaria de China; **he speaks German like a** ~ habla alemán como un alemán, habla alemán como si hubiera nacido allí.

(b) (*primitive*) nativo *m*, -a *f*, indígena *mf*.

Native American ['neɪtɪvə'merɪkən] **1** ADJ americano nativo. **2** N americano *m* nativo, americana *f* nativa.

nativity [nə'tɪvɪtɪ] N natividad *f*; **the N~** Navidad *f*; (*Art*) nacimiento *m*; ~ **play** auto *m* del nacimiento.

NATO ['neɪtəʊ] N ABBR *of* **North Atlantic Treaty Organization** OTAN *f*, Organización *f* del Tratado del Atlántico Norte.

NATSOPA [,næt'səʊpə] N (*Brit*) ABBR *of* **National Society of Operative Printers, Graphical and Media Personnel** *sindicato de tipógrafos.*

natter* ['nætər] (*Brit*) **1** N charla *f*; **to have a** ~ echar un párrafo*, cotillear (*with* con). **2** VI (*chat*) charlar; (*chatter*) parlotear, hablar mucho; (*keep on*) machacar; (*complain*) quejarse; **to** ~ **at sb** machacar en un tema con uno.

natterer* ['nætərər] N charlatán *m*, -ana *f*, cotorra* *mf*.

NATTKE N (*Brit*) ABBR *of* **National Association of Television, Theatrical and Kinematographic Employees** *sindicato de empleados de televisión, teatro y cine.*

natty* ['nætɪ] ADJ (*spruce*) majo, elegante, acicalado; (*deft*) diestro; *gadget etc* ingenioso.

natural ['nætʃrəl] **1** ADJ (*in most senses*) natural; normal; instintivo; *person* inafectado, sin afectación; *child* ilegítimo; ~ **break** (*TV etc*) interrupción *f* natural; **to die of** ~ **causes** morir de muerte natural; ~ **childbirth** parto *m* sin dolor; ~ **gas** gas *m* natural; ~ **history** historia *f* natural; ~ **justice** justicia *f* natural; **for the rest of one's** ~ **life** de por vida; ~ **parent** padre *m* biológico, madre *f* biológica; ~ **resources** recursos *mpl* naturales; ~ **sciences** ciencias *fpl* naturales; ~ **selection** selección *f* natural; ~ **wastage** desgaste *m* natural; **it is** ~ **that ...** es natural que ..., es lógico que ...; **it seems** ~ **enough to me** me parece totalmente normal; **he's a** ~ **painter** es un pintor nato, nació para pintor.

2 N **(a)** (*person*) imbécil *mf*. **(b)** (*Mus*) nota *f* natural; (*sign*) becuadro *m*; (*key*) tecla *f* blanca. **(c)** (*) cosa *f* de éxito seguro, persona *f* segura de tener éxito; **he's a** ~ tiene dotes innatas, nació para eso.

naturalism ['nætʃrəlɪzəm] N naturalismo *m*.

naturalist ['nætʃrəlɪst] N naturalista *mf*.

naturalistic [,nætʃrə'lɪstɪk] ADJ naturalista.

naturalization [,nætʃrəlaɪ'zeɪʃən] **1** N naturalización *f*. **2** ATTR: ~ **papers** carta *f* de ciudadanía.

naturalize ['nætʃrəlaɪz] **1** VT *person* naturalizar; *plant etc* aclimatar, establecer; **to become ~d** naturalizarse. **2** VI (*person*) naturalizarse; (*plant etc*) aclimatarse, establecerse.

naturally ['nætʃrəlɪ] ADV (a) (*in a natural way*) naturalmente; sin afectación, con naturalidad; instintivamente, por instinto; **a ~ optimistic person** una persona optimista por naturaleza; **to write ~** escribir con naturalidad; **to do what comes ~** actuar espontáneamente; **it happened ~** ocurrió de manera natural.
(b) (*of course*) naturalmente; desde luego ..., claro que ...; **~!** ¡naturalmente!; **~ it is not true** desde luego no es cierto.

naturalness ['nætʃrəlnɪs] N naturalidad f.

nature ['neɪtʃər] [1] N (a) (*essential quality, character*) naturaleza f; índole f; modo m de ser; esencia f; (*of person*) natural m, carácter m, temperamento m, genio m; **good ~** afabilidad f, amabilidad f; **to abuse sb's good ~** abusar de la amabilidad de uno; **he has a nice ~** tiene un temperamento agradable; **it is not in his ~ to say that** no es capaz de decir tal cosa, no es típico suyo el decir tal cosa; **that's very much in his ~** eso es muy de él; **to appeal to sb's better ~** apelar a los sentimientos nobles de uno; **the ~ of birds is to fly** las aves vuelan naturalmente, lo propio de las aves es volar; **outspokenness is second ~ with him** la franqueza le es completamente natural; **by its very ~** de por sí; **to be cautious by ~** ser cauteloso por naturaleza; **it's against ~, it's contrary to ~** es antinatural, es contrario a la naturaleza; **in the ~ of things it's impossible** lógicamente es imposible.
(b) (*kind*) género m, clase f; **~ of contents** (*Comm*) descripción f del contenido; **something of that ~** algo por el estilo; **of a technical ~** de carácter técnico; **of quite another ~** de otra índole; **some conclusions of a ~ to amaze one** unas conclusiones de tipo sorprendente; **in the ~ of** del género de, algo así como.
(c) (*Bio, Phys etc*) naturaleza f; **the laws of N~** las leyes de la Naturaleza; **a keen student of ~** un estudiante entusiasta de la naturaleza, un entusiasta de la historia natural); **in a state of ~** en su estado natural; **to draw from ~** dibujar del natural; **to return to ~** (*area*) volver a su estado natural, (*person*) volver a la naturaleza.
(d) **to relieve ~** hacer de cuerpo, hacer sus necesidades.
[2] ATTR: **N~ Conservancy Council** (*Brit*) ≈ Instituto m para la Conservación de la Naturaleza, ICONA m; **~ conservation** protección f de la naturaleza; **~ cure** cura f natural; **~ reserve** reserva f natural; **~ study** (estudio m de la) historia f natural; **~ trail** paseo m por la naturaleza, ruta f de interés para el estudio de la naturaleza; **~ worship** culto m de la naturaleza; (*ancient*) panteísmo m.

-natured ['neɪtʃəd] ADJ *ending in compounds* de carácter ..., de condición ...; **ill~** malévolo, malicioso; V **good-natured** *etc*.

nature-lover ['neɪtʃə,lʌvər] N amigo m, -a f de la naturaleza.

naturism ['neɪtʃərɪzəm] N naturismo m, naturalismo m.

naturist ['neɪtʃərɪst] N naturista mf, naturalista mf.

naturopath ['neɪtʃərə,pæθ] N naturópata mf.

naturopathy [,neɪtʃə'rɒpəθɪ] N naturopatía f.

naught [nɔːt] N nada; **there's ~ I can do about it** no hay nada que yo pueda hacer; **all for ~** todo en balde; **to bring to ~** *attempt, plan* frustrar, *hope* destruir; **to come to ~** fracasar, malograrse, no dar resultado; **to set at ~** no hacer caso de, despreciar; V *also* **nought**.

naughtily ['nɔːtɪlɪ] ADV traviesamente, mal; escabrosamente; con picardía, con malicia.

naughtiness ['nɔːtɪnɪs] N (a) (*of child etc*) travesuras fpl, mala conducta f, picardía f; desobediencia f. (b) (*of joke, song etc*) lo verde, lo escabroso; malicia f.

naughty ['nɔːtɪ] ADJ (a) *child etc* travieso, malo, pícaro; desobediente, revoltoso; **you've been very ~, that was very ~ of you, that was a ~ thing to do** has sido muy malo; **~!** ¡malo!; **don't be ~!** ¡no seas malo!; **you ~ boy!** ¡pillo!, **you ~ girl!** ¡picaruela!
(b) *joke, song etc* verde, escabroso, colorado (*LAm*); atrevido, picante; **that ~ jealousy of yours** esos pícaros celos tuyos; **she gave me a ~ look** me miró picaruela; **what ~ times we live in!** ¡qué tiempos más inmorales éstos!; **the N~ Nineties** la Bella Época; **~ bits:** alegrías: fpl, paquete: m.

nausea ['nɔːsɪə] N náusea f, bascas fpl; (*fig*) asco m, repugnancia f.

nauseate ['nɔːsɪeɪt] VT dar náuseas a; (*fig*) dar asco a, repugnar; **your conduct ~s me** me repugna tu conducta; **that cheese ~s me** ese queso me da asco.

nauseating ['nɔːsɪeɪtɪŋ] ADJ nauseabundo, repugnante, asqueroso.

nauseatingly ['nɔːsɪeɪtɪŋlɪ] ADV asquerosamente; **~ virtuous** tan virtuoso que da asco.

nauseous ['nɔːsɪəs] ADJ nauseabundo.

nautical ['nɔːtɪkəl] ADJ náutico, marítimo; **~ almanac** almanaque m náutico; **~ mile** milla f marina.

nautilus ['nɔːtɪləs] N nautilo m.

Navaho ['nævəhəʊ] N (a) (*also* **~ Indian**) Navajo mf. (b) (*Ling*) Navajo m.

naval ['neɪvəl] ADJ naval, de marina; de la marina de guerra; naval militar; *engagement* naval; *forces* de la marina; *power* marítimo; **~ academy** escuela f naval; **~ architecture** arquitectura f naval; **~ attaché** agregado m naval; **~ base** base f naval; **~ college** escuela f de

la Armada; **~ dockyard** astillero m naval; **~ officer** oficial m de marina; **~ port** puerto m naval; **~ power** potencia f marítima; **~ station** apostadero m naval; **~ warfare** guerra f naval.

Navarre [nə'vɑːr] N Navarra f.

Navarrese [,nævə'riːz] [1] ADJ navarro.
[2] N (a) navarro m, -a f. (b) (*Ling*) navarro m.

nave¹ [neɪv] N (*Archit*) nave f.

nave² [neɪv] N (*wheel*) cubo m; **~ plate** (*Aut*) tapacubos m.

navel ['neɪvəl] N ombligo m.

navel-gazing ['neɪvəlgeɪzɪŋ] N (*pej*) ombliguismo m, autocontemplación f.

navigable ['nævɪgəbl] ADJ (a) *river etc* navegable. (b) (*steerable*) gobernable, dirigible.

navigate ['nævɪgeɪt] [1] VT (a) *ship* marear, gobernar. (b) *river etc* navegar por. (c) (*fig*) conducir, guiar.
[2] VI navegar.

navigation [,nævɪ'geɪʃən] [1] N navegación f; (*science of ~*) náutica f, navegación f.
[2] ATTR: **~ lights** (*on ship*) luces fpl de navegación; (*in harbour*) baliza f.

navigational [,nævɪ'geɪʃənl] ADJ relativo a la navegación; **~ aids** ayudas fpl a la navegación.

navigator ['nævɪgeɪtər] N (*Naut*) navegador m, navegante m; (*Aer*) navegante m.

navvy ['nævɪ] N (*Brit*) peón m caminero, peón m zapador, bracero m.

navy ['neɪvɪ] [1] N marina f de guerra, armada f, flota f.
[2] ATTR: **N~ Department** (*US*) Ministerio m de Marina; **~ yard** (*US*) astillero m de la Armada.

navy-blue ['neɪvɪ'bluː] [1] N azul m marino, azul m de mar.
[2] ADJ azul marino.

nay [neɪ] [1] N nada; (†† *or prov*) ADV no; (*or rather*) más aun, mejor dicho, más bien; **bad, ~ terrible** malo, mejor dicho, horrible; **dozens, ~ hundreds** docenas, digo centenares.
[2] N (*refusal*) negativa f; (*in voting*) voto m negativo, voto m en contra; **to say sb ~** dar una respuesta negativa a uno.

Nazarene [,næzə'riːn] [1] ADJ nazareno.
[2] N nazareno m, -a f.

Nazareth ['næzərəθ] N Nazaret m.

Nazi ['nɑːtsɪ] [1] ADJ nazi, nazista.
[2] N nazi mf.

Nazism ['nɑːtsɪzəm] N nazismo m.

NB (a) ABBR *of* **nota bene; note well** nótese bien, N.B. (b) (*Canada*) ABBR *of* **New Brunswick.**

NBA N (*US*) ABBR *of* **National Basketball Association.** (b) ABBR *of* **National Boxing Association.**

NBC N (*US*) ABBR *of* **National Broadcasting Company.**

NBS N (*US*) ABBR *of* **National Bureau of Standards** ≈ Oficina f Nacional de Normas.

NC (a) (*US Post*) ABBR *of* **North Carolina.** (b) (*Comm etc*) ABBR *of* **no charge.**

NCB (*Brit: formerly*) N ABBR *of* **National Coal Board.**

NCC N (a) (*Brit*) ABBR *of* **Nature Conservancy Council** ≈ Instituto m para la Conservación de la Naturaleza, ICONA m. (b) (*US*) ABBR *of* **National Council of Churches.**

NCCL N (*Brit*) ABBR *of* **National Council for Civil Liberties.**

NCO N ABBR *of* **non-commissioned officer** suboficial m.

NCV ABBR *of* **no commercial value** sin valor comercial.

ND (*US Post*) ABBR *of* **North Dakota.**

n.d. ABBR *of* **no date** sin fecha, s.f.

N.Dak. ABBR *of* **North Dakota.**

NE (a) (*US Post*) ABBR *of* **Nebraska.** (b) (*Geog*) ABBR *of* **north east** NE m. (c) (*US Geog*) ABBR *of* **New England.**

NEA N (*US*) ABBR *of* **National Educational Association.**

Neanderthal [nɪ'ændətɑːl] [1] N (*Geog*) Neanderthal m.
[2] ADJ Neanderthal, de Neanderthal; **~ man** hombre m de Neanderthal.

neap [niːp] N (*also* **~ tide**) marea f muerta.

Neapolitan [nɪə'pɒlɪtən] [1] ADJ napolitano; **~ ice-cream** helado m napolitano.
[2] N napolitano m, -a f.

near [nɪər] [1] ADV cerca; **as ~ as I can recall** que yo recuerde; **~ on 30 books:** casi 30 libros; **that's ~ enough** (*fig*) ya basta, con eso vale; no merece la pena precisar más; **it's not anywhere ~ enough** no basta ni con mucho; **to bring sth ~** acercar algo; **to come ~, to draw ~** acercarse; **to come ~ to doing** llegar casi a hacer; **I came ~ to telling her everything** llegué casi a decírselo todo.
[2] PREP (*also* **~ to**) (*of place*) cerca de; junto a, próximo a, al lado de; (*of time*) cerca de, casi; (*of numbers*) casi, cerca de; **~ here** aquí cerca, cerca de aquí; **to be ~ (to) the fire** estar cerca del fuego; **the passage is ~ the end of the book** el trozo está hacia el final del libro; **~ the end of the century** hacia fines del siglo; **she was ~ her end** tocaba a su fin, estaba cerca de la muerte; **she was ~ to crying**

estaba a punto de llorar; **we were ~ to being drowned** por poco nos morimos ahogados.

3 ADJ *place etc* cercano; próximo, inmediato, vecino; *time* próximo; *relationship* estrecho, íntimo; *relative* cercano; *resemblance* grande; *translation etc* aproximativo; **the ~est way** el camino más corto; **the ~est I ever got to winning** lo más cerca que estuve de ganar; **the ~est I ever came to feeling that was when ...** la única vez que llegué a sentir algo parecido fue cuando ...; **work it out to the ~est pound** redondéalo a la libra entera; **one's ~est and dearest** los más allegados y queridos, sus parientes más cercanos; **it was a ~ guess** casi acertamos (*etc*) con la conjetura; **it's the ~est thing to murder** esto es casi un homicidio; V **miss 1**.

4 VT acercarse a, aproximarse a; **the building is ~ing completion** el edificio está casi terminado, el edificio se terminará dentro de poco; **he is ~ing 50** frisa en los 50, tiene casi 50 años; **the country is ~ing disaster** el país está al borde de la catástrofe.

nearby **1** ['nɪə'baɪ] ADV cerca.

2 ['nɪəbaɪ] ADJ cercano, próximo, inmediato.

Near East ['nɪər'iːst] N Próximo Oriente *m*, Cercano Oriente *m*.

nearly ['nɪəlɪ] ADV **(a)** (*closely*) **it touches me ~** me toca de cerca.
(b) (*numerals*) **~ 100** casi 100; **it's ~ 3 o'clock** son casi las 3; van a ser las 3; **she's ~ 40** tiene casi 40 años, frisa en los 40.
(c) (*with adj etc*) **~ finished** casi terminado; **~ black** casi negro, más o menos negro; **very ~!** ¡casi casi!; **it's pretty ~ dead** está casi muerto; **the same number or ~ so** el mismo número o casi.
(d) (*with negative*) **it's not ~ ready** no está listo ni con mucho; **it's not ~ good enough** no es bueno ni con mucho (*to* + *infin* para + *infin*); **she is not ~ so poor as she says** no es ni con mucho tan pobre como ella dice.
(e) (*with verb*) **I ~ lost it** por poco lo perdí; **I very ~ caught it** por poco lo cogí; **I ~ did it** estuve a punto de hacerlo.

near-money ['nɪə,mʌnɪ] N (*Comm*) NPL activos *mpl* realizables.

nearness ['nɪənɪs] N proximidad *f*, cercanía *f*, lo cercano; intimidad *f*; inminencia *f*; **because of its ~ to the station** por estar tan cerca de la estación.

near-side ['nɪəsaɪd] (*Aut etc*) **1** ADJ (*Brit*) izquierdo, (*most other countries*) derecho.

2 N (*Brit*) lado *m* izquierdo, (*most other countries*) lado *m* derecho.

near-sighted ['nɪə'saɪtɪd] ADJ corto de vista, miope.

near-sightedness ['nɪə'saɪtɪdnɪs] N miopía *f*.

neat [niːt] ADJ **(a)** (*clean and tidy*) *person etc* pulcro, esmerado, acicalado; *garden, room etc* bien cuidado, bien arreglado, ordenado; *work* primoroso; **her hair is always very ~** lleva el pelo siempre bien peinado; **he made a ~ job of it** lo hizo con esmero.
(b) (*pleasing to the eye*) *figure etc* atractivo, esbelto; bien proporcionado.
(c) (*skilful*) diestro; *phrase, writing, shot, solution* elegante; *plan* hábil, ingenioso; **that's ~!, very ~!** ¡muy bien!
(d) (*Brit*) *drink* puro, solo, sin mezcla; **~ gin** ginebra *f* pura; **I'll take it ~** lo tomo sin mezcla.
(e) (*US**) estupendo*, fantástico*.

neaten ['niːtn] VT *dress* alisarse; *desk* arreglar, ordenar; **to ~ one's hair** retocarse el peinado.

'neath [niːθ] PREP (*liter*) = **beneath**.

neatly ['niːtlɪ] ADV (*V* ADJ) **(a)** pulcramente, esmeradamente, con esmero; con primor, primorosamente. **(b)** atractivamente. **(c)** diestramente; elegantemente; hábilmente, ingeniosamente.

neatness ['niːtnɪs] N (*V* ADJ) **(a)** pulcritud *f*, esmero *m*; lo arreglado, lo cuidado; primor *m*. **(b)** lo atractivo, esbeltez *f*; buena proporción *f*. **(c)** destreza *f*; elegancia *f*; habilidad *f*.

NEB N ABBR of **New English Bible**.

Nebr. ABBR of **Nebraska**.

Nebuchadnezzar [,nebjukəd'nezər] NM Nabucodonosor.

nebula ['nebjulə] N, PL **nebulae** ['nebjuliː] nebulosa *f*.

nebulizer ['nebju,laɪzər] N nebulizador *m*

nebulous ['nebjuləs] ADJ (*also fig*) nebuloso.

NEC N ABBR of **National Executive Committee** comité *m* ejecutivo nacional.

necessarily ['nesɪsərɪlɪ] ADV necesariamente; forzosamente; **not ~** cabe otra posibilidad, eso no es cierto del todo, no tiene por qué ser así; **it is not ~ true that ...** no es necesariamente cierto que ...

necessary ['nesɪsərɪ] **1** ADJ necesario; forzoso, preciso, esencial, indispensable, imprescindible; **with the ~ enthusiasm** con el debido entusiasmo; **all the ~ ceremonies** todas las ceremonias obligatorias; **if ~** si es necesario, si es preciso; **it is ~ that ...** es necesario que + *subj*, es preciso que + *subj*; **it is ~ for us to go** es preciso que vayamos; **it made it ~ for us to sell them** hizo inevitable que los vendiésemos; **I shall do everything ~** haré todo lo necesario; **don't do more than is ~** no haga más de lo necesario.

2 N **(a)** cosa *f* necesaria, requisito *m* indispensable; (*also* **necessaries** PL) lo necesario; **to do the ~*** hacer lo que hace falta, hacer lo que hay que hacer. **(b)** (*: *money*) cumquibus *m*.

necessitate [nɪ'sesɪteɪt] VT necesitar, exigir.

necessitous [nɪ'sesɪtəs] ADJ necesitado, indigente.

necessity [nɪ'sesɪtɪ] N **(a)** (*need*) necesidad *f*; inevitabilidad *f*; **~ is the mother of invention** la necesidad estimula la invención, el hambre aguza el ingenio; **~ knows no law** la necesidad carece de ley; **the ~ for care** la necesidad del cuidado; **of ~** por necesidad, forzosamente; **out of sheer ~** por fuerza; **in case of ~** si fuese necesario, en caso de urgencia; **it's a case of sheer ~** es un caso de la mayor necesidad; **dire ~ leads me to ask** la más apremiante necesidad me obliga a pedirlo; **there is no ~ for you to do it** no es necesario que lo hagas; **to be under the ~ of** + *ger* verse obligado a + *infin*.
(b) (*article*) cosa *f* necesaria, requisito *m* indispensable; **necessities** artículos *mpl* de primera necesidad; **the necessities of life** las cosas necesarias para la vida; **a fridge is a ~ nowadays** hoy día una nevera es una necesidad, es indispensable ahora tener nevera.
(c) (*poverty*) indigencia *f*; **to be in ~** estar en la mayor necesidad, estar necesitado.

neck [nek] **1** N **(a)** (*Anat*) cuello *m*; garganta *f*; (*of animal*) pescuezo *m*; (*of bottle*) cuello *m*, gollete *m*; (*Geog*) istmo *m*; (*Sew*) cuello *m*, escote *m*; (*Mus: of guitar*) cuello *m*, (*of violin*) mástil *m*; **to race ~ and ~** ir muy iguales, correr parejos; **~ or nothing** (*Brit*) todo o nada; **in this ~ of the woods** en estos pagos; **to beat sb ~ and crop** vencer a uno fácilmente; **they threw him out ~ and crop** le pusieron de patitas en la calle; **to be up to one's ~** (*in work*) tener trabajo hasta la coronilla; **to be in sth up to one's ~** estar muy metido en un asunto; **to break one's ~** desnucarse; **to break sb's ~** romper el pescuezo a uno; **I'll break your ~!** ¡te parto la cara!; **she fell on his ~** ella se le colgó de su cuello; **to get it in the ~*** pagarlas, cargárselas*; (*be told off*) recibir un rapapolvo*; **he's got it all round his ~*** anda hecho un lío con esto*; **to have sb breathing down one's ~** tener a uno encima, tener a uno sobre sus talones; **the rain ran down my ~** la lluvia me corría por el cuello; **to risk one's ~, to stick one's ~ out** arriesgarse, jugarse el tipo; atreverse a expresar una opinión; **to win by a ~** ganar por una cabeza; **to wring a rabbit's ~** torcer el pescuezo a un conejo.
(b) (*Brit**) = **nerve 1(d)**.

2 VI (*) acariciarse, abrazarse amorosamente, besuquear; **to ~ with** acariciar a, besuquear a.

neckband ['nekbænd] N tirilla *f*.

neckerchief ['nekətʃiːf] N pañuelo *m*.

necking* ['nekɪŋ] N caricias *fpl*, abrazos *mpl* amorosos, besuqueo *m*.

necklace ['neklɪs] N, **necklet** ['neklɪt] N collar *m*.

neckline ['neklaɪn] N escote *m*.

necktie ['nektaɪ] N (*Brit*) corbata *f*.

necrological [,nekrəʊ'lɒdʒɪkəl] ADJ necrológico.

necrology [ne'krɒlədʒɪ] N necrología *f*.

necromancer ['nekrəʊmænsər] N nigromante *m*.

necromancy ['nekrəʊmænsɪ] N nigromancia *f*, nigromancía *f*.

necrophile ['nekrəʊ,faɪl] N necrófilo *m*, -a *f*.

necrophilia [,nekrəʊ'fɪlɪə] N necrofilia *f*.

necrophiliac [,nekrəʊ'fɪlɪæk] **1** ADJ necrófilo.

2 N necrófilo *m*, -a *f*.

necropolis [ne'krɒpəlɪs] N necrópolis *f*.

necrotising fasciitis ['nekrəʊtaɪzɪŋfæʃɪ'aɪtɪs] N (*Med*) fascitis *f* necrotizante.

nectar ['nektər] N néctar *m*.

nectarine ['nektəriːn] N nectarina *f*.

ned‡ [ned] N (*esp Scot*) chorizo‡ *m*, -a *f*, gamberro *m*, -a *f*.

NEDC, Neddy* ['nedɪ] N (*Brit*) ABBR of **National Economic Development Council** ≃ Consejo *m* Económico y Social.

née [neɪ] ADJ de soltera; **Mrs Minnie Crun, ~ Banister** Señora Minnie Crun, de soltera Banister; Señora Minnie Banister de Crun.

▼ **need** [niːd] **1** N **(a)** (*necessity*) necesidad *f* (*for, of* de); **if ~(s) be, in case of ~** si fuera necesario, en caso de urgencia; **there is every ~** es totalmente indispensable; **I see no ~** no veo la necesidad; **without the ~ to pay so much** sin necesidad de pagar tanto; **there is no ~ to** + *infin* no hace falta + *infin*; **there's no ~ to worry** no hay para qué inquietarse; **what ~ is there to buy it?** ¿qué necesidad hay de comprarlo?; **no ~ to say that ...** excusado es decir que ...; **no ~ to tell him what to do** no hace falta decirle qué hacer; **to be in ~ of, to have ~ of, to stand in ~ of** necesitar; **I have no ~ of advice** no necesito consejos, no me hacen falta consejos; **you have no ~ to go** no es preciso que vayas; **when I'm in ~ of a drink** cuando siento la necesidad de beber algo, cuando me hace falta tomar algo; **a house in ~ of painting** una casa que hay que pintar, una casa que necesita ser pintada.
(b) (*want, lack*) adversidad *f*; apuro *m*; (*absence*) carencia *f*; falta *f*, escasez *f*; **in times of ~** en tiempos de adversidad, en tiempos de carestía; **there is much ~ of food** hay una gran escasez de alimentos.
(c) (*poverty*) necesidad *f*, indigencia *f*; **my ~ is great** es grande mi necesidad; **to be in ~** estar necesitado.

(d) (*thing needed*) cosa *f* necesaria, requisito *m*; **bodily ~s** necesidades *fpl* corporales; **the ~s of industry** las necesidades de la industria; **my ~s are few** es poco lo que necesito, soy poco exigente; **to supply sb's ~s** proveer lo que necesita uno.

▼ **2** VT **(a)** (*person*) necesitar; **I ~ it** lo necesito, me hace falta; **it's just what I ~ed** es precisamente lo que necesitaba; **that's all we ~ed!** (*iro*) ¡lo que nos faltaba!; **I ~ this like I ~ a hole in the head** esto me sienta como un tiro; **I ~ two more to make up the series** me faltan dos para completar la serie; **he ~ed no bidding** no se hizo de rogar; **he ~s watching** hay que vigilarle, conviene vigilarle; **who ~s more motorways?** ¿para qué queremos más autopistas?

(b) (*thing*) exigir, requerir, reclamar; **it ~s care** requiere cuidado, exige cuidado; **a visa is ~ed** se exige visado; **the report ~s no comment** el informe no deja lugar a comentarios; **a much ~ed holiday** unas vacaciones muy necesarias; **I gave it a much ~ed wash** lo lavé pues le hacía mucha falta; **this will ~ some explaining** no va a ser fácil explicar esto.

▼ **(c)** (**to ~ to** + *infin*) **I ~ to do it** tengo que hacerlo, debo hacerlo; **he ~s to be told everything twice** hay que decírselo todo dos veces; **they don't ~ to be told all the details** no es preciso contarles todos los detalles; **you will hardly ~ to be reminded that ...** apenas es necesario recordarles que ...; **you only ~ed to ask** no había sino pedir; **this room ~s to be painted** hay que pintar este cuarto, conviene pintar este cuarto.

▼ **(d)** (V AUX) **~ I go?** ¿tengo que ir?; **he ~n't do it, ~ he?** ¿es esencial que lo haga?; **I ~ hardly add that ...** apenas hay que añadir que ...; **~ I say that this is untrue?** ni que decir tiene que esto no es cierto; **but I ~n't have bothered** pero era trabajo perdido; **it ~ not be done now** no es preciso hacerlo ahora.

(e) (*impersonal*) **it ~ed a war to alter that** fue necesaria una guerra para cambiar eso; **it doesn't ~ me to tell him** no hace falta que yo se lo diga.

needful ['niːdful] **1** ADJ necesario.
2 N: **the ~** el cumquibus*.

neediness ['niːdɪnɪs] N necesidad *f*, pobreza *f*.

needle ['niːdl] **1** N **(a)** aguja *f*; **to look for a ~ in a haystack** buscar una aguja en un pajar; **to be on the ~** pincharse*, ser drogadicto; **to get the ~** ponerse negro*.
(b) (*Bot*) aguja *f*, acícula *f*.
(c) (*) mala leche** *f*, rivalidad *f*; hostilidad *f*, rencor *m*.
(d) (‡: *drugs*) chuta‡ *f*.
2 ATTR: **~ match** partido *m* importantísimo, partido *m* muy emocionante, partido *m* muy reñido.
3 VT **(a)** (*) *person* pinchar, provocar, fastidiar.
(b) (US‡) *drink* añadir alcohol a.

needle-case ['niːdlkeɪs] N alfiletero *m*.

needlecraft ['niːdlkrɑːft] N arte *m* de la costura.

needle exchange ['niːdlɪks'tʃeɪndʒ] N cambio *m* de jeringuillas.

needlepoint ['niːdlpɔɪnt] N bordado *m* en arpillera.

needle-sharp ['niːdl'ʃɑːp] ADJ afiladísimo; (*fig*) agudísimo, de lo más penetrante.

needless ['niːdlɪs] ADJ innecesario, superfluo, inútil; **~ to say ...** excusado es decir que ..., está de más decir que ..., huelga decir que ...; **he was, ~ to say, drunk** ni que decir tiene que estaba borracho.

needlessly ['niːdlɪslɪ] ADV innecesariamente, inútilmente, en vano; **you worry quite ~** te inquietas sin motivo alguno.

needlessness ['niːdlɪsnɪs] N innecesariedad *f*; (*of remark*) inoportunidad *f*.

needlewoman ['niːdlˌwʊmən] N, PL **needlewomen** ['niːdlˌwɪmɪn] costurera *f*; **to be a good ~** coser bien.

needlework ['niːdlwɜːk] N labor *f* de aguja, costura *f*, bordado *m*; **to do ~** hacer costura, coser.

needn't ['niːdnt] = **need not**; V **need 2 (d)**.

needs [niːdz] ADV necesariamente, forzosamente; **if ~ must** si hace falta; **we must ~ walk** no tenemos más remedio que ir andando.

needy ['niːdɪ] **1** ADJ necesitado, pobre, indigente.
2 NPL: **the ~** los necesitados.

ne'er [nɛər] ADV (*poet*) nunca.

ne'er-do-well ['nɛədʊˌwel] **1** ADJ perdido.
2 N perdido *m*, perdulario *m*.

nefarious [nɪ'fɛərɪəs] ADJ nefario, vil, inicuo.

nefariousness [nɪ'fɛərɪəsnɪs] N vileza *f*.

neg. ABBR of **negative** negativo.

negate [nɪ'geɪt] VT anular, invalidar.

negation [nɪ'geɪʃən] N negación *f*.

negative ['negətɪv] **1** ADJ negativo; **~ cashflow** flujo *m* de fondos negativo; **~ feedback** reacción *f* negativa.
2 N **(a)** (*answer*) negativa *f*; **to answer in the ~** dar una respuesta negativa.
(b) (*Gram*) negación *f*.
(c) (*Phot*) negativo *m*, prueba *f* negativa.
(d) (*Elec*) polo *m* negativo.

3 VT (*veto*) poner veto a; (*vote down*) rechazar, desaprobar; *statement* negar, desmentir; *effect* anular.

negatively ['negətɪvlɪ] ADV negativamente.

neglect [nɪ'glekt] **1** N (*carelessness*) negligencia *f*, descuido *m*; (*of rule etc*) inobservancia *f*; (*of duty*) incumplimiento *m*; (*neglected state*) abandono *m*; (*of o.s.*) dejadez *f*; (*towards others*) desatención *f*; **to die in ~** morir abandonado.
2 VT *obligations etc* descuidar, desatender; tener descuidado, tener abandonado; *duty etc* no cumplir, faltar a; *friends* dejar de ver; desairar; *advice etc* no hacer caso de; (*omit*) omitir, olvidar; *opportunity* no aprovechar; *garden etc* no cuidar; *wife* dejar sola; **to ~ to** + *infin* olvidarse de + *infin*.

neglected [nɪ'glektɪd] ADJ *appearance* descuidado, desaliñado; *garden etc* sin cuidar; *wife* abandonada.

neglectful [nɪ'glektful] ADJ negligente, descuidado; **to be ~ of** descuidar, desatender.

neglectfully [nɪ'glektfəlɪ] ADV negligentemente.

negligée ['neglɪʒeɪ] N (*nightdress etc*) salto *m* de cama; (*housecoat*) bata *f*.

negligence ['neglɪdʒəns] N negligencia *f*, descuido *m*; **through ~** por descuido.

negligent ['neglɪdʒənt] ADJ negligente, descuidado; **to be ~ of** descuidar, desatender.

negligently ['neglɪdʒəntlɪ] ADV negligentemente, con descuido.

negligible ['neglɪdʒəbl] ADJ insignificante; despreciable; **a ~ quantity** una cantidad insignificante; **a by no means ~ opponent** un adversario nada despreciable.

negotiable [nɪ'gəʊʃɪəbl] ADJ **(a)** (*Fin*) negociable; **~ instrument** instrumento *m* negociable; **not ~** que no puede negociarse. **(b)** *road etc* transitable.

negotiate [nɪ'gəʊʃɪeɪt] **1** VT **(a)** *treaty* negociar; *loan, deal etc* negociar, gestionar, agenciar.
(b) *obstacle* salvar, franquear; *river etc* pasar, cruzar; *bend* tomar.
2 VI negociar; **to ~ for** negociar para obtener; **to ~ for peace** pedir la paz; **to ~ with sb** negociar con uno.

negotiating [nɪ'gəʊʃɪeɪtɪŋ] N negociación *f*, el negociar; **~ table** mesa *f* de negociaciones; **to sit (down) at the ~ table** sentarse a la mesa de negociaciones.

negotiation [nɪˌgəʊʃɪ'eɪʃən] N negociación *f*; gestión *f*; **to be in ~ with sb** estar negociando con uno; **the treaty is under ~** el tratado está siendo negociado; **that will be a matter for ~** eso tendrá que ser discutido, eso tendrá que someterse a discusión; **to break off ~s** romper las negociaciones; **to enter into ~s with sb** entrar en negociaciones con uno.

negotiator [nɪ'gəʊʃɪeɪtər] N negociador *m*, -ora *f*.

Negress ['niːgres] N († *pej in US*) negra *f*.

Negro ['niːgrəʊ] **1** ADJ negro; **~ spiritual** espiritual *m*.
2 N, PL **~es** ['niːgrəʊz] negro *m*.

negroid ['niːgrɔɪd] ADJ negroide.

neigh [neɪ] **1** N relincho *m*.
2 VI relinchar.

neighbour, (US) **neighbor** ['neɪbər] **1** N vecino *m*, -a *f*; (*fellow being*) prójimo *m*, -a *f*.
2 ATTR: **Good N~ Policy** (US) Política *f* del Buen Vecino.
3 VI: **to ~ upon** (*adjoin*) colindar con, estar contiguo a; (*be almost*) rayar en; **to ~ with sb** (US) comportarse como buen vecino de uno.

neighbourhood, (US) **neighborhood** ['neɪbəhʊd] **1** N **(a)** (*area*) vecindad *f*; barrio *m*, sección *f*, sector *m*; **all the girls of the ~** todas las jóvenes del barrio; **not a very nice ~** un barrio poco atractivo; **somewhere in the ~** por allí, cerca de allí; **anyone in the ~ of the crime** cualquier persona que estuviera cerca del lugar del crimen; **the soil in that ~** el suelo de aquel sector; **in the ~ of £80** alrededor de 80 libras.
(b) (*surrounding area*) alrededores *mpl*, cercanías *fpl*; **Málaga and its ~** Málaga y sus alrededores.
(c) (*persons*) vecinos *mpl*, vecindario *m*.
2 ATTR: **~ party** fiesta *f* de vecinos, fiesta *f* del barrio; **~ police** policía *f* de barrio; **~ watch** grupo *m* de vigilancia de los propios vecinos.

neighbouring, (US) **neighboring** ['neɪbərɪŋ] ADJ vecino; cercano, inmediato; (*Jur*) colindante.

neighbourliness, (US) **neighborliness** ['neɪbəlɪnɪs] N: **good ~** buena vecindad *f*.

neighbourly, (US) **neighborly** ['neɪbəlɪ] ADJ de buen vecino, amable, amistoso.

neighing ['neɪɪŋ] N relinchos *mpl*.

▼ **neither** ['naɪðər] **1** ADV, CONJ: **~ he nor I** ni él ni yo; **he ~ smokes nor drinks** no bebe ni fuma.
2 CONJ: **if you aren't going, ~ am I** si tú no vas, yo tampoco; **~ will he agree to sell it** ni consiente en venderlo tampoco.
3 PRON: **~ of them has any money** ninguno de los dos tiene dinero, ni el uno ni el otro tiene dinero; **~ of them saw it** ni el uno

ni el otro lo vio.

[4] ADJ: **on ~ side** por ninguno de los dos lados, en ningún lado; **~ car is for sale** no se vende ninguno de los dos coches.

nelly: ['nelɪ] N: **not on your ~!** ¡ni hablar!

nelson ['nelsən] N (*Wrestling*): **full ~** llave *f*; **half ~** media llave *f*; **to put a half ~ on sb** (*fig*) ponerle trabas a uno.

nem con ABBR *of* **nemine contradicente** nemine discrepante.

nemesis ['nemɪsɪs] N (*fig*) justo castigo *m*, justicia *f*.

neo... ['niːəʊ] PREF neo...

neoclassical ['niːəʊ'klæsɪkəl] ADJ neoclásico.

neoclassicism ['niːəʊ'klæsɪsɪzəm] N neoclasicismo *m*.

neocolonialism [ˌniːəʊkə'ləʊnɪəˌlɪzəm] N neocolonialismo *m*.

neodymium [ˌniːəʊ'dɪmɪəm] N neodimio *m*.

neofascism ['niːəʊ'fæʃɪzəm] N neofascismo *m*.

neofascist ['niːəʊ'fæʃɪst] [1] ADJ neofascista.
[2] N neofascista *mf*.

neogothic [ˌniːəʊ'gɒθɪk] ADJ neogótico.

neolithic [ˌniːəʊ'lɪθɪk] ADJ neolítico.

neological [ˌnɪə'lɒdʒɪkəl] ADJ neológico.

neologism [nɪ'ɒlədʒɪzəm] N neologismo *m*.

neomycin [ˌniːəʊ'maɪsɪn] N neomicina *f*.

neon ['niːɒn] [1] N neón *m*.
[2] ATTR: **~ lamp**, **~ light** lámpara *f* de neón; **~ sign** letrero *m* de neón.

neonatal ['niːəʊˌneɪtl] ADJ neonatal.

neonazi ['niːəʊ'nɑːtsɪ] [1] ADJ neonazi, neonazista.
[2] N neonazi *mf*.

neophyte ['niːəʊfaɪt] N neófito *m*, -a *f*.

neoplatonic ['niːəʊplə'tɒnɪk] ADJ neoplatónico.

neoplatonism ['niːəʊ'pleɪtənɪzəm] N neoplatonismo *m*.

neoplatonist ['niːəʊ'pleɪtənɪst] N neoplatonista *mf*.

Neozoic [ˌniːəʊ'zəʊɪk] ADJ neozoico.

Nepal [nɪ'pɔːl] N Nepal *m*.

Nepalese [ˌnepɔː'liːz] [1] ADJ nepalés.
[2] N INVAR nepalés *m*, -esa *f*.

nephew ['nevjuː] N sobrino *m*.

nephrectomy [nɪ'frektəmɪ] N nefrectomía *f*.

nephritic [ne'frɪtɪk] ADJ nefrítico.

nephritis [ne'fraɪtɪs] N nefritis *f*.

nephrology [nɪ'frɒlədʒɪ] N nefrología *f*.

nephrosis [nɪ'frəʊsɪs] N nefrosis *f*.

nepotism ['nepətɪzəm] N nepotismo *m*.

Neptune ['neptjuːn] NM Neptuno.

neptunium [nep'tjuːnɪəm] N neptunio *m*.

nerd: [nɜːd] N borde* *mf*.

nereid ['nɪəriːd] N nereida *f*.

Nero ['nɪərəʊ] NM Nerón.

nerve [nɜːv] [1] N (a) (*Anat, Bot*) nervio *m*; (*Ent*) nervadura *f*; **my ~s are on edge** tengo los nervios de punta; **it gets on my ~s** me pone los nervios de punta, me crispa los nervios, me saca de quicio; **he gets on my ~s** me fastidia terriblemente; **to be living on one's ~s** vivir en estado de nervios constante; **to strain every ~ to** + *infin* hacer un esfuerzo supremo por + *infin*.
(b) (*tension*) **~s** nerviosismo *m*, nerviosidad *f*, excitabilidad *f* nerviosa; **a fit of ~s** un ataque de nervios; **to be in a state of ~s** estar nervioso, estar hipertenso; **she suffers from ~s** padece de los nervios, sufre trastornos nerviosos.
(c) (*courage*) valor *m*, sangre *f* fría; **I hadn't the ~ to do it** no tuve el valor de hacerlo; **to lose one's ~** perder el valor, rajarse; **it takes some ~ to do that** hace falta mucha sangre fría para hacer eso.
(d) (*: cheek*) descaro *m*, valor* *m*, frescura* *f*, caradura* *f*; **of all the ~!**, **the ~ of it!**, **what a ~!** ¡qué frescura!*, ¡qué caradura!*; **you've got a ~!** ¡eres un caradura!*, ¡eres un fresco!*; **he had the ~ to ask for money** tuvo el valor de pedir dinero*.
[2] ATTR: **~ specialist** neurólogo *m*, -a *f*.
[3] VT: **to ~ sb to do sth** infundir a uno ánimo(s) para hacer algo.
[4] VR: **to ~ o.s. to do sth** animarse a hacer algo, esforzarse por hacer algo.

nerve-cell ['nɜːvsel] N neurona *f*.

nerve-centre, (*US*) **nerve-center** ['nɜːvˌsentər] N (*Anat*) centro *m* nervioso; (*fig*) punto *m* neurálgico.

nerve-gas ['nɜːvgæs] N gas *m* nervioso.

nerveless ['nɜːvlɪs] ADJ (*fig*) grasp flojo; *person* enervado, débil, soso.

nerve-racking ['nɜːvˌrækɪŋ] ADJ que crispa los nervios; horripilante, espantoso.

nerviness ['nɜːvɪnɪs] N nerviosidad *f*, nerviosismo *m*.

nervous ['nɜːvəs] ADJ (a) *person* nervioso; (*by nature*) tímido; miedoso, aprensivo, asustadizo; *market* nervioso, inquieto; **~ Nellie*** (*US*) miedica* *mf*; **to be ~ of** tener miedo a; **to be ~ of** + *ger* tener miedo a + *infin*; **I was ~ on his account** estaba inquieto por él; **I was ~ about speaking to her** me daba miedo la noción de hablar con ella; **to get ~** ponerse nervioso, sentir miedo; **I get ~ when I'm**

alone siento aprensión cuando estoy solo; **it makes me ~** me da miedo.
(b) (*Anat*) nervioso; **~ breakdown** colapso *m* nervioso; **~ exhaustion** postración *f* nerviosa; **~ system** sistema *m* nervioso.

nervously ['nɜːvəslɪ] ADV nerviosamente; tímidamente.

nervousness ['nɜːvəsnɪs] N nerviosidad *f*, nerviosismo *m*, timidez *f*, miedo *m*.

nervy* ['nɜːvɪ] ADJ (a) (*Brit: tense*) nervioso. (b) (*US*) = **cheeky**.

nest [nest] [1] N (*of bird*) nido *m*; (*of hen*) nidal *m*; (*of animal*) madriguera *f*; (*of wasps*) avispero *m*; (*of ants*) hormiguero *m*; (*clutch of eggs, young birds*) nidada *f*; (*person's house*) nido *m*; (*of thieves etc*) nido *m*, cueva *f*, guarida *f*; (*of boxes, drawers*) juego *m*; **to feather one's ~** ponerse las botas, hacer su agosto; **to foul one's own ~** manchar el propio nido.
[2] VT (*Comput*) anidar, encajar; **~ed loops** bucles *mpl* anidados.
[3] VI (a) (*bird*) anidar, hacer su nido, nidificar.
(b) (*collector*) buscar nidos.

nest-egg ['nesteg] N nidal *m*; (*fig*) ahorros *mpl*, cantidad *f* ahorrada, buena hucha *f*.

nesting ['nestɪŋ] [1] N (*Orn*) anidada *f*, anidación *f*; (*Gram, Comput*) anidamiento *m*.
[2] ATTR: **~ box** (*for hen*) nidal *m*, ponedero *m*; (*for wild bird*) caja *f* anidadera.

nestle ['nesl] VI (a) **to ~ among leaves** hacerse un nido entre las hojas; **to ~ down among the blankets** hacerse un ovillo entre las mantas; **to ~ up to sb** arrimarse cómodamente a uno, apretarse contra uno.
(b) **a house nestling beside a wood** una casa situada al abrigo de un bosque; **a village nestling among hills** un pueblecito protegido por las colinas.

nestling ['neslɪŋ] N pajarito *m* (en el nido).

NET N (*US*) ABBR *of* **National Educational Television**.

Net* [net] N: **the ~** (*Comput*) (el *or* la) Internet; **to surf the ~** navegar por Internet.

net¹ [net] [1] N red *f* (*also fig*); (*mesh*) malla *f*; (*fabric*) tul *m*; (*for hair etc*) redecilla *f*; **to cast one's ~ wider** ampliar el campo de acción, investigar otras posibilidades; **to slip through the ~** escapar de la red.
[2] ATTR: **~ curtains** visillos *mpl*.
[3] VT coger con red.

net² [net] (*Comm*) [1] ADJ neto, líquido; limpio; *amount, interest* neto; **~ assets** activo *m* neto; **~ income** renta *f* neta; **~ loss** pérdida *f* neta; **~ margin** margen *m* neto; **~ output** producción *f* neta; **~ payment** líquido *m*; **~ price** precio *m* neto; **~ profit** ganancia *f* neta; **~ wage** salario *m* neto; **~ weight** peso *m* neto; **at a ~ profit of 5%** con un beneficio neto de 5 por cien; **'terms strictly ~'** 'sin descuento'.
[2] VT ganar en limpio, producir en limpio; **he ~s £30,000 a year** tiene una renta neta de 30.000 libras al año.

netball ['netbɔːl] N baloncesto *m* (*or* básquet *m*) de mujeres.

nether ['neðər] ADJ inferior, más bajo, de abajo; **~ lip** labio *m* inferior; **~ regions** infierno *m*; **down in my ~ regions*** en la parte baja de mi persona.

Netherlander ['neðəˌlændər] N holandés *m*, -esa *f*, neerlandés *m*, -esa *f*.

Netherlands ['neðələndz] NPL Países *mpl* Bajos.

nethermost ['neðəməʊst] ADJ SUPERL (el *etc*) más bajo.

nett [net] = **net²**.

netting ['netɪŋ] N red *f*, redes *fpl*; (*obra f de*) malla *f*, mallas *fpl*.

nettle ['netl] [1] N ortiga *f*; **to grasp the ~** coger el toro por los cuernos.
[2] VT provocar, irritar, molestar; **somewhat ~d by this** algo molesto por esto.

nettle-rash ['netlræʃ] N urticaria *f*.

nettle-sting ['netlˌstɪŋ] N picadura *f* de ortiga.

network ['netwɜːk] [1] N (*fig*) red *f*; (*Rad, TV*) red *f*, cadena *f*; (*Comput*) red *f*; **the national railway ~** la red nacional de ferrocarriles; **a ~ of spies** una red de espías.
[2] VT (*Rad, TV*) difundir por la red de emisoras; (*Comput*) conectar a la red.
[3] VI hacer contactos en el mundo de los negocios.

networking ['netwɜːkɪŋ] N (*Comput*) conexión *f* de redes.

neural ['njʊərəl] ADJ neural.

neuralgia [njʊə'rældʒə] N neuralgia *f*.

neuralgic [njʊə'rældʒɪk] ADJ neurálgico.

neurasthenia [ˌnjʊərəs'θiːnɪə] N neurastenia *f*.

neurasthenic [ˌnjʊərəs'θenɪk] ADJ neurasténico.

neuritis [njʊə'raɪtɪs] N neuritis *f*.

neuro... ['njʊərəʊ] PREF neuro...

neurobiology [ˌnjʊərəʊbaɪ'ɒlədʒɪ] N neurobiología *f*.

neurological [ˌnjʊərə'lɒdʒɪkəl] ADJ neurológico.

neurologist [njʊə'rɒlədʒɪst] N neurólogo *m*, -a *f*.

neurology [njʊə'rɒlədʒɪ] N neurología *f*.

neuron ['njuərɒn] N neurona *f*.
neuropath ['njuərəpæθ] N neurópata *mf*.
neuropathology ['njuərəupə'θɒlədʒɪ] N neuropatología *f*.
neurophysiological [,njuərəu,fɪzɪə'lɒʒɪkəl] ADJ neurofisiológico.
neurophysiologist [,njuərəu,fɪzɪ'ɒlədʒɪst] N neurofisiólogo *m*, -a *f*.
neurophysiology [,njuərəu,fɪzɪ'ɒlədʒɪ] N neurofisiología *f*.
neuropsychiatric [,njuərəu,saɪkɪ'ætrɪk] ADJ neuropsiquiátrico.
neuropsychiatrist [,njuərəusaɪ'kaɪətrɪst] N neuropsiquiatra *mf*.
neuropsychiatry [,njuərəusaɪ'kaɪətrɪ] N neuropsiquiatría *f*.
neuropsychology ['njuərəusaɪ'kɒlədʒɪ] N neuropsicología *f*.
neurosis [njuə'rəusɪs] N, PL **neuroses** [njuə'rəusiːz] neurosis *f*.
neurosurgeon [,njuərəu'sɜːdʒən] N neurocirujano *m*, -a *f*.
neuro-surgery [,njuərəu'sɜːdʒərɪ] N neurocirugía *f*.
neurosurgical [,njuərəu'sɜːdʒɪkəl] ADJ neuroquirúrgico.
neurotic [njuə'rɒtɪk] **1** ADJ neurótico.
   2 N neurótico *m*, -a *f*.
neurotically [njuə'rɒtɪkəlɪ] ADV neuróticamente.
neuroticism [njuə'rɒtɪsɪzəm] N neuroticismo *m*.
neurovascular ['njuərəu'væskulər] ADJ neurovascular.
neuter ['njuːtər] **1** ADJ **(a)** (*Gram*) neutro.
   (b) *cat etc* sin sexo, castrado.
   2 N **(a)** (*Gram*) género *m* neutro.
   (b) (*cat etc*) macho *m* castrado, animal *m* sin sexo.
   3 VT *cat etc* castrar, capar.
neutral ['njuːtrəl] **1** ADJ *person, country, opinion* neutral; (*Zool, Bot, Elec, Chem etc*) neutro; *colour* neutro; **~ gear** punto *m* neutro; **to remain ~** permanecer neutral, mantener su neutralidad, no tomar partido.
   2 N **(a)** neutral *mf*; país *m* neutral.
   (b) (*Aut*) punto *m* muerto; **in ~** en punto muerto.
neutralism ['njuːtrəlɪzəm] N neutralismo *m*.
neutralist ['njuːtrəlɪst] **1** ADJ neutralista.
   2 N neutralista *mf*.
neutrality [njuː'trælɪtɪ] N neutralidad *f*.
neutralization [,njuːtrəlaɪ'zeɪʃən] N neutralización *f*.
neutralize ['njuːtrəlaɪz] VT neutralizar.
neutron ['njuːtrɒn] **1** N neutrón *m*.
   2 ATTR: **~ bomb** bomba *f* de neutrones; **~ star** estrella *f* de neutrones.
Nev. ABBR of **Nevada**.
▼ **never** ['nevər] ADV **(a)** nunca, jamás; **~!** ¡jamás!; **I ~ went** no fui nunca, no fui jamás; **you ~ saw anything like it** nunca se ha visto nada parecido; **I have ~ yet seen anything so horrible** en mi vida he visto cosa más horrible; **~ in all my life** jamás en la vida; **it had ~ been tried before** no se había intentado antes; **you must ~ ever come again** no vuelvas nunca jamás.
   (b) (*emphatic negative*) **~!, you ~ did!** ¿de veras?; **~ a one** ni uno siquiera; **~ a word did he say** no dijo ni una sola palabra; **I ~ expected it** no contaba con eso de ningún modo; **surely you ~ bought it?** ¿pero lo has comprado de veras?; **well I ~!** ¡caramba!, ¡no me digas!
never-ending ['nevər'endɪŋ] ADJ inacabable, interminable.
never-failing ['nevə'feɪlɪŋ] ADJ infalible; *supply* inagotable.
nevermore ['nevə'mɔːr] ADV nunca más.
never-never ['nevə'nevər] **1** ADJ: **~ land** país *m* de ensueños.
   2 N: **to buy sth on the ~*** comprar algo a plazos.
▼ **nevertheless** [,nevəðə'les] ADV sin embargo, no obstante, con todo; **it is ~ true that** ... con todo es verdad que ...
never-to-be-forgotten ['nevətəbi:,fə'gɒtn] ADJ inolvidable.
nevus ['niːvəs] N, PL **nevi** ['niːvaɪ] (*US*) = **naevus**.
new [njuː] ADJ nuevo; reciente; (*fresh*) fresco, nuevo; *bread* tierno; (*different*) nuevo, distinto; **a ~ car** (*different*) un nuevo coche, (*brand new*) un coche nuevo; **the ~ students** los nuevos estudiantes; **the ~ people in No. 5** la nueva familia del núm 5; **N~ Age** (*music*) música *f* de la Nueva Era; **~ look** nueva moda *f*; **the N~ Man** el nuevo hombre; **~ maths** matemáticas *fpl* modernas; **~ town** pueblo *m* nuevo, ciudad *f* nueva; **~ wool** lana *f* virgen; **'as ~'** (*advert*) 'como nuevo'; **she's very ~, poor girl** no está habituada todavía, la pobre; **are you ~ here?** ¿eres nuevo aquí?; **are you ~ to this?** ¿es nuevo para ti?; **he came ~ to us last year** empezó a trabajar con nosotros el año pasado nada más; **what's ~?*** ¿qué hay de nuevo?*; **it's as good as ~** está como nuevo; **there's nothing ~ under the sun** no hay nada nuevo bajo el sol.
new- [njuː] PREF (*in compounds*) recién ...
newborn ['njuːbɔːn] ADJ recién nacido.
New Caledonia [,njuː,kælɪ'dəunjə] N Nueva Caledonia *f*.
newcomer ['njuː,kʌmər] N recién llegado *m*, -a *f*, nuevo *m*, -a *f*.
New Delhi [,njuː'delɪ] N Nueva Delhi *f*.
newel ['njuːəl] N, **newel post** N poste *m* (de una escalera).
New England [,njuː'ɪŋglənd] N Nueva Inglaterra *f*.
New Englander [njuː'ɪŋgləndər] N habitante o nativo de Nueva Inglaterra.
new-fangled ['njuː,fæŋgld] ADJ (*pej*) recién inventado, moderno,

novedoso; que está tan de moda.
new-found ['njuː,faund] ADJ recién descubierto; **his ~ zeal** su recién estrenado entusiasmo.

┌───┐
│ **NEW**   *see also main entry* │

Position of "nuevo"
Nuevo tends to follow the noun when it means *new* in the sense of "brand-new" and to precede the noun when it means *new* in the sense of "another", "replacement" or "latest":
   ...the sales of new cars...
   ...las ventas de automóviles nuevos...
   ...the new prime minister...
   ...el nuevo primer ministro...
   ...the new model...
   ...el nuevo modelo...
For further uses and examples, see main entry.
└───┘

Newfoundland ['njuːfəndlənd] N **(a)** (*Geog*) Terranova *f*. **(b)** (*dog: also ~ dog*) perro *m* de Terranova.
Newfoundlander ['njuːfəndləndər] N habitante *mf* de Terranova.
New Guinea [,njuː'gɪniː] N Nueva Guinea *f*.
New Hampshire [njuː'hæmpʃɪər] N Nuevo Hampshire *m*, Nueva Hampshire *f*.
newish ['njuːɪʃ] ADJ bastante nuevo.
New Jersey [njuː'dʒɜːzɪ] N Nueva Jersey *f*.
new-laid [,njuː'leɪd] ADJ *egg* fresco, recién puesto.
new-look [,njuː'luk] ATTR nuevo; renovado; de estilo nuevo.
newly ['njuːlɪ] ADV nuevamente, recién ...; **~ made** recién hecho, acabado de hacer; **those ~ arrived** los recién llegados; **those ~ arrived from France** los que acaban de llegar de Francia.
newly-weds ['njuːlɪwedz] NPL recién casados *mpl*.
New Mexico [njuː'meksɪkəu] N Nuevo Méjico *m*.
new-mown ['njuː'məun] ADJ recién segado.
newness ['njuːnɪs] N novedad *f*; (*in a job etc*) inexperiencia *f*, falta *f* de práctica.
New Orleans [njuː'ɔːlɪənz] N Nueva Orléans *f*.
news [njuːz] **1** N **(a)** noticias *fpl*; nuevas *fpl*; **a piece of ~** una noticia, una nueva; **a sad piece of ~** una triste noticia; **that's good ~** es buena noticia; **no ~ is good ~** la falta de noticias es una buena señal; **it was ~ to me** me cogió de nuevas; **what ~?, what's the ~?** ¿qué hay de nuevo?; **a 700th anniversary is ~** un 700 aniversario es noticia; **they're in the ~** se oye hablar mucho de ellos, figuran mucho en los periódicos (*etc*); **to be bad ~*** (*person*) ser un ave de mal agüero, ser un liante*; (*thing*) ser mal asunto*; **to break the ~ to sb** comunicar una noticia a uno; **when the ~ broke** al saberse la noticia; **I have ~ for you** tengo que darte una noticia (*also iro*).
   (b) (*Press, Rad, TV*) informaciones *fpl*; **the ~** (*Rad*) noticiario *m*, diario *m* hablado; (*TV*) telediario *m*; **'N~ in Brief'** (*section in newspaper*) 'Brevedades' *fpl*.
   2 ATTR: **~ blackout** apagón *m* informativo; **~ conference** rueda *f* de prensa; **~ desk** redacción *f*, sección *f* de informaciones; **~ editor** jefe *mf* de información; **~ headlines** titulares *mpl*; **~ programme**, (*US*) **~ program** transmisión *f* de noticias, (*on TV*) telediario *m*; **~ vendor** vendedor *m*, -ora *f* de periódicos.
news agency ['njuːz,eɪdʒənsɪ] N agencia *f* de noticias.
newsagent ['njuːz,eɪdʒənt] N (*Brit*) vendedor *m*, -ora *f* de periódicos; **~'s** tienda *f* de periódicos, quiosco *m* de periódicos.
newsboy ['njuːzbɔɪ] N chico *m* que reparte (*or* vende) periódicos.
news-bulletin ['njuːz,bulɪtɪn] N (*Rad*) noticiario *m*, diario *m* hablado; (*TV*) telediario *m*.
newscast ['njuːzkɑːst] N telediario *m*.
newscaster ['njuːz'kɑːstər] N locutor *m*, -ora *f* de telediario.
newscopy ['njuːzkɒpɪ] N (*Press*) texto *m* de la noticia; (*TV, Rad*) resumen *m* de la noticia.
newsdealer ['njuːz'diːlər] N (*US*) vendedor *m*, -ora *f* de periódicos.
news-flash ['njuːzflæʃ] N flash *m*, noticia *f* de última hora.
newshound* ['njuːzhaund] N reportero *m*.
news-item ['njuːz,aɪtəm] N noticia *f*.
newsletter ['njuːz,letər] N hoja *f* informativa, informe *m*.
newsman ['njuːzmæn] N, PL **newsmen** ['njuːzmen] periodista *m*, reportero *m*.
New South Wales ['njuːsauθ'weɪlz] N Nueva Gales *f* del Sur.
newspaper ['njuːs,peɪpər] **1** N periódico *m*, diario *m*.
   2 ATTR de periódico, periodístico; **~ clipping**, **~ cutting** recorte *m* de periódico; **~ office** redacción *f* (de periódico); **~ report** reportaje *m*.
newspaperman ['njuːs,peɪpəmæn] N, PL **newspapermen** ['njuːs,peɪpəmen] periodista *m*.
newspeak ['njuːspiːk] N neolengua *f*.
newsprint ['njuːzprɪnt] N papel *m* prensa, papel *m* continuo.
newsreader ['njuːz,riːdər] N (*Brit TV*) locutor *m*, -ora *f* de telediario.
newsreel ['njuːzriːl] N noticiario *m*, película *f* de actualidades, (*in Spain*) Nodo *m* (*noticiario m documental*).

news-release ['nju:zrɪ,li:s] N (esp US) = **press-release**.

newsroom ['nju:zrʊm] N (of newspaper) (sala f de) redacción f; (of library) sala f de periódicos.

news-sheet ['nju:z,ʃi:t] N hoja f informativa.

news stand ['nju:zstænd] N (US) quiosco m de periódicos y revistas.

newsworthy ['nju:z,wɜ:ðɪ] ADJ noticioso, de interés periodístico, sensacional; **it's not ~** no es noticia, no tiene interés.

newsy* ['nju:zɪ] ADJ lleno de noticias.

newt [nju:t] N tritón m.

New Testament ['nju:'testəmənt] N Nuevo Testamento m.

newton ['nju:tn] N newton m, neutonio m.

Newtonian [nju:'təʊnɪən] ADJ newtoniano.

▼**New Year** ['nju:'jɪəʳ] ① N Año m Nuevo; **~'s Day** día m de Año Nuevo; **~'s Eve** noche f vieja; **happy ~!** ¡feliz año nuevo!; **to see the ~ in** festejar el año nuevo.
  ② ATTR: **~ resolutions** buenos propósitos mpl de fin de año.

New York ['nju:'jɔ:k] ① N Nueva York f.
  ② ATTR neoyorquino.

New Yorker ['nju:'jɔ:kəʳ] N neoyorquino m, -a f.

New Zealand [nju:'zi:lənd] ① N Nueva Zelanda f, Nueva Zelandia f.
  ② ATTR neozelandés.

New Zealander [nju:'zi:ləndəʳ] N neozelandés m, -esa f.

▼**next** [nekst] ① ADJ (a) (of place) próximo, inmediato, contiguo, vecino; **the ~ room** la habitación (de) al lado de ésta, la habitación inmediata; **the ~ house** la casa vecina, la casa de al lado; **on the ~ page** a la vuelta, a la página siguiente; **I get out at the ~ stop** yo bajo en la próxima parada.
  (b) (of order) próximo, siguiente; primero; **the ~ in order is ...** el próximo siguiendo el orden es ..., el primero según el orden es ...; **in the ~ volume** en el tomo siguiente, en el tomo después de éste; **the ~ life** la otra vida; **~ time** la próxima vez; **~ time you see him** la próxima vez que le veas; **the ~ but one** el segundo después de éste; **'see ~ page'** 'véase a la página siguiente'; **'continued in the ~ column'** 'sigue en la columna inmediata'; **'to be continued in our ~ ...'** 'continuará'; **as good as the ~ man** tan bueno como cada hijo de vecino; **he's ~ after me** es el primero después de mí; **~ please!** ¡el siguiente por favor!, ¡que pase el siguiente!; **what ~?** y ahora ¿qué?; **what ~, madam?** (in shop) ¿algo más, señora?; **who's ~?** ¿quién es el siguiente?; **whatever ~!** ¡qué horror!
  (c) (of time) próximo, siguiente; week, month, year próximo, que viene; **~ year** (looking to future) el año que viene, (in past time) el año siguiente; **~ day** el día siguiente; **the ~ day but one** dos días después, el segundo día después de éste; **the ~ 5 days** los 5 días que vienen; **~ morning** la mañana siguiente, a la mañana; **on 4th May ~** el próximo 4 de mayo; **the year after ~** el segundo año después de éste, en dos años; **by this time ~ year** por estas fechas del año que viene.
  ② ADV (a) (of place, order) inmediatamente después; **who comes ~?** ¿quién sigue?, ¿a quién le toca?; **what do we do ~?** ¿qué hacemos ahora?; **the ~ smaller size** el tamaño más pequeño después de éste; **the ~ best thing would be to + infin** lo mejor después de esto sería + infin; **to take the ~ best** tomar el segundo.
  ▼(b) (of time) luego, después; inmediatamente; la próxima vez; **~ we put the salt in** luego echamos la sal; **what did he do ~?** ¿qué hizo después?, ¿qué hizo entonces?; **when you ~ see him** cuando le veas la próxima vez; **when I ~ saw him** cuando le volví a ver.
  ③ PREP (a) (also ~ to) junto a, al lado de; **the car ~ to the door** el coche que está junto a la puerta; **his room is ~ to mine** su habitación está al lado de la mía; **to wear silk ~ (to) one's skin** llevar seda sobre la piel.
  (b) (fig) casi; **we got it for ~ to nothing** lo adquirimos por casi nada; **there was ~ to nobody there** no había casi nadie; **there is ~ to no news** apenas hay noticias, no hay noticias casi.

next-door ['neks'dɔ:ʳ] ADJ de al lado; **~ house** casa f de al lado; **~ neighbour** vecino m, -a f de al lado.

next-of-kin [,nekstəv'kɪn] N familiar mf (or pariente mf) más cercano, -a.

nexus ['neksəs] N nexo m.

NF (a) ABBR of **Newfoundland** Terranova f. **(b)** N (Brit Pol) ABBR of **National Front** partido político de la extrema derecha.

n/f (Fin) ABBR of **no funds**.

NFL N (US) ABBR of **National Football League**.

Nfld. ABBR of **Newfoundland**.

NFS N ABBR of **National Fire Service** servicio de bomberos.

NFT N (Brit) ABBR of **National Film Theatre**.

NFU N (Brit) ABBR of **National Farmers' Union**.

NG (US) ABBR of **National Guard**.

NGA N (Brit) ABBR of **National Graphical Association** sindicato de tipógrafos.

NGO N (US) ABBR of **non-governmental organization**.

NH (US Post) ABBR of **New Hampshire**.

NH(I) ABBR of **National Health (Insurance)**.

NHL N (US) ABBR of **National Hockey League**.

NHS N (Brit) ABBR of **National Health Service** Sistema m Nacional de Salud.

┌─ ⃞ **NHS** ─────────┐

ⓘ *El Sistema Nacional de Salud (**NHS** o **National Health Service**) es el sistema público sanitario que, desde 1948, ha proporcionado asistencia sanitaria gratuita a todos los residentes del Reino Unido. Financiado principalmente a través de los impuestos y de las cotizaciones a la Seguridad Social de trabajadores y empresarios, recibe también un porcentaje del dinero que se paga por las medicinas y por el tratamiento odontológico. Los sucesivos gobiernos del país han realizado una serie de cambios en la forma de operar del **NHS**, que han suscitado polémica y que han provocado abundantes quejas por el aumento de las listas de espera para intervenciones quirúrgicas y consultas de médicos especialistas, puesto que, al igual que en la sanidad española, para ser atendidos por el especialista los pacientes deben pasar primero por el médico de cabecera (**GP** o **General Practitioner**).*

NI (a) ABBR of **Northern Ireland**. **(b)** ABBR of **National Insurance** seguro social.

niacin ['naɪəsɪn] N ácido m nicotínico.

Niagara [naɪ'ægrə] ① N Niágara m.
  ② ATTR: **~ Falls** Catarata f del Niágara.

nib [nɪb] N punta f; (of fountain pen) plumilla f, plumín m.

nibble ['nɪbl] ① N (a) mordisco m; **I never had a ~ all day** (Fishing) el corcho no se movió en todo el día; **at £3000 he never got a ~** a las 3000 libras nadie le echó un tiento.
  (b) (food) bocado m; **I feel like a ~** podría comer algo, no me vendría mal un bocado.
  (c) **~s*** (at party etc) tapas fpl.
  ② VT mordiscar; food mordiscar, mordisquear, picar (LAm); (rat etc) roer; (horse) rozar; (fish) picar; **the cheese is all ~d** el queso está lleno de roeduras.
  ③ VI: **to ~ at** mordiscar etc (V VT); **to ~ at an offer** considerar una oferta, mostrar cierto interés por una oferta.

nibs [nɪbz] N: **his ~*** su señoría.

NIC N (Brit) ABBR of **National Insurance Contribution** contribuciones a la Seguridad Social.

NICAM ['naɪkæm] N ABBR of **near-instantaneous companding system**.

Nicaragua [,nɪkə'rægjʊə] N Nicaragua f.

Nicaraguan [,nɪkə'rægjʊən] ① ADJ nicaragüense.
  ② N nicaragüense mf.

Nice [ni:s] N Niza f.

nice [naɪs] ADJ (a) person (likeable) simpático; **he's a ~ man** es un hombre simpático.
  (b) person (kind) amable; **he was very ~ about it** estuvo muy amable; **it is ~ of you to help Vd** es muy amable ayudándome; **try to be ~ to him** procura ser amable con él; **I find it hard to be ~ to him** encuentro difícil hablar amistosamente con él.
  (c) person (attractive) guapo, mono, bonito, lindo (LAm); **how ~ you look!** ¡qué guapa estás!
  (d) thing (pleasant) agradable, ameno; (attractive) mono, bonito, precioso, lindo (LAm); weather etc bueno; **a ~ photo** una bonita foto; **that's a ~ ring** ¡qué anillo más mono!; **what a ~ idea that was!** ¡ésa sí fue una idea genial!; **what a ~ thing to do!** ¡qué detalle más fino!; **~ one!*** ¡bravo!; **it's ~ here** aquí se está bien; **we had a very ~ holiday in Ibiza** lo pasamos muy bien en Ibiza, hemos pasado unas vacaciones excelentes en Ibiza; **it smells ~** huele bien, tiene un olor agradable; **it doesn't taste at all ~** tiene un sabor nada agradable; **they give you ~ things to do** le dan cosas interesantes que hacer; **they give you ~ things to eat** le dan cosas deliciosas que comer; **it's not very ~ to have to + infin** no es muy agradable tener que + infin.
  (e) things, persons (refined) fino, culto; bien; delicado; **he has ~ manners** tiene modales muy finos; **where are all the ~ girls?** ¿adónde se habrán metido todas las chicas finas?; **only ~ people live here** aquí no vive sino gente culta, (pej) aquí no vive sino gente bien; **a ~ district** un barrio elegante; **that's not ~** aquello es feo, eso no es fino.
  (f) (intensive) muy, bastante, bien; **~ and sweet** bien dulce; **~ and early** tempranito; **it's ~ and warm here** aquí hace un calor agradable; **my feet are ~ and warm** tengo los pies a gusto y calientes; **a ~ long holiday** unas vacaciones bien largas; **a ~ cold drink** una bebida bien fría.
  (g) (fastidious) melindroso, delicado; difícil de contentar; (exacting) exigente; (precise) exacto, meticuloso; (scrupulous) escrupuloso; **he's not too ~ about his methods** no es demasiado escrupuloso en cuanto a sus métodos.
  (h) (requiring care etc) fino, delicado, sutil; **a ~ distinction** una distinción sutil; **a ~ point** un punto delicado; **it's a ~ question whether ... es** difícil determinar si ...

(i) (*discriminating*) fino, discernidor; **he has a ~ ear** tiene un oído fino.

(j) (*iro*) bonito, valiente; **a ~ friend you are!** ¡valiente amigo!; **that's a ~ thing to say!** ¡qué cosas más bonitas me dices!; **a ~ mess** un lío imponente; **a ~ mess!** ¡menudo lío!

nice-looking ['naɪs'lʊkɪŋ] ADJ atractivo; *person* bien parecido, mono, guapo, lindo (*LAm*).

nicely ['naɪslɪ] ADV (*V* ADJ) amablemente; agradablemente; con finura, bien; **very ~, thanks** muy bien, gracias; **a ~ situated house** una casa bien situada; **that will do ~** eso está muy bien; **he's doing very ~ (for himself)** levan bien las cosas, (*pej*) se está forrando; **he's getting on ~** hace buenos progresos; **she thanked me very ~** muy amablemente me dio las gracias; **the child behaves quite ~** el niño tiene modales bastante buenos.

niceness ['naɪsnɪs] N **(a)** (*of person*) simpatía *f*, lo simpático; amabilidad *f*. **(b)** (*of thing*) lo agradable, amenidad *f*. **(c)** (*refinement*) finura *f*, lo culto. **(d)** (*fastidiousness*) delicadeza *f*; meticulosidad *f*; escrupulosidad *f*; sutileza *f*; discernimiento *m*.

nicety ['naɪsɪtɪ] N **(a)** = **niceness**. **(b)** **to judge sth to a ~** juzgar algo con toda precisión; **niceties** detalles *mpl*, puntos *mpl* sutiles.

niche [niːʃ] N nicho *m*; hornacina *f*; (*fig*) colocación *f* conveniente, buena posición *f*; **to find a ~ for o.s.** encontrarse una buena posición.

Nicholas ['nɪkələs] NM Nicolás.

Nick [nɪk] NM *familiar form of* **Nicholas; Old ~** Patillas.

nick [nɪk] **1** N **(a)** mella *f*, muesca *f*, corte *m*; **in the ~ of time** a última hora, en el momento crítico.
(b) (*Brit‡*) (*prison*) chirona‡ *f*; (*police-station*) comisaría *f*.
(c) **in good ~*** (*Brit*) en buen estado.
2 VT **(a)** mellar, hacer muescas en, hacer cortes en; cortar; (*with sword etc*) pinchar.
(b) (*Brit‡*) (*steal*) robar, birlar*; (*arrest*) trincar‡; **you're ~ed!** ¡queda Vd detenido!
3 VR: **to ~ o.s.** cortarse.

nickel ['nɪkl] N níquel *m*; (*US*) moneda *f* de 5 centavos.

nickel-plated ['nɪkl'pleɪtɪd] ADJ niquelado.

nickel silver [,nɪkl'sɪlvər] N plata *f* alemana.

nicker‡ ['nɪkər] N INVAR (*Brit*) libra *f* esterlina.

nickname ['nɪkneɪm] **1** N apodo *m*, mote *m*.
2 VT apodar; **they ~d him Nobby** le dieron el apodo de Nobby; **Clark ~d Nobby** Clark apodado Nobby.

Nicosia [,nɪkəʊ'siːə] N Nicosia *f*.

nicotine ['nɪkətiːn] **1** N nicotina *f*.
2 ATTR: **~ poisoning** nicotinismo *m*.

nicotinic [,nɪkə'tɪnɪk] ADJ: **~ acid** ácido *m* nicotínico.

niece [niːs] N sobrina *f*.

niff‡ [nɪf] N (*Brit*) olorcito *m* (*of a*); tufillo *m*.

niffy‡ ['nɪfɪ] ADJ (*Brit*) maloliente, apestoso.

nifty* ['nɪftɪ] ADJ (*Brit*) (*smart*) elegante, muy pera*; (*skilful*) diestro, hábil, experto, ágil.

Niger ['naɪdʒər] N (*country, river*) Níger *m*.

Nigeria [naɪ'dʒɪərɪə] N Nigeria *f*.

Nigerian [naɪ'dʒɪərɪən] **1** ADJ nigeriano.
2 N nigeriano *m*, -a *f*.

niggardliness ['nɪgədlɪnɪs] N tacañería *f*.

niggardly ['nɪgədlɪ] ADJ *person* tacaño, avariento; *allowance etc* miserable.

nigger ['nɪgər] **1** N (**∷** *in US*) negro *m*, -a *f*; **to be the ~ in the woodpile** (*Brit*) ser el obstáculo, ser la cosa que estropea el todo.
2 ATTR: **~ brown** (*Brit*) (*colour*) café oscuro; **~ minstrel** cómico *m* disfrazado de negro.

niggle ['nɪgl] **1** N queja *f*; duda *f*.
2 VI (*worry*) inquietarse por pequeñeces; (*fuss*) perder el tiempo con detalles nimios, preocuparse por minucias; (*complain*) quejarse, murmurar.

niggling ['nɪglɪŋ] **1** ADJ *detail* nimio, insignificante; *doubt* persistente; (*small-minded*) de miras estrechas.
2 N quejas *fpl*; dudas *fpl*; murmurios *mpl*.

nigh [naɪ] (**†** *or prov*) **1** ADV cerca; casi; **it's ~ on finished** está casi terminado.
2 PREP cerca de.

night [naɪt] **1** N noche *f*; **a Beethoven ~** un concierto dedicado a Beethoven; **first ~** (*Theat etc*) estreno *m*; **good ~!** ¡buenas noches!; **last ~** anoche; **the ~ before last** anteanoche; **tomorrow ~** mañana por la noche; **the ~ before the ceremony** la víspera de la ceremonia; **all ~ (long)** toda la noche; **~ and day** noche y día; **at ~,** **by ~, in the ~** de noche, por la noche; **11 o'clock at ~** las 11 de la noche; **it is ~** es de noche; **it's the servant's ~ out** es la tarde libre de la criada; **to have a ~ out** salir de juerga (o de parranda) por la noche; **to have a bad ~** dormir mal, pasar una mala noche; **to have an early ~** acostarse temprano, retirarse pronto; **to have a late ~** no acostarse hasta (muy) tarde; **she's used to late ~s** ella está acostum-

brada a acostarse tarde; **to make a ~ of it** estar de juerga hasta muy entrada la noche; **are you planning to make a ~ of it?** ¿vais a estar fuera toda la noche?
2 ATTR nocturno, de noche; **~ blindness** ceguera *f* nocturna; **~ nurse** enfermera *f* de noche; **~ owl*** ave *f* nocturna; **~ porter** guardián *m* nocturno; **~ safe** caja *f* de seguridad nocturna, depósito *m* nocturno; **~ stand** (*US*) mesilla *f*, mesita *f* de noche; **~ storage heater** acumulador *m* eléctrico nocturno; **~ table** (*US*) = **~ stand; ~ watch** turno *m* de noche; (*Hist*) ronda *f* nocturna; **~ watchman** vigilante *m* nocturno, sereno *m*; **~ work** trabajo *m* nocturno.
3 ADV: **to work ~s** trabajar de noche, hacer el turno de noche; **I can't sleep ~s** (*US*) no puedo dormir la noche.

night-bird ['naɪtbɜːd] N pájaro *m* nocturno; (*person*) trasnochador *m*, -ora *f*.

nightcap ['naɪtkæp] N **(a)** gorro *m* de dormir. **(b)** (*drink*) sosiega *f*, bebida *f* que se toma antes de acostarse.

nightclothes ['naɪt,kləʊðz] NPL ropa *f* de dormir.

nightclub ['naɪtklʌb] N cabaret *m*, boite *f*, sala *f* de fiestas.

nightdress ['naɪtdres] N camisón *m* (de noche).

nightfall ['naɪtfɔːl] N anochecer *m*; **at ~** al anochecer; **by ~** antes del anochecer.

night-fighter ['naɪtfaɪtər] N caza *m* nocturno.

nightgown ['naɪtgaʊn] N, **nightie*** ['naɪtɪ] N camisón *m* (de noche).

nighthawk ['naɪthɔːk] N chotacabras *m*.

nightingale ['naɪtɪŋgeɪl] N ruiseñor *m*.

nightjar ['naɪtdʒɑːr] N chotacabras *m*.

night-life ['naɪtlaɪf] N vida *f* nocturna.

night-light ['naɪtlaɪt] N mariposa *f*, lamparilla *f*.

nightlong ['naɪt,lɒŋ] ADJ de toda la noche, que dura toda la noche.

nightly ['naɪtlɪ] **1** ADV todas las noches, cada noche.
2 ADJ de noche, nocturno; (*regular*) de todas las noches.

nightmare ['naɪtmeər] N pesadilla *f* (*also fig*).

nightmarish ['naɪtmeərɪʃ] ADJ de pesadilla, espeluznante.

night-night* ['naɪt,naɪt] N (*goodnight*) buenas noches *fpl*.

night-school ['naɪtskuːl] N escuela *f* nocturna.

nightshade ['naɪtʃeɪd] N dulcamara *f*, hierba *f* mora; **deadly ~** belladona *f*.

nightshift ['naɪtʃɪft] N turno *m* de noche; **to be** (*or* **to work**) **on ~** estar (*or* trabajar) en el turno de noche.

nightshirt ['naɪtʃɜːt] N camisa *f* de dormir (*de caballero*).

nightsight ['naɪtsaɪt] N visor *m* nocturno.

nightspot ['naɪt,spɒt] N lugar *m* de diversión nocturna, (*esp*) club *m* nocturno.

nightstick ['naɪtstɪk] N (*US*) porra *f* (de policía).

night-time ['naɪttaɪm] N noche *f*; **in the ~** de noche, durante la noche.

night-vision ['naɪtvɪʒən] ADJ *equipment, device* de vigilancia nocturna.

nightwear ['naɪtweər] N ropa *f* de dormir.

nig-nog‡ ['nignɒg] N (*pej*) negro *m*, -a *f*.

NIH N (*US*) ABBR *of* **National Institutes of Health**.

nihilism ['naɪlɪzəm] N nihilismo *m*.

nihilist ['naɪlɪst] N nihilista *mf*.

nihilistic [,naɪ'lɪstɪk] ADJ nihilista.

Nikkei average [nɪ,keɪ'ævərɪdʒ] N, **Nikkei index** [nɪ,keɪ'ɪndeks] N índice *m* Nikkei.

nil [nɪl] (*Brit*) **1** N cero *m*, nada *f*; **Granada beat Murcia two ~** el Granada venció al Murcia dos-cero; **its merits are ~** sus méritos son nulos, no tiene mérito alguno; *ver también* ⟨ZERO⟩.
2 ADJ nulo; **~ balance** (*Fin*) balance *m* nulo.

Nile [naɪl] N Nilo *m*.

nimble ['nɪmbl] ADJ (*in moving*) ágil, ligero; (*in wit*) listo; *fingers etc* diestro, experto.

nimbleness ['nɪmblnɪs] N agilidad *f*; ingenio *m*; destreza *f*.

nimbly ['nɪmblɪ] ADV ágilmente, ligeramente; diestramente.

nimbostratus [,nɪmbəʊ'streɪtəs] N, PL **nimbostrati** [,nɪmbəʊstreɪtaɪ] nimbostrato *m*.

nimbus ['nɪmbəs] N nimbo *m*.

NIMBY ['nɪmbɪ] N ABBR *of* **not in my backyard** *campaña contra depósito de residuos tóxicos (etc) 'en mi patio'*.

nincompoop ['nɪŋkəmpuːp] N bobo *m*, -a *f*, papirote *m*.

nine [naɪn] **1** ADJ nueve; **~-to-five job** trabajo *m* de nueve a cinco; **~ times out of ten** casi siempre; **a ~ days' wonder** una maravilla de un día.
2 N: **to be dressed up to the ~s** estar hecho un brazo de mar; **to get dressed up to the ~s** ponerse de punta en blanco.

ninepins ['naɪnpɪnz] NPL (*objects*) bolos *mpl*; (*game*) juego *m* de bolos; **to go down like ~** caer como bolos en bolera.

nineteen [naɪn'tiːn] ADJ diecinueve; **to talk ~ to the dozen** (*Brit*) hablar por los codos.

nineteenth ['naɪn'tiːnθ] ADJ decimonoveno, decimonono; **the ~ (hole)** (*hum*) el bar.

ninetieth ['naɪntɪɪθ] ADJ nonagésimo; noventa; **the ~ anniversary** el noventa aniversario.

ninety ['naɪntɪ] ADJ noventa; **the nineties** los años noventa; **to be in one's nineties** tener más de noventa años, ser noventón.

ninny ['nɪnɪ] N bobo *m*, -a *f*.

ninth [naɪnθ] ADJ noveno; **Pius IX** Pío Nono.

niobium [naɪ'əʊbɪəm] N niobio *m*.

Nip* [nɪp] N (*pej*) japonés *m*, -esa *f*.

nip¹ [nɪp] [1] N pellizco *m*; mordisco *m*; **there's a ~ in the air** hace un poco frío, hay helada.
[2] VT (*with fingers*) pellizcar, pinchar; (*bite*) mordiscar; (*cut*) cortar; *plant* helar; (*wind*) picar, helar; **to ~ one's fingers in a door** pillarse los dedos en una puerta.
[3] VI (*Brit*) correr, ir a toda velocidad; **I ~ped round to the shop*** fui a la tienda en una escapadita, me pegué un salto a la tienda.
◆**nip along*** VI: **we were ~ping along at 100 kph** (*Brit*) corríamos a 100 kph.
◆**nip in*** VI entrar, entrar un momento; entrar sin ser visto; **to ~ in and out of the traffic** colarse por entre el tráfico.
◆**nip off*** [1] VT cortar; despuntar.
[2] VI (*Brit*) pirarse*, largarse*.
◆**nip out*** VI: **I must ~ out for a moment** salgo un momento.

nip² [nɪp] N (*of drink*) trago *m*, traguito *m*.

nipper* ['nɪpəʳ] N (*Brit*) chiquillo *m*, -a *f*.

nipple ['nɪpl] N (*Anat*) pezón *m*; (*of male, bottle*) tetilla *f*; (*Mech*) boquilla *f* roscada, manguito *m* de unión; (*for greasing*) engrasador *m*, pezón *m* de engrase.

nippy* ['nɪpɪ] ADJ (**a**) (*Brit*) *person* ágil, listo; *car etc* rápido, veloz; **be ~ about it!** ¡corre!, ¡menearse!; **we shall have to be ~** tendremos que darnos prisa. (**b**) (*cold*) frío; **it's ~** hace frío.

NIREX ['naɪreks] N (*Brit*) ABBR *of* **Nuclear Industry Radioactive Waste Executive**.

nirvana [nɪə'vɑːnə] N nirvana *f*.

nit [nɪt] N (**a**) (*Zool*) liendre *f*. (**b**) (*Brit*) imbécil *mf*, idiota *mf*; **you ~!** ¡imbécil!

niter ['naɪtəʳ] N (*US*) = **nitre**.

nit-pick ['nɪtpɪk] VI sacarle faltas a todo, buscarle tres pies al gato.

nit-picker* ['nɪt,pɪkəʳ] N criticón *m*, -ona *f*, chinchorrero *m*, -a *f*.

nit-picking* ['nɪt,pɪkɪŋ] [1] ADJ criticón.
[2] N critiquería *f*, chinchorrería *f*.

nitrate ['naɪtreɪt] N nitrato *m*.

nitration [naɪ'treɪʃən] N nitratación *f*, nitración *f*.

nitre, (*US*) niter ['naɪtəʳ] N nitro *m*.

nitric ['naɪtrɪk] ADJ: **~ acid** ácido *m* nítrico.

nitrite ['naɪtraɪt] N nitrito *m*.

nitro- ['naɪtrəʊ-] PREF nitro-.

nitrobenzene [,naɪtrəʊben'ziːn] N nitrobenceno *m*.

nitrogen ['naɪtrədʒən] [1] N nitrógeno *m*.
[2] ATTR: **~ cycle** ciclo *m* de nitrógeno; **~ dioxide** dióxido *m* de nitrógeno; **~ oxide** óxido *m* de nitrógeno.

nitrogenous [naɪ'trɒdʒɪnəs] ADJ nitrogenado.

nitroglycerin(e) ['naɪtrəʊ'glɪsəriːn] N nitroglicerina *f*.

nitrous ['naɪtrəs] ADJ nitroso; **~ acid** ácido *m* nitroso; **~ oxide** óxido *m* nitroso.

nitty-gritty* ['nɪtɪgrɪtɪ] N realidad *f* básica, aspectos *mpl* esenciales; **let's get down to the ~** vamos a lo esencial.

nitwit* ['nɪtwɪt] N imbécil *mf*, idiota *mf*; **you ~!** ¡imbécil!

nix: [nɪks] [1] N nada.
[2] EXCL ¡ni hablar!

NJ (*US Post*) ABBR *of* **New Jersey**.

NLF N ABBR *of* **National Liberation Front**.

NLQ N (*Comput*) ABBR *of* **near letter quality** calidad *f* casi de correspondencia.

NLRB N (*US*) ABBR *of* **National Labor Relations Board**.

NLRB - NATIONAL LABOR RELATIONS BOARD

*(i) El **National Labor Relations Board** o **NLRB** es un organismo independiente del gobierno federal de Estados Unidos, creado por el Congreso en 1935 para mediar en las disputas entre empleados y patronos o sindicatos. También tiene como misión asegurarse de que ni los patronos ni los sindicatos lleven a cabo prácticas laborales injustas y que los empleados tengan la opción de ser o no representados por un sindicato en sus enfrentamientos con la patronal.*

NM (*US Post*) ABBR *of* **New Mexico**.

N. Mex. ABBR *of* **New Mexico**.

NMR N ABBR *of* **nuclear magnetic resonance**.

NNE ABBR *of* **north-north-east** NNE, nornoreste *m* (*also* ADJ).

NNR N (*Brit*) ABBR *of* **National Nature Reserve** reserva *f* natural nacional.

NNW ABBR *of* **north-north-west** NNO, nornoroeste *m* (*also* ADJ).

no [nəʊ] [1] ADV (**a**) no; **whether he comes or ~** si viene o no.
(**b**) (COMP) **I am ~ taller than you** yo no soy más alto que tú.

[2] ADJ (**a**) ninguno, no ... alguno; **no-one** V **nobody**; (*often not translated, eg*) **I have ~ money** no tengo dinero; **he made ~ reply** no contestó, no dio respuesta alguna; **~ two of them are alike** no hay dos iguales; **it's ~ distance** no está lejos; **it's ~ trouble** no es molestia; **details of little or ~ interest** detalles *mpl* de poco o ningún interés, detalles *mpl* de poquísimo interés; **problems of ~ easy solution** problemas que no tienen soluciones fáciles, problemas que no se resolverán fácilmente; **it is ~ easy task** es una tarea nada fácil; **he's ~ poet** de poeta no tiene nada; **he was ~ general** no era lo que se llama un general, no merecía el nombre de general; **judge or ~ judge, he's a fool** no importa que sea juez, es un tonto.
(**b**) (*prohibitions*) '**~ admittance**', '**~ entry**' 'se prohíbe la entrada'; **~ kidding?** ¿en serio?, ¿sin bromas?; **~ nonsense!** ¡déjate de tonterías!; '**~ parking**' 'prohibido estacionar'; '**~ smoking**' 'se prohíbe fumar'; **~ surrender!** ¡no nos rendimos nunca!
(**c**) (*with gerund*) **there's ~ denying it** es imposible negarlo; **there's ~ getting out of it** no hay posibilidad de evitarlo; **there's ~ pleasing him** resulta imposible contentarle, no hay modo de complacerle.
[3] N, PL **~es** [nəʊz] (**a**) no *m*; **I won't take ~ for an answer** no permito que lo rechaces, no acepto una respuesta negativa.
(**b**) (*Parl*) voto *m* negativo, voto *m* en contra; **there were 7 ~es** votaron 7 en contra; **the ~es have it** se ha rechazado la moción.

no. ABBR *of* **number** núm., nᵒ, número *m*.

no-account* ['nəʊə'kaʊnt] (*US*) [1] ADJ inútil, insignificante.
[2] N cero *m* a la izquierda.

Noah ['nəʊə] NM Noé; **~'s ark** arca *f* de Noé.

nob¹: [nɒb] N (*Anat*) cabeza *f*, cholla: *f*.

nob²: [nɒb] N (*Brit*) (*person of importance*) personaje *m*, pájaro *m* de cuenta; (*toff*) majo *m*, currutaco *m*.

nobble: ['nɒbl] VT (*Brit*) (**a**) *person* (*bribe*) sobornar; (*win over*) ejercer presión sobre, persuadir por medios nada rectos; (*accost*) procurar hablar con, abordar. (**b**) *horse* narcotizar, drogar, estropear. (**c**) (*arrest*) coger. (**d**) (*steal*) birlar*, pisar*.

Nobel [nəʊ'bel] ATTR: **~ prize** premio *m* Nóbel; **~ prizewinner** ganador *m*, -ora *f* del premio Nóbel.

nobelium [nəʊ'biːlɪəm] N nobelio *m*.

nobility [nəʊ'bɪlɪtɪ] N (*all senses*) nobleza *f*.

noble ['nəʊbl] [1] ADJ noble; *title* de nobleza; **the ~ art** el boxeo; **~ rot** (*of wine*) podredumbre *f* noble.
[2] N noble *mf*, aristócrata *mf*, (*Spanish Hist*) hidalgo *m*.

nobleman ['nəʊblmən] N, PL **noblemen** ['nəʊblmən] noble *m*, aristócrata *m*, (*Spanish Hist*) hidalgo *m*.

noble-minded [,nəʊbl'maɪndɪd] ADJ generoso.

nobleness ['nəʊblnɪs] N nobleza *f*.

noblewoman ['nəʊblwʊmən] N, PL **noblewomen** ['nəʊblwɪmɪn] dama *f* noble, aristócrata *f*, (*Spanish Hist*) hidalga *f*.

nobly ['nəʊblɪ] ADV noblemente, con nobleza; (*fig*) generosamente.

nobody ['nəʊbədɪ] [1] PRON nadie; **~ spoke** nadie habló, no habló nadie; **who spoke? — ~** ¿quién habló? — nadie; **~ has more right to it than she has** no hay nadie que tenga más derecho a ello que ella; **would ~ buy it?** ¿no había quién lo comprara?
[2] N: **a mere ~** un don nadie, un cero a la izquierda; **I knew him when he was ~** le conocí cuando no era nadie.

no-claim(s) bonus [,nəʊ'kleɪm(z),bəʊnəs] N, (*US*) **no-claims discount** [,nəʊ'kleɪmz,dɪskaʊnt] bonificación *f* por carencia de reclamaciones, prima *f* de no reclamación.

nocturnal [nɒk'tɜːnl] ADJ nocturno.

nocturne ['nɒktɜːn] N nocturno *m*.

nod [nɒd] [1] N (*sleepy etc*) cabezada *f*; (*sign*) señal *f* hecha con la cabeza, inclinación *f* de cabeza; **a ~ is as good as a wink** a buen entendedor (pocas palabras bastan); **he gave me a ~** me saludó inclinando la cabeza; **he agreed with a ~** asintió con la cabeza; **to give the ~ to** aprobar, dar luz verde a; **to go through on the ~** ser aprobado sin discusión, ser aprobado sin someterse a votación.
[2] VT *head* inclinar, mover, hacer una señal con; **he ~ded his agreement** asintió con la cabeza; **he ~ded a greeting** me saludó inclinando la cabeza; **he ~ded his head** (*saying yes*) asintió con la cabeza, movió la cabeza afirmativamente.
[3] VI (*sleepily*) dar cabezadas, cabecear; (*say yes*) decir que sí con la cabeza, asentir con la cabeza; (*trees*) mecerse, inclinarse; **Homer ~s** incluso Homero se duerme a veces; **we're on ~ding terms** nos conocemos justo para saludarnos.
◆**nod off** VI quedarse dormido.
◆**nod through** VT: **the porter ~ded us through** el conserje nos dejó pasar (inclinando la cabeza); **the delegates were ~ded through** los delegados fueron aprobados sin votación.

noddle* ['nɒdl] N mollera* *f*.

node [nəʊd] N (*Anat, Astron, Phys*) nodo *m*; (*Bot*) nudo *m*.

nodular ['nɒdjʊləʳ] ADJ nodular.

nodule ['nɒdjuːl] N nódulo *m*.

Noel [nəʊ'el] N Navidad f.

no-fault ['nəʊ'fɔːlt] ATTR: ~ **agreement** acuerdo m de pago respectivo; ~ **divorce** divorcio m en el que no se culpa a ninguno de los esposos; ~ **insurance** seguro m en el que no entra el factor de culpabilidad.

no-frills ['nəʊ,frɪlz] ADJ: **a** ~ **house** una casa sin adornos, una casa sin lujo.

noggin ['nɒgɪn] N (a) vaso m pequeño, (loosely) vaso m, caña f (de cerveza); **let's have a** ~ (Brit) tomemos algo.
(b) (measure) medida de licor (= 1,42 decilitros).
(c) (US‡: head) cabeza f, coco* m, calabaza‡ f.

no-go [,nəʊ'gəʊ] ATTR: ~ **area** (Brit) zona f prohibida.

no-good* ['nəʊgʊd] ADJ (US) malísimo, malvado.

no-growth ['nəʊ'grəʊθ] ATTR: ~ **economy** economía f sin crecimiento, economía f de crecimiento cero.

no-hoper* ['nəʊ,həʊpə'] N nulidad f.

nohow* ['nəʊhaʊ] ADV de ninguna manera, por ningún medio que sea.

noise [nɔɪz] ① N (a) ruido m; estrépito m; estruendo m; clamor m; tumulto m; alboroto m; (fig) escándalo m; ~ **pollution** contaminación f auditiva; ~ **prevention** medidas fpl para evitar el ruido; **to make a** ~ hacer ruido; **the book made a lot of** ~ **when it came out** el libro causó un escándalo cuando apareció, al aparecer se armó un escándalo en torno al libro; **they made a (lot of)** ~ **about it** protestaron (mucho) por ello, armaron un (tremendo) lío con este motivo; **he made** ~**s about changing it but did nothing** manifestó la intención de cambiarlo pero no hizo nada; **the minister is making all the right** ~**s** el ministro se muestra francamente favorable.
(b) (*) **big** ~ (person) pez m gordo*, pájaro m de cuenta; **he's a big** ~ **now** ahora es un personaje.
② VT: **to** ~ **sth abroad** divulgar la noticia de algo, hacer correr la voz de algo; **we don't want it** ~**d abroad** no queremos que se publique.

noiseless ['nɔɪzlɪs] ADJ silencioso, sin ruido.

noiselessly ['nɔɪzlɪslɪ] ADV en silencio, sin (hacer) ruido.

noisemaker ['nɔɪz,meɪkə'] N (US) matraca f.

noisily ['nɔɪzɪlɪ] ADV ruidosamente, estrepitosamente, clamorosamente; escandalosamente.

noisiness ['nɔɪzɪnɪs] N ruido m, estrépito m; lo ruidoso, lo estrepitoso.

noisome ['nɔɪsəm] ADJ (disgusting) asqueroso; (smelly) fétido, maloliente; (harmful) nocivo.

noisy ['nɔɪzɪ] ADJ ruidoso, estrepitoso, clamoroso; child etc escandaloso; protest ruidoso.

no-jump ['nəʊ,dʒʌmp] N salto m nulo.

nomad ['nəʊmæd] N nómada mf.

nomadic [nəʊ'mædɪk] ADJ nómada.

nomadism ['nəʊmædɪzəm] N nomadismo m.

no-man's ['nəʊmænz] ATTR: ~ **land** tierra f de nadie.

nom de plume ['nɒmdə'pluːm] N, PL **noms de plume** seudónimo m, nombre m artístico.

nomenclature [nəʊ'menklətʃə'] N nomenclatura f.

nomenklatura [,nəʊmenklə'tʊərə] N: **the** ~ la nomenklatura.

nominal ['nɒmɪnl] ADJ nominal; ~ **partner** socio mf nominal; ~ **value** valor m nominal; ~ **wage** salario m nominal.

nominalism ['nɒmɪnəlɪzəm] N nominalismo m.

nominalist ['nɒmɪnəlɪst] ADJ, N nominalista mf.

nominalization [,nɒmɪnəlaɪ'zeɪʃən] N nominalización f.

nominalize ['nɒmɪnəlaɪz] VT nominalizar.

nominally ['nɒmɪnəlɪ] ADV nominalmente.

nominate ['nɒmɪneɪt] VT proponer (la candidatura de); nombrar; **to** ~ **sb as chairman** proponer a uno como candidato a la presidencia, nombrar a uno para presidente; **to** ~ **sb for a job** nombrar a uno para un cargo.

nomination [,nɒmɪ'neɪʃən] N nombramiento m; propuesta f.

nominative ['nɒmɪnətɪv] ① ADJ nominativo; ~ **case** = 2.
② N nominativo m.

nominator ['nɒmɪneɪtə'] N persona que presenta o designa a un candidato.

nominee [,nɒmɪ'niː] N candidato m, -a f; persona f nombrada; **the** ~ **of sb** el candidato propuesto por uno, el candidato que apoya uno.

non- [nɒn] PREF in compounds: no..., des..., in...

non-academic ['nɒn,ækə'demɪk] ADJ staff no docente.

non-acceptance ['nɒnək'septəns] N rechazo m.

non-achiever ['nɒnə'tʃiːvə'] N persona f que no alcanza lo que se espera de ella.

non-addictive ['nɒnə'dɪktɪv] ADJ drug que no crea dependencia, no adictivo.

nonagenarian [,nɒnədʒɪ'neərɪən] ① ADJ nonagenario, noventón.
② N nonagenario m, -a f, noventón m, -ona f.

non-aggression ['nɒnə'greʃən] ① N no agresión f.
② ATTR: ~ **pact** pacto m de no agresión.

non-alcoholic ['nɒnælkə'hɒlɪk] ADJ no alcohólico, analcohólico; ~ **drink** refresco m.

non-aligned ['nɒnə'laɪnd] ADJ neutral, no comprometido; ~ **countries** países mpl no alineados.

non-alignment ['nɒnə'laɪnmənt] N no alineamiento m.

non-appearance ['nɒnə'pɪərəns] N ausencia f; (Jur) no comparecencia f.

non-arrival ['nɒnə'raɪvəl] N ausencia f; **the** ~ **of the mail** el hecho de no haber llegado el correo.

non-attendance ['nɒnə'tendəns] N ausencia f, falta f de asistencia.

non-availability ['nɒnə,veɪlə'bɪlɪtɪ] N no disponibilidad f.

non-believer ['nɒnbɪ'liːvə'] N no creyente mf.

non-belligerent ['nɒnbɪ'lɪdʒərənt] ① ADJ no beligerante.
② N no beligerante mf.

non-biological ['nɒnbaɪəʊ'lɒdʒɪkl] ADJ no biológico.

non-breakable ['nɒn'breɪkəbl] ADJ irrompible.

non-cash ['nɒn'kæʃ] ADJ: ~ **assets** activo m no líquido; ~ **payment** pago m no dinerario.

non-Catholic ['nɒn'kæθlɪk] ① ADJ no católico, acatólico.
② N no católico m, -a f.

nonce [nɒns] ADV: **for the** ~ por el momento.

nonce-word ['nɒnswɜːd] N palabra f efímera creada para un caso especial, hápax m.

nonchalance ['nɒnʃələns] N indiferencia f; negligencia f; aplomo m; sangre f fría, calma f.

nonchalant ['nɒnʃələnt] ADJ indiferente, impasible; negligente; despreocupado; **to be** ~ **about sth** no prestar atención a algo, no tomar algo en serio; **with** ~ **ease** con aplomo y facilidad, con desenvoltura.

nonchalantly ['nɒnʃələntlɪ] ADV con indiferencia; negligentemente; con aplomo, con calma; **a** ~ **knotted tie** una corbata negligentemente anudada.

non-Christian [,nɒn'krɪstɪən] ① ADJ no cristiano.
② N no cristiano m, -a f.

non-combatant ['nɒn'kɒmbətənt] ① ADJ no combatiente.
② N no combatiente mf.

non-combustible ['nɒnkəm'bʌstɪbl] ADJ incombustible.

non-commercial ['nɒnkə'mɜːʃl] ADJ no comercial, no lucrativo.

non-commissioned ['nɒnkə'mɪʃənd] ADJ: ~ **officer** suboficial m, sargento m or cabo m; ~ **officers** ≃ clases fpl.

non-committal ['nɒnkə'mɪtl] ADJ statement etc que no compromete a nada; (pej) evasivo, equívoco; **he was very** ~ **about it** se abstuvo de comprometerse a nada, no quiso concretar, evitó tomar una resolución definitiva.

non-committally [,nɒnkə'mɪtlɪ] ADV: **he said** ~ dijo como evitando tomar una resolución definitiva, dijo como si no quisiese comprometerse a nada.

non-completion ['nɒnkəm'pliːʃən] N incumplimiento m.

non-compliance ['nɒnkəm'plaɪəns] N incumplimiento m, infracción f (with de); desobediencia f (with de).

non compos mentis ['nɒn'kɒmpəs'mentɪs] ADJ (Jur: hum) desposeído de sus facultades mentales.

non-conductor ['nɒnkən'dʌktə'] N (Elec) aislante m, no conductor m, mal conductor m.

nonconformism ['nɒnkən'fɔːmɪzəm] N inconformismo m.

nonconformist ['nɒnkən'fɔːmɪst] ① ADJ inconformista.
② N inconformista mf.

nonconformity ['nɒnkən'fɔːmɪtɪ] N inconformismo m, disidencia f.

non-contagious ['nɒnkən'teɪdʒəs] ADJ no contagioso.

non-contributory [,nɒnkən'trɪbjʊtərɪ] ADJ: ~ **pension scheme** sistema m de pensión no contributiva, plan m de jubilación sin pago de primas.

non-controversial ['nɒnkɒntrə'vɜːʃl] ADJ no conflictivo.

non-conventional ['nɒnkən'venʃənl] ADJ no convencional.

non-convertible ['nɒnkən'vɜːtɪbl] ADJ currency no convertible.

non-cooperation ['nɒnkəʊ,ɒpə'reɪʃən] N (Pol) no cooperación f.

non-cooperative [,nɒnkəʊ'ɒpərətɪv] ADJ no cooperativo.

non-cumulative ['nɒn'kjuːmjʊlətɪv] ADJ no cumulativo.

non-custodial sentence ['nɒnkʌs'təʊdɪəl'sentəns] N sentencia que no implica privación de libertad.

non-delivery [,nɒndɪ'lɪvərɪ] N falta f de entrega.

non-denominational ['nɒndɪnɒmɪ'neɪʃənl] ADJ aconfesional.

nondescript ['nɒndɪskrɪpt] ADJ indeterminado, inclasificable; (pej) mediocre.

non-distinctive [,nɒndɪs'tɪŋktɪv] ADJ (Ling) no distintivo.

non-drinker ['nɒn'drɪŋkə'] N no bebedor m, -ora f, persona f que no bebe; **thanks, I'm a** ~ gracias, yo no bebo.

non-drip ['nɒn'drɪp] ADJ que no gotea.

non-durable ['nɒn'djʊərəbl] ADJ perecedero.

non-dutiable ['nɒn'djuːtɪəbl] ADJ libre de aranceles, no sujeto a derechos de aduana.

none [nʌn] ① PRON (person) nadie; (person, thing) ninguno; (thing) nada; **~ of them** ninguno de ellos; **~ of you can tell me** ninguno de vosotros sabe decirme; **we have ~ of your books** no tenemos ninguno de sus libros; **~ can tell** nadie lo sabe; **~ but he knows of this** sólo lo sabe él; **~ of this is true** nada de esto es verdad; **any news? — ~** ¿alguna noticia? — ninguna; **I'm sorry, there are ~** lo siento, pero no hay; **there are ~ left** no queda ninguno; **~ of that, now!** ¡déjate de eso!; **I want ~ of your lectures!** ¡basta ya de sermones!; **he is aware, ~ better, that ...** se da cuenta, cómo no, de que ...; **it was ~ other than the bishop** fue el obispo en persona, fue el mismo obispo.

2 ADJ († or hum): **riches have I ~** riqueza no la tengo; **reply came there ~** no hubo respuesta.

3 ADV de ningún modo; **I was ~ too comfortable** no me sentía muy cómodo; **they get on ~ too well** no se llevan del todo bien; **it was ~ too soon** ya era hora; **it's ~ the worse for that** no es peor por eso; **he was still ~ the better off** aun así no había mejorado su posición en lo más mínimo; *V also* **worse**.

nonentity [nɒ'nentɪtɪ] N nulidad *f*, cero *m* a la izquierda.

non-essential ['nɒnɪ'senʃəl] 1 ADJ no esencial.
2 N cosa *f* no esencial.

nonetheless [,nʌnðə'les] ADV = **nevertheless**.

non-event [,nɒnɪ'vent] N acontecimiento *m* fallido; fracaso *m*; **it was a ~** no pasó estrictamente nada.

non-executive [,nɒnɪg'zekjʊtɪv] ADJ: **~ director** vocal *mf*, consejero *m*, -a *f*.

non-existence ['nɒnɪg'zɪstəns] N inexistencia *f*, no existencia *f*.

non-existent ['nɒnɪg'zɪstənt] ADJ inexistente, no existente.

non-fattening [,nɒn'fætnɪŋ] ADJ que no engorda.

non-ferrous ['nɒn'ferəs] ADJ no ferroso, no férreo.

non-fiction ['nɒn'fɪkʃən] N literatura *f* no novelesca, no ficción *f*.

non-finite [,nɒn'faɪnaɪt] ADJ: **~ verb** verbo *m* no conjugado.

non-flammable ['nɒn'flæməbl] ADJ ininflamable.

non-fulfilment ['nɒnfʊl'fɪlmənt] N incumplimiento *m*.

non-governmental ['nɒn,gʌvn'mentl] ADJ no gubernamental.

non-impact ['nɒn'ɪmpækt] ADJ: **~ printer** impresora *f* de no impacto.

non-infectious ['nɒn,ɪn'fekʃəs] ADJ no contagioso.

non-inflammable ['nɒnɪn'flæməbl] ADJ ininflamable.

non-intervention ['nɒn,ɪntə'venʃən] N no intervención *f*.

non-iron ['nɒn'aɪən] ADJ de no planchar, que no necesita planchado.

non-laddering ['nɒn'lædərɪŋ] ADJ *stocking* indesmallable.

non-lethal ['nɒn'liːθl] ADJ *weapon* no mortífero; *wound* no mortal.

non-malignant ['nɒnmə'lɪgnənt] ADJ no maligno.

non-member ['nɒn'membər] N no miembro *m*, visitante *mf*.

non-metal ['nɒn'metl] N no metálico.

non-negotiable [,nɒnnɪ'gəʊʃɪəbl] ADJ *demand* innegociable.

non-nuclear ['nɒn'njuːklɪər] ADJ *defence, policy* no nuclear; *area* desnuclearizado.

no-no* ['nəʊnəʊ] N (*US*): **it's a ~** (*undesirable*) eso no se hace; eso es inaceptable; (*not an option*) no existe tal posibilidad.

no-nonsense [,nəʊ'nɒnsəns] ADJ sensato.

non-observance ['nɒnəb'zɜːvns] N no observancia *f*, incumplimiento *m*.

non obst. ABBR *of* **non obstante, notwithstanding** no obstante.

non-operational ['nɒn,ɒpə'reɪʃənl] ADJ que no funciona, incapaz de funcionar.

nonpareil ['nɒnpərəl] 1 ADJ sin par.
2 N persona *f* sin par, cosa *f* sin par; (*Typ*) nomparell *m*.

non-participating ['nɒnpɑː'tɪsɪpeɪtɪŋ] ADJ no participante.

non-partisan ['nɒn,pɑːtɪ'zæn] ADJ independiente, imparcial.

non-party ['nɒn'pɑːtɪ] ADJ (*Pol*) independiente.

non-paying ['nɒn'peɪɪŋ] ADJ *member* que no paga, que entra (*etc*) gratis.

non-payment ['nɒn'peɪmənt] N impago *m*, falta *f* de pago; **sued for ~ of debts** demandado por no pagar sus deudas.

non-person ['nɒn'pɜːsn] N persona *f* que no existe, ser *m* inexistente.

non-playing [,nɒn'pleɪɪŋ] ADJ *captain* no jugador.

nonplus ['nɒn'plʌs] VT dejar perplejo, confundir; **he was completely ~sed** estaba totalmente perplejo; **I confess myself ~sed** confieso que estoy perplejo.

non-poisonous [,nɒn'pɔɪznəs] ADJ no tóxico, atóxico; no venenoso.

non-political [,nɒnpə'lɪtɪkəl] ADJ apolítico.

non-polluting ['nɒnpə'luːtɪŋ] ADJ no contaminante.

non-practising ['nɒn'præktɪsɪŋ] ADJ no practicante.

non-productive [,nɒnprə'dʌktɪv] ADJ improductivo.

non-professional ['nɒnprə'feʃnəl] ADJ no profesional, aficionado.

non-profit [,nɒn'prɒfɪt] ADJ (*US*), **non-profitmaking** ['nɒn'prɒfɪtmeɪkɪŋ] ADJ no lucrativo, no comercial.

non-proliferation ['nɒnprəʊ'lɪfə'reɪʃn] ATTR: **~ treaty** tratado *m* de no proliferación.

non-recurring ['nɒnrɪ'kɜːrɪŋ] ADJ que no se repite, único; **~ expenditure** gasto *m* ocasional.

non-resident ['nɒn'rezɪdənt] 1 ADJ no residente, no fijo, transeúnte.
2 N no residente *mf*, huésped *m* no fijo, transeúnte *mf*.

non-residential ['nɒn,rezɪ'denʃl] ADJ no residencial.

non-returnable [,nɒnrɪ'tɜːnəbl] ADJ: **~ bottle** envase *m* sin vuelta, envase *m* no retornable; **~ deposit** depósito *m* sin devolución.

non-scheduled ['nɒn'ʃedjuːld] ADJ no programado; no previsto.

non-sectarian ['nɒnsek'teərɪən] ADJ no sectario.

nonsense ['nɒnsəns] 1 N disparates *mpl*, tonterías *fpl*, desatinos *mpl*; **a ~, a piece of ~** una tontería; **~!** ¡tonterías!; **what ~!** ¡qué ridículo!; **but that's ~!** ¡eso es absurdo!; **it is ~ to say that ...** es absurdo decir que ...; **this passage makes ~** este pasaje no tiene sentido; **this makes a ~ of our policy** esto es volver de arriba abajo nuestra política; **to talk ~** no decir más que tonterías; **it's just his ~** son cosas de él; **we don't want any of your ~** no queremos escuchar esas tonterías tuyas; **none of your ~!** ¡déjate de tonterías!; **I'll stand no ~ from you!** ¡no tolero tus tonterías!
2 ATTR: **~ verse** disparates *mpl* (en verso), versos *mpl* disparatados.

nonsensical [nɒn'sensɪkəl] ADJ disparatado, absurdo, tonto.

non seq. ABBR *of* **non sequitur**.

non sequitur [,nɒn'sekwɪtər] N incongruencia *f*, falta *f* de lógica; **it's a ~** aquí hay una falta de lógica.

non-sexist ['nɒn'seksɪst] ADJ *language etc* no sexista.

non-shrink ['nɒn'ʃrɪŋk] ADJ inencogible.

non-skid ['nɒn'skɪd] ADJ *surface etc* antideslizante, antirresbaladizo.

non-skilled ['nɒn'skɪld] ADJ *worker* no cualificado; *work* no especializado.

non-slip ['nɒn'slɪp] ADJ = **non-skid**.

non-smoker ['nɒn'sməʊkər] N (*person*) no fumador *m*, -ora *f*, persona *f* que no fuma; (*Rail*) departamento *m* de no fumadores; **I've always been a ~** no he fumado nunca.

non-smoking ['nɒn'sməʊkɪŋ] ADJ *person* que no fuma; (*Rail*) para no fumadores.

non-specialist ['nɒn'speʃəlɪst] N no especialista.

non-specific [,nɒnspə'sɪfɪk] ADJ (a) (*Med*) no específico, sin causa específica, sin sintomatología específica. (b) (*imprecise*) indeterminado, vago.

non-standard [,nɒn'stændəd] ADJ (*Ling*) no estándar.

non-starter [,nɒn'stɑːtər] N: **that idea is a ~** esa idea es imposible.

non-stick [,nɒn'stɪk] ADJ *coating, pan* antiadherente.

non-stop ['nɒn'stɒp] 1 ADV sin parar; (*Rail*) directamente; (*Aer etc*) sin escalas; **he talks ~** no para de hablar.
2 ADJ continuo, incesante; (*Rail*) directo; (*Aer*) sin escalas.

non-taxable ['nɒn'tæksəbl] ADJ no sujeto a impuestos, exento de impuestos, no imponible; **~ income** ingresos *mpl* exentos de impuestos.

non-teaching ['nɒn'tiːtʃɪŋ] ADJ *staff* no docente.

non-technical ['nɒn'teknɪkl] ADJ no técnico.

non-toxic ['nɒn'tɒksɪk] ADJ no tóxico.

non-trading ['nɒn'treɪdɪŋ] ADJ: **~ partnership** sociedad *f* no mercantil.

non-transferable ['nɒntræns'fɜːrəbl] ADJ intransferible.

non-U* [,nɒn'juː] ADJ (*Brit*) ABBR *of* **non-upper class** que no pertenece a la clase alta.

non-union ['nɒn'juːnjən] ADJ, **non-unionized** ['nɒn'juːnjənaizd] ADJ no sindicado.

non-verbal ['nɒn'vɜːbl] ADJ sin palabras.

non-viable ['nɒn'vaɪəbl] ADJ inviable.

non-violence ['nɒn'vaɪələns] N no violencia *f*.

non-violent ['nɒn'vaɪələnt] ADJ no violento, pacífico.

non-volatile [,nɒn'vɒlətaɪl] ADJ: **~ memory** memoria *f* permanente.

non-voting [,nɒn'vəʊtɪŋ] ADJ: **~ shares** acciones *fpl* sin derecho a votar.

non-white [,nɒn'waɪt] 1 ADJ de color.
2 N persona *f* de color.

non-yielding ['nɒn'jiːldɪŋ] ADJ improductivo.

noodle*1 ['nuːdl] N (a) (*head*) cabeza *f*. (b) (*fool*) bobo *m*, -a *f*.

noodle2 ['nuːdlz] 1 NPL: **~s** fideos *mpl*, tallarines *mpl*.
2 ATTR: **~ soup** sopa *f* de fideos.

nook [nʊk] N rincón *m*; **we looked in every ~ and cranny** buscamos en todos los sitios.

nookie* ['nʊkɪ] N: **to have ~** mojar*; **to want ~** querer mojar*.

noon [nuːn], **noonday** ['nuːndeɪ] 1 N mediodía *m*; **at ~** a mediodía; **high noon** (*fig*) apogeo *m*, punto *m* culminante.
2 ATTR de mediodía.

no-one ['nəʊwʌn] PRON = **nobody**.

noose [nuːs] 1 N lazo *m*, nudo *m* corredizo; (*hangman's*) dogal *m*.
2 VT coger con lazo.

no-par ['nəʊ'pɑːr] ADJ: **~ securities** títulos *mpl* sin valor nominal.

nope* [nəʊp] INTERJ (*esp US*) ¡no!

▼ **nor** [nɔːr] CONJ ni; **neither A ~ B** ni A ni B; **~ I** ni yo, ni yo tampoco; **I couldn't and ~ could he** yo no pude ni él tampoco; **I don't know, ~ can I guess** no lo sé, ni puedo conjeturarlo; **~ does it seem likely** ni tampoco parece probable; **~ was this all** y esto no fue todo.

Nordic ['nɔːdɪk] ADJ nórdico.

Norf N (*Brit*) ABBR of **Norfolk**.

norm [nɔːm] N norma *f*; pauta *f*; modelo *m*; (*Bio etc*) tipo *m*; **larger than the ~** más grande que lo normal, (*Bio*) más grande que el tipo; **to exceed one's ~** exceder de la norma.

normal ['nɔːməl] [1] ADJ normal; regular, corriente; **~ distribution** distribución *f* normal; **the child is not ~** el niño es anormal; **it is perfectly ~ to** + *infin* es muy normal + *infin*; **as per ~** como siempre, como es normal.

  [2] N estado *m* normal; nivel *m* normal; normalidad *f*; **the ~ is 20 degrees** lo normal es 20 grados; **things are returning to ~** la situación vuelve a la normalidad, la situación se está normalizando.

normalcy ['nɔːməlsɪ] N normalidad *f*.

normality [nɔː'mælɪtɪ] N normalidad *f*.

normalization [ˌnɔːməlaɪ'zeɪʃən] N normalización *f*.

normalize ['nɔːməlaɪz] VT normalizar.

normally ['nɔːməlɪ] ADV normalmente.

Norman ['nɔːmən] [1] ADJ normando; **~ architecture** arquitectura *f* románica; **the ~ Conquest** la conquista de los normandos.

  [2] N normando *m*, -a *f*.

Normandy ['nɔːməndɪ] N Normandía *f*.

normative ['nɔːmətɪv] ADJ normativo.

Norse [nɔːs] [1] ADJ nórdico, noruego, escandinavo.

  [2] N (*Ling*) nórdico *m*.

Norseman ['nɔːsmən] N, PL **Norsemen** ['nɔːsmən] vikingo *m*, escandinavo *m*.

north [nɔːθ] [1] N norte *m*; **N~ and South** (*Pol*) el Norte y el Sur.

  [2] ADJ del norte, septentrional; *wind* del norte; **the N~ Country** (*Brit*) los condados del norte (de Inglaterra); **~ star** estrella *f* polar, estrella *f* del norte.

  [3] ADV al norte, hacia el norte.

NORTH/SOUTH DIVIDE

🛈 *El término* **North/South divide** *se usa hablando de Gran Bretaña para hacer referencia a las diferencias sociales y económicas que existen entre el norte y el sur de la isla. En términos generales, se piensa que la gente del sur de Inglaterra posee una situación económica mejor, tiene mejores perspectivas de trabajo y lleva un estilo de vida más sano. También se piensa que en el sur, sobre todo en los alrededores de Londres, la población recibe un tratamiento privilegiado por parte del gobierno, en comparación con el resto del país. Muchas industrias manufactureras del norte han ido perdiendo importancia y a menudo se culpa al gobierno por no haber tomado medidas apropiadas para revitalizar la economía y la estructura de las áreas afectadas.*

North Africa ['nɔːθ'æfrɪkə] N África *f* del Norte.

North African ['nɔːθ'æfrɪkən] [1] ADJ norteafricano.

  [2] N norteafricano *m*, -a *f*.

North America ['nɔːθə'merɪkə] N América *f* del Norte, Norteamérica *f*.

North American ['nɔːθə'merɪkən] [1] ADJ norteamericano.

  [2] N norteamericano *m*, -a *f*.

Northants [nɔː'θænts] N ABBR of **Northamptonshire**.

North Atlantic ['nɔːθət'læntɪk] [1] N Atlántico *m* Norte.

  [2] ATTR: **~ Drift** Corriente *f* del Golfo; **~ Treaty Organization** Organización *f* del Tratado del Atlántico Norte.

northbound ['nɔːθbaʊnd] ADJ *traffic* que va hacia el norte; *carriageway* dirección norte.

north-country ['nɔːθˌkʌntrɪ] ADJ del norte de Inglaterra.

Northd N (*Brit*) ABBR of **Northumberland**.

north-east ['nɔːθ'iːst] [1] N nor(d)este *m*.

  [2] ADJ *point, direction* nor(d)este; *wind* del nor(d)este.

north-easterly ['nɔːθ'iːstəlɪ] ADJ *point, direction* nor(d)este; **~ wind** (viento *m* del) nor(d) este *m*.

north-eastern ['nɔːθ'iːstən] ADJ nor(d)este.

north-eastward(s) ['nɔːθ'iːstwəd(z)] ADV hacia el nor(d)este.

northerly ['nɔːðəlɪ] ADJ *point, direction* norte; *wind* del norte; **the most ~ point in Europe** el punto más septentrional de Europa, el punto más nórdico de Europa.

northern ['nɔːðən] ADJ del norte, septentrional, norteño; **~ hemisphere** hemisferio *m* norte; **~ lights** aurora *f* boreal.

northerner ['nɔːðənər] N habitante *mf* del norte; (*Nordic*) nórdico *m*, -a *f*; (*US Hist*) nortista *mf*; **he's a ~** es del norte.

Northern Ireland ['nɔːðən'aɪələnd] N Irlanda *f* del Norte.

Northern Irish [ˌnɔːðən'aɪərɪʃ] [1] ADJ norirlandés.

  [2] NPL norirlandeses *mpl*.

northernmost ['nɔːðənməʊst] ADJ (el) más norte, situado más al norte; **the ~ town in Europe** la ciudad más septentrional de Europa.

north-facing ['nɔːθˌfeɪsɪŋ] ADJ con cara al norte, orientado hacia el norte; **~ slope** vertiente *f* norte.

North Korea ['nɔːθkə'rɪə] N Corea *f* del Norte.

North Korean ['nɔːθkə'rɪən] [1] ADJ norcoreano.

  [2] N norcoreano *m*, -a *f*.

northland ['nɔːθlənd] N (*US*) región *f* septentrional.

Northman ['nɔːθmən] N, PL **Northmen** ['nɔːθmən] vikingo *m*, escandinavo *m*.

north-north-east [ˌnɔːθ,nɔːθ'iːst] [1] ADJ nornordeste.

  [2] N nornordeste *m*.

north-north-west [ˌnɔːθ,nɔːθ'west] [1] ADJ nornoroeste.

  [2] N nornoroeste *m*.

North Pole [ˌnɔːθ'pəʊl] N Polo *m* Norte.

North Sea ['nɔːθ'siː] [1] N Mar *m* del Norte.

  [2] ATTR: **~ gas** gas *m* del Mar del Norte; **~ oil** petróleo *m* del Mar del Norte.

Northumbria [nɔː'θʌmbrɪə] N *región del noroeste de Inglaterra*.

Northumbrian [nɔː'θʌmbrɪən] [1] ADJ de Northumbria.

  [2] N habitante *mf* or nativo *m*, -a *f* de Northumbria.

North Vietnam ['nɔːθvɪet'næm] N Vietnam *m* del Norte.

North Vietnamese ['nɔːθvɪetnə'miːz] [1] ADJ norvietnamita.

  [2] N INVAR norvietnamita *mf*.

northward ['nɔːθwəd] [1] ADJ *advance etc* hacia el norte, en dirección norte.

  [2] ADV (*also* **~s**) hacia el norte, en dirección norte.

north-west ['nɔːθ'west] [1] N noroeste *m*.

  [2] ADJ *point, direction* noroeste; *wind* del noroeste.

north-westerly ['nɔːθ'westəlɪ] ADJ *point, direction* noroeste; **~ wind** (viento *m* del) noroeste *m*.

north-western ['nɔːθ'westən] ADJ noroeste.

north-westward(s) ['nɔːθ'westwəd(z)] ADV hacia el noroeste.

Norway ['nɔːweɪ] N Noruega *f*; **~ lobster** cigala *f*.

Norwegian [nɔː'wiːdʒən] [1] ADJ noruego.

  [2] N (**a**) noruego *m*, -a *f*. (**b**) (*Ling*) noruego *m*.

nos. ABBR of **numbers** núms, números *mpl*.

no-score ['nəʊˌskɔːr] ADJ: **~ draw** empate *m* a cero.

nose [nəʊz] [1] N (**a**) (*Anat*) nariz *f*; (*pej*) narizota *f*, narices *fpl*; (*of animal*) hocico *m*; **right under one's ~** a ojos vistas, en las barbas de uno, bajo las narices de uno; **with his ~ in the air** con la frente levantada; **to bleed at the ~** echar sangre por las narices; **to blow one's ~** sonarse (las narices); **to count ~s** (*US*) hacer recuento de los presentes; **to cut off one's ~ to spite one's face** ir contra uno mismo; **to follow one's ~** (*go straight*) ir todo seguido, (*by instinct*) dejarse guiar por el instinto; **he gets up my ~:** me hace subir por las paredes*; **to have one's ~ in a book** estar enfrascado en un libro; **to hold one's ~** taparse las narices; **to keep one's ~ clean** (*fig*) mantener la reputación, no mancharse; **to keep one's ~ out of sth** no entrometerse en algo; **to lead sb by the ~** tener a uno agarrado por las narices; **to look down one's ~ at** desdeñar, mirar por encima del hombro a; **to make sb pay through the ~** desollar a uno, cobrar a uno un precio elevadísimo; **she paid through the ~ (for it)** pagó gusto y ganas, le costó un ojo de la cara; **to talk through one's ~** hablar por las narices, hablar con voz gangosa; **to poke** (*or* **stick**) **one's ~ into sth** meterse en algo; **who asked you to poke your ~ in?** ¿quién le manda meter las narices en esto?; **to rub sb's ~ in sth** refregar una cosa a uno por las narices; **to see no further than one's ~** no ver más allá de sus narices; **to turn up one's ~** torcer el morro (*at* ante, en presencia de).

  (**b**) (*sense of smell*) olfato *m*; **to have a good ~ for** tener buen olfato para.

  (**c**) (*of wine*) aroma *m*, buqué *m*.

  (**d**) (*Naut*) proa *f*; (*Aer*) morro *m*, proa *f*; (*Aut*) parte *f* delantera; **the traffic stood ~ to tail** los coches estaban pegados unos a otros.

  [2] VT: **to ~ one's way forward** avanzar con precaución.

  [3] VI: **to ~ past sth** pasar algo con mucho cuidado.

◆**nose about, nose around** VI curiosear, fisgonear.

◆**nose out** VT: **to ~ sth out** husmear algo, olfatear algo; *secret* lograr descubrir.

nosebag ['nəʊzbæg] N morral *m*.

noseband ['nəʊzbænd] N muserola *f*.

nosebleed ['nəʊzbliːd] N hemorragia *f* nasal; **to have a ~** tener una hemorragia nasal, reventarse la nariz*.

nose-cone ['nəʊzkəʊn] N cabeza *f* separable.

-nosed [nəʊzd] ADJ *ending in compounds* de nariz ...; **red~** de nariz colorada.

nose-dive ['nəʊzdaɪv] [1] N picado *m* vertical; (*involuntary*) caída *f* de narices; **to take a ~** (*fig*) caer en picado.

  [2] VI descender en picado; (*involuntarily*) caer de morro (*into* en).

nose-drops ['nəʊzdrɒps] NPL gotas *fpl* nasales.

nosegay ['nəʊzgeɪ] N ramillete *m*.

nosey* ['nəʊzɪ] ADJ curioso, fisgón; **don't be so ~!** ¡no seas tan entrometido!

nosey-parker* ['nəʊzɪ'pɑːkər] N (*Brit*) fisgón *m*, -ona *f*.

nosh: [nɒʃ] [1] N (*Brit*) papeo: *m*; **~ up!** ¡la comida está servida!

2 VI papear‡.

no-show ['nəʊʃəʊ] N ausente *mf*, persona *que no ocupa una plaza reservada previamente.*

nosh-up‡ ['nɒʃʌp] N (*Brit*) comilona* *f*, tragadera* *f* (*LAm*).

nosily ['nəʊzɪlɪ] ADV entrometidamente.

no-smoking ['nəʊ,sməʊkɪŋ] ADJ *area, carriage* de no fumadores; *policy* de prohibición del tabaco.

nostalgia [nɒs'tældʒɪə] N nostalgia *f*.

nostalgic [nɒs'tældʒɪk] ADJ nostálgico.

nostril ['nɒstrɪl] N nariz *f*, ventana *f* de la nariz; **~s** narices *fpl*.

nostrum ['nɒstrəm] N panacea *f* (*also fig*); remedio *m* secreto.

nosy* ['nəʊzɪ] = **nosey.**

not [nɒt] ADV **(a)** (*with verb*) no; **he is ~ here** no está aquí; **fear ~!** ¡no temas!; **is it ~ so?** ¿no es verdad?; **you owe me money, do you ~?** ¿me debes algo, no es verdad?; **he is a doctor, is he ~?** es (un) médico, ¿no?; **he asked me ~ to do it** me rogó no hacerlo.
(b) I wish it were ~ so ¡ojalá no fuera así!; **whether you go or ~** vayas o no; **let me know if ~** avísame en caso contrario; si no, me avisas; **I think ~** creo que no; **~ thinking that ...** sin pensar que ...; **~ that I don't like him** no es que me resulte antipático; **big, ~ to say enormous grande**, por no decir enorme; **why ~?** ¿por qué no?, ¿cómo no?; **~ without some regrets** no sin cierto sentimiento.
(c) absolutely ~! ¡en absoluto!; **certainly ~!**, **~ likely!** ¡de ninguna manera!, ¡ni hablar!; **of course ~!** ¡claro que no!
(d) (*with* PRON *etc*) **~ I!** ¡yo no!; **~ one** ni uno; **~ him either** él tampoco, ni él tampoco; **~ everybody can do it** no es cosa que todos sepan hacer; **~ any more** ya no.
(e) (*understatement*) **with ~ a little surprise** con no poca sorpresa; **there were ~ a few lions** había no pocos leones; *V* **even, much** *etc*.

notability [,nəʊtə'bɪlɪtɪ] N **(a)** notabilidad *f*. **(b)** (*person*) notabilidad *f*, personaje *m*.

notable ['nəʊtəbl] **1** ADJ notable; señalado, memorable; **it is ~ that ...** es de notar que ...
2 N notabilidad *f*, personaje *m*; **~s** notables *mpl*.

notably ['nəʊtəblɪ] ADV notablemente, señaladamente.

notarial [nəʊ'teərɪəl] ADJ notarial.

notarize ['nəʊtəraɪz] VT (*US*) autenticar (legalmente).

notary ['nəʊtərɪ] N (*also* **~ public**) notario *m*, -a *f*.

notate [nəʊ'teɪt] VT (*Mus*) notar.

notation [nəʊ'teɪʃən] N notación *f*.

notch [nɒtʃ] **1** N muesca *f*, mella *f*, corte *m*.
2 VT cortar muescas en, mellar; **to ~ up** apuntar.

note [nəʊt] **1** N **(a)** (*Mus etc*) nota *f*; **with a ~ of anxiety in his voice** con una nota de inquietud en la voz; **to hit the right ~** (*fig*) acertar, elegir acertadamente el tono (de un discurso *etc*); **to strike the wrong ~** (*fig*) desentonar.
(b) (*sign, stigma*) marca *f*, señal *f*; **~ of infamy** nota *f* de infamia.
(c) (*annotation*) nota *f*, apunte *m*; apuntación *f*; (*foot~*) nota *f* (en pie de página); **'N~s on Lucan'** 'Apuntes *mpl* sobre Lucano'; **'editor's ~'** (*in newspaper*) 'nota de la redacción'; **to compare ~s** cambiar impresiones, discutir los resultados; **to make a ~ of sth** apuntar algo, tomar nota de algo; **to speak from ~s** pronunciar un discurso a base de apuntes; **to take a ~ of sth** tomar nota de algo; **to take down ~s** tomar apuntes.
(d) (*letter etc*) nota *f*, carta *f*; recado *m*; esquela *f*; **take a ~, Miss Jones** toma nota, señorita.
(e) (*Comm*) vale *m*; (*Brit: bank~*) billete *m*; **~ of hand** pagaré *m*.
(f) (*eminence*) **of ~** notable, eminente, de importancia; **man of ~** hombre *m* notable.
(g) (*notice*) **worthy of ~** digno de atención; **nothing of ~** nada de particular, sin novedad; **to take ~ of** prestar atención a, ocuparse de; **only the critics took ~ of the book** solamente los críticos se ocuparon del libro.
2 VT **(a)** (*observe*) notar, observar, advertir.
(b) (*write down; also* **to ~ down**) apuntar, anotar.
(c) we duly ~ that ... nos hacemos cuenta de que ...; **your remarks have been ~d** hemos leído con atención sus observaciones.

notebook ['nəʊtbʊk] N libro *m* de apuntes, libreta *f*; (*student's etc*) cuaderno *m*.

note-case ['nəʊtkeɪs] N (*Brit*) cartera *f*, billetero *m*.

noted ['nəʊtɪd] ADJ célebre, conocido, famoso (*for* por).

note-pad ['nəʊtpæd] N (*Brit*) bloc *m*, libreta *f* para notas.

notepaper ['nəʊt,peɪpə*] N papel *m* para cartas, papel *m* de escribir.

noteworthiness ['nəʊt,wɜːðɪnɪs] N notabilidad *f*.

noteworthy ['nəʊt,wɜːðɪ] ADJ notable, digno de notarse; **it is ~ that ...** es notable que ...

nothing ['nʌθɪŋ] **1** N **(a)** nada *f*; (*nought*) cero *m*; **I have ~ to give you** no tengo nada que darte, nada tengo que darte; **I see ~ that I like** no veo nada que me guste; **~ else** nada más; **~ much** poca cosa; **there's ~ much to be said** poco es lo que hay que decir; **next to ~** casi nada; **there is ~ mean about him** no tiene nada de tacaño; **there's ~ special about it** no tiene nada de particular; **it's ~ to be**

proud of no es motivo para enorgullecerse; **there's ~ to fear** no hay de qué tener miedo; *ver también* **ZERO** .
(b) there is ~ in the rumours los rumores no tienen ni pizca de verdad; **there's ~ in it** (*in race*) van muy iguales; **there's ~ in it for us** de esto no vamos a sacar ningún provecho; **there's ~ for it but to pay** (*Brit*) no hay más remedio (*or* no nos queda otra *LAm*) que pagar; **there's ~ to it!** ¡es facilísimo!; **she is ~ to him** ella le es indiferente; **it's ~ more than a rumour** es simplemente un rumor; **it is ~ to me whether he comes or not** no me importa que venga o no; **he is ~ if not careful** es prudente por encima de todo; **I'm ~ of a swimmer** yo nado bastante mal.
(c) for ~ (*free*) gratis, (*unpaid*) gratuitamente, sin sueldo, (*in vain*) en vano, en balde; **it is not for ~ that ...** no es sin motivo que ..., por algo será que ...; **to get sth for ~** obtener algo gratis.
(d) to build up a business from ~ crear un negocio de la nada; **to come to ~** fracasar, parar en nada, quedarse en aguas de borraja; **to make ~ of** (*not understand*) no entender, no sacar nada en claro de; (*not use*) no aprovechar; (*not esteem*) no dar importancia a; **to say ~ of ...** sin mencionar ..., amén de ...; **to stop at ~** no pararse en barras; **to stop at ~ to + infin** emplear sin escrúpulo todos los medios para + *infin*; **to think ~ of** tener en poco, *task* tener por fácil; **he thinks ~ of walking 30 km** para él no tiene importancia recorrer 30 km a pie; **he thinks ~ of borrowing a fiver** con la mayor frescura pide prestado un billete de 5 libras; **think ~ of it!** ¡no hay de qué!; **he has ~ on her** (*comparison*) no le llega ni a la suela del zapato*.
(e) a mere ~ una friolera, una bagatela; **a mere ~!** ¡una bagatela!; **to whisper sweet ~s to sb** decir mil ternezas a una; *V* **do with, doing, kind** *etc*.
2 ADV de ninguna manera; **it's ~ like him** el retrato no se le parece en nada; **it was ~ like so big as we thought** era mucho menos grande de lo que nos imaginábamos; **pretty girl ~!*** ¡guapa, ni hablar!; **~ daunted** sin inmutarse.

nothingness ['nʌθɪŋnɪs] N nada *f*.

no throw [,nəʊ'θrəʊ] N (*Sport*) lanzamiento *m* nulo.

notice ['nəʊtɪs] **1** N **(a)** (*intimation, warning*) aviso *m*; **at short ~** a corto plazo, con poca antelación, con poco tiempo de anticipación; **at a moment's ~** en el acto, inmediatamente, casi sin aviso; **you must be ready to leave at a moment's ~** tienes que estar listo para partir en cuanto te avisen; **at 7 days' ~** con 7 días de antelación; **until further ~** hasta nuevo aviso, hasta nueva orden; **without previous ~** sin previo aviso; **he went without ~** se fue sin avisar a nadie; **to give sb at least a week's ~** avisar a uno lo menos con una semana de anticipación; **to give sb ~ that ...**, **to serve ~ on sb that ...** avisar a uno que ..., hacer saber a uno que ...; **~ is hereby given that ...** se pone en conocimiento del público que ...; **to give sb ~ to do sth** avisar a uno que haga algo; **I must have ~** es imprescindible que me avisen con anticipación; **we require 28 days' ~ for delivery** necesitamos 28 días de aviso para entrega; **we had no ~ of it** no nos habían avisado, no sabíamos nada de ello; **~ to quit** aviso *m* de desalojo.
(b) (*order to leave job etc: by employer*) despido *m*, (: *by employee*) dimisión *f*, renuncia *f* (*esp LAm*); (*period*) plazo *m*; **to be under ~** estar despedido; estar cesado; **to dismiss sb without ~** despedir a uno sin aviso; **to get one's ~** ser despedido; **to give sb ~** despedir a uno; **to give sb a week's ~** despedir a uno con una semana de plazo; **to hand in one's ~** dimitir; **a week's wages in lieu of ~** el salario de una semana como despido.
(c) (*announcement*) aviso *m*; (*in press*) anuncio *m*, nota *f*; comunicado *m*; (*sign*) letrero *m*; (*poster*) cartel *m*; **~ of a meeting** convocatoria *f*, llamada *f*; **to give out a ~** anunciar algo, comunicar algo.
(d) (*review*) reseña *f*, crítica *f*.
(e) (*attention*) atención *f*; interés *m*; **to be beneath one's ~** no merecer atención; **to attract one's ~** atraer la atención de uno, llamar la atención de uno; **it has attracted a lot of ~** ha suscitado gran interés; **to avoid ~** procurar pasar inadvertido; **to bring a matter to sb's ~** llamar la atención de uno sobre un asunto; **to come to sb's ~** llegar al conocimiento de uno; **it has come to my ~ that ...** ha llegado a mi conocimiento que ..., he llegado a saber que ...; **to escape ~** pasar inadvertido; **to take ~ of sb** hacer caso a uno; **a fat lot of ~ he takes of me!*** ¡maldito el caso que me hace!; **to take ~ of sth** hacer caso de algo, prestar atención a algo; **to take no ~ of sth** no hacer caso de algo; **he took no ~** no hizo caso; **take no ~!** ¡no hagas caso!, ¡no importa!; **I was not taking much ~ at the time** en ese momento iba algo distraído; **to sit up and take ~** aguzar las orejas, empezar a prestar atención.
2 VT **(a)** (*perceive*) notar, observar, reparar en, fijarse en; (*heed*) hacer caso de; (*recognize*) ver, reconocer; **I never ~d** no me había fijado; **I don't ~ such things** no me fijo en tales cosas; **eventually he deigned to ~ me** por fin se dignó reconocerme.
(b) (*review*) reseñar, escribir una reseña de.

noticeable ['nəʊtɪsəbl] ADJ evidente, obvio; sensible, perceptible; notable; **it was ~ that** ... era evidente que ..., se echaba de ver que ...; **there has been a ~ increase in** ... ha habido un aumento sensible de ...

noticeably ['nəʊtɪsəbl] ADV evidentemente, obviamente; sensiblemente; notablemente; **it has ~ improved** ha mejorado sensiblemente.

notice-board ['nəʊtɪsbɔːd] N (*Brit*) tablón *m* (de anuncios).

notifiable ['nəʊtɪfaɪəbl] ADJ de declaración obligatoria.

notification [,nəʊtɪfɪ'keɪʃən] N notificación *f*, aviso *m*.

notify ['nəʊtɪfaɪ] VT notificar, comunicar, avisar; **to ~ sb of sth** comunicar algo a uno, hacer saber algo a uno.

notion ['nəʊʃən] N **(a)** (*idea*) noción *f*, idea *f*; concepto *m*; (*view*) opinión *f*; (*whim*) idea *f*; capricho *m*; inclinación *f*; **what an odd ~!** ¡qué idea más rara!; **I have a ~ that** ... tengo la idea de que ..., se me ocurre pensar que ...; **to have no ~ of sth** no tener concepto alguno de algo; **you have no ~!** ¡no te lo puedes imaginar!; **I haven't the slightest ~** no tengo la más remota idea; **it's a ~ she has** es un capricho suyo, son cosas de ella; **to have a ~ to do sth** estar inclinado a hacer algo, estar dispuesto a hacer algo.
(b) **~s** (*US*) (artículos *mpl* de) mercería *f*.

notional ['nəʊʃənl] ADJ nocional; especulativo; hipotético; imaginario; **it is purely ~** existe en el pensamiento nada más, es teórico nada más.

notoriety [,nəʊtə'raɪətɪ] N celebridad *f*; (*pej*) mala fama *f*; escándalo *m*; **such was his ~ that** ... tan mala fama tuvo que ...

notorious [nəʊ'tɔːrɪəs] ADJ (*pej*) muy conocido, notorio; célebre (*for por*); de mala fama; escandaloso; **a ~ crime** un crimen muy sonado; **it is ~ that** ... es sabido que ..., es voz pública que ...; **he is ~ for his affairs** es archiconocido por sus amoríos.

notoriously [nəʊ'tɔːrɪəslɪ] ADJ notoriamente; **it is ~ difficult to** + *infin* se sabe perfectamente que es difícil + *infin*; **he is ~ unreliable** tiene fama de informal.

no-trumps ['nəʊ'trʌmps] N: **to bid 4 ~** marcar 4 sin triunfos.

Notts [nɒts] N ABBR *of* **Nottinghamshire**.

notwithstanding ['nɒtwɪð'stændɪŋ] **1** ADV no obstante, sin embargo; **this ~** no obstante esto, a pesar de esto; **this rule ~** no obstante esta regla; **I shall go ~** sin embargo iré, de todas formas iré.
2 PREP a pesar de.
3 CONJ (*also ~ that*) a pesar de que, por más que + *subj*.

nougat ['nuːgɑː] N ≈ turrón *m*.

nought [nɔːt] N nada *f*; (*Math etc*) cero *m*; **Murcia beat Granada two ~** el Murcia venció al Granada dos-cero; **~s and crosses** *juego parecido a tres en raya; see also* **naught**; *ver también* ZERO.

noun [naʊn] **1** N nombre *m*, sustantivo *m*.
2 ATTR: **~ clause** oración *f* sustantiva, cláusula *f* nominal; **~ phrase** frase *f* nominal.

nourish ['nʌrɪʃ] VT nutrir, alimentar, sustentar; (*fig*) fomentar, nutrir; **to ~ sb on sth** alimentar a uno con algo, dar a uno algo de comer.

nourishing ['nʌrɪʃɪŋ] ADJ nutritivo, rico; de gran valor alimenticio.

nourishment ['nʌrɪʃmənt] N alimento *m*, sustento *m*; nutrición *f*; **to derive ~ from** sustentarse de.

nous* [naʊs] N (*Brit*) chirumen* *m*, cacumen* *m*.

nouveau riche ['nuːvəʊ'riːʃ] N, PL **nouveaux riches** ['nuːvəʊ'riːʃ] nuevo rico *m*.

nouvelle cuisine ['nuːvelkwiː'ziːn] N nueva cocina *f*, nouvelle cuisine *f*.

Nov. ABBR *of* **November** nov.

Nova Scotia ['nəʊvə'skəʊʃə] N Nueva Escocia *f*.

Nova Scotian ['nəʊvə'skəʊʃən] **1** ADJ de Nueva Escocia.
2 N habitante *mf* de Nueva Escocia.

novel ['nɒvəl] **1** ADJ nuevo; original; insólito; **this is something ~** esto es nuevo.
2 N novela *f*.

novelette [,nɒvə'let] N novela *f* corta; (*pej*) novela *f* sentimental, novela *f* sin valor.

novelettish [,nɒvə'letɪʃ] ADJ sentimental, romántico.

novelist ['nɒvəlɪst] N novelista *mf*.

novella [nəʊ'velə] N novela *f* corta.

novelty ['nɒvəltɪ] N **(a)** (*newness*) novedad *f*; **once the ~ has worn off** cuando deja de parecer tan nuevo.
(b) (*new thing*) novedad *f*; innovación *f*; (*Comm*) novedad *f*.

November [nəʊ'vembər] N noviembre *m*.

novena [nəʊ'viːnə] N novena *f*.

novice ['nɒvɪs] N principiante *mf*, novato *m*, -a *f*; (*Eccl*) novicio *m*, -a *f*; (*Sport*) aprendiz *m*, -iza *f*; **a ~ painter** un pintor principiante, un aspirante a pintor; **he's no ~** no es ningún principiante; **to be a ~ at a job** ser nuevo en un oficio.

noviciate, novitiate [nəʊ'vɪʃɪt] N período *m* de aprendizaje; (*Eccl*) noviciado *m*.

novocaine ['nəʊvəʊkeɪn] N novocaína *f*.

NOW [naʊ] N (*US*) ABBR *of* **National Organization for Women**.

▼ **now** [naʊ] **1** ADV **(a)** (*at this time*) ahora; actualmente, al presente, hoy día; (*in past time*) luego, entonces; **just ~** (*right ~*) ahora mismo, en este momento, (*lately*) hace poco; **right ~** ahora mismo; **even ~** aun ahora; **even ~ we have no rifles** ni siquiera ahora tenemos fusiles; **not ~, dear** dejémoslo para después, querido; ahora no quiero, querido; **I must be off ~** me tengo que marchar ya; **they won't be long ~** ya no tardarán en venir; **it's ~ or never** es ahora o nunca; **~ I am committed** me he comprometido ya; **~ I'm ready** ya estoy listo; **(every) ~ and again, (every) ~ and then** de vez en cuando, cada cuando (*LAm*).
(b) (*alternation*) **~ she dances, ~ she sings** unas veces baila, otras veces canta; tan pronto baila como canta; **~ in France, ~ in Spain** ora en Francia, ora en España.
(c) (*with prep*) **before ~** (*already*) antes de ahora, antes, ya; (*at other times*) en otras ocasiones; **long before ~** hace tiempo ya, mucho tiempo ha; **between ~ and next Tuesday** entre hoy y el martes que viene; **by ~** ahora, ya; **they must be there by ~** habrán llegado ya; **by ~ everybody was tired** antes de eso todos se habían cansado; **3 weeks from ~** de hoy en 3 semanas; **a hundred years from ~** dentro de cien años; **from ~ on** a partir de ahora, de aquí en adelante; **as of ~** ahora; a partir de ahora; **until ~, up to ~** hasta ahora.
(d) (*without temporal force*) **~!** ¡a ver!; **come ~!** ¡vamos!, ¡no es para tanto!; **well ~** ahora bien; **~ then!** ¡vamos a ver!; **~ then, what's all this?** ¡eh! ¿qué hacéis aquí?; ¡eh! ¿qué es esto?; **~ ~, don't get so upset!** ¡oye, que no es para tanto!; **~ Johnny!** (*warning*) ¡oye, Juanito!
2 CONJ **(a)** **~ (that) you are 16** ahora que tienes 16 años; **take it, ~ that I've got 2** tómalo, pues tengo dos.
(b) (*without temporal force*) ahora bien, pues; **~ as you all know** ... pues como sabéis todos ...; **~ for the matter of your expenses** y por lo que respecta a sus gastos; **~ Peter was a fisherman** ahora bien, Pedro era pescador.

▼ **nowadays** ['naʊədeɪz] ADV hoy (en) día, actualmente, en la actualidad.

noways* ['nəʊweɪz] ADV (*US*) de ninguna manera.

nowhere ['nəʊwɛər] ADV **(a)** **I see it ~** no lo veo en ninguna parte; **you're going ~** no vas a ninguna parte; **~ in Europe** en ninguna parte de Europa; **~ else** en ninguna otra parte; **it's ~ you know** no es ningún sitio que conoces; **it's ~ you'll ever find it** está en un sitio donde no lo encontrarás nunca; **they seemed to come from** (*or* **out of**) **~** parecían haber salido de la nada.
(b) (*fig*) **it's ~ near as good** no es tan bueno ni con mucho, dista mucho de ser tan bueno; **A is ~ near as big as B** A no es tan grande como B ni con mucho; **the enemy looks ~ near giving in** el enemigo no da señales ni por aproximación de ceder; **the rest of the runners came ~** los demás atletas quedaron muy atrás; **in my opinion the rest come ~** en mi opinión los demás son muy inferiores; **without me he would be ~** sin mí no habría llegado a ninguna parte; **this is getting us ~** así no se llega a ninguna parte, esto no conduce a nada; **I'm getting ~ with this analysis** no consigo hacer carrera con este análisis.

no-win ['nəʊ'wɪn] ADJ: **a ~ situation** una situación imposible.

nowise ['nəʊwaɪz] ADV (*US*) de ninguna manera.

nowt [naʊt] N (*Brit dialectal*) = **nothing**.

noxious ['nɒkʃəs] ADJ nocivo, dañoso.

nozzle ['nɒzl] N (*Mech*) tobera *f*, inyector *m*; (*of hose, vacuum cleaner etc*) boquilla *f*; (*of spray*) pulverizador *m*.

NP N ABBR *of* **notary public**.

n.p. ABBR *of* **new paragraph** punto *m* y aparte.

n.p. or d. ABBR *of* **no place or date** s.l. ni f., sin lugar ni fecha.

NPV N (*Fin*) ABBR *of* **net present value**.

nr ABBR *of* **near** cerca de.

NRA **(a)** N (*Brit*) ABBR *of* **National Rivers Authority**. **(b)** N (*US*) ABBR *of* **National Rifle Association of America**.

NRA - NATIONAL RIFLE ASSOCIATION OF AMERICA

La **National Rifle Association of America** *o* **NRA** *(Asociación Nacional del Rifle) es uno de los grupos de presión más controvertidos y poderosos frente al Congreso de Estados Unidos. Cuenta con varios millones de socios, propietarios de armas de fuego para la caza o el tiro deportivo. La* **NRA** *promueve estos deportes al mismo tiempo que la conservación de la fauna, y organiza competiciones de tiro a nivel nacional. También se encarga de dar clases de seguridad para el uso de armas y apoya el derecho de todo estadounidense a tener armas de fuego para su propia defensa. La* **NRA** *ha recibido bastantes críticas por su oposición a las leyes de control de armas de fuego.*

NRV N (*Fin*) ABBR *of* **net realizable value**.

NS ABBR *of* **Nova Scotia** Nueva Escocia *f*.

NSB N (*Brit*) ABBR *of* **National Savings Bank**.

NSC N (*US*) ABBR *of* **National Security Council**.

NSF N (*US*) ABBR *of* **National Science Foundation**.

NSPCA N ABBR *of* **National Society for the Prevention of Cruelty to**

Animals.

NSPCC N ABBR of **National Society for the Prevention of Cruelty to Children**.

NSW ABBR of **New South Wales**.

NT N (a) ABBR of **New Testament**. (b) (*Brit*) ABBR of **National Trust**.

nth [enθ] ADJ V **N**.

NUAAW N (*Brit*) ABBR of **National Union of Agricultural and Allied Workers** sindicato de trabajadores del campo.

nuance ['njuːɑːns] N matiz *m*.

nub [nʌb] N pedazo *m*, trozo *m*; protuberancia *f*; (*fig*) lo esencial, parte *f* esencial; **that's the ~ of the question** ahí está el quid del asunto.

NUBE N (*Brit*) ABBR of **National Union of Bank Employees** sindicato de empleados bancarios.

nubile ['njuːbaɪl] ADJ núbil.

nuclear ['njuːklɪəʳ] ADJ nuclear; **~ age** era *f* nuclear; **~ bomb** bomba *f* nuclear; **~ confrontation** confrontación *f* nuclear; **~ device** ingenio *m* nuclear; **~ energy** energía *f* nuclear; **~ family** familia *f* nuclear; **~ fission** fisión *f* nuclear; **~ fuel** combustible *m* nuclear; **~ fusion** fusión *f* nuclear; **~ physics** física *f* nuclear; **~ power** fuerza *f* nuclear, energía *f* nuclear; **~ power station** central *f* nuclear; **~ reaction** reacción *f* nuclear; **~ reactor** reactor *m* nuclear; **~ shelter** refugio *m* antinuclear; **~ submarine** submarino *m* nuclear; **~ test** prueba *f* nuclear; **~ waste** vertidos *mpl* nucleares, residuos *mpl* nucleares; **~ weapon** arma *f* nuclear; **~ winter** invierno *m* nuclear.

nuclear-free ['njuːklɪə,friː] ADJ desnuclearizado, no nuclear; **~ zone** zona *f* desnuclearizada.

nuclei ['njuːklɪaɪ] NPL of **nucleus**.

nucleic ['njuːklɪɪk] ADJ: **~ acid** ácido *m* nucleico.

nucleo... ['njuːklɪəʊ] PREF nucleo....

nucleus ['njuːklɪəs] N, PL **nuclei** ['njuːklɪaɪ] núcleo *m*; **the ~ of a library** el núcleo de una biblioteca; **we have the ~ of a crew** tenemos los elementos indispensables para formar una tripulación.

NUCPS N (*Brit*) ABBR of **National Union of Civil and Public Servants** sindicato de funcionarios.

nude [njuːd] **1** ADJ desnudo.
2 N (a) (*Art*) desnudo *m*; **a ~ of Goya** un desnudo de Goya. (b) (*person*) desnudo *m*; mujer *f* desnuda. (c) **in the ~** desnudo.

nudge [nʌdʒ] **1** N codazo *m* (ligero); **he said 'she's his secretary, ~ ~'** dijo que 'ella es su secretaria, tú ya me entiendes'.
2 VT dar un codazo a; empujar (ligeramente); **to ~ sb's memory** refrescar la memoria de uno.

nudie: ['njuːdɪ] N (*also* **~ magazine**) revista *f* porno*.

nudism ['njuːdɪzəm] N nudismo *m*.

nudist ['njuːdɪst] **1** N nudista *mf*.
2 ATTR: **~ colony** colonia *f* de nudistas.

nudity ['njuːdɪtɪ] N desnudez *f*, desnudo *m*.

nugatory ['njuːgətərɪ] ADJ (*trivial*) insignificante; (*useless*) ineficaz, fútil, baladí.

nugget ['nʌgɪt] N (*Min*) pepita *f*; **gold ~** pepita *f* de oro.

▼ **nuisance** ['njuːsns] **1** N (a) (*thing, event*) molestia *f*, incomodidad *f*; fastidio *m*, lata* *f*; **what a ~!** ¡qué lata!*, ¡qué fastidio!; **this hat is a ~** este sombrero me está fastidiando, me estoy armando un lío con este sombrero; **the ~ of having to shave** la incomodidad de tener que afeitarse; **it's a ~ having to shave** es una lata tener que afeitarse; **'commit no ~'** 'mantenga limpio este sitio', (*more specifically*) 'prohibido hacer aguas'.
(b) (*person*) moscón *m*, pelmazo *m*; pesado *m*; **what a ~ you are!** ¡eres un pesado!; **you're being a ~** me estás dando la lata; **to make a ~ of o.s.** dar la lata.
(c) (*Jur*) perjuicio *m*, daño *m*.
2 ATTR: **~ value** valor *m* como irritante.

NUJ N (*Brit*) ABBR of **National Union of Journalists** sindicato de periodistas.

nuke* [njuːk] (*esp US*) **1** VT atacar con arma nuclear.
2 N bomba *f* atómica.

null [nʌl] ADJ nulo, inválido; **~ and void** nulo, sin efecto, sin fuerza legal; **to render sb's efforts ~** invalidar los esfuerzos de uno.

nullification [,nʌlɪfɪ'keɪʃən] N anulación *f*, invalidación *f*.

nullify ['nʌlɪfaɪ] VT anular, invalidar.

nullity ['nʌlɪtɪ] N nulidad *f*.

NUM N (*Brit*) ABBR of **National Union of Mineworkers** sindicato de mineros.

numb [nʌm] **1** ADJ entumecido; (*fig*) insensible; **my leg has gone ~** se me ha dormido la pierna; **to be ~ with cold** estar entumecido de frío, (*fig*) estar helado; **to be ~ with fright** estar paralizado de temor.
2 VT entumecer, entorpecer.

numbed [nʌmd] ADJ entumecido; (*fig*) insensible.

number ['nʌmbəʳ] **1** N (a) (*Math*) número *m*; (*figure*) número *m*, cifra *f*; (*Gram, Telec, etc*) número *m*; **a ~ of** algunos, varios, una porción de; **a ~ of people have protested** varias personas han protestado; **a large ~ of people** buen número de personas, muchas personas; **in a**

small ~ of cases en unos pocos casos, en contados casos; **on a ~ of occasions** en diversas ocasiones, varias veces; **any ~ of** la mar de; **any ~ of times** muchísimas veces; **to do sth by ~s** (*US*: **by the ~s**) hacer algo siguiendo las instrucciones; (*fig*) hacer algo paso a paso; **to be few in ~** ser pocos; **to be 8 in ~** ser 8; **to come in ~s** venir en tropel, venir en masa; **they exist in ~s in Africa** en África hay muchos, en África son frecuentes; **one of their ~** uno de ellos; **he is not of that ~** no es de ésos, no forma parte de ese grupo; **to the ~ of some 200** en número de unos 200; **times without ~** muchísimas veces; **his ~ is up*** todo se acabó para él; **his ~ came up** su número salió premiado; **I've got his ~ now*** le tengo calado ya.
(b) (*of house etc*) número *m*; (*of car etc*) matrícula *f*; **N~ Ten** el Número Diez (*de Downing Street, Londres, residencia del primer ministro*); **we live at No. 15** vivimos en el núm. 15; **the ~ one Spanish player** el jugador número uno de España; **to look after N~ One** mirar por sí, cuidar de sí mismo; **did you get his ~?** ¿has apuntado la matrícula?
(c) (*person*) **a nice little ~*** una chica monísima; **my opposite ~ in France** mi equivalente en Francia, mi homólogo francés.
(d) **a good ~:** (*job*) un buen chollo:.
(e) (*of journal*) número *m*.
(f) (*Theat etc*) número *m*; **and for my next ~...** ahora voy a cantar (*etc*) ...
(g) **~s** (*Poet*) versos *mpl*.
2 VT (a) (*count*) contar; **the library ~s 30,000 books** la biblioteca cuenta con 30.000 libros, la biblioteca posee 30.000 libros; **to ~ sb among one's friends** contar a uno entre sus amigos; **to be ~ed among** figurar entre, ser de; **his days are ~ed** tiene los días contados; **his days seem to be ~ed** sus días parecen contados.
(b) (*amount to*) ascender a, sumar; **they ~ 187** hay 187, ascienden a 187, suman 187; **they ~ several hundreds** hay varios centenares.
(c) (*assign ~ to*) numerar, poner número a; **MS pages** foliar; **the houses are not ~ed** las casas no están numeradas, las casas no tienen número; **~ed account** cuenta *f* numerada.
3 VI: **to ~ off** numerarse (*from the right* por la derecha).

number-cruncher* ['nʌmbə,krʌntʃəʳ] N (*machine*) machacadora *f* de números; **he's ~** él se encarga de los números.

number-crunching* ['nʌmbə,krʌntʃɪŋ] N machaqueo *m* de números, cálculo *m* a gran escala.

numbering ['nʌmbərɪŋ] **1** N numeración *f*.
2 ATTR: **~ machine** numerador *m*.

numberless ['nʌmbəlɪs] ADJ innumerable, sin número.

number plate ['nʌmbəpleɪt] N (*Brit Aut etc*) (placa *f* de) matrícula *f*.

numbers game ['nʌmbəz'geɪm] N, **numbers racket** ['nʌmbəz'rækɪt] N (*US*) lotería clandestina en Norteamérica.

numbhead* ['nʌmhed] N (*US*) tonto *m*, -a *f*, bobo *m*, -a *f*.

numbness ['nʌmnɪs] N entumecimiento *m*; (*fig*) insensibilidad *f*; parálisis *f*.

num(b)skull ['nʌmskʌl] N zote *m*, majadero *m*; **you ~!** ¡majadero!

numeracy ['njuːmərəsɪ] N competencia *f* en el cálculo, competencia *f* en matemáticas.

numeral ['njuːmərəl] **1** ADJ numeral.
2 N número *m*, cifra *f*, guarismo *m*.

numerate ['njuːmərɪt] ADJ competente en el cálculo, competente en las matemáticas.

numeration [,njuːmə'reɪʃən] N numeración *f*.

numerator ['njuːməreɪtəʳ] N numerador *m*.

numeric [njuː'merɪk] ADJ numérico; **~ field** campo *m* numérico; **~ keypad** teclado *m* numérico.

numerical [njuː'merɪkəl] ADJ numérico.

numerically [njuː'merɪkəlɪ] ADV numéricamente; **~ superior to** con superioridad numérica a, superiores en cuanto a su número a.

numerological [,njuːmərə'lɒdʒɪkəl] ADJ numerológico.

numerology [,njuːmə'rɒlədʒɪ] N numerología *f*.

numerous ['njuːmərəs] ADJ numeroso; muchos; **a ~ family** una familia numerosa; **in ~ cases** en muchos casos; **~ people believe that ...** mucha gente cree que ...

numismatic [,njuːmɪz'mætɪk] ADJ numismático.

numismatics [,njuːmɪz'mætɪks] N numismática *f*.

numismatist [njuː'mɪzmətɪst] N numismático *mf*, numismata *mf*.

nun [nʌn] N monja *f*, religiosa *f*; **to become a ~** tomar el hábito, meterse monja.

nunciature ['nʌnʃɪətjʊəʳ] N nunciatura *f*.

nuncio ['nʌnʃɪəʊ] N (*also* **papal ~**) nuncio *m* apostólico.

nunnery ['nʌnərɪ] N convento *m* de monjas.

NUPE ['njuːpɪ] N (*Brit*) ABBR of **National Union of Public Employees** sindicato de funcionarios.

nuptial ['nʌpʃəl] ADJ nupcial.

nuptials ['nʌpʃəlz] NPL (*hum*) nupcias *fpl*.

NUR N (*Brit*) ABBR of **National Union of Railwaymen** sindicato de ferroviarios.

nurd: [nɜːd] N borde* *mf*.

nurse [nɜːs] ①① N (Med) enfermera f; (male ~) enfermero m; (wet-~) nodriza f, ama f de leche; (children's) niñera f.
② VT (a) patient cuidar, atender, asistir; (US: suckle) criar, amamantar; (Brit: in arms) mecer; **to ~ sb back to health** cuidar a uno hasta que se reponga; **to ~ a cold** tratar de curarse de un resfriado.
(b) (fig) **to ~ a constituency** (Brit Parl) establecerse (entre elecciones) como candidato en un distrito electoral; **to ~ a business along** fomentar un negocio, promover un negocio.

nursemaid ['nɜːsmeɪd] N niñera f, chacha* f.

nursery ['nɜːsrɪ] ①① N (a) cuarto m de los niños; **from the ~** desde la niñez, desde niño. (b) (Agr etc) vivero m, semillero m, plantel m; (fig, Sport) cantera f; **a ~ for new players** una cantera de jóvenes jugadores.
② ATTR: **~ education** educación f preescolar; **~ nurse** puericultor m, -ora f; **~ schooling** = **~ education**; **~ school teacher** maestro m, -a f de preescolar; **~ slopes** (Brit Ski) pistas fpl para principiantes.

nurseryman ['nɜːsrɪmən] N, PL **nurserymen** ['nɜːsrɪmən] horticultor m.

nursery-rhyme ['nɜːsrɪraɪm] N canción f infantil.

nursery-school ['nɜːsrɪ,skuːl] N jardín m de infancia, parvulario m.

nursing ['nɜːsɪŋ] ①① ADJ (a) **~ auxiliary** (Brit) auxiliar mf de enfermería; **~ college** escuela f de enfermería; **~ officer** enfermero m jefe, enfermera f jefe (or jefa); **~ staff** enfermeras fpl.
(b) **~ mother** madre f lactante.
② N (of patient) asistencia f, cuidado m; (career, course, profession) enfermería f; (suckling) lactancia f; **to go in for ~** hacerse enfermera, dedicarse a la enfermería.

nursing-home ['nɜːsɪŋ,həʊm] N (esp Brit) clínica f (particular); (US) asilo m de ancianos.

nursling ['nɜːslɪŋ] N lactante mf, niño m, -a f de pecho.

nurture ['nɜːtʃəʳ] ①① N (nourishment) nutrición f; (bringing-up) educación f, crianza f.
② VT alimentar, nutrir (on de); educar, criar.

NUS N (Brit) (a) ABBR of **National Union of Students** sindicato de estudiantes. (b) ABBR of **National Union of Seamen** sindicato de marineros.

NUT N (Brit) ABBR of **National Union of Teachers** sindicato de profesores.

nut [nʌt] ①① N (a) (Bot) nuez f; **it's a hard ~ to crack** es un hueso duro de roer; **he's a tough ~** es un sujeto duro; **he can't play for ~s*** no juega nada.
(b) (‡: head) cholla‡ f; **he's off his ~** le falta un tornillo*; **you must be off your ~** ¿estás grillado?‡; **to do one's ~** (Brit) echar el resto*.
(c) (‡: madman) chiflado* m, -a f; (eccentric) excéntrico m, -a f; (enthusiast) entusiasta mf, maniático m, -a f.
(d) ~s‡‡ (esp US Anat) cojones‡‡ mpl.
(e) ~s!* (EXCL: US) ¡narices!*
(f) (Mech) tuerca f; **the ~s and bolts of a scheme** los aspectos prácticos de un proyecto.
② ATTR: **~ chocolate** chocolate m de nueces.

nut-brown ['nʌt'braʊn] ADJ café avellana; hair castaño claro.

nutcase‡ ['nʌtkeɪs] N pirado‡ m, -a f.

nutcracker(s) ['nʌt,krækəz] NPL cascanueces m; **a pair of nutcrackers** un cascanueces; **The Nutcracker** (Mus) El Cascanueces.

nuthatch ['nʌthætʃ] N trepador m, trepatroncos m.

nuthouse‡ ['nʌthaʊs] N, PL **nuthouses** ['nʌthaʊzɪz] manicomio m, casa f de locos.

nutmeg ['nʌtmeg] N nuez f moscada.

nutrasweet ['njuːtrəswiːt] ® N edulcorante m, sacarina f.

nutrient ['njuːtrɪənt] ①① ADJ nutritivo.
② N nutriente m.

nutriment ['njuːtrɪmənt] N nutrimento m, alimento m.

nutrition [njuːˈtrɪʃən] N nutrición f, alimentación f.

nutritional [njuːˈtrɪʃənl] ADJ value etc nutritivo, nutricional.

nutritionist [njuːˈtrɪʃənɪst] N nutricionista mf.

nutritious [njuːˈtrɪʃəs] ADJ, **nutritive** ['njuːtrɪtɪv] ADJ nutritivo, rico.

nuts‡ [nʌts] ADJ: **to be ~** estar chiflado*; **to be ~ about a girl** estar chalado por una*; **to be ~ about sth** pirrarse por algo‡; **to drive sb ~** volver loco a uno; **to go ~** volverse loco.

nutshell ['nʌtʃel] N cáscara f de nuez; **in a ~** en resumidas cuentas; **to put it in a ~** para decirlo brevemente; **that puts it in a ~** eso lo dice en pocas palabras.

nut-tree ['nʌttriː] N (hazel) avellano m, (walnut) nogal m.

nutter‡ ['nʌtəʳ] N (Brit) chiflado* m, -a f.

nutty ['nʌtɪ] ADJ (a) colour de nuez; cake con nueces; taste a nueces, que sabe a nueces; sherry almendrado, avellanado. (b) (‡) loco; **to be ~** estar loco; **to be ~ about sth** estar loco por algo.

nuzzle ['nʌzl] ①① VT acariciar con el hocico.
② VI = **snuggle, nestle**.

NV (US Post) ABBR of **Nevada**.

NVQ N (Brit) ABBR of **National Vocational Qualification**.

┌─ **NVQ – NATIONAL VOCATIONAL QUALIFICATION** ─┐

i La **National Vocational Qualification** o **NVQ** es una titulación profesional dirigida sobre todo a personas que ya han entrado en el mundo laboral, aunque en algunos casos puede cursarse también durante el período escolar, a la vez que o en vez de algún otro título académico como los **GCSEs** o los **A-levels**. La evaluación se hace a través del trabajo práctico realizado durante el curso y a través de exámenes orales y escritos. Este sistema funciona en Inglaterra, Gales e Irlanda del Norte, mientras que en Escocia funciona un sistema similar, el llamado **Scottish Vocational Qualification** o **SVQ**.
⇒ Ver también [GCSE], [ADVANCED LEVELS]
└─────────────────────────────────┘

NW ABBR of **north-west** NO m, noroeste m (also ADJ).

N.W.T. ABBR of **Northwest Territories**.

NY (US Post) ABBR of **New York**.

NYC (US Post) ABBR of **New York City**.

nylon ['naɪlɒn] ①① N nilón m, nailon m; **~s** medias fpl de nilón.
② ADJ de nilón, de nailon.

nymph [nɪmf] N ninfa f.

nymphet(te) [nɪmˈfet] N nínfula f.

nympho* ['nɪmfəʊ], **nymphomaniac** [,nɪmfəʊˈmeɪnɪæk] ①① ADJ ninfómano.
② N ninfómana f.

nymphomania [,nɪmfəʊˈmeɪnɪə] N ninfomanía f, furor m uterino.

NYPD N (US) ABBR of **New York Police Department**.

NYSE N (US) ABBR of **New York Stock Exchange**.

NZ ABBR of **New Zealand**.

O

O¹, o [əʊ] N (*letter*) O, o *f*; **O for Oliver, O for Oboe** (*US*) O de Oviedo; **O-grade** (*Scot Scol*), **O-Level** (*Brit Scol*) V **ordinary.**

O² [əʊ] = **oh.**

O & M N ABBR *of* **Organization and Methods** organización *f* y métodos.

o/a ABBR *of* **on account** a cuenta.

oaf [əʊf] N zoquete *m*, patán *m*.

oafish ['əʊfɪʃ] ADJ lerdo, zafio.

oak [əʊk] 1 N roble *m*; **to sport one's ~** (*Univ*) cerrar la puerta (para no recibir visitas). 2 ATTR de roble.

oak-apple ['əʊk‚æpl] N agalla *f* (de roble).

oaken ['əʊkən] ADJ de roble.

oakum ['əʊkəm] N estopa *f* (de calafatear).

oakwood ['əʊkwʊd] N robledo *m*.

O.A.P. N (*Brit*) **(a)** ABBR *of* **old age pension** subsidio *m* de vejez. **(b)** ABBR *of* **old age pensioner** pensionista *mf*.

OAPEC [əʊ'eɪpek] N ABBR *of* **Organization of Arab Petroleum Exporting Countries** Organización *f* de Países Árabes Exportadores de Petróleo, OPAEP *f*.

oar [ɔːʳ] N **(a)** remo *m*; **to lie** (*or* **rest**) **on one's ~s** dejar de remar, (*fig*) descansar, dormir sobre sus laureles; **to put** (*or* **shove**) **one's ~ in** meter su cuchara; **to ship the ~s** desarmar los remos. **(b)** (*person*) remero *m*, -a *f*; **to be a good ~** ser buen remero, remar bien.

oared [ɔːd] ADJ provisto de remos; (*in cpds*) de ... remos, *eg* **eight-~** de ocho remos.

oarlock ['ɔːlɒk] N (*US*) tolete *m*, escálamo *m*, chumacera *f*.

oarsman ['ɔːzmən] N, PL **oarsmen** ['ɔːzmən] remero *m*.

oarsmanship ['ɔːzmənʃɪp] N arte *m* de remar.

OAS N ABBR *of* **Organization of American States** Organización *f* de Estados Americanos, OEA *f*.

oasis [əʊ'eɪsɪs] N, PL **oases** [əʊ'eɪsiːz] oasis *m* (*also fig*).

oast-house ['əʊsthaʊs] N, PL **oast-houses** ['əʊsthaʊzɪz] secadero *m* para lúpulo.

oat bran ['əʊt‚bræn] N (*US*) salvado *m* de avena.

oatcake ['əʊtkeɪk] N torta *f* de avena.

oaten ['əʊtn] ADJ de avena.

oatfield ['əʊtfiːld] N avenal *m*.

oath [əʊθ] N, PL **oaths** [əʊðz] **(a)** (*solemn promise etc*) juramento *m*; **under ~, on ~,** bajo juramento; **to administer an ~ to sb** tomar juramento a uno; **to break one's ~** violar su juramento; **to put sb on ~** hacer prestar juramento a uno; **to take the** (*or* **an**) **~** prestar juramento (*on* sobre); **to take an ~ that** ... jurar que ...; **to take the ~ of allegiance** (*Mil*) jurar la bandera. **(b)** (*curse*) blasfemia *f*, reniego *m*, palabrota *f*.

oatmeal ['əʊtmiːl] N harina *f* de avena.

oats [əʊts] NPL avena *f*; **to be off one's ~** estar desganado, haber perdido el apetito; **to get one's ~**❡ mojar (con regularidad)❡.

OAU N ABBR *of* **Organization of African Unity** Organización *f* para la Unidad Africana, OUA *f*.

OB (*TV*) N ABBR *of* **outside broadcast** transmisión *f* exterior.

ob. ABBR *of* **obiit, died** murió, m.

Obadiah [‚əʊbə'daɪə] NM Abdías.

obbligato [‚ɒblɪ'ɡɑːtəʊ] N obligado *m*.

obduracy ['ɒbdjʊrəsɪ] N obstinación *f*, terquedad *f*; inflexibilidad *f*.

obdurate ['ɒbdjʊrɪt] ADJ obstinado, terco; (*in refusing etc*) inflexible.

OBE N (*Brit*) ABBR *of* **Officer of the Order of the British Empire**; *ver también* ⌈HONOURS LIST⌉.

obedience [ə'biːdɪəns] N obediencia *f*; sumisión *f*; docilidad *f*; **in ~ to** conforme a, de acuerdo con; **in ~ to your wishes** accediendo a sus deseos; **to compel ~** exigir obediencia (*from* a).

obedient [ə'biːdɪənt] ADJ obediente; sumiso, dócil; **to be ~ to** ser obediente a, obedecer a.

obediently [ə'biːdɪəntlɪ] ADV obedientemente; sumisamente, dócilmente; **yours ~** su atento servidor.

obeisance [əʊ'beɪsəns] N (*bow etc*) reverencia *f*; (*salutation*) saludo *m*; (*homage*) homenaje *m*; **to do** (*or* **make, pay**) **~ to** tributar homenaje a.

obelisk ['ɒbɪlɪsk] N obelisco *m*.

obese [əʊ'biːs] ADJ obeso.

obeseness [əʊ'biːsnɪs] N, **obesity** [əʊ'biːsɪtɪ] N obesidad *f*.

obey [ə'beɪ] VT (*person etc*) obedecer; (*pay heed to*) hacer caso a; *need, controls* responder a; *summons* acudir a; *law* cumplir, observar, obrar de acuerdo con; *instruction* cumplir; **I like to be ~ed** me gusta que se me obedezca.

obfuscate ['ɒbfəskeɪt] VT ofuscar.

obit* ['ɒbɪt] N = **obituary 2.**

obituary [ə'bɪtjʊərɪ] 1 ADJ necrológico; **~ column** sección *f* necrológica; **~ notice** necrología *f*; esquela *f* (mortuoria). 2 N necrología *f*, obituario *m*.

object 1 ['ɒbdʒɪkt] N **(a)** (*thing in general*) objeto *m*; cosa *f*, artículo *m*; (*pej: thing*) mamarracho *m*, (*person*) mamarracho *m*, espantajo *m*, estantigua *f*; **she was an ~ of pity to all** daba lástima a cuantos la veían; **he became an ~ of ridicule** se puso en ridículo. **(b)** (*aim*) objeto *m*, propósito *m*, intento *m*; **~ language** lengua *f* objeto; **~ programme** programa *m* objeto; **with this ~ in view** con este propósito; **with the ~ of** con el propósito de, al objeto de; **what is the ~ of the plan?** ¿qué finalidad tiene el plan?; **expense is no ~** no importan los gastos; **money is no ~** cueste lo que cueste. **(c)** (*Gram*) complemento *m*. 2 [əb'dʒekt] VT: **to ~ that** ... objetar que ...; **to this it was ~ed that** ... a esto se objetó que ... 3 [əb'dʒekt] VI hacer objeciones, oponerse; poner reparos; **I ~!** ¡protesto!; **I ~ most strongly!** ¡me opongo rotundamente a ello!; **if you don't ~** si no tienes inconveniente; **I ~ to that remark!** ¡protesto contra esa observación! **to ~ to sb doing sth** oponerse a que uno haga algo; **do you ~ to my going?** ¿te opones a que vaya yo?; **do you ~ to my smoking?** ¿te molesta que fume?; **I don't ~ to an occasional drink** no me opongo a que se tome algo de vez en cuando.

▼ **objection** [əb'dʒekʃən] N objeción *f*, reparo *m*; protesta *f*; (*difficulty*) inconveniente *m*; obstáculo *m*, dificultad *f*; **~!** ¡yo protesto!; **what are the ~s?** ¿qué obstáculo hay?, ¿cuáles son las dificultades?; **there is no ~** no hay inconveniente; **there is no ~ to your going** no hay inconveniente en que vayas; **I can find no ~ to it** no le encuentro ninguna dificultad; **I have no ~** no tengo inconveniente; **if you have no ~** si no tienes inconveniente; **have you any ~ to my smoking?** ¿te molesta que fume?; **have you any ~ to my going?** ¿tienes algún inconveniente en que vaya yo?; **he made no ~** no hizo ninguna objeción, no protestó, no se opuso a ello; **to raise ~s** poner reparos (*to* a), protestar (*to* contra); **I see no ~** no veo inconveniente.

objectionable [əb'dʒekʃnəbl] ADJ desagradable; *person* molesto, pesado; indeseable; *conduct etc* reprensible, censurable; **a most ~ person** una persona inaguantable.

objective [əb'dʒektɪv] 1 ADJ objetivo; **~ test** prueba *f* objetiva. 2 N objetivo *m*.

objectively [əb'dʒektɪvlɪ] ADV objetivamente.

objectivism [əb'dʒektɪvɪzəm] N objetivismo *m*.

objectivity [‚ɒbdʒɪk'tɪvɪtɪ] N objetividad *f*.

object-lesson ['ɒbdʒɪkt‚lesn] N lección *f* práctica, ejemplo *m*; **it was an ~ in good manners** fue una perfecta demostración de cortesía.

objector [əb'dʒektəʳ] N objetante *mf*.

objurgate ['ɒbdʒɜːgeɪt] VT increpar, reprender.

objurgation [‚ɒbdʒɜː'ɡeɪʃən] N increpación *f*, reprensión *f*.

oblation [əʊ'bleɪʃən] N oblación f; (gift) oblata f, ofrenda f.

obligate ['ɒblɪgeɪt] VT: **to ~ sb to do sth** obligar a uno a hacer algo; **to be ~d to** + infin estar obligado a + infin.

▼ **obligation** [ˌɒblɪ'geɪʃən] N obligación f; deber m; compromiso m; **of ~** (Eccl) de precepto; **without ~** (in advert) sin compromiso; '**no ~ to buy'** 'sin compromiso a comprar'; **it is your ~ to see that ...** le cumple a Vd comprobar que + subj, es su deber comprobar que + subj; **to be under an ~ to sb** deber favores a uno; **to be under an ~ to** + infin deber + infin, haberse comprometido a + infin, tener obligación de + infin; **to lay** (or **put**) **sb under an ~** poner a uno bajo una obligación; **to meet one's ~s** (Comm) cumplir sus compromisos; **to fail to meet one's ~s** no poder cumplir sus compromisos.

obligatory [ɒ'blɪgətərɪ] ADJ obligatorio; **to make it ~ for sb to do sth** imponer a uno la obligación de + infin.

▼ **oblige** [ə'blaɪdʒ] VT **(a)** (force) obligar, forzar; **to ~ sb to do sth** obligar a uno a hacer algo, forzar a uno a hacer algo; **to be ~d to do sth** verse obligado a hacer algo; **you are not ~d to do it** nada te obliga a hacerlo.
(b) (gratify) complacer, hacer un favor a; **you would greatly ~ me if ...** agradecería mucho que + subj; **anything to ~ a friend!** ¡lo que sea por complacer a un amigo!; **he did it to ~ us** lo hizo como favor, lo hizo para complacernos; **to ~ sb with a match** hacer a uno el favor de (prestarle, darle) una cerilla; **much ~d!** ¡muchísimas gracias!, ¡se agradece!; **I should be much ~d if ...** agradecería que + subj; **I am ~d to you for your help** agradezco su ayuda; **to be ~d to sb** estar en deuda con uno.

obligee [ˌɒblɪ'dʒiː] N tenedor m de una obligación.

obliging [ə'blaɪdʒɪŋ] ADJ servicial, atento, obsequioso.

obligingly [ə'blaɪdʒɪŋlɪ] ADV atentamente; **he very ~ helped us** muy amablemente nos ayudó.

oblique [ə'bliːk] ① ADJ oblicuo; reference etc indirecto, tangencial; **~ angle** ángulo m oblicuo.
② N (Typ) barra f (oblicua).

obliquely [ə'bliːklɪ] ADV ~ oblicuamente; indirectamente, tangencialmente.

obliqueness [ə'bliːknɪs] N, **obliquity** [ə'blɪkwɪtɪ] N oblicuidad f; lo indirecto, lo tangencial.

obliterate [ə'blɪtəreɪt] VT borrar, eliminar, destruir toda huella de; town etc arrasar, destruir; (Med) obliterar.

obliteration [əˌblɪtə'reɪʃən] N borradura f, eliminación f; arrasamiento m, destrucción f; (Med) obliteración f.

oblivion [ə'blɪvɪən] N olvido m; **to cast into ~** echar al olvido; **to fall** (or **sink**) **into ~** sumirse en el olvido.

oblivious [ə'blɪvɪəs] ADJ: **to be ~ of, to be ~ to** estar inconsciente de; **he, totally ~ of what was happening ...** él, totalmente inconsciente de lo que pasaba ...

oblong ['ɒblɒŋ] ① ADJ oblongo, apaisado.
② N oblongo m.

obloquy ['ɒbləkwɪ] N (abuse) injurias fpl, calumnia f; (shame) deshonra f; **to cover sb with ~** llenar a uno de injurias.

obnoxious [əb'nɒkʃəs] ADJ detestable, repugnante, odioso; fumes etc nocivo, desagradable; **it is ~ to me to** + infin me repugna + infin, me es repugnante + infin.

o.b.o. (US) ABBR of **or best offer** abierto ofertas.

oboe ['əʊbəʊ] N oboe m.

oboist ['əʊbəʊɪst] N oboe mf (persona).

obscene [əb'siːn] ADJ obsceno, indecente, escabroso, procaz.

obscenely [əb'siːnlɪ] ADV obscenamente, escabrosamente.

obscenity [əb'senɪtɪ] N obscenidad f, indecencia f, escabrosidad f, procacidad f; **to utter obscenities** proferir obscenidades.

obscurantism [ˌɒbskjʊə'ræntɪzəm] N oscurantismo m.

obscurantist [ˌɒbskjʊə'ræntɪst] ① ADJ oscurantista.
② N oscurantista mf.

obscure [əb'skjʊər] ① ADJ oscuro (also fig).
② VT oscurecer; (eclipse) eclipsar; (hide) esconder; issue entenebrecer, confundir; memory, glory etc oscurecer; **the house is ~d by the trees** la casa está escondida detrás de los árboles; **it served only to ~ the matter further** sirvió para complicar aun más el asunto.

obscurely [əb'skjʊəlɪ] ADV oscuramente.

obscurity [əb'skjʊərɪtɪ] N oscuridad f (also fig); **to live in ~** vivir en la oscuridad.

obsequies ['ɒbsɪkwɪz] NPL exequias fpl.

obsequious [əb'siːkwɪəs] ADJ servil.

obsequiously [əb'siːkwɪəslɪ] ADV servilmente.

obsequiousness [əb'siːkwɪəsnɪs] N servilismo m.

observable [əb'zɜːvəbl] ADJ observable, visible; **as is ~ in rabbits** según se puede apreciar en los conejos; **no ~ difference** ninguna diferencia perceptible.

observably [əb'zɜːvəblɪ] ADV visiblemente.

observance [əb'zɜːvəns] N **(a)** (of rule etc) observancia f (of de), cumplimiento m (of con); (rite etc) práctica f; **members of the strict ~** miembros mpl de la estricta observancia. **(b)** (custom) costumbre f.

observant [əb'zɜːvənt] ADJ observador, perspicaz; (watchful) vigilante; (attentive) atento; **the child is very ~** el niño es muy observador.

observation [ˌɒbzə'veɪʃən] ① N **(a)** (in most senses) observación f; (of rule etc) observancia f; **to be under ~** estar vigilado; (Med) estar en observación; **we can keep the valley under ~ from here** desde aquí dominamos el valle; **the police are keeping him under ~** la policía le está vigilando; **to escape ~** pasar inadvertido.
(b) (remark) observación f, comentario m; '**O~s on Sterne'** 'Apuntes mpl sobre Sterne'.
② ATTR: **~ car** (Rail) vagón-mirador m, coche m panorámico; **~ post** puesto m de observación; **~ tower** torre f (or torreta f) de observación.

observatory [əb'zɜːvətrɪ] N observatorio m.

observe [əb'zɜːv] VT **(a)** (obey) rule, custom observar; cumplir; Sabbath, silence guardar; care usar de, emplear; anniversary celebrar; **failure to ~ the law** incumplimiento m de la ley.
(b) (take note of, watch) observar; examinar; suspect vigilar; **I ~d him steal the duck** le vi robar el pato; **now ~ this closely** fijaos bien en esto.
(c) (say) observar, decir; **I ~d to him that ...** le hice observar que ...; **as Jeeves ~d** según dijo Jeeves.

observer [əb'zɜːvər] N observador m, -ora f.

obsess [əb'ses] VT obsesionar, causar obsesión a; **he is ~ed with this idea** está obsesionado por esta idea, le obsesiona esta idea.

obsession [əb'seʃən] N obsesión f; idea f fija, manía f; **the ~ about cleanliness** la obsesión de la limpieza, la manía de la limpieza; **to have an ~ about an idea** estar obsesionado por una idea; **it's an ~ with him** es una manía que tiene.

obsessional [əb'seʃənəl] ADJ obsesivo.

obsessive [əb'sesɪv] ADJ obsesionante.

obsessively [əb'sesɪvlɪ] ADV de modo obsesionante.

obsidian [ɒb'sɪdɪən] N obsidiana f.

obsolescence [ˌɒbsə'lesns] N caída f en desuso, obsolescencia f.

obsolescent [ˌɒbsə'lesnt] ADJ algo anticuado; **to be ~** irse haciendo anticuado, estar cayendo en desuso.

obsolete ['ɒbsəliːt] ADJ obsoleto.

obstacle ['ɒbstəkl] N obstáculo m; estorbo m, impedimento m, inconveniente m; **~s to independence** los factores que dificultan la independencia; **one of the ~s is money** uno de los obstáculos es el dinero; **to be an ~ to progress** ser un estorbo al progreso; **that is no ~ to our doing it** eso no impide que lo hagamos; **to put ~s in sb's way** crear dificultades a uno, dificultar el camino a uno.

obstacle course ['ɒbstəkl,kɔːs] N pista f americana.

obstacle race ['ɒbstəkl,reɪs] N carrera f de obstáculos.

obstetric(al) [ɒb'stetrɪk(əl)] ADJ obstétrico.

obstetrician [ˌɒbstə'trɪʃən] N obstétrico m, -a f.

obstetrics [ɒb'stetrɪks] N obstetricia f.

obstinacy ['ɒbstɪnəsɪ] N obstinación f, terquedad f, porfía f; tenacidad f.

obstinate ['ɒbstɪnɪt] ADJ obstinado, terco, porfiado; pursuit etc tenaz; **as ~ as a mule** tan terco como una mula; **to be ~ about sth** insistir con tesón en algo.

obstinately ['ɒbstɪnɪtlɪ] ADV obstinadamente, tercamente, porfiadamente; tenazmente.

obstreperous [əb'strepərəs] ADJ (noisy) ruidoso, estrepitoso; (unruly) turbulento, desmandado; protestón; **he became ~** empezó a desmandarse.

obstreperously [əb'strepərəslɪ] ADV ruidosamente, estrepitosamente; de modo turbulento.

obstruct [əb'strʌkt] ① VT obstruir; (Parl, Sport) obstruir; plan, progress etc dificultar, estorbar; person estorbar, impedir; road cerrar, bloquear, obstruir; pipe etc obstruir, atascar, atorar.
② VI estorbar.

obstruction [əb'strʌkʃən] N obstrucción f (also Parl); estorbo m, obstáculo m; (Med) oclusión f; **to cause an ~** causar un estorbo, (Aut etc) obstruir el tráfico.

obstructionism [əb'strʌkʃənɪzəm] N obstruccionismo m.

obstructionist [əb'strʌkʃənɪst] ① ADJ obstruccionista.
② N obstruccionista mf.

obstructive [əb'strʌktɪv] ADJ obstructivo, estorbador; **you're being ~** Vd nos está estorbando.

obstructiveness [əb'strʌktɪvnɪs] N carácter m obstructivo; obstructivismo m.

obtain [əb'teɪn] ① VT obtener; adquirir; lograr, conseguir; **oil can be ~ed from coal** el aceite se puede extraer del carbón; **his uncle ~ed the job for him** su tío le consiguió el puesto; **a work for which he ~ed a prize** un trabajo que le valió un premio, un trabajo por el que le dieron un premio.
② VI prevalecer, predominar; privar; regir; **the price which ~s now** el precio que rige ahora; **in the conditions then ~ing** en las condiciones que existían entonces; **that did not ~ in my day** en mis tiempos no existía eso, en mis tiempos no era así.

obtainable [əb'teɪnəbl] ADJ: **to be ~** ser asequible, poderse adquirir; (in shop) estar a la venta; **'~ at all chemists'** 'de venta en todas las farmacias'; **it is no longer ~** ya no se puede conseguir.

obtrude [əb'truːd] **1** VT tongue etc sacar, extender; **to ~ sth on sb** imponer algo a uno.

2 VI (person) entrometerse; **he does not let his opinions ~** no hace gala de sus opiniones, no impone sus opiniones a los demás.

obtrusion [əb'truːʒən] N imposición f; importunidad f; entrometimiento m.

obtrusive [əb'truːsɪv] ADJ importuno, molesto; intruso; indiscreto; building etc demasiado visible, llamativo; smell penetrante; person entrometido, intruso.

obtrusively [əb'truːsɪvlɪ] ADV importunamente; indiscretamente; de modo demasiado visible; de modo penetrante.

obtuse [əb'tjuːs] ADJ **(a)** (Math etc) obtuso. **(b)** person obtuso, estúpido, duro de mollera; remark poco inteligente; **now you're just being ~** te has empeñado en no comprender; **he can be very ~ at times** a veces puede ser muy obtuso.

obtuseness [əb'tjuːsnɪs] N (fig) estupidez f, torpeza f, obtusidad f.

obverse ['ɒbvɜːs] **1** ADJ del anverso.

2 N anverso m; (fig) complemento m.

obviate ['ɒbvɪeɪt] VT obviar, evitar, eliminar.

▼ **obvious** ['ɒbvɪəs] **1** ADJ (clear, perceptible) evidente, obvio, manifiesto, patente; (expected) obvio, natural; (unsubtle) poco sutil, transparente; (suitable) indicado; **the ~ thing to do is ...** lo lógico es ...; **he's the ~ man for the job** es el hombre más indicado para el puesto; **it's ~, isn't it?** ¿es obvio, no?; **it's not ~ to me** para mí no está tan claro; **we must not be too ~ about it** en esto conviene ser algo astuto.

2 N: **to state the ~** afirmar lo obvio.

obviously ['ɒbvɪəslɪ] ADV evidentemente, obviamente; **~!** ¡naturalmente!; **it's ~ the best** evidentemente es el mejor; **he was not ~ drunk** no estaba visiblemente borracho.

OC N ABBR of **Officer Commanding** jefe m.

o/c ABBR of **overcharge**.

ocarina [ˌɒkə'riːnə] N ocarina f.

OCAS N ABBR of **Organization of Central American States** Organización f de Estados Centroamericanos, ODECA f.

occasion [ə'keɪʒən] **1** N **(a)** (suitable juncture) coyuntura f; oportunidad f, ocasión f; **he was awaiting a suitable ~** aguardaba una coyuntura favorable, esperaba un momento propicio; **to take ~ to + infin** aprovechar la oportunidad de + infin.

(b) (reason) razón f, motivo m; **there is no ~ for alarm** no hay motivo para inquietarse, no hay por qué inquietarse; **there was no ~ for it** no había necesidad de eso; **to give ~ for scandal** provocar el escándalo; **he has given me no ~ for saying so** no me ha dado ocasión para decirlo; **I had ~ to reprimand him** tuve que reprenderle; **if you have ~ to use it** si te ves en el caso de usarlo.

(c) to go about one's lawful ~s ocuparse en sus negocios legítimos.

(d) (time, occurrence) ocasión f, vez f; **on the ~ of the cup final** cuando la final de copa; **on the ~ of his retirement** con motivo de su jubilación, para festejar su jubilación, para conmemorar su jubilación; **on ~** de vez en cuando; **on one ~** una vez; **on other ~s** otras veces; **on just such an ~** otra vez exactamente igual que ésta; **on that ~** esa vez, en aquella ocasión; **as the ~ requires** según el caso; **if the ~ arises** si se da el caso; **should the ~ so demand** si lo exigen las circunstancias; **to leave sth for another ~** dejar algo para otra vez; **to rise to the ~** ponerse a la altura de las circunstancias.

(e) (event, function) función f, acontecimiento m; **this is an important ~** esto es un acontecimiento importante; **it will be a big ~** será una función impresionante; **the three big ~s of the university year** las tres grandes funciones del año universitario; **it was quite an ~** realmente fue un acontecimiento; **music written for the ~** música f compuesta para la función.

2 VT ocasionar, causar.

occasional [ə'keɪʒənl] ADJ **(a) an ~ event** algo que pasa de vez en cuando, un acontecimiento poco frecuente; **~ paper** monografía f; **~ table** mesita f; **~ worker** (US) jornalero m temporero; **we have an ~ visitor** recibimos de vez en cuando una visita; **we're just ~ visitors** estamos de visita nada más.

(b) music etc de circunstancia, compuesto para una función determinada.

occasionally [ə'keɪʒnəlɪ] ADV de vez en cuando, a veces, cada cuando (LAm); **very ~** muy de tarde en tarde.

occident ['ɒksɪdənt] N occidente m.

occidental [ˌɒksɪ'dentl] ADJ occidental.

occipital [ɒk'sɪpɪtl] ADJ occipital.

occiput ['ɒksɪpʌt] N occipucio m.

occlude [ɒ'kluːd] VT obstruir.

occluded [ɒ'kluːdɪd] ADJ: **~ front** oclusión f.

occlusion [ɒ'kluːʒən] N oclusión f.

occlusive [ɒ'kluːsɪv] **1** ADJ oclusivo.

2 N oclusiva f.

occult [ɒ'kʌlt] **1** ADJ reason etc oculto, misterioso; (mystic) oculto, sobrenatural, mágico.

2 N: **the ~** lo oculto, lo sobrenatural; **to study the ~** dedicarse al ocultismo, estudiar las ciencias ocultas.

occultism ['ɒkəltɪzəm] N ocultismo m.

occultist ['ɒkəltɪst] N ocultista mf.

occupancy ['ɒkjʊpənsɪ] N ocupación f, tenencia f.

occupant ['ɒkjʊpənt] N (of boat, car etc) ocupante mf; pasajero m, -a f; (of house) habitante mf, inquilino m, -a f; **all the ~s were killed** perecieron todos los viajeros; **the ~s could not be reached** resultó imposible socorrer a los que iban dentro.

occupation [ˌɒkjʊ'peɪʃən] N **(a)** (of house etc) tenencia f, inquilinato m; (of country) ocupación f; (of office) tenencia f; **a house unfit for ~** una casa inhabitable; **to be in ~ of** ocupar; **we found them already in ~** encontramos que ya se habían instalado allí.

(b) (act of taking) ocupación f; **the ~ of Paris in 1940** la ocupación de París en 1940; **the house is ready for ~** la casa está lista para su ocupación.

(c) (work) trabajo m; (employment) empleo m; oficio m; (calling) oficio m; profesión f; (pastime) pasatiempo m; **a harmless enough ~** un pasatiempo inocente; **a tailor by ~** de oficio sastre; **what is he by ~?, what is his ~?** ¿cuál es su profesión?; **it gives ~ to 50 men** emplea a 50 hombres, da trabajo a 50 hombres; **this will give some ~ to your mind** esto le servirá para entretener la inteligencia.

occupational [ˌɒkjʊ'peɪʃənl] ADJ de oficio, relativo al oficio, profesional, laboral; ocupacional; **~ accident** accidente m laboral; **~ disease** enfermedad f profesional; **~ guidance** orientación f profesional; **~ hazard, ~ risk** (hum) gajes mpl del oficio; **~ pension plan, ~ pension scheme** plan m profesional de jubilación; **~ therapy** terapia f laboral, terapia f ocupacional; **~ training** formación f ocupacional.

occupier ['ɒkjʊpaɪər] N inquilino m, -a f.

occupy ['ɒkjʊpaɪ] VT ocupar (also Mil); house habitar, vivir en; time emplear, pasar; attention, mind entretener; **in occupied France** en la Francia ocupada (por los alemanes); **to be occupied in** (or with) ocuparse de (or en, con); **to be occupied** (US Telec) estar comunicando; **he is occupied in research** se dedica a la investigación; **he is very occupied at the moment** de momento está muy ocupado.

occur [ə'kɜːr] VI **(a)** (happen) ocurrir, suceder, acontecer, pasar; **to ~ again** volver a suceder, producirse de nuevo; **if a vacancy ~s** si se produce una vacante; **if the opportunity ~s** si se presenta la oportunidad; **don't let it ever ~ again** y que esto no vuelva a ocurrir nunca.

(b) (be found) encontrarse, existir; **the plant ~s all over Spain** la planta existe en todas partes en España.

(c) (come to mind) **it ~s to me that ...** se me ocurre que ...; **it ~red to me to ask him** se me ocurrió preguntárselo; **such an idea would never have ~red to her** tal idea no se le hubiera ocurrido nunca.

occurrence [ə'kʌrəns] N **(a)** (happening) acontecimiento m; incidente m; caso m; **a common ~** un caso frecuente; **an everyday ~** un suceso de todos los días; **that is a common ~** eso sucede a menudo, ese caso se da con frecuencia.

(b) (existence) existencia f; aparición f; **its ~ in the south is well known** se sabe que existe en el sur, es conocida su existencia en el sur; **its ~ here is unexpected** su aparición aquí es inesperada.

ocean ['əʊʃən] **1** N océano m; **~s of** (fig) la mar de.

2 ATTR: **~ bed** lecho m marino; **~ cruise** crucero m; **~ liner** transatlántico m.

oceanarium [ˌəʊʃə'neərɪəm] N oceanario m.

ocean-going ['əʊʃən,gəʊɪŋ] ADJ de alta mar, de altura.

Oceania [ˌəʊʃɪ'eɪnɪə] N Oceanía f.

oceanic [ˌəʊʃɪ'ænɪk] ADJ oceánico.

oceanographer [ˌəʊʃə'nɒgrəfər] N oceanógrafo m, -a f.

oceanographic [ˌəʊʃənəʊ'græfɪk] ADJ oceanográfico.

oceanography [ˌəʊʃə'nɒgrəfɪ] N oceanografía f.

ocelot ['əʊsɪlɒt] N ocelote m.

och [ɒx] EXCL (Scot) ¡oh!

ochre, (US) **ocher** ['əʊkər] **1** N ocre m.

2 ATTR: **red ~** ocre m rojo, almagre m; **yellow ~** ocre m amarillo.

ochreous ['əʊkrɪəs] ADJ de color ocre.

o'clock [ə'klɒk] **1** ADV: **it is 1 ~** es la una; **it is 3 ~** son las 3; **at 9 ~** a las 9; **at exactly 9 ~** a las 9 en punto; **it is just after 2 ~** son un poco más de las 2; **it is nearly 8 ~** son casi las 8.

2 as N: eg **the six ~** (train etc) el tren (etc) de las seis.

OCR (a) ABBR of **optical character reader** lector m óptico de caracteres, LOC m. **(b)** ABBR of **optical character recognition** reconocimiento m óptico de caracteres, ROC m.

Oct. ABBR of **October** octubre m, oct.

octagon ['ɒktəgən] N octágono m.

octagonal [ɒk'tægənl] ADJ octagonal.

octahedron [ˌɒktəˈhiːdrən] N octaedro m.
octal [ˈɒktəl] ① ADJ octal.
  ② N octal m.
octane [ˈɒkteɪn] N octano m; **~ number** grado m octánico.
octave [ˈɒktɪv] N (Mus, Poet) octava f.
Octavian [ɒkˈteɪvɪən] NM Octavio.
octavo [ɒkˈteɪvəʊ] ① ADJ en octavo.
  ② N libro m en octavo.
octet(te) [ɒkˈtet] N octeto m.
October [ɒkˈtəʊbəʳ] N octubre m.
octogenarian [ˌɒktəʊdʒɪˈnɛərɪən] ① ADJ octagenario.
  ② N octagenario m, -a f.
octopus [ˈɒktəpəs] N pulpo m.
octosyllabic [ˈɒktəʊsɪˈlæbɪk] ADJ octosílabo.
octosyllable [ˈɒktəʊˈsɪləbl] N octosílabo m.
ocular [ˈɒkjʊləʳ] ADJ ocular.
oculist [ˈɒkjʊlɪst] N oculista mf.
OD, O/D (a) ADV ABBR of **on demand** a solicitud. (b) N ABBR of **overdraft**. (c) ADJ ABBR of **overdrawn** en descubierto.
OD* [əʊˈdiː] (US) N ABBR of **overdose** ① N sobredosis f.
  ② VI administrarse una sobredosis de droga.
odalisk, odalisque [ˈəʊdəlɪsk] N odalisca f.
odd [ɒd] ADJ (a) (extra, left over) sobrante, de más; (isolated) suelto; (unpaired) sin pareja, desparejado, desparejo, de non; **the ~ dollar** el dólar que sobra, el dólar que hace falta; **the team and the ~ supporter** el equipo y algún hincha; **to be ~ man out** (surplus) estar de más, sobrar; (left out) quedar excluido; (different) ser distinto, diferenciarse de los demás.
  (b) (Math) impar; **~ or even** par o impar.
  (c) (and a few more) **30 ~** treinta y pico, treinta y tantos; **£20 ~** unas 20 libras.
  (d) (casual) **~ job** tarea f suelta, chapuza; **~ job man** hombre que hace de todo; **he has done the ~ job for us** ha trabajado para nosotros de vez en cuando; **~ lot** (St Ex) cantidad f irregular (y normalmente pequeña) de acciones (o valores); **at ~ times** de vez en cuando; **he has written the ~ article** ha escrito algún que otro artículo.
  (e) (strange) raro, extraño, singular; misterioso; estrambótico; **how ~!, very ~!, most ~!** ¡qué raro!; **the ~ thing about it is ...** lo raro es que ...; **he's very ~ in his ways** tiene manías; **he's got rather ~ lately** recientemente se ha vuelto algo raro; see also STRANGE, RARE .
oddball* [ˈɒdbɔːl] (esp US) ① ADJ raro, excéntrico.
  ② N bicho m raro, excéntrico m.
oddbod* [ˈɒdˌbɒd] N bicho m raro, excéntrico m.
oddity [ˈɒdɪtɪ] N (a) (strangeness) rareza f, singularidad f, excentricidad f. (b) (peculiar trait) rareza f, manía f; (odd person) genio m raro, original m; (odd thing) cosa f rara; **he has his oddities** tiene sus manías; **one of the oddities of the situation** uno de los aspectos raros que tiene la situación.
odd-looking [ˈɒdˌlʊkɪŋ] ADJ de aspecto singular.
oddly [ˈɒdlɪ] ADV singularmente, extrañamente; **they are ~ similar** tienen un extraño parecido; **~ attractive** extrañamente atractivo; **~ enough, ...** aunque parezca mentira, ...; **he is behaving most ~** se está comportando de una manera muy rara.
oddment [ˈɒdmənt] N artículo m suelto, artículo m que sobra, (pej) bagatela f, baratija f; (Brit Comm) retal m.
oddness [ˈɒdnɪs] N rareza f, singularidad f.
odds [ɒdz] NPL (a) (difference) **what's the ~?** ¿qué importa?, ¿qué más da?; **it makes no ~** no importa, lo mismo da; **it makes no ~ to me** me es igual.
  (b) (variance, strife) **to be at ~** estar reñidos (over por causa de), estar de punta; **to be at ~ with sb** estar reñido con uno (about, over con motivo de); estar incomodado con uno; **to set 2 people at ~** enemistar a 2 personas, hacer que riñan 2 personas.
  (c) (balance of advantage) ventaja f, superioridad f; **the ~ are in his favour** tiene muchas probabilidades (de ganar); **the ~ are too great** nuestra desventaja es insuperable; los peligros son demasiado grandes; **to fight against overwhelming ~** luchar contra fuerzas abrumadoras; **to succeed against all the ~** triunfar a pesar de todos los factores en contra.
  (d) (equalizing allowance) ventaja f; (in betting) puntos mpl de ventaja; **the ~ on the horse are 5 to 1** los puntos de ventaja del caballo son de 5 a 1; **to give ~ of 3 to 1** ofrecer 3 puntos de ventaja a 1; **what ~ will you give me?** ¿cuánta ventaja me da?; **to shout the ~*** (fig) vocear, gritar mucho; **to pay over the ~** (Brit) pagar en demasía.
  (e) (chances) probabilidades fpl; **the ~ are that ...** lo más probable es que + subj; **the ~ are against it** es poco probable.
  (f) **~ and ends** (of cloth etc) retazos mpl, materiales mpl sobrantes; (trinkets) baratijas fpl, chucherías fpl; (things in disorder) cosas fpl sin arreglar; (possessions) chismes mpl; **there were ~ and ends of machinery** había piezas sueltas de máquinas.
  (g) (:) **all the ~ and sods** todo quisque*, todo hijo de vecina*.

odds-on [ˈɒdzˈɒn] ADJ: **~ favourite** caballo m favorito, caballo m con puntos de ventaja; **he's ~ favourite for the job** él tiene las mejores posibilidades de ganar el puesto; **it's ~ he won't come** lo más probable es que no venga.
odd-sounding [ˈɒdˌsaʊndɪŋ] ADJ name etc raro, de sonido extraño.
ode [əʊd] N oda f.
odious [ˈəʊdɪəs] ADJ odioso, detestable.
odiously [ˈəʊdɪəslɪ] ADV odiosamente, detestablemente.
odium [ˈəʊdɪəm] N odio m; oprobio m; **to bring ~ on sb** hacer que uno sea odiado; **to incur the ~ of having + PTP** suscitar el odio de la gente por haber + PTP.
odometer [ɒˈdɒmɪtəʳ] N (US) cuentakilómetros m.
odontologist [ˌɒdɒnˈtɒlədʒɪst] N odontólogo m, -a f.
odontology [ˌɒdɒnˈtɒlədʒɪ] N odontología f.
odor [ˈəʊdəʳ] N (US) = **odour**.
odoriferous [ˌəʊdəˈrɪfərəs] ADJ odorífero.
odorless [ˈəʊdəlɪs] ADJ (US) = **odourless**.
odorous [ˈəʊdərəs] ADJ oloroso.
odour, (US) **odor** [ˈəʊdəʳ] N olor m (of a); fragancia f, perfume m; (fig) sospecha f; **~ of sanctity** olor m de santidad; **bad ~** mal olor m; **to be in bad ~** tener mala fama, estar bajo sospecha; **to be in bad ~ with sb** llevarse mal con uno.
odourless, (US) **odorless** [ˈəʊdəlɪs] ADJ inodoro.
Odysseus [əˈdɪsjuːs] NM Odiseo.
Odyssey [ˈɒdɪsɪ] N Odisea f; **o~** (fig) odisea f.
OE N (Ling) ABBR of **Old English** inglés m antiguo.
OECD N ABBR of **Organization for Economic Cooperation and Development** Organización f de Cooperación y Desarrollo Económico, OCDE f.
oecumenical, ecumenical [ˌiːkjuːˈmenɪkəl] ADJ ecuménico.
OED N ABBR of **Oxford English Dictionary**.
oedema, edema [ɪˈdiːmə] N edema m.
oedipal [ˈiːdɪpl] ADJ conflict, situation edípico.
Oedipus [ˈiːdɪpəs] ① NM Edipo.
  ② ATTR: **~ complex** complejo m de Edipo.
oenologist [iːˈnɒlədʒɪst] N enólogo m, -a f.
oenology [iːˈnɒlədʒɪ] N enología f.
oenophile [ˈiːnəʊfaɪl] N enófilo m, -a f.
o'er [ˈəʊəʳ] (poet) = **over**.
oesophagus, (US) **esophagus** [iːˈsɒfəgəs] N esófago m.
oestrogen, (US) **estrogen** [ˈiːstrəʊdʒən] N estrógeno m.
oestrous, (US) **estrous** [ˈiːstrəs] ADJ en celo; **~ cycle** ciclo m de celo.
oestrus, (US) **estrus** [ˈiːstrəs] N estro m.
œuvre [œvrə] N obra f.
of [ɒv, əv] PREP (a) (possession) de; **the pen ~ my aunt** la pluma de mi tía; **a friend ~ mine** un amigo mío; **love ~ country** el amor a la patria; **it's no business ~ yours** aquí no te metas, no tienes que ver con esto.
  (b) (partitive etc) de; **how much ~ this do you want?** ¿cuánto quieres de esto?; **there were 4 ~ us** éramos 4; **all ~ them** todos ellos; **~ the 12 two were bad** de los 12, dos estaban pasados; **most ~ all** más que nada; **you ~ all people ought to know** debieras saberlo más que nadie; **the best ~ friends** el mejor amigo; **they became the best ~ friends** se hicieron muy amigos; **the book ~ books** el libro de los libros; **king ~ kings** rey de reyes.
  (c) (descriptive genitive) **the city ~ Burgos** la ciudad de Burgos; **a boy ~ 8** un muchacho de 8 años; **cakes ~ her making** pasteles que ella había hecho; **by the name ~ Green** llamado Green; **bright ~ eye** de ojos claros; **hard ~ heart** duro de corazón; **that idiot ~ a minister** ese idiota de ministro; **a real palace ~ a house** una casa que es un verdadero palacio.
  (d) (origin, cause etc) **to buy sth ~ sb** comprar algo a uno; **'~ all chemists'** 'de venta en todas las farmacias'; **~ necessity** por necesidad, forzosamente; **~ itself** de por sí; **to die ~ a disease** morir de una enfermedad.
  (e) (material) de; **made ~ metal** hecho de metal.
  (f) (agent) **beloved ~ all** querido de todos; **it was very harsh ~ him to + infin** ha sido durísimo en + infin; **it is kind ~ you** eres muy amable.
  (g) (with certain verbs) **to dream ~ sth** soñar con algo; **to judge ~ sth** juzgar algo, opinar sobre algo; **to smell ~ sth** oler a algo; **he was robbed ~ his watch** le robaron el reloj, se le robó el reloj.
  (h) (*) **he died ~ a Friday** murió un viernes; **it was fine ~ a morning** por la mañana hacía buen tiempo.
  (i) (with hours: US) **it is 10 (minutes) ~ 4** son las 4 menos 10.
off [ɒf] ① ADV (a) (away) **a place 2 miles ~** un lugar a 2 millas (de distancia); **it landed not 50 metres ~** cayó a menos de 50 metros de nosotros; **noises ~** ruidos mpl de fondo, (Theat) efectos mpl sonoros; **a voice ~** voz de fondo, (Cine) voz en off.
  (b) (of removal) **with his hat ~** sin el sombrero puesto, sombrero en mano; **with his shoes ~** sin zapatos, descalzo; **hats ~!** ¡descúbranse!; **~ with those wet socks!** ¡quítate esos calcetines mojados!; **~ with**

his head! ¡que le corten la cabeza!; **hands ~!** ¡fuera las manos!; ¡no tocar!; **the lid is ~** la tapa está quitada; **~ with you!** ¡fuera de aquí!, (*tenderly*) ¡vete ya!; **~ we go!** ¡vamos!; **'10%⁻ ~'** 'descuento de 10 por cien'; **I'll give you 5% ~** te hago un descuento de 5 por cien; **to have a day ~** tomarse un día de asueto.

(c) **~ and on** de vez en cuando, a ratos, a intervalos; ya bien ya mal; **right ~, straight ~** sin parar, sin interrupción; **3 days straight ~** 3 días seguidos.

[2] ADV (*with* to be) **(a)** (*of distance, time*) **it's some way ~** está algo lejos; **the game is 3 days ~** faltan 3 días para el partido.

(b) (*depart*) **to be ~** irse; **I'm ~** me voy; **I must be ~** tengo que marcharme; **I'm ~ to Paris** voy a París, salgo para París; **she's ~ at 4** sale del trabajo a las 4; **be ~!** ¡fuera de aquí!, ¡lárgate!; **they're ~!** (*race etc*) ¡ya!; **he's ~ fishing every Sunday** todos los domingos sale a pescar, todos los domingos va de pesca.

(c) (*be absent*) **to be ~** estar fuera, no estar; estar libre, no trabajar; tener día franco; **to be ~ sick** estar de baja; **he's ~ fishing** ha ido a pescar; **she's ~ on Tuesdays** los martes no viene (a trabajar); **are you ~ this weekend?** ¿vas a estar fuera este fin de semana?; **salmon is ~** (*on menu*) no hay salmón ya, se acabó el salmón; **there are 2 buttons ~** faltan 2 botones; **the game is ~** se ha cancelado el partido; **sorry, but the party's ~** lo siento, pero no hay guateque; **their engagement is ~** han roto el noviazgo; **the talks are ~** se han cancelado las conversaciones.

(d) (*of switches etc*) **to be ~** estar en posición de desconectado; (*apparatus, radio, TV*) estar desenchufado, estar desconectado; (*light*) estar apagado; (*tap*) estar cerrado; (*Mech*) estar parado; (*water etc*) estar cortado; (*brake*) no estar puesto, estar quitado.

[3] ADJ **(a)** (*be bad*) **to be ~** estar pasado; (*milk*) estar cortado; (*fig*) **it's a bit ~, isn't it?** esto no lo apruebo, ¿sabes?; **I thought his behaviour was rather ~** me pareció que su conducta era bastante censurable; **she's feeling rather ~** se siente algo mal.

(b) (*financial etc*) **to be well ~** estar acomodado, tener dinero; **he's better ~ where he is** está mejor allí donde está ahora; **we should be no better ~** no ganaríamos nada; **to be badly ~** andar mal de dinero; **to be badly ~ for potatoes** andar escaso de patatas, sufrir escasez de patatas; **how are you ~ for money?** ¿qué tal andas de dinero?; V **well-off, worse ~** etc.

(c) (*non*) **to have an ~ day** tener un día malo; **~ season** temporada *f* baja, estación *f* muerta; **in the ~ season** fuera de temporada; **in the ~ position** en posición de cerrado (*etc*); V **off-side**.

[4] PREP **(a)** de; **height ~ the ground** altura *f* del suelo, altura *f* sobre el suelo; **to fall ~ a table** caer de una mesa; **to fall ~ a cliff** caer por un precipicio; **to eat ~ a dish** comer en un plato; **to dine ~ fish** cenar pescado; **to allow 5% ~ the price** rebajar el precio en un 5 por cien.

(b) **a street ~ the square** una calle que sale de la plaza; **a house ~ the main road** una casa algo apartada de la carretera.

(c) **~ Portland Bill** a la altura de Portland Bill, frente a Portland Bill.

(d) **there are 2 buttons ~ my coat** le faltan 2 botones a mi chaqueta; **to be ~ one's food** no tener apetito; **he was ~ work for 3 weeks** durante 3 semanas no pudo trabajar; **to take 3 days ~ work** tomarse 3 días libres.

[5] N (*) comienzo *m*: (*Sport*) salida *f*; **at the ~** en la salida; **ready for (the) ~** listos para comenzar, (*Sport*) listos para salir.

offal ['ɒfəl] N asaduras *fpl*, menudencias *fpl*.

offbeat ['ɒf,biːt] ADJ excéntrico, insólito; inconformista, nada convencional.

Off-Broadway ['ɔf'brɔːd,weɪ] ADJ *que no pertenece a las superproducciones de Broadway.*

┌─ **OFF-BROADWAY** ─┐

ⓘ *Off-Broadway es el término que se utiliza en la jerga del teatro para referirse a las producciones teatrales de Nueva York que no se representan en los famosos escenarios de Broadway. La primera vez que se utilizó esta expresión fue en los años cincuenta, al hablar de obras de bajo presupuesto pero con gran originalidad de dramaturgos como Tennessee Williams o Edward Albee. Estas producciones - tanto las amateurs como las más profesionales - suelen representarse en teatros con poco aforo y las entradas suelen ser bastante asequibles. También existe el término off-off Broadway, para referirse a los teatros que presentan obras aún más vanguardistas.*

off-centre, (*US*) **off-center** ['ɒf'sentər] ADJ: **to be ~** estar descentrado.

off-chance ['ɒftʃɑːns] N posibilidad *f* remota; **we'll go on the ~** iremos por si acaso, iremos aunque hay poca posibilidad; **he bought it on the ~ that it would come in useful** lo compró pensando que tal vez resultaría útil algún día.

off-colour, (*US*) **off-color** ['ɒf'kʌlər] ADJ *fabric etc* descolorido, desteñido; (*Brit: ill*) indispuesto, (*of child*) pachucho; (*of joke etc*) verde, su-

bido de tono.

offcut ['ɒf,kʌt] N trozo *m*; **~s** restos *mpl*, sobras *fpl*.

offence, (*US*) **offense** [ə'fens] N **(a)** (*insult*) ofensa *f*; **no ~!, no ~ meant** sin ofender a Vd; **no ~ was intended, he intended no ~** no quería ofender a nadie; **to give ~** ofender; **to take ~** ofenderse (*at* por), resentirse (*at* de).

(b) (*crime*) delito *m*, crimen *m*, infracción *f* de la ley; (*moral*) transgresión *f*, pecado *m*; **first ~** primer delito *m*; **second ~** reincidencia *f*; **it is an ~ to** + *infin* la ley castiga a los que ...; **to commit an ~** cometer un delito.

▼ **offend** [ə'fend] [1] VT ofender; **it ~s my sense of justice** ofende mi sentido de justicia; **to be ~ed** ofenderse (*at, by* por), tomarlo a mal; **he wasn't a bit ~ed** no se ofendió en lo más mínimo; **don't be ~ed** no te vayas a ofender, no lo tomes a mal; **he is easily ~ed** es algo picajoso; **to become ~ed** ofenderse.

[2] VI ofender; (*criminally*) cometer una infracción (de la ley *etc*); **to ~ again** reincidir.

◆**offend against** VT pecar contra.

offender [ə'fendər] N **(a)** (*insulter*) ofensor *m*, -ora *f*.

(b) (*criminal*) delincuente *mf*, culpable *mf*; (*against traffic code etc*) infractor *m*, -ora *f* (*against* de); **first ~**; V **first**.

(c) (*moral*) transgresor *m*, -ora *f*, pecador *m*, -ora *f*.

offending [ə'fendɪŋ] ADJ delincuente, culpable; **the ~ words are ...** las palabras ofensivas son ...

offense [ə'fens] N (*US*) = **offence**.

offensive [ə'fensɪv] [1] ADJ **(a)** *warfare etc* ofensivo.

(b) (*insulting*) ofensivo, injurioso; (*disgusting*) repugnante; **don't be ~!** ¡hable con más educación!; **to be ~ to sb** ser grosero con uno, decir injurias a uno.

[2] N ofensiva *f*; **to go over to the ~, to take the ~** tomar la ofensiva.

offensively [ə'fensɪvlɪ] ADV injuriosamente; repugnantemente; groseramente.

▼ **offer** ['ɒfər] [1] N oferta *f*, ofrecimiento *m*; (*Comm*) oferta *f*; **~ of marriage** oferta *f* de matrimonio, petición *f* de mano; **~ of peace** ofrecimiento *m* de paz; **to be on ~** estar en oferta, ofrecerse; **it was on ~ at £400** se ofrecía a 400 libras; **to be under ~** estar en oferta; **to make an ~ for sth** hacer una oferta por algo, ofrecerse a comprar algo; **make me an ~!** ¡hágame una oferta!; **it's the best ~ I can make** no puedo ofrecer más.

[2] ATTR: **~ price** precio *m* de oferta.

▼[3] VT **(a)** *help, love, money, services etc* ofrecer; *opportunity, prospect etc* brindar, facilitar, deparar; **to ~ sth to sb** ofrecer algo a uno; **to ~ one's flank to the enemy** exponer su flanco al enemigo; **to ~ resistance** ofrecer (*or* oponer) resistencia (*to* a); **he ~ed no resistance** no se resistió; **the plan ~s us nothing new** el plan no nos ofrece nada nuevo; **the garden ~s a fine spectacle** el jardín se muestra espléndido.

(b) **to ~ to do sth** ofrecerse a hacer algo; **he ~ed to strike me** hizo ademán de pegarme, hizo como si fuera a pegarme.

(c) *comment, remark* hacer; **he ~ed no comment** no hizo comentario alguno; **I wish to ~ two comments** quiero hacer dos observaciones.

(d) *prayers*; V **offer up**.

[4] VI: **if the opportunity ~s** si se me da la oportunidad, si se da el caso.

[5] VR: **to ~ o.s. for a mission** ofrecerse a ir a una misión; **to ~ o.s. for a post** presentarse para un puesto.

◆**offer up** VT *prayers* rezar, ofrecer.

offering ['ɒfərɪŋ] N ofrecimiento *m*; (*Rel*) ofrenda *f*; (*gift*) regalo *m*, don *m*; (*sacrifice*) sacrificio *m*.

offertory ['ɒfətərɪ] N ofertorio *m*.

offertory box ['ɒfətərɪ,bɒks] N cepillo *m*.

offhand ['ɒf'hænd] [1] ADJ informal, brusco, descortés; poco ceremonioso; **to treat sb in an ~ manner** tratar a uno con bastante informalidad; **he was very ~ about it** lo discutió sin darle importancia.

[2] ADV de improviso, sin pensarlo; **~ I couldn't tell you** así de improviso no te lo puedo decir.

offhanded ['ɒf'hændɪd] = **offhand 1**.

offhandedly ['ɒf'hændɪdlɪ] ADV con informalidad, bruscamente, descortésmente; sin ceremonias, sin miramientos; **to treat sb ~** tratar a uno con bastante informalidad; **he said ~** dijo en tono brusco.

offhandedness ['ɒf'hændɪdnɪs] N informalidad *f*; brusquedad *f*; descortesía *f*.

office ['ɒfɪs] [1] N **(a)** (*place*) oficina *f*; (*room*) despacho *m*; (*lawyer's*) bufete *m*; (*as part of organization*) sección *f*, departamento *m*; (*ministry*) ministerio *m*; (*branch*) sucursal *f*; (*US: Med etc*) consultorio *m*; **O~ of Fair Trading** (*Brit*) oficina de normas comerciales justas.

(b) (*function*) oficio *m*; (*post*) cargo *m*; **it is my ~ to** + *infin* yo tengo el deber de + *infin*, me incumbe + *infin*; **to be in ~, to hold ~** (*person*) estar en funciones, desempeñar un cargo, (*govt*) estar en el poder; **he is in ~ for one year** ocupa el cargo durante un año; **to be out of ~** no estar en el poder; **to come into ~, to take ~** (*person*) asumir un cargo, (*govt*) entrar en el poder; **to leave ~** (*person*) dimitir un cargo, (*govt*) salir del poder; **to perform the ~ of sb** hacer las veces de uno.

(c) **good ~s** buenos oficios *mpl*; **to offer one's good ~s** ofrecer sus buenos oficios; **through the ~s of** gracias a la mediación de.

(d) **O~ for the Dead** (*Eccl*) oficio *m* de difuntos.

[2] ATTR *work etc* de oficina; **~ automation** ofimática *f*, buromática *f*; **~ bearer** alto cargo *m*; **~ block** (*Brit*) bloque *m* de oficinas; **~ boy** chico *m* de los recados, ordenanza *m*, mandadero *m*; **~ building** edificio *m* de oficinas; **~ equipment, ~ furniture** muebles *m* de oficina, equipo *m* de oficina; **~ holder** funcionario *m*, -a *f*; **~ hours** (*Brit*) horas *fpl* de oficina, (*US*) horas *fpl* de consulta; **~ job** trabajo *m* de oficina; **~ manager** gerente *m*, jefe *m* de oficina; **~ party** fiesta *f* de oficina; **~ staff** personal *m* de oficina; **~ supplies** material *m* de oficina; **~ worker** oficinista *mf*.

officer [ˈɒfɪsər] [1] N (*Mil, Naut, Aer*) oficial *mf*; (*of society*) dignatario *m*, -a *f*; (*of local govt*) magistrado *m*, -a *f*; funcionario *m*, -a *f*; (*of company*) director *m*, -ora *f*; (*of police*) policía *m*, agente *mf* de policía; **~ of the day** oficial *mf* del día; **~ of the watch** oficial *m* de guardia; **the ~s of a company** los directores de una sociedad, la junta directiva de una sociedad; **an ~ and a gentleman** oficial y caballero; **'Yes, ~'** (*to policeman*) 'Sí, señor guardia'.

[2] VT (*command*) mandar; (*staff*) proveer de oficiales; **to be well ~ed** tener buena oficialidad.

official [əˈfɪʃəl] [1] ADJ oficial; autorizado; *voice, style etc* ceremonioso, solemne; **in ~ circles** en círculos oficiales; **is that ~?** ¿se ha confirmado eso (oficialmente)?; **O~ Receiver** (*Brit Fin*) síndico *m*, depositario *m* judicial; **O~ Secrets Act** (*Brit*) ley relativa a los secretos de Estado; **~ strike** huelga *f* oficial.

[2] N oficial *mf*, oficial *m* público, oficial *f* pública, funcionario *m*, -a *f*; **an ~ of the ministry** un funcionario del Ministerio.

officialdom [əˈfɪʃəldəm] N (*pej*) burocracia *f*.

officialese [ə,fɪʃəˈliːz] N lenguaje *m* burocrático, estilo *m* oficial burocrático.

officially [əˈfɪʃəlɪ] ADV oficialmente; de modo autorizado.

officiate [əˈfɪʃɪeɪt] VI oficiar (*as* de).

officious [əˈfɪʃəs] ADJ oficioso.

officiously [əˈfɪʃəslɪ] ADV oficiosamente.

officiousness [əˈfɪʃəsnɪs] N oficiosidad *f*.

offing [ˈɒfɪŋ] N: **to be in the ~** (*Naut*) estar a la vista, estar cerca, (*fig*) estar en perspectiva.

off-key [,ɒfˈkiː] [1] ADJ desafinado.

[2] ADV desafinadamente.

off-licence [ˈɒf,laɪsəns] N (*Brit*) *tienda donde se venden bebidas alcohólicas para llevar*.

off-limits [ˈɒfˈlɪmɪts] ADJ, ADV fuera de los límites.

off-line [ˈɒfˈlaɪn] [1] ADJ (*Comput*) off-line, fuera de línea; (*switched off*) desconectado.

[2] ADV fuera de línea, off-line.

offload [ˈɒfləʊd] VT = **unload**.

off-peak [,ɒfˈpiːk] ADJ *holiday* de temporada baja; *electricity* de banda económica.

off-piste [ˈɒfˈpiːst] [1] ADJ fuera de pista.

[2] ADV fuera de pista.

offprint [ˈɒfprɪnt] N separata *f*, tirada *f* aparte.

off-putting [ˈɒf,pʊtɪŋ] ADJ (*Brit*) poco atractivo, que quita las ganas; *person* difícil, poco amable; *reception* nada amistoso; **it's very ~ when ...** es desalentador cuando ..., es para desanimarse cuando ...

off ramp [ˈɒfræmp] N (*US*) vía *f* de salida.

off-road [ˈɒfrəʊd] ADJ *driving, racing* todoterreno; **~ vehicle** vehículo *m* todoterreno.

off sales [ˈɒfseɪlz] N (*Brit*) tienda *f* de bebidas alcohólicas.

offset [ˈɒfset] [1] N compensación *f*; (*Typ*) offset *m*; (*Hort: layer*) acodo *m*, (*bulb*) bulbo *m* reproductor; (*Archit*) retallo *m*.

[2] ATTR: **~ lithography ~ printing; ~ press** prensa *f* offset; **~ printing** impresión *f* en offset.

[3] VT (*irr: V* **set**) compensar; contrarrestar, contrapesar; **to ~ A against B** contrapesar A y B; **higher prices will be ~ by wage increases** los aumentos de precios serán compensados por incrementos salariales.

off-screen [ˈɒfskriːn] (*Cine, TV*) [1] ADV fuera de la pantalla, en la vida privada.

[2] ADJ real, en la vida privada.

offshoot [ˈɒfʃuːt] N (*Bot*) renuevo *m*, vástago *m*; (*fig*) ramal *m* (*from* de), retoño *m*.

offshore [ˈɒfˈʃɔːr] [1] ADV a cierta distancia, a lo largo; (*oil parlance*) off-shore, costa afuera.

[2] ADJ *breeze* terral, que sopla de tierra; *island* a poca distancia de la costa; **~ exploration** exploración *f* costa afuera; **~ fishing** pesca *f* de bajura; **~ investments** inversiones *fpl* off-shore; **~ oil** petróleo *m* de

costa afuera; **~ oilfield** campo *m* petrolífero submarino.

offside [ˈɒfˈsaɪd] [1] ADV: **to be ~** estar fuera de juego; **the goal was disallowed for ~** el gol fue anulado por fuera de banda (de un jugador).

[2] ADJ (a) **~ rule** regla *f* de fuera de juego; **~ trap** trampa *f* de fuera de juego.

(b) (*Aut etc*) (*Brit*) derecho, (*most other countries*) izquierdo.

[3] INTERJ ¡orsay!, ¡offside!

[4] N (*Aut etc*) (*Brit*) lado *m* derecho, (*most other countries*) lado *m* izquierdo.

offspring [ˈɒfsprɪŋ] N (*sing*) vástago *m*, descendiente *mf*; (PL) descendencia *f*, hijos *mpl*, prole *f*; **to die without ~** morir sin dejar descendencia.

offstage [ˈɒfˈsteɪdʒ] [1] ADV entre bastidores.

[2] ADJ de entre bastidores.

off-street parking [,ɒfstriːtˈpɑːkɪŋ] N aparcamiento *m* fuera de la vía pública, aparcamiento *m* privado.

off-the-cuff [,ɒfðəˈkʌf] [1] ADJ *remark* dicho sin pensar, espontáneo; *speech* improvisado.

[2] ADV de improviso; *see also* **cuff**².

off-the-job [ˈɒfðəˈdʒɒb] ADJ: **~ training** formación *f* fuera del trabajo.

off-the-peg [ˈɒfðəˈpeg] (*Brit*) ADJ, **off-the-rack** [ˈɒfðəˈræk] (*US*) ADJ confeccionado, de percha.

off-the-record [,ɒfðəˈrekəd] ADJ no oficial, extraoficial; confidencial.

off-the-wall• [,ɒfðəˈwɔːl] ADJ *idea etc* nuevo, inesperado; hecho de improviso; espontáneo.

off-white [ˈɒfˈwaɪt] ADJ blancuzco, color hueso.

Ofgas [ˈɒfgæs] N (*Brit*) ABBR of **Office of Gas Supply** *organismo que controla a las empresas del gas en Gran Bretaña*.

Oflot [ˈɒflɒt] N (*Brit*) *organismo nacional de control de loterías*, ≈ Organismo Nacional de Loterías y Apuestas del Estado, ≈ ONLAE *m* (*Sp*).

OFT N (*Brit*) ABBR of **Office of Fair Trading**.

oft [ɒft] ADV (*poet*) = **often**; **many a time and ~** repetidas veces.

Oftel [ˈɒftel] N (*Brit*) ABBR of **Office of Telecommunications** *organismo que controla a las telecomunicaciones británicas*.

▼ **often** [ˈɒfən] ADV con frecuencia, a menudo, mucho, muchas veces; **very ~** muchísimas veces, repetidas veces, muy a menudo; **not ~** pocas veces; **how ~?** ¿con qué frecuencia?; **so ~** tantas veces; **as ~ as** tantas veces como, siempre que; **as ~ as not, more ~ than not** las más veces; **every so ~** (*time*) cada cierto tiempo, (*distance, spacing*) cada cierta distancia; **it is not ~ that ...** no es corriente que ...; no es corriente que ...; **it cannot be said too ~ that ...** nunca huelga repetir que ...

oft-times [ˈɒftaɪmz] ADV (*liter*) a menudo.

Ofwat [ˈɒfwɒt] N (*Brit*) ABBR of **Office of Water Services** *organismo que controla a las empresas suministradores de agua en Inglaterra y Gales*.

ogival [əʊˈdʒaɪvəl] ADJ ojival.

ogive [ˈəʊdʒaɪv] N ojiva *f*.

ogle [ˈəʊgl] VT echar miradas amorosas (*or* incitantes) a, comerse con los ojos.

O-grade [ˈəʊgreɪd] N (*Scot Scol*) ABBR of **Ordinary grade**; V **ordinary 1**(b).

ogre [ˈəʊgər] N ogro *m*.

OH (*US Post*) ABBR of **Ohio**.

oh [əʊ] INTERJ (a) (*vocative*) **~ king!** ¡oh rey!

(b) (*pain*) ¡ay!

(c) (*preceding questions and excls*) **~ really?** ¿de veras?; **~ is he?** ¿en serio?; **~ what a surprise!** ¡qué sorpresa!; **~ yes?** ¿ah sí?; **~ no you don't!** ¡eso no!; **~ for a horse!** ¡quién tuviera un caballo!; **~ to be in Splotz!** ¡ojalá estuviera en Splotz!

ohm [əʊm] N ohmio *m*, ohm *m*.

OHMS (*Brit*) ABBR of **On Her (His) Majesty's Service**.

OHP N ABBR of **overhead projector** retroproyector *m*.

oik: [ɔɪk] N palurdo *m*, patán *m*.

oil [ɔɪl] [1] N (*in most senses*) aceite *m*, (*Geol, as mineral*) petróleo *m*; (*Art*) óleo *m*; (*holy ~*) crisma *f*, santo óleo *m*; **an ~ by Rembrandt** un óleo de Rembrandt; **to burn the midnight ~** quemarse las cejas; **to check the ~** (*Aut etc*) revisar el nivel del aceite; **to paint in ~s** pintar al óleo; **to pour ~ on troubled waters** tratar de calmar la tempestad (*or* las pasiones *etc*); **to strike ~** encontrar un pozo de petróleo, (*fig*) encontrar un filón, enriquecerse de súbito.

[2] ATTR: **~ deposits** yacimientos *mpl* de petróleo; **~ industry** industria *f* del petróleo, industria *f* petrolera; **~ pipeline** oleoducto *m*; **~ pollution** contaminación *f* de petróleo; **~ pressure** presión *f* del aceite; **~ spill** (*act*) fuga *f* de petróleo, (*slick*) marea *f* negra; **~ terminal** terminal *f* petrolífera.

[3] VT lubricar, lubrificar, engrasar; **to be well ~ed•** ir a la vela•.

oil-based [ˈɔɪlbeɪst] ADJ: **~ product** producto *m* derivado del petróleo.

oil-burning [ˈɔɪl,bɜːnɪŋ] ADJ (alimentado) al petróleo, de petróleo.

oilcake [ˈɔɪlkeɪk] N torta *f* de borujo, torta *f* de linaza.

oilcan [ˈɔɪlkæn] N aceitera *f*.

| OFTEN | *see also main entry* |

In statements

- When *often* means "on many occasions", you can usually translate it using *con frecuencia* or *a menudo*:

  He often came to my house
  Venía con frecuencia or *a menudo a mi casa*
  She doesn't often get angry
  No se enfada con frecuencia or *a menudo*
  You are late too often
  Llegas tarde con demasiada frecuencia or *demasiado a menudo*

- In informal contexts, particularly when *often* can be substituted by *a lot* or *much* with no change of meaning, *mucho* is an alternative translation:

  He doesn't often come to see me
  No viene mucho a verme
  He often hangs out in this bar
  Para mucho en este bar

- *Muchas veces* is another possible translation, but it should be used with the present only if the time, place or activity is restricted in some way:

  I've often heard him talk about the need for this law
  Le he oído muchas veces hablar de la necesidad de esta ley
  It can often be difficult to discuss this subject with one's partner
  Muchas veces es difícil hablar con la pareja sobre este tema

- When *often* describes a predictable, habitual or regular action, you can often translate it using the present or imperfect of *soler* as applicable:

  In England it is often cold in winter
  En Inglaterra suele hacer frío en invierno
  I often have a glass of sherry before dinner
  Suelo tomar un jerez antes de cenar
  We often went out for a walk in the evening
  Solíamos salir por la tarde a dar un paseo

- Use *soler* also when *often* means "in many cases":

  This heart condition is often very serious
  Esta enfermedad cardíaca suele ser muy grave

In questions

- You can usually use *con frecuencia* in questions, though there are other possibilities:

  How often do you go to Madrid?
  ¿Con qué frecuencia vas a Madrid?
  Do you often go to Spain?
  ¿Vas a España con frecuencia? ◊ *¿Vas a menudo* or *¿Vas mucho a España?*

  For further uses and examples, see main entry.

oil-change ['ɔɪlˌtʃeɪndʒ] N cambio *m* de aceite.
oilcloth ['ɔɪlklɒθ] N hule *m*, encerado *m*.
oildrum ['ɔɪldrʌm] N bidón *m* de aceite.
oiler ['ɔɪləʳ] N **(a)** (*ship*) petrolero *m*; (*can*) lata *f* de aceite or lubricante; (*person*) engrasador *m*. **(b)** ~s (*US: clothes*) hule *m*.
oilfield ['ɔɪlfiːld] N yacimiento *m* petrolífero.
oil-filter ['ɔɪlˌfɪltəʳ] N filtro *m* de aceite.
oil-fired ['ɔɪlfaɪəd] ADJ (alimentado) al petróleo; ~ **central heating** calefacción *f* central al petróleo; ~ **power-station** central *f* térmica de fuel.
oil-gauge ['ɔɪlɡeɪdʒ] N manómetro *m* de aceite; indicador *m* de nivel del aceite.
oiliness ['ɔɪlɪnɪs] N **(a)** lo aceitoso, oleaginosidad *f*; lo grasiento. **(b)** (*fig*) zalamería *f*.
oil-lamp ['ɔɪllæmp] N velón *m*, quinqué *m*, candil *m*.
oil-level ['ɔɪllevl] N nivel *m* del aceite.
oilman ['ɔɪlmæn] N, PL **oilmen** ['ɔɪlmen] petrolero *m*; magnate *m* del petróleo.
oil-painting ['ɔɪlˌpeɪntɪŋ] N pintura *f* al óleo; **she's no ~*** no es tan hermosa que digamos.
oilpan ['ɔɪlpæn] N (*US Aut*) cárter *m*.
oil platform ['ɔɪlˌplætfɔːm] N plataforma *f* petrolífera.
oil-refinery ['ɔɪlrɪˌfaɪnərɪ] N refinería *f* de petróleo.
oil-rig ['ɔɪlrɪɡ] N torre *f* de perforación; (*Naut*) plataforma *f* de perforación submarina.
oilskin ['ɔɪlskɪn] N hule *m*, encerado *m*; ~s (*Brit*) traje *m* de encerado, chubasquero *m*, ahulado *m* (*Mex*).
oil-slick ['ɔɪlslɪk] N (*large*) marea *f* negra; (*small*) mancha *f* de petróleo, capa *f* de petróleo (en el agua).
oil-stove ['ɔɪlstəʊv] N (*cooking*) cocina *f* de petróleo; (*heating*) estufa *f* de petróleo.
oil-tanker ['ɔɪltæŋkəʳ] N petrolero *m*.
oilwell ['ɔɪlwel] N pozo *m* de petróleo.
oily ['ɔɪlɪ] ADJ **(a)** (*liquid etc*) aceitoso, oleaginoso; *meal* grasiento, grasoso

(*LAm*). **(b)** *person* zalamero, empalagoso.
oink [ɔɪŋk] VI gruñir.
ointment ['ɔɪntmənt] N pomada *f*, ungüento *m*.
OJT N (*US*) ABBR of **on-the-job training** aprendizaje *m* en el trabajo.
OK (*US Post*) ABBR of **Oklahoma**.
O.K.* ['əʊ'keɪ] [1] INTERJ (*all right*) ¡está bien!; (*yes*) ¡sí!; (*understood*) ¡comprendo!; (*I agree*) ¡vale!; **I'm coming too, ~?** yo vengo también, ¿vale?
[2] ADJ (*agreed*) aprobado; (*satisfactory*) satisfactorio; **it's ~ with me** lo apruebo, estoy de acuerdo; **is it ~ with you if ...?** ¿te importa que ... + subj?, ¿me permites + infin ...?; **I'm ~, thanks** estoy bien, gracias; **that may have been ~ last year** eso puede haber estado bien el año pasado; **~ it's difficult but ~ ...** estoy de acuerdo que es difícil pero ...; **the ~ hair-do of 1999** el peinado elegante de 1999, el peinado que está de moda en 1999.
[3] ADV: **he's doing ~** las cosas le van bien.
[4] N visto *m* bueno; **to give sth one's ~** dar el visto bueno a algo, aprobar algo.
[5] VT dar el visto bueno a, aprobar.
okapi [əʊ'kɑːpɪ] N okapi *m*.
okay* [əʊ'keɪ] = **O.K.***
okey-doke(y)* [ˌəʊkɪ'dəʊk(ɪ)] EXCL de acuerdo, vale.
Okla. (*US*) ABBR of **Oklahoma**.
okra ['əʊkrə] N kimbombó *m*.
old [əʊld] *see also* OLD *on next page* [1] ADJ **(a)** (*person: aged*) viejo; anciano; **an ~ man** un viejo, un anciano; **an ~ woman** una vieja, una anciana; **~ and young** grandes y pequeños; **~ Peter** Pedro el viejo; **~ Mrs Brown** la vieja señora de Brown; **he's a good ~ horse** es un valiente caballo (aunque bastante viejo ya); **to grow ~** envejecerse; **to live to be ~** llegar a una edad avanzada; **if I live to be that ~** si llego a esa edad.
(b) (*ancient*) *thing* viejo; *clothes etc* viejo; usado, gastado; *bread* duro; *wine* añejo; **it's too ~ to be any use** es demasiado viejo para servir.
(c) (*with expression of years: person*) **how ~ are you?** ¿cuántos años tienes?, ¿qué edad tienes?; **I am 7 years ~** tengo 7 años; **she's 3 years ~ today** hoy cumple 3 años; **she is ~er than I** tiene más años que yo, es más vieja que yo; **she is the ~est** es la mayor; **to be 4 years ~er than sb** tener 4 años más que uno; **she's ~ enough to go alone** tiene bastante edad para ir sola; **he's ~ enough to know his own mind** tiene bastante edad para saber lo que quiere; **he's ~ enough to know better** a su edad debe portarse mejor; **he's ~ enough to be her father** tiene tanta edad como para ser su padre.
(d) (*with expression of years: thing*) **the building is 300 years ~** el edificio tiene 300 años (de construido); **the company is a century ~** la sociedad existe desde hace un siglo, la sociedad se fundó hace un siglo.
(e) (*old-established, long-standing*) viejo, antiguo; **an ~ friend of mine** un viejo amigo mío; **that's as ~ as the hills** eso es de tiempos de Maricastaña, eso es tan viejo como el mundo.
(f) (*former*) antiguo; **an ~ boy of the school** (*Brit*) un antiguo alumno (or ex alumno) del colegio; **my ~ school** mi antiguo colegio; **~ school tie** (*Brit*) corbata *f* del colegio; (*fig*) amiguismo* *m*, nepotismo *m* escolar; **in the ~ days** antaño, en el pasado; **O~ French** antiguo francés *m*.
(g) (*affectionate*) **the ~ country** la patria, (*mi etc*) país *m* natal; **O~ Glory** (*US*) bandera *f* de EE.UU.; **~ Lucas** el tío Lucas; **the ~ man*** el jefe, el patrón; **my ~ man*** el pariente*, **my ~ woman*** la parienta*; **I say, ~ man*** oye, chico; **any ~ thing does for me** me contento con cualquier cosa; **any ~ thing you like** lo que quieras; **it's not just any ~ painting, it's a Zurburán** no es un cuadro cualquiera, es un Zurburán; **he leaves his things any ~ how*** deja sus cosas de cualquier modo.
[2] N **(a)** **the ~** (*people*) los viejos, los mayores, los ancianos (*LAm*).
(b) **of ~** antiguamente, antaño; **knights of ~** los caballeros de antaño; **I know him of ~** le conozco de antiguo.
old-age ['əʊldeɪdʒ] ATTR: **~ pension** jubilación *f*; **~ pensioner** (*Brit*) pensionista *mf*.
Old Bailey ['əʊld'beɪlɪ] N (*Brit*): **the ~** el tribunal de lo penal de más alto rango de Inglaterra.
old-clothes ['əʊld'kləʊðz] ATTR: **~ dealer** ropavejero *m*, -a *f*, prendero *m*, -a *f*; **~ shop** ropavejería *f*, prendería *f*.
olden ['əʊldən] ADJ (†† or *liter*) antiguo; **in the ~ days** antaño, en el pasado.
Old English ['əʊld'ɪŋɡlɪʃ] [1] N (*Ling*) inglés *m* antiguo.
[2] ADJ: **~ sheepdog** pastor *m* ovejero inglés; *ver también* ANGLO-SAXON.
old-established ['əʊldɪ'stæblɪʃt] ADJ viejo, antiguo.
olde-worlde ['əʊldɪ'wɜːldɪ] ADJ (*hum*) viejísimo, antiquísimo; de antaño; arcaizante; **with ~ lettering** con letras al estilo antiguo; **a very ~ interior** un interior pintoresco de antaño; **Stratford is terribly ~** Stratford tiene sabor arcaico en exceso.

old-fashioned ['əʊld'fæʃnd] ADJ *thing* anticuado, pasado de moda; de estilo antiguo; *person* de ideas anticuadas, chapado a la antigua; **to give sb an ~ look*** mirar a uno con extrañeza.

```
┌─[ OLD ]──────────────────────── see also main entry ─┐
```

Position of "viejo" and "antiguo"

Viejo and *antiguo* can go either before or after the noun, depending on their meaning.

Viejo

- Put *viejo after* the noun when you are referring to age:

  ...boxes full of old clothes...

  ...cajas llenas de ropa vieja...

  Old cars are the ones that pollute the environment most

  Son los coches viejos los que más contaminan el medio ambiente

- Put *viejo before* the noun when you mean *old* in the sense of "long-standing" or "well-established":

  They got in touch with an old friend

  Se pusieron en contacto con un viejo amigo

  Many of the old customs have changed with the passing of time

  Muchas de las viejas costumbres han cambiado con el paso del tiempo

Antiguo

- Generally put *antiguo after* the noun to translate *ancient* or *old* in the sense of "ancient":

  ...one of Canada's most beautiful old houses...

  ...una de las más bellas casas antiguas de Canadá...

  ...the old part of the town...

  ...el barrio antiguo de la ciudad...

- Put *antiguo before* the noun to translate *former* or *old* in the sense of "former":

  My old colleagues are no longer my friends

  Mis antiguos compañeros ya no son mis amigos

  ...the former British colonies...

  ...las antiguas colonias británicas...

For further uses and examples, see main entry.

---

old folk's home* [,əʊld'fəʊks,həʊm] N asilo *m*, residencia *f* de ancianos.

oldie* ['əʊldɪ] N (*song*) melodía *f* del ayer; (*joke*) chiste *m* anticuado.

oldish ['əʊldɪʃ] ADJ algo viejo, más bien viejo, que va para viejo.

old-looking ['əʊld,lʊkɪŋ] ADJ de aspecto viejo.

old-maidish ['əʊld'meɪdɪʃ] ADJ de solterona; remilgado.

old people's home [,əʊldpiːplz'həʊm] N = **old folk's home**.

old-stager ['əʊld'steɪdʒəʳ] N veterano *m*, -a *f*.

oldster ['əʊldstəʳ] N (*US*) viejo *m*, vieja *f*.

old-style ['əʊld'staɪl] ADJ antiguo, al estilo antiguo, a la antigua; **~ calendar** calendario *m* juliano.

Old Testament [,əʊld'testəmənt] N Antiguo Testamento *m*.

old-time ['əʊldtaɪm] ADJ de antaño, del tiempo viejo; **~ dancing** bailes *mpl* de antaño.

old-timer [,əʊld'taɪməʳ] N veterano *m*, viejo *m*.

old-wives' tale ['əʊld'waɪvz,teɪl] N patraña *f*, cuento *m* de viejas.

old-world ['əʊld'wɜːld] ADJ (*Bio, Geog*) del Viejo Mundo; *character etc* antiguo, arcaico, rancio; **the ~ charm of Toledo** la atractiva ranciedad de Toledo, el sabor arcaico de Toledo.

oleaginous [əʊlɪ'ædʒɪnəs] ADJ oleaginoso.

oleander [,əʊlɪ'ændəʳ] N adelfa *f*.

oleo... ['əʊlɪəʊ] PREF oleo...

O-Level ['əʊ,levl] N (*Brit Scol*) ABBR of **Ordinary Level**; **to take 8 ~s** presentarse como candidato en 8 asignaturas de *Ordinary Level*; V **ordinary 1(b)**.

olfactory [ɒl'fæktərɪ] ADJ olfativo, olfatorio.

oligarchic(al) [,ɒlɪ'gɑːkɪk(əl)] ADJ oligárquico.

oligarchy ['ɒlɪgɑːkɪ] N oligarquía *f*.

oligo... ['ɒlɪgəʊ] PREF oligo...

Oligocene ['ɒlɪgəʊsiːn] ① ADJ oligocénico.

② N: **the ~** el Oligoceno.

oligopoly [,ɒlɪ'gɒpəlɪ] N oligopolio *m*.

oligopsony [,ɒlɪ'gɒpsənɪ] N oligopsonio *m*.

olive ['ɒlɪv] ① N (*fruit*) aceituna *f*, oliva *f*; (*tree*) olivo *m*.

② ADJ aceitunado, oliváceo; (*colour: also* **~green**) verdeoliva.

olive-branch ['ɒlɪvbrɑːntʃ] N ramo *m* de olivo (*also fig*); **to hold out the ~ to sb** ofrecer el ramo de olivo a uno.

olive-green ['ɒlɪv'griːn] ADJ verde oliva; **~ uniforms** uniformes *mpl* verde oliva.

olive-grove ['ɒlɪvgrəʊv] N olivar *m*.

olive-grower ['ɒlɪv,grəʊəʳ] N oleicultor *m*, -ora *f*, oleícola *mf*.

olive-growing ['ɒlɪv,grəʊɪŋ] ① N oleicultura *f*.

② ATTR: **~ region** región *f* olivera.

olive-oil ['ɒlɪv'ɔɪl] N aceite *m* (de oliva).

Oliver ['ɒlɪvəʳ] NM Oliverio.

Olympia [ə'lɪmpɪə] N Olimpia *f*.

Olympiad [əʊ'lɪmpɪæd] N olimpíada *f*.

Olympian [əʊ'lɪmpɪən] ADJ olímpico.

Olympic [əʊ'lɪmpɪk] ① ADJ olímpico; **O~ Games** Juegos *mpl* Olímpicos; **O~ medallist** medallero *m* olímpico, medallera *f* olímpica; **O~ torch** antorcha *f* olímpica.

② NPL: **O~s** Juegos *mpl* Olímpicos.

Olympus [əʊ'lɪmpəs] N Olimpo *m*.

OM N (*Brit*) ABBR of **Order of Merit** *título ceremonial*.

Oman [əʊ'mɑːn] N Omán *m*.

Omani [əʊ'mɑːnɪ] ① ADJ omaní.

② N omaní *mf*.

OMB N (*US*) ABBR of **Office of Management and Budget** servicio *m* que asesora al presidente en materia presupuestaria.

ombudsman ['ɒmbʊdzmən] N, PL **ombudsmen** ['ɒmbʊdzmən] ombudsman *m*, defensor *m* del pueblo (*Sp*).

```
┌─[ OMBUDSMAN ]────────────────────────────────────────┐
```

ⓘ *Se conoce con el nombre de* **ombudsman** *al funcionario encargado de investigar las quejas de los ciudadanos contra una institución determinada. En el Reino Unido, el* **ombudsman** *que se ocupa de los casos de administración fraudulenta en los ministerios del gobierno, el* **NHS** *y otros organismos institucionales es el* **Parliamentary Commissioner for Administration**. *Su jurisdicción se limita al área administrativa del gobierno, pero no afecta a su política o legislación. Otros* **ombudsmen** *se nombran para estudiar las quejas que provienen de los clientes de instituciones financieras, como por ejemplo el* **Banking Ombudsman**, *el* **Building Societies Ombudsman** *o el* **Insurance Ombudsman**. *En Estados Unidos, los* **ombudsmen** *llevan a cabo labores similares de investigación de instituciones, tanto en el sector público como en el privado.*

---

omega ['əʊmɪgə] N omega *f*.

omelet(te) ['ɒmlɪt] N tortilla *f*, tortilla *f* de huevo (*Méx*); **you can't make an ~ without breaking eggs** no se puede hacer tortillas sin romper huevos.

omen ['əʊmen] N agüero *m*, presagio *m*; **bird of ill ~** ave *f* de mal agüero; **it is a good ~ that ...** es un buen presagio que ...

ominous ['ɒmɪnəs] ADJ siniestro, de mal agüero, ominoso, amenazador; **the silence was ~** el silencio no auguraba nada bueno; **in an ~ tone** en tono amenazador; **that's ~** eso es mala señal.

ominously ['ɒmɪnəslɪ] ADV: **the thunder rumbled ~** retumbaba amenazador el trueno; **it was ~ familiar to us** nos era siniestramente familiar; **he spoke ~** habló en tono amenazador.

omission [əʊ'mɪʃən] N omisión *f*; supresión *f*; olvido *m*, descuido *m*; **it was an ~ on my part** fue un descuido mío.

omit [əʊ'mɪt] VT omitir; suprimir; olvidar, descuidar; *person, person's name* pasar por alto; **to ~ to** + *infin* olvidar de + *infin*, dejar de + *infin*; **don't ~ to visit her** no dejes de visitarla.

omni... ['ɒmnɪ] PREF omni...

omnibus ['ɒmnɪbəs] ① ADJ general, para todo; *edition* completo.

② N (a) (*Aut*) autobús *m*. (b) (*Liter*) antología *f*, tomo *m* colectivo. 3 ATTR: **~ edition** edición *f* colectiva.

omnidirectional [,ɒmnɪdɪ'rekʃənəl] ADJ omnidireccional.

omnipotence [ɒm'nɪpətəns] N omnipotencia *f*.

omnipotent [ɒm'nɪpətənt] ADJ omnipotente.

omnipresence ['ɒmnɪ'prezəns] N omnipresencia *f*.

omnipresent ['ɒmnɪ'prezənt] ADJ omnipresente.

omniscience [ɒm'nɪsɪəns] N omnisciencia *f*.

omniscient [ɒm'nɪsɪənt] ADJ omnisciente, omniscio.

omnivore ['ɒmnɪvɔːʳ] N omnívoro *m*, -a *f*.

omnivorous [ɒm'nɪvərəs] ADJ omnívoro; **she is an ~ reader** en sus lecturas lo devora todo, es lectora insaciable.

ON (*Canada*) ABBR of **Ontario**.

on [ɒn] ① ADV (a) **to have one's boots ~** llevar las botas puestas; **what had he got ~?** ¿cómo estaba vestido?; **she had not got much ~** iba muy ligera de ropa; **the lid is ~** la tapa está puesta; **it's not ~ properly** no está bien puesto.

(b) (*continuation*) **to drive ~, to go ~, to ride ~, to walk ~** *etc* seguir adelante (*see also* **go on** *etc*); **to read ~** seguir leyendo; **and so ~** y así sucesivamente, y así los demás; etcétera; **to talk ~ and ~** hablar sin parar, hablar incansablemente.

(c) (*time*) **from that time ~** desde entonces, a partir de entonces; **well ~ in June** bien entrado junio; **well ~ in years** entrado en años, que va para viejo.

(d) (*with to be: of switches etc*) **to be ~** estar conectado; (*apparatus, Rad, TV*) estar conectado, estar puesto, estar enchufado, estar prendido (*LAm*); (*light*) estar encendido, estar puesto, estar prendido (*LAm*); (*tap*) estar abierto; (*Mech*) estar en marcha, estar funcionando; (*brake*) estar puesto.

(e) (*with to be: of shows etc*) **the show is now ~** ha comenzado el espectáculo; **the show is now ~ in London** se ha estrenado el espectáculo en Londres; **the show was ~ for only 2 weeks** el show estuvo solamente 15 días en cartelera; ~ **with the show!** ¡que empiece (*or* continúe) el espectáculo!; ~ **with the dancing girls!** ¡que salgan las bailarinas!; **what's ~ at the cinema?** ¿qué ponen en el cine?; **what's ~ at the theatre?** ¿qué dan en el teatro?; **'what's ~ in London'** 'cartelera de los espectáculos londinenses'; **have you anything ~ this evening?** ¿tienes compromiso para esta noche?; **is the meeting ~ or not?** ¿se celebra la reunión o no?; **the deal is ~** se ha cerrado el trato, ya está concertado el trato; **that's not ~!*** ¡eso no se hace!, ¡no hay derecho!; eso es imposible.

(**f**) (*idioms with* to be) **to be ~** (*actor*) estar en escena; **you're ~ in 5 minutes** sales en 5 minutos; **are you ~ next?** ¿te toca a ti la próxima vez?; ¿viene ahora tu número?; **are you ~ tomorrow?** ¿estás de turno mañana?; **to be ~ to sth** creer haber encontrado algo, seguir una pista interesante; **he's ~ to sth good** se ha encontrado algo bueno; **he knows he's ~ to a good thing** sabe que ha encontrado algo que vale la pena; **the police are ~ to the villain** la policía tiene una pista que le conducirá al criminal; **we're ~ to them** los conocemos el juego; **they were ~ to him at once** le calaron en seguida, le identificaron en el acto; **he's always ~ to me about it*** me está majando continuamente con eso*.

(**g**) **~ and off** de vez en cuando, a intervalos; **to have one day ~ and the next off** trabajar un día y el otro no.

2 INTERJ ¡adelante!

3 PREP (**a**) (*of place etc*) en; sobre; encima de; **~ the Continent** en el continente; **~ the table** en la mesa, sobre la mesa; **a meal ~ the train** una comida en el tren; **~ all sides** por todas partes, por todos lados; **~ the ceiling** sobre el techo; **~ the high seas** en alta mar; **hanging ~ the wall** colgado de (*or* en) la pared; **with her hat ~ her head** con el sombrero puesto; **a house ~ the square** una casa en la plaza; **~ page 2** en la página 2; **~ the right** a la derecha; **~ foot** a pie; **~ horseback** a caballo; **I've no money ~ me** no llevo dinero encima, no llevo dinero; **to drift ~ to the shore** llegar a la deriva sobre la playa; **so they came ~ to me** así que los hicieron pasar a mí, así que vinieron a mis manos.

(**b**) (*fig*) **a story based ~ fact** una historia basada en hechos; **the march ~ Rome** la marcha sobre Roma; **an attack ~ the government** un ataque contra el gobierno; **to swear ~ the Bible** prestar juramento sobre la Biblia; **all the children play ~ the piano** todos los chicos saben tocar el piano; **so he played it ~ the violin** así que lo tocó al violín; **he's ~ the committee** es miembro del comité; **he's ~ the permanent staff** es de plantilla; **~ average** por término medio; **~ good authority** de buena tinta; **~ his authority** con su autorización; **~ my responsibility** bajo mi responsabilidad; **~ a charge of murder** acusado de homicidio; **~ pain of** so pena de; **~ account of** a causa de; **~ sale** de venta, en venta; **a student ~ a grant** un estudiante con beca; **I'm ~ £30,000** yo gano 30.000 libras (al año); **we're ~ irregular verbs** estamos estudiando los verbos irregulares; **I'm ~ a milk diet** sigo un régimen lácteo; **I'm ~ 3 pills a day** tomo 3 píldoras al día; **he's back ~ drugs** ha vuelto a drogarse; **many live ~ less than that** muchos viven con menos; (*for many expressions, eg* **~ duty, ~ hand,** V *the noun*).

(**c**) (*of time*) **~ Friday** el viernes; **~ Fridays** los viernes; **~ the next day** al día siguiente; **~ 14th May** el catorce de mayo; **~ the evening of the 2nd July** el 2 de julio por la tarde; **~ a day like this** un día como éste; **~ some days it is** hay días cuando lo es; **~ and after the 15th** el día 15 y a partir de la misma fecha; **~ or about the 8th** el día 8 o por ahí; **~ my arrival** al llegar yo, a mi llegada.

(**d**) (+ *ger*) **~ seeing him** al verle; **~ my calling to him** al llamarle yo.

(**e**) (*concerning*) sobre, acerca de; **a book ~ physics** un libro de física, un libro sobre física; **an examination ~ maths** un examen de matemáticas; **Eden ~ the events of 1956** lo que dice Eden acerca de los acontecimientos de 1956; **Bentley ~ Horace** los comentarios de Bentley sobre Horacio; **have you heard the boss ~ the new tax?** ¿has oído lo que dice el jefe acerca de la nueva contribución?; **while we're ~ the subject** como hablamos de esto.

(**f**) (*after, according to*) según; **~ this model** según este modelo.

(**g**) (*engaged in*) **he's away ~ business** está fuera por negocios; **the company is ~ tour** la compañía está en gira; **to be ~ holiday** estar de vacaciones; **I'm ~ a new project** trabajo sobre un nuevo proyecto.

(**h**) (*at the expense of*) **this round's ~ me** esto corre de mi cuenta, invito yo; **it's ~ the house** la casa invita, está pagado (por el dueño); **the tour was ~ the Council** la gira la pagó el Consejo, corrió el Consejo con los gastos de la gira.

(**i**) **woe ~ woe** dolor sobre dolor; **snow ~ snow** nieve y más nieve.

(**j**) (*as against*) **prices are down ~ last year's** los precios son inferiores a los del año pasado, han bajado los precios con relación al año pasado.

4 ADJ (**a**) **in the ~ position** tap abierto, en posición de abierto; (*Elec*) encendido, puesto, prendido; (*LAm*); **~-off switch** botón *m* de conexión.

(**b**) V **on-side.**

onanism ['əʊnənɪzəm] N onanismo *m*.

on-board [ˌɒn'bɔːd] ADJ: **~ computer** computadora *f* (*or* ordenador *m*) de a bordo.

ONC N (*Brit Scol*) ABBR *of* **Ordinary National Certificate**; V **ordinary 1** (b).

once [wʌns] **1** ADV (**a**) (*on one occasion*) una vez; **~ before** una vez antes; **we were here ~ before** estuvimos aquí una vez; **~ or twice** alguna que otra vez; **~ a week** una vez por semana; **~ only** una vez, una vez nada más; **~ again, ~ more** otra vez, una vez más; **~ in a while** de vez en cuando, cada cuando (*LAm*); **~ and for all** de una vez por todas; **just this ~** esta vez nada más; **for ~** por una vez; **more than ~** más de una vez; **not ~** ni una vez siquiera; **~ a thief always a thief** el ladrón siempre sigue ladrón.

(**b**) (*formerly*) antes, antiguamente, en otro tiempo; **~ when we were young** hace tiempo, cuando éramos jóvenes; **~ upon a time** en tiempos de Maricastaña, (*as start of story*) érase una vez ..., hubo una vez ...; **it had ~ been white** antes había sido blanco; **I knew him ~** le conocía hace tiempo.

(**c**) **at ~** en seguida, inmediatamente; sin pérdida de tiempo; (*in one go*) de una vez; **at ~ a food and a tonic** alimento y tónico a la vez, juntamente alimento y tónico; **all at ~** (*suddenly*) de repente, de golpe; (*in one go*) de una vez; (*all together*) todo junto, todos juntos, a un mismo tiempo.

2 CONJ una vez que ..., si ...; **~ allow this all is lost** en cuanto esto se permita se acaba todo; **~ you give him the chance** una vez que le des la oportunidad, si le das la oportunidad.

once-over* ['wʌnsˌəʊvəʳ] N (**a**) (*search etc*) **to give sth the ~** dar un vistazo a algo, examinar algo (rápidamente); **they gave the house the ~** registraron superficialmente la casa. (**b**) (*beating*) paliza *f*.

oncologist [ɒŋ'kɒlədʒɪst] N oncólogo *m*, -a *f*.

oncology [ɒŋ'kɒlədʒɪ] N oncología *f*.

oncoming ['ɒnˌkʌmɪŋ] ADJ (**a**) *event* que se acerca, venidero. (**b**) *traffic* que viene en dirección contraria.

oncosts ['ɒnˌkɒsts] NPL gastos *mpl* generales.

OND N (*Brit Scol*) ABBR *of* **Ordinary National Diploma**; V **ordinary 1** (b).

one [wʌn] **1** ADJ (**a**) (*numeral*) uno, una; (*before sing n*) un, *eg* **one man** un hombre; **~ or two people** algunas personas; **~ man out of two** uno de cada dos hombres; **there is only ~ left** queda uno solamente; **the last but ~** el penúltimo; **that's ~ way of doing it** es uno de los métodos de hacerlo; **you've got it in ~!** ¡has acertado la primera vez!; **they came in ~s and twos** entraron solos o en parejas; **they waited in ~s and twos** esperaban en pequeños grupos; V **number.**

(**b**) (*sole*) solo, único; **the ~ and only difficulty** la única dificultad; **the ~ and only Charlie Chaplin** el irrepetible Charlot, el inimitable Charlot; **his ~ care** su único cuidado; **the ~ way to do it** el único método de hacerlo; **no ~ man could do it** nadie podría hacerlo por sí sólo.

(**c**) (*same*) mismo; **all in ~ direction** todos en la misma dirección; **they are ~ and the same** son el mismo; **it's all ~** es lo mismo; **it's all ~ to me** me da igual, me da lo mismo; **God is ~** Dios es uno; **to be ~ with sth** formar un conjunto con algo; **to become ~** casarse; **they all shouted as ~** todos gritaron como un solo hombre.

2 N: **price of ~** precio *m* de la unidad; **it's made all in ~** está hecho en una sola pieza; **he's president and secretary all in ~** es presidente y secretario todo junto; **to be at ~ with sb** estar completamente de acuerdo con uno; **to be ~ up** tener la ventaja; tener un punto (*or* gol *etc*) de ventaja; haber ganado un partido más que los adversarios; **to be ~ up on sb** llevar ventaja a uno; **that puts us ~ up** eso nos da un punto (*or* gol *etc*) de ventaja; **to go ~ better than sb** quedar por encima de uno, aventajar a uno; **but John went ~ better** pero Juan hizo más; **he dotted her ~*** la pegó; **to have a quick ~*** echarse un traguito*; **to have ~ for the road*** beberse un trago antes de partir*, tomar la espuela*.

3 DEM PRON: **this ~** éste, ésta; **that ~** ése, ésa, aquél, aquélla; **this ~ is better than that** éste es mejor que ése; **~ or two** algunos; **which ~ do you want?** ¿cuál quieres?

4 REL PRON (**a**) **the ~ on the floor** el que está en el suelo; **the ~ who, the ~ that** el que, la que; **the ~s who, the ~s that** los que, las que; **they were the ~s who told us** ellos eran quienes nos lo dijeron.

(**b**) **the white dress and the grey ~** el traje blanco y el gris; **who wants these red ~s?** ¿quién quiere estos colorados?; **what about this little ~?** ¿y el pequeño éste?

(**c**) **that's a good ~!** ¡ésa sí que es buena!; **to pull a fast ~ on sb** jugar una mala pasada a uno, embaucar a uno; **that's a difficult ~** eso es un problema difícil; **our dear ~s** nuestros seres queridos; **the Evil O~** el demonio, el malo; **the little ~s** los pequeños, los chiquillos, la gente menuda; **he's a clever ~** es un taimado; **you're a fine ~!** ¡estás tú bueno!, ¡qué tío!; **you are a ~!** ¡qué cosas dices! (*or* haces *etc*); **he's the troublesome ~** él es el elemento revoltoso; **he's a**

great ~ for chess es estupendo para el ajedrez, es un entusiasta del ajedrez; **he's ~ for the ladies** es Perico entre ellas; **he's not much of a ~ for sweets** no le gustan mucho los dulces; **he is not the ~ to protest** no es de los que protestan.

5 INDEF ADJ: **~ day** un día, cierto día; **~ hot July evening** una tarde de julio de mucho calor.

6 INDEF PRON **(a) have you got ~?** ¿tienes uno?; **the book is ~ which I have never read** el libro es de los que no he leído nunca; **his message is ~ of pessimism** su mensaje es pesimista, su mensaje termina con tono de pesimismo; **~ of them** uno de ellos; **any ~ of us** cualquiera de nosotros; **he's ~ of the group** es del grupo, forma parte del grupo; **he's ~ of the family now** ya es de la familia; **I for ~ am not going** de todas formas yo no voy.
(b) never a ~ ni uno siquiera; **~ and all** todos sin excepción; **the ~..., the other ...** el uno ..., el otro ...; **you can't buy ~ without the other** no se puede comprar el uno sin el otro; **~ after the other** uno tras otro; **for ~ reason or another** por una razón u otra, por alguna razón; **~ by ~** uno a uno, uno tras otro.
(c) *(one another)* **they kissed ~ another** se besaron, se besaron el uno al otro; **they all kissed ~ another** se besaron unos a otros; **do you see ~ another much?** ¿os visitáis unos a otros?; **it's a year since we saw ~ another** hace un año que no nos vemos.
(d) he looked like ~ who had seen a ghost tenía el aspecto del que acababa de ver un fantasma; **~ more sensitive would have fainted** una persona de mayor sensibilidad se hubiera desmayado; **to ~ who can read between the lines** para el que sabe leer entre líneas; **~ Pérez** un tal Pérez.
(e) *(subject etc)* **~ never knows** nunca se sabe; **~ must wash** hay que lavarse; **~ has one's pride** uno tiene cierto amor propio.
(f) *(possessive)* **~'s life is not really safe** la vida de uno no es realmente segura; **~'s opinion does not count** la opinión de uno no cuenta; **to cut ~'s finger** cortarse el dedo.

one- [wʌn] PREF *in compounds*: de un ..., de un solo ..., uni-; un-, *eg* **a ~line message** un mensaje de una sola línea; **a ~celled animal** un animal unicelular; **he's a ~woman man** es un hombre para el que no existe más que una mujer; **a ~day excursion** *(US)* un billete de ida y vuelta en un día.

one-act ['wʌnækt] ADJ de un solo acto.

one-armed ['wʌnɑːmd] ADJ manco; **~ bandit** máquina *f* tragaperras.

one-eyed ['wʌnaɪd] ADJ tuerto.

one-handed ['wʌnhændɪd] 1 ADV: **to catch the ball ~** recoger la pelota con una sola mano. 2 ADJ manco.

one-horse ['wʌnhɔːs] ADJ **(a)** *carriage* de un solo caballo. **(b)** (*) insignificante, de poca monta; **~ town** pueblucho* *m*.

one-legged ['wʌnlegɪd] ADJ con una sola pierna.

one-liner [,wʌn'laɪnəʳ] N chiste *m* breve, observación *f* sucinta.

one-man ['wʌnmæn] ADJ individual, de un solo hombre; **~ band** hombre *m* orquesta; **~ exhibition, ~ show** exposición *f* de un solo artista; **~ woman** mujer *f* que dedica su vida a un solo hombre.

oneness ['wʌnnɪs] N unidad *f*; identidad *f*.

one-night ['wʌnnaɪt] ADJ: **~ stand** función *f* de una sola noche, representación *f* única; (*) ligue* *m*, cama *f* de una noche*.

one-off* ['wʌnɒf] 1 ADJ único; aislado; fuera de serie, excepcional, irrepetible; **~ job** acontecimiento *m* único. 2 N: **it's a ~** es un caso único; es una oportunidad *(etc)* fuera de serie; es una oferta *(etc)* irrepetible.

one-parent ['wʌn,peərənt] ADJ: **~ family** familia *f* monoparental, hogar *m* sin pareja.

one-party ['wʌn'pɑːtɪ] ADJ *state etc* de partido único.

one-piece ['wʌnpiːs] ADJ enterizo, de una pieza.

onerous ['ɒnərəs] ADJ oneroso.

oneself [wʌn'self] PRON *(subject)* uno mismo, una misma; *(acc, dative)* se; *(after prep)* sí (mismo, misma); **to wash ~** lavarse (a sí mismo); **to be ~** conducirse con naturalidad; ser fiel a su propia manera de ser; **to be by ~** estar solo, estar a solas; **to do sth by ~** hacer algo solo, hacer algo por sí mismo; **to look out for ~** mirar por sí; **to come to ~** volver en sí; **to say to ~** decir para sí, decir entre sí; **to talk to ~** hablar consigo mismo; **it's nice to have the museum to ~** es agradable estar solo en el museo.

one-shot* ['wʌnʃɒt] *(US)* 1 ADJ = **one-off**. 2 N artículo *m* fuera de serie.

one-sided ['wʌn'saɪdɪd] ADJ unilateral; asimétrico; *(unbalanced)* desequilibrado; *contest, game* desigual; *view etc* parcial, injusto.

one-sidedness [,wʌn'saɪdɪdnɪs] N carácter *m* unilateral; asimetría *f*; desequilibrio *m*; desigualdad *f*; parcialidad *f*, injusticia *f*.

one-stop ['wʌnstɒp] ADJ: **~ shopping** tiendas *fpl* y servicios *mpl* bajo el mismo techo.

one-time ['wʌntaɪm] ADJ antiguo; otrora; **~ butler to Lord Yaxley** antiguo mayordomo de Lord Yaxley; **~ prime minister** ex primer ministro *m*; **the ~ revolutionary** el otrora revolucionario.

one-to-one ['wʌntə'wʌn] *(Brit)* 1 ADJ exacto, en correspondencia

exacta; **~ relationship** relación *f* de uno a uno, relación *f* de persona a persona. 2 ADV exactamente, en correspondencia exacta.

one-track ['wʌntræk] ADJ *(Rail)* de vía única; *mind* que tiene un solo pensamiento.

one-two ['wʌn'tuː] N **(a)** *(Brit: Ftbl)* pared *f*; **to play a ~ with sb** hacer una pared con uno. **(b)** *(Boxing)* un-dos *m*.

one-upmanship [wʌn'ʌpmənʃɪp] N *(hum)* arte de llevar siempre la ventaja, arte de establecerse en una posición superior con respecto a otra persona (logrando una ventaja táctica en una conversación etc).

one-way ['wʌnweɪ] ADJ *admiration etc* que el otro *(etc)* no comparte, no correspondido; **~ journey** viaje *m* sin retorno; **~ street** calle *f* de dirección única, sentido *m* único *(LAm)*, calle *f* de un (solo) sentido *(Mex)*; **'~ traffic'** 'dirección única', 'dirección obligatoria'; **~ ticket** billete *m* sencillo.

one-woman ['wʌn'wʊmən] ADJ individual; de una sola mujer; **~ business** empresa *f* dirigida por una sola mujer; **~ man** hombre *m* que dedica su vida a una sola mujer.

one-year ['wʌnjɪəʳ] ADJ de un año; para un año; **~ unconditional warranty** garantía *f* incondicional de un año.

ongoing ['ɒn,gəʊɪŋ] ADJ que continúa, que sigue funcionando, que cursa, en marcha.

onion ['ʌnjən] 1 N cebolla *f*; (‡) cabeza *f*; **to know one's ~s** *(Brit)* conocer a fondo su oficio, conocer el paño. 2 ATTR: **~ johnny** vendedor *m* ambulante de cebollas; **~-shaped** acebollado, con forma de cebolla; **~ skin** papel *m* de cebolla.

on-line ['ɒnlaɪn] 1 ADJ *(Comput)* on-line, en línea; *(switched on)* conectado. 2 ADV on-line, en línea.

onlooker ['ɒn,lʊkəʳ] N espectador *m*, -ora *f*; observador *m*, -ora *f*; *(esp pej)* mirón *m*, -ona *f*; **I was a mere ~** yo era un simple espectador.

only ['əʊnlɪ] 1 ADV sólo, solamente, únicamente; no ... más que; nada más; **we have ~ 5** tenemos solamente 5, tenemos 5 solamente, tenemos 5 nada más; **what, ~ 5?** ¿cómo, 5 nada más?; **'Ladies ~'** 'Señoras'; **~ God can tell** sólo Dios lo sabe; **~ time will show** sólo el tiempo lo dirá; **I'm ~ the porter** yo soy simplemente el conserje, yo no soy más que el conserje; **I ~ touched it** no hice más que tocarlo; **you ~ have to ask** no hay sino preguntar; **I will ~ say that ...** diré solamente que ...; **~ to think of it!** ¡sólo pensar en ello!; **~ too glad!** ¡con mucho gusto!; **if ~ I could!** ¡ojalá!, ¡ojalá pudiese ...!; **~ just** apenas; **not ~ A but also B** no sólo A sino tambien B; *V* **if** *etc*. 2 ADJ único, solo; **their ~ son** su hijo único; **your ~ hope is to + infin** tu única posibilidad es + *infin*; **his ~ response was to laugh** por toda respuesta se rió; **to be the ~ one to + infin** ser el único en + *infin*; **you are not the ~ one** no eres el único en hacer *(etc)* eso. 3 CONJ: **it's very good ~ rather dear** es muy bueno pero algo caro; **I would gladly do it ~ I shall be away** lo haría de buena gana sólo que voy a estar fuera.

o.n.o. ABBR *of* **or near offer** abierto ofertas.

onomastic [,ɒnəʊ'mæstɪk] ADJ onomástico.

onomastics [,ɒnəʊ'mæstɪks] N SING onomástica *f*.

onomatopoeia [,ɒnəʊmætəʊ'piːə] N onomatopeya *f*.

onomatopoeic [,ɒnəʊmætəʊ'piːik] ADJ onomatopéyico.

onrush ['ɒnrʌʃ] N arremetida *f*, embestida *f*; avalancha *f*, riada *f*; fuerza *f*, ímpetu *m*.

onrushing ['ɒn,rʌʃɪŋ] ADJ *vehicle* embalado, sin freno; *water* creciente; **the ~ tide of migration** la creciente oleada de inmigrantes.

on-screen [,ɒn'skriːn] 1 ADJ **(a)** *(Comput etc)* en pantalla. **(b)** *(Cine, TV)* romance, kiss cinematográfico. 2 ADV *(Cine, TV)* en la pantalla.

onset ['ɒnset] N **(a)** *(attack)* ataque *m*, arremetida *f*. **(b)** *(beginning)* comienzo *m*; **the ~ of winter** el comienzo del invierno.

onshore ['ɒnʃɔːʳ] 1 ADV hacia la tierra. 2 ADJ *breeze* que sopla del mar hacia la tierra.

onside ['ɒnsaɪd] *(Aut etc)* 1 ADJ *(Brit)* izquierdo, *(most other countries)* derecho; *(Football etc:* [,ɒn'saɪd]*)* **to be ~** estar en posición correcta. 2 N *(Brit)* lado *m* izquierdo, *(most other countries)* lado *m* derecho.

on-site ['ɒn,saɪt] ADJ in situ.

onslaught ['ɒnslɔːt] N ataque *m* violento, embestida *f* furiosa; **to make a furious ~ on a critic** atacar violentamente a un crítico.

on-street parking [,ɒnstriːt'pɑːkɪŋ] N aparcamiento *m* en la vía pública.

Ont. *(Canada)* ABBR *of* **Ontario**.

on-the-job ['ɒnðə'dʒɒb] ADJ: **~ training** formación *f* en el trabajo (*or* sobre la práctica).

on-the-spot ['ɒnðə'spɒt] ADJ *decision* instantáneo; *investigation* en el terreno, en el propio lugar (del crimen *etc)*; *report* inmediato, de lo más actual; **our ~ reporter** nuestro reportero que está allí mismo.

onto* ['ɒntʊ] PREP = **on to**.

ontological [,ɒntə'lɒdʒɪkəl] ADJ ontológico.

ontology [ɒn'tɒlədʒɪ] N ontología *f*.

onus ['əʊnəs] N (*no* PL) carga *f*, responsabilidad *f*; **the ~ is upon the makers** la responsabilidad es de los fabricantes; **the ~ is upon him to** + *infin* le incumbe a él + *infin*; **the ~ of proof is on the prosecution** le incumbe al fiscal probar la acusación.

onward ['ɒnwəd] ADJ *march etc* progresivo, hacia adelante.

onward(s) ['ɒnwəd(z)] ① ADV adelante, hacia adelante; **from that time ~** desde entonces; **from the 12th century ~** desde el siglo XII en adelante, a partir del siglo XII.
② INTERJ ¡adelante!

onyx ['ɒnɪks] N ónice *m*, ónix *m*.

oodles* ['uːdlz] NPL: **we have ~** tenemos montones*, tenemos muchísimo; **we have ~ of** tenemos la mar de*, tenemos montones de*.

ooh [uː] ① EXCL ¡oh!
② VI exclamar con placer.

oolite ['əʊəlaɪt] N oolito *m*.

oolitic [,əʊə'lɪtɪk] ADJ oolítico.

oompah ['uːmpɑː] N chumpa *f*.

oomph* [ʊmf] N aquél* *m*, atracción *f* sexual, sexy *m*.

oophorectomy [,əʊəfə'rektəmɪ] N ooforectomía *f*, ovariotomía *f*.

oops* [ʊps] EXCL ¡ay!

ooze [uːz] ① N cieno *m*, lama *f*.
② VT rezumar; (*fig*) rezumar, rebosar de; **the wound was oozing blood** la herida sangraba lentamente; **he simply ~s confidence** rebosa confianza.
③ VI (*liquid*) rezumar, rezumarse; (*blood*) manar suavemente; (*barrel etc*) rezumar.
◆ **ooze away** VI rezumarse; agotarse poco a poco.
◆ **ooze out** VI rezumarse.

op* [ɒp] N = **operation**.

op (*Mus*) ABBR *of* **opus**.

opacity [əʊ'pæsɪtɪ] N opacidad *f*.

opal ['əʊpəl] N ópalo *m*.

opalescence [,əʊpə'lesns] N opalescencia *f*.

opalescent [,əʊpə'lesnt] ADJ opalescente.

opaque [əʊ'peɪk] ADJ opaco.

op art ['ɒpɑːt] N op-art *m*.

op.cit. ABBR *of* **opere citato, in the work cited** en la obra *f* citada, obr. cit.

OPEC ['əʊpek] N ABBR *of* **Organization of Petroleum Exporting Countries** Organización *f* de Países Exportadores de Petróleo, OPEP *f*.

Op-Ed ['ɒp'ed] ADJ, N (*esp US: Press*) ABBR *of* **opposite editorial**; **~ (page)** página *f* de tribuna.

open ['əʊpən] ① ADJ (a) (*not closed*) abierto; *book, grave, parcel, pores, wound etc* abierto; *bottle etc* destapado; **~ prison** cárcel *f* abierta, prisión *f* de régimen abierto; **~ and shut case** asunto *m* clarísimo; **the door is ~** la puerta está abierta; **a dress ~ at the neck** un vestido abierto por el cuello; **with his shirt ~** con la camisa desabotonada; **~ to the public on Mondays** se abre al público los lunes; **to break a safe ~** forzar una caja fuerte; **to cut a sack ~** abrir un saco cortándolo, abrir un saco de un tajo; **to fling** (*or* **throw**) **a door ~** abrir una puerta de golpe, abrir una puerta de par en par.
(b) (*unobstructed*) abierto, sin límites, no limitado; *road* franco, abierto, no obstruido; **~ country** campo *m* raso; **~ end trust** (*US*) sociedad *f* inversionista; **~ market** (*open-air*) mercado *m* al aire libre; (*Fin*) mercado *m* libre, mercado *m* abierto; **~ sea** mar *m* abierto; **in the ~ air** al aire libre; **with ~ views** con amplias vistas, con extensas vistas; **the way to Paris lay ~** el camino de París quedaba abierto.
(c) (*permissible*) **it is ~ to you to** + *infin* puedes perfectamente + *infin*, tienes derecho a + *infin*; **what choices are ~ to me?** ¿qué posibilidades hay?
(d) (*exposed*) abierto, descubierto; *town* abierto; *boat, car, carriage* descubierto; **the map was ~ on the table** el mapa estaba desplegado sobre la mesa; **the book was ~ at page 7** el libro estaba abierto por la página 7; **books on ~ access** libros *mpl* en libre acceso; **~ to every wind** expuesto a todos los vientos; **~ to influence from advertisers** accesible a la influencia de los anunciantes; **it is ~ to doubt whether ...** es discutible si ..., es dudoso que + *subj*; **it is ~ to criticism on several counts** se le puede criticar por diversas razones, es criticable desde diversos puntos de vista; **I am ~ to persuasion** estoy dispuesto a dejarme convencer; **I am ~ to advice** escucho de buena gana los consejos; **I am ~ to offers** estoy dispuesto a recibir ofertas; **to lay ~** abrir; *secret etc* poner al descubierto; **to lay o.s. ~ to criticism** exponerse a ser criticado.
(e) (*public, unrestricted*) público; para todos; *championship, competition, race, scholarship, ticket etc* abierto; *trial* público; **~ day, ~ house** día *m* para el público, jornada *f* de puertas abiertas; **~ letter** carta *f* abierta; **~ policy** (*Insurance*) póliza *f* abierta; **~ secret** secreto *m* a voces; **~ shop** (*factory etc*) empresa *f* con personal agremiado y no agremiado; **O~ University** (*Brit*) ≈ (*Sp*) Universidad *f* Nacional de Educación a Distancia; **he bought it on the ~ market** lo compró en el mercado público; **the competition is ~ to all** todos pueden participar en el certamen, el certamen se abre a todos; **membership is not ~ to**

women la sociedad no admite a las mujeres; *V* **house** *etc*.
(f) (*declared, frank*) abierto, franco; *admiration etc* franco; **an ~ enemy of the Church** un enemigo declarado de la Iglesia; **to be in ~ revolt** estar en franca rebeldía, estar en plena rebeldía; **he was not very ~ with us** no se portó del todo honradamente con nosotros, no fue muy sincero con nosotros.
(g) (*undecided*) *mind* receptivo; imparcial, sin prejuicios; *race* abierto, muy igual; *cheque* sin cruzar, abierto; **~ question** cuestión *f* pendiente, cuestión *f* sin resolver; **it is an ~ question whether ...** queda por resolver si ..., el tiempo dirá si ...; **~ verdict** juicio *m* en el que se determina el crimen sin designar el culpable; **let's leave it ~** dejémoslo sin decidir, dejémoslo pendiente.
② N (a) **to be out in the ~** (*in the country*) estar en el campo; (*in bare country*) estar al raso; (*out of doors*) estar al aire libre; **to sleep in the ~** dormir al raso, dormir a cielo abierto; **to bring a dispute into the ~** hacer que una disputa llegue a ser del dominio público; **their true feelings came into the ~** sus verdaderos sentimientos salieron a flor de piel; **why don't you come into the ~ about it?** ¿por qué no lo declara abiertamente?
(b) **the O~** (*Golf*) el campeonato 'open'.
③ VT (a) (*gen*) abrir; *arms, eyes, heart, mouth, case, letter etc* abrir; (*unfold*) desplegar, extender; *legs etc* abrir, separar; *abscess* cortar; *bottle etc* destapar; *parcel* abrir, desenvolver; *shop* abrir, poner; (*tear*) romper; (*leave exposed*) dejar al descubierto; **to ~ a road to traffic** abrir una carretera al tráfico.
(b) (*drive*) **to ~ a hole in a wall** hacer un agujero en una pared; **to ~ a road through a forest** construir una carretera a través de un bosque.
(c) (*begin*) *conversation, debate, negotiations etc* iniciar, empezar; **to ~ an account in sb's name** abrir una cuenta a nombre de uno; **to ~ the case** (*Jur*) exponer los detalles de la acusación, presentar los hechos en que se basa la acusación; **to ~ 3 hearts** (*Bridge*) abrir de 3 corazones.
(d) (*declare ~, inaugurate*) inaugurar; **the exhibition was ~ed by the Queen** la exposición fue inaugurada por la Reina.
④ VI (a) (*gen*) abrirse (*also* abrir); *flower etc* abrirse; **the door ~ed** se abrió la puerta; **a door that ~s on to the garden** una puerta que da al jardín; **this room ~s into a larger one** este cuarto se comunica con (*or* se junta con) otro más grande; **the shops ~ at 9** el comercio abre a las 9; **the heavens ~ed** se abrieron los cielos.
(b) (*begin*) empezar, comenzar, iniciarse; (*Bridge*) abrir (la declaración); **the season ~s in June** la temporada comienza en junio; **when we ~ed in Bradford** cuando dimos la primera representación en Bradford; **the play ~ed to great applause** el estreno de la obra fue muy aplaudido; **to ~ for the Crown** (*Jur*) exponer los detalles de la acusación, presentar los hechos en que se basa la acusación; **the book ~s with a long description** el libro comienza con una larga descripción; **to ~ with 2 hearts** (*Bridge*) abrir de 2 corazones.
◆ **open out** ① VT abrir; (*unfold*) extender, desplegar.
② VI (a) (*unfold*) extenderse, desplegarse; (*flower*) abrirse.
(b) (*widen*) hacerse más ancho.
(c) (*person*) hacerse menos reservado, perder la reserva; **the company is ~ing out a bit now** ahora la compañía está extendiendo el campo de sus actividades; **the team ~ed out in the second half** en el segundo tiempo el equipo se mostró más enérgico.
◆ **open up** ① VT (a) *box etc* abrir; *map etc* extender, desplegar; *jacket* abrir.
(b) *business, branch* abrir; inaugurar; **to ~ up a market** abrirse un mercado, conquistar un mercado.
(c) *route* abrir; *blocked road* franquear, despejar; *country* explorar; *secret, new vista* revelar; *new possibility* crear; **to ~ up a country for trade** abrir un país al comercio; **when the oilfield was ~ed up** cuando se empezó a explotar el campo petrolífero.
② VI (a) **~ up!** ¡abran!, (*police order*) ¡abran a la autoridad!
(b) (*Comm etc*) empezar, comenzar.
(c) (*Mil*) romper el fuego.
(d) (*emotionally*) franquearse, abrir su pecho.
(e) (*car*) acelerar (a fondo).

┌─ **OPEN UNIVERSITY** ─────────────────────────┐

i *La Open University u OU es el nombre que recibe en el Reino Unido la universidad a distancia para adultos, fundada en 1969. No se exigen requisitos formales de acceso para los primeros cursos y los alumnos estudian desde casa, con el apoyo de algunos programas de radio y televisión emitidos por la BBC, cursos por correspondencia y tutores en su localidad. Además, sobre todo en verano, se organizan algunos cursos a los que los alumnos tienen que asistir en persona.*

open-air ['əʊpn'eər] ADJ al aire libre.
opencast ['əʊpən'kɑːst] ADJ (*Brit*) a cielo abierto, de cielo abierto.
open-door ['əʊpən'dɔːr] ADJ: **~ policy** política *f* de puerta abierta.
open-ended ['əʊpən'endɪd] ADJ *discussion etc* abierto, sin límites fijos,

no limitado de antemano.

opener ['əupnəʳ] N **(a)** (*tin~*) abrelatas *m*. **(b)** (*Theat etc*) primer número *m*. **(c)** for **~s*** (*US*) de entrada.

open-eyed ['əupn'aɪd] ADJ con los ojos abiertos; (*amazed*) con ojos desorbitados.

open-handed ['əupn'hændɪd] ADJ liberal, generoso.

open-handedness ['əupn'hændɪdnɪs] N liberalidad *f*; generosidad *f*.

open-heart ['əupn,haːt] ATTR: **~ surgery** cirugía *f* de corazón abierto.

open-hearted [,əupn'haːtɪd] ADJ franco, generoso.

opening ['əupnɪŋ] **1** ADJ *remark etc* primero; *ceremony, speech*, de apertura; **~ hours** horas *fpl* de abrir; **~ night** primera noche *f*; (*Theat*) estreno *m*; (*of club etc*) inauguración *f*; **~ price** cotización *f* de apertura; **~ stock** existencias *fpl* iniciales; **~ time** (*Brit*) hora *f* de abrir.

2 N **(a)** (*gap*) abertura *f*; (*in walls etc*) brecha *f*; (*in wood*) claro *m*; (*in clouds*) abertura *f*, claro *m*. **(b)** (*beginning*) comienzo *m*, principio *m*; (*of play*) estreno *m*. **(c)** (*of exhibition etc*) inauguración *f*; (*Chess*) apertura *f*. **(d)** (*chance*) oportunidad *f*, entrada *f*; (*Comm*) salida *f*; (*post*) puesto *m*, vacante *f*; **an unusual ~ occurs for ...** se ofrece un puesto interesante de ...; **it's a fine ~ for a young man** es una magnífica oportunidad para un joven; **to give sb an ~ for sth** dar a uno la oportunidad de hacer algo.

openly ['əupənlɪ] ADV abiertamente, francamente; públicamente.

open-minded ['əupn'maɪndɪd] ADJ libre de prejuicios, imparcial; **I am still ~ about it** no me he decidido todavía, sigo sin resolverme.

open-mindedness ['əupn'maɪndɪdnɪs] N ausencia *f* de prejuicios, imparcialidad *f*.

open-mouthed ['əupn'mauðd] ADJ boquiabierto.

open-necked ['əupn'nekt] ADJ sin cuello, sin corbata.

openness ['əupnnɪs] N franqueza *f*.

open-plan ['əupn,plæn] ADJ: **~ office** oficina *f* de plan abierto.

open-top ['əupən,tɒp] ADJ *car, bus* descubierto.

openwork ['əupnwɜːk] N (*Sew*) calado *m*, enrejado *m*.

opera ['ɒpərə] N ópera *f*; (*building*) (teatro *m* de la) ópera *f*.

operable ['ɒpərəbl] ADJ operable.

opera-glasses ['ɒpərəglɑːsɪz] NPL gemelos *mpl* de teatro.

opera-goer ['ɒpərə,gəuəʳ] N aficionado *m*, -a *f* a la ópera.

opera-hat ['ɒpərəhæt] N clac *m*.

opera-house ['ɒpərəhaus] N, PL **opera-houses** ['ɒpərəhəuzɪz] teatro *m* de la ópera.

operand ['ɒpərænd] N operando *m*.

opera-singer ['ɒpərə,sɪŋəʳ] N cantante *mf* de (la) ópera, operista *mf*.

operate ['ɒpəreɪt] **1** VT *motor etc* impulsar; *machine* hacer funcionar, (*as driver etc*) manejar; *switchboard* atender a; *company etc* dirigir; *eg canal* explotar, administrar; **a machine ~d by electricity** una máquina que funciona con electricidad; **can you ~ this tool?** ¿sabes manejar esta herramienta?; **he has been operating a clever swindle** ha estado manejando una hábil estafa, ha andado en una estafa muy hábil.

2 VI **(a)** (*person etc*) obrar, actuar; (*Mech*) funcionar; *drug etc* surtir efecto (*on* en); (*Mil, St Ex etc*) operar; **to ~ on** producir efecto en, afectar, influir; **his words ~d on all our minds** sus palabras influyeron en nuestro ánimo; **it ~s on two levels** funciona a dos niveles.

(b) (*Med*) **to ~ on sb for sth** operar a uno de algo; **to ~ for appendicitis** operar a uno de apendicitis; **he has still not been ~d on** todavía no se le ha operado; **to ~ on sb's liver** operar de hígado a uno.

operatic [,ɒpə'rætɪk] ADJ de ópera, operístico.

operating ['ɒpəreɪtɪŋ] ADJ operante; **~ assets** activo *m* operante; **~ budget** presupuesto *m* operante; **~ costs**, **~ expenses** gastos *mpl* de funcionamiento, gastos *mpl* operacionales; **~ cycle** ciclo *m* de operaciones; **~ loss** pérdida *f* en operaciones; **~ margin** margen *m* operacional; **~ profit** beneficio *m* neto; **~ room** (*US*) **= ~ theatre**; **~ statement** (*Comm*) estado *m*, balance *m*, cuenta *f* (de pérdidas y ganancias); **~ system** (*Comput*) sistema *m* de explotación, sistema *m* operativo; **~ table** mesa *f* de operaciones; **~ theatre** (*Brit*) quirófano *m*, sala *f* de operaciones.

operation [,ɒpə'reɪʃən] **1** N **(a)** funcionamiento *m*; manejo *m*; dirección *f*; explotación *f*, administración *f*; (*Mil, St Ex etc*) operación *f*; (*of person*) actuación *f*; (*manoeuvre*) maniobra *f*; **the company's ~s during the year** las actividades de la compañía durante el año; **~s of doubtful legality** maniobras *fpl* de dudosa legalidad; **to be in ~** (*Mech*) funcionar, estar en funcionamiento, estar funcionando; (*Jur*) estar en vigor, ser vigente; **to be in full ~** estar en pleno funcionamiento; **to bring a machine into ~** poner una máquina en funcionamiento; **to come into ~** (*Jur*) entrar en vigor; **to put into ~** (*Jur*) hacer entrar en vigor, poner en obra.

(b) (*Med*) operación *f*, intervención *f* quirúrgica; **a liver ~** una operación de hígado; **to perform an ~ on sb for sth** operar a uno de algo; **to undergo an ~** ser operado (*for sth* de algo).

2 ATTR: **~ code** código *m* de operación; **~s research** investigaciones

fpl operacionales; **~s room** (*Police etc*) centro *m* de coordinación, sala *f* de dirección de operaciones.

operational [,ɒpə'reɪʃənl] ADJ **(a)** (*relating to operations*) de operaciones; **~ research** investigaciones *fpl* operacionales. **(b)** (*fit: Mil*) en condiciones de servicio, operacional; (*Mech*) en buen estado, capaz de funcionar; **it will not be ~ until next year** no será operacional hasta el año que viene; **when the service is fully ~** cuando el servicio esté en pleno funcionamiento.

operative ['ɒpərətɪv] **1** ADJ **(a)** **the ~ word is ...** la palabra clave es ...; **to be ~** (*Jur*) estar en vigor; **to become ~ from the 9th** (*Jur*) entrar en vigor a partir del 9. **(b)** (*Med*) operatorio. **2** N (*worker*) operario *m*, -a *f*; (*spy*) agente *mf*.

operator ['ɒpəreɪtəʳ] N **(a)** (*of machine*) operario *m*, -a *f*; maquinista *mf*; (*Cine, Med*) operador *m*; (*Telec*) telefonista *mf*; (*Comm*) agente *mf*, corredor *m*, -ora *f* de bolsa. **(b)** (*pej*) vivales *m*, vividor *m*; **he's a very clever ~** es un vividor de los más hábiles.

operetta [,ɒpə'retə] N opereta *f*; (*Sp*) zarzuela *f*.

Ophelia [ɒ'fiːlɪə] NF Ofelia.

ophthalmia [ɒf'θælmɪə] N oftalmía *f*.

ophthalmic [ɒf'θælmɪk] ADJ oftálmico.

ophthalmologist [,ɒfθæl'mɒlədʒɪst] N oftalmólogo *m*, -a *f*.

ophthalmology [,ɒfθæl'mɒlədʒɪ] N oftalmología *f*.

ophthalmoscope [ɒf'θælməskəup] N oftalmoscopio *m*.

opiate ['əupɪɪt] N opiata *f*, opiáceo *m*, narcótico *m* (*also fig*).

opine [əu'paɪn] VI opinar.

▼ **opinion** [ə'pɪnjən] **1** N opinión *f*, parecer *m*; juicio *m*; concepto *m*; **in my ~** en mi opinión, a mi juicio; **in the ~ of those who know** en la opinión de los que saben, según los que saben; **well, that's my ~** por lo menos eso pienso yo; **I am of the ~ that ...** soy del parecer de que; **I am entirely of your ~** estoy completamente de acuerdo contigo; **it's a matter of ~** es cuestión de opinión; **what is your ~ of him?** ¿qué concepto tienes de él?, ¿qué piensas de él?; **to ask sb's ~** pedir el parecer de uno; **his ~ doesn't count** no vale su opinión; **to echo sb's ~** compartir el sentir de uno; **to form an ~** formarse una opinión; **to give one's ~** dar su parecer; **to have a high ~ of sb** tener muy buen concepto de uno, tener a uno en mucho; **to have a high ~ of o.s.** estar pagado de sí mismo; **to have a low** (*or* **poor**) **~ of sb** tener un mal concepto de uno; **I do not share your ~** no comparto esa opinión.

2 ATTR: **~ poll**, **~ survey** sondeo *m* (de la opinión pública).

opinionated [ə'pɪnjəneɪtɪd] ADJ porfiado, terco, dogmático.

opium ['əupɪəm] **1** N opio *m*. **2** ATTR: **~ addict** opiómano *m*, -a *f*; **~ addiction** opiomanía *f*; **~ den** fumadero *m* de opio.

opossum [ə'pɒsəm] N zarigüeya *f*, opos(s)um *m*.

opp. ABBR *of* **opposite** en frente, enfrente de.

opponent [ə'pəunənt] N adversario *m*, -a *f*, contrario *m*, -a *f*, contrincante *m*.

opportune [ə'pɔːtjuːn] ADJ oportuno, a propósito; **to be ~** venir al caso, (*of time etc*) ser propicio; **at an ~ moment** en el momento oportuno; **his arrival was most ~** su llegada fue muy oportuna.

opportunely ['ɒpətjuːnlɪ] ADV oportunamente, a propósito; **this comes most ~** esto viene al pelo.

opportunism [,ɒpə'tjuːnɪzəm] N oportunismo *m*.

opportunist [,ɒpə'tjuːnɪst] **1** ADJ oportunista. **2** N oportunista *mf*.

opportunistic [,ɒpətjʊ'nɪstɪk] ADJ oportunista.

opportunity [ə'pə'tjuːnɪtɪ] N oportunidad *f*, ocasión *f*, chance *m* (*LAm*); **equality of ~** igualdad *f* de oportunidades; **at the earliest** (*or* **first**) **~** en la primera ocasión; cuanto antes; **they helped at every ~** ayudaban siempre cuando podían; **to have the ~ to** + *infin* tener la oportunidad (*or* el chance *LAm*) de + *infin*; **to make the most of one's ~** aprovechar la ocasión; **to miss one's ~** perder la ocasión, desperdiciar la ocasión; **I take this ~ to** + *infin* aprovecho esta ocasión para + *infin*.

oppose [ə'pəuz] VT oponerse a; resistir, combatir; **but he ~d it** pero él se opuso (a ello); **they ~d the motion** se opusieron a la moción; **we shall ~ this by all the means in our power** lucharemos contra esto por todos los medios.

opposed [ə'pəuzd] ADJ opuesto; **to be ~ to sth** oponerse a algo, hablar en contra de algo, resistirse a aceptar algo; **it is ~ to all our experience** va en contra de toda nuestra experiencia; **savings as ~ to investments** los ahorros y no las inversiones, los ahorros en comparación con las inversiones.

opposing [ə'pəuzɪŋ] ADJ opuesto, contrario; **~ team** equipo *m* adversario.

opposite ['ɒpəzɪt] **1** ADV en frente; **they sat ~** se sentaran frente a frente, se sentaron uno enfrente del otro; **it is immediately ~** está exactamente en frente; **they are directly ~** están enfrente por frente. **2** PREP (*also* **~ to**) enfrente de, frente a; **a house ~ the school** una casa enfrente de la escuela; **~ the bus stop** frente a la parada del autobús; **it was ~ the setting sun** estaba de cara al sol que se ponía; **to sit ~ sb** sentarse enfrente de uno; **we were ~ Calais at the time** (*Naut*) entonces estábamos a la altura de Calais.

3 ADJ **(a)** (*of position*) de enfrente; opuesto; **the house ~** la casa de enfrente; **on the ~ bank** en la ribera opuesta; **on the ~ page** en la página de enfrente; **in the ~ direction** en sentido contrario.

(b) (*point of view etc*) opuesto, contrario; (*hostile*) antagónico; **we take an ~ view** nosotros pensamos al contrario, nosotros creemos lo contrario; **of the ~ sex** del otro sexo; *V* **number.**

4 N: **the ~ is true** la verdad es al contrario; **quite the ~!** ¡todo lo contrario!; **he maintains the ~** él sostiene lo contrario; **it's the ~ of what we wanted** es totalmente distinto de lo que queríamos.

opposition [ˌɒpəˈzɪʃən] **1** N oposición *f* (*also Pol*); resistencia *f*; (*Comm*) competencia *f*; (*Sport: team*) equipo *m* contrario, equipo *m* opuesto; (*persons*) (demás) competidores *mpl*; **he made his ~ known** indicó su disconformidad; **to advance a kilometre without ~** avanzar un kilómetro sin encontrar resistencia; **to act in ~ to the chairman** obrar de modo contrario al presidente; **the party in ~** el partido de la oposición; **the O~** (*Pol*) la Oposición; **to be in ~** (*Pol*) estar en la oposición; **to start up a business in ~ to another** montar un negocio en competencia con otro.

2 ATTR *member, party* de la oposición; **the O~ benches** los escaños de la Oposición, la Oposición.

oppositionist [ˌɒpəˈzɪʃənɪst] N (*Pol*) militante *mf* de la oposición clandestina.

oppress [əˈpres] VT oprimir; (*of moral cause etc*) agobiar; (*heat etc*) agobiar, ahogar; **the ~ed** los oprimidos.

oppression [əˈpreʃən] N opresión *f*; agobio *m*.

oppressive [əˈpresɪv] ADJ (*Pol etc*) opresivo; tiránico, oprimente, cruel; *burden* agobiante, oneroso; *tax* gravoso; *heat etc* agobiante, agobiador, sofocante.

oppressively [əˈpresɪvlɪ] ADV opresivamente; cruelmente; de modo agobiante, de modo sofocante; **an ~ hot day** un día de calor agobiante.

oppressor [əˈpresəʳ] N opresor *m*, -ora *f*.

opprobrious [əˈprəʊbrɪəs] ADJ oprobioso.

opprobrium [əˈprəʊbrɪəm] N oprobio *m*.

opt [ɒpt] VI optar; **to ~ for sth** optar por algo, elegir algo, escoger algo; **to ~ to** + *infin* optar por + *infin.*

◆ **opt out** VI optar por no tomar parte (*of* en), decidir no participar (*of* en).

optative [ˈɒptətɪv] **1** ADJ optativo.
2 N optativo *m*.

optic [ˈɒptɪk] ADJ óptico; **~ nerve** nervio *m* óptico.

optical [ˈɒptɪkəl] ADJ óptico; **~ character reader** lector *m* óptico de caracteres; **~ character recognition** reconocimiento *m* óptico de caracteres; **~ disk** disco *m* óptico; **~ fiber** (*US*), **~ fibre** fibra *f* óptica; **~ illusion** ilusión *f* óptica; **~ reader** lector *m* óptico.

optician [ɒpˈtɪʃən] N óptico *mf*; **~'s** (*shop*) óptica *f*.

optics [ˈɒptɪks] N óptica *f*.

optimal [ˈɒptɪml] ADJ óptimo.

optimism [ˈɒptɪmɪzəm] N optimismo *m*.

optimist [ˈɒptɪmɪst] N optimista *mf*.

optimistic [ˌɒptɪˈmɪstɪk] ADJ optimista; **I am not ~ about it** no lo veo tan fácil, no soy optimista (respecto de ello).

optimistically [ˌɒptɪˈmɪstɪklɪ] ADV con optimismo; *speak etc* en tono optimista.

optimization [ˌɒptɪmaɪˈzeɪʃən] N optimización *f*.

optimize [ˈɒptɪmaɪz] VT optimizar.

optimum [ˈɒptɪməm] **1** ADJ óptimo, mejor; más favorable; **the ~ number is 8** el mejor número es 8; **in ~ conditions** en las condiciones más favorables.
2 N, PL **optima** [ˈɒptɪmə] lo óptimo, lo mejor; cantidad *f* óptima, grado *m* óptimo (*etc*).

▼ **option** [ˈɒpʃən] N opción *f* (*also Comm, Scol*); **~s** (*US Aut*) accesorios *mpl*, extras *mpl*; **with an ~ on 10 more aircraft** con opción para la compra de 10 aviones más; **6 months without the ~ (of a fine)** una condena de 6 meses sin la posibilidad de pagar una multa; **at the ~ of the purchaser** a opción del comprador; **to have the ~ of doing sth** tener la posibilidad de hacer algo; **I have no ~** no tengo otro recurso, no tengo más remedio; **to keep one's ~s open** no comprometerse; **to take out an ~ on another 100** suscribir una opción para la compra de otros 100.

optional [ˈɒpʃənl] ADJ discrecional, facultativo; potestativo; *part, fitting etc* opcional, de opción, optativo; (*Comm*) opcional; *dress ~* traje de etiqueta o de calle, traje a voluntad; **~ extras** (*Aut*) accesorios *mpl*, extras *mpl*; **the heater is ~** el calentador es de opción, el calentador es optativo; **that is completely ~** eso es según lo desee Vd.

optionally [ˈɒpʃənlɪ] ADV opcionalmente; **~ you can have a blue one** Vd puede optar por uno azul.

optometrist [ɒpˈtɒmətrɪst] N optometrista *mf*.

optometry [ɒpˈtɒmətrɪ] N optometría *f*.

opt-out [ˈɒptaʊt] **1** ADJ **(a)** (*Brit*) *school, hospital* autónomo (*transferido de la administración local al gobierno central*). **(b)** (*esp Brit*): **~ clause** cláusula *f* de exclusión voluntaria, cláusula *f* de no participación.
2 N (*from agreement, treaty*) opción *f* de exclusión voluntaria, opción *f* de no participación.

opulence [ˈɒpjʊləns] N opulencia *f*.

opulent [ˈɒpjʊlənt] ADJ opulento.

opus [ˈəʊpəs] N, PL **opera** [ˈɒpərə] (*Mus*) opus *m*, obra *f*; (*hum*) obra *f*.

OR (a) N ABBR *of* **operations research, operational research** investigaciones *fpl* operacionales. **(b)** (*US Post*) ABBR *of* **Oregon.**

▼ **or** [ɔːʳ] CONJ **(a)** o; (*before o-, ho-*) u; **7 ~ 8** siete u ocho; **this one ~ another** éste u otro; **either A ~ B** o A o B; **~ else** o bien, si no; de otro modo; **an hour ~ so** una hora más o menos; **20 ~ so** unos veinte, veinte más o menos; **let me go ~ I'll scream!** ¡suélteme, que voy a gritar!; **rain ~ no rain, you've got to go** con lluvia o sin lluvia, tienes que ir.

(b) (*after negative*) ni; **without relatives ~ friends** sin parientes ni amigos; **without fear ~ favour** imparcialmente; **he didn't write ~ telephone** no escribió ni telefoneó.

┌─ OR ─────────────────── see also main entry ─┐

"U" and "ó" instead of "o"

● While *or* is usually translated by *o*, use *u* instead before words beginning with *o* and *ho*:
  ...two or three photos...
  ...dos o tres fotos...
  ...for one reason or another...
  ...por un motivo u otro...
  She was accused of parricide or homicide
  Se le acusó de parricidio u homicidio

● Write *ó* instead of *o* between numerals to prevent confusion with zero:
  ...5 or 6...
  ...5 ó 6...

! Remember to use *ni* with negatives.
  For further uses and examples, see main entry.

└──┘

o.r. ABBR *of* **at owner's risk** a riesgo del propietario.

oracle [ˈɒrəkl] N oráculo *m*; **to work the ~** dirigirlo todo entre bastidores, ingeniárselas.

oracular [ɒˈrækjʊləʳ] ADJ profético, fatídico; sentencioso; misterioso.

oral [ˈɔːrəl] **1** ADJ oral; (*Anat*) bucal; *message* verbal, hablado; *examination, history* oral.
2 N examen *m* oral.

orally [ˈɔːrəlɪ] ADV oralmente; *tell etc* por boca, en palabras; (*Anat, Med*) por vía bucal.

orange [ˈɒrɪndʒ] **1** N (*fruit*) naranja *f*; (*tree*) naranjo *m*; (*colour*) color *m* naranja; (*orangeade*) naranjada *f*.
2 ADJ naranjado, anaranjado, color naranja.

orangeade [ˈɒrɪndʒˈeɪd] N naranjada *f*.

orange-blossom [ˈɒrɪndʒˌblɒsəm] N azahar *m*.

orange box [ˈɒrɪndʒˌbɒks] N, (*US*) **orange crate** [ˈɒrɪndʒkreɪt] N caja *f* de naranjas.

orange-coloured, (*US*) **orange-colored** [ˈɒrɪndʒˌkʌləd] ADJ = **orange 2.**

orange-grove [ˈɒrɪndʒɡrəʊv] N naranjal *m*.

orange-juice [ˈɒrɪndʒdʒuːs] N zumo *m* de naranja, jugo *m* de naranja (*LAm*).

Orangeman [ˈɒrɪndʒmən] N, PL **Orangemen** [ˈɒrɪndʒmən] (*Ir*) orangista *m* (*protestante de Irlanda del Norte*).

orangery [ˈɒrɪndʒərɪ] N invernadero *m* de naranjos.

orangey [ˈɒrɪndʒɪ] ADJ naranjilla, anaranjado.

orang-outang, orang-utan [ˈɔːræŋˈuːtæn] N orangután *m*.

orate [ɔːˈreɪt] VI (*hum*) perorar.

oration [ɔːˈreɪʃən] N oración *f*, discurso *m*.

orator [ˈɒrətəʳ] N orador *m*, -ora *f*.

oratorical [ˌɒrəˈtɒrɪkəl] ADJ oratorio; retórico.

oratorio [ˌɒrəˈtɔːrɪəʊ] N (*Mus*) oratorio *m*.

oratory¹ [ˈɒrətərɪ] N oratoria *f*.

oratory² [ˈɒrətərɪ] N (*Eccl*) oratorio *m*.

orb [ɔːb] N orbe *m*; esfera *f*, globo *m*.

orbit [ˈɔːbɪt] **1** N órbita *f* (*also fig*); **to be in ~** estar en órbita; **to go into ~ round the moon** entrar en órbita alrededor de la luna.
2 VT orbitar, girar alrededor de.
3 VI orbitar, girar.

orbital [ˈɔːbɪtl] **1** ADJ orbital; **~ space station** estación *f* orbital.
2 N (*also ~ motorway*) autopista *f* de circunvalación.

orbiter [ˈɔːbɪtəʳ] N (*Space*) orbitador *m*.

orchard [ˈɔːtʃəd] N huerto *m*; (*apple ~*) pomar *m*.

orchestra [ˈɔːkɪstrə] **1** N orquesta *f*; (*US: seating part of theatre*) platea *f*, patio *m* de butacas.
2 ATTR: **~ pit** foso *m* de orquesta; **~ stall** butaca *f* de platea.

orchestral [ɔ:'kestrəl] ADJ orquestal.

orchestrate ['ɔ:kɪstreɪt] VT orquestar, instrumentar; *campaign* orquestar.

orchestration [,ɔ:kɪs'treɪʃən] N orquestación *f*, instrumentación *f*.

orchid ['ɔ:kɪd] N, **orchis** ['ɔ:kɪs] N orquídea *f*.

ordain [ɔ:'deɪn] [1] VT (a) (*order*) ordenar, decretar; **to ~ that ...** ordenar que + *subj*; **to ~ sb's exile** decretar el destierro de uno.
(b) (*Eccl*) ordenar; **to ~ sb priest** ordenar a uno de sacerdote; **to be ~ed** ordenarse de sacerdote.
[2] VI mandar, disponer; **as God ~s** según Dios manda, como Dios manda.

ordeal [ɔ:'di:l] N (a) (*Hist*) ordalías *fpl*; **~ by fire** ordalías *fpl* del fuego.
(b) (*fig*) prueba *f* rigurosa, experiencia *f* penosa; sufrimiento *m*; **it was a terrible ~** fue una experiencia terrible; **after such an ~** después de tanto sufrir; **exams are an ~ for me** para mí los exámenes son una cosa horrible, sufro lo indecible con los exámenes.

▼ **order** ['ɔ:dər] [1] N (a) (*of society etc, Bio*) orden *m*; clase *f*, categoría *f*; **the lower ~s** la clase baja, la plebe; **talents of the first ~** talentos *mpl* de primer orden; **of the ~ of 500** del orden de 500.
(b) (*holy*) **~s** órdenes *fpl* sagradas.
(c) (*society, decoration*) (*Eccl*) orden *f*; (*secular*) orden *f*, sociedad *f*; (*worn on dress*) condecoración *f*, insignia *f*; **~ of knighthood** orden *f* de caballería; **O~ of the Garter** Orden *f* de la Jarretera.
(d) (*Archit*) orden *m*; **Doric ~** orden *m* dórico.
(e) (*succession, disposition*) orden *m*; clasificación *f*; método *m*; **in ~** en orden, por orden, por su orden; **in alphabetical ~** por orden alfabético; **in chronological ~** por orden cronológico; **in ~ of seniority** por orden de antigüedad; **to be out of ~** (*sequence*) estar mal arreglados; estar fuera de serie; **to get out of ~** desarreglarse; **to put in ~** poner en orden, arreglar, ordenar; clasificar.
(f) (*Mil*) **in close ~** en filas apretadas; **in battle ~** en orden de batalla; **in marching ~** en orden de marchar.
(g) (*good ~*) estado *m*; **in ~** en regla; **in good ~** en buen estado, en buenas condiciones; **his papers are in ~** tiene los papeles en regla; **everything is in ~** todo está en regla; **is this passport in ~?** ¿este pasaporte está en regla?; **beer would be in ~** sería indicado tomarse una cerveza; **what sort of an ~ is it in?** ¿en qué estado está?; **to put a matter in ~** arreglar un asunto; **a machine in working ~** una máquina en funcionamiento; **is it in ~ for me to go to Rome?** ¿tengo permiso para ir a Roma?; **'out of ~'** 'no funciona'; **to be out of ~** estar desarreglado; (*Mech*) no funcionar, estar descompuesto; **my liver is out of ~** no estoy bien del hígado; **to get out of ~** (*Mech*) descomponerse, estropearse, averiarse.
(h) (*Parl*) **~!** ¡orden! **to be out of ~** estar fuera de orden, estar fuera de la cuestión; ser improcedente; **it is not in ~ to discuss Ruritania** Ruritania está fuera de la cuestión; **to call sb to ~** llamar a uno al orden; **to call the meeting to ~** abrir la sesión; **to rise to a point of ~** levantarse para discutir una cuestión de procedimiento; **to rule a matter out of ~** decidir que un asunto no se puede discutir.
(i) (*peace*) orden *m*; **the forces of ~** las fuerzas del orden; **to keep ~** mantener el orden; **she can't keep ~** es incapaz de imponer la disciplina, no puede hacerse obedecer; **to keep children in ~** mantener a los niños en orden.
(j) **in ~ to** + *infin* para + *infin*; **in ~ that ...** para que + *subj*.
(k) (*command*) orden *f*; decreto *m*, mandato *m*; (*of court etc*) sentencia *f*, fallo *m*; **~ of the day** orden *f* del día; (*fig*) moda *f*, lo que es de rigor; **strikes are the ~ of the day** las huelgas están a la orden del día; **O~ in Council** Orden *f* Real; **~ of the court** sentencia *f* del tribunal; **by ~ of** por orden de; **by ~ of the king** por Real Orden; **on the ~s of** por orden de; **till further ~s** hasta nueva orden; **that's an ~!** ¡es una orden!; **~s are ~s** las órdenes no se discuten; **to be under the ~s of** estar bajo el mando de; **to be under starter's ~s** estar listo para la salida; **we are under ~s not to allow it** tenemos orden de no permitirlo; **to get one's marching ~s** ser despedido; **to give an ~** dar una orden; **to give sb ~s to do sth** ordenar a uno hacer algo; **to give ~s that sth should be done** mandar que se haga algo; **to obey ~s** cumplir las órdenes; **I don't take ~s from anyone** a mí no me da órdenes nadie.
▼ (l) (*Comm*) pedido *m*, encargo *m*; **~ department** sección *f* de pedidos; **~ number** número *m* de pedido; **made to ~** hecho por encargo especial, hecho a la orden; **to the ~ of** a la orden de; **we can't do things to ~** no podemos proveer en seguida todo cuanto se nos pide; **to give an ~ for sth** pedir algo, hacer un pedido de algo; **to place an ~ for sth with sb** pedir algo a uno; **we have it on ~ for you** está pedido para Vd; **we will put it on ~ for you** se lo pediremos para Vd al fabricante; **that's rather a tall ~** eso es mucho pedir; **an ~ of French fries** (*US*) una ración de patatas fritas.
(m) (*Fin*) libranza *f*; giro *m*.
[2] VT (a) (*put in ~*) disponer, arreglar, poner en orden; clasificar; **to ~ one's life properly** organizar bien su vida, vivir de acuerdo a cierto método.
(b) (*command*) **to ~ sb to do sth** mandar a uno hacer algo, ordenar

a uno hacer algo; **to ~ sb a new drug** recetar un nuevo medicamento para uno; **to ~ sb a complete rest** mandar a uno reposo absoluto; **to be ~ed to pay costs** ser condenado en costas.
(c) (*Comm*) pedir, encargar; *meal, taxi* encargar; **to ~ a suit of clothes** mandar hacer un traje; **have you ~ed yet?** ¿has escogido ya?, ¿has pedido ya?

◆ **order about, order around** VT mandar de acá para allá, marimandonear.

◆ **order back** VT mandar volver.

◆ **order in** VT mandar entrar.

◆ **order off** VT despedir, echar; decir que se vaya; (*Sport*) expulsar.

◆ **order out** VT echar; mandar que se vaya; *troops* llamar, enviar.

order-book ['ɔ:dəbʊk] N libro *m* de pedidos, cartera *f* de pedidos.

ordered ['ɔ:dəd] ADJ ordenado, metódico, disciplinado.

order-form ['ɔ:dəfɔ:m] N hoja *f* de pedido, boletín *m* de pedido.

ordering ['ɔ:dərɪŋ] N (*Comm*) pedido *m*; el pedir.

orderliness ['ɔ:dəlɪnɪs] N orden *m*, método *m*, disciplina *f*.

orderly ['ɔ:dəlɪ] [1] ADJ (*methodical*) ordenado, metódico; (*tidy*) aseado, en orden, en buen estado; (*well-behaved*) formal; *crowd etc* pacífico, obediente; disciplinado; **~ officer** oficial *m* del día.
[2] N (*Mil*) ordenanza *m*, asistente *m*; (*Med*) asistente *mf*.

orderly room ['ɔ:dəlɪ,rʊm] N oficina *f*.

order-paper ['ɔ:də,peɪpə'] N (*Brit Parl etc*) orden *m* del día.

ordinal ['ɔ:dɪnl] [1] ADJ ordinal; **~ number** número *m* ordinal.
[2] N ordinal *m*.

ordinance ['ɔ:dɪnəns] N ordenanza *f*, decreto *m*.

ordinand ['ɔ:dɪnænd] N ordenando *m*.

ordinarily [ɔ:dɪ'neərɪlɪ] ADV ordinariamente, de ordinario; **~ we buy 6 at a time** generalmente compramos 6 a la vez; **more than ~ polite** más cortés de lo común.

ordinary ['ɔ:dnrɪ] [1] ADJ (a) corriente, común, normal; **the ~ Frenchman** el francés corriente; **an ~ citizen** un simple ciudadano; **for the ~ reader** para el lector medio; **in the ~ way I wouldn't allow it** normalmente no lo permitiría; **it's not what you'd call an ~ present** no es lo que se diría un regalo de todos los días.
(b) **~ degree** (*Brit*) diploma *m*; **O~ grade** (*Scot Scol*), **O~ Level** (*Brit*) ≃ bachillerato *m* elemental (*examen oficial que se suele realizar en el cuarto curso de secundario*); **O~ National Certificate** (*Brit*) ≃ diploma *m* de técnico especialista; **O~ National Diploma** (*Brit*) *diploma profesional*, ≃ diploma *m* de técnico especialista; *ver también* DEGREE .
(c) *share* ordinario; **~ seaman** marinero *m*.
(d) (*pej*) vulgar, ordinario; mediocre; **just an ~ man** un hombre vulgar; **they're very ~ people** son gente muy modesta; **neither good nor bad, just ~** ni bueno ni malo, solamente regular.
[2] N: **a man above the ~** un hombre fuera de serie, un hombre que no es del montón; **sth out of the ~** algo fuera de lo común, algo extraordinario.

ordination [,ɔ:dɪ'neɪʃən] N (*Eccl*) ordenación *f*.

ordnance ['ɔ:dnəns] [1] N (*guns*) artillería *f*, cañones *mpl*; (*supplies*) pertrechos *mpl* de guerra.
[2] ATTR: **O~ Corps** Cuerpo *m* de Armamento y Material; **~ factory** fábrica *f* de artillería; **O~ Survey** (*Brit*) servicio oficial de topografía; **O~ (Survey) map** (*Brit*) ≃ mapa *m* del Estado Mayor.

Ordovician [,ɔ:dəʊ'vɪʃən] ADJ ordoviciense.

ordure ['ɔ:djʊə'] N inmundicia *f* (*also fig*).

ore [ɔ:'] N mineral *m*, mena *f*; **copper ~** mineral *m* de cobre (*etc*).

Ore. (*US*) ABBR *of* Oregon.

ore-carrier ['ɔ:kærɪə'] N mineralero *m*.

oregano [,ɒrɪ'gɑ:nəʊ] N orégano *m*.

organ ['ɔ:gən] N (*all senses*) órgano *m*.

organdie, (US) organdy ['ɔ:gəndɪ] N organdí *m*.

organ-grinder ['ɔ:gən,graɪndə'] N organillero *m*.

organic [ɔ:'gænɪk] ADJ (a) (*gen*) orgánico; **~ analysis** análisis *m* orgánico; **~ chemistry** química *f* orgánica. (b) (*free of chemicals*) orgánico, exento de productos químicos; **~ farming** agricultura *f* orgánica, agricultura *f* que no emplea productos químicos; **~ food products** alimentos *mpl* orgánicos (*or* naturales); **~ restaurant** restaurante *m* de cocina natural.

organically [ɔ:'gænɪkəlɪ] ADV orgánicamente; **he's farming ~** se dedica a la agricultura orgánica; **~ grown foods** alimentos *mpl* orgánicos; **there's nothing ~ wrong with you** Vd está en buen estado en cuanto a lo físico.

organism ['ɔ:gənɪzəm] N organismo *m*.

organist ['ɔ:gənɪst] N organista *mf*.

organization [,ɔ:gənaɪ'zeɪʃən] [1] N (a) (*act*) organización *f*.
(b) (*body*) organización *f*, organismo *m*.
[2] ATTR: **~ chart** organigrama *m*; **~ man** especialista *m* en ciencias administrativas.

organizational [,ɔ:gənaɪ'zeɪʃənl] ADJ organizativo.

organize ['ɔ:gənaɪz] [1] VT (a) (*gen*) organizar; **to get ~d** organizarse, arreglárselas.
(b) (*US Ind*) organizar en sindicatos, sindicar.

2 VI **(a)** (*gen*) organizarse (*for* para).
(b) (*US Ind*) sindicarse, afiliarse a un sindicato.
organized [ˈɔːgənaɪzd] ADJ **(a)** *crime etc* organizado. **(b)** *person* metódico, ordenado.
organizer [ˈɔːgənaɪzəʳ] N organizador *m*, -ora *f*.
organizing [ˈɔːgənaɪzɪŋ] ADJ: **~ committee** comisión *f* organizadora.
organ loft [ˈɔːgənlɒft] N tribuna *f* del órgano, galería *f* del órgano.
organ pipe [ˈɔːgənpaɪp] N cañón *m* de órgano.
organ stop [ˈɔːgənstɒp] N registro *m* de órgano.
organza [ɔːˈgænzə] N organza *f*, organdí *m* de seda.
orgasm [ˈɔːgæzəm] N orgasmo *m*.
orgasmic [ɔːˈgæzmɪk] ADJ orgásmico.
orgiastic [ˌɔːdʒɪˈæstɪk] ADJ orgiástico.
orgy [ˈɔːdʒɪ] N orgía *f*; **an ~ of destruction** una orgía de destrucción; **the flowers were an ~ of colour** las flores eran una explosión de colores.
oriel [ˈɔːrɪəl] N mirador *m*.
Orient [ˈɔːrɪənt] N Oriente *m*.
orient [ˈɔːrɪənt] VT *etc* = **orientate**.
oriental [ˌɔːrɪˈentəl] **1** ADJ oriental.
  2 N oriental *mf* (*also* **O~**).
orientalism [ˌɔːrɪˈentəlɪzəm] N orientalismo *m*.
orientalist [ˌɔːrɪˈentəlɪst] **1** ADJ orientalista.
  2 N orientalista *mf*.
orientate [ˈɔːrɪenteɪt] **1** VT orientar (*to, towards* hacia).
  2 VR: **to ~ o.s.** orientarse.
orientated [ˈɔːrɪenteɪtɪd] ADJ *in compounds eg* **career-~** orientado hacia una carrera; **commercially-~** orientado hacia el comercio.
orientation [ˌɔːrɪenˈteɪʃən] N orientación *f*; **~ course** curso *m* de orientación.
oriented [ˈɔːrɪentɪd] = **orientated**.
orienteering [ˌɔːrɪənˈtɪərɪŋ] N orientación *f*.
orifice [ˈɒrɪfɪs] N orificio *m*.
origami [ˌɒrɪˈgɑːmɪ] N papiroflexia *f*.
origin [ˈɒrɪdʒɪn] N origen *m*; (*point of departure*) procedencia *f*; **country of ~** país *m* de origen, país *m* de procedencia; **to be of humble ~**, **to have humble ~s** ser de nacimiento humilde.
original [əˈrɪdʒɪnl] **1** ADJ **(a)** (*first etc*) original, primero; *meaning, sin etc* original; (*earlier*) primitivo; **the ~ sense was ...** el sentido primitivo era ...; **one of the ~ members** uno de los primeros miembros, uno de los socios fundadores; **its ~ inventor** su inventor primitivo.
  (b) (*inventive, new*) original.
  2 N **(a)** (*manuscript, painting etc*) original *m*; (*archetype*) original *m*, prototipo *m*; **the ~ is lost** el original está perdido; **he reads Cervantes in the ~** lee a Cervantes en su idioma original, lee a Cervantes en su propia lengua.
  (b) (*person*) original *m*, excéntrico *m*.
originality [əˌrɪdʒɪˈnælɪtɪ] N originalidad *f*.
originally [əˈrɪdʒnəlɪ] ADV **(a)** (*at first*) al principio, en sus orígenes; originariamente, originalmente; **as they were ~ written** tal como fueron escritas originariamente; **~ they were in Athens** al principio estuvieron en Atenas, antiguamente estuvieron en Atenas.
  (b) (*in an original manner*) **it is quite ~ written** está escrito con bastante originalidad; **he deals with the subject ~** trata el asunto con inventiva.
originate [əˈrɪdʒɪneɪt] **1** VT producir, originar, dar lugar a; (*of person*) idear, inventar, crear.
  2 VI originarse, nacer, surgir; **to ~ from, to ~ in** traer su origen de; **to ~ with sb** ser obra de uno, ser invento de uno; **where did the fire ~?** ¿dónde empezó el incendio?; **with whom did the idea ~?** ¿quién tuvo la idea primero?
originator [əˈrɪdʒɪneɪtəʳ] N inventor *m*, -ora *f*, autor *m*, -ora *f*.
oriole [ˈɔːrɪəʊl] N: **golden ~** oropéndola *f*.
Orkney Islands [ˈɔːknɪˌaɪləndz] NPL, **Orkneys** [ˈɔːknɪz] NPL Órcadas *fpl*.
Orlon [ˈɔːlɒn] ® N orlón ® *m*.
ormolu [ˈɔːməʊluː] N similor *m*, bronce *m* dorado.
ornament **1** [ˈɔːnəmənt] N adorno *m*, ornato *m*, ornamento *m*; (*trinket*) chuchería *f*; (*vase etc*) objeto *m* de adorno; **he is the chief ~ of his country** es el máximo valor de su patria; **~s** (*Eccl*) ornamentos *mpl*.
  2 [ˈɔːnəment] VT adornar, ornamentar (*with* de).
ornamental [ˌɔːnəˈmentl] ADJ ornamental (*also Bot*); decorativo, de adorno.
ornamentation [ˌɔːnəmenˈteɪʃən] N ornamentación *f*.
ornate [ɔːˈneɪt] ADJ muy ornado, vistoso; *style* florido.
ornately [ɔːˈneɪtlɪ] ADV vistosamente; en estilo florido.
ornateness [ɔːˈneɪtnɪs] N vistosidad *f*; estilo *m* florido; lo florido.
ornithological [ˌɔːnɪθəˈlɒdʒɪkəl] ADJ ornitológico.
ornithologist [ˌɔːnɪˈθɒlədʒɪst] N ornitólogo *m*, -a *f*.
ornithology [ˌɔːnɪˈθɒlədʒɪ] N ornitología *f*.

orphan [ˈɔːfən] **1** ADJ huérfano.
  2 N huérfano *m*, -a *f*.
  3 VT dejar huérfano a; **the children were ~ed by the accident** el accidente dejó huérfanos a los niños; **she was ~ed at the age of 9** quedó huérfana a los 9 años.
orphanage [ˈɔːfənɪdʒ] N orfanato *m*, orfelinato *m*, asilo *m* de huérfanos.
Orpheus [ˈɔːfiuːs] NM Orfeo.
ortho... [ˈɔːθəʊ] PREF orto...
orthodontic [ˌɔːθəʊˈdɒntɪk] ADJ de ortodoncia, ortodoncista.
orthodontics [ˌɔːθəʊˈdɒntɪks] N ortodoncia *f*.
orthodontist [ˌɔːθəʊˈdɒntɪst] N ortodoncista *mf*.
orthodox [ˈɔːθədɒks] ADJ ortodoxo.
orthodoxy [ˈɔːθədɒksɪ] N ortodoxia *f*.
orthographic(al) [ˌɔːθəˈgræfɪk(əl)] ADJ ortográfico.
orthography [ɔːˈθɒgrəfɪ] N ortografía *f*.
orthopaedic, (*US*) **orthopedic** [ˌɔːθəʊˈpiːdɪk] ADJ ortopédico; **~ surgeon** cirujano *m* ortopédico, cirujana *f* ortopédica; **~ surgery** cirujía *f* ortopédica.
orthopaedics, (*US*) **orthopedics** [ˌɔːθəʊˈpiːdɪks] N ortopedia *f*.
orthopaedist, (*US*) **orthopedist** [ˌɔːθəʊˈpiːdɪst] N ortopedista *mf*.
oryx [ˈɒrɪks] N orix *m*.
OS (a) N (*Brit Geog*) ABBR *of* **Ordnance Survey** servicio oficial de topografía.
  (b) (*Hist*) ABBR *of* **old style** según el calendario juliano.
O.S. N (*Brit*) ABBR *of* **ordinary seaman**.
O/S ABBR *of* **out of stock**.
o/s (*Comm*) ABBR *of* **outsize** de tamaño extraordinario.
Oscar [ˈɒskəʳ] N (*Cine*) Oscar *m*.
oscillate [ˈɒsɪleɪt] **1** VT hacer oscilar.
  2 VI **(a)** oscilar (*between* entre; *from A to Z* de A a Z); fluctuar, variar.
  (b) (*person*) oscilar, vacilar; **he ~s between boredom and keenness** pasa del aburrimiento al entusiasmo, oscila entre el aburrimiento y el entusiasmo.
oscillating [ˈɒsɪleɪtɪŋ] ADJ oscilante.
oscillation [ˌɒsɪˈleɪʃən] N oscilación *f*; fluctuación *f*, variación *f*; vacilación *f*.
oscillator [ˈɒsɪleɪtəʳ] N oscilador *m*.
oscillatory [ˌɒsɪˈleɪtərɪ] ADJ oscilatorio.
oscilloscope [ɒˈsɪləˌskəʊp] N osciloscopio *m*.
osculate [ˈɒskjʊleɪt] (*hum*) **1** VT besar.
  2 VI besar(se).
osculation [ˌɒskjʊˈleɪʃən] N (*hum*) ósculo *m*.
OSHA N (*US*) ABBR *of* **Occupational Safety and Health Administration**.
osier [ˈəʊʒəʳ] **1** N mimbre *m* or *f*.
  2 ATTR: **~ bed** mimbrera *f*.
Oslo [ˈɒzləʊ] N Oslo *m*.
osmium [ˈɒzmɪəm] N osmio *m*.
osmosis [ɒzˈməʊsɪs] N ósmosis *f* (*also fig*).
osmotic [ɒzˈmɒtɪk] ADJ osmótico.
osprey [ˈɒspreɪ] N águila *f* pescadora, quebrantahuesos *m*.
osseous [ˈɒsɪəs] ADJ óseo.
ossification [ˌɒsɪfɪˈkeɪʃən] N osificación *f*.
ossify [ˈɒsɪfaɪ] **1** VT osificar.
  2 VI osificarse.
ossuary [ˈɒsjʊərɪ] N osario *m*.
OST N (*US*) ABBR *of* **Office of Science and Technology**.
Ostend [ɒsˈtend] N Ostende *m*.
ostensible [ɒsˈtensəbl] ADJ pretendido, aparente.
ostensibly [ɒsˈtensəblɪ] ADV aparentemente, en apariencia.
ostensive [ɒˈstensɪv] ADJ ostensivo.
ostentation [ˌɒstenˈteɪʃən] N ostentación *f*; aparato *m*, boato *m*; fausto *m*.
ostentatious [ˌɒstenˈteɪʃəs] ADJ ostentoso; aparatoso; *person* ostentativo.
ostentatiously [ˌɒstenˈteɪʃəslɪ] ADV ostentosamente, con ostentación; aparatosamente; con boato; **he remained ~ silent** permaneció ostentosamente silencioso.
osteo... [ˈɒstɪəʊ] PREF osteo...
osteoarthritis [ˈɒstɪəʊɑːˈθraɪtɪs] N osteoartritis *f*.
osteomalacia [ˌɒstɪəʊməˈleɪʃɪə] N osteomalacia *f*.
osteomyelitis [ˌɒstɪəʊmaɪɪˈlaɪtɪs] N osteomielitis *f*.
osteopath [ˈɒstɪəpæθ] N osteópata *mf*.
osteopathy [ˌɒstɪˈɒpəθɪ] N osteopatía *f*.
osteoporosis [ˌɒstɪəʊpɔːˈrəʊsɪs] N osteoporosis *f*.
ostler [ˈɒsləʳ] N (*esp Brit* ††) mozo *m* de cuadra.
ostmark [ˈɒstmɑːk] N marco *m* de la antigua RDA.
ostracism [ˈɒstrəsɪzəm] N ostracismo *m*.
ostracize [ˈɒstrəsaɪz] VT condenar al ostracismo, excluir de la sociedad (*or* del trato, del grupo *etc*); **he was ~d** vivió en el ostracismo.
ostrich [ˈɒstrɪtʃ] N avestruz *m*.
OT N ABBR *of* **Old Testament** Antiguo Testamento *m*, A.T.

OTB N (*US*) ABBR *of* **off-track betting** apuestas *fpl* ilegales hechas fuera del hipódromo.

OTC (**a**) ADV (*Comm*) ABBR *of* **over the counter** al contado. (**b**) N (*Brit*) ABBR *of* **Officer Training Corps** cuerpo *m* de cadetes militares.

OTE (*Brit*) ABBR *of* **on-target earnings** beneficios *mpl* según objetivos.

Othello [ə'θeləʊ] NM Otelo.

other ['ʌðər] **1** ADJ otro; **the ~ one** el otro; **the ~ five** los otros cinco; **the ~ day** el otro día; **come some ~ day** venga otro día; **all the ~ books have been sold** todos los otros libros se han vendido, todos los demás libros se han vendido; **~ people have done it** otros lo han hecho; **~ people's property** la propiedad ajena; **~ people's ideas** las ideas ajenas; **among ~ things she is a writer** entre otras cosas es escritora; **together with every ~ woman** así como todas las mujeres (*see also* **every**); **I do not wish him ~ than he is** no quiero que sea distinto de lo que es; **no book ~ than this** ningún libro que no sea éste; **he had no clothes ~ than those he stood up in** no tenía más ropa que la que llevaba puesta; **it was no ~ than the bishop** fue el obispo en persona, fue el mismo obispo.

2 PRON: **the ~** el otro; **the ~s** los otros, los demás; **one after the ~** uno tras otro; **among ~s** entre otros; **some do, ~s don't** algunos sí, otros no; los hay que sí, otros no; **are there any ~s?** ¿hay otros?; **and these 5 ~s** y estos otros 5; **she and no ~** ella y no otra; **some fool or ~** algún tonto; **somebody or ~** alguien, alguno, -a (*LAm*); **one or ~ of us** uno de nosotros; **no ~** ningún otro; **our happiness depends on that of ~s** nuestra felicidad depende de la de otros; **we must respect ~s' rights** hay que respetar los derechos ajenos; *V* **each**.

3 ADV: **~ than** de otra manera que; otra cosa que; **he could not act ~ than as he did** no podía hacer otra cosa que la que hizo; **I did not read it ~ than cursorily** no le di sino una lectura superficial.

otherness ['ʌðənɪs] N alteridad *f*.

otherwise ['ʌðəwaɪz] **1** ADV (**a**) (*in another way*) de otra manera; **it cannot be ~** no puede ser de otra manera; **we had no reason to think ~** no teníamos motivo para creer otra cosa; **Miller, ~ known as Dusty Miller**, por otro nombre Dusty; **goods whether sold or ~** géneros vendidos o sin vender.

(**b**) (*in other respects*) por lo demás, por otra parte; **~ it's a very good car** por lo demás es un coche muy bueno, aparte de esto es un coche muy bueno; **a car better than I would ~ have bought** un coche mejor que hubiera comprado normalmente.

2 CONJ (*if not*) si no; **~ we shall have to walk** pues si no (*or* pues de lo contrario) tendremos que ir a pie.

other-worldly ['ʌðə'wɜːldlɪ] ADJ (**a**) *person* espiritual, poco realista. (**b**) *experience* (como) de otro mundo; *being* extraterrestre.

otiose ['əʊtɪəʊs] ADJ ocioso, inútil.

otitis [əʊ'taɪtɪs] N otitis *f*.

OTT* ADJ ABBR *of* **over the top**.

otter ['ɒtər] N nutria *f*.

Otto ['ɒtəʊ] NM Otón.

Ottoman ['ɒtəmən] **1** ADJ otomano.

2 N otomano *m*, -a *f*.

ottoman ['ɒtəmən] N otomana *f*.

OU N (*Brit*) ABBR *of* **Open University** ≃ Universidad *f* Nacional de Educación a Distancia, UNED *f*; *ver también* OPEN UNIVERSITY .

ouch [aʊtʃ] EXCL ¡ay!

ought[1] [ɔːt] N = **aught**.

▼ **ought**[2] [ɔːt] V AUX (**a**) (*obligation*) deber; **I ~ to do it** debo hacerlo, debiera hacerlo; **I ~ to have done it** debiera haberlo hecho; **one ~ not to do it** no se debe hacer; **to behave as one ~** comportarse como se debe; **one ~ to be able to find it** ha de ser posible encontrarlo; **I thought I ~ to tell you** me creí en el deber de decírselo, pensé que debía decírselo.

▼ (**b**) (*vague desirability*) **you ~ to go and see it** vale la pena ir a verlo; **you ~ to have seen it!** ¡era de ver!; **you ~ to have seen him!** ¡había que verle!

(**c**) (*probability*) **that car ~ to win** ese coche tiene más probabilidades de ganar; **that ~ to be enough** eso ha de bastar; **he ~ to have arrived by now** debe de haber llegado ya.

Ouija ['wiːdʒə] ® N (*also* **~ board**) tabla *f* de espiritismo.

ounce [aʊns] N (**a**) onza *f* (= 28,35 *gr*); *ver también* IMPERIAL SYSTEM . (**b**) (*fig*) pizca *f*; **there's not an ~ of truth in it** no tiene ni pizca de verdad; **if you had an ~ of common sense** si tuvieras una gota de sentido común.

OUP N ABBR *of* **Oxford University Press**.

our [aʊər] POSS ADJ nuestro(s), nuestra(s).

ours [aʊəz] POSS PRON (el) nuestro, (la) nuestra *etc*.

ourselves [,aʊə'selvz] PRON (*subject*) nosotros mismos, nosotras mismas; (*acc, dat*) nos; (*after PREP*) nosotros (mismos), nosotras (mismas); *V* **oneself**.

oust [aʊst] VT desalojar; expulsar, echar; (*from house etc*) desahuciar; **to ~ sb from a post** lograr que uno renuncie a un puesto; **we ~ed them from the position** les hicimos abandonar la posición; **'fab'**

~ed 'smashing' 'fantástico' sustituyó a 'fabuloso'.

out [aʊt] **1** ADV (**a**) (*gen*) fuera, afuera; hacia fuera; **'~'** (*notice*) 'salida'; **~ you go!** ¡fuera!; **~ with him!** ¡fuera con él!, ¡que le echen fuera!; **~ with it!** ¡desembucha!*, ¡suelta la lengua! (*LAm*); **seconds ~!** (*Boxing*) ¡segundos fuera!; **you're ~** (*in games*) quedas fuera, te has eliminado; **I'm ~** (*in games*) termino; **the voyage ~** el viaje de ida; **murder will ~** el asesinato se descubrirá; **~ here** aquí fuera; aquí, aquí en este sitio tan remoto; **~ there** allí fuera; allí, allí en ese sitio tan remoto; **it carried us ~ to sea** nos llevó mar adentro; **to have a day ~** pasar un día fuera de casa, pasar un día en el campo, pasar un día al aire libre; **it's her evening ~** es su tarde libre; **to have a night ~** salir de juerga por la noche; *V* *other verbs, eg* **to come ~**, **to go ~** salir; **to run ~** salir corriendo.

(**b**) **to be ~** (*person*) no estar (en casa), estar fuera; haber salido; **Mr Green is ~** el Sr Green no está; **he's ~ a good deal** pasa bastante tiempo fuera; **to be ~ and about again** estar repuesto y activo, estar de nuevo en pie; **now that the Liberals are ~** ahora que los liberales están fuera del poder; **the railwaymen are ~** los ferroviarios están en huelga; **I was ~ for some minutes** (*unconscious*) estuve varios minutos sin conocimiento; **he was ~ cold** estuvo completamente sin conocimiento.

(**c**) (*incorrect*) **I'm 2 dollars ~** he perdido 2 dólares en el cálculo; **he was ~ in his reckoning** había hecho mal el cálculo, había calculado mal; **I was not far ~** lo acerté casi; **and he was not far ~ either** y su conjetura resultó ser casi exacta.

(**d**) (*fig*) **when the sun is ~** cuando brilla el sol; **the dahlias are ~** las dalias están en flor; **the book is ~** se ha publicado el libro, ha salido el libro; **the secret is ~** el secreto ha salido a luz; **the ball is ~** el balón está fuera del terreno; **the tide is ~** la marea está baja; **long dresses are ~** los vestidos largos ya no están de moda; **your watch is 5 minutes ~** su reloj lleva 5 minutos de atraso (*or* de adelanto); **before the week is ~** antes del fin de la semana; **to be ~** *fire, light, gas* estar apagado; **'lights ~ at 10 pm'** 'se apagan las luces a las 10'; **my pipe is ~** se me ha apagado la pipa.

(**e**) (*purpose*) **to be ~ for** buscar; ambicionar, aspirar a; **he's ~ for all he can get** está resuelto a hacerse con todo lo que pueda; **we're ~ for a quick decision** buscamos una pronta decisión; **they're ~ for trouble** quieren armar un escándalo; buscan camorra; **we are ~ after duck** estamos cazando ánades; **she's ~ to find a husband** se propone pescar un marido, está dedicada a conseguir marido.

(**f**) (*of clothes etc*) **the coat is ~ at the elbows** la chaqueta está rota por los codos.

(**g**) (*intensive*) **it's the biggest swindle ~** es la mayor estafa que hay; **he's the best footballer ~** es el mejor futbolista que se ha visto, es el mejor futbolista que se ha conocido jamás.

(**h**) **~ loud** en alta voz; **right ~, straight ~** francamente, sin rodeos.

2 ~ of PREP (**a**) (*outside, beyond*) fuera de; **to be ~ of range** estar fuera de alcance; **to be ~ of danger** estar fuera de peligro; **to be ~ of sight** estar invisible, no estar a la vista, no poderse ver; **to be ~ of season** estar fuera de temporada; **we're well ~ of it** de buena nos hemos librado; **to feel ~ of it** sentirse aislado, no tomar parte en las actividades sociales (*etc*).

(**b**) (*incompatible with*) **to be ~ of proportion with** no guardar proporción con; **~ of measure** fuera de medida; **times ~ of number** innumerables veces; *V* **mind, sort** *etc*.

(**c**) (*verbs of motion etc*) **to go ~ of the house** salir de la casa; **to go ~ of the door** salir por la puerta; **to throw sth ~ of a window** tirar algo por una ventana; **we looked ~ of the window** nos asomamos a la ventana, miramos por la ventana; **to turn sb ~ of the house** echar a uno de la casa.

(**d**) (*origin*) de; **a chapter ~ of a novel** un capítulo de una novela; **like a princess ~ of a fairy tale** como una princesa de un cuento de hadas; **to drink ~ of a glass** beber de un vaso; **to eat ~ of the same dish** comer del mismo plato; **to take sth ~ of a drawer** sacar algo de un cajón; **to read ~ of a novel** leer en una novela; **to copy sth ~ of a book** copiar algo de un libro.

(**e**) (*from among*) **1 ~ of 10** de cada 10, 1; **1 ~ of every 3 smokers** 1 de cada 3 fumadores.

(**f**) (*material*) de; **a box made ~ of wood** una caja hecha de madera.

(**g**) (*because of*) por; **~ of respect for you** por el respeto que te tengo; **~ of spite** por despecho; **~ of necessity** por necesidad; **to do sth ~ of sympathy** hacer algo por compasión.

(**h**) (*lacking*) **we're ~ of petrol** no hay gasolina, se acabó la gasolina, nos hemos quedado sin gasolina; **it's ~ of stock** no hay, no tenemos; **to be ~ of a suit** (*Bridge*) estar fallo; **to be ~ of hearts** tener fallo a corazones.

3 N: *V* **in 3**.

outage ['aʊtɪdʒ] N (*esp US Elec*) apagón *m*, corte *m*.

out-and-out ['aʊtən'aʊt] ADJ *believer etc* firme, acérrimo, cien por cien; de tomo y lomo; *scoundrel* consumado, redomado.

outback ['aʊtbæk] N (*Australia*) despoblado *m*, interior *m*, campo *m*.

outbid [aʊt'bɪd] (*irr: V* **bid**) VT licitar más que, hacer mejor oferta que;

sobrepujar.

outboard ['aʊtbɔːd] ADJ fuera de borda; **~ motor** motor *m* fuera de borda, motor *m* fuera-bordo, fuera bordo *m*, propela *f* (*Carib*).

outbound ['aʊt,baʊnd] (*US*) **1** ADV hacia fuera, hacia el exterior.

2 ADJ que va hacia fuera, que va hacia el exterior; *flight* de ida.

outbox [aʊt'bɒks] VT boxear mejor que.

outbreak ['aʊtbreɪk] N (*of spots*) erupción *f*; (*of disease*) epidemia *f*, brote *m*; (*of revolt*) estallido *m*; (*of war*) comienzo *m*, declaración *f*, (*of hostilities*) rompimiento *m*; (*of feeling, violence etc*) arranque *m*; (*of crimes etc*) ola *f*; **at the ~ of war** al declararse la guerra.

outbuilding ['aʊt,bɪldɪŋ] N dependencia *f*, edificio *m* accesorio; (*shed*) cobertizo *m*.

outburst ['aʊtbɜːst] N explosión *f*; arranque *m*, acceso *m*; **an ~ of anger** una explosión de cólera; **there was an ~ of applause** hubo una salva de aplausos, estallaron ruidosos los aplausos; **forgive my ~ last week** te ruego perdonar el que perdiera los estribos la semana pasada.

outcast ['aʊtkɑːst] N paria *mf*, proscrito *m*, -a *f*; marginado *m*, -a *f*; **he is a social ~** vive rechazado por la sociedad, ha sido marginado por la sociedad.

outclass [aʊt'klɑːs] VT ser netamente superior a, aventajar con mucho a.

outcome ['aʊtkʌm] N resultado *m*, consecuencia *f*.

outcrop ['aʊtkrɒp] **1** N afloramiento *m*, afloración *f*.

2 VI aflorar.

outcry ['aʊtkraɪ] N grito *m*, protesta *f* clamorosa; **to raise an ~ about sth** poner el grito en el cielo por motivo de algo; **there was a great ~** hubo fuertes protestas, se armó la gorda*.

outdated ['aʊt'deɪtɪd] ADJ anticuado, fuera de moda.

outdistance [aʊt'dɪstəns] VT dejar atrás.

outdo [aʊt'duː] (*irr: V* **do**) VT exceder, sobrepujar; **to ~ sb in sth** exceder a uno en algo; **he was not be outdone** no se quedó en menos; **I, not to be outdone ...** pues yo, para no quedar en menos ...; **not to be outdone, he added ...** ni corto ni perezoso, añadió que ...

outdoor ['aʊtdɔːʳ] ADJ al aire libre; **~ activities** actividades *fpl* al aire libre; **~ clothes** ropa *f* de calle; **the ~ life** la vida al aire libre; **~ market** mercado *m* al aire libre.

outdoors ['aʊt'dɔːz] **1** ADV al aire libre; fuera de casa; **go and play ~** id a jugar fuera.

2 N: **the great ~** el gran mundo al aire libre.

outer ['aʊtəʳ] ADJ exterior; externo; **~ leaves** hojas *fpl* de afuera; **O~ Mongolia** Mongolia *f* Exterior; **~ space** espacio *m* exterior.

outermost ['aʊtəməʊst] ADJ *place* extremo, (el) más remoto; *cover etc* (el) más exterior, primero.

outface [aʊt'feɪs] VT desafiar.

outfall ['aʊtfɔːl] N (*of drain*) desagüe *m*, desaguadero *m*; (*of river*) desembocadura *f*.

outfield ['aʊtfiːld] N (*Sport*) parte *f* más lejana del campo, (*Baseball*) jardín *m*.

outfielder ['aʊtfiːldəʳ] N (*Baseball, Cricket*) jugador en el extremo del campo.

outfit ['aʊtfɪt] N (a) (*gear*) equipo *m*; (*tools*) herramientas *fpl*, juego *m* de herramientas; (*of clothes*) traje *m*; **a complete camper's ~** un equipo completo de campista; **why are you wearing that ~?** ¿por qué te has trajeado así?

(b) (*) (*Mil*) unidad *f*, cuerpo *m*, equipo *m*; grupo *m*; organización *f*; (*Sport*) equipo *m*; **when I joined this ~** cuando vine a formar parte de esta unidad; **it's a rotten ~** es una sección horrible.

outfitter ['aʊtfɪtəʳ] N camisero *m*; **sports ~'s** tienda *f* especializada en ropa deportiva.

outflank [aʊt'flæŋk] VT (*Mil*) flanquear, rebasar; (*fig*) superar en táctica, burlar.

outflow ['aʊtfləʊ] N efusión *f*; desagüe *m*; pérdida *f*; (*of capital etc*) fuga *f*, salida *f*; (*Mech*) tubo *m* de salida.

outfox [aʊt'fɒks] VT ser más listo que.

outgeneral [aʊt'dʒenərəl] VT superar en estrategia (*or* táctica).

outgo ['aʊtgəʊ] N (*US*) gastos *mpl*.

outgoing ['aʊt,gəʊɪŋ] **1** ADJ (a) *president etc* saliente; *government* cesante; *ministry* que acaba de dimitir; *mail* que sale; *tide* que baja; *flight* de ida. (b) *character* extrovertido, abierto.

2 NPL: **~s** (*Brit*) gastos *mpl*.

outgrow [aʊt'grəʊ] (*irr: V* **grow**) VT (*person*) crecer más que; *habit etc* pasar la edad de, ser ya viejo para; *defect, illness* curarse de ... con la edad; *clothes* hacerse demasiado grande para; **she has ~n her gloves** se le han quedado chicos los guantes; **we've ~n all that** todo eso ha quedado ya a la espalda.

outgrowth ['aʊt,grəʊθ] N excrecencia *f*; (*fig*) extensión *f*.

outguess [aʊt'ges] VT adelantarse a, demostrar ser más rápido que.

outgun [,aʊt'gʌn] VT (*Mil*) sobrepasar en potencia de fuego a; (*fig*) vencer.

outhouse ['aʊthaʊs] N, PL **outhouses** ['aʊthaʊzɪz] (a) (*Brit*) = **out-**

building. (b) (*US*) retrete *m* fuera de la casa.

outing ['aʊtɪŋ] N (*walk*) paseo *m*; (*trip*) excursión *f*, jira *f* campestre; **I took a brief ~** di un pequeño paseo, di una vuelta; **everyone went on an ~ to Toledo** todos fueron de excursión a Toledo.

outlandish [aʊt'lændɪʃ] ADJ estrafalario, extravagante.

outlast [aʊt'lɑːst] VT durar más tiempo que; (*person*) sobrevivir a.

outlaw ['aʊtlɔː] **1** N proscrito *m*, forajido *m*.

2 VT proscribir; *drug etc* ilegalizar; *practice etc* declarar ilegal, declarar fuera de la ley.

outlawry ['aʊtlɔːrɪ] N bandolerismo *m*.

outlay ['aʊtleɪ] N desembolso *m*, inversión *f*.

outlet ['aʊtlet] N salida *f* (*also fig, Comm*); (*retail ~*) concesionario *m*; (*of drain etc*) desagüe *m*, desaguadero *m*; (*of stream etc*) desembocadura *f*; (*Mech*) salida *f*, tubo *m* de salida; (*US Elec*) toma *f* de corriente; **to find an ~ for a product** encontrar una salida (*or* un mercado) para un producto; **it provides an ~ for his energies** ofrece un empleo para sus energías.

outline ['aʊtlaɪn] **1** N (*profile*) contorno *m*, perfil *m*; (*of plan*) trazado *m*; (*sketch*) esbozo *m*, bosquejo *m*; (*general idea, also ~s*) idea *f* general, nociones *fpl* generales; **'O~s of History'** (*as title*) 'Introducción a la Historia'; **in broad ~** a grandes líneas, a grandes rasgos; **in broad ~ the plan is as follows ...** el trazado general del plan es el siguiente ...; **I'll give you a rapid ~ of the scheme** te esbozaré el proyecto, te daré un resumen del proyecto.

2 ADJ: **~ drawing** esbozo *m*; **~ history** resumen *m* de historia; **~ programme** borrador *m* de programa.

3 VT (*draw profile of*) perfilar; (*sketch*) trazar, bosquejar; *policy etc* explicar en términos generales, dar una idea general de; **to be ~d against** destacarse contra, dibujarse contra; **the building was ~d in the distance** el edificio se perfilaba a lo lejos; **let me ~ the scheme for you** te doy un resumen del proyecto.

outlive [aʊt'lɪv] VT **(a)** sobrevivir a; (*thing*) durar más tiempo que.

(b) (*live down*) hacer olvidar.

outlook ['aʊtlʊk] N **(a)** (*view, future promise*) perspectiva *f*, perspectivas *fpl*; panorama *m*; (*Met*) pronóstico *m*; **the ~ for the wheat crop is good** son favorables las perspectivas de la cosecha de trigo; **it's a grim ~** es una perspectiva nada halagüeña, el futuro no promete nada bueno.

(b) (*opinion*) punto *m* de vista; actitud *f*; **one's ~ on life** su concepto de la vida, la actitud de uno ante la vida; **what is his ~ on the matter?** ¿cuál es su punto de vista en este asunto?; **his ~ is always pessimistic** su actitud siempre es pesimista; **a person with a broad ~** una persona de amplias miras.

outlying ['aʊt,laɪɪŋ] ADJ (*distant*) remoto, lejano, aislado; *suburb etc* exterior, periférico.

outmanoeuvre, (*US*) **outmaneuver** [,aʊtmə'nuːvəʳ] VT superar en la táctica.

outmatch [aʊt'mætʃ] VT superar, aventajar.

outmoded [aʊt'məʊdɪd] ADJ anticuado, pasado de moda.

outnumber [aʊt'nʌmbəʳ] VT exceder en número, ser más numeroso que; **we were ~ed 10 to 1** ellos eran diez veces más que nosotros.

out-of-bounds [,aʊtəv'baʊndz] ADJ V **bound**[2].

out-of-court [aʊtəv'kɔːt] ADJ, ADV sin juicio.

out-of-date ['aʊtəv'deɪt] ADJ anticuado; *see also* **date**[1] **1.**

out-of-doors ['aʊtəv'dɔːz] ADV = **outdoors.**

out-of-pocket ['aʊtəv'pɒkɪt] ADJ: **~ expenses** gastos *mpl* realizados.

out-of-school [,aʊtəv'skuːl] ADJ: **~ activities** actividades *fpl* extraescolares.

out-of-the-way ['aʊtəvðə'weɪ] ADJ (*remote*) remoto, apartado, aislado; inaccesible; (*unusual*) insólito; poco conocido, poco común; (*recherché*) rebuscado.

out-of-towner [,aʊtəv'taʊnəʳ] N (*US*) forastero *m*, -a *f*.

outpace [aʊt'peɪs] VT dejar atrás.

outpatient ['aʊt,peɪʃənt] N paciente *m* externo, paciente *f* externa (del hospital); **~s' department** departamento *m* de consulta externa.

outperform ['aʊtpə'fɔːm] VT hacer mejor que, superar a.

outplay [aʊt'pleɪ] VT superar en la táctica, jugar mejor que; **we were ~ed in every department** ellos resultaron ser mejores que nosotros en todos los aspectos del juego, nos dominaron por completo.

outpoint [,aʊt'pɔɪnt] VT (*Boxing*) ganar por puntos a.

outpost ['aʊtpəʊst] N avanzada *f* (*also fig*), puesto *m* avanzado.

outpouring ['aʊt,pɔːrɪŋ] N efusión *f*; **the ~s of a sick mind** la efusión de una mente enferma; **an ~ of emotion** una efusión de emoción.

output ['aʊtpʊt] **1** N producción *f*, volumen *m* de producción; (*of machine*) rendimiento *m*; (*Elec*) potencia *f* de salida; (*Comput*) salida *f*, output *m*; **to raise ~** aumentar la producción.

2 ATTR: **~ bonus** prima *f* por rendimiento; **~ device** dispositivo *m* de salida.

3 VT (*Comput*) imprimir.

outrage **1** ['aʊtreɪdʒ] N atrocidad *f*; atropello *m*; (*by terrorists*) atentado *m*; (*committed during riot etc*) desmán *m*, desafuero *m*; (*public* *scandal*) escándalo *m*; (*suffered by sb*) indignidad *f*; **bomb ~** atentado *m* con bomba; **it's an ~!** ¡es un escándalo!, ¡qué barbaridad!, ¡no hay derecho!; **to commit an ~ against** (*or* **on**) **sb** cometer un desafuero contra uno.

　②[aʊtˈreɪdʒ] VT ultrajar, violentar, atropellar; (*rape*) violar; **it ~s justice** atropella la justicia.

outrageous [aʊtˈreɪdʒəs] ADJ atroz, terrible; monstruoso; escandaloso; indignante; **your ~ conduct** tu conducta escandalosa; **it is absolutely ~ that ...** es indignante que + *subj*; **it's ~!** ¡es un escándalo!, ¡qué barbaridad!, ¡no hay derecho!

outrageously [aʊtˈreɪdʒəslɪ] ADV *behave etc* de modo escandaloso.

outrank [aʊtˈræŋk] VT ser de categoría superior a.

outré [ˈuːtreɪ] ADJ extravagante, estrafalario.

outreach worker [ˈaʊtriːtʃˌwɜːkəʳ] N *funcionario dedicado a dar a conocer la existencia de ayudas sociales a las personas o grupos a quienes van dirigidas.*

outrider [ˈaʊtˌraɪdəʳ] N motociclista *m* de escolta.

outrigger [ˈaʊtˌrɪɡəʳ] N (*beam, spar*) batanga *f*, balancín *m*; (*rowlock*) portarremos *m* exterior; (*boat*) bote *m* con batanga, bote *m* con portarremos exterior.

outright ①[ˈaʊtraɪt] ADJ (*complete*) completo, entero, total; *sale etc* en su totalidad, definitivo; (*forthright*) franco; *supporter etc* incondicional, declarado; *refusal* rotundo.

　②[aʊtˈraɪt] ADV (*once and for all*) de una vez, de un golpe; (*forthrightly*) abiertamente, francamente; **to buy sth ~** comprar algo en su totalidad, comprar algo definitivamente; **to reject an offer ~** rechazar una oferta de pleno; **to laugh ~ at sth** reírse abiertamente de algo; **they won the cup ~** ganaron la copa definitivamente; **he was killed ~** murió en el acto, murió al instante.

outrun [aʊtˈrʌn] (*irr: V* **run**) VT correr más que; (*fig*) exceder, rebasar, pasar los límites de.

outsell [ˌaʊtˈsel] (*irr: V* **sell**) VT vender más que; superar en las ventas a; **this product ~s all the competition** este producto se vende más que todos los competidores.

outset [ˈaʊtset] N principio *m*, comienzo *m*; **at the ~** al principio; **from the ~** desde el principio.

outshine [aʊtˈʃaɪn] (*irr: V* **shine**) VT brillar más que; (*fig*) eclipsar, superar en brillantez.

outside [ˈaʊtsaɪd] ① ADV fuera; **to be ~** estar fuera; **to leave a car ~** dejar un coche fuera, (*at night etc*) dejar un coche en la calle, dejar un coche al descubierto; **to put the cat ~** hacer salir al gato; **seen from ~** visto desde fuera; **to ride ~** (*on bus*) viajar en el piso superior; **~ of =** **2**.

　②PREP fuera de; al exterior de; (*beyond*) más allá de, al otro lado de; **he's waiting ~ the door** espera a la puerta; **one could hear everything that was said ~ the door** se oía todo cuanto se estaba diciendo al otro lado de la puerta; **it's ~ the normal range** cae fuera del alcance normal; **it's ~ our scheme** no forma parte de nuestro proyecto; **that's ~ our terms of reference** eso no está comprendido en nuestro mandato.

　③ ADJ (*outer*) exterior, externo; (*outermost*) extremo; *chance etc* remoto, poco prometedor; (*relating to other people*) ajeno; (*brought from ~*) traído desde fuera; *TV broadcast* exterior; *forward* (*Sport*) extremo; **thanks to ~ influence** gracias a la influencia de personas ajenas al asunto, gracias a influencias extrañas; **to get an ~ opinion** buscar una opinión independiente; **~ call** llamada *f* de fuera; **~ contractor** contratista *mf* independiente; **~ lane** carril *m* de adelantamiento; **~ line** línea *f* exterior.

　④ N (*outer part*) exterior *m*; (*surface*) superficie *f*; (*outward aspect*) aspecto *m* exterior, apariencia *f*; (*of bus*) piso *m* superior; **at the ~** a lo sumo, cuando más; **from the ~** desde fuera, desde el exterior; **to open a window from the ~** abrir una ventana desde fuera; **on the ~** por fuera; **to pass sb on the ~** adelantar (*LAm*: rebasar) a uno por el exterior; **the window opens to the ~** la ventana se abre hacia fuera.

outside-forward [ˈaʊtsaɪdˈfɔːwəd] N delantero *m* extremo, delantera *f* extrema.

outside-left [ˈaʊtsaɪdˈleft] N extremo *m* izquierdo, extrema *f* izquierda.

outsider [ˈaʊtˈsaɪdəʳ] N (*stranger*) forastero *m*, -a *f*, desconocido *m*, -a *f*, (*pej*) intruso *m*, -a *f*; (*in racing*) caballo *m* que no figura entre los favoritos, (*in election*) candidato *m* poco conocido; (*cad*) canalla *m*, persona *f* indeseable; (*independent*) persona *f* independiente, persona *f* ajena al asunto, persona *f* no comprometida; **I'm an ~ in these matters** yo soy un profano en estos asuntos.

outside-right [ˈaʊtsaɪdˈraɪt] N extremo *m* derecho, extrema *f* derecha.

outsize [ˈaʊtsaɪz] ADJ muy grande, de tamaño extraordinario; (*hum*) enorme.

outskirts [ˈaʊtskɜːts] NPL afueras *fpl*; alrededores *mpl*; barrios *mpl* (exteriores).

outsmart [aʊtˈsmɑːt] VT ser más listo que, burlar; (*deceive*) engañar, burlar.

outsourcing [ˈaʊtsɔːsɪŋ] N (*Comm*) aprovisionamiento *m* del exterior; **the ~ of components** la adquisición de componentes de fuentes externas.

outspoken [aʊtˈspəʊkən] ADJ franco, abierto; **to be ~** no tener pelos en la lengua.

outspend [aʊtˈspend], PRET, PTP **outspent** VT: **to ~ sb** gastar más que uno.

outspokenly [aʊtˈspəʊkənlɪ] ADV francamente.

outspokenness [aʊtˈspəʊkənnɪs] N franqueza *f*.

outspread [ˈaʊtˈspred] ADJ extendido; desplegado.

outstanding [aʊtˈstændɪŋ] ADJ (a) (*exceptional*) destacado; excepcional, relevante, sobresaliente. (b) *problem* pendiente, no resuelto; *account* por pagar; *debt, interest, shares* pendiente.

outstandingly [aʊtˈstændɪŋlɪ] ADV excepcionalmente, extraordinariamente.

outstare [ˌaʊtˈstɛəʳ] VT: **to ~ sb** desconcertar a uno mirándole fijamente.

outstation [ˈaʊtˌsteɪʃən] N dependencia *f*.

outstay [aʊtˈsteɪ] VT *person* quedarse más tiempo que; **to ~ one's welcome** permanecer tanto tiempo que uno resulta pesado, quedarse más tiempo de lo conveniente; **I don't want to ~ my welcome** no quiero ser un pesado, no quiero abusar.

outstretched [ˈaʊtstretʃt] ADJ extendido; alargado; **with ~ arms** con los brazos tendidos.

outstrip [aʊtˈstrɪp] VT dejar atrás, aventajar, superar, adelantarse a.

out-take [ˈaʊtˌteɪk] N trozo *m* de película desechado.

out-tray [ˈaʊtˌtreɪ] N bandeja *f* de salida.

outturn [ˈaʊttɜːn] N (*US*) rendimiento *m*, producción *f*.

outvote [aʊtˈvəʊt] VT *person* vencer en las elecciones; *proposal* rechazar por votación; **but I was ~d** pero en la votación perdí.

outward [ˈaʊtwəd] ADJ exterior, externo, *journey* de ida.

outward-looking [ˈaʊtwədˌlʊkɪŋ] ADJ *person, organization, country* abierto al exterior; *policy, attitude* abierto, expansivo.

outwardly [ˈaʊtwədlɪ] ADV por fuera, aparentemente.

outward(s) [ˈaʊtwəd(z)] ADV hacia fuera; exteriormente; **to be ~ bound from Vigo** haber salido de Vigo; **to be ~ bound for Gijón** ir con rumbo a Gijón.

outwear [aʊtˈwɛəʳ] (*irr: V* **wear**) VT (*last longer than*) durar más tiempo que; (*wear out*) gastar.

outweigh [aʊtˈweɪ] VT pesar más que, tener mayor peso que; (*fig*) pesar más que; **this ~s all other considerations** éste vale más que todos los demás factores.

outwit [aʊtˈwɪt] VT ser más listo que, burlar.

outwith [ˌaʊtˈwɪθ] PREP (*Scot*) V **outside 2**.

outworn [aʊtˈwɔːn] ADJ gastado, cansado.

outworker [ˈaʊtwɜːkəʳ] N persona que trabaja en su propio domicilio.

ouzo [ˈuːzəʊ] N ouzo *m*.

ova [ˈəʊvə] NPL *of* **ovum**.

oval [ˈəʊvəl] ① ADJ oval, ovalado.

　② N óvalo *m*.

Oval Office [ˈəʊvəlˈɒfɪs] N: **the ~** (*US*) el Despacho Oval.

ovarian [əʊˈvɛərɪən] ADJ ovárico.

ovary [ˈəʊvərɪ] N ovario *m*.

ovate [ˈəʊveɪt] ADJ aovado.

ovation [əʊˈveɪʃən] N ovación *f*; **to give sb an ~** ovacionar a uno; **to receive an ~** ser ovacionado; **he got a standing ~ from the delegates** fue ovacionado por los delegados puestos de pie.

oven [ˈʌvn] N (*Tech*) horno *m*, (*Culin*) horno *m*, cocina *f* (*LAm*); **Huelva was like an ~** Huelva era un horno; **it's like an ~ in there** allí dentro es el mismo infierno.

oven-glove [ˈʌvnˌɡlʌv] N (*Brit*) guante *m* para el horno.

ovenproof [ˈʌvnpruːf] ADJ refractario, (a prueba) de horno.

oven-ready [ˌʌvnˈredɪ] ADJ listo para hornear.

oven-tray [ˈʌvntreɪ] N bandeja *f* para horno.

ovenware [ˈʌvnwɛəʳ] N utensilios *mpl* para horno, utensilios *mpl* termorresistentes.

over [ˈəʊvəʳ] ① ADV (a) (*of place*) encima; por encima; arriba (*LAm*); por arriba (*LAm*); **this goes under and that goes ~** éste pasa por debajo y ése por encima.

(b) (*in another place*) **~ here** acá; **~ there** allá; **~!** (*Radio*) ¡cambio!; **~ and out!** ¡cambio y corto!; **~ to you!** (*Telec etc*) ¡a ti!; **so now it's ~ to you** así que te toca a ti decidir, así que ahora dirás tú; **~ now to our reporter** (*Rad, TV*) ahora pasamos la palabra a nuestro reportero; **~ in France** allá en Francia; **they're ~ for the day** han venido a pasar el día; **when we were ~ in the States** cuando estábamos de visita en Estados Unidos; **~ against the wall** contra la pared; **~ against the church** al lado de la iglesia, junto a la iglesia.

(c) (*everywhere*: **all ~** *etc*) **the world ~** en todo el mundo; **to search the whole country ~** registrar el país de arriba abajo; **embroidered all ~** todo bordado; **to tremble all ~** estar todo tembloroso; **I ache all ~** me duele en todas partes; **I looked for you all ~** te busqué por todas partes; **it happens all ~** ocurre en todas partes, ocurre por doquier; **he was all ~ flour** estaba todo harina; **that's him all ~** eso es muy de él; **suddenly, he was all ~ me** de repente, se puso a manosearme.

(d) (*with verbs*) **to bend ~** inclinarse, encorvarse, doblarse (*LAm*); **to bend sth ~** doblar algo; **to boil ~** irse, rebosar; **to flow ~** desbordarse; *V* **fall over, lean over, look over** *etc.*

(e) (*of number, quantity*) **persons of 21 and ~** las personas de 21 años para arriba; **4 into 29 goes 7 and 1 ~** 29 dividido entre 4 son 7 y queda 1; **we have 4 pounds and a bit ~** tenemos 4 libras y algo más; **there are 3 ~** sobran 3, quedan 3; **I have a card ~** me sobra una carta, tengo una carta de más; **we did it two or three times ~** lo hicimos dos o tres veces (a fondo).

(f) (*finished*) **to be ~** (**and done with**) estar terminado; **when this is all ~** cuando esto haya terminado, cuando se acabe esto; **as soon as the war is ~** en cuanto termine la guerra; **the storm is ~** ya pasó la tormenta; **it's all ~!** ¡se acabó!; **it's all ~ with him** se acabó con él, está perdido, (*relationship*) he roto con él.

(g) **it happened (all) ~ again** volvió a ocurrir, ocurrió otra vez; **it's happening ~ and ~ (again)** esto pasa repetidas veces; **we shall have to start all ~ again** tendremos que volver a comenzar desde el principio.

2 PREP **(a)** (*place: above*) encima de, por encima de, arriba de (*LAm*); (*on, in contact with*) sobre; **~ our heads** por encima de nuestras cabezas; **to spread a sheet ~ sth** extender una sábana sobre algo; **to jump ~ sth** saltar por encima de algo; **we looked ~ the wall** miramos por encima de la tapia; **with a sign ~ the door** con un rótulo sobre la puerta; **it sticks out ~ the street** sobresale por encima de la calle; **to bend ~ a table** inclinarse sobre una mesa; **to fall ~ a cliff** caer por un precipicio; **to trip ~ sth** tropezar con algo; **to sit ~ the fire** estar sentado junto a la lumbre; **the water came ~ her knees** el agua le cubrió las rodillas; **a change came ~ him** se operó en él un cambio; **she's ~ it now** se ha repuesto de eso ya, eso queda ya a la espalda.

(b) (*place: across*) **the pub ~ the road** la taberna de enfrente; **it's just ~ the road from us** está justamente enfrente de nuestra casa; **it's ~ the river** está tras el río, está en la otra orilla del río; **the bridge ~ the river** el puente que cruza el río.

(c) (*place: with all*) **all ~ Spain** por toda España; **known all ~ the world** conocido en el mundo entero; **he had mud all ~ himself** estaba totalmente cubierto de lodo; **they were all ~ him** le recibieron con el mayor entusiasmo, le dieron grandes testimonios de su afecto; **Zaragoza were all ~ Bilbao** el Zaragoza dominó al Bilbao por completo.

(d) (*place: fig*) **to rule ~ a people** reinar sobre un pueblo; **he's ~ me** es mi superior; **they gave me the preference ~ him** me prefirieron a él; **to have an advantage ~ sb** llevar ventaja a uno.

(e) (*numbers*) **the numbers ~ 20** los números superiores a 20, los números más allá de 20; **~ 200** más de 200; **well ~ 200** 200 y muchos más; **she's ~ 21 now** tiene más de 21 años ya; **he must be ~ 60** tendrá más de 60 años; **~ and above last year's figure** en exceso de la cifra del año pasado; **an increase of 5% ~ last year's total** un aumento de 5 por cien sobre el año anterior; **~ and above what has been said** además de lo que se ha dicho; **~ and above our needs** más allá de nuestras necesidades.

(f) (*time*) **~ the last few years** durante los últimos años; **payments spread ~ some years** pagos espaciados por varios años; **we stayed on ~ the weekend** nos quedamos a pasar el fin de semana.

(g) (*motive*) **they fell out ~ money** riñeron por cuestión de dinero; **to pause ~ a difficulty** detenerse a considerar un punto difícil.

(h) (*means*) **I heard it ~ the radio** lo supe por la radio.

over- ['əʊvər] PREF sobre..., super...; demasiado...

overabundance ['əʊvərə'bʌndəns] N sobreabundancia *f*.

overabundant ['əʊvərə'bʌndənt] ADJ sobreabundante.

overact ['əʊvər'ækt] VI sobreactuar, exagerar (el papel).

overacting [,əʊvər'æktɪŋ] N sobreactuación *f*, exageración *f* (del papel).

overactive ['əʊvər'æktɪv] ADJ demasiado activo.

overage ['əʊvərɪdʒ] N (*US: Comm*) excedente *m* de mercancías.

overall **1** [,əʊvər'ɔːl] ADV en conjunto, en su totalidad; **~, we are well pleased** en resumen, estamos muy contentos. **2** ['əʊvərɔːl] ADJ *study, view etc* de conjunto; *length etc* total; (*total*) global.

overalls ['əʊvərɔːlz] NPL guardapolvo *m*, mono *m*, traje *m* de faena, bata *f*, overol *m* (*LAm*).

overambitious ['əʊvəræm'bɪʃəs] ADJ demasiado ambicioso.

overanxious ['əʊvər'æŋkʃəs] ADJ **(a)** (*worried*) demasiado preocupado, preocupado sin motivo.

(b) (*eager*) demasiado deseoso (*for* de; *to do* de hacer); **I'm not ~ to go** tengo pocas ganas de ir.

overarching [,əʊvər'ɑːtʃɪŋ] ADJ *question* global; *desire* general.

overarm ['əʊvərɑːm] ADV *throw, bowl* por encima de la cabeza.

overawe [,əʊvər'ɔː] VT intimidar; imponer respeto a.

overbalance [,əʊvə'bæləns] **1** VT hacer perder el equilibrio. **2** VI perder el equilibrio.

overbearing [,əʊvə'beərɪŋ] ADJ imperioso, altivo; déspótico.

overbid **1** ['əʊvəbɪd] N (*at auction*) mejor oferta *f*, mejor postura *f*; (*Bridge*) sobremarca *f*. **2** [,əʊvə'bɪd] (*irr: V* **bid**) VT (*at auction*) licitar más que, hacer mejor oferta que; (*Bridge*) marcar más que. **3** [,əʊvə'bɪd] VI (*Bridge*) hacer una sobremarca, (*foolishly*) declarar demasiado.

overbill ['əʊvəbɪl] VT (*US*) cobrar demasiado a, presentar una factura excesiva a; **I was ~ed** trataron de cobrarme demasiado.

overblown ['əʊvə'bləʊn] ADJ **(a)** *flower* marchito, pasado. **(b)** *style* pomposo, pretencioso.

overboard ['əʊvəbɔːd] ADV: **man ~!** ¡hombre al agua!; **to fall ~** caer al agua; **to throw sth ~** echar algo por la borda (*also fig*); **to go ~ for sth*** entusiasmarse locamente por algo.

overbold ['əʊvə'bəʊld] ADJ demasiado atrevido; temerario; descarado.

overbook [,əʊvə'bʊk] VT sobrereservar, reservar con exceso.

overbooking [,əʊvə'bʊkɪŋ] N sobrecontrata *f*, sobrecontratación *f*, exceso *m* de contratación.

overburden [,əʊvə'bɜːdn] VT sobrecargar; oprimir, agobiar (*with* de); **not exactly ~ed with worries** no precisamente agobiado de preocupaciones.

overcall [,əʊvə'kɔːl] VTI = **overbid**.

over-capacity ['əʊvəkə'pæsɪtɪ] N sobrecapacidad *f*.

overcapitalization [,əʊvə,kæpɪtəlaɪ'zeɪʃən] N sobrecapitalización *f*, capitalización *f* inflada.

overcapitalize [,əʊvə'kæpɪtəlaɪz] VT sobrecapitalizar.

overcast ['əʊvəkɑːst] ADJ *sky* encapotado, cubierto, nublado; **to grow ~** anublarse.

overcautious ['əʊvə'kɔːʃəs] ADJ demasiado cauteloso, prudente con exceso.

overcautiousness [,əʊvə'kɔːʃəsnɪs] N excesiva cautela *f*.

overcharge **1** [,əʊvə,tʃɑːdʒ] N precio *m* excesivo, cargo *m* excesivo. **2** ['əʊvə'tʃɑːdʒ] VT sobrecargar (*also Elec*); *person* cobrar demasiado a. **3** ['əʊvə'tʃɑːdʒ] VI cobrar un precio excesivo, hacer pagar demasiado.

overcoat ['əʊvəkəʊt] N abrigo *m*, sobretodo *m*, gabán *m*.

overcome [,əʊvə'kʌm] (*irr: V* **come**) **1** VT *enemy, temptation etc* vencer; *difficulty* salvar, superar; **sleep overcame him** le rindió el sueño; **he was ~ by remorse** le rindieron los remordimientos; **he was ~ by grief** estaba postrado de dolor. **2** VI vencer, triunfar; **we shall ~** venceremos.

WE SHALL OVERCOME

We Shall Overcome (Venceremos) es el título de una canción cantada por los miembros del llamado *US Civil Rights Movement* (movimiento por los derechos civiles en Estados Unidos). Se cantaba sobre todo en los años 50 y 60 durante las protestas contra la discriminación racial y aún hoy la usan quienes protestan en contra de la injusticia.

---

overcommit [,əʊvəkə'mɪt] VT: **to be ~ted** (*financially*) tener cargas financieras excesivas; (*at work*) comprometerse a trabajar más de lo que se puede.

overcompensate [,əʊvə'kɒmpen,seɪt] VI: **to ~ for sth** compensar algo excesivamente.

overcompensation ['əʊvə,kɒmpen'seɪʃən] N compensación *f* excesiva.

overconfidence ['əʊvə'kɒnfɪdəns] N confianza *f* excesiva, exceso *m* de confianza.

overconfident ['əʊvə'kɒnfɪdənt] ADJ demasiado confiado (*of* en).

overconsumption ['əʊvəkən'sʌmpʃən] N superconsumo *m*, exceso *m* de consumo.

overcook ['əʊvə'kʊk] VT cocer demasiado, recocer.

overcritical [,əʊvə'krɪtɪkəl] ADJ hipercrítico; **let's not be ~** seamos justos en nuestra crítica.

overcrowd [,əʊvə'kraʊd] VT atestar, superpoblar, congestionar.

overcrowded ['əʊvə'kraʊdɪd] ADJ *room etc* atestado de gente, muy lleno; *suburb etc* congestionado; *country* superpoblado.

overcrowding ['əʊvə'kraʊdɪŋ] N superpoblación *f*, congestionamiento *m*; masificación *f*; amontonamiento *m*; (*in tenement etc*) hacinamiento *m*, número *m* excesivo de inquilinos.

overdependence [,əʊvədɪ'pendəns] N dependencia *f* excesiva.

overdependent [,əʊvədɪ'pendənt] ADJ excesivamente dependiente (*on* de).

overdeveloped [,əʊvədɪ'veləpt] ADJ (*gen*) superdesarrollado; (*Phot*) sobreprocesado.

overdevelopment [,əʊvədɪ'veləpmənt] N superdesarrollo *m*.

overdo [,əʊvə'duː] (*irr: V* **do**) VT *food* cocer demasiado, recocer; (*exaggerate*) exagerar; (*use to excess*) usar demasiado; llevar a extremos, excederse en; **to ~ it, to ~ things** (*work too hard*) trabajar demasiado, fatigarse; (*exaggerate*) exagerar; pasarse, irse de la mano; (*in description, sentiment etc*) cargar la mano; **she rather overdoes the**

scent tiende a cargar la mano con el perfume; **see that you don't ~ it** cuidado con no fatigarte; **Espronceda overdoes the passion** Espronceda exagera la pasión.

overdone [ˌəʊvəˈdʌn] ADJ exagerado; *food* muy hecho, demasiado asado (*or* cocido *etc*).

overdose [ˈəʊvədəʊs] **1** N sobredosis *f*.
2 VI tomar una sobredosis (*on* de).

overdraft [ˈəʊvədrɑːft] **1** N (*Comm*) sobregiro *m*, (giro *m* en) descubierto *m*; (*on account*) saldo *m* deudor; (*loan*) préstamo *m*; **to have an ~ at the bank** tener un saldo deudor con el banco, deber dinero al banco.
2 ATTR: **~ charges** cargos *mpl* por descubierto; **~ facility** crédito *m* al descubierto; **~ limit** límite *m* del descubierto.

overdraw [ˈəʊvəˈdrɔː] (*irr: V* **draw**) VT girar en descubierto; **your account is ~n (by £50)** su cuenta tiene un saldo deudor (de 50 libras); **I'm ~n at the bank** tengo deudas en el banco, tengo un saldo deudor en el banco.

overdress [ˈəʊvəˈdres] VI vestirse con demasiada elegancia.

overdrive [ˈəʊvədraɪv] N sobremarcha *f*, superdirecta *f*; **to go into ~** (*fig*) ponerse en superdirecta.

overdue [ˈəʊvəˈdjuː] ADJ (*Comm*) vencido y no pagado; *train etc* atrasado, con retraso; **the bus is 30 minutes ~** el autobús tiene 30 minutos de retraso; **this baby is two weeks ~** este niño debió nacer hace quince días, se ha retrasado el parto quince días; **the book is 5 days ~** se acabó hace 5 días el plazo de préstamo de este libro; **that change was long ~** ese cambio debió hacerse mucho tiempo antes.

overeager [ˈəʊvərˈiːgəʳ] ADJ demasiado deseoso (*for* de; *to do* de hacer); demasiado entusiasta, entusiasta con exceso; muy afanado; **she was not ~ to help** tenía pocas ganas de ayudar.

overeat [ˈəʊvərˈiːt] (*irr: V* **eat**) VI comer con exceso; (*at 1 meal*) atracarse, darse un atracón.

overeating [ˌəʊvərˈiːtɪŋ] N comida *f* excesiva.

overelaborate [ˈəʊvərɪˈlæbərɪt] ADJ demasiado complicado; demasiado detallado; rebuscado; *courtesy etc* estudiado.

overemphasis [əʊvərˈemfəsɪs] N: **to put an ~ on** poner énfasis excesivo en.

overemphasize [ˌəʊvərˈemfəsaɪz] VT sobreenfatizar.

overemphatic [ˌəʊvərɪmˈfætɪk] ADJ demasiado enfático.

overemployment [ˈəʊvərɪmˈplɔɪmənt] N superempleo *m*.

overenthusiastic [ˈəʊvərɪnˌθjuːzɪˈæstɪk] ADJ demasiado entusiasta.

overenthusiastically [ˌəʊvərɪnˌθuːzɪˈæstɪkəlɪ] ADV con demasiado entusiasmo.

overestimate **1** [ˈəʊvərˈestɪmɪt] N sobre(e)stimación *f*, estimación *f* excesiva; (*Fin*) presupuesto *m* excesivo.
2 [ˈəʊvərˈestɪmeɪt] VT sobre(e)stimar, apreciar en una cantidad (*etc*) excesiva; estimar en valor excesivo; *person* tener un concepto exagerado de; **to ~ one's strength** creerse uno más fuerte de lo que es.

overexcite [ˈəʊvərɪkˈsaɪt] VT sobre(e)xcitar.

overexcited [ˈəʊvərɪkˈsaɪtɪd] ADJ sobre(e)xcitado; **to get ~** sobre(e)xcitarse.

overexcitement [ˈəʊvərɪkˈsaɪtmənt] N sobre(e)xcitación *f*.

overexert [ˈəʊvərɪgˈzɜːt] VR: **to ~ o.s.** hacer un esfuerzo excesivo.

overexertion [ˈəʊvərɪgˈzɜːʃən] N (*effort*) esfuerzo *m* excesivo; (*weariness*) fatiga *f*.

overexpenditure [ˌəʊvərɪksˈpendɪtʃəʳ] N gasto *m* excesivo.

overexpose [ˈəʊvərɪksˈpəʊz] VT sobre(e)xponer.

overexposure [ˈəʊvərɪksˈpəʊʒəʳ] N sobre(e)xposición *f*.

overextended [ˌəʊvərɪkˈstendɪd] ADJ *person, organization* desbordado (de obligaciones).

overfamiliar [ˈəʊvəfəˈmɪlɪəʳ] ADJ demasiado familiar, que emplea demasiada confianza.

overfeed [ˈəʊvəˈfiːd] (*irr: V* **feed**) **1** VT sobrealimentar; dar demasiado de comer a.
2 VI sobrealimentarse; comer demasiado, atracarse.

overfeeding [ˌəʊvəˈfiːdɪŋ] N sobrealimentación *f*.

overfishing [ˌəʊvəˈfɪʃɪŋ] N sobrepesca *f*, captura *f* abusiva (*de pescado*).

overflight [ˈəʊvəflaɪt] N sobrevuelo *m*.

overflow **1** [ˈəʊvəfləʊ] N (*liquid*) exceso *m* de líquido, líquido *m* derramado; (*pipe etc*) rebosadero *m*, cañería *f* de desagüe; (*of people*) exceso *m*, número *m* excesivo.
2 [ˈəʊvəfləʊ] ATTR: **~ meeting** reunión *f* para el público sobrante.
3 [ˌəʊvəˈfləʊ] VT *banks* desbordarse de, salir de; *fields, surrounds* inundar.
4 [ˌəʊvəˈfləʊ] VI (*vessel*) rebosar, desbordarse; (*river*) desbordarse, salir de madre; **to ~ with** (*fig*) rebosar de; **to fill a cup to ~ing** llenar una taza hasta que se derrame el líquido; **the crowd filled the stadium to ~ing** el estadio estaba a rebosar de público.

overfly [ˈəʊvəˈflaɪ] (*irr: V* **fly**) VT sobrevolar.

overfond [ˌəʊvəˈfɒnd] ADJ: **she is not ~ of dogs** no le dislocan los perros, no se vuelve loca por los perros.

overfull [ˈəʊvəˈfʊl] ADJ demasiado lleno (*of* de), más que lleno,

rebosante.

overgenerous [ˈəʊvəˈdʒenərəs] ADJ demasiado generoso; **an ~ helping** una porción excesivamente grande; **they were ~ in their praise of him** le elogiaron con exceso.

overground [ˈəʊvəgraʊnd] **1** ADJ de superficie.
2 ADV por la superficie, a cielo abierto.

overgrown [ˈəʊvəˈgrəʊn] ADJ (a) *boy etc* demasiado grande para su edad. (b) *garden etc* abandonado, descuidado; cubierto de malas hierbas; **~ with** cubierto de, revestido de; **the path is quite ~ now** la senda está ya totalmente cubierta de vegetación.

overhand [ˈəʊvəhænd] (*US*) **1** ADJ *stroke* hecho (*or* dado *etc*) por lo alto.
2 ADV por lo alto.

overhang **1** [ˈəʊvəhæŋ] N proyección *f*; (*of roof*) alero *m*; (*in rock climbing*) extraplomo *m*, panza *f* de burro, saliente *m*.
2 [ˌəʊvəˈhæŋ] (*irr: V* **hang**) VT sobresalir por encima de; estar pendiente sobre, estar colgado sobre; (*fig*) amenazar.
3 [ˌəʊvəˈhæŋ] VI sobresalir; estar pendiente, estar colgado.

overhanging [ˈəʊvəˈhæŋɪŋ] ADJ sobresaliente, voladizo.

overhastily [ˌəʊvəˈheɪstɪlɪ] ADV apresuradamente, precipitadamente.

overhasty [ˌəʊvəˈheɪstɪ] ADJ apresurado, precipitado.

overhaul **1** [ˈəʊvəhɔːl] N repaso *m* general, revisión *f*.
2 [ˌəʊvəˈhɔːl] VT (a) (*check*) *machine* revisar, repasar, dar un repaso general a; *plans etc* volver a pensar, rehacer, examinar. (b) (*overtake*) alcanzar, adelantar a.

overhead **1** [ˌəʊvəˈhed] ADV por lo alto, en alto, por encima de la cabeza; **a bird flew ~** pasó un pájaro.
2 [ˈəʊvəhed] ADJ de arriba, encima de la cabeza; *crane* de techo; *railway* elevado, aéreo, suspendido; *camshaft etc* superior, superpuesto; **~ cable** línea *f* eléctrica aérea; **~ expenses** gastos *mpl* generales; **~ kick** chilena *f*, tijereta *f*; **~ light** luz *f* de techo; **~ projector** retroproyector *m*.
3 [ˈəʊvəhed] N: ~ (*US*), ~s (*Brit*) gastos *mpl* generales.

overhear [ˌəʊvəˈhɪəʳ] (*irr: V* **hear**) VT oír, oír por casualidad; acertar a oír; **she was ~d complaining** le alcanzaron a oír quejándose.

overheat [ˈəʊvəˈhiːt] **1** VT recalentar, sobrecalentar (*also fig, Econ*); **to get ~ed** recalentarse.
2 VI recalentarse, sobrecalentarse.

overheating [ˌəʊvəˈhiːtɪŋ] N sobrecalentamiento *m* (*also fig, Econ*).

overindulge [ˈəʊvərɪnˈdʌldʒ] **1** VT *child* mimar con exceso; *passion etc* dar rienda suelta a; *taste etc* consentir.
2 VI darse demasiada buena vida; **to ~ in alcohol** (*etc*) abusar del alcohol (*etc*).

overindulgence [ˈəʊvərɪnˈdʌldʒəns] N (a) (*excess*) abuso *m* (*in* de), exceso *m* vicioso; **by his ~ in ...** por su abandono vicioso a ... (b) (*kindness*) exceso *m* de tolerancia (*towards* con).

overindulgent [ˈəʊvərɪnˈdʌldʒənt] ADJ demasiado indulgente (*towards* con).

overinvestment [ˌəʊvərɪnˈvestmənt] N sobreinversión *f*.

overissue [ˈəʊvərˌɪʃuː] (*St Ex*) **1** N emisión *f* excesiva.
2 VT emitir con exceso.

overjoyed [ˌəʊvəˈdʒɔɪd] ADJ: **they were ~** estuvieron llenos de alegría, se alegraron muchísimo; **he was ~ at the news** no cabía en sí de contento con la noticia; **she will be ~ to see you** estará encantada de veros.

overkill [ˈəʊvəkɪl] N capacidad *f* excesiva de destrucción; (*fig*) exceso *m* de medios; **there is a danger of ~ here** aquí hay peligro de excedernos en los medios.

overladen [ˌəʊvəˈleɪdn] ADJ sobrecargado (*with* de).

overland **1** [ˌəʊvəˈlænd] ADV por tierra, por vía terrestre.
2 [ˈəʊvəlænd] ADJ terrestre; **~ vehicle** vehículo *m* todo terreno; **by ~ mail** por vía terrestre.

overlap **1** [ˈəʊvəlæp] N traslapo *m*, solapo *m*; (*fig*) coincidencia *f* parcial; superposición *f*.
2 [ˌəʊvəˈlæp] VT traslapar.
3 [ˌəʊvəˈlæp] VI traslaparse; (*fig*) coincidir en parte.

overlay **1** [ˈəʊvəleɪ] N capa *f* sobrepuesta; incrustación *f*.
2 [ˌəʊvəˈleɪ] (*irr: V* **lay**[4]) VT cubrir (*with* con); **to get overlaid with** formarse una capa de, cubrirse con, incrustarse de.

overleaf [ˈəʊvəˈliːf] ADV a la vuelta; **'see ~'** 'véase al dorso'.

overlie [ˌəʊvəˈlaɪ] VT recubrir.

overload **1** [ˈəʊvələʊd] N sobrecarga *f*.
2 [ˈəʊvəˈləʊd] VT sobrecargar (*with* de); **to be ~ed with** estar sobrecargado de, estar agobiado de.

overlong [ˌəʊvəˈlɒŋ] ADJ demasiado largo, muy largo.

overlook **1** [ˈəʊvələʊd] VT (a) (*of view: person*) dominar; (*of building*) dar a, mirar hacia, tener vista a; **the house ~s the park** la casa tiene vistas al parque; **the garden is not ~ed** el jardín no tiene ningún edificio al lado que lo domine.
(b) (*watch over*) vigilar; (*inspect*) inspeccionar, examinar.
(c) (*leave out*) pasar por alto; olvidar; no hacer caso de; (*tolerate*) dejar pasar, disimular; (*forgive*) perdonar; (*wink at*) hacer la vista

gorda a; **we'll ~ it this time** se perdona esta vez; **the plant is easily ~ed** es fácil dejar de ver la planta.

overlord [ˈəʊvəlɔːd] N (*feudal etc*) señor *m*; (*leader*) jefe *m* supremo.

overlordship [ˈəʊvəlɔːdʃɪp] N señoría *f*; jefatura *f* suprema.

overly [ˈəʊvəlɪ] ADV (*US*) demasiado; **~ fond of** demasiado aficionado a.

overman [ˌəʊvəˈmæn] VT proveer exceso de mano de obra a; **an ~ned industry** una industria con exceso de mano de obra.

overmanning [ˌəʊvəˈmænɪŋ] N exceso *m* de mano de obra.

overmuch [ˈəʊvəˈmʌtʃ] 1 ADJ demasiado.
2 ADV demasiado; en demasía.

overnice [ˈəʊvəˈnaɪs] ADJ melindroso, remilgado.

overnight [ˈəʊvəˈnaɪt] 1 ADV: **it happened ~** ocurrió durante la noche, ocurrió de la noche a la mañana; **to stay ~** pasar la noche, pernoctar (*at* en); **we drove ~** viajamos por la noche; **will it keep ~?** ¿se conservará fresco hasta mañana?; **we can't solve this one ~** no podemos resolver este problema de la noche a la mañana.
2 ADJ: **~ bag** fin *m* de semana, neceser *m* de viaje; **~ journey** viaje *m* de noche; **~ stay** estancia *f* de una noche.

overoptimistic [ˌəʊvərɒptɪˈmɪstɪk] ADJ demasiado optimista.

overparticular [ˈəʊvəpəˈtɪkjʊləʳ] ADJ melindroso, remilgado; escrupuloso en exceso; **he's not ~ about money** le importa poco el dinero; (*pej*) es poco escrupuloso en asuntos de dinero; **I'm not ~** me da igual.

overpass [ˈəʊvəpɑːs] N (*US*) paso *m* superior, paso *m* a desnivel (*LAm*).

overpay [ˈəʊvəˈpeɪ] (*irr: V pay*) VT pagar demasiado a.

overpayment [ˈəʊvəˈpeɪmənt] N pago *m* excesivo.

overplay [ˌəʊvəˈpleɪ] VT: **to ~ (one's hand)** exagerar.

overpopulated [ˈəʊvəˈpɒpjʊleɪtɪd] ADJ superpoblado.

overpopulation [ˌəʊvəpɒpjʊˈleɪʃən] N superpoblación *f*.

overpower [ˌəʊvəˈpaʊəʳ] VT (*defeat*) sobreponerse a, vencer, subyugar; (*subdue physically*) dominar, asir y tener quieto; (*fig*) dominar; dejar estupefacto; *senses* embargar; **we were ~ed by a sense of tragedy** se apoderó de nosotros un sentimiento de tragedia.

overpowering [ˌəʊvəˈpaʊərɪŋ] ADJ abrumador, arrollador.

overpraise [ˈəʊvəˈpreɪz] VT elogiar demasiado.

overprescribe [əʊvəprɪsˈkraɪb] (*Pharm: Med*) 1 VI recetar demasiados medicamentos.
2 VT recetar sin control.

overprice [ˌəʊvəˈpraɪs] VT cargar demasiado sobre el precio de; **these goods are ~d** el precio de estas mercancías es excesivo.

overprint [ˈəʊvəˈprɪnt] 1 N sobrecarga *f*.
2 VT sobrecargar (*with* de).

overproduce [ˌəʊvəprəˈdjuːs] 1 VT producir demasiado.
2 VI producir demasiado.

overproduction [ˈəʊvəprəˈdʌkʃən] N superproducción *f*, exceso *m* de producción.

overprotect [ˌəʊvəprəˈtekt] VT proteger demasiado.

overprotection [ˌəʊvəprəˈtekʃən] N sobreprotección *f*.

overprotective [ˌəʊvəprəˈtektɪv] ADJ excesivamente solícito.

overqualified [ˌəʊvəˈkwɒlɪfaɪd] ADJ sobrecualificado.

overrate [ˈəʊvəˈreɪt] VT supervalorar, sobre(e)stimar.

overrated [ˌəʊvəˈreɪtɪd] ADJ sobre(e)stimado.

overreach [ˌəʊvəˈriːtʃ] VR: **to ~ o.s.** ir demasiado lejos, extralimitarse.

overreact [ˌəʊvərɪˈækt] VI reaccionar demasiado, sobrereaccionar.

overreaction [ˌəʊvərɪˈækʃən] N sobrerreacción *f*.

overreliance [ˌəʊvərɪˈlaɪəns] N confianza *f* excesiva (*on* en); dependencia *f* excesiva (*on* de).

overreliant [ˌəʊvərɪˈlaɪənt] ADJ excesivamente confiado (*on* en); excesivamente dependiente (*on* de).

override [ˌəʊvəˈraɪd] (*irr: V ride*) VT (*ignore*) no hacer caso de; (*invalidate*) anular, invalidar, restar valor a; desautorizar; (*set aside*) poner a un lado; **this fact ~s all others** este hecho domina todos los demás; **our protests were overridden** no hicieron caso de nuestras protestas; **the court can ~ all earlier decisions** el tribunal puede anular toda decisión anterior.

overriding [ˌəʊvəˈraɪdɪŋ] ADJ predominante, decisivo; *importance* primero, primordial; *need etc* imperioso.

overripe [ˈəʊvəˈraɪp] ADJ demasiado maduro, pasado; *fruit* pocho.

overrule [ˌəʊvəˈruːl] VT (*override*) desautorizar, anular; *request etc* denegar, rechazar; **but we were ~d** pero fuimos desautorizados.

overrun [ˈəʊvəˌrʌn] 1 N (*on costs*) exceso *m* de costos, costos *mpl* excesivos, sobrecoste *m*.
2 [ˌəʊvəˈrʌn] (*irr: V run*) VT (a) cubrir enteramente, invadir; **the field is ~ with weeds** las malas hierbas han invadido el campo, el campo está cubierto de malas hierbas; **the town is ~ with tourists** la ciudad ha sido invadida por los turistas.
(b) *costs, time limit etc* rebasar, exceder.
3 [ˌəʊvəˈrʌn] VI rebasar el límite; **his speech overran by 15 minutes** su discurso se excedió en 15 minutos.

overscrupulous [ˈəʊvəˈskruːpjʊləs] ADJ = **overparticular**.

overseas [ˈəʊvəˈsiːz] 1 ADV en ultramar, allende el mar; **to be ~** estar

en el extranjero; **to go ~** ir al extranjero; **to travel ~** viajar por el extranjero; **visitors from ~** visitantes *mpl* de ultramar; **to send a regiment to fight ~** enviar un regimiento a servir en el extranjero.
2 ADJ de ultramar; **~ agent** agente *m* extranjero; **~ debt** deuda *f* exterior; **~ market** mercado *m* exterior; **~ service** (*Mil etc*) servicio *m* en el extranjero; **~ trade** comercio *m* exterior.

oversee [ˈəʊvəˈsiː] (*irr: V see*) VT superentender, vigilar.

overseer [ˈəʊvəsɪəʳ] N superintendente *mf*; inspector *m*, -ora *f*; (*foreman*) capataz *m*.

oversell [ˈəʊvəˈsel] (*irr: V sell*) VT *product* hacer una propaganda excesiva a favor de; (*fig*) insistir demasiado en.

oversensitive [ˌəʊvəˈsensɪtɪv] ADJ hipersensible, demasiado sensible.

oversexed [ˌəʊvəˈsekst] ADJ de deseo sexual excesivo; sexualmente obsesionado.

overshadow [ˌəʊvəˈʃædəʊ] VT sombrear, ensombrecer; (*fig*) eclipsar; hacer minúsculo; **it was ~ed by greater events** fue eclipsado por sucesos de mayor trascendencia.

overshoe [ˈəʊvəʃuː] N chanclo *m*.

overshoot [ˈəʊvəˈʃuːt] (*irr: V shoot*) VTI: **to ~ (the mark)** pasar de la raya, excederse; **to ~ (the target) by 40 tons** producir 40 toneladas más de lo provisto; **to ~ (the runway)** aterrizar largo; **to ~ a turning** ir más allá de una bocacalle.

oversight [ˈəʊvəsaɪt] N (a) (*omission*) descuido *m*, inadvertencia *f*, equivocación *f*; **by an ~** por descuido; **it was an ~** ha sido una distracción.
(b) (*supervision*) superintendencia *f*, vigilancia *f*.

oversimplification [ˈəʊvəˌsɪmplɪfɪˈkeɪʃən] N simplificación *f* excesiva.

oversimplify [ˈəʊvəˈsɪmplɪfaɪ] VT simplificar demasiado.

oversize(d) [ˌəʊvəˈsaɪz(d)] ADJ demasiado grande, descomunal; (*US*) *clothes* de talla grande.

oversleep [ˈəʊvəˈsliːp] (*irr: V sleep*) VI dormir demasiado, no despertar a tiempo; **I overslept** durmiendo se me pasó la hora, se me pegaron las sábanas.

overspend [ˈəʊvəˈspend] (*irr: V spend*) 1 VT: **to ~ one's allowance** gastar más de lo que permite su pensión.
2 VI gastar demasiado, gastar más de la cuenta; **we have overspent by 50 dollars** hemos gastado 50 dólares más de lo que debíamos.

overspending [ˌəʊvəˈspendɪŋ] N gasto *m* excesivo.

overspill [ˈəʊvəspɪl] N (*Brit*) (*act*) desparramamiento *m* de población; (*quantity*) exceso *m* de población; **an ~ town for Manchester** una ciudad vecinal de absorción de Manchester.

overstaffed [ˌəʊvəˈstɑːft] ADJ con exceso de empleados.

overstaffing [ˌəʊvəˈstɑːfɪŋ] N exceso *m* de plantilla.

overstate [ˌəʊvəˈsteɪt] VT exagerar.

overstatement [ˈəʊvəˈsteɪtmənt] N exageración *f*.

overstay [ˌəʊvəˈsteɪ] VT: **to ~ one's leave** quedarse más tiempo de lo que la licencia permite; **to ~ one's welcome** quedarse más tiempo de lo conveniente.

overstep [ˌəʊvəˈstep] VT exceder, pasar de, traspasar; **to ~ the limit** pasarse de la raya; *V* **mark**² etc.

overstock [ˈəʊvəˈstɒk] VT abarrotar; **to be ~ed with** tener existencias excesivas de.

overstrain [ˈəʊvəˈstreɪn] 1 N fatiga *f* excesiva; (*nervous*) hipertensión *f*.
2 VT *person* fatigar excesivamente; provocar una hipertensión en; *metal* deformar, torcer; *resources* exigir demasiado de, someter a exigencias excesivas.
3 VR: **to ~ o.s.** fatigarse excesivamente.

overstretch [ˈəʊvəˈstretʃ] 1 VT (a) (*lit*) *muscles, legs* forzar demasiado.
(b) (*fig*) *resources, budget, finances* sobreexplotar; *abilities* forzar demasiado; **to ~ o.s.** excederse.
2 VI (*lit*) *person* estirarse más de la cuenta; *muscles, legs* forzarse demasiado.

overstrict [ˌəʊvəˈstrɪkt] ADJ demasiado estricto; excesivamente riguroso.

overstrike [ˌəʊvəˈstraɪk] (*Comput*) 1 N superposición *f*.
2 VT superponer.

overstrung [ˈəʊvəˈstrʌŋ] ADJ sobre(e)xcitado, hipertenso.

oversubscribed [ˌəʊvəsəbˈskraɪbd] ADJ suscrito en exceso; **the issue was ~** se pidieron más acciones de las que había; **the issue was ~ 4 times** la solicitud de acciones rebasó 4 veces la cantidad de títulos ofrecidos.

oversupply [ˈəʊvəsəˈplaɪ] VT proveer en exceso (*with* de); **we are over-supplied with cars** tenemos exceso de coches.

overt [əʊˈvɜːt] ADJ abierto, público; evidente.

overtake [ˌəʊvəˈteɪk] (*irr: V take*) VT (a) alcanzar; (*Brit Aut*) adelantar, rebasar; pasar, sobrepasar; **he doesn't want to be ~n** no quiere dejarse adelantar; **we overtook a lorry near Burgos** cerca de Burgos pasamos un camión; **you can't ~ that car on the bend** no puedes adelantar ese coche en la curva; **X has ~n Y in steel production** X se ha adelantado a Y en la producción de acero.
(b) (*fig*) coger de improviso, sorprender; **to be ~n by events** ser sor-

prendido por los sucesos.

[2] VI adelantar, pasar; **'no overtaking'** (Brit) 'prohibido adelantar', 'prohibido rebasar' (LAm).

overtaking [ˌəʊvəˈteɪkɪŋ] N adelantamiento m, paso m.

overtax [1] [ˈəʊvəˈtæks] VT (Fin) oprimir con tributos, exigir contribuciones excesivas a; (with effort) agobiar, exigir esfuerzos excesivos a.

[2] VR: **to ~ o.s.** fatigarse demasiado, exigirse demasiados esfuerzos a sí mismo.

over-the-counter [ˈəʊvəθəˈkaʊntəʳ] ADJ method etc limpio, honrado.

overthrow [1] [ˈəʊvəθrəʊ] N derrumbamiento m, derrocamiento m.

[2] [ˌəʊvəˈθrəʊ] VT (irr: V throw) echar abajo, tumbar, derribar; (overturn) volcar; dictator, system, empire etc derrumbar, derrocar.

overtime [ˈəʊvətaɪm] [1] N (a) horas fpl extra(ordinarias); tiempo m suplementario; **to do ~, to work ~** trabajar horas extra(ordinarias), hacer horas; **we shall have to work ~ to catch up** (fig) tendremos que esforzarnos al máximo para recuperar lo que hemos perdido. (b) (US: Sport) prórroga f.

[2] ATTR: **~ ban** prohibición f de horas extra(ordinarias); **~ pay, ~ rate** pago m de horas extra(ordinarias).

overtired [ˌəʊvəˈtaɪəd] ADJ muerto de cansancio.

overtly [əʊˈvɜːtlɪ] ADV abiertamente, públicamente.

overtone [ˈəʊvətəʊn] N (Mus) armónico m; (fig) trasfondo m; matiz m; sugestión f; **a speech with a hostile ~** un discurso con alguna nota de hostilidad.

overtop [ˈəʊvətɒp] VT descollar sobre.

overtrick [ˈəʊvətrɪk] N baza f de más.

overtrump [ˈəʊvəˈtrʌmp] VT contrafallar.

overture [ˈəʊvətjʊəʳ] N (Mus) obertura f; (fig) proposición f, propuesta f; sondeo m; **to make ~s to sb** hacer una propuesta a uno; **to make ~s for an armistice** hacer sondeos de armisticio, hacer propuestas de armisticio (to a).

overturn [ˌəʊvəˈtɜːn] [1] VT car, saucepan etc volcar; (disarrange) trastornar; government etc derrumbar, derrocar; decision revocar, anular; **they managed to have the ruling ~ed** lograron hacer anular la decisión.

[2] VI car, aircraft etc volcar, capotar, dar una vuelta de campana; boat zozobrar.

overuse [ˈəʊvəˈjuːz] VT usar demasiado.

overvalue [ˈəʊvəˈvæljuː] VT sobrevalorar, sobre(e)stimar.

overview [ˈəʊvəvjuː] N visión f de conjunto.

overweening [ˌəʊvəˈwiːnɪŋ] ADJ arrogante, presuntuoso, altivo; **~ pride** desmesurado orgullo m.

overweight [ˈəʊvəˈweɪt] [1] ADJ demasiado pesado; **to be ~** pesar demasiado, person ser gordo, tener exceso de carnes; **he is 8 kilos ~** tiene 8 kilos de más; **the parcel is a kilo ~** el paquete tiene un exceso de un kilo. [2] N exceso m de peso, sobrepeso m.

overwhelm [ˌəʊvəˈwelm] VT opponent, team etc arrollar, aplastar; (in argument) aplastar; (of waves etc) fundir, inundar; (of grief etc) vencer, postrar; (of work etc) abrumar, agobiar; **he speedily ~ed his opponent** arrolló a su contrincante en muy poco tiempo; **to ~ sb with favours** colmar a uno de favores; **to ~ sb with kindness** colmar a uno de atenciones; **he was ~ed with joy** rebosaba alegría, no cabía en sí de contento; **we have been ~ed with offers of help** estamos inundados de ofertas de ayuda; **Venice just ~s me** Venecia me deja boquiabierto, Venecia es pasmosa; **you ~ me!** ¡basta ya, te lo ruego!

overwhelming [ˌəʊvəˈwelmɪŋ] ADJ defeat etc arrollador, aplastante, contundente; success arrollador; majority abrumador; pressure etc irresistible; **one's ~ impression is of heat** la más fuerte impresión de todas es la del calor.

overwhelmingly [ˌəʊvəˈwelmɪŋlɪ] ADV de modo arrollador; abrumadoramente; irresistiblemente; **they voted ~ for X** la abrumadora mayoría de ellos votó por X; **he was ~ defeated** sufrió una derrota arrolladora.

overwind [ˈəʊvəˈwaɪnd] (irr: V wind²) VT watch dar demasiada cuerda a.

overwork [ˈəʊvəˈwɜːk] [1] N trabajo m excesivo; **to suffer from ~** haberse cansado trabajando demasiado.

[2] VT person hacer trabajar demasiado; exigir un esfuerzo excesivo a; word, concept usar en exceso, hacer uso excesivo de.

[3] VI trabajar demasiado, cansarse trabajando demasiado.

overwrite [ˌəʊvəˈraɪt] (irr: V write) VT (a) exagerar; cargar los efectos literarios de; **this passage is overwritten** este pasaje tiene un estilo recargado. (b) (Comput) sobreescribir.

overwrought [ˈəʊvəˈrɔːt] ADJ: **to be ~** estar nerviosísimo, haberse agotado por la emoción (etc), estar sobre(e)xcitado.

overzealous [ˈəʊvəˈzeləs] ADJ demasiado entusiasta, demasiado apasionado.

Ovid [ˈɒvɪd] NM Ovidio.

oviduct [ˈəʊvɪdʌkt] N oviducto m.

oviform [ˈəʊvɪfɔːm] ADJ oviforme.

ovine [ˈəʊvaɪn] ADJ ovino.

oviparous [əʊˈvɪpərəs] ADJ ovíparo.

ovoid [ˈəʊvɔɪd] [1] ADJ ovoide. [2] N ovoide m.

ovulate [ˈɒvjʊleɪt] VI ovular.

ovulation [ˌəʊvjʊˈleɪʃən] N ovulación f.

ovule [ˈəʊvjuːl] N óvulo m.

ovum [ˈəʊvəm] N, PL **ova** [ˈəʊvə] óvulo m.

ow [aʊ] EXCL ¡ay!

owe [əʊ] [1] VT deber; **to ~ sb £2** deber 2 libras a uno; **I'll ~ it to you** te lo quedo a deber; **to ~ allegiance to sb** deber lealtad a uno; **to ~ sb a grudge** guardar rencor a uno; **to ~ sb thanks for his help** estar agradecido a uno por su ayuda, deber las gracias a uno por su ayuda; **to ~ one's life to a lucky chance** deber su vida a una casualidad; **he ~s his talent to his mother** le debe su talento a su madre; **to whom do I ~ this honour?** ¿a quién le debo este honor?; **I ~ it to her to confess** mi deber con ella me obliga a confesarlo; **you ~ it to yourself to come** venir es un deber que tienes contigo mismo.

[2] VI tener deudas; **to ~ sb for a meal** estar en deuda con uno por una comida.

▼**owing** [ˈəʊɪŋ] [1] ADJ: **the £5 ~** las 5 libras que debemos, las 5 libras que se nos deben; **how much is ~ to you now?** ¿cuanto se te debe ahora?

▼[2]: **~ to** PREP debido a, por causa de; **~ to the bad weather** debido al mal tiempo, por el mal tiempo; **it is ~ to lack of time** se debe a la falta de tiempo.

owl [aʊl] N (barn ~) lechuza f; (little ~) mochuelo m; (long-eared ~) búho m; (tawny ~) cárabo m.

owlet [ˈaʊlɪt] N mochuelo m.

owlish [ˈaʊlɪʃ] ADJ look etc de búho; solemne.

own [əʊn] [1] ADJ propio; **it's all my ~ money** todo el dinero es el mío propio; **but his ~ brother said so** pero su propio hermano lo dijo; **in her ~ house** en su propia casa; **the house has its ~ garage** la casa tiene garaje propio; **~ goal** autogol m.

[2] PRON lo suyo etc; **all my ~** todo lo mío; **he has a style all his ~** tiene un estilo muy suyo; **the house is her (very) ~** la casa es la suya propia, la casa le pertenece únicamente a ella; **my time is my ~** dispongo de mi tiempo como quiero; **the decision was his ~** la decisión fue suya (y no de otro); **may I keep it for my (very) ~?** ¿me lo puedo guardar como mío propio?; **she has money of her ~** tiene dinero particular; **I'll give you a copy of your ~** te daré un ejemplar propio, te daré un ejemplar para guardar; **for reasons of his ~** por motivos particulares, por motivos propios; **a place of one's ~** una casa propia, una casa para sí; **to come into one's ~** entrar en posesión de lo suyo, (fig) justificarse, encontrar su plena justificación; obtener el éxito merecido; **to be on one's ~** estar a solas, estar solo; ser independiente; **now we're on our ~** ya estamos solos; **she was all on her ~ for a week** pasó una semana enteramente sola; **if I can get him on his ~** si puedo hablar con él a solas; **to do sth on one's ~** hacer algo por su cuenta, hacer algo sólo; **each to his ~** cada uno a lo suyo, cada cual a lo suyo; **to call sth one's ~** ser dueño de algo, disponer de algo como de cosa propia; **without a chair to call my ~** sin una silla que pueda decir que es mía; **I am so busy I can scarcely call my time my ~** estoy tan ocupado que apenas dispongo de mi tiempo; **he made the theory his ~** hizo suya la teoría, adoptó la teoría; **to get one's ~ back** desquitarse, tomar su revancha; **to hold one's ~** no cejar, mantenerse firme; no ceder terreno; mantenerse al nivel de los demás; poder competir; **he can hold his ~ with anybody** no le va a la zaga a nadie; **I can hold my ~ in German** me defiendo en alemán; **we all look after our ~** todos cuidamos lo nuestro.

[3] VT (a) (possess) poseer, tener; ser dueño de; **he ~s 2 tractors** posee 2 tractores; **he ~s 3 newspapers** es dueño de 3 periódicos; **who ~s the newspaper?** ¿quién es el dueño del periódico?; **who ~s this pen?** ¿a quién pertenece esta pluma?; **to come in as if one ~ed the place** entrar como Pedro en su casa; **a cat nobody wants to ~** un gato que nadie quiere reclamar.

(b) (acknowledge, recognize) reconocer; **he ~ed the child as his** reconoció al niño como suyo; **I ~ my mistake** reconozco mi error.

(c) (confess) confesar; **I ~ it** lo confieso; **I ~ I was wrong** confieso que me equivoqué.

[4] VI: **to ~ to a mistake** confesar un error, reconocer un error; **I ~ed to debts of £47** confesé tener deudas de 47 libras.

◆**own up** VI confesar, confesar de plano; **~ up!** ¡confésalo!; **she ~ed up to being 40** confesó tener 40 años; **they ~ed up to having stolen the apples** confesaron haber robado las manzanas.

own brand [ˈəʊnˌbrænd] [1] N marca f propia.

[2] ATTR: **~ products** productos mpl de establecimiento.

owner [ˈəʊnəʳ] [1] N dueño m, -a f, propietario m, -a f, amo m, -a f; poseedor m, -ora f; (Naut*) capitán m; **the ~ of car no. NBG 999** el dueño del coche matrícula NBG 999; **~'s equity** participación f del dueño; **is the ~ about?** ¿está el dueño?

[2] ATTR: **~ driver** conductor m propietario, conductora f propietaria;

there's a growing level of ~ **occupancy** hay cada vez más propietarios de la vivienda; ~ **occupier** ocupante *m* propietario, ocupante *f* propietaria.
owner-occupied [ˌəʊnəˈɒkjʊpaɪd] ADJ *property, house* ocupado por el dueño.
ownerless [ˈəʊnəlɪs] ADJ sin dueño.
ownership [ˈəʊnəʃɪp] N posesión *f*; propiedad *f*; '**under new ~**' 'nuevo propietario', 'nuevo dueño'; **books in** (*or* **under**) **the ~ of** ... libros que son de la propiedad de ...; **under his ~ the business flourished** el negocio prosperó bajo su dirección.
ownsome* [ˈəʊnsəm] N: **on one's ~** a solas.
owt [aʊt] N (*Brit dialect*) algo, alguna cosa.
ox [ɒks] N, PL **oxen** [ˈɒksən] buey *m*.
oxalic [ɒkˈsælɪk] ADJ: **~ acid** ácido *m* oxálico.
oxblood [ˈɒksblʌd] ADJ de color rojo oscuro.
oxbow lake [ˈɒksˌbəʊˈleɪk] N lago *m* en forma de herradura.
Oxbridge [ˈɒksbrɪdʒ] N (*Brit*) Universidades *fpl* de Oxford y Cambridge.

┌─── ⓘ **OXBRIDGE** ───┐

ⓘ *Oxbridge es el término que se usa para hacer referencia a las universidades de **Oxford** y **Cambridge**, sobre todo cuando se quiere destacar el ambiente de privilegio al que se las asocia, originado por su posición como las dos universidades más antiguas y prestigiosas del Reino Unido y por el hecho de que muchos licenciados de **Oxbridge** suelen acabar en puestos muy influyentes del ámbito empresarial, político o diplomático. Un buen número de estudiantes de estas universidades todavía proviene de institutos privados, aunque ambas instituciones tratan de aumentar el número de alumnos procedentes de centros estatales.*

oxcart [ˈɒkskɑːt] N carro *m* de bueyes.
oxen [ˈɒksən] NPL *of* **ox**.
ox-eye daisy [ˌɒksaɪˈdeɪzɪ] N margarita *f*.
Oxfam [ˈɒksfæm] N ABBR *of* **Oxford Committee for Famine Relief**.

┌─── ⓘ **OXFAM** ───┐

ⓘ *Oxfam es una organización benéfica cuyas siglas significan en inglés **Oxford Committee for Famine Relief**, muy conocida por sus campañas para recaudar fondos, su trabajo de ayuda al Tercer Mundo y su intento de*

*promocionar el uso de tecnología básica y de los recursos locales renovables. Además, el nombre **Oxfam** se asocia también a una cadena de tiendas gestionadas por esta organización, en las que se puede adquirir ropa y otros artículos de segunda mano, así como objetos hechos en talleres y cooperativas del Tercer Mundo.*

oxford [ˈɒksfəd] N (*US*) zapato *m* (de tacón bajo).
oxhide [ˈɒkshaɪd] N cuero *m* de buey.
oxidation [ˌɒksɪˈdeɪʃən] N oxidación *f*.
oxide [ˈɒksaɪd] N óxido *m*.
oxidize [ˈɒksɪdaɪz] ① VT oxidar.
  ② VI oxidarse.
oxlip [ˈɒkslɪp] N prímula *f*.
Oxon [ˈɒksən] ADJ (*Brit*) ABBR *of* **Oxoniensis, of Oxford**.
Oxonian [ɒkˈsəʊnɪən] ① ADJ oxoniense.
  ② N oxoniense *mf*.
oxtail [ˈɒksteɪl] N: **~ soup** sopa *f* de cola de buey.
oxter [ˈɒkstəʳ] N (*Scot*) axila *f*.
oxyacetylene [ˈɒksɪəˈsetɪliːn] ADJ oxiacetilénico; **~ burner**, **~ lamp**, **~ torch** soplete *m* oxiacetilénico; **~ welding** soldadura *f* oxiacetilénica.
oxygen [ˈɒksɪdʒən] N oxígeno *m*.
oxygenate [ɒkˈsɪdʒəneɪt] VT oxigenar.
oxygenation [ˌɒksɪdʒəˈneɪʃən] N oxigenación *f*.
oxygen-mask [ˈɒksɪdʒənˌmɑːsk] N máscara *f* de oxígeno, mascarilla *f* con oxígeno.
oxygen-tent [ˈɒksɪdʒənˌtent] N tienda *f* de oxígeno.
oxymoron [ˌɒksɪˈmɔːrɒn] N oxímoron *m*.
oyez [əʊˈjez] INTERJ ¡oíd!
oyster [ˈɔɪstəʳ] N ostra *f*; **the world is his ~** tiene el mundo a sus pies.
oysterbed [ˈɔɪstəbed] N criadero *m* (*o* vivero *m*) de ostras.
oystercatcher [ˈɔɪstəˌkætʃəʳ] N ostrero *m*.
oyster-farm [ˈɔɪstəfɑːm] N criadero *m* de ostras.
oyster-shell [ˈɔɪstəʃel] N concha *f* de ostra.
oz. ABBR *of* **ounce(s)** onza(s) *f(pl)*.
ozone [ˈəʊzəʊn] N ozono *m*; **~ hole** agujero *m* de ozono; **~ layer** capa *f* de ozono.
ozone-friendly [ˈəʊzəʊnˈfrendlɪ] ADJ que no daña la capa de ozono.
ozonosphere [əʊˈzəʊnəˌsfɪəʳ] N ozonosfera *f*.

P

P, p [piː] N (*letter*) P, p f; **P for Paris** P de París; **to mind one's Ps and Qs** cuidarse de no meter la pata.

P (a) ABBR *of* **president** presidente m, P. **(b)** ABBR *of* **prince** príncipe m, P.

p (a) N ABBR *of* **penny, pence** penique(s) m(pl). **(b)** ABBR *of* **page** página f, pág.

p.&h. (*US*) ABBR *of* **postage and handling** gastos mpl de envío.

P.&L. N ABBR *of* **profit and loss** pérdidas fpl y ganancias, Pérd. y Gan.

p.&p. N ABBR *of* **postage and packing** correo m y embalaje.

PA N **(a)** ABBR *of* **personal assistant** ayudante mf personal. **(b)** ABBR *of* **public address system** (sistema m de) megafonía f. **(c)** ABBR *of* **Press Association**. **(d)** (*US Post*) ABBR *of* **Pennsylvania**. **(e)** (*Theat etc*) ABBR *of* **personal appearance**.

p.a. ABBR *of* **per annum, yearly** por año, al año.

pa* [pɑː] N papá* m.

PAC N (*US*) ABBR *of* **political action committee**.

pace¹ [peɪs] ①① N **(a)** (*step*) paso m; **12 ~s off** a 12 pasos; **to put a horse through its ~** ejercitar un caballo, entrenar un caballo; **to put sb through his ~s** poner a uno a prueba, demostrar las cualidades de uno; **to show one's ~s** demostrar su capacidad, demostrar lo que puede uno.
(b) (*speed*) paso m, marcha f; ritmo m; **at a good ~, at a smart ~** a paso rápido; **at a slow ~** a paso lento; **at a walking ~** a la velocidad del que camina a pie; **at a snail's ~** a paso de tortuga; **we kept up a good ~ with the work** mantuvimos un buen ritmo de trabajo; **the present ~ of development** el actual ritmo del desarrollo; **to keep ~** ir al mismo paso; **he does it at his own ~** no lo hace a su propio ritmo; **to keep ~ with sb** llevar el mismo paso que uno; **industry has not kept ~ with technology** la industria no ha avanzado al mismo paso que la tecnología; **I can't keep ~ with events** no puedo mantenerme al corriente de los sucesos; **to make the ~, to set the ~** establecer el paso, marcar el ritmo; **to quicken one's ~** apretar el paso; **he can't stand the ~** no puede mantener el ritmo (de la marcha *etc*), (*fig*) las cosas se desarrollan demasiado rápidamente para él.
② VT *distance* medir a pasos; *floor, room* pasearse preocupado (*etc*) por; *competitor* marcar el paso para; **to ~ off 10 metres** medir 10 metros a pasos.
③ VI: **~ up and down** pasearse de un lado a otro.
◆ **pace out** VT *distance* mediar a pasos.

pace² ['peɪsɪ] PREP según, de acuerdo con.

-paced [peɪst] ADJ *ending in compounds*: **fast~** world, life trepidante; *action, environment* con un ritmo acelerado; **well~** film, novel con un ritmo adecuado.

pacemaker ['peɪs,meɪkəʳ] N **(a)** (*Sport*) liebre f. **(b)** (*Med*) marcapasos m.

pacer ['peɪsəʳ] N (*esp US: Sport*) liebre mf.

pacesetter ['peɪs,setəʳ] N (*Sport*) liebre f; (*fig*) persona f que da la pauta.

pacey, pacy ['peɪsɪ] ADJ **(a)** *production, thriller* rápido, con buen ritmo. **(b)** (*Sport*) *full-back, winger* rápido, con buen ritmo.

pachyderm ['pækɪdɜːm] N paquidermo m.

pacific [pə'sɪfɪk] ADJ pacífico.

pacifically [pə'sɪfɪkəlɪ] ADV pacíficamente.

pacification [,pæsɪfɪ'keɪʃən] N pacificación f.

Pacific Ocean [pə'sɪfɪk'əʊʃən] N Océano m Pacífico.

pacifier ['pæsɪfaɪəʳ] N (*US: baby's*) chupete m.

pacifism ['pæsɪfɪzəm] N pacifismo m.

pacifist ['pæsɪfɪst] ①① ADJ pacifista.
② N pacifista mf.

pacify ['pæsɪfaɪ] VT pacificar; apaciguar, calmar; **we managed to ~ him eventually** por fin logramos apaciguarle.

pack [pæk] ①① N **(a)** (*bundle*) lío m, fardo m; (*on animal*) carga f; (*ruck-*

sack, also Mil) mochila f; (*packet*) paquete m; (*of cigarettes: US*) paquete m, cajetilla f; (*wrapping*) envase m; (*Med*) compresa f; **a ~ of lies** un montón de mentiras; **it's a ~ of lies!** ¡mentira!, ¡es una sarta (*LAm:* bola f) de mentiras!
(b) (*of hounds*) jauría f; (*of wolves*) manada f; (*Rugby*) los delanteros; **they're a ~ of fools** son todos tontos; **they're like a ~ of kids** son como una pandilla de chavales.
(c) (*Cards*) baraja f.
② VT **(a)** *container* llenar, ir llenando; *case, trunk etc* hacer; *things in case etc* poner; *fish, meat in tin* enlatar; (*wrap*) envasar; (*put into parcel*) empaquetar; **~ed lunch** bolsa f de comida, merienda f, bocadillos mpl; **articles ~ed in dozens** artículos en caja de a docena; **it comes ~ed in polythene** viene envasado en politeno; **I'm ~ed and ready** tengo las maletas hechas y estoy listo para salir.
(b) (*excessively*) *container* llenar, atestar (*with* de); *articles* meter apretadamente; **to ~ earth round a plant** acollar una planta; **the place was ~ed (out)** el local estaba de bote en bote; **the Costa Brava is ~ed (out) with tourists** la Costa Brava está llena de turistas.
(c) *meeting* llenar de partidarios; *jury* nombrar de modo fraudulento.
(d) **he ~s a gun*** (*US*) lleva revólver.
(e) (*Comput*) comprimir.
③ VI **(a)** (*pack cases*) hacer las maletas, hacer el equipaje.
(b) (*form a mass*) endurecerse, consolidarse, formar una masa compacta; (*people*) apiñarse; **they ~ed round the speaker** se apiñaron en torno al orador.
(c) **to send sb ~ing** echar a uno con cajas destempladas; despedir a uno sin más.
◆ **pack away** VT guardar.
◆ **pack down** VT apretar, comprimir; (*with feet etc*) apisonar.
◆ **pack in** VT **(a)** **to ~ more people in** ir introduciendo más personas; **can you ~ 2 more in?** ¿caben 2 más?; **they were ~ed in like sardines** estaban como sardinas en banasta; **the show's ~ing them in*** el show tiene un lleno todas las noches.
(b) (*) dejarlo; **~ it in!** ¡déjalo!; **it's time we ~ed it in** es hora de dejarlo ya.
◆ **pack off** VT despachar, despedir, deshacerse de; **they ~ed him off to London** le enviaron sin más a Londres; **to ~ a child off to bed** mandar a un niño a la cama.
◆ **pack up** ① VT = **pack** ③ (a).
② VI **(a)** (*) terminar; (*and depart*) liar el petate*.
(b) (*: *engine etc*) averiarse, pararse.

package ['pækɪdʒ] ① N paquete m; bulto m; (*fig: of measures etc*) paquete m.
② ATTR: **~ bomb** (*US*) paquete-bomba m; **~ deal** paquete m, acuerdo m global; **~ holiday, ~ tour, ~ vacation** (*US*) vacaciones fpl todo pagado; **~ store** (*US*) = **off-licence**.
③ VT (*US: also to ~ up*) empaquetar, envasar.

packager ['pækɪdʒəʳ] N (*Publishing, TV*) productora f.

packaging ['pækɪdʒɪŋ] N envasado m, embalaje m; **~ material** material m de envasado.

pack-animal ['pæk,ænɪməl] N animal m de carga, acémila f.

packer ['pækəʳ] N embalador m, -ora f, empaquetador m, -ora f.

packet ['pækɪt] ① N **(a)** paquete m; (*of cigarettes*) paquete m, cajetilla f; (*of stamps*) sobre m; (*of crisps etc*) bolsa f; **a new ~ of proposals** un paquete de nuevas propuestas; **a whole ~ of trouble** la mar de disgustos; **to make a ~*** ganarse un dineral; **to make one's ~*** hacer su pacotilla; **that must have cost a ~*** eso habrá costado un dineral.
(b) (*Naut: also ~ boat*) paquebote m.
② ATTR: **~ switching** conmutación f de paquetes.

packhorse ['pækhɔːs] N caballo m de carga.

pack-ice ['pækaɪs] N témpanos mpl flotantes.

packing ['pækɪŋ] ① N **(a)** (*act*) embalaje m, envase m, envasado m; **to do one's ~** hacer sus maletas, arreglar el equipaje.

(b) (material) (outer) envase m; (inner) relleno m, empaquetadura f.

2 ATTR: **~ density** densidad f de compacidad; **~ house, ~ plant** fábrica f de conservas cárnicas.

packing-case ['pækɪŋkeɪs] N cajón m de embalaje.

packing-slip ['pækɪŋ‚slɪp] N hoja f de embalaje.

packsaddle ['pæk‚sædl] N albarda f.

pact [pækt] N pacto m; (on wages etc) convenio m; **to make a ~ with sb** pactar con uno.

pad¹ [pæd] VI: **to ~ about, to ~ along** andar, pisar (sin hacer ruido).

pad² [pæd] 1 N **(a)** (gen) almohadilla f, cojinete m; (of fox etc) pata f; (for inking) tampón m, almohadilla f para entintar; (of paper) bloc m, taco m; (blotting ~) secafirmas m; (on shoulder) hombrera f.
(b) (for helicopter) plataforma f; (launching) plataforma f de lanzamiento.
2 VT **(a)** (gen) almohadillar; acolchar; rellenar, forrar; shoulders etc acolchar, bombear; armour enguatar.
(b) book etc meter paja en, hinchar con mucha paja.

♦**pad out** VT book etc meter paja en, hinchar con mucha paja; **the speech was ~ded out with references to ...** el discurso estaba hinchado con referencias a ...

pad³ [pæd] N (home) casa f; (flat) piso m; (room) agujero m, habitación f; (bed) pulguero m, cama f.

padded ['pædɪd] ADJ shoulders acolchado, con hombrera(s), bombeado; dashboard etc almohadillado; armour enguatado; envelope acolchado; cell acolchado, de aislamiento.

padding ['pædɪŋ] N **(a)** relleno m, almohadilla f; acolchamiento m; (material) borra f. **(b)** (fig) paja f.

paddle ['pædl] 1 N **(a)** (oar) canalete m, zagual m; (blade of wheel) paleta f; (wheel) rueda f de paletas; (US) raqueta f.
(b) to go for a ~, to have a ~ ir a mojarse los pies, chapotear en el mar (etc).
2 VT **(a)** boat impulsar con canalete, remar con canalete.
(b) to ~ one's feet in the sea mojarse los pies en el mar, chapotear en el mar.
(c) (US*) child azotar, zurrar*.
3 VI **(a)** (in boat) palear, remar con canalete; **they ~d to the bank** dirigieron el bote a la orilla.
(b) (with feet) mojarse los pies, chapotear.

paddle-boat ['pædlbəʊt] N, **paddle-steamer** ['pædl‚stiːmər] N (Brit) vapor m de ruedas, vapor m de paletas.

paddle-wheel ['pædlwiːl] N rueda f de paletas.

paddling-pool ['pædlɪŋpuːl] N (Brit) estanque m para chapotear, estanque m (or piscina f) para niños.

paddock ['pædək] N (field) prado m; (of racecourse) corral m, explanada f de ensillado, paddock m; (of cars) parque m.

Paddy ['pædɪ] NM familiar form of **Patrick**; (pej) irlandés m.

paddy¹ ['pædɪ] N (rice) arroz m; (field) arrozal m.

paddy²* ['pædɪ] N rabieta* f; **to get into a ~** coger una rabieta.

paddy waggon* ['pædɪ‚wægən] N (US) coche m celular.

paddywhack* ['pædɪwæk] N rabieta* f.

padlock ['pædlɒk] 1 N candado m.
2 VT cerrar con candado.

padre* ['pɑːdrɪ] N (Mil) capellán m militar; (Univ) capellán m de colegio; (in direct address) padre.

paean ['piːən] N himno m de alegría; **~s of praise** alabanzas fpl.

paederast ['pedəræst] = **pederast**.

paediatric, (US) **pediatric** [‚piːdɪ'ætrɪk] ADJ pediátrico; **~ ward** sala f de pediatría.

paediatrician, (US) **pediatrician** [‚piːdɪə'trɪʃən] N pediatra mf, pedíatra mf, médico m puericultor.

paediatrics, (US) **pediatrics** [‚piːdɪ'ætrɪks] N pediatría f.

paedological, (US) **pedological** [‚piːdə'lɒdʒɪkl] ADJ pedológico.

paedology, (US) **pedology** [pɪ'dɒlədʒɪ] N pedología f.

paedophile, (US) **pedophile** ['piːdəʊfaɪl] N pedófilo m.

paedophilia, (US) **pedophilia** [‚piːdəʊ'fɪlɪə] N pedofilia f.

pagan ['peɪgən] 1 ADJ pagano.
2 N pagano m, -a f.

paganism ['peɪgənɪzəm] N paganismo m.

page¹ [peɪdʒ] 1 N (boy-servant) paje m; (squire) escudero m.
2 VT: **to ~ sb** buscar a uno llamando (su nombre), hacer llamar a uno por el altavoz.

page² [peɪdʒ] 1 N página f; (Typ, of newspaper) plana f; **a glorious ~ in our history** una página gloriosa de nuestra historia; **the news was on the front ~** la noticia figuraba en la primera plana; **on ~ 14** a la página 14, en la página 14; **'see ~ 20'** 'véase la página 20'.
2 ATTR: **~ break** (Comput) límite m de la página.
3 VT paginar.

⌐ **PAGE THREE** ⌐

ⓘ Durante años, en la página tres del periódico **The Sun**, el diario sensacionalista de más venta en el Reino Unido, ha aparecido una foto a toda página de una chica en topless, conocida como la **page three girl**.

De ahí que el término haya pasado a usarse también, en sentido extenso, para referirse a las modelos que posan semidesnudas en otros periódicos sensacionalistas.

-page [peɪdʒ] N ending in compounds: **a 4-~ pamphlet** un folleto de 4 páginas.

pageant ['pædʒənt] N (show) espectáculo m brillante; representación f escénica; (procession) desfile m; **a ~ of Elizabethan times** una representación de la época isabelina en una serie de cuadros; **the town held a ~ to mark the anniversary** la ciudad organizó una serie de fiestas públicas para celebrar el aniversario.

pageantry ['pædʒəntrɪ] N pompa f, boato m; **the ~ of the occasion** lo espectacular del acontecimiento, lo vistoso del acontecimiento; **all the ~ of History** toda la magnificencia de la Historia; **it was celebrated with much ~** se celebró con gran boato.

pageboy ['peɪdʒbɔɪ] N paje m; **~ hairstyle** peinado m de paje.

page-proofs ['peɪdʒpruːfs] NPL pruebas fpl de planas.

pager ['peɪdʒər] N localizador m, busca* m.

paginate ['pædʒɪneɪt] VT paginar.

pagination [‚pædʒɪ'neɪʃən] N paginación f; **without ~** sin paginar.

paging ['peɪdʒɪŋ] 1 N (Comput, Typ) paginación f.
2 ATTR: **~ device** localizador m, busca* m.

pagoda [pə'gəʊdə] N pagoda f.

pah [pæ] EXCL (†) ¡bah!

paid [peɪd] 1 PRET AND PTP of **pay**.
2 ADJ **(a)** official asalariado, que recibe un sueldo; work remunerado, rentado (SC); **a ~ hack** un escritorzuelo a sueldo.
(b) bill, holiday etc pagado; **to put ~ to sth** acabar con algo.

paid-up ['peɪd'ʌp] ADJ, (US) **paid-in** ['peɪd'ɪn] ADJ share liberado; **fully ~ share** acción f totalmente liberada; **~ capital** capital m pagado; **a fully ~ member** miembro m que ha pagado su cuota.

pail [peɪl] N cubo m, balde m; (child's) cubito m.

pailful ['peɪlfʊl] N cubo m, contenido m de un cubo.

paillasse ['pælɪæs] N jergón m.

pain [peɪn] 1 N **(a)** (Med) dolor m; sufrimiento m; **~ barrier** barrera f del dolor; **to be in ~** estar con dolor; **to be in great ~** tener mucho dolor, sufrir mucho; **cucumber gives me a ~** el pepino me sienta mal; **I have a ~ in my leg** me duele la pierna; **to put a wounded animal out of its ~** acortar la agonía de un animal herido, despachar un animal herido.
(b) ~s (efforts) trabajos mpl, cuidados mpl, esfuerzos mpl; **to be at great ~s over sth, to take ~s over sth** esmerarse en algo, tomarse trabajo en algo; **he was at ~s to be reasonable** se esforzó por parecer razonable; **all he got for his ~s was ...** lo único que logró después de tantos trabajos fue ...; **to spare no ~s** no perdonar esfuerzos (to + infin por + infin); **to take ~s to** + infin poner especial cuidado en + infin.
(c) (penalty) pena f; **on ~ of death** so pena de muerte; **with all the ~s and penalties of fame** con todas las dificultades y disgustos que acarrea la fama.
(d) (*: nuisance) (person) persona f latosa*; **she's a real ~** es una persona realmente latosa*; **what a ~!** ¡qué lata!*; **it's a ~ having to** + infin es una lata tener que* + infin; **he's a ~ in the arse** (Brit), **he's a ~ in the ass** (US) es más pesado que el plomo*, da mucho la tabarra*; **he's a ~ in the neck, it gives me a ~ in the neck** me da cien patadas*.
2 VT (physically) doler; (mentally) dar lástima a; **my leg ~s me** me duele la pierna; **you ~ me!** (iro) ¡me das lástima!; **where does it ~ you?** ¿dónde te duele?

pained [peɪnd] ADJ expression de disgusto, afligido; ofendido; voice dolorido; **he looked ~** hizo una mueca, torció el gesto.

painful ['peɪnfʊl] ADJ **(a)** (physically) doloroso, dolorido; (difficult) difícil, penoso, angustioso; duty desagradable, nada grato; **it is my ~ duty to tell you that ...** tengo el deber desagradable de decirle que ...; **my arm was becoming ~** empezaba a dolerme el brazo; **it was ~ to behold** daba lástima verlo.
(b) (*) horrible, malísimo; **~, isn't it?** ¿es horrible, no?; **she gave a ~ performance** dio una actuación lamentable, actuó pésimamente.

painfully ['peɪnfəlɪ] ADV **(a)** dolorosamente, con dolor; penosamente.
(b) (fig) terriblemente.

painkiller ['peɪnkɪlər] N analgésico m.

painkilling ['peɪn‚kɪlɪŋ] ADJ drug analgésico.

painless ['peɪnlɪs] ADJ (without pain) indoloro, sin dolor; (easy) fácil; **~ childbirth** parto m sin dolor.

painlessly ['peɪnlɪslɪ] ADV (without pain) sin causar dolor; (easily) fácilmente.

painstaking ['peɪnz‚teɪkɪŋ] ADJ person laborioso, concienzudo, esmerado; work hecho con cuidado, esmerado.

painstakingly ['peɪnz‚teɪkɪŋlɪ] ADV laboriosamente, concienzudamente, esmeradamente.

paint [peɪnt] 1 N pintura f; (for face) colorete m; **box of ~s** caja f de pinturas; **'wet ~'** ¡(ojo,) recién pintado!

2 VT pintar; **to ~ sth black** pintar algo de negro; **to ~ one's face** pintarse, ponerse colorete.

3 VI pintar; ser pintor.

◆**paint in** VT pintar; añadir (con pintura).

◆**paint out** VT tachar (or tapar) con una mano de pintura.

◆**paint over** VT (a) = paint out. (b) (repaint) repintar, volver a pintar.

paintbox ['peɪntbɒks] N caja f de pinturas.

paintbrush ['peɪntbrʌʃ] N (Art) pincel m; (for decorating) brocha f.

painter¹ ['peɪntəʳ] N (Art) pintor m, -ora f; (decorator) pintor m (de brocha gorda).

painter² ['peɪntəʳ] N (Naut) amarra f; **to cut the ~** (fig) cortar las amarras, independizarse.

painterly ['peɪntəlɪ] ADJ style, talents pictoricista.

painting ['peɪntɪŋ] N (art) pintura f; (picture) cuadro m, pintura f.

paintpot ['peɪntpɒt] N bote m de pintura.

paint-remover ['peɪntrɪ,muːvəʳ] N quitapintura f.

paint-roller ['peɪnt,rəʊləʳ] N rodillo m (pintor).

paint-spray ['peɪntspreɪ] N pistola f (rociadora) de pintura.

paint-stripper ['peɪnt,strɪpəʳ] N quitapintura f.

paintwork ['peɪntwɜːk] N pintura f.

pair [peəʳ] **1** N (of gloves, shoes, etc) par m; (of people, animals, cards, stamps) pareja f; (of oxen) yunta f; **a ~ of trousers** un pantalón, unos pantalones; **a carriage and ~** un landó con dos caballos; **a ~ of scissors** unas tijeras; **the happy ~** la feliz pareja, los novios; **arranged in ~s** arreglados (or colocados) de dos en dos.

2 VT aparear (also Bio).

3 VI aparearse (also Bio); **to ~ with** aparearse con, juntarse con.

◆**pair off, pair up** VI aparearse, formar pareja (with con).

pair-bond(ing) ['peə,bɒnd(ɪŋ)] N unión f de pareja, emparejamiento m.

pairing ['peərɪŋ] N (Bio) apareamiento m.

paisley ['peɪzlɪ] **1** N (fabric) cachemira f; (design: also ~ **pattern**) cachemira f.

2 ATTR: **~ shawl** chal m de cachemira.

pajamas [pə'dʒɑːməz] NPL (US) pijama m.

Pakiː ['pækɪ] N (Brit pej) ABBR of **Pakistani**.

Pakistan [,pɑːkɪs'tɑːn] N Pakistán m, Paquistán m.

Pakistani [,pɑːkɪs'tɑːnɪ] **1** ADJ pakistaní, paquistaní.

2 N pakistaní mf, paquistaní mf.

pakora [pə'kɔːrə] N plato indio consistente en bolas de cebolla fritas en pasta de harina de garbanzos.

PAL [pæl] N ABBR of **phase alternation line** línea f de fase alternante.

palˣ [pæl] N camarada mf, compinche m, compañero m, -a f, cuate mf (Mex); **old ~'s act** acto m de amiguismo*; **be a ~!** ¡vamos, pórtate como un amigo!; **you've always been a ~ to me** siempre has sido muy amable conmigo; **they're great ~s** son íntimos amigos.

◆**pal up** VI hacerse amigos; **to ~ up with sb** hacerse amigo de uno.

palace ['pælɪs] N palacio m.

palaeo- ['pælɪəʊ] etc = **paleo-** etc.

Palaeozoic [,pælɪəʊ'zəʊɪk] ADJ, N (Geol) paleozoico m.

palatable ['pælətəbl] ADJ sabroso, apetitoso; (just passable) comible; (fig) aceptable (to a); **it may not be ~ to the government** puede no ser del gusto (or agrado) del gobierno.

palatal ['pælətl] **1** ADJ palatal.

2 N palatal f.

palatalize ['pælətəlaɪz] **1** VT palatalizar.

2 VI palatalizarse.

palate ['pælɪt] N paladar m (also fig); **hard ~** paladar m; **soft ~** velo m del paladar; **to have a delicate ~** tener un paladar delicado; **to have no ~ for wine** no tener paladar para el vino; **I have no ~ for that kind of activity** no aguanto (or no puedo tragar) ese tipo de actividad.

palatial [pə'leɪʃəl] ADJ suntuoso, espléndido.

palatinate [pə'lætɪnɪt] N palatinado m.

palaver [pə'lɑːvəʳ] **1** N (a) (conference) conferencia f, parlamento m. (b) (*) (fuss) lío* m; (trouble) molestias fpl, trámites mpl engorrosos; (US: chatter) palabrería f; **that ~ about the car** aquel lío que se armó acerca del coche*; **can't we do it without a lot of ~?** ¿no podemos hacerlo sin tantas molestias?, ¿no podemos hacerlo sin meternos en tantos líos*?

2 VI parlamentar.

pale¹ [peɪl] **1** ADJ complexion, face pálido; colour claro; light tenue; **a ~ blue dress** un vestido azul claro; **she was deathly ~** estaba pálida como la muerte; **to go ~, to grow ~, to turn ~** palidecer, ponerse pálido.

2 VI palidecer, ponerse pálido; **but X ~s beside Y** pero X pierde al lado de Y.

pale² [peɪl] N (stake) estaca f; **to be beyond the ~** estar excluido de la buena sociedad; ser inaceptable, ser un indeseable; **to be outside the ~ of** quedar fuera de los límites de.

paleface ['peɪlfeɪs] N rostropálido m, -a f; (US term) blanco m, -a f.

pale-faced [,peɪl'feɪst] ADJ pálido.

paleness ['peɪlnɪs] N palidez f; tenuidad f.

paleo... ['pælɪəʊ] PREF paleo...

paleographer [,pælɪ'ɒgrəfəʳ] N paleógrafo m, -a f.

paleography [,pælɪ'ɒgrəfɪ] N paleografía f.

paleolithic [,pælɪəʊ'lɪθɪk] **1** ADJ paleolítico.

2 N: **the P~** el Paleolítico.

paleontologist [,pælɪɒn'tɒlədʒɪst] N paleontólogo m, -a f.

paleontology [,pælɪɒn'tɒlədʒɪ] N paleontología f.

Palestine ['pælɪstaɪn] N Palestina f.

Palestinian [,pæləs'tɪnɪən] **1** ADJ palestino.

2 N palestino m, -a f.

palette ['pælɪt] N paleta f.

palette knife ['pælɪtnaɪf] N, PL **palette knives** ['pælɪtnaɪvz] espátula f.

palfrey ['pɔːlfrɪ] N palafrén m.

palimony* ['pælɪmənɪ] N alimentos mpl pagados a una ex compañera.

palimpsest ['pælɪmpsest] N palimpsesto m.

palindrome ['pælɪndrəʊm] N palindromo m.

paling ['peɪlɪŋ] N (stake) estaca f; (fence) valla f, estacada f, (em)palizada f.

palisade [,pælɪ'seɪd] N palizada f, estacada f, vallada f.

pall¹ [pɔːl] N (on coffin) paño m mortuorio; (robe, Eccl) palio m; (fig) manto m, capa f; **a ~ of smoke** una capa de humo.

pall² [pɔːl] VI perder su sabor (on para), dejar de gustar (on a); empalagar (on a); **it ~s after a time** después de cierto tiempo deja de gustar; **it never ~s** nunca pierde su sabor; **I found the book ~ed** encontré que el libro empezaba a aburrirme.

palladium [pə'leɪdɪəm] N paladio m.

pallbearer ['pɔːl,beərəʳ] N portador m del féretro.

pallet ['pælɪt] N (bed) jergón m; (platform) paleta f, plataforma f.

palletization [pælɪtaɪ'zeɪʃən] N paletización f.

pallet truck ['pælɪttrʌk] N carretilla f elevadora de paletas.

palliasse ['pælɪæs] N = **paillasse**.

palliate ['pælɪeɪt] VT paliar, mitigar.

palliative ['pælɪətɪv] **1** ADJ paliativo, lenitivo.

2 N paliativo m, lenitivo m.

pallid ['pælɪd] ADJ pálido.

pallidness ['pælɪdnɪs] N, **pallor** ['pæləʳ] N palidez f.

pally* ['pælɪ] ADJ: **he's a ~ sort** es una persona afable; **they're very ~** son muy amigos; **to be pretty ~ with sb** ser muy amigo de uno.

palm¹ [pɑːm] **1** N (Bot) palma f, palmera f; (English sallow) sauce m; (as carried at Easter) ramo m; **to bear the ~** llevarse la palma; **to yield the ~ to sb** reconocer la superioridad de uno, conceder la victoria a uno.

2 ATTR: **P~ Sunday** Domingo m de Ramos.

palm² [pɑːm] (Anat) **1** N palma f; **you must cross the gipsy's ~ with silver** hay que pagar a la gitana con una moneda de plata; **to grease sb's ~** untar la mano a uno; **to have an itching ~** ser muy codicioso; (be bribable) estar dispuesto a dejarse sobornar; **to read sb's ~** leer la mano a uno.

2 VT card escamotear.

◆**palm off** VT (a) **to ~ sth off on sb** encajar algo a uno; **I managed to ~ the visitor off on John** logré que Juan se encargara de la visita. (b) **I ~ed him off with the excuse that ...** logré satisfacerle con la excusa de que ...; **I will not be ~ed off with such nonsense** a mí no se me aparta del propósito con tonterías así.

palmcorder ['pɑːmkɔːdəʳ] N videocámara f portátil, minicámara f de vídeo.

palm-grove [,pɑːm'grəʊv] N palmar m, palmeral m.

palmist ['pɑːmɪst] N quiromántico m, -a f, palmista mf (Carib, Mex).

palmistry ['pɑːmɪstrɪ] N quiromancia f.

palm-oil ['pɑːmɔɪl] N aceite m de palma.

palmtop ['pɑːmtɒp] N (Comput) ordenador m de bolsillo, palmtop m.

palm-tree ['pɑːmtriː] N palma f, palmera f, palmero m (And, SC, Mex).

palmy ['pɑːmɪ] ADJ floreciente; próspero, feliz; **those ~ days** aquellos días tan prósperos.

palomino [pælə'miːnəʊ] N caballo de color tostado con crin y cola blancas.

palpable ['pælpəbl] ADJ palpable; (fig) palpable, sensible.

palpably ['pælpəblɪ] ADV palpablemente; sensiblemente; **a ~ unjust sentence** una condena manifiestamente injusta; **that is ~ untrue** eso es a todas luces falso.

palpate ['pælpeɪt] VT (Med) palpar.

palpitate ['pælpɪteɪt] VI palpitar.

palpitating ['pælpɪteɪtɪŋ] ADJ palpitante.

palpitation [,pælpɪ'teɪʃən] N palpitación f; **to have ~s** tener vahidos.

palsied ['pɔːlzɪd] ADJ paralítico.

palsy ['pɔːlzɪ] N perlesía f, parálisis f.

paltry ['pɔːltrɪ] ADJ insignificante, baladí; vil; miserable; **for a few ~ pesetas** por unas pesetillas, por unas miserables pesetas; **for some ~ reason** por alguna razón insignificante.

pampas ['pæmpəs] NPL pampa f, pampas fpl; **the P~** la Pampa.

pamper ['pæmpəʳ] VT mimar.

pampered ['pæmpəd] ADJ *child etc* mimado, consentido; *life* regalado; **he had a ~ childhood** se crió entre algodones.

pamphlet ['pæmflɪt] N (*informative, brochure*) folleto *m*, impreso *m*; (*literary*) panfleto *m*; (*political, handed out in street*) octavilla *f*, hoja *f* de propaganda.

pamphleteer [,pæmflɪ'tɪəʳ] N folletista *mf*, panfletista *mf*.

pan¹ [pæn] [1] N (*utensil*) cazuela *f*, cacerola *f*; perol *m*; (*frying* ~) sartén *f*; (*of lavatory*) taza *f*; (*of firearm*) cazoleta *f*.
[2] VT (**a**) *gold* separar en la gamella.
(**b**) (*) *play* dar un palo a.
[3] VI: **to ~ for gold** lavar con batea para obtener el oro.
◆ **pan out** [1] VT repartir.
[2] VI resultar, salir (bien *etc*); **if it ~s out as we hope** si sale como nosotros lo esperamos; **it didn't ~ out at all well** no dio ningún resultado satisfactorio; **we must wait and see how it ~s out** tenemos que esperar hasta ver cómo sale esto.

pan² [pæn] (*Cine*) VTI panoramizar.

pan... [pæn] PREF pan...; **pan-African** panafricano.

panacea [,pænə'sɪə] N panacea *f*.

panache [pə'næʃ] N aire *m*, garbo *m*, brío *m*, brillantez *f*; **to do sth with ~** hacer algo con brío, hacer algo con aire triunfal.

Pan-African ['pæn'æfrɪkən] ADJ panafricano.

Pan-Africanism ['pæn'æfrɪkənɪzəm] N panafricanismo *m*.

Pan-Asian ['pæn'eɪʃn] ADJ panasiático.

Panama [,pænə'mɑː] [1] N Panamá *m*.
[2] ATTR: **~ Canal** Canal *m* de Panamá; **~ hat** (sombrero *m* de) jipijapa *f*, panamá *m*.

Panamanian [,pænə'meɪnɪən] [1] ADJ panameño.
[2] N panameño *m*, -a *f*.

Pan-American ['pænə'merɪkən] ADJ panamericano; **~ Union** Unión *f* Panamericana.

Pan-Americanism ['pænə'merɪkənɪzəm] N panamericanismo *m*.

pancake ['pænkeɪk] [1] N crep *m*, hojuela *f*, tortita *f*, panqueque *m* (*LAm*).
[2] ATTR: **~ day** martes *m* de carnaval (*en que en Inglaterra se sirven hojuelas*); **~ landing** aterrizaje *m* de panza.

panchromatic ['pænkrəʊ'mætɪk] ADJ pancromático.

pancreas ['pæŋkrɪəs] N páncreas *m*.

pancreatic [,pæŋkrɪ'ætɪk] ADJ pancreático.

panda ['pændə] N panda *mf*; **~ car** coche *m* patrulla.

pandemic [pæn'demɪk] [1] ADJ pandémico.
[2] N pandemia *f*.

pandemonium [,pændɪ'məʊnɪəm] N pandemonio *m*, ruido *m* de todos los diablos, estruendo *m* infernal; **it's sheer ~!** ¡es la monda!; **at this there was ~** en esto se armó las de Caín, en esto se armó un tremendo jaleo.

pander ['pændəʳ] [1] N alcahuete *m*.
[2] VI alcahuetear; **to ~ to sb** consentir a uno, mimar a uno, desvivirse por complacer a uno; **to ~ to sb's desires** tratar por todos los medios de satisfacer los deseos de uno; **this is ~ing to the public's worst tastes** esto es condescender con los peores gustos del público.

Pandora [pæn'dɔːrə] NF: **~'s box** caja *f* de Pandora.

pandrop ['pændrɒp] N (*Scot*) pastilla *f* de menta.

pane [peɪn] N cristal *m*, (hoja *f* de) vidrio *m*.

panegyric [,pænɪ'dʒɪrɪk] N panegírico *m*.

panel ['pænl] [1] N (**a**) panel *m*; (*of wall*) panel *m*; (*of ceiling*) artesón *m*; (*of door*) entrepaño *m*, panel *m*; (*Sew*) paño *m*; (*Art*) tabla *f*; (*of instruments, switches*) tablero *m*, panel *m*.
(**b**) (*Brit Med etc*) lista *f* de pacientes; (*in competition*) jurado *m*; (*TV etc*) panel *m*; (*of assessors*) grupo *m* de asesores.
[2] ATTR: **~ discussion** mesa *f* redonda; **~ game** concurso *m* por equipos.
[3] VT poner paneles (*etc*) a, adornar con paneles (*etc*).

panel-beater ['pænl,biːtəʳ] N chapista *m*.

panel-beating ['pænl,biːtɪŋ] N chapistería *f*.

panelled, (*US*) **paneled** ['pænld] ADJ con paneles, adornado de paneles; artesonado.

panelling, (*US*) **paneling** ['pænəlɪŋ] N paneles *mpl*; artesonado *m*; entrepaños *mpl*.

panellist, (*US*) **panelist** ['pænəlɪst] N miembro *mf* del jurado (de un concurso *etc*), miembro *mf* del panel.

Pan-European ['pæn,jʊərə'piːən] ADJ paneuropeo.

pang [pæŋ] N punzada *f*, dolor *m* súbito, dolor *m* agudo; **~ of conscience** remordimiento *m*; **I felt a ~ of conscience** me remordió la conciencia; **~s of childbirth** dolores *mpl* del parto; **the ~s of hunger** el acometimiento del hambre.

panhandle ['pænhændl] (*US*) [1] N faja angosta de territorio de un estado que entra en el de otro.
[2] VI (*US*) mendigar, pedir limosna.

panhandler* ['pænhændləʳ] N (*US: beggar*) pordiosero *m*, -a *f*.

panic ['pænɪk] [1] N pánico *m*, terror *m* pánico; **to flee in ~** huir ate-

rrado; **the country was thrown into a ~** el pánico cundió en el país, el país fue preso del pánico; **there's no ~, tomorrow will do** no hay ninguna prisa loca, lo haremos mañana; **they were in their usual mad ~** todos corrían de acá para allá como locos.
[2] ATTR: **~ button** botón *m* de alarma; **~ buying** compras *fpl* debidas al pánico; **~ measures** medidas *fpl* inducidas por el pánico; **it was ~ stations*** reinaba el pánico.
[3] VT aterrar, infundir pánico a.
[4] VI llenarse de terror, aterrarse, ser preso de un terror pánico; **the crew ~ked** la tripulación se abandonó al terror; **don't ~!** ¡con calma!, ¡no te asustes!

panicky ['pænɪkɪ] ADJ (**a**) *person* asustadizo; lleno de pánico; **to get ~** llenarse de pánico; **don't get ~!** ¡con calma!, ¡no te asustes!
(**b**) *act, measure etc* influido por el terror.

panic-stricken ['pænɪk,strɪkən] ADJ preso de pánico, muerto de miedo.

panjandrum [pæn'dʒændrəm] N jefazo *m*, mandamás *m*; **he's the great ~** es el archipámpano.

pannier ['pænɪəʳ] [1] N cuévano *m*, serón *m*, banasta *f*.
[2] ATTR: **~ bag** (*on cycle etc*) cartera *f*, bolsa *f* (para equipaje); (*for mule etc*) alforja *f*.

panoply ['pænəplɪ] N (*armour*) panoplia *f*; (*fig*) pompa *f*, esplendor *m*.

panorama [,pænə'rɑːmə] N panorama *m*.

panoramic [,pænə'ræmɪk] ADJ panorámico; **~ screen** pantalla *f* panorámica; **~ view** visión *f* panorámica.

panpipes ['pænpaɪps] NPL flauta *f* de pan.

pansy ['pænzɪ] N (**a**) (*Bot*) pensamiento *m*. (**b**) (‡) maricón‡ *m*.

pant [pænt] [1] N jadeo *m*; resuello *m*.
[2] VT: **to ~ out** decir jadeando, decir con palabras entrecortadas.
[3] VI jadear; resollar; (*heart*) palpitar; **to ~ for water** jadear sediento; **to ~ for breath** jadear; **to ~ with desire for sth** desear algo ardientemente.
◆ **pant for** VT (*fig*) suspirar por, anhelar.

pantaloons [,pæntə'luːns] NPL (*also* **pair of ~**) (pantalones *mpl*) bombachos *mpl*.

pantechnicon [pæn'teknɪkən] N (*Brit*) camión *m* de mudanzas.

pantheism ['pænθiːɪzəm] N panteísmo *m*.

pantheist ['pænθiːɪst] N panteísta *mf*.

pantheistic [,pænθiː'ɪstɪk] ADJ panteísta.

pantheon ['pænθɪən] N panteón *m*.

panther ['pænθəʳ] N pantera *f*.

panties ['pæntɪz] NPL bragas *fpl*, braga *f*, braguitas *fpl*; **a pair of ~** unas bragas.

pantihose ['pæntɪhəʊz] NPL (*esp US*) = **panty hose**.

panting ['pæntɪŋ] N jadeo *m*; respiración *f* difícil.

panto* ['pæntəʊ] N ABBR of **pantomime**.

pantomime ['pæntəmaɪm] N (*classical*) pantomima *f*; (*Brit*) revista musical en época de Navidades, a base de cuentos de hadas *etc*; **what a ~!** ¡qué farsa!; **it was a real ~** fue una verdadera comedia.

┌─────────────┐
│ **PANTOMIME** │
└─────────────┘

ⓘ Una **pantomime***, abreviada en inglés como* **panto***, es una obra teatral que se representa normalmente en Navidades ante un público familiar. Suele estar basada en un cuento de hadas u otra historia conocida y en ella nunca faltan personajes como la dama (***dame***), papel que siempre interpreta un actor, el protagonista joven (***principal boy***), normalmente interpretado por una actriz, y el malvado (***villain***). Aunque es un espectáculo familiar dirigido fundamentalmente a los niños, en él se alienta la participación de todo el público y posee una gran dosis de humor para adultos.*

pantry ['pæntrɪ] N despensa *f*.

pants [pænts] NPL (*Brit*) (*man's*) calzoncillos *mpl*; (*US*) pantalones *mpl*; (*woman's*) bragas *fpl*; **a pair of ~** (*Brit*) unos calzoncillos, (*US*) unos pantalones, un pantalón; **to bore the ~ off sb*** aburrir terriblemente a uno; **to catch sb with his ~ down*** coger a uno desprevenido; **she wears the ~*** ella manda.

pants press ['pænts,pres] N (*US*) prensa *f* para pantalones.

pantsuit ['pæntsuːt] N (*US*) traje *m* de chaqueta y pantalón.

panty ['pæntɪ] ATTR: **~ girdle** faja *f* pantalón; **~ hose** pantys *mpl*, pantimedias *fpl*.

Panzer ['pæntsəʳ] (*German army*) [1] ADJ motorizado; **~ division** división *f* motorizada.
[2] N: **the ~s** las tropas motorizadas.

pap [pæp] N papilla *f*, gachas *fpl*.

papa [pə'pɑː] N papá *m*.

papacy ['peɪpəsɪ] N papado *m*, pontificado *m*.

papadum ['pæpədəm] N torta *f* india.

papal ['peɪpəl] ADJ papal, pontificio; **~ nuncio** nuncio *m* apostólico.

paparazzi [pæpə'rætsiː] NPL paparazzi *mpl*.

papaya [pə'paɪə] N (*fruit*) papaya *f*, mamón *m* (*And, SC*); (*tree*) árbol *m* de la papaya.

▼ **paper** ['peɪpər] **1** N **(a)** (*material, gen*) papel *m*; (*wall~*) papel *m* pintado; **a piece of ~** un papel, una hoja de papel, un trozo de papel; **on ~** sobre el papel, teóricamente; **to commit sth to ~, to get** (*or* **put**) **sth down on ~** poner algo por escrito; **it's not worth the ~ it's written on** no vale para nada.
(b) (*document*) papel *m*, documento *m*; **~s** (*identity etc*) papeles *mpl*, documentación *f*; **your ~s, please** la documentación, por favor; **ship's ~s** documentación *f* del barco; **Churchill's private ~s** los papeles personales de Churchill.
(c) (*Univ etc exercise*) ejercicio *m*, ensayo *m*; (*exam*) cuestionario *m* de examen; **to do a good ~ in maths** hacer un buen examen de matemáticas; **to set a ~ in physics** poner un examen de física.
▼ **(d)** (*learned: written*) artículo *m*, (*read aloud*) comunicación *f*, ponencia *f*; **we heard a good ~ on place-names** escuchamos una buena ponencia sobre toponimia.
(e) (*newspaper*) periódico *m*; **to write for the ~s** colaborar en los periódicos, escribir artículos para los periódicos; **to write to the ~ about sth** escribir una carta al director de un periódico.
2 ATTR de papel; **~ advance** avance *m* de papel; **~ bag** saco *m* de papel, bolsa *f* de papel; **~ credit** papel *m* crédito; **~ cup** vaso *m* de cartón; **~ currency** papel *m* moneda; **~ handkerchief, ~ hankie** pañuelo *m* de papel; **~ industry** industria *f* papelera; **~ lantern** farolillo *m* de papel; **~ loss** pérdida *f* que tiene lugar cuando baja el valor de una acción (*etc*) sin venderse ésta; **~ money** papel *m* moneda, billetes *mpl* de banco; **~ profit** beneficio *m* no realizado; **~ round** reparto *m* de periódicos (por las casas); **~ tape** cinta *f* de papel; **~ tiger** tigre *m* de papel; **~ tissue** pañuelo *m* de papel, tisú *m*; **~ towel** toallita *f* de papel.
3 VT *wall, room* empapelar, tapizar (*LAm*).
◆ **paper over** VT (*fig*) disimular.
paperback ['peɪpəbæk] N libro *m* en rústica, (*loosely*) libro *m* de bolsillo.
paperbacked ['peɪpəbækt] ADJ, **paperbound** ['peɪpəbaʊnd] ADJ en rústica.
paperboy ['peɪpəbɔɪ] N repartidor *m* de periódicos.
paper-chain ['peɪpətʃeɪn] N cadeneta *f* de papel.
paperchase ['peɪpətʃeɪs] N rallye-paper *m*.
paperclip ['peɪpəklɪp] N clip *m*, sujetapapeles *m*, broche *m* (*SC*), ataché *m* (*Carib*).
paper-fastener ['peɪpə,fɑːsnər] N grapa *f*.
paper-feed(er) ['peɪpəˈfiːd(ər)] N alimentador *m* de papel.
papergirl ['peɪpəgɜːl] N repartidora *f* de periódicos.
paperhanger ['peɪpə,hæŋər] N (*Brit*) empapelador *m*.
paper-knife ['peɪpənaɪf] N, PL **paper-knives** ['peɪpənaɪvz] abrecartas *m*, plegadera *f*, cortapapeles *m*.
paperless ['peɪpəlɪs] ADJ sin papel; **the ~ society** la sociedad sin papel.
paper-mill ['peɪpəmɪl] N fábrica *f* de papel, papelera *f*.
paper-shop ['peɪpəʃɒp] N ≈ kiosco *m* (de periódicos).
paper trail N (*US*) pruebas *fpl* documentales.
paperweight ['peɪpəweɪt] N pisapapeles *m*.
paperwork ['peɪpəwɜːk] N trabajo *m* administrativo; trabajo *m* de oficina; aspecto *m* teórico; (*pej*) papeleo *m*, trámites *mpl* burocráticos.
papery ['peɪpərɪ] ADJ parecido al papel; delgado como el papel.
papier-mâché ['pæpɪeɪˈmæʃeɪ] **1** ADJ de cartón piedra.
2 N cartón *m* piedra.
papist ['peɪpɪst] N papista *mf*.
papistry ['peɪpɪstrɪ] N papismo *m*.
papoose [pəˈpuːs] N **(a)** (*baby*) niño *m* indio norteamericano, niña *f* india norteamericana. **(b)** (*for carrying baby*) mochila *f* portabebés.
paprika ['pæprɪkə] N pimienta *f* húngara, paprika *f*.
Pap test ['pæptest] N frotis *m* (cervical).
Papua New Guinea ['pæpjʊənjuːˈgɪnɪ] **1** N Nueva Guinea *f* Papúa.
2 ADJ de Nueva Guinea Papúa.
Papua New Guinean ['pæpjʊənjuːˈgɪnɪən] N papú *mf*.
papyrus [pəˈpaɪərəs] N, PL **papyruses** *or* **papyri** [pəˈpaɪəraɪ] papiro *m*.
par [pɑːr] **1** ADJ *value etc* nominal, a la par; **~ value** valor *m* a la par.
2 N (*Comm*) par *f*; (*Golf*) par *m*; **~ for the course** par *m* del campo; **it's about ~ for the course** (*fig*) es más o menos normal, es más o menos lo que era de esperar; **5 under ~** 5 bajo par; **2 over ~** 2 sobre par; **to be above** (*or* **over**) **~** (*Comm*) estar por encima de (*or* sobre) la par; **to be under** (*or* **below**) **~** (*Comm*) estar por debajo de (*or* bajo) la par, (*Med*) estar indispuesto, sentirse mal, (*thing: also* **to be not up to ~**) ser inferior a la calidad normal; **to be at ~** (*Comm*) estar a la par; **to be on a ~ with** ser equivalente a, correr parejas con; **to place sth on a ~ with** parangonar algo con, equiparar algo con.
para. N ABBR *of* **paragraph** párrafo *m*.
parable ['pærəbl] N parábola *f*.
parabola [pəˈræbələ] N parábola *f*.

parabolic [,pærəˈbɒlɪk] ADJ parabólico; **~ aerial** antena *f* parabólica.
paracetamol [,pærəˈsiːtəmɒl] N paracetamol *m*.
parachute ['pærəʃuːt] **1** N paracaídas *m*.
2 ATTR **~ drop** lanzamiento *m* en paracaídas; **~ jump** salto *m* en paracaídas; **~ regiment** regimiento *m* de paracaidistas.
3 VT lanzar en paracaídas; **to ~ food to sb** suministrar víveres a uno en paracaídas.
4 VI lanzarse en paracaídas; (*also* **to ~ down**) bajar en paracaídas; **to ~ to safety** salvarse utilizando el paracaídas.
parachutist ['pærəʃuːtɪst] N paracaidista *mf*.
Paraclete ['pærəkliːt] N: **the ~** el Paráclito.
parade [pəˈreɪd] **1** N (*procession*) desfile *m*; (*Mil*) desfile *m*, parada *f*; (*of models*) desfile *m*, presentación *f*; (*road*) paseo *m*; (*fig*) alarde *m*; **to be on ~** (*fig*) estar visible, estar a la vista del público; **to make a ~ of** hacer alarde de, ostentar.
2 VT *troops* formar, formar en parada; *streets* recorrer, desfilar por; *placard, image etc* pasear (*through the streets* por las calles); (*show off*) hacer alarde de, hacer ostentación de, lucir; **to ~ one's learning** hacer alarde de su erudición.
3 VI (*Mil*) formar en parada, pasar revista; (*group of people*) desfilar; (*one person*) pasearse; **the strikers ~d through the town** los huelguistas desfilaron por la ciudad; **she ~d up and down with the hat on** se paseó de un lado a otro con el sombrero puesto, andaba de acá para allá para lucir el sombrero.
◆ **parade about, parade around** VI pavonearse.
parade-ground [pəˈreɪdgraʊnd] N plaza *f* de armas.
paradigm ['pærədaɪm] N paradigma *m*.
paradigmatic [,pærədɪgˈmætɪk] ADJ paradigmático.
paradise ['pærədaɪs] N paraíso *m*; **this is ~!** ¡esto es jauja!; V **fool¹, earthly**.
paradisiac [,pærədɪˈseɪɪk] ADJ, **paradisiacal** [,pærədɪˈsaɪəkəl] ADJ paradisíaco.
paradox ['pærədɒks] N paradoja *f*.
paradoxical ['pærəˈdɒksɪkəl] ADJ paradójico.
paradoxically [,pærəˈdɒksɪkəlɪ] ADV paradójicamente.
paraffin ['pærəfɪn] **1** N (*Brit: also* **~ oil**) petróleo *m* (de alumbrado), queroseno *m*; (*wax*) parafina *f*.
2 ATTR **~ lamp** quinqué *m* de petróleo; **~ wax** parafina *f*.
paragon ['pærəgən] N dechado *m*; **a ~ of virtue** un dechado de virtudes.
paragraph ['pærəgrɑːf] **1** N párrafo *m*, acápite *m* (*LAm*); (*Typ: short article in newspaper*) suelto *m*; **'new ~'** '(punto y) aparte'.
2 VT dividir en párrafos.
Paraguay ['pærəgwaɪ] N el Paraguay.
Paraguayan [,pærəˈgwaɪən] **1** ADJ paraguayo.
2 N paraguayo *m*, -a *f*.
parakeet ['pærəkiːt] N perico *m*, periquito *m*.
paralanguage ['pærə,læŋgwɪdʒ] N paralenguaje *m*.
paralegal [,pærəˈliːgəl] **1** N ayudante *mf* de abogado.
2 ATTR que trabaja como ayudante de abogado.
paralinguistic [,pærəlɪŋˈgwɪstɪk] ADJ paralingüístico.
parallel ['pærəlel] **1** ADJ paralelo; (*Comput, Elec*) en paralelo; (*fig*) semejante, análogo (*to* a); **~ bars** paralelas *fpl*; **~ printer** impresora *f* en paralelo; **in a ~ direction to** en dirección paralela a; **to run ~ to** ir en línea paralela a, correr paralelo con;; **this is a ~ case to the last one** este caso es análogo al anterior.
2 N (*Geom*) paralela *f*, línea *f* paralela; (*Geog, fig*) paralelo *m*; **the 49th ~** el paralelo 49; **in ~** (*Elec*) en paralelo; **a case without ~** un caso sin paralelo, un caso nunca visto; **it has no ~ as far as I know** que yo sepa no tiene paralelo, que yo sepa no hay nada parecido; **to draw a ~ between X and Y** establecer un paralelo entre X e Y; **these things occur in ~** estas cosas corren parejas (*with* con), estas cosas ocurren paralelamente.
3 VT (*fig*) ser paralelo a, ser análogo a, correr parejas con; **it is ~led by ...** corre parejas con ..., tiene su paralelo en ...
parallelepiped [,pærə,lelə'paɪped] N paralelepípedo *m*.
parallelism ['pærəlelɪzəm] N paralelismo *m*.
parallelogram [,pærəˈleləʊgræm] N paralelogramo *m*.
Paralympic [pærə'lɪmpɪk] ADJ paralímpico; **the ~ Games, the Paralympics** los juegos paralímpicos.
paralysis [pəˈræləsɪs] N parálisis *f*; (*fig*) paralización *f*, parálisis *f*.
paralytic [,pærəˈlɪtɪk] **1** ADJ **(a)** paralítico. **(b)** **he was ~** (*Brit**) estaba como una cuba*.
2 N paralítico *m*, -a *f*.
paralyzation [,pærəlaɪˈzeɪʃən] N paralización *f*.
paralyze ['pærəlaɪz] VT paralizar (*also fig*); **to be ~d in both legs** estar paralizado de las dos piernas; **to be ~d with fright** estar paralizado de miedo.
paramedic [,pærəˈmedɪk] N paramédico *m*, -a *f*.
paramedical [,pærəˈmedɪkəl] ADJ paramédico.
parameter [pəˈræmɪtər] N parámetro *m*.
paramilitary [,pærəˈmɪlɪtərɪ] ADJ paramilitar.

paramount ['pærəmaʊnt] ADJ supremo; **of ~ importance** de la mayor importancia, primordial; **solvency must be ~** la solvencia es lo más importante, ante todo la solvencia.
paramour ['pærəmʊəʳ] N (*esp hum*) amante *mf*, querido *m*, -a *f*.
paranoia [,pærə'nɔɪə] N paranoia *f*.
paranoiac [,pærə'nɔɪɪk] ① ADJ paranoico.
　② N paranoico *m*, -a *f*.
paranoid ['pærənɔɪd] ADJ paranoide.
paranormal [,pærə'nɔːməl] ① ADJ paranormal.
　② N: **the ~** lo paranormal.
parapet ['pærəpɪt] N parapeto *m*; (*of well etc*) brocal *m*.
paraphernalia ['pærəfə'neɪlɪə] N parafernalia *f*.
paraphrase ['pærəfreɪz] ① N paráfrasis *f*.
　② VT parafrasear.
paraplegia [,pærə'pliːdʒə] N paraplejía *f*.
paraplegic [,pærə'pliːdʒɪk] ① ADJ parapléjico.
　② N parapléjico *m*, -a *f*.
parapsychological [,pærəsaɪkə'lɒdʒɪkəl] ADJ parapsicológico.
parapsychologist [,pærəsaɪ'kɒlədʒɪst] N parapsicólogo *m*, -a *f*.
parapsychology [,pærəsaɪ'kɒlədʒɪ] N parapsicología *f*.
Paraquat ['pærəkwɒt] ® N herbicida *m*.
Paras* ['pærəz] NPL ABBR *of* **Parachute Regiment** paras* *mpl*, paracas* *mpl*.
parasite ['pærəsaɪt] N parásito *m* (*also fig: on* de).
parasitic(al) [,pærə'sɪtɪk(əl)] ADJ parasítico, parasitario; **to be ~ on** ser parásito de.
parasitism ['pærəsɪtɪzəm] N parasitismo *m*.
parasitize ['pærəsɪ,taɪz] VT parasitar (en).
parasitologist [,pærəsaɪ'tɒlədʒɪst] N parasitólogo *m*, -a *f*.
parasitology [,pærəsɪ'tɒlədʒɪ] N parasitología *f*.
parasol [,pærə'sɒl] N sombrilla *f*, quitasol *m*, parasol *m*.
parasuicide [,pærə'sʊɪsaɪd] N parasuicidio *m*.
parataxis [,pærə'tæksɪs] N parataxis *f*.
paratrooper ['pærətruːpəʳ] N paracaidista *m*.
paratroops ['pærətruːps] NPL paracaidistas *mpl*.
paratyphoid ['pærə'taɪfɔɪd] N paratifoidea *f*.
parboil ['pɑːbɔɪl] VT sancochar.
Parcae ['pɑːkiː] NPL: **the ~** las Parcas.
parcel ['pɑːsl] N paquete *m*; (*of land*) parcela *f*.
◆ **parcel out** VT repartir; dividir; *land* parcelar.
◆ **parcel up** VT empaquetar, embalar.
parcel-bomb ['pɑːslbɒm] N paquete-bomba *m*.
parcel-office ['pɑːsl,ɒfɪs] N departamento *m* de paquetes.
parcel-post ['pɑːslpəʊst] N servicio *m* de paquetes postales.
parch [pɑːtʃ] ① VT secar, resecar; agostar; quemar.
　② VI secarse.
parched [pɑːtʃt] ADJ *land etc* seco; **to be ~** (**with thirst**) estar muerto de sed.
parchment ['pɑːtʃmənt] N pergamino *m*.
parchment-like ['pɑːtʃmənt,laɪk] ADJ apergaminado.
pardon ['pɑːdn] ① N perdón *m*; (*Jur*) indulto *m*; **free ~** indulto *m* absoluto; **general ~** amnistía *f*; **to beg sb's ~** pedir perdón a uno; **I beg your ~, but could you …?** perdone la molestia, pero ¿podría Vd …?; **I beg your ~!** ¡perdone Vd!, ¡ay perdone!, ¡disculpe! (*LAm*); **~?, (I beg your) ~?, (US) ~ me?** ¿cómo?, ¿mande? (*Mex*).
　② VT perdonar, dispensar; (*Jur*) indultar; **to ~ sb sth** perdonar algo a uno; dispensar a uno de hacer (*etc*) algo; **~ me, but could you …?** perdone la molestia, pero ¿podría Vd …?; **~ me!** ¡perdone Vd!, ¡ay perdone!; **~ my mentioning it** siento tener que decirlo, perdona que te lo diga.
pardonable ['pɑːdnəbl] ADJ perdonable.
pardonably ['pɑːdnəblɪ] ADV: **he was ~ angry** es fácil disculpar su enojo, se comprende fácilmente que se encolerizara.
pare [peəʳ] VT *nails* cortar; *fruit etc* mondar; *stick etc* adelgazar; **to ~ away, to ~ down** (*fig*) reducir, ir reduciendo; **to ~ sth down to the minimum** reducir algo al mínimo.
parent ['peərənt] ① N padre *m*, madre *f*; **~s** padres *mpl*.
　② ADJ, ATTR: **the ~ plant** la planta madre; **the ~ company** la casa matriz; **~-teacher association** ≃ asociación *f* de padres de alumnos.
parentage ['peərəntɪdʒ] N familia *f*, linaje *m*; **of humble ~** de nacimiento humilde; **of unknown ~** de padres desconocidos.
parental [pə'rentl] ADJ *care etc* de padre y madre, de los padres; paternal, maternal; **~ authority** patria potestad *f*.
parenteral [pæ'rentərəl] ADJ parenteral.
parenthesis [pə'renθɪsɪs] N, PL **parentheses** [pə'renθɪsiːz] paréntesis *m*; **in ~** entre paréntesis.
parenthetic(al) [,pærən'θetɪk(əl)] ADJ entre paréntesis; explicativo.
parenthetically [,pærən'θetɪkəlɪ] ADV entre paréntesis; a modo de explicación.
parenthood ['peərənthʊd] N el ser padre (*or* madre), el tener hijos; paternidad *f*, maternidad *f*.
parenting ['peərəntɪŋ] N el ser padres; **shared ~** participación *f*

conjunta en la vida familiar; **~ is a full-time occupation** el cuidar de los hijos es una labor de plena dedicación.
parer ['peərəʳ] N pelalegumbres *m*.
par excellence [pɑːr'eksələːns] ADV por excelencia.
pariah ['pærɪə] N paria *mf*.
parietal [pə'raɪɪtl] ADJ parietal.
paring ['peərɪŋ] ATTR: **~ knife** cuchillo *m* de mondar.
parings ['peərɪŋz] NPL peladuras *fpl*, mondaduras *fpl*; desperdicios *mpl*.
pari passu ['pærɪ'pæsuː] ADV a ritmo parecido, al igual; **~ with** a ritmo parecido al de, al igual que.
Paris ['pærɪs] ① N París *m*.
　② ATTR parisiense.
parish ['pærɪʃ] ① N parroquia *f*.
　② ATTR parroquial, de la parroquia; **~ church** iglesia *f* parroquial; **~ council** concejo *m* parroquial; **~ priest** párroco *m*; **~ register** libro *m* parroquial, registro *m* parroquial.
parishioner [pə'rɪʃənəʳ] N feligrés *m*, -esa *f*.
parish-pump ['pærɪʃpʌmp] ATTR (*Brit pej*) de campanario, de aldea, pueblerino; **~ attitude** espíritu *m* de campanario.
Parisian [pə'rɪzɪən] ① ADJ parisiense, parisino, parisién.
　② N parisiense *mf*.
parity ['pærɪtɪ] N paridad *f*, igualdad *f*; (*Fin*) paridad *f*; **exchange at ~** cambio *m* a la par.
park [pɑːk] ① N parque *m*; jardines *mpl*; (*Sport**) campo *m*; (*Aut*) aparcamiento *m*, parque *m* (de automóviles).
　② VT (*Aut*) estacionar, aparcar (*Sp*); (*) poner, dejar, depositar; **can I ~ my car here?** ¿puedo aparcar mi coche aquí?
　③ VI (*Aut*) estacionarse, aparcar (*Sp*); (*) quedarse.
parka ['pɑːkə] N anorak *m*.
park-and-ride [,pɑːkənd'raɪd] N, **park-ride** [,pɑːk'raɪd] N *aparcamiento en estaciones periféricas conectadas con el transporte urbano colectivo*.
parking ['pɑːkɪŋ] ① N estacionamiento *m*; aparcamiento *m*; '**no ~**' 'prohibido estacionar'; '**good ~ for cars**' 'amplio aparcamiento para coches'; '**~ for 50 cars**' 'aparcamiento para 50 coches'.
　② ATTR: **~ attendant** guardacoches *mf*; **~ bay** área *f* de aparcamiento (*or* estacionamiento *m LAm*) de coches; **~ lights** luces *fpl* de estacionamiento; **~ lot** (*esp US*) aparcamiento *m*, estacionamiento *m* (*LAm*); **~ meter** parquímetro *m*, contador *m* de aparcamiento, estacionómetro *m* (*Mex*); **~ offence, ~ violation** (*US*) ofensa *f* por aparcamiento indebido; **~ place, ~ space** sitio *m* para aparcar, aparcamiento *m*; **~ ticket** multa *f* de aparcamiento (*or* estacionamiento *LAm*).
Parkinson ['pɑːkɪnsən] N: **~'s disease** enfermedad *f* de Parkinson; **~'s law** ley *f* de Parkinson.
park-keeper ['pɑːk,kiːpəʳ] N guardián *m* (de parque), guardabosque *m*.
parkland ['pɑːklænd] N zonas *fpl* verdes.
parkway ['pɑːkweɪ] N (*US*) carretera *f* principal, alameda *f*.
parky* ['pɑːkɪ] ADJ (*Brit*) frío; **it's pretty ~** hace un frío glacial.
parlance ['pɑːləns] N lenguaje *m*; **in common ~** en lenguaje corriente; **in technical ~** en lenguaje técnico.
parley ['pɑːlɪ] ① N parlamento *m*.
　② VI parlamentar (*with* con).
parliament ['pɑːləmənt] N parlamento *m*; (*Spanish*) Cortes *fpl*; **to get into ~** llegar a ser diputado, ser elegido (a las Cortes *etc*).
parliamentarian [,pɑːləmen'teərɪən] ① ADJ parlamentario.
　② N parlamentario *m*, -a *f*.
parliamentary [,pɑːlə'mentərɪ] ADJ parlamentario; **~ agent** agente *m* parlamentario, agente *f* parlamentaria; **~ democracy** democracia *f* parlamentaria; **~ election** elecciones *fpl* parlamentarias; **~ government** gobierno *m* parlamentario; **~ immunity** inmunidad *f* parlamentaria; **~ privilege** privilegio *m* parlamentario.
parlour, (US) parlor ['pɑːləʳ] ① N sala *f* de recibo, salón *m*, living *m* (*LAm*); (*Eccl*) locutorio *m*.
　② ATTR: **~ car** (*US*) coche-salón *m*.
parlour game, (US) parlor game ['pɑːləgeɪm] N juego *m* de salón.
parlourmaid, (US) parlormaid ['pɑːləmeɪd] N camarera *f*.
parlous ['pɑːləs] ADJ *state* lamentable, crítico, pésimo, peligroso, alarmante.
Parma ['pɑːmə] ATTR: **~ ham** jamón *m* de Parma; **~ violet** violeta *f* de Parma.
Parmesan [,pɑːmɪ'zæn] N (*cheese*) parmesano *m*.
Parnassus [pɑː'næsəs] N Parnaso *m*.
parochial [pə'rəʊkɪəl] ADJ (*Eccl*) parroquial; (*fig*) estrecho, limitado, restringido; de miras estrechas.
parochialism [pə'rəʊkɪəlɪzəm] N (*fig*) estrechez *f*, lo limitado, lo restringido; estrechez *f* de miras; mentalidad *f* pueblerina.
parodic [pə'rɒdɪk] ADJ paródico.
parodist ['pærədɪst] N parodista *mf*.
parody ['pærədɪ] ① N parodia *f*.
　② VT parodiar.
parole [pə'rəʊl] ① N (*promise*) palabra *f*, palabra *f* de honor; (*freedom*)

libertad *f* bajo palabra, libertad *f* condicional; **to be on ~** estar libre bajo palabra; **to break one's ~** faltar a su palabra; **to put sb on ~** dejar a uno libre bajo palabra.
  2 VT dejar libre bajo palabra.

paroxysm ['pærəksɪzəm] N paroxismo *m*.

parquet ['pɑːkeɪ] N parquet *m*, parqué *m*; entarimado *m* (de hojas quebradas *or* de maderas finas).

parquetry ['pɑːkɪtrɪ] N entarimado *m*, obra *f* de entarimado.

parricide ['pærɪsaɪd] N (a) (*act*) parricidio *m*. (b) (*person*) parricida *mf*.

parrot ['pærət] 1 N loro *m*, papagayo *m*; **they repeated it like ~s** lo repitieron como loros.
  2 VT *words* repetir como un loro, (*person*) imitar como un loro.

parrot-cry ['pærətkraɪ] N eslogan *m* (*etc*) que se repite mecánicamente; cantilena *f*.

parrot-fashion ['pærət,fæʃən] ADV *learn etc* mecánicamente.

parry ['pærɪ] VT (*Fencing*) parar, quitar; *blow* parar, desviar; *attack* rechazar, defenderse de; (*fig*) esquivar, eludir, desviar hábilmente.

parse [pɑːz] VT analizar.

parsec ['pɑːsek] N parsec *m*.

Parsee [pɑːˈsiː] N parsi *mf*.

parser ['pɑːzəʳ] N analizador *m* sintáctico.

parsimonious [,pɑːsɪˈməʊnɪəs] ADJ parco; escaso, corto; frugal.

parsimoniously [,pɑːsɪˈməʊnɪəslɪ] ADV parcamente; escasamente; frugalmente.

parsimony ['pɑːsɪmənɪ] N parquedad *f*; escasez *f*; frugalidad *f*.

parsing ['pɑːzɪŋ] N análisis *m* gramatical, análisis *m* sintáctico.

parsley ['pɑːslɪ] N perejil *m*.

parsnip ['pɑːsnɪp] N chirivía *f*, pastinaca *f*.

parson ['pɑːsn] N clérigo *m*, cura *m*; (*esp*) párroco *m*, (*Protestant*) pastor *m*; **~'s nose** (*of chicken*) rabadilla *f*.

parsonage ['pɑːsnɪdʒ] N casa *f* del párroco; casa *f* del pastor.

parsonical [pɑːˈsɒnɪkəl] ADJ (*hum*) frailuno.

part [pɑːt] 1 N (a) (*portion, fragment*) parte *f*; porción *f*; trozo *m*; **this ~ is blue** esta parte es azul; **the funny ~ of it is that ...** lo gracioso es que ...; **you haven't heard the best ~ yet** todavía no te he dicho lo mejor; **that's the awkward ~** eso es lo difícil; **it is ~ and parcel of the scheme** es parte esencial del proyecto, es parte integrante del proyecto; **the book is good in ~s** hay partes del libro que son buenas; **a good ~ of, a large ~ of** buena parte de; **the greater ~ of it is done** la mayor parte está hecha; **this is in great ~ due to ...** esto se debe ante todo a ..., más que nada esto se debe a ...; **for the most ~** por la mayor parte; **it went on for the best ~ of an hour** continuó casi una hora; **we lost the best ~ of a month** perdimos casi un mes; **for the better ~ of the day** durante la mayor parte del día; **in the latter ~ of the year** en los últimos meses del año; **in ~** en parte; **it is ready in ~** en parte está listo; **to pay a debt in ~** pagar parte de una deuda; **5 ~s of sand to 1 of cement** 5 partes de arena y 1 de cemento; **three ~s** tres cuartos; **it's 3 ~s gone** las tres cuartas partes se han usado ya.
  (b) (*Mech*) pieza *f*.
  (c) (*Gram*) parte *f*; **~ of speech** parte *f* de la oración; **principal ~s of a verb** partes *fpl* principales de un verbo.
  (d) (*of journal*) número *m*; (*of series*) tomo *m*; (*of serial*) entrega *f*; (*of reference work*) fascículo *m*.
  (e) (*share*) parte *f*; **to do one's ~** cumplir con sus obligaciones; **each one did his ~** cada uno hizo lo que le tocaba; **to have no ~ in sth** (*not be active*) no participar en algo, (*have nothing to do with*) no tener nada que ver con algo, ser ajeno a algo, desentenderse de algo; **he had no ~ in stealing it** no tuvo que ver con el robo; **to take (a) ~ in** tomar parte en, intervenir en, participar en; **are you taking ~?** ¿vas a tomar parte?
  (f) (*Theat, fig*) papel *m*; **it is not my ~ to +** *infin* no me toca a mí + *infin*; **to look the ~** vestir el cargo; **to play a ~** hacer un papel, (*fig*) desempeñar un papel; **what ~ do you play?** ¿qué papel haces?; **he's just playing a ~** está haciendo un papel, nada más; **the climate has played a ~ in +** *ger* el clima ha contribuido a + *infin*.
  (g) (*Mus*) parte *f*; **the soprano ~** la parte de soprano; **to sing in ~s** cantar por partes.
  (h) (*region*) ~s lugar *m*; comarca *f*, región *f*; **from all ~s** de todas partes; **in these ~s** por aquí; en estos pagos, en estos contornos; **the biggest thief in these ~s** el mayor ladrón en estos contornos; **in foreign ~s** en el extranjero; **what ~ are you from?** ¿de dónde es Vd?; **he's not from these ~s** no es de aquí; **it's a lovely ~** es una región hermosa.
  (i) (*side*) parte *f*; **for my ~, on my ~** por mi parte; **a mistake on the ~ of ...** un error por parte de ..., un error debido a ...; **on the one ~..., on the other ...** por una parte ..., por otra ...; **there is opposition on the ~ of some** hay oposición por parte de algunos; **to take sb's ~** ponerse del lado de uno, tomar el partido de uno.
  (j) **to take sth in good ~** tomar algo en buena parte.
  (k) **a man of ~s** un hombre de talento.
  (l) (*US: in hair*) raya *f*, vereda *f* (*Mex*).

  2 ADV: **~ one and ~ the other** parte esto y parte lo otro; **it is ~ brass and ~ copper** parte es latón y parte es cobre; **it was ~ eaten** había sido comido en parte; **she is ~ French** ella es en parte francesa.
  3 ATTR: **a 4 ~ song** una canción a 4 voces; **~ load** carga *f* parcial; **~ work** revista *f* con entregas coleccionables.
  4 ADJ parcial; co..., con...; **~-author** coautor *m*, -ora *f*; **~-owner** condueño *m*, -a *f*, copropietario *m*, -a *f*.
  5 VT separar, dividir (*from* de); (*break*) romper, partir; **to ~ sth in two** partir algo en dos; **he ~ed the grass with his hand** con la mano apartó la hierba; **to ~ one's hair** hacerse la raya.
  6 VI (a) (*crowd etc*) apartarse; **the branches ~ed** se apartaron las ramas; **the people ~ed to let her through** la gente se hizo a un lado para dejarla pasar.
  (b) (*2 persons*) separarse; **they ~ed 5 years ago** se separaron hace 5 años; **the best of friends must ~** los mejores amigos han de separarse alguna vez; **to ~ from sb** separarse de uno, despedirse de uno; **when we ~ed from Seville** cuando nos despedimos de Sevilla.
  (c) (*roads etc*) bifurcarse.
  (d) (*snap, break*) romperse, partirse (*LAm*); (*fall away*) separarse, desprenderse.
  (e) **to ~ with** ceder, entregar; *money* pagar, dar, soltar; (*get rid of*) deshacerse de; **I hate ~ing with it** siento mucho tener que cederlo, me da pena partirme.

partake [pɑːˈteɪk] (*irr: V take*) VTI (a) **to ~ of** *food* comer, comer de, aceptar; *drink* tomar, beber; **do you ~?** ¿bebes vino? (*etc*); **will you ~?** ¿quieres de esto?
  (b) **to ~ of a quality** tener algo de una cualidad, tener rasgos de una cualidad.
  (c) **to ~ in** tomar parte en, participar en; **are you partaking?** ¿vas a tomar parte?

parterre [pɑːˈteə] N parterre *m*.

part-exchange ['pɑːtɪksˈtʃeɪndʒ] N (*Brit*): **to offer sth in ~** ofrecer algo como parte del pago; **'we take your old car in ~'** 'admitimos su coche usado a cambio'.

parthenogenesis ['pɑːθɪnəʊˈdʒenɪsɪs] N partenogénesis *f*.

Parthenon ['pɑːθənɒn] N Partenón *m*.

partial ['pɑːʃəl] ADJ (a) (*in part*) parcial. (b) (*biased*) parcial. (c) **to be ~ to sth·** ser aficionado a algo, tener gusto por algo.

partiality [,pɑːʃɪˈælɪtɪ] N (a) (*bias*) parcialidad *f*; predisposición *f*, prejuicio *m*. (b) (*liking*) **~ for, ~ to** afición *f* a, gusto *m* por.

partially ['pɑːʃəlɪ] ADV (a) (*partly*) parcialmente, en parte. (b) (*with bias*) con parcialidad.

participant [pɑːˈtɪsɪpənt] N partícipe *mf*, participante *mf*; (*in competition*) concursante *mf*; (*in fight*) combatiente *mf*.

participate [pɑːˈtɪsɪpeɪt] VI participar, tomar parte (*in* en); **participating countries** países *mpl* participantes.

participation [pɑːˌtɪsɪˈpeɪʃən] N participación *f*.

participative [pɑːˈtɪsɪpətɪv] ADJ (*frm*) *management, democracy* participativo.

participatory [pɑːtɪsɪˈpeɪtərɪ] ADJ *democracy, sport* participativo.

participial [,pɑːtɪˈsɪpɪəl] ADJ participial.

participle ['pɑːtɪsɪpl] N participio *m*; **past ~** participio *m* pasivo, participio *m* pasado, participio *m* (de) pretérito; **present ~** participio *m* activo, participio *m* (de) presente.

particle ['pɑːtɪkl] N (a) partícula *f*; (*of dust etc*) átomo *m*, grano *m*; (*fig*) pizca *f*; **~ accelerator** acelerador *m* de partículas; **~ physics** física *f* de partículas; **there's not a ~ of truth in it** eso no tiene ni pizca de verdad. (b) (*Gram*) partícula *f*.

particleboard ['pɑːtɪklbɔːd] N (*US*) madera *f* aglomerada.

parti-coloured, (*US*) **parti-colored** ['pɑːtɪ,kʌləd] ADJ de diversos colores, multicolor, abigarrado.

▼ **particular** [pəˈtɪkjʊləʳ] 1 ADJ (a) (*special*) particular; especial; concreto; determinado; individual; **that ~ person** esa persona en particular, esa persona (y no otra); **a ~ thing** una cosa determinada; **in ~ cases** en casos especiales; **it varies according to the ~ case** varía según el caso individual; **in this ~ case** en este caso concreto; **for no ~ reason** por ninguna razón especial; **to take ~ care** tomar especial cuidado, ser especialmente cuidadoso.
  (b) *account etc* detallado, minucioso.
  (c) (*fastidious*) exigente, quisquilloso (*about, as to, as to what* en cuanto a, en asuntos de, para); (*scrupulous*) escrupuloso; (*about food etc*) delicado; **he's ~ about his food** es delicado con lo que come; **he is very ~ about cleanliness** es muy exigente para la limpieza; **he's ~ about his car** cuida mucho del coche; **I'm ~ about my friends** escojo mis amigos con cierto cuidado; **I'm not too ~ (about it)** lo mismo da, me es igual; **he was most ~ about it** insistió mucho sobre esto; **he was very ~ to say that ...** subrayó que ..., dijo con toda claridad que ...

▼ 2 N (a) (*detail*) detalle *m*, pormenor *m*, dato *m*; **~s** detalles *mpl*; **in this ~** en este caso particular; **correct in every ~** correcto en todos los detalles; **for further ~s apply to ...** para más informes escriban a

...; **to give ~s** citar los detalles; **please give full ~s** se ruega hacer constar todos los detalles, se ruega dar un informe detallado.

(b) in ~ en particular; en concreto, concretamente; **nothing in ~** nada concreto, nada en particular; **are you looking for anything in ~?** ¿busca Vd algo en concreto?

particularity [pə,tɪkjʊ'lærɪtɪ] N particularidad f.

particularize [pə'tɪkjʊləraɪz] ① VT particularizar, especificar, señalar; **he did not ~ which one he wanted** no especificó cuál quería.

② VI dar todos los detalles, concretar; **he did not ~** no concretó.

particularly [pə'tɪkjʊləlɪ] ADV: **this is ~ true of his later novels** sobre todo es esto verdad de sus novelas de última época; **notice ~ that ...** observen Vds sobre todo que ...; **he said most ~ not to do it** dijo de modo particular que no se hiciera; **do you want it ~ for tomorrow?** ¿lo necesitas especialmente para mañana?; **he was not ~ pleased** no se puso loco de contento que digamos; **not ~!** ¡no mucho!

parting ['pɑːtɪŋ] ① ADJ de despedida; **a ~ present** un regalo de despedida; **~ shot** última observación, palabra f dicha al despedirse, golpe m final; **his ~ words** sus palabras al despedirse; **he made a ~ threat** al separarse de nosotros pronunció una amenaza, nos dejó con una amenaza.

② N **(a)** separación f; despedida f; **the ~ of the ways** el momento de la separación, (fig) el punto decisivo.

(b) (Brit: in hair) raya f, vereda f (Mex).

partisan [,pɑːtɪ'zæn] ① ADJ partidista; (Mil) de partisanos, de guerrilleros; **~ spirit** partidismo m; **~ warfare** guerra f de guerrilleros.

② N partidario m, -a f, (of de); (Mil) partisano m, -a f, guerrillero m, -a f.

partisanship [,pɑːtɪ'zænʃɪp] N partidismo m.

partition [pɑː'tɪʃən] ① N **(a)** (Pol etc) partición f, división f.

(b) (wall) tabique m, medianía f (LAm).

② VT **(a)** country etc partir, dividir; (share) repartir (among entre).

(b) room etc tabicar, dividir con tabique; **to ~ a part off** separar una parte con tabique.

partitive ['pɑːtɪtɪv] ADJ partitivo.

partly ['pɑːtlɪ] ADV en parte; en cierto modo; **only ~ true** verdad sólo en parte; **it was ~ destroyed** quedaba destruido en parte, quedaba parcialmente destruido.

partner ['pɑːtnəʳ] ① N compañero m, -a f (also Cards); (Comm) socio mf; (in dance, at tennis etc) pareja f; (in crime) codelincuente mf; (spouse) cónyuge mf; (sexual) pareja f; (lover) compañero m, -a f; **Britain's EC ~s** los socios comunitarios de Gran Bretaña.

② VT acompañar; **to be ~ed by** ir acompañado de; tener a uno por pareja (etc).

partnership ['pɑːtnəʃɪp] N asociación f, (Comm) sociedad f (comanditaria); (of spouses) vida f conyugal, vida f en común; **A is in ~ with Z** A es socio de Z; **to enter into ~, to form a ~** asociarse (with con); **to take sb into ~** tomar a uno como socio.

part-owner ['pɑːt'əʊnəʳ] N condueño m, -a f, copropietario m, -a f.

part-payment ['pɑːt'peɪmənt] N pago m parcial; **to offer sth in ~** ofrecer algo como parte del pago.

partridge ['pɑːtrɪdʒ] N perdiz f.

part-song ['pɑːtsɒŋ] N canción f a varias voces.

part-time ['pɑːt'taɪm] ① ADV: **to work ~** trabajar en horario de jornada reducida, trabajar parte de la jornada.

② ADJ person en dedicación parcial, que trabaja por horas; **work** por horas, de horario partido.

③ N jornada f reducida; **to be on ~** trabajar en horario de jornada reducida.

part-timer [,pɑːt'taɪməʳ] N trabajador m, -ora f a tiempo partido.

parturition [,pɑːtjʊə'rɪʃən] N parturición f, parto m.

part-way ['pɑːt,weɪ] ADV: **~ through the week** a mitad de la semana; **we're only ~ into** (or **through**) **the work** hemos hecho sólo una parte del trabajo; **the window was ~ open** la ventana estaba medio abierta.

▼ **party** ['pɑːtɪ] ① N **(a)** (Pol) partido m; **to be a member of the ~** ser miembro del partido; **to join the ~** hacerse miembro del partido.

(b) (group) grupo m; (Mil) pelotón m, destacamento m; **a ~ of travellers** un grupo de viajeros; **hunting ~** partida f de caza; **we were a ~ of 5** éramos un grupo de 5; **we were only a small ~** éramos pocos; **I was one of the ~** yo formaba parte del grupo; **to join sb's ~** unirse al grupo de uno.

▼ **(c)** (gathering) reunión f; (tea ~ etc) tertulia f; (merry) fiesta f, guateque m; **that little ~ at El Alamein*** la fiestecita de El Alamain*; **that was quite a ~*!** ¡eso fue de miedo*!; **the ~'s over** se acabó la fiesta; **to crash a ~*** colarse, entrar de rondón; **to give a ~** ofrecer una fiesta, organizar una fiesta; **to go to a ~** ir a una fiesta; **keep the ~ clean!** ¡nada de chistes verdes!

(d) (Jur etc) parte f; interesado m, -a f; **third ~** tercera persona f, tercero m; **the parties to a dispute** las partes de una disputa, los interesados; **the high contracting parties** las altas partes contratantes; **to be a ~ to an agreement** firmar un acuerdo; **to be a ~ to a crime** ser cómplice en un crimen; **were you a ~ to this?** ¿tuvo

Vd algo que ver con esto?; **I will not be a ~ to any violence** no quiero tener nada que ver con la violencia; **I will not be a ~ to any such attempt** no me presto a ninguna tentativa de ese tipo.

(e) (*: person) individuo m, -a* f; **a ~ of the name of Pérez** un individuo llamado Pérez*.

② ATTR **(a)** (Pol) **~ line** línea f de partido; **~ machine** aparato m del partido; **~ politics** política f de partidos, (pej) partidismo m, politiqueo m.

(b) **~ dress** traje m de fiesta; **~ piece, ~ trick** numerito m (de fiesta); **~ pooper*** (US) aguafiestas mf.

(c) **~ line** (Telec) línea f compartida.

(d) **~ wall** pared f medianera.

(e) **~ plan** venta f directa a través de círculos sociales.

③ (*) VI ir a fiestas, ir (mucho) a guateques; **we partied at John's** fuimos a la fiesta de Juan; **where shall we ~ tonight?** ¿a qué fiesta vamos esta noche?

party-goer ['pɑːtɪ,gəʊəʳ] N (gen) asiduo m, -a f a fiestas; (on specific occasion) invitado m, -a f; **I'm not much of a ~** yo voy poco a las fiestas.

party-going ['pɑːtɪ,gəʊɪŋ] N: **he spends his time ~ instead of working** se pasa el tiempo en ir a fiestas y no en trabajar.

partying* ['pɑːtɪɪŋ] N: **I'm not a great one for ~** no me gustan mucho las fiestas.

party-political [,pɑːtɪpə'lɪtɪkəl] ADJ advantage, issue de(l) partido; **~ broadcast** ≃ espacio m electoral.

parvenu ['pɑːvənjuː] N advenedizo m, -a f.

paschal ['pɑːskəl] ADJ pascual; **the P~ Lamb** el cordero pascual.

pas de deux ['pɑːdə'dɜː] N paso m a dos.

pasha ['pæʃə] N bajá m, pachá m.

pass [pɑːs] ① N **(a)** (permit) permiso m, pase m; (Mil etc) salvoconducto m; (of journalist, worker etc) permiso m; (Theat) entrada f de favor; (Rail etc) billete m de favor; (membership card) carnet m.

(b) (Sport, Fencing, by conjuror, mesmerist) pase m; **forward ~** pase m adelantado.

(c) (in exams) aprobado m, nota f de aprobado; **to get a ~ in German** aprobar en alemán; **I need a ~ in physics still** todavía tengo que aprobar la física.

(d) **things have come to a pretty ~** las cosas han llegado a una situación crítica, estamos en una situación crítica.

(e) **to make a ~ at*** echar un tiento a*.

(f) (Geog) puerto m, paso m (LAm); (small) desfiladero m; **to sell the ~** tracionar la causa; ceder lo que bien podría ser defendido.

② VT **(a)** (move past) pasar; pasar por delante de; person (on street etc) cruzarse con; competitor pasar; (Aut: overtake) pasar, adelantar a, rebasar (LAm); **they ~ed each other on the way** se cruzaron en el camino; **we are now ~ing the Tower of London** pasamos ahora delante de la Torre de Londres.

(b) (cross) frontier etc cruzar.

(c) **it ~es belief** es increíble (that que); **it ~es my comprehension that ...** para mí resulta incomprensible que ...

(d) (Univ etc) exam aprobar, ser aprobado en.

(e) censor ser aprobado por; critic merecer la aprobación de.

(f) (approve) motion, plan, candidate etc aprobar; **to ~ sb fit** dar a uno de alta; **to ~ sb for the army** declarar a uno apto para el servicio militar.

(g) ball etc pasar; **to ~ sth from hand to hand** pasar algo de mano a mano; **~ me the salt, please** ¿me haces el favor de pasar (or alcanzar SC) la sal?

(h) false coin pasar.

(i) **to ~ a cloth over sth** limpiar algo con un paño, frotar algo con un trapo; **to ~ one's hand between two bars** introducir la mano entre dos rejas.

(j) (spend) time pasar; **we ~ed the weekend pleasantly** pasamos el fin de semana agradablemente; **just to ~ the time** para pasar el rato; **I ~ed the time of day with him** me detuve un rato a charlar con él, cambié algunas palabras con él.

(k) remark hacer; opinion expresar; sentence pronunciar, dictar (on sobre, en el asunto de).

(l) blood, water evacuar.

③ VI **(a)** (come, go) pasar; **to ~ into a tunnel** entrar en un túnel; **to ~ into oblivion** ser olvidado; **to ~ out of sight** perderse de vista; **~ along the car please!** ¡vayan pasando por delante!; **words ~ed between them** se cambiaron algunas palabras (fuertes); **no money has ~ed** ningún dinero ha cambiado de dueño; **to let sth ~** no hacer caso de algo, no protestar contra algo; **we can't let that ~!** ¡eso no lo podemos consentir!; **let it ~** conviene dejarlo, conviene no protestar.

(b) (of time) (also **to ~ by**) pasar; **how time ~es!** ¡cómo pasa el tiempo!

(c) (disappear) pasar; desaparecer; (clouds etc) disiparse; **it'll ~** eso pasará, eso se olvidará.

(d) (be acceptable) ser aceptable, aprobarse; **what ~es in New York**

may not be good enough here lo que se aprueba en Nueva York puede resultar inaceptable aquí.
(e) (*be considered as*) **it ~es for a restaurant** pasa por ser restaurante; **in her day she ~ed for a great beauty** en sus tiempos se le consideraba una gran belleza; **or what ~es nowadays for a hat** o lo que se llama sombrero hoy día.
(f) (*Univ etc*) aprobar, ser aprobado; **I ~ed!** ¡aprobé!; **did you ~ in chemistry?** ¿aprobaste en química?
(g) it came to ~ that ... (*liter*) aconteció que ...
(h) (*Cards etc*) **I ~** paso.
◆ **pass about, pass around** VT = **pass round**.
◆ **pass along** 1 VT pasar de uno a otro, hacer circular.
2 VI pasar, circular.
◆ **pass away** VI **(a)** (*die*) fallecer. **(b)** = **pass 3 (c)**.
◆ **pass back** VT devolver (*to* a).
◆ **pass by** 1 VT no hacer caso de, no fijarse en, pasar por alto.
2 VI pasar de largo; pasar cerca.
◆ **pass down** 1 VT transmitir, pasar.
2 VI transmitirse, pasar.
◆ **pass off** 1 VT **(a)** *coin* pasar; *offence* disimular; **to ~ sth off as a joke** pasar algo por chiste; **he ~ed the girl off as his sister** hizo creer que la chica era su hermana, hizo pasar a la chica por su hermana.
(b) to ~ sth off on sb encajar algo a uno.
2 VI **(a)** (*subside*) pasar, desaparecer.
(b) (*occur*) pasar, tener lugar; **it all ~ed off without incident** todo transcurrió normalmente.
3 VR: **to ~ o.s. off as a doctor** hacerse pasar por médico.
◆ **pass on** 1 VT (*hand down*) pasar, transmitir; *message* dar, decir, comunicar; **we shall have to ~ the increase on to the consumer** tendremos que hacer que el consumidor cargue con el incremento.
2 VI **(a)** (*die*) fallecer. **(b)** (*continue*) pasar adelante; seguir su camino; **to ~ on to a new subject** pasar a un nuevo asunto.
◆ **pass out** 1 VT *leaflets etc* distribuir, repartir.
2 VI **(a)** (*emerge*) salir (*of* de).
(b) (*Mil*) graduarse; (*US Scol*) salir, terminar los estudios.
(c) (*: faint*) caer redondo*, perder el conocimiento.
◆ **pass over** 1 VT (*neglect*) pasar por alto, omitir; **I think we can ~ that bit over** creo que podemos dejar ese trozo a un lado; **he was ~ed over again for promotion** en los ascensos volvieron a postergarle.
2 VI (*die*) fallecer.
◆ **pass round** VT *bottle etc* pasar de uno a otro; pasar de mano en mano; *note* hacer circular.
◆ **pass through** 1 VT *hardships* pasar por, aguantar.
2 VI pasar; **I'm just ~ing through** estoy de paso nada más.
◆ **pass up** VT *chance* no aprovechar; *claim* renunciar a.
passable ['pɑːsəbl] ADJ **(a)** (*tolerable*) pasable; tolerable, admisible. **(b)** (*usable, crossable*) transitable.
passably ['pɑːsəblɪ] ADV medianamente, pasablemente.
passage ['pæsɪdʒ] N **(a)** (*act of passing*) paso *m*, tránsito *m*; (*voyage*) viaje *m*, travesía *f*; (*fare*) pasaje *m*; (*Parl: process*) trámites *mpl*, (*final*) aprobación *f*; **the ~ of time** el paso del tiempo; **in the ~ of time** andando el tiempo, con el tiempo.
(b) (*corridor*) pasillo *m*, galería *f*, pasadizo *m*; (*alley*) callejón *m*; (*Mech*) tubo *m*, conducto *m*; (*Anat*) tubo *m*.
(c) ~ of arms combate *m*.
(d) (*Liter, Mus etc*) pasaje *m*; trozo *m*; episodio *m*, sección *f*; **'selected ~s from Caesar'** 'selecciones de César'.
passage money ['pæsɪdʒˌmʌnɪ] N pasaje *m*.
passageway ['pæsɪdʒweɪ] N pasillo *m*, galería *f*, pasadizo *m*.
passbook ['pɑːsbʊk] N libreta *f* de depósitos.
passé ['pæseɪ] ADJ pasado de moda.
passel ['pæsəl] N (*US*) muchedumbre *f*.
passenger ['pæsndʒəʳ] 1 N **(a)** pasajero *m*, -a *f*; viajero *m*, -a *f*; **the ~s** (*collectively*) el pasaje, los pasajeros; **will ~s please rejoin the train?** ¡señores viajeros, al tren! **(b)** (*pej*) **for many years he was a ~** durante muchos años fue una nulidad; **there's no room for ~s in this company** en esta empresa no toleramos a los gandules.
2 ATTR de pasajeros; **~ list** lista *f* de pasajeros; **~ seat** (*Aut*) asiento *m* de pasajero; **~ ship** buque *m* de pasajeros; **~ train** tren *m* de pasajeros.
passenger-miles ['pæsndʒəʳˌmaɪlz] NPL millas-pasajero *fpl*.
passe-partout ['pæspɑːtuː] N paspartú *m*, passe partout *m*.
passer-by ['pɑːsəˈbaɪ] N, PL **passers-by** ['pɑːsəzˈbaɪ] transeúnte *mf*.
passim ['pæsɪm] ADV passim.
passing ['pɑːsɪŋ] 1 ADJ (*fleeting*) pasajero; *glance etc* rápido, superficial; **a ~ car** un coche que pasaba; **~ fancy** capricho *m*; **~ grade** (*US*) aprobado *m*; **~ lane** (*US Aut*) carril *m* de adelantamiento; **~ place** (*Brit Aut*) apartadero *m*; **~ remark** comentario *m* hecho de paso; **~ shot** (*Sport*) tiro *m* pasado; **with each ~ day it gets more difficult** día tras día se hace más difícil.
2 N **(a)** paso *m*; (*Parl*) aprobación *f*; (*disappearance*) desaparición *f*;

(*euph: death*) fallecimiento *m*; **in ~** de paso, de pasada. **(b)** (*US Aut*) adelantamiento *m*, paso *m*.
passing bell ['pɑːsɪŋbel] N toque *m* de difuntos.
passing-out [ˌpɑːsɪŋˈaʊt] ATTR: **~ parade** desfile *m* de promoción.
passion ['pæʃən] 1 N **(a)** pasión *f*; (*anger*) cólera *f*, arranque *m* de cólera; **crime of ~** crimen *m* pasional; **he said with ~** dijo con pasión; **political ~s are strong here** aquí son muy fuertes las pasiones políticas; **to be in a ~** estar encolerizado; **to burst** (*or* **fly**) **into a ~** montar en cólera, encolerizarse; **to conceive a ~ for sb** enamorarse con verdadera pasión de uno, apasionarse por uno; **I have a ~ for shellfish** adoro los mariscos, me apasionan los mariscos.
(b) the P~ la Pasión.
2 ATTR: **P~ play** drama *m* de la Pasión; **P~ Sunday** domingo *m* de la Pasión.
passionate ['pæʃənɪt] ADJ *embrace, speech, temperament etc* apasionado; *believer, desire* vehemente, ardiente; (*angry*) colérico.
passionately ['pæʃənɪtlɪ] ADV apasionadamente, con pasión; con vehemencia, ardientemente; coléricamente; **to love sb ~** amar a uno con pasión.
passionflower ['pæʃənˌflaʊəʳ] N pasionaria *f*.
passionfruit ['pæʃənfruːt] N granadilla *f*, fruta *f* de la pasión.
passionless ['pæʃənlɪs] ADJ *affair etc* sin pasión, frío; desapasionado; (*dispassionate*) imparcial.
passive ['pæsɪv] 1 ADJ pasivo (*also Gram*); inactivo, inerte; **~ resistance** resistencia *f* pasiva; **~ smoking** fumar *m* pasivo.
2 N VOZ *f* pasiva.
passively ['pæsɪvlɪ] ADV pasivamente.
passiveness ['pæsɪvnɪs] N, **passivity** [pæˈsɪvɪtɪ] N pasividad *f*; inercia *f*.
passkey ['pɑːskiː] N llave *f* maestra.
passmark ['pɑːsmɑːk] N aprobado *m*.
Passover ['pɑːsəʊvəʳ] N Pascua *f* (de los judíos).
passport ['pɑːspɔːt] N pasaporte *m*; **the ~ to fame** el pasaporte de la fama.
passport control ['pɑːspɔːtkənˈtrəʊl] N control *m* de pasaportes.
password ['pɑːswɜːd] N santo *m* y seña, contraseña *f*; (*Comput*) contraseña *f* de acceso.
past [pɑːst] 1 ADV por delante; **to fly ~** pasar volando; **to march ~** desfilar; **to rush ~** pasar precipitadamente; **he went ~ without stopping** pasó sin detenerse; **she walked slowly ~** pasó despacio.
2 PREP **(a)** (*place: in front of*) por delante de; (*beyond*) más allá de; **just ~ the town hall** un poco más allá del Ayuntamiento; **to run ~ sb** pasar a uno corriendo; alcanzar y pasar a uno corriendo.
(b) (*with numbers*) más de; **we're ~ 100 already** ya vamos a más de 100; hemos contado más de 100 ya; **she's ~ 40** tiene más de 40 años.
(c) (*with time*) después de; **10 ~ 3** (*Brit*) las 3 y 10; **half ~ 4** (*Brit*) las 4 y media; **at a quarter ~ 9** (*Brit*) a las 9 y cuarto; **it's ~ 12** dieron las 12 ya, son las 12 dadas.
(d) (*other expressions*) **it is ~ belief** es increíble; **it is ~ endurance** es intolerable; **we're ~ caring** ya nos trae sin cuidado, ya no tenemos por qué preocuparnos de eso; **he's ~ it** ya no puede, ya no tiene fuerzas para eso; **I wouldn't put it ~ him** le creo capaz hasta de eso, no me extrañaría en él.
3 ADJ pasado (*also Gram*); (*former*) antiguo, ex ..., que fue; *master etc* consumado; **~ perfect** pluscuamperfecto *m*; **~ tense** tiempo *m* pasado; **for some time ~** de algún tiempo a esta parte; **in times ~** en otro tiempo, antiguamente; **all that is now ~** todo eso ha quedado ya a la espalda; **in ~ years** en otros años, en años pasados; **~ president of ...** antiguo presidente de ..., ex presidente de ..., presidente que fue de ...
4 N el pasado (*also Gram*), lo pasado; (*early history*) historia *f*, antecedentes *mpl*; **in the ~** en el pasado, antes, antiguamente; **as we did in the ~** como hacíamos antes; **it's a thing of the ~** pertenece a la historia; **silent pictures are things of the ~** las películas mudas han quedado anticuadas; **that belongs to my murky ~** eso pertenece a mi turbio pasado; **what's his ~?** ¿cuáles son sus antecedentes?; **a town with a ~** una ciudad de abolengo histórico, una ciudad llena de historia; **she's a woman with a ~** es una mujer que tiene historia.
pasta ['pæstə] N pastas *fpl* alimenticias.
paste [peɪst] 1 N **(a)** (*material in general*) pasta *f*; (*for sticking*) engrudo *m*; (*fish-~*) pasta *f*. **(b)** (*gems*) diamante *m* de imitación, bisutería *f*.
2 VT **(a)** (*apply ~ to*) engrudar; engomar; (*affix, stick together*) pegar; **to ~ sth to a wall** pegar algo a una pared.
(b) (*: beat*) pegar; (*Sport*) cascar*, dar una paliza a.
◆ **paste up** VT: **to ~ up a notice** pegar un anuncio.
pasteboard ['peɪstbɔːd] 1 N cartón *m*.
2 ATTR de cartón.
pastel ['pæstəl] 1 N **(a)** (*material*) pastel *m*; (*crayon*) lápiz *m* de color; (*drawing etc*) pintura *f* al pastel. **(b) ~s** (*colours*) colores *mpl* pastel.

2 ATTR: ~ **blue** azul *m* pastel; ~ **drawing** pintura *f* al pastel; ~ **shade** tono *m* pastel.
pastern ['pæstə:n] N cuartilla *f* (del caballo).
pasteurization [,pæstəraɪ'zeɪʃən] N paste(u)rización *f*.
pasteurize ['pæstəraɪz] VT paste(u)rizar.
pasteurized ['pæstəraɪzd] ADJ paste(u)rizado.
pastiche [pæs'ti:ʃ] N pastiche *m*, imitación *f*.
pastille ['pæstɪl] N pastilla *f*.
pastime ['pɑ:staɪm] N pasatiempo *m*.
pasting* ['peɪstɪŋ] N paliza *f*; **to give sb a ~** dar una paliza a uno; **he got a ~ from the critics** los críticos le dieron una paliza.
pastor ['pɑ:stəʳ] N pastor *m*.
pastoral ['pɑ:stərəl] **1** ADJ *care, economy* pastoral; (*Eccl*) pastoral; (*Liter*) pastoril; ~ **letter = 2**.
2 N (*Eccl*) pastoral *f*.
pastrami [pə'strɑ:mɪ] N *especie de embutido ahumado a base de carne de vaca con especias*.
pastry ['peɪstrɪ] N (*dough*) pasta *f*; (*collectively*) pastas *fpl*, pasteles *mpl*; (*art*) pastelería *f*; **pastries** pastas *fpl*, pasteles *mpl*.
pastryboard ['peɪstrɪ,bɔ:d] N tabla *f* de amasar.
pastrybrush ['peɪstrɪ,brʌʃ] N cepillo *m* de repostería.
pastrycase ['peɪstrɪ,keɪs] N cobertura *f* de pasta.
pastrycook ['peɪstrɪkʊk] N pastelero *m*, -a *f*, repostero *m*, -a *f*.
pastry cutter ['peɪstrɪ,kʌtəʳ] N cortador *m* de masa.
pastry shop ['peɪstrɪʃɒp] N pastelería *f*, repostería *f*.
pasturage ['pɑ:stjʊrɪdʒ] N = **pasture 1**.
pasture ['pɑ:stʃəʳ] **1** N (*grass*) pasto *m*; (*land*) pasto *m*, prado *m*, dehesa *f*; **to put** (*or* **send**) **animals out to ~** echar los animales al pasto; **they're putting me out to ~** me echan al pasto (como a caballo viejo); **he's gone to ~s new** (*euph, hum*) ha pasado a mejor vida.
2 VT *animals* apacentar, pastorear; *grass* comer, pacer.
3 VI pastar, pacer.
pastureland ['pɑ:stʃəlænd] N pasto *m*, prado *m*, dehesa *f*.
pasty **1** ['peɪstɪ] ADJ *material* pastoso; *colour* pálido; **to look ~** estar pálido.
2 ['pæstɪ] N (*Brit*) pastel *m* (de carne), empanada *f*.
pasty-faced ['peɪstɪ,feɪst] ADJ pálido, de cara pálida.
Pat [pæt] NM AND NF *familiar form of* **Patrick, Patricia**.
pat¹ [pæt] **1** N (**a**) (*with hand*) palmadita *f*, golpecito *m*; (*on shoulder*) palmada *f*; (*caress*) caricia *f*; **to give sb a ~ on the back** dar a uno una palmada en la espalda, (*fig*) pronunciar unas palabras elogiosas para uno, felicitar a uno; **to give o.s. a ~ on the back** felicitarse a sí mismo.
(**b**) (*of butter*) pastelillo *m*.
2 VT (*touch*) tocar, pasar la mano por, posar la mano sobre; (*tap, with hand*) dar una palmadita en, *shoulder* dar una palmada en; *child's head, dog etc* acariciar; **he ~ted the chair with the book** tocó la silla con el libro; **to ~ sb on the back** dar a uno una palmada en la espalda, (*fig*) pronunciar unas palabras elogiosas para uno, felicitar a uno.
3 VR: **to ~ o.s. on the back** (*fig*) felicitarse a sí mismo.
pat² [pæt] **1** ADV: **he knows it** (*off*) ~ lo sabe al dedillo; **he always has an excuse just ~** siempre tiene su excusa lista; **the answer came too ~** dio su respuesta con demasiada prontitud; **to stand ~** (*US*) mantenerse firme, mantenerse en sus trece.
2 ADJ *answer etc* oportuno, a propósito; pronto; convincente.
Patagonia [,pætə'gəʊnɪə] N Patagonia *f*.
Patagonian [,pætə'gəʊnɪən] **1** ADJ patagón, patagónico.
2 N patagón *m*, -ona *f*.
patch [pætʃ] **1** N (**a**) (*piece of cloth etc*) pedazo *m*; (*mend*) remiendo *m*; (*on tyre, wound*) parche *m*, guarache *m* (*Mex*); (*beauty-spot*) lunar *m* postizo; (*Comput*) ajuste *m*. (**b**) (*stain etc*) mancha *f*; (*small area*) pedazo *m*, pequeña extensión *f*; (*Agr*) terreno *m*, parcela *f*; **they must get off our ~*** tienen que largarse de lo nuestro*; **but this is their ~*** pero éste es territorio de ellos; **a ~ of oil** una mancha de aceite; **a ~ of blue flowers** una masa de flores azules, una extensión de flores azules; **a ~ of blue sky** un pedazo de cielo azul, un claro. (**c**) **the team is having a bad ~** el equipo pasa por un momento difícil, el equipo tiene una mala racha; **we have had our bad ~es** hemos tenido nuestros momentos malos; **then we hit a bad ~ of road** dimos luego con un tramo de carretera bastante malo; **it's not a ~ on the other one** no se puede comparar con el otro.
2 VT remendar, poner remiendo a.
◆ **patch together** VT *materials* ir componiendo (de modo provisional); *coalition etc* formar (de modo poco satisfactorio).
◆ **patch up** VT: **to ~ sth up** componer algo de modo provisional; **we'll see if we can ~ sth up for you** trataremos de arreglarlo para Vd; **after a time they ~ed things up** después de un rato se la arreglaron; **to ~ up a quarrel** hacer las paces (*with* con).
patchwork ['pætʃwɜ:k] **1** N labor *f* de retazos; (*fig*) masa *f* confusa; mosaico *m*; **a ~ of fields** un mosaico de campos.

2 ATTR: ~ **quilt** centón *m*, edredón *m* de trozos multicolores.
patchy ['pætʃɪ] ADJ desigual, poco uniforme; *pattern etc* manchado.
pate [peɪt] N mollera *f*; testa *f*; **bald ~** calva *f*.
pâté ['pæteɪ] N paté *m*; pastel *m* (de carne *etc*).
patella [pə'telə] N rótula *f*.
paten ['pætən] N patena *f*.
patent ['peɪtənt] **1** ADJ (**a**) (*obvious*) patente, evidente, palmario. (**b**) (*Comm*) de patente, patentado.
2 N (**a**) (*also* ~ **leather**) charol *m*. (**b**) (*Comm*) patente *f*; ~ **applied for**, ~ **pending** patente en trámite; **to take out a ~** obtener una patente.
3 ATTR de patentes; ~ **agent** agente *m* de patentes; ~ **law** derecho *m* de patentes; ~ **leather = 2** (**a**); ~ **medicine** específico *m*; ~ **office** oficina *f* de patentes; **P~ Office** (*Brit*), **P~ and Trademark Office** (*US*) registro de la propiedad industrial; ~ **rights** derechos *mpl* de patente.
4 VT patentar.
patentable ['peɪtəntəbl] ADJ patentable.
patentee [,peɪtən'ti:] N poseedor *m*, -ora *f* de patente, concesionario *m*, -a *f* de la patente.
patently ['peɪtəntlɪ] ADV evidentemente, a las claras; **a ~ untrue statement** una declaración de evidente falsedad.
patentor ['peɪtəntəʳ] N dueño *m*, -a *f* de patente.
pater* ['peɪtəʳ] N: **the ~** (*esp Brit*) el viejo*.
paterfamilias ['peɪtəfə'mɪlɪæs] N padre *m* de familia.
paternal [pə'tɜ:nl] ADJ *quality* paternal; *relation* paterno.
paternalism [pə'tɜ:nəlɪzəm] N gobierno *m* paternal.
paternalist [pə'tɜ:nəlɪst] N paternalista *m*.
paternalistic [pə,tɜ:nə'lɪstɪk] ADJ paternalista.
paternally [pə'tɜ:nəlɪ] ADV paternalmente; **he said ~** dijo paternal.
paternity [pə'tɜ:nɪtɪ] **1** N paternidad *f*.
2 ATTR: ~ **leave** licencia *f* de paternidad; ~ **suit** litigio *m* de paternidad.
paternoster ['pætə'nɒstəʳ] N padrenuestro *m*.
path [pɑ:θ] N, PL **paths** [pɑ:ðz] camino *m*, senda *f*, sendero *m*, vereda *f*; (*fig*) camino *m*; trayectoria *f*, curso *m*; (*person's track*) pista *f*; (*of bullet*) trayectoria *f*; (*of hurricane etc*) rastro *m*, marcha *f*; (*Comput*) camino *m*; **the ~ to power** el camino del poder; **to beat a ~ to sb's door** asediar a uno; **to cross sb's ~** tropezar con uno, parar dificultades a uno; **to keep to the straight and narrow ~** ir por la vereda, no apartarse del buen camino; **to smooth sb's ~ for him** allanarle el camino a uno; **to tread the ~ of moderation** ir por el camino de la moderación.
pathetic [pə'θetɪk] ADJ (**a**) patético, lastimoso, conmovedor; **a ~ sight** una escena lastimosa; **a ~ creature** un infeliz, un pobre hombre; **it was ~ to see it** daba pena verlo.
(**b**) (*very bad*) horrible, malísimo; ~, **isn't it?** ¿es horrible, no?; **it was a ~ performance** fue una exhibición que daba pena.
(**c**) ~ **fallacy** (*Liter*) engaño *m* sentimental.
pathetically [pə'θetɪklɪ] ADV patéticamente, lastimosamente; **a ~ inadequate answer** una respuesta tan poco satisfactoria que da pena.
pathfinder ['pɑ:θ,faɪndəʳ] N explorador *m*, piloto *m*; pionero *m*.
pathogen ['pæθəʊdʒen] N patógeno *m*.
pathogenic [pæθə'dʒenɪk] ADJ patógeno.
pathological [,pæθə'lɒdʒɪkəl] ADJ patológico.
pathologist [pə'θɒlədʒɪst] N patólogo *m*, -a *f*.
pathology [pə'θɒlədʒɪ] N patología *f*.
pathos ['peɪθɒs] N patetismo *m*, lo patético.
pathway ['pɑ:θweɪ] N = **path**.
patience ['peɪʃəns] N (**a**) paciencia *f*; **my ~ is exhausted** se me ha acabado la paciencia, no tengo más paciencia; **you must have ~** hay que tener paciencia; **I have no ~ with you** ya no aguanto más, estoy para desesperarme; **to lose one's ~** perder la paciencia; **to possess one's soul in ~** armarse de paciencia; **she taxes** (*or* **tries**) **my ~ very much** me cuesta no impacientarme con ella.
(**b**) (*Brit Cards*) solitario *m*.
patient ['peɪʃənt] **1** ADJ paciente; sufrido; **to be ~ with sb** ser paciente con uno; **you must be very ~ about it** hay que tener mucha paciencia; **we have been ~ long enough!** ¡ya no aguantamos más!, ¡se nos agota la paciencia!
2 N paciente *mf*, enfermo *m*, -a *f*.
patiently ['peɪʃəntlɪ] ADV pacientemente, con paciencia.
patina ['pætɪnə] N pátina *f*.
patio ['pætɪəʊ] **1** N patio *m*.
2 ATTR: ~ **doors** puertas *fpl* que dan al patio.
patois ['pætwɑ:] N dialecto *m*, jerga *f*.
pat. pend. ABBR *of* **patent pending**.
patriarch ['peɪtrɪɑ:k] N patriarca *m*.
patriarchal [,peɪtrɪ'ɑ:kəl] ADJ patriarcal.
patriarchy ['peɪtrɪ,ɑ:kɪ] N patriarcado *m*.
Patricia [pə'trɪʃə] NF Patricia.
patrician [pə'trɪʃən] **1** ADJ patricio.
2 N patricio *m*, -a *f*.

patricide ['pætrɪsaɪd] N (*crime*) patricidio *m*; (*person*) patricida *mf*.
Patrick ['pætrɪk] NM Patricio.
patrimony ['pætrɪmənɪ] N patrimonio *m*.
patriot ['peɪtrɪət] N patriota *mf*.
patriotic [ˌpætrɪ'ɒtɪk] ADJ patriótico.
patriotically ['pætrɪ'ɒtɪkəlɪ] ADV patrióticamente.
patriotism ['pætrɪətɪzəm] N patriotismo *m*.
patrol [pə'trəʊl] ① N patrulla *f*; **to be on ~** estar de patrulla, patrullar.
② VT (**a**) patrullar por; *frontier etc* guardar, defender; **they ~led the streets at night** patrullaban por las calles de noche; **the frontier is not ~led** la frontera no tiene patrullas.
(**b**) (*fig*) rondar, pasearse por.
③ VI (**a**) patrullar.
(**b**) (*fig*) rondar, pasearse; **he ~s up and down** se pasea de un lado a otro.
patrol-boat [pə'trəʊlbəʊt] N patrullero *m*, (lancha *f*) patrullera *f*.
patrol-car [pə'trəʊlkɑːʳ] N coche *m* patrulla.
patrol leader [pə'trəʊl'liːdəʳ] N jefe *m* de patrulla.
patrolman [pə'trəʊlmən] N, PL **patrolmen** [pə'trəʊlmən] (*Brit Aut*) mecánico *m* del servicio de ayuda en carretera; (*US*) guardia *m*, policía *m*.
patrol wagon [pə'trəʊlˌwægən] N (*US*) coche *m* celular.
patrolwoman [pə'trəʊlˌwʊmən] N, PL **patrolwomen** (*Brit: Aut*) mecánica *f* del servicio de ayuda en carretera; (*US*) mujer *f* policía.
patron ['peɪtrən] N (*Comm*) cliente *mf*; (*of enterprise*) patrocinador *m*; (*Liter, Art*) mecenas *m*; (*Eccl, also* **~ saint**) patrón *m*, patrono *m*, patrona *f*.
patronage ['pætrənɪdʒ] N (*of enterprise*) patrocinio *m*; (*Liter, Art*) mecenazgo *m*, protección *f*; (*Eccl*) patronato *m*; **under the ~ of** bajo el patronato de, patrocinado por, bajo los auspicios de.
patroness ['peɪtrənes] N (*of enterprise*) patrocinadora *f*; (*Liter, Art*) mecenas *f*; **~ of the arts** patrona de las artes.
patronize ['pætrənaɪz] VT (**a**) *shop* ser cliente de, comprar en; *services etc* usar, utilizar; *enterprise* patrocinar, favorecer, fomentar, apoyar; **the shop is well ~d** la tienda tiene mucha clientela, la tienda está muy acreditada.
(**b**) (*treat condescendingly*) tratar con condescendencia.
patronizing ['pætrənaɪzɪŋ] ADJ paternalista, desdeñoso, altivo; superior, lleno de superioridad; **a few ~ remarks** algunas observaciones dichas con aire protector; **he's a ~ person** es una persona llena de superioridad.
patronizingly ['pætrənaɪzɪŋlɪ] ADV protectoramente, con aire paternalista, con aire de superioridad; desdeñosamente, altivamente.
patronymic [ˌpætrə'nɪmɪk] ① ADJ patronímico.
② N patronímico *m*.
patsy* ['pætsɪ] N (*US*) bobo *m*, -a *f*, primo* *m*.
patten ['pætn] N zueco *m*, chanclo *m*.
patter¹ ['pætəʳ] ① N (*jargon*) jerga *f*; labia *f*; (*of salesman*) jerga *f* publicitaria; (*rapid speech*) parloteo *m*; **~ song** aria *f* (*or* canción *f*) de letra rapidísima; **the fellow has some very clever ~** el tío tiene unos argumentos muy hábiles, hablando el tío es muy listo.
② VI (*also* **to ~ on**) charlar, parlotear (*about* de).
patter² ['pætəʳ] ① N (*of feet*) pasos *mpl* ligeros, pataditas *fpl*, ruido *m* sordo; (*taps*) golpecitos *mpl*; golpeteo *m*; (*of rain*) tamborileo *m*; **we shall soon hear the ~ of tiny feet** pronto habrá un niño en la casa, pronto sentiremos pataditas.
② VI (*also* **to ~ about**) andar con pasos ligeros, pisar con ruido sordo; (*rain*) tamborilear; **he ~ed over to the door** fue con pasos ligeros a la puerta.
pattern ['pætən] ① N modelo *m*; (*sample*) muestra *f*; (*design*) diseño *m*, dibujo *m*; (*Sew*) patrón *m*, modelo *m*, molde *m* (*SC*); (*fig*) pauta *f*, norma *f*; **~ of distribution** patrón *m* de distribución; **~ of expenditure** composición *f* de los gastos; **~ of trade** estructura *f* del comercio; **~ recognition** reconocimiento *m* de modelos; **on the ~ of** sobre el modelo de, según el diseño de; **it set a ~ for other conferences** estableció una pauta para otros congresos; **it is following the usual ~** se está desarrollando como siempre, sigue la norma.
② VT modelar (*on* sobre), diseñar (*on* según).
pattern-book ['pætənbʊk] N libro *m* de muestras.
patterned ['pætənd] ADJ *material, fabric, china* estampado.
patterning ['pætənɪŋ] N diseño *m*, dibujo *m*.
pattern-maker ['pætən'meɪkəʳ] N carpintero *m* modelista.
patty ['pætɪ] N empanada *f*.
paucity ['pɔːsɪtɪ] N escasez *f*, insuficiencia *f*, corto número *m*.
Paul [pɔːl] NM Pablo; (*Saint*) Pablo; (*Pope*) Paulo (*see also* **John**).
Pauline¹ ['pɔːlaɪn] ADJ: **the ~ Epistles** las Epístolas de San Pablo.
Pauline² ['pɔːliːn] NF Paulina.
paunch [pɔːntʃ] ① N panza *f*, barriga *f*.
② VT *rabbit etc* destripar.
paunchy ['pɔːntʃɪ] ADJ panzudo, barrigudo.
pauper ['pɔːpəʳ] N pobre *mf*, indigente *mf*.

pauperism ['pɔːpərɪzəm] N pauperismo *m*.
pauperization [ˌpɔːpəraɪ'zeɪʃən] N empobrecimiento *m*.
pauperize ['pɔːpəraɪz] VT empobrecer, reducir a la miseria.
pause [pɔːz] ① N pausa *f* (*also Mus*); intervalo *m*; interrupción *f*; silencio *m*; **there was a ~ while ...** hubo un silencio mientras ...; **we carried on without ~** continuamos sin interrupción, seguíamos trabajando (*etc*) sin descansar; **to give sb ~** dar que pensar a uno, hacer vacilar a uno.
② VI hacer una pausa; (*speaker etc*) detenerse (brevemente), callarse (momentáneamente), interrumpirse; **~ before you act** reflexione antes de obrar; **he ~d for breath** se calló para cobrar aliento; **he spoke for 30 minutes without once pausing** habló durante 30 minutos sin interrumpirse una sola vez; **let's ~ here** detengámonos aquí un rato; **it made him ~** le hizo vacilar.
pave [peɪv] VT pavimentar; (*with flags*) enlosar, solar; (*with stones*) empedrar; adoquinar; (*with bricks*) enladrillar; **to ~ the way** preparar el terreno (*for* a); **the streets are ~d with gold** las calles tienen pavimento de oro.
paved [peɪvd] ADJ pavimentado; enlosado; empedrado; enladrillado; *road* asfaltado, afirmado.
pavement ['peɪvmənt] ① N (*Brit*) pavimento *m*; (*sidewalk*) acera *f*, vereda *f* (*LAm*), andén *m* (*CAm*), banqueta *f* (*CAm, Mex*); (*US*) calzada *f*, camino *m* asfaltado; **brick ~** enladrillado *m*; **stone ~** empedrado *m*; **to leave the ~** (*US Aut*) salir de la calzada.
② ATTR: **~ artist** pintor *m* callejero; **~ café** café *m* con terraza, café *m* al aire libre.
pavilion [pə'vɪlɪən] N pabellón *m*; (*for band etc*) quiosco *m*; (*Sport*) caseta *f*, vestuario *m*; (*at trade-fair etc*) pabellón *m*.
paving ['peɪvɪŋ] N pavimento *m*, pavimentación *f*, enlosado *m*, adoquinado *m*, enladrillado *m*.
paving-stone ['peɪvɪŋstəʊn] N adoquín *m*; (*flagstone*) losa *f*.
Pavlovian [pæv'ləʊvɪən] ADJ pavloviano.
paw [pɔː] ① N (**a**) (*of animal*) pata *f*; (*of cat*) garra *f*; (*of lion*) zarpa *f*.
(**b**) (*: *hand*) manaza *f*, manota *f*.
② VT (**a**) (*animal*) tocar con la pata; (*lion*) dar zarpazos a; **to ~ the ground** (*horse*) piafar.
(**b**) (*) (*person: pej*) tocar, manosear, (*amorously*) sobar, palpar; **stop ~ing me!** ¡fuera las manos!, ¡manos quietas!
③ VI: **to ~ at sth** tocar algo con la pata, (*to wound*) dar zarpazos a algo.
pawl [pɔːl] N trinquete *m*.
pawn¹ [pɔːn] N (*Chess*) peón *m*; (*fig*) instrumento *m*; **they simply used me as a ~** se aprovecharon de mí como mero instrumento.
pawn² [pɔːn] ① N: **in ~** en prenda; **to leave** (*or* **put**) **sth in ~** dejar algo en prenda; **the country is in ~ to foreigners** el país está empeñado a extranjeros.
② VT empeñar, pignorar, dejar en prenda.
pawnbroker ['pɔːnˌbrəʊkəʳ] N prestamista *m*, prendero *m*, agenciero *m* (*SC*); **~'s** (**shop**) casa *f* de empeños, prendería *f*, monte *m* de piedad.
pawnshop ['pɔːnʃɒp] N casa *f* de empeños, prendería *f*, monte *m* de piedad, agencia *f* (*SC*).
pawn-ticket ['pɔːnˌtɪkɪt] N papeleta *f* de empeño.
pawpaw ['pɔːpɔː] N papaya *f*.
pax [pæks] N (**a**) **~!** (*Brit*) ¡me rindo! (**b**) (*Eccl*) beso *m* de la paz.
pay [peɪ] ① N paga *f*; remuneración *f*, retribución *f*; (*of professional person*) sueldo *m*; (*of worker*) salario *m*, sueldo *m*; (*of day labourer*) jornal *m*; **equal ~** igualdad *f* de retribución (para hombres y mujeres); **to be in sb's ~** ser asalariado de uno, estar al servicio de uno; **agents in the enemy's ~** agentes *mpl* al servicio del enemigo; **to draw** (*or* **get**) **one's ~** cobrar.
② ATTR: **~ as you earn** (*Brit*), **~-as-you-go** (*US*) retención *f* fiscal (*hecha por la empresa*); **~ award** adjudicación *f* de aumento de salarios; **~ bargaining** negociación *f* salarial; **~ increase, ~ rise** incremento *m* salarial, subida *f* de salario; **~ negotiations** negociaciones *fpl* salariales; **~ policy** política *f* salarial; **~ round** serie *f* de negociaciones salariales; **~ structure** estructura *f* salarial; **~ talks = ~ negotiations**; **~ TV** TV *f* de pago.
③ (*irr*: PRET AND PTP **paid**) VT (**a**) pagar (*for* por); **to ~ sb £10** pagar 10 libras a uno; **what did you ~ for it?** ¿cuánto pagaste por él?; **it's a service that has to be paid for** es un servicio que hay que pagar; **to ~ money into an account** ingresar dinero en una cuenta; **how much is there to ~?** ¿cuánto hay que pagar?; **to be** (*or* **get**) **paid on Fridays** cobrar los viernes; **when do you get paid?** ¿cuándo cobras?; **to ~ cash** (**down**) pagar al contado; **shares that ~ 5%** acciones *fpl* que producen un 5 por 100; **the company paid 12% last year** el año pasado la sociedad pagó 12 por 100; **to ~ sb to do a job** pagar a uno para que haga un trabajo; **a badly paid worker** un obrero mal retribuido; **a badly paid job** un empleo mal remunerado; *V also* **paid**.
(**b**) *account, debt* liquidar; satisfacer; *bill, duty, fee* pagar; **'paid'** (*on receipted bill*) 'pagado'.

(c) (*be profitable to*) ser provechoso a; **it wouldn't ~ him to do it** no le saldría a cuenta hacerlo, (*fig*) no le sería aconsejable hacerlo, no le valdría la pena hacerlo; **it doesn't ~ you to be kind nowadays** hoy día no vale la pena mostrarse amable; **but it paid him in the long run** pero a la larga le fue provechoso.

(d) *attention* prestar (*to* a); *homage* rendir (*to* a); *respects* ofrecer, presentar; *visit* hacer; *V also* **address** *etc*.

4 VI **(a)** pagar; **who ~s?** ¿quién paga?; **to ~ on account** pagar a cuenta; **to ~ in advance** pagar por adelantado; **to ~ in full** pagarlo todo, pagar la cantidad íntegra; **to ~ in instalments** pagar a plazos; **'please ~ at the door'** 'por favor: paguen a la entrada'; **to ~ for sth** pagar algo; costear algo, correr con los gastos de algo; **they made him ~ dearly for it** le hicieron pagarlo muy caro; **she paid for it with her life** lo pagó con la vida; **he paid for his rashness with his life** su temeridad le costó la vida; **they paid for her to go** pagaron para que fuera; **I'll make you ~ for this!** ¡me las pagarás!

(b) (*be profitable*) rendir, rendir bien, ser provechoso; **it's a business that ~s** es un negocio que rinde, es un negocio rentable; **it's ~ing at last** por fin produce ganancias; **his job ~s well** tiene un buen sueldo, el trabajo le paga bien; **it ~s to be courteous** vale la pena mostrarse cortés; **it doesn't ~ to paint it** vale más no pintarlo, es mejor no pintarlo; **it ~s to advertise** compensa hacer publicidad.

◆ **pay away** VT pagar, desembolsar.

◆ **pay back** VT **(a)** *money* devolver; restituir, reintegrar.
(b) *person* pagar. **(c) to ~ sb back (in his own coin)** (*fig*) pagar a uno en la misma moneda.

◆ **pay down** VT (*cash*) pagar al contado; (*deposit*) pagar como desembolso inicial.

◆ **pay in** **1** VT *cheque, money* ingresar.
2 VI **(a)** (*at bank*) ingresar dinero.
(b) (*to scheme etc*) pagar contribuciones; **he was ~ing in for 20 years** llevaba 20 años pagando contribuciones.

◆ **pay off** **1** VT **(a)** *debt* pagar, liquidar, saldar; *mortgage etc* amortizar, redimir; *old score* ajustar.
(b) *workers, crew* pagar y despedir.
2 VI (*fig*) valer la pena, merecer la pena; tener éxito; reportar beneficios, dar buenos resultados; **the rule paid off** la estratagema salió bien; **it has paid off many times over** ha demostrado su valor muchísimas veces; **when do you think it will begin to ~ off?** ¿cuándo piensas que empezará a dar resultado?

◆ **pay out** **1** VT **(a)** *money* pagar, desembolsar.
(b) (*fig*) *person* pagar en la misma moneda; desquitarse con; **I'll ~ you out for this!** ¡me las pagarás!
(c) *rope* ir dando.
2 VI: **to ~ out on a policy** pagar una póliza.

◆ **pay over** VT pagar, entregar.

◆ **pay up** **1** VT pagar de mala gana).
2 VI pagar; pagar lo que se debe; **~ up!** ¡a pagar!

payable ['peɪəbl] ADJ pagadero; **~ to bearer** pagadero al portador; **~ on demand** pagadero a presentación; **~ at sight** pagadero a vista; **to make a cheque ~ to sb** extender un cheque a favor de uno.

payback ['peɪbæk] N restitución f; **~ period** período m de restitución.

paybed ['peɪbed] N cama f de pago.

paycheck ['peɪtʃek] N (*US*) sueldo m, pago m.

payday ['peɪdeɪ] N día m de paga.

paydesk ['peɪdesk] N caja f.

paydirt ['peɪdɜːt] N (*US*) grava f provechosa (*also fig*).

PAYE N (*Brit*) ABBR of **pay as you earn**; *V* **pay 2.**

payee [peɪ'iː] N portador m, -ora f, tenedor m, -ora f; (*on cheque*) orden f, beneficiario m, -a f; **account ~ only** (*on cheque*) cuenta f nominal.

pay envelope ['peɪˌenvələʊp] N (*US*) sobre m de paga.

payer ['peɪər] N pagador m, -ora f; **slow ~, bad ~** moroso m, -a f.

paying ['peɪɪŋ] ADJ provechoso, que rinde bien; rentable; **~ bank** banco m pagador; **~ guest** huésped m, -a f de pago, pensionista mf; **it's a ~ proposition** es un negocio provechoso.

paying-in slip [ˌpeɪɪŋ'ɪnˌslɪp] N, **pay-in slip** [ˌpeɪ'ɪnˌslɪp] N hoja f de ingreso.

payload ['peɪləʊd] N carga f útil.

paymaster ['peɪmɑːstər] N (*Mil etc*) (oficial m) pagador m; **the spy's Ruritanian ~s** los oficiales ruritanios que pagaban al espía.

▼ **payment** ['peɪmənt] N pago m; remuneración f, retribución f; **~ on account** pago m a cuenta; **~ card** tarjeta f de pago; **~ in cash** pago m al contado; **~ after delivery** pago m a la entrega; **~ by instalments** pago m a plazos; **~ on invoice** pago m a la presentación de factura; **~ by results** pago m por resultados; **~ terms** condiciones fpl de pago; **as ~ for, in ~ for** en pago de; **as ~ for your services** en concepto de sus servicios; **on ~ of £5** pagando 5 libras, mediante el pago de 5 libras; **without ~** sin remuneración; **to make a ~** efectuar un pago; **to present sth for ~** presentar algo al cobro; **to stop ~s** (*bank*) suspender los pagos; **to stop ~ of a cheque** detener el cobro de un cheque.

payoff ['peɪɒf] N **(a)** (*payment*) pago m; (*of debt*) liquidación f (total).
(b) **~ card** tarjeta f de pago; (*reward*) recompensa f; retribución f; (*vengeance*) ajuste m de cuentas, castigo m; (*bribe*) soborno m; (*spin-off*) beneficios mpl. **(c)** (*outcome*) resultado m, consecuencia f; (*climax*) momento m de la verdad.

pay office ['peɪˌɒfɪs] N caja f, pagaduría f.

payola* [peɪ'əʊlə] N (*US*) soborno m.

pay-out ['peɪaʊt] N pago m; (*share-out*) reparto m.

pay packet ['peɪˌpækɪt] N (*Brit*) sobre m de paga.

pay pause ['peɪpɔːz] N congelación f de sueldos y salarios.

pay-per-view [ˌpeɪpə'vjuː] ADJ de pago; **~ television** televisión f de pago.

payphone ['peɪfəʊn] N teléfono m público.

payroll ['peɪrəʊl] **1** N nómina f (de sueldos); **to be on a firm's ~** estar en la nómina f de una empresa; **he has 1000 people on his ~** tiene una nómina de 1000 personas.
2 ATTR: **~ tax** impuesto m sobre la nómina.

paysheet ['peɪʃiːt] N nómina f.

payslip ['peɪslɪp] N hoja f de sueldo.

pay station ['peɪˌsteɪʃən] N (*US*) teléfono m público.

pay-television ['peɪˌtelɪˌvɪʒən] N televisión f de pago.

PB N ABBR of **personal best** marca f personal.

PBAB ABBR of **please bring a bottle.**

PBS N (*US*) ABBR of **Public Broadcasting Service.**

PBX N (*Telec*) ABBR of **private branch exchange** centralita para extensiones.

PC **1** N **(a)** (*Brit*) ABBR of **police constable** policía mf. **(b)** ABBR of **personal computer** ordenador m (*or* computadora f) personal, CP, PC. **(c)** (*Brit*) ABBR of **Privy Councillor.**
2 ABBR of **politically correct** políticamente correcto; *ver también* POLITICALLY CORRECT.

p.c. **(a)** ABBR of **postcard** tarjeta f postal. **(b)** ABBR of **per cent** por cien, por ciento, p.c.

P/C **(a)** (*St Ex*) ABBR of **prices current** cotizaciones fpl. **(b)** (*Comm*) ABBR of **petty cash.**

PCA **(a)** (*Brit*) ABBR of **Police Complaints Authority.** **(b)** N ABBR of **Professional Chess Association.**

PCB N **(a)** ABBR of **printed circuit board** tarjeta f de circuito(s) impreso(s), TCI f. **(b)** ABBR of **polychlorinated biphenyl** bifenilo m policlorinado.

PCC N (*Brit*) ABBR of **Press Complaints Commission.**

PCFC N ABBR of **Polytechnics and Colleges Funding Council.**

pcm ADV ABBR of **per calendar month** por mes, p/mes.

PCP **(a)** (*Drugs*) ABBR of **phencyclidine** fenciclidina f. **(b)** (*Med*) ABBR of **pneumocystis carinii** neumocistis f carinii.

PD N (*US*) ABBR of **police department.**

pd ABBR of **paid** pagado, pgdo.

pdq* ADV ABBR of **pretty damn quick** en un momento.

PDSA N ABBR of **People's Dispensary for Sick Animals.**

PDT N (*US*) ABBR of **Pacific Daylight Time.**

PE N ABBR of **physical education** cultura f física, educación f física, ed. física.

pea [piː] **1** N guisante m, arveja f (*LAm*), chícharo m (*LAm*).
2 ATTR: **~ soup** sopa f de guisantes.

peace [piːs] **1** N paz f; (*peacefulness*) paz f, tranquilidad f, sosiego m; **~ of mind** tranquilidad f de ánimo; **the (King's) ~** el orden público; **to be at ~** estar en paz; **to break (or disturb) the ~** perturbar la paz, alterar el orden público; **to hold one's ~** guardar silencio, callarse; **to keep the ~** mantener el orden; mantener la paz; **he was bound over to keep the ~** se le ordenó respetar el orden público; **to make ~** hacer las paces (*with* con).
2 ATTR: **~ campaign** campaña f pacifista; **~ campaigner** persona que participa en una campaña pacifista; **P~ Corps** (*US*) Cuerpo m de la Paz; **~ dividend** dividendos mpl de la paz, beneficios mpl de la paz; **~ initiative** iniciativa f de paz; **P~ Movement** Movimiento m Pacifista; **~ sign** señal f de paz; **~ talks** negociaciones fpl de paz; **~ treaty** tratado m de paz.

peaceable ['piːsəbl] ADJ pacífico.

peaceably ['piːsəblɪ] ADV live, settle pacíficamente.

peaceful ['piːsfʊl] ADJ (*not warlike*) pacífico; (*quiet*) tranquilo, sosegado; coexistence pacífico; **it's very ~ here** aquí todo está perfectamente tranquilo; **on a ~ June evening** una tranquila tarde de junio.

peacefully ['piːsfəlɪ] ADV pacíficamente, en paz; tranquilamente; **to die ~** morirse tranquilamente.

peacefulness ['piːsfʊlnɪs] N tranquilidad f, sosiego m, calma f; (*of nation*) carácter m pacífico.

peacekeeper ['piːsˌkiːpər] N (*Mil*) pacificador m.

peace-keeping ['piːsˌkiːpɪŋ] **1** ADJ: **~ force** fuerzas fpl de pacificación; **~ operation** operación f pacificadora.
2 N pacificación f; mantenimiento m de la paz.

peace-loving ['piːsˌlʌvɪŋ] ADJ nation amante de la paz.

peacemaker ['piːsˌmeɪkər] N pacificador m, -ora f; (*between 2 sides*) árbitro *m*, conciliador *m*, -ora *f*.

peacemaking ['pi:smeɪkɪŋ] **1** N pacificación *f*, negociaciones *mpl* de paz.
2 ATTR *efforts, process, role* pacificador.

peacenik* ['pi:snɪk] N pacifista *mf*, milikaka*₂ mf* (*Sp*).

peace-offering ['pi:s,ɒfərɪŋ] N prenda *f* de paz, ramo *m* de olivo; (*to gods*) sacrificio *m* propiciatorio.

peacetime ['pi:staɪm] N: **in ~** en tiempo de paz.

peach¹ [pi:tʃ] **1** N (a) (*fruit*) melocotón *m*, durazno *m* (*LAm*); (*tree*) melocotonero *m*, durazno *m* (*LAm*).
(b) (*) **she's a ~** es un bombón*, es una monada*; **it's a ~** es una monada*; **a ~ of a girl** una real moza; **a ~ of a dress** un vestido monísimo.
(c) (*colour*) color *m* de melocotón.
2 ADJ color melocotón.

peach²₂ [pi:tʃ] VI soplar (*on contra*)*.

peach-tree ['pi:tʃtri:] N melocotonero *m*, durazno (*LAm*).

peacock ['pi:kɒk] N pavo *m* real, pavón *m*; **~ blue** azul *m* pavo.

pea-green ['pi:'gri:n] ADJ verde claro.

peahen ['pi:hen] N pava *f* real.

peak [pi:k] **1** N (*point*) punta *f*; (*of mountain*) cumbre *f*, cima *f*; (*mountain*) pico *m*; (*of cap*) visera *f*; (*fig*) cumbre *f*; apogeo *m*, punto *m* más alto; **when the empire was at its ~** cuando el imperio estaba en su apogeo; **when demand is at its ~** cuando la demanda alcanza su punto más alto; **he was at the ~ of his fame** estaba en la cumbre de su fama.
2 ADJ: **~ hours** horas *fpl* punta; **~ load** carga *f* máxima; **~ period** período *m* de máxima actividad; **~ production** producción *f* máxima; **~ season** temporada *f* más popular del año, temporada *f* alta; **~(-hour) traffic** movimiento *m* máximo (de tráfico), tráfico *m* de horas punta; **~ viewing time** banda *f* horaria caliente.
3 VI alcanzar su punto más alto, llegar al máximo.

peaked¹ [pi:kt] ADJ: **~ cap** gorra *f* de visera.

peaked² [pi:kt] ADJ, **peaky** ['pi:kɪ] ADJ pálido, enfermizo; **to look ~** tener la cara pálida.

peaktime ['pi:ktaɪm] ADJ (*Brit: TV*) horas *fpl* de máxima audiencia.

peal [pi:l] **1** N (*sound of bells*) repique *m*, campanillazo *m*, toque *m* de campanas; **~ of bells** (*set*) juego *m* de campanas; **~ of laughter** carcajada *f*; **~ of the organ** sonido *m* del órgano; **~ of thunder** trueno *m*.
2 VT repicar, tocar a vuelo.
3 VI (*bell*) repicar, tocar a vuelo; (*organ*) sonar.

peanut ['pi:nʌt] **1** N cacahuete *m*, maní *m* (*LAm*); **it's mere ~s to him*** para él es una bagatela; **we're not playing for ~s*** esto no es ninguna bagatela, esto va en serio.
2 ATTR: **~ butter** manteca *f* de cacahuete; **~ oil** aceite *m* de cacahuete.

peapod ['pi:pɒd] N vaina *f* de guisante.

pear [peər] N (*fruit*) pera *f*; (*tree*) peral *m*.

pearl [pɜ:l] **1** N perla *f* (*also fig*); (*mother-of-pearl*) nácar *m*; **to cast ~s before swine** echar margaritas a los puercos.
2 ATTR *necklace etc* de perla, de perlas; (*in colour*) color de perla; **~ barley** cebada *f* perlada; **~ diver** pescador *m* de perlas; **~ fishery** pescadería *f* de perlas; **~ necklace** collar *m* de perlas; **~ oyster** madre perla *f*.

pearl-grey ['pɜ:l'greɪ] ADJ gris perla.

pearly ['pɜ:lɪ] ADJ (*made of pearl*) de perla, de perlas; (*in colour*) color de perla, perlino; *mother of pearl* nacarado; **the P~ Gates** (*hum*) las puertas del Paraíso.

pear-shaped ['peəʃeɪpt] ADJ de forma de pera.

pear-tree ['peətri:] N peral *m*.

peasant ['pezənt] **1** N campesino *m*, -a *f*; labrador *m*, -ora *f*; (*pej*) palurdo *m*, -a *f*.
2 ATTR campesino; rústico; **~ farmer** campesino *m*.

peasantry ['pezəntrɪ] N campesinos *mpl*, campesinado *m*.

peashooter ['pi:ʃu:tər] N cerbatana *f*.

pea-souper* ['pi:'su:pər] N puré *m* de guisantes*, niebla *f* muy densa.

peat [pi:t] N turba *f*.

peatbog ['pi:tbɒg] N turbera *f*, turbal *m*.

peaty ['pi:tɪ] ADJ turboso.

pebble ['pebl] N guija *f*, guijarro *m*, china *f*; **he's not the only ~ on the beach** no es el único en el mundo.

pebbledash [,pebl'dæʃ] **1** N enguijarrado *m*.
2 VT enguijarrar.

pebbly ['peblɪ] ADJ guijarroso.

pecan ['pi:kæn] N pacana *f*.

peccadillo [,pekə'dɪləʊ] N falta *f* leve, pecadillo *m*.

peck¹ [pek] N *medida de áridos*: = 9,087 *litros*; (*fig*) montón *m*; **a ~ of troubles** la mar de disgustos.

peck² [pek] **1** N picotazo *m*; (*kiss*) besito *m*, beso *m* rápido.
2 VT picotear; (*kiss*) dar un besito a, dar un beso rápido a.
3 VI picotear; **to ~ at** (*bird*) intentar picotear, (*in eating*) comer

melindrosamente.

pecker ['pekər] N (a) (*Brit**) **to keep one's ~ up** no dejarse desanimar; **keep your ~ up!** ¡ánimo! (b) (*US*₂*) polla₂* *f*.

pecking-order ['pekɪŋ'ɔ:dər] N (*Bio*) orden *m* en que picotean las gallinas; (*fig*) jerarquía *f* social.

peckish* ['pekɪʃ] ADJ (a) hambriento, con hambre; **I'm ~, I feel ~** me anda el gusanillo. (b) (*US*) irritable.

pecs* [peks] NPL ABBR *of* **pectorals** pectorales *mpl*.

pectin ['pektɪn] N pectina *f*.

pectoral ['pektərəl] **1** ADJ pectoral.
2 **~s** NPL (*músculos mpl*) pectorales *mpl*.

peculate ['pekjʊleɪt] VI desfalcar.

peculation [,pekjʊ'leɪʃən] N desfalco *m*, peculado *m*.

peculiar [pɪ'kju:lɪər] ADJ (a) (*belonging exclusively*) peculiar; propio, característico; (*marked*) particular, especial; **an animal ~ to Africa** un animal autóctono de África, un animal que existe únicamente en África; **it is a phrase ~ to him** es una frase propia de él; **the region has its ~ dialect** la región tiene su dialecto especial.
(b) (*strange*) singular, extraño, raro; sui generis; **a most ~ flavour** un sabor muy extraño; **he's a ~ chap** es un tío raro; **how very ~!** ¡qué raro!; **it's really most ~** es realmente extraño; **I'm feeling a bit ~** no me siento del todo bien.

peculiarity [pɪ,kju:lɪ'ærɪtɪ] N (*V ADJ*) (a) peculiaridad *f*; particularidad *f*; rasgo *m* característico; **it has the ~ that ...** tiene la particularidad de que ...; **'special peculiarities'** (*on passport etc*) 'señas *fpl* particulares'.
(b) singularidad *f*, rareza *f*; extravagancia *f*, manía *f*; **there is some ~ which I cannot quite define** hay alguna rareza que no puedo precisar; **it's a ~ he has** es una manía que tiene; **he has his peculiarities** tiene sus manías.

peculiarly [pɪ'kju:lɪəlɪ] ADV (*V ADJ*) (a) particularmente, especialmente; **a ~ difficult work** una obra particularmente difícil.
(b) extrañamente, de modo raro; **he has been acting very ~** se ha comportado de modo rarísimo.

pecuniary [pɪ'kju:nɪərɪ] ADJ pecuniario.

pedagogic(al) [,pedə'gɒdʒɪk(əl)] ADJ pedagógico.

pedagogically [,pedə'gɒdʒɪkəlɪ] ADV pedagógicamente.

pedagogue, (*US sometimes*) **pedagog** ['pedəgɒg] N pedagogo *m*, -a *f*.

pedagogy ['pedəgɒgɪ] N pedagogía *f*.

pedal ['pedl] **1** N pedal *m* (*also Mus*); **loud ~** pedal *m* fuerte; **soft ~** sordina *f*.
2 VT impulsar pedaleando; **he came up ~ling his bicycle furiously** llegó en su bicicleta dándoles duro a los pedales.
3 VI pedalear.
4 ATTR: **~ (bi)cycle** bicicleta *f* a pedales; **~ bin** cubo *m* con pedal; **~ cyclist** ciclista *mf*.

pedal-boat ['pedl,bəʊt] N, **pedalo** ['pedələʊ] N patín *m* a pedal, pedaló *m*.

pedant ['pedənt] N pedante *mf*.

pedantic [pɪ'dæntɪk] ADJ *person* pedante; *manner etc* pedantesco.

pedantically [pɪ'dæntɪkəlɪ] ADV con pedantería, pedantescamente.

pedantry ['pedəntrɪ] N pedantería *f*.

peddle ['pedl] VT vender como buhonero, vender por las casas, andar vendiendo (de puerta en puerta); (*fig*) *scandal etc* contar, repetir, difundir.

peddler ['pedlər] N (*US*) = **pedlar**.

pederast ['pedəræst] N pederasta *m*.

pederasty ['pedəræstɪ] N pederastia *f*.

pedestal ['pedɪstl] **1** N pedestal *m*, basa *f*; **to knock sb off his ~** tumbar a uno, derrocar a uno; **to put sb on a ~** poner a uno sobre un pedestal.
2 ATTR: **~ lamp** lámpara *f* de pie.

pedestrian [pɪ'destrɪən] **1** ADJ (a) (*lit*) pedestre. (b) (*fig*) prosaico, pedestre.
2 N peatón *m*.
3 ATTR de peatones, para peatones; **~ area** zona *f* peatonal, zona *f* peatonizada; **~ crossing** paso *m* para peatones; **~ precinct** (*Brit*) = **~ area**; **~ traffic** circulación *f* de peatones.

pedestrianize [pɪ'destrɪənaɪz] VT peatonizar.

pediatrician *etc* = **paediatrician** *etc*.

pedicure ['pedɪkjʊər] N pedicura *f*, quiropedia *f*.

pedigree ['pedɪgri:] **1** N (*lineage*) genealogía *f*, linaje *m*; (*of animal*) pedigree *m*, pedigrí *m*; (*tree*) árbol *m* genealógico; (*document*) certificado *m* de genealogía.
2 ATTR de raza, de casta, de pura sangre; (*fig*) certificado, garantizado.

pediment ['pedɪmənt] N frontón *m*.

pedlar ['pedlər] N vendedor *m* ambulante, buhonero *m*, pacotillero *m* (*And, Carib*).

pedological [,pi:də'lɒdʒɪkl] ADJ (*US*) = **paedological**.

pedology [pɪ'dɒlədʒɪ] N (*US*) = **paedology**.

pedometer [pɪ'dɒmɪtər] N podómetro *m*.

pedophile ['pi:dəʊfaɪl] N (US) = **paedophile**.
pedophilia ['pi:dəʊ'fɪlɪə] N (US) = **paedophilia**.
pee [pi:] = **piss**.
peek [pi:k] ① N mirada f rápida, mirada f furtiva; **to take a ~ at** echar una mirada rápida (or furtiva) a.
② VI mirar a hurtadillas; **to ~ at** echar una mirada rápida (or furtiva) a.
peel [pi:l] ① N piel f; (after removal) pieles fpl, monda f, cáscara f, peladuras fpl; (fragment in cocktail etc) corteza f.
② VT fruit etc pelar, mondar, quitar la piel a; bark descortezar; layer of paper etc quitar, quitar una capa de.
③ VI (layer of paper etc) quitarse, despegarse, desprenderse; (paint etc) desconcharse; (bark) descortezarse; **I'm ~ing** se me despega la piel.
◆ **peel away** ① VT rind, skin mondar; film, covering pelar.
② VI (Med, skin) pelarse; (paint) caerse a tiras; (wallpaper) despegarse.
◆ **peel back** VT film, covering despegar.
◆ **peel off** ① VT dress etc quitarse rápidamente, quitarse lisamente.
② VI (a) (separate) separarse (from de); desviarse (from de); **this is where we ~ off from the main road** aquí es donde salimos de la carretera principal. (b) (*) desnudarse rápidamente.
peeler ['pi:lər] N (a) (gadget) mondador m; (electric) pelacables m. (b) (US*) estriptista f.
peelie-wally ['pi:lɪ'wælɪ] ADJ: **to be ~** (Scot) tener mala cara.
peeling ['pi:lɪŋ] N (Med: of face etc) descamación f; (cosmetic trade) peeling m; **~s** monda f, peladuras fpl.
peep¹ [pi:p] ① N (of bird etc) pío m; **there hasn't been a ~ out of them** no han dicho ni pío; **we can't get a ~ out of them** no les podemos hacer contestar; **I don't want a single ~ out of you** tú ni chistar, tú ni pío.
② VI piar.
peep² [pi:p] ① N mirada f rápida, mirada f furtiva, ojeada f; **at ~ of day** al primer amanecer; **to get a ~ at sth** lograr ver algo brevemente; **let's take a ~** vamos a verlo; **take a ~ at this** echa una ojeada a esto.
② VI mirar rápidamente, mirar furtivamente; **to ~ at sth** echar una mirada rápida (or furtiva) a algo; **to ~ from behind a tree** mirar a hurtadillas desde detrás de un árbol; **to ~ over a wall** atisbar por encima de una tapia, asomar cuidadosamente la cabeza por encima de una tapia para mirar; **to ~ through a window** atisbar a través de una ventana.
◆ **peep out** ① VT asomar; **she ~ed her head out** asomó la cabeza.
② VI asomar; **the book is ~ing out of his pocket** se deja ver en su bolsillo, asoma el libro por su bolsillo; **a head ~ed out** se asomó una cabeza; **the sun ~ed out from behind the clouds** el sol atisbó por las nubes.
peepers* ['pi:pəz] NPL ojos mpl.
peephole ['pi:phəʊl] N mirilla f, atisbadero m.
Peeping Tom [,pi:pɪŋ'tɒm] NM curioso m, mirón m.
peepshow ['pi:pʃəʊ] N mundonuevo m; (*) vistas fpl sicalípticas, espectáculo m deshonesto.
peeptoe ['pi:ptəʊ] ADJ: **~ sandal** sandalia f abierta; **~ shoe** zapato m abierto.
peer¹ [pɪər] ① N (a) (noble) par m; **~ of the realm** par m del reino. (b) (equal) igual mf, par mf; **as a musician he has no ~** como músico no tiene par.
② ATTR: **~ group** grupo m paritario; **~ review** evaluación f por los iguales.
peer² [pɪər] VI (a) (person) mirar con ojos de miope; **to ~ at sth** mirar algo de cerca, mirar algo con ojos de miope; **to ~ into a room** mirar dentro de un cuarto; **to ~ out of a window** asomarse (curioso) a una ventana; **to ~ over a wall** atisbar por encima de una tapia. (b) (fig) **two eyes ~ed out** aparecieron dos ojos, se asomaron dos ojos.
peerage ['pɪərɪdʒ] N (persons) nobleza f, aristocracia f; (rank) título m de nobleza, dignidad f de par; (book) (libro m) nobiliario m, guía f nobiliaria; **to get a ~** recibir un título de nobleza; **so they gave him a ~** así que le dieron un título de nobleza; **to marry into the ~** casarse con un título.
peeress ['pɪərɪs] N paresa f.
peerless ['pɪəlɪs] ADJ sin par, incomparable.
peeve* [pi:v] VT enojar, irritar.
peeved* [pi:vd] ADJ: **to be ~** estar enojado, estar furioso; **to get ~** sulfurarse*; ofenderse; **he got a bit ~** se ofendió.
peevish ['pi:vɪʃ] ADJ malhumorado, displicente, picajoso; impaciente.
peevishly ['pi:vɪʃlɪ] ADV malhumoradamente, con mal humor; impacientemente; **he said ~** dijo malhumorado.
peevishness ['pi:vɪʃnɪs] N mal humor m, displicencia f; impaciencia f.
peewee* [pi:wi:] ADJ (US) diminuto, pequeñito.
peewit ['pi:wɪt] N avefría f.
peg [peg] ① N clavija f, claveta f; (Mus) clavija f; (in ground) estaca f, estaquilla f; (tent-~) estaca f; (clothes-~) pinza f, broche m (LAm); (for

coat) gancho m, colgadero m, percha f (LAm); (in barrel) estaquilla f; (fig) pretexto m; (for argument etc) punto m de apoyo, punto m de partida; **a ~ of whisky** (Brit) un trago de whiskey; **clothes off the ~** (Brit) ropa f de percha; **to buy a suit off the ~** (Brit) comprar un traje de percha; **it was just a ~ on which to hang personal rivalries** era simplemente un clavo en que colgar las rivalidades personales; **to be a square ~ in a round hole** no cuadrar (donde se está); ser un inadaptado; **to take sb down a ~** bajar los humos a uno.
② VT (a) (fix ~s to) enclavijar.
(b) currency vincular (to a); prices fijar, estabilizar (a cierto nivel).
◆ **peg away*** VI machacar, batir el yunque; **to ~ away at sth** persistir en algo, afanarse por lograr algo.
◆ **peg down** VT estaquillar, fijar con estacas, sujetar con estacas.
◆ **peg out** ① VT area señalar con estacas; clothes tender (con pinzas).
② VI (‡) estirar la pata*.
Pegasus ['pegəsəs] N Pegaso m.
pegboard ['pegbɔ:d] N tablero m de clavijas.
pegleg ['pegleg] N pata f de palo.
PEI (Canada) ABBR of **Prince Edward Island**.
peignoir ['peɪnwɑ:r] N bata f (de señora), peinador m.
pejorative [pɪ'dʒɒrɪtɪv] ADJ peyorativo (also Gram), despectivo.
peke* [pi:k] N, **pekinese** [,pi:kɪ'ni:z] N pequinés m, -esa f.
Pekin [pi:'kɪn] N, **Peking** [pi:'kɪŋ] N Pekín m.
pelagic [pɪ'lædʒɪk] ADJ pelágico.
pelican ['pelɪkən] N pelícano m; **~ crossing** semáforo m sonoro.
pellagra [pə'lægrə] N pelagra f.
pellet ['pelɪt] N bolita f; (pill etc) píldora f; (shot) perdigón m; (of fertilizer etc) gránulo m.
pell-mell ['pel'mel] ADV en tropel, atropelladamente.
pellucid [pe'lu:sɪd] ADJ diáfano, translúcido.
pelmet ['pelmɪt] N galería f (para cubrir la barra de las cortinas).
Peloponnese [,peləpə'ni:s] N: **the ~** el Peloponeso.
Peloponnesian [,peləpə'ni:ʃən] ADJ peloponense.
pelota [pɪ'ləʊtə] ① N pelota f (vasca).
② ATTR: **~ player** pelotari m.
pelt¹ [pelt] N (skin) pellejo m; (fur) piel f.
pelt² [pelt] ① VT (a) (throw) tirar, arrojar (at a).
(b) **to ~ sb with eggs** tirar huevos a uno; **to ~ sb with stones** apedrear a uno; **they ~ed him with questions** le acribillaron a preguntas.
② VI (a) (of rain: also **to ~ with rain**) llover a cántaros.
(b) (*) a máxima velocidad; **to go ~ing past** pasar como un rayo; **to go ~ing off** partir como un rayo.
③ N: **to go full ~** ir a todo correr, ir a máxima velocidad.
◆ **pelt down** VI: **it was ~ing down** (rain) llovía de verdad, diluviaba.
pelvic ['pelvɪk] ADJ pélvico.
pelvis ['pelvɪs] N pelvis f.
pen¹ [pen] ① N (enclosure) corral m; (sheep-~) redil m, aprisco m; (bull-~) toril m; (play-~) parque m (de niño); (US*) chirona f.
② VT encerrar, acorralar.
pen² [pen] ① N pluma f; (fountain ~) estilográfica f, plumafuente f (LAm); **to put ~ to paper** empuñar la pluma, escribir algo; **to wield a ~** menear cálamo.
② ATTR: **~-and-ink drawing** dibujo m a pluma.
③ VT escribir; redactar, formular.
pen³ [pen] N (Orn) cisne m hembra.
penal ['pi:nl] ADJ (a) (gen) penal; **~ code** código m penal; **~ colony** colonia f penal; **~ servitude** trabajos mpl forzados; **~ settlement** = **~ colony**. (b) taxation etc muy gravoso, perjudicial.
penalization [,pi:nəlaɪ'zeɪʃn] N castigo m.
penalize ['pi:nəlaɪz] VT penar; (accidentally, unfairly) perjudicar; (Sport) castigar, sancionar, penalizar; **to be ~d for a foul** ser castigado por una falta; **we are ~d by not having a car** somos perjudicados por no tener coche; **the decision ~s those who ...** la decisión perjudica a los que ....
penalty ['penltɪ] ① N pena f, castigo m; (fine) multa f; (Sport) castigo m, sanción f, (football etc) penálty m, penalti m; (golf) penalización f, (Bridge) multa f, castigo m; **'~ £5'** 'la infracción se castigará con una multa de 5 libras'; **on ~ of** so pena de; **the ~ for this is death** esto se castiga con la muerte; **to pay the ~** sufrir el castigo (for de).
② ATTR: **~ area, ~ box** área f de castigo; **~ clause** cláusula f penal; **~ goal** gol m de penálty (or de tiro de castigo); **~ kick** penálty m, penalti m; **~ point** punto m de castigo; **~ shoot-out** desempate m a penaltis, tanda f de penaltis; **~ spot** punto m del penálty.
penance ['penəns] N penitencia f; **to do ~** hacer penitencia (for por).
pence [pens] NPL of **penny**.
penchant [,pɑ̃:ŋʃɑ̃:ŋ] N predilección f (for por), inclinación f (for hacia); **to have a ~ for** tener predilección por.
pencil ['pensl] ① N lápiz m, lapicero m (LAm); (propelling ~) lapicero m; (for eyebrows) lápiz m de cejas; (of light) rayo m delgado; **to draw in ~** dibujar con lápiz.
② ATTR: **~ drawing** dibujo m a lápiz; **~ mark** señal f hecha a lápiz.

3 VT (*also* **to ~ in**) escribir con lápiz; **a ~led note** un apunte escrito a lápiz.

◆**pencil in** VT apuntar (con lápiz); (*fig*) apuntar con carácter provisional.

pencil-box ['penslbɒks] N cajita *f* de lápices.

pencil-case ['penslkeɪs] N plumier *m*.

pencil-sharpener ['pensl.ʃɑːpnəʳ] N sacapuntas *m*.

pendant ['pendənt] N pendiente *m*, medallón *m*.

pending ['pendɪŋ] **1** ADJ pendiente; **~ tray** cajón *m* para documentos pendientes; **to be ~** estar pendiente, estar en trámite; **and other matters ~** y otros asuntos todavía por resolver. **2** PREP: **~ the arrival of ...** hasta que llegue ...; **~ your decision** mientras se decida Vd.

pendulous ['pendjʊləs] ADJ colgante.

pendulum ['pendjʊləm] N péndulo *m*.

Penelope [pə'neləpɪ] NF Penélope.

penetrable ['penɪtrəbl] ADJ penetrable.

penetrate ['penɪtreɪt] VT penetrar (por).

penetrating ['penɪtreɪtɪŋ] ADJ penetrante (*also fig*).

penetratingly ['penɪtreɪtɪŋlɪ] ADV con penetración, de manera penetrante.

penetration [.penɪ'treɪʃən] N penetración *f* (*also fig*).

penetrative ['penɪtrətɪv] ADJ penetrante.

penfriend ['penfrend] N (*Brit*) amigo *m*, -a *f* por correspondencia.

penguin ['peŋgwɪn] N pingüino *m*.

penholder ['pen.həʊldəʳ] N portaplumas *m*.

penicillin [.penɪ'sɪlɪn] N penicilina *f*.

penile ['piːnaɪl] ADJ del pene.

peninsula [pɪ'nɪnsjʊlə] N península *f*.

peninsular [pɪ'nɪnsjʊləʳ] ADJ peninsular; **the P~ War** la Guerra de Independencia.

penis ['piːnɪs] N pene *m*.

penitence ['penɪtəns] N penitencia *f*, arrepentimiento *m*.

penitent ['penɪtənt] **1** ADJ penitente (*also Eccl*); arrepentido, compungido. **2** N penitente *mf*.

penitential [.penɪ'tenʃəl] ADJ penitencial.

penitentiary [.penɪ'tenʃərɪ] N (*US*) cárcel *f*, presidio *m*, penitenciaria *f*.

penitently ['penɪtəntlɪ] N penitentemente; arrepentidamente, compungidamente.

penknife ['pennaɪf] N, PL **penknives** ['pennaɪvz] navaja *f* (pequeña), cortaplumas *m*.

penman ['penmən] N, PL **penmen** ['penmən] pendolista *m*, calígrafo *m*.

penmanship ['penmənʃɪp] N caligrafía *f*.

Penn., Penna. (*US*) ABBR *of* **Pennsylvania**.

pen-name ['penneɪm] N seudónimo *m*, nombre *m* de guerra.

pennant ['penənt] N banderola *f*; banderín *m*; (*Naut*) gallardete *m*.

pen-nib ['pennɪb] N punta *f* (de pluma); plumilla *f*, plumín *m* (de estilográfica).

penniless ['penɪlɪs] ADJ pobre; sin dinero; **to be ~** no tener un céntimo; **to be left ~** quedar completamente sin dinero.

Pennine ['penaɪn] N: **the ~s** los (Montes) Peninos.

pennon ['penən] N pendón *m*.

Pennsylvania [.pensɪl'veɪnɪə] N Pensilvania *f*.

penny ['penɪ] N, PL **pennies** ['penɪz] *or* **pence** [pens] penique *m*; (*US*) centavo *m*; (*Spanish equivalent*) perra *f*; **~ arcade** (*US*) galería *f* de máquinas tragaperras; **for two pence I'd ...** por menos de nada yo ...; **in for a ~, in for a pound** preso por mil, preso por mil quinientos; **a ~ for your thoughts!** ¿en qué piensas?; **I'm not a ~ the wiser** lo entiendo menos que antes; **that must have cost a pretty ~** eso habrá costado un dineral; **to earn an honest ~** emplearse en un oficio honrado; ganarse unos duros honradamente; **he hasn't a ~ to his name, he hasn't two pennies to rub together** no tiene donde caerse muerto; **take care of the pennies and the pounds will take care of themselves** muchos pocos hacen un montón; **then the ~ dropped** luego se dio cuenta, por fin cayó en la cuenta; **to spend a ~*** cambiar el agua al canario*; **he turns up like a bad ~** aparece una y otra vez como la falsa moneda.

Penny ['penɪ] NF familiar form of **Penelope**.

penny-a-liner ['penɪə'laɪnəʳ] N escritorzuelo *m*, -a *f*, gacetillero *m*, -a *f*.

penny dreadful ['penɪ'dredfʊl] N (*Brit*) tebeo *m* (*or* revista *f* juvenil) de bajísima calidad.

penny-in-the-slot ['penɪɪnðə'slɒt] ATTR: **~ machine** (máquina *f*) tragaperras *m*.

penny-pinching ['penɪ.pɪntʃɪŋ] **1** N tacañería *f*. **2** ADJ *person* tacaño, avaro.

pennyweight ['penweɪt] N *peso de 24 granos* (= 1,555 gramos).

penny whistle [.penɪ'wɪsl] N flauta *f* metálica.

pennyworth ['penəθ] N valor *m* de un penique, cantidad *f* que se

---

compra con un penique; (*fig*) pizca *f*.

penologist [piː'nɒlədʒɪst] N penalista *mf*, criminólogo *m*, -a *f*.

penology [piː'nɒlədʒɪ] N ciencia *f* penal, criminología *f*.

pen-pal* ['penpæl] N = **penfriend**.

penpusher ['pen.pʊʃəʳ] N (*Liter*) plumífero *m*; (*clerk*) empleadillo *m*, -a *f*.

pension ['penʃən] **1** N pensión *f*; (*Mil*) retiro *m*; (*superannuation etc*) jubilación *f*; **to retire on a ~** jubilarse. **2** ATTR: **~ book** libreta *f* de pensión; **~ fund** caja *f* de pensiones; **~ rights** derechos *mpl* de pensión; **~ scheme** plan *m* de pensiones. **3** VT pensionar, dar una pensión a.

◆**pension off** VT: **to ~ sb off** jubilar a uno.

pensionable ['penʃənəbl] ADJ: **~ age** edad *f* de jubilación; **~ post** empleo *m* con derecho a pensión.

pensioner ['penʃənəʳ] N pensionado *m*, -a *f*, pensionista *mf*; (*Mil*) inválido *m*; **~s** clases *fpl* pasivas.

pensive ['pensɪv] ADJ pensativo, meditabundo; preocupado; triste.

pensively ['pensɪvlɪ] ADV pensativamente; tristemente; **he said ~** dijo pensativo.

pent [pent] ADJ V **pent-up**.

pentagon ['pentəgən] N pentágono *m*; **the P~** (*Washington*) el Pentágono.

pentagonal [pen'tægənl] ADJ pentagonal.

pentagram ['pentəgræm] N estrella *f* de cinco puntas.

pentameter [pen'tæmɪtəʳ] N pentámetro *m*.

Pentateuch ['pentətjuːk] N Pentateuco *m*.

pentathlete [pen'tæθliːt] N pentatleta *mf*.

pentathlon [pen'tæθlən] N pentatlón *m*.

pentatonic [.pentə'tɒnɪk] ADJ pentatónico; **~ scale** escala *f* pentatónica.

Pentecost ['pentɪkɒst] N Pentecostés *m*.

Pentecostal [.pentɪ'kɒstl] ADJ de Pentecostés.

Pentecostalism [.pentɪ'kɒstlɪzəm] N pentecostalismo *m*.

penthouse ['penthaʊs] N, PL **penthouses** ['penthaʊzɪz] cobertizo *m*; (*flat*) ático *m*, casa *f* de azotea.

Pentium processor [.pentɪəm'prəʊsesəʳ] ℞ N procesador *m* Pentium.

pent-up ['pentʌp] ADJ **(a) to be ~, to feel ~** (*person etc*) estar encerrado, sentirse como enjaulado. **(b)** *emotion etc* reprimido; **~ demand** demanda *f* reprimida.

penult [pɪ'nʌlt] N penúltima *f*.

penultimate [pɪ'nʌltɪmɪt] ADJ penúltimo.

penumbra [pɪ'nʌmbrə] N penumbra *f*.

penurious [pɪ'njʊərɪəs] ADJ miserable, pobrísimo.

penury ['penjʊrɪ] N **(a)** (*poverty*) miseria *f*, pobreza *f*; **to live in ~** vivir en la miseria. **(b)** (*lack*) falta *f*, escasez *f* (*of* de).

penwiper ['pen.waɪpəʳ] N limpiaplumas *m*.

peon ['piːən] N peón *m*.

peonage ['piːənɪdʒ] N condición *f* de peón; estado *m* en que viven los peones; (*fig*) servidumbre *f*, esclavitud *f*.

peony ['pɪənɪ] N peonía *f*, saltaojos *m*.

people ['piːpl] **1** N **(a)** (*Pol etc*) pueblo *m*; ciudadanos *mpl*; **the ~** (*pej*), **the common ~** el pueblo, la plebe; **the ~ at large** el pueblo en general; **a man of the ~** un hombre del pueblo; **the king and his ~** el rey y su pueblo, el rey y sus súbditos; **government by the ~** gobierno *m* por el pueblo; **~'s democracy** democracia *f* popular; **Chinese P~s' Republic** República *f* Popular China.
(b) (*race*) pueblo *m*, nación *f*; **English ~** los ingleses; **the English ~** el pueblo inglés; **the British ~** la nación británica; **the Beaker P~** la gente de las copas, el pueblo de las copas.
(c) (*parents*) padres *mpl*; (*relatives*) parientes *mpl*, familia *f*; **my ~** mis padres, mi familia; **how are your ~?** ¿cómo están los tuyos?, ¿cómo está tu familia?; **have you met his ~?** ¿conoces a sus padres?
(d) (*persons*) gente *f*; **the good ~, the little ~** las hadas; **old ~** los viejos; **young ~** los jóvenes, la juventud; **what do you ~ think?** y ustedes, ¿qué opinan?; **the place was full of ~** el local estaba lleno de gente; **they're strange ~** son gente rara; **I like the ~ here** aquí la gente es simpática, la gente de aquí me gusta; **the gas ~ are coming tomorrow** los del gas vienen mañana; **try the idea with our design ~** prueba la idea con la gente de diseño.
(e) (*inhabitants*) habitantes *mpl*; **the ~ of London** los habitantes de Londres, los londinenses; **Madrid has over 4 million ~** Madrid tiene más de 4 millones de habitantes.
(f) (*with numerals*) **20 ~** 20 personas; **many ~ think that ...** muchas personas creen que ..., son muchos los que creen que ...; **some ~** algunos, algunas personas.
(g) (*vague subject use*) **~ say that ...** dicen que ..., se dice que ..., la gente dice que ...; **here ~ quarrel a lot** aquí se riñe mucho; **~ get worried** la gente se inquieta; **it's enough to worry ~** basta para inquietar a la gente.
2 VT poblar; **the country is ~d by ...** el país está poblado por ..., el país está habitado por ...

people mover ['piːpl,muːvəʳ] N (a) (car) monovolumen m. (b) (US: walkway) cinta f transbordadora, pasillo m móvil.
pep* [pep] N empuje m, dinamismo m, ímpetu m, energía f.
◆**pep up*** VT estimular, animar, hacer más dinámico; drink etc fortalecer.

┌─── **PEP RALLY** ───────────────────────────────────┐

🛈 Pep Rally es un término usado en Estados Unidos para referirse a las concentraciones que se realizan antes de la celebración de un partido de fútbol americano o baloncesto en los institutos de enseñanza secundaria o en la universidad. En estas celebraciones, que tienen lugar uno o varios días antes del partido, participan animadores de grupo, una banda de música y tanto los jugadores como los entrenadores tienen que pronunciar unas palabras ante los demás. También se emplea a veces el término **Pep Rally** con referencia a los mítines políticos o a encuentros entre los miembros de una empresa para alentar la motivación entre sus afiliados o empleados por medio de la adulación pública o el anuncio de nuevos proyectos o de éxitos futuros.

└──┘

pepper ['pepəʳ] ① N (spice) pimienta f; (vegetable) pimiento m; (~ plant) pimentero m; **~ steak** filete m a la pimienta.
② VT (a) (spice) sazonar con pimienta, añadir pimienta a. (b) **to ~ a work with quotations** salpicar una obra de citas; **to ~ sb with shot** acribillar a uno a tiros.
pepperbox ['pepəbɒks] N pimentero m.
peppercorn ['pepəkɔːn] ① N grano m de pimienta.
② ATTR: **~ rent** alquiler m nominal.
peppermill ['pepəmɪl] N molinillo m de pimienta.
peppermint ['pepəmɪnt] N (plant, flavour) menta f, hierbabuena f; (sweet) pastilla f de menta.
pepperoni [pepə'rəʊni] N salchichón m a la pimienta, pepperoni m.
pepperpot ['pepəpɒt] N, **pepper shaker** ['pepə,ʃeɪkəʳ] N (US) pimentero m.
peppery ['pepəri] ADJ taste picante; mordiscante; (fig) enojadizo, de malas pulgas.
pep-pill ['peppɪl] N píldora f antifatiga, estimulante m.
pep rally ['pep,ræli] N (US) encuentro de motivación.
pepsin ['pepsɪn] N pepsina f.
pep-talk* ['peptɔːk] N: **to give a ~ to** dar ánimos a, arengar a.
peptic ['peptɪk] ADJ péptico; **~ ulcer** úlcera f péptica.
peptone ['peptəʊn] N peptona f.
per [pɜːʳ] PREP por; (with year etc) a; **£20 ~ annum** 20 libras al año; **£7 ~ week** 7 libras a la semana; **45p ~ dozen** 45 peniques la docena; **60 miles ~ hour** 60 millas por hora; **4 litres ~ 100 km** 4 litros por 100 km; **~ cent, ~cent** por ciento, por cien; **20 ~ cent** 20 por cien(to); **it has increased by 8 ~ cent** ha aumentado en un 8 por cien(to); **there is a 10 ~ cent discount** hay un descuento de un 10 por cien(to); **at so much ~ cent** a un tanto por ciento; **~ person** por persona; **~ se** de por sí; **as ~ invoice** según factura; V usual.
perambulate [pə'ræmbjʊleɪt] ① VT recorrer (para inspeccionar).
② VI pasearse, deambular.
perambulation [pə,ræmbjʊ'leɪʃən] N (visit) visita f de inspección; (stroll) paseo m; (journey) viaje m.
perambulator ['præmbjʊleɪtəʳ] N (Brit) cochecito m de niño.
perborate [pə'bɔːreɪt] N perborato m.
per capita [pə'kæpɪtə] ADV per cápita; **~ income** ingresos mpl per cápita.
perceive [pə'siːv] VT percibir; (see) notar, observar; divisar; (hear) percibir; (understand) comprender; (realize) darse cuenta de; **now I ~ that ...** ahora veo que ...; **do you ~ anything strange?** ¿notas algo raro?; **I do not ~ how it can be done** no comprendo cómo se puede hacer.
percentage [pə'sentɪdʒ] ① N porcentaje m, tanto m por ciento; proporción f; (*: rake-off) tajada* f; (commission) comisión f porcentual; **the figure is expressed as a ~** la cifra está expresada como un tanto por ciento; **a high ~ are girls** un elevado porcentaje son chicas; **to get a ~ on all sales** recibir un tanto por ciento sobre todas las ventas.
② ATTR porcentual; **on a ~ basis** según un sistema porcentual; **~ increase** aumento m porcentual; **~ point** punto m porcentual; **~ sign** signo m del tanto por ciento.
percentile [pə'sentaɪl] N percentil m.
perceptible [pə'septəbl] ADJ perceptible; sensible.
perceptibly [pə'septəbli] ADV perceptiblemente; sensiblemente; **it has improved ~** ha mejorado sensiblemente.
perception [pə'sepʃən] N percepción f; perspicacia f; penetración f; agudeza f.
perceptive [pə'septɪv] ADJ perspicaz; penetrante, agudo; function perceptivo.
perceptiveness [pə'septɪvnɪs] N penetración f; sensibilidad f; facultad f perceptiva.

perceptual [pə'septjʊəl] ADJ skills, problems de percepción, perceptual.
perch¹ [pɜːtʃ] N, PL INVAR or **perches** ['pɜːtʃɪz] (fish) perca f.
perch² [pɜːtʃ] ① N (a) medida de longitud = 5,029 m.
(b) (of bird) percha f; (fig) posición f elevada; posición f peligrosa; posición f poco segura; **to knock sb off his ~** (fig) destronar a uno, tumbar a uno.
② VT encaramar, colocar (en una posición elevada, poco segura etc); **he ~ed his hat on his head** posó el sombrero en la cabeza; **we ~ed the child on the wall** encaramamos al niño en la tapia.
③ VI (bird) posarse (on en); (person etc) sentarse (en un sitio elevado, poco seguro etc); colocarse en una posición elevada; **we ~ed in a tree to see the procession** nos subimos a un árbol para ver el desfile; **the village ~es on a hilltop** el pueblo ocupa la cumbre de una colina; **she ~ed on the arm of my chair** se acomodó en el brazo de mi butaca.
perchance [pə'tʃɑːns] ADV (liter) por ventura, acaso.
percipient [pə'sɪpɪənt] ADJ perspicaz; penetrante, agudo.
percolate ['pɜːkəleɪt] ① VT filtrar, colar; (fig) filtrarse en, filtrarse por; coffee preparar, filtrar.
② VI (a) filtrarse, colarse; **to ~ down to** penetrar hasta; **to ~ through** penetrar por.
(b) (coffee) prepararse.
percolator ['pɜːkəleɪtəʳ] N percolador m.
percussion [pə'kʌʃən] ① N percusión f.
② ATTR instrument etc de percusión; **~ cap** cápsula f fulminante.
percussionist [pə'kʌʃənɪst] N percusionista mf.
per diem ['pɜː'diːem] ADV por día.
perdition [pɜː'dɪʃən] N perdición f.
peregrination [,perɪgrɪ'neɪʃən] N peregrinación f; **~s** (hum) vagabundeo m, periplo m.
peregrine ['perɪgrɪn] ① N halcón m común, neblí m.
② ATTR: **~ falcon** halcón m peregrino.
peremptory [pə'remptəri] ADJ perentorio; person imperioso, autoritario.
perennial [pə'renɪəl] ① ADJ perenne (also Bot); eterno, perpetuo; **it's a ~ complaint** es una queja constante.
② N (Bot) perenne m, planta f vivaz.
perennially [pə'renɪəli] ADV perennemente; perpetuamente; constantemente.
perestroika [perə'strɔɪkə] N perestroika f.
perfect ① ['pɜːfɪkt] ADJ (a) perfecto; host etc perfecto, modélico, ejemplar; **it's just ~!** ¡qué maravilla!; **with ~ assurance** con la más completa confianza; **she's a ~ terror** es una arpía; **he's a ~ stranger to me** me es completamente desconocido; **he's a ~ idiot** es un idiota completo; **he's a ~ gentleman** es un cumplido caballero; **his Spanish is far from ~** su español dista mucho de ser perfecto.
(b) (Gram) perfecto.
② ['pɜːfɪkt] N (Gram) perfecto m.
③ [pə'fekt] VT perfeccionar.
perfectibility [pə,fektɪ'bɪlɪti] N perfectibilidad f.
perfectible [pə'fektəbl] ADJ perfectible.
perfection [pə'fekʃən] N perfección f; **she does it to ~** lo hace a la perfección, lo hace a las mil maravillas.
perfectionism [pə'fekʃənɪzm] N perfeccionismo m.
perfectionist [pə'fekʃənɪst] N perfeccionista mf.
perfective [pə'fektɪv] ① ADJ aspect, verb perfectivo.
② N perfectivo m.
perfectly ['pɜːfɪktli] ADV (a) perfectamente; **she does it ~** lo hace perfectamente, lo hace a la perfección.
(b) **it's ~ marvellous** es de lo más maravilloso; **how ~ marvellous!** ¡qué maravilla!; **it's ~ ridiculous** es completamente absurdo; **we're ~ happy about it** estamos completamente contentos con esto.
perfidious [pɜː'fɪdɪəs] ADJ pérfido.
perfidiously [pɜː'fɪdɪəsli] ADV pérfidamente.
perfidy ['pɜːfɪdi] N perfidia f.
perforate ['pɜːfəreɪt] VT perforar, horadar, agujerear; **to ~ holes in sth** practicar agujeros en algo.
perforated ['pɜːfəreɪtɪd] ADJ stamp dentado.
perforation [,pɜːfə'reɪʃən] N perforación f; agujero m; (of stamp) trepado m, dentado m.
perforce [pə'fɔːs] ADV (liter) forzosamente.
perform [pə'fɔːm] ① VT (a) task etc hacer, cumplir, realizar; duty cumplir; function desempeñar; ejercer; operation llevar a cabo, realizar; (Ling) realizar. (b) (Theat) play representar, dar, poner, part interpretar, hacer; (Mus) ejecutar, interpretar.
② VI (a) (Mus: play) tocar, (sing) cantar; (Theat) representar, actuar; trabajar; hacer un papel, tener un papel; (trained animal) hacer trucos; **to ~ on the violin** tocar el violín, interpretar una obra al violín; **how did he ~?** ¿qué tal lo hizo?; **he ~ed brilliantly as Hamlet** interpretó brillantemente el papel de Hamlet, en el papel de Hamlet se lució; **when we ~ed in Seville** cuando nos presentamos en Sevilla; **I'm not ~ing this time** esta vez no hago ningún papel,

esta vez no tomo parte.

(b) (*Mech etc*) funcionar, comportarse; **the car is not ~ing properly** el coche no funciona bien; **how does the metal ~ under pressure?** ¿cómo se comporta el metal bajo presión?

performance [pə'fɔ:məns] N **(a)** (*of task etc*) cumplimiento *m*, ejecución *f*, realización *f*; resultado *m*; (*of function*) desempeño *m*; ejercicio *m*; acción *f*, actuación *f*; (*Ling*) realización *f*; **in the ~ of his duties** en el ejercicio de su cargo.

(b) (*Theat: of play*) representación *f*, (*by actor, of a part*) actuación *f*, desempeño *m*; interpretación *f*; (*Mus*) ejecución *f*; interpretación *f*; (*sitting: Theat*) función *f*, (*cinema*) sesión *f*; **the late ~** la función de la noche, la sesión de la noche; **'no ~ tonight'** 'no hay representación esta noche'; **first ~** estreno *m*; **we didn't like his ~ as Don Juan** no nos gustó su interpretación del papel de don Juan, su modo de entender el papel de don Juan no nos gustó; **he gave a splendid ~** su actuación fue estupenda; **the play had 300 ~s** la obra tuvo 300 representaciones, la obra siguió en la cartelera durante 300 representaciones; **it has not had a ~ since 1950** no se ha representado desde 1950.

(c) (*Mech etc*) comportamiento *m*; funcionamiento *m*; (*economic, of person, by motor*) rendimiento *m*; (*Aut etc*) prestaciones *fpl*; (*of team in match*) actuación *f*, desempeño *m*; (*of athlete, car, horse in race*) performance *f*; **the team gave a poor ~** el equipo tuvo una actuación nada satisfactoria; **they eventually put up a good ~** por fin estuvieron a su altura.

(d) (*: fuss*) lío* *m*, jaleo *m*; **what a ~!** ¡qué lata!*; **it's such a ~ getting here** llegar aquí supone un tremendo jaleo.

performance art [pə'fɔ:mənsɑ:t] N performance art *m*.

performance-related pay [pə'fɔ:mənsrɪ'leɪtɪd'peɪ] N *sistema salarial que incluye un plus de productividad*

performative [pə'fɔ:mətɪv] N: **~ (verb)** (verbo *m*) performativo *m*.

performer [pə'fɔ:məʳ] N (*Theat*) actor *m*, actriz *f*; artista *mf*; (*Mus*) intérprete *mf*, ejecutante *mf*, músico *m*; **a skilled ~ on the piano** un pianista experto.

performing [pə'fɔ:mɪŋ] ADJ **(a)** *animal* amaestrado, sabio. **(b)** **~ arts** artes *fpl* teatrales.

perfume [1] ['pɜ:fju:m] N perfume *m*.
[2] [pə'fju:m] VT perfumar.

perfumery [pə'fju:məri] N (*perfumes*) perfumes *mpl*; (*factory*) perfumería *f*.

perfunctorily [pə'fʌŋktərɪlɪ] ADV superficialmente, someramente, a la ligera.

perfunctory [pə'fʌŋktəri] ADJ superficial, somero; hecho (*etc*) a la ligera; *service etc* rutinario; **he gave a ~ performance** tocó (*etc*) por cumplir.

pergola ['pɜ:gələ] N pérgola *f*.

▼ **perhaps** [pə'hæps, præps] ADV tal vez, quizá(s), puede que; **~!** ¡quizá!; **~ not** puede que no; **~ so** quizá, quizá sea así; **~ he did it** quizá lo hizo; **~ he's in Segovia** puede que esté en Segovia; **~ he'll come** quizá venga, puede que venga.

peri... ['peri] PREF peri...

pericardium [,peri'kɑ:diəm] N, PL **pericardia** [,peri'kɑ:diə] pericardio *m*.

perigee ['perɪdʒi:] N perigeo *m*.

peril ['peril] N peligro *m*, riesgo *m*; **to be in ~** estar en peligro; **to be in ~ of one's life** correr riesgo de perder la vida; **do it at your ~** hágalo a su riesgo.

perilous ['periləs] ADJ peligroso, arriesgado; **it would be ~ to** + *infin* sería arriesgado + *infin*.

perilously ['periləslı] ADV peligrosamente; **to come ~ close to ...** acercarse de modo peligroso a ..., (*fig*) rayar en ....

perimeter [pə'rɪmɪtəʳ] N perímetro *m*.

perinatal [,peri'neɪtl] ADJ perinatal.

perineum [,peri'ni:əm] N perineo *m*.

period ['pɪəriəd] [1] N **(a)** período *m*; época *f*, edad *f*; (*time limit*) plazo *m*; (*Sport*) tiempo *m*; **at that ~** en aquel entonces; **within a 3 month ~** en 3 meses; dentro de un plazo de 3 meses; **this is a bad ~ for ...** ésta es una mala época para ...; **a painting of his early ~** un cuadro de su primera época, un cuadro de su juventud; **the postwar ~** la posguerra.

(b) (*Scol*) hora *f*, clase *f*; **we have two French ~s** tenemos dos clases de francés.

(c) (*Gram*) período *m*; (*full stop: esp US*) punto *m*; **I said no, ~** he dicho que no, y punto.

(d) (*menstruation*) período *m*, regla *f*.

[2] ATTR: **~ cost** costo *m* fijo; **in ~ dress** en traje de la época; **~ furniture** muebles *mpl* de época, muebles *mpl* clásicos; **~ piece** mueble *m* (*etc*) clásico.

periodic [,pɪərɪ'ɒdɪk] ADJ periódico; **~ table** tabla *f* periódica.

periodical [,pɪərɪ'ɒdɪkəl] [1] ADJ periódico.
[2] N revista *f*, publicación *f* periódica.
[3] ATTR: **~s library** hemeroteca *f*.

periodically [,pɪərɪ'ɒdɪkəlɪ] ADV periódicamente; (*from time to time*) de vez en cuando, cada cierto tiempo.

periodicity [,pɪərɪə'dɪsɪtɪ] N periodicidad *f*.

periodontal [,peri'dɒntl] ADJ periodontal.

peripatetic [,perɪpə'tetɪk] ADJ ambulante, que no tiene residencia fija; (*Philos*) peripatético; **to lead a ~ existence** cambiar mucho de domicilio, no tener residencia fija.

peripheral [pə'rɪfərəl] [1] ADJ periférico; **~ device** dispositivo *m* periférico; **~ unit** unidad *f* periférica.
[2] N periférico *m*, unidad *f* periférica.

peripheralize [pə'rɪfərəlaɪz] VT marginar.

periphery [pə'rɪfəri] N periferia *f*.

periphrasis [pə'rɪfrəsɪs] N, PL **periphrases** [pə'rɪfrəsi:z] perífrasis *f*.

periphrastic [,peri'fræstɪk] ADJ perifrástico.

periscope ['periskəup] N periscopio *m*.

perish ['periʃ] [1] VT deteriorar, estropear, echar a perder; **to be ~ed (with cold)*** estar helado.
[2] VI **(a)** (*person*) *etc* perecer, fallecer; **we shall do it or ~ in the attempt** lo conseguiremos o moriremos intentándolo; **he ~ed at sea** murió en el mar; **~ the thought!** ¡ni por pensamiento!, ¡Dios me libre!
(b) (*food, material*) deteriorarse, estropearse.

perishable ['periʃəbl] [1] ADJ perecedero.
[2] N: **~s** artículos *mpl* perecederos, productos *mpl* perecederos.

perisher: ['periʃəʳ] N (*Brit*) tío* *m*; **little ~** tunante *m*; **you little ~!** ¡tunante!

perishing* ['periʃɪŋ] ADJ **(a)** (*) **it's ~ (cold)** hace un frío glacial; **I'm ~** estoy helado. **(b)** (*Brit* :) condenado*.

peristalsis [,peri'stælsɪs] N, PL **peristalses** [,peri'stælsi:z] peristalsis *f*.

peristyle ['peristaɪl] N peristilo *m*.

peritoneum [,perito'ni:əm] N peritoneo *m*.

peritonitis [,perito'naɪtɪs] N peritonitis *f*.

periwig ['periwɪg] N peluca *f*.

periwinkle ['peri,wɪŋkl] N (*Bot*) vincapervinca *f*; (*Zool*) litorina *f*, caracol *m* de mar.

perjure ['pɜ:dʒəʳ] VT: **to ~ o.s.** perjurar, perjurarse.

perjured ['pɜ:dʒəd] ADJ *evidence* falso.

perjurer ['pɜ:dʒərəʳ] N perjuro *m*, -a *f*.

perjury ['pɜ:dʒəri] N perjurio *m*; **to commit ~** jurar en falso, perjurar.

perk¹ [pɜ:k] [1] VT: **to ~ sb up** reanimar a uno, infundir nuevo vigor a uno; **this will ~ you up!** ¡anímate con esto!, ¡esto te animará!; **to ~ one's ears up** aguzar las orejas; **to ~ one's head up** levantar la cabeza.
[2] VI: **to ~ up** (*person*) reanimarse, cobrar ánimo; (*in health*) sentirse mejor, reponerse; **business is ~ing up** los negocios van mejor.

perk²* [pɜ:k] N gaje *m*, prebenda* *f*; **~s** gajes *mpl* (y emolumentos *mpl*), beneficios *mpl* adicionales; (*tips*) propinas *fpl*; **a salary and ~s** un sueldo y otros beneficios; **company ~s** beneficios *mpl* corporativos; **there are no ~s in this job** en este empleo no hay nada aparte del sueldo.

perk³ [pɜ:k] VI (ABBR of **percolate**) (*coffee*) filtrarse.

perkiness ['pɜ:kɪnɪs] N alegría *f*, buen humor *m*; despejo *m*; frescura *f*.

perky ['pɜ:kɪ] ADJ (*gay*) alegre, de excelente humor; (*wide-awake*) despabilado; (*pert*) fresco; **to feel ~** estar alegre, estar de buen humor.

perm¹* [pɜ:m] [1] N permanente *f*; **to have a ~** hacerse una permanente.
[2] VT: **to ~ sb's hair** hacer una permanente a una; **to have one's hair ~ed** hacerse una permanente.

perm² [pɜ:m] N ABBR of **permute, permutation**.

permafrost ['pɜ:məfrɒst] N permagel *m*.

permanence ['pɜ:mənəns] N permanencia *f*.

permanency ['pɜ:mənənsi] N (*permanence*) permanencia *f*; (*permanent arrangement*) arreglo *m* permanente, cosa *f* fija; **the post is not a ~** no es un puesto permanente; **I hope this is now a ~** espero que esto sea un arreglo definitivo.

permanent ['pɜ:mənənt] ADJ permanente (*also Comput*); estable, fijo; *finish on steel etc* inalterable; *wave* permanente; **~ staff** personal *m* de plantilla; **I'm not ~ here** yo no estoy fijo aquí; **we cannot make any ~ arrangements** no podemos arreglar las cosas de modo definitivo.

permanently ['pɜ:mənəntli] ADV permanentemente; de modo estable, de modo definitivo; **we seem to be ~ stuck here** parece que nos vamos a quedar aquí para siempre; **he is ~ drunk** está borracho todo el tiempo.

permanent-press [,pɜ:mənənt'pres] ADJ *trousers* de raya permanente; *skirt* inarrugable.

permanganate [pɜ:'mæŋgənɪt] N permanganato *m*; **~ of potash** permanganato *m* de potasio.

permeability [,pɜ:mɪə'bɪlɪtɪ] N permeabilidad *f*.

permeable ['pɜ:mɪəbl] ADJ permeable.

permeate ['pɜ:mɪeɪt] [1] VT penetrar; calar; saturar, impregnar (*with* de); **to be ~d with** estar impregnado de.

➤ LANGUAGE IN USE: perhaps → 15.3

2 VI penetrar, filtrarse; (*fig*) extenderse, propagarse.

permissible [pə'mɪsəbl] ADJ permisible, lícito; **it is not ~ to** + *infin* no se permite + *infin*; **would it be ~ to say that ...?** ¿podemos decir que ...? ¿sería lícito decir que ...?

▼ **permission** [pə'mɪʃən] N permiso *m*; licencia *f*; autorización *f*; **with your ~** con permiso de Vds; **without ~** sin licencia; **'by kind ~ of Pérez Ltd'** 'con permiso de la Cía. Pérez'; **to give sb ~ to** + *infin* autorizar a uno para que + *subj*; **no ~ is needed** no hay que pedir permiso; **to withhold one's ~** negar su permiso.

permissive [pə'mɪsɪv] ADJ (a) (*tolerant*) permisivo; **~ society** sociedad *f* permisiva. (b) (*optional*) facultativo, opcional.

permissively [pə'mɪsɪvlɪ] ADV permisivamente; facultativamente.

permissiveness [pə'mɪsɪvnɪs] N permisividad *f*.

permit **1** ['pɜːmɪt] N permiso *m*, licencia *f*; (*allowing free entry etc*) pase *m*; **~ holder** titular *mf* de un permiso.

2 [pə'mɪt] VT permitir; autorizar; tolerar, sufrir; **to ~ sb to do sth** permitir a uno hacer algo; **is it ~ted to smoke?** ¿se puede fumar?; **whoever ~ted this was a fool** el que dio permiso para eso fue un tonto; **we could never ~ it to happen** no podríamos nunca tolerar eso; **~ me!** ¡permítame!

3 [pə'mɪt] VI (a) permitir; **weather ~ing** si el tiempo lo permite. (b) **to ~ of** permitir; dar lugar a; posibilitar; **it ~s of certain changes** nos permite hacer varios cambios; **it does not ~ of doubt** no deja lugar a dudas.

permutation [,pɜːmjʊ'teɪʃən] N permutación *f*.

permute [pə'mjuːt] VT permutar.

pernicious [pɜː'nɪʃəs] ADJ pernicioso (*also Med*); nocivo, dañoso; peligroso; funesto; **~ anaemia** anemia *f* perniciosa; **the ~ custom of ...** la funesta costumbre de ...

perniciously [pɜː'nɪʃəslɪ] ADV perniciosamente.

pernickety* [pə'nɪkɪtɪ] ADJ (*person*) quisquilloso, remirado; *talk* delicado; **he's very ~ about clocks** tiene ideas raras sobre los relojes; **he's terribly ~ about punctuality** tiene la manía de la puntualidad; **she's ~ about food** es exigente para la comida.

peroration [,perə'reɪʃən] N peroración *f*.

peroxide [pə'rɒksaɪd] **1** N peróxido *m*.

2 ATTR: **~ blonde** rubia *f* de bote, rubia *f* oxigenada.

perpendicular [,pɜːpən'dɪkjʊləʳ] **1** ADJ perpendicular.

2 N perpendicular *f*; **to be out of (the) ~** salir de la perpendicular, no estar a plomo.

perpetrate ['pɜːpɪtreɪt] VT cometer; (*Jur*) perpetrar.

perpetration [,pɜːpɪ'treɪʃən] N comisión *f*; (*Jur*) perpetración *f*.

perpetrator ['pɜːpɪtreɪtəʳ] N autor *m*, -ora *f*; responsable *mf*; (*Jur*) perpetrador *m*, -ora *f*.

perpetual [pə'petjʊəl] ADJ perpetuo; incesante, constante, continuo; *motion etc* perpetuo, continuo; **~ motion** movimiento *m* perpetua; **these ~ complaints** este continuo quejarse.

perpetually [pə'petjʊəlɪ] ADV perpetuamente; constantemente, continuamente; **we were ~ hungry** teníamos hambre siempre; **they complain ~** se quejan constantemente.

perpetuate [pə'petjʊeɪt] VT perpetuar.

perpetuation [pə,petjʊ'eɪʃən] N perpetuación *f*.

perpetuity [,pɜːpɪ'tjuːɪtɪ] N perpetuidad *f*; **in ~** para siempre.

Perpignan ['pɜːpiːnjɒn] N Perpiñán *m*.

perplex [pə'pleks] VT dejar perplejo, confundir.

perplexed [pə'plekst] ADJ perplejo; confuso, desconcertado; **to look ~** parecer confuso.

perplexedly [pə'pleksɪdlɪ] ADV perplejamente.

perplexing [pə'pleksɪŋ] ADJ confuso, que causa perplejidad; complicado; misterioso; **it's all very ~** no entiendo nada; **it's a ~ situation** es una situación complicada, es una situación que deja a todos perplejos.

perplexity [pə'pleksɪtɪ] N perplejidad *f*, confusión *f*; **to be in some ~** estar algo perplejo.

per pro. ABBR *of* **per procurationem, by proxy** por poder, p.p.

perquisite ['pɜːkwɪzɪt] N gaje *m*, prebenda *f*.

perry ['perɪ] N sidra *f* de peras.

persecute ['pɜːsɪkjuːt] VT perseguir; (*harass*) atormentar, importunar, molestar, acosar; **under the Nazis they were ~d** bajo los nazis se les persiguió, bajo los nazis sufrieron la persecución.

persecution [,pɜːsɪ'kjuːʃən] **1** N persecución *f*.

2 ATTR: **~ complex** complejo *m* persecutorio; **~ mania** manía *f* persecutoria.

persecutor ['pɜːsɪkjuːtəʳ] N perseguidor *m*, -ora *f*.

Persephone [pə'sefənɪ] N Perséfone *f*.

Perseus ['pɜːsjuːs] N Perseo *m*.

perseverance [,pɜːsɪ'vɪərəns] N perseverancia *f*, tenacidad *f*.

persevere [,pɜːsɪ'vɪəʳ] VI perseverar, persistir (*in* en); **to ~ with** continuar con, no abandonar.

persevering [,pɜːsɪ'vɪərɪŋ] ADJ perseverante, tenaz.

perseveringly [,pɜːsɪ'vɪərɪŋlɪ] ADV con perseverancia, perseverantemente.

Persia ['pɜːʃə] N (*Hist*) Persia *f*.

Persian ['pɜːʃən] **1** ADJ persa; **~ carpet** alfombra *f* persa; **~ cat** gato *m* de Angora, gata *f* de Angora; **~ lamb** (*animal*) oveja *f* caracul, (*skin*) caracul *m*.

2 N (a) (*person*) persa *mf*. (b) (*Ling*) persa *m*.

Persian Gulf ['pɜːʃən'gʌlf] N Golfo *m* Pérsico.

persiflage [,pɜːsɪ'flɑːʒ] N burlas *fpl*, zumba *f*, guasa *f*.

persimmon [pɜː'sɪmən] N placaminero *m*, caqui *m*.

persist [pə'sɪst] VI (a) persistir; continuar; **we must ~** hay que persistir, tenemos que mantenernos firmes; **we shall ~ in our efforts to** + *infin* seguiremos esforzándonos por + *infin*; **it will ~ some time yet** durará todavía algún tiempo.

(b) (*insist*) porfiar, empeñarse, obstinarse; **if he ~s** si se empeña en ello, si se obstina; **to ~ in doing sth** empeñarse en hacer algo, obstinarse en hacer algo.

persistence [pə'sɪstəns] N, **persistency** [pə'sɪstənsɪ] N persistencia *f*; porfía *f*, empeño *m*; (*of disease etc*) pertinacia *f*; **as a reward for her ~** en premio a su perseverancia.

persistent [pə'sɪstənt] ADJ persistente; continuo; porfiado; *disease etc* pertinaz; **~ offender** multirreincidente *mf*, delincuente *mf* habitual; **~ vegetative state** estado *m* vegetativo persistente; **he is most ~** es muy porfiado, se porfía mucho; **despite our ~ warnings** a pesar de nuestras continuas advertencias.

persistently [pə'sɪstəntlɪ] ADV con persistencia, persistentemente; constantemente; **he ~ refuses to help** se niega constantemente a prestar su ayuda.

persnickety [pɜː'snɪkɪtɪ] ADJ (*US*) = **pernickety**.

person ['pɜːsn] **1** N (a) persona *f*; **private ~** particular *m*; **in ~** en persona; **in the ~ of** en la persona de; **he is neat in his ~** es muy pulcro; **per ~** por persona; **murder by ~ or ~s unknown** homicidio *m* por mano desconocida.

(b) (*Gram*) persona *f*; **in the first ~** en primera persona.

2 ATTR: **~ to ~ call** (*US*) llamada *f* de persona a persona.

persona [pɜː'səʊnə] N, PL **personae** [pɜː'səʊnaɪ] persona *f*; **~ grata** persona *f* grata; **~ non grata** persona *f* no grata.

personable ['pɜːsnəbl] ADJ bien parecido, atractivo.

personage ['pɜːsnɪdʒ] N personaje *m*.

personal ['pɜːsnl] **1** ADJ personal; (*private*) privado, íntimo, particular; (*for one's sole use*) de uso personal; *liberty etc* individual; *interview* en persona; **~ account** (*story*) narración *f* personal; (*Fin*) cuenta *f* personal; **~ allowance** desgravación *f* personal; **~ appearance** aspecto *m* personal, aspecto *m* físico; (*Theat etc*) presentación *f* en directo, presentación *f* en vivo; **to make a ~ appearance** aparecer en persona; **~ assets** bienes *mpl* muebles; **~ assistant** ayudante *mf* personal; **~ best** (*Sport*) marca *f* personal; **~ call** (*Brit Telec*) llamada *f* a una persona especificada; **~ check** (*US*), **~ cheque** cheque *m* personal; **~ cleanliness** aseo *m* personal; **~ column** (sección *f* de) anuncios *mpl* personales; **~ computer** ordenador *m* personal; **~ effects** efectos *mpl* personales; **~ foul** falta *f* personal; **~ identification number** número *m* personal de identificación; **~ income tax** impuesto *m* sobre la renta de las personas físicas; **~ investment** inversión *f* personal; **~ letter** carta *f* particular; **~ loan** préstamo *m* personal; **~ organizer** organizador *m* personal; **~ pronoun** pronombre *m* personal; **~ property** cosas *fpl* personales; bienes *mpl* muebles; **~ questions** hacer preguntas sobre asuntos íntimos; **~ relief** (*on tax*) desgravación *f* (de impuestos) personal; **~ secretary** secretario *m*, -a *f* particular; **~ security** (*on loan*) garantía *f* personal; **I need my own ~ space** necesito tiempo para mí; **to invade sb's ~ space** acercarse demasiado a uno; **~ stereo** estéreo *m* personal; **~ trainer** preparador *m*, -ora *f* personal; **don't be ~!** ¡Vd es un maleducado!; **to become ~** pasar a hacer crítica personal, empezar a hacer referencias de tipo personal; **I have no ~ knowledge of it** no lo conozco directamente; **my ~ view is that ...** creo para mí que ...; **to make a ~ application for sth** solicitar algo en persona.

2 N (*US : in magazine etc*) nota *f* de sociedad; (*message*) mensaje *m* personal.

personality [,pɜːsə'nælɪtɪ] **1** N (*character*) personalidad *f*; (*person, figure*) personaje *m*; figura *f*; **a well-known radio ~** una conocida figura de la radio; **to indulge in personalities** hacer crítica personal, cambiar personalismos, hacer referencias de tipo personal.

2 ATTR: **~ cult** culto *m* a la personalidad.

personalize ['pɜːsənəlaɪz] VT (a) *garment etc* marcar con iniciales (*etc*). (b) *argument etc* llevar al terreno de lo personal.

personalized ['pɜːsənəlaɪzd] ADJ *garment etc* con las iniciales (*etc*) de uno; *service etc* personal, creado para el individuo.

▼ **personally** ['pɜːsnəlɪ] ADV (a) (*for my etc part*) personalmente; **~ I think that ...** creo personalmente que ..., creo para mí que ...; **~ I am willing, but others ...** en cuanto a mí digo que sí, pero otros ...; **don't take it too ~** no vayas a creer que lo digo contra ti, no te des por aludido.

(b) (*in person*) **to hand sth over ~** entregar algo en persona; **the**

manager saw her ~ el gerente habló con ella en persona.

personalty ['pɜːsnltɪ] N bienes *mpl* muebles.

personate ['pɜːsəneɪt] VT (*impersonate*) hacerse pasar por; (*Theat*) hacer el papel de.

personification [pɜːˌsɒnɪfɪ'keɪʃən] N personificación *f*; **he is the ~ of good taste** es la personificación del buen gusto, es el buen gusto en persona.

personify [pɜː'sɒnɪfaɪ] VT personificar; representar; **he personified the spirit of resistance** encarnó el espíritu de la resistencia; **he is greed personified** es la codicia en persona, es la personificación de la codicia.

person mover ['pɜːsənˌmuːvəʳ] N (*US*) cinta *f* transbordadora, pasillo *m* móvil.

personnel [ˌpɜːsə'nel] ① N personal *m*.
  ② ATTR: **~ agency** agencia *f* de personal; **~ carrier** transporte *m* de tropas; camión *m* blindado; **~ department** sección *f* de personal; **~ management** administración *f* del personal, gestión *f* de personal; **~ manager, ~ officer** jefe *mf* del personal.

perspective [pə'spektɪv] N perspectiva *f*; **from our ~** desde nuestro punto de vista; **in ~** en perspectiva; **let's get things in ~** pongamos las cosas en su sitio; **to see things in their proper ~** apreciar debidamente las cosas, apreciar las cosas en su justo valor; **he gets things out of ~** ve las cosas distorsionadas.

Perspex ['pɜːspeks] ® N (*esp Brit*) plexiglás ® *m*.

perspicacious [ˌpɜːspɪ'keɪʃəs] ADJ perspicaz.

perspicacity [ˌpɜːspɪ'kæsɪtɪ] N perspicacia *f*.

perspicuous [ˌpə'spɪkjʊəs] ADJ perspicuo.

perspicuity [ˌpɜːspɪ'kjuːɪtɪ] N perspicuidad *f*.

perspiration [ˌpɜːspə'reɪʃən] N transpiración *f*; sudor *m*; **beads of ~** gotitas *fpl* de sudor; **to be bathed in ~** estar bañado en sudor, estar todo sudoroso.

perspire [pəs'paɪəʳ] VI transpirar, sudar; **to ~ freely** sudar mucho.

perspiring [pəs'paɪərɪŋ] ADJ sudoroso.

persuadable [pə'sweɪdəbl] ADJ influenciable, persuasible; **he may be ~** quizá le podamos persuadir.

persuade [pə'sweɪd] VT persuadir, convencer; **to ~ sb to do sth** persuadir a uno a hacer algo, convencer a uno para que haga algo, inducir a uno a hacer algo; **but they ~d me not to** pero ellos me disuadieron, pero ellos me persuadieron a dejarlo; **to ~ sb that sth is true** convencer a uno de que algo es verdad; **I am ~d that ...** estoy convencido de que ...; **to ~ sb of the truth of a theory** convencer a uno de que una teoría es verdadera; **she is easily ~d** se deja convencer fácilmente; **it does not take much to ~ him** no se necesita mucho esfuerzo para persuadirle.

persuasion [pə'sweɪʒən] N (**a**) (*act*) persuasión *f*.
  (**b**) (*persuasiveness*; *also* **power of ~**) persuasiva *f*; **he needed a lot of ~** había que ejercer mucha persuasiva; **I don't need much ~ to stop working** me cuesta poco dejar el trabajo.
  (**c**) (*creed*) creencia *f*, secta *f*; opinión *f*; **I am not of that ~** no es ésa mi opinión, yo lo veo de otro modo; **the Methodist ~** la secta metodista; **and others of that ~** y otros que creen así.

persuasive [pə'sweɪsɪv] ADJ persuasivo; **I had to be very ~** tuve que ejercer mucha persuasión.

persuasively [pə'sweɪsɪvlɪ] ADV de modo persuasivo.

persuasiveness [pə'sweɪsɪvnɪs] N persuasiva *f*.

PERT [pɜːt] N ABBR *of* **programme evaluation and review technique** técnica *f* de evaluación y revisión de proyectos.

pert [pɜːt] ADJ (**a**) (*saucy*) impertinente, respondón, fresco*. (**b**) (*jaunty*) elegante, coqueto.

pertain [pɜː'teɪn] VI: **to ~ to** (*concern*) tener que ver con, estar relacionado con; (*belong to*) pertenecer a; (*be the province of*) incumbir a; **and other matters ~ing to it** y otros asuntos relacionados, y otros asuntos pertenecientes.

pertinacious [ˌpɜːtɪ'neɪʃəs] ADJ pertinaz.

pertinaciously [ˌpɜːtɪ'neɪʃəslɪ] ADV con pertinacia.

pertinacity [ˌpɜːtɪ'næsɪtɪ] N pertinacia *f*.

pertinence ['pɜːtɪnəns] N pertinencia *f*, oportunidad *f*.

pertinent ['pɜːtɪnənt] ADJ pertinente, oportuno, a propósito; **not very ~** poco oportuno, no muy a propósito.

pertinently ['pɜːtɪnəntlɪ] ADV oportunamente, a propósito, atinadamente.

pertly ['pɜːtlɪ] ADV de modo impertinente, descaradamente, con frescura.

pertness ['pɜːtnɪs] N (**a**) impertinencia *f*, frescura *f*. (**b**) elegancia *f*.

perturb [pə'tɜːb] VT perturbar, inquietar; **we are all very ~ed** todos estamos muy inquietos.

perturbation [ˌpɜːtɜː'beɪʃən] N perturbación *f*, inquietud *f*; **she asked in some ~** preguntó algo perturbada.

perturbing [pə'tɜːbɪŋ] ADJ perturbador, inquietante.

Peru [pə'ruː] N el Perú.

perusal [pə'ruːzəl] N lectura *f* (cuidadosa), examen *m* (detenido).

peruse [pə'ruːz] VT leer (con atención), examinar (con detenimiento).

Peruvian [pə'ruːvɪən] ① ADJ peruano; **~ bark** quina *f*.
  ② N peruano *m*, -a *f*.

perv* [pɜːv] N pervertido *m*, -a *f*.

pervade [pɜː'veɪd] VT extenderse por, difundirse por, empapar (de), impregnar, saturar; **to be ~d with** estar impregnado de, estar saturado de.

pervasive [pɜː'veɪsɪv] ADJ penetrante; omnipresente, generalizado.

perverse [pə'vɜːs] ADJ (*wicked*) perverso; (*obstinate*) terco, contumaz; (*wayward*) travieso, díscolo.

perversely [pə'vɜːslɪ] ADV perversamente; tercamente; traviesamente.

perverseness [pə'vɜːsnɪs] N perversidad *f*; terquedad *f*, contumacia *f*; lo travieso.

perversion [pə'vɜːʃən] N perversión *f* (*also Med*); (*of facts, truth*) desnaturalización *f*, tergiversación *f*.

perversity [pə'vɜːsɪtɪ] N = **perverseness**.

pervert ① [pə'vɜːt] N pervertido *m*, -a *f*.
  ② [pə'vɜːt] VT pervertir (*also Med*); *taste etc* estragar, estropear; *words* torcer, forzar; *facts, truth* desnaturalizar, tergiversar; *talent* emplear mal.

perverted [pə'vɜːtɪd] ADJ (*all senses*) pervertido.

pervious ['pɜːvɪəs] ADJ permeable (*to* a).

peseta [pə'setə] N peseta *f*.

pesky* ['peskɪ] ADJ (*US*) molesto, fastidioso.

peso ['peɪsəʊ] N peso *m*.

pessary ['pesərɪ] N pesario *m*, óvalo *m* (*Mex*).

pessimism ['pesɪmɪzəm] N pesimismo *m*.

pessimist ['pesɪmɪst] N pesimista *mf*.

pessimistic [ˌpesɪ'mɪstɪk] ADJ pesimista.

pessimistically [ˌpesɪ'mɪstɪkəlɪ] ADV con pesimismo.

pest [pest] N (**a**) (*Zool*) plaga *f*; insecto *m* nocivo, animal *m* dañino; **the moth is a ~ of pinewoods** la mariposa es una plaga de los pinares; **rabbits are a ~ in Australia** el conejo es muy dañino en Australia; **this will kill the ~s on your roses** esto matará los insectos nocivos de sus rosas.
  (**b**) (*fig*) (*person*) machaca *f*, mosca *f*, pelma *m*; (*thing*) molestia *f*, lata *f*; **what a ~ that child is!** ¡cómo me fastidia ese niño!; **it's a ~ having to go** es una lata tener que ir.

pest-control ['pestkənˌtrəʊl] ① N lucha *f* contra los insectos nocivos, lucha *f* contra las plagas.
  ② ATTR: **~ officer** oficial *m* del departamento de lucha contra plagas.

pester ['pestəʳ] VT molestar, acosar, importunar; **he's constantly ~ing me** no me deja a sol ni a sombra; **is this man ~ing you?** ¿le molesta este hombre?; **she ~ed me for the book** me pidió el libro repetidas veces; **he ~s me with his questions** me molesta con sus preguntas, me fastidia haciendo tantas preguntas; **stop ~ing!** ¡no machaques!; **to ~ sb to do sth** insistir constantemente en que uno haga algo, rogar repetidas veces que uno haga algo.

pesticide ['pestɪsaɪd] N pesticida *m*.

pestilence ['pestɪləns] N pestilencia *f*, peste *f*.

pestilent ['pestɪlənt] ADJ pestilente.

pestilential [ˌpestɪ'lenʃəl] ADJ pestilente; (*) engorroso, latoso*.

pestle ['pesl] N mano *f* (de mortero).

pesto ['pestəʊ] N pesto *m*.

pet¹ [pet] ① ADJ *animal* doméstico, domesticado, de casa, familiar; (*favourite*) favorito; *name etc* cariñoso; **a ~ lion** un león domesticado; **a ~ rabbit** un conejo casero; **her two ~ dogs** sus dos perros de casa; **it's my ~ subject** es mi tema predilecto; **~ aversion** bestia *f* negra, pesadilla *f*; **~ name** nombre *m* cariñoso, nombre *m* hipocorístico, (*short form*) diminutivo *m* cariñoso.
  ② N (**a**) (*animal*) animal *m* doméstico, animal *m* de casa; animal *m* de compañía; perro *m*, gato *m* (*etc*); **no ~s are allowed in school** no se permite llevar animales a la escuela.
  (**b**) (*person*) favorito *m*, -a *f*; persona *f* querida; persona *f* muy mimada; **yes, my ~** sí, mi cielo; **she's teacher's ~** es la favorita de la maestra; **he's rather a ~** es simpatiquísimo, es un ángel.
  ③ VT acariciar; (*: *amorously*) acariciar, sobar, magrear⁑; (*spoil*) mimar.
  ④ VI (*) acariciarse, besuquearse, sobarse, hacerse arrumacos.

pet² [pet] N rabieta* *f*; **to be in a ~** estar de mal humor, estar enojado.

petal ['petl] N pétalo *m*.

petard [pe'tɑːd] N petardo *m*; **he was hoist with his own ~** le salió el tiro por la culata.

pet door [pet'dɔːʳ] N (*US*) gatera *f*.

Pete [piːt] NM *familiar form of* **Peter** (Perico); **for ~'s sake!*** ¡por Dios!

Peter ['piːtəʳ] NM San Pedro; **~'s pence** dinero *m* de San Pedro; **to rob ~ to pay Paul** desnudar a un santo para vestir a otro; **~ the Great** Pedro el Grande; **~ Rabbit** el Conejo Peter.

peter¹ ['piːtəʳ] VI: **to ~ out** (*supply*) agotarse, acabarse; (*vein of metal etc*) desaparecer; (*plan etc*) quedar en agua de borrajas, parar en nada.

peter²⁑ ['piːtəʳ] N (*US*) verga⁑ *f*, picha⁑ *f*.

peter³ ['piːtər] N (safe) caja f de caudales; (cell) celda f.
petfood ['petfuːd] N comida f para animales.
pethidine ['peθɪdiːn] N petidina f.
petit bourgeois [ˌpetɪ'bʊəʒwɑː] **1** ADJ pequeñoburgués.
  2 N pequeñoburgués m, -esa f.
petite bourgeoisie [ˌpetɪˌbʊəʒwɑː'ziː] N pequeña burguesía f.
petite [pə'tiːt] ADJ chiquita.
petit four [ˌpetɪ'fɔː] N pastelito m de mazapán.
petition [pə'tɪʃən] **1** N petición f, instancia f, demanda f; súplica f; ~ **for divorce** petición f de divorcio; **to file a ~** presentar una petición.
  2 VT person dirigir una instancia a; **to ~ for sth** pedir algo, solicitar algo; **to ~ sb to do sth** rogar a uno hacer algo, pedir que uno haga algo.
  3 VI: **to ~ for** pedir, solicitar.
petitioner [pə'tɪʃnər] N suplicante mf, demandante mf.
petits pois ['petiː'pwaː] NPL petits pois mpl.
Petrarch ['petraːk] NM Petrarca.
Petrarchan [pe'traːkən] ADJ petrarquista.
Petrarchism ['petraːkɪzəm] N petrarquismo m.
petrel ['petrəl] N petrel m, paíño m.
petrifaction [ˌpetrɪ'fækʃən] N, **petrification** [ˌpetrɪfɪ'keɪʃən] N petrificación f.
petrified ['petrɪfaɪd] ADJ petrificado; V petrify.
petrify ['petrɪfaɪ] **1** VT (a) (lit) petrificar; **to become petrified** petrificarse.
  (b) (fig) pasmar, horrorizar; **I was simply petrified** me quedé de piedra; **to be petrified with fear** estar muerto de miedo.
  2 VI petrificarse.
petro... ['petrəʊ] PREF petro...
petrochemical [ˌpetrəʊ'kemɪkəl] **1** ADJ petroquímico.
  2 N: ~s productos mpl petroquímicos.
petrodollar ['petrəʊˌdɒlər] N petrodólar m.
petrol ['petrəl] N (Brit) gasolina f, gas m (Carib), nafta f (Argentina), bencina f (Chile); (for lighter) bencina f; **to run out of ~** quedarse sin gasolina.
petrol-bomb ['petrəlbɒm] N (Brit) bomba f de gasolina.
petrol-can ['petrəlkæn] N (Brit) bidón m de gasolina.
petrol-engine ['petrəlˌendʒɪn] N (Brit) motor m de gasolina.
petroleum [pɪ'trəʊlɪəm] **1** N petróleo m.
  2 ATTR: ~ **jelly** jalea f de petróleo; ~ **products** derivados mpl del petróleo.
petrol (filler)-cap ['petrəl(ˌfɪlə)ˌkæp] N tapón m de depósito.
petrol-gauge ['petrəlgeɪdʒ] N (Brit) indicador m de nivel de gasolina.
petrology [pe'trɒlɪdʒɪ] N petrología f.
petrol-pump ['petrəlpʌmp] N (Brit) (in engine) bomba f de gasolina; (at garage) surtidor m de gasolina.
petrol-station ['petrəlˌsteɪʃən] N (Brit) estación f de gasolina, gasolinera f, grifo m (And), estación f de servicio (SC).
petrol-tank ['petrəltæŋk] N (Brit) depósito m de gasolina.
petrol-tanker ['petrəlˌtæŋkər] N (Brit) gasolinero m.
petshop ['petʃɒp] N pajarería f.
petticoat ['petɪkəʊt] N enaguas fpl; (slip) combinación f; (stiff) falda f can-can.
pettifogging ['petɪfɒgɪŋ] ADJ detail etc insignificante, pequeño, nimio; lawyer etc pedante, charlatán; suggestion etc hecho para entenebrecer el asunto.
pettily ['petɪlɪ] ADV mezquinamente.
pettiness ['petɪnɪs] N (V ADJ) (a) insignificancia f, pequeñez f; nimiedad f; frivolidad f.
  (b) mezquindad f; estrechez f de miras; rencor m; manía f de criticar; intolerancia f.
petting ['petɪŋ] N caricias fpl, magreo m.
pettish ['petɪʃ] ADJ malhumorado.
petty ['petɪ] ADJ (a) detail etc insignificante, pequeño, nimio; de poca monta; excuse frívolo, baladí; **the ~ wars of the time** las pequeñas guerras de la época; **the ~ kings of Moslem Spain** los reyezuelos de la España musulmana.
  (b) (Brit: minor) ~ **cash** (dinero m para) gastos mpl menores; caja f chica; ~ **cash book** libro m de caja auxiliar; ~ **claims** reclamaciones mpl menores; ~ **expenses** gastos mpl menores; ~ **larceny** robo m de menor cuantía; ~ **officer** suboficial m de marina; ~ **sessions** tribunal m de primera instancia.
  (c) (small-minded) mezquino; de miras estrechas; (preoccupied with detail) quisquilloso; (spiteful) rencoroso; (faultfinding) reparón, criticón; (intolerant) intolerante; **you're being very ~ about it** en esto te estás mostrando poco comprensivo, en esto muestras que guardas rencor.
petulance ['petjʊləns] N mal humor m, irritabilidad f.
petulant ['petjʊlənt] ADJ malhumorado, irritable.
petulantly ['petjʊləntlɪ] ADV malhumoradamente, con mal humor.
petunia [pɪ'tjuːnɪə] N petunia f.
pew [pjuː] N (Eccl) banco m (de iglesia, de los fieles); (*) asiento

m; **take a ~!** ¡siéntate!; **can you find a ~?** ¿puedes buscarte un asiento?
pewter ['pjuːtər] **1** N peltre m.
  2 ATTR de peltre.
peyote [peɪ'əʊtɪ] N peyote m.
Pfc (US Mil) ABBR of **private first class**.
pfennig ['fenɪg] N pfennig m.
PFLP N ABBR of **Popular Front for the Liberation of Palestine** Frente m Popular de Liberación Palestina, FPLP m.
PG N (Cine) ABBR of **Parental Guidance** ≃ menores acompañados.
PGA N ABBR of **Professional Golfers' Association**.
PGCE N (Brit) ABBR of **Postgraduate Certificate of Education** ≃ CAP m.
PH N (US Mil) ABBR of **Purple Heart**.
pH N ABBR of **potential of hydrogen** potencial m de hidrógeno.
PHA N (US) ABBR of **Public Housing Administration**.
phagocyte ['fægəʊsaɪt] N fagocito m.
phalange ['fælændʒ] N falange f; **P~** (Spain) Falange f.
phalangist [fæ'lændʒɪst] **1** ADJ falangista.
  2 N falangista mf.
phalanx ['fælæŋks] N falange f.
phalarope ['fælərəʊp] N falaropo m.
phallic ['fælɪk] ADJ fálico.
phallus ['fæləs] N, PL **phalli** ['fælaɪ] or **phalluses** ['fæləsɪz] falo m.
phantasm ['fæntæzəm] N fantasma m.
phantasmagoria [ˌfæntæzmə'gɔːrɪə] N fantasmagoría f.
phantasmagoric [ˌfæntæzmə'gɒrɪk] ADJ fantasmagórico.
phantasy ['fæntəzɪ] N fantasía f.
phantom ['fæntəm] **1** N fantasma m.
  2 ADJ fantasmal; ~ **pregnancy** embarazo m nervioso, pseudoembarazo m; ~ **ship** buque m fantasma.
Pharaoh ['feərəʊ] NM Faraón.
Pharisaic(al) [ˌfærɪ'seɪɪk(əl)] ADJ farisaico.
Pharisee ['færɪsiː] N fariseo m.
pharmaceutical [ˌfɑːmə'sjuːtɪkəl] **1** ADJ farmacéutico.
  2 ~s NPL productos mpl farmacéuticos.
pharmacist ['fɑːməsɪst] N farmacéutico m, -a f; **to go to the ~'s** ir a la farmacia.
pharmacological [ˌfɑːməkə'lɒdʒɪkəl] ADJ farmacológico.
pharmacologist [ˌfɑːmə'kɒlədʒɪst] N farmacólogo m, -a f.
pharmacology [ˌfɑːmə'kɒlədʒɪ] N farmacología f.
pharmacopoeia, (US sometimes) **pharmacopeia** [ˌfɑːməkə'piːə] N farmacopea f.
pharmacy ['fɑːməsɪ] N farmacia f.
pharyngitis [ˌfærɪn'dʒaɪtɪs] N faringitis f.
pharynx ['færɪŋks] N faringe f.
phase [feɪz] **1** N fase f (also Astron); etapa f; **to be in ~** estar en fase; **to be out of ~** estar desfasado, estar fuera de fase.
  2 VT plan etc proyectar en una serie de etapas, escalonar; arreglar, organizar; **we must ~ this carefully** hay que organizar esto con cuidado; ~**d development** desarrollo m por etapas; **a ~d withdrawal** una retirada progresiva, una retirada programada.
♦ **phase in** VT escalonar; introducir poco a poco.
♦ **phase out** VT reducir progresivamente, eliminar (or retirar) por etapas.
phase-out ['feɪzˌaʊt] N (esp US) reducción f progresiva.
phatic ['fætɪk] ADJ fático.
PhD N ABBR of **Doctor of Philosophy** doctor m, -ora f en filosofía; ver también DEGREE.
pheasant ['feznt] N faisán m.
phenobarbitone ['fiːnəʊ'bɑːbɪtəʊn] N fenobarbitona f.
phenol ['fiːnɒl] N fenol m.
phenomena [fɪ'nɒmɪnə] NPL of **phenomenon**.
phenomenal [fɪ'nɒmɪnl] ADJ fenomenal.
phenomenally [fɪ'nɒmɪnəlɪ] ADV de modo fenomenal; ~ **rich** rico en un grado fenomenal.
phenomenological [fəˌnɒmənə'lɒdʒɪkəl] ADJ fenomenológico.
phenomenologist [fəˌnɒmə'nɒlədʒɪst] N fenomenólogo m, -a f.
phenomenology [fəˌnɒmɪ'nɒlədʒɪ] N fenomenología f.
phenomenon [fɪ'nɒmɪnən] N, PL **phenomena** [fɪ'nɒmɪnə] fenómeno m.
pheromone ['ferəməʊn] N feromona f.
phew [fjuː] INTERJ ¡puf!
phial ['faɪəl] N ampolla f, redoma f, frasco m.
Phi Beta Kappa [ˌfaɪ'beɪtə'kæpə] N (US Univ) asociación de antiguos alumnos sobresalientes.

PHI BETA KAPPA

La sociedad honorífica Phi Beta Kappa fue fundada en Estados Unidos en 1776 para estudiantes universitarios con aptitudes académicas sobresalientes. Los miembros se eligen durante el tercer o cuarto año de sus estudios y el nombre proviene de las iniciales griegas que forman el lema de la asociación: philosophia biou kubernetes (la filosofía como motor de *vida). A cada miembro se le conoce como un **Phi Beta Kappa** o un **Phi Beta Kappa** student.*

Phil [fɪl] NM *familiar form of* **Philip.**
Philadelphia [ˌfɪlə'delfɪə] N Filadelfia *f.*
philander [fɪ'lændəʳ] VI flirtear, mariposear (*with* con).
philanderer [fɪ'lændərəʳ] N tenorio *m,* mariposón *m.*
philandering [fɪ'lændərɪŋ] ① ADJ mariposón.
　② N flirteo *m.*
philanthropic [ˌfɪlən'θrɒpɪk] ADJ filantrópico.
philanthropist [fɪ'lænθrəpɪst] N filántropo *m,* -a *f.*
philanthropy [fɪ'lænθrəpɪ] N filantropía *f.*
philatelic [ˌfɪlə'telɪk] ADJ filatélico.
philatelist [fɪ'lætəlɪst] N filatelista *mf.*
philately [fɪ'lætəlɪ] N filatelia *f.*
-phile [faɪl] SUF -filo, *eg* **francophile** francófilo *m,* -a *f.*
philharmonic [ˌfɪlɑ:'mɒnɪk] ADJ filarmónico.
-philia ['fɪlɪə] SUF -filia, *eg* **francophilia** francofilia *f.*
Philip ['fɪlɪp] NM Felipe.
philippic [fɪ'lɪpɪk] N filípica *f.*
Philippine ['fɪlɪpi:n] ① ADJ filipino.
　② N filipino *m,* -a *f.*
Philippines ['fɪlɪpi:nz] NPL, **Philippine Islands** ['fɪlɪpi:n,aɪləndz] NPL Filipinas *fpl.*
Philistine ['fɪlɪstaɪn] ① ADJ filisteo (*also fig*).
　② N filisteo *m,* -a *f* (*also fig*).
philistinism ['fɪlɪstɪnɪzəm] N filisteísmo *m.*
Phillips ['fɪlɪps] ® ATTR: ~ **screw** tornillo *m* de cabeza cruciforme; ~ **screwdriver** destornillador *m* cruciforme.
philological [ˌfɪlə'lɒdʒɪkəl] ADJ filológico.
philologist [fɪ'lɒlədʒɪst] N filólogo *m,* -a *f.*
philology [fɪ'lɒlədʒɪ] N filología *f.*
philosopher [fɪ'lɒsəfəʳ] N filósofo *m,* -a *f;* **~'s stone** piedra *f* filosofal.
philosophic(al) [ˌfɪlə'sɒfɪk(əl)] ADJ filosófico.
philosophically [ˌfɪlə'sɒfɪkəlɪ] ADV filosóficamente.
philosophize [fɪ'lɒsəfaɪz] VI filosofar.
philosophy [fɪ'lɒsəfɪ] N filosofía *f;* **~ of life** filosofía *f* de la vida.
philtre, (US) **philter** ['fɪltəʳ] N filtro *m,* poción *f.*
phiz* [fɪz] N jeta* *f.*
phlebitis [flɪ'baɪtɪs] N flebitis *f.*
phlegm [flem] N flema *f* (*also fig*).
phlegmatic [fleg'mætɪk] ADJ flemático.
phlegmatically [fleg'mætɪkəlɪ] ADV con flema; **he said** ~ dijo flemático.
phlox [flɒks] N flox *m.*
Phnom Penh, Pnom Penh ['nom'pen] N Phnom Penh *m.*
-phobe [fəub] SUF -fobo, *eg* **francophobe** francófobo *m,* -a *f.*
phobia ['fəubɪə] N fobia *f.*
-phobia ['fəubɪə] SUF -fobia, *eg* **anglophobia** anglofobia *f.*
phobic ['fəubɪk] ADJ fóbico.
Phoebus ['fi:bəs] NM Febo.
Phoenicia [fɪ'nɪʃɪə] N Fenicia *f.*
Phoenician [fɪ'nɪʃɪən] ① ADJ fenicio.
　② N fenicio *m,* -a *f.*
phoenix ['fi:nɪks] N fénix *m.*
phone[1]* [fəun] ① N = **telephone.**
　② ATTR: ~ **book** *etc* = **telephone book** *etc.*
◆ **phone up** VTI llamar (al teléfono).
phone[2] [fəun] N (*Ling*) fono *m.*
phonecard ['fəunkɑ:d] N tarjeta *f* telefónica.
phone-in ['fəunɪn] N (*also* ~ **programme**) (programa *m*) coloquio *m* (por teléfono).
phoneme ['fəuni:m] N fonema *m.*
phonemic [fəu'ni:mɪk] ADJ fonémico.
phonetic [fəu'netɪk] ADJ fonético.
phonetically [fəu'netɪkəlɪ] ADV fonéticamente.
phonetician [ˌfəunɪ'tɪʃən] N fonetista *mf.*
phonetics [fəu'netɪks] N fonética *f.*
phon(e)y* ['fəunɪ] ① ADJ falso, postizo; fingido, simulado; mixtificado; sospechoso; insincero; **the** ~ **war** (*1939*) la extraña guerra; **it's completely** ~ no es lo que parece ser en absoluto; **there's sth** ~ **about it** esto huele a camelo.
　② N (*person*) farsante* *mf;* (*thing*) cosa *f* falsa, cosa *f* postiza; **it's a** ~ es falso, es un engaño.
phonic ['fɒnɪk] ADJ fónico.
phono... ['fəunəu] PREF fono...
phonograph ['fəunəgrɑ:f] N (US) gramófono *m,* fonógrafo *m,* tocadiscos *m.*
phonological [ˌfəunə'lɒdʒɪkəl] ADJ fonológico.
phonologically [ˌfəunə'lɒdʒɪklɪ] ADV fonológicamente.
phonologist [fə'nɒlədʒɪst] N fonólogo *m,* -a *f.*
phonology [fəu'nɒlədʒɪ] N fonología *f.*

phony* ['fəunɪ] ADJ = **phoney.**
phooey* ['fu:ɪ] EXCL (*rubbish*) ¡bobadas!; (*annoyance*) ¡qué tonto soy!; (*disappointment*) ¡ay!
phosgene ['fɒzdʒi:n] N fosgeno *m.*
phosphate ['fɒsfeɪt] N fosfato *m.*
phosphene ['fɒsfi:n] N fosfeno *m.*
phosphide ['fɒsfaɪd] N fosfito *m.*
phosphine ['fɒsfi:n] N fosfino *m.*
phosphoresce [ˌfɒsfə'res] VI fosforecer.
phosphorescence [ˌfɒsfə'resns] N fosforescencia *f.*
phosphorescent [ˌfɒsfə'resnt] ADJ fosforescente.
phosphoric [fɒs'fɒrɪk] ADJ fosfórico.
phosphorous ['fɒsfərəs] ADJ fosforoso.
phosphorus ['fɒsfərəs] N fósforo *m.*
photo ['fəutəu] N foto *f;* ~ **booth** fotomatón *m,* cabina *f* de fotos; ~ **opportunity** = **photocall;** = **photograph.**
photo... ['fəutəu] PREF foto...
photocall ['fəutəukɔ:l] N rueda *f* fotográfica, oportunidad *f* fotográfica.
photochemical [ˌfəutəu'kemɪkəl] ADJ fotoquímico.
photocompose [ˌfəutəukəm'pəuz] VT fotocomponer.
photocomposer [ˌfəutəukəm'pəuzəʳ] N fotocomponedora *f.*
photocomposition [ˌfəutəukɒmpə'zɪʃən] N fotocomposición *f.*
photocopier ['fəutəu,kɒpɪəʳ] N fotocopiadora *f.*
photocopy ['fəutəu,kɒpɪ] ① N fotocopia *f.*
　② VT fotocopiar.
photocopying ['fəutəu,kɒpɪɪŋ] N fotocopia *f.*
photocoverage ['fəutəu,kʌvərɪdʒ] N reportaje *m* gráfico.
photodisk ['fəutəu,dɪsk] N fotodisco *m.*
photoelectric ['fəutəuɪ'lektrɪk] ADJ fotoeléctrico; ~ **cell** célula *f* fotoeléctrica.
photoelectron [ˌfəutəuɪ'lektrɒn] N fotoelectrón *m.*
photoengrave [ˌfəutəuɪn'greɪv] VT fotograbar.
photoengraving ['fəutəuen'greɪvɪŋ] N fotograbado *m.*
photo-finish ['fəutəu'fɪnɪʃ] N resultado *m* comprobado por fotocontrol; (*fig*) final *m* muy reñido.
Photofit ['fəutəufɪt] ® ATTR: ~ **picture** retrato *m* robot.
photoflash ['fəutəuflæʃ] N flash *m,* relámpago *m.*
photogenic [ˌfəutəu'dʒenɪk] ADJ fotogénico.
photograph ['fəutəgræf] ① N fotografía *f* (*foto*); **to take a** ~ sacar una foto.
　② ATTR: ~ **album** álbum *m* de fotos.
　③ VT fotografiar, hacer una fotografía de, sacar una foto de; '~**ed by X'** 'fotografía de X'.
　④ VI: **to** ~ **well** ser fotogénico, sacar buena foto.
photographer [fə'tɒgrəfəʳ] N fotógrafo *m,* -a *f.*
photographic [ˌfəutə'græfɪk] ADJ fotográfico.
photographically [ˌfəutə'græfɪkəlɪ] ADV fotográficamente; **to record sth** ~ registrar algo por medio de fotografías, hacer una historia fotográfica de algo.
photography [fə'tɒgrəfɪ] N fotografía *f.*
photogravure [ˌfəutəgrə'vjuəʳ] N fotograbado *m.*
photojournalism ['fəutəu'dʒɜ:nə,lɪzəm] N fotoperiodismo *m.*
photojournalist ['fəutəu'dʒɜ:nəlɪst] N fotoperiodista *mf.*
photokit ['fəutəukɪt] N retrato *m* robot.
photolitho [ˌfəutəu'laɪθəu] N fotolito *m.*
photolithograph [ˌfəutəu'lɪθə,grɑ:f] N grabado *m* fotolitográfico.
photolithography [ˌfəutəu'lɪθɒgrəfɪ] N fotolitografía *f.*
photometer [fə'tɒmətəʳ] N fotómetro *m.*
photometric [ˌfəutə'metrɪk] ADJ fotométrico.
photometry [fəu'tɒmɪtrɪ] N fotometría *f.*
photomontage [ˌfəutəumɒn'tɑ:ʒ] N fotomontaje *m.*
photon ['fəutɒn] N fotón *m.*
photosensitive [ˌfəutəu'sensɪtɪv] ADJ fotosensible.
photosensitivity [ˌfəutəusensɪ'tɪvɪtɪ] N fotosensibilidad *f.*
photosensitize [ˌfəutəu'sensɪ,taɪz] VT fotosensibilizar.
photosetting ['fəutəu,setɪŋ] ① N fotocomposición *f.*
　② ATTR: ~ **machine** fotocompositora *f.*
photostat ['fəutəustæt] (® *in US*) ① N fotóstato *m.*
　② VT fotostatar.
photosynthesis [ˌfəutəu'sɪnθəsɪs] N fotosíntesis *f.*
phototropism ['fəutəu'trəupɪzəm] N fototropismo *m.*
phototype ['fəutəu,taɪp] N fototipo *m.*
phototypesetting [ˌfəutəu'taɪp,setɪŋ] N (US: *Typ*) fotocomposición *f.*
phototypography [ˌfəutəutaɪ'pɒgrəfɪ] N fototipografía *f.*
photovoltaic [ˌfəutəuvɒl'teɪɪk] ADJ fotovoltaico; ~ **cell** célula *f* fotovoltaica.
phrasal ['freɪzəl] ADJ frasal; ~ **verb** verbo *m* frasal, verbo *m* con preposición (or adverbio).
phrase [freɪz] ① N frase *f* (*also Mus*), expresión *f,* locución *f;* **to coin a** ~ para decirlo así; si se me permite la frase; **he knows how to turn a** ~ a veces es muy elocuente, sabe crear frases muy expresivas.

[2] VT expresar; **a carefully ~d letter** una carta redactada con cuidado; **can we ~ that differently?** ¿podemos poner eso de otro modo?

[3] ATTR: **~ marker** marcador *m* de frase; **~ structure** estructura *f* de frase.

phrasebook ['freɪzbʊk] N libro *m* de frases.

phraseology [ˌfreɪzɪ'ɒlədʒɪ] N fraseología *f*.

phrasing ['freɪzɪŋ] N (*act*) redacción *f*; (*style*) estilo *m*, fraseología *f*, términos *mpl*; (*Mus*) fraseo *m*; **the ~ is rather unfortunate** la forma de expresarse no es apropiada.

phrenetic [frɪ'netɪk] ADJ frenético.

phrenologist [frɪ'nɒlədʒɪst] N frenólogo *m*, -a *f*.

phrenology [frɪ'nɒlədʒɪ] N frenología *f*.

phthisis ['θaɪsɪs] N tisis *f*.

phut* [fʌt] ADJ: **to go ~** estropearse, romperse, hacer kaput*; (*fig*) fracasar, acabarse.

phylactery [fɪ'læktərɪ] N filacteria *f*.

phylloxera [ˌfɪlɒk'sɪərə] N filoxera *f*.

physic ['fɪzɪk] N (††) medicina *f*.

physical ['fɪzɪkəl] ADJ (a) (*of the body*) físico; **~ condition** estado *m* físico; **~ culture** cultura *f* física; **~ education** educación *f* física; **~ examination** reconocimiento *m* físico; **~ geography** geografía *f* física; **~ jerks*** (*Brit*) ejercicios *mpl* físicos, gimnasia *f*; **~ record** registro *m* físico; **~ science** ciencias *fpl* físicas; **~ training** gimnasia *f*.
(b) (*fig*) material; **a ~ impossibility** una imposibilidad material; **~ inspection** inspección *f* material.
(c) (*Sport: euph*) play duro.

physically ['fɪzɪkəlɪ] ADV físicamente.

physician [fɪ'zɪʃən] N médico *m*, -a *f*.

physicist ['fɪzɪsɪst] N físico *m*, -a *f*.

physics ['fɪzɪks] N física *f*.

physio* ['fɪzɪəʊ] N (*Sport*) = **physiotherapist**.

physio... ['fɪzɪəʊ] PREF fisio...

physiognomy [ˌfɪzɪ'ɒnəmɪ] N fisonomía *f*.

physiological ['fɪzɪə'lɒdʒɪkəl] ADJ fisiológico.

physiologist [ˌfɪzɪ'ɒlədʒɪst] N fisiólogo *m*, -a *f*.

physiology [ˌfɪzɪ'ɒlədʒɪ] N fisiología *f*.

physiotherapist [ˌfɪzɪə'θerəpɪst] N fisioterapeuta *mf*, fisioterapista *mf*.

physiotherapy [ˌfɪzɪə'θerəpɪ] N fisioterapia *f*.

physique [fɪ'ziːk] N físico *m*, complexión *f*.

phytobiology [ˌfaɪtəʊbaɪ'ɒlədʒɪ] N fitobiología *f*.

phytofagous [faɪ'tɒfəgəs] ADJ fitófago.

phytopathology [ˌfaɪtəʊpə'θɒlədʒɪ] N fitopatología *f*.

pi¹* [paɪ] ADJ piadoso, devoto.

pi² [paɪ] N (*Math*) pi *m*.

pianist ['pɪənɪst] N pianista *mf*.

piano ['pjɑːnəʊ] [1] N piano *m*.
[2] ATTR: **~ concerto** concierto *m* para piano; **~ duet** dúo *m* de piano; **~ lesson** lección *f* de piano; **~ piece** música *f* para piano; **~ teacher** profesor *m*, -ora *f* de piano.

piano-accordion ['pjɑːnəʊə'kɔːdɪən] N acordeón-piano *m*.

pianoforte [ˌpjɑːnəʊ'fɔːtɪ] N = **piano**.

pianola [pɪə'nəʊlə] N pianola *f*.

piano-stool ['pjɑːnəʊˌstuːl] N taburete *m* de piano.

piano-tuner ['pjɑːnəʊˌtjuːnəʳ] N afinador *m*, -ora *f* de pianos.

piastre, (*US*) **piaster** [pɪ'æstəʳ] N piastra *f*.

piazza [pɪ'ætsə] N (*US*) pórtico *m*, galería *f*.

pic* [pɪk] N, PL **pics** or **pix** [pɪks] ABBR of **picture** foto *f*.

pica ['paɪkə] N (*Med, Vet*) pica *f*; (*Typ*) cícero *m*.

picador ['pɪkə'dɔː] N picador *m*.

Picardy ['pɪkədɪ] N Picardía *f*.

picaresque [ˌpɪkə'resk] ADJ picaresco; **~ novel** novela *f* picaresca.

picayune [ˌpɪkə'juːn] (*US*) [1] ADJ de poca monta.
[2] N (*person*) persona *f* insignificante; (*thing*) bagatela *f*.

piccalilli ['pɪkəˌlɪlɪ] N legumbres *fpl* en escabeche, encurtidos *mpl* picantes.

piccaninny ['pɪkəˌnɪnɪ] N negrito *m*, -a *f*.

piccolo ['pɪkələʊ] N flautín *m*, píccolo *m*.

pick [pɪk] [1] N (a) (*tool*) pico *m*, zapapico *m*, piqueta *f*.
(b) (*choice, right to choose*) derecho *m* de elección; **it's your ~** a ti te toca elegir; **whose ~ is it?** ¿a quién le toca elegir?; **he had his ~ of the books** él escogió los libros que quería; él pudo llevarse los mejores libros; **take your ~!** ¡a elegir!
(c) (*best*) lo mejor, lo más escogido; flor *f* y nata; **it's the ~ of the bunch** es el mejor del grupo.
[2] VT (a) *hole etc* picar, hacer; *teeth* mondarse, limpiarse; *nose* hurgarse; *bone* roer; *bird* desplumar; *sore etc* rascar; manosear; *lock* forzar, abrir con ganzúa.
(b) (*choose*) escoger, elegir; escoger con cuidado; *team* seleccionar; **to ~ one's way** andar con mucho tiento (*across* por), abrirse camino (*among* entre, *through* por).
(c) **to ~ pockets** ratear, robar carteras, ser carterista; **to ~ sb's pock-**

et robar algo del bolsillo de uno; **he had his pocket ~ed** le robaron la cartera (*etc*).
(d) (*pluck*) coger (*Sp*), recoger (*LAm*).
[3] VI: **to ~ and choose** tardar en decidirse; hacer melindres al escoger, mostrarse difícil; **I like to ~ and choose** me gusta elegir con cuidado.

◆**pick at** VT (a) *sore etc* rascar; manosear; **to ~ at one's food** comer con poco apetito, picar.
(b) (*US**) = **pick on** (b).

◆**pick off** VT (a) *paint* arrancar, separar; **to ~ sth off the ground** recoger algo del suelo.
(b) (*shoot*) matar de un tiro; matar con tiros sucesivos; *opponents* acabar uno a uno con.

◆**pick on** VT (a) (*single out*) esoger; designar, nombrar; **why ~ on me?** ¿por qué lo dices a mí y no a otro?
(b) (*harass*) perseguir; criticar mucho; fastidiar; **he's always ~ing on me** me tiene manía.
(c) (*US: choose*) = **pick out** (a).

◆**pick out** VT (a) (*choose*) elegir, escoger; entresacar.
(b) (*distinguish*) distinguir (*among* entre, *from* de); (*recognize*) conocer, identificar (*by* por); (*discern*) alcanzar a ver.
(c) *tune* tocar de oído (*on the piano* al piano).
(d) (*highlight*) destacar, hacer resaltar.

◆**pick over, pick through** VT ir revolviendo y examinando.

◆**pick up** [1] VT (a) (*lift*) recoger; levantar, alzar; *telephone* descolgar; *child* levantar en los brazos.
(b) (*collect*) recoger, buscar (*esp LAm*); **I'll call and ~ it up** pasaré por casa a recogerlo.
(c) (*Aut*) *hitch-hiker* recoger.
(d) (*: sexually*) ligar*, ligar con*.
(e) (*acquire*) adquirir; (*buy*) comprar, adquirir; (*find*) encontrar; (*learn*) aprender, adquirir; *information* saber, indagar; saber por casualidad; *disease* contagiarse con; *habit* adquirir; **he ~s up £400 a week** gana 400 libras a la semana; **he ~s up a living selling antiques** se gana la vida vendiendo antigüedades.
(f) (*Rad*) captar, sintonizar; **the dog ~ed up the scent** el perro cogió el rastro; **our ears cannot ~ up that sound** nuestro oído no percibe ese sonido.
(g) (*Naut etc: rescue*) recoger, rescatar.
(h) (*arrest*) detener.
(i) (*focus on*) destacar; subrayar; **I want to ~ up three points** quiero subrayar tres temas.
(j) (*reprimand*) reprender; **he ~ed me up on my grammar** me señaló diversas faltas de gramática; **may I ~ you up on one point?** ¿me permites criticarte en un punto?
(k) **to ~ up speed** acelerar, cobrar velocidad.
(l) (*: steal*) birlar*.
[2] VI (a) (*improve*) mejorar; (*Med*) reponerse; (*business etc*) ir mejor; **the game ~ed up in the second half** se jugó mejor en el segundo tiempo.
(b) (*put on speed*) acelerarse, ir cobrando velocidad.
(c) **we ~ed up where we had left off** reanudamos la conversación (*etc*) donde la habíamos dejado.
[3] VR: **to ~ o.s. up** ponerse de pie, levantarse; (*fig*) restablecerse.

pickaback ['pɪkəbæk] ADV: **to carry sb ~** llevar a uno sobre los hombros, llevar a uno a cuestas.

pickaxe, (*US*) **pickax** ['pɪkæks] N pico *m*, zapapico *m*, piqueta *f*.

picked [pɪkt] ADJ escogido, selecto.

picker ['pɪkəʳ] N (*of fruit etc*) recolector *m*, -ora *f*.

picket ['pɪkɪt] [1] N (a) (*stake*) estaca *f*.
(b) (*all other senses*) piquete *m*.
[2] ATTR: **~ duty** servicio *m* de piquetes.
[3] VT *factory* piquetear, estacionar piquetes a la puerta de.
[4] VI estar de guardia (los piquetes).

picketing ['pɪkɪtɪŋ] N piquete *m*, el piquetear.

picket-line ['pɪkɪtlaɪn] N piquete *m*; **to cross a ~** no hacer caso de un piquete.

picking ['pɪkɪŋ] N (a) (*of fruit etc*) recolección *f*, cosecha *f*; (*act of choosing*) elección *f*, selección *f*.
(b) **~s** (*leftovers*) sobras *fpl*, desperdicios *mpl*; (*profits*) ganancias *fpl*; (*stolen goods*) artículos *mpl* robados.

pickle ['pɪkl] [1] N (a) (*as condiment: also* **~s**) encurtido *m*; (*of fish, olives*) escabeche *m*; (*of meat*) adobo *m*; (*in salt solution*) salmuera *f*.
(b) (*) (*plight*) apuro *m*; **to be in a ~** (*person*) estar en un apuro, (*room*) estar en desorden, estar revuelto; **to get into a ~** meterse en líos*; **what a ~!** ¡qué lío!*
(c) (*: child*) diablillo *m*, pillo *m*.
[2] VT encurtir; escabechar; adobar; conservar, conservar en vinagre; (*Bio*) conservar en alcohol, conservar en formalina.

pickled ['pɪkld] ADJ (a) *food* escabechado, encurtido, en conserva; **~ onions** cebollas *fpl* en vinagre; **~ herrings** arenques *mpl* en escabeche; **~ walnuts** nueces *fpl* adobadas.

(b) to be ~: (*drunk*) estar jumado*.

picklock ['pɪklɒk] N ganzúa f.

pick-me-up ['pɪkmiːʌp] N (*Brit*) (*Med*) tónico m; (*alcohol*) bebida f, trago m.

pickpocket ['pɪkˌpɒkɪt] N carterista m, ratero m, bolsista m (*Mex*).

pick-up ['pɪkʌp] **1** N **(a)** (*Mus*) pick-up m.
(b) (*Aut: also* ~ **truck**, (*Brit*) ~ **van**) furgoneta f, camioneta f (de reparto).
(c) (*) ligue* m.
2 ATTR: ~ **arm** pick-up m, fonocaptor m; ~ **point** punto m de recogida.

picky* ['pɪkɪ] ADJ (*US*) **(a)** (*critical*) criticón. **(b)** (*choosy*) melindroso, delicado.

picnic ['pɪknɪk] **1** N jira f, excursión f campestre, merienda f en el campo, picnic m; **to go for a ~, to go on a ~** ir de jira, merendar en el campo; **we found a nice place for a ~** encontramos un buen sitio para merendar; **it was no ~*** no era nada fácil; no tenía nada de agradable.
2 ATTR: ~ **basket** canasta f para bocadillos; ~ **site** lugar m destinado para picnics.
3 VI ir de jira, merendar en el campo; llevar la merienda al campo; **we ~ked by the river** merendamos junto al río; **we go ~king every Sunday** todos los domingos vamos de jira.

picnicker ['pɪknɪkəʳ] N excursionista mf.

pics* [pɪks] NPL ABBR *of* **pictures (a)** (*Cine*) cine m, películas fpl. **(b)** (*Phot*) fotos fpl.

Pict [pɪkt] N picto m, -a f.

Pictish ['pɪktɪʃ] **1** ADJ picto.
2 N picto m.

pictogram ['pɪktəʊgræm] N pictograma m.

pictograph ['pɪktəgraːf] N **(a)** (*record, chart etc*) pictografía f. **(b)** (*Ling*) (*symbol*) pictograma m; (*writing*) pictografía f.

pictorial [pɪk'tɔːrɪəl] **1** ADJ pictórico; *magazine* gráfico, ilustrado.
2 N revista f ilustrada.

pictorially [pɪk'tɔːrɪəlɪ] ADV pictóricamente; *represent etc* gráficamente, por imágenes.

picture ['pɪktʃəʳ] **1** N **(a)** (*Art*) cuadro m, pintura f; (*portrait*) retrato m; (*photo*) fotografía f; (*in book*) lámina f, estampa f, grabado m.
(b) (*TV*) cuadro m, imagen f.
(c) (*Cine*) película f, film m; **the ~s** (*esp Brit*) el cine; **to go to a ~** ir a ver una película; **to go to the ~s** (*esp Brit*) ir al cine.
(d) (*spoken etc*) descripción f; (*mental*) imagen f; recuerdo m; (*outlook*) perspectiva f; (*overall view*) visión f de conjunto; **the other side of the ~** el reverso de la medalla; **she looked a ~!** ¡estaba guapísima!; **the garden is a ~ in June** en junio el jardín es de lo más hermoso; **his face was a ~!** ¡había que ver la cara que puso!; **it was a ~ of devastation** todo fue devastación; **she looked a ~ of health** era la salud personificada; **he gave us a grim ~** nos hizo una descripción horrorosa; **he painted a black ~ of the future** nos hizo un cuadro muy negro del porvenir; **I have no very clear ~ of it** no lo recuerdo con claridad; **these figures give the general ~** estas cifras ofrecen una visión de conjunto; **are you in the ~?*** ¿estás enterado?; **I get the ~*** ya comprendo; **to put sb in the ~*** poner a uno al corriente, poner a uno en antecedentes.
2 ATTR: de pinturas, de cuadros; *paper* gráfico, ilustrado; ~ **card** (*Cards*) carta f de figura; ~ **hat** pamela f; ~ **window** ventanal m, ventana f grande.
3 VT (*paint*) pintar; (*describe*) pintar, describir; **to ~ sth to o.s.** imaginarse algo, representarse algo en la imaginación; ~ **the scene** figúraos la escena; ~ **if you can a winkle** imaginaos, si podéis, un bígaro.

picture-book ['pɪktʃəbʊk] N libro m de imágenes.

picture-frame ['pɪktʃəfreɪm] N marco m (para cuadro).

picture gallery ['pɪktʃə'gæləɪ] N museo m de pintura, museo m de bellas artes, pinacoteca f; **the Prado ~** el Museo del Prado.

picturegoer ['pɪktʃəˌɡəʊəʳ] N aficionado m, -a f al cine.

picture-in-picture [ˌpɪktʃərɪn'pɪktʃəʳ] N (*TV, Comput*) imagen f en imagen.

picture-palace ['pɪktʃəˌpælɪs] N (†) cine m.

picture postcard ['pɪktʃə'pəʊstkaːd] N tarjeta f postal.

picture-rail ['pɪktʃəreɪl] N moldura f (*pegada a la pared para colgar cuadros*).

picturesque [ˌpɪktʃə'resk] ADJ pintoresco; (*quaint, of tourist interest*) típico.

picturesquely [ˌpɪktʃə'resklɪ] ADV de modo pintoresco.

picturesqueness [ˌpɪktʃə'resknɪs] N lo pintoresco; pintoresquismo m.

piddle ['pɪdl] = **piss**.

piddling* ['pɪdlɪŋ] ADJ de poca monta, insignificante.

pidgin ['pɪdʒɪn] N (*also* ~ **English**) lengua franca (inglés-chino) comercial del Lejano Oriente.

pie [paɪ] N (*of fruit etc*) pastel m, tarta f, pay m (*LAm*); (*of meat*) empanada f, pastel m; **it's ~ in the sky** es como prometer la luna; **to**

eat humble ~ humillarse y pedir perdón, morder el polvo.

piebald ['paɪbɔːld] **1** ADJ pío, de varios colores.
2 N caballo m pío.

piece [piːs] **1** N **(a)** (*fragment*) pedazo m, trozo m, fragmento m; (*Mech, Mil*) pieza f; (*coin*) moneda f, pieza f; (*Liter, Theat, Mus*) obra f, pieza f; (*Chess*) pieza f; **a 50-pence ~** una moneda de 50 peniques; **that nice ~ in the third movement** aquel pasaje tan bonito del tercer tiempo; **to buy sth by the ~** comprar algo por piezas; **it is made all in one ~** está hecho de una pieza, forma pieza única, las partes no son separables; **the back is all of a ~ with the seat** el respaldo forma pieza única con el asiento; **to get back all in one ~** volver sano y salvo; **we got it back all in one ~** nos lo devolvieron en buen estado; **this is of a ~ with the other** éste es de la misma clase que el otro, éste se parece al otro; **this is of a ~ with what he told us** esto es conforme con lo que nos dijo, esto concuerda con lo que nos dijo; **to pick up the ~s** recoger los platos rotos; **to leave sb to pick up the ~s** dejar que otro pague los platos rotos; **I said my ~ and left** dije lo que tenía que decir y salí; **when do I say my ~?** ¿cuándo digo lo mío?
(b) a nice little ~: (*girl*) una pizpireta*, una chica muy mona.
(c) (*examples of a ~ of*) **a ~ of paper** un trozo de papel, una hoja de papel, un papel; **a ~ of soap** un cacho de jabón; **a ~ of string** un cabo; **a ~ of bread** un pedazo de pan; **a ~ of cake** una porción de tarta; **it's a ~ of cake*** es pan comido, está tirado; **another ~ of cake?** ¿quieres más tarta?; **a ~ of my work** una de mis obras, una muestra de mi trabajo; **a ~ out of a book** un trozo de un libro; **a ~ of advice** un consejo; **a ~ of carelessness** un descuido, un acto de imprudencia; **a ~ of clothing** una prenda (de vestir); **a ~ of folly** una locura, un acto de locura; **a ~ of furniture** un mueble; **a ~ of ground** un lote de terreno, un terreno, (*for building*) un solar; **by a ~ of good luck** por suerte; **a ~ of luggage** un bulto; **3 ~s of luggage** 3 bultos; **a ~ of news** una noticia, una nueva; **a ~ of poetry** una poesía; **to give sb a ~ of one's mind** decir cuatro verdades a uno, cantar las cuarenta a uno.
(d) to be in ~s (*taken apart*) estar desmontado, (*broken*) estar hecho pedazos, estar roto; **to break sth to** (*or* **in**) **~s** hacer algo pedazos; **to break** (VI) **in ~s** hacerse pedazos; **to come to ~s, to fall to ~s** hacerse pedazos, romperse; **it comes to ~s** se desmonta, es desmontable; **to go to ~s** (*person*) sufrir un ataque de nervios, perder el control, (*government etc*) venirse abajo, (*Med*) perder la salud, (*team etc*) desanimarse por completo; **to hack sth to ~s** cortar algo en pedazos (*violentamente, despiadadamente etc*); **to pull to ~s** deshacer, despedazar, hacer pedazos, *argument* deshacer, *person* criticar duramente; **to say one's ~** decir lo que uno quiere decir; **to smash sth to ~s** destrozar algo violentamente, romper algo a golpes; **the boat was smashed to ~s on the rocks** el barco se estrelló contra las rocas y se hizo astillas; **to take sth to ~s** desmontar algo; **it takes to ~s** se desmonta, es desmontable; **to tear sth to ~s** romper algo violentamente, (*prey etc*) desgarrar algo; **the crowd will tear him to ~s** la gente le hará pedazos; **he tore the theory to ~s** destrozó la teoría por completo.
2 ATTR: ~ **rate** (*Comm*) tarifa f a destajo.

◆piece together VT juntar, juntar las partes de; (*Mech*) montar, ir montando; (*fig*) atar cabos e ir comprendiendo; **we eventually ~d the story together** por fin logramos saber toda la historia, por fin logramos atar todos los cabos.

pièce de résistance [ˌpjesdərezis'tãːs] N lo principal, lo más importante; (*on menu*) plato m principal; (*in programme*) atracción f principal, número m más importante.

piecemeal ['piːsmiːl] **1** ADV (*bit by bit*) poco a poco, a pedacitos, a trozos, por etapas; (*haphazard*) sin sistema fijo.
2 ADJ poco sistemático.

piecework ['piːswɜːk] N trabajo m a destajo; **to be on ~, to do ~** trabajar a destajo.

pieceworker ['piːswɜːkəʳ] N destajista mf.

pie-chart ['paɪtʃaːt] N (*Math*) gráfico m circular, gráfico m de sectores (*or* de tarta); (*Comput*) tarta f.

piecrust ['paɪkrʌst] **1** N pasta f de pastel.
2 ATTR: ~ **pastry** (*US*) pasta f quebradiza.

pied [paɪd] ADJ *animal* pío, de varios colores; *bird* manchado; **the P~ Piper of Hamelin** el flautista de Hamelin.

pied-à-terre [ˌpɪeɪdæ'teəʳ] N apeadero m.

Piedmont ['piːdmɒnt] N Piamonte m.

Piedmontese [ˌpiːdmɒn'tiːz] **1** ADJ piamontés.
2 N piamontés m, -esa f.

pie-eyed* ['paɪ'aɪd] ADJ jumado*.

pier [pɪəʳ] N **(a)** (*Archit*) pilar m, columna f; (*of bridge*) estribo m, pila f. **(b)** (*Naut*) dique m, malecón m, embarcadero m; paseo m marítimo (sobre malecón).

pierce [pɪəs] VT penetrar; atravesar, traspasar; (*hole*) agujerear; (*bore*) horadar, perforar; (*punch*) taladrar; (*puncture*) pinchar; **the bullet ~d the armour** la bala penetró en la coraza; **the bullet ~d his lung** la bala le atravesó el pulmón, la bala entró en el pulmón; **to have one's ears ~d** hacerse abrir las orejas; **the rock is ~d by numerous holes** la roca está agujereada (*or* horadada) en muchos sitios; **a nail ~d the tyre** un clavo pinchó el neumático; **the dam had been ~d in various places** se habían abierto brechas en distintas partes de la presa; **a wall ~d with loopholes** un muro en el que se abrían aspilleras; **to ~ sth through and through** perforar algo una y otra vez; **a cry ~d the silence** un grito desgarró el silencio; **a light ~d the darkness** una luz hendió la oscuridad; **the news ~d him to the heart** la noticia le hirió en el alma.

piercing ['pɪəsɪŋ] ADJ *wind* cortante; *cry* agudo, desgarrador, penetrante; *look* penetrante; *pain* lancinante.

piercingly ['pɪəsɪŋlɪ] ADV *blow* de modo cortante; *cry* agudamente, en tono penetrante.

pierhead ['pɪəhed] N punta *f* del muelle.

pierrot ['pɪərəʊ] N pierrot *m*.

pietism ['paɪətɪzəm] N piedad *f*, devoción *f*; (*pej*) beatería *f*, mojigatería *f*.

pietistic [paɪə'tɪstɪk] ADJ (*pej*) pietista, beato, mojigato.

piety ['paɪətɪ] N piedad *f*, devoción *f*; **affected ~** beatería *f*.

piffle* ['pɪfl] N disparates *mpl*, tonterías *fpl*; **~!** ¡tonterías!

piffling* ['pɪflɪŋ] ADJ de poca monta, insignificante.

pig [pɪg] **1** N (a) cerdo *m*, puerco *m*, cochino *m*, chancho *m* (*LAm*); **roast ~** cochinillo *m* asado, lechón *m* asado; **to buy a ~ in a poke** cerrar un trato a ciegas; **to sell sb a ~ in a poke** dar gato por liebre; **when ~s (learn to) fly** cuando las ranas críen pelos; **it was a ~ of a job** fue un trabajo horrible; **he made a right ~'s ear of it** se armó un tremendo lío con eso; lo hizo malísimamente; **in a ~'s eye!*** (*US*) ¡ni hablar!, ¡que te lo has creído!
(b) (*fig: person*) cochino *m*, marrano *m*, chancho *m* (*LAm*); (‡: *policeman*) poli* *m*; **you ~!** (*hum*) ¡bandido!; **the boss is a ~** el jefe es un bruto; **you're a ~, sir!** ¡Vd es un maleducado!; **to make a ~ of o.s.** comer demasiado; darse un atracón* (*over* de).
(c) (*Metal*) lingote *m*.
2 VT: **to ~ it** vivir como cerdos.

pig-breeding ['pɪg,briːdɪŋ] N cría *f* de cerdos.

pigeon ['pɪdʒən] N (a) paloma *f*, palomo *m*; (*young*) palomino *m*, pichón *m*; (*as food*) pichón *m*. (b) (*) **that's his ~** allá él; **it's not my ~** eso no tiene que ver conmigo.

pigeon-fancier ['pɪdʒən,fænsɪə'] N colombófilo *m*, -a *f*.

pigeon-fancying ['pɪdʒən,fænsɪŋ] N colombofilia *f*.

pigeonhole ['pɪdʒənhəʊl] **1** N casilla *f*; **set of ~s** casillas *fpl*, casillero *m*.
2 VT (*classify*) encasillar, clasificar; (*store away*) archivar; archivar en la memoria; (*shelve*) dar carpetazo a.

pigeon-house ['pɪdʒənhaʊs] N, PL **pigeon-houses** ['pɪdʒən,haʊzɪz], **pigeon-loft** ['pɪdʒənlɒft] N palomar *m*.

pigeon-post ['pɪdʒən,pəʊst] N correo *m* de palomas; **by ~** por paloma mensajera.

pigeon-shooting ['pɪdʒən,ʃuːtɪŋ] N tiro *m* de pichón.

pigeon-toed ['pɪdʒən'təʊd] ADJ con los pies torcidos hacia dentro.

piggery ['pɪgərɪ] N pocilga *f*, porqueriza *f*, cochiquera *f*.

piggish ['pɪgɪʃ] ADJ (*in manners*) puerco; (*greedy*) glotón; (*stubborn*) tozudo, testarudo.

piggy ['pɪgɪ] **1** N cerdito *m*, cochinillo *m*, lechón *m*; **to be ~ in the middle** sufrir por estar entre otros dos que se riñen (*etc*).
2 ADJ: **with little ~ eyes** con ojos pequeños como de cerdo.

piggy-back ['pɪgɪbæk] N: **to give a child a ~** llevar a un niño sobre los hombros, llevar a un niño a cuestas.

piggy-bank ['pɪgɪbæŋk] N hucha *f* (en forma de cerdito).

pigheaded ['pɪg'hedɪd] ADJ *person* terco, testarudo; *attitude etc* obstinado; **it was a ~ thing to do** fue un acto que reveló su terquedad.

pigheadedly ['pɪg'hedɪdlɪ] ADV tercamente; obstinadamente.

pigheadedness ['pɪg'hedɪdnɪs] N terquedad *f*, testarudez *f*; obstinación *f*.

pig-ignorant* [,pɪg'ɪgnərənt] ADJ bruto.

pig-iron ['pɪg,aɪən] N hierro *m* en lingotes.

piglet ['pɪglɪt] N cerdito *m*, cochinillo *m*, lechón *m*.

pigman ['pɪgmæn] N, PL **pigmen** ['pɪgmen] porquerizo *m*, porquero *m*.

pigmeat ['pɪgmiːt] N carne *f* de cerdo.

pigment ['pɪgmənt] N pigmento *m*.

pigmentation [,pɪgmən'teɪʃən] N pigmentación *f*.

pigmented [pɪg'mentɪd] ADJ pigmentado.

pigmy ['pɪgmɪ] **1** ADJ pigmeo; (*fig*) enano; miniatura, pequeñito.
2 N pigmeo *m*, -a *f*, enano *m*, -a *f*.

pigpen ['pɪgpen] N (*US*) = **pigsty**.

pigskin ['pɪgskɪn] N piel *f* de cerdo.

pigsty ['pɪgstaɪ] N (*Brit*) pocilga *f*, porqueriza *f*, cochiquera *f* (*also fig*).

pigswill ['pɪgswɪl] N bazofia *f* (*also fig*).

pigtail ['pɪgteɪl] N (*of Chinese, bullfighter etc*) coleta *f*; (*girl's*) trenza *f*.

pike¹ [paɪk] N (*Mil*) pica *f*, chuzo *m*.

pike² [paɪk] N, PL INVAR (*Fish*) lucio *m*.

pikeman ['paɪkmən] N, PL **pikemen** ['paɪkmən] piquero *m*.

piker‡ ['paɪkə'] N (*US*) (*mean person*) cicatero *m*; (*unimportant person*) persona *f* de poco fuste; (*coward*) cobarde *m*.

pikestaff ['paɪkstɑːf] N V **plain 1**.

pilaf(f) ['pɪlæf] N *plato oriental a base de arroz*.

pilaster [pɪ'læstə'] N pilastra *f*.

Pilate ['paɪlət] NM Pilatos.

pilau [pɪ'laʊ] N = **pilaff**.

pilchard ['pɪltʃəd] N sardina *f*.

pile¹ [paɪl] N (*Archit*) pilote *m*.

pile² [paɪl] **1** N (a) (*heap*) montón *m*, pila *f*, rimero *m*; **to make a ~ of things**, **to put things in a ~** amontonar cosas, juntar cosas en un montón.
(b) (*) fortuna *f*; **to make one's ~** hacer su agosto; **he made his ~ in oil** se hizo una fortuna en el petróleo; **~s of*** montones de*.
(c) (*of buildings*) mole *f*, masa *f* imponente, conjunto *m* grandioso; **the Escorial, that noble ~** El Escorial, aquel edificio tan imponente.
(d) (*Phys etc*) pila *f*; **atomic ~** pila *f* atómica.
2 VT amontonar, apilar, juntar en un montón; acumular; **a table ~d high with books** una mesa cargada de libros; **to ~ coal on the fire** echar carbón al fuego.
3 VI (a) amontonarse, apilarse; acumularse.
(b) **we all ~d into the car*** entramos todos en el coche.
◆ **pile in*** VI: **~ in!** ¡dentro todos, que nos vamos!
◆ **pile off*** VI (*of people*) salir en avalancha.
◆ **pile on** VT: **to ~ it on** exagerar; **he does rather ~ it on** es un exagerado; **to ~ on the agony** aumentar el dolor, añadir dolor sobre dolor; **to ~ on the pressure** ir aumentando la presión, (*fig*) presionar cada vez más fuerte.
◆ **pile out*** VI: **everybody ~d out** todos salieron en desorden.
◆ **pile up** **1** VT amontonar, apilar, juntar en un montón; acumular; **we ~d it all up high** lo amontonamos todo muy alto; **he went on piling up the evidence** fue acumulando los datos, fue amontonando las pruebas; **to ~ the fire up with coal** echar carbón al fuego.
2 VI (a) amontonarse, apilarse; acumularse; **the evidence is piling up** las pruebas van acumulándose.
(b) (*) **the car ~d up against the wall** el coche se estrelló contra el muro; **the ship ~d up on the rocks** el buque se estrelló contra las rocas.

pile³ [paɪl] N (*of carpet*) pelo *m*.

pile-driver ['paɪl,draɪvə'] N martinete *m*.

pile-dwelling ['paɪl,dwelɪŋ] N (*Hist*) vivienda *f* construida sobre pilotes.

piles [paɪlz] NPL (*Med*) almorranas *fpl*, hemorroides *fpl*.

pile-up* ['paɪlʌp] N (*Aut etc*) accidente *m* múltiple, colisión *f* (*or* choque *m*) en cadena; **there was a ~ at the corner** chocaron varios coches en la esquina, hubo un accidente múltiple en la esquina.

pilfer ['pɪlfə'] **1** VT *article* ratear, hurtar; (*by servant etc*) sisar; **the crate had been ~ed** algunos artículos habían sido robados del cajón; **they often ~ the trucks** con frecuencia roban cosas de los vagones.
2 VI ratear, robar cosas.

pilferage ['pɪlfərɪdʒ] N hurto *m*, robo *m*.

pilferer ['pɪlfərə'] N ratero *m*, -a *f*, ladronzuelo *m*, -a *f*.

pilfering ['pɪlfərɪŋ] N ratería *f*, hurto *m*.

pilgrim ['pɪlgrɪm] **1** N peregrino *m*, -a *f*, romero *m*, -a *f*.
2 ATTR: **the P~ Fathers** los padres peregrinos.

┌─ *PILGRIM FATHERS* ─┐

ⓘ Los *Pilgrim Fathers* fueron un grupo de puritanos que abandonaron Inglaterra en 1620 huyendo de las persecuciones religiosas y que, después de cruzar el Atlántico en el *Mayflower*, fundaron una colonia en Nueva Inglaterra (New Plymouth, Massachusetts), dando así comienzo a la colonización británica en Norteamérica. Se les considera como los fundadores de Estados Unidos y el éxito de su primera cosecha se conmemora cada año en el Día de Acción de Gracias (*Thanksgiving Day*).
⇨ *Ver también* | THANKSGIVING |

pilgrimage ['pɪlgrɪmɪdʒ] N peregrinación *f*, romería *f*; **to go on a ~**, **to make a ~** ir en peregrinación, ir en romería (*to* a).

pill [pɪl] N gragea *f*; píldora *f*; **the ~** (*contraceptive*) la píldora; **she's on the ~** toma la píldora; **it was a bitter ~ (to swallow)** fue una píldora amarga, fue un trago amargo; **to sugar (*or* sweeten) the ~** dorar la píldora.

pillage ['pɪlɪdʒ] **1** N pillaje *m*, saqueo *m*.
2 VT pillar, saquear.

pillar ['pɪlə'] N pilar *m*, columna *f*; (*fig*) sostén *m*, pilar *m*; **~ of salt** estatua *f* de sal; **the P~s of Hercules** las Columnas de Hércules; **to be a ~ of strength** ser firme como una roca, ser una columna de sostén; **to chase sb from ~ to post** acosar a uno, no dejar a uno a sol ni a sombra.

pillarbox ['pɪləbɒks] N (*Brit*) buzón *m*.

pillbox ['pɪlbɒks] N (*Med*) pastillero *m*, cajita *f* de píldoras; (*Mil*) fortín *m*.

pillion ['pɪljən] ⒈ N (*also* **~ seat**) asiento *m* de atrás, asiento *m* de pasajero; (*on horse*) grupera *f*.
⒉ ATTR: **~ passenger** pasajero *m*, -a *f* que va detrás.
⒊ ADV: **to ride ~** ir en el asiento de atrás.

pillock‡ ['pɪlək] N (*Brit*) gili* *mf*.

pillory ['pɪlərɪ] ⒈ N picota *f*.
⒉ VT (*fig*) poner en ridículo, satirizar; censurar duramente.

pillow ['pɪləʊ] ⒈ N almohada *f*.
⒉ VT apoyar sobre una almohada; apoyar, servir de almohada a; **she ~ed her head on my shoulder** apoyó la cabeza en mi hombro.

pillowcase ['pɪləʊkeɪs] N, ↓ **pillowslip** ['pɪləʊslɪp] N funda *f* de almohada.

pillow-talk ['pɪləʊˌtɔːk] N charla *f* de enamorados (en la cama).

pilot ['paɪlət] ⒈ N (a) (*Aer*) piloto *mf*, aviadora *f*; (*Naut*) práctico *m*, piloto *m*. (b) = **~ light**. (c) = **~ programme**.
⒉ ADJ piloto, experimental; **~ jet, ~ light** (*on stove*) mechero *m*, encendedor *m*; **~ light** (*Aut*) luz *f* de situación; **~ plant** planta *f* piloto; **~ program** (*US*), **~ programme** programa *m* piloto; **~ scheme** proyecto *m* experimental; **~ series** serie *f* piloto; **~ study** estudio *m* piloto.
⒊ VT pilotar; (*fig*) guiar, conducir; dirigir; **a plane ~ed by ...** un avión pilotado por ...; **he ~ed the negotiations through** dirigió las negociaciones, condujo las negociaciones a buen fin; **to ~ a bill through the House** encargarse de un proyecto de ley durante los debates parlamentarios, asegurar la aprobación de un proyecto de ley.

pilot boat ['paɪlətbəʊt] N bote *m* del práctico.

pilot house ['paɪləthaʊs] N, PL **pilot houses** ['paɪləthaʊzɪz] (*Naut*) timonera *f*.

pilot officer ['paɪlətˌɒfɪsəʳ] N oficial *m* piloto.

pimento [pɪ'mentəʊ] N pimiento *m*.

pimp [pɪmp] ⒈ N alcahuete *m*; coime *m*, chulo *m* de putas, cafiche *m* (*LAm*).
⒉ VI alcahuetear; ser coime, ser chulo de putas; **to ~ for sb** servir de alcahuete a uno.

pimpernel ['pɪmpənel] N muraje *mpl*, pimpinela *f*.

pimple ['pɪmpl] N grano *m*; **she came out in ~s** le salieron granos.

pimply ['pɪmplɪ] ADJ lleno de granos, cubierto de granos; granujiento; **~ youth** (*fig*) mocoso *m*, mozalbete *m*.

PIMS N ABBR *of* **personal information management system**.

PIN [pɪn] N (*Comput, Fin*) ABBR *of* **personal identification number**; **~ number** número *m* personal de identificación, NPI *m*.

pin [pɪn] ⒈ N (a) (*Sew etc*) alfiler *m*; (*Mech*: *bolt*) perno *m*, (*cotter*) chaveta *f*; (*of grenade*) arandela *f*; (*wooden*) clavija *f*; **~s and needles** hormiguillo *m*, hormigueo *m*; **like a new ~** como una patena; **for two ~s I'd knock his head off** por menos de nada le rompo la crisma; **you could have heard a ~ drop** se oía el vuelo de una mosca.
(b) (*Elec*) polo *m*.
(c) **~s*** (*legs*) piernas *fpl*.
⒉ ATTR: **two ~ plug** clavija *f* bipolar; **three ~ plug** clavija *f* de 3 polos.
⒊ VT (a) (*put pin in*) prender con alfiler, prender con alfileres; (*with bolt*) sujetar (con perno *etc*); **to ~ a medal to sb's uniform** prender una medalla al uniforme de uno; **to ~ sb's arms to his side** sujetar los brazos de uno; **to ~ sb against a wall** apretar a uno contra una pared; **the battalion was ~ned against the river** el batallón estaba copado junto al río, el batallón quedó inmovilizado junto al río.
(b) **to ~ one's hopes** (*or* **faith**) **on sb** cifrar sus esperanzas en uno.
(c) (*) **to ~ sth on sb** acusar (falsamente) a uno de algo; **you can't ~ it on me** no podéis lograr que yo cargue con la culpa, es imposible probar que lo hiciera; **they ~ned a number of robberies on him** le acusaron (falsamente) de haber participado en una serie de robos.

♦**pin back** VT (*lit*) doblar hacia atrás y sujetar con alfileres; **now ~ your ears back** escuchadme muy atentos; **to ~ sb's ears back** (*fig*: *startle*) meter a uno el susto en el cuerpo*; (*US**: *scold*) reñir a uno, regañar a uno (*US**: *beat up*) darle una zurra a uno*.

♦**pin down** VT (*fig*) **to ~ sb down** obligar a uno a que concrete; **we were ~ned down by the bombardment** el bombardeo nos inmovilizó; **it's impossible to ~ him down** es imposible hacerle concretar; **you can't ~ him down to a date** es imposible lograr que nos diga una fecha concreta; **there's something odd I can't quite ~ down** hay algo raro que no puedo precisar; **the idea is rather hard to ~ down** es un concepto de difícil concreción.

♦**pin on** VT prender.

♦**pin together** VT: **to ~ papers together** prender unos papeles con una grapa, grapar papeles.

♦**pin up** VT *clothing* recoger con alfileres (*or* imperdible); *hair* recoger con horquilla; **to ~ a notice up** fijar un anuncio con chinches; poner un anuncio, pegar un anuncio.

pina colada ['piːnəkə'lɑːdə] N piña *f* colada.

pinafore ['pɪnəfɔːʳ] N delantal *m* (de niña); **~ dress** mandil *m*.

pinball ['pɪnbɔːl] N (*also* **~ machine**) millón *m*, flíper *m*.

pince-nez ['pɛːnsneɪ] NPL quevedos *mpl*.

pincer ['pɪnsəʳ] ⒈ N (a) (*Zool*) pinza *f*. (b) (*Tech*) **~s** tenazas *fpl*, pinzas *fpl*; **a pair of ~s** unas tenazas.
⒉ ATTR: **~ movement** (*Mil*) movimiento *m* de pinza.

pinch [pɪntʃ] ⒈ N (a) (*with fingers*) pellizco *m*; **to give sb a ~ on the arm** pellizcar el brazo a uno.
(b) (*small quantity*) pizca *f*; pulgarada *f*; **a ~ of salt** una pizca de sal; **to take sth with a ~ of salt** tomar algo con un grano de sal; **a ~ of snuff** un polvo de rapé.
(c) (*fig*) apuro *m*; **to feel the ~** (empezar a) pasar apuros; **to feel the ~ of hunger** empezar a tener hambre; **to feel the ~ of poverty** saber lo que significa ser pobre; **at a ~** si es realmente necesario, en caso de necesidad.
⒉ VT (a) (*with fingers*) pellizcar, dar un pellizcón a; (*squeeze, crush*) apretar, estrujar, aplastar; (*of shoe*) apretar; **to ~ one's finger in the door** pillarse el dedo en la puerta.
(b) (*: *steal*) birlar*, guindar‡, pisar*; **I had my pen ~ed** me guindaron la pluma; **he ~ed that idea from Shaw** esa idea la robó de Shaw; **A ~ed B's girl** A le pisó la novia a B.
(c) (‡: *arrest etc*) coger (*Sp*), pescar*; **he got ~ed for a parking offence** le pescaron en una infracción de aparcamiento.
⒊ VI (a) (*shoe*) apretar; **to know where the shoe ~es** (*fig*) saber dónde aprieta el zapato.
(b) (*economize*) economizar; privarse de lo necesario; **we had to ~ and scrape** tuvimos que hacer muchas economías; **they ~ed and scraped to send her to college** se privaron de muchas cosas a fin de poder enviarla a la universidad.

♦**pinch back, pinch off** VT: **to ~ off a bud** quitar un brote con los dedos, separar un brote con la uña.

pinchbeck ['pɪntʃbek] ⒈ N similor *m*.
⒉ ATTR de similor; (*fig*) falso.

pinched ['pɪntʃt] ADJ (a) (*drawn*) **to look ~** tener la cara pálida; **to look ~ with cold** estar aterido, estar chupado. (b) **to be ~ for money** andar escaso de dinero; **we're very ~ for space** tenemos muy poco espacio.

pinch-hit ['pɪntʃhɪt] VI (*US*) batear de suplente; (*fig*) sustituir a otro en un apuro.

pinchpenny ['pɪntʃpenɪ] ADJ tacaño.

pincushion ['pɪnˌkʊʃən] N acerico *m*, almohadilla *f*.

Pindar ['pɪndəʳ] NM Píndaro.

Pindaric [pɪn'dærɪk] ADJ pindárico.

pine¹ [paɪn] N pino *m*.

pine² [paɪn] VI (*also* **to ~ away**) languidecer, consumirse; **to ~ for** suspirar por, perecer por, consumirse pensando en.

pineal ['pɪnɪəl] ADJ: **~ body, ~ gland** glándula *f* pineal.

pineapple ['paɪnˌæpl] N piña *f* (de América), ananás *m*.

pinecone ['paɪnkəʊn] N piña *f*.

pine-grove ['paɪngrəʊv] N pinar *m*.

pine-kernel ['paɪnˌkɜːnl] N piñón *m*.

pine-marten ['paɪnˌmɑːtɪn] N marta *f*.

pine-needle ['paɪnˌniːdl] N aguja *f* de pino.

pine-nut ['paɪnˌnʌt] N piña *f*, piñón *m*.

pine-tree ['paɪntriː] N pino *m*.

pinewood ['paɪnwʊd] N pinar *m*.

ping [pɪŋ] ⒈ N (*of bullet, through air*) silbido *m*, (*on striking*) sonido *m* metálico; (*of bell*) tintín *m*.
⒉ VI silbar (como una bala); hacer un sonido metálico (como una bala); tintinear, hacer tintín.

ping-pong ['pɪŋpɒŋ] ® ⒈ N ping-pong *m*, pimpón *m*.
⒉ ATTR: **~ ball** pelota *f* de ping-pong.

pinhead ['pɪnhed] N (*lit*) cabeza *f* de alfiler; (*) mentecato *m*, cabeza de chorlito*.

pinhole ['pɪnhəʊl] N agujero *m* de alfiler; **~ camera** cámara *f* de agujero de alfiler.

pinion¹ ['pɪnjən] ⒈ N (*poet*) ala *f*.
⒉ VT *bird* cortar las alas a; *person* atar los brazos a; **he was ~ed against the wall** estaba contra la pared sin poderse mover, le tuvieron apretado contra la pared.

pinion² ['pɪnjən] N (*Mech*) piñón *m*.

pink¹ [pɪŋk] ⒈ N (a) (*Bot*) clavel *m*, clavellina *f*.
(b) (*colour*) color *m* de rosa.
(c) **hunting ~** levitín *m* rojo de caza.
(d) (*Pol*) rojillo *m*, -a *f*.
(e) (*fig*) **to be in the ~** vender salud, rebosar salud; estar como un reloj; **to be in the ~ of condition** estar en perfecto estado.
⒉ ADJ (*colour*) rosado, color de rosa; (*Pol*) rojillo; **~ gin** ginebra *f* con

angostura; **~ slip** (US) notificación f de despido; **strike me ~!ː** ¡caray!*; **to be tickled ~ about sth*** (pleased) estar encantado con algo, (joke) reírse mucho con algo.

pink² [pɪŋk] VT (Sew) ondear, picar; **to ~ sb with a sword** herir a uno levemente con un florete.

pink³ [pɪŋk] VI (Brit Aut) picar.

pinkie*, pinky ['pɪŋkɪ] N meñique m, dedo m chico.

pinking ['pɪŋkɪŋ] N (Brit: Aut) piqueteo m.

pinking shears ['pɪŋkɪŋˌʃiːəz] NPL tijeras fpl dentadas.

pinkish ['pɪŋkɪʃ] ADJ rosáceo; (Pol) rojillo.

pinko* ['pɪŋkəʊ] (Pol pej) [1] ADJ rojillo.
[2] N rojillo m, -a f.

pin-money ['pɪnˌmʌnɪ] N alfileres mpl, dinero m para gastos menores.

pinnace ['pɪnɪs] N pinaza f.

pinnacle ['pɪnəkl] N (Archit) pináculo m, remate m; chapitel m; (of rock etc) punta f; (of mountain) pico m, cumbre f; (fig) cumbre f, cúspide f; **the ~ of fame** la cumbre de la fama.

pinny* ['pɪnɪ] N = **pinafore**.

Pinocchio [pɪ'nɒkɪəʊ] NM Pinocho.

pinpoint ['pɪnpɔɪnt] [1] N punta f de alfiler; (fig) punto m muy pequeño.
[2] VT indicar con toda precisión; concretar; poner el dedo en.

pinprick ['pɪnprɪk] N alfilerazo m; pinchazo m; (fig) alfilerazo m, molestia f pequeña.

pinstripe ['pɪnstraɪp] [1] ADJ a rayas, rayado; **~ suit** traje m a rayas.
[2] N traje m (etc) a rayas.

pint [paɪnt] [1] N (a) pinta f (= 0,57 litros, US = 0,47 litros); ver también IMPERIAL SYSTEM.
(b) (Brit: loosely) vaso m grande de cerveza, caña f de cerveza; **we had a ~ together** tomamos una caña; **he likes his ~** le gusta la cerveza, es algo aficionado a la cerveza; **we had a few ~s** bebimos unas cuantas; ver también BEER.
[2] ATTR: **~-size(d)*** diminuto, pequeñito.

pinta* ['paɪntə] N pinta f (de leche).

pin-table ['pɪnteɪbl] N billar m romano, billar m automático.

pintail ['pɪnteɪl] N ánade m rabudo.

pinto bean ['pɪntəʊbiːn] N judía f pinta, alubia f pinta.

pin-up ['pɪnʌp] N pin-up mf.

pinwheel ['pɪnˌwiːl] N (esp US) rueda f catalina.

pioneer [ˌpaɪə'nɪər] [1] N pionero m, -a f; (explorer) explorador m, -ora f; (early settler) colonizador m, -ora f; (Mil) zapador m; (of scheme, in study) iniciador m, -ora f; promotor m, -ora f; **he was one of the ~s** él era de los pioneros; **he was a ~ in the study of bats** fue uno de los primeros en estudiar los murciélagos.
[2] ATTR: **~ corps** cuerpo m de zapadores; **~ work** trabajo m de pioneros.
[3] VT settlement etc preparar el terreno para, hacer los preparativos para; scheme, study iniciar, promover; echar los cimientos de, sentar las bases de.
[4] VI explorar, abrir nuevos caminos.

pioneering [ˌpaɪə'nɪərɪŋ] ADJ work, research, study pionero.

pious ['paɪəs] ADJ piadoso, devoto; **~ hopes** esperanzas fpl piadosas.

piously ['paɪəslɪ] ADV piadosamente, devotamente.

pip¹ [pɪp] N (Med) pepita f; **it gives me the ~*** me fastidia terriblemente; **it's enough to give you the ~*** es para volverse loco; **he's got the ~*** está de muy mal humor.

pip² [pɪp] N (a) (Bot) pepita f, pepa f (LAm); (on card, dice) punto m; (Brit: on uniform) estrella f.
(b) (sound) bip m, pitido m; **the 6 ~s** (Rad) los 6 pitidos; **wait till you hear the ~** espera a que se oiga el pitido.

pip³* [pɪp] [1] VT (wound) herir (levemente); (defeat) vencer; **A ~ped B at the post** A le ganó a B en el último momento; **he was ~ped at the post by another candidate** por muy escaso margen dieron el puesto a otro; **I ~ped French again** volvieron a escabecharme en francés*.
[2] VI (*) (lose) perder; (fail) fracasar; (in exam) catearse*, cargarse*.

pipe [paɪp] [1] N (a) (tube) tubo m, caño m, conducto m; (also **~s**) tubería f, cañería f; (of a hose etc) manga f; (of wine) pipa f.
(b) (Mus: of organ) cañón m, tubo m; (instrument) caramillo m, (boatswain's) pito m; **~s** (Scot) gaita f, (Pan's) flauta f.
(c) (smoker's) pipa f; **~ of peace** pipa f de la paz; **to fill one's ~** cargar la pipa; **put that in your ~ and smoke it!*** ¡chúpate eso!*
[2] VT (a) water etc conducir en cañerías; **~d music** hilo m musical, música f ambiental; **water is ~d to the farm** se conduce el agua a la granja por unas cañerías; **the oil is ~d across the desert** el petróleo es conducido a través del desierto en un oleoducto.
(b) (Mus) tune tocar; **to ~ the admiral aboard** tocar el pito al subir el almirante a bordo.
(c) (Sew) adornar con rib etc.
[3] VI (Mus) tocar el caramillo, tocar la flauta; tocar la gaita; (bird) trinar.

◆ **pipe down*** VI callarse.

◆ **pipe up*** VI decir (inesperadamente), echar a hablar (inesperadamente).

pipe bomb ['paɪpbɒm] N bomba de mano casera en forma de tubo.

pipeclay ['paɪpkleɪ] [1] N albero m.
[2] VT blanquear con albero.

pipe-cleaner ['paɪpˌkliːnər] N limpiapipas m, limpiador m de pipa.

pipe-dream ['paɪpdriːm] N esperanza f imposible, sueño m imposible, castillos mpl en el aire.

pipefitter ['paɪpˌfɪtər] N fontanero m.

pipeful ['paɪpfʊl] N pipa f; **a ~ of tobacco** una pipa de tabaco.

pipeline ['paɪplaɪn] N tubería f, cañería f; tubería f de distribución; (for oil) oleoducto m; (for gas) gasoducto m; **it is in the ~** (fig) está en trámite, se está tramitando.

piper ['paɪpər] N flautista mf; (Scot) gaitero m; **to pay the ~** cargar con los gastos; **he who pays the ~ calls the tune** el que paga tiene derecho a escoger.

pipe-rack ['paɪpræk] N soporte m para pipas.

pipe-smoker ['paɪpˌsməʊkər] N fumador m de pipa, pipero m.

pipe-tobacco ['paɪptəˌbækəʊ] N tabaco m de pipa.

pipette [pɪ'pet] N pipeta f.

pipework ['paɪpwɜːk] N tuberías fpl.

piping ['paɪpɪŋ] [1] N (a) (in house etc) tubería f, cañería f.
(b) (Mus) sonido m del caramillo, música f de flauta; (of bird) trinar m, trinos mpl.
(c) (Sew) ribete m, cordoncillo m.
[2] ADJ voice agudo.
[3] ADV: **~ hot** bien caliente, que casi quema.

pipistrelle [ˌpɪpɪ'strel] N pipistrelo m.

pipit ['pɪpɪt] N bisbita f, pitpit m.

pipkin ['pɪpkɪn] N ollita f de barro.

pippin ['pɪpɪn] N camuesa f, manzana f reineta.

pipsqueak ['pɪpskwiːk] N persona f insignificante, fantoche m.

piquancy ['piːkənsɪ] N picante m, lo picante.

piquant ['piːkənt] ADJ (a) (Culin) picante. (b) (fig) picante; attitude, remark agudo, provocativo; situation picante.

piquantly ['piːkəntlɪ] ADV de modo picante.

pique [piːk] [1] N pique m, resentimiento m; **to be in a ~** estar resentido; **to do sth in a fit of ~, to do sth out of ~** hacer algo motivado por el rencor.
[2] VT picar, herir; **to be ~d at** ofenderse por, estar resentido por.
[3] VR: **to ~ o.s. on sth** preciarse de algo, enorgullecerse de algo.

piquet [pɪ'ket] N piquet m.

piracy ['paɪərəsɪ] N piratería f; (of book) publicación f pirata.

piranha [pɪ'rɑːnjə] N piraña f.

pirate ['paɪərɪt] [1] N pirata m.
[2] ADJ: **~ broadcasting** radiodifusión f no autorizada; **~ radio** emisora f pirata.
[3] VT book, tape piratear.

pirated ['paɪərɪtɪd] ADJ: **~ edition** edición f pirata.

piratical [paɪ'rætɪkəl] ADJ pirático.

pirouette [ˌpɪrʊ'et] [1] N pirueta f.
[2] VI piruetear.

Piscean ['paɪsɪən] N: **to be a ~** ser Piscis.

Pisces ['paɪsiːz] N (Zodiac) Piscis m.

piss:ː [pɪs] [1] N orina f, meados:ː mpl; **~ artist** privota:ː mf; **to have a ~ mear:ː**; **to take the ~ out of sb** cachondearse de uno*.
[2] VT mear:ː.
[3] VI mear:ː; **it's ~ing with rain** está lloviendo a chuzos.

◆ **piss about:ː** VI hacer el oso.

◆ **piss down:ː** VI: **it's fair ~ing down** llueve a torrentes.

◆ **piss off:ː** [1] VT (annoy) irritar; sacar de quicio; (depress) desalentar; (disappoint) decepcionar; **I feel thoroughly ~ed off about it** estoy hasta la coronilla con esto*; **he's feeling ~ed off** está de mala leche:ː.
[2] VI largarse*; **~ off!** ¡vete al cuerno!*

pissed:ː [pɪst] ADJ: **to be ~** (Brit) estar ajumado*, (US) estar de mala leche:ː.

piss-take:ː ['pɪsteɪk] N broma f, tomadura f de pelo*; **come on it was only a ~!** ¡venga ya era sólo de pitorreo!*; **the movie's a ~ of other cop movies** la película se pitorrea de otras películas policiacas.

piss-up:ː ['pɪsʌp] N juerga f de borrachera*.

pistachio [pɪs'tɑːʃɪəʊ] N pistacho m.

piste [piːst] N (Ski) pista f.

pistil ['pɪstɪl] N pistilo m.

pistol ['pɪstl] [1] N pistola f, revólver m.
[2] ATTR: **at ~ point** a punta de pistola.

pistol-shot ['pɪstlˌʃɒt] N pistoletazo m; **to be within ~** estar a tiro de pistola.

pistol-whip ['pɪstlwɪp] VT golpear con una pistola.

piston ['pɪstən] [1] N pistón m, émbolo m; (Mus) pistón m, llave f.
[2] ATTR: **~ engine** motor m de pistón.

piston-engined ['pɪstənˌendʒɪnd] ADJ con motor de pistón.

piston-ring ['pɪstən,rɪŋ] N aro *m* de pistón, segmento *m* de pistón.
piston-rod ['pɪstən,rɒd] N vástago *m* de émbolo.
piston-stroke ['pɪstən,strəʊk] N carrera *f* del émbolo.
pit¹ [pɪt] ①① N (a) (*hole in ground*) hoyo *m*, hoya *f*, foso *m*; (*small depression in surface*) hoyo *m*; (*as trap*) trampa *f*; (*at garage*) foso *m* de inspección, foso *m* de reparación; (*in motor-racing*) box *m*; (*of stomach*) boca *f*; (*Min*) mina *f*, (*quarry*) cantera *f*; (*fig*) abismo *m*; **the ~** (*fig: hell*) el infierno; **the ~ of hell** lo más profundo del infierno.
(b) (*Brit Theat*) platea *f*; (*for cockfighting*) cancha *f*, reñidero *m*; (*US St Ex*) parquet *m* de la Bolsa; **the cotton ~** la bolsa del algodón.
(c) (*US**) **the ~s** (*gloom*) estado *m* de depresión; (*low point*) punto *m* más bajo; **this game is the ~s** este partido es una basura; **he's the ~s** es la reoca*; **it really sent her to the ~s** la mandó a lo último.
② VT (a) *surface* hacer hoyos en, marcar con hoyos; (*with smallpox*) marcar con viruelas; **the surface was ~ted with ...** en la superficie había hoyos formados por ...
(b) **to ~ A against B** oponer A a B; **we ~ted all our strength against him** nos opusimos a él con todas nuestras fuerzas; **we are ~ting our wits against the experts** nos enfrentamos a los expertos en un certamen de inteligencia; **he found himself ~ted against the champion** encontró que tenía que habérselas con el campeón.
③ VR: **to ~ o.s. against an opponent** medirse con un contrario.
pit² [pɪt] (*US*) ①① N (*Bot*) hueso *m*.
② VT deshuesar, quitar el hueso a.
pitapat ['pɪtə'pæt] ADV: **my heart went ~** mi corazón latía rápidamente, mi corazón palpitaba.
pitch¹ [pɪtʃ] ①① N pez *f*, brea *f*.
② VT embrear.
pitch² [pɪtʃ] ①① N (a) (*throw*) tiro *m*, lanzamiento *m*; echada *f*; **it came full ~ into my hands** llegó a mis manos sin tocar el suelo; **it fell full ~ into the garden** cayó de plano en el jardín.
(b) (*Naut*) cabezada *f*.
(c) (*Brit Sport*) campo *m*, terreno *m*, cancha *f* (*LAm*).
(d) (*place in market etc*) puesto *m*; (*fig*) terreno *m*; **this is my usual ~** éste es mi puesto habitual; **keep off our ~!** ¡cuidado con no meteros en lo nuestro!
(e) (*slope*) grado *m* de inclinación; (*of roof*) pendiente *f*.
(f) (*height, degree*) punto *m*, extremo *m*; (*height*) elevación *f*; (*of propeller etc*) paso *m*; **to such a ~ that ...** a tal punto que ...; **excitement is at a high ~** la emoción está al rojo vivo; **matters reached such a ~ that ...** las cosas llegaron a tal extremo que ...
(g) (*Mus*) tono *m*; diapasón *m*; **to adjust the ~ of an instrument** ajustar el tono de un instrumento; **to have perfect ~** tener oído perfecto, poder dar el tono exacto; **to queer sb's ~** chafar la guitarra a uno; frustrar el intento de uno.
(h) (*: *spiel*) rollo* *m*, explicaciones *fpl*.
(i) (*) **to make a ~ for sth** tratar de asegurarse algo; **he made a ~ for the women's vote** procuró acaparar los votos de las mujeres; **he made a ~ for her** (*US*) le dio un tiento.
② VT (a) (*throw*) arrojar, lanzar, tirar; (*Baseball etc*) lanzar.
(b) (*Mus*) *note* dar, producir, entonar; (*play*) tocar, (*sing*) cantar; *instrument* graduar el tono de; **she can't ~ a note properly** es incapaz de producir una nota buena; **I'll ~ you a note** os doy la nota para empezar; **you're ~ing it too high for me** lo tocas demasiado alto para mí; **to ~ one's aspirations too high** picar muy alto; **it is ~ed in rather high-flown terms** está redactado en términos algo retóricos; **it must be ~ed at the right level for the audience** el tono ha de ajustarse al público.
(c) *tent* armar.
(d) (*) **to ~ it strong** exagerar, no perdonar detalle; **to ~ sb a story** contar a uno un cuento (*inverosímil*); **he ~ed me this hard-luck story** me contó esta historia tan trágica.
③ VI (a) (*fall*) caer, caerse; **the ball ~ed in front of him** la pelota cayó delante de él, la pelota vino a parar a sus pies; **after ~ing it bounced high** después de tocar el suelo rebotó muy alto; **the aircraft ~ed into the sea** el avión se precipitó en el mar.
(b) (*Naut*) cabecear.
◆ **pitch forward** VI caer de bruces, caer de cabeza.
◆ **pitch in*** VI (a) (*start*) empezar, (*esp*) empezar a comer; **~ in!** ¡vamos!; ¡a ello!; ¡manos a la obra! (b) (*cooperate*) cooperar; (*contribute*) contribuir; **so we all ~ed in together** así que todos nos pusimos a trabajar (*etc*) juntos.
◆ **pitch into*** VT (a) **to ~ into the work** emprender enérgicamente el trabajo, ponerse enérgicamente a trabajar; **they ~ed into the food** atacaron las viandas.
(b) (*attack*) atacar; (*verbally*) arremeter contra; (*scold*) poner como un trapo*.
◆ **pitch off** ① VT quitar de encima, sacudir; **he was ~ed off his horse** fue desarzonado, cayó del caballo.
② VI caer; **he ~ed off the roof** cayó del techo.
◆ **pitch out** VT *object* tirar; *person* echar, expulsar, poner de patitas en la calle.

◆ **pitch over** ① VT tirar; **~ it over!** ¡tíramelo!
② VI (*vehicle etc*) volcarse.
◆ **pitch (up)on** VT (a) (*choose*) elegir, escoger.
(b) (*find*) encontrar, dar con.
pitch-and-putt [,pɪtʃən'pʌt] N minigolf *m*.
pitch-and-toss ['pɪtʃən'tɒs] N (juego *m* de) cara *f* o cruz, chapas *fpl*.
pitch-black ['pɪtʃ'blæk] ADJ negro como boca de lobo.
pitchblende ['pɪtʃblend] N pec(h)blenda *f*.
pitch-dark ['pɪtʃ'dɑːk] ADJ negro como boca de lobo.
pitched [pɪtʃt] ADJ: **~ battle** batalla *f* campal.
pitcher¹ ['pɪtʃəʳ] N (*jug*) cántaro *m*, jarro *m*.
pitcher² ['pɪtʃəʳ] N (*Baseball*) lanzador *m*; *ver también* BASEBALL .
pitchfork ['pɪtʃfɔːk] ① N horca *f*, bielda *f*.
② VT (*fig*) **to ~ sb into a job** imponer inesperadamente a uno una tarea, hacer que uno se encargue de algo de buena o mala gana; **I was ~ed into it** tuve que aceptarlo a la fuerza, me metieron en esto a la fuerza.
pitchpine ['pɪtʃpaɪn] N pino *m* de tea.
pitch pipe ['pɪtʃpaɪp] N (*Mus*) diapasón *m*.
piteous ['pɪtɪəs] ADJ lastimero, lastimoso, patético.
piteously ['pɪtɪəslɪ] ADV lastimosamente.
pitfall ['pɪtfɔːl] N escollo *m*, peligro *m*; trampa *f*; **it's a ~ for the unwary** es una trampa para los imprudentes; **'P~s of English'** 'Escollos *mpl* del inglés'; **there are many ~s ahead** hay muchos peligros por delante.
pith [pɪθ] N (*Bot*) médula *f*; (*fig*) meollo *m*, médula *f*, jugo *m*, esencia *f*.
pithead ['pɪthed] N bocamina *f*.
pithiness ['pɪθɪnɪs] N jugosidad *f*; lo sentencioso, lo expresivo; lo sucinto, lo lacónico, concisión *f*.
pithy ['pɪθɪ] ADJ (*full of sense*) jugoso; sentencioso, expresivo; (*terse*) sucinto, lacónico, conciso; **~ saying** dicho *m* sentencioso.
pitiable ['pɪtɪəbl] ADJ lastimoso, digno de compasión; **in a ~ state** en un estado que da lástima; **it was most ~ to see** daba lástima verlo.
pitiably ['pɪtɪəblɪ] ADV *low, small, weak* lamentablemente.
pitiful ['pɪtɪfʊl] ADJ (a) (*moving to pity*) lastimero, lastimoso; conmovedor. (b) (*contemptible*) lamentable, miserable, despreciable; **a ~ display** una exhibición lamentable; **it was just ~** daba lástima.
pitifully ['pɪtɪfəlɪ] ADV (a) (*pathetically*) lastimosamente; de modo conmovedor; **she was crying most ~** lloraba que daba lástima. (b) (*contemptibly*) lamentablemente; **a ~ bad play** una comedia tan mala que da lástima.
pitiless ['pɪtɪlɪs] ADJ despiadado, implacable, inmisericorde.
pitilessly ['pɪtɪlɪslɪ] ADV despiadadamente, implacablemente.
pitman ['pɪtmən] N, PL **pitmen** ['pɪtmən] minero *m*.
piton ['piːtɒn] N pitón *m*, clavija *f* de escala.
pit pony ['pɪt,pəʊnɪ] N poney usado antiguamente en las minas.
pit-prop ['pɪtprɒp] N puntal *m*, peón *m*.
pit-stop ['pɪtstɒp] N (*motor racing*) entrada *f* a boxes; (*: *on journey*) parada *f* en ruta.
pitta ['pɪtə] N (*also* **~ bread**) pan *m* árabe.
pittance ['pɪtəns] N miseria *f*, renta *f* miserable; **a mere ~!** ¡una miseria!; **to live on a ~** vivir de una renta miserable.
pitted ['pɪtɪd] ADJ (a) *skin* picado (de viruelas), cacarañado; *surface* picado. (b) (*US*) *fruit* deshuesado, sin hueso.
pitter-patter ['pɪtə'pætəʳ] N *etc* = **patter²**.
pituitary [pɪ'tjuːɪtərɪ] ① ADJ pituitario; **~ gland** = 2.
② N glándula *f* pituitaria.
pit worker ['pɪt,wɜːkəʳ] N minero *m*.
pity ['pɪtɪ] ① N (a) (*compassion*) compasión *f*, piedad *f*; **for ~'s sake!** ¡por piedad!; (*less seriously*) ¡por Dios!, ¡por el amor de Dios!; **I did it out of ~ for him** se lo hice por compasión; **to feel no ~ for sb** no sentir compasión por uno; **to move sb to ~** mover a uno a compasión, dar lástima a uno; **to take ~ on sb** tener piedad de uno, apiadarse de uno, compadecerse de uno.
(b) (*misfortune*) lástima *f*; **what a ~!** ¡qué lástima!, ¡qué pena!; **more's the ~!** ¡desgraciadamente!; **it is a ~ that ...** es una lástima que + *subj*, es una pena que + *subj*; **the ~ of it was that ...** lo lamentable fue que ..., lo peor del caso fue que ...; **it is a thousand pities that ...** es muy de lamentar que + *subj*.
② VT compadecer(se de), tener lástima a; apiadarse de.
pitying ['pɪtɪɪŋ] ADJ *glance etc* de lástima, lleno de compasión, compasivo.
pityingly ['pɪtɪɪŋlɪ] ADV con lástima, compasivamente.
Pius ['paɪəs] NM Pío.
pivot ['pɪvət] ① N pivote *m*, gorrón *m*; (*fig*) eje *m*, punto *m* central.
② VT montar sobre un pivote; **he ~ed it on his hand** lo hizo girar sobre la mano, lo mantuvo en equilibrio sobre la mano.
③ VI girar (*on* sobre); **to ~ on** (*fig*) depender de.
pivotal ['pɪvətl] ADJ (*fig*) central, fundamental.
pix* [pɪks] = **pics.**
pixel ['pɪksel] N pixel *m*, punto *m*.
pixie, pixy ['pɪksɪ] N duendecito *m*.

pixie hood ['pɪksɪhʊd] N caperucita f.

pizza ['piːtsə] N pizza f.

piz(z)azz* [pə'zæz] N energía f, dinamismo m.

pizzeria [ˌpiːtsə'rɪə] N pizzería f.

pizzicato [ˌpɪtsɪ'kɑːtəʊ] ADJ, ADV pizzicato.

pkt ABBR *of* **packet** paquete m.

Pl. ABBR *of* **Place** Plaza f.

PL a/c ABBR *of* **profit and loss account** cuenta f de pérdidas y ganancias.

placard ['plækɑːd] ① N (*on wall etc*) cartel m; (*sign, announcement*) letrero m; (*carried in procession etc*) pancarta f.

② VT: **the wall is ~ed all over** la pared está llena de carteles; **the town is ~ed with slogans** en todas partes de la ciudad se ven carteles con slogans.

placate [plə'keɪt] VT aplacar, apaciguar.

placatory [plə'keɪtərɪ] ADJ *act, gesture, smile* apaciguador.

place [pleɪs] ① N (a) (*gen*) sitio m, lugar m; **a ~ in the sun** (*fig*) una posición envidiable; **this is the ~** éste es el lugar, aquí es; **we came to a ~ where …** llegamos a un sitio donde …; **any ~ will do** cualquier lugar será conveniente, donde quiera sirve; **I don't see it any ~** (*US*) no lo veo en ninguna parte; **it must be some ~ else** (*US*) estará en otra parte; **it's a pretty low sort of ~** no es un lugar muy decente; **people in high ~s** los que ocupan puestos relevantes; **this is no ~ for you** éste no es sitio conveniente para ti; **from ~ to ~** de lugar en lugar; de un lugar para otro; **in another ~** en otra parte, (*Brit Parl*) en la otra cámara; **in high ~s** allá arriba, en las altas esferas, en el gobierno (*etc*); **when the new law is in ~** cuando la nueva ley entre en vigor; **the furniture was all over the ~** los muebles estaban por todas partes; **we're all over the ~** vivimos en la mayor confusión; **your work is all over the ~** haces tu trabajo de cualquier modo; **it all began to fall into ~** todo empezó a tener sentido; todo empezó a parecer lógico; **to find one's ~ in a book** encontrar la página; **to lose one's ~** no encontrar el lugar, (*in reading*) no encontrar la página; perder el hilo; **to mark one's ~ in a book** registrar un libro; **to laugh at the right ~** reírse en el momento oportuno; **to go ~s** (*travel*) viajar, visitar muchos países (*etc*); **we like to go ~s at weekends** durante los fines de semana nos gusta salir de excursión; **he's going ~s** es un ambicioso; llegará lejos; es un hombre de empuje; **we're going ~s at last** por fin empezamos a hacer progresos; **to run in ~** (*US*) correr en parada.

(b) (*specific*) sitio m, local m; **~ of amusement** lugar m de diversión; **~ of business** oficina f, (*shop*) comercio m; **~ of employment, ~ of work** lugar m de trabajo; **~ of refuge** refugio m, asilo m; **~ of residence** residencia f, domicilio m; **~ of worship** templo m, edificio m de culto.

(c) (*town etc*) lugar m; ciudad f (*etc*); **fortified ~** plaza f, fortaleza f; **find a native of the ~** busca un natural de aquí, busca a uno que sea realmente de aquí; **it's a small ~** es un pueblo pequeño; **it's just a small country ~** no es más que un pequeño pueblo rural.

(d) (*house*) casa f; **his ~ in the country** su casa de campo; **they have a new ~ now** tienen una nueva casa ya; **it's a vast great ~** es una casa inmensa; **we were at Peter's ~** estuvimos en casa de Pedro, estuvimos donde Pedro*; **come to our ~** ven (a visitarnos) a casa; **my ~ or yours?** ¿en mi cama o en la tuya?

(e) (*in street names*) plaza f.

(f) (*~ in relation to owner etc*) sitio m, lugar m, puesto m; **does this have a ~?** ¿tiene esto un sitio determinado?; **to be in ~** estar en su lugar; **to put sth back in its ~** volver algo a su sitio; **to hold sth in ~** sujetar algo en su lugar; **in ~ of** en lugar de, en vez de; **if I were in your ~** yo en tu lugar, yo que tú; **to be out of ~** estar fuera de lugar; desentonar; estar fuera de serie; haberse equivocado de sitio; **that remark was quite out of ~** esa observación estaba fuera de propósito, no cabía tal observación; **it looks out of ~ here** aquí no está bien, aquí parece que está fuera de (su) lugar; **I feel rather out of ~ here** aquí me siento algo desplazado, me siento como que estoy de más aquí; **to change ~s** cambiar de sitio; **to change ~s with sb** trocarse con uno; **to give ~ to** ceder el paso a; **to take ~** tener lugar, verificarse; (*meeting etc*) celebrarse; **the marriage will not now take ~** ahora la boda no se celebrará, ahora no habrá boda; **Z has taken the ~ of A** Z ha sustituido a A; **nobody could ever take his ~** nadie sería capaz de sustituirle; **he managed to keep his ~ in the team** logró conservar su puesto en el equipo.

(g) (*seat*) plaza f, asiento m; (*at table*) cubierto m; **a theatre with 2000 ~s** un teatro de 2000 asientos, un teatro que tiene un aforo de 2000; **are there any ~s left?** ¿quedan plazas?; **is this ~ taken?** ¿está ocupado este asiento?; **to lay an extra ~ for sb** poner otro cubierto para uno.

(h) (*post*) puesto m, empleo m; colocación f; **~s for 500 workers** 500 puestos mpl de trabajo; **school ~** puesto m escolar; **it is not my ~ to +** *infin* no me cumple a mí + *infin*; **he found a ~ for his nephew in the firm** le dio un puesto en la compañía a su sobrino; **to seek a ~ in publishing** buscarse una colocación en una casa

editorial.

(i) (*in series, as rank etc*) lugar m, puesto m; (*in exam*) calificación f; (*rank*) posición f, rango m; **in the first ~** en primer lugar; **in the second ~** en segundo lugar; **in the next ~** luego, después; **to three ~s of decimals** en milésimas; **to work sth out to three ~s of decimals** calcular algo hasta las milésimas; **P won, with Q in second ~** ganó P, con Q en segunda posición; **to attain a high ~** llegar muy alto, alcanzar un rango alto; **to back a horse for a ~** apostar algo a un caballo para colocado; **to give up one's ~** (*in a queue*) ceder la vez, ceder su turno; **to keep one's ~** mantenerse en la misma posición, lograr seguir como antes; **to know one's ~** ser respetuoso, guardar las distancias; **to put sb in his ~** bajar los humos a uno; **if he gets fresh put him in his ~** si se pone fresco vuélvele a su sitio; **that properly put him in his ~** eso sí le hizo sentirse humilde; **A took (over) B's ~** A ocupó el lugar de B.

② VT (a) (*gen*) poner, colocar; fijar; situar, emplazar; **~ it on the table** ponlo en la mesa; **it is ~d rather high up** está en una posición más bien alta, se ha fijado un poco alto; **the house is well ~d** la casa está bien situada; **the shop is awkwardly ~d** la tienda está en una posición de difícil acceso; **the town is ~d on a hill** la ciudad está emplazada en una colina; **to ~ confidence in sb** poner confianza en uno, confiar a uno; **we should ~ no trust in that** no hay que fiarse de eso.

(b) (*of orders etc*) **to ~ an advert in a paper** poner un anuncio en un periódico; **to ~ a book with a publisher** colocar un libro con una editorial; **I shall ~ the book elsewhere** ofreceré el libro a otra editorial; **to ~ a contract for machinery with a French firm** firmar un contrato con una compañía francesa para adquirir unas máquinas; **to ~ money** invertir dinero; **to ~ money at interest** colocar dinero a interés; **to ~ an order** colocar un pedido (*for* de), pedir; **goods that are difficult to ~** unos géneros que no encuentran salida; **Cuba was trying to ~ her sugar** Cuba trataba de colocar su azúcar; **the child was ~d with a loving family** el niño fue a vivir con una familia muy cariñosa.

(c) (*of jobs*) dar un puesto a, emplear, colocar; **we could ~ 200 men if we had them** de tenerlos podríamos colocar a 200 hombres.

(d) (*of series, rank etc*) colocar, clasificar; **to be ~d** (*in race*) colocarse; **to be ~d second** colocarse en segundo lugar; **Vigo is well ~d in the League** Vigo tiene un buen puesto en la Liga; **she was ~d in the first class in maths** le dieron un sobresaliente en matemáticas; **where shall we ~ this candidate?** ¿cómo clasificamos a este candidato?; **he is well ~d to see it** está en una buena posición para observarlo todo; **we are better ~d than a month ago** estamos mejor colocados que hacía un mes; **we are well ~d to attack** estamos en una buena posición para pasar a la ofensiva.

(e) (*recall etc*) recordar, traer a la memoria; (*recognize*) reconocer; (*identify*) identificar, ubicar (*LAm*); **I can't ~ him** no le recuerdo; **I can't quite ~ it** no puedo identificarlo con precisión; **she ~d him at once** le reconoció en seguida.

placebo [plə'siːbəʊ] N (*Med, fig*) placebo m.

placebo effect [plə'siːbəʊ'fekt] N efecto m placebo.

placecard ['pleɪskɑːd] N tarjeta f que indica el puesto que uno ha de ocupar en la mesa.

placekick ['pleɪskɪk] N puntapié m colocado, tiro m libre.

placeman ['pleɪsmæn] N, pl **placemen** (*pej*) cargo m de confianza.

placemat ['pleɪsmæt] N tapete m individual, reposaplatos m.

placement ['pleɪsmənt] N colocación f.

place-name ['pleɪsneɪm] N nombre m de lugar, topónimo m; **~s** (*as study, in general*) toponimia f; **the ~s of Aragon** la toponimia aragonesa.

placenta [plə'sentə] N placenta f.

place-setting ['pleɪsˌsetɪŋ] N cubierto m.

placid ['plæsɪd] ADJ plácido; apacible; tranquilo, sosegado.

placidity [plə'sɪdɪtɪ] N placidez f; apacibilidad f; tranquilidad f; sosiego m.

placidly ['plæsɪdlɪ] ADV plácidamente; apaciblemente; tranquilamente; sosegadamente.

placing ['pleɪsɪŋ] N (*act*) colocación f; clasificación f; (*~ in table, rank*) puesto m, calificación f.

plagal ['pleɪgəl] ADJ plagal.

plagiarism ['pleɪdʒɪərɪzəm] N plagio m.

plagiarist ['pleɪdʒɪərɪst] N plagiario m, -a f.

plagiarize ['pleɪdʒɪəraɪz] VT plagiar.

plague [pleɪg] ① N (*Med*) peste f; (*fig*) plaga f; **what a ~ he is!** ¡es un pesado!; **to avoid sth like the ~** huir de algo como de la peste, evitar algo a toda costa; **to hate sth like the ~** tener un odio visceral a algo.

② VT plagar, infestar; (*fig*) acosar, atormentar; fastidiar; **a thought is plaguing me** me atormenta una idea; **to ~ the life out of sb** fastidiar a uno terriblemente, amargar la vida a uno; **to ~ sb with questions** importunar a uno con preguntas.

plague-ridden ['pleɪgˌrɪdn] ADJ, **plague-stricken** ['pleɪgˌstrɪkən] ADJ apestado.

plaguey* ['pleɪgɪ] ADJ latoso*, engorroso.

plaice [pleɪs] N, PL INVAR platija f, solla f.

plaid [plæd] N (cloth) tela f a cuadros, tartán m; (cloak) manta f escocesa, plaid m; ver también KILT .

plain [pleɪn] 1 ADJ (a) (clear) claro, evidente; **a ~ case of jealousy** un caso evidente de celos; **it is ~ that ...** es evidente que ..., está claro que ...; **it must be ~ to all that ...** ha de ser obvio para todos que ...; **it's as ~ as a pikestaff** está claro como la luz del día; **to make sth ~ to sb** explicar algo a uno con toda claridad; decir algo a uno de modo que no quede lugar a dudas; **I must make it ~ that ...** conste que ..., quede bien claro que ..., tengo que subrayar que ...; **to make one's meaning ~** explicar lo que uno quiere decir; **do I make myself ~?** ¿me entiendes?

(b) (outspoken) franco, abierto; **to be ~ with sb** hablar claro a uno; **let me be ~ with you** dejémonos de rodeos, pongamos las cosas en su sitio.

(c) (unadorned) sencillo, llano; sin adornos; answer franco; dealing honrado; language, style corriente, llano; living sencillo, sin lujo; cooking corriente, casero; truth liso y llano; **in ~ clothes** en traje de calle, de paisano; **under ~ cover** en un paquete discreto; **~ knitting** punto m de media, punto m del derecho; **in ~ language** hablando sin rodeos; para decirlo como es, para llamar las cosas por su nombre; **~ speaking** franqueza f; **they're very ~ people** son gente muy sencilla; **I'm a ~ man** soy un hombre llano; **it's a ~ guess** evidentemente es una conjetura; **they used to be called ~ Smith** antes se llamaban Smith sin más.

(d) (unmixed) natural, puro, sin mezcla; **~ chocolate** chocolate m negro, chocolate m sin leche; **~ flour** harina f normal; **I like ~ whisky** me gusta el whisky sin añadidura, me gusta el whisky sin mezcla.

(e) (of appearance) sin atractivo, algo feo, ordinario; **she's terribly ~, poor girl** no tiene atractivo alguno, la pobre; **pretty girls and ~ ones** las guapas y las feas.

2 ADV claro, claramente; **so I told him pretty ~** así que se lo dije con toda claridad; **I can't say it any ~er** no lo puedo decir de modo más claro; **he's ~ wrong** no tiene razón, y punto.

3 N llano m, llanura f; **the Great P~s** (US) la Pradera (norteamericana).

plain-clothes ['pleɪn'kləʊðz] ADJ: **~ policeman** policía m en paisano, policía m no uniformado.

plainly ['pleɪnlɪ] ADV (a) (clearly) claramente, evidentemente; **~ I was not welcome** evidentemente no iban a recibirme con placer; **to put sth ~** explicar algo con claridad; **to speak ~ to sb** hablar claro a uno.

(b) (frankly) francamente, con franqueza; categóricamente.

(c) (simply) sencillamente, claramente.

plainness ['pleɪnnɪs] N (a) (clarity) claridad f; evidencia f.

(b) (frankness) franqueza f.

(c) (simplicity) sencillez f, llaneza f.

(d) (of face) falta f de atractivo, fealdad f.

plainsman ['pleɪnzmən] N, PL **plainsmen** ['pleɪnzmən] llanero m, hombre m de la llanura.

plainsong ['pleɪnsɒŋ] N canto m llano.

plain-spoken ['pleɪn'spəʊkən] ADJ franco, llano.

plaintiff ['pleɪntɪf] N demandante mf, querellante mf.

plaintive ['pleɪntɪv] ADJ lastimero, dolorido, quejumbroso.

plaintively ['pleɪntɪvlɪ] ADV lastimeramente, con dolor.

plait [plæt] 1 N trenza f; **in ~s** trenzado, en trenzas.

2 VT trenzar.

▼ **plan** [plæn] 1 N (a) (Archit) plano m; **to make a ~ of** trazar el plano de.

(b) (schedule etc) programa m; (system) sistema m; **if everything goes according to ~** si todo se realiza tal como se prevé; **everything went according to ~** todo salió bien, todo resultó como se había previsto.

(c) (Pol, Econ etc) plan m; **~ of action** plan m de acción, (loosely) propósito m, programa m; **what's our ~ of action?** ¿qué nos proponemos hacer?; **~ of campaign** plan m de campaña; **the Badajoz P~** el Plan Badajoz; **the Marshall P~** el Plan Marshall; **the Divine P~** el Diseño Divino; **to draw up a ~** hacer un plan, redactar un plan.

▼ (d) (personal project etc) proyecto m; **the ~ is to come back later** pensamos volver más tarde, tenemos la idea de volver más tarde; **the best ~ is to** + infin lo mejor es + infin; **to change one's ~** cambiar de proyecto, cambiar de idea; **what ~s have you for the holiday?** ¿qué proyectos tienes para las vacaciones?; **have you any ~s for tonight?** ¿tienes programa para esta noche?; **I have no fixed ~s** no he arreglado nada en definitivo; **what ~s have you for Jim?** ¿qué proyectos hay para Jaimito?, ¿qué ideas tienes sobre el porvenir de Jaimito?; **to make ~s** hacer proyectos; **to upset sb's ~s** dar al traste con los proyectos de uno.

2 VT (a) (devise, work out) planear, planificar; proyectar; preparar;

idear; **to ~ a robbery** planear un robo; **to ~ the future of an industry** planificar el porvenir de una industria; **the mania of ~ning everything** la manía de planificarlo todo; **this trip was ~ned by him** este viaje lo preparó él, fue él quien hizo los preparativos para este viaje.

▼ (b) (intend) **to ~ to do sth, to ~ on doing sth** proponerse hacer algo, pensar hacer algo, proyectar hacer algo; **we weren't ~ning to** no teníamos tal intención; no se nos había ocurrido; **how long do you ~ to stay?** ¿cuánto tiempo piensas quedarte?

3 VI hacer proyectos; hacer los preparativos; **to ~ for months** hacer proyectos durante meses enteros; **we are ~ning for next April** hacemos proyectos para el abril que viene; **one has to ~ months ahead** hay que hacer los preparativos con varios meses de antelación.

♦ **plan out** VT planear detalladamente.

planchette [plɑːnˈʃet] N tabla f de escritura espiritista.

plane¹ [pleɪn] N (Bot: also **~ tree**) plátano m.

plane² [pleɪn] 1 ADJ plano; **~ geometry** geometría f plana.

2 N (a) (Math) plano m.

(b) (fig) nivel m, esfera f; **he seems to exist on another ~** parece existir en una esfera distinta; **on this ~** en este nivel, a esta altura.

(c) (tool) (small) cepillo m (de carpintero); (large) garlopa f.

(d) (Aer) avión m; **to go by ~** ir en avión; **to send goods by ~** enviar artículos por avión.

3 VT acepillar; **to ~ down** acepillar, desbastar, alisar.

plane³ [pleɪn] VI (bird, glider, boat) planear; (car) aquaplanear.

planet ['plænɪt] N planeta m.

planetarium [ˌplænɪˈtɛərɪəm] N planetario m.

planetary ['plænɪtərɪ] ADJ planetario.

plangent ['plændʒənt] ADJ plañidero.

plank [plæŋk] 1 N tabla f (gruesa), tablón m; (fig: Pol) principio m, artículo m (de un programa político); **~s** (planking) tablaje m; **deck ~s** tablazón f de la cubierta.

2 VT (a) entablar, entarimar.

(b) **to ~ sth down** tirar algo violentamente, arrojar algo violentamente.

3 VR: **to ~ o.s. down** sentarse (etc) de modo agresivo.

planking ['plæŋkɪŋ] N tablas fpl, tablaje m; (Naut) tablazón f de la cubierta.

plankton ['plæŋktən] N plancton m.

planned [plænd] ADJ economy dirigido; development, redundancy etc programado; crime, murder premeditado.

planner ['plænər] 1 N planificador m, -ora f.

2 ATTR: **~ board** diagrama m de planificación.

planning ['plænɪŋ] 1 N (Pol, Econ etc) planificación f; (personal projects) proyectos mpl.

2 ATTR: **~ board** comisión f planificadora; **~ permission** permiso m de construcción; **we're still in the ~ stage** estamos todavía en la etapa de la planificación.

plant [plɑːnt] 1 N (a) (Bot) planta f.

(b) (Tech: machinery) equipo m, maquinaria f, instalación f; (factory) planta f, fábrica f.

(c) (*: trick) truco m para incriminar a uno; **it's a ~** aquí hay trampa.

(d) (*: person) agente mf, espía f.

2 ATTR vegetal; **~ life** vida f vegetal, las plantas; **~ kingdom** reino m vegetal; **~ louse** pulgón m.

3 VT (a) plant plantar; seed sembrar; **to ~ a field with turnips** sembrar un campo de nabos; **the field is ~ed with wheat** el campo está sembrado de trigo.

(b) (place) poner, colocar; fijar; people establecer; informer, spy colar, colocar, introducir (on en); blow plantar, asestar; idea etc inculcar (in en), imbuir (in con); **to ~ sth on sb** ocultar algo en la ropa (or en la habitación etc) de uno para incriminarle.

4 VR: **to ~ o.s. in the middle of the road** ponerse en medio de la calle.

♦ **plant out** VT seedlings trasplantar.

♦ **plant up** VT land plantar, sembrar.

plantain ['plæntɪn] N llantén m, plátano m (LAm).

plantation [plænˈteɪʃən] N (of tea, sugar etc) plantación f; (large estate) hacienda f; (of trees) arboleda f; (of young trees) plantel m; (Hist) colonia f.

planter ['plɑːntər] N plantador m, -ora f; cultivador m, -ora f; (loosely) colono m.

planting ['plɑːntɪŋ] N plantación f, el plantar; **~ season** estación f de plantar.

plantpot ['plɑːntpɒt] N tiesto m, maceta f.

plaque [plæk] N placa f; (on teeth) sarro m.

plash [plæʃ] N = splash.

plasm ['plæzəm] N, **plasma** ['plæzmə] N plasma m.

plaster ['plɑːstər] 1 N (a) (lime material) yeso m; (in building) argamasa f, (layer on wall) enlucido m.

(b) (*Brit Med*: *applied to wound*) emplasto *m*, parche *m*; (*for injured arm etc*) escayola *f*, tablilla *f* de yeso; (*Brit*: *adhesive* ~) esparadrapo *m*, tirita *f*; **~ of Paris** yeso *m* mate; **with his leg in ~** con la pierna escayolada; **to have one's neck in ~** tener el cuello escayolado.

2 ATTR: **~ cast** vaciado *m*; (*death mask*) mascarilla *f* mortuoria; (*Med*) escayola *f*.

3 VT **(a)** *wall* enyesar, enlucir; (*Med*) emplastar, aplicar un emplasto a; **to ~ a wall with posters** llenar (*or* cubrir) una pared de carteles; **to ~ posters on a wall** pegar carteles a una pared; **to ~ over a hole** llenar un hoyo de argamasa; **the story was ~ed all over the front page** el reportaje llenaba la primera plana; **the children came back ~ed with mud** los niños volvieron cubiertos de lodo.

(b) (*) dar una paliza a, pegar.

plasterboard ['plɑːstəbɔːd] N cartón *m* de yeso y fieltro.

plastered ['plɑːstəd] ADJ: **to be ~** estar ajumado*, estar tomado* (*LAm*).

plasterer ['plɑːstərər] N yesero *m*, enlucidor *m*.

plastering ['plɑːstərɪŋ] N enlucido *m*.

plastic ['plæstɪk] 1 ADJ **(a)** (*gen*) plástico; **~ bag** bolsa *f* de plástico; **~ bomb** bomba *f* de goma 2; **~ bullet** bala *f* de goma; **~ explosive** goma *f* 2; **~ money** dinero *m* plástico; **~ surgeon** cirujano *m* especializado en cirugía plástica; **~ surgery** cirugía *f* plástica, cirugía *f* estética. **(b)** (*: sham*) falso, de imitación.

2 N plástico *m*; (*credit cards*) dinero *m* plástico.

Plasticine ['plæstɪsiːn] ® N plasticina ® *f*, plastilina *f*, arcilla *f* de modelar.

plasticity [plæs'tɪsɪtɪ] N plasticidad *f*.

plate [pleɪt] 1 N (*dish*) plato *m*; (*of metal etc*) lámina *f*, chapa *f*, plancha *f*; (*on cooker*) quemador *m*, fuego *m*, placa *f*; (*plaque*) placa *f*; (*silver*) vajilla *f* de plata; (*for taking collection*) platillo *m*; (*Geol*) placa *f*; (*Typ*) lámina *f*; (*Phot: of microscope*) placa *f*; (*prize, in racing*) premio *m*; (*also* **dental ~**) placa *f* de la dentadura postiza; (*US Baseball*) plato *m*; **~s‡** (*feet*) tachines‡ *mpl*; **gold ~** vajilla *f* de oro; **to hand sb sth on a ~** (*fig*) servir algo a uno en bandeja de plata; **to go to the ~** (*US*) entrar a batear; (*fig*) afrontar el problema; reconocer sus responsabilidades; **to have a lot on one's ~** estar muy ocupado, tener muchos asuntos entre manos, tener grandes responsabilidades.

2 ATTR: **~ armor** (*US*), **~ armour** blindaje *m*; **~ glass** vidrio *m* cilindrado, luna *f*.

3 VT (*with metal*) planchear, chapear; (*with armour*) blindar; (*with silver*) platear; (*with nickel*) niquelar.

Plate [pleɪt] N: **the River ~** el Río de la Plata.

plateau ['plætəʊ] N, PL **plateaux** ['plætəʊz] meseta *f*, altiplanicie *f*, altiplano *m* (*LAm*).

plated ['pleɪtɪd] ADJ chapeado (*with* de); niquelado; (*armoured*) blindado.

plateful ['pleɪtfʊl] N plato *m*.

plateholder ['pleɪtˌhəʊldər] N (*Phot*) portaplacas *m*.

platelayer ['pleɪtˌleɪər] N obrero *m* (de ferrocarriles).

platen ['plætən] N rodillo *m*.

plate-rack ['pleɪtræk] N portaplatos *m*.

plate-warmer ['pleɪtˌwɔːmər] N calentador *m* de platos.

platform ['plætfɔːm] 1 N **(a)** plataforma *f*; (*at meeting*) tribuna *f*; (*for band etc*) estrado *m*; (*roughly-built*) tarima *f*, tablado *m*; (*Pol*) programa *m* electoral, plataforma *f* ~ **the society offered him a ~** la sociedad le ofreció una tribuna (para exponer sus ideas); **last year they shared a ~** el año pasado ocuparon la misma tribuna.

(b) (*Brit Rail*) andén *m*; (*with number mentioned*) vía *f*; **the 5.15 is at** (*or* **on**) **~ 8** el tren de las 5.15 está en la vía número 8.

2 ATTR: **the ~ speakers** los oradores de la tribuna; **~ ticket** (*Brit*) billete *m* (*LAm*: boleto *m*) de andén.

plating ['pleɪtɪŋ] N enchapado *m*; capa *f* metálica; (*armour-*~) blindaje *m*; (*of nickel*) niquelado *m*.

platinum ['plætɪnəm] 1 N platino *m*.

2 ATTR: **~ blonde** rubia *f* platino.

platitude ['plætɪtjuːd] N lugar *m* común, tópico *m*, perogrullada *f*; **it is a ~ to say that ...** es un tópico decir que ...

platitudinize [ˌplætɪ'tjuːdɪnaɪz] VI decir tópicos.

platitudinous [ˌplætɪ'tjuːdɪnəs] ADJ *speech* lleno de lugares comunes (*etc*); *speaker* aficionado a los lugares comunes (*etc*), que peca por exceso de tópicos.

Plato ['pleɪtəʊ] NM Platón.

platonic [plə'tɒnɪk] ADJ platónico; **~ love** amor *m* platónico.

platonism ['pleɪtənɪzəm] N platonismo *m*.

platonist ['pleɪtənɪst] N platonista *mf*.

platoon [plə'tuːn] N pelotón *m*, sección *f*.

platter ['plætər] N **(a)** (*dish*) fuente *f*. **(b)** (*US*) disco *m*.

platypus ['plætɪpəs] N ornitorrinco *m*.

plaudits ['plɔːdɪts] NPL aplausos *mpl*.

plausibility [ˌplɔːzə'bɪlɪtɪ] N verosimilitud *f*, admisibilidad *f*, credibilidad *f*; **his ~ is such that ...** habla tan bien que ..., tiene tanto cuento que ...

plausible ['plɔːzəbl] ADJ *argument etc* verosímil, admisible, creíble; *person* bien hablado pero no del todo confiable, que casi convence; **he's a ~ sort** tiene mucho cuento.

plausibly ['plɔːzəblɪ] ADV de modo verosímil, creíblemente; **he tells it most ~** lo cuenta de modo que casi convence.

play [pleɪ] 1 N **(a)** (*amusement etc*) juego *m*, recreo *m*, diversión *f*; **~ on words** juego *m* de palabras; **to be at ~** estar jugando; **to make ~ of** burlarse de; **to say sth in ~** decir algo en broma.

(b) (*Sport etc: act of ~ing*) jugada *f*; **neat ~** una bonita jugada; **a clever piece of ~** una hábil jugada; **fair ~** juego *m* limpio; **foul ~** juego *m* sucio; **to be in ~** estar en juego; **to be out of ~** estar fuera de juego; **~ began at 3 o'clock** el partido comenzó a las 3, se empezó a jugar a las 3.

(c) (*activity etc*) juego *m*, actividad *f*; **to bring into ~** poner en juego; **to come into ~** entrar en juego; **to give full ~ to one's imagination** dar rienda suelta a la imaginación; **to make great ~ with sth** recalcar algo, insistir en algo.

(d) (*Mech*) juego *m*, holgura *f*, movimiento *m* libre.

(e) **the ~ of light on the water** el rielar de la luz sobre el agua; **the ~ of light and dark in this picture** el efecto de luz y sombra en este cuadro.

(f) (*Theat*) obra *f*, obra *f* dramática, comedia *f*; **the ~s of Lope** las obras dramáticas de Lope, el teatro de Lope; **to go to the ~** ir al teatro.

(g) **to make a ~ for sth** tratar de conseguir algo, hacer una tentativa de obtener algo; **he made a ~ for her** le echó un tiento.

2 VT **(a)** (*Theat etc*) *play* representar, poner, dar; *part* hacer, hacer el papel de, (*fig*) desempeñar; **when we ~ed 'Hamlet'** cuando representamos 'Hamlet'; **when I ~ed Hamlet** cuando hice el papel de Hamlet; **what did you ~?** ¿qué papel tuviste?; **we shall be ~ing the West End** pondremos la obra en el West End; **when we last ~ed Blackpool** cuando representamos la última vez en Blackpool; **we ~ed 'Lear' as a comedy** representamos 'Lear' como comedia; **we ~ed 'Charley's Aunt' straight** representamos 'Charley's Aunt' como obra seria; **let's ~ it for laughs** hagámoslo de manera burlesca; **he likes to ~ the soldier** se las echa de soldado, se da aires de militar; V **fool**[1] *etc*.

(b) **to ~ a joke on sb** gastar una broma a uno; **to ~ a dirty trick on sb** hacer una mala pasada a uno.

(c) *card* jugar; *ball* golpear; *chess piece etc* mover; *fish* dejar que se canse, agotar; **to ~ the market** jugar a la bolsa; **to ~ both ends against the middle** beneficiarse de la diversidad de factores en juego.

(d) *cards, game etc* jugar a; **to ~ a game of tennis** jugar un partido de tenis; **to ~ a game of cards with sb** echar una partida de cartas con uno; **do you ~ football?** ¿juegas al fútbol?

(e) *opponent* jugar con, jugar contra; **I ~ed him at chess** jugué contra él al ajedrez; **I ~ed him twice** jugué contra él dos veces; **I'll ~ you for the drinks** quien pierde paga.

(f) (*make member of team*) incluir, incluir en el equipo; **are they ~ing Wooster?** ¿juega Wooster?, ¿van a incluir a Wooster?

(g) (*Sport: in position*) jugar de; **I ~ed back** jugué de defensa; **can you ~ goalkeeper?** ¿puedes jugar de portero?

(h) **to ~ sb false** traicionar a uno.

(i) (*direct*) dirigir (*on* hacia, sobre); **to ~ hoses on a fire** dirigir mangueras sobre un incendio; **~ the hose this way a bit** dirige la manguera más hacia este lado; **to ~ a searchlight on an aircraft** dirigir un reflector hacia un avión, hacer de un avión el blanco de un reflector.

(j) (*Mus*) *instrument* tocar; *record, tape* poner; **to learn to ~ the piano** aprender a tocar el piano; **they ~ed the 5th Symphony** tocaron la Quinta Sinfonía, interpretaron la Quinta Sinfonía.

3 VI **(a)** (*amuse o.s.*) jugar; divertirse; (*frolic*) jugar, juguetear; (*gambol*) retozar; **run away and ~!** ¡idos a jugar!; **to ~ with a stick** jugar con un palo; **to ~ with fire** jugar con fuego; **to ~ with one's food** comiscar, jugar con la comida; **he's just ~ing with you** se está burlando de ti; **to ~ with an idea** acariciar una idea; **he's got money to ~ with** tiene dinero de sobra; **this is not a question to be ~ed with** éste no es asunto para reírse, éste no es asunto para tomar en broma; V **fast**[1] *etc*.

(b) (*at a game etc*) **to ~ at chess** jugar al ajedrez; **he just ~s at it** lo hace con poca seriedad; **the little girl ~s at being a woman** la niña juega a ser mujer; **to ~ at soldiers** jugar a los soldados; **to ~ at trains** jugar con los trenes; **what are you ~ing at?** ¿a qué esto?; **~!** ¡listo!; **who ~s first?** ¿quién juega primero?; **are you ~ing today?** ¿tu juegas hoy?; **I've not ~ed for a long time** hace mucho tiempo que no juego; **to ~ fair** jugar limpio; **to ~ for time** tratar de ganar tiempo; **to ~ into sb's hands** hacer el caldo gordo a uno, hacer el juego a uno.

(c) (*Mus*) tocar; **to ~ on the piano** tocar el piano; **do you ~?** ¿sabes tocar?; **to ~ to sb** tocar para uno; **when the organ ~s** cuando suena el órgano.

(d) (*light*) rielar; **the sun was ~ing on the water** rielaba el sol sobre el agua.

(e) *(fountain)* correr; funcionar.

(f) *(act)* **to ~ in a film** tener *(or* hacer*)* un papel en una película; **we have ~ed all over the South** hemos representado en todas partes del Sur; **to ~ ill** fingirse enfermo; **to ~ hard to get** hacerse de rogar; *(woman)* hacerse la difícil; **to ~ safe** obrar con cautela, ser prudente.

◆**play about, play around** VI **(a)** *(children)* jugar, divertirse; *(sleep around)* dormir con cualquiera.

(b) to ~ about with *(fiddle)* jugar con, manosear; *(damage)* estropear; *(test)* explorar, ensayar (de varias maneras); **I ~ed around with the programme till it worked** ensayé el programa de varias maneras hasta hacerle funcionar bien.

◆**play along** VI: **to ~ along with sb** seguir el humor a uno; ajustarse a las ideas de uno.

◆**play back** VT repetir, reproducir.

◆**play down** VT quitar *(or* restar*)* importancia a, tratar de minimizar, relativizar.

◆**play in** ① VT: **the band ~ed the procession in** tocaba la orquesta mientras entraba el desfile.

② VR: **to ~ o.s. in** acostumbrarse a las condiciones de juego.

◆**play off** ① VT **(a) to ~ off A against B** contraponer A a B.

(b) to ~ off a tie jugar el desempate.

② VI *(Sport)* jugar el desempate.

◆**play on** ① VT: **to ~ on words** jugar con las palabras; **to ~ on sb's emotions** jugar con las emociones de uno; **to ~ on sb's nerves** poner los nervios de uno de punta; **to ~ on sb's credulity** explotar la credulidad de uno.

② VT *(Mus)* seguir tocando; *(Sport)* seguir jugando; **~ on!** ¡adelante!

◆**play out** VT **(a) to ~ out time** entretener el tiempo que queda, seguir jugando por pura fórmula hasta el fin.

(b) the organ ~ed the congregation out tocaba el órgano mientras salían los fieles.

(c) to be ~ed out* *(person, seam etc)* estar agotado.

(d) *fantasy etc* realizar, dar forma práctica a, expresar en la realidad; **they are ~ing out a drama of revenge** están representando un drama de venganza.

◆**play over, play through** VT *music* tocar, ensayar.

◆**play up** ① VT **(a)** *(give trouble)* dar guerra a; causar molestias a; **the kids ~ her up dreadfully** los chavales le dan guerra de mala manera.

(b) *(magnify)* exagerar, encarecer.

② VI **(a)** *(Sport)* jugar mejor, jugar con más ánimo; **~ up!** ¡ánimo!, ¡aúpa!

(b) *(Brit*)* dar guerra; causar problemas, causar molestias; **my stomach is ~ing up again** mi estómago vuelve a darme problemas; **the car is ~ing up** el coche no marcha bien.

(c) to ~ up to sb* hacer la pelotilla a uno*, bailar el agua a uno.

◆**play upon** VT = **play on** 2.

playact ['pleɪækt] VI hacer la comedia; *(exaggerate)* hacer teatro.

playacting ['pleɪ,æktɪŋ] N comedia *f*, farsa *f*; **this is mere ~** esto es puro teatro, no es más que una comedia.

playactor ['pleɪ,æktəʳ] N actor *m* *(also fig)*.

playback ['pleɪbæk] N repetición *f*, reproducción *f*; *(TV etc)* playback *m*, previo *m*.

playbill ['pleɪbɪl] N cartel *m* (de teatro).

playboy ['pleɪbɔɪ] N señorito *m*, córrelas *m*, botarate *m*.

played-out* ['pleɪd'aʊt] ADJ *person, seam etc* agotado, rendido; quemado.

player ['pleɪəʳ] N **(a)** *(Theat)* actor *m*, actriz *f*, representante *mf*. **(b)** *(Mus)* músico *m*, -a *f*. **(c)** *(Sport)* jugador *m*, -ora *f*; **football ~** jugador *m* de fútbol.

playfellow ['pleɪ,feləʊ] N compañero *m*, -a *f* de juego.

playful ['pleɪfʊl] ADJ *person* juguetón; *mood* alegre; *remark* dicho en broma, festivo.

playfully ['pleɪfəlɪ] ADV jugando, en juego; alegremente; en broma; **he said ~** dijo guasón.

playfulness ['pleɪfʊlnɪs] N carácter *m* juguetón; alegría *f*; tono *m* guasón.

playgoer ['pleɪ,gəʊəʳ] N aficionado *m*, -a *f* al teatro; **we are regular ~s** vamos con regularidad al teatro.

playground ['pleɪgraʊnd] N *(in school)* patio *m*; campo *m* de recreo; *(of millionaires)* paraíso *m*, lugar *m* favorito.

playgroup ['pleɪ,gruːp] N guardería *f* infantil, jardín *m* de infancia.

playhouse ['pleɪhaʊs] N, PL **playhouses** ['pleɪ,haʊzɪz] teatro *m*; *(US)* casita *f* de muñecas.

playing ['pleɪɪŋ] N **(a)** *(Sport)* juego *m*; **~ in the wet is tricky** es difícil jugar cuando llueve. **(b)** *(Mus)* **the orchestra's ~ of the symphony was uninspired** la interpretación de la orquesta de la sinfonía fue poco inspirada; **there was some fine ~ in the violin concerto** el concierto de violín estuvo muy bien interpretado.

playing-card ['pleɪɪŋkɑːd] N carta *f*, naipe *m*.

playing-field ['pleɪɪŋfiːld] N campo *m* *(LAm:* cancha *f)* de deportes.

playlist ['pleɪlɪst] N *(Radio)* lista *f* discográfica.

playmaker ['pleɪmeɪkəʳ] N *(Sport)* jugador *encargado de facilitar buenas jugadas a sus compañeros.*

playmate ['pleɪmeɪt] N camarada *mf*, compañero *m*, -a *f* de juego.

play-off ['pleɪɒf] N (partido *m* de) desempate *m*; *(of top teams in league)* liguilla *f*.

playpen ['pleɪpen] N parque *m* de jugar, corralito *m* (de niño).

play-reading ['pleɪ,riːdɪŋ] N lectura *f* (de una obra dramática).

playroom ['pleɪrʊm] N cuarto *m* de los niños.

playschool ['pleɪ,skuːl] N parvulario *m*.

plaything ['pleɪθɪŋ] N juguete *m* *(also fig)*.

playtime ['pleɪtaɪm] N recreo *m*.

playwright ['pleɪraɪt] N dramaturgo *mf* *(also* -a *f)*, autor *m* dramático, autora *f* dramática.

plaza ['plɑːzə] N *(US)* **(a)** *(motorway services)* zona *f* de servicios. **(b)** *(toll)* peaje *m*.

PLC, plc N *(Brit)* ABBR of **public limited company** Sociedad *f* Anónima por acciones, S.A.

plea [pliː] N **(a)** *(excuse)* pretexto *m*, disculpa *f*. **(b)** *(entreaty)* ruego *m*, súplica *f*, petición *f*; **he made a ~ for mercy** pidió clemencia. **(c)** *(Jur)* alegato *m*, defensa *f*; contestación *f* a la demanda, declaración *f*; **a ~ of insanity** un alegato de desequilibrio mental.

plea bargaining ['pliː,bɑːgɪnɪŋ] N *acuerdo táctico entre fiscal y defensor para agilizar los trámites judiciales.*

plead [pliːd] *(irr in US:* PRET, PTP **pled**) ① VT **(a) to ~ sb's cause** hablar por uno, interceder por uno; *(Jur)* defender a uno en juicio.

(b) *(give as excuse)* alegar; pretextar; **to ~ ignorance** pretextar ignorancia; **he ~ed certain difficulties** alegó ciertas dificultades; **to ~ that ...** alegar que ..., pretextar que ...

② VI **(a)** suplicar, rogar; **to ~ with sb** suplicar a uno; **to ~ with sb for sth** rogar a uno que conceda *(or* permita *etc)* algo; **I ~ed and ~ed but it was no use** le supliqué mil veces pero de nada sirvió; **the village has ~ed for a new bridge for 10 years** durante 10 años el pueblo viene reclamando un nuevo puente.

(b) *(Jur: as barrister)* abogar.

(c) *(Jur: as defendant)* declarar; **how do you ~?** ¿qué contestación hace Vd a la demanda?; **to ~ guilty** confesarse culpable; **to ~ not guilty** negar la acusación.

pleading ['pliːdɪŋ] ① N súplicas *fpl*; *(Jur)* alegatos *mpl*; **special ~** argumentos *mpl* especiosos.

② ADJ *tone etc* suplicante, de súplica.

pleasant ['pleznt] ADJ agradable; *surprise etc* grato; *manner, style* ameno; *person* simpático, afable, amable; **we had a ~ time** lo pasamos muy bien; **it's very ~ here** aquí se está muy bien; **it made a ~ change from our usual holiday** fueron unas vacaciones distintas de las acostumbradas y muy agradables; **it's a ~ surprise to find that ...** es una grata sorpresa descubrir que ...; **it did not make ~ reading** su lectura no fue nada agradable; **to make o.s. ~ to sb** procurar ser amable con uno.

pleasantly ['plezntlɪ] ADV agradablemente; gratamente; en estilo ameno; afablemente, amablemente; **I am ~ surprised that ...** para mí es una grata sorpresa que + *subj*; **it is ~ warm** hace un calor agradable.

pleasantness ['plezntnɪs] N agrado *m*, lo agradable; amenidad *f*; simpatía *f*, amabilidad *f*.

pleasantry ['plezntrɪ] N chiste *m*, dicho *m* gracioso.

▼ **please** [pliːz] ① VTI **(a)** *(give pleasure to)* dar gusto a, dar satisfacción a, agradar, contentar; caer en gracia a; **I did it just to ~ you** lo hice únicamente para darte gusto; **there's no pleasing him** es imposible contentarle; **he is easily ~d** se contenta con cualquier cosa; **she's hard to ~** es muy exigente; **the joke ~d him** el chiste le cayó en gracia; **he is anxious to ~** procura dar satisfacción; **a gift that is sure to ~** un regalo que siempre agrada; **music that ~s the ear** una música grata para el oído; **to lay o.s. out to ~ sb** desvivirse por contentar a uno; **it ~d him to order that ...** tuvo a bien ordenar que + *subj*.

(b) *(impers)* **~ God!** ¡plegue a Dios!; **~ God that ...!** ¡plegue a Dios que + *subj*!

▼**(c)** *(expressing wish)* **~!** ¡por favor!, *(as protest)* ¡por Dios!; **my bill ~** la cuenta, por favor; **two pints ~!** ¡dos cañas (por favor)!; **two to Victoria ~** a Victoria, dos (por favor); **~ pass the salt, pass the salt ~** ¿me haces el favor de pasar la sal?; **~ tell me** haz el favor de decírmelo, dímelo por favor; **~ be seated** siéntense; **~ sit down!** ¡hagan el favor de sentarse!; **~ accept this book** le ruego acepte este libro; **'~ do not open this door'** 'se ruega no abrir esta puerta'; **~ don't cry!** ¡no llores, te lo suplico!; **now ~ DO let me know if ...** no dejes de decirme si ...; **may I? ... ~ do!** ¿se puede? ... ¡por supuesto!

(d) *(think fit)* **if you ~** si te parece; con tu permiso; **he wanted 10, if you ~!** quería llevarse 10, ¡fíjate!; **to do as one ~s** hacer lo que le da la gana; **I shall do what I ~** haré lo que me parezca bien; **as you ~** como quieras; **do as you ~** haz lo que quieras.

② VR: **to ~ o.s.** hacer lo que le da la gana; **~ yourself!** ¡como quieras!; **he has always ~d himself about holidays** en asunto de vacaciones siempre ha hecho lo que le venía en gana.

▼ **pleased** [pliːzd] ADJ **(a)** (*happy*) alegre, contento; **to be ~** estar contento; **to be as ~ as Punch** estar como unas pascuas; **to look ~** estar alegre, parece estar contento; tener aire satisfecho.

▼ **(b) to be ~ with sth** estar satisfecho de algo; **to be ~ with sb** mostrarse satisfecho con uno; **to be ~ with o.s.** estar satisfecho de sí mismo; **they were anything but ~ with the news** no estaban nada contentos con la noticia, distaban mucho de estar contentos con la noticia; **I am ~ at the decision** me alegro de la decisión; **I am ~ to hear it** me alegro de saberlo; (**I am**) **~ to meet you** (tengo) mucho gusto en conocerle, (estoy) encantado de conocerle; **I am ~ to be able to announce that ...** me es grato poderles anunciar que ...; **we are ~ to inform you that ...** (*Comm*) nos complacemos en comunicarles que ..., nos es grato informarles que ...

(c) (*royal usage*) **Her Majesty has been graciously ~ to accept ...** su Majestad aceptó sumamente complacida ...

pleasing ['pliːzɪŋ] ADJ agradable; grato; halagüeño; **with ~ results** con resultados halagüeños; **a most ~ piece of news** una noticia muy grata.

pleasingly ['pliːzɪŋlɪ] ADV agradablemente; gratamente.

pleasurable ['pleʒərəbl] ADJ agradable, deleitoso.

pleasurably ['pleʒərəblɪ] ADV agradablemente, deleitosamente; **we were ~ surprised** para nosotros fue una grata sorpresa.

▼ **pleasure** ['pleʒəʳ] **1** N **(a)** (*in general*) placer *m*, gusto *m*, satisfacción *f*; **with ~** con mucho gusto; **it's a ~ to see him** da gusto verle; **it's a ~ to know that ...** es un motivo de satisfacción saber que ...; **it's a real ~** es un verdadero placer; **~!, the ~ is mine!** (*returning thanks*) ¡no hay de qué!; **to find ~ in chess** disfrutar jugando al ajedrez; **what ~ can you find in shooting partridges?** ¿qué placer encuentras en matar perdices?; **to give sb ~** dar gusto a uno; **if it gives you any ~** si te gusta; **I have much ~ in informing you that ...** me es grato informarle que ...; **may I have the ~?** (*at dance*) ¿quieres bailar?; **to take ~ in books** disfrutar leyendo; **I take great ~ in watching them grow** disfruto muchísimo viéndolos crecer; **to take ~ in doing damage** complacerse en hacer daño; **Mr and Mrs X request the ~ of Y's company** los señores de X solicitan el placer de la compañía del Sr Y.

(b) (*amusements*) placeres *mpl*; diversión *f*, recreo *m*; **all the ~s of London** todos los placeres de Londres, todas las diversiones de Londres; **sexual ~** placer *m* sexual; **to be fond of ~** ser amante de los placeres.

(c) (*will*) voluntad *f*; **at ~** a voluntad; **do it at your ~** hazlo cuando quieras, hazlo cuando tengas tiempo; **during the royal ~** mientras quiera el monarca; **what is your ~, sir?** ¿en qué puedo servirle, señor?, ¿qué manda Vd, señor?

2 ATTR de recreo; **~ trip** viaje *m* de recreo.

pleasure-boat ['pleʒəbəʊt] N, **pleasure-craft** ['pleʒəkrɑːft] N barco *m* de recreo; embarcación *f* deportiva.

pleasure-cruise ['pleʒəkruːz] N crucero *m* de recreo.

pleasure-ground ['pleʒəgraʊnd] N parque *m* de atracciones.

pleasure-loving ['pleʒə,lʌvɪŋ] ADJ amante de los placeres.

pleasure-seeker ['pleʒə,siːkəʳ] N hedonista *mf*.

pleasure-seeking ['pleʒə,siːkɪŋ] ADJ hedonista, que busca el placer.

pleasure-steamer ['pleʒə,stiːməʳ] N vapor *m* de recreo.

pleat [pliːt] **1** N pliegue *m*, doblez *m*; (*of skirt*) tabla *f*. **2** VT plegar, plisar.

pleb* [pleb] **1** N plebeyo *m*, -a *f*, persona *f* ordinaria; **the ~s** la plebe. **2** ADJ plebeyo, aplebeyado.

plebeian [plɪ'biːən] **1** ADJ plebeyo. **2** N plebeyo *m*, -a *f*.

plebiscite ['plebɪsɪt] N plebiscito *m*.

plectrum ['plektrəm] N plectro *m*.

pled [pled] (*US*) *irr*: PRET, PTP *of* **plead**.

pledge [pledʒ] **1** N (*given as security*) prenda *f*; (*promise*) promesa *f*, voto *m*; garantía *f*; (*to flag etc*) acto *m* de acatamiento; (*between governments etc*) compromiso *m*; (*toast*) brindis *m*; **~ of allegiance** (*US*) juramento de lealtad a la nación; **as a ~ of** en señal de, como garantía de; **I give you this ~** os hago esta promesa; **the government will honour its ~s** el gobierno hará honor a sus compromisos; **to sign the ~** jurar abstenerse del alcohol.

2 VT **(a)** (*pawn*) empeñar, pignorar, dejar en prenda.

(b) (*promise*) prometer; *one's word* dar; **to ~ support for sb** prometer su apoyo a uno, prometer apoyar a uno; **to ~ one's allegiance to sb** jurar ser fiel a uno; **I am ~d to secrecy** he jurado guardarlo secreto; **we are ~d to go to their aid** hemos prometido ir a ayudarles, nos hemos comprometido a ayudarles.

(c) (*toast*) brindar por.

3 VR: **to ~ o.s.** *to* + *infin* comprometerse a + *infin*.

┌─────────────────────────┐
│ **PLEDGE OF ALLEGIANCE** │
└─────────────────────────┘

ⓘ *El **Pledge of Allegiance** es un juramento de lealtad a la nación, considerado como un elemento de gran importancia en la educación norteamericana. Fue escrito en 1892 y desde entonces lo recitan*

diariamente todos los alumnos estadounidenses (especialmente en los centros de educación primaria) mirando a la bandera y con la mano en el corazón.

Pleiades ['plaɪədiːz] NPL Pléyades *fpl*.

plenary ['pliːnərɪ] **1** ADJ plenario; **~ paper** ponencia *f* en sesión plenaria, ponencia *f* general; **~ session** sesión *f* plenaria, pleno *m*. **2** N = **~ paper**.

plenipotentiary [,plenɪpə'tenʃərɪ] N plenipotenciario *m*, -a *f*.

plenitude ['plenɪtjuːd] N plenitud *f*.

plenteous ['plentɪəs] ADJ, **plentiful** ['plentɪfʊl] ADJ copioso, abundante; **a ~ supply of ...** una buena provisión de ..., un buen surtido de ...; **eggs are now ~** hay abundancia de huevos, abundan los huevos.

plentifully ['plentɪfəlɪ] ADV copiosamente, abundantemente.

plenty ['plentɪ] **1** N **(a)** abundancia *f*; cantidad *f* suficiente; **land of ~** tierra *f* de la abundancia; **in ~** en abundancia; **it rained in ~** llovió copiosamente; **it grows here in ~** por aquí existe en abundancia; **to live in ~** vivir en el lujo; **that's ~, thanks!** ¡basta, gracias!; **we have ~** tenemos bastante; **there's ~ to go on** hay suficientes datos, son muchas las pruebas; **we know ~ about you** sabemos mucho acerca de Vd.

(b) ~ of bastante; muchos, muchísimos; una cantidad suficiente de; **we have ~ of money** tenemos bastante dinero; **they have ~ of money** tienen mucho dinero; **we have ~ of tea** tenemos mucho té; **there are ~ of them** los hay en cantidad; **we see ~ of them** (*numbers*) vemos muchos de ellos, (*as friends*) les vemos mucho, nos vemos con frecuencia; **we have ~ of time** tenemos tiempo de sobra; **it takes ~ of courage** exige bastante valor; **~ of people do** hay muchos que lo hacen, son muchos los que lo hacen.

2 ADV (*) **it's ~ big enough** claro que es bastante grande; **they're ~ rich enough to pay for two** son lo bastante ricos para pagar por dos de ellos; **it rained ~** (*US*) y ¡cómo llovió!; **we like it ~** (*US*) nos gusta mucho.

plenum ['pliːnəm] N pleno *m*.

pleonasm ['pliːənæzəm] N pleonasmo *m*.

pleonastic [plɪə'næstɪk] ADJ pleonástico.

plethora ['pleθərə] N plétora *f*.

plethoric [ple'θɒrɪk] ADJ pletórico.

pleurisy ['plʊərɪsɪ] N pleuresía *f*, pleuritis *f*.

Plexiglas ['pleksɪglɑːs] ® N (*US*) plexiglás ® *m*.

pliability [,plaɪə'bɪlɪtɪ] N flexibilidad *f* (*also fig*).

pliable ['plaɪəbl] ADJ, **pliant** ['plaɪənt] ADJ flexible (*also fig*); plegable.

pliers ['plaɪəz] NPL alicates *mpl*, tenazas *fpl*; **a pair of ~, some ~** unos alicates, unas tenazas.

plight¹ [plaɪt] VT *word* dar, empeñar; **to ~ one's troth** (†† *or hum*) prometerse, dar su palabra de casamiento (*to* a).

plight² [plaɪt] N condición *f* (inquietante), situación *f* (difícil), situación *f* apremiante; crisis *f*; **the ~ of the shellfish industry** la crisis de la industria marisquera; **the country's economic ~** la situación económica del país; los apuros económicos del país; **to be in a sad** (*or* **sorry**) **~** estar en un estado lamentable.

Plimsoll ['plɪmsəl] ATTR: **~ line** línea *f* de máxima carga.

plimsolls ['plɪmsəlz] NPL (*Brit*) zapatos *mpl* de tenis.

plinth [plɪnθ] N plinto *m*.

Pliny ['plɪnɪ] NM Plinio *m*; **~ the Elder** Plinio el Viejo; **~ the Younger** Plinio el Joven.

PLO N ABBR *of* **Palestine Liberation Organization** Organización *f* para la Liberación de Palestina, OLP *f*.

plod [plɒd] **1** N **(a) to go at a steady ~** caminar despacio pero sin desanimarse.

(b) it's a long ~ to the village queda mucho camino para llegar al pueblo.

2 VT recorrer despacio; **we ~ded the road for another hour** seguimos andando con dificultad durante una hora más; **we ~ded our way homeward** volvimos penosamente hacia casa.

3 VI **(a)** (*also* **to ~ along, to ~ on**) caminar despacio, andar penosamente, avanzar con dificultad; **keep ~ding!** ¡ánimo!, ¡no os dejéis desanimar!

(b) (*at work etc*) trabajar laboriosamente, trabajar lentamente pero sin desanimarse; **to ~ away at a task** dedicarse laboriosamente a un trabajo, seguir trabajando a pesar de las dificultades.

plodder ['plɒdəʳ] N estudiante *mf* más aplicado que brillante, persona *f* que trabaja con más aplicación que talento.

plodding ['plɒdɪŋ] ADJ perseverante, laborioso; *student* empollón; *worker* más aplicado que brillante.

plonk¹ [plɒŋk] **1** N golpe *m* seco, ruido *m* seco; **it fell with a ~ to the floor** cayó al suelo con un ruido seco.

2 ADV: **he went ~ into the stream** cayó ¡zas! en el arroyo; **it landed ~ on his cheek** le dio de lleno en la mejilla.

3 VT **(a)** (*Mus*) puntear.

(b) to ~ sth down arrojar algo con fuerza, dejar caer algo pesadamente.

4 VR: **to ~ o.s. down in a chair** dejarse caer pesadamente en una silla, desplomarse en una silla.

plonk²* [plɒŋk] N (*Brit*) vino *m* corriente, vino *m* peleón, purrela* *f*.

plonker: [ˈplɒŋkəʳ] N (*Brit*) gili* *mf*.

plop [plɒp] **1** N paf *m*; **~!** ¡paf!

2 VT (*also* **to ~ down**) arrojar dejando oír un paf.

3 VI caer dejando oír un paf.

plosive [ˈpləʊsɪv] **1** ADJ explosivo.

2 N explosiva *f*.

plot¹ [plɒt] N (*Agr*) terreno *m*; parcela *f*; (*of vegetables, flowers etc*) cuadro *m*; (*for building*) solar *m*; **~ of grass** cuadro *m* de cesped; **vegetable ~** cuadro *m* de hortalizas.

plot² [plɒt] **1** N (**a**) (*conspiracy*) complot *m*, compló *m*, conspiración *f*, conjura *f*.

(b) (*Liter, Theat*) argumento *m*; estructura *f*; trama *f*, intriga *f*; **the ~ thickens** (*fig*) la cosa se complica.

2 VT (**a**) *progress, course* (*on graph etc*) trazar; **to ~ A against Z** trazar A como función de Z.

(b) *downfall etc* urdir, tramar, maquinar.

3 VI conspirar, conjurarse; intrigar; **to ~ to do sth** conspirar para hacer algo, conjurarse para hacer algo.

plotter¹ [ˈplɒtəʳ] N conspirador *m*, -ora *f*, conjurado *m*, -a *f*.

plotter² [ˈplɒtəʳ] N (*Comput*) trazador *m* (de gráficos), tabla *f* trazadora, plotter *m*.

plotting [ˈplɒtɪŋ] **1** N conspiración *f*, intrigas *fpl*, maquinaciones *fpl*.

2 ATTR: **~ board** tablero *m* trazador; **~ paper** (*US*) papel *m* cuadriculado; **~ table** mesa *f* trazadora.

plough, (*US*) **plow** [plaʊ] **1** N arado *m*; **the P~** (*Astron*) el Carro, la Osa Mayor.

2 ATTR: **~ horse** caballo *m* de labranza.

3 VT (**a**) arar; (*fig*) surcar; **to ~ one's way through snow** abrirse con dificultad paso por la nieve; **to ~ one's way through a book** leer un libro con dificultad; **I ~ed my way through it eventually** por fin acabé de leerlo pero resultó pesadísimo.

(b) to ~ money into a project invertir (grandes cantidades de) dinero en un proyecto.

(c) (*Brit Univ**) cargar*, dar calabazas a*; **I was ~ed in German, they ~ed me in German** me cargaron en alemán.

4 VI (**a**) arar; **to ~ through = to ~ one's way; the lorry ~ed into the crowd** el camión se lanzó (violentamente) en medio de la multitud, el camión se metió en la multitud; *V* **3** (**a**).

(b) (*Brit Univ**) **I ~ed again** volvieron a cargarme*.

♦ **plough back** VT *profits* reinvertir.

♦ **plough in, plough under** VT cubrir arando, enterar arando.

♦ **plough up** VT *new ground* roturar; *bushes etc* arrancar con el arado, *pathway* hacer desaparecer arando; **the train ~ed up the track for 100 metres** el tren destrozó unos 100 metros de la vía.

ploughing, (*US*) **plowing** [ˈplaʊɪŋ] N arada *f*; **~ back** inversión *f* de ganancias.

ploughland, (*US*) **plowland** [ˈplaʊlænd] N tierra *f* de labrantío, tierra *f* labrantía.

ploughman, (*US*) **plowman** [ˈplaʊmən] N, PL **ploughmen,** (*US*) **plowmen** [ˈplaʊmən] arador *m*, labrador *m*; **~'s lunch** almuerzo de pub consistente en pan con queso y encurtidos.

ploughshare, (*US*) **plowshare** [ˈplaʊʃɛəʳ] N reja *f* del arado.

plover [ˈplʌvəʳ] N chorlito *m*.

plow [plaʊ] (*US*) etc = **plough** etc.

ploy [plɔɪ] N truco *m*, estratagema *f*, táctica *f*.

PLP N ABBR *of* **Parliamentary Labour Party.**

PLR N ABBR *of* **Public Lending Right.**

pluck¹ [plʌk] N (*courage*) valor *m*, ánimo *m*; (*guts*) agallas *fpl*; **it takes ~ to do that** hace falta mucho valor para conseguir eso; **he's got plenty of ~** sí tiene agallas; **I didn't have the ~ to own up** no tuve el valor para confesar.

pluck² [plʌk] **1** N (*tug*) tirón *m*.

2 VT *fruit, flower* coger, recoger (*LAm*); *bird* desplumar; *guitar* pulsar, puntear; **to ~ one's eyebrows** depilarse las cejas; **the helicopter ~ed him from the sea** el helicóptero le recogió del mar; **he seemed to ~ the answer out of the air** parecía sacar la solución de la nada; **it's an idea I've just ~ed out of the air** es una idea que he cogido al vuelo.

3 VI: **to ~ at** tirar de, dar un tirón a; **to ~ at sb's sleeve** tirar ligeramente de la manga de uno.

♦ **pluck off, pluck out** VT arrancar con los dedos, arrancar de un tirón.

♦ **pluck up** VT (**a**) = **pluck off; he ~ed it up off the table** lo recogió bruscamente de la mesa. (**b**) **to ~ up courage** cobrar ánimo.

pluckily [ˈplʌkɪlɪ] ADV valientemente; con resolución.

pluckiness [ˈplʌkɪnɪs] N valor *m*, ánimo *m*; resolución *f*.

plucky [ˈplʌkɪ] ADJ valiente, valeroso; resuelto.

plug [plʌg] **1** N (**a**) (*bung*) tapón *m*, taco *m*; (*in bath etc*) tapón *m*; (*Med: of cotton wool etc*) tampón *m*; (*US: of tobacco*) rollo *m*, tableta *f* (de tabaco de mascar); **the bank pulled the ~ on my overdraft*** el banco dejó de tolerar mi saldo deudor.

(b) (*Elec: free, on wire, on apparatus*) clavija *f*, enchufe *m*; (*in wall*) toma *f*; (*Telec*) clavija *f*; (*Aut*) bujía *f*.

(c) (*) enchufe* *m*; anuncio *m* (incidental), publicidad *f* (incidental); **to give sb a ~** dar publicidad a uno; **to put in a ~ for a product** lograr anunciar un producto (de modo solapado).

2 VT (**a**) *hole etc* tapar, llenar, obturar; (*Archit*) rellenar; *tooth* empastar; **to ~ a lead into a socket** enchufar un hilo en una toma; **~ this cloth into the hole** tapa el agujero con este trapo; **to ~ the drain on the reserves** acabar con las pérdidas de divisas.

(b) (:) (*hit*) pegar; (*shoot*) pegar un tiro a.

(c) (*) (*Comm*) anunciar (de modo solapado), dar publicidad (incidental) a; (*repeat*) repetir, machacar en; **he's been ~ging that line for years** hace años que viene diciendo lo mismo.

♦ **plug away*** VI seguir trabajando (*etc*) a pesar de todo, batir el yunque; no dejarse desanimar.

♦ **plug in** **1** VT (*Elec*) enchufar, conectar; **to ~ in a radio** conectar una radio.

2 VI (*esp US*) ponerse en la onda; **~ in to** ponerse en la onda de, sintonizar, compenetrarse de.

♦ **plug up** VT tapar, obturar.

plug-and-play [ˌplʌgənˈpleɪ] ADJ (*Comput*) fácil de conectar.

plughole [ˈplʌghəʊl] N tubo *m* de salida, salida *f*; **all that work has gone down the ~** todo ese trabajo se perdió, todo ese trabajo vale para nada.

plug-in [ˈplʌgˈɪn] ADJ (*Elec*) enchufable, con enchufe.

plum [plʌm] N (**a**) (*fruit*) ciruela *f*; (*tree*) ciruelo *m*. (**b**) (*fig: the best*) lo mejor; (*also* **~ job**) pingüe destino *m*, turrón *m**, breva* *f*.

plumage [ˈpluːmɪdʒ] N plumaje *m*.

plumb [plʌm] **1** N plomada *f*.

2 ADJ vertical, a plomo.

3 ADV (**a**) (*vertically*) verticalmente, a plomo.

(b) (*wholly*) totalmente, completamente; **~ crazy** completamente loco; **~ in the middle** exactamente en el centro; **it hit him ~ on the nose** le dio de lleno en las narices.

4 VT (*also fig*) sondar, sondear; **to ~ the depths of despair** conocer la mayor desesperación.

♦ **plumb in** VT conectar (con el suministro de agua).

plumbago [plʌmˈbeɪgəʊ] N plombagina *f*.

plumber [ˈplʌməʳ] N fontanero *m*, plomero *m* (*LAm*), gasfitero *m* (*SC*); **~'s helper** (*US*), **~'s mate** desatascador *m* de fregaderos.

plumbic [ˈplʌmbɪk] ADJ plúmbico, plúmbeo.

plumbing [ˈplʌmɪŋ] N (**a**) (*craft*) fontanería *f*, plomería *f* (*LAm*), gasfitería *f* (*SC*). (**b**) (*piping*) instalación *f* de cañerías; (*bathroom fittings*) aparatos *mpl* sanitarios.

plumbline [ˈplʌmlaɪn] N (cuerda *f* de) plomada *f*.

plume [pluːm] **1** N pluma *f*; (*on helmet*) penacho *m*; (*of smoke etc*) penacho *m*, hilo *m*.

2 VR: **the bird ~s itself** el ave se limpia las plumas, el ave se arregla las plumas.

plumed [pluːmd] ADJ plumado; con plumas; *helmet* empenachado.

plummet [ˈplʌmɪt] **1** N plomada *f*.

2 VI: **to ~ down, to come ~ing down** caer a plomo (*also fig*).

plummeting [ˈplʌmɪtɪŋ] ADJ *prices, profits, sales* que cae(n) en picado; *popularity* que se va a pique; *temperatures* que baja(n) drásticamente.

plummy* [ˈplʌmɪ] ADJ *voice* pastoso.

plump¹ [plʌmp] **1** ADJ *body* rechoncho, rollizo; *face* mofletudo; *chicken etc* gordo.

2 VT (*fatten*) engordar; (*swell*) hinchar.

3 VI engordar; hincharse.

plump² [plʌmp] **1** ADV de lleno; **it fell ~ on the roof** cayó de lleno en el techo.

2 VI (*fall*) caer pesadamente, dejarse caer pesadamente.

♦ **plump down** **1** VT: **to ~ sth down** arrojar algo pesadamente, dejar caer algo pesadamente (en el suelo *etc*).

2 VI: **to ~ down on to a chair** dejarse caer pesadamente en un sillón, desplomarse en un sillón.

3 VR: **to ~ o.s. down** dejarse caer pesadamente, desplomarse.

♦ **plump for** VT decidir por, optar por; (*vote*) votar por.

♦ **plump up** VT hinchar.

plumpness [ˈplʌmpnɪs] N gordura *f*; lo rollizo.

plum-pudding [ˈplʌmˈpʊdɪŋ] N budín *m*.

plum tomato [ˌplʌmtəˈmɑːtəʊ] N tomate *m* pera.

plum-tree [ˈplʌmtriː] N ciruelo *m*.

plunder [ˈplʌndəʳ] **1** N (*act*) pillaje *m*, saqueo *m*; (*loot*) botín *m*.

2 VT saquear, pillar; *tomb* robar; *safe* robar el contenido de, robar (las alhajas de); **they ~ed my cellar** saquearon mi bodega.

plunderer [ˈplʌndərəʳ] N saqueador *m*, -ora *f*.

plundering [ˈplʌndərɪŋ] N saqueo *m*.

plunge [plʌndʒ] **1** N **(a)** (*dive from bank etc*) salto *m*; (*submersion by swimmer, bird etc*) zambullida *f*; (*by professional diver*) inmersión *f*; (*bathe*) baño *m*; **the diver rested after each ~** el buzo descansó después de cada inmersión; **he had a ~ before breakfast** se fue a bañar antes de desayunar.
(b) (*bath*) baño *m*; (*pool*) piscina *f*; **cold ~** baño *m* frío.
(c) (*fig: fall*) baja *f*, caída *f*, descenso *m*.
(d) (*fig*) **to take the ~** dar el paso decisivo, aventurarse; resolverse; jugarse el todo; (*esp hum: get married*) decidir casarse; **we are about to take the ~** estamos al punto de dar el paso decisivo; **I took the ~ and bought it** por fin me resolví a comprarlo.
2 VT **(a)** (*immerse*) sumergir; hundir (*into* en); **he ~d his hands into the water** hundió las manos en el agua; **he ~d his hand into his pocket** metió la mano bien dentro del bolsillo; **to ~ a dagger into sb's chest** hundir (*or* clavar) un puñal en el pecho de uno.
(b) **to ~ a room into darkness** sumir un cuarto en la oscuridad; **New York was suddenly ~d into darkness** Nueva York se encontró de repente sumida en la oscuridad; **to ~ sb into sadness** hundir (*or* sumir, abismar) a uno en la tristeza; **we were ~d into gloom by the news** la noticia nos sumió en la tristeza.
3 VI **(a)** (*dive*) saltar; zambullirse; sumergirse; (*sink*) hundirse; **then the submarine ~d** luego se sumergió el submarino; **she ~d into 10 metres of water** se zambulló en 10 metros de agua.
(b) (*fall*) caer; (*road, cliff*) precipitarse; **he ~d to his death** tuvo una caída mortal; **he ~d from a 5th storey window** se arrojó desde una ventana del 5° piso; **the aircraft ~d into the sea off Dover** el avión cayó al (*or* se precipitó en el) mar a la altura de Dover.
(c) (*dress*) tener mucho escote, ser muy escotado.
(d) (*ship*) cabecear; (*horse*) corcovear.
(e) (*person: rush*) arrojarse, lanzarse, precipitarse; **to ~ forward** precipitarse hacia adelante; **to ~ into one's work** emprender resuelto su trabajo, engolfarse en el trabajo; **to ~ heedlessly into danger** meterse en los peligros sin hacer caso de ellos; **he ~d into a discussion of Plato** se lanzó a una discusión de Platón.
(f) (*: gamble*) apostar el todo; jugar fuerte; (*Comm*) arriesgar mucho dinero.
(g) (*: decide*) resolverse, dar el paso decisivo.
plunger ['plʌndʒər] N (*Mech*) émbolo *m*; (*for sink*) desatascador *m* (de fregaderos).
plunging ['plʌndʒɪŋ] ADJ: **~ neckline** escote *m* muy bajo.
plunk [plʌŋk] N *etc* (*US*) = **plonk**[1].
pluperfect ['plu:'pɜ:fɪkt] N pluscuamperfecto *m*.
plural ['plʊərəl] **1** ADJ plural; **the ~ form of the noun** la forma del sustantivo en plural.
2 N plural *m*; **in the ~** en el plural.
pluralism ['plʊərəlɪzəm] N pluralismo *m*.
pluralist ['plʊərəlɪst] **1** ADJ pluralista.
2 N pluralista *mf*.
pluralistic [,plʊərə'lɪstɪk] ADJ pluralista.
plurality [,plʊə'rælɪtɪ] N pluralidad *f*.
plus [plʌs] **1** PREP más, y; además de; juntamente con; **3 ~ 4** 3 más 4; **~ what I have to do already** además de (*or* más) lo que tengo que hacer ya; **we're ~ 500** (*Bridge*) tenemos una ventaja de 500 puntos.
2 ADJ **(a)** (*Math, Elec: quantity*) positivo, de signo positivo; **~ sign** signo *m* de más, signo *m* de sumar.
(b) **two pounds ~** dos libras y algo más, más de dos libras; **twenty ~** veinte y pico, veintitantos.
3 N **(a)** (*Math: sign*) signo *m* de más, signo *m* de sumar; (*amount*) cantidad *f* positiva.
(b) (*fig*) punto *m* a favor; aspecto *m* positivo; **that is a ~ for him** es un punto a su favor.
4 CONJ (*esp US*) además; **~ we haven't got the money** además no tenemos el dinero.
plus fours ['plʌs'fɔ:z] NPL pantalones *mpl* de golf, pantalones *mpl* holgados de media pierna.
plush [plʌʃ] **1** N felpa *f*.
2 ADJ de felpa; felpado; (***) V **plushy**.
plushy* ['plʌʃɪ] ADJ lujoso, elegante, de buen tono.
Plutarch ['plu:tɑ:k] NM Plutarco.
Pluto ['plu:təʊ] NM Plutón.
plutocracy [,plu:'tɒkrəsɪ] N plutocracia *f*.
plutocrat ['plu:təʊkræt] N plutócrata *mf*.
plutocratic [,plu:təʊ'krætɪk] ADJ plutocrático.
plutonium [plu:'təʊnɪəm] N plutonio *m*.
pluviometer [,plu:vɪ'ɒmɪtər] N pluviómetro *m*.
ply[1] [plaɪ] N: **three ~** (*wood*) de tres capas; (*wool*) triple, de tres hebras.
ply[2] [plaɪ] **1** VT **(a)** (*needle, tool etc*) manejar, menear (vigorosamente); *oars etc* emplear; *trade* ejercer; *seas, river* navegar por.
(b) **to ~ sb with questions** acosar a uno con preguntas, importunar a uno haciéndole muchas preguntas; **to ~ sb for information** importunar a uno pidiéndole informes; **to ~ sb with drink** dar a

uno repetidas veces de beber, emborrachar a uno; **to ~ sb with cakes** ofrecer repetidas veces los pastelitos a uno.
2 VI: **to ~ between** hacer el servicio entre, ir y venir entre; **to ~ for hire** ofrecerse para alquilar.
plywood ['plaɪwʊd] N madera *f* contrachapada, madera *f* multilaminar, panel *m*.
PM N **(a)** (*Brit*) ABBR of **Prime Minister. (b)** (*Jur, Med*) ABBR of **postmortem.**
p.m. ADV ABBR of **post meridiem** después del mediodía, de la tarde.
PMG N (*Brit*) ABBR of **Postmaster General** Director *m* General de Correos.
PMS N ABBR of **premenstrual syndrome** síndrome *m* premenstrual.
PMT N ABBR of **premenstrual tension** síndrome *m* premenstrual, SPM.
PN, P/N N ABBR of **promissory note** pagaré *m*.
PND N ABBR of **postnatal depression** depresión *f* posparto.
pneumatic [nju:'mætɪk] ADJ neumático; **~ drill** taladradora *f* neumática.
pneumoconiosis [,nju:məʊ,kəʊnɪ'əʊsɪs] N neumoconiosis *f*.
pneumonia [nju:'məʊnɪə] N pulmonía *f*.
Pnom Penh ['nɒm'pen] N = **Phnom Penh.**
PO N **(a)** ABBR of **Post Office** oficina *f* de correos. **(b)** ABBR of **PO Box** apartado *m*, apdo, casilla *f*. **(c)** (*Aer*) ABBR of **Pilot Officer** oficial *m* piloto. **(d)** (*Naut*) ABBR of **Petty Officer** suboficial *m* de marina.
po: [pəʊ] N (*Brit*) orinal *m*.
p.o. ABBR of **postal order** giro *m* postal.
POA N **(a)** (*Brit*) ABBR of **Prison Officers' Association** sindicato de empleados de cárcel. **(b)** (*Comm*) ABBR of **prices on application** los precios, a solicitud.
poach[1] [pəʊtʃ] VT (*Culin*) *egg* escalfar; *fish etc* hervir.
poach[2] [pəʊtʃ] **1** VT cazar (*or* pescar *etc*) en vedado; cazar (*or* pescar *etc*) ilegalmente; (*fig: steal*) robar, *advantage etc* pisar, tomar.
2 VI cazar (*or* pescar *etc*) en finca ajena; cazar furtivamente; **to ~ on sb's preserves** (*fig*) cazar en finca ajena, meterse en los asuntos ajenos.
poached [pəʊtʃt] ADJ *egg* escalfado; *fish etc* hervido.
poacher[1] ['pəʊtʃər] N cazador *m* furtivo.
poacher[2] ['pəʊtʃər] N (*for eggs*) escalfador *m* (de huevos).
poaching ['pəʊtʃɪŋ] N furtivismo *m*, caza *f* furtiva, pesca *f* furtiva.
POB ABBR of **post office box** apartado *m* de correos.
pochard ['pəʊtʃəd] N porrón *m* común.
pock [pɒk] N (*also ~mark*) pústula *f*; picadura *f*, hoyuelo *m*.
pocked [pɒkt] ADJ = **pockmarked.**
pocket ['pɒkɪt] **1** N bolsillo *m*, bolsa *f* (*Méx*); (*Billiards*) tronera *f*; (*fig: Geol, Mil etc*) bolsa *f*; hoyo *m*, cavidad *f*, hueco *m*; (*Aer*) bolsa *f* de aire; **~ of resistance** bolsa *f* de resistencia; **to be in ~** salir ganando; **to be £5 in ~** haber ganado 5 libras; **to be out of ~** salir perdiendo; **to be £5 out of ~** haber perdido 5 libras; **he has the game in his ~** tiene el partido en el bote; **to have sb in one's ~** tener a uno en el bolsillo; **that hurts his ~** eso le duele en el bolsillo; **to line one's ~s** ponerse las botas; V **pick.**
2 ATTR de bolsillo; **~ battleship** acorazado *m* de bolsillo; **~ calculator** calculadora *f* de bolsillo; **~ diary** agenda *f* de bolsillo; **~ edition** edición *f* de bolsillo.
3 VT meter en el bolsillo, guardar en el bolsillo; (*Billiards*) entronerar; (*earn, make*) ganar; (*pej*) apropiarse, alzarse con, embolsar; **he ~ed half the takings** se embolsó la mitad de la recaudación; V **pride** *etc*.
pocketbook ['pɒkɪtbʊk] N (*US*) **(a)** (*wallet*) cartera *f*, portamonedas *m*; (*handbag*) bolso *m* (de mano), cartera *f* (*LAm*). **(b)** (*book*) libro *m* de bolsillo.
pocketful ['pɒkɪtfʊl] N bolsillo *m*; cantidad *f* que cabe en el bolsillo; **a ~ of nuts** un bolsillo de nueces.
pocket-handkerchief [,pɒkɪt'hæŋkətʃɪf] N pañuelo *m*.
pocketknife ['pɒkɪtnaɪf] N, PL **pocketknives** ['pɒkɪtnaɪvz] navaja *f*.
pocket-money ['pɒkɪt,mʌnɪ] N (*Brit*) asignación *f*, dinero *m* para pequeños gastos personales.
pocket-size ['pɒkɪtsaɪz] ADJ de bolsillo.
pockmark ['pɒkmɑ:k] N picadura *f*, hoyuelo *m*.
pockmarked ['pɒkmɑ:kt] ADJ *face* picado de viruelas; *surface* marcado de hoyuelos; **to be ~ with** estar marcado de, estar acribillado de.
POD N ABBR of **payment on delivery** pago *m* a la entrega.
pod [pɒd] N vaina *f*.
podgy ['pɒdʒɪ] ADJ gordinflón; *face* mofletudo.
podiatrist [pɒ'dɪətrɪst] N (*US*) pedicuro *mf*.
podiatry [pɒ'dɪətrɪ] N (*US*) pedicura *f*.
podium ['pəʊdɪəm] N, PL **podia** ['pəʊdɪə] podio *m*.
POE N **(a)** ABBR of **port of embarkation** puerto *m* de embarque. **(b)** ABBR of **port of entry** puerto *m* de entrada.
poem ['pəʊɪm] N (*short*) poesía *f*; (*long, narrative*) poema *m*; **P~ of the Cid** Poema *m* de mío Cid, Cantar *m* de mío Cid; **Lorca's ~s** las poesías de Lorca, la obra poética de Lorca, las obras en verso de Lorca.
poet ['pəʊɪt] N poeta *mf*; **P~ Laureate** (*Brit*) Poeta *m* laureado.

poetaster [ˌpəʊɪˈtæstəʳ] N poetastro *m*.

poetess [ˈpəʊɪtes] N poetisa *f*.

poetic(al) [pəʊˈetɪk(əl)] ADJ poético; **~ justice** justicia *f* poética; **~ licence**, **~ license** (*US*) licencia *f* poética.

poetically [pəʊˈetɪkəlɪ] ADV poéticamente.

poeticize [pəʊˈetɪsaɪz] VT (*enhance*) poetizar, adornar con detalles poéticos; (*translate into verse*) hacer un poema de, hacer una versión poética de.

poetics [pəʊˈetɪks] N poética *f*.

poetry [ˈpəʊɪtrɪ] ① N poesía *f*.
② ATTR: **~ magazine** revista *f* de poesía; **~ reading** lectura *f* de poemas.

POEU N (*Brit*) ABBR *of* **Post Office Engineering Union**.

po-faced [ˌpəʊˈfeɪst] ADJ que mira con desaprobación, severo.

pogrom [ˈpɒgrəm] N pogrom *m*, pogromo *m*, persecución *f* antisemítica.

poignancy [ˈpɔɪnjənsɪ] N patetismo *m*; intensidad *f*, profundidad *f*.

poignant [ˈpɔɪnjənt] ADJ (*moving*) conmovedor, patético; (*profound*) intenso, agudo, profundo.

poignantly [ˈpɔɪnjəntlɪ] ADV de modo conmovedor, patéticamente; intensamente, agudamente.

poinsettia [pɔɪnˈsetɪə] N flor *f* de pascua.

▼ **point** [pɔɪnt] ① N **(a)** (*Typ etc: dot*) punto *m*; **7.6** (**seven ~ six**) 7,6 (siete coma seis, seite con seis, siete enteros con seis décimos).
(b) (*on scale: place, time*) punto *m*; **~ of the compass** cuarta *f*; **~ of departure** punto *m* de partida; **Slough and all ~s west** Slough y las
▼ estaciones más hacia el oeste; **~ of reference** punto *m* de referencia; **~ of no return** punto *m* de no retorno; **at the ~ where the road forks** donde se bifurca el camino; **at this ~** en esto, llegado a este punto; **at that ~ in time** en aquel momento; **at all ~s** por todas partes, en todos los sitios; **matters are at such a ~ that ...** las cosas han llegado a tal extremo que ...; **to be on the ~ of** + *ger* estar a punto de + *infin*; **delivered free to all ~s in Spain** entrega gratuita en cualquier punto de España; **he is severe to the ~ of cruelty** es
▼ tan severo que resulta cruel, su severidad raya en la crueldad; **up to a ~** hasta cierto punto; en cierto modo.
(c) (*aspect*) punto *m*, aspecto *m*; **~ of interest** punto *m* interesante, aspecto *m* interesante; **~ of honour** cuestión *f* de honor, punto *m* de honor; **~ of order** cuestión *f* de procedimiento, cuestión *f* de orden; **in ~ of** en cuanto a, por lo que se refiere a; **in ~ of fact** en realidad; **in ~ of numbers** en cuanto al número; **in ~ of sheer strength** en cuanto a la fuerza sola.
(d) **~ of view** punto *m* de vista; **from the ~ of view of** desde el punto de vista de; **to come round to sb's ~ of view** adoptar el criterio de uno, llegar a compartir la opinión de uno; **to look at a matter from all ~s of view** considerar una cuestión bajo todos sus aspectos; **to see** (*or* **understand**) **sb's ~ of view** comprender el punto de vista de uno.
▼ **(e)** (*of argument etc*) punto *m*; **to argue ~ by ~** razonar punto por punto; **the ~ at issue** el punto en cuestión, el asunto en litigio; **the ~s to remember are ...** los puntos a retener son los siguientes ...; **to be beside the ~** no venir al caso; **it is beside the ~ that ...** no importa que + *subj*; **it's off the ~** está fuera de propósito; **to get off the ~**, **to wander off the ~** salirse del tema, apartarse del tema; **on this ~** sobre este punto; **on that ~** en cuanto a eso; **on that ~ we agree** sobre eso estamos de acuerdo; **to differ on a ~** no estar de acuerdo en un particular; **an argument very much to the ~** un argumento muy a propósito; **that is hardly to the ~** eso apenas hace al caso; **to come to the ~** ir al grano; **let's come to the ~!** ¡vamos al grano!, ¡dejémonos de historias!; **to get back to the ~** volver al tema; **now, to get back to the ~** bueno, para volver al tema; **to keep to the ~** no salirse del tema; **to carry one's ~** salirse con la suya; **it gave ~ to the argument** hizo ver la importancia del argumento; **to speak to the ~** (*relevantly*) hablar acertadamente, hablar con tino; **I think she has a ~** creo que tiene un poco de razón; **to make a ~** establecer un punto, hacer aceptar una opinión; **you've made your ~** nos (*etc*) has convencido; **he made the following ~s** dijo lo siguiente; **to make the ~ that ...** hacer ver que ...; **to make a ~ of** + *ger* no dejar de + *infin*, insistir en + *infin*; **to press the ~** insistir (*that* en que); **to pursue one's ~** seguir su tema; **to stretch a ~** hacer una excepción, hacer una concesión; **I take your ~** acepto lo que dices; **~ taken!** ¡de acuerdo!, ¡tienes razón!
(f) (*significant part, important thing*) lo significativo, lo importante;

this is the ~ esto es lo importante; **the ~ is, ...** lo importante es ...; **the whole ~ is ...** lo único que importa es ...; **the ~ is that ...** el hecho es que ...; **that's just the ~!** ¡sí eso es lo más importante!, ¡eso es!; **that's not the ~** no es eso; **the ~ of the joke is that ...** la gracia del chiste consiste en que ...; **to get the ~** comprender; **to miss the ~** no comprender; no ver lo esencial.
(g) (*purpose*) fin *m*, finalidad *f*, objeto *m*; (*usefulness*) utilidad *f*; **what's the ~ of railways?** ¿qué utilidad tienen los ferrocarriles?, ¿de qué sirven los ferrocarriles?; **what's the ~ of trying?** ¿de qué sirve esforzarse?; **there is no ~ in** + *ger* no vale la pena + *infin*, no hay para qué + *infin*; **I don't see the ~ of doing it** no entiendo por qué sea necesario hacerlo, no veo el motivo por hacerlo.
(h) (*of character*) rasgo *m*, característica *f*; cualidad *f*; **weak ~** flaco *m*, punto *m* flaco, punto *m* débil; **~s of a horse** características *fpl* de un caballo; **he has his ~s** tiene algunas cualidades buenas; **it was always his strong ~** siempre ha sido su punto fuerte; **maths is not a strong ~ of mine** nunca he sido muy fuerte en matemáticas; **what ~s should I look for?** ¿qué puntos debo buscar?
(i) (*Games*) punto *m*, tanto *m*; **~s against** puntos *mpl* en contra; **~s for** puntos *mpl* a favor; **to give sb ~s** dar una ventaja a uno; **to score 10 ~s** marcar 10 puntos; **to win on ~s** ganar a los puntos.
(j) (*unit*) **the thermometer went up 3 ~s** el termómetro subió 3 grados; **the shares went down 2 ~s** las acciones bajaron 2 enteros.
(k) (*sharp end*) (*of needle etc*) punta *f*; (*of pen*) puntilla *f*; (*Geog*) punta *f*, promontorio *m*, cabo *m*; (*Elec*) enchufe *m*, toma *f*; **~s** (*Brit Rail*) agujas *fpl*; **to dance on ~s** bailar sobre las puntas; **to put a ~ on a pencil** sacar punta a un lápiz; **not to put too fine a ~ on it** para decirlo como es, hablando sin rodeos.
(l) (*Typ*) cuerpo *m*; **9 ~ black** negritas *fpl* del cuerpo 9.
(m) (*Brit Elec: also* **power ~**) toma *f* de corriente.
② ATTR: **~s decision** (*Boxing*) decisión *f* a los puntos; **a five-~ star** una estrella de cinco puntas; **~s system** sistema *m* de puntos; **~s win** victoria *f* a los puntos.
③ VT **(a)** (*sharpen*) afilar, aguzar; *pencil* sacar punta a.
(b) **to ~ a moral** inculcar una lección, subrayar una moraleja.
(c) *gun, telescope etc* apuntar (*at* a); **to ~ a gun at sb** apuntar a uno con un fusil; **to ~ a finger at sb** señalar a uno con el dedo; **would you ~ me in the direction of the town hall?** ¿me quiere decir dónde está el ayuntamiento?; **we ~ed him in the right direction** le indicamos el camino.
(d) *path, way* indicar, señalar.
(e) *wall* rejuntar.
(f) *text* puntuar; *Hebrew etc* puntar.
④ VI **(a)** **to ~ at sb** señalar (*or* indicar) a uno con el dedo.
(b) (*of dog*) mostrar la caza, parar.
(c) **it ~s north** está orientado hacia el norte; **the hand ~ed to midnight** la aguja marcaba las 12; **this ~s to the fact that ...** esto indica que ...; **everything ~s that way** todo parece indicarlo; **everything ~s to his success** todo anuncia su éxito; **everything ~s to the festival being a lively one** el festival se anuncia animado; **the evidence ~s to her** las pruebas indican que ella es la culpable.

▼◆ **point out** VT indicar, señalar; **to ~ out sth to sb** señalar algo a uno, enseñar algo a uno; (*in speaking*) hacer ver algo a uno, indicar algo a uno; **to ~ out sb's mistakes** señalar los errores de uno; **to ~ out to sb the advantages of a car** explicar a uno las ventajas de tener coche; **to ~ out that ...** indicar que ..., señalar que ...; **may I ~ out that ...** permítaseme observar que ...

◆ **point up** VT destacar, poner de relieve.

point-blank [ˈpɔɪntˈblæŋk] ① ADV a quemarropa (*also fig*); **to ask sb sth** ~ preguntar algo a uno a quemarropa; **to refuse ~** dar una negativa rotunda.
② ADJ *question, shot* hecho a quemarropa.

point-by-point [ˈpɔɪntbarˈpɔɪnt] ADJ punto por punto.

point duty [ˈpɔɪntˌdjuːtɪ] N (*Brit*) control *m* de la circulación.

pointed [ˈpɔɪntɪd] ADJ **(a)** *shape* puntiagudo; (*sharp*) afilado, agudo; (*Archit*) *arch, window* ojival. **(b)** *remark etc* intencionado, lleno de intención; inequívoco, directo; enfático.

pointedly [ˈpɔɪntɪdlɪ] ADV *say etc* con intención; inequívocamente, directamente; enfáticamente.

pointer [ˈpɔɪntəʳ] N **(a)** (*needle*) indicador *m*, aguja *f*; (*of balance*) fiel *m*; (*long stick*) puntero *m*. **(b)** (*dog*) perro *m* de muestra, braco *m*. **(c)** (*fig*) índice *m* (*to* de); indicación *f*; pista *f*; **it is a ~ to a possible solution** es una indicación de una solución posible; **there is at present no ~ to the outcome** por ahora nada indica qué resultado tendrá; **this is a ~ to the guilty man** es una pista que conducirá al criminal.

pointillism [ˈpwæntɪlɪzəm] N puntillismo *m*.

pointing [ˈpɔɪntɪŋ] N (*Constr*) rejuntado *m*.

pointless [ˈpɔɪntlɪs] ADJ (*useless*) inútil; (*motiveless*) sin motivo, inmotivado; (*meaningless*) sin sentido; insensato; **it is ~ to complain** es inútil quejarse, de nada sirve quejarse; **an apparently ~ crime** un crimen que parece carecer de motivo; **a ~ existence** una vida sin sentido, una vida que carece de propósito.

pointlessly ['pɔɪntlɪslɪ] ADV inútilmente; sin motivo.

pointlessness ['pɔɪntlɪsnɪs] N inutilidad *f*; falta *f* de motivo; falta *f* de sentido; **the ~ of war** la insensatez de la guerra.

point of sale [,pɔɪntəv'seɪl] [1] N punto *m* de venta.

[2] **point-of-sale** ATTR *advertising etc* en el punto de venta.

pointsman ['pɔɪntsmən] N, PL **pointsmen** ['pɔɪntsmən] (*Rail*) encargado *m* del cambio de agujas.

point-to-point ['pɔɪnttə'pɔɪnt] N (*also* **~ race**) carrera de caballos a campo traviesa.

pointy* ['pɔɪntɪ] ADJ *hat, ears, shoes* picudo, puntiagudo.

poise [pɔɪz] [1] N (a) (*balance*) equilibrio *m*.

(b) (*fig: of body*) aire *m*, porte *m*; elegancia *f*; **she dances with such ~** baila con tanta elegancia, baila con tal garbo.

(c) (*of mind*) serenidad *f*; aplomo *m*; confianza *f* en sí mismo; **she does it with great ~** lo hace con el mayor aplomo; **he lacks ~** le falta confianza en sí mismo.

[2] VT equilibrar; balancear; **he ~d it on his hand** lo puso en equilibrio sobre la mano; **to be ~d** estar suspendido; (*hover*) cernerse, estar inmóvil (en el aire *etc*); **they are ~d to attack, they are ~d for the attack** están listos para atacar, están aprestados para el ataque.

poised [pɔɪzd] ADJ (*in temperament*) sereno, ecuánime, confiado en sí mismo.

poison ['pɔɪzn] [1] N veneno *m*; tóxico *m*; (*fig*) ponzoña *f*, veneno *m*; **to die of ~** morir envenenado; **to take ~** envenenarse; **they hate each other like ~** se odian a muerte.

[2] ATTR **~ gas** gas *m* tóxico, gas *m* asfixiante.

[3] VT envenenar; (*chemically*) intoxicar; (*fig*) envenenar, emponzoñar; corromper; **to ~ sb's mind** envenenar el pensamiento de uno (*against* contra); **the wells were ~ed** echaron sustancias tóxicas a los pozos.

poisoner ['pɔɪznər] N envenenador *m*, -ora *f*.

poisoning ['pɔɪznɪŋ] N envenenamiento *m*; intoxicación *f*.

poisonous ['pɔɪznəs] ADJ *snake etc* venenoso; *substance, plant, fumes etc* tóxico; (*fig: damaging*) pernicioso, (*very bad*) horrible, malísimo; **this ~ propaganda** esta propaganda perniciosa; **the play was ~** la obra fue horrible; **he's a ~ individual** es una persona odiosa.

poison-pen ['pɔɪzn'pen] ADJ: **~ letter** anónimo *m* ofensivo.

poke¹ [pəʊk] N (*esp Scot: sack*) saco *m*, bolsa *f*.

poke² [pəʊk] [1] N (a) (*push*) empuje *m*, empujón *m*; (*with elbow*) codazo *m*; (*jab*) pinchazo *m*; hurgonazo *m*; (*with poker*) hurgonada *f*, hurgonazo *m*; **to give the fire a ~** atizar la lumbre, remover la lumbre; **to give sb a ~ in the ribs** dar a uno un codazo en las costillas.

(b) **to have a ~⁎** (*Brit*) echar un polvo⁎.

[2] VT (*push*) empujar; *fire* hurgar, atizar, remover; (*Comput*) almacenar; **to ~ sb in the ribs** dar a uno un codazo en las costillas; **to ~ sb in the ribs with a stick** dar a uno un empujón con un palo en las costillas; **to ~ a stick into a crack** meter un palo en una grieta; **to ~ a rag into a tube** introducir un trapo en un tubo; **to ~ a stick into the ground** clavar un palo en el suelo; **to ~ a hole in a picture** hacer un agujero en un cuadro; **to ~ fun at sb** ridiculizar a uno.

[3] VI: **to ~ at sth with a stick** tratar de remover (*etc*) algo con un bastón; **to ~ into sb's business** meterse en los asuntos de uno.

♦**poke about, poke around** VI andar buscando; (*pej*) fisgar, hacer indagaciones a hurtadillas; **we spent a day poking about in the shops** pasamos un día curioseando en las tiendas; **and now you come poking about!** ¡y ahora te metes a husmear!

♦**poke out** VT: **to ~ sb's eye out** sacar el ojo a uno, quebrar el ojo a uno; **to ~ one's head out** sacar la cabeza, asomar la cabeza.

poker¹ ['pəʊkər] N atizador *m*, hurgón *m*.

poker² ['pəʊkər] N (*Cards*) póquer *m*, póker *m*; **to have a ~ face** tener una cara impasible.

poker-faced ['pəʊkə'feɪst] ADJ de cara impasible; **they looked on ~** miraron impasibles, miraron sin expresión.

poky ['pəʊkɪ] ADJ *room* estrecho, muy pequeño; **a ~ little room** un cuartucho.

Polack⁎ ['pəʊlæk] N (*US pej*) polaco *m*, -a *f*.

Poland ['pəʊlənd] N Polonia *f*.

polar ['pəʊlər] ADJ polar; **~ bear** oso *m* blanco, oso *m* polar; **~ cap** casquete *m* polar; **P~ Circle** Círculo *m* Polar.

polarity [pəʊ'lærɪtɪ] N polaridad *f*.

polarization [,pəʊlərai'zeɪʃən] N polarización *f*.

polarize ['pəʊləraɪz] [1] VT polarizar.

[2] VI polarizarse.

Polaroid ['pəʊlərɔɪd] ® [1] ADJ Polaroid ®.

[2] N (*also* **~ camera**) Polaroid ® *f*.

Pole [pəʊl] N polaco *m*, -a *f*.

pole¹ [pəʊl] [1] N (a) *medida de longitud* = 5,029 *m*.

(b) palo *m*, palo *m* largo, vara *f* larga; (*flag~*) asta *f*; (*tent~*) mástil *m*; (*for fencing*) estaca *f*; (*Telec*) poste *m*; (*for gymnastics*) percha *f*; (*for vaulting*) pértiga *f*; (*for punting*) pértiga *f*; (*of cart*) vara *f*, lanza *f*; **to**

be up the **~⁎** estar chiflado⁎.

[2] VT *punt etc* impeler con pértiga.

pole² [pəʊl] N (*Elec, Geog etc*) polo *m*; **~ star** estrella *f* polar; **North P~** Polo *m* Norte; **South P~** Polo *m* Sur; **from ~ to ~** de polo a polo; **they're ~s apart** son polos opuestos.

poleaxe, (*US*) **poleax** ['pəʊlæks] VT desnucar; (*fig*) pasmar, aturdir.

pole bean ['pəʊl,biːn] N (*US*) judía *f* trepadora.

polecat ['pəʊlkæt] N turón *m*; (*US*) mofeta *f*.

Pol. Econ. ['pɒlɪkɒn] N ABBR *of* **political economy**.

polemic [pɒ'lemɪk] [1] ADJ polémico.

[2] N polémica *f*; **~s** polémica *f*.

polemical [pɒ'lemɪkəl] ADJ polémico.

polemicist [pɒ'lemɪsɪst] N polemista *mf*.

pole position ['pəʊlpə'zɪʃn] N posición *f* de cabeza, pole *f*; (*fig*) posición *f* de ventaja.

polevault ['pəʊlvɔːlt] [1] N salto *m* de pértiga.

[2] VI saltar con pértiga.

polevaulter ['pəʊl,vɔːltər] N saltador *m* de pértiga, pertiguista *m*.

polevaulting ['pəʊl,vɔːltɪŋ] N salto *m* de pértiga.

police [pə'liːs] N policía *f*.

[2] ATTR **~ captain** (*US*) subjefe *mf*; **~ car** coche *m* de policía, coche-patrulla *m*; **~ constable** policía *m*, guardia *m*; **~ court** tribunal *m* de policía, tribunal *m* correccional; **in ~ custody** bajo custodia policial; **~ department** (*US*) policía *f*; **~ dog** perro *m* policía; **~ escort** escolta *f* policial; **~ force** policía *f*; **~ inspector** inspector *m*, -ora *f* de policía; **~ officer** policía *m*; **~ protection** protección *f* policial; **~ record** antecedentes *mpl* penales; **~ state** estado *m* policíaco; **~ station** comisaría *f*; delegación *f* (*Mex*); **~ work** trabajo *m* policial, trabajo *m* de la policía.

[3] VT *frontier* vigilar, patrullar por; *area* mantener servicio de policía en, mantener el orden público en; *process* vigilar, controlar; **the frontier is ~d by UN patrols** la frontera la vigilan las patrullas de la ONU; **the area used to be ~d by Britain** antes Gran Bretaña proveía la policía para la región.

policeman [pə'liːsmən] N, PL **policemen** [pə'liːsmən] policía *m*, guardia *m*.

policewoman [pə'liːs,wʊmən] N, PL **policewomen** [pə'liːs,wɪmɪn] mujer *f* policía, agente *f*.

policing [pə'liːsɪŋ] N servicio *m* policial.

policy¹ ['pɒlɪsɪ] N (a) política *f*; (*loosely*) principios *mpl*; criterio *m*, actitud *f*; sistema *m*; (*of party, at election*) programa *m*; (*of newspaper*) normas *fpl* de conducta; **~ decision** decisión *f* de principio; **~ statement** declaración *f* de política; **that's not my ~** ése no es mi sistema; **to change one's ~** cambiar de táctica; **it would be contrary to public ~ to +** *infin* no sería conforme con el interés nacional **+** *infin*.

(b) (*wisdom*) prudencia *f*; **it is ~ to +** *infin* es prudente **+** *infin*.

policy² ['pɒlɪsɪ] N (*insurance*) póliza *f*; **to take out a ~** hacerse un seguro, sacar un seguro.

policyholder ['pɒlɪsɪ,həʊldər] N tenedor *m*, -ora *f* de una póliza, asegurado *m*, -a *f*.

policy-making ['pɒlɪsɪ,meɪkɪŋ] [1] N elaboración *f* de la política a seguir.

[2] ATTR *body, process* que organiza la política a seguir; *role* en la organización de la política a seguir.

polio ['pəʊlɪəʊ] N polio *f*.

poliomyelitis ['pəʊlɪəʊmaɪə'laɪtɪs] N poliomielitis *f*.

Polish ['pəʊlɪʃ] [1] ADJ polaco.

[2] N (*Ling*) polaco *m*.

polish ['pɒlɪʃ] [1] N (a) (*material*) (*shoe* ~) betún *m*; (*floor ~, furniture* ~) cera *f* (de lustrar); (*metal* ~) líquido *m* para limpiar metales; (*nail* ~) esmalte *m* para las uñas, laca *f* para las uñas.

(b) (*act*) pulimento *m*; **to give sth a ~** sacar brillo a algo, pulir algo; **my shoes need a ~** hace falta limpiar mis zapatos.

(c) (*shine*) brillo *m*, bruñido *m*, lustre *m*; **high ~** lustre *m* brillante; **the buttons have lost their ~** los botones han perdido su brillo, los botones se han deslustrado; **to put a ~ on sth** sacar brillo a algo; **the water takes the ~ off** el agua quita el brillo.

(d) (*fig: refinement*) finura *f*, cultura *f*, urbanidad *f*; (*of artistry etc*) elegancia *f*; perfección *f*; **his style needs ~** le hace falta limar el estilo; **he lacks ~** le falta finura.

[2] VT (a) *shoes* limpiar, bolear (*Mex*); *floor, furniture* encerar, sacar brillo a; *pans, metal, silver* pulir; (*mechanically, industrially*) pulimentar.

(b) (*also* **to ~ up**) *person* civilizar; *manners* refinar; *style etc* pulir, limar; **one's French etc** repasar, refrescar.

♦**polish off** VT *work* despachar; *person etc* acabar con; *food, drink* despachar, dar cuenta de.

♦**polish up** VT = **polish 2 (b)**.

polished ['pɒlɪʃt] ADJ pulido; *style etc* limado, elegante; *person* culto, distinguido, fino; *manners* fino.

polisher ['pɒlɪʃər] N (*person*) pulidor *m*, -ora *f*; (*machine*) enceradora *f*.

polishing machine ['pɒlɪʃɪŋmə,ʃiːn] N pulidor *m*; (*for floors*)

enceradora f.
Politburo ['pɒlɪtbjʊərəʊ] N Politburó m.
polite [pə'laɪt] ADJ cortés, atento, fino; educado, correcto; **that's not very ~** eso no es fino; **I can't deny he was very ~ to me** no niego que estuvo muy correcto conmigo; **in ~ society** en la buena sociedad.
politely [pə'laɪtlɪ] ADV cortésmente, atentamente; correctamente.
politeness [pə'laɪtnɪs] N cortesía f, finura f; educación f, corrección f; **with exquisite ~** con la mayor finura; **to do sth out of ~** hacer algo por cortesía.
politic ['pɒlɪtɪk] ADJ prudente.
political [pə'lɪtɪkəl] ADJ político; **~ correctness** lo políticamente correcto; **~ correspondent** corresponsal m político, corresponsal f política; **~ economy** economía f política; **~ editor** editor m político, editora f política; **~ levy** impuesto m político; **~ prisoner** preso m político, presa f política; **~ science** ciencias fpl políticas; **~ scientist** experto m, -a f en ciencias políticas.
politically [pə'lɪtɪkəlɪ] ADV políticamente; **~ correct** políticamente correcto.

┌─ **POLITICALLY CORRECT** ─────────────────┐

ⓘ *Se dice que una persona o su comportamiento es **politically correct** o **PC** cuando sus actitudes o palabras no reflejan ningún desprecio o insulto hacia grupos minoritarios o con algún tipo de desventaja física o social, tales como disminuidos físicos o psíquicos, minorías étnicas, homosexuales, mujeres, etc. Los que propugnan el uso de este tipo de lenguaje y actitud políticamente correctos creen que con ello desafían los valores que la sociedad occidental ha tratado de imponer sobre el resto del mundo a lo largo de la historia. Sin embargo, el término **politically correct** se emplea también de forma irónica por las personas que se burlan de este tipo de lenguaje y actitudes por considerarlas excesivas. Entre las expresiones políticamente correctas, algunas de las más conocidas son: **Native American** en vez de **Red Indian** (indio americano), **visually impaired** en vez de **blind** (ciego) y **vertically challenged** en vez de **short** (bajo).*

└───┘

politician [,pɒlɪ'tɪʃən] N político mf; (pej) politicastro m; (manipulator) politiquero m, -a f.
politicization [pə,lɪtɪsaɪ'zeɪʃən] N politización f.
politicize [pə'lɪtɪsaɪz] VT politizar.
politicking ['pɒlɪtɪkɪŋ] N politiqueo m.
politico [pə'lɪtɪkəʊ] N (hum) político m.
politics ['pɒlɪtɪks] N política f; (Univ etc) estudios mpl políticos; **to go into ~** dedicarse a la política; **to talk ~** hablar de política.
polity ['pɒlɪtɪ] N gobierno m, forma f de gobierno; estado m.
polka ['pɒlkə] N polca f.
polka dot ['pɒlkədɒt] N punto m; diseño m de puntos.
poll [pəʊl] **1** N **(a)** (election) votación f; elección f; **in the ~ of 1945, at the ~s in 1945** en las elecciones de 1945; **a ~ was demanded** reclamaron una votación, insistieron en una votación; **to go to the ~s** acudir a las urnas; **to head the ~** obtener la mayoría de los votos, ser elegido, ocupar el primer puesto en la elección; **to take a ~** someter un asunto a votación; **a ~ was taken among those present** votaron los asistentes.
(b) (total votes) votos mpl; **the candidate achieved a ~ of 5000 votes** el candidato obtuvo 5000 votos; **there was a ~ of 84%** votaron el 84 por cien; **the ~ has been a heavy one** ha votado un elevado porcentaje del electorado.
(c) (public opinion organization) organismo m de sondaje; (inquiry) encuesta f, sondeo m; **the Gallup ~** la encuesta Gallup, el sondeo Gallup; **to take a ~** hacer una encuesta.
(d) (Telec) interrogación f.
2 VT **(a)** cattle descornar.
(b) votes obtener, recibir; **he ~ed only 50 votes** obtuvo solamente 50 votos.
(c) persons encuestar, hacer una encuesta de; **1068 people were ~ed** figuraron 1068 personas en la encuesta.
3 VI: **he ~ed badly** recibió pocos votos, tuvo escaso apoyo; **we shall ~ heavily** obtendremos muchos votos.
pollack ['pɒlək] N abadejo m.
pollard ['pɒləd] **1** N árbol m desmochado.
2 VT desmochar.
pollen ['pɒlən] N polen m; **~ allergy** alergia f polínica; **~ count** recuento m polínico; **~ grain** grano m de polen.
pollinate ['pɒlɪneɪt] VT fecundar (con polen), polinizar.
pollination [,pɒlɪ'neɪʃən] N polinización f, fecundación f.
pollinator ['pɒlɪneɪtə^r] N (Zool) polinizador m, -ora f.
polling ['pəʊlɪŋ] N votación f; **~ will be on Thursday** las elecciones se celebrarán el jueves, se votará el jueves; **~ has been heavy** ha votado un elevado porcentaje de los electores.
polling-booth ['pəʊlɪŋ,buːð] N cabina f de votar.
polling-day ['pəʊlɪŋ,deɪ] N día m de elecciones.
polling-station ['pəʊlɪŋ,steɪʃən] N (Brit) colegio m electoral, centro m

electoral.
polliwog ['pɒlɪwɒg] N (US) renacuajo m.
pollster ['pəʊlstə^r] N encuestador m, -ora f.
poll-tax ['pəʊltæks] N (contribución f de) capitación f, impuesto m (municipal etc) por cabeza.
pollutant [pə'luːtənt] N contaminante m, agente m contaminador.
pollute [pə'luːt] VT contaminar; ensuciar; (fig) corromper; **to become ~d** contaminarse (with de).
polluter [pə'luːtə^r] N contaminador m, -ora f.
pollution [pə'luːʃən] N contaminación f, polución f; (fig) corrupción f.
Pollyanna [pɒlɪ'ænə] N (US) persona f que todo lo ve color de rosa, optimista m redomado, optimista f redomada.
pollywog ['pɒlɪwɒg] N (US) renacuajo m.
polo ['pəʊləʊ] N polo m.
polonaise [,pɒlə'neɪz] N polonesa f.
poloneck ['pəʊləʊnek] N cuello m cisne; **~ sweater** suéter m con cuello cisne.
polonecked ['pəʊləʊnekt] ADJ con cuello cisne.
polonium [pə'ləʊnɪəm] N polonio m.
poltergeist ['pɔːltəgaɪst] N poltergeist m, duende m travieso.
poltroon [pɒl'truːn] N cobarde m.
poly... [pɒlɪ] PREF poli...
poly* ['pɒlɪ] N = polytechnic.
polyandrous [,pɒlɪ'ændrəs] ADJ poliándrico.
polyandry ['pɒlɪændrɪ] N poliandria f.
polyanthus [,pɒlɪ'ænθəs] N prímula f, primavera f, hierba f de San Pablo mayor.
poly bag* ['pɒlɪbæg] N bolsa f de politeno.
polychromatic [,pɒlɪkrəʊ'mætɪk] ADJ policromo.
polyester [,pɒlɪ'estə^r] N poliéster m.
polyethylene [,pɒlɪ'eθəliːn] N (US) polietileno m.
polygamist [pɒ'lɪgəmɪst] N polígamo m.
polygamous [pə'lɪgəməs] ADJ polígamo.
polygamy [pə'lɪgəmɪ] N poligamia f.
polygenesis [,pɒlɪ'dʒenɪsɪs] N poligénesis f.
polyglot ['pɒlɪglɒt] **1** ADJ polígloto.
2 N polígloto m, -a f.
polygon ['pɒlɪgən] N polígono m.
polygonal [pɒ'lɪgənl] ADJ poligonal.
polygraph ['pɒlɪgrɑːf] N polígrafo m, detector m de mentiras.
polyhedron [,pɒlɪ'hiːdrən] N poliedro m.
polymath ['pɒlɪmæθ] N polímata mf, erudito m, -a f.
polymer ['pɒlɪmə^r] N polímero m.
polymerization [,pɒlɪməraɪ'zeɪʃən] N polimerización f.
polymorphic [,pɒlɪ'mɔːfɪk] ADJ polimorfo.
polymorphism [,pɒlɪ'mɔːfɪzəm] N polimorfismo m.
Polynesia [,pɒlɪ'niːzɪə] N la Polinesia.
Polynesian [,pɒlɪ'niːzɪən] **1** ADJ polinesio.
2 N polinesio m, -a f.
polynomial [,pɒlɪ'nəʊmɪəl] ADJ, N polinomio m.
polyp ['pɒlɪp] N (Med, Zool) pólipo m.
Polyphemus [,pɒlɪ'fiːməs] NM Polifemo.
polyphonic [,pɒlɪ'fɒnɪk] ADJ polifónico.
polyphony [pə'lɪfənɪ] N polifonía f.
polypropylene [,pɒlɪ'prɒpɪliːn] N polipropileno m.
polypus ['pɒlɪpəs] N (Zool) pólipo m.
polysemic [,pɒlɪ'siːmɪk] ADJ polisémico.
polysemy [pɒ'lɪsəmɪ] N polisemia f.
polystyrene [,pɒlɪ'staɪriːn] N poliestireno m.
polysyllabic ['pɒlɪsɪ'læbɪk] ADJ polisílabo.
polysyllable ['pɒlɪ,sɪləbl] N polisílabo m.
polytechnic [,pɒlɪ'teknɪk] N (Brit) politécnico m, escuela f politécnica.
polytheism ['pɒlɪθiːɪzəm] N politeísmo m.
polytheistic [,pɒlɪθiː'ɪstɪk] ADJ politeísta.
polythene ['pɒlɪθiːn] N (Brit) politene m, politeno m.
polyunsaturate [,pɒlɪʌn'sætʃərɪt] N poliinsaturado m.
polyunsaturated [,pɒlɪʌn'sætʃəreɪtɪd] ADJ poliinsaturado.
polyurethane [,pɒlɪ'jʊərɪθeɪn] N poliuretano m.
polyvalent [pə'lɪvələnt] ADJ polivalente.
polyvinyl ['pɒlɪvaɪnl] N polivinilo m.
pom¹* [pɒm] N = pommy.
pom²* [pɒm] N (dog) perro m de Pomerania, lulú mf (de Pomerania).
pomade [pə'mɑːd] N pomada f.
pomander [pəʊ'mændə^r] N recipiente de porcelana que contiene hierbas perfumadas.
pomegranate ['pɒməgrænɪt] N (fruit) granada f; (tree) granado m.
pomelo ['pɒmɪ,ləʊ] N pomelo m.
Pomeranian [,pɒmə'reɪnɪən] N (dog) pomeranio m.
pommel ['pʌml] **1** N pomo m.
2 VT apuñear, dar de puñetazos; aporrear.
pommy* ['pɒmɪ] (pej) **1** N inglés m, -esa f (inmigrante en Australia).

2 ADJ inglés.

pomp [pɒmp] N pompa f; fausto m, boato m, ostentación f; **~ and circumstance** pompa f y solemnidad.

Pompeii [pɒm'peɪɪ] N Pompeya f.

Pompey ['pɒmpɪ] NM Pompeyo.

pompom ['pɒmpɒm] N, **pompon** ['pɒmpɒn] N pompón m, borla f.

pomposity [pɒm'pɒsɪtɪ] N pomposidad f; fausto m, ostentación f; ampulosidad f, hinchazón f.

pompous ['pɒmpəs] ADJ pomposo; fastuoso, ostentoso; language ampuloso, hinchado.

pompously ['pɒmpəslɪ] ADV pomposamente; ampulosamente, hinchadamente.

ponce [pɒns] N (Brit) coime m, chulo m de putas, rufián m.
◆**ponce about*, ponce around*** VI chulear*.

poncho ['pɒntʃəʊ] N poncho m.

poncy* ['pɒnsɪ] ADJ (Brit) cursi.

pond [pɒnd] N (natural) charca f; (artificial) estanque m; (fish~) vivero m.

ponder ['pɒndər] 1 VT ponderar, meditar, considerar con especial cuidado.
2 VI reflexionar, pensar; **to ~ on sth, to ~ over sth** meditar algo.

ponderable ['pɒndərəbl] ADJ ponderable.

ponderous ['pɒndərəs] ADJ (all senses) pesado.

ponderously ['pɒndərəslɪ] ADV pesadamente; say etc en tono pesado, lentamente y con énfasis.

pondlife ['pɒndlaɪf] N fauna f de las charcas.

pondweed ['pɒndwiːd] N planta f acuática.

pone [pəʊn] N (US) pan m de maíz.

pong* [pɒŋ] (Brit) 1 N hedor m, tufo m.
2 VI apestar, heder.

pongy* ['pɒŋɪ] ADJ foche*, maloliente.

poniard ['pɒnjəd] N (liter) puñal m.

pontiff ['pɒntɪf] N pontífice m.

pontifical [pɒn'tɪfɪkəl] ADJ pontificio, pontifical; (fig) dogmático, autoritario.

pontificate 1 [pɒn'tɪfɪkɪt] N pontificado m.
2 [pɒn'tɪfɪkeɪt] VI pontificar (also fig).

Pontius Pilate ['pɒnʃəs'paɪlət] NM Poncio Pilato.

pontoon[1] [pɒn'tuːn] 1 N pontón m.
2 ATTR **~ bridge** puente m de pontones.

pontoon[2] [pɒn'tuːn] N (Brit Cards) veintiuna f.

pony ['pəʊnɪ] N **(a)** caballito m, jaca f, poni m, poney m, potro m (LAm). **(b)** (Brit*) 25 libras. **(c)** (US*) chuleta* f.

ponytail ['pəʊnɪteɪl] N trenza f, (peinado m de) cola f de caballo.

pony trekking ['pəʊnɪ,trekɪŋ] N excursión f en poney.

pooch* [puːtʃ] N (US) perro m.

poodle ['puːdl] N perro m de lanas, caniche m.

poof* [puf] N (Brit), **poofter*** ['puftər] N (Brit) maricón* m.

poofy* ['pufɪ] ADJ (Brit) de maricón*, afeminado.

pooh [puː] INTERJ ¡bah!, ¡qué va!

pooh-pooh [puː'puː] VT proposal etc rechazar con desdén; danger etc negar la importancia de.

pool[1] [puːl] N (natural) charca f; (artifical) estanque m; (swimming ~) piscina f, alberca f (LAm), pileta f (SC); (in river) pozo m, remanso m; (of spilt liquid) charco m.

pool[2] [puːl] 1 N **(a)** (game) chapolín m; (Cards) polla f; (football ~) quinielas fpl; (Comm) consorcio m, asociación f; mancomunidad f; fusión f de intereses; (of typists) sala f de mecanógrafas; servicio m de mecanógrafas; **coal and steel ~** comunidad f de carbón y acero; **that's dirty ~*** (US) eso no es jugar limpio; **to shoot ~** (US) jugar al chapolín.
(b) (reserve) reserva f; (source) fuente f; (of genes etc) fondo m, reserva f; **an untapped ~ of ability** una reserva de inteligencia no utilizada aún.
2 VT juntar, mancomunar; resources consociar, utilizar (etc) en forma consociada.

pooling ['puːlɪŋ] N consocio m, utilización f en forma consociada.

poolroom ['puːlruːm] N (US) sala f de billar.

pool table ['puːl,teɪbl] N mesa f de billar.

poop[1] [puːp] N (Naut) popa f.

poop[2]* [puːp] N (excrement) caca** f.

poop[3]* [puːp] N (US: information) onda* f, información f.

pooped* [puːpt] ADJ: **to be ~** (esp US) (tired) estar hecho polvo; (drunk) estar ajumado*.

pooper-scooper* ['puːpə'skuːpər] N caca-can* m.

poo-poo* ['puː'puː] N caca** f.

poor [pʊər] 1 ADJ **(a)** (not rich) pobre; soil etc pobre, estéril; **a ~ man** un pobre; **a ~ woman** una mujer pobre; **~ law** ley f de asistencia pública; **~ white** (US etc) blanco m, -a f pobre; **an ore ~ in metal** un mineral de escaso contenido metálico; **a food ~ in vitamins** un alimento pobre en vitaminas; **to be as ~ as a church-mouse** ser más pobre que las ratas, ser pobre de solemnidad.

(b) (bad) malo; de baja calidad; (in spirit) apocado, mezquino; **my ~ memory** mi mala memoria; **it's ~ stuff** no es bueno; **the game was pretty ~** el partido fue bastante malo; **to be in ~ health** estar mal (de salud); **to be ~ at maths** ser malo en matemáticas; **to have a ~ opinion of sb** tener un concepto poco favorable de uno.

(c) (unfortunate) pobre; **~ me!** ¡pobre de mí!; **~ you!, ~ old you!, you ~ old thing!** ¡pobrecito!; **~ Mary!** ¡pobre María!; **~ Mary's lost all her money** la pobre de María ha perdido todo su dinero; **he's very ill, ~ old chap** está grave el pobre.

2 NPL: **the ~** los pobres.

POOR | see also main entry

Position of "pobre"
You should generally put **pobre** after the noun when you mean **poor** in the sense of "not rich" and before the noun in the sense of "unfortunate".

It's a poor area
Es una región pobre
The poor boy was trembling
El pobre chico estaba temblando
For further uses and examples, see main entry.

---

poorbox ['pʊəbɒks] N cepillo m de los pobres.

poorhouse ['pʊəhaʊs] N, PL **poorhouses** ['pʊəhaʊzɪz] asilo m de los pobres.

poorly ['pʊəlɪ] 1 ADV **(a)** pobremente; **they live very ~** viven en la mayor pobreza.
(b) (badly) mal; **the team is doing ~** el equipo juega mal; **exports are doing ~** las exportaciones no van bien; **I used to do ~ at chemistry** tenía malas notas en química.
2 ADJ (ill) mal, enfermo, malucho; en mal estado; **to be ~, to look ~** estar malo; **I found him very ~** le encontré en muy mal estado.

poorness ['pʊənɪs] N **(a)** (lack of wealth) pobreza f. **(b)** (badness) mala calidad f; **~ of spirit** apocamiento m, mezquindad f.

poor-spirited ['pʊə'spɪrɪtɪd] ADJ apocado, mezquino.

poove* [puːv] N = poof.

POP **(a)** ABBR of **publish or perish** publica o perece. **(b)** ABBR of **Post Office Preferred.**

pop[1] [pɒp] 1 N **(a)** (sound) ligera detonación f; (of cork) taponazo m; (of fastener etc) ruido m seco; (imitative sound) ¡pum!; **to go ~** (bottle etc) hacer ¡pum!
(b) (*: drink) gaseosa f.
(c) (*) **to have** (or **take**) **a ~ at sb** (criticize) hacer un repaso a uno.
2 VT **(a)** balloon hacer reventar; pinchar.
(b) (place) poner, poner rápidamente; **to ~ sth into a drawer** poner algo (rápidamente, sin ser visto etc) en un cajón; **to ~ pills** drogarse (con pastillas).
(c) (*: pawn) empeñar.
(d) (*) **to ~ the question** declararse.
3 VI **(a)** (burst etc) estallar, reventar (con ligera detonación); pincharse; **there were corks ~ping all over** por todas partes saltaban los tapones; **my ears ~ped on landing** al aterrizar se me han taponado los oídos; **to make sb's eyes ~** dejar a uno con los ojos fuera de órbita.
(b) **we ~ped over to see them** fuimos a hacerles una breve visita; **let's ~ round to Joe's** vamos a casa de Pepe.
◆**pop back** 1 VT lid etc poner de nuevo, volver a poner.
2 VI volver un momento.
◆**pop in** VI entrar de sopetón, dar un vistazo; **to ~ in to see sb** ir a saludar a uno, pasar por la casa de uno; **I just ~ped in** me acerqué a veros, me asomé a veros, no tuve la intención de quedarme.
◆**pop off*** VI estirar la pata*.
◆**pop on** VT light, oven poner, encender; kettle poner (a calentar); clothing ponerse (de prisa); **I'll just ~ my hat on** voy a ponerme el sombrero.
◆**pop out** 1 VT: **she ~ped her head out** asomó de repente la cabeza.
2 VI salir un momento; **he ~ped out for some cigarettes** fue en una escapadita a buscar tabaco; **he ~ped out from his hiding place** salió de repente de su escondite.
◆**pop up** VI aparecer inesperadamente.

pop[2]* [pɒp] ADJ ABBR of **popular** pop; **~ art** arte m pop; **~ artist** artista mf pop; **~ music** música f pop; **~ star** estrella f de la música pop.

pop[3]* [pɒp] N (esp US) papá* m.

pop. ABBR of **population** habitantes mpl, h.

popcorn ['pɒpkɔːn] N rosetas fpl, palomitas fpl (de maíz).

pope [pəʊp] N papa m; **P~ John XXIII** el Papa Juan XXIII.

popemobile ['pəʊpməʊ,biːl] N papamóvil m.

popery ['pəʊpərɪ] N (pej) papismo m; **no ~!** ¡abajo el papa!, ¡papa no!

pop-eyed ['pɒp'aɪd] ADJ (permanently) de ojos saltones; **they were ~ with amazement** se les desorbitaron los ojos con el asombro; **they looked at me ~** me miraron con los ojos desorbitados.

popgun ['pɒpgʌn] N fusil m de juguete, taco m.

popinjay ['pɒpɪndʒeɪ] N pisaverde *m*.
popish ['pəʊpɪʃ] ADJ (*pej*) papista, católico.
poplar ['pɒplər] N (*black*) chopo *m*, álamo *m*; (*white*) álamo *m* blanco.
poplin ['pɒplɪn] N popelina *f*.
poppa* ['pɒpə] N (*US*) papá* *m*.
poppadum ['pɒpədəm] N = **papadum**.
popper‡ ['pɒpər] N cápsula *f* de nitrito amílico.
poppet* ['pɒpɪt] N (*Brit*): **yes, my ~** sí, hija; sí, querida; **hullo, ~!** ¡oye, ricura!*; **isn't she a ~?** ¡qué preciosidad!; **the boss is a ~** el jefe es muy amable.
poppy ['pɒpɪ] N amapola *f*, adormidera *f*; **P~ Day** *día en el que se recuerda a los caídos en las dos guerras mundiales*; **~ seed** semilla *f* de amapola.

┌─ **POPPY DAY** ─────────────────────────────┐

ⓘ *Poppy Day* es la expresión coloquial para referirse al **Remembrance Day** o **Remembrance Sunday**, *día en que se recuerdan los caídos en las dos grandes guerras mundiales del siglo XX. La celebración se hace el segundo domingo de noviembre y en los días que preceden a este día se venden amapolas de papel con el fin de recaudar fondos destinados a las instituciones de caridad que prestan ayuda a los veteranos de guerra y a sus familias. Las amapolas representan las que florecieron en los campos franceses, donde tantos soldados perecieron durante la Primera Guerra Mundial.*

⇨ *Ver también* [LEGION - AMERICAN LEGION/BRITISH LEGION]
└──┘

poppycock* ['pɒpɪkɒk] N tonterías *fpl*; **~!** ¡tonterías!
Popsicle ['pɒpsɪkl] ® N (*US*) polo *m*.
popsy‡ ['pɒpsɪ] N chica *f*.
populace ['pɒpjʊlɪs] N pueblo *m*; (*pej*) plebe *f*, populacho *m*.
popular ['pɒpjʊlər] ADJ (a) (*well-liked*) popular; **to be ~** (*enjoy wide esteem*) ser popular, (*be in fashion*) estar de moda; **it's a ~ work** una obra popular; **the show is proving very ~** el espectáculo está muy concurrido; **there is a ~ belief that ...** muchos creen que ..., se cree generalmente que ...; **he's ~ with the girls** tiene mucho éxito con las chicas; **I'm not very ~ in the office just now** por ahora no me quieren mucho en la oficina.
(b) (*of the people*) popular; **~ front** frente *m* popular; **by ~ request, we offer ...** respondiendo a la demanda general, ofrecemos ...; **it's a ~ work** es una obra de vulgarización.
popularist ['pɒpjʊlərɪst] ADJ popularista.
popularity [,pɒpjʊ'lærɪtɪ] N popularidad *f*.
popularization ['pɒpjʊləraɪ'zeɪʃən] N popularización *f*; vulgarización *f*.
popularize ['pɒpjʊləraɪz] VT (*make popular*) popularizar; (*make available to laymen*) vulgarizar.
popularly ['pɒpjʊləlɪ] ADV: **X ~ known as Y** X conocido por regla general como Y, X al que se llama vulgarmente Y; **it is ~ thought that ...** muchos creen que ...
populate ['pɒpjʊleɪt] VT poblar.
population [,pɒpjʊ'leɪʃən] N población *f*; (*in numbering inhabitants*) habitantes *mpl*; **~ explosion** explosión *f* demográfica; **~ growth** crecimiento *m* demográfico; **~ pressures** presiones *fpl* demográficas.
populism ['pɒpjʊlɪzəm] N populismo *m*.
populist ['pɒpjʊlɪst] ① ADJ populista.
② N populista *mf*.
populous ['pɒpjʊləs] ADJ populoso; **the most ~ city in the world** la ciudad más poblada del mundo.
pop-up ['pɒpʌp] ATTR: **~ book** libro *m* con dibujos en relieve; **~ toaster** tostador *m* automático.
porcelain ['pɔːslɪn] N porcelana *f*.
porch [pɔːtʃ] N pórtico *m*; entrada *f*; (*of house, church*) porche *m*.
porcine ['pɔːsaɪn] ADJ porcino, porcuno.
porcupine ['pɔːkjʊpaɪn] N puerco *m* espín.
porcupine fish ['pɔːkjʊpaɪn,fɪʃ] N pez *m* globo.
pore¹ [pɔːr] N poro *m*.
pore² [pɔːr] VI: **to ~ over sth** estar absorto en el estudio de algo, estudiar algo larga y detenidamente; **we ~d over it for hours** lo estudiamos durante horas y horas.
pork [pɔːk] N (carne *f* de) cerdo *m*, (carne *f* de) chancho *m* (*LAm*); **~ butcher** tocinero *m*; **~ sausage** salchicha *f* de cerdo.
porker ['pɔːkər] N cerdo *m*, cochino *m*.
porkies‡ ['pɔːkɪz] NPL mentiras *fpl*.
porkpie ['pɔːkpaɪ] N pastel *m* de carne de cerdo.
porky* ['pɔːkɪ] ADJ gordo, gordinflón*.
porn* [pɔːn] N ABBR of **pornography**; **~ merchant** traficante *m* en pornografía; **~ shop** tienda *f* de pornografía, tienda *f* porno*.
porno* ['pɔːnəʊ] (*esp US*) = **porn**.
pornographer [pɔː'nɒgrəfər] N editor *m* (or artista *m* etc) porno, pornografista *mf*.
pornographic [,pɔːnə'græfɪk] ADJ pornográfico.
pornography [pɔː'nɒgrəfɪ] N pornografía *f*.

porosity [pɔː'rɒsɪtɪ] N porosidad *f*.
porous ['pɔːrəs] ADJ poroso.
porousness ['pɔːrəsnɪs] N porosidad *f*.
porphyria [pɔː'fɪrɪə] N porfirismo *m*.
porphyry ['pɔːfɪrɪ] N pórfido *m*.
porpoise ['pɔːpəs] N marsopa *f*, puerco *m* de mar.
porridge ['pɒrɪdʒ] N (a) (*approx*) gachas *fpl* de avena; (*baby's*) papilla *f*; **~ oats** copos *mpl* de avena. (b) **to do 2 years' ~‡** (*Brit*) pasar 2 años a la sombra‡.
port¹ [pɔːt] ① N (a) (*Naut: harbour*) puerto *m*; **~ of call** puerto *m* de escala; **his next ~ of call was the chemist's** luego fue a la farmacia; **which is your next ~ of call?** ¿adónde se dirige ahora?; **~ of entry** puerto *m* de entrada; **any ~ in a storm** en el peligro cualquier refugio es bueno; la necesidad carece de ley; **to come into ~, to put into ~** entrar a puerto; **to leave ~** hacerse a la mar, zarpar.
(b) (*Comput*) puerta *f*, puerto *m*, port *m*.
② ATTR de puerto, portuario; **~ authority** autoridad *f* portuaria; **~ dues** derechos *mpl* de puerto; **~ facilities** facilidades *fpl* portuarias.
port² [pɔːt] N (*Naut: ~hole*) portilla *f*; (*Mech*) lumbrera *f*; (*Mil* ††) tronera *f*.
port³ [pɔːt] (*Naut: also ~ side*) ① N babor *m*; **the sea to ~** la mar a babor; **land to ~!** ¡tierra a babor!
② ATTR lighter etc de babor; **on the ~ side** a babor.
③ VT: **to ~ the helm** poner el timón a babor, virar a babor.
port⁴ [pɔːt] N (*wine*) vino *m* de Oporto, oporto *m*.
portability [,pɔːtə'bɪlɪtɪ] N (*esp Comput*) portabilidad *f*, portatilidad *f*; (*of software*) transferibilidad *f*.
portable ['pɔːtəbl] ① ADJ portátil.
② N máquina *f* (*etc*) portátil.
portage ['pɔːtɪdʒ] N porteo *m*.
Portakabin ['pɔːtə,kæbɪn] ® N (*gen*) caseta *f* prefabricada; (*extension to office etc*) anexo *m* prefabricado; (*works office etc*) barracón *m* de obras.
portal ['pɔːtl] N puerta *f* (grande, imponente).
portcullis [pɔːt'kʌlɪs] N rastrillo *m*.
portend [pɔː'tend] VT presagiar, anunciar; **what does this ~?** ¿qué quiere decir esto?
portent ['pɔːtent] N presagio *m*, augurio *m*, señal *f*; (*prodigy*) portento *m*; **a ~ of doom** un presagio de la catástrofe.
portentous [pɔː'tentəs] ADJ (a) (*ominous, prodigious*) portentoso. (b) (*pompous*) pomposo.
portentously [pɔː'tentəslɪ] ADV (a) portentosamente. (b) pomposamente.
porter ['pɔːtər] N (a) (*Brit: of hotel, office etc*) portero *m*, conserje *m*; (*Brit Rail: uniformed*) mozo *m* de estación, (*US Rail*) mozo *m* de los coches-cama, (*touting for custom*) mozo *m* de cuerda; (*Sherpa*) porteador *m*; **~'s lodge** portería *f*, conserjería *f*.
(b) (*beer*) cerveza *f* negra.
porterage ['pɔːtərɪdʒ] N porte *m*.
porterhouse ['pɔːtəhaʊs] ① N, PL **porterhouses** ['pɔːtəhaʊzɪz] (††) mesón *m*.
② ATTR: **~ steak** (*Brit*) biftec *m* de filete.
portfolio [pɔːt'fəʊlɪəʊ] N cartera *f*, carpeta *f*; (*Pol*) cartera *f*; **~ management** administración *f* de la cartera de acciones; **~ of shares** cartera *f* de acciones; **minister without ~** ministro *m* sin cartera.
porthole ['pɔːthəʊl] N portilla *f*.
Portia ['pɔːʃə] NF Porcia.
portico ['pɔːtɪkəʊ] N pórtico *m*.
portion ['pɔːʃən] ① N porción *f*, parte *f*; (*helping*) ración *f*; (*also marriage ~*) dote *f*; (*quantity, in relation to a whole*) porción *f*; sección *f*; porcentaje *m*.
② VT (*also to ~ out*) repartir, dividir.
portliness ['pɔːtlɪnɪs] N gordura *f*, corpulencia *f*.
portly ['pɔːtlɪ] ADJ gordo, corpulento.
portmanteau [pɔːt'mæntəʊ] N baúl *m* de viaje; **~ word** palabra *f* híbrida, palabra *f* entrecruzada (*p.ej. motel, smog*).
Porto Rico [,pɔːtəʊ'riːkəʊ] etc = **Puerto Rico** etc.
portrait ['pɔːtrɪt] N (a) **gallery** museo *m* de retratos, galería *f* iconográfica; **National P~ Gallery** Museo *m* Iconográfico Nacional; **~ orientation** formato *m* vertical; **to have one's ~ painted, to sit for one's ~** retratarse, hacerse retratar.
portraitist ['pɔːtrɪtɪst] N, **portrait painter** ['pɔːtrɪt,peɪntər] N retratista *mf*.
portraiture ['pɔːtrɪtʃər] N (*portrait*) retrato *m*; (*portraits collectively*) retratos *mpl*; (*art of ~*) arte *m* de retratar; **Spanish ~ in the 16th century** retratos *mpl* españoles del siglo XVI.
portray [pɔː'treɪ] VT (*Art*) retratar; (*fig*) pintar, describir; representar.
portrayal [pɔː'treɪəl] N (*Art*) retrato *m*; (*fig*) descripción *f*; descripción *f* gráfica, representación *f*; **a most unflattering ~** una representación nada halagüeña.
portress ['pɔːtrɪs] N portera *f*.
Portugal ['pɔːtjʊgəl] N Portugal *m*.
Portuguese [,pɔːtjʊ'giːz] ① ADJ portugués.

⟨2⟩ N **(a)** portugués *m*, -esa *f.* **(b)** (*Ling*) portugués *m.*
POS N ABBR *of* **point of sale** punto *m* de venta.
pos. ABBR *of* **positive** positivo.
pose [pəʊz] ⟨1⟩ N **(a)** (*of body*) postura *f*, actitud *f.*
(b) (*fig*) afectación *f*, pose *f*; **it's just a big ~** todo esto no es más que afectación.
⟨2⟩ VT **(a)** (*place*) colocar; **he ~d the model in the position he wanted** hizo que la modelo adoptara la postura que él quería.
(b) *problem* plantear; *question* hacer, formular; *threat* representar, encerrar.
⟨3⟩ VI **(a)** (*place o.s.*) colocarse; (*as model*) posar; **she once ~d for Picasso** una vez posó para Picasso.
(b) (*affectedly*) darse tono; tomar una postura afectada; **to ~ as** hacerse pasar por, echárselas de.
Poseidon [pə'saɪdən] NM Poseidón.
poser [ˈpəʊzəʳ] N **(a)** (*problem*) pregunta *f* difícil, problema *m* difícil.
(b) (*person*) = **poseur.**
poseur [pəʊˈzɜːʳ] N persona *f* afectada, farsante *mf*, vacilón* *m*, -ona *f*, maniquí *mf.*
posh [pɒʃ] ⟨1⟩ ADJ elegante, de lujo, lujoso; (**~** *but in bad taste*) cursi; *wedding etc* de mucho rumbo; *accent* afectado; *school* de buen tono; **~ people** gente *f* bien; **a ~ car** un coche de lujo; **it's a very ~ neighbourhood** es un barrio de lo más elegante.
⟨2⟩ ADV: **to talk ~** hablar con acento afectado.
⟨3⟩ VT: **to ~ a place up** procurar que un local parezca más elegante, renovar la pintura (*etc*) de un local; **it's all ~ed up** está totalmente renovado, se ha reformado por completo.
⟨4⟩ VR: **to ~ o.s. up** arreglarse, ataviarse, emperejilarse.
posing pouch [ˈpəʊzɪŋˌpaʊtʃ] N tanga *m*, marcapaquete *m.*
posit [ˈpɒzɪt] VT proponer como principio (*that* que), postular.
▼ **position** [pəˈzɪʃən] ⟨1⟩ N **(a)** (*place, in physical sense*) posición *f*, situación *f*; (*of body, posture*) posición *f*, postura *f*, actitud *f*; (*sexual*) postura *f*; (*Sport*) posición *f*; **to be in ~** estar en posición, estar en su lugar; **to be in a dangerous ~** estar en una posición peligrosa; **what ~ was the body in?** ¿cuál era la postura del cadáver?; **you are in the best ~ to see it** estás en la mejor posición para verlo, estás en el mejor sitio para verlo; **to place sth in ~** colocar algo, poner algo en su lugar; **put yourself in my ~** ponte en mi lugar; **to be out of ~** estar fuera de su lugar, estar desplazado; **what ~ do you play (in)?** ¿qué posición tienes?; **my usual ~ is goalkeeper** en general yo juego de portero.
(b) (*Naut*) posición *f*; **to fix one's ~** determinar su posición, averiguar su posición; **to take up ~ astern** ponerse a popa.
(c) (*Mil*) posición *f*; (*post*) puesto *m*; (*for gun*) emplazamiento *m*; **our ~s before the attack** nuestras posiciones antes del ataque; **to manoeuvre for ~** hacer maniobras para mejorar de posición; **to storm an enemy ~** tomar una posición enemiga al asalto.
(d) (*rank*) posición *f*; (*social*) posición *f*, rango *m*, categoría *f*; (*in class, league etc*) puesto *m*; **of good social ~** de buena posición social, de categoría; **to have a high social ~** ocupar una posición social elevada; **to lose one's ~ at the top of the league** perder su puesto a la cabeza de la liga.
▼ **(e)** (*post*) puesto *m*, empleo *m*; colocación *f*; situación *f*; cargo *m*; **the ~ of ambassador in Bogotá** el puesto de embajador en Bogotá; **to have a good ~ in a bank** tener un buen puesto en un banco; **to look for a ~** buscar una colocación.
(f) (*state*) situación *f*; **the country's economic ~** la situación económica del país; **the ~ is that ...** es que ..., el hecho es que ...; **our ~ is improving** estamos mejorando de situación; **to be in a ~ to + infin** estar en condiciones de + *infin*; **to be in no ~ to + infin** no estar en condiciones de + *infin*; **to consider one's ~** (*euph*) pensar en dimitir, estudiar la conveniencia de dimitir.
▼ **(g)** (*opinion*) postura *f*, opinión *f*; actitud *f*; **what is our ~ on Greece?** ¿cuál es nuestra actitud hacia (*or* para con) Grecia?, ¿cuál es nuestra política con Grecia?; **to take up a ~ on a matter** adoptar una postura en un asunto; **to change one's ~** cambiar de opinión, cambiar de idea.
⟨2⟩ VT colocar, disponer.
positive [ˈpɒzɪtɪv] ⟨1⟩ ADJ **(a)** (*definite*) positivo; definitivo; real, verdadero; **~ proof** prueba *f* concluyente; **there are some ~ results at last** por fin hay unos resultados positivos; **it's a ~ miracle!** ¡es un auténtico milagro!; **he's a ~ nuisance** realmente es un pesado.
(b) (*of person: sure*) seguro; **he is ~ about it** está seguro de ello; **I'm quite ~ on that point** estoy completamente convencido de ello; **you don't sound very ~** no pareces estar muy seguro.
(c) (*of things: sure*) enfático, categórico; **in a ~ tone of voice** con énfasis.
(d) (*of character*) de fuerte personalidad, enérgico, activo; **she's a ~ sort of person** es una persona enérgica, es una persona que sabe lo que quiere.
(e) (*Gram*) *degree* positivo; (*affirmative*) afirmativo; **~ cash flow** flujo *m* positivo de efectivo; **~ discrimination** discriminación *f* positiva; **~**

vetting investigación *f* positiva.
(f) (*Elec, Math, Phot*) positivo.
⟨2⟩ N (*Phot*) positiva *f.*
positively [ˈpɒzɪtɪvlɪ] ADV **(a)** (*definitely*) positivamente; definitivamente; verdaderamente; **it's ~ marvellous!** ¡es realmente maravilloso!
(b) (*emphatically*) con énfasis, categóricamente.
(c) (*energetically*) con energía, enérgicamente.
positivism [ˈpɒzɪtɪvɪzəm] N positivismo *m.*
positivist [ˈpɒzɪtɪvɪst] ⟨1⟩ ADJ positivista.
⟨2⟩ N positivista *mf.*
positron [ˈpɒzɪˌtrɒn] N positrón *m.*
poss.* [pɒs] ADJ, ADV ABBR *of* **possible, possibly.**
posse [ˈpɒsɪ] N (*US*) pelotón *m*, grupo *m* (*esp fuerza civil armada bajo el mando del Sheriff*).
possess [pəˈzes] ⟨1⟩ VT **(a)** (*have, own, also* **to be ~ed of**) poseer; **it ~es many advantages** posee muchas ventajas; **they ~ a fortune** poseen una fortuna, tienen una fortuna.
(b) **to be ~ed by demons** estar poseso (*or* poseído) por los demonios; **to be ~ed by an idea** estar dominado por una idea; **we are ~ed by many doubts** son muchas las dudas que tenemos; **whatever can have ~ed you?** ¿cómo lo has podido hacer?; **what can have ~ed you to think like that?** ¿cómo has podido pensar así?
⟨2⟩ VR **(a)** **to ~ o.s. of** tomar posesión de; (*violently*) apoderarse de.
(b) **to ~ o.s. in patience** armarse de paciencia.
possessed [pəˈzest] ADJ poseso, poseído; **like one ~** como un poseso, como un energúmeno.
possession [pəˈzeʃən] N **(a)** (*act, state*) posesión *f*; **~ of arms** tenencia *f* de armas; **to get ~ of** adquirir, hacerse con; (*improperly*) apoderarse de; **to take ~ of** tomar posesión de; *house etc* ocupar, entrar en; (*improperly*) apoderarse de, hacerse dueño de; (*confiscate*) incautarse de; **to be in ~ of** poseer, tener; **to be in full ~ of one's faculties** poseer todas sus facultades; **to be in the ~ of** estar en manos de, ser de la propiedad de, pertenecer a; **to come into ~ of** adquirir; **to come (or pass) into the ~ of** pasar a manos de; **to have ~ (of the ball)** estar en posesión (del balón); **to have sth in one's ~** poseer algo; **a house with vacant ~** una casa (que se vende) desocupada; **'with vacant ~'** 'llave en mano'.
(b) (*object*) posesión *f*; **~s** posesiones *fpl*; (*as legal term*) bienes *mpl*; **Spain's overseas ~s** las posesiones de España en ultramar.
(c) (*by devil*) posesión *f.*
possessive [pəˈzesɪv] ⟨1⟩ ADJ **(a)** *love etc* dominante, tiránico, absorbente; **to be ~ towards sb** ser absorbente con uno.
(b) (*Gram*) posesivo; **~ pronoun** pronombre *m* posesivo.
⟨2⟩ N posesivo *m.*
possessively [pəˈzesɪvlɪ] ADV tiránicamente; de modo absorbente.
possessiveness [pəˈzesɪvnɪs] N posesividad *f.*
possessor [pəˈzesəʳ] N poseedor *m*, -ora *f*; dueño *m*, -a *f*; **he was the proud ~ of ...** se preciaba de poseer ...
▼ **possibility** [ˌpɒsəˈbɪlɪtɪ] N **(a)** (*chance*) posibilidad *f*; (*outlook*) perspectiva *f*; **the ~ of severe losses** la posibilidad de sufrir pérdidas cuantiosas; **there is no ~ of his agreeing to it** no existe posibilidad alguna de que consienta en ello; **if by any ~...** si por casualidad ...; **it is within the bounds of ~** cabe dentro de lo posible; **it's a grim ~** es una perspectiva aterradora.
▼ **(b)** (*event etc*) acontecimiento *m* posible; posibilidad *f*; **to allow for the ~ that it may happen** tener en cuenta la posibilidad de que una cosa ocurra; **to foresee all the possibilities** prever todas las posibilidades.
(c) (*promise*) **he has possibilities** promete, es prometedor; **the subject has possibilities** es un tema prometedor, es un tema de gran potencial.
▼ **possible** [ˈpɒsəbl] ⟨1⟩ ADJ **(a)** posible; **a ~ defeat** una posible derrota; **a ~ candidate** un candidato aceptable; **all ~ concessions** todas las concesiones posibles; **one has to foresee all ~ outcomes** hay que prever todos los resultados posibles; **to make sth ~** hacer algo posible, posibilitar algo; **we will help whenever ~** ayudaremos siempre cuando sea posible; **where ~, wherever ~** donde sea posible.
▼ **(b)** (*with verb* to be *etc*) **if ~** si es posible, de ser posible, a ser posible; si cabe; **it is just ~** existe una pequeña posibilidad (*that* de que + *subj*); **it is ~ that ...** es posible que + *subj*, puede ser que + *subj*; **it is ~ to + infin** es posible + *infin*; **it is not ~ to do more** es imposible hacer más; **it will be ~ for you to return the same day** te será posible volver el mismo día, podrás volver el mismo día.
(c) (*with* as) **we will help as far as ~** ayudaremos en lo posible, ayudaremos en cuanto podamos; **as much as ~** todo lo posible; **as often as ~** lo más frecuentemente posible; **as well as ~** lo mejor posible; **as soon as ~** cuanto antes, lo antes posible, lo más pronto posible; **as heavy as ~** lo más pesado que pueda ser, todo lo pesado que pueda ser; **as ~** el más pesado que haya.
⟨2⟩ N: **a list of ~s for the job** una lista de candidatos aceptables para el puesto; **he's a ~ for the team** tiene posibilidades de formar parte

---

del equipo; **P~s versus Probables** la selección B contra la selección A.

▼ **possibly** ['pɒsəblɪ] ADV posiblemente; tal vez; **yes, ~** sí, es posible; **if I ~ can** si me es posible; **~ they've gone already** es posible que hayan ido ya, puede que hayan ido ya, han ido ya quizá; **he did all he ~ could** hizo todo lo que pudo; **I come as often as I ~ can** vengo todas las veces que puedo, vengo lo más a menudo posible; **I cannot ~ allow it** no lo puedo permitir de ninguna manera, me es totalmente imposible autorizarlo; **it can't ~ be true!** ¡no puede ser!, ¡no es posible!

possum ['pɒsəm] N zarigüeya f; **to play ~** (sleeping) fingir estar dormido; (dead) hacerse el muerto.

post¹ [pəʊst] ① N (of timber etc) poste m; (goal ~) poste m (de la portería); (for fencing, marking) estaca f; **the ~** (Sport) (starting) poste m de salida, (finishing) poste m de llegada, meta f; **to be left at the ~** quedar atrás desde la salida; **to win on the ~** ganar junto al mismo poste de llegada.
② VT (announce) anunciar; bills etc (also **to ~ up**) fijar, pegar; **'~ no bills'** 'prohibido fijar carteles'; **to ~ sb missing** declarar a uno desaparecido.

▼ **post²** [pəʊst] ① N (Brit) (a) (mail) correo m; (office) casa f de correos, correos mpl; (numbered: collection) recogida f, (delivery) entrega f; **first ~** primera recogida f; **last ~** última recogida f, última entrega f; **by ~** por correo; **free ~** libre de franqueo; **~ paid** porte m pagado; **your cheque is in the ~** su cheque está en el correo; **the ~ has come** ha llegado el correo; **it came with the ~** vino con el correo; **to drop a card in the ~** echar una postal al buzón; **to go to the ~** ir a correos, ir al buzón; **to open one's ~** abrir sus cartas; **to sort the ~** clasificar las cartas; **to take a parcel to the ~** llevar un paquete a correos.
(b) **there has been a general ~ among the staff** muchos miembros del personal han intercambiado sus puestos.
② VT (a) (Brit) mail echar al buzón, llevar a correos; **this was ~ed on Monday** esto se echó al buzón el lunes; **to ~ sth to sb** mandar algo a uno por correo.
(b) (inform) **to keep sb ~ed** tener a uno al corriente; **please keep me ~ed** no dejes de mantenerme al corriente.
③ VI (††) viajar en posta; **he went ~ing off to India** se fue (inesperadamente, a toda prisa etc) a la India.

▼ **post³** [pəʊst] ① N (a) (job) puesto m, empleo m; destino m; cargo m; **to look for a ~** buscar un puesto; **the duties of the ~** las funciones del cargo; **to take up one's ~** ocupar el puesto, entrar en funciones.
(b) (Mil) puesto m; **Last P~** toque m de retreta; **to die at one's ~** morir en su puesto.
② VT (a) (station) situar, apostar; **to ~ sentries** apostar centinelas; **to ~ a man at the gate** apostar un hombre a la puerta.
(b) (Brit: send) **to ~ sb to Buenos Aires** enviar a uno a Buenos Aires, nombrar a uno en Buenos Aires, destinar a uno para Buenos Aires; **to be ~ed to a regiment** ser ordenado a incorporarse a un regimiento; **he was ~ed first to a destroyer** se le mandó primero a un destructor; **to be ~ed captain** ser ascendido a capitán.

post... [pəʊst] PREF post..., pos...

postage ['pəʊstɪdʒ] N porte m, franqueo m; **~s** (in account) gastos mpl de correo; **~ due** a pagar; **~ machine** (US), **~ meter** (US) franqueadora f; **~ paid** porte pagado, franco de porte; **~ rates** tarifa f de correo.

postage-stamp ['pəʊstɪdʒˌstæmp] N sello m (de correo), estampilla f (LAm), timbre m (Mex).

postal ['pəʊstəl] ADJ postal, de correos; **~ area, ~ district** distrito m postal; **~ charges, ~ rates** tarifa f de correo; **~ order** giro m postal; **~ packet** paquete m postal; **~ service** servicio m postal; **~ system** sistema m postal, correo m; **~ vote** voto m postal; **~ worker** empleado m, -a f de correos.

postbag ['pəʊstbæg] N (Brit) saco m postal; **it arrived in my ~** llegó en mi correo; **he received a heavy ~** recibió muchas cartas.

postbox ['pəʊstbɒks] N (Brit) buzón m.

postcard ['pəʊstkɑːd] N tarjeta f postal, postal f.

postcode ['pəʊstkəʊd] N (Brit) código m postal.

post-coital [pəʊst'kɔɪtəl] ADJ de después del coito.

postdate [pəʊst'deɪt] VT poner fecha adelantada a, posfechar.

postdated [pəʊst'deɪtɪd] ADJ cheque con fecha adelantada.

post-doctoral [pəʊst'dɒktərəl] ADJ posdoctoral; **~ fellow** becario m, -a f posdoctoral; **~ fellowship** beca f posdoctoral.

poster ['pəʊstər] N cartel m; póster m, afiche m (And, Mex, SC); **~ artist, ~ designer** cartelista mf; **~ paint** pintura f al agua.

poste restante ['pəʊst'restɑːnt] N (Brit) lista f de correos, poste f restante (LAm).

posterior [pɒs'tɪərɪər] ① ADJ posterior.
② N trasero m.

posterity [pɒs'terɪtɪ] N posteridad f.

postern ['pəʊstɜːn] N postigo m.

post-free ['pəʊst'friː] ADV porte pagado, franco de porte, libre de

franqueo.

postglacial ['pəʊst'gleɪsɪəl] ADJ posglacial.

postgrad* ['pəʊst'græd] ADJ, N ABBR of **postgraduate** posgraduado m, -a f.

postgraduate ['pəʊst'grædjʊɪt] ① ADJ (pos)graduado; **~ course** curso m para (pos)graduados.
② N (pos)graduado m, -a f.

post-haste ['pəʊst'heɪst] ADV a toda prisa, con toda urgencia.

post-hole ['pəʊsthəʊl] N agujero m de poste.

post-horn ['pəʊstˌhɔːn] N corneta f del correo.

posthumous ['pɒstjʊməs] ADJ póstumo.

posthumously ['pɒstjʊməslɪ] ADV póstumamente, con carácter póstumo, después de la muerte.

postie* ['pəʊstɪ] N cartero m, -a f.

postilion [pəs'tɪlɪən] N postillón m.

post-imperial ['pəʊstɪm'pɪərɪəl] ADJ posimperial.

post-impressionism ['pəʊstɪm'preʃənɪzəm] N posimpresionismo m.

post-impressionist ['pəʊstɪm'preʃənɪst] ① ADJ posimpresionista.
② N posimpresionista mf.

post-industrial [ˌpəʊstɪn'dʌstrɪəl] ADJ posindustrial.

posting ['pəʊstɪŋ] N (a) (Brit Mil etc) destino m. (b) (Fin) asiento m, traspaso m al libro mayor.

postman ['pəʊstmən] N, PL **postmen** ['pəʊstmən] cartero m.

postmark ['pəʊstmɑːk] ① N matasellos m; **date as ~** según fecha del matasellos.
② VT matar (el sello de), timbrar; **it is ~ed 'León'** lleva el matasellos de León.

postmaster ['pəʊstˌmɑːstər] N administrador m de correos; **P~ General** (Brit) Director m, -ora f General de Correos.

postmistress ['pəʊstˌmɪstrɪs] N administradora f de correos.

postmodern ['pəʊst'mɒdən] ADJ posmoderno.

postmodernism ['pəʊst'mɒdənɪzəm] N posmodernismo m.

postmodernist ['pəʊst'mɒdənɪst] ① ADJ posmodernista.
② N posmodernista mf.

post-mortem ['pəʊst'mɔːtəm] N autopsia f; **to carry out a ~** practicar una autopsia; **to hold a ~ on sth** (fig) analizar los resultados de algo, examinar algo críticamente, pasar algo en revista.

postnatal ['pəʊst'neɪtl] ADJ posnatal; **~ depression** depresión f posparto.

post office ['pəʊst'ɒfɪs] ① N (oficina f, casa f de) correos; **General P~** Administración f General de Correos; **I was in the ~** estaba en correos; **I'm going to the ~** voy a correos.
② ATTR: **~ box** apartado m de correos, casilla f de correos (LAm); **~ savings-bank** caja f postal de ahorros; **~ worker** empleado m, -a f de correos.

post-operative [ˌpəʊst'ɒpərətɪv] ADJ posoperativo, posoperatorio.

post-paid ['pəʊst'peɪd] ADV porte pagado, franco de porte.

postpartum [pəʊst'pɑːtəm] N postparto, posparto m; **~ depression** depresión f pos(t)parto.

postpone [pəʊst'pəʊn] VT aplazar; diferir; **to ~ sth for a month** aplazar algo por un mes; **it has been ~d till Tuesday** ha sido aplazado hasta el martes.

postponement [pəʊst'pəʊnmənt] N aplazamiento m.

postpositive [pəʊst'pɒzɪtɪv] ADJ pospositivo.

postprandial ['pəʊst'prændɪəl] ADJ speech, talk etc de sobremesa; walk etc que se da después de comer.

postscript ['pəʊsskrɪpt] N posdata f; (fig) añadidura f; epílogo m; **there is a ~ to this story** esta historia tiene epílogo.

poststructuralism ['pəʊst'strʌktʃərəlɪzm] N posestructuralismo m.

poststructuralist [ˌpəʊst'strʌktʃərəlɪst] ADJ, N postestructuralista mf.

postulant ['pɒstjʊlənt] N postulante m, -a f.

postulate ① ['pɒstjʊlɪt] N postulado m.
② ['pɒstjʊleɪt] VT postular.

postulation [ˌpɒstjʊ'leɪʃən] N postulación f.

postural ['pɒstʃərəl] ADJ (frm) habits, exercises postural.

posture ['pɒstʃər] ① N postura f, actitud f.
② VI tomar una postura, adoptar una actitud; (pej) adoptar una actitud afectada.

posturing ['pɒstʃə'rɪŋ] N fachada f; **there was a lot of political ~ going on** había mucho de fachada política.

postviral [ˌpəʊst'vaɪrəl] ADJ: **~ syndrome** síndrome m posvírico.

postvocalic [ˌpəʊstvəʊ'kælɪk] ADJ posvocálico.

postwar ['pəʊst'wɔːr] ADJ de pos(t)guerra, de la pos(t)guerra, posbélico; **the ~ period** la pos(t)guerra.

posy ['pəʊzɪ] N ramillete m.

pot¹ [pɒt] ① N (a) (for cooking) olla f, puchero m, marmita f; (for preserving) tarro m, pote m; (coffee~) cafetera f; (tea~) tetera f; (US: kitty) bote m; (flower~) tiesto m, maceta f; (chamber~) orinal m; **big ~*** pez m gordo*, personaje m; **the ~ calling the kettle black** el puchero dijo a la sartén 'apártate de mí que me tiznas'; **a ~ of coffee for two** café m para dos; **~s and pans** cacharros mpl; (modern) batería f

de cocina; **we have ~s of it*** tenemos montones*; **to have ~s of money*** ser muy rico; **to go to ~*** echarse a perder, arruinarse; **to keep the ~ boiling** (*earn living*) ganarse la vida; (*make things progress*) mantener las cosas en marcha; **to make a ~ of tea** hacer el té.
(b) (*Sport**) copa *f*.
(c) (*Anat**) barriga *f*, panza *f*.
(d) (*Snooker*) golpe *m*; (*~shot*) tiro *m*; **he took a ~ at the wolf** tiró al lobo.
2 ATTR: **~ cheese** (*US*) ≃ requesón *m*.
3 VT **(a)** *food* conservar (en botes *etc*); (*also* **to ~ up**) *seedling* enmacetar, *plant* poner en tiesto.
(b) *game* derribar; abatir (a tiros); *person* herir; (*Snooker*) *ball* embolsar, entronerar.
4 VI: **to ~ at sb** disparar sobre uno; **to ~ away** seguir disparando.
pot²* [pɒt] N marijuana *f*.
potable ['pəʊtəbl] ADJ potable.
potash ['pɒtæʃ] N potasa *f*.
potassium [pə'tæsɪəm] N potasio *m*; **~ cyanide** cianuro *m* de potasio; **~ nitrate** nitrato *m* de potasio; **~ sulphate** sulfato *m* potásico.
potations [pəʊ'teɪʃənz] NPL libaciones *fpl*.
potato [pə'teɪtəʊ] **1** N, PL **potatoes** [pə'teɪtəʊz] patata *f*, papa *f* (*LAm*); **potatoes in their jackets** patatas *fpl* enteras, patatas *fpl* con su piel.
2 ATTR: **~ beetle** dorífora *f*, escarabajo *m* de la patata; **~ blight** roña *f* de la patata; **~ cake** croqueta *f* de patata; **~ chips** (*US*), **~ crisps** (*Brit*) patatas *fpl* fritas (a la inglesa), papas *fpl* fritas (*LAm*); **~ field** patatal *m*; **~ masher** utensilio para aplastar las patatas al hacer puré; **~ peeler** pelapatatas *m*.
potbellied ['pɒt,belɪd] ADJ barrigón, tripudo, panzudo; (*from malnutrition*) con la barriga hinchada.
potbelly [,pɒt'belɪ] N (*from overeating*) panza *f*; (*from malnutrition*) barriga *f* hinchada.
potboiler ['pɒt,bɔɪlər] N obra *f* (mediocre) compuesta para ganar dinero.
pot-bound ['pɒtbaʊnd] ADJ: **this plant is ~** esta planta ya no cabe en la maceta, esta planta ha crecido demasiado para esta maceta.
poteen [pɒ'tiːn, pɒ'tʃiːn] N aguardiente *m*, whiskey *m* (*irlandés, destilado ilegalmente*).
potency ['pəʊtənsɪ] N potencia *f*; fuerza *f*; eficacia *f*; (*Physiol*) potencia *f*.
potent ['pəʊtənt] ADJ potente, poderoso; *drink* fuerte; *remedy* eficaz.
potentate ['pəʊtənteɪt] N potentado *m*.
potential [pə'tenʃəl] **1** ADJ potencial; posible, eventual, en potencia; futuro; **~ earnings** ganancias *fpl* potenciales; **a ~ prime minister** un primer ministro en ciernes, un primer ministro en potencia; **a ~ threat** una posible amenaza.
2 N potencial *m* (*also Elec, Math, Phys*); potencialidad *f*, capacidad *f*; **the war ~ of Ruritania** el potencial bélico de Ruritania.
potentiality [pə,tenʃɪ'ælɪtɪ] N potencialidad *f*; aptitud *f*, capacidad *f*.
potentially [pə'tenʃəlɪ] ADV potencialmente, en potencia.
potentiate [pə'tenʃɪ,eɪt] VT potenciar.
pother ['pɒðər] N alharaca *f*, aspaviento *m*; lío *m*; **all this ~!** ¡qué lío!; **to make a ~ about sth** armar un lío a causa de algo.
pot-herb ['pɒthɜːb] N hierba *f* de (*or* para) cocina.
pothole ['pɒthəʊl] **1** N (*in road*) bache *m*; (*Geol*) sima *f*, marmita *f* de gigante, (*loosely*) cueva *f*, caverna *f* profunda, gruta *f*.
2 VI: **to ~, to go potholing** dedicarse a la espeleología; ir a explorar una gruta.
pot-holed ['pɒt,həʊld] ADJ lleno de baches.
potholer ['pɒthəʊlər] N espeleólogo *m*, -a *f*.
potholing ['pɒthəʊlɪŋ] N espeleología *f*.
pothunter ['pɒthʌntər] N cazador *m*, -ora *f* de premios.
potion ['pəʊʃən] N poción *f*, pócima *f*.
potluck ['pɒt'lʌk] N: **to take ~** comer lo que haya; (*fig*) tomar lo que haya, contentarse con lo que haya.
pot-plant ['pɒtplɑːnt] N planta *f* de maceta, planta *f* de interior.
potpourri [pəʊ'pʊrɪ] N (*leaves, Mus*) popurrí *m*; (*Liter etc*) mezcla *f*, centón *m*, popurrí *m*.
pot-roast ['pɒtrəʊst] **1** N carne *f* asada.
2 VT asar.
potsherd ['pɒtʃɜːd] N tiesto *m*, casco *m*.
potshot ['pɒt,ʃɒt] N tiro *m* sin apuntar, tiro *m* al azar; **to take a ~ at sth** tirar a algo sin apuntar.
potted ['pɒtɪd] ADJ **(a)** *food* en conserva, cocido y conservado en bote; *plant* en tiesto, en maceta. **(b)** (*fig*) *account, version* resumido, breve.
potter¹ ['pɒtər] N alfarero *m*; (*artistic*) ceramista *mf*; **~'s clay** arcilla *f* de alfarería; **~'s field** (*US*) cementerio *m* de pobres; **~'s wheel** torno *m* de alfarero.
potter² ['pɒtər] VI ocuparse en fruslerías; no hacer nada de particular; **I ~ed round the house all day** hice bagatelas en casa todo el día; **I ~ed round to see him** fui a verle; **we ~ed round the shops** nos paseamos por las tiendas.

♦**potter about** VI ocuparse en fruslerías; no hacer nada de particular; **he likes ~ing about in the garden** le gusta pasar el tiempo haciendo pequeños trabajos en el jardín.
♦**potter along** VI hacerse el remolón; **we ~ along** vamos tirando.
♦**potter around, potter away** VI = **potter along**.
pottery ['pɒtərɪ] N **(a)** (*workshop*) alfar *m*, alfarería *f*. **(b)** (*craft*) alfarería *f*, (*art*) cerámica *f*. **(c)** (*pots*) cacharros *mpl*, (*of fine quality*) loza *f*; (*archaeological remains*) cerámicas *fpl*.
potting compost ['pɒtɪŋ,kɒmpɒst] N compost *m* para macetas.
potting-shed ['pɒtɪŋʃed] N cobertizo *m* de enmacetar.
potty¹ ['pɒtɪ] N orinal *m* de niño, orinal *m* pequeño, bacinica *f*.
potty²* ['pɒtɪ] ADJ (*Brit*) **(a)** (*small*) insignificante, fútil, miserable.
(b) (*mad*) chiflado*; **you must be ~!** ¿has perdido el juicio?; **to drive sb ~** volver loco a uno; **it's enough to drive you ~** es para volverse loco; **she's ~ about him** se chifla por él*, anda loca por él.
potty-trained ['pɒtɪ,treɪnd] ADJ acostumbrado a la bacinica, que ya no necesita pañales.
pouch [paʊtʃ] N bolsa *f* (*also Anat, Zool*); (*hunter's*) morral *m*, zurrón *m*; (*tobacco ~*) petaca *f*; (*Mil*) cartuchera *f*.
pouf(fe) [puːf] N pouf *m*, puff *m*.
poulterer ['pəʊltərər] N pollero *m*, -a *f*; **~'s (shop)** pollería *f*.
poultice ['pəʊltɪs] **1** N cataplasma *f*, emplasto *m*.
2 VT poner una cataplasma a, emplastar (*with* con).
poultry ['pəʊltrɪ] N (*alive*) aves *fpl* de corral; (*dead*) pollos *mpl*, volatería *f*; **~ breeding** avicultura *f*; **~ dealer** recovero *m*, -a *f*, pollero *m*, -a *f*; **~ shop** (*US*) pollería *f*.
poultry-farm ['pəʊltrɪfɑːm] N granja *f* avícola.
poultry-farmer ['pəʊltrɪ,fɑːmər] N avicultor *m*, -ora *f*.
poultry-farming ['pəʊltrɪ,fɑːmɪŋ] N avicultura *f*.
poultry-house ['pəʊltrɪhaʊs] N, PL **poultry-houses** ['pəʊltrɪhaʊzɪz] gallinero *m*.
poultry-keeper ['pəʊltrɪ,kiːpər] N avicultor *m*, -ora *f*.
poultry-keeping ['pəʊltrɪ,kiːpɪŋ] N avicultura *f*.
pounce [paʊns] **1** N salto *m*; ataque *m* súbito; (*swoop by bird*) calada *f*.
2 VI atacar súbitamente; saltar, precipitarse; (*by bird*) calarse; **to ~ on sth** saltar sobre algo, precipitarse sobre algo, arrojarse sobre algo; **to ~ on sb's mistake** saltar sobre el error de uno.
pound¹ [paʊnd] **1** N **(a)** (*weight*) libra *f* (= 453,6 *gr*); **half a ~** media libra *f*; **two dollars a ~** dos dólares la libra; **they sell it by the ~** lo venden por libras; **to have one's ~ of flesh** (*fig*) exigir el cumplimiento completo (de un contrato *etc*); exprimir a uno hasta la última gota; *ver también* [IMPERIAL SYSTEM]
(b) (*money*) libra *f*; **~ sterling** libra *f* esterlina; **it must have cost ~s** habrá costado un dineral.
2 ATTR: **~ note** billete *m* de a libra.
pound² [paʊnd] N corral *m* de concejo; (*police ~, for cars*) depósito *m*.
pound³ [paʊnd] **1** VT (*crush etc*) machacar, majar; (*with hammer*) martillar; (*grind*) moler; (*beat*) golpear, aporrear; (*of sea*) azotar, batir; (*Mil*) bombardear; **he used to ~ the table with his fists** aporreaba la mesa con los puños, golpeaba la mesa con los puños; **to ~ sb.with one's fists** dar de puñetazos a uno; **he was ~ing the piano** aporreaba el piano; **to ~ sth to pieces** romper algo a martillazos; **to ~ a fort into surrender** bombardear una fortaleza hasta que se rinda.
2 VI (*heart*) palpitar; **to ~ at, to ~ on** aporrear, dar golpes en, descargar golpes sobre; **the sea was ~ing against the rocks** el mar azotaba las rocas; **he was ~ing along the road** corría pesadamente por la carretera; **the train ~ed past us** el tren pasó estrepitosamente delante de nosotros.
♦**pound away** VI: **to ~ away at** (*also fig*) machacar en, seguir machacando en.
♦**pound down** VT *drugs, spices* moler; *rocks* machacar; *earth* apisonar; **to ~ sth down to a pulp** hacer algo papilla.
♦**pound out** VT: **he was ~ing out a tune on the piano** a golpes violentos tocaba una melodía al piano.
♦**pound up** VT = **pound down**.
poundage ['paʊndɪdʒ] N impuesto *m* (*or* comisión *f etc*) que se exige por cada libra (esterlina) (*or* de peso).
-pounder ['paʊndər] N *ending in compounds*: **four~** (pez *m etc*) de cuatro libras; **twenty-five~** (*Mil*) cañón *m* de veinticinco.
pounding ['paʊndɪŋ] N (*of heart*) palpitación *f*; (*noise*) martilleo *m*, golpeo *m*, el aporrear *etc*; (*of sea*) azote *m*, embate *m*; (*Mil*) bombardeo *m*; **the ship took a ~ from the waves** el barco tuvo que aguantar la violencia de las olas; **the city took a ~ last night** la ciudad sufrió terriblemente en el bombardeo de anoche; **Barcelona gave us a real ~** el Barça nos dio una paliza de las buenas.
pour [pɔːr] **1** VT **(a)** verter, echar; derramar; *a drink, tea etc* servir, echar; preparar; **he ~ed me a sherry** me sirvió un jerez; **shall I ~ the tea?** ¿sirvo el té?, ¿echo el té?; **he ~ed himself some coffee** se sirvió café; **to ~ money into a project** invertir muchísimo dinero en un proyecto, proveer abundantes fondos para un proyecto; **he has ~ed good ideas into the book** ha llenado el libro de excelentes

ideas; **to ~ it on*** (*US*) volcarse, echar el resto*.
(b) (*of rain*) **to ~ cats and dogs, to ~ torrents** llover a cántaros.
[2] VI **(a)** (*rain*) llover mucho, diluviar, llover a cántaros; (*of water etc*) correr, fluir (abundantemente); **it's ~ing, it's ~ing with rain** está lloviendo a cántaros; **it ~ed for 4 days** llovió seguido durante 4 días; **water came ~ing into the room** el agua entraba a raudales en el cuarto; **water ~ed from the broken pipe** el agua salía a raudales del tubo roto; **blood ~ed from the wound** la sangre salía a borbotones de la herida, la herida sangraba a chorros; **confessions ~ed from his lips** las confesiones salían atropelladamente de su boca.
(b) they came ~ing into the shop entraban a raudales en la tienda.
♦ **pour away** VT vaciar, verter.
♦ **pour down** VI: **the rain** (*or* it) **was ~ing down** llovía a cántaros.
♦ **pour in** [1] VT: **to ~ in a broadside** hacer fuego con todos los cañones.
[2] VI (*persons etc*) entrar a raudales, entrar en tropel; **tourists are ~ing in from all sides** acuden los turistas en tropel de todas partes; **requests are ~ing in** nos llegan las solicitudes a montones.
♦ **pour off** VT vaciar, verter.
♦ **pour out** [1] VT *coffee etc* servir, echar; *unwanted remainder* vaciar; *smoke* arrojar; **to ~ out one's feelings** expresar tumultuosamente sus sentimientos; **to ~ out one's heart to sb** abrir su pecho a uno; **to ~ out one's thanks** expresar efusivamente sus gracias; **to ~ out threats against sb** desatarse en amenazas contra uno.
[2] VI (*persons etc*) salir a raudales, salir en tropel; **they ~ed out into the streets** invadieron las calles; **secrets came ~ing out of the inquiry** los secretos se revelaron a docenas en la investigación.
pouring ['pɔːrɪŋ] [1] ADJ: **~ rain** lluvia *f* torrencial.
[2] ADV: **a ~ wet day** un día de lluvia torrencial.
pout [paʊt] [1] N puchero *m*, mala cara *f*; **to say with a ~** decir con mala cara.
[2] VT: **'Never!', she ~ed** '¡Nunca!', dijo con mala cara; **to ~ one's lips = 3.**
[3] VI hacer pucheros, poner mala cara, hacer morros.
poverty ['pɒvətɪ] [1] N pobreza *f*, miseria *f*; (*of ideas etc*) falta *f*, escasez *f*; **~ is no crime** pobreza no es vileza; **to live in ~** vivir en la miseria; **~ of ideas** carencia *f* de ideas; **~ of resources** escasez *f* de recursos.
[2] ATTR: **~ line** mínimo *m* vital; **to live below the ~ line** vivir en la indigencia; **to live on the ~ line** vivir del salario mínimo; **~ trap** (*Brit*) trampa *f* de la pobreza.
poverty-stricken ['pɒvətɪ,strɪkn] ADJ menesteroso, indigente, necesitado.
P.O.W. N ABBR *of prisoner of war* prisionero *m*.
powder ['paʊdər] [1] N polvo *m*; (*face ~*) polvos *mpl*; (*gun ~*) pólvora *f*; **to keep one's ~ dry** no gastar la pólvora en salvas, reservarse para mejor ocasión; **to reduce sth to ~** reducir algo a polvo, pulverizar algo.
[2] VT **(a)** (*reduce to ~*) reducir a polvo, pulverizar.
(b) (*apply ~ to*) polvorear, (*Culin etc*) espolvorear (*with* de); **to ~ one's face, to ~ one's nose** ponerse polvos, empolvarse; **I must go and ~ my nose** (*euph*) voy donde la propia reina que tiene que ir en persona.
[3] VI **(a)** pulverizarse, hacerse polvo.
(b) (*person*) **= 4.**
[4] VR: **to ~ o.s.** ponerse polvos, empolvarse.
powder-blue ['paʊdə'bluː] [1] ADJ azul pálido.
[2] N azul *m* pálido.
powder-compact ['paʊdə,kɒmpækt] N polvera *f*.
powdered ['paʊdəd] ADJ en polvo; **~ milk** leche *f* en polvo; **~ sugar** (*US*) azúcar *m* extrafino.
powdering ['paʊdərɪŋ] N: **a ~ of snow** una leve capa de nieve.
powder-keg ['paʊdəkeg] N (*fig*) polvorín *m*, barril *m* de pólvora; **the country is a ~** el país es un polvorín.
powder magazine ['paʊdəmægə,ziːn] N santabárbara *f*.
powder-puff ['paʊdəpʌf] N borla *f* (para empolvarse).
powder-room ['paʊdərʊm] N aseos *mpl* (de señora), tocador *m*; **'P~'** 'Señoras'.
powdery ['paʊdərɪ] ADJ *substance* en polvo, polvoriento; *snow* polvoriento; *surface* polvoriento, empolvado.
power ['paʊər] [1] N **(a)** (*gen*) poder *m*; (*physical strength*) fuerza *f*, energía *f*, vigor *m*; (*Mil*) potencia *f*, poder *m*; **a painting of great ~** un cuadro de gran impacto, un cuadro que causa honda impresión; **our ~ in the air** nuestra potencia en el aire; **more ~ to your elbow!** ¡que tengas éxito!; **it is beyond his ~ to save her** no está dentro de sus posibilidades salvarla, no puede hacer nada para salvarla; **to be in the ~ of** estar en manos de; **to do all in one's ~ to** + *infin* hacer lo posible por + *infin*; **to have sb in one's ~** tener a uno en su poder; **to fall into sb's ~** caer en manos de uno; **it does not lie within my ~** no está dentro de mis posibilidades, eso no es de mi competencia; **as far as lies within my ~** en cuanto me sea posible; **to the utmost of one's ~** hasta más no poder.

(b) (*mental*) facultad *f* (*of* de); (*drive*) empuje *m*, energía *f*; **mental ~s** facultades *fpl* mentales; **to be at the height of one's ~s** estar en la cumbre de sus facultades mentales; **his ~s are failing** decaen sus facultades; **to lose the ~ of speech** perder el habla.
(c) (*Mech etc*) potencia *f*; energía *f*, fuerza *f*; (*output*) rendimiento *m*; **engines at half ~** motores *mpl* a medio vapor, motores *mpl* a potencia mitad; **the ship returned to port under her own ~** el buque volvió al puerto impulsado por sus propios motores.
(d) (*Elec*) fuerza *f*, energía *f*, fluido *m*; (*electric ~*) electricidad *f*, fuerza *f* eléctrica, energía *f* eléctrica; **they cut off the ~** cortaron la corriente.
(e) (*Pol etc*) poder *m*; poderío *m*; autoridad *f*; influencia *f*; **~ to the people!** ¡el pueblo al poder!; **~ of life and death** poder *m* de vida y de muerte; **the ~s of darkness** las fuerzas del mal; **the ~s that be** los poderes fácticos, los que mandan, las autoridades (actuales); **he's a ~ in the land** es de los que mandan en el país; **in that year the Prime Minister was at the height of her ~** aquel año fue la cumbre del poderío de la primera ministra; **to be in ~** estar en el poder; **to come to ~** subir al poder, empezar a gobernar, tomar el mando; **to raise sb to ~** alzar a uno al poder; **to share ~** compartir el poder.
(f) (*specific ~*) **~ of attorney** poder *m*, procuración *f*; **full ~s** plenos poderes *mpl*; **to exceed one's ~s** excederse, ir demasiado lejos.
(g) (*nation*) potencia *f*; **the Great P~s** las Grandes Potencias.
(h) (*) **a ~ of people** muchísima gente; **to make a ~ of money** hacerse una pingüe ganancia; **that did me a ~ of good!** ¡con eso me siento mucho mejor!, ¡ahora sí que estoy mucho mejor!; **beer does you a ~ of good** la cerveza le hace pero que mucho bien*.
(i) (*Math*) potencia *f*; **7 to the ~ of 3** 7 elevado al cubo, 7 elevado a la 3ª potencia; **to the nth ~** a la enésima potencia.
[2] ATTR **(a)** (*Pol etc*) **~ base** base *f* de poder; **~ game** juego *m* del poder; **~ structure** estructura *f* del poder; **~ struggle** lucha *f* por el poder.
(b) (*Mech*) **~ cable** cable *m* de energía eléctrica; **~ consumption** consumo *m* de energía; **~ cut** (*Brit*), **~ outage** (*US*) corte *m* de corriente, apagón *m*; **~ drill** taladro *m* mecánico, taladradora *f* de fuerza; **~ failure** fallo *m* del suministro de electricidad; **~ hammer** martillo *m* mecánico; **~ line** línea *f* de conducción eléctrica; **~ loader** rompedora-cargadora *f*; **~ plant** grupo *m* electrógeno, (*US*) central *f* eléctrica; **~ point** (*Brit*) toma *f* de corriente; **~ saw** motosierra *f*, sierra *f* mecánica; **~ shovel** excavadora *f*; **~ station** central *f* eléctrica; **~ steering** dirección *f* asistida; **~ tool** herramienta *f* mecánica; **~ unit** grupo *m* electrógeno; **~ workers** trabajadores *mpl* del sector energético.
[3] VT accionar, impulsar; **a car ~ed by electricity** un coche impulsado por electricidad; **a plane ~ed by 4 jets** un avión impulsado por 4 motores a reacción.
power-assisted ['paʊərə,sɪstɪd] ADJ: **~ brakes** servofrenos *mpl*; **~ steering** dirección *f* asistida.
powerboat ['paʊə,bəʊt] N motora *f*, motorbote *m*.
powerboating ['paʊə,bəʊtɪŋ] N motonáutica *f*.
power-driven ['paʊədrɪvn] ADJ con motor; *tool, saw etc* mecánico.
powered ['paʊəd] ADJ con motor; mecánico.
-powered ['paʊəd] ADJ *ending in compounds*: **wind~** impulsado por el viento, que funciona con energía eólica.
powerful ['paʊəfʊl] ADJ *person, government etc* poderoso; *engine etc* potente; *build* fuerte, fornido; *blow, kick* fuerte; *light, smell, swimmer, voice* fuerte; *emotion* intenso, profundo; *argument* convincente; *painting etc* de gran impacto, que produce honda emoción; **a ~ lot of people*** muchísima gente; **it is a ~ film** es una película muy emocionante; **he gave a ~ performance** su actuación fue magistral.
powerfully ['paʊəfʊlɪ] ADV poderosamente; fuertemente; intensamente; profundamente; de modo convincente; **to be ~ built** ser fornido; **I was ~ affected by the book** el libro me conmovió profundamente.
powerhouse ['paʊəhaʊs] N, PL **powerhouses** ['paʊəhaʊzɪz] central *f* eléctrica; (*fig*) fuente *f* de energía; **he's a ~ of ideas** es una fuente inagotable de ideas.
powerless ['paʊəlɪs] ADJ impotente; ineficaz; **to be ~ to resist** no tener fuerzas para resistir, no poder resistir; **we are ~ to help you** estamos sin fuerzas para ayudarle, somos incapaces de prestarle ayuda; **they are ~ in the matter** no tienen autoridad para intervenir en el asunto, el asunto no es de su competencia.
powerlessness ['paʊəlɪsnɪs] N impotencia *f*; ineficacia *f*.
power-sharing ['paʊə,ʃeərɪŋ] [1] ADJ: **a ~ government** un gobierno de poder compartido.
[2] N compartimiento *m* del poder.
powwow ['paʊwaʊ] [1] N conferencia *f*.
[2] VI conferenciar.
pox* [pɒks] N (*VD*) sífilis *f*; (*small~*) viruelas *fpl*; **a ~ on them!** (††) ¡malditos sean!
poxy: ['pɒksɪ] ADJ puñetero:.
pp (a) ABBR *of* parcel post.

(b) ABBR of **post-paid**.

(c) ABBR of **prepaid**.

pp. ABBR of **pages** páginas *fpl*, págs.

p.p. ADV ABBR of **per procurationem, by proxy** por poder, p.p.

PPE N ABBR of **philosophy, politics, economics** grupo de asignaturas de la Universidad de Oxford.

ppm NPL ABBR of **parts per million** partes *fpl* por millón.

PPP N ABBR of **personal pension plan**.

PPS N (a) (*Brit*) ABBR of **Parliamentary Private Secretary**. (b) ABBR of **post-postscriptum** posdata *f* adicional.

PPV N ABBR of **pay-per-view** de pago.

PQ N (*Canada*) ABBR of **Province of Quebec**.

PR (a) N (*Pol*) ABBR of **proportional representation**. (b) N (*Comm*) ABBR of **public relations** relaciones *fpl* públicas, R.P. (c) (*US Post*) ABBR of **Puerto Rico**.

Pr. ABBR of **prince** príncipe, P.

practicability [ˌpræktɪkəˈbɪlɪtɪ] N practicabilidad *f*, factibilidad *f*; **I doubt its ~** dudo que sea factible.

▼ **practicable** [ˈpræktɪkəbl] ADJ factible, practicable, hacedero.

practical [ˈpræktɪkəl] [1] ADJ (a) práctico; **for all ~ purposes** en la práctica, desde el punto de vista práctico; **~ joke** broma *f* pesada, trastada *f*, mistificación *f*; **~ nurse** (*US*) enfermera *f* práctica, enfermera *f* sin título. (b) **it's a ~ certainty** es prácticamente cierto; **it's a ~ sell-out** es casi una traición. [2] NM (*Univ etc*) examen *m* práctico.

practicality [ˌpræktɪˈkælɪtɪ] N (a) (*of temperament*) espíritu *m* práctico; (*of scheme etc*) factibilidad *f*; **I doubt its ~** dudo que sea factible. (b) (*thing*) cosa *f* práctica; **practicalities** aspectos *mpl* prácticos.

practically [ˈpræktɪklɪ] ADV (a) (*in a practical way*) prácticamente. (b) (*almost*) prácticamente, casi; **~ everybody** casi todos; **~ nothing** casi nada; **there has been ~ no rain** casi no ha llovido.

practice [ˈpræktɪs] [1] N (a) (*habit*) costumbre *f*, uso *m*; **according to his usual ~** según su costumbre; **it is not our ~ to + infin** no acostumbramos a + *infin*; **to make a ~ of + ger, to make it a ~ to + infin** acostumbrar + *infin*.

(b) (*exercise*) ejercicio *m*; (*training*) adiestramiento *m*, (*period*) período *m* de entrenamiento; clase *f* práctica; (*Sport*) entrenamiento *m*; **to be in ~** estar entrenado, estar en forma; **to be out of ~** estar desentrenado, no estar en forma; **to learn by ~** aprender por la práctica, aprender por la experiencia; **~ makes perfect** la práctica (*or* el uso) hace maestro; **it needs a lot of ~** hace falta bastante experiencia.

(c) (*reality*) práctica *f*; **in ~** en la práctica; **to put sth into ~** poner algo en obra.

(d) (*of profession etc*) práctica *f*, ejercicio *m*; **the ~ of medicine** el ejercicio de la medicina; **he was in ~ in Bilbao** ejercía en Bilbao; **he is no longer in ~** ya no ejerce; **to set up in ~** (*Jur*) poner su bufete; (*Med*) empezar a ejercer de médico; **to set up in ~ as** empezar a trabajar como.

(e) (*Med, Jur: patients, clients*) clientela *f*.

[2] ATTR: **~ flight** vuelo *m* de entrenamiento; **~ run** carrera *f* de entrenamiento.

practise, (*US*) **practice** [ˈpræktɪs] [1] VT (a) (*carry out in action*) practicar; tener por costumbre; **we ~ this method** nosotros empleamos (*or* seguimos) este método; **to ~ charity** ejercitar la caridad; **to ~ patience** tener paciencia; **to ~ what one preaches** predicar con el ejemplo.

(b) *profession* ejercer; **to ~ medicine** practicar la medicina, ejercer de médico.

(c) (*train o.s. at*) hacer ejercicios de, hacer prácticas de; **to ~ the piano** hacer ejercicios en el piano, estudiar el piano; **to ~ football** entrenarse en el fútbol; **to ~ a shot at golf** ensayar un golpe de golf; **to ~ + ger** ensayarse + *infin*.

[2] VI (a) (*Mus*) tocar, estudiar, hacer ejercicios; (*Sport*) ejercitarse, entrenarse, adiestrarse; ensayarse; **to ~ every day** hacer ejercicios todos los días; **one has to ~ a lot** hace falta estudiar mucho.

(b) **to ~ as a doctor** ejercer de médico, practicar la medicina.

practised, (*US*) **practiced** [ˈpræktɪst] ADJ *eye etc* experto; *teacher etc* experto, de gran experiencia; *performance* pulido.

practising, (*US*) **practicing** [ˈpræktɪsɪŋ] ADJ activo, que ejerce, practicante; **a ~ Christian** un cristiano practicante.

practitioner [prækˈtɪʃənər] N (*of an art*) practicante *mf*; (*Med: also* **medical ~**) médico *m*, -a *f*; V **general**.

pr(a)esidium [prɪˈsɪdɪəm] N (*Pol*) presidio *m*.

praetorian, (*US*) **pretorian** [prɪˈtɔːrɪən] ADJ: **~ guard** guardia *f* pretoriana.

pragmatic [prægˈmætɪk] [1] ADJ pragmático. [2] **~s** N SING pragmática *f*.

pragmatically [prægˈmætɪklɪ] ADV pragmáticamente.

pragmatism [ˈprægmətɪzəm] N pragmatismo *m*.

pragmatist [ˈprægmətɪst] N pragmatista *mf*.

Prague [prɑːg] N Praga *f*.

prairie [ˈprɛərɪ] [1] N pradera *f*, llanura *f*, pampa *f* (*LAm*).

[2] ATTR (*US*): **~ oyster** huevo crudo y sazonado que se toma en una bebida alcohólica; **~ wolf** coyote *m*.

praise [preɪz] [1] N alabanza *f*, elogio *m*; alabanzas *fpl*, elogios *mpl*; **in ~ of** en alabanza de; **all ~ to him!** ¡enhorabuena!; **~ be!, ~ be to God!** ¡gracias a Dios!; **it's beyond ~** queda por encima de todo elogio; **to be loud** (*or* **warm**) **in one's ~s of sth** alabar algo sinceramente, elogiar algo con entusiasmo; **he is not much given to ~** no acostumbra pronunciar palabras de elogio; **I have nothing but ~ for him** merece todos mis elogios; **to heap ~s on sb** amontonar alabanzas sobre uno; **to sing the ~s of sb** cantar las alabanzas de uno, elogiar con efusión a uno; **to sound** (*or* **sing**) **one's own ~s** cantar sus propias alabanzas.

[2] VT alabar, elogiar; **to ~ God** glorificar a Dios.

◆ **praise up** VT: **to ~ sth up** poner algo por las nubes.

praiseworthily [ˈpreɪzˌwɜːðɪlɪ] ADV loablemente, plausiblemente, de modo digno de elogio.

praiseworthiness [ˈpreɪzˌwɜːðɪnɪs] N lo loable, lo plausible, mérito *m*.

praiseworthy [ˈpreɪzˌwɜːðɪ] ADJ loable, plausible, digno de elogio.

praline [ˈprɑːliːn] N praliné *m*.

pram [præm] N (*Brit*) cochecito *m* de niño.

prance [prɑːns] VI (*horse*) hacer cabriolas, hacer corvetas, encabritarse; (*person*) saltar, bailar; andar con cierta afectación; **he came prancing into the room** entró en la habitación como cabriolando; **to ~ with rage** saltar de rabia.

prang [præŋ] VT (*Brit*) (a) *town etc* bombardear, destruir. (b) *plane* estrellar; *car etc* estropear.

prank [præŋk] N travesura *f*; broma *f*; **a childish ~** una travesura, una diablura; **a student ~** una broma estudiantil; **to play a ~ on sb** gastar una broma a uno.

prankish [ˈpræŋkɪʃ] ADJ travieso, pícaro.

prankster [ˈpræŋkstər] N bromista *mf*.

praseodymium [ˌpreɪzɪəʊˈdɪmɪəm] N praseodimio *m*.

prat [præt] N inútil* *mf*; imbécil *mf*; **you ~!** ¡imbécil!

prate [preɪt] VI parlotear, charlar; **to ~ of** hablar interminablemente de.

pratfall [ˈprætfɔːl] N (*US*) culada* *f*, caída *f* de culo*.

prating [ˈpreɪtɪŋ] ADJ parlanchín.

prattle [ˈprætl] [1] N parloteo *m*; (*child's*) balbuceo *m*.

[2] VI parlotear; balbucear.

prawn [prɔːn] [1] N gamba *f*; (*small*) quisquilla *f*, camarón *m*; (*Dublin Bay ~, large ~*) langostino *m*.

[2] ATTR: **~ cocktail** cóctel *m* de gambas.

pray [preɪ] [1] VT (*liter*) rogar, suplicar; **I ~ you** se lo suplico; **~ tell me, I ~ you tell me ...** le ruego decirme ...; **to ~ sb to do sth** rogar a uno hacer algo, rogar a uno que haga algo; **~ be seated, ~ take a seat** siéntese, por favor.

[2] VI (a) (*say prayers*) rezar, orar; **to ~ to God** rogar a Dios; **to ~ for sth** rogar algo, orar por algo; **to ~ for sb's soul** orar por el alma de uno; **to ~ for sb** orar por uno, rezar por uno; **to ~ that sth may not happen** hacer votos para que algo no ocurra, hacer rogativas para que algo no ocurra; **he's past ~ing for** es un caso desahuciado, ya no le valen oraciones.

(b) **what good is that, ~?** ¿de qué sirve eso, pues?

prayer [prɛər] N (a) (*to God*) oración *f*, rezo *m*; **~s** (*as service*) rezo *m*, oficio *m*; **~s for peace** oraciones *fpl* por la paz; **Book of Common P~** liturgia de la Iglesia Anglicana; **to be at one's ~s** estar rezando, estar en oración; **to offer up ~s for** orar por, rezar por; **to say one's ~s** orar, rezar; **he didn't have a ~*** (*US*) no tenía nada que hacer, no tenía ni la menor posibilidad.

(b) (*entreaty*) ruego *m*, súplica *f*; (*Jur*) petición *f*.

prayer-beads [ˈprɛəˌbiːdz] NPL rosario *m*.

prayerbook [ˈprɛəbʊk] N devocionario *m*, misal *m*.

prayer-mat [ˈprɛəˌmæt] N alfombra *f* de oración.

prayer meeting [ˈprɛəˌmiːtɪŋ] N reunión *f* para rezar.

praying [ˈpreɪɪŋ] ADJ: **~ mantis** mantis *f* religiosa.

pre... [priː] PREF pre...; ante...

preach [priːtʃ] [1] VT (a) predicar; **to ~ a sermon** predicar un sermón; **to ~ the gospel** predicar el Evangelio.

(b) *advantages etc* celebrar; *patience etc* aconsejar.

[2] VI predicar; **to ~ at sb** predicar a uno, dar un sermón a uno; **to ~ to a congregation** predicar a los fieles.

preacher [ˈpriːtʃər] N predicador *m*, -ora *f*; (*US*) pastor *m*, -ora *f*.

preachify* [ˈpriːtʃɪfaɪ] VI sermonear largamente; (*fig*) disertar largamente.

preaching [ˈpriːtʃɪŋ] N predicación *f*; (*pej*) sermoneo *m*.

preachy* [ˈpriːtʃɪ] ADJ dado a sermonear.

preamble [priːˈæmbl] N preámbulo *m*.

prearrange [ˈpriːəˈreɪndʒ] VT arreglar de antemano, predeterminar.

prearranged [ˌpriːəˈreɪndʒd] ADJ predeterminado.

prearrangement [priːəˈreɪndʒmənt] N: **by ~** por previo acuerdo.

prebend [ˈprebənd] N (*stipend*) prebenda *f*; (*person*) prebendado *m*.

prebendary ['prebəndərɪ] N prebendado *m*.

precarious [prɪ'keərɪəs] ADJ precario.

precariously [prɪ'keərɪəslɪ] ADV precariamente.

precariousness [prɪ'keərɪəsnɪs] N precariedad *f*.

precast ['priː'kɑːst] ADJ: ~ **concrete** hormigón *m* precolado.

precaution [prɪ'kɔːʃən] N precaución *f*; **by way of ~** como precaución, para mayor seguridad; **to take ~s** tomar precauciones; **to take the ~ of** + *ger* tomar la precaución de + *infin*.

precautionary [prɪ'kɔːʃənərɪ] ADJ de precaución, precautorio; **~ measure** medida *f* de precaución, medida *f* cautelar.

precede [prɪ'siːd] VTI preceder; **for a month preceding this** durante un mes antes de esto; **to ~ a lecture with a joke** empezar una conferencia contando un chiste.

precedence ['presɪdəns] N precedencia *f*; prioridad *f*; primacía *f*; **to take ~ over sb** preceder a uno, tener precedencia sobre uno, primar sobre uno.

precedent ['presɪdənt] N precedente *m*; **according to ~** de acuerdo con los precedentes; **against all the ~s** contra todos los precedentes; **without ~** sin precedentes; **to establish** (*or* **lay down, set up**) **a ~** establecer un precedente, sentar un precedente (**for** a).

preceding [prɪ'siːdɪŋ] ADJ precedente; **the ~ day** el día anterior.

precentor [prɪ'sentəʳ] N chantre *m*.

precept ['priːsept] N precepto *m*.

preceptor [prɪ'septəʳ] N preceptor *m*.

pre-Christian [priː'krɪstʃən] ADJ precristiano.

precinct ['priːsɪŋkt] N recinto *m*; (*US: area*) barrio *m*; (*US Pol*) distrito *m* electoral, circunscripción *f*; (*US: of policeman*) ronda *f*; **~s** contornos *mpl*; **within the ~s of** dentro de los límites de.

preciosity [presɪ'ɒsɪtɪ] N preciosidad *f*.

precious ['preʃəs] **1** ADJ (a) precioso; *metal, stone* precioso; *person etc* amado, querido; **the book is very ~ to me** para mí el libro tiene gran valor.
(b) *style etc* preciosista, afectado, rebuscado.
(c) (*: iro*) **that ~ marrow of yours** aquel estimable calabacín tuyo; **your ~ son** tu magnífico hijo.
2 ADV (*) muy; **there are ~ few left** quedan bien pocos; **to take ~ good care to see that ...** velar de modo muy particular para que + *subj*; **~ little has been gained** se ha logrado muy poco.
3 N: (**my**) **~!** ¡querida!

precipice ['presɪpɪs] N precipicio *m*, despeñadero *m*.

precipitance [prɪ'sɪpɪtəns] N, **precipitancy** [prɪ'sɪpɪtənsɪ] N precipitación *f*.

precipitancy [prɪ'sɪpɪtənsɪ] N precipitación *f*.

precipitate **1** [prɪ'sɪpɪtɪt] N (*Chem*) precipitado *m*.
2 [prɪ'sɪpɪteɪt] VT precipitar (*also Chem*); (*hasten*) acelerar; *trouble etc* causar, motivar, producir.
3 [prɪ'sɪpɪtɪt] ADJ precipitado, apresurado.

precipitately [prɪ'sɪpɪtɪtlɪ] ADV precipitadamente.

precipitation [prɪ,sɪpɪ'teɪʃən] N (*all senses*) precipitación *f*; **to act with ~** obrar con precipitación.

precipitous [prɪ'sɪpɪtəs] ADJ (a) (*steep*) escarpado, cortado a pico. (b) (*hasty*) precipitado, apresurado.

precipitously [prɪ'sɪpɪtəslɪ] ADV en escarpa, en precipicio.

précis ['preɪsiː] **1** N resumen *m*; **to make a ~ of** = 3.
2 ATTR: ~ **writer** redactor *m*, -ora *f* de actas resumidas.
3 VT hacer un resumen de, resumir.

▼ **precise** [prɪ'saɪs] ADJ (a) *thing* preciso, exacto; (*clearly stated*) claro; **at that ~ moment** en ese mismo momento; **they gave me the ~ book I wanted** me dieron justo el libro que buscaba; **let's be ~ about this** pongamos las cosas en su punto, concretemos; **well, to be ~...** bueno, en rigor ...; **there were 6, to be ~** había 6, para ser exacto.
(b) (*meticulous*) meticuloso, puntual, escrupuloso; (*over~*) afectado, pedante; **he's very ~ in everything** es meticuloso en todo; **in that ~ voice of hers** con su tono un poco pedante, con ese tono suyo un tanto afectado.

▼ **precisely** [prɪ'saɪslɪ] ADV (*V ADJ*) (a) precisamente, con precisión, exactamente; claramente; **~!** ¡perfectamente!, ¡eso es!, ¡justo!; **at ~ 7 o'clock** a las 7 en punto; **~ what was it you wanted?** ¿qué era lo que quería Vd exactamente?
(b) meticulosamente, puntualmente; (*over ~*) afectadamente, con pedantería; **he said very ~** dijo con énfasis.

preciseness [prɪ'saɪsnɪs] N (*V ADJ*) (a) precisión *f*, exactitud *f*. (b) puntualidad *f*, escrupulosidad *f*; afectación *f*, pedantería *f*.

precision [prɪ'sɪʒən] **1** N = **preciseness**.
2 ATTR de precisión; **~ bombing** bombardeo *m* de precisión; **~ instrument** instrumento *m* de precisión; **~-made** de precisión.

preclude [prɪ'kluːd] VT excluir; imposibilitar; **this does not ~ the possibility of ...** esto no excluye (*or* quita) la posibilidad de ...; **so as to ~ all doubt** para disipar cualquier duda; **we are ~d from** + *ger* nos vemos imposibilitados para + *infin*; nos está vedado + *infin*.

precocious [prɪ'kəʊʃəs] ADJ precoz.

precociously [prɪ'kəʊʃəslɪ] ADV de modo precoz, con precocidad.

precociousness [prɪ'kəʊʃəsnɪs] N precocidad *f*.

precocity [prə'kɒsɪtɪ] N precocidad *f*.

precognition [,priːkɒg'nɪʃən] N precognición *f*.

pre-Columbian ['priːkə'lʌmbɪən] ADJ precolombino.

preconceived ['priːkən'siːvd] ADJ preconcebido.

preconception ['priːkən'sepʃən] N preconcepción *f*, idea *f* preconcebida.

preconcerted ['priːkən'sɜːtɪd] ADJ preconcertado.

precondition ['priːkən'dɪʃən] N condición *f* previa, estipulación *f* hecha de antemano; **without ~s** sin condiciones previas.

precook [,priː'kʊk] VT precocinar.

precooked [,priː'kʊkt] ADJ precocinado.

precool ['priː'kuːl] VT preenfriar.

precursor [priː'kɜːsəʳ] N precursor *m*, -ora *f*.

precursory [prɪ'kɜːsərɪ] ADJ preliminar.

predate ['priː'deɪt] VT preceder, ser anterior a, antedatar.

predator ['predətəʳ] N depredador *m*, animal *m* (*etc*) de rapiña.

predatory ['predətərɪ] ADJ *animal* rapaz, de rapiña; *person* agresivo, depredador.

predecease ['priːdɪ'siːs] VT morir antes que.

predecessor ['priːdɪsesəʳ] N predecesor *m*, -ora *f*, antecesor *m*, -ora *f*.

predestination [priː,destɪ'neɪʃən] N predestinación *f*.

predestine ['priː'destɪn] VT predestinar; **to be ~d to** + *infin* ser predestinado a + *infin*.

predetermination ['priː,dɪˌtɜːmɪ'neɪʃən] N predeterminación *f*.

predetermine ['priːdɪ'tɜːmɪn] VT predeterminar.

predicament [prɪ'dɪkəmənt] N apuro *m*, situación *f* difícil; **to be in a ~** estar en un apuro; **what a ~ to be in!** ¡qué lío!

predicate **1** ['predɪkɪt] N predicado *m*.
2 ['predɪkeɪt] VT (a) (*base*) basar, fundar (**on** en); **to be ~d on** estar basado en. (b) (*imply*) implicar.

predicative [prɪ'dɪkətɪv] ADJ predicativo.

predicatively [prɪ'dɪkətɪvlɪ] ADV predicativamente.

predict [prɪ'dɪkt] VT pronosticar, profetizar, predecir.

predictability [prɪdɪktə'bɪlɪtɪ] N previsibilidad *f*.

predictable [prɪ'dɪktəbl] ADJ previsible, que se puede prever; *person* de reacciones previsibles; **it is ~ that ...** se prevé que ...

predictably [prɪ'dɪktəblɪ] ADV previsiblemente; **he was ~ angry** como era de esperar, se enfadó.

prediction [prɪ'dɪkʃən] N pronóstico *m*, profecía *f*, predicción *f*.

predictive [prɪ'dɪktɪv] ADJ profético, que vale como pronóstico.

predictor [prɪ'dɪktəʳ] N indicador *m*.

predigested [,priːdaɪ'dʒestɪd] ADJ predigerido.

predilection [,priːdɪ'lekʃən] N predilección *f*; **to have a ~ for** tener predilección por.

predispose ['priːdɪs'pəʊz] VT predisponer.

predisposition ['priː,dɪspə'zɪʃən] N predisposición *f*.

predominance [prɪ'dɒmɪnəns] N predominio *m*.

predominant [prɪ'dɒmɪnənt] ADJ predominante.

predominantly [prɪ'dɒmɪnəntlɪ] ADV de modo predominante, en un grado predominante; en su mayor parte.

predominate [prɪ'dɒmɪneɪt] VI predominar.

predominately [prɪ'dɒmɪnətlɪ] = **predominantly**.

pre-eclampsia [,priːɪ'klæmpsɪə] N pre-eclampsia *f*.

preemie* ['priːmɪ] N (*US Med*) bebé *m* prematuro.

pre-eminence [priː'emɪnəns] N preeminencia *f*.

pre-eminent [priː'emɪnənt] ADJ preeminente.

pre-eminently [priː'emɪnəntlɪ] ADV especialmente; **a ~ political stance** una actitud sumamente política; **it was ~ created for ...** fue creado especialmente para ...

pre-empt [priː'empt] VT (*Brit*) (a) *person* adelantarse a; **we found they had ~ed us in buying it** encontramos que se nos habían adelantado a comprarlo. (b) **to ~ sth** asegurarse de algo adelantándose a otros; hacer valer sus derechos sobre algo.

pre-emption [priː'empʃən] N preempción *f*; prioridad *f*; derecho *m* de preferencia (de compra); anticipación *f*.

pre-emptive [prɪ(ː)'emptɪv] ADJ *claim etc* por derecho de prioridad, preferente; **~ bid** oferta *f* con derecho preferente; propuesta *f* hecha con intención de excluir cualquier otra; **~ right** derecho *m* preferencial; **~ strike** ataque *m* anticipado; ataque *m* preventivo.

preen [priːn] **1** VT *feather* limpiar, arreglar con el pico.
2 VR: **to ~ o.s.** (*bird*) limpiarse, arreglarse las plumas con el pico; (*person*) pavonearse, atildarse; **to ~ o.s. on** enorgullecerse de, jactarse de.

pre-establish ['priːɪs'tæblɪʃ] VT preestablecer.

pre-established ['priːɪs'tæblɪʃt] ADJ establecido de antemano.

pre-exist ['priːɪg'zɪst] VI preexistir.

pre-existence ['priːɪg'zɪstəns] N preexistencia *f*.

pre-existent ['priːɪg'zɪstənt] ADJ preexistente.

prefab* ['priːfæb] N casa *f* prefabricada.

prefabricate ['priː'fæbrɪkeɪt] VT prefabricar.

prefabricated ['priː'fæbrɪkeɪtɪd] ADJ prefabricado.

preface ['prefɪs] **1** N prólogo *m*, prefacio *m*.
2 VT: **he ~d this by saying that ...** a modo de prólogo a esto dijo que ..., introdujo este tema diciendo que ...; **the book is ~d by an essay** el libro tiene un ensayo a modo de prólogo.
prefaded [,priː'feɪdɪd] ADJ *jeans etc* desteñido de origen.
prefatory ['prefətərɪ] ADJ preliminar, a modo de prólogo.
prefect ['priːfekt] N prefecto *m*; (*Brit Scol*) tutor *m*, monitor *m*.
prefecture ['priːfektjʊəʳ] N prefectura *f*.
▼ **prefer** [prɪ'fɜːʳ] **1** VT (a) preferir; **to ~ coffee to tea** preferir el café al té; **to ~ walking to going by car** preferir ir a pie a ir en coche; **to ~ to +** *infin* preferir **+** *infin*; **I ~ not to say** prefiero no decirlo; **which do you ~?** ¿cuál prefieres?, ¿cuál te gusta más?; **A is much to be ~red over B** A es mucho mejor que B.
(b) (*esp Eccl: promote*) ascender, promover; (*appoint*) nombrar; **he was ~red to the see of Toledo** le nombraron al arzobispado de Toledo.
(c) (*charge*) hacer, presentar; **to ~ a charge against sb** poner a uno un juicio, acusar a uno.
(d) **~red stock** (*US*) acciones *fpl* preferentes.
2 VI: **as you ~** como Vd quiera.
preferable ['prefərəbl] ADJ preferible (*to* a).
preferably ['prefərəblɪ] ADV preferentemente, más bien.
preference ['prefərəns] **1** N preferencia *f*, prioridad *f*; **for ~** de preferencia; **A in ~ to B** A más que B, A antes que B; **to give sth ~** preferir algo, tener preferencia por algo; **to give sth ~ over sth else** anteponer algo a otra cosa; **what is your ~?** ¿cuál te gusta más?; **I have no ~** no tengo preferencia.
2 ATTR (*Brit*) *share* preferente.
preferential [,prefə'renʃəl] ADJ preferente, de preferencia, preferencial; **on ~ terms** con condiciones preferenciales.
preferentially [,prefə'renʃəlɪ] ADV de manera preferente.
preferment [prɪ'fɜːmənt] N (*esp Eccl*) ascenso *m*, promoción *f*; nombramiento *m* (*to* a); **to get ~** ser ascendido.
prefiguration [,priːfɪgə'reɪʃən] N prefiguración *f*.
prefigure [priː'fɪgəʳ] VT prefigurar.
prefix **1** ['priːfɪks] N prefijo *m*. **2** [priː'fɪks] VT prefijar.
preflight ['priːflaɪt] ADJ anterior al despegue.
preggers* ['pregəz] ADJ: **to be ~ = to be pregnant**.
pregnancy ['pregnənsɪ] **1** N embarazo *m*, preñez *f*.
2 ATTR: **~ test** test *m* de embarazo.
pregnant ['pregnənt] ADJ (a) embarazada; **to be ~** estar embarazada, estar en estado, estar encinta; **to be 6 months ~** estar embarazada de 6 meses; **to become ~**, **to get ~** quedarse embarazada.
(b) (*fig*) **~ with** cargado de, preñado de; **a ~ pause** una pausa llena de expectación; **a ~ silence** un silencio elocuente (*or* significativo).
preheat ['priː'hiːt] VT precalentar.
prehensile [prɪ'hensaɪl] ADJ prensil.
prehistoric ['priːhɪs'tɒrɪk] ADJ prehistórico.
prehistory ['priː'hɪstərɪ] N prehistoria *f*.
preignition ['priːɪg'nɪʃən] N preignición *f*.
prejudge ['priː'dʒʌdʒ] VT prejuzgar.
prejudice ['predʒʊdɪs] **1** N (a) (*bias*) parcialidad *f*; (*biased view*) prejuicio *m*; (*hostility*) mala voluntad *f*, prevención *f*; **there are many ~s about this** sobre esto existen muchos prejuicios; **to have a ~ against sb** tener mala voluntad contra uno, tener prevención contra uno, estar predispuesto contra uno.
(b) (*injury, detriment*) perjuicio *m*; daño *m*; **to the ~ of** con perjuicio de, con menoscabo de; **without ~** (*Jur*) sin detrimento de sus propios derechos; **without ~ to** sin perjuicio de.
2 VT (a) (*predispose, bias*) prevenir, predisponer (*against* contra).
(b) (*damage*) perjudicar; **to ~ one's chances** perjudicar las posibilidades de uno.
prejudiced ['predʒʊdɪst] ADJ (a) *view etc* parcial, interesado; **he's very ~** tiene muchos prejuicios.
(b) **to be ~d against sb** tener mala voluntad contra uno, tener prevención contra uno, estar predispuesto contra uno.
prejudicial [,predʒʊ'dɪʃəl] ADJ perjudicial (*to* para).
prelate ['prelɪt] N prelado *m*.
prelim ['priːlɪm] N ABBR *of* **preliminary**.
preliminary [prɪ'lɪmɪnərɪ] **1** ADJ preliminar.
2 N preliminar *m*; **preliminaries** preliminares *mpl*, preparativos *mpl*.
prelude ['preljuːd] **1** N preludio *m* (*also Mus*; *to* de).
2 VT preludiar.
premarital ['priː'mærɪtl] ADJ premarital, prematrimonial, prenupcial.
premature ['premətʃʊəʳ] ADJ prematuro; **~ baby** niño *m* prematuro, niña *f* prematura; **~ baldness** calvicie *f* precoz; **it seems ~ to think of it** parece prematuro pensar en ello; **he was (born) 5 weeks ~** nació con 5 semanas de antelación; **I think you're being a little ~** creo que te has adelantado.
prematurely ['premətʃʊəlɪ] ADV prematuramente; antes de su debido tiempo; **~ bald** con calvicie precoz.
pre-med ['priː'med] **1** N (*Brit*) ABBR *of* **premedication**.
2 ADJ (*US*) ABBR *of* **premedical**; **~ course** curso *m* preparatorio a los

estudios en la Facultad de Medicina.
premedication [,priːmedɪ'keɪʃən] N premedicación *f*, medicación *f* previa.
premeditate [priː'medɪteɪt] VT premeditar.
premeditated [priː'medɪteɪtɪd] ADJ premeditado.
premeditation [priː,medɪ'teɪʃən] N premeditación *f*.
premenstrual [priː'menstrʊəl] ADJ premenstrual; **~ tension** síndrome *m* premenstrual.
premier ['premɪəʳ] **1** ADJ primero, principal.
2 N primer ministro *m*, primera ministra *f*.
première [,premɪ'eəʳ] **1** N estreno *m*; **world ~** estreno *m* mundial; **the film had its ~** se estrenó la película. **2** VT estrenar.
premiership ['premɪəʃɪp] N cargo *m* del primer ministro, puesto *m* de primer ministro; período *m* de gobierno.
▼ **premise** ['premɪs] **1** N (a) (*gen, Philos: also* **premiss**) premisa *f*. (b) **~s** local *m*; (*house*) casa *f*; (*building*) edificio *m*; (*shop etc*) tienda *f*, establecimiento *m*; (*as property*) local *m*, propiedad *f*; **on the ~s** en el local (*etc*); **for consumption on the ~s** para tomarse en el local.
2 VT: **to be ~d on** estar basado en, tener como premisa.
premium ['priːmɪəm] **1** N (*prize*) premio *m*; (*Comm, insurance*) prima *f*; **~ price** precio *m* con prima; **to be at a ~** (*Comm*) estar sobre la par, (*fig*) tener mucha demanda, ser muy solicitado; **to put a ~ on sth** estimular algo, fomentar algo; hacer que suba el valor de algo (debido a su escasez); **to sell sth at a ~** vender algo en más de su valor nominal.
2 ATTR: **~ bond** (*Brit*) bono *m* de la caja de ahorros; **~ deal** oferta *f* extraordinaria; **~ gasoline** (*US*) (gasolina *f*) súper *f*.
premium-rate ['priːmɪəm,reɪt] ADJ (*Telec*) con aplicación *f* de la máxima tarifa.
premolar [priː'məʊləʳ] N premolar *m*.
premonition [,priːmə'nɪʃən] N presentimiento *m*, premonición *f*; **to have a ~ that ...** presentir que ...
premonitory [prɪ'mɒnɪtərɪ] ADJ premonitorio.
prenatal ['priː'neɪtl] ADJ prenatal, antenatal; **~ clinic** clínica *f* prenatal.
prenuptial [,priː'nʌpʃəl] ADJ prematrimonial, prenupcial; **~ agreement** contrato *m* matrimonial.
preoccupation [priː,ɒkjʊ'peɪʃən] N preocupación *f*.
preoccupied [priː'ɒkjʊpaɪd] ADJ preocupado; absorto; abstraído; **to be ~ about** estar preocupado por, inquietarse por; **to be ~ with sth** estar absorto en algo; **he was too ~ to notice** estaba demasiado absorto para darse cuenta.
preoccupy [priː'ɒkjʊpaɪ] VT preocupar.
pre-op* ['priː'ɒp] ADJ preoperatorio; **~ medication** medicación *f* preoperatoria.
preordain ['priːɔː'deɪn] VT predestinar.
preordained ['priːɔː'deɪnd] ADJ predestinado.
pre-owned ['priː'əʊnd] ADJ (*US*) seminuevo.
prep* [prep] **1** N (*Brit Scol*) ABBR *of* **preparation** tareas *fpl*, deberes *mpl*.
2 ADJ: **~ school** = **preparatory school**; *V* **preparatory**.
3 VI (*US**) (a) **to ~ for sth** prepararse para algo.
(b) (*Scol*) hacer el curso de preparación a los estudios universitarios.
4 VR: **to ~ o.s.** (*US*) prepararse.
prepack [,priː'pæk] VT, **prepackage** [,priː'pækɪdʒ] VT preempaquetar.
prepackaged ['priː'pækɪdʒd] ADJ, **prepacked** [,priː'pækt] ADJ empaquetado.
prepaid ['priː'peɪd] ADJ pagado con antelación; (*Post*) porte pagado, franco de porte.
preparation [,prepə'reɪʃən] N preparación *f*; **~s** preparativos *mpl* (*for* para); **to be in ~** (*book*) estar en preparación; **to do sth without ~** hacer algo sin preparación; **to make one's ~s** hacer sus preparativos (*to +* *infin* para **+** *infin*); **Latin is a good ~ for Greek** el latín es buena preparación para el griego.
preparatory [prɪ'pærətərɪ] **1** ADJ preparatorio, preliminar; **~ school** (*Brit*) escuela privada para alumnos de 6 a 11 años (*que pasan después a una* public school), (*US*) colegio *m* privado.
2 **~ to** as PREP como preparación para; con miras a, antes de.

────────────────

PREPARATORY SCHOOL

En el Reino Unido una **preparatory school** *o* **prep school** *es una escuela privada de educación primaria, normalmente no mixta, para alumnos de edades comprendidas entre los 6 y los 11 años. Estos centros exigen uniforme y su objetivo es preparar a los alumnos para que prosigan su formación en centros privados.*
En Estados Unidos una **preparatory** *o* **prep school** *es un centro privado de enseñanza secundaria que prepara a sus alumnos para su ingreso en la universidad. Tanto en el Reino Unido como en Estados Unidos las* **preparatory schools** *se asocian con las clases sociales más pudientes y privilegiadas. La palabra* **preppy**, *usada como sustantivo o adjetivo, designa a los alumnos de las* **prep schools** *estadounidenses o la forma de vestir y apariencia pulcra, discreta y conservadora que normalmente se les atribuye.*

────────────────

► LANGUAGE IN USE: **prefer: 1a** → 7.1, 7.4   **premise: 1a** → 26.3

prepare [prɪ'peəʳ] **1** VT preparar; disponer; aparejar; **how is it ~d?** ¿cómo se prepara?; ¿cómo se hace?; **to ~ a surprise for sb** preparar una sorpresa para uno; **to ~ the way for a treaty** preparar el terreno para un tratado; **to ~ sb for bad news** prevenir a uno para recibir una mala noticia.

2 VI prepararse; disponerse; hacer preparativos; prevenirse; **to ~ for sb's arrival** hacer preparativos para recibir a uno; **to ~ for a storm** prepararse para una tempestad; **to ~ for an examination** estudiar para un examen; **to ~ to +** *infin* disponerse a + *infin*, hacer preparativos para + *infin*.

▼ **prepared** [prɪ'peəd] ADJ (a) listo; **~ food** producto *m* previamente elaborado; **'be ~'** (*motto*) '¡está preparado!'

▼ (b) to be ~ **for anything** estar preparado para todo; no dejarse sorprender por nada; **we were not ~ for this** esto no lo esperábamos, no contábamos con esto; **we were ~ for it** lo habíamos previsto; **to be ~ to +** *infin* estar dispuesto a + *infin*; **he was not ~ to listen to us** no estaba dispuesto a escucharnos.

preparedness [prɪ'peərɪdnɪs] N preparación *f*, estado *m* de preparación; **military ~** preparación *f* militar.

prepay ['priː'peɪ] (*irr: V* **pay**) VT pagar por adelantado.

prepayment ['priː'peɪmənt] N pago *m* adelantado, pago *m* anticipado.

preponderance [prɪ'pɒndərəns] N preponderancia *f*, predominio *m*.

preponderant [prɪ'pɒndərənt] ADJ preponderante, predominante.

preponderantly [prɪ'pɒndərəntlɪ] ADV de modo predominante, en un grado predominante; en su mayor parte.

preponderate [prɪ'pɒndəreɪt] VI preponderar, predominar.

preposition [ˌprepə'zɪʃən] N preposición *f*.

prepositional [ˌprepə'zɪʃənl] ADJ preposicional.

prepositionally [ˌprepə'zɪʃənəlɪ] ADV como preposición.

prepossess [ˌpriːpə'zes] VT (*preoccupy*) preocupar; (*bias, impress favourably*) predisponer.

prepossessing [ˌpriːpə'zesɪŋ] ADJ atractivo, agradable; **not very ~** no muy atractivo.

preposterous [prɪ'pɒstərəs] ADJ absurdo, ridículo.

preposterously [prɪ'pɒstərəslɪ] ADV absurdamente.

preposterousness [prɪ'pɒstərəsnɪs] N lo absurdo.

preppy* ['prepɪ] ADJ (*US*) de muy buen tono; guapón*, elegantón*.

preprandial [ˌpriː'prændɪəl] ADJ (*frm*) *drink* para abrir boca.

preprepared [ˌpriːprɪ'peəd] ADJ preprepared.

preproduction [ˌpriːprə'dʌkʃən] **1** N preproducción *f*.

2 ATTR: **~ model** prototipo *m*; **~ trial** ensayo *f* con prototipo.

preprogramme, (*US, freq Comput*) **preprogram** [ˌpriː'prəʊgræm] VT preprogramar.

preprogrammed, (*US*) **preprogramed** [ˌpriː'prəʊgræmd] ADJ preprogramado.

prepubescent [ˌpriːpjuː'besənt] ADJ prepúber.

prepuce ['priːpjuːs] N prepucio *m*.

prequel ['priːkwəl] N película hecha para ser la primera parte de otra aparecida antes.

pre-Raphaelite ['priː'ræfəlaɪt] **1** ADJ prerrafaelista.

2 N prerrafaelista *mf*.

prerecord ['priːrɪ(ː)'kɔːd] VT grabar (*or* registrar) de antemano.

prerecorded ['priːrɪ'kɔːdɪd] ADJ pregrabado, ya grabado.

prerelease ['priːrɪ'liːs] ADJ: **~ showing** (*Cine*) preestreno *m*.

prerequisite ['priː'rekwɪzɪt] **1** ADJ previamente necesario.

2 N requisito *m* previo; condición *f* previa; cosa *f* necesaria, esencial *m*; **~s for success** las cosas necesarias para asegurar el éxito.

prerogative [prɪ'rɒgətɪv] N prerrogativa *f*.

Pres ABBR *of* **President** Presidente *m*, -a *f*.

presage ['presɪdʒ] **1** N presagio *m*.

2 VT presagiar.

Presbyterian [ˌprezbɪ'tɪərɪən] **1** ADJ presbiteriano.

2 N presbiteriano *m*, -a *f*.

Presbyterianism [ˌprezbɪ'tɪərɪənɪzəm] N presbiterianismo *m*.

presbytery ['prezbɪtərɪ] N casa *f* parroquial; (*Archit*) presbiterio *m*.

preschool ['priː'skuːl] ADJ preescolar; **~ education** educación *f* preescolar.

prescience ['presɪəns] N presciencia *f*.

prescient ['presɪənt] ADJ presciente.

prescribe [prɪs'kraɪb] **1** VT (a) (*also Jur*) prescribir; ordenar; **in the ~d way** de conformidad con la ley, en el modo que ordena la ley; **in the ~d time** dentro del plazo que fija la ley.

(b) (*Med*) recetar; **to ~ a medicine for sb** recetar una medicina para uno; **he ~d complete rest** recomendó el reposo completo; **what do you ~?** ¿qué me recomiendas?

2 VI (a) prescribir (*also Jur*); ordenar.

(b) (*Med*) recetar; **to ~ for boils** recetar una medicina para curar los diviesos.

prescription [prɪs'krɪpʃən] **1** N (a) prescripción *f* (*also Jur*); precepto *m*.

(b) (*Med*) receta *f*, prescripción *f*; **made according to ~** hecho según receta; **available only on ~** obtenible sólo con receta.

2 ATTR: **~ lenses** (*US*) lentes *fpl* graduadas.

prescriptive [prɪs'krɪptɪv] ADJ legal; sancionado por la costumbre; (*Ling*) prescriptivo.

prescriptivism [prɪ'skrɪptɪˌvɪzəm] N prescriptivismo *m*.

presealed ['priː'siːld] ADJ precintado (de antemano).

pre-select [priːsɪ'lekt] VT preseleccionar.

presence ['prezns] N (a) presencia *f*; (*attendance*) asistencia *f* (*at* a); **~ of mind** aplomo *m*, serenidad *f*, sangre *f* fría; **saving your ~** con perdón de los presentes, con la venia de los presentes; **in the ~ of** en presencia de, (*fig*) ante; **to be admitted to the P~** ser conducido ante el rey (*etc*); **to make one's ~ felt** (saber) imponerse, hacerse notar; **your ~ is requested** se ruega su asistencia.

(b) (*bearing etc*) presencia *f*.

present **1** ['preznt] ADJ (a) (*in attendance*) presente; **~!** ¡presente!; **those ~** los presentes, los asistentes; **to be ~** asistir (*at* a); **all were ~ to hear it** todos asistieron para oírlo, acudieron todos a oírlo; **he was ~ at the accident** fue testigo del accidente; **he was ~ at the foundation** presenció la fundación; **nobody else was ~** no había nadie más; **how many others were ~?** ¿cuántos más había?

(b) (*of time, current*) actual; presente; *month etc* corriente; **~ methods include ...** los métodos actuales incluyen ..., los métodos en uso incluyen ...; **the ~ Queen of England** la actual Reina de Inglaterra; **the ~ letter** la presente; **the ~ writer** el que esto escribe; **its ~ value** su valor actual; **in the ~ year** en el año que corre.

(c) (*Gram*) *tense* presente; *participle* activo, (de) presente.

2 ['preznt] N (a) (*of time*) presente *m*, actualidad *f*; **the ~** el presente; **at ~** al presente, actualmente; **for the ~** por ahora, por el momento; **up to the ~** hasta ahora.

(b) (*gift*) regalo *m*, presente *m*; obsequio *m*; **to make sb a ~ of sth** regalar algo a uno, (*fig*) dar algo a uno medio regalado, servir algo a uno en bandeja.

(c) (*Gram*) (tiempo *m*) presente *m*; **~ perfect** pretérito *m* perfecto.

3 [prɪ'zent] VT (a) (*introduce*) presentar; **to ~ X to Y** presentar a X a Y; **may I ~ Miss Blandish?** permítame presentarle a la señorita Blandish; **to be ~ed at court** ser presentado en la corte.

(b) (*Theat*) **to ~ a play** representar una obra; **'~ing Garbo as Mimi'** 'con Garbo en el papel de Mimi'.

(c) (*expound*) *case etc* exponer; **to ~ a plan to a meeting** exponer (*or* explicar) un proyecto a una reunión.

(d) (*give*) presentar, ofrecer, dar; (*show*) *documents, tickets etc* presentar, mostrar; (*TV*) *programme* presentar; (*represent, portray*) presentar; **to ~ sth to sb, to ~ sb with sth** regalar algo a uno, (*more formally*) obsequiar a uno con algo; **to ~ an account** (*Comm*) pasar factura; **to ~ a report** presentar un informe; **to ~ one's compliments to sb** cumplimentar a uno, saludar a uno, ofrecer sus saludos a uno; **the report ~s him in a favourable light** el informe le presenta bajo una luz favorable.

(e) (*provide*) ofrecer; **it ~s a magnificent sight** ofrece un espectáculo maravilloso; **the case ~s some odd features** el caso tiene ciertas características algo raras; **it ~s some difficulties** nos plantea algunas dificultades; **the boy ~s a problem** el chico nos plantea un problema.

(f) (*Mil*) **to ~ arms** presentar las armas; **~ arms!** ¡presenten armas!

4 [prɪ'zent] VR: **to ~ o.s.** presentarse (*at a time* a una hora, *at a place* en un sitio); **to ~ o.s. for examination** examinarse (*in* de); **when the chance ~s itself** cuando se ofrece la ocasión; **a problem has ~ed itself** ha surgido un problema.

presentable [prɪ'zentəbl] ADJ presentable; **are you ~?** (*dressed etc*) ¿estás visible?; **I must go and make myself ~** voy a arreglarme un poco.

presentably [prɪ'zentəblɪ] ADV: **~ dressed** vestido de manera presentable.

presentation [ˌprezən'teɪʃən] **1** N (a) (*act*) presentación *f*; (*of case etc*) exposición *f*; (*Theat*) representación *f*; **on ~ of the voucher** al presentarse el vale.

(b) (*present*) obsequio *m*; (*ceremony*) entrega *f* ceremoniosa de un regalo; **to make sb a ~ on his retirement** hacer un obsequio a uno en su jubilación.

(c) (*Scol, Univ*) exposición *f* oral de un ejercicio escrito.

2 ATTR: **~ case** estuche *m* de regalo; **~ copy** ejemplar *m* con dedicatoria del autor.

presentational [ˌprezən'teɪʃənəl] ADJ relativo a la presentación.

present-day ['prezntdeɪ] ADJ actual, de hoy en día.

presenter [prɪ'zentəʳ] N (*Brit TV etc*) presentador *m*, -ora *f*.

presentiment [prɪ'zentɪmənt] N presentimiento *m*, corazonada *f*; **to have a ~ about sth** tener un presentimiento acerca de algo; **to have a ~ that ...** presentir que ...

presently ['prezntlɪ] ADV (*Brit*) luego, dentro de poco; (*esp US*) ahora, actualmente; en el momento presente.

preservation [,prezə'veɪʃən] ① N conservación f; preservación f; **in a good state of ~, in good ~** bien conservado, en buen estado.

② ATTR: **~ order** (Brit) orden f de preservación; **~ society** (Brit) sociedad f para la preservación.

preservative [prɪ'zɜ:vətɪv] ① ADJ preservativo.

② N preservativo m.

preserve [prɪ'zɜ:v] ① N **(a)** (Brit Culin) conserva f; confitura f; compota f.

(b) (Hunting) coto m, vedado m; (game ~) coto m de caza; (fig) dominio m, territorio m; **it's a female ~** es un coto cerrado femenino.

② VT **(a)** (keep) conservar; mantener en buen estado; (keep from harm) preservar (against, from contra), guardar, proteger (against, from de); **may God ~ you** que Dios os guarde.

(b) (Culin) hacer una conserva de; (in syrup) almibarar, (in salt) salar, salpresar.

preserved [prɪ'zɜ:vd] ADJ food en conserva.

preset ['pri:'set] VT (irr: V set) programar.

pre-shrunk ['pri:'ʃrʌŋk] ADJ inencogible.

preside [prɪ'zaɪd] VI presidir; **to ~ at** (or **over**) **a meeting** presidir una reunión.

presidency ['prezɪdənsɪ] N presidencia f.

president ['prezɪdənt] N (Pol etc) presidente m, -a f; (US Comm) director m, -ora f; (US Univ) rector m, -ora f; **~-elect** presidente m electo, presidenta f electa; **~'s list** (US Univ) lista de honor académica; ver también DEAN'S LIST .

presidential [,prezɪ'denʃəl] ADJ presidencial.

presidium [prɪ'sɪdɪəm] N (Pol) presidio m.

press [pres] ① N **(a)** (pressure) presión f; (of hand etc) apretón m, presión f; (Weightlifting) presa f; **give it a ~ here** presione aquí.

(b) (crush etc of people) apiñamiento m, agolpamiento m; (of affairs) urgencia f; **there was such a ~ of people** había tal multitud de gente, era tal el apiñamiento; **in the ~ of the battle** en lo más reñido de la batalla.

(c) (Mech) prensa f.

(d) (Typ) (printing press, publishing firm) imprenta f; (newspapers in general) prensa f; **the P~** la Prensa; **to be in ~** estar en prensa; **to get** (or **have**) **a bad ~** tener mala prensa; **to get** (or **have**) **a good ~** tener buena prensa; **to go to ~** entrar en prensa, entrar en máquina; **to pass sth for the ~** aprobar algo para la prensa.

② ATTR: **~ baron** magnate m de la prensa; **~ card** tarjeta f de periodista, pase m de periodista; **~ corps** cuerpo m de periodistas; **~ office** oficina f de prensa; **~ officer, ~ secretary** secretario m, -a f de prensa.

③ VT **(a)** button, switch, doorbell etc apretar, pulsar, presionar, empujar; hand, trigger apretar; hand (painfully) apretujar; grapes pisar, prensar; metal, olives etc (Tech) prensar; suit planchar; (crush, squeeze) estrujar; **to ~ sb's hand** apretar la mano a uno; **to ~ the juice out of an orange** exprimir el zumo de una naranja; **it ~es me here** me aprieta aquí; **he ~ed his face to the window** pegó la cara al cristal; **to ~ sb to one's heart** abrazar a uno estrechamente; **to ~ books into a case** meter libros apretadamente en una maleta.

(b) (put pressure on enemy etc) acosar, hostigar, (in game) apretar, (in pursuit) seguir muy de cerca, pisar los talones de; **to ~ sb hard** apretar mucho a uno; **to ~ sb for payment** insistir en que uno pague algo, exigir el pago a uno, apremiar a uno a que pague; **to ~ sb for an answer** pedir insistentemente que uno conteste a algo; **to ~ charges against sb** hacer acusaciones contra uno; **to ~ a claim** insistir en una demanda; **to ~ a point** insistir en su punto de vista; **to ~ home an advantage** aprovechar todo lo posible de una ventaja; **to ~ a gift on sb** insistir en que uno acepte un regalo; **to ~ sb to do sth** instar a uno a que haga algo, apremiar a uno para que haga algo, hacer presión sobre uno para que haga algo; **he didn't need much ~ing** no hacía falta convencerle; **he was being ~ed by creditors** le acosaban los acreedores; **to be ~ed for money** andar muy escaso de dinero; **to be ~ed for time** tener poco tiempo, tener mucha prisa.

④ VI **(a)** (in physical sense) apretar; ejercer presión; **to ~ hard** apretar mucho; **to ~ close up to sb** arrimarse a uno; **to ~ on one's pen** escribir haciendo más presión con la pluma; **the people ~ed round him** la gente se apiñó en torno a él.

(b) (fig) ejercer presión, hacer presión; presionar; **time ~es** el tiempo apremia; **responsibilities ~ hard on him** las responsabilidades pesan sobre él.

(c) to ~ for sth presionar por algo, presionar para conseguir algo; reclamar algo, exigir algo, pedir algo con urgencia; **to ~ for sb to resign** presionar para que uno dimita.

◆**press ahead** VI = **press forward**.

◆**press back** VT crowd, enemy rechazar.

◆**press down** ① VT: **to ~ sth down** comprimir algo.

② VI: **to ~ down on sth** apretar algo comprimiéndolo; pesar sobre algo.

◆**press forward, press on** VI avanzar; seguir su camino; (hasten) apretar el paso; **~ on!** ¡adelante!

◆**press out** VT: **to ~ the juice out of an orange** exprimir el zumo de una naranja.

press-agency ['pres,eɪdʒənsɪ] N agencia f de prensa.

press-agent ['pres,eɪdʒənt] N agente mf de publicidad.

press attaché ['presə'tæʃeɪ] N agregado m de prensa.

press-box ['presbɒks] N tribuna f de la prensa.

press-button ['pres'bʌtn] ① N botón m (de control).

② ATTR mandado por botón.

press-clipping ['pres,klɪpɪŋ] = **press-cutting.**

press-conference ['pres,kɒnfərəns] N rueda f de prensa, conferencia f de prensa.

press-cutting ['pres,kʌtɪŋ] N recorte m (de periódico).

press gallery ['pres,gælərɪ] N tribuna f de la prensa.

press-gang ['presgæŋ] ① N leva f, ronda f de enganche.

② VT: **to ~ sb into sth** obligar a uno muy contra su voluntad a hacer algo.

pressing ['presɪŋ] ADJ urgente, apremiante, acuciante.

pressman ['presmæn] N, PL **pressmen** ['presmen] (Brit) periodista m; (US) tipógrafo m.

pressmark ['presmɑ:k] N (Brit) signatura f.

press photographer ['presfə'tɒgrəfər] N fótografo m, -a f de prensa.

press-release ['presrɪ,li:s] N boletín m de prensa, comunicado m de prensa, nota f de prensa.

press-report ['presrɪ,pɔ:t] N reportaje m de prensa.

press run ['presrʌn] N (US) tirada f.

press-stud ['presstʌd] N (Brit) botón m de presión.

press-up ['presʌp] N flexión f, abdominal m, plancha f.

pressure ['preʃər] ① N **(a)** (Met, Phys, Tech) (weight) peso m; (strength) fuerza f; **a ~ of x kilogrammes to the square metre** una presión de x kg al m².

(b) (urgency) urgencia f, apremio m; (influence) influencia f, persuasión f; (Med) tensión f nerviosa; **because of the ~ of business** (Comm) debido a la cantidad de negocios, (at meeting etc) por el número de los asuntos a tratar; **to act under ~** obrar bajo persuasión; **he is under ~ to sign the agreement** le están presionando para que firme el acuerdo; **to do sth under ~ from the bankers** hacer algo presionado por los banqueros; **to bring ~ to bear on sb** hacer presión sobre uno (to do sth para que haga algo); **to live at high ~** tener una vida muy activa; **to work under ~** trabajar con urgencia.

② VT = **pressurize.**

pressure-cook ['preʃə,kʊk] VT cocer en olla a presión.

pressure-cooker ['preʃə,kʊkər] N olla f a presión.

pressure-feed ['preʃəfi:d] N tubo m de alimentación a presión.

pressure-gauge ['preʃəgeɪdʒ] N manómetro m.

pressure-group ['preʃəgru:p] N grupo m de presión.

pressure pan ['preʃəpæn] N (US) olla f a presión.

pressure-point ['preʃə,pɔɪnt] N (Anat) punto m de presión.

pressure-suit ['preʃə,su:t] N traje m de presión compensada.

pressurize ['preʃəraɪz] VT presionar, hacer presión sobre, ejercer presión sobre; **to ~ sb into doing sth** forzar a uno a hacer algo, presionar a uno para que haga algo.

pressurized ['preʃəraɪzd] ADJ cabin a presión, presurizado; **~ water reactor** reactor m de agua a presión.

press view ['presvju:] N preestreno m (para prensa).

Prestel ['prestel] ® N videotex m.

prestidigitation ['prestɪ,dɪdʒɪ'teɪʃən] N prestidigitación f.

prestige [pres'ti:ʒ] N prestigio m.

prestigious [pres'tɪdʒəs] ADJ prestigioso.

presto ['prestəʊ] ADV: **hey ~!** ¡abracadabra!

prestressed ['pri:'strest] ADJ: **~ concrete** hormigón m pretensado.

presumably [prɪ'zju:məblɪ] ADV probablemente, presumiblemente, según cabe presumir; **~ he will come** imagino que vendrá; **~ he did** cabe presumir que lo hizo.

presume [prɪ'zju:m] ① VT **(a)** (suppose) presumir; suponer; **his death must be ~d** hay que presumir que ha muerto, es de suponer que murió; **to ~ that ... suponer que ...; it may be ~d that ... es de** suponer que ...; **to ~ sb to be innocent** suponer que uno es inocente; **Dr Livingstone, I ~** Dr Livingstone según creo, cabe conjeturar que Vd es el Dr Livingstone.

(b) (venture) **to ~ to ~** atreverse a + infin; pretender + infin, tomarse la libertad de + infin; **if I may ~ to advise you** si me permites ofrecerte un consejo.

② VI: **to ~ on sb's friendship** abusar de la amistad de uno; **you ~ too much** no sabes lo que pides, eso es mucho pedir.

presumption [prɪ'zʌmpʃən] N **(a)** (arrogance) presunción f; atrevimiento m; **pardon my ~** le ruego perdonar mi atrevimiento.

(b) (thing presumed) suposición f; pretensión f; **the ~ is that ...** es de suponer que ..., puede presumirse que ...

presumptive [prɪ'zʌmptɪv] ADJ heir presunto; **~ evidence** pruebas fpl presuntivas.

presumptuous [prɪˈzʌmptjʊəs] ADJ presumido, presuntuoso; atrevido; **in that I was rather ~** en eso fui algo atrevido; **it would be ~ of me to express an opinion** sería osado que yo opinara.

presumptuously [prɪˈzʌmptjʊəslɪ] ADV con presunción, presuntuosamente.

presumptuousness [prɪˈzʌmptjʊəsnɪs] N presunción f, atrevimiento m.

presuppose [ˌpriːsəˈpəʊz] VT presuponer.

presupposition [ˌpriːsʌpəˈzɪʃən] N presuposición f.

pre-tax [ˌpriːˈtæks] ADJ anterior al impuesto; **~ profits** beneficios mpl preimpositivos.

pre-teen [ˌpriːˈtiːn] (US) ① ADJ preadolescente.
② NPL: **the ~s** los preadolescentes.

pretence, (US) **pretense** [prɪˈtens] N (a) (claim) pretensión f; **to make no ~ to learning** no pretender ser erudito.
(b) (display) ostentación f; afectación f; **without ~, devoid of all ~** sin ostentación, sin afectación.
(c) (pretext) pretexto m; **on the ~ of, under the ~ of** so pretexto de.
(d) (make-believe) fingimiento m; ficción f; fraude m, engaño m; **it's all a ~** todo es fingido; **to make a ~ of sth** fingir algo.

pretend [prɪˈtend] ① VT (a) (feign) fingir, aparentar, simular; **to ~ ignorance** fingir ignorancia, fingir ignorar, aparentar no saber; **to ~ that ...** (querer) hacer creer que ...; **let's ~ I'm the doctor and you're the nurse** yo era el médico y tú eras la enfermera; **to ~ to go away** fingir marcharse; **to ~ to be mad** fingirse loco; **to ~ to be asleep, to ~ to sleep** fingir dormir, fingirse dormido, hacerse el dormido; **he ~s to be a poet** se dice poeta, se hace el poeta, las echa de poeta; **to ~ not to be listening** hacerse el distraído; **to ~ not to understand** hacerse el desentendido.
(b) (claim) pretender; **I do not ~ to know the answer** no pretendo saber la respuesta; **I don't ~ to understand art** no pretendo entender de arte.
② VI (a) (feign) fingir; **it's just ~, we're only ~ing** (to child etc) es de mentirijillas; **let's ~** imaginémoslo; **let's not ~ to each other** no nos engañemos uno a otro.
(b) (claim) **to ~ to the throne** pretender el trono; **to ~ to intelligence** afirmar tener inteligencia, pretender ser inteligente.
③ ADJ: **~ money*** dinero m de juego.

pretended [prɪˈtendɪd] ADJ pretendido.

pretender [prɪˈtendəʳ] N pretendiente mf; **~ to the throne** pretendiente mf al trono; **the Young P~** el joven Pretendiente.

pretense [prɪˈtens] N (US) = **pretence**.

pretension [prɪˈtenʃən] N (a) (claim) pretensión f; **to have ~s to culture** tener pretensiones de cultura, pretender ser culto.
(b) (pretentiousness) presunción f; afectación f.

pretentious [prɪˈtenʃəs] ADJ pretencioso; person presumido; (ostentatious) ostentoso, aparatoso, ambicioso; (and vulgar) cursi.

pretentiously [prɪˈtenʃəslɪ] ADV con presunción; ostentosamente, aparatosamente.

pretentiousness [prɪˈtenʃəsnɪs] N pretenciosidad f; presunción f; lo ostentoso, lo aparatoso; cursilería f.

preterite [ˈpretərɪt] N pretérito m.

preterm [ˌpriːˈtɜːm] ① ADJ prematuro.
② ADV prematuramente.

preternatural [ˌpriːtəˈnætʃrəl] ADJ preternatural.

pretext [ˈpriːtekst] N pretexto m; **under ~ of** so pretexto de; **it's just a ~** es sólo un pretexto.

pretorian [prɪˈtɔːrɪən] ADJ (US) = **praetorian**.

prettify [ˈprɪtɪfaɪ] VT (pej) embellecer, adornar (de modo ridículo); ataviar.

prettily [ˈprɪtɪlɪ] ADV con gracia, elegantemente; preciosamente; **~ adorned with** con adornos elegantes de.

pretty [ˈprɪtɪ] ① ADJ (a) person guapo, bonito, lindo (LAm); dress, object etc precioso, mono, bonito; scene hermoso; **a ~ girl** una muchacha guapa; **a ~ little house** una casita preciosa; **what a ~ hat!** ¡qué sombrero más mono!, ¡qué monada de sombrero!; **yes, my ~** (to child) sí, ricura; **she's as ~ as a picture** es guapísima; **he has a ~ wit** (liter) tiene un ingenio muy vivo, es muy ingenioso.
(b) sum etc importante, considerable.
(c) (iro) bueno; **a ~ mess we're in!** ¡vaya lío!
② ADV bastante; casi; **~ good** bastante bueno, muy bueno; **~ hard** bastante difícil; **it's ~ much the same** llega a ser como lo mismo, es lo mismo más o menos; **he got ~ cross** se enfadó bastante; **I have a ~ fair idea who did it** yo sé casi seguramente quién lo hizo; **it's ~ near ruined** está casi arruinado; **that's ~ well everything** eso es todo más o menos; **~ well, thanks!** ¡regular, gracias!; **to be sitting ~** estar bien sentado.

♦ **pretty up** VT = **prettify**.

pretty-pretty* [ˈprɪtɪˈprɪtɪ] ADJ (pej): **he's very ~** es un guapito de cara*; **she's very ~** es una niña mona.

pretzel [ˈpretsl] N (US) galleta tostada en forma de rosquilla, polvoreada con sal.

prevail [prɪˈveɪl] VI (a) (gain mastery) prevalecer, imponerse; **to ~ against** (or **over**) **one's enemies** triunfar sobre los enemigos; **finally good sense ~ed** por fin se impuso el buen sentido; **eventually peace ~ed** por fin se restableció la paz.
(b) (be current) reinar, imperar; predominar; (be in fashion) estar de moda, estar en boga; **the conditions that now ~** las condiciones que ahora imperan.
(c) (persuade) **to ~ upon sb to do sth** convencer a uno para que haga algo, inducir a uno a hacer algo; **he was eventually ~ed upon to + infin** por fin se dejó persuadir a + infin; **he could not be ~ed upon** era imposible persuadirle, no se convenció.

prevailing [prɪˈveɪlɪŋ] ADJ reinante, imperante; vigente; predominante; usual, corriente; price imperante; **the ~ fashion** la moda actual, la moda reinante; **under ~ conditions** bajo las condiciones actuales; **the ~ wind** el viento predominante.

prevalence [ˈprevələns] N predominio m; frecuencia f; uso m corriente, costumbre f.

prevalent [ˈprevələnt] ADJ predominante; frecuente, común, corriente; (fashionable) en boga, de moda; custom etc extendido; (present-day) actual.

prevaricate [prɪˈværɪkeɪt] VI buscar evasivas, usar sofismas, tergiversar.

prevarication [prɪˌværɪˈkeɪʃən] N evasivas fpl, sofismas mpl, tergiversación f.

prevent [prɪˈvent] VT person impedir, estorbar; event etc impedir, evitar; estorbar; prevenir; illness etc evitar; **it was impossible to ~ it** fue imposible impedirlo; **to ~ sb + ger, to ~ sb from + ger** impedir a uno + infin.

preventable [prɪˈventəbl] ADJ evitable.

preventative [prɪˈventətɪv] ADJ = **preventive**.

prevention [prɪˈvenʃən] N prevención f; el impedir, el evitar; **~ is better than cure** es más fácil prevenir que curar; **the ~ of errors is not easy** no es fácil evitar los errores; **for the ~ of accidents** para evitar los accidentes; **a society for the ~ of cruelty to animals** una sociedad protectora de animales.

preventive [prɪˈventɪv] ADJ preventivo, impeditivo; **~ dentistry** odontología f preventiva; **~ detention** arresto m preventivo; **~ measure** medida f preventiva; **~ medicine** medicina f preventiva.

preview [ˈpriːvjuː] ① N preestreno m; (fig) anticipo m, vista f anticipada; (Cine) tráiler m, avance m; **to have a ~ of sth** ver algo con anticipación, lograr ver algo antes que otros.
② VT preestrenar.

previous [ˈpriːvɪəs] ① ADJ (a) previo, anterior; **in ~ years** en años anteriores; **no ~ experience necessary** no hace falta experiencia previa; **because of a ~ engagement** por tener compromiso anterior.
(b) (hasty) prematuro; **this seems somewhat ~** esto parece algo prematuro; **you have been rather ~** has obrado con cierta prisa.
② PREP: **~ to** antes de; **~ to doing this** antes de hacer esto.

previously [ˈpriːvɪəslɪ] ADV (already) previamente, con anticipación, anteriormente; (in early times) antes.

prewar [ˈpriːwɔːʳ] ADJ de antes de la guerra, de (la) preguerra, prebélico; **the ~ period** la preguerra.

prewash [ˈpriːwɒʃ] N prelavado m.

prey [preɪ] ① N presa f, víctima f; **bird of ~** ave f de rapiña; **to be a ~ to** ser víctima de; **he fell (a) ~ to the disease** llegó a ser víctima de la enfermedad.
② VI (a) **to ~ on** (feed on) atacar, alimentarse de, comer, devorar; (plunder) robar, pillar; (sponge on) vivir a costa de; **rabbits are ~ed on by foxes** los conejos son presa de los zorros.
(b) **to ~ on** (mind) atormentar, remorder, preocupar; **doubts ~ed on him** le obsesionaban las dudas; **the tragedy so ~ed on his mind that ...** la tragedia le afectó de tal modo que ...

prezzie* [ˈprezɪ] N ABBR of **present** regalo m.

price [praɪs] ① N precio m; (quotation, Fin) cotización f; (in betting) puntos mpl de ventaja; **at a ~ of £500** a un precio de 500 libras; **at a reduced ~** a un precio reducido, con descuento; **at any ~** (fig) a toda costa; **peace at any ~** la paz a toda costa; **they need to win at any ~** tienen que ganar a cualquier precio; **you can buy it at a ~** se puede comprar pero cuesta bastante; **not at any ~!** de ningún modo; **I don't want that at any ~** eso no lo quiero ni regalado; **what ~ these pigs?** ¿cuánto se me ofrece por estos cerdos?; **what ~ liberty?** y la libertad, ¿qué?; **what ~ Joe Soap now?** ¿qué me dicen ahora sobre Joe Soap?; **what ~ she'll change her mind?** ¿qué posibilidades hay de que cambie de opinión?; **what's the ~ of this?** ¿cuánto vale esto?; **to pay top ~ for sth** pagar algo al precio máximo; **she paid a high ~ for her success** compró muy caro su triunfo; **that was the ~ that had to be paid for progress** así había que pagar el progreso; **that is a small ~ to pay for independence** ése es un precio módico para comprar la independencia; **to rise in ~** subir de precio; **houses have risen in ~** ha aumentado el valor de las casas.

2 ATTR: **~ bracket** categoría *f* de precio; **~ control** control *m* de precios; **~ cut** rebaja *f*; **~ cutting** reducción *f* de precios; **~ fixing** fijación *f* de precios; **~ freeze** congelación *f* de los precios; **~ index** (*Brit*) índice *m* de precios; **~ level** nivel *m* de precios; **to put a ~ limit on sth** poner un precio límite a algo; **~ range** escala *f* de precios; **~ ring** confabulación *f* de comerciantes (formada para fijar los precios de los productos); **~ support** subsidio *m* de precios; **~ sticker, ~ tag, ~ ticket** etiqueta *f* del precio; **~ war** guerra *f* de precios; **~s and incomes policy** política *f* de ingresos y precios.

3 VT estimar, valuar, valorar (*at* en); tasar (*at* en), fijar el precio de; **it is ~d rather high at £80** está valorado en 80 libras, lo cual es mucho; **it's not ~d in the window** en el escaparate no lleva precio.

♦ **price down** VT rebajar.

♦ **price out** **1** VT: **to be ~d out of the market** dejar de ser competitivo (en el mercado), perder competetividad de precios.
2 VR: **to ~ o.s. out of the market = 1**.

♦ **price up** VT aumentar el precio de.

-priced [praɪst] ADJ *ending in compounds:* **high~** muy caro; *V* **low**.

priceless ['praɪslɪs] ADJ (**a**) inapreciable, que no tiene precio. (**b**) (*) divertidísimo, impagable; **it was ~!** ¡fue para morirse de risa!*

price-list ['praɪslɪst] N lista *f* de precios.

price-rigging ['praɪsˌrɪgɪŋ] N (*pej*) manipulación *f* de precios.

price-tag ['praɪstæg] N etiqueta *f* de precio, escandallo *m*.

pricey* ['praɪsɪ] ADJ caro.

pricing ['praɪsɪŋ] **1** N fijación *f* de precios.
2 ATTR: **~ policy** política *f* tarifaria.

prick [prɪk] **1** N (**a**) pinchazo *m*, punzada *f*; (*sting etc*) picadura *f*; (*with pin*) alfilerazo *m*; (*of spur*) espolada *f*; (*with goad*) aguijonazo *m*; **~ of conscience** escrúpulo *m* de conciencia, remordimiento *m*; **to kick against the ~s** dar coces contra el aguijón.
(**b**) (**‡**: *penis*) polla‡ *f*.
(**c**) (**‡**: *person*) gilipollas‡ *m*.
2 VT (**a**) pinchar, punzar, picar; (*sting*) picar; (*with spur*) dar con las espuelas; (*goad*) aguijar; (*make hole in*) agujerear; (*mark with holes*) marcar con agujerillos.
(**b**) **it ~ed his conscience** le remordió la conciencia, le dio un escrúpulo de conciencia.
3 VI: **= prickle 3**.

♦ **prick out** VT (*Hort*) plantar.

♦ **prick up** **1** VT: **to ~ up one's ears** aguzar el oído.
2 VI aguzar el oído, empezar a prestar atención.

pricked [prɪkt] ADJ wine picado.

prickings ['prɪkɪŋz] NPL: **~ of conscience** remordimientos *mpl*.

prickle ['prɪkl] **1** N (**a**) (*Bot*) espina *f*; (*Zool*) púa *f*. (**b**) (*on skin etc*) escozor *m*.
2 VT picar.
3 VI hormiguear; picar; **my eyes are prickling** me duelen los ojos; **I could feel my skin prickling** me escocía la piel.

prickly ['prɪklɪ] ADJ espinoso, lleno de espinas; lleno de púas; *person* poco afable, malhumorado, difícil; **~ heat** salpullido *m* causado por exceso de calor; **~ pear** higo *m* chumbo, chumbera *f*; **he's rather ~ about that** sobre ese tema es algo quisquilloso.

pride [praɪd] **1** N (**a**) orgullo *m*; (*pej*) orgullo *m*, soberbia *f*, arrogancia *f*; **it's the ~ of Navarre** es el blasón de Navarra; **he's the ~ of the family** es el orgullo de la familia; **his roses are his ~ and joy** sus rosas son su tesoro, sus rosas son un gran motivo de orgullo; **~ comes before a fall, ~ must have a fall** el orgullo excesivo conduce a la caída; **it is a source of ~ to us that ...** es para nosotros un motivo de orgullo el que ...; **to nurse one's ~** conservar el amor propio; tratar de restaurar el amor propio; **to swallow one's ~** tragarse el amor propio; tragar una afrenta; **to take (a) ~ in sth** enorgullecerse de algo, ufanarse de algo; **to take ~ of place** venir primero, ocupar el primer puesto.
(**b**) (*of lions*) grupo *m*, manada *f*.
2 VR: **to ~ o.s. on sth** enorgullecerse de algo, ufanarse de algo; **he ~s himself on his punctuality** se precia de puntual; **to ~ o.s. on +** *ger* enorgullecerse de + *infin*.

priest [priːst] N (*gen, pagan*) sacerdote *m*; (*Christian*) sacerdote *m*, cura *m*.

priestess ['priːstɪs] N sacerdotisa *f*.

priesthood ['priːsthʊd] N (*function*) sacerdocio *m*; (*priests collectively*) clero *m*; **to enter the ~** ordenarse de sacerdote.

priestly ['priːstlɪ] ADJ sacerdotal.

prig [prɪg] N presumido *m*, -a *f*; pedante *mf*; mojigato *m*, -a *f*, gazmoño *m*, -a *f*; **don't be such a ~!** ¡no seas tan pedante!; ¡no presumas!

priggish ['prɪgɪʃ] ADJ presumido; pedante; mojigato, gazmoño.

priggishness ['prɪgɪʃnɪs] N presunción *f*; pedantería *f*; mojigatería *f*, gazmoñería *f*.

prim [prɪm] ADJ (*formal*) etiquetero, estirado; (*affected*) remilgado; (*prudish*) gazmoño.

primacy ['praɪməsɪ] N primacía *f*.

prima donna ['priːmə'dɒnə] N primadonna *f*, diva *f*; (*fig*) persona *f* difícil, persona *f* de reacciones imprevisibles.

primaeval [praɪ'miːvl] (*Brit*) = **primeval**.

prima facie ['praɪmə'feɪʃɪ] **1** ADV a primera vista.
2 ADJ (*Jur*): **~ case** presunciones *fpl* razonables; **~ evidence** prueba *f* semiplena; **there are ~ reasons why ...** hay suficientes razones que justifican el que + *subj*; **he has a ~ case** (*fig*) a primera vista parece que tiene razón.

primal ['praɪməl] ADJ (*first in time*) original; (*first in importance*) principal; **~ scream** grito *m* primal.

primarily ['praɪmərɪlɪ] ADV ante todo; en primer lugar; principalmente.

primary ['praɪmərɪ] **1** ADJ primario; principal; central; *colour, education* primario; **~ education** educación *f* primaria, educación *f* primera; **~ products** productos *mpl* primarios; **~ school** (*Brit*) escuela *f* primaria; **~ storage** almacenamiento *m* primario; **that is not the ~ reason** ésa no es la razón principal; *ver también* EDUCATION .
2 N (*US Pol: also* **~ election**) (elección *f*) primaria *f*.

┌─ PRIMARIES ─┐

ⓘ *Las elecciones primarias (**primaries**) sirven para preseleccionar a los candidatos de los partidos demócrata (**Democratic**) y republicano (**Republican**) durante la campaña que precede a las elecciones a Presidente de Estados Unidos. Se inician en New Hampshire y tienen lugar en 35 estados entre los meses de febrero y junio. El número de votos obtenidos por cada candidato determina el número de delegados que votarán en el congreso general (**National Convention**) de julio y agosto, en el que se decide el candidato definitivo de cada partido.*
---

primate¹ ['praɪmɪt] N (*Eccl*) primado *m*.

primate² ['praɪmeɪt] N (*Zool*) primate *m*.

prime [praɪm] **1** ADJ (**a**) (*Math*) primo.
(**b**) (*chief*) primero, principal; fundamental; **the ~ reason** la razón principal; **of ~ importance** de primera importancia; **of ~ necessity** de primera necesidad; **~ cost** costo *m* neto, costo *m* de producción; **~ factor** factor *m* primordial; **~ minister** primer ministro *m*, primera ministra *f*; (*Sp*) presidencial; (*elsewhere*) del primer ministro; **~ ministerial** (*Sp*) presidencial; (*elsewhere*) del primer ministro; **~ ministership** (*tenure*) (*Sp*) presidencia *f*, (*elsewhere*) período *m* de funciones de primer ministro; (*office*) cargo *m* de(l) primer ministro; **~ mover** (*Mech*) máquina *f* motriz; (*Philos*) primer motor *m*; (*person*) promotor *m*, -ora *f*; **~ rate** tipo *m* de interés preferente; **~ suspect** principal sospechoso *m*, -a *f*; **~ time** (*TV*) banda *f* horaria caliente, horas *fpl* de mayor sintonía; (*Comm*) tiempo *m* preferencial.
(**c**) (*excellent*) selecto, de primera clase; **~ quality beef** carne *f* de vaca de primera calidad; **in ~ condition** en excelente estado.
2 N (**a**) flor *f*, lo mejor; **the ~ of life** la flor de la vida, la edad viril; **to be in one's ~** estar en la flor de la vida; **to be past one's ~** haber dado lo mejor de sí, estar en decadencia; **to be cut off in one's ~** morir en la flor de la vida.
(**b**) (*Eccl*) prima *f*.
3 VT *gun, pump* cebar; *surface etc* preparar, aprestar; **to ~ sb** informar a uno de antemano; **they ~d him about what he should say** le dieron instrucciones acerca de lo que había de decir; **to ~ sb with drink** emborrachar a uno, hacer que uno beba; **he arrived well ~d** llegó ya medio borracho.

primer ['praɪmər] N (**a**) (*book*) cartilla *f*, libro *m* de texto elemental; **a French ~** un libro elemental de francés. (**b**) (*paint*) apresto *m*. (**c**) (*of bomb*) iniciador *m*.

primeval [praɪ'miːvəl] ADJ primitivo.

priming ['praɪmɪŋ] **1** N preparación *f*; (*of pump etc*) cebo *m*; (*Art*) primera capa *f*.
2 ATTR: **~ device** iniciador *m*.

primitive ['prɪmɪtɪv] **1** ADJ (*early, original, primary*) primitivo; (*old-fashioned*) anticuado; (*simple, rude*) rudimentario, sencillo; (*uncivilized*) inculto; (*sordid*) sucio, miserable, asqueroso; (*Art*) primitivo.
2 N (*Art*) primitivo *m*.

primly ['prɪmlɪ] ADV remilgadamente; con gazmoñería.

primness ['prɪmnɪs] N lo etiquetero, lo estirado; remilgo *m*; gazmoñería *f*.

primogeniture [ˌpraɪməʊ'dʒenɪtʃər] N primogenitura *f*.

primordial [praɪ'mɔːdɪəl] ADJ primordial.

primp [prɪmp] = **prink**.

primrose ['prɪmrəʊz] **1** N (*Bot*) primavera *f*; (*colour*) color *m* amarillo pálido.
2 ADJ amarillo pálido.
3 ATTR: **~ path** caminito *m* de rosas.

primula ['prɪmjʊlə] N oreja *f* de oso.

Primus (stove) ['praɪməs(stəʊv)] ® N cocinilla *f* de camping, hornillo *m*, infernillo *m* campestre.

prince [prɪns] N príncipe *m*; **P~ Charming** el Príncipe Azul, el Príncipe Encantador; **the ~ of darkness** el príncipe de las tinieblas,

Satanás *m*; ~ **consort** príncipe *m* consorte; ~ **regent** príncipe *m* regente; **P~ of Wales** Príncipe *m* de Gales (*heredero del trono del Reino Unido, equivalente al Príncipe de Asturias en España*).

princely ['prɪnslɪ] ADJ principesco; magnífico, noble; **a ~ gesture** un gesto magnífico, un gesto digno de un príncipe; **the ~ sum of 5 dollars** (*iro*) la bonita cantidad de 5 dólares.

princess [prɪn'ses] N princesa *f*; ~ **royal** hija *f* mayor del soberano.

principal ['prɪnsɪpəl] ① ADJ principal; mayor; ~ **boy** joven héroe *m* (*papel de actriz en la 'pantomime' navideña*).
② N (**a**) principal *mf*, jefe *m*, -a *f*; (*of school, college*) director *m*, -ora *f*; (*Univ*) rector *m*, -ora *f*. (**b**) (*Fin*) principal *m*, capital *m*.

principality ['prɪnsɪ'pælɪtɪ] N principado *m*.

principally ['prɪnsɪpəlɪ] ADV principalmente.

▼ **principle** ['prɪnsəpl] N principio *m*; **in ~** en principio; **agreement in ~** acuerdo *m* de principio; **on ~** por principio; **to argue from first ~s** construir su argumento sobre los principios (fundamentales); **to go back to first ~s** volver a los principios (fundamentales); **to have high ~s** tener principios nobles; **to lay it down as a ~ that ...** sentar el principio de que ...; **I make it a ~ never to + infin** me hago una regla de nunca + *infin*.

principled ['prɪnsɪpld] ADJ *person* de fuertes principios; *behaviour, stand* basado en fuertes principios.

prink [prɪŋk] ① VT acicalar, ataviar; arreglar elegantemente.
② VI acicalarse, ataviarse; arreglarse elegantemente.

print [prɪnt] ① N (**a**) (*mark, imprint*) marca *f*, señal *f*, impresión *f*; (*foot~*) huella *f*, pisada *f*; (*finger~*) huella *f* dactilar.
(**b**) (*Typ*) tipo *m*, letra *f* de molde; caracteres *mpl*; (*printed matter*) impreso *m*; **large ~** tipo *m* grande; **fine ~, small ~** tipo *m* menudo; **one must read the small ~** hay que leer la letra menuda; **in (cold) ~** en letras de molde; **books in ~** libros *mpl* en venta; **to be in ~** (*be published as book etc*) estar impreso; (*be available*) estar disponible, estar en existencia; **to be out of ~** estar fuera de catálogo, estar agotado; **he likes to see himself in ~** se enorgullece de que se impriman sus artículos (*etc*); le agrada que le mencionen en los periódicos; **to get into ~** imprimirse, publicarse; **we don't want that to get into ~** no queremos que eso se publique; **I've got into ~ at last!** ¡por fin me van a publicar el artículo! (*etc*); **to rush into ~** publicar una obra sin reflexionar, lanzarse a publicar.
(**c**) (*Art*) estampa *f*, grabado *m*; (*Phot*) positiva *f*, copia *f*; (*dress, fabric*) estampado *m*.
② ATTR *dress* estampado; ~ **queue** cola *f* de espera para impresión; ~ **speed** velocidad *f* de impresión; ~ **wheel** rueda *f* impresora.
③ VT imprimir; (*on the mind etc*) grabar; *book etc* imprimir; sacar a luz, dar a la estampa, publicar; (*Phot*) imprimir; *cloth, pattern* estampar; (*write plainly*) escribir en caracteres de imprenta, escribir en letras de molde; **the ~ed word** la palabra impresa; **~ed by** impreso por; **they ~ed 300 copies** tiraron 300 ejemplares, hicieron una tirada de 300 ejemplares.

◆ **print off** VT imprimir.

◆ **print out** VT imprimir.

printable ['prɪntəbl] ADJ imprimible.

printed ['prɪntɪd] ADJ impreso; *dress* estampado; ~ **circuit** circuito *m* impreso; ~ **matter** impresos *mpl*; ~ **paper rate** (*Brit*) tarifa *f* de impreso.

printer ['prɪntər] N (**a**) (*person*) impresor *m*; ~**'s ink** tinta *f* de imprenta; ~**'s mark** pie *m* de imprenta. (**b**) (*Comput*) impresora *f*.

printhead ['prɪnthed] N cabeza *f* impresora.

printing ['prɪntɪŋ] ① N (**a**) (*art*) tipografía *f*, imprenta *f*; '**16th century ~ in Toledo**' 'la imprenta en Toledo en el siglo XVI'.
(**b**) (*act*) impresión *f*; (*quantity*) **4ᵗʰ ~** 4ª impresión; **a ~ of 500 copies** una tirada de 500 ejemplares.
② ATTR: ~ **frame** prensa *f* de copiar; ~ **ink** tinta *f* de imprenta; ~ **office** imprenta *f*; ~ **press** imprenta *f*, prensa *f*; ~ **queue** cola *f* de impresión; ~ **works** imprenta *f*.

printmaking ['prɪntmeɪkɪŋ] N grabado *m*.

printout ['prɪntaʊt] N print-out *m*, output *m*, listado *m*, impresión *f*.

print-run ['prɪntrʌn] N tirada *f*.

print-shop ['prɪntʃɒp] N (*Typ*) taller *m* de impresión; (*art shop*) tienda *f* de cuadros.

▼ **prior** ['praɪər] ① ADJ anterior, previo; *claim etc* preferente.
② ADV (**a**) ~ **to** antes de; hasta; ~ **to this discovery** antes de este descubrimiento. (**b**) (*US*) antes; **it happened 2 days ~** ocurrió 2 días antes.
③ N (*Eccl*) prior *m*.

prioress ['praɪərɪs] N priora *f*.

prioritize [praɪ'ɒrɪtaɪz] VT (*esp US*) priorizar.

priority [praɪ'ɒrɪtɪ] ① N prioridad *f*; (*in time*) anterioridad *f*, antelación *f*, precedencia *f*; **to give sth first** (*or* **top**) ~ dar la máxima prioridad a algo, priorizar algo de modo absoluto; **to have** (*or* **take**) ~ tener prioridad (*over sb* sobre uno); **they will be given out in strict order of** ~ se distribuirán estrictamente de acuerdo con prioridades; **we must get our priorities right** hemos de establecer

un justo orden de prioridades.
② ATTR prioritario; preferente; ~ **case** caso *m* prioritario; ~ **share** acción *f* prioritaria; ~ **treatment** trato *m* preferente.

priory ['praɪərɪ] N priorato *m*.

prise [praɪz] VT (*Brit*): **to ~ open** abrir por fuerza, abrir con una palanca; **to ~ a lid up** levantar una tapa con una palanca; **we had to ~ the secret out of him** tuvimos que sacarle el secreto a la fuerza; **to ~ sb out of his post** lograr que uno renuncie a su puesto, desahuciar a uno.

◆ **prise off** VT arrancar.

prism ['prɪzəm] N prisma *m*.

prismatic [prɪz'mætɪk] ADJ prismático.

prison ['prɪzn] ① N cárcel *f*, prisión *f*; **to be in ~** estar en la cárcel; **to go to ~ for 5 years** ser condenado a 5 años de prisión; pasar 5 años en la cárcel; **to put sb in ~, to send sb to ~** encarcelar a uno; **to send sb to ~ for 2 years** condenar a uno a 2 años de prisión.
② ATTR carcelario; ~ **break** fuga *f* (de la cárcel); ~ **camp** campamento *m* para prisioneros; ~ **governor** (*Brit*), ~ **warden** (*US*) director *m*, -ora *f* de (la) prisión; ~ **life** vida *f* en la cárcel; ~ **officer** carcelero *m*, -a *f*; ~ **population** población *f* reclusa; ~ **riot** motín *m* carcelario; ~ **system** sistema *m* penitenciario; ~ **term** condena *f*; ~ **van** coche *m* celular; ~ **visitor** visitante *mf* de un prisionero; ~ **yard** patio *m* de (la) cárcel.

prisoner ['prɪznər] N (*under arrest*) detenido *m*, -a *f*; (*facing charge*, ~ **at the bar**) acusado *m*, -a *f*; (*convicted*) preso *m*, -a *f*; (*Mil*) prisionero *m*, -a *f*; ~ **of conscience** preso *m*, -a *f* de conciencia; ~ **of war** prisionero *m*, -a *f* de guerra; **to hold sb ~** detener a uno; **to take sb ~** hacer prisionero a uno.

prissy* ['prɪsɪ] ADJ remilgado, repipi*.

pristine ['prɪstaɪn] ADJ prístino.

prithee ['prɪðiː] (††) EXCL le ruego.

privacy ['prɪvəsɪ] N soledad *f*, retiro *m*, aislamiento *m*; vida *f* privada; intimidad *f*; (*secrecy*) secreto *m*, reserva *f*; sigilo *m*; (*Comput*) privacidad *f*, confidencialidad *f*; **desire for ~** deseo *m* de estar a solas; **in search of some ~** en busca de soledad; **there is no ~ in these flats** en estos pisos no hay vida privada; **in the ~ of one's home** en la intimidad de su casa; **in the strictest ~** en el mayor secreto, con el mayor sigilo; **to invade sb's ~** invadir la soledad de uno; **P~ Act** ≃ Ley *f* del Derecho a la Intimidad.

private ['praɪvɪt] ① ADJ privado; particular; (*for ~ use*) propio, personal; (*confidential*) secreto, reservado, confidencial; *life* privado, íntimo; *conversation, letter* íntimo, entre los dos; *opinion* personal; *arrangement, car, company, entrance, house, interview, lesson, room, school, etc* particular; *hearing, sitting* secreto, a puertas cerradas; *report* secreto, confidencial; '**~**' 'propiedad particular'; '**~ and confidential**' 'privado y confidencial'; ~ **detective** detective *m* privado; ~ **enterprise** iniciativa *f* privada; ~ **eye*** detective *m*; ~ **finance** finanzas *fpl* privadas; ~ **income, ~ means** renta *f* de fuente particular; ~ **limited company** sociedad *f* de responsabilidad limitada; ~ **health care** servicio *m* médico privado; ~ **line** (*Telec*) línea *f* particular; ~ **member** miembro *mf* (que no es ministro); ~ **member's bill** proyecto *m* de ley presentado por un miembro (no por el gobierno); ~ **patient** paciente *m* privado, paciente *f* privada; ~ **parts** partes *fpl* pudendas; ~ **practice** (*Med*) consulta *f* privada; ~ **property** propiedad *f* privada; ~ **prosecution** demanda *f* civil; ~ **secretary** secretario *m*, -a *f* particular; ~ **sector** sector *m* privado; ~ **soldier** soldado *m* raso; ~ **view** inauguración *f*; **my ~ opinion is that ...** yo creo para mí que ..., mi opinión personal es que ...; **the wedding was ~** la ceremonia se celebró en la intimidad; **to keep a matter ~** guardar el secreto de un asunto, no divulgar un asunto; **he's a very ~ person** es una persona muy reservada; **they want to be ~** quieren estar a solas; **to go ~** (*Med*) ir a lo privado, ir a particular.
② N (**a**) (*Mil*) soldado *m* raso; **P~ Jones** el soldado Jones; **P~ Jones!** ¡Jones!
(**b**) **in ~** en privado; en secreto; de persona a persona, entre los dos; confidencialmente; **I have been told in ~ that ...** me han dicho confidencialmente que ...; **the committee sat in ~** la comisión se reunió puerta cerrada; **the wedding was held in ~** la ceremonia se celebró en la intimidad.
(**c**) ~**s** (*Anat*) partes *fpl* pudendas.

privateer [ˌpraɪvə'tɪər] N corsario *m*.

privately ['praɪvɪtlɪ] ADV privadamente, en privado; en secreto; particularmente; **the meeting was held ~** la reunión fue a puerta cerrada; **the wedding took place ~** la ceremonia se celebró en la intimidad; ~ **I think that ...** personalmente creo que ...; **I have been told ~ that ...** me han dicho confidencialmente que ...; **but ~ he was very upset** pero en su corazón se sintió muy molesto; **so he spoke ~ to me** así que me habló privadamente; **he is being ~ educated** está en un colegio particular; tiene un profesor particular.

privation [praɪ'veɪʃən] N (**a**) (*state*) privación *f*, miseria *f*, estrechez *f*; **to live in ~** vivir en la miseria. (**b**) (*hardship*) privaciones *fpl*, apuro *m*; **to suffer many ~s** pasar muchos apuros.

privative ['prɪvətɪv] **1** ADJ privativo.
2 N privativo *m*.
privatization [ˌpraɪvətaɪˈzeɪʃən] N privatización *f*.
privatize ['praɪvətaɪz] VT privatizar.
privatizing ['praɪvətaɪzɪŋ] N privatización *f*.
privet ['prɪvɪt] N ligustro *m*, alheña *f*.
privilege ['prɪvɪlɪdʒ] **1** N privilegio *m*; prerrogativa *f*; (*Jur, Parl*) inmunidad *f*; **to have parliamentary ~** gozar de la inmunidad parlamentaria.
2 VT: **to be ~d to** + *infin* tener el privilegio de + *infin*.
privileged ['prɪvɪlɪdʒd] ADJ privilegiado; *information* confidencial; *speech* que goza de la inmunidad parlamentaria (*etc*); **for a ~ few** para unos pocos afortunados.
privily ['prɪvɪlɪ] ADV privadamente, en privado; *tell etc* confidencialmente.
privy ['prɪvɪ] **1** ADJ (a) **to be ~ to sth** estar enterado secretamente de algo. (b) (*Brit*) **P~ Council** Consejo *m* Privado (del monarca); **P~ Councillor** consejero *m*, -a *f* del Consejo Privado; **P~ Purse** gastos *mpl* personales del monarca.
2 N retrete *m*.

┌─── **PRIVY COUNCIL** ───┐

ⓘ *El consejo de asesores de la Corona, conocido como* **Privy Council**, *tuvo su origen en la época de los normandos, y fue adquiriendo mayor importancia hasta ser substituido en 1688 por el actual Consejo de Ministros (***Cabinet***). Hoy día sigue existiendo con un carácter fundamentalmente honorífico que se concede de forma automática a los ministros del gobierno, así como a otras personalidades políticas, eclesiásticas y jurídicas.*

prize¹ [praɪz] **1** N (a) premio *m*; galardón *m*; **first ~** primer premio *m*; (*in lottery*) el gordo; **~ day** día *m* de distribución de premios; **to carry off the ~, to win the ~** ganar el premio.
(b) (*Naut*) presa *f*; **~ court** tribunal *m* de presas marítimas.
2 ADJ *entry, rose etc* galardonado, premiado; (*fig*) digno de premio; excelente, de primera clase; **he's a ~ idiot** es un tonto de capirote; **what a ~ idiot you are!** ¡imbécil!
3 VT apreciar, estimar; **to ~ sth highly** estimar algo en mucho.
prize² [praɪz] VT = **prise**.
prize draw ['praɪzˌdrɔː] N tómbola *f*.
prize fight ['praɪzfaɪt] N partido *m* de boxeo profesional.
prize fighter ['praɪzfaɪtər] N boxeador *m* profesional.
prize fighting ['praɪzˌfaɪtɪŋ] N boxeo *m* profesional.
prize-giving ['praɪzˌɡɪvɪŋ] N distribución *f* de premios.
prize money ['praɪzˌmʌnɪ] N (*Naut*) parte *f* de presa; (*cash*) premio *m* en metálico; (*Boxing*) bolsa *f*.
prize ring ['praɪzˌrɪŋ] N (*Boxing*) ring *m*.
prizewinner ['praɪzˌwɪnər] N premiado *m*, -a *f*.
prizewinning ['praɪzˌwɪnɪŋ] ADJ premiado.
PRO N (a) ABBR of **Public Record Office** Archivo *m* Nacional. (b) (*Comm etc*) ABBR of **public relations officer**.
pro¹ [prəʊ] **1** PREP (a) (*in favour of*) pro; en pro de.
(b) (*in compounds*) pro-; *eg* **~-Soviet** pro-soviético; **~-Spanish** hispanófilo; **~-European** europeísta; **they were terribly ~-Franco** eran unos franquistas furibundos, eran partidarios acérrimos de Franco.
(c) **~ forma** pro forma; **~ forma invoice** factura *f* pro forma, factura *f* simulada; **~ forma letter** carta *f* pro forma; **~ rata** a prorrateo, proporcionalmente; **the money will be shared out ~ rata** el dinero será repartido a prorrateo, se prorrateará el dinero; **a ~ rate agreement** (*US*) un acuerdo a prorrateo; **~ tempore, ~ tem*** por ahora, por el momento, interinamente.
2 N: **the ~s and the cons** el pro y el contra; **we are weighing up the ~s and the cons** estudiamos los argumentos a favor y en contra.
pro²* [prəʊ] N profesional *mf*.
pro³* [prəʊ] N (*prostitute*) puta *f*.
pro-abortion [ˌprəʊəˈbɔːʃən] ADJ pro-aborto, proabortista.
pro-abortionist [ˌprəʊəˈbɔːʃənɪst] N proabortista *mf*.
probabilistic [ˌprɒbəbəˈlɪstɪk] ADJ probabilístico.
probability [ˌprɒbəˈbɪlɪtɪ] N probabilidad *f*; **in all ~** sin duda, según toda probabilidad; **the ~ is that ...** es probable que + *subj*.
probable ['prɒbəbl] ADJ (a) (*likely*) probable; **it is ~ that ...** es probable que + *subj*. (b) (*credible*) verosímil.
▼ **probably** ['prɒbəblɪ] ADV probablemente; **he will ~ come, ~ he will come** es probable que venga; **he ~ forgot** lo habrá olvidado, a lo mejor lo olvidó; **~ not** quizá no; **very ~, but ...** bien puede ser, pero ...
probate ['prəʊbɪt] N verificación *f* oficial de los testamentos; **~ court** tribunal *m* de testamentarías; **to value sth for ~** evaluar algo para la verificación oficial de testamentos.
probation [prəˈbeɪʃən] **1** N (*Jur*) libertad *f* condicional, libertad *f* vigilada; **release on ~** libertad *f* a prueba; **to be on ~** estar en libertad condicional; **to put sb on ~** (*fig*) asignar a uno un período a prueba; **to take sth on ~** tomar algo a prueba.
2 ATTR: **~ officer** oficial *m* que vigila las personas que están en libertad condicional.
probationary [prəˈbeɪʃnərɪ] ADJ de prueba; **~ period** (*Jur*) período *m* de libertad condicional, (*fig*) período *m* a (*or* de) prueba.
probationer [prəˈbeɪʃnər] N (*Jur*) persona *f* en libertad condicional; (*Med*) aprendiz *mf* de ATS (*Sp*), aprendiz *mf* de enfermero; (*Eccl*) novicio *m*, -a *f*.
probe [prəʊb] **1** N (a) (*Med*) sonda *f*, tienta *f*; (*rocket*) cohete *m*, proyectil *m*; (*space ~*) vehículo *m* espacial, sonda *f*.
(b) (*inquiry*) investigación *f*, indagación *f*, encuesta *f*; **a ~ into the drug traffic** una investigación del tráfico de drogas.
2 VT (*Med*) sondar, tentar; *ground etc* sondar; (*explore*) explorar; (*search*) registrar; (*investigate*) investigar, indagar; **to ~ a mystery** investigar un misterio.
3 VI investigar; **to ~ into sb's past** investigar el pasado de uno; **you should have ~d more deeply** convenía hacer una investigación más a fondo.
probing ['prəʊbɪŋ] **1** ADJ *question etc* agudo, penetrante.
2 N sondeo *m*; investigación *f*; exploración *f*.
probity ['prəʊbɪtɪ] N probidad *f*.
▼ **problem** ['prɒbləm] **1** N problema *m*; **the housing ~** el problema de la vivienda; (*more serious*) la crisis de la vivienda; **it's not my ~** no tiene que ver conmigo; **no ~!** ¡no hay problema!
2 ATTR: **~ child** niño *m*, -a *f* difícil, niño *m*, -a *f* problema; **~ page** consultorio *m*; **~ play** drama *m* de tesis.
problematic(al) [ˌprɒblɪˈmætɪk(əl)] ADJ problemático, dudoso; **it is ~ whether ...** es dudoso si ...
problem-solving ['prɒbləmˌsɒlvɪŋ] N resolución *f* de problemas; **~ skills** habilidad *f* para la resolución de problemas.
proboscis [prəʊˈbɒsɪs] N probóscide *f*, trompa *f*; (*: *hum*) trompa* *f*.
procedural [prəˈsiːdjʊrəl] ADJ relativo al procedimiento; (*Jur*) procesal; **a ~ question** una cuestión de procedimiento.
procedure [prəˈsiːdʒər] N procedimiento *m*; proceder *m*; trámites *mpl*, tramitación *f*; **the usual ~ is to** + *infin* lo que se hace por lo general es + *infin*; **the correct ~ would be to** + *infin* lo correcto sería + *infin*.
proceed [prəˈsiːd] VI (a) (*go*) proceder; **before we ~ any further** antes de ir más lejos, antes de seguir; **to ~ on one's way** seguir adelante, seguir su camino; **we ~ed to London** seguimos (viaje) a Londres; **we ~ed to the bar** nos trasladamos al bar; **the ship ~ed at 10 knots** el barco continuó a una velocidad de 10 nudos, el barco reanudó el viaje a una velocidad de 10 nudos; **cars should ~ slowly** los automóviles deberán seguir despacio; **let us ~ with caution** avancemos con precaución.
(b) (*go on to*) **how should we ~?** ¿cómo hemos de proceder?; **to ~ to blows** llegar a las manos; **to ~ to business** pasar a discutir los asuntos a tratar; **let us ~ to the next item** pasemos al punto siguiente; **to ~ to do sth** pasar a hacer algo, ponerse a hacer algo, empezar a hacer algo; **he ~ed to drink the lot** en seguida se lo bebió todo; **he ~ed to say that ...** dijo a continuación que ...
(c) (*continue*) continuar, seguir; **the text ~s thus** el texto sigue así; **things are ~ing according to plan** las cosas se están desarrollando según previsto; **how does the story ~ after that?** ¿cómo se desarrolla el argumento después de eso?; **they ~ed with their plan** prosiguieron su proyecto; **~!** ¡siga!
(d) **to ~ against sb** (*Jur etc*) proceder contra uno, procesar a uno.
(e) (*emerge*) **to ~ from** salir de; (*fig*) proceder de, provenir de; **sounds ~ed from the box** unos ruidos salían de la caja; **this ~s from ignorance** esto proviene de la ignorancia.
proceeding [prəˈsiːdɪŋ] N (a) (*way*) procedimiento *m*, modo *m* de proceder; proceder *m*; **the best ~** el mejor modo de proceder; **a somewhat dubious ~** un proceder sospechoso.
(b) **~s** (*ceremony etc*) acto *m*, actos *mpl*, función *f*; **the ~s began at 7 o'clock** el acto comenzó a las 7; **the ~s were orderly** en estos actos no sufrió alteración el orden público.
(c) **~s** (*of learned society*) actas *fpl*, transacciones *fpl*; **P~s of the Royal Society** Actas *fpl* de la Real Sociedad.
(d) **~s** (*measures*) medidas *fpl*; **to take ~s** tomar medidas; **to take ~s against sb** (*Jur*) proceder contra uno, procesar a uno; **to take legal ~s** entablar demanda, instruir causa.
proceeds ['prəʊsiːdz] NPL importe *m* (de la recaudación *etc*); producto *m*, ingresos *mpl*.
process¹ ['prəʊses] **1** N (a) (*proceeding*) procedimiento *m*; proceso *m*; **the ~es of government** los trámites gubernamentales; **the ~es of the mind** los procedimientos de la mente; **by due ~ of law** por los justos procedimientos de la ley; **by a ~ of elimination** por un proceso de eliminación; **it's a very slow ~** es un proceso muy lento.
(b) (*course*) **in ~ of construction** bajo construcción, en construcción; **it is in ~ of reform** está siendo reformado; **it is in ~ of demolition** está siendo derribado; **in the ~ of time** con el tiempo,

➤ LANGUAGE IN USE: **probably** → 15.2   **problem:** 1 → 13, 26.1, 26.3

andando el tiempo; **in the ~ of cleaning the picture, they discovered ...** mientras limpiaban el cuadro, descubrieron ...; **we are in ~ of removal to ...** estamos en vía de trasladarnos a ...
(c) (*method*) método *m*, sistema *m*; (*Tech*) proceso *m*; **the Bessemer ~** el proceso de Bessemer.
(d) (*Jur*) proceso *m*.
(e) (*Anat, Bot etc*) proceso *m*.
[2] VT (*Tech*) preparar; tratar; someter a un tratamiento especial; elaborar; *food* procesar, tratar; (*Phot*) revelar; *application* tramitar; *data* tratar, manejar.
process² [prə'ses] VI (*Brit*) desfilar.
process³ ['prəuses] ADJ (*US*), **processed** ['prəusest] ADJ *food* procesado, tratado.
processing ['prəusesɪŋ] N preparación *f*; tratamiento *m*; elaboración *f*; **~ language** lenguaje *m* de procesamiento; **~ speed** velocidad *f* de procesamiento; **~ plant** planta *f* depuradora; **~ unit** unidad *f* central de proceso.
procession [prə'seʃən] N desfile *m*; (*Eccl*) procesión *f*; (*of funeral*) cortejo *m*, comitiva *f*; **to go** (*or* **walk**) **in ~** desfilar; (*Eccl*) ir en procesión.
processional [prə'seʃənl] ADJ procesional.
processor ['prəusesəʳ] N unidad *f* central, procesador *m*.
process-server ['prəuses,sɜ:vəʳ] N notificador *m*, -ora *f*, ujier *m*.
pro-choice [,prəu'tʃɔɪs] ADJ en favor de la libertad de elección.
proclaim [prə'kleɪm] [1] VT (a) (*announce*) proclamar; **to ~ sb king** proclamar a uno rey.
(b) (*reveal*) revelar, anunciar; **his tone ~ed his confidence** su tono declaraba su optimismo; **their faces ~ed their guilt** su culpabilidad se revelaba en las caras.
[2] VR: **to ~ o.s. king** proclamarse rey.
proclamation [,prɒklə'meɪʃən] N (*act*) proclamación *f*; (*document*) proclama *f*.
proclivity [prə'klɪvɪtɪ] N propensión *f*, inclinación *f*.
proconsul [,prəu'kɒnsəl] N procónsul *m*.
procrastinate [prəu'kræstɪneɪt] VI aplazar una decisión, no resolverse; andarse con dilaciones; procurar ganar tiempo.
procrastination [prəu,kræstɪ'neɪʃən] N dilación *f*, falta *f* de resolución.
procrastinator [prəu,kræstɪ'neɪtəʳ] N (*frm*): **he's too much of a ~** es demasiado dejado.
procreate ['prəukrɪeɪt] VT procrear.
procreation [,prəukrɪ'eɪʃən] N procreación *f*.
Procrustean [prəu'krʌstɪən] ADJ de Procusto.
Procrustes [prəu'krʌstiːz] NM Procusto.
proctor ['prɒktəʳ] [1] N (*Jur*) procurador *m*; (*Brit Univ*) censor *m*, oficial que cuida de la disciplina, (*US Univ*) celador *m*, -ora *f*.
[2] VTI (*US*) vigilar.
procurable [prə'kjuərəbl] ADJ asequible; **easily ~** muy asequible.
procurator ['prɒkjureɪtəʳ] N procurador *m*, -ora *f*; **P~ Fiscal** (*Scot*) fiscal *mf*.
procure [prə'kjuəʳ] [1] VT (a) (*obtain*) obtener, conseguir; lograr; gestionar; **to ~ sb sth, to ~ sth for sb** obtener algo para uno; **to ~ some relief** conseguir cierto alivio.
(b) **to ~ a girl** (*Jur*) obtener una joven para una casa de prostitución.
[2] VI alcahuetear, dedicarse al proxenetismo.
procurement [prə'kjuəmənt] [1] N obtención *f*, consecución *f*.
[2] ATTR: **~ agency** agencia *f* de aprovisionamiento; **~ price** precio *m* al productor.
procurer [prə'kjuərəʳ] N alcahuete *m*, proxeneta *m*.
procuress [prə'kjuəris] N alcahueta *f*, proxeneta *f*.
procuring [prə'kjuərɪŋ] N alcahuetería *f*, proxenetismo *m*.
prod [prɒd] [1] N (*push*) empuje *m*; (*with elbow*) codazo *m*; (*jab*) pinchazo *m*; **to give sb a ~** dar un pinchazo a uno (*also fig*); **he needs an occasional ~** hay que pincharle de vez en cuando.
[2] VT (*push*) empujar; (*with elbow*) codear, dar un codazo a; (*jab*) pinchar, punzar; (*with goad*) aguijar; **he has to be ~ded along** hay que empujarle constantemente hacia adelante; **he needs to be ~ded** hay que pincharle; **to ~ sb to do sth** instar a uno a hacer algo.
[3] VI: **he ~ded at the picture with a finger** indicó el cuadro con un movimiento brusco del dedo, dio con el dedo en el cuadro.
prodigal ['prɒdɪgəl] [1] ADJ pródigo; **~ of** pródigo de, pródigo en; **the ~ son** el hijo pródigo.
[2] N pródigo *m*, -a *f*.
prodigality [,prɒdɪ'gælɪtɪ] N prodigalidad *f*.
prodigious [prə'dɪdʒəs] ADJ prodigioso; enorme, vasto, ingente.
prodigiously [prə'dɪdʒəslɪ] ADV prodigiosamente, maravillosamente.
prodigy ['prɒdɪdʒɪ] N prodigio *m*; portento *m*; **child ~, infant ~** niño *m* prodigio.
produce [1] ['prɒdjuːs] N producto *m*; (*Agr*) productos *mpl* agrícolas; **'~ of Spain'** 'producto *m* de España'.
[2] ['prɒdjuːs] ATTR: **~ dealer** (*US*) verdulero *m*, -a *f*.

[3] [prə'djuːs] VT (a) (*bring forward, show*) presentar, mostrar; *proof* aducir, presentar; **he ~d it from his pocket** lo sacó del bolsillo; **he seemed to ~ it out of thin air** parece que lo sacó de la nada; **how can I ~ £500?** ¿dónde voy yo a buscar 500 libras?; **'please ~ your tickets'** 'se ruega mostrar los billetes'; **he could ~ no witnesses** no pudo nombrar ningún testigo.
(b) (*Theat*) *play* presentar, poner en escena; representar, dar; (*Cine, TV*) realizar; *actors* dirigir; **when we last ~d 'Hamlet'** cuando representamos 'Hamlet' la última vez; **a well ~d play** una obra bien montada, una obra bien realizada.
(c) *line* prolongar.
(d) (*manufacture*) producir, fabricar; (*yield*) producir; *crop, fruit* dar; *interest, profit* rendir; *offspring* dar a luz, tener; **he ~s 3 novels a year** escribe (*or* publica) 3 novelas al año; **it ~s 200 watts** da 200 vatios, produce 200 vatios; **the mine ~s 20 tons of lead** la mina produce 20 toneladas de plomo; **Ireland does not ~ atomic bombs** Irlanda no fabrica bombas atómicas.
(e) (*cause*) causar, motivar, ocasionar, producir; acarrear; **it ~d great alarm** causó mucha alarma; **this ~d a sensation** esto causó una sensación; **what impression does it ~ on you?** ¿qué impresión te produce?
[4] [prə'djuːs] VI (a) (*mine etc*) producir.
(b) (*Theat etc*) dirigir; **who is going to ~?** ¿quién va a dirigir?
producer [prə'djuːsəʳ] N productor *m*, -ora *f*; (*Theat*) director *m*, -ora *f* de escena; (*Cine*) productor *m*, -ora *f*; (*TV*) productor *m*, -ora *f*, realizador *m*, -ora *f*.
-producing [prə'djuːsɪŋ] ADJ *ending in compounds* productor de ...; **oil~** productor de petróleo; **one of the most important coal~ countries** uno de los principales países productores de carbón.
product ['prɒdʌkt] [1] N (a) (*thing produced*) producto *m*; (*result*) fruto *m*, resultado *m*, consecuencia *f*; **meat ~** derivado *m* cárnico. (b) (*Math*) producto *m*.
[2] ATTR: **~ liability** responsabilidad *f* del fabricante; **~ placement** publicidad *f* encubierta; **~ research** investigación *f* del producto.
production [prə'dʌkʃən] [1] N (a) (*act of showing*) presentación *f*; **on ~ of this card** presentando esta tarjeta, mediante presentación de esta tarjeta.
(b) (*Tech etc*) producción *f*, rendimiento *m*; **the country's steel ~** la producción nacional de acero; **the factory is in full ~** la fábrica trabaja a plena capacidad.
(c) (*product*) producto *m*; (*Art, Liter etc*) obra *f*.
(d) (*Theat: performance*) presentación *f*; representación *f*; (*by producer, of actor*) dirección *f*; (*Cine, TV*) realización *f*; **'Peribáñez: a new ~ by ...'** 'Peribáñez: nueva presentación a cargo de ...'.
[2] ATTR (a) **~ agreement** (*US*) acuerdo *m* de productividad; (*Comm*) **~ bonus** prima *f* por rendimiento; **~ control** control *m* de producción; **~ line** línea *f* de montaje; **~ manager** encargado *m*, -a *f* (*or* jefe *mf*) de producción.
(b) (*Cine, TV*) **~ assistant** ayudante *mf* de realización; **~ manager** jefe *mf* de realización.
productive [prə'dʌktɪv] ADJ (a) productivo; provechoso; eficaz; **the factory is not yet fully ~** la fábrica todavía no trabaja a plena capacidad.
(b) **~ of** fértil en, prolífico en; **to be ~ of error** tener tendencia a causar errores; **it is ~ of nothing but trouble** no produce sino disgustos.
productively [prə'dʌktɪvlɪ] ADV de manera productiva; provechosamente, de manera provechosa; eficazmente.
productivity [,prɒdʌk'tɪvɪtɪ] [1] N productividad *f*; rendimiento *m*; **when it is in full ~** cuando esté trabajando a plena capacidad.
[2] ATTR: **~ agreement** (*Brit*) acuerdo *m* de productividad; **~ bonus** prima *f* por rendimiento, bono *m* de productividad.
Prof. [prɒf] N ABBR of **professor** profesor *m*, -ora *f*, Prof.
prof* [prɒf] N profe *m*.
profanation [,prɒfə'neɪʃən] N profanación *f*.
profane [prə'feɪn] [1] ADJ (a) (*secular, uninitiated, lay*) profano; (*irreverent*) profano, sacrílego, blasfemo.
(b) *language etc* fuerte, indecente; **he's very ~** es un malhablado; **don't be ~!** ¡no digas palabrotas!; **he became ~** empezó a jurar.
[2] VT profanar.
profanity [prə'fænɪtɪ] N (*V ADJ*) (a) profanidad *f*; blasfemia *f*, impiedad *f*.
(b) lenguaje *m* indecente, palabrotas *fpl*; **to utter a string of profanities** soltar una serie de palabrotas.
profess [prə'fes] [1] VT *faith, belief etc* profesar; (*assent*) afirmar, declarar; *regret etc* manifestar; *ignorance etc* confesar; **I do not ~ to be an expert** no pretendo ser un experto; **he ~es to know all about it** afirma estar enterado de ello; **she ~es to be 25** dice tener 25 años, afirma tener 25 años.
[2] VR: **to ~ o.s. satisfied** declararse satisfecho; **to ~ o.s. unable to +** *infin* declararse incapaz de + *infin*.
professed [prə'fest] ADJ declarado; (*pej*) supuesto, ostensible; (*Eccl*)

profeso.

professedly [prə'fesɪdlɪ] ADV declaradamente; (*pej*) supuestamente.

profession [prə'feʃən] N (a) (*declaration*) profesión *f*, declaración *f*; ~ of faith profesión *f* de fe. (b) (*calling*) profesión *f*; oficio *m*; carrera *f*; by ~ he is an engineer es ingeniero de oficio.

professional [prə'feʃənl] ① ADJ (a) profesional; de profesión, de oficio; ~ charges, ~ fees honorarios *mpl*, derechos *mpl*; ~ diplomat diplomático *m*, -a *f* de carrera; ~ foul falta *f* profesional; ~ liability responsabilidad *f* profesional; ~ man hombre *m* profesional; ~ qualifications títulos *mpl* profesionales; ~ services servicios *mpl* profesionales; ~ standing reputación *f* profesional; he's a ~ thug es un matón de oficio.

(b) (*competent*) experto, perito.

② N profesional *mf*; (*of golf-club*) maestro *m*, -a *f*.

professionalism [prə'feʃnəlɪzəm] N (a) (*of person, employment*) profesionalismo *m*. (b) (*of book etc*) excelencia *f*, alta calidad *f*, pericia *f*.

professionally [prə'feʃnəlɪ] ADV (a) profesionalmente; I never met him ~ no le conocí nunca en su cargo profesional; X, known ~ as Y X conocido por Y en la profesión.

(b) (*fig*) expertamente, con pericia; they did it most ~ lo hicieron expertamente.

professor [prə'fesər] N profesor *m* (universitario), profesora *f* (universitaria), catedrático *m*, -a *f*.

professorial [ˌprɒfə'sɔ:rɪəl] ADJ de profesor, de catedrático; profesoral.

professorship [prə'fesəʃɪp] N cátedra *f*; to be appointed to a ~ obtener una cátedra, ser nombrado a una cátedra.

proffer ['prɒfər] VT ofrecer.

proficiency [prə'fɪʃənsɪ] ① N pericia *f*, habilidad *f*, competencia *f*.

② ATTR: ~ test examen *m* de suficiencia.

proficient [prə'fɪʃənt] ADJ perito, hábil, competente (at, in en).

profile ['prəʊfaɪl] ① N perfil *m* (*also fig*); in ~ de perfil; to keep (or maintain) a high ~ tratar de llamar la atención; to keep (or maintain) a low ~ tratar de pasar inadvertido, adoptar una actitud discreta.

② VT (*fig*) *person* retratar, hacer el retrato de; *situation* describir, analizar.

profit ['prɒfɪt] ① N (*Comm*) ganancia *f*; (*fig*) provecho *m*, beneficio *m*; utilidad *f*, ventaja *f*; ~s ganancias *fpl*, utilidades *fpl*, beneficios *mpl*; ~ and loss ganancias *fpl* y pérdidas; to make a ~ of two millions ganar dos millones, sacar una ganancia de dos millones; to make a ~ on a deal salir ganando en un negocio; to show (or yield) a ~ dar dinero, rendir una ganancia; to sell sth at a ~ vender algo con ganancia; to turn sth to ~ aprovecharse de algo.

② ATTR: ~ and loss account cuenta *f* de ganancias y pérdidas; ~ center (*US*), ~ centre centro *m* de beneficios; ~ margin margen *m* de beneficios, margen *m* de utilidad; ~ motive afán *m* de lucro; ~ squeeze reducción *f* de los márgenes de beneficio; ~s tax impuesto *m* sobre los beneficios, impuesto *m* sobre las utilidades.

③ VT servir a, aprovechar a, ser de utilidad a; what will it ~ him to go? ¿qué le aprovechará ir?

④ VI ganar; (*Comm*) sacar ganancia; he does not seem to have ~ed no parece haber sacado provecho de ello; to ~ by, to ~ from aprovechar, beneficiarse de, sacar partido de; to ~ by the mistakes of others escarmentar en cabeza ajena.

profitability [ˌprɒfɪtə'bɪlɪtɪ] N rentabilidad *f*.

profitable ['prɒfɪtəbl] ADJ provechoso, útil; ventajoso; (*Comm*) lucrativo; (*economic to run etc*) rentable; a most ~ trip un viaje sumamente provechoso; a ~ investment una inversión lucrativa; the line is no longer ~ la línea ya no es rentable; it would be ~ to you to read this te beneficiarás de leer esto, te sería útil leer esto.

profitably ['prɒfɪtəblɪ] ADV con provecho, provechosamente; (*Comm*) lucrativamente, con lucro.

profiteer [ˌprɒfɪ'tɪər] ① N acaparador *m*, -ora *f*, él (or la) que hace ganancias excesivas; (*black marketeer*) estraperlista *mf*.

② VI hacer ganancias excesivas, cobrar más de lo justo.

profiteering [ˌprɒfɪ'tɪərɪŋ] N ganancias *fpl* excesivas.

profitless ['prɒfɪtlɪs] ADJ inútil.

profitlessly ['prɒfɪtlɪslɪ] ADV inútilmente.

profit-making ['prɒfɪtˌmeɪkɪŋ] ADJ: a ~ organization una organización lucrativa.

profit-related ['prɒfɪtrɪ'leɪtɪd] ADJ: ~ bonus prima *f* relacionada con los beneficios.

profit-seeking ['prɒfɪtˌsiːkɪŋ] ADJ de fines lucrativos, lucrativo.

profit-sharing ['prɒfɪtˌʃeərɪŋ] N (*by workers*) participación *f* directa en los beneficios; (*by company*) reparto *m* de los beneficios.

profit-taking ['prɒfɪtˌteɪkɪŋ] N realización *f* de beneficios.

profligacy ['prɒflɪɡəsɪ] N libertinaje *m*; prodigalidad *f*.

profligate ['prɒflɪɡɪt] ① ADJ (*dissolute*) libertino, disoluto; (*extravagant*) manirroto, pródigo.

② N libertino *m*; manirroto *m*, despilfarrador *m*.

pro-form ['prəʊˌfɔːm] N (*Ling*) pro forma *f*.

profound [prə'faʊnd] ADJ profundo.

profoundly [prə'faʊndlɪ] ADV profundamente.

profundity [prə'fʌndɪtɪ] N profundidad *f*.

profuse [prə'fjuːs] ADJ profuso; pródigo (*in* en); to be ~ in one's apologies disculparse con efusión.

profusely [prə'fjuːslɪ] ADV profusamente; pródigamente; he apologized ~ se disculpó con efusión; to sweat ~ sudar muchísimo.

profusion [prə'fjuːʒən] N profusión *f*, abundancia *f*; prodigalidad *f*; derroche *m*; a ~ of colour un derroche de color; a ~ of flowers una abundancia de flores; trees in ~ árboles *mpl* abundantes, muchísimos árboles *mpl*.

prog.* [prɒɡ] (*Brit*: *TV etc*) N ABBR of **programme** programación *f*, programa *m*.

progenitor [prəʊ'dʒenɪtər] N progenitor *m*.

progeny ['prɒdʒɪnɪ] N progenie *f*, prole *f*.

progesterone [prəʊ'dʒestərəʊn] N progesterona *f*.

prognosis [prɒɡ'nəʊsɪs] N, PL **prognoses** [prɒɡ'nəʊsiːz] pronóstico *m*.

prognostic [prɒɡ'nɒstɪk] N pronóstico *m*.

prognosticate [prɒɡ'nɒstɪkeɪt] VT pronosticar.

prognostication [prɒɡˌnɒstɪ'keɪʃən] N (*act, art*) pronosticación *f*; (*forecast*) pronóstico *m*.

programmable, (*US, also freq Comput*) **programable** ['prəʊɡræməbl] ADJ programable.

programme, (*US, also freq Comput*) **program** ['prəʊɡræm] ① N programa *m*.

② ATTR: ~ music música *f* de programa; ~ notes notas *fpl* de programa.

③ VT (*Comput*) programar; it is ~d to + *infin* está programado para + *infin*.

programmed, (*US*) **programed** ['prəʊɡræmd] ADJ programado; ~ learning, ~ teaching enseñanza *f* programada.

programmer, (*US*) **programer** ['prəʊɡræmər] N programador *m*, -ora *f*.

programming, (*US*) **programing** ['prəʊɡræmɪŋ] ① N programación *f*.

② ATTR: ~ environment entorno *m* de programación; ~ language lenguaje *m* de programación.

progress ① ['prəʊɡres] N progreso *m*; progresos *mpl*; (*of events etc*) marcha *f*, desarrollo *m*; (*of disease*) desarrollo *m*, evolución *f*; the ~ of events la marcha de los acontecimientos; the ~ of a student los progresos de un estudiante; it is in ~ está en vía de realizarse (*etc*); harvesting is in full ~ la cosecha está en plena marcha; the game was already in ~ había comenzado ya el partido; to make (some) ~ hacer progresos, progresar; to make slow ~ avanzar despacio; I can't make any ~ with this child no hago carrera con este niño.

② ['prəʊɡres] ATTR: ~ report informe *m* sobre la labor realizada; informe *m* interino.

③ [prə'ɡres] VI hacer progresos, progresar; avanzar; desarrollarse; as the game ~ed a medida que iba desarrollándose el partido; matters are ~ing slowly las cosas avanzan lentamente; how is the student ~ing? ¿qué progresos hace el estudiante?; the patient is ~ing favourably el enfermo está mejorando de modo satisfactorio.

④ [prə'ɡres] VT seguir adelante con.

progression [prə'ɡreʃən] N progresión *f*.

progressive [prə'ɡresɪv] ① ADJ progresivo; (*Pol*) progresista; ~ tax impuesto *m* progresivo.

② N progresista *mf*.

progressively [prə'ɡresɪvlɪ] ADV progresivamente; (*Pol*) de modo progresista; it diminishes ~ disminuye progresivamente; it's getting ~ better se va haciendo cada vez mejor.

progressiveness [prə'ɡresɪvnɪs] N carácter *m* progresista.

prohibit [prə'hɪbɪt] VT (a) (*forbid*) prohibir; to ~ sb from doing sth prohibir a uno hacer algo; 'it is ~d to feed the animals' 'se prohibe dar de comer a los animales'; 'smoking ~d' 'se prohibe fumar', 'prohibido fumar'; ~d area zona *f* prohibida.

(b) (*prevent*) impedir; to ~ sb from doing sth impedir a uno hacer algo; his health ~s him from swimming su salud le impide nadar.

prohibition ['prəʊɪ'bɪʃən] N prohibición *f*; (*US*) prohibicionismo *m*; ley *f* seca.

prohibitionism [ˌprəʊɪ'bɪʃənɪzəm] N prohibicionismo *m*.

prohibitionist [ˌprəʊɪ'bɪʃənɪst] ① ADJ prohibicionista.

② N prohibicionista *mf*.

prohibitive [prə'hɪbɪtɪv] ADJ prohibitivo; *price* imposible.

prohibitively [prə'hɪbɪtɪvlɪ] ADV: ~ expensive imposiblemente caro.

prohibitory [prə'hɪbɪtərɪ] ADJ prohibitorio.

project ① ['prɒdʒekt] N proyecto *m*.

② [prə'dʒekt] VT proyectar; ~ed costs gastos *mpl* previstos, gastos *mpl* presupuestados.

③ [prə'dʒekt] VI salir, sobresalir, resaltar; to ~ beyond sobresalir más allá de; to ~ over sobresalir por encima de.

projectile [prə'dʒektaɪl] N proyectil *m*.

projecting [prə'dʒektɪŋ] ADJ saliente, saledizo.
projection [prə'dʒekʃən] N **(a)** proyección *f*; *(overhang etc)* saliente *m*, resalto *m*; *(knob etc)* protuberancia *f*. **(b)** *(Fin)* proyección *f*.
projectionist [prə'dʒekʃnɪst] N operador *m*, -ora *f* (de proyector), proyectista *mf*.
projection room [prə'dʒekʃən,rʊm] N cabina *f* (de proyección).
project manager ['prɒdʒekt,mænɪdʒəʳ] N director *m*, -ora *f* de proyecto.
projector [prə'dʒektəʳ] N proyector *m* (de películas).
prolapse ['prəʊlæps] N prolapso *m*.
proles [prəʊlz] NPL proletarios *mpl*.
proletarian [,prəʊlə'teərɪən] [1] ADJ proletario.
[2] N proletario *m*, -a *f*.
proletarianize [,prəʊlə'teərɪənaɪz] VT proletariar.
proletariat [,prəʊlə'teərɪət] N proletariado *m*.
pro-life [,prəʊ'laɪf] ADJ pro-vida.
proliferate [prə'lɪfəreɪt] [1] VT multiplicar; extender.
[2] VI proliferar, multiplicarse; extenderse.
proliferation [prə,lɪfə'reɪʃən] N proliferación *f*, multiplicación *f*; extensión *f*.
prolific [prə'lɪfɪk] ADJ prolífico *(of* en).
prolix ['prəʊlɪks] ADJ prolijo.
prolixity [prəʊ'lɪksɪtɪ] N prolijidad *f*.
prologue, *(US)* **prolog** ['prəʊlɒg] N prólogo *m* *(to* de).
prolong [prə'lɒŋ] VT *(in space)* prolongar, extender; *(in time)* alargar, extender.
prolongation [,prəʊlɒŋ'geɪʃən] N prolongación *f*, alargamiento *m*, extensión *f*.
prolonged [prə'lɒŋd] ADJ *absence, leave etc* prolongado; *event, period, struggle* (muy) largo; **at this there was ~ applause** esto fue aplaudido durante varios minutos.
prom* [prɒm] N **(a)** *(Brit)* = **promenade concert**. **(b)** *(seaside* ~) paseo *m* marítimo. **(c)** *(US) baile de gala bajo los auspicios de los alumnos de un colegio.*

┌─── PROM ───────────────────────────────────┐

i *En Gran Bretaña el término* **prom** *es la forma abreviada de* **promenade concert,** *y hace referencia a un concierto de música clásica en el que una parte del público permanece de pie en una zona del auditorio reservada al efecto. La serie de conciertos de este tipo más conocida es la que se celebra cada verano en el* **Royal Albert Hall** *de Londres, y que tuvo su origen en 1895 a partir de una idea del director de orquesta Henry Wood. Actualmente convertidos en una institución nacional, destaca entre todas las actuaciones la llamada* **Last Night of the Proms** *en la que se interpretan piezas de carácter patriótico, entre otras de repertorio.*

En los Estados Unidos un **prom** *es un baile de gala que se celebra para los alumnos de un centro de educación secundaria o universitaria. De todos estos bailes el más famoso es el* **senior prom,** *al que asisten los alumnos del último año de una* **high school** *y que se considera un acontecimiento de gran importancia para los adolescentes estadounidenses. Los alumnos acuden normalmente con su pareja y visten de etiqueta: esmoquin los chicos y traje de noche las chicas.*

promenade [,prɒmɪ'nɑːd] [1] N **(a)** *(act)* paseo *m*.
(b) *(avenue)* paseo *m*, avenida *f*; *(at seaside)* paseo *m* marítimo.
[2] ATTR: **~ concert** *(Brit) concierto en el que una parte del público permanece de pie*; **~ deck** cubierta *f* de paseo.
[3] VT pasear.
[4] VI pasearse.
Prometheus [prə'miːθjuːs] NM Prometeo.
prominence ['prɒmɪnəns] N prominencia *f*; *(fig)* eminencia *f*, importancia *f*; **to bring sth into ~** hacer que algo destaque; **he came into ~ in the Cuba affair** empezó a sobresalir cuando lo de Cuba; **that aspect is coming into ~** ese aspecto está adquiriendo importancia.
prominent ['prɒmɪnənt] ADJ *(jutting out)* prominente; *cheekbone, tooth etc* saliente; *eye* saltón; *(fig)* eminente, importante, notable, destacado; **the most ~ article in the window** el objeto que más salta a la vista en el escaparate; **the most ~ feature of this theory** el aspecto más notable de esta teoría; **put it in a ~ position** ponlo muy a la vista; **to be ~ in a deal** desempeñar un papel importante en un negocio; **she is ~ in London society** es una figura destacada de la buena sociedad londinense.
prominently ['prɒmɪnəntlɪ] ADV: **to display sth ~** exponer algo muy a la vista, poner algo en un sitio donde resulta perfectamente visible; **he figured ~ in the case** desempeñó un papel importante en el proceso.
promiscuity [,prɒmɪs'kjuːɪtɪ] N *(V ADJ)* **(a)** libertad *f* en las relaciones sexuales, inmoralidad *f*, libertinaje *m*. **(b)** promiscuidad *f*.
promiscuous [prə'mɪskjʊəs] ADJ **(a)** *person* libre en las relaciones sexuales, inmoral, libertino; *relationship* ilícito; *conduct* inmoral, libre.
(b) *(mixed)* promiscuo.

promiscuously [prə'mɪskjʊəslɪ] ADV *(V ADJ)* **(a)** libremente, de modo inmoral; ilícitamente. **(b)** promiscuamente.
promise ['prɒmɪs] [1] N **(a)** *(pledge)* promesa *f*; **~ of marriage** palabra *f* de matrimonio; **under ~ of** bajo palabra de; **a ~ is a ~** lo prometido es deuda; **to break one's ~** faltar a su palabra; **to hold** (or **keep) sb to his ~** obligar a uno a cumplir su promesa, hacer que uno cumpla su promesa; **to keep one's ~** cumplir su promesa; **to release sb from his ~** absolver a uno de su promesa.
(b) *(hope)* promesa *f*; esperanza *f*; porvenir *m*; **full of ~** muy prometedor; **a young man of ~** un joven que promete, un joven de porvenir; **to hold out a ~ of** dar esperanzas de; **to show ~** prometer, demostrar tener aptitudes.
[2] VT prometer; *(forecast)* prometer, augurar, pronosticar; **no, I ~ you** no, se lo aseguro; **to ~ to do sth** prometer hacer algo; **to ~ sb sth, to ~ sth to sb** prometer dar algo a uno; **it ~s trouble** nos augura algo malo; **they ~ us rain tomorrow** nos pronostican lluvia para mañana; **this does not ~ to be easy** esto me parece que no va a ser fácil.
[3] VI **(a)** prometer; **~?** ¿me lo prometes?; **I can't ~** no lo puedo prometer.
(b) *(fig)* **to ~ well** prometer, ser prometedor; **the crop ~s well** la cosecha se muestra buena, la cosecha se anuncia espléndida; **this does not ~ well** esto no nos anuncia nada bueno.
[4] VR: **to ~ o.s. sth** prometerse algo.
promised ['prɒmɪst] ADJ prometido; **the P~ Land** la tierra de promisión.
promising ['prɒmɪsɪŋ] ADJ prometedor, que promete; *future prospect* esperanzador, halagüeño; **a ~ young man** un joven que promete, un joven de porvenir; **two ~ candidates** dos candidatos buenos; **it doesn't look very ~** no parece muy halagüeño, es una perspectiva poco atractiva.
promisingly ['prɒmɪsɪŋlɪ] ADV de manera prometedora; esperanzadoramente; **it's going quite ~** va bastante bien; **she plays ~** tocando se ve que promete, toca lo bastante bien para demostrar que tiene aptitudes.
promissory ['prɒmɪsərɪ] ADJ: **~ note** pagaré *m*.
promo* ['prəʊməʊ] N *(Comm)* ABBR of **promotion** promoción *f*.
promontory ['prɒməntrɪ] N promontorio *m*.
promote [prə'məʊt] VT **(a)** *trade etc* promover, fomentar; *good feeling* fomentar; *campaign* apoyar; *product (advertise)* dar publicidad a, hacer propaganda por, *(sell)* promover, impulsar, aumentar las ventas de; *discussion etc* estimular, favorecer, facilitar; *(Parl) bill* presentar; *company* fundar, crear, financiar.
(b) *(in rank)* ascender; **to be ~d** ser ascendido *(to colonel* a coronel); **Tarifa was ~d to the first division** Tarifa fue promovida a primera división, Tarifa ascendió a primera división.
(c) *(Chem) reaction* provocar.
promoter [prə'məʊtəʳ] N promotor *m*, -ora *f*; agente *mf* de negocios; *(of company)* fundador *m*, -ora *f*; *(Boxing)* empresario *m*, promotor *m*; **sales ~** promotor *m*, -ora *f* de ventas.
promotion [prə'məʊʃən] N **(a)** promoción *f*, fomento *m*; apoyo *m*; gestión *f*; facilitación *f*; presentación *f*; fundación *f*, creación *f*; **sales ~** promoción *f* de ventas; **'a ~ by Bloggs Enterprises'** 'presentación de la Empresa Bloggs'.
(b) *(in rank)* ascenso *m*; promoción *f*; **to get ~** ser ascendido *(to* a); **to move up the ~ ladder** subir en el escalafón; **to win ~** *(Sport)* ser promovido, ganar la promoción, ascender.
(c) *(Chem)* provocación *f*.
promotional [prə'məʊʃənl] ADJ promocional.
prompt [prɒmpt] [1] ADJ pronto; *action, delivery, reply etc* pronto, inmediato; *service* rápido; *payment* puntual; *person's character* puntual; **they're very ~** son muy puntuales; **'please be ~'** 'se ruega mucha puntualidad'.
[2] ADV puntualmente; **at 6 o'clock ~** a las 6 en punto.
[3] VT **(a)** *(urge)* **to ~ sb to do sth** mover a uno a hacer algo, incitar a uno a hacer algo; **I felt ~ed to protest** me encontré en la necesidad de protestar; **what ~ed you to do it?** ¿qué te movió a hacerlo?
(b) *(suggest)* inspirar; provocar; sugerir; **what ~ed that question?** ¿cuál fue el motivo de esa pregunta?; **a decision ~ed by fear** una decisión influida por el temor; **a poem ~ed by a memory** una poesía inspirada por un recuerdo; **it ~s the thought that ...** sugiere la noción de que ..., hace pensar que ...
(c) *(Theat)* apuntar; **don't ~ her!** ¡no la ayudes a recordar!, ¡no le soples cosas al oído!; **the witness had to be ~ed** fue necesario recordar unos hechos al testigo, hubo que traer ciertas cosas a la memoria del testigo.
[4] VI *(Theat)* apuntar.
[5] N **(a)** *(Theat)* apuntador *m*, -ora *f*.
(b) *(Comput)* aviso *m*, guía *f*, carácter *m* de petición.
[6] ATTR: **~ side** *(Theat)* lado *m* izquierdo (del actor).
prompt-box ['prɒmptbɒks] N concha *f* (del apuntador).
prompter ['prɒmptəʳ] N apuntador *m*, -ora *f*.

prompting ['prɒmptɪŋ] N: **without ~** sin ayuda de nadie, sin tener que consultar el texto (etc); **the ~s of conscience** los escrúpulos de la conciencia; **the ~s of love** los dictados del amor.

promptitude ['prɒmptɪtjuːd] N = **promptness**.

promptly ['prɒmptlɪ] ADV puntualmente, con prontitud; inmediatamente; rápidamente; **they do it very ~** lo hacen con toda prontitud; **they left ~ at 6** partieron a las 6 en punto.

promptness ['prɒmptnɪs] N prontitud f, puntualidad f; rapidez f.

promulgate ['prɒmʌlgeɪt] VT promulgar.

promulgation [,prɒmʌl'geɪʃən] N promulgación f.

prone [prəʊn] ADJ **(a)** (face down) **to be ~** estar postrado (boca abajo).
(b) (liable) **to be ~ to** + N ser propenso a + N, estar inclinado a + N; **to be ~ to** + infin ser propenso a + infin.

proneness ['prəʊnnɪs] N propensión f (to a), predisposición f (to a).

prong [prɒŋ] N punta f, púa f, diente m.

-pronged [prɒŋd] ADJ ending in compounds: **three~** de tres puntas.

pronominal [prəʊ'nɒmɪnl] ADJ pronominal.

pronoun ['prəʊnaʊn] N pronombre m.

pronounce [prə'naʊns] **1** VT **(a)** (Ling) pronunciar. **(b)** (Jur) pronunciar; (with adj) declarar; **they ~d him unfit to** + infin le declararon incapaz de + infin.
2 VI: **to ~ in favour of sth** pronunciarse en favor de algo; **to ~ on sth** expresar una opinión sobre algo, juzgar algo.

pronounceable [prə'naʊnsəbl] ADJ pronunciable.

pronounced [prə'naʊnst] ADJ marcado, acusado, fuerte; pronunciado; decidido.

pronouncement [prə'naʊnsmənt] N declaración f; opinión f; **to make a ~** pronunciarse, hacer una declaración (about sobre).

pronto* ['prɒntəʊ] ADV pronto.

pronunciation [prə,nʌnsɪ'eɪʃən] N pronunciación f.

proof [pruːf] **1** N **(a)** (gen) prueba f (also Math etc); comprobación f; **~ positive** prueba f concluyente; ..., **~ positive that** ......, lo cual es prueba concluyente de que ...; **in ~ of** en prueba de, en comprobación de; **as señal de; in ~ whereof** en fe de lo cual; **it is ~ that he is poor** es prueba de su pobreza; **to adduce ~ to the contrary** aducir hechos que prueban lo contrario; **to give** (or **show**) **~ of** dar prueba de; **the onus of ~ lies with the accuser** le cumple al acusador probar lo que dice; **the ~ of the pudding is in the eating** al probar se ve el mosto; los melones, a cata.
(b) (Typ) prueba f; **~s**, **~ sheets** pruebas fpl; **to read the ~s** corregir las pruebas.
(c) (of alcohol) graduación f normal; **this drink is 40% ~** esta bebida tiene una graduación de 40 por 100.
2 ADJ **(a)** alcohol de graduación normal; **~ spirit** licor m de graduación normal.
(b) **to be ~ against sth** ser (or estar) a prueba de algo; **it is ~ against moisture** está a prueba de la humedad; **I'm not ~ against temptation** yo no soy insensible a la tentación.
(c) eg **bullet-~** a prueba de balas.
3 VT impermeabilizar.

proofread ['pruːfriːd] (irr: V **read**) VT corregir las pruebas de.

proofreader ['pruːf,riːdər] N corrector m, -ora f de pruebas.

proofreading ['pruːf,riːdɪŋ] N corrección f de pruebas.

prop [prɒp] **1** N apoyo m; (Archit) puntal m; (Hort) horca f, rodrigón m; (Min) peón m, entibo m, puntal m; (Naut) escora f; (fig) sostén m; **~ forward** pilier m.
2 VT (also **to ~ up**) apoyar; apuntalar; apoyar con rodrigón (etc); (fig) apoyar, sostener; **to ~ a ladder against a wall** apoyar una escalera contra una pared; **the company was ~ped up by a big loan** la compañía recibió el apoyo de un préstamo cuantioso.
3 VR: **to ~ o.s. against a tree** apoyarse contra un árbol.

prop. **(a)** (Comm) ABBR of **proprietor** propietario m, -a f. **(b)** [prɒp] N (Theat*) ABBR of **property** accesorio m. **(c)** [prɒp] N (Aer*) ABBR of **propeller** hélice f.

propaganda [,prɒpə'gændə] N propaganda f.

propagandist [,prɒpə'gændɪst] N propagandista mf.

propagandize [,prɒpə'gændaɪz] **1** VT doctrine propagar; person hacer propaganda a.
2 VI hacer propaganda.

propagate ['prɒpəgeɪt] **1** VT propagar.
2 VI propagarse.

propagation [,prɒpə'geɪʃən] N propagación f.

propane ['prəʊpeɪn] N propano m.

propel [prə'pel] VT impulsar, propulsar; (push) empujar; **it is ~led by turbines** está propulsado por turbinas.

propellant, propellent [prə'pelənt] N propulsor m; (aerosol etc) propelente m.

propeller [prə'pelər] N hélice f.

propeller shaft [prə'peləʃɑːft] N (Aer) eje m de la hélice; (Aut) árbol m de mando, eje m cardán; (Naut) eje m portahélice.

propelling pencil [prə'pelɪŋ'pensl] N (Brit) lapicero m, portaminas m.

propensity [prə'pensɪtɪ] N propensión f (to a).

proper ['prɒpər] **1** ADJ **(a)** (peculiar, characteristic) propio, peculiar; característico; **~ name, ~ noun** nombre m propio; **the qualities which are ~ to it** las cualidades que le son propias, las cualidades que son propias de él.
(b) (correct) verdadero, exacto, apropiado; **physics ~** la física propiamente dicha; **in the ~ sense of the word** en el sentido estricto de la palabra; **I'm not a ~ Londoner** no soy un auténtico londinense, no soy un londinense de verdad.
(c) (*) **he's a ~ rogue** es un verdadero pillo; **it's a ~ nuisance** es una verdadera molestia; **he's a ~ gentleman now** ya es un caballero hecho y derecho; **we got a ~ beating** nos dieron una paliza de las buenas; **there was a ~ row** hubo un lío de todos los diablos*.
(d) (right, suitable) apropiado, conveniente; oportuno; debido; justo, exacto; **in ~ condition** en buen estado; **at the ~ time** en el momento oportuno; **in the ~ way** convenientemente, del modo conveniente; **as you think ~** según te parezca, según tu criterio; **do as you think ~** haz lo que te parezca bien; **to do the ~ thing by sb** tratar a uno con justicia, cumplir con uno; **to say the ~ thing** decir lo que piden las circunstancias; **it was the ~ thing to say** fue lo que había que decir; **in a style ~ to his station** en un estilo que conviene a su rango; **I think it ~ to** + infin creo hacer bien en + infin.
(e) (seemly) decente; correcto; **~ behaviour** conducta f correcta; **what is ~** lo que está bien, lo que conviene; **it is not ~ for you to** + infin no está bien que + subj; **it's not ~ with children about** no es decente si hay niños delante.
(f) (prim and ~) etiquetero, relamido; formal.
(g) (Her) natural.
2 ADV (*) **(a)** (really) **it's ~ difficult** es realmente difícil, es dificilísimo; **we were ~ puzzled** quedamos francamente perplejos.
(b) = **properly (b)**.

properly ['prɒpəlɪ] ADV **(a)** (correctly etc) correctamente, apropiadamente, debidamente; **a word ~ used** una palabra correctamente empleada; **~ speaking** propiamente dicho; en el sentido estricto de la palabra; **it is not ~ so called** no es correcto llamarlo así, no se llama así en propiedad, en propiedad no se dice así; **she very ~ refused** se negó a ello e hizo bien; **to do sth ~** hacer algo bien, hacer algo como se debe, hacer algo como Dios manda.
(b) (in seemly fashion) decentemente; correctamente; **not ~ dressed** incorrectamente vestido; **to behave ~** portarse correctamente; **behave ~!** ¡pórtate bien!, ¡estáte formal!
(c) (intensive) **we were ~ ashamed** nos avergonzamos de verdad; **we got ~ beaten** nos dieron una paliza de las buenas; **we were ~ puzzled** quedamos requeteperplejos.

propertied ['prɒpətɪd] ADJ adinerado, acaudalado; **the ~ classes** la clase acaudalada.

property ['prɒpətɪ] **1** N **(a)** (quality) propiedad f; **the properties of this substance** las propiedades de esta sustancia.
(b) (thing owned) propiedad f; bienes mpl; (estate) hacienda f, finca f, propiedad f; **that's my ~** eso es mío; **whose ~ is this?** ¿de quién es esto?; **it doesn't seem to be anyone's ~** no parece que tenga dueño, no parece que pertenezca a nadie; **that news is common ~** eso lo saben todos ya, esa noticia es ya del dominio público; **it is common ~ that ...** todos saben que ...; **it became the ~ of Mr Jones** pasó a ser propiedad del Sr Jones; **she left her ~ to X** dejó sus bienes a X.
(c) (Theat) accesorio m; **properties** accesorios mpl, at(t)rezzo m.
2 ATTR inmobiliario; **~ company** compañía f inmobiliaria; **~ developer** promotor m inmobiliario, promotora f inmobiliaria, promotor m, -ora f (de construcciones); **~ market** mercado m inmobiliario, mercado m de bienes raíces; **~ mart** sección f de ventas de inmuebles y viviendas (de un periódico); **~ mistress** accesorista f, attrezzista f; **~ owner** hacendado m, -a f, terrateniente mf; **~ speculation** especulación f inmobiliaria; **~ tax** contribución f territorial, impuesto m sobre la propiedad; **~ transfer tax** impuesto m sobre transmisiones patrimoniales.

prophecy ['prɒfɪsɪ] N profecía f.

prophesy ['prɒfɪsaɪ] VT profetizar; (fig) predecir, prever, augurar (that que).

prophet ['prɒfɪt] N profeta m.

prophetess ['prɒfɪtɪs] N profetisa f.

prophetic [prə'fetɪk] ADJ profético.

prophetically [prə'fetɪkəlɪ] ADV proféticamente.

prophylactic [,prɒfɪ'læktɪk] **1** ADJ profiláctico.
2 N profiláctico m.

prophylaxis ['prɒfɪ'læksɪs] N profilaxis f.

propinquity [prə'pɪŋkwɪtɪ] N (nearness) propincuidad f; (kinship) consanguinidad f, parentesco m.

propitiate [prə'pɪʃɪeɪt] VT propiciar.

propitiation [prə,pɪʃɪ'eɪʃən] N propiciación f.

propitiatory [prə'pɪʃɪətərɪ] ADJ propiciatorio, conciliatorio.

propitious [prə'pɪʃəs] ADJ propicio, favorable.

propitiously [prəˈpɪʃəslɪ] ADV de modo propicio, bajo signo propicio, favorablemente.

proponent [prəˈpəʊnənt] N defensor *m*, -ora *f*.

proportion [prəˈpɔːʃən] N (a) (*ratio, relationship: also Math*) proporción *f*; parte *f*, porción *f*, porcentaje *m*; **the ~ of blacks to whites** la proporción entre negros y blancos; **what ~ is in private hands?** ¿qué porción queda en manos de particulares?; **in equal ~s** por partes iguales; **in due ~** en su justa medida; **in ~ as** a medida que; **in ~ to** en proporción con, a medida de; **and the rest in ~** y lo demás en proporción, (*Comm*) y lo demás a prorrata; **to be out of ~** ser desproporcionado; **to be out of ~ with** (*or* **to**) no guardar proporción con; **it has been magnified out of all ~** se ha exagerado mucho.
(b) **sense of ~** (*lit, fig*) sentido *m* de la medida.
(c) **~s** (*size*) dimensiones *fpl*.

proportional [prəˈpɔːʃənl] ADJ proporcional; **~ representation** representación *f* proporcional; **~ to** en proporción con, a medida de; **X is not ~ to Y** X no guarda proporción con Y; **~ spacing** (*Comput: on printer*) espaciado *m* proporcional.

proportionality [ˌprəpɔːʃəˈnælɪtɪ] N proporcionalidad *f*.

proportionally [prəˈpɔːʃnəlɪ] ADV proporcionalmente, en proporción.

proportionate [prəˈpɔːʃnɪt] ADJ proporcionado.

proportionately [prəˈpɔːʃnɪtlɪ] ADV proporcionadamente, en proporción.

proportioned [prəˈpɔːʃnd] ADJ: **well ~** bien proporcionado.

proposal [prəˈpəʊzl] N (a) (*offer*) propuesta *f*, proposición *f*; oferta *f*; (*to girl*) declaración *f* (de amor); **~ of marriage** oferta *f* de matrimonio, (*formally*) petición *f* de mano; **to make a ~** hacer una propuesta; **to make the ~ that ...** proponer que ...
(b) (*plan*) proyecto *m*; (*notion*) idea *f*; (*suggestion*) sugerencia *f*; **my ~ was to + infin** mi idea era de + *infin*; **it is a new ~ to reform the currency** es un nuevo proyecto para reformar la moneda.

propose [prəˈpəʊz] ① VT (a) (*suggest*) proponer; ofrecer; *motion* proponer; *candidate* proponer (la candidatura de); **the ~d motorway** la autopista que se propone; **to ~ marriage to sb** hacer una oferta de matrimonio a una, (*formally*) pedir la mano de una a su padre; **to ~ sb for membership of a club** proponer la candidatura de uno para socio de un club; **what course do you ~?** ¿qué línea de acción nos recomiendas?
(b) **to ~ sb's health** brindar por uno, beber a la salud de uno.
(c) **to ~ to + infin** proponerse + *infin*; pensar + *infin*, tener la intención de + *infin*; **what do you ~ doing?** ¿qué piensas hacer?
② VI (a) **Man ~s, God disposes** el hombre propone y Dios dispone.
(b) (*to girl*) declararse (*to* a); **to ~ to sb** (*formally*) hacer una oferta de matrimonio a una, pedir la mano de una a su padre.

proposer [prəˈpəʊzər] N (*Parl etc*) proponente *mf* autor *m*, -ora *f* (de una moción).

proposition [ˌprɒpəˈzɪʃən] ① N (a) (*statement, Math, Logic etc*) proposición *f*; (*proposal*) propuesta *f*, proposición *f*; oferta *f*; (*plan*) proyecto *m*.
(b) (*job*) tarea *f*; (*enterprise*) empresa *f*; (*problem*) problema *m*; (*objective*) propósito *m*; (*opponent*) adversario *m*, -a *f*; (*prospect*) perspectiva *f*; **it's a tough ~** es mucho pedir; **he's a tough ~** es un adversario formidable; **the journey alone is quite a ~** sólo el viaje pide grandes esfuerzos; **it will be a paying ~** dará dinero; **it's not an economic ~** no es rentable.
② VT *girl* echar un tiento a*.

propound [prəˈpaʊnd] VT proponer, exponer, presentar.

proprietary [prəˈpraɪətərɪ] ADJ propietario; *article* patentado; **~ brand** marca *f* comercial; **~ goods** artículos *mpl* de marca; **~ interest** interés *m* patrimonial; **~ name** nombre *m* propietario.

proprietor [prəˈpraɪətər] N propietario *m*, -a *f*, dueño *m*, -a *f*.

proprietorial [prəˌpraɪəˈtɔːrɪəl] ADJ *attitude etc* protector.

proprietorship [prəˈpraɪətəʃɪp] N propiedad *f*, posesión *f*.

proprietress [prəˈpraɪətrɪs] N propietaria *f*, dueña *f*.

propriety [prəˈpraɪətɪ] N (*seemliness*) decoro *m*, decencia *f*, corrección *f*; (*fitness*) conveniencia *f*; **the proprieties** las convenciones, los cánones sociales, el decoro; **breach of ~** ofensa *f* contra el decoro, incorrección *f*; **to observe the proprieties** atenerse a los cánones sociales; **to throw ~ to the winds** abandonar totalmente el decoro.

props* [prɒps] NPL (*Theat*) V **property 1 (c)**.

propulsion [prəˈpʌlʃən] N propulsión *f*.

pro rata [ˌprəʊˈrɑːtə] ADJ, ADV V **pro 1 (c)**.

prorate [ˈprəʊreɪt] (*US*) ① N prorrata *f*.
② VT prorratear.

prorogation [ˌprəʊrəˈgeɪʃən] N prorrogación *f*.

prorogue [prəˈrəʊg] VT prorrogar.

prosaic [prəʊˈzeɪɪk] ADJ prosaico.

prosaically [prəʊˈzeɪɪkəlɪ] ADV prosaicamente.

Pros. Atty. (*US*) ABBR *of* **prosecuting attorney**.

proscenium [prəʊˈsiːnɪəm] N proscenio *m*; **~ arch** embocadura *f*; **~ box** palco *m* de proscenio.

proscribe [prəʊsˈkraɪb] VT proscribir.

proscription [prəʊsˈkrɪpʃən] N proscripción *f*.

prose [prəʊz] ① N (a) (*Liter*) prosa *f*. (b) (*Scol etc: also ~ composition*) traducción *f* inversa.
② ATTR de prosa; en prosa, prosístico.

prosecute [ˈprɒsɪkjuːt] VT (a) (*Jur*) procesar; enjuiciar; *claim* demandar en juicio; **to ~ sb for theft** procesar a uno por ladrón; **to be ~d for a traffic offence** ser procesado por una infracción del código; **'trespassers will be ~d'** 'se procederá contra los intrusos'.
(b) (*follow up*) proseguir, continuar, llevar adelante.

prosecuting [ˈprɒsɪkjuːtɪŋ] ADJ: **~ counsel** fiscal *mf*.

prosecution [ˌprɒsɪˈkjuːʃən] N (a) (*Jur: case*) proceso *m*, causa *f*, juicio *m*; (*act*) acusación *f*, procesamiento *m*; (*side*) parte *f* actora; **counsel for the ~** fiscal *mf*; **~ witness** testigo *mf* de cargo; **to start a ~ against sb** entablar juicio contra uno, entablar una acción judicial contra uno.
(b) (*furtherance*) prosecución *f*; **in the ~ of his duty** en el cumplimiento de su deber.

prosecutor [ˈprɒsɪkjuːtər] N acusador *m*, -ora *f*; (*also* **public ~**) fiscal *mf*.

proselyte [ˈprɒsɪlaɪt] N prosélito *m*, -a *f*.

proselytism [ˈprɒsɪlɪtɪzəm] N proselitismo *m*.

proselytize [ˈprɒsɪlɪtaɪz] VI ganar prosélitos.

prose writer [ˈprəʊzˌraɪtər] N prosista *mf*.

prosody [ˈprɒsədɪ] N métrica *f*.

prospect ① [ˈprɒspekt] N (a) (*view*) vista *f*, panorama *m*; **the ~ from the window** la vista desde la ventana; **a ~ of Toledo** una vista de Toledo; **where every ~ pleases** donde todo deleita la vista.
(b) (*outlook*) perspectiva *f*; (*hope*) esperanza *f*; expectativa *f*; (*future*) porvenir *m*; **what a ~!** (*iro*) ¡qué perspectiva!; **future ~s** perspectivas *fpl* del futuro; **~s are really good** las perspectivas son francamente buenas; **'good ~s'** (*advert for job*) 'buen provenir', 'porvenir risueño', 'posibilidades de superación'; **it's a grim ~** es una perspectiva nada atractiva; **there are ~s of a fine day** el día se presenta muy bueno; **~s for the harvest are poor** la cosecha se anuncia más bien mediocre; **his ~s are outstandingly good** le espera un gran porvenir; **he has no ~s** no tiene porvenir; **this ~ cheered him up** se alegró con esta perspectiva; **we are faced with the ~ of + ger** nos encontramos ante la perspectiva de + *infin*; **to have sth in ~** esperar algo; **to hold out a ~ of** dar esperanzas de.
(c) (*chance*) probabilidad *f*, **the ~ of an early peace** la posibilidad de una pronta paz; **there is little ~ of his coming** hay pocas posibilidades de que venga; **to dangle a ~ before sb** ofrecer a uno la posibilidad de + *infin*, tentar a uno con la posibilidad de + *infin*; **I see no ~ of that** eso no lo creo probable.
(d) (*person*) persona *f* en perspectiva; (*Comm*) cliente *m* posible, comprador *m* (*etc*) probable; **is he a ~ for the team?** ¿vale considerarle como posible miembro del equipo?; **he's not much of a ~ for her** no vale gran cosa como partido para ella.
② [prəsˈpekt] VT explorar.
③ [prəsˈpekt] VI: **to ~ for** buscar.

prospecting [prəsˈpektɪŋ] N (*Min*) prospección *f*.

prospective [prəsˈpektɪv] ADJ anticipado, prospectivo, esperado; probable; *son-in-law etc* futuro; *heir* presunto; *legislation etc* en perspectiva.

prospector [prəsˈpektər] N explorador *m*; **gold ~** buscador *m* de oro.

prospectus [prəsˈpektəs] N prospecto *m*; programa *m*; folleto *m* informativo.

prosper [ˈprɒspər] ① VT favorecer, fomentar.
② VI prosperar; medrar; florecer.

prosperity [prɒsˈpɛrɪtɪ] N prosperidad *f*.

▼ **prosperous** [ˈprɒspərəs] ADJ próspero.

prosperously [ˈprɒspərəslɪ] ADV prósperamente.

prostaglandin [ˌprɒstəˈglændɪn] N prostaglandina *f*.

prostate [ˈprɒsteɪt] N próstata *f*.

prosthesis [prɒsˈθiːsɪs] N, PL **prostheses** [prɒsˈθiːsiːs] prótesis *f*.

prosthetic [prɒsˈθetɪk] ADJ prostético.

prostitute [ˈprɒstɪtjuːt] ① N prostituta *f*.
② VT prostituir (*also fig*).

prostitution [ˌprɒstɪˈtjuːʃən] N prostitución *f*.

prostrate ① [ˈprɒstreɪt] ADJ postrado; (*Bot*) procumbente; (*fig*) postrado, abatido (*with* por).
② [prɒsˈtreɪt] VT postrar, abatir; (*fig*) postrar, abatir; **to be ~d by grief** estar postrado por el dolor.
③ [prɒsˈtreɪt] VR: **to ~ o.s.** postrarse.

prostration [prɒsˈtreɪʃən] N postración *f*; (*fig*) postración *f*, abatimiento *m*.

prosy [ˈprəʊzɪ] ADJ prosaico, aburrido, monótono.

Prot. ABBR *of* **Protestant**.

protagonist [prəʊˈtægənɪst] N protagonista *mf*.

protean [ˈprəʊtɪən] ADJ proteico.

protect [prəˈtekt] VT proteger (*against, from* contra, de); amparar, resguardar.

protection [prə'tekʃən] [1] N protección f; (Comm) protección f, proteccionismo m; **the policy gives ~ against ...** la póliza protege contra ...; **to be under sb's ~** estar bajo la protección de uno. [2] ATTR: **he pays 200 dollars a week ~ money** paga 200 dólares de protección a la semana; **~ factor** factor m de protección; **~ racket** chantaje m ejercido contra un comerciante so pretexto de protegerle.

protectionism [prə'tekʃənızəm] N proteccionismo m.

protectionist [prə'tekʃənıst] [1] ADJ proteccionista. [2] N proteccionista mf.

protective [prə'tektıv] ADJ protector; (Comm) proteccionista; **~ coloration** colores mpl protectores; **~ cream** crema f protectora; **~ custody** detención f preventiva; **~ duty** impuesto m proteccionista; **~ mimicry** mimetismo m protector.

protectively [prə'tektıvlı] ADV protectoramente, de modo protector.

protectiveness [prə'tektıvnıs] N actitud f (or cualidad f etc) protectora.

protector [prə'tektər] N protector m, -ora f.

protectorate [prə'tektərıt] N protectorado m.

protectress [prə'tektrıs] N protectora f.

protégé ['prɒteʒeı] N protegido m, ahijado m.

protégée ['prɒteʒeı] N protegida f, ahijada f.

protein ['prəutiːn] [1] N proteína f. [2] ATTR: **~ content** contenido m proteínico.

pro tem ['prəu'tem] ADV ABBR of **pro tempore** = **for the time being** provisionalmente.

▼ **protest** [1] ['prəutest] N protesta f; **under ~** bajo protesta, haciendo objeciones; **I'll do it but under ~** lo haré pero que conste mi protesta; **to make a ~** hacer una protesta. [2] ['prəutest] ATTR: **~ demonstration** manifestación f de protesta; **~ march** marcha f de protesta; **~ movement** movimiento m de protesta, movimiento m contestatario; **~ song** canción f (de) protesta; **~ vote** voto m de protesta. [3] [prə'test] VT (a) (complain) protestar; **to ~ that ...** protestar de que ... (b) (affirm) afirmar, declarar (enérgicamente, solemnemente etc). ▼[4] [prə'test] VI protestar; **to ~ at** (or **against**) protestar de, protestar contra.

Protestant ['prɒtıstənt] [1] ADJ protestante. [2] N protestante mf.

Protestantism ['prɒtıstəntızəm] N protestantismo m.

protestation [ˌprɒtes'teıʃən] N (a) (complaint) protesta f. (b) (affirmation) afirmación f, declaración f (enérgica, solemne etc).

protester, protestor [prə'testər] N protestador m, -ora f; (on march, in demonstration etc) manifestante mf.

proto... ['prəutəu] PREF proto...

protocol ['prəutəkɒl] N protocolo m.

proton ['prəutɒn] N protón m.

protoplasm ['prəutəuplæzəm] N protoplasma m.

prototype ['prəutəutaıp] N prototipo m.

prototypical [ˌprəutə'tıpıkəl] ADJ prototípico.

protozoan [ˌprəutə'zəuən] ADJ protozoico.

protract [prə'trækt] VT prolongar; extender, alargar.

protracted [prə'træktıd] ADJ largo, prolongado.

protraction [prə'trækʃən] N prolongación f; extensión f, alargamiento m.

protractor [prə'træktər] N transportador m.

protrude [prə'truːd] [1] VT sacar fuera. [2] VI salir (fuera), sobresalir.

protruding [prə'truːdıŋ] ADJ saliente; eye, tooth saltón.

protrusion [prə'truːʒən] N saliente m, protuberancia f.

protuberance [prə'tjuːbərəns] N protuberancia f, saliente m.

protuberant [prə'tjuːbərənt] ADJ protuberante, saliente; prominente; eye, tooth saltón.

proud [praud] ADJ (a) (of person etc) orgulloso; (pej) soberbio, arrogante, altanero; **as ~ as a peacock** más orgulloso que un pavo real; **to be ~ of** estar orgulloso de, enorgullecerse de, preciarse de, ufanarse de; **to be ~ that ...** estar orgulloso de que ...; **to be ~ to +** infin tener el honor de + infin, estar orgulloso de + infin; **to do o.s. ~** permitirse toda clase de lujos; darse buena vida, vivir a cuerpo de rey; **to do sb ~*** hacer muchas fiestas a uno, regalar a uno, (with food) dar de comer opíparamente a uno. (b) (imposing) espléndido, imponente; (glorious) glorioso; **it is a ~ day for us** es un día glorioso para nosotros; **a ~ ship** un magnífico buque, un soberbio buque; **it is the town's ~est possession** es la posesión más importante de la ciudad. (c) **~ flesh** bezo m.

proudly ['praudlı] ADV (V ADJ) (a) orgullosamente; say etc con orgullo; arrogantemente. (b) de modo imponente.

prove [pruːv] [1] VT demostrar; probar; (verify) comprobar; (show) demostrar; (confirm) confirmar; will verificar; **this ~s that ...** esto demuestra que ...; **the exception ~s the rule** la excepción confirma la regla; **can you ~ it?** ¿tiene Vd prueba (de ello)?; **you can't ~ anything against me** Vd no puede demostrar nada contra mí; **it remains to be ~d whether ...** queda por demostrar si ...; **it all goes to ~ that ...** todo sirve para demostrar que ...; **he was ~d right in the end** al fin se demostró que tenía razón; **to ~ sb innocent** demostrar la inocencia de uno. [2] VI resultar; **if it ~s useful** si resulta útil; **the news ~d false** resultó que la noticia era falsa; **she ~d unequal to the job** ella resultó no estar al nivel del puesto; **if it ~s otherwise** si sale al contrario, si resulta que no es así. [3] VR: **to ~ o.s.** dar prueba de su valor, probar su valor.

proven ['pruːvən] ADJ probado; **of ~ quality** de calidad probada; **it's a ~ fact that ...** es un hecho comprobado que ...; **he's a ~ liar** es un mentiroso probado como tal; **the case was found not ~** el acusado fue absuelto por falta de pruebas; **there are ~ oil reserves** hay reservas de petróleo conocidas.

provenance ['prɒvınəns] N procedencia f, origen m, punto m de origen.

Provençal [ˌprɒvaːn'saːl] [1] ADJ provenzal. [2] N (a) provenzal mf. (b) (Ling) provenzal m.

Provence [prɒ'vaːns] N Provenza f.

provender ['prɒvındər] N forraje m; (hum) provisiones fpl, comida f.

proverb ['prɒvɜːb] N refrán m, proverbio m.

proverbial [prə'vɜːbıəl] ADJ proverbial.

proverbially [prə'vɜːbıəlı] ADV proverbialmente.

provide [prə'vaıd] [1] VT (a) (supply, furnish) suministrar, surtir; dar, proporcionar; **to ~ sb with sth** (supply) proveer a uno de algo, suministrar algo a uno; (give) proporcionar algo a uno; **the car is ~d with a heater** el coche está provisto de un calentador; **can you ~ a substitute?** ¿podéis encontrar un suplente?; **the government ~d half the money** el gobierno proporcionó la mitad del dinero; **the plant will ~ an output of ...** la fábrica permitirá una producción de ...; **it ~s shade for the cows** da sombra para las vacas. (b) **to ~ that ...** (stipulate) estipular que ..., disponer que ... [2] VI (a) **God will ~** Dios proveerá; **a husband who ~s well** un marido que mantiene debidamente a su familia. (b) **to ~ against** precaverse de, tomar precauciones contra; **to ~ for sb** mantener a uno, proporcionar medios de vida a uno, (with an allowance) señalar una pensión a uno; **they are well ~d for** tienen medios adecuados; **to ~ for one's dependants** asegurar el porvenir de su familia; **to ~ for every contingency** prevenir cualquier posibilidad; **we have ~d for that** eso lo hemos previsto. (c) **the treaty ~s for ...** el tratado estipula ...; **as ~d for in the 1990 contract** de acuerdo con lo estipulado en el contrato de 1990. [3] VR: **to ~ o.s. with sth** proveerse de algo.

provided [prə'vaıdıd] CONJ: **~, ~ that** con tal que + subj, siempre que + subj; a condición de que + subj.

providence ['prɒvıdəns] N (all senses) providencia f; **P~** Divina Providencia f.

provident ['prɒvıdənt] ADJ providente, previsor, próvido; **~ fund** fondo m de previsión; **~ society** (Brit) sociedad f de socorro mutuo, mutualidad f.

providential [ˌprɒvı'denʃəl] ADJ providencial; (lucky) afortunado, milagroso.

providentially [ˌprɒvı'denʃəlı] ADV providencialmente; afortunadamente, milagrosamente.

providently ['prɒvıdəntlı] ADV próvidamente.

provider [prə'vaıdər] N proveedor m, -ora f.

providing [prə'vaıdıŋ] CONJ = **provided.**

province ['prɒvıns] N (a) provincia f; **they live in the ~s** viven en provincia. (b) (fig: field) esfera f; especialidad f; (jurisdiction etc) competencia f; **it's not within my ~** no es de mi competencia. (c) (Eccl) arzobispado m.

provincial [prə'vınʃəl] [1] ADJ provincial, de provincia; (pej) provinciano. [2] N provinciano m, -a f.

provincialism [prə'vınʃəlızəm] N provincialismo m.

proving ground ['pruːvıŋˌgraund] N terreno m de prueba.

provision [prə'vıʒən] [1] N (a) (gen) provisión f; (supply) provisión f, suministro m; abastecimiento m; **the ~ of new capital** la provisión de nuevos capitales; **the ~ of new housing** la provisión de nuevas viviendas; **to make ~ for** prevenir, prever; **to make ~ for one's family** asegurar el porvenir de su familia. (b) **~s** (food) provisiones fpl, comestibles mpl, víveres mpl. (c) (stipulation) estipulación f, disposición f; **according to the ~s of the treaty** de acuerdo con lo estipulado en el tratado; **there is no ~ to the contrary** no hay estipulación que lo prohíba; **it comes within the ~s of this law** está comprendido dentro de lo estipulado por esta ley. [2] VT aprovisionar, abastecer.

provisional [prə'vɪʒənl] [1] ADJ provisional; interino; **~ (driving) licence** (*Brit*) carnet *m* de conducir provisional; *ver también* DRIVING LICENCE/DRIVER'S LICENSE .
  [2] N = **~ (driving) licence**.
  [3] NPL: **the P~s** los Provisionales (*tendencia activista del IRA*).

provisionally [prə'vɪʒnəlɪ] ADV provisionalmente; con carácter provisional; interinamente.

proviso [prə'vaɪzəʊ] N condición *f*, estipulación *f*; salvedad *f*; **with the ~ that ...** con la condición de que + *subj*.

Provo* ['prəʊvəʊ] N = **provisional 2**.

provocation [,prɒvə'keɪʃən] N provocación *f*; **to act under ~** obrar bajo provocación; **to suffer great ~** sufrir una gran provocación.

provocative [prə'vɒkətɪv] ADJ *remark etc* provocador, provocativo; *title* provocador; *book etc* sugestivo, que invita a pensar; *person* seductor; **now you're trying to be ~** ahora sí que intentas provocarme.

provocatively [prə'vɒkətɪvlɪ] ADV de modo provocador, de modo provocativo.

provoke [prə'vəʊk] VT **(a)** (*cause*) provocar, causar, producir, motivar; facilitar; (*rouse, move*) provocar, incitar, mover (*to* a); **it ~d us to action** nos incitó a obrar; **it ~d the town to revolt** incitó la ciudad a sublevarse.
  (b) (*anger*) provocar; irritar; **he is easily ~d** se irrita por cualquier cosa.

provoking [prə'vəʊkɪŋ] ADJ provocativo; irritante, fastidioso; **how very ~!** ¡qué lata!*

provost ['prɒvəst] [1] N (*Univ*) rector *m*, -ora *f*; director *m*, -ora *f*; (*Scot*) alcalde *m*, -esa *f*.
  [2] ATTR: **~ marshal** capitán *m* preboste.

prow [praʊ] N proa *f*.

prowess ['praʊɪs] N (*skill*) destreza *f*, habilidad *f*; (*courage*) valor *m*.

prowl [praʊl] [1] N ronda *f* (en busca de presa, botín *etc*); **to be on the ~** merodear, rondar.
  [2] ATTR: **~ car** (*US*) coche-patrulla *m*.
  [3] VT: **to ~ the streets** rondar las calles, vagar por las calles.
  [4] VI rondar (en busca de presa, botín *etc*), merodear; **he ~s round the house at night** (*outside*) ronda la casa de noche, (*inside*) se pasea por la casa de noche.

prowler ['praʊləʳ] N rondador *m*, hombre *m* que ronda en busca de presa (*or mujeres etc*); merodeador *m*; ladrón *m*.

prox. ABBR *of* **proximo** próximo futuro, pr. fr.

proximity [prɒk'sɪmɪtɪ] N proximidad *f*; **in ~ to** cerca de, junto a.

proximo ['prɒksɪməʊ] ADV (*Comm*) del mes próximo; **before the 7th ~** antes del 7 del mes que viene.

proxy ['prɒksɪ] [1] N (*power*) poder *m*, procuración *f*; (*person*) apoderado *m*, -a *f*; sustituto *m*, -a *f*; **by ~** por poder, por poderes; **to be married by ~** casarse por poderes.
  [2] ATTR: **~ vote** voto *m* por poderes.

Prozac ['prəʊzæk] ® N Prozac ® *m*.

PRP N (*Brit*) **(a)** ABBR *of* **performance-related pay** *sistema salarial que incluye un plus de productividad*. **(b)** ABBR *of* **profit-related pay** *sistema salarial en el que los empleados reciben un porcentaje de los beneficios de la empresa*.

PRS N ABBR *of* **Performing Rights Society** sociedad de derechos de autor, ≃ SGAE *f*.

prude [pruːd] N remilgado *m*, -a *f*, mojigato *m*, -a *f*, gazmoño *m*, -a *f*.

prudence ['pruːdəns] N prudencia *f*.

prudent ['pruːdənt] ADJ prudente.

prudential [pru(ː)'denʃəl] ADJ prudencial.

prudently ['pruːdəntlɪ] ADV prudentemente, con prudencia.

prudery ['pruːdərɪ] N remilgo *m*, mojigatería *f*, gazmoñería *f*.

prudish ['pruːdɪʃ] ADJ remilgado, mojigato, gazmoño.

prudishness ['pruːdɪʃnɪs] N = **prudery**.

prune¹ [pruːn] N **(a)** (*fruit*) ciruela *f* pasa. **(b)** (*) bobo *m*, -a *f*, majadero *m*, -a *f*.

prune² [pruːn] VT podar; (*fig*) reducir, recortar.
◆ **prune away** VT *branches* podar; (*fig*) *words* cortar.

pruning ['pruːnɪŋ] N poda *f*.

pruning-hook ['pruːnɪŋhʊk] N, **pruning-knife** ['pruːnɪŋnaɪf] N, PL **pruning-knives** ['pruːnɪŋnaɪvz], **pruning-shears** ['pruːnɪŋʃɪəz] NPL podadera *f*.

prurience ['prʊərɪəns] N salacidad *f*, lascivia *f*.

prurient ['prʊərɪənt] ADJ salaz, lascivo.

Prussia ['prʌʃə] N Prusia *f*.

Prussian ['prʌʃən] [1] ADJ prusiano; **~ blue** azul *m* de Prusia.
  [2] N prusiano *m*, -a *f*.

prussic ['prʌsɪk] ADJ: **~ acid** ácido *m* prúsico.

pry¹ [praɪ] VI (*watch*) fisgonear, curiosear; (*meddle*) entrometerse; **to ~ into sb's affairs** entrometerse en lo ajeno; **to ~ into sb's secrets** ir curioseando los secretos de uno.

pry² [praɪ] VT (*US*) = **prise**.

prying ['praɪɪŋ] ADJ fisgón, curioso; entrometido.

PS N **(a)** ABBR *of* **postscript** posdata *f*, P.D. **(b)** (*Parl*) ABBR *of* **Parliamen-** tary Secretary.

psalm [sɑːm] N salmo *m*.

psalmist ['sɑːmɪst] N salmista *m*.

psalmody ['sælmədɪ] N salmodia *f*.

psalter ['sɔːltəʳ] N salterio *m*.

PSAT N (*US*) ABBR *of* **Preliminary Scholastic Aptitude Test**.

PSBR N (*Econ*) ABBR *of* **public sector borrowing requirement** necesidades *fpl* de endeudamiento del sector público.

psephologist [se'fɒlədʒɪst] N psefólogo *m*, -a *f*.

psephology [se'fɒlədʒɪ] N psefología *f*.

pseud* [sjuːd] N (*Brit*) farsante* *mf*.

pseudo* ['sjuːdəʊ] ADJ falso, fraudulento; *person* fingido; (*of person's character*) artificial, afectado.

pseudo... ['sjuːdəʊ] PREF seudo...; falso, fingido; **a ~-artist** un seudo artista.

pseudohistory [,sjuːdəʊ'hɪstərɪ] N seudohistoria *f*.

pseudonym ['sjuːdənɪm] N seudónimo *m*.

pseudonymous [sjuː'dɒnɪməs] ADJ seudónimo.

pshaw [pʃɔː] INTERJ ¡bah!

psi N ABBR *of* **pounds per square inch** ≃ kg/cm².

psittacosis [,psɪtə'kəʊsɪs] N psitacosis *f*.

psoriasis [sə'raɪəsɪs] N soriasis *f*.

psst [pst] EXCL ¡oye!, ¡eh!

PST (*US*) ABBR *of* **Pacific Standard Time**.

PSV N ABBR *of* **public service vehicle** vehículo *m* de servicio público.

psych* [saɪk] (ABBR *of* **psychoanalyse**) VT **(a)** (*guess, anticipate*) *reactions etc* adivinar, anticipar. **(b)** (*make uneasy: also* **to ~ out**) poner nervioso; **that doesn't ~ me** no me da ni frío ni calor, me tiene sin cuidado. **(c)** (*prepare psychologically: also* **to ~ up**) mentalizar; **to get o.s. ~ed up for sth** mentalizarse para algo; **he was all ~ed up to start, when ...** ya estaba mentalizado para empezar, cuando ...
◆ **psych out*** [1] VT (*unhinge*) desquiciar.
  [2] VI **(a)** desquiciarse. **(b)** (*make uneasy*) = **psych (b)**.
◆ **psych up*** VT *V* **psych (c)**.

psych... [saɪk] PREF psic..., psiqu..., sic..., siqu...

Psyche ['saɪkɪ] NF Psique.

psyche ['saɪkɪ] N psique *f*.

psychedelic [,saɪkə'delɪk] ADJ psiquedélico, psicodélico.

psychiatric [,saɪkɪ'ætrɪk] ADJ psiquiátrico.

psychiatrist [saɪ'kaɪətrɪst] N psiquiatra *mf*.

psychiatry [saɪ'kaɪətrɪ] N psiquiatría *f*.

psychic(al) ['saɪkɪk(əl)] ADJ psíquico; **I'm not psychic*** no soy psicológico, no tengo psicología; **you must be ~*** tienes que ser psicológico.

psycho* ['saɪkəʊ] N caso *m* psicológico, persona *f* anormal.

psycho... ['saɪkəʊ] PREF psico...

psychoactive [,saɪkəʊ'æktɪv] ADJ: **~ drug** droga *f* psicoactiva.

psychoanalyse, (*US*) **psychoanalyze** [,saɪkəʊ'ænəlaɪz] VT psicoanalizar.

psychoanalysis [,saɪkəʊə'næ lɪsɪs] N psicoanálisis *m*.

psychoanalyst [,saɪkəʊ'ænəlɪst] N psicoanalista *mf*.

psychoanalytic(al) [,saɪkəʊ,ænə'lɪtɪk(əl)] ADJ psicoanalítico.

psychobabble* ['saɪkəʊ,bæbl] N verborrea *f*, jerga *f* de psicólogos.

psychodrama ['saɪkəʊ,drɑːmə] N psicodrama *m*.

psychodynamics [,saɪkəʊdaɪ'næmɪks] N SING psicodinámica *f*.

psychokinesis [,saɪkəʊkɪ'niːsɪs] N psicoquinesis *f*.

psychokinetic [,saɪkəʊkɪ'netɪk] ADJ psicoquinético.

psycholinguistic [,saɪkəʊlɪŋ'gwɪstɪk] ADJ psicolingüístico.

psycholinguistics [,saɪkəʊlɪŋ'gwɪstɪks] N psicolingüística *f*.

psychological [,saɪkə'lɒdʒɪkəl] ADJ psicológico; **~ block** bloqueo *m* psicológico; **~ make-up** perfil *m* psicológico; **~ moment** momento *m* psicológico; **~ profile** perfil *m* psicológico; **~ profiling** trazado *m* de perfil psicológio; **~ warfare** guerra *f* psicológica.

psychologically [,saɪkə'lɒdʒɪkəlɪ] ADV psicológicamente.

psychologist [saɪ'kɒlədʒɪst] N psicólogo *m*, -a *f*.

psychology [saɪ'kɒlədʒɪ] N psicología *f*.

psychometric ['saɪkəʊ'metrɪk] [1] ADJ psicométrico.
  [2] N: **~s** psicometría *f*.

psychometry [saɪ'kɒmɪtrɪ] N psicometría *f*.

psychomotor ['saɪkəʊ'məʊtəʳ] ADJ psicomotor.

psychoneurosis ['saɪkəʊnjʊə'rəʊsɪs] N, PL **psychoneuroses** ['saɪkəʊnjʊə'rəʊsiːz] psiconeurosis *f*.

psychopath ['saɪkəʊpæθ] N psicópata *mf*.

psychopathic [,saɪkəʊ'pæθɪk] ADJ psicopático.

psychopathology ['saɪkəʊpə'θɒlədʒɪ] N psicopatología *f*.

psychosexual [,saɪkəʊ'seksjʊəl] ADJ psicosexual.

psychosis [saɪ'kəʊsɪs] N psicosis *f*.

psychosocial ['saɪkəʊ'səʊʃəl] ADJ psicosocial.

psychosociological ['saɪkəʊ,səʊsɪə'lɒdʒɪkəl] ADJ psicosociológico.

psychosomatic ['saɪkəʊsəʊ'mætɪk] ADJ psicosomático.

psychosurgery [,saɪkəʊ'sɜːdʒərɪ] N psicocirugía *f*.

psychotherapist [,saɪkəʊ'θerəpɪst] N psicoterapeuta *mf*.

psychotherapy [ˈsaɪkəʊˈθerəpɪ] N psicoterapia f.
psychotic [saɪˈkɒtɪk] **1** ADJ psicótico. **2** N psicótico m, -a f.
psychotropic [ˌsaɪkəʊˈtrɒpɪk] ADJ psicotrópico.
PT N ABBR of **physical training** gimnasia f, cultura f física.
Pt (Geog) ABBR of **Point** Punta f, Pta.
pt **(a)** ABBR of **part** parte f. **(b)** ABBR of **pint(s)**. **(c)** ABBR of **point** punto m. **(d)** (Comm) ABBR of **payment** pago m.
P/T ABBR of **part-time**.
PTA N ABBR of **Parent-Teacher Association** ≃ Asociación f de Padres de Alumnos, APA f.
ptarmigan [ˈtɑːmɪgən] N perdiz f blanca, perdiz f nival.
Pte ABBR of **Private** soldado m raso.
pterodactyl [ˌterəʊˈdæktɪl] N pterodáctilo m.
PTO ABBR of **please turn over** véase al dorso, sigue.
Ptolemaic [ˌtɒləˈmeɪɪk] ADJ: ~ **system** sistema m de Tolomeo, sistema m tolemaico.
Ptolemy [ˈtɒləmɪ] NM Tolomeo.
ptomaine [ˈtəʊmeɪn] N (p)tomaína f; ~ **poisoning** envenenamiento m (p)tomaínico.
PTV N (US) ABBR of **pay television, public television**.
pub [pʌb] N (Brit) taberna f, tasca f, bar m.
pub-crawl [ˈpʌbkrɔːl] (Brit) **1** N chateo* m (de tasca* en tasca); **to go on a ~ = 2**.
 2 VI ir de chateo* (or parranda* LAm), copear*, alternar*.
puberty [ˈpjuːbətɪ] N pubertad f.
pubes: [ˈpjuːbiːz] NPL vello m púbico.
pubescence [pjuːˈbesəns] N pubescencia f.
pubescent [pjuːˈbesənt] ADJ pubescente.
pubic [ˈpjuːbɪk] ADJ púbico; ~ **hair** vello m púbico.
pubis [ˈpjuːbɪs] N pubis m.
public [ˈpʌblɪk] **1** ADJ público; ~ **access television** (US) televisión abierta al público; ~ **address system** sistema m de altavoces, sistema m amplificador; ~ **bar** bar m; ~ **body** corporación f estatal; ~ **company** compañía f pública; ~ **convenience** (Brit) aseos mpl públicos, sanitarios mpl (LAm); ~ **debt** deuda f pública; ~ **defender** (US) abogado m, -a f de oficio; ~ **enemy** enemigo m público; ~ **enemy number one** enemigo m público número uno; ~ **enterprise** (firm) empresa f pública, (endeavour) iniciativa f pública; ~ **expenditure** gastos mpl públicos; ~ **health** salud f pública, sanidad f pública; ~ **holiday** fiesta f oficial; ~ **house** (Brit) taberna f; ~ **housing** (US) viviendas fpl protegidas; ~ **issue** (St Ex) emisión f pública; ~ **lavatory** urinarios mpl; ~ **library** biblioteca f pública; ~ **life** vida f pública; ~ **limited company** sociedad f anónima; ~ **nuisance** (Jur) perjuicio m público, daño m público; **he's a ~ nuisance** perjudica al bienestar público; ~ **opinion** opinión f pública; ~ **ownership** nacionalización f, propiedad f pública; ~ **property** (land etc) dominio m público; (fig: private life) dominio m público; **he couldn't handle being ~ property** no podía soportar ser un personaje público; ~ **prosecutor** (esp Brit) fiscal mf; **P~ Records Office** (Brit) Archivo m Nacional; ~ **relations** relaciones fpl públicas; ~ **relations adviser** asesor m, -ora f de imagen; ~ **relations officer** encargado m, -a f de relaciones públicas, public relations* mf; ~ **school** (Brit: approx) internado m privado, (Scot, US) escuela f pública; ~ **sector** sector m público; ~ **servant** funcionario mf; ~ **service vehicle** vehículo m de servicio público; ~ **speaking** oratoria f; ~ **spending** gastos mpl públicos; ~ **spirit** civismo m; ~ **transport, ~ transportation** (US) transportes mpl públicos; ~ **utilities** empresas fpl del servicio público; ~ **utility** servicio m público; ~ **works** obras fpl públicas; **it's too ~ here** aquí la gente nos mira, aquí estamos a la vista de todos; **to be in the ~ eye** estar muy a la vista; **to go ~** (Comm) hacerse cotizar en la Bolsa, ofrecer acciones a la venta pública; (*: reveal) hablar en público, revelar secretos al público; **to make a matter ~** publicar un asunto, hacer público un asunto.
 2 N público m; **in ~** en público; **the general ~** el gran público; **the sporting ~** los aficionados al deporte; **the great British ~** (hum) los ingleses, los súbditos de su Majestad.

┌─ **PUBLIC ACCESS TELEVISION** ─┐

En Estados Unidos, el término Public Access Television *hace referencia a una serie de cadenas no comerciales de televisión por cable que emiten programas de ámbito local o programas dedicados a organizaciones humanitarias sin ánimo de lucro. Entre sus emisiones se incluyen charlas sobre actividades escolares, programas sobre aficiones diversas e incluso discursos de organizaciones racistas. Estas emisiones de acceso público se crearon para dar cabida a temas de interés local e impedir que los canales por cable estuvieran dominados por unos cuantos privilegiados. En virtud de la* Ley de Emisiones por Cable, *el* Cable Act *de 1984, cualquier población en que haya algún canal por cable puede obligar a los propietarios de dicho canal a que instalen una cadena adicional de acceso público y provean el equipo, el estudio, los medios técnicos y el personal necesarios para la emisión.*

publican [ˈpʌblɪkən] N **(a)** (Brit) tabernero m. **(b)** (Bible) publicano m.
publication [ˌpʌblɪˈkeɪʃən] **1** N publicación f.
 2 ATTR: ~ **date** fecha f de publicación; ~ **details** detalles mpl de publicación.
publicist [ˈpʌblɪsɪst] N publicista mf.
publicity [pʌbˈlɪsɪtɪ] **1** N publicidad f.
 2 ATTR: ~ **agent** agente mf de publicidad; ~ **campaign** campaña f publicitaria; ~ **manager** director m, -ora f de publicidad; **~-shy** reacio a la publicidad; ~ **stunt** truco m publicitario.
publicize [ˈpʌblɪsaɪz] VT publicar, dar publicidad a, anunciar.
publicly [ˈpʌblɪklɪ] ADV públicamente, en público.
public-spirited [ˈpʌblɪkˈspɪrɪtɪd] ADJ de buen ciudadano; person lleno de civismo, consciente del bien público.
publish [ˈpʌblɪʃ] VT publicar; banns correr.
publisher [ˈpʌblɪʃəʳ] N editor m, -ora f.
publishing [ˈpʌblɪʃɪŋ] **1** N publicación f (de libros); **he's in ~** publica libros, está con una casa editorial.
 2 ATTR: ~ **company, ~ house** casa f editorial.
puce [pjuːs] **1** N color m castaño rojizo.
 2 ADJ de color castaño rojizo; (with shame etc) colorado.
puck¹ [pʌk] N (imp) duende m (malicioso).
puck² [pʌk] N (Sport) puck m, disco m.
pucker [ˈpʌkəʳ] **1** N arruga f; (Sew) frunce m, fruncido m; (accidentally formed) buche m.
 2 VT (also **to ~ up**) arrugar; (brow, Sew) fruncir.
 3 VI (also **to ~ up**) arrugarse, formar buches.
puckish [ˈpʌkɪʃ] ADJ malicioso, juguetón.
pud* [pʊd] N = **pudding**.
pudding [ˈpʊdɪŋ] N púding m; (as course) postre m (dulce).
pudding-basin [ˈpʊdɪŋˌbeɪsn] N cuenco m.
pudding-rice [ˈpʊdɪŋˌraɪs] N arroz m redondo.
puddingstone [ˈpʊdɪŋstəʊn] N pudinga f.
puddle [ˈpʌdl] **1** N charco m.
 2 VT (Tech) pudelar.
pudenda [puːˈdendə] NPL partes fpl pudendas.
pudgy [ˈpʌdʒɪ] ADJ = **podgy**.
puerile [ˈpjʊəraɪl] ADJ pueril.
puerility [pjʊəˈrɪlɪtɪ] N puerilidad f.
puerperal [pjʊ(ː)ˈɜːpərəl] ADJ puerperal; ~ **fever** fiebre f puerperal; ~ **psychosis** psicosis f puerperal.
Puerto Rican [ˈpwɜːtəʊˈriːkən] **1** ADJ puertorriqueño.
 2 N puertorriqueño m, -a f.
Puerto Rico [ˈpwɜːtəʊˈriːkəʊ] N Puerto m Rico.
puff [pʌf] **1** N **(a)** (of air) soplo m, (of wind) soplo m, racha f; (of smoke) humareda f, (at cigarette, pipe) chupada f, fumada f; (from mouth) bocanada f; (sound: of breathing, of engine) resoplido m, resuello m, bufido m.
 (b) (powder ~) borla f; (Culin: cream ~) petisú m, pastelillo m de crema.
 (c) (advert) bombo m.
 (d) (‡: drug) canabis m.
 2 VT (blow) soplar; pipe etc chupar; **to ~ smoke in sb's face** echar humo a la cara de uno.
 3 VI (blow) soplar; (~ and blow) jadear, resollar, acezar; **to ~ (away) at one's pipe** chupar su pipa.
◆ **puff along** VI (train) avanzar bufando; (person) correr (etc) jadeando.
◆ **puff away** VI V **puff 3**.
◆ **puff out 1** VT **(a)** smoke etc echar, arrojar, despedir. **(b)** cheeks, chest, sails hinchar, inflar (LAm); feathers erizar.
 2 VI: **the train ~ed out of the station** el tren salió bufando, el tren salió echando humo.
◆ **puff up 1** VT **(a)** = **puff out (b)**. **(b)** tyre etc inflar, hinchar. **(c)** (fig*) dar bombo a.
 2 VR: **to ~ o.s. up** darse bombo, engreírse.
puff-adder [ˈpʌfˌædəʳ] N víbora f puff.
puffball [ˈpʌfbɔːl] N bejín m, pedo m de lobo.
puffed [pʌft] ADJ eye hinchado (also ~ **up**); **to be ~*** (out of breath) estar sin aliento, estar acezando; **to be ~ up** (with pride) estar engreído.
puffer* [ˈpʌfəʳ] N locomotora f.
puffin [ˈpʌfɪn] N frailecillo m.
puffiness [ˈpʌfɪnɪs] N hinchazón f.
puff-pastry [ˈpʌfˈpeɪstrɪ] N, (US) **puff paste** [ˈpʌfˈpeɪst] N hojaldre m.
puff sleeves [ˌpʌfˈsliːvz] NPL mangas fpl filipinas.
puffy [ˈpʌfɪ] ADJ eye etc hinchado.
pug [pʌg] N doguillo m; ~ **nose** nariz f chata.
pugilism [ˈpjuːdʒɪlɪzəm] N pugilato m, pugilismo m.
pugilist [ˈpjuːdʒɪlɪst] N púgil m, pugilista m.
pugnacious [pʌgˈneɪʃəs] ADJ belicoso, agresivo, pugnaz.
pugnaciously [pʌgˈneɪʃəslɪ] ADV con pugnacidad, agresivamente.
pugnacity [pʌgˈnæsɪtɪ] N pugnacidad f, belicosidad f, agresividad f, pugnacidad f.
pug-nosed [ˈpʌgˈnəʊzd] ADJ chato, braco.

puke: [pjuːk] **1** N **(a)** (*matter*) vómito *m*. **(b) to have a ~** = **2**.
2 VI cambiar la peseta*, vomitar; **it makes me ~** me da asco.
pukka* ['pʌkə] ADJ (*real*) auténtico, genuino; (*posh*) esnob, elegante, lujoso.
pulchritude ['pʌlkrɪtjuːd] N (*hum*) belleza *f*.
pulchritudinous [ˌpʌlkrɪ'tjuːdɪnəs] ADJ (*hum*) bello.

PULITZER
---

*ℹ️ Los premios **Pulitzer** se conceden anualmente en Estados Unidos a trabajos periodísticos, literarios y musicales excepcionales, y gozan de un enorme prestigio. En periodismo se conceden trece premios, entre ellos los destinados al periodismo de investigación y crítica. En literatura existen seis categorías, entre las que destacan las de novela, poesía y teatro. Los premios llevan el nombre del editor periodístico norteamericano Joseph Pulitzer (1847-1911), quien inicialmente aportó el dinero de los premios.*

pull [pʊl] **1** N **(a)** (*tug*) tirón *m*, jalón *m* (*LAm*), jalada *f* (*Mex*); estirón *m*; (*with oar etc*) golpe *m*; (*of a magnet, also fig*) atracción *f*, fuerza *f* atractiva; (*of current*) fuerza *f*, ímpetu *m*; **the ~ of the south** la atracción del Sur, lo atractivo del Sur; **it was a long ~** fue mucho camino; **we had a long ~ up the hill** nos costó mucho trabajo subir la cuesta; **give the rope a ~** tira de la cuerda; **suddenly it gave a ~** de repente dio un tirón.
(b) (*advantage*) ventaja *f*; (*influence*) enchufe* *m*; palanca* *f* (*LAm*), influencia *f*, poder *m*; **they have a ~ over us now** ahora nos llevan ventaja; **he has a slight ~** tiene una pequeña ventaja; **he has ~ in the right places** tiene influencia donde hace falta.
(c) (*at one's pipe*) chupada *f*; (*drink*) trago *m*; **he took a ~ at his pipe** chupó la pipa; **he took a ~ from the bottle** dio un tiento a la botella.
(d) (*handle of drawer etc*) tirador *m*; (*of bell*) cuerda *f*.
(e) (*Typ*) primeras pruebas *fpl*.
2 VT **(a)** (*tug at*) bell rope, hair etc tirar de, jalar (*LAm*); *trigger* apretar; *oar* tirar de; *boat* remar; (*Naut*) *rope* halar, jalar; *weeds* arrancar; *muscle* torcerse, dislocarse; **to ~ a gun on sb** sacar una pistola para amenazar a uno; **his ideas ~ed me the same way** sus ideas me llevaron por el mismo camino; **~ the other one!:** ¡cuéntaselo a tu abuela*!
(b) (*extract, take out*) sacar; *beer* servir.
(c) (*draw along*) tirar, arrastrar, remolcar; **the engine ~s 6 coaches** la locomotora arrastra 6 vagones; **~ your chair over** acerca la silla.
(d) (*Typ*) proof imprimir.
(e) *ball* (*at golf, etc*) golpear oblicuamente (a la izquierda).
(f) (*): **he knows how to ~ the birds** sabe ligar con las chicas; **this will really ~ the punters** esto seguramente atraerá clientela.
(g) to ~ a fast one (*or* **a trick**) **on sb** jugar una mala pasada a uno, embaucar a uno.
3 VI **(a)** tirar (*at* de); dar un tirón; **to ~ at a rope** tirar de una cuerda; **the steering ~s to the right** la dirección tira a la derecha.
(b) (*vehicle*) ir; (*oarsmen etc*) remar; **we ~ed for the shore** remamos hacia la orilla; **he ~ed sharply to one side to avoid the lorry** torció bruscamente a un lado para no chocar con el camión; **the car ~ed slowly up the hill** el coche subía despacio la cuesta; **it ~ed to a stop** se paró, se detuvo.
(c) to ~ at one's pipe dar chupadas a la pipa; **to ~ at a bottle** dar un tiento a una botella.
◆ **pull about** VT manosear, estropear.
◆ **pull ahead** VI (*in race etc*) tomar la delantera; (*in poll, contest*) ponerse por delante; **to pull ahead of sb/sth** (*in race etc*) tomarle la delantera a uno/algo; (*in poll, contest*) ponerse por delante de uno/algo.
◆ **pull along** **1** VT arrastrar.
2 VR: **to ~ o.s. along** arrastrarse.
◆ **pull apart** **1** VT **(a)** (*pull to pieces*) romper; partir en dos; (*take to pieces*) desmontar; (*criticize*) criticar duramente.
(b) (*separate*) separar; despegar, desunir.
2 VI: **they ~ apart easily** se separan fácilmente.
◆ **pull away** **1** VT arrancar (*from* a), quitar arrancando (*from* a).
2 VI (*vehicle*) adelantarse (*from* a); **boat A ~ed away from B** el bote A dejaba atrás a B.
(b) to ~ away at the oars seguir remando; tirar (enérgicamente) de los remos.
(c) to ~ away from sb apartarse bruscamente de uno.
◆ **pull back** **1** VT **(a)** (*withdraw*) retirar; (*hold back*) retener, tirar hacia atrás.
(b) *lever etc* tirar hacia sí; *curtains* descorrer.
(b) (*Sport*) **to ~ one back** remontar un gol.
2 VI (*withdraw*) retirarse; (*refrain*) contenerse, (*pej*) rajarse.
◆ **pull down** VT **(a)** (*lower*) bajar; tirar hacia abajo; *price etc* rebajar; *person* hacer caer, tumbar; **he ~ed his hat down** se caló el sombrero, se encasquetó el sombrero.
(b) (*demolish*) derribar, demoler; *government* derribar.
(c) (*weaken*) debilitar; **the mark in chemistry ~s her down** la nota

de química es la razón de que salga mal.
(d) (*US**: *earn*) ganar.
◆ **pull in** **1** VT **(a)** tirar hacia sí; *net* recoger; *rope* cobrar.
(b) *suspect* detener.
(c) *horse* enfrenar.
(d) (*: *earn*) ganar.
(e) (*: *attract*) **the film is ~ing them in** la película atrae un público numeroso, la película es muy popular; **this will ~ them in** esto les hará venir en masa.
2 VI (*Aut*) parar (junto a la acera); (*Rail*) llegar (a la estación).
3 VR: **to ~ o.s. in** apretarse el cinturón.
◆ **pull off** **1** VT **(a)** (*remove*) arrancar, separar; quitar de un tirón; *clothes* quitarse (de prisa); **the buses were ~ed off the road at once** en seguida los autobuses dejaron de circular.
(b) *plan etc* llevar a cabo; *deal* cerrar, concluir con éxito (algo inesperadamente); *game* ganar (algo inesperadamente); **to ~ it off** lograrlo, llevarlo a cabo, vencer.
2 VI (*Aut*) **we ~ed off (the road) into a layby** salimos de la carretera y paramos en un apartadero.
◆ **pull on** **1** VT *gloves etc* ponerse (de prisa).
2 VI tirar de.
◆ **pull out** **1** VT **(a)** (*take out*) sacar; *tooth* sacar, extraer; *lever etc* tirar hacia fuera; **to ~ sb out of a hole** tirar a uno de un hoyo a estirones; **to ~ sb out of a river** sacar a uno de un río.
(b) (*stretch*) estirar, extender.
(c) (*withdraw*) retirar; **everybody was ~ed out on strike** todos fueron llamados a la huelga.
2 VI **(a)** (*leave*) irse, marcharse (*from* de); (*Mil*) retirarse (*from* de); **we're ~ing out** nos marchamos ya.
(b) (*Aut*) salirse; (*Rail*) salir (de la estación); **he ~ed out and disappeared into the traffic** arrancó y se perdió en el tráfico; **the red car ~ed out from behind that black one** el coche rojo se salió de detrás de aquel negro.
(c) it ~s out easily (*drawer etc*) sale fácilmente.
◆ **pull over** **1** VT **(a)** (*move*) acercar tirando.
(b) (*topple*) derribar; volcar.
2 VI (*Aut*) hacerse a un lado, desviarse hacia un lado.
◆ **pull round** **1** VT: **to ~ sb round** ayudar a uno a reponerse.
2 VI reponerse.
◆ **pull through** **1** VT: **to ~ sb through** sacar a uno de un apuro (*or* de una enfermedad *etc*).
2 VI salir de un apuro; (*Med*) reponerse, recobrar la salud.
◆ **pull together** **1** VT: **this essay needs ~ing together** hay que reorganizar este ensayo, este ensayo conviene remodelarlo; **he has ~ed the team together** gracias a él los jugadores han recuperado su espíritu de equipo.
2 VI (*fig*) trabajar con un propósito común, trabajar (*etc*) con espíritu de equipo.
3 VR: **to ~ o.s. together** sobreponerse, serenarse, recobrar la calma; **~ yourself together!** ¡cálmate!, ¡anímate!
◆ **pull up** **1** VT **(a)** (*raise*) alzar, levantar; tirar hacia arriba; *socks etc* alzar; *chair* acercar.
(b) *plant* arrancar, desarraigar.
(c) (*strengthen*) fortalecer; **his mark in French has ~ed him up** la nota de francés es la razón de que salga bien; **it has ~ed the pound up** ha fortalecido la libra.
(d) (*halt*) parar; *horse* refrenar.
(e) (*scold*) reprender.
2 VI **(a)** (*stop*) pararse, detenerse; (*Aut*) parar(se); (*restrain o.s.*) contenerse; (*stop talking etc*) interrumpirse.
(b) (*improve position*) mejorar, mejorar su posición.
pull-back ['pʊlbæk] N (*Mil*) retirada *f*.
pull-down ['pʊl,daʊn] ADJ: **~ menu** menú *m* desplegable.
pullet ['pʊlɪt] N polla *f*, pollita *f*.
pulley ['pʊlɪ] N polea *f*.
pull-in ['pʊl,ɪn] N (*Brit Aut*: *lay-by*) apartadero *m*; (*for food*) café *m* de carretera, restaurante *m* de carretera.
Pullman car ['pʊlmən,kɑːr] N coche *m* Pullman, (*US*) coche-cama *m*.
pull-off ['pʊlɒf] N (*US Aut*) apartadero *m*.
pull-out ['pʊlaʊt] **1** N (*of magazine*) separable *m*, suplemento *m*.
2 ATTR separable.
pullover ['pʊləʊvə^r] N pullover *m*, pull *m*.
pull-ring ['pʊlrɪŋ] N, **pull-tab** ['pʊltæb] N anilla *f*.
pullulate ['pʌljʊleɪt] VI pulular.
pull-up ['pʊlʌp] N **(a)** (*Brit*) = **pull-in**. **(b)** (*US*) = **press-up**.
pulmonary ['pʌlmənərɪ] ADJ pulmonar.
pulp [pʌlp] **1** N pulpa *f*; (*Bot*) pulpa *f*, carne *f*; (*paper ~, wood~*) pasta *f*; (*also* **~ magazines** *etc*) prensa *f* amarilla; **~ literature** literatura *f* para tirar, literatura *f* de bajísima calidad; **a leg crushed to ~** una pierna hecha trizas; **to beat sb to a ~** dar a uno una tremenda paliza; **to reduce sth to ~** hacer algo pulpa, reducir algo a pulpa.
2 VT hacer pulpa, reducir a pulpa.

pulping ['pʌlpɪŋ] N reducción f a pulpa.
pulpit ['pʊlpɪt] N púlpito m.
pulpy ['pʌlpɪ] ADJ (a) pulposo. (b) *literature* para tirar, de bajísima calidad.
pulsar ['pʌlsɑ:ʳ] N pulsar m.
pulsate [pʌl'seɪt] VI pulsar, latir.
pulsating [pʌl'seɪtɪŋ] ADJ *heart* palpitante; *music* vibrante; (*fig: exciting*) palpitante, excitante.
pulsation [pʌl'seɪʃən] N pulsación f, latido m.
pulse¹ [pʌls] [1] N (*Anat*) pulso m; (*throb*) pulsación f, latido m; **to feel** (*or* **take**) **sb's ~** tomar el pulso a uno; **he keeps his finger on the company's ~** está tomando constantemente el pulso a la compañía.
[2] VI pulsar, latir.
pulse² [pʌls] N (*Bot*) legumbre f, legumbres fpl.
pulsebeat ['pʌlsbi:t] N latido m del pulso.
pulse rate ['pʌlsreɪt] N frecuencia f del pulso.
pulverization [ˌpʌlvəraɪ'zeɪʃən] N pulverización f.
pulverize ['pʌlvəraɪz] [1] VT pulverizar; (*fig*) hacer polvo; anonadar; (*) cascar*.
[2] VI pulverizarse.
puma ['pju:mə] N puma m.
pumice ['pʌmɪs] N, **pumice-stone** ['pʌmɪsstəun] N piedra f pómez.
pummel ['pʌml] = **pommel.**
pump¹ [pʌmp] [1] N bomba f; (*Naut*) pompa f; (*Aut: at garage*) surtidor m de gasolina.
[2] VT (a) sacar (*or* elevar, llevar *etc*) con una bomba; bombear; **to ~ shots into sb** pegar muchos tiros a uno, acribillar a uno a tiros; **to ~ air along a tube** hacer que pase el aire por un tubo por medio de una bomba; **to ~ a tank dry** secar (*or* vaciar) un tanque con una bomba; **to ~ money into a company** invertir (grandes cantidades de) dinero en una compañía.
(b) *arm, handle* mover rápidamente de arriba para abajo; **to ~ hands** (*US*) estrechar la mano con fuerza; estrechar muchas manos.
(c) (*) *person* sonsacar (*for information* para obtener información); **it's no good trying to ~ me** es inútil tratar de sonsacarme.
[3] VI (*person*) dar a la bomba; (*heart: also* **to ~ away**) pulsar, latir (fuertemente).
♦ **pump in** VT *water etc* introducir bombeando; **~ some more air in** pon más aire.
♦ **pump out** [1] VT (a) *liquid* sacar con una bomba. (b) *flooded cellar etc* sacar el agua de (con bomba); *stomach* vaciar (bombeando).
[2] VI: **the blood was ~ing out of the wound** la sangre salía a borbotones de la herida.
♦ **pump up** VT *tyre* inflar (con una bomba), bombear (*LAm*).
pump² [pʌmp] N (*shoe*) zapatilla f; (*US*) escarpín m.
pumper ['pʌmpəʳ] N (*US*) coche m bomba.
pumpernickel ['pʌmpənɪkl] N (*US*) pan m de centeno entero.
pumphouse ['pʌmphaʊs] N, PL **pumphouses** ['pʌmphaʊzɪz] casa f de bombas.
pumping-station ['pʌmpɪŋˌsteɪʃən] N estación f de bombeo.
pumpkin ['pʌmpkɪn] N (*vegetable*) calabaza f; (*plant*) calabacera f.
pump-priming ['pʌmp'praɪmɪŋ] N (*fig*) inversión f inicial con carácter de estímulo; (*US*) inversión f estatal en nuevos proyectos que se espera beneficien la economía.
pumproom ['pʌmprʊm] N pabellón m de hidroterapia.
pun [pʌn] [1] N juego m de palabras (*on* sobre), equívoco m, retruécano m, albur m (*Mex*).
[2] VI hacer un juego de palabras (*on* sobre), jugar del vocablo, alburear (*Mex*).
Punch [pʌntʃ] NM Polichinela; **~-and-Judy show** guiñol m, teatro m de polichinelas.
punch¹ [pʌntʃ] [1] N (a) (*tool*) punzón m; (*for tickets*) sacabocados m, taladro m.
(b) (*blow*) puñetazo m, golpe m; **he packs a ~*** pega duro*; **to pull one's ~es** no emplear toda su fuerza; **he didn't pull any ~es** (*fig*) no se mordió la lengua, no anduvo con chiquitas.
(c) (*fig*) empuje m, vigor m, fuerza f; **he has ~** es hombre de empuje; **he's a speaker with some ~** es un orador dinámico; **think of a phrase that's got some ~** to le dame una frase que tenga garra.
[2] VT (a) (*with tool*) punzar, taladrar; agujerear; perforar; *card* perforar; *ticket* picar, ponchar (*Carib*); **~ed tape** cinta f perforada; **to ~ holes in a sheet** practicar agujeros en una lámina.
(b) (*with fist*) dar un puñetazo a, pegar, golpear.
(c) *button, key* presionar, tocar; **you have to ~ the code in first** primero hay que introducir el código.
[3] VI pegar.
♦ **punch in** VI fichar, picar.
♦ **punch out** [1] VT *hole* taladrar, perforar; (*machine parts*) troquelar; (*design*) estampar.
[2] VI (a) (*on time clock*) fichar al salir, picar la salida. (b) (*US*) estirar la pata*.
punch² [pʌntʃ] N (*drink*) ponche m.

punchball ['pʌntʃbɔ:l] N (*Brit*) saco m de arena, punching m.
punchbowl ['pʌntʃbəul] N ponchera f.
punch-drunk ['pʌntʃ'drʌŋk] ADJ: **to be ~** estar groggy, estar grogui, estar sonado*.
punch(ed) card ['pʌntʃ(t)kɑ:d] N tarjeta f perforada.
puncher ['pʌntʃəʳ] N (a) (*tool*) perforador m. (b) **he's a hard ~** pega fuerte.
punch(ing)-bag ['pʌntʃ(ɪŋ)bæg] N saco m de arena, punching m.
punch-line ['pʌntʃlaɪn] N frase f clave; **the ~ of his speech was ...** remató su discurso con la frase ...
punch-operator ['pʌntʃɒpəreɪtəʳ] N operador m, -ora f de máquina perforadora.
punch-up: ['pʌntʃʌp] N (*Brit*) riña f, pendencia f.
punchy* ['pʌntʃɪ] ADJ (*US*) *person etc* de empuje, dinámico; *phrase, remark* tajante, contundente; *style* vigoroso.
punctilio [pʌŋk'tɪlɪəʊ] N puntillo m, etiqueta f; puntualidad f.
punctilious [pʌŋk'tɪlɪəs] ADJ puntilloso, etiquetero, puntual.
punctiliously [pʌŋk'tɪlɪəslɪ] ADV de modo puntilloso; puntualmente.
punctual ['pʌŋktjʊəl] ADJ puntual; **'please be ~'** 'se ruega la mayor puntualidad'; **will the train be ~?** ¿llegará el tren a la hora?
punctuality [ˌpʌŋktjʊ'ælɪtɪ] N puntualidad f.
punctually ['pʌŋktjʊəlɪ] ADV puntualmente; **~ at 6 o'clock** a las 6 en punto; **the bus arrived ~** el autobús llegó a la hora.
punctuate ['pʌŋktjʊeɪt] VT puntuar; (*fig*) interrumpir; **his speech was ~d by bursts of applause** su discurso fue interrumpido por salvas de aplausos.
punctuation [ˌpʌŋktjʊ'eɪʃən] [1] N puntuación f.
[2] ATTR: **~ mark** signo m de puntuación.
puncture ['pʌŋktʃəʳ] [1] N perforación f; (*of skin etc*) puntura f, punzada f; (*Aut*) pinchazo m; (*Med*) punción f; **I have a ~** tengo un neumático pinchado, se me ha reventado un neumático (una llanta LAm).
[2] VT (*gen*) perforar; *leather, paper etc* punzar, pinchar; *balloon, tyre* pinchar, ponchar (*Carib*); (*Med*) perforar; **this ~d his confidence** esto destruyó su confianza; **we'll see if it ~s his pride** veremos si esto le baja los humos.
[3] VI (*tyre*) pincharse.
pundit ['pʌndɪt] N (*iro*) lumbrera f, erudito m a la violeta.
pungency ['pʌndʒənsɪ] N lo acre; picante m; mordacidad f, acerbidad f.
pungent ['pʌndʒənt] ADJ *smell* acre; (*piquant*) picante; *satire etc* mordaz, acerbo.
pungently ['pʌndʒəntlɪ] ADV acremente; de modo picante; mordazmente, acerbamente.
Punic ['pju:nɪk] [1] ADJ púnico.
[2] N púnico m.
punish ['pʌnɪʃ] VT (a) castigar; **to ~ sb for sth** castigar a uno por algo; **to ~ sb for doing sth** castigar a uno por haber hecho algo.
(b) (*fig*) (*maltreat*) maltratar; (*in race etc*) exigir esfuerzos sobrehumanos a; (*Boxing*) castigar; (*take advantage of*) aprovecharse al máximo de; *food* devorar, no perdonar.
punishable ['pʌnɪʃəbl] ADJ punible, castigable; **a ~ offence** una infracción que castiga la ley; **a crime ~ by death** un delito que merece la pena de muerte.
punishing ['pʌnɪʃɪŋ] [1] ADJ *race etc* duro, agotador.
[2] N castigo m; (*fig*) castigo m, malos tratos mpl; **to take a ~** sufrir un duro castigo.
punishment ['pʌnɪʃmənt] N castigo m; **to make the ~ fit the crime** señalar un castigo de acuerdo con el crimen; **the boxer took a lot of ~** el boxeador sufrió un duro castigo; **to take one's ~ like a man** sufrir el castigo sin quejarse.
punitive ['pju:nɪtɪv] ADJ punitivo; (*Jur*) *damages* punitorio.
Punjabi [pʌn'dʒɑ:bɪ] [1] ADJ punjabí.
[2] N (a) punjabí mf. (b) (*Ling*) punjabí m.
punk [pʌŋk] [1] ADJ (a) (*) malo, baladí, de baja calidad. (b) (*1980s*) punki.
[2] N (a) (*US:*) pobre hombre m; novato m; bobo m; (*hoodlum*) matón m. (b) (:: *nonsense*) bobadas fpl. (c) (*1980s*) punki mf.
punnet ['pʌnɪt] N (*Brit*) canastilla f.
punster ['pʌnstəʳ] N persona f aficionada a los juegos de palabras, equivoquista mf.
punt¹ [pʌnt] [1] N batea f.
[2] VT impulsar con percha.
[3] VI ir en batea, pasearse en batea.
punt² [pʌnt] [1] N puntapié m de volea.
[2] VT dar un puntapié de volea a.
punt³ [pʌnt] VI (*Brit: bet*) jugar, hacer apuestas.
punter ['pʌntəʳ] N (*Brit*) (a) (*who bets*) apostante mf. (b) (*person**) tío* m, sujeto m; (*Comm, also of prostitute*) cliente m.
puntpole ['pʌntpəul] N percha f, pértiga f (de batea).
puny ['pju:nɪ] ADJ *person etc* débil, encanijado; *effort* débil, flojo; (*petty*) insignificante.

PUP N (*Brit*) ABBR *of* **Progressive Unionist Party**.
pup [pʌp] **1** N cachorro *m*, -a *f*; **to sell sb a ~** dar a uno gato por liebre.
   2 VI parir (*la perra*).
pupa ['pjuːpə] N, PL **pupae** ['pjuːpiː] crisálida *f*.
pupate ['pjuːpeɪt] VI crisalidar.
pupil[1] ['pjuːpl] N alumno *m*, -a *f*, escolar *mf*, educando *m*, -a *f*.
pupil[2] ['pjuːpl] N (*Anat*) pupila *f*.
puppet ['pʌpɪt] **1** N títere *m*; (*fig*) títere *m*, marioneta *mf*.
   2 ATTR: **~ régime** gobierno *m* títere; **~ show, ~ theater** (*US*), **~ theatre** (*Brit*) títeres *mpl*, teatro *m* de títeres.
puppeteer ['pʌpɪ'tɪəʳ] N titiritero *m*, -a *f*.
puppetry ['pʌpɪtrɪ] N títeres *mpl*, arte *m* del titiritero.
puppy ['pʌpɪ] **1** N cachorro *m*, -a *f*, perrito *m*, -a *f*.
   2 ATTR: **~ fat** carnes *fpl* de adolescente; **~ love** amor *m* de jóvenes.
purblind ['pɜːblaɪnd] ADJ cegato; (*fig*) ciego, falto de comprensión.
purchase ['pɜːtʃɪs] **1** N **(a)** (*Comm etc*) compra *f*; adquisición *f*; **to make a ~** hacer una compra.
   (b) (*on rock etc*) agarre *m* firme, pie *m* firme; (*Mech*) apalancamiento *m*; **to get a ~ on the surface** tener donde agarrarse a la superficie, lograr pegarse a la superficie.
   2 ATTR: **~ order** orden *f* de compra; **~ price** precio *m* de compra; **~ tax** (*Brit*) impuesto *m* de venta.
   3 VT comprar, adquirir.
purchaser ['pɜːtʃɪsəʳ] N comprador *m*, -ora *f*.
purchasing ['pɜːtʃɪsɪŋ] N compra *f*, el comprar; **~ power** poder *m* de compra, poder *m* adquisitivo.
purdah ['pɜːdə] N (*India etc*) costumbre *f* de mantener recluida a la mujer, reclusión *f* femenina; **to be in ~** (*fig*) estar en cuarentena.
pure [pjʊəʳ] ADJ puro; **~ mathematics** matemáticas *fpl* puras; **~ science** ciencias *fpl* puras; **~ and simple** puro y sencillo; **it's a ~ waste of time** es sencillamente perder el tiempo; **as ~ as the driven snow** puro como la nieve.

```
┌─[PURE]──────────────────────────[see also main entry]─┐
│                                                         │
│  Position of "puro"                                     │
│    You should generally put puro after the noun when    │
│    you mean pure in the sense of "uncontaminated" or    │
│    "unadulterated" and before the noun in the sense of  │
│    "sheer" or "plain":                                  │
│        ...pure olive oil...                             │
│        ...aceite puro de oliva...                       │
│        It's pure coincidence                            │
│        Es pura coincidencia                             │
│    For further uses and examples, see main entry.       │
└─────────────────────────────────────────────────────────┘
```

purebred ['pjʊə'bred] **1** ADJ de pura sangre, de raza.
   2 N pura sangre *mf*.
purée ['pjʊəreɪ] N puré *m*.
purely ['pjʊəlɪ] ADV puramente; **~ and simply** sencillamente, simplemente.
pure-minded ['pjʊə'maɪndɪd] ADJ de mente pura.
pureness ['pjʊənɪs] N pureza *f*.
purgation [pɜː'geɪʃən] N purgación *f*.
purgative ['pɜːgətɪv] **1** ADJ purgativo, purgante.
   2 N purgante *m*.
purgatory ['pɜːgətərɪ] N purgatorio *m*; **it was ~!** ¡fue un purgatorio!
purge [pɜːdʒ] **1** N (*act*) purga *f*; (*medicine*) purga *f*, purgante *m*; (*Pol*) purga *f*, depuración *f*.
   2 VT purgar; purificar, depurar; *offence, sin* purgar; (*Pol*) *party* purgar, depurar, *member* liquidar.
purification [pjʊərɪfɪ'keɪʃən] N purificación *f*, depuración *f*.
purifier ['pjʊərɪfaɪəʳ] N depurador *m*.
purify ['pjʊərɪfaɪ] VT purificar, depurar; *metal* acrisolar, refinar; *town etc* depurar.
purism ['pjʊərɪzəm] N purismo *m*.
purist ['pjʊərɪst] N purista *mf*, casticista *mf*.
puritan ['pjʊərɪtən] **1** ADJ puritano.
   2 N puritano *m*, -a *f*.
puritanical [pjʊərɪ'tænɪkəl] ADJ puritano.
puritanism ['pjʊərɪtənɪzəm] N puritanismo *m*.
purity ['pjʊərɪtɪ] N pureza *f*.
purl [pɜːl] **1** N puntada *f* invertida, punto *m* del revés.
   2 VT hacer a puntadas invertidas; **'~ two'** 'dos puntadas invertidas'.
purler ['pɜːləʳ] N: **to come a ~** caer pesadamente, caer aparatosamente; (*fig*) fracasar estrepitosamente, darse un batacazo.
purlieus ['pɜːljuːz] NPL alrededores *mpl*, inmediaciones *fpl*.
purloin [pɜː'lɔɪn] VT robar, hurtar.
purple ['pɜːpl] **1** ADJ purpúreo; *bruise etc* morado; **~ heart** (píldora *f* de) anfetamina *f*; **P~ Heart** (*US Mil*) condecoración otorgada a los heridos de guerra; **~ passage, ~ patch** trozo *m* de estilo hinchado; **to go ~** (*in the face*) enrojecerse.
   2 N púrpura *f*.

   3 VT purpurar.
purplish ['pɜːplɪʃ] ADJ purpurino, algo purpúreo.
purport **1** ['pɜːpət] N (*meaning*) significado *m*, sentido *m*; (*purpose*) intención *f*.
   2 [pɜː'pɔːt] VT (*mean*) significar; (*convey meaning*) dar a entender (*that* que); (*profess*) pretender (*to be* ser); **this ~s to be a statement of ...** esto pretende ser una declaración de ...
purportedly [pɜː'pɔːtɪdlɪ] ADV supuestamente; **~ written by ...** supuestamente escrito por ...
▼ **purpose** ['pɜːpəs] **1** N **(a)** (*intention*) propósito *m*, intención *f*, objeto *m*; **'~ of visit'** (*official form*) 'motivo *m* del viaje'; **novel with a ~** novela *f* de tesis, novela *f* de intención seria; **my ~ in doing this** mi propósito al hacer esto; **for the ~** al efecto; **for this ~** para este fin; **in a box placed for that ~** en una caja colocada a ese efecto; **for our ~s we may disregard this** para nuestros fines podemos hacer caso omiso de esto; **for the ~ of** + *ger* con el fin de + *infin*, al efecto de + *infin*; **for the ~s of this meeting** por lo que toca a esta reunión; **on ~** a propósito, aposta, adrede; **to speak to the ~** hablar oportunamente, hablar muy a propósito; **to good ~, to some ~** con buenos resultados, provechosamente; **to little ~** para poco; **to no ~** inútilmente, en vano; **to answer** (*or* **serve**) **sb's ~** servir para el caso, servir para lo que quiere uno; **it serves no useful ~** no tiene utilidad práctica; **it serves a variety of ~s** sirve para diversos efectos.
   (b) (*sense of ~*) resolución *f*; **infirmity of ~** falta *f* de resolución; **strength of ~** resolución *f*, firmeza *f*.
   2 VT proponerse, proyectar, intentar; **to ~ to do sth** proponerse hacer algo.
purpose-built [pɜːpəs'bɪlt] ADJ construido con propósitos específicos.
purposeful ['pɜːpəsfʊl] ADJ resuelto, determinado; *activity* intencionado.
purposefully ['pɜːpəsfəlɪ] ADV resueltamente.
purposefulness ['pɜːpəsfʊlnɪs] N resolución *f*.
purposeless ['pɜːpəslɪs] ADJ *person's character* irresoluto; *person's state* indeciso; *act* sin propósito, sin objeto, sin finalidad.
purposely ['pɜːpəslɪ] ADV a propósito, adrede, expresamente; **a ~ vague statement** una declaración hecha adrede en términos vagos.
purposive ['pɜːpəsɪv] ADJ = **purposeful**.
purr [pɜːʳ] **1** N ronroneo *m*.
   2 VT (*say*) decir suavemente, susurrar.
   3 VI (*cat, engine*) ronronear; (*person*) estar satisfecho.
purse [pɜːs] **1** N bolsa *f*; monedero *m*, portamonedas *m*; (*handbag: US*) bolso *m*, cartera *f* (*LAm*); (*prize*) premio *m*; (*collection*) colecta *f*; **a well-lined ~** una bolsa llena; **it is beyond my ~** mis recursos no llegan a tanto, está fuera de mi alcance.
   2 VT: **to ~ (up) one's lips** fruncir los labios.
purser ['pɜːsəʳ] N contador *m* (de navío), comisario *m*, -a *f*.
purse-snatcher ['pɜːssnætʃəʳ] N (*US*) tironista *mf*.
purse-strings ['pɜːsstrɪŋz] NPL: **to hold the ~** manejar los cuartos.
pursuance [pə'sjuːəns] N prosecución *f*, cumplimiento *m*; **in ~ of** con arreglo a, en cumplimiento de.
pursuant [pə'sjuːənt] ADV: **~ to** de acuerdo con, conforme a.
pursue [pə'sjuː] VT (*hunt*) seguir, seguir la pista de, perseguir, cazar, dar caza a; (*chase, molest*) acosar, dar caza a, asediar; *line of conduct, inquiry* seguir; *aim, objective* buscar, aspirar a; *study* proseguir; *profession* dedicarse a, ejercer; *plan* proceder de acuerdo con, obrar con arreglo a; *pleasures etc* dedicarse a; **they ~d the fox into the wood** siguieron la zorra dentro del bosque; **he ~d the girl home** siguió a la chica hasta casa; **he won't stop pursuing me!** ¡no me deja a sol ni a sombra!
pursuer [pə'sjuːəʳ] N perseguidor *m*, -ora *f*.
pursuit [pə'sjuːt] N **(a)** (*chase*) caza *f*; perseguimiento *m*, persecución *f*; (*search*) busca *f*; **in ~ of** en busca de, en pos de; **with two policemen in hot ~** con dos policías que le seguían muy de cerca; **to go in ~ of sb** ir en pos de uno; **to set out in ~ of sb** salir a buscar a uno.
   (b) the ~ of happiness la busca de la felicidad; **the ~ of wealth** el afán de riqueza.
   (c) (*occupation*) ocupación *f*, carrera *f*, empleo *m*; (*pastime*) pasatiempo *m*; **her favourite ~** su pasatiempo predilecto; **literary ~s** intereses *mpl* literarios, actividades *fpl* literarias.
pursuit plane [pə'sjuːtpleɪn] N avión *m* de caza.
purulence ['pjʊərʊləns] N purulencia *f*.
purulent ['pjʊərʊlənt] ADJ purulento.
purvey [pɜː'veɪ] VT proveer, suministrar, abastecer.
purveyance [pɜː'veəns] N provisión *f*, suministro *m*, abastecimiento *m*.
purveyor [pɜː'veəʳ] N proveedor *m*, -ora *f*, abastecedor *m*, -ora *f*.
purview ['pɜːvjuː] N alcance *m*, esfera *f*; **it comes within the ~ of the law** está comprendido dentro de los límites de la ley.
pus [pʌs] N pus *m*, postema *f* (*Mex*).
push [pʊʃ] **1** N **(a)** (*shove*) empuje *m*, empujón *m*; **with one ~** de un empuje; **to give sb a ~** dar un empujón a uno; **to give sb a helping**

~ ayudar a uno empujando su coche (*etc*).

(b) (*Mil*) ataque *m*, ofensiva *f*; avance *m*; **the final** ~ el último esfuerzo.

(c) (*Brit**) **to get the** ~ (*worker*) ser despedido; (*lover*) recibir calabazas; **to give sb the** ~ (*member, worker*) poner a uno de patitas en la calle, (*lover*) dar calabazas a uno*.

(d) (*pushfulness*) dinamismo *m*, empuje *m*, energía *f*; **he's got no** ~ no tiene empuje, le falta energía; **he's a man with plenty of** ~ es hombre de empuje.

(e) (*) **at a** ~ si es necesario, en caso de necesidad; **when it comes to the** ~ en el momento de la verdad, llegado el punto crítico.

2 VT (a) (*press*) empujar; (*down, with foot*) pisar, apretar; *button etc* apretar, pulsar, presionar; **to** ~ **a car into the garage** empujar un coche dentro del garaje; **to** ~ **one's finger into a hole** introducir el dedo en un agujero; **he** ~**ed his finger into my eye** me metió el dedo en el ojo.

(b) *person* empujar; **don't** ~ **me!** ¡no me empujes!; **to** ~ **sb off the pavement** echar a uno de la acera a empujones; **they** ~**ed me off the ball** me quitaron el balón a empujones.

(c) (*press*) *advantage* aprovecharse de; *claim* proseguir, insistir en; *enterprise* promover, fomentar; *person* proteger, ayudar, ayudar en su carrera; *product etc* promocionar; **to** ~ **an attack home** esforzarse por asegurar el éxito de un ataque; **don't** ~ **your luck** no te fíes demasiado de tu buena suerte, no te arriesgues demasiado.

(d) (*force*) empujar; **to** ~ **sb to do sth** empujar a uno a hacer algo; incitar a uno a hacer algo; **I was** ~**ed into it** me obligaron a ello; **when we** ~**ed her, she explained it all** cuando insistimos con ella, lo explicó todo; **to** ~ **sb for payment** ejercer presión sobre uno para que pague; **we are** ~**ed for time** tenemos poco tiempo, tenemos mucha prisa; **to be** ~**ed for money** andar muy escaso de dinero; **I'm rather** ~**ed for boxes just now** ahora ando algo escaso de cajas; **we shall be (hard)** ~**ed to finish it** tendremos grandes dificultades para terminarlo.

(e) *drugs* vender, traficar en.

(f) (*) **he's** ~**ing 60** tiene casi 60 años.

3 VI (a) empujar; dar un empujón, dar empujones; '~' (*on doors*) 'empujad'; **don't** ~! ¡no empujen!

(b) (*fig*) hacer esfuerzos, obrar con energía; **they're** ~**ing for better conditions** hacen campaña para mejorar sus condiciones (de trabajo).

(c) **to** ~ **into enemy territory** avanzar en territorio enemigo.

◆**push along** 1 VT (a) *object* empujar.

(b) *work* acelerar, agilizar.

2 VI (a) (*Aut etc*) rodar, circular, ir.

(b) (*: *leave*) largarse*.

◆**push around** VT (a) empujar (de acá para allá).

(b) (*bully*) mandar, dar órdenes a; tratar brutalmente; **he's not one to be** ~**ed around** no da su brazo a torcer.

◆**push aside, push away** VT *object* apartar (con la mano); **to** ~ **sb aside** apartar a uno empujándole, (*fig*) arrinconar a uno.

◆**push at** VT *door etc* empujar.

◆**push back** VT *enemy* echar atrás, rechazar; *crowd* hacer retroceder; *hair etc* echar hacia atrás; **he's** ~**ing back the frontiers of knowledge** está ampliando nuestros conocimientos.

◆**push down** VT (a) (*press down*) comprimir; (*lower*) bajar, hacer bajar; *price, value* hacer bajar.

(b) (*topple*) derribar, hacer caer.

◆**push forward** 1 VT (a) *person etc* empujar hacia adelante.

(b) *plan, work* llevar adelante.

2 VI avanzar.

3 VR: **to** ~ **o.s. forward** ofrecer (con poca modestia) sus servicios; ofrecerse, proponerse; darse mucha importancia.

◆**push in** 1 VT (a) *screw etc* introducir a la fuerza; empujar; clavar, hincar.

(b) **to** ~ **one's way in** = 2 (a).

2 VI (a) entrar a empujones; introducirse a la fuerza.

(b) (*interfere*) injerirse, entrometerse.

◆**push off** 1 VT (a) *lid etc* quitar a la fuerza.

(b) (*Naut*) desatracar.

2 VI (a) (*Naut*) desatracar; apartarse de la orilla.

(b) (*) largarse*; ~ **off!** ¡lárgate*!

(c) **the top** ~**es off** la tapa se quita empujando.

◆**push on** 1 VT (a) *lid etc* poner (presionando).

(b) (*incite*) empujar, incitar (*to* + *infin* a + *infin*).

(c) *work* acelerar, agilizar.

2 VI seguir adelante, continuar (a pesar de todo); **they** ~**ed on another 5 km** avanzaron 5 km más; **we** ~**ed on to the camp** seguimos hasta el campamento; **it's time to** ~ **on** es hora de ponernos otra vez en camino.

◆**push out** 1 VT (a) *person* empujar hacia fuera; expulsar, hacer salir; *boat* desatracar.

(b) *tentacle etc* sacar, extender.

(c) (*produce*) producir.

2 VI (*root etc*) extenderse.

◆**push over** VT (a) **to** ~ **one's way over** acercarse a empujones.

(b) *object* empujar (*to* hacia).

(c) (*topple*) derribar, hacer caer; *car* volcar.

◆**push through** 1 VT (a) *hand etc* pasar (a la fuerza); hacer pasar (empujando).

(b) *deal* concluir rápidamente, concluir a pesar de la oposición; (*Parl*) *bill* hacer aceptar a la fuerza.

(c) **to** ~ **one's way through a crowd** abrirse camino a empujones por la muchedumbre, abrirse paso empujando a través de una multitud.

2 VI (*plant*) aparecer; **to** ~ **through** (*also* **to** ~ **one's way through**) abrirse camino a empujones.

◆**push to** VT *door* cerrar.

◆**push up** VT (a) *lever etc* alzar, levantar; empujar hacia arriba.

(b) (*increase*) hacer subir, aumentar.

pushbike* ['puʃbaik] N (*Brit*) bici* *f*.

push-button ['puʃˌbʌtn] 1 N pulsador *m*, botón *m* (de control *etc*).

2 ATTR dotado de pulsador, con botón (de mando *etc*), de botones; **with** ~ **control** con mando de botón.

pushcart ['puʃkaːt] N carretilla *f* de mano.

pushchair ['puʃtʃeəʳ] N (*Brit*) sillita *f* de ruedas.

pusher ['puʃəʳ] N (a) persona *f* emprendedora; (*pej*) persona *f* de ambición desmesurada. (b) (*: *of drugs*) camello* *m*, traficante *m* de drogas.

pushful ['puʃfʊl] ADJ emprendedor, dinámico, enérgico; ambicioso; (*pej*) agresivo.

pushfulness ['puʃfʊlnɪs] N empuje *m*, dinamismo *m*, espíritu *m* emprendedor; ambición *f*; (*pej*) agresividad *f*.

pushing ['puʃɪŋ] ADJ = **pushful**.

pushover* ['puʃˌəuvəʳ] N: **it's a** ~ es pan comido*, está tirado*; **he was a** ~ era fácil convencerle (*or* sonsacarle *etc*); **I'm a** ~ **when a woman asks me** no resisto cuando me lo pide una mujer.

push-pull ['puʃpʊl] ATTR: ~ **circuit** circuito *m* de contrafase, circuito *m* equilibrado.

push-rod ['puʃrɒd] N (*Aut*) barra *f* de presión.

push-up ['puʃʌp] N (*US*) = **press-up**.

pushy* ['puʃi] ADJ = **pushful**.

pusillanimity [ˌpjuːsɪləˈnɪmɪti] N pusilanimidad *f*.

pusillanimous [ˌpjuːsɪˈlænɪməs] ADJ pusilánime.

puss [pus] N (a) minino *m*, micho *m*; ~, ~! ¡miz, miz!; **P~ in Boots** el gato con botas. (b) (‡) jeta* *f*.

pussy ['pusi] N (a) = **puss** (a). (b) (**) coño** *m*.

pussycat ['pusikæt] N minino *m*.

pussyfoot* ['pusifut] VI (*esp US*) (*also* **to** ~ **around**) andar sigilosamente, moverse a paso de gato; andar a tientas; (*fig*) no decidirse, no declararse.

pussy-willow [ˌpusiˈwɪləu] N sauce *m*.

pustule ['pʌstjuːl] N pústula *f*.

put [put] (*irr*: PRET AND PTP **put**) 1 VT (a) (*place*) poner; colocar; (*esp into, inside*) meter; ~ **it here** ponlo aquí; ~ **it there*!** (*handshake*) ¡chócala*!, ¡vengan esos cinco!; **to** ~ **milk in one's coffee** echar (*or* añadir) leche a su café; **to** ~ **sth to one's ear** acercar algo al oído; **to** ~ **one's signature to sth** poner su firma en algo, firmar algo; **I've** ~ **a lot of time into this** he dedicado mucho tiempo a esto; **to** ~ **a field under oats** sembrar un campo de avena; **to** ~ **sb under an obligation** poner a uno bajo una obligación; **to** ~ **virtue before success** anteponer la virtud al éxito, preferir la virtud al éxito; **he** ~**s the Italians before the Spaniards** estima a los italianos más que a los españoles.

(b) (*versions*) **to** ~ **a text into verse** poner un texto en verso, versificar un texto; **to** ~ **a passage into Greek** traducir un pasaje al griego.

(c) (*invest etc*) **to** ~ **money into a company** invertir dinero en una sociedad; **to** ~ **one's money into shares** comprar acciones con su dinero; **to** ~ **one's savings into marks** cambiar sus ahorros en marcos; **to** ~ **money on a horse** apostar dinero a un caballo.

(d) (*state etc*) declarar; (*express*) expresar; (*in writing*) redactar; *plan etc* exponer, explicar (*to* a); *problem* plantear; **as Lope** ~**s it** como lo expresa Lope; **if I may** ~ **it so** si se me permite decirlo así; **all that can be** ~ **in 2 sentences** todo eso se puede expresar en 2 frases; **as the Portuguese** ~ **it** como dicen los portugueses; **to** ~ **it bluntly** para decirlo como es, hablando sin rodeos; **to** ~ **it briefly** para decirlo en pocas palabras; **to** ~ **it simply** para decirlo sencillamente; ~ **it to him nicely** díselo de buen modo, díselo con finura; **how will you** ~ **it to him?** ¿cómo se lo vas a explicar?; **he** ~**s a convincing case** se explica con argumentos convincentes; **I** ~ **it to you that** ... les sugiero que ..., me veo en el caso de decirles que ...; **to** ~ **a question to sb** hacer una pregunta a uno; **I should like to** ~ **a resolution** quiero proponer una moción; **the chairman** ~ **it to the committee** el presidente lo sometió a votación en el comité.

(e) (*estimate*) calcular; computar, estimar (*at* en); **the population is ~ at 2500** se calcula la población en 2500; **what would you ~ it at?** ¿en cuánto lo estimas?; **I would ~ her at about 40** diría que tiene unos 40 años.

(f) (*with personal object*) **to ~ sb to bed** acostar a uno; **to ~ the enemy to flight** poner en fuga al enemigo; **they ~ the lad to a trade** le pusieron al muchacho de aprendiz en un oficio; **to ~ sb to a new kind of work** poner a uno a trabajar en un nuevo oficio; **to ~ sb through his paces** poner a uno a prueba, demostrar las cualidades de uno; **to ~ sb through a test** hacer pasar a uno por una prueba, someter a uno a una prueba; **they really ~ him through it** le sometieron a las pruebas más rigurosas; de veras le dieron un mal rato; **to ~ a horse at a fence** hacer que un caballo salte una valla.

(g) (*direct*) **to ~ a bullet through sb** atravesar a uno de una bala; **to ~ one's pen through a word** tachar una palabra; **to ~ the weight** lanzar el peso.

(h) (*ptp*) **~ option** opción *f* de venta a precio fijado; **to stay ~** no moverse, seguir en el mismo sitio.

2 VR: **where would you like me to ~ myself?** ¿dónde quieres que me coloque?, (*at meal*) ¿dónde quieres que me siente?; **I didn't know where to ~ myself** creí morir de vergüenza.

◆**put about, put around** **1** VT **(a)** *rumour* diseminar, hacer correr; **to ~ it about that ...** dar a entender que ..., hacer creer que ...; hacer correr el rumor de que ...; **she's ~ting it about a bit:** se está ofreciendo a todo quisque*.

(b) (*Naut*) hacer virar.

2 VI (*Naut*) virar, cambiar de bordada.

◆**put across** **1** VT **(a)** *information* comunicar; *meaning* hacer entender; *idea, product* hacer aceptar; *personality* presentar.

(b) *deal etc* cerrar.

(c) **to ~ it across sb*** (*deceive*) engañar a uno, embaucar a uno; (*defeat*) dar una paliza a uno.

2 VR: **to ~ o.s. across** impresionar con su personalidad, presentarse de manera eficaz; comunicar eficazmente lo que uno quiere decir.

◆**put apart** VT: **that ~s him apart from the others** (*fig*) eso le separa de los demás.

◆**put aside** VT **(a)** (*reject*) rechazar; *fears etc* desechar; *work* dejar, poner a un lado.

(b) (*save*) dejar de lado, poner aparte.

◆**put away** VT **(a)** (*store*) guardar, poner aparte; *money* ahorrar.

(b) (*replace*) devolver a su lugar; *car* poner en el garaje; *sword* envainar; (*in pocket etc*) guardar.

(c) (*reject*) *thought* desechar, descartar; *wife* repudiar.

(d) (*imprison*) encarcelar; *lunatic* recluir en un manicomio; (*banish*) alojar.

(e) (*) *food* zamparse; **he can certainly ~ it away** ése sí sabe comer.

◆**put back** **1** VT **(a)** (*replace*) devolver a su lugar; restituir, volver a poner; (*in pocket, drawer etc*) guardar, volver; (*to post*) restituir; **~ that back!** ¡déjalo!

(b) (*retard*) retrasar; **this will ~ us back 10 years** esto nos retrasará 10 años; **to ~ a clock back one hour** retrasar un reloj una hora.

(c) (*postpone*) aplazar.

(d) (*) *drink* beber(se); **I've already ~ back seven gins** me he bebido siete copitas de ginebra ya.

2 VI: **to ~ back to port** volver a puerto.

◆**put by** VT: **to have money ~ by** tener ahorros, tener dinero ahorrado; **I had it ~ by for you** te lo tenía guardado; **see also put away** **(a)**.

◆**put down** VT **(a)** *burden* poner en tierra, poner en el suelo, depositar; *blinds etc* bajar; (*let go*) soltar, dejar; *passengers* dejar apearse; **~ it down!** ¡déjalo!, ¡suéltalo!; **I couldn't ~ the book down** me era imposible dejar de leer el libro.

(b) (*Aer*) poner en tierra.

(c) *umbrella etc* cerrar.

(d) (*pay*) pagar como desembolso inicial.

(e) *wine* poner en cava.

(f) (*suppress*) *abuse etc* suprimir; *revolt* sofocar, dominar.

(g) (*silence*) hacer callar, dejar sin réplica posible; (*humiliate*) humillar.

(h) (*record*) apuntar; poner por escrito; *name on list* poner, inscribir; **~ me down for two, please** por favor, apúntame para dos.

(i) (*reduce in rank*) degradar; (*Sport etc*) pasar a una división inferior.

(j) (*attribute*) **we ~ it down to his account** lo sentamos en su cuenta; **we ~ it down to nerves** lo atribuimos a los nervios; **what do you ~ it down to?** ¿a qué lo atribuyes?, ¿cuál crees que es la causa?

(k) (*consider*) **I ~ him down as a disaster** le creí una calamidad; **I used to ~ her down as a troublemaker** la creía revoltosa, la tenía por revoltosa; **I should ~ her down as about 30** le daría unos 30 años, creo que tendría unos 30 años.

(l) (*Brit: kill*) sacrificar.

◆**put forth** VT *hand* alargar, tender; *arm* extender; *leaves etc* echar; *effort*

emplear, desplegar.

◆**put forward** **1** VT **(a)** (*propose*) *candidate* nombrar, presentar; *idea* proponer; *suggestion* hacer; *case, theory* presentar, proponer, exponer.

(b) (*advance*) adelantar; **to ~ a clock forward one hour** adelantar un reloj una hora.

2 VR: **to ~ o.s. forward** ofrecerse (con poca modestia); ponerse en evidencia; llamar la atención sobre sí.

◆**put in** **1** VT **(a)** (*into box etc*) meter, introducir.

(b) (*insert*) insertar; *remark* interponer.

(c) (*present*) *claim etc* presentar; *evidence* aducir.

(d) (*Pol*) *party* votar a, elegir.

(e) (*devote*) dedicar; **I ~ in 2 hours reading** pasé 2 horas leyendo; **to ~ in time on a project** invertir tiempo en un proyecto, dedicar tiempo a un proyecto; **you've ~ in a good day's work** has trabajado bien hoy; **more effort has to be ~ in** hay que esforzarse más.

(f) (*instal*) instalar; conectar; (*plant*) plantar; (*sow*) sembrar.

2 VI **(a)** **to ~ in to a port** entrar a puerto, (*on route*) hacer escala en un puerto.

(b) (*apply*) **to ~ in for a post** presentarse a un puesto, solicitar un puesto; **are you ~ting in?** ¿te vas a presentar?

◆**put off** **1** VT **(a)** (*postpone*) aplazar, posponer, dejar para después.

(b) (*dissuade*) disuadir; (*confuse*) desconcertar; (*discourage*) desanimar; **to ~ sb off with a promise** dar largas a uno con una promesa; **he's not easily ~ off** no es fácil apartarle de su propósito; **we shall have to ~ the guests off** tendremos que decir a los invitados que no vengan; **he tried to ~ me off my stroke** trató de distraerme en el golpe, trató de hacerme errar el golpe; **her face is enough to ~ anyone off** su cara basta para desanimar al más fuerte; **you quite ~ me off my meal** me has quitado todo el apetito; **what you say ~s me off prawns** lo que dices me quita las ganas de las gambas; **it almost ~ me off opera for good** casi mató mi gusto por la ópera para siempre; **we managed to ~ them off the scent** logramos despistarlos.

(c) *passenger* dejar; *dress* quitarse.

(d) (*extinguish*) apagar.

2 VI (*Naut*) hacerse a la mar; salir (*from* de).

◆**put on** VT **(a)** *clothes, make-up* ponerse; *ointment etc* aplicar.

(b) (*add*) **to ~ on speed** acelerar; (*cobrar velocidad*); **they ~ £2 on (to) the price** añadieron 2 libras al precio; *V* **weight** etc.

(c) (*assume*) asumir; *accent* poner; **to ~ on an innocent air** adoptar una postura de inocencia; **to ~ it on** (*exaggerate*) exagerar, (*overact*) exagerar el papel; **she does ~ it on (so)** se emociona demasiado, es una persona muy exagerada; se da tanto tono.

(d) (*present*) *play* representar, poner en escena; *extra train* poner; *dish on menu* poner.

(e) *light, radio etc* poner, encender; *disc, tape* poner; *brake* aplicar, echar; *kettle, stew etc* poner (a calentar).

(f) *clock* adelantar; **to ~ a clock on one hour** adelantar un reloj una hora.

(g) **Sue ~ us on to you** Sue nos dio su nombre, Sue nos sugirió su nombre; **what ~ you on to it?** ¿qué te hizo pensar en esto?; ¿qué te dio la pista?; **one of the thieves ~ the police on to the others** uno de los ladrones denunció a los otros a la policía.

(h) (*: *kid, esp US*) tomar el pelo a.

◆**put out** **1** VT **(a)** (*put outside*) *chairs etc* sacar, poner fuera; *cat* mandar a pasearse; (*eject*) echar, expulsar; poner en la calle; *tenant, squatter* desahuciar; **to ~ clothes out to dry** tender la ropa, poner la ropa a secar.

(b) (*Naut*) *boat* echar al mar.

(c) (*extend*) *hand* alargar, tender, (*Aut*) sacar; *arm* extender; *tongue* sacar; *head* asomar, sacar; *horns* sacar; *leaves etc* echar.

(d) (*set out*) ordenar, disponer; desplegar.

(e) (*extinguish*) *light* apagar; *fire* apagar, sofocar.

(f) (*disconcert*) desconcertar; (*anger*) enojar, irritar; (*inconvenience*) incomodar; **I don't want to ~ you out at all** no quiero molestarte en lo más mínimo; **she was very ~ out** estaba muy enfadada; **she never seems to be ~ out** no parece alterarse por nada.

(g) (*dislocate*) dislocarse.

(h) (*publish*) *book etc* publicar, sacar a luz; *announcement* hacer; *rumour* diseminar, hacer correr.

(i) **to ~ money out at interest** poner el dinero a interés.

2 VI (*Naut*) hacerse a la mar; salir (*from* de).

3 VR: **to ~ o.s. out** tomarse la molestia, molestarse; **don't ~ yourself out!** ¡no te molestes!, ¡no te incomodes!

◆**put over** VT **(a)** = **put across**.

(b) **to ~ one over on sb*** (*forestall*) ganar por la mano a uno, (*deceive*) engañar a uno, dar a uno gato por liebre.

◆**put through** VT **(a)** *deal* cerrar; *business* despachar; *proposal* hacer aprobar.

(b) (*Telec*) **to ~ a call through** poner una llamada; **~ me through to Sr Blanco** póngame (comuníqueme *LAm*) con el Sr Blanco.

(c) **to ~ sb through a test** someter a uno a una prueba; **we'll ~**

him through the course le haremos estudiar el curso; **they really ~ him through it at the interview** en la entrevista le han hecho sudar la gota gorda.

◆**put together** VT (a) (*place together*) poner juntos; juntar; reunir; (*add*) añadir, (*Math*) sumar; **more than all the rest ~ together** más que todos los demás reunidos; **if all the cigars in the world are ~ together end to end** si se ponen uno tras otro todos los puros del mundo.

(b) (*assemble*) *machine* montar, armar; *collection* juntar, reunir, formar; *scheme* crear, formar, organizar; *meal* confeccionar; **I like to know how it's ~ together** me gusta saber cómo está hecho.

(c) **then the team really ~ it together*** luego el equipo jugó realmente bien.

▼◆**put up** ⊡ VT (a) (*raise*) *hand* alzar, levantar, poner en alto; *window etc* levantar; *umbrella* abrir; *collar* alzar; *ladder* montar, poner; *flag, sail* izar; *picture* colgar; *notice* pegar, fijar, poner; *sword* envainar; *building* construir; **~ your hands up!** ¡arriba las manos!; **to ~ one's hair up** recoger el pelo, (*stylishly*) hacerse un peinado alto.

(b) (*increase*) aumentar, subir.

(c) (*offer*) *prayer, prize* ofrecer; *plan* presentar; *suggestion* hacer; *resistance* oponer; *candidate* nombrar, proponer (*for* a); **to ~ a house up for sale** poner una casa en venta.

(d) (*provide*) dar, poner; **to ~ up the money for sth** poner el dinero para algo.

(e) (*prepare*) *meal etc* preparar, hacer.

(f) (*lodge*) hospedar, alojar.

(g) (*incite*) incitar; **to ~ sb up to sth** incitar a uno a hacer algo; **sb must have ~ him up to it** alguien ha debido sugerírselo.

(h) *game* levantar.

(i) *petition* presentar.

⊡ VI (a) **to ~ up at a hotel** hospedarse en un hotel.

(b) (*offer o.s.*) **to ~ up for president** ser candidato a la presidencia; **to ~ up for the Greens** ser candidato de los Verdes; **to ~ up for Bognor** ser candidato por Bognor.

▼(c) **to ~ up with** aguantar; resignarse a, conformarse con; **I can't ~ up with her** no la puedo ver, no la aguanto; **I can't ~ up with it any longer** no aguanto más; **she ~s up with a lot** es muy tolerante, tiene mucho aguante.

◆**put upon** VT: **to ~ upon sb** molestar a uno, incomodar a uno; pedir mucho a uno; abusar de la amabilidad de uno.

putative ['pjuːtətɪv] ADJ supuesto; *relation* putativo.

put-down* ['pʊt,daʊn] N (*act*) humillación *f*; (*words*) frase *f* despectiva.

put-in ['pʊt,ɪn] N (*Rugby*) introducción *f*.

put-on* ['pʊt,ɒn] ⊡ N (*pretence*) burla *f*, cachondeo* *m*; (*hoax*) broma *f* (de mal gusto). ⊡ ADJ (*feigned*) fingido.

putrefaction [,pjuːtrɪ'fækʃən] N putrefacción *f*.

putrefy ['pjuːtrɪfaɪ] ⊡ VT pudrir. ⊡ VI pudrirse.

putrescence [pjuː'tresns] N pudrición *f*.

putrescent [pjuː'tresnt] ADJ putrescente, podrido.

putrid ['pjuːtrɪd] ADJ (a) podrido, putrefacto. (b) (*) horrible, malísimo.

putsch [pʊtʃ] N golpe *m* de estado.

putt [pʌt] ⊡ N putt *m*, pat *m*, golpe *m* corto. ⊡ VTI patear.

putter ['pʌtər] ⊡ N putter *m*. ⊡ VI (*US*) = **potter²**.

putting ['pʊtɪŋ] N: **~ the weight** lanzamiento *m* del peso.

putting green ['pʌtɪŋɡriːn] N green *m*, minigolf *m*.

putty ['pʌtɪ] N masilla *f*.

putty-knife ['pʌtɪnaɪf] N, PL **putty-knives** ['pʌtɪnaɪvz] espátula *f* para masilla.

put-up* ['pʊtʌp] ADJ: **~ job** cosa *f* proyectada y preparada de

antemano; asunto *m* fraudulento; **it was a ~ job to give him the post** fue un truco para darle el puesto.

put-upon ['pʊtə'pɒn] ADJ: **she's feeling very ~** cree que los demás la están explotando; se siente agobiada por las muchas exigencias (*etc*).

put-you-up ['pʊtjuˌʌp] N (*Brit*) cama *f* plegable, sofá-cama *m*.

puzzle ['pʌzl] ⊡ N (a) (*game*) rompecabezas *m*, puzzle *m*; (*riddle*) acertijo *m*; (*crossword*) crucigrama *m*; (*jigsaw*) rompecabezas *m*.

(b) (*mystery*) problema *m*, enigma *m*, misterio *m*; **it's a real ~** es un verdadero problema; **the ~ of their origin** el enigma de su origen; **your friends are ~s to me** no llego a entender a tus amigos.

⊡ VT dejar perplejo, confundir; **that properly ~d him** eso le dejó totalmente perplejo; **I am ~d to know why** no llego a comprender por qué, no acabo de entender por qué; **I was ~d to know what to answer** no sabía en absoluto lo que debía contestar.

⊡ VI: **to ~ over sth** esforzarse por resolver algo, devanarse los sesos para descifrar algo; tratar de comprender algo.

◆**puzzle out** VT: **to ~ sth out** resolver algo, descifrar algo; **we're still trying to ~ out why he did it** seguimos tratando de comprender por qué lo hizo.

puzzle book ['pʌzl,bʊk] N libro *m* de puzzles.

puzzled ['pʌzld] ADJ *look etc* perplejo.

puzzlement ['pʌzlmənt] N perplejidad *f*, confusión *f*.

puzzler ['pʌzlər] N problema *m*, enigma *m*, misterio *m*.

puzzling ['pʌzlɪŋ] ADJ enigmático, misterioso; incomprensible; **it is ~ that ...** es curioso que ...

PVC N ABBR *of* **polyvinyl chloride** cloruro *m* de polivinilo.

PVS N ABBR *of* **persistent vegetative state** estado *m* vegetativo persistente; ABBR *of* **postviral syndrome**.

Pvt. (*US*) ABBR *of* **Private** soldado *m* raso.

PW N (*US*) ABBR *of* **prisoner of war** prisionero *m*.

p.w. ABBR *of* **per week** por semana, a la semana.

PWR ABBR *of* **pressurized water reactor** reactor *m* de agua a presión.

PX N (*US Mil*) ABBR *of* **Post Exchange** economato militar.

pygmy ['pɪɡmɪ] ⊡ ADJ pigmeo; (*fig*) miniatura, minúsculo. ⊡ N pigmeo *m*, -a *f*.

pyjamas [pɪ'dʒɑːməz] NPL (*Brit*) pijama *m*.

pylon ['paɪlən] N pilón *m*, poste *m*; (*Elec*) torre *f* (de conducción eléctrica, de alta tensión).

pyorrhoea, (*US*) **pyorrhea** [,paɪə'rɪə] N piorrea *f*.

pyramid ['pɪrəmɪd] ⊡ N pirámide *f*. ⊡ ATTR: **~ selling** venta *f* piramidal.

pyramidal [pɪ'ræmɪdl] ADJ piramidal.

pyre ['paɪər] N pira *f*; (*fig*) hoguera *f*.

Pyrenean [,pɪrə'niːən] ADJ pirenaico, pirineo.

Pyrenees [,pɪrə'niːz] NPL Pirineo *m*, Pirineos *mpl*.

pyrethrum [paɪ'riːθrəm] N piretro *m*.

pyretic [paɪ'retɪk] ADJ pirético.

Pyrex ['paɪreks] ® ⊡ N pírex ® *m*. ⊡ ATTR *dish* de pírex ®.

pyrites [paɪ'raɪtiːz] N pirita *f*.

pyro- ['paɪərəʊ] PREF piro...

pyromania [,paɪrəʊ'meɪnɪə] N piromanía *f*, incendiarismo *m*.

pyromaniac ['paɪərəʊ'meɪnɪæk] N pirómano *m*, -a *f*, incendiario *m*, -a *f*.

pyrotechnic [,paɪərəʊ'teknɪk] ⊡ ADJ pirotécnico. ⊡ NPL: **~s** pirotecnia *f*.

Pyrrhic ['pɪrɪk] ADJ: **~ victory** victoria *f* pírrica.

Pyrrhus ['pɪrəs] NM Pirro.

Pythagoras [paɪ'θæɡərəs] NM Pitágoras.

Pythagorean [paɪ,θæɡə'rɪən] ADJ pitagóreo.

python ['paɪθən] N pitón *m*.

pythonesque [,paɪθə'nesk] ADJ pitonesco (*del estilo de Monty Python*).

pyx [pɪks] N píxide *f*.

pzazz* [pə'zæz] N = **piz(z)azz**.

Q, q [kjuː] N (*letter*) Q, q *f*; **Q for Queen** Q de Quebec.
Q. (a) ABBR of **Queen** reina *f*. (b) ABBR of **question** pregunta *f*, p.
Qatar [kæˈtɑːʳ] N Katar *m*, Qatar *m*.
QC N (*Brit*) ABBR of **Queen's Counsel.**

┌──── QC/KC ────┐

ℹ️ *QC o KC, abreviaturas de **Queen's** o **King's Counsel**, es el título que se les da a los abogados de más alto rango en el Reino Unido. Los letrados denominados **barristers** (o **advocates** en Escocia) que hayan practicado la abogacía durante al menos diez años pueden solicitar este título al **Lord Chancellor**, quien a su vez los recomienda a la Corona para su designación. Pasar a ser un **QC** o **KC** se conoce como **taking silk** (recibir la seda), haciendo referencia al material de la túnica que llevan estos letrados.*

⇨ *Ver también* ⟨LAWYERS⟩ , ⟨LORD⟩

QED (*Math etc*) ABBR of **quod erat demonstrandum** que es lo que había que probar, Q.E.D.
QM ABBR of **Quartermaster.**
qr ABBR of **quarter(s).**
q.t. [kjuːˈtiː] N ABBR of **quiet; on the ~*** a hurtadillas.
qty ABBR of **quantity** cantidad *f*, ctdad.
Qu. ABBR of **Queen** reina *f*.
qua [kweɪ] PREP como, en cuanto; **let us consider man ~ animal** consideremos al hombre en cuanto animal.
quack¹ [kwæk] ① N graznido *m* (del pato).
② VI graznar.
quack² [kwæk] ① N charlatán *m*; (*Med*) curandero *m*, matasanos *m*.
② ADJ falso, fingido; *remedy* de curandero; **~ doctor** medicucho *m*, curandero *m*.
quackery [ˈkwækərɪ] N charlatanismo *m*; curanderismo *m*.
quack-quack [ˈkwækˈkwæk] N cuac cuac *m*.
quad [kwɒd] N (a) (*Archit**) = **quadrangle.** (b) (*Typ*) cuadratín *m*. (c) ABBR of **quadruple.** (d) (*) ABBR of **quadruplet.**
Quadragesima [ˌkwɒdrəˈdʒesɪmə] N Cuadragésima *f*.
quadrangle [ˈkwɒdræŋgl] N cuadrilátero *m*, cuadrángulo *m*; (*court*) patio *m*.
quadrangular [kwɒˈdræŋgjʊləʳ] ADJ cuadrangular.
quadrant [ˈkwɒdrənt] N cuadrante *m*.
quadraphonic [ˌkwɒdrəˈfɒnɪk] ADJ cuatrifónico.
quadratic [kwɒˈdrætɪk] ADJ: **~ equation** ecuación *f* de segundo grado, cuadrática *f*.
quadrature [ˈkwɒdrətʃəʳ] N cuadratura *f*.
quadrennial [kwɒˈdrenɪəl] ADJ cuatrienal.
quadrilateral [ˌkwɒdrɪˈlætərəl] ① ADJ cuadrilátero.
② N cuadrilátero *m*.
quadrille [kwəˈdrɪl] N cuadrilla *f*.
quadripartite [ˈkwɒdrɪˈpɑːtaɪt] ADJ cuadripartido.
quadriplegia [ˌkwɒdrɪˈpliːdʒə] N cuadriplegia *f*, tetraplegia *f*.
quadriplegic [ˌkwɒdrɪˈpliːdʒɪk] ① ADJ cuadriplégico.
② N cuadriplégico *m*, -a *f*.
quadrivium [kwɒˈdrɪvɪəm] N cuadrivio *m*.
quadroon [kwɒˈdruːn] N cuarterón *m*.
quadrophonic [ˌkwɒdrəˈfɒnɪk] ADJ cuadrafónico.
quadruped [ˈkwɒdrʊped] N cuadrúpedo *m*.
quadruple ① [ˈkwɒdrʊpl] ADJ cuádruple, cuádruplo.
② [ˈkwɒdrʊpl] N cuádruple *m*, cuádruplo *m*.
③ [ˈkwɒdrʊpl] VT cuadruplicar.
④ [ˈkwɒdrʊpl] VI cuadruplicarse.
quadruplet [kwɒˈdruːplɪt] N cuatrillizo *m*, -a *f*.
quadruplicate ① [kwɒˈdruːplɪkɪt] ADJ cuadruplicado.
② [kwɒˈdruːplɪkɪt] N: **in ~** por cuadruplicado.
③ [kwɒˈdruːplɪkeɪt] VT cuadruplicar.

quaestor, (*US sometimes*) **questor** [ˈkwiːstəʳ] N cuestor *m*.
quaff [kwɒf] VT (†† *or hum*) beber(se).
quagmire [ˈkwægmaɪəʳ] N tremedal *m*, cenegal *m*, lodazal *m*; (*fig*) atolladero *m*, cenegal *m*.
quail¹ [kweɪl] N codorniz *f*.
quail² [kweɪl] VI acobardarse, amedrentarse (*before* ante); **her heart ~ed** se le desfalleció el corazón.
quaint [kweɪnt] ADJ (*odd*) curioso, original, singular; *workmanship etc* rebuscado; *person* singular, original; (*picturesque, of tourist interest etc*) típico, pintoresco.
quaintly [ˈkweɪntlɪ] ADV curiosamente; singularmente; típicamente; **he described it ~ as ...** le dio la calificación curiosa de ...
quaintness [ˈkweɪntnɪs] N curiosidad *f*, originalidad *f*, singularidad *f*; lo rebuscado; tipismo *m*, lo pintoresco.
quake [kweɪk] ① N = **earthquake.**
② VI temblar, estremecerse; **to ~ at the knees** flaquearle a uno las piernas, temblarle a uno las rodillas; **to ~ at the sight** estremecerse viendo tal cosa; **to ~ with fright** temblar de miedo; **the earth ~d 3 times** la tierra tembló 3 veces.
Quaker [ˈkweɪkəʳ] ① ADJ cuáquero.
② N cuáquero *m*, -a *f*.
Quakerism [ˈkweɪkərɪzəm] N cuaquerismo *m*.
qualification [ˌkwɒlɪfɪˈkeɪʃən] N (a) (*reservation*) reserva *f*; salvedad *f*; modificación *f*, restricción *f*; **to accept sth without ~** aceptar algo sin reserva.
(b) (*for a post etc*) requisito *m*, calificación *f* (*LAm*); **the ~s for the post are ...** los requisitos del puesto son ...; **the ~s for membership** lo que se requiere para ser socio.
(c) (*of person*) **~s** aptitud *f*, capacidad *f*; (*paper ~s*) títulos *mpl*; **to have the ~s for a post** llenar los requisitos de un puesto, tener los títulos exigidos para un puesto, estar capacitado para ocupar un puesto; **what are his ~s?** ¿qué títulos tiene?
(d) (*act, description*) calificación *f*; **without ~** sin reserva; (*pej*) sin paliativos.
qualified [ˈkwɒlɪfaɪd] ADJ (a) *person* (*fit*) apto, competente (*to + infin* para + *infin*); (*trained*) capacitado, cualificado, calificado, habilitado; (*professionally*) titulado, que tiene título, con título; **a ~ engineer** un ingeniero titulado; **to be ~ to do sth** estar capacitado para hacer algo; ser competente para hacer algo; **to be ~ to vote** tener los requisitos para votar; **I don't feel ~ to judge that** no me creo calificado para juzgar eso.
(b) (*limited*) modificado, limitado; **~ acceptance** aceptación *f* condicional; **he gave it his ~ approval** lo aprobó pero con reservas; **it was a ~ success** obtuvo un éxito moderado.
qualifier [ˈkwɒlɪfaɪəʳ] N calificador *m*.
qualify [ˈkwɒlɪfaɪ] ① VT (a) (*describe*) calificar (*as* de); (*Gram*) calificar a.
(b) (*make competent*) habilitar, capacitar; **this should ~ you for the post** esto deberá darte los requisitos para el puesto; **her skills ~ her for the job** reúne las condiciones necesarias para el puesto; **to ~ sb to do sth** habilitar a uno para hacer algo; **that doesn't ~ him to speak on this** eso no le da derecho para hablar sobre este asunto.
(c) (*modify*) modificar; restringir; **I think you should ~ that** creo que te conviene modificar eso.
(d) (*diminish*) atenuar, moderar, disminuir.
② VI habilitarse, capacitarse; ser apto; reunir las condiciones necesarias; (*professionally*) cursar los estudios profesionales, estudiar; (*graduate*) obtener el título, graduarse; **to ~ as an engineer** (*as student*) estudiar para ingeniero, (*finally*) obtener el título de ingeniero, calificarse de ingeniero (*LAm*); **to ~ for a post** llenar los requisitos para un puesto; reunir las condiciones necesarias para un puesto; **does he ~?** ¿tiene los requisitos?; **I qualified in 1968** yo saqué el título en 1968; **we shall marry when he qualifies** nos

casaremos en cuanto termine la carrera; **he hardly qualifies as a poet** apenas se le puede calificar de poeta.

qualifying ['kwɒlɪfaɪɪŋ] ADJ (a) (*Gram*) calificativo. (b) *round etc* eliminatorio; **~ examination** examen *m* eliminatorio, examen *m* de ingreso.

qualitative ['kwɒlɪtətɪv] ADJ cualitativo.

qualitatively ['kwɒlɪtətɪvlɪ] ADV bajo el aspecto cualitativo.

quality ['kwɒlɪtɪ] ① N (a) (*nature, kind*) calidad *f*; categoría *f*, clase *f*; **~ of life** calidad *f* de la vida; **of the best ~** de la mejor calidad; **of good ~, of high ~** de buena calidad; **of low ~** de baja calidad; **fibres of ~** fibras *fpl* de calidad; **he's a man of some ~** es hombre de cierta categoría; **he has real ~** tiene verdadera excelencia.
(b) (*characteristic, moral ~ etc*) cualidad *f*; **among her qualities** entre sus cualidades; **he has many good qualities** tiene muchas buenas cualidades.
(c) (††) **the ~** la aristocracia; **people of ~** la gente bien nacida, las personas cultas.
(d) (*of sound*) timbre *m*, tono *m*.
② ATTR: **a ~ carpet** una alfombra de calidad; **~ control** control *m* de (la) calidad; **the ~ papers, the ~ press** los periódicos serios; **~ product** producto *m* de calidad; **~ time** *tiempo dedicado a la familia y a los amigos*; **I need to spend some ~ time with my family** necesito dedicarle más tiempo a mi familia.
ver también TABLOIDS AND BROADSHEETS .

qualm [kwɑːm] N (a) (*Med*) bascas *fpl*, náusea *f*; mareo *m*.
(b) (*scruple*) escrúpulo *m*, duda *f*; **to have ~s about doing sth** sentir escrúpulo al hacer algo; **now she's having ~s about it** ahora le está remordiendo la conciencia por ello, ahora le están asaltando las dudas; **to have no ~s about doing sth** no dudar en hacer algo, hacer algo sin escrúpulos, hacer algo sin remordimientos.

quandary ['kwɒndərɪ] N dilema *m*, apuro *m*; **to be in a ~** estar perplejo, estar en un dilema; encontrarse ante una encrucijada; **to get sb out of a ~** sacar a uno de un apuro.

quango ['kwæŋgəʊ] N (*Brit*) ABBR *of* **quasi-autonomous non-governmental organization**.

┌─────────────────────┐
│   QUANGO   │
└─────────────────────┘

ⓘ *El término* **quango**, *que corresponde a las siglas de* **quasi-autonomous non-governmental organization**, *se empezó a usar en el Reino Unido para referirse a organizaciones tales como la* **Equal Opportunities Commission** *o la* **Race Relations Board**, *que fueron establecidas por el gobierno pero que no dependen de ningún ministerio. Algunos* **quangos** *poseen funciones ejecutivas, mientras que otros son meramente consultivos. La práctica de poner demasiadas responsabilidades en manos de* **quangos** *ha sido criticada debido al hecho de que sus miembros son a menudo nombrados a dedo por el gobierno y no tienen la obligación de responder de sus actividades ante el electorado.*

quanta ['kwɒntə] NPL *of* **quantum**.

quantifiable ['kwɒntɪfaɪəbl] ADJ cuantificable.

quantifier ['kwɒntɪfaɪəʳ] N cuantificador *m*.

quantify ['kwɒntɪfaɪ] VT cuantificar.

quantitative ['kwɒntɪtətɪv] ADJ cuantitativo.

quantitatively ['kwɒntɪtətɪvlɪ] ADV bajo el aspecto cuantitativo.

quantity ['kwɒntɪtɪ] ① N cantidad *f*; **unknown ~** incógnita *f*; **in large quantities, in ~** en grandes cantidades; **what ~ do you want?** ¿cuánto quiere?
② ATTR: **~ discount** descuento *m* por cantidad; **~ mark** signo *m* prosódico; **~ surveyor** (*Brit*) aparejador *m*, medidor *m* de cantidad de obra.

quantum ['kwɒntəm] ① N, PL **quanta** ['kwɒntə] cuanto *m*, quántum *m*.
② ATTR: **~ leap** salto *m* espectacular; **~ mechanics** mecánica *f* cuántica; **~ number** número *m* cuántico; **~ physics** física *f* cuántica; **~ theory** teoría *f* cuántica.

quarantine ['kwɒrəntiːn] ① N cuarentena *f*; **to be in ~** estar en cuarentena; **to place a dog in ~** poner un perro en cuarentena.
② VT poner en cuarentena.

quark [kwɑːk] N cuark *m*.

quarrel ['kwɒrəl] ① N (a) (*argument*) riña *f*, disputa *f*; (*with blows*) reyerta *f*, pendencia *f*, pelea *f*; **to have a ~ with sb** reñir con uno, pelearse con uno (*esp LAm*); **we had a ~** reñimos; **I have no ~ with you** no tengo nada en contra de Vd, no tengo queja de Vd; **to ~ pick a ~ with sb** buscar camorra; **to pick a ~ with sb** meterse con uno, armar pleito con uno; **to take up sb's ~** ponerse de la parte de uno.
② VI reñir, pelearse (*esp LAm*); disputar; **they ~led about** (*or* **over**) **money** riñeron por cuestión de dinero; **to ~ with sb** reñir con uno, pelearse con uno; **we ~led and I never saw him again** reñimos y no volví a verle; **to ~ with sb for doing sth** reñir a uno por haber hecho algo; **you can't ~ with that** es imposible quejarse de eso; **what we ~ with is ...** nuestro motivo de queja es ...

quarrelling, (*US*) **quarreling** ['kwɒrəlɪŋ] N disputas *fpl*, altercados

mpl; **there was constant ~** se reñía constantemente.

quarrelsome ['kwɒrəlsəm] ADJ pendenciero, discutón, peleón.

quarrelsomeness ['kwɒrəlsəmnɪs] N espíritu *m* pendenciero.

quarrier ['kwɒrɪəʳ] N cantero *m*.

quarry¹ ['kwɒrɪ] N (*Hunting*) presa *f*; (*fig*) presa *f*, víctima *f*.

quarry² ['kwɒrɪ] ① N cantera *f*; (*fig*) mina *f*, cantera *f*; **~ tile** baldosa *f* (no vidriada).
② VT sacar, extraer.
③ VI explotar una cantera, extraer piedra (*etc*) de una cantera; **to ~ for marble** sacar mármol de una cantera.
◆ **quarry out** VT extraer.

quarryman ['kwɒrɪmən] N, PL **quarrymen** ['kwɒrɪmən] cantero *m*, picapedrero *m*.

quart [kwɔːt] N *cuarto de galón* (*Brit = 1,136 litros*); **we drank ~s** bebimos cantidades.

quarter ['kwɔːtəʳ] ① N (a) (*fourth part*) cuarto *m*, cuarta parte *f*; (*Brit weight*) = 28 libras (= 12.7 kg, *approx* = arroba *f*); (*US, Can Fin*) moneda de 25 centavos, cuarto *m* de dólar; (*Her*) cuartel *m*; **~s** (*of horse*) anca *f*; **a ~ of a century** un cuarto de siglo; **for a ~ of the price** por la cuarta parte del precio; **it's a ~ gone already** ya se ha gastado la cuarta parte; **it's only a ~ as long** tiene solamente la cuarta parte de largo; **to divide sth into ~s** dividir algo en cuartos.
(b) (*of moon*) cuarto *m*; (*3 months*) trimestre *m*; **to pay by the ~** pagar cada 3 meses, pagar trimestralmente.
(c) (*time*) **a ~ of an hour** un cuarto de hora; **it's a ~ to 3, it's a ~ of 3** (*US*) son las 3 menos cuarto, es un cuarto para las 3 (*LAm*); **it's a ~ past 3, it's a ~ after 3** (*US*) son las 3 y cuarto.
(d) (*of compass*) cuarta *f*; (*region*) región *f*; (*fig*) fuente *f*, origen *m*; procedencia *f*; dirección *f*; **the 4 ~s of the globe** las 4 partes del mundo; **from all ~s** de todas partes; **at close ~s** de cerca, (*fight*) casi cuerpo a cuerpo; **from an unknown ~** de procedencia desconocida, de origen desconocido; **we may expect trouble in that ~** podemos tener dificultades en esa región; **the wind is in the right ~** el viento sopla en dirección favorable; **what ~ is the wind in?** ¿qué dirección lleva el viento?
(e) (*of town*) barrio *m*; **the business ~** el barrio comercial.
(f) (*lodging*) **~s** vivienda *f*; alojamiento *m*; (*Mil*) alojamiento *m*; (*barracks*) cuartel *m*; **to have free ~s** tener alojamiento gratis; **to live in cramped ~s** tener un cuarto (*etc*) muy estrecho; **to shift one's ~s** cambiar de alojamiento; **to take up one's ~s** ocupar su cuarto (*etc*); establecerse, alojarse.
(g) **to give no ~** no dar cuartel.
② ADJ: **for a ~ century** durante un cuarto de siglo; **a ~ mile** un cuarto de milla; **~ note** (*US*) negra *f*; **the ~ part of** la cuarta parte de; **he has a ~ share** tiene una cuarta parte.
③ VT (a) (*divide into 4*) cuartear, dividir en cuartos; *meat* descuartizar; (*Her*) cuartelar.
(b) (*Mil*) acuartelar, alojar; **to be ~ed on sb** estar alojado en casa de uno.
(c) **to ~ the ground** (*dog*) buscar olfateando.

quarterback ['kwɔːtəbæk] N (*US: Ftbl*) estratega *m*.

quarter-day ['kwɔːtədeɪ] N primer día *m* del trimestre; (*Fin*) día *m* en que se paga un trimestre.

quarter-deck ['kwɔːtədek] N alcázar *m*.

quarter-final ['kwɔːtəˌfaɪnl] N cuarto *m* de final.

quarter-finalist ['kwɔːtəˈfaɪnəlɪst] N cuartofinalista *mf*.

quarter-hour ['kwɔːtəˈaʊəʳ] N cuarto *m* de hora.

quarter-hourly ['kwɔːtəˈaʊəlɪ] ① ADV cada cuarto de hora.
② ADJ: **at ~ intervals** cada cuarto de hora.

quartering ['kwɔːtərɪŋ] N (*Her*) cuartel *m*.

quarter light ['kwɔːtəˌlaɪt] N (*Brit*) ventanilla *f* direccional.

quarterly ['kwɔːtəlɪ] ① ADV cada tres meses, trimestralmente, por trimestres.
② ADJ trimestral; **~ account** cuenta *f* trimestral; **~ return** informe *m* trimestral; **~ statement** relato *m* trimestral.
③ N publicación *f* trimestral.

quartermaster ['kwɔːtəˌmɑːstəʳ] ① N (*approx*) furriel *m*, comisario *m*.
② ATTR: **~ general** intendente *m* general; **~ sergeant** ≃ brigada *m*.

quartern ['kwɔːtən] N cuarta *f*; **~ loaf** pan *m* de 4 libras.

quarterstaff ['kwɔːtəstɑːf] N (*Hist*) barra *f*.

quarter-tone ['kwɔːtətəʊn] N cuarto *m* de tono.

quartet(te) [kwɔː'tet] N (*Mus*) cuarteto *m*; (*set of 4*) grupo *m* de cuatro.

quartile ['kwɔːtaɪl] N cuartil *m*.

quarto ['kwɔːtəʊ] ① ADJ en cuarto; (*paper size*) tamaño *m* holandesa.
② N libro *m* en cuarto.

quartz ['kwɔːts] ① N cuarzo *m*.
② ATTR: **~ clock, ~ watch** reloj *m* de cuarzo; **~ crystal** cristal *m* de cuarzo; **~ lamp** lámpara *f* de cuarzo.

quartzite ['kwɔːtsaɪt] N cuarcita *f*.

quasar ['kweɪzɑːʳ] N cuasar *m*.

quash [kwɒʃ] VT *verdict* anular, invalidar; *rebellion* sofocar, reprimir;

proposal rechazar.

quasi ['kweɪzaɪ, 'kwɑːzɪ] ADV cuasi; **a ~ monarch** un cuasi monarca.

quatercentenary [ˌkwɒtəsen'tiːnərɪ] N cuarto centenario *m*.

quaternary [kwə'tɜːnərɪ] ① ADJ cuaternario.
　② N cuaternario *m*.

quatrain ['kwɒtreɪn] N cuarteto *m*, estrofa *f* de cuatro versos.

quaver ['kweɪvə'] ① N temblor *m*; vibración *f*; (*esp Brit Mus: trill*) trémolo *m*, (*note*) corchea *f*; **with a ~ in her voice** con voz trémula.
　② VT decir con voz temblorosa; **'yes', she ~ed** 'sí', dijo temblorosa.
　③ VI temblar; vibrar.

quavering ['kweɪvərɪŋ] ADJ tembloroso, trémulo; **in ~ tones** en tono tembloroso.

quaver rest ['kweɪvə'rest] N (*Brit*) pausa *f* de corchea.

quavery ['kweɪvərɪ] ADJ = **quavering**.

quay [kiː] N, **quayside** ['kiːsaɪd] N muelle *m*; **on the ~** en el muelle.

Que. (*Canada*) ABBR of **Quebec**.

queasiness ['kwiːzɪnɪs] N (*Med*) bascas *fpl*; propensión *f* a la náusea; (*of conscience*) delicadeza *f*, escrupulosidad *f*.

queasy ['kwiːzɪ] ADJ (*Med*) bascoso; *stomach* delicado; *conscience* delicado, escrupuloso; **I feel ~** me siento mal.

Quebec [kwɪ'bek] N Quebec *m*.

queen [kwiːn] ① N (a) reina *f*; (*Chess*) reina *f*; (*Cards*) dama *f*, (*in Spanish pack*) caballo *m*; **~ consort** reina *f* consorte; **she was ~ to Charles II** era la reina de Carlos II; **Q~'s Bench** (*Brit*) *departamento del Tribunal Supremo de Justicia*; **Q~'s Counsel** (*Brit*) abogado *mf* (*de categoría superior*); *ver también* QC/KC.
　(b) (*Zool*) (*also* **~ bee**) abeja *f* reina, (*ant*) hormiga *f* reina.
　(c) (ⵣ) marica⚨ *m*, homosexual *m*.
　② ATTR: **~ mother** reina *f* madre.
　③ VT *pawn* coronar; **to ~ it** conducirse como una reina, (*fig*) pavonearse.
　④ VI (*Chess*) ser coronado.

┌─────────────────────────────┐
│　　**QUEEN'S/KING'S SPEECH**　　│
└─────────────────────────────┘

ⓘ *En el Reino Unido, el* **Queen's** o **King's Speech** *es el discurso que el monarca dirige cada año a las dos cámaras del Estado en la apertura del nuevo curso parlamentario. El discurso se retransmite por radio y televisión y es preparado por el gobierno, ya que en él se indican las directrices del programa de gobierno para el curso que comienza, así como la nueva legislación que se introducirá ese año. Para seguir con la tradición, en este discurso el monarca sigue refiriéndose al gobierno como* **my government**.

queenly ['kwiːnlɪ] ADJ regio, de reina.

queer [kwɪə'] ① ADJ (a) (*odd*) raro, extraño, singular; misterioso; excéntrico; sospechoso; **~ fish*** tío *m* raro*; **it's very ~** es muy raro; **there's something ~ going on** pasa algo raro; **what's ~ about it?** ¿qué tiene esto de raro?; **to be in Q~ Street** (*Brit*) estar en la miseria.
　(b) (ⵣ) maricón⚨.
　(c) (*Brit Med*) malucho; **to come over ~, to feel ~** tener vahídos, sentirse mal, sentirse indispuesto.
　② N (ⵣ) maricón *m*.
　③ VT estropear; *V* **pitch 1** (g).

queer-bashing⚨ ['kwɪə,bæʃɪŋ] N: **to go in for ~** atacar a homosexuales.

queerly ['kwɪəlɪ] ADV de modo raro, extrañamente; misteriosamente; **to behave ~** comportarse de modo raro.

queerness ['kwɪənɪs] N rareza *f*, singularidad *f*; lo misterioso; lo excéntrico.

quell [kwel] VT *passion etc* reprimir; calmar; *revolt* sofocar, dominar; *opposition* sobreponerse a, dominar; *fears* desechar.

quench [kwentʃ] VT *flames, thirst etc* apagar; *desire, hope* matar, sofocar; *enthusiasm* enfriar.

quenchless ['kwentʃlɪs] ADJ inapagable.

quern [kwɜːn] N molinillo *m* de mano.

querulous ['kwerʊləs] ADJ quejumbroso.

querulously ['kwerʊləslɪ] ADV quejumbrosamente; en tono quejumbroso.

query ['kwɪərɪ] ① N (a) (*question*) pregunta *f*; interrogante *m*; (*doubt*) duda *f*; **~ language** lenguaje *m* de interrogación; **there are many queries about it** hay muchos interrogantes acerca de esto; **did you have a ~?** ¿querías preguntar algo?; **~: who killed Cock Robin?** pregunta: ¿quién mató a Cock Robin?
　(b) (*Gram*) signo *m* de interrogación.
　② VT (*ask*) preguntar; (*doubt*) dudar de, expresar dudas acerca de; (*Comput*) interrogar; (*disagree with*) no estar conforme con; **to ~ whether ...** dudar si ...; **I ~ that** dudo si eso es cierto, tengo mis dudas acerca de eso; **do you ~ the evidence?** ¿tienes dudas acerca del testimonio?

quest [kwest] ① N busca *f*, búsqueda *f* (*for* de); (*Hist*) demanda *f* (*for* de); **to go in ~ of** ir en busca de.
　② VTI buscar (*for sth* algo).

▼ **question** ['kwestʃən] ① N (a) (*interrogative*) pregunta *f*; interrogante *m*; **~s and answers** preguntas *fpl* y respuestas; **are there any ~s?** ¿hay alguna pregunta?; **to ask sb a ~, to put a ~ to sb** hacer una pregunta a uno; **many ~s were left unanswered** muchas preguntas quedaron sin contestar; **to pop the ~*** declararse.
　▼ (b) (*matter*) asunto *m*, cuestión *f*; problema *m*; **the German ~** el problema alemán; **the ~ is, ...** el caso es, ...; **it is a ~ of** se trata de ...; **it is a ~ of whether ...** se trata de saber si ...; **that is the ~** ahí está la dificultad; **that is not the ~** no se trata de eso; **it is not simply a ~ of money** no se trata simplemente de dinero, no es cuestión de dinero y nada más; **there is no ~ of outside help** no hay posibilidad de ayuda exterior; **there can be no ~ of your resigning** no se puede consentir en que dimitas; **there was some ~ of John coming** se hablaba de que pudiera venir Juan; **at the time in ~** a la hora que nos (*etc*) interesa; **the person in ~** la persona de quien hablamos (*etc*); **it's out of the ~** es imposible; **that begs the ~** eso es una petición de principio.
　(c) (*at meeting*) asunto *m*; interpelación *f*; **~!** ¡que se vuelva al tema de la discusión!; **~ time** (*Brit Parl*) sesión *f* de interpelaciones (dirigidas a ministros); **to move the previous ~** plantear la cuestión previa; **to put the ~** someter la moción a votación.
　(d) (*doubt etc*) **beyond ~, past ~** incuestionable, fuera de toda duda; **in ~** en cuestión; **without ~** sin duda, indudablemente; **there is no ~ about it** no existen dudas sobre ello; **it is open to ~ whether ...** es discutible si ...; **to bring** (*or* **call**) **sth in(to) ~** poner algo en duda; **to come into ~** empezar a discutirse; **I make no ~ but that it is so** no dudo que es así.
　② VT (a) (*interrogate*) hacer preguntas a; (*by police etc*) interrogar; (*by examiner etc*) examinar; (*at meeting*) interpelar; **we ~ed him closely to find out whether ...** le interrogamos del modo más apremiante para saber si ...; **I will not be ~ed about it** no permito que se me interrogue sobre eso.
　▼ (b) (*doubt*) cuestionar, poner en duda; dudar de, desconfiar de; **I ~ whether it is worthwhile** me pregunto si vale la pena; **I don't ~ your honesty** no dudo de tu honradez.

▼ **questionable** ['kwestʃənəbl] ADJ cuestionable, dudoso, discutible; **it is ~ whether ...** es dudoso si ...; **in ~ taste** de gusto dudoso.

questionary ['kwestʃənərɪ] N cuestionario *m*, encuesta *f*.

questioner ['kwestʃənə'] N interrogador *m*, -ora *f*; (*at meeting*) interpelante *mf*.

questioning ['kwestʃənɪŋ] ① ADJ interrogativo.
　② N preguntas *fpl*; (*by police etc*) interrogatorio *m*.

question-mark ['kwestʃənmɑːk] N signo *m* de interrogación; (*fig*) interrogante *m*; **a big ~ hangs over him** sobre él pende un interrogante mayúsculo.

question-master ['kwestʃən,mɑːstə'] N interrogador *m*.

questionnaire [ˌkwestʃə'nɛə'] N cuestionario *m*, encuesta *f*.

question tag ['kwestʃəntæg] N pregunta *f* coletilla.

questor ['kwiːstə'] N (*US*) = **quaestor**.

queue [kjuː] ① N (*Brit*) cola *f*; **to form a ~, to stand in a ~** hacer cola; **to jump the ~** salirse de su turno, colarse.
　② VI (*Brit: also* **to ~ up**) hacer cola; **to ~ for sth** hacer cola para comprar (*etc*) algo; **to ~ for 3 hours** pasar 3 horas haciendo cola.

queue-jump ['kjuː,dʒʌmp] VI salirse de su turno, colarse.

queue-jumper ['kjuː,dʒʌmpə'] N colón *m*, -ona *f*.

queue-jumping ['kjuː,dʒʌmpɪŋ] N colarse *m*.

quibble ['kwɪbl] ① N sofistería *f*, sutileza *f*; objeción *f* de poca monta; **that's just a ~** eso es pura sofistería, eso es mucho sutilizar.
　② VI usar sofisterías, sutilizar, buscar objeciones evasivas; hacer objeciones de poca monta; **he always ~s** es un quisquilloso, es un sofista; **you can't ~ about that** no puedes hacer objeciones acerca de eso.

quibbler ['kwɪblə'] N sofista *mf*.

quibbling ['kwɪblɪŋ] ① ADJ quisquilloso, sofista.
　② N sofistería *f*, sofismas *mpl*; sutilezas *fpl*; objeciones *fpl* de poca monta.

quiche [kiːʃ] N quiche *m*.

quick [kwɪk] ① ADJ (*speedy*) rápido; veloz; (*early*) pronto; (*of foot*) ligero, veloz; (*agile*) ágil; (*in mind*) listo, inteligente; *ear* fino; *eye, wit etc* agudo; *temper* vivo; **a ~ train** un tren rápido; **the ~est method** el método más rápido; **a ~ reply** una pronta contestación; **for a ~ sale** para poder venderlo pronto; **as ~ as a flash, as ~ as lightning** como un relámpago, como un rayo (*LAm*); **~ on the draw** rápido en sacar la pistola; **be ~!** ¡pronto! ¡date prisa!; **and just be ~ about it!** ¡no te entretengas!; **you have been very ~ about it** lo has hecho con la mayor prontitud; **he's too ~ for me** (*in speech*) habla demasiado de prisa para mí; (*in escaping*) corre más que yo; (*in intelligence*) es demasiado listo para mí; **to be ~ to act** obrar con prontitud; **to be ~ to take offence** ofenderse por poca cosa; **to be ~ to anger** tener repentinos enojos; **to be ~ to pity** tener repentina compasión; **to have a ~ one** echarse un traguito; **let's have a ~ one** entremos a tomar algo.
　② N (a) (*Anat*) carne *f* viva; **to cut sb to the ~** herir a uno en lo

vivo.

(b) (*liter*) **the ~** (*living*) los vivos; **the ~ and the dead** los vivos y los muertos.

⟨3⟩ ADV = **quickly**.

quick-acting ['kwɪk'æktɪŋ] ADJ extrarrápido, de acción rápida.

quick-change ['kwɪk'tʃeɪndʒ] ADJ: **~ actor, ~ artist** transformista *m.*

quick-eared ['kwɪk'ɪəd] ADJ de oído fino.

quicken ['kwɪkən] ⟨1⟩ VT acelerar, apresurar; avivar; **to ~ one's pace** apretar (*LAm:* acelerar) el paso.

⟨2⟩ VI acelerarse, apresurarse; avivarse; (*embryo*) empezar a moverse.

quick-eyed ['kwɪk'aɪd] ADJ de vista aguda.

quick-fire ['kwɪk'faɪə'] ADJ *gun* de tiro rápido; *question etc* rápido, hecho a quemarropa.

quick-firing ['kwɪk,faɪərɪŋ] ADJ de tiro rápido.

quick-freeze ['kwɪk'friːz] VT congelar rápidamente.

quickie* ['kwɪkɪ] N (*question*) pregunta *f* relámpago; (*drink*) trago* *m* (*etc*) rápido.

quicklime ['kwɪklaɪm] N cal *f* viva.

quickly ['kwɪklɪ] ADV rápidamente; de prisa; pronto; **~!** ¡pronto!; **they answered ~** contestaron pronto; **the next phase followed ~** la etapa siguiente empezó inmediatamente; **he talks too ~ for me to understand** habla demasiado rápidamente para que pueda entenderle; **come as ~ as you can** ven cuanto antes, ven lo más pronto que puedas; **the firemen were ~ on the spot** los bomberos se presentaron sin pérdida de tiempo.

quickness ['kwɪknɪs] N rapidez *f*, velocidad *f*; prontitud *f*, presteza *f*; agilidad *f*; inteligencia *f*; penetración *f*, finura *f*; agudeza *f*; viveza *f.*

quicksand ['kwɪksænd] N arena *f* movediza.

quickset ['kwɪkset] ⟨1⟩ ADJ compuesto de plantas vivas (*esp* de espinos).

⟨2⟩ N (*slip*) plantón *m*; (*hawthorn*) espino *m*; (*hedge*) seto *m* vivo (*esp* de espinos).

quick-setting ['kwɪk,setɪŋ] ADJ: **~ glue** pegamento *m* rápido.

quick-sighted ['kwɪk'saɪtɪd] ADJ de vista aguda; (*fig*) perspicaz.

quicksilver ['kwɪk,sɪlvə'] ⟨1⟩ N azogue *m*, mercurio *m.*

⟨2⟩ ADJ azogado; (*fig*) inconstante, caprichoso.

⟨3⟩ VT azogar.

quickstep ['kwɪkstep] N *baile formal a ritmo rápido.*

quick-tempered ['kwɪk'tempəd] ADJ de genio vivo, irascible, de prontos enojos.

quick-witted ['kwɪk'wɪtɪd] ADJ agudo, perspicaz; **that was very ~ of you** en eso ha estado muy listo.

quid¹* [kwɪd] N (*Brit*) libra *f* esterlina; **3 ~** 3 libras; **to be ~s in** haber ganado bastante.

quid² [kwɪd] N mascada *f* (de tabaco).

quiddity ['kwɪdɪtɪ] N (*Philos*) esencia *f*; (*quibble*) sutileza *f*, sofistería *f.*

quid pro quo ['kwɪdprəʊ'kwəʊ] N quid pro quo *m*, compensación *f*, recompensa *f* (*for* de).

quiescence [kwaɪ'esns] N quietud *f*, inactividad *f*; reposo *m.*

quiescent [kwaɪ'esnt] ADJ quieto, inactivo; reposado.

quiet ['kwaɪət] ⟨1⟩ ADJ **(a)** (*silent*) silencioso, callado; *person* (*by nature*) callado, reservado; *place, town etc* tranquilo; (*pej*) *town, life etc* aburrido; *engine etc* sin ruido, que no hace ruido, silencioso; (*not excited*) tranquilo, reposado; **~!, be ~!** (*to people*) ¡silencio!, (*more forcefully*) ¡a callar!, (*to 1 person*) ¡cállate!; **to be ~** (*person: after speaking*) callarse, (*in moving about*) no hacer ruido; **isn't it ~?** ¡qué silencio!; **it was as ~ as the grave** había un silencio sepulcral; **to keep ~** no hacer ruido; no decir nada, quedar callado, callarse; **keep those bottles ~!** ¡no hagas tanto ruido con esas botellas!; **to keep as ~ as a mouse** estar a la chita callando; **they paid £100 to keep him ~** pagaron 100 libras para callarle.

(b) *temperament* tranquilo, sosegado; *animal* manso; 'The Q~ American' 'El americano impasible'.

(c) *dress etc* no llamativo, discreto; *colour* suave, apagado.

(d) (*not overt*) discreto; (*private*) más bien privado; íntimo, que se celebra en la intimidad; (*informal*) íntimo, sin ceremonias; **with ~ humour he said ...** con su humor discreto dijo ...; **all ~ here** aquí sin novedad; **all ~ on the Western Front** sin novedad en el frente del oeste; **it was a ~ wedding** la boda se celebró en la intimidad; **we had a ~ supper** cenamos en la intimidad; **business is very ~** el negocio está muy flojo; **to have a ~ dig at sb** burlarse discretamente de uno; **they lead a ~ life** llevan una vida tranquila.

⟨2⟩ N silencio *m*; paz *f*; tranquilidad *f*; reposo *m*; **an hour of blessed ~** una hora de paz bendita; **on the ~** a la sordina, a hurtadillas; **let's have complete ~** quiero que se callen completamente todos.

⟨3⟩ VT calmar; V **quieten**.

quieten ['kwaɪətn] ⟨1⟩ VT (*esp Brit*) (*also* **to ~ down**) (*calm*) calmar, tranquilizar; (*silence*) hacer callar; **he managed to ~ the crowd** logró tranquilizar a la multitud.

⟨2⟩ VI (*also* **to ~ down**) calmarse, tranquilizarse; callarse; (*after unruly youth etc*) sentar los cascos, hacerse más juicioso.

quietism ['kwaɪətɪzəm] N quietismo *m.*

quietist ['kwaɪətɪst] N quietista *mf.*

quietly ['kwaɪətlɪ] ADV (*V* ADJ) **(a)** silenciosamente, en silencio, calladamente; tranquilamente; sin hacer ruido; **he said ~** dijo dulcemente, dijo en tono bajo; **please play more ~** procure tocar con menos ruido, por favor; **she came in ~** entró sin hacer ruido.

(b) sosegadamente; mansamente; **are you coming ~ or are you going to make trouble?** ¿nos acompaña Vd pacíficamente o va a armar un lío*?

(c) discretamente; **to be ~ dressed** ir vestido con discreción.

(d) discretamente; en la intimidad, en privado; sin ceremonias; **let's get married ~** casémonos sin ceremonias; **we dined ~ at home** cenamos en la intimidad del hogar.

quietness ['kwaɪətnɪs] N (*V* ADJ) **(a)** silencio *m*; paz *f*; tranquilidad *f*; reposo *m*; **the ~ of her voice** lo dulce de su voz, su voz dulce.

(b) sosiego *m*, lo sosegado; mansedumbre *f.*

(c) discreción *f.*

(d) discreción *f*; intimidad *f.*

quietude ['kwaɪətjuːd] N quietud *f.*

quietus [kwaɪ'iːtəs] N golpe *m* de gracia; (*death*) muerte *f*; (*Comm*) quitanza *f*, finiquito *m.*

quiff [kwɪf] N copete *m.*

quill [kwɪl] N (*Zool*) pluma *f* de ave; (*part of feather*) cañón *m* de pluma; (*pen*) pluma *f* (de ganso); (*in fishing*) cañón *m* de pluma; (*of hedgehog etc*) púa *f*; (*bobbin*) canilla *f*; **~ pen** pluma *f* (de ganso).

quilt [kwɪlt] ⟨1⟩ N (*Brit*) colcha *f*, edredón *m.*

⟨2⟩ VT acolchar.

quilted ['kwɪltɪd] ADJ acolchado.

quilting ['kwɪltɪŋ] N colchadura *f*; (*Sew*) piqué *m*, acolchado *m.*

quim* [kwɪm] N coño* *m.*

quin* [kwɪn] N (*Brit*) = **quintuplet**.

quince [kwɪns] ⟨1⟩ N (*fruit, tree*) membrillo *m.*

⟨2⟩ ATTR: **~ cheese, ~ jelly** carne *f* de membrillo.

quincentenary [,kwɪnsen'tiːnərɪ] N quinto centenario *m.*

quinine [kwɪ'niːn] N quinina *f.*

Quinquagesima [,kwɪnkwə'dʒesɪmə] N Quincuagésima *f.*

quinquennial [kwɪn'kwenɪəl] ADJ quinquenal.

quinquennium [kwɪn'kwenɪəm] N quinquenio *m.*

quinsy ['kwɪnzɪ] N angina *f.*

quint* [kwɪnt] N (*US*) quintillizo *m*, -a *f.*

quintessence [kwɪn'tesns] N quintaesencia *f.*

quintessential [,kwɪntɪ'senʃəl] ADJ quintaesencial.

quintet(te) [kwɪn'tet] N quinteto *m.*

quintuple ⟨1⟩ ['kwɪntjʊpl] ADJ quíntuplo.

⟨2⟩ ['kwɪntjʊpl] N quíntuplo *m.*

⟨3⟩ ['kwɪn'tjuːpl] VT quintuplicar.

⟨4⟩ ['kwɪn'tjuːpl] VI quintuplicarse.

quintuplet [kwɪn'tjuːplɪt] N quintillizo *m*, -a *f.*

quip [kwɪp] ⟨1⟩ N chiste *m*, agudeza *f*, ocurrencia *f*, pulla *f.*

⟨2⟩ VT: **'~', he ~ped '~'**, dijo humorísticamente.

⟨3⟩ VI hacer un chiste.

quire ['kwaɪə'] N mano *f* (de papel).

quirk [kwɜːk] N **(a)** (*oddity*) peculiaridad *f*, rasgo *m* peculiar; capricho *m*; **by some ~ of fate** por algún capricho de la suerte; **it's just a ~ he has** son cosas suyas, es un rasgo peculiar suyo.

(b) (*flourish*) rasgo *m*; (*Archit*) avivador *m.*

quirkiness ['kwɜːkɪnɪs] N carácter *m* caprichoso; rareza *f*, lo estrafalario.

quirky ['kwɜːkɪ] ADJ caprichoso; raro, estrafalario.

quisling ['kwɪzlɪŋ] N quisling *mf*; colaboracionista *mf.*

quit [kwɪt] (*irr*: PRET AND PTP **quit** *or* **quitted**) ⟨1⟩ VT dejar, abandonar (*also Comput*); *place* abandonar, salir de; *premises etc* desocupar; **to ~ one's job** abandonar su puesto, dimitir; **to ~ work** suspender el trabajo, dejar de trabajar; **to ~ + ger** (*US*) dejar de + *infin*, desistir de + *infin*; **~ fooling!** ¡déjate de tonterías!; **it's time to ~ dreaming** es hora de renunciar a los sueños.

⟨2⟩ VI (*esp US*) (*go away*) irse, marcharse; (*withdraw*) retirarse; (*Comput*) terminar, abandonar; (*resign*) dimitir; (*give up, in game etc*) rajarse, abandonar; *stop work* suspender el trabajo, dejar de trabajar; (*be a quitter*) renunciar a una empresa, abandonar, rajarse; **I ~!** ¡me rajo!

⟨3⟩ ADJ: **to be ~ of sb** estar libre de uno, haberse librado de uno.

quite [kwaɪt] ADV **(a)** (*completely*) totalmente, completamente; **~ new** completamente nuevo; **~ a hero** todo un héroe (*also iro*); **~!, ~ so!** ¡se comprende!, ¡así es!, perfectamente; **oh, ~ that!** ¡lo menos eso!; **that's ~ enough** eso basta y sobra; **that's ~ enough for me** eso me basta a mí; **not ~ as many as last time** algo menos que la última vez; **I ~ understand** lo comprendo perfectamente; **I don't ~ understand it** no acabo de entenderlo; **that's not ~ right** eso no está del todo bien; **he has not ~ recovered yet** no se ha repuesto todavía del todo; **it was ~ 3 months** era lo menos 3 meses; **it's not ~ what we wanted** no es exactamente lo que buscábamos; **we don't ~ know** no sabemos exactamente; **he's ~ grown up now** ahora está hecho un hombre; es todo un hombre.

(b) (*rather*) bastante; **it's ~ good** es bastante bueno; **it was ~ a** (*or* **some**) **surprise** me sorprendió bastante; **I ~ believe that** ... casi tengo la certeza de que ...

Quito ['kiːtəʊ] N Quito *m*.

quits [kwɪts] ADV: **to be ~ with sb** estar en paz con uno, estar desquitado con uno; **now we're ~!** ¡ahora no nos debemos nada!; **let's call it ~** hagamos las paces; **to cry ~** (querer) hacer las paces.

quitter ['kwɪtəʳ] N remolón *m*, -ona *f*; persona *f* que deja fácilmente lo empezado; inconstante *mf*, rajado *m*, -a *f*.

quiver[1] ['kwɪvəʳ] N carcaj *m*, aljaba *f*.

quiver[2] ['kwɪvəʳ] **1** N temblor *m*, estremecimiento *m*, palpitación *f*. **2** VI temblar, estremecerse, palpitar (*with* de).

qui vive [kiːˈviːv] N: **to be on the ~** estar alerta.

Quixote ['kwɪksət] NM Quijote.

quixotic [kwɪkˈsɒtɪk] ADJ quijotesco.

quixotically [kwɪkˈsɒtɪkəlɪ] ADV de manera quijotesca; **to behave ~** comportarse como un quijote.

quixotism ['kwɪksətɪzəm] N quijotismo *m*.

quiz [kwɪz] **1** N (*interrogation*) interrogatorio *m*; examen *m*; (*US*) test *m*; (*inquiry*) encuesta *f*; (*Rad etc*; *also* **~ programme, ~ show**) concurso *m* de preguntas y respuestas; **~ master** moderador *m*. **2** VT (*stare at*) mirar con curiosidad; (*question*) interrogar (*about* sobre).

quizzical ['kwɪzɪkəl] ADJ burlón.

quizzically ['kwɪzɪkəlɪ] ADV: **he looked at me ~** me miró burlón.

quod: [kwɒd] N (*Brit*) chirona: *f*.

quoin [kɔɪn] N (*angle*) esquina *f*, ángulo *m*; (*stone*) piedra *f* angular; (*Typ*) cuña *f*.

quoit [kwɔɪt] N aro *m*, tejo *m*; **~s** juego *m* de aros, juego *m* de tejos.

quondam ['kwɒndæm] ADJ (††) antiguo.

quorate ['kwɔːreɪt] ADJ: **the meeting was not ~** no había suficiente quórum en la reunión.

Quorn [kwɔːn] ® N *sustituto de comidas a base de proteínas vegetales*.

quorum ['kwɔːrəm] N quórum *m*; **to constitute a ~** constituir un quórum; **what number constitutes a ~?** ¿cuántos constituyen un quórum?

quot. N ABBR *of* **quotation** (**b**).

quota ['kwəʊtə] N cuota *f*; (*Comm etc*) contingente *m*, cupo *m*; (*of production*) cuota *f*, cupo *m*; **import ~** cupo *m* de importación; **~ system** sistema *m* de cuota.

quotable ['kwəʊtəbl] ADJ citable; digno de citarse; (*Fin*) cotizable.

quotation [kwəʊˈteɪʃən] N (**a**) (*words*) cita *f*; (*act*) citación *f*; **~ marks** comillas *fpl*; **in ~ marks** entre comillas; **dictionary of ~s** diccionario *m* de frases. (**b**) (*Fin*) cotización *f*; (*Comm*) presupuesto *m*.

quote [kwəʊt] **1** VT (**a**) citar; *reference number etc* dar, expresar; *example* dar, aducir; **he ~d Góngora** citó a Góngora; **he can ~ Góngora all day long** es capaz de seguir recitando versos de Góngora hasta cuando sea; **he said, and I ~,** ... dijo textualmente ...; **but don't ~ me** pero no me menciones, pero sin mencionar mi nombre; **please ~ the number of the postal order** por favor exprese el número del giro postal; **can you ~ me an example?** ¿puedes darme un ejemplo? (**b**) (*Fin*) cotizar (*at* en); (*Comm*) estimar; **~d company** empresa *f* cotizada en la Bolsa; **it is not ~d on the Stock Exchange** no se cotiza en la Bolsa.
2 VI (**a**) citar; **to ~ from an author** citar versos (*etc*) de un autor, repetir las palabras de un autor; **and I ~** y aquí cito sus propias palabras.
(**b**) **to ~ for** (*Comm*) preparar el presupuesto para, presupuestar; estimar el precio de.
3 N cita *f*; **~s** (*inverted commas*) comillas *fpl*; **in ~s** entre comillas; **'~'** 'comienza la cita'; **'close the ~', 'end of ~'** 'fin de la cita'; **she said the minister was (~) "as tired as a newt" (un~)** dijo que el ministro estaba — entre comillas — "más cansado que una cuba".

quoth [kwəʊθ] VI (††): **~ I** dije yo; **~ he** dijo él.

quotidian [kwəʊˈtɪdɪən] ADJ (*liter*) cotidiano.

quotient ['kwəʊʃənt] N cociente *m*.

q.v. ABBR *of* **quod vide** = 'which see' véase, q.v.

qwerty ['kwɜːtɪ] ATTR: **~ keyboard** teclado *m* QWERTY.

R

R, r [ɑːʳ] N (*letter*) R *f*, r *f*; **R for Robert, R for Roger** (*US*) R de Ramón; **the 3 Rs** (= *reading, writing, [a]rithmetic*) las enseñanzas básicas; *ver también* ⟨THREE RS⟩.

R (a) (*Brit*) ABBR of **Rex** Rey *m*, R.
(b) (*Brit*) ABBR of **Regina** Reina *f*, R.
(c) (*Geog*) ABBR of **river** río *m*, R.
(d) ABBR of **right** derecha *f*, dcha.
(e) ADJ (*US Cine*) ABBR of **restricted** sólo mayores.
(f) ABBR of **Réaumur (scale)**.
(g) (*US Pol*) ABBR of **Republican**.

Ⓡ N ABBR of **registered trade mark** marca *f* registrada.

R&B N ABBR of **Rhythm and Blues**.

R&D N ABBR of **research and development** investigación *f* y desarrollo, I. y D.

R&R N (*US Mil*) ABBR of **rest and recreation** descanso *m*.

RA N (a) (*Brit Art*) ABBR of **Royal Academy (of Arts)** Real Academia *f* de Bellas Artes. (b) (*Brit Art*) ABBR of **Royal Academician** miembro *mf* de la Real Academia de Bellas Artes. (c) (*Mil*) ABBR of **Royal Artillery**. (d) ABBR of **Rear Admiral**.

⸺ RA - ROYAL ACADEMY OF ARTS ⸺

 *La **Royal Academy of Arts** o **RA** es la más famosa de las fundaciones de arte británicas. Con sede en Londres, la **Royal Academy** presenta exposiciones de artistas modernos y de todas las épocas, y también imparte algunas clases a futuros artistas. Cada verano tiene lugar la **Summer Exhibition**, que es la mayor exposición abierta de arte contemporáneo en el mundo. Cualquier artista puede enviar su trabajo y la selección final de obras concentra una amplia gama de estilos, tanto de artistas conocidos como de principiantes. Los artistas miembros de la **Royal Academy of Arts** pueden escribir las iniciales **RA** después de sus nombres, como si de un título académico se tratase.*

RAAF N ABBR of **Royal Australian Air Force**.

Rabat [rə'bɑːt] N Rabat *m*.

rabbi ['ræbaɪ] N rabino *m*; (*before name*) rabí *m*; **chief ~** gran rabino *m*.

Rabbinic [rə'bɪnɪk] N (*Ling*) hebreo *m* rabínico.

rabbinical [rə'bɪnɪkəl] ADJ rabínico.

rabbit ['ræbɪt] **1** N conejo *m*; (*Sport**) jugador *m*, -ora *f* inhábil; **~ ears*** (*US TV*) antena *f* de conejo.
2 VI (a) **to go ~ing** (ir a) cazar conejos.
(b) **to ~ on*** (*Brit*) dar el rollo*, no parar de hablar, hablar sin ton ni son.

rabbit burrow ['ræbɪt,bʌrəʊ] N madriguera *f* (de conejos).

rabbit-hole ['ræbɪthəʊl] N hura *f* de conejos.

rabbit-hutch ['ræbɪthʌtʃ] N conejera *f*.

rabbit punch ['ræbɪtpʌntʃ] N golpe *m* de nuca.

rabbit warren ['ræbɪt,wɒrən] N conejera *f*, madriguera *f* (de conejos).

rabble ['ræbl] N (*the ~*) canalla *f*, chusma *f*; **a ~ of** una multitud turbulenta de.

rabble-rouser ['ræbl,raʊzəʳ] N agitador *m*, -ora *f*, demagogo *m*, -a *f*.

rabble-rousing ['ræbl'raʊzɪŋ] **1** ADJ demagógico.
2 N agitación *f*, demagogia *f*.

Rabelaisian [,ræbə'leɪzɪən] ADJ rabelasiano.

rabid ['ræbɪd] ADJ (*Med*) rabioso; (*fig*) rabioso, fanático.

rabies ['reɪbiːz] N rabia *f*.

RAC N (*Brit*) (a) (*Aut*) ABBR of **Royal Automobile Club** ≃ Real Automóvil Club *m* de España, RACE *m*. (b) (*Mil*) ABBR of **Royal Armoured Corps**.

raccoon [rə'kuːn] N mapache *m*.

race¹ [reɪs] **1** N (a) (*contest*) carrera *f*, prueba *f*; (*on water*) regata *f*; **~s** carreras *fpl*; **the ~ for the moon** la carrera hacia la luna; **~ against the clock**, (*fig*) **~ against time** carrera *f* contra (el) reloj; **to go to the ~s** ir a las carreras; **to run a ~** tomar parte en una carrera; **you**

ran a good **~** corriste muy bien.
(b) (*rush*) carrera *f*, corrida *f*; **the ~ to the bus** la carrera precipitada para coger el autobús; **it was a ~ to finish it in time** nos costó para terminarlo a tiempo.
(c) (*current*) corriente *f* fuerte; (*of mill*) caz *m*, saetín *m*.
2 ATTR: **~ car** coche *m* de carreras; **~ (car) driver** (*US*) corredor *m*, -ora *f* de coches.
3 VT (a) *horse etc* hacer correr, (*at race meeting*) presentar.
(b) **to ~ sb** competir con uno en una carrera (*or* regata); **I'll ~ you!** ¡te echo una carrera!, ¡a ver quién corre más!; **I'll ~ you home!** ¡a ver quién llega primero a casa!
(c) **to ~ an engine** acelerar un motor al máximo, hacer funcionar un motor a velocidad excesiva.
(d) **to ~ a plan through** hacer que se apruebe un proyecto de prisa; no permitir que se discuta debidamente un proyecto.
4 VI (a) (*go fast*) correr de prisa, (*Aut etc*) ir a máxima velocidad; **to ~ along** ir corriendo; **to ~ down a hill** ir cuesta abajo a toda carrera; **he ~d past us** pasó delante de nosotros corriendo como un demonio, nos pasó a toda carrera.
(b) (*pulse*) latir a ritmo acelerado; (*engine*) girar a velocidad excesiva.
(c) (*in contest*) competir; presentarse; **they will ~ at 3 o'clock** empezarán la carrera a las 3; **we're not racing today** no tomamos parte hoy; **when did you last ~?** ¿cuándo corriste (*etc*) la última vez?

race² [reɪs] **1** N (*Bio*) raza *f*; casta *f*, estirpe *f*, familia *f*; **the white ~** la raza blanca; **he comes from a ~ of smugglers** es de linaje de contrabandistas.
2 ATTR: **~ relations** relaciones *fpl* raciales; **~ riot** disturbio *m* racial.

racecard ['reɪskɑːd] N programa *m* de carreras.

racecourse ['reɪskɔːs] N (*esp Brit*) hipódromo *m*.

racegoer ['reɪsgəʊəʳ] N el *m* (*or* la *f*) que asiste a las carreras, aficionado *m*, -a *f* a las carreras (de caballos).

race-hatred ['reɪs'heɪtrɪd] N odio *m* racial, racismo *m*.

racehorse ['reɪshɔːs] N caballo *m* de carreras.

raceme ['ræsiːm] N racimo *m*.

race-meeting ['reɪs,miːtɪŋ] N carreras *fpl* (de caballos).

racer ['reɪsəʳ] N corredor *m*, -ora *f*; (*horse*) caballo *m* de carreras; (*Aut*) coche *m* de carreras.

racetrack ['reɪstræk] N (*Brit: horses*) pista *f*, (*US*) hipódromo *m*; (*Aut etc*) autódromo *m*.

Rachel ['reɪtʃəl] NF Raquel.

rachitic [ræ'kɪtɪk] ADJ raquítico.

racial ['reɪʃəl] ADJ racial; racista; **~ discrimination** discriminación *f* racial; **~ integration** integración *f* racial.

racialism ['reɪʃəlɪzəm] N racismo *m*.

racialist ['reɪʃəlɪst] **1** ADJ racista.
2 N racista *mf*.

racially ['reɪʃəlɪ] ADV racialmente; de manera racista; **children of ~ mixed parents** hijos *mpl* de padres racialmente mixtos.

raciness ['reɪsɪnɪs] N picante *m*, sal *f*, vivacidad *f*.

racing ['reɪsɪŋ] **1** N carreras *fpl*.
2 ATTR de carreras; **~ bicycle** bicicleta *f* de carreras; **~ calendar** calendario *m* de carreras (de caballos); **~ car** coche *m* de carreras; **~ cyclist** corredor *m*, -ora *f* ciclista; **~ driver**, **~ motorist** piloto *m*, corredor *m*, -ora *f* automovilista; **~ man** aficionado *m* a las carreras (de caballos); experto *m* en caballos; **~ pigeon** paloma *f* de carreras; **the ~ world** el mundo de las carreras (de caballos); **~ yacht** yate *m* de regatas.

racism ['reɪsɪzəm] N racismo *m*.

racist ['reɪsɪst] **1** ADJ racista.
2 N racista *mf*.

rack¹ [ræk] **1** N (*shelf*) estante *m*, estantería *f*, anaquel *m*; (*for clothes etc*) percha *f*, perchero *m*, cuelgacapas *m*, colgadero *m* (*LAm*); (*Aut*) baca *f*; (*Rail*) rejilla *f*; (*Mech*) cremallera *f*; (*for torture*) potro *m*; (*for arms*) armero *m*; (*for billiard cues*) taquera *f*; **~ and pinion** cremallera *f* y piñón; **to be on the ~** (*fig*) estar en ascuas; **to buy clothes off the ~** (*US*) comprar ropa de percha.

2 VT **(a)** atormentar; **to be ~ed by pains** tener dolores atroces por todas partes; **to be ~ed by remorse** estar atormentado por el remordimiento; *V* **brain**.

(b) *wine* (*also* **to ~ off**) trasegar.

♦**rack up** VT (*accumulate*) conseguir, ganar.

rack² [ræk] N: **to go to ~ and ruin** arruinarse, echarse a perder.

racket¹ ['rækɪt] N, **racquet** ['rækɪt] N raqueta *f*; **~s** (*game*) especie de tenis jugado contra frontón.

racket² ['rækɪt] **1** N **(a)** (*din*) ruido *m*, estrépito *m*; (*confused noise*) barahúnda *f*, jaleo *m*; **you never heard such a ~!** ¡no se había oído nunca tal ruido!; **to kick up** (*or* **make**) **a ~** armar un jaleo, meter ruido.

(b) (*: trick*) trampa *f*, trapacería *f*; (*criminal*) fraude *m* sistematizado, estafa *f*, timo *m*; (*blackmail, protection*) chantaje *m*; **the drug ~** el tráfico de drogas; **the car ~** (*hum*) el negocio del automóvil; **it's a ~!** ¡aquí hay trampa!; **what ~ are you in?** ¿a qué se dedica Vd?; **he was in on the ~** era de los que operaban la trampa; **to stand the ~** pagar los platos rotos.

2 VI (*make noise*) (*also* **to ~ about**) hacer ruido, armar un jaleo.

racketeer [,rækɪ'tɪəʳ] N estafador *m*, timador *m*; chantajista *m*.

racketeering [,rækɪ'tɪərɪŋ] N chantaje *m* sistematizado, crimen *m* organizado.

racking ['rækɪŋ] ADJ *pain* atroz.

rack railway ['ræk'reɪlweɪ] N ferrocarril *m* de cremallera.

rack-rent ['rækrent] N alquiler *m* exorbitante.

raconteur [,rækɒn'tɜːʳ] N anecdotista *m*, narrador *m*, (*esp*) el que cuenta con gracia los chistes.

racoon [rə'kuːn] N mapache *m*.

racquet ['rækɪt] N = **racket¹**.

racy ['reɪsɪ] ADJ picante, salado, vivo.

rad: [ræd] ADJ (*esp US*) = **radical (b)**.

RADA ['rɑːdə] N (*Brit*) ABBR *of* **Royal Academy of Dramatic Art**.

radar ['reɪdɑːʳ] **1** N radar *m*.

2 ATTR: **~ beacon** faro *m* de radar; **~ scanner** antena *f* giratoria de radar; **~ screen** pantalla *f* de radar; **~ station** estación *f* de radar; **~ trap** trampa *f* de radar.

raddled ['rædld] ADJ depravado, decaído.

radial ['reɪdɪəl] ADJ radial; **~ engine** motor *m* radial; **~ tyre** (*Brit*), **~-ply (tire)** (*US*) neumático *m* radial.

radiance ['reɪdɪəns] N brillantez *f*, brillo *m*, resplandor *m*.

radiant ['reɪdɪənt] ADJ radiante, brillante, resplandeciente; **a ~ smile** una sonrisa radiante; **the bride was ~** la novia estaba hermosísima; **to be ~ with happiness** estar radiante de felicidad, rebosar felicidad.

radiantly ['reɪdɪəntlɪ] ADV brillantemente; **to be ~ happy** irradiar felicidad; **to smile ~ at sb** echar una sonrisa radiante a uno.

radiate **1** ['reɪdɪeɪt] VT radiar, irradiar; *happiness etc* difundir; **lines that ~ from the centre** líneas *fpl* que se extienden desde el centro.

2 ['reɪdɪeɪt] VI irradiar, radiar (*from* de); (*roads etc*) salir (*from* de).

3 ['reɪdɪɪt] ADJ radiado.

radiation [,reɪdɪ'eɪʃən] N radiación *f*; **~ sickness** enfermedad *f* de radiación; **~ therapy** terapéutica *f* por radiaciones; **~ treatment** tratamiento *m* por radiaciones.

radiator ['reɪdɪeɪtəʳ] N radiador *m*; **~ cap** tapón *m* de radiador; **~ grille** reja *f* de radiador.

radical ['rædɪkəl] **1** ADJ **(a)** radical. **(b)** (*US:*) guay*, súper*.

2 N (*all senses*) radical *m*.

radicalism ['rædɪkəlɪzəm] N radicalismo *m*.

radicalize ['rædɪkə,laɪz] VT radicalizar.

radically ['rædɪkəlɪ] ADV radicalmente.

radicchio [ræ'diːkɪəʊ] N achicoria *f* roja.

radicle ['rædɪkl] N (*Bot*) radícula *f*; (*Chem*) radical *m*.

radii ['reɪdɪaɪ] NPL *of* **radius**.

radio ['reɪdɪəʊ] **1** N (*as science etc*) radio *f*, radiofonía *f*; (*set*) radio *f* (*m in parts of LAm*), receptor *m* de radio, radiorreceptor *m*; **by ~, on the ~, over the ~** por radio; **to talk on the ~** hablar por radio.

2 ATTR: **~-alarm clock** radio-reloj *m* despertador; **~ announcer** locutor *m*, -ora *f* de radio; **~ astronomy** radioastronomía *f*; **~ beacon, ~ beam** radiofaro *m*; **~ broadcast** emisión *f* de radio; **~ contact** radiocomunicación *f*; **~ engineer** radiotécnico *m*; **~ engineering** radiotécnica *f*; **~ frequency** frecuencia *f* de radio; **~ ham** radioaficionado *m*, -a *f*; **~ link** enlace *m* radiofónico; **~ mast, ~ tower** (*US*) torre *f* de radio; **~ network** cadena *f* (*or* red *f*) de emisoras; **~ operator** radiotelegrafista *mf*; **~ play** comedia *f* radiofónica; **~ program** (*US*), **~ programme** programa *m* de radio; **~ set** radio *f*; **~ silence** silencio *m* radiofónico; **~ station** emisora *f*; **~ taxi** radiotaxi *m*; **~ telescope** radiotelescopio *m*; **~ transmitter** emisora *f*; **~ wave** onda *f* de radio.

3 VT radiar, transmitir por radio.

4 VI: **to ~ for help** pedir socorro por radio; **to ~ to sb** enviar un mensaje a uno por radio.

radio... ['reɪdɪəʊ] PREF radio...

radioactive ['reɪdɪəʊ'æktɪv] ADJ radiactivo; **~ waste** residuos *mpl* radiactivos.

radioactivity ['reɪdɪəʊæk'tɪvɪtɪ] N radiactividad *f*.

radiobiology [,reɪdɪəʊbaɪ'ɒlədʒɪ] N radiobiología *f*.

radiocarbon [,reɪdɪəʊ'kɑːbən] N radiocarbono *m*; **~ analysis** análisis *m* por radiocarbono; **~ test** test *m* por radiocarbono.

radiocassette [,reɪdɪəʊkə'set] N (*also* **~ recorder**) radiocaset(t)e *m*.

radio-controlled [,reɪdɪəʊkən'trəʊld] ADJ teledirigido.

radiogram ['reɪdɪəʊgræm] N (*Brit: set*) radiogramola *f*; (*message*) radiograma *m*.

radiograph ['reɪdɪəʊgrɑːf] **1** N radiografía *f*.

2 VT radiografiar.

radiographer [,reɪdɪ'ɒgrəfəʳ] N radiógrafo *m*, -a *f*.

radiography [,reɪdɪ'ɒgrəfɪ] N radiografía *f*.

radioisotope ['reɪdɪəʊ'aɪsətəʊp] N radioisótopo *m*.

radiolocation [,reɪdɪəʊlə'keɪʃən] N radiolocalización *f*.

radiological [,reɪdɪə'lɒdʒɪkəl] ADJ radiológico.

radiologist [,reɪdɪ'ɒlədʒɪst] N radiólogo *m*, -a *f*.

radiology [,reɪdɪ'ɒlədʒɪ] N radiología *f*.

radiopager ['reɪdɪəʊ,peɪdʒəʳ] N localizador *m*, busca* *m*.

radioscopy [,reɪdɪ'ɒskəpɪ] N radioscopia *f*.

radiotelephone ['reɪdɪəʊ'telɪfəʊn] N radioteléfono *m*.

radiotelephony [,reɪdɪəʊtə'lefənɪ] N radiotelefonía *f*.

radiotherapist [,reɪdɪəʊ'θerəpɪst] N radioterapeuta *mf*.

radiotherapy ['reɪdɪəʊ'θerəpɪ] N radioterapia *f*.

radish ['rædɪʃ] N rábano *m*.

radium ['reɪdɪəm] N radio *m*.

radius ['reɪdɪəs] N, PL **radii** ['reɪdɪaɪ] (*most senses*) radio *m*; (*Aer. also* **operational ~**) autonomía *f*; **within a ~ of 50 km** en un radio de 50 km.

radix ['reɪdɪks] N, PL **radices** ['reɪdɪsiːz] (*Bot, Gram*) raíz *f*; (*Math*) base *f*.

radon ['reɪdɒn] N radón *m*.

RAF N (*Brit*) ABBR *of* **Royal Air Force** fuerzas *fpl* aéreas británicas.

raffia ['ræfɪə] N rafia *f*.

raffish ['ræfɪʃ] ADJ disipado, disoluto.

raffle ['ræfl] **1** N rifa *f*, sorteo *m*.

2 VT rifar, sortear; **10 bottles will be ~d for charity** se sortearán 10 botellas con fines benéficos.

raft [rɑːft] N **(a)** balsa *f*, almadía *f*. **(b)** (*) (*quantity*) cantidad *f*; montón *m*; (*set*) serie *f*; grupo *m*.

rafter ['rɑːftəʳ] N par *m*; **the ~s** (*loosely*) el techo.

rag¹ [ræg] **1** N **(a)** (*piece of cloth*) trapo *m*; (*for cleaning*) trapo *m*, paño *m*; (*shred of clothing*) andrajo *m*, harapo *m*; **~s** (*: clothes*) trapos* *mpl*; **from ~s to riches** de los andrajos a la riqueza; **to be in ~s** estar harapiento, estar en andrajos; **to chew the ~** (*US: chat*) charlar, pasar el rato, (*argue*) discutir; **to feel like a ~** estar hecho cisco; **she hasn't a ~ to her back** no tiene con qué vestirse; **to put on one's glad ~s** endomingarse; **it's like a red ~ to a bull** es lo que más le provoca a cólera, no hay nada que más le enfurezca.

(b) (*: newspaper*) periodicucho* *m*.

2 ATTR: **~ doll** muñeca *f* de trapo; **~ fair** rastro *m*, feria *f* de ropa y objetos usados; **~ trade*** industria *f* del vestido.

rag² [ræg] (*Brit*) **1** N (*practical joke*) broma *f* pesada; (*Univ*) broma *f* estudiantil; novatada *f*, (*for charity*) función *f* estudiantil benéfica; **~ week** semana *f* de funciones benéficas (estudiantiles); **we did it just for a ~** lo hicimos en broma nada más.

2 (*) VT dar guerra a, tomar el pelo a*; **they were ~ging him about his new tie** le estaban tomando el pelo por la nueva corbata*.

3 VI guasearse, bromearse; **I was only ~ging** lo dije en broma.

───── *RAG WEEK* ─────

ⓘ Los universitarios británicos suelen organizar cada año lo que llaman **rag week**. Es costumbre que, durante esa semana, los estudiantes se disfracen y salgan así vestidos a la calle, pidiendo dinero a los transeúntes con el fin de recaudar fondos para fines benéficos.

ragamuffin ['rægə,mʌfɪn] N granuja *m*, galopín *m*.

rag-and-bone man [,rægən'bəʊnmæn] N, PL **rag-and-bone men** [,rægən'bəʊnmen] (*Brit*) trapero *m*.

ragbag ['rægbæg] N talego *m* de recortes; (*Brit fig*) mezclanza *f*, cajón *m* de sastre; **it's a ~ of a book** es un libro todo revuelto, el libro es todo un fárrago.

rage [reɪdʒ] **1** N **(a)** (*anger*) rabia *f*, furor *m*, ira *f*; (*of wind etc*) furia *f*; **to be in a ~** estar furioso (*about* por, *with sb* contra uno); **to fly into a ~** montar en cólera, encolerizarse; **to vent one's ~ on sb** descargar su indignación sobre uno.

(b) (*fashion*) boga *f*, moda *f* (*for* de); (*craze*) manía *f* (*for* de); **it's all the ~** es la moda, es la última; **his dresses are all the ~ in New**

York sus vestidos hacen furor en Nueva York.

[2] VI (a) (*be angry*) estar furioso, rabiar; **to ~ against sb** estar furioso con uno; culpar amargamente a uno; **to ~ against sth** protestar furiosamente contra algo.

(b) (*of pain*) doler atrozmente; (*sea etc*) embravecerse, enfurecerse; (*wind*) bramar; (*fire, plague etc*) desencadenarse; continuar con pleno vigor; **fire ~d in the building for 3 hours** durante 3 horas el fuego hizo estragos en el edificio.

ragged ['rægɪd] ADJ (a) *dress* roto; *person* andrajoso, harapiento; *edge* desigual, mellado; *coastline etc* accidentado; *line, procession* confuso, desordenado, sin orden; *style* desigual, descuidado; (*Mus*) *note* poco suave, imperfecto.

(b) (*text*) **~ left** margen *m* izquierdo irregular; **~ right** margen *m* derecho irregular.

(c) (*US**) **to run sb ~** cansar a uno, agobiar a uno.

raggedly ['rægɪdlɪ] ADV: **he was ~ dressed** estaba muy mal vestido, estaba en andrajos; **the engine is running ~** el motor marcha mal.

ragged robin ['rægɪd'rɒbɪn] N (*Bot*) cuclillo *m*.

raging ['reɪdʒɪŋ] ADJ rabioso, furioso; *storm etc* violento; *pain* atroz, agudo; **to be in a ~ temper** estar furiosísimo.

raglan ['ræglən] N raglán *m*.

ragman ['rægmæn] N, PL **ragmen** ['rægmen] trapero *m*.

ragout [ræ'guː] N guisado *m*.

ragpicker ['rægpɪkəʳ] N trapero *m*.

rag-tag* ['rægtæg] N chusma *f* (*also* **~ and bobtail**).

ragtime ['rægtaɪm] N tiempo *m* sincopado, rag-time *m*; **in ~** sincopado.

ragweed ['rægwiːd] N ambrosía *f*.

ragwort ['rægwɜːt] N hierba *f* cana, zuzón *m*, hierba *f* de Santiago.

raid [reɪd] [1] N (*into territory, across border etc*) incursión *f*, correría *f*, razzia *f*; (*Aer*) ataque *m* (*on* contra), bombardeo *m* (*on* de); (*sweep by police*) redada *f*, batida *f*; (*by criminals*) asalto *m* (*on* a); **the men are away on a ~** los hombres están fuera en una correría; **only 5 aircraft returned from the ~** solamente 5 aviones regresaron después del ataque; **there was a ~ on the jeweller's last night** anoche fue asaltada la joyería.

[2] VT (*by land*) invadir, atacar, hacer una incursión en; (*Aer*) atacar, bombardear; (*by criminals*) asaltar; **the boys ~ed the orchard** los muchachos pillaron el huerto; **the police ~ed the club** la policía registró el club; **shall we ~ the larder?** ¿asaltamos la despensa?, ¿vamos a coger algo en la despensa?; **the king's tomb had already been ~ed** la tumba del rey había sido ya saqueada.

[3] VI hacer una incursión, ir en razzia, razziar; **they ~ed deep into enemy territory** penetraron profundamente en tierras enemigas.

raider ['reɪdəʳ] N (*across frontier*) invasor *m*, incursor *m*; (*Aer*) bombardero *m*; (*Naut*) buque *m* corsario; (*criminal*) criminal *m*, asaltante *m*, ladrón *m*.

raiding party ['reɪdɪŋˌpɑːtɪ] N grupo *m* de ataque.

rail¹ [reɪl] [1] N (a) (*hand~*) baranda *f*, barandilla *f*, pasamanos *m*; (*Naut*) barandilla *f*; borda *f*; (*of bar*) apoyo *m* para los pies; **~s** (*fence*) cerca *f*, palizada *f*.

(b) (*Rail*) carril *m*, raíl *m*, riel *m*; **~s** (*freq*) vía *f*; **~s** (*Fin*) acciones *fpl* de sociedades ferroviarias; **to come off** (*or* **run off, jump, leave**) **the ~s** descarrilar; **to go** (*or* **run**) **off the ~s** (*fig*) extraviarse; (*morally*) echarse a perder; **by ~** por ferrocarril.

[2] ATTR: **~ accident** accidente *m* de ferrocarril; **~ journey** viaje *m* por ferrocarril; **~ strike** huelga *f* de ferroviarios; **~ system** red *f* ferroviaria, sistema *m* ferroviario; **~ traffic** tráfico *m* por ferrocarril.

[3] VT (a) (*also* **to ~ in, to ~ off**) cercar con una barandilla, poner barandilla a.

(b) (*Rail*) transportar por ferrocarril, mandar por ferrocarril.

rail² [reɪl] N (*Orn*) rascón *m*.

rail³ [reɪl] VI: **to ~ at, to ~ against** denostar, despotricar contra, maldecir de.

railcar ['reɪlkɑːʳ] N automotor *m*.

railcard ['reɪlkɑːd] N carnet *m* para obtener descuento en los ferrocarriles; **family ~** carnet *m* de familia (de la RENFE); **student's ~** carnet *m* de estudiante.

railhead ['reɪlhed] N estación *f* terminal, cabeza *f* de línea.

railing ['reɪlɪŋ] N baranda *f*, barandilla *f*, pasamanos *m*; **~s** verja *f*, enrejado *m*.

raillery ['reɪlərɪ] N burlas *fpl*, chanzas *fpl*.

railroad ['reɪlrəʊd] [1] N, ATTR (*US*) = **railway**.

[2] VT: **to ~ sth through** llevar algo a cabo muy precipitadamente; **to ~ a bill through** hacer que se apruebe un decreto de ley sin discutirse; **to ~ sb into doing sth** obligar a uno a hacer algo (sin darle tiempo para reflexionar).

railroader ['reɪlrəʊdəʳ] N (*US*) = **railwayman**.

railway ['reɪlweɪ] [1] N (*Brit*) ferrocarril *m*; (*as track*) vía *f*, vía *f* férrea; (*as route*) línea *f* (de ferrocarril).

[2] ATTR ferroviario; de ferrocarril; **~ bridge** puente *m* de ferrocarril; **~ carriage** vagón *m*, coche *m* (de ferrocarril); **~ engine** máquina *f*,

locomotora *f*; **~ line** (*track*) vía *f*, vía *f* férrea, (*route*) línea *f* (de ferrocarril); **~ network** red *f* ferroviaria; **~ porter** mozo *m*; **~ station** estación *f* (de ferrocarril); **~ ticket** billete *m* de ferrocarril; **~ timetable** horario *m* de trenes; **~ track** vía *f* (de ferrocarril); **~ yard** cochera *f*.

railwayman ['reɪlweɪmən] N, PL **railwaymen** ['reɪlweɪmən], **railworker** ['reɪlˌwɜːkəʳ] N ferroviario *m*, ferrocarrilero *m* (*LAm*).

raiment ['reɪmənt] N (*liter*) vestido *m*, vestimenta *f*.

rain [reɪn] [1] N lluvia *f* (*also fig*); **the ~s** la época de las lluvias; **a ~ of gifts** una lluvia de regalos; **a walk in the ~** un paseo bajo la lluvia; **to be out in the ~** estar fuera aguantando la lluvia; **come in out of the ~!** ¡entra, que te vas a mojar!; **come ~ or shine** pase lo que pase, contra viento y marea; **if the ~ keeps off** si no llueve; **it looks like ~** parece que va a llover.

[2] VT llover; **to ~ blows on sb** llover golpes sobre uno; **to ~ gifts on sb** colmar a uno de regalos; **hereabouts it ~s soot** por aquí llueve hollín; **to ~ cats and dogs** llover a cántaros.

[3] VI llover; **blows ~ed upon him** llovieron sobre él los golpes; **gifts ~ed upon him** le llovieron regalos encima; **it ~s on the just as well as on the unjust** la lluvia cae sobre los buenos como sobre los malos; **it never ~s but it pours** (*fig*) llueve sobre mojado, las desgracias nunca vienen solas.

◆**rain down** VI llover.

◆**rain off**, (*US*) **rain out** VT: **the match was ~ed off** se canceló (*or* se abandonó) el partido debido a la lluvia; **we were ~ed off** tuvimos que abandonarlo por la lluvia.

rainbelt ['reɪnbelt] N zona *f* de lluvias.

rainbow ['reɪnbəʊ] [1] N arco *m* iris.

[2] ATTR: **the ~ coalition** la coalición multicolor; **~ trout** trucha *f* arco iris.

raincheck ['reɪntʃek] N (*US*) contraseña *f* para usar otro día (en caso de cancelación por lluvia); **to take a ~** (*fig*) esperar que la invitación se renueve para otro día, apuntarse para la próxima vez.

raincloud ['reɪnklaʊd] N nubarrón *m*.

raincoat ['reɪnkəʊt] N impermeable *m*, gabardina *f*.

raindrop ['reɪndrɒp] N gota *f* de agua.

rainfall ['reɪnfɔːl] N (*act*) precipitación *f*; (*quantity*) lluvia *f*, cantidad *f* de lluvia; **the region has 3" of ~ a year** la región tiene 3 pulgadas de lluvia al año.

rain-forest ['reɪnˌfɒrɪst] N (*also* **tropical ~**) pluviselva *f*, selva *f* tropical.

rain-gauge ['reɪngeɪdʒ] N pluviómetro *m*.

rain-hood ['reɪnhʊd] N capucha *f* impermeable.

raininess ['reɪnɪnɪs] N lo lluvioso, pluviosidad *f*.

rainless ['reɪnlɪs] ADJ sin lluvia, seco.

rainproof ['reɪnpruːf] ADJ impermeable.

rainstorm ['reɪnstɔːm] N tempestad *f* de lluvia, temporal *m*.

rain-swept ['reɪnswept] ADJ barrido con lluvia.

rainwater ['reɪnwɔːtəʳ] N agua *f* llovediza, agua *f* de lluvia.

rainwear ['reɪnweəʳ] N ropa *f* impermeable.

rainy ['reɪnɪ] ADJ *climate, region* lluvioso; **~ day** día *m* de lluvia, (*fig*) tiempo (futuro) *m* de escasez; **~ season** estación *f* de las lluvias; **it was so ~ yesterday** llovió tanto ayer.

raise [reɪz] [1] N (*esp US*) aumento *m*, subida *f*; (*of salary*) aumento *m*; (*Cards*) sobremarca *f*.

[2] VT (a) (*lift*) *fallen object, weight, arm, eyes etc* levantar, alzar, elevar; *hat* quitarse; *flag* izar, enarbolar; *dust* levantar; *dough* fermentar; *sunken ship* sacar a flote; *camp, siege* levantar; *spirits* (*conjure*) evocar; *embargo etc* levantar; (*from the dead*) resucitar; (*Math*) elevar (a una potencia); **to ~ one's glass** alzar el vaso; **to ~ sb to power** alzar a uno al poder; **to ~ the standard of revolt** pronunciarse, sublevarse; **to ~ tribesmen in revolt** sublevar a las tribus; **to ~ the people against a tyrant** hacer que el pueblo se subleve contra un tirano; **to ~ sb's hopes excessively** hacer a uno concebir esperanzas desmesuradas; **to ~ sb's spirits** dar aliento a uno, reanimar a uno.

(b) (*erect*) *building* erigir, edificar; *statue* erigir.

(c) (*increase*) *price, salary* aumentar, subir; *production* aumentar; *person* (*in rank*) ascender (*to* a); *voice* levantar; **don't ~ your voice!** ¡no levantes la voz!; **you are not to ~ your voice to me** Vd no me levanta a mí la voz; **I'll ~ you 10 dollars** (*bet*) apuesto 10 dólares más, (*bid*) ofrezco 10 dólares más.

(d) (*bring up etc*) *family, livestock* criar; *crop* cultivar.

(e) (*produce*) causar, producir; dar lugar a; *bump etc* causar; *laughter* suscitar, provocar; *doubts* suscitar; *problem, question* plantear; *objection* poner, hacer; *cry etc* dar; *outcry* armar; **I'll ~ the point with them** se lo mencionaré; **it ~s many problems for us** nos plantea muchos problemas; **this ~s the question of whether ...** esto plantea el problema de si ...; **can't you ~ a smile?** ¿no sonríes siquiera?

(f) (*get together*) *army* reclutar; *funds* reunir; obtener, movilizar; *loan* lograr, obtener; *new taxes* imponer; **to ~ money on an estate** obtener un préstamo sobre una propiedad.

(g) (*) (*contact*) contactar con; (*find*) localizar; **I'll see if I can ~ him** by phone trataré de localizarle por teléfono.

(h) (*improve*) mejorar; **to ~ one's game** mejorar su juego, jugar mejor.

3 VR: **to ~ o.s.** alzarse, levantarse.

◆**raise up** 1 VT (*lift*) levantar, alzar, elevar; **to ~ sb up from poverty** sacar a uno de la pobreza, ayudar a uno a salir de la miseria.

2 VR: **he ~d himself up on one elbow** se apoyó en un codo; **he has ~d himself up from nothing** ha salido de la nada.

raised [reɪzd] ADJ (*in relief*) en relieve.

raisin ['reɪzən] N pasa *f*, uva *f* pasa.

raison d'être ['reɪzɔːn'deːtr] N razón *f* de ser.

raj [rɑːdʒ] N: **the British ~** el imperio británico (en la India); la soberanía británica (en la India).

rajah ['rɑːdʒə] N rajá *m*.

rake¹ [reɪk] 1 N (*garden ~*) rastrillo *m*; (*Agr*) rastro *m*; (*fire ~*) hurgón *m*.

2 VT (*Agr etc*) rastrillar; *fire* hurgar; (*with shots etc*) barrer; (*with eyes*) examinar, escudriñar; (*search, ransack*) registrar, buscar en.

◆**rake in** VT **(a)** *gambling chips* recoger. **(b)** (*) **they ~d in a profit of £1000** se sacaron 1000 libras de ganancia limpia; **he ~s in £50 on every deal** se toma una tajada de 50 libras de cada negocio*; **he must be raking it in** está acuñando dinero.

◆**rake off** VT quitar con el rastrillo.

◆**rake over** VT *flowerbed* rastrillar; *memories, past* remover.

◆**rake together** VT reunir (*or* recoger) con el rastrillo; (*fig*) reunir (con dificultad); **we managed to ~ a team together** por fin logramos formar un equipo.

◆**rake up** VT *subject* sacar a relucir; *the past etc* remover; **why did you have to ~ that up?** ¿para qué has vuelto a mencionar eso?

rake² [reɪk] N (*person*) libertino *m*, calavera *m*; **old ~** viejo *m* verde.

rake³ [reɪk] 1 N (*Archit, Naut*) inclinación *f*.

2 VT inclinar.

rake-off* ['reɪkɔf] N comisión *f*, tajada* *f*, porcentaje *m*.

rakish¹ ['reɪkɪʃ] ADJ (*dissolute*) libertino, disoluto.

rakish² ['reɪkɪʃ] ADJ *ship* de palos inclinados; (*fast-looking*) veloz, ligero; (*smart*) elegante, gallardo; desenvuelto; de mucho garbo; **with his hat at a ~ angle** con el sombrero echado de lado, con el sombrero a lo chulo.

rakishly ['reɪkɪʃlɪ] ADV (*of hat etc*) echado al lado, a lo chulo; elegantemente.

rally¹ ['rælɪ] 1 N **(a)** (*Pol etc*) reunión *f*, mitin *m*, manifestación *f*; (*of scouts etc*) reunión *f*, congreso *m*; (*Aut*) rallye *m*.

(b) (*Tennis*) peloteo *m*.

(c) (*Mil*) repliegue *m*; (*Med, Fin etc*) recuperación *f*.

2 VT (*gather*) reunir; (*Mil*) rehacer; *faculties* concentrar; (*encourage*) reanimar, infundir ánimo a, fortalecer.

3 VI **(a)** (*gather*) reunirse (*around sb, to sb* en torno a uno); (*demonstrate*) manifestarse; **they rallied to him** se reunieron en torno a él, afirmaron su adhesión, se solidarizaron con él; **to ~ to the call** responder a la llamada.

(b) (*Mil*) replegarse, rehacerse; (*Med, Fin etc*) recuperarse, mejorar.

◆**rally round** VI: **everyone must ~ round** todos hemos de afirmar nuestra unidad; todos tenemos que cooperar; **they have all rallied round nobly** todos han hecho maravillas en un esfuerzo común.

rally² ['rælɪ] VT (*tease*) tomar el pelo a.

rallycross ['rælɪkrɒs] N *rally sobre un circuito de cross con tramos de asfalto*.

rallying-cry ['rælɪɪŋ,kraɪ] N llamamiento *m* (para reanimar la resistencia *etc*).

rallying-point ['rælɪɪŋ,pɔɪnt] N punto *m* de reunión.

RAM [ræm] N ABBR of **random access memory**.

ram [ræm] 1 N **(a)** (*Zool*) carnero *m*, morueco *m*; (*Astron*) Aries *m*.

(b) (*Mil*) ariete *m*; (*Naut*) espolón *m*; (*Tech: rammer*) pisón *m*, (*pile driver*) martillo *m* pilón.

2 VT **(a)** (*tread down*) (*also* **to ~ down**) apisonar; (*squeeze*) apretar; (*fill*) rellenar (*with* de); **to ~ a charge home** atacar una carga; **they ~med it down his throat** se lo hicieron tragar a la fuerza; **to ~ clothes into a case** poner la ropa apretadamente en una maleta; **to ~ sth into a hole** meter algo apretadamente en un agujero, introducir algo a la fuerza en un agujero; **we had Campoamor ~med into us at school** nos dimos un atracón de Campoamor en el colegio.

(b) (*collide with*) chocar con, dar contra; (*Naut: deliberately*) atacar con el espolón; **the car ~med the lamppost** el coche chocó con el farol.

Ramadan [,ræmə'dæn] N ramadán *m*.

ramble ['ræmbl] 1 N paseo *m* por el campo, excursión *f* a pie, caminata *f*; **to go for a ~** salir de excursión a pie, dar una caminata.

2 VI **(a)** (*walk*) salir de excursión a pie, dar una caminata; pasearse, ir de paseo (en el campo); **we spent a week rambling in the hills** pasamos una semana explorando la montaña a pie (*or* paseándonos por la montaña).

(b) (*in speech*) divagar; (*lose thread*) perder el hilo, salirse del tema; (*of river etc*) serpentear; (*of plant*) trepar, enredarse; extenderse una enredadera; **he just ~d on and on** siguió divagando.

rambler ['ræmblər] N **(a)** (*person*) excursionista *mf* (a pie). **(b)** (*Bot*) trepadora *f*; **~ rose** rosal *m* trepador.

rambling ['ræmblɪŋ] 1 ADJ *plant* trepador; *speech* divagador, prolijo y confuso, enmarañado; *house* laberíntico, sin plan.

2 N **(a)** excursionismo *m* a pie; excursiones *fpl* a pie.

(b) (*also* **~s**) desvaríos *mpl*, divagaciones *fpl*.

rambunctious* [ræm'bʌŋkʃəs] ADJ bullicioso, pendenciero.

RAMC N (*Brit*) ABBR of **Royal Army Medical Corps.**

ramification [,ræmɪfɪ'keɪʃən] N ramificación *f*; **in all its ~s** en toda su complejidad; **with numerous ~s** con innumerables ramificaciones.

ramify ['ræmɪfaɪ] VI ramificarse.

ramjet ['ræmdʒet] N estatorreactor *m*.

rammer ['ræmər] N (*roadmaking*) pisón *m*; (*for rifle*) baqueta *f*.

ramp¹ [ræmp] N (*incline*) rampa *f*; (*on road*) desnivel *m*.

ramp²* [ræmp] N (*Brit*) estafa *f*, timo *m*; **the housing ~** el escándalo (del precio) de la vivienda; **it's a ~!** ¡no hay derecho!, ¡esto no se puede consentir!

rampage [ræm'peɪdʒ] 1 N: **to be on the ~** = 2.

2 VI desbocarse, desmandarse; alborotar; comportarse como un loco; **the crowd ~d through the market** la multitud corrió alocada por el mercado.

rampancy ['ræmpənsɪ] N exuberancia *f*, lozanía *f*; furia *f*, desenfreno *m*; agresividad *f*; predominio *m*.

rampant ['ræmpənt] ADJ (*Her*) rampante; (*Bot*) exuberante, lozano; *person* furioso, desenfrenado; agresivo; *inflation* galopante; **to be ~** (*be common*) cundir, predominar; **he's a ~ anarchist** es un anarquista furibundo; **anarchism is ~ here** aquí el anarquismo está muy extendido, aquí ha cundido mucho el anarquismo.

rampart ['ræmpɑːt] N terraplén *m*, defensa *f*; (*city wall*) muralla *f*; **the ~s of York** la muralla de York.

ram-raider ['ræmreɪdər] N *ladrón que rompe el escaparate con un coche*.

ramrod ['ræmrɒd] N baqueta *f*, atacador *m*.

ramshackle ['ræm,ʃækl] ADJ desvencijado, destartalado.

ram's-horn ['ræmzhɔːn] N cuerno *m* de carnero.

ran [ræn] PRET of **run**; V also **~**.

ranch [rɑːntʃ] 1 N (*US*) hacienda *f*; estancia *f*, rancho *m* (*LAm*).

2 ATTR: **~ hand** peón *m*; **~ house** casa *f* de rancho.

rancher ['rɑːntʃər] N (*US*) ganadero *m*, estanciero *m* (*LAm*), ranchero *m* (*LAm*).

ranching ['rɑːntʃɪŋ] N (*US*) ganadería *f*.

rancid ['rænsɪd] ADJ rancio.

rancidity [ræn'sɪdɪtɪ] N, **rancidness** ['rænsɪdnɪs] N rancidez *f*, ranciedad *f*.

rancorous ['ræŋkərəs] ADJ rencoroso.

rancour, (*US*) **rancor** ['ræŋkər] N rencor *m*.

rand [rænd] N rand *m*.

randiness* ['rændɪnɪs] N cachondez *f*, rijosidad *f*.

random ['rændəm] 1 ADJ fortuito, casual; hecho al azar, hecho sin pensar; sin orden ni concierto; (*Math*) *distribution, variant* aleatorio; *sample* seleccionado al azar; **~ access** acceso *m* aleatorio; **~ access memory** memoria *f* de acceso aleatorio; **~ shot** disparo *m* hecho sin apuntar, bala *f* perdida.

2 N: **at ~** al azar; sin pensar; **to choose sth at ~** escoger algo sin pensar; **to hit out at ~** repartir golpes por todos lados; **to talk at ~** hablar sin pesar las palabras.

randomize ['rændəmaɪz] VT aleatorizar.

randomly ['rændəmlɪ] ADV: **~ chosen** elegidos al azar.

randomness ['rændəmnɪs] N aleatoriedad *f*.

randy* ['rændɪ] ADJ cachondo, rijoso, con ganas (*LAm*); **to feel ~** estar cachondo.

rang [ræŋ] PRET of **ring²**.

range [reɪndʒ] 1 N **(a)** (*row*) línea *f*, hilera *f*; (*of buildings*) grupo *m*; (*of mountains*) sierra *f*, cadena *f*, cordillera *f*.

(b) (*US Agr*) dehesa *f*, terreno *m* de pasto.

(c) (*for shooting: in open*) campo *m* de tiro, (*at fair*) galería *f* de tiro, barraca *f* de tiro.

(d) (*extent*) extensión *f*; intervalo *m*, banda *f*; recorrido *m*; (*of voice*) extensión *f*, alcance *m*, compás *m*; (*series*) serie *f*; escala *f*, abanico *m*, gama *f*; (*Comm*) surtido *m*; **~ of action** esfera *f* de acción; **~ of vision** campo *m* visual; **the present ~ of knowledge** la extensión de los conocimientos actuales; **~ of variation** gama *f* de variación (permisible); **~ of colours** gama *f* de colores; **~ of prices** escala *f* de precios; **~ of speeds** escala *f* de velocidades; **~ of possibilities** abanico *m* de posibilidades; **~ of frequencies** gama *f* de frecuencias; **the ~ of sb's mind** el alcance de la inteligencia de uno; **over the whole ~ of politics** sobre todo el campo de la política; **that's outside my ~** eso no pertenece a mi esfera de actividades; **to go outside one's normal ~** salir de su acostumbrada esfera de actividades; **she has a wide ~ of interests** tiene una extensa gama de intereses; **they have a new**

~ of models tienen una nueva gama (or un nuevo surtido) de modelos.

(e) (*Bio*) distribución *f*, zona *f* de distribución; **the plant has a limited ~** la planta tiene una distribución restringida; **this is outside its normal ~** este sitio queda fuera de su zona acostumbrada; **its ~ extends to León** alcanza la provincia de León.

(f) (*distance attainable*: *Mil*) alcance *m*, alcance *m* de tiro; distancia *f*; **a gun with a ~ of 3 miles** un cañón con un alcance de 3 millas; **at a ~ of 5 miles** a una distancia de 5 millas; **at close ~** de cerca, (*point-blank*) a quemarropa; **within ~** al alcance, a tiro, a tiro de fusil (*etc*); **the plane is out of ~** el avión está fuera de alcance; **to correct the ~** corregir la puntería (*or* la distancia; **to take the ~** averiguar la distancia.

(g) (*of plane, ship*) autonomía *f*, radio *m* de acción; **the ~ is 3,000 miles** la autonomía es de 3.000 millas.

(h) (*kitchen ~*) cocina *f* económica, fogón *m*.

[2] ATTR: **intermediate ~ missile** misil *m* de medio alcance; **shorter ~ missile** misil *m* de corto alcance.

[3] VT **(a)** (*arrange*) arreglar, ordenar; clasificar; (*line up*) alinear; (*place*) colocar; **he ~d them along the wall** los colocó a lo largo de la pared.

(b) (*go about*) recorrer; **they ~d the countryside** recorrieron el campo; **his eye ~d the horizon** escudriñó el horizonte.

(c) **to ~ a gun** apuntar un cañón.

(d) (*text*) **~d left** alineado a la izquierda; **~d right** alineado a la derecha.

[4] VI **(a)** (*extend*) extenderse; (*wander over*) recorrer; vagar por; **the insect ~s from Andalusia to Burgos** el insecto se extiende desde Andalucía hasta Burgos; **research ranging over a wide field** investigaciones *fpl* que se extienden sobre un ancho campo; investigaciones *fpl* de gran alcance; **his mind ~s widely** tiene una mentalidad de gran alcance; **the troops ~d over the whole province** las tropas recorrieron toda la provincia.

(b) (*of numbers etc*) oscilar, variar, fluctuar; **temperatures ~ from 5 to 30 degrees** las temperaturas oscilan entre los 5 y 30 grados; **they ~ as high as 40 degrees at times** a veces suben hasta los 40 grados.

[5] VR: **to ~ o.s. with sb** ponerse al lado de uno; **to ~ o.s. with a group** sumarse a un grupo.

rangefinder ['reɪndʒ,faɪndə'] N telémetro *m*.

ranger ['reɪndʒə'] N guardabosque *m*.

Rangoon [ræŋ'guːn] N Rangún *m*.

rangy ['reɪndʒɪ] ADJ (*US*) alto y delgado.

rank¹ [ræŋk] [1] N **(a)** (*row*) fila *f*, hilera *f*, línea *f*; (*Mil*) fila *f*; **the ~s of poplars** las hileras de álamos; **in serried ~s** en filas apretadas; **the ~s, the ~ and file** las masas, la gente común, (*of club*) los socios ordinarios, (*Mil*) los soldados rasos; **in the ~s of the party** en las filas del partido; **to break ~s** romper filas; **to close (the) ~s** (*Mil, fig*) apretar las filas, cerrar filas; **to join the ~s of** (*fig*) unirse con, llegar a ser uno de; **to reduce sb to the ~s** degradar a uno a soldado raso; **to rise from the ~s** ascender desde soldado raso, llegar a oficial.

(b) (*status*) posición *f*, categoría *f*, dignidad *f*, calidad *f*; (*Mil*) graduación *f*, grado *m*, rango *m*; **persons of ~** gente *f* de calidad; **other ~s** (*esp Brit*) soldados *mpl* que no son oficiales; **a writer of the first ~** un escritor de primera categoría; **4 officers of high ~** 4 oficiales de alta graduación; **their ~s range from lieutenant to colonel** sus graduaciones van de teniente a coronel; **to attain the ~ of major** ser ascendido a comandante, llegar a comandante; **to pull ~*** tratar de conseguir una ventaja (*or* colocarse en situación superior *etc*) empleando su categoría más alta.

(c) (*taxi ~*) (*Brit*) parada *f*.

[2] ATTR: **as a ~ and file policeman I must say ...** como policía de filas, debo decir ...

[3] VT clasificar, ordenar; jerarquizar; **I ~ him 6th** le pongo en 6ª posición; **to ~ A with B** considerar iguales A y B, poner A y B en el mismo nivel; **where would you ~ him?** ¿qué posición le darías?

[4] VI clasificarse; figurar; **to ~ 4th** ocupar el 4° puesto; **to ~ 2nd to sb else** tener el segundo lugar después de otra persona; **to ~ high** ocupar una alta posición; **where does she ~?** ¿qué posición ocupa?; **the shares will ~ for dividend** se pagará el dividendo que corresponda a estas acciones; **to ~ above** ser superior a; **to ~ among** figurar entre; estar al nivel de; **to ~ as** equivaler a, figurar como; **to ~ with** ser igual a, equipararse con, estar al nivel de.

rank² [ræŋk] ADJ **(a)** (*Bot*) lozano, exuberante; (*soil*) fértil; (*thick*) espeso, tupido.

(b) (*smelly*) maloliente, fétido, rancio; **to smell ~** oler mal.

(c) (*fig*) beginner, outsider *etc* completo, puro; **that's ~ nonsense!** ¡puras tonterías!; **it's a ~ bad play** es una obra francamente mala; **it's ~ injustice** es una injusticia manifiesta; **he's a ~ liar** es un mentiroso redomado.

ranker ['ræŋkə'] N (*Mil*) oficial *m* patatero*.

ranking ['ræŋkɪŋ] [1] ADJ (*chiefly US*) superior, de (mucha) categoría; **a ~ scientist** un científico de categoría.

[2] N ránking *m*; categoría *f*, clase *f*, posición *f*; jerarquización *f*; (*Mil*)

graduación *f*.

rankle ['ræŋkl] VI doler; **to ~ with sb** afligir continuamente a uno, roer a uno, amargar la vida a uno; **it still ~s** duele todavía.

rankly ['ræŋklɪ] ADV lozanamente, con exuberancia; espesamente.

rankness ['ræŋknɪs] N (*V* **rank²**) **(a)** lozanía *f*, exuberancia *f*; fertilidad *f*; espesura *f*. **(b)** mal olor *m*, fetidez *f*, ranciedad *f*. **(c)** (*of injustice etc*) enormidad *f*.

ransack ['rænsæk] VT (*search*) registrar (de arriba abajo); escudriñar (minuciosamente); (*pillage*) desvalijar; saquear; **they ~ed the house for arms** registraron toda la casa buscando armas; **the place had been ~ed** el local había sido saqueado.

ransom ['rænsəm] [1] N rescate *m*; (*Rel*) redención *f*; **~ money** rescate *m*, dinero *m* exigido a cambio del rehén; **to hold sb to ~** pedir un rescate por uno, (*fig*) hacer chantaje a uno.

[2] VT rescatar; (*Rel*) redimir.

ransoming ['rænsəmɪŋ] N rescate *m*; redención *f*.

rant [rænt] [1] N lenguaje *m* campanudo, lenguaje *m* declamatorio.

[2] VI vociferar, despotricar; hablar en tono violento, hablar en un estilo hinchado; **he ~ed and raved for hours** despotricó durante varias horas; **he ~ed on about the Pope** siguió vociferando injurias (*or* echando pestes) contra el papa.

ranter ['ræntə'] N fanfarrón *m*; orador *m* campanudo, orador *m* populachero.

ranting ['ræntɪŋ] [1] ADJ fanfarrón; campanudo, vociferador, chillón.

[2] N lenguaje *m* campanudo, lenguaje *m* declamatorio; vociferación *f*; **for all his ~** por más que despotrique.

ranunculus [rə'nʌŋkjʊləs] N ranúnculo *m*.

rap [ræp] [1] N **(a)** golpecito *m*, golpe *m* seco; (*at door*) llamada *f*, aldabada *f*; **there was a ~ at the door** llamaron a la puerta.

(b) (*) **to take the ~** pagar el pato*; **to take the ~ for sth** sufrir las consecuencias de algo; cargar con la culpa de algo.

(c) (*esp US**) acusación *f*; **murder ~** acusación *f* de homicidio; **to beat the ~** (lograr) ser absuelto.

(d) (*Mus*) rap *m*.

[2] VT **(a)** golpear, dar un golpecito en, tocar. **(b)** (*) criticar severamente.

[3] VI **(a)** (*US**) charlar. **(b)** **to ~ at the door** llamar a la puerta. **(c)** (*Mus*) hacer rap.

◆**rap out** VT decir en tono brusco; **to ~ out an order** espetar una orden.

rapacious [rə'peɪʃəs] ADJ rapaz.

rapaciously [rə'peɪʃəslɪ] ADV con rapacidad.

rapacity [rə'pæsɪtɪ] N rapacidad *f*.

rape¹ [reɪp] [1] N violación *f*, estupro *m*; (*fig*) destrucción *f*, ruina *f*; **attempted ~** intento *m* de violación; **the ~ of Poland** la destrucción de Polonia.

[2] VT violar, estuprar, forzar.

rape² [reɪp] N (*Bio*) colza *f*; **~ oil** (*also* **~seed oil**) aceite *m* de colza.

rapeseed ['reɪpsiːd] N semilla *f* de colza.

Raphael ['ræfeəl] NM Rafael.

rapid ['ræpɪd] ADJ rápido.

rapid-fire ['ræpɪd,faɪə] ADJ gun de fuego racheado; (*fig*) trepidante; **a ~ succession of questions** una sucesión trepidante de preguntas.

rapidity [rə'pɪdɪtɪ] N rapidez *f*.

rapidly ['ræpɪdlɪ] ADV rápidamente.

rapids ['ræpɪdz] NPL rápido(s) *m(pl)*, rabión *m*, rabiones *mpl*.

rapier ['reɪpɪə'] N estoque *m*.

rapine ['ræpaɪn] N rapiña *f*.

rapist ['reɪpɪst] N violador *m*.

rapper ['ræpə'] N músico *mf* de rap.

rapping ['ræpɪŋ] N golpecitos *mpl*, golpes *mpl* secos; llamadas *fpl*, aldabadas *fpl*.

rapport [ræ'pɔ:'] N buena relación *f*; entendimiento *m*; conformidad *f*; compenetración *f*; **we often find ourselves in ~** nos entendemos casi siempre bien; **to be in ~ with** estar conforme con, estar de acuerdo con.

rapprochement [ræ'prɒʃmɑ̃:ŋ] N acercamiento *m*, aproximación *f*.

rapscallion [ræp'skælɪən] N bribón *m*, golfo *m*.

rapt [ræpt] ADJ arrebatado; (*absorbed*) absorto, ensimismado; (*enraptured*) extático, extasiado; **with ~ attention** con atención fija; **to be ~ in contemplation** estar absorto en la contemplación.

raptor ['ræptə'] N ave *f* raptora.

rapture ['ræptʃə'] N éxtasis *m*, rapto *m*, arrobamiento *m*; **what ~!** ¡qué encanto!; **to be in ~s** estar extasiado, extasiarse; **to go into ~s** extasiarse (*over, about* ante, con).

rapturous ['ræptʃərəs] ADJ extático; applause *etc* delirante, extático.

rapturously ['ræptʃərəslɪ] ADV extáticamente; con entusiasmo.

rare¹ [reə'] ADJ **(a)** raro, poco común, nada frecuente; excepcional; (*Phys*) ralo; **at ~ intervals** muy de tarde en tarde; **in a moment of ~ generosity** en un momento de generosidad poco frecuente en él; **it is ~ to find that ...** es poco frecuente encontrar que ...; **the plant is ~ in Wales** la planta es poco común en Gales.

(b) (*) maravilloso, estupendo*; **we had a ~ old time last night** lo pasamos pipa anoche*; **we had a ~ old time getting here** nos ha costado un ojo de la cara llegar aquí*; **you gave me a ~ old fright!** ¡vaya susto que me diste!; *see also* STRANGE, RARE .

rare² [reə¹] ADJ *meat* poco hecho, algo crudo.

rarebit ['reəbɪt] N: Welsh ~ pan *m* con queso tostado.

rarefaction [ˌreərɪ'fækʃən] N rarefacción *f*.

rarefied ['reərɪfaɪd] ADJ *atmosphere* enrarecido (*also fig*).

rarefy ['reərɪfaɪ] 1 VT enrarecer.
2 VI enrarecerse.

rarely ['reəlɪ] ADV raramente, con poca frecuencia; rara vez, pocas veces, casi nunca; **it is ~ found here** aquí se encuentra con poca frecuencia; **that method is ~ satisfactory** ese método no es satisfactorio casi nunca.

rareness ['reənɪs] N, **rarity** ['reərɪtɪ] N rareza *f*; **it's a rarity here** aquí es una rareza.

raring ['reərɪŋ] ADJ: **to be ~ to do sth** tener muchas ganas de hacer algo; **to be ~ to go** tener muchas ganas de empezar.

rascal ['rɑːskəl] N pillo *m*, pícaro *m*.

rascality [rɑːs'kælɪtɪ] N picardía *f*.

rascally ['rɑːskəlɪ] ADJ pícaro, truhanesco.

rash¹ [ræʃ] N **(a)** (*Med*) erupción *f* (cutánea); sarpullido *m*; **she came out in a ~** le salieron erupciones en la piel. **(b)** (*fig*) brote *m*; serie *f*, racha *f*; **a ~ of complaints** una serie de quejas.

rash² [ræʃ] ADJ temerario; imprudente; precipitado; **that was very ~ of you** en eso has sido muy imprudente.

rasher ['ræʃə¹] N (*Brit*) lonja *f*, loncha *f*.

rashly ['ræʃlɪ] ADV temerariamente; imprudentemente; precipitadamente, a la ligera.

rashness ['ræʃnɪs] N temeridad *f*; imprudencia *f*; precipitación *f*.

rasp [rɑːsp] 1 N **(a)** (*tool*) escofina *f*, raspador *m*. **(b)** (*sound*) sonido *m* desapacible; (*of voice*) tono *m* áspero.
2 VT **(a)** (*Tech*) escofinar, raspar. **(b)** (*say*) decir con tono áspero; *order* (*also* **to ~ out**) espetar.
3 VI hacer un sonido desapacible.

raspberry ['rɑːzbərɪ] N **(a)** (*fruit*) frambuesa *f*; (*bush*) frambueso *m* (*also* **~ bush, ~ cane**).
(b) (*) sonido *m* grosero, sonido *m* despectivo, sonido *m* ofensivo; **to blow sb a ~** hacer un gesto grosero a uno; **to get the ~** recibir una bronca, sufrir una repulsa.

rasping ['rɑːspɪŋ] ADJ *voice etc* áspero, desapacible.

raspy ['rɑːspɪ] ADJ *voice* ronco, áspero; tono quebrado.

Rasta* ['ræstə], **Rastafarian** [ˌræstə'feərɪən] 1 ADJ rastafario.
2 N rastafario *m*, -a *f*.

rat [ræt] 1 N rata *f*; (*) (*rotter*) canalla *m*; (*deserter*) desertor *m*; **~s!*** (*Brit*) ¡narices!*; **you ~!*** ¡bestia!*; **to smell a ~** oler el poste; **I smell a ~** aquí hay gato encerrado.
2 VI **(a)** cazar ratas, matar ratas.
(b) (*) chaquetear, desertar; **to ~ on sb** (*abandon*) abandonar a uno, (*inform*) chivarse de uno‡, soplar contra uno*.

ratable ['reɪtəbl] ADJ = **rateable**.

rat-a-tat [ˌrætə'tæt] N (*at door*) golpecitos *mpl*; (*imitating sound*) ¡toc, toc!; (*of machine-gun*) tableteo *m*.

ratatouille [ˌrætə'twiː] N ≈ pisto *m*.

ratcatcher ['rætˌkætʃə¹] N cazarratas *m*, cazador *m* de ratas.

ratchet ['rætʃɪt] N trinquete *m*; **~ wheel** rueda *f* de trinquete.

rate¹ [reɪt] 1 N **(a)** (*proportion, ratio*) proporción *f*, relación *f*, razón *f*; tanto *m* por ciento; **~ of births** (índice *m* de) natalidad *f*; **at a ~ of 5%** a un 5 por ciento; **at a ~ of 5 in every 30** a razón de 5 por cada 30; **at the ~ of 3 per person** a razón de 3 por persona; **at any ~** de todas formas, de todos modos; por lo menos; **at that ~** de ese modo; **if things go on at this ~** de seguir las cosas así.
(b) (*price etc*) precio *m*, tasa *f*; tarifa *f*; (*of interest etc*) tipo *m*; (*of hotel etc*) tarifa *f*; **at a cheap ~** a un precio reducido; **the ~ for the job** el pago por el trabajo; **advertising ~s** tarifa *f* de anuncios; **~ of exchange** (tipo *m* de) cambio *m*; **~ of interest** tipo *m* de interés; **~s of pay** escala *f* de sueldos, escalafón *m*; **~ of return** (*Fin*) tasa *f* de rentabilidad (*or* rendimiento); **~ of taxation** nivel *m* de impuestos.
(c) **~s** (*Brit: local tax*) contribución *f* municipal, impuestos *mpl* municipales; **~s and taxes** contribuciones *fpl* e impuestos; **we pay £900 in ~s** pagamos 900 libras de contribuciones.
(d) **first-~** de primera clase; **some third-~ author** algún autor de baja categoría, algún escritorcillo.
(e) (*speed*) velocidad *f*; (*of work etc*) ritmo *m*; **~ of climb** (*Aer*) velocidad *f* de subida; **~ of flow** velocidad *f* de flujo; **~ of growth** ritmo *m* de expansión; **a high ~ of growth** un elevado ritmo de crecimiento; **at a great ~** rapidísimamente, (*of vehicle*) a gran velocidad; **at a ~ of 20 knots** a una velocidad de 20 nudos.
2 ATTR: **~ rebate** devolución *f* de contribución municipal.
3 VT **(a)** (*estimate*) estimar; (*estimate value*) tasar, valorar (*at* en); (*classify*) clasificar; **I ~ it at £20** lo valoro en 20 libras; **I don't ~ your chances** creo que tienes pocas posibilidades; **I ~ the book highly**

estimo el libro en mucho; **I ~ him highly** tengo un muy buen concepto de él; **how do you ~ her?** ¿qué opinas de ella?; **I ~ him among my best 3 pupils** le pongo entre mis 3 mejores alumnos.
(b) (*Fin*) imponer contribución municipal a; **we are highly ~d here** aquí nos exigen una contribución elevada; **the house is ~d at £840 per annum** se impone una contribución de 840 libras al año a esta casa, pagamos por esta casa una contribución de 840 libras al año.
(c) (*deserve*) merecer; **it didn't ~ a mention** no mereció ser mencionado, no logró una mención; **this hotel doesn't ~ 4 stars** este hotel no merece 4 estrellas.
4 VI: **to ~ as** ser considerado como, ser tenido por; **he just doesn't ~** no cuenta para nada, no vale para nada; **this case does not ~ for a grant** en este caso no se justifica un subsidio.

rate² [reɪt] VT regañar, reñir.

-rate [reɪt] SUF V **rate¹** 1 (d).

rateable ['reɪtəbl] ADJ *property* imponible; **~ value** valor *m* catastral.

rate-capping ['reɪtˌkæpɪŋ] N (*Brit Pol*) limitación de la contribución municipal impuesta por el Estado.

ratepayer ['reɪtpeə¹] N contribuyente *mf*.

▼ **rather** ['rɑːðə¹] 1 ADV **(a)** (*more accurately*) antes, más bien; mejor dicho; **or ~** mejor dicho; **~ it is a matter of money** antes es cuestión de dinero, es al contrario cuestión de dinero, es más bien cuestión de dinero.
(b) (*somewhat*) algo, un poco, bastante; **~ good** bastante bueno; **~ difficult** algo difícil; **it's ~ wet** está un poco mojado; **I'm ~ tired** estoy un poco cansado; **there's ~ a lot** hay bastante; **I ~ think he won't come** me inclino a creer que no vendrá; **I ~ expected as much** ya lo preveía; **are you keen to go?... yes, I am ~** ¿quieres ir en efecto?... sí quiero; **isn't she pretty?... yes, she is ~** ¿es guapa, eh?... sí, bastante.
▼**(c)** (*for preference*) **A ~ than B** A antes que B, más bien A que B; **this ~ than that** esto antes que eso; **anything ~ than that!** ¡todo menos eso!; **play anything ~ than that** toca cualquier cosa no sea eso; **'I'm going to have it out with the boss' — '~ you than I!'** 'voy a planteárselo al jefe' — '¡allá tú!'; **I would ~ not say** prefiero no decirlo; **I would ~ have sherry** me gustaría más un jerez; **I would ~ not** más bien no quiero hacerlo (*etc*).
2 INTERJ **would you like some? ... ~!** ¿quieres algo de esto? ... ¡ya lo creo! (*or* ¡por supuesto!).

ratification [ˌrætɪfɪ'keɪʃən] N ratificación *f*.

ratify ['rætɪfaɪ] VT ratificar.

rating¹ ['reɪtɪŋ] 1 N **(a)** (*act of valuing*) tasación *f*, valuación *f*; derrama *f*; (*value*) valor *m*; (*Brit: local tax*) contribución *f*.
(b) (*standing*) clasificación *f*; puesto *m*, posición *f*; (*of audience, TV etc: also* **~s**) índice *m*; (*of ship*) clase *f*; **~s** (*Comm, Fin*) clasificación *f*, ránking *m*; **what's his ~?** ¿qué puesto ocupa?; ¿qué opinión hay de él?
(c) (*Brit Naut*) marinero *m*.
2 ATTR: **~ service** servicio *m* de clasificación de valores.

rating² ['reɪtɪŋ] N represión *f*.

ratio ['reɪʃɪəʊ] N razón *f*, relación *f*, proporción *f*; **in direct ~ to** en razón directa con; **in the ~ of 5 to 2** a razón de 5 a 2; **the ~ of wages to raw materials** la relación entre los sueldos y las materias primas.

ratiocinate [ˌrætɪ'ɒsɪneɪt] VI raciocinar.

ratiocination [ˌrætɪɒsɪ'neɪʃən] N raciocinación *f*.

ration ['ræʃən] 1 N ración *f*; **~s** (*Mil etc*) víveres *mpl*, suministro *m*; **it's off the ~ now** ya no está racionado; **to be on short ~s** andar escaso de víveres, tener poco que comer; **to draw one's ~s** recibir los víveres; **when they put bread on the ~** cuando racionaron el pan.
2 VT (*also* **to ~ out**) racionar; **they are ~ed to 1 kilo a day** están racionados a 1 kilo por día.

rational ['ræʃənl] ADJ racional; lógico, razonable; (*sane, of person*) sensato, cuerdo; **~ number** número *m* racional; **the ~ thing to do would be ...** lo lógico sería ...; **he seemed quite ~** parecía estar perfectamente cuerdo; **a long skirt is hardly ~ dress for the beach** una falda larga es poco práctica en la playa; **let's be ~ about this** seamos razonables.

rationale [ræʃə'nɑːl] N razón *f* fundamental, base *f* lógica.

rationalism ['ræʃnəlɪzəm] N racionalismo *m*.

rationalist ['ræʃnəlɪst] 1 ADJ racionalista.
2 N racionalista *mf*.

rationalistic [ˌræʃnə'lɪstɪk] ADJ racionalista.

rationality [ˌræʃə'nælɪtɪ] N racionalidad *f*; lógica *f*.

rationalization [ˌræʃnəlaɪ'zeɪʃən] N racionalización *f*; **industrial ~** (*euph*) reconversión *f* industrial.

rationalize ['ræʃnəlaɪz] VT racionalizar; (*Math*) quitar los radicales a, racionalizar.

rationally ['ræʃnəlɪ] ADV racionalmente; lógicamente, razonablemente; **he spoke quite ~** habló cuerdamente, habló de modo juicioso.

ration-book ['ræʃənbʊk] N, **ration-card** ['ræʃənkɑːd] N cartilla f de racionamiento.

rationing ['ræʃnɪŋ] N racionamiento m.

Ratisbon ['rætɪzbɒn] N Ratisbona f.

ratpack* ['ræt,pæk] N (Brit: pej) periodistas que persiguen a los famosos.

rat-poison ['ræt'pɔɪzn] N matarratas m, raticida m.

rat-race ['rætreɪs] N lucha f incesante por adelantar, competencia f sin tregua para adelantar; **it's a ~** es una arrebatiña.

rat run* ['rætrʌn] N (Brit) calle residencial usada para evitar atascos.

rats'-tails [,ræts'teɪlz] NPL greñas fpl.

rattan [rə'tæn] N rota f, junco m (or caña f) de Indias.

rat-tat-tat ['rættættæt] N = **rat-a-tat.**

ratter ['rætəʳ] N cazarratones m invar.

rattle ['rætl] **1** N (a) (noise: banging) golpeteo m; (of cart, train etc) traqueteo m; (of machine gun etc) traqueteo m, tableteo m; (eg of stone in tin) ruido m, castañeteo m; (of hail, rain) tamborileo m; (of window etc) crujido m; (of teeth) castañeteo m; (in throat) estertoɾ m.
(b) (instrument) carraca f, matraca f; (child's) sonajero m; (snake's) cascabel m.
2 VT (a) (shake) agitar, sacudir; (play) hacer sonar; (vibrate) hacer vibrar; (jolt) traquetear; **the wind ~d the window** el viento hacía crujir la ventana; **he ~d the tin** agitó la lata, sacudió la lata.
(b) (*: disconcert) desconcertar, confundir; poner nervioso; **he was badly ~d** quedó muy desconcertado; **that ~d him badly** eso le desconcertó de mala manera; **to get ~d** ponerse nervioso; **he never gets ~d** nunca pierde la calma.
3 VI (a) golpear; traquetear; tabletear; sonar, hacer ruido; tamborilear; crujir; castañetear.
(b) **we were rattling along at 50** corríamos a 50 (kilómetros por hora).
♦**rattle away** VI = **rattle on.**
♦**rattle off** VT enumerar rápidamente, decir de carretilla.
♦**rattle on** VI: **he ~d on** seguía parloteando; **he was rattling on about the war** seguía hablando incansablemente de la guerra.
♦**rattle through** VT darse prisa con.

rattler* ['rætləʳ] N (US), **rattlesnake** ['rætlsneɪk] N serpiente f de cascabel, yarará f (And).

rattletrap ['rætltræp] **1** ADJ desvencijado.
2 N armatoste m.

rattling ['rætlɪŋ] **1** ADJ: **at a ~ pace** muy rápidamente, a gran velocidad.
2 ADV: **~ good*** realmente estupendo*.

rattrap ['rættræp] N trampa f para ratas, ratonera f.

ratty* ['rætɪ] ADJ: (a) (Brit) **he was pretty ~ about it** se picó mucho por ello; **to get ~** ponerse negro*. (b) (US) andrajoso.

raucous ['rɔːkəs] ADJ estridente, ronco, chillón.

raucously ['rɔːkəslɪ] ADV de modo estridente, roncamente, en tono chillón.

raucousness ['rɔːkəsnɪs] N estridencia f, ronquedad f.

raunchy* ['rɔːntʃɪ] ADJ (US: smutty) lascivo, verde; (randy) cachondo.

ravage ['rævɪdʒ] **1** N estrago m, destrozo m; **~s** destrucción f, estragos mpl; **the ~s of time** los estragos del tiempo.
2 VT estragar, destruir, destrozar; (plunder) saquear, pillar; **the region was ~d by floods** la región fue asolada por las inundaciones; **a picture ~d by time** un cuadro muy deteriorado por el tiempo; **a body ~d by disease** un cuerpo desfigurado por la enfermedad.

rave [reɪv] **1** N (*) **it's a ~** es lo último*, es la monda*.
2 ADJ: **the play got ~ notices*** la obra fue reseñada con el mayor entusiasmo, se escribieron reseñas entusiastas de la obra; **the film got ~ reviews** la película obtuvo críticas excelentes.
3 VI delirar, desvariar; **to ~ about sb** pirrarse por uno, hablar en términos entusiastas de uno; **to ~ about sth** entusiasmarse por algo; **to ~ at sb** despotricar contra uno.

rave-in* ['reɪvɪn] N orgía f.

ravel ['rævəl] VT enredar, enmarañar (also fig).

raven ['reɪvn] **1** N cuervo m.
2 ADJ hair negro.

raven-haired [,reɪvn'heəd] ADJ de pelo negro.

ravening ['rævnɪŋ] ADJ rapaz, salvaje.

ravenous ['rævənəs] ADJ (starving) famélico, hambriento; (voracious) voraz; **I'm ~!** ¡me comería un toro!; **he was ~** tenía un hambre canina.

ravenously ['rævənəslɪ] ADV vorazmente; **to be ~ hungry** tener una hambre canina.

raver* ['reɪvəʳ] N juerguista* mf; persona f totalmente desinhibida.

rave-up* ['reɪvʌp] N (Brit) juerga* f.

ravine [rə'viːn] N barranco m, garganta f, quebrada f (LAm).

raving ['reɪvɪŋ] **1** ADJ: **~ lunatic** loco m de atar.
2 ADV: **~ mad** loco m de atar.

ravings ['reɪvɪŋz] NPL delirio m, desvarío m.

ravioli [,rævɪ'əʊlɪ] NPL ravioles mpl.

ravish ['rævɪʃ] VT (a) (charm) encantar, embelesar. (b) (liter: carry off)

raptar, robar; (rape) violar.

ravisher ['rævɪʃəʳ] N raptor m; violador m.

ravishing ['rævɪʃɪŋ] ADJ encantador, embelesador.

ravishingly ['rævɪʃɪŋlɪ] ADV encantadoramente, embelesadoramente; **~ beautiful** bellísimo.

ravishment ['rævɪʃmənt] N (V vt) (a) embeleso m, éxtasis m. (b) rapto m, robo m; violación f.

raw [rɔː] **1** ADJ (a) (uncooked) food crudo; spirit puro, sin mezcla; de baja calidad; leather, silk etc bruto, sin refinar, crudo; cotton en rama; account, piece of writing sin pulir, sin refinar; tosco; **~ data** datos mpl brutos, datos mpl en bruto; **~ material** materia f prima.
(b) (inexperienced) novato, inexperto; (socially coarse) tosco, grosero; **~ recruit** (Mil) soldado m bisoño, quinto m, (fig) novicio m.
(c) (sore) flesh sensible; wound abierto; **in the ~ flesh** en carne viva; **I touched a ~ nerve** le di en lo más sensible, le herí en lo vivo; **his nerves are very ~** tiene los nervios a flor de piel.
(d) day, weather crudo, áspero; wind fuerte.
(e) (unfair) inequitativo; **~ deal** injusticia f, trato m inequitativo; **he got a ~ deal** le trataron mal; **that's pretty ~** eso es injusto, no hay derecho a eso.
2 N carne f viva; **in the ~** (US*) desnudo; **life in the ~** la vida tal como es, la vida bajo su aspecto más inculto; **it got him on the ~** le hirió en lo más vivo.

rawboned ['rɔː'bəʊnd] ADJ huesudo.

rawhide ['rɔːhaɪd] **1** ADJ de cuero crudo.
2 N (US) cuero m de vaca.

Rawlplug ['rɔːlplʌg] ® N taco m.

rawness ['rɔːnɪs] N (a) crudeza f. (b) (inexperience) inexperiencia f; tosquedad f.

Ray [reɪ] NM familiar form of **Raymond.**

ray¹ [reɪ] N rayo m; **~ of light** rayo m de luz; **without a ~ of hope** sin la más tenue esperanza; **I see a ~ of hope** (or light) hay un rayo de esperanza.

ray² [reɪ] N (Fish) raya f.

ray³ [reɪ] N (Mus) re m.

Raymond ['reɪmənd] NM Raimundo, Ramón.

rayon ['reɪɒn] N rayón m.

raze [reɪz] VT (also **~ to the ground**) arrasar, asolar.

razor ['reɪzəʳ] N (open) navaja f, chaveta f (Mex); (safety ~) maquinilla f de afeitar, gillette f; (electric ~) maquinilla f eléctrica, rasuradora f; **~ burn** erosión f cutánea; **it's on a ~'s edge** está al filo de la navaja.

razorbill ['reɪzəbɪl] N alca f (común).

razorblade ['reɪzəbleɪd] N hoja f de afeitar, cuchilla f de afeitar.

razor-cut ['reɪzə,kʌt] N (Hairdressing) corte m a la navaja.

razor-sharp ['reɪzə'ʃɑːp] ADJ afiladísimo; mind agudísimo, de lo más penetrante.

razor-strop ['reɪzəstrɒp] N suavizador m.

razz* [ræz] VT (US) tomar el pelo a*.

razzle* ['ræzl] N borrachera f; **to go on the ~** ir de juerga*, ir de borrachera; **to be on the ~** estar de juerga*.

razzle-dazzle* ['ræzl,dæzl] N (a) = **razzle.** (b) = **razzmatazz.**

razzmatazz* [,ræzmə'tæz] N (US) bombo m publicitario, actividad f frenética, juerga* f (con que se lanza a un candidato, un producto etc); animación f, bullicio m.

RC N ABBR of **Roman Catholic** católico m, -a f; also adj.

RCAF N ABBR of **Royal Canadian Air Force.**

RCMP N ABBR of **Royal Canadian Mounted Police** fuerza de policía canadiense montada.

RCN N ABBR of **Royal Canadian Navy.**

RD (US Post) ABBR of **rural delivery.**

Rd ABBR of **road** calle f, c/.

R/D VT ABBR of **refer to drawer** protestar este cheque por falta de fondos.

RDA ABBR of **recommended daily allowance** ingesta f diaria recomendada.

RDC N (a) ABBR of **Rural District Council.** (b) ABBR of **regional distribution centre.**

RE N (a) (Scol) ABBR of **religious education** educación f religiosa, ed. religiosa. (b) (Brit Mil) ABBR of **Royal Engineers.**

re¹ [riː] PREP respecto a, con referencia a; **~ yours of the 8th** me refiero a su carta del día 8.

re² [reɪ] N (Mus) re m.

re... [riː] PREF re...

reabsorb ['riːəb'zɔːb] VT reabsorber.

reabsorption ['riːəb'zɔːpʃən] N reabsorción f.

reach [riːtʃ] **1** N (a) (accessibility) alcance m; extensión f; distancia f; (Boxing etc) envergadura f; **to have a long ~** tener brazos largos; **to be beyond sb's ~, to be out of sb's ~** estar fuera del alcance de uno; **to be within ~ of the hand** estar al alcance de la mano; **to be within (easy) ~** estar al alcance, estar a la mano; **cars within the ~ of all families** coches mpl al alcance de todas las familias; **a house within easy ~ of the station** una casa a corta distancia de la estación; **it's within easy ~ by bus** es fácilmente accesible en autobús.

(b) (*of river*) recto *m*, extensión *f* entre dos recodos; (*of canal*) recto *m*, extensión *f* entre dos compuertas; **the upper ~es of the Seine** la parte alta del Sena.

2 VT (a) (*stretch out*) alargar, extender; **he ~ed out a hand** alargó la mano.

(b) (*pass*) alcanzar, pasar, dar; **please ~ me down that case** por favor bájeme la maleta esa; **can you ~ me (over) the oil?** ¿me das (*LAm*: alcanzas) el aceite, por favor?

(c) (*arrive at, attain*) alcanzar; llegar a, llegar hasta; lograr; extenderse a, abarcar; **to ~ home** llegar a casa; **it doesn't ~ the bottom** no llega al fondo; **the child hardly ~ed my waist** el niño apenas me llegaba a la cintura; **the door is ~ed by a long staircase** se sube a la puerta por una larga escalera; **your letter ~ed me this morning** su carta me llegó esta mañana; **when this news ~ed my ears** cuando supe esta noticia; **to ~ 21** cumplir los 21 años; **to ~ perfection** lograr la perfección; **to ~ a compromise** llegar a un arreglo; **production now ~es 3,400 megawatts** la producción actual alcanza 3.400 megavatios; **the law does not ~ such cases** la ley no se extiende a tales casos.

(d) *person* ponerse en contacto con, contactar (*esp LAm*); **to ~ sb by telephone** hablar con uno por teléfono; **you can always ~ me at the office** me puedes llamar en todo momento en la oficina.

(e) (*US Jur*) *witness* sobornar.

3 VI (a) to ~ out (with one's hand) for sth alargar (*or* tender) la mano para tomar algo; **don't ~ over people** no alargues la mano delante de otros; **see if you can ~ up for it** a ver si puedes alcanzarlo; **to ~ for the sky** aspirar al cielo; **~ for the sky!** (*US*) ¡arriba las manos!

(b) (*stretch*) alcanzar; extenderse; llegar; **it won't ~** no llega; **it ~es to the sea** se extiende hasta el mar; **as far as the eye could ~** hasta donde alcanzaba la vista; **the beer won't ~ till Friday** la cerveza no llega al viernes; **it ~es back to 1700** se remonta a 1700; **it's a tradition that ~es back for centuries** es una tradición de varios siglos; **the water ~ed up to the windows** el agua llegó a las ventanas.

reachable ['riːtʃəbl] ADJ alcanzable; accesible.

reach-me-down ['riːtʃmɪˌdaʊn] **1** ADJ *clothes, ideas* común y corriente; de segunda mano.

2 ~s NPL ropa *f* burda, traje *m* de segunda mano; ropa *f* de percha.

react [riː'ækt] VI reaccionar (*against* contra; *on* sobre; *to* a, ante; *with* (*Chem*) con); **how did she ~?** ¿cómo reaccionó?

reaction [riː'ækʃən] N reacción *f*; **what was your ~?** ¿cómo reaccionaste?, ¿qué impresión te produjo?; **it produced no ~** no surtió efecto.

reactionary [riː'ækʃənrɪ] **1** ADJ reaccionario; retrógrado.

2 N reaccionario *m*, -a *f*.

reactivate [riː'æktɪveɪt] VT reactivar.

reactivation [riːˌæktɪ'veɪʃən] N reactivación *f*.

reactive [riː'æktɪv] ADJ reactivo.

reactor [riː'æktər] N reactor *m*.

read [riːd] (*irr*: PRET AND PTP **read** [red]) **1** VT **(a)** leer; (*with difficulty*) lograr leer, interpretar, descifrar; **do you ~ Russian?** ¿sabes leer el ruso?; **I ~ it differently** lo entiendo de otro modo; **I ~ you loud and clear** (*Aer etc*) te oigo perfectamente; **do you ~ me?** (*Aer etc*) ¿me oyes?; **to take the minutes as ~** dar las actas por leídas; **we can take that as ~** (*fig*) eso lo podemos dar por sentado.

(b) to ~ sth aloud leer algo en voz alta; **to ~ the news** leer las noticias; **to ~ a report to a meeting** leer un informe a una reunión.

(c) to ~ sb to sleep adormecer a uno leyéndole.

(d) (*Univ*) estudiar, cursar; **to ~ Romance languages** estudiar lenguas románicas; **what are you ~ing?** ¿qué asignatura estudias?

(e) to ~ music leer música; **to ~ sb's hand** leer la mano a uno; **she can ~ me like a book** me conoce a fondo; **to ~ the future** adivinar el porvenir; **to ~ sb's thoughts** adivinar el pensamiento de uno.

(f) (*take a reading from*) leer, consultar; **when I ~ the thermometer** cuando consulté el termómetro; **they come to ~ the meter once a month** vienen una vez al mes a leer el contador; **he wants to ~ the gas meter** quiere ver el contador de gas.

(g) you're ~ing too much into it le atribuyes demasiada importancia; **to ~ into a sentence what is not there** ver en una frase un significado que no tiene.

2 VI (a) leer; **to ~ aloud** leer en voz alta; **I ~ about it in the papers** lo leí en los periódicos; **I'm ~ing about Napoleon** me estoy documentando sobre Napoleón; estoy leyendo acerca de Napoleón; **to ~ between the lines** leer entre líneas; **to ~ to sb** leer un libro (*etc*) a uno.

(b) (*notice etc*) decir, rezar; (*of thermometer etc*) indicar, marcar; **it should ~ 'Urraca'** debiera decir 'Urraca'.

(c) (*of text*) **how does the letter ~ now?** ¿qué tal te parece la carta ahora?, ¿a ver cómo te suena la carta ahora?; **the book ~s well** el libro está bien escrito; **it would ~ better if you said ...** causaría mejor

impresión si pusieras ..., sería más elegante si escribieras ...; **the play acts better than it ~s** la obra es mejor representada que leída.

(d) (*study*) estudiar; **to ~ for a degree** estudiar la licenciatura; **to ~ for the Bar** estudiar derecho (para hacerse abogado).

3 N: **I was having a quiet ~ in the garden** leía tranquilamente en el jardín; **I like a good ~** me gusta leer; **it's a good solid ~** el libro dará muchas horas de lectura amena; **I managed to have a good ~ whilst waiting** pude leer bastante mientras esperaba.

◆**read back** VT releer, volver a leer.

◆**read off** VT leer; leer de un tirón.

◆**read on** VI seguir leyendo; **'now ~ on'** 'prosigue el cuento'.

◆**read out** VT leer, leer en voz alta; leer para que lo oigan todos (*etc*); **please ~ it out** por favor léenoslo.

◆**read over** VT repasar, volver a leer.

◆**read through** VT leer (de cabo a rabo); repasar.

◆**read up** VT estudiar; preparar; repasar.

◆**read up on** VT leer bibliografía sobre.

readability [ˌriːdə'bɪlɪtɪ] N legibilidad *f* (*also Comput*); amenidad *f*, interés *m*.

readable ['riːdəbl] ADJ *writing* legible; que se deja leer; *book etc* digno de leerse, ameno, interesante.

readdress ['riːə'dres] VT *letter* poner señas nuevas (*or* correctas) en, reexpedir; **to ~ a letter to sb** volver a dirigir una carta a uno.

reader ['riːdər] N **(a)** lector *m*, -ora *f*; (*in library*) usuario *m*, -a *f*; (*Typ*) corrector *m*, -a *f*; **he's a great ~** lee mucho, es muy aficionado a la lectura; **I'm not much of a ~** leo poco, no me interesan mucho los libros.

(b) (*Brit Univ*) profesor *m* adjunto, profesora *f* adjunta.

(c) (*book*) libro *m* de lectura.

(d) (*machine*) máquina *f* lectora, aparato *m* lector.

readership ['riːdəʃɪp] N **(a)** lectorado *m*, número *m* total de lectores (de un periódico). **(b)** (*Brit Univ*) puesto del **reader**.

read head ['riːdhed] N cabeza *f* de lectura.

readily ['redɪlɪ] ADV (*quickly*) en seguida, pronto; (*willingly*) de buena gana; (*easily*) fácilmente.

readiness ['redɪnɪs] N prontitud *f*; disponibilidad *f*; buena disposición *f*, buena voluntad *f*; (*preparedness*) preparación *f*; **~ of wit** viveza *f* de ingenio; **everything is in ~** todo está listo, todo está preparado; **to hold o.s. in ~ for sth** estar listo para algo; **hold yourself in ~ for ...** prepárese para ...

reading ['riːdɪŋ] **1** N **(a)** (*gen*) lectura *f*; (*aloud*) lectura *f*, recitación *f*.

(b) (*understanding*) interpretación *f*.

(c) (*of thermometer etc*) indicación *f*, lectura *f*; medición *f*.

(d) (*in text*) lección *f*.

(e) (*Parl*) lectura *f*; **second ~** segunda lectura *f*; **to give a bill a second ~** leer un proyecto de ley por segunda vez.

2 ADJ: **the ~ public** el público que lee, ei público lector; **he's a great ~ man** es un hombre que lee mucho, es hombre muy aficionado a la lectura.

3 ATTR de lectura; **he has a ~ age of 8** tiene el nivel de lecturas de un niño de ocho años; **~ book** libro *m* de lectura; **~ comprehension test** ejercicio *m* de comprensión lectora; **~ glass** lente *m* para leer; **~ glasses** gafas *fpl* de leer (*or* de lectura); **she has a ~ knowledge of Spanish** sabe leer el español; **~ lamp** lámpara *f* para ieer (en la cama *etc*), lámpara *f* portátil; **~ list** lista *f* de lecturas; **~ matter** lectura *f*; **~ room** sala *f* de lectura; **~ speed** velocidad *f* de lectura.

readjust ['riːə'dʒʌst] **1** VT reajustar; reorientar.

2 VI reajustarse; reorientarse.

readjustment ['riːə'dʒʌstmənt] N reajuste *m*; reorientación *f*.

readmit ['riːəd'mɪt] VT readmitir, volver a admitir.

read-only [ˌriːd'əʊnlɪ] ADJ: **~ memory** memoria *f* muerta, memoria *f* de sola lectura.

read-out ['riːdaʊt] N lectura *f* de salida.

read-write [ˌriːd'raɪt] ADJ: **~ head** cabeza *f* de lectura-escritura; **~ window** ventana *f* de lectura-escritura.

ready ['redɪ] **1** ADJ **(a)** (*prepared*) listo, preparado; pronto; (*available*) disponible; **~?, are you ~?** ¿estás listo?, ¿vamos?; **~, steady, go!** ¡preparados, listos, ya!; **~ when you are!** ¡todo listo!; **we're all ~ and waiting** todos estamos listos y dispuestos; **~ for action** dispuesto para el combate, (*fig*) lanza en ristre; **~ for use** listo para usar; **I'm ~ for bed** tengo sueño; **I'm ~ for a drink** muero por echarme un trago; **~ cash, ~ money** dinero *m* contante, dinero *m* efectivo, fondos *mpl* disponibles; **to be ~ to hand** estar a la mano, estar disponible; **to be ~ to do sth** estar listo para hacer algo; **the aircraft will be ~ to fly in 6 months** el avión estará listo para volar en 6 meses; **I am ~ to face him now** ahora estoy con ánimo para enfrentarme con él; **~ to serve** preparado; **~ to use** listo para usar; **to get ~, to make ~** prepararse; disponerse (*to* + *infin* a + *infin*); **to get sth ~, to make sth ~** preparar algo, disponer algo; **to hold o.s. ~ (for)** estar listo (*for* para); **hold yourselves ~ to leave at any moment** prepárense para partir en cualquier momento.

(b) (*willing*) dispuesto (*to* + *infin* a + *infin*); **he's a ~ helper** presta su ayuda de buena gana.

(c) (*about*) **I was ~ to die of hunger** estaba para morirme de hambre; **we were ~ to give up there and then** estábamos a punto de abandonarlo sin más.

(d) (*prompt*) fácil, pronto; *wit* agudo, vivo; **to have a ~ wit** ser ingenioso, tener chispa; **to have a ~ pen** escribir con soltura; **to have a ~ tongue** no morderse la lengua; **to find a ~ sale** venderse fácilmente, tener una salida fácil.

[2] N **(a) with rifles at the ~** con los fusiles listos para tirar, con los fusiles apercibidos; **pen at the ~** pluma en ristre.

(b) some of the ~: algo de parné:, algún dinero *m* contante.

[3] VT (*esp US*) preparar, disponer; poner a punto.

ready-cooked ['redɪ'kʊkt] ADJ listo para comer.

ready-made ['redɪ'meɪd] ADJ hecho, confeccionado; *clothing* hecho, de percha.

ready-mixed ['redɪmɪkst], (*US*) **ready-mix** ['redɪmiks] ADJ *concrete* preparado; *cake* de paquete.

ready-reckoner ['redɪ'reknər] N baremo *m*, libro *m* de cálculos hechos.

ready-to-serve [,redɪtə'sɜːv] ADJ preparado.

ready-to-wear ['redɪtə'weər] ADJ hecho, confeccionado, de percha.

reaffirm ['riːə'fɜːm] VT reafirmar, reiterar, afirmar de nuevo.

reaffirmation ['riːæfə'meɪʃən] N reafirmación *f*, reiteración *f*.

reafforest ['riːə'fɒrɪst], (*US*) **reforest** ['riː'fɒrɪst] VT repoblar de árboles.

reafforestation ['riːə,fɒrɪs'teɪʃən], (*US*) **reforestation** [,riːfɒrɪs'teɪʃən] N repoblación *f* forestal.

reagent [riː'eɪdʒənt] N reactivo *m*.

real [rɪəl] [1] ADJ **(a)** real; verdadero; auténtico; legítimo; *income, value, wages* real; **the ~ world** el mundo real; **a ~ man** todo un hombre; **~ ale** cerveza *f* legítima; **in ~ terms** en términos reales; **the ~ McCoy** lo auténtico, lo realmente genuino; **you're a ~ friend** eres un verdadero amigo; **the ~ power is in the hands of X** el poder efectivo está en manos de X; **this is ~ coffee** esto es auténtico café, esto es lo que se llama café; **we have had days of ~ heat** hemos tenido días de auténtico calor; **is he the ~ king?** ¿él es el rey legítimo?; **this is the ~ thing at last** por fin lo tenemos sin trampa ni cartón.

(b) ~ assets propiedad *f* inmueble, bienes *mpl* raíces; **~ estate, ~ property** bienes *mpl* raíces; **~ estate agent** (*US*) agente *m* inmobiliario, agente *f* inmobiliaria; **~ estate market** (*US*) mercado *m* inmobiliario.

(c) ~ time tiempo *m* real.

[2] ADV (*) **~ good** muy bueno, realmente bueno; **a ~ nice guy** un chico de los más amables; **it's ~ heavy** pesa una barbaridad.

[3] N **(a) the ~** (*Philos*) lo real.

(b) (*) **it's for ~** esto va de veras; **don't worry, it's not for ~** no te preocupes, no es de veras.

realign [riːə'laɪn] VT reordenar.

realignment [riːə'laɪnmənt] N reordenación *f*.

realism ['rɪəlɪzəm] N realismo *m*; autenticidad *f*.

realist ['rɪəlɪst] N realista *mf*.

realistic [rɪə'lɪstɪk] ADJ realista; auténtico; objetivo.

realistically [rɪə'lɪstɪkəlɪ] ADV de modo realista; auténticamente.

reality [riː'ælɪtɪ] N realidad *f*; **in ~** en realidad; **the realities of power** la realidad del poder; **let's get back to ~** volvamos a la realidad; **let's stick to realities** atengámonos a la realidad.

realizable ['rɪəlaɪzəbl] ADJ realizable, factible.

realization [,rɪəlaɪ'zeɪʃən] N **(a)** comprensión *f*; **this ~ came too late** esto lo comprendió tarde; **it was a sudden ~** cayó de repente en la cuenta. **(b)** (*Comm*) realización *f*.

realize ['rɪəlaɪz] VT **(a)** (*comprehend*) darse cuenta de, hacerse cargo de, comprender; caer en la cuenta de; **without realizing it** sin darse cuenta; **I ~ that ...** me doy cuenta de que ..., comprendo que ..., reconozco que ...; **once I ~d how it was done** tan pronto como caí en la cuenta de cómo se hacía; **do you ~ what you've done?** ¿te das cuenta de lo que has hecho?

(b) (*carry out*) realizar, llevar a cabo, poner por obra; *one's potential* realizar; **my worst fears were ~d** resultaron ser ciertos mis temores.

(c) (*Comm*) *assets etc* realizar.

real-life [,rɪəl'laɪf] ADJ de la vida real, auténtico.

reallocate [riː'ælə,keɪt] VT *resources* redistribuir.

really ['rɪəlɪ] ADV **(a)** (*used alone*) **~?** ¿de veras?, ¿ah sí?; **not ~?** ¿lo dices en serio?; **~!** ¡ca!; ¡eh!; ¡mire Vd!; **~, whatever next!** ¡qué cosas pasan!

(b) (*with adj*) verdaderamente, realmente, francamente; **a ~ good film** una película realmente buena, una película francamente buena; **~ ugly** lo que se dice feo, lo que se llama feo; **I'm ~ very cross with you** estoy francamente disgustado contigo; **now it's ~ true** ahora sí es verdad; **this time we're ~ done for*** esta vez hemos pringado de verdad*.

(c) (*with verb*) en realidad; realmente; en el fondo; en rigor; **I don't**

~ know en realidad no lo sé; **you ~ must see it** realmente tienes que verlo; **can it ~ be expected that ...?** ¿cabe realmente esperar que ...?; **has he ~ gone?** ¿es cierto que se ha ido?; **how a gentleman who is ~ a gentleman lives** cómo vive un señor señor; **as for ~ talking Chinese, I can't** hablar chino, lo que se dice hablar chino, no sé.

realm [relm] N reino *m*; (*fig*) esfera *f*, campo *m*; dominio *m*; **in the ~ of speculation** en la esfera de la especulación; **in the ~s of fantasy** en el país de la fantasía.

realtor ['rɪəltɔːr] N (*US*) corredor *m* de bienes raíces, corredor *m* de fincas.

realty ['rɪəltɪ] N bienes *mpl* raíces.

ream¹ [riːm] N resma *f*; (*fig*) montón *m*, gran cantidad *f*.

ream² [riːm] VT (*Tech: also to ~ out*) escariar.

reamer ['riːmər] N escariador *m*.

reanimate [riː'ænɪmeɪt] VT reanimar.

reap [riːp] VT segar; (*fig*) cosechar, recoger; **to ~ what one has sown** cosechar lo que uno ha sembrado; **to ~ no profit from sth** no obtener ganancia de algo, (*fig*) no sacarse ventaja de algo; **who ~s the reward?** ¿quién se lleva el beneficio?

reaper ['riːpər] N **(a)** (*person*) segador *m*, -ora *f*. **(b)** (*machine*) segadora *f*, agavilladora *f*.

reaping ['riːpɪŋ] N siega *f*.

reaping hook ['riːpɪŋhʊk] N hoz *f*.

reappear ['riːə'pɪər] VI reaparecer, volver a aparecer.

reappearance ['riːə'pɪərəns] N reaparición *f*.

reapply ['riːə'plaɪ] [1] VT aplicar de nuevo; *paint etc* dar otra capa de. [2] VI volver a presentarse, mandar una nueva solicitud (*for* pidiendo).

reappoint ['riːə'pɔɪnt] VT volver a nombrar.

reappointment ['riːə'pɔɪntmənt] N nuevo nombramiento *m*.

reapportion ['riːə'pɔːʃən] VT volver a repartir (*among* entre).

reappraisal ['riːə'preɪzəl] N reevaluación *f*.

reappraise ['riːə'preɪz] VT reevaluar.

rear¹ [rɪər] [1] ADJ trasero, posterior; de cola; (*Mil*) de retaguardia; **~ door** puerta *f* de atrás; **~ gunner** artillero *m* de cola; **~ lamp, ~ light** luz *f* trasera, calavera *f* (*Mex*); **~ wheel** rueda *f* trasera; **~-wheel drive** tracción *f* trasera; **~ window** ventanilla *f* de atrás, (*Aut*) luneta *f* trasera.

[2] N parte *f* trasera, parte *f* posterior; cola *f*; (*Anat**) trasero *m*; (*Mil: row*) última fila *f*, (*rearguard*) retaguardia *f*; **at the ~ of, in (the) ~ of** detrás de; **in the ~** (*Mil*) a retaguardia; **3 miles to the ~** 3 millas a retaguardia; **to be well to the ~** quedar muy atrasado; **to bring up the ~** cerrar la marcha; **to take the enemy in the ~** atacar al enemigo por detrás.

rear² [rɪər] [1] VT **(a)** (*build*) erigir. **(b)** (*raise*) levantar, alzar; **violence ~s its ugly head again** la violencia vuelve a levantar la cabeza. **(c)** (*bring up*) criar.

[2] VI (*also to ~ up*) encabritarse, ponerse de manos.

rear-admiral ['rɪər'ædmərəl] N contraalmirante *m*.

rear-end* [,rɪə'end] VT dar un golpe por detrás (*a un coche*).

rear-engined ['rɪər,endʒɪnd] ADJ con motor trasero.

rearguard ['rɪəgɑːd] [1] N retaguardia *f*. [2] ATTR: **~ action** combate *m* para cubrir una retirada; **to fight a ~ action** (*fig*) resistir en lo posible.

rearm ['riː'ɑːm] [1] VT rearmar. . [2] VI rearmarse.

rearmament ['riː'ɑːməmənt] N rearme *m*.

rearmost ['rɪəməʊst] ADJ trasero, último de todos.

rear-mounted ['rɪə'maʊntɪd] ADJ: **~ engine** motor *m* trasero, motor *m* posterior.

rearrange ['riːə'reɪndʒ] VT volver a arreglar; ordenar de nuevo, arreglar de otro modo; refundir.

rearrangement ['riːə'reɪndʒmənt] N nuevo arreglo *m*, nueva disposición *f*; (*Liter*) refundición *f*.

rear-view ['rɪə,vjuː] ATTR retrovisor; **~ mirror** espejo *m* retrovisor.

rearward ['rɪəwəd] ADJ trasero, de atrás, posterior.

rearward(s) ['rɪəwəd(z)] ADV hacia atrás.

▼ **reason** ['riːzn] [1] N **(a)** (*motive*) razón *f*; motivo *m*; causa *f*; **the ~ for my departure** el motivo de mi ida; **the ~ for my going** la razón por la que me marcho; **the ~ why** la razón por qué, el por qué; **~s of state** razón *f* de estado; **by ~ of** a causa de; en virtud de; **for this ~** por eso, por esta razón; **for that very ~** por esa misma razón; **for some ~ or other** por alguna razón que otra; **for no good ~, for no ~ at all** sin razón, sin motivo; **for ~s best known to himself** por motivos que se sabe él; **with good ~** con razón; **all the more ~ why you should not sell it** razón de más para no venderlo, motivo más que sobrado para no venderlo; **what ~ can there be for it?** ¿qué razón puede haber?; **you had ~ to complain** Vd tuvo motivo de queja; **we have ~ to believe that ...** tenemos motivo para creer que ...; **as I have good ~ to know** según ciertos indicios que tengo.

(b) (*faculty*) razón *f*; **to lose one's ~** perder la razón.

(c) (*good sense*) sensatez *f*; moderación *f*; **everything in ~** todo con moderación; **we cannot in ~ agree** no podemos razonablemente consentir; **it's out of all ~** está fuera de razón; **to listen to ~, to see ~** ponerse en razón; **we'll make him see ~** le haremos entrar en razón; **it stands to ~** es evidente, es lógico (*that* que); **within ~** dentro de lo razonable.

2 VT **(a) to ~ that** ... razonar que ..., calcular que ..., estimar que ...; **ours not to ~ why** no nos cumple a nosotros averiguar por qué.

(b) to ~ out a problem resolver un problema meditándolo.

(c) to ~ sb out of sth disuadir a uno de algo (alegando razones en contra).

3 VI razonar, discurrir; **to ~ about the universe** especular acerca del universo; **to ~ from data** razonar partiendo de ciertos datos; **to ~ with sb** alegar razones para convencer a uno, tratar de convencer a uno.

▼ **reasonable** ['ri:znəbl] ADJ (*in most senses*) razonable; *person* sensato, juicioso; tolerante; **be ~!** ¡sé razonable!

reasonableness ['ri:znəblnɪs] N lo razonable; sensatez *f*; juicio *m*; tolerancia *f*; **in an atmosphere of sweet ~** en un ambiente de moderación, en un ambiente de tolerancia.

reasonably ['ri:znəblɪ] ADV razonablemente; **a ~ good price** un precio razonable; **a ~ accurate report** un informe bastante exacto; **he acted very ~** obró con mucho tino.

reasoned ['ri:znd] ADJ razonado.

reasoning ['ri:znɪŋ] **1** ADJ racional.

2 N razonamiento *m*; argumentos *mpl*; **I don't follow your ~** no comprendo tus argumentos.

reassemble ['ri:ə'sembl] **1** VT volver a reunir; (*Tech*) montar de nuevo.

2 VI volver a reunirse; (*Parl etc*) volver a celebrar sesión.

reassembly [,ri:ə'semblɪ] N **(a)** (*Parl etc*) (inauguración *f* de la) nueva sesión *f*. **(b)** (*Tech*) nuevo montaje *m*.

reassert ['ri:ə'sɜ:t] VT reafirmar, reiterar.

reassertion [,ri:ə'sɜ:ʃən] N reafirmación *f*, reiteración *f*.

reassess ['ri:ə'ses] VT (*Fin*) tasar de nuevo, revalorar, valorar de nuevo (*at* en); *amount of tax* fijar de nuevo (*at* en); (*Liter etc*) hacer una nueva apreciación de; .**we shall have to ~ the situation** tendremos que estudiar la situación de nuevo.

reassessment [,ri:ə'sesmənt] N (*Fin*) revaloración *f*; (*Liter etc*) nueva apreciación *f*.

reassurance ['ri:əʃʊərəns] N **(a)** noticia *f* tranquilizadora, promesa *f* tranquilizadora; alivio *m*, seguridades *fpl*. **(b)** (*Fin*) reaseguro *m*.

reassure ['ri:ə'ʃʊər] VT **(a)** tranquilizar; alentar; **to feel ~d** estar más tranquilo. **(b)** (*Fin*) reasegurar.

reassuring ['ri:ə'ʃʊərɪŋ] ADJ tranquilizador; alentador; **to make ~ noises** decir cosas tranquilizadoras.

reassuringly ['ri:ə'ʃʊərɪŋlɪ] ADV de modo tranquilizador; **he spoke ~** nos alentó con sus palabras; **a ~ strong performance** una actuación cuya fuerza nos alentó.

reawaken ['ri:ə'weɪkən] **1** VT volver a despertar.

2 VI (volver a) despertarse.

reawakening ['ri:ə'weɪknɪŋ] N despertar *m*.

REB N ABBR of **Revised English Bible** *versión revisada de la Biblia*.

rebarbative [rɪ'bɑ:bətɪv] ADJ repugnante, repelente.

rebate ['ri:beɪt] **1** N rebaja *f*, descuento *m*.

2 VT rebajar, descontar.

Rebecca [rɪ'bekə] NF Rebeca.

rebel **1** ['rebl] ADJ rebelde; **the ~ government** el gobierno rebelde; **~ leader** cabecilla *m*.

2 ['rebl] N rebelde *mf*.

3 [rɪ'bel] VI rebelarse, sublevarse; (*legs, stomach etc*) rebelarse, negarse a funcionar.

rebellion [rɪ'beljən] N rebelión *f*, sublevación *f*.

rebellious [rɪ'beljəs] ADJ rebelde; *child etc* revoltoso, díscolo.

rebelliousness [rɪ'beljəsnɪs] N rebeldía *f*; carácter *m* revoltoso, naturaleza *f* díscola.

rebind ['ri:'baɪnd] (*irr: V bind*) VT volver a atar; *book* reencuadernar.

rebirth ['ri:'bɜ:θ] N renacimiento *m*.

reboot [,ri:'bu:t] VTI reinicializar, reiniciar.

rebore ['ri:'bɔ:r] (*Tech*) **1** N rectificado *m*.

2 VT rectificar.

reborn ['ri:'bɔ:n] PTP: **to be ~** renacer.

rebound **1** N ['ri:baʊnd] rebote *m*; **on the ~** de rebote, de rechazo; **she married him on the ~** se casó con él de rechazo.

2 [rɪ'baʊnd] VI rebotar (*off* después de chocar con), dar un rebote; (*fig*) repercutir (*on* en).

rebroadcast ['ri:'brɔ:dkɑ:st] **1** N retransmisión *f*.

2 VT retransmitir.

rebuff [rɪ'bʌf] **1** N repulsa *f*, desaire *m*; **to meet with a ~** ser repulsado, aguantar un desaire.

2 VT rechazar; desairar.

rebuild ['ri:'bɪld] (*irr: V build*) VT reconstruir, reedificar; reconstituir.

rebuilding ['ri:'bɪldɪŋ] N reconstrucción *f*, reedificación *f*; reconstitución *f*.

rebuilt ['ri:'bɪlt] PRET, PTP of **rebuild**.

rebuke [rɪ'bju:k] **1** N reprensión *f*; reprimenda *f*.

2 VT reprender, censurar; **to ~ sb for having done sth** reprender a uno por haber hecho algo.

rebus ['ri:bəs] N jeroglífico *m*.

rebut [rɪ'bʌt] VT rebatir, refutar, rechazar.

rebuttal [rɪ'bʌtl] N refutación *f*.

recalcitrance [rɪ'kælsɪtrəns] N obstinación *f*, terquedad *f*.

recalcitrant [rɪ'kælsɪtrənt] ADJ reacio, refractorio, recalcitrante.

recall [rɪ'kɔ:l] **1** N aviso *m*, llamada *f* (para hacer volver a uno); retirada *f*; destitución *f*; **to be beyond** (*or past*) **~** ser irrevocable; (*person*) haberse ido definitivamente; **those days are gone beyond ~** aquellos días son irrevocables; **to have total ~** poder recordarlo todo, tener una memoria infalible.

2 VT **(a)** (*call back*) *person* llamar, hacer volver; *ambassador, capital* retirar; (*dismiss*) destituir; *library book* reclamar; *defective product* retirar del mercado; (*Comput*) volver a llamar.

(b) (*remember*) recordar, traer a la memoria; **I can't quite ~ whether** ... no recuerdo del todo si ...; **it ~s the time when** ... hace pensar en aquella ocasión cuando ...

recant [rɪ'kænt] **1** VT retractar, desdecirse de; renunciar a.

2 VI retractarse, desdecirse; confesar su error.

recantation [,ri:kæn'teɪʃən] N retractación *f*; confesión *f* de error.

recap* ['ri:kæp] **1** N recapitulación *f*, resumen *m*.

2 VTI recapitular, resumir.

recapitalization [,ri:kæpɪtəlaɪ'zeɪʃən] N recapitalización *f*.

recapitalize [,ri:'kæpɪtəlaɪz] VT recapitalizar.

recapitulate [,ri:kə'pɪtjʊleɪt] VTI recapitular, resumir.

recapitulation ['ri:kə,pɪtjʊ'leɪʃən] N recapitulación *f*, resumen *m*.

recapture ['ri:'kæptʃər] **1** N recobro *m*; reconquista *f*.

2 VT *prisoner etc* recobrar, volver a prender; *town* reconquistar, volver a tomar; *memory, scene* hacer revivir.

recast ['ri:'kɑ:st] (*irr: V cast*) VT (*Tech, Liter etc*) refundir; *play* repartir de otra manera los papeles de.

recce* ['reki] (*Mil*) **1** ABBR of **(a)** N **reconnaissance** reconocimiento *m*. **(b)** VT **reconnoitre** reconocer.

recd, rec'd (*Comm*) ABBR of **received** recibido, rbdo.

recede [rɪ'si:d] VI retroceder, retirarse; (*floods, price*) bajar; (*danger etc*) alejarse, disminuir; (*memory*) desvanecerse; **his hair is receding** se le están formando entradas.

receding [rɪ'si:dɪŋ] ADJ *prospect* que va disminuyendo; *tide* que está bajando; *forehead* huidizo, achatado; **with a ~ hairline** con acusadas entradas capilares.

▼ **receipt** [rɪ'si:t] **1** N **(a)** (*act of receiving*) recepción *f*, recibo *m*; **to acknowledge ~ of** acusar recibo de; **I am in ~ of your letter** he recibido su carta, (*more formally*) obra su carta en mi poder; **on ~ of** al recibo de; **on ~ of these goods** a la recepción de estas mercancías; **on ~ of this news** al saber esta noticia, al recibir esta noticia; **pay on ~** pago *m* contra entrega, pago *m* al recibo.

(b) (*document*) recibo *m*, abono *m* (*Mex*); **please give me a ~** haga el favor de darme un recibo.

(c) ~s (*Comm, Fin: money taken*) ingresos *mpl*; (*of function, game etc*) entrada *f*.

2 VT *goods* dar recibo por; *bill* poner el 'recibí' en.

receipt book [rɪ'si:tbʊk] N libro *m* talonario.

receivable [rɪ'si:vəbl] **1** ADJ recibidero; (*Comm*) por (*or* a) cobrar.

2 ~s NPL cuentas *fpl* por cobrar.

receive [rɪ'si:v] **1** VT recibir; *money* recibir, *payment, salary* cobrar, recibir; (*accept*) aceptar, admitir; *guests* acoger, (*to stay*) hospedar, alojar; *broadcast* captar; *stolen goods* encubrir, ocultar, receptar; *wound* sufrir; *blow, thrashing* cobrar; (*stand weight of*) sufrir, apoyar; *ball* restar; (*approve*) aprobar; **'~d with thanks'** 'recibí'; **are you receiving me?** (*Rad*) ¿me oye?; **to ~ sb into the Academy** recibir a uno en la Academia; **to ~ sb as a partner** admitir a uno como socio; **to ~ sb into the Church** bautizar a uno, recibir a uno en el seno de la Iglesia; **to ~ sb into one's home** hospedar a uno en su casa; **the idea was well ~d** la idea tuvo buena acogida; **the book was not well ~d** el libro tuvo una acogida poco entusiasta; **he ~d a wound in the leg** sufrió una herida en la pierna; **to ~ a blank refusal** encontrar una negativa rotunda; **what treatment did you ~?** ¿qué tratamiento te dieron?

2 VI **(a)** (*Jur*) receptar, ser receptador.

(b) (*Sport*) ser restador.

(c) (*socially*) recibir; **the Duchess ~s on Thursdays** la duquesa recibe los jueves.

received [rɪ'si:vd] ADJ (*Brit*) *pronunciation* estándar; *opinion* admitido, aceptado, recibido; *ver también* ‿ENGLISH‿.

receiver [rɪ'si:vər] N **(a)** (*person*) recibidor *m*, -ora *f*; (*addressee*) destinatario *m*, -a *f*; (*of stolen goods*) receptador *m*, -ora *f*, perista* *mf*; (*in bankruptcy, also* **official ~**) síndico *m*, administrador *m* jurídico;

(*Sport*) restador *m*, -ora *f*; **to call in the ~** entrar en liquidación.

(**b**) (*Rad*) receptor *m*, radiorreceptor *m*; (*Telec*) auricular *m*, fono *m* (*SC*).

(**c**) (*Chem etc*) recipiente *m*.

receivership [rɪˈsiːvəʃɪp] N: **to go into ~** entrar en liquidación.

receiving [rɪˈsiːvɪŋ] ① N recepción *f*; (*of stolen goods*) receptación *f*, encubrimiento *m*.

② ADJ (**a**) **~ set** receptor *m*, radiorreceptor *m*. (**b**) **to be at the ~ end** ser la víctima, ser el blanco.

recension [rɪˈsenʃən] N recensión *f*.

recent [ˈriːsnt] ADJ reciente; nuevo; **in ~ years** en estos últimos años; **in the ~ past** en el próximo pasado.

recently [ˈriːsntlɪ] ADV (**a**) recientemente; hace poco, últimamente; **as ~ as 1990** todavía en 1990; **until ~** hasta hace poco, hasta fecha reciente. (**b**) (*before ptps*) recién; **~ arrived** recién llegado.

receptacle [rɪˈseptəkl] N recipiente *m*.

▼ **reception** [rɪˈsepʃən] ① N (**a**) (*act*) recepción *f*, recibimiento *m*; (*welcome*) acogida *f*; **to get a warm ~** tener buena acogida, ser recibido con entusiasmo; **they'll get a warm ~ if they come here** (*iro*) estamos listos para recibirles si se presentan aquí.

▼ (**b**) (*social function*) recepción *f*.

(**c**) (*Rad etc*) recepción *f*.

(**d**) (*in hotel etc*) recepción *f*.

② ATTR: **~ center** (*US*), **~ centre** centro *m* de recepción; **~ class** clase *f* de primer año; **~ desk** (mesa *f* de) recepción *f*; **~ room** sala *f* de recibo.

receptionist [rɪˈsepʃənɪst] N (*hotel*) recepcionista *f*; (*dentist's etc*) chica *f*, chica *f* enfermera; (*other*) secretaria *f*.

receptive [rɪˈseptɪv] ADJ receptivo.

receptiveness [rɪˈseptɪvnɪs] N, **receptivity** [rɪsepˈtɪvɪtɪ] N receptividad *f*.

receptor [rɪˈseptəʳ] N (*Physiol, Rad*) receptor *m*.

recess [rɪˈses] ① N (**a**) (*vacation*) vacaciones *fpl*; (*US: short rest*) descanso *m*; (*esp US: in school*) recreo *m*; (*Parl*) suspensión *f*, (*between sittings*) intermedio *m*; **parliament is in ~** la sesión del parlamento está suspendida.

(**b**) (*Tech*) rebajo *m*; (*Archit*) hueco *m*; nicho *m*; (*hiding place*) escondrijo *m*.

(**c**) **~es** (*fig*) seno *m*; lo más hondo, lo más recóndito.

② VI (*US Jur, Parl*) prorrogarse, suspenderse la sesión.

recession [rɪˈseʃən] N retroceso *m*, retirada *f*; (*fall*) baja *f*; (*lessening*) disminución *f*; (*Fin, Comm*) recesión *f*.

recessional [rɪˈseʃənl] N himno *m* de fin de oficio.

recessionary [rɪˈseʃənərɪ] ADJ *factors etc* recesivo.

recessive [rɪˈsesɪv] ADJ recesivo.

recharge [ˈriːtʃɑːdʒ] VT volver a cargar, recargar; **to ~ one's batteries** (*fig*) reponerse.

rechargeable [rɪˈtʃɑːdʒəbl] ADJ recargable.

recherché [rəˈʃeəʃeɪ] ADJ rebuscado.

rechristen [ˈriːˈkrɪsn] VT (*Eccl*) rebautizar; (*rename*) poner nuevo nombre a; **they have ~ed the boat 'Gloria'** han puesto al barco el nuevo nombre de 'Gloria'.

recidivism [rɪˈsɪdɪvɪzəm] N reincidencia *f*.

recidivist [rɪˈsɪdɪvɪst] N reincidente *mf*.

recipe [ˈresɪpɪ] N receta *f* (*for* de); **it's a ~ for disaster** es una receta para el desastre.

recipient [rɪˈsɪpɪənt] N recibidor *m*, -ora *f*, recipiente *mf*; el que recibe, la que recibe; (*of gift etc*) beneficiario *m*, -a *f*.

reciprocal [rɪˈsɪprəkəl] ① ADJ recíproco, mutuo.

② N (*Math*) recíproca *f*.

reciprocally [rɪˈsɪprəkəlɪ] ADV recíprocamente, mutuamente.

reciprocate [rɪˈsɪprəkeɪt] ① VT *good wishes etc* intercambiar, devolver; corresponder, y a; **and this feeling is ~d** y correspondemos plenamente, y queremos expresar idénticos sentimientos; **her kindness was not ~d** no correspondieron a su amabilidad.

② VI (**a**) (*Mech*) oscilar, alternar.

(**b**) (*fig*) usar de reciprocidad, corresponder; **but they did not ~** pero ellos no correspondieron a esto; **he ~d with a short speech** pronunció un breve discurso a modo de contestación.

reciprocation [rɪsɪprəˈkeɪʃən] N reciprocación *f*; reciprocidad *f*, correspondencia *f*.

reciprocity [resɪˈprɒsɪtɪ] N reciprocidad *f*.

recital [rɪˈsaɪtl] N relación *f*, narración *f*; (*Mus*) recital *m*.

recitation [resɪˈteɪʃən] N (*act*) recitación *f*; (*text, piece for ~*) recitado *m*; **with humorous ~s** con recitados humorísticos.

recitative [resɪtəˈtiːv] ① ADJ recitativo.

② NM recitado *m*.

recite [rɪˈsaɪt] ① VT narrar, referir; enumerar; (*recitation*) recitar; **she ~d her troubles all over again** volvió a enumerar todas sus dificultades.

② VI dar un recitado.

reckless [ˈreklɪs] ADJ *person* temerario, imprudente; *act* imprudente;

speed etc excesivo, peligroso; *statement* inconsiderado; (*daring*) osado; (*scatterbrained*) atolondrado; **~ driver** conductor *m* temerario, conductora *f* temeraria; **~ driving** conducción *f* temeraria.

recklessly [ˈreklɪslɪ] ADV temerariamente, imprudentemente; **to drive ~** conducir temerariamente; **to spend ~** derrochar dinero.

recklessness [ˈreklɪsnɪs] N temeridad *f*, imprudencia *f*; inconsideración *f*; **the ~ of youth** la temeridad de la juventud; **the ~ of her driving** su modo imprudente de conducir.

reckon [ˈrekən] ① VT (**a**) (*count number*) contar, calcular; computar; (*ascertain quantity*) calcular, estimar.

(**b**) (*believe*) considerar, estimar; **to ~ sb among one's friends** contar a uno entre los amigos; **to ~ sb as** considerar a uno como.

(**c**) (*think*) pensar, creer; considerar; **I ~ we can start** creo que podemos empezar; **to ~ that ...** estimar que ..., considerar que ..., creer que ...; **I ~ he's worth more** considero que vale más; **she'll come, I ~** según creo vendrá; **I ~ so** así lo creo, creo que sí; cierto.

② VI (**a**) (*do sum*) calcular; hacer cálculos; **to learn to ~** aprender a calcular; **~ing from today** contando desde hoy.

(**b**) **you ~?** ¿tú crees?; **to ~ on** contar con; **to ~ on** + *ger* contar con + *infin*; **to ~ to** + *infin* contar con poder + *infin*, esperar poder + *infin*; **to ~ with** tener en cuenta, contar con; **he's a person to be ~ed with** es una persona de cuenta; **if you offend him you'll have to ~ with the whole family** si le ofendes tendrás que ver con toda la familia; **we didn't ~ with that** no contábamos con eso; **we hadn't ~ed with having to walk** no habíamos contado con ir a pie; **to ~ without sb** dejar fuera a uno, omitir a uno en sus cálculos; **we ~ed without that** no contábamos con eso.

◆ **reckon in** VT incluir.

◆ **reckon up** VT calcular, computar; **to ~ up one's losses** calcular sus pérdidas.

reckoner [ˈrekənəʳ] V ready-reckoner.

reckoning [ˈrekənɪŋ] N (**a**) (*calculation*) cálculo *m*, cuenta *f*; **by any ~** a todas luces; **according to my ~** según mis cálculos; **to be out in one's ~** hacer mal el cálculo, calcular mal.

(**b**) (*bill*) cuenta *f*.

(**c**) (*fig*) ajuste *m* de cuentas.

reclaim [rɪˈkleɪm] ① N: **to be beyond** (*or* **past**) **~** ser irremediable, no tener remedio; estar definitivamente perdido.

② VT (*claim back*) reclamar; *baggage* recoger, reclamar; *sinner etc* reformar; (*tame*) amansar, domesticar; *land* recuperar, hacer utilizable; (*from sea*) ganar, rescatar; *swamp* sanear, entarquinar; *rubber etc* regenerar, volver a hacer utilizable.

reclaimable [rɪˈkleɪməbl] ADJ reclamable; utilizable.

reclamation [rekləˈmeɪʃən] N reclamación *f*; reformación *f*; domesticación *f*; recuperación *f*; utilización *f*; **land ~** rescate *m* de terrenos, entarquinamiento *m*.

reclassify [riːˈklæsɪfaɪ] VT reclasificar.

recline [rɪˈklaɪn] ① VT (*lean, lay*) apoyar, recostar, reclinar; (*rest*) descansar.

② VI reclinarse, recostarse; apoyarse; descansar; **to ~ upon** (*fig*) contar con, fiarse de.

recliner [rɪˈklaɪnəʳ] N butaca *f* reclinable.

reclining [rɪˈklaɪnɪŋ] ADJ acostado; tumbado; *figure, statue* yacente; **~ chair** sillón *m* reclinable; (*Med*) silla *f* de extensión; **~ seat** asiento *m* abatible.

recluse [rɪˈkluːs] N solitario *m*, -a *f*, recluso *m*, -a *f*.

reclusion [rɪˈkluːʒən] N reclusión *f*.

reclusive [rɪˈkluːzɪv] ADJ dado a la reclusión, solitario.

recognition [rekəgˈnɪʃən] N reconocimiento *m*; **a smile of ~** una sonrisa de reconocimiento; **in ~ of** en reconocimiento de, en premio de; en señal de; **in ~ of this fact** reconociendo este hecho; **to change sth beyond ~** cambiar algo de modo que resulta irreconocible.

recognizable [ˈrekəgnaɪzəbl] ADJ reconocible; identificable; **it is ~ as** se puede reconocer como, se puede identificar como.

recognizably [rekəgˈnaɪzəblɪ] ADV: **it is ~ different/better** *etc* se ve a las claras que es diferente/mejor *etc*.

recognizance [rɪˈkɒgnɪzəns] N reconocimiento *m*; obligación *f* contraída; (*sum*) fianza *f*; **to enter into ~s to** + *infin* comprometerse legalmente a + *infin*.

▼ **recognize** [ˈrekəgnaɪz] VT (**a**) (*know again*) reconocer, identificar; conocer; **you don't ~ me** no me reconoce; **I ~d him by his walk** le conocí por su modo de andar; **his own mother would not have ~d him** su propia madre no le hubiera conocido; **he was ~d by 2 policemen** le reconocieron 2 policías; **do you ~ this handbag?** ¿conoce Vd este bolso?

▼ (**b**) (*acknowledge*) admitir, confesar; reconocer; **we ~ that ...** reconocemos que ..., confesamos que ...; **we do not ~ the government of Ruritania** no reconocemos el gobierno de Ruritania; **does the Academy ~ the word?** ¿admite la Academia la palabra?; **we do not ~ your claim** no admitimos (*or* aceptamos) su pretensión; **to ~ sb as king** reconocer a uno por rey.

➤ LANGUAGE IN USE: **reception: 1b** → 25.1, 25.2 **recognize: b** → 26.3

(c) the Chair ~s Mr X (*US Parl*) el Sr X tiene la palabra.

recognized [ˈrekəgnaɪzd] ADJ *expert etc* reconocido como tal; *feature* conocido; *agent etc* acreditado, oficial; **it's the ~ method** es el sistema normal.

recoil [rɪˈkɔɪl] 1 N retroceso *m*; (*of gun*) retroceso *m*, rebufo *m*, culatazo *m*.
2 VI recular, retroceder; (*Mil*) retroceder, rebufar; **to ~ in fear** retroceder espantado; **to ~ from sth** retroceder ante algo, cejar ante la perspectiva de algo; **to ~ from doing sth** sentir repugnancia por hacer algo, no animarse a hacer algo; **it ~ed on him** recayó sobre él, resultó contraproducente para él.

recoilless [rɪˈkɔɪllɪs] ADJ *gun* sin retroceso.

recollect [ˌrekəˈlekt] 1 VT recordar, acordarse de.
2 VI recordar, acordarse.

recollection [ˌrekəˈlekʃən] N recuerdo *m*; **to the best of my ~** que yo recuerde.

recommence [ˈriːkəˈmens] 1 VT reanudar, recomenzar, volver a comenzar.
2 VI reanudarse, recomenzar, volver a comenzar.

▼ **recommend** [ˌrekəˈmend] VT recomendar; **to ~ a candidate for a post** recomendar a un candidato para un puesto; **I ~ him to you most warmly** se lo recomiendo con el mayor confianza; **to ~ sb to do sth** recomendar a uno que haga algo, aconsejar a uno hacer algo; **~ed retail price** precio *m* de venta recomendado, precio *m* de venta al público.

recommendable [ˌrekəˈmendəbl] ADJ recomendable.

recommendation [ˌrekəmenˈdeɪʃən] N recomendación *f*; **the ~s of a report** las recomendaciones de un informe.

recommendatory [ˌrekəˈmendətərɪ] ADJ recomendatorio.

recompense [ˈrekəmpens] 1 N recompensa *f*.
2 VT recompensar (*for* por).

reconcilable [ˈrekənsaɪləbl] ADJ conciliable, reconciliable.

reconcile [ˈrekənsaɪl] 1 VT *persons* reconciliar; *theories etc* conciliar; *quarrel* componer; **to become ~d to sth** resignarse a algo, acomodarse con algo; **what ~d him to the place was the weather** lo que le hizo conformarse con el lugar fue el tiempo.
2 VR: **to ~ o.s. to sth** resignarse a algo, acomodarse con algo, conformarse con algo.

reconciliation [ˌrekənsɪlɪˈeɪʃən] N reconciliación *f*; conciliación *f*; composición *f*; **~ statement** (*Fin*) estado *m* de reconciliación.

recondite [rɪˈkɒndaɪt] ADJ recóndito.

recondition [ˈriːkənˈdɪʃən] VT reacondicionar.

reconditioned [ˈriːkənˈdɪʃənd] ADJ renovado, reparado.

reconnaissance [rɪˈkɒnɪsəns] N reconocimiento *m*; **~ flight** vuelo *m* de reconocimiento; **to make a ~** reconocer el terreno, explorar el terreno.

reconnoitre, (*US*) **reconnoiter** [ˌrekəˈnɔɪtər] 1 VT reconocer, explorar.
2 VI reconocer el terreno, explorar el terreno.

reconquer [ˈriːˈkɒŋkər] VT reconquistar.

reconquest [ˈriːˈkɒŋkwest] N reconquista *f*; **the R~** (*of Spain*) la Reconquista.

reconsider [ˈriːkənˈsɪdər] 1 VT volver a considerar, volver a examinar; reconsiderar, repensar.
2 VI volver a considerarlo.

reconsideration [ˈriːkənˌsɪdəˈreɪʃən] N reconsideración *f*; **on ~** después de volver sobre ello.

reconstitute [ˈriːˈkɒnstɪtjuːt] VT reconstituir.

reconstitution [ˈriːˌkɒnstɪˈtjuːʃən] N reconstitución *f*.

reconstruct [ˈriːkənˈstrʌkt] VT reconstruir; reedificar; *crime etc* reconstituir.

reconstruction [ˈriːkənˈstrʌkʃən] N reconstrucción *f*; reedificación *f*; reconstitución *f*.

reconstructive [ˌriːkənˈstrʌktɪv] ADJ *surgery, treatment* reparador.

reconvene [riːkənˈviːn] 1 VT volver a convocar.
2 VI volver a reunirse.

reconvert [ˈriːkənˈvɜːt] VT volver a convertir (*to* en); reorganizar.

record 1 [ˈrekɔːd] N (a) (*document, report etc*) documento *m*; registro *m*, partida *f*; relación *f*; (*Jur*) acta *f*; (*note*) nota *f*, apunte *m*; (*Comput*) registro *m*; **~ of attendances** registro *m* de asistencias; **~ of a case** acta *f* de un proceso; **for the ~, I disagree** que conste, no estoy de acuerdo; **to write sth into the ~** añadir algo a la relación escrita; **off the ~** (ADJ) no oficial, extraoficial, confidencial; (ADV) de modo no oficial, extraoficialmente, confidencialmente; **it is on ~ that ..., it is a matter of ~ that ...** consta que ...; **the fact is on ~** consta el hecho; **the highest temperatures on ~** las temperaturas más altas de que hay constancia; **the minister is on ~ as saying that ...** consta que el ministro ha dicho que ...; **to place** (*or* **put**) **sth on ~** hacer constar algo, dejar constancia de algo; **there is no ~ of it** no hay constancia de ello, no consta en los documentos; **to keep** (*or* **make**) **a ~ of** apuntar, tomar nota de; **he left no ~ of it** no dejó relación de ello; **let me put** (*or* **set**) **the ~ straight** que consten los hechos;

les diré la verdad de los hechos.
(b) ~s archivos *mpl*; (*of police*) archivo *m* del servicio de identificación; **the ~s of a society** los archivos de una sociedad; **I will have the ~s searched** mandaré buscar en los archivos.
(c) (*person's past in general*) historia *f*; reputación *f*; antecedentes *mpl*; (*as dossier*) expediente *m*; (*written with application for post*) carrera *f*, curriculum *m* vitae; (*Jur*) acta *f*; (*note*) nota *f*, historial *m*; (*Mil*) hoja *f* de servicios; **criminal ~** antecedentes *mpl* delictivos; **her past ~** su historia, su historial; **this company's splendid ~** el brillante historial de esta compañía; **his ~ is against him** su historial obra en perjuicio suyo; **has he a ~?** ¿tiene antecedentes penales?, ¿tiene ficha? (*esp LAm*); **he has a clean ~** no hay nada en su historial que le perjudique; **he left behind a splendid ~ of achievements** dejó un magnífico historial de éxitos.
(d) (*Sport etc*) récord *m*, marca *f*; **is this a ~?** ¿es esto un récord?; ¿es excepcional esto?; **to beat** (*or* **break**) **the ~** batir el récord, superar la marca; **to establish** (*or* **set up**) **a ~** establecer un récord; **to hold the ~ for the 100 metres** ostentar el récord de los 100 metros.
(e) (*Mus etc*) disco *m*; **to make a ~** grabar un disco.
2 [ˈrekɔːd] ATTR: **~ album** álbum *m* de discos; **~ cabinet** armario *m* para discos; **~ company** casa *f* discográfica; **~ dealer** (*person*) vendedor *m*, -ora *f* de discos; (*shop*) tienda *f* de discos; **~ library** discoteca *f*; **~ player** tocadiscos *m*; **~ token** cupón *m* para discos.
3 [ˈrekɔːd] ADJ récord (*invar*), sin precedentes, máximo, nuevo; **a ~ output** una producción sin precedentes; **in a ~ time** en un tiempo récord; **in the ~ time of 12 seconds** en el tiempo récord de 12 segundos.
4 [rɪˈkɔːd] VT **(a)** (*set down*) registrar; inscribir; apuntar; hacer constar, dejar constancia de, consignar; **it is not ~ed anywhere** no consta en ninguna parte; **I will ~ your order** apuntaré su pedido.
(b) (*on dial etc*) indicar, marcar.
(c) (*Mus etc*) grabar, registrar; **she ~ed the song in 1989** grabó la canción en 1989; **to have one's voice ~ed** hacer grabar su voz.
(d) (*Comput*) registrar.
5 [rɪˈkɔːd] VI (*Mus etc*) grabar, hacer una grabación.

record-breaker [ˈrekɔːdˌbreɪkər] N recordman *m*, plusmarquista *mf*.

record-breaking [ˈrekɔːdˌbreɪkɪŋ] ADJ *person, team* brillante, excepcional; que tantos récords ostenta; *effort, run* récord (*invar*).

record-card [ˈrekɔːdˌkɑːd] N ficha *f*.

record-changer [ˈrekɔːdˌtʃeɪndʒər] N cambiadiscos *m*.

recorded [rɪˈkɔːdɪd] ADJ **(a) ~ music** música *f* grabada. **(b) never in ~ history** nunca en la historia escrita; **it is a ~ fact that ...** consta el hecho de que ...; **~ delivery** (*Brit Post*) entrega *f* con acuse de recibo.

recorder [rɪˈkɔːdər] N **(a)** (*person*) registrador *m*, -ora *f*, archivero *m*, -a *f*; **he was a faithful ~ of the facts** registró puntualmente los hechos.
(b) (*Brit Jur*) juez *m* municipal.
(c) (*Mus*) flauta *f* dulce, flauta *f* de pico.
(d) (*Mech*) contador *m*, indicador *m*; (*tape~*) magnetofón *m*.

record-holder [ˈrekɔːdˌhəʊldər] N recordman *m*, titular *mf*, plusmarquista *mf*; **the 100 metres ~** el (*or* la) que ostenta el récord de los 100 metros.

recording [rɪˈkɔːdɪŋ] 1 N grabación *f*; registro *m*.
2 ATTR: **~ angel** ángel *m* que registra las acciones buenas o malas de los hombres; **~ artist** músico *m* (*etc*) que hace grabaciones; **~ density** densidad *f* de grabación; **~ studio** estudio *m* de grabación, sala *f* de grabaciones; **~ tape** cinta *f* de grabación, cinta *f* magnetofónica; **~ van** camión *m* de grabación.

recordist [rɪˈkɔːdɪst] N (*Cine, TV*) sonista *mf*.

recount [rɪˈkaʊnt] VT contar, referir.

re-count [ˈriːˈkaʊnt] 1 N (*Parl*) segundo escrutinio *m*; **to have a ~** someter los votos a un segundo escrutinio.
2 VT volver a contar.

recoup [rɪˈkuːp] VT recobrar, recuperar; indemnizarse por.

recourse [rɪˈkɔːs] N recurso *m*; **to have ~ to** recurrir a.

recover [rɪˈkʌvər] 1 VT recobrar, recuperar (*also Comput*); *money* reembolsarse; *stolen property* recuperar; (*rescue*) rescatar; **to ~ lost time** recuperar el tiempo perdido; **to ~ consciousness** recobrar el conocimiento, volver en sí; **to ~ one's health** recobrar la salud, reponerse; **to ~ sth from sb** hacer que uno devuelva algo; **to ~ one's property** (*Jur*) reivindicar su propiedad; **to ~ damages from sb** ser indemnizado por daños y perjuicios por uno.
2 VI (*Med, Fin etc*) restablecerse, reponerse; (*Econ etc*) reactivarse; **to ~ from an illness** reponerse de una enfermedad; **has she quite ~ed?** ¿se ha curado del todo?; **shares have ~ed** las acciones han vuelto a subir; **when I had ~ed from my astonishment** cuando me había sobrepuesto a mi asombro.
3 VR: **to ~ o.s.** reponerse, sobreponerse.

re-cover [ˈriːˈkʌvər] VT volver a cubrir.

recoverable [rɪˈkʌvərəbl] ADJ recuperable; (*at law*) reivindicable.

recovery [rɪˈkʌvərɪ] 1 N recobro *m*, recuperación *f*; (*Comput, Fin*) recuperación *f*; (*Econ*) reactivación *f*; (*rescue*) rescate *m*; (*Med etc*) restablecimiento *m*, mejoría *f*; (*Jur*) reivindicación *f*; **an action for ~ of damages** una demanda del pago de daños y perjuicios; **to be past ~** haberse perdido definitivamente, ser irrecuperable, (*Med*) estar desahuciado; **to make a rapid ~** restablecerse rápidamente; **to make a slow ~** restablecerse lentamente; **prices made a slow ~** las cotizaciones tardaron en restablecerse.

2 ATTR: **~ room** (*Med*) sala *f* de posoperatorio; **~ service** (*Aut*) servicio *m* de rescate; **~ ship**, **~ vessel** nave *f* de salvamento.

recreant†† ['rekrɪənt] 1 N cobarde *mf*.

2 ADJ cobarde.

recreate ['rekrɪeɪt] VT recrear.

re-create ['ri:krɪ'eɪt] VT (*create again*) recrear, volver a crear.

recreation [,rekrɪ'eɪʃən] 1 N (**a**) (*act*) recreación *f*. (**b**) (*play, amusement*) recreo *m*; (*Scol*) recreo *m*, hora *f* de recreo.

2 ATTR: **~ center** (*US*), **~ centre** centro *m* de recreo; **~ ground** campo *m* de deportes; **~ room** salón *m* de recreo.

recreational [,rekrɪ'eɪʃənəl] ADJ recreativo; **~ facilities** facilidades *fpl* de recreo, instalaciones *fpl* recreativas; **~ vehicle** (*US*) caravana *f* pequeña, rulota *f* pequeña; **this is only ~** esto es sólo un pasatiempo.

recreative ['rekrɪ,eɪtɪv] ADJ recreativo.

recriminate [rɪ'krɪmɪneɪt] VI recriminar.

recrimination [rɪ,krɪmɪ'neɪʃən] N recriminación *f*.

recross ['ri:'krɒs] VTI volver a cruzar.

recrudesce [,ri:kru:'des] VI recrudecer.

recrudescence [,ri:kru:'desns] N recrudescencia *f*, recrudecimiento *m*.

recrudescent [,ri:kru:'desnt] ADJ recrudescente.

recruit [rɪ'kru:t] 1 N recluta *m*.

2 VT (*Mil*) reclutar; *strength etc* restablecer.

3 VI alistar reclutas.

recruiting [rɪ'kru:tɪŋ] 1 N reclutamiento *m*.

2 ATTR: **~ office** caja *f* de reclutas; **~ officer** oficial *m* de reclutamiento.

recruitment [rɪ'kru:tmənt] N reclutamiento *m*; **~ agency** agencia *f* de colocaciones, agencia *f* de selección de personal.

rec't N ABBR of **receipt**.

rectal ['rektəl] ADJ rectal.

rectangle ['rek,tæŋgl] N rectángulo *m*.

rectangular [rek'tæŋgjʊlər] ADJ rectangular.

rectifiable ['rektɪfaɪəbl] ADJ rectificable.

rectification [,rektɪfɪ'keɪʃən] N rectificación *f*.

rectifier ['rektɪfaɪər] N (*Elec, Chem etc*) rectificador *m*; (*Mech*) rectificadora *f*.

rectify ['rektɪfaɪ] VT (*all senses*) rectificar.

rectilinear [,rektɪ'lɪnɪər] ADJ rectilíneo.

rectitude ['rektɪtju:d] N rectitud *f*.

rector ['rektər] N (*Eccl*) párroco *m*, -ora *f*; (*Univ etc*) rector *m*, -ora *f*; (*Scot Scol*) director *m*, -ora *f*.

rectorship ['rektəʃɪp] N (*Scot: Scol*) parroquia *f*; (*Univ*) ≈ rectorado *m*.

rectory ['rektərɪ] N casa *f* del párroco.

rectum ['rektəm] N recto *m*.

recumbent [rɪ'kʌmbənt] ADJ recostado, acostado; *statue* yacente.

recuperate [rɪ'ku:pəreɪt] 1 VT recuperar.

2 VI restablecerse, reponerse; **to ~ after an illness** reponerse de una enfermedad.

recuperation [rɪ,ku:pə'reɪʃən] N recuperación *f*; (*Med*) restablecimiento *m*.

recuperative [rɪ'ku:pərətɪv] ADJ recuperativo.

recur [rɪ'kɜːr] VI repetirse, producirse de nuevo, volver a producirse; (*revert to*) volver a; (*come to mind again*) volver a la mente; **the idea ~s constantly in his work** la idea se repite constantemente en su obra.

recurrence [rɪ'kʌrəns] N repetición *f*, reaparición *f*.

recurrent [rɪ'kʌrənt] ADJ repetido; constante; (*Anat, Med*) recurrente; **it is a ~ theme** es un tema constante, es un tema que se repite a menudo.

recurring [rɪ'kɜːrɪŋ] ADJ: **~ decimal** decimal *f* periódica.

recursive [rɪ'kɜːsɪv] ADJ recursivo.

recursively [rɪ'kɜːsɪvlɪ] ADV recursivamente.

recusant ['rekjʊzənt] 1 ADJ recusante.

2 N recusante *mf*.

recyclable [,ri:'saɪkləbl] ADJ reciclable.

recycle [,ri:'saɪkl] VT reciclar.

recycling [,ri:'saɪklɪŋ] N reciclado *m*, reciclaje *m*; **~ plant** planta *f* de reciclaje.

red [red] 1 ADJ rojo, colorado; *face* (*high-coloured*) encarnado; (*with anger*) encendido (de ira); (*with shame*) encendido, ruboroso; *hair* rojo; *wine* tinto; *ink* colorado; (*Pol*) rojo; **~ admiral** (*butterfly*) vanesa *f* roja; **~ alert** alarma *f* roja; **R~ Army** Ejército *m* Rojo; **~ cabbage** col *f* lombarda; **~ card** tarjeta *f* roja, cartulina *f* roja; **R~ Cross** Cruz *f* Roja; **~ deer** ciervo *m* (común); **~ diesel** (*oil*) gasóleo *m* B; **~ flag**

bandera *f* roja; **~ heat** calor *m* rojo; **~ herring** pista *f* falsa, ardid *m* para apartar la atención del asunto principal; **R~ Indian** piel roja *mf*; **~ lead** minio *m*; **~ light** luz *f* roja; **~ pepper** pimiento *m* rojo, chile *m* rojo (*LAm*); **~ squirrel** ardilla *f* roja; **~ tape** (*rules*) reglas *fpl*; (*formalities*) formalidades *fpl* burocráticas, trámites *mpl*; (*paperwork*) papeleo *m*; **to be ~ in the face** tener la cara encendida, tener el rostro sofocado; **was my face ~ !** ¡cómo me avergoncé!; **to go** (*or* turn) **as ~ as a beetroot** (*or* lobster *or* tomato) ponerse como un tomate; **to go** (*or* turn) **~ with shame** ponerse colorado, ruborizarse.

2 N (**a**) rojo *m*, color *m* rojo; (*Pol*) rojo *m*, -a *f*; **to be in the ~** estar en números rojos; **to be £1000 in the ~** deber 1000 libras; **to get into the ~** contraer deudas; **to get out of the ~** salirse de deudas, liquidar sus deudas; **to see ~** sulfurarse, salirse de sus casillas; **this makes me see ~** esto me saca de quicio.

(**b**) (*Pol*) rojo *m*, -a *f*.

(**c**) (*wine*) (vino *m*) tinto *m*.

redact [rɪ'dækt] VT redactar.

redaction [rɪ'dækʃən] N redacción *f*.

red-berried ['red'berɪd] ADJ con bayas rojas.

red-blooded ['red'blʌdɪd] ADJ viril, vigoroso, enérgico, de pelo en pecho.

redbreast ['redbrest] N (*also* robin ~) petirrojo *m*.

redbrick ['redbrɪk] ADJ: **~ building** edificio *m* de ladrillo; **~ university** (*Brit*) universidad *f* de ladrillo fundada en el siglo XIX.

redcap ['redkæp] N (*Brit Mil*) policía *m* militar; (*US*) mozo *m* de estación.

▐ **REDBRICK UNIVERSITY** ▌

ⓘ *El término* **redbrick university** *se aplica a las universidades británicas construidas en los grandes centros urbanos industriales como Birmingham, Liverpool o Manchester a finales del siglo XIX o principios del XX. Deben su nombre a que sus edificios son normalmente de ladrillo, a diferencia de las universidades tradicionales de Oxford y Cambridge, cuyos edificios suelen ser de piedra.*

redcoat ['redkəʊt] N (*Brit*) soldado *m* inglés (del siglo XVIII *etc*).

redcurrant ['red'kʌrənt] N (*fruit*) grosella *f* roja, (*bush*) grosellero *m* rojo.

redden ['redn] 1 VT enrojecer, teñir de rojo.

2 VI enrojecerse, ponerse rojo; (*person: with anger*) enrojecerse, (*with shame*) ponerse colorado, ruborizarse.

reddish ['redɪʃ] ADJ rojizo.

redecorate ['ri:'dekəreɪt] VT *room* renovar, pintar de nuevo, volver a decorar.

redecoration [ri:,dekə'reɪʃən] N renovación *f*.

redeem [rɪ'di:m] 1 VT redimir (*also Rel*), rescatar; *mortgage, bonds* amortizar; (*from pawn*) desempeñar; *promise* cumplir; *fault* expiar.

2 VR: **to ~ o.s.** salvarse, expiar su falta.

redeemable [rɪ'di:məbl] ADJ redimible; (*Fin*) amortizable; (*Comm*) reembolsable.

Redeemer [rɪ'di:mər] N Redentor *m*.

redeeming [rɪ'di:mɪŋ] ADJ: **~ feature** rasgo *m* bueno, (*fig*) punto *m* favorable; **~ virtue** virtud *f* compensadora; **I see no ~ feature in it** no le encuentro ningún aspecto bueno.

redefine [,ri:dɪ'faɪn] VT redefinir.

redemption [rɪ'dempʃən] N redención *f* (*also Rel*), rescate *m*; (*Fin*) amortización *f*; desempeño *m*; cumplimiento *m*; expiación *f*; **~ price** precio *m* de retroventa; **to be beyond** (*or* past) **~** no tener remedio, ser irremediable.

redemptive [rɪ'demptɪv] ADJ redentor.

redeploy ['ri:dɪ'plɔɪ] VT *resources, men* disponer de otro modo, reorganizar; utilizar de modo distinto.

redeployment ['ri:dɪ'plɔɪmənt] N nueva disposición *f*, reorganización *f*; utilización *f* más económica (*or* lógica).

redesign [,ri:dɪ'zaɪn] VT rediseñar.

redevelop [,ri:dɪ'veləp] VT reorganizar.

redevelopment [,ri:dɪ'veləpmənt] N reorganización *f*.

redeye* ['red,aɪ] N (*esp US*) vuelo *m* de noche.

red-eyed ['red'aɪd] ADJ con los ojos enrojecidos.

red-faced ['red'feɪst] ADJ (*with anger*) con la cara encendida, con la cara colorada; (*with shame*) colorado, ruboroso, avergonzado.

red-haired ['red'heəd] ADJ pelirrojo.

red-handed ['red'hændɪd] ADJ: **to catch sb ~** coger (*LAm*: pillar) a uno con las manos en la masa, coger (*LAm*: pillar) a uno in fraganti.

redhead ['redhed] N pelirroja *f*.

red-headed ['red'hedɪd] ADJ pelirrojo.

red-hot ['red'hɒt] ADJ (*lit*) candente; (*fig*) *news* de última hora; *issue* peligrosísimo; de máxima importancia, de la mayor actualidad; *supporter etc* vehemente, acérrimo; **~ player** as *m*.

redial [ri:'daɪəl] 1 VTI volver a marcar.

2 N: **automatic ~** marcación *f* automática.

redid [,ri:'dɪd] PRET of **redo**.

redirect ['riːdaɪ'rekt] VT *letter* reexpedir; *energies* emplear de otro modo; *traffic* desviar, dirigir por otra ruta.

rediscover ['riːdɪs'kʌvəʳ] VT volver a descubrir, redescubrir.

rediscovery ['riːdɪs'kʌvərɪ] N redescubrimiento *m*.

redistribute ['riː'dɪs'trɪbjuːt] VT distribuir de nuevo, volver a distribuir.

redistribution ['riːˌdɪstrɪ'bjuːʃən] N redistribución *f*, nueva distribución *f*.

red-letter ['red'letəʳ] ADJ: ~ **day** día *m* señalado, día *m* especial.

red-light ['red'laɪt] ADJ: ~ **district** barrio *m* chino, barrio *m* de los lupanares, zona *f* de tolerancia.

redneck ['rednek] N (*US*) campesino *m* blanco (de los estados del Sur); patán *m*.

redness ['rednɪs] N rojez *f*, color *m* rojo, lo rojo, lo encarnado.

redo ['riː'duː] (*irr: V do*) VT rehacer, volver a hacer.

redolence ['redəʊləns] N fragancia *f*, perfume *m*.

redolent ['redəʊlənt] ADJ: ~ **of** perfumado como, con perfume como el de; **to be** ~ **of** (*fig*) recordar, hacer pensar en.

redone [ˌriː'dʌn] PTP *of* redo.

redouble [riː'dʌbl] [1] VT redoblar, intensificar; (*Bridge*) redoblar.
[2] VI redoblarse, intensificarse; (*Bridge*) redoblar.

redoubt [rɪ'daʊt] N reducto *m*; **the last** ~ **of** ... el último reducto de ...

redoubtable [rɪ'daʊtəbl] ADJ temible, formidable.

redound [rɪ'daʊnd] VI: **to** ~ **to** redundar en, redundar en beneficio de; **this will hardly** ~ **to his credit** esto no va a beneficiar su buen nombre.

redraft ['riː'drɑːft] VT volver a redactar, hacer un nuevo borrador de, rehacer.

redraw ['riː'drɔː] (*irr: V draw*) VT volver a dibujar; *map, plan* volver a trazar.

redress [rɪ'dres] [1] N reparación *f*, compensación *f*; remedio *m* (*legal*), derecho *m* a satisfacción; **in such a case you have no** ~ en tal caso Vd no tiene ningún derecho a satisfacción; **to seek** ~ **for** solicitar compensación por, reclamar satisfacción por.
[2] VT (*readjust*) reajustar; *balance etc* rectificar, corregir; (*make up for*) reparar, compensar; *fault* remediar; *offence* desagraviar, enmendar.

Red Riding Hood ['red'raɪdɪŋhʊd] NF Caperucita *f* Roja.

Red Sea ['red'siː] N Mar *m* Rojo.

redshank ['redʃæŋk] N archibebe *m*.

redskin ['redskɪn] N piel roja *mf*.

redstart ['redstɑːt] N colirrojo *m* real.

reduce [rɪ'djuːs] [1] VT (a) reducir (*to* a; *also Math etc*), disminuir; *price* rebajar; (*in rank*) degradar; (*Culin*) hervir y espesar; **to** ~ **an article by a quarter** abreviar un artículo en la cuarta parte; **to** ~ **everything to simple terms** expresarlo todo en términos sencillos; **to** ~ **sth to ashes** reducir algo a cenizas; **to** ~ **speed** reducir la velocidad; **this ~d him to silence** esto le hizo callar; **we were ~d to begging in the streets** nos vimos sin otro recurso que el de pedir por las calles.
(b) (*Mil: capture*) tomar, conquistar.
[2] VI (a) reducirse, disminuir; (*Culin*) espesarse.
(b) (*slim*) adelgazar.

reduced [rɪ'djuːst] ADJ: **a** ~ **income** una renta mermada, unos ingresos disminuidos; **at a** ~ **price** con rebaja, con descuento; ~ **goods** mercancías *fpl* rebajadas; '**greatly** ~ **prices**' 'grandes rebajas'; '~ **to clear**' 'rebajas por liquidación'.

reducer [rɪ'djuːsəʳ] N (*Phot, Elec*) reductor *m*.

reducible [rɪ'djuːsəbl] ADJ reducible.

reduction [rɪ'dʌkʃən] N (a) reducción *f* (*in, of* de), disminución *f*; (*in price*) rebaja *f*; (*in rank*) degradación *f*; (*shortening*) abreviación *f*; '**great** ~s' (*Comm*) 'grandes rebajas'; **there has been no** ~ **in demand** no ha disminuido la demanda.
(b) (*Mil*) toma *f*, conquista *f*.

reductive [rɪ'dʌktɪv] ADJ reduccionista.

redundance [rɪ'dʌndəns] N redundancia *f*.

redundancy [rɪ'dʌndənsɪ] [1] N exceso *m*, superfluidad *f*; (*of worker: euph*) despido *m*; (*among workers*) desempleo *m*; V **compulsory** etc.
[2] ATTR: ~ **compensation**, ~ **payment** (*Brit*) (compensación *f* por) despido *m*, indemnización *f* por desempleo.

redundant [rɪ'dʌndənt] ADJ excesivo, superfluo; (*Gram*) redundante; **to be** ~ (*Brit*) estar de más; **the workers now made** ~ (*Brit*) los obreros que quedan ahora sin trabajo; **automation may make some workers** ~ (*Brit*) la automatización puede hacer que varios obreros pierdan sus puestos.

reduplicate [rɪ'djuːplɪkeɪt] VT reduplicar.

reduplication [rɪˌdjuːplɪ'keɪʃən] N reduplicación *f*.

reduplicative [rɪ'djuːplɪkətɪv] ADJ reduplicativo.

redwing ['redwɪŋ] N malvís *m*.

redwood ['redwʊd] N secoya *f*.

redye ['riː'daɪ] VT reteñir, volver a teñir.

re-echo ['riː'ekəʊ] [1] VT repetir, resonar con.
[2] VI resonar, repercutirse.

reed [riːd] [1] N (*Bot*) carrizo *m*, junco *m*, caña *f*; (*Mus: in mouthpiece*) lengüeta *f*, (*pipe*) caramillo *m*; **broken** ~ (*fig*) persona *f* quemada.
[2] ATTR: ~ **instrument** instrumento *m* de lengüeta; ~ **stop** registro *m* de lengüetas.

reedbed ['riːdbed] N carrizal *m*, juncal *m*, cañaveral *m*.

reed bunting ['riːd'bʌntɪŋ] N verderón *m* común.

re-edit ['riː'edɪt] VT reeditar.

reedmace ['riːdmeɪs] N anea *f*, espadaña *f*.

re-educate ['riː'edjʊkeɪt] VT reeducar.

re-education ['riːˌedjʊ'keɪʃən] N reeducación *f*.

reed-warbler ['riːd'wɔːbləʳ] N carricero *m* común.

reedy ['riːdɪ] ADJ (a) *place* lleno de cañas, cubierto de carrizos (*etc*). (b) (*Mus*) aflautado, atiplado.

reef[1] [riːf] (*Naut*) [1] N rizo *m*; **to let out a** ~ largar rizos, (*fig*) aflojar el cinturón (*etc*); **to take in a** ~ tomar rizos, (*fig*) apretar el cinturón (*etc*).
[2] VT arrizar.

reef[2] [riːf] N (*Geog*) escollo *m*, arrecife *m*.

reefer[1] ['riːfəʳ] N chaquetón *m*.

reefer[2] ['riːfəʳ] N porro; *m*.

reefknot ['riːfnɒt] N nudo *m* de marino.

reek [riːk] [1] N mal olor *m*, hedor *m* (*of* a).
[2] VI (*smoke*) humear, vahear; (*smell*) oler, heder, apestar (*of* a); trascender (*of* a); **this ~s of treachery** esto huele a traición; **she ~s with affectation** su afectación es inaguantable; **he comes home simply ~ing** (*of drink*) vuelve a casa que apesta a vino.

reel [riːl] [1] N (*in fishing etc*) carrete *m*; (*for tape recorder etc*) carrete *m*, bobina *f*; (*Sew*) broca *f*, devanadera *f*; (*Phot: for small camera*) carrete *m*, película *f*, rollo *m*, (*of cine film*) bobina *f*, cinta *f*; (*Mus*) baile escocés muy vivo; **about 20 right off the** ~ (*US*) unos 20 seguidos, unos 20 sin parar.
[2] VT (*Sew*) devanar.
[3] VI tambalear, tambalearse; (*retreat*) cejar, retroceder; **he was ~ing about drunkenly** andaba haciendo eses; **the boxer ~ed to his corner** el boxeador se fue tambaleando a su rincón; **the mind ~s** la mente queda atolondrada; **we ~ed at the news** la noticia nos atolondró; **to make sb's mind** ~ atolondrar a uno; **my head is ~ing** mi cabeza está dando vueltas.
◆**reel in** VT: **to** ~ **in one's line** ir cobrando el sedal; **to** ~ **in a fish** tirar de un pez haciendo girar el carrete.
◆**reel off** VT enumerar rápidamente, recitar de una tirada, ensartar.

re-elect ['riːɪ'lekt] VT reelegir.

re-election ['riːɪ'lekʃən] N reelección *f*.

re-eligible ['riː'elɪdʒəbl] ADJ reelegible.

reel-to-reel ['riːltə'riːl] ADJ: ~ **tape-recorder** grabadora *f* de bobina.

re-embark [ˌriːɪm'bɑːk] VTI reembarcar.

re-embarkation ['riːˌembɑː'keɪʃən] N reembarco *m*.

re-emerge ['riːɪ'mɜːdʒ] VI volver a salir, reaparecer.

re-employ [ˌriːɪm'plɔɪ] VT volver a emplear.

re-enact ['riːɪ'nækt] VT (a) (*Parl*) volver a promulgar; decretar de nuevo. (b) (*Theat etc*) volver a representar; *crime* reconstruir.

re-enactment [ˌriːɪ'næktmənt] N reconstrucción *f*.

re-engage ['riːɪn'geɪdʒ] VT contratar de nuevo.

re-enlist ['riːɪn'lɪst] VI reengancharse, alistarse de nuevo.

re-enter ['riːɪn'entəʳ] VT reingresar en, volver a entrar en.

re-entry ['riː'entrɪ] N reingreso *m*, segunda entrada *f*; (*of spacecraft*) reentrada *f*, reingreso *m*.

re-equip ['riːɪ'kwɪp] VT equipar de nuevo (*with* con).

re-erect ['riːɪ'rekt] VT reerigir.

re-establish ['riːɪs'tæblɪʃ] VT restablecer.

re-establishment ['riːɪs'tæblɪʃmənt] N restablecimiento *m*.

reeve[1] [riːv] VT (*Naut*) asegurar (con cabo); pasar por un ojal.

reeve[2] [riːv] N (*Hist*) baile *m*, juez *m* local.

re-examination ['riːɪgˌzæmɪ'neɪʃən] N reexaminación *f*.

re-examine ['riːɪg'zæmɪn] VT reexaminar.

re-export ['riː'ekspɔːt] [1] VT reexportar.
[2] N reexportación *f*.

ref[1] [ref] N (*Sport*) árbitro *m*.

ref[2] (a) PREP ABBR *of* **with reference to** respecto de. (b) (*in letter-head*) N ABBR *of* **reference** referencia *f*.

reface ['riː'feɪs] VT revestir de nuevo, forrar de nuevo (*with* de), poner un nuevo revestimiento a.

refashion ['riː'fæʃən] VT formar de nuevo, rehacer.

refectory [rɪ'fektərɪ] N refectorio *m*.

refer [rɪ'fɜːʳ] [1] VT (a) (*send, direct*) remitir; **to** ~ **sth (back) to sb** remitir algo a uno; **to** ~ **sb to sth** remitir a uno a algo; **the reader is ~red to page 15** remito al lector a la página 15; **it is ~red to us for decision** se remite a nosotros para que decidamos; **to** ~ **a matter to a lawyer** entregar un asunto a un abogado; **a cheque ~red to drawer (R/D)** un cheque protestado por falta de fondos.
(b) (*ascribe*) atribuir, referir (*to* a); relacionar (*to* con); **he ~s his mistake to tiredness** el error lo achaca a su cansancio; **he ~s the paint-**

ing to the **14th century** atribuye el cuadro al siglo XIV; **this insect is to be ~red to the genus Pieris** este insecto ha de clasificarse en el género Pieris.

2 VI: **to ~ to** referirse a, aludir a, mencionar, hacer referencia a; **I ~ to our worthy president** me refiero a nuestro digno presidente; **we will not ~ to it again** no lo volveremos a mencionar; **~ring to yours of the 5th** me refiero a su carta del 5; **please ~ to section 3** véase la sección 3; **you must ~ to the original** hay que recurrir al original; **to ~ to one's notes** consultar sus notas.

◆**refer back** VT remitir.

referable [rɪˈfɜːrəbl] ADJ: **~ to** referible a; atribuible a; que ha de clasificarse en.

referee [ˌrefəˈriː] 1 N **(a)** (*in dispute, Sport etc*) árbitro *mf*; (*of learned paper*) evaluador *m*, -ora *f*.

(b) (*Brit: of person, for post*) referencia *f*; **Pérez has named you as a ~** Pérez dice que Vd está dispuesto a dar informes sobre él.

2 VT **(a)** *game* dirigir, arbitrar en. **(b)** *learned paper* evaluar.

3 VI arbitrar.

▼ **reference** [ˈrefrəns] 1 N **(a)** (*act of referring*) remisión *f*; **it was agreed without ~ to me** se acordó sin consultarme, se decidió sin que se pidiera mi parecer.

(b) (*bearing*) relación *f* (*to* con); **for future ~, please note that ...** por si importa en el futuro, obsérvese que ...; **I'll keep it for future**

▼ **~** lo guardo por si importa en el futuro; **with ~ to** en cuanto a, respecto de; **with ~ to yours of the 8th** me refiero a su carta del 8; **without ~ to any particular case** sin referirme a ningún caso concreto; **what ~ has A to B?** ¿qué tiene que ver A con B?; **it has no ~ to what I asked** no tiene que ver con lo que yo pregunté.

(c) (*allusion*) referencia *f*, alusión *f*, mención *f*; **he spoke without any ~ to you** habló sin mencionarte para nada; **to make ~ to** referirse a, hacer referencia a.

(d) (*directive*) referencia *f*; número *m* de referencia *f*; sigla *f*; (*Typ: also ~* **mark**) llamada *f*; **'~ XYZ2'** 'número de referencia: XYZ2'; **a ~ in the margin** una referencia al margen.

(e) (*testimonial*) referencia *f*; informe *m*; (*person*) persona *f* a quien se puede acudir para pedir una referencia; **to have good ~s** tener buenas referencias; **to take up sb's ~s** pedir referencias (*or* informes) acerca de uno.

2 ATTR de referencia; **~ book** libro *m* de consulta; **~ library** biblioteca *f* de consulta; **~ number** número *m* de referencia; **~ point** punto *m* de referencia; **~ price** (*Agr*) precio *m* de referencia.

referendum [ˌrefəˈrendəm] N, PL **~s** *or* **referenda** [ˌrefəˈrendə] referéndum *m*.

referential [ˌrefəˈrenʃəl] ADJ referencial.

refill 1 [ˈriːfɪl] N repuesto *m*, recambio *m*; (*for pencil*) mina *f*; **would you like a ~?** ¿te pongo más vino? (*etc*), ¿otro vaso?

2 [ˈriːfɪl] VT rellenar, volver a llenar.

refinance [rɪˈfaɪnæns] VT refinanciar.

refine [rɪˈfaɪn] 1 VT refinar; purificar; *society etc* refinar, educar, hacer más culto; *methods* refinar; *style* limar, purificar; *oil etc* refinar; *metal* acrisolar, acendrar; *fats* clarificar.

2 VI: **to ~ upon sth** refinar algo, mejorar algo; (*discuss*) discutir algo con mucha sutileza.

refined [rɪˈfaɪnd] ADJ **(a)** refinado. **(b)** *society, person* fino, culto; (*pej*) redicho, afectado; *style* elegante, pulido.

refinement [rɪˈfaɪnmənt] N **(a)** refinamiento *m*; (*act, Tech*) refinación *f*; purificación *f*.

(b) (*of society, person*) finura *f*, cultura *f*, educación *f*; (*pej*) afectación *f*; (*of style*) elegancia *f*, urbanidad *f*; **a person of some ~** una persona fina; **that is a ~ of cruelty** eso es ser más cruel todavía; **with every possible ~ of cruelty** con las formas más refinadas de la crueldad.

refiner [rɪˈfaɪnər] N refinador *m*.

refinery [rɪˈfaɪnərɪ] N refinería *f*.

refit [ˈriːfɪt] 1 N reparación *f*, compostura *f*; (*Naut*) reparación *f*, carenadura *f*.

2 VT reparar, componer; (*Naut*) reparar, carenar; **to ~ sth with a device** volver a equipar algo con un dispositivo.

3 VI (*Naut*) repararse.

refitting [ˈriːfɪtɪŋ] N, **refitment** [ˈriːfɪtmənt] N reparación *f*, compostura *f*; (*Naut*) reparación *f*, carenadura *f*.

reflate [ˌriːˈfleɪt] VT reflacionar.

reflation [riːˈfleɪʃən] N reflación *f*.

reflationary [riːˈfleɪʃnərɪ] ADJ reactivador, reflacionario.

reflect [rɪˈflekt] 1 VT **(a)** reflejar; **plants ~ed in the water** plantas *fpl* reflejadas en el agua; **the difficulties are ~ed in his report** el informe se hace eco de las dificultades, las dificultades se reflejan en su informe; **the speech ~s credit on him** el discurso le hace honor.

(b) to ~ that ... pensar que ...

2 VI (*think*) reflexionar, pensar; meditar; **~ before you act** reflexione antes de obrar; **if we but ~ a moment** sí sólo reflexionamos un instante.

◆**reflect (up)on** VT: **~ (up)on it!** ¡medítelo!; **that ~s well (up)on him** eso le hace honor; **that ~s ill (up)on him** eso le muestra bajo una luz poco favorable; **it ~s (up)on all of us** eso tiende a perjudicarnos (*or* desprestigiarnos) a todos; **it ~s (up)on her reputation** eso pone en tela de duda su fama.

reflection [rɪˈflekʃən] N **(a)** (*of light: act*) reflexión *f*, (*image*) reflejo *m*; **the ~ of the light in the mirror** el reflejo de la luz en el espejo; **a pale ~ of former glories** un pálido reflejo de glorias pasadas; **to see one's ~ in a shop window** verse reflejado en un escaparate.

(b) (*aspersion*) reproche *m* (*on* a), crítica *f*; **this is no ~ on your honesty** esto no dice nada en contra de su honradez, esto no es ningún reproche a su honradez; **to cast ~s on sb** reprochar a uno.

(c) (*reconsideration*) **on ~** después de volver a pensarlo, pensándolo bien; **without due ~** sin pensarlo bastante; **mature ~ suggests that ...** una meditación más profunda indica que ...

(d) (*idea*) pensamiento *m*, idea *f*; **'R~s on Ortega'** 'Meditación *f* sobre Ortega'.

reflective [rɪˈflektɪv] ADJ **(a)** *surface* brillante, lustroso. **(b)** (*thoughtful*) pensativo, meditabundo. **(c) to be ~ of** reflejar.

reflectively [rɪˈflektɪvlɪ] ADV pensativamente; **he said ~** dijo pensativo; **she looked at me ~** me miró pensativa.

reflectiveness [rɪˈflektɪvnɪs] N **(a)** (*of surface*) brillo *m*. **(b)** (*thoughtfulness*) carácter *m* pensativo.

reflector [rɪˈflektər] N reflector *m*; (*Aut: also rear ~*) reflectante *m*, captafaros *m*.

reflex [ˈriːfleks] 1 ADJ reflejo.

2 N reflejo *m*.

reflexive [rɪˈfleksɪv] 1 ADJ reflexivo; **~ pronoun** pronombre *m* reflexivo; **~ verb** verbo *m* reflexivo.

2 N pronombre *m* reflexivo; verbo *m* reflexivo.

reflexively [rɪˈfleksɪvlɪ] ADV reflexivamente.

reflexology [ˌriːflekˈsɒlədʒɪ] N reflexología *f*, reflejoterapia *f*.

refloat [ˈriːˈfləʊt] VT desencallar, desvarar, poner a flote, reflotar.

reflux [ˈriːflʌks] N reflujo *m*.

reforest [ˈriːˈfɒrɪst] VT repoblar de árboles.

reforestation [ˈriːˌfɒrɪsˈteɪʃən] N repoblación *f* forestal.

reform [rɪˈfɔːm] 1 N reforma *f*; **~ school** (*US*) reformatorio *m*.

2 VT reformar.

3 VI reformarse.

re-form [ˈriːˈfɔːm] 1 VT formar de nuevo, volver a formar; reorganizar, reconstituir.

2 VI formarse de nuevo, volver a formarse; reconstituirse; (*Mil*) rehacerse.

reformat [ˈriːˈfɔːmæt] VT reformatear.

reformation [ˌrefəˈmeɪʃən] N reformación *f*; **R~** (*Eccl*) Reforma *f*.

reformatory [rɪˈfɔːmətərɪ] N (*Brit*) reformatorio *m*.

reformed [rɪˈfɔːmd] ADJ reformado.

reformer [rɪˈfɔːmər] N reformador *m*, -ora *f*.

reformist [rɪˈfɔːmɪst] 1 ADJ reformista.

2 N reformista *mf*.

refract [rɪˈfrækt] VT refractar.

refracting [rɪˈfræktɪŋ] ADJ: **~ telescope** telescopio *m* de refracción, telescopio *m* refractor.

refraction [rɪˈfrækʃən] N refracción *f*.

refractive [rɪˈfræktɪv] ADJ refractivo.

refractor [rɪˈfræktər] N refractor *m*.

refractoriness [rɪˈfræktərɪnɪs] N obstinacia *f*.

refractory [rɪˈfræktərɪ] ADJ **(a)** refractario, obstinado. **(b)** (*Tech*) refractario.

refrain¹ [rɪˈfreɪn] N estribillo *m*; **his constant ~ is ...** siempre está con la misma canción ...

refrain² [rɪˈfreɪn] VI: **to ~ from sth** abstenerse de algo; **to ~ from + ger** abstenerse de + *infin*; **I couldn't ~ from laughing** no pude menos de reír, no pude contener la risa, no pude dejar de reír.

refresh [rɪˈfreʃ] 1 VT refrescar; **to ~ sb's memory** recordar algo a uno.

2 VR: **to ~ o.s.** refrescarse, tomar un refresco.

refresher [rɪˈfreʃər] 1 N **(a)** refresco *m*. **(b)** (*Jur*) honorarios *mpl* suplementarios.

2 ATTR: **~ course** curso *m* de actualización, curso *m* de repaso.

refreshing [rɪˈfreʃɪŋ] ADJ **(a)** refrescante. **(b)** (*fig*) interesante, estimulante; **it's a ~ change to find this** es interesante encontrar esta novedad, es alentador encontrar esto; **it's ~ to hear some new ideas** da gusto escuchar nuevas ideas.

refreshingly [rɪˈfreʃɪŋlɪ] ADV: **~ different** tan nuevo que resulta alentador.

refreshment [rɪˈfreʃmənt] 1 N refresco *m*; refrigerio *m*; **'R~s'** 'Refrescos'; **'R~s will be served'** 'se servirá un refrigerio'; **to take some ~** tomar algo, comer (*or* beber *etc*).

2 ATTR: **~ bar** chiringuito *m* de refrescos; **~ room** (*Rail*) cantina *f*, comedor *m* (*LAm*); **~ stall, ~ stand** puesto *m* de refrescos.

refried beans [ˌriːfraɪdˈbiːnz] NPL frijoles *mpl* refritos.

▶ LANGUAGE IN USE: **reference: 1b** → 21.1

refrigerant [rɪˈfrɪdʒərənt] N refrigerante *m*.
refrigerate [rɪˈfrɪdʒəreɪt] VT refrigerar.
refrigeration [rɪˌfrɪdʒəˈreɪʃən] N refrigeración *f*.
refrigerator [rɪˈfrɪdʒəreɪtəʳ] ① N frigorífico *m*, refrigerador *m*, nevera *f*, refrigeradora *f* (*LAm*), heladera *f* (*SC*).
  ② ATTR: **~ lorry** camión *m* frigorífico; **~ ship** buque *m* frigorífico.
refuel [ˈriːˈfjʊəl] ① VT reabastecer (*or* rellenar) de combustible; *speculation etc* renovar, volver a despertar.
  ② VI repostar, repostar combustible.
refuelling, (*US*) **refueling** [ˈriːˈfjʊəlɪŋ] N reabastecimiento *m* (*or* rellenado *m*) de combustible, repostaje *m*; **~ stop** escala *f* para repostar.
refuge [ˈrefjuːdʒ] N refugio *m*, asilo *m*; (*resort*) recurso *m*; (*hut*) albergue *m*; **God is my ~** Dios es mi amparo; **to seek ~** buscar dónde guarecerse; **to take ~** ponerse al abrigo, guarecerse; **to take ~ in** refugiarse en, (*fig*) acogerse a, recurrir a.
refugee [ˌrefjʊˈdʒiː] N refugiado *m*, -a *f*; **~ camp** campamento *m* de refugiados; **~ from justice** prófugo *m* de la justicia; **~ status** status *m* de refugiado.
refulgence [rɪˈfʌldʒəns] N refulgencia *f*.
refulgent [rɪˈfʌldʒənt] ADJ refulgente.
refund ① [ˈriːfʌnd] N (*act*) devolución *f*; (*amount*) reembolso *m*.
  ② [rɪˈfʌnd] VT devolver, reintegrar, reembolsar.
refundable [rɪˈfʌndəbl] ADJ reintegrable, reembolsable.
refurbish [ˈriːˈfɜːbɪʃ] VT restaurar; (*decorate*) renovar; *literary work* refundir.
refurnish [ˈriːˈfɜːnɪʃ] VT amueblar de nuevo.
refusal [rɪˈfjuːzəl] N (**a**) negativa *f*, denegación *f*; **a blank** (*or* **flat**) **~** una rotunda negativa; **the offer met a flat ~** rechazaron la oferta de plano.
  (**b**) (*Comm etc*) opción *f*, opción *f* exclusiva; **you have first ~** Vd tiene opción al artículo, lo ofreceré primero a Vd.
refuse¹ [ˈrefjuːs] ① N basura *f*, desperdicios *mpl*, desecho *m*.
  ② ATTR: **~ bin** cubo *m* (*LAm*: bote *m*) de la basura; **~ chute** rampa *f* de desperdicios, rampa *f* de la basura; **~ collection** recolección *f* de basuras; **~ collector** basurero *m*; **~ disposal** eliminación *f* de basuras; **~ disposal unit** triturador *m* de basura; **~ dump** vertedero *m*; **~ lorry** camión *m* de la basura.
▼**refuse²** [rɪˈfjuːz] ① VT rehusar, rechazar, denegar; no querer aceptar; negar; **to ~ to** + *infin* negarse a + *infin*, rehusar + *infin*; **to ~ sb sth** negar algo a uno; **they can ~ her nothing** son incapaces de privarla de nada; **I have never been ~d here** aquí no se han negado nunca a servirme; **she ~d my offer** rechazó mi oferta; **I regret to have to ~ your invitation** siento no poder aceptar su invitación.
  ② VI (**a**) **he ~d** se negó a hacerlo.
  (**b**) (*of horse*) rehusar, plantarse, resistirse a saltar.
  ③ VR: **to ~ o.s. sth** privarse de algo.
refusenik [rɪˈfjuːznɪk] N refusenik *mf*.
refutable [rɪˈfjuːtəbl] ADJ refutable.
refutation [ˌrefjʊˈteɪʃən] N refutación *f*.
refute [rɪˈfjuːt] VT refutar, rebatir.
regain [rɪˈgeɪn] VT cobrar, recobrar, recuperar; *breath* cobrar; **to ~ consciousness** recobrar el conocimiento, volver en sí.
regal [ˈriːgəl] ADJ regio, real.
regale [rɪˈgeɪl] ① VT agasajar, festejar; **to ~ sb on oysters** agasajar a uno con ostras; **he ~d the company with a funny story** para divertirles les contó a los comensales un chiste.
  ② VR: **to ~ o.s. on** (*or* **with**) **sth** regalarse con algo, darse el lujo de algo.
regalia [rɪˈgeɪlɪə] N insignias *fpl* (*esp* reales).
regally [ˈriːgəlɪ] ADV regiamente; con pompa (*etc*) regia.
▼ **regard** [rɪˈgɑːd] ① N (**a**) (*gaze*) mirada *f*.
  (**b**) (*aspect, point*) respecto *m*; aspecto *m*; **in ~ to, with ~ to** con ▼ respecto a, en cuanto a, por lo que se refiere a, in this ~ con respecto a esto.
  (**c**) (*attention, care*) atención *f*; **without ~ to** sin hacer caso de, sin considerar; **having ~ to** en atención a, teniendo en cuenta; **to have no ~ to** (*of person*) no prestar atención a, no tener en cuenta; (*of relationship*) no guardar relación con, no tener que ver con; **~ must be had to this matter** hay que tener en cuenta este asunto.
  (**d**) (*esteem*) respeto *m*, consideración *f*, estimación *f*; **my ~ for him** el respeto que le tengo; **out of ~ for** por respeto a; **to have a high ~ for sb, to hold sb in high ~** tener un gran concepto de uno, estimar mucho a uno; **to show ~ for sb** mostrar respeto por uno; **he shows little ~ for their feelings** le importan poco sus susceptibilidades.
  (**e**) (*in messages*) **~s** recuerdos *mpl*; **~s to X, please give my ~s to X** recuerdos a X, saluda de mi parte a X; **with kind ~s** con muchos recuerdos.
  ② VT (**a**) (*look at*) mirar; observar; **she ~ed me with astonishment** me miró atónita.
  (**b**) (*consider*) considerar; **we ~ it as worth doing** consideramos que

vale la pena hacerlo; **we don't ~ it as necessary** no creemos que sea necesario; **they ~ it with horror** lo ven con horror; **to ~ sb with suspicion** recelarse de uno.
  (**c**) **as ~s** (*regarding*) en cuanto a, por lo que se refiere a.
  (**d**) **highly ~ed** muy estimado, muy bien reputado.
regardful [rɪˈgɑːdfʊl] ADJ: **~ of** atento a.
regarding [rɪˈgɑːdɪŋ] PREP en cuanto a, por lo que se refiere a; **and other things ~ money** y otras cosas relativas al dinero.
regardless [rɪˈgɑːdlɪs] ① ADJ: **~ of** indiferente a; insensible a; sin hacer caso de, sin pensar para nada en, sin miramientos de; **buy it ~ of the cost** cómpralo cueste lo que cueste; **they shot them all ~ of rank** los fusilaron a todos sin miramientos a su graduación; **we did it ~ of the consequences** lo hicimos sin tener en cuenta las consecuencias.
  ② ADV a pesar de todo; pese a quien pese; **he went on ~** continuó sin prestar atención a esto, a pesar de esto siguió adelante; **press on ~!** ¡echa por la calle de en medio!
regatta [rɪˈgætə] N regata *f*.
regd ADJ (**a**) (*Comm*) ABBR *of* **registered** registrado. (**b**) (*Post*) ABBR *of* **registered**.
regency [ˈriːdʒənsɪ] N regencia *f*; **R~ furniture** mobiliario *m* Regencia, mobiliario *m* estilo Regencia.
regenerate ① [rɪˈdʒenərɪt] ADJ regenerado.
  ② [rɪˈdʒenəreɪt] VT regenerar.
regeneration [rɪˌdʒenəˈreɪʃən] N regeneración *f*.
regenerative [rɪˈdʒenərətɪv] ADJ regenerador.
regent [ˈriːdʒənt] ① ADJ: **prince ~** príncipe *m* regente.
  ② N regente *mf*.
reggae [ˈregeɪ] N reggae *m*.
regicide [ˈredʒɪsaɪd] N (**a**) (*act*) regicidio *m*. (**b**) (*person*) regicida *mf*.
régime [reɪˈʒiːm] N régimen *m*; **ancien ~** antiguo régimen *m*; **under the Nazi ~** bajo el régimen de los nazis.
regimen [ˈredʒɪmən] N régimen *m*.
regiment ① [ˈredʒɪmənt] N (*Mil*) regimiento *m*; **a whole ~ of mice** todo un ejército de ratones.
  ② [ˈredʒɪment] VT organizar muy estrictamente; reglamentar; **we are very ~ed at the college** en el colegio nuestra vida está muy reglamentada.
regimental [ˌredʒɪˈmentl] ① ADJ de regimiento, del regimiento; (*fig*) militar; **with ~ precision** con precisión militar.
  ② NPL: **~s** (*Mil*) uniforme *m*.
regimentation [ˌredʒɪmenˈteɪʃən] N reglamentación *f*, organización *f* estricta.
Reginald [ˈredʒɪnld] NM Reinaldo, Reginaldo.
region [ˈriːdʒən] N región *f*; comarca *f*; zona *f*; **a fertile ~** una región fértil; **the lower ~s** (*fig*) el infierno; **in the ~ of 40** alrededor de 40, unos 40; **I felt a pain in the kidney ~** sentí un dolor a la altura de los riñones, sentí un dolor a la altura de los riñones.
regional [ˈriːdʒənl] ADJ regional; **~ council** (*Scot*) consejo *m* regional; **~ development** desarrollo *m* regional; **~ development grant** subsidio *m* para el desarrollo regional.
regionalism [ˈriːdʒənəlɪzəm] N regionalismo *m*.
regionalist [ˈriːdʒənəlɪst] ① ADJ regionalista.
  ② N regionalista *mf*.
register [ˈredʒɪstəʳ] ① N registro *m*; (*Mus, Typ, of hotel*) registro *m*; (*in school*) lista *f*; (*of members*) lista *f*, padrón *m*; (*Univ, Naut*) matrícula *f*; (*Tech*) indicador *m*; (*Ling*) registro *m*, estilo *m*; (*US: cash ~*) caja *f* registradora; **~ of births** registro *m* de nacimientos; **R~ of Companies** Registro *m* de Empresas; **~ of deaths** registro *m* de defunciones; **~ of marriages** registro *m* de casamientos; **~ of voters** registro *m* electoral; **to be in ~** (*Typ*) estar en registro; **to call the ~** (*Scol*) pasar lista; **to sign the ~** (*in hotel*) firmar el registro.
  ② ATTR: **~ office** V **registry**; **a ship of 50,000 gross ~ tons** un buque de 50.000 toneladas de registro bruto.
  ③ VT (**a**) (*record*) registrar; *birth etc* declarar; *trademark etc* registrar; (*record*) apuntar, registrar, hacer constar; (*Univ, Naut*) matricular; (*by post*) certificar, (*by rail*) facturar.
  (**b**) (*show, indicate*) marcar, indicar; *emotion* acusar, mostrar, manifestar; **the thermometer ~s 40 degrees** el termómetro marca 40 grados; **he ~ed no surprise** no acusó sorpresa alguna; **the patient has ~ed a marked improvement** el enfermo ha acusado una notable mejoría; **production has ~ed a big fall** la producción ha experimentado un descenso considerable.
  (**c**) (*take note of*) darse cuenta de; **I ~ed the fact that she had gone** me di cuenta de que se había ido.
  ④ VI (**a**) (*sign on etc*) inscribirse, matricularse; (*for conference*) inscribirse; **to ~ at an hotel** registrarse en un hotel; **to ~ for a course** matricularse en un curso; **to ~ with a doctor** inscribirse en la lista de un médico.
  (**b**) (*Typ*) estar en registro.
  (**c**) (*be understood*) producir impresión (*with* en); **it doesn't seem to have ~ed with her** parece no haber producido impresión en ella;

when it finally ~ed cuando por fin cayó en la cuenta, cuando por fin comprendió; **things like that just don't ~** las cosas así pasan inadvertidas.

registered ['redʒɪstəd] ADJ *letter, mail, post* certificado, *baggage* facturado; *design, trademark etc* registrado; *student etc* matriculado; *charity* legalizado, legalmente constituido; **~ company** sociedad *f* legalmente constituida; **~ nurse** (*US*) enfermero *m* calificado, enfermera *f* calificada; **~ office** domicilio *m* social.

registrar [,redʒɪs'trɑːʳ] N registrador *m*, -ora *f*; archivero *m*, -a *f*; (*of society*) secretario *m*, -a *f*; (*Brit Univ*) secretario *m*, -a *f* general; (*Brit: of births etc*) secretario *m*, -a *f* del registro civil; (*Brit Med*) médico *m*, -a *f* asistente.

registration [,redʒɪs'treɪʃən] ① N (*act*) registro *m*; inscripción *f*; matrícula *f*; declaración *f*; certificación *f*, facturación *f*; (*Aut, Naut, Univ etc: number*) matrícula *f*.
② ATTR: **~ document** (*Brit Aut*) documento *m* de matriculación; **~ fee** derechos *mpl* de matriculación; **~ form** formulario *m* de inscripción; **~ number** (*Brit Aut*) matrícula *f*; **~ tag** (*US Aut*) (placa *f* de) matrícula *f*.

registry ['redʒɪstrɪ] ① N registro *m*, archivo *m*; (*Univ etc*) secretaría *f* general; **servants' ~** agencia *f* de colocaciones.
② ATTR: **~ office** (*Brit*) juzgado *m* municipal, registro *m* civil; **to get married at a ~ office** casarse por lo civil, casarse por el juzgado.

Regius ['riːdʒəs] ADJ (*Brit Univ*) regio.

regress ① ['riːgres] N regreso *m*.
② [rɪ'gres] VI regresar.

regression [rɪ'greʃən] N regresión *f*.

regressive [rɪ'gresɪv] ADJ regresivo.

▼**regret** [rɪ'gret] ① N (a) sentimiento *m*, pesar *m*; remordimiento *m*; **much to my ~, to my great ~** con gran pesar mío; **to express one's ~ to sb** (*for act*) expresar su sentimiento a uno, disculparse con uno, (*for death etc*) enviar el pésame a uno; **to feel ~** sentirlo, sentir pesar; **I have no ~s** no me arrepiento de ello; **I say it with ~** lo digo con pesar.
(b) (*in messages*) **~s** (*excuses*) excusas *fpl*; **to send one's ~s for not being able to come** mandar sus excusas por no poder venir.
▼② VT sentir, lamentar; arrepentirse de; **I ~ the error** lamento el error; **it is to be ~ted** es de sentir, es de lamentar; **to ~ that ...** sentir que + *subj*, lamentar que + *subj*; **we ~ to inform you that ...** lamentamos tener que informarle que ...; **he ~s saying it** lamenta haberlo dicho, se arrepiente de haberlo dicho.

regretful [rɪ'gretful] ADJ pesaroso; arrepentido; **to be ~ that ...** lamentar que + *subj*; **he was most ~ about it** lo lamentó profundamente; **we are not ~ about leaving** no nos pesa tener que partir.

regretfully [rɪ'gretfəlɪ] ADV con pesar, sentidamente; **she spoke ~** habló con sentimiento; **I have to tell you that ...** siento tener que decirles que ...

regrettable [rɪ'gretəbl] ADJ lamentable, deplorable; *loss etc* sensible.

regrettably [rɪ'gretəblɪ] ADV lamentablemente; **there were ~ few replies** hubo tan pocas respuestas que daba lástima.

regroup ['riː'gruːp] ① VT reagrupar; (*Mil etc*) reorganizar.
② VI reagruparse; (*Mil etc*) reorganizarse.

regrouping ['riː'gruːpɪŋ] N reagrupación *f*; reorganización *f*.

Regt. ABBR of **Regiment** regimiento *m*, regto.

regular ['regjʊləʳ] ① ADJ (a) (*gen*) regular; (*Eccl, Mil, Gram etc*) uniforme; normal, corriente, constante; *meeting* ordinario; *attender, reader etc* habitual, asiduo; **our ~ waiter** el camarero que suele servirnos; **the ~ travellers on a train** los que siempre viajan en un tren; **~ customer** cliente *mf* habitual; **~ feature** (*of newspaper*) crónica *f* regular; **~ size** (*US*) tamaño *m* normal; **the ~ staff** los empleados permanentes; **~ troops** tropas *fpl* regulares; **as a ~ reader of your journal, may I ...** como lector habitual de su revista, me permito ...; **as ~ as clockwork** como un reloj; **X has been Y's ~ escort** X ha sido el acompañante fijo de Y; **to have a ~ time for doing sth** tener hora fija para hacer algo, hacer algo siempre a la misma hora; **to make ~ use of sth** usar algo con regularidad.
(b) (*systematic*) sistemático, regular; *consistent* constante; **~ features** facciones *fpl* correctas; **a man of ~ habits** un hombre ordenado (en sus costumbres).
(c) (*normal*) normal, corriente; **the ~ word is 'looking glass'** la palabra corriente es 'espejo'; **it's perfectly ~** es completamente normal; **it's quite ~ to see deer here** es corriente ver ciervos por aquí.
(d) (*) cabal, verdadero; **a ~ feast** un verdadero banquete; **there was a ~ quarrel** se riñó de verdad; **he's a ~ guy** (*US*) es buen chico, es un tipo estupendo*.
② N (*Eccl*) regular *m*; (*Mil*) soldado *m* de línea; (*client etc*) parroquiano *m*, -a *f*, cliente *mf* habitual; (*US: gas*) gasolina *f* normal; **one of the café ~s** un asiduo del café; **we keep the best goods for our ~s** guardamos lo mejor para nuestros clientes habituales.

regularity [,regjʊ'lærɪtɪ] N regularidad *f*; **with great ~** con la mayor regularidad.

regularize ['regjʊləraɪz] VT regularizar; formalizar; normalizar; arreglar, poner en orden; **in order to ~ your position** para arreglar su situación.

regularly ['regjʊləlɪ] ADV regularmente, con regularidad; **'use brand X ~'** 'use la marca X con regularidad'; **he's ~ late** siempre llega con retraso; **a ~ declined noun** un sustantivo de declinación regular; **this ground has been ~ fought over** sobre este terreno se ha luchado constantemente.

regulate ['regjʊleɪt] VT regular (*also Mech etc*); arreglar, ajustar; (*make regulations for*) reglamentar; **to ~ one's life by ...** vivir según las normas establecidas por ..., vivir con arreglo a ...; **a well ~d life** una vida ordenada; **to ~ prices** regular los precios.

regulation [,regjʊ'leɪʃən] ① N (a) (*act*) regulación *f*; arreglo *m*. (b) (*rule*) regla *f*; reglamento *m*.
② ATTR reglamentario, de reglamento; normal; **it's ~ wear in school** es el uniforme del reglamento en la escuela.

regulative ['regjʊlətɪv] ADJ reglamentario.

regulator ['regjʊleɪtəʳ] N regulador *m*.

regulatory ['regjʊ,leɪtərɪ] ADJ regulador.

regulo ['regjʊləʊ] N *número del mando de temperatura de un horno a gas.*

regurgitate [rɪ'gɜːdʒɪteɪt] ① VT volver a arrojar, vomitar (sin esfuerzo); (*fig*) reproducir maquinalmente.
② VI regurgitar.

regurgitation [rɪ'gɜːdʒɪ'teɪʃən] N regurgitación *f*; (*fig*) reproducción *f* maquinal.

rehab* ['riːhæb] N ABBR of **rehabilitation** (*esp US: of drug user, alcoholic*) rehabilitación *f*.

rehabilitate [,riːə'bɪlɪteɪt] VT rehabilitar.

rehabilitation ['riːə,bɪlɪ'teɪʃən] N rehabilitación *f*.

rehash ['riː'hæʃ] ① N refrito *m*.
② VT hacer un refrito de.

rehearsal [rɪ'hɜːsəl] N enumeración *f*, repetición *f*; (*Mus, Theat etc*) ensayo *m*; **it was just a ~ for bigger things to come** fue a modo de ensayo para las empresas mayores que habían de venir después.

rehearse [rɪ'hɜːs] VT enumerar, repetir; (*Mus, Theat etc*) ensayar.

rehouse ['riː'haʊz] VT *family* dar nueva vivienda a, proveer de vivienda nueva; trasladar a otra casa; **200 families have been ~d** 200 familias tienen vivienda nueva ya.

reification [,riːɪfɪ'keɪʃən] N cosificación *f*.

reify ['riːɪ,faɪ] VT cosificar.

reign [reɪn] ① N reinado *m*; (*fig*) dominio *m*, predominio *m*; **the ~ of the miniskirt** la moda de la minifalda; **~ of terror** régimen *m* del terror; **in** (*or* **under**) **the ~ of** bajo el reinado de.
② VI reinar; (*fig*) predominar, imperar, prevalecer; **total silence ~ed** reinaba el silencio más absoluto; **it is better to ~ in hell than serve in heaven** más vale ser cabeza de ratón que cola de león.

reigning ['reɪnɪŋ] ADJ *monarch* reinante, actual; (*fig*) predominante, que impera.

reimburse [,riːɪm'bɜːs] VT reembolsar; **to ~ sb for sth** pagar (*or* reembolsar) a uno por algo.

reimbursement [,riːɪm'bɜːsmənt] N reembolso *m*.

reimpose ['riːɪm'pəʊz] VT volver a imponer, reimponer.

rein [reɪn] N rienda *f*; **to draw ~** detenerse, tirar de la rienda (*also fig*); **to give** (**free**) **~ to** dar rienda suelta a; **to keep a tight ~ on sb** atar corto a uno; **we must keep a tight ~ on expenditure** tenemos que restringir los gastos.
♦**rein back** VT refrenar.
♦**rein in** ① VT refrenar.
② VI detenerse.

reincarnate [,riːɪn'kɑːneɪt] VT reencarnar; **to be ~d** reencarnar, volver a encarnar.

reincarnation ['riːɪnkɑː'neɪʃən] N reencarnación *f*.

reindeer ['reɪndɪəʳ] N reno *m*.

reinforce [,riːɪn'fɔːs] VT reforzar (*also fig*); *concrete etc* armar.

reinforced [,riːɪn'fɔːst] ADJ reforzado; *concrete* armado.

reinforcement [,riːɪn'fɔːsmənt] N (*act*) reforzamiento *m*; **~s** refuerzos *mpl*.

reinsert ['riːɪn'sɜːt] VT volver a insertar, reinsertar; volver a introducir.

reinstate ['riːɪn'steɪt] VT *suppressed passage etc* reintegrar (*in* a), volver a incluir; (*rehabilitate*) rehabilitar; *dismissed worker* volver a emplear; *dismissed official* restituir a su puesto, reintegrar, reinstalar.

reinstatement ['riːɪn'steɪtmənt] N reintegración *f* (*in* a); rehabilitación *f*; vuelta *f* a su empleo; restitución *f* a su puesto, reinstalación *f*.

reinsurance ['riːɪn'ʃʊərəns] N reaseguro *m*.

reinsure ['riːɪn'ʃʊəʳ] VT reasegurar.

reintegrate ['riːɪn'tɪgreɪt] VT volver a integrar; (*socially*) reinsertar (*into* en).

reintegration ['riːɪntɪ'greɪʃən] N reintegración *f*; reinserción *f*.

reinter ['riːɪn'tɜːʳ] VT enterrar de nuevo.

reinvest ['riːɪn'vest] VT reinvertir, volver a invertir.

reinvestment ['riːɪn'vestmənt] N reinversión *f*.

reinvigorate ['riːɪn'vɪgəreɪt] VT vigorizar, infundir nuevo vigor a; **to**

feel **~d** sentirse con nuevas fuerzas, sentirse vigorizado.

reissue [ˈriːˈɪʃuː] **1** N nueva emisión *f*; reedición *f*; reimpresión *f*; reexpedición *f*; reestreno *m*.
2 VT *stamp* volver a emitir; *book* reeditar; reimprimir; *patent etc* reexpedir; *film* reestrenar.

reiterate [riːˈɪtəreɪt] VT reiterar, repetir; subrayar; **I must ~ that ...** tengo que subrayar que ...

reiteration [riːˌɪtəˈreɪʃən] N reiteración *f*, repetición *f*.

reiterative [riːˈɪtərətɪv] ADJ reiterativo.

reject 1 [ˈriːdʒekt] N cosa *f* rechazada, cosa *f* defectuosa; producto *m* defectuoso; persona *f* rechazada.
2 [ˈriːdʒekt] ATTR: **~ shop** tienda *f* de taras.
3 [rɪˈdʒekt] VT *offer etc* rechazar; *application* denegar; *motion* rechazar, desestimar; *plan etc* desechar; *solution* descartar; *advance* repulsar; *bad coin, damaged goods* rechazar, no aceptar; *(of stomach etc)* arrojar; *(Med) tissue* rechazar; *person* rechazar; marginar.

rejection [rɪˈdʒekʃən] **1** N rechazamiento *m*, rechazo *m*; denegación *f*; desestimación *f*; **to meet with a ~** sufrir una repulsa; **the novel has already had 3 ~s** ya han rechazado la novela 3 veces.
2 ATTR: **~ slip** nota *f* de rechazo.

rejig [riːˈdʒɪg] VT *schedule, structure, programme* recomponer, reajustar.

rejoice [rɪˈdʒɔɪs] **1** VT alegrar, regocijar, causar alegría a; **to ~ that ...** alegrarse de que + *subj*.
2 VI (a) alegrarse, regocijarse *(at, about, over* de); **let us not ~ too soon** es aconsejable no alegrarse demasiado pronto.
(b) **to ~ in the name of Anastasius** *(hum, iro)* ser el afortunado poseedor del nombre de Anastasio.

rejoicing [rɪˈdʒɔɪsɪŋ] N *(also* **~s** PL) regocijo *m*, júbilo *m*, alegría *f*; *(general, public)* fiestas *fpl*; **the ~ lasted far into the night** continuaron las fiestas hasta una hora avanzada.

rejoin[1] [rɪˈdʒɔɪn] VT replicar, contestar.

rejoin[2] [ˈriːˈdʒɔɪn] VT reunirse con, volver a juntarse con; *regiment etc* reincorporarse a.

rejoinder [rɪˈdʒɔɪndər] N réplica *f*; **as a ~ to ...** como contestación a ...

rejuvenate [rɪˈdʒuːvɪneɪt] VT rejuvenecer.

rejuvenating [rɪˈdʒuːvɪneɪtɪŋ] ADJ *effect etc* rejuvenecedor.

rejuvenation [rɪˌdʒuːvɪˈneɪʃən] N rejuvenecimiento *m*.

rekindle [ˈriːˈkɪndl] VT volver a encender, reencender; *(fig)* despertar, reavivar.

relapse [rɪˈlæps] **1** N *(Med)* recaída *f*; *(into crime, error)* reincidencia *f*, recaída *f*; **to have a ~** *(Med)* recaer, tener una recaída.
2 VI *(Med)* recaer; *(into crime, error)* reincidir *(into* en).

relate [rɪˈleɪt] **1** VT (a) *(tell)* contar, narrar, relatar; **strange to ~** aunque parece mentira, por raro que parezca.
(b) *(establish relation between)* relacionar *(to, with* con), establecer una conexión entre.
2 VI: **to ~ to** relacionarse con, tener que ver con, referirse a; **this ~s to what I said yesterday** esto se refiere a lo que dije ayer.

related [rɪˈleɪtɪd] ADJ (a) *subject* afín, conexo; **~ to** relativo a, referente a; **these ~ subjects** son temas afines; **this murder is not ~ to the other** este asesinato no tiene que ver con el otro, no hay relación entre este asesinato y el otro.
(b) *person* emparentado; **they are ~** son parientes, están emparentados; **they are closely ~** son parientes cercanos; **we are ~ but only distantly** somos parientes pero lejanos; **are you ~ to the prisoner?** ¿es Vd pariente del acusado?; **they became ~ by marriage to the Borgias** emparentaron con los Borja.

-related [rɪˈleɪtɪd] ADJ *in compounds: eg* **football~ hooliganism** gamberrismo *m* relacionado con el fútbol.

relating [rɪˈleɪtɪŋ] *as* PREP: **details ~ to X** detalles *mpl* acerca de X, detalles *mpl* relativos a X; **and other matters ~ to Y** y otros asuntos concernientes a Y.

relation [rɪˈleɪʃən] N (a) *(narration)* narración *f*; relato *m*, relación *f*.
(b) *(relationship)* conexión *f*, relación *f*, nexo *m* *(to, with* con); *(between persons)* parentesco *m*; **the ~ between A and B** la relación entre A y B; **in ~ to** respecto de, con relación a; **Proust in ~ to the French novel** Proust en relación con la novela francesa; **to bear a certain ~ to ...** guardar cierta relación con ...; **it bears no ~ to the facts** no tiene que ver con los hechos, se desentiende por completo de los hechos.
(c) *(contact)* **~s** relaciones *fpl*; **good ~s** buenas relaciones *fpl*; **~s are rather strained** las relaciones están algo tirantes; **to break off ~s with sb** romper con uno; **we have broken off ~s with Ruritania** hemos roto las relaciones con Ruritania; **to enter into ~s with sb** establecer relaciones con uno; **we have business ~s with them** tenemos relaciones comerciales con ellos; **to have sexual ~s with sb** tener relaciones sexuales con uno.
(d) *(relative)* pariente *m*, -a *f*, familiar *mf*; **friends and ~s** amigos *mpl* y familiares; **close ~** pariente *m* cercano, parienta *f* cercana; **two distant ~s** dos parientes lejanos; **all my ~s** todos mis parientes, toda mi familia; **what ~ is she to you?** ¿qué parentesco hay entre ella y

Vd?; **she's no ~** no es parienta mía.

relational [rɪˈleɪʃənl] ADJ relacional.

relationship [rɪˈleɪʃənʃɪp] N relación *f* *(to, with* con); afinidad *f*; *(kinship)* parentesco *m*; *(between persons)* relaciones *fpl*; amistad *f*; trato *m*; **~ by marriage** parentesco *m* por enlace matrimonial, parentesco *m* político; **~ by blood** consanguinidad *f*, parentesco *m* natural; **our ~ lasted 5 years** nuestras relaciones continuaron durante 5 años; **they have a beautiful ~** *(US)* les unen los lazos de la más fina amistad; se llevan maravillosamente bien; **what is your ~ to the prisoner?** ¿qué parentesco hay entre Vd y el acusado?; **the ~ of A to B, the ~ between A and B** la relación entre A y B.

relative [ˈrelətɪv] **1** ADJ (a) relativo *(to* a); *(respective)* respectivo; **with ~ ease** con relativa facilidad. (b) *(Gram)* relativo; **~ clause** oración *f* relativa; **~ pronoun** pronombre *m* relativo.
2 N (a) *(Gram)* relativo *m*. (b) *(person)* pariente *m*, -a *f*, familiar *mf*; **= relation** (d).

relatively [ˈrelətɪvlɪ] ADV relativamente; **there are ~ few** hay relativamente pocos.

relativism [ˈrelətɪvɪzəm] N relativismo *m*.

relativist [ˈrelətɪvɪst] N relativista *mf*.

relativistic [ˌrelətɪvˈɪstɪk] ADJ relativista.

relativity [ˌreləˈtɪvɪtɪ] N relatividad *f*.

relaunch [ˈriːˈlɔːntʃ] VT *plan etc* relanzar.

relaunching [ˈriːˈlɔːntʃɪŋ] N relanzamiento *m*.

relax [rɪˈlæks] **1** VT *grip etc* relajar, aflojar; *restrictions, severity* relajar, mitigar, suavizar; **to ~ one's muscles** aflojar los músculos; **to ~ one's hold on sth** dejar de agarrarse de *(or* a) algo tan apretadamente, soltar algo.
2 VI (a) *(grip etc)* relajarse, aflojarse; *(restrictions, severity)* mitigarse, suavizarse; **his face ~ed into a smile** se le aflojaron los músculos de la cara y empezó a sonreír; **we must not ~ in our efforts** es preciso no cejar en nuestros esfuerzos *(to + infin* por + *infin)*.
(b) *(rest)* relajarse; descansar; *(amuse o.s.)* esparcirse, expansionarse; **~!** ¡cálmate!; ¡no te apures!; ¡tranquilo!; **now there is time to ~ a little** ahora hay tiempo para esparcirse un poco; **we ~ed in the sun of Majorca** nos expansionamos bajo el sol de Mallorca; **I like to ~ with a book** me gusta relajarme leyendo.

relaxant [rɪˈlæksənt] N relajante *m*.

relaxation [ˌriːlækˈseɪʃən] N (a) *(act)* relajación *f*, aflojamiento *m*; mitigación *f*.
(b) *(rest)* relajamiento *m*; descanso *m*; *(amusement)* esparcimiento *m*, recreo *m*; **to seek ~ in painting** esparcirse dedicándose a la pintura; **to take some ~** esparcirse, expansionarse.
(c) *(pastime)* pasatiempo *m*, recreo *m*, diversión *f*; **a favourite ~ of the wealthy** un pasatiempo favorito de los ricos.

relaxed [rɪˈlækst] ADJ relajado, tranquilo, sosegado, ecuánime; **in a ~ atmosphere** en un clima de distensión; **he always seems so ~** siempre parece tan sosegado; **try to be more ~** procura ser más tranquilo.

relaxing [rɪˈlæksɪŋ] ADJ relajante.

relay [ˈriːleɪ] **1** N (a) *(of workmen)* tanda *f*; *(of horses)* parada *f*, posta *f*; **to work in ~s** trabajar por tandas.
(b) *(Sport: also* **~ race**) carrera *f* de relevos; **the 400 metres ~** los 400 metros relevos.
(c) *(Elec)* relaí(s) *m*, relé *m*.
2 ATTR: **~ station** *(Elec)* estación *f* retransmisora, estación *f* repetidora.
3 VT *(Rad etc)* retransmitir; **to ~ a message to sb** pasar un mensaje a uno, hacer llegar un mensaje a uno.

re-lay [ˈriːˈleɪ] VT volver a colocar; *cable, rail etc* volver a tender.

release [rɪˈliːs] **1** N (a) *(freeing etc)* liberación *f*; excarcelación *f*; libertad *f*; emisión *f*; lanzamiento *m*; disparo *m*; aflojamiento *m*; descargo *m*, absolución *f*; **a sudden ~ of gas** un súbito escape de gas; **a sudden ~ of creative energy** un repentino estallar de energía creadora; **death came as a merciful ~** la muerte fue una liberación feliz; **his ~ came through on Monday** se aprobó su excarcelación el lunes, la orden de su puesta en libertad llegó el lunes.
(b) *(Mech, Phot etc)* disparador *m*.
(c) *(for press etc)* boletín *m*, comunicado *m*; *(book, film etc)* novedad *f*.
(d) *(act of publishing)* publicación *f*; *(of news)* divulgación *f*; *(of film)* estreno *m*; *(of record, video)* puesta *f* en venta, puesta *f* en circulación; **to be on general ~** exhibirse en todos los cines.
2 VT (a) *(set free)* soltar, libertar; *prisoner* poner en libertad, *convict* excarcelar; *person from obligation* descargar, absolver; **~ me, sir!** ¡suélteme, señor!; **to ~ sb on bail** poner a uno en libertad bajo fianza; **to ~ sb from a debt** absolver a uno de una deuda; **they ~d him to go to a new post** permitieron que se fuera a ocupar un nuevo puesto; **can you ~ him for a few hours each week?** ¿nos lo ceden algunas horas cada semana?
(b) *(let go)* soltar; *bomb* lanzar; *gas, smoke* despedir, arrojar, emitir; *(Phot)* disparar; *(Mech)* desenganchar, disparar; *brake* soltar; *grip, hold*

soltar, aflojar.

(c) *book* publicar; *record, video* poner a la venta; *film* estrenar; *news, report* publicar, autorizar la publicación de; divulgar, dar a conocer.

relegate ['relɪgeɪt] VT relegar (*to* a); **Mérida is ~d to the second division** Mérida pasa a la segunda división, Mérida desciende a la segunda división.

relegation [ˌrelɪ'geɪʃən] N relegación *f*; (*Sport*) descenso *m*.

relent [rɪ'lent] VI ablandarse, apiadarse, ceder.

relentless [rɪ'lentlɪs] ADJ implacable, inexorable; despiadado; **with ~ severity** con implacable severidad; **he is quite ~ about it** en esto se muestra totalmente implacable.

relentlessly [rɪ'lentlɪslɪ] ADV implacablemente, inexorablemente; **he presses on ~** avanza implacable.

relet ['riː'let] VT realquilar.

relevance ['reləvəns], (*US*) **relevancy** ['reləvənsɪ] N pertinencia *f*; conexión *f*, relación *f*; aplicabilidad *f*; **matters of doubtful ~** asuntos *mpl* de dudosa pertinencia; **what is the ~ of that?** y eso ¿tiene que ver (con lo que estamos discutiendo)?

relevant ['reləvənt] ADJ (a) (*related*) pertinente; conexo, relacionado (*to* con); aplicable; **details ~ to this affair** detalles *mpl* relacionados con este asunto, detalles *mpl* concernientes a este asunto; **that is hardly ~** eso apenas tiene que ver (con lo que estamos discutiendo).
(b) (*fitting*) apropiado, oportuno, adecuado; **bring the ~ papers** traiga los documentos pertinentes; **we have all the ~ data** tenemos todos los datos que hacen al caso.

reliability [rɪˌlaɪə'bɪlɪtɪ] N exactitud *f*, veracidad *f*; seguridad *f*; confianza *f*; confiabilidad *f*, fiabilidad *f*; formalidad *f*, seriedad *f*.

reliable [rɪ'laɪəbl] ADJ *news etc* fidedigno, fehaciente, digno de crédito; *account* exacto, veraz; *machine etc* seguro; *person* (*trustworthy*) de confianza, de fiar, fiable; (*businesslike*) formal, serio; **it's a most ~ firm** es una casa de toda confianza; **I have it from a ~ source** lo sé de fuente fidedigna (*or* competente, solvente); **he's not very ~** no es de fiar, no hay que fiarse de él; **I've always found him very ~** siempre me ha parecido de mucha formalidad.

reliably [rɪ'laɪəblɪ] ADV: **I am ~ informed that ...** sé de fuente fidedigna que ...

reliance [rɪ'laɪəns] N confianza *f* (*on* en); dependencia *f* (*on* de); **our excessive ~ on him** nuestra excesiva dependencia con respecto de él, el que dependamos tanto de él; **you can place no ~ on that** eso no es de fiar, no hay que tener confianza en eso.

reliant [rɪ'laɪənt] ADJ confiado; **to be ~ on sth** confiar en algo, tener confianza en algo.

relic ['relɪk] N reliquia *f*, vestigio *m*; (*Eccl*) reliquia *f*.

relict ['relɪkt] N (††) viuda *f*.

relief [rɪ'liːf] ① N (a) (*alleviation*) alivio *m*; desahogo *m*; consuelo *m*; aligeramiento *m*; (*of taxation*) desgravación *f*; (*of congestion*) descongestión *f*; **by way of light ~** a modo de diversión; **there is a comic scene by way of ~** para aliviar la tensión sigue una escena cómica; **that's a ~!** ¡menos mal!, ¡qué alivio!; **it is a ~ to find that ...** me consuela encontrar que ..., me alegro de encontrar que ...; **the medicine brings ~** la medicina alivia; **it came as a general ~ when they left** se aliviaron todos cuando ellos se marcharon; **to heave a sigh of ~** dar un suspiro de alivio.
(b) (*aid*) socorro *m*, ayuda *f*; **poor ~** socorro *m*, beneficencia *f*; **to be on ~** vivir de la beneficencia, cobrar del seguro; **to go to sb's ~** acudir a socorrer a uno.
(c) (*Mil: of town*) descerco *m*, socorro *m*.
(d) (*Mil: also ~ party, ~ troops*) relevo *m*; (*substitute*) relevo *m*, sustituto *m*.
(e) (*Jur*) satisfacción *f*, remedio *m*.
(f) (*Art, Geog*) relieve *m*, realce *m*; **high ~** alto relieve *m*; **low ~** bajo relieve *m*; **to stand out in ~** destacar; **to throw sth into ~** hacer resaltar algo, (*fig*) servir para destacar (*or* subrayar) algo.
② ATTR: **~ fund** fondo *m* de auxilio (a los damnificados); **~ map** mapa *m* en relieve; **~ organization** organización *f* de beneficencia, beneficencia *f*; **~ road** (*Brit*) carretera *f* de descongestión; **~ supplies** provisiones *fpl* de auxilio; **~ work** trabajos *mpl* de socorro; **~ works** obras *fpl* públicas (de alivio al paro).

relieve [rɪ'liːv] ① VT (a) (*mitigate*) *sufferings etc* aliviar, mitigar; *person's mind* tranquilizar; *feelings* desahogar; *burden* aligerar; *pain, headache etc* quitar, suprimir, aliviar; **to feel ~d** sentirse aliviado, sentir un alivio; **I am ~d to hear that ...** me alegro de saber que ...; **to ~ one's feelings** desahogarse; **I ~ed my feelings in a letter** desahogué escribiendo una carta; **to ~ the boredom of the journey** para aliviar el aburrimiento del viaje; **the plain is ~d by an occasional hill** de vez en cuando una colina alivia la monotonía de la llanura.
(b) **to ~ the poor** (*help*) socorrer a los pobres.
(c) (*release*) **to ~ sb from doing sth** librar a uno de la necesidad de hacer algo; **to ~ sb of anxiety** tranquilizar a uno; **this ~s us of financial worries** esto acaba con nuestras preocupaciones económicas; **to ~ sb of a duty** exonerar a uno de un deber; **to ~ sb**

of a post destituir a uno; **he was ~d of his command** fue relevado de su mando; **to ~ sb of his wallet** quitar la cartera a uno, robar la cartera a uno; **let me ~ you of your coat** permítame tomarle el abrigo.
(d) (*Mil*) *city* descercar, socorrer; *troops* relevar; **I'll come and ~ you at 6** vengo a las 6 a relevarte.
② VR (a) **to ~ o.s.** (*euph*) hacer del cuerpo, hacer sus necesidades.
(b) **to ~ o.s. of a burden** deshacerse de un peso, quitarse un peso de encima.

religion [rɪ'lɪdʒən] N religión *f*; **to get ~*** darse a la religión.

religiosity [rɪˌlɪdʒɪ'ɒsɪtɪ] N religiosidad *f*.

religious [rɪ'lɪdʒəs] ① ADJ (a) religioso; **~ instruction** enseñanza *f* religiosa; **~ toleration** libertad *f* de cultos.
(b) (*fig*) puntual; exacto, fiel.
② N religioso *m*, -a *f*.

religiously [rɪ'lɪdʒəslɪ] ADV (a) religiosamente. (b) (*fig*) puntualmente, exactamente, fielmente.

religiousness [rɪ'lɪdʒəsnɪs] N religiosidad *f*.

reline ['riː'laɪn] VT reforrar, poner nuevo forro a.

relinquish [rɪ'lɪŋkwɪʃ] VT abandonar, renunciar a; *grip* soltar; *post* renunciar a, dimitir de.

relinquishment [rɪ'lɪŋkwɪʃmənt] N abandono *m*, renuncia *f*; dimisión *f*.

reliquary ['relɪkwərɪ] N relicario *m*.

relish ['relɪʃ] ① N (a) (*flavour*) sabor *m*, gusto *m*; (*smack*) dejo *m* (*of* de), sabor *m* (*of* a).
(b) (*Culin: sauce*) salsa *f*, condimento *m*.
(c) (*enjoyment*) gusto *m*; (*attractive quality*) apetencia *f*; (*appetite*) apetito *m*; (*zest*) entusiasmo *m*; (*liking*) afición *f*; **to eat sth with ~** comer algo con apetito; **to do sth with ~** hacer algo de buena gana, hacer algo con entusiasmo; **to have a ~ for sth** apetecer algo, gustar de algo, ser aficionado a algo; **hunting has no ~ for me now** ya no me apetece la caza; **the ~ for hunting does not seem to be so strong** no parece que la caza atraiga tanto, parece que hay menos afición a la caza.
② VT *taste, savour* paladear, saborear; (*like*) gustar de, tener buen apetito para; **I don't ~ the idea** no me gusta la idea; **I ~ a day's fishing** apetece salir de pesca un día, me gusta pasar el día pescando; **do you ~ some fishing?** ¿quieres ir a pescar?; **I don't ~ the idea of staying up all night** no me hace gracia la idea de estar levantado toda la noche.

relive ['riː'lɪv] VT vivir de nuevo, volver a vivir.

reload ['riː'ləud] VT recargar, volver a cargar.

relocate ['riː'ləu'keɪt] ① VT volver a colocar, volver a situar.
② VI moverse (a otro solar), trasladarse.

relocation [riːləu'keɪʃən] N nueva ubicación *f*, nueva colocación *f*; **~ package** prima *f* de traslado.

reluctance [rɪ'lʌktəns] N desgana *f*, renuencia *f*, reticencia *f*; repugnancia *f*; **with ~** a desgana, de mala gana; **to affect ~** aparentar no querer.

reluctant [rɪ'lʌktənt] ADJ (a) (*unwilling, disinclined*) **he was ~** no quiso, se mostró poco dispuesto a hacerlo; **to be ~ to do sth** estar poco dispuesto a hacer algo, tener pocas ganas de hacer algo; **he was ~ to decide** vaciló en decidirse; **I should be most ~ to let you go** me resistiría a permitirte ir, no consentiría de buena gana en que fueras.
(b) (*done etc unwillingly*) **it had his ~ agreement** consintió pero de mala gana; **the ~ dragon** el dragón que no quería; **I should make a ~ secretary** yo, de ser secretario, sería a desgana.

reluctantly [rɪ'lʌktəntlɪ] ADV de mala gana, a regañadientes; **she went ~** se fue de mala gana; **I ~ agree** consiento pero contra mi voluntad.

rely [rɪ'laɪ] VI: **to ~ on** confiar en, fiarse de, contar con; **you can't ~ on the trains** es imposible fiarse de los trenes; **one can't ~ on the weather** no puede uno fiarse del tiempo; **we are ~ing on you to do it** contamos con Vd para hacerlo, confiamos en que Vd lo haga.

REM [rem] N (a) (*Physiol*) ABBR **of rapid eye movement** movimiento *m* rápido del ojo. (b) (*Phys*) ABBR **of roentgen equivalent man**.

remain [rɪ'meɪn] VI (a) (*be left over*) sobrar; (*survive*) quedar; **if any ~** si sobra alguno; **few ~** quedan pocos; **the few pleasures that ~ to me** los pocos placeres que me quedan; **nothing ~s but to sell up** no queda otro remedio sino venderlo todo; **it ~s to be done** queda por hacer; **it ~s to be seen whether ...** queda por ver si ...; **more than half ~s to be built** queda por construir más de la mitad.
(b) (*continue*) quedar, quedarse, permanecer; seguir, continuar; **we ~ed there 3 weeks** nos quedamos allí 3 semanas; **how long do you expect to ~?** ¿cuánto tiempo piensas quedarte aquí?; **that objection ~s** queda (en pie) esa objeción; **it will ~ in my memory** quedará grabado en mi memoria; **the fact ~s that ...** sigue siendo un hecho que ..., no es menos cierto que ...; **to ~ behind** quedarse; **to ~ seated, to ~ sitting** permanecer sentado; **to ~ standing** permanecer de pie.
(c) (*with adj complement*) **to ~ faithful to** seguir fiel a; **the problem**

~s unsolved el problema sigue sin solucionarse; **it ~s true that ...** no es menos cierto que ...; **it ~s the same** sigue siendo lo mismo; **if the weather ~s fine** si el tiempo sigue bueno.

(d) *(in letters)* **I ~ yours faithfully** le saluda atentamente.

◆ **remain behind** VI *(fall back)* quedarse atrás, rezagarse; *(after school)* quedarse después de la clase.

remainder [rɪ'meɪndəʳ] **1** N **(a)** *(sth left over)* resto *m*; *(Math)* residuo *m*, resto *m*, resta *f*; **the ~** lo que sobra, lo que queda; los *(etc)* demás; **the ~ of the debt** el resto de la deuda; **during the ~ of the day** durante el resto del día; **the ~ would not come** los otros *(or los demás)* no quisieron venir.

(b) ~s *(Comm)* artículos *mpl* no vendidos; *(books)* restos *mpl* de edición.

2 VT *books etc* saldar.

remaining [rɪ'meɪnɪŋ] ADJ que queda; **the 3 ~ possibilities** las 3 posibilidades que quedan; **the ~ passengers** los otros pasajeros, los demás pasajeros.

remains [rɪ'meɪnz] NPL *(human, archaeological etc)* restos *mpl*; *(left-overs)* sobras *fpl*, desperdicios *mpl*; restos *mpl*, despojos *mpl*.

remake *(irr: V make)* **1** ['riː'meɪk] VT rehacer, volver a hacer.

2 ['riː'meɪk] N *(Cine)* nueva versión *f*, refundición *f*.

remand [rɪ'mɑːnd] **1** N: **prisoner on ~** preso *m* preventivo, presa *f* preventiva; **to be on ~** **(in custody)** estar en prisión preventiva, estar detenido (mientras se investiga una acusación *or* se prepara el proceso).

2 ATTR *(Brit)*: **~ centre** cárcel *f* transitoria; **~ home** cárcel *f* transitoria para menores; **~ wing** galería *f* de prisión preventiva.

3 VT: **to ~ sb (in custody)** poner a uno en prisión preventiva, reencarcelar a uno (para que se investigue una acusación *or* se prepare el proceso); **to ~ sb on bail** libertar a uno bajo fianza (mientras se prepara el proceso); **to ~ sb for a week** reencarcelar a uno durante una semana; **he was ~ed to Brixton** volvieron a encarcelarle en Brixton.

remark [rɪ'mɑːk] **1** N **(a)** *(notice)* **worthy of ~** notable, digno de notar; **to let sth pass without ~** dejar pasar algo sin comentario.

(b) *(comment)* observación *f*; comentario *m*; **'R~s on the Press'** 'Observaciones *fpl* sobre la Prensa'; **after some introductory ~s** después de hacer algunas observaciones a modo de prefacio; **to make a ~** hacer una observación; **to make the ~ that ...** observar que ...; **to pass ~s on sb** hacer observaciones acerca de uno, *(freq)* hacer un comentario desfavorable sobre uno.

2 VT **(a)** *(notice)* observar, notar.

(b) *(say)* **to ~ that ...** decir que ..., observar que ...; **'it's a pity'** she **~ed** 'es una lástima' dijo.

3 VI: **to ~ on sth** hacer una observación sobre algo, comentar algo.

remarkable [rɪ'mɑːkəbl] ADJ notable, singular, extraordinario; **~!, most ~!** ¡qué raro!; **with ~ skill** con singular habilidad; **it is in no way ~** no tiene nada que sea digno de notar; **what's ~ about that?** ¿es que eso te parece singular?, y eso ¿qué tiene de raro?; **he's a most ~ man** es un hombre extraordinario.

remarkably [rɪ'mɑːkəblɪ] ADV extraordinariamente.

remarriage ['riː'mærɪdʒ] N segundas nupcias *fpl*, segundo casamiento *m*.

remarry ['riː'mærɪ] VI volver a casarse, casarse en segundas nupcias.

rematch ['riː'mætʃ] N partido *m* de vuelta, revancha *f*.

remediable [rɪ'miːdɪəbl] ADJ remediable.

remedial [rɪ'miːdɪəl] ADJ remediador; *(Med)* curativo, terapéutico; **~ course** curso *m* correctivo; **~ exercises** gimnasia *f* terapéutica; **~ teaching** enseñanza *f* de los niños *(etc)* atrasados.

remedy ['remədɪ] **1** N remedio *m* (**for** para curar); *(Jur etc)* recurso *m*; **there's no ~ for that** eso no tiene remedio; **the best ~ for that is to protest** eso se remedia protestando; **to have no ~ at law** no tener recurso legal.

2 VT remediar; curar; **that's soon remedied** eso es fácil remediarlo, eso fácilmente queda arreglado.

▼ **remember** [rɪ'membəʳ] **1** VT **(a)** *(recall)* acordarse de, recordar; *(commemorate)* conmemorar; **I ~ seeing it, I ~ having seen it** recuerdo haberlo visto; **she ~ed to do it** se acordó de hacerlo; **don't you ~ me?** ¿no se acuerda Vd de mí?; **it is worth ~ing that ...** vale la pena recordar que ...; **give me sth to ~ you by** dame algún recuerdo tuyo; **so I gave him sth to ~ me by** *(fig)* así que le di algo para que no me olvidara; **to ~ sb in one's will** mencionar a uno en su testamento.

(b) *(bear in mind)* tener presente, no olvidar; **~ that he carries a gun** ten presente que lleva revólver; **~ what happened before** no te olvides de lo que pasó antes, acuérdate de lo que pasó antes; **~ to turn out the light** no te olvides de apagar la luz; **'please ~ the guide'** 'se ruega no olvidar los servicios del guía'; **~ who you're with!** ¡piensa con quién estás!

(c) *(with wishes)* **~ me to him!** ¡dale recuerdos míos!, salúdale de mi parte; **she asks to be ~ed to you all** ella manda recuerdos para todos.

2 VI: **yes, I ~** sí, me acuerdo; **if I ~ aright** si bien me acuerdo; **as far as I can ~** que yo recuerde.

REMEMBER   *see also main entry*

"Acordarse de" or "recordar"?

● Both *acordarse de* and *recordar* can be used to translate *to remember* (used transitively). Provided the object of *remember* is not another verb, translate using *acordarse* in everyday contexts and *recordar* in formal or written ones:

> Do you remember where he lives?
> *¿Tú te acuerdas de dónde vive?* ◊ *¿Recuerda usted dónde vive él?*
> Do you remember me?
> *¿Te acuerdas de mí?* ◊ *¿Me recuerda usted?*

● Use *acordarse de* + INFINITIVE to translate *to remember to* + VERB:

> Did you remember to close the door?
> *¿Te acordaste de cerrar la puerta?*

! Don't use *recordar* for *remembering to do sth*.

● Use *recordar* + PERFECT INFINITIVE/CLAUSE or *acordarse de* + CLAUSE to translate *to remember* + -ING:

> I remember closing the door
> *Recuerdo haber cerrado* or *Recuerdo que cerré* or *Me acuerdo de que cerré la puerta*

NOTE: *Recordar* also translates *remind*:

> I must remind Richard to pay the rent
> *Tengo que recordarle a Richard que pague el alquiler*

For further uses and examples, see main entry.

---

remembrance [rɪ'membrəns] **1** N *(remembering)* recordación *f*; memoria *f*; *(souvenir)* recuerdo *m*; **~s** recuerdos *mpl*; **in ~ of** en conmemoración de, para conmemorar; **I have no ~ of it** no lo recuerdo en absoluto.

2 ATTR: **R~ Day, R~ Sunday** *(Brit)* día *m* en el que se recuerda a los caídos en las dos guerras mundiales; ver también POPPY DAY.

▼ **remind** [rɪ'maɪnd] **1** VT recordar; **to ~ sb of sth** recordar algo a uno; **that ~s me of last time** eso me recuerda la vez pasada; **she ~s me of Anne** me recuerda a Ana, me hace pensar en Ana, tiene mucho parecido con Ana; **that ~s me!** y a propósito ...; **to ~ sb to do sth** recordar a uno que haga algo; **you have to keep ~ing him to do it** hay que traérselo constantemente a la memoria.

2 VR: **to ~ o.s. that ...** recordarse que ...; **I ~ myself about it all the time** me lo recuerdo constantemente; *see also* REMEMBER.

reminder [rɪ'maɪndəʳ] **1** N *(note etc)* recordatorio *m*; advertencia *f*; *(Comm)* notificación *f*; **it's a gentle ~** es una advertencia amistosa, **we will send a ~** le enviaremos un recordatorio.

(b) *(memento)* recuerdo *m*; **it's a ~ of the good old days** recuerda los buenos tiempos pasados.

2 ATTR: **subscription ~ card** tarjeta *f* recordatoria de renovación de suscripción.

reminisce [ˌremɪ'nɪs] VI contar los recuerdos, recordar viejas historias *(about* de).

reminiscence [ˌremɪ'nɪsəns] N reminiscencia *f*, recuerdo *m*; **'R~s of life in the Congo'** 'Recuerdos *mpl* de la vida en el Congo'; **the symphony has ~s of Mozart** la sinfonía tiene reminiscencias de Mozart.

reminiscent [ˌremɪ'nɪsənt] ADJ **(a)** **it's a ~ work** es una obra evocadora; es una obra llena de reminiscencias; **to be in a ~ mood** estar de humor para contar los recuerdos, estar de humor para evocar el pasado.

(b) **to be ~ of sth** recordar algo; *(pej)* oler a algo, sonar a algo; **that bit is ~ of Rossini** ese trozo recuerda a Rossini, ese trozo tiene reminiscencia de Rossini; **that's ~ of another old joke** eso suena a otro chiste viejo.

reminiscently [ˌremɪ'nɪsəntlɪ] ADV: **he spoke ~** habló pensando en el pasado.

remiss [rɪ'mɪs] ADJ negligente, descuidado; **I have been very ~ about it** he sido muy descuidado en eso; **you have been ~ in not attending to it** Vd merece que se le censure por no atenderlo, el no atenderlo ha sido un descuido suyo.

remission [rɪ'mɪʃən] N *(all senses)* remisión *f*; **~ of sins** remisión *f* de los pecados.

remissness [rɪ'mɪsnɪs] N negligencia *f*, descuido *m*.

remit **1** ['riːmɪt] N cometido *m*, deber *m*; *(of committee etc)* puntos *mpl* de consulta.

2 [rɪ'mɪt] VT **(a)** *(send)* remitir, enviar. **(b)** *(excuse)* perdonar; **3 months of the sentence were ~ted** se le redujo la pena en 3 meses.

3 [rɪ'mɪt] VI disminuir, reducirse.

remittal [rɪ'mɪtl] N *(Jur)* remisión *f*.

remittance [rɪ'mɪtəns] **1** N remesa *f*, envío *m*.

2 ATTR: **~ advice** aviso *m* de pago.

remittee [rɪmɪ'tiː] N consignatario *m*, -a *f*.

remittent [rɪ'mɪtənt] ADJ *fever etc* remitente.

remitter [rɪ'mɪtəʳ] N remitente *mf*.

---

remix [,ri:'mıks] (*Mus*) ① N remix *m*.
② VT mezclar.

remnant ['remnənt] ① N (*remainder*) resto *m*, residuo *m*; (*of cloth*) retazo *m*.
② ATTR: ~ **day** (*Comm*) día *m* de venta de restos de serie; ~ **sale** venta *f* de restos de serie, remate *m* total.

remodel ['ri:'mɒdl] VT modelar de nuevo, remodelar; reestructurar; reorganizar; (*Liter etc*) refundir.

remold ['ri:'məʊld] (*US*) = **remould**.

remonstrance [rı'mɒnstrəns] N protesta *f*, reconvención *f*.

remonstrate ['remənstreɪt] VI protestar, objetar; **to ~ about sth** protestar contra algo, poner reparos a algo; **to ~ with sb** reconvenir a uno.

remorse [rı'mɔːs] N remordimiento *m*; **to feel ~** arrepentirse, compungirse.

remorseful [rı'mɔːsfʊl] ADJ arrepentido, compungido; **now he's ~** ahora está lleno de remordimientos, ahora le remuerde la conciencia.

remorsefully [rı'mɔːsfəlɪ] ADV con remordimiento; **he said ~** dijo compungido.

remorsefulness [rı'mɔːsfʊlnɪs] N remordimiento *m*, compunción *f*.

remorseless [rı'mɔːslɪs] ADJ implacable, despiadado, inexorable.

remorselessly [rı'mɔːslɪslɪ] ADV implacablemente, despiadadamente, inexorablemente.

remorselessness [rı'mɔːslɪsnɪs] N inexorabilidad *f*.

remote [rı'məʊt] ADJ (a) (*distant*) remoto (*also Comput*); distante, lejano; aislado; ~ **control** mando *m* a distancia, telecontrol *m*; telemando *m*; ~ **job entry** entrada *f* de trabajos a distancia; ~ **learning** aprendizaje *m* a distancia; ~ **viewing** (*US*) clarividencia *f*; **in a ~ spot** en un lugar remoto; **in a ~ farmstead** en una alquería aislada, en una alquería apartada; **it's ~ from the town** está lejos de la ciudad; **she is ~ from such things** queda alejada de tales cosas, tales cosas le son ajenas; **in some ~ future** en un futuro lejano.
(b) (*slight*) ligero; leve, tenue; **it's a ~ prospect** es poco probable, de eso existe poca probabilidad; **there is a ~ resemblance** hay un ligero parecido; **he hasn't the ~st chance** no tiene la más remota posibilidad; **I haven't the ~st idea** no tengo la más remota idea; **all the while there remains a ~ chance** mientras haya una tenue posibilidad.

remote-controlled [rı'məʊtkən'trəʊld] ADJ con mando a distancia, teledirigido.

remotely [rı'məʊtlɪ] ADV (a) remotamente; **it is ~ situated** está situado en un lugar remoto; **they are ~ related** hay un parentesco lejano entre ellos. (b) **it's not even ~ likely** de eso no hay la más remota posibilidad.

remoteness [rı'məʊtnɪs] N distancia *f*; aislamiento *m*, alejamiento *m*; **her ~ from everyday life** su alejamiento de la vida diaria.

remote sensing [rı,məʊt'sensɪŋ] ① N detección *f* a distancia.
② ADJ de detección a distancia.

remould, (*US*) **remold** ① ['ri:məʊld] N recauchutado *m*.
② ['ri:'məʊld] VT *tyre* recauchutar.

remount ['ri:'maʊnt] ① N (*Mil etc*) remonta *f*.
② VT volver a subir (a), subir de nuevo (a); *horse* montar de nuevo.
③ VI subir de nuevo.

removable [rı'mu:vəbl] ADJ separable, amovible; desmontable; *collar etc* de quita y pon.

removal [rı'mu:vəl] ① N remoción *f*, el quitar (*etc*); supresión *f*; separación *f*; eliminación *f*; extirpación *f*; destitución *f*; el tachar; solución *f*; disipación *f*; apartamiento *m*, alejamiento *m*; (*of house*) mudanza *f*; **his ~ to a new post** su traslado a un nuevo puesto; **the ~ of this threat** la eliminación de esta amenaza.
② ATTR: ~ **allowance** subvención *f* de mudanza; ~ **expenses** gastos *mpl* de traslado de efectos personales; ~ **man** mozo *m* de mudanzas; ~ **van** (*Brit*) camión *m* de mudanzas.

remove [rı'mu:v] ① N: **this is but one ~ from disaster** esto raya en la catástrofe; **this is several ~s from our official policy** en esto nos apartamos bastante de nuestra política oficial.
② VT (*take away*) quitar; llevarse; (*take off*) quitar, *clothes etc* quitarse; (*steal*) llevarse, robar; (*get out of the way*) quitar de en medio; *letter, passage, tax etc* suprimir; *name from list* tachar, borrar (*from* de); (*Mech*) *part* separar, retirar, quitar; *obstacle, threat, waste* eliminar; (*Med*) *appendix etc* extirpar; *person from post* destituir; *problem* solucionar; *doubt* disipar; *fear* acabar con; (*do away with*) *person* quitar de en medio, eliminar; *competitor* apartar, alejar, deshacerse de; ~ **hats on entering** se ruega descubrirse al entrar; **he ~d his hat** se descubrió, se quitó el sombrero; **first ~ the lid** primero quitar la tapa; ~ **that bauble** que se quite esa chuchería de en medio; **this effectively ~d him from the scene** esto terminó de alejarle de allí; **illness ~d him from politics** la enfermedad le hizo abandonar la política; **to ~ sth to another place** trasladar algo a otro sitio, cambiar algo de sitio; **that is far ~d from what we wanted** eso se aparta mucho de lo que

queríamos; **cousin once ~d** hijo *m*, -a *f* de primo carnal, sobrino *m* segundo, sobrina *f* segunda.
③ VI mudarse, trasladarse (*to* a), cambiarse (*Mex*).
④ VR: **to ~ o.s.** irse, marcharse; quitarse de en medio; **kindly ~ yourself at once** haga el favor de irse inmediatamente; **to ~ o.s. to another place** irse a otro sitio; **I must ~ myself** tengo que marcharme.

remover [rı'mu:vər] N (*owner*) agente *m* de mudanzas; (*workman*) mozo *m* de mudanzas.

remunerate [rı'mju:nəreɪt] VT remunerar.

remuneration [rı,mju:nə'reɪʃən] N remuneración *f*.

remunerative [rı'mju:nərətɪv] ADJ remunerador, remunerativo, lucrativo.

renaissance [rə'neɪsɑːns] ① N renacimiento *m*; **R~** (*Hist*) Renacimiento *m*; **the 12th century R~** el Renacimiento del siglo XII.
② ATTR: **R~** renacentista, del Renacimiento.

renal ['ri:nl] ADJ renal; ~ **failure** insuficiencia *f* renal.

rename ['ri:'neɪm] VT poner nuevo nombre a, rebautizar; **they have ~d it 'Mon Repos'** le han puesto el nuevo nombre de 'Mon Repos'.

renascence [rı'næsns] N renacimiento *m*; **a spiritual ~** un renacimiento espiritual, un despertar espiritual.

renascent [rı'næsnt] ADJ renaciente, que renace.

renationalization ['ri:,næʃnəlaɪ'zeɪʃən] N renacionalización *f*.

renationalize ['ri:'næʃnəlaɪz] VT renacionalizar.

rend [rend] (*irr*: PRET AND PTP **rent**) VT (*liter*) (*tear*) rasgar, desgarrar; (*split*) hender, rajar; **to ~ sth in twain** partir algo por medio, hender algo; **to ~ one's dress** rasgar su ropa; **to turn and ~ sb** perder por fin la paciencia y arremeter contra uno; **a cry rent the air** un grito desgarró los aires; **the air was rent with cries** los gritos hendieron el aire.

render ['rendər] VT (a) (*return*) **to ~ good for evil** devolver bien por mal; **to ~ thanks to sb** dar las gracias a uno.
(b) (*hand over*) entregar; ~ **unto Caesar ...** al César lo que es del César (y a Dios lo que es de Dios).
(c) (*give*) *service* hacer, prestar; *assistance* dar, prestar; *honour* dar.
(d) (*send in*) **to ~ an account** (*Comm*) pasar factura; **to account ~ed** según factura anterior; **to ~ an account of one's stewardship** dar cuenta de su gobierno, justificar su conducta durante su mando; **to ~ an account to God** dar cuenta de sí ante Dios.
(e) (*reproduce*) reproducir, representar; (*Mus*) interpretar, ejecutar; (*translate*) traducir, verter (*into* a); **no photograph could adequately ~ the scene** ninguna fotografía podría representar adecuadamente la escena; **how does one ~ 'cursi'?** ¿cómo se traduce 'cursi'?
(f) (*make*) hacer, volver; **this ~s it impossible** esto lo hace imposible, esto lo imposibilita; **you have ~ed our efforts useless** Vd ha inutilizado nuestros esfuerzos, Vd ha hecho inútiles nuestros esfuerzos.
(g) *fat* derretir.
(h) *building etc* enlucir.
◆ **render down** VT *fat* derretir.
◆ **render up** VT ceder, entregar; **the earth ~s up its treasures** la tierra rinde sus tesoros.

rendering ['rendərɪŋ] N reproducción *f*, representación *f*; (*Mus*) interpretación *f*; traducción *f*, versión *f*; **her ~ of the sonata** su interpretación de la sonata; **an elegant ~ of Machado** una elegante versión de Machado.

rendezvous ['rɒndɪvu:] ① N, PL **rendezvous** ['rɒndɪvu:z] cita *f*; lugar *m* de una cita; ~ **in space** cita *f* espacial; **to have a ~ with sb** tener cita con uno; **to make a ~ with another ship at sea** efectuar un enlace con otro buque en el mar.
② VI reunirse, verse; (*spaceship*) efectuar una reunión espacial (*with* con); **we will ~ at 8** nos reuniremos a las 8; **the ships will ~ off Vigo** los buques efectuarán el enlace a la altura de Vigo.

rendition [ren'dɪʃən] N (*Mus*) interpretación *f*, ejecución *f*.

renegade ['renɪgeɪd] ① ADJ renegado.
② N renegado *m*, -a *f*.

renege [rı'ni:g] VI faltar a su palabra; **to ~ on a promise** no cumplir una promesa.

renew [rı'nju:] VT renovar; (*resume*) reanudar; *lease, loan etc* extender, prorrogar; *subscription* renovar; *promise* reafirmar; *attack etc* volver a; *effort etc* volver a hacer, redoblar; **to ~ acquaintance with sb** reanudar la amistad con uno; **to ~ the attack on sb** volver a arremeter contra uno; **to ~ the attack on a town** volver a atacar una ciudad; **to ~ one's strength** restablecer sus fuerzas, cobrar nuevo vigor.

renewable [rı'nju:əbl] ADJ renovable; ~ **energy** energías *fpl* alternativas.

renewal [rı'nju:əl] N renovación *f*; reanudación *f*; extensión *f*; prorrogación *f*; reafirmación *f*; ~ **of subscriptions** renovación *f* de suscripciones; **the ~ of the attack** el nuevo ataque; **a spiritual ~** una renovación espiritual; **urban ~** renovación *f* urbana.

renewed [rı'nju:d] ADJ renovado; nuevo; **with ~ vigour** con nuevo vigor, con redoblado vigor; con nuevos bríos; **to feel spiritually ~** sentirse con nuevas fuerzas espirituales.

rennet ['renɪt] N cuajo *m*.

renounce [rɪ'naʊns] [1] VT *right, inheritance, offer etc* renunciar; *plan, post, the world etc* renunciar a.
  [2] VI (*Cards*) renunciar.

renouncement [rɪ'naʊnsmənt] N renuncia *f*.

renovate ['renəʊveɪt] VT renovar, restaurar.

renovation [,renəʊ'veɪʃən] N renovación *f*, restauración *f*.

renown [rɪ'naʊn] N renombre *m*, nombradía *f*, fama *f*.

renowned [rɪ'naʊnd] ADJ renombrado; **it is ~ for** ... es famoso por ..., es célebre por ...

rent¹ [rent] [1] PRET AND PTP *of* rend. [2] N (*tear*) rasgón *m*, rasgadura *f*; (*split*) abertura *f*, raja *f*, hendedura *f*; (*fig*) escisión *f*, cisma *m*.

rent² [rent] [1] N alquiler *m*, arriendo *m*; **we pay £350 in ~** pagamos 350 libras de alquiler; **to build flats for ~** construir pisos para alquilarlos; **'for ~'** (*US*) 'se alquila'.
  [2] ATTR: **~ book** librito *m* del alquiler; **~ rebate** devolución *f* de alquiler.
  [3] VT (*also* **to ~ out**) alquilar, rentar (*Mex*); **to ~ a flat from sb** alquilar un piso de uno; **to ~ a house (out) to sb** alquilar una casa a uno; **it is ~ed out at £400 a week** está alquilado a 400 libras por semana.

rental ['rentl] [1] N alquiler *m*, arriendo *m*.
  [2] ATTR: **~ car** (*US*) coche *m* de alquiler; **~ value** valor *m* de alquiler.

rent-a-mob ['rentəmɒb] N turba *f* alquilada.

rentboy* ['rentbɔɪ] N chapero♯ *m*.

rent-collector ['rentkə,lektər] N recaudador *m*, -ora *f* de alquileres.

rent-control ['rentkən,trəʊl] N control *m* de alquileres.

rent-controlled ['rentkən,trəʊld] ADJ: **a ~ flat** un piso de alquiler controlado.

rent-free ['rent'friː] [1] ADJ *house etc* exento de alquiler, gratuito.
  [2] ADV: **to live ~** ocupar una casa (*etc*) sin pagar alquiler.

rentier ['rɒntɪeɪ] N rentista *m*.

renting ['rentɪŋ] N arrendamiento *m*.

rent-roll ['rentrəʊl] N lista *f* de alquileres; (*total m de*) ingresos *mpl* de alquileres.

renumber ['riː'nʌmbər] VT volver a numerar; corregir la numeración de.

renunciation [rɪ,nʌnsɪ'eɪʃən] N renuncia *f*.

reoccupy ['riː'ɒkjʊpaɪ] VT volver a ocupar.

reopen ['riː'əʊpən] [1] VT volver a abrir, reabrir; **to ~ a case** (*Jur*) rever un pleito, rever un proceso, (*fig*) reconsiderar un asunto.
  [2] VI volver a abrirse, reabrirse; **school ~s on the 8th** el nuevo curso comienza el día 8.

reopening ['riː'əʊpnɪŋ] N reapertura *f*; (*Jur*) revisión *f*; reconsideración *f*.

reorder ['riː'ɔːdər] VT (a) *objects* ordenar (*or* arreglar *etc*) de nuevo, volver a poner en orden. (b) (*Comm*) volver a pedir, repetir el pedido de.

reorganization ['riː,ɔːgənaɪ'zeɪʃən] N reorganización *f*.

reorganize ['riː'ɔːgənaɪz] [1] VT reorganizar.
  [2] VT reorganizarse.

rep¹ [rep] N (*fabric*) reps *m*.

rep²* [rep] [1] N (*Comm*) viajante *mf*, agente *mf*; (*of union etc*) representante *mf*.
  [2] VI: **to ~ for** ser agente de.

rep³* [rep] N (*Theat*) = **repertory.**

Rep. (a) ABBR *of* **Republic** República *f*. (b) (*US Pol*) ABBR *of* **Republican** republicano *m*, -a *f* (*also adj*). (c) (*US Pol*) ABBR *of* **Representative** diputado *m*, -a *f*.

repack ['riː'pæk] VT *object* reembalar, reenvasar, devolver a su caja (*etc*); *suitcase* volver a hacer.

repackage [,riː'pækɪdʒ] VT *product* reempaquetar; *parcel* reembalar; (*fig*) *proposal, scheme* reformular.

repaid [riː'peɪd] PRET, PTP *of* **repay.**

repaint ['riː'peɪnt] VT repintar; **to ~ sth blue** repintar algo de azul.

repair¹ [rɪ'peər] VI: **to ~ to** (*move to*) trasladarse a, dirigirse a; (*go regularly to*) acudir a, reunirse en.

repair² [rɪ'peər] [1] N (a) (*act*) reparación *f*, compostura *f*; (*patch etc*) remiendo *m*; **~s** reparaciones *fpl*, (*Archit*) obras *fpl*, reformas *fpl*; **'closed for ~s'** 'cerrado por obras', 'cerrado por reformas'; **cost of ~s** coste *m* de las reparaciones; **to be under ~** estar siendo reparado; (*Archit*) estar en obras; **it is beyond ~** no tiene arreglo, no se puede reparar; (*fig*) no tiene remedio; **it is damaged beyond ~** ha sufrido tantos desperfectos que no se puede reparar.
  (b) (*state*) **to be in good ~** estar en buen estado; **it's in very bad ~** está en muy mal estado.
  [2] ATTR: **~ kit** caja *f* de herramientas (para reparaciones); **~ shop** taller *m* de reparaciones.
  [3] VT reparar, componer; *shoes etc* remendar.

repairable [rɪ'peərəbl] ADJ que se puede reparar.

repairer [rɪ'peərər] N reparador *m*, -ora *f*.

repairman [rɪ'peəmæn] N, PL **repairmen** [rɪ'peəmen] reparador *m*,

mecánico *m*, técnico *m*.

repaper ['riː'peɪpər] VT empapelar de nuevo.

reparable ['repərəbl] ADJ reparable.

reparation [,repə'reɪʃən] N reparación *f*; satisfacción *f*; **~s** (*Fin*) indemnización *f*; **to make ~s** dar satisfacción (*for* por).

repartee [,repɑː'tiː] N (intercambio *m* de) réplicas *fpl* agudas, réplicas *fpl* chistosas.

repass ['riː'pɑːs] VT repasar.

repast [rɪ'pɑːst] N comida *f*.

repatriate [1] [riː'pætrɪət] N repatriado *m*, -a *f*.
  [2] [riː'pætrɪeɪt] VT repatriar.

repatriation [riː,pætrɪ'eɪʃən] N repatriación *f*.

repay [riː'peɪ] (*irr*: *V* **pay**) VT *money* devolver, reembolsar, reintegrar; *person* pagar; *debt* pagar, liquidar; *person* (*in compensation*) resarcir, compensar; *person* (*pej*) pagar en la misma moneda; *kindness etc* devolver, corresponder a; *visit* devolver, pagar; **to ~ sb in full** pagar a uno todo lo que se le debe, devolver a uno la suma entera; **how can I ever ~ you?** ¿cómo podré nunca corresponder?; **it ~s a visit** vale la pena visitarlo; **it ~s study** merece que se le estudie; **it ~s reading** vale la pena leerlo.

repayable [riː'peəbl] ADJ reembolsable, reintegrable; **£5 deposit not ~** desembolso *m* inicial de 5 libras no reembolsable; **~ in 10 instalments** a pagar en 10 cuotas; **~ on demand** reembolsable a petición; **the money is ~ on the 5th of June** el dinero ha de ser devuelto el 5 de junio.

repayment [riː'peɪmənt] [1] N devolución *f*, reembolso *m*; pago *m*; **now he asks for ~** ahora pide que se le devuelva el dinero; **in 6 ~s of £8** en 6 cuotas de 8 libras cada uno.
  [2] ATTR: **~ schedule** plan *m* de amortización.

repeal [rɪ'piːl] [1] N revocación *f*, abrogación *f*.
  [2] VT revocar, abrogar.

repeat [rɪ'piːt] [1] N repetición *f*; (*Rad etc*) retransmisión *f*.
  [2] ATTR: **~ broadcast** retransmisión *f*; **~ mark(s)** (*Mus*) símbolo(s) *m(pl)* de repetición; **~ mortgage** hipoteca *f* amortizable; **~ order** (*Brit*) pedido *m* de repetición; **~ performance** repetición *f*; **~ sign** (*Mus*) = **~ mark.**
  [3] VT repetir; *thanks etc* reiterar, volver a dar; (*aloud*) recitar; **she went and ~ed it to the boss** fue a contárselo al jefe; **don't ~ it to anybody** no lo digas a nadie; **this offer cannot be ~ed** esta oferta no se repetirá; **can you ~ the design of this house?** ¿puede Vd construir otra casa igual que ésta?
  [4] VI repetirse; (*clock, rifle, taste*) repetir; **radishes ~ on me** me repite el rábano.

repeated [rɪ'piːtɪd] ADJ repetido; reiterado; **in spite of ~ reminders** a pesar de habérselo recordado infinitas veces.

repeatedly [rɪ'piːtɪdlɪ] ADV repetidamente, repetidas veces; reiteradamente; **I have told you so ~** te lo he dicho repetidas veces.

repeater [rɪ'piːtər] N (a) (*watch*) reloj *m* de repetición; (*rifle*) rifle *m* de repetición. (b) (*US Jur*) reincidente *mf*.

repeating [rɪ'piːtɪŋ] ADJ (*Math*) periódico.

repechage [,repɪ'ʃɑːʒ] N repesca *f*.

repel [rɪ'pel] [1] VT rechazar, repeler; (*fig*) repugnar; **he ~s me** me da asco; **it ~s me to have to + *infin*** me repugna tener que + *infin*.
  [2] VI repelerse mutuamente.

repellent [rɪ'pelənt] [1] ADJ repugnante; **it is ~ to insects** ahuyenta los insectos.
  [2] N: **insect ~** repelente *m* de insectos, crema *f* anti-insectos.

repent [rɪ'pent] [1] VT arrepentirse de.
  [2] VI arrepentirse.

repentance [rɪ'pentəns] N arrepentimiento *m*.

repentant [rɪ'pentənt] ADJ arrepentido; contrito, compungido.

repeople ['riː'piːpl] VT repoblar.

repercussion [,riːpə'kʌʃən] N repercusión *f*; **~s** (*fig*) repercusiones *fpl*; resonancia *f*; **as for the political ~s** en cuanto a las repercusiones políticas; **it had great ~s in Ruritania** tuvo gran resonancia en Ruritania.

repertoire ['repətwɑːr] N repertorio *m*.

repertory ['repətərɪ] [1] N repertorio *m*; **to be** (*or* **act**) **in ~** formar parte de una compañía de repertorio.
  [2] ATTR: **~ company** compañía *f* de repertorio; **~ theater** (*US*), **~ theatre** (*Brit*) teatro *m* de repertorio.

repetition [,repɪ'tɪʃən] N repetición *f*; recitación *f*.

repetitious [,repɪ'tɪʃəs] ADJ repetidor, que se repite; monótono.

repetitive [rɪ'petɪtɪv] ADJ reiterativo; **the book is a bit ~** el libro tiene sus repeticiones.

rephrase [riː'freɪz] VT expresar de otro modo, decir con otras palabras.

repine [rɪ'paɪn] VI quejarse (*at* de), afligirse (*at* por).

replace [rɪ'pleɪs] VT (a) (*put back*) reponer, poner en su lugar, devolver a su sitio, colocar nuevamente; **please ~ the receiver** cuelgue, por favor.
  (b) (*take the place of*) reemplazar, sustituir; **to ~ sth by** (*or* **with**) **sth**

else sustituir a algo por otra cosa; **the Matisse was ~d by a Klee** el Matisse fue sustituido por un Klee, un cuadro de Klee sustituyó al de Matisse; **nobody could ever ~ him in my heart** nadie podría reemplazarle en mi corazón; **he asked to be ~d** rogó que se le sustituyera (or relevara); **he had to be ~d** tuvo que ser destituido; **we will ~ the broken glasses** nosotros pagaremos los vasos rotos.

replaceable [rɪ'pleɪsəbl] ADJ reemplazable, sustituible; **it will not easily be ~** no será fácil encontrar un repuesto; **he will not easily be ~** no será fácil encontrar un sustituto.

replacement [rɪ'pleɪsmənt] ① N **(a)** *(act)* reposición *f*; devolución *f*; reemplazo *m*, sustitución *f*.

(b) *(substitute: thing)* reemplazo *m*, repuesto *m*, *(person)* sustituto *m*, suplente *mf*; **it took 3 days to find a ~** tardaron 3 días en encontrar un repuesto.

② ATTR: **~ cost** costo *m* de sustitución; **~ engine** motor *m* de repuesto; **~ part** repuesto *m*; **~ value** valor *m* de sustitución.

replant [ri:'plɑːnt] VT replantar.

replay ① ['riːpleɪ] N *(TV)* repetición *f*; *(Sport)* (partido *m* de) desempate *m*.

② [ˌriː'pleɪ] VT *(TV)* repetir; *(Sport)* volver a jugar; *(Mus)* volver a tocar.

③ [ˌriː'pleɪ] VI *(Sport)* jugar el desempate.

replenish [rɪ'plenɪʃ] VT *(refill)* rellenar; *(with supplies)* reaprovisionar, repostar *(with* de); *stocks* reponer; *(with fuel)* repostar.

replenishment [rɪ'plenɪʃmənt] N rellenado *m*; reaprovisionamiento *m*; reposición *f*.

replete [rɪ'pliːt] ADJ repleto, totalmente lleno *(with* de).

repletion [rɪ'pliːʃən] N saciedad *f*, repleción *f*; **to eat to ~** darse un atracón, comer realmente bien.

replica ['replɪkə] N *(Art etc)* copia *f*, reproducción *f* (exacta); réplica *f*; *(fig: person etc)* segunda edición *f*.

replicate ['replɪˌkeɪt] VT reproducir exactamente.

reply [rɪ'plaɪ] ① N respuesta *f*, contestación *f*; **~ card** tarjeta *f* respuesta; **'~ paid'** 'porte pagado'; **~ paid postcard** tarjeta *f* de respuesta pagada; **in ~ he said ...** contestando a esto dijo que ...; **he had nothing to say in ~** no podía darme *(etc)* respuesta; **what is your ~ to this?** ¿qué contestas a esto?; **we await your ~** *(ending letter)* en espera de sus noticias.

② ATTR: **~ coupon** cupón-respuesta *m*; **international ~ coupon** cupón-respuesta *m* internacional.

③ VI responder, contestar; **to ~ to sb** contestar a uno; **to ~ to a letter** contestar una carta.

repoint [ri:'pɔɪnt] VT rejuntar.

repointing [ri:'pɔɪntɪŋ] N rejuntamiento *m*.

repopulate ['riː'pɒpjʊleɪt] VT repoblar.

repopulation ['riːˌpɒpjʊ'leɪʃən] N repoblación *f*.

report [rɪ'pɔːt] ① N **(a)** *(account)* relato *m*, relación *f*; *(Mil etc)* parte *m*; *(official)* informe *m*; *(piece of news)* noticia *f*; *(in newspaper)* reportaje *m*, crónica *f*, información *f*; *(school)* papeleta *f*, nota *f*, certificado *m* escolar; *(annual ~)* memoria *f* anual; **the Robbins R~** el Informe Robbins; **'R~ on the Motor Industry'** 'Informe *m* sobre la Industria del Automóvil'; **the ~ of his death upset us** la noticia de su muerte nos causó pesar; **to present a ~** presentar un informe.

(b) *(rumour)* rumor *m*, voz *f*; **there is a ~ that ...** corre la voz de que ..., se rumorea que ...; **I only know of it by ~** lo sé de oídas nada más.

(c) *(reputation: liter)* reputación *f*, fama *f*; **a person of good ~** una persona de buena fama.

(d) *(bang)* estampido *m*, estallido *m*; explosión *f*; **there was a ~** se oyó una explosión.

② VT *(recount)* relatar, narrar, dar cuenta de; *(Mil)* dar parte de; *event etc* informar acerca de; *crime etc* denunciar *(to* a); *meeting (as secretary)* levantar las actas de, *(as reporter)* escribir la crónica de; **to ~ that ...** informar que ..., comunicar que ...; **it is ~ed from Berlin that ...** se informa desde Berlín que ..., comunican desde Berlín que ...; **he is ~ed to have said that ...** parece que dijo que ..., habría dicho que ...; **she is ~ed to be in Italy** se cree que está en Italia; **~ed speech** discurso *m* indirecto, discurso *m* referido; **what have you to ~?** ¿qué tienes que decirnos?; **nothing to ~** sin novedad; **nothing to ~ from the front** sin novedad en el frente; **to ~ progress** dar cuenta de los progresos; **I shall have to ~ this** tendré que denunciar esto; **you have been ~ed for idleness** Vd ha sido denunciado por vago, le han acusado de ser holgazán; **he was ~ed for swearing at the referee** se le denunció por dirigir palabrotas al árbitro.

③ VI **(a)** *(make report)* hacer un informe, presentar un informe *(on* acerca de); **a committee was set up to ~ on the pill** se creó una comisión para investigar la píldora; **Professor X ~s on his discovery in the next issue** el Profesor X informará de su descubrimiento en el próximo número; **the committee will ~ to the cabinet** la comisión elevará su informe al consejo de ministros; **he ~s to the marketing director** es responsable al director de márketing; **Jim Bloggs ~s from Chicago** *(Rad, TV)* Jim Bloggs informa desde Chicago.

(b) *(as reporter)* ser reportero; **he ~ed for the 'Daily Echo' for 40**

years durante 40 años fue reportero del 'Daily Echo'.

(c) *(present o.s.)* presentarse; personarse; **to ~ at a place at 18.00 hours** presentarse en un sitio a las 18.00 horas; **~ to me when you are better** venga a verme cuando te hayas repuesto; **he is to ~ to the court tomorrow** tiene que personarse mañana ante el tribunal; **to ~ sick** darse de baja por enfermo; **to ~ fit** darse de alta; **to ~ to one's unit** reincorporarse a su unidad.

◆**report back** VI: **to ~ back to sb** rendir cuentas a uno; presentarse para informar a uno; **~ back at 6 o'clock** preséntese a las 6.

reportage [ˌrepɔː'tɑːʒ] N reportaje *m*.

report card [rɪ'pɔːt,kɑːd] N *(Scol)* cartilla *f* escolar.

reportedly [rɪ'pɔːtɪdlɪ] ADV según se dice, según se informa; **he is ~ living in Australia** se dice que está viviendo en Australia.

reporter [rɪ'pɔːtəʳ] N reportero *m*, -a *f*, periodista *mf*; *(TV, Radio)* locutor *m*, -ora *f*.

reporting [rɪ'pɔːtɪŋ] ① N reportaje *m*.

② ADJ: **~ structure** estructura *f* laboral jerárquica.

report stage [rɪ'pɔːt,steɪdʒ] N *(Brit: Parl)* fase de debate de las enmiendas propuestas por las comisiones legislativas a un proyecto de ley.

repose [rɪ'pəʊz] ① N reposo *m*.

② VT *(lay etc)* reposar, descansar; recostar; **to ~ confidence in sb** poner confianza en uno.

③ VI reposar, descansar; **to ~ on** descansar sobre, *(fig)* descansar en, estribar en, estar basado en.

repository [rɪ'pɒzɪtərɪ] N depósito *m*, almacén *m*; *(furniture ~)* guardamuebles *m*; *(person)* depositario *m*, -a *f*.

repossess ['riːpə'zes] ① VT recobrar.

② VR: **to ~ o.s. of sth** recobrar algo, volver a tomar algo.

repossession [ˌriːpə'zeʃən] N recuperación *f* de un artículo no pagado.

repot [ri:'pɒt] VT poner en nueva maceta, cambiar de maceta.

reprehend [ˌreprɪ'hend] VT reprender.

reprehensible [ˌreprɪ'hensɪbl] ADJ reprensible, censurable.

reprehensibly [ˌreprɪ'hensɪblɪ] ADV censurablemente.

reprehension [ˌreprɪ'henʃən] N reprensión *f*.

represent [ˌreprɪ'zent] VT representar; *(Jur)* ser apoderado de, *(fig)* hablar en nombre de; *(Comm)* ser agente de; **the goods are not as ~ed** las mercancías no son como nos las describieron; **his early work is well ~ed in the exhibition** su obra juvenil tiene una fuerte representación en la exposición; **you ~ed it falsely to us** Vd nos lo describió falsamente; **it has been ~ed to us that ...** se ha pretendido que ..., se nos ha dicho que ...; **he ~s nobody but himself** no representa a nadie sino a sí mismo.

re-present ['riːprɪ'zent] VT volver a presentar.

representation [ˌreprɪzen'teɪʃən] N **(a)** representación *f* *(also Pol)*.

(b) *(protest etc)* petición *f*; declaración *f*; **to make ~s to sb** presentar una petición a uno, dirigir un memorial a uno, *(complain)* quejarse ante uno; **to make ~s about sth** quejarse de algo.

(c) to make false ~s describir algo falsamente.

representational [ˌreprɪzen'teɪʃənəl] ADJ *(Art)* figurativo.

representative [ˌreprɪ'zentətɪv] ① ADJ representativo; **~ government** gobierno *m* representativo; **these figures are more ~** estas cifras son más representativas; **a person not fully ~ of the group** una persona que no representa adecuadamente el grupo.

② N representante *mf* *(also Comm)*; *(Jur)* apoderado *m*; *(US Pol)* diputado *m*, -a *f*.

repress [rɪ'pres] VT reprimir.

repressed [rɪ'prest] ADJ reprimido.

repression [rɪ'preʃən] N represión *f*.

repressive [rɪ'presɪv] ADJ represivo.

reprieve [rɪ'priːv] ① N *(breathing space)* respiro *m*, alivio *m* temporal; *(Jur)* indulto *m*, suspensión *f* (*esp* de la pena de muerte); **to win a last-minute ~** ser indultado a última hora; **the wood got a ~** se retiró la orden de talar el bosque.

② VT indultar, suspender la pena de; **to ~ sb from death** indultar a uno de muerte, suspender la pena de muerte de uno.

reprimand ['reprɪmɑːnd] ① N reprimenda *f*, reprensión *f*.

② VT reprender, reconvenir.

reprint ① ['riːprɪnt] N reimpresión *f*; *(offprint)* tirada *f* aparte, separata *f*.

② ['riː'prɪnt] VT reimprimir; **'~ed from the Transactions of ...'** 'tirada aparte de las Actas de ...'

reprisal [rɪ'praɪzəl] N represalia *f*; **as a ~ for** como represalia por; **by way of ~** a modo de represalia; **to take ~s** tomar represalias.

reprise [rɪ'priːz] ① N repetición *f*.

② VT repetir.

repro* ['riːprəʊ] ① N ABBR of **reprographics, reprography**.

② ATTR ABBR of **reproduction**; **~ furniture** muebles *mpl* de imitación.

reproach [rɪ'prəʊtʃ] ① N *(spoken etc)* reproche *m*, censura *f*; *(stain, disgrace)* tacha *f*, baldón *m*, oprobio *m*; **beyond ~** por encima de toda crítica, intachable; **term of ~** término *m* oprobioso; **this is a ~ to us all** esto es deshonroso para todos nosotros; **poverty is a ~ to civili-**

zation la pobreza es una vergüenza para la civilización.

[2] VT: **to ~ sb for sth, to ~ sb with sth** reprochar algo a uno, censurar algo a uno, echar algo en cara a uno.

[3] VR: **to ~ o.s. for sth** reprocharse algo; **you have no reason to ~ yourself** Vd no tiene motivo para reprocharse (nada).

reproachful [rɪˈprəʊtʃʊl] ADJ *look etc* acusador, lleno de reproches; **next day she was ~** el día siguiente me reprochó.

reproachfully [rɪˈprəʊtʃəlɪ] ADV *look etc* con reproche; *speak etc* en tono acusador.

reprobate [ˈreprəʊbeɪt] N réprobo *m*, -a *f*.

reprobation [ˌreprəʊˈbeɪʃən] N reprobación *f*.

reprocess [ˌriːˈprəʊses] VT reprocesar.

reprocessing [ˌriːˈprəʊsesɪŋ] N reprocesamiento *m*; **~ plant** planta *f* de reprocesamiento.

reproduce [ˌriːprəˈdjuːs] [1] VT reproducir.

[2] VI reproducirse.

reproducible [ˌriːprəˈdjuːsɪbl] ADJ reproducible.

reproduction [ˌriːprəˈdʌkʃən] [1] N reproducción *f*.

[2] ATTR: **~ furniture** mobiliario *m* estilo.

reproductive [ˌriːprəˈdʌktɪv] ADJ reproductor.

reprographic [ˌriːprəˈɡræfɪk] ADJ de reprografía; **~s** reprografía.

reprography [rɪˈprɒɡrəfɪ] N reprografía *f*.

reproof [rɪˈpruːf] N reprensión *f*, reconvención *f*; **to administer a ~ to sb** reprender a uno.

re-proof [ˌriːˈpruːf] VT reimpermeabilizar.

reproval [rɪˈpruːvəl] N reprobación *f*.

reprove [rɪˈpruːv] VT reprender, reconvenir; **to ~ sb for sth** reprender algo a uno.

reproving [rɪˈpruːvɪŋ] ADJ reprobador, lleno de reproches.

reprovingly [rɪˈpruːvɪŋlɪ] ADV en tono reprobador, reprobadoramente, con reprobación; **she looked at me ~** me miró severa, me reprendió con la mirada.

reptile [ˈreptaɪl] N reptil *m*.

reptilian [repˈtɪlɪən] [1] ADJ reptil.

[2] N reptil *m*.

Repub. ABBR **(a)** *of* **Republic. (b)** *of* **Republican.**

republic [rɪˈpʌblɪk] N república *f*.

republican [rɪˈpʌblɪkən] [1] ADJ republicano.

[2] N republicano *m*, -a *f*.

republicanism [rɪˈpʌblɪkənɪzəm] N republicanismo *m*.

republication [ˈriːˌpʌblɪˈkeɪʃən] N reedición *f*.

republish [ˈriːˈpʌblɪʃ] VT reeditar.

repudiate [rɪˈpjuːdɪeɪt] VT *charge etc* rechazar, negar, desechar; *attitude etc* repudiar; *possibility* descartar; *obligation etc* rechazar, desconocer; *wife* repudiar; *debt, treaty* anular, cancelar.

repudiation [rɪˌpjuːdɪˈeɪʃən] N rechazamiento *m*; desconocimiento *m*; repudio *m*; incumplimiento *m*; anulación *f*, cancelación *f*.

repugnance [rɪˈpʌɡnəns] N repugnancia *f*.

repugnant [rɪˈpʌɡnənt] ADJ repugnante; **it is ~ to me** me repugna.

repulse [rɪˈpʌls] [1] N repulsa *f*, repulsión *f*; rechazo *m*; **to suffer a ~** ser repulsado, ser rechazado.

[2] VT rechazar, repulsar.

repulsion [rɪˈpʌlʃən] N repulsión *f*, repugnancia *f*; (*Phys*) repulsión *f*.

repulsive [rɪˈpʌlsɪv] ADJ repulsivo, repelente.

repulsively [rɪˈpʌlsɪvlɪ] ADV de modo repulsivo; **~ ugly** terriblemente feo.

repulsiveness [rɪˈpʌlsɪvnɪs] N lo repulsivo; lo repelente; **of such ~** tan repelente.

repurchase [ˈriːˈpɜːtʃɪs] [1] N readquisición *f*.

[2] VT readquirir, volver a comprar.

reputable [ˈrepjʊtəbl] ADJ *firm, brand etc* acreditado, de toda confianza; *person* honroso, formal, estimable.

reputation [ˌrepjʊˈteɪʃən] N reputación *f*, fama *f*; **of good ~** de buena fama; **to have a bad ~** tener mala fama; **to have a ~ for meanness** tener fama de tacaño; **the hotel has a ~ for good food** el hotel es célebre por su buena comida; **he has the ~ of being awkward** se dice que es difícil, tiene fama de difícil; **to ruin a girl's ~** acabar con la buena fama de una joven.

repute [rɪˈpjuːt] [1] N reputación *f*, fama *f*; **by ~** según la opinión común, según se dice; **a firm of (good) ~** una casa acreditada; **a café of ill ~** un café de mala fama; **a house of ill ~** (*euph*) una casa de mala fama; **to hold sb in (high) ~** tener un alto concepto de uno; **his skill was held in high ~** su destreza era muy estimada; **to know sb by ~ only** conocer a uno sólo por su reputación, conocer a uno de oídas nada más.

[2] VT reputar; **to be ~d as** tener fama de, pasar por; **to be ~d to be clever** tener fama de inteligente, pasar por ser inteligente; **he is ~d to be a millionaire** se dice que es millonario.

reputed [rɪˈpjuːtɪd] ADJ supuesto, presunto.

reputedly [rɪˈpjuːtɪdlɪ] ADV según se dice, según la opinión común.

▼ **request** [rɪˈkwest] [1] N ruego *m*, petición *f*; instancia *f*; (*formal*) solicitud *f*; **a ~ for help** una petición de socorro; **at the ~ of** a

petición de, a instancia de; **at the urgent ~ of X I have decided to + *infin*** accediendo al ruego insistente de X he decidido + *infin*; **by ~** a petición; **to play a record by ~** tocar un disco a petición de un oyente; **it is much in ~** tiene mucha demanda, está muy solicitado; **on ~** a solicitud; **to grant sb's ~** acceder al ruego de uno; **to make a ~ for sth** pedir algo, hacer una petición de algo.

[2] ATTR *programme* a petición de los radioyentes; *stop* discrecional, a petición.

▼ [3] VT pedir, rogar; solicitar; **to ~ sth of sb** pedir algo a uno; **to ~ sb to do sth** rogar a uno hacer algo, pedir que uno haga algo; **'visitors are ~ed not to talk'** 'se ruega a los visitantes respetar el silencio'.

requiem [ˈrekwɪem] N réquiem *m*.

▼ **require** [rɪˈkwaɪəʳ] VT **(a)** (*need*) necesitar; exigir; pedir, requerir; **we ~ another chair** necesitamos otra silla más; **it ~s great care** exige mucho cuidado; **the lock ~s attention** hace falta reparar la cerradura; **the battery ~s regular attention** hay que comprobar la pila con regularidad; **no maintenance ~d** no necesita manutención alguna; **it ~d all his strength to lift it** hacía falta que emplease todas sus fuerzas para levantarlo; **this plant ~s watering frequently** esta planta hay que regarla con frecuencia; **is my presence ~d?** ¿es necesario que asista yo?; **your presence is ~d** se exige que asista Vd; **if ~d** en caso de necesidad, si es necesario; **when ~d** cuando hace falta; **as the situation may ~** según lo exija la situación; **we will do all that is ~d** haremos todo lo que haga falta; **what qualifications are ~d?** ¿qué títulos se requieren?

(b) to ~ sth of sb pedir algo a uno; **what do you ~ of me?** ¿qué piden Vds que haga?

▼ **(c)** (*demand*) **to ~ that ...** exigir que + *subj*, requerir que + *subj*, insistir en que + *subj*; **the law ~s that it should be done** la ley exige que se haga.

required [rɪˈkwaɪəd] ADJ necesario, obligatorio, que hace falta; **a pipe of the ~ length** un tubo del largo que hace falta; **by the ~ date** antes de la fecha prescrita; **within the ~ time** dentro del plazo establecido; **has he got the ~ qualities?** ¿tiene las cualidades necesarias?; **the qualities ~ for the job** las cualidades que se requieren para el puesto; **it is a ~ course for the degree** (*US*) es una asignatura obligatoria para el título.

requirement [rɪˈkwaɪəmənt] N requisito *m*; estipulación *f*; necesidad *f*; condición *f*; exigencia *f*; **~s** requisitos *mpl*; **our ~s are few** nuestras necesidades son pocas, necesitamos poco; **Latin is a ~ for the course** el latín es un requisito para este curso, para este curso se exige el latín; **it is one of the ~s of the contract** es una de las estipulaciones del contrato; **to meet all the ~s for sth** llenar todos los requisitos para algo.

requisite [ˈrekwɪzɪt] [1] ADJ preciso, indispensable, imprescindible.

[2] N requisito *m*; **office ~s** material *m* de oficina; **toilet ~s** artículos *mpl* de tocador.

requisition [ˌrekwɪˈzɪʃən] [1] N pedido *m*, solicitud *f* (*for* de); (*Mil*) requisa *f*, requisición *f*.

[2] VT (*Mil*) requisar.

requital [rɪˈkwaɪtl] N compensación *f*, satisfacción *f*; desquite *m*.

requite [rɪˈkwaɪt] VT (*make return for*) compensar, recompensar, pagar; **to ~ sb's love** corresponder al amor de uno; **that love was not ~d** ese amor no fue correspondido.

reran [ˌriːˈræn] PRET *of* **rerun.**

reread [ˈriːˈriːd] (*irr: V* **read**) VT releer, volver a leer.

reredos [ˈrɪədɒs] N retablo *m*.

reroof [ˌriːˈruːf] VT poner un tejado nuevo en *or* a, poner un techo nuevo en *or* a.

reroute [ˈriːˈruːt] VT desviar; **the train was ~ed through Burgos** el tren se desvió de la ruta normal y pasó por Burgos.

rerun [1] [ˈriːrʌn] N repetición *f*; (*Theat etc*) reestreno *m*, reposición *f*.

[2] [ˈriːˈrʌn] (*irr: V* **run**) VT *race* correr de nuevo; (*Theat etc*) reestrenar, reponer.

resale [ˈriːˈseɪl] [1] N reventa *f*.

[2] ATTR: **~ price maintenance** mantenimiento *m* del precio de venta; **~ value** valor *m* de reventa.

resat [ˈriːˈsæt] PRET, PTP *of* **resit.**

reschedule [riːˈʃedjuːl] VT reprogramar.

rescind [rɪˈsɪnd] VT rescindir, anular, revocar.

rescission [rɪˈsɪʒən] N rescisión *f*, anulación *f*, revocación *f*.

rescue [ˈreskjuː] [1] N salvamento *m*, rescate *m*; liberación *f* (*from* de); **the hero of the ~ was ...** el héroe del salvamento fue ...; **to come** (*or* **go**) **to the ~ of** ir al socorro de, acudir al rescate de; **to the ~!** ¡al socorro!; **Batman to the ~!** ¡Batman acude a la llamada!

[2] ATTR: **~ attempt** tentativa *f* de salvamento; **~ dig** excavación *f* de urgencia; **~ operations** operaciones *fpl* de salvamento; **~ party, ~ team** equipo *m* de salvamento; **~ services** servicios *mpl* de rescate; **~ vessel** buque *m* de salvamento; **~ work** operación *f* de salvamento.

[3] VT salvar, rescatar; librar, libertar (*from* de); **three men were ~d** tres hombres fueron salvados; **they waited 3 days to be ~d** esperaron 3 días hasta ser rescatados; **to ~ sb from death** librar a

uno de la muerte; **the ~d man is in hospital** el hombre rescatado está en el hospital.

rescuer ['reskjʊəʳ] N salvador *m*, -ora *f*.

resealable [ˌriː'siːləbl] ADJ *container* que se puede volver a cerrar.

research [rɪ'sɜːtʃ] **1** N investigación *f*, investigaciones *fpl* (*in, into* de); **~ and development** investigación *f* y desarrollo; **atomic ~** investigaciones *fpl* atómicas; **our ~ shows that ...** nuestras investigaciones demuestran que ...; **a piece of ~** una investigación.
2 ATTR: **~ establishment** instituto *m* de investigaciones; **~ fellow** investigador *m*, -ora *f*; **~ laboratory** laboratorio *m* de investigación; **~ staff** personal *m* investigador; **~ student** estudiante *m* investigador, estudiante *f* investigadora; **~ team** equipo *m* de investigación; **~ work** investigaciones *fpl*, trabajos *mpl* de investigación; **~ worker** investigador *m*, -ora *f*.
3 VI investigar; **to ~ into sth** investigar algo, hacer investigaciones de algo.
4 VT (*US*) investigar; **to ~ an article** preparar el material para un estudio, reunir datos para escribir un artículo; **a well ~ed study** un estudio bien preparado.

researcher [rɪ'sɜːtʃəʳ] N investigador *m*, -ora *f*.

reseat [ˌriː'siːt] VT *chair* poner nuevo asiento a.

resection [riː'sekʃən] N (a) (*Survey*) triangulación *f*. (b) (*Med*) resección *f*.

resell ['riː'sel] (*irr: V* sell) VT revender, volver a vender.

resemblance [rɪ'zembləns] N semejanza *f*, parecido *m*; **to bear a strong ~ to sb** parecerse mucho a uno; **to bear no ~ to sb** no parecerse en absoluto a uno; **there is no ~ between them** los dos no se parecen en absoluto; **there is hardly any ~ between this version and the one I gave you** apenas existe parecido entre esta versión y la que te di.

resemble [rɪ'zembl] VT parecerse a; **he doesn't ~ his father** no se parece a su padre; **they do ~ one another** sí se parecen uno a otro.

resent [rɪ'zent] VT ofenderse por, tomar a mal, resentirse de (*or* por); **I ~ that!** ¡protesto contra esa observación!, ¡no permito que se diga eso!, ¡eso no!; **he ~s my being here** se ofende por mi presencia aquí, no está conforme con mi presencia aquí; **I don't ~ your saying it** no me ofende que lo digas.

resentful [rɪ'zentfʊl] ADJ *person* resentido, ofendido, agraviado; *tone* resentido, ofendido; **to be** (*or* **feel**) **~ of** ofenderse por, sentirse agraviado por; **no wonder she feels ~** no me extraña que se sienta ofendida; **he is still ~ about it** todavía guarda rencor por ello.

resentfully [rɪ'zentfəlɪ] ADV con resentimiento; **he said ~** dijo resentido.

resentment [rɪ'zentmənt] N resentimiento *m* (*about, at* por).

reservation [ˌrezə'veɪʃən] N (a) (*act*) reservación *f*, reserva *f*; (*mental*) reserva *f*, (*in contract etc*) salvedad *f*, (*in argument*) distingo *m*; **with certain ~s** con ciertas reservas; **to accept sth without ~** aceptar algo sin reserva; **I had ~s about it** tenía ciertas dudas sobre ese punto.
(b) (*booking*) reservación *f*; (*seat*) plaza *f* reservada; (*in restaurant*) mesa *f* reservada; **to make a ~ in a hotel** reservar una habitación en un hotel.
(c) (*on road*) mediana *f*, franja *f* central.
(d) (*US*) reserva *f* (de pieles rojas).

reservation desk [ˌrezə'veɪʃən,desk] N (*Brit*) mostrador *m* de reservas, (*US: in hotels*) recepción *f*.

▼ **reserve** [rɪ'zɜːv] **1** N (a) (*of money etc*) reserva *f*; **to have sth in ~** tener algo de reserva; **to have a ~ of strength** tener una reserva de fuerzas; **there are untapped ~s of energy** hay reservas de energía que quedan sin explotar; **Spain possesses half the world's ~s of pyrites** España tiene la mitad de las reservas mundiales de piritas.
(b) (*Mil*) **the ~** la reserva.
(c) (*Sport etc*) suplente *mf*; **to play in** (*or* **with**) **the ~s** jugar en el segundo equipo.
(d) (*land*) reserva *f*; (*game*) coto *m* (de caza); (*nature*) reserva *f* natural.
(e) (*restriction*) **without ~** sin reserva.
(f) (*shyness*) reserva *f*.
2 ATTR: **~ currency** divisa *f* de reserva; **~ fund** fondo *m* de reserva; **~ gas tank** (*US*), **~ petrol tank** (*Brit*) depósito *m* de gasolina de reserva; **~ player** suplente *mf*; **~ price** (*Brit*) precio *m* mínimo (fijado en una subasta); **~ team** segundo equipo *m*.
▼ **3** VT (a) (*keep, book*) reservar; **that's being ~d for me** eso está reservado para mí; **I ~ the right to** + *infin* me reservo el derecho de + *infin*; **did you ~ the seats?** ¿has reservado las plazas?
(b) (*Jur*) aplazar, diferir; **the judge ~d sentence** el juez difirió la sentencia.
4 VR: **I'm reserving myself for later** me reservo para más tarde.

reserved [rɪ'zɜːvd] ADJ (*all senses*) reservado.

reservedly [rɪ'zɜːvɪdlɪ] ADV con reserva.

reservist [rɪ'zɜːvɪst] N reservista *mf*.

reservoir ['rezəvwɑːʳ] N (a) (*small*) depósito *m*, represa *f*; (*tank*) depósito *m*, cisterna *f*; (*large, for irrigation, hydroelectric power*) pantano

m, embalse *m*, represa *f* (*LAm*); **natural underground ~** embalse *m* subterráneo natural.
(b) (*fig: of strength etc*) reserva *f*.

reset ['riː'set] (*irr: V* set) **1** VT *machine etc* reajustar; (*Typ*) recomponer; (*Comput*) reinicializar; *bone* volver a encajar; *jewel* reengastar.
2 ATTR: **~ switch** conmutador *m* de reajuste.

resettle ['riː'setl] **1** VT *persons* restablecer, volver a establecer; *land* volver a colonizar, volver a poblar; **the lands were ~d by the Poles** las tierras fueron nuevamente colonizadas por los polacos.
2 VI restablecerse, volver a establecerse.

resettlement ['riː'setlmənt] N restablecimiento *m*; nueva colonización *f*, repoblación *f*.

reshape ['riː'ʃeɪp] VT reformar, formar de nuevo, rehacer; reorganizar.

reshuffle ['riː'ʃʌfl] **1** N (*Pol*) reconstrucción *f*, remodelación *f*, reajuste *m*.
2 VT *cards* volver a barajar; (*Pol*) reconstruir, remodelar, reajustar.

reside [rɪ'zaɪd] VI residir, vivir; **to ~ in** (*fig*) residir en.

residence ['rezɪdəns] **1** N (a) (*stay*) residencia *f*; (*stay, in official parlance*) permanencia *f*, estancia *f*; **after 6 months' ~** después de 6 meses de permanencia; **when the students are in ~** cuando están los estudiantes; **there is a doctor in ~** hay un médico interno; **to take up one's ~** establecerse.
(b) (*house*) residencia *f*, domicilio *m*; (*Univ: also* **hall of ~**) residencia *f*; **'town and country ~s for sale'** 'se ofrecen fincas urbanas y rurales'; **the minister's official ~** la residencia oficial del ministro.
2 ATTR: **~ permit** (*Brit*) permiso *m* de permanencia.

residency ['rezɪdənsɪ] N residencia *f*.

resident ['rezɪdənt] **1** ADJ (*gen, Comput*) residente; *population etc* fijo, permanente; *doctor etc* interno; *servant* permanente, que duerme en casa; *bird* no migratorio; **to be ~ in a town** residir en una ciudad, tener domicilio fijo en una ciudad; **we were ~ there for some years** residimos allí durante varios años.
2 N residente *mf*; vecino *m*, -a *f*; (*in hotel etc*) huésped *m*, -eda *f*; **~s' association** asociación *f* de vecinos; **the ~s got together to protest** los vecinos se reunieron para protestar.

residential [ˌrezɪ'denʃəl] ADJ residencial; **~ area** barrio *m* residencial.

residual [rɪ'zɪdjʊəl] **1** ADJ residual.
2 N: **~s** derechos *mpl* residuales de autor.

residuary [rɪ'zɪdjʊərɪ] ADJ restante, remanente, residual; **~ legatee** legatario *m*, -a *f* universal.

residue ['rezɪdjuː] N resto *m*, residuo *m*; (*Fin etc*) saldo *m*, superávit *m*; **a ~ of bad feeling** un residuo de rencor, un rencor que queda.

residuum [rɪ'zɪdjʊəm] N residuo *m*.

resign [rɪ'zaɪn] **1** VT *office etc* dimitir, renunciar a; *claim, task etc* renunciar a; **to ~ a task to others** ceder un cometido a otros; **when he ~ed the leadership** cuando dimitió la jefatura.
2 VI (a) dimitir; renunciar; **to ~ in favour of sb else** renunciar en favor de otro.
(b) (*Chess*) abandonar.
3 VR: **to ~ o.s.** resignarse; **to ~ o.s. to** resignarse a, conformarse con; **I ~ed myself to never seeing her again** me resigné a no volverla a ver jamás.

resignation [ˌrezɪg'neɪʃən] N (a) (*act*) dimisión *f* (*from* de), renuncia *f*; **to offer** (*or* **send in, submit, tender**) **one's ~** dimitir, presentar su dimisión.
(b) (*state*) resignación *f* (*to* a), conformidad *f* (*to* con); **to await sth with ~** esperar algo resignado, esperar algo con resignación.

resigned [rɪ'zaɪnd] ADJ resignado.

resignedly [rɪ'zaɪnɪdlɪ] ADV con resignación.

resilience [rɪ'zɪlɪəns] N elasticidad *f*, (*fig*) resistencia *f*; poder *m* de recuperación; flexibilidad *f*, capacidad *f* para adaptarse.

resilient [rɪ'zɪlɪənt] ADJ elástico; (*fig*) resistente; que tiene poder de recuperación; flexible, que tiene capacidad para adaptarse.

resin ['rezɪn] N resina *f*.

resinous ['rezɪnəs] ADJ resinoso.

resist [rɪ'zɪst] **1** VT resistir (a); oponerse a; oponer resistencia a; **to ~ arrest** resistirse a ser detenido, oponer resistencia a la policía; **to ~ temptation** resistir la tentación; **they ~ed the attack vigorously** resistieron vigorosamente el ataque; **we ~ this change** nos oponemos a este cambio; **I can't ~ squid** me apasionan los calamares; **I couldn't ~ buying it** no me resistí a comprarlo, no pude menos de comprarlo, me fue imposible dejar de comprarlo; **I can't ~ saying that ...** no resisto al impulso de decir que ...
2 VI resistirse, oponer resistencia.

resistance [rɪ'zɪstəns] **1** N (*all senses*) resistencia *f*; **the R~** (*Pol*) la Resistencia; **to offer ~** oponer resistencia (*to* a); **to have good ~ to disease** tener mucha resistencia a la enfermedad; **to take the line of least ~** seguir la línea de menor resistencia, optar por lo más fácil.
2 ATTR: **~ fighter, ~ worker** militante *mf* de la Resistencia; **~ movement** (movimiento *m* de) resistencia *f*.

resistant [rɪ'zɪstənt] ADJ resistente (*to* a).

resister ['rɪzɪstəʳ] N insumiso *m*, -a *f*.

resistible [rɪ'zɪstɪbl] ADJ resistible.
resistor [rɪ'zɪstəʳ] N resistor *m*.
resit (*Brit*) ① ['riːsɪt] N reválida *f*.
  ② ['riːˈsɪt] (*irr: V* **sit**) VT *exam* presentarse otra vez a; *subject* examinarse otra vez de.
  ③ ['riːsɪt] VI presentarse otra vez, volver a examinarse.
resold [ˌriːˈsəʊld] PRET, PTP *of* **resell**.
resole ['riːˈsəʊl] VT sobresolar, remontar.
resolute ['rezəluːt] ADJ resuelto.
resolutely ['rezəluːtlɪ] ADV resueltamente.
resoluteness ['rezəluːtnɪs] N resolución *f*.
resolution [ˌrezə'luːʃən] N (a) (*resoluteness*) resolución *f*; **to show ~** mostrarse resuelto.
  (b) (*separation, solving*) resolución *f*.
  (c) (*motion*) resolución *f*, proposición *f*; (*Parl*) acuerdo *m*; **to pass a ~** tomar un acuerdo; **to put a ~ to a meeting** someter una moción a votación.
  (d) (*resolve*) propósito *m*; **good ~s** buenos propósitos *mpl*; **to make a ~ to** + *infin* resolverse a + *infin*.
  (e) (*Comput*) resolución *f*, definición *f* (de la pantalla).
resolvable [rɪ'zɒlvəbl] ADJ soluble.
resolve [rɪ'zɒlv] ① N (a) (*resoluteness*) resolución *f*; **unshakeable ~** resolución *f* inquebrantable.
  (b) (*decision*) propósito *m*; **to make a ~ to** + *infin* resolverse a + *infin*.
  ② VT (*all senses*) resolver (*into* en); **this will ~ your doubts** esto ha de resolver sus dudas; **the problem is still not ~d** el problema queda por resolver; **it was ~d that ...** se acordó que ...
  ③ VI (a) (*separate*) resolverse (*into* en); **the question ~s into 4 parts** la cuestión se resuelve en 4 partes.
  (b) (*decide*) **to ~ on sth** optar por algo, resolverse por algo; **to ~ on** + *ger* acordar + *infin*; **to ~ to** + *infin* resolverse a + *infin*; **to ~ that ...** acordar que ...
resolved [rɪ'zɒlvd] ADJ resuelto; **to be ~ to** + *infin* estar resuelto a + *infin*.
resonance ['rezənəns] N resonancia *f*.
resonant ['rezənənt] ADJ resonante.
resonate ['rezəneɪt] VI resonar (*with* de).
resonator ['rezəneɪtəʳ] N resonador *m*.
resorption [rɪ'zɔːpʃən] N resorción *f*.
resort [rɪ'zɔːt] ① N (a) (*recourse*) recurso *m*; **as a last ~, in the last ~** en último caso; **without ~ to force** sin recurrir a la fuerza.
  (b) (*place*) punto *m* de reunión, lugar *m* de reunión; (*holiday ~*) punto *m* de veraneo; (*coastal, seaside*) playa *f*, punto *m* marítimo (de veraneo); **it is a ~ of thieves** es lugar frecuentado por los ladrones, es donde se reúnen los ladrones.
  ② VI: **to ~ to** (a) *place* frecuentar, concurrir a, acudir a.
  (b) (*have recourse to*) recurrir a; acudir a; hacer uso de; **to ~ to violence** recurrir a la violencia; **then they ~ed to throwing stones** pasaron luego a tirar piedras; **then you ~ to me for help** así que acudes a mí a pedir ayuda.
resound [rɪ'zaʊnd] VI resonar, retumbar; **the valley ~ed with shouts** resonaron los gritos por el valle; **the whole house ~s with laughter** resuenan las risas por toda la casa.
resounding [rɪ'zaʊndɪŋ] ADJ sonoro; (*fig*) *success etc* clamoroso, resonante; *failure* estrepitoso.
resoundingly [rɪ'zaʊndɪŋlɪ] ADV: **to defeat sb ~** obtener una victoria resonante sobre uno.
resource [rɪ'sɔːs] ① N (a) (*expedient*) recurso *m*, expediente *m*.
  (b) **~s** (*wealth, supplies etc*) recursos *mpl*; **financial ~s** recursos *mpl* financieros; **natural ~s** recursos *mpl* naturales; **to be at the end of one's ~s** haber agotado sus recursos; **he has great ~s of energy** tiene una gran reserva de energía; **those ~s are as yet untapped** esos recursos quedan todavía sin explotar.
  (c) (*resourcefulness*) inventiva *f*.
  ② VT proveer fondos para, financiar; **we are ~d by X** nuestra fuente de fondos es X; **they are generously ~d** su fuente de fondos los trata generosamente; **an inadequately ~d project** un proyecto insuficientemente financiado.
resourceful [rɪ'sɔːsfʊl] ADJ inventivo, ingenioso.
resourcefully [rɪ'sɔːsfəlɪ] ADV ingeniosamente, mostrando tener inventiva.
resourcefulness [rɪ'sɔːsfʊlnɪs] N inventiva *f*, iniciativa *f*, ingeniosidad *f*.
re-sow [ˌriːˈsəʊ] VT resembrar, volver a sembrar.
re-sowing [ˌriːˈsəʊɪŋ] N resembrado *m*.
respect [rɪs'pekt] ① N (a) (*relation*) respecto *m*; **in every ~** desde todos los puntos de vista; **in many ~s** desde muchos puntos de vista; en cierto modo; **in one ~** desde un punto de vista; bajo uno de los aspectos; **in other ~s** por lo demás; **in some ~s** desde varios puntos de vista; **in this ~** por lo que se refiere a esto; en cuanto a esto; **in ~ of** respecto a, respecto de; **with ~ to** con respecto a.

  (b) (*frm*) **without ~ of persons** sin acepción de personas.
  (c) (*consideration*) respeto *m*, consideración *f*; **~ for one's parents** respeto *m* a sus padres; **~ for the truth** respeto *m* por la verdad; **out of ~ for sb** por consideración a uno; **with all ~ to you** sin menoscabo del respeto que se le debe a Vd; **with all due ~** con el respeto debido; **if I may say so with ~** si puedo decirlo con el mayor respeto; **worthy of ~** digno de respeto, respetable; **to command ~** imponer respeto, hacerse respetar; **to have ~ for sb, to hold sb in ~** tener respeto a uno, respetar a uno; **we have the greatest ~ for him** le respetamos muchísimo; **to pay ~ to sb** respetar a uno; **to pay one's last ~s to sb** hacer honor al muerto, acompañar por última vez a uno; (*in official ceremony*) rendir el último homenaje a uno; **to show no ~ to sb** faltar al respeto debido a uno; **he shows scant ~ for our opinions** poco respeta nuestras opiniones; **to treat sb with ~** tratar a uno respetuosamente; **to win sb's ~** ganarse el respeto de uno.
  (d) (*in messages*) **~s** recuerdos *mpl*, saludos *mpl*; **to pay one's ~s to sb** cumplimentar a uno, presentar sus respetos a uno; **to send one's ~s to sb** mandar recuerdos a uno.
  ② VT respetar; acatar; **to ~ sb's opinions** respetar las opiniones de uno; **to ~ sb's wishes** atenerse a los deseos de uno; **to make o.s. ~ed** hacerse respetar.
respectability [rɪsˌpektə'bɪlɪtɪ] N respetabilidad *f*.
respectable [rɪs'pektəbl] ADJ (a) (*deserving respect*) respetable; **for perfectly ~ reasons** por motivos perfectamente respetables.
  (b) (*of fair social standing, decent*) respetable, decente, honrado; **~ people** gente *f* bien; **in ~ society** en la buena sociedad, entre personas educadas; **that's not ~** eso no se hace, eso no es decente, eso es de mala educación; **that skirt isn't ~** esa falda no es decente.
  (c) *amount etc* respetable; apreciable, importante; **at a ~ distance** a respetable distancia; a distancia prudencial; **she lost a ~ sum** perdió una cantidad importante.
  (d) (*passable*) pasable, tolerable; **we made a ~ showing** lo hicimos pasablemente; **his work is ~ but not brilliant** su obra es pasable pero no brillante.
respectably [rɪs'pektəblɪ] ADV (a) (*decently*) respetablemente; decentemente. (b) (*passably*) pasablemente.
respected [rɪs'pektɪd] ADJ respetado, estimado; **a much ~ person** una persona muy respetada.
respecter [rɪs'pektəʳ] N: **to be no ~ of persons** no ser aceptador de personas.
respectful [rɪs'pektfʊl] ADJ respetuoso.
respectfully [rɪs'pektfəlɪ] ADV respetuosamente; **Yours ~** le saluda respetuosamente.
respectfulness [rɪs'pektfʊlnɪs] N respetuosidad *f*, acatamiento *m*.
respecting [rɪs'pektɪŋ] PREP (con) respecto a; en cuanto a; por lo que se refiere a.
respective [rɪs'pektɪv] ADJ respectivo.
respectively [rɪs'pektɪvlɪ] ADV respectivamente.
respiration [ˌrespɪ'reɪʃən] N respiración *f*.
respirator ['respɪreɪtəʳ] N (*Mil etc*) careta *f* antigás; (*Med*) resucitador *m*.
respiratory [rɪs'paɪərətərɪ] ADJ respiratorio; **~ tract** vías *fpl* respiratorias.
respire [rɪs'paɪəʳ] VTI respirar.
respite ['respaɪt] N respiro *m*, respiradero *m*; (*Jur*) plazo *m*, prórroga *f*; **without ~** sin tregua, sin respirar; **to get no ~** no tener alivio, no poder descansar; **we got no ~ from the heat** el calor apenas nos dejó respirar; **they gave us no ~** nos hicieron trabajar (*etc*) sin tregua, no nos dejaron respirar.
resplendence [rɪs'plendəns] N resplandor *m*, refulgencia *f*.
resplendent [rɪs'plendənt] ADJ resplandeciente, refulgente; **to be ~** resplandecer, refulgir; **to be ~ in a new dress** lucir un nuevo vestido; **the car is ~ in green** luce el coche su pintura verde.
respond [rɪs'pɒnd] VI (a) (*answer*) responder. (b) (*be responsive*) reaccionar, ser sensible (*to* a); atender (*to* a); **it ~s to sunlight** reacciona a la luz solar, es sensible a la luz solar; **it is ~ing to treatment** responde al tratamiento; **the cat ~s to kindness** el gato es sensible a los buenos tratos.
respondent [rɪs'pɒndənt] N (*Jur*) demandado *m*, -a *f*, acusado *m*, -a *f*; (*to questionnaire*) persona *f* que responde.
response [rɪs'pɒns] N (a) (*answer*) respuesta *f*; (*Eccl*) responsorio *m*; **~ time** tiempo *m* de respuesta; **his only ~ was to yawn** por toda respuesta dio un bostezo. (b) (*reaction*) reacción *f*, correspondencia *f* (*to* a); (*to charity appeal*) acogida *f*; **in ~ to many requests ...** accediendo a muchos ruegos ...; **the ~ was not favourable** la reacción no fue favorable; **we got a 73% ~** respondió el 73 por cien; **we had hoped for a bigger ~** habíamos esperado más correspondencia; **it found no ~** no tuvo correspondencia alguna, no encontró eco alguno; **it met with a generous ~** tuvo una generosa acogida.

▼ **responsibility** [rɪsˌpɒnsə'bɪlɪtɪ] ① N (a) (*liability*) responsabilidad *f* (*for* de); **joint ~** responsabilidad *f* solidaria; **on one's own ~** bajo su propia responsabilidad; **to accept ~ for sth** hacerse responsable de algo; **that's his ~** eso le incumbe a él, eso le toca a él; **it is my ~ to decide** me toca a mí decidir; **to claim ~ for an outrage** reivindicar un atentado, responsabilizarse de un atentado.

(b) (*sense of ~*) seriedad *f*; formalidad *f*; **try to show some ~** procure tener un poco de seriedad.

2 ATTR: **~ payment** (*Brit Scol*) *prima de responsabilidad basada en el número de alumnos a su cargo*.

▼ **responsible** [rɪs'pɒnsəbl] ADJ **(a)** (*liable*) responsable (*for* de); **to be ~ to sb for sth** ser responsable ante uno de algo; **those ~ will be punished** se castigará a las personas responsables; **who was ~ for the delay?** ¿a quién se debe el retraso?; **the fog was not ~ this time** no se puede culpar a la niebla esta vez; **she is ~ for 40 children** tiene a su cargo 40 niños; **the committee is ~ to the council** la comisión depende del consejo; **he is not ~ for his actions** no es responsable de sus actos; **to hold sb ~ for an accident** echar a uno la culpa de un accidente, hacer a uno responsable de un accidente; **to make o.s. ~** responsabilizarse, tomar sobre sí la responsabilidad.

(b) (*of character*) serio, formal; **he is a fully ~ person** es una persona de toda formalidad; **to act in a ~ fashion** obrar con seriedad.

(c) *post etc* de confianza, de gran responsabilidad, de autoridad.

responsibly [rɪs'pɒnsəblɪ] ADV: **to act ~** obrar con seriedad, obrar con formalidad.

responsive [rɪs'pɒnsɪv] ADJ *audience etc* que reacciona con entusiasmo (*or* interés *etc*); **he was not very ~** apenas dio indicio de interés, apenas parecía interesarle la cosa; **to be ~ to sth** ser sensible a algo.

responsiveness [rɪs'pɒnsɪvnɪs] N interés *m*; sensibilidad *f* (*to* a); grado *m* de reacción.

respray ['riː'spreɪ] **1** VT *car* volver a pintar (a pistola).

2 ['riː'spreɪ] N: **the car needs a ~** el coche necesita que lo pinten.

rest[1] [rest] **1** N **(a)** (*repose*) descanso *m*, reposo *m*; (*fig*) paz *f*; **day of ~** día *m* de descanso, asueto *m*, (*as calendar item*) día *m* festivo; **to be at ~** estar en reposo, descansar; (*of insect etc*) estar posado; (*of the dead*) estar en paz; **to come to ~** (*vehicle*) pararse, detenerse, (*machine*) pararse, (*insect etc*) posarse; **give it a ~!*** ¡déjalo!, ¡no machaques!; **give the piano a ~!*** ¡deja el piano!; **to go to (one's) ~** ir a acostarse; **to have a 10-minute ~** descansar durante 10 minutos; **to have a good night's ~** dormir bien, pasar una buena noche; **to lay sb to ~** enterrar a uno; **this puts that theory to ~** esto permite enterrar esa teoría; **to set sb's mind at ~** tranquilizar a uno; **to take a ~** descansar, descansar un rato.

(b) (*Mus*) silencio *m*, pausa *f*.

(c) (*support*) apoyo *m*, soporte *m*; (*base*) base *f*; (*Telec*) horquilla *f*; (*for lance etc*) ristre *m*.

2 ATTR: **~ area, ~ stop** (*US Aut*) apartadero *m*; **~ camp** campamento *m* de reposo; **~ cure** cura *f* de reposo; **~ day** día *m* de descanso; **~ home** casa *f* de reposo; asilo *m* (de ancianos), residencia *f* para jubilados.

3 VT **(a)** (*give ~ to*) descansar; dejar descansar; **to ~ one's men** dejar descansar a sus hombres; **horses have to be ~ed** hay que dejar descansar a los caballos; **I feel very ~ed** he descansado mucho; me encuentro mejor con el descanso; **these colours ~ your eyes** estos colores descansan la vista; **God ~ his soul!** ¡Dios le acoja en su seno!; **to ~ one's case** (*Jur*) terminar la presentación de su alegato.

(b) (*support*) descansar, apoyar (*against* contra, *on* sobre); **~ your head on the pillow** apoya la cabeza en la almohada; **~ the ladder against the tree** apoya la escalera contra el árbol; **she ~ed her eyes on the picture** clavó la vista en el cuadro.

4 VI **(a)** (*repose*) descansar (*from* de), reposar; (*stop*) detenerse, pararse; (*Theat: euph*) no tener trabajo, estar sin trabajo; **where my caravan has ~ed** donde se ha detenido mi caravana; **he never ~s** no descansa nunca; **the waves never ~** las olas no descansan nunca; **may he ~ in peace** descanse en paz; **we shall never ~ until it is settled** no nos tranquilizaremos hasta que se arregle el asunto; **let us not ~ until he is avenged** no descansemos hasta vengarle.

(b) (*lean, be supported*) **to ~ on** (*perch*) posar en, posarse en; (*be supported*) descansar sobre, apoyarse en; (*fig*) estribar en, estar basado en; **her arm ~ed on my chair** su brazo estaba apoyado en mi silla; **her head ~ed on her hand** su cabeza se apoyaba en la mano; **the case ~s on the following facts** la teoría está basada en los siguientes datos; **his eye ~ed on me** su mirada se clavó en mí, clavó su mirada en mí; **a heavy responsibility ~s on him** pesa sobre él una grave responsabilidad.

(c) (*remain*) quedar; **and there the matter ~s** así que ahí queda el asunto; **we cannot let the matter ~ there** no podemos permitir que las cosas sigan en ese punto, no podemos dejar ahí el asunto; **please ~ assured that ...** tenga la seguridad de que ...; **to ~ with** depender de; residir en; **it does not ~ with me** no depende de mí; **the authority ~s with him** la autoridad reside en él.

◆ **rest up*** VI tomar un descanso.

rest[2] [rest] N resto *m*; **the ~** el resto, lo demás, los demás (*etc*); she

was a deb and all the **~ of it*** era debutante y todo lo demás; **for the ~** por lo demás; **the ~ stayed outside** los demás quedaron fuera; **what shall we give the ~ of them?** ¿qué daremos a los otros?; **the ~ of them couldn't care less** a los otros les trae sin cuidado; **the ~ of the soldiers** los otros soldados, los demás soldados.

restart ['riː'stɑːt] **1** VT empezar de nuevo, volver a empezar; reanudar; (*engine*) volver a arrancar.

2 VI empezar de nuevo, reempezar; reanudarse.

restate ['riː'steɪt] VT repetir, reafirmar; *case* volver a exponer; *problem* volver a plantear.

restatement ['riː'steɪtmənt] N repetición *f*, reafirmación *f*; nueva exposición *f*; nuevo planteamiento *m*.

restaurant ['restərɒŋ] N restaurante *m*, restorán *m*.

restaurant car ['restərɒŋ,kɑː[r]] N (*Brit*) coche-comedor *m*.

restaurateur [,restərə'tɜː[r]] N propietario *m* de un restaurante, restaurador *m*, restorador *m*.

restful ['restfʊl] ADJ descansado, reposado, sosegado.

restfully ['restfəlɪ] ADV reposadamente, sosegadamente.

resting-place ['restɪŋpleɪs] N (*also* last ~) última morada *f*.

restitution [,restɪ'tjuːʃən] N restitución *f*; **to make ~ for sth** indemnizar a uno por algo.

restive ['restɪv] ADJ inquieto, intranquilo; *horse* repropio; **to get ~** agitarse, impacientarse, (*horse*) ponerse repropio.

restiveness ['restɪvnɪs] N inquietud *f*, intranquilidad *f*; agitación *f*, impaciencia *f*.

restless ['restlɪs] ADJ inquieto, intranquilo, desasosegado; descontentadizo; (*sleepless*) insomne, desvelado; (*Pol etc*) turbulento; (*roving*) andariego; **the poet's ~ genius** el genio inquieto del poeta; **he's the ~ sort** es un tipo inquieto*, (*pej*) es un culo de mal asiento*; **he is ~ to be gone** se impacienta por partir; **he's been ~ in the job** no ha estado contento en el puesto; **the spectators were getting ~** los espectadores se estaban impacientando; **the unions are getting ~** se están agitando los sindicatos; **I had a ~ night** pasé una mala noche, pasé una noche agitada.

restlessly ['restlɪslɪ] ADV inquietamente, desasosegadamente; turbulentamente; **she moved ~ in her sleep** se movió inquieta mientras dormía.

restlessness ['restlɪsnɪs] N inquietud *f*, intranquilidad *f*, desasosiego *m*; agitación *f*, impaciencia *f*; descontento *m*; insomnio *m*, desvelo *m*; turbulencia *f*; lo andariego; **there is much ~ in the provinces** existe gran descontento en las provincias.

restock ['riː'stɒk] VT *larder etc* reaprovisionar, repostar; *pond etc* repoblar (*with* de); **we ~ed with Brand X** renovamos las existencias de Marca X.

restoration [,restə'reɪʃən] N restauración *f*; devolución *f*; restablecimiento *m*; **the R~** (*Brit Hist*) la Restauración (*de la monarquía inglesa en 1660*).

restorative [rɪs'tɔːrətɪv] **1** ADJ reconstituyente, regenerador, fortalecedor.

2 N reconstituyente *m*.

restore [rɪs'tɔː[r]] VT **(a)** (*return*) *object to owner etc* devolver (*to* a); *strength etc* restablecer; *law, tax* reimponer, volver a imponer; **to ~ sth to sb** devolver algo a uno; **to ~ sth to its place** devolver algo a su lugar; **to ~ sb to health** devolver la salud a uno; **to ~ sb to liberty** devolver la libertad a uno; **to ~ sb's sight** devolver la vista a uno; **to ~ sb's strength** restaurar las fuerzas a uno, reconstituir las fuerzas de uno; **to ~ the value of the pound** restablecer el valor de la libra; **they ~d the king to his throne** volvieron a poner al rey sobre su trono; **order was soon ~d** pronto se restableció el orden, se volvió pronto a la normalidad.

(b) *building, painting etc* restaurar.

restorer [rɪs'tɔːrə[r]] N **(a)** (*Art etc*) restaurador *m*, -ora *f*. **(b)** (*hair ~*) loción *f* capilar, regenerador *m* del cabello.

restrain [rɪs'treɪn] **1** VT contener, refrenar, reprimir; moderar; tener a raya; **to ~ sb from** + *ger* disuadir a uno de + *infin*, (*physically etc*) impedir a uno + *infin*; **kindly ~ your friend** haga el favor de refrenar a su amigo; **I managed to ~ my anger** logré contener mi enojo.

2 VR: **to ~ o.s.** contenerse, dominarse; **but I ~ed myself** pero me contuve, pero me dominé; **please ~ yourself!** ¡por favor, cálmese!; **to ~ o.s. from** + *ger* dominarse para que no + *subj*.

restrained [rɪs'treɪnd] ADJ moderado, comedido; *style etc* refrenado, moderado; **he was very ~ about it** estuvo muy comedido.

restraining order [rɪs'treɪnɪŋ,ɔːdə[r]] N (*Jur*) interdicto *m*.

restraint [rɪs'treɪnt] N **(a)** (*check, control*) freno *m*, control *m*; restricción *f*, limitación *f*; (*on wages etc*) moderación *f*; **a ~ on trade** una restricción del comercio, (*on free enterprise*) una limitación de la libre competencia; **without ~** sin restricción, libremente; **to be under a ~** estar cohibido; **to fret under a ~** impacientarse por una restricción; **to put sb under a ~** refrenar a uno; (*Jur*) imponer una restricción legal a uno.

(b) (*constraint*) (*of manner*) reserva *f*, (*of character*) moderación *f*, comedimiento *m*; (*self-control*) dominio *m* de sí mismo, autodominio *m*; **to cast aside all ~** abandonar toda moderación, abandonar toda reserva; **he showed great ~** mostró poseer gran autodominio, se mostró muy comedido.

restrict [rɪs'trɪkt] ① VT restringir, limitar (*to* a).

② VR: **I ~ myself to the facts** me limito a exponer los hechos; **nowadays I ~ myself to a litre a day** hoy día me limito a beber un litro diario.

restricted [rɪs'trɪktɪd] ADJ (*small*) *area, circulation etc* reducido; *distribution etc* restringido; *horizon* limitado; (*prohibited*) prohibido; (*Mil*) **~ area** zona *f* prohibida; **~ document** documento *m* de circulación restringida; **~ market** mercado *m* restringido; **he has rather a ~ outlook** tiene miras más bien estrechas; **the plant is ~ to Andalusia** la planta está restringida a Andalucía; **his output is ~ to novels** su producción consiste únicamente en novelas.

restriction [rɪs'trɪkʃən] N restricción *f*, limitación *f*; **without ~ as to ...** sin restricción de ...; **to place ~ on the sale of a drug** restringir la venta de una droga; **to place ~s on sb's liberty** restringir la libertad de uno.

restrictive [rɪs'trɪktɪv] ADJ restrictivo; **~ practices** normas *fpl* restrictivas, prácticas *fpl* restrictivas.

re-string [,riː'strɪŋ] (*irr*: PRET, PTP **re-strung**) VT *pearls, necklace* ensartar de nuevo; *violin, racket* poner nuevas cuerdas a; *bow* poner una nueva cuerda a.

rest room ['restrʊm] N cuarto *m* de descanso; (*US euph*) aseos *mpl*, sanitarios *mpl* (*LAm*); *ver también* [TOILET].

restructure [,riː'strʌktʃər] VT reestructurar; (*Econ etc*) sanear.

restructuring [,riː'strʌktʃərɪŋ] N reestructuración *f*; saneamiento *m*.

restyle [,riː'staɪl] VT *car etc* remodelar.

restyling [,riː'staɪlɪŋ] N remodelación *f*.

▼ **result** [rɪ'zʌlt] ① N resultado *m*; **~s** (*of election, exam etc*) resultados *mpl*; **as a ~** por consiguiente; **as a ~ of** de resultas de, a consecuencia de; **as a ~ of a misunderstanding** debido a un malentendido; **in the ~** finalmente; **with the ~ that ...** resultando que ..., con la consecuencia de que ...; **without ~** sin resultado; **the ~ is that ...** el resultado es que ...; **what will be the ~ of it all?** ¿en qué va a parar todo esto?

② ATTR: **~s bonus** bonificación *f* según resultados.

▼ ③ VI: **to ~ from** resultar de; **to ~ in** producir, motivar, terminar en, dar por resultado, dar como resultado; traducirse en; acarrear; **it ~ed in his death** causó su muerte, condujo a su muerte; **it ~ed in a large increase** produjo un aumento apreciable; **it didn't ~ in anything useful** no produjo nada útil, no dio ningún resultado útil.

resultant [rɪ'zʌltənt] ADJ consiguiente, resultante.

resume [rɪ'zjuːm] ① VT (a) (*continue*) reanudar, continuar; *office etc* reasumir; **to ~ one's seat** volver a sentarse; **to ~ one's work** reanudar su trabajo; **'Now then', he ~d** 'Ahora bien', dijo reanudando la conversación (*or* su discurso *etc*).

(b) (*summarize*) resumir.

② VI continuar; comenzar de nuevo.

résumé ['reɪzjuːmeɪ] N resumen *m*; (*US*) currículum *m* (vitae).

resumption [rɪ'zʌmpʃən] N reanudación *f*, continuación *f*; reasunción *f*; **on the ~ of the sitting** al reanudarse la sesión.

resurface ['riː'sɜːfɪs] ① VT poner nueva superficie a; volver a allanar; *road* rehacer el firme de.

② VI (*submarine*) volver a emerger, volver a salir a la superficie; (*person*) reaparecer, presentarse de nuevo.

resurgence [rɪ'sɜːdʒəns] N resurgimiento *m*.

resurgent [rɪ'sɜːdʒənt] ADJ resurgente, renaciente, que está en trance de renacer.

resurrect [,rezə'rekt] VT resucitar.

resurrection [,rezə'rekʃən] N resurrección *f*.

resuscitate [rɪ'sʌsɪteɪt] VTI resucitar.

resuscitation [rɪ,sʌsɪ'teɪʃən] N resucitación *f*.

resuscitator [rɪ'sʌsɪteɪtər] N resucitador *m*.

ret. ABBR of **retired** jubilado, (*Mil*) retirado.

retail ['riːteɪl] ① N venta *f* al por menor, venta *f* al detalle.

② ATTR: **~ business** comercio *m* (*or* negocio *m*) al por menor (*or* al detalle); **~ dealer, ~ trader** comerciante *mf* al por menor, detallista *mf*; **~ outlet** punto *m* de venta al por menor (*or* al detalle); **~ park** zona de hipermercados; **~ price** precio *m* al por menor, precio *m* al detalle; **~ price index** índice *m* de precios al consumo (*or* al por menor); **~ sales** ventas *fpl* al detalle; **~ trade** comercio *m* al por menor, comercio *m* detallista, comercio *m* menorista (*LAm*).

③ ADV: **to sell sth ~** vender algo al por menor, vender algo al detalle.

④ VT (a) (*Comm*) vender al por menor, vender al detalle.

(b) [rɪ'teɪl] *gossip* repetir, *story* contar.

⑤ VI venderse al por menor (*at* a).

retailer ['riːteɪlər] N comerciante *mf* al por menor, detallista *mf*, menorista *mf* (*LAm*).

retain [rɪ'teɪn] VT (a) (*keep*) retener, conservar; (*keep in one's possession*) guardar, quedarse con; (*in memory*) retener; **~ed earnings, ~ed profit** beneficios *mpl* retenidos; **the sponge ~s the water** la esponja retiene el agua; **it ~s sth of its past glories** conserva una parte de sus viejas glorias; **the customer ~s that part** el cliente se queda con esa porción.

(b) (*sign up*) *lawyer* ajustar; *player* contratar, fichar.

retainer [rɪ'teɪnər] N (a) (*follower*) secuaz *m*; adherente *m*, partidario *m*, -a *f*; (*servant*) criado *m*; **family ~, old ~** viejo criado *m* (que lleva muchos años sirviendo en la misma familia).

(b) (*Jur*) anticipo *m* (sobre los honorarios); (*on flat etc*) depósito *m*, señal *f* (para que se guarde el piso *etc*).

retake ① ['riːteɪk] N (*Cine*) repetición *f*, nueva toma *f*.

② [,riː'teɪk] (*irr*: V **take**) VT (a) (*Mil*) volver a tomar, reconquistar. (b) (*Cine*) repetir, volver a tomar. (c) *exam* presentarse segunda vez a; *subject* examinarse otra vez de.

retaliate [rɪ'tælɪeɪt] VI desquitarse, tomar represalias, tomar su revancha; **to ~ by** + *ger* vengarse + *ger*; **to ~ on sb** tomar represalias contra uno; vengarse de uno.

retaliation [rɪ,tælɪ'eɪʃən] N desquite *m*, represalias *fpl*, revancha *f*; venganza *f*; **by way of ~, in ~** en revancha, para desquitarse, para vengarse.

retaliatory [rɪ'tælɪətərɪ] ADJ: **~ raid** ataque *m* vengativo, ataque *m* de desquite; **to take ~ measures** tomar medidas para desquitarse, tomar represalias.

retard [rɪ'tɑːd] VT retardar, retrasar.

retarded [rɪ'tɑːdɪd] ① ADJ retardado, retrasado.

② NPL: **the ~** los retrasados (mentales).

retch [retʃ] VI vomitar; esforzarse por vomitar; darle a uno arcadas.

retching ['retʃɪŋ] N esfuerzo *m* por vomitar; náusea *f*, bascas *fpl*.

retd ABBR of **retired** jubilado, (*Mil*) retirado.

retell ['riː'tel] (*irr*: V **tell**) VT volver a contar.

retention [rɪ'tenʃən] N retención *f* (*also Med*); conservación *f*.

retentive [rɪ'tentɪv] ADJ retentivo.

retentiveness [rɪ'tentɪvnɪs] N retentiva *f*, poder *m* de retención.

rethink ['riː'θɪŋk] ① N: **to have a ~** volver a pensarlo.

② (*irr*: V **think**) VT repensar, volver a pensar; reformular.

reticence ['retɪsəns] N reticencia *f*, reserva *f*.

reticent ['retɪsənt] ADJ reticente, reservado; **he has been very ~ about it** no ha querido decirnos nada acerca de ello, ha tratado el asunto con la mayor reserva.

reticently ['retɪsəntlɪ] ADV con reserva.

reticle ['retɪkl] N retículo *m*.

reticulate [rɪ'tɪkjʊlɪt] ADJ, **reticulated** [rɪ'tɪkjʊleɪtɪd] ADJ reticular.

reticule ['retɪkjuːl] N (a) (*Opt etc*) retículo *m*. (b) (*Hist: bag*) ridículo *m*.

retina ['retɪnə] N retina *f*.

retinue ['retɪnjuː] N séquito *m*, comitiva *f*.

retire [rɪ'taɪər] ① VT jubilar; **he was compulsorily ~d** le obligaron a jubilarse.

② VI (a) (*withdraw*) retirarse (*also Mil*); **to ~ to bed, to ~ for the night** ir a dormir, ir a acostarse, recogerse; **to ~ from the world** retirarse del mundo; **to ~ into o.s.** encerrarse en sus pensamientos, huir del mundo exterior.

(b) (*of age limit*) jubilarse; (*Mil*) retirarse; **to ~ from business** dejar los negocios; **to ~ from a post** dimitir un cargo, renunciar a un puesto; **to ~ on a pension** jubilarse; **they ~d to the countryside** se jubiló él (*or* ella) y fueron a vivir en el campo.

(c) (*Sport*) abandonar; **he had to ~ in the 5th lap** tuvo que abandonar en la 5ª vuelta.

retired [rɪ'taɪəd] ADJ jubilado, (*esp Mil*) retirado; **a ~ person** un jubilado, una jubilada; **to place sb on the ~ list** dar el retiro a uno.

retiree [rɪ'taɪə,riː] N (*US*) jubilado *m*, -a *f*.

retirement [rɪ'taɪəmənt] ① N (a) (*state of being retired*) retiro *m*; **to live in ~** vivir en el retiro; **to spend one's ~ growing roses** ocuparse después de la jubilación cultivando rosas; **how will you spend your ~?** ¿qué piensa hacer después de jubilarse?

(b) (*act of retiring*) jubilación *f*; (*esp Mil*) retiro *m*.

(c) (*Mil: withdrawal*) retirada *f*.

② ATTR: **~ age** edad *f* de jubilación, (*Mil*) edad *f* de retiro; **~ benefit** prestaciones *fpl* por jubilación; **~ pay, ~ pension** jubilación *f*, (*Mil*) retiro *m*.

retiring [rɪ'taɪərɪŋ] ADJ (a) *member etc* saliente, dimitente; *age, pay etc* de jubilación, (*Mil*) de retiro; **the ~ members of staff** los miembros que se jubilan.

(b) *character* reservado, retraído, modesto.

retook [,riː'tʊk] PRET of **retake**.

retort [rɪ'tɔːt] ① N (a) (*answer*) réplica *f*. (b) (*Chem*) retorta *f*.

② VT *insult etc* devolver; **he ~ed that ...** replicó que ...

retouch ['riː'tʌtʃ] VT retocar.

retrace [riː'treɪs] VT volver a trazar; (*in memory*) recordar, ir recordando, rememorar; *sb's journey etc* seguir las huellas de; **to ~ one's steps** desandar lo andado, volver sobre los pasos.

retract [rɪ'trækt] ① VT retractar, retirar; (*draw in*) retraer, encoger;

undercarriage etc replegar.
[2] VI retractarse; (*be drawn in*) retraerse; (*undercarriage etc*) replegarse; **he refuses to ~** se niega a retractarse.
retractable [rɪ'træktəbl] ADJ retractable; (*Aer etc*) replegable, retráctil.
retraction [rɪ'trækʃən] N retractación *f*, retracción *f*.
retrain ['riː'treɪn] VT *workers* recapacitar, reciclar, reeducar.
retraining ['riː'treɪnɪŋ] N recapacitación *f*, reciclaje *m*, reeducación *f* profesional.
retransmit ['riː'trænzmɪt] VT retransmitir.
retread (*Brit*) [1] ['riː'tred] N recauchutado *m*, reencauchado *m* (*CAm*).
[2] ['riː'tred] VT *tyre* recauchutar, reencauchar (*CAm*).
re-tread [ˌriː'tred] VT *path etc* volver a pisar.
retreat [rɪ'triːt] [1] N (a) (*place*) retiro *m*; refugio *m*, asilo *m*; (*state*) retraimiento *m*, apartamiento *m*.
(b) (*Mil*) retirada *f*; (*fig*) vuelta *f* atrás, marcha *f* hacia atrás; **the ~ from Mons** la retirada de Mons; **to beat the ~** dar el toque de retreta; **to beat a ~** retirarse, batirse en retirada; (*fig*) emprender la retirada; **to beat a hasty ~** retirarse precipitadamente; **the government is in ~ on this issue** en este asunto el gobierno se está echando atrás; **this represents a ~ from his promise** con esto se está volviendo atrás de su promesa; **to be in full ~** retirarse en masa, retirarse en todo el frente.
(c) (*Eccl: house*) retiro *m*; casa *f* de ejercicios; (*act*) ejercicios *mpl*.
[2] VI retirarse, batirse en retirada; **they ~ed to Dunkirk** se retiraron a Dunquerque; **the waters are ~ing** las aguas están bajando.
retrench [rɪ'trentʃ] [1] VT reducir, cercenar.
[2] VI economizar, hacer economías.
retrenchment [rɪ'trentʃmənt] N reducción *f*, cercenadura *f*; economías *fpl*.
retrial ['riː'traɪəl] N (*of person*) nuevo proceso *m*; (*of case*) revisión *f*.
retribution [ˌretrɪ'bjuːʃən] N justo castigo *m*, pena *f* merecida; desquite *m*.
retributive [rɪ'trɪbjʊtɪv] ADJ castigador, de castigo.
retrievable [rɪ'triːvəbl] ADJ recuperable; *error etc* reparable.
retrieval [rɪ'triːvəl] N recuperación *f*; (*Hunting*) cobra *f*; reparación *f*; subsanación *f*; rescate *m*; (*Comput*) recuperación *f*.
retrieve [rɪ'triːv] VT (*recover*) cobrar, recobrar, recuperar; (*Hunting*) cobrar; *information, loss* recuperar; *fortunes* reparar; *error* reparar, subsanar; **to ~ sth from the water** rescatar algo del agua; **she ~d her handkerchief** recogió su pañuelo, volvió a tomar su pañuelo; **we shall ~ nothing from this disaster** no salvaremos nada de esta catástrofe.
retriever [rɪ'triːvəʳ] N perro *m* cobrador, perdiguero *m*.
retro ['retrəʊ] ADJ *fashion, music* retro.
retro... ['retrəʊ] PREF retro...
retroactive [ˌretrəʊ'æktɪv] ADJ retroactivo.
retroflex ['retrəʊfleks] ADJ vuelto hacia atrás.
retrograde ['retrəʊgreɪd] ADJ retrógrado; **a ~ step** un paso hacia atrás, una medida reaccionaria.
retrogress [ˌretrəʊ'gres] VI retroceder; (*fig*) empeorar, degenerar, decaer.
retrogression [ˌretrəʊ'greʃən] N retroceso *m*, retrogradación *f*.
retrogressive [ˌretrəʊ'gresɪv] ADJ retrógrado.
retrorocket ['retrəʊ'rɒkɪt] N retrocohete *m*.
retrospect ['retrəʊspekt] N retrospección *f*, mirada *f* retrospectiva; **in ~** retrospectivamente; mirando hacia atrás, volviendo a considerar el pasado; **in ~ it seems a happy time** visto desde esta altura parece haber sido un período feliz.
retrospection [ˌretrəʊ'spekʃən] N retrospección *f*, consideración *f* del pasado.
retrospective [ˌretrəʊ'spektɪv] [1] ADJ retrospectivo; *law etc* retroactivo, de efecto retroactivo.
[2] N (*Art*) (exposición *f*) retrospectiva *f*.
retrospectively [ˌretrəʊ'spektɪvlɪ] ADV retrospectivamente; de modo retroactivo.
retroussé [rə'truːseɪ] ADJ: **~ nose** nariz *f* respingona.
retrovirus ['retrəʊˌvaɪrəs] N retrovirus *m*.
retry ['riː'traɪ] VT *person* procesar de nuevo, volver a procesar; *case* rever.
retune [ˌriː'tjuːn] VT afinar de nuevo.
▼ **return** [rɪ'tɜːn] [1] N (a) (*going back*) vuelta *f*, regreso *m*; (*Med etc*) reaparición *f*; **the ~ home** la vuelta a casa; **the ~ to school** la vuelta al colegio; **the ~ of King Kong** la vuelta de King Kong; **his ~ to his old habits** su vuelta a sus costumbres de antes; **by ~ (of post), by ~ mail** (*US*) a vuelta de correo; **on my ~** a mi regreso, a la vuelta; **many happy ~s (of the day)!** ¡feliz cumpleaños!, ¡felicidades!
(b) (*Comm*) ganancia *f*, retorno *m*; ingresos *mpl*; (*interest*) rédito *m*; **~ on capital** rendimiento *m* del capital; **the ~ on investments is only 2%** las inversiones rinden sólo el 2 por ciento; **~ on sales** rendimiento *m* de las ventas; **law of diminishing ~s** ley *f* de rendimiento decreciente; **to bring in a good ~** rendir bien, dar un buen rédito.

(c) (*of thing borrowed, of merchandise*) devolución *f*; restitución *f*; **3 dozen on a sale or ~ basis** 3 docenas a devolver si no se venden.
(d) (*Tennis etc*) resto *m*.
(e) (*reward*) recompensa *f*; **in ~** en cambio; **in ~ for** en cambio de, en recompensa de; **in ~ you ...** en cambio Vd ...; **in ~ for this service** en recompensa de este servicio.
(f) (*report*) informe *m*, relación *f*; (*answer*) respuesta *f*; (*figures*) estadística *f*; (*tax* ~) declaración *f*; **~s** estadísticas *fpl*, tablas *fpl* de estadísticas (*for* de); **~ of income** declaración *f* de renta.
(g) (*Parl etc: of member*) elección *f*; (*voting*) resultado *m* (del escrutinio).
(h) (*Brit*: **~ ticket**) billete *m* de ida y vuelta.
(i) **= ~ key**.
[2] ATTR (a) **~ fare** (*Brit*), **~ half** parte *f* de vuelta; **~ flight** vuelo *m* de regreso; **~ journey** viaje *m* de vuelta, viaje *m* de regreso; **~ key** tecla *f* de retorno; **~ ticket** (*Brit*) billete *m* de ida y vuelta.
(b) **~ match** (partido *m* de) desquite *m*, partido *m* de vuelta, revancha *f*.
(c) **~ address** señas *fpl* del remitente.
[3] VT (a) (*give back*) devolver, regresar (*LAm*); restituir; (*send back*) *light* reflejar; *ball* restar; (*Mil*) *fire* devolver, responder a; *suit of cards* devolver; *answer, thanks* dar; *favour, kindness, love* corresponder a; *visit* pagar; **to ~ sth to its place** devolver algo a su lugar; **to ~ partner's lead** devolver el palo que sirvió el compañero; **'~ to sender'** 'devuélvase al remitente'; **to ~ blow for blow** devolver golpe por golpe; **to ~ like for like** pagar a uno en la misma moneda; **I hope to ~ your kindness** espero poder corresponder a su amabilidad; **her love was not ~ed** su amor no fue correspondido.
(b) (*declare*) declarar; **to ~ an income of £X** declarar tener una renta de X libras; **to ~ a verdict** pronunciar una sentencia, dar un fallo; **to ~ a verdict of guilty on sb** declarar culpable a uno.
(c) (*Parl etc*) elegir, votar a; **he was ~ed by an overwhelming majority** resultó elegido por una abrumadora mayoría; **Old Sarum used to ~ two members to Parliament** Old Sarum tenía antes el derecho a dos escaños en el Parlamento.
(d) (*reply*) responder, contestar.
(e) (*Fin*) *profit etc* producir, dar.
[4] VI (a) (*go back*) volver, regresar (*to* a); (*Jur*) revertir (*to* a); **to ~ home** volver a casa; **to ~ from town** volver de la ciudad; **to ~ from a journey** volver de un viaje, regresar después de un viaje; **his good spirits ~ed** renació su alegría, se restableció su buen humor.
(b) **to ~ to a task** volver a una tarea, emprender de nuevo una tarea; **to ~ to a theme** volver a un asunto.
(c) (*Med: symptoms etc*) reaparecer.
returnable [rɪ'tɜːnəbl] ADJ restituible; *deposit* reintegrable, reembolsable; *bottle etc* retornable; (*Jur*) devolutivo; (*on approval*) a prueba; **~ empties** envases *mpl* a devolver; **the book is ~ on the 14th** el libro deberá devolverse el 14; **the deposit is not ~** no se reembolsa el depósito.
returnee [rɪtɜː'niː] N (*US*) persona *f* que vuelve.
returner [rɪ'tɜːnəʳ] N *mujer que vuelve a trabajar tras un tiempo dedicada a la familia.*
returning officer [rɪ'tɜːnɪŋ ˌɒfɪsəʳ] N escrutador *m*, -ora *f*.
retype [ˌriː'taɪp] VT reescribir (a máquina).
reunification ['riːˌjuːnɪfɪ'keɪʃən] N reunificación *f*.
reunify ['riː'juːnɪfaɪ] VT reunificar.
reunion [riː'juːnjən] N reunión *f*.
reunite ['riːjuː'naɪt] [1] VT reunir; (*in friendship etc*) reconciliar; **eventually the family was ~d** por fin la familia volvió a verse unida; **she was ~d with her husband** volvió a verse al lado de su marido.
[2] VI reunirse; reconciliarse; volver a verse unido.
re-usable [ˌriː'juːzəbl] ADJ reutilizable, que se puede volver a emplear.
re-use [ˌriː'juːz] VT volver a usar, reutilizar.
rev* [rev] (*Aut etc*) [1] N revolución *f*.
[2] VT (*also* **to ~ up**) girar (el motor de); acelerar (la marcha de).
[3] VI (*also* **to ~ up**) girar (rápidamente); acelerarse; **the plane was ~ving up** se aceleraban los motores del avión.
Rev(d). ABBR *of* **Reverend** Reverendo, R., Rdo., Rvdo.; **the ~*** (*Catholic*) el cura, (*Protestant*) el pastor.
revaluation [riːˌvæljʊ'eɪʃən] N revaluación *f*, revalorización *f*.
revalue ['riː'væljuː] VT revaluar, revalorizar.
revamp ['riː'væmp] VT remendar; (*fig*) rehacer, refundir, renovar; modernizar.
revanchism [rɪ'væntʃɪzəm] N revanchismo *m*.
revanchist [rɪ'væntʃɪst] [1] ADJ revanchista.
[2] N revanchista *mf*.
reveal [rɪ'viːl] VT revelar; desplegar, demostrar; *feelings* exteriorizar; **on that occasion he ~ed great astuteness** en aquella ocasión desplegó gran astucia.
revealing [rɪ'viːlɪŋ] ADJ revelador.
revealingly [rɪ'viːlɪŋlɪ] ADV de modo revelador.
reveille [rɪ'vælɪ] N diana *f*, toque *m* de diana.

revel ['revl] ⬚1 VI jaranear, estar de parranda, divertirse tumultuosamente; **to ~ in** deleitarse en, deleitarse con; **to ~ in +** *ger* deleitarse en + *infin.*
⬚2 **~s** NPL jolgorio *m,* jarana *f,* diversión *f* tumultuosa; *(organized)* fiestas *fpl,* festividades *fpl;* **let the ~s begin!** ¡que comience la fiesta!; **the ~s lasted for 3 days** continuaron las fiestas durante 3 días.
revelation [,revə'leɪʃən] N revelación *f;* *(Book of)* **R~s** el Apocalipsis; **it was a ~ to me** fue una revelación para mí.
revelatory ['revələtəri] ADJ revelador.
reveller, *(US)* **reveler** ['revləʳ] N jaranero *m,* juerguista *mf;* *(drunk)* borracho *m.*
revelry ['revlrɪ] N jolgorio *m,* juerga *f,* jarana *f,* diversión *f* tumultuosa; *(organized)* fiestas *fpl,* festividades *fpl;* **the spirit of ~** el espíritu de carnaval.
revenge [rɪ'vendʒ] ⬚1 N venganza *f;* **in ~** para vengarse *(for* de); **to take ~ on sb for sth** vengarse de algo en uno.
⬚2 VT vengar; **to be ~d on sb** vengarse en uno.
⬚3 VI: **to ~ o.s.** vengarse *(on sb* en uno, *for sth* de algo).
revengeful [rɪ'vendʒful] ADJ vengativo.
revengefully [rɪ'vendʒfəlɪ] ADV vengativamente.
revenger [rɪ'vendʒəʳ] N vengador *m,* -ora *f.*
revenue ['revənjuː] ⬚1 N **(a)** *(income: also* **~s)** ingresos *mpl;* renta *f;* *(on investments)* rédito *m;* *(profit)* ganancia *f,* beneficio *m (from* de).
(b) *(of state)* rentas *fpl* públicas; *(Inland ~, US Internal ~)* Fisco *m,* Hacienda *f.*
⬚2 ATTR: **~ account** cuenta *f* de ingresos presupuestarios; **~ expenditure** gasto *m* corriente; **~ stamp** timbre *m* fiscal.
reverb ['riːvɜːb] N reverberación *f.*
reverberate [rɪ'vɜːbəreɪt] VI **(a)** *(sound)* resonar, retumbar; **the sound ~d in the distance** el sonido retumbaba a lo lejos; **the valley ~d with the sound** el ruido resonaba por el valle.
(b) *(Tech: light)* reverberar.
reverberation [rɪ,vɜːbə'reɪʃən] N **(a)** *(of sound)* retumbo *m,* el retumbar, eco *m.* **(b)** *(of light)* reverberación *f.*
reverberator [rɪ'vɜːbəreɪtəʳ] N reverberador *m.*
revere [rɪ'vɪəʳ] VT reverenciar, venerar; **a ~d figure** una figura venerada.
reverence ['revərəns] ⬚1 N reverencia *f;* **Your R~** Reverencia.
⬚2 VT reverenciar.
reverend ['revərənd] ⬚1 ADJ reverendo; **right ~** reverendísimo.
⬚2 N *(*: Catholic)* padre *m,* cura *m;* *(Protestant)* pastor *m.*
reverent ['revərənt] ADJ reverente.
reverential [,revə'renʃəl] ADJ reverencial.
reverently ['revərəntlɪ] ADV reverentemente, con reverencia.
reverie ['revərɪ] N ensueño *m;* **to be lost in ~** estar absorto, estar ensimismado.
revers [rɪ'vɪəʳ] N solapa *f.*
reversal [rɪ'vɜːsəl] N *(of order)* inversión *f;* *(of direction, policy)* cambio *m* completo; *(of decision)* revocación *f.*
reverse [rɪ'vɜːs] ⬚1 ADJ **(a)** *order* inverso, invertido; *direction* contrario, opuesto; **in the ~ order** en orden inverso, al revés; **in the ~ direction** en sentido contrario; **~ turn** vuelta *f* al revés; **~ video** vídeo *m* inverso.
(b) *(Mech)* gear de marcha atrás.
⬚2 N **(a)** *(opposite)* **the ~** lo contrario; **quite the ~** todo lo contrario; **but the ~ is true** pero es al contrario; **it was the ~ of what we had expected** fue todo lo contrario de lo que habíamos esperado; **his remarks were the ~ of flattering** sus observaciones eran poco halagüeñas, todo lo contrario; **it's the same process in ~** es el mismo proceso al revés, es una forma invertida del mismo proceso.
(b) *(face: of coin)* reverso *m;* *(of cloth)* revés *m;* *(of paper etc)* dorso *m.*
(c) *(Mech)* marcha *f* atrás, contramarcha *f,* reversa *f (LAm);* **to go into ~** dar marcha atrás; **my luck went into ~** mi suerte dio marcha atrás; **to put a car into ~** dar marcha atrás a un coche.
(d) *(setback)* revés *m,* contratiempo *m;* *(defeat)* derrota *f.*
⬚3 VT **(a)** *(invert order of)* invertir, invertir el orden de; trastrocar; *(turn other way)* volver al revés; *arms* llevar a la funerala; **to ~ A and B** invertir el orden de A y B, anteponer B a A; **~(d) charge call** *(Brit)* llamada *f* a cobro revertido; *V* **charge.**
(b) *(change)* opinion cambiar completamente de; *decision* revocar, anular, cancelar.
(c) *(Mech)* poner en marcha atrás; invertir la marcha de; **he ~d the car into the garage** dio marcha atrás y entró en el garaje; **he ~d the car into a pillarbox** al dar marcha atrás chocó con un buzón.
⬚4 VI *(Brit)* dar marcha atrás; **I ~d into a van** al dar marcha atrás choqué con una furgoneta.
reversible [rɪ'vɜːsəbl] ADJ reversible.
reversing [rɪ'vɜːsɪŋ] N marcha *f* atrás; **~ light** luz *f* de marcha atrás.
reversion [rɪ'vɜːʃən] N reversión *f (also Bio, Jur);* **~ to type** reversión *f* al tipo, salto *m* atrás.
reversionary [rɪ'vɜːʃnərɪ] ADJ reversionario, reversible.
revert [rɪ'vɜːt] VI *(Jur)* revertir *(to* a); *(Bio)* saltar atrás; **to ~ to a subject**

volver a un tema; **~ing to the matter under discussion ...** volviendo al tema de la discusión ...; **to ~ to type** saltar atrás en la cadena natural.
revetment [rɪ'vetmənt] N revestimiento *m.*
revictual [riː'vɪtl] ⬚1 VT reabastecer.
⬚2 VI reabastecerse.
review [rɪ'vjuː] ⬚1 N **(a)** *(Jur. revision)* revisión *f;* *(examination)* repaso *m;* examen *m;* análisis *m;* *(of research etc)* evaluación *f;* **the annual ~ of expenditure** el examen anual de los gastos; **the sentence is subject to ~ in the high court** la sentencia puede volver a ser vista en el tribunal supremo; **salaries are under ~** los sueldos están sujetos a revisión; **we shall keep your case under ~** volveremos a considerar su caso; **when the case comes up for ~** cuando el asunto se someta a revisión.
(b) *(Mil etc)* revista *f;* **the Spithead R~** la revista naval de Spithead; **the general passed the troops in ~** el general pasó revista a las tropas; **the troops passed in ~ before the general** las tropas desfilaron en revista ante el general.
(c) *(critique)* reseña *f;* **~ copy** ejemplar *m* para reseñar.
(d) *(journal)* revista *f.*
(e) *(show)* revista *f.*
⬚2 VT **(a)** *(Jur)* rever; *(US Scol: take stock of)* repasar; examinar, analizar, estudiar; *research etc* evaluar; **we will ~ the position in a month** volveremos a estudiar la situación dentro de un mes; **we shall have to ~ our policy** tendremos que reconsiderar nuestra política.
(b) *(Mil etc)* pasar revista a, revistar.
(c) *(write ~ of)* reseñar.
reviewer [rɪ'vjuːəʳ] N crítico *m,* -a *f;* *(of book)* reseñante *mf.*
reviewing stand [rɪ'vjuːɪŋ,stænd] N tribuna *f* de autoridades en los desfiles militares.
revile [rɪ'vaɪl] VT injuriar, llenar de injurias, vilipendiar.
revise [rɪ'vaɪz] ⬚1 VT *(look over)* revisar, volver a examinar, volver a estudiar; *(Brit) lesson etc* repasar; *(amend)* modificar, corregir; *proofs* corregir; *text* refundir; *decision* modificar.
⬚2 VI: **to ~ for exams** repasar para los exámenes.
revised [rɪ'vaɪzd] ADJ *text* refundido; **R~ Version** *(Brit)* Versión *f* Revisada *(traducción inglesa de la Biblia, 1884).*
reviser [rɪ'vaɪzəʳ] N revisor *m,* -ora *f;* refundidor *m,* -ora *f;* *(Typ)* corrector *m,* -ora *f.*
revision [rɪ'vɪʒən] N revisión *f;* repaso *m;* modificación *f,* corrección *f;* refundición *f;* **I need 2 weeks for ~** necesito 2 semanas para repasar mis libros *(etc).*
revisionism [rɪ'vɪʒənɪzəm] N revisionismo *m.*
revisionist [rɪ'vɪʒənɪst] ⬚1 ADJ revisionista.
⬚2 N revisionista *mf.*
revisit ['riː'vɪzɪt] VT volver a visitar; **'Brideshead R~ed'** 'Retorno *m* a Brideshead'.
revitalize ['riː'vaɪtəlaɪz] VT revivificar; vigorizar; infundir fuerzas a.
revival [rɪ'vaɪvəl] N resucitación *f;* reanimación *f;* restablecimiento *m;* despertamiento *m;* *(Theat)* reposición *f,* reestreno *m;* *(of learning, art)* renacimiento *m;* *(Pol etc)* resurgimiento *m;* **the R~ of Learning** el Renacimiento.
revivalism [rɪ'vaɪvə,lɪzəm] N evangelismo *m.*
revivalist [rɪ'vaɪvəlɪst] ⬚1 N evangelista *mf;* *(preacher)* predicador *m* evangelista.
⬚2 ATTR: **~ meeting** reunión *f* evangelista.
revive [rɪ'vaɪv] ⬚1 VT *(restore to life)* resucitar; *(fig)* reanimar; restablecer; *fire* avivar; *accusation* volver a, volver a hacer; *hopes* despertar; *suspicion* hacer revivir; *play* reponer, reestrenar; **this will ~ you** esto te reanimará; **to ~ sb's courage** infundir nuevo ánimo a uno.
⬚2 VI *(come back to life)* resucitar; *(recover)* reponerse, restablecerse; cobrar fuerzas; *(after unconsciousness)* volver en sí; *(after apparent death)* revivir; **the pound has ~d** la libra se ha repuesto; **interest in Gongora has ~d** ha renacido el interés por Góngora; **his courage ~d** se sintió con nuevo ánimo.
reviver [rɪ'vaɪvəʳ] N *(drink)* bebida *f* que da fuerzas.
revivify [riː'vɪvɪfaɪ] VT revivificar.
revocation [,revə'keɪʃən] N revocación *f.*
revoke [rɪ'vəuk] ⬚1 N *(Cards)* renuncio *m.*
⬚2 VT revocar.
⬚3 VI *(Cards)* renunciar.
revolt [rɪ'vəult] ⬚1 N rebelión *f,* sublevación *f;* **to be in open ~** estar en franca *(o plena)* rebeldía; **to rise in ~** rebelarse, sublevarse.
⬚2 VT repugnar, dar asco a; **the book ~ed me** el libro me dio asco.
⬚3 VI rebelarse, sublevarse *(against* contra).
revolting [rɪ'vəultɪŋ] ADJ asqueroso, repugnante.
revoltingly [rɪ'vəultɪŋlɪ] ADV asquerosamente, de modo repugnante; **they're ~ rich** son tan ricos que da asco.
revolution [,revə'luːʃən] N **(a)** *(Pol)* revolución *f.*
(b) *(turn)* revolución *f;* vuelta *f,* rotación *f;* **600 ~s per minute** 600 revoluciones por minuto.
revolutionary [,revə'luːʃənərɪ] ⬚1 ADJ revolucionario.

2 N revolucionario *m*, -a *f*.
revolutionize [,revə'luːʃənaɪz] VT revolucionar.
revolve [rɪ'vɒlv] 1 VT girar, hacer girar; (*in the mind*) dar vueltas a, revolver, meditar.
2 VI (**a**) (*Mech etc*) girar (*on* sobre, *round* alrededor de); dar vueltas; (*Astron*) revolverse.
(**b**) (*fig*) **everything ~s round him** todo depende de él, todo se centra en él; **the discussion ~d round 3 topics** el debate se centró en 3 temas.
revolver [rɪ'vɒlvəʳ] N revólver *m*.
revolving [rɪ'vɒlvɪŋ] ADJ giratorio; **~ credit** crédito *m* rotativo (*or* renovable); **~ door** puerta *f* giratoria; **~ stage** escena *f* giratoria.
revue [rɪ'vjuː] N revista *f*.
revulsion [rɪ'vʌlʃən] N (**a**) (*disgust*) asco *m*, repugnancia *f*; (*Med*) revulsión *f*. (**b**) (*change*) reacción *f*, cambio *m* repentino.
reward [rɪ'wɔːd] 1 N recompensa *f*, premio *m*; (*for finding sth*) gratificación *f*, hallazgo *m*; **as a ~ for** en recompensa de, como premio a; '**£50 ~**' '50 libras de hallazgo', '50 libras de recompensa'; '**a ~ will be paid for information about ...**' 'se recompensará al que dé informes acerca de ...'
2 VT recompensar, premiar; **to ~ sb for his services** recompensar a uno por sus servicios; **she ~ed me with a smile** me premió con una sonrisa; **it might ~ your attention** podría valer la pena ir a verlo (*etc*); **the case would ~ your investigation** le valdría la pena investigar el asunto.
rewarding [rɪ'wɔːdɪŋ] ADJ remunerador, (*fig*) provechoso, útil, valioso.
rewind ['riː'waɪnd] (*irr: V* **wind**) VT *watch* dar cuerda a; *wool etc* devanar; (*Elec, Cine*) rebobinar.
rewinding ['riː'waɪndɪŋ] N (*Elec*) rebobinado *m*.
rewire ['riː'waɪəʳ] VT *house* renovar (completamente) el alambrado de.
reword ['riː'wɜːd] VT expresar en otras palabras, redactar en otra forma.
rework [riː'wɜːk] VT rehacer; refundir.
rewrite 1 ['riː'raɪt] (*irr: V* **write**) VT volver a escribir, escribir de nuevo; *text* rehacer, refundir; redactar en otras palabras.
2 ['riːraɪt] N nueva versión *f*, refundición *f*.
Reykjavik ['reɪkjəviːk] N Reíkiavik *m*.
RFD N (*US Post*) ABBR *of* **rural free delivery**.
RFU N (*England*) ABBR *of* **Rugby Football Union**; *ver también* ⟨RUGBY⟩.
RGN N (*Brit*) ABBR *of* **Registered General Nurse** enfermero *m* colegiado, enfermera *f* colegiada.
Rgt ABBR *of* **Regiment** Regimiento *m*.
Rh N ABBR *of* **Rhesus** Rhesus *m*, Rh.
r.h. ABBR *of* **right hand** derecha *f*, der., derª.
rhapsodic [ræp'sɒdɪk] ADJ rapsódico; (*fig*) extático, locamente entusiasmado, delirante.
rhapsodize ['ræpsədaɪz] VI: **to ~ over sth** extasiarse ante algo, entusiasmarse por algo; hablar de algo en términos elogiosos.
rhapsody ['ræpsədɪ] N rapsodia *f*; (*fig*) transporte *m* de admiración (*etc*); **to be in rhapsodies** estar extasiado; **to go into rhapsodies over sth** extasiarse ante algo, entusiasmarse por algo; hablar de algo en términos elogiosos.
rhea ['riːə] N ñandú *m*.
Rhenish ['renɪʃ] 1 ADJ renano.
2 N vino *m* del Rin.
rhenium ['riːnɪəm] N renio *m*.
rheostat ['riːəʊstæt] N reóstato *m*.
rhesus ['riːsəs] 1 N macaco *m* de la India; **~ negative** Rhesus negativo; **~ positive** Rhesus positivo.
2 ATTR: **~ baby** bebé *m* con factor Rhesus; **~ factor** factor *m* Rhesus; **~ monkey** macaco *m* de la India.
rhetic ['riːtɪk] ADJ rético.
rhetoric ['retərɪk] N retórica *f*.
rhetorical [rɪ'tɒrɪkəl] ADJ retórico; **~ question** pregunta *f* a la que no se espera contestación.
rhetorically [rɪ'tɒrɪkəlɪ] ADV retóricamente; **I speak ~** hablo en metáfora.
rhetorician [,retə'rɪʃən] N retórico *m*.
rheumatic [ruː'mætɪk] 1 ADJ reumático; **~ fever** fiebre *f* reumática.
2 NPL: **~s*** reumatismo *m*.
rheumaticky* [ruː'mætɪkɪ] ADJ reumático.
rheumatism ['ruːmətɪzəm] N reumatismo *m*.
rheumatoid ['ruːmətɔɪd] ADJ reumatoideo; **~ arthritis** reumatismo *m* articular crónico, reúma *m* articular.
rheumatologist [,ruːmə'tɒlədʒɪst] N reumatólogo *m*, -a *f*.
rheumatology [,ruːmə'tɒlədʒɪ] N reumatología *f*.
rheumy ['ruːmɪ] ADJ *eyes* legañoso, pitañoso.
Rhine [raɪn] 1 N Rin *m*.
2 ATTR: **~ wine** vino *m* blanco del Rin.
Rhineland ['raɪnlənd] N Renania *f*.
rhinestone ['raɪn,stəʊn] N diamante *m* de imitación.

rhinitis [raɪ'naɪtɪs] N rinitis *f*.
rhino* ['raɪnəʊ] N, **rhinoceros** [raɪ'nɒsərəs] N rinoceronte *m*.
rhizome ['raɪzəʊm] N rizoma *m*.
Rhodes [rəʊdz] N Rodas *f*.
Rhodesia [rəʊ'diːʒə] N (*Hist*) Rodesia *f*.
Rhodesian [rəʊ'diːʒən] (*Hist*) 1 ADJ rodesiano.
2 N rodesiano *m*, -a *f*.
rhodium ['rəʊdɪəm] N rodio *m*.
rhododendron [,rəʊdə'dendrən] N rododendro *m*.
rhomb [rɒm] N rombo *m*.
rhomboid ['rɒmbɔɪd] 1 ADJ romboidal.
2 N romboide *m*.
rhombus ['rɒmbəs] N rombo *m*.
Rhône [rəʊn] N Ródano *m*.
rhubarb ['ruːbɑːb] N (**a**) (*Bot, Culin*) ruibarbo *m*. (**b**) (*Theat*) palabra que se repite para representar la conversación callada en escenas de comparsas.
rhyme [raɪm] 1 N (**a**) (*identical sound*) rima *f*; **without ~ or reason** sin ton ni son. (**b**) (*poem*) poesía *f*, versos *mpl*; **in ~** en verso.
2 VTI rimar; **rhyming slang** argot *m* basado en rimas (*p.ej.*, '**apples and pears**' = '**stairs**').
3 ATTR: **~ scheme** esquema *m* de la rima, combinación *f* de rimas.

⎡ **RHYMING SLANG** ⎤

ⓘ *El* **rhyming slang** *(jerga rimada) es un tipo muy peculiar de jerga que usan los habitantes de un barrio en el este de Londres, los* **cockneys**, *en la que una palabra o frase determinada se sustituye por otra que rima con ella; por ejemplo, dicen* **apples and pears** *en vez de* **stairs**. *Puede resultar muy confuso para las personas que no lo conocen bien, sobre todo porque, además, muchas veces se establece un doble juego de palabras en el que la palabra que rima no se dice; por ejemplo,* **butcher's hook** *quiere decir* **look**, *pero a menudo sólo se dice* **butcher's**, *como en la frase* **let's have a butcher's**. *El uso de algunas de estas expresiones se ha extendido al inglés coloquial habitual, como* **use your loaf**, *donde* **loaf**, *que viene de* **loaf of bread**, *quiere decir* **head**.

rhymed [raɪmd] ADJ rimado.
rhymer ['raɪməʳ] N, **rhymester** ['raɪmstəʳ] N rimador *m*, -ora *f*.
rhythm ['rɪðəm] N ritmo *m*; **~ method** método *m* de Ogino-Knaus.
rhythmic(al) ['rɪðmɪk(əl)] ADJ rítmico.
rhythmically ['rɪðmɪkəlɪ] ADV rítmicamente, de modo rítmico.
RI N (**a**) (*US*) ABBR *of* **Rhode Island.** (**b**) (*Scol*) ABBR *of* **religious instruction** religión *f*.
rib [rɪb] 1 N (*Anat, Culin*) costilla *f*; (*Bot*) nervio *m*, nervadura *f*; (*in fabric*) cordoncillo *m*; (*Archit*) nervadura *f*; (*of umbrella*) varilla *f*; (*Naut*) costilla *f*, cuaderna *f*; **~ cage** tórax *m*.
2 VT: **to ~ sb*** tomar el pelo a uno*.
RIBA N ABBR *of* **Royal Institute of British Architects.**
riband ['rɪbənd] (††) = **ribbon**.
ribald ['rɪbəld] ADJ verde, obsceno, escabroso; irreverente y regocijado.
ribaldry ['rɪbəldrɪ] N (*character*) lo verde, obscenidad *f*, escabrosidad *f*; (*jokes etc*) cosas *fpl* verdes, cosas *fpl* obscenas.
ribbed [rɪbd] ADJ: **~ sweater** jersey *m* de cordoncillo.
ribbing ['rɪbɪŋ] N (*in fabric*) cordoncillos *mpl*; (*Archit*) nervaduras *fpl*.
ribbon ['rɪbən] 1 N cinta *f*; (*Mil*) galón *m*; **to tear sth to ~s** hacer algo trizas; **with his jacket torn to ~s** con su chaqueta hecha trizas.
2 ATTR: **~ development** desarrollo *m* línea, desarrollo *m* a lo largo de la carretera.
riboflavin [,raɪbəʊ'fleɪvɪn] N riboflavina *f*.
ribonucleic [,raɪbəʊnjuː'kleɪk] ADJ: **~ acid** ácido *m* ribonucleico.
rib-tickler* ['rɪb'tɪkləʳ] N (*Brit*) chiste *m* desternillante*, historia *f* desternillante*.
rib-tickling* ['rɪbtɪklɪŋ] ADJ desternillante.
rice [raɪs] 1 N arroz *m*.
2 ATTR: **~ paddy** (*US*) arrozal *m*; **~ paper** papel *m* de paja de arroz; **~ pudding** arroz *m* con leche, arequipa *f* (*Méx*); **~ wine** vino *m* de arroz.
ricefield ['raɪsfiːld] N arrozal *m*.
rice-growing ['raɪs,grəʊɪŋ] ADJ arrocero.
rich [rɪtʃ] 1 ADJ rico; (*in price, workmanship*) costoso, precioso, exquisito; *colour* vivo, brillante; *profit* pingüe; *smell* rico; *soil* fértil; *voice* sonoro; *clothing, fabric* rico; *banquet* suntuoso, opíparo; *food* sabroso, suculento, (*pej*) pesado, fuerte, muy dulce, empalagoso; *wine* generoso; *style* copioso; *experience, history* rico; (*: funny*) muy divertido; **that's ~!** ¡qué gracioso!; **to be ~ in** abundar de, abundar en; **a gallery ~ in Impressionists** un museo que posee gran caudal de impresionistas; **a style ~ in metaphors** un estilo en el que abundan las metáforas; **the soil is ~ in nitrates** el suelo tiene abundantes nitratos; **to become** (*or* **get, grow**) **~** enriquecerse (*on* con); **to get ~ quick** enriquecerse pronto; **to strike it ~*** ponerse las botas.
2 NPL (**a**) **the ~** (*people*) los ricos.
(**b**) **~es** (*wealth*) riqueza *f*, riquezas *fpl*; **the earth's ~es** las riquezas

de la tierra.

Richard ['rɪtʃəd] NM Ricardo; **~ (the) Lionheart** Ricardo Corazón de León.

richly ['rɪtʃlɪ] ADV (V adj) ricamente; preciosamente, exquisitamente; suntuosamente; sabrosamente; copiosamente; **a ~ adorned chair** una silla de exquisitos adornos; **a ~ humorous situation** una situación divertidísima; **a ~ endowed library** una biblioteca de fondos copiosos; **she ~ deserves it** muy bien merecido lo tiene.

richness ['rɪtʃnɪs] N (V adj) riqueza f; preciosidad f, exquisitez f; viveza f, brillantez f; fertilidad f; sonoridad f; suntuosidad f; suculencia f; lo pesado, lo fuerte; copia f; abundancia f.

Richter ['rɪktə'] N: **~ scale** escala f (de) Richter.

rick¹ [rɪk] (Agr) **1** N almiar m, niara f.
2 VT almiarar, recoger en niaras (etc), amontonar.

rick² [rɪk] VT = **wrick**.

rickets ['rɪkɪts] N raquitismo m, raquitis f.

rickety ['rɪkɪtɪ] ADJ (a) (Med) raquítico. (b) (unsafe) desvencijado; (unsteady) tambaleante, inseguro.

rickshaw ['rɪkʃɔː] N jinrikisha f, carro m de culí.

ricochet ['rɪkəʃeɪ] **1** N rebote m.
2 VI rebotar (off de).

rictus ['rɪktəs] N rictus m.

rid [rɪd] (irr: PRET **rid, ridded,** PTP **rid**) **1** VT (a) **to ~ a place of rats** librar un lugar de ratas, eliminar las ratas de un lugar; **to ~ sb of a difficulty** librar a uno de una dificultad; **the medicine ~ me of the cough** la medicina me curó (or quitó) la tos.
(b) **to be ~ of** estar libre de; **we're ~ of him at last!** ¡por fin nos vemos libres de él!
(c) **to get ~ of** deshacerse de, desembarazarse de; hacer desaparecer; **the body gets ~ of waste** el cuerpo elimina los desechos; **get ~ of it at any price** véndelo a cualquier precio; **to get ~ of sb** deshacerse de uno, (euph) eliminar a uno matándole.
2 VR: **to ~ o.s. of** librarse de, desembarazarse de; **to ~ o.s. of evil thoughts** librarse de los malos pensamientos.

riddance ['rɪdəns] N: **good ~ (to bad rubbish)!** (iro) ¡enhoramala!; ¡vete con viento fresco!; **it was a good ~** de buena nos libramos; **and good ~ to him** que se pudra.

ridden ['rɪdn] PTP of **ride**; **a horse ~ by ...** un caballo montado por ...

riddle¹ ['rɪdl] N (conundrum) acertijo m, adivinanza f; (mystery) enigma m, misterio m; (person etc) enigma m; **to ask sb a ~** proponer un acertijo a uno; **to speak in ~s** hablar en enigmas.

riddle² ['rɪdl] **1** N (sieve) criba f, criba f gruesa; (potato sorter etc) escogedor m.
2 VT (a) (sieve) cribar; potatoes etc pasar por el escogedor.
(b) **to ~ a door with bullets** acribillar una puerta a balazos; **the organization is ~d with communists** el organismo está plagado de comunistas; **the army is ~d with subversion** el ejército está lleno de subversionismo.

ride [raɪd] **1** N (a) (on horse) cabalgata f, paseo m a caballo; (in car etc) paseo m en coche, viaje m en coche (or bicicleta etc); (US) viaje m gratuito, aventón m (LAm); (distance ridden) viaje m, recorrido m; **the ~ of the Valkyries** la cabalgata de las valquirias; **'50p a ~'** '50 peniques por persona', '50 peniques la vuelta'; **it was a rough ~** fue un viaje nada cómodo; **to give sb a rough ~** (fig) hacer pasar un mal rato a uno; **it's only a short ~** es poco camino, es poca distancia; **it's a 10-minute ~ by bus** el viaje dura 10 minutos en autobús; **it's a 70p ~ from the station** el viaje desde la estación cuesta 70 peniques; **they gave me a ~ into town** me llevaron (en coche) a la ciudad; **it's my first ~ in a Rolls** es la primera vez que viajo en un Rolls; **to take a ~ in a helicopter** dar un paseo en helicóptero; **to take sb for a ~*** dar gato por liebre a uno, embaucar a uno, (US*) dar el paseo a uno‡; **to be taken for a ~*** hacer el primo*.
(b) (in a wood) vereda f.
2 (irr: PRET **rode,** PTP **ridden**) VT (a) **to ~ a horse** montar a caballo; **to ~ a bicycle** ir en bicicleta; **to ~ an elephant** ir montado en un elefante; **he rode his horse up the stairs** hizo que el caballo subiese la escalera; **he rode his horse into the shop** entró a caballo en la tienda; **it has never been ridden** hasta ahora nadie ha montado en él; **he rode it in two races** lo corrió en dos carreras; **to ~ a horse hard** castigar mucho a un caballo; **can you ~ a bicycle?** ¿sabes montar en bicicleta?
(b) (esp US fig) **to ~ sb** tiranizar a uno, dominar a uno; **don't ~ him too hard** no seas demasiado severo con él; **to ~ an idea to death** explotar una idea con demasiado entusiasmo, acabar con una idea a fuerza de repetirla demasiado.
(c) (Naut) waves hender, surcar.
(d) **to ~ a good race** hacer bien una carrera, dar buena cuenta de sí (en una carrera).

3 VI (a) (on animal) montar, cabalgar; (on a bicycle, in a car) ir; pasearse, viajar; **to ~ on an elephant** ir montado en un elefante; **to ~ in a car** ir en coche; **some rode but I had to walk** algunos fueron en coche pero yo tuve que ir a pie; **to ~ astride** montar a horcajadas; **to ~ like mad** correr como el demonio; **to ~ home on sb's shoulders** ser llevado a casa en los hombros de uno; **she ~s every day** monta a diario; **he ~s for a different stable** monta para otra cuadra.
(b) (with expressions of distance and time, often not translated) **to ~ to Jaén** ir (a caballo) a Jaén; **we'll ~ over to see you** vendremos a verte; **he rode straight at me** arremetió contra mí; **he rode 12 miles** recorrió 12 millas, hizo 12 millas.
(c) (fig) **to ~ at anchor** estar al ancla, estar anclado; **the moon was riding high in the sky** la luna estaba en lo alto del cielo; **to be riding high** (person) estar alegre, estar en la cumbre de la felicidad; **when I'm riding high** cuando mis cosas van bien, cuando todo me va bien.

◆**ride about, ride around** VI pasearse a caballo (or en coche, en bicicleta etc).
◆**ride away** VI alejarse, irse, partir.
◆**ride back** VI volver (a caballo, en bicicleta etc).
◆**ride behind** VI ir después, caminar a la zaga; (in rear seat) ir en el asiento de atrás; (on same horse) cabalgar a la grupa.
◆**ride by** VI pasar (a caballo).
◆**ride down** VT (a) (trample) atropellar. (b) (catch) coger, alcanzar.
◆**ride off** VI = **ride away**.
◆**ride on** VI seguir adelante.
◆**ride out** VT storm aguantar (also fig).
◆**ride up** VI (a) (horseman, motorcyclist etc) llegar, acercarse. (b) (dress) subirse.

rider ['raɪdə'] N (a) (horse ~) jinete m, -a f; caballero m; (cyclist) ciclista mf; (motorcyclist) motociclista mf; (US Aut) pasajero m, -a f, viajero m, -a f; **I'm not much of a ~** apenas sé montar; **he's a fine ~** es un jinete destacado.
(b) (clause) aditamento m; corolario m; **I must add the ~ that ...** tengo que añadir que ...

ridge [rɪdʒ] N (of hills) cadena f, sierra f; estribación f; (of hill) cresta f; (of nose, roof) caballete m; (on cloth etc) cordoncillo m; (wrinkle) arruga f; (Agr) caballón m, camellón m; **~ of high pressure** zona f de alta presión.

ridgepole ['rɪdʒpəʊl] N parhilera f, cumbrera f.

ridge tent ['rɪdʒˌtent] N tienda f canadiense.

ridgetile ['rɪdʒtaɪl] N teja f de caballete.

ridgeway ['rɪdʒweɪ] N ruta f de las crestas.

ridicule ['rɪdɪkjuːl] **1** N irrisión f; burlas fpl, mofa f; **to expose sb to public ~** exponer a uno a la mofa pública; **to hold sb up to ~** ridiculizar a uno, mofarse de uno; **to lay o.s. open to ~** exponerse al ridículo.
2 VT ridiculizar, poner en ridículo, mofarse de.

▼ **ridiculous** [rɪ'dɪkjʊləs] ADJ ridículo, absurdo; **~!, how ~!** ¡qué ridículo!; **to make o.s. ~** ponerse en ridículo.

ridiculously [rɪ'dɪkjʊləslɪ] ADV ridículamente, absurdamente; de modo ridículo; **it is ~ easy** es ridículamente fácil.

riding ['raɪdɪŋ] **1** N equitación f, montar m a caballo.
2 ATTR de montar; de equitación.

riding-boots ['raɪdɪŋbuːts] NPL botas fpl de montar.

riding-breeches ['raɪdɪŋˌbrɪtʃɪz] NPL pantalones mpl de montar.

riding-crop ['raɪdɪŋkrɒp] N fusta f.

riding-habit ['raɪdɪŋˌhæbɪt] N amazona f, traje m de montar.

riding-jacket ['raɪdɪŋˌdʒækɪt] N chaqueta f de montar.

riding-master ['raɪdɪŋˌmɑːstə'] N profesor m de equitación.

riding-school ['raɪdɪŋskuːl] N picadero m, escuela f de equitación, escuela f hípica.

riding-stables ['raɪdɪŋˌsteɪblz] NPL cuadras fpl.

riding-whip ['raɪdɪŋwɪp] N fusta f.

rife [raɪf] ADJ (a) (widespread) **to be ~** abundar, ser muy común; ser endémico; **corruption is ~** la corrupción existe en todas partes; **measles is ~** hay mucho sarampión; **the abuse has become ~ of late** recientemente ha cundido el abuso, recientemente se ha extendido mucho el abuso.
(b) **to be ~ with** estar lleno de, abundar de (or en).

riff [rɪf] N (Mus) riff m, frase de dos o cuatro compases que se repite continuamente a lo largo de la canción.

riffle ['rɪfəl] VI: **to ~ through a book** hojear (rápidamente) un libro, volver rápidamente las hojas de un libro.

riffraff ['rɪfræf] N gentuza f, chusma f; **and all the ~ of the neighbourhood** y todos los sinvergüenzas del barrio.

rifle¹ ['raɪfl] VT robar, saquear; desvalijar; **to ~ a case** desvalijar una maleta; **the house had been ~d** habían saqueado la casa; **they ~d the house in search of money** saquearon la casa buscando dinero.

rifle² ['raɪfl] **1** N (a) rifle m, fusil m. (b) **~s** (as regiment etc) fusileros mpl.

2 VT estriar, rayar.

rifle-butt ['raɪflbʌt] N culata *f* de rifle.

rifled ['raɪfld] ADJ (*Tech*) estriado, rayado.

rifle-fire ['raɪflfaɪəʳ] N fuego *m* de fusilería.

rifleman ['raɪflmən] N, PL **riflemen** ['raɪflmən] fusilero *m*.

rifle-range ['raɪflreɪndʒ] N campo *m* de tiro, polígono *m* de tiro; (*at fair*) barraca *f* de tiro al blanco.

rifle-shot ['raɪflʃɒt] N tiro *m* de fusil; **within ~** a tiro de fusil.

rifling ['raɪflɪŋ] N (*Tech*) estría *f*, estriado *m*, rayado *m*.

rift [rɪft] N hendedura *f*, grieta *f*, rendija *f*; (*in clouds etc*) claro *m*, abertura *f*; (*in relations etc*) grieta *f*; (*between friends*) desavenencia *f*; (*in party*) escisión *f*, cisma *m*.

rig [rɪg] **1** N (a) (*Naut*) aparejo *m*.
(b) (*: *dress*) atuendo *m*.
(c) (*oil~*) torre *f* de perforación; (*Naut*) plataforma *f* de perforación submarina.
2 VT (a) (*Naut*) aparejar, enjarciar.
(b) (*falsify*) amañar; falsificar; **to ~ an election** amañar unas elecciones, dar pucherazo; **the government had got it all ~ged** el gobierno lo había arreglado de modo fraudulento; **to ~ the market** manipular la lonja; **it's been ~ged!** ¡aquí hay tongo!
◆ **rig out** VT (*Naut*) proveer (*with* de), equipar (*with* con); **to ~ sb out in sth** ataviar a uno de algo; **to be ~ged out in a new dress** lucir un vestido nuevo.
◆ **rig up** VT (*build*) armar, construir; (*arrange*) arreglar; (*improvise*) improvisar; **we'll see what we can ~ up** veremos si podemos arreglar algo.

rigger ['rɪgəʳ] N (*Naut*) aparejador *m*; (*Aer*) mecánico *m*.

rigging ['rɪgɪŋ] N jarcia *f*, cordaje *m*, aparejo *m*.

▼ **right** [raɪt] **1** ADJ (a) (*just*) justo, equitativo; (*suitable*) debido, indicado; (*proper*) apropiado, propio, conveniente; (*reasonable*) razonable; **it is ~ that ...** es justo que ...; **it is only ~ to add that ...** es de justicia añadir que ...; **it is only ~ and proper to** + *infin* la justicia exige que + *subj*; **it cannot be ~ for you to** + *infin* no puede ser justo que Vd + *subj*; **would it be ~ for me to ask him?** ¿conviene que yo se lo pregunte?; **it's not ~!** ¡no hay derecho!; **I thought it ~ to** + *infin* me pareció conveniente + *infin*; **to do the ~ thing** hacer lo que hay que hacer; **to do the ~ thing by sb** tratar a uno con justicia, obrar honradamente con respecto a uno; **she's on the ~ side of 40** tiene menos de 40 años; **if the price is ~** si el precio es razonable; **we'll do it when the time is ~** lo haremos en el momento oportuno.
▼ (b) (*correct*) correcto, exacto; (*true*) verdadero; *conditions etc* favorable, propicio; *thing sought etc* que hace falta, que se busca; **Mr R~** el novio soñado, el marido ideal; **~!** ¡conforme!, ¡bueno!, ¡muy bien!; sí, eso es; ¡justo!; (*answering call*) ¡voy!; **~ you are!** ¡bueno!; **quite ~!** ¡exacto!, ¡perfectamente!; **that's ~** eso es; **the ~ answer** la respuesta correcta; (*Math: to problem etc*) la solución correcta; **the ~ word** la palabra exacta, la palabra apropiada; **the ~ time** la hora exacta; **have you the ~ time?** ¿tienes la hora exacta?; **~ side of cloth** lado *m* derecho de un paño, haz *f* de un paño; **to choose the ~ moment** elegir el momento oportuno (*or* favorable); **is this the ~ house?** ¿es ésta la casa?; **is this the ~ road for Segovia?** ¿es éste el camino de Segovia?, ¿por aquí se va a Segovia?; **are we on the ~ road?** ¿vamos por buen camino?; **am I ~ for the station?** ¿por aquí se va a la estación?; **he's the ~ man for the job** es el hombre más indicado para el cargo, es el hombre que hace falta para el puesto; **he knows all the ~ people** conoce a todas las personas que pueden serle útiles; **they holiday in all the ~ places** toman sus vacaciones en todos los sitios que están de moda; **it's not the ~ length** de largo no sirve, de largo no vale; **he's one of the ~ sort** es buen chico, es un tío simpático; **he's clever but not the ~ sort for us** es inteligente pero no nos conviene; **to say the ~ thing** decir lo que conviene, decir lo que se debe decir; **we must get it ~ this time** esta vez tenemos que acertarlo, tenemos que hacerlo bien esta vez; **to put a clock ~** poner un reloj en hora; **to put (or set) sth ~** arreglar algo, poner algo en orden; **that's soon put ~** eso se corrige fácilmente; **to put a mistake ~** corregir un error, rectificar un error; **to put sb ~** corregir a uno, señalar a uno su error, (*unpleasantly*) enmendar la plana a uno.
▼ (c) **to be ~** (*person*) tener razón, estar en lo cierto (*esp LAm*); **you're dead ~, you're quite ~** estás en lo cierto; **to be ~ to** + *infin* hacer bien en + *infin*; **am I ~ in thinking that ...?** ¿me equivoco al afirmar que ...?
(d) (*in mind*) cuerdo; **to be in one's ~ mind** estar en su cabal juicio; **she's not ~ in the head** no está en sus cabales.
(e) (*in order, settled*) **all's ~ with the world** todo le va bien al mundo; **to be as ~ as rain** (*Brit*) estar perfectamente; **I'm as ~ as rain, thanks** gracias, estoy perfectamente; **she'll be as ~ as rain in a few days** en unos pocos días se repondrá completamente de esto; **it all came ~ in the end** al fin todo se arregló, al fin todo salió bien; **it will all come ~ in the end** todo se arreglará.

(f) *V* **all right**.
(g) (*not left*) derecho; (*Pol*) derechista; **~ back** defensa *m* derecho, defensa *f* derecha; **~ half** medio *m* derecho, medio *m* volante derecho; **~ wing** (*Mil, Sport*) ala *f* derecha.
(h) (*Math*) *angle* recto.
(i) (*) **he's a ~ idiot** es un puro idiota; **a ~ twit I should feel if ...** bien tonto me creería si ...; **he made a ~ mess of it** lo hizo malísimamente, lo embrolló todo de mala manera.
2 ADV (a) (*straight etc*) derecho; directamente; **~ away** en seguida, ahorita mismo (*Mex*); **~ away!** (*Rail etc*) ¡en marcha!; **~ here** aquí mismo; **~ now** ahora mismo; **I'll be ~ over** voy en seguida; **to go ~ on** seguir, seguir derecho, seguir adelante; **~ on!** ¡eso es!, ¡de acuerdo!; **he just went ~ on talking** siguió hablando tan fresco; **to speak ~ out** hablar claramente, hablar sin rodeos.
(b) (*quite, exactly*) completamente; exactamente; **~ in the middle** exactamente en el centro, por toda la mitad; **~ at the top** en todo lo alto; **it hit him ~ on the chest** le dio de lleno en el pecho; **he filled it ~ up** lo llenó del todo; **the wind is ~ behind us** sopla el viento precisamente detrás de nosotros; **~ at the end of his speech** precisamente al fin de su discurso; **there is a fence ~ round the house** hay una valla que rodea la casa por completo; **it goes ~ to the end** llega hasta el final (sin dejar espacio *etc*); **he put his hand in ~ to the bottom** introdujo la mano hasta el mismo fondo.
(c) (*rightly*) bien; correctamente; **to do ~** obrar bien, obrar correctamente; **you did ~** hiciste bien; **if I remember ~** si no recuerdo mal; **nothing goes ~ with them** nada les sale bien; **it was him all ~** fue él sin sombra de duda; **it's a big one all ~** ya lo creo que es grande; **~ enough!** ¡muy bien!; ¡razón tienes!; **it was there ~ enough** sí estaba allí; *V* **serve**.
(d) (*not left*) a la derecha, hacia la derecha; **~ (about) turn!** ¡media vuelta a la derecha!; **to turn ~** torcer a la derecha; **he looked neither ~ nor left** no miró a ningún lado; **they owe money ~ and left** deben dinero a todos, tienen deudas por doquier; **we are a ~ of centre party** somos un partido del centro derecho.
(e) **R~** Reverend Reverendísimo *m*.
3 N (a) (*what is lawful*) derecho *m*; (*what is just*) justicia *f*; (*what is morally ~*) bien *m*; **~ and wrong** el bien y el mal; **might and ~** la fuerza y el derecho; **to be in the ~** tener razón; **to fight for the ~** luchar por la justicia; **to have ~ on one's side** tener la razón de su parte; **to know ~ from wrong** saber distinguir el bien del mal.
▼ (b) (*title, claim*) derecho *m*; título *m*; privilegio *m*; **~ of abode** derecho *m* a domicilio; **~ of assembly** derecho *m* de reunión; **~s of the citizen** derechos *mpl* del ciudadano; **~s of man** derechos *mpl* del hombre; **~ to reply** derecho *m* de réplica; **~ of way** derecho *m* de paso, (*Jur*) servidumbre *f* de paso, (*Aut etc*) prioridad *f*; **sole ~** (*Comm*) exclusiva *f*; **as of ~** por derecho propio; de oficio; **by ~ de derecho**, en justicia; **by ~ of** por razón de; **by what ~?** ¿con qué derecho ...?; **to be within one's ~s** estar en su derecho; **to exercise one's ~** usar de su derecho (*to* + *infin* de + *infin*); **to have a ~ to sth** tener derecho a algo; **to have the ~ to** + *infin* tener el derecho de + *infin*; **you had no ~ to** + *infin* no le correspondía a Vd + *infin*; **to own sth in one's own ~** poseer algo por derecho propio; **to reserve the ~ to** + *infin* reservarse el derecho de + *infin*.
(c) (*of authorship etc*) derechos *mpl*; propiedad *f*; **film ~s** derechos *mpl* cinematográficos; **'all ~s reserved'** 'es propiedad', 'reservados todos los derechos'.
(d) **~s: I don't know the ~s of the matter** no sé quién tiene razón en el asunto; **to set sth to ~s** arreglar algo; componer algo.
(e) (*not left*) derecha *f*; (*Pol: also ~ wing*) derecha *f*; (*Boxing*) derechazo *m*; **on the ~, to the ~** a la derecha; **to keep to the ~** (*Aut*) circular por la derecha; **reading from ~ to left** leyendo de derecha a izquierda; **he is of the ~** es de derechas; **he's further to the ~ than I am** es más derechista que yo.
4 ATTR: **~s issue** emisión *f* gratuita de acciones.
5 VT (a) (*set upright etc*) enderezar.
(b) (*correct*) corregir, rectificar; **to ~ a wrong** deshacer un agravio, acabar con un abuso.

right angle ['raɪt,æŋgl] N ángulo *m* recto; **to be at ~s to** estar en (*or* formar) ángulo recto con.

right-angled ['raɪt,æŋgld] ADJ rectangular; *triangle* rectángulo; *bend etc* en ángulo recto.

righteous ['raɪtʃəs] ADJ justo, honrado, recto; *indignation etc* virtuoso, justificado.

righteously ['raɪtʃəslɪ] ADV honradamente, rectamente; virtuosamente; con justicia.

righteousness ['raɪtʃəsnɪs] N honradez *f*, rectitud *f*; virtud *f*; justicia *f*.

rightful ['raɪtfʊl] ADJ legítimo; verdadero; **~ claimant** derechohabiente *mf*.

rightfully ['raɪtfəlɪ] ADV legítimamente; verdaderamente.

right-hand ['raɪthænd] ADJ: **~ drive** conducción *f* por la derecha; **~ man** brazo *m* derecho, hombre *m* de confianza; **~ side** derecha *f*; **~**

turn vuelta *f* a la derecha.

right-handed ['raɪt'hændɪd] ADJ diestro, que usa la mano derecha; *tool* para persona que usa la mano derecha.

right-hander [,raɪt'hændər] N (*Sport*) diestro *m*, -a *f*.

right-ho* [,raɪt'həʊ] EXCL ¡vale!, ¡bien!

rightism ['raɪtɪzəm] N derechismo *m*.

rightist ['raɪtɪst] [1] ADJ derechista.
　　[2] N derechista *mf*.

▼ **rightly** ['raɪtlɪ] ADV correctamente; debidamente; bien; ~ **or wrongly** mal que bien; con razón o sin ella; **and ~ so** y con razón, a justo título; **to act ~** obrar correctamente, obrar bien; **as he ~ believed** según creía correctamente; **he was ~ dismissed** con toda justicia le despidieron; **I don't ~ know, I couldn't ~ say** no lo sé muy bien, no estoy muy seguro.

right-minded ['raɪt'maɪndɪd] ADJ (*sensible*) prudente; (*decent*) honrado.

rightness ['raɪtnɪs] N (*correctness*) exactitud *f*; (*justice*) justicia *f*.

right-thinking ['raɪt'θɪŋkɪŋ] ADJ juicioso, sensato; honrado.

right-to-life [,raɪttə'laɪf] ADJ *movement, group* pro derecho a la vida.

rightward ['raɪtwəd] ADJ *movement etc* a (*or* hacia) la derecha.

rightward(s) ['raɪtwəd(z)] ADV *move etc* a (*or* hacia) la derecha.

right-wing ['raɪt'wɪŋ] ADJ derechista.

right-winger ['raɪt'wɪŋər] N derechista *mf*.

rigid ['rɪdʒɪd] ADJ rígido; yerto; (*in attitude*) inflexible, severo; **he is quite ~ about it** es inflexible sobre ese punto; **we were ~ with fear** quedamos helados de miedo; **to shake sb ~*** pasmar a uno, dejar frío a uno*.

rigidity [rɪ'dʒɪdɪtɪ] N rigidez *f*; inflexibilidad *f*, severidad *f*.

rigidly ['rɪdʒɪdlɪ] ADV rígidamente; inflexiblemente, severamente; **he is ~ opposed to it** está totalmente en contra de esto.

rigmarole ['rɪgmərəʊl] N galimatías *m*, relación *f* disparatada.

rigor ['rɪgər] N (*US*) = **rigour.**

rigor mortis ['rɪgə'mɔːtɪs] N rigidez *f* cadavérica.

rigorous ['rɪgərəs] ADJ riguroso.

rigorously ['rɪgərəslɪ] ADV rigurosamente.

rigour, (*US*) **rigor** ['rɪgər] N rigor *m*, severidad *f*; **the full ~ of the law** el máximo rigor de la ley; **the ~s of the climate** los rigores del clima.

rig-out* ['rɪgaʊt] N atuendo *m*, atavío *m*.

rile* [raɪl] VT sulfurar*, reventar*, sacar de quicio a; **it ~s me terribly** me irrita muchísimo; **there's nothing that ~s me more** no hay nada que me reviente más*.

rill [rɪl] N (*liter*) arroyo *m*, riachuelo *m*.

rim [rɪm] N (*of cup etc*) borde *m*, canto *m*; (*of wheel*) llanta *f*; (*of spectacles*) montura *f*, aro *m*; (*of dirt etc*) cerco *m*; **the ~ of the sun** el borde del sol.

rime¹ [raɪm] N (*poet*) rima *f*.

rime² [raɪm] N (*frost*) escarcha *f*.

rimless ['rɪmlɪs] ADJ *glasses* sin aros.

rimmed [rɪmd] ADJ: ~ **with ...** con un borde de ..., bordeado de ...; **glasses ~ with gold** gafas *fpl* con montura de oro.

rind [raɪnd] N (*of fruit etc*) corteza *f*, cáscara *f*, piel *f*; (*of cheese*) costra *f*; (*of bacon*) piel *f*.

ring¹ [rɪŋ] [1] N (a) (*circle: of metal etc*) aro *m*; argolla *f*; (*on finger*) anillo *m*, sortija *f*; alianza *f*; (*on bird's leg, for curtain*) anilla *f*; (*ear~*) arete *m*; (*on stove*) hornillo *m*, quemador *m*; (*Bot: annual ~*) anillo *m* anual, cerco *m* anual; **~s** (*Gymnastics*) anillas *fpl*; **~ of smoke** anillo *m* de humo, (*from mouth*) bocanada *f* de humo; **~s of Saturn** anillos *mpl* de Saturno; **to have ~s round one's eyes** tener ojeras.

(b) (*of people*) círculo *m*, grupo *m*; (*of children, gossips etc*) corro *m*; (*coterie*) camarilla *f*; (*gang*) pandilla *f*; (*Comm*) confabulación *f*, (*on large scale*) cartel *m*; **there was a ~ of children round her** los niños estaban reunidos en torno suyo, ella estaba rodeada de niños; **they were sitting in a ~** estaban sentados en círculo; **to make** (*or* run) **~s round sb** dar quince y raya a uno.

(c) (*Boxing: arena etc*) cuadrilátero *m*; (*at circus*) pista *f*; (*bull~*) ruedo *m*, redondel *m*, plaza *f*; (*at horse race*) cercado *m*; **the ~** (*fig*) el boxeo.

　　[2] ATTR: ~ **exercise** anillas *fpl*; ~ **finger** dedo *m* anular.

　　[3] VT cercar, rodear (*by, with* de); *bird* anillar, poner anilla a; **the town is ~ed by hills** la ciudad está rodeada de colinas; **we are ~ed by enemies** estamos rodeados de enemigos, nos cercan los enemigos.

◆ **ring round** VT rodear (*with* de).

▼ **ring²** [rɪŋ] [1] N (a) (*metallic sound*) sonido *m* metálico; (*resonance*) resonancia *f*; (*tinkle*) retintín *m*; (*of voice*) timbre *m*; (*tone*) tono *m*, entonación *f*; (*of large bell*) repique *m*, tañido *m*; (*of handbell*) campanilleo *m*; (*of electric bell*) toque *m* de timbre; (*at door*) llamada *f*; **there was a ~ at the door** llamaron a la puerta; **give 3 ~s for the maid** tocar el timbre 3 veces para llamar a la camarera; **with a ~ of defiance** en son de reto; **with a sarcastic ~ in his voice** con retintín, con énfasis sarcástico; **that has the ~ of truth about it** eso tiene traza de ser verdad.

(b) **a ~ of bells** (*set*) un juego de campanas.

(c) (*Telec*) llamada *f* telefónica, telefonazo *m*; **I'll give you a ~** te llamaré.

　　[2] (*irr*: PRET **rang**, PTP **rung**) VT (a) (*strike, make sound*) hacer sonar; *large bell* repicar, tañer; *electric bell* tocar; ~ **the bell, please** por favor toque el timbre.

▼ (b) **to ~ sb** (*Brit Telec*) llamar a uno al (*or* por) teléfono, telefonear a uno.

▼ [3] VI (*sound*) sonar; resonar (*with* con); (*large bell*) repicar; (*small bell*) sonar; (*tinkle*) campanillear, tintinear; (*at door*) llamar; (*ears*) zumbar; **the telephone rang** (*Brit*) sonó el teléfono; **the valley rang with cries** resonaron los gritos por el valle; **his words were ~ing in my head** sus palabras resonaban en mi cabeza; **you rang, madam?** ¿me llama Vd, señora?; **we'll ~ for some sugar** llamaremos para pedir azúcar; **his words rang false** sus palabras sonaban falsas; **his story ~s true** su narración parece verídica.

◆ **ring back** [1] VT volver a llamar a, llamar otra vez a.
　　[2] VI volver a llamar.

◆ **ring down** VT *curtain* bajar.

◆ **ring in** [1] VT anunciar; **to ~ in the New Year** celebrar el Año Nuevo (con campanas).
　　[2] VI (a) telefonear (una noticia *etc*).
　　(b) (*US Ind*) fichar.

◆ **ring off** VI colgar.

◆ **ring out** [1] VT: **to ~ out the old year** tañer las campanas para señalar el fin del año.
　　[2] VI (a) oírse, sonar; **a shot rang out** se oyó un tiro, sonó un tiro.
　　(b) (*US Ind*) fichar la salida.

◆ **ring round** VT llamar (al teléfono).

◆ **ring up** VT (a) (*Telec*) llamar (por teléfono).
　　(b) *curtain* levantar; **to ~ up the curtain on** (*fig*) dar comienzo a, iniciar.
　　(c) *amount* (*on cash-register*) registrar.

ring-a-ring-a-roses ['rɪŋə'rɪŋə'rəʊzɪz] N corro *m*; **to play ~** jugar al corro.

ring binder ['rɪŋbaɪndər] N carpeta *f* de anillos.

ringbolt ['rɪŋbəʊlt] N perno *m* con anillo, (*Naut*) cáncamo *m*.

ringdove ['rɪŋdʌv] N paloma *f* torcaz.

ringer ['rɪŋər] N (a) campanero *m*, -a *f*. (b) (:) **dead ~** doble *m*, viva imagen *f*; **A is a dead ~ for B** A se le parece en todo a B. (c) (*US Racing*) caballo *m* sustituido.

ringing¹ ['rɪŋɪŋ] N (*Orn*) anillado *m*, anillamiento *m*.

ringing² ['rɪŋɪŋ] [1] ADJ resonante, sonoro; **in ~ tones** en tono vibrante, en tono enérgico; ~ **tone** (*Brit Telec*) tono *m* de llamada.
　　[2] N (*of large bell*) repique *m*, tañido *m*; (*of handbell*) campanilleo *m*; (*of electric bell*) toque *m* de timbre; (*in ears*) zumbido *m*.

ringleader ['rɪŋ,liːdər] N cabecilla *m*.

ringlet ['rɪŋlɪt] N rizo *m*, bucle *m*, tirabuzón *m*.

ringmaster ['rɪŋ,mɑːstər] N jefe *m* de pista, director *m* de circo; (*trainer*) domador *m*.

ring-pull ['rɪŋpʊl] N anilla *f*; ~ **can** lata *f* de anilla.

ringroad ['rɪŋrəʊd] N (*Brit*) carretera *f* de circunvalación, carretera *f* radial, periférico *m* (*LAm*).

ringside ['rɪŋsaɪd] N: **to be at the ~** estar junto al cuadrilátero; **a ~ seat** una butaca de primera fila; **to have a ~ seat** (*fig*) verlo todo desde muy cerca.

ring-spanner ['rɪŋ,spænər] N llave *f* dentada.

ringway ['rɪŋweɪ] N (*US*) = **ringroad.**

ringworm ['rɪŋwɜːm] N tiña *f*.

rink [rɪŋk] N pista *f*.

rinse [rɪns] [1] N (a) (*of dishes etc*) enjuague *m*; (*of clothes*) aclarado *m*; **to give one's stockings a ~** aclarar las medias.
　　(b) (*colouring*) reflejo *m*; **to give one's hair a blue ~** dar reflejos azules a su pelo.
　　[2] VT (a) (*also* to ~ out) enjuagar; aclarar; *mouth* lavar, limpiar.
　　(b) (*colour*) dar reflejos a.

Rio de Janeiro [,riːəʊdədʒə'nɪərəʊ] N Río *m* de Janeiro.

riot ['raɪət] [1] N motín *m*, disturbio *m*; tumulto *m*; (*fig*) orgía *f*; alboroto *m*; (*in prison*) amotinamiento *m*, sublevación *f*; **a ~ of colour** había una exhibición brillante de colores; **there was nearly a ~** hubo casi un motín; **it was a ~!** (*fig*) ¡fue divertidísimo!, ¡fue la monda!*; **to run ~** desmandarse, cometer excesos, librarse de toda traba; (*spread*) extenderse por todas partes, cubrirlo todo; **to let one's imagination run ~** dejar volar la imaginación, dar rienda suelta a la imaginación.
　　[2] ATTR: **to read the ~ act** mandar que cese el disturbio, imponer la paz; **to read the ~ act to sb** leerle la cartilla a uno; ~ **gear** uniforme *m* antidisturbios; ~ **police** brigada *f* antidisturbios; ~ **shield** escudo *m* antidisturbios; ~ **squad** = ~ **police.**
　　[3] VI amotinarse.

rioter ['raɪətər] N amotinado *m*, -a *f*, manifestante *mf*, revoltoso *m*.

riotous ['raɪətəs] ADJ *person, populace* amotinado; *assembly* desordenado, alborotado; *party* bullicioso, ruidoso; *life* desenfrenado; **it was a ~ success** obtuvo un éxito ruidoso; **we had a ~ time** nos divertimos una barbaridad.

riotously ['raɪətəsli] ADV con desorden, alborotadamente; bulliciosamente, ruidosamente; desenfrenadamente; **a ~ funny play** una comedia tremendamente divertida.

▼ **R.I.P.** ABBR *of* **requiescat in pace, (may he** (*etc*) **rest in peace)** que en paz descanse, E.P.D., D.E.P.

rip [rɪp] **1** N rasgón *m*, rasgadura *f*.
2 VT rasgar, desgarrar; **to ~ a box open** abrir una caja rompiéndola, quitar violentamente la tapa de una caja; **to ~ an envelope open** abrir un sobre rompiéndolo.
3 VI **(a)** (*cloth*) rasgarse, romperse.
(b) (*) **to ~ along** correr a toda mecha, ir a buen tren; **let her ~!** ¡más rápido!, ¡más gas!*
♦ **rip off** VT **(a)** arrancar, quitar (de un tirón). **(b)** (‡) *person* timar, robar; *object* pulir‡, birlar*.
♦ **rip out** VT arrancar.
♦ **rip through** VT desgarrar, romper (violentamente); destrozar.
♦ **rip up** VT (*tear*) desgarrar, romper; **the train ~ped up 100 metres of track** el tren destrozó 100 metros de la vía.

riparian [raɪ'pɛərɪən] ADJ ribereño.
ripcord ['rɪpkɔːd] N cabo *m* de desgarre.
ripe [raɪp] ADJ **(a)** *fruit etc* maduro; **to be ~ for picking** estar bastante maduro para poderse coger; **to grow ~** madurar.
(b) (*fig*) listo; perfecto, en su punto; **a plan ~ for execution** un plan listo para ponerse en obra; **to be ~ for mischief** estar dispuesto a emprender cualquier diablura; **the company is ~ for a takeover** la empresa está en su punto para que la adquiera otro; **the country is ~ for revolution** la revolución está a punto de estallar en el país; **to live to a ~ old age** llegar a muy viejo; **when the time is ~** cuando se nos depare la oportunidad, cuando llegue el momento oportuno.
(c) (*) *language* grosero, verde; *smell* fuerte, desagradable; **that's pretty ~!** ¡eso no se puede consentir!

ripen ['raɪpən] VTI madurar.
ripeness ['raɪpnɪs] N madurez *f*.
rip-off‡ ['rɪpɒf] N timo *m*, robo *m*, estafa *f*.
riposte [rɪ'pɒst] **1** N (*Fencing*) estocada *f*; (*reply*) respuesta *f* aguda, réplica *f*.
2 VI replicar, responder con viveza.
ripper ['rɪpəʳ] N: **Jack the R~** Juanito el Destripador.
ripping*† ['rɪpɪŋ] ADJ (*Brit*) estupendo*, bárbaro*.
ripple ['rɪpl] **1** N (*wave*) rizo *m*, onda *f*; (*sound*) murmullo *m*; **~ effect = knock-on effect; a ~ of excitement** un susurro de emoción; **a ~ of applause** unos cuantos aplausos.
2 VT rizar.
3 VI rizarse; correr con rizos; murmurar; **the crowd ~d with excitement** el público se estremeció emocionado.
rip-roaring* ['rɪp,rɔːrɪŋ] ADJ *party etc* bullicioso, animadísimo, de lo más ruidoso; *speech* apasionado, violento; *success* apoteósico.
riptide ['rɪptaɪd] N aguas *fpl* revueltas.
RISC N (*Comput*) ABBR *of* **reduced instruction set computer** o **computing**.
rise [raɪz] **1** N **(a)** (*act of rising*) subida *f*, ascensión *f*, elevación *f*; (*of sun, moon*) salida *f*; (*of river*) crecida *f*; **a ~ in the voice** una elevación de tono; **~ and fall** (*of water etc*) subida *f* y bajada; (*of music, voice*) cadencia *f*.
(b) (*act of rising, fig*) **the ~ of the middle class** el desarrollo de la clase media; **the ~ of Bristol** el crecimiento de Bristol; **Napoleon's ~ to power** la subida de Napoleón al poder; **the ~ and fall of the empire** la grandeza y caída del imperio; **inflation is on the ~ again** la inflación vuelve a subir; **to take a ~ out of sb*** burlarse de uno; poner a uno en ridículo; **nobody takes a ~ out of me*** a mí nadie me tose.
(c) (*in price, temperature*) subida *f*, alza *f*; (*in value*) aumento *m*; (*in salary*) aumento *m*, subida *f*; (*promotion*) ascenso *m*; **to ask for a ~** (*Brit*) pedir un aumento de sueldo; **they got a ~ of 50 dollars** les aumentaron el sueldo en 50 dólares; **prices are on the ~** los precios están subiendo; **a ~ of 5 degrees in temperature** una subida de temperatura de 5 grados.
(d) (*of spring, river*) nacimiento *m*; (*fig*) origen *m*; **the river takes its ~ in the mountains** el río nace en las montañas; **to give ~ to** dar origen a, motivar, ocasionar, (*doubts etc*) suscitar, dar lugar a.
(e) (*high ground*) altura *f*, eminencia *f*; (*slope*) cuesta *f*, pendiente *f*.
2 (*irr*: PRET **rose**, PTP **risen**) VI **(a)** (*of person*: *to one's feet etc*) levantarse, ponerse en pie; **he rose to greet us** se levantó para recibirnos; **to ~ from table** levantarse de la mesa; **to ~ at 6** levantarse a las 6; **to ~ early** levantarse temprano, madrugar; **to ~ (again) from the dead** resucitar; **Slobodia shall ~ again** Eslobodia renacerá.
(b) to ~ (in revolt) sublevarse, rebelarse (*against* contra); **to ~ (up) in arms** alzarse en armas.
(c) (*sun, moon*) salir; (*smoke etc*) subir, elevarse, alzarse; (*building*,

mountain) elevarse; **it rose 3 metres off the ground** se elevó 3 metros sobre el suelo; **the mountain ~s to 3,500 metres** la montaña alcanza 3.500 metros, la montaña se eleva a 3.500 metros; **to ~ to the surface** salir a la superficie; **she could feel a blush rising to her cheeks** sentía que sus mejillas se ponían coloradas; **the partridge rose** se levantó la perdiz, la perdiz alzó el vuelo; **to ~ to the bait** picar, morder el anzuelo (*also fig*); **he wouldn't ~ (to the bait)** no quería picar; **to ~ to the challenge** ponerse a la altura del reto, responder al desafío como se debe.
(d) (*ground*) subir (en pendiente); (*dough*) leudarse; (*barometer, temperature, sea etc*) subir; (*river*) crecer; (*sound, voice*) hacerse más fuerte, sonar más fuerte; (*wind*) hacerse más fuerte, soplar más fuerte; (*swell*) hincharse, crecer; (*price*) subir, avanzar; (*St Ex*) estar en alza, cotizarse en alza; (*number*) subir, aumentar; **prices are rising** suben los precios; **tension is rising** aumenta la tensión; **it has risen 20% in price** su precio ha subido en un 20 por cien; **a thought rose in my mind** se me ocurrió algo; **laughter rose from the audience** en el público estallaron las risas; **our spirits rose** volvimos a animarnos, nos reanimamos.
(e) to ~ above petty rancour mostrarse superior a los pequeños rencores; **to ~ to the occasion** ponerse a la altura de las circunstancias.
(f) (*in rank*) ascender, avanzar; **he rose to colonel** ascendió a coronel; **he rose from nothing** salió de la nada; **to ~ in the world** hacer carrera, avanzar en su carrera; **to ~ in sb's opinion** ganar en la opinión de uno.
(g) (*river*) nacer.
(h) then the House rose luego se suspendió la sesión.
♦ **rise up** VI V **rise 2**.
risen ['rɪzn] PTP *of* **rise**.
riser ['raɪzəʳ] N: **to be an early ~** madrugar, ser madrugador; **to be a late ~** levantarse tarde.
risibility [,rɪzɪ'bɪlɪtɪ] N risibilidad *f*.
risible ['rɪzɪbl] ADJ risible.
rising ['raɪzɪŋ] **1** ADJ *number, quantity* creciente; *tide* creciente; *sun etc* naciente; *trend* (*Fin*) alcista; (*promising*) prometedor, que promete, de porvenir; **the ~ number of murders** el creciente número de homicidios; **with ~ alarm** con creciente alarma; **~ damp** humedad *f*; **the ~ generation** las nuevas generaciones; **~ ground** terreno *m* ascendente; **~ politician** político *m* en alza.
2 N **(a)** (*rebellion*) sublevación *f*, rebelión *f*.
(b) (*of river*) nacimiento *m*; (*of sun etc*) salida *f*.
(c) **on the ~ of the House** al suspenderse la sesión.
3 ADV: **he's ~ 12*** pronto tendrá 12 años.
▼ **risk** [rɪsk] **1** N riesgo *m*, peligro *m*; **against all ~s** contra todo riesgo; **persons at ~** personas *fpl* en peligro, personas *fpl* vulnerables; **at the ~ of** a riesgo de; **at the ~ of one's life** con peligro de la vida, arriesgando la vida; **at one's own ~** bajo su propia responsabilidad; **at owner's ~** bajo la responsabilidad del dueño; **there is a fire ~** hay peligro de provocar un incendio; **it's not worth the ~** no vale la pena correr tanto peligro; **to put sth at ~** poner algo en peligro; **to run the ~ of defeat** correr riesgo de ser derrotado; **to run the ~ of +** *ger* correr el riesgo de + *infin*; **to take ~s** arriesgarse; **he takes a lot of ~s** se arriesga mucho; **will you take the ~?** ¿te atreves?; **I can't take the ~** no me puedo exponer a eso.
2 ATTR: **~ capital** capital *m* (de) riesgo.
3 VT arriesgar; atreverse a, exponerse a; **I'll ~ it** acepto; **I can't ~ it** no me puedo exponer a eso; **shall we ~ it?** ¿nos atrevemos?; **to ~ defeat** correr riesgo de ser derrotado, exponerse a una posible derrota; **to ~ +** *ger* arriesgarse a + *infin*; **I can't ~ going alone** no puedo arriesgarme a ir solo, no me atrevo a ir solo.
riskiness ['rɪskɪnɪs] N peligro *m*, lo peligroso, lo arriesgado; **in view of the ~ of the plan** visto lo peligroso del plan.
risky ['rɪskɪ] ADJ **(a)** *plan, deed etc* peligroso, arriesgado, aventurado; **a ~ enterprise** una empresa arriesgada; **it is ~ to suppose that ...** es arriesgado (*or* temerario) suponer que ... **(b)** = **risqué**.
risotto [rɪ'zɒtəʊ] N arroz *m* (con pollo, verduras, etc).
risqué ['riːskeɪ] ADJ verde, indecente, de color subido.
rissole ['rɪsəʊl] N (*Brit*) ≈ croqueta *f*.
rite [raɪt] N rito *m*; (*funeral* ~s) exequias *fpl*; **last ~s** extremaunción *f*; **'The R~ of Spring'** 'La Consagración de la Primavera'.
ritual ['rɪtjʊəl] **1** ADJ ritual; (*fig*) consagrado, formulario; **in the ~ phrase** en la expresión consagrada.
2 N ritual *m*, ceremonia *f*.
ritualism ['rɪtjʊəlɪzəm] N ritualismo *m*.
ritualist ['rɪtjʊəlɪst] N ritualista *mf*.
ritualistic [,rɪtjʊə'lɪstɪk] ADJ ritualista; (*fig*) consagrado, sacramental.
ritualize ['rɪtjʊə,laɪz] VT: **to ~ sth** hacer de algo un ritual; **it's a highly ~d event** es un acontecimiento de marcado carácter ritualístico.
ritually ['rɪtjʊəlɪ] ADV ritualmente.
ritzy* ['rɪtsɪ] ADJ (*US*) muy pera*, lujoso.
rival ['raɪvəl] **1** ADJ rival, opuesto; **a ~ firm** una firma competidora.

2 N rival *mf*, competidor *m*, -ora *f*.
3 VT rivalizar con, competir con.

rivalry ['raɪvəlrɪ] N rivalidad *f*; competencia *f*; **to enter into ~ with sb** empezar a competir con uno.

riven ['rɪvən] ADJ, PTP (*liter*) rajado, hendido; **~ by** desgarrado por, dividido por, escindido por.

river ['rɪvəʳ] **1** N río *m*; **down ~** río abajo; **up ~** río arriba; **up ~ from Toledo** aguas arriba de Toledo; **to sell sb down the ~*** traicionar a uno.
2 ATTR de río, del río; fluvial; **~ fish** pez *m* de río; **~ fishing** pesca *f* de río; **~ police** brigada *f* fluvial; **~ traffic** tráfico *m* fluvial.

riverbank ['rɪvəbæŋk] **1** N orilla *f* del río, margen *f* del río.
2 ATTR ribereño.

riverbasin ['rɪvə,beɪsn] N cuenca *f* de río.

riverbed ['rɪvəbed] N lecho *m*, cauce *m* (del río).

riverboat ['rɪvəbəʊt] N embarcación *f* fluvial, barcaza *f*.

riverine ['rɪvəraɪn] ADJ fluvial, ribereño.

rivermouth ['rɪvəmaʊθ] N, PL **rivermouths** ['rɪvəmaʊðz] estuario *m*, ría *f*.

riverside ['rɪvəsaɪd] **1** N ribera *f*, orilla *f* (del río).
2 ATTR ribereño.

rivet ['rɪvɪt] **1** N roblón *m*, remache *m*.
2 VT remachar; (*fig*) clavar (*on, to* en); **to ~ one's eyes on sth** clavar la vista en algo; **it ~ed our attention** nos llamó fuertemente la atención, lo miramos fascinados.

riveter ['rɪvɪtəʳ] N remachador *m*.

rivet(t)ing ['rɪvɪtɪŋ] **1** N remachado *m*.
2 ADJ fascinante, cautivador.

Riviera [,rɪvɪ'eərə] N (*French*) Riviera *f* (francesa), Costa *f* Azul; (*Italian*) Riviera *f* italiana.

rivulet ['rɪvjʊlɪt] N riachuelo *m*, arroyuelo *m*.

Riyadh [rɪ'yɑːd] N Riyadh *m*.

riyal [riː'ɑːl] N riyal *m*.

RK N (*Scol*) ABBR *of* **Religious Knowledge** instrucción *f* religiosa.

RL N ABBR *of* **Rugby League** *rugby profesional*.

Rly ABBR *of* **Railway** ferrocarril, f.c.

RM N ABBR *of* **Royal Marines**.

RMT N ABBR *of* **Rail, Maritime and Transport**.

RN N (**a**) (*Brit*) ABBR *of* **Royal Navy**. (**b**) (*US*) ABBR *of* **registered nurse**.

RNA N ABBR *of* **ribonucleic acid** ácido *m* ribonucleico, ARN *m*.

RNAS N (*Brit*) ABBR *of* **Royal Naval Air Services**.

RNLI N ABBR *of* **Royal National Lifeboat Institution** *servicio de lanchas de socorro*.

RNR N (*Brit*) ABBR *of* **Royal Naval Reserve**.

RNVR N ABBR *of* **Royal Naval Volunteer Reserve**.

RNZAF N ABBR *of* **Royal New Zealand Air Force**.

RNZN N ABBR *of* **Royal New Zealand Navy**.

roach [rəʊtʃ] N (**a**) (*Fish*) escarcho *m*; (*US*) cucaracha *f*. (**b**) (*US‡: drug*) cucaracha‡ *f*.

road [rəʊd] **1** N camino *m* (*to* de; *also fig*); (*main ~*) carretera *f*; (*in town*) calle *f*; (*surface*) firme *m*; (*roadway, not pavement*) calzada *f*; **~s** (*Naut*) rada *f*; **'~ narrows'** 'estrechamiento de la calzada'; **'~ up'** 'cerrado por obras'; **the ~ to Teruel** el camino de Teruel; **at the 23rd kilometre on the Valencia ~** en el kilómetro 23 de la carretera de Valencia; **the ~ to success** el camino del éxito; **one for the ~*** el trago del estribo*, la del estribo; **across the ~** al otro lado de la calle, enfrente; **she lives across the ~ from us** vive en frente de nosotros; **by ~** por carretera; **my car is off the ~** mi coche está en el garaje; **to be on the ~** estar en camino; (*Comm*) ser viajante; (*Theat*) estar de gira; **my car is on the ~ again** he vuelto a tener coche en carretera; **he's on the ~ to recovery** se está reponiendo; **we're on the ~ to disaster** vamos camino del desastre; **the dog was wandering on the ~** el perro andaba por la calzada; **to get (*or* take) a show on the ~,** to take to the ~ echarse a la carretera; **to be on the right ~** ir por buen camino (*also fig*); **to get out of the ~** (*fig*) quitarse de en medio; **our relationship has reached the end of the ~** nuestras relaciones han llegado al punto final; **to hold the ~** (*Aut*) agarrarse al camino; **to take the ~** ponerse en camino (*to X* para ir a X).
2 ATTR de carretera; vial; **~ accident** accidente *m* de tráfico, accidente *m* de tránsito; **~ construction** construcción *f* de carreteras; **~ haulage** transportes *mpl* por carretera; **~ haulier** compañía *f* de transportes por carretera; transportista *mf*; **~ hump** banda *f* de desaceleración; **~ junction** empalme *m*; **~ racer** (*Cycling*) ciclista *mf* de fondo en carretera; **~ rage** *conducta agresiva de los conductores*; **~ safety** seguridad *f* en la carretera, seguridad *f* vial; **~ sense** instinto *m* del automovilista; **~ tax** impuesto *m* de rodaje; **~ test, ~ trial** prueba *f* en carretera; **~ traffic** circulación *f* por carretera; tránsito *m* rodado; **~ transport** transportes *mpl* por carretera; **~ vehicle** vehículo *m* carretero.

roadbed ['rəʊdbed] N (*US*) firme *m*; (*Rail*) capa *f* de balasto.

roadblock ['rəʊdblɒk] N control *m*; barricada *f*.

roadbook ['rəʊdbʊk] N (*Aut*) libro *m* de mapas e itinerarios (*etc*).

roadbridge ['rəʊdbrɪdʒ] N puente *m* de carretera.

roadhog ['rəʊdhɒg] N loco *m* del volante, loca *f* del volante.

roadholding ['rəʊd,həʊldɪŋ] N agarre *m*.

roadhouse ['rəʊdhaʊs] N, PL **roadhouses** ['rəʊdhaʊzɪz] albergue *m* de carretera, motel *m*.

roadie* ['rəʊdɪ] N (*Mus*) encargado *m* del transporte del equipo.

roadmaking ['rəʊd,meɪkɪŋ] N construcción *f* de carreteras.

roadmap ['rəʊdmæp] N mapa *m* de carreteras, mapa *m* vial.

roadmender ['rəʊdmendəʳ] N peón *m* caminero.

road metal ['rəʊdmetl] N grava *f*, lastre *m*.

roadrace ['rəʊdreɪs] N carrera *f* en carretera.

roadroller ['rəʊd,rəʊləʳ] N apisonadora *f*.

roadshow ['rəʊdʃəʊ] N (*Theat*) bolo* *m*.

roadside ['rəʊdsaɪd] **1** N borde *m* (*LAm*: orilla *f*) del camino, borde *m* (*LAm*: orilla *f*) de la carretera.
2 ATTR de camino, de carretera; **~ inn** fonda *f* de carretera; **~ repairs** reparaciones *fpl* al borde de la carretera; **~ restaurant** (*US*) café-restaurante *m* (de carretera).

roadsign ['rəʊdsaɪn] N señal *f* de tráfico, señal *f* de carretera, señal *f* vertical.

roadstead ['rəʊdsted] N rada *f*.

roadster ['rəʊdstəʳ] N (*car*) coche *m* de turismo; (*cycle*) bicicleta *f* de turismo.

roadsweeper ['rəʊd,swiːpəʳ] N barrendero *m*.

roaduser ['rəʊd,juːzəʳ] N usuario *m* de la vía pública.

roadway ['rəʊdweɪ] N calzada *f*.

roadworks ['rəʊdwɜːks] NPL obras *fpl* de carretera.

roadworthy ['rəʊd,wɜːðɪ] ADJ *car* en condiciones para circular, apto para circular.

roam [rəʊm] **1** VT vagar por, errar por, recorrer.
2 VI vagar.
♦ **roam about, roam around** VI andar sin propósito fijo.

roamer ['rəʊməʳ] N hombre *m* errante, andariego *m*; (*tramp*) vagabundo *m*.

roaming ['rəʊmɪŋ] N vagabundeo *m*; (*as tourist etc*) excursiones *fpl*, paseos *mpl*.

roan [rəʊn] **1** ADJ ruano.
2 N caballo *m* ruano.

roar [rɔːʳ] **1** N (*of animal*) rugido *m*, bramido *m*; (*of person*) rugido *m*; (*loud noise*) estruendo *m*, fragor *m*; (*of fire*) crepitación *f*; (*of river, storm etc*) estruendo *m*; (*of laughter*) carcajada *f*; **with great ~s of laughter** con grandes carcajadas; **he said with a ~** dijo rugiendo; **to set the room in a ~** hacer reír a todo el mundo a carcajadas.
2 VT rugir, decir a gritos; **to ~ one's disapproval** manifestar su disconformidad a gritos; **he ~ed out an order** lanzó una orden a voz en grito.
3 VI rugir, bramar; hacer estruendo; (*of guns, thunder*) retumbar; (*with laughter*) reírse a carcajadas; **to ~ with pain** rugir de dolor; **the lorry ~ed past** el camión pasó ruidosamente; **this will make you ~** esto os hará moriros de risa.
4 VR: **to ~ o.s. hoarse** ponerse ronco gritando, gritar hasta enronquecerse.

roaring ['rɔːrɪŋ] ADJ: **the R~ Forties** los cuarenta rugientes; **he was ~ drunk** estaba borracho y despotricaba; **in front of a ~ fire** junto a la lumbre que arde furiosamente; **it was a ~ success** fue un éxito clamoroso; **to do a ~ trade** hacer un tremendo negocio.

roast [rəʊst] **1** N carne *f* asada, asado *m*.
2 ADJ asado; *coffee* torrefacto, tostado; **~ beef** rosbif *m*.
3 VT *meat* (**a**) asar; *coffee* tostar; **the sun which was ~ing the city** el sol que achicharraba la ciudad; **to ~ one's feet by the fire** asarse los pies junto al fuego.
(**b**) (*) **to ~ sb** (*mock*) mofarse de uno; (*criticize*) criticar a uno, censurar a uno; (*scold*) desollar vivo a uno, poner a uno como un trapo*.
4 VI (*meat*) asarse; (*person*) tostarse; **we ~ed there for a whole month** nos asamos allí durante un mes entero.

roaster ['rəʊstəʳ] N (**a**) (*implement*) asador *m*, tostador *m*. (**b**) (*bird*) pollo *m* para asar.

roasting ['rəʊstɪŋ] **1** ADJ (**a**) *chicken etc* para asar. (**b**) *day, heat* abrasador.
2 N (**a**) (*Culin*) asado *m*; (*of coffee*) tostadura *f*, tueste *m*. (**b**) **to give sb a ~*** = roast 3 (**b**).

roasting-jack ['rəʊstɪŋdʒæk] N, **roasting-spit** ['rəʊstɪŋspɪt] N asador *m*.

rob [rɒb] VT robar; *bank etc* atracar; **to ~ sb of sth** robar algo a uno; **I've been ~bed!** ¡me han robado!; **we were ~bed!*** (*Sport*) ¡hubo tongo!

robber ['rɒbəʳ] N ladrón *m*; (*bank~*) atracador *m*; (*footpad*) salteador *m* (de caminos); (*brigand*) bandido *m*.

robbery ['rɒbərɪ] N robo *m*; latrocinio *m*; **~ with violence** robo *m* a mano armada, atraco *m*, asalto *m*.

robe [rəʊb] **1** N (††) manto *m*, túnica *f*; (*monk's*) hábito *m*; (*priest's*) sotana *f*; (*lawyer's, Univ*) toga *f*, traje *m* talar; (*bath~*) albornoz *m*; (*christening ~*) traje *m* de bautismo; **~s** traje *m* de ceremonia, traje *m* talar.

[2] VT: **to ~ sb in black** vestir a uno de negro; **to appear ~d in a long dress** aparecer vestido de un traje largo.

[3] VR: **to ~ o.s.** vestirse.

Robert ['rɒbət] NM Roberto.

robin ['rɒbɪn] N (*Orn*) petirrojo *m*.

robot ['rəʊbɒt] N robot *m*, autómata *m*.

robotic [rəʊ'bɒtɪk] ADJ (a) (*automated*) arm, equipment robótico, robotizado. (b) (*mechanical*) movements, tone robótico.

robotics [rəʊ'bɒtɪks] N robótica *f*.

robust [rəʊ'bʌst] ADJ robusto; fuerte, vigoroso; **a ~ defence** una defensa vigorosa, una defensa enérgica; **a ~ sense of humour** un fuerte sentido del humor.

robustly [rəʊ'bʌstlɪ] ADV robustamente; fuertemente, vigorosamente.

robustness [rəʊ'bʌstnɪs] N robustez *f*; fuerza *f*, vigor *m*, energía *f*.

rock¹ [rɒk] N roca *f*; (*standing stone, ~face*) peña *f*, peñasco *m*; (*US*) piedra *f*, piedrecilla *f*; (*Naut*) escollo *m*; (¢: *diamond*) diamante *m*; (¢: *drug*) crack *m*; **the R~ (of Gibraltar)** el Peñón (de Gibraltar); **whisky on the ~s*** whisky *m* con (cubitos de) hielo; **to be on the ~s*** (*broke*) no tener un céntimo; **their marriage is on the ~s*** su matrimonio anda mal; **to run on to the ~s** (*Naut*) dar en un escollo, (*fig*) peligrar, estar en peligro.

rock² [rɒk] [1] VT (*gently*) mecer, balancear; (*violently*) sacudir; **to ~ a child to sleep** arrullar a un niño, adormecer a un niño meciéndole en la cuna (*etc*); **the country was ~ed by strikes** el país fue sacudido por las huelgas; **the news ~ed us all** la noticia pasmó a todos.

[2] VI mecerse, balancearse; sacudirse; **the ship ~ed gently on the waves** el buque se balanceaba en las olas; **the train ~ed violently** el tren se sacudió violentamente; **we just ~ed (with laughter)** nos morimos de risa; **the theatre ~ed with laughter** las risas estremecieron el teatro.

[3] N (*Mus*) rock *m*; **~ concert** concierto *m* de rock; **~ festival** festival *m* de rock; **~ music** música *f* rock; **~ and roll** rocanrol *m*.

rock-bottom ['rɒk'bɒtəm] [1] N fondo *m*, parte *f* más profunda; (*fig*) punto *m* más bajo; **prices are at ~** los precios están por los suelos; **to reach ~, to touch ~** (*fig*) llegar a su punto más bajo.

[2] ATTR price más bajo, mínimo.

rock cake ['rɒk,keɪk] N (*Brit*) pastel de frutos secos y especias.

rock-carving ['rɒk,kɑːvɪŋ] N escultura *f* rupestre.

rock-climber ['rɒk,klaɪməʳ] N escalador *m*, -ora *f* (de rocas).

rock-climbing ['rɒk,klaɪmɪŋ] N escalada *f* en rocas.

rock crystal ['rɒk,krɪstl] N cristal *m* de roca, cuarzo *m*.

rocker ['rɒkəʳ] N (a) (*Mech*) balancín *m*, eje *m* de balancín; (*chair*) mecedora *f*. (b) (¢) cabeza *f*; **he's off his ~** le falta un tornillo*; **you must be off your ~!** ¡estás majareta!* (c) (*Mus*) rockero *m*, -a *f*.

rockery ['rɒkərɪ] N jardincito *m* rocoso, cuadro *m* alpino.

rocket¹ ['rɒkɪt] N (*Bot*) oruga *f*.

rocket² ['rɒkɪt] [1] N (a) cohete *m*.

(b) (*) peluca* *f*; **to get a ~ from sb** (*Brit*) recibir una peluca de uno; **to give sb a ~** echar un rapapolvo a uno* (*for the mistake* por el error).

[2] VT (*Mil*) atacar con cohetes.

[3] VI: **to ~ upwards** subir como un cohete; **to ~ to the moon** ir en cohete a la luna; **to ~ to fame** hacerse famoso de la noche a la mañana, llegar repentinamente a la fama; **prices have ~ed** los precios se han puesto por las nubes.

rocket attack ['rɒkɪtə,tæk] N ataque *m* con cohetes.

rocket-launcher ['rɒkɪt,lɔːntʃəʳ] N lanzacohetes *m*.

rocket-propelled ['rɒkɪtprə,peld] ADJ propulsado por cohete(s).

rocket propulsion ['rɒkɪtprə,pʌlʃən] N propulsión *f* a cohete.

rocket-range ['rɒkɪtreɪndʒ] N base *f* de lanzamiento de cohetes.

rocketry ['rɒkɪtrɪ] N cohetería *f*.

rockface ['rɒkfeɪs] N pared *f* de roca.

rockfall ['rɒkfɔːl] N deslizamiento *m* de montaña.

rock-garden ['rɒk,gɑːdn] N jardincito *m* rocoso, cuadro *m* alpino.

rock-hard ['rɒk'hɑːd] ADJ duro como la roca.

Rockies ['rɒkɪz] NPL Montañas *fpl* Rocosas.

rocking ['rɒkɪŋ] N balanceo *m*.

rocking-chair ['rɒkɪŋtʃeəʳ] N mecedora *f*.

rocking-horse ['rɒkɪŋhɔːs] N caballo *m* de balancín.

rock-painting ['rɒk,peɪntɪŋ] N pintura *f* rupestre.

rock-plant ['rɒkplɑːnt] N planta *f* rupestre, planta *f* rupícola.

rock-pool ['rɒkpuːl] N charca *f* (de agua de mar) entre rocas.

rockrose ['rɒkrəʊz] N jara *f*, heliantemo *m*.

rock-salmon ['rɒk'sæmən] N (*Brit*) perro *m* marino, cazón *m*.

rock-salt ['rɒksɔːlt] N sal *f* gema, sal *f* sin refinar.

rock-solid [,rɒk'sɒlɪd] ADJ sólido como una piedra, inamovible; *alliance* indisoluble; **the ~ franc is under attack** la solidez del franco se encuentra en peligro.

rock-steady ['rɒk'stedɪ] ADJ hand muy firme; voice firme, muy seguro; car muy estable; camera, gun muy preciso.

rocky¹ ['rɒkɪ] ADJ substance de roca, parecido a roca; slope etc rocoso; fragoso, escabroso.

rocky² ['rɒkɪ] ADJ (a) (*unstable*) que se bambolea, inestable. (b) (*) débil, flojo, nada firme.

Rocky Mountains ['rɒkɪ'maʊntɪnz] NPL Montañas *fpl* Rocosas.

rococo [rəʊ'kəʊkəʊ] [1] ADJ rococó.

[2] N rococó *m*.

rod [rɒd] N (*Mech etc*) vara *f*, varilla *f*, barra *f*; (*stick, of authority*) vara *f*; (*fishing ~*) caña *f*; (*Survey*) jalón *m*; (*curtain ~*) barra *f*; (*connecting ~*) biela *f*; (*measure*) medida de longitud = 5,029 metros; (*US* ¢) pipa¢ *f*, pistola *f*; **to have a ~ in pickle for sb** guardársela a uno; **to make a ~ for one's own back** hacer algo que después resultará contraproducente; **to rule with a ~ of iron** gobernar con mano de hierro; **to spare the ~** excusar la vara; **this is to spare the ~ and spoil the child** quien bien te quiere te hará llorar.

Rod [rɒd] NM, **Roddy** ['rɒdɪ] NM *familiar forms of* **Roderick**.

rode [rəʊd] PRET *of* **ride**.

rodent ['rəʊdənt] N roedor *m*.

rodeo ['rəʊdɪəʊ] N rodeo *m*.

Roderick ['rɒdərɪk] NM Rodrigo; **~, the last of the Goths** Rodrigo el último godo.

rodomontade [,rɒdəmɒn'teɪd] N fanfarronada *f*.

roe¹ [rəʊ] N (*Zool*: *also ~ deer*) corzo *m*, -a *f*.

roe² [rəʊ] N (*Fish*): **hard ~** hueva *f*; **soft ~** lecha *f*.

roebuck ['rəʊbʌk] N corzo *m*.

Rogation [rəʊ'geɪʃən]: **~ Days** Rogativas *fpl* de la Ascensión; **~ Sunday** Domingo *m* de la Ascensión.

rogations [rəʊ'geɪʃənz] NPL (*Eccl*) rogativas *fpl*.

Roger ['rɒdʒəʳ] NM Rogelio; **~!** (*Telec etc*) ¡bien!, ¡de acuerdo!

roger¢ ['rɒdʒəʳ] VT joder¢.

rogue [rəʊg] [1] N pícaro *m*, pillo *m*; (*hum*) picaruelo *m*; **you ~!** ¡canalla!; **~s' gallery** fichero *m* de delincuentes.

[2] ADJ solitario; (*que actúa solo (y de modo sospechoso)*); **~ elephant** elefante *m* solitario (y peligroso).

roguery ['rəʊgərɪ] N picardía *f*, truhanería *f*; (*mischief*) travesuras *fpl*, diabluras *fpl*; **they're up to some ~** están haciendo alguna diablura.

roguish ['rəʊgɪʃ] ADJ picaresco; (*mischievous*) pillo, travieso; look, smile etc picaruelo, malicioso.

roguishly ['rəʊgɪʃlɪ] ADV look, smile etc con malicia; **she looked at me ~** me miró picaruela.

ROI N ABBR of **return on investments** rendimiento *m* de las inversiones.

roil [rɔɪl] VT (*US*) = **rile**.

roister ['rɔɪstəʳ] VI jaranear.

roisterer ['rɔɪstərəʳ] N jaranero *m*.

Roland ['rəʊlənd] NM Roldán, Rolando.

role, rôle [rəʊl] N (*Theat, fig*) papel *m*; **to cast sb in the ~ of** dar a uno el papel de (*also fig*); **to play** (or **take**) **a ~** (*Theat*) hacer un papel, (*fig*) desempeñar un papel.

role-model ['rəʊl,mɒdl] N modelo *m* a imitar.

role-playing ['rəʊl,pleɪɪŋ] N juego *m* de imitación, juego *m* de roles.

roll [rəʊl] [1] N (a) (*of paper, tobacco, film etc*) rollo *m*; (*of cloth*) pieza *f*; (*of fat on body*) rodete *m*, rosca *f*, michelín *m* (*hum*); (*US*: *of banknotes*) fajo *m*; (*of bread*) panecillo *m*, bolillo *m* (*Méx*).

(b) (*list*) lista *f*; rol *m*, nómina *f*; **~s** (*Hist*) archivos *mpl*; **~ of honour** lista *f* de honor; **to call the ~** pasar lista; **to have 500 pupils on ~** tener inscritos 500 alumnos; **to strike sb off the ~** tachar a uno de la lista.

(c) (*sound*) (*of thunder*) retumbo *m*; (*of drum*) redoble *m*.

(d) (*movement*) (*of gait*) bamboleo *m*; (*of ship*) balanceo *m*; **to walk with a ~** andar bamboleándose; **the ship gave a sudden ~** el buque se balanceó de repente.

[2] VT vehicle, furniture etc hacer rodar; (*move*) mover; (*push*) empujar; eyes poner en blanco; soil allanar; lawn, pitch apisonar; pastry aplanar; metal laminar; cigarette liar, hacer; tongue vibrar; one's Rs pronunciar con énfasis, exagerar, (*in Spanish*) pronunciar bien; **to ~ a car to the side of the road** empujar un coche al borde de la carretera; **to ~ a ball along the pavement** hacer rodar una pelota sobre la acera; **to ~ a stone downhill** hacer rodar una piedra cuesta abajo; **he's judge and jury ~ed into one** es a la vez juez y jurado.

[3] VI (a) (*go ~ing*) rodar, ir rodando, dar vueltas; (*on ground, in pain etc*) revolcarse; (*land*) ondular; (*camera, machine*) funcionar; **it ~ed under the chair** rodó debajo de la silla; **it went ~ing downhill** fue rodando cuesta abajo; **when the tanks ~ed into the city** cuando los tanques entraron en la ciudad; **the bus ~ed to a stop** el autobús se paró; **to be ~ing in plenty** nadar en la abundancia; **they're ~ing in money***, **they're ~ing in it*** nadan en oro.

(b) (*sound*) (*thunder*) retumbar; (*drum*) redoblar; (*organ*) sonar.

(c) (*in walking*) bambolearse; (*Naut*) balancearse; **he ~ed from side to side as he walked** iba bamboleándose de un lado para otro.

◆**roll about, roll around** VI (*coins etc*) rodar, ir rodando; (*dog etc*) rodar por el suelo; (*ship*) balancearse.

◆**roll along** VI (**a**) (*ball etc*) rodar, ir.
(**b**) (*: *arrive*) llegar, venir, presentarse.

◆**roll away** [1] VT *table etc* apartar, quitar.
[2] VI (*mist etc*) disiparse; (*ball*) alejarse (rodando).

◆**roll back** VT *carpet* quitar, enrollar; **to ~ back the years** remontarse en el tiempo, volver a los tiempos pasados.

◆**roll by** VI (*cart, procession, years*) pasar.

◆**roll down** [1] VT *sleeve etc* bajar; desenrollar.
[2] VI rodar por, bajar rodando por; **tears ~ed down her cheeks** las lágrimas le corrieron por las mejillas.

◆**roll in** VI (**a**) llegar; **the waves came ~ing in** llegaban grandes olas a la playa; **the money is ~ing in*** nos entra el dinero a raudales.
(**b**) (*: *person*) llegar, volver, presentarse; **he ~ed in at 2 am** entró en la casa (*etc*) a las 2.

◆**roll off** VI caer rodando.

◆**roll on** VI (*vehicle*) seguir su marcha; (*river*) correr, seguir su curso; (*offensive, time*) avanzar; **~ on the summer!*** ¡que venga el verano!

◆**roll out** VT (**a**) *barrel, table* sacar (rodando).
(**b**) *excuse etc* ensartar; presentar (otra vez); *speech* pronunciar (pesadamente).
(**c**) *pastry* extender (con el rodillo); *metal* laminar.

◆**roll over** [1] VT (**a**) remover; volver.
(**b**) *debt* extender el plazo de.
[2] VI dar una vuelta, volverse al otro lado.

◆**roll past** VI = **roll by.**

◆**roll up** [1] VT *map, umbrella* arrollar, enrollar; *sleeve* arremangar, remangar; **to ~ sth up in paper** envolver algo en papel; **he was ~ed up in the blankets** estaba envuelto en las mantas.
[2] VI (**a**) (*hedgehog etc*) enroscarse, arrollarse, hacerse un ovillo.
(**b**) (*car etc*) llegar; (*: *person*) aparecer, presentarse, llegar; acudir, venir; **~ up, ~ up!** ¡vengan todos!
[3] VR: **to ~ o.s. up into a ball** arrollarse, hacerse un ovillo; **to ~ o.s. up in a blanket** envolverse en una manta.

rollaway ['rəʊləweɪ] N (*US: also ~ **bed**) cama *f* desmontable (sobre ruedas), cama *f* abatible (sobre ruedas).

rollbar ['rəʊlbɑː^r] N (*Aut*) barra *f* estabilizadora.

rollcall ['rəʊlkɔːl] N lista *f*, acto *m* de pasar lista.

rolled [rəʊld] ADJ *umbrella etc* arrollado; *metal* laminado; **~ gold** oro *m* laminado; **~ oats** copos *mpl* de avena.

roller ['rəʊlə^r] N (**a**) (*Agr, Tech*) rodillo *m*; (*castor*) rueda *f*; (*steam~*) apisonadora *f*; (*for hair, sports field*) rulo *m*. (**b**) (*wave*) ola *f* larga, ola *f* grande.

roller bandage ['rəʊlə'bændɪdʒ] N venda *f* enrollada.

roller blind ['rəʊlə,blaɪnd] N persiana *f* enrollable.

roller-coaster ['rəʊlə'kəʊstə^r] N montaña *f* rusa.

roller-skate ['rəʊlə,skeɪt] [1] N patín *m* de ruedas.
[2] VI ir en patines de ruedas.

roller-skating ['rəʊlə,skeɪtɪŋ] N patinaje *m* sobre ruedas.

roller towel ['rəʊlə'taʊəl] N toalla *f* de rodillo, toalla *f* sin fin.

rollick ['rɒlɪk] VI jugar, divertirse; jaranear.

rollicking ['rɒlɪkɪŋ] [1] ADJ alegre, divertido; **we had a ~ time** nos divertimos una barbaridad; **it was a ~ party** fue una fiesta animadísima; **it's ~ nonsense** son disparates de los más divertidos; **it's a ~ farce** es una farsa de lo más divertido.
[2] N (*Brit*): **to give sb a ~** poner a uno como un trapo*.

rolling ['rəʊlɪŋ] [1] ADJ rodante; *countryside* ondulado; *programme* continuo; **~ stone** (*fig*) canto *m* rodante; **a ~ stone gathers no moss** piedra movediza nunca moho la cobija; **to walk with a ~ gait** andar bamboleándose.
[2] N (*Naut*) balanceo *m*.

rolling-mill ['rəʊlɪŋmɪl] N taller *m* de laminación; tren *m* de laminaje.

rolling-pin ['rəʊlɪŋpɪn] N rodillo *m* (de cocina).

rolling-stock ['rəʊlɪŋstɒk] N material *m* rodante, material *m* móvil.

rollmop ['rəʊlmɒp] N arenque *m* adobado.

roll-neck ['rəʊlnek] N (*Brit*) jersey *m* cuello cisne.

roll-on ['rəʊlɒn] [1] N faja *f* elástica, tubular *m*.
[2] ADJ elástico.
[3] ATTR: **~ deodorant** bola *f* desodorante; **roll-on-roll-off facility** facilidad *f* para la carga y descarga autopropulsada; **roll-on-roll-off ship** ro-ro *m*, rolón *m*.

rollover ['rəʊləʊvə^r] [1] N (**a**) (*Fin: of loan, debt*) aplazamiento *m*. (**b**) (*Brit: of lottery*) bote *m*.
[2] ATTR (*Brit: lottery*) *week, jackpot* con bote.

roll-top ['rəʊltɒp] ADJ: **~ desk** buró *m*, escritorio *m* de tapa rodadera.

Rolodex ['rəʊlədeks] ® N archivo *m* de fichas giratorio.

roly-poly ['rəʊlɪ'pəʊlɪ] [1] N (*Brit: also ~ **pudding**) brazo *m* de gitano.
[2] ADJ regordete.

ROM [rɒm] N ABBR *of* **read-only-memory** ROM *f*, memoria *f* muerta, memoria *f* de sola lectura.

romaine [rəʊ'meɪn] N (*US, Canada: also ~ **lettuce**) lechuga *f* romana, lechuga *f* cos.

Roman ['rəʊmən] [1] ADJ romano; **~ alphabet** alfabeto *m* romano; **~ candle** candela *f* romana; **~ Catholic** (ADJ) católico (romano), (N) católico *m* (romano), católica *f* (romana); **~ Catholicism** catolicismo *m*; **~ law** derecho *m* romano; **~ nose** nariz *f* aguileña; **~ numeral** número *m* romano.
[2] N (**a**) romano *m*, -a *f*. (**b**) (*Typ*) tipo *m* romano.

romance [rəʊ'mæns] [1] N (**a**) (*tale*) novela *f* (sentimental), cuento *m* (de amor); (*medieval*) libro *m* de caballerías, poema *m* caballeresco; libro *m* de aventuras; (*Mus*) romanza *f*.
(**b**) (*love-affair*) amores *mpl*, amorío *m*, aventura *f* sentimental; **their ~ lasted exactly 6 months** sus amores duraron exactamente 6 meses; **a young girl waiting for ~** una joven que espera su primer amor; **I've finished with ~** para mí no más amores.
(**c**) (*romantic character*) lo romántico, lo pintoresco, lo poético; **the ~ of the sea** el encanto del mar; **the ~ of travel** lo romántico del viajar; **the ~ of history** lo atractivo de la historia, lo poético de la historia.
(**d**) (*Ling*) romance *m*.
[2] ADJ *language* romance, románico, neolatino.
[3] VI soñar, inventar fábulas; exagerar; fantasear.

Romanesque [,rəʊmə'nesk] ADJ, **Romanic** [rəʊ'mænɪk] ADJ románico.

Romania [rəʊ'meɪnɪə] N Rumania *f*, Rumanía *f*.

Romanian [rəʊ'meɪnɪən] [1] ADJ rumano.
[2] N (**a**) rumano *m*, -a *f*. (**b**) (*Ling*) rumano *m*.

romanize ['rəʊmənaɪz] VT romanizar.

Romansch [rəʊ'mænʃ] [1] ADJ rético.
[2] N (**a**) rético *m*, -a *f*. (**b**) (*Ling*) rético *m*.

romantic [rəʊ'mæntɪk] [1] ADJ romántico.
[2] N romántico *m*, -a *f*.

romantically [rəʊ'mæntɪkəlɪ] ADV románticamente, de modo romántico.

romanticism [rəʊ'mæntɪsɪzəm] N romanticismo *m*.

romanticist [rəʊ'mæntɪsɪst] N: **he's a bit of a ~** es un romántico.

romanticize [rəʊ'mæntɪsaɪz] [1] VT hacer romántico; añadir detalles románticos (*or* ambiente romántico) a.
[2] VI hablar (*or* escribir *etc*) de modo romántico; soñar, fantasear.

Romany ['rɒmənɪ] [1] ADJ gitano.
[2] N (**a**) gitano *m*, -a *f*. (**b**) (*Ling*) romanó *m*, lengua *f* gitana; (*in Spain*) caló *m*.

Rome [rəʊm] N (**a**) Roma *f*; **~ was not built in a day** no se ganó Zamora en una hora; **all roads lead to ~** por todas partes se va a Roma; **when in ~ do as the Romans do** allí donde fueres haz lo que vieres.
(**b**) (*Eccl*) la Iglesia, el catolicismo; **Manning turned to ~** Manning se convirtió al catolicismo.

Romeo ['rəʊmɪəʊ] NM Romeo.

Romish ['rəʊmɪʃ] ADJ (*pej*) católico.

romp [rɒmp] [1] N retozo *m*, juego *m*; **to have a ~ in the hay** retozar en el heno, revolcarse en el pajar; **the play was just a ~** la obra era una farsa alegre nada más.
[2] VI retozar, jugar, divertirse; (*lambs etc*) brincar, correr alegremente; **the horse ~ed home to win by 19 lengths** el caballo ganó fácilmente por 19 cuerpos; **she ~ed through the examination** encontró que el examen era muy fácil.

rompers ['rɒmpəz] NPL pelele *m*, mono *m*.

romper suit ['rɒmpə,suːt] N pelele *m*.

Romulus ['rɒmjʊləs] NM Rómulo.

rondeau ['rɒndəʊ] N (*Liter*) rondó *m*.

rondo ['rɒndəʊ] N (*Mus*) rondó *m*.

Roneo ['rəʊnɪəʊ] ® VT reproducir con multicopista.

rood [ruːd] N cruz *f*, crucifijo *m*.

roodscreen ['ruːdskriːn] N reja *f* entre la nave y el coro.

roof [ruːf] [1] N, PL **roofs** [ruːfs *or* ruːvz] techo *m*, tejado *m*; (*outside of bus, car*) baca *f*; (*of coach*) imperial *f*; (*tiled*) tejado *m*; (*of heaven*) bóveda *f* celeste; **~ of the mouth** paladar *m*, cielo *m* de la boca; **prices are going through the ~** los precios están por las nubes; **they haven't a ~ over their heads** no tienen donde cobijarse; **he hit the ~*** se subió por las paredes*; **they live under the same ~** viven bajo el mismo techo; **to raise the ~** (*protest*) poner el grito en el cielo; (*sing etc*) cantar (*etc*) como para levantar el techo.
[2] VT (*also* **to ~ in**, **to ~ over**) techar, poner techo a; **it is ~ed in wood** tiene techo de madera; **to ~ a hut in wood** (*or* **with wood**) poner techo de madera a una caseta.

roof-garden ['ruːf,gɑːdn] N azotea *f* con flores y plantas.

roofing ['ruːfɪŋ] [1] N techumbre *f*; material *m* para techado.
[2] ATTR *felt etc* para techos.

roofless ['ruːflɪs] ADJ sin techo.

roof-rack ['ruːfræk] N (*Brit*) baca *f*, portaequipajes *m*.

rooftop ['ruːftɒp] [1] N techo *m*; azotea *f*; **we will proclaim it from the ~s** lo proclamaremos a los cuatro vientos.

2 ATTR: **~ restaurant** restaurante *m* de azotea.

rook¹ [rʊk] 1 N (*Orn*) grajo *m*, -a *f*.

2 VT estafar, timar; **you've been ~ed** te han cobrado demasiado, te han desollado; **they always ~ the customer in that shop** en esa tienda siempre le timan al cliente.

rook² [rʊk] N (*Chess*) torre *f*.

rookery ['rʊkərɪ] N colonia *f* de grajos.

rookie* ['rʊkɪ] N (*Mil*) bisoño *m*, novato *m*.

▼ **room** [rʊm] 1 N (a) (*in house*) cuarto *m*, habitación *f*; pieza *f*; (*large, public*) sala *f*; **~s** (*lodging*) alojamiento *m*, (*flat*) piso *m*; **this is my ~** ésta es mi habitación; **in ~ 504** (*hotel*) en la habitación número 504; **in the professor's ~** en el cuarto del profesor; **he has ~s in college** tiene un cuarto en el colegio; **they've always lived in ~s** han vivido siempre en pisos alquilados.

(b) (*space*) sitio *m*, espacio *m*; cabida *f*, cupo *m* (*Méx*); **is there ~?** ¿hay sitio?; **is there ~ for this?** ¿cabe esto?; **there is no ~ for that** eso no cabe; **there's no ~ for anything else** no cabe más; **is there ~ for me?** ¿quepo yo?, ¿hay sitio para mí?; **there is plenty of ~** queda mucho espacio libre; **there is still ~ on Tuesday** quedan todavía localidades para el martes; **to be cramped for ~** tener poco espacio; **to make ~ for sb** hacer sitio para uno, hacer lugar para uno; **make ~!** ¡abran paso!

(c) (*fig*) **there is no ~ for doubt** no queda lugar a dudas; **there is ~ for improvement** esto se puede mejorar todavía; **to leave ~ for imponderables** dar cabida a un margen de imponderables.

2 ATTR: **~ clerk** (*US*) recepcionista *mf* (de hotel); **~ temperature** temperatura *f* ambiente.

3 VI: **to ~ with a landlady** alojarse en casa de una patrona; **to ~ with 3 other students** estar en una pensión con otros 3 estudiantes, compartir un piso con otros 3 estudiantes.

room divider ['rʊmdɪˌvaɪdəʳ] N biombo *m*; tabique *m*.

-roomed [rʊmd] ADJ de ... piezas, *eg* **seven~** de siete piezas.

roomer ['rʊməʳ] N (*US*) inquilino *m*, -a *f*; huésped *m*, -eda *f*.

roomette [ruːˈmet] N (*US*) departamento *m* de coche-cama.

roomful ['rʊmfʊl] N: **a ~ of priests** un cuarto lleno de curas; **they have Picassos by the ~** tienen salas enteras llenas de cuadros de Picasso.

roominess ['rʊmɪnɪs] N espaciosidad *f*, amplitud *f*; holgura *f*.

rooming house ['rʊmɪŋhaʊs] N, PL **rooming houses** ['rʊmɪŋˌhaʊzɪz] (*US*) casa *f* de huéspedes, pensión *f*.

roommate ['rʊmmeɪt] N compañero *m*, -a *f* de cuarto.

room-service ['rʊmˌsɜːvɪs] N servicio *m* en la habitación, servicio *m* de habitación.

roomy ['rʊmɪ] ADJ *room* espacioso, amplio; *garment* capaz, holgado.

roost [ruːst] 1 N percha *f*; (*hen~*) gallinero *m*; **to rule the ~** mandar, dirigir el cotarro.

2 VI dormir (*or* descansar) en una percha; (*fig*) pasar la noche; **the birds ~ in that tree** los pájaros pasan la noche en ese árbol; **now his policies have come home to ~** ahora su política produce su fruto amargo, ahora se están viendo los malos resultados de su política.

rooster ['ruːstəʳ] N gallo *m*.

root [ruːt] 1 N raíz *f* (*also fig*); (*Gram*) radical *m*; **~ and branch** de raíz, completamente, del todo; **money is the ~ of all evil** el dinero es la raíz de todos los males; **the ~ of the problem is that ...** lo fundamental del problema es que ..., la esencia del problema es que ...; **what lies at the ~ of his attitude?** ¿qué razón fundamental tiene su actitud?; **to put down one's ~s in a country** radicarse en un país, echar raíces en un país; **to strike** (*or* **take**) **~** echar raíces, arraigar; **to strike at the ~ of sth** afectar la parte fundamental de algo, atacar la misma esencia de algo.

2 ADJ: **~ beer** (*US*) cerveza *f* no alcohólica; **~ cause** causa *f* primordial; **~ crops** (cultivos *mpl* de) raíces *fpl*; **~ idea** idea *f* fundamental, idea *f* esencial; **~ sign** (*Math*) raíz *f*; **~ vegetable** raíz *f*; **~ word** palabra *f* radical.

3 VT (a) (*plant*) hacer arraigar.

(b) (*fig*) **to be** (*or* **stand**) **~ed to the spot** quedar helado (de miedo *etc*), quedar inmovilizado, estar sin poderse mover; **it is firmly ~ed in all minds that ...** está grabado en la mente de todos que ..., todos creen firmemente que ...; **a ~ed prejudice** un prejuicio muy arraigado.

4 VI (a) (*Bot*) echar raíces, arraigar(se). (b) (*animal*) hozar, hocicar.

◆**root about, root around** VI (*pig*) hozar, hocicar, (*fig*) andar buscando por todas partes (*for sth* algo); investigar.

◆**root for*** VT (*esp US*) *team etc* gritar por; *cause etc* hacer propaganda por, apoyar a.

◆**root out** VT arrancar (de raíz), desarraigar; (*fig*) desarraigar, extirpar; suprimir del todo.

◆**root through** VT hocicar; (*fig*) examinar, explorar.

◆**root up** VT arrancar.

rootless ['ruːtlɪs] ADJ *person etc* desarraigado.

rootstock ['ruːtstɒk] N rizoma *m*.

rope [rəʊp] 1 N cuerda *f*, mecate *m* (*Mex*); soga *f*; (*Naut: hawser*) maroma *f*, cable *m*, (*in rigging*) cabo *m*; (*hangman's*) dogal *m*; (*of pearls*) collar *m*; (*of onions etc*) ristra *f*; **the ~s** (*Boxing*) las cuerdas; **to be on the ~s** (*fig*) estar en las cuerdas; **to give sb more ~** dar a uno mayor libertad de acción; **if you give him enough ~ he'll hang himself** déjale actuar y él se condenará a sí mismo; **to jump ~, to skip ~** (*US*) saltar a la comba; **to know the ~s** conocer un negocio a fondo, saber cuántas son dos y dos; **to learn the ~s** aprender el oficio; **I'll show you the ~s** te voy a mostrar lo que hay que hacer, te enseñaré el oficio; **there were 3 of us on the ~** (*Mountaineering*) éramos 3 los encordados.

2 ATTR: **~ burn** quemadura *f* por fricción; **~ ladder** escala *f* de cuerda; **~ trick** truco *m* de la cuerda.

3 VT atar con una cuerda, amarrar con una cuerda; (*US*) *animal* coger con lazo; **to ~ two things together** atar dos cosas con una cuerda; **there were 4 ~d together** había 4 que iban encordados.

4 VR: **they are roping themselves together** se están encordando.

◆**rope in*** VT: **to ~ sb in** enganchar a uno (*to do sth* para hacer algo); **they managed to ~ in their friends** consiguieron arrastrar a sus amigos.

◆**rope off** VT: **to ~ off a space** acordonar un espacio, cercar un espacio con cuerdas.

◆**rope up** VT cordar.

ropemaker ['rəʊpˌmeɪkəʳ] N cordelero *m*.

ropewalker ['rəʊpˌwɔːkəʳ] N funámbulo *m*, -a *f*, volatinero *m*, -a *f*.

rop(e)y ['rəʊpɪ] ADJ (a) *liquid* viscoso. (b) (*) deteriorado, desvencijado; inestable; *plan, argument etc* nada convincente, flojo; **I feel a bit ~** no me siento del todo bien.

RO/RO ABBR *of* roll-on/roll-off.

rosary ['rəʊzərɪ] N rosario *m*; **to say one's ~** rezar el rosario.

Rose [rəʊz] NF Rosa.

rose¹ [rəʊz] 1 N (a) (*Bot*) rosa *f*; (*colour*) color *m* de rosa; **wild ~** rosal *m* silvestre; **life isn't all ~s** la vida no es un lecho de rosas; **there's no ~ without a thorn** no hay rosa sin espina.

(b) (*of watering-can*) roseta *f*.

(c) (*Archit*) rosetón *m*.

2 ADJ color de rosa, rosado, rosáceo; **~ pink** rosa.

rose² [rəʊz] PRET *of* rise.

rosé ['rəʊzeɪ] 1 ADJ rosado.

2 N rosado *m*.

roseate ['rəʊzɪɪt] ADJ róseo, rosado.

rosebay ['rəʊzbeɪ] N adelfa *f*.

rosebed ['rəʊzbed] N rosaleda *f*.

rosebowl ['rəʊzbəʊl] N jarrón *m* (*or* florero *m*) para rosas.

rosebud ['rəʊzbʌd] N capullo *m* de rosa, botón *m* de rosa.

rosebush ['rəʊzbʊʃ] N rosal *m*.

rose-coloured, (*US*) **rose-colored** ['rəʊzˌkʌləd] ADJ color de rosa, rosado, rosáceo; **to see everything through ~ spectacles** verlo todo color de rosa.

rose garden ['rəʊzˌgɑːdn] N rosaleda *f*.

rose hip ['rəʊzhɪp] 1 N escaramujo *m*.

2 ATTR: **~ syrup** jarabe *m* de escaramujo.

rosemary ['rəʊzmərɪ] N romero *m*.

rose-red ['rəʊzˈred] ADJ color de rosa.

rosetree ['rəʊztriː] N rosal *m*.

rosette [rəʊˈzet] N (*Archit*) rosetón *m*; (*emblem*) escarapela *f*.

rosewater ['rəʊzˌwɔːtəʳ] N agua *f* de rosas.

rose window ['rəʊzˈwɪndəʊ] N rosetón *m*.

rosewood ['rəʊzwʊd] N palo *m* de rosa, palisandro *m*.

Rosicrucian [ˌrəʊzɪˈkruːʃən] 1 N rosacruz *mf*.

2 ADJ rosacruz.

rosin ['rɒzɪn] N colofonia *f*.

ROSPA ['rɒspə] N ABBR *of* **Royal Society for the Prevention of Accidents**.

roster ['rɒstəʳ] 1 N lista *f*.

2 ATTR: **~ duty** lista *f* de deberes.

rostrum ['rɒstrəm], PL **~s** *or* **rostra** ['rɒstrə] 1 N tribuna *f*.

2 ATTR: **~ cameraman** (*TV*) cámara-truca *m*.

rosy ['rəʊzɪ] ADJ (a) rosado, sonrosado; **with ~ cheeks** con mejillas sonrosadas. (b) (*fig*) *prospects etc* prometedor, halagüeño.

rot [rɒt] 1 N (a) putrefacción *f*, podredumbre *f*; **it has ~** está podrido.

(b) (*fig*) decadencia *f*; **a ~ set in** comenzó un período de decadencia, todo empezó a decaer; **to stop the ~** acabar con la degeneración, impedir que la situación vaya de mal en peor, reformarlo todo.

(c) (*:* *nonsense*) tonterías *fpl*, bobadas *fpl*, babosadas *fpl* (*LAm*); **oh ~!, what ~!** ¡tonterías!; **don't talk ~!** ¡no digas bobadas!; **it is utter ~ to say that ...** es una sandez decir que ...

2 VT pudrir, corromper, descomponer (*also fig*).

3 VI pudrirse, corromperse, descomponerse; **to ~ in jail** pudrirse en la cárcel; **you can ~ for all I care!** ¡que te pudras!

◆**rot away** vi pudrirse, corromperse, descomponerse; **it had ~ted away with the passage of time** con el tiempo se había descompuesto; **it had quite ~ted away** se había descompuesto del todo.

rota ['rəʊtə] N lista *f* (de tandas *etc*).

Rotarian [rəʊ'tɛərɪən] ① ADJ rotario.
  ② N rotario *m*.

rotary ['rəʊtərɪ] ADJ rotativo; giratorio; **R~ Club** Sociedad *f* Rotaria; **~ press** prensa *f* rotativa.

rotate [rəʊ'teɪt] ① VT *wheel etc* hacer girar; dar vueltas a; (*Comput*) *graphics* rotar, girar; *crops* alternar, cultivar en rotación; (*vary*) alternar; **to ~ A and B** alternar A con B.
  ② VI girar; dar vueltas; alternarse.

rotating [rəʊ'teɪtɪŋ] ADJ rotativo; giratorio.

rotation [rəʊ'teɪʃən] N rotación *f* (*also Agr, Astron*); alternación *f*; **~ of crops** rotación *f* de cultivos; **in ~** por turno; **A and B in ~** A y B alternadamente; **orders are dealt with in strict ~** los pedidos se sirven por riguroso orden.

rotational [rəʊ'teɪʃənəl] ADJ rotacional.

rotatory [rəʊ'teɪtərɪ] ADJ rotativo; giratorio.

rotavate ['rəʊtəveɪt] VT trabajar con motocultor.

rotavator ['rəʊtəveɪtər] N (*Brit*) motocultor *m*.

rote [rəʊt] N: **by ~** de memoria; **to learn sth by ~** aprender algo maquinalmente, aprender algo a fuerza de repetirlo (en coro); **~ learning was the fashion** era costumbre aprender cosas a fuerza de repetirlas.

rotgut* ['rɒtgʌt] N matarratas *m*.

rotisserie [rəʊ'tɪsərɪ] N rotisserie *f*.

rotor ['rəʊtər] ① N rotor *m*.
  ② ATTR: **~ arm** (*Aut*) rotor *m*; **~ blade** paleta *f* de rotor.

rotproof ['rɒtpruːf] ADJ a prueba de putrefacción, imputrescible.

rotten ['rɒtn] ① ADJ (a) podrido, putrefacto, corrompido; *tooth* cariado; *wood* carcomido; (*fig*) corrompido; **to smell ~** oler a podredumbre.
  (b) (*) (*morally*) vil, despreciable; (*of bad quality*) malísimo, lamentable, fatal*; (*Med*) malo; **what a ~ thing to do!** ¡qué cosa más vil!; **what a ~ thing to happen!** ¡qué mala suerte!; **how ~ for you!** ¡cuánto te compadezco!, ¡lo que habrás sufrido!; **what ~ weather!** ¡qué tiempo de perros!; **his English is ~** tiene un inglés fatal*; **he's ~ at chess** para el ajedrez es un desastre; **it's a ~ novel** es una novela que huele*, es una novela lamentable; **I feel ~** me siento fatal*; **beer always makes me feel ~** la cerveza siempre me pone malo; **he's ~ with money** está que huele de dinero*, está podrido de dinero*; **to be ~ to sb*** portarse como un canalla con uno.
  ② ADV (‡) malísimamente, fatal*; **they played real ~** jugaron fatal*; **they made me suffer something ~** me hicieron pasarlas negras.

rottenly* ['rɒtnlɪ] ADV: **to behave ~ to sb** portarse como un canalla con uno.

rottenness ['rɒtnɪs] N podredumbre *f*, putrefacción *f*; (*fig*) corrupción *f*.

rotter* ['rɒtər] N (*Brit*) caradura* *m*, sinvergüenza *m*; **you ~!** ¡canalla!

rotting ['rɒtɪŋ] ADJ podrido, que se está pudriendo.

Rottweiler ['rɒt,vaɪlər] N Rottweiler *m*.

rotund [rəʊ'tʌnd] ADJ rotundo; (*fat*) gordo.

rotunda [rəʊ'tʌndə] N rotonda *f*.

rotundity [rəʊ'tʌndɪtɪ] N rotundidad *f*; gordura *f*.

rouble, (*US*) **ruble** ['ruːbl] N rublo *m*.

roué ['ruːeɪ] N libertino *m*.

Rouen ['ruːɑ̃:ŋ] N Ruán *m*.

rouge [ruːʒ] ① N colorete *m*, carmín *m*.
  ② VT: **to ~ one's cheeks** ponerse colorete.

rough [rʌf] ① ADJ (a) *surface, skin etc* áspero; *ground* quebrado, fragoso, escabroso; *road* desigual, lleno de baches; *cloth* basto; *hand* calloso; *hair* despeinado; *edge* desigual; **~ to the touch** áspero al tacto; **~ diamond** diamante *m* (en) bruto (*also fig*).
  (b) *treatment, behaviour etc* brutal; inconsiderado; *person* inculto, sin educación; *sea* bravo; encrespado, picado; *weather* borrascoso, tormentoso; *wind* violento; *play, sport* duro; *neighbourhood* malo, de mala vida, peligroso; **to be ~ with sb** tratar a uno de modo brutal; **to get ~** (*sea*) embravecerse; **to get ~ with sb** empezar a pegar a uno; **he got a ~ handling in the press** le dieron una paliza en la prensa; **he got ~ justice** recibió un castigo duro pero apropiado.
  (c) *manners* tosco, grosero; *voice* bronco, áspero; *speech* rudo; *style* tosco; *work* chapucero; *workman* torpe, desmañado; *material* crudo, bruto.
  (d) *calculation, estimate* aproximado; *guess* aproximativo; *plan, sketch* a grandes rasgos; *draft* primero; *work* de preparación, preliminar; *translation* no muy exacto; preliminar; aproximativo; **~ copy** borrador *m*; **I would say 50 at a ~ guess** diría que 50 aproximadamente.
  ② ADV: **to cut up ~** (*Brit**) cabrearse*; **to live ~** vivir sin comodidades, vivir como un vagabundo; **to play ~** jugar duro; **to sleep ~** pasar la noche al raso, dormir al descubierto, dormir a la

intemperie.
  ③ N (a) (*ground etc*) terreno *m* quebrado, superficie *f* áspera; (*Golf*) rough *m*, zona *f* de matojos; **in (the) ~** en bruto, (*plan etc*) a grandes rasgos; **we'll do it first in ~** lo haremos primero sólo en forma preliminar (*or* en forma de bosquejo); **to take the ~ with the smooth** tomar las duras con las maduras, aceptar la vida como es.
  (b) (*person*) matón *m*.
  ④ VT: **to ~ it** pasar apuros, luchar contra dificultades, vivir sin comodidades.

◆**rough out** VT: **to ~ out a plan** esbozar un plan, bosquejar un plan, trazar un plan a grandes rasgos.

◆**rough up*** VT *hair* despeinar; *person* dar una paliza a.

roughage ['rʌfɪdʒ] N sustancia *f* celulósica, forraje *m*.

rough-and-ready ['rʌfən'redɪ] ADJ tosco pero eficaz; improvisado; provisional; (*person*) inculto pero estimable.

rough-and-tumble ['rʌfən'tʌmbl] N (*quarrel, fight*) riña *f*, pendencia *f*; (*activity etc*) actividad *f* frenética; **the ~ of life** la confusión y violencia de la vida; **the ~ of politics** los avatares de la política, los altibajos de la política.

roughcast ['rʌfkɑːst] N mezcla *f* gruesa.

roughen ['rʌfn] ① VT poner áspero; hacer más tosco.
  ② VI ponerse áspero; hacerse más tosco; (*sea*) embravecerse.

rough-hew ['rʌf'hjuː] (*irr: V* **hew**) VT desbastar.

rough-hewn ['rʌf'hjuːn] ADJ toscamente labrado; desbastado; (*fig*) tosco, inculto.

roughhouse* ['rʌfhaʊs] N, PL **roughhouses** ['rʌfhaʊzɪz] trifulca* *f*, riña *f* general, reyerta *f*.

roughly ['rʌflɪ] ADV (*V adj*) (a) ásperamente. (b) brutalmente; incultamente; violentamente; duramente. (c) toscamente; groseramente; broncamente; torpemente. (d) aproximadamente, más o menos; de modo preliminar.

roughneck ['rʌfnek] N matón *m*.

roughness ['rʌfnɪs] N (*V adj*) (a) aspereza *f*; lo quebrado, fragosidad *f*; desigualdad *f*; callosidad *f*.
  (b) brutalidad *f*; incultura *f*; falta *f* de educación; braveza *f*; violencia *f*; dureza *f*.
  (c) tosquedad *f*; rudeza *f*; lo chapucero; torpeza *f*, desmaña *f*.

rough puff pastry [,rʌf,pʌf'peɪstrɪ] N hojaldre *m*.

roughrider ['rʌf,raɪdər] N domador *m* de caballos.

roughshod ['rʌfʃɒd] ADV: **to ride ~ over sb** tratar a uno sin miramientos, no hacer caso alguno de uno.

rough-spoken ['rʌf'spəʊkən] ADJ inculto, de habla inculta, malhablado.

roulette [ruː'let] N ruleta *f*.

Roumania [ruː'meɪnɪə] *etc* = **Romania** *etc*.

round [raʊnd] ① ADJ redondo; *sum* redondo; *denial etc* rotundo, terminante; *trip* de ida y vuelta, completo; *dance* en ruedo; **a ~ dozen** una docena redonda; **~ arch** arco *m* redondo; **in ~ figures** en números redondos; **~ number** número *m* redondo; **in ~ numbers** en números redondos; **~ robin** (*request*) petición *f* firmada en rueda, (*protest*) protesta *f* firmada en rueda; **R~ Table** (*Hist*) Mesa *f* Redonda; **~ table conference** conferencia *f* de mesa redonda; **~ trip** ida *f* y vuelta, viaje *m* redondo (*LAm*); **~ trip ticket** (*US*) billete *m* de ida y vuelta.
  ② ADV alrededor; **all ~** por todos lados; **all the year ~** durante todo el año; **it has a fence all ~** tiene una cerca que lo rodea completamente; **taking it all ~** (considerándolo) en conjunto; **drinks all ~!** ¡pago la ronda para todos!; **it is 200 metres ~** tiene 200 metros en redondo; **for 5 miles ~ about** en 5 millas a la redonda, en 5 millas en torno; **it's a long way ~** es mucho rodeo; **when you're ~ this way** cuando pases por aquí; **we were ~ at John's** estábamos en casa de Juan; **we shall be ~ at the pub** estaremos en el bar; **it flew ~ and ~** voló dando vueltas.
  ③ PREP (a) (*place etc*) alrededor de; **a trip ~ the world** un viaje alrededor del mundo; **the wall ~ the town** la muralla que rodea la ciudad; **a walk ~ the town** un paseo por la ciudad; **all the people ~ about** toda la gente alrededor; **it's just ~ the corner** está precisamente a la vuelta de la esquina; **we were sitting ~ the table** estábamos sentados alrededor de la mesa; **we were sitting ~ the fire** estábamos sentados al amor de la lumbre; **it's written ~ the Suez episode** tiene por tema principal el episodio de Suez; **she's 36 inches ~ the bust** mide de pecho 36 pulgadas; **to sing hymns ~ the pubs** cantar himnos de bar en bar; **to deliver papers ~ the houses** repartir periódicos por las casas.
  (b) (*approximately*) alrededor de; cerca de, cosa de; **~ 2 o'clock** a eso de las 2; **~ about £50** cerca de 50 libras, cosa de 50 libras, 50 libras más o menos; **somewhere ~ that sum** esa cantidad más o menos.
  ④ N (a) (*circle*) círculo *m*; esfera *f*; (*slice*) tajada *f*, rodaja *f*; **a ~ of toast** una tostada.
  (b) (*routine*) rutina *f*; **one long ~ of pleasures** una sucesión de placeres, una serie sin fin de placeres.
  (c) (*esp Brit: beat: of watchman etc*) ronda *f*; (*of postman, milkman etc*)

recorrido *m*; (*of golf etc*) recorrido *m*, ronda *f*, vuelta *f*; (*of doctor*) visitas *fpl*; **a ~ of talks** una serie de conferencias; **the first ~ of negotiations** la primera ronda de negociaciones; **he's out on his ~s** está fuera visitando sus enfermos; **she did** (*or* **went, made**) **the ~s of the agencies** visitó todas las agencias, recorrió todas las agencias; **to go the ~s** (*watchman etc*) estar de ronda, hacer su ronda de inspección; **the story is going the ~s that ...** se dice que ..., se rumorea que ...; **the story went the ~s of the club** el chiste se contó en todos los corrillos del club.

(d) (*Boxing*) asalto *m*; (*Golf*) round *m*; (*in tournament*) vuelta *f*, rueda *f*; (*of election*) vuelta *f*; (*lap*) circuito *m*; (*in show jumping*) recorrido *m*; **to have a clear ~** hacer un recorrido sin penalizaciones.

(e) **~** (*of drinks*) ronda *f* (de bebidas); **~ of applause** salva *f* de aplausos; **~ of ammunition** tiro *m*, cartucho *m*, bala *f*; **whose ~ is it?** ¿a quién le toca (pagar)?

(f) **in the ~** (*Theat*) en redondo; (*fig*) **develop etc** en conjunto, en su totalidad, globalmente.

⑤ VT: **to ~ a corner** doblar una esquina; **the ship ~ed the headland** el buque dobló el promontorio.

♦ **round down** VT *price etc* redondear (rebajando).

♦ **round off** VT redondear; acabar, terminar; perfeccionar; **to ~ the series off** para completar la serie.

♦ **round on** VT volverse contra.

♦ **round out** VT redondear, completar.

♦ **round up** VT **(a)** (*bring together*) acorralar, rodear (*LAm*); **we ~ed up a few friends to help** reunimos a unos amigos para ayudar.

(b) *figure etc* redondear.

♦ **round upon** VT volverse contra.

roundabout ['raʊndəbaʊt] ① ADJ indirecto; **by a ~ way** dando un rodeo, por una ruta indirecta; **to speak in a ~ way** ir con rodeos, hablar con circunloquios.

② N (*Brit*) (*at fair*) tiovivo *m*; (*Aut*) glorieta *f*, (cruce *m* de) circulación *f* giratoria, redoma *f* (*Carib*), rotonda *f* (*SC*).

rounded ['raʊndɪd] ADJ *end* redondeado; esférico; *end of boat* redondo; *style* maduro, expresivo.

roundelay ['raʊndɪleɪ] N (*song*) canción *f* que se canta en rueda; (*dance*) baile *m* en círculo.

rounders ['raʊndəz] N (*Brit*) *juego similar al béisbol*.

round-eyed ['raʊnd'aɪd] ADJ, ADV: **to look at sb ~** mirar a uno con los ojos desorbitados.

round-faced ['raʊnd'feɪst] ADJ de cara redonda.

Roundhead ['raʊndhed] N (*Brit Hist*) cabeza *f* pelada.

roundhouse ['raʊndhaʊs] N, PL **roundhouses** ['raʊndhaʊzɪz] (*US Rail*) cocherón *m* circular, rotonda *f* para locomotoras; (*Naut*) chupeta *f*.

roundly ['raʊndlɪ] ADV (*fig*) rotundamente, terminantemente.

round-necked ['raʊnd‚nekt] ADJ: **~ pullover** jersey *m* de cuello cerrado (*or* redondo).

roundness ['raʊndnɪs] N redondez *f*.

round-shouldered ['raʊnd'ʃəʊldəd] ADJ cargado de espaldas.

roundsman ['raʊndzmən] N, PL **roundsmen** ['raʊndzmən] (*Brit*) repartidor *m*, proveedor *m* casero.

round-the-clock ['raʊndðə'klɒk] ADJ *surveillance etc* de veinticuatro horas, permanente.

round-up ['raʊndʌp] N (*Agr*) rodeo *m*; (*of suspects etc*) detención *f*; (*by police*) redada *f*; **~ of the latest news** resumen *m* de las últimas noticias.

roundworm ['raʊndwɜːm] N lombriz *f* intestinal.

rouse [raʊz] ① VT (*wake*) despertar; *emotion* excitar, suscitar, despertar; (*from torpor*) animar, reanimar; *game* levantar; **to ~ sb from sleep** despertar a uno; **to ~ sb to action** mover a uno a la acción; **to ~ sb to fury** provocar a uno a la furia; **it ~d the whole house** despertó a todo el mundo.

② VI despertar(se).

③ VR: **to ~ o.s.** despertarse; (*to act etc*) animarse a hacer algo.

rousing ['raʊzɪŋ] ADJ *welcome etc* emocionado, entusiasta; *song etc* vivo, lleno de vigor; *speech* conmovedor.

Roussillon ['ruːsijɔ̃] N Rosellón *m*.

roust [raʊst] VT (*also* **~ out**) (*US*) hacer salir bruscamente.

roustabout* ['raʊstəbaʊt] N (*US*) peón *m*.

rout [raʊt] ① N (*defeat*) derrota *f* (completa); (*flight*) fuga *f* desordenada.

② VT derrotar (completamente).

♦ **rout out** VT: **to ~ sb out** hacer salir a uno; **to ~ sb out of bed** hacer que uno se levante apresuradamente, hacer que uno abandone la cama.

route [ruːt] ① N **(a)** (*gen*) ruta *f*, camino *m*; itinerario *m*; (*of bus*) recorrido *m*, línea *f*; (*Naut*) rumbo *m*, derrota *f*; **R~ 31** (*US*) Ruta *f* 31; **to go by a new ~** seguir una nueva ruta; **the ~ to the coast** el camino de la costa. **(b)** (*US: often* [raʊt]: *delivery round*) recorrido *m*.

② VT fijar el itinerario de; (*Comput*) encaminar; **the train is now ~ed through X** ahora el tren pasa por X.

route-map ['ruːtmæp] N mapa *m* de carreteras.

route-march ['ruːtmɑːtʃ] N marcha *f* de entrenamiento, marcha *f* de maniobras.

routine [ruː'tiːn] ① N rutina *f*; **the daily ~** la rutina cotidiana; **as a matter of ~** por rutina.

② ADJ rutinario, de rutina; **a ~ inspection** una inspección rutinaria; **it's just ~** es cosa de rutina.

routinely [ruː'tiːnlɪ] ADV rutinariamente, por rutina.

routing ['raʊtɪŋ] N (*Comput*) encaminamiento *m*.

rove [raʊv] ① VT vagar por, errar por, recorrer.

② VI vagar; **to ~ about** andar sin propósito fijo; **his eye ~d over the room** su mirada pasó por todo el cuarto.

rover ['raʊvər] N vagabundo *m*, andariego *m*; (*Naut*) pirata *m*; (*Scout*) escultista *m*.

roving ['raʊvɪŋ] ADJ (*wandering*) errante; *salesman etc* ambulante; *ambassador* itinerante; *reporter* volante; *disposition* andariego; **to have a ~ commission** no tener puesto fijo, tener el cometido de hacer investigaciones (*etc*) donde le parezca a uno; **he has a ~ eye** se le van los ojos tras las mujeres.

row¹ [raʊ] ① N (*line*) fila *f*, hilera *f*; renglón *m*; (*Theat etc*) fila *f*; (*of books, houses etc*) hilera *f*; (*in knitting*) pasada *f*; vuelta *f*; **in the front ~** en primera fila; **in the fourth ~** en la cuarta fila, en la fila cuatro; **he killed four in a ~** mató cuatro seguidos, mató cuatro uno tras otro; **for 5 days in a ~** durante 5 días seguidos.

② ATTR: **~ houses** (*US*) casas *fpl* adosadas.

row² [raʊ] ① N **(a)** (*trip*) paseo *m* en bote de remos; **to go for a ~** pasearse en bote, hacer una excursión en bote.

(b) **it was a hard ~ to the shore** nos costó llegar a la playa remando; **you'll have a hard ~ upstream** os costará trabajo remar contra la corriente.

② VT *boat* conducir remando; **to ~ a race** tomar parte en una regata (de botes de remos); **you ~ed a good race** habéis remado muy bien; **he ~ed the Atlantic** cruzó el Atlántico a remo; **to ~ sb across a river** llevar a uno en bote a través de un río; **can you ~ me out to the yacht?** ¿me lleva en bote al yate?

③ VI remar, bogar; **to ~ hard** esforzarse remando, hacer fuerza de remos; **to ~ against sb** competir con uno en una regata a remo; **we ~ed for the shore** remamos (para llegar) a la playa, remamos hacia la playa; **he ~ed for Oxford** remó en el bote de Oxford; **to ~ round an island** dar la vuelta a una isla a remo.

row³ [raʊ] ① N **(a)** (*noise*) ruido *m*, estrépito *m*, estruendo *m*; **hold your ~!, stop your ~!** ¡cállate!; **the ~ from the engine** el ruido del motor; **it makes a devil of a ~** hace un ruido de todos los demonios.

(b) (*dispute*) bronca *f*, pelea *f*; **the ~ about wages** la disputa acerca de los salarios; **now don't let's start a ~** no riñamos.

(c) (*fuss, disturbance, incident*) jaleo *m*, lío *m*, follón *m* (*Sp*), bronca *f* (*LAm*); escándalo *m*; **what's the ~ about?** ¿a qué se debe el lío?; **there was a devil of a ~ about it** sobre esto se armó un tremendo follón (*LAm*: lío); **to kick up a ~, to make a ~** armar un jaleo, armar un follón, armar bronca (*LAm*); (*protest*) poner el grito en el cielo; **he makes a ~ about nothing** se queja por nada; **make a ~ with your member of parliament** quéjese a su diputado.

(d) (*scolding*) regaño *m*; **you'll get into a ~** te van a regañar (*for* por).

② VT: **to ~ sb** echar un rapapolvo a uno.

③ VI reñir, reñirse, pelear (*esp LAm*); **they're always ~ing** siempre están riñendo; **to ~ with sb** pelearse con uno.

rowan ['raʊən] N (*also* **~ tree**) serbal *m*; (*berry*) serba *f*.

rowboat ['rəʊbəʊt] N (*US*) bote *m* de remos.

rowdiness ['raʊdɪnɪs] N lo ruidoso, ruido *m*; carácter *m* pendenciero; alboroto *m*, desorden *m*.

rowdy ['raʊdɪ] ① ADJ *person* (*noisy*) ruidoso; (*quarrelsome*) pendenciero, quimerista; *meeting etc* alborotado, desordenado.

② N quimerista *mf*.

rowdyism ['raʊdɪzəm] N disturbios *mpl*, pendencias *fpl*; gamberrismo *m*.

rower ['rəʊər] N remero *m*, -a *f*.

rowing ['rəʊɪŋ] N remo *m*; **~ machine** máquina *f* de remo.

rowing-boat ['rəʊɪŋbəʊt] N (*Brit*) bote *m* de remos.

rowing-club ['rəʊɪŋklʌb] N club *m* de remo.

rowlock ['rɒlək] N tolete *m*, escálamo *m*, chumacera *f*.

royal ['rɔɪəl] ① ADJ **(a)** (*gen*) real; (*esp fig*) regio; **R~ Academy (of Arts)** (*Brit*) Real Academia *f* de Bellas Artes; **~ blue** azul *m* marino; **R~ Commission** (*Brit*) Comisión *f* Real; **R~ Engineers** (*Brit*) Cuerpo *m* de Ingenieros; **~ family** familia *f* real; **~ household** casa *f* real; **~ line** familia *f* real, casa *f* real; **R~ Society** Real Academia *f* de Ciencias; **the ~ 'we'** el plural mayestático; *ver también*
RA - ROYAL ACADEMY OF ARTS .

(b) (*splendid*) magnífico, espléndido, suntuoso; **a ~ feast** un banquete suntuoso; **to have a right ~ time** pasarlo en grande.

② N (*) personaje *m* real, miembro *m* de la familia real; **the ~s** la realeza.

royalism ['rɔɪəlɪzəm] N sentimiento *m* monárquico, monarquismo *m*.

royalist ['rɔɪəlɪst] 1 ADJ monárquico.
　2 N monárquico *m*, -a *f*.

royally ['rɔɪəlɪ] ADV *(fig)* magníficamente, espléndidamente.

royalty ['rɔɪəltɪ] N **(a)** realeza *f*; personajes *mpl* reales, familia *f* real; **in the presence of ~** estando presente un miembro de la familia real; **a shop patronized by ~** una tienda que visita la familia real, una tienda donde la familia real hace compras.
　(b) *(payment; also* **royalties**) derechos *mpl* de autor, regalías *fpl (LAm)*; derechos *mpl* de patente; **the royalties on oil** los derechos del petróleo.

rozzer ['rɒzər] N *(Brit)* guindilla* *m*, guiri* *m*.

RP N **(a)** *(Brit Ling)* ABBR *of* **Received Pronunciation** *pronunciación estándar del inglés; ver también* ENGLISH , HOME COUNTIES . **(b)** *(Post)* ABBR *of* **reply paid** contestación *f* pagada, CP.

RPI N ABBR *of* **Retail Price Index** Índice *m* de precios al consumidor, IPC *m*.

RPM N ABBR *of* **resale price maintenance** mantenimiento *m* del precio de venta.

rpm N ABBR *of* **revolutions per minute** revoluciones *fpl* por minuto, r.p.m.

RR *(US)* ABBR *of* **Railroad** ferrocarril *m*, FC *m*.

RRP N ABBR *of* **recommended retail price** precio *m* al por menor recomendado, precio *m* orientativo de venta al público, PVP *m*.

RSA N **(a)** ABBR *of* **Republic of South Africa**. **(b)** *(Brit)* ABBR *of* **Royal Society of Arts**. **(c)** ABBR *of* **Royal Scottish Academy**.

RSC N *(Brit)* ABBR *of* **Royal Shakespeare Company**.

RSI N ABBR *of* **repetitive strain injury** lesión *f* de la tensión repetida.

RSM N ABBR *of* **Regimental Sergeant-Major** ≃ brigada *m* de regimiento.

RSPB N *(Brit)* ABBR *of* **Royal Society for the Protection of Birds**.

RSPCA N *(Brit)* ABBR *of* **Royal Society for the Prevention of Cruelty to Animals**.

RSV N ABBR *of* **Revised Standard Version**.

▼ **RSVP** ABBR *of* **répondez s'il vous plaît** = *please reply* se ruega contestación, S.R.C.

rt ABBR *of* **right**.

RTA N ABBR *of* **road traffic accident** accidente *m* de carretera.

RTE N *(Ireland)* ABBR *of* **Raidió Teilifís Éireann** Radio y Televisión Nacional Irlandesa.

Rt.Hon. *(Brit)* ABBR *of* **Right Honourable** título honorífico de diputado.

Rt Rev. ABBR *of* **Right Reverend** reverendo, Rvdo.

RU ABBR *of* **Rugby Union**.

rub [rʌb] 1 N **(a)** frotamiento *m*; *(accidental friction)* roce *m*, rozadura *f*; **to give sb's back a ~** frotar las espaldas de uno; **to give one's shoes a ~ (up)** limpiar los zapatos; **to give the silver a ~** sacar brillo a la plata.
　(b) *(fig)* **there's the ~** ahí está el problema, ésa es la dificultad; **but here we come to the ~** pero aquí tropezamos con la dificultad principal; **the ~ is that ...** la dificultad es que ...
　2 VT *(apply friction)* frotar, *(Med etc)* friccionar; *(hard)* estregar, restregar; *(to clean)* limpiar frotando; *(polish)* sacar brillo a; **to ~ sth dry** secar algo frotándolo; **to ~ a surface bare** alisar una superficie a fuerza de frotarla; **to ~ one's hands together** frotarse las manos.

◆ **rub against** VT rozar.

◆ **rub along*** VI ir tirando; **I can ~ along in Arabic** me defiendo en árabe.

◆ **rub away** VT quitar frotando; desgastar.

◆ **rub down** 1 VT *body* secar frotando, *horse* almohazar, *wall etc* alisar frotando.
　2 VI *(person)* secarse frotándose con una toalla.

◆ **rub in** VT: **to ~ an ointment in** frotar con un ungüento, dar fricciones con un ungüento; **to ~ an idea in** reiterar una idea; *(pej)* insistir en una idea; **the lesson has to be ~bed in** hay que insistir en la lección; **don't ~ it in!** ¡no machaques!, ¡no insistas!

◆ **rub off** 1 VT quitar, frotar; hacer desaparecer.
　2 VI borrarse debido al roce; **some of their ideas have ~bed off on him** una parte de sus opiniones ha influido en él, él ha hecho suyas algunas de las opiniones de ellos.

◆ **rub on** VT **(a)** *ointment etc* aplicar frotando.
　(b) *(~ against)* rozar.

◆ **rub out** 1 VT *(erase)* borrar; **to ~ sb out*** cargarse a uno*, despenar a uno*.
　2 VI borrarse; **it ~s out easily** es fácil quitarlo.

◆ **rub up** VT limpiar; pulir, sacar brillo a; *(fig)* refrescar; *V* **way 1** (h).

rub-a-dub ['rʌbə'dʌb] N rataplán *m*.

rubber¹ ['rʌbər] 1 N *(material)* caucho *m*, goma *f*, hule *m (LAm)*; *(Brit: eraser)* goma *f* de borrar; *(Mech etc)* paño *m* de pulir; *(*)* condón *m*, goma *f*; **~s** *(shoes)* chanclos *mpl*, zapatos *mpl* de goma.
　2 ATTR de caucho, de goma; **~ band** goma *f*, gomita *f*; **~ bullet** bala *f* de goma; **~ cement** adhesivo *m* de goma; **~ cheque*** *(Brit)* cheque *m* sin fondos; **~ dinghy** lancha *f* neumática; **~ goods** artículos *mpl* de goma; *(euph)* gomas *fpl* higiénicas; **~ industry** industria *f* gomera; **~ plant** ficus *m*; **~ plantation** cauchal *m*; **~ raft** balsa *f* neumática; **~ solution** disolución *f* de goma; **~ stamp** estampilla *f* (de goma) *(see also* **~-stamp**); **~ tree** árbol *m* gomero, árbol *m* de caucho.

rubber² ['rʌbər] N *(Bridge etc)* juego *m*, coto *m*.

rubberize ['rʌbəraɪz] VT engomar, cauchutar.

rubberized ['rʌbəraɪzd] ADJ engomado, cauchutado, cubierto de goma.

rubberneck* ['rʌbənek] *(US)* 1 N mirón *m*, -ona *f*.
　2 VI curiosear.

rubber-stamp [,rʌbə'stæmp] VT *(fig)* aprobar maquinalmente; aprobar con carácter oficial; poner su firma a.

rubbery ['rʌbərɪ] ADJ gomoso, parecido a la goma.

rubbing ['rʌbɪŋ] 1 N **(a)** *(act)* frotamiento *m*. **(b)** *(brass ~)* calco *m*.
　2 ATTR: **~ alcohol** *(US)* alcohol *m*.

rubbish ['rʌbɪʃ] 1 N **(a)** *(waste)* basura *f*; desperdicios *mpl*, desecho *m*, desechos *mpl*.
　(b) *(fig: goods)* pacotilla *f*; *(production, work of art etc)* basura *f*, porquería *f*; *(spoken, written)* tonterías *fpl*, bobadas *fpl*; **~!, what ~!** ¡tonterías!; **he talks a lot of ~** no dice más que tonterías; **it's all ~** todo son bobadas; **the novel is ~** la novela es una basura.
　2 VT *(*)* condenar como inútil, criticar duramente, poner por los suelos.

rubbish-bin ['rʌbɪʃbɪn] N *(Brit)* cubo *m* de la basura, basurero *m*.

rubbish-chute ['rʌbɪʃʃuːt] N rampa *f* de la basura.

rubbish collection ['rʌbɪʃkə,lekʃən] N recogida *f* de basuras, recolección *f* de la basura.

rubbish-dump ['rʌbɪʃdʌmp] N, **rubbish-heap** ['rʌbɪʃhiːp] N vertedero *m*, basurero *m*.

rubbishy ['rʌbɪʃɪ] ADJ *goods* de pacotilla; *production, work of art etc* que no vale para nada, de bajísima calidad.

rubble ['rʌbl] N escombros *mpl*, cascote *m*; *(filling)* cascajo *m*; **the town was reduced to ~** el pueblo quedó reducido a escombros.

rub-down ['rʌbdaʊn] N masaje *m*; secada *f* con toalla; frotación *f*, frotada *f*; **to give o.s. a ~** secarse (con toalla).

rube* [ruːb] N *(US)* patán *m*, palurdo *m*.

rubella [rʊ'belə] N rubéola *f*.

Rubicon ['ruːbɪkən] N Rubicón *m*; **to cross the ~** pasar el Rubicón.

rubicund ['ruːbɪkənd] ADJ rubicundo.

rubidium [ruː'bɪdɪəm] N rubidio *m*.

ruble ['ruːbl] N *(US)* = **rouble**.

rubric ['ruːbrɪk] N rúbrica *f*.

rub-up ['rʌbʌp] N frotada *f*; **to give a table a ~** encerar una mesa, sacar brillo a una mesa.

ruby ['ruːbɪ] 1 N rubí *m*.
　2 ADJ *necklace etc* de rubíes; *ring* de rubí, con un rubí; *colour* color de rubí.

RUC N ABBR *of* **Royal Ulster Constabulary** Policía de Irlanda del Norte.

ruched [ruːʃt] ADJ fruncido.

ruck¹ [rʌk] N *(Racing)* grueso *m* del pelotón; *(Rugby)* melé *f*; *(fig)* gente *f* común, personas *fpl* corrientes; **to get out of the ~** empezar a destacar, adelantarse a los demás.

ruck² [rʌk], **ruckle** ['rʌkl] 1 N *(in clothing etc)* arruga *f*.
　2 *(also* **to ~ up**) VT arrugar.
　3 VI arrugarse.

rucksack ['rʌksæk] N mochila *f*.

ruckus* ['rʌkəs] N *(US)* = **ruction**.

ruction* ['rʌkʃən] N lío* *m*, jaleo *m*, bronca *f*; **there will be ~s** se va a armar la gorda*.

rudder ['rʌdər] N *(Naut)* timón *m*, gobernalle *m*; *(Aer)* timón *m*.

rudderless ['rʌdəlɪs] ADJ sin timón.
ruddiness ['rʌdɪnɪs] N rubicundez *f*; lo rojizo; lo frescote, frescura *f*.
ruddy¹ ['rʌdɪ] ADJ rubicundo; rojizo; *complexion* coloradote, frescote.
ruddy²‡ ['rʌdɪ] ADJ (*Brit euph*) condenado*, puñetero‡.
rude [ruːd] ADJ (a) (*offensive*) grosero, descortés, ofensivo; **don't be ~!** ¡Vd es un maleducado!, ¡Vd es un fresco!; **you were very ~ to me once** Vd estuvo muy descortés conmigo una vez; **it's ~ to eat noisily** es de mala educación hacer ruido al comer; **would it be ~ of me to ask if ...?** ¿puedo sin ser descortés preguntar si ...?; **how ~!** ¡qué ordinario!
(b) (*indecent*) indecente; *joke etc* verde, colorado (*LAm*); **they sing ~ songs** cantan canciones verdes; **there's nothing ~ about that picture** ese cuadro no tiene nada de indecente.
(c) (*uncivilized etc*) rudo, grosero, tosco; inculto.
(d) (*sudden*) repentino; (*violent*) violento; **a ~ shock** un golpe inesperado; **a ~ awakening** una sorpresa desagradable.
(e) (*vigorous*) **to be in ~ health** gastar salud, vender salud.
rudely ['ruːdlɪ] ADV (a) (*offensively*) groseramente, con descortesía, de modo ofensivo. (b) (*indecently*) toscamente. (c) (*suddenly*) de repente; violentamente.
rudeness ['ruːdnɪs] N (a) grosería *f*, descortesía *f*. (b) indecencia *f*. (c) rudeza *f*, tosquedad *f*. (d) violencia *f*.
rudiment ['ruːdɪmənt] N (*Bio*) rudimento *m*; **~s** rudimentos *mpl*, primeras nociones *fpl*.
rudimentary [ˌruːdɪ'mentərɪ] ADJ (*Bio*) rudimental, (*fig*) rudimentario; **he has ~ Latin** tiene las primeras nociones de latín, sabe un poquito de latín.
rue¹ [ruː] VT arrepentirse de, lamentar; **you shall ~ it** te arrepentirás de haberlo hecho; **I ~ the day when I did it** ojalá no lo hubiera hecho nunca; **he lived to ~ it** vivió para arrepentirse.
rue² [ruː] N (*Bot*) ruda *f*.
rueful ['ruːful] ADJ triste; arrepentido; lamentable.
ruefully ['ruːfəlɪ] ADV tristemente.
ruefulness ['ruːfulnɪs] N tristeza *f*.
ruff¹ [rʌf] N gorguera *f*, gola *f*; (*Orn, Zool*) collarín *m*.
ruff² [rʌf] (*Cards*) ① N fallada *f*.
② VT fallar.
ruffian ['rʌfɪən] N matón *m*, criminal *m*; **you ~!** ¡canalla!
ruffianly ['rʌfɪənlɪ] ADJ brutal, criminal.
ruffle ['rʌfl] ① N arruga *f*; (*Sew*) volante *m* fruncido; (*ripple*) rizo *m*.
② VT (*wrinkle*) arrugar; *surface* agitar, rizar; (*Sew*) fruncir; *hair* despeinar; *feathers* encrespar, erizar; *sb's composure* descomponer, perturbar; **to ~ sb's feelings** ofender a uno, herir los sentimientos de uno; **nothing ~s him** no se altera por nada; **she wasn't at all ~d** no se perturbó en lo más mínimo; **to smooth sb's ~d feathers** (*fig*) alisar las plumas erizadas de uno.
③ VI arrugarse; agitarse, rizarse.
rug [rʌg] N (*on floor*) tapete *m*, alfombrilla *f*; (*travelling ~*) manta *f* (de viaje); **to pull the ~ from under sb** (*fig*) mover la silla para que uno se caiga.
rugby ['rʌgbɪ] N (*also ~ football*) rugby *m*; **~ player** jugador *m* de rugby.

┌─ *RUGBY* ─┐

🛈 *Se cree que el rugby comenzó a jugarse en el colegio **Rugby** de Inglaterra en 1823. Sin embargo, cuando la **Rugby Football Union** estableció las reglas de este deporte, el juego profesional quedó prohibido, por lo que un grupo decidió formar el **Rugby League**, lo que dio origen a dos tipos distintos de rugby. El **Rugby League** se juega con 13 jugadores por equipo, tiene sus propias reglas y sistema de tanteo y sus jugadores pueden ser profesionales. Se juega sobre todo en el norte de Inglaterra y Australia. Por su parte, el **Rugby Union** se juega con equipos compuestos por 15 jugadores y es un deporte muy popular en todo el mundo. El carácter amateur de esta versión del rugby se mantuvo hasta 1995, año en que la Federación Internacional de este deporte (**International Rugby Board**) decidió permitir que los jugadores y directivos pudiesen cobrar. Como deporte escolar en el Reino Unido, el rugby es frecuente en los colegios privados, mientras que, en los colegios públicos, el fútbol es el deporte más extendido.*

Rugby League [ˌrʌgbɪ'liːg] N *tipo de rugby en que los equipos tienen trece jugadores.*
Rugby Union [ˌrʌgbɪ'juːnjən] N *tipo de rugby en que los equipos tienen quince jugadores.*
rugged ['rʌgɪd] ADJ *terrain* escabroso, áspero, accidentado, bravo; (*harsh*) duro, severo; *character* robusto; *construction* fuerte, robusto; *features* fuerte, acentuado; *workmanship* tosco; *independence etc* vigoroso; *style* desigual.
ruggedness ['rʌgɪdnɪs] N escabrosidad *f*, aspereza *f*, lo accidentado; severidad *f*; robustez *f*; lo fuerte; tosquedad *f*; vigor *m*; desigualdad *f*.
rugger* ['rʌgəʳ] N (*Brit*) rugby *m*.

ruin ['ruːɪn] ① N (a) ruina *f*; **~s** ruinas *fpl*; restos *mpl*; **to be in ~s** estar en ruinas, estar arruinado; **her hopes were in ~s** sus esperanzas estaban arruinadas; **to lay a town in ~s** asolar una ciudad; **the city rose from the ~s** la ciudad volvió a nacer sobre las ruinas.
(b) (*act*) ruina *f*, arruinamiento *m*.
(c) (*fig*) ruina *f*; perdición *f*; **the ~ of sb's hopes** la destrucción de las esperanzas de uno; **it will be the ~ of him** será su ruina; **drink will be his ~** el alcohol le perderá, el alcohol será su perdición; **to bring sb to ~** arruinar a uno; **~ stared us in the face** nos encontramos frente a la ruina.
② VT arruinar; asolar; (*spoil*) estropear; *taste etc* estragar; (*morally*) perder; **her extravagance ~ed him** sus despilfarros le arruinaron; **what ~ed him was gambling** lo que le perdió fue el juego; **he ~ed my new car** estropeó mi nuevo coche.
ruination [ˌruːɪ'neɪʃən] N ruina *f*, arruinamiento *m*, perdición *f*.
ruined ['ruːɪnd] ADJ arruinado (*also fig*), en ruinas, ruinoso.
ruinous ['ruːɪnəs] ADJ (*all senses*) ruinoso.
ruinously ['ruːɪnəslɪ] ADV de modo ruinoso; **~ expensive** carísimo, de lo más caro.
rule [ruːl] ① N (a) (*ruling*) regla *f*; norma *f*; costumbre *f*; principio *m*; **~s** (*of competition*) bases *fpl*; **as a ~** en general, por regla general; normalmente; **~ of the road** reglamento *m* del tráfico; **~ of three** (*Math*) regla *f* de tres; **~ of thumb** regla *f* empírica; **by ~ of thumb** por experiencia, por rutina; mediante una prueba práctica; **the ~s of the game** las reglas del juego; **~s and regulations** reglamento *m*; **it's the ~** es de regla; **it's against the ~s** es contra la regla, eso no se permite; **our ~ is ...** nuestro principio es ...; **bad weather is the ~ here** el mal tiempo es normal aquí; **the golden ~ is ...** la regla principal es ...; **there is no hard-and-fast ~ about it** sobre eso no existe ninguna regla terminante; **to bend** (*or* **stretch**) **the ~** ajustar la regla; **to do everything by ~** obrar siempre por sistema; **to make it a ~ to** + *infin* hacerse una regla de + *infin*; **I make it a ~ never to drink** yo por sistema nunca bebo; **to work to ~** trabajar al mínimo legal, hacer huelga de celo, estar en paro técnico.
(b) (*Jur*) fallo *m*; decisión *f*.
(c) (*dominion etc*) dominio *m*, imperio *m*; autoridad *f*; mando *m*; **under British ~** bajo la autoridad británica; **under the ~ of Louis XV** bajo el reinado de Luis XV; **~ of law** imperio *m* de la ley; **under the ~ of fear** bajo el imperio del miedo.
(d) (*ruler*) metro *m*.
(e) (*Eccl*) regla *f*; **the Benedictine ~** la regla benedictina.
② VT (a) (*govern: also* **to ~ over**) gobernar, mandar, regir; **to ~ an empire** gobernar un imperio; **he ~d the company for 40 years** durante 40 años rigió la compañía; **he's ~d by his wife** le domina su mujer; **be ~d by my advice** déjate guiar por mis consejos, guíate por mí.
(b) (*Jur*) decidir; (*of chairman etc*) disponer, determinar; **to ~ that ...** decidir que ..., decretar que ...; **to ~ sth out of order** decidir que un asunto no se puede discutir.
(c) (*draw*) *line* trazar, tirar; *paper* rayar, reglar.
③ VI (a) (*govern*) gobernar; (*of monarch*) reinar.
(b) (*decide*) fallar, decidir (*against* contra, en contra de, *for* en favor de).
(c) (*of price*) regir.
◆ **rule off** VT cerrar con una línea, tirar una línea debajo de.
◆ **rule out** VT: **to ~ sth out** excluir algo, descartar algo; **we can't ~ out the possibility that ...** no podemos excluir la posibilidad de que + *subj*; **you are not ~d out because of that** no se te excluye por eso.

┌─ *RULE BRITANNIA* ─┐

🛈 ***Rule Britannia** es una canción patriótica que data de 1740. La letra, escrita por el poeta escocés James Thomson, celebra el control marítimo del que Gran Bretaña disfrutaba en aquella época. Aunque algunos critican el tono excesivamente chovinista de la canción, **Rule Britannia** aún se canta en algunas celebraciones de carácter patriótico, como la **Last Night of the Proms**. El estribillo reza así: **Rule Britannia, Britannia rule the waves, Britons never never never will be slaves.***
⇨ *Ver también* │PROM│

rulebook ['ruːlbʊk] N libro *m* de normas, libro *m* de reglamento; **we'll do it by the ~** lo haremos de acuerdo con el reglamento.
ruled [ruːld] ADJ *paper* rayado.
ruler ['ruːləʳ] N (a) (*person*) gobernante *mf*, gobernador *m*, -ora *f*; soberano *m*, -a *f*. (b) (*for measuring*) regla *f*.
ruling ['ruːlɪŋ] ① ADJ *passion* dominante, predominante; *price* que rige; **the ~ classes** la clase que gobierna, la clase que manda.
② N fallo *m*, decisión *f*; **to give a ~** fallar, decidir; **to give a ~ on a dispute** pronunciar un fallo sobre una disputa.
rum¹ [rʌm] ① N ron *m*.
② ATTR: **~ toddy** *ron con agua caliente y azúcar.*
rum²* [rʌm] ADJ (*Brit*) extraño, raro.

Rumania *etc* (*Brit*) = **Romania** *etc.*

rumba ['rʌmbə] N rumba *f.*

rumble¹ ['rʌmbl] ⓵ N retumbo *m*, ruido *m* sordo, rumor *m*; (*of thunder etc*) redoble *m*; (*in stomach*) ruido *m* (de tripas); (*of tank etc*) rodar *m*; **~s of discontent** ruidos *mpl* sordos de descontento.
⓶ VI retumbar; hacer un ruido sordo; redoblar; rodar; (*stomach*) sonar, hacer ruidos; **the train ~d past** el tren pasó con estruendo; **the talk ~d on** se siguió charlando pesadamente; **he ~d on another half-hour** continuó media hora más con el rollo*.

rumble²* ['rʌmbl] VT (*Brit*) calar; **he's ~d us** nos ha calado, nos ha pillado (*LAm*); **I soon ~d what was going on** pronto me olí lo que estaban haciendo.

rumble seat ['rʌmbl'si:t] N (*US Aut*) asiento *m* trasero exterior.

rumble strip ['rʌmbl,strɪp] N *superficie rugosa en la calzada para frenado.*

rumbling ['rʌmblɪŋ] N = **rumble¹**.

rumbustious [rʌm'bʌstʃəs] ADJ bullicioso, ruidoso.

ruminant ['ru:mɪnənt] ⓵ ADJ rumiante.
⓶ N rumiante *m.*

ruminate ['ru:mɪneɪt] VTI rumiar (*also fig*).

rumination [,ru:mɪ'neɪʃən] N (*act*) rumia *f*; (*thought*) meditación *f*, reflexión *f.*

ruminative ['ru:mɪnətɪv] ADJ (*Bio*) rumiante; (*fig*) pensativo, meditabundo.

ruminatively ['ru:mɪnətɪvlɪ] ADV pensativamente; **'I hope so', he said ~** 'espero que sí', dijo pensativo.

rummage ['rʌmɪdʒ] VI hurgar; **to ~ about** revolverlo todo, buscar revolviéndolo todo; **he was rummaging about in the drawer** estaba hurgando en el cajón; **he ~d in his pocket and produced a key** hurgando en el bolsillo sacó una llave.

rummage sale ['rʌmɪdʒseɪl] N (*US*) venta *f* de objetos usados (con fines benéficos); *ver también* JUMBLE SALE/RUMMAGE SALE .

rummy¹* ['rʌmɪ] ⓵ ADJ extraño, raro.
⓶ N (*US*: *drunk*) borracho *m*, -a *f.*

rummy² ['rʌmɪ] N (*Cards*) rummy *m.*

rumour, (*US*) **rumor** ['ru:mər] ⓵ N rumor *m*; **as ~ has it** según se dice; **~ has it that ...** se rumorea que ...
⓶ VT: **it is ~ed that ...** se rumorea que ..., se dice que ...; **he is ~ed to be rich** se dice que es rico.

rump [rʌmp] N (**a**) (*Anat*) (*of horse etc*) ancas *fpl*, grupa *f*; (*of bird*) rabadilla *f*; (*: of person*) trasero *m*; (*Culin*) cuarto *m* trasero, cadera *f.*
(**b**) (*of party etc*) parte *f* que queda; núcleo *m* irreductible; **there's just a ~ left** quedan solamente unos pocos miembros.

rumple ['rʌmpl] VT ajar, arrugar, chafar.

rumpsteak ['rʌmp'steɪk] N filete *m.*

rumpus* ['rʌmpəs] N lío* *m*, jaleo *m*; batahóla* *f*, revuelo *m*; **to have a ~ with sb** pelearse con uno; **to kick up a ~** armar un lío*, armar una bronca (*LAm*).

rumpus room ['rʌmpəs,rʊm] N (*US*) cuarto *m* de los niños, cuarto *m* de juegos.

rumpy-pumpy* ['rʌmpɪpʌmpɪ] N (*Brit*: *hum*) chiquichín *m*, ñakañaka *m.*

run [rʌn] ⓵ N (**a**) (*act of running*) corrida *f*, carrera *f*; (*Athletics, Baseball, Cricket*) carrera *f*; (*in stocking*) carrera *f*, acarraladura *f* (*And, SC*); (*of fish*) migración *f*; **at a ~** corriendo; **to go at a steady ~** correr a un paso regular; **to break into a ~** echar a correr, empezar a correr; **to be on the ~** estar huido; **a prisoner on the ~** un preso fugado, un preso evadido; **he's on the ~ from prison** escapó de la cárcel; **he was on the ~ for 6 weeks** estuvo libre durante 6 semanas; **he's on the ~ from his creditors** se está escapando de sus acreedores; **to keep sb on the ~** hacer que uno corra de acá para allá; mantener a uno en constante actividad; acosar a uno, (*Mil*) hostigar a uno; **we soon had the enemy on the ~** pronto pusimos al enemigo en fuga; **we've got them on the ~ now** ya están casi vencidos; **it came down with a ~** bajó repentinamente, cayó todo junto; **prices came down with a ~** los precios bajaron de golpe; **I had a ~ to catch it** tuve que correr bastante para cogerlo; **I have a ~ before breakfast** corro antes del desayuno; **to make a ~ for it** tratar de fugar, tratar de escaparse; **we shall have to make a ~ for it** tendremos que correr; **they gave us** (or **we had**) **a (good) ~ for our money** nos dieron bastante satisfacción por nuestro dinero; **never mind, we gave him a (good) ~ for his money** no importa, le hicimos sudar; *ver también* CRICKET .
(**b**) (*Aut etc: outing*) paseo *m* (en coche), excursión *f* (en coche); (*Aer etc: raid*) ataque *m*; **it was a very pleasant ~** fue un viaje muy agradable; **to go for a ~**, **to have a ~** dar un paseo (en coche), dar una vuelta (en coche); **we'll have a ~ down to the coast** iremos de excursión a la costa.
(**c**) (*Rail etc: distance travelled*) trayecto *m*, recorrido *m*; **day's ~** (*Naut*) singladura *f*; **the Plymouth-Santander ~** el servicio de Plymouth a Santander, la línea de Plymouth a Santander; **it's a short car ~** es un breve viaje en coche.
(**d**) (*Typ*) tirada *f*; **a ~ of 5,000 copies** una tirada de 5.000

ejemplares.
(**e**) (*tendency*) tendencia *f*; **the ~ of the market** la tendencia del mercado; **the ~ of the play was favourable to us** el partido se desarrolló de modo favorable para nosotros; **they scored against the ~ of play** marcaron un gol cuando menos se podía esperar.
(**f**) (*series*) serie *f*; (*of product*) cantidad *f*, total *m*; **a ~ of four** (*Cards*) una escalera de cuatro; **a ~ of luck** una racha de suerte; **a ~ of bad luck** una temporada de mala suerte; **a ~ of 5 wins** una racha de 5 victorias; **to have a long ~** (*fashion*) estar en boga mucho tiempo, conservar su popularidad durante mucho tiempo; **the play had a long ~** la obra se mantuvo mucho tiempo en la cartelera; **when the London ~ was over** al terminarse la serie de representaciones en Londres; **in the long ~** a la larga; **in the short ~** a plazo corto.
(**g**) (*Comm*) **~ on a bank** asedio *m* de un banco; **there is a ~ on soap** hay una gran demanda de jabón, el jabón tiene mucha demanda.
(**h**) (*generality*) **the common ~ of people** el común de las gentes; **the common ~ of books** la generalidad de los libros; **it's above the common ~** es superior al nivel general.
(**i**) (*access*) **to have the ~ of sb's house** poder entrar libremente en la casa de uno; **to have the ~ of sb's library** tener libre uso de la biblioteca de uno, poder usar a discreción la biblioteca de uno.
(**j**) (*Agr etc*) terreno *m* de pasto; (*hen~*) corral *m*, gallinero *m*; (*ski~*) pista *f* de esquí.
(**k**) (*Mus*) fermata *f*; carrerilla *f.*
(**l**) **to have the ~s**‡ tener el vientre descompuesto, tener cagueruelas‡.
⓶ (*irr*: PRET **ran**, PTP **run**) VT (**a**) (*gen*) correr; **she ran 20 km** corrió 20 km; **to ~ a race** tomar parte en una carrera; **you ran a good race** corriste muy bien; **they're not ~ning the race this year** este año no hay carrera; **the race is ~ over 4 km** la distancia de la carrera es de 4 km.
(**b**) **to ~ a risk** correr un riesgo.
(**c**) (*cause to run*) hacer correr; (*hunt, chase*) cazar, dar caza a; **to ~ sb off his legs** correr hasta cansar al compañero; agotar a uno corriendo; **to ~ sb close**, **to ~ sb hard** casi alcanzar a uno, ir pisándole los talones a uno (*also fig*); **to ~ it close**, **to ~ it fine** llegar con muy poco tiempo, dejarse muy poco margen.
(**d**) **to ~ sheep in a field** pacer las ovejas en un campo.
(**e**) (*move, transport etc*) llevar; transportar; **he ran the car into the garage** puso el coche en el garaje; **he ran the car into a tree** chocó con un árbol; **this will ~ you into debt** esto te endeudará; **it ran him into a lot of trouble** le causó muchas molestias; **I'll ~ you up to town** te llevo a la ciudad; **to ~ a boat ashore** varar una embarcación; **to ~ guns across a frontier** pasar fusiles de contrabando a través de una frontera; **the stream ran blood** el arroyo iba tinto de sangre; **to ~ messages** llevar recados; **to ~ a new bus service** establecer un nuevo servicio de autobuses; **they're ~ning an extra train** ponen un tren suplementario; **they don't ~ that bus on Sundays** no ponen ese autobús los domingos.
(**f**) **to ~ the blockade** forzar el bloqueo, burlar el bloqueo; **to ~ a stoplight** (*US*) saltarse un semáforo en rojo.
(**g**) (*have, possess*) tener, poseer; **he ~s two cars** tiene dos coches; **we don't ~ a car** no tenemos coche; **to ~ a (high) temperature** tener fiebre; **to ~ a temperature of 104°** tener 4 grados de fiebre.
(**h**) (*direct, operate etc*) *business* dirigir; controlar, gobernar, regir; *machine* hacer funcionar, manejar; (*Comput*) *program* ejecutar, rodar; *campaign* dirigir, organizar; *course* ofrecer, organizar; **to ~ the house for sb** llevar la casa a uno; **a house which is easy to ~** (or **easily ~**) una casa de fácil manejo; **she's the one who really ~s everything** la que en realidad lo dirige todo es ella; **I want to ~ my own life** quiero organizar mi propia vida; **you can ~ this machine on gas** puedes hacer funcionar esta máquina a gas; **you can ~ it on** (or **off**) **the mains** funciona con corriente de la red.
(**i**) (*present in contest*) **to ~ a horse** correr un caballo; **he ran 3 horses last season** en la última temporada corrió 3 caballos; **to ~ a candidate** presentar un candidato; **the liberals are not ~ning anybody this time** esta vez los liberales no tienen candidato.
(**j**) (*pass*) pasar; (*pierce*) traspasar; (*introduce*) introducir; **to ~ one's hand over a chair** pasar la mano por un sillón, recorrer un sillón con la mano; **to ~ one's eye over a text** dar una ojeada a un texto; **~ your eye over this** mira esto un poco; **let me ~ this idea past you** (*US*) a ver qué piensas de esta idea; **to ~ a line round sth** trazar una línea alrededor de algo; **to ~ water into a bath** hacer correr agua en un baño, llenar un baño de agua; **would you ~ my bath?** ¿me preparas el baño?; **we'll ~ a fence round it** pondremos un cerco alrededor de él; **to ~ a pipe through a wall** pasar un tubo a través de una pared; **he ran his pencil through the phrase** tachó la frase con el lápiz; **I ran a thorn into my finger** me clavé una espina en el dedo.
(**k**) *report, story* publicar, imprimir, presentar; *product* vender, poner

a la venta.

3 VI (**a**) (*gen*) correr; (*hasten*) correr, darse prisa, apresurarse; (*in race*) competir, tomar parte; **to ~ for all one is worth, to ~ like the devil** correr a todo correr; **to ~ downstairs** bajar la escalera corriendo; **to ~ down the garden** correr por el jardín; **to ~ for a bus** correr para coger un autobús; **to ~ to meet sb** correr al encuentro de uno, acudir corriendo para recibir a uno; **to ~ to help sb** acudir corriendo en ayuda de uno.

(**b**) (*flee*) huir; **we shall have to ~ for it** tendremos que correr; **~ for your lives!** ¡sálvese el que pueda!

(**c**) (*present o.s.*) **to ~ for office** ser candidato para un puesto, presentarse como candidato para un puesto; **are you ~ning?** ¿vas a presentar tu candidatura?

(**d**) (*Naut*) **to ~ before the wind** navegar con viento a popa; **to ~ aground** encallar, embarrancar.

(**e**) (*function: engine etc*) funcionar, marchar, andar; estar en marcha; **the lift isn't ~ning** el ascensor no funciona; **the car ~s smoothly** el coche marcha bien; **things did not ~ smoothly for them** las cosas no les fueron bien; **it ~s on petrol** funciona con gasolina, tiene motor de gasolina; **it ~s off the mains** funciona con corriente de la red.

(**f**) (*function: service etc*) circular, ir; **the trains ~ning between Madrid and Ávila** los trenes que circulan entre Madrid y Ávila, los trenes que hacen el servicio entre Madrid y Ávila; **there are no trains ~ning to Toboso** no hay servicio de trenes a Toboso; **that train does not ~ on Sundays** ese tren no circula los domingos; **the buses ~ every 10 minutes** los autobuses salen cada 10 minutos; **the train is ~ning late** el tren lleva retraso; **the service usually ~s on time** el servicio generalmente es puntual; **steamers ~ daily between X and Y** hay servicio diario de vapores entre X e Y.

(**g**) (*pass*) **a rumour ran round the school** un rumor corrió por la escuela; **a ripple ran through the crowd** la multitud se estremeció (de emoción *etc*); **it ~s through the whole history of art** afecta toda la historia del arte, se observa en toda la historia del arte; **it ~s in the family** viene de familia; **the thought ran through my head that ...** se me ocurrió pensar que ...; **that tune keeps ~ning in my head** esa melodía la tengo metida en la cabeza; **the conversation ran on wine** el tema de la conversación era el vino; **my thoughts ran on Mary** mi pensamiento se concentró en María.

(**h**) (*go, continue*) seguir; **the contract ran for 7 years** el contrato fue válido durante 7 años; **the play ran for 40 performances** la obra tuvo 40 representaciones seguidas; **the play ~ for 3 months** la obra se mantuvo en la cartelera durante 3 meses; **things must ~ their course** las cosas tienen que seguir su curso; **the affair has ~ its course** el asunto ha terminado; **where his writ does not ~** donde su autoridad no vale, donde él no tiene jurisdicción.

(**i**) (*extend*) **to ~ to** extenderse a; (*of amounts*) subir a, ascender a, sumar; **the book has ~ into 20 editions** el libro ha alcanzado 20 ediciones; **the cost will ~ into millions** el coste se elevará a varios millones; **the talk ran to 2 hours** la charla se extendió a 2 horas; **the book will ~ to 700 pages** el libro tendrá 700 páginas en total; **my salary won't ~ to a second car** mi sueldo no me permite adquirir un segundo coche; **we can't possibly ~ to a grand piano** nos es imposible comprar un piano de cola.

(**j**) (*colour*) desteñirse, correrse; (*melt*) derretirse; (*Med: sore*) supurar; **colours that will not ~** colores *mpl* sólidos, colores *mpl* inalterables, colores *mpl* que no se corren; **my ice is ~ning** mi helado se está derritiendo.

(**k**) (*flow*) correr, fluir; (*tears*) correr; (*drip*) gotear; **the milk ran all over the floor** la leche se derramó por todo el suelo; **tears ran down her cheeks** las lágrimas le corrían por las mejillas; **my pen ~s** mi pluma gotea; **the streets were ~ning with water** el agua corría por las calles; **we were ~ning with sweat** chorreábamos de sudor; **a land ~ning with milk and honey** una tierra que abunda en leche y miel; **to leave a tap ~ning** dejar abierto un grifo, dejar abierta una llave (*LAm*); **the Tagus ~s past Toledo** el Tajo pasa por Toledo; **the river ~s for 300 miles** el río corre 300 millas; **it ~s into the sea at Lisbon** desemboca en el mar en Lisboa; **the street ~s into the square** la calle desemboca en la plaza; **blood ran from the wound** la sangre manaba de la herida, la herida manaba sangre; **a heavy sea was ~ning** el mar estaba muy picado; había una fuerte corriente; **when the tide is ~ning strongly** cuando sube la marea rápidamente; **to ~ dry** (*river*) secarse, (*resources*) agotarse.

(**l**) (*go, pass*) ir; **the road ~s along the river** la carretera sigue el río, la carretera va a lo largo del río; **a fence ~s along that side** hay un cerco por ese lado; **a balcony ~s round the hall** una galería se extiende todo lo largo de la sala; **a fence ~s round the field** el campo está rodeado por una cerca; **York has walls that ~ right round it** York tiene una muralla que la rodea completamente; **the road ~s by our house** la carretera pasa junto a nuestra casa; **it ~s north and south** va de norte a sur.

(**m**) (*say*) **so the story ~s** así dice el cuento; **the text ~s like this** el

texto dice así, el texto reza así.

(**n**) (*develop*) **to ~ to seed** granar; **to ~ to fat** engordar; tener tendencia a engordar; *V* **high, low¹** *etc.*

(**o**) (*stocking*) hacerse una carrera.

(**p**) (*Comput*) ejecutarse.

♦**run about, run around** VI correr (por todas partes); (*have fun*) divertirse corriendo; **to ~ around with** (*fig*) salir con, alternar con; ser compañero de, acompañar (mucho) a.

♦**run across** **1** VT (*encounter*) *person* toparse con; *object etc* encontrar.
2 VI cruzar corriendo; **the water ran across the road** el agua cruzó la calle.

♦**run after** VT correr tras; *girl* correr detrás de, dar caza a, perseguir.

♦**run along** VI correr; (*depart*) marcharse; **~ along (now)!** ¡anda ya!

♦**run at** VT lanzarse sobre, precipitarse sobre.

♦**run away** VI (**a**) (*escape*) evadirse, huir, escaparse; (*horse*) dispararse; **to ~ away from home** huir de casa; **to ~ away from prison** fugarse de la cárcel; **to ~ away from the facts** no prestar atención a los hechos, no hacer caso de los hechos; **to ~ away from one's responsibilities** evadir sus responsabilidades; **to ~ away with sb** fugarse con uno; **to ~ away with the cash** alzarse con el dinero; **to ~ away with a race** ganar fácilmente una carrera; **it simply ~s away with the money** es que devora el dinero; **don't let your feelings ~ away with you** no te dejes dominar por las emociones; **don't ~ away with the idea that ...** no te imagines que ..., no te dejes arrastrar por la idea de que ...; *V also* **~ along.**
(**b**) (*water etc*) irse, salir.

♦**run back** **1** VT (**a**) *person* llevar (a su casa *etc*) en coche.
(**b**) *film* rebobinar.
2 VI volver corriendo.

♦**run down** **1** VT (**a**) (*Aut*) atropellar.
(**b**) (*Naut*) hundir.
(**c**) (*reduce*) reducir, restringir; *battery etc* agotar, descargar; *company* restringir la producción de; *supply* reducir; (*Med*) agotar; **to be ~ down** (*Med*) no estar bien de salud, estar agotado, estar debilitado; (*battery*) estar descargado; (*clock*) estar parado.
(**d**) (*: denigrate*) hablar mal de, vilipendiar; desacreditar.
(**e**) (*find*) localizar, encontrar; (*catch up with*) alcanzar; (*capture*) coger, cazar.
(**f**) **he ran down the list** pasó (rápidamente) el ojo por la lista.
2 VI (**a**) bajar corriendo.
(**b**) (*clock*) parar; (*battery*) acabarse; ir perdiendo fuerza; **the spring has ~ down** se ha acabado la cuerda.

♦**run in** **1** VT (**a**) (*Brit Aut*) rodar; **'~ning in'** 'en rodaje'.
(**b**) (*: arrest*) detener, meter en la cárcel.
2 VI entrar corriendo.

♦**run into** VT (**a**) (*crash*) chocar con, dar contra; **the two cars ran into each other** chocaron los dos coches.
(**b**) (*meet*) topar a, tropezar con.
(**c**) (*fig*) **to ~ into debt** contraer deudas, endeudarse, endrogarse (*LAm*); **to ~ into trouble** tropezar con dificultades, encontrar problemas; **to ~ into danger** exponerse a un peligro.

♦**run off** **1** VT (**a**) *water etc* vaciar; dejar correr, dejar salir.
(**b**) (*recite*) enumerar rápidamente; (*compose*) componer en el acto; (*print*) tirar, imprimir.
(**c**) (*Sport*) *heats* decidir, correr.
2 VI **~ away** (**a**).

♦**run on** **1** VT (*Typ*) continuar sin dejar espacio; unir al párrafo anterior.
2 VI (**a**) seguir corriendo.
(**b**) (*in talking etc*) continuar, continuar sin interrupción; **the Wagner ran on for 9 hours** el Wagner continuó durante 9 horas; **he's good but he does ~ on** es bueno pero continúa más de lo necesario; **she does ~ on so** es tan habladora, no termina de hablar.

♦**run out** **1** VT *rope* ir dando; pasar, extender.
2 VI (**a**) (*person etc*) salir corriendo; (*liquid*) irse; (*tide*) bajar.
(**b**) (*come to an end*) acabarse, agotarse; (*time*) acabarse, vencerse (*LAm*); (*lease, term*) expirar; (*contract, permit*) vencer, caducar; (*stock, supply*) acabarse; **when the money ~s out** cuando se acabe el dinero; **the tide is ~ning out, the sands are ~ning out** (*fig*) queda poco tiempo.
(**c**) **we ran out of petrol** nos quedamos sin gasolina; **I ran out of patience** se me acabó la paciencia; **I ran out of road on the bend** se me acabó la carretera en la curva.
(**d**) **she ran out on her husband** abandonó a su marido; **you're not going to ~ out on us now?** ¿ahora nos abandonas?

♦**run over** **1** VT (**a**) (*Aut*) atropellar.
(**b**) (*rehearse*) volver a hacer, repasar, volver a ensayar; (*read rapidly*) repasar, leer por encima.
2 VI (**a**) (*go*) ir; **to ~ over to** ir (corriendo) a; (*Aut*) ir (en coche) a visitar a, ir en una escapada a.
(**b**) (*overflow*) irse, desbordarse, rebosar.
(**c**) (*in time*) rebasar el límite; **the show ran over by 5 minutes** la

función duró 5 minutos más de lo debido; **this text ~s over by 200 words** este texto tiene 200 palabras más de lo estipulado.

◆ **run through** VT **(a)** (*with sword etc*) traspasar.
(b) (*use up*) gastar, consumir.
(c) (*read*) *book* hojear, leer a la ligera; *instructions etc* repasar; (*rehearse*) repasar.

◆ **run up** 1 VT **(a)** *flag* izar.
(b) *account, bill* crear, hacerse; *debt* incurrir en, contraer.
(c) *dress* hacer de prisa; *building* construir.
2 VI **(a)** subir corriendo; (*approach*) acudir corriendo; **to ~ up to sb** acercarse corriendo a uno; **to ~ up a hill** subir un cerro corriendo.
(b) (*plant*) trepar por.
(c) (*fig: encounter*) **to ~ up against sb** tener que habérselas con uno; **to ~ up against difficulties** tropezar con dificultades.

runabout ['rʌnəbaʊt] N **(a)** (*Aut*) coche *m* pequeño. **(b)** (*Rail etc*) billete *m* kilométrico.

runaround* ['rʌnəraʊnd] N: **to give sb the ~** traer a uno al retortero.

runaway ['rʌnəweɪ] 1 ADJ *prisoner, slave* fugitivo; *soldier* desertor; *horse* desbocado; *lorry* sin frenos, fuera de control; *inflation* galopante, desenfrenado; *success* arrollador; *victory* abrumador, fácil; *marriage* clandestino, fugitivo.
2 N (*person*) fugitivo *m*, -a *f*; (*horse*) caballo *m* desbocado.

run-down ['rʌn'daʊn] ADJ *battery* descargado; *health* debilitado; *building* descuidado, mal cuidado; *organization etc* en decadencia.

rundown ['rʌndaʊn] N **(a)** (*of industry etc*) cierre *m* gradual; (*of activity*) disminución *f*, reducción *f*; decline *m*; deterioro *m*. **(b)** (*briefing*) resumen *m* (oral) (*on* de), informe *m* (oral); **to give sb a ~** poner a uno al día.

rune [ruːn] N runa *f*.

rung[1] [rʌŋ] N escalón *m*, peldaño *m*.

rung[2] [rʌŋ] PTP of **ring**[2].

runic ['ruːnɪk] ADJ rúnico.

run-in ['rʌnɪn] N **(a)** (*Typ*) palabras *fpl* insertadas en un párrafo. **(b)** (*in contest, election*) desempate *m*. **(c)** (*rehearsal*) ensayo *m*. **(d)** (*approach*) aproximación *f*; etapa *f* previa. **(e)** (*: argument*) altercado *m*.

runlet ['rʌnlɪt] N, **runnel** ['rʌnl] N arroyuelo *m*.

runner ['rʌnər] 1 N **(a)** (*athlete*) corredor *m*, -ora *f*, atleta *mf*; (*horse, in race*) caballo *m*; (*messenger*) mensajero *m*, (*Mil*) ordenanza *m*, (*Fin*) corredor *m*.
(b) (*ring: of curtain etc*) anillo *m* movible; (*wheel*) ruedecilla *f*; (*of sledge, aircraft*) patín *m*.
(c) (*carpet*) alfombra *f* de pasillo; (*table ~*) tapete *m*.
(d) (*Bot*) tallo *m* rastrero, estolón *m*.
(e) (‡) **to do a ~** largarse*.
2 ATTR: **~ bean** (*Brit*) judía *f* (escarlata), habichuela *f*.

runner-up ['rʌnər'ʌp] N subcampeón *m*, -ona *f*, segundo *m*, -a *f*.

running ['rʌnɪŋ] 1 ADJ *water* corriente; *knot* corredizo; *writing* cursivo; *commentary* en directo; *start* lanzado; **~ costs** gastos *mpl* de explotación, gastos *mpl* corrientes; **~ fight** acción *f* de retirada; combate *m* continuo; **~ head** encabezamiento *m* normal; **~ kick** puntapié *m* dado mientras corre el jugador (*etc*); **~ mate** (*Pol etc*) compañero *m*, -a *f* de candidatura; **~ repairs** reparaciones *fpl* provisionales; **~ sore** úlcera *f*, (*fig*) llaga *f*; **~ total** suma *f* parcial; suma y sigue; **in ~ order** en buen estado; **5 days ~** 5 días seguidos; **for the sixth time ~** por sexta vez consecutiva.
2 N **(a)** (*act of ~*) el correr; *footing m*, *jogging m*; **to be in the ~** tener posibilidades de ganar; **to be in the ~ for a chair** tener posibilidades de ganar una cátedra; **to be out of the ~** no tener posibilidad de ganar; **to make (all) the ~** ir a la cabeza, ir delante; ser el promotor (principal).
(b) (*of business etc*) dirección *f*; control *m*; gobierno *m*; administración *f*; organización *f*; manejo *m*.
(c) (*of machine*) marcha *f*, funcionamiento *m*.

running-board ['rʌnɪŋbɔːd] N estribo *m*.

running-in ['rʌnɪŋ'ɪn] N rodaje *m*.

running mate ['rʌnɪŋ'meɪt] N (*US Pol*) candidato *m*, -a *f* a la vicepresidencia.

running-shoe ['rʌnɪŋ,ʃuː] N zapatilla *f* para correr.

running-track ['rʌnɪŋ,træk] N pista *f* (de atletismo).

runny ['rʌnɪ] ADJ líquido; derretido; **~ nose** narices *fpl* que moquean.

run-off ['rʌnɒf] N **(a)** (*Sport*) carrera *f* de desempate; (*Pol*) desempate *m*, segunda vuelta *f*. **(b)** (*Agr*) escorrentía *f*; **~ water** aguas *fpl* de escorrentía.

run-of-the-mill ['rʌnəvðə'mɪl] ADJ corriente y moliente, ordinario.

runproof ['rʌnpruːf] ADJ *mascara* que no se corre; *tights* indesmallable.

runt [rʌnt] N (*also fig*) redrojo *m*, enano *m*; **you little ~!** ¡canalla!

run-through ['rʌnθruː] N prueba *f* preliminar, ensayo *m*.

run-up ['rʌnʌp] N **(a)** (*Brit*) período *m* previo (*to* a); preparativos *mpl* (*to* para). **(b)** (*Sport*) corrida *f*.

runway ['rʌnweɪ] N (*Aer*) pista *f*; (*US: Theat etc*) pasarela *f*; **~ lights** baliza *f*.

rupee [ruː'piː] N rupia *f*.

rupture ['rʌptʃər] 1 N (*Med*) hernia *f*, quebradura *f*; (*fig*) ruptura *f*, rompimiento *m*.
2 VT **(a)** causar una hernia en, quebrarse. **(b)** (*fig*) romper, destruir.
3 VR: **to ~ o.s.** causarse una hernia, quebrarse.

rural ['rʊərəl] ADJ rural; **~ free delivery** (*US*) entrega *f* gratuita en zona rural.

ruse [ruːz] N ardid *m*, treta *f*, estratagema *f*.

rush[1] [rʌʃ] 1 N (*Bot*) junco *m*.
2 ATTR: **~ mat** estera *f*; **~ matting** esteras *fpl*.

rush[2] [rʌʃ] 1 N **(a)** (*act of ~ing*) ímpetu *m*; (*Mil*) ataque *m*; acometida *f*; asalto *m*; **general ~** desbandada *f* general; **the gold ~** la rebatiña del oro; **there was a ~ to the door** se precipitaron todos hacia la puerta; **there was a ~ for safety** todos hicieron lo posible por ponerse a salvo; **to make a ~ at sb** arremeter contra uno, precipitarse sobre uno; **it got lost in the ~** se perdió en la confusión; **2 were injured in the ~** al precipitarse todos 2 resultaron heridos.
(b) (*haste*) prisa *f*, precipitación *f*, apuro *m* (*LAm*); (*tumult*) bullicio *m*, ajetreo *m*; **the ~ of modern life** el ajetreo de la vida moderna; **the ~ of London** el bullicio de Londres; **what's all the ~ about?** ¿por qué tanta prisa?; **is there any ~ for this?** ¿te corre prisa esto?; **we're in a ~** tenemos prisa, tenemos apuro (*LAm*), llevamos prisa; **we're in a ~ to finish** tenemos prisa por terminarlo; **I did it in a ~** lo hice de prisa; **we had a ~ to get it ready** tuvimos que darnos prisa para tenerlo listo; **everything happened with a ~** todo ocurrió de repente; **it came down with a ~** cayó de repente.
(c) (*Comm*) demanda *f* (*for, on* de); **there has been a ~ on matches** ha habido una demanda extraordinaria de cerillas.
(d) (*current*) **a ~ of air** una fuerte corriente de aire, una ráfaga de aire; **a ~ of water** un torrente de agua; **a ~ of words** un torrente de palabras; **a ~ of people** un tropel; **in a ~ of sympathy** en un arrebato de compasión; **we've had a ~ of orders** estamos inundados de pedidos; **he had a ~ of blood to the head** (*fig*) le pasó algo totalmente inesperado; tuvo un momento de locura.
(e) **~es** (*Cine*) primeras pruebas *fpl*.
2 ADJ: **~ hours** horas *fpl* punta, horas *fpl* de máximo tránsito; **~ hour traffic** tráfico *m* de hora punta; **Barcelona in the ~ hour** Barcelona a la hora punta; **~ job** trabajo *m* urgente; trabajo *m* hecho de prisa; **~ order** pedido *m* urgente; **~ work** trabajo *m* hecho precipitadamente.
3 VT **(a)** *person* dar prisa a, apresurar; **I hate being ~ed** me ofende que me metan prisa, no aguanto a los que piden que vaya más de prisa; **we're ~ed off our feet** tenemos trabajo (*etc*) hasta encima de la coronilla; **I don't want to ~ you** quiero que lo hagas con tranquilidad.
(b) *work* hacer precipitadamente, ejecutar de mucha prisa.
(c) (*carry etc*) llevar rápidamente; **to ~ medicine to sb** llevar con toda prisa medicina a uno; **he was ~ed to hospital** le llevaron al hospital con la mayor urgencia.
(d) (*Mil*) *position etc* asaltar, tomar al asalto; *troops* atacar repentinamente; **the crowd ~ed the barriers** el público asaltó las barreras.
(e) (‡) **how much did they ~ you?** ¿cuánto te cobraron?; **they ~ed me £20** me hicieron pagar 20 libras.
4 VI precipitarse, lanzarse; correr (*etc*) rápidamente, ir de prisa, ir a máxima velocidad; **I must ~** me voy corriendo; tengo mucha prisa; **to ~ across a road** cruzar una calle a toda prisa; **you mustn't ~ across roads like that** es peligroso cruzar las calles con tanta precipitación; **everyone ~ed to the windows** se precipitaron todos hacia las ventanas; **the rocket was ~ing through space** el cohete iba a gran velocidad por el espacio; **don't ~!** ¡con calma!; **to ~ past** pasar como un rayo; **to ~ into the fray** lanzarse a la batalla; **I ~ed to her side** corrí a su lado; **I was ~ing to finish it** me daba prisa por terminarlo.

◆ **rush about, rush around** VI correr de acá para allá.
◆ **rush at** VT precipitarse hacia, lanzarse sobre; **to ~ at sb** arremeter contra uno, abalanzarse sobre uno.
◆ **rush away** VI partir como un rayo.
◆ **rush by** VI pasar como un rayo.
◆ **rush down** VI bajar corriendo.
◆ **rush in** VI entrar precipitadamente.
◆ **rush off** VI = **rush away**.
◆ **rush out** 1 VT *book etc* publicar con toda prisa.
2 VI salir precipitadamente.
◆ **rush through** VT *work etc* hacer apresuradamente, hacer urgentemente; **to ~ a bill through** (*Parl*) hacer aprobar de prisa un proyecto de ley.
◆ **rush up** VI subir corriendo; **he ~ed up to a policeman** se acercó corriendo a un policía.

rushed [rʌʃt] ADJ: **it was a ~ job** el trabajo se hizo con mucha prisa.

rushlight ['rʌʃlaɪt] N vela *f* de junco.

rushy ['rʌʃɪ] ADJ juncoso.

rusk [rʌsk] N bizcocho *m* tostado, tostada *f*, biscote *m*.

russet ['rʌsɪt] ① N color *m* bermejo, color *m* rojizo.
② ADJ bermejo, rojizo.
Russia ['rʌʃə] N Rusia *f*.
Russian ['rʌʃən] ① ADJ ruso; ~ **roulette** ruleta *f* rusa; ~ **salad** ensalada *f* rusa.
② N (a) ruso *m*, -a *f*. (b) (*Ling*) ruso *m*.
Russian Federation ['rʌʃən,fedə'reɪʃən] N: **the ~** la Federación Rusa.
Russki* ['rʌski] ADJ, N = **Russian**.
rust [rʌst] ① N (*action*) oxidación *f*, corrosión *f*; (*visible*) óxido *m*, herrumbre *f*, moho *m*; (*colour*) color *m* de orín; (*Agr*) roya *f*.
② VT oxidar, corroer; aherrumbrar.
③ VI oxidarse, corroerse; aherrumbrarse, tomarse de orín.
Rust Belt, rustbelt ['rʌstbelt] N (*US*): **the ~** el cinturón industrial; *ver también* SUNBELT .
rust-coloured, (*US*) **rust-colored** ['rʌst,kʌləd] ADJ color *m* de orín.
rusted ['rʌstɪd] ADJ oxidado, aherrumbrado.
rustic ['rʌstɪk] ① ADJ rústico; aldeano; (*pej*) rústico; (*person*) palurdo.
② N rústico *m*, palurdo *m*.
rusticate ['rʌstɪkeɪt] ① VT (*Brit Univ*) suspender temporalmente.
② VI rusticar.
rustication [,rʌstɪ'keɪʃən] N (*Univ*) suspensión *f* temporal.
rusticity [rʌs'tɪsɪtɪ] N rusticidad *f*.
rustiness ['rʌstɪnɪs] N (a) herrumbre *f*, lo aherrumbrado. (b) (*fig*) falta *f* de práctica, torpeza *f*.
rustle¹ ['rʌsl] ① N (*of leaves, wind*) susurro *m*; (*of paper*) crujido *m*; (*of silk, dress*) frufrú *m*.
② VT (*V n*) hacer susurrar, mover ligeramente; hacer crujir.
③ VI susurrar; crujir; hacer frufrú.
◆ **rustle up*** VT (*find*) buscar; (*obtain*) conseguir, (lograr) reunir; *meal etc* improvisar; **I'll see what I can ~ up** veré lo que hay; **can you ~ up some coffee?** ¿podrías hacerme un café?
rustle²* ['rʌsl] VT (*US*) robar, hurtar.
rustler ['rʌslər] N (*US*) ladrón *m* de ganado; (*) persona *f* dinámica.

rustless ['rʌstlɪs] ADJ inoxidable.
rustling¹ ['rʌslɪŋ] N = **rustle**¹ **1.**
rustling² ['rʌslɪŋ] N: **cattle ~** (*US*) robo *m* de ganado.
rustproof ['rʌstpruːf] ① ADJ inoxidable.
② VT tratar contra la corrosión.
rustproofing ['rʌst,pruːfɪŋ] N tratamiento *m* anticorrosión.
rust-resistant ['rʌstrɪzɪstənt] ADJ inoxidable.
rusty ['rʌstɪ] ADJ (a) (*lit*) oxidado, herrumbroso, aherrumbrado, mohoso; *colour* color de orín. (b) (*fig*) falto de práctica, torpe; **my Catalan is pretty ~** mi catalán está bastante oxidado.
rut¹ [rʌt] N rodera *f*, rodada *f*, carril *m*; bache *m*; (*fig*) rutina *f*, sendero *m* trillado; **to be in a ~** estar sin poder salir de la rutina, ir encarrilado; **you've got into a ~** te has hecho esclavo de la rutina; **to get out of the ~** salir del bache.
rut² [rʌt] (*Bio*) ① N celo *m*; **to be in ~** estar en celo.
② VI (*be*) estar en celo; (*begin to ~*) caer en celo.
rutabaga [,ruːtə'beɪgə] N (*US*) nabo *m* sueco, naba *f*.
ruthenium [ruː'θiːnɪəm] N rutenio *m*.
ruthless ['ruːθlɪs] ADJ despiadado; sin piedad; implacable, inexorable.
ruthlessly ['ruːθlɪslɪ] ADV despiadadamente; implacablemente, inexorablemente.
ruthlessness ['ruːθlɪsnɪs] N crueldad *f*; implacabilidad *f*.
rutinize [ruː'tiːnaɪz] VT (*US*) organizar de manera rutinaria.
rutted ['rʌtɪd] ADJ lleno de baches.
rutting ['rʌtɪŋ] ADJ (*Bio*) en celo; ~ **season** época *f* de celo.
rutty ['rʌtɪ] ADJ lleno de baches.
RV N (a) ABBR *of* **Revised Version** versión revisada de la Biblia. (b) N (*US*) ABBR *of* **recreational vehicle.**
Rwanda [rʊ'ændə] N Ruanda *f*.
rye [raɪ] ① N centeno *m*.
② ATTR: ~ (**bread**) pan *m* de centeno; ~ (**whisky**) (*US*) whisky *m* de centeno.
ryegrass ['raɪgrɑːs] N ballico *m*, joyo *m*.

S

S, s [es] N (*letter*) S, s *f*; **S for sugar** S de Soria; **S-bend** curva *f* en S.
S **(a)** ABBR of **south** sur *m*; *also adj.* **(b)** ABBR of **Saint** santo *m*, santa *f*, Sto., Sta. **(c)** (*US Scol*) ABBR of **satisfactory** suficiente.
s. **(a)** ABBR of **second** segundo *m*. **(b)** ABBR of **son** hijo *m*. **(c)** (*Brit Fin* †) ABBR of **shilling(s)** chelín *m*, chelines *mpl*.
SA **(a)** ABBR of **South Africa** África *f* del Sur. **(b)** ABBR of **South America** América *f* del Sur. **(c)** ABBR of **South Australia.**
Saar [zɑːʳ] N Sarre *m*.
sab* [sæb] N (*Brit*) ABBR of **saboteur** saboteador *m*, -ora *f* (*de una caza de zorros*).
sabbatarian [ˌsæbəˈtɛərɪən] **1** ADJ sabatario.
2 N sabatario *m*, -a *f*, partidario *m* de guardar estrictamente el domingo.
Sabbath [ˈsæbəθ] N (*Christian*) domingo *m*; (*Jewish*) sábado *m*.
sabbatical [səˈbætɪkəl] **1** ADJ (*Rel*) sabático; dominical; **~ year** = **2.**
2 N año *m* sabático.
saber [ˈseɪbəʳ] (*US*) = **sabre.**
sabbing* [ˈsæbɪŋ] N (*Brit*) sabotaje *m* (*de una caza de zorros*).
sable [ˈseɪbl] **1** N (*animal, fur*) marta *f* (cebellina); (*colour*) negro *m*; (*Her*) sable *m*.
2 ADJ negro.
sabot [ˈsæbəʊ] N zueco *m*.
sabotage [ˈsæbətɑːʒ] **1** N sabotaje *m*.
2 VT sabotear (*also fig*).
saboteur [ˌsæbəˈtɜːʳ] N saboteador *m*.
sabre, (*US*) **saber** [ˈseɪbəʳ] **1** N sable *m*.
2 VT herir (*or* matar *etc*) a sablazos.
sabre-rattler, (*US*) **saber-rattler** [ˈseɪbəˌrætləʳ] N patriotero *m*, jingoísta *m*.
sabre-rattling, (*US*) **saber-rattling** [ˈseɪbəˌrætlɪŋ] N patriotería *f*, jingoísmo *m*.
sac [sæk] N (*Anat etc*) saco *m*.
saccharin [ˈsækərɪn] N (*US*) = **saccharine 2.**
saccharine [ˈsækəriːn] **1** ADJ sacarino; (*fig*) azucarado, empalagoso.
2 N sacarina *f*.
sacerdotal [ˌsæsəˈdəʊtl] ADJ sacerdotal.
sachet [ˈsæʃeɪ] N saquito *m*, bolsita *f*; (*of perfume*) almohadilla *f* perfumada.
sack¹ [sæk] **1** N **(a)** (*bag*) saco *m*, costal *m*.
(b) (*) (*dismissal*) despido *m*; **to get the ~** ser despedido; **to give sb the ~** despedir a uno.
(c) (‡: *esp US: bed*) pulguero‡ *m*; **to hit the ~** acostarse.
2 VT **(a)** ensacar, meter en sacos.
(b) (*) despedir.
sack² [sæk] (*Mil*) **1** N saqueo *m*.
2 VT saquear.
sackbut [ˈsækbʌt] N sacabuche *m*.
sackcloth [ˈsækklɒθ] N (h)arpillera *f*; **to wear ~ and ashes** ponerse el hábito de penitencia, ponerse cenizas en la cabeza.
sackful [ˈsækfʊl] N saco *m*, contenido *m* de un saco.
sacking¹ [ˈsækɪŋ] N **(a)** (*material*) (h)arpillera *f*. **(b)** (*) despido *m*.
sacking² [ˈsækɪŋ] N (*Mil*) saqueo *m*.
sack race [ˈsækreɪs] N carrera *f* de sacos.
sacral [ˈseɪkrəl] ADJ sacral.
sacrament [ˈsækrəmənt] N sacramento *m*; Eucaristía *f*; **to receive the last ~s** recibir los últimos sacramentos.
sacramental [ˌsækrəˈmentl] ADJ sacramental.
sacred [ˈseɪkrɪd] ADJ sagrado; santo; consagrado; **~ cow** vaca *f* sagrada (*also fig*); **S~ History** Historia *f* Sagrada; **~ music** música *f* sacra; **~ to the memory of ...** consagrado a la memoria de ...; **is nothing ~ to you?** ¿no hay nada sagrado para ti?, ¿no respetas nada?
sacredness [ˈseɪkrɪdnɪs] N santidad *f*.
sacrifice [ˈsækrɪfaɪs] **1** N sacrificio *m*; (*person etc*) víctima *f*; **the ~ of**

the mass el sacrificio de la misa; **to make ~s** privarse de algo, renunciar a algo; **to sell sth at a ~** vender algo con pérdida.
2 VT sacrificar; (*Comm*) vender con pérdida, vender a precio de sacrificio.
3 VR: **to ~ o.s.** sacrificarse.
sacrificial [ˌsækrɪˈfɪʃəl] ADJ de sacrificio.
sacrilege [ˈsækrɪlɪdʒ] N sacrilegio *m*.
sacrilegious [ˌsækrɪˈlɪdʒəs] ADJ sacrílego.
sacrist [ˈsækrɪst] N, **sacristan** [ˈsækrɪstən] N sacristán *m*.
sacristy [ˈsækrɪstɪ] N sacristía *f*.
sacrosanct [ˈsækrəʊsæŋkt] ADJ sacrosanto.
sacrum [ˈsækrəm] N (*Anat*) sacro *m*.
sad [sæd] ADJ **(a)** (*unhappy*) triste; melancólico; **how ~!** ¡qué triste!; **to be ~ at heart** estar profundamente triste, tener el corazón oprimido; **to grow ~** entristecerse, ponerse triste; **to make sb ~** entristecer a uno, poner triste a uno; **he left a ~der and a wiser man** partió habiendo aprendido una dura lección.
(b) (*unfortunate*) lamentable; **a ~ mistake** un error lamentable; **it's a ~ business** es un asunto lamentable.

┌───┐
| **SAD**   *see also main entry* |
| |
| **Position of "triste"** |
| You should generally put *triste* after the noun when translating |
| *sad* in the sense of "unhappy", and before the noun in the sense |
| of "unfortunate": |
| He always seemed a sad little boy |
| *Siempre pareció un niño triste* |
| ...the sad reality... |
| *...la triste realidad...* |
| *For further uses and examples, see main entry.* |
└───┘

sadden [ˈsædn] VT entristecer; afligir.
saddle [ˈsædl] **1** N **(a)** silla *f* (de montar); (*cycle* ~) asiento *m*, sillín *m*; **Red Rum won with X in the ~** ganó Red Rum montado por X; **to be in the ~** (*fig*) estar en el poder, mandar; **to leap into the ~** saltar a la silla.
(b) (*hill*) collado *m*.
(c) (*of meat*) cuarto *m* trasero.
2 VT **(a)** *horse* (*also* **to ~ up**) ensillar. **(b)** (*) **to ~ sb with sth** echar algo a cuestas a uno, echar a uno la responsabilidad de algo; **now we're ~d with it** ahora tenemos que cargar con ello; **to get ~d with sth** tener que cargar con algo.
3 VR: **to ~ o.s. with sth** cargar con algo.
saddle-backed [ˈsædlbækt] ADJ (*Zool*) ensillado.
saddlebag [ˈsædlbæg] N alforja *f*.
saddlebow [ˈsædlbəʊ] N arzón *m* delantero.
saddlecloth [ˈsædlklɒθ] N sudadero *m*.
saddler [ˈsædləʳ] N talabartero *m*, guarnicionero *m*.
saddlery [ˈsædlərɪ] N talabartería *f*, guarnicionería *f*.
saddle-sore [ˈsædlˌsɔːʳ] ADJ: **he was ~** le dolían las posaderas de tanto montar.
sadism [ˈseɪdɪzəm] N sadismo *m*.
sadist [ˈseɪdɪst] N sadista *mf*, sádico *m*, -a *f*.
sadistic [səˈdɪstɪk] ADJ sádico.
sadly [ˈsædlɪ] ADV **(a)** (*unhappily*) tristemente. **(b)** (*regrettably*) muy; **~ lacking in** muy deficiente en; **a ~ incompetent headmaster** un director (de colegio) de lo más ineficaz; **you are ~ mistaken** estás muy equivocado, te equivocas gravemente.
sadness [ˈsædnɪs] N tristeza *f*, melancolía *f*.
sadomasochism [ˌseɪdəʊˈmæsəˌkɪzəm] N sadomasoquismo *m*.
sadomasochist [ˌseɪdəʊˈmæsəkɪst] N sadomasoquista *mf*.
sadomasochistic [ˌseɪdəʊˌmæsəˈkɪstɪk] ADJ sadomasoquista.
s.a.e. N ABBR of **stamped addressed envelope** sobre *m* con las propias

señas de uno y con sello.

safari [sə'fɑːrɪ] ① N safari m; **to be on ~** estar de safari.

② ATTR: **~ jacket** chaqueta f safari; **~ park** parque m de fieras.

safe [seɪf] ① ADJ seguro; salvo, fuera de peligro; (from injury) ileso, incólume; journey, trip feliz; sin novedad; birth feliz; (Parl) seat, investment seguro; bet etc seguro, cierto; person (trustworthy) digno de confianza, formal; (sound) prudente, sensato; **~ and sound** sano y salvo; **~ from** a salvo de, al abrigo de; **~ house** piso m franco, vivienda f segura; **~ period** período m sin peligro; **~ sex** sexo m seguro; **better ~ than sorry!** ¡la prudencia ante todo!; **as ~ as houses** completamente seguro; **the ~st thing is to** + infin lo más seguro es + infin; **just to be ~** por precaución, para mayor seguridad; **all the passengers are ~** todos los pasajeros están ilesos, no ha habido víctimas entre los pasajeros; **these stairs are not very ~** esta escalera no es muy segura; **it's a ~ beach** es una playa sin peligro; **no girl is ~ with him** ninguna joven está sin peligro estando con él; **is that dog ~?** ¿es peligroso ese perro?; **he's ~ with children** es de fiar con los niños, no es un peligro para los niños; **your reputation is ~** su reputación está a salvo; **the secret is ~ with me** el secreto seguirá siéndolo conmigo; **the book is ~ now** ahora el libro está en buenas manos; **you'll be perfectly ~ here** aquí estás fuera de todo peligro; **his life was not ~** no estaba seguro de su vida; **is it ~ to go out?** ¿se puede salir sin peligro?; **the ice isn't ~** el hielo no es sólido, el hielo no es de fiar; **there is ~ bathing here** aquí se baña sin peligro; **it is in ~ hands** está en buenas manos; **it is ~ to say that ...** se puede decir con confianza que ...; **to come ~ home** volver a casa sin novedad; **I don't feel very ~ up here** no me siento muy seguro aquí arriba; **to keep sth ~** tener algo seguro; **he plays a ~ game** es un jugador prudente.

② ADV: V **play 3(f)**.

③ N caja f de caudales; (for meat) fresquera f.

safe-blower ['seɪf,bləʊər] N, **safe-breaker** ['seɪf,breɪkər] N ladrón m, -ona f de cajas fuertes.

safe-conduct ['seɪf'kɒndəkt] N salvoconducto m.

safe-cracker ['seɪf,krækər] N (US) ladrón m, -ona f de cajas fuertes.

safe deposit ['seɪfdɪ,pɒzɪt] N (vault) cámara f acorazada; (box: also **~ box**) caja f fuerte, caja f de seguridad.

safeguard ['seɪfgɑːd] ① N salvaguardia f; protección f, garantía f; **as a ~** por precaución; **as a ~ against ...** como defensa contra ..., para evitar ...

② VT salvaguardar, proteger, defender.

safe-keeping [,seɪf'kiːpɪŋ] N custodia f; **in his ~** bajo su custodia.

safely ['seɪflɪ] ADV seguramente, con seguridad; sin peligro; arrive, travel etc sin novedad, sin accidente; **you may ~ do it now** ahora puedes hacerlo sin peligro; **to put sth away ~** guardar algo en un lugar seguro; **we can ~ say that ...** podemos decir con confianza que ...

safeness ['seɪfnɪs] N seguridad f.

safety ['seɪftɪ] ① N seguridad f; **~ on the roads** seguridad f en la carretera; **'~ first!'** (as slogan) '¡prudencia ante todo!'; **~ first campaign** campaña f pro seguridad; **~ first policy** política f de seguridad; **in a place of ~** en un lugar seguro; **for ~'s sake** por precaución, para mayor seguridad, en interés de la seguridad; **with complete ~** con la mayor seguridad; **there's ~ in numbers** cuantos más, menos peligro; **to play for ~** obrar prudentemente; **to reach ~** ponerse a salvo; **to seek ~ in flight** salvarse huyendo.

② ATTR de seguridad; **~ belt** cinturón m de seguridad; **~ catch** fiador m; (on door) cadena f de seguridad; (on gun) seguro m; **~ chain** seguro m de pulsera; **~ curtain** (Theat) telón m de seguridad; **~ deposit box** caja f fuerte, caja f de seguridad; **~ device** dispositivo m de seguridad; **~ factor** factor m de seguridad; **~ glass** vidrio m inastillable; **~ harness** arnés m de seguridad; **~ lamp** lámpara f de seguridad; **~ lock** seguro m, cerradura f de seguridad; **~ margin** margen m de seguridad; **~ match** cerilla f de seguridad; **~ measure** medida f de seguridad, precaución f, prevención f; **~ mechanism** mecanismo m de seguridad; **~ net** red f de seguridad; **~ officer** encargado m, -a f de seguridad; **~ pin** imperdible m, seguro m (LAm); (of grenade) arandela f; **~ precaution** medida f de seguridad; **~ razor** maquinilla f de afeitar, gillette f; **~ regulations** normas fpl de seguridad; **~ valve** válvula f de seguridad.

saffron ['sæfrən] ① N azafrán m.

② ADJ azafranado, color azafrán.

sag [sæg] ① N comba f.

② VI (bulge, warp) combarse, hundirse, pandear; (slacken) aflojarse, ceder; (price etc) bajar; (spirit) flaquear.

saga ['sɑːgə] N saga f; (fig) saga f, epopeya f; (novel) saga f, novela f río.

sagacious [sə'geɪʃəs] ADJ sagaz.

sagaciously [sə'geɪʃəslɪ] ADV sagazmente.

sagacity [sə'gæsɪtɪ] N sagacidad f.

sage¹ [seɪdʒ] N (Bot) salvia f; **~ green** verde salvia.

sage² [seɪdʒ] ① ADJ sabio.

② N sabio m.

sagebrush ['seɪdʒbrʌʃ] N (US) artemisa f.

sagely ['seɪdʒlɪ] ADV sabiamente.

sagging ['sægɪŋ] ADJ ground hundido; beam pandeado; cheek fofo; rope flojo; gate, hemline caído.

saggy ['sægɪ] ADJ mattress, sofa, deformado, hundido; garment deformado, dado de sí, colgón; bottom, breasts colgón, caído.

Sagittarian [,sædʒɪ'teərɪən] N: **to be (a) ~** ser Sagitario.

Sagittarius [,sædʒɪ'terɪəs] N (Zodiac) Sagitario m.

sago ['seɪgəʊ] ① N sagú m.

② ATTR: **~ palm** palmera f sagú.

Sahara [sə'hɑːrə] N Sáhara m, Sájara m.

Sahel [sɑː'hel] N Sahel m.

sahib ['sɑːhɪb] N (India) (a) señor m; **Smith S~** (el) señor Smith. (b) (hum) caballero m; **pukka ~** caballero m de verdad.

said [sed] ① PRET AND PTP of **say**. ② ADJ dicho, antedicho; **the ~ animals** dichos animales, los cuales animales; **the ~ general** dicho general.

Saigon [saɪ'gɒn] N Saigón m.

sail [seɪl] ① N (a) (cloth) vela f; **in full ~, under full ~, with all ~s set** a toda vela, a vela llena; **to set ~** hacerse a la vela, zarpar (for con rumbo a); **to lower the ~s** arriar las velas; **to take in the ~s** amainar.

(b) (of mill) aspa f.

(c) (trip) paseo m (en barco), paseo m en balandro (etc); **it is 3 days' ~ from here** desde aquí es un viaje de 3 días en barco; **to go for a ~** dar un paseo en barco, salir en balandro (etc).

(d) (boat) barco m de vela, velero m; **20 ~** 20 barcos.

② VT (a) ship (steer) gobernar; boat manejar; **they ~ed the ship to Cadiz** fueron con el barco a Cádiz, fueron en el barco a Cádiz; **he ~s his own boat** tiene barco propio.

(b) **to ~ the seas** navegar los mares; **to ~ the Atlantic** cruzar el Atlántico.

③ VI (a) (Naut) navegar; **to ~ at 12 knots** navegar a 12 nudos, ir a 12 nudos; **we ~ed into Lisbon** llegamos a Lisboa; **we ~ed into harbour** entramos a puerto; **to go ~ing** (as sport) hacer vela; **to ~ round the world** dar la vuelta al mundo; **to ~ round a headland** doblar un cabo; **to ~ up the Tagus** entrar en el Tajo, subir el Tajo.

(b) (Naut: leave) hacerse a la vela, zarpar (for con rumbo a); (gen) salir, partir; **she ~s on Monday** sale el lunes; **we ~ for Australia** partimos para Australia.

(c) (fig: swan etc) deslizarse; (cloud) flotar; (object) volar; **it ~ed over my head** voló por encima de mi cabeza; **it ~ed over into the next garden** voló por los aires y cayó en el jardín de al lado.

◆ **sail into** VT (a) **to ~ into sb** (*: scold) poner a uno como un trapo*, (attack) arremeter contra uno, atacar a uno. (b) **she ~ed into the room*** entró en la sala a vela tendida.

◆ **sail through** VT: **she ~ed through the exam** aprobó el examen volando; **don't worry, you'll ~ through it** no te preocupes, todo será facilísimo.

sailboard ['seɪlbɔːd] ① N plancha f de windsurf.

② VI hacer windsurf.

sailboarder ['seɪlbɔːdər] N windsurfista mf.

sailboarding ['seɪlbɔːdɪŋ] N windsurf m, surf m a vela.

sailboat ['seɪlbəʊt] N (US) barco m de vela.

sailcloth ['seɪlklɒθ] N lona f.

sailfish ['seɪlfɪʃ] N aguja f de mar, pez m vela.

sailing ['seɪlɪŋ] ① N (a) (gen) navegación f; (as sport) (deporte m de la) vela f, balandrismo m; **to go ~** salir en balandro; **now it's all plain ~** ahora es muy sencillo, ahora es cosa de coser y cantar; **it's not exactly plain ~** no es tan sencillo que digamos.

(b) (departure) salida f, partida f.

② ATTR: **~ boat** (Brit) barco m de vela; **~ date** fecha f de salida; **~ orders** últimas instrucciones fpl (dadas al capitán de un buque); **~ time** hora f de salida (de un barco).

sailing ship ['seɪlɪŋʃɪp] N velero m, buque m de vela.

sailmaker ['seɪl,meɪkər] N velero m.

sailor ['seɪlər] ① N marinero m, marino m; **to be a bad ~** marearse fácilmente; **to be a good ~** no marearse.

② ATTR: **~ hat** sombrero m de marinero; **~ suit** traje m de marinero (de niño).

sailplane ['seɪlpleɪn] N planeador m.

sainfoin ['sænfɔɪn] N pipirigallo m.

▼ **saint** [seɪnt] N (a) santo m, -a f; **~'s day** fiesta f (de santo).

(b) before m names abbreviated to San, eg **St John** San Juan; except **St Dominic** Santo Domingo, **St Thomas** Santo Tomás.

(c) (as name of church) **at St Mark's** en San Marcos, en la iglesia de San Marcos.

(d) **St Andrew** (patrón de Escocia) San Andrés; **St Bernard** (dog) perro m de San Bernardo; **St Elmo's fire** fuego m de Santelmo; **St George** (patrón de Inglaterra) San Jorge; **St James** (patrón de España) Santiago; **St John the Baptist** San Juan Bautista; **St Kitts** (WI) San Cristóbal; **St Patrick** (patrón de Irlanda) San Patricio; **St Theresa** Santa Teresa; **St**

Valentine's Day día *m* de San Valentín (*14 febrero, día de los enamorados*); **St Vitus' dance** baile *m* de San Vito.

sainted ['seɪntɪd] ADJ santo; bendito; (*of dead*) que en santa gloria esté; **my ~ aunt!*** (*hum*) ¡caray!*

sainthood ['seɪnthʊd] N santidad *f*.

saint-like ['seɪntlaɪk] ADJ = **saintly**.

saintliness ['seɪntlɪnɪs] N santidad *f*.

saintly ['seɪntlɪ] ADJ santo, piadoso.

sake¹ [seɪk] N: **for the ~ of** por; por motivo de; en consideración a, en atención a; **for God's ~** por el amor de Dios; **for God's ~!, for heaven's ~!** ¡por Dios!; **for my ~** por mí; **for your own ~** por tu propio bien, en interés propio; **for old times' ~** por respeto al pasado, por los tiempos pasados; **for the ~ of peace** por amor a la paz, en interés de la paz; para obtener la paz; **art for art's ~** el arte por el arte; **to talk for talking's ~** hablar por hablar; **she likes this kind of music for its own ~** le gusta este tipo de música por sí misma.

sake² ['sɑːkɪ] N sake *m*.

sal [sæl] N sal *f*.

salaam [sə'lɑːm] **1** N zalema *f*.
  2 VI hacer zalemas.

salable ['seɪləbl] ADJ (*US*) = **saleable**.

salacious [sə'leɪʃəs] ADJ salaz.

salaciousness [sə'leɪʃəsnɪs] N, **salacity** [sə'læsɪtɪ] N salacidad *f*.

salad ['sæləd] N ensalada *f*.

salad-bowl ['sælədbəʊl] N ensaladera *f*.

salad-cream ['sæləd,kriːm] N (*Brit*) mayonesa *f*.

salad-days ['sælədðeɪz] NPL juventud *f*; ingenuidad *f* juvenil.

salad-dish ['sælədðɪʃ] N ensaladera *f*.

salad-dressing ['sæləd,dresɪŋ] N mayonesa *f*, aliño *m*.

salad-oil ['sælədɔɪl] N aceite *m* para ensaladas.

salamander ['sælə,mændə'] N salamandra *f*.

salami [sə'lɑːmɪ] N salami *m*.

sal ammoniac [,sælə'məʊnɪæk] N sal *f* amoníaca.

salaried ['sælərɪd] ADJ asalariado; **~ person** persona *f* asalariada; **~ post** puesto *m* retribuido; **~ staff** personal *m* asalariado.

▼ **salary** ['sælərɪ] **1** N sueldo *m*.
  2 ATTR: **~ bracket** categoría *f* salarial; **~ package** paquete *m* salarial; **~ range** margen *m* salarial; **~ review** revisión *f* de sueldos; **~ scale** banda *f* salarial; **~ structure** estructuración *f* salarial.

salary-earner ['sælərɪ,ɜːnə'] N persona *f* que gana un sueldo, persona *f* que cobra cada mes.

sale [seɪl] **1** N (**a**) (*act*) venta *f*; **~ and lease back** venta *f* y arrendamiento al vendedor; **'for ~'** 'se vende'; **'horse for ~'** 'se vende caballo'; **is it for ~?** ¿se vende?; **'not for ~'** 'no se vende'; **it's going cheap for a quick ~** se ofrece a un precio módico para venderlo pronto; **it found a ready ~** se vendió pronto; **to put a house up for ~** ofrecer una casa en venta; **on a ~ or return basis** a base de vender o devolver; **to be on ~** estar en venta; **'on ~ at all fishmongers'** 'de venta en todas las pescaderías'.
  (**b**) (*event*: *clearance ~*) liquidación *f*; (*annual etc*) saldo *m*, rebaja *f* (*LAm*); (*auction, public ~*) subasta *f*; **'~'** (*in shop window*) 'grandes rebajas'; **the ~s are on** es la temporada de los saldos.
  2 ATTR: **~s agent** agente *mf* de ventas; **~s assistant** (*Brit*), **~s clerk** (*US*) vendedor *m*, -ora *f*, dependiente *m*, -a *f*; **~ brochure** folleto *m* publicitario; **~ budget** presupuesto *m* de ventas; **~s campaign** campaña *f* de ventas; **~s check** (*US*) hoja *f* de venta; **~s conference** conferencia *f* de ventas; **~s department** sección *f* de ventas; **~s drive** promoción *f* de ventas; **~s executive** ejecutivo *m*, -a *f* de ventas; **~s figures** cifras *fpl* de ventas; **~s force** personal *m* de ventas; **~s forecast** previsión *f* de ventas; **~(s) invoice** factura *f* de venta(s); **~s leaflet** folleto *m* publicitario; **~s ledger** libro *m* de ventas; **~s literature** folletos *mpl* de venta; propaganda *f* de venta; **~s manager** jefe *mf* de ventas; **~s meeting** reunión *f* de ventas; **~s office** oficina *f* de ventas; **~s pitch*** rollo* *m* publicitario; **~s potential** potencial *m* de ventas; **~ price** precio *m* de venta; **~ promotion** promoción *f* de ventas; **~s rep(resentative)** agente *mf* de ventas; **~s resistance** resistencia *f* a comprar; **~s slip** hoja *f* de venta; **~s talk** jerga *f* de vendedor; **~ value** valor *m* comercial, valor *m* en el mercado.

saleability [,seɪlə'bɪlɪtɪ] N vendibilidad *f*.

saleable ['seɪləbl] ADJ vendible.

saleroom ['seɪlrʊm] N, (*US*) **salesroom** ['seɪlzrʊm] N sala *f* de subastas.

salesgirl ['seɪlzgɜːl] N dependienta *f*, vendedora *f*.

salesman ['seɪlzmən] N, PL **salesmen** ['seɪlzmən] (*in shop*) dependiente *m*, vendedor *m*; (*traveller*) viajante *m*; **'Death of a S~'** 'La muerte de un viajante'.

salesmanship ['seɪlzmənʃɪp] N arte *m* de vender.

salesperson ['seɪlz,pɜːsn] N (*esp US*) vendedor *m*, -ora *f*, dependiente *m*, -a *f*.

sales tax ['seɪlztæks] N (*US*) impuesto *m* sobre las ventas.

saleswoman ['seɪlzwʊmən] N, PL **saleswomen** ['seɪlzwɪmɪn] dependienta *f*, vendedora *f*.

salient ['seɪlɪənt] **1** ADJ saliente; (*fig*) sobresaliente, destacado, notable; **~ points** puntos *mpl* principales.
  2 N saliente *m*.

salina [sə'liːnə] N (*marsh etc, saltworks*) salina *f*; (*mine*) mina *f* de sal, salina *f*.

saline ['seɪlaɪn] ADJ salino; **~ drip** gota-a-gota *m* salino.

salinity [sə'lɪnɪtɪ] N salinidad *f*.

saliva [sə'laɪvə] N saliva *f*.

salivary ['sælɪvərɪ] ADJ salival; **~ gland** glándula *f* salival.

salivate ['sælɪveɪt] VI salivar.

salivation [,sælɪ'veɪʃən] N salivación *f*.

sallow¹ ['sæləʊ] N (*Bot*) sauce *m* cabruno.

sallow² ['sæləʊ] ADJ cetrino, amarillento.

sallowness ['sæləʊnɪs] N lo cetrino, amarillez *f*.

Sallust ['sæləst] NM Salustio.

Sally ['sælɪ] NF *familiar form of* **Sarah**.

sally ['sælɪ] **1** N (*all senses*) salida *f*; **to make a ~** hacer una salida.
  2 VI hacer una salida.

◆ **sally forth, sally out** VI salir resueltamente.

salmon ['sæmən] **1** N, PL INVAR salmón *m*; (*colour*) color *m* salmón.
  2 ADJ color salmón.
  3 ATTR: **~ fishing** pesca *f* de salmón; **~ ladder** paso *m* salmonero; **~ trout** trucha *f* asalmonada, trucha *f* de mar.

salmonella [,sælmə'nelə] N salmonela *f*; **~ food-poisoning** salmonelosis *f*.

salmonellosis [,sælmənə'ləʊsɪs] N salmonelosis *f*.

Salome [sə'ləʊmɪ] NF Salomé.

salon ['sælɒn] N salón *m*.

saloon [sə'luːn] N salón *m*; (*Naut*) cámara *f*, salón *m*; (*Brit Aut*) turismo *m*; (*US: bar*) bar *m*; taberna *f*, cantina *f* (*Mex*).

saloon-car [sə'luːnkɑː'] N (*Rail*) coche-salón *m*; (*Aut*) turismo *m*.

salopettes [,sælə'pets] NPL peto *m* de esquiar.

salsify ['sælsɪfɪ] N salsifí *m*.

SALT [sɔːlt] N ABBR *of* **Strategic Arms Limitation Talks**.

salt [sɔːlt] **1** N sal *f*; **~s** sales *fpl* medicinales; **~ of the earth** (*fig*) sal *f* de la tierra; **to rub ~ in the wound** (*fig*) poner sal en la llaga; **to be worth one's ~** (*fig*) merecer el pan que se come.
  2 ADJ *meat, water etc* salado; *taste* salobre; **~ beef** carne *f* de vaca salada; **~ lake** lago *m* de agua salada; **it's very ~** está muy salado.
  3 VT (*cure*) salar; (*flavour*) poner sal en, añadir sal a; *road* poner sal en, tratar con sal; **to ~ a dig** poner objetos en una excavación para que se encuentren después.

◆ **salt away** VT ahorrar, ocultar para uso futuro.

◆ **salt down** VT conservar en sal, salar.

salt-cellar ['sɔːlt,selə'] N salero *m*.

salted ['sɔːltɪd] ADJ salado, con sal.

salt-flats ['sɔːltflæts] NPL salinas *fpl*.

salt-free ['sɔːltfriː] ADJ sin sal.

saltiness ['sɔːltɪnɪs] N salinidad *f*; sabor *m* de sal; salobridad *f*.

saltings ['sɔːltɪŋz] NPL saladar *m*.

saltmarsh ['sɔːltmɑːʃ] N saladar *m*, salina *f*.

saltmine ['sɔːltmaɪn] N mina *f* de sal.

saltpan ['sɔːltpæn] N salina *f*.

saltpetre, (*US*) **saltpeter** ['sɔːlt,piːtə'] N salitre *m*.

salt-shaker ['sɔːltʃeɪkə'] N salero *m*.

salt-spoon ['sɔːltspuːn] N cucharita *f* de sal.

saltwater ['sɔːlt,wɔːtə'] ATTR *fish etc* de mar, de agua salada.

saltworks ['sɔːltwɜːks] N salinas *fpl*.

salty ['sɔːltɪ] ADJ salado (*also fig*); salobre.

salubrious [sə'luːbrɪəs] ADJ salubre, sano.

salubrity [sə'luːbrɪtɪ] N salubridad *f*.

salutary ['sæljʊtərɪ] ADJ saludable.

salutation [,sæljʊ'teɪʃən] N salutación *f*, saludo *m*.

salute [sə'luːt] **1** N (*with hand etc*) saludo *m*; (*of guns*) salva *f*; **to fire a ~ of 21 guns for sb** saludar a uno con una salva de 21 cañonazos; **to take the ~** tomar el saludo.
  2 VTI saludar.

Salvadorian [,sælvə'dɔːrɪən] **1** ADJ salvadoreño.
  2 N salvadoreño *m*, -a *f*.

salvage ['sælvɪdʒ] **1** N (**a**) (*act*) salvamento *m*; recuperación *f*.
  (**b**) (*objects*) objetos *mpl* salvados; (*material*) material *m* aprovechable.
  (**c**) (*fee*) derechos *mpl* de salvamento.
  2 ATTR: **~ operation** salvamento *m*; **~ value** valor *m* de desecho; **~ vessel** buque *m* de salvamento.
  3 VT salvar; recuperar; **to ~ sth from the wreckage** salvar algo de las ruinas.

salvation [sæl'veɪʃən] N salvación *f*; **S~ Army** Ejército *m* de Salvación.

salvationist [sæl'veɪʃnɪst] N miembro *mf* del Ejército de Salvación.

salve¹ [sælv] VT (*Naut etc*) salvar; recuperar.

salve² [sælv] **1** N (*fig*) ungüento *m*, bálsamo *m*.

2 VT curar (con ungüento); **to ~ one's conscience** tranquilizar la conciencia.

salver ['sælvə^r] N bandeja f.

salvia ['sælvɪə] N salvia f.

salvo[1] ['sælvəʊ] N salvedad f, reserva f.

salvo[2] ['sælvəʊ] N (Mil) salva f; **a ~ of applause** una salva de aplausos.

sal volatile [,sælvə'lætəlɪ] N sal f volátil.

Salzburg ['sæltsbɜːɡ] N Salsburgo m.

SAM [sæm] N ABBR of **surface-(to)-air missile**.

Sam [sæm], **Sammy** ['sæmɪ] NM familiar form of **Samuel**; **Sam Browne (belt)** correaje m de oficial.

Samaritan [sə'mærɪtn] [1] ADJ samaritano.
[2] N samaritano m, -a f; **good ~** buen samaritano m.

samarium [sə'mɛərɪəm] N samario m.

samba ['sæmbə] N samba f.

sambo ['sæmbəʊ] N (pej) mestizo m; negro m.

▼ **same** [seɪm] [1] ADJ mismo; igual; idéntico; **the ~ day** el mismo día; **~ day delivery** entrega f en el mismo día, entrega f inmediata; **it's the very ~ dog** es el mismísimo perro; **we sat at the ~ table as usual** nos sentamos a la mesa de siempre; **it's the ~ thing again** es lo mismo, es lo de siempre; **it comes to the ~ thing** viene a ser lo mismo.

▼[2] PRON el mismo, la misma; **the ~ as ...** el mismo que ...; **we all have the ~** todos tenemos lo mismo; **do the ~ as he does** haz lo que él, haz lo mismo que él; **(the) ~ again, please** lo mismo, por favor; **it's the ~ with us** es igual para nosotros, nosotros tenemos lo mismo; **and I did the ~** y yo hice lo mismo; **I'd do the ~ again** yo volvería a hacer lo mismo; **and the ~ to you!** ¡igualmente!; ¡a Vd!; **all the ~** con todo, de todas formas; a pesar de todo; **it's all the ~** es lo mismo, es todo uno; **it's all the ~ to me** me es igual, lo mismo me da; **if it's all the ~ to you** si a ti te da lo mismo; **no, but thanks all the ~** no, pero en todo caso, gracias; **it's just the ~** es exactamente igual; **they are much the ~** son más o menos idénticos; **she's much about the ~** sigue más o menos igual; **I still feel the ~ about you** yo para contigo sigo igual; **to repair of door and repainting ~ ...** reparación de la puerta y pintar lo mismo ...; **~ here!** ¡yo también!

[3] ADV igual; **things go on just the ~** las cosas siguen igual.

sameness ['seɪmnɪs] N igualdad f; identidad f; (pej) monotonía f.

samey* ['seɪmɪ] ADJ (pej) song machacón*; **I find her books very ~** me parece que sus libros son todos iguales.

samizdat [sæmiz'dat] N samizdat m.

Samoa [sə'məʊə] N Samoa f.

Samoan [sə'məʊən] [1] ADJ samoano.
[2] N samoano m, -a f.

samosa [sə'məʊsə] N, PL **samosas** or **samosa** empanadilla picante.

samovar [sæmə'vɑː^r] N samovar m.

sampan ['sæmpæn] N sampán m.

sample ['sɑːmpl] [1] N (all senses) muestra f; **free ~** muestra f gratuita; **~ pack** paquete m de muestra; **~ survey** estudio m de muestra.
[2] VT probar; (in blending) catar; (Statistics) muestrear.

sample book ['sɑːmplbʊk] N muestrario m.

sampler ['sɑːmplə^r] N (a) (person) catador m. (b) (Sew) dechado m.

sampling ['sɑːmplɪŋ] N muestreo m; **~ technique** método m de muestreo.

Samson ['sæmsn] NM Sansón.

Samuel ['sæmjʊəl] NM Samuel.

samurai ['sæmʊ,raɪ] N, PL **samurai** or **samurais** samurai m.

San Andreas [,sænæn'dreɪəs] N: **~ Fault** falla f de San Andrés.

sanatorium [,sænə'tɔːrɪəm] N, PL **sanatoriums** or **sanatoria** [,sænə'tɔːrɪə] (Brit) sanatorio m.

sanctification [,sæŋktɪfɪ'keɪʃən] N santificación f.

sanctify ['sæŋktɪfaɪ] VT santificar.

sanctimonious [,sæŋktɪ'məʊnɪəs] ADJ mojigato, santurrón, beato.

sanctimoniously [,sæŋktɪ'məʊnɪəslɪ] ADV con mojigatería; **she said ~** dijo mojigata.

sanctimoniousness [,sæŋktɪ'məʊnɪəsnɪs] N mojigatería f, santurronería f, beatería f.

sanction ['sæŋkʃən] [1] N (a) (permission) sanción f, autorización f, aprobación f. (b) (penalty) sanción f; **~ busting** ruptura f de sanciones; **to impose trade ~s against a country** imponer sanciones comerciales contra un país.
[2] VT (a) (permit) sancionar, autorizar, aprobar. (b) (penalize) sancionar.

sanctity ['sæŋktɪtɪ] N santidad f; inviolabilidad f.

sanctuary ['sæŋktjʊərɪ] N santuario m; (high altar) sagrario m; (Hist: place of refuge) sagrado m, (modern) refugio m, asilo m; (for wildlife) reserva f; **to seek ~** acogerse a sagrado; **to seek ~ in** refugiarse en; **to seek ~ with** acogerse a.

sanctum ['sæŋktəm] N lugar m sagrado; (fig) despacho m particular.

sand [sænd] [1] N arena f; **~s** (of desert) arenas fpl, (beach) playa f (arenosa); **the plan ran into the ~** el proyecto quedó estancado; **the**

~s are running out queda poco tiempo.
[2] VT enarenar.

♦ **sand down** VT alisar con arena.

sandal ['sændl] N sandalia f; (rope-soled) alpargata f.

sandal(wood) ['sændl(wʊd)] N sándalo m.

sandbag ['sændbæg] [1] N saco m de arena, saco m terrero.
[2] VT proteger con sacos de arena.

sandbank ['sændbæŋk] N banco m de arena.

sand-bar ['sændbɑː^r] N barra f de arena, banco m de arena.

sandblast ['sændblɑːst] N chorro m de arena.

sandbox ['sændbɒks] N (US) cajón m de arena.

sand-boy ['sændbɔɪ] N: **to be as happy as a ~** estar como unas pascuas.

sandcastle ['sænd,kɑːsl] N castillo m de arena.

sand-dune ['sænddjuːn] N duna f.

sander ['sændə^r] N (tool) pulidora f.

sand flea ['sændfliː] N pulga f de mar.

sand fly ['sændflaɪ] N jején m, mosquito m.

sandglass ['sændglɑːs] N reloj m de arena.

sanding ['sændɪŋ] N (of road) enarenamiento m; (of floor) pulimiento m; (sandpapering) lijamiento m.

sandlot ['sændlɒt] (US) [1] N terreno en una ciudad que se usa para el béisbol (etc).
[2] ADJ (Sport) de barrio, de vecindad; **~ baseball** béisbol m de barrio.

sandman ['sændmæn] N ser imaginario que les trae el sueño a los niños.

sand-martin ['sænd,mɑːtɪn] N avión m zapador.

sandpaper ['sænd,peɪpə^r] [1] N papel m de lija.
[2] VT lijar.

sandpiper ['sænd'paɪpə^r] N andarríos m, lavandera f.

sandpit ['sændpɪt] N (esp Brit) arenal m; (in garden) cuadro m de arena.

sandshoes ['sændʃuːz] NPL playeras fpl.

sandstone ['sændstəʊn] N piedra f arenisca.

sandstorm ['sændstɔːm] N tempestad f (or tormenta f) de arena.

sandwich ['sænwɪdʒ] [1] N sándwich m, emparedado m, bocadillo m; **~ course** (Univ etc) programa que intercala períodos de estudio con prácticas profesionales.
[2] VT insertar; intercalar; (Sport) apretujar; **to ~ sth between two things** poner algo (apretadamente) entre dos cosas; **the house is ~ed between two big hotels** la casa se encuentra entre dos grandes hoteles, la casa ocupa un espacio estrecho entre dos grandes hoteles; **I was ~ed between two fat ladies** me tocó estar apretujado entre dos señoras gordas.

sandwich-bar ['sænwɪdʒ,bɑː^r] N bocadillería f.

sandwich-board ['sænwɪdʒ,bɔːd] N cartelón m (que lleva el hombre-anuncio).

sandwich-man ['sænwɪdʒmæn] N, PL **sandwich-men** ['sænwɪdʒmen] hombre-anuncio m, anuncio m ambulante.

sandworm ['sændwɜːm] N gusano m de arena.

sandy ['sændɪ] ADJ (a) arenoso. (b) (in colour) rojizo, dorado; hair rojo.

sane [seɪn] ADJ person cuerdo, sensato, de juicio sano; policy etc prudente.

sanely ['seɪnlɪ] ADV sensatamente; prudentemente.

Sanforized ['sænfəraɪzd] ® ADJ sanforizado ®.

sang [sæŋ] PRET of **sing**.

sangfroid ['sãːŋ'frwɑː] N sangre f fría.

sangria [sæŋ'griːə] N sangría f.

sanguinary ['sæŋgwɪnərɪ] ADJ sanguinario; sangriento.

sanguine ['sæŋgwɪn] ADJ (fig) optimista.

sanguineous [sæŋ'gwɪnɪəs] ADJ sanguíneo.

sanitarium [,sænɪ'tɛərɪəm] N (esp US) sanatorio m.

sanitary ['sænɪtərɪ] ADJ (a) (clean) higiénico. (b) system etc sanitario; **~ engineer** ingeniero m sanitario; **~ inspector** inspector m de sanidad; **~ napkin** (US), **~ towel** (Brit) paño m higiénico, compresa f (higiénica).

sanitation [,sænɪ'teɪʃən] [1] N sanidad f; higiene f; (domestic ~) instalación f sanitaria, saneamiento m, (euph) servicios mpl higiénicos; (in town) servicio m de desinfección.
[2] ATTR: **~ department** (US) departamento m de limpieza y recogida de basuras.

sanitize ['sænɪtaɪz] VT sanear; **to ~ the image of war** sanear la imagen de la guerra.

sanitized ['sænɪtaɪzd] ADJ saneado.

sanity ['sænɪtɪ] N cordura f, sensatez f, juicio m sano; prudencia f; **~ demands that ...** la razón exige que ...; **fortunately ~ prevailed** afortunadamente se impuso el buen juicio; **to be restored to ~** recobrar su juicio; **to return to ~** ponerse en razón, volver a la razón.

sank [sæŋk] PRET of **sink**[1].

San Marino [,sænmə'riːnəʊ] N San Marino m.

Sanskrit ['sænskrɪt] [1] ADJ sánscrito.
[2] N sánscrito m.

sans serif [,sæn'serɪf] N grotesca f.

➤ LANGUAGE IN USE: **same:** 1 → 5.2 **2** → 5.2, 5.3

Santa Claus [ˌsæntəˈklɔːz] NM San Nicolás, Papá Noel.
Santiago [ˌsæntɪˈɑːgəʊ] N (*Chile*) Santiago *m* (de Chile); (*Spain*) **~ de Compostela** Santiago *m* (de Compostela).
sap¹ [sæp] N (*Bot*) savia *f*; (*fig*) jugo *m* (vital), vitalidad *f*.
sap² [sæp] (*Mil*) ① N zapa *f*.
  ② VT zapar; socavar; *strength etc* minar, agotar.
sap³: [sæp] N bobo *m*; **you ~!** ¡bobo!
sapling [ˈsæplɪŋ] N pimpollo *m*, árbol *m* nuevo, arbolito *m*.
sapper [ˈsæpəʳ] N (*Brit*) zapador *m*.
Sapphic, sapphic [ˈsæfɪk] ADJ (*lesbian*) sáfico.
sapphire [ˈsæfaɪəʳ] ① N zafiro *m*.
  ② ATTR: **~ blue** azul zafiro; **~ (blue) sky** cielo *m* azul zafiro.
sappiness [ˈsæpɪnɪs] N jugosidad *f*.
sappy¹ [ˈsæpɪ] ADJ (*Bot*) lleno de savia, jugoso.
sappy²: [ˈsæpɪ] ADJ bobo.
SAR N ABBR *of* **Search and Rescue** Servicio *m* de Búsqueda y Salvamento.
saraband [ˈsærəbænd] N zarabanda *f*.
Saracen [ˈsærəsn] ① ADJ sarraceno.
  ② N sarraceno *m*, -a *f*.
Saragossa [ˌsærəˈgɒsə] N Zaragoza *f*.
Sarah [ˈsɛərə] NF Sara.
sarcasm [ˈsɑːkæzəm] N sarcasmo *m*.
sarcastic [sɑːˈkæstɪk] ADJ sarcástico.
sarcastically [sɑːˈkæstɪkəlɪ] ADV con sarcasmo, sarcásticamente.
sarcoma [sɑːˈkəʊmə] N sarcoma *m*.
sarcophagus [sɑːˈkɒfəgəs] N, PL **sarcophagi** [sɑːˈkɒfəgaɪ] sarcófago *m*.
sardine [sɑːˈdiːn] N sardina *f*.
Sardinia [sɑːˈdɪnɪə] N Cerdeña *f*.
Sardinian [sɑːˈdɪnɪən] ① ADJ sardo.
  ② N sardo *m*, -a *f*.
sardonic [sɑːˈdɒnɪk] ADJ burlón, irónico, sarcástico, sardónico.
sardonically [sɑːˈdɒnɪkəlɪ] ADV con aire burlón, irónicamente, con sarcasmo.
sarge: [sɑːdʒ] N = **sergeant; yes ~** sí, mi sargento.
sari [ˈsɑːrɪ] N sari *m*.
sarky: [ˈsɑːkɪ] ADJ = **sarcastic.**
sarnie: [ˈsɑːnɪ] N (*Brit*) bocata* *f*.
sarong [səˈrɒŋ] N sarong *m*.
sarsaparilla [ˌsɑːsəpəˈrɪlə] N zarzaparrilla *f*.
sartorial [sɑːˈtɔːrɪəl] ADJ relativo al vestido; **~ elegance** elegancia *f* en el vestido; **~ taste** gusto *m* en vestidos.
SAS N (*Brit Mil*) ABBR *of* **Special Air Service.**
s.a.s.e. N (*US*) ABBR *of* **self-addressed stamped envelope** sobre *m* con las propias señas de uno y con sello.
sash¹ [sæʃ] N faja *f*; (*Mil: of order*) fajín *m*.
sash² [sæʃ] N (*window ~*) marco *m* corredizo de ventana.
sashay: [sæˈʃeɪ] VI pasearse; **to ~ off** largarse*.
sashcord [ˈsæʃkɔːd] N cuerda *f* de ventana (de guillotina).
sash-window [ˈsæʃˌwɪndəʊ] N ventana *f* de guillotina.
Sask. (*Canada*) ABBR *of* **Saskatchewan.**
sass: [sæs] (*US*) ① N réplicas *fpl*, descoco *m*.
  ② VT: **to ~ sb** replicar a uno.
sassafras [ˈsæsəfræs] N sasafrás *m*.
Sassenach [ˈsæsənæx] N (*Scot: sometimes pej*) inglés *m*, -esa *f*.
sassy: [ˈsæsɪ] ADJ (*US*) fresco, descarado.
SAT N (*US*) ABBR *of* **Scholastic Aptitude Test.**

| SCHOLASTIC APTITUDE TEST |

ⓘ En Estados Unidos los exámenes de acceso a la universidad se conocen como Scholastic Aptitude Tests o SATS. Estos exámenes evalúan la capacidad de razonamiento verbal y matemático, siendo el resultado máximo 1.600 puntos, aunque la media se sitúa en torno a los 900. Los alumnos pueden hacer también otros exámenes adicionales si desean acceder a las universidades de más prestigio. Los resultados, conocidos como SAT scores, se envían a la universidad en la que el alumno ha presentado la solicitud de ingreso y la admisión se hace atendiendo a los resultados de estos exámenes y al expediente académico. Aunque las pruebas intentan ser objetivas y justas, se las ha criticado por favorecer en teoría a los estudiantes de clase media. Los estudiantes pueden volver a examinarse cuantas veces lo deseen, pero tienen que pagar tasas extras cada vez que hacen el examen.

---

sat [sæt] PRET AND PTP *of* **sit.**
Sat. N ABBR *of* **Saturday** sábado *m*, sáb.
Satan [ˈseɪtn] NM Satanás, Satán.
satanic [səˈtænɪk] ADJ satánico.
Satanism [ˈseɪtəˌnɪzəm] N satanismo *m*.
Satanist [ˈseɪtənɪst] ① ADJ satánico.
  ② N satanista *mf*.
satchel [ˈsætʃəl] N bolsa *f*, cartera *f*; (*schoolboy's*) cartera *f*, cabás *m*,

mochila *f* (*LAm*).
sate [seɪt] VT saciar, hartar.
sateen [sæˈtiːn] N satén *m*.
satellite [ˈsætəlaɪt] ① N satélite *m*.
  ② ATTR: **~ broadcasting** transmisión *f* por satélite; **~ country** país *m* satélite; **~ dish** antena *f* parabólica para TV por satélite; **~ state** estado *m* satélite; **~ town** ciudad *f* satélite; **~ TV** TV *f* por satélite.
satiate [ˈseɪʃɪeɪt] VT saciar, hartar.
satiated [ˈseɪʃɪeɪtɪd] ADJ (*with food*) harto; (*with pleasures*) saciado.
satiation [ˌseɪʃɪˈeɪʃən] N, **satiety** [səˈtaɪətɪ] N saciedad *f*, hartura *f*; **to ~** hasta la saciedad.
satin [ˈsætɪn] ① N raso *m*.
  ② ADJ (*also* **satiny** [ˈsætɪnɪ]) terso, liso; lustroso; **with a ~ finish** satinado.
satinwood [ˈsætɪnwʊd] N madera *f* satinada de las Indias, doradillo *m*, satín *m*.
satire [ˈsætaɪəʳ] N sátira *f*.
satiric(al) [səˈtɪrɪk(əl)] ADJ satírico.
satirically [səˈtɪrɪkəlɪ] ADV satíricamente.
satirist [ˈsætərɪst] N escritor *m* satírico, escritora *f* satírica.
satirize [ˈsætəraɪz] VT satirizar.
satisfaction [ˌsætɪsˈfækʃən] N satisfacción *f*; (*of debt*) pago *m*, liquidación *f*; **to the general ~** con la satisfacción de todos; **has it been done to your ~?** ¿se ha hecho a tu satisfacción?; **to demand ~** pedir satisfacción; **to express one's ~ at a result** expresar su satisfacción con un resultado, declararse satisfecho con un resultado; **it gives every (or full) ~** es completamente satisfactorio; **it gives me much ~ to introduce ...** es para mí un verdadero placer presentar a ...
satisfactorily [ˌsætɪsˈfæktərɪlɪ] ADV satisfactoriamente, de modo satisfactorio.
satisfactory [ˌsætɪsˈfæktərɪ] ADJ satisfactorio.
▼ **satisfy** [ˈsætɪsfaɪ] ① VT satisfacer; *debt* pagar, liquidar; *condition* satisfacer, llenar; (*convince*) convencer; **he is never satisfied** no está contento nunca, no se da nunca por satisfecho; **it completely satisfies me** me satisface completamente; **to ~ sb that ...** convencer a uno de que ...; **I am not satisfied that ...** no estoy convencido de que ...; **to ~ the requirements** llenar los requisitos; **to ~ the examiners** aprobar; **you'll have to be satisfied with that** tendrás que contentarte con eso; **we are very satisfied with it** estamos perfectamente satisfechos con él, nos satisface completamente.
  ② VR: **to ~ o.s. about sth** satisfacerse con algo; **to ~ o.s. that ...** convencerse de que ...
satisfying [ˈsætɪsfaɪɪŋ] ADJ satisfactorio, que satisface; agradable; *food, meal* bueno, que llena.
satsuma [ˌsætˈsuːmə] N satsuma *f*.
saturate [ˈsætʃəreɪt] ① VT saturar, empapar (*with* de); **to be ~d with** (*fig*) estar empapado de.
  ② VR: **to ~ o.s. in** (*fig*) empaparse en.
saturated [ˈsætʃəreɪtɪd] ADJ: **~ fat** grasa *f* saturada.
saturation [ˌsætʃəˈreɪʃən] ① N saturación *f*.
  ② ATTR: **~ bombing** bombardeo *m* por saturación; **~ diving** buceo *m* de saturación; **~ point** punto *m* de saturación.
Saturday [ˈsætədɪ] N sábado *m*.
Saturn [ˈsætən] NM Saturno.
Saturnalia [ˌsætəˈneɪlɪə] NPL saturnales *fpl*.
saturnine [ˈsætənaɪn] ADJ saturnino.
satyr [ˈsætəʳ] N sátiro *m*.
sauce [sɔːs] N (**a**) (*Culin*) salsa *f*; (*sweet*) crema *f*; (*apple ~*) compota *f*; **what's ~ for the goose is ~ for the gander** lo que es bueno para uno es bueno para el otro.
  (**b**) (*) frescura *f*; **what ~!** ¡qué fresco*!; **none of your ~!** ¡eres un fresco*!
sauceboat [ˈsɔːsbəʊt] N salsera *f*.
saucepan [ˈsɔːspən] N cacerola *f*, cazo *m*.
saucer [ˈsɔːsəʳ] N platillo *m*.
saucily [ˈsɔːsɪlɪ] ADV *reply etc* con frescura; con coquetería.
sauciness [ˈsɔːsɪnɪs] N frescura *f*, descaro *m*, desfachatez *f*; coquetería *f*.
saucy [ˈsɔːsɪ] ADJ fresco, descarado, desfachatado; *girl* coqueta; *hat etc* coquetón; **don't be ~!** ¡qué fresco!
Saudi [ˈsaʊdɪ] ① ADJ saudí, saudita.
  ② N saudí *mf*, saudita *mf*.
Saudi Arabia [ˈsaʊdɪəˈreɪbɪə] N Arabia *f* Saudí, Arabia *f* Saudita.
Saudi Arabian [ˈsaʊdɪəˈreɪbɪən] ADJ = **Saudi.**
sauerkraut [ˈsaʊəkraʊt] N chucrut *m*, chucrú *m*.
Saul [sɔːl] NM Saúl.
sauna [ˈsɔːnə] N sauna *f*.
saunter [ˈsɔːntəʳ] ① N paseo *m* (lento y tranquilo); **to have a ~ in the park** dar un paseo tranquilo en el parque.
  ② VI pasearse (despacio y tranquilamente); **to ~ up and down** deambular, pasearse despacio de acá para allá; **he ~ed up to me** se

acercó a mí con mucha calma.

saurian ['sɔ:rɪən] N saurio *m*.

sausage ['sɒsɪdʒ] N (*gen*) embutido *m*; (*small*) salchicha *f*; **not a ~*!** ¡ni un botón!, ¡nada de nada!

sausage dog* ['sɒsɪdʒ,dɒg] N perro *m* salchicha*.

sausage-machine ['sɒsɪdʒmə,ʃi:n] N embutidora *f*.

sausage-meat ['sɒsɪdʒmi:t] N masa *f* del embutido; carne *f* de salchicha.

sausage-roll ['sɒsɪdʒ'rəul] N (*esp Brit*) empanadilla *f* de salchicha.

sauté ['səuteɪ] ① ADJ salteado.
② VT saltear.

savage ['sævɪdʒ] ① ADJ salvaje; *attack* feroz, furioso, violento; **to be ~*** estar rabioso; **to get ~*** ponerse negro*.
② N salvaje *mf*.
③ VT (*of animal*) embestir, atacar, morder; (*fig*) atacar ferozmente.

savagely ['sævɪdʒlɪ] ADV de modo salvaje; ferozmente, furiosamente, violentamente; **he said ~** dijo furioso.

savageness ['sævɪdʒnɪs] N, **savagery** ['sævɪdʒrɪ] N salvajismo *m*, salvajería *f*; ferocidad *f*, furia *f*, violencia *f*.

savannah [sə'vænə] N sabana *f*.

savant ['sævənt] N sabio *m*, erudito *m*, intelectual *m*.

save¹ [seɪv] ① VT (a) (*rescue*) salvar; rescatar; **to ~ sb's life** salvar la vida a uno; **to ~ sb from death** salvar a uno de la muerte, rescatar a uno de la muerte; **to ~ sb from falling** impedir que caiga uno, agarrarse a uno para que no se caiga; **to ~ appearances** salvar las apariencias; **to ~ the situation** salvar la situación; **to ~ one's soul** salvarse; **I couldn't do it to ~ my soul** (*or* life) no lo podría hacer por nada del mundo; **God ~ the Queen** Dios guarde a la Reina, Dios salve a la Reina; **God ~ us all!** ¡que Dios nos ayude!; **to ~ a building for posterity** lograr conservar un edificio para la posteridad; **to ~ one's eyes** cuidarse la vista; **to ~ sth from the wreck** salvar algo de las ruinas.
(b) (*put by; also* **to ~ up**) guardar, reservar; (*preserve*) conservar; *money etc* ahorrar; *stamps etc* (*Comput*) salvar, grabar, guardar; **~ as you earn** (*savings scheme*) ahorre mientras gana; **I ~d this for you** guardé esto para ti; **~ me a seat** resérvame un asiento; **she has £2000 ~d** sus ahorros suman 2000 libras.
(c) (*avoid using up*) *time etc* ahorrar; economizar; **to ~ time ...** para ahorrar tiempo ..., para ganar tiempo ...; **this way you ~ £8** por este sistema te ahorras 8 libras; **this way you ~ 4 miles** por esta ruta te ahorras 4 millas; **it ~s fuel** economiza combustible; **he's saving his strength for tomorrow** se reserva para mañana.
(d) (*prevent*) evitar, impedir; **to ~ a goal** parar un tiro, impedir que se marque un gol; **it ~d a lot of trouble** evitó muchas molestias, evitó muchos disgustos; **to ~ sb trouble** evitar molestias a uno.
② VI ahorrar, economizar, hacer economías; **to ~ on petrol** ahorrar gasolina.
③ VR: **to ~ o.s. for** reservarse para.
④ N (*Sport*) parada *f*.
◆ **save up** ① VT *dinero* ahorrar.
② VI: **to ~ up for a new bicycle** ahorrar dinero para comprar una bicicleta.

┌──────────────────────────────┐
│ **SAVE THE CHILDREN** │
└──────────────────────────────┘

ⓘ *Save the Children es una organización benéfica fundada en el Reino Unido en 1919 para ayudar a los niños que sufrieron las secuelas de la Revolución Rusa y de la Segunda Guerra Mundial. Hoy en día se dedica a ofrecer ayuda de emergencia a los niños de todo el mundo que sufren de inanición o son víctimas de los efectos de guerras y desastres naturales, y desarrolla proyectos a largo plazo para mejorar la higiene, la nutrición y la educación, además de luchar para que los gobiernos den prioridad a los derechos de los niños.*

save² [seɪv] PREP AND CONJ (*esp liter*) salvo, excepto, con excepción de; **all ~ one** todos excepto uno, todos menos uno; **~ for** excepto; si no fuera por; **~ that ...** excepto que ...

saveloy ['sævəlɔɪ] N *salchicha seca muy sazonada*.

saver ['seɪvəʳ] N (a) (*having account*) ahorrador *m*, -ora *f*; **small ~** ahorrador *m* pequeño, ahorradora *f* pequeña. (b) (*by nature*) persona *f* ahorrativa. (c) (*ticket*) billete-abono *m*.

Saville Row ['sævɪl'rəu] N (*Brit*) *calle londinense donde están las mejores sastrerías*.

saving ['seɪvɪŋ] ① ADJ (a) económico; (*pej*) tacaño; **she's not the ~ sort** no es de las que economizan.
(b) **~ clause** cláusula *f* que contiene una salvedad; **~ grace** virtud *f*, mérito *m*; **it has the ~ grace that ...** tiene el mérito excepcional de que ...
② N (a) (*act: rescue*) salvamento *m*, rescate *m*; (*Eccl*) salvación *f*.
(b) (*of money etc*) ahorro *m*; (*of cost etc*) economía *f*; **~s** ahorros *mpl*; **she has ~s of £3000** sus ahorros suman 3000 libras; **to live on one's ~s** vivir de sus ahorros; **we must make ~s** tenemos que economizar.

③ ATTR: **~s account** cuenta *f* de ahorros; **~s bond** bono *m* de ahorros; **~s certificate** bono *m* de caja de ahorros; **~s and loan association** (*US*) sociedad *f* inmobiliaria, cooperativa *f* de construcciones.

savings-bank ['seɪvɪŋzbæŋk] N caja *f* de ahorros.

savings-stamp ['seɪvɪŋz,stæmp] N sello *m* de ahorros.

saviour, (*US*) **savior** ['seɪvjəʳ] N salvador *m*, -ora *f*; **S~** Salvador *m*.

savoir-faire ['sævwɑː'fɛəʳ] N desparpajo *m*; habilidad *f* práctica; sentido *m* común; don *m* de gentes.

savor ['seɪvəʳ] *etc* (*US*) = **savour** *etc*.

savory¹ ['seɪvərɪ] N (*Bot*) tomillo *m* salsero.

savory² ['seɪvərɪ] (*US*) = **savoury**.

savour, (*US*) **savor** ['seɪvəʳ] ① N sabor *m*, gusto *m*; (*aftertaste*) dejo *m*; (*fig*) sabor *m* (*of* a); **it has lost its ~** ha perdido su sabor, fama.
② VT saborear, paladear; (*fig*) saborear.
③ VI: **to ~ of** saber a, oler a (*also fig*).

savouriness, (*US*) **savoriness** ['seɪvərɪnɪs] N sabor *m*, buen sabor *m*, lo sabroso.

savourless, (*US*) **savorless** ['seɪvəlɪs] ADJ soso, insípido.

savoury, (*US*) **savory²** ['seɪvərɪ] ① ADJ (*appetizing*) sabroso, apetitoso; (*not sweet*) no dulce; (*salted*) salado; **not very ~** (*fig*) no muy respetable, poco decente; **it's not a very ~ district** es un barrio de mala fama.
② N plato *m* salado (*que empieza o termina una comida*).

Savoy [sə'vɔɪ] N Saboya *f*.

savoy [sə'vɔɪ] N berza *f* de Saboya.

savvy* ['sævɪ] ① N inteligencia *f*; desparpajo *m*.
② VT comprender; **~?** ¿comprende?

saw¹ [sɔː] ① N sierra *f*.
② ATTR: **~ edge** filo *m* dentado (*or* de sierra).
③ (*irr*: PRET **sawed**, PTP **sawed** *or* **sawn**) VT serrar.
◆ **saw away** ① VT quitar con la sierra.
② VI: **she was ~ing away at the violin** iba rascando el violín.
◆ **saw off** VT quitar con la sierra.
◆ **saw up** VT cortar con la sierra.

saw² [sɔː] N refrán *m*, dicho *m*.

saw³ [sɔː] PRET *of* **see¹**.

sawbench ['sɔːbentʃ] N, **sawbuck** ['sɔːbʌk] N (*US*) caballete *m* para serrar.

sawbones* ['sɔːbəunz] N matasanos *m*.

sawdust ['sɔːdʌst] N serrín *m*.

sawed-off ['sɔːdɒf] ADJ (*US*), **sawn-off** ['sɔːnɒf] ADJ: **~ shotgun** escopeta *f* de cañones recortados, recortada *f*, recortado *m* (*SC*).

sawfish ['sɔːfɪʃ] N pez *m* sierra.

sawhorse ['sɔːhɔːs] N caballete *m* para serrar.

sawmill ['sɔːmɪl] N aserradero *m*.

sawn [sɔːn] PTP *of* **saw¹** 3.

sawyer ['sɔːjəʳ] N aserrador *m*.

sax* [sæks] N saxo* *m*.

saxhorn ['sækshɔːn] N bombardino *m*.

saxifrage ['sæksɪfrɪdʒ] N saxífraga *f*.

Saxon ['sæksn] ① ADJ sajón.
② N sajón *m*, -ona *f*.

Saxony ['sæksənɪ] N Sajonia *f*.

saxophone ['sæksəfəun] N saxofón *m*, saxófono *m*.

saxophonist [,sæk'sɒfənɪst] N saxofón *m*, saxófono *m*, saxofonista *mf*.

say [seɪ] ① N: **to have a** (*or* **some**) **~ in sth** tener voz y voto; **to have no ~ in sth** no tener voz ni voto en capítulo; **I had no ~ in it** no tuve nada que ver con ello, no pidieron mi parecer acerca de ello; **if I had had a ~ in it** si hubieran pedido mi parecer; **I have had my ~** he dicho lo que quería; **to let sb have his ~** dejar hablar a uno; **let him have his ~!** ¡que hable él!
② (*irr*: PRET AND PTP **said**) VT (a) (*gen*) decir; *mass* decir; *prayer* rezar; *lesson* recitar; **to ~ yes** decir que sí; **to ~ no** decir que no; **to ~ yes to an invitation** aceptar una invitación; **to ~ no to a proposal** rechazar una propuesta; **to ~ good-bye to sb** despedirse de uno; **to ~ good morning to sb** dar los buenos días a uno; **they ~** se dice, dicen; **to ~ to o.s.** decir para sí; **who shall I ~?** ¿qué nombre digo?
(b) (*idioms*) **that is to ~** es decir, esto es; **to ~ nothing of the rest** y no digamos de los demás; **to ~ nothing of swearing** sin mencionar lo de decir palabrotas (*and V* **nothing 1** (d)); **his suit ~s a lot about him** su traje dice mucho de él; **I will ~ this about him: he's bright** reconozco (a pesar de todo) que es listo; **it's an original, not to ~ revolutionary, idea** la idea es original y hasta revolucionaria; **~ what you like about her hat, she's charming** dígase lo que se quiera acerca de su sombrero, es encantadora; **to ~ the least** para no decir más; **as one might ~** como si dijéramos; **that's ~ing a lot** ya es decir; **would you really ~ so?** ¿lo crees de veras?; **what would you ~ to that?** ¿qué contestas a eso?; **what would you ~ to a cup of tea?** ¿te apetece una taza de té?, ¿se te antoja una taza de té? (*LAm*); **I wouldn't ~ no to a gin** no me vendría mal una ginebra; **what have you got to ~ for yourself?** ¿qué puedes decir en tu defensa?; ¿cómo te vas a justificar?; **she hasn't much to ~ for her-**

self es muy reservada, no es nada habladora; **that doesn't ~ much for her** eso no dice mucho en su favor; **it doesn't ~ much for his intelligence** eso no dice mucho a favor de su inteligencia; **it ~s much for his courage that he stayed** el que permaneciera allí demuestra su valor; **it goes without ~ing that ...** ni que decir tiene que ...; **that goes without ~ing** eso cae de su peso; **there's no ~ing** nadie lo sabe; **there's no ~ing what he'll do** podría hacer cualquier cosa; **though I ~ (or ~s*) it myself, though I ~ (or ~s*) it as shouldn't** aunque soy yo el que lo dice.

(c) (*exclamatory idioms*) **~!** (*US*), **I ~!** (*calling attention*) ¡oiga!, (*in surprise*) ¡caramba!; **you don't ~ (so)!** ¡parece mentira!, ¿de veras?; **I should ~ so!**, **you can ~ that again!** ¡ya lo creo!; ¡bien dicho!; **you've said it!** ¡eso es!; **so you ~!** ¡es Vd quien lo dice!; **~ no more!** ¡basta!, ¡ni una palabra más!

(d) (*phrases with ptp said*) **it is said that ...** se dice que ...; **he is said to be worth a million** se dice que es millonario; **there is sth to be said for it** hay algunas razones a favor de esa opinión (*etc*); **there is a lot to be said for doing it now** hay buenas razones por las que conviene hacerlo ahora; **there is sth to be said on both sides** hay algo que decir en pro y en contra; **when all is said and done there's no money for it** total que no hay dinero para ello, a fin de cuentas no hay dinero para ello; **it's easier said than done** eso se dice muy pronto; del dicho al hecho hay gran trecho; **no sooner said than done** dicho y hecho; **well said!** ¡muy bien dicho!; **enough said!** ¡basta!; al buen entendedor pocas palabras le bastan.

(e) (*suppose*) **~ it is worth £20** pongamos por caso que vale 20 libras; **we sell it at ~ £25** pongamos que lo vendemos por 25 libras; **we were going at ~ 80 kph** íbamos a 80 kph más o menos; **shall we ~ £5?** ¿convenimos en 5 libras?; **shall we ~ Tuesday?** ¿para el martes, pues?

(f) (*admit*) decir; confesar, admitir; **I must ~ she's very pretty** tengo que reconocer que es muy guapa; **it's difficult, I must ~** es difícil, lo confieso.

(g) (*register: dial etc*) marear, señalar; (*text*) decir, rezar; **my watch ~s 3 o'clock** mi reloj marca las 3; **it ~s 30 degrees** marca 30 grados.

SAYE ABBR of **save as you earn**.

▼ **saying** ['seɪŋ] N dicho *m*, refrán *m*; **as the ~ goes** como dice el refrán, como dijo el otro; **it's just a ~** es un refrán, es un decir.

say-so* ['seɪsəʊ] N **(a)** (*rumour*) rumor *m* (infundado); (*statement*) aserto *m*; **we have only his ~ for this accusation** esta acusación depende solamente de su aserto.
(b) (*authority*) autoridad *f*; aprobación *f*; decisión *f*; **it depends on his ~** necesita su visto bueno.

SBA N (*US*) ABBR of **Small Business Administration**.

SC (a) N (*US*) ABBR of **Supreme Court**. **(b)** (*US Post*) ABBR of **South Carolina**.

s.c. ABBR of **self-contained**.

scab [skæb] N **(a)** (*Med*) costra *f*. **(b)** (*Vet*) roña *f*. **(c)** (*) esquirol *m*.
scabbard ['skæbəd] N vaina *f* (de espada).
scabby ['skæbɪ] ADJ **(a)** costroso; lleno de costras. **(b)** (*Vet*) roñoso.
scabies ['skeɪbiːz] N sarna *f*.
scabious¹ ['skeɪbɪəs] ADJ (*Med*) sarnoso.
scabious² ['skeɪbɪəs] N (*Bot*) escabiosa *f*.
scabrous ['skeɪbrəs] ADJ escabroso.
scads* [skædz] NPL montones* *mpl*; **we have ~ of it** lo tenemos a montones*, tenemos montones de eso*.
scaffold ['skæfəld] N (*Archit*) andamio *m*; (*for execution*) cadalso *m*, patíbulo *m*.
scaffolding ['skæfəldɪŋ] N andamio *m*, andamiaje *m*.
scag: [skæg] N (*US: Drugs*) heroína *f*, caballo *m*:.
scalawag ['skæləwæg] N (*US*) = **scallywag**.
scald [skɔːld] **1** N escaldadura *f*.
2 VT *o.s., skin etc* escaldar, quemar con agua caliente; *milk* calentar; *instruments* esterilizar con agua caliente; **to ~ out a saucepan** escaldar una cacerola.
scalding ['skɔːldɪŋ] ADJ: **~ hot** hirviendo, hirviente; **the soup is ~** la sopa está muy caliente.
scale¹ [skeɪl] **1** N (*of fish etc*) escama *f*; (*flake*) hojuela *f*; laminita *f*; (*of skin*) costra *f*; (*on teeth*) sarro *m*.
2 VT *fish* escamar; (*Tech*) raspar; *teeth* quitar el sarro a.
3 VI (*also to ~ off*) descamarse; desconcharse.
scale² [skeɪl] **1** N (*of balance*) platillo *m*; **~s** balanza *f*, (*for heavy weights*) báscula *f*; **the S~** (*Zodiac*) Libra *f*; **to turn (or tip) the ~** (*fig*) inclinar la balanza, decidirlo; **he turns the ~s at 80 kilos** pesa 80 kilos.
2 VI pesar; **it ~s 4 kilos** pesa 4 kilos.
scale³ [skeɪl] **1** N escala *f* (*also Math, Mus*); (*of salaries*) escalafón *m*, banda *f*; **~ of charges** tarifa *f*, lista *f* de precios; **on a ~ of 5 km to the centimetre** a escala de 5 km al centímetro; **on a big (or large) ~** a gran escala, a grande escala; **on a small ~** a pequeña escala; **on a national ~** a escala nacional; **to draw sth to ~** dibujar algo a escala; **the drawing is not to ~** el dibujo no está a escala.

2 ATTR: **~ drawing** dibujo *m* a escala; **~ model** modelo *m* a escala, maqueta *f*.
3 VT *mountain etc* escalar; *tree etc* trepar a.
♦ **scale back** (*US*), **scale down** VT (*gen*) reducir a escala, reducir proporcionalmente; (*Econ*) reducir, rebajar; (*Comput*) escalar.
♦ **scale up** VT aumentar a escala, aumentar proporcionalmente; (*Comput*) escalar.
scallion ['skæljən] N cebolleta *f* (para ensalada), cebollita *f* (*LAm*), chalote *m*.
scallop ['skɒləp] **1** N **(a)** (*Zool*) venera *f*, vieira *f*; **~ shell** venera *f*. **(b)** (*Sew*) festón *m*.
2 VT **(a)** (*Culin*) guisar en conchas. **(b)** (*Sew*) festonear.
scallywag ['skælɪwæg] N = **scamp¹**.
scalp [skælp] **1** N cuero *m* cabelludo, cabellera *f*; (*Anat*) pericráneo *m*; (*fig*) trofeo *m*.
2 VT **(a)** escalpar, quitar el cuero cabelludo a. **(b)** (*US**) revender.
3 VI (*US**) revender.
scalpel ['skælpəl] N escalpelo *m*.
scalper* ['skælpəʳ] N (*US*) revendedor *m*, -ora *f*.
scalping ['skælpɪŋ] N (*US**) reventa *f*.
scaly ['skeɪlɪ] ADJ escamoso.
scam: [skæm] N estafa *f*, timo *m*.
scamp¹ [skæmp] N tunante *mf*, bribón *m*, -ona *f*; (*child*) diablillo *m*, travieso *m* (*LAm*); **you little ~!** ¡pícaro!
scamp² [skæmp] VT chapucear, frangollar.
scamper ['skæmpəʳ] **1** N carrera *f* rápida; huida *f* precipitada.
2 VI correr, darse prisa; **to ~ along** ir corriendo; **to ~ for the bus** correr para coger el autobús; **to ~ past** pasar corriendo.
♦ **scamper about** VI corretear.
♦ **scamper away, scamper off** VI escabullirse, escaparse corriendo.
scampi ['skæmpɪ] NPL gambas *fpl*.
scan [skæn] **1** VT **(a)** (*examine*) escudriñar, examinar; (*Comput*) examinar, explorar; (*glance at*) dar un vistazo a; *horizon etc* explorar con la vista; (*by radar etc*) explorar, registrar.
(b) *verse* medir, escandir.
2 VI estar bien medido; **it does not ~** no está bien medido.
3 N escáner *m*; **to go for a ~, to have a ~** hacerse un escáner.
scandal ['skændl] N **(a)** (*disgrace*) escándalo *m*; (*Jur*) difamación *f*; **the groundnuts ~** el escándalo de los cacahuetes; **to cause a ~, to create a ~** hacer un escándalo, armar un lío; **what a ~!, it's a ~!** ¡qué vergüenza!; **it is a ~ that ...** es una vergüenza que ...
(b) (*gossip*) chismorreo *m*, murmuración *f*; (*pieces of gossip*) habladurías *fpl*, chismes *mpl*; **the local ~** los chismes del pueblo (*or* del barrio *etc*); **have you heard the latest ~?** ¿te han contado el último chisme?, ¿has oído lo que están diciendo ahora?; **there's a lot of ~ going round about the vicar** se cuentan muchos chismes acerca del pastor; **to talk ~** murmurar, contar chismes.
scandalize ['skændəlaɪz] VT escandalizar; **she was ~d** se escandalizó.
scandalmonger ['skændl,mʌŋgəʳ] N chismoso *m*, -a *f*.
scandalous ['skændələs] ADJ escandaloso; (*libellous*) difamatorio, calumnioso; **~ talk** habladurías *fpl*, chismes *mpl*; **it's simply ~!** ¡es una vergüenza!, ¡no hay derecho!
scandalously ['skændələslɪ] ADV escandalosamente.
Scandinavia [,skændɪ'neɪvɪə] N Escandinavia *f*.
Scandinavian [,skændɪ'neɪvɪən] **1** ADJ escandinavo.
2 N escandinavo *m*, -a *f*.
scandium ['skændɪəm] N escandio *m*.
scanner ['skænəʳ] N (*Radar*) antena *f* direccional giratoria; (*TV*) dispositivo *m* explorador; (*Comput, Med*) escáner *m*.
scanning ['skænɪŋ] N (*Med*) visualización *f* radiográfica; **~ device** detector *m*.
scansion ['skænʃən] N escansión *f*; medida *f*.
scant [skænt] ADJ escaso.
scantily ['skæntɪlɪ] ADV insuficientemente; **~ provided with ...** con escasa provisión de...; **~ dressed** ligeramente vestido, ligero de ropa.
scantiness ['skæntɪnɪs] N escasez *f*, cortedad *f*, insuficiencia *f*.
scanty ['skæntɪ] ADJ escaso, corto, insuficiente; *clothing* ligero.
scapegoat ['skeɪpgəʊt] N cabeza *f* de turco, chivo *m* expiatorio, víctima *f* propiciatoria; **to be a ~ for** pagar el pato por, pagar los cristales rotos por.
scapegrace ['skeɪpgreɪs] N pícaro *m*, bribón *m*.
scapula ['skæpjʊlə] N escápula *f*.
scapular ['skæpjʊləʳ] ADJ, N escapulario *m*.
scar¹ [skɑːʳ] **1** N (*Med*) cicatriz *f*, señal *f*; (*fig*) señal *f*; **it left a deep ~ on his mind** dejó una profunda señal en su espíritu.
2 VT dejar una cicatriz en; marcar con una cicatriz, marcar con cicatrices; (*fig*) señalar, dejar señales en; **he was ~red with many wounds** llevaba las cicatrices de muchas heridas; **he was ~red for life** quedó marcado para toda la vida; **the walls are ~red with bullets** las balas han dejado señales en las paredes.
3 VI (*also to ~ over*) cicatrizarse.
scar² [skɑːʳ] N (*Geog*) paraje *m* rocoso, pendiente *f* rocosa.

scarab ['skærəb] N escarabajo *m*.

scarce ['skɛəs] [1] ADJ escaso; poco común, poco frecuente; **money is ~** escasca el dinero, hay poco dinero; **such people are ~** tales personas son poco frecuentes; **the plant is ~ in the north** en el norte la planta es poco común; **to grow ~** ir escaseando; **to make o.s.* ~** largarse*, esfumarse, rajarse (*LAm*); no dejarse ver.
[2] ADV = **scarcely**.

scarcely ['skɛəslɪ] ADV apenas; **~ 200** apenas 200; **~ anybody** casi nadie; **~ ever** casi nunca; **it will ~ be enough** escasamente alcanzará, apenas bastará; **I could ~ stand up** apenas (si) pude levantarme; **I ~ know what to say** en realidad no sé qué decir.

scarceness ['skɛəsnɪs] N escasez *f*; poca frecuencia *f*.

scarcity ['skɛəsɪtɪ] [1] N escasez *f*; poca frecuencia *f*; (*shortage*) carestía *f*; **in years of ~** en años de carestía; **due to the ~ of money** debido a la escasez de dinero.
[2] ATTR: **~ value** valor *m* de escasez, valor *m* excesivo debido a la poca frecuencia (de un artículo *etc*).

scare ['skɛəʳ] [1] N susto *m*, sobresalto *m*; **the invasion ~** el pánico de la invasión; los rumores alarmistas de una invasión; **to create (or raise) a ~** infundir miedo a la gente, alarmar a las personas; **to give sb a ~** dar un susto a uno; **what a ~ you gave me!** ¡qué susto me diste!
[2] ATTR: **~ campaign** campaña *f* alarmista, campaña *f* de intimidación; **it's only a ~ story** se trata de un reportaje alarmista.
[3] VT asustar, espantar, infundir miedo a; **to be ~d to death, to be ~d stiff** estar muerto de miedo; **to ~ the hell (or life) out of sb*** meter a uno el ombligo para dentro*; **she was too ~d to talk** estaba demasiado asustada para poder hablar, no podía hablar por el susto; **he's ~d of women** tiene miedo a las mujeres; **don't be ~d** no te asustes, no tengas miedo.
[4] VI: **he doesn't ~ easily** no se asusta por poca cosa.
♦ **scare away, scare off** VT ahuyentar.

scarecrow ['skɛəkrəʊ] N espantapájaros *m*; (*fig*) espantajo *m*.

scaredy cat* ['skɛədɪˌkæt] N (*Brit: children's talk*) cagueta: *mf*, miedica* *mf*.

scarehead ['skɛəhed] N (*US*) titulares *mpl* sensacionales.

scaremonger ['skɛəmʌŋgəʳ] N alarmista *mf*.

scaremongering ['skɛəˌmʌŋgərɪŋ] N alarmismo *m*.

scarf [skɑːf] N, PL **scarfs** or **scarves** [skɑːvz] bufanda *f*; (head~) pañuelo *m*.

scarface ['skɑːfeɪs] N (*as nickname*) caracortada *mf*.

scarify ['skɛərɪfaɪ] VT (*Med, Agr*) escarificar; (*fig*) despellejar, desollar, criticar severamente.

scarifying ['skɛərɪfaɪɪŋ] ADJ *attack etc* mordaz, severo.

scarlatina [ˌskɑːləˈtiːnə] N escarlatina *f*.

scarlet ['skɑːlɪt] [1] N escarlata *f*.
[2] ADJ color escarlata; **~ fever** escarlatina *f*; **~ pimpernel** mujares *mpl*; **~ runner** judía *f* escarlata; **to blush ~, to turn ~** enrojecer, ponerse colorado; **he was ~ with rage** se puso rojo de furia.

scarp [skɑːp] N escarpa *f*, declive *m*.

scarper: ['skɑːpəʳ] VI (*Brit*) largarse*.

scarves [skɑːvz] NPL of **scarf**.

scary* ['skɛərɪ] ADJ *person etc* asustadizo; *experience* espeluznante; *place* que infunde miedo.

scat* [skæt] INTERJ ¡zape!

scathing ['skeɪðɪŋ] ADJ *attack, criticism* mordaz, duro; **he was ~ about our trains** criticó duramente nuestros trenes; **he was pretty ~** tuvo cosas bastante duras que decir.

scathingly ['skeɪðɪŋlɪ] ADV mordazmente, duramente; **he spoke ~ of ...** criticó duramente ...

scatological [ˌskætəˈlɒdʒɪkəl] ADJ escatológico.

scatology [skæˈtɒlədʒɪ] N escatología *f*.

scatter ['skætəʳ] [1] N (*Math, Tech*) dispersión *f*; **a ~ of houses** unas casas dispersas; **a ~ of raindrops** unas cuantas gotas de lluvia.
[2] VT (*dot about*) esparcir, desparramar; salpicar; *benefits etc* (*also* **to ~ about**) derramar aquí y allá; (*put to flight*) dispersar; *clouds etc* disipar; **the flowers were ~ed about on the floor** las flores estaban desparramadas por el suelo; **the floor was ~ed with flowers** el suelo estaba sembrado de flores dispersas.
[3] VI desparramarse; dispersarse; **the family ~ed to distant parts** los miembros de la familia se desparramaron por sitios lejanos; **the crowd ~ed** la multitud se dispersó.
[4] ATTR: **~ cushions** almohadones *mpl*.

scatterbrain ['skætəbreɪn] N cabeza *mf* de chorlito.

scatterbrained ['skætəbreɪnd] ADJ ligero de cascos, atolondrado.

scattered ['skætəd] ADJ disperso; **~ showers** lluvias *fpl* aisladas; **the village is very ~** las casas del pueblo son muy dispersas.

scattering ['skætərɪŋ] N: **a ~ of books** unos cuantos libros aquí y allá.

scattershot ['skætəʃɒt] ADJ: **the money has been spent in ~ fashion** el dinero se ha gastado sin ton ni son; **the message is somewhat ~** el mensaje es muy poco consistente.

scattiness* ['skætɪnɪs] N (*Brit*) ligereza *f* de cascos, atolondramiento *m*.

scatty* ['skætɪ] ADJ (*Brit*) ligero de cascos, atolondrado; **to drive sb ~** volver majareta a uno*, poner chalupa a uno*.

scavenge ['skævɪndʒ] [1] VT limpiar las calles (*etc*), recoger la basura.
[2] VI: **to ~ for food** andar buscando comida (entre la basura).

scavenger ['skævɪndʒəʳ] N (a) basurero *m*, barrendero *m*. (b) (*Zool*) animal *m* (or ave *f etc*) que se alimenta de carroña.

Sc.D. N ABBR of **Doctor of Science**.

SCE N ABBR of **Scottish Certificate of Education**.

scenario [sɪˈnɑːrɪəʊ] N (a) (*Cine*) guión *m*. (b) (*forecast*) pronóstico *m*; marco *m* hipotético.

scenarist ['siːnərɪst] N guionista *mf*.

scene [siːn] [1] N (a) (*Theat*) escena *f*; **the bedroom ~** la escena del dormitorio; **the big ~ in the film** la principal escena de la película; **behind the ~s** entre bastidores; **the ~ is set in a castle** la acción se desarrolla en un castillo, la escena es en un castillo; **to set the ~ for a love affair** (*fig*) crear el ambiente para una aventura sentimental; **now let our reporter set the ~ for you** ahora permitan que nuestro reportero les describa la escena; **there were unhappy ~s at the meeting** en la reunión pasaron cosas nada agradables.
(b) (*place in general*) escenario *m*, teatro *m*, lugar *m*; **the ~ of operations** el teatro de las operaciones; **the ~ of the disaster** el lugar de la catástrofe; **the ~ of the crime** el lugar del crimen, el escenario del crimen; **the ~s of one's early life** los lugares frecuentados por uno en su juventud; **the political ~ in Italy** el escenario político italiano; **to appear (or come etc) on the ~** presentarse, llegar; **when I came on the ~** cuando llegué; **he appeared unexpectedly on the ~** se presentó inesperadamente; **to disappear from the political ~** desaparecer del escenario político.
(c) (*sight, vision*) vista *f*, perspectiva *f*, panorama *m*; (*landscape*) paisaje *m*; **the ~ from the top is marvellous** desde la cumbre se abarca un panorama maravilloso; **the ~ spread out before you** el panorama que se extiende delante de uno; **it was a ~ of utter destruction** fue una perspectiva de destrucción total; **it is a lonely ~** es un paisaje solitario; **a change of ~ would do you good** le vendría bien un cambio de aire.
(d) (*: environment etc*) ambiente *m*; panorama *m*; movida* *f*; **the pop ~** el mundo pop; **it's not my ~** esto no es lo mío, en este ambiente no estoy bien; **to be part of the Madrid ~** estar en la movida madrileña*.
(e) (*: fuss*) escándalo *m*, lío* *m*, jaleo *m*; **try to avoid a ~** procura no armar un lío*; **I hate ~s** detesto los jaleos; **to make a ~** armar un lío*, armar un escándalo; **she had a ~ with her husband** riñó con su marido.
[2] ATTR: **~ change** (*Theat*) cambio *m* de escena.

scene-painter ['siːnˌpeɪntəʳ] N (*designer*) escenógrafo *m*, -a *f*, (*workman*) pintor *m*, -ora *f* de decoraciones.

scenery ['siːnərɪ] N (a) (*landscape*) paisaje *m*. (b) (*Theat*) decoraciones *fpl*, decorado *m*.

scene-shifter ['siːnˌʃɪftəʳ] N tramoyista *mf*.

scenic ['siːnɪk] ADJ (a) (*Theat*) escénico, dramático. (b) (*picturesque*) pintoresco; **~ railway** montaña *f* rusa; **~ road** (*US*) ruta *f* turística; **an area of ~ beauty** una región de bellos paisajes.

scenography [siːˈnɒgrəfɪ] N escenografía *f*.

scent [sent] [1] N (a) (*smell*) olor *m*; (*pleasant smell*) perfume *m*, aroma *m*, fragancia *f*; (*Hunting*) rastro *m*, pista *f*; **to be on the ~** seguir la pista (*also fig; of de*); **to lose the ~** perder la pista; **to throw sb off the ~** despistar a uno.
(b) (*liquid*) perfume *m*.
(c) (*sense of smell*) olfato *m*.
[2] VT (a) (*add ~ to*) perfumar (*with de*).
(b) (*smell*) oler; *danger etc* percibir, sospechar; **to ~ sth out** olfatear algo, husmear algo.

scent-bottle ['sentˌbɒtl] N frasco *m* de perfume.

scented ['sentɪd] ADJ perfumado.

scentless ['sentlɪs] ADJ inodoro.

scent-spray ['sentspreɪ] N atomizador *m* (de perfume), pulverizador *m* (de perfume).

scepter ['septəʳ] N (*US*) = **sceptre**.

sceptic, (*US*) **skeptic** ['skeptɪk] N escéptico *m*, -a *f*.

sceptical, (*US*) **skeptical** ['skeptɪkəl] ADJ escéptico; **he was ~ about it** se mostró escéptico acerca de ello, tenía dudas sobre ello.

sceptically, (*US*) **skeptically** ['skeptɪkəlɪ] ADV escépticamente.

scepticism, (*US*) **skepticism** ['skeptɪsɪzəm] N escepticismo *m*.

sceptre, (*US*) **scepter** ['septəʳ] N cetro *m*.

schedule ['ʃedjuːl, *US* 'skedjuːl] [1] N (*list*) lista *f*; (*timetable*) horario *m*; (*of events etc*) programa *m*; (*of charges, prices*) lista *f*; (*of questions*) cuestionario *m*; (*legal document*) inventario *m*, apéndice *m*; (*of work to be done etc*) programa *m*, plan *m*; **the train is behind ~** el tren lleva un retraso; **the bus was on ~** el autobús llegó a la hora debida, el autobús llegó sin retraso; **the work is up to ~** los trabajos llevan el ritmo adecuado, los trabajos avanzan de acuerdo con lo previsto;

we are working to a very tight ~ trabajamos de acuerdo con un plan riguroso; **our ~ did not include the Prado** nuestro programa de visitas no incluía la del Museo del Prado.

  2 VT (*list*) poner en una lista, hacer una lista de; catalogar, inventariar; (*plan*) proyectar, redactar el plan de; *trains etc* establecer el horario de; (*Rad, TV etc*) programar; *visit, lecture etc* fijar la hora de, programar; **as ~d** según (lo) previsto; **~d building** monumento *m* histórico, edificio *m* declarado de interés histórico-artístico; **~d flight** vuelo *m* regular; **~d stop** parada *f* prevista, escala *f* prevista; **this stop is not ~d** esta parada no es oficial; **the plane is ~d for 2 o'clock, the plane is ~d to land at 2 o'clock** según el horario el avión debe llegar a las 2; **you are ~d to speak for 20 minutes** según el programa hablarás durante 20 minutos; **this building is ~d for demolition** se prevé la demolición de este edificio.

scheduling ['ʃedjuːlɪŋ] N (*Comput*) planificación *f*.

Scheldt [ʃelt] N Escalda *m*.

schema ['skiːmə] N, PL **schemata** ['skiːmətə] esquema *m*.

schematic [skɪ'mætɪk] ADJ esquemático.

schematically [skɪ'mætɪkəlɪ] ADV esquemáticamente.

scheme [skiːm] **1** N (a) (*arrangement*) disposición *f*; combinación *f*; (*of colours etc*) combinación *f*; (*of rhymes*) esquema *m*, combinación *f*; **man's place in the ~ of things** el puesto del hombre en el diseño divino; **in the government's ~ of things there is no place for protest** la política del gobierno no deja espacio para la protesta.
  (b) (*systematic table*) plan *m*, esquema *m*; (*diagram*) diagrama *m*; (*summary*) resumen *m*.
  (c) (*plan*) plan *m*, proyecto *m*; (*idea*) idea *f*; (*US: shady deal*) asunto *m* poco limpio, negocio *m* turbio; **the ~ for the new bridge** el proyecto del nuevo puente; **it's some crazy ~ of his** es una idea estrafalaria de las de él; **it's not a bad ~** no es mala idea.
  (d) (*plot*) intriga *f*; (*ruse*) treta *f*, ardid *m*; **it's a ~ to get him out of the way** es una jugada para quitarle de en medio.
  2 VT (*plan*) proyectar; (*pej*) tramar, urdir.
  3 VI (*plan*) hacer proyectos, formar planes; (*pej*) intrigar; **they're scheming to get me out** están intrigando para expulsarme.

schemer ['skiːmər] N intrigante *mf*.

scheming ['skiːmɪŋ] **1** ADJ intrigante; astuto, mañoso.
  2 N intrigas *fpl*.

scherzo ['skɜːtsəʊ] N scherzo *m*.

schilling ['ʃɪlɪŋ] N chelín *m* austríaco.

schism ['sɪzəm, 'skɪzəm] N cisma *m*.

schismatic [sɪz'mætɪk, skɪz'mætɪk] **1** ADJ cismático.
  2 N cismático *m*.

schismatical [sɪz'mætɪkəl, skɪz'mætɪkəl] ADJ cismático.

schist [ʃɪst] N esquisto *m*.

schizo* ['skɪtsəʊ] N (*Brit*) esquizo* *m*, -a *f*.

schizoid ['skɪtsɔɪd] **1** ADJ esquizoide.
  2 N esquizoide *mf*.

schizophrenia [ˌskɪtsəʊ'friːnɪə] N esquizofrenia *f*.

schizophrenic [ˌskɪtsəʊ'frenɪk] **1** ADJ esquizofrénico.
  2 N esquizofrénico *m*, -a *f*.

schlemiel* [ʃlə'miːl] N (*US*) (*clumsy*) persona *f* desmañada; (*unlucky*) persona *f* desgraciada.

schmaltz* [ʃmɔːlts] N (*US*) sentimentalismo *m*, sensiblería *f*.

schmaltzy* [ʃmɔːltsɪ] ADJ (*US*) sentimental, sensiblero, empalagoso.

schmo* [ʃməʊ] N, PL **schmoes** (*US*) chiquilicuatro* *mf*.

schmooze* [ʃmuːz] VI (*US*) cascar*, estar de cháchara*.

schmuck⁑ [ʃmʌk] N (*US*) imbécil *mf*.

schnapps [ʃnæps] N schnapps *m*.

schnitzel ['ʃnɪtsəl] N escalope *m*; *V also* **wiener ~**.

schnozzle⁑ ['ʃnɒzəl] N (*esp US*) napia⁑ *f*, nariz *f*.

scholar ['skɒlər] N (a) (*pupil*) colegial *m*, -ala *f*, alumno *m*, -a *f*, escolar *mf*.
  (b) (*learned person*) erudito *m*, -a *f*; sabio *m*, -a *f*; **~'s list** (*US Univ*) lista de honor académica **he's a Tirso ~** es especialista en Tirso; **the famous Cervantes ~** el docto cervantista; **I'm no ~** yo apenas sé nada, yo no soy nada intelectual; *ver también* DEAN'S LIST .
  (c) (*scholarship holder*) becario *m*, -a *f*.

scholarly ['skɒləlɪ] ADJ erudito.

scholarship ['skɒləʃɪp] **1** N (a) (*learning*) erudición *f*. (b) (*money award*) beca *f*.
  2 ATTR: **~ holder** becario *m*, -a *f*.

scholastic [skə'læstɪk] **1** ADJ (a) (*relative to school*) escolar; **S~ Aptitude Test** (*US*) examen *m* de acceso a la universidad; **~ books** libros *mpl* escolares; **the ~ year** el año escolar; **the ~ profession** el magisterio. (b) (*relative to scholasticism*) escolástico.
  2 N escolástico *m*.

scholasticism [skə'læstɪsɪzəm] N escolasticismo *m*.

school¹ [skuːl] **1** N (a) (*gen*) escuela *f*; (*primary, specialist, military etc*) escuela *f*; colegio *m*; academia *f*; **the ~s** (*Hist*) las escuelas; **~ of art** escuela *f* de bellas artes; **~ of dancing** escuela *f* de baile, escuela *f* de ballet; **~ of music** academia *f* de música, conservatorio *m*; **to be at**

~ estar en la escuela; **we have to be at ~ by 9** tenemos que estar en la clase para las 9; **you weren't at ~ yesterday** ayer faltaste a la clase; **which ~ were you at?** ¿dónde cursó Vd los estudios (del bachillerato)?; **we were at ~ together** fuimos al mismo instituto (*etc*); **to go to ~** ir a la escuela; **to learn in a tough ~** formarse en una escuela dura.
  (b) (*lessons*) clases *fpl*, clase *f*; curso *m*; **~ starts again in September** el curso empieza de nuevo en septiembre; **there's no ~ today** hoy no hay clase.
  (c) (*Univ*) departamento *m*, facultad *f*; **in the History ~** en el departamento de Historia; **S~ of Arabic Studies** Escuela *f* de Estudios Árabes.
  (d) (*US freq*) universidad *f*; **I went back to ~ at 35** a la edad de 35 volví a la universidad.
  (e) (*of thought etc*) escuela *f*; **Plato and his ~** Platón y su escuela, Platón y sus discípulos; **the Dutch ~** la escuela holandesa; **I am not of that ~** yo no sigo esa opinión; **I am not of the ~ that ...** yo no soy de los que ...; **people of the old ~** gente *f* de la vieja escuela, gente *f* chapada a la antigua.
  2 ATTR: **~-age child** niño *m* en edad escolar; **~ attendance** asistencia *f* a la escuela; **~ attendance officer** funcionario encargado del cumplimiento del reglamento de asistencia; **~ board** comité *m* educativo; **~ bus** bus *m* escolar; **~ dinner** comida *f* escolar; **~ doctor** médico *mf* de escuela; **~ fees** cuota *f* de enseñanza; pensión *f* (escolar); **~ holidays** vacaciones *fpl* escolares; **~ hours** horas *fpl* de escuela; **~ inspector** inspector *m*, -ora *f* de enseñanza; **~ life** vida *f* escolar; **~ lunch** almuerzo *m* proveído por la escuela; **to take ~ lunches** comer (*or* almorzar) en la escuela; **~ meal** comida *f* proveída por la escuela; **~ population** población *f* escolar, (cifra *f* de) escolaridad *f*; **~ report** informe *m* escolar, nota *f* escolar; **in ~ time** durante las horas de escuela; **~ uniform** uniforme *m* escolar; **to go on a ~ visit** (*or* outing *or* trip) **to the zoo** ir de visita al zoo con el colegio; **~ year** año *m* escolar.
  3 VT instruir, enseñar; disciplinar; **to ~ sb in a technique** instruir a uno en una técnica; **to ~ sb to do sth** enseñar a uno a hacer algo; entrenar a uno para que haga algo; **he has been well ~ed** ha sido bien instruido.
  4 VR: **to ~ o.s.** instruirse, enseñarse; disciplinarse; **to ~ o.s. in patience** aprender paciencia, disciplinarse para ser paciente.

school² [skuːl] N (*Fish*) banco *m*, cardumen *m*.

schoolbag ['skuːlbæg] N bolso *m*, cabás *m*.

schoolbook ['skuːlbʊk] N libro *m* escolar.

schoolboy ['skuːlbɔɪ] N colegial *m*, escolar *m*.

schoolchild ['skuːltʃaɪld] N alumno *m*, -a *f*, escolar *mf*.

schooldays ['skuːldeɪz] NPL años *mpl* de colegio.

schoolfellow ['skuːlˌfeləʊ] N compañero *m*, -a *f* de clase.

schoolfriend ['skuːlfrend] N amigo *m*, -a *f* de clase.

schoolgirl ['skuːlgɜːl] **1** N colegiala *f*, escolar *f*.
  2 ATTR: **~ complexion** cutis *m* de colegiala; **~ crush*** amartelamiento *m* de colegiala.

schoolhouse ['skuːlhaʊs] N, PL **schoolhouses** ['skuːlhaʊzɪz] escuela *f*.

schooling ['skuːlɪŋ] N (*teaching etc*) instrucción *f*, enseñanza *f*; disciplina *f*; **compulsory ~ up to 16** escolaridad *f* obligatoria hasta los 16 años; **~ is free** la enseñanza es gratuita; **he had little formal ~** apenas asistió a la escuela.

schoolkid* ['skuːlkɪd] N colegial *m*, colegiala *f*, niño *m* de colegio, niña *f* de colegio.

school-leaver ['skuːlˌliːvər] N joven *mf* que ha terminado los estudios.

school-leaving age [ˌskuːl'liːvɪŋˌeɪdʒ] N fin *m* de la escolaridad obligatoria; **to raise the ~** elevar el fin de la escolaridad obligatoria.

schoolman ['skuːlmən] N, PL **schoolmen** ['skuːlmən] escolástico *m*.

schoolmarm* ['skuːlmɑːm] N (*pej*) institutriz *f*.

schoolmaster ['skuːlˌmɑːstər] N (*secondary school*) profesor *m* (de instituto); (*other*) maestro *m*.

schoolmate ['skuːlmeɪt] N compañero *m*, -a *f* de clase.

schoolmistress ['skuːlˌmɪstrɪs] N (*secondary school*) profesora *f* (de instituto); (*other*) maestra *f*.

schoolroom ['skuːlrʊm] N clase *f*.

schoolteacher ['skuːlˌtiːtʃər] N maestro *m*, -a *f*, profesor *m*, -ora *f*.

schoolteaching ['skuːlˌtiːtʃɪŋ] N enseñanza *f*; pedagogía *f*; magisterio *m*; **to go in for ~** dedicarse al magisterio.

schoolwork ['skuːlwɜːk] N trabajo *m* de clase.

schoolyard ['skuːljɑːd] N patio *m* (de recreo).

schooner ['skuːnər] N goleta *f*.

schwah [ʃwɑː] N vocal *f* neutra.

sciatic [saɪ'ætɪk] ADJ ciático.

sciatica [saɪ'ætɪkə] N ciática *f*.

science ['saɪəns] **1** N ciencia *f*; **to blind sb with ~** impresionar (*or* deslumbrar) a uno citándole muchos datos científicos; lucir sus conocimientos para impresionar a uno.

2 ATTR: ~ **park** zona *f* de ciencias; ~ **teacher** profesor *m*, -ora *f* de ciencias.

science-fiction ['saɪən,fɪkʃən] N ciencia-ficción *f*.

scientific [,saɪən'tɪfɪk] ADJ científico.

scientifically [,saɪən'tɪfɪkəlɪ] ADV científicamente.

scientist ['saɪəntɪst] N científico *m*, -a *f*.

scientologist [,saɪən'tɒlədʒɪst] N cientólogo *m*, -a *f*.

scientology [,saɪən'tɒlədʒɪ] N cienciología *f*, cientología *f*.

sci-fi* ['saɪ'faɪ] N ABBR *of* **science-fiction.**

Scillies ['sɪlɪz] NPL, **Scilly Isles** ['sɪlɪaɪlz] NPL Islas *fpl* Sorlinga.

scimitar ['sɪmɪtər] N cimitarra *f*.

scintillate ['sɪntɪleɪt] VI centellear, chispear; (*fig*) brillar.

scintillating ['sɪntɪleɪtɪŋ] ADJ (*fig*) brillante; ingenioso; de lo más vivo, animadísimo.

scion ['saɪən] N (*Bot, fig*) vástago *m*; ~ **of a noble family** vástago *m* de una familia noble.

Scipio ['skɪpɪəʊ] NM Escipión.

scissors ['sɪzəz] NPL tijeras *fpl*; **a pair of** ~ unas tijeras; ~ **jump** tijera *f*; ~ **kick** chilena *f*, tijereta *f*.

scissors-and-paste [,sɪzəzən'peɪst] ADJ (*Brit*): **a** ~ **job** un refrito.

sclerosis [sklɪ'rəʊsɪs] N esclerosis *f*.

scoff¹ [skɒf] VI mofarse, burlarse (*at* de).

scoff²* [skɒf] **1** N comida *f*; ~ **up!** ¡la comida está servida!
2 VT (*esp Brit*) zamparse, engullir; **she** ~**ed the lot** se lo comió todo.

scoffer ['skɒfər] N mofador *m*, -ora *f*.

scoffing ['skɒfɪŋ] N mofas *fpl*, burlas *fpl*.

scold [skəʊld] **1** N virago *f*.
2 VT reprender, regañar (*for* por).

scolding ['skəʊldɪŋ] N reprensión *f*, regaño *m*; **to give sb a** ~ reprender a uno.

scoliosis [,skəʊlɪ'əʊsɪs] N escoliosis *f*.

scollop ['skɒləp] = **scallop.**

sconce [skɒns] N candelabro *m* de pared.

scone [skɒn] N bollo *m*.

scoop [skuːp] **1** N (**a**) (*instrument*) pala *f*, paleta *f*, cuchara *f*; (*for bailing*) achicador *m*; (*kitchen implement*) paleta *f*; (*carpenter's*) gubia *f*; (*of dredger*) cuchara *f* (de draga), cangilón *m*; (*Med*) espátula *f*.
(**b**) (*profit*) ganancia *f* grande; golpe *m* financiero; (*by newspaper*) primicia *f* informativa, exclusiva *f*, pisotón* *m*, escupe* *m*; **it was a** ~ **for the paper** fue un gran éxito para el periódico; **we brought off the** ~ logramos un triunfo con la exclusiva.
2 VT (**a**) *grain, liquid etc* (*also* **to** ~ **out, to** ~ **up**) sacar con pala, sacar con cuchara; sacar con achicador.
(**b**) **to** ~ **the pool** llevar las diez de últimas; ganar todas las bazas; **we** ~**ed the other papers** nos adelantamos a los demás periódicos con nuestra exclusiva.
♦**scoop out** VT (*hollow*) excavar, ahuecar; hacer; V **scoop 2.**
♦**scoop up** VT *cards etc* recoger rápidamente; V **scoop 2.**

scoot* [skuːt] VI (*also* **to** ~ **away, to** ~ **off**) escabullirse, largarse*; correr precipitadamente; ir en una escapadita; **I must** ~ tengo que marcharme.

scooter ['skuːtər] N (*child's*) patinete *m*; (*adult's*) scooter *m*, escúter *m*, moto *f*, motoneta *f* (*CAm*).

scope [skəʊp] N alcance *m*; envergadura *f*; esfera *f* de acción; ámbito *m*; campo *m*, campo *m* de aplicación; **there is** ~ **for** hay campo para; **a programme of considerable** ~ un programa de gran alcance, un programa de ancha envergadura; **the** ~ **of the new measures must be defined** conviene delimitar el campo de aplicación de las nuevas medidas; **I'm looking for a job with more** ~ busco un puesto que ofrezca más posibilidades; **to give sb full** ~ dar carta blanca a uno; **this should give you plenty of** ~ **for your talents** esto ha de darte grandes posibilidades para explotar tus talentos; **it is outside my** ~ eso está fuera de mi alcance; **it is well within his** ~ está dentro de su alcance, está bien dentro de su competencia.

scorbutic [skɔː'bjuːtɪk] ADJ escorbútico.

scorch [skɔːtʃ] **1** VT chamuscar; (*of sun, wind*) abrasar; *plants etc* quemar, secar; ~ **mark** señal *f* que deja una quemadura; ~**ed earth policy** política *f* de tierra quemada; **to** ~ **the earth** quemar la tierra, destruir todo lo útil; arrasarlo todo.
2 VI (**a**) chamuscarse; quemarse, secarse.
(**b**) **to** ~ **along*** (*Brit*) ir volando, correr a gran velocidad.

scorcher* ['skɔːtʃər] N día *m* de mucho calor.

scorching ['skɔːtʃɪŋ] ADJ *sun etc* abrasador; *day* de mucho calor; *speed* grande, excesivo; **it's** ~ **hot** hace un tremendo calor; **a few** ~ **remarks** algunas observaciones mordaces.

score [skɔːr] **1** N (**a**) (*notch*) muesca *f*, entalladura *f*; señal *f*; (*line*) raya *f*, línea *f*.
(**b**) (*reckoning*) cuenta *f*; **to pay one's** ~ pagar la cuenta; **to pay off old** ~**s** ajustar cuentas viejas; **to settle an old** ~ **with sb** desquitarse con uno; **I have a** ~ **to settle with him** tengo cuentas pendientes con él.

(**c**) (*in exam, test*) puntuación *f*; (*Sport*) tanteo *m*; tantos *mpl*, puntos *mpl* (*etc*); **what's the** ~? ¿cómo estamos?, ¿cómo va esto?; **the** ~ **was Toboso 9, Barataria 1** el resultado fue Toboso 9, Barataria 1; **there was no** ~ **at half-time** en el primer tiempo no hubo goles; **to keep (the)** ~ tantear, llevar la cuenta (*LAm*); **do you know the** ~? ¿sabes cuántos goles han marcado?; **he doesn't know the** ~* no está al tanto, (*pej*) es un despistado, es un pobre hombre; **we all know what the** ~ **is*** todos estamos al cabo de la calle (en cuanto a eso); **to make a** ~ marcar un tanto, marcar un gol (*etc*).
(**d**) (*Mus*) partitura *f*; (*of film etc*) música *f*; **piano** ~ partitura *f* para piano.
(**e**) (*twenty*) veinte, veintena *f*; **a** ~ **of people** veinte personas, una veintena de personas; **3** ~ **years and 10** 70 años; **there were** ~**s of mistakes** había muchísimas erratas, había erratas a granel; **actresses by the** ~ actrices en cantidades.
(**f**) (*ground, reason*) **on the** ~ **of illness** por enfermedad, con motivo de su enfermedad; **on that** ~ a ese respecto, por lo que se refiere a eso; **on what** ~? ¿con qué motivo?
2 VT (**a**) (*notch*) hacer muescas en, hacer cortes en; señalar; (*line*) rayar; **the wall is heavily** ~**d with lines** las paredes están profundamente rayadas; **the plane** ~**d the runway as it landed** al aterrizar el avión hizo rayas en la pista; **to** ~ **sth through** tachar algo.
(**b**) (*in exam, test*) obtener una puntuación ...; obtener una nota...; ser calificado de...; (*Sport*) *goal, points* ganar, apuntar; marcar; *runs* hacer; **to** ~ **70%** obtener una puntuación de 70 por ciento; **to** ~ **well in a test** obtener buena nota en un test; **to** ~ **a goal** marcar un gol; **they went 5 games without scoring a point** en 5 partidos no apuntaron un solo punto; **they had 14 goals** ~**d against them** sus adversarios metieron 14 goles contra ellos; **to** ~ **a great success** marcar un gran triunfo.
(**c**) (*Mus*) instrumentar, orquestar; **it is** ~**d for 5 bassoons** está instrumentado para 5 fagots; **the film was** ~**d by X** la banda musical de la película es de X.
(**d**) (:) *drugs* comprar, obtener.
3 VI (**a**) (*Sport etc*) marcar un tanto, marcar un gol, ganar puntos (*etc*); **to fail to** ~ no marcar ningún gol; **that's where he** ~**s** en eso es donde tiene más ventajas (*over the others* sobre los otros), es en ese aspecto donde sobresale; **to** ~ **with a girl*** ligar con una chica*; **to** ~ **off sb** triunfar a costa de uno, (*with witty remark*) hacer un chiste a costa de uno; **she's easy to** ~ **off** es fácil hacer chistes a costa suya.
(**b**) (*keep* ~) tantear, llevar el tanteo.
(**c**) (*count*) puntuar; **that doesn't** ~ eso no puntúa, eso no vale.
(**d**) (:) comprar droga.
♦**score off, score out, score through** VT tachar.
♦**score up** VT: ~ **it up to me** apúntelo en mi cuenta.

scoreboard ['skɔːbɔːd] N tanteador *m*, marcador *m*.

scorebook ['skɔːbʊk] N cuaderno *m* de tanteo.

scorecard ['skɔːkɑːd] N marcador *m*, tarjeta *f* en que se lleva el tanteo.

scorekeeper ['skɔː,kiːpər] N tanteador *m*, -ora *f*.

scoreless ['skɔːlɪs] ADJ: ~ **draw** empate *m* a cero.

scorer ['skɔːrər] N (*player*) marcador *m*, -ora *f*; (*recorder*) tanteador *m*, -ora *f*; **he is top** ~ **in the league** es el principal goleador en la liga, ha marcado más goles que ningún otro en la liga; **the** ~**s were A and B** marcaron los goles A y B.

scoresheet ['skɔːʃiːt] N acta *f* (*or* hoja *f*) de tanteo.

scoring ['skɔːrɪŋ] N (**a**) (*Sport*) tanteo *m*; **rules for** ~ reglas *fpl* para el tanteo; **a low** ~ **match** un partido de pocos goles (*etc*); **all the** ~ **was in the second half** todos los goles se marcaron en el segundo tiempo.
(**b**) (*cuts*) muescas *fpl*, cortes *mpl*.
(**c**) (*Mus*) orquestación *f*.

scorn ['skɔːn] **1** N desprecio *m*, desdén *m* (*for* de); **to laugh sth to** ~, **to pour** ~ **on sth** ridiculizar algo, poner algo en ridículo.
2 VT despreciar, desdeñar; **to** ~ **to do sth** desdeñarse de hacer algo, no dignarse hacer algo.

scornful ['skɔːnfʊl] ADJ desdeñoso; **to be** ~ **about sth** desdeñar algo.

scornfully ['skɔːnfəlɪ] ADV desdeñosamente, con desprecio.

Scorpio ['skɔːpɪəʊ] N (*Zodiac*) Escorpión *m*.

scorpion ['skɔːpɪən] N escorpión *m*, alacrán *m*.

Scot [skɒt] N escocés *m*, -esa *f*.

Scotch [skɒtʃ] **1** ADJ escocés; ~ **broth** sopa *f* escocesa; ~ **egg** huevo *m* escocés; ~ **mist** llovizna *f*; ~ **tape** (*US*) ® escotch *m* ®, cinta *f* adhesiva, durex *m* (*Mex*); ~ **terrier** terrier *m* escocés; ~ **whisky** = **2** (**a**).
2 N (**a**) whisky *m* (escocés). (**b**) **the** ~ los escoceses.

scotch [skɒtʃ] **1** N calza *f*, cuña *f*.
2 VT *wheel* calzar, engalgar; *rumour* desmentir; *idea* hacer abandonar; *plan etc* frustrar.

scot-free ['skɒt'friː] ADJ impune; **to get off** ~ (*unpunished*) salir impune, quedar sin castigo, (*unhurt*) salir ileso.

Scotland ['skɒtlənd] **1** N Escocia f.
  2 ATTR: ~ **Yard** oficina central de la policía de Londres.
Scots [skɒts] **1** ADJ escocés; ~ **pine** pino m escocés.
  2 N (Ling) escocés m.
Scotsman ['skɒtsmən] N, PL **Scotsmen** ['skɒtsmən] escocés m.
Scotswoman ['skɒts,wumən] N, PL **Scotswomen** ['skɒts,wɪmɪn] escocesa f.
Scotticism ['skɒtɪsɪzəm] N giro m escocés, escocesismo m.
scottie ['skɒtɪ] N terrier m escocés.
Scottish ['skɒtɪʃ] ADJ escocés; ~ **Office** Ministerio m de Asuntos Escoceses.
scoundrel ['skaʊndrəl] N canalla m, sinvergüenza m.
scoundrelly ['skaʊndrəlɪ] ADJ canallesco, vil.
scour¹ ['skaʊəʳ] VT pan etc fregar, estregar, limpiar fregando, restregar (esp LAm); channel limpiar; (Med) purgar.
  ◆**scour out** VT pan etc fregar, estregar, limpiar fregando; channel limpiar; (Med) purgar; **the river had ~ed out part of the bank** el río se había llevado una parte de la orilla.
scour² ['skaʊəʳ] **1** VT area recorrer, registrar; **we are ~ing the countryside for him** recorremos el campo buscándole.
  2 VI: **to ~ about for sth** buscar algo por todas partes.
scourer ['skaʊrəʳ] N (pad) estropajo m; (powder) limpiador m, desgrasador m.
scourge [skɜːdʒ] **1** N azote m; (fig) azote m, flagelo m; plaga f; **the ~ of malaria** el azote del paludismo; **Attila, the ~ of God** Atila, el azote de Dios; **it is the ~ of our times** es la plaga de nuestros tiempos; **God sent it as a ~** Dios lo envió como castigo.
  2 VT azotar, flagelar; (fig) hostigar.
scouring pad ['skaʊrɪŋpæd] N estropajo m.
scouring powder ['skaʊrɪŋpaʊdəʳ] N limpiador m, desgrasador m.
Scouse* [skaʊs] **1** ADJ de Liverpool.
  2 N (a) habitante mf de Liverpool. (b) (Ling) dialecto m de Liverpool.
scout¹ [skaʊt] **1** N (a) (person: Mil) explorador m, escucha m; (Univ) criado m; **boy ~** explorador m.
  (b) (*) (reconnaissance) reconocimiento m; (search) búsqueda f; **to have a ~ round** reconocer el terreno; **we'll have a ~ for it** lo buscaremos.
  2 VT explorar; reconocer el terreno; hacer una batida; **to ~ for sth** buscar algo.
  ◆**scout about, scout around** VI (Mil) ir de reconocimiento, reconocer el terreno.
  ◆**scout round** VI: **to ~ round for sth** buscar algo.
scout² [skaʊt] VT proposal rechazar con desdén; rumour etc desmentir.
scout-car ['skaʊtkɑːʳ] N (Mil) vehículo m de reconocimiento.
scouting ['skaʊtɪŋ] N escutismo m.
scoutmaster ['skaʊt,mɑːstəʳ] N jefe m de sección de exploradores.
scow [skaʊ] N gabarra f.
scowl [skaʊl] **1** N ceño m; **he said with a ~** dijo ceñudo.
  2 VI fruncir el ceño, poner mal gesto; **to ~ at sb** mirar con ceño a uno.
scowling ['skaʊlɪŋ] ADJ ceñudo.
scrabble ['skræbl] VI (in writing) garrapatear; **to ~ about** escarbar; revolverlo todo al buscar algo; **she was scrabbling about in the coal** iba revolviendo el carbón mientras buscaba.
scrag [skræg] **1** N pescuezo m.
  2 VT animal torcer el pescuezo a; (*) person dar una paliza a.
scragginess ['skrægɪnɪs] N flaqueza f.
scraggly ['skræglɪ] ADJ (US) beard descuidado; hair revuelto; plant asalvajado, de aspecto salvaje.
scraggy ['skrægɪ] ADJ flaco, descarnado, escuálido, esquelético.
scram* [skræm] VI largarse*, rajarse (LAm); ~! ¡lárgate*!
scramble ['skræmbl] **1** N (a) (climb) subida f; (outing) excursión f (de montaña, sobre terreno escabroso etc).
  (b) (fight etc) arrebatiña f, pelea f (for por); (race) carrera f (confusa).
  (c) (Sport) carrera f de motocross.
  2 VT (a) eggs revolver, hacer un revoltillo de; **~d eggs** huevos mpl revueltos or pericos (And).
  (b) message cifrar, poner en cifra; (Rad, Telec) desmodular; (TV) codificar.
  (c) aircraft hacer despegar con urgencia (por alarma).
  3 VI (a) **to ~ out** salir de prisa, salir con dificultad, salir a gatas; **to ~ through a hedge** abrirse paso con dificultad a través de un seto; **to ~ up** trepar a, subir gateando a.
  (b) **to ~ for coins** andar a la rebatiña por unas monedas, disputarse unas monedas a gritos, pelearse entre sí para recoger unas monedas.
scrambler ['skræmbləʳ] N (a) (Telec: device) scrambler m, aparato m de interferencia radiofónica. (b) (motorcyclist) motociclista mf de motocross.
scrambling ['skræmblɪŋ] N (Sport) motocross m campo a través; (TV) codificación f.
scran* [skræn] N comida f.

scrap¹ [skræp] **1** N (a) (small piece) pedacito m, fragmento m; ~ **of paper** papel m mojado.
  (b) (fig) pizca f; **a few ~s of news** algunas noticias de escasa importancia; **it's a ~ of comfort** es una migaja de consolación; **I overheard a ~ of conversation** logré escuchar algunas palabras de la conversación; **there is not a ~ of truth in it** eso no tiene ni pizca de verdad; **not a ~!** ¡ni pizca!, ¡en absoluto!
  (c) ~**s** (left-overs) sobras fpl, desperdicios mpl; **the dog feeds on ~s** el perro come las sobras de la mesa.
  (d) (~ iron) chatarra f, hierro m viejo; **to sell a ship for ~** vender un barco para chatarra; **what is it worth as ~?** ¿cuánto vale como chatarra?
  2 ATTR iron etc viejo; ~ **metal** chatarra f, desecho m de metal; ~ **paper** (waste) papeles mpl viejos; (for notes) papel m para apuntes; **its ~ value is £30** como chatarra vale 30 libras.
  3 VT car, ship etc desguazar, reducir a chatarra; vender para chatarra; old equipment etc tirar; plan etc desechar, descartar; **we had to ~ that idea** tuvimos que descartar esa idea.
scrap²* [skræp] **1** N riña f, camorra f, bronca f; **to get into** (or **have**) **a ~ with sb** armar una bronca con uno, pelear-se con uno; **there was a tremendous ~ over the steel bill** se armó una bronca fenomenal sobre el proyecto de ley del acero.
  2 VI reñir, armar una bronca, pelearse; **they were ~ping in the street** se estaban peleando en la calle.
scrapbook ['skræpbʊk] N álbum m de recortes.
scrap dealer ['skræp,diːləʳ] N chatarrero m.
scrape [skreɪp] **1** N (a) (act) raspadura f; **to give sth a ~** raspar algo, limpiar algo raspándolo; **to give one's knee a ~** rasguñarse la rodilla.
  (b) (*) lío* m; apuro m; **to get into a ~** armarse un lío*, meterse en un lío*; **to get sb out of a ~** ayudar a uno a salir de un apuro.
  2 VT raspar, raer; (flesh etc) rasguñar, raer; surface (in decorating) rascar; (~ against) rozar; (Mus, hum) rascar; shoes restregar; **the lorry ~d the wall** el camión rozó la pared; **the ship ~d the bottom** el barco rozó el fondo; **to ~ one's boots** limpiarse las botas; **to ~ one's feet across the floor** arrastrar los pies por el suelo.
  3 VI (a) (make noise) rechinar. (b) (economize) hacer economías; vivir muy justo. (c) **to ~ past** pasar rozando; **we just managed to ~ through the gap** pudimos con dificultad pasar por la abertura sin tocar las paredes.
  ◆**scrape along** VI rozar; (fig) ir tirando; **I can ~ along in Arabic** me defiendo en árabe.
  ◆**scrape away** **1** VT raspar, quitar raspando.
  2 VI: **to ~ away at the violin** ir rascando el violín.
  ◆**scrape by** VI arreglárselas, vivir con lo justo.
  ◆**scrape off** VT = scrape away 1.
  ◆**scrape out** VT contents remover raspando.
  ◆**scrape through** **1** VT: **to ~ through an exam** aprobar un examen por los pelos.
  2 VI: **I just ~d through** aprobé por los pelos.
  ◆**scrape together, scrape up** VT arañar, (fig) reunir poco a poco, rebañar.
scraper ['skreɪpəʳ] N (tool) rascador m, raspador m; (in roadmaking) niveladora f; (at door) limpiabarros m.
scraperboard ['skreɪpəbɔːd] N cartulina entintada sobre la cual se realiza un dibujo rascando la capa de tinta.
scrap-heap ['skræphiːp] N montón m de desechos; **this is for the ~** esto es para tirar; **to throw sth on the ~** desechar algo, descartar algo; **workers are being thrown on the ~** los obreros van al basurero.
scrapie ['skreɪpɪ] N scrapie m.
scrapings ['skreɪpɪŋz] NPL raspaduras fpl; ~ **of the gutter** (fig) hez f de la sociedad.
scrap-iron ['skræp'aɪən] N chatarra f, hierro m viejo.
scrap merchant ['skræp,mɜːtʃənt] N chatarrero m.
scrappy ['skræpɪ] ADJ meal etc pobre, escaso; text etc muy imperfecto, fragmentario; speech inconexo, descosido; knowledge superficial.
scrapyard ['skræpjɑːd] N depósito m de chatarra; (for cars) cementerio m de coches.
scratch ['skrætʃ] **1** N (a) (from claw, on flesh etc) rasguño m, arañazo m; (on surface) raya f, marca f; **it's just a ~** es un rasguño nada más; **the cat gave her a ~** el gato la arañó; **he hadn't a ~ on him** no tuvo la más leve herida; **to have a good ~** rascarse vigorosamente.
  (b) (Sport) línea f de salida; **to be** (or **come**) **up to ~** (thing) estar en buen estado, llenar los requisitos, ser de buena calidad, (person) ser tan bueno como siempre, estar a la altura de las circunstancias; **to start from ~** (with no resources) empezar sin nada, empezar sin ventaja alguna, (from beginning) empezar desde el principio; **we shall have to start from ~ again** tendremos que partir nuevamente de cero, tendremos que comenzar desde el principio otra vez.
  2 ADJ competitor sin ventaja; team improvisado, sin experiencia, reunido de prisa; ~ **meal** comida f improvisada, comistrajo m.

3 VT (a) (*with claw etc*) rasguñar, arañar; (*to relieve itch*) rascar; *hard surface* rayar, marcar; (*of chicken etc*) escarbar; **to ~ a hole in sth** hacer un agujero en algo rascándolo; **she ~ed the dog's ear** le rascó la oreja al perro; **he ~ed his head** se rascó la cabeza; **the glass of this watch cannot be ~ed** el cristal de este reloj no puede rayarse; **we ~ed our names on the wood** grabamos nuestros nombres en la madera; **to ~ sb's eyes out** sacar los ojos a uno con las uñas; **to ~ sb off a list** tachar el nombre de uno de una lista.

(b) (*Sport*) retirar (tachando el nombre de); **that horse has been ~ed** ese caballo ha sido retirado.

(c) (*Comput: erase*) borrar.

4 VI (a) rasguñar; (*to relieve itch*) rascarse; (*of chicken etc*) escarbar; (*pen*) raspear; **the dog ~ed at the door** el perro arañó la puerta.

(b) (*Sport*) retirarse.

◆ **scratch together** VT (*fig*) *money* arañar.

scratch card ['skr[ae]tʃkɑːd] N (*Brit*) papeleta *f* de lotería (*que se rasca*).

scratch file ['skrætʃfaɪl] N fichero *m* de trabajo.

scratchpad ['skrætʃpæd] N (*US*) cuadernillo *m* de apuntes, bloc *m*.

scratch score [ˌskrætʃˈskɔːʳ] N (*Golf*) puntuación *f* par.

scratch tape ['skrætʃteɪp] N cinta *f* reutilizable.

scratchy ['skrætʃɪ] ADJ *pen* que raspea; *tone* áspero; *writing* flojo, irregular.

scrawl [skrɔːl] **1** N garabatos *mpl*, garrapatos *mpl*; **the word finished in a ~** la palabra terminó en un garabato; **I can't read her ~** no soy capaz de leer sus garabatos.

2 VT: **to ~ a note to sb** garabatear una nota para uno; **a wall ~ed all over with rude words** una pared llena de palabras feas.

3 VI garrapatear, hacer garabatos.

scrawny ['skrɔːnɪ] ADJ descarnado, escuálido.

scream [skriːm] **1** N (a) chillido *m*, grito *m* (agudo); **there were ~s of laughter** hubo grandes carcajadas; **to give a ~** chillar, dar un grito.

(b) (*) **it was a ~** fue para morirse de risa*; **he's a ~** es célebre, es impagable.

2 VT *abuse etc* vociferar (*at* contra).

3 VI chillar, gritar; **to ~ with pain** lanzar gritos de dolor; **to ~ with laughter** reírse a carcajadas.

4 VR: **to ~ o.s. hoarse** enronquecer a fuerza de gritar.

◆ **scream out** **1** VT = **scream 2**.

2 VI = **scream 3**.

screamer* ['skriːməʳ] N (*US*) (a) (*headline*) titular *m* muy grande. (b) (*joke*) chiste *m* desternillante; **he's a ~** es la monda*. (c) (*Sport: shot*) trallazo *m*.

screamingly* ['skriːmɪŋlɪ] ADV: **a ~ funny joke** un chiste de lo más divertido; **it was ~ funny** fue para morirse de risa*.

scree [skriː] N cono *m* de desmoronamiento.

screech [skriːtʃ] = **scream** (*in most senses*); VI (*brakes, wheels etc*) chirriar.

screech-owl ['skriːtʃaʊl] N lechuza *f*.

screed [skriːd] N escrito *m* largo y pesado, documento *m* aburrido; **to write ~s** escribir esta vida y la otra.

screen [skriːn] **1** N (a) (*protective*) pantalla *f*; (*folding*) biombo *m*; (*Mil etc*) cortina *f*; (*Phot*) retícula *f*; (*on window*) red *f* metálica; (*sieve*) tamiz *m*, criba *f*.

(b) (*Cine, TV*) pantalla *f*; **the small ~** la pequeña pantalla; **stars of the ~** las estrellas *fpl* de la pantalla, estrellas *fpl* del cine; **to write for the ~** escribir para el cine.

2 ATTR: **~ actor** actor *m* de cine, **~ actress** actriz *f* de cine; **~ editing** corrección *f* en pantalla; **~ memory** memoria *f* de la pantalla; **~play** guión *m* (cinematográfico); **~ rights** derechos *mpl* cinematográficos; **~ test** prueba *f* cinematográfica; **~ writer** guionista *mf*.

3 VT (a) (*hide*) ocultar, esconder; tapar; (*protect*) proteger (con una pantalla), abrigar; **the house is ~ed by trees** la casa se oculta detrás de unos árboles; **in order to ~ our movements from the enemy** para impedir que el enemigo observara nuestros movimientos.

(b) (*sift*) tamizar, pasar por una criba; *suspects etc* investigar; (*select*) seleccionar, pasar por el tamiz; **he was ~ed by Security** la Seguridad le investigó, tuvo que someterse a las investigaciones de la Seguridad.

(c) (*Cine, TV*) *film* proyectar; *novel etc* adaptar para el cine, hacer una película de, hacer una versión cinematográfica de.

(d) (*Med*) hacer una exploración a.

◆ **screen off** VT tapar.

screening ['skriːnɪŋ] N (a) ocultación *f*; protección *f*. (b) (*by security etc*) investigación *f*; (*selection*) selección *f*. (c) (*Cine, TV*) proyección *f*. (d) (*Med*) exploración *f*.

screenwriting ['skriːnraɪtɪŋ] N escritura *f* de guiones.

screw [skruː] **1** N (a) (*Mech*) tornillo *m*; rosca *f* (*also* **~ thread**); (*Sport: of ball*) efecto *m*; **he's got a ~ loose*** le falta un tornillo*; **to put the ~s on sb*** apretar los tornillos a uno.

(b) (*Aer, Naut*) hélice *f*.

(c) (‡: *income*) sueldo *m*; **he gets a good ~** tiene un buen sueldo.

(d) (‡: *warder*) boca‡ *m*.

(e) (⁎⁎) polvo⁎⁎ *m*; **to have a ~** echar un polvo⁎⁎.

2 VT (a) *screw* atornillar; *nut* apretar; *ball* torcer, dar efecto a.

(b) **to ~ money out of sb** arrancar dinero a uno; **to ~ the truth out of sb** arrancar la verdad a uno.

(c) (⁎⁎) joder⁎⁎, tirarse a⁎⁎; **~ the government!** ¡que se joda el gobierno⁎⁎!; **~ the cost, it's got to be done!** ¡no importa el gasto, hay que hacerlo!

(d) (*: *defraud*) timar, estafar.

3 VI (*ball*) torcerse.

◆ **screw around** VI (a) (‡: *waste time*) hacer el vago.

(b) (⁎⁎: *sexually*) ligar*.

◆ **screw down** VT: **to ~ sth down** fijar algo con tornillos.

◆ **screw off** **1** VT desenroscar.

2 VI desenroscarse; **the lid ~s off** la tapadera se desenrosca.

◆ **screw on** **1** VT: **to ~ sth on to a board** fijar algo en un tablón con tornillos; **he's got his head ~ed on** sabe cuántas son cinco.

2 VI: **it ~s on here** se fija aquí con tornillos.

◆ **screw together** VT unir con tornillos.

◆ **screw up** **1** VT (a) *screw* atornillar; *nut* apretar; **V courage**.

(b) *paper* arrugar; **to ~ up one's eyes** entornar los ojos; **to ~ up one's face** arrugar la cara, hacer visajes.

(c) (‡: *spoil*) estropear, arruinar, joder‡; armarse un lío con*; **the experience really ~ed him up** la experiencia le afectó de mala manera.

2 VI: **it will ~ up tighter than that** se puede apretar todavía más.

3 VR: **to ~ o.s. up to do sth** obligarse a hacer algo; cobrar bastante ánimo para hacer algo.

screwball* ['skruːbɔːl] (*US*) **1** ADJ excéntrico, estrafalario.

2 N chalado* *m*, -a *f*, tarado* *m*, -a *f* (*LAm*).

screwdriver ['skruːˌdraɪvəʳ] N destornillador *m*, desarmador *m* (*CAm*); (*: *drink*) destornillador *m*.

screw-top ['skruːtɒp] N tapa *f* de tornillo; **~ jar** pote *m* con tapa de tornillo.

screw-up‡ ['skruːʌp] N lío* *m*, embrollo *m*, cacao* *m*.

screwy* ['skruːɪ] ADJ chiflado*.

scribble ['skrɪbl] **1** N garabatos *mpl*; **I can't read her ~** no soy capaz de leer sus garabatos; **a wall covered in ~s** una pared llena de garabatos.

2 VT: **to ~ one's signature** escribir con mucha prisa su firma; **a word ~d on a wall** una palabra mal escrita en una pared; **a sheet of paper ~d (over) with notes** una hoja de papel emborronada de notas.

3 VI garrapatear, hacer garabatos; escribir con mucha prisa; (*pej, hum*) ser escritor, ser periodista.

◆ **scribble down** VT *notes* escribir de prisa.

scribbler ['skrɪbləʳ] N escritorzuelo *m*, -a *f*, plumífero *m*.

scribbling ['skrɪblɪŋ] N garabato *m*.

scribbling pad ['skrɪblɪŋˌpæd] N borrador *m*, bloc *m*.

scribe [skraɪb] N (*professional letter-writer etc*) escribiente *m*; amanuense *m*; (*of manuscript*) copista *m*; (*Bible*) escriba *m*; (*pej, hum*) escritorzuelo *m*, -a *f*, plumífero *m*.

scrimmage ['skrɪmɪdʒ] N (a) (*fight*) arrebatiña *f*, pelea *f*. (b) (*US Sport*) = **scrum**.

scrimp [skrɪmp] **1** VT escatimar.

2 VI economizar, escatimar, hacer economías; **to ~ and save** hacer grandes economías, vivir muy justo.

scrimpy ['skrɪmpɪ] ADJ *person* tacaño; *supply etc* escaso.

scrimshank* ['skrɪmʃæŋk] VI (*Brit Mil*) racanear*, hacer el rácano*.

scrimshanker* ['skrɪmˌʃæŋkəʳ] N (*Brit Mil*) rácano* *m*.

scrip [skrɪp] N (*Fin*) vale *m*, abonaré *m*.

script [skrɪpt] **1** N (a) (*writing*) escritura *f*, letra *f* (cursiva).

(b) (*manuscript*) manuscrito *m*; (*Scol, Univ*) trabajo *m* escrito, examen *m*; (*Cine*) guión *m*.

2 ATTR: **~ editor** (*Cine, TV*) revisor *m*, -ora *f* de guión; **~ girl** (*Cine*) script *f*, anotadora *f*, secretaria *f* de dirección.

3 VT *film* escribir el guión de; **the film was not well ~ed** la película no tenía un buen guión.

scriptural ['skrɪptʃərəl] ADJ escriturario, bíblico.

Scripture ['skrɪptʃəʳ] N (*also* **Holy ~**) Sagrada Escritura *f*; (*as school subject, lesson*) Historia *f* Sagrada.

scriptwriter ['skrɪptˌraɪtəʳ] N guionista *mf*.

scrofula ['skrɒfjʊlə] N escrófula *f*.

scrofulous ['skrɒfjʊləs] ADJ escrofuloso.

scroll [skrəʊl] **1** N rollo *m*; (*ancient*) rollo *m* de escritura; rollo *m* de pergamino; (*Art, Archit*) voluta *f*; **~ of fame** lista *f* de la fama; **~ key** tecla *f* de desplazamiento; **the Dead Sea ~s** los manuscritos del Mar Muerto.

2 VTI desplazar.

◆ **scroll down** **1** VT desplazar hacia abajo.

2 VI desplazarse hacia abajo.

◆ **scroll up** **1** VT desplazar hacia arriba.

2 VI desplazarse hacia arriba.
scrolling ['skrəʊlɪŋ] N (Comput) corrimiento m.
Scrooge [skruːdʒ] N el avariento típico (personaje del 'Christmas Carol', de Dickens).
scrotum ['skrəʊtəm] N escroto m.
scrounge* [skraʊndʒ] **1** N: **to be on the ~** ir de gorra*, ir sableando*; tratar de adquirir cosas sin pagar; tratar de pedir algo prestado; **to have a ~ round for sth** buscar algo.
2 VT obtener por medio de gorronería*, obtener sin pagar, agenciarse*; **can I ~ a drink from you?** ¿me invitas a un trago?*; **I ~d a ticket** me agencié una entrada; **to ~ sth from sb** gorronear algo a uno*.
3 VI ir de gorra*, gorronear*, sablear*; **to ~ around for sth** buscar algo; **to ~ on sb** vivir a costa de uno.
scrounger* ['skraʊndʒər] N gorrón* m, sablista* mf.
scrub¹ [skrʌb] N (Bot) maleza f, monte m bajo, matas fpl; **~ fire** incendio m de monte bajo.
scrub² [skrʌb] **1** N fregado m, fregadura f; **to give sth a ~** limpiar algo fregándolo; **it needs a hard ~** hay que fregarlo con fuerza.
2 VT **(a)** fregar, restregar; limpiar fregando.
(b) (*: cancel) cancelar, borrar; **let's ~ it** bueno, lo borramos.
3 VI (fig) **let's ~ round it*** pasemos la esponja, borrón y cuenta nueva.
♦ **scrub away** VT dirt quitar restregando; stain quitar frotando.
♦ **scrub down 1** VT room, walls fregar a fondo.
2 VR: **to ~ o.s. down** lavarse a fondo.
♦ **scrub off** VT = **scrub away.**
♦ **scrub out** VT stain limpiar restregando; pan fregar; name tachar.
♦ **scrub up** VI (of surgeon etc) lavarse las manos.
scrubber ['skrʌbər] N **(a)** (also pan-~) estropajo m. **(b)** (‡) tía f fea*; (whore) putilla‡ f.
scrubbing-brush ['skrʌbɪŋˌbrʌʃ] N, (US) **scrub brush** ['skrʌbˌbrʌʃ] N cepillo m de fregar.
scrubby ['skrʌbɪ] ADJ **(a)** person achaparrado, enano. **(b)** land cubierto de maleza.
scrubland ['skrʌblænd] N monte m bajo.
scrubwoman ['skrʌbˌwʊmən] N, PL **scrubwomen** ['skrʌbˌwɪmɪn] (US) fregona f.
scruff¹ [skrʌf] N: **~ of the neck** pescuezo m; **to take sb by the ~ of the neck** agarrar a uno por el pescuezo.
scruff²* [skrʌf] N persona f desaliñada.
scruffily ['skrʌfɪlɪ] ADV: **~ dressed** mal vestido, vestido con desaliño.
scruffiness ['skrʌfɪnɪs] N desaliño m; suciedad f.
scruffy ['skrʌfɪ] ADJ desaliñado, dejado (LAm); sucio, piojoso.
scrum [skrʌm] N, **scrummage** ['skrʌmɪdʒ] N melé f; **loose ~** melé f abierta; **set ~** melé f cerrada.
♦ **scrum down** VI formar la melé cerrada.
scrum-half [ˌskrʌm'hɑːf] N medio m (de) melé.
scrumptious* ['skrʌmpʃəs] ADJ de rechupete*, riquísimo.
scrumpy ['skrʌmpɪ] N (Brit) sidra f muy seca.
scrunch [skrʌntʃ] VT (also **to ~ up**) ronzar.
scruple ['skruːpl] **1** N **(a)** (weight) escrúpulo m (Pharm = 20 granos = 1.296 gramos).
(b) (fig) escrúpulo m; **a person of no ~s** una persona sin escrúpulos; **he is entirely without ~** no tiene conciencia en absoluto; **to have no ~s about ...** no tener escrúpulos acerca de ...; **to make no ~ to + infin** no vacilar en + infin.
2 VI: **not to ~ to + infin** no vacilar en + infin.
scrupulous ['skruːpjʊləs] ADJ escrupuloso (about en cuanto a).
scrupulously ['skruːpjʊləslɪ] ADV escrupulosamente; **a ~ fair decision** una decisión completamente justa; **a ~ clean room** un cuarto completamente limpio.
scrupulousness ['skruːpjʊləsnɪs] N escrupulosidad f.
scrutineer [ˌskruːtɪ'nɪər] N (Brit) escudriñador m, -ora f.
scrutinize ['skruːtɪnaɪz] VT escudriñar, examinar; votes escrutar.
scrutiny ['skruːtɪnɪ] N escrutinio m, examen m; **it does not stand up to ~** no resiste al examen; **to submit sth to a close ~** someter algo a un cuidadoso examen; **under his ~ she felt nervous** bajo su mirada se sintió nerviosa; **to keep sb under close ~** vigilar a uno de cerca.
SCSI N (Comput) ABBR of **small computer systems interface.**
scuba ['skuːbə] ATTR: **~ diving** buceo m con escafandra autónoma; **~ suit** escafandra f autónoma.
scud [skʌd] VI: **to ~ along** correr (llevado por el viento), deslizarse rápidamente; **the clouds were ~ding across the sky** las nubes pasaban rápidamente a través del cielo; **the ship ~ded before the wind** el barco iba viento en popa.
scuff [skʌf] **1** VT shoes desgastar, rayar; feet arrastrar.
2 ATTR: **~ marks** rozaduras fpl.
3 VI andar arrastrando los pies.
scuffle ['skʌfl] **1** N refriega f, pelea f.
2 VI pelearse; **to ~ with the police** pelearse con la policía.

scull [skʌl] **1** N espadilla f.
2 VTI remar (con espadilla).
scullery ['skʌlərɪ] N (esp Brit) trascocina f, fregadero m, office m.
scullery-maid ['skʌlərɪmeɪd] N fregona f.
sculpt [skʌlpt] VT esculpir.
sculptor ['skʌlptər] N escultor m, -ora f.
sculptress ['skʌlptrɪs] N escultora f.
sculptural ['skʌlptʃərəl] ADJ escultural.
sculpture ['skʌlptʃər] **1** N (art, object) escultura f.
2 VT esculpir.
scum [skʌm] N **(a)** (on liquid) espuma f, nata f; (on pond) verdín m; (on metal) escoria f. **(b)** (fig) heces fpl; **the ~ of the earth** las heces de la sociedad; **you ~!** ¡canalla!
scumbag‡ ['skʌmˌbæg] N cabronazo‡ m, puta mierda*‡ mf.
scummy ['skʌmɪ] ADJ (V n) **(a)** lleno de espuma; cubierto de verdín. **(b)** (fig) canallesco, vil.
scunner ['skʌnər] N (esp N Engl, Scot): **to take a ~ to sb/sth** tomarla con uno/algo*, tenerle ojeriza a uno/algo*.
scupper ['skʌpər] **1** N imbornal m.
2 VT (Naut) abrir los imbornales de; (loosely) hundir; (fig: ruin) arruinar, destruir, acabar con; (fig: frustrate) frustrar.
scurf [skɜːf] N caspa f.
scurfy ['skɜːfɪ] ADJ casposo.
scurrility [skʌ'rɪlɪtɪ] N grosería f, procacidad f, chocarrería f; lo difamatorio.
scurrilous ['skʌrɪləs] ADJ grosero, procaz, chocarrero; difamatorio; **a ~ journal** una revista chocarrera; **to make a ~ attack on sb** atacar a uno de modo grosero.
scurrilously ['skʌrɪləslɪ] ADV groseramente, con procacidad; de modo difamatorio.
scurry ['skʌrɪ] VI correr, ir a toda prisa; **to ~ along** ir corriendo; **to ~ for shelter** correr para ponerse al abrigo.
♦ **scurry away, scurry off** VI escabullirse.
scurvy ['skɜːvɪ] **1** ADJ vil, canallesco; ruin.
2 N escorbuto m.
scut [skʌt] N rabito m (esp de conejo).
scutcheon ['skʌtʃən] N = **escutcheon.**
scuttle¹ ['skʌtl] N cubo m, carbonera f.
scuttle² ['skʌtl] **1** VT (Naut) barrenar, dar barreno a, echar a pique.
2 VI (fig) abandonar, renunciar; **a policy of ~** una política de abandonarlo todo.
scuttle³ ['skʌtl] **1** N huida f precipitada, retirada f precipitada.
2 VI: **to ~ along** correr, ir a toda prisa; **we must ~** tenemos que marcharnos.
♦ **scuttle away, scuttle off** VI escabullirse.
scuzzy‡ ['skʌzɪ] ADJ (esp US) cutre*.
Scylla ['sɪlə] NF: **~ and Charybdis** Escila y Caribdis.
scythe [saɪð] **1** N guadaña f.
2 VT guadañar, segar con guadaña.
SD (US Post) ABBR of **South Dakota.**
S.Dak. (US) ABBR of **South Dakota.**
SDI N ABBR of **Strategic Defence Initiative** Iniciativa f de Defensa Estratégica, IDE f.
SDLP N ABBR of **Social Democratic and Labour Party** partido político de Irlanda del Norte.
SDP N (Brit Pol, formerly) ABBR of **Social Democratic Party.**
SDR N ABBR of **special drawing rights** derechos mpl especiales de giro, DEG mpl.
SE ABBR of **south east** sudeste m, also adj, SE.
sea [siː] **1** N **(a)** (not land) mar m (or f in some phrases; V below); **the seven ~s** todos los mares del mundo; **in Spanish ~s** en aguas españolas; **at ~** en el mar; **beyond the ~s** allende el mar; **from beyond the ~s** desde allende el mar; **by ~** por mar, por vía marítima; **by the ~** a la orilla del mar, junto al mar; **out at ~** en alta mar; **to be all at ~** estar despistado, estar en un mar de confusiones; **to be all at ~ about sth** (or **with sth**) no saber nada en absoluto de algo; **on the high ~s** en alta mar; **to follow the ~, to go to ~** hacerse marinero; **to put to ~** hacerse a la mar; **to remain 2 months at ~** estar navegando durante 2 meses, pasar 2 meses en el mar; **to stand out to ~** apartarse de la costa.
(b) (state of the ~) **heavy ~, strong ~** oleada f, marejada f; **to ship a heavy** (or **green**) **~** ser inundado por una ola grande.
(c) (fig) **a ~ of faces** una multitud de caras; **a ~ of corn** un mar de espigas; **a ~ of flame** una vasta extensión de llamas; **a ~ of troubles** un piélago de penas; **~s of blood** ríos mpl de sangre.
2 ATTR de mar; marino, marítimo; **~ air** aire m de mar; **~ battle** batalla f naval; **~ change** (fig) viraje m, cambiazo m; **~ power** potencia f naval; **~ transport** transporte m por mar, transporte m marítimo; **~ trip** viaje m por mar.
sea-anemone ['siːə'nemənɪ] N anémona f de mar.
sea-bass ['siːbæs] N corvina f.
sea-bathing ['siːˌbeɪðɪŋ] N baños mpl de mar.

seabed ['siːbed] N lecho *m* del mar, lecho *m* marino.

seabird ['siːbɜːd] N ave *f* marina.

seaboard ['siːbɔːd] N litoral *m*.

seaboots ['siːbuːts] NPL botas *fpl* de marinero.

seaborne ['siːbɔːn] ADJ transportado por mar.

seborrhoea [ˌsebəˈrɪə] N seborrea *f*.

seabream ['siːbriːm] N besugo *m*.

sea-breeze ['siːˈbriːz] N brisa *f* de mar.

seacoast ['siːkəʊst] N litoral *m*, costa *f* marítima, orilla *f* del mar.

sea-cow ['siːˈkaʊ] N manatí *m*.

sea-crossing ['siːkrɒsɪŋ] N travesía *f*.

sea-dog ['siːdɒg] N lobo *m* de mar.

seafarer ['siːˌfeərəʳ] N marinero *m*.

seafaring ['siːˌfeərɪŋ] **1** ADJ *community* marinero, *life* de marinero.

[2] N marinería *f*; vida *f* de marinero.

sea-fight ['siːfaɪt] N combate *m* naval.

sea-fish ['siːfɪʃ] N pez *m* de mar.

seafood ['siːfuːd] N mariscos *mpl*; **~ restaurant** marisquería *f*.

seafront ['siːfrʌnt] N *(beach)* playa *f*; *(promenade)* paseo *m* marítimo.

seagirt [siːgɜːt] ADJ *(liter)* rodeado por el mar.

seagoing ['siːˌgəʊɪŋ] ADJ de alta mar, de altura.

sea-green ['siːgriːn] ADJ verdemar.

seagull ['siːgʌl] N gaviota *f*.

seahorse ['siːhɔːs] N caballito *m* de mar, hipocampo *m*.

seakale ['siːkeɪl] N col *f* marina.

seal[1] [siːl] **1** N *(Zool)* foca *f*.

[2] ATTR: **~ cull, ~ culling** matanza *f* (selectiva) de focas.

[3] VI: **to go ~ing** ir a cazar focas.

seal[2] [siːl] **1** N sello *m*; precinto *m*; *(Mec)* sello *m*; **under the ~ of secrecy** bajo promesa de guardar el secreto; **under my hand and ~** firmado y sellado por mí; **he gave it his ~ of approval** lo aprobó, le dio su aprobación; **to set** *(or* **put***)* **one's ~ to sth** sellar algo, poner su sello en algo.

[2] VT **(a)** sellar; precintar; cerrar, cerrar herméticamente; *(with wax)* lacrar; *(with lead)* emplomar; **~ed bid** oferta *f* cerrada; **~ed orders** órdenes *fpl* secretas; **to ~ a letter** cerrar una carta; **my lips are ~ed** he prometido no decir nada, soy una tumba.

(b) *(fig) fate etc* decidir; **this ~ed his fate** esto acabó de perderle; **the ship's fate is ~ed** la suerte del barco está decidida.

◆ **seal in** VT encerrar herméticamente.

◆ **seal off** VT obturar; separar, aislar.

◆ **seal up** VT cerrar; *(Comm) packet* precintar.

sea lamprey ['siːˈlæmpreɪ] N lamprea *f* marina.

sea-lane ['siːleɪn] N ruta *f* marítima.

sealant ['siːlənt] N *(device)* sellador *m*, tapador *m*; *(substance)* silicona *f* selladora.

sea-legs ['siːlegz] NPL: **to get one's ~** acostumbrarse a la vida de a bordo.

sealer ['siːləʳ] N *(person)* cazador *m* de focas; *(boat)* barco *m* para la caza de focas.

sea-level ['siːlevl] N nivel *m* del mar; **800 metres above ~** 800 metros sobre el nivel del mar.

sealing ['siːlɪŋ] N caza *f* de focas.

sealing-wax ['siːlɪŋwæks] N lacre *m*.

sealion ['siːlaɪən] N león *m* marino.

sealskin ['siːlskɪn] N piel *f* de foca.

seam [siːm] **1** N **(a)** *(Sew)* costura *f*; *(Tech)* juntura *f*; *(line on skin)* arruga *f*; *(Anat)* sutura *f*; *(Naut)* costura *f* de los tablones; **to burst** *(or* **come apart***)* **at the ~s** descoserse; **we're bursting at the ~s in the office** en la oficina ya no cabemos.

(b) *(Geol)* filón *m*, veta *f*.

[2] VT *(Sew)* coser; *(Tech)* juntar; *face* arrugar.

seaman ['siːmən] N, PL **seamen** ['siːmən] marinero *m*.

seamanlike ['siːmənlaɪk] ADJ de buen marinero.

seamanship ['siːmənʃɪp] N náutica *f*, marinería *f*.

sea-mist ['siːmɪst] N bruma *f*.

seamless ['siːmlɪs] ADJ sin costura.

seamstress ['semstrɪs] N costurera *f*.

seamy ['siːmɪ] ADJ miserable, vil; asqueroso; **the ~ side** *(fig)* el revés de la medalla.

séance ['seɪɑːns] N sesión *f* de espiritismo.

sea-perch ['siːˌpɜːtʃ] N perca *f* de mar.

seapiece ['siːpiːs] N *(Art)* marina *f*.

seaplane ['siːpleɪn] N hidroavión *m*.

seaport ['siːpɔːt] N puerto *m* de mar.

SEAQ ['siːˌæk] N ABBR *of* **Stock Exchange Automated Quotations**.

sear [sɪəʳ] VT *(wither)* secar, marchitar; *(Med)* cauterizar; *(of pain etc)* punzar; *(of sun, wind)* abrasar; *(scorch)* chamuscar, quemar; **it was ~ed into my memory** quedó grabado en la memoria.

◆ **sear through** VT *walls, metal* penetrar a través de.

search [sɜːtʃ] **1** N *(quest)* busca *f*, búsqueda *f* *(for* de); *(of person, of house etc)* registro *m*, cateo *m* *(Mex)*; *(inspection)* reconocimiento *m*; *(Comput)* búsqueda *f*; *(Video)* búsqueda *f* de imagen; **right of ~** derecho *m* de visita; **in ~ of** en busca de; en demanda de; **to do a ~ and replace** hacer una operación de buscar y reemplazar; **to make a ~ in a house** practicar un registro en una casa; **a ~ is being made for the missing child** se está buscando al niño desaparecido; **I am having a ~ made in the archives** estoy organizando un registro de los archivos.

[2] ATTR: **~ and destroy operation** operación *f* de acoso y derribo.

[3] VT *(scan)* examinar, escudriñar; *place* explorar, registrar; buscar en; *conscience* examinar; *house, luggage etc* registrar, catear *(Mex)*; *person* registrar, *(for weapon)* cachear; **we have ~ed the whole library for it** lo hemos buscado en todas partes de la biblioteca, hemos registrado la biblioteca de arriba abajo; **the police are ~ing the woods** la policía está registrando el bosque; **~ me!*** ¡yo qué sé!, ¡ni idea!

[4] VI buscar *(also Comput)*; *(Med)* tentar, sondar; **'~ and replace'** *(Comput)* 'buscar y reemplazar'; **to ~ after, to ~ for** buscar; **to ~ into** investigar.

◆ **search about, search around** VI buscar por todas partes.

◆ **search out** VT: **to ~ sb out** buscar a uno, *(and find)* descubrir a uno tras una búsqueda; **it ~es out the weak spots** identifica los puntos débiles.

searcher ['sɜːtʃəʳ] N buscador *m*, -ora *f*; investigador *m*, -ora *f*.

searching ['sɜːtʃɪŋ] ADJ *look* penetrante; *question* agudo, perspicaz.

searchingly ['sɜːtʃɪŋlɪ] ADV con penetración; agudamente, con perspicacia.

searchlight ['sɜːtʃlaɪt] N reflector *m*, proyector *m*.

search-party ['sɜːtʃˌpɑːtɪ] N pelotón *m* de salvamento.

search-warrant ['sɜːtʃˌwɒrənt] N mandamiento *m* judicial de registro, auto *m* de registro domiciliario.

searing ['sɪərɪŋ] ADJ *heat etc* abrasador; *pain* punzante; *criticism* mordaz, acerbo.

sea-room ['siːrʊm] N espacio *m* para maniobrar.

seascape ['siːskeɪp] N marina *f*.

sea-serpent ['siːˌsɜːpənt] N serpiente *f* de mar.

sea-shanty ['siːˌʃæntɪ] N saloma *f*.

seashell ['siːʃel] N concha *f* (marina), caracol *m* (marino).

seashore ['siːʃɔːʳ] N playa *f*; orilla *f* del mar.

seasick ['siːsɪk] ADJ mareado; **to be ~** estar mareado; **to get ~** marearse.

seasickness ['siːsɪknɪs] N mareo *m*.

seaside ['siːsaɪd] **1** N playa *f*; costa *f*; orilla *f* del mar; **to go to the ~** ir a una playa (a veranear); **to take the family to the ~ for a day** llevar a la familia a pasar un día junto al mar.

[2] ATTR: **~ resort** playa *f*, punto *m* marítimo de veraneo; **we like ~ holidays** nos gusta pasar las vacaciones en la costa, nos gusta veranear junto al mar.

season ['siːzn] **1** N *(of the year)* estación *f*; *(indefinite)* época *f*, período *m*; *(eg social ~, sporting ~)* temporada *f*; *(opportune time)* sazón *f*; **at this ~** en esta época del año; **at that ~** a la sazón; **at the height of the ~** en plena temporada; **for a ~** durante una temporada; **in due ~** a su tiempo; **a word in ~** una palabra a propósito; **in ~ and out of ~** a tiempo y a destiempo; **to be in ~** *(fruit)* estar en sazón; *(animal)* estar en celo; **prices are higher in (the) ~** suben los precios en la temporada alta; **the open ~** *(Hunting)* la temporada de caza, *(Fishing)* la temporada de pesca; **to be out of ~** estar fuera de temporada; **the London ~** la temporada social de Londres; **it was not the ~ for jokes** no era el momento oportuno para chistes; **we did a ~ at La Scala** representamos en la Scala durante una temporada; **did you have a good ~?** ¿qué tal la temporada?

[2] ATTR: **~ ticket** billete *m* de abono; *(Theat)* abono *m* (de temporada); **~ ticket holder** abonado *m*, -a *f*.

[3] VT **(a)** *food* sazonar, condimentar; **a speech ~ed with wit** un discurso salpicado de agudezas.

(b) *wood* curar; *(moderate)* moderar, templar; *person etc* acostumbrar *(to* a); ejercitar *(to* en).

seasonable ['siːznəbl] ADJ *(suitable)* oportuno; *weather etc* propio de la estación.

seasonal ['siːzənl] ADJ *unemployment etc* estacional; *worker* temporal; *dress etc* apropiado a la estación; **it's very ~** varía mucho según la estación.

seasonally ['siːzənlɪ] ADV estacionalmente, según la estación; **~ adjusted** ajustado a la estación.

seasoned ['siːznd] ADJ **(a)** *food* sazonado. **(b)** *timber* curado, maduro; *person* experto, perito; *(Mil)* veterano, aguerrido; **a ~ campaigner** un veterano, una veterana.

seasong ['siːsɒŋ] N canción *f* de marineros; *(shanty)* saloma *f*.

seasoning ['siːznɪŋ] N **(a)** *(Culin)* condimento *m*; *(fig)* salsa *f*, sal *f*; **with a ~ of jokes** con una salpicadura de chistes. **(b)** *(of timber)* cura *f*.

seat [siːt] **1** N **(a)** *(chair)* asiento *m*, silla *f*; *(bench)* banco *m*; *(in counting numbers of ~s in bus, plane etc)* plaza *f*, asiento *m*; *(Theat etc)* localidad *f*, *(as ticket)* localidad *f*, entrada *f*; *(of cycle)* asiento *m*, sillín *m;* **an aircraft with 250 ~s** un avión de 250 plazas; **are there any ~s left?** ¿quedan entradas?; **to have a ~ on the board** ser miembro de la junta directiva; **to keep one's ~** permanecer sentado; **we need 2 ~s on an early flight** necesitamos 2 plazas en el primer vuelo disponible; **to take a ~** sentarse, tomar asiento; **please take your ~s for supper** la cena está servida; **do take a ~** siéntese por favor.

(b) *(Parl)* escaño *m;* **a majority of 50 ~s** una mayoría de 50 (miembros, votos *etc);* **to gain a ~ for the liberals** ganar un escaño para los liberales; **to keep one's ~** retener su escaño; **to win 4 ~s from the nationalists** ganar 4 escaños a los nacionalistas; **to take one's ~** prestar juramento como diputado.

(c) *(of chair)* fondo *m;* *(of trousers)* fondillos *mpl;* *(Anat*)* trasero *m;* **he does it by the ~ of his pants** lo hace por instinto; **to get a bump on one's ~** darse un golpe en el trasero.

(d) *(centre: of government etc)* sede *f;* *(of governor etc)* residencia *f;* *(of nobleman)* casa *f* solariega; *(of infection, fire, trouble)* foco *m;* **~ of learning** centro *m* de estudios.

(e) *(of rider)* **to have a good ~** montar bien, **to keep one's ~** seguir en la silla; **to lose one's ~** caer del caballo.

2 VT **(a)** *person etc* sentar; **to be ~ed** estar sentado; **please be ~ed** siéntese por favor; **where shall we ~ the bishop?** ¿dónde ponemos al obispo?; **to remain ~ed** permanecer sentado, no levantarse; **when you are comfortably ~ed** cuando estén sentados cómodamente.

(b) *(of capacity)* tener asientos para; **the car ~s 5** el coche tiene 5 asientos, caben 5 personas en el coche; **the table ~s 12** hay sitio para 12 en esta mesa; **the theatre ~s 900** el teatro tiene un aforo de 900.

(c) *(Mech)* valve *etc* asentar, ajustar.

3 VR: **to ~ o.s.** sentarse.

seatback ['siːtbæk] N respaldo *m.*

seatbelt ['siːtbelt] N cinturón *m* de seguridad.

-seater ['siːtəʳ] ADJ, N *ending in compounds:* **a 10~ plane** un avión de 10 plazas, un avión con capacidad para 10 plazas.

seating ['siːtɪŋ] **1** N asientos *mpl.*

2 ATTR: **~ accommodation** plazas *fpl,* asientos *mpl;* **~ arrangements, ~ plan** distribución *f* de asientos; **~ capacity** cabida *f,* número *m* de asientos.

SEATO ['siːtəu] N ABBR *of* **Southeast Asia Treaty Organization** Organización *f* del Tratado de Asia Sudeste, OTASE *f.*

sea-trout ['siːtraut] N trucha *f* marina, reo *m.*

sea-urchin ['siːˌɜːtʃɪn] N erizo *m* de mar.

sea-wall ['siːˈwɔːl] N dique *m* marítimo.

seaward ['siːwəd] ADJ de hacia el mar, de la parte del mar; **on the ~ side** en el lado del mar.

seaward(s) ['siːwəd(z)] ADV hacia el mar; **to ~** en la dirección del mar.

sea-water ['siːˌwɔːtəʳ] N agua *f* de mar.

seaway ['siːweɪ] N vía *f* marítima.

seaweed ['siːwiːd] N alga *f* (marina).

seaworthiness ['siːˌwɜːðɪnɪs] N navegabilidad *f.*

seaworthy ['siːˌwɜːðɪ] ADJ marinero, navegable, en condiciones de navegar.

sea-wrack ['siːræk] N algas *fpl* (en la playa).

sebaceous [sɪ'beɪʃəs] ADJ sebáceo.

seborrhoea [ˌsebə'rɪə] N seborrea *f.*

sebum ['siːbəm] N sebo *m.*

SEC N *(US)* ABBR *of* **Securities and Exchange Commission.**

Sec. ABBR *of* **Secretary** Secretario *m,* -a *f,* Srio, Sria.

sec. N ABBR *of* **second(s)** segundo *m,* segundos *mpl;* V **second 3 (a).**

SECAM ['siːˌkæm] *(TV)* N ABBR *of* **séquentiel couleur à mémoire** SECAM *m.*

secant ['siːkənt] N secante *f.*

secateurs [ˌsekə'tɜːz] NPL tijeras *fpl* de podar, podadera *f.*

secede [sɪ'siːd] VI secesionarse, separarse *(from* de).

secession [sɪ'seʃən] N secesión *f,* separación *f.*

secessionist [sɪ'seʃnɪst] **1** ADJ secesionista, separatista.

2 N secesionista *m,* separatista *m.*

secluded [sɪ'kluːdɪd] ADJ retirado, apartado.

seclusion [sɪ'kluːʒən] N retiro *m,* apartamiento *m;* **to live in ~** vivir en el retiro, vivir lejos del tumulto.

second **1** ['sekənd] ADJ segundo; otro; **a ~ Manolete** otro Manolete; **every ~ post** cada dos postes, un poste sí y otro no; **the ~ largest fish** el mayor pez después del primero; **this is the ~ largest fish** este pez es el segundo en tamaño; **this is the ~ largest city of Slobodia** ésta es la segunda ciudad de Eslobodia; **to be ~ to none** no ser inferior a nadie; no ir a la zaga a nadie *(in* en); **A is ~ only to B as a tourist attraction** como atracción turística A vale casi lo que B; **to be ~ in command** ser el segundo después del jefe, *(fig)* ser el segundo de a bordo; **will you have a ~ cup?** ¿quieres otra taza?; **you won't get a ~ chance** no tendrás otra oportunidad; **~ coming** segundo advenimiento *m;* **~ cousin** primo *m* segundo, prima *f*

segunda; **~ floor** *(Brit)* segundo piso *m,* tercer piso *m* *(LAm);* *(US)* primer piso *m,* segundo piso *m* *(LAm);* **~ gear** segunda velocidad *f;* **~ generation** segunda generación *f;* **a ~ generation model** un modelo de segunda generación; **~ half** *(Sport)* segundo tiempo *m;* *(Fin)* segundo semestre *m* (del año económico); **~ home** segunda vivienda *f,* casa *f* de veraneo; **~ language** segunda lengua *f;* **~ lieutenant** *(Mil)* alférez *m,* subteniente *m;* **~ mate, ~ officer** *(Naut)* segundo *m* de a bordo; **~ mortgage** segunda hipoteca *f;* **~ person** segunda persona *f;* **~ sight** doble vista *f;* clarividencia *f.*

2 ADV en segundo lugar; **to come ~** *(in race)* ocupar el segundo puesto; **to go ~, to travel ~** *(Rail)* viajar en segunda.

3 N **(a)** *(time)* segundo *m;* **~ hand** *(of watch)* segundero *m;* **just a ~!** ¡un momento!, ¡momentito! *(LAm);* **it won't take a ~** es cosa de unos momentos; **at that very ~** en ese mismo instante; **I'll be with you in (just) a ~** un momento y estoy contigo; **in a split ~** en un instante, en un abrir y cerrar de ojos; **the operation is timed to a split ~** la operación está concebida con la mayor precisión en cuanto al tiempo.

(b) *(Mus)* segunda *f.*

(c) *(Brit Univ)* segunda clase *f;* *ver también* DEGREE.

(d) *(Boxing)* segundo *m,* cuidador *m;* *(in duel)* padrino *m.*

(e) *(Aut)* segunda velocidad *f;* **in ~** en segunda.

(f) *(in race, exam etc)* **to come in ~** llegar el segundo, ocupar el segundo puesto; **to come a poor ~** resultar ser muy inferior al que gana.

(g) *(Comm)* **~s** artículos *mpl* de segunda calidad, artículos *mpl* con algún desperfecto.

(h) *(Culin*)* **will you have some ~s?** ¿quieres más?, ¿quieres servirte otra porción?

4 VT **(a)** secundar, apoyar; ayudar; *motion* apoyar; **I ~ that!** ¡yo digo lo mismo!

(b) [sɪ'kɒnd] *(Brit)* trasladar temporalmente *(to* a).

secondary ['sekəndərɪ] ADJ secundario; **~ education** segunda enseñanza *f;* **~ explosion** explosión *f* por simpatía; **~ modern school** *(Brit)* centro de educación secundaria enfocado a la formación profesional **~ picket(ing)** piquete *m* secundario; **~ production** producción *f* secundaria; **~ school** instituto *m* (de segunda enseñanza); **~ storage** almacenamiento *m* secundario; *ver también* COMPREHENSIVE SCHOOLS , EDUCATION .

second-best ['sekənd'best] **1** ADJ segundo; (el) mejor después del primero; **our ~ car** nuestro coche número dos.

2 ADV **to come off ~** quedarse en segundo lugar.

3 N expediente *m;* sustituto *m;* **it's a ~** es un sustituto, no es todo lo que hubiéramos deseado, sabemos que es inferior.

second-class ['sekənd'klɑːs] **1** ADJ de segunda clase; inferior, más bien mediocre; **~ citizen** ciudadano *m* de segunda clase; **~ mail, ~ post** correo *m* de segunda clase; **~ ticket** billete *m* de segunda clase.

2 ADV: **to send a letter ~** enviar una carta por correo de segunda clase.

seconder ['sekəndəʳ] N el (la) que apoya una moción; **there was no ~** nadie apoyó la moción.

secondhand ['sekənd'hænd] **1** ADJ de segunda mano, de lance; usado, no nuevo; **~ bookseller** librero *m* de viejo; **~ bookshop** librería *f* de viejo; **~ car** coche *m* de segunda mano; **~ clothes** ropa *f* usada; **~ information** información *f* de segunda mano; **~ shop** compraventa *f.*

2 ADV: **to buy sth ~** comprar algo de segunda mano (*or* usado *etc);* **I heard it only ~** yo lo supe solamente por otro.

second-in-command ['sekəndɪnkə'mɑːnd] N *(Mil)* subjefe *m,* segundo *m* en el mando.

▼ **secondly** ['sekəndlɪ] ADV en segundo lugar.

secondment [sɪ'kɒndmənt] N *(Brit)* traslado *m* temporal *(to* a); **she is on ~ to section B** se ha trasladado temporalmente a la Sección B.

second-rate ['sekənd'reɪt] ADJ de segunda categoría; inferior, más bien mediocre; **some ~ writer** algún escritor de segunda categoría.

second-string [ˌsekənd'strɪŋ] **1** ADJ suplente.

2 N sustituto *m.*

secrecy ['siːkrəsɪ] N secreto *m;* reserva *f,* discreción *f;* **in ~** en secreto; **in strict ~** en el mayor secreto; **to swear sb to ~** hacer que uno jure no revelar algo.

secret ['siːkrɪt] **1** ADJ secreto; *information etc* secreto, confidencial; *(secretive)* reservado; *(hidden)* oculto, encubierto; **~ agent** agente *m* secreto, agente *f* secreta; **~ drawer** secreto *m;* **~ police** policía *f* secreta; **~ service** servicio *m* secreto, servicio *m* de contraespionaje; **to keep sth ~** tener algo secreto, no revelar algo; **it's all highly ~** todo es de lo más secreto.

2 N secreto *m;* **the ~s of nature** los misterios de la naturaleza; **in ~** en secreto; clandestinamente; **to be in on the ~** estar en el secreto; **there's no ~ about it** esto no tiene nada de secreto; **to keep a ~** guardar un secreto, no revelar un secreto; **to let sb into a ~** revelar a uno un secreto; **shall I let you into a ~?** ¿quieres que te revele un secreto?; **to make no ~ of sth** no tratar de tener algo secreto; **he**

made no ~ **that** ... no trató de negar que ...; **to tell sb sth as a ~** contar algo a uno como un secreto, decir algo a uno en confianza.

secretarial [ˌsekrəˈteərɪəl] ADJ de secretaria; ~ **college** colegio m de secretaría; ~ **course** curso m de secretaria; ~ **services** servicios mpl de secretaria; ~ **skills** técnicas fpl de secretaria; ~ **work** trabajo m de secretaria, trabajo m de oficina.

secretariat [ˌsekrəˈteərɪət] N secretaría f, secretariado m.

secretary [ˈsekrətrɪ] ① N secretario m, -a f; **S~ of State** (Brit) Ministro m, -a f (for de); (US) Ministro m, -a f de Asuntos Exteriores.
② ATTR: ~ **pool** (US) servicio m de mecanógrafas.

secretary-general [ˈsekrətrɪˈdʒenərəl] N secretario m, -a f general.

secretaryship [ˈsekrətrɪʃɪp] N secretaría f, secretariado m.

secrete [sɪˈkriːt] VT (a) (hide) esconder, ocultar. (b) (Med) secretar, segregar.

secretion [sɪˈkriːʃən] N (a) escondimiento m, ocultación f. (b) (Med) secreción f, segregación f.

secretive [ˈsiːkrətɪv] ADJ reservado, callado; sigiloso; **to be ~ about sth** hacer un secreto de algo, hacer algo con secreto.

secretively [ˈsiːkrətɪvlɪ] ADV calladamente; sigilosamente.

secretiveness [ˈsiːkrətɪvnɪs] N reserva f; sigilo m.

secretly [ˈsiːkrɪtlɪ] ADV secretamente, en secreto; a escondidas; **to be ~ pleased about sth** alegrarse en el fondo de su corazón de algo.

sect [sekt] N secta f.

sectarian [sekˈteərɪən] ① ADJ sectario.
② N sectario m, -a f.

sectarianism [sekˈteərɪənɪzəm] N sectarismo m.

section [ˈsekʃən] N sección f; parte f, porción f; (of city) barrio m; (of country) región f; (of code, document, law etc) artículo m; (of pipeline, road etc) tramo m; (of opinion) sector m; (in diagram, dissection) sección f, corte m; (of orange etc) gajo m; (~ mark) párrafo m; **passports ~** sección f de pasaportes; **in all ~s of the public** en todos los sectores del público.

◆ **section off** VT cortar, seccionar, vallar.

sectional [ˈsekʃənl] ADJ seccional; relativo a una sección; regional, local; furniture combinado, desmontable, fabricado en secciones.

sectionalism [ˈsekʃənəlɪzəm] N faccionalismo m.

section mark [ˈsekʃənmɑːk] N párrafo m.

sector [ˈsektər] N sector m (also Comput).

sectoral [ˈsektərəl] ADJ (Econ) sectorial.

secular [ˈsekjʊlər] ADJ secular, seglar; ~ **school** escuela f laica.

secularism [ˈsekjʊlərɪzəm] N laicismo m.

secularization [ˌsekjʊlərɑrˈzeɪʃən] N secularización f.

secularize [ˈsekjʊlərɑɪz] VT secularizar.

secure [sɪˈkjʊər] ① ADJ (safe, certain) seguro; (firm) firme, fijo, estable; ~ **in the knowledge that** ... sabiendo perfectamente que ...; **to be ~ against, to be ~ from** estar asegurado contra, estar protegido contra; **to feel ~** sentirse seguro; **to make a door ~** asegurar una puerta.
② VT (a) (make firm) asegurar, fijar, afianzar, cerrar; loan asegurar, garantizar; ~**d creditor** acreedor m con garantía; ~**d loan** préstamo m con garantía.
(b) (obtain) obtener, conseguir; **to ~ the services of sb** obtener los servicios de uno; **I ~d two fine specimens** obtuve dos bellos ejemplares; **he ~d it for £900** lo adquirió por 900 libras.

securely [sɪˈkjʊəlɪ] ADV seguramente; firmemente, fijamente; **it is ~ fastened** está bien sujetado; **we are now ~ established** ahora estamos firmemente establecidos.

security [sɪˈkjʊərɪtɪ] ① N (a) seguridad f; protección f; (against spying etc) seguridad f; (Fin: on loan) fianza f; (on small loan) prenda f; (person) fiador m, -ora f; **to live on** (social) ~ vivir del Seguro; ~ **of tenure** tenencia f asegurada; **up to £100 without ~** hasta 100 libras sin fianza; **to lend money on ~** prestar dinero sobre fianza; **to stand ~ for sb** (Fin) salir fiador de uno, (fig) salir por uno.
(b) **securities** (Fin) títulos mpl, valores mpl, obligaciones fpl.
② ATTR: ~ **agreement** (Fin) acuerdo m de garantía; ~ **blanket** (Psych: of a child) manta f de seguridad; (secrecy) colchón m de seguridad; **S~ Council** Consejo m de Seguridad; ~ **firm** empresa f de seguridad; ~ **forces** fuerzas fpl de seguridad; ~ **guard** guarda m jurado; ~ **leak** filtración f de información secreta; ~ **man** hombre m de seguridad; **securities market** mercado m bursátil; ~ **officer** oficial mf de seguridad; ~ **police** policía f de seguridad; **securities portfolio** cartera f de valores; **a ~ risk** persona f de dudosa lealtad, persona f no enteramente confiable (desde el punto de vista de la seguridad nacional); ~ **services** servicios mpl de seguridad; ~ **system** sistema m de seguridad; ~ **vetting** acreditación f por la Seguridad.

Secy. ABBR of **Secretary** Secretario m, -a f, Srio, Sria.

sedan [sɪˈdæn] N (also ~ **chair**) silla f de manos; (US Aut) sedán m.

sedate [sɪˈdeɪt] ① ADJ tranquilo, sosegado; serio.
② VT (Med) administrar sedantes a, sedar.

sedately [sɪˈdeɪtlɪ] ADV tranquilamente; sosegadamente, seriamente.

sedateness [sɪˈdeɪtnɪs] N tranquilidad f, sosiego m; seriedad f.

sedation [sɪˈdeɪʃən] N sedación f, tratamiento m con calmantes; un-

der ~ bajo calmantes, bajo sedación.

sedative [ˈsedətɪv] ① ADJ sedante, calmante.
② N sedante m, calmante m.

sedentary [ˈsedntrɪ] ADJ sedentario.

sedge [sedʒ] N junco m, juncia f.

sediment [ˈsedɪmənt] N sedimento m (also Geol); poso m.

sedimentary [ˌsedɪˈmentərɪ] ADJ sedimentario.

sedimentation [ˌsedɪmenˈteɪʃən] N sedimentación f.

sedition [səˈdɪʃən] N sedición f.

seditious [səˈdɪʃəs] ADJ sedicioso.

seduce [sɪˈdjuːs] VT seducir; **to ~ sb from his duty** apartar a uno de su deber.

seducer [sɪˈdjuːsər] N seductor m.

seduction [sɪˈdʌkʃən] N seducción f.

seductive [sɪˈdʌktɪv] ADJ seductor.

seductively [sɪˈdʌktɪvlɪ] ADV de modo seductor; en tono seductor.

seductiveness [sɪˈdʌktɪvnɪs] N atractivo m.

seductress [sɪˈdʌktrɪs] N seductora f.

sedulous [ˈsedjʊləs] ADJ asiduo, diligente.

sedulously [ˈsedjʊləslɪ] ADV asiduamente, diligentemente.

▼ **see¹** [siː] (irr. PRET **saw**, PTP **seen**) ① VT (a) (gen) ver; **'~ page 8'** 'véase la página 8'; **he's ~n a lot of the world** ha visto mucho mundo; **she'll not ~ 40 again** los 40 ya no los cumple; **I'll ~ what I can do** veré si puedo hacer algo; **I can ~ to read** veo bastante bien para poder leer; **to ~ sb do sth** ver a uno hacer algo; **I saw him coming** lo vi venir; **he was ~n to fall** se le vio caer; **I saw it done in 1968** lo vi hacer en 1968; **I'll ~ him damned first** antes le veré colgado; **there was not a house to be ~n** no se veía ni una sola casa; **this dress is not fit to be ~n** este vestido no se puede ver; **he's not fit to be ~n in public** no se le puede presentar a los ojos del público.
(b) (accompany) acompañar; **to ~ sb to the door** acompañar a uno a la puerta; **to ~ a girl home** acompañar a una chica a su casa; **may I ~ you home?** ¿puedo acompañarte a casa?; **he was so drunk we had to ~ him to bed** estaba tan borracho que tuvimos que llevarle a la cama.

▼ (c) (understand) comprender, entender, ver; **I don't ~ why** no veo por qué, no comprendo por qué; **I fail to ~ how** no comprendo cómo; **as far as I can ~** según mi modo de entender las cosas; a mi ver; **this is how I ~ it** éste es mi modo de entenderlo, yo lo entiendo así; **the Russians ~ it differently** los rusos lo miran desde otro punto de vista, el criterio de los rusos es distinto; **I don't ~ it** (fig) no creo que sea posible; no veo cómo se podría hacer.
(d) (look, learn, perceive) mirar; observar; percibir; **I saw only too clearly that ...** percibí demasiado bien que ...; **I ~ in the paper that ...** veo en el periódico que ...; **did you ~ that Queen Anne is dead?** ¿has oído que ha muerto la reina Ana?; **I ~ nothing wrong in it** no le encuentro nada indebido; **I don't know what she ~s in him** no sé lo que ella le encuentra.
(e) (ensure) **to ~ (to it) that ...** procurar que + subj, asegurar que + subj; ~ **that he has all he needs** cuida que tenga todo lo que necesita; ~ **that it does not happen again** y que no vuelva a ocurrir; ~ **that you have it ready for Monday** procura tenerlo listo para el lunes; **to ~ that sth is done** procurar que algo se haga.
(f) (visit, frequent) ver, visitar; **to ~ the doctor** consultar al médico; **I want to ~ you about my daughter** quiero hablar con Vd acerca de mi hija; **what did he want to ~ you about?** ¿qué asunto quería discutir contigo?, ¿qué motivo tuvo su visita?; **we don't ~ much of them nowadays** ahora les vemos bastante poco; **we shall be ~ing them for dinner** vamos a cenar con ellos; **to call** (or **go**) **and ~ sb** ir a visitar a uno; **the minister saw the Queen yesterday** el ministro se entrevistó con la Reina ayer; **I'm afraid I can't ~ you tomorrow** lamento no poder verle mañana; **~ you*!, ~ you soon!, ~ you later!, be ~ing you*!** ¡hasta pronto!; **~ you on Sunday!** ¡hasta el domingo!
(g) (imagine) **I don't ~ her as a minister** no me imagino verla como ministra; **I can't ~ myself doing that** no me imagino con capacidad para hacer eso; **I can't really ~ myself being elected** en realidad no creo que me vayan a elegir.
(h) (experience) **he's ~n it all** está de vuelta de todo; **this hat has ~n better days** este sombrero ha conocido mejores días; **I never thought I'd ~ the day when ...** parece imposible que llegara el día en que ...; **she's certainly ~ing life** es seguro que está viendo muchas cosas; **we'll not ~ his like again** no veremos otro como él.
② VI (a) (gen) ver; **let me ~** déjame ver; (fig: also **let's ~**) vamos a ver, veamos; a ver; **I'll go and ~** voy a ver; ~ **for yourself!** ¡véalo Vd!; **now just ~ here!** ¡mire!; **so I ~** lo veo, lo estoy viendo; **as far as the eye can ~** hasta donde alcanza la vista; **from here you can ~ for miles** desde aquí se ve muy lejos; desde aquí se domina un gran panorama; **he was trying to ~** in uno se esforzaba por ver el interior; **we shan't be able to ~ out** no podremos ver el exterior.
(b) (understand) comprender; **I ~** lo veo; **I ~!** ¡ya!, ¡ya caigo!, ¡ya comprendo!; **it's all over, ~?*** se acabó, ¿comprendes?; **he's dead, don't you ~?** está muerto, me entiendes?; **as far as I can ~** a mi ver,

► LANGUAGE IN USE: **see¹: 1c** → 26.2

según mi modo de entender las cosas.

◆ **see about** VT **(a)** (*attend to*) atender a, encargarse de; **I'll ~ about it** lo haré, me encargo de eso; **he came to ~ about our TV** vino a ver nuestra televisión; (*and repair*) vino a reparar nuestra televisión.

(b) (*consider*) **I'll ~ about it** lo veré, lo pensaré; **we'll ~ about that!** ¡es lo que hay que ver!; ¡y cómo!; **we must ~ about getting a new car** tenemos que pensar en comprar un nuevo coche.

◆ **see in** VT *person* hacer entrar, hacer pasar; **to ~ the New Year in** celebrar (*LAm*: festejar) el Año Nuevo.

◆ **see into** VT investigar, examinar.

◆ **see off** VT **(a)** (*say goodbye*) despedirse de; **we went to ~ him off at the station** fuimos a despedirnos de él en la estación.

(b) (*: *send away*) **the policeman saw them off** el policía los acompañó a la puerta; el policía les dijo que se fueran.

(c) (*: *defeat*) vencer, cascar*; deshacerse de; acabar con; **the minister saw the miners off** el ministro acabó con los mineros.

◆ **see out** VT **(a)** *person* acompañar a la puerta.

(b) to ~ a film out quedarse hasta el fin de una película, permanecer sentado hasta que termine una película; **we wondered if he would ~ the month out** nos preguntábamos si viviría hasta el fin del mes.

◆ **see over** VT visitar, hacer la visita de; recorrer.

◆ **see through** VT **(a)** *deal* llevar a cabo; **don't worry, we'll ~ it through** no te preocupes, nosotros lo haremos todo.

(b) to ~ sb through ayudar a uno a salir de un apuro, ayudar a uno en un trance difícil; **£100 should ~ you through** tendrás bastante con 100 libras, con 100 libras estarás bien.

(c) to ~ through sb calar a uno, conocer el juego de uno; **to ~ through a mystery** penetrar un misterio.

◆ **see to** VT atender a; encargarse de; (*repair*) reparar, componer; **he ~s to everything** se encarga de todo, lo hace todo; **the rats saw to that** las ratas se encargaron de eso; **to ~ to it that ...** procurar que + *subj*, asegurar que + *subj*.

see² [siː] N sede *f*; (*of archbishop*) arzobispado *m*; (*of bishop*) obispado *m*; **V holy**.

seed [siːd] **1** N **(a)** (*Bot*; *for sowing*) semilla *f*, simiente *f*; (*within fruit*) pepita *f*; (*grain*) grano *m*; **to go to ~, to run to ~** granar, dar en grana; (*fig*) echarse a perder; ir a menos; **to sow ~s of doubt in sb's mind** sembrar la duda en la mente de uno.

(b) (*sperm*) simiente *f*; (*offspring*) descendencia *f*.

(c) (*of idea etc*) germen *m*.

(d) (*Sport*) preseleccionado *m*, -a *f*.

2 VT **(a)** *land* sembrar (*with* de); (*extract* ~*s from*) despepitar.

(b) (*Sport*) preseleccionar.

3 VI granar, dar en grana; dejar caer semillas.

seedbed ['siːdbed] N semillero *m*.

seedbox ['siːdbɒks] N caja *f* de simientes, semillero *m*.

seedcake ['siːdkeɪk] N torta *f* de alcaravea.

seedcorn ['siːdkɔːn] N trigo *m* de siembra.

seed-drill ['siːddrɪl] N sembradora *f*.

seedily ['siːdɪlɪ] ADV *dress* andrajosamente.

seediness ['siːdɪnɪs] N (*shabbiness*) desaseo *m*; (*illness*) indisposición *f*.

seedless ['siːdlɪs] ADJ sin semillas.

seedling ['siːdlɪŋ] N plántula *f*.

seed merchant ['siːd,mɜːtʃənt] N comerciante *mf* de semillas.

seed pearl ['siːdpɜːl] N aljófar *m*.

seed pod ['siːdpɒd] N vaina *f*.

seed potato ['siːdpə,teɪtəʊ] N, PL **seed potatoes** ['siːdpə,teɪtəʊz] patata *f* (*or* papa *f LAm*) de siembra.

seedsman ['siːdzmən] N, PL **seedsmen** ['siːdzmən] vendedor *m* de semillas.

seed-time ['siːdtaɪm] N siembra *f*.

seedy ['siːdɪ] ADJ **(a)** (*Med*) enfermo, indispuesto; pachucho, ojeroso.

(b) *appearance* desaseado; *clothing* raído; *place* pobre, sórdido.

seeing ['siːɪŋ] **1** N vista *f*, visión *f*; **~ is believing** ver y creer; **a film worth ~** una película que vale la pena de verse.

2 CONJ **~ that ..., ~ as* ...** visto que ..., puesto que ...

seek [siːk] (*irr*: PRET AND PTP **sought**) **1** VT **(a)** buscar; *post* pretender, solicitar; *honour* ambicionar; (*search*) registrar, recorrer buscando; **to ~ death** buscar la muerte; **to ~ shelter** buscar dónde refugiarse; **to ~ advice from sb** pedir consejos a uno; **it is much sought after** está muy cotizado; **the reason is not far to ~** no es difícil indicar la causa; **he has been sought in many countries** se le ha buscado en muchos países.

(b) (*attempt*) **to ~ to +** *infin* intentar + *infin*, procurar + *infin*; esforzarse por + *infin*.

2 VI buscar; **to ~ after, to ~ for** buscar; **to ~ to +** *infin* intentar + *infin*, procurar + *infin*; esforzarse por + *infin*.

◆ **seek out** VT buscar.

seeker ['siːkər] N buscador *m*, -ora *f*.

▼ **seem** [siːm] VI parecer; **so it ~s** así parece; **how does it ~ to you?** ¿qué te parece?; **it ~s that ...** parece que ...; **it does not ~ that ...** no

parece que + *subj*; **he ~s honest** parece honrado; **he ~ed absorbed in ...** parecía estar absorto en ...; **she ~s not to want to go** parece que no quiere ir; **I ~ to have heard that before** me parece que ya me contaron eso antes; **what ~s to be the trouble?** ¿pasa algo?

seeming ['siːmɪŋ] **1** ADJ aparente.

2 N apariencia *f*; **to all ~** según todas las apariencias.

seemingly ['siːmɪŋlɪ] ADV aparentemente, según parece (*or* parecía *etc*); **it is ~ finished** parece que está terminado.

seemliness ['siːmlɪnɪs] N decoro *m*, decencia *f*, corrección *f*.

seemly ['siːmlɪ] ADJ decoroso, decente, correcto.

seen [siːn] PTP *of* **see¹**.

seep [siːp] VI filtrarse, rezumarse.

◆ **seep away** VI escurrirse.

◆ **seep in** VI filtrarse.

◆ **seep out** VI escurrirse.

seepage ['siːpɪdʒ] N filtración *f*.

seer [sɪər] N vidente *mf*, profeta *mf*.

seersucker ['sɪə,sʌkər] N sirsaca *f*.

seesaw ['siːsɔː] **1** N balancín *m*, columpio *m* de tabla, subibaja *m*; (*fig*) vaivén *m*.

2 ADJ *movement* de vaivén, oscilante; **~ motion** movimiento *m* oscilante (*or* de balanceo).

3 VI columpiarse; (*fig*) oscilar.

seethe [siːð] VI hervir; **to ~ with** hervir de, hervir en; **he's seething** está furioso; **to ~ with anger** indignarse muchísimo, estar furioso.

see-through ['siːθruː] ADJ *dress* diáfano, transparente.

segment ['segmənt] N segmento *m*.

segmentation [,segmən'teɪʃən] N segmentación *f*.

segregate ['segrɪgeɪt] VT segregar, separar (*from* de); **to be ~d from** estar separado de.

segregated ['segrɪgeɪtɪd] ADJ segregado, separado.

segregation ['segrɪ'geɪʃən] N segregación *f*, separación *f*; (*esp*) segregación *f* racial.

segregationist [,segrɪ'geɪʃnɪst] N segregacionista *mf*.

Seine [seɪn] N Sena *m*.

seine [seɪn] N jábega *f*.

seismic ['saɪzmɪk] ADJ sísmico.

seismograph ['saɪzməgrɑːf] N sismógrafo *m*.

seismography [saɪz'mɒgrəfɪ] N sismografía *f*.

seismologist [saɪz'mɒlədʒɪst] N sismólogo *m*, -a *f*.

seismology [saɪz'mɒlədʒɪ] N sismología *f*.

seize [siːz] VT (*clutch*) agarrar, asir, coger; (*Jur*) *person* detener, prender, *property* embargar, secuestrar; *contraband etc* incautarse de; *territory etc* apoderarse de; *opportunity* aprovechar sin vacilar; **to ~ sb by the arm** asir a uno por el brazo; **to be ~d with fear** sobrecogerse, ser preso del miedo; **he was ~d with a desire to +** *infin* le entró un súbito deseo de + *infin*.

◆ **seize up** VI (*Mech*) agarrotarse (*also fig*).

◆ **seize (up)on** VT fijarse en; *pretext etc* valerse de.

seizure ['siːʒər] N **(a)** (*V vt*) asimiento *m*; detención *f*; prendimiento *m*; embargo *m*, secuestro *m*; incautación *f*; **the ~ of Slobodia** el acto de apoderarse de Eslobodia. **(b)** (*Med*) ataque *m*; convulsión *f*, crisis *f*; acceso *m*; **to have a ~** sufrir un ataque (*esp* epiléptico).

seldom ['seldəm] ADV rara vez, raramente; **~ if ever** rara vez por no decir jamás.

select [sɪ'lekt] **1** VT escoger, elegir; (*Sport*) seleccionar.

2 ADJ selecto, escogido; exclusivista; *tobacco etc* fino; **~ committee** comité *m* de investigación; **a very ~ neighbourhood** un barrio de muy buen tono; **a ~ group of people** un grupo selecto de personas.

selection [sɪ'lekʃən] N selección *f*; elección *f*; (*Sport*) surtido *m*; **'~s from Rossini'** 'selecciones *fpl* de Rossini'; **'~s from Cervantes'** 'páginas *fpl* escogidas de Cervantes'; **~s for the big race** pronósticos *mpl* para la carrera principal; **one has to make a ~** hay que escoger, hay que tomar unos y dejar otros.

2 ATTR: **~ committee** tribunal *m* de selección, jurado *m*.

selective [sɪ'lektɪv] ADJ selectivo; **one has to be ~** hay que escoger, hay que tomar unos y dejar otros.

selectively [sɪ'lektɪvlɪ] ADV selectivamente.

selectivity [sɪlek'tɪvɪtɪ] N selectividad *f*.

selector [sɪ'lektər] N (*Tech*) selector *m*; (*Sport*) seleccionador *m*, -ora *f*.

selenium [sɪ'liːnɪəm] N selenio *m*.

self [self] **1** REFLEXIVE PRON se (*etc*); (*after prep*) sí mismo (*etc*); (*Comm, hum**) = **myself** *etc*; **a room reserved for wife and ~** una habitación reservada para mi esposa y yo.

2 ADJ (*esp Bot*) unicolor.

3 N, PL **selves** [selvz] uno mismo, una misma; **the ~** el yo; **my better ~** mi mejor parte; **my former ~** mi ser anterior; **one's other ~** su otro yo; **if your good ~ could possibly ...** si Vd tuviera tanta amabilidad como para ...; **my humble ~** este servidor; **is it for ~ or someone else?** ¿es para Vd o para otra persona?; **he's quite his old ~ again** vuelve a ser el mismo de antes, se ha repuesto completamente; **he thinks of nothing but ~** no piensa sino en sí

➤ LANGUAGE IN USE: **seem** → 15.2, 16.3

mismo.

self- [self] PREF auto...; ... de sí mismo.

self-abasement ['selfə'beɪsmənt] N rebajamiento *m* de sí mismo, autodegradación *f*.

self-absorbed ['selfəb'zɔːbd] ADJ absorto en sí mismo; ensimismado.

self-abuse ['selfə'bjuːs] N (*euph*) masturbación *f*.

self-acting ['self'æktɪŋ] ADJ automático.

self-addressed ['selfə'drest] ADJ: ~ **envelope** sobre *m* con el nombre y dirección de uno mismo.

self-adhesive ['selfəd'hiːzɪv] ADJ autoadhesivo.

self-advertisement ['selfəd'vɜːtɪsmənt] N autobombo *m*.

self-aggrandizement [,selfə'grændɪzmənt] N autobombo *m*.

self-analysis [,selfə'næləsɪs] N autoanálisis *m*.

self-apparent ['selfə'pærənt] ADJ evidente, patente.

self-appointed ['selfə'pɔɪntɪd] ADJ que se ha nombrado a sí mismo.

self-appraisal [,selfə'preɪzl] N autovaloración *f*.

self-assembly [selfə'semblɪ] ADJ *furniture etc* automontable.

self-assertion ['selfə'sɜːʃən] N asertividad *f*.

self-assertive ['selfə'sɜːtɪv] ADJ asertivo; que insiste en reafirmarse, que trata de imponerse.

self-assertiveness ['selfə'sɜːtɪvnɪs] N asertividad *f*; insistencia *f* en reafirmarse.

self-assessment ['selfə'sesmənt] N autoevaluación *f*.

self-assurance ['selfə'ʃʊərəns] N confianza *f* en sí mismo.

self-assured ['selfə'ʃʊəd] ADJ seguro de sí mismo.

self-awareness [,selfə'weənɪs] N conocimiento *m* (*or* conciencia *f*) de sí mismo.

self-catering ['self'keɪtərɪŋ] ATTR: ~ **apartment** piso *m* sin pensión; ~ **holiday** vacaciones *fpl* en piso (*or* chalet *or* casita *etc*) con cocina propia.

self-centred, (*US*) **self-centered** ['self'sentəd] ADJ egocéntrico.

self-cleaning [,self'kliːnɪŋ] ADJ *oven etc* autolimpiable.

self-closing [,self'kləʊzɪŋ] ADJ de cierre automático.

self-coloured, (*US*) **self-colored** ['self'kʌləd] ADJ de color uniforme, unicolor.

self-command ['selfkə'mɑːnd] N dominio *m* sobre sí mismo, autodominio *m*.

self-complacent ['selfkəm'pleɪsənt] ADJ satisfecho de sí mismo.

self-composed ['selfkəm'pəʊzd] ADJ ecuánime, dueño de sí mismo, sereno.

self-composure ['selfkəm'pəʊʒər] N ecuanimidad *f*, serenidad *f*.

self-conceit ['selfkən'siːt] N presunción *f*, vanidad *f*, engreimiento *m*.

self-conceited [,selfkən'siːtɪd] ADJ presumido, vanidoso, engreído.

self-confessed [,selfkən'fest] ADJ confeso, autoconfesado.

self-confidence ['self'kɒnfɪdəns] N confianza *f* en sí mismo.

self-confident ['self'kɒnfɪdənt] ADJ seguro de sí mismo, lleno de confianza en sí mismo.

self-congratulation ['selfkən,grætjʊ'leɪʃən] N autofelicitación *f*.

self-conscious ['self'kɒnʃəs] ADJ cohibido, tímido, encogido, inseguro.

self-consciously [,self'kɒnʃəslɪ] ADV cohibidamente, tímidamente.

self-consciousness ['self'kɒnʃəsnɪs] N timidez *f*, encogimiento *m*, inseguridad *f*.

self-contained ['selfkən'teɪnd] ADJ independiente; que tiene sus propios recursos, que no necesita ayuda de afuera; (*Brit*) *flat* independiente, con entrada particular; *person* independiente; reservado, poco comunicativo.

self-contradiction ['self,kɒntrə'dɪkʃən] N contradicción *f* en sí.

self-contradictory ['self,kɒntrə'dɪktərɪ] ADJ que se contradice a sí mismo, que lleva implícita una contradicción.

self-control ['selfkən'trəʊl] N autodominio *m*, dominio *m* sobre sí mismo, control *m* de sí mismo; **to exercise one's** ~ contenerse, dominarse; **to lose one's** ~ perder la calma, ponerse nervioso.

self-controlled ['selfkən'trəʊld] ADJ ecuánime, sereno.

self-correcting [,selfkə'rektɪŋ] ADJ autocorrector.

self-critical [,self'krɪtɪkl] ADJ autocrítico.

self-criticism ['self'krɪtɪsɪzəm] N autocrítica *f*.

self-deception ['selfdɪ'sepʃən] N engaño *m* de sí mismo; **this is mere** ~ son ilusiones, esto es engañarse a sí mismo.

self-defeating ['selfdɪ'fiːtɪŋ] ADJ contraproducente.

self-defence, (*US*) **self-defense** ['selfdɪ'fens] N autodefensa *f*, defensa *f* propia; **to act in** ~ obrar en defensa propia.

self-delusion [,selfdɪ'luːʒən] N autoengaño *m*.

self-denial ['selfdɪ'naɪəl] N abnegación *f*.

self-denying ['selfdɪ'naɪɪŋ] ADJ abnegado; ~ **ordinance** resolución *f* abnegada.

self-destruct [,selfdɪs'trʌkt] VI autodestruirse.

self-destruction ['selfdɪs'trʌkʃən] N suicidio *m*; (*of weapon*) autodestrucción *f*.

self-destructive [,selfdɪs'trʌktɪv] ADJ autodestructivo.

self-determination ['selfdɪ,tɜːmɪ'neɪʃən] N autodeterminación *f*.

self-determined [,selfdɪ'tɜːmɪnd] ADJ autodeterminado, indepen-

diente.

self-discipline ['self'dɪsɪplɪn] N autodisciplina *f*, autodominio *m*.

self-disciplined ['self'dɪsɪplɪnd] ADJ autodisciplinado.

self-doubt [,self'daʊt] N desconfianza *f* de sí mismo.

self-drive [,self'draɪv] ATTR: ~ **hire** (*Brit Aut*) alquiler *m* sin chófer.

self-educated ['self'edjʊketɪd] ADJ autodidacta.

self-effacement ['selfɪ'feɪsmənt] N modestia *f*, humildad *f*.

self-effacing ['selfɪ'feɪsɪŋ] ADJ modesto, humilde.

self-employed ['selfɪm'plɔɪd] ADJ autónomo, que trabaja por cuenta propia.

self-employment ['selfɪm'plɔɪmənt] N trabajo *m* autónomo, trabajo *m* por cuenta propia.

self-esteem ['selfɪs'tiːm] N amor *m* propio, autoestima *f*.

self-evident ['self'evɪdənt] ADJ evidente, patente.

self-examination [,selfɪg,zæmɪ'neɪʃən] N autoexamen *m*, introspección *f*, examen *m* de conciencia.

self-explanatory ['selfɪks'plænɪtərɪ] ADJ que se explica por sí mismo.

self-expression ['selfɪks'preʃən] N autoexpresión *f*; arte *m* de expresarse, expresión *f* de la personalidad de uno.

self-filling ['self'fɪlɪŋ] ADJ de relleno automático.

self-financing [,selffaɪ'nænsɪŋ] ① N autofinanciación *f*, autofinanzamiento *m*.
② ADJ autofinanciado.

self-fulfilling ['selffʊl'fɪlɪŋ] ADJ: ~ **prophecy** profecía *f* que por su propia naturaleza contribuye a cumplirse.

self-fulfilment, (*US*) **self-fulfillment** ['selffʊl'fɪlmənt] N realización *f* de los más íntimos deseos de uno, realización *f* completa de la potencialidad de uno.

self-governing ['self'gʌvənɪŋ] ADJ autónomo.

self-government ['self'gʌvnmənt] N autonomía *f*, autogobierno *m*.

self-help ['self'help] N ayuda *f* propia, autoayuda *f*, esfuerzo *m* personal; ~ **group** grupo *m* de apoyo mutuo.

self-image ['self'ɪmɪdʒ] N autoimagen *f*, imagen *f* del propio ego.

self-importance ['selfɪm'pɔːtəns] N presunción *f*, vanidad *f*, engreimiento *m*.

self-important ['selfɪm'pɔːtənt] ADJ presumido, vanidoso, engreído.

self-imposed ['selfɪm'pəʊzd] ADJ *punishment etc* autoimpuesto, que uno se impone a sí mismo, voluntario.

self-improvement [,selfɪm'pruːvmənt] N autosuperación *f*.

self-induced ['selfɪn'djuːst] ADJ autoinducido.

self-indulgence ['selfɪn'dʌldʒəns] N falta *f* de moderación, excesos *mpl* (en el comer *etc*); egoísmo *m*; comodonería *f*.

self-indulgent ['selfɪn'dʌldʒənt] ADJ inmoderado, que se permite excesos (en el comer *etc*); egoísta; comodón, regalón.

self-inflicted ['selfɪn'flɪktɪd] ADJ *wound* autoinfligido, infligido a sí mismo.

self-interest ['self'ɪntrɪst] N egoísmo *m*; interés *m* propio.

self-interested ['self'ɪntrɪstɪd] ADJ egoísta.

selfish ['selfɪʃ] ADJ egoísta; interesado.

selfishly ['selfɪʃlɪ] ADV con egoísmo, de modo egoísta.

selfishness ['selfɪʃnɪs] N egoísmo *m*.

self-justification [,self,dʒʌstɪfɪ'keɪʃən] N autojustificación *f*.

self-knowledge ['self'nɒlɪdʒ] N conocimiento *m* de sí mismo.

selfless ['selflɪs] ADJ desinteresado.

selflessly ['selflɪslɪ] ADV desinteresadamente.

selflessness ['selflɪsnɪs] N desinterés *m*.

self-loading ['self'ləʊdɪŋ] ADJ autocargador, de autocarga.

self-locking ['self'lɒkɪŋ] ADJ de cierre automático.

self-love ['self'lʌv] N egoísmo *m*; narcisismo *m*; egolatría *f*.

self-made ['self'meɪd] ADJ: ~ **man** hombre *m* que ha llegado a su posición actual por sus propios esfuerzos, hijo *m* de sus propias obras.

self-management ['self'mænɪdʒmənt] N autogestión *f*.

self-mockery ['self'mɒkərɪ] N burla *f* de sí mismo.

self-neglect ['selfnɪ'glekt] N abandono *m* de sí mismo.

self-opinionated ['selfə'pɪnjəneɪtɪd] ADJ terco.

self-perpetuating [,selfpə'petjʊeɪtɪŋ] ADJ autoperpetuable.

self-pity ['self'pɪtɪ] N compasión *f* de sí mismo, lástima *f* de sí mismo, autocompasión *f*.

self-pitying [,self'pɪtɪɪŋ] N autocompasión *f*.

self-pollination ['self,pɒlɪ'neɪʃən] N autopolinización *f*.

self-portrait ['self'pɔːtrɪt] N autorretrato *m*.

self-possessed ['selfpə'zest] ADJ sereno, dueño de sí mismo.

self-possession ['selfpə'zeʃən] N serenidad *f*, dominio *m* de sí mismo, autodominio *m*.

self-praise ['self'preɪz] N autobombo *m*.

self-preservation ['self,prezə'veɪʃən] N autopreservación *f*, propia conservación *f*.

self-proclaimed [,selfprə'kleɪmd] ADJ autoproclamado.

self-propelled ['selfprə'peld] ADJ autopropulsado, automotor (*f* automotriz).

self-raising ['self,reɪzɪŋ] ADJ (*Brit*): ~ **flour** harina *f* con levadura, harina _f_ de fuerza.

self-regard ['selfrɪ'gɑːd] N amor _m_ propio; (_pej_) egoísmo _m_.

self-regulating ['self'regjʊleɪtɪŋ] ADJ de regulación automática.

self-regulation ['self'regjʊleɪʃən] N autorregulación _f_.

self-regulatory [,self'regjʊlətərɪ] ADJ autorregulado.

self-reliance ['selfrɪ'laɪəns] N confianza _f_ en sí mismo; independencia _f_.

self-reliant ['selfrɪ'laɪənt] ADJ seguro de sí mismo; independiente.

self-reproach ['selfrɪ'prəʊtʃ] N remordimiento _m_.

self-respect ['selfrɪs'pekt] N amor _m_ propio, dignidad _f_.

self-respecting ['selfrɪs'pektɪŋ] ADJ que tiene amor propio, consciente de su dignidad personal.

self-restraint ['selfrɪs'treɪnt] N = **self-control**.

self-righteous ['self'raɪtʃəs] ADJ santurrón, farisaico.

self-righteousness [,self'raɪtʃəsnɪs] N santurronería _f_, farisaísmo _m_.

self-rising ['self'raɪzɪŋ] ADJ (_US_): ~ **flour** harina _f_ con levadura.

self-rule [,self'ruːl] N autonomía _f_.

self-sacrifice ['self'sækrɪfaɪs] N (_act_) sacrificio _m_ de sí mismo; (_spirit_) abnegación _f_.

self-sacrificing ['self'sækrɪfaɪsɪŋ] ADJ abnegado.

selfsame ['selfseɪm] ADJ mismo, mismísimo.

self-satisfaction ['self,sætɪs'fækʃən] N satisfacción _f_ de sí mismo; suficiencia _f_.

self-satisfied ['self'sætɪsfaɪd] ADJ satisfecho de sí mismo, pagado de sí mismo; suficiente.

self-sealing ['self'siːlɪŋ] ADJ _tank_ de cierre automático; _envelope_ autoadhesivo, autopegado.

self-seeking ['self'siːkɪŋ] ① ADJ egoísta.

② N egoísmo _m_.

self-service ['self'sɜːvɪs] ADJ: ~ **laundry** lavandería _f_ de autoservicio; ~ **restaurant** autoservicio _m_, self-service _m_, automático _m_ (_SC_).

self-serving ['self'sɜːvɪŋ] ADJ egoísta, interesado.

self-starter ['self'stɑːtər] N (a) (_Aut_) arranque _m_ automático. (b) (_Comm etc_) persona _f_ dinámica.

self-styled ['self'staɪld] ADJ supuesto, sediciente.

self-sufficiency ['selfsə'fɪʃənsɪ] N independencia _f_; (_economic_) autosuficiencia _f_, autarquía _f_; (_of person_) confianza _f_ en sí mismo.

self-sufficient ['selfsə'fɪʃənt] ADJ independiente; (_economically_) autosuficiente; _person_ seguro de sí mismo.

self-supporting ['selfsə'pɔːtɪŋ] ADJ independiente; que tiene sus propios recursos (económicos); que vive de su propio trabajo; **you can marry her when you are** ~ te puedes casar con ella cuando ganes un sueldo adecuado.

self-taught ['self'tɔːt] ADJ autodidacta.

self-test ['self,test] ① N autocomprobación _f_.

② VI autocomprobarse.

self-willed ['self'wɪld] ADJ terco, voluntarioso.

self-winding ['self'waɪndɪŋ] ADJ: ~ **watch** reloj _m_ de cuerda automática.

sell [sel] (_irr_: PRET AND PTP **sold**) ① VT (a) vender (_at_ a, _for_ por); **'car to** ~' 'se vende coche'; **'to be sold'** 'se vende'; **to** ~ **one's life dearly** vender cara la vida; **I was sold this in Valencia** esto me lo vendieron en Valencia; **to** ~ **sb for a slave, to** ~ **sb into slavery** vender a uno como esclavo; _V_ **auction, loss** etc.

(b) (*: _put over_) comunicar, hacer aceptar; **if we can** ~ **coexistence to Ruritania** si podemos hacer aceptar en Ruritania la idea de la coexistencia; **he doesn't manage to** ~ **his personality** no consigue comunicar su personalidad.

(c) (*: _cheat, betray_) vender, traicionar; **sold again!** ¡la estafa de siempre!; **you've been sold** te han dado gato por liebre.

(d) (*) **to be sold on** estar cautivado por; **I'm not exactly sold on the idea** no me estusiasma la idea, estoy lejos de dejarme cautivar por la idea.

② VI (a) venderse (_at_ a, _for_ por); estar de venta; **it** ~**s well** tiene buena venta, se vende bien, tiene mucha demanda; **that line doesn't** ~ ese género no tiene demanda.

(b) (_fig_) ser aceptable; **the idea didn't** ~ la idea no resultó aceptable.

③ VR: **to** ~ **o.s.** venderse; (_fig_) comunicar con el público, comunicar su personalidad.

④ N (a) (*) decepción _f_; engaño _m_, estafa _f_; **what a** ~! ¡cómo nos han decepcionado!; ¡todo ha sido engaño!

(b) (_Comm_) _V_ **hard, soft**.

◆ **sell back** VT: **to** ~ **sth back to sb** revender algo a uno.

◆ **sell off** VT vender (todas las existencias de); liquidar, saldar.

◆ **sell on** VT revender.

◆ **sell out** ① VT (_Comm_) vender (todas las existencias de); liquidar, saldar; **we are sold out of bananas** hemos agotado las existencias de plátanos; **stocks of umbrellas are sold out** las existencias de paraguas están agotadas.

② VI (a) (_Comm_) venderlo todo, vender todas las existencias; realizar.

(b) (_fig_) abandonar, renunciar; (_compromise_) transigir, transar (_LAm_);

to ~ **out to the Slobodians** abandonar y dejar el paso a los eslobodios.

◆ **sell up** VI (_esp Brit_) venderlo todo; vender todas las existencias; realizar.

sell-by date ['selbaɪ,deɪt] N fecha _f_ de caducidad; fecha _f_ límite de venta.

seller ['selər] N (a) (_person who sells_) vendedor _m_, -ora _f_; (_dealer_) comerciante _m_ (_of_ en); ~'s **market** mercado _m_ de demanda, mercado _m_ de signo favorable al vendedor, mercado _m_ de vendedores. (b) **good** ~ artículo _m_ que tiene mucha demanda.

selling ['selɪŋ] ① N venta _f_, el vender; **a career in** ~ una carrera en el márketing.

② ATTR: ~ **point** punto _m_ fuerte, aspecto _m_ interesante; ~ **price** precio _m_ de venta; ~ **rate** (_Fin_) precio _m_ de venta medio.

Sellotape ['seləʊteɪp] ® (_Brit_) ① N Sellotape ® _m_, cinta _f_ adhesiva, scotch _m_ (_LAm_), durex _m_ (_Mex_).

② VT cerrar (_or_ pegar _etc_) con cinta adhesiva.

sellout ['selaʊt] N (a) (_betrayal_) traición _f_; abandono _m_, renuncia _f_. (b) (_Theat, Sport etc_) lleno _m_, venta _f_ total.

seltzer (water) ['seltsər(,wɔːtər)] N agua _f_ de seltz.

selvage, selvedge ['selvɪdʒ] N orillo _m_, borde _m_.

selves [selvz] PL of **self**.

semantic [sɪ'mæntɪk] ADJ semántico.

semantically [sɪ'mæntɪkəlɪ] ADV semánticamente.

semanticist [sɪ'mæntɪsɪst] N semasiólogo _m_, -a _f_, semantista _mf_.

semantics [sɪ'mæntɪks] N semántica _f_.

semaphore ['seməfɔːr] ① N semáforo _m_.

② VT comunicar por semáforo.

semblance ['sembləns] N apariencia _f_; **without a** ~ **of regret** sin mostrar siquiera el remordimiento; **without a** ~ **of fear** sin dar señal alguna de miedo; **to put on a** ~ **of gaiety** procurar parecer alegre, fingir alegría.

seme [siːm] N sema _m_.

semen ['siːmən] N semen _m_.

semester [sɪ'mestər] N (_esp US_) semestre _m_.

semi... ['semɪ] PREF semi...; medio...

semi* ['semɪ] N (a) (_Brit_) casa _f_ semiseparada, chalet _m_ adosado, dúplex _m_. (b) (_US, also_ ~ **trailer**) trailer _m_.

semiautomatic [,semɪ,ɔːtə'mætɪk] ① ADJ semiautomático.

② N arma _f_ semiautomática.

semibasement ['semɪ'beɪsmənt] N semisótano _m_.

semibreve ['semɪbriːv] N (_esp Brit_) semibreve _f_.

semicircle ['semɪ,sɜːkl] N semicírculo _m_.

semicircular ['semɪ'sɜːkjʊlər] ADJ semicircular; _archway_ de medio punto.

semicolon ['semɪ'kəʊlən] N punto _m_ y coma.

semiconductor [,semɪkən'dʌktər] N semiconductor _m_.

semiconscious ['semɪ'kɒnʃəs] ADJ semiconsciente.

semiconsonant ['semɪ'kɒnsənənt] N semiconsonante _f_.

semidarkness ['semɪ'dɑːknɪs] N: **in the** ~ en la casi oscuridad.

semidetached ['semɪdɪ'tætʃt] ADJ: ~ **house** casa _f_ semiseparada, chalet _m_ adosado, dúplex _m_.

semifinal ['semɪ'faɪnl] N semifinal _f_.

semifinalist ['semɪ'faɪnəlɪst] N semifinalista _mf_.

semifinished [,semɪ'fɪnɪʃt] ADJ _product_ semiacabado, semielaborado.

semiliterate [,semɪ'lɪtərɪt] ADJ semialfabetizado.

seminal ['semɪnl] ADJ seminal.

seminar ['semɪnɑːr] N (_Univ: class_) seminario _m_, clase _f_ de discusión; (_group_) grupo _m_ de investigadores; (_conference_) congreso _m_; reunión _f_; (_institute_) instituto _m_.

seminarian [semɪ'nɛərɪən] N seminarista _m_.

seminarist ['semɪnərɪst] N seminarista _m_.

seminary ['semɪnərɪ] N seminario _m_.

semiofficial ['semɪə'fɪʃəl] ADJ semioficial.

semiology [,semɪ'ɒlədʒɪ] N semiología _f_.

semiotic [,semɪ'ɒtɪk] ADJ semiótico.

semiotics [,semɪ'ɒtɪks] N semiótica _f_.

semiprecious ['semɪ,preʃəs] ADJ fino, semiprecioso; ~ **stone** piedra _f_ semipreciosa.

semiquaver ['semɪ,kweɪvər] N (_esp Brit_) semicorchea _f_.

semiskilled ['semɪ'skɪld] ADJ _person_ semiexperto, semicualificado; _work_ para persona semiexperta.

semi-skimmed ['semɪ'skɪmd] ADJ: ~ **milk** leche _f_ semidesnatada.

Semite ['siːmaɪt] N semita _mf_.

Semitic [sɪ'mɪtɪk] ADJ semítico.

semitone ['semɪtəʊn] N semitono _m_.

semitrailer ['semɪ'treɪlər] N (_US_) trailer _m_.

semivowel ['semɪ'vaʊəl] N semivocal _f_.

semolina [,semə'liːnə] N sémola _f_.

sempiternal [,sempɪ'tɜːnl] ADJ sempiterno.

sempstress ['sempstrɪs] N costurera _f_.

SEN N (_Brit_) ABBR of **State Enrolled Nurse**.

Sen. (a) ABBR of **Senior.** (b) (*US Pol*) ABBR of **Senator.** (c) (*US Pol*) ABBR of **Senate.**

senate ['senɪt] N senado *m*; (*Univ*) ≈ claustro *m*; **the S~** (*US*) el Senado; *ver también* CABINET , CONGRESS .

senator ['senɪtəʳ] N senador *m*, -ora *f*; *ver también* CONGRESS .

senatorial [ˌsenə'tɔːrɪəl] ADJ senatorial.

▼ **send** [send] (*irr*: PRET AND PTP **sent**) 1 VT (a) (*gen*) enviar, mandar; despachar; remitir; *message, signal* enviar; *telegram* poner; **the gods ~ it as a punishment** los dioses nos lo envían como castigo; **to ~ a child to school** poner a un niño en la escuela; **in Britain children are sent to school at 5** en Gran Bretaña los niños van a la escuela a los 5 años; **some children are sent to school without breakfast** hay niños que van a la escuela sin desayunar; **I wrote the letter but didn't ~ it** escribí la carta pero no la eché al correo; **to ~ sb for sth** enviar a uno a buscar algo; enviar a uno a comprar algo; **they sent him here to help** le enviaron para que nos ayudara; **the rain sent us indoors** la lluvia nos obligó a buscar abrigo; **please ~ me further details** le ruego enviarme más detalles; **they sent a party to look for him** enviaron un pelotón a buscarle; **the sight sent her running to her mother** viendo esto se echó a correr a su madre.

(b) (*propel*) *ball etc* lanzar; *arrow* enviar, lanzar, arrojar; **he sent everything flying** lo echó todo a rodar; **the blow sent him sprawling** el golpe le hizo caer redondo.

(c) (*with adj*) hacer, volver, poner; **it ~s the wool green** vuelve la lana verde; **it's enough to ~ you barmy:** es para volverse loco; **the speech sent everybody wild** el discurso llenó a todos de entusiasmo.

(d) (:) entusiasmar, llenar de emoción, chiflar*, embelesar; **that tune ~s me** esa melodía me chifla*; **he ~s me** me vuelve loca; **it doesn't ~ me** me trae sin cuidado.

2 VI mandar; **she sent to say that ...** envió un recado diciendo que ..., mandó a decir que ...

◆**send away** 1 VT (a) enviar (fuera).
(b) (*dismiss*) despedir.
(c) *goods* despachar, expedir; enviar.
2 VI: **to ~ away for** pedir (por correo), encargar (por correo).

◆**send back** VT *goods etc* devolver; *person* hacer volver.

◆**send down** VT (a) (hacer) bajar; *diver* enviar.
(b) *price etc* hacer bajar.
(c) (*Brit Univ*) expulsar; *criminal* encarcelar; **they sent him down for 2 years** le condenaron a 2 años de prisión.

◆**send for** VT (a) *doctor etc* llamar; enviar por.
(b) (*order*) pedir, encargar; requerir; mandar buscar, mandar traer.

◆**send forth** VT *smoke etc* emitir, arrojar; *sparks* lanzar; **to ~ sb forth into the world** enviar a uno a vivir en el mundo.

◆**send in** VT (a) *person* hacer entrar; *visitor* hacer pasar; **~ him in!** ¡que pase!; **to ~ in the troops** enviar los soldados.
(b) *bill, name, resignation* presentar.

◆**send off** 1 VT (a) *person* enviar; (*say goodbye to*) despedir.
(b) *goods* despachar, expedir; (*by post*) enviar por correo; echar al correo.
(c) (*Sport*) expulsar.
2 VI: **to ~ off for** pedir, encargar.

◆**send on** VT (*Brit*) *letter* hacer seguir; *application etc* dar curso a; *instructions* dar, transmitir.

◆**send out** 1 VT (a) *person* enviar; (*of room*) mandar fuera.
(b) *invitations etc* mandar.
(c) (*emit*) *smoke etc* arrojar, despedir; *signal* emitir; (*Bot*) *shoot* echar.
2 VI: **to ~ out for** mandar traer, mandar buscar.

◆**send round** VT (a) (*circulate*) hacer circular; pasar; distribuir.
(b) **I'll ~ it round to you** te lo enviaré; **to ~ sb round to the shop** enviar a uno a la tienda.

◆**send up** VT (a) (hacer) subir; *balloon* lanzar; **~ him up!** ¡que suba!
(b) *price etc* hacer subir, aumentar.
(c) (*Brit**: *parody*) parodiar, satirizar.
(d) (*blow up*) volar, destruir.

sender ['sendəʳ] N remitente *mf*; (*Elec*) transmisor *m*.

sending-off ['sendɪŋ,ɒf] N (*Sport*) expulsión *f*.

send-off ['sendɒf] N (*farewell*) despedida *f*; (*start*) inauguración *f*, apertura *f*; principio *m*; **to give a project a good ~** inaugurar felizmente un proyecto, hacer que un proyecto comience felizmente.

send-up* ['sendʌp] N (*Brit*) parodia *f*, sátira *f*.

Seneca ['senɪkə] NM Séneca.

Senegal [ˌsenɪ'gɔːl] N el Senegal.

Senegalese [ˌsenɪgə'liːz] 1 ADJ senegalés.
2 N senegalés *m*, -esa *f*.

senile ['siːnaɪl] ADJ senil; **~ dementia** demencia *f* senil; **to go ~** padecer debilidad senil.

senility [sɪ'nɪlɪti] N senilidad *f*.

senior ['siːnɪəʳ] 1 ADJ (*in age*) mayor (de edad), más viejo; (*on a staff*) más antiguo (*to* que); *position, rank* superior, de categoría superior;

section (*in competition etc*) para mayores; **Joseph Bloggs, ~** Joseph Bloggs, padre; **~ citizen** (*euph*) ciudadano *m*, -a *f* de la tercera edad; **~ high school** (*US*) ≈ instituto *m* de enseñanza media, instituto *m* de BUP (*Sp*); **~ management** altos cargos *mpl* directivos; **~ partner** socio *mf* principal, socio *mf* más antiguo; **S~ Service** marina *f*; **he is ~ to me** (*in age*) tiene más años que yo, es más viejo que yo; (*in rank*) tiene categoría superior a la mía.

2 N mayor *mf*; (*in group*) miembro *mf* más antiguo, -a; decano *m*; (*in company etc*) socio *mf* más antiguo, -a; (*US*) alumno *m*, -a *f* del último año; **he is my ~** (*in age*) tiene más años que yo, es más viejo que yo; (*in rank*) tiene categoría superior a la mía; **he is 2 years my ~, he is my ~ by 2 years** tiene 2 años más que yo, él me lleva 2 años; *ver también* GRADE .

seniority [ˌsiːnɪ'ɒrɪti] N antigüedad *f*.

senna ['senə] N sena *f*.

sensation [sen'seɪʃən] N sensación *f*; **to be a ~, to cause a ~, to create a ~** causar sensación; **it was a ~ in New York** en Nueva York causó sensación; **it's a ~!** ¡es formidable*!, ¡es una bomba!

sensational [sen'seɪʃənl] ADJ sensacional.

sensationalism [sen'seɪʃnəlɪzəm] N sensacionalismo *m*.

sensationalist [sen'seɪʃnəlɪst] ADJ, N sensacionalista *mf*.

sensationalize [sen'seɪʃnəlaɪz] VT sensacionalizar, presentar en términos sensacionales.

sensationally [sen'seɪʃnəlɪ] ADV *report, describe* sensacionalmente; **it was ~ successful** tuvo un éxito sensacional; **it was ~ popular** era increíblemente popular.

sense [sens] 1 N (a) (*bodily*) sentido *m*; **the 5 ~s** los 5 sentidos; **~ of hearing** oído *m*; **~ of sight** vista *f*; **~ of smell** olfato *m*; **~ of taste** gusto *m*; **~ of touch** tacto *m*; **to have a keen ~ of smell** tener buen olfato; **sixth ~** sexto sentido *m*.

(b) **~s** (*right mind*) juicio *m*; **any man in his ~s** cualquier hombre sensato; **to be out of one's ~s** haber perdido el juicio, no estar en sus cabales; **to bring sb to his ~s** obligar a uno a sentar la cabeza, hacer entrar en razón a uno; (*Med*) hacer a uno volver en sí; **to come to one's ~s** sentar la cabeza; (*Med*) volver en sí; **to take leave of one's ~s** perder el juicio; **have you taken leave of your ~s?** ¿se te ha vuelto el juicio?

(c) (*good ~*) buen sentido *m*, juicio *m*; inteligencia *f*; **good ~, sound ~** sentido *m* común; **a man of ~** un hombre sensato, un hombre juicioso; **there is no ~ in that** eso no sirve para nada, eso es inútil; **there is no ~ in** + *ger* es inútil + *infin*; **what is the ~ of** + *ger*? ¿de qué sirve + *infin*?; **I couldn't get any ~ out of him** no pude sacar nada en claro de él; **he had the ~ to call the doctor** tuvo bastante inteligencia como para llamar al médico; **didn't you have the ~ to shout?** ¿no se te ocurrió gritar?; **it doesn't make ~** no tiene sentido; **it doesn't make ~ to me** para mí no tiene sentido; **can you make any ~ of it?** ¿has logrado descifrar el misterio?; **to make sb see ~** hacer que uno entre en razón; **I can't see any ~ in it** no encuentro ningún sentido en eso, no veo para qué vale eso; **to talk ~** hablar con juicio, hablar razonablemente; **now you're talking ~** esto es más razonable.

(d) (*feeling*) sensación *f*; **a ~ of pleasure** una sensación de placer; **the picture conveys a ~ of occasion** el cuadro comunica una sensación de acontecimiento importante; **there was a real ~ of occasion in the stadium** había una atmósfera muy especial en el estadio; **to labour under a ~ of injustice** creer que uno ha sido tratado injustamente.

(e) (*instinct, insight*) sentido *m*; talento *m*, instinto *m*; aptitud *f*; **~ of colour** sentido *m* del color; **~ of direction** sentido *m* de la dirección; **~ of humour** sentido *m* del humor; **she lacks all ~ of humour** no tiene sentido del humor en absoluto; **~ of proportion** sentido *m* de la medida; **business ~** aptitud *f* para los negocios.

(f) (*sentiment*) opinión *f*; **to take the ~ of the meeting** interpretar la opinión colectiva de la reunión.

(g) (*meaning*) sentido *m*, significado *m*; acepción *f*; significación *f*; **in a ~** hasta cierto punto; **in the broad ~** en el sentido amplio; **in the full ~ of that word** en toda la extensión de la palabra; **in the strict ~** en el sentido estricto; **in what ~ do you use the word?** ¿qué significado le das a la palabra?; **in no ~ can it be said that ...** de ninguna manera se puede decir que ...; **it has various ~s** tiene diversas acepciones; **there are ~s in which that may be true** desde algunos puntos de vista eso puede ser cierto; **he's an amateur in the best ~** es un aficionado en el buen sentido de la palabra.

2 VT sentir, percibir, barruntar; **to ~ that ...** percibir que ..., barruntar(se) que ..., darse cuenta de que ..., formarse la impresión de que ...

senseless ['senslɪs] ADJ (a) (*stupid*) estúpido, insensato. (b) (*Med*) sin sentido, sin conocimiento; **to fall ~** caer sin sentido; **to knock sb ~** derribar a uno y dejarle sin sentido.

senselessly ['senslɪslɪ] ADV estúpidamente, insensatamente.

senselessness ['senslɪsnɪs] N insensatez *f*.

sense organ ['sens,ɔːgən] N órgano *m* sensorio.

➤ LANGUAGE IN USE: **send:** 1a → 20.1, 20.3, 21.1, 21.3

sensibility [ˌsensɪ'bɪlɪtɪ] N sensibilidad *f* (*to* a); **sensibilities** delicadeza *f*, sentimientos *mpl* delicados.

sensible ['sensəbl] ADJ **(a)** (*having good sense*) juicioso, sensato; prudente, discreto; inteligente; **he's a ~ sort** es una persona sensata, es una persona de buen criterio; **try to be ~ about it** procura ser razonable.
(b) (*reasonable*) *act, decision etc* prudente; razonable, lógico; *reply, taste* acertado; *clothing etc* práctico; **that's a ~ thing to do** eso me parece razonable; **the ~ course would be to** + *infin* lo más prudente sería + *infin*; **that is very ~ of you** en eso haces muy bien, me parece muy lógico.
(c) (*appreciable*) apreciable, perceptible.
(d) (†: *aware*) **to be ~ of** ser consciente de, darse cuenta de; **I am ~ of the honour you do me** agradezco el honor que se me hace.

sensibleness ['sensəblnɪs] N (*V adj*) **(a)** juicio *m*, sensatez *f*; prudencia *f*, discreción *f*; inteligencia *f*. **(b)** lo razonable, lógica *f*; lo práctico.

sensibly ['sensəblɪ] ADV sensatamente; prudentemente; discretamente; inteligentemente; razonablemente, lógicamente; acertadamente; **she acted very ~** obró muy prudentemente; **he ~ answered that ...** contestó con tino que ...; **try to behave ~** procura ser más formal.

sensitive ['sensɪtɪv] ADJ **(a)** (*impressionable*) impresionable, susceptible, sensible, delicado; (*touchy*) susceptible; (*quick to react*) sensible; **to be ~ to** ser sensible a; **to be ~ about one's hair** preocuparse mucho por su pelo, tener vergüenza de (*LAm*: pena por) su pelo; **you're too ~ about your suit** te preocupas demasiado por el traje.
(b) *skin etc* delicado, sensible; (*Phot*) *paper etc* sensibilizado; *market* volátil.
(c) (*relating to the senses*) sensitivo, sensorio.
(d) (*secret*) secreto, confidencial.

sensitively ['sensɪtɪvlɪ] ADV susceptiblemente, sensiblemente, impresionablemente.

sensitiveness ['sensɪtɪvnɪs] N, **sensitivity** [ˌsensɪ'tɪvɪtɪ] N **(a)** lo impresionable, susceptibilidad *f*. **(b)** delicadeza *f*; sensibilidad *f* (*to* a).

sensitize ['sensɪtaɪz] VT sensibilizar; (*US*) mentalizar, concienciar.

sensitized ['sensɪtaɪzd] ADJ sensibilizado.

sensor ['sensə'] N sensor *m*.

sensory ['sensərɪ] ADJ sensorio, sensorial; **~ deprivation** aislamiento *m* sensorial.

sensual ['sensjʊəl] ADJ sensual.

sensualism ['sensjʊəlɪzəm] N sensualismo *m*.

sensualist ['sensjʊəlɪst] N sensualista *mf*.

sensuality [ˌsensjʊ'ælɪtɪ] N sensualidad *f*.

sensually ['sensjʊəlɪ] ADV sensualmente.

sensuous ['sensjʊəs] ADJ sensual, sensorio.

sensuously ['sensjʊəslɪ] ADV sensualmente, con sensualidad.

sensuousness ['sensjʊəsnɪs] N sensualidad *f*.

sent [sent] PRET and PTP of **send**.

sentence ['sentəns] ☐1 N **(a)** (*Gram*) frase *f*; oración *f*; **he writes very long ~s** escribe frases larguísimas.
(b) (*Jur*) sentencia *f*, fallo *m*; (*with expression of time etc*) condena *f*; **~ of death** (condena *f* a la) pena *f* de muerte; **to be under ~ of death** estar condenado a muerte; **the judge gave him a 6-month ~** el juez le condenó a 6 meses de prisión; **he got a 5-year ~** se le condenó a 5 años de prisión; **to pass ~** pronunciar sentencia, fallar (*on sb* en el proceso de uno); **to serve one's ~** cumplir su condena.
☐2 ATTR **~ structure** estructura *f* de la frase.
☐3 VT condenar (*to* a).

sententious [sen'tenʃəs] ADJ sentencioso.

sententiously [sen'tenʃəslɪ] ADV sentenciosamente.

sententiousness [sen'tenʃəsnɪs] N sentenciosidad *f*, estilo *m* sentencioso.

sentient ['senʃənt] ADJ sensitivo, sensible.

sentiment ['sentɪmənt] N **(a)** (*feeling*) sentimiento *m*; (*opinion*) opinión *f*, sentir *m*; **those are my ~s too** ése es mi criterio también, así lo pienso yo también. **(b)** (*sentimentality*) sentimentalismo *m*, sensiblería *f*; **to wallow in ~** nadar en el sentimentalismo.

sentimental [ˌsentɪ'mentl] ADJ sentimental; (*pej*) sentimental, sensiblero; romántico; **~ value** valor *m* sentimental.

sentimentalism [ˌsentɪ'mentəlɪzəm] N sentimentalismo *m*.

sentimentalist [ˌsentɪ'mentəlɪst] N persona *f* sentimental, romántico *m*, -a *f*.

sentimentality [ˌsentɪmen'tælɪtɪ] N sentimentalismo *m*, sensiblería *f*.

sentimentalize [ˌsentɪ'mentəlaɪz] ☐1 VT sentimentalizar, imbuir de sentimiento.
☐2 VI dejarse llevar por el sentimentalismo.

sentimentally [ˌsentɪ'mentəlɪ] ADV de modo sentimental; *say* en tono sentimental.

sentinel ['sentɪnl] N centinela *m*.

sentry ['sentrɪ] N centinela *m*, guardia *m*; **to be on ~ duty** estar de guardia, hacer guardia.

sentry-box ['sentrɪbɒks] N garita *f* de centinela.

sentry-go ['sentrɪgəʊ] N turno *m* de centinela; **to be on ~** estar de

guardia.

Seoul [səʊl] N Seúl *m*.

Sep. ABBR of **September** se(p)tiembre *m*, sep.

sepal ['sepəl] N sépalo *m*.

separable ['sepərəbl] ADJ separable.

separate ☐1 ['seprɪt] ADJ separado (*from* de); distinto; suelto; independiente (*from* de); **under ~ cover** por separado; **they sleep in ~ rooms** duermen en habitaciones distintas; **could we have ~ bills?** queremos cuentas individuales; **I wrote it on a ~ sheet** lo escribí en otra hoja; **take a ~ sheet for the next part** toma una nueva hoja para lo que viene después; **everybody has a ~ cup** cada uno tiene su taza particular (*or* individual); **they live very ~ lives** viven muy independientes uno de otro; **they went their ~ ways** fueron cada uno por su lado; **to sign a ~ peace** firmar un tratado de paz por separado; **'with ~ toilet'** 'con inodoro separado'; **this is quite ~ from his profession** esto no tiene nada que ver con su profesión.
☐2 ['seprɪt] N **(a)** (*US*) separata *f*. **(b)** **~s** PL (*clothes*) coordinados *mpl*.
☐3 ['sepəreɪt] VT separar (*from* de); dividir, desunir; **to ~ truth from error** separar lo falso de lo verdadero, distinguir entre lo falso y lo verdadero; **he is ~d from his wife** está separado de su mujer.
☐4 ['sepəreɪt] VI separarse; **they ~d in 1990** se separaron en 1990.
♦ **separate out** VT apartar.

separately ['seprɪtlɪ] ADV separadamente; por separado; aparte.

separation [ˌsepə'reɪʃən] N separación *f*.

separatism ['sepərətɪzəm] N separatismo *m*.

separatist ['sepərətɪst] ☐1 ADJ separatista.
☐2 N separatista *mf*.

separator ['sepəreɪtə'] N separador *m*.

Sephardi [se'fɑːdɪ] N, PL **Sephardim** [se'fɑːdɪm] sefardí *mf*.

Sephardic [se'fɑːdɪk] ADJ sefardí.

sepia ['siːpɪə] ☐1 N (*fish*) sepia *f*, jibia *f*; (*colour*) sepia *f*.
☐2 ATTR color sepia.

sepoy ['siːpɔɪ] N cipayo *m*.

sepsis ['sepsɪs] N sepsis *f*.

Sept. ABBR of **September** se(p)tiembre *m*, sep.

September [sep'tembə'] N se(p)tiembre *m*.

septet [sep'tet] N septeto *m*.

septic ['septɪk] ADJ séptico; **~ tank** pozo *m* séptico; **to go ~, to turn ~** infectarse.

septicaemia, (*US*) **septicemia** [ˌseptɪ'siːmɪə] N septicemia *f*.

septuagenarian [ˌseptjʊədʒɪ'neərɪən] ☐1 ADJ septuagenario.
☐2 N septuagenario *m*, -a *f*.

Septuagesima [ˌseptjʊə'dʒesɪmə] N Septuagésima *f*.

Septuagint ['septjʊədʒɪnt] N versión *f* de los setenta.

septuplet [sep'tjʊplɪt] N septillizo *m*, -a *f*.

sepulchral [sɪ'pʌlkrəl] ADJ sepulcral (*also fig*).

sepulchre, (*US*) **sepulcher** ['sepəlkə'] N (*liter*) sepulcro *m*; **whited ~** sepulcro *m* blanqueado.

sequel ['siːkwəl] N consecuencia *f*, resultado *m*; desenlace *m*; (*of story*) continuación *f*; **in the ~** como consecuencia; **it had a tragic ~** tuvo un desenlace trágico, la cosa terminó trágicamente.

sequence ['siːkwəns] N sucesión *f*, orden *m* de sucesión; serie *f*; (*Cards*) serie *f*, escalera *f*; (*Cine*) secuencia *f*; **~ of tenses** concordancia *f* de tiempos; **to arrange things in ~** ordenar cosas secuencialmente.

sequential [sɪ'kwenʃəl] ADJ secuencial; **~ access** acceso *m* secuencial.

sequester [sɪ'kwestə'] VT **(a)** (*isolate, shut up*) aislar. **(b)** (*Jur*) *property* secuestrar, confiscar.

sequestered [sɪ'kwestəd] ADJ **(a)** (*isolated*) aislado, remoto. **(b)** *property* secuestrado, confiscado.

sequestrate [sɪ'kwestreɪt] VT secuestrar.

sequestration [ˌsiːkwes'treɪʃən] N secuestración *f*.

sequin ['siːkwɪn] N lentejuela *f*.

sequinned ['siːkwɪnd] ADJ con lentejuelas, cubierto de lentejuelas.

sequoia [sɪ'kwɔɪə] N secoya *f*.

seraglio [se'rɑːlɪəʊ] N serallo *m*.

seraph ['serəf] N, PL **seraphim** ['serəfɪm] serafín *m*.

seraphic [sə'ræfɪk] ADJ seráfico.

Serb [sɜːb] N serbio *m*, -a *f*.

Serbia ['sɜːbɪə] N Serbia *f*.

Serbian ['sɜːbɪən] ☐1 ADJ serbio.
☐2 N serbio *m*, -a *f*.

Serbo-Croat ['sɜːbəʊ'krəʊæt] N (*Ling*) serbocroata *m*.

Serbo-Croatian ['sɜːbəʊkrəʊ'eɪʃən] ☐1 ADJ serbocroata.
☐2 N serbocroata *mf*.

SERC N (*Brit*) ABBR of **Science and Engineering Research Council**.

sere [sɪə'] ADJ seco, marchito.

serenade [ˌserə'neɪd] ☐1 N serenata *f*.
☐2 VT dar serenata a.

serendipity [ˌserən'dɪpɪtɪ] N serendipia *f*.

serene [sə'riːn] ADJ sereno, tranquilo; **all ~!** ¡sin novedad!

serenely [sə'riːnlɪ] ADV serenamente, tranquilamente; **~ indifferent to**

the noise sin molestarse en lo más mínimo por el ruido; **'No' he said** ~ 'No' dijo con mucha tranquilidad.

serenity [sɪ'renɪtɪ] N serenidad *f*, tranquilidad *f*.

serf [sɜ:f] N siervo *m*, -a *f* (de la gleba).

serfdom ['sɜ:fdəm] N servidumbre *f* (de la gleba); *(fig)* servidumbre *f*.

serge [sɜ:dʒ] N estameña *f*, sarga *f*.

sergeant ['sɑ:dʒənt] N sargento *m*; ~ **at arms** *(Parl)* oficial *m* de orden, ujier *m*; ~ **first class, top** ~ *(US)* primer sargento *m*; **yes,** ~ sí, mi sargento.

sergeant-major ['sɑ:dʒənt'meɪdʒəʳ] N *(Brit)* ≈ brigada *m*.

serial ['sɪərɪəl] [1] ADJ consecutivo, en serie; ~ **access** acceso *m* en serie; ~ **interface** interface *m* en serie; ~ **number** número *m* de serie; ~ **printer** impresora *f* en serie; ~ **rights** derechos *mpl* de publicación por entregas; ~ **story** = 2.
[2] N *(Liter)* serial *m*, novela por entregas; *(TV)* serial *m*, telenovela *f*, serie *f* televisiva.

serialization [ˌsɪərɪəlaɪ'zeɪʃən] N serialización *f*, publicación *f* por entregas.

serialize ['sɪərɪəlaɪz] VT serializar, publicar como serial, publicar por entregas; **it has been ~d in the papers** ha aparecido en una serie de entregas en los periódicos.

serially ['sɪərɪəlɪ] ADV en serie.

seriatim [ˌsɪərɪ'eɪtɪm] ADV en serie.

sericulture [ˌserɪ'kʌltʃəʳ] N sericultura *f*.

series ['sɪəriːz] [1] N, PL **series** serie *f*; sucesión *f*; *(Math)* serie *f*, progresión *f*; *(of lectures etc)* ciclo *m*; **to connect in** ~ *(Elec)* conectar en serie.
[2] ATTR: ~ **producer** *(TV)* productor *m*, -ora *f* de la serie.

series-wound ['sɪəriːz'waʊnd] ADJ arrollado en serie.

▼ **serious** ['sɪərɪəs] ADJ **(a)** *(in earnest)* serio; *character* serio, formal; **are you** ~ **(about it)?, you can't be ~!** ¿lo dices en serio?; **gentlemen, let's be** ~ señores, un poco de formalidad; **he's** ~ **about her** está enamorado de verdad de ella; **when we're alone he gets** ~ cuando estamos a solas se pone muy serio; **to give** ~ **thought to** pensar seriamente en; **the** ~ **student of jazz would say that ...** el que se interese seriamente en el jazz diría que ...
(b) *(causing concern)* grave; de consideración, importante; **the injury is not** ~ la lesión no es de gravedad; **things are getting** ~ las cosas van poniéndose graves.
(c) (*) **that's a** ~ **wine** ése es un vino de verdad; **now, that's** ~ **money!** ¡eso sí que es dinero!

seriously ['sɪərɪəslɪ] ADV **(a)** seriamente; en serio; ~, **though ...** pero en serio ...; **do you say so** ~? ¿me lo dices en serio?; **I can't take Campoamor** ~ no puedo tomar a Campoamor en serio; **he takes himself** ~ se toma muy en serio.
(b) *(dangerously)* gravemente; ~ **wounded** herido de gravedad; **he is** ~ **ill** está grave; **we are** ~ **worried** estamos gravemente preocupados.

seriousness ['sɪərɪəsnɪs] N *(V adj)* **(a)** seriedad *f*; **in all** ~ en serio, seriamente. **(b)** gravedad *f*; **the** ~ **of the situation** la gravedad de la situación.

sermon ['sɜ:mən] N sermón *m* *(also fig)*; **the S~ on the Mount** el Sermón de la Montaña.

sermonize ['sɜ:mənaɪz] VTI sermonear.

serology [sɪ'rɒlədʒɪ] N serología *f*.

seropositive [ˌsɪərəʊ'pɒzɪtɪv] ADJ seropositivo.

serous ['sɪərəs] ADJ seroso.

serpent ['sɜ:pənt] N serpiente *f*, sierpe *f*; *(fig)* serpiente *f*.

serpentine ['sɜ:pəntaɪn] [1] ADJ serpentino.
[2] N *(Min)* serpentina *f*.

SERPS [sɜ:ps] N ABBR of **state earnings-related pension scheme**.

serrated [se'reɪtɪd] ADJ serrado, dentellado.

serration [se'reɪʃən] N borde *m* dentado.

serried ['serɪd] ADJ apretado; **in** ~ **ranks** en filas apretadas.

serum ['sɪərəm] N suero *m*.

servant ['sɜ:vənt] [1] N *(domestic)* criado *m*, -a *f*, muchacho *m*, -a *f* *(LAm)*; *(of company etc)* empleado *m*, -a *f*; *(gen fig)* servidor *m*, -ora *f*; **your devoted** ~, **your humble** ~ un servidor, servidor de Vd; **your obedient** ~ *(in letters)* suyo afmo., att. y s.s. (= atento y seguro servidor); **the** ~**s** *(collectively)* la servidumbre.
[2] ATTR: ~ **girl** criada *f*; **the** ~ **problem** el problema del servicio.

serve [sɜ:v] [1] VT **(a)** *(of person)* servir; estar al servicio de; **to** ~ **the Queen** servir a la Reina; **he ~d his country well** sirvió dignamente a la patria, prestó valiosos servicios a la patria.
(b) *(of thing)* servir; ser útil a; **if my memory ~s me** si mi memoria no me falla, si tengo buena memoria.
(c) *(Rail etc)* **in towns ~d by this line** en las ciudades por donde pasa esta línea; **the villages used to be ~d by buses** antes en estos pueblos había servicio de autobuses.
(d) *(in shop)* *goods* vender; despachar; *customer* servir, atender; *food, meal* servir; **to** ~ **sb with 5 kilos of potatoes** vender 5 kilos de patatas a uno; **to** ~ **sb with hors d'oeuvres** servir los entremeses a uno; **dinner is ~d** la cena está servida; **this recipe ~s 6** esta receta es

suficiente para 6 personas; **are you being ~d, madam?** ¿le están despachando, señora?; **they ~d cod as halibut** hicieron pasar bacalao por halibut.
(e) *(Tennis etc)* sacar.
(f) *writ* entregar.
(g) *(treat)* tratar; **he ~d me very ill** me trató muy mal; **it ~s her right** le está bien empleado, se lo ha buscado; **it ~s you right!** ¡bien merecido lo tienes!; **it ~d him right for being so greedy** lo mereció por ser tan glotón; **it would have ~d them right if he had** bien merecido lo hubieran tenido ellos si lo hubiese hecho él.
(h) *(of stallion etc)* cubrir.
(i) *(work out)* *apprenticeship, time* hacer; *sentence* cumplir; **to** ~ **one's time** *(Mil)* hacer su servicio.
[2] VI **(a)** servir; **to** ~ **10 years in the army** servir 10 años en el ejército; **to** ~ **at table** servir a la mesa; **to** ~ **on the jury** formar parte del jurado, ser miembro del jurado; **to** ~ **on the council** ser concejal; **to** ~ **in parliament** ser diputado; **he is not willing to** ~ no quiere servir, no está dispuesto a ofrecer sus servicios.
(b) **to** ~ **as, to** ~ **for** servir de; servir para; **it will** ~ servirá para el caso; **when the occasion ~s** cuando se presente una ocasión propicia; **it ~s to show that ...** sirve para demostrar que ...
(c) *(Tennis etc)* sacar.
[3] N *(Tennis etc)* saque *m*; **whose** ~ **is it?** ¿quién saca?; **he has a strong** ~ saca muy fuerte.

◆ **serve out** VT **(a)** *meal* servir; *rations etc* repartir, distribuir.
(b) **to** ~ **sb out** ajustar cuentas con uno; **I'll** ~ **you out for this!** ¡me las pagarás!
(c) *period, time* hacer, cumplir.

◆ **serve up** VT *food* servir; presentar; **he ~d that up as an excuse*** eso lo ofreció como excusa.

server ['sɜ:vəʳ] N **(a)** *(Tennis)* saque *mf*; *(Eccl)* acólito *m*. **(b)** *(US)* camarero *m*, -a *f*. **(c)** *(for fish etc)* pala *f*.

service ['sɜ:vɪs] [1] N **(a)** *(gen)* servicio *m*; **he has 10 years'** ~ lleva 10 años en el servicio, sirve desde hace 10 años; **he saw long** ~ sirvió durante muchos años; **to see** ~ **as** prestar servicio de; **is** ~ **included in the bill?** ¿se incluye el servicio en la cuenta?; **15%** ~ **is included** se incluye un 15 por ciento de servicio.
(b) *(branch, department etc)* servicio *m*; **the S~** *(Mil)* el ejército; *(Aer)* la aviación; *(Naut)* la marina; **the (three) S~s** las fuerzas armadas, los tres ejércitos; **'all main ~s'** 'todos servicios'; **the train** ~ **to Pamplona** el servicio de trenes a Pamplona; **the number 13 bus** ~ el servicio de autobuses número 13; **to be on government** ~ estar al servicio del gobierno.
(c) *(domestic)* **to be in** ~ ser criado, ser criada; servir; **she was in** ~ **at Lord Copper's** era criada en la casa de Lord Copper; **to go into** ~ entrar a servir *(with* a).
(d) *(act of serving etc)* servicio *m*; **for ~s to education** en premio a sus servicios a la educación; **his ~s to industry were most valuable** prestó valiosísimos servicios a la industria; **I don't need any lawyer's ~s** no necesito los servicios de ningún abogado; **the** ~ **is really poor in this hotel** en este hotel el servicio es francamente malo; **to dispense with sb's ~s** despedir a uno; **to do sb a** ~ prestar un servicio a uno; **to do good** ~ servir bien, ser muy útil; **Tristram Shandy, at your** ~ Tristram Shandy, para servirle *(or* a su disposición): **I am at your** ~ estoy a su disposición; **Brand X is always at your** ~ la marca X está siempre lista para servirle; **to bring into** ~ empezar a usar, introducir; **to come into** ~ entrar en servicio; **to press into** ~ *thing* utilizar; echar mano de; *person* hacer trabajar, hacer prestar servicio; **to be of** ~ servir, ayudar; **can I be of** ~? ¿puedo ayudarle?, ¿puedo servirle? *(LAm)*; **it's of no** ~ **in an emergency** en caso de urgencia no sirve para nada; **to be out of** ~ *(Mech)* no funcionar.
(e) *(Eccl)* *(Catholic)* misa *f*; *(other)* culto *m*, oficio *m* divino.
(f) *(Tennis)* saque *m*, servicio *m*.
(g) *(Jur)* entrega *f*.
(h) *(set)* vajilla *f*, juego *m*, servicio *m* de mesa.
(i) *(Aut, Mech)* revisión *f*, mantenimiento *m*; **the car is in for a** ~ están revisando el coche; **to send one's car in for a** ~ mandar el coche a revisar.
[2] ATTR: ~ **agreement** contrato *m* de mantenimiento; ~ **area** área *f* de servicios; ~ **bus** coche *m* de línea; ~ **charge** *(Brit)* servicio *m*; *(of flat etc)* gastos *mpl* de servicio, gastos *mpl* de escalera; ~ **corps** cuerpo *m* de intendencia; ~ **department** *(office etc)* departamento *m* *(or* sección *f)* de mantenimiento; *(repair shop)* taller *m* de reparaciones; ~ **families** familias *fpl* de miembros de las fuerzas armadas; ~ **flat** *(Brit)* piso *m* con servicio de criada, conserje *etc;* ~ **industry** industria *f* de servicios; ~ **lift** *(Brit)*, ~ **elevator** *(US)* ascensor *m* de carga; ~ **line** *(Tennis)* línea *f* de saque; ~ **road** vía *f* de acceso; ~ **sector** *(Econ)* sector *m* de servicios, sector *m* terciario; ~ **station** estación *f* de servicio.
[3] VT **(a)** *(Aut, Mech)* revisar, mantener. **(b)** *debt* pagar el interés de. **(c)** *committee etc* proveer a las necesidades de, atender.

serviceable ['sɜːvɪsəbl] ADJ servible, utilizable, útil; práctico; *(lasting)* duradero.

serviceman ['sɜːvɪsmən] N, PL **servicemen** ['sɜːvɪsmən] militar *m*.

service tree ['sɜːvɪstriː] N serbal *m*.

servicewoman ['sɜːvɪsˌwʊmən] N, PL **servicewomen** mujer *f* soldado, miembro *m* femenino del ejército.

servicing ['sɜːvɪsɪŋ] N *(of car)* revisión *f*; *(of washing machine etc)* servicio *m* de reparaciones.

serviette [ˌsɜːvɪ'et] N servilleta *f*.

serviette-ring [ˌsɜːvɪ'etrɪŋ] N servilletero *m*.

servile ['sɜːvaɪl] ADJ servil.

servility [sɜː'vɪlɪtɪ] N servilismo *m*.

serving ['sɜːvɪŋ] ① ADJ *officer* en activo; ~ **cart** *(US)*, ~ **trolley** carrito *m*; ~ **dish** plato *m* de servir.
② N *(of meal etc)* servicio *m*.

servitude ['sɜːvɪtjuːd] N servidumbre *f*.

servo ['sɜːvəʊ] N servo *m*.

servoassisted ['sɜːvəʊəˈsɪstɪd] ADJ servoasistido.

sesame ['sesəmɪ] ① N *(Bot)* sésamo *m*; **open ~!** ¡ábrete sésamo!
② ATTR: ~ **oil** aceite *m* de sésamo; ~ **seeds** semillas *fpl* de sésamo.

sesquipedalian [ˌseskwɪpɪ'deɪlɪən] ADJ sesquipedal; polisilábico; ~ **word** palabra *f* kilométrica.

sessile ['sesaɪl] ADJ sésil.

session ['seʃən] N sesión *f* *(also Comput)*; *(Scol, Univ)* curso *m*; **to be in ~** estar celebrando sesión, sesionar; **to go into secret ~** celebrar una sesión secreta.

sessional ['seʃənl] ADJ de una sesión; *exam* de fin de curso.

sestet [ses'tet] N sesteto *m*.

set [set] ① N **(a)** *(group: of tools, cups, chairs, golf clubs etc)* juego *m*; *(of kitchen utensils)* batería *f*; *(of cutlery)* cubierto *m*; *(of turbines etc)* equipo *m*; *(of gears)* tren *m*; *(of stamps)* serie *f*; *(of rooms)* grupo *m*; apartamento *m*; *(of books, works)* colección *f*; *(of songs etc)* grupo *m*, serie *f*; *(Math)* conjunto *m*; ~ **of teeth** dentadura *f*; **a complete ~ of Galdós novels** una colección completa de las novelas de Galdós; **that one makes up the ~** ése completa la serie; **it makes a ~ with those over there** hace juego con los que ves allá; **I need two to make up the ~** me faltan dos para completar la serie *(or* colección*)*.
(b) *(Tennis)* set *m*, manga *f*.
(c) *(Elec etc)* aparato *m*; *(Rad)* aparato *m* de radio, radiorreceptor *m*; *(TV)* televisión *f*, televisor *m*.
(d) *(of persons)* grupo *m*; clase *f*; *(pej)* pandilla *f*, camarilla *f*; **the fast ~** la gente de vida airada; **the literary ~** los literatos, la gente literaria; **the smart ~** el mundo elegante, los elegantes; **we're not in their ~** no formamos parte de su mundo; **they're a ~ of thieves** son unos ladrones; **they form a ~ by themselves** forman un grupo aparte.
(e) *(Brit Scol)* clase *f*; **the mathematics ~** la clase de matemáticas.
(f) **to make a dead ~ at sb** *(pick on)* emprenderla resueltamente con uno, escoger a uno como víctima; *(amorously)* proponerse conquistar a uno.
(g) **to have a shampoo and ~** hacerse lavar y marcar el pelo.
(h) *(of fabric)* caída *f*; *(of dress)* corte *m*, ajuste *m*; *(of head)* porte *m*, manera *f* de llevar; *(of saw)* triscamiento *m*; *(of tide, wind)* dirección *f*; *(of person's mind etc)* inclinación *f*, sesgo *m*, tendencia *f*.
(i) *(Hort)* planta *f* de transplantar; esqueje *m*; **onion ~s** cebollitas *fpl* de transplantar.
(j) *(Theat)* decorado *m*, decorados *mpl*; *(Cine)* plató *m*; **to be on the ~** estar en plató.
② ATTR: ~ **designer** director *m*, -ora *f* de arte, decorador *m*, -ora *f*; ~ **point** punto *m* de set.
③ ADJ AND PTP **(a)** *(rigid)* rígido, inflexible; *face* rígido, sin expresión; *smile* forzado; *permanente; (in belief)* inflexible; **the fruit is ~** el fruto está formado.
(b) *(ready)* listo; **all ~?, are we all ~?** ¿estamos?, ¿estamos listos?; **to be all ~ for** estar listo para; **with their cameras all ~ to shoot** con las máquinas a punto para disparar.
(c) *(fixed, decided in advance)* fijo; decidido de antemano; *menu, price, purpose* fijo; *task* asignado; *subject* prescrito, establecido; *time* señalado; *(usual)* reglamentario; *(customary)* acostumbrado; ~ **phrase** frase *f* hecha, frase *f* estereotipada; ~ **piece** *(Art)* grupo *m*; *(fireworks)* cuadro *m*; *(Liter etc)* escena *f* importante, episodio *m* central; **at a ~ time** a la hora señalada; **there is no ~ time for it** para eso no hay hora fija; ~ **books** autores *mpl* del programa; **with no ~ limits** sin límites determinados; **he gave us a ~ speech** pronunció un discurso preparado de antemano *(or* formal*)*; **he has a ~ speech for these occasions** para estas ocasiones tiene un discurso estereotipado.
(d) *(resolved)* resuelto, decidido; **to be ~ in one's purpose** tener un propósito firme, mantenerse firme en su propósito; **to be ~ in one's ways** tener costumbres profundamente arraigadas; **to be ~ on sth** estar empeñado en algo; **to be ~ on + ger** estar resuelto a + infin; **since you are so ~ on it** puesto que te empeñas en ello; **to be dead**

~ **against sth** estar completamente opuesto a algo.
(e) **the tide is ~ in our favour** la marea fluye para llevarnos adelante; *(fig)* la tendencia actual nos favorece, llevamos el viento en popa; **the wind is ~ strong from the north** el viento sopla recio del norte.

④ *(irr:* PRET AND PTP **set)** VT **(a)** *(place)* poner, colocar; situar; *jewel* engastar, montar; **bricks ~ in mortar** ladrillos puestos en argamasa; **to ~ places for 14** poner cubiertos para 14 personas; **to ~ the table** poner la mesa; ~ **the chairs by the window** pon las sillas junto a la ventana; **to ~ a poem to music** poner música a un poema; **she ~ the dish before me** puso el plato delante de mí; **to ~ a plan before a committee** exponer un plan ante una comisión; **I ~ him above Greene** le creo superior a Greene, le antepongo a Greene; **what value do you ~ on it?** ¿en cuánto lo valoras?; *(fig)* ¿qué valor tiene para ti?; **the ruins are ~ in a valley** las ruinas están enclavadas en un valle; **the scene is ~ in Rome** la escena es Roma, la acción pasa en Roma; **his stories, ~ in the society of 1890 ...** sus cuentos, ambientados en la sociedad de 1890 ...
(b) *(adjust)* ajustar, arreglar; *clock* poner en hora; *alarm clock* poner; *bone* reducir, encasar, componer; *specimen* montar; *hair* marcar, fijar; *sail* desplegar; *saw* triscar; *trap* armar; *snare* tender *(also fig)*; *type* componer; *cement etc* solidificar, endurecer; *jelly* cuajar; *teeth* apretar; **the alarm clock is ~ for 7** el despertador está puesto para las 7; **he ~s his watch by Big Ben** pone su reloj por el Big Ben; **I'll ~ your room** *(US)* voy a limpiar y arreglar su habitación.
(c) *(fix)* fijar, señalar; **to ~ a time for a meeting** fijar una hora para una reunión; **to ~ limits to sth** señalar límites a algo; **to ~ a period of 3 months** señalar un plazo de 3 meses; **to ~ the fashion** imponer la moda *(for* de*)*; **to ~ a record of 10 seconds** establecer un récord de 10 segundos; **to ~ course for** hacer rumbo a; **the meeting is ~ for Tuesday** *(US)* la reunión se celebrará el martes.
(d) *(give)* *example* dar; *task* imponer, asignar; *problem* plantear, *(as test etc)* poner; **to ~ Lorca for 1999** poner una obra de Lorca en el programa de estudios para 1999; **Cela is not ~ this year** este año Cela no figura en el programa; **to ~ an exam paper in German** poner un examen en alemán.
(e) **to ~ a dog on sb** azuzar un perro contra uno; **I was ~ on by 3 dogs** me atacaron 3 perros; **we ~ the police on to him** le denunciamos a la policía; **what ~ the police on the trail?** ¿qué puso a la policía sobre la pista?
(f) *(start)* **the noise ~ the dogs barking** el ruido hizo ladrar a los perros; **to ~ sth going** poner algo en marcha; **to ~ sb laughing** hacer reír a uno; **to ~ everyone talking** dar que hablar a todos; **this ~ me thinking** esto me hizo pensar; **to ~ sb to work** poner a uno a trabajar; **to ~ a fire** *(US)* provocar un incendio.
⑤ VI **(a)** *(sun etc)* ponerse.
(b) *(bone)* componerse.
(c) *(jelly etc)* cuajarse; *(blood)* coagularse; *(cement)* fraguar; *(gum, mud)* endurecerse, solidificarse; *(fruit, seed)* formarse.
(d) *(dog)* estar de muestra.
(e) **to ~ to work** *(start)* ponerse a trabajar; poner manos a la obra.

◆**set about** VT **(a)** *task* emprender, comenzar; **to ~ about + ger** ponerse a + infin.
(b) *(attack)* atacar, agredir; empezar a pegar.

◆**set against** VT **(a)** *(provoke enmity)* **to ~ A against B** indisponer a A con B, enemistar a A con B.
(b) *(contrast)* compensar; **these costs can be ~ against tax** estos gastos son desgravables; **one has to ~ X against Z** hay que contrapesar X y Z, hay que pesar X contra Z.
(c) **to ~ sb against an idea** hacer que uno se oponga a una idea; **he is very ~ against it** se opone rotundamente a ello.

◆**set apart** VT **(a)** = set aside (a), (b).
(b) *(make difference)* diferenciar, hacer distinto *(from* de*)*.

◆**set aside** VT **(a)** *(save)* poner aparte; reservar, guardar; *land* abandonar definitivamente, retirar de la producción.
(b) *(put away)* poner a un lado.
(c) *(reject)* *proposal* desechar, rechazar; *petition* desestimar; *law, sentence, will* anular.

◆**set back** VT **(a)** *(replace)* devolver a su lugar.
(b) **a house ~ back from the road** una casa algo apartada de la carretera.
(c) *(retard)* *clock* retrasar; *progress* detener, entorpecer; poner obstáculos a; **this has ~ us back some years** esto representa una pérdida de varios años, esto nos ha costado varios años de progreso.
(d) *(*: cost)* costar; **the dinner ~ me back £40** la cena me costó 40 libras.

◆**set by** VT = set aside (a).

◆**set down** VT **(a)** *(put down)* dejar; poner en tierra, poner en el suelo; depositar; **the taxi ~ us down here** el taxi nos dejó aquí; **the train ~s down passengers at ...** los viajeros se apean en ...
(b) *(Aer)* poner en tierra.
(c) *(in writing)* poner por escrito; consignar, registrar.

(d) (*attribute*) **we ~ it down to ...** lo atribuimos a ..., lo achacamos a ...; **I ~ him down as a liar** le juzgué mentiroso.

◆ **set forth** 1 VT *theory* exponer, explicar; (*display*) mostrar.
2 VI = **set out 2 (a)**.

◆ **set in** VI (*begin*) comenzar; (*night, winter*) cerrar; **the reaction ~ in after the war** la reacción se afianzó después de la guerra; **the rain has ~ in for the night** la lluvia continuará toda la noche; **the rain has really ~ in now** ahora está lloviendo de verdad.

◆ **set off** 1 VT (**a**) *bomb* explotar, hacer estallar; accionar.
(**b**) (*enhance*) hacer resaltar, dar énfasis a; **the black ~s off the red** el negro hace resaltar el rojo, el negro pone de relieve el rojo; **her dress ~s off her figure** su vestido le acentúa el tipo.
(**c**) (*balance*) contraponer; **to ~ off profits against losses** contraponer las ganancias a las pérdidas; **these expenses are ~ off against tax** estos gastos son desgravables.
(**d**) (*start*) causar, provocar, motivar; **that was what ~ off the riot** eso fue lo que provocó el motín; **to ~ sb off** (*laughing*) hacer reír a uno; (*talking*) dar a uno la oportunidad de hablar; **that really ~ him off** con eso se puso furioso.
2 VI (*leave*) partir, ponerse en camino.

◆ **set on** VT (*attack*) agredir, atacar; **he was ~ on by 4 of them** fue agredido por 4 de ellos.

◆ **set out** 1 VT (*arrange*) arreglar, ordenar; sacar y disponer; clasificar; (*on paper etc*) disponer; (*state*) exponer, explicar.
2 VI (**a**) (*leave*) partir, salir (*for* para); ponerse en camino.
(**b**) (*intend*) **to ~ out to** + *infin* ponerse a + *infin*; proponerse + *infin*; **what are you ~ting out to do?** ¿qué os proponéis?, ¿cuál es vuestro objetivo?; **we did not ~ out to do that, we did not ~ out with that idea** no teníamos esa intención al principio.

◆ **set to** VI (**a**) (*start*) empezar; (*work*) ponerse (resueltamente) a trabajar; aplicarse con vigor; (*start eating*) empezar a comer (con buen apetito); **~ to!** ¡a ello!
(**b**) **they ~ to with their fists** empezaron a pegarse, se liaron a golpes.

◆ **set up** 1 VT (**a**) (*place*) *monument* erigir, levantar; *fence etc* construir, poner.
(**b**) (*start*) *company etc* crear, fundar, establecer; *committee* constituir; *fund* crear; (*Tech*) armar, montar; *house* poner; *government* establecer, instaurar; *record* establecer; *precedent* sentar; **he ~ her up in a flat** la instaló en un piso; **to ~ sb up in business** establecer a uno en un negocio, ayudar a uno a establecerse en un negocio; **to ~ sb up as a model** poner a uno como modelo; **to ~ sb up as a judge** erigir a uno como juez.
(**c**) (*after illness etc*) fortalecer; **now he's ~ up for life** ahora tiene una carrera (*or* recursos etc) para toda la vida, ahora tiene el porvenir asegurado.
(**d**) (*equip*) equipar, proveer (*with* de); **to be well ~ up for** estar bien provisto de, tener buena provisión de.
(**e**) (*Typ*) componer.
(**f**) *cry* levantar, lanzar, dar; *protest* levantar, formular.
(**g**) (*) (*select*) escoger como víctima; (*frame*) incriminar dolosamente.
2 VI: **to ~ up in business** establecerse en un negocio; **to ~ up as a plumber** establecerse como fontanero, empezar a trabajar como fontanero.
3 VR: **to ~ o.s. up as a model** ofrecerse como modelo; **to ~ o.s. up as judge** erigirse en juez, constituirse en juez.

◆ **set upon** VT = **set on**.

set-aside ['setə'saɪd] ADJ: **~ land** tierras *fpl* en abandono definitivo, tierras *fpl* retiradas de la producción.

setback ['setbæk] N revés *m*, contratiempo *m*; **to suffer a ~** sufrir un revés.

setscrew ['setskruː] N tornillo *m* de presión.

setsquare ['setskweəʳ] N cartabón *m*, escuadra *f*.

sett [set] N madriguera *f* (*de tejón*).

settee [se'tiː] N sofá *m*.

settee-bed [se'tiːˈbed] N sofá-cama *m*.

setter ['setəʳ] N (**a**) (*of puzzle etc*) autor *m*, -ora *f*. (**b**) (*dog*) perro *m* de muestra inglés, setter *m*.

setting ['setɪŋ] N (**a**) (*of sun*) puesta *f*; (*act of placing*) colocación *f*; (*of bone*) reducción *f*, composición *f*; (*of machine etc*) ajuste *m*; (*Typ*) composición *f*.
(**b**) (*of jewel*) engaste *m*, montadura *f*, montura *f*.
(**c**) (*Theat etc*) escena *f*, escenario *m*; (*of action etc*) marco *m*; encuadre *m*; (*natural ~, landscape etc*) marco *m*.
(**d**) (*Mus*) arreglo *m*, versión *f*; **a ~ for 2 violins** un arreglo para 2 violines.

setting-up ['setɪŋˈʌp] N (*of monument*) erección *f*; (*of institution, company*) creación *f*, fundación *f*, establecimiento *m*; (*Typ*) composición *f*.

settle¹ ['setl] N banco *m*.

settle² ['setl] 1 VT (**a**) (*place*) colocar; (*place firmly*) asentar; (*fix*)

asegurar, fijar, afirmar; *gaze* fijar; **to ~ one's feet in the stirrups** afirmarse en los estribos.
(**b**) (*persons*) establecer; *land* colonizar, poblar (*with* de); **it was first ~d by the French** los primeros colonos fueron los franceses; **he ~d her in a little flat** la instaló en un modesto piso.
(**c**) **to ~ an income on sb** (*assign*) asignar (*or* señalar) una renta a uno.
(**d**) (*arrange*) **to ~ one's affairs** arreglar sus asuntos; **to ~ an invalid for the night** poner a un enfermo cómodamente para la noche.
(**e**) (*calm*) *nerves* calmar, sosegar; *doubts* disipar, desvanecer; *stomach* asentar.
(**f**) (*resolve*) *account* ajustar, liquidar, saldar; *claim* satisfacer; *differences, quarrel* componer; *date etc* fijar, acordar; *deal* firmar; *problem* resolver, solucionar; **several points remain to be ~d** quedan varios puntos por resolver; **the terms were ~d by negotiation** se acordaron las condiciones mediante una negociación; **to ~ an affair out of court** arreglar una disputa; **the result was ~d in the first half** se decidió el resultado en el primer tiempo; **it's all ~d** todo está resuelto; ya no hay problema; **so that's ~d then** así que todo está arreglado; **that ~s it!** ¡ya no hay más que decir!; **~ it among yourselves!** ¡allá vosotros!, ¡arregladlo vosotros!
(**g**) (*) **I'll soon ~ him** me lo cargaré*; **that ~d him** ya no hay problema con él, ya no volverá a molestarnos.
2 VI (**a**) (*establish o.s.: in a house etc*) establecerse, instalarse; (*in a country*) arraigarse; (*first settlers*) asentarse; (*bird, insect*) posarse; **to ~ comfortably in an armchair** sentarse cómodamente en una butaca; **the snow is settling** la nieve cuaja; **the wind ~d in the east** el viento siguió soplando del este; **a deep gloom has ~d on the party** un profundo pesimismo se ha apoderado del partido; **a smile ~d on his face** siguió con su sonrisa fija; **my eyes ~d on her immediately** en seguida se fijó mi mirada en ella.
(**b**) (*building*) asentarse; (*liquid*) clarificarse; (*sediment*) depositarse, sedimentarse; (*food*) digerirse, asimilarse; asentarse en el estómago; (*ship*) hundirse lentamente; **things are settling into shape** las cosas empiezan a adquirir una forma.
(**c**) (*calm down: passion etc*) calmarse; (*weather*) serenarse; (*conditions*) normalizarse, volver a la normalidad.
(**d**) (*resolve*) **to ~ on sth** decidirse por algo; (*choose*) escoger algo, optar por algo; **to ~ on a date** fijar una fecha.
(**e**) (*agree*) llegar a un arreglo, llegar a un acuerdo; transigir; **now they want to ~** ahora quieren llegar a un arreglo; **I'll ~ for all of us** pago la cuenta para todos, pago por todos; **to ~ for** *solution etc* decidir por, aceptar; **to ~ for £250** convenir en aceptar 250 libras; **will you ~ for a draw?** ¿quedamos en empate?; **I'll ~ for the smaller one** me conformo con el pequeño.

◆ **settle down** 1 VI (**a**) (*establish o.s.: in a house etc*) establecerse, instalarse; (*in a country*) arraigarse; (*first settlers*) asentarse; (*of bird, insect*) posarse; **to ~ down comfortably in an armchair** sentarse cómodamente en una butaca.
(**b**) (*after wild period etc*) sentar la cabeza; **to marry and ~ down** casarse y empezar a tomar las cosas en serio; **to ~ down to a new life** adaptarse a una vida nueva; **he's settling down at school** se está acostumbrando a la escuela; **things are beginning to ~ down** las cosas empiezan a volver a la normalidad; **he ~d down with two mistresses** se las arregló para vivir con dos queridas; **he can't ~ down anywhere** es un culo de mal asiento*; **to ~ down to work** aplicarse al trabajo, dedicarse a trabajar (en serio).
2 VR: **to ~ o.s. down in an armchair** sentarse cómodamente en una butaca; **to ~ o.s. down for the night** arreglarse para pasar la noche.

◆ **settle in** VI (*get things straight*) acostumbrarse, habituarse; (*get used to things*) adaptarse bien.

◆ **settle up** VI (*also fig*) ajustar cuentas (*with sb* con uno).

settled ['setld] ADJ fijo; permanente; **a ~ social order** un orden social fijo; **the first ~ civilization** la primera civilización de carácter fijo; **I feel very ~ in this job** me siento perfectamente establecido en este puesto.

▼ **settlement** ['setlmənt] N (**a**) (*of account*) ajuste *m*, liquidación *f*; (*of claim*) satisfacción *f*; (*of difference, quarrel*) arreglo *m*; (*of problem*) solución *f*; **please find enclosed my cheque in full ~ of ...** adjunto le remito el talón a cuenta de la total liquidación de ...
(**b**) (*agreement*) acuerdo *m*, convenio *m*; composición *f*; (*of marriage*) contrato *m*; **to reach a ~** llegar a un acuerdo.
(**c**) (*act of settling persons*) establecimiento *m*; (*of land*) colonización *f*; asentamiento *m*.
(**d**) (*colony*) colonia *f*; (*village*) pueblo *m*; núcleo *m* rural; (*homestead*) caserío *m*; (*for social work*) centro *m* social; (*archaeological site*) asentamiento *m*.

settler ['setləʳ] N colono *m*, -a *f*; (*pioneer*) colonizador *m*, -ora *f*.

set-to* ['set'tuː] N bronca *f*, pelea *f*, agarrada *f*; **to have a ~ with sb** pelearse con uno.

set-up* ['setʌp] N tinglado *m*, sistema *m*, organización *f*; estructura *f*; plan *m*; (*persons*) equipo *m*; **it's an odd ~ here** aquí tienen un extraño sistema; **you have to know the ~** hay que conocer el tinglado; **what's the ~?** ¿cuál es el sistema?, ¿cómo está organizado?; **he's joining our ~** formará parte de nuestro equipo.

seven ['sevn] [1] ADJ siete.
  [2] N siete m.

sevenfold ['sevnfəʊld] [1] ADJ séptuplo.
  [2] ADV siete veces.

seventeen ['sevn'tiːn] ADJ diecisiete.

seventeenth ['sevn'tiːnθ] ADJ decimoséptimo.

seventh ['sevnθ] [1] ADJ séptimo; **S~ Cavalry** (US) Séptimo m de Caballería.
  [2] N séptimo m, séptima parte f; (Mus) séptima f.

seventieth ['sevntɪɪθ] ADJ septuagésimo; setenta; **the ~ anniversary** el setenta aniversario.

seventy ['sevntɪ] ADJ setenta; **the seventies** (eg 1970s) los años setenta; **to be in one's seventies** tener más de setenta años, ser setentón.

sever ['sevər] VT cortar; separar, dividir; relations romper.

several ['sevrəl] [1] ADJ (a) (of number) varios, algunos; diversos; **~ times already** varias veces ya; **I bought ~ books** compré algunos libros.
  (b) (respective) respectivos, distintos; **they have their ~ colours** tienen sus respectivos colores; **they went their ~ ways** se fueron cada uno por su lado; **joint and ~** (Jur) solidario.
  [2] PRON algunos; varios; **~ of them wore hats** algunos de ellos llevaban sombrero; **~ were dead** algunos estaban muertos.

severally ['sevrəlɪ] ADV respectivamente; (one by one) por separado, individualmente.

severance ['sevərəns] [1] N corte m; separación f, división f; (of relations) ruptura f; (from work) despido m.
  [2] ATTR: **~ pay** (indemnización f por) despido m.

severe [sɪ'vɪər] ADJ severo; riguroso, fuerte; duro; weather, winter, critic, restriction etc riguroso; illness, loss, wound grave; pain intenso, agudo; storm violento; reprimand áspero; blow duro; style adusto, austero; **to be ~ on sb** tratar a uno con rigor; **to be too ~ (on sb)** cargar la mano.

severely [sɪ'vɪəlɪ] ADV severamente; rigurosamente, fuertemente; duramente; gravemente; intensamente; agudamente; ásperamente; austeramente; **~ wounded** herido de gravedad; **a ~ plain style** un estilo de lo más austero; **to leave sth ~ alone** no tener nada en absoluto que ver con algo.

severity [sɪ'verɪtɪ] N severidad f; rigor m; gravedad f; intensidad f, agudeza f; aspereza f; austeridad f.

Seville [sə'vɪl] [1] N Sevilla f.
  [2] ATTR: **~ orange** naranja f amarga.

Sevillian [sə'vɪlɪən] [1] ADJ sevillano.
  [2] N sevillano m, -a f.

sew [səʊ] (irr: PRET **sewed**, PTP **sewn**) [1] VT coser.
  [2] VI coser.

◆**sew on** VT coser, pegar.

◆**sew up** VT (a) coser, zurcir. (b) (*) **to get a matter all ~n up*** arreglar un asunto de modo definitivo; **the deal is all ~n up** el negocio está hecho definitivamente; **we've got the game all ~n up now*** tenemos el partido en el bote*.

sewage ['sjuːɪdʒ] [1] N aguas fpl residuales, aguas fpl fecales.
  [2] ATTR: **~ disposal** depuración f de aguas residuales; **~ farm**, **~ works** estación f depuradora (de aguas residuales).

sewer ['sjʊər] N albañal m, alcantarilla f, cloaca f; (fig) letrina f, sentina f.

sewerage ['sjʊərɪdʒ] N alcantarillado m; (as service on estate etc) saneamiento m.

sewing ['səʊɪŋ] [1] N costura f; labor f de costura.
  [2] ATTR de coser.

sewing-basket ['səʊɪŋˌbɑːskɪt] N cesta f de costura.

sewing-machine ['səʊɪŋməˌʃiːn] N máquina f de coser.

sewing-silk ['səʊɪŋsɪlk] N torzal m, seda f de coser.

sewn [səʊn] PTP of **sew**.

sex [seks] [1] N sexo m; **to have ~** tener relaciones sexuales (con with).
  [2] ATTR sexual; **~ act** acto m carnal, coito m; **~ aids** ayudas fpl sexuales; **~ crime** crimen m sexual; **~ discrimination** discriminación f sexual; **~ education** educación f sexual; **~ hormone** hormona f sexual; **~ maniac** maníaco m sexual; **~ object** objeto m sexual; **~ offender** delincuente m sexual; **~ organ** órgano m sexual (or genital); **~ symbol** sex-símbol mf.
  [3] VT chicks sexar, determinar el sexo de.

sexagenarian [ˌseksədʒɪ'neərɪən] [1] ADJ sexagenario.
  [2] N sexagenario m, -a f.

Sexagesima [ˌseksə'dʒesɪmə] N Sexagésima f.

sex-appeal ['seksəˌpiːl] N sexy m, sex-appeal m, sexapel m.

sex-change ['sekstʃeɪndʒ] [1] N cambio m de sexo.
  [2] ATTR: **~ operation** operación f de cambio de sexo.

sex-crazed ['sekskreɪzd] ADJ obsesionado por el sexo.

sexed [sekst] ADJ (Bio, Zool) sexuado; **to be highly ~** estar obsesionado con el sexo.

sexiness ['seksɪnɪs] N sexy m; carácter m sexual; cachondez f.

sexism ['seksɪzəm] N sexismo m.

sexist ['seksɪst] [1] ADJ sexista.
  [2] N sexista mf.

sexless ['sekslɪs] ADJ asexuado, desprovisto de instinto sexual; desprovisto de atractivo sexual; (Bio) sin sexo, asexual.

sex-life ['sekslaɪf] N vida f sexual.

sex-linked ['seks'lɪŋkt] ADJ (Bio) ligado al sexo.

sex-mad [ˌseks'mæd] ADJ obsesionado por el sexo.

sexologist [sek'sɒlədʒɪst] N sexólogo m, -a f.

sexology [sek'sɒlədʒɪ] N sexología f.

sexpot* ['sekspɒt] N (hum) cachonda f.

sex-shop ['seksʃɒp] N sexería f, sex-shop m.

sex-starved ['seksstɑːvd] ADJ sexualmente frustrado.

sextant ['sekstənt] N sextante m.

sextet(te) [seks'tet] N sexteto m.

sex therapist ['seksˌθerəpɪst] N sexólogo m, -a f.

sexton ['sekstən] N sacristán m; (gravedigger) sepulturero m.

sextuplet ['sekstjʊplɪt] N sextillizo m, -a f.

sexual ['seksjʊəl] ADJ sexual; **~ abuse** abuso m sexual; **~ act** acto m carnal, coito m; **~ assault** atentado m contra el pudor; **~ desire** deseo m sexual; **~ harassment** importunación f sexual, acoso m sexual; **~ intercourse** comercio m sexual, trato m sexual, coito m; **~ organs** órganos mpl sexuales; **~ orientation** orientación f sexual.

sexuality [ˌseksjʊ'ælɪtɪ] N sexualidad f.

sexually ['seksjʊəlɪ] ADV sexualmente; **~ transmitted disease** enfermedad f de transmisión sexual.

sexy ['seksɪ] ADJ person sexy; cachondo; dress etc sexy, provocativo; joke, film etc verde, escabroso.

Seychelles [seɪ'ʃelz] NPL Seychelles fpl.

sez: [sez] = **says**; **~ you!** ¡lo dices tú!

SF (a) N ABBR of **science-fiction** ciencia-ficción f. (b) ABBR (Ireland: Pol) of **Sinn Féin**.

SFA N (Scot) ABBR of **Scottish Football Association**; (:) ABBR of **sweet Fanny Adams**.

SFO N (Brit) ABBR of **Serious Fraud Office**.

SG N (US) ABBR of **Surgeon General** jefe m del servicio federal de sanidad.

sgd ABBR of **signed** firmado.

Sgt ABBR of **Sergeant** sargento m.

sh [ʃ] INTERJ ¡chitón!, ¡chist!

shabbily ['ʃæbɪlɪ] ADV (a) (lit) pobremente. (b) (fig) injustamente; vilmente; de manera poco honrada.

shabbiness ['ʃæbɪnɪs] N (a) (lit) pobreza f, lo desharrapado; lo raído, lo viejo; mal estado m. (b) (fig) injusticia f; vileza f.

shabby ['ʃæbɪ] ADJ (a) person pobremente vestido, desharrapado; garment raído, gastado, viejo; area pobre; building etc de aspecto pobre, en mal estado; **to feel ~** sentirse mal vestido; **to look ~** tener aspecto pobre, tener aspecto poco elegante.
  (b) treatment etc injusto; trick vil, malo; behaviour poco honrado; excuse poco convincente.

shabby-looking ['ʃæbɪˌlʊkɪŋ] ADJ de aspecto pobre.

shack [ʃæk] N chabola f, choza f, jacal m (Carib), bohío m (CAm).

◆**shack up:** VI: **to ~ up with sb** amontonarse con uno*; **to ~ up together** vivir amontonados*.

shackle ['ʃækl] [1] VT encadenar; poner grilletes a; (fig) poner trabas a, estorbar; **we are ~d by tradition** las trabas de la tradición nos tienen presos.
  [2] NPL: **~s** grillos mpl, grilletes mpl; (fig) trabas fpl; **the ~s of convention** las trabas de la convención.

shad [ʃæd] N sábalo m.

shade [ʃeɪd] [1] N (a) (shadow) sombra f; **~s of night** tinieblas fpl, oscuridad f; **the ~s of night were falling fast** se hacía rápidamente de noche; **in the ~** a la sombra (of de); **temperature in the ~** temperatura f a la sombra; **35° in the ~** 35 grados a la sombra; **to put sth in the ~** (fig) eclipsar algo, dejar algo chico; **to put sb in the ~** (fig) hacer sombra a uno.
  (b) (lamp~) pantalla f; (eye~) visera f; (US: blind) persiana f; **~s** (esp US: glasses) gafas fpl de sol.
  (c) (of colour) matiz m; tonalidad f, tono m; (of meaning, opinion) matiz m, modalidad f; **a new ~ of lipstick** una nueva tonalidad de lápiz labial; **have you a lighter ~?** ¿tiene una tonalidad más clara?; **all ~s of opinion are represented** todas las modalidades de la opinión están representadas.
  (d) (small quantity) poquito m; pizca f; **just a ~ more** un poquito más; **he's a ~ better** está un poquito mejor; **it's a ~ awkward** es un tanto difícil.
  (e) (ghost) fantasma m; **the S~s** el Averno, el infierno; **~s of Professor X!** ¡eso recuerda al profesor X!
  [2] VT (a) dar sombra a, sombrear; face etc proteger contra el sol (etc);

resguardar de la luz; **to ~ one's eyes with one's hand** llevar la mano a los ojos para protegerlos contra el sol; **to ~ a light** poner pantalla a una lámpara; **her face was ~d by a big hat** un sombrero ancho le daba sombra a la cara; **the garden is ~d by a large tree** el jardín está sombreado por un árbol grande.

(b) (*Art*) sombrear, esfumar; (*cross-hatch*) sombrear; *eyes* poner sombreador en, sombrear; **the dark ~d area** (*Typ etc*) la zona en trama oscura.

◆ **shade away = shade off.**

◆ **shade off** [1] VT (*Art*) *colours* degradar.

[2] VI cambiar poco a poco (*into* hasta hacerse), transformarse gradualmente (*into* en); **blue that ~s off into black** azul que se transforma (*or* se funde) gradualmente en negro.

shadeless ['ʃeɪdlɪs] ADJ sin sombra, privado de sombra.

shadiness ['ʃeɪdɪnɪs] N **(a)** (*shade*) sombra *f*, lo umbroso. **(b)** (*fig*) dudosa honradez *f*; tenebrosidad *f*.

shading ['ʃeɪdɪŋ] N (*for eyes*) sombreado *m*; (*of colours*) degradación *f*; transformación *f* gradual (*into* en); (*cross-hatching*) sombreado *m*; trama *f* oscura.

shadow ['ʃædəʊ] [1] N **(a)** sombra *f*; **the ~s** la oscuridad, las tinieblas; **the ~ of death** la sombra de la muerte; **in the ~ of** dentro de la sombra de, (*fig*) amenazado por; **under the ~ of serious charges** amenazado por unas acusaciones graves; **without a ~ of doubt** sin sombra de duda, sin la menor duda; **without a ~ of truth** sin tener la más pequeña parte de verdad; **he is but a ~ of his former self** es apenas una sombra de lo que fue; **to cast a ~** proyectar una sombra; **to cast a ~ over the festivities** ser una nota triste en la fiesta; **to wear o.s. to a ~** extenuarse, agotarse.

(b) (*person: tail*) sombra *f*, policía *m* (*or* detective *m etc*) que sigue a un sospechoso; (*companion*) sombra *f*.

[2] ADJ **~ cabinet** (*Brit*) gobierno *m* en la sombra; **~ leader** (*Brit*) dirigente *mf* en la sombra; **~ Foreign Secretary** (*Brit*) portavoz *mf* de Asuntos Exteriores del gobierno en la sombra.

[3] VT **(a)** (*darken*) oscurecer; (*Art*) sombrear; **to ~ forth** anunciar, indicar vagamente, simbolizar.

(b) (*follow*) seguir y vigilar; **have that man ~ed** que se vigile a ese hombre; **I was ~ed all the way home** me siguieron todo el camino hasta mi casa.

┌─ **SHADOW CABINET** ─┐

ⓘ *El **Shadow Cabinet** (gobierno en la sombra) está constituido por los parlamentarios británicos del principal partido de la oposición que tendrían cargos ministeriales si su partido llegase al poder. Cada ministro del gobierno tiene su homólogo en la oposición, por ejemplo al Ministro de Economía se opone el **Shadow Chancellor** y al Ministro del Interior el **Shadow Home Secretary**. Su misión consiste en juzgar la política del Gobierno en lo que se refiere al área de la que se ocupan ellos y en actuar como portavoces del programa de su partido.*

⇨ *Ver también* |CABINET| , |FRONT BENCH|

shadow-box ['ʃædəʊbɒks] VI boxear con un adversario imaginario; (*fig*) disputar con un adversario imaginario.

shadow-boxing ['ʃædəʊˌbɒksɪŋ] N boxeo *m* con un adversario imaginario; (*fig*) disputa *f* con un adversario imaginario.

shadowy ['ʃædəʊɪ] ADJ oscuro; (*fig*) oscuro; indistinto, vago, indefinido; **a ~ form** un bulto, una forma indistinta; **the company leads a ~ existence** la compañía tiene una existencia misteriosa.

shady ['ʃeɪdɪ] ADJ **(a)** *place* sombreado, umbroso, de sombra; a la sombra; **a ~ tree** un árbol que da sombra; **it's ~ here** aquí hay sombra.

(b) (*fig*) *person* sospechoso; *deal* turbio; *past etc* tenebroso; **the ~ side of politics** el aspecto turbio de la política; **to be on the ~ side of 40** tener más de 40 años.

shaft [ʃɑːft] [1] N **(a)** (*arrow etc*) flecha *f*, dardo *m*, saeta *f*; (*part of arrow*) astil *m*; (*of column*) caña *f*, fuste *m*; (*of tool, golf-club etc*) mango *m*; (*of cart, carriage*) vara *f*; (*Mech*) eje *m*, árbol *m*; (*of light*) rayo *m*; **the ~s of Cupid** las flechas de Cupido; **~ of wit** agudeza *f*.

(b) (*Min*) pozo *m*.

[2] VT (*US‡*) timar, joder‡.

shag¹ [ʃæg] N tabaco *m* picado, picadura *f*.

shag² [ʃæg] N (*Orn*) cormorán *m* moñudo.

shag³‡ [ʃæg] [1] N polvo‡ *m*; **to have a ~** echar un polvo‡.

[2] VT joder‡.

[3] VI joder‡.

shag⁴ [ʃæg] N (*carpet*) tripe *m*.

shagged‡ [ʃægd] ADJ (*also ~ out‡*) hecho polvo*.

shaggy ['ʃægɪ] ADJ velludo, peludo, lanudo; **~ dog story** chiste *m* goma.

shagreen [ʃæ'griːn] N chagrín *m*, zapa *f*.

Shah [ʃɑː] N cha *m*, chah *m*, sha *m*.

shake [ʃeɪk] [1] N **(a)** sacudida *f*, sacudimiento *m*; (*quiver*) temblor *m*; (*of vehicle etc*) vibración *f*; (*Mus*) trino *m*; (*of head*) movimiento *m*; **with a ~ in his voice** con voz temblorosa; **with a ~ of her head**

moviendo la cabeza, con un movimiento de la cabeza; **to be all of a ~** estar todo tembloroso; **to give sb a good ~** sacudir violentamente a uno; **to give a rug a good ~** sacudir bien una alfombrilla; **to have the ~s** temblar como un azogado.

(b) (*milk ~*) batido *m*.

(c) **he's no great ~s* at swimming, he's no great ~s* as a swimmer** como nadador no vale mucho; **in a brace of ~s*, in two ~s*** en un decir Jesús, en un abrir y cerrar de ojos.

[2] (*irr*: PRET **shook**, PTP **shaken**) VT **(a)** sacudir; *building etc* hacer temblar, hacer retemblar; *head* mover, menear; *hand* estrechar; *bottle* agitar; *cocktail etc* agitar, remover; **'~ the bottle'** 'agitar la botella'; **'~ well before using'** 'agítese bien antes de usar'; **we had to ~ him to rouse him** tuvimos que sacudirle para despertarle; **to ~ one's finger at sb** negar con el dedo lo que dice (*etc*) uno; **to ~ one's fist at sb** amenazar a uno con el puño; **to ~ hands** estrecharse la mano, darse las manos; **to ~ hands on a deal** darse las manos para cerrar un trato; **to ~ hands with sb** estrechar la mano a uno; **to ~ one's head** negar con la cabeza, mover la cabeza negativamente.

(b) (*fig*) (*weaken*) debilitar; hacer flaquear; (*impair*) perjudicar, afectar; **it has ~n his health** ha afectado su salud; **nothing will ~ our resolve** nada hará flaquear nuestra resolución; **the firm's credit has been badly ~n** ha sido perjudicada la buena fama de la casa; **the prosecutor could not ~ his evidence** el fiscal no logró hacerle modificar su testimonio; el fiscal no pudo desacreditar su testimonio.

(c) (*fig: alarm*) inquietar, perturbar; (*amaze*) sorprender, pasmar, dejar estupefacto; (*upset composure of*) desconcertar; (*shock*) dar una sacudida a; **the news shook me** la noticia me pasmó; **that shook him** eso le desconcertó; **7 days which shook the world** 7 días que estremecieron el mundo; **it shook me rigid** (*or solid*)* me pasmó, me dejó frío; **he needs to be ~n out of his smugness** hay que darle una sacudida para que deje su presunción.

[3] VI estremecerse; temblar, retemblar (*at, with* de); (*of voice*) temblar; (*Mus*) trinar; **to ~ like a leaf** temblar como un azogado; **to ~ with fear** temblar de miedo; **to ~ with laughter** desternillarse de risa; **the house shook with merry singing** la casa retemblaba con alegres canciones; **the walls shook at the sound** se estremecían las paredes con el ruido; **to ~ in one's shoes** temblar de aprensión; **it shook in the wind** bamboleaba al viento; **his voice shook** le tembló la voz; **~*!, ~ on it*!** ¡chócala*!; **to ~ on a deal** darse las manos para cerrar un trato.

[4] VR: **to ~ o.s. free** librarse de una sacudida.

◆ **shake down** [1] VT *fruit etc* hacer caer, sacudir; bajar sacudiendo.

(b) (*US**) **to ~ sb down** sacar dinero a uno por chantaje; **they shook him down for 5000 dollars** le sacaron 5000 dólares.

(c) **to ~ sb down for weapons*** cachear a uno.

[2] VI (**: settle for sleep*) acostarse, echarse a dormir; **I can ~ down anywhere** yo me duermo en cualquier sitio.

◆ **shake off** VT **(a)** *dust etc* sacudirse.

(b) *cold etc* quitarse (de encima); deshacerse de, librarse de; *habit* dejar; *yoke* sacudirse; *pursuer* zafarse de, dar esquinazo a.

◆ **shake out** VT **(a)** *flag etc* desplegar; *blanket etc* abrir y sacudir; **to ~ dust out** sacudir el polvo.

(b) *company* reorganizar, reestructurar; *work-force* reducir.

◆ **shake up** VT **(a)** *bottle etc, contents* agitar, remover; *travellers* sacudir.

(b) (*emotionally*) chocar; perturbar, desconcertar; **she was badly ~n up** sufrió una profunda conmoción.

(c) (*rouse, stir up*) *person etc* dar una sacudida a, dar un pinchazo a; estimular, reanimar; infundir nueva energía a; *organization* reorganizar, reestructurar.

shakedown* ['ʃeɪkdaʊn] N **(a)** (*bed*) cama *f* improvisada. **(b)** (*US*) exacción *f* de dinero; chantaje *m*. **(c)** (*search*) registro *m* a fondo.

shaken ['ʃeɪkən] PTP *of* **shake**.

shake-out ['ʃeɪkaʊt] N reorganización *f*, reestructuración *f*; reducción *f*.

shaker ['ʃeɪkər] N (*cocktail* ~) coctelera *f*.

Shakespeare ['ʃeɪkspɪər] NM Shakespeare, Chéspir.

Shakespearian [ʃeɪks'pɪərɪən] ADJ shakespeariano, chespiriano.

shake-up ['ʃeɪkʌp] N conmoción *f*; reorganización *f*; sacudida *f*, pinchazo *m*; infusión *f* de nueva energía; **the company needs a big ~** la compañía necesita una reorganización completa.

shakily ['ʃeɪkɪlɪ] ADV de modo inestable; con poca firmeza; **he said ~** dijo en voz trémula; **to walk ~** andar con paso vacilante.

shakiness ['ʃeɪkɪnɪs] N inestabilidad *f*, falta *f* de firmeza; temblor *m*; debilidad *f*; (*of knowledge*) deficiencia *f*, mala calidad *f*.

shaking ['ʃeɪkɪŋ] [1] ADJ: **a ~ experience** una experiencia desconcertante.

[2] N: **to give sb a good ~** sacudir violentamente a uno; **he needs a good ~** (*fig*) hay que darle un pinchazo.

shako ['ʃækəʊ] N chacó *m*.

shaky ['ʃeɪkɪ] ADJ (*unstable*) inestable, poco firme, poco sólido; movedizo; *hands etc* tembloroso; *health* delicado; *voice* trémula, débil;

writing poco firme; *start* incierto; *situation* precario; **his Spanish is rather ~** su español es algo defectuoso; **to be ~ on one's legs** tener las piernas débiles, andar con paso vacilante.

shale [ʃeɪl] N esquisto *m*.

shale oil [ˈʃeɪlɔɪl] N petróleo *m* de esquisto.

▼ **shall** [ʃæl] (*irr: see also* **should**) V AUX (a) (*used to form future tense*) **I ~ go** iré; **no I ~ not, no I shan't** no, yo no; **it ~ be done** así se hará; **~ I hear from you soon?** ¿me escribirás pronto?
(b) (*emphatic*) **you ~ pay for this!** ¡me las pagarás!; **they ~ not pass!** ¡no pasarán!
(c) (*in commands, of duty etc*) **passengers ~ not cross the line** se prohíbe a los señores viajeros cruzar la vía; **it ~ be done this way** ha de hacerse de este modo; **you ~ do it!** ¡sí lo harás!; **thou shalt not kill** no matarás.
▼(d) (*in questions*) **~ I go now?** ¿me voy ahora?, ¿quieres que me vaya ahora?; **I'll buy 3, ~ I?** compro 3, ¿no te parece?; **let's go in, ~ we?** ¿entramos?; **~ we let him?** ¿se lo permitimos?

shallot [ʃəˈlɒt] N chalote *m*, cebollita *f*, cebolleta *f* (*LAm*).

shallow [ˈʃæləʊ] ① ADJ (a) *water etc* poco profundo, no muy profundo, bajo; *dish etc* llano; *breathing* poco profundo.
(b) *person* superficial, frívolo, sin carácter; *knowledge etc* superficial, somero.
② N: **~s** bajos *mpl*, bajío *m*.
③ VI hacerse menos profundo.

shallowness [ˈʃæləʊnɪs] N (a) (*lit*) poca profundidad *f*. (b) (*fig*) superficialidad *f*, frivolidad *f*, falta *f* de carácter.

shalt†† [ʃælt] = **shall**.

sham [ʃæm] ① ADJ falso, fingido, simulado; **~ fight** simulacro *m* de combate; **she's terribly ~** es la mar de afectada; **with ~ politeness** con fingida cortesía.
② N (a) (*imposture*) impostura *f*, fraude *m*, engaño *m*; imitación *f*; **it's all a ~** todo es engaño; **the ~ of these elections** el fraude de estas elecciones; **the declaration was a mere ~** la declaración no fue sino una impostura.
(b) (*person*) impostor *m*, -ora *f*; **he's just a big ~** es un grandísimo farsante.
③ VT fingir, simular; **to ~ illness** fingirse enfermo.
④ VI fingir, fingirse; **he's just ~ming** lo está fingiendo; **to ~ dead** fingir estar muerto; **to ~ ill** fingirse enfermo.

shaman [ˈʃæmən] N chamán *m*.

shamanism [ˈʃæmə,nɪzəm] N chamanismo *m*.

shamateur* [ˈʃæmətər] N amateur *m* fingido, amateur *f* fingida.

shamble [ˈʃæmbl] VI (*also* **to ~ along**) andar arrastrando los pies; **he ~d across to the window** fue arrastrando los pies a la ventana.

shambles [ˈʃæmblz] N SING (*scene of carnage*) lugar *m* de gran matanza; (*carnage*) matanza *f*, carnicería *f*; (*ruined place*) ruina *f*, escombrera *f*; (*muddle*) caos *m*, confusión *f*; **the place was a ~** el sitio era todo escombros; **this room is a ~!** ¡has visto qué desorden en este cuarto!; **the game was a ~** el partido degeneró en follón.

shambolic* [ʃæmˈbɒlɪk] ADJ caótico.

shame [ʃeɪm] ① N (a) (*feeling, humiliation*) vergüenza *f*; deshonra *f*; **the ~ of that defeat** la vergüenza de esa derrota; **the street is the ~ of the town** la calle es la vergüenza (*or* el baldón) de la ciudad; **~!, for ~!, ~ on you!, the ~ of it!** ¡qué vergüenza!; **to my eternal** (*or* **lasting**) **~ I did nothing** con gran vergüenza mía no hice nada; **to be without ~, to be lost to all sense of ~** no tener vergüenza; **to bring ~ upon sb** deshonrar a uno; **have you no ~?** ¿no te da vergüenza esto?; ¡qué cinismo!; **to put sb to ~** avergonzar a uno, (*fig*) superar con mucho a uno, dejar chico a uno.
(b) (*pity*) lástima *f*, pena *f*; **it's a ~ that ...** es una lástima que + *subj*, es una pena que + *subj*; **it's a ~ to have to ~** es una pena tener que + *infin*; **what a ~!** ¡qué lástima!, ¡qué pena!
② VT avergonzar; deshonrar; **they ~d me into contributing** me obligaron a contribuir por vergüenza.

shamefaced [ˈʃeɪmfeɪst] ADJ avergonzado; vergonzoso, tímido.

shamefacedly [ˈʃeɪmfeɪsɪdlɪ] ADV con vergüenza, avergonzado; tímidamente.

shamefacedness [ˈʃeɪmfeɪstnɪs] N vergüenza *f*; timidez *f*.

shameful [ˈʃeɪmfʊl] ADJ vergonzoso; **how ~!** ¡qué vergüenza!

shamefully [ˈʃeɪmfəlɪ] ADV vergonzosamente; **~ ignorant** tan ignorante que da vergüenza; **they are ~ underpaid** se les paga terriblemente mal.

shamefulness [ˈʃeɪmfʊlnɪs] N vergüenza *f*; ignominia *f*.

shameless [ˈʃeɪmlɪs] ADJ desvergonzado, descarado, descocado; impúdico; cínico; **~ person** sinvergüenza *mf*; **are you completely ~?** ¿no tienes vergüenza?; ¡qué cinismo!

shamelessly [ˈʃeɪmlɪslɪ] ADV desvergonzadamente, descaradamente; impúdicamente; cínicamente.

shamelessness [ˈʃeɪmlɪsnɪs] N desvergüenza *f*, descaro *m*, descoco *m*; impudor *m*; cinismo *m*.

shaming [ˈʃeɪmɪŋ] ADJ vergonzoso; **this is too ~!** ¡qué vergüenza!

shammy [ˈʃæmɪ] N gamuza *f*.

shampoo [ʃæmˈpuː] ① N champú *m*; **to give o.s. a ~** lavarse la cabeza, darse un champú; **a ~ and set** un lavado y marcado.
② VT *person* lavar la cabeza a, dar un champú a; *hair* lavar; *carpet* limpiar, lavar; **to have one's hair ~ed and set** hacerse lavar y marcar el pelo.

shamrock [ˈʃæmrɒk] N trébol *m* (*emblema nacional irlandés*).

shandy [ˈʃændɪ] N (*Brit*), **shandygaff** [ˈʃændɪ,gæf] N (*US*) cerveza *f* con gaseosa.

Shanghai [ʃæŋˈhaɪ] N Shanghai *m*.

shanghai* [ʃæŋˈhaɪ] VT: **to ~ sb** (*Naut*) narcotizar (*or* emborrachar) a uno y llevarle como marinero; (*fig*) secuestrar a uno.

Shangri-la [ˈʃæŋrɪˈlɑː] N jauja *f*, paraíso *m* terrestre.

shank [ʃæŋk] N (*part of leg*) caña *f*; (*bird's leg*) zanca *f*; (*Bot*) tallo *m*; (*handle*) mango *m*; **~s*** piernas *fpl*; **to go on S~s' pony** ir en el coche de San Francisco, ir a golpe de calcetín.

shan't [ʃɑːnt] = **shall not**.

shantung [ʃænˈtʌŋ] N shantung *m*.

shanty¹ [ˈʃæntɪ] N (*hut*) choza *f*, chabola *f*.

shanty² [ˈʃæntɪ] N (*Brit Mus*) saloma *f*.

shanty-town [ˈʃæntɪˌtaʊn] N barrio *m* de chabolas, suburbio *m*; callampas *fpl* (*Chile*), colonia *f* proletaria (*Mex*), barriadas *fpl* (*Perú*), cantegriles *mpl* (*Uruguay*), ranchos *mpl* (*Venezuela*), villa *f* miseria (*Argentina*).

shape [ʃeɪp] ① N forma *f*; figura *f*; configuración *f*; (*of garment*) corte *m*; (*of person*) talle *m*, tipo *m*; (*for jelly etc*) molde *m*; (*thing dimly seen*) bulto *m*, forma *f*; **the ~ of things to come** la configuración del futuro; **not in any ~ or form** de ningún modo, en absoluto; **they come in all ~s and sizes** se sirven en todas las formas y todos los tamaños; **royalty was present in the ~ of Princess Ida** asistió la Realeza, en persona de la Princesa Ida; **stamps of all ~s** sellos *mpl* de todas las formas; **it is rectangular in ~** es de forma rectangular, tiene forma rectangular; **what ~ is it?** ¿de qué forma es?; **to be in good ~** estar en buenas condiciones, (*person*) estar bien de salud, estar en forma; **to be in bad ~** estar en mal estado, (*person*) estar enfermo, estar en malas condiciones físicas; **to beat sth into ~** dar forma a algo a martillazos; **to keep in ~** mantener(se) en forma; **to knock** (*or* **lick**) **sb into ~** desbastar a uno; disciplinar a uno; adiestrar a uno; **to lick a team into ~** ir entrenando un equipo; **to put an essay into ~** corregir un ensayo, preparar un ensayo para publicarlo (*etc*); **to get out of ~, to lose ~** perder la forma; **to take ~** tomar forma, irse formando, (*fig*) irse perfilando.
② VT formar, dar forma a; moldear; *stone* labrar; *wood* tallar; *jug etc* modelar, hacer; *course etc* condicionar, determinar; plasmar, amoldar; **~d like a tank** de forma de un carro de combate; **Plato helped to ~ his ideas** Platón ayudó a formar sus ideas; **the factors which ~ one's life** los factores que determinan el desarrollo de la vida de uno; **he did not ~ the course of events** él no influyó en la marcha de los acontecimientos; **there is a destiny which ~s our ends** hay un destino que gobierna nuestra vida.
③ VI formarse, tomar forma; **to ~ well** desarrollarse de modo esperanzador, prometer; **he is shaping (up) nicely as a goalkeeper** como guardameta promete, es un guardameta que promete; **how are things shaping?** ¿cómo van las cosas?; **as things are shaping** tal y como van las cosas.

◆ **shape up** VI (*US*) comportarse mejor; trabajar mejor, rendir más.

-shaped [ˈʃeɪpt] ADJ *ending in compounds* en forma de, *eg* **heart~** acorazonado, en forma de corazón; **U~** en forma de U.

shapeless [ˈʃeɪplɪs] ADJ informe, sin forma definida.

shapelessness [ˈʃeɪplɪsnɪs] N falta *f* de forma.

shapeliness [ˈʃeɪplɪnɪs] N proporción *f*; elegancia *f* (de forma).

shapely [ˈʃeɪplɪ] ADJ bien formado, bien proporcionado; *leg etc* torneado; *person* de buen talle; **~ columns** columnas *fpl* elegantes; **the ~ Miss Galicia** la bien modelada Miss Galicia.

shard [ʃɑːd] N tiesto *m*, casco *m*, fragmento *m* (de loza *etc*).

▼**share¹** [ʃeər] ① N (a) (*thing received*) parte *f*, porción *f*; (*proportion*) cuota *f*; participación *f*; proporción *f*; **~ in the market** participación *f* del mercado; **~ in the profits** participación *f* en los beneficios; **the lion's ~** la parte del león; **fair ~s for all** la equidad para todos, un trato equitativo para todos; **in equal ~s** por partes iguales; **your ~ is £5** le tocan a Vd 5 libras; **how much will my ~ be?** ¿cuánto me corresponderá a mí?; **to come in for one's full ~ of work** tener que hacer una buena parte del trabajo; **the minister came in for a full ~ of criticism** el ministro recibió una amplia dosis de críticas; **it fell to my ~** me tocó a mí, me correspondió a mí; **to go ~s** dividir lo recibido; contribuir por partes iguales; **to go half ~s with sb** dividir lo recibido con otro por partes iguales; **we've had our ~ of misfortunes** hemos sufrido bastante infortunio.
(b) (*contribution*) contribución *f*; cuota *f*; parte *f*; **to bear one's ~ of the cost** pagar la parte del coste que le corresponde a uno; **to do one's ~** cumplir con su obligación; **he doesn't do his ~** no hace todo lo que debiera, no hace todo lo que le cumple; **to have a ~ in sth** participar en algo; **I had no ~ in that** no tuve nada que ver con

eso; **to go ~s** ir a escote, escotar cada uno lo suyo; **to pay one's ~** pagar su cuota.

(c) (*Brit Fin*) acción *f*; **to hold 1000 ~s in a company** tener 1000 acciones en una compañía, poseer 1000 acciones de una compañía.

2 ATTR: **~ capital** capital *m* social en acciones; **~ certificate** (*Brit*) (certificado *m or* título *m* de una) acción *f*; **~ index** índice *m* de cotización en bolsa; **~ issue** emisión *f* de acciones; **~ option** plan *m* de compra de acciones de una empresa por sus empleados (*a precios ventajosos*); **~ premium** prima *f* de emisión; **~ prices** cotizaciones *fpl* (de acciones); **~ prospectus** prospecto *m* de acciones; **~ warrant** certificado *m* de acción.

▼**3** VT **(a)** (*have in common*) compartir, poseer en común; usar juntos de; **they ~ a room** comparten un cuarto; **to ~ certain characteristics** poseer en común ciertas características; **I do not ~ that view** no comparto ese criterio.

(b) (*divide*) partir (*with sb* con uno), dividir.

4 VI: **to ~ and ~ alike** participar por partes iguales; **children have to learn to ~** los niños tienen que aprender a compartir con otros; **there were no rooms free so I had to ~** no había habitación libre y por tanto tuve que compartir una con otra persona; **to ~ in** tener parte en, participar en, (*fig*) participar de; **to ~ in sb's success** contribuir al éxito de uno.

♦**share out** VT repartir, distribuir.

share² [ʃeəʳ] N (*Agr*) reja *f*.

sharecropper [ˈʃeəˌkrɒpəʳ] N (*US*) aparcero *m*, mediero *m* (*Mex*).

sharecropping [ˈʃeəˌkrɒpɪŋ] N (*US*) aparcería *f*.

shared [ʃeəd] ADJ compartido; *facilities etc* comunitario; **~ line** línea *f* compartida.

shareholder [ˈʃeəˌhəʊldəʳ] N (*Brit*) accionista *mf*.

shareholding [ˈʃeəˌhəʊldɪŋ] N accionariado *m*, acciones *fpl*; participación *f* accionaria.

share-out [ˈʃeəraʊt] N reparto *m*, distribución *f*.

shark [ʃɑːk] N **(a)** (*Fish*) tiburón *m*. **(b)** (*: swindler*) estafador *m*; **the ~s of the building trade** los piratas de la construcción. **(c)** (*US**) experto *m*, -a *f*, as* *m*.

sharkskin [ˈʃɑːkskɪn] N zapa *f*.

sharon [ˈʃærən] N (*also* **~ fruit**) sharon *m*.

sharp [ʃɑːp] **1** ADJ **(a)** (*cutting*) afilado, cortante; *point* puntiagudo; *angle* agudo; *curve, bend* cerrado, fuerte; *turn by car* repentino, brusco; *feature* bien marcado, anguloso; *outline* definido; *photo* nítido; *contrast* neto, marcado; **to be at the ~ end*** estar en situación peligrosa; ser el que va a sufrir las consecuencias; ser la víctima, ser el blanco.

(b) (*of person*) *mind* listo, vivo, despabilido, inteligente; *hearing* fino; *sight* agudo, penetrante; *glance* penetrante; **the child is quite ~** el niño es bastante listo; **he's as ~ as they come** es de lo más avispado; **that was pretty ~ of you** en eso has estado muy perspicaz; **you'll have to be ~er than that** tendrás que espabilarte.

(c) (*of person: pej*) astuto, mañoso; poco escrupuloso; *trick* poco honrado; **he's too ~ for me** es demasiado astuto para mi gusto; **~ practice** trampa *f*, maña *f*.

(d) (*fig*) *shower, storm* fuerte, repentino; *frost* fuerte; *wind* penetrante; *pain* agudo, intenso; *fight* encarnizado; *pace* rápido, vivo; *walk* rápido; *fall in price* brusco; *temper* áspero, vivo; *retort* áspero; *tongue* mordaz; *rebuke* severo; *tone* acerbo, áspero, severo; **that was ~ work!** ¡qué rápido!

(e) *taste* acerbo, acre; *wine* ácido.

(f) *sound* agudo, penetrante; (*Mus*) sostenido; **C ~** (*Mus*) do *m* sostenido.

2 ADV **(a)** (*Mus*) desafinadamente.

(b) **at 5 o'clock ~** a las 5 en punto; **and be ~ about it** y date prisa; **look ~!** ¡pronto!, ¡rápido!; **look ~ about it!** ¡menéarse!; **if you don't look ~** si no te meneas; **to pull up ~** frenar en seco; **you turn ~ left at the lights** a las luces se tuerce muy cerrado a la izquierda.

3 N **(a)** (*Mus*) sostenido *m*.

(b) (*: person*) estafador *m*, (*card~*) fullero *m*.

sharp-edged [ˈʃɑːpˈedʒd] ADJ afilado, de filo cortante.

sharpen [ˈʃɑːpən] **1** VT **(a)** *tool* afilar, aguzar; amolar; *pencil* sacar punta a.

(b) *appetite* (*also* **to ~ up**) abrir; *wits* despabilar; *conflict, emotion, sensation* aguzar.

2 VI (*fig*) agudizarse.

sharpener [ˈʃɑːpnəʳ] N afilador *m*, máquina *f* de afilar; (*pencil ~*) sacapuntas *m*.

sharper [ˈʃɑːpəʳ] N estafador *m*; (*card~*) fullero *m*.

sharp-eyed [ˈʃɑːpˈaɪd] ADJ de vista aguda, de ojos de lince.

sharp-faced [ˈʃɑːpˈfeɪst] ADJ de facciones angulosas.

sharpish* [ˈʃɑːpɪʃ] ADV prontito, bien pronto; **we'll be leaving ~ tomorrow** mañana partimos tempranito; **it needs to be ready ~** hay que tenerlo listo bien pronto.

sharply [ˈʃɑːplɪ] ADV (*abruptly*) bruscamente; (*clearly*) claramente; (*harshly*) severamente; **~ pointed** puntiagudo; **shares rose ~** las acciones subieron bruscamente.

sharpness [ˈʃɑːpnɪs] N (*V adj*) **(a)** lo afilado, lo cortante; lo puntiagudo; lo cerrado; lo repentino, brusquedad *f*; definición *f*; nitidez *f*; lo marcado.

(b) viveza *f*, inteligencia *f*; finura *f*; agudeza *f*.

(c) fuerza *f*, lo fuerte, lo repentino; agudeza *f*, intensidad *f*; brusquedad *f*, aspereza *f*; mordacidad *f*; severidad *f*; **there was a note of ~ in his voice** se notaba cierta aspereza en su tono; **there is a ~ in the air** empieza a notarse el frío.

sharpshooter [ˈʃɑːpˌʃuːtəʳ] N tirador *m* certero.

sharp-sighted [ˈʃɑːpˈsaɪtɪd] ADJ de vista aguda, de ojos de lince.

sharp-tempered [ˌʃɑːpˈtempəd] ADJ de genio áspero.

sharp-tongued [ˈʃɑːpˈtʌŋd] ADJ de lengua mordaz.

sharp-witted [ˈʃɑːpˈwɪtɪd] ADJ listo, perspicaz.

shat⁺ [ʃæt] PRET AND PTP *of* **shit.**

shatter [ˈʃætəʳ] **1** VT romper, hacer añicos, hacer pedazos; *health* quebrantar; *nerves* destrozar; *hopes etc* destruir, acabar con; **to ~ sth against a wall** estrellar algo contra una pared; **I was ~ed to hear it** al saberlo quedé estupefacto; **this will ~ you** tengo que decirte algo pasmoso; **she was ~ed by his death** su muerte la anonadó.

2 VI romperse, hacerse añicos; hacerse pedazos; estrellarse (*against* contra); **the windscreen ~ed** el parabrisas se hizo añicos.

shattered [ˈʃætəd] ADJ (*grief-stricken*) destrozado; (*aghast, overwhelmed*) abrumado, confundido; (*: exhausted*) hecho polvo*.

shattering [ˈʃætərɪŋ] ADJ *attack* demoledor; *news etc* pasmoso, fulgurante; *defeat* contundente; *experience* fulgurante; *day, journey* agotador.

shatterproof [ˈʃætəpruːf] ADJ *glass* inastillable.

shave [ʃeɪv] **1** N **(a)** afeitado *m*, rasurado *m*; **to have a ~** afeitarse.

(b) **close ~** (*lit*) afeitado *m* apurado; (*fig*) **to have a close** (*or* **narrow**) **~** escaparse por un pelo; **that was a close ~** eso fue cosa de milagro.

2 (*irr*: PRET **shaved**, PTP **shaved** *or* **shaven**) VT *face* afeitar, rasurar; *wood* acepillar; (*skim*) casi tocar, pasar rozando; *price etc* reducir; **to ~ one's legs** afeitarse las piernas, depilarse las piernas.

3 VI (*person*) afeitarse, rasurarse; **that razor ~s well** esa navaja afeita bien.

♦**shave off** VT: **to ~ off one's beard** afeitarse la barba, quitarse la barba.

shaven [ˈʃeɪvn] **1** PTP *of* **shave. 2** ADJ *head etc* rapado.

shaver [ˈʃeɪvəʳ] N **(a)** (*electric ~*) máquina *f* de afeitar eléctrica, afeitadora *f* eléctrica, rasuradora *f*. **(b)** **young ~*†** muchachuelo *m*, rapaz *m*, chaval* *m*.

Shavian [ˈʃeɪvɪən] ADJ shaviano, típico de G.B. Shaw.

shaving [ˈʃeɪvɪŋ] **1** N **(a)** (*with razor etc*) afeitado *m*, el afeitarse, rasurado *m*; **~ is a nuisance** es una pesadez tener que afeitarse.

(b) (*piece of wood, metal etc*) **~s** virutas *fpl*, acepilladuras *fpl*; **wood ~s** virutas *fpl* de madera.

2 ATTR de afeitar.

shaving-brush [ˈʃeɪvɪŋbrʌʃ] N brocha *f* (de afeitar).

shaving-cream [ˈʃeɪvɪŋkriːm] N crema *f* de afeitar.

shaving-foam [ˈʃeɪvɪŋfəʊm] N espuma *f* de afeitar.

shaving-lotion [ˈʃeɪvɪŋˌləʊʃən] N loción *f* para el afeitado.

shaving-mirror [ˈʃeɪvɪŋmɪrəʳ] N espejo *m* de bolsillo.

shaving point [ˈʃeɪvɪŋpɔɪnt] N enchufe *m* para máquinas de afeitar.

shaving-soap [ˈʃeɪvɪŋsəʊp] N jabón *m* de afeitar.

shaving-stick [ˈʃeɪvɪŋstɪk] N barra *f* de jabón de afeitar.

shawl [ʃɔːl] N chal *m*.

shawm [ʃɔːm] N chirimía *f*.

s/he ABBR *of* **he** *or* **she** él o ella.

she [ʃiː] **1** PRON ella; **~ who** la que, quien.

2 N hembra *f*.

3 ATTR hembra, *eg* **the ~-hedgehog** el erizo hembra, la hembra del erizo; **~-bear** osa *f*; **~-cat** gata *f*.

sheaf [ʃiːf] N, PL **sheaves** [ʃiːvz] (*Agr*) gavilla *f*; (*of arrows etc*) haz *m*; (*of papers*) fajo *m*, lío *m*.

shear [ʃɪəʳ] (*irr*: PRET **sheared**, PTP **shorn**) **1** VT *sheep* esquilar, trasquilar; *cloth* tundir.

2 N: **~s** tijeras *fpl* (grandes); (*Hort*) tijeras *fpl* de jardín; (*for metals*) cizalla *f*.

♦**shear off** VT cortar, quitar cortando; **the machine ~ed off two fingers** la máquina cercenó dos dedos; **the ship had its bows shorn off in the collision** la colisión cortó la proa al buque.

♦**shear through** VT cortar, hender.

shearer [ˈʃɪərəʳ] N esquilador *m*, -ora *f*.

shearing [ˈʃɪərɪŋ] N esquileo *m*; **~s** lana *f* esquilada.

shearing machine [ˈʃɪərɪŋməˌʃiːn] N esquiladora *f*.

shearwater [ˈʃɪəwɔːtəʳ] N pardela *f*.

sheath [ʃiːθ] N vaina *f*; funda *f*, cubierta *f*; (*Bot etc*) vaina *f*; (*Brit*) (*contraceptive*) condón *m*, preservativo *m*.

sheathe [ʃiːð] VT *sword* envainar; enfundar; **to ~ sth in metal** revestir algo de metal, poner cubierta metálica a algo.

sheathing [ˈʃiːðɪŋ] N revestimiento *m*, cubierta *f*.

sheath-knife [ˈʃiːθnaɪf] N, PL **sheath-knives** [ˈʃiːθnaɪvz] cuchillo *m* de

---

▶ LANGUAGE IN USE: **share: 3a → 12.1**

funda.

sheaves [ʃiːvz] PL of **sheaf**.

Sheba [ˈʃiːbə] N Sabá; **Queen of ~** reina f de Sabá.

shebang*: [ʃəˈbæŋ] N: **the whole ~** (esp US) todo ello, todo el negocio.

shebeen [ʃɪˈbiːn] N (Ir) taberna f ilícita.

shed[1] [ʃed] (irr: PRET AND PTP **shed**) VT **(a)** (get rid of) clothes, leaves etc despojarse de; skin mudar; unwanted thing deshacerse de; desprenderse de, quitarse; **the party tried to ~ its leader** el partido intentó deshacerse de su jefe; **the lorry ~ its load** la carga cayó del camión; **the roof is built to ~ water** el techo está construido para que el agua no quede en él; **I'm trying to ~ 5 kilos** estoy tratando de perder 5 kilos.

(b) (send out) tears verter; blood verter, derramar; light dar, (fig) echar, arrojar; happiness etc difundir, irradiar; **much blood has been ~** se ha vertido mucha sangre; **no blood was ~** no hubo efusión de sangre.

shed[2] [ʃed] N (garden ~ etc) cobertizo m, alpende m; (workmen's) barraca f; (industrial) nave f.

she'd [ʃiːd] = **she would; she had**.

sheen [ʃiːn] N lustre m; brillo m; **to take the ~ off sth** deslustrar algo.

sheeny [ˈʃiːnɪ] ADJ lustroso, brillante.

sheep [ʃiːp] N, PL INVAR oveja f; (ram) carnero m; (pl, collectively) ganado m lanar; **to count ~** fingir contar ovejas (para dormirse); **to separate the ~ from the goats** (fig) apartar las ovejas de los cabritos; **to make ~'s eyes at sb** mirar tiernamente a uno; **they followed like a lot of ~** le (etc) siguieron como manada de borregos; V **black 1**.

sheep-dip [ˈʃiːpdɪp] N (baño m) desinfectante m para ovejas.

sheepdog [ˈʃiːpdɒg] N perro m pastor; **~ trials** pruebas fpl de trabajo para perros pastores, concurso m de pastoreo.

sheep-farm [ˈʃiːpfɑːm] N granja f de ovejas.

sheep-farmer [ˈʃiːpˌfɑːməʳ] N dueño m de ganado lanar, ganadero m.

sheep-farming [ˈʃiːpˌfɑːmɪŋ] N pastoreo m, industria f del ganado lanar, ganadería f.

sheepfold [ˈʃiːpfəʊld] N redil m, aprisco m.

sheepish [ˈʃiːpɪʃ] ADJ tímido, vergonzoso.

sheepishly [ˈʃiːpɪʃlɪ] ADV tímidamente.

sheepishness [ˈʃiːpɪʃnɪs] N timidez f, vergüenza f.

sheepmeat [ˈʃiːpmiːt] N carne f de oveja.

sheep-run [ˈʃiːprʌn] N pasto m de ovejas, dehesa f de ovejas.

sheepshearer [ˈʃiːpˌʃɪərəʳ] N (person) esquilador m, -ora f; (machine) esquiladora f.

sheepskin [ˈʃiːpskɪn] N piel f de carnero; zamarra f, badana f; **~ jacket** zamarra f, gamulán m (SC).

sheep-track [ˈʃiːptræk] N cañada f.

sheepwalk [ˈʃiːpwɔːk] N = **sheep-run**.

sheep-worrying [ˈʃiːpˌwʌrɪɪŋ] N acoso m de ovejas.

sheer[1] [ʃɪəʳ] [1] ADJ **(a)** (absolute) puro, completo, absoluto; **the ~ impossibility of ...** la total imposibilidad de ...; **~ nonsense!** ¡puro disparate!; **this is ~ robbery** esto es puro robo; **by ~ force** a viva fuerza; **by ~ hard work** gracias simplemente al trabajo, por puro esfuerzo de trabajo; **in ~ desperation** en último extremo; see also PURE.

(b) (steep) escarpado, cortado a pico; perpendicular; **there is a ~ fall of 200 metres** hay una caída de 200 metros sin obstáculo alguno.

(c) (of cloth etc) diáfano; **~ curtain** visillos mpl.

[2] ADV: **it falls ~ to the sea** baja sin obstáculo alguno hasta el mar; **it rises ~ above the town** está cortado a pico por encima de la ciudad; **it rises ~ for 100 metres** se levanta verticalmente unos 100 metros.

[3] NPL: **~s** (US) visillos mpl.

sheer[2] [ʃɪəʳ] VI: **to ~ away from a topic** desviarse de un tema, evitar hablar de un tema.

♦**sheer off** VI (Naut) desviarse; (fig) largarse.

sheet [ʃiːt] [1] N (bed~) sábana f; (shroud) mortaja f; (of paper, newspaper) hoja f; (of tin) hoja f, (of other metal) chapa f, lámina f; (of glass) lámina f; (of water etc) extensión f; (Naut) escota f; (cover) cubierta f; (tarpaulin) alquitranado m; **a ~ of flame** unas lenguas de fuego; **a ~ of ice** una capa de hielo; **to start again with a clean ~** volver a comenzar sin nota adversa.

[2] ATTR: **~ feed** alimentador m de papel; **~ glass** vidrio m plano; **~ lightning** relámpago m difuso, fucilazo m; **~ music** (hojas fpl de) partitura f; **~ steel** chapa f de acero; láminas fpl de acero, acero m en láminas.

[3] VT: **to ~ sth in, to ~ sth over** cubrir algo con un alquitranado.

sheet anchor [ˈʃiːtˌæŋkəʳ] N ancla f de la esperanza.

sheeting [ˈʃiːtɪŋ] N (cloth) lencería f para sábanas; (metal) placas fpl de metal, laminado m, cobertura f metálica.

sheik(h) [ʃeɪk] N jeque.

sheik(h)dom [ˈʃeɪkdəm] N reino m (or territorio m) de un jeque.

shekel [ˈʃekl] N siclo m; **~s*** pasta* f, parné: m.

sheldrake [ˈʃeldreɪk] N, **shelduck** [ˈʃeldʌk] N tadorna f.

shelf [ʃelf] [1] N, PL **shelves** [ʃelvz] **(a)** tabla f, anaquel m; (of cupboard, kitchen) repisa f; **shelves** (collectively) estante m, estantería f; **to be (left) on the ~** (girl) quedarse para vestir santos; (proposal etc) quedar arrinconado; **to leave sth on the ~** (fig) arrinconar algo, dar carpetazo a algo; **to buy a product off the ~** comprar un producto ya hecho.

(b) (Geog: on rock face) repisa f; (Naut) banco m de arena, bajo m; plataforma f.

[2] ATTR (Comm) **~ life** tiempo m de durabilidad antes de la venta; **~ mark** código m; **~ space** cantidad f de estanterías (para exponer la mercancía).

she'll [ʃiːl] = **she will, she shall**.

shell [ʃel] [1] N **(a)** (Zool: of egg) cáscara f, cascarón m; (of nut) cáscara f; (of mollusc) concha f; (of tortoise, turtle) caparazón m; (of insect, lobster etc) caparazón m, carapacho m; (of pea) vaina f; **to come out of one's ~** salir de su concha; **to retire into one's ~** meterse en su concha.

(b) (Tech: framework) armazón f, esqueleto m; (of house, after bombardment etc) casco m; (Naut) casco m; (outer covering) cubierta f, exterior m.

(c) (boat) bote m de construcción lisa.

(d) (Mil) proyectil m, obús m, granada f; (US) cartucho m.

[2] VT **(a)** peas desenvainar; eggs, nuts descascarar, quitar la cáscara a.

(b) (Mil) bombardear.

♦**shell out*** [1] VT money aflojar*, desembolsar.

[2] VI retratarse* (for sth para pagar algo).

shellac [ʃəˈlæk] N laca f, goma f laca.

shelled [ʃeld] ADJ: **~ nuts** nueces fpl sin cáscara.

shellfire [ˈʃelfaɪəʳ] N cañoneo m, fuego m de artillería, bombardeo m; **to be under ~** sufrir un bombardeo; **the ~ lasted all night** el cañoneo duró toda la noche.

shellfish [ˈʃelfɪʃ] N (Zool) crustáceo m; (as food) marisco m, (collectively) mariscos mpl.

shell-hole [ˈʃelhəʊl] N hoyo m que forma un obús al explotar.

shelling [ˈʃelɪŋ] N bombardeo m.

shellproof [ˈʃelpruːf] ADJ a prueba de bombas.

shellshock [ˈʃelʃɒk] N neurosis f de guerra, shock m (causado por bombardeos).

shell-shocked [ˈʃelʃɒkt] ADJ que padece neurosis de guerra; (fig) que sufre estrés.

shell suit [ˈʃelsuːt] N chandal m holgado.

shelter [ˈʃeltəʳ] [1] N abrigo m, asilo m, refugio m; (air-raid ~ etc) refugio m; (bus ~) refugio m (de espera); (mountain ~) albergue m; (fig) protección f, resguardo m; **under ~** al abrigo; **under the ~ of the mountain** al abrigo de la montaña; **to seek ~** buscar dónde cobijarse; **to seek ~ for the night** buscar dónde pasar la noche; **to take ~** ponerse al abrigo (from de), cobijarse (from de).

[2] VT abrigar (from de); (aid) amparar, proteger (from de); (hide) esconder, ocultar; **to ~ a criminal** proteger a un criminal, dar albergue a un criminal.

[3] VI abrigarse, ponerse al abrigo, cobijarse (from de); refugiarse; **to ~ from the rain** ponerse al abrigo de la lluvia.

sheltered [ˈʃeltəd] ADJ place abrigado; industry protegido (contra la competencia extranjera); **~ accommodation** residencia f vigilada; **~ life** vida f protegida; **she has led a very ~ life** se ha criado bajo las faldas de mamá, se ha criado en la inocencia; **a spot ~ from the wind** un sitio al abrigo del viento.

shelve [ʃelv] [1] VT (fig) dar carpetazo a, arrinconar, aplazar indefinidamente; (Parl etc) aparcar*.

[2] VI formar declive, estar en declive; **the beach ~s rapidly** el fondo está en fuerte declive; **it ~s down to the sea** baja hacia el mar.

shelves [ʃelvz] PL of **shelf**.

shelving [ˈʃelvɪŋ] N estante m, estantería f.

shemozzle* [ʃəˈmɒzl] N (Brit) lío* m; bronca f, follón* m.

shenanigans* [ʃəˈnænɪgənz] NPL trampas fpl, artimañas fpl; travesuras fpl; bromas fpl.

shepherd [ˈʃepəd] [1] N pastor m; **the Good S~** el Buen Pastor; **~'s crook** cayado m; **~'s pie** (Brit) plato a base de carne picada y puré de patatas; **~'s purse** (Bot) zurrón m de pastor.

[2] VT guiar, conducir; **to ~ children across a road** conducir niños a través de una calle.

shepherd-boy [ˈʃepədbɔɪ] N zagal m.

shepherdess [ˈʃepədɪs] N pastora f, zagala f.

sherbet [ˈʃɜːbət] N = **sherbet**.

sherbet [ˈʃɜːbət] N polvos mpl de limón; gaseosa f en polvo; (US) sorbete m.

sherd [ʃɜːd] N = **shard**.

sheriff [ˈʃerɪf] N sheriff m, alguacil m (oficial de justicia inglés, escocés, o norteamericano); ver también COURTS.

sheriff court [ˌʃerɪfˈkɔːt] N (Scot) tribunal m de distrito.

Sherpa [ˈʃɜːpə] N sherpa mf.

sherry [ˈʃerɪ] N jerez m.

she's [ʃiːz] = she is; she has.

Shetland Islands ['ʃetlənd,aɪləndz] NPL, **Shetlands** ['ʃetləndz] NPL Islas *fpl* Shetland, Islas *fpl* de Zetlandia.

shew [ʃəʊ] VTI (††) = **show**.

shewn [ʃəʊn] PTP (††) of **show**.

shiatsu [ʃiː'ætsuː] N shiatsu *m*, digitopuntura *f*.

shibboleth ['ʃɪbəleθ] N (*Bible*) lema *m*, santo *m* y seña; (*fig*) dogma *m* hoy desacreditado, doctrina *f* que ha quedado anticuada.

shield [ʃiːld] **1** N (*also Her*) escudo *m*; (*round*) rodela *f*; (*Tech*) blindaje *m*, capa *f* protectora; (*fig*) escudo *m*, defensa *f*.
2 VT proteger, resguardar, amparar; *criminal* proteger; (*Tech*) blindar, revestir de una capa protectora; **to ~ one's eyes from the sun** proteger los ojos contra el sol.

shieling ['ʃiːlɪŋ] N (*Scot*) (*pasture*) pasto *m*, prado *m*; (*hut*) choza *f*, cabaña *f*; albergue *m*; (*sheepfold*) aprisco *m*.

shift [ʃɪft] **1** N (a) (*change*) cambio *m* (*in, of* de); cambio *m* de sitio, traslado *m*, movimiento *m*; desplazamiento *m*; **~ of emphasis** cambio *m* de énfasis; **~ of wind** cambio *m* (de dirección) del viento; **consonant ~** cambio *m* consonántico; **~ in demand** desplazamiento *m* de la demanda; **there has been a ~ in policy** ha habido un cambio de política; **the ~ from north to south is increasing** el movimiento de norte a sur se acelera; **to make a ~** cambiar de sitio, (*person*) irse, largarse; **it's time we made a ~** ya es hora de cambiar de sitio.
(b) (*at work*) turno *m*; (*of workers*) tanda *f*; **an 8-hour ~** un turno de 8 horas; **to work in ~s** trabajar por turnos.
(c) (*expedient*) recurso *m*, expediente *m*; (*pej*) maña *f*, astucia *f*; **to make ~ with** arreglárselas con, contentarse con; **to make ~ without** arreglárselas sin, prescindir de, pasarse sin; **to make ~ to** + *infin* arreglárselas para + *infin*, ingeniarse por + *infin*.
(d) (††) camisa *f* (de mujer).
(e) (*US Aut: gear ~*) palanca *f* de velocidades, cambio *m* de marcha (*LAm*).
2 ATTR: **three-~ system** (*work*) sistema *m* de tres turnos.
3 VT cambiar; (*move*) cambiar de sitio, trasladar a otro sitio, mover; (*budge*) mover; *stain etc* quitar, hacer salir; (*get rid of*) quitarse de encima, librarse de; *gears* (*US*) cambiar de; **to ~ scenery** cambiar el decorado; **~ it over to the wall** ponlo contra la pared; **we could not ~ him (from his opinion)** no logramos hacerle cambiar de opinión; **I can't ~ this cold** no me quito este catarro; **they ~ed him to Valencia** le trasladaron a Valencia; **we shall have to ~ 20 tons** hará falta mover 20 toneladas; **to ~ the blame on to sb else** echar (*or* pasar) la culpa a otro.
4 VI (a) (*move*) moverse; cambiar; cambiar de sitio; (*person*) cambiar de puesto, trasladarse a otro sitio; (*move house*) mudar; (*of ballast, cargo*) correrse; (*of wind*) cambiar; (*in attitude etc*) cambiar de actitud, modificar su postura; **can you please ~ along a little?** ¿te corres un poco a ese lado?; **to ~ into second (gear)** (*US*) cambiar a segunda (velocidad); **the scene ~s to Burgos** la escena cambia a Burgos; **he ~ed to Lima** se trasladó a Lima; **we couldn't get him to ~** no logramos hacerle cambiar de actitud.
(b) (*: car etc*) ir a gran velocidad, correr; (*person*) darse prisa, menearse; **~!** ¡menearse!
(c) **to ~ for o.s.** valerse por sí mismo, arreglárselas solo.
♦**shift about, shift around** VI cambiar (mucho) de sitio, (*in job*) cambiar de empleo.
♦**shift over** VI correrse.

shiftily ['ʃɪftɪlɪ] ADV astutamente; furtivamente; **to behave ~** comportarse de modo sospechoso.

shiftiness ['ʃɪftɪnɪs] N lo tramposo, lo taimado, astucia *f*; lo sospechoso; lo furtivo.

shifting ['ʃɪftɪŋ] ADJ *sand etc* movedizo.

shift-key ['ʃɪftkiː] N tecla *f* de mayúsculas.

shiftless ['ʃɪftlɪs] ADJ (*lazy*) vago, holgazán; (*useless*) inútil, incompetente.

shiftlessness ['ʃɪftlɪsnɪs] N holgazanería *f*; inutilidad *f*.

shift register ['ʃɪft,redʒɪstəʳ] N registro *m* de desplazamiento.

shift-worker ['ʃɪft,wɜːkəʳ] N (*Brit*) trabajador *m*, -ora *f* por turnos.

shift-work(ing) ['ʃɪftwɜːk(ɪŋ)] N (*Brit*) trabajo *m* por turno.

shifty ['ʃɪftɪ] ADJ tramposo, taimado, astuto; *conduct* sospechoso; *glance etc* furtivo.

shifty-eyed ['ʃɪftɪ'aɪd] ADJ de mirada furtiva.

Shi'ite ['ʃiːaɪt] **1** ADJ chiíta.
2 N chiíta *mf*.

shillelagh [ʃə'leɪlə, ʃə'leɪlɪ] N (*Ir*) cachiporra *f*.

shilling ['ʃɪlɪŋ] N chelín *m*; **6 ~s in the pound** 6 chelines por libra; **to cut sb off with a ~** desheredar a uno; **to take the Queen's** (*or* **King's**) **~** (*Hist*) alistarse en el ejército.

shilly-shally ['ʃɪlɪ,ʃælɪ] VI vacilar, no resolverse, no saber qué hacer; **you've shilly-shallied long enough** has estado bastante tiempo ya sin resolverte.

shilly-shallying ['ʃɪlɪ,ʃælɪŋ] N vacilación *f*, titubeos *mpl*.

shimmer ['ʃɪməʳ] **1** N reflejo *m* trémulo, resplandor *m* trémulo.
2 VI rielar, relucir.

shimmering ['ʃɪmərɪŋ] ADJ, **shimmery** ['ʃɪmərɪ] ADJ reluciente; *light* trémulo.

shimmy* ['ʃɪmɪ] N camisa *f* (de mujer).

shin [ʃɪn] N espinilla *f*; (*of meat*) jarrete *m*, corvejón *m*.
♦**shin up** VI trepar; **to ~ up a tree** trepar a un árbol.

shinbone ['ʃɪnbəʊn] N espinilla *f*, tibia *f*.

shindig* ['ʃɪndɪg] N juerga* *f*, guateque *m*.

shindy* ['ʃɪndɪ] N (*noise*) ruido *m* grande, conmoción *f*; (*dispute*) lío* *m*, bronca *f*; **to kick up a ~** meter ruido; armar un lío*.

shine [ʃaɪn] **1** N (a) (*brilliance*) brillo *m*, lustre *m*; **to give one's shoes a ~** sacar brillo a los zapatos, limpiar los zapatos; **to take the ~ off** sth deslustrar algo; (*fig*) quitarle el encanto a algo; **to take the ~ out of sb** eclipsar a uno, dejar a uno muy atrás; **to take a ~ to*** tomar simpatía por, encontrar simpático a.
(b) (*Met*) buen tiempo *m*, tiempo *m* de sol; **we'll go rain or ~** iremos no importa el tiempo que haga.
2 (*irr*: PRET AND PTP **shone**) VT (a) *shoes* sacar brillo a, limpiar, bolear (*Mex*); *silver etc* pulir.
(b) **to ~ a light on sth** proyectar una luz sobre algo; **~ the torch this way** dirige la linterna hacia este lado.
3 VI (a) brillar; relucir, resplandecer; **a lamp was shining** brillaba una lámpara; **the sun is shining** hay sol; **the metal shone in the sun** el metal relucía al sol; **her face shone with happiness** su cara irradiaba felicidad; **a certain quiet confidence ~s through** trasciende cierta confianza.
(b) (*fig*) brillar, lucirse, distinguirse; **he doesn't exactly ~ at his work** no brilla en sus estudios que digamos; **he shone as a footballer** se distinguió como futbolista.
♦**shine down** VI (*of sun, moon, stars*) brillar.

shiner* ['ʃaɪnəʳ] N (*black eye*) ojo *m* a la funerala.

shingle¹ ['ʃɪŋgl] **1** N (a) (*Archit*) ripia *f*. (b) (†: *hair style*) corte *m* a lo garçon. (c) (*US*) rótulo *m* de oficina (*or* de consultorio *etc*); **to hang out one's ~** colgar un cartel; abrir una oficina (*etc*).
2 VT (†) *hair* cortar a lo garçon.

shingle² ['ʃɪŋgl] N (*pebbles*) guijos *mpl*, guijarral *m*; (*beach*) playa *f* guijarrosa.

shingles ['ʃɪŋglz] N (*Med*) herpes *m or fpl*.

shingly ['ʃɪŋglɪ] ADJ guijarroso.

shinguard ['ʃɪŋgɑːd] N espinillera *f*.

shininess ['ʃaɪnɪnɪs] N brillo *m*.

shining ['ʃaɪnɪŋ] ADJ brillante, lustroso; *face etc* radiante; *example* notable; **their ~ hour** su momento cumbre.

shinpad ['ʃɪnpæd] N espinillera *f*.

Shinto ['ʃɪntəʊ] N shinto *m*.

Shintoism ['ʃɪntəʊɪzəm] N shintoísmo *m*.

Shintoist ['ʃɪntəʊɪst] ADJ, N shintoísta *mf*.

shinty ['ʃɪntɪ] N (*Scot*) especie de hockey.

shiny ['ʃaɪnɪ] ADJ brillante, lustroso; *cloth* (*with wear*) gastado, con brillo.

ship [ʃɪp] **1** N buque *m*, barco *m*, navío *m*; **the good ~ Venus** el buque Venus, el Venus; **Her** (*or* **His**) **Majesty's S~** (ABBR **HMS**) buque *m* de guerra inglés; **to serve on HMS Warspite** servir en el Warspite; **~'s boat** lancha *f*, bote *m* salvavidas; **~'s company** tripulación *f*; **~'s doctor** médico *m* de a bordo; **~'s manifest** manifesto *m* del buque; **~'s papers** documentación *f* del buque; **the ~ of the desert** el camello; **~ of the line** buque *m* de línea; **on board ~** a bordo; **to abandon ~** abandonar el barco; **to clear a ~ for action** alistar un buque para el combate; **when my ~ comes in** cuando lleguen las vacas gordas, cuando la suerte me favorezca; **to jump ~** desertar del buque; **to pump ~**❋ mear❋; **to take ~ for** embarcarse para.
2 VT (a) (*put on board*) *goods, passengers* embarcar; *mast* izar; *oars* desarmar; **to ~ a sea** embarcar agua.
(b) (*transport*) transportar (por vía marítima), enviar, expedir.
3 VI embarcarse (*on* en).
♦**ship off** VT expedir.
♦**ship out** VT enviar, mandar; **a new engine had to be ~ped out to them** hubo que enviarles un nuevo motor.

shipboard ['ʃɪpbɔːd] N: **on ~** a bordo.

shipbreaker ['ʃɪp,breɪkəʳ] N desguazador *m*.

ship-broker ['ʃɪp,brəʊkəʳ] N agente *m* marítimo.

shipbuilder ['ʃɪp,bɪldəʳ] N constructor *m* de buques, arquitecto *m* naval.

shipbuilding ['ʃɪp,bɪldɪŋ] N construcción *f* de buques, construcción *f* naval.

ship canal ['ʃɪpkə,næl] N canal *m* de navegación.

shipload ['ʃɪpləʊd] N cargamento *m* (entero) de un buque; (*loosely*) envío *m*, cantidad *f* enviada; (*) montón* *m*; **we have jam by the ~*** tenemos mermelada a montones*; **the tourists are arriving by the ~*** los turistas vienen en masa.

shipmate ['ʃɪpmeɪt] N camarada *m* de a bordo.

shipment ['ʃɪpmənt] N (act) embarque m; transporte m; (quantity) envío m, remesa f.

shipowner ['ʃɪpəʊnəʳ] N naviero m, armador m.

shipper ['ʃɪpəʳ] N exportador m; importador m; (sender) remitente m, transportista m.

shipping ['ʃɪpɪŋ] ① N (a) (act) embarque m; transporte m (por vía marítima).

(b) (ships) buques mpl, barcos mpl; (ships of a country) flota f, marina f; **dangerous to ~** peligroso para la navegación; **~ losses in 1942** cantidad f (or tonelaje m) de buques perdidos en 1942; **the canal is closed to British ~** el canal está cerrado para la marina británica.

② ATTR: **~ agent** agente m marítimo; **~ company** compañía f naviera; **~ department** departamento m de envíos; **~ instructions** instrucciones fpl de embarque; **~ lane** ruta f de navegación; **~ line** compañía f naviera; **~ office** oficina f de compañía naviera; **~ specification** especificaciones fpl de embarque.

ship's chandler ['ʃɪps,tʃɑːndləʳ] N (also **ship chandler**) abastecedor m de buques, proveedor m de efectos navales.

shipshape ['ʃɪpʃeɪp] ADV, ADJ en buen orden, en regla; **to get everything ~** ponerlo todo en orden.

ship-to-shore ['ʃɪptə,ʃɔːʳ] ATTR: **~ radio** radio f de barco a costa.

shipwreck ['ʃɪprek] ① N naufragio m (also fig).

② VT: **to be ~ed** naufragar; **~ person** náufrago m, -a f.

shipwright ['ʃɪpraɪt] N carpintero m de navío.

shipyard ['ʃɪpjɑːd] N astillero m.

shire ['ʃaɪəʳ] ① N (Brit) condado m; **the S~s** los condados centrales de Inglaterra.

② ATTR: **~ horse** percherón m.

-shire [ʃɪəʳ] N ending in compounds: condado m.

shirk [ʃɜːk] ① VT eludir, esquivar; obligation faltar a; work no hacer, rehuir; difficulty, issue escamotear; **to ~ doing sth** esquivar el deber de hacer algo.

② VI faltar al deber; ponerse al socaire; escamotear; (not work) gandulear; **you're ~ing!** ¡eres un gandul!

shirker ['ʃɜːkəʳ] N gandul m, flojo m (LAm).

shirr [ʃɜːʳ] VT (a) (Sew) fruncir. (b) **~ed eggs** (US) huevos mpl al plato.

shirring ['ʃɜːrɪŋ] N frunce m.

shirt [ʃɜːt] N camisa f; (Sport) camiseta f; **to keep one's ~ on*** quedarse sereno; **keep your ~ on!*** ¡con calma!; **to put one's ~ on a horse** apostar todo lo que tiene uno a un caballo.

shirt-collar ['ʃɜːt,kɒləʳ] N cuello m de camisa.

shirtdress ['ʃɜːtdres] N camisa f vestido.

shirt-front ['ʃɜːtfrʌnt] N pechera f.

shirtless ['ʃɜːtlɪs] ADJ sin camisa, descamisado.

shirt-sleeves ['ʃɜːtsliːvz] NPL: **to be in ~** estar en mangas de camisa.

shirttail ['ʃɜːteɪl] N faldón m (de camisa).

shirtwaist ['ʃɜːtweɪst] N (US) blusa f (de mujer).

shirty* ['ʃɜːtɪ] ADJ (esp Brit): **he was pretty ~ about it** la cosa no le gustó en absoluto, la cosa no le cayó en gracia; **to get ~** ponerse negro*, amostazarse*.

shish kebab ['ʃiːʃkə'bæb] N V **kebab**.

shit⚠ [ʃɪt] ① N (a) (excrement) mierda⚠ f, caca⚠ f; **~!, oh ~!** ¡mierda!⚠; **tough ~!** ¡mala suerte!; **to beat** (or **knock** etc) **the ~ out of sb** dar una tremenda paliza a uno*; **I don't give a ~** me importa un rábano; **to have the ~s** tener el vientre descompuesto; **he landed** (or **dropped**) **us in the ~** nos dejó en la mierda⚠.

(b) (person) mierda⚠ f, cabrón⚠ m.

(c) (nonsense) cagadas⚠ fpl.

② (PRET AND PTP **shit**, **shitted** or **shat**) VT cagar⚠; **to ~ bricks** (etc) cagarse de miedo⚠.

③ VI cagar⚠.

④ VR: **to ~ o.s.** cagarse de miedo⚠.

shite⚠ [ʃaɪt] (Brit) = **shit**.

shitless⚠ ['ʃɪtlɪs] ADJ: **to be scared ~** estar acojonado⚠; **to be bored ~** estar más harto que la hostia⚠.

shitlist⚠ ['ʃɪtlɪst] N lista f negra.

shitty⚠ ['ʃɪtɪ] ADJ (fig) de mierda⚠.

shiver¹ ['ʃɪvəʳ] ① N (a) temblor m, estremecimiento m; (with cold) tiritón m; (of horror etc) escalofrío m; **to give a ~** estremecerse; **it sent ~s down my back** me dio escalofríos.

(b) **the ~s** (fig) dentera f, grima f; **it gives me the ~s** (of fear) me da miedo; (of taste etc) me da dentera.

② VI temblar, estremecerse; vibrar; (with fear) temblar, dar diente con diente; (with cold) tiritar.

shiver² ['ʃɪvəʳ] ① VT (break) romper, hacer añicos.

② VI romperse, hacerse añicos.

shivery ['ʃɪvərɪ] ADJ estremecido; (sensitive to cold) friolero, friolento (LAm); **to feel ~** tener frío, tener escalofríos.

shoal¹ [ʃəʊl] ① N (sandbank etc) banco m de arena, bajío m, bajo m.

② VI disminuir en profundidad, hacerse menos profundo.

shoal² [ʃəʊl] N (of fish) banco m, cardumen m; (of people etc) multitud f; muchedumbre f; **to come in ~s** venir en tropel; **we have ~s of**

---

applications tenemos montones de solicitudes.

shock¹ [ʃɒk] ① N (a) (Elec) descarga f (eléctrica); sacudida f, calambre m; (collision) choque m, colisión f; (jolt) sacudida f; (of earthquake) seísmo m, temblor m de tierra; **she got a ~ from the refrigerator** la nevera le dio una descarga; **the ~ of the explosion was felt 5 miles away** se sintió el choque de la explosión a una distancia de 5 millas; **the house collapsed at the first ~** al primer seísmo se hundió la casa.

(b) (emotional) conmoción f (desagradable); impresión f (fuerte); (start) sobresalto m, susto m; **our feeling is one of ~** lo que sentimos es un enorme disgusto; **the ~ was too much for him** la conmoción que le produjo la noticia le anonadó; **the ~ killed him** el disgusto le mató; **it comes as a ~ to hear that ...** nos asombramos al saber que ...; **to give sb a ~** sobresaltar a uno; asombrar a uno; **it gave me a nasty ~** me produjo una conmoción desagradable; **the news gave me quite a ~** la noticia me afectó muchísimo, la noticia me disgustó bastante; **what a ~ you gave me!** ¡qué susto me diste!

(c) (Med) shock m, postración f nerviosa, conmoción f; **to be in** (a **state of**) **~** estar conmocionado; **to be suffering from ~** padecer una postración nerviosa.

② ATTR: **~ result** resultado m sorprendente; **~ tactics** táctica f de ataque repentino; **~ therapy**, **~ treatment** terapia f de choque (also fig); **~ troops** tropas fpl de asalto; **~ wave** onda f de choque, onda f expansiva.

③ VT (startle) sobresaltar, dar un susto a; (affect emotionally) dar un disgusto a, producir una conmoción desagradable a; impresionar (fuertemente); (make indignant) indignar; (because of impropriety) escandalizar; ofender; **she is easily ~ed** se ofende por cualquier cosa, se escandaliza por poca cosa; **I was ~ed to hear the news** la noticia me dio un enorme disgusto, la noticia me asombró; **now don't be ~ed at what I'm going to say** no te escandalices de lo que te voy a decir; **you can't ~ me** yo no me asombro de nada; **to ~ sb into doing sth** dar una sacudida a uno para animarle a hacer algo; **we managed to ~ him out of his complacency** con el susto pudimos sacarle de su suficiencia.

shock² [ʃɒk] ① N (Agr) tresnal m, garbera f.

② VT poner en tresnales.

shock³ [ʃɒk] N: **~ of hair** greña f; melena f.

shockable ['ʃɒkəbl] ADJ impresionable; sensible; **she's very ~** se escandaliza por poca cosa; **I am not easily ~** yo no me asombro de nada.

shock-absorber ['ʃɒkəb,zɔːbəʳ] N amortiguador m.

shocked [ʃɒkt] ADJ (taken aback) sorprendido; (disgusted) ofendido; (scandalized) escandalizado; (Med) en estado de shock, conmocionado; **a ~ silence** un silencio conmocionado.

shocker* ['ʃɒkəʳ] N (a) (Liter) novelucha f. (b) **it's a ~** es horrible; es de lo más vil; **he's a ~** es un sinvergüenza, es un canalla; **you ~!** (hum) ¡canalla!

shock-headed ['ʃɒk'hedɪd] ADJ greñudo; melenudo.

shocking ['ʃɒkɪŋ] ① ADJ (appalling) espantoso, horrible; (morally improper) escandaloso, vergonzoso, ofensivo, chocante (esp LAm); **~ pink** rosa m estridente; **how ~!** ¡qué horror!; **isn't it ~?** ¿es espantoso, eh?; **it was a ~ sight** fue un espectáculo horrible; **she has ~ taste** tiene un pésimo gusto; **the book is not all that ~** el libro es menos escandaloso de lo que se dice.

② ADV (*) **a ~ bad film** una película de bajísima calidad; **it was ~ awful** fue de lo más horrible.

shockingly ['ʃɒkɪŋlɪ] ADV horriblemente; escandalosamente; **~ dear** terriblemente caro; **a ~ bad film** una película de bajísima calidad; **to behave ~** comportarse de modo escandaloso.

shock jock* ['ʃɒkdʒɒk] N (esp US) presentador(a) polémico/a de coloquios radiofónicos abiertos al público.

shockproof ['ʃɒkpruːf] ADJ a prueba de choques; person imperturbable.

shod [ʃɒd] PRET AND PTP of **shoe**; **~ with** calzado de.

shoddily ['ʃɒdɪlɪ] ADV (behave) ruínmente; **~ made** mal hecho.

shoddiness ['ʃɒdɪnɪs] N baja calidad f; mala hechura f.

shoddy ['ʃɒdɪ] ① ADJ de pacotilla, de bajísima calidad; muy mal hecho.

② N (cloth) paño m burdo de lana; (wool) lana f regenerada; (as waste, fertilizer) desechos mpl de lana.

shoe [ʃuː] ① N zapato m; (horse~) herradura f; (brake~) zapata f; **I wouldn't like to be in his ~s** no quisiera estar en su pellejo; **to cast a ~** (horse) perder una herradura; **to know where the ~ pinches** saber dónde aprieta el zapato; **to put on one's ~s** calzarse; **to take off one's ~s** quitarse los zapatos, descalzarse; **to step into sb's ~s** pasar a ocupar el puesto de uno; **to be waiting for dead men's ~s** esperar a que muera uno (para pasar luego a ocupar su puesto).

② (irr: PRET AND PTP **shod**) VT calzar (with de); horse herrar.

shoeblack ['ʃuːblæk] N limpiabotas m, lustrabotas m (LAm).

shoeblacking ['ʃuːblækɪŋ] N betún m, lustre m (LAm).

shoebrush ['ʃuːbrʌʃ] N cepillo m para zapatos.

shoecap ['ʃuːkæp] N puntera f.

shoehorn ['ʃuːhɔːn] N calzador m.

shoelace ['ʃuːleɪs] N cordón m, agujeta f (Mex), trenza f (Carib).

shoe-leather ['ʃuːˌleðəʳ] N cuero m para zapatos; **to wear out one's ~** gastarse el calzado (andando de acá para allá).

shoemaker ['ʃuːˌmeɪkəʳ] N zapatero m; **~'s** (**shop**) zapatería f.

shoe-polish ['ʃuːˌpɒlɪʃ] N betún m, crema f (para el calzado), lustre m (LAm).

shoe-repairer ['ʃuːrɪˌpɛərəʳ] N zapatero m remendón.

shoe-repairs ['ʃuːrɪˌpɛəz] NPL reparación f de calzado.

shoeshine ['ʃuːʃaɪn] (US) **1** N: **to have a ~** hacerse limpiar los zapatos.

2 ATTR: **~ boy** limpiabotas m, lustrabotas m (LAm).

shoeshop ['ʃuːʃɒp] N zapatería f, tienda f de calzado, peletería f (Carib).

shoestring ['ʃuːstrɪŋ] **1** N (US) cordón m; **on a ~** a lo barato; con cuatro cuartos; **to do sth on a ~** hacer algo con muy poco dinero; **to live on a ~** vivir muy justo (or con escasos recursos).

2 ATTR: **~ budget** presupuesto m muy limitado.

shoetree ['ʃuːtriː] N horma f.

shone [ʃɒn] PRET AND PTP of **shine**.

shoo [ʃuː] **1** INTERJ ¡zape!, ¡ox!, ¡os!; (to child) ¡vete!, ¡fuera de aquí!

2 VT (also **to ~ away**, **to ~ off**) ahuyentar; **I had to ~ the children away** tuve que mandar a los niños ir a otra parte; **sb ~ed us away** alguien nos mandó ir a otra parte.

3 ATTR: **it's a ~-in** (US*) es cosa de coser y cantar.

shook [ʃʊk] PRET of **shake**.

shoot [ʃuːt] **1** N (a) (Bot) renuevo m, retoño m, vástago m.

(b) (inclined plane) conducto m inclinado; (on ice) resbaladero m; V **chute**.

(c) (shooting party, hunt) partida f de caza, cacería f; (competition) certamen m de tiro al blanco.

(d) (preserve) coto m, vedado m.

2 INTERJ: **oh, ~!** (*: euph) ¡caracoles!

3 (irr: PRET AND PTP **shot**) VT (a) (Mil etc) bullet disparar, tirar; arrow etc disparar; gun disparar, descargar; lava etc arrojar.

(b) person, animal matar con arma de fuego, herir con arma de fuego; (execute) fusilar; **to ~ sb dead**, **to ~ sb to death** matar a uno a tiros; **he was shot dead by a policeman** fue muerto a tiros por un policía; **he was shot in the leg** una bala le hirió en la pierna; **he had been shot through the heart** la bala le había atravesado el corazón; **I'll ~ you a rabbit** te cazaré un conejo; **he shot his wife** pegó un tiro a su mujer; **he was shot as a spy** le fusilaron por espía; **you'll get me shot** si hago esto me harás fusilar; **people have been shot for less** han fusilado a muchos por menos motivos.

(c) (fig) film rodar; film scene fotografiar, filmar; subject of snapshot tomar, sacar una instantánea de; goal marcar, meter; bolt correr; coal, rubbish etc verter, vaciar; dice echar; net echar; ray of light echar; glance echar, lanzar; **'~ no rubbish'** (US) 'prohibido verter basuras'; **to ~ the sun** tomar la altura del sol; **to ~ a question at sb** disparar una pregunta inesperada a uno.

(d) (pass) rapids salvar, atravesar; bridge pasar por debajo de; **to ~ the lights** (Aut*) saltarse un semáforo en rojo.

4 VI (a) (with gun: as sport) practicar el deporte del tiro al blanco, (as hunter) cazar; **do you ~?** ¿Vd caza?; **I haven't shot for years** hace tiempo que no manejo la escopeta; **to ~ for Oxford** forma parte del equipo de tiro de Oxford; **we can ~ over Lord Emsworth's ground** podemos cazar en la finca de Lord Emsworth; **if they attack you, ~** si os atacan, disparad; **~ to kill** tirad a matar; **~ to kill policy** programa m de tirar a matar; **don't ~!** ¡no dispare!; **to ~ at sb** tirar a uno, disparar a uno; pegar un tiro a uno; **he shot at me but missed** disparó contra mí pero erró el tiro; **to ~ wide of the mark** errar el tiro.

(b) **~!*** (in conversation) ¡adelante!, ¡suelta!, ¡bien, dime!

(c) (Ftbl etc) chutar, tirar; **~!** ¡chuta!; **to ~ at goal** tirar a gol.

(d) (pain) punzar, dar punzadas.

(e) (Bot) brotar.

(f) (move rapidly: person) lanzarse, precipitarse; **he shot to the door** se lanzó hacia la puerta; **to ~ ahead** adelantarse rápidamente; **we were ~ing along** íbamos a gran velocidad; **to ~ by**, **to ~ past** pasar como un meteoro; **to ~ in** entrar como una bala; **he shot into space** se lanzó al espacio; **the car shot past us** el coche pasó como un rayo.

(g) (Phot) disparar.

◆**shoot away** **1** VT = **shoot off 1** (b).

2 VI (a) (Mil) seguir tirando.

(b) (move) partir como una bala, salir disparado.

◆**shoot back** **1** VT devolver rápidamente, devolver en el acto.

2 VI (a) (Mil) devolver el tiro, responder con disparos.

(b) (move) volver como una bala (to a).

◆**shoot down** VT (a) (Aer) derribar, abatir; argument rebatir, destruir; arguer anonadar.

(b) (kill) matar de un tiro, balear (Mex).

◆**shoot off** **1** VT (a) gun disparar; V **mouth**.

(b) **he had a leg shot off** un disparo le cercenó una pierna.

2 VI = **shoot away 2** (b).

◆**shoot out** **1** VT (a) arm extender rápidamente; extender inesperadamente; tongue sacar; sparks etc arrojar.

(b) lights apagar a tiros.

(c) **to ~ it out** resolverlo a tiros.

(d) **we were literally shot out of bed by the noise** nos vimos materialmente arrancados de la cama por el estruendo.

2 VI (flame, water) salir (con gran fuerza); (arm) extenderse rápidamente (or inesperadamente); (person) salir como una bala, salir disparado.

◆**shoot up** **1** VT aerodrome destrozar a tiros; town, district aterrorizar a tiros; person acribillar a tiros, balacear (Mex).

2 VI (a) (flame etc) salir (con gran fuerza); (hand) alzarse rápidamente; (price etc) subir vertiginosamente.

(b) (grow quickly) crecer, espigar.

(c) (‡: drugs) chutarse‡, inyectarse.

shooter* ['ʃuːtəʳ] N (pistol) pistola f; (shotgun) escopeta f.

shooting ['ʃuːtɪŋ] **1** N (a) (shots) tiros mpl, disparos mpl; (continuous ~) tiroteo m; (by artillery) cañoneo m, bombardeo m.

(b) (act: murder) asesinato m; (execution) fusilamiento m.

(c) (Hunting) caza f (con escopeta); **he comes each year for the ~** viene cada año para la caza; **there is good ~ in Asturias** Asturias es buen terreno para la caza; **to go ~** ir de caza, ir a cazar; **good ~!** ¡buen tiro!; ¡bravo!

(d) (Cine) rodaje m.

2 ATTR de tiro; de caza; pain punzante; **~ affray** refriega f con tiros; **~ incident** incidente m de tiroteo; **within ~ range** a tiro; **~ war** guerra f a tiros.

shooting-box ['ʃuːtɪŋbɒks] N, **shooting-lodge** ['ʃuːtɪŋlɒdʒ] N pabellón m de caza.

shooting-brake ['ʃuːtɪŋbreɪk] N (Brit: †) rubia f, furgoneta f, camioneta f (LAm).

shooting-gallery ['ʃuːtɪŋˌgæləri] N galería f de tiro al blanco.

shooting-jacket ['ʃuːtɪŋˌdʒækɪt] N chaquetón m.

shooting-match ['ʃuːtɪŋmætʃ] N certamen m de tiro al blanco; **the whole ~*** (Brit) el todo, todo el negocio.

shooting-party ['ʃuːtɪŋˌpɑːtɪ] N partida f de caza.

shooting-range ['ʃuːtɪŋreɪdʒ] N campo m de tiro.

shooting-star [ʃuːtɪŋ'stɑːʳ] N estrella f fugaz.

shooting-stick ['ʃuːtɪŋstɪk] N bastón m taburete.

shoot-out ['ʃuːtaʊt] N (a) tiroteo m, balacera f (Mex). (b) (Sport) desempate m a penaltis.

shop [ʃɒp] **1** N (a) (esp Brit: Comm) tienda f, negocio m (And, SC); (large store) almacén m; **~!** ¿quién despacha?; **to keep a ~** poseer un negocio; **to set up ~** poner una tienda; **to shut up ~** cerrar; (fig) dar por terminado un asunto; desistir de una empresa; **to talk ~** hablar del propio trabajo, hablar de asuntos profesionales; **it's all over the ~*** está en el mayor desorden; **she leaves things all over the ~*** deja sus cosas de cualquier modo; **they're all over the ~*** no tienen ni idea, carecen de todo sentido del buen orden; **the papers were all over the ~*** los papeles estaban en la mayor confusión.

(b) (Tech) taller m.

2 ATTR (a) (Comm) **~ assistant** (Brit) vendedor m, -ora f, dependiente m, -a f, empleado m, -a f (de una tienda) (LAm); **~ hours** horas fpl de apertura; **~ talk** temas mpl del oficio, conversación f sobre el trabajo, asuntos mpl de interés profesional.

(b) (Brit Tech) **~ floor** (fig) taller m, fábrica f; **~ floor (workers)** obreros mpl; **~ floor opinion** opinión f de las bases sindicales, opinión f de los obreros; **~ steward** enlace mf sindical.

3 VT **to ~ sb‡** (esp Brit) traicionar a uno, delatar a uno; denunciar a uno a la policía.

4 VI comprar, hacer compras; **to go ~ping** ir de compras, ir de tiendas; **to send sb ~ping** enviar a uno a hacer compras; **to ~ at Joe's** hacer sus compras en la tienda de Joe; **to ~ for fish** ir a buscar pescado en las tiendas.

◆**shop around** VI comparar los precios en diversas tiendas (for sth antes de comprar algo).

shopfront ['ʃɒpfrʌnt] N escaparate m.

shopgirl ['ʃɒpɡɜːl] N (Brit) dependienta f, empleada f (de una tienda) (LAm).

shopkeeper ['ʃɒpˌkiːpəʳ] N tendero m, -a f.

shoplift ['ʃɒplɪft] VI hurtar en tiendas.

shoplifter ['ʃɒpˌlɪftəʳ] N mechera f, ratero m de tiendas.

shoplifting ['ʃɒpˌlɪftɪŋ] N ratería f, hurto m (en las tiendas).

shopper ['ʃɒpəʳ] N comprador m, -ora f.

shopping ['ʃɒpɪŋ] **1** N (a) (act) **I like ~** me gusta ir de tiendas; **we have to go a long way for our ~** para comprar cosas tenemos que ir muy lejos. (b) (goods bought) compras fpl.

2 ATTR: **~ bag** bolsa f de compras; **~ basket** cesta f de compras; **~**

cart (US), **~ trolley** carrito m de la compra; **~ centre**, (US) **~ center**, **~ mall** centro m comercial, zona f de tiendas; **~ list** lista f de compras; **~ precinct** centro m comercial; **~ trip** viaje m de compras.

shop-soiled ['ʃɒpsɔɪld] ADJ (Brit) usado, deteriorado; (fig) trasnochado.

shopwalker ['ʃɒp,wɔːkəʳ] N (Brit) vigilante m, -a f.

shopwindow ['ʃɒp,wɪndəʊ] N escaparate m, vitrina f (LAm), vidriera f (SC).

shopworn ['ʃɒpwɔːn] ADJ (US) = shop-soiled.

shore¹ [ʃɔːʳ] **1** N playa f; orilla f, ribera f; **these ~s** (fig) estas tierras, esta parte; **on ~** en tierra.

2 ATTR: **~ leave** licencia f para ir a tierra.

shore² [ʃɔːʳ] **1** N puntal m; (Min) entibo m.

2 VT (also to **~ up**) apuntalar; entibar.

◆**shore up** VT (fig) apoyar, reforzar, sostener.

shoreline ['ʃɔːlaɪn] N línea f de la costa.

shoreward(s) ['ʃɔːwəd(z)] ADV hacia la costa, hacia la playa.

shorn [ʃɔːn] PTP of **shear** mocho; **~ of** sin, desprovisto de; despojado de; **~ of its verbiage, this means ...** quitando la palabrería, esto quiere decir ...; **~ of outside aid we cannot go on** sin la ayuda exterior no podemos continuar.

▼ **short** [ʃɔːt] **1** ADJ **(a)** (in length, distance) corto; message etc breve, sucinto; person bajo, chaparro (Mex); radio wave corto; **~ sight** miopía f; **to have ~ sight** ser míope, ser corto de vista; **~ story** cuento m; **~ story writer** escritor m, -ora f de cuentos; **the ~est route** la ruta más corta; **a few ~ words** algunas palabritas; **a ~ way off** a poca distancia, no muy lejos; **by a ~ head** por una cabeza escasa; **to be ~ in the leg** tener las piernas cortas; **these trousers are a bit ~ in the leg** estos pantalones tienen la pierna algo pequeña; **the ~ answer is that ...** en pocas palabras la razón es que ...; **to have a ~ back-and-sides** llevar el pelo corto por detrás y por los lados; **to have sb by the ~ and curlies**: tener a alguien por los huevos·; **to take ~ steps** dar pequeños pasos; **to take a ~ walk** dar un paseíto.

(b) (of words) **'Joss' is ~ for 'Jocelyn'** 'Joss' es diminutivo de 'Jocelyn'; **'living' is ~ for 'living room'** 'living' es apócope de 'living room'; **he's called Fred for ~** su diminutivo es Fred; **'TV' is ~ for 'television'** 'TV' es abreviatura de 'televisión'.

(c) (in time) corto, breve; de poca duración; vowel breve; memory flaco, malo; **for a ~ time** por poco tiempo; **in ~ order** con toda rapidez; sin demora; **it was ~ and sweet** fue corto y bueno; **February is a ~ month** febrero es un mes corto; **the days are getting ~er** los días se hacen más breves; **time is getting ~er** nos queda poco tiempo.

(d) (curt) reply brusco, seco; manner brusco, corto (LAm); temper vivo; **to be ~ with sb** tratar a uno con sequedad.

(e) (insufficient) insuficiente; **~ delivery** (Comm) entrega f incompleta; **~ ton** (US: = 2,000 lb) tonelada f corta; **5 ~** faltan 5, 5 de menos; **I'm £3 ~** me faltan 3 libras; **it's 2 kilos ~** faltan 2 kilos; **we were ~ last week** la semana pasada nos faltó; **oranges are in ~ supply** escasean las naranjas, hay escasez de naranjas, hay poca naranja; **to give ~ weight** vender algo con peso insuficiente; **to give sb ~ change** faltarle a uno en la vuelta; **to be on ~ time** trabajar jornadas reducidas; **not far ~ of £100** poco menos de 100 libras; **nothing ~ of total surrender** nada menos que la rendición incondicional; **it's little ~ of madness** dista poco de la locura; **nothing ~ of a bomb would stop him** fuera de una bomba nada le impediría.

(f) (lacking) **to be ~ of** estar falto de, andar escaso de; **we are ~ of petrol** andamos escasos de gasolina; **we're not ~ of volunteers** se han ofrecido muchos voluntarios, no andamos escasos de voluntarios; **I was ~ of clubs** tenía poco trébol; **the plan is ~ on details** el proyecto tiene pocos detalles; **he's ~ on brains·** le falta chirumen·; **bananas are very ~** escasean los plátanos, casi no hay plátanos; **to go ~ of** pasarse sin; **no one goes ~ in this house** en esta casa nadie padece hambre; **to run ~** escasear; **we ran ~ of petrol** se nos acabó la gasolina, quedamos sin gasolina.

(g) pastry quebradizo.

▼ **2** ADV **(a)** **in ~** en resumen; en fin; **to cut ~** acortar, abreviar; interrumpir; terminar inesperadamente; **they had to cut ~ their holiday** tuvieron que interrumpir sus vacaciones; **to fall ~** resultar ser insuficiente, no alcanzar; **production has fallen ~ by 100 tons** la producción arroja un déficit de 100 toneladas; **to fall ~ of the target** no alcanzar el blanco, no llegar al blanco; **to fall ~ of expectations** no cumplir las esperanzas; **it falls far ~ of what we require** dista mucho de satisfacer nuestras exigencias; **to sell ~** vender al descubierto; **to sell sb ~** (deceive) engañar a uno en un negocio; (belittle) despreciar a uno, quitar méritos a uno; **to stop ~** parar en seco; parar de repente; **to stop ~ of** detenerse antes de llegar a; **to be taken ~** necesitar urgentemente ir al wáter.

(b) **~ of blowing it up** a menos que lo volemos, a no ser que lo volemos; **~ of murder I'll do anything** lo haré todo menos matar; **it's nothing ~ of robbery** es nada menos que un robo.

3 N **(a)** (Cine) cortometraje m; complemento m.

(b) (Elec) cortocircuito m.

(c) (drink) licor m, bebida f corta, copa f (de licor).

(d) (garment) **~s** pantalón m corto; (US) calzoncillos mpl.

4 VT (Elec) poner en cortocircuito.

5 VI ponerse en cortocircuito.

shortage ['ʃɔːtɪdʒ] N escasez f, falta f; insuficiencia f; penuria f; **the housing ~** la crisis de la vivienda; **~ of staff** insuficiencia f de personal; **in times of ~** en las épocas de escasez; **there is no ~ of advice** no es que falten los consejos.

shortbread ['ʃɔːtbred] N torta dulce seca y quebradiza.

shortcake ['ʃɔːtkeɪk] N torta f de frutas; = shortbread.

short-change ['ʃɔːt'tʃeɪndʒ] VT: **to ~ sb** faltarle a uno en la vuelta; (fig) defraudar a uno, decepcionar a uno; **to do this is to ~ the project** (esp US) hacer esto es tratar inadecuadamente el proyecto.

short-circuit ['ʃɔːt'sɜːkɪt] **1** N cortocircuito m.

2 VT **(a)** (Elec) poner en cortocircuito. **(b)** (fig: bypass) evitar (la necesidad de pasar por); (cause to fail) dar al traste con, arruinar, estropear.

3 VI ponerse en cortocircuito.

shortcoming ['ʃɔːtkʌmɪŋ] N defecto m, deficiencia f, fallo m.

shortcrust pastry ['ʃɔːtkrʌst,peɪstrɪ] N (Brit) pasta f quebradiza; V also short 1 (g).

short-dated ['ʃɔːt'deɪtɪd] ADJ a corto plazo.

shorten ['ʃɔːtn] **1** VT acortar; abreviar; reducir; holiday, journey etc acortar.

2 VI acortarse; abreviarse; reducirse; **the odds have ~ed** los puntos de ventaja se han reducido.

shortening ['ʃɔːtnɪŋ] N (V vt) **(a)** acortamiento m; abreviación f; reducción f. **(b)** (Culin) manteca f (de hojaldre).

shortfall ['ʃɔːtfɔːl] N déficit m, deficiencia f.

short-haired ['ʃɔːt'heəd] ADJ pelicorto.

shorthand ['ʃɔːthænd] (Brit) **1** N taquigrafía f; **to take ~** escribir en taquigrafía; **to take sth down in ~** apuntar algo taquigráficamente.

2 ATTR: **~ note** nota f taquigráfica; **~ notebook** cuaderno m de taquigrafía; **~ speed** palabras fpl por minuto (en taquigrafía); **~ typing** taquimecanografía f; **~ typist** taquimeca(nógrafa) f; **~ writer** taquígrafo m, -a f.

short-handed ['ʃɔːt'hændɪd] ADJ falto de personal, falto de mano de obra.

short-haul ['ʃɔːthɔːl] ADJ de corto recorrido.

shortie* ['ʃɔːtɪ] = shorty.

shortish ['ʃɔːtɪʃ] ADJ algo pequeño, más bien bajo, bajito.

shortlist ['ʃɔːt'lɪst] **1** N (Brit) preselección f, terna f, lista f de candidatos escogidos.

2 VT: **to ~ sb** poner a uno en la lista de candidatos escogidos, preseleccionar a uno.

short-lived ['ʃɔːt'lɪvd] ADJ efímero.

shortly ['ʃɔːtlɪ] ADV **(a)** (soon) en breve, dentro de poco; luego; próximamente; **~ after** poco después; **~ before this** poco tiempo antes de esto; **you shall see it very ~** lo va a ver muy pronto.

(b) (curtly) bruscamente, secamente.

shortness ['ʃɔːtnɪs] N **(a)** (in length, distance) cortedad f; (of message etc) brevedad f; (of person) pequeñez f; (in time) brevedad f, poca duración f; **because of the ~ of my memory** debido a mi mala memoria; **~ of sight** miopía f; **~ of breath** falta f de aliento, respiración f difícil.

(b) (curtness) brusquedad f, sequedad f.

short-order cook [,ʃɔːtɔːdə'kʊk] N (esp US) cocinero m de comida rápida, cocinera f de comida rápida.

short-range ['ʃɔːt'reɪndʒ] ADJ gun de corto alcance; aircraft de autonomía limitada, de corto radio en acción.

short-run ['ʃɔːt'rʌn] ADJ breve, de alcance limitado.

short-sighted ['ʃɔːt'saɪtɪd] ADJ (esp Brit) miope, corto de vista; (fig) miope, person falto de previsión, imprevisor; measure etc imprudente.

short-sightedly ['ʃɔːt'saɪtɪdlɪ] ADV con ojos de miope; (fig) imprudentemente.

short-sightedness ['ʃɔːt'saɪtɪdnɪs] N miopía f; cortedad f de vista; (fig) falta f de previsión, imprevisión f; imprudencia f.

short-sleeved ['ʃɔːtsliːvd] ADJ de manga corta.

short-staffed [,ʃɔːt'stɑːft] ADJ falto de personal.

short-stay ['ʃɔːtsteɪ] ADJ car park de tiempo limitado; ward de hospitalización breve; visitor, student de estancia limitada.

short-tempered ['ʃɔːt'tempəd] ADJ de genio vivo, enojadizo.

short-term ['ʃɔːttɜːm] ADJ a corto plazo; **~ car park** zona f de estacionamiento limitado.

short-time ['ʃɔːt'taɪm] **1** ADJ: **~ working** sistema m de jornadas reducidas, sistema m de jornada limitada, trabajo m de horario reducido; **to be on ~ working** trabajar jornadas reducidas.

2 ADV: **to work ~** trabajar jornadas reducidas.

shortwave ['ʃɔːt,weɪv] ADJ de onda corta.

short-winded ['ʃɔːt'wɪndɪd] ADJ corto de resuello.

shorty* ['ʃɔːtɪ] N tapón* m (de alberca), enano* m, -a f; **hey ~!** ¡hola enano!

shot [ʃɒt] **1** N **(a)** (*missile*) bala f; proyectil m; (*sound of ~*) tiro m, disparo m; (*causing wound*) balazo m; (*pellets*) perdigones mpl; (*weight, Sport*) peso m; **~ across the bows** cañonazo m de advertencia; **~ in the dark** (*fig*) tiro m al azar; **good ~!** ¡muy bien!; **I'll do it like a ~** lo haré de buena gana; **he did it like a ~** lo hizo como un relámpago, lo hizo como un resorte; **he was off like a ~** partió como una bala; **it's a long ~, but we could try** no es fácil, pero podemos probar; **that guess was a very long ~** fue una conjetura muy arriesgada; **to fire a ~ at sb** disparar sobre uno, tirar a uno; **who fired that ~?** ¿quién disparó?; **it surrendered without firing a ~** (*or* **without a ~ being fired**) se rindió sin resistencia alguna; **we captured it without firing a ~** lo tomamos sin disparar una sola vez; **to exchange ~s** tirotearse; **to put the ~** lanzar el peso; **to take a ~ at sb** tirar a uno.

(b) (*person*) tirador m, -ora f; **to be a crack ~** ser un tirador experto; **I'm rather a poor ~** no tiro muy bien; V **big 1**.

(c) (*in space exploration*) lanzamiento m; cohete m, vehículo m espacial.

(d) (*Sport*: *with club etc*) golpe m; (*Snooker etc*) golpe m, jugada f; (*throw*) tirada f, echada f; (*at goal*) tiro m, disparo m; **to call the ~s** (*fig*) mandar, dirigirlo todo.

(e) (*attempt*) tentativa f; (*guess*) conjetura f; **it's your ~** te toca a ti; **to have a ~** probar suerte; **to have a ~ at** + *ger* hacer una tentativa de + *infin*; **will you have a ~ at it?** ¿quieres probar?

(f) (*injection*) inyección f; (*dose*) dosis f; (*: *of drug*) pico⁑ m, chute⁑ m; **a ~ of rum** un trago de ron*; **it's a ~ in the arm for ...** es un estimulazo para ...; **the industry needs a ~ in the arm** la industria necesita una fuerte ayuda económica.

(g) (*Phot*) foto f, instantánea f; (*in film*) fotograma m, toma f, plano m.

2 PRET AND PTP *of* **shoot**; **~ silk** seda f tornasolada; **to get ~ of*** deshacerse de, quitarse de encima; **black ~ (through) with blue** negro con visos azules; **his story is ~ through with inconsistencies** su narración está plagada de incongruencias.

shotgun ['ʃɒtɡʌn] **1** N escopeta f.

2 ATTR: **~ marriage**, **~ wedding** casamiento m a la fuerza; **to have a ~ wedding** casarse a la fuerza, casarse de penalty*.

shot-put ['ʃɒtpʊt] N (*Sport*) lanzamiento m de pesos.

shot-putter ['ʃɒtˌpʊtəʳ] N lanzador m, -ora f de pesos.

▼ **should** [ʃʊd] (*irr*: PRET AND CONDITIONAL *of* **shall**) V AUX **(a)** (*used to form conditional tense*) **I ~ go if they sent for me** iría si me llamasen; **~ I be out at the time** si estoy fuera en aquel momento; **I ~n't be surprised if ...** no me sorprendería si ...; **I ~n't if I were you** yo en tu lugar no lo haría; **he ordered that it ~ be done** mandó que se hiciera así; **thanks, I ~ like to** gracias, me gustaría; **I ~n't like to say** prefiero no decirlo.

▼ **(b)** (*statements of duty and command*) **all cars ~ carry lights** todos los coches deben llevar luces; **you ~n't do that** no debes hacer eso; **all is as it ~ be** todo está en regla; ..., **which is as it ~ be** ... como es razonable; **why ~I?** ¿por qué lo voy a hacer?; **why ~ he (have done it)?** ¿por qué lo iba a hacer?; **why ~ you want to know?** ¿por qué has de saberlo tú?; **he ~ know that ...** debiera saber que ...; **he ~ have paid it** debiera haberlo pagado.

(c) (*statements of probability*) **he ~ be there by now** debe haber llegado ya; **they ~ arrive tomorrow** deberán llegar mañana; **this ~ be good** esto promete ser bueno.

shoulder ['ʃəʊldəʳ] **1** N **(a)** (*Anat*) hombro m; espaldas fpl; (*of meat*) espalda f; (*of coat etc*) hombrera f; **to carry sth on one's ~s** llevar algo a hombros; **he was carried out on their ~s** le sacaron a hombros; **all the responsibilities fell on his ~s** tuvo que cargar con todas las responsabilidades; **they carried him ~ high** le llevaron a hombros; **to give sb the cold ~, turn a cold ~ on** (*or* **to**) **sb** (*US*) volver la espalda a uno; **to give sb sth straight from the ~** decir algo a uno sin rodeos; **to look over one's ~** mirar por encima del hombro; **to put one's ~ to the wheel** arrimar el hombro; **to rub ~s with sb** codearse con uno; **to stand ~ to ~** estar hombro con hombro.

(b) (*of hill*) lomo m; (*Brit*: *of motorway*) arcén m.

2 VT **(a)** (*carry*) llevar al hombro; (*pick up*) poner al hombro; (*fig*) responsibilities etc cargar con; **~ arms!** ¡armas al hombro!

(b) to ~ sb aside apartar a uno con el hombro; abrirse paso empujando a uno con el hombro; (*fig*) dejar a uno al lado; **to ~ one's way through** abrirse paso a empujones.

shoulder-bag ['ʃəʊldəˌbæɡ] N bolso m de bandolera.

shoulderblade ['ʃəʊldəbleɪd] N omóplato m.

shoulder-flash ['ʃəʊldəˌflæʃ] N charretera f.

shoulder-holster ['ʃəʊldəˌhəʊlstəʳ] N pistolera f.

shoulder-joint ['ʃəʊldəˌdʒɔɪnt] N articulación f del hombro.

shoulderknot ['ʃəʊldənɒt] N dragona f, charretera f.

shoulder-length ['ʃəʊldəˌleŋθ] ADJ *hair* hasta el hombro.

shoulderpad ['ʃəʊldəpæd] N hombrera f.

shoulder-strap ['ʃəʊldəstræp] N (*Mil*) dragona f; (*of dress*) tirante m; (*of satchel etc*) correa f, bandolera f.

shouldn't ['ʃʊdnt] = **should not**.

should've ['ʃʊdəv] = **should have**; V **should**.

shout [ʃaʊt] **1** N grito m, voz f; **a ~ of protest** un grito de protesta; **there were ~s of applause** hubo grandes aplausos; **there were ~s of laughter** hubo grandes carcajadas; **to give sb a ~** llamar a uno; **it's my ~*** me toca a mí; **he's still in with a ~*** todavía tiene una posibilidad de ganar.

2 VT gritar; **to ~ abuse at sb** lanzar improperios contra uno; **to ~ a protest** protestar en alta voz.

3 VI gritar; dar voces; (*talk loudly*) hablar a voz en grito; **he ~ed for his servant** llamó a su criado a voz en grito; **to ~ for help** pedir socorro a voces; **to ~ with laughter** reírse a grandes carcajadas.

4 VR: **to ~ o.s. hoarse** enronquecer gritando.

◆ **shout down** VT: **to ~ sb down** abuchear a uno, hundir a uno en gritos; **to ~ a play down** hundir una obra a gritos.

◆ **shout out 1** VT gritar, decir a voz en grito.

2 VI gritar, dar gritos.

shouting ['ʃaʊtɪŋ] **1** N gritos mpl, vocerío m, clamoreo m; V **bar 3**.

2 ATTR: **within ~ distance** al alcance de la voz.

shove [ʃʌv] **1** N empujón m; **to give sb a ~** empujar a uno; **can you give me a ~, please?** (*Aut etc*) ¿por favor, me ayuda a arrancar empujándolo?; **one more ~ and we're there** empujad una vez más y ya está; **give it a good ~** dale un buen empujón.

2 VT **(a)** (*push*) empujar; **to ~ sb aside** apartar a uno empujándole, apartar a uno a codazos; **his friends ~d him forward** sus amigos le empujaron hacia adelante.

(b) (*) poner, meter; dejar; **~ it here** ponlo aquí.

3 VI empujar, dar empujones; **stop shoving!** ¡dejen de empujar!

◆ **shove about, shove around** VT (*lit*) *object* empujar de un lado a otro; *person* mandar de un lado a otro; (*) tiranizar.

◆ **shove away** VT *person, object* empujar.

◆ **shove back** VT: **to ~ sb back** hacer retroceder a uno empujándole.

◆ **shove off 1** VT: **to ~ a boat off** echar afuera un bote.

2 VI (*Naut*) alejarse del muelle (*etc*); (*) largarse*; **~ off!** ¡lárgate*!

◆ **shove on*** VT *hat, coat etc* ponerse; **~ another record on** pon otro disco.

◆ **shove out** VT: **to ~ a boat out** echar afuera un bote; **they ~d him out** le empujaron fuera, (*fig*) le obligaron a salir de su puesto (*etc*).

◆ **shove over 1** VT **(a)** (*knock over*) *chair etc* derribar; *person* derribar de un golpe.

(b) they ~d the car over the cliff fueron empujando el coche hasta que cayó por el acantilado.

(c) ~ **it over to me*** trae pa'acá*.

2 (*) VI correrse; **~ over!** ¡córrete!, ¡échate pa'allá*!

◆ **shove up*** VI = **shove over 2**.

shovel ['ʃʌvl] **1** N pala f; (*mechanical*) pala f mecánica.

2 VT traspalar, mover con pala; **to ~ earth into a pile** amontonar tierra con una pala; **he was ~ling food into his mouth** iba zampando la comida; **to ~ coal on to a fire** añadir carbón a la lumbre con pala; **they were ~ling out the mud** estaban sacando el lodo con palas.

◆ **shovel up** VT *coal etc* levantar con una pala; *snow* quitar con pala.

shovelboard ['ʃʌvlbɔːd] N juego m de tejo.

shoveler ['ʃʌvləʳ] N **(a)** (*Orn*) espátula f común, pato m cuchareta. **(b)** (*tool*) paleador m.

shovelful ['ʃʌvlfʊl] N paletada f.

show [ʃəʊ] **1** N **(a)** (*showing*) demostración f; **~ of hands** votación f a mano alzada; **an impressive ~ of power** una impresionante exhibición de poder; **the garden is a splendid ~** el jardín está muy vistoso; **the dahlias make a fine ~** las dalias se muestran espléndidas.

(b) (*exhibition*) exposición f; (*of agriculture, trade*) feria f; **to be on ~** estar expuesto; **he's holding his first London ~** está organizando su primera exposición en Londres; V **horse ~, motor ~** etc.

(c) (*Theat etc*) función f, espectáculo m; show m; **on with the ~!** ¡que comience (*or* continúe) la función!; **the ~ goes on** (*Theat*) la función continúa, (*fig*) seguimos adelante a pesar de todo; **the last ~ starts at 11** la última función empieza a las 11; **there is no ~ on Sundays** el domingo no hay función; **let's get this ~ on the road** (*fig*) echémosnos a la carretera; **to go to a ~** ir a un teatro, ir a un espectáculo; **to steal the ~** acaparar toda la atención; **Lord Mayor's S~** desfile m del alcalde de Londres (el día de su inauguración).

(d) (*: *undertaking, organization*) negocio m, empresa f, cosa f, organización f; **who's in charge of this ~?** ¿quién manda aquí?; **this is my ~** esto es mío, aquí mando yo; **he runs the ~** manda él, él es el amo.

(e) (*Brit**: *performance*) **bad ~!** ¡malo!; **good ~!** ¡muy bien!, ¡bravo!; **to put up a good ~** hacer un buen papel, dar buena cuenta de sí; **it's a pretty poor ~, isn't it?** esto es un desastre, ¿no?; **to give the ~**

away (*deliberately*) tirar de la manta, (*involuntarily*) clarearse.
(**f**) (*outward* ~) apariencia *f*; ostentación *f*; (*pomp*) boato *m*, aparato *m*, pompa *f*; **it's just for** ~ es sólo para impresionar; **it's all** ~ **with him** todo lo hace para impresionar; **to do sth for** ~ hacer algo para impresionar; **to make a** ~ **of resistance** aparentar resistir, fingir resistir; **to make a** ~ **of unwillingness** fingir no querer; **to make a great** ~ **of sympathy** hacer alarde de su mucha compasión.
2 ATTR: ~ **bill** cartel *m*; ~ **house** (*Brit*) casa *f* piloto, casa *f* modelo; ~ **trial** proceso *m* organizado con fines propagandísticos, proceso *m* espectacular.
3 (*irr*: PRET **showed**, PTP **shown**) VT (**a**) (*manifest*) mostrar, enseñar; *film* proyectar, poner; *slides* proyectar; *picture* exhibir; *goods* exponer; **to** ~ **sb sth, to** ~ **sth to sb** mostrar (*or* enseñar) algo a uno; **to** ~ **one's passport** mostrar su pasaporte, presentar su pasaporte; **to** ~ **a picture at the Academy** exhibir un cuadro en la Academia; **to** ~ **a film at Cannes** presentar una película en Cannes; **the film was first ~n in 1968** la película se estrenó en 1968; **to** ~ **a light** alumbrar a uno, dar luz a uno; **he had nothing to** ~ **for his trouble** se quedó sin nada después de tantos trabajos, no sacó provecho alguno de tantos trabajos; **they ~ed us round the garden** nos mostraron el jardín, con ellos visitamos el jardín; **who is going to** ~ **us round?** ¿quién actuará de guía?
(**b**) (*indicate*) indicar; (*Comm*) arrojar; **it ~s 200°** indica 200°, marca 200°; **it ~s a speed of ...** indica una velocidad de ...; **as ~n in the illustration** según se indica en la lámina, como lo indica el grabado; **the roads are ~n in red** las carreteras están marcadas en rojo; **to** ~ **a loss** dejar una pérdida; **to** ~ **a profit** arrojar un saldo positivo; **the figures** ~ **a rise** las cifras arrojan un aumento.
(**c**) (*demonstrate*) mostrar, manifestar; acusar; (*prove*) probar, demostrar; **I'll** ~ **you!** (*indignant*) ¡ya lo verás!; **to** ~ **intelligence** mostrar tener inteligencia, mostrar ser inteligente; **to** ~ **his disagreement, he ...** para mostrar su disconformidad, él ...; **she ~ed no reaction** no acusó reacción alguna; **her face ~ed her happiness** su felicidad se acusaba en la cara; **to** ~ **one's affection** demostrar su cariño; **a big crowd turned up to** ~ **its feeling for him** una gran multitud acudió para testimoniarle su simpatía; **the choice of dishes ~s excellent taste** la selección de platos demuestra un gusto muy fino; **she's beginning to** ~ **her age** ya empieza a aparentar su edad; **to** ~ **that ...** demostrar que ...; **I ~ed him that this could not be true** le hice ver que esto no podía ser cierto.
(**d**) (*reveal*) revelar; **the gap ~s her legs** el espacio deja ver sus piernas; **she likes to** ~ **her legs** le gusta hacer exhibición de sus piernas; **a dress which ~s the slip** un vestido que deja ver la combinación; **this ~s him to be a swindler** esto le revela como estafador, esto demuestra que es estafador.
(**e**) (*direct*) **to** ~ **sb the way** enseñar a uno el camino; **let me** ~ **you** se lo voy a enseñar; **to** ~ **sb into a room** hacer que pase uno, hacer entrar a uno en un cuarto; **I was ~n into a large hall** me hicieron pasar a un vestíbulo grande; **to** ~ **sb to his seat** enseñar a uno su asiento, acompañar a uno a su asiento.
4 VI mostrarse, verse, revelarse; aparecer; (*film*) proyectarse; **your slip's ~ing, madam** señora, se le ve la combinación; **it doesn't** ~ no se nota; **don't worry, it won't** ~ no te preocupes, no se notará; **the tulips are beginning to** ~ empiezan a brotar los tulipanes; **a little colour is beginning to** ~ **now** ahora se empieza a verles un poco de color; **it just goes to** ~! ¡hay que ver!: **it all goes to** ~ **that ...** todo sirve para demostrar que ...
5 VR: **to** ~ **o.s.** presentarse; hacer acto de presencia; **to** ~ **o.s. incompetent** descubrir su incompetencia, mostrarse incompetente; **it ~s itself in his speech** se revela en su forma de hablar, se le nota en el habla.
◆ **show in** VT hacer pasar; ~ **him in!** ¡que pase!
◆ **show off** **1** VT (**a**) (*display*) hacer gala de, lucir; *beauty etc* hacer resaltar, destacar.
(**b**) (*pej*) hacer ostentación de.
2 VI darse importancia, presumir; fachendear; **to** ~ **off in front of one's friends** presumir ante las amistades; **stop ~ing off!** ¡no presumas!
◆ **show out** VT acompañar a la puerta.
◆ **show through** VI verse; transparentarse, trascender; clarearse.
◆ **show up** **1** VT (**a**) *visitor* hacer subir; ~ **her up!** ¡que suba!
(**b**) *fraud etc* descubrir; *person* desenmascarar; *defect etc* revelar, patentizar.
(**c**) (*present*) presentar; *beauty etc* hacer resaltar, destacar.
(**d**) (*embarrass*) avergonzar.
2 VI (**a**) (*stand out*) destacar.
(**b**) (*: appear*) acudir, presentarse, aparecer.
show biz* [ˈʃəʊbɪz] N = **show business**.
showboat [ˈʃəʊbəʊt] N (*US*) barco-teatro *m*.
show business [ˈʃəʊbɪznɪs] N los espectáculos, el mundo del espectáculo, el negocio del espectáculo; la vida de actor.
showcase [ˈʃəʊkeɪs] **1** N vitrina *f* (de exposición), (*fig*) escaparate *m*.

2 ATTR: ~ **project** proyecto *m* modelo.
3 VT exhibir
showdown [ˈʃəʊdaʊn] N confrontación *f*, enfrentamiento *m* decisivo; ajuste *m* de cuentas definitivo; momento *m* decisivo; hora *f* de la verdad; **the Suez** ~ la crisis de Suez; **if it comes to a** ~ si llega a un conflicto, si llega el momento decisivo; **to have a** ~ **with sb** enfrentarse con uno, confrontarse con uno; **I'm going to have a** ~ **with the boss** le voy a decir cuatro verdades al jefe.
shower [ˈʃaʊəʳ] **1** N (**a**) (*of rain*) chaparrón *m*, chubasco *m*, aguacero *m*.
(**b**) (*fig: of arrows, stones etc*) lluvia *f*.
(**c**) (*Brit*) gentuza *f*; **they were an utter** ~ eran horribles, eran unos pesados; **what a** ~! ¡qué pesados!
(**d**) (*~bath*) ducha *f*, regadera *f* (*Mex*); **to take** (*or* **have**) **a** ~ ducharse, tomar una ducha.
(**e**) (*US*) fiesta *f* con motivo de un nacimiento (*or* matrimonio etc).
2 ATTR: ~ **gel** gel *m* de baño; ~ **unit** ducha *f*.
3 VT (*fig: also* **to** ~ **down**) llover, derramar; **to** ~ **sb with honours, to** ~ **honours on sb** colmar a uno de honores; **he was ~ed with invitations** le llovieron encima las invitaciones, le abrumaron de invitaciones.
4 VI (**a**) (*rain*) llover, caer un chaparrón. (**b**) (*in ~bath*) ducharse, tomar una ducha.
showerbath [ˈʃaʊəbɑːθ] N, PL **showerbaths** [ˈʃaʊəbɑːðz] ducha *f*; **to take a** ~ ducharse, tomar una ducha.
showercap [ˈʃaʊəkæp] N gorro *m* de ducha.
shower-curtain [ˈʃaʊəˌkɜːtən] N cortina *f* de ducha.
shower-head [ˈʃaʊəhed] N alcachofa *f* de ducha.
showerproof [ˈʃaʊəpruːf] ADJ impermeable.
showery [ˈʃaʊərɪ] ADJ *day etc* de chaparrones; *weather* lluvioso; **it will be** ~ **tomorrow** mañana habrá chaparrones.
showgirl [ˈʃəʊɡɜːl] N corista *f*.
showground [ˈʃəʊɡraʊnd] N real *m* (de la feria), ferial *m*.
showily [ˈʃəʊɪlɪ] ADV vistosamente, llamativamente; aparatosamente; de modo espectacular; ostentosamente.
showiness [ˈʃəʊɪnɪs] N vistosidad *f*, lo llamativo; espectacularidad *f*, ostentación *f*; boato *m*.
showing [ˈʃəʊɪŋ] N (**a**) (*of pictures etc*) exposición *f*; (*of film*) proyección *f*, presentación *f*; **a second** ~ **of 'The Blue Angel'** un reestreno de 'El Ángel Azul'.
(**b**) (*performance*) actuación *f*; **the team's** ~ **this season** la actuación del equipo durante la temporada actual; **the poor** ~ **of the team** la pobre actuación del equipo; **to make a good** ~ hacer un buen papel, dar buena cuenta de sí.
(**c**) **on his own** ~ según él mismo confiesa.
showing-off [ˌʃəʊɪŋˈɒf] N lucimiento *m*; (*pej*) fachenda *f*.
show-jumper [ˈʃəʊˌdʒʌmpəʳ] N participante *mf* en concursos de saltos.
show-jumping [ˈʃəʊˌdʒʌmpɪŋ] N concurso *m* de saltos.
showman [ˈʃəʊmən] N, PL **showmen** [ˈʃəʊmən] empresario *m*, director *m* de espectáculos; (*fig*) persona *f* ostentosa, exhibicionista *m*; (*pej*) comediante *m*, fantoche *m*, charlatán *m*; **the prime minister is a consummate** ~ el primer ministro es un brillante actor.
showmanship [ˈʃəʊmənʃɪp] N instinto *m* del buen actor; teatralidad *f*; talento *m* para organizar grandes espectáculos.
shown [ʃəʊn] PTP of **show**.
show-off* [ˈʃəʊɒf] N fantasmón*, comediante *m*, fantoche *m*.
showpiece [ˈʃəʊpiːs] N objeto *m* de valor (*or* interés etc) excepcional; **the** ~ **of the exhibition is ...** la joya de la exposición es ...; **this vase is a real** ~ este florero es realmente excepcional.
showplace [ˈʃəʊpleɪs] N lugar *m* de gran atractivo, centro *m* turístico, monumento *m*; **Granada is a** ~ Granada es una ciudad de gran atractivo, Granada es un monumento artístico e histórico; **the new school is not typical but is a** ~ el nuevo colegio no es un colegio corriente, es más bien una cosa excepcional para mostrar a los visitantes.
showroom [ˈʃəʊrʊm] N salón *m* de demostraciones; (*in shop*) sala *f* de muestras; (*Art*) sala *f* de exposición.
show-stopper* [ˈʃəʊˌstɒpəʳ] N: **he** (*or* **it**) **was a** ~ fue un éxito clamoroso.
show-stopping [ˌʃəʊˈstɒpɪŋ] ADJ *performance* sensacional, impresionante; *product* sensacional.
showtime [ˈʃəʊtaɪm] N (*Theat, TV*) comienzo *m* del espectáculo.
show window [ˈʃəʊˌwɪndəʊ] N escaparate *m*.
showy [ˈʃəʊɪ] ADJ vistoso, llamativo; aparatoso, espectacular; *person* ostentoso.
shpt N (*Comm*) ABBR of **shipment**.
shrank [ʃræŋk] PRET of **shrink**.
shrapnel [ˈʃræpnl] N metralla *f*.
shred [ʃred] **1** N (*bit*) fragmento *m*, pedazo *m*; (*of cloth*) triza *f*, jirón *m*; (*narrow strip*) tira *f*; **there isn't a** ~ **of truth in it** eso no tiene ni pizca de verdad; **if you had a** ~ **of decency** si Vd tuviese una gota

de honradez; **without a ~ of clothing on** sin ni asomo de vestido; **to be in ~s** estar roto, estar destrozado; **her dress hung in ~s** su vestido estaba hecho jirones; **to tear sth to ~s** hacer algo trizas; **to tear an argument to ~s** hacer un argumento pedazos; **the crowd will tear him to ~s** la gente le hará pedazos.

[2] VT hacer trizas, hacer tiras; *food etc* desmenuzar; *meat* deshilar; *paper* desfibrar, triturar.

shredder ['ʃredəʳ] N, **shredding-machine** ['ʃredɪŋməˌʃiːn] N (*document ~*) desfibradora *f*, trituradora *f*; (*vegetable ~*) picadora *f*.

shrew [ʃruː] N (a) (*Zool*) musaraña *f*. (b) (*fig*) arpía *f*, fiera *f*; **'The Taming of the S~'** 'La fierecilla domada'.

shrewd [ʃruːd] ADJ *person* sagaz, perspicaz; listo; *plan etc* prudente, astuto; **~ reasoning** razonamiento *m* inteligente; **that is a ~ thing to do** eso es lo más prudente; **that was very ~ of you** en eso has sido muy perspicaz; **I have a ~ idea that ...** se me ocurre pensar que ..., me parece razonable suponer que ...

shrewdly ['ʃruːdlɪ] ADV sagazmente, con perspicacia; prudentemente, astutamente.

shrewdness ['ʃruːdnɪs] N sagacidad *f*, perspicacia *f*; inteligencia *f*; prudencia *f*, astucia *f*.

shrewish ['ʃruːɪʃ] ADJ regañona, de mal genio.

shriek [ʃriːk] [1] N chillido *m*, grito *m* agudo; **a ~ of pain** un grito de dolor; **with ~s of laughter** con grandes carcajadas.

[2] VT gritar; **to ~ abuse at sb** lanzar improperios contra uno.

[3] VI chillar, gritar; **to ~ with pain** chillar de dolor; **to ~ with laughter** reírse a grandes carcajadas; **the colour simply ~s at one** es un color de lo más chillón.

shrieking ['ʃriːkɪŋ] [1] ADJ *child, colour* chillón.

[2] N chillidos *mpl*, gritos *mpl*.

shrift [ʃrɪft] N: **to give sb short ~** echar a uno con cajas destempladas; **he gave that idea short ~** mostró su completa disconformidad con tal idea, desechó muy pronto tal posibilidad; **he got short ~ from the boss** el jefe se mostró poco compasivo con él; **he'll get short ~ from me!** ¡que no venga a mí a pedir compasión!

shrike [ʃraɪk] N alcaudón *m*.

shrill [ʃrɪl] [1] ADJ chillón, agudo, estridente.

[2] VT gritar (con voz estridente).

[3] VI chillar.

shrillness ['ʃrɪlnɪs] N lo chillón, estridencia *f*.

shrilly ['ʃrɪlɪ] ADV agudamente, de modo estridente.

shrimp [ʃrɪmp] [1] N (a) (*Zool*) camarón *m*. (b) (*fig*) enano *m*, renacuajo *m*.

[2] ATTR: **~ cocktail** cóctel *m* de camarones; **~ sauce** salsa *f* de camarones.

[3] VI (*also* **to go ~ing**) pescar camarones.

shrine [ʃraɪn] N (*tomb*) sepulcro *m* (de santo), santuario *m*; relicario *m*; (*chapel*) capilla *f*; (*altar*) altar *m*; (*fig*) lugar *m* sagrado.

shrink [ʃrɪŋk] (*irr*: PRET **shrank**, PTP **shrunk**) [1] VT encoger; contraer; *quality* reducir, disminuir; **to ~ a part on** (*Tech*) montar una pieza en caliente.

[2] VI (a) (*get smaller*) encoger(se); contraerse; (*quantity*) reducirse, disminuir, mermar; **to ~ in the wash** encogerse al lavar; **'will not ~'** 'no (se) encoge', 'inencogible'; **to ~ away to nothing** reducirse a nada, desaparecer.

(b) (*recoil: also* **to ~ away, to ~ back**) retroceder (*from* ante); acobardarse, retirarse (*from, at* ante); **I ~ from doing it** no me atrevo a hacerlo, me repugna hacerlo; **he did not ~ from touching it** no vaciló en tocarlo.

[3] N (*esp US*) psiquiatra *mf*.

shrinkage ['ʃrɪŋkɪdʒ] N encogimiento *m*; contracción *f*; reducción *f*, disminución *f*.

shrinking ['ʃrɪŋkɪŋ] ADJ *clothes* que se encoge; *resources etc* que escasea; **~ violet** (*fig*) tímido *m*, -a *f*, vergonzoso *m*, -a *f*.

shrink-wrap ['ʃrɪŋkræp] VT empaquetar (*or* envasar) al vacío.

shrink-wrapped ['ʃrɪŋkræpt] ADJ empaquetado (*or* envasado) al vacío.

shrink-wrapping ['ʃrɪŋkræpɪŋ] N envasado *m* al vacío.

shrivel ['ʃrɪvl] [1] VT (*also* **to ~ up**) secar, marchitar; *skin* arrugar.

[2] VI (*also* **to ~ up**) secarse, marchitarse; (*skin etc*) arrugarse, avellanarse, apergaminarse; (*fruit*) consumirse.

shrivelled, (*US*) **shriveled** ['ʃrɪvld] ADJ *plant etc* seco, marchito; *skin* arrugado, apergaminado.

shroud [ʃraʊd] [1] N (a) sudario *m*, mortaja *f*; (*fig*) velo *m*; **the S~ of Turin** el Santo Sudario de Turín; **a ~ of mystery** un velo de misterio.

(b) **~s** (*Naut*) obenques *mpl*.

[2] VT amortajar; (*fig*) velar, cubrir; **the castle was ~ed in mist** el castillo estaba envuelto en niebla; **the whole thing is ~ed in mystery** el asunto entero está envuelto en un velo de misterio.

Shrovetide ['ʃraʊvtaɪd] N carnestolendas *fpl*.

Shrove Tuesday ['ʃraʊv'tjuːzdɪ] N martes *m* de carnaval.

shrub [ʃrʌb] N arbusto *m*.

shrubbery ['ʃrʌbərɪ] N arbustos *mpl*, plantío *m* de arbustos.

shrubby ['ʃrʌbɪ] ADJ *tree* con forma de arbusto; *area* con muchos matojos.

shrug [ʃrʌg] [1] N encogimiento *m* de hombros; **he said with a ~** dijo encogiéndose de hombros.

[2] VT: **to ~ one's shoulders** = **3**.

[3] VI encogerse de hombros.

◆ **shrug off** VT: **to ~ sth off** negar importancia a algo, minimizar algo; **you can't just ~ that off** no puedes negar la importancia de eso.

shrunk [ʃrʌŋk] PTP *of* **shrink**.

shrunken ['ʃrʌŋkən] ADJ encogido; (*shrivelled*) seco; marchito; apergaminado; *head* reducido; *quantity* reducido, mermado.

shtoom: [ʃtʊm] ADJ: **to keep ~** achantar*, estar achantado*.

shuck [ʃʌk] [1] N (a) (*husk*) vaina *f*, hollejo *m*. (b) (*US: of shellfish*) concha *f* (de marisco); **~s!** (*US*) ¡cáscaras!

[2] VT (a) *peas etc* desenvainar. (b) (*US*) *shellfish* desbullar.

shudder ['ʃʌdəʳ] [1] N estremecimiento *m*, escalofrío *m*; (*of vehicle etc*) vibración *f*, sacudida *f*; **a ~ ran through her** se estremeció; **she realized with a ~ that ...** se estremeció al darse cuenta de que ...; **it gives me the ~s** me da escalofríos.

[2] VI estremecerse (*with* de); vibrar, sacudirse; **I ~ to think of it** sólo pensar en eso me da escalofríos; **I ~ to think what he will do next** me da escalofríos pensar en lo que hará luego.

shuffle ['ʃʌfl] [1] N (a) **to walk with a ~** caminar arrastrando los pies. (b) (*Cards*) barajadura *f*; **to give the cards a ~** barajar las cartas; **whose ~ is it?** ¿a quién le toca barajar?

[2] VT (a) *feet* arrastrar.

(b) (*mix up*) mezclar, revolver; *cards* barajar, mezclar.

(c) **to ~ sb aside** apartar a uno, relegar a uno a un puesto menos importante.

[3] VI (a) (*walk*) arrastrar los pies; caminar (*or* bailar *etc*) arrastrando los pies; **he ~d across to the door** fue hacia la puerta arrastrando los pies; **he managed to ~ out of the job** logró zafarse del compromiso.

(b) (*Cards*) barajar.

◆ **shuffle off** [1] VI marcharse arrastrando los pies.

[2] VT *garment* despojarse de; (*fig*) *responsibility* rechazar; **to ~ sth off** deshacerse de algo.

shuffleboard ['ʃʌflbɔːd] N juego *m* de tejo.

shufti: ['ʃʊftɪ] N ojeada *f*; **let's have a ~** a ver, déjame ver; **we went to take a ~** fuimos a echar un vistazo.

shun [ʃʌn] VT evitar, esquivar, rehuir; volver la espalda a; **to ~ doing sth** evitar hacer algo; **to feel ~ned by the world** sentirse rechazado por la gente.

shunt [ʃʌnt] [1] VT (*Rail*) maniobrar; **to ~ sb aside** apartar a uno, relegar a uno a un puesto menos importante; **to ~ sb off** apartar a uno de su propósito; **he was ~ed into retirement** lograron con maña que se jubilase; **to ~ sb to and fro** mandar a uno de acá para allá.

[2] VI: **to ~ to and fro** trajinar de acá para allá.

shunter ['ʃʌntəʳ] N (*Brit*) guardagujas *m*.

shunting ['ʃʌntɪŋ] [1] N maniobras *fpl*.

[2] ATTR: **~ engine** locomotora *f* de maniobra; **~ yard** estación *f* de maniobras, playa *f* de clasificación.

shush [ʃʊʃ] [1] INTERJ ¡chitón!

[2] VT hacer callar, imponer silencio a.

shut [ʃʌt] (*irr*: PRET AND PTP **shut**) [1] VT cerrar; **to find the door ~** encontrar que la puerta está cerrada; **he had the door ~ in his face** le dieron con la puerta en las narices; **to ~ one's fingers in the door** pillarse los dedos en la puerta.

[2] VI cerrarse; **we ~ at 5** cerramos a las 5; **the lid doesn't ~** la tapa no cierra (bien).

◆ **shut away** [1] VT encerrar; recluir.

[2] VR: **to ~ o.s. away** encerrarse; recluirse; **he ~s himself away all day in his room** permanece encerrado todo el día en su habitación.

◆ **shut down** [1] VT (a) *lid etc* cerrar.

(b) *business, factory* cerrar.

(c) *machine* parar.

[2] VI (*business etc*) cerrar, cerrarse.

◆ **shut in** VT *person etc* encerrar; (*surround*) cercar, rodear; **to feel ~ in** sentirse encerrado; **the runner was ~ in** el atleta se encontró tapado.

◆ **shut off** VT (a) (*stop, cut*) *water etc* cortar; interrumpir; *engine* parar; *pipe etc* obturar, cegar.

(b) (*isolate*) aislar, separar (*from* de); **to be ~ off from** estar aislado de.

◆ **shut out** VT (a) (*by door etc*) excluir; negar la entrada a; *workers* dejar sin trabajo por lock-out.

(b) (*block*) tapar, ocultar; impedir ver.

◆ **shut to** [1] VT cerrar.

[2] VI cerrarse.

◆ **shut up** [1] VT (a) (*close*) cerrar.

(b) (*block*) cegar, obturar.
(c) *person etc* encerrar; recluir.
(d) *factory etc* cerrar.
(e) (*: *silence*) hacer callar, reducir al silencio.
[2] VI (*: *be quiet*) callarse; ~ **up!** ¡calla!, ¡cállate!; **to ~ up like a clam** callarse como un muerto.

shutdown ['ʃʌtdaʊn] N cierre *m*.
shut-eye* ['ʃʌtaɪ] N sueño *m*; **to get some ~** echar un sueñecito*.
shut-in ['ʃʌtɪn] ADJ encerrado.
shutoff ['ʃʌtɒf] N interruptor *m*.
shut-out ['ʃʌtaʊt] N cierre *m* (para impedir la entrada); (*US Sport*) victoria *f* fácil, victoria *f* abrumadora; (*Brit Sport*) **the goalkeeper had 10 successive ~s** el portero salió imbatido en 10 partidos sucesivos; **~ record** récord *m* de imbatibilidad; **~ bid** declaración *f* aplastante.
shutter ['ʃʌtə] [1] N (*of window*) contraventana *f*; (*Phot*) obturador *m*; **to put up the ~s** (*shop*) cerrar del todo, (*fig*) abandonar, (*Sport etc*) resolverse a no correr riesgo alguno.
[2] ATTR: **~ speed** velocidad *f* de obturación.
shuttered ['ʃʌtəd] ADJ (*having shutters*) con contraventanas; (*with shutters closed*) con las contraventanas cerradas.
shuttle ['ʃʌtl] [1] N (a) (*of loom, sewing machine*) lanzadera *f*.
(b) (*Aer*) puente *m* aéreo.
(c) (*Space*) transbordador *m* espacial.
[2] ATTR: **~ diplomacy** viajes *mpl* diplomáticos; **~ service** (*Aer*) puente *m* aéreo; (*Rail etc*) servicio *m* de lanzadera.
[3] VT: **to ~ sb about** mandar a uno de acá para allá; **we were ~d about all day** pasamos todo el día trajinando de acá para allá; **the form was ~d about between different departments** la solicitud fue enviada de departamento a departamento (sin que nadie la atendiese).
[4] VI (*Aer, Rail etc*) hacer el servicio rápido y continuo (*between 2 points* entre 2 puntos).
shuttlecock ['ʃʌtlkɒk] N volante *m*, rehilete *m*.
shy¹ [ʃaɪ] [1] ADJ (a) (*bashful*) vergonzoso; (*reserved*) reservado; (*unsociable*) huraño; *animal* huraño, asustadizo; **I can't do it, I'm ~** no puedo hacerlo, me da vergüenza; **to be ~ of, to fight ~ of** procurar evitar; **to be ~ of** + *ger* procurar evitar + *infin*, no atreverse a + *infin*; **don't be ~** no tengas miedo; **he makes me ~** él me hace sentirme miedoso.
(b) I'm 10 dollars ~ (*US*) me faltan 10 dólares, he perdido 10 dólares.
[2] VI (*of horse*) espantarse, respingar (*at sth* al ver algo); **to ~ at a fence** negarse a saltar una valla.
◆**shy away** VI: **to ~ away from sth** alejarse asustado de algo; **they shied away from the idea** se asustaron de la idea; **to ~ away from** + *ger* asustarse y negarse a + *infin*.
shy² [ʃaɪ] (*Brit*) [1] N (*throw*) tirada *f*; (*fig*) tentativa *f*; **to have a ~ at sth** probar algo; **to have a ~ at** + *ger* hacer una tentativa de + *infin*; '**50 pesetas a ~**' '50 pesetas la tirada'.
[2] VT lanzar, echar.
shyly ['ʃaɪlɪ] ADV tímidamente; con vergüenza, vergonzosamente.
shyness ['ʃaɪnɪs] N timidez *f*; vergüenza *f*; reserva *f*; lo huraño, lo asustadizo.
shyster* ['ʃaɪstə'] N (*US*) abogado *m* trampista; persona *f* poco honrada.
SI N ABBR of **Système Internationale** *system of metric units*.
Siam [saɪ'æm] N Siam *m*.
Siamese [,saɪə'miːz] [1] ADJ siamés; **~ cat** gato *m* siamés, gata *f* siamesa; **~ twins** gemelos *mpl* siameses, gemelas *fpl* siamesas.
[2] N (a) siamés *m*, -esa *f*. (b) (*Ling*) siamés *m*.
SIB N (*Brit*) ABBR of **Securities and Investments Board**.
Siberia [saɪ'bɪərɪə] N Siberia *f*.
Siberian [saɪ'bɪərɪən] [1] ADJ siberiano.
[2] N siberiano *m*, -a *f*.
sibilant ['sɪbɪlənt] [1] ADJ sibilante.
[2] N sibilante *f*.
sibling ['sɪblɪŋ] [1] N hermano *m* (*or* hermana *f*); **it turned out they were ~s** resultó que eran hermanos.
[2] ATTR: **~ rivalry** rivalidad *f* de hermanos.
Sibyl ['sɪbɪl] NF Sibila *f*.
sibyl ['sɪbɪl] N sibila *f*.
sibylline ['sɪbɪlaɪn] ADJ sibilino.
sic [sɪk] ADV: **he said '...'** dijo '...' (palabras textuales *or* la cita es textual).
Sicilian [sɪ'sɪlɪən] [1] ADJ siciliano.
[2] N (a) siciliano *m*, -a *f*. (b) (*Ling*) siciliano *m*.
Sicily ['sɪsɪlɪ] N Sicilia *f*.
sick [sɪk] [1] ADJ (a) (*ill*) enfermo; **~ building syndrome** síndrome *m* causado por el aire acondicionado; **to be (off) ~** estar enfermo; **to fall ~, to go ~, to take ~** caer enfermo, enfermar; (*be absent*) ausentarse debido a enfermedad; **the cow took ~ and died** la vaca cayó enferma y murió; **to report ~** darse de baja por enfermo.

(b) (*Brit: dizzy, about to vomit*) mareado; **to be ~** vomitar; arrojar*; **to feel ~** estar mareado; **I get ~ in aeroplanes** me mareo en los aviones; **too much beer makes me ~** un exceso de cerveza me da ganas de vomitar.
(c) (*fig*) **to be ~ at heart** estar muy deprimido, sentirlo en el alma; **they were all as ~ as parrots*** todos arrojaron hasta los huesos*; **to be ~ (and tired) of, to be ~ to death of** estar harto de; **I get ~ of that** eso se me hace pesado, cojo asco a eso; **he just did look ~** estaba la mar de abatido; estaba furioso consigo mismo; **it's enough to make you ~** es para volverse loco; **you make me ~!** ¡me das asco!; **it makes me ~ to think that ...** me da asco pensar que ...; **she worried herself ~ about it** se inquietó terriblemente por esto.
(d) *humour* negro, malsano; **~ joke** chiste *m* negro.
[2] NPL (a) **the ~** los enfermos. (b) (*) vómito *m*.
◆**sick up*** VT arrojar*, devolver*.
sickbay ['sɪkbeɪ] N enfermería *f*.
sickbed ['sɪkbed] N lecho *m* de enfermo.
sicken ['sɪkn] [1] VT dar asco a (*also fig*); **it ~s me** me da asco, me repugna.
[2] VI caer enfermo, enfermar; **to ~ at sth** sentir náuseas ante algo; **I ~ at the sight of blood** el ver sangre me da náuseas; **to ~ for, to be ~ing for** (*Med*) mostrar síntomas de; **to ~ for want of** enfermar por.
sickening ['sɪknɪŋ] ADJ nauseabundo; (*fig*) asqueroso, repugnante; **it's ~ that ...** me ofende en el alma que + *subj*.
sickeningly ['sɪknɪŋlɪ] ADV (*fig*) asquerosamente; **~ sentimental** tan sensiblero que da asco.
sickle ['sɪkl] N hoz *f*.
sick-leave ['sɪkliːv] N permiso *m* por enfermedad; **to be on ~** estar ausente con permiso por enfermedad.
sickle-cell ['sɪkl,sel] ATTR: **~ anaemia, ~ anemia** (*US*) anemia *f* de células falciformes, drepanocitosis *f*.
sickliness ['sɪklɪnɪs] N lo enfermizo, lo achacoso; palidez *f*; lo nauseabundo; debilidad *f*; lo empalagoso.
sick-list ['sɪklɪst] N lista *f* de enfermos; **to be on the ~** estar enfermo.
sickly ['sɪklɪ] ADJ *person* enfermizo, achacoso; *plant* débil, de mal aspecto; *appearance* pálido; (*Brit*) *smell* nauseabundo; *smile* débil, forzado; *cake, sweet* empalagoso; **~ sweet** dulzón, empalagoso.
sick-making* ['sɪkmeɪkɪŋ] ADJ asqueroso.
sickness ['sɪknɪs] N (*Med*) enfermedad *f*, mal *m*; (*fig*) mal *m*, malestar *m*; **~ benefit** subsidio *m* por invalidez; **there is ~ on board** hay epidemia a bordo, hay enfermedad contagiosa a bordo.
sick-out ['sɪkaʊt] N (*US: Ind*) baja colectiva por enfermedad como forma de protesta.
sick-pay ['sɪkpeɪ] N subsidio *m* de enfermedad; **to be on ~** recibir el subsidio de enfermedad.
sickroom ['sɪkrʊm] N cuarto *m* del enfermo.
side [saɪd] [1] N (a) (*Anat etc*) costado *m*, lado *m*; (*of animal*) flanco *m*, ijada *f*; **~ of bacon** hoja *f* de tocino; **the assistant was at (or by) his ~** el ayudante estaba a su lado; **by the ~ of** al lado de; **he had the telephone by his ~** tenía el teléfono a su lado; **to sit by sb's ~** estar sentado al lado de uno; **to sit ~ by ~ with sb** estar sentado al lado de uno; **to sleep on one's ~** dormir de costado; **to split one's ~s** desternillarse de risa.
(b) (*flank etc, fig*) lado *m*, flanco *m*; (*of triangle*) lado *m*; (*of ship*) costado *m*; (*of hill*) falda *f*, ladera *f*; (*of lake*) orilla *f*; (*of small pond etc*) borde *m*; (*of wood*) límite *m*, borde *m*.
(c) (*face, surface*) lado *m*, superficie *f*; (*of record, slice of bread, solid etc*) cara *f*; **wrong ~** revés *m*, envés *m*; **to be wrong ~ out** estar al revés; **what's on the other ~?** (*of record*) ¿qué hay a la vuelta?; **these are two ~s of the same coin** son dos caras de la misma moneda; **let us look at the other ~ of the coin** véamos el revés de la medalla; **please write on both ~s of the paper** escribir en ambas caras del papel.
(d) (*part, region*) lado *m*; **left-hand ~** izquierda *f*; **right-hand ~** derecha *f*; **to be on the left-hand ~** estar a la izquierda; **on one ~..., on the other ...** por una parte ..., por otra ...; **on this ~** por este lado; **on all ~s** por todas partes, por todos lados; **on both ~s** por ambos lados; **on my mother's ~** por parte de mi madre; **on the ~** (*as adv*) incidentalmente; de paso; (*unofficially*) de modo extraoficial; **to make a bit on the ~** ganarse algo bajo cuerda; **to get out of bed on the wrong ~** levantarse con el pie izquierdo; **to be on the right ~ of 40** no haber cumplido todavía los 40 años; **to put sth on one ~** poner algo aparte, guardarse algo; ahorrar; **I'll put it on one ~ for you** te lo guardaré; **from ~ to ~** de un lado al otro; **leaving that to one ~ for the moment, ...** dejando eso a un lado por ahora, ...; **to move to one ~** apartarse, hacerse a un lado; **it's this ~ of Segovia** está más acá de Segovia; **it's the other ~ of Illescas** está más allá de Illescas; **it won't happen this ~ of Christmas** no será antes de Navidades; **he's the wrong ~ of 40** tiene más de 40 años, ha pasado ya de los 40.
(e) (*aspect*) aspecto *m*, lado *m*; **the other ~** (*of the picture*), **the seamy ~** el reverso de la medalla; **to be on the safe ~ ...** para

mayor seguridad ..., por precaución ...; **let's be on the safe ~** atengámonos a lo más seguro; **to hear both ~s of the question** escuchar los argumentos en pro y en contra; **to see only one ~ of the question** sólo ver un aspecto de la cuestión; **to get on the good ~ of sb** procurar congraciarse con uno; **to get on the wrong ~ of sb** ponerse a malas con uno; **to look on the bright ~** ser optimista, ver el lado risueño de las cosas.

(f) *(fig)* **it's on the large ~** es algo grande; **the results are on the poor ~** los resultados son más bien mediocres; **the weather's on the cold ~** el tiempo es algo frío.

(g) *(Brit*: conceit, superiority)* tono *m*, postín* *m*; **there's no ~ about** *(or* **to) him** no presume, no se da aires de superioridad; **to put on ~** darse tono.

(h) *(party)* partido *m*; *(team)* equipo *m*; *(Bridge etc)* bando *m*, campo *m*; **our ~** nuestro campo *(etc)*, los nuestros; **the science ~ of the school** los estudios científicos en el instituto; **he went on the science ~** optó por estudiar ciencias; **to change ~s** pasar al otro bando, cambiar de partido; cambiar de opinión; **to let the ~ down** hacer algo indigno de su colegio *(etc)*, hacer algo que desmerece de su partido *(etc)*; **to pick a ~** seleccionar un equipo; **to take ~s** tomar partido; **he's on our ~** es de los nuestros, es partidario nuestro; **whose ~ are you on?** ¿a quiénes apoyas?; **you have tradition on your ~** la tradición está de parte de Vd, la tradición le apoya a Vd; **with a few concessions on the government ~** con algunas concesiones por parte del gobierno.

2 ATTR lateral, de lado; *entrance* accesorio; *elevation* lateral; **~ door** puerta *f* accesoria; **~ effect** efecto *m* secundario; **~ entrance** entrada *f* lateral; **~ issue** cuestión *f* secundaria; **~ plate** plato *m* pequeño.

◆**side against** VT: **to ~ against sb** tomar el partido contrario a uno, alinearse con los que se oponen a uno.

◆**side with** VT: **to ~ with sb** declararse por uno, tomar el partido de uno; **I'm siding with nobody** yo no tomo partido.

side-arms ['saɪdɑːmz] NPL armas *fpl* de cinto.

sideboard ['saɪdbɔːd] N aparador *m*.

sideboards ['saɪdbɔːdz] NPL *(Brit)*, **sideburns** ['saɪdbɜːnz] NPL patillas *fpl*.

sidecar ['saɪdkɑːʳ] N sidecar *m*.

-sided ['saɪdɪd] ADJ *ending in compounds* de ... lados, *eg* **six~** de seis lados.

side dish ['saɪddɪʃ] N plato *m* adicional (servido con el principal).

side drum ['saɪddrʌm] N tamboril *m*.

side face ['saɪdfeɪs] **1** N perfil *m*.
2 ATTR de perfil.
3 ADV de perfil.

side glance ['saɪdglɑːns] N mirada *f* de soslayo.

side-impact protection [ˌsaɪdɪmpæktprəˈtekʃən] N *(Auto)* protección *f* contra impactos laterales.

sidekick* ['saɪdkɪk] N compañero *m* (de trabajo *etc)*, compinche *m*.

sidelight ['saɪdlaɪt] N **(a)** *(Brit Aut etc)* luz *f* lateral, luz *f* de posición. **(b)** *(fig)* detalle *m* incidental, información *f* incidental *(on* relativo a).

sideline ['saɪdlaɪn] **1** N **(a)** *(Rail)* apartadero *m*, vía *f* secundaria. **(b)** *(Sport, Ftbl etc)* línea *f* lateral, *(Tennis etc)* línea *f* de banda; **to stand** *(or* **stay) on the ~s** *(fig)* no tomar parte, mantenerse aparte; mantener su neutralidad. **(c)** *(fig)* empleo *m* suplementario, negocio *m* suplementario; **it's just a ~** es solamente una cosa secundaria; **he breeds parrots as a ~** como negocio suplementario se dedica a criar loros.
2 VT *(esp US)* apartar, marginar, dejar a un lado; **we won't be ~d** no permitimos que se nos margine; **he was ~d by injury the whole season** quedó fuera del equipo durante toda la temporada debido a una lesión.

sidelong ['saɪdlɒŋ] **1** ADV de lado, lateralmente; oblicuamente; *glance* de soslayo.
2 ADJ lateral; oblicuo; *glance* de soslayo.

sidereal [saɪˈdɪrɪəl] ADJ sidéreo.

side road ['saɪdrəʊd] N *(Brit)* calle *f* lateral; calle *f* secundaria.

sidesaddle ['saɪdˌsædl] **1** N silla *f* de mujer.
2 ADV: **to ride ~** montar a mujeriegas, montar a asentadillas.

sideshow ['saɪdʃəʊ] N *(at fair)* barraca *f*, caseta *f* (de feria); *(fig)* función *f* secundaria.

sideslip ['saɪdslɪp] N *(Aer)* deslizamiento *m* lateral.

side-slipping ['saɪdˌslɪpɪŋ] N *(Ski)* derrapaje *m*.

sidesman ['saɪdzmən] N, PL **sidesmen** ['saɪdzmən] acólito *m*.

side-splitting ['saɪdˌsplɪtɪŋ] ADJ *joke* divertidísimo.

side-step ['saɪdstep] **1** N paso *m* hacia un lado; *(dodge)* esquivada *f*.
2 VT *(fig)* evitar, esquivar; **he neatly ~ped the question** esquivó hábilmente la pregunta.
3 VI dar un paso hacia un lado, moverse a un lado.

side street ['saɪdstriːt] N calle *f* lateral; calle *f* secundaria.

sidestroke ['saɪdstrəʊk] N natación *f* de costado.

side-swipe ['saɪdswaɪp] N golpe *m* de refilón *(also fig)*.

sidetable ['saɪdˌteɪbl] N trinchero *m*.

sidetrack ['saɪdtræk] **1** N *(Rail)* apartadero *m*, vía *f* muerta; *(fig)* cuestión *f* secundaria.
2 VT *person* apartar de su propósito, desviar del asunto principal; *discussion* conducir por cuestiones de poca importancia; **I got ~ed** me aparté del asunto principal, me despisté.

side view ['saɪdvjuː] N perfil *m*.

sidewalk ['saɪdwɔːk] N *(US)* acera *f*, vereda *f* *(LAm)*, andén *m* *(CAm)*, banqueta *f* *(CAm, Mex)*.

sidewards ['saɪdwədz] ADV de lado; hacia un lado; oblicuamente; **it goes in ~** entra de lado.

sideways ['saɪdˌweɪz] ADV **(a)** = **sidewards**. **(b)** *(fig)* **to move ~** *(in career etc)* trasladarse a otro puesto equivalente al actual, ir a tomar un puesto de la misma categoría.

side whiskers ['saɪdˌwɪskəz] NPL patillas *fpl*.

sidewind ['saɪdwɪnd] N viento *m* lateral.

siding ['saɪdɪŋ] N apartadero *m*, vía *f* muerta.

sidle ['saɪdl] VI: **to ~ up** acercarse cautelosamente *(or* sigilosamente, servilmente; *to* a).

Sidon ['saɪdən] N Sidón *m*.

SIDS N ABBR *of* **sudden infant death syndrome** muerte *f* en la cuna.

siege [siːdʒ] **1** N cerco *m*, sitio *m*; **to lay ~ to** poner sitio a, sitiar, cercar; *person* asediar; **to raise the ~** levantar el cerco.
2 ATTR: **~ economy** economía *f* de sitio *(or* de asedio).

sienna [sɪˈenə] N siena *f*.

Sierra Leone [sɪˈerəlɪˈəʊn] N Sierra *f* Leona.

Sierra Leonean [sɪˌerəlɪˈəʊnɪən] **1** ADJ sierraleonés.
2 N sierraleonés *m*, -esa *f*.

siesta [sɪˈestə] N siesta *f*; **to have a ~** dormir la siesta.

sieve [sɪv] **1** N tamiz *m*, cedazo *m*, criba *f*; *(Culin)* coladera *f*.
2 VT = **sift**.

sift [sɪft] VT tamizar, cerner, cribar; *(fig)* escudriñar, examinar.

sigh [saɪ] **1** N suspiro *m*; *(of wind)* susurro *m*; **to breathe a ~ of relief** suspirar, suspirar aliviado; **to heave a ~** dar un suspiro.
2 VI suspirar; *(wind)* susurrar; **to ~ for** suspirar por.

sighing ['saɪɪŋ] N suspiros *mpl*; *(of wind)* susurro *m*.

sight [saɪt] **1** N **(a)** *(faculty, act of seeing)* vista *f*; visión *f*; **30 days' (after) ~** *(a)* 30 días vista; **at ~, at first ~** a primera vista, a la vista; **to hate sb at first ~ on** *(or* at) detestar a uno desde el principio, odiar a uno desde el primer momento; **payable at ~** pagadero a la vista; **to shoot at ~** disparar nada más ver; **to translate at ~** traducir oralmente, traducir a libro abierto; **it was love at first ~** fue un flechazo; **to know sb by ~** conocer a uno de vista; **land in ~!** ¡tierra a la vista!; **to be in** *(or* within) **~** estar a la vista *(of* de); **our goal is in ~** ya vemos la meta; **we are in ~ of victory** estamos a las puertas de la victoria; **to keep sb in ~** no perder a uno de vista; **to find favour in sb's ~** *(plan etc)* ser aceptable a uno, *(person)* merecerse la aprobación de uno; **to come into ~** aparecer, asomarse; **to heave in(to) ~** aparecer; **on ~ = at ~; to be out of ~** estar invisible, no estar a la vista, no poderse ver; **to drop out of ~** desaparecer; **not to let sb out of one's ~** no perder a uno de vista, vigilar constantemente a uno; **out of ~*** *(US)* fabuloso*, fantástico*; **out of ~, out of mind** ojos que no ven, corazón que no siente; **to be lost to ~** desaparecer, perderse de vista; **I can't bear the ~ of blood** no aguanto la vista de la sangre; **I can't bear the ~ of him** no le puedo ver; **to buy sth ~ unseen** comprar algo sin verlo; **to catch ~ of** *(glimpse)* vislumbrar; *(happen to see)* ver por casualidad; *(on appearance of object)* alcanzar a ver; **to get a ~ of sth** lograr ver algo; **I hate the ~ of him** no le puedo ver; **to lose ~ of sb** perder a uno de vista; **to lose ~ of the fact that ...** no tener presente el hecho de que ...; **to lose one's ~** perder la vista, quedar ciego; **to regain one's ~** recobrar la vista.

(b) *(on gun)* mira *f*, alza *f*, guión *m* de mira; visor *m*; **to set one's ~s too high** *(fig)* apuntar muy alto, ser demasiado ambicioso; **to set one's ~s on sth** resolverse a adquirir *(or* obtener *etc)* algo.

(c) *(scene, spectacle)* vista *f*, escena *f*, espectáculo *m*; **it is a ~ to see** es cosa digna de verse; **it's a sad ~** es una cosa triste; **it's not a pretty ~** no es muy agradable para la vista; **it was a ~ for sore eyes** daba gusto verlo; **his face was a ~!** ¡había que ver su cara!, *(after injury etc)* ¡había que ver el estado en que quedaba su cara!

(d) *(spectacle: of person)* **I must look a ~** debo parecer horroroso, ¿no?; **doesn't she look a ~ in that hat!** ¡con ese sombrero parece un espantajo!; **what a ~ you are!** ¡qué adefesio!

(e) *(for tourists etc)* **~s** monumentos *mpl*, cosas *fpl* de interés *(turístico)*, curiosidades *fpl*; **the ~s of Córdoba** los monumentos de Córdoba; **to see the ~s** visitar los monumentos, visitar los puntos de interés.

2 ATTR: **~ draft** letra *f* a la vista; **~ translation** traducción *f* oral, traducción *f* a libro abierto.

3 ADV **(*)** **it's a (long) ~ better than the other one** es muchísimo mejor que el otro; **he's a ~ too clever** es demasiado listo; **it's a ~ dearer** es mucho más caro.

4 VT **(a)** *(see)* ver, divisar, avistar; **to ~ land** ver tierra; **we ~ed him**

coming down the street le vimos bajar la calle.
  (**b**) (*aim*) **to ~ a gun** apuntar un cañón (*at, on* a).

sighted ['saɪtɪd] ADJ vidente, que ve, de vista normal; **a blind man and a ~ companion** un ciego y su compañero de vista normal.

-sighted ['saɪtɪd] ADJ *ending in compounds*: **weak~** corto de vista, miope.

sighting ['saɪtɪŋ] N observación *f*.

sightless ['saɪtlɪs] ADJ ciego, invidente.

sightly ['saɪtlɪ] ADJ: **not very ~** no muy agradable para la vista.

sight-read ['saɪtriːd] (*irr: V* **read**) VTI leer sin preparación; (*Mus*) ejecutar a la primera lectura, repentizar.

sight-reading ['saɪtˌriːdɪŋ] N lectura *f* sin preparación; (*Mus*) ejecución *f* a la primera vista.

sightseeing ['saɪtˌsiːɪŋ] N excursionismo *m*, turismo *m*, visita *f* de puntos de interés; **'S~ in Ruritania'** 'Monumentos *mpl* de Ruritania'; **to go ~** visitar los monumentos.

sightseer ['saɪtˌsɪər] N excursionista *mf*, turista *mf*; visitante *mf*.

sight-singing ['saɪtˌsɪŋɪŋ] N ejecución *f* a la primera lectura.

sign [saɪn] ① N (**a**) (*with hand etc*) señal *f*, seña *f*; **~ of recognition** señal *f* de reconocimiento *m*; **to communicate by ~s** hablar por señas; **to make a ~ to sb** hacer una señal a uno; **to make a rude ~** hacer una señal grosera; **to make the ~ of the Cross** hacer la señal de la cruz; **to make the ~ of the Cross over sth** santiguar algo.
  (**b**) (*indication*) señal *f*, indicio *m*; asomo *m*; (*Med*) síntoma *m*; **the ~s of measles are ...** los síntomas del sarampión son ...; **at the slightest ~ of disagreement** ante cualquier asomo de discrepancia; **it's a ~ of rain** es indicio de lluvia; **it's a sure ~** es un indicio inconfundible; **it's a ~ of the true expert** esto indica el verdadero experto; **it's a ~ of the times** así son los tiempos actuales; **there's no ~ of their agreeing** no hay indicio de que se vayan a poner de acuerdo; **it's a good ~** es buena señal; **to show ~s of** dar muestras de, dar indicios de; **as a ~ of, in ~ of** en señal de.
  (**c**) (*trace*) huella *f*, vestigio *m*, rastro *m*; **there was no ~ of it** no quedaba rastro de él; **there was no ~ of him anywhere** no se le veía en ninguna parte; **there was no ~ of the former inhabitants** no quedaba huella de los antiguos habitantes; **there was no ~ of life in the village** no había vestigio de ser viviente en el pueblo.
  (**d**) (*road ~*) señal *f* de carretera; indicador *m*; (*inn ~*) letrero *m*; (*shop ~*) rótulo *m*; (*US: carried in demonstration*) pancarta *f*; **there was a big ~ which said 'Danger'** había un grande letrero que decía 'Peligro (de muerte)'.
  (**e**) (*written symbol*) signo *m*; símbolo *m*; (*Astron, Math, Mus, Zodiac*) signo *m*.
  ② VT firmar; **~ed and sealed** firmado y lacrado, firmado y sellado.
  ③ VI (**a**) **to ~ to sb to do sth** hacer señas a uno para que haga algo, decir a uno por medio de señas que haga algo.
  (**b**) (*with signature*) firmar, firmar su nombre.
  ④ VR: **he ~s himself Joe Soap** usa la firma Joe Soap, firma con el nombre Joe Soap.
◆**sign away** VT firmar la cesión de, (*fig*) ceder, abandonar.
◆**sign for** VT *key, parcel etc* firmar el recibo de; **he ~ed for Real Madrid** fichó por el Madrid.
◆**sign in** ① VT: **to ~ sb in** (*at club etc*) firmar el registro para avalar la admisión de uno.
  ② VI (*in factory*) firmar la entrada; (*in hotel*) firmar en el registro, registrarse.
◆**sign off** VI terminar; (*Rad, TV*) terminar el programa, terminar la emisión; (*Bridge*) terminar la declaración; (*ending letter*) terminar.
◆**sign on** ① VT: **to ~ sb on** contratar a uno.
  ② VI (*Comm*) contratarse; apuntarse, inscribirse; firmar un contrato; (*Sport etc*) fichar (*for* por); (*as unemployed*) registrarse (para cobrar el subsidio de paro); **to ~ on at a hotel** firmar el registro (de un hotel).
◆**sign out** ① VT: **the book is ~ed out to Professor Q** el libro está prestado al profesor Q; **you must ~ all books out** tienes que firmar al tomar prestado cualquier libro.
  ② VI: **to ~ out of a hotel** firmar el registro al salir de un hotel.
◆**sign over** VT: **to ~ sth over to sb** firmar el traspaso de algo a uno.
◆**sign up** = **sign on**.

signal ['sɪɡnl] ① N (**a**) (*sign*) señal *f*, seña *f*; (*Rad, TV*) señal *f*; **it was the ~ for revolt** fue la señal para la sublevación; **to give the ~ for** dar la señal de (*or* para); **to make a ~ to sb** hacer una señal a uno.
  (**b**) (*apparatus*) señal *f*; **the ~ is at red** la señal está en rojo.
  (**c**) **S~s** (*Mil*) transmisiones *fpl*, cuerpo *m* de transmisiones.
  ② ADJ notable, señalado, insigne.
  ③ VT: **to ~ one's approval** hacer una seña de aprobación; **to ~ sb to do sth** hacer señas a uno para que haga algo; **to ~ sb on** hacer señas a uno para que avance; **to ~ that ...** comunicar por señales que ...; **to ~ a turn to the right** indicar que uno va a torcer a la derecha; **to ~ a train** anunciar por señales la llegada de un tren; **the train is ~led** la señal indica la llegada del tren.
  ④ VI hacer una señal, hacer señales; **to ~ before stopping** hacer

una señal antes de parar.
signal book ['sɪɡnlbʊk] N (*Naut*) código *m* de señales.
signalbox ['sɪɡnlbɒks] N garita *f* de señales; casilla *f* de maniobras.
signal flag ['sɪɡnlflæɡ] N bandera *f* de señales.
signalize ['sɪɡnəlaɪz] VT distinguir, señalar.
signal lamp ['sɪɡnllæmp] N reflector *m* de señales, lámpara *f* de señales.
signally ['sɪɡnəlɪ] ADV notablemente, señaladamente; **he has ~ failed to do it** ha sufrido un notable fracaso al tratar de hacerlo.
signalman ['sɪɡnlmən] N, PL **signalmen** ['sɪɡnlmən] guardavía *m*.
signatory ['sɪɡnətərɪ] ① ADJ firmante, signatario; **the ~ powers to an agreement** las potencias firmantes de un acuerdo.
  ② N firmante *mf*, signatario *m*, -a *f*.
signature ['sɪɡnətʃər] N firma *f*; (*Mus, Typ*) signatura *f*; **to put one's ~ to a document** firmar un documento, poner su firma en un documento.
signature-tune ['sɪɡnətʃə,tjuːn] N (*esp Brit*) sintonía *f*.
signboard ['saɪnbɔːd] N letrero *m*, muestra *f*.
signer ['saɪnər] N firmante *mf*.
signet ['sɪɡnɪt] ① N sello *m*.
  ② ATTR: **~ ring** anillo *m* de sello.
significance [sɪɡ'nɪfɪkəns] N significación *f*, significado *m*; trascendencia *f*.
significant [sɪɡ'nɪfɪkənt] ADJ significativo; trascendente, importante; *improvement etc* sensible; *look* expresivo; **calculate it to 4 ~ figures** calcúlelo a 4 cifras significativas; **it is ~ that ...** es significativo que ...
significantly [sɪɡ'nɪfɪkəntlɪ] ADV significativamente; expresivamente; **it has improved ~** ha mejorado sensiblemente; **it is not ~ different** no hay diferencia importante; **she looked at me ~** me lanzó una mirada expresiva.
signify ['sɪɡnɪfaɪ] ① VT (**a**) (*mean*) significar, querer decir; **it signifies that ...** significa que ...; **what does it ~?** ¿qué quiere decir?
  (**b**) (*make known*) indicar; *opinion* comunicar, hacer saber; **to ~ that ...** dar a entender que ...; **to ~ one's approval** indicar su aprobación.
  ② VI: **it does not ~** no importa; **in the wider context it does not ~** en el contexto más amplio no tiene importancia.
signing ['saɪnɪŋ] N (*esp Ftbl, Rugby*) fichaje *m*.
sign-language ['saɪn,læŋɡwɪdʒ] N lenguaje *m* de señas, lenguaje *m* mímico, mímica *f*; **to talk in ~** hablar por señas.
sign-painter ['saɪn,peɪntər] N rotulista *mf*.
signpost ['saɪnpəʊst] ① N poste *m* indicador, indicador *m* de dirección.
  ② VT señalizar; **the road is well ~ed** la carretera tiene buena señalización.
signposting ['saɪnpəʊstɪŋ] N señalización *f*.
sign-writer ['saɪn,raɪtər] N rotulista *mf*.
Sikh [siːk] ① ADJ sij.
  ② N sij *mf*.
Sikhism ['siːkɪzəm] N sijismo *m*.
silage ['saɪlɪdʒ] N ensilaje *m*.
silence ['saɪləns] ① N silencio *m*; **~!** ¡silencio!; **~ is golden** el silencio es de oro; **in dead ~** en el silencio más absoluto; **there was ~** hubo un silencio; **~ gives consent** quien calla otorga; **to pass over sth in ~** silenciar algo; pasar algo por alto; **to reduce sb to ~** hacer callar a uno; **to reduce guns to ~** reducir los cañones al silencio.
  ② VT hacer callar, acallar; *guns etc* reducir al silencio; (*Tech*) silenciar; *critic* imponer silencio a, amordazar.
silencer ['saɪlənsər] N (*Brit*) silenciador *m*.
silent ['saɪlənt] ADJ silencioso; callado; *letter* mudo; **~ film, ~ picture** película *f* muda; **~ majority** mayoría *f* silenciosa; **~ partner** (*esp US*) socio *m* comanditario; **to be ~, to keep ~, to remain ~** callarse, guardar silencio, permanecer silencioso; **to become ~** callarse, enmudecer; **it was as ~ as the grave** había un silencio sepulcral.
silently ['saɪləntlɪ] ADV silenciosamente, en silencio.
silhouette [,sɪluː'et] ① N silueta *f*; **in ~** en silueta.
  ② VT destacar, hacer aparecer en silueta; **to be ~d against** destacarse contra, destacarse sobre.
silica ['sɪlɪkə] N sílice *f*.
silicate ['sɪlɪkɪt] N silicato *m*.
siliceous [sɪ'lɪʃəs] ADJ silíceo.
silicon ['sɪlɪkən] ① N silicio *m*.
  ② ATTR: **~ carbide** carburo *m* de silicio; **~ chip** chip *m* de silicio, pastilla *f* de silicio.
silicone ['sɪlɪkəʊn] N silicona *f*.
silicosis [,sɪlɪ'kəʊsɪs] N silicosis *f*.
silk [sɪlk] ① N seda *f*; **to take ~** (*Brit*) ser ascendido a la abogacía superior; *ver también* ⟨QC/KC⟩.
  ② ATTR de seda; **with a ~ finish** *cloth, paintwork* satinado; **~ hat** sombrero *m* de copa; **~ industry** industria *f* sedera; **~ screen printing** serigrafía *f*; **~ thread** hilo *m* de seda.
silken ['sɪlkən] ADJ (*of silk*) de seda; (*like silk*) sedoso, sedeño; *manner,*

silkiness ['sɪlkɪnɪs] N sedosidad *f*, lo sedoso; suavidad *f*, lo mimoso.

silkmoth ['sɪlkmɒθ] N mariposa *f* de seda.

silk-raising ['sɪlk,reɪzɪŋ] N sericultura *f*.

silkworm ['sɪlkwɜːm] N gusano *m* de seda.

silky ['sɪlkɪ] ADJ sedoso.

sill [sɪl] N antepecho *m*; (*window~*) alféizar *m*, repisa *f* (*LAm*); (*door ~*) umbral *m*.

silliness ['sɪlɪnɪs] N tontería *f*, necedad *f*; insensatez *f*; lo absurdo.

silly ['sɪlɪ] ADJ *person* tonto, bobo, necio; *act* tonto, insensato; *idea etc* absurdo; **~ season** temporada *f* boba, canícula *f*; **~ (of) me!** ¡qué tonto soy!; **you ~ child!**, **you big ~!** ¡bobo!; **don't be ~** no seas bobo; **that was ~ of you**, **that was a ~ thing to do** eso fue muy bobo, eso fue una estupidez; **I've done a ~ thing** he hecho una tontería, he sido un tonto; **I feel ~ in this hat** temo hacer el ridículo con este sombrero; **you look ~ carrying that fish** pareces un tonto llevando ese pez; **to knock sb ~*** dar una paliza a uno; **the blow knocked him ~** el golpe le dejó sin sentido; **to laugh o.s. ~*** desternillarse de risa*; **to make sb look ~** poner a uno en ridículo.

silo ['saɪləʊ] N (*Agr*) silo *m*, ensiladora *f*; (*Mil*) silo *m*.

silt [sɪlt] [1] N sedimento *m*, aluvión *m*.
[2] VT (*also to ~ up*) obstruir con sedimentos.
[3] VI (*also to ~ up*) obstruirse con sedimentos.

silting [sɪltɪŋ] N (*also ~ up*) obstrucción *f* con sedimentos.

silver ['sɪlvər] [1] N (a) (*metal*) plata *f*.
(b) (*Fin*) monedas *fpl* de plata.
(c) (*US: cutlery*) cubertería *f*.
[2] ATTR de plata, plateado; **~ beet** (*US*) acelga *f*, acelgas *fpl*; **~ birch** abedul *m* (plateado); '**~ collection**' 'contribuya generosamente'; **~ fir** abeto *m* blanco, pinabete *m*; **~ foil** hoja *f* de plata, (*paper*) papel *m* de plata; **~ fox** zorro *m* plateado; **~ gilt** plata *f* dorada; **~ jubilee** vigésimo quinto aniversario *m*; **~ lining** (*fig*) resquicio *m* de esperanza; **~ medal** medalla *f* de plata; **~ medallist** medallero *m*, -a *f* de plata; **~ paper** (*Brit*) papel *m* de plata, papel *m* de estaño; **~ plate** vajilla *f* de plata; **the ~ screen** la pantalla cinematográfica; **~ wedding** bodas *fpl* de plata.
[3] VT *metal* platear; *mirror* azogar; *hair* blanquear.
[4] VI (*hair*) blanquear.

silverfish ['sɪlvəfɪʃ] N lepisma *f*.

silver-grey ['sɪlvə'greɪ] ADJ gris perla.

silver-haired ['sɪlvə'heəd] ADJ de pelo entrecano.

silver-plate ['sɪlvə'pleɪt] VT platear.

silver-plated ['sɪlvə'pleɪtɪd] ADJ chapado en plata, plateado.

silversmith ['sɪlvəsmɪθ] N platero *m*; **~'s** (**shop**) platería *f*.

silver-tongued ['sɪlvə'tʌŋd] ADJ elocuente, con pico de oro.

silverware ['sɪlvəweər] N plata *f*, vajilla *f* de plata.

silvery ['sɪlvərɪ] ADJ plateado; *voice etc* argentino.

silviculture ['sɪlvɪ,kʌltʃər] N silvicultura *f*.

simian ['sɪmɪən] ADJ símico.

▼ **similar** ['sɪmɪlər] ADJ parecido, semejante; **A and B are ~**, **A is ~ to B** A y B se parecen; **they are not at all ~** no se parecen en absoluto; **they are ~ in size** son de tamaño parecido; **this is ~ to what happened before** esto es parecido a lo que pasó antes.

similarity [,sɪmɪ'lærɪtɪ] N parecido *m*, semejanza *f*; **there is a certain ~** hay cierto parecido.

similarly ['sɪmɪləlɪ] ADV de un modo parecido; **and ~, ...** y asimismo, ...

simile ['sɪmɪlɪ] N símil *m*.

similitude [sɪ'mɪlɪtjuːd] N similitud *f*, semejanza *f*.

simmer ['sɪmər] [1] N: **to be on the ~**, **to keep on the ~** hervir a fuego lento.
[2] VT cocer a fuego lento.
[3] VI (a) (*Culin*) hervir a fuego lento.
(b) (*fig*) estar hirviendo, estar a punto de estallar (*with rage* de ira).
◆**simmer down** VI (*fig*) calmarse poco a poco, tranquilizarse lentamente; **~ down!** ¡cálmate!

Simon ['saɪmən] NM Simón.

simony ['saɪmənɪ] N simonía *f*.

simp* [sɪmp] N (*US*) bobo *m*, -a *f*.

simper ['sɪmpər] [1] N sonrisa *f* afectada, sonrisa *f* boba.
[2] VI sonreírse afectadamente, sonreírse bobamente.
[3] VT: '**Yes**, **she ~ed** 'Sí', dijo sonriendo afectada.

simpering ['sɪmpərɪŋ] ADJ afectado; bobo y remilgado.

simperingly ['sɪmpərɪŋlɪ] ADV afectadamente; bobamente.

simple ['sɪmpl] ADJ (a) (*uncomplicated, easy, plain*) sencillo; **it's as ~ as ABC** es de lo más sencillo; **the ~ life** la vida sencilla; **I'm a ~ soul** soy un hombre sencillo; **it's very ~** es muy sencillo; **it's ~ madness** es una locura ni más ni menos; **he's a ~ craftsman** es un simple artesano.
(b) (*not compound*) *fracture, interest, sentence etc* simple.
(c) (*foolish*) simple; imbécil; (*innocent*) ingenuo, inocente; crédulo; **S~ Simon** Simón el Bobito; **he's a bit ~** es algo bobo, está algo

tocado; **I am not so ~ as to believe that ...** no soy lo bastante ingenuo como para creer que ...

simple-hearted ['sɪmpl'hɑːtɪd] ADJ candoroso, ingenuo.

simple-minded ['sɪmpl'maɪndɪd] ADJ candoroso, ingenuo; (*pej*) simple, mentecato; **I am not so ~** no soy tan ingenuo; **in their ~ way** en su modo ingenuo.

simple-mindedness ['sɪmpl'maɪndɪdnɪs] N candor *m*, ingenuidad *f*; (*pej*) simpleza *f*, mentecatez *f*.

simpleton ['sɪmpltən] N inocentón *m*, -ona *f*, simplón *m*, -ona *f*, bobalicón *m*, -ona *f*.

simplicity [sɪm'plɪsɪtɪ] N sencillez *f*; simpleza *f*, ingenuidad *f*, credulidad *f*; **it's ~ itself** es de lo más sencillo.

simplifiable ['sɪmplɪfaɪəbl] ADJ simplificable.

simplification [,sɪmplɪfɪ'keɪʃən] N simplificación *f*.

simplify ['sɪmplɪfaɪ] VT simplificar.

simplistic [sɪm'plɪstɪk] ADJ simplista.

simply ['sɪmplɪ] ADV sencillamente; simplemente; **a ~ furnished room** un cuarto amueblado sencillamente; **I ~ said that ...** dije sencillamente que ...; **it's ~ impossible!** ¡es sencillamente imposible!; **but you ~ must!** ¡pero no tienes más remedio que hacerlo!; **I was ~ amazed** me quedé completamente asombrado.

simulacrum [,sɪmjʊ'leɪkrəm] N, PL **simulacra** [,sɪmjʊ'leɪkrə] simulacro *m*.

simulate ['sɪmjʊleɪt] VT simular, fingir.

simulated ['sɪmjʊ,leɪtɪd] ADJ simulado; **~ attack** simulacro *m* de ataque; **~ leather** cuero *m* de imitación.

simulation [,sɪmjʊ'leɪʃən] N simulación *f*, fingimiento *m*; (*Comput*) simulación *f*.

simulator ['sɪmjʊleɪtər] N simulador *m*.

simulcast ['sɪməl,kɑːst] [1] N emisión *f* simultánea por radio y televisión.
[2] VT emitir simultáneamente por radio y televisión.

simultaneity [,sɪməltə'nɪətɪ] N simultaneidad *f*.

simultaneous [,sɪməl'teɪnɪəs] ADJ simultáneo; **~ equations** sistema *m* de ecuaciones; **~ interpreting** interpretación *f* simultánea; **~ processing** procesamiento *m* simultáneo; **~ translation** traducción *f* simultánea.

simultaneously [,sɪməl'teɪnɪəslɪ] ADV simultáneamente.

sin [sɪn] [1] N pecado *m*; **like ~** con vehemencia; **for my ~s** por mis pecados; **his besetting ~ is ...** su mayor defecto es ..., tiene la manía de ...; **it would be a ~ to** + *infin* sería un crimen + *infin*, sería un pecado + *infin*; **to fall into ~** caer en el pecado; **to live in ~** estar amancebados.
[2] VI pecar; **he was more ~ned against than ~ning** era más bien el ofendido y no el ofensor.

Sinai ['saɪnɪaɪ] [1] N Sinaí *m*; **Mount ~** el monte Sinaí.
[2] ATTR: **the ~ Desert** el desierto del Sinaí.

Sinbad ['sɪnbæd] NM Simbad; **the Sailor** Simbad el marino.

sin bin* ['sɪnbɪn] N banquillo *m* de los expulsados.

▼ **since** [sɪns] [1] ADV desde entonces, después; **ever ~** desde entonces; **long ~** hace tiempo; **a long time ~** hace mucho (tiempo); **not long ~**, **a short time ~** hace poco.
[2] PREP desde; a partir de, después de; **~ Monday** desde el lunes; **~ arriving** desde que llegué, desde mi llegada; **I've been waiting ~ 10** espero desde las 10; **ever ~ 1900** a partir de 1900, de 1900 acá; **how long is it ~ the accident?** ¿cuánto tiempo ha pasado desde el accidente?; *V* then.
[3] CONJ (a) (*time*) desde que; **~ I arrived** desde que llegué; **it is a week ~ he left** hace una semana que salió, salió hace una semana; **~ I've been here** desde que estoy aquí.
▼(b) (*because*) ya que, puesto que; **~ you can't come** puesto que no puedes venir; **~ he is Spanish** como es español, siendo él español.

sincere [sɪn'sɪər] ADJ sincero.

sincerely [sɪn'sɪəlɪ] ADV sinceramente; **Yours ~** le saluda atentamente, le saluda cordialmente.

sincerity [sɪn'serɪtɪ] N sinceridad *f*; **in all ~** con toda sinceridad, con toda franqueza.

sine [saɪn] N (*Math*) seno *m*.

sinecure ['saɪnɪkjʊər] N sinecura *f*; canonjía *f*, prebenda *f*.

sine qua non ['saɪnɪkweɪ'nɒn] N sine qua non *m*.

sinew ['sɪnjuː] N tendón *m*; **~s** (*fig*) nervio *m*, fibra *f*; recursos *mpl*; **the ~s of war** el dinero.

sinewy ['sɪnjuːɪ] ADJ nervudo, nervioso, vigoroso.

sinfonietta [,sɪnfən'jetə] N sinfonieta *f*.

sinful ['sɪnfʊl] ADJ *person* pecador; *act*, *thought* pecaminoso; *town etc* inmoral, depravado.

sinfully ['sɪnfʊlɪ] ADV de modo pecaminoso.

sinfulness ['sɪnfʊlnɪs] N maldad *f*; pecaminosidad *f*; vicio *m*, depravación *f*.

sing [sɪŋ] (*irr. PRET* **sang**, *PTP* **sung**) [1] VT cantar; **~ us a song!** ¡cántanos algo!; **to ~ a child to sleep** arrullar a un niño, adormecer a un niño cantando.

2 VI **(a)** cantar; (*bird*) trinar, gorjear; (*ears*) zumbar; (*wind*) susurrar; (*kettle*) silbar (al hervir); **to ~ flat, to ~ out of tune** desafinar, cantar mal; **to ~ small** achantarse, ser más humilde.
(b) (*US⁕*) cantar*.
◆**sing along** VI: **to sing along with sth/sb** cantar a coro con algo/uno; **to sing along to a song** acompañar una canción.
◆**sing out** VI cantar más fuerte; (*fig*) vocear, gritar; **if you want anything ~ out*** si necesitas algo me llamas; **to ~ out for sth** reclamar algo a gritos.
◆**sing up** VI cantar más fuerte; **~ up!** ¡más fuerte!

┌─────────── SINCE ────────────────── see also main entry ──┐

Time
• When *since* is followed by a noun or noun phrase, you can usually translate it as *desde*:
   Spain has changed a lot since Franco's death
   España ha cambiado mucho desde la muerte de Franco
• When *since* is followed by a verb phrase, use *desde que* instead:
   Since I saw you a fortnight ago a lot of things have happened
   Desde que te vi hace quince días han pasado muchas cosas
! Use the *present tense* in Spanish to describe a situation that started in the past and has continued up to now (present perfect or present perfect continuous in English):
   I have been here since this morning
   Estoy aquí or *Llevo aquí desde esta mañana*
   They've been waiting since nine o'clock
   Están esperando or *Llevan esperando desde las nueve*
   He has been taking more exercise since he talked to his doctor
   Hace más ejercicio desde que habló con el médico
• Translate *since then* or *ever since* using *desde entonces*:
   She came home at 5 and has been studying ever since
   Llegó a casa a las cinco y está estudiando desde entonces
• Translate *long since* using *hace tiempo* (+ *que* + PAST TENSE) or *hacía tiempo* (+ *que* + PAST/PAST PERFECT) as relevant:
   His wife has long since died
   Hace tiempo que murió su mujer ◊ *Su mujer murió hace tiempo*

Meaning "as", "because"
• In formal contexts you can usually translate *since* using *ya que* or *puesto que*. In more everyday Spanish, use *como*, which must go at the beginning of the sentence:
   They could not afford the house since they were not earning enough
   No podían pagar la casa puesto que or *ya que no ganaban bastante*
   Since I hadn't heard from you, I decided to give you a call
   Como no sabía nada de ti, decidí llamarte
For further uses and examples, see main entry.

└──┘

singalong, sing-along ['sɪŋəlɒŋ] N canción *f* a coro; **how about a sing-along around the piano?** ¿por qué no cantamos una canción a coro junto al piano?
Singapore [,sɪŋə'pɔ:ʳ] N Singapur *m*.
Singaporean [,sɪŋgə'pɔ:rɪən] **1** ADJ de Singapur.
   2 N nativo *m*, -a *f* (*or* habitante *mf*) de Singapur.
singe [sɪndʒ] VT chamuscar; *hair* quemar las puntas de.
singer ['sɪŋəʳ] N cantor *m*, -ora *f*; (*professional*) cantante *mf*; (*in cabaret etc*) vocalista *mf*.
singer-songwriter [,sɪŋəʳ'sɒŋraɪtəʳ] N cantautor *m*, -ora *f*.
Singhalese [,sɪŋgə'li:z] **1** ADJ cingalés.
   2 N **(a)** cingalés *m*, -esa *f*. **(b)** (*Ling*) cingalés *m*.
singing ['sɪŋɪŋ] **1** N canto *m*; cantos *mpl*, canciones *fpl*; (*in the ears*) zumbido *m*.
   2 ATTR: **~ lesson** lección *f* de canto; **~ teacher** profesor *m*, -ora *f* de canto; **~ telegram** telegrama *m* cantado; **to have a good ~ voice** tener una buena voz para cantar.
single ['sɪŋgl] **1** ADJ **(a)** (*only*) único, solo; (*not double*) simple, sencillo; *bed, room* individual, sencillo (*LAm*); *ticket, spacing* sencillo; **~ combat** combate *m* singular; **~ density disk** disco *m* de densidad sencilla; **S~ European Act** Acta *f* Única Europea; **in ~ file** en fila de a uno; **~ market** mercado *m* único; **~ track** vía *f* única; **~ user** (ADJ) monousuario; **the greatest ~ problem** el mayor problema; **every ~ day** todos los días sin excepción; **every ~ book I looked at** todos los libros que miré sin excepción; **not a ~ one spoke up** no habló ni uno solo; **there was a ~ rose in the garden** en el jardín había una rosa única.
(b) (*unmarried*) soltero, no casado; **~ parent** madre *f* sin pareja, madre *f* sola, padre *m* sin pareja, padre *m* solo; **~ parent family** familia *f* monoparental, hogar *m* sin pareja; **~ parenthood** monoparentalidad *f*; **~ people** personas *fpl* no casadas; **the ~ state** el estado célibe; **she's a ~ woman** es soltera; **she remained ~** siguió sin casarse.
   2 N **(a)** (*Brit Rail etc*) billete *m* sencillo.

(b) (*Mus*) single *m*, sencillo *m*.
(c) **~s** solteros *mpl*; **~s bar** bar *m* para solteros.
(d) **~s** (*Tennis*) juego *m* de individuales; **ladies' ~s** individual *m* femenino; **men's ~s** individual *m* masculino.
(e) (*record*) single *m*.
(f) (*Fin*) moneda *f* de una libra, billete *m* de un dólar, *etc*; **he paid me 200 dollars in ~s** me pagó 200 dólares en billetes de a uno.
(g) (*measure of drink*) ración *f* normal.
◆**single out** VT (*choose*) escoger; (*distinguish*) distinguir, singularizar; **he was ~d out to lead the team** se le escogió para ser capitán del equipo; **to ~ (out) plants** entresacar plantas.
single-barrelled ['sɪŋgl'bærəld] ADJ *gun* de cañón único.
single-breasted ['sɪŋgl'brestɪd] ADJ *jacket* sin cruzar, recto.
single-cell(ed) ['sɪŋgl'sel(d)] ADJ unicelular.
single-chamber ['sɪŋgl'tʃeɪmbəʳ] ADJ unicameral.
single-engined ['sɪŋgl'endʒɪnd] ADJ monomotor.
single-entry ['sɪŋgl'entrɪ] **1** N partida *f* simple.
   2 ATTR: **~ book-keeping** contabilidad *f* por partida simple.
single-family ['sɪŋgl,fæmlɪ] ATTR unifamiliar.
single-figure ['sɪŋgl,fɪgəʳ] ATTR: **~ inflation** inflación *f* de un solo dígito.
single-handed ['sɪŋgl'hændɪd] ADJ, ADV sin ayuda (de nadie).
single-hearted ['sɪŋgl'hɑːtɪd] ADJ sincero, leal; resuelto.
single-masted ['sɪŋgl'mɑːstɪd] ADJ de palo único.
single-minded ['sɪŋgl'maɪndɪd] ADJ resuelto, firme.
single-mindedness [,sɪŋgl'maɪndɪdnɪs] N resolución *f*, firmeza *f*.
singleness ['sɪŋglnɪs] N: **~ of purpose** resolución *f*, firmeza *f*.
single-party ['sɪŋgl'pɑːtɪ] ADJ *state etc* de partido único.
single-seater ['sɪŋgl'siːtəʳ] N monoplaza *m*.
single-sex ['sɪŋglseks] ADJ: **~ school** escuela *f* para sólo niños (*or* sólo niñas).
single-sided ['sɪŋgl,saɪdɪd] ADJ: **~ disk** disco *m* de una cara.
single-space ['sɪŋgl'speɪs] VT *text* mecanografiar a espacio sencillo.
single spacing ['sɪŋgl'speɪsɪŋ] N interlineado *m* simple; **in ~** a espacio sencillo.
singlet ['sɪŋglɪt] N (*Brit*) camiseta *f*.
singleton ['sɪŋgltən] N semifallo *m* (*in a*).
single-track ['sɪŋgl'træk] ADJ de vía única.
singly ['sɪŋglɪ] ADV uno a uno, individualmente, separadamente.
singsong ['sɪŋ,sɒŋ] **1** ADJ *tone* monótono, cantarín.
   2 N (*tone*) salmodia *f*, sonsonete *m*; (*songs*) concierto *m* espontáneo; **to get together for a ~** reunirse para cantar (canciones populares, folklóricas *etc*).
singular ['sɪŋgjʊləʳ] **1** ADJ **(a)** (*Gram*) singular; **a ~ noun** un sustantivo en singular.
(b) (*odd*) raro, extraño, singular; **a most ~ occurrence** un acontecimiento muy extraño; **how very ~!** ¡qué raro!
   2 N singular *f*; **in the ~** en singular.
singularity [,sɪŋgjʊ'lærɪtɪ] N singularidad *f*, particularidad *f*.
singularize ['sɪŋgjʊlə,raɪz] VT singularizar.
singularly ['sɪŋgjʊləlɪ] ADV singularmente; **a ~ inappropriate remark** una observación de lo más inoportuno.
Sinhalese [,sɪnə'liːz] = **Singhalese**.
sinister ['sɪnɪstəʳ] ADJ siniestro.
sinisterly ['sɪnɪstəlɪ] ADV siniestramente.
sink¹ [sɪŋk] (*irr*: PRET **sank**, PTP **sunk**) **1** VT **(a)** *ship* hundir, echar a pique; sumergir; (*fig*) *theory* destruir, acabar con; *person* acabar con.
(b) *mine* abrir, excavar; *hole* hacer, excavar; *well* perforar; (*) *drink* tragarse, embaular*; *ball, putt* embocar; **to ~ a post 2 metres in the ground** fijar un poste 2 metros bajo tierra; **to ~ one's teeth into sth** hincar los dientes en algo; **he can ~ a glass of beer in 12 seconds** se traga una caña de cerveza en 12 segundos.
(c) *differences* suprimir, olvidar; **to ~ one's identity in that of a group** olvidar su individualidad en la solidaridad de un grupo.
(d) **to ~ money in an enterprise** invertir dinero en una empresa.
(e) (*phrases with* **sunk**) **to be sunk in thought** estar absorto en la meditación, estar ensimismado; **to be sunk in depression** estar sumido en el abatimiento; **to be sunk in debt** estar agobiado por las deudas; **now we're sunk!** ¡estamos perdidos!
   2 VI **(a)** (*ship etc*) hundirse; irse a pique, naufragar; sumergirse; **to ~ by the bow** hundirse de proa; **to ~ to the bottom** ir al fondo; **it ~s instead of floating** se hunde en lugar de flotar; **he was left to ~ or swim** (*fig*) le abandonaron a su suerte.
(b) (*subside*) hundirse; (*building, land etc*) hundirse; (*fire*) estarse apagando, morir; (*person*) debilitarse, morirse; (*sun*) ponerse; **he sank in the mud up to his knees** se hundió en el lodo hasta las rodillas; **to ~ into a chair** dejarse caer en una silla, arrellanarse en una silla; **to ~ into insignificance** perder su importancia; **to ~ deeper into degradation** hundirse cada vez más en la degradación, envilecerse más y más; **to ~ into poverty** caer en la miseria; **to ~ to one's knees** caer de rodillas; **his voice sank to a whisper** pasó a hablar en

tono muy bajo; **my spirits sank, my heart sank** se me cayeron las alas del corazón; **to ~ out of sight** desaparecer.

(c) (*in quantity*) disminuir; (*in value*) perder su valor; (*decline*) declinar, menguar; **he has sunk in my estimation** ha bajado en mi estima; **the shares have sunk to 3 dollars** las acciones han bajado a 3 dólares.

◆**sink away** VI (*liquid*) irse, desaparecer.

◆**sink back** VI arrellanarse, arrepanchigarse; **he sank back into his chair** se arrellanó en la silla.

◆**sink down** VI: **to ~ down into a chair** dejarse caer en una silla, arrellanarse en una silla.

◆**sink in** VI penetrar, calar; **to let the paint ~ in** dejar que penetre la pintura; **the water ~s in in time** con el tiempo va penetrando el agua; **his words seem to have sunk in** sus palabras parecen haber surtido efecto, parece que sus palabras han hecho mella.

sink² [sɪŋk] N fregadero *m*, pila *f*; (*Tech*) sumidero *m*; (*fig*) sentina *f*; **~ of iniquity** sentina *f*, lugar *m* de todos los vicios; **~ tidy** cubeta *f* para basura.

sinker ['sɪŋkəʳ] N (*Fishing*) plomo *m*.

sinking ['sɪŋkɪŋ] [1] ADJ: **~ fund** fondo *m* de amortización; **that ~ feeling** esa sensación de que todo se va a pique; **with ~ heart** con alma aprensiva.
[2] N hundimiento *m*.

sink-unit ['sɪŋk'juːnɪt] N lavadero *m*, fregadero *m* (de cocina).

sinless ['sɪnlɪs] ADJ libre de pecado, puro, inmaculado.

sinner ['sɪnəʳ] N pecador *m*, -ora *f*.

Sinn Fein [ˌʃɪn'feːn] N Sinn Fein *m*.

Sino... ['saɪnəʊ] PREF sino..., chino...

Sinologist [ˌsaɪ'nɒlədʒɪst] N sinólogo *m*, -a *f*.

Sinology [ˌsaɪ'nɒlədʒɪ] N sinología *f*.

sinuosity [ˌsɪnjʊ'ɒsɪtɪ] N sinuosidad *f*.

sinuous ['sɪnjʊəs] ADJ sinuoso.

sinus ['saɪnəs] N (*Anat*) seno *m*.

sinusitis [ˌsaɪnə'saɪtɪs] N sinusitis *f*.

sip [sɪp] [1] N sorbo *m*.
[2] VT sorber, beber a sorbitos; probar.
[3] VI (*also* **to ~ at**) sorber, beber a sorbitos.

siphon ['saɪfən] [1] N sifón *m*.
[2] VT sacar con sifón; *funds etc* (*also* **to ~ off**) desviar, malversar.

◆**siphon off** VT (*lit*) sacar con sifón; (*fig*) quitar poco a poco, reducir gradualmente; separar; desviar; *funds etc* (*illegally*) malversar.

◆**siphon out** VT sacar con sifón.

SIPS [sɪps] N ABBR *of* **side impact protection system** sistema *m* de protección contra impactos laterales.

sir [sɜːʳ] N (*in direct address*) señor *m*; (*as title*) sir *m*; **yes, ~** (*Mil*) sí, mi capitán (*etc*); **S~** (*to editor of paper*) señor director; **S~s** (*US*) muy señores nuestros; **Dear S~** muy señor mío; **my dear ~!, my good ~!** ¡pero amigo ...!

sire ['saɪəʳ] [1] N (*Zool*) padre *m*; (*stallion*) semental *m*, caballo *m* padre; **S~** (*to monarch*: ††) Señor *m*.
[2] VT ser el padre de; engendrar; **he ~d 49 children** tuvo 49 hijos; **the horse A, ~d by B** el caballo A, cuyo padre fue B.

siree* [sɪ'riː] N (*US: emphatic*) **yes/no ~!** ¡sí/no señor!

siren ['saɪərən] N (*all senses*) sirena *f*; **~ song** canto *m* de sirena.

Sirius ['sɪrɪəs] NM Sirio.

sirloin ['sɜːlɔɪn] N solomillo *m*, diezmillo *m* (*Mex*).

sirocco [sɪ'rɒkəʊ] N siroco *m*.

sis* [sɪs] N = **sister**.

sisal ['saɪsəl] N henequén *m*, fique *m*, pita *f*.

sissy‡ [sɪsɪ] N (a) (*effeminate*) marica‡ *m*, mariquita‡ *m*; **the last one's a ~!** ¡maricón el último‡! (b) (*coward*) gallina* *f*.

sister ['sɪstəʳ] [1] N (a) hermana *f*. (b) (*Eccl*) hermana *f*; **S~ Manuela** Sor Manuela. (c) (*Brit Med*) enfermera *f*, hermana *f* enfermera, (*of higher rank*) enfermera *f* jefa.
[2] ADJ: **~ city** (*US*) ciudad *f* gemela; **~ college** colegio *m* hermano; **~ company** empresa *f* hermana; **~ organizations** organizaciones *fpl* hermanas.

sisterhood ['sɪstəhʊd] N hermandad *f*.

sister-in-law ['sɪstərɪnlɔː] N, PL **sisters-in-law** cuñada *f*, hermana *f* política.

sisterly ['sɪstəlɪ] ADJ de hermana, como hermana.

sister-ship ['sɪstəʃɪp] N buque *m* gemelo; **X is the ~ of Z** X es buque gemelo de Z.

Sistine ['sɪstiːn] ADJ: **the ~ Chapel** la Capilla Sixtina.

Sisyphus ['sɪsɪfəs] NM Sísifo.

sit [sɪt] (*irr*: PRET AND PTP **sat**) [1] VT (a) (*also* **to ~ down**) sentar; **to ~ sb (down) in a chair** sentar a uno en una silla; **to ~ a child (down) on one's knees** sentar a un niño sobre las rodillas.
(b) **to ~ a horse well** montar bien (a caballo).
(c) (*esp Brit*) **to ~ an examination** presentarse a un examen, pasar un examen (*LAm*); **to ~ an examination in French** examinarse de francés.

[2] VI (a) (*gen: act*) sentarse; (*state*) estar sentado; **~!** (*to dog*) ¡quieto!; **~ here** siéntate aquí; **I was ~ting there** estaba sentado allí; **~ by me** siéntate a mi lado, siéntate conmigo; **to ~ at home all day** pasar todo el día en casa (sin hacer nada); **to ~ at table** sentarse a la mesa; **he ~s on the board** (*Comm etc*) es miembro de la junta directiva, forma parte de la junta directiva; **he sat over his books all night** pasó toda la noche con sus libros; **don't just ~ there, do something!** ¡no te quedes ahí sin hacer nada!
(b) (*assembly*) reunirse; celebrar junta, celebrar sesión; **the House sat all night** la sesión de la Cámara duró toda la noche; **the House sat for 22 hours** la Cámara tuvo una sesión de 22 horas.
(c) (*bird, insect*) posarse; (*hen*) empollar, incubar; **the hen is ~ting on 12 eggs** la gallina empolla 12 huevos.
(d) (*fig: dress*) caer, sentar (*on sb* a uno); **that pie ~s heavy on the stomach** la empanada esa no me sienta; **how ~s the wind?** ¿de dónde sopla el viento?; **it sat heavy on his conscience** le remordió la conciencia.
(e) (*model*) **to ~ for a painter** posar para un pintor, servir de modelo a un pintor; **she sat for Goya** se hizo retratar por Goya; **to ~ for one's portrait** hacerse retratar, hacerse un retrato.
(f) (*esp Brit: candidate*) presentarse (*for an exam* a un examen).
(g) (*Brit Pol*) **to ~ for Bury** representar a Bury, ser diputado por Bury; **to ~ in Parliament** ser diputado (*Sp*: a Cortes), ser miembro del Parlamento.

◆**sit about, sit around** VI estar sin hacer nada.

◆**sit back** VI sentarse cómodamente; **to ~ back (and do nothing)** cruzarse de brazos.

◆**sit down** [1] VT = **sit 1 (a)**.
[2] VI sentarse; **do ~ down!** ¡siéntese, por favor!; **to ~ down to table** sentarse a la mesa; **to ~ down to a big supper** sentarse a comer una cena fuerte; **to ~ down under an insult** tragar un insulto, aguantar un insulto; **we sat down 13 to supper** éramos 13 a la mesa para cenar.
[3] VR: **to ~ o.s. down** sentarse.

◆**sit in** VI (*students, workers*) hacer una sentada, ocupar las aulas (*or* la fábrica *etc*); **to ~ in for a friend** sustituir a un amigo; **to ~ in on talks** asistir a una conferencia (sin ser delegado oficial), participar como observador en unas discusiones.

◆**sit on** VT (a) (*) *secret* guardar secreto, no revelar; no publicar; guardar para sí; *plan etc* dar carpetazo a.
(b) (*) *person* (*silence*) hacer callar; (*suppress*) reprimir a; (*be hard on*) ser severo con; **he won't be sat on** no quiere callar, no da su brazo a torcer.
[2] VI permanecer sentado, seguir en su asiento.

◆**sit out** [1] VT (a) **to ~ a lecture out** aguantar hasta el fin de una conferencia; **to ~ sb out** resistir más tiempo que uno, demostrar tener más aguante que uno; **to ~ out a strike** aguantar una huelga (sin ofrecer concesiones).
(b) **to ~ out a dance** no bailar; **let's ~ this one out** no bailemos esta vez.
[2] VI sentarse fuera; estar sentado al aire libre.

◆**sit through** VT *concert, lecture* permanecer hasta el fin de, aguantar toda la extensión de.

◆**sit up** [1] VT *doll, patient* sentar, poner derecho; **to ~ an invalid up** incorporar a un enfermo (en la cama).
[2] VI (a) (*after lying*) incorporarse; **to ~ up in bed** incorporarse en la cama; **to ~ up with a start** incorporarse sobresaltado; **to ~ up at the table** sentarse a la mesa.
(b) (*straighten o.s.*) ponerse derecho, erguirse en la silla.
(c) (*stay awake*) velar, trasnochar, no acostarse; **to ~ up for sb** esperar a que vuelva uno, estar sin acostarse hasta que vuelva uno; **to ~ up with a child** velar a un niño.
(d) **to ~ up (and take notice)** empezar a prestar atención; darse cuenta; **to make sb ~ up** dar en qué pensar a uno; impresionar fuertemente a uno; sorprender a uno.

sitar [sɪ'tɑːʳ] N sitar *m*.

sitcom* ['sɪtkɒm] N (*TV*) ABBR *of* **situation comedy**.

sit-down ['sɪtdaʊn] [1] N: **I must have a ~*** tengo que descansar (sentado).
[2] ATTR: **we had a ~ lunch** hemos comido a la mesa; **~ strike** sentada *f*, huelga *f* de brazos caídos.

site [saɪt] [1] N sitio *m*, local *m*; (*for building*) solar *m*; (*archaeological, Geol*) yacimiento *m*; **the ~ of the battle** el lugar de la batalla; **a late Roman ~** un emplazamiento romano tardío; **the only ~ for the plant in Spain** la única localidad para la planta en España.
[2] VT situar; localizar; **a badly ~d building** un edificio mal situado.

sit-in ['sɪtɪn] N sentada *f*, ocupación *f*, encierro *m*.

siting ['saɪtɪŋ] N situación *f*, emplazamiento *m*; **the ~ of new industries** la localización de las nuevas industrias.

Sits Vac. [ˌsɪts'væk] N ABBR *of* **Situations Vacant** Ofrecen trabajo.

sitter ['sɪtəʳ] N (a) (*Art*) modelo *mf* de pintor. (b) (*baby~*) canguro* *mf*. (c) (*) cosa *f* fácil; **it was a ~*** (*Sport*) fue un gol (*etc*) que se canta*;

you missed a ~* erraste un tiro de lo más fácil.
sitting ['sɪtɪŋ] **1** ADJ sentado; **a ~ bird** una ave que está posada, una ave que está inmóvil; **a ~ hen** una gallina clueca; **~ duck** *(fig)* blanco *m* fácil, presa *f* fácil; **~ member** miembro *mf* actual, miembro *mf* en funciones; **~ tenant** inquilino *m*, -a *f* en posesión.
   2 N *(Pol etc)* sesión *f*; *(of eggs)* nidada *f*; **~ and standing room** sitio *m* para sentarse y para estar de pie; **at one ~** en una sesión; de una vez, de un tirón; **second ~ for lunch** segundo turno *m* de comedor.
sitting-room ['sɪtɪŋrʊm] N cuarto *m* de estar, living *m*.
situ ['sɪtjuː] *(frm)* V **in ~**.
situate ['sɪtjʊeɪt] VT situar; **it is ~d in the High Street** está situado en la Calle Mayor; **how are you ~d?** ¿cuál es su situación actual?; **a pleasantly ~d house** una casa bien situada.
situation [ˌsɪtjʊ'eɪʃən] **1** N **(a)** *(location)* situación *f*; emplazamiento *m*.
   (b) *(circumstances)* situación *f*; *(Econ, Pol etc)* coyuntura *f*: **to save the ~** salvar la situación.
   (c) *(job)* puesto *m*, empleo *m*, colocación *f*; **'S~s Vacant'** 'Ofrecen trabajo'; **'S~s Wanted'** 'Buscan trabajo'.
   2 ATTR: **~ comedy** comedia *f* de situación.
situational [ˌsɪtjʊ'eɪʃənl] ADJ situacional.
Situationism [sɪtjʊ'eɪʃənɪzəm] N *(Philos)* situacionismo *m*.
Situationist [sɪtjʊ'eɪʃənɪst] *(Philos)* **1** ADJ situacionista.
   2 N situacionista *mf*.
sit-up ['sɪtʌp] N ejercicio *m* de abdominales boca arriba.
six [sɪks] **1** ADJ seis; **~ of the best** *(Brit)* seis azotes *mpl* *(castigo escolar)*; **it's ~ of one and half-a-dozen of the other** lo mismo da; olivo y aceituno es todo uno.
   2 N seis *m*; **to be at ~es and sevens** *(things)* estar en confusión, estar en desorden, *(persons)* estar reñidos; **to knock sb for ~*** dejar pasmado a uno.
six-eight ['sɪks'eɪt] ATTR: **in ~ time** en un compás de seis por ocho.
sixfold ['sɪksfəʊld] **1** ADJ séxtuplo.
   2 ADV seis veces.
six-footer ['sɪks'fʊtəʳ] N hombre *m* *(or mujer f)* que mide 6 pies.
six-pack ['sɪkspæk] N paquete *m* de seis.
sixpence ['sɪkspəns] N *(Brit †)* 6 peniques *mpl*.
sixpenny ['sɪkspənɪ] ADJ *(Brit †)* de 6 peniques; *(pej)* insignificante, inútil.
six-shooter ['sɪks'ʃuːtəʳ] N revólver *m* de 6 tiros.
sixteen ['sɪks'tiːn] ADJ dieciséis.
sixteenth ['sɪks'tiːnθ] ADJ decimosexto; **~ note** *(US)* semicorchea *f*.
sixth [sɪksθ] **1** ADJ sexto; **~ form** clase *f* de alumnos del sexto año *(de 16 a 18 años de edad)*; **~ former** alumno *m*, -a *f* de 16 a 18 años.
   2 N sexto *m*, sexta parte *f*.
sixth-form [sɪksθfɔːm] ATTR: **~ college** instituto *m* para alumnos de 16 a 18 años; *ver también* EDUCATION .
sixtieth ['sɪkstɪɪθ] ADJ sexagésimo; sesenta; **the ~ anniversary** el sesenta aniversario.
sixty ['sɪkstɪ] ADJ sesenta; **the sixties** *(eg 1960s)* los años sesenta; **to be in one's sixties** tener más de sesenta años, ser sesentón.
sixtyish ['sɪkstɪɪʃ] ADJ de unos sesenta años.
sizable ['saɪzəbl] = **sizeable**.
sizably ['saɪzəblɪ] = **sizeably**.
size¹ [saɪz] **1** N tamaño *m*; dimensiones *fpl*; extensión *f*; magnitud *f*; *(of person)* talla *f*, estatura *f*; *(measurement: of gloves, shoes etc)* número *m*; *(of dress, shirt etc)* talla *f*; **a hall of immense ~** una sala de vastas dimensiones; **the ~ of the problem daunted him** la magnitud del problema le asombró; **the great ~ of the operation** la gran envergadura de la operación; **it's the ~ of a brick** del tamaño de un ladrillo; **what ~ is it?** ¿de qué tamaño es?, ¿cómo es de grande?; **it's quite a ~** es bastante grande; **it's 2 ~s too big** lo quisiera 2 números más pequeño; **he's about your ~** tiene más o menos la talla de Vd; **that's about the ~ of it** eso es lo que puedo decirle acerca del asunto, es más o menos eso, *(as answer)* así es; **to be of a ~** ser del mismo tamaño, tener el mismo tamaño; **they're all of a ~** tienen todos el mismo tamaño; **to cut sth to ~** cortar algo del tamaño preciso que se necesita; **to cut sb down to ~** bajarle los humos a uno, ponerle a uno en su sitio; **it is drawn to natural ~** está dibujado a tamaño natural; **what ~ shoe do you take?** ¿qué número calza Vd?; **I take ~ 9** uso el número 9; **what ~ shirt do you take?** ¿qué talla de camisa es la de Vd?; **try this (on) for ~** prueba esto a ver si te conviene, a ver si esta medida es la tuya.
   2 VT clasificar según el tamaño.
♦ **size up** VT: **to ~ sb up** medir a uno con la vista; **to ~ up a problem** formarse una idea de un problema, tomar la medida de un problema; **I've got him all ~d up** le tengo calado; **I can't quite ~ him up** no llego a entenderle bien.
size² [saɪz] **1** N cola *f*, apresto *m*.
   2 VT encolar, aprestar.
sizeable ['saɪzəbl] ADJ bastante grande, considerable, importante; **a ~ sum** una cantidad importante; **it's quite a ~ house** es una casa

bastante grande.
sizeably ['saɪzəblɪ] ADV considerablemente.
-sized [saɪzd] ADJ *ending in compounds* de tamaño ...; **medium~** de tamaño mediano.
sizzle ['sɪzl] VI chisporrotear, churruscar, crepitar; *(in frying)* crepitar (al freírse).
sizzling ['sɪzlɪŋ] **1** ADJ *heat* sofocante; *shot etc* fulminante.
   2 N chisporroteo *m*, crepitación *f*.
S.J. ABBR *of* **Society of Jesus** C. de J.
SK *(Canada)* ABBR *of* **Saskatchewan**.
skate¹ [skeɪt] N *(Brit: fish)* raya *f*.
skate² [skeɪt] **1** N patín *m*; **get your ~s on!*** ¡date prisa!, ¡apúrate!
   2 VI patinar; **it went skating across the floor** se deslizó velozmente sobre el suelo; **I ~d into a tree** (en un patinazo) di contra un árbol.
♦ **skate around, skate over, skate round** VT *problem* evitar, esquivar.
skateboard ['skeɪtbɔːd] N monopatín *m*.
skateboarder ['skeɪtbɔːdəʳ] N monopatinador *m*, -ora *f*.
skateboarding ['skeɪtbɔːdɪŋ] N monopatinaje *m*.
skater ['skeɪtəʳ] N patinador *m*, -ora *f*.
skating ['skeɪtɪŋ] N patinaje *m*.
skating-rink ['skeɪtɪŋrɪŋk] N pista *f* de patinaje.
skean dhu ['skiːən'duː] N *(Scot)* puñal *m* *(que se lleva en el calcetín del traje típico escocés)*.
skedaddle* [skɪ'dædl] VI escabullirse, salir pitando*, poner pies en polvorosa*; **they ~d in all directions** huyeron por todos lados.
skein [skeɪn] N madeja *f*; **a tangled ~** *(fig)* un asunto enmarañado.
skeletal ['skelɪtl] ADJ esquelético.
skeleton ['skelɪtn] **1** N *(Anat)* esqueleto *m*; *(fig)* esquema *m*, plan *m*; *(Tech)* armazón *f*, armadura *f*; **the ~ at the feast** el aguafiestas; **~ in the cupboard, ~ in the closet** *(US)* secreto *m* vergonzoso de la familia, cadáver *m* en el armario.
   2 ADJ *staff etc* reducido; *outline* esquemático; **~ key** llave *f* maestra, ganzúa *f*.
skeptic ['skeptɪk] *etc (US)* = **sceptic** *etc*.
sketch [sketʃ] **1** N **(a)** *(rough draft)* esbozo *m*, boceto *m*, bosquejo *m*, croquis *m* *(for de)*; *(drawing)* dibujo *m*, diseño *m*; **~ for a costume** diseño *m* de un traje.
   (b) *(Theat)* sketch *m*.
   2 ATTR: **~ map** mapa *m* esbozado.
   3 VT *(also* **to ~ out)** *(outline)* esbozar, trazar a grandes líneas; *(draw)* bosquejar, dibujar; hacer un dibujo de.
   4 VI dibujar, hacer dibujos.
♦ **sketch in** VT: **he ~ed in the details for me** me explicó los detalles.
sketchbook ['sketʃbʊk] N libro *m* de dibujos.
sketchily ['sketʃɪlɪ] ADV incompletamente, superficialmente.
sketching ['sketʃɪŋ] N dibujo *m*, arte *m* de dibujar.
sketch(ing)-pad ['sketʃ(ɪŋ)pæd] N bloc *m* de dibujo.
sketchy ['sketʃɪ] ADJ incompleto, superficial, somero; difuminado; impreciso.
skew [skjuː] **1** N: **to be on the ~** estar desviado, estar sesgado; estar puesto mal.
   2 ADJ sesgado, oblicuo, torcido.
   3 VT sesgar, desviar; poner mal.
   4 VI *(also* **to ~ round)** desviarse, ponerse al sesgo, torcerse.
skewbald ['skjuːbɔːld] **1** ADJ pintado, con pintas.
   2 N pinto *m*.
skewed ['skjuːd] ADJ sesgado, torcido *(also fig)*.
skewer ['skjuəʳ] **1** N broqueta *f*, espetón *m*.
   2 VT espetar; pasar una broqueta por.
skew-whiff [ˌskjuː'wɪf] ADJ *(Brit)* sesgado, oblicuo, torcido; **to be on ~** estar puesto mal.
ski [skiː] **1** N esquí *m*.
   2 ATTR: **~ instructor** instructor *m*, -ora *f* de esquí; **~ rack** baca *f* portaesquís; **~ resort** estación *f* de esquí; **~ stick** bastón *m* de esquiar.
   3 VI esquiar.
ski-boot ['skiːbuːt] N bota *f* de esquí.
skid [skɪd] **1** N **(a)** *(Aut etc)* patinazo *m*, derrape *m*, deslizamiento *m*.
   (b) *(Aer)* patín *m*; **to grease the ~s*** *(US)* engrasar el mecanismo; **to put the ~s under sb*** deshacerse de uno con maña, lograr con maña que uno abandone un puesto *(etc)*.
   2 ATTR: **~ row*** *(US)* barrio *m* de mala vida; calles *fpl* donde se refugian los borrachos, drogadictos *etc*.
   3 VI *(Aut etc)* patinar, derrapar; *(of person)* resbalar; **it went ~ding across the floor** se deslizó velozmente sobre el suelo; **I ~ded into a tree** de un patinazo di contra un árbol; **the car ~ded to a halt** el coche se resbaló y paró.
skiddoo* [skɪ'duː] VI *(US)* largarse*.
skidlid* ['skɪdlɪd] N casco *m* protector (de motorista).
skidmark ['skɪdmɑːk] N huella *f* del patinazo.
skidproof ['skɪdpruːf] ADV a prueba de patinazos.
skier ['skɪːəʳ] N esquiador *m*, -ora *f*.
skiff [skɪf] N esquife *m*.

skiffle ['skɪfl] N estilo de música popular de los años cincuenta de guitarra y percusión.

skiing ['ski:ɪŋ] **1** N esquí *m*; **to go ~** ir a esquiar.

2 ATTR: **~ holiday** vacaciones *fpl* de esquí; **~ resort** estación *f* de esquí.

ski-jump ['ski:dʒʌmp] N pista *f* para saltos de esquí.

ski-jumper ['ski:ˌdʒʌmpəʳ] N saltador *m*, -ora *f* de esquí.

ski-jumping ['ski:ˌdʒʌmpɪŋ] N salto *m* de esquí.

skilful, (*US*) **skillful** ['skɪlfʊl] ADJ hábil, diestro, experto (*at, in* en).

skilfully, (*US*) **skillfully** ['skɪləlɪ] ADV hábilmente, diestramente.

skilfulness, (*US*) **skillfulness** ['skɪlfʊlnɪs] N habilidad *f*, destreza *f*.

ski-lift ['ski:lɪft] N remonte *m*, telesquí *m*, telesilla *m*.

skill [skɪl] N (a) (*ability*) habilidad *f*, destreza *f*; pericia *f*; **linguistic ~s** destrezas *fpl* lingüísticas; **his ~ at billiards** su habilidad en el billar; **he shows no small ~** muestra tener no poca habilidad; **we could make good use of his ~** podríamos utilizar su pericia.

(b) (*in craft etc*) arte *m*, técnica *f*; oficio *m*; **it's a ~ that has to be acquired** es una técnica que se aprende.

skilled [skɪld] ADJ (*skilful*) hábil, diestro; (*qualified*) cualificado, especializado; *work* especializado, que requiere técnicas especiales; **~ labor** (*US*), **~ labour** mano *f* de obra cualificada (*or* especializada); **to be ~ in a craft** ser perito en una artesanía; **a man ~ in diplomacy** un hombre de gran habilidad diplomática.

skillet ['skɪlɪt] N sartén *f*; cacerola *f* de mango largo.

skillful ['skɪlfʊl] ADJ *etc* (*US*) = **skilful** *etc*.

skim [skɪm] **1** VT (a) *liquid* espumar; *milk* desnatar, descremar.

(b) (*graze*) rozar, rasar, casi tocar al pasar.

2 VI: **to ~ over** pasar rasando, pasar casi tocando; **to ~ through** examinar superficialmente, hojear.

3 ADJ: **~(med) milk** leche *f* desnatada, leche *f* descremada.

◆ **skim off** VT *cream, grease* desnatar, despumar, espumar; **they ~med off the brightest pupils** separaron a la flor y nata de los alumnos.

ski-mask ['ski:mɑ:sk] N (*US*) pasamontaña(s) *m*.

skimmer ['skɪməʳ] N (*Orn*) picotijera *m*, rayador *m*.

skimp [skɪmp] **1** VT *escatimar*; *work* chapucear, frangollar.

2 VI economizar, ser parsimonioso (*on* con).

skimpily ['skɪmpɪlɪ] ADV *serve, provide* escasamente; *live* mezquinamente.

skimpy ['skɪmpɪ] ADJ *allowance etc* escaso, pequeño; mezquino; *skirt etc* muy abreviado, muy corto; *person* tacaño.

skin [skɪn] **1** N (a) piel *f*; (*with reference to texture etc*) cutis *m*; **by the ~ of one's teeth** por los pelos; **it's no ~ off my nose:** no me va ni me viene; **he's nothing but ~ and bone** está en los huesos; **to have a thick ~** ser bastante insensible, tener mucha cara dura; **to have a thin ~** ser muy susceptible; **he gets under my ~:** me hace subir por las paredes:; **I've got you under my ~:** el recuerdo de ti no se me quita de la cabeza; **to jump out of one's ~** llevarse un tremendo susto; **to save one's ~** salvar el pellejo; **to wear wool next to one's ~** llevar prenda de lana sobre la piel.

(b) (*Zool*) piel *f*, pellejo *m*; (*as hide*) piel *f*, cuero *m*; (*for wine*) odre *m*.

(c) (*Bot*) piel *f*, pellejo *m*; corteza *f*.

(d) (*fig*) (*on milk*) nata *f*; (*for duplicating*) clisé *m*; (*Aer, Naut*) revestimiento *m*.

(e) (*) = **skinhead**.

2 ATTR de la piel; **~ disease** enfermedad *f* cutánea, enfermedad *f* dérmica; **~ trade** publicación *f* de revistas porno; **~ wound** herida *f* superficial.

3 VT (a) *animal* despellejar, desollar; *fruit* pelar, quitar la piel a; *tree* descortezar; **to ~ sb alive** desollar vivo a uno; **to ~ one's knee** despellejarse la rodilla.

(b) (: *steal from*) despellejar, esquilmar.

◆ **skin over** VI (*Med*) cicatrizarse.

◆ **skin up:** VI liar (*un porro*).

skin-deep ['skɪn'di:p] ADJ epidérmico, superficial; **beauty is only ~** la hermosura es cosa pasajera, la hermosura atañe a lo superficial.

skindiver ['skɪndaɪvəʳ] N buceador *m*, -ora *f*.

skindiving ['skɪnˌdaɪvɪŋ] N natación *f* submarina, exploración *f* submarina, pesca *f* submarina.

skinflick: ['skɪnflɪk] N película *f* porno*.

skinflint ['skɪnflɪnt] N tacaño *m*, cicatero *m*.

skinful* ['skɪnfʊl] N: **to have had a ~** llevar una copa de más, haber bebido más de la cuenta.

skin game ['skɪngeɪm] N (*US*) estafa *f*.

skin graft(ing) ['skɪnˌgrɑ:ft(ɪŋ)] N injerto *m* de piel.

skinhead ['skɪnhed] N (*Brit*) pelado *m*, cabeza rapada *m*.

skinless ['skɪnlɪs] ADJ *chicken, sausages* sin piel.

-skinned [skɪnd] ADJ *ending in compounds* de piel ...; **dark~** de piel morena; **rough~** de piel áspera.

skinny ['skɪnɪ] ADJ flaco, magro, escuálido, descarnado.

skinny-dipping* ['skɪnɪdɪpɪŋ] N: **to go ~** bañarse en bolas*.

skint: [skɪnt] ADJ (*Brit*): **to be ~** no tener ni un céntimo, estar pelado* (*LAm*).

skin-tight ['skɪntaɪt] ADJ muy ajustado, muy ceñido.

skip¹ [skɪp] **1** N brinco *m*, salto *m* (pequeño).

2 VT *passage* (*in reading etc*) omitir, pasar por alto; (*) *class, work* fumarse*; **to ~ lunch** saltarse el almuerzo, no almorzar; **~ it!** ¡déjalo!, ¡no te preocupes más de eso!; **oh, ~ it!** bueno, ¡no importa!

3 VI (a) brincar, saltar; (*with rope*) saltar a la comba; **to ~ with joy** brincar de alegría; **he ~ped out of the way** se apartó de un salto; **to ~ from one subject to another** saltar de un tema a otro; **the book ~s about a lot** el libro da muchos saltos; **to ~ over sth** saltar por encima de algo; (*omit*) omitir algo, pasar algo por alto.

(b) (*) largarse*, escabullirse; **we ~ped up to London yesterday** ayer fuimos en una escapadita a Londres.

skip² [skɪp] N (*cage*) jaula *f*; (*bucket*) cuba *f*; (*basket*) cesta *f*, canasta *f*; (*builder's*) contenedor *m* de escombros.

ski-pants ['ski:'pænts] NPL pantalones *mpl* de esquí.

skipper ['skɪpəʳ] **1** N capitán *m* (*also Sport*); (*Naut*) patrón *m*; **well, you're the ~** bueno, tú eres el jefe.

2 VT *boat* patronear.

skipping ['skɪpɪŋ] N saltar *m* a la comba.

skipping-rope ['skɪpɪŋrəʊp] N, (*US*) **skip rope** ['skɪprəʊp] N comba *f*, cuerda *f* de saltar.

skirl [skɜːl] N (*Scot*): **the ~ of the pipes** el son de la gaita, la música de la gaita.

skirmish ['skɜːmɪʃ] **1** N escaramuza *f*; (*fig*) roce *m*; **to have a ~ with** (*fig*) tener un roce con.

2 VI escaramuzar.

skirmisher ['skɜːmɪʃəʳ] N escaramuzador *m*.

skirt [skɜːt] **1** N falda *f*, pollera *f* (*LAm*); (*of coat etc*) faldón *m*; (:: *girl*) falda* *f*.

2 ATTR: **a ~ length** tela *f* suficiente para una falda.

3 VT (*surround*) ceñir, rodear; (*go round*) orillar, ladear, seguir el borde (*or* la orilla) de; (*avoid*) evitar entrar en, mantenerse a distancia de; **we ~ed Seville to the north** pasamos al norte de Sevilla.

4 VI: **to ~ round = 3**.

skirting(-board) ['skɜːtɪŋ(bɔːd)] N rodapié *m*, cenefa *f*.

ski-run ['ski:rʌn] N, **ski-slope** ['ski:sləʊp] N pista *f* de esquí.

ski-suit ['ski:su:t] N traje *m* de esquiar.

skit [skɪt] N sátira *f*, parodia *f* (*on* de); (*Theat*) número *m* corto satírico.

skitter ['skɪtəʳ] VI: **to ~ across the water/along the ground** (*bird*) volar rozando el agua/el suelo; (*stone*) saltar por encima del agua/por el suelo.

skittish ['skɪtɪʃ] ADJ *horse etc* nervioso, asustadizo; *playful* juguetón; *girl* coqueta; caprichoso.

skittishly ['skɪtɪʃlɪ] ADV nerviosamente; de modo juguetón; con coquetería; caprichosamente.

skittle ['skɪtl] N bolo *m*; **~s** juego *m* de bolos, boliche *m*.

skittle alley ['skɪtlˌælɪ] N bolera *f*.

skive: [skaɪv] (*Brit*) **1** N: **to be on the ~, to have a good ~** gandulear, no hacer nada.

2 VI gandulear, no hacer nada.

◆ **skive off:** VI (*Brit*) escabullirse, rajarse (*LAm*).

skiver: ['skaɪvəʳ] N (*Brit*) gandul *m*.

skivvy* ['skɪvɪ] N (*Brit*) fregona *f*.

skua ['skju:ə] N págalo *m*.

skulduggery* [skʌl'dʌgərɪ] N trampas *fpl*, embustes *mpl*; **piece of ~** trampa *f*, embuste *m*.

skulk [skʌlk] VI estar escondido, permanecer oculto; acechar sin ser visto, procurar no ser visto.

skull [skʌl] N calavera *f*; (*Anat*) cráneo *m*; **~ and crossbones** calavera *f*, bandera *f* negra (*de los piratas*).

skullcap ['skʌlkæp] N casquete *m*, solideo *m*.

skunk [skʌŋk] N (*Zool*) mofeta *f*; (*) canalla *m*; **you ~!** ¡canalla!

sky [skaɪ] N cielo *m*; **under blue skies** bajo un cielo azul; **the skies over England** el cielo sobre Inglaterra; **out of a clear blue ~** (*fig*) de repente, inesperadamente; **the ~'s the limit** no hay límite; **to praise sb to the skies** poner a uno por las nubes.

sky-blue ['skaɪ'blu:] **1** N azul *m* celeste.

2 ADJ azul celeste.

sky-dive ['skaɪdaɪv] **1** N caída *f* libre.

2 VI saltar en caída libre.

sky-diver ['skaɪdaɪvəʳ] N paracaidista *mf* de caída libre, paracaidista *m* acrobático, paracaidista *f* acrobática.

sky-diving ['skaɪdaɪvɪŋ] N caída *f* libre, paracaidismo *m* acrobático.

sky-high ['skaɪ'haɪ] ADV hasta las nubes; por las nubes; **the smoke rose ~** el humo se elevaba hasta las nubes; **to blow sth ~** volar algo en mil pedazos; **to blow a theory ~** refutar completamente una teoría; **prices have gone ~** los precios se han puesto por las nubes.

skyjack* ['skaɪdʒæk] VT *plane* atracar, piratear.

skyjacking* ['skaɪdʒækɪŋ] N atraco *m* (aéreo), piratería *f* (aérea).

skylab ['skaɪlæb] N skylab *m*, laboratorio *m* espacial.

skylark ['skaɪlɑːk] **1** N alondra *f*.

2 (*) VI jaranear, juguetear.

skylarking* ['skaɪlɑːkɪŋ] N jarana f; bromas fpl; pelea f amistosa.

skylight ['skaɪlaɪt] N tragaluz m, claraboya f.

skyline ['skaɪlaɪn] N horizonte m, línea f del horizonte; (of building) silueta f, perfil m; (of city) perfil m.

skyrocket ['skaɪˌrɒkɪt] [1] N cohete m.
[2] VI subir (como un cohete); (fig, of price etc) ponerse por las nubes, dispararse.

skyscraper ['skaɪˌskreɪpəʳ] N rascacielos m.

skytrain ['skaɪtreɪn] N puente m aéreo.

skyward(s) ['skaɪwəd(z)] ADV hacia el cielo.

skyway ['skaɪweɪ] N ruta f aérea.

skywriting ['skaɪˌraɪtɪŋ] N escritura f aérea, publicidad f aérea.

SL N ABBR of **source language** lenguaje m fuente.

slab [slæb] N bloque m; (of wood etc) plancha f, tabla f; (of stone) bloque m, (flat) losa f; (of meat etc) tajada f (gruesa); (of cake) porción f gruesa; (of chocolate) tableta f.

slack [slæk] [1] ADJ (a) (not tight) flojo; ~ **tide**, ~ **water** repunte m de la marea.
(b) (lax) descuidado, negligente; (lazy) vago, perezoso; student desaplicado, inerte, poco serio; **to be** ~ (student etc) gandulear, racanear*; **to be** ~ **about one's work** desatender su trabajo, ser negligente en su trabajo; **to be** ~ **about** (or **in**) **doing sth** dejar de hacer algo por desidia.
(c) (inactive) demand flojo; market flojo, encalmado; period de inactividad; season muerto; **business is** ~ el mercado está flojo, hay poca actividad en el mercado.
[2] N (a) (part of rope etc) lo flojo, parte f floja; **to take up the** ~ quitar la parte floja, tensar la cuerda (etc); **to take up the** ~ **in the economy** utilizar toda la capacidad productiva de la economía.
(b) (period) período m de inactividad; (season) estación f muerta.
(c) (Min) cisco m.
(d) (trousers) ~s pantalones mpl (flojos).
[3] VT (a) = **slacken**.
(b) = **slake**.
[4] VI gandulear, racanear*, flojear (LAm); **he's been** ~**ing** ha sido muy gandul.

slacken ['slækn] [1] VT (also **to** ~ **off**) aflojar; (reduce) disminuir; **to** ~ **speed** (person) aflojar el paso, ir más despacio, (car etc) disminuir la velocidad, moderar la marcha.
[2] VI aflojarse; disminuir, reducirse; (wind) amainar; (activity etc) hacerse menos intenso; (Comm) aflojarse.
◆ **slacken off** [1] VI dejar de trabajar (etc) tanto.
[2] VT = **slacken 1**.
◆ **slacken up** VI (person) aflojar el paso, ir más despacio.

slackening ['slækənɪŋ] N aflojamiento m; disminución f.

slacker ['slækəʳ] N vago m, -a f, gandul m, rácano* m.

slackly ['slæklɪ] ADV hang flojamente, laxamente; (fig) work negligentemente.

slackness ['slæknɪs] N (V adj) (a) flojedad f, lo flojo; (b) descuido m, negligencia f; vaguedad f, pereza f; desaplicación f, inercia f, falta f de seriedad. (c) inactividad f; (Comm) flojedad f, inactividad f.

slag¹ [slæg] N (of metal) escoria f.

slag²: [slæg] N (whore) putilla: f.

slag³: [slæg] VT (also **to** ~ **off**: criticize) poner como un trapo*, dar una paliza a; (get rid of) deshacerse de.

slagheap ['slæghiːp] N escorial m, escombrera f.

slain [sleɪn] [1] PTP of **slay**.
[2] NPL: **the** ~ los muertos, los caídos.

slake [sleɪk] VT lime, thirst apagar; ~**d lime** cal f muerta.

slalom ['slɑːləm] N eslálom m, eslalon m.

slam [slæm] [1] N (a) golpe m; (of door) portazo m; **to close the door with a** ~ dar un portazo, cerrar la puerta ruidosamente.
(b) (Cards) bola f, capote m; slam m; **grand** ~ gran slam m; **small** ~ pequeño slam m.
[2] (a) VT (strike) golpear; **to** ~ **the door** dar un portazo, cerrar la puerta ruidosamente (see also **door**); **he** ~**med the ball into the net** disparó la pelota a la red; **Ruritania** ~**med in 5 goals*** Ruritania marcó 5 goles.
(b) (*: defeat) cascar*, dar una paliza a.
(c) (*: criticize) vapulear, dar una paliza a; condenar, criticar duramente.
(d) (:) **to get** ~**med** (drunk) ajumarse*.
[3] VI (of door) cerrarse de golpe; **the door** ~**med shut** la puerta se cerró de golpe.
◆ **slam down** VT: **to** ~ **sth down on the table** arrojar algo violentamente sobre la mesa.
◆ **slam on** VT: **she** ~**med the brakes on** frenó violentamente.
◆ **slam to** VI: **the door** ~**med to** la puerta se cerró de golpe.

slammer: ['slæməʳ] N trena: f, talego: m.

slander ['slɑːndəʳ] [1] N calumnia f, difamación f; **to sue sb for** ~ demandar a uno por calumnia.
[2] VT calumniar, difamar; decir mal de, hablar mal de.

slanderer ['slɑːndərəʳ] N calumniador m, -ora f, defamador m, -ora f.

slanderous ['slɑːndərəs] ADJ calumnioso, difamatorio.

slanderously ['slɑːndərəslɪ] ADV calumniosamente.

slang [slæŋ] [1] N argot m; (of a group, trade etc) jerga f; (thieves' ~) germanía f; (gipsy ~) caló m; **that word is** ~ esa palabra es del argot; **to talk** ~ hablar en argot.
[2] ADJ: ~ **word** palabra f del argot, palabra f argótica.
[3] VT (*) (insult) llenar de insultos; (criticize) criticar duramente, poner como un trapo*, poner verde*.

slangily ['slæŋɪlɪ] ADV: **to talk** ~ hablar con mucho argot.

slanging-match* ['slæŋɪŋ'mætʃ] N discusión f violenta.

slangy ['slæŋɪ] ADJ person que emplea mucho argot, que habla en argot; style etc lleno de argot.

slant [slɑːnt] [1] N (a) inclinación f, sesgo m; **to be on the** ~ estar inclinado, estar sesgado; **the situation is taking on a new** ~ la situación está tomando un nuevo giro.
(b) (fig) punto m de vista; modo m de ver una cosa, modo m de enfocar un problema; **what is your** ~ **on this?** ¿cuál es su punto de vista en esto?; **to get a** ~ **on a topic** pedir pareceres sobre un asunto.
[2] VT inclinar, sesgar; **to** ~ **a report** escribir un informe parcial, escribir un informe desde un punto de vista particular.
[3] VI inclinarse, sesgarse; **the light** ~**ed in at the window** la luz entraba oblicuamente por la ventana.

slant-eyed ['slɑːnt'aɪd] ADJ de ojos almendrados.

slanting ['slɑːntɪŋ] ADJ inclinado, oblicuo, sesgado.

slantwise ['slɑːntwaɪz] ADJ oblicuamente, al sesgo.

slap [slæp] [1] N palmada f, manotada f; ~ **in the face** cachete m, bofetada f, (fig) palmetazo m, golpe m rudo, desaire m; ~ **on the back** espaldarazo m; **they were having a bit of the old** ~ **and tickle*** los dos se estaban sobando; **to give sb a** ~ **on the wrist** (fig) dar un aviso a uno.
[2] INTERJ ¡zas!
[3] ADV de lleno, de plano; directamente; **it fell** ~ **in the middle** cayó en todo el medio, cayó en el mismo centro; **he ran** ~ **into a tree** dio de lleno contra un árbol.
[4] VT (a) (strike) dar una palmada (or bofetada) a; pegar, golpear; **to** ~ **sb's face**, **to** ~ **sb on the face** dar una bofetada a uno, pegar un tortazo a uno; **to** ~ **sb on the back** dar un espaldarazo a uno; **to** ~ **one's knees** palmotearse las rodillas.
(b) (place) **he** ~**ped the book on the table** arrojó el libro en la mesa.
◆ **slap down** VT: **to** ~ **sb down** derribar a uno de una bofetada; (fig) aplastar a uno, apabullar a uno.
◆ **slap on** VT: **they've** ~**ped another storey on the house** han añadido un piso a la casa (como si tal cosa); **the judge** ~**ped £100 on the fine** el juez aumentó la multa en 100 libras; ~ **a coat of paint on it** échale una mano de pintura.

slap-bang ['slæp'bæŋ] ADV ruidosamente, violentamente; directamente, exactamente.

slapdash ['slæpdæʃ] ADJ person descuidado; despreocupado; work de brocha gorda, descuidado, chapucero.

slap-happy* ['slæp'hæpɪ] ADJ alegre y despreocupado; totalmente inconsciente.

slapper: ['slæpəʳ] N guarra: f, furcia* f.

slapstick ['slæpstɪk] N payasadas fpl; ~ **comedy** comedia f de payasadas, comedia f de golpe y porrazo.

slap-up* ['slæpʌp] ADJ (Brit) muy pera*, de lujo, de primera; ~ **meal** banquetazo* m, comilona* f; **it was** ~ fue un banquetazo.

slash [slæʃ] [1] N (a) (with knife) cuchillada f; (with whip) latigazo m.
(b) (US Typ) barra f oblicua.
(c) (:) **to go for a** ~, **to have a** ~ cambiar el agua al canario:.
[2] VT (a) (with knife etc) acuchillar; rasgar; tyre rajar; (Sew) acuchillar; (with whip) azotar; ~ **and burn agriculture** agricultura f de rozas y quema.
(b) (reduce) price machacar, quemar; estimate etc reducir radicalmente; speech, text abreviar sensiblemente.
(c) (*: attack) atacar, criticar severamente.
[3] VI: **to** ~ **at sb** tirar tajos a uno, tratar de acuchillar a uno.

slasher movie* ['slæʃəˌmuːvɪ], **slasher film*** ['slæʃəˌfɪlm] N película f de cuchilladas.

slashing ['slæʃɪŋ] ADJ attack etc fulminante.

slat [slæt] N tablilla f, hoja f, listón m; (of blind) lama f.

slate [sleɪt] [1] N (a) pizarra f; **put it on the** ~* (Brit) apúntalo en mi cuenta; **to start with a clean** ~, **to wipe the** ~ **clean** hacer borrón y cuenta nueva.
(b) (US Pol) lista f de candidatos.
[2] ATTR de pizarra; color pizarra; ~ **pencil** pizarrín m; ~ **roof** empizarrado m.
[3] VT (a) cubrir de pizarras.
(b) (US) anunciar; **it is** ~**d to start at 9** según el programa comienza a las 9, deberá comenzar a las 9.

(c) (*US Pol*) *candidate* nombrar.
(d) (*Brit**) vapulear, dar una paliza a.
slate-blue ['sleɪt'bluː] ADJ color azul pizarra.
slate-coloured, (*US*) **slate-colored** ['sleɪt,kʌləd] ADJ color pizarra.
slate-grey [,sleɪt'greɪ] [1] ADJ gris pizarra.
  [2] N gris *m* pizarra.
slate quarry ['sleɪt,kwɒrɪ] N pizarral *m*.
slater ['sleɪtəʳ] N pizarrero *m*.
slatted ['slætɪd] ADJ de tablillas, hecho de listones.
slattern ['slætən] N mujer *f* dejada, mujer *f* sucia, pazpuerca *f*.
slatternly ['slætənlɪ] ADJ sucio, puerco, desaseado.
slaty ['sleɪtɪ] ADJ (*of material*) parecido a pizarra, pizarroso; (*in colour*) color pizarra.
slaughter ['slɔːtəʳ] [1] N (*of animals*) matanza *f*, sacrificio *m*; (*of persons*) carnicería *f*, mortandad *f*; **the ~ on the roads** la carnicería en las carreteras; **the S~ of the Innocents** la Degollación de los Inocentes; **like a lamb to the ~** como borrego al matadero; **there was great ~** hubo gran mortandad.
  [2] VT *animals* matar, sacrificar, carnear (*LAm*); *persons* matar (brutalmente), hacer una carnicería de; (*: *Sport etc*) cascar*.
slaughterer ['slɔːtərəʳ] N jifero *m*, matarife *m*.
slaughterhouse ['slɔːtəhaʊs] N, PL **slaughterhouses** ['slɔːtəhaʊzɪz] matadero *m*.
slaughterman ['slɔːtəmən] N, PL **slaughtermen** ['slɔːtəmən] jifero *m*, matarife *m*.
Slav [slɑːv] [1] ADJ eslavo.
  [2] N eslavo *m*, -a *f*.
slave [sleɪv] [1] N esclavo *m*, -a *f*; **to be a ~ to tobacco** ser esclavo del tabaco; **to be a ~ to duty** ser esclavo del deber.
  [2] ATTR: **~ labour** (*work*) trabajo *m* de esclavos; (*persons*) esclavos *mpl*.
  [3] VI (*also* **to ~ away**) trabajar como un negro (*at* en), sudar tinta.
slavedriver ['sleɪv,draɪvəʳ] N negrero *m* (*also fig*).
slaver¹ ['sleɪvəʳ] N (*ship*) barco *m* negrero; (*person*) negrero *m*.
slaver² ['slævəʳ] [1] N baba *f*.
  [2] VI babear.
slavery ['sleɪvərɪ] N esclavitud *f*; **his ~ to tobacco** la esclavitud en que el tabaco le tiene; **to sell sb into ~** vender a uno como esclavo.
slave-trade ['sleɪvtreɪd] N comercio *m* de esclavos, tráfico *m* de esclavos.
slave-trader ['sleɪv,treɪdəʳ] N traficante *m* en esclavos; negrero *m*.
slavey* ['sleɪvɪ] N fregona *f*.
Slavic ['slævɪk] [1] ADJ eslavo.
  [2] N eslavo *m*.
slavish ['sleɪvɪʃ] ADJ servil.
slavishly ['sleɪvɪʃlɪ] ADV servilmente.
slavishness ['sleɪvɪʃnɪs] N servilismo *m*.
Slavonic [slə'vɒnɪk] [1] ADJ eslavo.
  [2] N eslavo *m*.
slaw [slɔː] N (*US*) ensalada *f* de col.
slay [sleɪ] (*irr*: PRET **slew**, PTP **slain**) VT **(a)** (*lit, hum*) matar, asesinar. **(b)** (*) hacer morir de risa*; **this will ~ you** esto os hará morir de risa*; **you ~ me!** (*iro*) ¡qué divertido!
slayer ['sleɪəʳ] N asesino *m*.
SLD N (*Brit*) ABBR *of* **Social and Liberal Democratic (Party)**.
sleaze* ['sliːz] N, **sleaziness*** ['sliːzɪnɪs] N deseaso *m*, desaliño *m*; sordidez *f*, asco *m*; mala fama *f*; **the ~ factor in these dealings** la poca limpieza de estas operaciones (*de la Bolsa etc*).
sleazeball* ['sliːzbɔːl] N depravado *m*, -a *f*.
sleazy* ['sliːzɪ] ADJ *person* desaseado, desaliñado; *place* sórdido, asqueroso; de mala fama; *deal etc* poco limpio, moralmente sospechoso.
sled [sled] (*esp US*), **sledge¹** [sledʒ] [1] N trineo *m*.
  [2] VT transportar por trineo, llevar en trineo.
  [3] VI ir en trineo.
sledge² [sledʒ] N, **sledgehammer** ['sledʒ,hæməʳ] N macho *m*, acotillo *m*, almádena *f*.
sleek [sliːk] [1] ADJ liso y brillante, lustroso; (*of general appearance*) pulcro, muy aseado; *boat, car* de líneas puras; *animal* gordo y de buen aspecto.
  [2] VT alisar, pulir.
◆ **sleek down** VT: **to ~ one's hair down** alisar y arreglarse el pelo.
sleekly ['sliːklɪ] ADV *smile, reply* zalameramente.
sleekness ['sliːknɪs] N lisura *f* y brillantez, lustre *m*; pulcritud *f*, aseo *m*; pureza *f* de líneas; gordura *f*.
sleep [sliːp] [1] N sueño *m*; **to drop off to ~, to go to ~** dormirse, quedarse dormido; **to go to ~** (*limb*) dormirse; **to have a ~** dormir, (*briefly*) descabezar un sueño; **to have a good night's ~** dormir bien durante la noche; **I shan't lose any ~ over it** eso no me hará desvelarme; **to put sb to ~** acostar a uno; dormir a uno, adormecer a uno; **to put an animal to ~** sacrificar un animal; **to send sb to ~** dormir a uno; **to sleep the ~ of the just** dormir con la conciencia tranquila; dormir a pierna suelta; **to walk in one's ~** ser sonámbulo,

pasearse dormido; **she walked downstairs in her ~** estando dormida bajó la escalera.
  [2] (*irr*: PRET AND PTP **slept**) VT **we can ~ 4** tenemos camas para 4; **can you ~ all of us?** ¿hay camas para todos nosotros?
  [3] VI dormir; **to ~ like a log** (*or* **top**) dormir como un lirón; **to ~ heavily, to ~ soundly** dormir profundamente; **he was ~ing soundly** estaba profundamente dormido; **to ~ with sb** dormir con uno; **to get to ~** conciliar el sueño.
◆ **sleep around*** VI dormir con todo el mundo, acostarse con cualquiera.
◆ **sleep away** VT: **to ~ the hours away** pasar las horas durmiendo.
◆ **sleep in** VI **(a)** (*late*) dormir tarde, seguir dormido. **(b)** (*in house*) dormir en casa.
◆ **sleep off** VT: **to ~ it off, to ~ off a hangover** dormir la mona*, dormir la cruda* (*LAm*); **she's ~ing off the effects of the drug** duerme hasta que desaparezcan los efectos de la droga.
◆ **sleep on** [1] VT: **to ~ on a problem** consultar algo con la almohada.
  [2] VI = **sleep in (a)**.
◆ **sleep out** VI (*not at home*) dormir fuera de casa; (*in open air*) dormir al aire libre, pasar la noche al raso.
◆ **sleep through** [1] VT: **he slept through the alarm clock** no oyó el despertador.
  [2] VI: **I slept through till the afternoon** dormí hasta la tarde.
◆ **sleep together** VI dormir juntos, acostarse juntos.
sleeper ['sliːpəʳ] N **(a)** (*person*) durmiente *mf*, persona *f* dormida; **to be a heavy ~** tener el sueño profundo; **to be a light ~** tener el sueño ligero.
  (b) (*Brit Rail: tie*) traviesa *f*, durmiente *m*; (*coach*) coche-cama *m*.
  (c) (*US: for baby*) pijama *m* de niño.
sleepily ['sliːpɪlɪ] ADV soñolientamente; **she said ~** dijo soñolienta.
sleepiness ['sliːpɪnɪs] N somnolencia *f*; (*fig*) letargo *m*, carácter *m* soporífero.
sleeping ['sliːpɪŋ] [1] ADJ durmiente, dormido; *pill etc* para dormir; **S~ Beauty** la Bella Durmiente (del Bosque); **~ partner** (*Brit*) socio *m* comanditario, socia *f* comanditaria; **~ policeman** policía *m* muerto.
  [2] N sueño *m*, el dormir; **between ~ and waking** entre duerme y vela.
sleeping-bag ['sliːpɪŋbæg] N saco-manta *m*, saco *m* de dormir; (*baby's*) camiseta *f* de dormir.
sleeping-car ['sliːpɪŋkɑːʳ] N coche-cama *m*.
sleeping-draught ['sliːpɪŋdrɑːft] N soporífero *m*.
sleeping-pill ['sliːpɪŋpɪl] N comprimido *m* para dormir, somnífero *m*.
sleeping-quarters ['sliːpɪŋ,kwɔːtəz] NPL dormitorio *m*; espacio *m* para dormir.
sleeping sickness ['sliːpɪŋ,sɪknɪs] N enfermedad *f* del sueño, encefalitis *f* letárgica.
sleeping-tablet ['sliːpɪŋ,tæblɪt] N comprimido *m* para dormir, somnífero *m*.
sleepless ['sliːplɪs] ADJ *person* insomne, desvelado; **to have a ~ night** pasar la noche en blanco.
sleeplessness ['sliːplɪsnɪs] N insomnio *m*.
sleep-talk ['sliːptɔːk] VI (*US*) hablar estando dormido.
sleepwalk ['sliːpwɔːk] VI ser sonámbulo, pasearse dormido.
sleepwalker ['sliːp,wɔːkəʳ] N sonámbulo *m*, -a *f*.
sleepwalking ['sliːp,wɔːkɪŋ] N sonambulismo *m*.
sleepwear ['sliːpwɛəʳ] N (*US*) ropa *f* de dormir.
sleepy ['sliːpɪ] ADJ *person, voice etc* soñoliento; *place* soporífero; *pear* pasado, fofo; **to be ~** (*person*) tener sueño; **to feel ~** sentirse con sueño; **I feel very ~ at midnight** a medianoche empiezo a tener mucho sueño.
sleepyhead ['sliːpɪhed] N dormilón *m*, -ona *f*.
sleet [sliːt] [1] N aguanieve *f*.
  [2] VI: **it was ~ing** caía aguanieve.
sleeve [sliːv] N (*of dress*) manga *f*; (*of record*) portada *f*, funda *f*; (*Mech*) manguito *m*, enchufe *m*; **to have sth up one's ~** guardar una carta en la manga, tener algo en reserva; **to laugh up one's ~** reírse para su capote; **to roll up one's ~s** arremangarse.
sleeved [sliːvd] ADJ con mangas.
-sleeved [sliːvd] ADJ *ending in compounds* con mangas ..., *eg* **long~** con mangas largas.
sleeveless ['sliːvlɪs] ADJ sin mangas.
sleigh [sleɪ] [1] N, VTI = **sled**. [2] ATTR: **~ bell** cascabel *m*; **to go for a ~ ride** ir a pasear en trineo.
sleight [slaɪt] N: **~ of hand** escamoteo *m*, prestidigitación *f*; destreza *f*; **by ~ of hand** con maña, mañosamente.
slender ['slendəʳ] ADJ (*not thick*) delgado, tenue; fino; *hand, waist etc* delgado; *figure* esbelto; *resources etc* escaso, limitado, reducido; *chance* pequeño, escaso; *hope* remoto; *excuse* poco convincente.
slenderize ['slendəraɪz] VT (*US*) adelgazar.
slenderly ['slendəlɪ] ADV: **~ built** (*person*) delgado; de talle esbelto; **~ made** de construcción delicada.
slenderness ['slendənɪs] N delgadez *f*, tenuidad *f*; esbeltez *f*; escasez

f, lo limitado; lo remoto.

slept [slept] PRET AND PTP *of* **sleep**.

sleuth [slu:θ] N detective *m*, sabueso *m*.

slew¹ [slu:] **1** VT (*also* **to ~ round**) torcer; girar; **to ~ sth to the left** torcer algo a la izquierda; girar algo a la izquierda; **to be ~ed:** estar ajumado*.

2 VI (*also* **to ~ round**) torcerse.

slew² [slu:] PRET *of* **slay**.

slew³* [slu:] N (*US*) montón* *m*.

slice [slaɪs] **1** N (**a**) (*of meat etc*) tajada *f*, lonja *f*; (*of sausage*) raja *f*; (*of bread*) rebanada *f*, trozo *m*; (*of lemon, cucumber etc*) rodaja *f*.

(**b**) (*fig: portion*) parte *f*, porción *f*; **a ~ of life** un trozo de la vida tal como es; **it took quite a ~ of our profits** nos quitó una buena parte de nuestras ganancias; **it affects a large ~ of the population** afecta a buena parte de la población.

(**c**) (*tool*) estrelladera *f*, pala *f*.

(**d**) (*Golf*) golpe *m* con efecto a la derecha.

2 VT (**a**) cortar, tajar; cortar en rodajas; *bread* rebanar; **to ~ sth in two** cortar algo en dos.

(**b**) *ball* cortar, torcer, dar efecto a; (*Golf*) golpear oblicuamente (a derecha).

◆ **slice off** VT cercenar.

◆ **slice through** VT *rope* cortar; (*fig*) *restrictions etc* pasarse por encima; **to ~ through the air/the waves** cortar el aire/las olas.

◆ **slice up** VT cortar en rebanadas.

sliced [slaɪst] ADJ *bread* rebanado, en rebanadas; **it's the best thing since ~ bread** (*hum*) es un magnífico parto del ingenio humano; **~ lemon** limón *m* en rodajas.

slicer [ˈslaɪsəʳ] N rebanadora *f*, máquina *f* de cortar.

slick [slɪk] **1** ADJ (*skilful*) hábil, diestro; (*quick*) rápido; (*pej*) *person* astuto, mañoso; **he's the ~ sort** es un astuto; **he's too ~ for me** es demasiado hábil para mi gusto; **be ~ about it!** ¡date prisa!

2 N (*of oil etc*) masa *f* flotante, mancha *f*, capa *f* (en el agua).

3 VT = **sleek 2**.

slicker [ˈslɪkəʳ] N embaucador *m*, tramposo *m*; **city ~*** capitalino* *m*.

slickly [ˈslɪklɪ] ADV hábilmente, diestramente; rápidamente; astutamente, mañosamente.

slickness [ˈslɪknɪs] N habilidad *f*, destreza *f*; rapidez *f*; maña *f*.

slid [slɪd] PRET AND PTP *of* **slide**.

slide [slaɪd] **1** N (**a**) (*place: on ice, mud etc*) resbaladero *m*; (*for logs etc*) deslizadero *m*; (*in playground, swimming pool*) tobogán *m*.

(**b**) (*Tech: part*) corredera *f*, cursor *m*; (*for hair*) pasador *m*; (*Mus*) vara *f*, corredera *f*.

(**c**) (*microscope ~*) platina *f*, portaobjeto *m*; (*Phot*) diapositiva *f*, filmina *f*; **a lecture with ~s** una conferencia con diapositivas, una conferencia con proyecciones.

(**d**) (*act*) resbalón *m*; (*of land*) desprendimiento *m*; **the ~ in share prices** la baja de las cotizaciones; **the ~ in temperature** el descenso de la temperatura.

2 (*irr: PRET AND PTP* **slid**) VT correr, pasar, deslizar; **to ~ furniture across the floor** deslizar un mueble sobre el suelo; **~ the top on when you've finished** pon la tapa cuando termines.

3 VI (*slip*) resbalar; (*glide*) deslizarse; **they were sliding across the floor** se deslizaban sobre el suelo; **it ought to ~ gently into place** debiera correr suavemente a su lugar; **to ~ into a habit** caer en un hábito (sin darse cuenta); **to let things ~** no ocuparse de las cosas, no prestar atención a lo que pasa, dejar rodar la bola; **these last months he's let everything ~** estos últimos meses se ha desatendido de todo.

◆ **slide down** VT: **to ~ down the banisters** bajar deslizándose por la barandilla; **the ring ~s down this rope** el anillo corre por esta cuerda.

◆ **slide off** VI *top, lid etc* resbalar.

slideholder [ˈslaɪd,həʊldəʳ] N portadiapositiva *m*.

slide-magazine [ˈslaɪd,mægə,zi:n] N cartucho *m* (*or* guía *f*) para diapositivas.

slide-projector [ˈslaɪdprə,dʒektəʳ] N proyector *m* de diapositivas.

sliderule [ˈslaɪdru:l] N regla *f* de cálculo.

sliding [ˈslaɪdɪŋ] ADJ *part* corredizo; **~ door** puerta *f* deslizante, puerta *f* de corredera; **~ roof** techo *m* corredizo, techo *m* de corredera; **~ scale** escala *f* móvil; **~ seat** bancada *f* corrediza.

slight [slaɪt] **1** ADJ (**a**) *figure* delgado, fino; *stature* pequeño, bajo; (*of weak appearance*) débil, frágil, delicado.

(**b**) (*trivial*) leve; insignificante, de poca importancia; (*small*) leve; pequeño, escaso; **a ~ pain in the arm** un leve dolor de brazo; **the wound is only ~** la herida es más bien leve, la herida no es de consideración; **of ~ importance** de escasa importancia; **a ~ improvement** una pequeña mejora; **of ~ intelligence** de escasa inteligencia; **to a ~ extent** en un grado pequeño; **he showed some ~ optimism** mostró cierto optimismo; **the future does not justify the ~est optimism** el futuro no autoriza el más leve optimismo; **there's not the ~est possibility of that** de eso no existe la más

remota posibilidad; **not in the ~est** en absoluto, ni en lo más mínimo.

2 N desaire *m*, insulto *m* (*on* a, para).

3 VT desairar, ofender, insultar.

slighting [ˈslaɪtɪŋ] ADJ despreciativo, menospreciativo, despectivo.

slightingly [ˈslaɪtɪŋlɪ] ADV con desprecio, despectivamente.

slightly [ˈslaɪtlɪ] ADV un poco; **yes, ~** sí, un poco; **~ better** un poco mejor; **~ built** de talle delgado, menudo; **to know sb ~** conocer a uno ligeramente, conocer a uno un poco.

slightness [ˈslaɪtnɪs] N (**a**) (*of size etc*) delgadez *f*, finura *f*; pequeñez *f*; fragilidad *f*. (**b**) (*of importance etc*) insignificancia *f*, poca importancia *f*.

slim [slɪm] **1** ADJ (**a**) (*of figure*) delgado, esbelto; **to get ~** adelgazar. (**b**) *resources etc* escaso, insuficiente; **his chances are pretty ~** sus posibilidades son escasas.

2 VT adelgazar.

3 VI adelgazar.

◆ **slim down** **1** VT (**a**) = **slim 2**.

(**b**) (*fig*) **~med down** *business, industry* reconvertido, saneado.

2 VI bajar de peso, adelgazar.

slime [slaɪm] N limo *m*, légamo *m*, cieno *m*; (*of snail*) baba *f*; (*fig*) lodo *m*.

sliminess [ˈslaɪmɪnɪs] N (**a**) (*lit*) lo limoso; lo baboso; viscosidad *f*. (**b**) (*of person*) lo rastrero; zalamería *f*.

slimline [ˈslɪm,laɪn] ADJ: **~ food** alimento *m* reductivo, alimento *m* que no engorda.

slimmer [ˈslɪməʳ] N persona *f* que está a dieta.

slimming [ˈslɪmɪŋ] **1** N adelgazamiento *m*.

2 ATTR reductivo; **to be on a ~ diet** seguir un régimen para adelgazar, estar a dieta; **to eat only ~ foods** comer solamente cosas que no engordan.

slimness [ˈslɪmnɪs] N delgadez *f*.

slimy [ˈslaɪmɪ] ADJ (**a**) limoso, legamoso; *snail* baboso; viscoso. (**b**) *person* rastrero; zalamero; odioso.

sling [slɪŋ] **1** N (*weapon*) honda *f*; (*Med*) cabestrillo *m*; (*for rifle etc*) portafusil *m*; (*Naut*) eslinga *f*; (*toy*) tirador *m*; **to have one's arm in a ~** llevar el brazo en cabestrillo.

2 VT (*irr: PRET AND PTP* **slung**) (**a**) (*throw*) lanzar, tirar, arrojar.

(**b**) (*hang*) colgar, suspender; alzar; (*Naut*) eslingar; **with a rifle slung across his shoulder** con un fusil en bandolera.

◆ **sling away*** VT: **to ~ sth away** tirar algo.

◆ **sling out*** VT *object* tirar, botar*; *person* echar, botar, expulsar.

◆ **sling over*** VT: **to ~ sth over to sb** tirar algo a uno, pasar algo a uno.

slingshot [ˈslɪŋʃɒt] N (*weapon*) honda *f*, tirador *m*; (*US*) tirador *m*, tirachinas *m*, (*shot*) hondazo *m*.

slink [slɪŋk] (*irr: PRET AND PTP* **slunk**) VI: **to ~ along** andar furtivamente; **to ~ away, to ~ off** largarse*, escabullirse, irse cabizbajo.

slinky* [ˈslɪŋkɪ] ADJ seductor, provocativo; *walk etc* sinuoso, ondulante.

slip¹ [slɪp] **1** N (**a**) (*slide*) resbalón *m*; (*trip*) traspié *m*, tropezón *m*; (*of earth*) desprendimiento *m* (de tierras).

(**b**) (*mistake*) falta *f*, error *m*, equivocación *f*; (*moral*) desliz *m*; (*by neglect*) descuido *m*; **~ of the pen** lapsus *m* calami; **~ of the tongue** lapsus *m* linguae; **it was a bad ~** fue una grave equivocación; **there's many a ~ 'twixt cup and lip** de la mano a la boca desaparece la sopa.

(**c**) (*pillow~*) funda *f*; (*undergarment*) combinación *f*; (*gym~ etc*) túnica *f*.

(**d**) (*Naut*) **~s** grada *f*, gradas *fpl*.

(**e**) **to give sb the ~** dar esquinazo a uno, zafarse de uno.

2 VT (**a**) (*slide*) deslizar; **to ~ a coin into a slot** introducir una moneda en una ranura; **~ that nut on here** pon esa tuerca aquí; **to ~ sth across to sb** pasar algo (furtivamente) a uno; **would you ~ the salt across, please?** ¿me das la sal, por favor?; **to ~ an arm round sb's waist** pasar el brazo por la cintura de una; **to ~ sb a fiver** pasar a uno un billete de 5 libras (como propina o para comprar su ayuda).

(**b**) (*escape from*) eludir, escaparse de; **to ~ a disc** dislocarse una vértebra; **to ~ a cable** soltar una amarra; **the dog ~ped its chain** el perro soltó la cadena; **it ~ped my memory** se me olvidó, se me fue de la cabeza; **to ~ sb's notice** no ser advertido por uno, pasar inadvertido ante uno.

3 VI (**a**) (*glide*) deslizarse (*along* por, sobre); (*stumble*) tropezar, resbalar; (*of bone etc*) dislocarse; (*of earth*) caer, correrse; **I ~ped on the ice** resbalé en el hielo; **my foot ~ed** se me fue el pie; **it ~s easily along the wire** se desliza suavemente por el hilo; **the knot has ~ped** el nudo se ha desatado; **it ~ped from her hand** se le escapó de entre las manos; **the clutch ~s** el embrague patina.

(**b**) (*move quickly*) ir (rápidamente); **I'll ~ round to the shop** voy a la tienda en una escapadita; **to ~ into bed** meterse en la cama; **she ~ped into the room** se coló dentro del cuarto, se introdujo (sin llamar la atención) en el cuarto; **to ~ into a dress** ponerse un vestido; **the motorcycle ~s through the traffic** la moto se cuela por entre la circulación.

(c) (with let) **to let it ~ that ...** revelar inadvertidamente que ...; **he let a secret ~** se le escapó un secreto; **to let a chance ~** perder una oportunidad, no aprovechar una oportunidad.

(d) (decline) declinar, decaer; **you're ~ping** no eres lo que eras antes; se te nota un ir a menos.

◆ **slip away** VI marcharse desapercibido, irse sin ser notado; (pej) largarse*, escabullirse; **time is ~ping away** se nos escapa el tiempo, el tiempo corre; **her life was ~ping away** se le estaba acabando la vida.

◆ **slip back** VI regresar con sigilo.

◆ **slip by** VI pasar inadvertido.

◆ **slip down** VI object, car resbalar pendiente abajo; person resbalar; **I'll just ~ down and get it** bajo un momento y lo traigo.

◆ **slip in** ① VT deslizar, introducir suavemente (or sin ruido etc); comment, word insinuar.

② VI entrar desapercibido; colarse dentro.

◆ **slip off** ① VT dress quitarse; cover, lid quitar.

② VI (a) = **slip away**.

(b) (cover, lid) quitarse, deslizarse.

◆ **slip on** VT dress, ring etc ponerse; cover, lid poner.

◆ **slip out** VI (person) salir un instante; salir en una escapada; **the name ~ped out** se me escapó el nombre, dije el nombre sin querer; **to ~ out of a dress** quitarse un vestido.

◆ **slip over** ① VT: **to ~ one over on sb*** jugar una mala pasada a uno; ganar por la mano a uno; encajar algo a uno.

② VI = **slip up (a)**.

◆ **slip past** VI pasar desapercibido.

◆ **slip up** VI (a) resbalar, tropezar.

(b) (fig: make mistake) equivocarse; cometer un desliz; meter la pata*.

slip² [slɪp] N estaca f, plantón m; **~ of paper** papeleta f, papelito m; (in filing system etc) ficha f; (packer's) hoja f de embalaje, hoja f de control; **a ~ of a girl** una jovenzuela, una chicuela.

slipcase ['slɪpkeɪs] N estuche m.

slipcovers ['slɪp,kʌvəz] NPL (US) fundas fpl que se pueden quitar.

slipknot ['slɪpnɒt] N nudo m corredizo.

slip-on ['slɪpɒn] ADJ que se pone por la cabeza; de quitaipón; **~ shoes** zapatos mpl sin cordón.

slipover ['slɪpəʊvəʳ] N pullover m sin mangas.

slippage ['slɪpɪdʒ] N (slip) deslizamiento m; (loss) pérdida f; (shortage) déficit m; (delay) retraso m.

slipped ['slɪpt] ADJ: **~ disc** hernia f discal, vértebra f dislocada.

slipper ['slɪpəʳ] N zapatilla f; babucha f, pantufla f (LAm), chancla f (Mex).

slippery ['slɪpərɪ] ADJ (a) surface resbaladizo; skin etc viscoso; **to be on a ~ slope** (fig) estar en terreno resbaladizo. (b) person astuto, escurridizo, evasivo, (pej) escurridizo, nada confiable; **he's as ~ as they come** (or **as an eel**) tiene más conchas que un galápago.

slippy* ['slɪpɪ] ADV (Brit): **to be ~**, **to look ~ about it** darse prisa, menearse; **look ~!** ¡menearse!; **we shall have to look ~** tendremos que darnos prisa.

slip-road ['slɪprəʊd] N (Brit) carretera f de acceso.

slipshod ['slɪpʃɒd] ADJ descuidado, poco correcto.

slipstream ['slɪpstriːm] N viento m de la hélice, estela f.

slip-up ['slɪpʌp] N (mistake) falta f, error m, equivocación f; metedura f de pata*; (moral) desliz m; (by neglect) descuido m.

slipway ['slɪpweɪ] N grada f, gradas fpl.

slit [slɪt] ① N hendedura f, raja f; resquicio m; corte m largo; **to make a ~ in sth** hacer un corte en algo.

② (irr: PRET AND PTP **slit**) VT hender, rajar; cortar; **to ~ a sack open** abrir un saco con un cuchillo (etc); **to ~ sb's throat** degollar a uno.

slit-eyed [,slɪt'aɪd] ADJ de ojos rasgados.

slither ['slɪðəʳ] VI deslizarse (down a rope por una cuerda); ir rodando (down a slope por una pendiente); **to ~ about on ice** ir resbalando sobre el hielo.

sliver ['slɪvəʳ] N raja f; (of wood etc) astilla f.

Sloane Ranger* ['sləʊn'reɪndʒəʳ] N niño m bien* (londinense), niña f bien.

┌─ SLOANE RANGER ─┐

ⓘ El término **Sloane Ranger** o **Sloane** se usa para referirse a los jóvenes de clase alta que viven en las zonas más refinadas de Londres, como por ejemplo Chelsea o Kensington, y que visten ropa muy cara de estilo campero. Los **Sloane** hablan con un acento típico de su clase, tienen, en general, ideas conservadoras y le dan mucha importancia al rango social y a la apariencia. Este término fue acuñado por un escritor de moda en los años 70 y se usa en la actualidad con un tono despectivo para referirse a las personas con valores superficiales. La expresión proviene de un juego de palabras hecho con **Lone Ranger** (el Llanero Solitario) y el nombre de una zona elegante del centro de Londres, **Sloane Square**.

slob* [slɒb] N haragán m, -ana f, gandul m, gandula f; **you ~!** ¡patán!

◆ **slob out*** VI holgazanear, zanganear, haraganear.

slobber ['slɒbəʳ] ① N baba f.

② VI babear; **to ~ over** besuquear; (fig) caerse la baba por; tratar con mucha sensiblería, entusiasmarse tontamente por.

slobbery ['slɒbərɪ] ADJ kiss mojado, baboso; person sensiblero, tontamente sentimental.

sloe [sləʊ] ① N (fruit) endrina f; (tree) endrino m.

② ATTR: **~ gin** licor m de endrinas.

slog [slɒg] ① N: **it was a ~** me costó trabajo; **it's a hard ~ to the top** cuesta mucho trabajo llegar a la cumbre.

② VT ball golpear (sin arte).

③ VI (a) (work etc) afanarse, sudar tinta.

(b) (walk etc) caminar penosamente.

◆ **slog along** VI = **slog on**.

◆ **slog away** VI: **to ~ away at sth** afanarse por hacer algo, trabajar como un negro para terminar algo.

◆ **slog on** VI: **we ~ged on for 8 kilometres** caminamos con dificultad 8 kilómetros más.

◆ **slog out** VI: **to ~ it out** (fighting) luchar hasta el fin, seguir luchando; (arguing) discutir sin ceder terreno; (working etc) aguantarlo todo, no cejar.

slogan ['sləʊgən] N slogan m, eslogan m; (graffiti) pintada f.

sloganeering [,sləʊgə'nɪərɪŋ] N abuso m de eslóganes.

slogger ['slɒgəʳ] N trabajador m, -ora f.

slo-mo* ['sləʊməʊ] N ABBR of **slow-motion**.

sloop [sluːp] N balandra f; corbeta f.

slop [slɒp] ① NPL: **~s** (food) gachas fpl; (of wine) heces fpl; (waste) agua f sucia, lavazas fpl.

② VT derramar, verter.

③ VI (also **to ~ over**) derramarse; desbordarse.

◆ **slop about** VI: **to ~ about in the mud** chapotear en el lodo; **the water was ~ping about in the bucket** el agua chapoteaba en el cubo.

◆ **slop out** VI vaciar los cubos usados como retretes por los prisioneros en sus celdas.

◆ **slop over** VI = **slop 3**.

slop-basin ['slɒp,beɪsn] N recipiente m para agua sucia; (at table) taza f para los posos del té.

slope [sləʊp] ① N inclinación f; (up) cuesta f, pendiente f; (down) declive m; (of hill) falda f; vertiente f, ladera f; **the ~s of Mulacén** las laderas de Mulacén; **the southern ~ of the Guadarrama** la vertiente sur del Guadarrama; **the car got stuck on a ~** el coche se quedó parado en una cuesta; **there is a ~ down to the town** la tierra está en declive hacia la ciudad.

② VT inclinar; sesgar; **~ arms!** ¡armas al hombro!

③ VI inclinarse, estar inclinado; declinar, estar en declive; **to ~ forwards** estar inclinado hacia delante.

◆ **slope away**, **slope down** VI estar en declive; **the garden ~s down to the sea** el jardín baja hacia el mar.

◆ **slope off*** VI largarse*.

◆ **slope up** VI estar en pendiente, subir, ascender.

sloping ['sləʊpɪŋ] ADJ inclinado; (up) en pendiente, (down) en declive.

slop-pail ['slɒppeɪl] N cubeta f para agua sucia.

sloppily ['slɒpɪlɪ] ADV (a) (carelessly) descuidadamente, de modo poco sistemático; **to dress ~** vestir con poca elegancia. (b) (sentimentally) de modo sentimental, con sensiblería.

sloppiness ['slɒpɪnɪs] N (a) (carelessness) descuido m, lo descuidado, falta f de sistema; desaseo m. (b) (sentimentality) sentimentalismo m, sensiblería f.

slopping out [,slɒpɪŋ'aʊt] N vaciado de los cubos usados como retretes por los prisioneros en sus celdas.

sloppy ['slɒpɪ] ADJ (a) (in consistency) poco sólido, casi líquido; road etc lleno de charcos, lleno de barro; (wet) mojado. (b) work etc descuidado, poco sistemático; thought poco riguroso; mal presentado; dress desgalichado; appearance desaseado. (c) (sentimental) sentimental, sensiblero.

slop shop ['slɒpʃɒp] N (US*) bazar m de ropa barata, tienda f de pacotilla.

slosh* [slɒʃ] VT (esp Brit) person pegar; **to ~ some water over sth** echar agua sobre algo.

◆ **slosh about**, **slosh around** VI: **to ~ about in the puddles** chapotear en los charcos; **the water was ~ing about in the pail** el agua chapoteaba en el cubo.

sloshed* [slɒʃt] ADJ (esp Brit): **to be ~** estar ajumado*; **to get ~** ajumarse*, agarrar una trompa*.

slot [slɒt] ① N (a) muesca f, ranura f; **to put a coin in the ~** meter una moneda en la ranura.

(b) (job ~) vacante f; (in programme etc) espacio m; lugar m; (advertising ~) cuña f (publicitaria).

(c) (for aircraft) espacio m.

② VT: **to ~ a part into another part** encajar una pieza en (la ranura de) otra pieza; **to ~ sth into place** colocar algo en su lugar; **we can**

~ you into the programme te podemos dar un espacio en el programa, te podemos incluir en el programa.
◆**slot in** VI: **it ~s in here** entra en esta ranura, encaja aquí.
sloth [sləʊθ] N **(a)** (idleness) pereza f, indolencia f, desidia f. **(b)** (Zool) perezoso m.
slothful ['sləʊfʊl] ADJ perezoso.
slot-machine ['slɒtməˌʃiːn] N (Comm) aparato m vendedor automático; (in fun fair etc) tragaperras m.
slotted spoon ['slɒtɪd'spuːn] N cucharón m perforado.
slouch [slaʊtʃ] [1] N **(a) to walk with a ~** andar con un aire gacho, caminar arrastrando los pies.
(b) he's no ~* (in skill) no es ningún principiante, (at work) no es ningún vago; **he's no ~ in the kitchen** tiene buena mano para cocina.
[2] ADJ: **~ hat** sombrero m flexible.
[3] VI andar con un aire gacho, caminar con los hombros caídos; **to sit ~ed in a chair** repanchigarse en un sillón; **he was ~ed over his desk** estaba inclinado sobre su mesa de trabajo en postura desgarbada.
◆**slouch about, slouch around** VI **(a)** andar con un aire gacho, caminar arrastrando los pies; andar de un lado para otro (sin saber qué hacer). **(b)** (fig) gandulear, golfear.
◆**slouch along** VI = **slouch about, slouch around** (a).
◆**slouch off** VI irse cabizbajo, alejarse con un aire gacho.
slough[1] [slaʊ] N fangal m, cenegal m; (fig) abismo m; **the ~ of despond** el abatimiento más profundo, el abismo de la desesperación.
slough[2] [slʌf] [1] N (Zool) camisa f, piel f vieja (que muda la serpiente); (Med) escara f.
[2] VT mudar, echar de sí; (fig) deshacerse de, desechar.
[3] VI desprenderse, caerse.
◆**slough off** [1] VT mudar, echar de sí; (fig) deshacerse de, desechar.
[2] VI = **slough**[2] 3.
Slovak ['sləʊvæk] [1] ADJ eslovaco.
[2] N eslovaco m, -a f.
Slovakia [sləʊ'vækɪə] N Eslovaquia f.
Slovakian [sləʊ'vækɪən] ADJ eslovaco.
Slovak Republic ['sləʊvækrɪ'pʌblɪk] N: **the ~** la República Eslovaca.
sloven ['slʌvn] N (in appearance) persona f desgarbada, persona f desaseada; (at work) vago m, -a f.
Slovene ['sləʊviːn] [1] ADJ esloveno.
[2] N esloveno m, -a f.
Slovenia [sləʊ'viːnɪə] N Eslovenia f.
Slovenian [sləʊ'viːnɪən] [1] ADJ esloveno.
[2] N **(a)** esloveno m, -a f. **(b)** (Ling) esloveno.
slovenliness ['slʌvnlɪnɪs] N desaseo m; despreocupación f, dejadez f; descuido m, chapucería f.
slovenly ['slʌvnlɪ] ADJ appearance desgarbado, desaseado; person despreocupado, dejado, descuidado; work descuidado, chapucero.
slow [sləʊ] [1] ADJ **(a)** person, progress, vehicle etc lento; pausado; **~ fuse** espoleta f retardada; **~ lane** (Brit Aut) carril m de la izquierda, (most countries) carril m de la derecha; carril m de los lentos; **~ match** mecha f tardía; **~ train** (Brit) tren m correo, tren m ómnibus; **~ but sure!** ¡despacio pero seguro!; **it's ~ work** es (un) trabajo lento; **he's a ~ worker** trabaja despacio; **this car is ~er than my old one** este coche anda menos que el que tenía antes; **business is very ~** el negocio está muy flojo; **life here is ~** aquí se vive a un ritmo lento.
(b) (not prompt) **to be ~ to do sth** tardar en hacer algo; **they were ~ to act** tardaron en obrar; **he was not ~ to notice that ...** no tardó en observar que ...; **to be ~ to anger** ser ecuánime, tener mucho aguante; **to be ~ to pay** ser moroso.
(c) clock atrasado; **my watch is ~** mi reloj (se) atrasa; **my watch is 20 minutes ~** mi reloj (se) atrasa 20 minutos, mi reloj lleva 20 minutos de atraso.
(d) character (phlegmatic) flemático, cachazudo; (stupid) torpe, lerdo.
(e) (boring) aburrido; **the game is very ~** el partido es la mar de aburrido.
(f) surface, pitch pesado.
[2] ADV despacio, lentamente; **to go ~** ir despacio, (in industrial dispute) trabajar a ritmo lento, trabajar al mínimo legal.
[3] VT (also **to ~ down, to ~ up**) retardar; engine, machine reducir la velocidad de, moderar la marcha de; economy etc ralentizar; development retardar; **that car ~s up the traffic** ese coche entorpece la circulación.
[4] VI (also **to ~ down, to ~ up**) ir más despacio, (in walking etc) aflojar el paso; (Aut) moderar la marcha, desacelerar, reducir la velocidad; (economy etc) ralentizarse; **'S~ down'** (road sign) 'Disminuir velocidad'; **the car ~ed to a stop** el coche moderó su marcha y paró; **production has ~ed to almost nothing** la producción se ha reducido casi a cero.
◆**slow down** VT, VI = **slow** 3, 4.
◆**slow up** VT, VI = **slow** 3, 4.
slow-acting ['sləʊˌæktɪŋ] ADJ de efecto retardado.

slow-burning ['sləʊ'bɜːnɪŋ] ADJ que se quema lentamente; **~ fuse** espoleta f retardada.
slowcoach* ['sləʊkəʊtʃ] N (Brit) (idler) perezoso m, -a f, vago m, -a f; (stupid person) torpe mf.
slow cooker ['sləʊˌkʊkəʳ] N bote m eléctrico de cocción lenta.
slowdown ['sləʊdaʊn] N (US: strike) huelga f de manos caídas; = **slowing-down**.
slowing-down ['sləʊɪŋ'daʊn] N disminución f de velocidad; retardación f; (of economy etc) ralentización f.
slowly ['sləʊlɪ] ADV despacio, lentamente; poco a poco; **~ but surely** lenta pero seguramente.
slow-mo*, slomo* ['sləʊˌməʊ] ADJ, N = **slow-motion**.
slow-motion ['sləʊ'məʊʃən] [1] ADJ: **~ film** película f a cámara lenta.
[2] N: **to show a film in ~** pasar una película a cámara lenta, pasar una película ralentizada.
slow-moving [ˌsləʊ'muːvɪŋ] ADJ lento; de acción lenta; de movimiento pesado.
slowness ['sləʊnɪs] N (V ADJ) **(a)** lentitud f. **(b)** flema f; torpeza f; aburrimiento m. **(c)** pesadez f.
slowpoke* ['sləʊˌpəʊk] N (US) = **slowcoach**.
slow-witted ['sləʊ'wɪtɪd] ADJ torpe, lerdo.
slowworm ['sləʊwɜːm] N lución m.
SLR N (Phot) ABBR of **single lens reflex (camera)**.
sludge [slʌdʒ] N (mud) lodo m, fango m; (sediment) sedimento m fangoso; (sewage) aguas fpl de albañal.
slue [sluː] VTI (US) = **slew**[1], **slew**[3].
slug[1] [slʌg] N (Zool) babosa f; (bullet) posta f; (Typ) lingote m; (US: for slot-machine) ficha f; (US*: of drink) trago m.
slug[2]; [slʌg] VT pegar, aporrear.
◆**slug out** VT: **to ~ it out (with sb)** pegarse, aporrearse; resolver un asunto con los puños.
sluggard ['slʌgəd] N haragán m, -ana f.
slugger ['slʌgəʳ] N (Baseball) bateador que golpea la bola muy fuerte.
sluggish ['slʌgɪʃ] ADJ (indolent) perezoso; (slow-moving) lento; animal etc inactivo, inerte, perezoso; business, market flojo; person's temperament flemático, cachazudo.
sluggishly ['slʌgɪʃlɪ] ADV perezosamente; lentamente; inactivamente; flojamente; con flema.
sluggishness ['slʌgɪʃnɪs] N pereza f; lentitud f; inactividad f, inercia f; flojedad f; flema f.
sluice [sluːs] N **(a)** (gate) compuerta f, esclusa f; (barrier) dique m de contención; (waterway) canal m. **(b) to give sth a ~ down** echar agua sobre algo (para lavarlo), regar algo; **to give sb a ~ down** dar una ducha a uno.
◆**sluice down** VT: **to ~ sth down (with water)** echar agua sobre algo (para lavarlo), regar algo con agua.
sluicegate ['sluːsgeɪt] N compuerta f.
sluiceway ['sluːsweɪ] N canal m.
slum [slʌm] [1] N (area) barrio m bajo, barrio m pobre, barriada f (LAm); (house) casucha f, tugurio m; **the ~s** los barrios bajos, los suburbios; **they live in a ~** viven en una casucha; **this house will be a ~ in 10 years** dentro de 10 años esta casa será una ruina; **they've made their house a ~** su casa es un desastre.
[2] ATTR: **~ area** barrio m bajo; **~ clearance programme** programa m de demolición y reconstrucción de los barrios pobres; **~ dwelling** tugurio m.
[3] VT: **to ~ it*** (esp Brit) vivir como pobres; vivir muy barato.
[4] VI: **to ~, to go ~ming** visitar los barrios bajos; investigar los bajos fondos sociales, conocer los lugares de la baja vida.
slumber ['slʌmbəʳ] [1] N (lit) sueño m; (fig) inactividad f, inercia f; **~s** sueño m; **my ~s were rudely interrupted** mis sueños fueron bruscamente interrumpidos.
[2] VI dormir; estar dormido; (fig) permanecer inactivo, estar inerte.
slumb(e)rous ['slʌmbərəs] ADJ soñoliento; (fig) inactivo, inerte.
slum-dweller ['slʌmˌdweləʳ] N barriobajero m, -a f.
slummy* ['slʌmɪ] ADJ muy pobre, sórdido.
slump [slʌmp] [1] N (economic) depresión f, declive m económico, retroceso m; **the 1929 ~** la depresión de 1929, la crisis económica de 1929; **~ in prices** hundimiento m de los precios; **the ~ in the price of copper** la baja repentina del precio del cobre; **~ in morale** bajón m en la moral.
[2] VI **(a)** (price etc) hundirse, bajar repentinamente; (production) bajar catastróficamente; (morale etc) sufrir un bajón, decaer gravemente.
(b) to ~ into a chair dejarse caer pesadamente en un sillón; **he was ~ed over the wheel** se había desplomado sobre el volante; **he was ~ed on the floor** estaba tumbado en el suelo.
slung [slʌŋ] PRET AND PTP of **sling**.
slunk [slʌŋk] PRET AND PTP of **slink**.
slur [slɜːʳ] [1] N **(a)** (stigma) borrón m, mancha f, nota f infamante; calumnia f; **to cast a ~ on sb** calumniar a uno, hacer un reparo (injustificado) a uno; **it is no ~ on him to say that ...** no es hacer un reparo a él decir que ... no es baldonarle a él decir que ...

(b) (*Mus*) ligado *m*.

2 VT (*also* **to ~ over**) pasar por alto de, omitir, suprimir; (*hide*) ocultar; *word* articular mal, *syllable* comerse; (*Mus*) ligar.

◆ **slur over** VT = **slur** 2.

slurp [slɜːp] 1 VT sorber.

2 VI sorber.

slurred [slɜːd] ADJ *speech* indistinto, poco correcto.

slurry [ˈslʌrɪ] N compuesto *m* acuoso; lodo *m* (*etc*) líquido; (*Agr*) estiércol *m* líquido.

slush [slʌʃ] 1 N **(a)** (*watery snow*) nieve *f* a medio derretir; (*mud*) fango *m*, lodo *m* (líquido).

(b) (*) sentimentalismo *m*, tonterías *fpl* sentimentales, cursilería *f*.

2 ATTR: **~ fund** caja *f* B, fondos *mpl* para sobornar.

slushy [ˈslʌʃɪ] ADJ **(a)** *snow* a medio derretir, casi líquido; *mud* casi líquido; *path etc* lleno de lodo, fangoso. **(b)** (*) sentimentaloide*, sensiblero, cursi.

slut [slʌt] N tía *f* guarra, marrana *f*.

sluttish [ˈslʌtɪʃ] ADJ puerco, desaliñado.

sly [slaɪ] 1 ADJ (*wily*) astuto; (*hypocritical*) taimado; (*secretive*) furtivo, disimulado, sigiloso; (*arch*) malicioso; (*bantering*) guasón; (*insinuating*) intencionado.

2 N: **on the ~** a hurtadillas; disimuladamente, sigilosamente.

slyboots [ˈslaɪˌbuːts] N SING taimado *m*, -a *f*.

slyly [ˈslaɪlɪ] ADV astutamente; furtivamente, disimuladamente, sigilosamente; maliciosamente; con intención.

slyness [ˈslaɪnɪs] N astucia *f*; lo taimado, carácter *m* taimado; disimulo *m*, sigilo *m*; malicia *f*; guasa *f*; intención *f*.

smack¹ [smæk] 1 N (*taste*) sabor *m*, saborcillo *m*, dejo *m* (*of* a).

2 VI tener un saborcillo un poco raro; saber mal; **to ~ of** saber a, tener un saborcillo a; (*fig, pej*) tener resabios de; oler a; **the whole thing ~s of bribery** el asunto entero huele a corrupción.

smack² [smæk] 1 N **(a)** (*slap*) manotada *f*, palmada *f*; (*blow, stroke*) golpe *m*; (*sound*) ruido *m* de un golpe, chasquido *m*; **it hit the wall with a great ~** dio ¡zas! contra la pared; **the ~ of firm government** la mano dura del gobierno resuelto; **it was a ~ in the eye for them*** (*esp Brit*) fue un golpe duro para ellos; **to give a child a ~** dar una manotada a un niño; **stop it or you'll get a ~** déjalo o te pego.

(b) (*esp Brit**) tentativa *f*; **I'll have a ~ at it** lo voy a tentar, probaré.

2 VT (*slap*) dar una manotada a, pegar (con la mano); **he ~ed it on to the table** dio con él ¡zas! en la mesa; **to ~ one's lips** relamerse, chuparse los labios.

3 ADV: **it fell ~ in the middle** cayó en el mismo centro; **he went ~ into a tree** dio de golpe contra un árbol, dio de lleno contra un árbol.

4 INTERJ ¡zas!

smack³ [smæk] N (*Naut*) queche *m*, barco *m* de pesca.

smack⁴ [smæk] N (*US*) heroína *f*.

smacker [ˈsmækəʳ] N **(a)** (*kiss*) beso *m* sonado; (*blow*) golpe *m* ruidoso. **(b)** (*Brit Fin*) libra *f*; (*US*) dólar *m*.

smacking [ˈsmækɪŋ] 1 ADJ: **at a ~ pace** a gran velocidad, muy rápidamente.

2 N zurra *f*, paliza *f*; **to give sb a ~** dar una paliza a uno.

small [smɔːl] 1 ADJ pequeño; chico; menudo; (*person*) pequeño, bajo (de estatura), chaparro (*Mex*); *stock, supply etc* escaso, corto, exiguo; (*lesser*) menor; (*unimportant*) insignificante; *voice* humilde; (*the idea of ~ is often expressed by a diminutive, eg*) **a ~ house** una casita, **a ~ book** un librillo; **I'm sorry it's so ~** siento que sea tan chiquito; **the fish here are very ~** aquí los peces son chiquitines; **~ ad*** (*Brit*) anuncio *m* breve; **~ business** negocio *m* pequeño; **~ capitals** (*Typ: also ~ caps*) versalitas *fpl*; **~ change** cambio *m*, calderilla *f*, sencillo *m* (*LAm*), feria *f* (*Mex*); **~ claims court** tribunal *m* de instancia (que se ocupa de asuntos menores); **he's just ~ fry** es un don nadie; **~ hours** altas horas *fpl*; **~ intestine** intestino *m* delgado; **~ investor** pequeño inversionista *m*, pequeño inversionista *f*; **~ letter** minúscula *f*; **~ print** letra *f* menuda; **the ~ screen** la pequeña pantalla; **with no ~ surprise** con no poca sorpresa; **~ trader** comerciante *mf* minorista; **to be in business in a ~ way** tener un negocio modesto; **we started in just a ~ way** empezamos a escala pequeña; **I do my best in my own ~ way** hago lo que puedo con mis modestos objetivos; **when we were ~** cuando éramos pequeños; **to be a ~ eater** comer poco; **to feel ~** sentirse humillado, tener vergüenza; **it made me feel pretty ~** me hizo sentirme poca cosa; **to make sb look ~** humillar a uno, dar vergüenza a uno; **this house makes the other one look ~** esta casa hace que la otra quede pequeña; **to make o.s. ~** achicarse, agacharse; **the ~er of the two** el menor (de los dos); **the Earth is 75 times ~er than Uranus** la Tierra es 75 veces menor que Urano.

2 N **(a)** **~ of the back** parte *f* más estrecha de la espalda.

(b) **~s** (*Brit**) paños *mpl* menores, ropa *f* interior, ropa *f* íntima (*LAm*).

small-arms [ˈsmɔːlˌɑːmz] NPL armas *fpl* cortas, armas *fpl* portátiles.

small-boned [ˌsmɔːlˈbəʊnd] ADJ de huesos pequeños.

small-bore [ˈsmɔːlˌbɔːʳ] ADJ de bajo calibre.

smallholder [ˈsmɔːlˌhəʊldəʳ] N (*Brit*) cultivador *m*, -ora *f* de una granja pequeña, minifundista *mf*.

smallholding [ˈsmɔːlˌhəʊldɪŋ] N (*Brit*) parcela *f*, granja *f* pequeña; minifundio *m*.

SMALL   *see also main entry*

Position of "pequeño"

● *Pequeño* usually follows the noun when making implicit or explicit comparison with something bigger:

He picked out a small melon
Escogió un melón pequeño
At that time, Madrid was a small city
En aquella época Madrid era una ciudad pequeña

● When used more subjectively with no attempt at comparison, *pequeño* usually precedes the noun:

But there's one small problem...
Pero existe un pequeño problema...
She lives in the little village of La Granada
Vive en el pequeño pueblo de La Granada
For further uses and examples, see main entry.

---

smallish [ˈsmɔːlɪʃ] ADJ más bien pequeño.

small-minded [ˌsmɔːlˈmaɪndɪd] ADJ de miras estrechas; mezquino.

small-mindedness [ˌsmɔːlˈmaɪndɪdnɪs] N estrechez *f* de miras; mezquindad *f*.

smallness [ˈsmɔːlnɪs] N (*V* **small**) pequeñez *f*, pequeño tamaño *m*, tamaño *m* reducido; escasez *f*; insignificancia *f*.

smallpox [ˈsmɔːlpɒks] N viruela *f*, viruelas *fpl*.

small-scale [ˈsmɔːlˈskeɪl] ADJ en pequeña escala.

small-talk [ˈsmɔːlˌtɔːk] N conversación *f* sin trascendencia, cháchara *f*, palique *m*; banalidades *fpl*; **she has no ~** no sabe hablar de trivialidades; **to swap ~ with sb** intercambiar banalidades con uno.

small-time [ˈsmɔːlˈtaɪm] ADJ de poca monta; de escasa importancia; en pequeña escala.

small-town [ˈsmɔːlˈtaʊn] ADJ pueblerino, provinciano.

SMALL TOWN

ℹ️ *EL término* **small town** *(ciudad pequeña) se usa en Estados Unidos para referirse a las localidades de menos de 10.000 habitantes. La palabra* **village** *(pueblo) no se suele usar por tener connotaciones del Viejo Continente o del Tercer Mundo. Los valores de estas ciudades pequeñas, que se ven como algo positivo, representan sobre todo la amabilidad, la honradez, la ayuda entre vecinos y el patriotismo, aunque a veces la expresión se usa en un sentido negativo, como por ejemplo cuando se habla de* **small-town attitudes** *(actitudes provincianas), haciendo referencia a las mentes estrechas o con prejuicios.*

---

smarm* [smɑːm] VT: **to ~ one's hair down** alisarse y fijarse el pelo.

smarmy* [ˈsmɑːmɪ] ADJ (*Brit*) cobista*; **he's a ~ sort** es un cobista*.

smart [smɑːt] 1 ADJ **(a)** (*elegant*) elegante; pulcro; (*not shabby*) aseado; *society* elegante, de buen tono; **that's a ~ car** qué coche más elegante; **in a ~ shop on Serrano** en una tienda elegante de Serrano; **you're looking very ~!** ¡qué elegante estás!, ¡qué guapo estás!

(b) (*bright*) listo, vivo, inteligente; *computer, missile etc* inteligente; (*pej*) ladino, astuto, cuco; **~ Alec(k)*, ~ ass** (*US*) sabelotodo*, *m*, listillo *m*; **~ card** tarjeta *f* electrónica, tarjeta *f* de cajero automático, tarjeta *f* inteligente; **~ money** dinero *m* en busca de utilidades excepcionales; dinero *m* del inversionista con información confidencial; **he's a ~ one** es un cuco; **he was too ~ for me** era muy listo para mí; **that's a ~ trick** es un truco hábil; **he thinks it's ~ to + infin** él se cree la mar de listo al + *infin*; **that was pretty ~ of you** listo fuiste.

(c) (*quick*) pronto, rápido, vivo; *pace* vivo; *attack etc* repentino; **that's ~ work** lo has hecho con toda rapidez; **~ work by the police led to ...** una pronta acción de parte de la policía condujo a ...; **and look ~ about it!** ¡y dáte prisa!, y ¡menearse!, ¡apúrate! (*LAm*).

2 N **(a)** escozor *m*; (*fig*) dolor *m*, resentimiento *m*.

(b) **~s** (*US**) picardía *f*.

3 VI **(a)** (*Med*) escocer, picar; **it makes my mouth ~** escuece en la boca; **my eyes are ~ing** me duelen los ojos; **it ~s for a few minutes** escuece durante algunos minutos.

(b) (*fig*) **to ~ under, to ~ with** sufrir bajo, resentirse de; **to ~ under criticism** resentirse de la crítica; **you shall ~ for this!** ¡me las pagarás!

smartarse [ˈsmɑːtɑːs], **smartass** [ˈsmɑːtæs] N sabelotodo* *mf*, listillo *m*, -a *f*; **smartass comments** comentarios de sabelotodo.

smarten [ˈsmɑːtn] = **smarten up**.

◆ **smarten up** 1 VT arreglar, mejorar el aspecto de; hermosear; **we'll ~ the house up for the summer** arreglaremos la casa para el verano.

2 VR: **to ~ o.s. up** arreglarse; mejorarse de aspecto; **I must go and ~ myself up** tengo que ir a arreglarme un poco; **she has ~ed herself**

up a lot in the last year durante el año pasado ha mejorado mucho de aspecto.

smartly ['smɑːtlɪ] ADV (*V adj*) **(a)** elegantemente; pulcramente, de modo distinguido; **she dresses very ~** viste con mucha elegancia. **(b)** inteligentemente; (*pej*) astutamente. **(c)** pronto, rápidamente; a paso vivo; de repente, repentinamente; **they marched him ~ off to the police station** le llevaron sin más a la comisaría.

smartness ['smɑːtnɪs] N (*V adj*) **(a)** elegancia *f;* pulcritud *f,* distinción *f;* aseo *m;* buen tono *m.* **(b)** viveza *f,* inteligencia *f;* (*pej*) astucia *f,* cuquería *f.* **(c)** viveza *f,* rapidez *f.*

smarty* ['smɑːtɪ] N sabelotodo* *m.*

smartypants* ['smɑːtɪpænts] N sabelotodo *mf,* listillo *m,* -a *f.*

smash [smæʃ] **1** N **(a)** (*collision, also* ~-**up**) choque *m* (violento), colisión *f,* encontronazo *m;* accidente *m;* (*breakage*) rotura *f,* quiebra *f* (*LAm*); (*noise of* ~) estruendo *m;* **he died in a car ~** murió en accidente de automóvil; **the 1969 rail ~** el accidente de ferrocarril de 1969. **(b)** (*Tennis etc*) smash *m,* mate *m.* **(c)** (*Fin*) quiebra *f,* crisis *f* económica; **the 1929 ~** la crisis de 1929. **2** ADJ (*) **~ hit** éxito *m* fulminante, exitazo *m;* **the ~ hit of 1920** el mayor éxito de 1920. **3** ADV: **to go ~ into sth** dar de lleno contra algo, dar violentamente contra algo. **4** VT (*break*) romper, quebrar (*esp LAm*); (*shatter*) hacer pedazos; (*annihilate*) destruir; *ball* golpear violentamente; *attack* desbaratar; *opponent* aplastar; *crime ring, conspiracy* deshacer, acabar con, descoyuntar; **when they ~ed the atom** cuando desintegraron el átomo; **he ~ed it against the wall** lo estrelló contra la pared; **the waves threatened to ~ the boat on the rocks** las olas amenazaban con estrellar el barco contra las rocas; **I've ~ed my watch** he estropeado mi reloj; **A ~ed his fist into B's face** A dio a B un puñetazo violento en la cara. **5** VI (*break*) romperse; hacerse pedazos, quebrarse (*esp LAm*); estropearse; (*collide*) chocar (*against, into* con, contra), estrellarse (*against, into* contra); (*Fin*) quebrar.

♦ **smash down** VT *door etc* romper.
♦ **smash in** VT *door etc* romper; **I'll ~ your face in** te rompo la cara.
♦ **smash up** VT *car* hacer pedazos; *room* destrozar; **he was all ~ed up in the accident** sufrió grandes lesiones en el accidente.

smash-and-grab raid ['smæʃən'græb,reɪd] N robo *m* relámpago (*con rotura de escaparate; en joyería etc*).

smashed [smæʃt] ADJ (*drunk*) colocado;* (*drugged*) flipado;*.

smasher ['smæʃəʳ] N (*esp Brit*) cosa *f* estupenda, (*esp girl*) bombón* *m,* guayabo* *m;* **it's a ~!** ¡es estupendo!

smashing* ['smæʃɪŋ] ADJ (*esp Brit*) imponente*, bárbaro*, pistonudo*; **a ~ dress** un vestido monísimo; **we had a ~ time** lo pasamos en grande*; **isn't it ~?** ¿es estupendo, no?

smash-up ['smæʃʌp] N choque *m* violento, colisión *f* violenta, accidente *m.*

smattering ['smætərɪŋ] N conocimientos *mpl* elementales, conocimiento *m* superficial, nociones *fpl;* **I have a ~ of Catalan** tengo algunas nociones de catalán.

smear [smɪəʳ] **1** N mancha *f;* (*fig*) calumnia *f,* mancha *f;* (*Med*) frotis *m.* **2** ATTR: **~ campaign** campaña *f* denigratoria, campaña *f* de desprestigio; **~ tactics** tácticas *fpl* de difamación; **~ test** citología *f,* análisis *m* citológico. **3** VT **(a)** manchar (*with* de), untar (*with* de); **to ~ one's face with blood** untarse la cara de sangre; **to ~ wet paint** manchar la pintura fresca. **(b)** (*fig*) calumniar, difamar; desprestigiar; **to ~ sb as a traitor** tachar a uno de traidor; **to ~ sb because of his past** tachar a uno por su pasado. **(c)** (*US**) derrotar sin esfuerzo. **4** VI mancharse.

smell [smel] **1** N **(a)** (*sense of* ~) olfato *m;* **to have a keen sense of ~** tener buen olfato. **(b)** (*odour*) olor *m* (*of a*); **bad ~** mal olor *m,* hedor *m;* **it has a nice ~** tiene un olor agradable. **(c)** **let's have a ~** déjame olerlo. **2** (*irr*: PRET AND PTP **smelled** *or* **smelt**) VT oler; *danger, difficulty etc* percibir, presentir; (*esp of animals*) olfatear. **3** VI **(a)** oler (*of a*); **it ~s good** huele bien; **it ~s bad** huele mal, tiene mal olor; **that flower doesn't ~** esa flor no tiene olor; **it's a gas which doesn't ~** es un gas inodoro; **it ~s damp in here** aquí dentro huele a húmedo. **(b)** **since the accident he cannot ~** después del accidente no tiene olfato; **the dog ~ed at my shoes** el perro olfateó mis zapatos.

♦ **smell out** VT **(a)** (*find by scent*) olfatear, husmear; (*identify*) identificar, descubrir. **(b)** (*cause to smell*) apestar; **it's ~ing the room out** hace

oler mal todo el cuarto, apesta el cuarto.

smelliness ['smelɪnɪs] N hediondez *f.*

smelling-bottle ['smelɪŋ,bɒtl] N frasco *m* de sales.

smelling-salts ['smelɪŋsɔːlts] NPL sales *fpl* (aromáticas).

smelly ['smelɪ] ADJ que huele mal, de mal olor, apestoso, hediondo; **it's ~ in here** aquí dentro huele (mal).

smelt¹ [smelt] PRET AND PTP *of* **smell.**

smelt² [smelt] VT fundir.

smelt³ [smelt] N (*Fish*) eperlano *m.*

smelter ['smeltəʳ] N horno *m* de fundición.

smelting ['smeltɪŋ] **1** N fundición *f.* **2** ATTR: **~ furnace** horno *m* de fundición.

smidgen*, smidgin* ['smɪdʒən] N: **a ~ of** un poquito de, un poquitín de, una pizca de; (*of truth*) una pizca de.

smile [smaɪl] **1** N sonrisa *f;* **with a ~ on one's lips** con una sonrisa en los labios; **a face wreathed in ~s** una cara con una sonrisa radiante; **to give sb a ~** sonreír a uno; **come on, give me a ~!** ¡vamos, una sonrisa!; **to knock the ~ off sb's face** quitarle a uno las ganas de sonreír; **to raise a ~** forzar una sonrisa; **can't you even raise a ~?** ¿no sonríes siquiera? **2** VT *emotion* expresar con una sonrisa; **she ~d her thanks** dio las gracias con una sonrisa; **to ~ a bitter ~** sonreír amargamente. **3** VI sonreír, sonreírse (*at* de); **to keep smiling** seguir con la sonrisa en los labios; **to ~ at danger** reírse del peligro; **fortune ~d on him** le favoreció la fortuna; **if she ~s on me** si me mira con buenos ojos.

smiley ['smaɪlɪ] **1** ADJ **(a)** *face, eyes* sonriente, risueño; *person* sonriente, jovial. **(b)** *badge, symbol, e-mail* smiley. **2** N (*in e-mail etc*) smiley *m.*

smiling ['smaɪlɪŋ] ADJ sonriente, risueño.

smilingly ['smaɪlɪŋlɪ] ADV sonriendo, con cara risueña, con una sonrisa.

smirch [smɜːtʃ] VT (*liter*) mancillar, desdorar.

smirk [smɜːk] **1** N sonrisa *f* satisfecha; sonrisa *f* afectada. **2** VI sonreírse satisfecho; sonreírse afectadamente.

smirkingly ['smɜːkɪŋlɪ] ADV con una sonrisa satisfecha (*or* afectada).

smite [smaɪt] (*irr*: PRET **smote**, PTP **smitten**) VT (*liter*) (*strike*) golpear; (*punish*) castigar; (*pain*) doler, afligir; (*of light, sound etc*) herir; **an idea smote me** se me ocurrió una idea; **my conscience smote me** me remordió la conciencia; **he smote the ball hard** golpeó la pelota duro; *V also* **smitten.**

smith [smɪθ] N herrero *m.*

smithereens ['smɪðə'riːnz] NPL: **to smash sth to ~** hacer algo añicos; **it was in ~** estaba hecho añicos.

┌─ **SMITHSONIAN INSTITUTION** ─┐

*La **Smithsonian Institution**, en Washington DC, es el complejo de museos más grande del mundo. Fue fundado por el Congreso en 1846 gracias a fondos donados por el científico inglés James Smithson (de ahí su nombre) y en la actualidad está patrocinado por el gobierno estadounidense como centro para la ciencia y el arte. Posee alrededor de cien millones de piezas y catorce museos, que incluyen el **National Museum of American History**, la **National Gallery of Art** y el **National Portrait Gallery**. También cuenta con un zoológico y lleva a cabo labores de investigación. A esta institución se la conoce como **the nation's attic** (la buhardilla de la nación).*

smithy ['smɪðɪ] N herrería *f.*

smitten ['smɪtn] PTP *of* **smite**; **to be ~ with the plague** sufrir el azote de la peste, ser afligido por la peste; **to be ~ with an idea** entusiasmarse por una idea; **to be ~ with sb** estar chalado por uno; **I was ~ by the urge to** + infin me entraron deseos vehementes de + infin.

smock [smɒk] **1** N (*artist's, labourer's*) blusa *f;* (*child's*) delantal *m;* (*expectant mother's*) bata *f* corta, tontón *m;* (*US: overall*) guardapolvo *m.* **2** VT fruncir, adornar con frunces.

smocking ['smɒkɪŋ] N adorno *m* de frunces.

smog [smɒg] N niebla *f* con humo, calina *f;* niebla *f* tóxica.

smoggy ['smɒgɪ] ADJ *city* envuelto de niebla tóxica; *sky* cubierto de niebla tóxica; *air* cargado con niebla tóxica.

smoke [sməʊk] **1** N **(a)** humo *m;* **the S~;** (*Brit*) Londres; **there's no ~ without fire** cuando el río suena agua lleva, lo que hace humo es porque está ardiendo; **to go up in ~** (*building etc*) quedar destruido en un incendio, quemarse totalmente; (*: *person*) subirse por las paredes*; (*plans*) fracasar, quedar en agua de borrajas; **his fortune went up in ~** su fortuna se hizo humo. **(b)** (*cigarette etc*) pitillo *m,* tabaco *m,* cigarro *m* (*LAm*); **to have a ~** echar un pitillo, fumar un cigarrillo; **I like to have a ~ after meals** me gusta fumar después de comer; **will you have a ~?** ¿quieres fumar?; **I've no ~;** no tengo tabaco. **2** VT *tobacco* fumar; *bacon, glass etc* ahumar; **he ~s a pipe** fuma en pipa; **he's smoking his pipe** está fumando su pipa. **3** VI **(a)** (*chimney etc*) humear, echar humo. **(b)** (*smoker*) fumar; (*esp US**) fumar marijuana; **do you ~?** ¿fuma

Vd?; **will you ~?** ¿quieres fumar?; **do you mind if I ~?** ¿te molesta que fume?; **he ~s like a chimney** fuma como un carretero.
◆**smoke out** VT: **to ~ insects out** ahuyentar insectos con humo; **to ~ a gang out** hacer que salga una pandilla de su escondite pegándole fuego; **to ~ out a beehive** ahumar una colmena; **that lamp is smoking the room out** esa lámpara está llenando el cuarto de humo.
smoke-bomb ['sməʊkbɒm] N bomba f de humo, granada f de humo.
smoked [sməʊkt] ADJ *bacon, glass etc* ahumado.
smoke-detector ['sməʊkdɪ,tektəʳ] N detector m de humo.
smoke-dried ['sməʊkdraɪd] ADJ ahumado, curado al humo.
smoke-filled ['sməʊkfɪld] ADJ lleno de humo.
smokehood ['sməʊkhʊd] N capucha f antihumo.
smokeless ['sməʊklɪs] ADJ sin humo; **~ fuel** combustible m sin humo; **~ zone** zona f libre de humo.
smoker ['sməʊkəʳ] N **(a)** (*person*) fumador m, -ora f; **~'s cough** tos f de fumador; **I'm not a ~** no fumo; **to be a heavy ~** fumar mucho. **(b)** (*Rail*) coche m fumador.
smoke ring ['sməʊkrɪŋ] N anillo m de humo; **to blow a ~** hacer una "o", hacer un anillo de humo.
smokescreen ['sməʊkskriːn] N (*also fig*) cortina f de humo; **to put up a ~** (*fig*) entenebrecer un asunto, enmarañar un asunto (para despistar a la gente).
smoke shop ['sməʊkʃɒp] N (*US*) estanco m, tabaquería f.
smokesignal ['sməʊk,sɪgnl] N ahumada f.
smokestack ['sməʊkstæk] N chimenea f; **~ industries** industrias fpl con chimeneas.
smokey ['sməʊkɪ] = smoky.
smoking ['sməʊkɪŋ] **1** ADJ humeante, que humea.
2 N el humar; **~ is bad for you** el fumar te hace daño; **'no ~'** 'se prohíbe fumar'; **no ~ area** zona f de no fumar; **to give up ~** dejar de fumar.
3 ATTR de fumar; de (*or* para) fumador; **~ compartment**, (*US*) **~ car** departamento m de fumadores, coche m fumador; **~ jacket** chaqueta f casera, medio batín m; **~ room** salón m de fumar.
smoky ['sməʊkɪ] ADJ *chimney, fire* humeante, que humea; *room* lleno de humo; *flavour, surface etc* ahumado; **it's ~ in here** aquí hay mucho humo.
smolder ['sməʊldəʳ] VI (*US*) = smoulder.
smooch* [smuːtʃ] VI besuquearse, manosearse, acariciarse, abrazarse amorosamente.
smoochy* ['smuːtʃɪ] ADJ *record etc* sentimental; erótico.
smooth [smuːð] **1** ADJ **(a)** *surface* liso, terso; suave; llano, igual, uniforme, parejo (*LAm*); *skin etc* liso, suave; *brow* sin arrugas; *sea* tranquilo, en calma.
(b) (*in consistency*) *paste etc* liso, sin grumos; *running of engine, take-off etc* suave; *voice* suave; *style* fluido, suave; *passage, trip* tranquilo, sin novedad; *person's manner* afable.
(c) *person* afable, culto; (*pej*) zalamero, meloso; **he's a ~ operator** es muy persuasivo; **he's a ~ talker** tiene pico de oro.
2 VT *hair etc* alisar; *surface* allanar, igualar; *dress etc* arreglar; *wood* desbastar; *style etc* suavizar; **to ~ the way** (*or* **path**) **for sb** allanar el camino a uno, preparar el terreno para uno.
◆**smooth away** VT = smooth over.
◆**smooth back** VT *hair* peinarse hacia atrás, alisarse; *sheet* estirar, alisar.
◆**smooth down** VT *hair etc* alisar; *surface* allanar, igualar; *wood* desbastar; **to ~ sb down** calmar a uno, apaciguar a uno.
◆**smooth out** VT *dress* arreglar.
◆**smooth over** VT: **to ~ over difficulties** allanar dificultades, zanjar dificultades.
smooth-chinned ['smuːð'tʃɪnd] ADJ, **smooth-faced** ['smuːð'feɪst] ADJ barbilampiño; bien afeitado; **some ~ youth** algún joven imberbe.
smoothie* ['smuːðɪ] N zalamero m; lameculos* m.
smoothing-iron ['smuːðɪŋ,aɪən] N plancha f.
smoothly ['smuːðlɪ] ADV (*V adj*) **(a)** lisamente; suavemente; de modo uniforme; tranquilamente; **everything went ~** todo fue sobre ruedas, todo fue viento en popa. **(b)** afablemente; **he said ~** dijo sin alterarse.
smoothness ['smuːðnɪs] N (*V adj*) lisura f, tersura f; suavidad f; igualdad f, uniformidad f; tranquilidad f, calma f; fluidez f; afabilidad f; (*pej*) zalamería f.
smooth-running ['smuːð'rʌnɪŋ] ADJ *engine etc* que funciona bien.
smooth-shaven ['smuːð'ʃeɪvn] ADJ apurado.
smooth-spoken ['smuːð'spəʊkən] ADJ, **smooth-talking** ['smuːð'tɔːkɪŋ] ADJ afable; (*pej*) zalamero, meloso.
smooth-tongued ['smuːð'tʌŋd] ADJ zalamero, meloso.
smorgasbord ['smɔːgəs,bɔːd] N smorgasbord m; ambigú m escandinavo.
smote [sməʊt] PRET *of* smite.
smother ['smʌðəʳ] **1** VT (*stifle*) ahogar, sofocar, asfixiar; *fire* apagar; *yawn* contener; *criticism, doubt etc* ahogar, suprimir; **fruit ~ed in**

cream fruta f cubierta de crema; **a book ~ed in dust** un libro cubierto de polvo; **the child was ~ed in dirt** el niño estaba todo sucio; **she ~ed the child with kisses** cubrió al nino de besos.
2 VI ahogarse, sofocarse.
smoulder, (*US*) **smolder** ['sməʊldəʳ] VI arder sin llama, arder lentamente; (*fig: hatred etc*) estar latente, estar sin apagarse.
smouldering, (*US*) **smoldering** ['sməʊldərɪŋ] ADJ que arde lentamente; (*fig*) latente; **she gave me a ~ look** me miró provocativa.
smudge [smʌdʒ] **1** N mancha f, tiznón m.
2 VT manchar; tiznar (*with* de).
3 VI mancharse.
smudgy ['smʌdʒɪ] ADJ manchado; lleno de manchas; *writing etc* borroso.
smug [smʌg] ADJ pagado de sí (mismo), suficiente; presumido; **he said with ~ satisfaction** dijo muy pagado de sí; **don't be so ~!** ¡no presumas!
smuggle ['smʌgl] **1** VT pasar (de contrabando); **~d goods** géneros mpl de contrabando; **to ~ goods in** introducir artículos de contrabando; **to ~ sth past** (*or* **through**) **the customs** pasar algo por la aduana sin declararlo; **to ~ sb out in disguise** pasar a uno disfrazado.
2 VI hacer contrabando, dedicarse a pasar cosas de contrabando.
smuggler ['smʌgləʳ] N contrabandista mf.
smuggling ['smʌglɪŋ] **1** N contrabando m.
2 ATTR: **~ ring** red f de contrabando, red f de contrabandistas.
smugness ['smʌgnɪs] N satisfacción f de sí (mismo), suficiencia f; presunción f.
smut [smʌt] N **(a)** (*piece of dirt*) tizne m; (*in eye*) mota f de carbonilla; (*on paper*) tiznón m, mancha f. **(b)** (*Bot*) tizón m. **(c)** (*fig*) obscenidades fpl, cosas fpl verdes; **to talk ~** contar cosas verdes.
smuttiness ['smʌtɪnɪs] N (*fig*) obscenidad f.
smutty ['smʌtɪ] ADJ **(a)** tiznado. **(b)** (*Bot*) atizonado. **(c)** (*fig*) obsceno, verde; **a lot of ~ talk** muchos cuentos verdes.
Smyrna ['smɜːnə] N Esmirna f.
snack [snæk] N bocadillo m, tentempié m, piscolabis m; **to have a ~** tomar un bocadillo, comer algo.
snackbar ['snækbɑːʳ] N cafetería f, bar m, lonchería f (*LAm*).
snaffle¹ ['snæfl] N bridón m.
snaffle²* ['snæfl] VT (*Brit*) afanar*, birlar*.
snag [snæg] **1** N **(a)** (*in wood*) nudo m; (*of tree*) tocón m; (*of tooth*) raigón m.
(b) (*fig*) dificultad f, obstáculo m, estorbo m, pega f; **there's a ~** hay una dificultad; **the ~ is that ...** la dificultad es que ...; **that's the ~** ahí está el problema; **what's the ~?** ¿qué obstáculo hay?; **to hit** (*or* **run into**) **a ~** encontrar una pega, tropezar con una dificultad.
2 VT enganchar, coger (*on* en).
3 VI engancharse, quedar cogido (*on* en).
snail [sneɪl] **1** N caracol m; **at a ~'s pace** a paso de tortuga.
2 ATTR: **~ shell** concha f de caracol.
snail mail ['sneɪlmeɪl] N (*Comput: hum*) correo m no electrónico.
snake [sneɪk] **1** N culebra f, víbora f; **the** (**European Monetary**) **S~** la Serpiente; **he's the ~ in the grass** él es el traidor, él es el enemigo oculto, él es el peligro oculto; **~s and ladders** juego m de escaleras y serpientes.
2 VI: **a hand ~d out of the curtain** una mano se deslizó de la cortina.
◆**snake about, snake along** VI serpentear.
snakebite ['sneɪkbaɪt] N mordedura f de serpiente.
snake-charmer ['sneɪk,tʃɑːməʳ] N encantador m de serpientes.
snakepit ['sneɪkpɪt] N nido m de serpientes.
snakeskin ['sneɪkskɪn] N piel f de serpiente.
snaky ['sneɪkɪ] ADJ serpentino, tortuoso.
snap [snæp] **1** N **(a)** (*sound: of fingers*) castañetazo m; (*of whip etc*) chasquido m; (*report*) estallido m; (*click*) golpe m seco, ruido m seco; **it shut with a ~** se cerró de golpe, se cerró con un ruido seco.
(b) **cold ~** ola f de frío, período m breve de frío.
(c) (*) vigor m, energía f; **put some ~ into it!** ¡menearse!
(d) (*US: fastener*) automático m, clec m.
(e) (*Phot*) foto f, instantánea f; **to take a ~ of sb** tomar una foto de uno; **these are our holiday ~s** éstas son las fotos de nuestras vacaciones.
(f) **it's a ~** (*US**) eso está tirado*, es muy fácil.
2 ADJ repentino; **~ answer** respuesta f sin pensar, respuesta f instantánea; **~ decision** decisión f tomada de repente; **~ judgement** juicio m instantáneo; **~ vote** votación f improvista.
3 ADV: **~!** ¡crac!; **to go ~** hacer crac.
4 EXCL ¡lo mismo!; ¡yo también!
5 VT **(a)** *fingers* castañetear (*see also* **finger**); *whip* chasquear; **to ~ a box shut** cerrar una caja de golpe; **to ~ sth into place** colocar algo con un golpe seco.
(b) (*break*) romper, quebrar, hacer saltar.

(c) (*Phot*) **to ~ sb** tomar una foto de uno.

6 VI **(a)** **to ~ at sb** (*dog*) querer morder a uno, tratar de morder a uno; (*person*) contestar (*or* hablar *etc*) bruscamente (*or* con brusquedad) a uno; **don't ~ at me!** ¡habla con más educación!

(b) (*whip etc*) chasquear; (*fastener etc*) hacer un ruido seco; **it ~ped shut** se cerró de golpe.

(c) (*break*) romperse, quebrarse; separarse, desprenderse; saltar.

(d) **she ~ped into action** echó a trabajar (*etc*) en seguida.

◆ **snap back** VI: **to ~ back at sb** contestar (*or* hablar *etc*) bruscamente a uno.

◆ **snap off** 1 VT romper, separar; (*dog etc*) morder y separar, separar con los dientes; **to ~ sb's head off** echar un rapapolvo a uno; interrumpir bruscamente a uno.

2 VI: **it ~ped off** se desprendió, se partió.

◆ **snap out** 1 VT: **to ~ out an order** espetar una orden.

2 VI (*) **to ~ out of sth** dejarse de algo, quitarse algo de encima; **~ out of it!** ¡déjate de eso!, ¡ánimo!

◆ **snap up** VT: **to ~ up a bargain** lanzarse sobre un saldo, agarrarse de una ganga; **our stock was ~ped up at once** nuestras existencias quedaron agotadas al instante.

snapdragon ['snæp.drægən] N dragón *m*, boca *f* de dragón.

snap fastener ['snæp'fɑːsnəʳ] N (*US*) automático *m*, clec *m*.

snappish ['snæpɪʃ] ADJ brusco, abrupto; irritable.

snappishness ['snæpɪʃnɪs] N brusquedad *f*; irritabilidad *f*.

snappy* ['snæpɪ] ADJ **(a)** (*quick*) rápido, (*energetic*) enérgico, vigoroso; *answer* instantáneo; *slogan* conciso; **to be ~ about sth** hacer algo con toda rapidez; **and be ~ about it!** ¡y date prisa!; **make it ~!** ¡rápido! **(b)** (*smart*) elegante; **he's a ~ dresser** se viste con elegancia.

snapshot ['snæpʃɒt] N foto *f*, instantánea *f*.

snare [snɛəʳ] 1 N lazo *m*, trampa *f*; (*fig*) trampa *f*, engaño *m*; **it's a ~ and delusion** es una pura trampa.

2 VT coger (*LAm*: agarrar) con trampas; (*fig*) hacer caer en el lazo, engañar.

snare drum ['snɛədrʌm] N tambor *m* militar pequeño.

snarl[1] [snɑːl] 1 N gruñido *m*; **he said with a ~** dijo gruñendo.

2 VT gruñir, decir gruñendo.

3 VI gruñir; **to ~ at sb** decir algo a uno gruñendo.

snarl[2] [snɑːl] 1 VT (*also* **to ~ up**) enmarañar, enredar; **it's got all ~ed up** ha quedado en la mayor confusión; **the traffic was all ~ed up** la circulación quedó bloqueada.

2 VI (*also* **to ~ up**) enmarañarse, enredarse.

◆ **snarl up** VT, VI = **snarl 1, 2.**

snarl-up ['snɑːlʌp] N **(a)** (*Aut etc*) congestión *f*, embotellamiento *m*; bloque *m*. **(b)** lío *m*; caos *m*, confusión *f*.

snatch [snætʃ] 1 N **(a)** (*act*) arrebatamiento *m*; (*Weight-lifting*) arrancada *f*; **~ squad** unidad *f* de arresto; **to make a ~ at sth** tratar de arrebatar algo.

(b) (*: robbery*) robo *m*; (*of handbag*) tirón *m* (de bolso); (*kidnapping*) secuestro *m*; **jewellery ~** robo *m* de joyas.

(c) (*Mus etc*) trocito *m*; **to whistle ~es of Mozart** silbar trocitos de Mozart.

(d) (*US⁑*) coño⁑ *m*.

2 VT **(a)** (*pick up*) asir, coger, agarrar; (*from sb's hold*) arrebatar (*from* a); (*out of the air*) coger al vuelo; **to ~ a meal** comer algo a toda prisa; **to ~ an opportunity** asir una ocasión; **to ~ an hour of happiness** procurarse (*a pesar de todo*) una hora de felicidad.

(b) (*: steal*) robar, (*kidnap*) secuestrar.

3 VI: **don't ~!** ¡no arrebates las cosas!; **to ~ at sth** tratar de arrebatar algo; tratar de coger algo al vuelo; **to ~ at an opportunity** agarrar una ocasión al vuelo.

◆ **snatch away** VT: **to ~ sth away** arrebatar algo (*from* a).

◆ **snatch up** VT agarrar; **to ~ up a knife** asir un cuchillo; **to ~ up a child** coger a un niño en brazos.

snatchy* ['snætʃɪ] ADJ *work* irregular, intermitente; *conversation* intermitente, inconexo.

snazzy⁑ ['snæzɪ] ADJ: **a ~ dress** un vestido de lo más elegante.

sneak [sniːk] 1 N soplón* *m*, -ona *f*; (*Brit*) acusón* *m*, -ona *f*.

2 ADJ furtivo; imprevisto; **~ preview** anticipo *m* no autorizado; **~ visit** visita *f* furtiva.

3 VT **(a)** (*steal*) robar a hurtadillas, afanar, birlar.

(b) **to ~ a look at sth** ver algo de tapadillo; **I managed to ~ one in** logré meter uno sin ser visto.

4 VI **(a)** **to ~ about** ir a hurtadillas, moverse furtivamente; **to ~ away, to ~ off** largarse a hurtadillas*; **to ~ in** entrar a hurtadillas, entrar sin ser visto.

(b) **to ~ on sb*** (*Brit*) soplarse de uno*; **to ~ to the teacher** soplarse al profesor*.

◆ **sneak away, sneak off** VI escabullirse; **to ~ off with sth** alzarse con algo.

sneakers* ['sniːkəz] NPL zapatos *mpl* de lona, deportivos *mpl*, zapatillas *fpl*.

sneaking ['sniːkɪŋ] ADJ *manner* furtivo, sigiloso; **to have a ~ regard for sb** respetar a uno a pesar de todo, respetar a uno sin querer confesarlo abiertamente.

sneak-thief ['sniːkθiːf] N, PL **sneak-thieves** ['sniːkθiːvz] ratero *m*, garduño *m*.

sneaky ['sniːkɪ] ADJ *manner* furtivo, sigiloso; (*of character*) soplón *m*.

sneer [snɪəʳ] 1 N (*expression*) visaje *m* de burla y desprecio, sonrisa *f* de sarcasmo; (*remark*) burla *f*, mofa *f*; comentario *m* despreciativo; **he said with a ~** dijo con desprecio; **the book is full of ~s about ...** el libro se mofa constantemente de ...

2 VI hacer un visaje de burla y desprecio; **to ~ at sb** mofarse de uno, hablar con desprecio de uno.

sneerer ['snɪərəʳ] N mofador *m*, -ora *f*.

sneering ['snɪərɪŋ] ADJ *tone etc* burlador y despreciativo, lleno de desprecio.

sneeringly ['snɪərɪŋlɪ] ADV en tono burlador y despreciativo; con una sonrisa de desprecio.

sneeze [sniːz] 1 N estornudo *m*.

2 VI estornudar; **an offer not to be ~d at** una oferta que no es de despreciar.

snick [snɪk] 1 N **(a)** (*cut*) corte *m*, tijeretada *f*.

(b) (*Sport*) toque *m* ligero.

2 VT **(a)** (*cut*) cortar (un poco), tijeretear; **to ~ sth off** cortar algo con un movimiento rápido.

(b) *ball* desviar ligeramente.

snicker ['snɪkəʳ] = **snigger**.

snide [snaɪd] ADJ despreciativo, sarcástico.

sniff [snɪf] 1 N sorbo *m* por las narices; inhalación *f*; (*of dog etc*) husmeo *m*; **to go out for a ~ of air** salir a tomar el fresco; **we never got a ~ of the vodka*** no llegamos siquiera a oler la vodka*; **one ~ of that would kill you** una inhalación de eso te mataría.

2 VT sorber por las narices; inhalar; *glue etc* esnifar, inhalar; (*of dog etc, also* **to ~ out**) husmear, olfatear; **just ~ these flowers** huele un poco estas flores; **you can ~ the sea air here** aquí se huele ese aire de mar; **~ the gas deeply** aspire profundamente el gas.

3 VI **(a)** (*person*) sorber por las narices; inhalar; **to ~ at** oler; **don't ~!** ¡no hagas ese ruido con las narices!

(b) (*dog etc*) oler, husmear, olfatear; **the dog ~ed at my shoes** el perro olió mis zapatos.

(c) **to ~ at sth** (*fig*) despreciar algo, tratar algo con desdén; **an offer not to be ~ed at** una oferta que no es de despreciar.

◆ **sniff out*** VT **(a)** *explosives, drugs* detectar (con el olfato); **a police dog, trained to ~ explosives** un perro policía, entrenado para detectar explosivos. **(b)** (*fig*) olerse; **the reporter who sniffs out the truth** el reportero que se huele la verdad.

sniffer ['snɪfəʳ] ADJ: **~ dog** (*drugs*) perro *m* antidroga; (*explosives*) perro *m* antiexplosivos.

sniffle ['snɪfl] 1 N: **to have the ~s** hacer ruido con las narices; estar un poco acatarrado.

2 VI = **1.**

sniffy* ['snɪfɪ] ADJ estirado, desdeñoso; **he was pretty ~ about it** trató el asunto con bastante desdén.

snifter ['snɪftəʳ] N **(a)** (*) trago *m*. **(b)** (*US*) copita *f* para coñac.

snigger ['snɪgəʳ] 1 N risa *f* disimulada.

2 VI reírse con disimulo (*at* de).

sniggering ['snɪgərɪŋ] 1 N risitas *fpl*, cachondeo* *m*.

2 ADJ que se ríe tontamente.

snip [snɪp] 1 N **(a)** (*cut*) tijeretada *f*, tijeretazo *m*; (*incision*) tijeretada *f*; (*piece of material etc*) recorte *m*; **to have the ~*** esterilizarse.

(b) (*Brit*) ganga *f*.

2 VT tijeretear.

◆ **snip off** VT recortar.

snipe [snaɪp] 1 N (*Orn*) agachadiza *f*, becacina *f*.

2 VI: **to ~ at sb** tirar a uno desde un escondite; **to ~ from the shelter of ...** tirar desde la protección de ...; **to ~ at one's critics** contestar (con precaución) a los críticos de uno; **he was really sniping at the Minister** en realidad sus ataques iban dirigidos contra el Ministro.

sniper ['snaɪpəʳ] N tirador *m* escondido, francotirador *m*.

snippet ['snɪpɪt] N (*of cloth*) retazo *m*, retal *m*; (*of information etc*) retazo *m*; **~s** retazos *mpl*; **'S~s'** (*heading in press etc*) 'Breverías'.

snitch⁑ [snɪtʃ] 1 N (*nose*) napias⁑ *fpl*; (*informer*) soplón* *m*, -ona *f*.

2 VT birlar*.

3 VI soplarse* (*on sb* de uno).

snivel ['snɪvl] VI lloriquear.

sniveller ['snɪvləʳ], (*US*) **sniveler** N quejica* *mf*.

snivelling ['snɪvlɪŋ], (*US*) **sniveling** 1 ADJ llorón.

2 N lloriqueo *m*.

snob [snɒb] N (e)snob *mf*.

snobbery ['snɒbərɪ] N (e)snobismo *m*.

snobbish ['snɒbɪʃ] ADJ (e)snob.

snobbishness ['snɒbɪʃnɪs] N (e)snobismo *m*.

snobby* ['snɒbɪ] ADJ (e)snob.

snog‡ [snɒg] [1] N: **to have a ~ = 2.**
[2] VI sobarse, besuquearse*.

snood [snu:d] N (*band*) cintillo *m*; (*net*) redecilla *f*.

snook* [snu:k] N: **to cock a ~ at sb** hacer burla de uno con la mano; (*fig*) dejar a uno con un palmo de narices; mofarse abiertamente de uno.

snooker ['snu:kə^r] [1] N (*Brit*) snooker *m*.
[2] VT (*) **to ~ sb** (*US*) poner a uno en un aprieto; **now we're properly ~ed** (*Brit*) ahora no hay nada que hacer, en buen lío nos hemos metido*.

snoop* [snu:p] [1] N (a) (*person*) fisgón *m*, -ona *f*; **he's a regular ~** (*US*) es un cuzo*.
(b) (*act*) **I'll have a ~ round** voy a reconocer el terreno; **I had a ~ round the kitchen** fui fisgando por la cocina, estuve husmeando por la cocina.
[2] VI (*also* **to ~ about, to ~ around**) curiosear, fisgonear; practicar un registro furtivo, hacer una investigación furtiva; **he comes ~ing around here** viene aquí a fisgonear.

snooper* ['snu:pə^r] N (*official*) investigador *m* (*or* inspector *m*) encubierto, investigadora *f* (*or* inspectora *f*) encubierta; (*nosey person*) fisgón *m*, -ona *f*; (*spy*) espía *mf*.

snooty* ['snu:tɪ] ADJ fachendoso*, presumido; **people hereabouts are very ~** por aquí la gente se da mucho tono; **there's no call to be ~ about it** Vd no tiene motivo para presumir.

snooze* [snu:z] [1] N siestecita *f*, sueñecillo *m*; **to have a ~ = 2.**
[2] VI dormitar, echar una siestecita.

snore [snɔ:^r] [1] N ronquido *m*.
[2] VI roncar.

snorer ['snɔ:rə^r] N persona *f* que ronca mucho.

snoring ['snɔ:rɪŋ] N ronquidos *mpl*.

snorkel ['snɔ:kl] [1] N tubo *m* snorkel, esnórquel *m*, tubo *m* de respiración.
[2] VI nadar respirando por un tubo.

snort [snɔ:t] [1] N (a) bufido *m*; **with a ~ of rage** con un bufido de enojo. (b) (‡) (*drink*) trago *m*; (*drug*) esnife* *m*.
[2] VT (a) bufar; **'No!' he ~ed** '¡No!' dijo bufando. (b) (*Drugs‡*) inhalar, esnifar*.
[3] VI esnifar*.

snorter‡ ['snɔ:tə^r] N (a) **a real ~ of a song** una canción estupenda*; **a ~ of a question** una pregunta dificilísima; **it was a ~ of a game** fue un partido maravilloso. (b) (‡) **= snort 1 (b).**

snot* [snɒt] (a) N (*mucus*) mocarro *m*. (b) (*person*) mocoso *m*, -a *f* insolente*.

snotty* ['snɒtɪ] ADJ (a) mocoso. (b) (*fig*) (*snooty*) fachendoso*, presumido; (*angry*) enojado.

snotty-faced* ['snɒtɪˌfeɪst] ADJ mocoso.

snotty-nosed* ['snɒtɪˌnəʊzd] ADJ (a) (*lit*) **= snotty-faced*.** (b) (*fig*) engreído.

snout [snaʊt] N (a) hocico *m*, morro *m*; (‡: *of person*) napias* *fpl*. (b) (‡) tabaco *m*, cigarrillos *mpl*.

snow [snəʊ] [1] N (a) nieve *f*. (b) (‡) nieve‡ *f*, cocaína *f*. (c) (*TV*) nieve *f*.
[2] VT: **to ~ sb*** (*US*) camelar a uno*.
[3] VI nevar.

◆**snow in** VT: **to be ~ed in** estar encerrado (*or* aprisionado) por la nieve.

◆**snow under** VT: **to be ~ed under** (*fig*) estar inundado (*by, with* por).

◆**snow up** VT (*Brit*) **= snow in.**

snowball ['snəʊbɔ:l] [1] N bola *f* de nieve.
[2] VT lanzar bolas de nieve a.
[3] VI (*fig*) aumentar progresivamente, aumentar rápidamente.

snow-blind ['snəʊˌblaɪnd] ADJ cegado por la nieve.

snow-blindness ['snəʊˌblaɪndnɪs] N ceguera *f* causada por la nieve.

snowbound ['snəʊbaʊnd] ADJ aprisionado por la nieve.

snow-cap ['snəʊˌkæp] N casquete *m* de nieve, corona *f* de nieve.

snow-capped ['snəʊkæpt] ADJ coronado de nieve, nevado.

snow-covered ['snəʊˌkʌvəd] ADJ cubierto de nieve, nevado.

snowdrift ['snəʊdrɪft] N montón *m* de nieve, nieve *f* amontonada, (*on mountain*) ventisquero *m*.

snowdrop ['snəʊdrɒp] N campanilla *f* de febrero, flor *f* de nieve, campanilla *f* blanca.

snowfall ['snəʊfɔ:l] N nevada *f*.

snowfence ['snəʊfens] N valla *f* paranieves.

snowfield ['snəʊfi:ld] N campo *m* de nieve.

snowflake ['snəʊfleɪk] N copo *m* de nieve.

snowgoose ['snəʊˌgu:s] N, PL **snowgeese** ['snəʊˌgi:s] ánsar *m* nival.

snow-leopard ['snəʊˌlepəd] N onza *f*.

snowline ['snəʊlaɪn] N límite *m* de las nieves perpetuas.

snow machine ['snəʊməˌʃi:n] N cañón *m* de nieve artificial.

snowman ['snəʊmæn] N, PL **snowmen** ['snəʊmen] figura *f* de nieve, monigote *m* de nieve; **the abominable ~** el abominable hombre de las nieves.

snowmobile ['snəʊməˌbi:l] N motonieve *f*.

snowplough, (*US*) **snowplow** ['snəʊplaʊ] N quitanieves *m*.

Snow Queen ['snəʊˌkwi:n] N Reina *f* de las nieves.

snowshoe ['snəʊʃu:] N raqueta *f* (de nieve).

snowslide ['snəʊslaɪd] N (*US*) alud *m* (de nieve), avalancha *f*.

snowstorm ['snəʊstɔ:m] N nevada *f*, nevasca *f*.

snowsuit ['snəʊsu:t] N mono *m* acolchado de nieve.

snow-tyre, (*US*) **snow tire** ['snəʊˌtaɪə^r] N neumático *m* antideslizante.

Snow White ['snəʊwaɪt] NF Blancanieves *f*; **'~ and the Seven Dwarfs'** 'Blancanieves y los siete enanitos'.

snow-white ['snəʊ'waɪt] ADJ blanco como la nieve; (*poet*) níveo, cándido.

snowy ['snəʊɪ] ADJ (a) (*Met*) *climate, region* de mucha nieve, que tiene mucha nieve; *countryside etc* cubierto de nieve; **~ day** día *m* de nieve; **~ season** estación *f* de las nieves; **it was very ~ yesterday** ayer nevó mucho, ayer cayó mucha nieve.
(b) (*fig*) blanco como la nieve, (*poet*) níveo, cándido.

SNP N ABBR of **Scottish National Party.**

Snr ABBR of **Senior.**

snub¹ [snʌb] [1] N desaire *m*; repulsa *f*.
[2] VT *person* desairar, ofender; repulsar; *offer etc* despreciar.

snub² [snʌb] ADJ: **~ nose** nariz *f* respingona.

snub-nosed ['snʌb'nəʊzd] ADJ chato, de nariz respingona, ñato (*LAm*).

snuff [snʌf] [1] N rapé *m*, tabaco *m* en polvo; **to take ~** tomar rapé.
[2] VT (a) (*breathe in*) aspirar, sorber por la nariz.
(b) *candle* despabilar; **to ~ it‡** estirar la pata*.

◆**snuff out** VT apagar; (*fig*) extinguir.

snuffbox ['snʌfbɒks] N tabaquera *f*.

snuffer ['snʌfə^r] N matacandelas *m*; **~s** (*scissors; also* **pair of ~s**) apagaderas *fpl*.

snuffle ['snʌfl] [1] N ruido *m* de la nariz; (*twang*) gangueo *m*.
[2] VI respirar con ruido, hacer ruido con la nariz; (*in speaking*) ganguear.

snuff movie* ['snʌfˌmu:vɪ] N película *f* porno en que muere realmente uno de los participantes.

snug [snʌg] [1] ADJ (*cosy*) cómodo y bien caliente; (*sheltered*) abrigado, al abrigo; (*of dress*) ajustado; *income etc* respetable, nada despreciable; **to be ~ in bed** estar cómodamente acostado; **it's nice and ~ here** aquí se está bien.
[2] N (*Brit*) salón *m* pequeño.

◆**snuggle down** VI: **to ~ down in bed** acomodarse en la cama, hacerse un ovillo en la cama; **they'll ~ down together** se acurrucarán juntos.

◆**snuggle up** VI: **to ~ up to sb** arrimarse (*or* abrazarse) (*amorosamente etc*) a uno, apretarse contra uno; **~ up to me** arrímate a mí; **I like to ~ up with a book** me gusta ponerme cómodamente y leer.

snugly ['snʌglɪ] ADV cómodamente; al abrigo; **it fits ~** se ajusta perfectamente.

SO, S/O ABBR of **standing order** giro *m* regular.

▼**so¹** [səʊ] [1] ADV (a) (*in comparisons: before adj and adv*) tan; **~ quick** tan rápido, **~ quickly** tan rápidamente; **it's about ~ high** es más o menos así de alto; **it is ~ big that ...** es tan grande que ...; **it's not ~ very difficult** no es tan difícil, la dificultad no es tan grande; **he's not ~ silly as to do that** no es bastante tonto para hacer eso, no es tan tonto como para hacer eso; **~ many flies** tantas moscas; **~ much tea** tanto té (*and V* **many, much**); **we spent ~ much** gastamos tanto; **I love you ~ much** te quiero tanto; **he who ~ loved Spain** él que amó tanto a España; V **kind, sure** etc.
(b) (*thus*) así; (*in this way*) de este modo, de esta manera; **he does it ~** lo hace de este modo; **if ~** si es así; en ese caso; **only more ~** pero en mayor grado; **how ~?** ¿cómo es eso?; **why ~?** ¿por qué?, ¿cómo?; **just ~!** ¡eso!, ¡eso es!, ¡perfectamente!, ¡precisamente!; **he likes things just ~** quiere tener cada cosa en su lugar, le gusta una vida bien ordenada; **you do it like ~*** se hace así, se hace de esta manera; **not ~!** ¡nada de eso!; **~ would I** yo también; **~ do I** yo también, yo hago lo mismo; **he's wrong and ~ are you** él se equivoca y tú también; **and ~ forth, and ~ on** y así sucesivamente, y así los demás; etcétera; **it is ~** es así; **~ it is!, ~ it does!** ¡es verdad!, ¡es cierto!; **that's ~** eso es; **is that ~?** ¿de veras?, ¿es cierto eso?; **isn't that ~?** ¿no es así?; ¿no es verdad?; **~ be it** así sea; **~ it was that ...** así fue que ...; **we ~ arranged things that ...** lo arreglamos de modo que ...; **and he did ~** y lo hizo; **by ~ doing** haciéndolo así; **it ~ happens that ...** da la casualidad que ...; **I hope ~** espero que sí; **~ saying, he walked out** diciendo esto, se marchó; **~ to speak** por decirlo así; **I think ~** creo que sí, lo creo; **I told you ~** te lo dije ya; **I tell you it is ~** te digo que es así; **30 or ~** unos 30, 30 o así.
(c) **~ that** (*purpose*) para que + *subj*, a fin de que + *subj*; **I brought it ~ that you should see it** lo traje para que lo vieras.
▼(d) **~ that** (*result*) de modo que + *indic*; **he stood ~ that nobody could get past** estaba en tal posición que nadie podía pasar.

► LANGUAGE IN USE: **so¹: 1a** → 5.1, 17.2 **1d** → 17.2

(e) ~ **as to** + *infin* para + *infin*, a fin de + *infin*; **we hurried ~ as not to be late** nos dimos prisa para no llegar tarde.

▼②︎ CONJ **(a) it rained and ~ we could not go out** llovió y por tanto (*or* por consiguiente) no pudimos salir.

(b) (*exclamatory etc*) **~?, ~ what?** ¿y qué?; **~ you're Spanish?** ¿conque Vd es español?, así que ¿Vd es español?; **~ you're not going?** ¿de suerte que no vas?; **~ there you are!** ¡ahí estás!; **~ you're not selling?** ¿de modo que no lo vende?, así que ¿no lo vende?; V **there** *etc*.

so² [səʊ] N (*Mus*) = **soh**.

soak [səʊk] ①︎ VT **(a) to ~ sth in a liquid** remojar algo en un líquido, empapar algo en un líquido; **to be ~ed (to the skin)** estar calado hasta los huesos; **to get ~ed (to the skin)** calarse hasta los huesos.

(b) (*) **to ~ sb** desplumar a uno*, clavar un precio excesivo a uno*; **to ~ sb for a loan** pedir prestado dinero a uno; **to ~ the rich** cargar la mano con los ricos; **~ the rich!** ¡que paguen los ricos!

②︎ VI **(a)** remojarse, estar a remojo; **to leave sth to ~** dejar algo a remojo.

(b) (‡) beber mucho; emborracharse.

③︎ VR: **to ~ o.s.** calarse hasta los huesos; **to ~ o.s. in** (*fig*) empaparse en.

④︎ N **(a)** (*rain*) diluvio *m*; **to have a good ~ in the bath** descansar bañándose largamente; **give your shirt a ~ overnight** deja la camisa en remojo por la noche.

(b) (‡) borrachín *m*.

◆**soak in** VI (*liquid*) calar, penetrar; (*fig*) penetrar; hacer mella, tener efecto.

◆**soak through** VI calar, penetrar.

◆**soak up** VT (*absorb*) absorber, embeber.

soaking ['səʊkɪŋ] ①︎ ADJ: **to be ~ (wet)** (*person*) estar hecho una sopa, (*object*) estar totalmente mojado, estar empapado; **a ~ wet day** un día de muchísima lluvia.

②︎ N (*in liquid*) remojo *m*; (*of rain*) diluvio *m*; **to get a ~** calarse hasta los huesos.

so-and-so ['səʊənsəʊ] N **(a) Mr ~** don Fulano (de Tal); **old ~ up at the shop** fulano el de la tienda; **any ~ could pinch it*** cualquiera pudiera apañarlo*.

(b) he's a ~* (*pej*) es un tío*; **you old ~!** (*hum*) ¡sinvergüenza!

soap [səʊp] ①︎ N **(a)** jabón *m*. **(b)** (*) = **soap-opera**.

②︎ VT jabonar, enjabonar.

◆**soap up** VT: **to ~ sb up*** dar coba a uno*.

soapbox ['səʊpbɒks] ①︎ N caja *f* vacía empleada como tribuna (en la calle).

②︎ ATTR: **~ orator** orador *m* callejero.

soapdish ['səʊpdɪʃ] N jabonera *f*.

soapflakes ['səʊpfleɪks] NPL jabón *m* en escamas.

soap-opera* ['səʊp,ɒpərə] N (*Rad*) radionovela *f*; (*TV*) telenovela *f*, serial *m* (doméstico, sentimental *etc*), culebrón* *m*.

soap-powder ['səʊp,paʊdər] N jabón *m* en polvo.

soapstone ['səʊpstəʊn] N esteatita *f*.

soapsuds ['səʊpsʌdz] NPL jabonaduras *fpl*, espuma *f* de jabón.

soapy ['səʊpɪ] ADJ **(a)** jabonoso; cubierto de jabón; (*like soap*) parecido a jabón, jabonoso; **it tastes ~** sabe a jabón. **(b)** (*) zalamero, cobista*.

soar [sɔːr] VI **(a)** (*rise*) remontarse, encumbrarse, subir muy alto; (*hover*) cernerse.

(b) (*fig: tower etc*) elevarse mucho sobre el suelo, elevarse hacia el cielo; (*price etc*) subir vertiginosamente, ponerse por las nubes; **the new tower ~s over the city** la nueva torre se eleva sobre la ciudad; **after this his ambition ~ed** después de esto se extendió mucho más su ambición; **our spirits ~ed** nos reanimamos de golpe; renació nuestra esperanza.

soaraway* ['sɔːrəweɪ] ADJ *success, career* fulminante; **~ sales** ventas que se disparan.

soaring ['sɔːrɪŋ] ADJ *flight* encumbrado, por lo alto; *building* altísimo; *ambition* inmenso; *price* que va subiendo vertiginosamente.

sob [sɒb] ①︎ N sollozo *m*; **she said with a ~** dijo sollozando.

②︎ ATTR: **~ story*** historia *f* sentimental; dramón* *m*; narración *f* patética; **~ stuff*** sentimentalismo *m*, sensiblería *f*.

③︎ VT: **'No'**, **she ~bed** 'no', dijo sollozando; **to ~ o.s. to sleep** dormirse sollozando.

④︎ VI sollozar.

◆**sob out** VT: **to ~ one's heart out** llorar a lágrima viva; **she ~bed out her woes** contó sus penas llorando.

S.O.B.‡ N (*US*) ABBR *of* **son of a bitch** hijo *m* de puta‡.

sobbing ['sɒbɪŋ] N sollozos *mpl*.

sober ['səʊbər] ADJ **(a)** (*moderate, sedate*) sobrio, serio, moderado; (*sensible*) sensato, juicioso; *colour* discreto; **a ~ assessment of the facts** una seria valoración de los hechos; **a ~ statement** una declaración razonada.

(b) (*not drunk*) no embriagado, que no ha bebido, sereno; **I'm perfectly ~ as a judge, to be stone-cold ~** estar totalmente sereno; **I'm perfect-**

---

ly ~ no he bebido en absoluto, tengo la cabeza perfectamente despejada; **one has to be ~ to drive** para conducir es necesario no haber bebido nada; **tomorrow, when you're ~** mañana, cuando te hayas despejado de la borrachera.

◆**sober down** ①︎ VT: **to ~ sb down** calmar a uno.

②︎ VI calmarse; **he's ~ed down recently** recientemente ha sentado la cabeza.

◆**sober up** ①︎ VT: **to ~ sb up** quitar la sopa a uno*; **this will ~ you up** esto te quitará la merluza*.

②︎ VI (*after drinking*) espabilar la borrachera; (*calm o.s.*) recuperar la sobriedad.

sober-headed ['səʊbə'hedɪd] ADJ *person* sensato, sobrio; *decision* sensato.

sobering ['səʊbərɪŋ] ADJ: **it had a ~ effect** moderó el entusiasmo (*etc*); hizo que la gente (*etc*) pensara en las consecuencias; **it's a ~ thought** eso hace reflexionar, eso da en qué pensar.

soberly ['səʊbəlɪ] ADV sobriamente, seriamente, moderadamente; sensatamente; discretamente; **~ dressed** discretamente vestido.

sober-minded ['səʊbə'maɪndɪd] ADJ serio, formal.

soberness ['səʊbənɪs] N, **sobriety** [səʊ'braɪətɪ] N **(a)** sobriedad *f*, seriedad *f*; moderación *f*; sensatez *f*; discreción *f*. **(b)** estado *m* del que no ha bebido, serenidad *f*; moderación *f* en beber.

sobersides* ['səʊbəsaɪdz] N persona *f* muy reservada.

sobriquet ['səʊbrɪkeɪ] N apodo *m*, mote *m*.

Soc. (a) ABBR *of* **society** sociedad *f*. **(b)** ABBR *of* **Socialist** socialista *mf*, *also adj*.

so-called ['səʊ'kɔːld] ADJ llamado, denominado; supuesto, presunto; **in the ~ rush hours** en las llamadas horas punta; **all these ~ journalists** todos estos presuntos periodistas.

soccer ['sɒkər] ①︎ N fútbol *m*.

②︎ ATTR futbolístico; **~ player** futbolista *mf*.

sociability [,səʊʃə'bɪlɪtɪ] N sociabilidad *f*; afabilidad *f*.

sociable ['səʊʃəbl] ADJ sociable; afable; amistoso.

sociably ['səʊʃəblɪ] ADV sociablemente; afablemente; amistosamente; **to live ~ together** vivir juntos amistosamente.

social ['səʊʃəl] ①︎ ADJ social; sociable; **a ~ outcast** una persona desterrada de la sociedad; **man is a ~ animal** el hombre es un animal sociable; **~ administration** administración *f* social; **~ anthropology** antropología *f* social; **the S~ Chapter** la Carta Social; **~ class** clase *f* social; **~ climber** trepador *m*, -ora *f*; **~ climbing** arribismo *m* (social); **~ club** club *m* social; **~ column** notas *fpl* de sociedad; **~ contract** contrato *m* social; **~ cost** costo *m* en términos sociales; **S~ Democrat** socialdemócrata *mf*; **S~ Democratic** socialdemocrático; **I'm a ~ drinker only** yo no bebo a solas, yo bebo solamente en compañía de los amigos; **~ engineering** ingeniería *f* social; **~ insurance** (*US*), **~ welfare** seguro *m* social; **~ life** vida *f* social; **~ mobility** movilidad *f* social; **~ science** ciencia *f* social; **~ scientist** sociólogo *m*, -a *f*; **~ secretary** secretario *m*, -a *f* social; **~ security** seguridad *f* social; **~ security benefit** subsidio *m* del seguro social; **to be on ~ security** cobrar el seguro de desempleo; **~ services** servicios *mpl* sociales; **~ studies** estudios *mpl* sociales; **one's ~ superiors** los socialmente superiores a uno; **~ work** asistencia *f* social; **~ worker** trabajador *m*, -ora *f* social, asistente *mf* social.

②︎ N velada *f*, tertulia *f*, peña *f* (*LAm*).

socialism ['səʊʃəlɪzəm] N socialismo *m*.

socialist ['səʊʃəlɪst] ①︎ ADJ socialista.

②︎ N socialista *mf*.

socialistic [,səʊʃə'lɪstɪk] ADJ socialista.

socialite ['səʊʃəlaɪt] N persona *f* mundana, persona *f* conocidísima en la buena sociedad.

socialization [,səʊʃəlaɪ'zeɪʃən] N socialización *f*.

socialize ['səʊʃəlaɪz] ①︎ VT socializar.

②︎ VI alternar con la gente, mezclarse con la gente; conversar, charlar; **you should ~ more** debes ver más gente; **we don't ~ much these days** no salimos mucho estos días.

socializing ['səʊʃəlaɪzɪŋ] N: **he doesn't like ~** no le gusta hacer vida social.

socially ['səʊʃəlɪ] ADV socialmente; sociablemente; **we meet ~** nos vemos en las reuniones de tipo social.

societal [sə'saɪətəl] ADJ societal.

society [sə'saɪətɪ] ①︎ N **(a)** (*community*) sociedad *f*; **to live in ~** vivir en la sociedad; **he's a danger to ~** es un peligro para la sociedad.

(b) (*high ~*) alta sociedad *f*, buena sociedad *f*, mundo *m* elegante; **to go into ~** (*girl*) ponerse de largo; **to move in ~** frecuentar la buena sociedad.

(c) (*companionship*) sociedad *f*, compañía *f*; **in the ~ of** en compañía de, acompañado por; **I enjoy his ~** me gusta su compañía.

(d) (*group*) sociedad *f*; asociación *f*; **S~ of Friends** los cuáqueros; **S~ of Jesus** Compañía *f* de Jesús.

②︎ ATTR: **~ news** notas *fpl* de sociedad; **~ wedding** boda *f* de la buena sociedad; **~ woman** mujer *f* conocida en la buena sociedad.

socio... ['səʊsɪəʊ] PREF socio...

sociobiology [ˌsəʊsɪəʊbaɪˈɒlədʒɪ] N sociobiología f.
sociocultural [ˌsəʊsɪəʊˈkʌltʃərəl] ADJ sociocultural.
socioeconomic [ˈsəʊsɪəʊˌiːkəˈnɒmɪk] ADJ socioeconómico.
sociolect [ˈsəʊsɪəʊˌlekt] N sociolecto m.
sociolinguistic [ˌsəʊsɪəʊlɪŋˈgwɪstɪk] ADJ sociolingüístico.
sociolinguistics [ˌsəʊsɪəʊlɪŋˈgwɪstɪks] N sociolingüística f.
sociological [ˌsəʊsɪəˈlɒdʒɪkəl] ADJ sociológico.
sociologically [ˌsəʊsɪəˈlɒdʒɪkəlɪ] ADV sociológicamente.
sociologist [ˌsəʊsɪˈɒlədʒɪst] N sociólogo m, -a f.
sociology [ˌsəʊsɪˈɒlədʒɪ] N sociología f.
sociopath [ˈsəʊsɪəʊpæθ] N sociópata mf, inadaptado m, -a f social.
sociopathic [ˌsəʊsɪəʊˈpæθɪk] ADJ sociopático, anti-social.
sociopolitical [ˌsəʊsɪəʊpəˈlɪtɪkəl] ADJ sociopolítico.
sock[1] [sɒk] N calcetín m, media f (LAm); (insole) plantilla f; **to pull one's ~s up** (fig) hacer un esfuerzo, procurar hacer mejor; **put (or shove) a ~ in it!*** ¡a callar!, ¡cállate!
sock[2]* [sɒk] [1] N tortazo* m.
  [2] VT pegar; **~ him one!** ¡pégale!; **~ it to me!** ¡dímelo!
socket [ˈsɒkɪt] N (of eye) cuenca f, órbita f; (of tooth) alvéolo m; (of joint) fosa f; (Brit Elec) enchufe m, toma f; (Mech) encaje m, cubo m.
socket joint [ˈsɒkɪtˌdʒɔɪnt] N (Carp) machihembrado m; (Anat) articulación f esférica.
socko* [ˈsɒkəʊ] (US) [1] ADJ estupendo*, extraordinario.
  [2] N gran éxito m.
Socrates [ˈsɒkrətiːz] NM Sócrates f.
Socratic [sɒˈkrætɪk] ADJ socrático.
sod[1] [sɒd] N césped m.
sod[2]*⚉ [sɒd] (Brit) [1] N bestia* f, bruto m; **you ~!** ¡cabrón!⚉; **~'s law** ley f de la indefectible mala voluntad de los objetos inanimados; **he's a real ~** es una mala bestia; **this job is a real ~** este trabajo es la monda*; **the lid is a ~ to get off** quitar la tapa hace sudar la gota gorda; **some poor ~** algún pobre diablo.
  [2] VT: **~ it!** ¡mierda!⚉; **~ him!** ¡que se joda!⚉
◆ **sod off**⚉ VI irse a la porra*, ir a hacer puñetas⚉; **~ off!** ¡vete a la porra!*
soda [ˈsəʊdə] N (a) (Chem) sosa f, soda f; (Culin) bicarbonato m (sódico).
  (b) (drink) soda f, agua f de seltz, gaseosa f; **gin and ~** ginebra f con sifón; **do you like ~ with it?** ¿te echo un poco de sifón?, ¿con soda?
soda bread [ˈsəʊdəbred] N pan hecho con levadura de bicarbonato.
sod-all⚉ [ˈsɒdɔːl] = **damn-all**.
soda ash [ˈsəʊdəˌæʃ] N sosa f comercial, ceniza f de soda.
soda fountain [ˈsəʊdəˌfaʊntɪn] N (US) sifón m; bar m de bebidas no alcohólicas.
sodality [səʊˈdælɪtɪ] N hermandad f, cofradía f.
soda-siphon [ˈsəʊdəˌsaɪfən] N sifón m.
soda-water [ˈsəʊdəˌwɔːtəʳ] N soda f, agua f de seltz, gaseosa f; **...with ~ ...** con sifón, ... con soda.
sodden [ˈsɒdn] ADJ empapado, mojado, saturado; **to be ~ with drink** estar embrutecido por el alcohol.
sodding⚉ [ˈsɒdɪŋ] ADJ jodido⚉, puñetero⚉.
sodium [ˈsəʊdɪəm] [1] N sodio m.
  [2] ATTR: **~ bicarbonate** bicarbonato m sódico; **~ carbonate** carbonato m sódico; **~ chloride** cloruro m sódico; **~ nitrate** nitrato m sódico; **~ sulphate** sulfato m sódico.
Sodom [ˈsɒdəm] N Sodoma f.
sodomite [ˈsɒdəmaɪt] N sodomita m.
sodomize [ˈsɒdəmaɪz] VT sodomizar.
sodomy [ˈsɒdəmɪ] N sodomía f.
sofa [ˈsəʊfə] N sofá m.
sofa-bed [ˈsəʊfəbed] N sofá-cama m.
Sofia [ˈsəʊfɪə] N Sofía f.
soft [sɒft] ADJ (a) material etc blando; muelle; (flabby) flojo; skin suave, terso, fino; metal dúctil; hat flexible; fruit blando; **~ centre** centro m blando; **~ coal** huella f grasa; **~ collar** cuello m blando; **~ furnishings** tejidos mpl para casa (cortinas, fundas, etc); **~ goods** géneros mpl textiles; **~ ice cream** helado m de máquina; **~ money** (US) papel m moneda; **~ palate** velo m del paladar; **~ shoulder** = **~ verge**; **~ top** (esp US) descapotable m; **~ toy** muñeco m de peluche; **~ verge** (Brit) borde m blando; **~ to the touch** blando al tacto; **as ~ as silk, as ~ as velvet** tan suave como la seda; **to go ~** ablandarse, ponerse blando; **his muscles have gone ~** sus músculos han perdido su fuerza, sus músculos ya están flojos.
  (b) (fig) air, sound suave; voice dulce; step suave; water blando; rain suave; colour delicado; loan favorable, privilegiado; heart, words tierno, compasivo; job fácil; character débil, muelle, afeminado; (lenient) indulgente, tolerante; **~ copy** copia f transitoria; **~ currency** moneda f blanda; **~ drink** bebida f no alcohólica, bebida f refrescante, gaseosa f; **~ drug** droga f suave, droga f blanda; **~ focus** flou m, desenfoque m; **in ~ focus** desenfocado; **~ job*** prebenda* f, chollo* m; **~ landing** aterrizaje m suave; **~ lighting** luz f baja; **lights and sweet music** poca luz y música sentimental; **~ option**

alternativa f más fácil; **~ porn*** pornografía f blanda; **~ sell*** venta f persuasiva, venta f con publicidad discreta; venta f fácil; **~ soap*** coba* f; **~ touch*** persona f que se deja convencer fácilmente; **~ water** agua f blanda; **to be ~ on sb** tratar a uno con demasiada indulgencia; **to be ~ on crime** ser blando con el delito; **he's ~ on communism** es demasiado tolerante para con el comunismo.
  (c) (foolish) estúpido, tonto; **you must be ~!** ¿has perdido el juicio?; **he's ~ (in the head)** es un poco tocado; **he's going ~ (in the head)** está perdiendo el juicio.
softback [ˈsɒftbæk] ATTR = **soft-bound**.
softball [ˈsɒftbɔːl] N (US) especie de béisbol sobre un terreno más pequeño que el normal, con pelota grande y blanda.
soft-boiled [ˈsɒftˌbɔɪld] ADJ: **~ egg** huevo m pasado por agua, huevo m tibio (And), huevo m amelcochado (Carib).
soft-bound [ˈsɒftbaʊnd] ADJ, **soft-cover** [ˈsɒftkʌvəʳ] ATTR: **~ book** libro m en rústica.
soften [ˈsɒfn] [1] VT ablandar, reblandecer; (weaken) debilitar; (mitigate) mitigar, suavizar, templar; blow amortiguar.
  [2] VI ablandarse, reblandecerse; debilitarse, aflojarse; suavizarse, templarse.
◆ **soften up** [1] VT: **to ~ up resistance** debilitar la resistencia.
  [2] VI: **to ~ up on sb** hacerse menos severo con uno, mitigar su severidad con uno; **we must not ~ up on communism** tenemos que seguir tan opuestos como siempre al comunismo.
softener [ˈsɒfnəʳ] N (water ~) descalcificador m; (fabric ~) suavizante m.
softening [ˈsɒfnɪŋ] N reblandecimiento m; debilitación f; mitigación f, suavización f; **~ of the brain** reblandecimiento m cerebral; **there has been a ~ of his attitude** se ha suavizado su actitud.
soft-headed [ˈsɒftˌhedɪd] ADJ bobo, tonto.
soft-hearted [ˈsɒftˈhɑːtɪd] ADJ compasivo, bondadoso.
soft-heartedness [ˈsɒftˈhɑːtɪdnɪs] N bondad f.
softie* [ˈsɒftɪ] N = **softy**.
soft-liner [ˌsɒftˈlaɪnəʳ] N blando m, -a f.
softly [ˈsɒftlɪ] ADV blandamente; suavemente; dulcemente; delicadamente; **she said ~** dijo dulcemente; **to move ~** moverse silenciosamente, moverse sin ruido; **to adopt a ~ ~ approach** avanzar con cautela, ir con pies de plomo.
softness [ˈsɒftnɪs] N (V adj) (a) blandura f; flojedad f; suavidad f, tersura f; ductilidad f. (b) dulzura f; delicadeza f; ternura f; debilidad f; indulgencia f, tolerancia f. (c) estupidez f.
soft-pedal [ˈsɒftˈpedl] VT (fig) no dar tanto énfasis a, dejar de insistir en, conceder menos importancia a.
soft-soap* [ˌsɒftˈsəʊp] VT dar coba a*.
soft-spoken [ˈsɒftˈspəʊkən] ADJ de voz suave, de tono dulce.
software [ˈsɒftweəʳ] [1] N software m, elementos mpl de programación, logicial m, soporte m lógico, componentes mpl lógicos.
  [2] ATTR: **~ engineering** ingeniería f de software; **~ house** compañía f especializada en programación; **~ package** paquete m de programas.
softwood [ˈsɒftwʊd] N madera f blanda.
SOGAT [ˈsəʊgæt] N (Brit) ABBR of **Society of Graphical and Allied Trades** sindicato de tipógrafos.
softy* [ˈsɒftɪ] N mollejón* m, -ona f; memo m, -a f.
soggy [ˈsɒgɪ] ADJ empapado, saturado; esponjoso.
soh [səʊ] N sol m.
soi-disant [ˈswɑːdiːˈsɔːŋ] ADJ supuesto, presunto, sediciente.
soigné [ˈswɑːnjeɪ] ADJ pulcro, acicalado.
soil[1] [sɔɪl] N tierra f, suelo m; **one's native ~** su tierra, su patria.
soil[2] [sɔɪl] [1] VT ensuciar; manchar (also fig).
  [2] VI ensuciarse.
  [3] VR: **to ~ o.s.** ensuciarse; **I would not ~ myself by contact with ...** no me rebajaría a tener contacto con ...
soiled [sɔɪld] ADJ sucio.
soilpipe [ˈsɔɪlpaɪp] N tubo m de desagüe sanitario.
soirée [ˈswɑːreɪ] N velada f.
sojourn [ˈsɒdʒɜːn] [1] N permanencia f, estancia f.
  [2] VI permanecer, residir, morar; pasar una temporada.
solace [ˈsɒlɪs] [1] N consuelo m; **to seek ~ with ...** procurar consolarse con ...
  [2] VT consolar.
  [3] VR: **to ~ o.s.** consolarse (with con).
solar [ˈsəʊləʳ] ADJ solar, del sol; **~ battery** pila f solar; **~ calculator** calculadora f solar; **~ cell** célula f solar; **~ eclipse** eclipse m solar; **~ energy** energía f solar; **~ flare** erupción f solar; **~ heat** calor m solar; **~ heating** calefacción f solar; **~ panel** panel m solar; **~ plexus** plexo m solar; **~ system** sistema m solar; **~ wind** viento m solar.
solarium [səʊˈlɛərɪəm] N, PL **solaria** [səʊˈlɛərɪə] solario m, solárium m, solana f.
solar-powered [ˈsəʊləˈpaʊəd] ADJ que funciona con energía solar.
sold [səʊld] PRET AND PTP of **sell**.
solder [ˈsəʊldəʳ] [1] N soldadura f.
  [2] VT soldar.

soldering-iron ['səʊldərɪŋ,aɪən] N soldador *m*.

soldier ['səʊldʒər] [1] N soldado *mf*; militar *m*; ~ **of fortune** aventurero *m* militar; **common** ~ soldado *m* raso; **old** ~ veterano *m*, excombatiente *m*; **a young woman** ~ una joven soldado; **to come the old** ~ **with sb*** tratar de imponerse a uno (por más experimentado).
[2] VI militar, ser soldado; servir; **he ~ed for 10 years in the East** sirvió durante 10 años en el Oriente.
◆ **soldier on** VI (*Brit*) continuar a pesar de todo.

soldierly ['səʊldʒəlɪ] ADJ militar.

soldiery ['səʊldʒərɪ] N soldadesca *f*; **a brutal and licentious** ~ la soldadesca indisciplinada.

sole¹ [səʊl] [1] N (*Anat*) planta *f*; (*of shoe*) suela *f*, piso *m*.
[2] VT poner suela a, poner piso a.

sole² [səʊl] N (*Fish*) lenguado *m*.

sole³ [səʊl] ADJ único, solo; exclusivo; ~ **agency** agencia *f* única; ~ **agent** agente *m* único, agente *f* única; **to be** ~ **agent for** tener la representación exclusiva de; ~ **owner** propietario *m* único, propietaria *f* única; ~ **trader** comerciante *m* exclusivo; **the** ~ **reason is that ...** la única razón es que ...

solecism ['sɒləsɪzəm] N solecismo *m*.

solely ['səʊllɪ] ADV únicamente, solamente, sólo.

solemn ['sɒləm] ADJ solemne.

solemnity [sə'lemnɪtɪ] N solemnidad *f*.

solemnization [,sɒləmnaɪ'zeɪʃən] N solemnización *f*.

solemnize ['sɒləmnaɪz] VT solemnizar.

solemnly ['sɒləmlɪ] ADV solemnemente.

solenoid ['səʊlənɔɪd] N solenoide *m*.

solfa ['sɒl'faː] N solfa *f*.

solicit [sə'lɪsɪt] [1] VT (*request*) solicitar; implorar, pedir insistentemente; (*importune*) importunar; (*prostitute*) abordar, importunar; **to** ~ **sb for sth**, **to** ~ **sth of sb** solicitar algo a uno.
[2] VI (*prostitute*) importunar.

solicitation [sə,lɪsɪ'teɪʃən] N solicitación *f*.

soliciting [sə'lɪsɪtɪŋ] N abordamiento *m*.

solicitor [sə'lɪsɪtər] N (a) (*US*) representante *mf*, agente *mf*; (*US Jur*) abogado *m* asesor adscrito a un municipio (*etc*).
(b) (*Brit Jur*) procurador *m*, abogado *m*; (*for oaths, wills etc*) notario *m*; **S~ General** (*Brit*) subfiscal *m* de la Corona, (*US*) fiscal *m* general del Estado; *ver también* LAWYERS .

solicitous [sə'lɪsɪtəs] ADJ solícito (*about, for* por); preocupado, N solicitud *f*; preocupación *f*, ansiedad *f*; atención *f*.

solid ['sɒlɪd] [1] ADJ (a) (*gen*) sólido; *gold, silver, oak etc* macizo; *tyre* macizo, sin cámara; (*of consistency of soup etc*) sustancioso; *meal* fuerte; *crowd* denso, apretado; *vote* unánime; *person's character* enteramente serio, muy formal; *conviction* firme; *argument* sólido, fundado; *supporter* incondicional; **the** ~ **South** (*US*) el bloque sólido constituido por los estados del Sur (que apoyaban siempre al Partido Democrático); ~ **compound** (*Ling*) compuesto *m* cuyos términos están gráficamente soldados; ~ **fuel** combustible *m* sólido; ~ **fuel heater** calentador *m* de combustible sólido; ~ **geometry** geometría *f* del espacio; ~ **word** palabra *f* simple; **Slobodia is** ~ **for Smith** Eslobodia apoya unánimemente a Smith; **the house is** ~ **enough** la casa es perfectamente sólida; **the square was** ~ **with cars** la plaza estaba totalmente llena de coches, la plaza estaba atestada de coches; **to be frozen** ~ estar completamente helado; **it was cut into** ~ **rock** se excavó en peña viva; **to have** ~ **grounds for thinking that ...** tener buenos motivos para creer que ...; **it makes good** ~ **sense** hace muy buen sentido; **we walked 14** ~ **miles** anduvimos 14 millas largas; **we waited 2** ~ **hours** esperamos dos horas enteras.
(b) (*US: excellent*) excelente, extraordinario.
[2] N sólido *m*; ~**s** (*food*) alimentos *mpl* sólidos.

solidarity [,sɒlɪ'dærɪtɪ] N solidaridad *f*; ~ **strike** huelga *f* por solidaridad; **out of** ~ **with the workers** por solidaridad con los obreros.

solidification [sə,lɪdɪfɪ'keɪʃən] N solidificación *f*.

solidify [sə'lɪdɪfaɪ] [1] VT solidificar.
[2] VI solidificarse.

solidity [sə'lɪdɪtɪ] N solidez *f*.

solidly ['sɒlɪdlɪ] ADV sólidamente; densamente, apretadamente; unánimemente; **a** ~ **reasoned argument** un argumento sólidamente razonado; **to vote** ~ **for sb** votar unánimemente por uno; **we were** ~ **for Smith** apoyamos unánimemente a Smith; **a** ~**-built house** una casa de sólida construcción.

solid-state ['sɒlɪd'steɪt] ATTR del estado sólido; ~ **physics** física *f* del estado sólido.

solidus ['sɒlɪdəs] N (*Typ*) barra *f*.

soliloquize [sə'lɪləkwaɪz] VI soliloquiar; '~', **he ~d** '~' dijo para sí.

soliloquy [sə'lɪləkwɪ] N soliloquio *m*.

solipsism ['səʊlɪpsɪzəm] N solipsismo *m*.

solitaire [,sɒlɪ'teər] N (*game, gem*) solitario *m*.

solitary ['sɒlɪtərɪ] [1] ADJ (a) (*living alone*) solitario, solo; (*secluded*)

retirado, apartado; **to be in** ~ **confinement** estar incomunicado, estar en pelota‡; **to take a** ~ **walk** dar un paseo solo, pasearse sin compañía; **to feel rather** ~ sentirse solo, sentirse aislado.
(b) (*sole*) único, solo; **not a** ~ **one** ni uno (solo); **there has been one** ~ **case** ha habido un caso único; **there has not been one** ~ **case** no ha habido ni un solo caso.
[2] N (a) (*person*) solitario *m*, -a *f*.
(b) (*) = ~ **confinement**; *V* 1a.

solitude ['sɒlɪtjuːd] N soledad *f*.

solo ['səʊləʊ] [1] N, PL **solos** ['səʊləʊz] (*Cards, Mus*) solo *m*; **to sing a** ~ cantar un solo; **a tenor** ~ un solo para tenor.
[2] ADJ: ~ **flight** vuelo *m* a solas; **passage for** ~ **violin** pasaje *m* para violín solo; ~ **trip round the world** vuelta *f* al mundo en solitario.
[3] ADV: **to fly** ~ volar a solas; **to sing** ~ cantar solo.

soloist ['səʊləʊɪst] N solista *mf*.

Solomon ['sɒləmən] [1] NM Salomón.
[2] ATTR: ~ **Islands** Islas *fpl* Salomón.

solstice ['sɒlstɪs] N solsticio *m*; **summer** ~ solsticio *m* de verano; **winter** ~ solsticio *m* de invierno.

solubility [,sɒljʊ'bɪlɪtɪ] N solubilidad *f*.

soluble ['sɒljʊbl] ADJ soluble; ~ **in water** soluble en agua.

solution [sə'luːʃən] N (*all senses*) solución *f* (*to a problem* de un problema); **in** ~ en solución.

solvable ['sɒlvəbl] ADJ soluble, que se puede resolver.

solve [sɒlv] VT resolver, solucionar; *riddle* adivinar.

solvency ['sɒlvənsɪ] N solvencia *f*.

solvent ['sɒlvənt] [1] ADJ solvente.
[2] N solvente *m*.
[3] ATTR: ~ **abuse** esnifamiento *m* de disolvente.

solver ['sɒlvər] N solucionista *mf*.

Som. N (*Brit*) ABBR of **Somerset**.

Somali [səʊ'maːlɪ] [1] ADJ somalí.
[2] N somalí *mf*.

Somalia [səʊ'maːlɪə] N Somalia *f*.

Somalian [səʊ'maːlɪən] [1] ADJ somalí.
[2] N somalí *mf*.

Somaliland [səʊ'maːlɪlænd] N Somalia *f*.

somatic [səʊ'mætɪk] ADJ somático.

sombre, (*US*) **somber** ['sɒmbər] ADJ sombrío; pesimista; **in** ~ **hues** en colores sombríos; **a** ~ **prospect** una perspectiva sombría; **he was** ~ **about our chances** se mostró pesimista acerca de nuestras posibilidades.

sombrely, (*US*) **somberly** ['sɒmbəlɪ] ADV sombríamente; con pesimismo, en tono pesimista.

sombreness, (*US*) **somberness** ['sɒmbənɪs] N lo sombrío; pesimismo *m*.

sombrero [sɒm'breərəʊ] N sombrero *m* mejicano.

some [sʌm] [1] ADJ (a) alguno, (*before m sing n*) algún; unos, unos cuantos; ~ **day** algún día; ~ **man** algún hombre; ~ **people** algunos, algunas personas; ~ **very big cars** unos coches muy grandes, unos coches muy grandes; ~ **distance away** a cierta distancia; **after** ~ **time** después de cierto tiempo; **it took** ~ **courage to do that** hacer eso exigió bastante valor, quien hizo eso tenía bastante valor; ~ **books I could name** ciertos libros que pudiera mencionar; ~ **days ago** hace unos días; **in** ~ **form or other** en alguna forma; **for** ~ **reason or other** por alguna razón; ~ **politician or other** algún político; ~ **other time** otro día; ~ **idiot of a driver** algún imbécil de conductor; ~ **people just don't care** hay gente que no se preocupa en lo más mínimo.
(b) (*partitive*) un poco de, algo de; (*freq not translated, eg*) **have you** ~ **money?** ¿tienes dinero?, **will you have** ~ **tea?** ¿quieres té?; **all I have left is** ~ **chocolate** solamente me queda un poco de chocolate; **here is** ~ **water for you** te he traído un poco de agua; ~ **water, please** agua, por favor.
(c) (*intensive*) **that's** ~ **fish!** ¡eso es lo que se llama un pez!; ¡eso es un pez de verdad!; ~ **expert!** (*iro*) ¡valiente experto!; **that's** ~ **woman** es mucha mujer; **it was** ~ **party** menuda fiesta fue; **you're** ~ **friend!** ¡menudo amigo tú!
[2] PRON (a) (*a certain number*) algunos; ~ **went this way and** ~ **that** algunos fueron por aquí y otros por allá; ~ **say yes and** ~ **say no** algunos dicen que sí y otros que no; ~ **of them are crazy** algunos de ellos están locos; ~ **believe that ...** algunos creen que ..., hay quien cree que ...
(b) (*a certain amount*) algunos; algo, un poco; **do take** ~ (PL) toma algunos, (*sing*) toma algo, toma un poco; **thanks, I have** ~ gracias, ya tengo; **could I have** ~ **of that cheese?** ¿me puedes servir un poco de ese queso?; **I like** ~ **of what you said in the speech** me gusta una parte de lo que Vd dijo en el discurso; ~ **of what you say is true** parte de lo que dices es cierto; **and then** ~*** y luego más, y más todavía.
[3] ADV (a) (*about*) ~ **20 people** unas 20 personas, aproximadamente 20 personas, una veintena de personas; ~ **£30** unas 30 libras, más o

menos 30 libras; **~ few difficulties** unas pocas dificultades.

(b) (*esp US**) mucho; **we laughed ~** nos reímos mucho; **it sure bothered us ~** ya lo creo que nos preocupó bastante; **he's travelling ~** lleva gran velocidad.

-some [səm] N *ending in compounds* grupo *m* de ...; **three~** grupo *m* de tres personas; **we'll go in a three~** iremos los tres, iremos como grupo de tres; **have we a four~ for bridge?** ¿tenemos cuatro para jugar al bridge?; **to make up a four~** formar un grupo de cuatro.

somebody ['sʌmbədɪ] 1 PRON alguien; **~ else** algún otro, otra persona; **~ told me so** alguien me lo dijo, me lo dijo alguno; **~ or other must have taken it** alguien se lo habrá llevado; **~ up there loves me** tengo una buena racha; **~ up there hates me** tengo una mala racha.

2 N: **to be ~** ser un personaje, ser alguien; **he thinks he's ~ now** ahora se cree un personaje.

someday ['sʌmdeɪ] ADV algún día.

somehow ['sʌmhaʊ] ADV (a) (*in some way*) de algún modo, de un modo u otro; **it must be done ~ or other** de un modo u otro tiene que hacerse; **~ or other I never liked him** por alguna razón no me era simpático.

(b) **it seems ~ odd, it seems odd ~** no sé por qué pero me parece extraño.

someone ['sʌmwʌn] PRON = **somebody**.

someplace ['sʌmpleɪs] ADV (*US*) = **somewhere**.

somersault ['sʌməsɔːlt] 1 N (*by person*) salto *m* mortal; (*by car etc*) vuelco *m*, vuelta *f* de campana; **to turn a ~** dar un salto mortal; volcar; **to turn ~s** dar saltos mortales; dar vueltas de campana.

2 VI dar un salto mortal; dar una vuelta de campana.

something ['sʌmθɪŋ] 1 PRON (a) algo; alguna cosa; **~ else** otra cosa; **~ or other is bothering him** algo le trae preocupado; **there's ~ the matter** pasa algo; **did you say ~?** ¿dijiste algo?; **there's ~ odd here** aquí hay algo raro; **~ of the kind** algo por el estilo; **it's come to ~ when ...** llegamos a un punto grave cuando ...; **there's ~ in what you say** hay gran parte de verdad en lo que dices; **well, that's ~** eso ya es algo; **she has a certain ~** tiene un no sé qué (de atractivo); **that certain ~ that makes all the difference** ese no sé qué que importa tanto; **her hat was quite ~** su sombrero era de ver; **her win was quite ~** su victoria era extraordinaria; **that's quite (or really) ~!** ¡eso sí que es algo!; **you've got ~ there*** no es mala idea (*etc*); es un punto clave; **he's called John ~** se llama Juan y no sé qué más; **there were 30 ~** había treinta y algunos más; **will you have ~ to drink?** ¿quieres tomar algo?; **I need ~ to eat** necesito comer; **I gave him ~ for himself** le di algo para sí; **it gives her ~ to live for** le da un motivo para vivir; **do you want to make ~ of it?** ¿quién le mete a Vd en esto?; y a Vd ¿qué le importa?

(b) (*or* **~**) **are you mad or ~?** ¿estás loco o qué?; **her name is Camilla or ~** se llama algo así como Camila; **he's got flu or ~** tiene gripe o algo parecido.

(c) **it's ~ of a problem** en cierto sentido representa un problema, viene a ser un problema; **he's ~ of a musician** es en cierto modo un músico, tiene cierto talento para la música; **let's see ~ of you soon** ven a vernos pronto.

2 ADV (a) **~ over 200** algo más de 200; **he left ~ over £10,000** dejó más de 10.000 libras; **he left ~ like £10,000** dejó algo así como 10.000 libras; **now that's ~ like a rose!** ¡eso es lo que se llama una rosa!

(b) (*) **it's ~ chronic** es horrible, es fatal*; **the weather was ~ shocking** el tiempo fue asqueroso.

-something ['sʌmθɪŋ] 1 ADJ *ending in compounds*: **thirty~** treinta y tantos, treinta y algo, treinta y pico.

2 N *ending in compounds*: **thirty~s** treintañeros *m*, -as *f*.

sometime ['sʌmtaɪm] 1 ADV (a) (*in future*) algún día; alguna vez; **~ or other it will have to be done** tarde o temprano tendrá que hacerse; **write to me ~ soon** escríbeme pronto, escríbeme algún día de éstos; **~ before tomorrow** antes de mañana; **~ next year** el año que viene.

(b) (*in past*) **~ last month** el mes pasado; **~ last century** en el siglo pasado, durante el siglo pasado; **it was ~ before 1950** fue antes de 1950 (no lo sé más exactamente).

2 ADJ (a) ex ..., antiguo; **~ mayor of Wapping** ex alcalde de Wapping.

(b) (*US: occasional*) intermitente.

sometimes ['sʌmtaɪmz] ADV algunas veces; a veces.

somewhat ['sʌmwɒt] ADV algo, algún tanto; **we are ~ worried** estamos algo inquietos; **it was done ~ hastily** se hizo con demasiada prisa.

somewhere ['sʌmwɛəʳ] ADV (a) (*be*) en alguna parte; (*go*) a alguna parte; **~ else** (*be*) en otra parte; (*go*) a otra parte; **I left it ~ or other** lo dejé en alguna parte, lo dejé por ahí; **he's ~ around** anda por ahí; **now we're getting ~** estamos haciendo progresos; **~ near Huesca** cerca de Huesca; **~ in Aragón** en alguna parte de Aragón; **to broadcast from ~ in Europe** emitir de algún lugar de Europa.

(b) (*approximately*) alrededor de; **~ about 3 o'clock** alrededor de las 3, a eso de las 3; **he paid ~ about £12** pagó alrededor de 12 libras; **she's ~ about 50** tiene 50 años más o menos.

Somme [sɒm] N Somme *m*; **the Battle of the ~** la batalla del Somme.

somnambulism [sɒm'næmbjʊlɪzəm] N so(m)nambulismo *m*.

somnambulist [sɒm'næmbjʊlɪst] N so(m)námbulo *m*, -a *f*.

somniferous [sɒm'nɪfərəs] ADJ somnífero.

somnolence ['sɒmnələns] N somnolencia *f*.

somnolent ['sɒmnələnt] ADJ soñoliento.

son [sʌn] N hijo *m*; **~ of a bitch‡** hijo *m* de puta‡; **S~ of God** Hijo *m* de Dios; **S~ of Man** Hijo *m* del Hombre.

sonar ['səʊnɑːʳ] N sonar *m*.

sonata [sə'nɑːtə] N sonata *f*.

son et lumière [ˌsɔ̃eɪlym'jɛːr] N (espectáculo *m* de) luz *f* y sonido.

song [sɒŋ] 1 N (*a ~*) canción *f*; (*art of singing*) canto *m*; (*epic*) cantar *m*; **festival of Spanish ~** festival *m* de la canción española; **'A S~ for Europe'** 'Canción *f* para Europa'; **S~ of Roland** Cantar *m* de Roldán; **S~ of Solomon, S~ of S~s** Cantar *m* de los Cantares; **to burst into ~** romper a cantar; **give us a ~!** ¡cántanos algo!; **to make a great ~ and dance about sth** hacer algo a bombo y platillos; **he made a ~ and dance about the carpet** armó la gorda por lo de la alfombra; **there's no need to make a ~ and dance** no es para tanto; **to give sb the same old ~ and dance*** (*US*) andar siempre con las mismas disculpas; **to sell sth for a (mere) ~** vender algo medio regalado; **I got it for a ~** lo adquirí muy barato; **to sing another ~** (*fig*) bajar el tono, desdecirse.

2 ATTR: **~ and dance routine** número *m* de canción y baile.

songbird ['sɒŋbɜːd] N pájaro *m* cantor, ave *f* cantora.

songbook ['sɒŋbʊk] N cancionero *m*.

song-cycle ['sɒŋˌsaɪkl] N ciclo *m* de canciones.

songfest ['sɒŋfest] N festival *m* de canciones.

song-hit ['sɒŋhɪt] N canción *f* de moda, canción *f* popular del momento, impacto *m*.

songster ['sɒŋstəʳ] N pájaro *m* cantor.

songstress ['sɒŋstrɪs] N cantante *f*.

songthrush ['sɒŋθrʌʃ] N tordo *m* cantor, tordo *m* melodioso.

songwriter ['sɒŋˌraɪtəʳ] N compositor *m*, -ora *f* de canciones.

sonic ['sɒnɪk] ADJ sónico; **~ boom** estampido *m* sónico.

sonics ['sɒnɪks] N sónica *f*.

son-in-law ['sʌnɪnlɔː] N, PL **sons-in-law** ['sʌnzɪnlɔː] yerno *m*, hijo *m* político.

sonnet ['sɒnɪt] N soneto *m*.

sonny* ['sʌnɪ] N hijito *m*; (*in direct address*) hijo *m*.

son-of-a-gun‡ [ˌsʌnəvə'gʌn] N hijo *m* de tu madre*, hijo *m* de la gran pu‡.

sonority [sə'nɒrɪtɪ] N sonoridad *f*.

sonorous ['sɒnərəs] ADJ sonoro.

sonorousness ['sɒnərəsnɪs] N sonoridad *f*.

soon [suːn] ADV (a) (*before long*) pronto, dentro de poco; (*early*) temprano; **come back ~** vuelve pronto; **~ afterwards** poco después; **how ~ can you come?** ¿cuándo puedes venir?; **how ~ can you be ready?** ¿para cuando estarás listo?; **we got there too ~** llegamos demasiado pronto; **Friday is too ~** el viernes es muy pronto; **all too ~ it was over** la función terminó demasiado pronto; **we were none too ~** llegamos en el momento oportuno; no llegamos antes de tiempo.

(b) (*with as*) **as ~ as** en cuanto, tan pronto como; **as ~ as you've seen him** en cuanto le veas, en cuanto le hayas visto; **as ~ as it was finished** en cuanto se terminó; **as ~ as possible** cuanto antes, lo antes posible, lo más pronto posible; **I would as ~ not go** más que prefiero no ir, más me gustaría no ir; **she'd marry him as ~ as not** se casaría con él y tan contenta; V *also* **sooner**.

sooner ['suːnəʳ] ADV (a) (*time*) más temprano, antes; **we got there ~** nosotros llegamos antes; **~ or later** tarde o temprano; **the ~ the better** cuanto antes, mejor; **no ~ had we arrived, than ...** apenas habíamos llegado, cuando ..., no bien llegamos, cuando ...; **no ~ said than done** dicho y hecho; **in 5 years or at his death, whichever is the ~** al cabo de 5 años o a su muerte, lo que suceda antes; **the ~ we start the ~ we finish** cuanto más pronto empecemos, más pronto podremos concluir.

(b) (*preference*) **I had ~ not do it, I would ~ not do it** preferiría no hacerlo; **which would you ~?** ¿cuál prefieres?; **~ you than me!** ¡me alegro de no estar en tu lugar!

soot [sʊt] N hollín *m*.

sooth†† [suːθ] N: **in ~** en realidad.

soothe [suːð] VT tranquilizar, calmar; *pain* aliviar.

soothing ['suːðɪŋ] ADJ tranquilizador, calmante; (*pain-killing*) analgésico; *tone, words etc* dulce, consolador.

soothingly ['suːðɪŋlɪ] ADV *speak etc* dulcemente, con dulzura, en tono consolador.

soothsayer ['suːθˌseɪəʳ] N adivino *m*, -a *f*.

soothsaying ['suːθˌseɪɪŋ] N adivinación *f*.

sooty ['sutɪ] ADJ hollinoso, cubierto de hollín; (fig) negro como el hollín.

┌─ AS SOON AS ──────────────── see also main entry ─┐

- As with other time conjunctions, *en cuanto* and *tan pronto como* are used with the *subjunctive* if the action which follows hasn't happened yet or hadn't happened at the time of speaking:
  As soon as *or* The moment we finish, I've got to write an editorial
  En cuanto terminemos *or* ***Tan pronto como terminemos, tengo que escribir un editorial***
  As soon as I know the dates, I'll let you know
  En cuanto sepa *or* ***Tan pronto como sepa las fechas, te lo diré***
- *En cuanto* and *tan pronto como* are used with the *indicative* when the action in the time clause has already taken place:
  He left the podium as soon as *or* the moment he received his prize
  Se bajó del podio en cuanto recibió *or* ***tan pronto como recibió el premio***
- *En cuanto* and *tan pronto como* are also used with the *indicative* when describing habitual actions:
  As soon as any faxes arrive, they're put in a special box
  En cuanto llegan *or* ***Tan pronto como llegan los faxes, se guardan en una caja especial***
  For further uses and examples, see main entry at soon.

SOP N ABBR *of* **standard operating procedure.**

sop [sɒp] N **(a)** (*food*) sopa *f.* **(b)** (*fig*) regalo *m*, dádiva *f*; compensación *f*; **as a ~ to his pride** para ayudarle a salvar las apariencias, como compensación a su amor propio; **this is a ~ to Cerberus** esto es para comprar la benevolencia de ... **(c)** (*) bobo *m*, -a *f.*

◆ **sop up** VT absorber.

Sophia [səʊ'faɪə] NF Sofía.

sophism ['sɒfɪzəm] N sofisma *m.*

sophist ['sɒfɪst] N sofista *mf.*

sophistical [sə'fɪstɪkəl] ADJ sofístico.

sophisticate [sə'fɪstɪkeɪt] N persona *f* sofisticada.

sophisticated [sə'fɪstɪkeɪtɪd] ADJ (*all senses*) sofisticado.

sophistication [sə,fɪstɪ'keɪʃən] N sofisticación *f.*

sophistry ['sɒfɪstrɪ] N sofistería *f*; **a ~** un sofisma.

Sophocles ['sɒfəkliːz] NM Sófocles.

sophomore ['sɒfəmɔːr] N (*US*) estudiante *mf* de segundo año; *ver también* ┌GRADE┐.

soporific [,sɒpə'rɪfɪk] ADJ soporífero.

sopping ['sɒpɪŋ] ADJ: **it's ~ (wet)** está empapado, está totalmente mojado; **he was ~ wet** estaba hecho una sopa.

soppy* ['sɒpɪ] ADJ (*Brit*) **(a)** (*foolish*) bobo, tonto. **(b)** (*mushy*) sentimental, sensiblero.

soprano [sə'prɑːnəʊ] ①① N, PL **sopranos** [sə'prɑːnəʊz] N (*person*) soprano *f*, tiple *f*; (*voice and part*) soprano *m.*
② ADJ *part etc* de soprano, para soprano; *voice* de soprano.

sorb [sɔːb] N (*tree*) serbal *m*; (*fruit*) serba *f.*

sorbet ['sɔːbeɪ, 'sɔːbɪt] N (*water ice*) sorbete *m*; **lemon ~** sorbete *m* de limón.

sorbic acid [,sɔːbɪk'æsɪd] N ácido *m* sórbico.

sorbitol ['sɔːbɪtɒl] N sorbitol *m.*

sorcerer ['sɔːsərər] N hechicero *m*, brujo *m*; **~'s apprentice** aprendiz *m* de brujo.

sorceress ['sɔːsərɪs] N hechicera *f*, bruja *f.*

sorcery ['sɔːsərɪ] N hechicería *f*, brujería *f.*

sordid ['sɔːdɪd] ADJ (*squalid, dirty*) sórdido, asqueroso, sucio; *place, room* miserable; *deal, motive etc* vil; **it's a pretty ~ business** es un asunto de lo más desagradable.

sordidly ['sɔːdɪdlɪ] ADV sórdidamente.

sordidness ['sɔːdɪdnɪs] N sordidez *f*, lo asqueroso, suciedad *f*; lo miserable; vileza *f.*

sore [sɔːr] ①① ADJ **(a)** (*Med*) inflamado, dolorido, que duele; **~ throat** dolor *m* de garganta; **my eyes are ~, I have ~ eyes** me duelen los ojos; **I'm ~ all over** me duele todo el cuerpo; **where are you ~?** ¿dónde te duele?
(b) (*fig*) **to be ~ at heart** dolerle a uno el corazón; **to be ~ about sth** estar resentido por algo; **to be ~ with sb** estar enojado con uno; **what are you so ~ about?** ¿por qué estás tan ofendido?; **now don't get ~** no te vayas a ofender; **it's a ~ point** es un asunto delicado.
(c) (*liter*) **there is a ~ need of ...** hay gran necesidad de ...; **it was a ~ temptation** era una gran tentación.
② N (*Med*) llaga *f*, úlcera *f*; (*caused by harness etc*) matadura *f*; (*fig*) llaga *f*, herida *f*; recuerdo *m* doloroso; **to open an old ~** (*fig*) renovar la herida.

sorehead* ['sɔːhed] N (*US*) persona *f* resentida, resentido *m*, -a *f.*

sorely ['sɔːlɪ] ADV: **~ wounded** herido de gravedad, gravemente herido; **I am ~ tempted** tengo grandes tentaciones; **I am ~ tempted**

---

to + *infin* casi estoy por + *infin*; **he has been ~ tried** ha sufrido lo indecible.

soreness ['sɔːnɪs] N (*Med*) inflamación *f*, dolor *m.*

sorghum ['sɔːgəm] N sorgo *m.*

sorority [sə'rɒrɪtɪ] N (*US Univ*) hermandad *f* de mujeres.

┌─ SORORITY/FRATERNITY ──────────────┐

ⓘ *Muchas universidades estadounidenses poseen dentro del campus hermandades conocidas como* **fraternities** *o* **frats** *(de hombres) o* **sororities** *(de mujeres). Estas hermandades, a las que sólo se puede ingresar mediante invitación, organizan fiestas, recogen fondos con fines benéficos e intentan hacer que su hermandad sobresalga entre las demás. Suelen tener nombres compuestos de letras del alfabeto griego, como por ejemplo* **Kappa Kappa Gamma.** *Existe división de opiniones en cuanto a los beneficios o ventajas de estas hermandades: para los miembros es una buena manera de hacer amigos, pero la mayoría de los estudiantes piensan que son elitistas y discriminatorias. Durante las ceremonias secretas de iniciación, que incluyen varias pruebas físicas y novatadas que se denominan* **hazing,** *se ha producido la muerte de varios estudiantes, lo cual ha aumentado la polémica.*

---

sorrel[1] ['sɒrəl] N (*Bot*) acedera *f.*

sorrel[2] ['sɒrəl] ① ADJ alazán.
② N alazán *m*, caballo *m* alazán.

sorrow ['sɒrəʊ] ① N pesar *m*, pena *f*, dolor *m*; tristeza *f*; **more in ~ than in anger** con más pesar que enojo; **to my (great) ~** con gran pesar mío, con gran sentimiento mío; **this was a great ~ to me** esto me causó mucha pena; **the ~s of their race** las aflicciones de su raza; **to drown one's ~s** olvidar su tristeza emborrachándose, ahogar sus penas en alcohol.
② VI apenarse, afligirse (*at, for, over* de, por), dolerse (*at, for, over* de).

sorrowful ['sɒrəfʊl] ADJ afligido, triste, pesaroso.

sorrowfully ['sɒrəflɪ] ADV con pena, tristemente.

sorrowing ['sɒrəʊɪŋ] ADJ afligido.

▼ **sorry** ['sɒrɪ] ADJ **(a)** (*regretful*) arrepentido; (*sad*) triste, afligido, apenado; **~!** ¡perdón!, ¡perdone!; **awfully ~!, so ~!, very ~!** lo siento mucho, lo siento en el alma, ¡cuánto lo siento!; **to be ~** sentirlo; **I am very ~** lo siento mucho; **I can't say I'm ~** no puedo decir que lo sienta; **he wasn't in the least bit ~** no se arrepintió en lo más mínimo; **I'm ~ to say it was no use** desgraciadamente no sirvió para nada; **to be ~ about sth** afligirse por algo; **I'm ~ about that vase** te pido perdón por lo del florero; me da pena el florero ese; **to be (*or* feel) ~ for sb** compadecer a uno, tener lástima a uno; **I feel ~ for the child** el niño me da lástima; **to feel ~ for o.s.** sentirse desgraciado; **there's no need to be ~ for him** no hace falta compadecerle; **you'll be ~ for this!** ¡lo arrepentirás!, ¡me las pagarás!; **to be (*or* feel, look) ~ for o.s.** estar muy abatido; **to be that ... sentir que + *subj*; **to be ~ to + *infin*** sentir + *infin*, lamentar + *infin*; **I am ~ to have to tell you that ...** lamento tener que decirle que ...; **we are ~ to inform you that ...** lamentamos informarle que ...; **I am ~ for the inconvenience caused by ...** lamento las molestias que se han debido a ...
(b) (*bad*) *condition, plight* lastimoso; *sight* triste; *figure* ridículo; *excuse* nada convincente; *joke* pobre; **it was a ~ tale of defeat** fue una triste narración de derrotas.

sort [sɔːt] ① N **(a)** (*class, kind*) clase *f*, género *m*, especie *f*; tipo *m*; **what ~ do you want?** ¿qué clase quiere Vd?; **the ~ you gave me last time** la misma que Vd me dio la última vez; **but not that ~** pero no de ese tipo, pero no como eso; **I know his ~** ésos me los conozco, conozco el paño; **he's the ~ who will cheat you** es de los que te engañarán; **books of all ~s** toda clase de libros, libros de toda clase; **he's a painter of a ~, he's a painter of ~s** es en cierto modo pintor; **it's coffee of a ~** es café pero bastante inferior, es lo que apenas se puede llamar café; **perfect of its ~** perfecto en su línea; **something of the ~** algo por el estilo; **nothing of the ~!** ¡nada de eso!, ¡ni hablar!; **I shall do nothing of the ~** no haré eso bajo ningún concepto; **in some ~** en cierta medida; **it takes all ~s (to make a world)** de todo hay en la viña del Señor.
(b) (*with of*) **what ~ of car?** ¿qué clase de coche?; **what ~ of man is he?** ¿qué tipo de hombre es?; **this ~ of house** una casa de este tipo; **an odd ~ of novel** una novela rara, una novela de tipo extraño; **all ~s of dogs** toda clase de perros, perros de toda clase; **he's a ~ of agent** es algo así como un agente; **he's some ~ of painter** es pintor pero no sé de qué género; **I felt a ~ of shame** sentí algo parecido a la vergüenza, en cierto modo sentí vergüenza; **it's a ~ of dance** es una especie de baile; **I have a ~ of idea that ...** tengo cierta idea de que ...; **that's the ~ of thing I need** eso es lo que me hace falta; **that's the ~ of thing I mean** eso es precisamente lo que quiero decir; **and all that ~ of thing** y otras cosas por el estilo; **that's the ~ of person I am** yo soy así; **he's not that ~ of person** no es capaz de hacer eso, no es de los que hacen tales cosas; **I'm not that ~ of girl** yo no soy de ésas.

(c) (*: ~ **of**) **it's ~ of awkward** es bastante (*LAm*: medio) difícil; **it's ~ of blue** es más bien azul; **I'm ~ of lost** estoy como perdido; **it's ~ of finished** está más o menos terminado; **I ~ of feel that ...** en cierto modo creo que ...; **it ~ of made me laugh** no sé por qué pero me hizo reír; **aren't you pleased? ... ~ of** ¿no te alegras? ... en cierto modo.

(d) (*person*) **he's a good ~** es buena persona, es buena gente (*LAm*), es un buen chico; **she sounds a good ~** da la impresión de ser buena persona; **he's an odd ~** es un tipo extraño; **your ~ never did any good** las personas como Vd nunca hicieron nada bueno.

(e) to be out of ~s (*Med*) estar indispuesto, no estar del todo bien; (*in mood*) estar molesto, sentirse incómodo.

(f) (*Comput*) ordenación *f*.

2 VT *problems* arreglar; *papers* clasificar; (*Comput*) ordenar.

◆**sort out** VT **(a)** (*classify*) clasificar; **to ~ out the bad ones** (*select*) separar los malos, quitar los malos.

(b) (*fig*) *problem etc* arreglar; solucionar; **we've got it ~ed out now** lo hemos arreglado ya; **can you ~ this out for me?** ¿puede ayudarme con esto?; **to ~ sb out*** (*Brit*) ajustar cuentas con uno; **I'll come down there and ~ you out!*** ¡si bajo allá te pego una paliza!

(c) (*explain*) **to ~ sth out for sb** explicar algo a uno, aclarar algo a uno.

◆**sort through** VT revisar.

sort code ['sɔːtkəʊd] N número *m* de agencia.

sorter ['sɔːtəʳ] N clasificador *m*, -ora *f*; (*Post*) oficial *mf* de correos.

sortie ['sɔːtɪ] N salida *f*; **to make a ~** hacer una salida.

sorting ['sɔːtɪŋ] N clasificación *f*; (*Comput*) ordenación *f*.

sorting-office ['sɔːtɪŋ,ɒfɪs] N sala *f* de batalla.

sort-out* ['sɔːtaʊt] N: **to have a ~** hacer limpieza; arreglar las cosas.

SOS N (*signal*) s.o.s. *m*; (*fig*) llamada *f* de socorro.

so-so ['səʊsəʊ] ADV regular, así así.

sot [sɒt] N borrachín *m*.

sottish ['sɒtɪʃ] ADJ embrutecido (por el alcohol).

sotto voce ['sɒtəʊ'vəʊtʃɪ] ADV en voz baja.

soubriquet ['suːbrɪkeɪ] N V **sobriquet**.

Soudan [suːdɑːn] *etc* = **Sudan** *etc*.

soufflé ['suːfleɪ] 1 N suflé *m*, soufflé *m*.

2 ATTR: **~ dish** fuente *f* de soufflé.

sough [saʊ] 1 N susurro *m*.

2 VI susurrar.

sought [sɔːt] PRET AND PTP **of seek.**

sought-after ['sɔːt,ɑːftəʳ] ADJ codiciado; solicitado, deseado, que tiene mucha demanda; **this much ~ title** este codiciado título.

souk [suːk] N zoco *m*.

soul [səʊl] N **(a)** alma *f*; **like a lost ~** como alma en pena; **upon my ~!**, (**God**) **bless my ~!** ¡caramba!; ¡Dios mío!; **with all one's ~** con toda el alma; **God rest his ~!** ¡Dios le tenga en su gloria!; **to bare one's ~** abrir su pecho (*to sb* a uno); **to possess one's ~ in patience** armarse de paciencia.

(b) (*fig: person*) alma *f*; **3,000 ~s** 3.000 almas; **poor ~!** ¡pobrecito!; **the poor ~ had nowhere to sleep** el pobre no tenía dónde dormir; **he's a good ~** es un bendito; **she's a simple ~** es un alma de Dios; **without seeing a ~** sin ver bicho viviente; **every living ~** todo ser viviente; **the ship was lost with all ~s** el buque se hundió con toda la tripulación (y pasajeros); **he's the ~ of discretion** es la misma discreción, es la discreción en persona.

(c) (*US*) *se aplica a la cultura de los negros de EE.UU*; **~ food** cocina *f* negra del sur de EE.UU; **~ music** soul *m*.

╔══ **SOUL FOOD** ══

ⓘ *La comida conocida como* **soul food** *tiene su origen en la población negra de escasos recursos económicos que vivía en el sur de Estados Unidos, aunque hoy día se come en todas partes. Son típicos, por ejemplo, los* **chitlins**, *hechos de intestinos de cerdo fritos, los* **pig's trotters** *(manitas de cerdo) o la sopa llamada* **cow pea soup**, *hecha de verduras cocidas con huesos de jamón y cebollas. Un plato típico completo es el* **blackplate**, *que consiste en revuelto de sesos de cerdo acompañados, entre otros ingredientes, de* **chitlins**, **dumplings** *(bolas de masa cocidas),* **baked grits** *(sémola al horno) y* **corn bread** *(pan de maíz).*

soul-destroying ['səʊldɪs'trɔɪɪŋ] ADJ (*fig*) de lo más aburrido (*or* monótono *etc*); totalmente desprovisto de interés, de nulo interés intelectual (*or* estético *etc*).

soulful ['səʊlfʊl] ADJ sentimental; conmovedor; (*pej*) patético, lacrimoso.

soulfully ['səʊlfəlɪ] ADV de modo sentimental; de modo conmovedor.

soulless ['səʊllɪs] ADJ *person* sin alma, desalmado; *work etc* mecánico, monótono, sin interés humano.

soulmate ['səʊlmeɪt] N perfecto compañero *m* espiritual, perfecta compañera *f* espiritual.

soul-searching ['səʊl,sɜːtʃɪŋ] N examen *m* de conciencia, examen *m* introspectivo.

soul-stirring ['səʊl,stɜːrɪŋ] ADJ conmovedor, emocionante, inspirador.

sound¹ [saʊnd] 1 ADJ sano; firme, sólido; *constitution* robusto; (*Comm*) solvente; *person* formal, digno de confianza; *argument, idea, opinion* razonable, lógico, bien fundado; *ortodoxo*; *policy* prudente; *investment* bueno, seguro; *move* acertado, lógico; *rule* bueno; *training etc* sólido; *sleep* profundo; **in ~ condition** en buenas condiciones; **to be as ~ as a bell** estar en perfecta salud; **to be ~ in wind and limb** estar en buen estado físico; **to be ~ in mind and body** ser sano de cuerpo y de espíritu; **he's a very ~ man** es persona de la mayor confianza; **he's a ~ worker** es buen trabajador, trabaja con toda seriedad; **he is ~ enough on the theory** tiene una preparación sólida en cuanto a la teoría; tiene opiniones ortodoxas acerca de la teoría.

2 ADV: **to be ~ asleep** estar profundamente dormido; **I shall sleep the ~er for it** por eso dormiré más tranquilamente.

sound² [saʊnd] 1 N sonido *m*, son *m*; ruido *m*; **to the ~(s) of the national anthem** a los sones del himno nacional; **by the ~ of it** según parece, al parecer; **within ~ of** al alcance de; **they were within ~ of the camp** el campamento estaba al alcance del oído; **the Glenn Miller ~** la música de Glenn Miller; **not a ~ was heard** no hubo ruido alguno; **there came the ~ of breaking glass** se oyó el ruido de cristales que se rompían; **I don't like the ~ of it** esto no nos promete nada bueno, me inquieta la noticia, no me gusta la idea.

2 ATTR: **~ archive** archivo *m* del sonido; **~ bite** frase *f* pegadiza; **~ engineer** sonista *mf*; **~ law** ley *f* fonética; **~ library** fonoteca *f*; **~-producing** productor de sonido; **~ shift** cambio *m* de pronunciación; **~ system** (*of language*) sistema *m* fonológico, (*hi-fi*) cadena *f* de sonido; **~ truck** (*US*) furgón *m* publicitario.

3 VT *sonar*; *alarm, bell, horn, trumpet* tocar; *warning* dar; *praises* cantar, entonar; **to ~ the 'd' in 'hablado'** pronunciar la 'd' en 'hablado'; **to ~ the charge** tocar la carga; **to ~ the retreat** tocar a retirada.

4 VI **(a)** sonar, resonar; **the bell ~ed** sonó el timbre; **it ~s hollow** suena a hueco; **it ~s like Dutch to me** me suena a holandés; **a gun ~ed a long way off** se oyó un cañón a lo lejos.

(b) (*fig: seem*) sonar, parecer; **that ~s very odd** eso parece muy raro; **he ~s like a good sort** parece buena persona, da la impresión de ser buena persona; **how does it ~ to you?** ¿a ti qué te parece?; **it ~s as if she's not coming** parece que no viene.

◆**sound off*** VI (*speak firmly*) hablar en tono autoritario; (*complain*) quejarse; (*protest*) protestar, poner el grito en el cielo.

sound³ [saʊnd] 1 N (*Med*) sonda *f*.

2 VT (*Med, Naut*) sondar; *chest* auscultar.

◆**sound out** VT *person, intentions* sondear, tantear; **to ~ sb out about sth** tratar de averiguar lo que piensa uno acerca de un asunto; **to ~ out one's conscience** consultar su conciencia.

sound⁴ [saʊnd] N (*Geog*) estrecho *m*, brazo *m* de mar.

sound-barrier ['saʊnd,bærɪəʳ] N barrera *f* del sonido.

soundbox ['saʊndbɒks] N (*Mus*) caja *f* de resonancia.

sound card ['saʊndkɑːd] N (*Comput*) tarjeta *f* de sonido.

sound-effects ['saʊndɪ,fekts] NPL efectos *mpl* sonoros.

sounding¹ ['saʊndɪŋ] N **(a)** (*of trumpet, bell etc*) sonido *m*, son *m*; **the ~ of the retreat/the alarm** el toque de retirada/de generala. **(b)** (*Med*) sondeo *m*.

sounding² ['saʊndɪŋ] N (*Naut*) sondeo *m*; **~s** (*for oil etc*) sondeos *mpl*; **to take ~s** (*fig*) sondear la opinión, pulsar las opiniones.

sounding-board ['saʊndɪŋbɔːd] N (*Mus*) secreto *m*, tabla *f* armónica, tablero *m* sonoro, caja *f* de resonancia; (*fig*) piedra *f* de toque, caja *f* de resonancia.

soundless ['saʊndlɪs] ADJ silencioso, sin ruido; insonoro.

soundlessly ['saʊndlɪslɪ] ADV silenciosamente, sin ruido.

soundly ['saʊndlɪ] ADV sólidamente; razonablemente, lógicamente, prudentemente; **to beat sb ~** derrotar a uno completamente; **to thrash sb ~** dar a uno una paliza de verdad; **to sleep ~** dormir bien, dormir profundamente.

soundness ['saʊndnɪs] N firmeza *f*, solidez *f*; robustez *f*; solvencia *f*; formalidad *f*; lo razonable, lógica *f*, sólida fundación *f*; ortodoxia *f*; prudencia *f*; seguridad *f*; **the ~ of sb's health** la buena salud de uno; **the ~ of a proposal** la solidez de una proposición.

soundproof ['saʊndpruːf] 1 ADJ insonorizado, a prueba de ruidos.

2 VT insonorizar.

soundproofing ['saʊndpruːfɪŋ] N insonorización *f*.

sound recording ['saʊndrɪ,kɔːdɪŋ] N grabación *f* sonora.

sound recordist ['saʊndrɪ,kɔːdɪst] N (*TV*) registrador *m*, -ora *f* de sonido.

soundtrack ['saʊndtræk] N banda *f* sonora.

soundwave ['saʊndweɪv] N onda *f* sonora, onda *f* acústica.

soup [suːp] N (*clear, thin*) caldo *m*, consomé *m*; (*thick*) puré *m*, sopa *f*; **to be in the ~*** estar en apuros; **now we're properly in the ~*** ahora la hemos pringado de verdad*.

◆**soup up*** VT (*Aut*) sobrealimentar, trucar*; (*fig*) mejorar, aumentar la eficacia de.

soupçon ['suːpsɔ̃] N pizca *f*; olorcillo *m* (*of a*); **with a ~ of ginger** con una pizca de jengibre.

souped-up* ['su:pt,ʌp] ADJ (Aut) sobrealimentado, trucado*.

soup-kitchen ['su:p,kɪtʃɪn] N comedor m de beneficencia, olla f común.

soup-plate ['su:ppleɪt] N plato m sopero.

soupspoon ['su:pspu:n] N cuchara f sopera.

soup tureen ['su:ptə,ri:n] N sopera f.

soupy ['su:pɪ] ADJ liquid espeso, turbio; atmosphere pesado, espeso; viciado.

sour ['saʊər] 1 ADJ agrio, acre; milk cortado; land maleado; person agrio, desabrido, poco afable; tone, reply áspero, desabrido; **~ cream** (Culin) nata f cortada, crema f agria; **to go ~** (milk) cortarse; **to turn ~** agriarse, volverse agrio.
　2 VT agriar; land malear; person agriar, amargar.
　3 VI agriarse, volverse agrio; (land) malearse.

source [sɔ:s] 1 N (of river) fuente f, nacimiento m; (fig) fuente f, origen m; procedencia f; (Liter etc) fuente f; (of infection) foco m; **what is the ~ of this information?** ¿de dónde proceden estos informes?; **I have it from a good ~ that ...** sé de fuente fidedigna que ...; **we have other ~s of supply** tenemos otras fuentes de suministro.
　2 ATTR: **~ file** archivo m fuente; **~ language** lengua f de partida, lengua f original, lengua f (de) base; (Comput) lenguaje m fuente; **~ materials** materiales mpl de referencia; **~ program(me)** programa m fuente.

sourdine [sʊə'di:n] N sordina f.

sourdough ['saʊə,dəʊ] ATTR: **~ bread** (US) pan m de masa fermentada.

sour-faced ['saʊəfeɪst] ADJ con cara de pocos amigos.

sourish ['saʊərɪʃ] ADJ agrete.

sourly ['saʊəlɪ] ADV (fig) agriamente; **to answer ~** contestar en tono áspero.

sourness ['saʊənɪs] N agrura f, acidez f; (fig) agrura f, aspereza f.

sourpuss* ['saʊəpʊs] N persona f desabrida, persona f poco afable.

souse [saʊs] 1 VT (a) (pickle) escabechar. (b) (plunge) zambullir (into en); (soak) empapar (with de, en), mojar (with de); **to ~ sb with soup** empapar a uno de sopa; **to get ~d** mojarse, calarse. (c) **to be ~d**‡ estar ajumado*.
　2 N (US‡) borracho m, -a f.

soutane [su:'tɑ:n] N sotana f.

south [saʊθ] 1 N sur m; mediodía m.
　2 ADJ del sur, meridional; wind del sur.
　3 ADV al sur, hacia el sur.

South Africa [saʊθ'æfrɪkə] N África f del Sur.

South African [saʊθ'æfrɪkən] 1 ADJ sudafricano.
　2 N sudafricano m, -a f.

South America [,saʊθə'merɪkə] N América f del Sur, Sudamérica f.

South American [,saʊθə'merɪkən] 1 ADJ sudamericano.
　2 N sudamericano m, -a f.

South Australia [,saʊθɒs'treɪlɪə] N Australia f del Sur.

southbound ['saʊθbaʊnd] ADJ traffic que va hacia el sur; carriageway dirección sur.

South Carolina [,saʊθkærə'laɪnə] N Carolina f del Sur.

South Dakota [,saʊθdə'kəʊtə] N Dakota f del Sur.

south-east ['saʊθ'i:st] 1 N sudeste m.
　2 ADJ point, direction sudeste; wind del sudeste.

South-East Asia [,saʊθi:st'eɪʃə] N Asia f Sudoriental.

south-easterly [saʊθ'i:stəlɪ] ADJ point, direction sudeste; wind del sudeste.

south-eastern [saʊθ'i:stən] ADJ sudeste.

south-eastward(s) [saʊθ'i:stwəd(z)] ADV hacia el sudeste.

southerly ['sʌðəlɪ] ADJ point, direction sur; wind del sur; **the most ~ point in Europe** el punto más meridional de Europa.

southern ['sʌðən] ADJ del sur, meridional; **S~ Cross** Cruz f del Sur; **~ hemisphere** hemisferio m sur.

southerner ['sʌðənər] N habitante mf del sur; meridional mf, sureño m, -a f (LAm); (US Hist) sudista mf; **she's a ~** es del Sur; **~s are shorter than northerners** los meridionales son menos altos que los septentrionales.

southernmost ['sʌðənməʊst] ADJ (el) más meridional, situado más al sur; **the ~ town in Europe** la ciudad más meridional de Europa.

south-facing ['saʊθ,feɪsɪŋ] ADJ con cara al sur, orientado hacia el sur; **~ slope** vertiente f sur.

South Georgia [,saʊθ'dʒɔ:dʒɪə] N Georgia f del Sur.

South Korea ['saʊθkə'rɪə] N Corea f del Sur.

South Korean ['saʊθkə'rɪən] 1 ADJ surcoreano.
　2 N surcoreano m, -a f.

South Pacific [,saʊθpə'sɪfɪk] N Pacífico m Sur.

southpaw ['saʊθpɔ:] N (esp US) zurdo m.

South Pole [,saʊθ'pəʊl] N Polo m Sur.

South Sea Islands [,saʊθsi:'aɪləndz] NPL Islas fpl de los mares del Sur.

South Seas ['saʊθ'si:z] NPL mares mpl del Sur.

south-south-east [,saʊθsaʊθ'i:st] 1 N sudsudeste m.
　2 ADJ sudsudoriental, sudsudeste.
　3 ADV hacia el sudsudeste.

south-south-west [,saʊθsaʊθ'west] 1 N sudsudoeste m.
　2 ADJ sudsudoccidental, sudsudoeste.
　3 ADV hacia el sudsudoeste.

South Vietnam [saʊθ,vjet'næm] N Vietnam m del Sur.

South Vietnamese ['saʊθ,vjetnə'mi:z] 1 ADJ survietnamita.
　2 N survietnamita mf.

southward ['saʊθwəd] 1 ADJ advance etc hacia el sur, en dirección sur.
　2 ADV (also **~s**) hacia el sur, en dirección sur.

south-west ['saʊθ'west] 1 N suroeste m.
　2 ADJ point, direction suroeste; wind del suroeste.

South West Africa [,saʊθwest'æfrɪkə] N África f del Suroeste.

south-wester [saʊθ'westər] N (wind) suroeste m; (hat) sueste m.

south-westerly [saʊθ'westəlɪ] ADJ point, direction suroeste; wind del suroeste.

south-western [saʊθ'westən] ADJ suroeste.

south-westward(s) [saʊθ'westwəd(z)] ADV hacia el suroeste.

souvenir [,su:və'nɪər] N recuerdo m.

sou'wester [saʊ'westər] N sueste m.

sovereign ['sɒvrɪn] 1 ADJ soberano; **~ state** estado m soberano.
　2 N soberano m, -a f; (Brit: coin) soberano m.

sovereignty ['sɒvrəntɪ] N soberanía f.

soviet ['saʊvɪət] 1 N (a) soviet m. (b) **S~** (person) soviético m, -a f, ruso m, -a f.
　2 ADJ soviético; **S~ Russia** Rusia f Soviética; **S~ Union** Unión f Soviética.

Sovietologist [,saʊvɪə'tɒlədʒɪst] N sovietólogo m, -a f.

sow¹ [səʊ] (irr: PRET **sowed**, PTP **sown**) VT sembrar (with de; also fig); esparcir; doubts sembrar; **to ~ mines in a strait, to ~ a strait with mines** sembrar un estrecho de minas, colocar minas en un estrecho.

sow² [saʊ] N cerda f, puerca f, marrana f; (of wild boar) jabalina f; (of badger) tejón m hembra; (Tech) galápago m.

sower ['səʊər] N sembrador m, -ora f.

sowing ['səʊɪŋ] N siembra f.

sowing-machine ['səʊɪŋmə,ʃi:n] N sembradora f.

sowing time ['səʊɪŋtaɪm] N época f de la siembra, sementera f.

sown [səʊn] PTP of **sow**.

sow-thistle ['saʊθɪsl] N cerraja f.

soy [sɔɪ] (esp US), **soya** ['sɔɪə] (esp Brit) 1 N soja f.
　2 ATTR: **~ bean** haba f de soja, fríjol m de soja; **~ flour** harina f de soja; **~ oil** aceite m de soja; **~ sauce** salsa f de soja.

sozzled‡ ['sɒzld] ADJ: **to be ~** estar ajumado*; **to get ~** ajumarse*.

SP N ABBR of **starting price** precio m inicial.

spa [spɑ:] N balneario m, estación f termal.

space [speɪs] 1 N (a) (gen) espacio m; (room) espacio m, sitio m; **for a ~** durante cierta distancia, durante cierto tiempo; **in a confined ~** en un espacio restringido; **in the ~ of one hour** en el espacio de una hora; **in the ~ of 3 generations** en el espacio de 3 generaciones; **to buy ~ in a newspaper** comprar un espacio en un periódico; **to clear a (or make) ~ for** hacer un sitio para, hacer lugar para; **to leave ~ for** dejar un sitio para; **leave a ~ for the name** deje un espacio para el nombre; **to stare into ~** mirar al vacío; mirar distraído; **it takes up a lot of ~** ocupa bastante espacio.
　(b) (Astron, Phys) espacio m.
　2 ATTR espacial; **~ age** era f espacial; **~ exploration** exploración f espacial; **S~ Invaders** (game) Marcianitos mpl; **~ lab** laboratorio m espacial; **~ platform** plataforma f espacial; **~ probe** sonda f espacial; **~ race** carrera f espacial; **~ research** investigaciones fpl espaciales; **~ sickness** enfermedad f espacial; **~ travel** viajes mpl espaciales.
　3 VT (a) (also **to ~ out**) espaciar (also Typ); **well ~d out** bastante distanciados.
　(b) **to be ~d out**‡ (on drugs) estar colocado‡; (drunk) estar ajumado*.

space-bar ['speɪsbɑ:r] N barra f espaciadora, espaciador m.

space-capsule ['speɪs,kæpsju:l] N cápsula f espacial.

space-centre, (US) **space-center** ['speɪs,sentər] N centro m espacial.

spacecraft ['speɪskrɑ:ft] N, PL INVAR nave f espacial, astronave f.

space-flight ['speɪsflaɪt] N vuelo m espacial.

space-helmet ['speɪs,helmɪt] N casco m espacial.

spaceman ['speɪsmæn] N, PL **spacemen** ['speɪsmen] astronauta m, cosmonauta m.

space-saving ['speɪs,seɪvɪŋ] ADJ que economiza espacio; de tamaño reducido.

spaceship ['speɪsʃɪp] N nave f espacial, astronave f.

space-shot ['speɪsʃɒt] N (lanzamiento m de un) vehículo m espacial.

space-shuttle ['speɪs,ʃʌtl] N transbordador m espacial, lanzadera f espacial.

space-station ['speɪs,steɪʃən] N estación f espacial, cosmódromo m.

spacesuit ['speɪssu:t] N traje m espacial.

space-time ['speɪs'taɪm] N (*also* ~ **continuum**) continuo *m* espacio-tiempo.

space-vehicle ['speɪsˌviːɪkl] N vehículo *m* espacial.

spacewalk ['speɪswɔːk] 1 N paseo *m* espacial.

2 VI pasear por el espacio.

spacewoman ['speɪsˌwʊmən] N, PL **spacewomen** ['speɪsˌwɪmɪn] astronauta *f*, cosmonauta *f*.

spacey* ['speɪsɪ] ADJ *music* psicodélico, sideral; *person* ausente, en babia.

spacing ['speɪsɪŋ] N espaciamiento *m*; (*Typ*) espaciado *m*; **with double ~** a doble espacio; **in single ~** a espacio sencillo.

spacing-bar ['speɪsɪŋbɑːʳ] N barra *f* espaciadora, espaciador *m*.

spacious ['speɪʃəs] ADJ espacioso, amplio; extenso; *living* holgado, lujoso.

spaciousness ['speɪʃəsnɪs] N espaciosidad *f*, amplitud *f*; extensión *f*.

spade [speɪd] N (**a**) (*tool*) pala *f*, laya *f*; **to call a ~ a ~** llamar al pan pan y al vino vino. (**b**) **~s** (*Cards*) picas *fpl*, picos *mpl*, (*in Spanish pack*) espadas *fpl*. (**c**) (*pej*‡) negro *m*, -a *f*.

spadeful ['speɪdfʊl] N pala *f*; **by the ~** (*fig*) en grandes cantidades.

spadework ['speɪdwɜːk] N (*fig*) trabajo *m* preliminar.

spaghetti [spə'getɪ] N espaguetis *mpl*; fideos *mpl*; **~ junction*** scalextric *m*; **~ western** película *f* de vaqueros hecha por un director italiano, spaghetti western *m*.

Spain [speɪn] N España *f*.

spake†† [speɪk] PRET *of* **speak.**

Spam [spæm] ® N carne *f* de cerdo en conserva.

span[1] [spæn] 1 N (**a**) (*extent*) (*of time*) lapso *m*, espacio *m*; duración *f*; (*of wing*) envergadura *f*; (*of bridge: referring to space*) ojo *m*, luz *f*, (*referring to structure*) arcada *f*, tramo *m*; (*of roof*) vano *m*; **a ~ of 50 metres** (*bridge*) una luz de 50 metros; **a bridge with 7 ~s** un puente de 7 arcadas, un puente de 7 ojos; **the longest single-~ bridge in the world** el puente más largo del mundo de una sola arcada; **the average ~ of life** la duración media de la vida; **for a brief ~** durante una breve temporada; **the whole ~ of world affairs** toda la extensión de los asuntos mundiales, los asuntos mundiales en toda su amplitud.

(**b**) (††: *measure*) palmo *m*.

(**c**) (*yoke: of oxen*) yunta *f*, (*horses*) pareja *f*.

2 VT (**a**) (*bridge*) extenderse sobre, cruzar; (*builder*) tender un puente sobre; (*in time etc*) abarcar; **his life ~ned 4 reigns** su vida abarcó 4 reinados.

(**b**) (*measure*) medir (a palmos).

span[2] [spæn] PRET *of* **spin.**

spangle ['spæŋgl] 1 N lentejuela *f*.

2 VT adornar con lentejuelas; **~d with** (*fig*) sembrado de.

Spanglish ['spæŋglɪʃ] N (*hum*) angliparla *f*, hispinglés *m*, espinglés *m*.

spangly ['spæŋglɪ] ADJ cubierto con lentejuelas, de lentejuelas.

Spaniard ['spænjəd] N español *m*, -ola *f*.

spaniel ['spænjəl] N perro *m* de aguas.

Spanish ['spænɪʃ] 1 ADJ español; **~ America** Hispanoamérica *f*; **~ Armada** la Invencible (*1588*); **~ chestnut** castaña *f* dulce; **~ fly** cantárida *f*; **~ guitar** guitarra *f* española.

2 N (**a**) **the ~** los españoles. (**b**) (*Ling*) español *m*, castellano *m*.

Spanish-American ['spænɪʃə'merɪkən] 1 ADJ hispanoamericano.

2 N hispanoamericano *m*, -a *f*.

Spanishness ['spænɪʃnɪs] N carácter *m* español, cualidad *f* española; españolismo *m*.

Spanish-speaking ['spænɪʃ'spiːkɪŋ] ADJ hispanohablante, hispanoparlante, de habla española.

spank [spæŋk] 1 N azote *m*, manotada *f* (en las nalgas); **to give sb a ~** dar un azote a uno (en las nalgas).

2 VT zurrar, manotear; **I'll ~ you!** ¡te voy a pegar!

3 VI: **to ~ along** correr, ir volando.

spanking ['spæŋkɪŋ] 1 ADJ (*) *pace* grande, rápido; *breeze* fuerte; **we had a ~ (good) time** lo pasamos en grande*.

2 N zurra* *f*; **to give sb a ~** zurrar a uno*.

spanner ['spænəʳ] N (*Brit*) llave *f*, llave *f* de tuercas; **to throw** (*or* **put**) **a ~ in the works** meter un palo en la rueda.

spar[1] [spɑːʳ] N (*Naut*) palo *m*, verga *f*.

spar[2] [spɑːʳ] VI (*Boxing*) hacer fintas, fintar; entrenarse en el boxeo, hacer ejercicios de boxeo; **to ~ at sb** amagar a uno; **to ~ with sb about sth** (*fig*) disputar algo amistosamente con uno; **he's only ~ring with the problem** no intenta seriamente resolver el problema.

spar[3] [spɑːʳ] N (*Min*) espato *m*.

spare [speəʳ] 1 ADJ (**a**) (*left over*) sobrante, que sobra, de más; (*available*) disponible; *room* para convidados; *time* libre, desocupado; *part* (*Mech*) de repuesto, de recambio; **~ collar** cuello *m* de repuesto; **~ part = 2; ~ part surgery*** cirugía *f* de trasplantes; **~ time** ratos *mpl* libres, ratos *mpl* de ocio; horas *fpl* libres; **if you have any ~ time** si dispones de tiempo, si tienes tiempo; **~ tire** (*US*), **~ tyre** neumático *m* de repuesto, (*hum*) michelín *m*, rosca *f*, rodete *m*; **there are 2 go-**

ing ~ sobran 2, quedan 2; **if you have any ~ bottles** si dispones de algunas botellas; **it's all the ~ cash I have** es todo el dinero que me sobra.

(**b**) (*of build etc*) enjuto; **~ rib** costilla *f* de cerdo (con poca carne).

(**c**) **to go ~** (*Brit*‡) enloquecerse, subirse por las paredes*.

2 N pieza *f* de repuesto, repuesto *m*, recambio *m*, refacción *f* (*Mex*); **we stock ~s** tenemos existencia de repuestos.

3 VT (**a**) (*be grudging with*) excusar; escatimar; **to ~ no expense** no escatimar dinero; **to ~ no pains to do sth** no escatimar esfuerzos por hacer algo.

(**b**) (*do without*) pasarse sin, prescindir de; ahorrar; economizar; **we can't ~ him now** ahora no podemos estar sin él, ahora no podemos prescindir de él; **can you ~ this for a moment?** ¿me puedo llevar esto un momento?, ¿me permite llevarme esto un momento?; **if you can ~ it** si puedes pasarte sin él, si puedes cedérmelo; **can you ~ the time?** ¿dispones del tiempo?; **I can ~ you 5 minutes** estoy libre para verle durante 5 minutos, le puedo dedicar 5 minutos.

(**c**) (*left over*) **to ~** de sobra; **there is none to ~** apenas queda nada; no tenemos nada de sobra, no nos sobra nada; **we have 9 bottles to ~** nos sobran 9 botellas; **there's enough and to ~** basta y sobra, hay más que suficiente para todos.

(**d**) (*show mercy to*) *life* perdonar; **the fire ~d nothing** el incendio no perdonó nada; **he was ~d another 3 years** Dios le dio 3 años más de vida; **he ~s nobody** hace trabajar a todos; es severo con todos sin excepción; **to ~ sb's feelings** procurar no herir los sentimientos de uno; **I will ~ you the details** te evitaré los detalles; **to ~ sb the trouble of doing sth** evitar a uno la molestia de hacer algo; **~ my blushes!** ¡considera mi modestia!, ¡qué cosas me dices!

spare-time ['speətaɪm] ATTR: **~ job** actividad *f* que ocupa las horas libres.

sparing ['speərɪŋ] ADJ escaso; (*thrifty*) económico; controlado, limitado; **his ~ use of colour** su parquedad con los colores; **to be ~ of, to be ~ with** ser parco en, ser avaro de; **to be ~ of praise** escatimar los elogios; **to be ~ of words** ser persona de pocas palabras; ser parco en hablar.

sparingly ['speərɪŋlɪ] ADV escasamente; económicamente; **we used water ~** empleamos poca agua; **he uses colour ~** es parco en el uso de los colores; **use it very ~** úselo en pequeñas cantidades, úselo con moderación; **to eat ~** comer poco, comer frugalmente.

sparingness ['speərɪŋnɪs] N parquedad *f*; economía *f*, moderación *f*.

spark [spɑːk] 1 N (**a**) chispa *f*; (*of wit*) chispazo *m*; **bright ~*** tipo *m* muy listo*; **there's not a ~ of life about it** no tiene ni un átomo de vida; **the book hasn't a ~ of interest** el libro no tiene ni pizca de interés; **to make the ~s fly** provocar una bronca; **they struck ~s off each other** por efecto mutuo hacían chispear el ingenio.

(**b**) **~s*** (*Naut*) telegrafista *m*; (*Film, TV*) iluminista *mf*.

2 VT (*also* **to ~ off**) hacer estallar; (*fig*) hacer estallar, precipitar, provocar.

3 VI chispear, echar chispas.

spark-gap ['spɑːkgæp] N entrehierro *m*.

sparking-plug ['spɑːkɪŋplʌg] N, **spark-plug** ['spɑːkplʌg] N bujía *f*, chispero *m* (*CAm*).

sparkle ['spɑːkl] 1 N centelleo *m*, destello *m*; (*fig*) brillo *m*, viveza *f*, vida *f*; **a person without ~** una persona sin viveza.

2 VI centellear, destellar, chispear; (*shine*) brillar, relucir; **she doesn't exactly ~** no tiene mucha viveza que digamos; **the conversation ~d** la conversación fue animadísima, en la conversación hubo muchas salidas ingeniosas.

sparkler ['spɑːkləʳ] N (*firework*) bengala *f*; (‡) diamante *m*.

sparkling ['spɑːklɪŋ] ADJ centelleante; brillante, reluciente; *wine* espumoso; *eyes, wit, conversation* chispeante.

sparkly* ['spɑːklɪ] ADJ *necklace, eyes* brillante, centelleante.

sparky ['spɑːkɪ] ADJ vivaracho, marchoso*.

sparring match ['spɑːrɪŋˌmætʃ] N combate *m* con spárring.

sparring-partner ['spɑːrɪŋˌpɑːtnəʳ] N spárring *m*; (*hum*) contertulio *m*, -a *f*.

sparrow ['spærəʊ] N gorrión *m*.

sparrowhawk ['spærəʊhɔːk] N gavilán *m*.

sparse [spɑːs] ADJ disperso, esparcido; poco denso; escaso; *hair* ralo; **~ furnishings** muebles *mpl* escasos; **~ population** población *f* poco densa.

sparsely ['spɑːslɪ] ADV de modo poco denso; escasamente; **a ~ furnished room** un cuarto con pocos muebles; **a ~ inhabited area** una región de población poco densa.

Sparta ['spɑːtə] N Esparta *f*.

Spartacus ['spɑːtəkəs] NM Espartaco.

Spartan ['spɑːtən] 1 ADJ espartano (*also fig*).

2 N espartano *m*, -a *f*.

spasm ['spæzəm] N (*Med*) espasmo *m*; (*fig*) acceso *m*, arranque *m*; **in a ~ of fear** en un acceso de miedo; **a sudden ~ of activity** un arranque repentino de actividad; **to work in ~s** trabajar a rachas.

spasmodic [spæz'mɒdɪk] ADJ espasmódico; irregular, intermitente.

spasmodically [spæz'mɒdɪkəlɪ] ADV de modo espasmódico; de modo irregular, de modo intermitente; a rachas.
spastic ['spæstɪk] **1** ADJ espástico.
   2 N espástico *m*, -a *f*.
spasticity [spæs'tɪsɪtɪ] N espasticidad *f*.
spat¹ [spæt] N (*Fish*) freza *f*; (*of oysters*) hueva *f* de ostras.
spat² [spæt] N (*gaiter*) polaina *f* corta, botín *m*.
spat³* [spæt] (*US*) **1** N riña *f*, disputa *f* (sin trascendencia).
   2 VI reñir.
spat⁴ [spæt] PRET AND PTP *of* spit.
spate [speɪt] N avenida *f*, crecida *f*; (*fig*) torrente *m*; avalancha *f*; **to be in ~** estar crecido; **to be in full ~** estar muy crecido.
spatial ['speɪʃəl] ADJ espacial.
spatio-temporal [speɪʃɪəʊ'tempərəl] ADJ espaciotemporal.
spatter ['spætəʳ] VT salpicar, rociar (*with* de); **a dress ~ed with mud** un vestido manchado de lodo; **a wall ~ed with blood** una pared salpicada de sangre.
spatula ['spætjʊlə] N espátula *f*.
spavin ['spævɪn] N esparaván *m*.
spawn [spɔːn] **1** N (*Fish*) freza *f*, hueva *f*; (*of frog etc*) huevas *fpl*; (*of mushroom*) semillas *fpl*; (*fig: pej*) prole *f*.
   2 VT (*pej*) engendrar, producir.
   3 VI desovar, frezar.
spawning ['spɔːnɪŋ] N desove *m*, freza *f*.
spay [speɪ] VT *animal* sacar los ovarios a.
S.P.C.A. N (*US*) ABBR *of* **Society for the Prevention of Cruelty to Animals**.
S.P.C.C. N (*US*) ABBR *of* **Society for the Prevention of Cruelty to Children**.
speak [spiːk] (*irr*: PRET **spoke**, PTP **spoken**) **1** VT **(a)** (*gen*) decir, hablar; **to ~ the truth** decir la verdad; **to ~ one's mind** hablar con franqueza, hablar claro; **nobody spoke a word** nadie habló, nadie dijo palabra.
   (b) *language* hablar; **do you ~ Arabic?** ¿hablas árabe?; **'English spoken here'** 'se habla inglés'.
   2 VI **(a)** (*gen*) hablar; **did you ~?** ¿dijiste algo?; **since they quarrelled they don't ~** desde que riñeron no se hablan; **to ~ to sb** hablar con uno; **she never spoke to me again** no volvió a dirigirme la palabra; **I'll ~ to him about it** hablaré con él sobre eso; discutiré el asunto con él; **to ~ harshly to sb** hablar a uno en tono severo; **I don't know him to ~ to** no le conozco bastante como para hablar con él; **I know him to ~ to** le conozco bastante bien para cambiar algunas palabras con él; **so to ~** por decirlo así, como quien dice; **roughly ~ing** más o menos, aproximadamente; **technically** (*etc*) **~ing** en términos técnicos (*etc*), desde el punto de vista técnico (*etc*); **~ing personally,** ... en cuanto a mí ..., yo por mi parte; **~ing as a member,** ... como miembro, digo que ...; **to ~ of** hablar de; **~ing of lions** ... a propósito de los leones ...; ... **lions, not to ~ of tigers** ... leones, para no hablar de tigres; **it's nothing to ~ of** no tiene importancia, no es nada; **there are no trees to ~ of** no hay árboles que digamos; **everything ~s of hatred** por todas partes late el odio; **everything ~s of luxury** todo indica el lujo; **to ~ well of sb** hablar bien de uno; **~ now or forever hold your peace** hable ahora o guarde para siempre silencio.
   (b) to ~ for sb hablar por uno; hablar en nombre de uno; interceder por uno; **he ~s for the miners** habla por los mineros, representa a los mineros; **~ing for myself** en cuanto a mí, yo por mi parte; **~ for yourself!** ¡eso lo dices tú!; **it ~s for itself** es evidente, habla por sí mismo; **the facts ~ for themselves** los datos hablan por sí solos; **that is already spoken for** eso está reservado ya.
   (c) (*gun*) oírse, sonar; (*dog*) ladrar; **the gun spoke** se oyó un tiro.
   (d) (*formally, in assembly*) hablar, pronunciar un discurso; intervenir (en un debate); (*begin to ~*) tomar la palabra, hacer uso de la palabra; **are you ~ing in the debate?** ¿interviene Vd en el debate?; **it's years since he spoke** hace años que no pronuncia ningún discurso; **the member rose to ~** el diputado se levantó para tomar la palabra; **the speaker asked Mr X to ~** el presidente le concedió la palabra al Sr X.
   (e) (*Telec*) **~ing!** ¡al aparato!, ¡al habla!; **John ~ing!** ¡soy Juan!; **who is that ~ing?** ¿quién habla?, ¿de parte de (quién)?
◆**speak out** VI hablar claro; hablar francamente; osar hablar; **~ out!** ¡más fuerte!
◆**speak up** VI **(a)** hablar alto; **to ~ up for sb** (*fig*) hablar en favor de uno.
   (b) = **speak out**.
-speak [spiːk] N (*pej*) *ending in compounds*: **computer~** lenguaje *m* de los ordenadores, jerga *f* informática.
speakeasy* ['spiːk,iːzɪ] N (*US*) taberna *f* (clandestina).
speaker ['spiːkəʳ] N **(a)** (*gen*) el (*or* la) que habla; (*public ~*) orador *m*, -ora *f*; (*lecturer*) conferenciante *mf*; (*at conference*) ponente *mf*; (*Parl*) presidente *mf* (*de la Cámara de los Comunes*); **as the last ~ said** como dijo el señor (*or* la señora) que acaba de hablar; **he's a good ~** es

buen orador, habla bien; *ver también* FRONT BENCH .
   (b) (*of language*) hablante *mf*; **are you a Welsh ~?** ¿habla Vd galés?; **all ~s of Spanish** todos los que hablan español, todos los hispanohablantes; **Catalan has several million ~s** el catalán es hablado por varios millones.
   (c) (*loud~*) altavoz *m*; **~s** (*of hi-fi system*) pantallas *fpl* acústicas.

┌─────────────────────────┐
│ **SPEAKER** │
└─────────────────────────┘

*ⓘ En el sistema parlamentario británico el **Speaker** es la máxima autoridad de la Cámara de los Comunes (**House of Commons**) y su misión es presidirla y hacer que se guarde el orden y que se acaten las normas establecidas. Es elegido al comienzo de la legislatura por parlamentarios (**MPs**) de todos los partidos y puede pertenecer a cualquiera de ellos. Una vez que toma posesión de su cargo, el **Speaker** no vota ni toma la palabra (excepto a nivel oficial) y ha de ser totalmente imparcial. Los parlamentarios suelen comenzar sus discursos dirigiéndose al **Speaker** en vez de a toda la Cámara, como por ejemplo en: **Mister/Madam Speaker, I feel very strongly about this.***

*En Estados Unidos, el **Speaker** es el encargado de presidir la Cámara de los Representantes (**House of Representatives**) y es también el dirigente del partido mayoritario, además de miembro de la Cámara. Es elegido por los miembros de su partido y se encarga de las actas de las sesiones de la Cámara y de actuar como portavoz de su partido. Es uno de los puestos más influyentes del gobierno federal, además de ser el que sigue al Vicepresidente (**Vice-President**) en la sucesión a la presidencia.*

speaking ['spiːkɪŋ] ADJ hablante; **~ likeness** retrato *m* vivo; **~ part** papel *m* hablado; **to be within ~ distance** estar al habla, estar al alcance de la voz; **to be on ~ terms with sb** estar en buenas relaciones con uno; **we're not on ~ terms** no nos hablamos; **a pleasant ~ voice** una voz agradable.
-speaking ['spiːkɪŋ] ADJ *ending in compounds*: **English~** anglófono, anglohablante, de habla inglesa.
speaking clock [spiːkɪŋ'klɒk] N (*Brit*) servicio *m* telefónico de información horaria.
speaking trumpet ['spiːkɪŋ,trʌmpɪt] N bocina *f*.
speaking-tube ['spiːkɪŋtjuːb] N tubo *m* acústico.
spear [spɪəʳ] **1** N (*Mil*) lanza *f*; (*fishing ~*) arpón *m*.
   2 VT alancear, herir (*or* matar) con lanza; *fish* arponear; (*fig*) pasar, atravesar, pinchar; **he ~ed the paper on his fork** atravesó el papel en su tenedor.
speargun ['spɪəgʌn] N harpón *m* submarino.
spearhead ['spɪəhed] **1** N punta *f* de lanza (*also fig*).
   2 ATTR: **~ industry** sector *m* puntero, industria *f* de vanguardia.
   3 VT *attack etc* encabezar, dirigir.
spearmint ['spɪəmɪnt] N menta *f* verde, menta *f* romana.
spec* [spek] N (*Comm*): **to buy sth on ~** comprar algo como especulación; **to go along on ~** ir a ver lo que sale, ir a probar fortuna.
special ['speʃəl] **1** ADJ especial, particular; *edition etc* extraordinario; **~ agent** agente *mf* especial; **S~ Branch** (*Brit*) sección *f* de la policía que vigila la seguridad política; **~ correspondent** enviado *m*, -a *f* especial; **~ delivery** (*Post*) entrega *f* urgente; **~ effects** efectos *mpl* especiales; **~ feature** (*Press*) artículo *m*, crónica *f*; (*of product*) característica *f*, prestación *f*; **~ general meeting** junta *f* general extraordinaria; **~ interest group** grupo *m* de presión que persigue un tema específico; **~ jury** jurado *m* especial; **~ licence** licencia *f* especial de matrimonio; una tasa especial; **~ measures** medidas *fpl* especiales; **~ offer** oferta *f* especial; **~ price** precio *m* de ocasión; **my ~ friend** mi mejor amigo, uno de mis amigos más íntimos; **we can offer you a ~ rate** podemos ofrecerle una tasa especial; **what happened? ... nothing ~** ¿qué tal? ... sin novedad (*or* nada de particular); **what's so ~ about this house?** ¿qué tiene de particular esta casa?; **what's so ~ about that?** y eso ¿qué tiene de particular?
   2 N (*constable*) guardia *m* auxiliar; (*edition*) número *m* extraordinario; (*train*) tren *m* extraordinario, tren *m* especial; (*US Comm*) oferta *f* extraordinaria, ganga *f*; (*US Culin*) plato *m* del día.
specialism ['speʃə,lɪzəm] N especialidad *f*, campo *m* de conocimiento (*or* estudios *etc*) especializados.
specialist ['speʃəlɪst] **1** N especialista *mf*.
   2 ATTR: **~ knowledge** conocimientos *mpl* especializados; **~ teacher** (*primary*) maestro *m* especializado, maestra *f* especializada; (*secondary*) profesor *m* especializado, profesora *f* especializada; **that's ~ work** es trabajo para un profesional, es trabajo que pide conocimientos especializados.
speciality [speʃɪ'ælɪtɪ] N, (*US*) **specialty** ['speʃəltɪ] N especialidad *f*; **it's a ~ of the house** es una especialidad de la casa, es un plato especial de la casa; **to make a ~ of sth** especializarse en algo, dedicarse a algo de modo especial.
specialization [speʃəlaɪ'zeɪʃən] N especialización *f*.
specialize ['speʃəlaɪz] VI especializarse (*in*, (*US*) *on* en).
specialized ['speʃəlaɪzd] ADJ: **~ knowledge** conocimientos *mpl*

especializados.

specially ['speʃəlɪ] ADV especialmente, particularmente; sobre todo, ante todo; **a ~ difficult task** un cometido especialmente difícil; **we asked for it ~** lo pedimos especialmente; **~ the yellow ones** sobre todo los amarillos.

specialty ['speʃəltɪ] N (US) = **speciality**.

specie ['spiːʃiː] N, en metálico m, efectivo m; **in ~** en metálico.

species ['spiːʃiːz] N, PL **species** especie f.

specific [spə'sɪfɪk] 1 ADJ específico; expreso, explícito; **~ gravity** peso m específico.
2 N (a) específico m. (b) **~s** (esp US) detalles mpl; aspectos mpl concretos.

-specific [spə'sɪfɪk] ADJ ending in compounds: **country~** específico del país; **job~** específico para el puesto de trabajo.

specifically [spə'sɪfɪkəlɪ] ADV específicamente; expresamente, explícitamente.

specification [,spesɪfɪ'keɪʃən] N especificación f; **~s** (plan) presupuesto m, plan m detallado.

▼ **specify** ['spesɪfaɪ] VTI especificar; designar (en un plan); concretar, precisar, indicar, puntualizar; **he did not ~** no concretó, no mencionó nada concreto; **at a specified time** a una hora indicada; **unless otherwise specified** a no ser que se especifique lo contrario, salvo indicación al contrario.

specimen ['spesɪmɪn] 1 N ejemplar m, espécimen m; muestra f; **a fine ~ of trout** un bello ejemplar de trucha; **he's an odd ~** es un tipo extraño; **you're a pretty poor ~** no vales para mucho.
2 ATTR: **~ copy** ejemplar m de muestra; **~ page** página f que sirve de muestra; **~ signature** espécimen m de firma.

specious ['spiːʃəs] ADJ especioso.

speciousness ['spiːʃəsnɪs] N lo especioso.

speck [spek] 1 N (of dirt) pequeña mancha f, manchita f; (of dust) grano m; (smut) mota f (de carbonilla etc); (small portion) partícula f, pizca f; (dot, point) punto m; **just a ~ on the horizon** solamente un punto en el horizonte; **just a ~, thanks** (of drink etc) un poquitín, gracias; **there's not a ~ of truth in it** no tiene ni pizca de verdad.
2 VT = **speckle**.

speckle ['spekl] 1 N punto m, mota f.
2 VT salpicar, motear (with de); salpicar de manchitas.

speckled ['spekld] ADJ con puntos, con manchas, moteado.

specs* [speks] NPL (a) gafas fpl, lentes mpl (LAm). (b) ABBR of **specifications**.

spectacle ['spektəkl] N (a) (sight) espectáculo m; **a sad ~** un triste espectáculo; **to make a ~ of o.s.** ponerse en ridículo.
(b) **~s** (Brit) gafas fpl, anteojos mpl, lentes mpl (LAm); **a pair of ~s** unas gafas; **to see everything through rose-coloured ~s** verlo todo color de rosa.

spectacle-case ['spektəkl,keɪs] N estuche m de gafas.

spectacled ['spektəkld] ADJ con gafas.

spectacular [spek'tækjʊləʳ] ADJ espectacular; fall etc aparatoso; show, success etc impresionante.

spectacularly [spek'tækjʊləlɪ] ADV de manera espectacular, espectacularmente; aparatosamente; de manera impresionante.

spectate [spek'teɪt] VI hacer de espectador.

spectator [spek'teɪtəʳ] N espectador m, -ora f; **~s** (collectively, at game etc) público m; **~ sport** deporte m para espectadores.

spectral ['spektrəl] ADJ espectral.

spectre, (US) **specter** ['spektəʳ] N espectro m, fantasma m.

spectrogram ['spektrəʊgræm] N espectrograma m.

spectrograph ['spektrəʊgrɑːf] N espectrógrafo m.

spectrometer [spek'trɒmɪtəʳ] N espectrómetro m.

spectrometry [spek'trɒmɪtrɪ] N espectrometría f.

spectroscope ['spektrəskəʊp] N espectroscopio m.

spectroscopic [spektrə'skɒpɪk] ADJ espectroscópico.

spectroscopy [spek'trɒskəpɪ] N espectroscopia f.

spectrum ['spektrəm] N, PL **spectra** ['spektrə] espectro m; (fig) gama f, abanico m; **~ analysis** análisis m espectral; **a wide ~ of opinions** un amplio abanico de opiniones.

speculate ['spekjʊleɪt] VI especular (on en); **to ~ about** especular sobre, hacer conjeturas acerca de, formular teorías acerca de. (b) (Fin) especular (in en).

speculation [,spekjʊ'leɪʃən] N (a) especulación f; **it is the subject of much ~** es tema de muchas conjeturas, sobre esto existen muchas teorías. (b) (Fin) especulación f; **to buy sth on ~** comprar algo como especulación; **it's a good ~** vale como especulación.

speculative ['spekjʊlətɪv] ADJ especulativo.

speculator ['spekjʊleɪtəʳ] N especulador m, -ora f.

speculum ['spekjʊləm] N espéculo m.

sped [sped] PRET AND PTP of **speed**.

speech [spiːtʃ] 1 N (a) (faculty of ~) habla f; palabra f; **to be slow of ~** hablar lentamente, ser torpe de palabra; **to lose the power of ~** perder el habla, perder la palabra; **to recover one's ~** recobrar el habla, recobrar la palabra.

(b) (words) palabras fpl; **without further ~** sin decir más.
(c) (language) (national) idioma m; (of class etc) lenguaje m; (of region) dialecto m, habla f regional; **in dockers' ~** en el lenguaje de los portuarios; **in the ~ of Leon** en el dialecto de León, en leonés.
(d) (oration) discurso m, oración f; parlamento m; **to deliver a ~, to make a ~** pronunciar un discurso.
(e) (Gram) oración f.
2 ATTR: **~ act** acto m de habla; **~ analysis** análisis m de la voz; **~ command** comando m vocal; **~ community** comunidad f lingüística; **~ day** (Brit) (día m de) distribución f de premios; **~ defect** defecto m del habla; **~ impediment** impedimento m del habla; **~ organ** órgano m del habla; **~ synthesizer** sintetizador m de la voz humana; **~ therapist** logopeda mf, logoterapeuta mf; **~ therapy** terapia f lingüística, logopedia f, logoterapia f; **~ training** lecciones fpl de elocución.

speechify ['spiːtʃɪfaɪ] VI (pej) disertar prolijamente, perorar.

speechifying ['spiːtʃɪfaɪɪŋ] N (pej) disertaciones fpl prolijas, peroratas fpl.

speechless ['spiːtʃlɪs] ADJ mudo, estupefacto; **I'm ~!** ¡estoy mudo!; **everybody was ~ at this** con esto todos quedaron estupefactos; **to be ~ with rage** enmudecer de rabia.

speechmaking ['spiːtʃ,meɪkɪŋ] N (a) pronunciación f de discursos; (speeches collectively) discursos mpl. (b) (pej) = **speechifying**.

speechwriter ['spiːtʃ,raɪtəʳ] N escritor m, -ora f de discursos, redactor m, -ora f de discursos.

speed [spiːd] 1 N (a) velocidad f; rapidez f; (haste) prisa f; (promptness) prontitud f; **at ~** a gran velocidad; **at full ~, at top ~** a máxima velocidad, a toda máquina, a todo correr; **full ~ ahead!** ¡avante toda!*, ¡avante a toda máquina!; **with all possible ~** con toda prontitud; **the maximum ~ is 90 mph** la velocidad máxima es de 90 mph; **what ~ were you doing?** ¿a qué velocidad ibas?; **to pick up ~** acelerar, cobrar velocidad.
(b) (gear) velocidad f; **four forward ~s** cuatro velocidades hacia adelante; **five-~ gearbox** caja f de cambios de cinco velocidades.
(c) **good ~!††** ¡buen viaje!
(d) (:) anfetamina f.
2 VT (regular) **to ~ sb on his way** despedir a uno, desear un feliz viaje a uno.
3 VI (irr: PRET AND PTP **sped**) (a) (person etc) darse prisa, apresurarse; **he sped down the street** corrió a toda prisa por la calle; **to ~ off** irse a toda prisa.
(b) (Aut) exceder la velocidad permitida.

◆ **speed along** VI (pret, ptp **sped along**) ir a gran velocidad, ir a toda rapidez.

◆ **speed up** 1 VT (pret, ptp **speeded up**) engine acelerar; process acelerar, agilizar, activar; fomentar; person dar prisa a, apurar (LAm).
2 VI (process) acelerarse; (person) darse prisa, apurarse (LAm).

speedball ['spiːdbɔːl] N (a) (game) speedball m. (b) (:: drugs) chute m de cocaína con heroína‡.

speedboat ['spiːd,bəʊt] N motora f, lancha f rápida.

speed bump ['spiːd,bʌmp] N banda f de frenado.

speed cop* ['spiːdkɒp] N (Brit) policía m de tráfico, policía m de tránsito (LAm).

speeder ['spiːdəʳ] N (fast driver) automovilista mf que conduce a gran velocidad; (convicted) infractor m, -ora f de los límites de velocidad.

speedily ['spiːdɪlɪ] ADV rápidamente; prontamente, con toda prontitud; **it ~ became obvious that ...** pronto se hizo manifiesto que ...; **as ~ as possible** lo más pronto posible.

speediness ['spiːdɪnɪs] N velocidad f, rapidez f; prontitud f.

speeding ['spiːdɪŋ] N (Aut) exceso m de velocidad; **he was fined for ~** se le impuso una multa por exceso de velocidad.

speed-limit ['spiːd,lɪmɪt] N velocidad f máxima, límite m de velocidad; **to exceed the ~** exceder la velocidad permitida.

speedometer [spɪ'dɒmɪtəʳ] N velocímetro m, cuentakilómetros m.

speed restriction ['spiːdrɪs,trɪkʃən] N limitación f de velocidad.

speed skater ['spiːdskeɪtəʳ] N patinador m, -ora f de velocidad.

speed-skating ['spiːd,skeɪtɪŋ] N patinaje m de velocidad.

speed trap ['spiːdtræp] N control m por radar.

speed-up ['spiːdʌp] N aceleración f, agilización f.

speedway ['spiːdweɪ] N (a) (track) pista f de ceniza, carretera f para carreras. (b) (motor-cycle racing) carreras fpl de motocicleta. (c) (US) autopista f.

speedwell ['spiːdwel] N verónica f.

speedy ['spiːdɪ] ADJ veloz, rápido; answer etc pronto; service etc rápido.

speleologist [,spiːlɪ'ɒlədʒɪst] N espeleólogo m, -a f.

speleology [,spiːlɪ'ɒlədʒɪ] N espeleología f.

spell¹ [spel] N encanto m, hechizo m; ensalmo m; **to be under a ~** estar hechizado; **to be under sb's ~** estar hechizado por uno; **to break the ~** romper el encanto; **to cast a ~ over sb, to put sb under a ~** hechizar a uno (also fig); **Seville casts its ~ over the tourists** Sevilla hechiza a los turistas.

spell² [spel] (irr: PRET AND PTP **spelled** or **spelt**) VTI (a) escribir; **she can't**

~ no sabe escribir correctamente, sabe poco de ortografía; **how do you ~ 'onyx'?** ¿cómo se escribe 'ónice'?; **what do these letters ~?** ¿qué palabra se forma con estas letras?; **c-a-t ~s 'cat'** c-a-t hacen 'cat'.
(b) (*denote*) anunciar, presagiar; significar; **it ~s disaster for us** representa un desastre para nosotros; **it ~s ruin** significa la ruina.
◆ **spell out** VT **(a)** (*read letter by letter*) deletrear.
(b) to ~ sth out for sb (*fig*) explicar algo a uno de un modo muy sencillo, explicar algo a uno detalladamente.
spell³ [spel] N **(a)** (*at work*) tanda *f*, turno *m*; **to take a ~ with the saw** trabajar su turno con la sierra.
(b) (*period in general*) rato *m*; temporada *f*, período *m*; **by ~s** a rachas, a ratos; **cold ~** período *m* de frío; **a prolonged ~ of bad weather** una larga temporada de mal tiempo; **we had a ~ in Chile** pasamos una temporada en Chile; **I had a ~ as a traveller** durante cierto tiempo trabajé como viajante; **they're going through a bad ~** atraviesan un mal rato.
spellbinder ['spel,baɪndə^r] N orador *m*, -ora *f* fascinante.
spellbinding ['spel,baɪndɪŋ] ADJ cautivador, fascinante.
spellbound ['spelbaʊnd] ADJ embelesado, hechizado; **to hold one's audience ~** tener a sus oyentes embelesados.
spellchecker ['spel,tʃekə^r] N (*Comput*) corrector *m* ortográfico.
speller ['spelə^r] N: **to be a bad ~** no saber escribir correctamente, tener mala ortografía.
spelling ['spelɪŋ] N ortografía *f*; **~ checker** corrector *m* ortográfico, consultor *m* de ortografía; **~ error** error *m* de ortografía; **~ pronunciation** pronunciación *f* ortográfica; **the correct ~ is ...** la buena ortografía es ...
spelling bee ['spelɪŋ,biː] N certamen *m* de ortografía.
spelt¹ [spelt] N (*Bot*) espelta *f*.
spelt² [spelt] PRET AND PTP of **spell²**.
spelunker [spɪ'lʌŋkə^r] N (*esp US*) espeleólogo *m*, -a *f*.
spelunking [spɪ'lʌŋkɪŋ] N (*esp US*) espeleología *f*.
spend [spend] (*irr*: PRET AND PTP **spent**) ① VT **(a)** (*money*) gastar (*on* en).
(b) *time* pasar; (*on journey, project etc*) invertir (*on* en), dedicar (*on* a); **I spent an hour reading** pasé una hora leyendo; **where are you ~ing your holiday?** ¿dónde vas a pasar tus vacaciones?
(c) (*consume*) *anger, emotion* agotar, consumir; *effort* gastar; **the storm has spent its fury** la tempestad ha agotado su violencia.
② VI gastar dinero; **he ~s freely** gasta mucho, gasta bastante.
spender ['spendə^r] N gastador *m*, -ora *f*; **big ~** persona *f* generosa, (*pej*) derrochador *m*, -ora *f*; **to be a free ~** gastar libremente su dinero, ser derrochador.
spending ['spendɪŋ] ① N gasto *m*; gastos *mpl*.
② ATTR: **~ limit** límite *m* de gastos; **~ money** dinero *m* para gastos personales; **~ power** poder *m* de compra, poder *m* adquisitivo; **~ spree** derroche *m* de dinero; **we went on a ~ spree** gastamos como locos.
spendthrift ['spendθrɪft] ① ADJ derrochador, pródigo.
② N derrochador *m*, -ora *f*, pródigo *m*, -a *f*.
spent [spent] PRET AND PTP of **spend**.
② ADJ agotado; *bullet* frío; **he's a ~ force** es una vieja gloria, ya no vale lo que antes.
sperm [spɜːm] N esperma *f*; **~ bank** banco *m* de espermas; **~ count** recuento *m* de espermas; **~ whale** cachalote *m*.
spermaceti [,spɜːmə'setɪ] N esperma *f* de ballena.
spermatozoon [,spɜːmətəʊ'zəʊɒn] N, PL **spermatozoa** [,spɜːmətəʊ'zəʊə] espermatozoo *m*.
spermicidal [,spɜːmɪ'saɪdl] ADJ espermicida.
spermicide ['spɜːmɪsaɪd] N espermicida *m*.
spew [spjuː] VT (*also* **to ~ forth, to ~ out, to ~ up**) vomitar; (*fig*) vomitar, arrojar, echar fuera; **it makes me ~** (*fig*) me da asco.
SPG N (*Brit: Police*) ABBR of **Special Patrol Group**.
sphagnum ['sfægnəm] N esfagno *m*.
sphere [sfɪə^r] N **(a)** (*lit*) esfera *f*. **(b)** (*fig*) esfera *f*, campo *m*; competencia *f*; **~ of influence** esfera *f* de influencia; **~ of activity** campo *m* de actividad; **in the ~ of music** en la esfera de la música, en el mundo de la música; **that's outside my ~** eso no es de mi competencia.
spherical ['sferɪkəl] ADJ esférico.
spheroid ['sfɪərɔɪd] N esferoide *m*.
sphincter ['sfɪŋktə^r] N esfínter *m*.
sphinx [sfɪŋks] N esfinge *f*.
spice [spaɪs] ① N (*Culin*) especia *f*, olor *m* (*Mex, SC*); (*fig*) sabor *m*, picante *m*; **it's the ~ of life** es la sal de la vida; **the detail added ~ to the story** el detalle dio más sabor a la narración; **the papers like stories with some ~** a los periódicos les gusta reportajes con cierto picante.
② VT condimentar; (*fig*) dar picante a; **gossip ~d with scandal** unos chismes con el sabor adicional de detalles escandalosos; **a highly ~d account** un relato de mucho picante.
spice-rack ['spaɪs,ræk] N especiero *m*.

spiciness ['spaɪsɪnɪs] N lo picante, picante *m*, sabor *m* (*also fig*).
Spick [spɪk] N (*US*) hispano *m*, -a *f*.
spick-and-span ['spɪkən'spæn] ADJ impecablemente limpio; *house etc* como una tacita de plata; *person* pulcro, aseado, acicalado.
spicy ['spaɪsɪ] ADJ condimentado, picante; (*fig*) picante, sabroso.
spider ['spaɪdə^r] N araña *f*; **~ crab** centollo *m*, centolla *f*; **~'s web** telaraña *f*.
spiderman ['spaɪdəmæn] N, PL **spidermen** ['spaɪdəmen] obrero *m* que trabaja en la construcción de edificios altos.
spider-plant ['spaɪdəplɑːnt] N arañonero *m*.
spidery ['spaɪdərɪ] ADJ delgado; *writing* de patas de araña.
spiel [spiːl] N (*speech*) arenga *f*, discurso *m*; (*of salesman etc*) rollo* *m*, material *m* publicitario; (*tale*) relato *m* con que uno procura convencer a otro.
spiffing*† ['spɪfɪŋ] ADJ fetén†*, estupendo*, fenomenal*.
spigot ['spɪgət] N (*of cask*) espita *f*, grifo *m*; (*Tech*) espiga *f*, macho *m*.
spike [spaɪk] ① N **(a)** (*point*) punta *f*; (*tool*) escarpia *f*; (*on shoes, for letters etc*) clavo *m*; (*Zool: of hedgehog etc*) pincho *m*, púa *f*; (*Elec*) pico *m* parásito; (*Bot*) espiga *f*; (*US*) **~ heel** talón *m* de aguja.
(b) NPL (*Sport*) **~s** zapatillas *fpl* con clavos.
② VT **(a)** atravesar con un pincho; sujetar con un clavo (*etc*); *gun* clavar, (*fig*) inutilizar, hacer inútil; (*) *news item etc* rechazar, desestimar; **to ~ a quote** cancelar una cita.
(b) (*US*) *drink* echar licor a, fortalecer.
spiked [spaɪkt] ADJ *shoe* claveteado.
spikenard ['spaɪknɑːd] N nardo *m*.
spiky ['spaɪkɪ] ADJ **(a)** puntiagudo; armado de púas, cubierto de púas, erizado. **(b)** *person* quisquilloso, susceptible.
spill¹ [spɪl] ① N **(a)** caída *f*; vuelco *m*; **to have a ~** sufrir una caída, tener un accidente.
(b) (*US*) vertido *m*, vertidos *mpl*.
② (*irr*: PRET AND PTP **spilled** or **spilt**) VT derramar, verter; *rider* hacer caer, desarzonar.
③ VI derramarse, verterse.
◆ **spill out** ① VT derramar.
② VI derramarse, desparramarse; (*people etc*) salir en avalancha; **the crowd ~ed out into the streets** la gente salió a la calle en avalancha.
◆ **spill over** VI irse, desbordarse; (*fig*) desbordarse.
spill² [spɪl] N pajuela *f*.
spillage ['spɪlɪdʒ] N vertido *m*.
spillover ['spɪləʊvə^r] N (*act of spilling*) derrame *m*; (*quantity spilt*) cantidad *f* derramada; (*fig: excess part*) excedente *m*; (*Econ: effect*) incidencia *f* indirecta en el gasto público.
spillway ['spɪlweɪ] N (*US*) derramadero *m*, aliviadero *m*.
spilt [spɪlt] PRET AND PTP of **spill**.
spin [spɪn] ① N **(a)** (*revolution*) vuelta *f*, revolución *f*; **to give a wheel a ~** poner una rueda en movimiento, hacer que una rueda gire.
(b) (*: trip*) paseo *m* (en coche *etc*); **to go for a ~** dar un paseo (en coche), salir de excursión en coche.
(c) (*Aer*) barrena *f*; **to go into a ~** entrar en barrena; **to be in a flat ~*** estar completamente confuso, estar totalmente despistado.
(d) (*on ball*) efecto *m*, torcimiento *m*; **to put a ~ on a ball** dar efecto a una pelota, torcer una pelota.
② (*irr*: PRET **spun** or **span**, PTP **spun**) VT **(a)** *thread* hilar; *cocoon* devanar, hacer.
(b) (*turn*) girar, hacer girar; dar una vuelta a; *top* hacer bailar; *ball* dar efecto a, torcer; *coin* echar a cara o cruz; *clothes* (*Brit*) centrifugar.
(c) *story* contar.
③ VI **(a)** (*revolve: also* **to ~ round**) girar, dar vueltas; (*top*) girar, bailar; (*Aer*) entrar en barrena; descender en barrena; **to ~ along** correr rápidamente, ir a buen tren; **my head is ~ning** estoy mareado; **it makes my head ~** me marea; **to send sth ~ning** echar algo a rodar; **the blow sent him ~ning** el golpe le echó a rodar por los suelos.
◆ **spin out** VT alargar, prolongar.
spina bifida [,spaɪnə'bɪfɪdə] N espina *f* bífida.
spinach ['spɪnɪdʒ] N (*plant*) espinaca *f*; (*dish*) espinacas *fpl*.
spinal ['spaɪnl] ADJ espinal; **~ column** columna *f* vertebral; **~ cord** médula *f* espinal.
spindle ['spɪndl] N (*for spinning*) huso *m*; (*Mech*) eje *m*.
spindleshanks* ['spɪndlʃæŋks] N zanquivano *m*, -a *f*.
spindly ['spɪndlɪ] ADJ largo y delgado, larguirucho; *leg* zanquivano.
spindrift ['spɪndrɪft] N rocío *m* del mar, espuma *f*.
spin-dry [,spɪn'draɪ] VT *washing* centrifugar.
spin-dryer ['spɪn'draɪə^r] N (*Brit*) secador *m* centrífugo.
spine [spaɪn] N **(a)** (*Anat*) espinazo *m*, columna *f* vertebral; (*Zool*) púa *f*; (*Bot*) espina *f*; (*of book*) lomo *m*. **(b)** (*US fig*) decisión *f*, valor *m*.
spine-chiller ['spaɪn,tʃɪlə^r] N libro *m* (or película *f etc*) escalofriante.
spine-chilling ['spaɪn,tʃɪlɪŋ] ADJ escalofriante.
spineless ['spaɪnlɪs] ADJ débil, flojo, falto de voluntad, sin carácter.
spinelessly ['spaɪnlɪslɪ] ADV débilmente, flojamente.
spinet [spɪ'net] N espineta *f*.

spine-tingling ['spaɪn,tɪŋglɪŋ] ADJ (*frightening*) inquietante; (*moving*) emocionante.

spinnaker ['spɪnəkəʳ] N balón *m*, espinaquer *m*.

spinner ['spɪnəʳ] N hilandero *m*, -a *f*.

spinneret [,spɪnə'ret] N pezón *m* hilador.

spinney ['spɪnɪ] N bosquecillo *m*.

spinning ['spɪnɪŋ] N (**a**) (*motion*) rotación *f*, girar *m*. (**b**) (*of thread*) (*act*) hilado *m*, hilatura *f*; (*art*) hilandería *f*; arte *m* de hilar.

spinning-jenny ['spɪnɪŋ'dʒenɪ] N máquina *f* de hilar de husos múltiples.

spinning-mill ['spɪnɪŋmɪl] N hilandería *f*.

spinning-top ['spɪnɪŋtɒp] N peonza *f*.

spinning-wheel ['spɪnɪŋwiːl] N torno *m* de hilar, rueca *f*.

spin-off ['spɪnɒf] N subproducto *m*; efecto *m* indirecto, producto *m* suplementario (*or* adicional); beneficios *mpl* incidentales, beneficios *mpl* indirectos.

spinster ['spɪnstəʳ] N soltera *f*; (*pej*) solterona *f*.

spiny ['spaɪnɪ] ADJ con púas, erizado de púas; espinoso.

spiracle ['spɪrəkl] N espiráculo *m*.

spiraea, (*US*) **spirea** [spaɪ'rɪə] N espirea *f*.

spiral ['spaɪərəl] ① ADJ espiral, helicoidal; en espiral; **~ staircase** escalera *f* de caracol.
② N espiral *f*; hélice *f*; **the inflationary ~** la espiral inflacionista.
③ VI dar vueltas en espiral.
◆ **spiral down** VI: **the plane ~led down** el avión bajó en espiral.
◆ **spiral up** VI: **the smoke ~led up, the smoke went ~ling up** el humo subió en espiral; **prices have ~led up** los precios han subido vertiginosamente.

spirally ['spaɪərəlɪ] ADV en espiral.

spire ['spaɪəʳ] N aguja *f*, chapitel *m*.

spirit ['spɪrɪt] ① N (**a**) (*soul*) espíritu *m*, alma *f*; ánima *f*; **an unquiet ~** un alma inquieta; **to be vexed in ~** sentirlo en el alma.
(**b**) (*ghost*) aparecido *m*, fantasma *m*; (*evil etc*) espíritu *m* (*maligno*); **to cast out ~s** exorcizar espíritus.
(**c**) (*person*) alma *f*; **the leading** (*or* **moving**) **~ in the party** el alma del partido, la figura más destacada del partido; **a few restless ~s** algunas personas descontentadizas.
(**d**) (*humour, mood*) espíritu *m*; temple *m*, humor *m*; **the ~ of the age** el espíritu de la época; **in a ~ of friendship** con espíritu de amistad; **in a ~ of mischief** estando de humor para hacer alguna travesura; **we are with you in ~** os acompañamos en el sentimiento; nos alineamos con vosotros; **everyone is in a party ~** todo el mundo quiere divertirse; **it's in the ~ of the book** representa bien el espíritu del libro; **that's the ~!** ¡muy bien!; **to enter into the ~ of sth** dejarse emocionar por algo; empaparse en el ambiente de algo; **to take sth in the wrong ~** interpretar mal el espíritu con que se ha hecho algo; **it depends on the ~ in which it is done** depende del humor con que se hace.
(**e**) (*courage*) valor *m*; (*energy*) energía *f*; (*panache*) brío *m*, ánimo *m*; **a man of some ~** un hombre de cierta energía; **to catch sb's ~** ser influido por el valor de uno; **they lack ~** carecen de energía, no tienen carácter; **to show some ~** mostrar algún brío; **to sing with ~** cantar con brío.
(**f**) **~s** (*frame of mind*) ánimo *m*; humor *m*; **high ~s** optimismo *m*; alegría *f*; **to be in high ~s** estar animadísimo, estar muy alegre; **low ~s** pesimismo *m*, abatimiento *m*; **to be in low ~s** estar abatido; **to keep up one's ~s** no dejarse desanimar, no perder su optimismo; **we kept our ~s up by singing** nos animamos cantando; **to raise sb's ~s** dar aliento a uno, reanimar a uno; **to recover one's ~s** volver a estar alegre, reanimarse; **my ~s rose somewhat** me sentí algo más alegre, me sentí un poco más optimista.
(**g**) (*Chem*) alcohol *m*; (*Aut: also* **motor ~**) gasolina *f*; (*drink*) licor *m*; **~s of wine** espíritu *m* de vino; **I keep off ~s** no bebo licores.
② ATTR: **~ duplicator** copiadora *f* al alcohol.
◆ **spirit away, spirit off** VT llevarse misteriosamente, hacer desaparecer.

spirited ['spɪrɪtɪd] ADJ *person* animoso, brioso; *attack etc* enérgico, vigoroso; *horse* fogoso; *other animal* bravo.

spirit-lamp ['spɪrɪtlæmp] N lamparilla *f* de alcohol.

spiritless ['spɪrɪtlɪs] ADJ apocado, sin ánimo.

spirit-level ['spɪrɪt,levl] N nivel *m* de aire.

spirit-stove ['spɪrɪtstəʊv] N infiernillo *m* de alcohol.

spiritual ['spɪrɪtjʊəl] ① ADJ espiritual.
② N (*Mus*: **negro ~**) espiritual *m* negro.

spiritualism ['spɪrɪtjʊəlɪzəm] N espiritismo *m*.

spiritualist ['spɪrɪtjʊəlɪst] N espiritista *mf*.

spirituality [,spɪrɪtjʊ'ælɪtɪ] N espiritualidad *f*.

spiritually ['spɪrɪtjʊəlɪ] ADV espiritualmente.

spirituous ['spɪrɪtjʊəs] ADJ espirit(u)oso.

spirt [spɜːt] ① N chorro *m*, chorretada *f*.
② VT hacer salir en chorro, arrojar un chorro de.
③ VI (*also* **to ~ out, to ~ up**) salir en chorro, salir a chorros; brotar a

borbotones; *V also* **spurt**.

spit¹ [spɪt] ① N (*Culin*) asador *m*, espetón *m*; (*of land*) lengua *f*; (*sandbank*) banco *m* de arena; **~ roast** asado *m*.
② VT espetar.

spit² [spɪt] ① N saliva *f*; esputo *m*; **a ~ of rain** unas gotas de lluvia; **that table needs a bit of ~ and polish*** esa mesa hay que limpiarla (y sacarle brillo); **they're very keen on ~ and polish here*** aquí lo tienen todo relimpio; **to be the dead** (*or* **very**) **~ of sb** ser la segunda edición de uno, ser la viva imagen de uno.
② (*irr*: PRET AND PTP **spat**) VT escupir.
③ VI escupir (*at* a, *on* en); (*cat*) bufar; (*fat, fire*) chisporrotear; **to ~ in sb's face** escupir a la cara a uno; **the fish is ~ting in the pan** chisporrotea el pescado en la sartén; **it is ~ting** (**with rain**) caen algunas gotas de lluvia, empieza a llover.
◆ **spit forth** VT = **spit out**.
◆ **spit out** VT escupir (*also fig*); **~ it out!*** ¡dilo!, ¡desembucha!
◆ **spit up** VT *blood* soltar un esputo de.

spit³ [spɪt] N (*Agr*) azadada *f*; **to dig 3 ~s deep** excavar a una profundidad de 3 azadadas.

▼ **spite** [spaɪt] ① N rencor *m*, ojeriza *f*, despecho *m*; **in ~ of** a pesar de, a despecho de; **in ~ of all he says** a pesar de todo lo que dice; **to do sth out of** (*or* **from**) **~** hacer algo por despecho.
② VT mortificar, herir, causar pena a; **she just does it to ~ me** lo hace solamente para causarme pena.

spiteful ['spaɪtfʊl] ADJ rencoroso, malévolo; **to be ~ to sb** tratar a uno con malevolencia.

spitefully ['spaɪtfəlɪ] ADV con rencor, malévolamente; por despecho; **she said ~** dijo malévola.

spitefulness ['spaɪtfʊlnɪs] N rencor *m*, malevolencia *f*.

spitfire ['spɪt,faɪəʳ] N fierabrás *m*.

spitroast ['spɪtrəʊst] VT rostizar.

spitting ['spɪtɪŋ] ① N: **'~ prohibited'** 'prohibido escupir'.
② ADJ: **it's within ~ distance*** está muy cerca, está justo al lado; *V* **image**.

spittle ['spɪtl] N saliva *f*, baba *f*.

spittoon [spɪ'tuːn] N escupidera *f*.

spiv* [spɪv] N (*Brit*) chanchullero* *m*, caballero *m* de industria; (*slacker*) gandul *m*; (*black marketeer*) estraperlista *m*.

splash [splæʃ] ① N (*spray*) salpicadura *f*, rociada *f*; (**~ing noise**) chapoteo *m*; (*of colour*) mancha *f*; **whisky with a ~ of water** whisky *m* con un poquitín de agua; **it fell with a great ~ into the water** cayó ruidosamente al agua, cayó al agua levantando mucha espuma; **with a great ~ of publicity*** con mucho bombo publicitario*; **to make a ~*** causar una sensación, impresionar; hacer algo en grande*.
② VT (**a**) salpicar (*with* de). (**b**) (*fig*) **they ~ed the news across the front page** publicaron la noticia con mucho bombo en la primera plana.
③ VI (*liquid*) esparcirse, rociarse; (*person in water*) chapotear.
◆ **splash about** ① VT: **to ~ water about** desparramar (el) agua; **to ~ one's money about** derrochar su dinero por todas partes.
② VI (*person in water*) chapotear; **to ~ about in the water** chapotear en el agua.
◆ **splash down** VI (*Aer*) amerizar.
◆ **splash out*** VI derrochar dinero; **so we ~ed out and bought it** así que en un derroche lo compramos.
◆ **splash up** ① VT salpicar.
② VI salpicar.

splashback ['splæʃbæk] N salpicadero *m*.

splashboard ['splæʃbɔːd] N guardabarros *m*, alero *m*.

splashdown ['splæʃdaʊn] N amaraje *m*, amerizaje *m*, chapuzón *m*.

splashy ['splæʃɪ] ADJ líquido; fangoso.

splat [splæt] ① N: **with a ~** con un plaf.
② EXCL ¡plaf!

splatter ['splætəʳ] = **spatter**.

splay [spleɪ] VT extender (sin gracia); (*Tech*) biselar, achaflanar.

spleen [spliːn] N (*Anat*) bazo *m*; (*fig*) spleen *m*, esplín *m*, rencor *m*; **to vent one's ~** descargar la bilis (*on* contra).

splendid ['splendɪd] ADJ espléndido; **~!** ¡magnífico!; **that's simply ~!** ¡pero qué bien!; **but how ~ for you!** ¡cuánto me alegro por ti!; **a ~ joke** un chiste excelente; **he has done ~ work** ha hecho una magnífica labor.

splendidly ['splendɪdlɪ] ADV espléndidamente; magníficamente; **a ~ dressed man** un hombre brillantemente vestido; **you did ~** hiciste muy bien, lo has hecho rebién; **everything went ~** todo fue a las mil maravillas; **we get along ~** nos llevamos muy bien.

splendiferous* [splen'dɪfərəs] ADJ = **splendid**.

splendour, (*US*) **splendor** ['splendəʳ] N esplendor *m*; magnificencia *f*; (*of achievement etc*) brillo *m*, gloria *f*.

splenetic [splɪ'netɪk] ADJ (*Anat*) esplénico; (*fig*) enojadizo, de genio vivo; malhumorado.

splice [splaɪs] ① N empalme *m*, junta *f*.

2 VT empalmar, juntar; (*Naut*) ayustar; **to get ~d:** casarse.
splicer ['splaɪsər] N (*for film*) máquina *f* de montaje.
spliff* [splɪf] N (*Brit*) canuto: *m*, porro: *m* (*Sp*).
splint [splɪnt] 1 N tablilla *f*; (*Vet*) sobrecaña *f*; **to put sb's arm in ~s** entablillar el brazo a uno.
2 VT entablillar.
splinter ['splɪntər] 1 N astilla *f*; (*in finger*) espigón *m*.
2 ATTR: **~ group** grupo *m* disidente, facción *f*; **~ party** partido *m* nuevo formado a raíz de la escisión de otro.
3 VT astillar, hacer astillas.
4 VI astillarse, hacerse astillas; **to ~ off** separarse.
splinterbone ['splɪntəbəʊn] N peroné *m*.
splinterless ['splɪntəlɪs] ADJ inastillable.
splinterproof ['splɪntəpruːf] ADJ: **~ glass** cristal *m* inastillable.
split [splɪt] 1 N (*crack*) hendedura *f*, raja *f*, grieta *f*; (*fig*) división *f*; cisma *m*; (*Pol*) escisión *f*; (*quarrel*) ruptura *f*; **a three-way ~** una división en tres partes; **there are threats of a ~ in the progressive party** hay amenazas de escisión en el partido progresista; **to do the ~s** despatarrarse, esparrancarse.
2 ADJ partido, hendido; *party etc* escindido, dividido; **~ infinitive** infinitivo en el que un adverbio o una frase se intercala entre 'to' y el verbo; **~ pea** guisante *m* majado; **~ personality** personalidad *f* desdoblada; **~ pin** (*Brit*) chaveta *f*, pasador *m*; **~ screen** pantalla *f* partida; **~-screen facility** capacidad *f* de pantalla partida; **the party was ~** el partido estaba escindido; **the party is ~ 3 ways** el partido está escindido en 3 grupos; **the votes are ~ 5-3** los votos están repartidos 5 a 3; **it was a ~ decision** la decisión no fue unánime; V **second 3** (a).
3 (*irr*: PRET AND PTP **split**) VT (*cleave*) partir, hender, rajar; dividir; repartir; **to ~ the atom** desintegrar el átomo; **to ~ the difference** partir la diferencia; **the sea had ~ the ship in two** el mar había partido el barco en dos; **the blow ~ his head open** el golpe le abrió la cabeza; **the dispute ~ the party** la disputa escindió el partido.
4 VI (a) (*also* **to ~ up**) partirse, henderse, rajarse; dividirse; (*party*) escindirse; **the ship ~ on the rocks** el buque se estrelló contra las rocas; **my head is ~ting** me duele terriblemente la cabeza.
(b) (*Brit**) soplar:, chivatear: (*on sb* contra uno); **don't ~ on me** de esto no digas ni pío.
(c) (*esp US**) largarse:, irse.
◆ **split off** 1 VT separar.
2 VI separarse, desprenderse, (*Pol*) escindirse.
◆ **split up** 1 VT partir, dividir; *estate* parcelar; **we'll ~ the work up among us** dividiremos el trabajo entre nosotros.
2 VI (a) = **split 4** (a).
(b) (*persons*) separarse; (*crowd*) dispersarse; **let's ~ up for safety** separémonos para mayor seguridad; **they were married 14 years but then they ~ up** estuvieron casados durante 14 años pero luego se separaron.
split-level ['splɪt,levl] ADJ *house* construido sobre dos niveles, con planta baja de dos niveles, a desnivel; **~ cooker** cocina *f* encimera.
split-off ['splɪtɒf] N separación *f*; (*Pol etc*) escisión *f*.
splitting ['splɪtɪŋ] 1 ADJ *headache* terrible, enloquecedor.
2 N: **~ of the atom** desintegración *f* del átomo.
split-up ['splɪtʌp] N ruptura *f*; separación *f*.
splodge [splɒdʒ] N, **splotch** [splɒtʃ] N mancha *f*, borrón *m*.
splurge* [splɜːdʒ] 1 N (a) (*show*) fachenda* *f*, ostentación *f*. (b) (*excess*) derroche *m*, exceso *m*.
2 VI: **to ~ on sth** derrochar dinero comprando algo.
splutter ['splʌtər] 1 N (*of fat etc*) chisporroteo *m*; (*of speech*) farfulla *f*.
2 VT decir balbuceando; **'Yes', he ~ed** 'Sí', balbuceó.
3 VI chisporrotear; farfullar, balbucear; (*engine*) renquear.
spoil [spɔɪl] 1 N (*also* **~s**) despojo *m*, botín *m*; trofeo *m*; **~ system** (*US*) sistema *m* de repartirse los empleos entre los del partido victorioso; **the ~s of war** el botín de la guerra, los trofeos de la guerra.
2 (*irr*: PRET AND PTP **spoiled** *or* **spoilt**) VT (a) echar a perder, estropear, malograr, arruinar; deteriorar; *voting paper* invalidar; **to ~ sb's fun** aguar la fiesta a uno; **it quite ~ed our holiday** arruinó completamente nuestras vacaciones; **it would ~ my appetite** me quitaría el apetito; **the coast has been ~ed by development** la costa ha sido arruinada por la urbanización; **and there were 20 ~ed papers** y hubo 20 votos inválidos; **to get ~ed** echarse a perder, estropearse.
(b) (*pamper*) *child* mimar, consentir.
3 VI (a) echarse a perder, estropearse; arruinarse; dañarse; deteriorarse; **if we leave it here it will ~** si lo dejamos aquí se estropeará.
(b) **to be ~ing for a fight** querer de todos modos luchar, tener ganas de pelearse.
spoilage ['spɔɪlɪdʒ] N (*process*) deterioro *m*; (*thing, amount spoilt*) desperdicio *m*.
spoiled [spɔɪld] 1 ADJ (*US*) *food* pasado, malo; *milk* cortado; =

spoilt 2.
2 PRET AND PTP = **spoilt 1.**
spoiler ['spɔɪlər] N (*Aut, Aer*) alerón *m*, spoiler *m*.
spoilsport ['spɔɪlspɔːt] N aguafiestas *m*; **to be a ~** aguar la fiesta.
spoilt [spɔɪlt] 1 PRET AND PTP *of* **spoil**.
2 ADJ (a) estropeado; dañado, deteriorado; *vote* nulo. (b) *child* consentido, muy mimado.
spoke¹ [spəʊk] N rayo *m*, radio *m*; **to put a ~ in sb's wheel** meter un palo en la rueda de uno.
spoke² [spəʊk] PRET *of* **speak**.
spoken ['spəʊkən] 1 PTP *of* **speak**. 2 ADJ hablado; **the ~ language** la lengua hablada, la lengua oral.
spokeshave ['spəʊkʃeɪv] N raedera *f*.
spokesman ['spəʊksmən] N, PL **spokesmen** ['spəʊksmən] portavoz *m*, vocero *m* (*esp LAm*); **to act as ~ for** hablar en nombre de; **they made him ~** le eligieron para hablar en su nombre.
spokesperson ['spəʊkspɜːsn] N portavoz *mf*.
spokeswoman ['spəʊkswʊmən] N, PL **spokeswomen** ['spəʊkswɪmɪn] portavoz *f*.
spoliation [,spəʊlɪ'eɪʃən] N despojo *m*.
spondee ['spɒndiː] N espondeo *m*.
sponge [spʌndʒ] 1 N (a) esponja *f*; **to throw in the ~** arrojar (*or* tirar) la toalla.
(b) (*Culin*) bizcocho *m*.
2 VT (a) (*wash*: *also* **to ~ down**) lavar con esponja, lavar con trapo, limpiar con esponja; **to ~ a stain off** quitar una mancha con una esponja.
(b) (*) **he ~d £5 off me** me sacó 5 libras de gorra*.
3 VI (*) dar sablazos*, vivir de gorra*, gorrear; **to ~ on sb** vivir a costa de uno; **to ~ on sb for sth** sacar algo de gorra a uno*.
◆ **sponge down** VT = **sponge 2** (a).
◆ **sponge up** VT absorber.
spongebag ['spʌndʒbæg] N (*Brit*) esponjera *f*.
spongecake ['spʌndʒkeɪk] N bizcocho *m*.
sponge pudding [,spʌndʒ'pʊdɪŋ] N pudín *m* de bizcocho.
sponger* ['spʌndʒər] N gorrón* *m*, sablista* *mf*.
sponginess ['spʌndʒɪnɪs] N esponjosidad *f*.
sponging* ['spʌndʒɪŋ] N gorronería* *f*.
spongy ['spʌndʒɪ] ADJ esponjoso.
sponsor ['spɒnsər] 1 N patrocinador *m*, -ora *f* (*also Rad, Sport, TV*); (*godparent*) padrino *m*, madrina *f*; (*of membership etc*) padrino *m*; (*Comm*) fiador *m*, garante *m*; (*Parl: of bill*) promotor *m*, -ora *f*.
2 VT patrocinar; (*Rad, TV*) patrocinar, costear, presentar; *idea, plan etc* fomentar, promover; (*Parl*) *bill* promover; (*as godparent, for membership etc*) apadrinar, actuar de padrino a; **~ed walk** marcha emprendida a cambio de donaciones a una obra benéfica.
sponsorship ['spɒnsəʃɪp] N patrocinio *m*, patrocinazgo *m*; **under the ~ of** patrocinado por, bajo los auspicios de.
spontaneity [,spɒntə'neɪɪtɪ] N espontaneidad *f*.
spontaneous [spɒn'teɪnɪəs] ADJ espontáneo.
spontaneously [spɒn'teɪnɪəslɪ] ADV espontáneamente.
spoof* [spuːf] 1 N (*trick*) trampa *f*, truco *m*, mistificación *f*; (*Liter etc*) parodia *f* (*on* de); documento *m* (*etc*) apócrifo.
2 ADJ: **~ letter** carta *f* paródica, carta *f* apócrifa.
3 VT engañar, burlar, mistificar.
4 VI bromear.
spook* [spuːk] 1 N (a) espectro *m*. (b) (*US**) espía *mf*, agente *m* secreto, agente *f* secreta.
2 VT (*US*) asustar, pegar un susto a.
spooky* [spuːkɪ] ADJ (*like a ghost*) fantasmal, espectral; (*mysterious*) misterioso; (*frightening*) escalofriante, horripilante.
SPOOL [spuːl] N ABBR *of* **simultaneous peripherical operation on-line** operación *f* simultánea de periféricos en línea.
spool [spuːl] N (*Sew, Phot, Fishing*) carrete *m*; (*of sewing machine*) canilla *f*.
spoon [spuːn] 1 N cuchara *f*; (*Fishing*) cucharilla *f*; **to be born with a silver ~ in one's mouth** nacer en buena cuna, criarse en buenos pañales.
2 VT (*also* **to ~ out**) cucharear, sacar con cuchara; (*fig*) sacar como en cuchara.
3 VI (*) acariciarse amorosamente, besuquearse*.
◆ **spoon off** VT *fat, cream etc* quitar con la cuchara.
◆ **spoon out** VT = **spoon 2.**
◆ **spoon up** VT recoger con cuchara.
spoonbill ['spuːnbɪl] N espátula *f*.
spoonerism ['spuːnərɪzəm] N juego de palabras (*o* error divertido) que consiste en trastrocar los sonidos iniciales de dos o más vocablos.
spoon-feed ['spuːnfiːd] (*irr*: V **feed**) VT dar de comer con cuchara a; (*fig*) tratar como a un niño a, ayudar hasta con las cosas más sencillas a.
spoon-fed ['spuːnfed] ADJ muy mimado.
spoonful ['spuːnfʊl] N cucharada *f*.

spoor [spʊəʳ] N pista f, rastro m.

sporadic [spə'rædɪk] ADJ esporádico.

sporadically [spə'rædɪkəlɪ] ADV esporádicamente.

spore [spɔːt] N espora f.

sporran ['spɒrən] N (Scot) sporran m (escarcela que se lleva sobre la falda escocesa); ver también [KILT] .

sport [spɔːt] **1** N **(a)** (games in general) deporte m; (hunting) caza f; deporte m; (amusement) juego m, diversión f; (plaything) víctima f, juguete m; **the ~ of kings** el deporte de los reyes (el hipismo); **in ~** en broma; **to have some good ~** tener éxito en la caza, lograr unas cuantas piezas hermosas; **the trout here give good ~** aquí las truchas no se rinden fácilmente; **to make ~ of sb** burlarse de uno.
(b) (person) buen chico m; buen perdedor m; **yes, ~*** (Australia) sí, macho*; **be a ~!** ¡como amigo!; **he's a real ~** es una persona realmente buena.
(c) (Bio) mutación f.
2 ATTR: deportivo; de deportes; **~s car** coche m deportivo, deportivo m, coche m sport; **~s centre, ~s complex, ~s hall** polideportivo m; **~(s) coat** (US) = **~s jacket**; **~s day** (Brit) día m de competiciones deportivas (de un colegio); **~s desk** sección f de deportes; **~s editor** jefe mf de la redacción deportiva; **~s facilities** instalaciones fpl deportivas; **~s field, ~s ground** campo m deportivo, campo m de deportes, centro m deportivo (LAm); **~s jacket** chaqueta f sport, americana f de sport; **~s page** página f deportiva.
3 VT llevar; gastar; lucir, ostentar.
4 VI divertirse; jugar, juguetear.

sportiness ['spɔːtɪnɪs] N (lit) deportividad f; (fig) cursilería f.

sporting ['spɔːtɪŋ] ADJ deportivo; conduct, spirit etc deportivo, caballeroso; chance, offer que da cierta posibilidad de éxito; dog, gun de caza; **that's very ~ of you** es una oferta (etc) muy caballerosa; **I'm a ~ man** me gusta hacer apuestas arriesgadas.

sportingly ['spɔːtɪŋlɪ] ADV de modo deportivo.

sportive ['spɔːtɪv] ADJ juguetón.

sportscast ['spɔːtskɑːst] N (US) programa m deportivo.

sportsman ['spɔːtsmən] N, PL **sportsmen** ['spɔːtsmən] (player, hunter) deportista m; (honourable person) persona f honrada, caballero m; **the ~ of the year** el deportista del año.

sportsmanlike ['spɔːtsmənlaɪk] ADJ deportivo; honrado, caballeroso.

sportsmanship ['spɔːtsmənʃɪp] N deportividad f.

sportswear ['spɔːtsweəʳ] N ropa f de deporte.

sportswoman ['spɔːtswʊmən] N, PL **sportswomen** ['spɔːtswɪmɪn] deportista f.

sports-writer ['spɔːtsraɪtəʳ] N cronista m deportivo, cronista f deportiva.

sporty ['spɔːtɪ] ADJ **(a)** (liking sport) deportivo; aficionado a los deportes.
(b) (fig) alegre; guasón, jovial.
(c) (US) disipado, libertino; elegante, guapo.

spot [spɒt] **1** N **(a)** (place in general) sitio m, lugar m; **a pleasant ~** un lugar agradable; **a good ~ for trout** un buen lugar para las truchas; **high ~** cumbre; **to be in a (tight) ~** estar en un aprieto; **to have a soft ~ for sb** tener una debilidad por uno; **to know sb's weak ~s** saber de qué pie cojea uno; **to put one's finger on the weak ~** poner el dedo en la llaga.
(b) (phrases with on) **on this very ~** en este mismo sitio; **our man on the ~** nuestro hombre sobre el terreno; **the reporter was on the ~** el reportero estaba allí mismo; **the firemen were on the ~ in 3 minutes** los bomberos llegaron dentro de 3 minutos, acudieron los bomberos a los 3 minutos; **I always have to be on the ~** estoy de servicio siempre; **to do sth on the ~** hacer algo en el acto, hacer algo acto seguido; hacer algo sin demora; **to pay cash on the ~** (US) pagar al contado; **to put sb on the ~** poner a uno en la encrucijada, poner a uno en un aprieto (or un apuro); **now I'm really on the ~** ahora me veo de verdad entre la espada y la pared; **to run on the ~** correr en parada.
(c) (Med etc) grano m, lunar m; (freckle) peca f; (stain) mancha f; **measles ~s** manchas fpl de sarampión; **to break (or come) out in ~s** salir a uno granos en la piel; **it made a ~ on the table** hizo una mancha en la mesa.
(d) (of colour) punto m; pinta f, mancha f; **a cloth with blue ~s** un paño con puntos azules; **to knock ~s off sb*** dar ciento y raya a uno; **this can knock ~s off yours any time*** éste da ciento y raya al tuyo en cualquier momento; **five ~*** (US) billete m de 5 dólares; **ten ~*** (US) billete m de 10 dólares.
(e) (esp Brit: small quantity) poquito m, poquitín m; (of rain) gota f; **just a ~, thanks** un poquitín, gracias; **we had a few ~s** tuvimos algunas gotitas; **a ~ of bother** cierto disgusto, un poco de dificultad; **he had a ~ of bother with the police** se armó un lío con la policía; **we're in a ~ of trouble** tenemos cierta dificultad; **without a ~ of trouble** sin dificultad alguna.
(f) (Rad, TV) espacio m, cuña f.
(g) **~s** (Comm) géneros mpl vendidos al contado; géneros mpl para entrega inmediata.
(h) **night ~*** sala f de fiestas; lugar m de diversión nocturna.
(i) **(*) = spotlight**.
2 ATTR **(a)** **~ cash** dinero m contante; **~ goods** géneros mpl vendidos al contado; géneros mpl para entrega inmediata; **~ market** mercado m al contado; **~ price** precio m al contado (or de entrega inmediata).
(b) **~ check** comprobación f en el acto, reconocimiento m rápido; **~ survey** inspección f sorpresa; **~ test** prueba f superficial.
3 VT **(a)** (speckle) manchar, motear, salpicar (with de); **to ~ sb with mud** salpicar a uno de lodo.
(b) (notice, see) notar, observar; encontrar; descubrir; error reparar en; (recognize) reconocer; (select) elegir, escoger; **I ~ted him at once** le reconocí en seguida; **did you ~ the winner?** ¿has adivinado el ganador?; ¿has pronosticado el ganador?
4 VI: **to ~** (with rain) chispear.

spot-check ['spɒt,tʃek] VT revisar en el acto.

spotless ['spɒtlɪs] ADJ nítido; sin manchas, inmaculado; (clean) perfectamente limpio, como una tacita de plata.

spotlessly ['spɒtlɪslɪ] ADV: **~ clean** limpísimo, como una tacita.

spotlessness ['spɒtlɪsnɪs] N nitidez f; perfecta limpieza f.

spotlight ['spɒtlaɪt] **1** N (Theat: lamp) foco m, reflector m, proyector m, (light) luz f del foco; (Aut) faro m auxiliar; (fig) luz f concentrada; **to be in the ~** (fig) estar bajo la luz de la publicidad, ser el foco de la atención pública; **to turn the ~ on sb** (fig) volver sobre uno la luz de la publicidad (or de la atención pública etc).
2 VT iluminar; destacar, subrayar.

spotlit ['spɒtlɪt] ADJ iluminado.

spot-on* [,spɒt'ɒn] **1** ADJ: **what he said was ~** lo que dijo era muy justo.
2 ADV: **she guessed ~** lo adivinó exactamente.

spotted ['spɒtɪd] ADJ manchado; moteado; **a dress ~ with blue** un vestido con puntos azules; **a dress ~ with mud** un vestido manchado de lodo.

spotter ['spɒtəʳ] N (Aer etc) observador m, -ora f; (Brit Rail) coleccionista mf de números de locomotoras.

spotting ['spɒtɪŋ] N punteo m, moteamiento m; **to go train/plane ~** ir a ver trenes/aviones.

spotty ['spɒtɪ] ADJ manchado, lleno de manchas; (Med) (pimply) con granos; (of infection) con manchas; **some ~ herbert*** algún criajo*; **to be all ~** estar cubierto de manchas.

spot-weld ['spɒt,weld] VT soldar por puntos.

spouse [spaʊs] N cónyuge mf.

spout [spaʊt] **1** N (of jar) pico m; (of teapot, wine jug) pitón m, pitorro m; (of guttering) canalón m; (pipe) caño m, conducto m; (jet of water) chorro m; (column of water) surtidor m; **to be up the ~*** (Brit: person, in a jam) estar en un apuro, (pregnant) estar en estado; **my holiday's up the ~*** (Brit) mis vacaciones se hicieron pedazos.
2 VT arrojar en chorro; levantar un surtidor de; (fig) declamar, recitar; soltar; **he can ~ figures about it** es capaz de soltarte una retahíla de cifras.
3 VI chorrear; (fig) recitar, perorar; **he was still ~ing when we left** seguía perorando cuando salimos.

sprain [spreɪn] **1** N torcedura f, desgarro m (LAm).
2 VT torcer; **to ~ one's wrist** torcerse la muñeca.

sprang [spræŋ] PRET de **spring**.

sprat [spræt] N espadín m, sardineta f.

sprawl [sprɔːl] **1** N (of body) postura f desgarbada; (of town etc) extensión f; **an endless ~ of suburbs** una interminable extensión de barrios exteriores; **urban ~** urbanización f caótica.
2 VI arrellanarse, repanchigarse; extenderse (en postura desgarbada), tumbarse (de modo poco elegante); (plant, town) extenderse; **he was ~ed in a chair** estaba tumbado de modo poco elegante en un sillón; **the body was ~ed on the floor** el cadáver estaba tumbado en el suelo; **to send sb ~ing (with a blow)** derribar a uno por el suelo; **the jolt sent him ~ing** la sacudida le hizo ir rodando por el suelo.

sprawling ['sprɔːlɪŋ] ADJ person, position desmadejado; handwriting desgarbado; city desparramado.

spray¹ [spreɪ] N (Bot) ramita f, ramo m.

spray² [spreɪ] **1** N **(a)** (liquid) rociada f; (of sea) espuma f; (as irrigation) riego m por aspersión; (of insecticide etc) pulverización f.
(b) (implement) (scent ~) atomizador m; (paint ~) pistola f (rociadora) de pintura; (Med) rociador m; (insecticide ~) pulverizador m; **to paint with a ~** pintar con pistola.
2 VT rociar, regar (with de); atomizar, pulverizar; **to ~ the roses with insecticide** rociar las rosas de insecticida; **to ~ paint on to a car** pintar un coche con una pistola rociadora; **to ~ a house with bullets** rociar una casa de balas.
◆ spray out VI (liquid etc) salir a chorro; **water ~ed out all over them** el agua les caló.

spraycan ['spreɪkæn] N espray m, pulverizador m.

sprayer ['spreɪəʳ] N = **spray²** 1 (b).

spraygun ['spreɪɡʌn] N pistola f rociadora; pulverizador m.

spray-on ['spreɪɒn] ADJ **(a)** (lit) en aerosol, en spray. **(b)** (*: hum) jeans, dress etc apretadísimo; **he was wearing ~ jeans** llevaba unos vaqueros apretadísimos or que le iban a reventar.

spray-paint ['spreɪpeɪnt] N pintura f para pistola (or de espray).

spread [spred] **1** N **(a)** (act) extensión f; propagación f, diseminación f, difusión f; generalización f; proliferación f; **the ~ of education** la extensión de la educación; **the ~ of nuclear weapons** la proliferación de armas nucleares.

(b) (of wings) envergadura f; (of figures, marks etc) extensión f; abanico m, gama f, escala f; **middle-age ~** gordura f de la mediana edad.

(c) (*: meal) comilona* f, banquetazo* m.

(d) (Culin: cheese ~ etc) pasta f.

(e) (Typ) anuncio m (or artículo m etc) a doble página.

2 (irr: PRET AND PTP **spread**) VT extender, tender; intangible things propagar, diseminar, difundir; divulgar; generalizar; butter etc untar; banner, sails, wings desplegar; net tender; table poner; (scatter) esparcir, desparramar; **to ~ butter on one's bread** untar el pan con mantequilla, extender mantequilla sobre el pan; **to ~ cream on one's face** extender crema sobre el rostro; **to ~ oil on the sea** tender una capa de aceite sobre el mar; **to ~ the sea with oil** cubrir el mar con una capa de aceite; **meadows ~ with flowers** prados cubiertos de flores; **the peacock ~s its tail** el pavo real hace la rueda; **repayments will be ~ over 18 months** los pagos se efectuarán a lo largo de 18 meses; **to ~ news about** divulgar una noticia; **our resources are very thinly ~** tenemos poco margen en la distribución de nuestros recursos; **the book ~s error** el libro disemina el error.

3 VI extenderse; cundir; propagarse, difundirse; divulgarse; generalizarse; desplegarse; (scatter) esparcirse, desparramarse; **the fire ~ rapidly** el incendio se extendió rápidamente; **the strike ~ to other workers** la huelga se extendió a otros obreros; **a knowledge of this ~ widely** el conocimiento de esto se divulgó a muchas partes; **the disease ~** la enfermedad se propagó.

4 VR: **to ~ o.s. (a)** (physically) arrellanarse; ponerse a sus anchas, tomar una postura cómoda; **I like to ~ myself** me gusta tener mucho espacio (para trabajar cómodamente etc).

(b) (*: in speech) explayarse, hablar prolijamente.

(c) to ~ o.s. too thin traerse demasiadas cosas entre manos, dispersar esfuerzos en demasía.

◆**spread out 1** VT separar; abrir, extender, desplegar; **to ~ a map out on a table** extender un mapa sobre una mesa.

2 VI (persons) separarse; desparramarse.

spread-eagle ['spred'iːɡl] VT extender (completamente), despatarrar.

spread-eagled ['spred'iːɡld] ADJ despatarrado.

spreader ['spredər] N (for butter etc) cuchillo m para esparcir; (for glue etc) paleta f; (for scatter) paleta f.

spreadsheet ['spredʃiːt] N hoja f electrónica, hoja f de cálculo.

spree [spriː] N juerga f, parranda f; excursión f; **to be (out) on a ~** estar de juerga; **to go on a ~** ir de juerga; **let's have a ~** echemos una cana al aire.

sprig [sprɪɡ] N (Bot) ramita f; (of heather etc) espiga f; (Tech) puntilla f.

sprightliness ['spraɪtlɪnɪs] N viveza f, energía f, animación f.

sprightly ['spraɪtlɪ] ADJ vivo, enérgico, animado.

spring [sprɪŋ] **1** N **(a)** (of water) fuente f, manantial f; **hot ~** fuente f termal; **~ water** agua f de manantial.

(b) (season) primavera f; **in ~, in the ~** en la primavera; **~ is in the air** se nota la llegada de la primavera.

(c) (leap) salto m, brinco m; **in one ~** de un salto; **to take a ~ into the air** dar un salto.

(d) (bounciness) elasticidad f; **to walk with a ~ in one's step** andar con pasos alegres, caminar alegre y confiado.

(e) (Mech: of watch etc) resorte m, (of mattress, seat etc) muelle m; **~s** (Aut) ballestas fpl.

2 ATTR: **~ break** (US: Educ) ≃ vacaciones fpl de Semana Santa; **~ chicken** polluelo m; **she's no ~ chicken*** V chicken 1; **~ onion** (Brit) cebollita f; **~ sunshine** sol m de primavera, sol m primaveral.

3 (irr: PRET **sprang**, PTP **sprung**) VT **(a)** (leap) saltar, saltar por encima de.

(b) (warp) torcer, combar.

(c) mine volar; trap hacer saltar; **to ~ a leak** abrirse una vía de agua; **to ~ a piece of news on sb** comunicar una noticia imprevista a uno; **to ~ a surprise on sb** coger a uno de improviso; **to ~ an idea on sb** espetar una idea a uno, sugerir una idea a uno de buenas a primeras.

(d) (Hunting) game levantar; **to ~ a prisoner from jail*** ayudar a un preso a salir de la cárcel.

4 VI **(a)** (water etc) brotar, nacer; salir en chorro; (Bot) brotar; **to ~ into existence** nacer de la noche a la mañana, aparecer repentinamente; **to ~ from** (fig) nacer de, proceder de, provenir de; family ser de, nacer de; **a man sprung from the people** un hombre surgido de la plebe.

(b) (leap) saltar, brincar; **the lid sprang open** la tapa se abrió de golpe; **to ~ aside** hacerse de prisa a un lado; **to ~ at sb** abalanzarse sobre uno; **to ~ back** saltar para atrás; **the branch sprang back** la rama volvió a su posición como un látigo; **where on earth did you ~ from?** ¿de dónde diablos has salido?; **to ~ into the air** saltar en el aire; **to ~ into the saddle** saltar a la silla; **to ~ out of bed** saltar de la cama; **to ~ to one's feet** levantarse de un salto; **to ~ to sb's aid** acudir con toda rapidez a ayudar a uno.

(c) (warp) torcerse, combarse.

◆**spring up** VI **(a)** (grow) (plant) brotar; crecer rápidamente; (problem) surgir, presentarse; (friendship etc) nacer; **the weeds ~ up all over** las malas hierbas aparecen por todas las partes.

(b) (person, animal) levantarse de un salto; (of breeze etc) levantarse de pronto.

> ┌─ **SPRING BREAK** ─┐
>
> 𝒊 Durante la primavera, normalmente alrededor de Semana Santa, las universidades estadounidenses cierran por un periodo vacacional llamado **spring break**. Estos días de descanso se han convertido en un rito social para los universitarios, muchos de los cuales se van a las playas de Florida o California para disfrutar de una semana de diversión total. La invasión de tantos estudiantes puede llegar a veces a causarle problemas a la policía local.

spring balance ['sprɪŋ'bæləns] N peso m de muelle.

spring binder [ˌsprɪŋ'baɪndər] N carpeta f de pinza.

springboard ['sprɪŋbɔːd] N trampolín m; (fig) plataforma f de lanzamiento; **~ dive** salto m de trampolín.

springbok ['sprɪŋbɒk] N gacela f (del sur de África).

spring-bolt ['sprɪŋbəult] N pestillo m de golpe.

spring-clean ['sprɪŋ'kliːn] **1** VT limpiar completamente.

2 VI limpiarlo todo, limpiar toda la casa.

spring-cleaning ['sprɪŋ'kliːnɪŋ] N limpieza f general; **to do the ~** limpiar toda la casa.

spring fever ['sprɪŋ'fiːvər] N desasosiego m primaveral, sentimiento m de malestar (or intranquilidad etc); deseo m fuerte de cambiar de estilo de vida; (hum) celo m amoroso.

spring-gun ['sprɪŋɡʌn] N trampa f de alambre y escopeta.

springiness ['sprɪŋɪnɪs] N elasticidad f.

spring-like ['sprɪŋlaɪk] ADJ day, weather primaveral.

spring-loaded ['sprɪŋˌləudɪd] ADJ con resorte.

spring-lock ['sprɪŋlɒk] N cerradura f de resorte.

spring mattress ['sprɪŋ'mætrɪs] N colchón m de muelles, somier m.

spring-tide ['sprɪŋ'taɪd] N marea f viva.

springtime ['sprɪŋtaɪm] N primavera f.

springy ['sprɪŋɪ] ADJ elástico; turf etc muelle; movement, step ligero.

sprinkle ['sprɪŋkl] **1** N rociada f; salpicadura f; **a ~ of rain** unas gotitas de lluvia; **a ~ of salt** un poquito de sal.

2 VT salpicar, rociar (with de); sembrar (with de); (with holy water) asperjar; esparcir; **to ~ water on a plant, to ~ a plant with water** rociar una planta de agua; **a rose ~d with dew** una rosa cubierta de rocío; **they are ~d about here and there** están esparcidos aquí y allá.

3 VI (with rain) lloviznar.

sprinkler ['sprɪŋklər] N (Agr) rociadera f, aparato m de lluvia artificial; (for lawn) aspersor m; (of watering can etc) regadera f; (in fire-fighting) aparato m de rociadura automática; (Eccl) hisopo m; (Agr) **~ system** sistema m de regadío por aspersión.

sprinkling ['sprɪŋklɪŋ] N rociada f, salpicadura f; aspersión f; **a ~ of knowledge** unos pocos conocimientos; **there was a ~ of young people** había unos cuantos jóvenes.

sprint [sprɪnt] **1** N (in race) (e)sprint m; (dash) carrera f.

2 VI (in race) (e)sprintar; (dash) correr a todo correr, precipitarse; **he ~ed for the bus** corrió a toda prisa para coger el autobús; **we shall have to ~** tendremos que correr.

sprinter ['sprɪntər] N (e)sprínter mf, velocista mf.

sprit [sprɪt] N botavara f, verga f de abanico.

sprite [spraɪt] N duende m, trasgo m; hada f.

spritsail ['sprɪtseɪl, Naut 'sprɪtsl] N cebadera f, vela f de abanico.

spritzer ['sprɪtsər] N vino m blanco con soda.

sprocket ['sprɒkɪt] **1** N rueda f de espigas.

2 ATTR: **~ feed** avance m por rueda de espigas.

sprocket wheel ['sprɒkɪtwiːl] N rueda f de cadena.

sprog* [sprɒɡ] N rorro* m, bebé m.

sprout [spraut] **1** N brote m, retoño m; **~s** coles fpl de Bruselas.

2 VT echar, hacerse; **to ~ new leaves** echar nuevas hojas; **the calf is ~ing horns** le salen los cuernos al ternero; **the town is ~ing new buildings** en la ciudad surgen nuevos edificios.

3 VI brotar, retoñar, echar retoños; (shoot up) crecer rápidamente; **skyscrapers are ~ing up** se levantan rápidamente los rascacielos.

spruce¹ [spruːs] ADJ aseado, acicalado, pulcro.

◆**spruce up 1** VT arreglar, componer; **all ~d up** muy acicalado.

2 VR: **to ~ o.s. up** arreglarse; ataviarse; mejorar de aspecto, hacerse más elegante.

spruce² [spruːs] N (*Bot: also* **~ tree**) picea *f*.

sprucely ['spruːslɪ] ADV: **~ dressed** elegantemente vestido.

spruceness ['spruːsnɪs] N aseo *m*, pulcritud *f*; elegancia *f*.

sprung [sprʌŋ] 1 PTP *of* **spring**.
2 ADJ: **~ bed** cama *f* de muelles; **interior ~ mattress** somier *m*, colchón *m* de muelles; **~ seat** asiento *m* de ballesta.

spry [spraɪ] ADJ ágil, activo.

SPUC [spʌk] N ABBR *of* **Society for the Protection of Unborn Children** ≈ Federación *f* Española de Asociaciones Pro-Vida.

spud [spʌd] 1 N (a) (*Agr*) escarda *f*. (b) (*) patata *f*, papa *f* (*LAm*).
2 VT escardar.

spume [spjuːm] N (*liter*) espuma *f*.

spun [spʌn] 1 PRET AND PTP *of* **spin**.
2 ADJ: **~ glass** lana *f* de vidrio; **~ silk** seda *f* hilada; **~ yarn** meollar *m*.

spunk [spʌŋk] N (a) (‡: *courage*) agallas* *fpl*; arrojo *m*, coraje *m*. (b) (‡‡: *semen*) leche‡‡ *f*. (c) (*esp Australia*) guaperas* *m*.

spunky ['spʌŋkɪ] ADJ (a) valiente, arrojado. (b) (*esp Australia*) guaperas*.

spur [spɜːr] 1 N espuela *f*; (*Zool*) espolón *m*; (*Geog*) espolón *m*; (*fig*) estímulo *m*, aguijón *m*; (*Rail*) ramal *m* corto; **the ~ of hunger** el estímulo del hambre; **it will be a ~ to further progress** estimulará a más progresos; **on the ~ of the moment** sin reflexión, en un arranque, de improviso; **it was a ~ of the moment decision** fue una decisión tomada al instante; **to win one's ~s** distinguirse, demostrar de modo concluyente lo que vale uno.
2 VT (*also* **~ on**) espolear, picar con las espuelas; **to ~ on** (*fig*) estimular, incitar, acuciar; **to ~ sb (on) to do sth** incitar a uno a hacer algo, dar a uno aliento para que haga algo; **this ~red him (on) to greater efforts** esto le incitó a hacer mayores esfuerzos; **~red on by greed** bajo el aguijón de la codicia, acuciado por la codicia.
3 VI: **to ~ on** picar el caballo con las espuelas; apretar el paso.

spurge [spɜːdʒ] N euforbio *m*.

spur-gear ['spɜːgɪər] N rueda *f* dentada recta.

spurge laurel ['spɜːdʒ,lɒrəl] N lauréola *f*, torvisco *m*.

spurious ['spjʊərɪəs] ADJ falso, espurio.

spuriously ['spjʊərɪəslɪ] ADV falsamente.

spuriousness ['spjʊərɪəsnɪs] N falsedad *f*.

spurn [spɜːn] VT desdeñar, rechazar.

spurt [spɜːt] 1 N esfuerzo *m* supremo; **final ~** esfuerzo *m* final (para ganar una carrera); **to put in** (*or* on) **a ~** hacer un esfuerzo supremo, acelerar; *see also* **spirt**.
2 VI hacer un esfuerzo supremo, acelerar; *see also* **spirt**.

spur-wheel ['spɜːwiːl] N engranaje *m* cilíndrico.

sputnik ['spʊtnɪk] N sputnik *m*.

sputter ['spʌtər] = **splutter**.

sputum ['spjuːtəm] N esputo *m*.

spy [spaɪ] 1 N espía *mf*; **~ plane** avión *m* espía; **~ ring** red *f* de espionaje; **~ satellite** satélite *m* espía; **~ ship** buque *m* espía; **~ story** novela *f* de espionaje.
2 VT divisar, columbrar; lograr ver; observar; descubrir; **finally I spied him** conseguí al fin poder verle viniendo.
3 VI espiar, ser espía: **I ~** (*game*) veo-veo (*m*); **he spied for Slobodia** fue espía al servicio de Eslobodia; **to ~ on sb** espiar a uno, observar a uno clandestinamente; seguir los pasos a uno.
♦ **spy out** VT: **to ~ out the land** reconocer el terreno.

spycatcher ['spaɪkætʃər] N agente *mf* de contraespionaje.

spyglass ['spaɪglɑːs] N catalejo *m*.

spyhole ['spaɪhəʊl] N mirilla *f*.

spying ['spaɪɪŋ] N espionaje *m*.

spy-in-the-sky* [,spaɪɪnðə'skaɪ] N (*satellite*) satélite *m* espía.

spymaster ['spaɪmæstər] N jefe *m*, -a *f* de espías.

spy-plane ['spaɪpleɪn] N avión *m* espía.

Sq. ABBR *of* **Square** plaza *f*.

sq. (*Math*) ABBR *of* **square** cuadrado.

sq.ft. ABBR *of* **square foot** pie *m* cuadrado, ABBR *of* **square feet** pies *mpl* cuadrados.

squab [skwɒb] N (a) (*Orn*) pichón *m*; pollito *m*, polluelo *m*; (*fig*) persona *f* regordeta. (b) (*cushion*) cojín *m*; (*sofa*) sofá *m*, canapé *m*.

squabble ['skwɒbl] 1 N riña *f*, disputa *f*.
2 VI reñir (*about*, *over* por cuestión de), disputar, pelearse.

squabbler ['skwɒblər] N pendenciero *m* -a *f*.

squabbling ['skwɒblɪŋ] N riñas *fpl*, disputas *fpl*.

squad [skwɒd] N (*Mil*) pelotón *m*; escuadra *f*; (*of police*) brigada *f*, grupo *m*, escuadrón *m*; (*Sport*) equipo *m*.

squad-car ['skwɒd,kɑːr] N coche-patrulla *m*.

squaddie* ['skwɒdɪ] N soldado *m* raso.

squadron ['skwɒdrən] N (*Aer*, *Mil*) escuadrón *m*; (*Naut*) escuadra *f*.

squadron-leader ['skwɒdrən'liːdər] N (*Brit*) comandante *m* (de

aviación).

squalid ['skwɒlɪd] ADJ (*dirty*) miserable, vil, asqueroso; *motive etc* vil; *affair* asqueroso.

squall¹ [skwɔːl] 1 N (*cry*) chillido *m*, grito *m*, berrido *m*.
2 VI chillar, gritar, berrear.

squall² [skwɔːl] N (*Naut*: *gust*) ráfaga *f*; (*brief storm*) chubasco *m*, turbión *m*; (*fig*) tempestad *f*; **there are ~s ahead** (*fig*) el futuro se anuncia no muy tranquilo.

squalling ['skwɔːlɪŋ] ADJ *child* chillón, berreador.

squally ['skwɔːlɪ] ADJ *wind* que viene a ráfagas; *day* de chubascos; (*fig*) turbulento, lleno de dificultades.

squalor ['skwɒlər] N miseria *f*; suciedad *f*; **to live in ~** vivir en la miseria, vivir en la sordidez.

squander ['skwɒndər] VT *money* malgastar, derrochar, despilfarrar; disipar (*on* en); *opportunity* desperdiciar; *time*, *resources* emplear mal.

square [skwɛər] 1 ADJ (a) (*in shape*) cuadrado; *corner* en ángulo recto; *edge* escuadrado; *build* robusto, fornido; *jaw*, *shoulder* cuadrado.
(b) (*Math*) cuadrado; **~ kilometre** kilómetro *m* cuadrado; **~ measure** medida *f* cuadrada; **~ root** raíz *f* cuadrada; **2 metres ~** 2 metros en cuadro.
(c) (*fig*) *treatment etc* justo, equitativo; *person* honrado, formal; *refusal* rotundo; **~ deal** justicia *f*, trato *m* equitativo; **I want a ~ deal** yo pido justicia; **he didn't get a ~ deal** le trataron injustamente; **~ meal** comida *f* realmente buena; **it's 3 days since I had a ~ meal** hace 3 días que no como decentemente; **it met with a ~ refusal** fue rechazado de plano.
(d) (*even*, *balanced*) **to be ~ with sb** estar en paz con uno, no deber nada a uno; (*Sport*) ir iguales, ir empatados; **now we're all ~** ahora vamos iguales; **we can start again all ~** podemos volver a comenzar en pie de igualdad; **if you pay me a pound we'll call it ~** si me pagas una libra diremos que no hay más deuda; **to get ~ with sb** ajustar cuentas con uno, desquitarse con uno; **I'll get ~ with him yet!** ¡ya le ajustaré las cuentas!
(e) (*) *person* carca*; *idea etc* anticuado.
2 ADV: **~ to**, **~ with** en ángulo recto con; **it fell ~ in the middle** cayó de lleno en el centro, cayó exactamente en el centro.
3 N (a) (*shape*) cuadrado *m*; cuadro *m* (*also Mil*); (*of chessboard*, *graph paper*) casilla *f*; **a 6-metre ~** un cuadrado de 6 metros de lado; **we're back to ~ one** estamos de nuevo en el punto de partida; **to divide sth into ~s** dividir algo en cuadrados.
(b) (*of town*) plaza *f*, zócalo *m* (*Mex*); (*US*) manzana *f*, cuadra *f* (*LAm*).
(c) (*Math*) cuadrado *m*; **4 is the ~ of 2** 4 es el cuadrado de 2.
(d) (*Archit*, *Tech*) escuadra *f*.
(e) (*Univ*) birrete *m*; (*kerchief*) pañuelo *m*.
(f) (*) carroza* *mf*, carca* *mf*.
4 VT (a) (*make ~*) cuadrar; (*Archit*, *Tech*) escuadrar.
(b) (*arrange*) arreglar; (*reconcile*) ajustar, acomodar; *account* ajustar, pagar; (*bribe*) sobornar, comprar el silencio (*or* la ayuda *etc*) de; **can you ~ it with your conscience?** ¿lo puedes acomodar con tu conciencia?; **I'll ~ (it with) the porter*** lo arreglaré con el conserje.
(c) (*Math*) cuadrar.
5 VI cuadrar, conformarse (*with* con); **it doesn't ~ with what you said before** esto no cuadra con lo que dijiste antes; **it doesn't ~ with the facts** esto no cuadra con los hechos.
♦ **square up** VI (a) **to ~ up to sb** ponerse en actitud para defenderse contra uno, mostrarse resuelto a defenderse contra uno.
(b) **to ~ up with sb** ajustar cuentas con uno, pagar a uno.

squarebashing* ['skwɛə,bæʃɪŋ] N (*Brit*) instrucción *f*.

squared [skwɛəd] ADJ *paper* cuadriculado.

square dance ['skwɛə,dɑːns] N cuadrilla *f* (*baile*).

┌─ **SQUARE DANCE** ─┐

ⓘ *Se llama* **square dance** *a un baile folklórico tradicional de origen francés en el que cuatro parejas de bailarines se colocan formando un cuadrado. Es un baile muy popular en Estados Unidos y Canadá y a veces se enseña en la escuela. En algunas ocasiones alguien se encarga de explicar los pasos que se han de seguir, de modo que los que no los conocen bien puedan participar. El instrumento musical más utilizado en ellos es el violín, aunque también se usan a veces la guitarra, el banjo o el acordeón.*

square-faced [,skwɛə'feɪst] ADJ de cara cuadrada.

squarely ['skwɛəlɪ] ADV (a) en cuadro. (b) *refuse* rotundamente; honradamente. (c) de lleno, directamente; **we must face this ~** tenemos que hacer frente a esto sin pestañear; **it hit ~ in the middle** dio de lleno en el centro.

square-rigged ['skwɛə'rɪgd] ADJ con aparejo de cruz.

square rigger ['skwɛə'rɪgər] N buque *m* de vela con aparejo de cruz.

square-toed [,skwɛə'təʊd] ADJ *shoes* de punta cuadrada.

squarial ['skwɛərɪəl] N antena *f* cuadrada.

squash¹ [skwɒʃ] 1 N (a) (*Brit*: *drink*) zumo *m*, jugo *m* (*LAm*); **orange ~** naranjada *f*, zumo *m* de naranja, jugo *m* de naranja (*LAm*).
(b) (*crowd*) apiñamiento *m*, agolpamiento *m*; **there was such a ~ in**

the doorway había tantísima gente en la puerta, se apiñaba tanto la gente en la puerta.
[2] VT (*flatten*) aplastar; *argument* confutar; *person* apabullar, reducir a silencio.
[3] VI (*get crushed*) aplastarse.
♦ **squash in** [1] VT apretar; apiñar; **can you ~ my shoes in?** ¿puedes hacer caber mis zapatos?; **can you ~ 2 more in the car?** ¿caben 2 más en el coche?
[2] VI entrar (apretadamente, a pesar de la muchedumbre *etc*); **we all ~ed in** entramos todos aunque con dificultad.
♦ **squash together** [1] VT apretar; apiñar.
[2] VI apiñarse, estar muy juntos.
♦ **squash up** VI apretarse (más); correrse a un lado, hacer lugar.
squash² [skwɒʃ] N, **squash-rackets** ['skwɒʃ,rækɪts] N squash *m*.
squash³ [skwɒʃ] N (*US Bot*) calabacín *m*, calabacita *f*.
squashy ['skwɒʃɪ] ADJ blando y algo líquido, muelle y húmedo.
squat [skwɒt] [1] ADJ *person* rechoncho, achaparrado; *building* desproporcionadamente bajo.
[2] N (*) comunidad *f* de '*squatters*'; vivienda *f* ocupada por '*squatters*'.
[3] VI (a) (*also* **to ~ down**) agacharse, sentarse en cuclillas; (*) sentarse.
(b) (*on property*) establecerse sin derecho, apropiarse sin derecho.
squatter ['skwɒtəʳ] N (*Hist*) colono *m* usurpador, intruso *m*, -a *f*, persona *f* que se establece en un terreno público sin derecho; (*in house*) squátter *mf*, ocupante *mf* ilegal (de vivienda), paracaidista *mf* (*Mex*).
squatting ['skwɒtɪŋ] N ocupación *f* ilegal de una propiedad.
squaw [skwɔː] N india *f* norteamericana, piel roja *f*.
squawk [skwɔːk] [1] N graznido *m*, chillido *m*.
[2] VI graznar, chillar.
squeak [skwiːk] [1] N (*of hinge, wheel etc*) chirrido *m*, rechinamiento *m*; (*of shoe*) crujido *m*; (*of mouse etc*) chillido *m*, grito *m* agudo; (*of pen*) raspear *m*; **to have a narrow ~** escaparse por un pelo; **I couldn't get a ~ out of him** no pude sacarle palabra alguna; **we don't want a ~ out of you about this** de esto no digas ni pío.
[2] VI (a) chirriar, rechinar; crujir; chillar, dar chillidos, dar gritos agudos; raspear.
(b) **to ~ by*** pasar muy justo; arreglárselas.
squeaker ['skwiːkəʳ] N (*in toy etc*) chirriador *m*.
squeaky ['skwiːkɪ] ADJ chirriador; que cruje; chillón; que raspea; **~ clean** relimpio, perfectamente limpio; (*fig*) perfectamente honrado, sin sospecha alguna.
squeal [skwiːl] [1] N chillido *m*, grito *m* agudo; **with a ~ of pain** con un chillido de dolor; **with a ~ of brakes** con un chirriar de frenos.
[2] VT: **'Yes', he ~ed** 'Sí', dijo chillando.
[3] VI (a) chillar, dar gritos agudos; (*brakes, tyres*) chirriar.
(b) (*: complain*) quejarse; **don't come ~ing to me** no vengas a quejarte a mí.
(c) (*: inform*) cantar*, chivatear* (*on* contra).
squeamish ['skwiːmɪʃ] ADJ remilgado, delicado, susceptible; aprensivo; **I'm not ~** no tengo esa delicadeza, eso me trae sin cuidado; **I'm ~ about spiders** tengo horror a las arañas; **don't be so ~** no seas tan aprensivo, quítate esos remilgos; **to feel ~** sentir náuseas.
squeamishness ['skwiːmɪʃnɪs] N remilgos *mpl*, delicadeza *f*, susceptibilidad *f*; aprensión *f*; náuseas *fpl*; **to feel a certain ~** sentir cierta repugnancia.
squeegee ['skwiːdʒiː] N enjugador *m* de goma, escobilla *f* de goma.
squeeze [skwiːz] [1] N (a) (*act, pressure*) estrujón *m*, estrujadura *f*; presión *f*; (*of hand*) apretón *m*; (*in bus etc*) apiñamiento *m*, apretura *f*; **a ~ of lemon** unas gotas de limón; **it was a tight ~ in the bus** íbamos muy apretados en el autobús; **it was a tight ~ to get through** había muy poco espacio para pasar; **to give sb's hand a little ~** apretar suavemente la mano a uno; **to give sth a ~** apretar algo.
(b) (*Econ etc*) apretón *m*; (*of credit*) restricción *f*; (*difficulty*) apuro *m*, aprieto *m*; **to put the ~ on sb*** apretar las tuercas a uno.
(c) (*Bridge*) tenaza *f* (*in diamonds* a diamantes).
[2] VT (*painfully*) estrujar, apretar; *hand etc* apretar; presionar; **to ~ out juice** exprimir, *person* excluir; **3 were ~d to death** 3 murieron estrujados; **I ~d my finger in the door** me pillé el dedo en la puerta; **to ~ a lemon, to ~ the juice out of a lemon** exprimir el zumo (*LAm*: el jugo) de un limón; **to ~ money out of sb** sacar dinero a uno; **to ~ information out of sb** arrancar información a uno; **to ~ clothes into a case** meter ropa apretadamente en una maleta; **to ~ sb in hearts** atenazar a uno a corazones.
[3] VI: **to ~ through a crowd** abrirse paso (a codazos) por entre una multitud; **to ~ through a hole** lograr pasar por un agujero.
♦ **squeeze in** [1] VT: **can you ~ 2 more in?** ¿caben 2 más?; ¿puedes meter a 2 más?; **I'll see if we can ~ you in for Thursday** (*Theat etc*) veremos si quedan por casualidad entradas para el jueves, (*for appointment*) veremos si es posible ofrecerles hora el jueves.
[2] VI introducirse con dificultad en, deslizarse en.

♦ **squeeze past** VI deslizarse; lograr pasar.
♦ **squeeze up** VI apretarse (más); correrse a un lado, hacer lugar.
squeeze-box ['skwiːzbɒks] N concertina *f*.
squeezer ['skwiːzəʳ] N exprimelimones *m*, exprimidor *m*.
squelch [skwelʃ] [1] VT aplastar, despachurrar; **to ~ one's way through mud** ir chapoteando por el lodo.
[2] VI (*person*, ir chapoteando; **to ~ through the mud** ir chapoteando por el lodo.
squib [skwɪb] N buscapiés *m*.
squid [skwɪd] N calamar *m*.
squidgy* ['skwɪdʒɪ] ADJ (*Brit*) blanducho.
squiffy* ['skwɪfɪ] ADJ (*Brit*): **to be ~** estar achispado*.
squiggle ['skwɪgl] N garabato *m*.
squiggly ['skwɪglɪ] ADJ *line* garrapatoso.
squint [skwɪnt] [1] N (a) (*Med*) estrabismo *m*; (*~ing look*) mirada *f* bizca; (*sidelong glance*) mirada *f* de soslayo, mirada *f* furtiva; **he has a terrible ~** tiene un marcado estrabismo.
(b) (*) vistazo *m*; **have a ~ at this** mírame esto; **let's have a ~** dame un vistazo, déjame ver.
[2] VI (a) (*Med*) bizquear, ser bizco; (*look sidelong*) mirar de soslayo, torcer la vista; (*narrow eyes*) entornar (*or* entrecerrar) los ojos; cerrar casi los ojos; **to ~ at sth** mirar algo de soslayo; **he ~ed in the sunlight** entornó los ojos en el sol.
(b) (*) **to ~ at sth** echar un vistazo (*or* una ojeada) a algo.
squint-eyed ['skwɪnt'aɪd] ADJ bizco.
squire ['skwaɪəʳ] [1] N (*landowner*) propietario *m*, hacendado *m*; (*Hist*) escudero *m*; (*lady's escort*) galán *m*, acompañante *m*; **the ~** (*in relation to villagers etc*) el señor; **the ~ of Ambridge** el señor de Ambridge, el mayor terrateniente de Ambridge; **yes, ~!*** (*Brit*) ¡sí, jefe!; **which way, ~?*** ¿por dónde, caballero?
[2] VT *lady* acompañar.
squirearchy ['skwaɪərɑːkɪ] N aristocracia *f* rural, terratenientes *mpl*.
squirm [skwɜːm] VI retorcerse, revolverse; **to ~ with embarrassment** estar violento, avergonzarse mucho; **I'll make him ~** yo le haré sufrir.
squirrel ['skwɪrəl] N ardilla *f*.
♦ **squirrel away** VT *nuts etc* almacenar.
squirt [skwɜːt] [1] N (a) (*jet*) chorro *m*, jeringazo *m*; (*implement*) jeringa *f*.
(b) (*) farolero* *m*, farsante* *m*, mequetrefe *m*.
[2] VT arrojar un chorro de, arrojar a chorros; jeringar; **to ~ water at sb** lanzar un chorro de agua hacia uno.
[3] VI salir a chorros, chorrear; **the water ~ed into my eye** salió un chorro de agua que me dio en los ojos.
squirter ['skwɜːtəʳ] N atomizador *m*.
squishy ['skwɪʃɪ] ADJ *fruit* blando; **~ wet fields** campos como barrizales.
Sr ABBR *of* **Senior**.
SRC N (*Brit*) ABBR *of* **Students' Representative Council**.
Sri Lanka [,sriː'læŋkə] N Sri Lanka *m*.
Sri Lankan [,sriː'læŋkən] [1] ADJ de Sri Lanka.
[2] N nativo *m*, -a *f* (*or* habitante *mf*) de Sri Lanka.
SRN N (*Brit*) ABBR *of* **state registered nurse** enfermera *f* diplomada.
SRO (*US*) ABBR *of* **standing room only**.
SRU N (*Scot*) ABBR *of* **Scottish Rugby Union**.
SS (a) N (*Brit*) ABBR *of* **steamship** vapor *m*. (b) ABBR *of* **Saints**.
SSA N (*US*) ABBR *of* **Social Security Administration** ≃ Seguro *m* Social.
SSE ABBR *of* **south-south-east** sudsudeste *m*, *also* ADJ, SSE.
SSI N ABBR *of* **small-scale integration** integración *f* a pequeña escala.
SSSI N ABBR *of* **site of special scientific interest**.
SST N (*US*) ABBR *of* **supersonic transport**.
SSW ABBR *of* **south-south-west** sudsudoeste *m*, *also* ADJ, SSO.
St (a) (*Rel*) ABBR *of* **Saint** San, Santa, Sto., Sta., S. (b) (*Geog*) ABBR *of* **Strait** estrecho *m*. (c) ABBR *of* **Street** Calle *f*, C. (d) ABBR *of* **stone** (= 14 *libras = 6,348 kg*). (e) ABBR *of* **summer time** hora *f* de verano.
St. ABBR *of* **Station** estación *f*.
stab [stæb] [1] N (a) (*with knife etc*) puñalada *f*; (*wound in general*) herida *f*; (*of pain*) pinchazo *m*, punzada *f*, dolor *m* agudo; **~ in the back** (*fig*) puñalada *f* por la espalda, puñalada *f* encubierta.
(b) (*) tentativa *f*; **to have a ~ at sth** intentar algo, probar a hacer algo.
[2] VT apuñalar, dar de puñaladas a; **to ~ sb with a knife** herir a uno con un cuchillo; **to ~ sb in the back** (*fig*) apuñalar a uno por la espalda, apuñalar a uno encubiertamente; **to ~ sb to death** matar a uno a puñaladas.
[3] VI: **to ~ at sb** tratar de apuñalar a uno; **he ~bed at the picture with his finger** señaló el cuadro con un movimiento brusco del dedo.
stabbing ['stæbɪŋ] [1] N puñalada *f*, puñaladas *fpl*, el apuñalar; muerte *f* a puñaladas.
[2] ADJ: **~ pain** dolor *m* punzante.
stability [stə'bɪlɪtɪ] N estabilidad *f*.

stabilization [ˌsteɪbəlaɪˈzeɪʃən] N estabilización f.
stabilize [ˈsteɪbəlaɪz] **1** VT estabilizar.
2 VI estabilizarse.
stabilizer [ˈsteɪbəlaɪzəʳ] N (Culin) estabilizante m; (Tech) estabilizador m.
stable¹ [ˈsteɪbl] ADJ estable, firme; (Med) estacionario; job permanente; relationship, marriage etc sólido, firme; character equilibrado.
stable² [ˈsteɪbl] **1** N cuadra f, caballeriza f; (group of racehorses) cuadra .f; **to shut** (or **close**) **the ~ door after the horse has bolted** (or **gone**) a buenas horas, mangas verdes.
2 VT poner en una cuadra, guardar en una cuadra.
stableboy [ˈsteɪblbɔɪ] N, **stable-lad** [ˈsteɪblæd] N mozo m de cuadra.
stableman [ˈsteɪblmən] N, PL **stablemen** [ˈsteɪblmən] mozo m de cuadra.
stablemate [ˈsteɪblmeɪt] N (horse) caballo m de la misma cuadra; (fig) camarada m.
stab wound [ˈstæbwuːnd] N puñalada f.
staccato [stəˈkɑːtəʊ] **1** ADV staccato.
2 ADJ staccato.
stack [stæk] **1** N (a) montón m, rimero m, pila f; (Agr) almiar m, hacina f; (Mil) pabellón m de fusiles; (book ~) estantería f de libros.
(b) (*) montón* m; **we have ~s, thanks** gracias, tenemos montones; **we have ~s of time** nos sobra tiempo; **I have ~s of work to do** tengo un montón de trabajo que hacer.
(c) (of chimney) cañón m de chimenea, fuste m de chimenea.
2 VT (a) amontonar, apilar; recoger en un montón, formar una pila de; (Agr) hacinar; (**well**) **~ed**: (US) woman bien formada, muy buena*.
(b) **the cards are ~ed against us** (fig) la suerte está en contra nuestra.
stacker [ˈstækəʳ] N (for printer) apiladora f.
stadium [ˈsteɪdɪəm] N, PL **stadia** [ˈsteɪdɪə] or **stadiums** estadio m.
staff [stɑːf] **1** N (a) (PL **staves** [steɪvz] or **staffs**) (stick) palo m; (walking stick) bastón m, (pilgrim's) bordón m; (symbol of authority) bastón m de mando; (Eccl) báculo m; (of flag, lance etc) asta f; (fig) sostén m, apoyo m.
(b) (persons: PL **staffs**) personal m; (establishment) plantilla f de personal; (Mil) estado m mayor; (of company) equipo m directivo; (Scol, Univ) profesorado m, personal m docente; **to be on the ~** ser de plantilla, ser de planta (LAm); tener un puesto (permanente); **to join the ~** entrar a formar parte del personal; **to leave the ~** dimitir; **they keep a ~ of 5** (servants) tienen 5 criados.
(c) (Mus: PL **staves**) pentagrama m.
2 ATTR: **~ association** asociación f del personal; **~ canteen** comedor m del personal; **~ college** escuela f militar superior; **~ meeting** reunión f del personal; **~ nurse** enfermera f cualificada; **~ officer** oficial m del Estado Mayor; **~-student ratio** proporción f alumnos-profesor; **~ training** formación f de personal.
3 VT proveer de personal; **to be well ~ed** tener un buen personal.
staffer [ˈstɑːfəʳ] N (esp US) miembro mf del personal, empleado m, -a f de plantilla.
staffing [ˈstɑːfɪŋ] N empleo m de personal; **~ ratio** proporción f alumnos-profesor.
staffroom [ˈstɑːfruːm] N sala f de profesores.
Staffs [stæfs] N (Brit) ABBR of **Staffordshire**.
stag [stæɡ] **1** N (a) (Zool) ciervo m, venado m. (b) (Fin) especulador m con nuevas emisiones. (c) (man) soltero m.
2 ADJ de hombres, para hombres; masculino; **~ party** fiesta f de despedida de soltero; **to go ~ to a party** (US) ir sin compañía a una fiesta.
stag-beetle [ˈstæɡbiːtl] N ciervo m volante.
stage [steɪdʒ] **1** N (a) (platform) plataforma f, estrado m, tablado m; (of microscope) portaobjeto m; (of rocket) escalón m, piso m; **a 4-~ rocket** un cohete de 4 pisos; **the second ~ fell away** se separó el segundo escalón.
(b) (Theat) escena f; (fig) escenario m, teatro m; **~ left** parte f de la escena a la izquierda del actor (que mira al público); **~ right** parte f de la escena a la derecha del actor (que mira al público); **I get nervous on ~** me pongo nervioso en la escena; **you're on ~ in 2 minutes** sales en 2 minutos; **to go on the ~** hacerse actor, hacerse actriz; **to put a play on the ~** poner una obra; **to put a novel on the ~** dramatizar una novela, llevar una novela a la escena; **don't put your daughter on the ~** no permita que su hija se haga actriz; **to set the ~ for** (fig) disponer el escenario para; **to write for the ~** escribir para el teatro.
(c) (point, section: of journey) etapa f, jornada f; (of road, pipeline etc) tramo m; (fig) fase f, etapa f; grado m; **in ~s** por etapas; **in** (or **by**) **easy ~s** en cortas etapas; gradualmente, poco a poco; **at this ~ in the negotiations** en esta fase de las negociaciones; **what ~ have we reached?** ¿a qué punto hemos llegado?; **to go through a difficult ~** pasar por una fase difícil; **to have a work in the final ~s** tener un trabajo ultimado; **~ race** carrera f por etapas.

2 VT play representar, poner (en escena); escenificar; (bring about) efectuar, lograr, llevar a cabo; recovery efectuar; (arrange) arreglar; organizar; **that was no accident, it was ~d** eso no fue accidente, fue organizado; **to ~ a comeback** restablecerse, rehabilitarse; **to ~ a demonstration** organizar una manifestación.
stage box [ˈsteɪdʒbɒks] N palco m de proscenio.
stagecoach [ˈsteɪdʒkəʊtʃ] N diligencia f.
stagecraft [ˈsteɪdʒkrɑːft] N arte m teatral, escenotecnia f.
stage designer [ˈsteɪdʒdɪˌzaɪnəʳ] N decorador m, -ora f de teatro, escenógrafo m, -a f.
stage direction [ˈsteɪdʒdɪˌrekʃən] N acotación f.
stage director [ˈsteɪdʒdɪˌrektəʳ] N director m, -ora f de escena.
stage door [ˈsteɪdʒdɔːʳ] N entrada f de artistas.
stage fright [ˈsteɪdʒfraɪt] N miedo m al público.
stagehand [ˈsteɪdʒhænd] N tramoyista m, sacasillas m.
stage-manage [ˈsteɪdʒˌmænɪdʒ] VT play, production dirigir; (fig) event, confrontation etc orquestar.
stage manager [ˈsteɪdʒˌmænɪdʒəʳ] N director m, -ora f de escena; (TV) regidor m, -ora f.
stage name [ˈsteɪdʒˌneɪm] N nombre m artístico.
stage-struck [ˈsteɪdʒstrʌk] ADJ apasionado por el teatro.
stage whisper [ˈsteɪdʒˈwɪspəʳ] N aparte m.
stagey [ˈsteɪdʒɪ] ADJ teatral, dramático.
stagflation [stæɡˈfleɪʃən] N (e)stagflación f, estanflación f.
stagger [ˈstæɡəʳ] **1** N tambaleo m; ~s (Vet) modorra f.
2 VT (a) (amaze) asombrar, consternar, sorprender; (cause to waver) hacer dudar, hacer vacilar; **you ~ me!** ¡me asombras!, ¡me asustas!; **I was ~ed to hear that ...** me consterné al saber que ...
(b) hours, holidays, payments escalonar; spokes etc alternar.
3 VI tambalear, titubear, hacer eses; **he ~ed to the door** fue tambaleando a la puerta; **he was ~ing about** iba tambaleando.
staggering [ˈstæɡərɪŋ] ADJ asombroso, pasmoso.
staghound [ˈstæɡhaʊnd] N perro m de caza, sabueso m.
staghunt [ˈstæɡhʌnt] N cacería f de venado.
staghunting [ˈstæɡˌhʌntɪŋ] N caza f de venado.
staging [ˈsteɪdʒɪŋ] **1** N (a) (scaffolding) andamiaje m. (b) (Theat) escenificación f, puesta f en escena. (c) (Space) desprendimiento m (de una sección de un cohete).
2 ATTR: **~ post** (Mil, also gen) escala f.
stagnancy [ˈstæɡnənsɪ] N estancamiento m.
stagnant [ˈstæɡnənt] ADJ estancado; (fig) estancado, paralizado, inmóvil; society etc anquilosado; (Fin) inactivo.
stagnate [stæɡˈneɪt] VI estancarse; estar estancado, quedar estancado (also fig); (fig) estar paralizado.
stagnation [stæɡˈneɪʃən] N estancamiento m; (fig) estancamiento m, paralización f, inmovilismo m; anquilosamiento m; inactividad f.
stagy [ˈsteɪdʒɪ] ADJ = **stagey**.
staid [steɪd] ADJ serio, formal.
staidness [ˈsteɪdnɪs] N seriedad f, formalidad f.
stain [steɪn] **1** N (a) (mark) mancha f; (dye) tinte m, tintura f; (paint) pintura f.
(b) (fig) mancha f; **without a ~ on one's character** sin una sola mancha en la reputación.
2 VT manchar; (dye) teñir, colorar; (paint) pintar; **her hands were ~ed with blood** sus manos estaban manchadas de sangre; **~ed glass** vidrio m de color; **~ed glass window** vidriera f (de colores).
3 VI mancharse.
stainless [ˈsteɪnlɪs] ADJ inmaculado; inmanchable; steel inoxidable.
stain-remover [ˈsteɪnrɪˌmuːvəʳ] N quitamanchas m.
stair [steəʳ] N peldaño m, escalón m; (stairway) escalera f; ~s escalera f; **flight of ~s** tramo m de escalera; **life below ~s** vida f de los criados; **gossip below ~s** habladurías fpl de la servidumbre.
staircarpet [ˈsteəˌkɑːpɪt] N alfombra f de escalera.
staircase [ˈsteəkeɪs] N escalera f; caja f de escalera.
stair-rod [ˈsteərɒd] N varilla f (sujetadora de alfombra de escalera).
stairway [ˈsteəweɪ] N = **staircase**.
stairwell [ˈsteəwel] N hueco m de la escalera.
stake [steɪk] **1** N (a) (post) estaca f, poste m; (for plant) rodrigón m.
(b) (for execution) poste m; hoguera f; **to burn sb at the ~** quemar a uno en el poste; **to die at the ~** morir en la hoguera; **to be condemned to the ~** ser condenado a morir en la hoguera.
(c) (bet) puesta f, apuesta f, parada f; ~s (prize) premio m, (race) carrera f; **the issue at ~** el punto en cuestión; **to be at ~** estar en juego, estar en litigio; estar en peligro; **there is a lot at ~ here** esto nos importa muchísimo, esto nos interesa muchísimo; **to have a ~ in** tener interés en; **Britain had a big ~ in Ruritania** Gran Bretaña tuvo muchos intereses en Ruritania; **X is top in the popularity ~s** en la popularidad X va en cabeza.
2 VT (a) (also **to ~ off, to ~ out**) estacar; cercar con estacas, señalar con estacas; plant rodrigar.
(b) (bet) apostar (on a); (Fin) aventurar, arriesgar; invertir (on en); **to ~ one's all** jugar el todo por el todo; aventurarlo todo; **to ~ one's**

reputation on sth jurar como hombre honrado que algo es así; **to ~ a claim** hacer una reclamación; **to ~ one's claim to a job** afirmar su derecho a un puesto.

◆ **stake off** VT = **stake 2 (a)**.

◆ **stake out** VT (a) = **stake 2 (a)**.
(b) *property etc* poner bajo vigilancia.

stakeholder ['steɪk,həʊldəʳ] N *persona que guarda las apuestas.*

stake-out ['steɪkaʊt] N vigilancia *f*.

stalactite ['stæləktaɪt] N estalactita *f*.

stalagmite ['stæləgmaɪt] N estalagmita *f*.

stale [steɪl] ADJ *food* no fresco, pasado, rancio; *bread* duro; *air* viciado; *news* viejo; *joke* viejo, mohoso; *cheque* caducado; (*old-fashioned*) anticuado, pasado de moda; *person* cansado; **I'm getting ~** me estoy cansando; ya no tengo la inventiva de antes.

stalemate ['steɪlmeɪt] [1] N (*Chess*) tablas *fpl* (por ahogado); (*fig*) paralización *f*, estancamiento *m*; **the ~ is complete** la paralización es completa; **to reach ~** llegar a un punto muerto; **there is ~ between the two powers** las relaciones entre las dos potencias están en un punto muerto.
[2] VT (*Chess*) ahogar, dar tablas por ahogado a; (*fig*) paralizar.

stalemated ['steɪlmeɪtɪd] ADJ *discussions* estancado, en un punto muerto; *project* en un punto muerto; *person* en tablas.

staleness ['steɪlnɪs] N rancidez *f*; dureza *f*; lo viciado; lo viejo, lo mohoso; lo anticuado; cansancio *m*, falta *f* de inventiva.

Stalin ['stɑːlɪn] NM Stalin.

Stalinism ['stɑːlɪnɪzəm] N estalinismo *m*.

Stalinist ['stɑːlɪnɪst] [1] ADJ estalinista.
[2] N estalinista *mf*.

stalk¹ [stɔːk] [1] VT *game* cazar al acecho, acechar; *person* seguir los pasos a.
[2] VI (*also* **to ~ along**) andar con paso majestuoso; **to ~ away, to ~ off** irse con paso airado; **to ~ out** salir ofendido, salir con paso airado.

stalk² [stɔːk] N (*Bot*) tallo *m*, caña *f*; (*cabbage ~*) troncho *m*; (*of glass*) pie *m*.

stalker ['stɔːkəʳ] N *persona que acecha a otra furtivamente.*

stalk-eyed ['stɔːkaɪd] ADJ (*Zool*) de ojos pedunculares.

stalking ['stɔːkɪŋ] N *acecho furtivo a una persona.*

stalking-horse ['stɔːkɪŋhɔːs] N pretexto *m*.

stall [stɔːl] [1] N (*Agr: stable*) establo *m*, (*part of stable*) casilla *f* de establo, (*manger*) pesebre *m*; (*in market etc*) puesto *m*, caseta *f*; (*Brit Theat*) butaca *f*, luneta *f* (*Mex*); (*Eccl*) silla *f* de coro; (*US: in car park*) emplazamiento *m*; **to set out one's ~** (*fig*) exponer lo que se ofrece (a la venta).
[2] VT (a) (*Aut etc*) parar, cortar accidentalmente, atascar.
(b) **to ~ sb off** deshacerse de uno mediante algún pretexto, tener a uno a raya.
[3] VI (a) (*Aut etc*) pararse, calar(se), atascarse; **we ~ed on a steep hill** quedamos parados en una cuesta abrupta, se nos atascó el motor en una cuesta abrupta; **the talks are** (*or* **have**) **~ed** las negociaciones están en un callejón sin salida.
(b) (*fig*) buscar evasivas, evitar contestar directamente, ir con rodeos; **stop ~ing!** ¡déjese de evasivas!; **the minister ~ed for 20 minutes** durante 20 minutos el ministro evitó contestar directamente.

stall-fed ['stɔːlfed] ADJ engordado en establo.

stallholder ['stɔːl,həʊldəʳ] N dueño *m*, -a *f* de un puesto (de mercado etc).

stallion ['stælɪən] N caballo *m* padre, semental *m*.

stalwart ['stɔːlwət] [1] ADJ (*in build*) fornido, robusto; (*in spirit*) leal; valiente; cien por cien, incondicional; **a ~ supporter of ...** partidario incondicional de ...
[2] N partidario *m*, -a *f* leal.

stamen ['steɪmen] N estambre *m*.

stamina ['stæmɪnə] N resistencia *f*, aguante *m*; nervio *m*, vigor *m*; **intellectual ~** vigor *m* intelectual; **has he enough ~ for the job?** ¿tiene bastante resistencia para el puesto?; **you need ~** hace falta tener nervio.

stammer ['stæməʳ] [1] N tartamudeo *m*, balbuceo *m*; **he has a bad ~** tartamudea terriblemente.
[2] VT (*also* **to ~ out**) balbucir, decir tartamudeando.
[3] VI tartamudear; balbucir.

stammerer ['stæmərəʳ] N tartamudo *m*, -a *f*.

stammering ['stæmərɪŋ] [1] ADJ tartamudo.
[2] N tartamudeo *m*.

stammeringly ['stæmərɪŋlɪ] ADV: **he said ~** dijo tartamudeando.

stamp [stæmp] [1] N (a) (*with foot*) patada *f*; **with a ~ of her foot** dando una patada.
(b) (*rubber ~*) estampilla *f*; (*die*) cuño *m*, troquel *m*.
(c) (*mark*) marca *f*, huella *f*, impresión *f*; **a man of his ~** un hombre de su temple, (*pej*) un hombre de esa calaña; **it bears the ~ of genius** lleva el sello de la genialidad; **to leave** (*or* **put**) **one's ~ on sth**

poner (*or* dejar) su sello en algo.
(d) (*postage ~*) sello *m* (de correos), estampilla *f* (*LAm*); (*fiscal ~, revenue ~*) timbre *m*, póliza *f*; (*trading ~*) cupón *m*; (*for free food etc*) bono *m*, vale *m*.
[2] VT (a) **to ~ one's foot** patear, golpear con el pie; (*in dancing*) zapatear; (*horse*) piafar.
(b) (*impress mark etc on*) estampar, imprimir; *coin, design* estampar; *passport* sellar; (*fig*) marcar, señalar; sellar; **paper ~ed with one's name** papel *m* con el nombre de uno impreso, papel *m* con membrete; **to ~ sth on one's memory** grabar algo en la memoria de uno; **his manners ~ him a gentleman** sus modales le señalan como caballero.
(c) (*mark with rubber ~*) estampillar; (*mark with fiscal ~*) timbrar; *letter* pegar un sello a, poner un sello en; franquear; **~ed addressed envelope** sobre *m* con las propias señas de uno y con sello; **the letter is insufficiently ~ed** la carta no lleva suficiente franqueo; **they ~ed my passport at the frontier** sellaron mi pasaporte en la frontera.
[3] VI patear, golpear con los pies; pisar muy fuerte; (*disapprovingly*) patalear; (*of horse*) piafar; **he ~s about the house** anda por la casa pisando muy fuerte; **to ~ on** pisotear, hollar; **sb ~ed on my foot** alguien me pisoteó el pie.
[4] VR: **to ~ o.s. on sth** poner (*or* dejar) su sello en algo.

◆ **stamp down** VT: **to ~ sth down** apisonar algo, comprimir algo con los pies.

◆ **stamp out** VT (a) (*extinguish*) *fire* apagar pateando; (*fig*) extirpar, acabar con, desarraigar; **we must ~ out this abuse** tenemos que acabar con esta injusticia; **the doctors ~ed out the epidemic** los médicos dominaron la epidemia.
(b) **they ~ed out the rhythm** marcaron el ritmo con los pies.

stamp-album ['stæmp,ælbəm] N álbum *m* para sellos.

stamp-book ['stæmpbʊk] N (*collection*) álbum *m* de sellos; (*for posting*) libro *m* de sellos.

stamp-collecting ['stæmpkə,lektɪŋ] N filatelia *f*.

stamp-collection ['stæmpkə,lekʃən] N colección *f* de sellos.

stamp-collector ['stæmpkə,lektəʳ] N filatelista *mf*.

stamp-dealer ['stæmp,diːləʳ] N comerciante *mf* en sellos (de correo).

stamp-duty ['stæmp,djuːtɪ] N impuesto *m* (*or* derecho *m*) del timbre.

stamped [stæmpt] ADJ *paper* sellado, timbrado; *envelope* con sello, que lleva sello.

stampede [stæm,piːd] [1] N espantada *f*, desbandada *f*, estampida *f* (*LAm*); **there was a sudden ~ for the door** de repente se precipitaron todos hacia la puerta; **the exodus turned into a ~** el éxodo se transformó en una fuga precipitada.
[2] VT hacer huir en desorden; hacer desbandarse; infundir un terror pánico a; **to ~ sb into doing sth** infundir terror a uno para que haga algo; hacer que uno haga algo sin la debida reflexión; **let's not be ~d** no obremos precipitadamente.
[3] VI huir en desorden, huir precipitadamente; desbandarse.

stamping-ground* ['stæmpɪŋ,graʊnd] N territorio *m* personal; lugar *m* predilecto; guarida *f*; **this is his private ~** éste es terreno particular suyo, éste es coto cerrado de su propiedad; **to keep off sb's ~** no invadir el territorio de uno.

stamp-machine ['stæmpmə,ʃiːn] N expendedor *m* automático de sellos (de correo).

Stan [stæn] NM *familiar form of* **Stanley.**

stance [stæns] N postura *f*; **to take up a ~** adoptar una postura.

stanch [stɑːntʃ] VT *blood* restañar.

stanchion ['stɑːnʃən] N puntal *m*, montante *m*.

▼ **stand** [stænd] [1] N (a) (*position*) posición *f*, postura *f*; **to take up one's ~ by the door** ponerse cerca de la puerta; **to take one's ~ on a principle** aferrarse a un principio, sentar cátedra sobre un principio; **to take a firm ~** adoptar una actitud firme.
(b) (*Mil*) parada *f*, alto *m*; resistencia *f*; **the ~ of the Australians at Tobruk** la resistencia de los australianos en Tobruk; **they turned and made a ~** hicieron alto para resistir de nuevo; **to make a ~ against sth** oponer resistencia a algo, hacer frente a algo.
(c) (*for taxis*) parada *f*.
(d) (*Theat*) función *f*, representación *f*.
(e) (*support: for lamp etc*) sostén *m*; pie *m*, pedestal *m*; (*for display*) mesilla *f*; (*hall~*) perchero *m*; (*Mus*) atril *m*.
(f) (*in market etc*) puesto *m*; barraca *f*, caseta *f*; (*news~*) quiosco *m*; (*band~*) quiosco *m*; (*at exhibition*) stand *m*; (*Sport*) tribuna *f*; **to take the ~** (*esp US*) subir a la tribuna de los testigos, (*fig*) prestar declaración.
(g) (⁝) empalme⁝ *m*.
(h) (*of trees*) línea *f*, grupo *m*, hilera *f*; plantación *f*.
[2] (*irr*. PRET AND PTP **stood**) VT (a) (*place*) poner, colocar (de pie); **to ~ sth** (**up**) **against a wall** poner algo contra una pared; **to ~ a vase on a table** poner un florero sobre una mesa.
(b) **to ~ one's ground** mantenerse firme, mantenerse en sus trece.
▼ (c) (*tolerate*) tolerar, aguantar, soportar; resistir (a); *test* salir muy bien de; *cost* pagar, sufragar, correr con; **it won't ~ the cold** no

resiste el (or al) frío; **his heart couldn't ~ the shock** su corazón no resistió el (or al) choque; **the company will have to ~ the loss** la compañía tendrá que encargarse de las pérdidas; **I can't ~ him** no le puedo ver; **I can't ~ Debussy** no aguanto a Debussy; **I can ~ anything but that** lo aguanto todo menos eso; **I can't ~ it any longer!** ¡no aguanto más!, ¡no puedo más!; *V* **chance.**

(d) (*pay for*) **to ~ sb a drink** invitar a uno a beber, pagar la bebida de uno; **he stood beers all round** invitó a todos a tomar cerveza; **he stood me lunch** me pagó la comida.

3 VI **(a)** (*be upright*) estar de pie, estar parado (*LAm*); (*get up*) levantarse, ponerse de pie; **all ~!** ¡levántense!; **~ at ease!** en su lugar ¡descanso!; **he could hardly ~** apenas podía mantenerse de pie; **to ~ at the bar** estar junto al bar; **to ~ in the doorway** estar en la puerta; **to ~ talking** seguir hablando; quedarse a hablar; **we stood chatting for half an hour** charlamos durante media hora, pasamos media hora charlando; **he left everybody else ~ing** (*fig*) dejó a todos muy atrás, dejó a todos parados (*LAm*); superó fácilmente a los demás; *V* **end, leg** *etc.*

(b) (*of measurement*) medir; **the tree ~s 30 metres high** el árbol mide 30 metros, el árbol tiene 30 metros de alto; **he ~s a good 6 feet** mide 6 pies largos; **the mountain ~s 3000 metres high** la montaña tiene una altura de 3000 metros.

(c) (*be, be placed*) estar, estar situado, encontrarse; **it ~s beside the town hall** está junto al ayuntamiento; **to buy a house as it ~s** comprar una casa tal como está; **to let sth ~ in the sun** poner algo al sol, dejar algo al sol; **the car has been ~ing in the sun** el coche ha estado expuesto al sol; **nothing now ~s between us** ya no existe ningún estorbo entre nosotros.

(d) (*remain*) quedar en pie, mantenerse en vigor; (*last*) perdurar, durar; **the record ~s at 10 minutes** el record está en 10 minutos, el tiempo récord sigue siendo de 10 minutos; **the objection ~s** la objeción es válida, la objeción vale; **the contract ~s** el contrato sigue en vigor; **the theory ~s or falls by this** con esto o se confirma o se destruye la teoría; **it has stood for 600 years** ha durado 600 años ya, lleva ya 600 años de vida; *V* **fast¹, firm¹** *etc.*

(e) (*temporary conditions*) **as things ~, as it ~s** tal como están las cosas; **how do we ~?** ¿cómo estamos?; **I like to know where I ~** me gusta estar enterado de mi situación (con relación a otras personas); **where do you ~ with him?** ¿cuáles son tus relaciones con él?; **to ~ well with sb** llevarse bien con uno, ser tenido en mucho por uno.

(f) (*remain undisturbed*) estar; sedimentar; **to allow a liquid to ~** dejar estar un líquido; **let it ~ for 3 days** dejarlo así durante 3 días; **don't let the tea ~** no dejes que se pase el té.

(g) (*special cases*) **to ~ as a candidate** (*Brit*) presentarse como candidato; **to ~ (as) security for sb** (*Fin*) salir fiador de uno, (*fig*) salir por uno; **the thermometer ~s at 40°** el termómetro marca 40 grados; **there is £50 ~ing to your credit** Vd tiene 50 libras en el haber; **sales ~ at 5% more than last year** las ventas han aumentado en un 5 por cien en relación con el año pasado; **we ~ to lose a lot** para nosotros supondría una pérdida importante, estamos en peligro de perder bastante; **what do we ~ to gain by it?** ¿qué posibilidades hay para nosotros de ganar algo?, ¿qué ventaja nos daría esto?; **he ~s to win £5** tiene la posibilidad de ganar 5 libras; *V* **need** *etc.*

◆**stand about, stand around** VI estar; esperar; seguir en un sitio sin propósito fijo; **they just ~ about all day** pasan todo el día por ahí sin hacer nada; **they kept us ~ing about for hours** nos hicieron esperar (de pie) durante horas enteras.

◆**stand aside** VI apartarse, quitarse de en medio, hacerse a un lado; **~ aside, please!** ¡apártense, por favor!; **we cannot ~ aside and do nothing** no podemos estar sin hacer nada; **he stood aside when he could have helped** se mantuvo aparte cuando pudo ayudar.

◆**stand back** VI **(a)** (*person*) retroceder, moverse hacia atrás; **~ back, please!** ¡más atrás, por favor!; *V also* **stand aside.**

(b) (*house etc*) estar algo apartado (*from* de).

◆**stand by** **1** VT *promise* cumplir, atenerse a; *person* apoyar, defender; no abandonar; **the Minister stood by his decision** el Ministro mantuvo su decisión; **I ~ by what I said** reafirmo lo que dije, lo dicho dicho.

2 VI **(a)** (*as onlooker*) estar presente (sin intervenir); estar de mirón; *V also* **stand aside.**

(b) (*on alert*) estar alerta, mantenerse listo; estar dispuesto para el combate (*etc*); estar a la expectativa; **~ by for further news** estén listos para recibir más noticias; **the Navy is ~ing by to help** unidades de la Flota están listas para prestar ayuda; **~ by for take-off!** ¡listos para despegar!

◆**stand down** VI **(a)** retirarse; ceder (su puesto *etc*); renunciar a su oportunidad (*etc*); **someone has to ~ down** alguien tiene que ceder; **the candidate is ~ing down in favour of a younger person** el candidato se retira a favor de una persona más joven; **you may ~ down** (*Jur etc*) Vd puede retirarse.

(b) **the troops have stood down** (*Mil*) ha terminado el estado de alerta (militar).

◆**stand for** VT **(a)** (*represent*) representar; (*mean*) significar; **'A ~s for apple'** 'M es de manzana'; **here a dash ~s for a word** aquí una raya representa una palabra.

(b) *post* proponerse para, ofrecerse para, presentarse como candidato a; **he stood for Parliament in 1987** se presentó en las elecciones parlamentarias de 1987; **he stood for Castroforte** fue uno de los candidatos en Castroforte; **he stood for Labour** fue candidato laborista.

(c) (*support*) apoyar, defender; hablar por; creer en; afirmar su adhesión a.

(d) (*tolerate*) aguantar; permitir, consentir; **I'll not ~ for that** eso no lo permito, eso no se debe consentir; **I'll not ~ for your whims any longer** no aguanto tus caprichos un momento más.

◆**stand in** VI **(a)** **to ~ in to the shore** acercarse a la costa.

(b) **to ~ in for sb** suplir a uno.

(c) **to ~ in with sb** apoyar a uno; declararse por uno; (*financially*) compartir el gasto con uno.

◆**stand off** **1** VT *workers* despedir (temporalmente, por falta de trabajo), suspender.

2 VI apartarse, guardar las distancias; (*Naut*) apartarse.

◆**stand out** VI **(a)** (*project*) salir, sobresalir; destacar (*against* contra, sobre).

(b) (*be outstanding*) destacarse, descollar, sobresalir; llamar la atención, impresionar.

(c) **to ~ out to sea** hacerse a la mar.

(d) (*remain firm*) mantenerse firme; **to ~ out against** oponerse (resueltamente) a; **to ~ out for** insistir en, no ceder hasta obtener.

◆**stand over** **1** VT: **to ~ over sb to see that he works** vigilar a uno para asegurar que trabaja.

2 VI (*remain in suspense*) quedar en suspenso; **to let an item ~ over** dejar un asunto para la próxima vez.

◆**stand to** VI estar alerta, estar sobre las armas.

◆**stand up** **1** VT **(a)** (*place*) = **stand 2 (a).**

(b) (*) dar plantón a*, dejar plantado*.

2 VI **(a)** (*rise*) levantarse, ponerse de pie; (*be standing*) estar de pie; **a brew so strong that a spoon could ~ up in it** un brebaje en el cual se podría mantener de pie una cuchara; **we must ~ up and be counted** (*fig*) tenemos que declararnos abiertamente.

(b) (*argument etc*) ser sólido, ser lógico; convencer; **the case did not ~ up in court** la acusación no se mantuvo en el tribunal.

(c) **to ~ up for sb** defender a uno; **to ~ up for o.s.** no achantarse; defenderse a sí mismo.

(d) **to ~ up to sb** resistir (resueltamente) a uno, hacer frente a uno; **to ~ up to a test** salir bien de una prueba; **it ~s up to hard wear** es muy resistente; **it won't ~ up to close examination** no resiste al examen cuidadoso.

stand-alone ['stændələʊn] ADJ: **~ (computer) system** sistema *m* autónomo.

standard ['stændəd] **1** N **(a)** (*flag*) estandarte *m*, bandera *f*; **to raise the ~ of revolt** pronunciarse, sublevarse.

(b) (*measure etc used as norm*) patrón *m*; pauta *f*, norma *f*, estándar *m*; (*fig*) modelo *m*, regla *f*.

(c) (*moral*) criterio *m*; **~s** valores *mpl* morales; **double ~s** doble tabla *f* de valores; **by any ~** por cualquier criterio; **he has good ~s** tiene buen criterio; **she has no ~s** carece de valores morales; **to apply a double ~** medir a dos raseros; **to judge by that ~ ...** si lo juzgamos desde ese criterio ...

(d) (*degree of excellence*) nivel *m*, grado *m*; **~ of living** nivel *m* de vida; **~ of culture** nivel *m* de cultura; **at first-year university ~** al nivel del primer año universitario; **of low ~** de baja calidad; inferior; **to be below ~** estar por debajo del nivel correcto, ser inferior; **to be up to ~** estar conforme con el debido nivel; **to set a good ~** establecer un buen nivel.

(e) (*Bot*) árbol *m* (*etc*) de tronco derecho; (*of small lamp*) pie *m*; (*of street lamp*) poste *m*.

2 ADJ normal, corriente; estándar; uniforme, estereotipado; de serie; **5th gear now ~ on this car** 5ª velocidad ahora de serie en este coche; **~ agreement** acuerdo *m* normal; **~ costs** costos *mpl* normales; **~ deviation** desviación *f* normal; **~ English** inglés *m* normativo; **~ error** error *m* estándar; **~ gauge** vía *f* normal; **S~ Grade** (*Scot Scol*) *certificado obtenido tras aprobar los exámenes al final de la educación secundaria;* **~ lamp** (*Brit*) lámpara *f* de pie; **~ mark** (*on silver*) contraste *m*; **~ measure** medida *f* tipo; **~ model** modelo *m* estándar; (*car*) coche *m* de serie; **~ nomenclature** nomenclatura *f* oficial; **~ pitch** diapasón *m* normal; **~ practice** norma *f*, práctica *f* común; **~ price** precio *m* oficial, precio *m* normal; **~ quality** calidad *f* normal; **~ rate** tipo *m* de interés vigente; **~ time** hora *f* legal; **~ unit** (*Elec, Gas*) paso *m* (de contador); **~ weight** peso *m* legal; **~ work of reference** obra *f* clásica de consulta; **that word is hardly ~** esa palabra apenas pertenece al léxico oficial; **the practice became ~ in the 1940s** la práctica llegó a ser corriente en los años 40; *ver también* ⎹ENGLISH⎸ ,

$\boxed{GCSE}$.

standard-bearer [ˈstændəd‚bɛərəʳ] N abanderado *m*; (*fig*) jefe *m*, adalid *m*.

standardization [‚stændədaɪˈzeɪʃən] N normalización *f*, estandarización *f*.

standardize [ˈstændədaɪz] VT normalizar, regularizar, estandarizar, uniformar.

stand-by [ˈstændbaɪ] $\boxed{1}$ N **(a)** (*person*) persona *f* de toda confianza, persona *f* siempre dispuesta a prestar su ayuda; reserva *f*; paño *m* de lágrimas; (*thing*) recurso *m* seguro, recurso *m* favorito, artículo *m* de toda confianza; (*loan*) crédito *m* contingente, stand-by *m*.
(b) (*alert*) alerta *m*; aviso *m* (para partir); (*Aer*) stand-by *m*, lista *f* de espera; **to be on ~** estar sobre aviso, estar preparado, (*doctor*) estar listo para acudir; **to be on 24-hours ~** estar listo para partir dentro de 24 horas; **to put sb on 3-day ~** avisar a uno para que esté listo para partir dentro de 3 días.
$\boxed{2}$ ATTR: **~ aircraft** avión *m* de reserva; **~ air ticket** billete *m* para la lista de reserva; **~ arrangements** (*Fin*) acuerdo *m* de reserva; **~ credit** crédito *m* disponible, crédito *m* stand-by; **~ facility** stand-by *m*, lista *f* de reserva; **~ generator** generador *m* de reserva; **~ passenger** pasajero *m*, -a *f* en la lista de espera; **~ (ticket)** billete *m* stand-by.

standee* [stænˈdiː] N (*US*) espectador *m*, -ora *f* que asiste de pie.

stand-in [ˈstændɪn] N suplente *mf* (for de); (*Cine*) doble *mf* (for de).

standing [ˈstændɪŋ] $\boxed{1}$ ADJ **(a)** (*upright*) derecho; (*on foot*) de pie, en pie; *stone* derecho, vertical; *crop* que sigue creciendo, que está sin segar; *water* estancado, encharcado; **~ start** salida *f* parada; **to leave sb ~** dejar a uno muy atrás, (*fig*) aventajar a uno con mucho, resultar ser muy superior a uno; *V* **ovation**.
(b) (*permanent*) *army, committee, rule etc* permanente; *custom* arraigado; *grievance, joke* constante, eterno; **~ order** (*Brit: at bank*) orden *f* bancaria, (*Comm*) pedido *m* permanente, pedido *m* regular; **~ orders** (*of meeting*) reglamento *m*, estatuto *m*.
$\boxed{2}$ N **(a)** (*position*) posición *f*, situación *f*; (*repute*) reputación *f*; categoría *f*; importancia *f*; **financial ~** solvencia *f*; **social ~** posición *f* social; **of high ~** de categoría; **the restaurant has a high ~** el restaurante tiene una buena reputación; **a man of some ~** un hombre de cierta categoría; **the relative ~ of these problems** la relativa importancia de estos problemas; **to be in good ~** gozar de buen crédito; tener buena reputación; **what is his ~ locally?** ¿qué reputación tiene en la ciudad? (*etc*); **he has no ~ in this matter** no tiene voz ni voto en este asunto.
(b) (*duration*) duración *f*; existencia *f*; (*seniority*) antigüedad *f*; **of only 6 months' ~** que existe desde hace 6 meses solamente; **a captain of only a month's ~** un capitán que lleva solamente un mes en el puesto (*or* en tal graduación); **of long ~** de mucho tiempo, existente desde hace mucho tiempo, viejo.
(c) (*US Aut*) **'no ~'** 'prohibido estacionarse'.

standing room [ˈstændɪŋrʊm] N sitio *m* para estar de pie.

stand-off [ˈstændɒf] N **(a)** (*US: deadlock*) punto *m* muerto; (*paralysis*) parálisis *f*; situación *f* estancada; (*stalemate*) empate *m*. **(b)** **~ half** medio *m* de apertura.

stand-offish [‚stændˈɒfɪʃ] ADJ reservado, endiosado, que se da aires de superioridad; poco amable, frío.

stand-offishly [‚stændˈɒfɪʃlɪ] ADV con poca amabilidad, fríamente.

stand-offishness [‚stændˈɒfɪʃnɪs] N reserva *f*; endiosamiento *m*, superioridad *f*; falta *f* de amabilidad, frialdad *f*.

standpat [ˈstændpæt] ADJ inmovilista.

standpipe [ˈstændpaɪp] N columna *f* de alimentación; (*in street*) tubo *m* vertical.

standpoint [ˈstændpɔɪnt] N punto *m* de vista; **from the ~ of ...** desde el punto de vista de ...

standstill [ˈstændstɪl] N parada *f*; paro *m*; alto *m*; paralización *f*; **to be at a ~** estar parado; estar paralizado; **negotiations are at a ~** las negociaciones están paralizadas; **to bring a car to a ~** parar un coche; **to bring an industry to a ~** paralizar una industria; **to bring traffic to a ~** paralizar el tráfico, parar totalmente el tráfico; **to come to a ~** (*persons*) pararse, hacer alto, (*vehicle*) pararse, (*industry etc*) quedar paralizado.

stand-to [ˈstændˈtuː] N alerta *m*.

stand-up [ˈstændʌp] ADJ: **~ buffet** comida *f* tomada de pie; **~ collar** cuello *m* alto; **~ comic** cómico *m* caricato; **~ fight** pelea *f* violenta, riña *f* a puñetazos, (*fig*) altercado *m* violento.

stank [stæŋk] PRET of **stink**.

stanley knife [ˈstænlɪ‚naɪf] N, PL **stanley knives** [ˈstænlɪ‚naɪvz] cuchilla *f* para moqueta.

stannic [ˈstænɪk] ADJ estánnico.

stanza [ˈstænzə] N estrofa *f*, estancia *f*.

stapes [ˈsteɪpiːz] N, PL **stapedes** [stəˈpiːdiːz] (*Anat*) estribo *m*.

staphylococcus [‚stæfɪləˈkɒkəs] N, PL **staphylococci** [‚stæfɪləˈkɒkaɪ] estafilococo *m*.

staple¹ [ˈsteɪpl] $\boxed{1}$ N (*fastener*) grapa *f*, corchete *m* (*SC*); **~ gun** grapadora *f*.

$\boxed{2}$ VT (*also* **to ~ together**) grapar.

staple² [ˈsteɪpl] $\boxed{1}$ ADJ principal; establecido; corriente; **their ~ food** (*or diet*) su comida corriente, su alimento de primera necesidad.
$\boxed{2}$ N (*chief product*) producto *m* principal; (*raw material*) materia *f* prima; (*of wool*) fibra *f* (textil); (*of conversation etc*) asunto *m* principal, elemento *m* esencial.

stapler [ˈsteɪpləʳ] N, **stapling machine** [ˈsteɪplɪŋməˌʃiːn] N grapadora *f*.

star [stɑːʳ] $\boxed{1}$ N **(a)** (*Astron*) estrella *f*, astro *m*; (*Typ*) asterisco *m*; **S~s and Stripes** (*US*) (bandera *f* de) las barras y las estrellas, Bandera *f* Estrellada; **S~ of David** estrella *f* de David; **to be born under a lucky ~** nacer con estrella; **to believe in one's lucky ~** creer en su buena estrella; **you can thank your lucky ~s that ...** puedes dar las gracias a Dios porque ...; **to see ~s** (*fig*) ver las estrellas.
(b) (*person*) figura *f* destacada, figura *f* más brillante; (*Cine etc*) astro *m*, estrella *f*, vedette *f*; **the ~ of the team was X** la figura más destacada del equipo fue X.
$\boxed{2}$ ATTR principal; destacado, más brillante; **their ~ player** su jugador más destacado, su jugador más brillante; **~ role** papel *m* estelar; **~ screwdriver** destornillador *m* de estrella; **~ show** programa *m* estelar; **~ sign** signo *m* del Zodíaco; **~ turn** atracción *f* especial, número *m* más destacado; **'S~ Wars'** 'Guerra *f* de las Galaxias'.
$\boxed{3}$ VT **(a)** (*adorn with ~s*) estrellar, adornar con estrellas, sembrar de estrellas; (*mark with ~*) señalar con asterisco.
(b) (*Cine etc*) presentar como estrella; **a film ~ring Greta Garbo** una película que presenta a Greta Garbo en el papel principal.
$\boxed{4}$ VI (*Cine etc*) ser el astro, ser la estrella; tener el papel principal; (*be outstanding*) destacar, descollar, actuar brillantemente; **the 3 films in which James Dean ~red** las 3 películas que protagonizó James Dean; **he didn't exactly ~ in that game** en ese partido no destacó que digamos.

-star [stɑːʳ] ATTR *ending in compounds: eg* **4~ hotel** hotel *m* de 4 estrellas; **4~ (petrol)** gasolina *f* extra, súper *f*.

starboard [ˈstɑːbɔːd] $\boxed{1}$ N estribor *m*; **the sea to ~** la mar a estribor; **land to ~!** ¡tierra a estribor!
$\boxed{2}$ ADJ *lights etc* de estribor; **on the ~ side** a estribor.
$\boxed{3}$ VT: **to ~ the helm** poner el timón a estribor, virar a estribor.

starburst [ˈstɑːˌbɜːst] N (*liter*) explosión *f* de color.

starch [stɑːtʃ] $\boxed{1}$ N almidón *m*; (*in food*) fécula *f*.
$\boxed{2}$ VT almidonar.

star-chamber [ˈstɑːˌtʃeɪmbəʳ] ADJ (*fig*) secreto y arbitrario.

starched [stɑːtʃt] ADJ almidonado.

starch-reduced [ˈstɑːtʃrɪˌdjuːst] ADJ *bread etc* de régimen, con menos fécula.

starchy [ˈstɑːtʃɪ] ADJ feculento; (*fig*) estirado, entonado, etiquetero.

star-crossed [ˈstɑːˌkrɒst] ADJ malhadado, desventurado.

stardom [ˈstɑːdəm] N estrellato *m*; **to reach ~** alcanzar el estrellato.

stardust [ˈstɑːdʌst] N (*fig*) encanto *m*, embeleso *m*.

stare [stɛəʳ] $\boxed{1}$ N mirada *f* fija; **to give sb a ~** mirar fijamente a uno.
$\boxed{2}$ VT: **to ~ sb out of countenance** desconcertar a uno mirándole fijamente; **it's staring you in the face** salta a la vista.
$\boxed{3}$ VI mirar fijamente; **don't ~!** ¡no mires tan fijo!; **it's rude to ~** es de mala educación mostrar tanta curiosidad; **to ~ at sb** mirar fijamente a uno, clavar la vista en uno, (*in surprise*) mirar a uno con sorpresa; **to ~ into the distance, to ~ into space** estar mirando a las nubes.

starfish [ˈstɑːfɪʃ] N, PL INVAR estrella *f* de mar.

stargaze [ˈstɑːgeɪz] VI mirar las estrellas; (*fig*) distraerse, mirar las telarañas.

stargazer [ˈstɑːˌgeɪzəʳ] N astrónomo *m*, -a *f*.

stargazing [ˈstɑːˌgeɪzɪŋ] N estudio *m* de las estrellas; astronomía *f*; (*fig*) distracción *f*.

stargrass [ˈstɑːgrɑːs] N azucena *f*.

staring [ˈstɛərɪŋ] ADJ que mira fijamente, curioso; *eyes* saltón, (*in fear*) lleno de espanto.

stark [stɑːk] $\boxed{1}$ ADJ (*stiff*) rígido; (*utter*) completo, puro; (*unadorned*) escueto, severo; *cliff etc* espantoso, ceñudo.
$\boxed{2}$ ADV: **~ staring mad, ~ raving mad** loco de atar; **~ naked** en cueros, en pelota, como le parió su madre.

starkers* [ˈstɑːkəz] ADJ: **to be ~** (*Brit*) estar en cueros*.

starkly [ˈstɑːklɪ] ADV completamente; **~ evident** completamente claro; **he put the choice ~** nos ofreció la alternativa y nada más.

starkness [ˈstɑːknɪs] N desolación *f*, severidad *f*.

starless [ˈstɑːlɪs] ADJ sin estrellas.

starlet [ˈstɑːlɪt] N estrella *f* joven, estrella *f* en ciernes, aspirante *f* a estrella.

starlight [ˈstɑːlaɪt] N luz *f* de las estrellas; **by ~** a la luz de las estrellas.

starling [ˈstɑːlɪŋ] N estornino *m*.

starlit [ˈstɑːlɪt] ADJ iluminado por las estrellas.

star-of-Bethlehem [‚stɑːrəvˈbeθlɪhem] N (*Bot*) leche *f* de gallina, matacandiles *m*.

starry ['stɑːrɪ] ADJ estrellado, sembrado de estrellas.

starry-eyed ['stɑːrɪ'aɪd] ADJ inocentón, ingenuo; idealista, poco práctico; lleno de amor (or entusiasmo etc) candoroso.

star shell ['stɑːʃel] N cohete m luminoso, bengala f.

star-spangled ['stɑːˌspæŋgld] ADJ estrellado; **the S~ Banner** la Bandera Estrellada.

star-studded ['stɑːˌstʌdɪd] ADJ sky estrellado; (fig) play, cast lleno de estrellas.

START [stɑːt] N ABBR of **Strategic Arms Reduction Treaty** Tratado m de Reducción de Armas Estratégicas, START m.

▼ **start** [stɑːt] ① N **(a)** (fright etc) susto m, sobresalto m; (of horse) respingo m; **to give a sudden ~** sobresaltarse; **to give sb a ~** asustar a uno, dar un susto a uno; **what a ~ you gave me!** ¡qué susto me diste!; **to wake with a ~** despertarse sobresaltado; V **fit²**.
(b) (beginning) principio m, comienzo m; (departure) salida f, partida f; (of race) salida f; (point of starting) punto m de arranque; **at the ~** al principio; **at the very ~** muy al principio, en los mismos comienzos; **at the ~ of the century** a principios del siglo; **we are at the ~ of sth big** estamos en los comienzos de algo grandioso; **for a ~** en primer lugar, para empezar; **from the ~** desde el principio; **from ~ to finish** desde el principio hasta el fin, de cabo a rabo; **to get off to a bad ~** comenzar mal; **to get off to a good ~** empezar bien, (fig) comenzar felizmente, entrar con buen pie; **to give sb a ~ in life** ayudar a uno a situarse en la vida; **the review gave the book a good ~** la reseña ayudó al libro a venderse bien desde el principio; **to make a ~** empezar; **to make an early ~** ponerse en camino temprano; **to make a fresh (or new) ~ in life** hacer vida nueva, empezar de nuevo; **to make a good ~ (in life)** emprender felizmente su carrera.
(c) (advantage) ventaja f; **to give sb a 5 minute ~** dar a uno una ventaja de 5 minutos; **to have a ~ on sb** tener ventaja sobre uno.
② VT **(a)** (begin) comenzar, empezar; iniciar; principiar; discussion etc abrir, iniciar; (undertake) emprender; bottle abrir; **to ~ negotiations** iniciar las negociaciones; **to ~ a new life** comenzar una vida nueva; **to ~ a novel** empezar a escribir (or leer) una novela; **to ~ a family** (empezar a) tener hijos; **don't ~ that again!** ¡no vuelvas a eso!; **now she's ~ed a baby*** ahora está encinta; **we can't ~ a baby yet*** todavía no podemos tener un niño; **to ~ to** + infin, **to ~** + ger comenzar a + infin, empezar a + infin; **~ moving!** ¡menéarse!; **~ talking!** ¡desembucha!
(b) (give signal for: also **to ~ off**) **to ~ (off) a race** dar la señal de salida para una carrera.
(c) (disturb: also **to ~ up**) **to ~ a partridge** levantar una perdiz.
(d) (cause) causar, provocar; **to ~ a fire** causar un incendio; **it ~ed the collapse of the empire** dio comienzo al derrumbamiento del imperio.
(e) (found: also **to ~ up**) fundar, crear; **to ~ (up) an enterprise** fundar una empresa; **to ~ (up) a newspaper** fundar un periódico.
(f) (Mech: also **to ~ up**) poner en marcha, hacer funcionar; car, engine arrancar; clock poner en marcha.
(g) (with personal object: also **to ~ off**) **to ~ sb reminiscing** hacer que uno empiece a contar sus recuerdos; **once you ~ him (off) on that** en cuanto le pones a hablar de eso; **to ~ sb (off) on a career** ayudar a uno a emprender una carrera; **they ~ed her (off) in the sales department** la emplearon primero en la sección de ventas.
③ VI **(a)** (in fright) asustarse, sobresaltarse, sobrecogerse (at a, with de); **to ~ from one's chair** levantarse asustado de su silla; **to ~ out of one's sleep** despertarse sobresaltado; **his eyes were ~ing out of his head** se le saltaban los ojos de la cabeza.
(b) (timber etc) combarse, torcerse; (rivets etc) soltarse.
▼ **(c)** (begin: also **to ~ off**) comenzar, empezar; principiar; iniciarse; (on journey) partir, ponerse en camino; (of bus, train) salir; (in race) salir; (car, engine etc) arrancar, ponerse en marchar; empezar a funcionar; **to ~ by** + ger comenzar + ger; **~ing from Tuesday** a partir del martes; **the route ~s from here** la ruta sale de aquí; **to ~ afresh** volver a empezar, comenzar de nuevo; **to ~ at the beginning** empezar desde el principio; **to ~ on a task** empezar un cometido; emprender una tarea; **to ~ on something new** emprender algo nuevo; **to ~ with a prayer** empezar con una oración; **what shall we ~ (off) with?** ¿con qué empezamos?; **to ~ with** (as adv phrase) en primer lugar, para empezar; en el principio.
(d) (Mech: also **to ~ up**) ponerse en marcha, empezar a funcionar; (car, engine) arrancar(se).

◆**start after** VT: **to ~ after sb** salir en busca de uno; ir en pos de uno.
◆**start back** VI **(a)** (return) emprender el viaje de regreso; **it's time we ~ed back** es hora de volvernos.
(b) (recoil) retroceder; **to ~ back in horror** retroceder horrorizado.
◆**start in** VI empezar; poner manos a la obra, empezar a trabajar (etc); **then she ~ed in** luego ella metió su cuchara.
◆**start off** ① VT V **start 2 (b), 2 (g)**.
② VI (begin) comenzar, empezar; (on journey) partir, ponerse en camino; (bus, train etc) salir.

◆**start on*** VT (quarrel with) meterse con; (scold) regañar.
◆**start out** VI = **start off 2**.
◆**start over** VI (US) volver a empezar.
◆**start up** ① VT V **start 2 (c), 2 (e), 2 (f)**.
② VI **(a)** (begin) comenzar, empezar; (Mus) empezar a tocar; (Mech) arrancar(se).
(b) (jump etc) incorporarse bruscamente, ponerse de pie de un salto; see also **start 3 (d)**.

starter ['stɑːtər] N **(a)** (person) (judge) juez m de salida; (competitor) corredor m, -ora f; caballo m (etc). **(b)** (Aut etc) (motor) motor m de arranque; (button) botón m de arranque. **(c)** (Brit Culin) entremés m; **for ~s*** de entrada, para empezar.

starting-block ['stɑːtɪŋˌblɒk] N taco m de salida; **to be on the ~s** (fig) estar en la recámara.

starting-gate ['stɑːtɪŋgeɪt] N cajón m de salida, parrilla f de salida.

starting-grid ['stɑːtɪŋˌgrɪd] N parrilla f de arranque.

starting-handle ['stɑːtɪŋˌhændl] N (Brit) manivela f de arranque.

starting-line ['stɑːtɪŋlaɪn] N línea f de salida.

starting-motor ['stɑːtɪŋˌməʊtər] N motor m de arranque.

▼ **starting-point** ['stɑːtɪŋpɔɪnt] N punto m de partida, punto m de arranque.

starting-post ['stɑːtɪŋpəʊst] N poste m de salida.

starting-price ['stɑːtɪŋpraɪs] N cotización f, puntos mpl de ventaja al empezar la carrera.

starting salary ['stɑːtɪŋˌsælərɪ] N sueldo m incial.

starting stalls ['stɑːtɪŋˈstɔːlz] NPL (Brit) cajones mpl de salida.

starting-switch ['stɑːtɪŋswɪtʃ] N botón m de arranque.

startle ['stɑːtl] VT asustar, sobrecoger; alarmar; **you quite ~d me!** ¡vaya susto que me has dado!; **it ~d him out of his serenity** le hizo perder su serenidad.

startled ['stɑːtld] ADJ animal asustado, espantado; person sorprendido; expression, voice de sobresalto, sobresaltado.

startling ['stɑːtlɪŋ] ADJ asombroso, sorprendente; alarmante; sobrecogedor; colour etc chillón; dress etc llamativo, exagerado.

start-up ['stɑːtʌp] ATTR: **~ costs** gastos mpl de puesta en marcha.

starvation [stɑːˈveɪʃən] ① N hambre f, (Med) inanición f; muerte f por hambre; (fig) privación f; **to die of ~** morir de hambre; **they are threatened with ~** les amenaza el hambre.
② ATTR: **~ diet** régimen m de hambre; **~ wages** sueldo m de hambre.

starve [stɑːv] ① VT **(a)** (kill) hacer morir de hambre; (deprive of food) privar de comida, hacer pasar hambre; **to ~ sb to death** hacer a uno morir de hambre; **to ~ a town into surrender** hacer que una ciudad se rinda por hambre.
(b) (fig) **to ~ sb of sth** privar a uno de algo; **to be ~d of affection** estar privado de cariño (paternal etc).
② VI **(a)** (die) morir de hambre; (lack food) pasar hambre, padecer hambre; **to ~ to death** morir de hambre.
(b) (fig) morir de hambre; **I'm simply starving!** ¡estoy muerto de hambre!, ¡qué hambre tengo!

◆**starve out** VT: **to ~ a garrison out** hacer que una guarnición se rinda por hambre.

starving ['stɑːvɪŋ] ADJ hambriento, famélico.

stash* [stæʃ] ① N escondite m; alijo m.
② VT: **to ~ away** ir acumulando; ocultar para uso futuro.

stasis ['steɪsɪs] N estasis f.

state [steɪt] ① N **(a)** (condition) estado m, condición f; **in this ~ of affairs** (estando) así las cosas, en estas circunstancias; **if this ~ of affairs continues** si las cosas siguen así; **~ of emergency** estado m de emergencia, estado m de excepción; **to declare a ~ of emergency** declarar el estado de emergencia; **~ of health** salud f, estado m físico; **~ of mind** estado m de ánimo; **~ of play** (Sport) situación f del juego, (fig) situación f; **~ of siege** estado m de sitio; **~ of war** estado m de guerra; **~ of weightlessness** estado m de ingravidez; **in a comatose ~** en estado comatoso; **races still in a savage ~** razas fpl todavía en estado de salvajismo; **to be in a bad ~** estar en mal estado; **to be in a good ~** estar en buenas condiciones; **he's not in a (fit) ~ to do it** no está en condiciones para hacerlo; **he arrived home in a shocking ~** llegó a casa en un estado espantoso; **she was in no ~ to talk** no estaba en condiciones para hablar.
(b) (anxiety) agitación f; estado m nervioso; **to be in a great ~** estar muy agitado, estar aturrulado; **now don't get into a ~ about it** no te pongas nervioso.
(c) (rank) rango m, dignidad f; **he attained the ~ of bishop** llegó a la dignidad de obispo.
(d) (pomp) pompa f, fausto m; ceremonia f; **in ~** con gran pompa; **to dine in ~** cenar con mucha ceremonia; **to live in ~** vivir lujosamente; **to travel in ~** viajar con gran pompa; **to lie in ~** estar expuesto en capilla ardiente.
(e) (Pol) estado m; **the S~** el Estado; **the S~s** (US) los Estados Unidos; **~ line** (US) frontera f de estado, frontera f entre dos estados; **a ~ within a ~** un estado dentro del estado; **Secretary of S~** (US) Ministro m, -a f de Asuntos Exteriores; **Secretary of S~ for ...** Minis-

tro *m*, -a *f* de ...

[2] ATTR (*Pol etc*) estatal, del Estado; público; **~ aid** ayuda *f* estatal; **~ apartments** apartamentos *mpl* oficiales; **~ banquet** banquete *m* de gala; **~ control** control *m* estatal, control *m* público; **S~ Department** (*US*) Ministerio *m* de Asuntos Exteriores; **~ education** (*Brit*) enseñanza *f* pública; **~ fair** (*US*) feria *f* estatal; **~ funding** financiación *f* pública; **~ funeral** funeral *m* de Estado; **~ highway** (*US*) ≃ carretera *f* nacional; **~ papers** documentos *mpl* de Estado; **~ pension** pensión *f* estatal; **~ school** (*Brit*) escuela *f* pública; **~ secret** secreto *m* de Estado; **~ subsidy** subvención *f* estatal; **~ tax** (*US*) impuesto *m* del Estado (*p.ej. de Ohio*); **~ trooper** (*US*) policía *m* del Estado (*p.ej. de Idaho*); **~ visit** visita *f* de Estado; *ver también* STATE FAIR.

[3] VT **(a)** declarar, afirmar, decir; manifestar; consignar, hacer constar; **as ~d above** como se ha dicho arriba; **it is nowhere ~d that ...** no se dice en ninguna parte que ...; **I have seen it ~d that ...** he visto afirmarse que ...; **he is ~d to have been there** se afirma que estuvo allí; **~ your name** escriba su nombre; **cheques must ~ the amount clearly** los cheques han de consignar claramente la cantidad; **it must be ~d in the records** tiene que hacerse constar en los archivos.

(b) *case* exponer, explicar; *law* formular; *problem* plantear, exponer; **to ~ the case for the prosecution** explicar los hechos en que se basa la acusación.

STATE OF THE UNION ADDRESS

i Se denomina **State of the Union Address** *al discurso que el Presidente de Estados Unidos dirige cada mes de enero al Congreso y al pueblo estadounidense, en que muestra su visión de la nación y la economía y explica sus planes para el futuro. Como el discurso recibe una amplia cobertura informativa, el mensaje del Presidente va dirigido no sólo a los parlamentarios sino a todo el país. Esta tradición de dirigirse al Congreso poco después de la vuelta de éste de las vacaciones de Navidad el día 3 de enero se debe a que es un requisito de la Constitución que el Presidente informe al Congreso de vez en cuando sobre el* **State of the Union**.

STATES' RIGHTS

i Al hablar de **States' Rights** *los estadounidenses se refieren a los derechos que tienen los estados en relación al gobierno federal, como por ejemplo la capacidad de recaudar impuestos, aprobar leyes o controlar la educación pública. En la Décima Enmienda de la Constitución estadounidense se dice que los poderes que la Constitución no delega a los Estados Unidos "se reservan a cada estado particular o al pueblo", aunque ha habido mucha polémica a la hora de interpretar esta enmienda. Este principio se usó para justificar la secesión de los estados sureños antes de la Guerra Civil y se convirtió en una consigna sureña contra la integración racial durante los años 50. Recientemente esta idea se ha ido extendiendo por todo el país debido a la falta de confianza de la gente en el gobierno federal, que está acaparando cada vez más poderes pero cuyos gastos son también mayores.*

---

state-controlled ['steɪtkən'trəʊld] ADJ controlado por el Estado, estatal.

statecraft ['steɪtkrɑːft] N arte *m* de gobernar; política *f*; diplomacia *f*.

stated ['steɪtɪd] ADJ dicho; indicado; fijo, establecido; **the sum ~** la cantidad dicha; **on the ~ date** en la fecha indicada; **within ~ limits** dentro de límites fijos.

state-funded [,steɪt'fʌndɪd] ADJ *schools, education* estatal; *services, projects* realizado con fondos públicos.

statehood ['steɪthʊd] N categoría *f* de estado, dignidad *f* de estado; **when the country achieves ~** cuando el país alcance la categoría de estado.

stateless ['steɪtlɪs] ADJ desnacionalizado, apátrida, sin patria.

statelet ['steɪtlət] N (*Pol*) pequeño estado *m*.

stateliness ['steɪtlɪnɪs] N majestad *f*, majestuosidad *f*.

stately ['steɪtlɪ] ADJ majestuoso; imponente; augusto; **~ home** casa *f* solariega.

statement ['steɪtmənt] N declaración *f*, afirmación *f*, manifestación *f*; informe *m*, relación *f*; exposición *f*; (*Fin*) estado *m* de cuenta; (*Comput*) sentencia *f*; (*Jur*) declaración *f*; **~ of account** estado *m* (*Mex*: extracto *m*) de cuenta; **official ~** informe *m* oficial, nota *f* oficial; **according to his own ~** según su propia declaración; **to make a ~** (*Jur*) prestar declaración.

state-of-the-art [,steɪtəvðɪ'ɑːt] ADJ moderno, al día; de vanguardia; **it's ~** es lo más moderno (*or* reciente).

state-owned [,steɪt'əʊnd] ADJ nacional, estatal.

stateroom ['steɪtrʊm] N camarote *m*.

stateside* ['steɪtsaɪd] ADV (*US*) (*be*) en Estados Unidos; (*go*) a Estados Unidos, hacia Estados Unidos.

statesman ['steɪtsmən] N, PL **statesmen** ['steɪtsmən] estadista *m*, hombre *m* de estado.

statesmanlike ['steɪtsmənlaɪk] ADJ (digno) de estadista.

statesmanship ['steɪtsmənʃɪp] N arte *m* de gobernar; habilidad *f* de estadista; **that showed true ~** eso demostró su verdadera capacidad de estadista; **~ alone will not solve the problem** la habilidad de los estadistas no resolverá el problema por sí sola.

state-subsidized [,steɪt'sʌbsɪdaɪzd] ADJ subvencionado por el Estado.

state-trading countries ['steɪt,treɪdɪŋ'kʌntrɪz] NPL países *mpl* de comercio estatal.

static ['stætɪk] [1] ADJ inactivo, inmóvil, estancado; (*Phys*) estático.

[2] N (*also* **~s**) (*Phys*) estática *f*; (*Rad*) parásitos *mpl*.

station ['steɪʃən] [1] N **(a)** (*place*) puesto *m*, sitio *m*; situación *f*; **Roman ~** sitio *m* ocupado por los romanos; **the only ~ for this rare plant** el único sitio donde existe esta planta tan poco frecuente; **action ~s!** ¡a sus puestos!; **from my ~ by the window** desde el sitio donde estaba junto a la ventana; **to take up one's ~** colocarse, ir a su puesto.

(b) (*~ in life*) posición *f* social; puesto *m* en la sociedad; **of humble ~** de baja posición social, de condición humilde; **a man of exalted ~** un hombre de rango elevado; **to marry below one's ~** casarse con un hombre (*or* una mujer) de posición social inferior; **to get ideas above one's ~** darse aires de superioridad, darse tono.

(c) (*specific*) estación *f*; (*Rad*) emisora *f*; (*Rail*) estación *f* (de ferrocarril); (*police ~*) comisaría *f*; **S~s of the Cross** Vía *f* Crucis.

[2] VT colocar, situar; (*Mil*) estacionar, destinar; *missile etc* emplazar.

[3] VR: **to ~ o.s.** colocarse, situarse.

stationary ['steɪʃənərɪ] ADJ estacionario; inmóvil; *engine etc* estacionario, fijo; **to remain ~** (*person*) quedar inmóvil, estar sin moverse.

stationer ['steɪʃənəʳ] N papelero *m*, -a *f*; **~'s (shop)** papelería *f*.

stationery ['steɪʃənərɪ] [1] N papelería *f*, papel *m* de escribir, efectos *mpl* de escritorio.

[2] ATTR: **S~ Office** Imprenta *f* Nacional.

station house ['steɪʃən,haʊs] N, PL **station houses** ['steɪʃən,haʊzɪz] (*US Rail*) estación *f* de ferrocarril; (*police*) comisaría *f*.

stationmaster ['steɪʃən,mɑːstəʳ] N jefe *m* de estación.

station wagon ['steɪʃən,wægən] N (*US*) furgoneta *f*, rubia *f*, camioneta *f*.

statist ['steɪtɪst] ADJ (*Pol*) controlado por el estado.

statistic [stə'tɪstɪk] N estadística *f*, número *m*; **~s** (*as subject*) estadística *f*; (*numbers*) estadísticas *fpl*.

statistical [stə'tɪstɪkəl] ADJ estadístico; **~ package** paquete *m* estadístico.

statistically [stə'tɪstɪkəlɪ] ADV: **to prove sth ~** probar algo por medios estadísticos; **~ that may be true** en cuanto a la estadística eso puede ser cierto.

statistician [,stætɪs'tɪʃən] N estadístico *mf*.

stative ['steɪtɪv] ADJ: **~ verb** verbo *m* de estado.

stator ['steɪtəʳ] N estator *m*.

stats* [stæts] NPL ABBR of **statistics**. **(a)** (*figures*) estadísticas *fpl*. **(b)** (*as subject*) estadística *f*.

statuary ['stætjʊərɪ] [1] ADJ estatuario.

[2] N (*art*) estatuaria *f*; (*statues*) estatuas *fpl*.

statue ['stætjuː] N estatua *f*.

statuesque [,stætjʊ'esk] ADJ escultural.

statuette [,stætjʊ'et] N figurilla *f*, estatuilla *f*.

stature ['stætʃəʳ] N **(a)** (*lit*) estatura *f*, talla *f*; **to be of short ~** ser de estatura baja, tener poca talla.

(b) (*fig*) talla *f*; valor *m*, carácter *m*; **to have sufficient ~ for a post** estar a la altura de un cargo; **he lacks moral ~** le falta carácter.

status ['steɪtəs] [1] N posición *f*, condición *f*; (e)status *m*; rango *m*, categoría *f*; prestigio *m*; reputación *f*; (*Jur*) estado *m*; (*civil etc*) estado *m*; **social ~** posición *f* social; **the ~ of the Negro population** la posición social de la población negra; **what is his ~ in the profession?** ¿qué rango ocupa en la profesión?, ¿cómo se le considera en la profesión?; **he has not sufficient ~ for the job** no tiene categoría bastante alta para este cargo.

[2] ATTR: **~ inquiry** comprobación *f* de valoración crediticia; **~ line** línea *f* de situación, línea *f* de estado; **~ report** informe *m* situacional; **~ symbol** signo *m* exterior de prestigio social.

status quo ['steɪtəs'kwəʊ] N statu *m* quo.

statute ['stætjuːt] [1] N ley *f*, estatuto *m*; **by ~** según la ley, de acuerdo con la ley.

[2] ATTR: **~ law** derecho *m* escrito.

statute book ['stætjuːtbʊk] N código *m* de leyes; **to be on the ~** ser ley.

statutory ['stætjʊtərɪ] ADJ estatutario; *holiday, right etc* legal; **~ meeting** junta *f* constitutiva.

staunch¹ [stɔːntʃ] ADJ leal, firme, incondicional.

staunch² [stɔːntʃ] VT = **stanch**.

staunchly ['stɔːntʃlɪ] ADV lealmente, firmemente, incondicionalmente.

staunchness ['stɔːntʃnɪs] N lealtad *f*, firmeza *f*.

stave [steɪv] [1] N (*of barrel*) duela *f*; (*of ladder*) peldaño *m*; (*Mus*) pentagrama *m*; (*Liter*) estrofa *f*.

[2] (*irr:* PRET AND PTP **stove** *or* **staved**) VT = **stave in, stave off.**

◆ **stave in** VT romper, quebrar a golpes; desfondar.

◆ **stave off** VT *attack* rechazar; apartar, mantener a distancia; *threat etc* evitar, conjurar; (*delay*) diferir; aplazar.

staves [steɪvz] NPL *of* **staff.**

stay¹ [steɪ] [1] N (**a**) estancia *f*, permanencia *f*; visita *f*; **a ~ of 10 days** una estancia de 10 días; **~ in hospital** estancia *f* hospitalaria; **our second ~ in Murcia** nuestra segunda visita a Murcia; **come for a longer ~ next year** ven a estar más tiempo el año que viene.

(**b**) (*Jur*) suspensión *f*, prórroga *f*; **~ of execution** aplazamiento *m* de una sentencia; **~ of proceedings** sobreseimiento *m*.

[2] VT (**a**) (*check*) detener; controlar; poner freno a; *epidemic etc* tener a raya; *hunger* matar, engañar; **to ~ one's hand** contenerse, detenerse; **to ~ sb's hand** parar la mano a uno.

(**b**) (*Jur*) suspender, prorrogar; aplazar.

(**c**) (*last out*) *race* terminar; *distance* cubrir, cubrir toda la extensión de.

[3] VI (**a**) (*wait*) esperar; **~!** ¡espera!

(**b**) (*remain*) quedarse, permanecer; (*as guest etc*) estar, quedarse, hospedarse; **you ~ right there** tú te quedas ahí, no te muevas de ahí; **to ~ at home** quedarse en casa; **to ~ in bed** guardar cama; **how long can you ~?** ¿hasta cuándo te puedes quedar?; **what? you ~ed for the Debussy?** ¿cómo? ¿os quedasteis a escuchar el Debussy?; **to ~ for supper, to ~ to supper** quedarse a cenar; **to ~ at an hotel** hospedarse en un hotel; **to ~ with friends** quedarse con unos amigos; **where are you ~ing?** ¿dónde vives?; **she came for a weekend and ~ed 3 years** vino a pasar el fin de semana y permaneció 3 años; **it has clearly come to ~** evidentemente tiene carácter permanente; **things can't be allowed to ~ like that** no podemos permitir que las cosas sigan así.

(**c**) (*remain, with adj*) **it ~s red** sigue tan rojo como antes; **if it ~s fine** si continúa el buen tiempo, si el tiempo sigue bueno; **it ~s motionless for hours** sigue durante horas enteras sin moverse; **he ~ed faithful to his wife** siguió fiel a su mujer.

(**d**) (*last out*) resistir; **the horse doesn't ~** el caballo no resiste esa distancia, el caballo no tiene bastante resistencia; **~ with it!*** ¡sigue adelante!, ¡no te dejes desanimar!

◆ **stay away** VI ausentarse (*from* de), no asistir (*from* a); **you ~ away from my daughter!** ¡no vengas más por aquí a molestar a mi hija!; **~ away from that machine** no te acerques a esa máquina.

◆ **stay behind** VI quedarse; quedarse en casa, no salir; **they made him ~ behind after school** le hicieron quedar en la escuela después de las clases; **we told him to ~ behind till the last lap** dijimos que quedase atrás hasta la última vuelta.

◆ **stay down** VI (**a**) permanecer abajo; (*bending*) permanecer doblado; (*lying down*) permanecer en el suelo; (*under water*) permanecer bajo el agua; (*Scol*) seguir en la misma clase.

(**b**) **nothing he eats will ~ down** no retiene nada de lo que come.

◆ **stay in** VI (**a**) (*cork etc*) quedarse puesto.

(**b**) (*person: at home*) quedarse en casa, no salir.

◆ **stay off** VT: **to stay off school/work** no ir al colegio/trabajo; **to stay off drink/drugs** (*stop taking*) dejar de beber/drogarse; (*avoid taking*) no beber/drogar; **I have stayed off the booze for more than a year now** llevo más de un año sin probar la bebida.

◆ **stay on** VI (**a**) (*lid etc*) quedarse puesto, seguir en su lugar.

(**b**) (*person*) quedarse; permanecer, continuar en su lugar; **he ~ed on as manager** siguió en su puesto de gerente, (*after change*) pasó a ser gerente (de la misma compañía); **they ~ed on after everyone else had left** se quedaron después de que todos los demás se habían marchado.

◆ **stay out** VI (**a**) (*person*) quedarse fuera, no volver a casa; **she ~s out till midnight** no vuelve a casa hasta medianoche.

(**b**) (*striker*) mantenerse en huelga, no volver al trabajo.

(**c**) **to ~ out of** no tomar parte en; **you ~ out of this!** ¡no te metas en esto!, ¡tú fuera!

◆ **stay over** VI pasar la noche, pernoctar; quedarse un poco.

◆ **stay up** VI (**a**) (*remain standing etc*) mantenerse de pie; seguir en buen estado; **the team ~s up** el equipo sigue en la división superior.

(**b**) (*person*) velar, no acostarse; seguir sin acostarse; **to ~ up all night** trasnochar; **don't ~ up for me** no os quedéis esperándome hasta muy tarde.

stay² [steɪ] [1] N (**a**) (*Mech*) sostén *m*, soporte *m*, puntal *m*; (*Naut*) estay *m*; **~s** corsé *m*.

(**b**) (*fig*) sostén *m*, apoyo *m*; **the ~ of one's old age** el sostén de su vejez.

[2] VT sostener, apoyar, apuntalar; **this will ~ you till lunchtime** esto te engañará a resistir hasta la comida, esto engañará el hambre hasta la comida.

stay-at-home ['steɪəthəʊm] [1] ADJ casero, hogareño.

[2] N persona *f* casera, persona *f* hogareña.

stayer ['steɪəʳ] N (*horse*) caballo *m* apto para carreras de distancia; (*per-*

son) persona *f* de carácter firme, persona *f* de mucho aguante.

staying-power ['steɪɪŋˌpaʊəʳ] N resistencia *f*, aguante *m*.

| STAY | see also main entry |

In a place

Meaning "remain"

- Use ***quedarse*** or, in more formal language, ***permanecer*** to translate *stay* in this sense:

  Stay here
  Quédate aquí
  We stayed at home that summer
  Aquel verano nos quedamos en casa
  They stayed in France until the end of the war
  Permanecieron en Francia hasta el final de la guerra

Meaning "lodge"

- Use ***estar*** or ***quedarse*** in everyday language and ***alojarse*** or ***hospedarse*** in formal language to translate *stay* meaning being temporarily in a hotel or at someone's house. *Hospedarse* usually implies payment:

  He's staying at my house
  Está or ***Se queda en mi casa***
  Where are you going to stay?
  ¿Dónde vas a quedarte? ◊ ***¿Dónde vas a estar?***
  I'm staying at the Europa Hotel
  Estoy or ***Me alojo*** or ***Me hospedo en el Hotel Europa***
  I shall be staying with some friends
  Me quedaré or ***Me alojaré con unos amigos***

With adjective

- When *stay* is followed by an adjective, you can usually translate it using ***seguir*** (*estando/siendo*):

  I want to stay healthy
  Quiero seguir (estando) bien de salud

- ***Mantenerse*** is often another possibility in the sense of "keep", but other translations may also be possible depending on the adjective:

  She tries to stay active
  Trata de seguir or ***mantenerse activa***

  For further uses and examples, see main entry.

---

staysail ['steɪseɪl], (*Naut*) 'steɪsl] N vela *f* de estay.

STD N (**a**) (*Brit Telec*) ABBR *of* **Subscriber Trunk Dialling; ~ code** prefijo *m* para conferencias interurbanas (automáticas). (**b**) (*Med*) ABBR *of* **sexually transmitted disease** enfermedad *f* de transmisión sexual, ETS *f*.

stead [sted] N: **in his ~** en su lugar; **to stand sb in good ~** ser útil a uno, aprovechar a uno.

steadfast ['stedfəst] ADJ firme, resuelto; constante; tenaz; *gaze* fijo; **~ in adversity** firme en el infortunio; **~ in danger** impertérrito; **~ in love** constante en el amor.

steadfastly ['stedfəstlɪ] ADV firmemente, resueltamente; con constancia; tenazmente; fijamente.

steadfastness ['stedfəstnɪs] N firmeza *f*, resolución *f*; constancia *f*; tenacidad *f*; fijeza *f*.

steadicam ['stedɪkæm] ® N *cámara con estabilizador óptico de imagen*.

steadily ['stedɪlɪ] ADV firmemente, fijamente; de modo estable; regularmente, constantemente, uniformemente; continuamente; sin parar, ininterrumpidamente; sensatamente; seriamente; diligentemente; tranquilamente; resueltamente; imperturbablemente; **it gets ~ worse** se hace cada vez peor; **the temperature goes ~ up** la temperatura sube constantemente, la temperatura no deja de subir; **to work ~** trabajar ininterrumpidamente; **she looked at me ~** me miró sin pestañear.

steadiness ['stedɪnɪs] N firmeza *f*, fijeza *f*; estabilidad *f*; regularidad *f*, constancia *f*, uniformidad *f*; sensatez *f*, juicio *m*; seriedad *f*, formalidad *f*; diligencia *f*; serenidad *f*, ecuanimidad *f*; sangre *f* fría; imperturbabilidad *f*.

steady ['stedɪ] [1] ADJ firme, fijo; estable; regular, constante, uniforme; continuo, ininterrumpido; (*in character*) sensato, juicioso; serio, formal; (*at work*) diligente, trabajador; aplicado; *boyfriend etc* fijo; formal; (*not nervous*) sereno, tranquilo, ecuánime; resuelto; imperturbable; **~ demand** demanda *f* constante; **~ job** empleo *m* seguro, empleo *m* fijo; **~ progress** progreso *m* ininterrumpido; **~-state theory** teoría *f* de la creación continua; **~ temperature** temperatura *f* constante, temperatura *f* uniforme; **with a ~ hand** con mano firme; **at a ~ pace** a paso regular; **as ~ as a rock** firme como una roca; **the car is very ~ at corners** el coche es muy estable en las curvas; **there was a ~ downpour for 3 hours** llovió sin interrupción durante 3 horas; **we were going at a ~ 90 kph** íbamos a una velocidad uniforme de 90 kph; **he plays a very ~ game** juega muy sensatamente.

[2] ADV: **~!** ¡con calma!, ¡despacio!; **they are going ~ now*** son novios formales ya; **they've been going ~ for 6 months*** llevan 6

meses de relaciones; **is he going ~ with her?*** ¿es novio formal de ella?

3 N (*) novio *m*, -a *f* formal.

4 VT (*hold*) mantener firme, sujetar en posición firme; (*stabilize*) estabilizar, hacer más estable; uniformar, regularizar; *nerves* calmar; *nervous person* (*also* **to ~ down**, **to ~ up**) tranquilizar, *wild person* hacer que siente la cabeza.

5 VI (*also* **to ~ down**, **to ~ up**) (*market, price etc*) estabilizarse, hacerse más estable; uniformarse, regularizarse; (*person*) calmarse; tranquilizarse; sentar la cabeza.

6 VR: **to ~ o.s.** afirmarse, recobrar el equilibrio; **to ~ o.s. against sth** apoyarse en algo.

steak [steɪk] N biftec *m*; filete *m*; (*of meat other than beef*) tajada *f*; **~ and kidney pie** pastel *m* de biftec y riñones.

steakhouse ['steɪkhaʊs] N, PL **steakhouses** ['steɪk,haʊzɪz] parrilla *f*.

steak-knife ['steɪknaɪf] N, PL **steak-knives** ['steɪknaɪvz] cuchillo *m* para el biftec.

steal [stiːl] (*irr*: PRET **stole**, PTP **stolen**) **1** VT robar, hurtar; (*fig*) robar; **to ~ a glance at sb** mirar de soslayo a uno, echar una mirada furtiva a uno.

2 VI (a) (*thieve*) robar, hurtar; **to live by ~ing** vivir del robo.

(b) to ~ into a room deslizarse en un cuarto, entrar en un cuarto a hurtadillas; **to ~ up on sb** acercarse a uno sin ruido.

◆**steal away, steal off** VI marcharse sigilosamente, escabullirse.

stealing ['stiːlɪŋ] N robo *m*, hurto *m*.

stealth [stelθ] N cautela *f*, sigilo *m*; **by ~** a escondidas, a hurtadillas, sigilosamente.

stealthily ['stelθɪlɪ] ADV clandestinamente, a hurtadillas.

stealthiness ['stelθɪnɪs] N cautela *f*, sigilo *m*; cárácter *m* furtivo.

stealthy ['stelθɪ] ADJ cauteloso, sigiloso, furtivo; clandestino.

steam [stiːm] **1** N vapor *m*; vaho *m*, humo *m*; **full ~ ahead!** ¡todo avante!; **to get up ~** acumular vapor, dar presión; **to let off ~** descargar vapor, (*fig*) desahogarse; **the ship went on under its own ~** el buque siguió adelante con sus propios motores; **to come under one's own ~** venir por los propios medios; **to run out of ~** (*fig*) perder vigor, perder su fuerza; **to take the ~ out of a situation** reducir la tensión de una situación.

2 ATTR de vapor; **~ bath** baño *m* de vapor; **~ heat** calor *m* por vapor; **~ iron** plancha *f* de vapor.

3 VT (a) (*Culin*) cocer al vapor.

(b) *window* empañar.

(c) to ~ open an envelope abrir un sobre por medio de vapor; **to ~ a stamp off** separar un sello por medio de vapor.

4 VI (a) (*give out ~*) echar vapor; **the bowl was ~ing on the table** la cacerola humeaba en la mesa.

(b) (*move etc, function*) **to ~ ahead** avanzar, (*fig*) adelantarse mucho; **to ~ along** ir, avanzar (echando vapor); **we were ~ing at 12 knots** íbamos a 12 nudos, navegábamos a 12 nudos; **the ship ~ed into harbour** el buque entró al puerto; **the train ~ed out** salió el tren.

◆**steam up** **1** VT *window* empañar; **the windows quickly get ~ed up** las ventanas se empañan pronto; **to get ~ed up about sth** (*fig*) excitarse por algo, exaltarse por algo; **don't get ~ed up!*** ¡no te exaltes!, ¡cálmate!

2 VI (*window*) empañarse.

steamboat ['stiːmbəʊt] N vapor *m*, buque *m* de vapor.

steam-driven ['stiːm,drɪvn] ADJ impulsado por vapor, a vapor.

steam-engine ['stiːm,enʤɪn] N máquina *f* de vapor.

steam-hammer ['stiːm'hæməʳ] N maza *f* a vapor, maza *f* mecánica.

steamer ['stiːməʳ] N (a) (*ship*) vapor *m*, buque *m* de vapor. (b) (*Culin*) vaporera *f*.

steaming ['stiːmɪŋ] **1** ADJ (a) *kettle, plate* humeante. (b) (*: *angry*) furioso. (c) (‡: *drunk*) ajumado‡.

2 N (*) atraco en transportes públicos.

steam-organ ['stiːm,ɔːgən] N órgano *m* de vapor.

steamroller ['stiːm,rəʊləʳ] **1** N apisonadora *f*.

2 VT allanar con apisonadora; (*fig*) aplastar, arrollar; **to ~ a bill through parliament** hacer aprobar un proyecto de ley a rajatabla.

steamship ['stiːmʃɪp] N vapor *m*, buque *m* de vapor; **~ company**, **~ line** compañía *f* naviera.

steam shovel ['stiːm,ʃʌvl] N (*US*) pala *f* mecánica de vapor, excavadora *f*.

steam turbine ['stiːm'tɜːbaɪn] N turbina *f* de vapor.

steamy ['stiːmɪ] ADJ (a) vaporoso; *room etc* lleno de vapor; *atmosphere* húmedo y de mucho calor; *window* empañado. (b) (*) *film etc* erótico; *relationship* apasionado.

steed [stiːd] N (*liter*) corcel *m*.

steel [stiːl] **1** N (a) acero *m*; **to be made of ~** (*fig*) ser de bronce; **to fight with cold ~** luchar con armas blancas.

(b) (*sharpener*) chaira *f*, eslabón *m*; (*for striking spark*) eslabón *m*.

2 ATTR de acero; acerado; **~ band** banda *f* de percusión del Caribe; **~ guitar** guitarra *f* de cordaje metálico; **~ helmet** casco *m* (de acero); **~ industry** industria *f* siderúrgica; **~ maker**, **~ manufacturer** fa-

bricante *m* de acero; **~ tape** cinta *f* métrica de acero; **~ wool** virutas *fpl* de acero.

3 VT acerar; revestir de acero; **to ~ one's heart** hacerse duro de corazón; **to ~ one's men** infundir valor a los suyos.

4 VR: **to ~ o.s.** fortalecerse (*against* contra); **to ~ o.s. to do sth** cobrar bastante ánimo para hacer algo, persuadirse a hacer algo.

steel-clad ['stiːlklæd] ADJ revestido de acero, acorazado.

steel-grey [,stiːl'greɪ] ADJ gris metálico.

steel mill ['stiːlmɪl] N acería *f*, fábrica *f* de acero; fábrica *f* siderúrgica, fundidora *f* (*LAm*).

steel-plated [,stiːl'pleɪtɪd] ADJ chapado en acero.

steelworker ['stiːl,wɜːkəʳ] N trabajador *m* siderúrgico.

steelworks ['stiːlwɜːks] N, PL INVAR acería *f*, fábrica *f* de acero, fábrica *f* siderúrgica.

steely ['stiːlɪ] ADJ acerado; (*fig*) inflexible, duro; *gaze* duro; **~ blue** azul metálico.

steelyard ['stiːljɑːd] N romana *f*, báscula *f*.

steely-eyed [,stiːlɪ'aɪd] ADJ de mirada penetrante.

steep¹ [stiːp] ADJ (a) (*lit*) escarpado, abrupto; *cliff etc* cortado a pico, precipitoso; *stairs etc* empinado; **a ~ slope** una fuerte pendiente; **it's too ~ for the tractor** la pendiente es demasiado fuerte para el tractor; **it's a ~ climb** es una cuesta empinada.

(b) (*) *price etc* exorbitante, excesivo; *story etc* difícil de creer, increíble; **that's pretty ~!** ¡eso es demasiado!, ¡no hay derecho!; **it seems a bit ~ that ...** no parece razonable que + *subj*.

steep² [stiːp] **1** VT empapar, remojar (*in* en); **~ed in** (*fig*) saturado de, impregnado de, empapado en; **a town ~ed in history** una ciudad saturada de historia.

2 VI: **to leave sth to ~** dejar algo en remojo.

steeple ['stiːpl] N aguja *f*, campanario *m*, torre *f*.

steeplechase ['stiːpl,tʃeɪs] N carrera *f* de obstáculos, carrera *f* de vallas.

steeplechasing ['stiːpl,tʃeɪsɪŋ] N deporte *m* de las carreras de obstáculos.

steeplejack ['stiːpldʒæk] N reparador *m* de chimeneas, torres *etc*.

steeply ['stiːplɪ] ADV: **the mountain rises ~** la montaña está cortada a pico; **the road climbs ~** la carretera sube muy empinada; **prices have risen ~** los precios han subido muchísimo.

steepness ['stiːpnɪs] N lo escarpado, lo abrupto; lo precipitoso; lo fuerte.

steer¹ [stɪəʳ] **1** VT guiar, dirigir; *car etc* conducir, manejar (*LAm*); *ship* gobernar; **to ~ one's way through a crowd** abrirse paso por entre una multitud; **you nearly ~ed us into that rock** por poco dimos con aquella roca; **I ~ed her across to the bar** la llevé hacia el bar; **he ~ed me on to a good job*** me enchufó para un buen trabajo.

2 VI conducir, manejar (*LAm*); gobernar; **who's going to ~?** ¿quién manejará el volante (*or* timón *etc*)?; **can you ~?** ¿sabes gobernar el barco (*etc*)?; **to ~ for** dirigirse a, dirigirse hacia, ir con rumbo a; **to ~ clear of** evitar cualquier contacto con.

steer² [stɪəʳ] N buey *m*; novillo *m*; **to sell sb a bum ~*** (*US*) dar información falsa a uno, embaucar a uno.

steerage ['stɪərɪdʒ] N entrepuente *m*; **to go ~** viajar en tercera clase.

steering ['stɪərɪŋ] **1** N (*Aut etc*) dirección *f*, conducción *f*; (*Naut*) gobierno *m*.

2 ADJ: **~ committee** comité *m* directivo.

steering-arm ['stɪərɪŋɑːm] N brazo *m* de dirección.

steering-column ['stɪərɪŋ,kɒləm] N columna *f* de dirección.

steering-lock ['stɪərɪŋlɒk] N (*Aut*) (*anti-theft device*) dispositivo *m* antirrobo; cierre *m* de dirección; (*turning circle*) capacidad *f* de giro.

steering-wheel ['stɪərɪŋwiːl] N volante *m* (de dirección).

steersman ['stɪəzmən] N, PL **steersmen** ['stɪəzmən] timonero *m*.

stellar ['steləʳ] ADJ estelar.

stem¹ [stem] **1** N (a) (*of plant*) tallo *m*, (*of tree*) tronco *m*, (*of leaf etc*) pedúnculo *m*; (*of glass*) pie *m*; (*of pipe*) cañón *m*, tubo *m*, (*Mech*) vástago *m*; (*of word*) tema *m*.

(b) (*Naut*) roda *f*, tajamar *m*; **from ~ to stern** de proa a popa.

2 VI: **to ~ from** provenir de, proceder de, resultar de.

stem² [stem] VT (*check, stop*) refrenar, detener; *flood* represar; *attack* rechazar, parar; *flow of blood* restañar.

stench [stentʃ] N hedor *m*.

stencil ['stensl] **1** N (*Tech*) patrón *m* picado, estarcido *m*; (*for lettering*) plantilla *f*; (*for typing*) cliché *m*, clisé *m*.

2 VT estarcir; (*in typing*) hacer un cliché de.

Sten gun ['stengʌn] N metralleta *f* Sten.

stenographer [ste'nɒgrəfəʳ] N (*US*) taquígrafo *m*, -a *f*, estenógrafo *m*, -a *f*.

stenography [ste'nɒgrəfɪ] N (*US*) taquigrafía *f*, estenografía *f*.

stentorian [sten'tɔːrɪən] ADJ estentóreo.

STEP [step] N ABBR of **Science and Technology for Environmental Protection** Ciencia *f* y Tecnología para la Protección del Medio Ambiente.

step [step] **1** N (a) (*pace*) paso *m*; (*sound*) paso *m*, pisada *f*; (*footprint*)

huella *f*; (*of dance*) paso *m*; (*Comput*) paso *m*; **at every ~** a cada paso; **~ by ~** paso a paso, poco a poco; **it's a good ~** es bastante camino, está algo lejos; **it's quite a ~ to the village** el pueblo queda algo lejos, hay mucho camino para ir al pueblo; **to be in ~ with** llevar el paso con, (*fig*) estar conforme a, estar de acuerdo con; **to be out of ~ with** no ir al paso de, no llevar el paso con, (*fig*) estar en desacuerdo con; estar desfasado de; **to break ~** romper el paso; **to fall into ~** empezar a llevar el paso, (*fig*) conformarse; **to follow in sb's ~s** seguir los pasos de uno; **to keep in ~** llevar el paso; **to retrace one's ~s** desandar lo andado, volver sobre los pasos; **to take a ~** dar un paso; **to turn one's ~s towards** dirigirse hacia; **to watch one's ~** ir con tiento.
(b) (*measure*) paso *m*; medida *f*, gestión *f*; **~s to deal with the problem** medidas *fpl* para resolver el problema; **the first ~ is to ...** la primera medida a tomar es ...; **it's a great** (*or* **big**) **~ forward** esto significa un gran avance; es un paso gigante; **it's a ~ in the right direction** es una medida plausible; **what's the next ~?** ¿qué hacemos después?; **the next ~ is to** + *infin* luego hay que + *infin*, lo que se hace luego es + *infin*; **to take ~s to** + *infin* tomar medidas para + *infin*; **one can't take a single ~ without ...** no se puede dar un solo paso sin ...
(c) (*stair*) peldaño *m*, escalón *m*, grada *f*; (*of vehicle*) estribo *m*.
(d) **~s** (*stairs*) escalera *f*; (*outside building*) escalinata *f*; **folding ~s, pair of ~s** (*Brit*) escalera *f* de tijera, escalera *f* doble.
2 VT **(a)** (*place at intervals*) escalonar, colocar de trecho en trecho.
(b) *distance* (*also* **to ~ out**) medir a pasos; **to ~ it out** apretar el paso, andar más rápidamente.
3 VI dar un paso; (*walk*) ir, andar, caminar; (*with care, heavily etc*) pisar; **~ this way** haga el favor de pasar por aquí; **to ~ on sth** pisar algo; **~ on it!** ¡date prisa!, ¡apúrate! (*LAm*); **to ~ on board** ir a bordo; **just ~ outside a moment** (*challenge*) pues salga un momento; **to ~ over sth** evitar pisar algo, evitar chocar con algo; **he ~ped carefully over the cable** pasó por encima del cable con cuidado.
♦ **step aside** VI hacerse a un lado, apartarse.
♦ **step back** VI retroceder, dar un paso hacia atrás; **we ~ back into the 18th century** volvemos al siglo XVIII.
♦ **step down 1** VT reducir, disminuir.
2 VI bajar (*from de*); (*fig*) ceder su puesto; darse de baja; retirarse; renunciar a sus pretensiones; **to ~ down for someone else** retirarse en favor de otro.
♦ **step forward** VI dar un paso (hacia adelante).
♦ **step in** VI entrar; (*fig*) intervenir; **~ in!** ¡adelante!, ¡pasa!
♦ **step inside** VI: **~ inside!** ¡adelante!, ¡pasa!
♦ **step out 1** VT *distance* medir a pasos.
2 VI (*go out*) salir; (*hurry*) apretar el paso, andar más rápidamente.
♦ **step up 1** VT aumentar, elevar; *campaign* reforzar; *production, current* aumentar.
2 VI subir (*on a*); **to ~ up to sb** acercarse a uno; **to ~ up to receive a prize** avanzar a recibir un premio.
stepbrother ['step,brʌðəʳ] N hermanastro *m*.
step-by-step [ˌstepbaɪ'step] ADJ: **~ instructions** instrucciones *fpl* paso a paso.
stepchild ['steptʃaɪld] N, PL **stepchildren** ['step,tʃɪldrən] hijastro *m*, -a *f*, alnado *m*, -a *f*.
stepdaughter ['step,dɔːtəʳ] N hijastra *f*.
stepfather ['step,fɑːðəʳ] N padrastro *m*.
Stephen ['stiːvn] NM Esteban.
stepladder ['step,lædəʳ] N escalera *f* de tijera, escalera *f* doble.
stepmother ['step,mʌðəʳ] N madrastra *f*.
step-parent ['step,pɛərənt] N (*father*) padrastro *m*, (*mother*) madrastra *f*.
steppe [step] N estepa *f*.
stepping-stone ['stepɪŋstəʊn] N pasadera *f*; (*fig*) escalón *m* (*to* para llegar a).
stepsister ['step,sɪstəʳ] N hermanastra *f*.
stepson ['stepsʌn] N hijastro *m*.
step-up ['stepʌp] N elevación *f*; aumento *m*; aceleración *f*; refuerzo *m*; (*promotion*) ascenso *m*.
ster. ABBR *of* **sterling**.
stereo... ['steriəʊ] PREF estereo...
stereo ['steriəʊ] N **(a)** ABBR *of* **stereophonic**: (*all senses*) estéreo *m*; **recorded in ~** grabado en estéreo; **~ sound** sonido *m* estéreo, sonido *m* estereofónico.
(b) ABBR *of* **stereoscope, stereotype** *etc* estéreo *m*.
stereogram ['steriəgræm] N, **stereograph** ['steriəgræf] N estereografía *f*.
stereophonic [ˌsteriə'fɒnɪk] ADJ estereofónico.
stereophony [steri'ɒfənɪ] N estereofonía *f*.
stereoscope ['steriəskəʊp] N estereoscopio *m*.
stereoscopic [ˌsteriəs'kɒpɪk] ADJ estereoscópico; *film* tridimensional, en relieve.
stereotype ['steriətaɪp] **1** N clisé *m*, estereotipo *m*.

2 VT clisar, estereotipar; (*fig*) estereotipar.
stereotypical [ˌsteriə'tɪpɪkəl] ADJ estereotípico.
sterile ['steraɪl] ADJ estéril.
sterility [ste'rɪlɪtɪ] N esterilidad *f*.
sterilization [ˌsterɪlaɪ,zeɪʃən] N esterilización *f*.
sterilize ['sterɪlaɪz] VT esterilizar.
sterling ['stɜːlɪŋ] **1** ADJ **(a)** (*fig*) verdadero, excelente; **a ~ character** una persona de toda confianza; **a person of ~ worth** una persona de grandes méritos.
(b) (*Econ*) **pound ~** libra *f* esterlina; **~ area** zona *f* de la libra esterlina; **~ balances** balances *mpl* de libras esterlinas.
(c) **~ silver** plata *f* de ley.
2 N libras *fpl* esterlinas.
stern¹ [stɜːn] ADJ severo; duro; austero; **a ~ glance** una mirada severa; **a ~ warning** un aviso terminante; **he was very ~ with me** fue muy duro conmigo; **but he was made of ~er stuff** pero él tenía más carácter.
stern² [stɜːn] N popa *f* (*also Anat*).
sternly ['stɜːnlɪ] ADV severamente; duramente; austeramente; terminantemente; **she looked at me ~** me miró severamente.
sternness ['stɜːnnɪs] N severidad *f*; dureza *f*; austeridad *f*; lo terminante.
sternum ['stɜːnəm] N esternón *m*.
steroid ['stɪərɔɪd] N esteroide *m*.
stertorous ['stɜːtərəs] ADJ estertoroso.
stet [stet] VI (*Typ*) vale, deje como está.
stethoscope ['steθəskəʊp] N estetoscopio *m*.
Stetson ['stetsən] ® N sombrero *m* (de hombre) de alas anchas.
stevedore ['stiːvɪdɔːʳ] N estibador *m*.
Steve [stiːv] NM *familiar form of* **Stephen, Steven**.
Steven ['stiːvn] NM Esteban.
stew [stjuː] **1** N cocido *m*; estofado *m*, guisado *m* (*LAm*); **to be in a ~** pasar apuros, sudar la gota gorda; **now we're properly in the ~** la hemos pringado de verdad*.
2 ATTR: **~ meat** (*US*) carne *f* de vaca.
3 VT estofar; guisar; *fruit* cocer, hacer una compota de; **~ed apples** compota *f* de manzanas.
4 VI (*tea*) pasarse; **to let sb ~ in his own juice** dejar a uno cocer en su propia salsa.
steward ['stjuːəd] N (*on estate etc*) administrador *m*; (*butler*) mayordomo *m*; (*Naut, in club etc*) camarero *m*; (*bouncer*) portero *m*, encargado *m*, -a *f* del servicio de orden y entrada; (*Aer*) auxiliar *m* de vuelo.
stewardess ['stjʊədes] N (*Naut*) camarera *f*; (*Aer*) auxiliar *f* de vuelo, azafata *f*, aeromoza *f* (*LAm*).
stewardship ['stjʊədʃɪp] N administración *f*, gobierno *m*.
stewing steak ['stjuːɪŋ,steɪk] N (*Brit*) carne *f* de vaca.
stewpan ['stjuːpæn] N, **stewpot** ['stjuːpɒt] N cazuela *f*, cacerola *f*, puchero *m*.
St. Ex., St. Exch. ABBR *of* **Stock Exchange** Bolsa *f*.
Stg ABBR *of* **sterling** esterlina, ester.
stick¹ [stɪk] **1** N **(a)** palo *m*, vara *f*; (*as weapon*) palo *m*, porra *f*; (*walking ~*) bastón *m*; (*Aer*) palanca *f* de mando; (*of wax, gum etc*) barra *f*; (*of bombs*) grupo *m*; (*of celery*) tallo *m*; **~s** (*for the fire*) astillas *fpl*, leña *f*; **~ of furniture** mueble *m*; **policy of the big ~** política *f* del palo grueso; **policy of the ~ and the carrot** política *f* del garrote y la zanahoria; **to be in a cleft ~** estar entre la espada y la pared; **to give sb the ~, to take the ~ to sb** dar palo a uno; **the critics gave him a lot of ~** los críticos le dieron una buena paliza; **to get** (*or* **take**) **a lot of ~** recibir una buena paliza; tener que aguantar mucho; **I got the dirty end of the ~** me tocó bailar con la más fea; **they live out in the ~s** viven en el quinto pino.
(b) **old ~** (*Brit*) tío* *m*; **he's a funny old ~** es un tío raro (*or* divertido)*.
2 ATTR: **~ shift** (*US*) palanca *f* de marchas.
stick² [stɪk] (*irr*: PRET AND PTP **stuck**) **1** VT **(a)** (*gum*) pegar, encolar; **to ~ a poster on the wall** pegar un póster a la pared; **'~ no bills'** 'prohibido fijar carteles'; **he tried to ~ the crime on his brother** trató de colgar el crimen a su hermano*.
(b) (*thrust*) clavar, hincar; **to ~ a knife into a table** clavar un cuchillo en una mesa.
(c) (*place, put*) poner, meter; **~ it on the shelf** ponlo en el estante; **~ it in your case** métela en la maleta; **we'll ~ an advert in the paper*** pondremos un anuncio en el periódico; **they've stuck £5 on the price*** han subido el precio en 5 libras; **you know where you can ~ that!⁑** ¡que te jodas!⁑
(d) (*pierce*) picar; **to ~ sb with a bayonet** herir a uno con bayoneta, clavar la bayoneta a uno; **a cork stuck all over with pins** un corcho lleno de alfileres, un corcho todo cubierto de alfileres; **I've stuck the needle into my finger** me he picado el dedo con la aguja.
(e) (*esp Brit: tolerate*) resistir, aguantar; **I can't ~ him at any price** no le puedo ver de ninguna manera; **I can't ~ it any longer** no

aguanto más, no resisto más.

(f) (*passive: stop*) **to get stuck in the snow** quedar sin poderse mover en la nieve; **he's stuck in France** sigue en Francia sin poder moverse; **he's stuck in a boring job** tiene un trabajo muy aburrido (y no puede buscarse otro); **the mechanism was stuck** el mecanismo estaba bloqueado; **the lift is stuck at the 9th floor** el ascensor se ha atrancado en el piso 9.

(g) (*fig phrases*) **let's get stuck in!** ¡vamos!; ¡a trabajar!; **to get stuck into sth** emprender algo en serio, dedicarse seriamente a algo; **now we're stuck** estamos clavados; **to be stuck with sth** tener que cargar con algo; **we got stuck with this problem** nos quedamos con este problema; **and now we're stuck with it** y ahora no lo podemos quitar de encima, y ahora no hay manera de deshacernos de eso; **he's never stuck for an answer** siempre tiene una contestación pronta; **I was stuck with him for 2 hours** tuve que soportar su compañía durante 2 horas; **the problem had them all stuck** el problema les tenía a todos perplejos; **we're stuck at No. 13** no logramos pasar más allá del núm. 13; **to be stuck on sb** estar enamorado de uno.

2 VI **(a)** (*gum etc*) pegarse, adherirse; **this stamp won't ~** este sello no se pega; **the name stuck to him** el apodo se le pegó; **the charge seems to have stuck** la acusación no ha sido olvidada nunca; **to make an agreement ~** hacer que un acuerdo sea efectivo (*or* duradero); **to make a charge ~** hacer que una acusación tenga efecto.

(b) (*in mud*) atascarse, quedar atascado; (*mechanism etc*) bloquearse, trabarse, no poder moverse; pegarse; (*pin etc*) prender, estar prendido; **it stuck to the wall** quedó pegado a la pared; **to ~ fast in the mud** quedar clavado en el barro; **the door ~s in wet weather** en tiempo de lluvia la puerta se pega.

(c) (*remain*) pararse, quedarse parado; (*stay*) quedarse, permanecer; **I ~** (*Cards*) me planto; **here I am and here I ~** aquí estoy y aquí me quedo; **this thought stuck in my mind** esto se clavó en mi pensamiento; **to ~ at sth** (*not give up*) persistir en algo, no abandonar algo, seguir trabajando (*etc*) en algo; **to ~ by sb** (*follow*) pegarse a uno, pisar los talones a uno; (*support*) apoyar a uno, defender a uno, ser fiel a uno; **to ~ to one's principles** seguir fiel a sus principios, aferrarse a sus principios; **to ~ to a promise** cumplir una promesa; **to ~ to it** persistir, no cejar, seguir trabajando (*etc*); **~ to it!** ¡ánimo!; **let's ~ to the matter in hand** ciñámonos al asunto, no perdamos de vista el tema principal, volvamos al grano; **to ~ to sb = to ~ by sb**; **to ~ to sb like a limpet** (*or* **leech**) pegarse a uno como una lapa; **to ~ with sb = to ~ by sb**; **~ with us and you'll be all right** quédate con nosotros y todo saldrá bien; **you'll have to ~ with it** tendrás que seguir del mismo modo.

(d) (*balk*) plantarse; retroceder (*at* ante); **he ~s at nothing** no siente escrúpulo por nada, no se para en barras; **he wouldn't ~ at murder** hasta cometería un asesinato, no se arredraría ante el homicidio; **that's where I ~** yo de ahí no paso.

◆**stick around** VI esperar por ahí, quedarse.

◆**stick back** VT **(a)** (*replace*) volver a su lugar.
(b) (*gum etc*) volver a pegar.

◆**stick down** **(a)** VT (*gum etc*) pegar.
(b) (*put down*) poner, dejar; *note* apuntar (rápidamente).

◆**stick in** VT **(a)** (*thrust in*) clavar, hincar; meter; introducir; (*add, insert*) introducir, añadir.
(b) (*) **to get stuck in(to it)** poner manos a la obra, empezar a trabajar (*etc*) en serio; **get stuck in!** ¡a ello!, ¡apúrate!

◆**stick on** **1** VT **(a)** *stamp etc* pegar.
(b) *hat* ponerse, calarse; *coat etc* ponerse.
(c) *extra cost etc* añadir; **they've stuck 10p on a litre** han subido el precio del litro en 10p.
2 VI adherirse, pegarse; quedar pegado.

◆**stick out** **1** VT **(a)** *tongue* asomar, sacar; *leg etc* extender; *chest* sacar; *head* asomar.
(b) (*) aguantar; **to ~ it out** aguantar (hasta el final).
2 VI **(a)** (*project*) salir, sobresalir; asomarse.
(b) (*fig*) ser evidente; **it ~s out a mile** salta a los ojos, se ve a la legua; **it ~s out like a sore thumb** resalta como una mosca en la leche.
(c) (*insist*) **to ~ out for sth** insistir en algo, no ceder hasta obtener algo; **they're ~ing out for more money** porfían en reclamar más dinero, se empeñan en pedir más dinero.

◆**stick together** **1** VT pegar, unir con cola (*etc*).
2 VI **(a)** (*adhere*) pegarse, quedar pegados.
(b) (*persons etc*) mantenerse unidos; no separarse; (*fig*) cerrar las filas.

◆**stick up** **1** VT **(a)** *notice etc* fijar, pegar; *hand etc* levantar, alzar; **~ 'em up!** ¡arriba las manos!
(b) (‡) *person* atracar, encañonar‡; *bank etc* asaltar.
2 VI **(a)** (*show above*) salir, sobresalir (por encima), asomarse (por encima); (*hair etc*) estar de punta.
(b) **to ~ up for sb** defender a uno, sacar la cara por uno.

sticker ['stɪkəʳ] N **(a)** (*person*) persona *f* aplicada, persona *f* perseverante. **(b)** (*label*) etiqueta *f* engomada; pegatina *f*, pegatín *m*.

stickiness ['stɪkɪnɪs] N **(a)** (*lit*) pegajosidad *f*; viscosidad *f*; bochorno *m*, humedad *f* (con calor). **(b)** (*fig*) lo difícil.

sticking-plaster ['stɪkɪŋ,plɑːstəʳ] N (*Brit*) esparadrapo *m*, curita *f* (*LAm*), tirita *f* (*LAm*).

sticking-point ['stɪkɪŋ,pɔɪnt] N punto *m* de fricción.

stick-insect ['stɪkɪnsekt] N insecto *m* palo.

stick-in-the-mud ['stɪkɪnðəmʌd] N persona *f* pesada; persona *f* rutinaria; reaccionario *m*, -a *f*, persona *f* chapada a la antigua, retrógrado *m*.

stickleback ['stɪklbæk] N espinoso *m*.

stickler ['stɪkləʳ] N rigorista *mf* (*for* en cuanto a), persona *f* etiquetera; **he's a real ~ for correct spelling** insiste terminantemente en la correcta ortografía.

stick-on ['stɪkɒn] ADJ adhesivo.

stickpin ['stɪkpɪn] N (*US*) alfiler *m* de corbata.

stick-up‡ ['stɪkʌp] N atraco *m*, asalto *m*.

sticky ['stɪkɪ] ADJ **(a)** pegajoso; viscoso; *label* engomado; *atmosphere* bochornoso, húmedo (y con calor); **~ tape** cinta *f* adhesiva; **to have ~ fingers** ser largo de uñas. **(b)** (*) *problem, person* difícil; *situation* difícil, violento; **to come to a ~ end** tener mal fin, ir a acabar mal; **to have a ~ time** pasar un mal rato; **he was very ~ about signing it** se puso muy difícil al firmarlo.

stiff [stɪf] **1** ADJ **(a)** (*unbending*) rígido, inflexible, tieso; *door, joint* duro, tieso; *collar, shirt front* duro, (*starched*) almidonado; *brush* duro; *paste, soil* espeso, consistente; **as ~ as a poker** tieso como un ajo; **to be ~ in the legs** tener las piernas entumecidas; **to be ~ with cold** estar aterido; **you'll feel ~ tomorrow** mañana te van a doler los músculos, mañana tendrás agujetas.
(b) (*fig*) *breeze* fuerte; *climb, examination, task, test etc* difícil; *resistance* tenaz; *price* exorbitante, subido; *bow* frío; *person* etiquetero, ceremonioso; *manner* estirado; **she poured herself a ~ whisky** se sirvió una copa grande de whisky.
2 ADV: **to be worried ~** estar muy preocupado.
3 N (‡) fiambre *m*, cadáver *m*.

stiffen ['stɪfn] **1** VT hacer más rígido, atiesar; endurecer; hacer más espeso; *limb* entumecer, agarrotar; *morale, resistance etc* fortalecer.
2 VI hacerse más rígido, atiesarse; endurecerse; hacerse más espeso, espesarse; entumecerse; fortalecerse, robustecerse; hacerse más tenaz; **when I said this she ~ed** al decir yo esto, se volvió menos cordial; **the breeze ~ed** refrescó el viento; **resistance to the idea seems to have ~ed** parece que ha aumentado la oposición a esta idea.

stiffener ['stɪfənəʳ] N (*starch etc*) apresto *m*; (*plastic strip*) lengüeta *f*.

stiffly ['stɪflɪ] ADV rígidamente, tiesamente; **to move ~** moverse con dificultad, moverse despacio con los miembros entumecidos; **she said ~** dijo fríamente, dijo estirada; **this was ~ resisted** a esto opusieron una tenaz resistencia.

stiff-necked ['stɪf'nekt] ADJ (*fig*) terco, obstinado; estirado.

stiffness ['stɪfnɪs] N (V *adj*) **(a)** rigidez *f*, inflexibilidad *f*, tiesura *f*; dureza *f*; espesura *f*, espesor *m*; consistencia *f*; entumecimiento *m*. **(b)** fuerza *f*; dificultad *f*, lo difícil; tenacidad *f*; lo exorbitante; frialdad *f*, carácter *m* etiquetero, carácter *m* estirado.

stifle ['staɪfl] **1** VT ahogar, sofocar; (*fig*) suprimir; **to ~ a yawn** ahogar un bostezo, contener un bostezo; **to ~ opposition** suprimir la oposición.
2 VI ahogarse, sofocarse.

stifling ['staɪflɪŋ] ADJ sofocante (*also fig*), bochornoso; **it's ~ in here** aquí dentro hay un calor sofocante; **the atmosphere in the company is ~** en la compañía hay una atmósfera sofocante.

stigma ['stɪgmə] N, PL **stigmas** (*Bot, Med*), PL **stigmata** [stɪg'mɑːtə] (*Rel*) estigma *m*; (*moral stain*) estigma *m*, tacha *f*, baldón *m*.

stigmatic [stɪg'mætɪk] (*Rel*) **1** ADJ estigmatizado.
2 N estigmatizado *m*, -a *f*.

stigmatize ['stɪgmətaɪz] VT estigmatizar; **to ~ sb as** calificar a uno de, tachar a uno de.

stile [staɪl] N escalera *f* para pasar una cerca.

stiletto [stɪ'letəʊ] N estilete *m*; (*tool*) pinzón *m*; **~ heel** (*Brit*) tacón *m* de aguja.

still¹ [stɪl] **1** ADJ (*motionless*) inmóvil; quieto; (*and quiet*) tranquilo, silencioso; *wine* no espumoso; **~ life** bodegón *m*, naturaleza *f* muerta; **~ life painter** bodegonista *mf*; **to keep ~** estar inmóvil, no moverse; **keep ~!** ¡estáte quieto!; **he fell and lay ~** cayó y permaneció inmóvil; **to sit ~** estarse quieto en su silla; **sit ~!** ¡quieto!; **to stand ~** estarse quieto; **my heart stood ~** se me paró el corazón.
2 N **(a)** (*liter*) silencio *m*, calma *f*; **in the ~ of the night** en el silencio de la noche.
(b) (*Cine*) fotograma *m*.
3 VT calmar, tranquilizar; aquietar; (*silence*) acallar.

still² [stɪl] **1** ADV todavía, aún; **~ more** aún más, más aún; **~ better** mejor aún, aún mejor; **there are ~ 2 more** quedan 2 más; **he ~**

hasn't come no ha venido todavía; **I can ~ recall it** todavía lo recuerdo, lo recuerdo aún; **I ~ play a bit** sigo jugando un poco; **do you ~ believe that?** ¿sigues creyendo eso?; **~ and all*** (*esp US*) en resumidas cuentas, bien mirado todo.
[2] CONJ sin embargo, con todo, a pesar de todo; **~, it was worth it** sin embargo, valió la pena.

┌─ *STILL* ─────────────────── *see also main entry* ─┐

• Translate *still* relating to time using *todavía* or *aún* (with an accent):
  They are still working for the same company
  Todavía or *Aún están trabajando en la misma empresa*
  NOTE: Both *todavía* and *aún* normally come before the verb group in this meaning.
• Alternatively, use *seguir* + GERUND (with or without *todavía/aún*):
  Siguen or *Todavía siguen* or *Aún siguen trabajando en la misma empresa*
• *Still* with *more, less* and other comparatives is normally translated by *todavía* or *aún* (with an accent):
  More important still are the peace talks
  Todavía or *Aún más importantes son las negociaciones de paz*
  He lowered his voice still further
  Bajó la voz todavía or *aún más*
  Within a couple of weeks matters got still worse
  Al cabo de dos semanas los problemas empeoraron todavía or *aún más*
! Whenever it is synonymous with *todavía*, *aún* carries an accent. *For further uses and examples, see main entry.*

└──┘

still³ [stɪl] N alambique *m*.
stillbirth [ˈstɪlˌbɜːθ] N nacimiento *m* de un niño muerto.
stillborn [ˈstɪlˌbɔːn] ADJ **(a)** nacido muerto, mortinato; **the child was ~** el niño nació muerto. **(b)** (*fig*) fracasado, malogrado.
stillness [ˈstɪlnɪs] N inmovilidad *f*; quietud *f*; tranquilidad *f*, silencio *m*.
stilt [stɪlt] N zanco *m*; (*Archit*) pilar *m*, soporte *m*; pilote *m*.
stilted [ˈstɪltɪd] ADJ afectado, hinchado, artificial.
stimulant [ˈstɪmjʊlənt] [1] ADJ estimulante.
[2] N estimulante *m*, excitante *m*; (*drink*) bebida *f* alcohólica.
stimulate [ˈstɪmjʊleɪt] VT estimular; *growth etc* favorecer, fomentar, promover; *demand* estimular; **to ~ sb to do sth** estimular a uno a hacer algo, incitar a uno a hacer algo.
stimulating [ˈstɪmjʊleɪtɪŋ] ADJ (*Med etc*) estimulador, estimulante; *experience, book etc* sugestivo; alentador; inspirador.
stimulation [ˌstɪmjʊˈleɪʃən] N (*stimulus*) estímulo *m*; (*state*) excitación *f*.
stimulative [ˈstɪmjʊlətɪv] ADJ *effect* estimulador; *measure, policy* alentador.
stimulus [ˈstɪmjʊləs] N, PL **stimuli** [ˈstɪmjʊlaɪ] estímulo *m*, incentivo *m*.
stimy [ˈstaɪmɪ] VT = **stymie**.
sting [stɪŋ] [1] N **(a)** (*Zool, Bot: organ*) aguijón *m*; **but there's a ~ in the tail** pero viene algo no tan agradable al final.
(b) (*act, wound*) picadura *f*; (*pain*) escozor *m*; picazón *f*; (*pain, fig*) punzada *f*; **a ~ of remorse** una punzada de remordimiento; **the ~ of the rain in one's face** el azote de la lluvia en la cara; **I felt the ~ of his irony** su ironía me hirió en lo vivo; **this will take the ~ out of it** esto lo hará más aceptable, esto servirá para dorar la píldora.
(c) (*esp US⁑*) timo *m*.
[2] (*irr*: PRET AND PTP **stung**) VT **(a)** picar; punzar; (*make smart*) picar, escocer en; (*of hot dishes*) resquemar; (*of hail etc*) azotar; **the bee stung him** la abeja le picó; **my conscience stung me** me remordió la conciencia; **the reply stung him to the quick** la respuesta le hirió en lo vivo; **he was clearly stung by this remark** era evidente que este comentario hizo mella en él.
(b) to ~ sb to do sth incitar a uno a hacer algo, provocar a uno a hacer algo.
(c) (*) **they stung me for £4** me clavaron 4 libras*; **how much did they ~ you (for)?** ¿cuánto te clavaron?*
[3] VI picar; escocer; **moths don't ~** las mariposas no pican; **my eyes ~ me** me pican los ojos; **that mouthful stung me** ese bocado me quemó la lengua; **that blow really stung** ese golpe me dolió de verdad.
stingily [ˈstɪndʒɪlɪ] ADV con tacañería.
stinginess [ˈstɪndʒɪnɪs] N tacañería *f*.
stinging [ˈstɪŋɪŋ] [1] ADJ *insect etc* que pica, que tiene aguijón; *pain* punzante; *remark etc* mordaz.
[2] N (*sensation*) escozor *m*; picazón *m*; punzada *f*.
stinging-nettle [ˈstɪŋɪŋˌnetl] N ortiga *f*.
sting-ray [ˈstɪŋreɪ] N pastinaca *f*.
stingy [ˈstɪndʒɪ] ADJ tacaño; **to be ~ with sth** ser tacaño con algo.
stink [stɪŋk] [1] N **(a)** hedor *m*, mal olor *m*; tufo *m*; **a ~ of ...** un hedor a ...; **the ~ of corruption** el olor a corrupción.

(b) (*) lío *m**, follón* *m*; **there was a tremendous ~ about it** se armó un tremendo follón*; **to kick up** (or **make** *etc*) **a ~** armar un escándalo, armar un follón*.
[2] (*irr*: PRET **stank**, PTP **stunk**) VT: **to ~ out** *room* apestar, hacer oler mal; **to ~ sb out** ahuyentar a uno con un mal olor.
[3] VI **(a)** heder, oler mal (*of a*); **it ~s in here** aquí huele que apesta.
(b) (*) **the idea ~s** es una idea horrible; **I think the plan ~s** creo que es un proyecto abominable; **as a headmaster he ~s** como director es fatal*; **they are ~ing with money** son unos ricachos*, tienen tanto dinero que da asco.
stink-bomb [ˈstɪŋkˌbɒm] N bomba *f* fétida.
stinker⁑ [ˈstɪŋkə⁺] N (*person*) mal bicho *m*, canalla *m*; **you ~!** ¡bestia!*; **this problem is a ~** problema endiablado es éste.
stinking [ˈstɪŋkɪŋ] [1] ADJ **(a)** hediondo, fétido. **(b)** (*) horrible, bestial, asqueroso.
[2] ADV: **to be ~ rich⁑** ser un ricacho, tener tanto dinero que da asco.
stinky* [ˈstɪŋkɪ] ADJ apestoso, maloliente.
stint [stɪnt] [1] N **(a)** (*amount of work*) destajo *m*; tarea *f*; **to do one's ~** hacer su parte, trabajar (*etc*) como se debe, (*fig*) cumplir con las obligaciones que uno tiene, hacer su contribución; **to finish one's ~** terminar el trabajo que le corresponde a uno.
(b) without ~ libremente, generosamente; sin restricción.
[2] VT limitar, restringir; escatimar; **he did not ~ his praises** no escatimó sus elogios, prodigó sus elogios; **to ~ sb of sth** privar a uno de algo, dar a uno menor cantidad de algo de la que pide (*or* necesita).
[3] VR: **to ~ o.s.** estrecharse, privarse de cosas; **don't ~ yourself!** ¡no te prives de nada!, ¡sírvete (*etc*) cuanto quieras!; **to ~ o.s. of sth** privarse de algo, negarse algo, no permitirse algo.
stipend [ˈstaɪpend] N estipendio *m*, sueldo *m*.
stipendiary [staɪˈpendɪərɪ] [1] ADJ estipendiario.
[2] N estipendiario *m*.
stipple [ˈstɪpl] VT puntear; granear.
▼ **stipulate** [ˈstɪpjʊleɪt] [1] VT estipular, poner como condición; especificar.
[2] VI: **to ~ for sth** estipular algo, poner algo como condición.
stipulation [ˌstɪpjʊˈleɪʃən] N estipulación *f*, condición *f*.
stir¹ [stɜː⁺] [1] N **(a)** acto *m* de agitar (*etc*); hurgonada *f*; **to give one's tea a ~** remover su té; **give the fire a ~** remueve un poco la lumbre.
(b) (*fig*) conmoción *f*, revuelo *m*; sensación *f*; agitación *f*; **to cause a ~** causar una sensación, armar gran revuelo; provocar mucho interés; **it didn't make much of a ~** apenas despertó interés alguno; **there was a great ~ in parliament** hubo una gran conmoción en el parlamento.
[2] VT **(a)** *liquid etc* remover, agitar, revolver, menear; *fire* atizar, hurgar; **to ~ sugar into coffee** añadir azúcar a su café removiéndolo; **'~ before using'** 'agítese antes de usar'.
(b) (*move*) mover, agitar; **a breeze ~red the leaves** una brisa movió las hojas; **he never ~ed a foot all day** no movió el pie en todo el día.
(c) (*fig*) *emotions* conmover, despertar; *imagination* estimular; **to ~ to do sth** incitar a uno a hacer algo; **to ~ sb to pity** provocar a uno a lástima, excitar compasión en uno; **to feel deeply ~red** conmoverse profundamente, estar muy emocionado; **we were all ~red by the speech** el discurso nos conmovió a todos.
[3] VI **(a)** (*move*) moverse, menearse; **she hasn't ~red all day** no se ha movido en todo el día; **he never ~red from the spot** no abandonó el sitio ni un solo momento; **don't you ~ from here** no te muevas de aquí; **nobody is ~ring yet** están todavía en cama.
(b) (*) acizañar, meter cizaña.
◆ **stir up** VT **(a)** *liquid etc* remover, agitar, menear.
(b) (*fig*) *passions* excitar; *revolt* fomentar; *trouble* armar; **to ~ up the past** remover el pasado.
stir² [stɜː⁺] N (*esp US*) chirona⁑ *f*.
stir-fry [ˈstɜːfraɪ] [1] VT sofreír.
[2] N sofrito *m* (chino).
stirring [ˈstɜːrɪŋ] [1] ADJ *speech etc* emocionante, conmovedor; inspirador; *period etc* turbulento, agitado.
[2] N: **there were ~s of protest** la gente empezó a protestar; **I sense no ~ of interest** no creo que se esté despertando el interés.
stirrup [ˈstɪrəp] N estribo *m*.
stirrup cup [ˈstɪrəpcʌp] N copa *f* del estribo.
stirrup-pump [ˈstɪrəppʌmp] N bomba *f* de mano.
stitch [stɪtʃ] [1] N **(a)** (*Sew*) puntada *f*, punto *m*; (*Med: in surgery*) punto *m* de sutura; **a ~ in time saves 9** una puntada a tiempo ahorra ciento, quien acude a la gotera acude a la casa; **she hadn't a ~ on** estaba en pelota; **he hadn't a dry ~ on him** estaba calado hasta los huesos; **to put ~es in a wound** suturar una herida.
(b) (*pain*) punto *m*, punzada *f*; **to have a ~** tener flato; **we were in ~es*** nos moríamos de risa*.
[2] VT (*also* **to ~ down**, **to ~ together**, **to ~ up**) coser; (*Med*) suturar.

◆**stitch up:** VT incriminar dolosamente, vender*.

stitching ['stɪtʃɪŋ] N puntadas *fpl*, puntos *mpl*.

stoat [stəʊt] N armiño *m*.

stock [stɒk] ① N **(a)** (*of tree*) tronco *m*, (*of vine*) cepa *f*, (*for grafting*) patrón *m*.
(b) (*Bot: species*) alhelí *m*.
(c) (*family*) estirpe *f*, linaje *m*, raza *f*; **of good ~** de buen linaje; **of good Castilian ~** de buena cepa castellana.
(d) (*handle*) mango *m*; (*of gun*) caja *f*, culata *f*.
(e) ~s (*Hist: punishment*) cepo *m*.
(f) ~s (*Naut*) astillero *m*, grada *f* de construcción; **to be on the ~s** (*ship*) estar en vía de construcción, (*boat etc*) estar en preparación; **he has 3 plays on the ~s** tiene 3 obras entre manos.
(g) (*supply*) provisión *f*, (*Comm*) surtido *m*, existencias *fpl*, stock *m*; **~ of spares** stock *m* de recambios; **to be in ~** estar en existencia, estar en almacén; **to be out of ~** estar agotado; **we are out of ~ of umbrellas** no nos quedan paraguas, están agotados los paraguas; **to have sth in ~** tener algo en existencia; **to lay in a ~ of** proveerse de, hacer provisión de; **to take ~** hacer inventario (*of* de); **to take ~ of** (*fig*) asesorarse de, considerar; evaluar.
(h) (*Agr*) (*live ~*) ganado *m*, ganadería *f*; (*dead ~*) aperos *mpl*; V **rolling** *etc*.
(i) (*Culin*) caldo *m*.
(j) (*Fin: of company*) capital *m* (comercial); (*shares*) acciones *fpl*, valores *mpl*; **~s and shares** valores *mpl*; **his ~ is going up** su reputación crece, su crédito aumenta.
② ATTR (*Comm*) de surtido, en existencia; *size etc* de serie, corriente, normal; (*Theat*) de repertorio; *phrase* hecho; *remark* banal, vulgar; *response etc* que se espera, acostumbrado, consagrado; **~ control** control *m* de existencias; **~ option plan** plan *m* que permite que los ejecutivos de una empresa compren acciones en ella a un precio favorable; **~ warrant** certificado *m* de derechos (para compra de acciones a precio fijo).
③ VT **(a)** (*also* **to ~ up**) (*supply*) surtir, proveer, abastecer (*with* de); **to ~ a pond with fish** poblar un charco de peces.
(b) (*keep*) tener existencias de, tener el almacén; **we don't ~ that brand** no tenemos esa marca; **do you ~ bananas?** ¿vende Vd plátanos?

◆**stock up** ① VT = **stock 3 (a)**.
② VI: **to ~ up with** proveerse de, adquirir existencias de, (*fig*) ir acumulando.

stockade [stɒ'keɪd] N estacada *f*; (*US**) prisión *f* militar.

stockbreeder ['stɒk,briːdəʳ] N ganadero *m*.

stockbreeding ['stɒk,briːdɪŋ] N ganadería *f*.

stockbroker ['stɒk,brəʊkəʳ] N bolsista *mf*, agente *mf* de bolsa, corredor *m* de bolsa; **~ belt** zona *f* residencial de los bolsistas.

stockbroking ['stɒk,brəʊkɪŋ] N correduría *f* de bolsa.

stock car ['stɒkkɑːʳ] N (*Rail*) borreguero *m*, vagón *m* de ganado; (*Aut, Sport*) stock-car *m*.

stock-car racing ['stɒkkɑː,reɪsɪŋ] N carreras *fpl* de stock-car.

stock company ['stɒk,kʌmpənɪ] N sociedad *f* anónima, sociedad *f* (*or* compañía *f*) de acciones.

stock-cube ['stɒkkjuːb] N cubito *m*.

stock exchange ['stɒkɪks,tʃeɪndʒ] ① N bolsa *f*; **to be on the ~** ser bolsista, ser miembro de la bolsa, dedicarse a negocios de bolsa; **prices on the ~** cotizaciones *fpl* de bolsa.
② ATTR bursátil.

stockfish ['stɒkfɪʃ] N pescado *m* de seco.

stockholder ['stɒk,həʊldəʳ] N (*US*) accionista *mf*.

Stockholm ['stɒkhəʊm] N Estocolmo *m*.

stockily ['stɒkɪlɪ] ADV: **~ built** de complexión robusta.

stockiness ['stɒkɪnɪs] N robustez *f*.

stockinet [,stɒkɪ'net] N tela *f* de punto.

stocking ['stɒkɪŋ] N media *f*; (*knee-length*) calceta *f*; **a pair of ~s** un par de medias; **in one's ~ed feet** sin zapatos.

stocking-filler ['stɒkɪŋ,fɪləʳ] N pequeño regalo *m* de Navidad (*que completa la 'media' de los regalos*).

stock-in-trade ['stɒkɪn'treɪd] N (*Comm*) capital *m*; existencias *fpl*, existencia *f* de mercancías; (*fig*) repertorio *m*; **that joke is part of his ~** es un chiste de su repertorio.

stockist ['stɒkɪst] N (*Brit*) distribuidor *m*, -ora *f*.

stockjobber ['stɒk,dʒɒbəʳ] N (*Brit*) agiotista *mf*.

stockjobbing ['stɒk,dʒɒbɪŋ] N agiotaje *m*.

stockkeeper ['stɒkkiːpəʳ] N almacenero *m*, -a *f*.

stocklist ['stɒklɪst] N (*Fin*) lista *f* de valores y acciones; (*Comm*) lista *f* de existencias.

stock market ['stɒk,mɑːkɪt] N = **stock exchange**.

stockpile ['stɒkpaɪl] ① N reservas *fpl* (de materias primas).
② VT acumular, poner en reserva, formar una reserva de.

stock raising ['stɒk,reɪzɪŋ] N ganadería *f*.

stockroom ['stɒkrʊm] N almacén *m*, depósito *m*.

stock-still ['stɒk'stɪl] ADV: **to be** (*or* **stand**) **~** estar completamente

inmóvil.

stocktaking ['stɒk,teɪkɪŋ] N (*Brit*) inventario *m*, balance *m*; **~ sale** venta *f* postbalance; **to do the ~** hacer el inventario.

stocky ['stɒkɪ] ADJ rechoncho, bajo pero fuerte.

stockyard ['stɒkjɑːd] N corral *m* de ganado.

stodge* [stɒdʒ] N (*Brit*) comida *f* indigesta, cosas *fpl* indigestas.

stodgy ['stɒdʒɪ] ADJ *food* indigesto, pesado; *book, style etc* pesado.

stogie, stogy ['stəʊgɪ] N (*US*) cigarro *m*, puro *m*.

stoic ['stəʊɪk] ① ADJ estoico.
② N estoico *m*.

stoical ['stəʊɪkəl] ADJ estoico.

stoically ['stəʊɪklɪ] ADV estoicamente, impasiblemente.

stoicism ['stəʊɪsɪzəm] N estoicismo *m*.

stoke [stəʊk] (*also* **to ~ up**) ① VT *furnace* cargar, cebar; *fire* echar carbón a; (*fig*) cebar; (*hum*) atiborrarse de.
② VI cebar el hogar, echar carbón a la lumbre; (*hum*) atiborrarse.

stoker ['stəʊkəʳ] N fogonero *m*.

stokehold ['stəʊkhəʊld] N cuarto *m* de calderas.

stokehole ['stəʊkhəʊl] N boca *f* del horno.

STOL [stɒl] N ABBR *of* **short take-off and landing** despegue *m* y aterrizaje cortos.

stole[1] [stəʊl] N estola *f*.

stole[2] [stəʊl] PRET *of* **steal**.

stolen ['stəʊlən] PTP *of* **steal**; **~ goods** géneros *mpl* robados.

stolid ['stɒlɪd] ADJ impasible, imperturbable; flemático; (*pej*) terco.

stolidity [stɒ'lɪdɪtɪ] N impasibilidad *f*, imperturbabilidad *f*; flema *f*; terquedad *f*.

stolidly ['stɒlɪdlɪ] ADV impasiblemente, imperturbablemente.

stomach ['stʌmək] ① N estómago *m*; vientre *m*; (*fig*) deseo *m*, apetito *m* (*for* de); **they have no ~ for the fight** no tienen valor para la pelea; **it turns my ~** me revuelve el estómago.
② ATTR estomacal, de(l) estómago; **~ upset** trastorno *m* estomacal.
③ VT (*fig*) tragar, aguantar.

stomach-ache ['stʌmək,eɪk] N dolor *m* de estómago.

stomach-pump ['stʌmək,pʌmp] N bomba *f* estomacal.

stomp [stɒmp] ① VT (*US*) = **stamp 2 (a)**.
② VI pisar muy fuerte.

stone [stəʊn] ① N **(a)** piedra *f*; (*commemorative*) lápida *f*; **within a ~'s throw** a tiro de piedra, a dos pasos; **to cast the first ~** lanzar la primera piedra; **which of you shall cast the first ~?** ¿cuál de vosotros se atreve a lanzar la primera piedra?; **to leave no ~ unturned** no dejar piedra por mover, revolver Roma con Santiago.
(b) (*of fruit*) hueso *m*.
(c) (*Med*) cálculo *m*, piedra *f*; (*as complaint*) mal *m* de piedra.
(d) (*Brit: weight*) PL **stone** = *14 libras = 6,348 kg*; *ver también* ⟦IMPERIAL SYSTEM⟧ .
② ADJ de piedra; **S~ Age** Edad *f* de (la) Piedra.
③ VT **(a)** apedrear, lapidar; **~ me!:** ¡caray!*
(b) *fruit* deshuesar.

stone-blind ['stəʊn'blaɪnd] ADJ completamente ciego.

stone-broke* ['stəʊn'brəʊk] ADJ (*US*) = **stony-broke**.

stonechat ['stəʊntʃæt] N culiblanco *m*.

stone-cold [,stəʊn'kəʊld] ADJ muy frío, totalmente frío; **to be ~ sober** no estar borracho en lo más mínimo.

stonecrop ['stəʊnkrɒp] N uva *f* de gato.

stonecutter ['stəʊn,kʌtəʳ] N = **stonemason**.

stoned: [stəʊnd] ADJ (*drunk*) trompa:, borracho, como una cuba*; (*Drugs*) colocado:.

stone-dead ['stəʊn'ded] ADJ más muerto que una piedra; **it killed the idea ~** acabó completamente con la idea.

stone-deaf ['stəʊn'def] ADJ completamente sordo, más sordo que una tapia.

stone-ground ['stəʊn,graʊnd] ADJ *flour* molido por piedras.

stonemason ['stəʊn'meɪsn] N albañil *m*; (*in quarry*) cantero *m*.

stone-pit ['stəʊnpɪt] N, **stone-quarry** ['stəʊn,kwɒrɪ] N cantera *f*.

stonewall ['stəʊn'wɔːl] VI emplear una táctica de cerrojo; (*fig*) negarse a contestar claramente, prolongar un asunto mediante evasivas.

stonewalling ['stəʊn'wɔːlɪŋ] N táctica *f* de cerrojo.

stoneware ['stəʊnwɛəʳ] ① N gres *m*.
② ADJ de gres.

stonewashed ['stəʊn,wɒʃt] ADJ *jeans* lavado a la piedra.

stonework ['stəʊnwɜːk] N cantería *f*, obra *f* de sillería; piedras *fpl*.

stonily ['stəʊnɪlɪ] ADV (*fig*) glacialmente, fríamente.

stonking: ['stɒŋkɪŋ] ADJ (*Brit*) cojonudo:, de puta madre:.

stony ['stəʊnɪ] ADJ **(a)** *material* pétreo; como piedra, parecido a piedra; *ground* pedregoso, cubierto de piedras. **(b)** *glance* glacial, frío; *heart* empedernido; *stare* duro; *silence* sepulcral.

stony-broke* ['stəʊnɪ'brəʊk] ADJ: **to be ~** (*Brit*) no tener un céntimo, estar tronado*.

stony-faced [,stəʊnɪ'feɪst] ADJ de expresión pétrea.

stony-hearted ['stəʊnɪ'hɑːtɪd] ADJ de corazón empedernido.

stood [stʊd] PRET AND PTP *of* **stand**.

stooge* [stuːdʒ] ① N hombre *m* de paja*; secuaz *m*, partidario *m*; paniaguado *m*; (*of comedian*) compañero *m*.

② VI: **to ~ for sb** ayudar a uno; servir humildemente a uno.

◆**stooge about, stooge around** VI estar sin hacer nada, estar por ahí; vagabundear.

stook [stuːk] ① N tresnal *m*, garbera *f*.

② VT poner en tresnales.

stool [stuːl] N **(a)** (*seat*) taburete *m*, escabel *m*; (*folding*) silla *f* de tijera; **to fall between two ~s** quedarse sin el pan y sin la torta.

(b) (*Bot*) planta *f* madre.

(c) (*Med*) cámaras *fpl*.

stool-pigeon* [ˈstuːlˌpɪdʒən] N soplón* *m*, chivato* *m*.

stoop¹ [stuːp] ① N inclinación *f*; (*defect*) cargazón *f* de espaldas; **to walk with a ~** andar encorvado.

② VT inclinar, bajar.

③ VI inclinarse, encorvarse; (*permanently, as defect*) ser cargado de espaldas, andar encorvado; **to ~ to pick sth up** inclinarse para recoger algo; **to ~ to** + *infin* (*fig*) rebajarse a + *infin*.

stoop² [stuːp] N (*US*) pórtico *m*, pequeña veranda *f*.

stooping [ˈstuːpɪŋ] ADJ inclinado, encorvado; cargado de espaldas.

stop [stɒp] ① N **(a)** (*gen*) parada *f*; alto *m*; pausa *f*, interrupción *f*; **a 20-minute ~ for coffee** un alto de 20 minutos para tomar café; **to be at a ~** estar parado; quedar paralizado; **to bring to a ~** *vehicle* parar; *production, progress etc* parar, paralizar; **to come to a ~** venir a parar, pararse; **to come to a dead** (*or* **sudden**) **~** pararse en seco, detenerse repentinamente; **to come to a full ~** pararse, paralizarse, quedar detenido en un punto muerto; **to go on for 2 hours without a ~** continuar durante 2 horas sin parar (*or* sin interrupción); **to put a ~ to sth** poner fin a algo, acabar con algo.

(b) (*stay*) estancia *f*; **a ~ of a few days** una estancia de unos días.

(c) (*of bus, tram etc*) parada *f*; (*Aer, Naut*) escala *f*; **to make a ~ at Bordeaux** hacer escala en Burdeos.

(d) (*Typ: also* **full ~**) punto *m*.

(e) (*Mus*) (*of organ*) registro *m*; (*of guitar*) traste *m*; (*of other instrument*) llave *f*; **to pull out all the ~s** (*fig*) desplegar todos sus recursos, tocar todos los registros.

(f) (*Mech*) tope *m*, retén *m*.

(g) (*Phon: also* **~ consonant**) (consonante *f*) oclusiva *f*.

② VT **(a)** (*block: also* **~ up**) *leak, hole etc* tapar; cegar; *road etc* cerrar, obstruir, bloquear; *tooth* empastar; *flow of blood* restañar; *cheque* anular, cancelar; **to ~ one's ears** taparse los oídos; **to ~ a gap** tapar un agujero, (*fig*) llenar un vacío.

(b) (*arrest progress of*) parar, detener; *ball, bullet, engine, car, charge, traffic etc* parar; *blow* rechazar, parar; *aggression* rechazar, contener; *danger, threat* evitar, estorbar; *process* terminar; *abuse* poner fin a, acabar con; (*forbid*) prohibir, poner fin a; **~ thief!** ¡al ladrón!; **and there is nothing to ~ him** y no hay nada que se lo impida; **the walls ~ some of the noise** las paredes suprimen una parte del ruido; **the curtains ~ the light** las cortinas impiden la entrada de la luz; **this should ~ any further trouble** esto habrá de evitar cualquier dificultad en el futuro; **to ~ sb (from) doing sth** (*prevent*) impedir a uno hacer algo, (*forbid*) prohibir a uno hacer algo; **to ~ sth being done** impedir que algo se haga; **to ~ sth happening** evitar que algo ocurra.

(c) (*cease*) terminar; **~ it!** ¡basta!, ¡basta ya!, ¡párate! (*LAm*); **~ that noise!** ¡basta ya de ruido!; **~ the nonsense!** ¡déjate de tonterías!; **to ~ work** suspender el trabajo, dejar de trabajar.

(d) (*suspend*) *payments etc* suspender; *supply* cortar, interrumpir; **to ~ sb's electricity** cortar la electricidad de uno; **to ~ sb's wages** suspender el pago del sueldo de uno; **to ~ a pound out of sb's wages** retener una libra del sueldo de uno; **all leave is ~ped** han sido cancelados todos los permisos; **to ~ the milk for a fortnight** cancelar la leche durante quince días.

③ VI **(a)** (*cease motion*) parar, pararse; detenerse; hacer alto; (*finish, run out*) terminarse, acabarse; (*supply etc*) cortarse, interrumpirse; (*process, rain etc*) cesar; **the car ~ped** se paró el coche; **where does the bus ~?** ¿dónde para el autobús?; **the clock has ~ped** el reloj se ha parado; **~!** ¡pare!, ¡alto!; **when the programme ~s** cuando termine el programa; **payments have ~ped** (*temporarily*) se han suspendido los pagos, (*permanently*) han terminado los pagos; **the rain has ~ped** la lluvia ha cesado, ha dejado de llover; **he seems not to know when to ~** parece no saber cuándo conviene hacer alto; **to ~ to do sth** detenerse a hacer algo.

(b) (*stay*) hospedarse, alojarse (*at* en, *with* con); quedarse; **she's ~ping with her aunt** se hospeda en casa de su tía; vive con su tía; **did you ~ till the end?** ¿te quedaste hasta el fin?

(c) (*with verb constructions*) **to ~ doing sth** dejar de hacer algo; **she never ~s talking** habla incansablemente, no termina de hablar; **it has ~ped raining** ha dejado de llover, ya no llueve.

④ VR **(a) I ~ped myself in time** me detuve a tiempo.

(b) to ~ o.s. doing sth abstenerse de hacer algo, guardarse de hacer algo; **I can't seem to ~ myself doing it** parece que no puedo dejar

de hacerlo.

◆**stop away** VI ausentarse (*from* de); no asistir (*from* a); **you ~ away from my sister!** ¡no vengas más por aquí a molestar a mi hermana!

◆**stop behind** VI quedarse; quedarse en casa, no salir; **they made him ~ behind after school** le hicieron quedar en la escuela después de las clases.

◆**stop by** VI detenerse brevemente; **I'll ~ by your house** pasaré por tu casa; **I'll ~ by on the way to school** me asomaré de paso al colegio.

◆**stop in** VI quedarse en casa, no salir; **don't ~ in for me** no te quedes esperándome en casa.

◆**stop off** VI interrumpir el viaje (*at* en); hacer escala (*at* en).

◆**stop out** VI quedarse fuera; no volver a casa.

◆**stop over** VI pasar la noche, pernoctar; quedarse un poco.

◆**stop up** ① VT V **stop 2 (a)**.

② VI (*Brit*) velar, no acostarse, seguir sin acostarse; **don't ~ up for me** no os quedéis esperándome hasta muy tarde.

stop-and-go [ˈstɒpənˈgəʊ] N (*US*) = **stop-go**.

stopcock [ˈstɒpkɒk] N llave *f* de cierre.

stopgap [ˈstɒpgæp] ① N (*thing*) recurso *m* provisional, expediente *m*; (*person*) tapagujeros *m*, sustituto *m*, tapaboquetes *m*.

② ATTR: **~ measure** medida *f* interina.

stop-go [ˈstɒpˈgəʊ] N: **period of ~** período *m* cuando una política de expansión económica alterna con otra de restricción.

stoplights [ˈstɒplaɪts] NPL (*Aut*) luces *fpl* de freno; (*US*) luces *fpl* de tráfico, semáforo *m*.

stop-off [ˈstɒpɒf] N, **stopover** [ˈstɒpəʊvəʳ] N parada *f* intermedia; escala *f*; interrupción *f* de un viaje.

stoppage [ˈstɒpɪdʒ] N **(a)** parada *f*, cesación *f*, detención *f*; interrupción *f*; (*of work*) paro *m*, suspensión *f*; (*of pay*) suspensión *f*; (*from pay*) descuento *m*; (*in game*) detención *f*; (*strike*) huelga *f*. **(b)** (*blockage*) obstrucción *f*.

stopper [ˈstɒpəʳ] ① N tapón *m*; (*Tech*) taco *m*, tarugo *m*.

② VT tapar, taponar.

stopping [ˈstɒpɪŋ] ① N **(a)** parada *f*; suspensión *f*. **(b)** (*of tooth*) empaste *m*.

② ADJ: **~ train** tren *m* correo, tren *m* ómnibus.

stopping-place [ˈstɒpɪŋpleɪs] N paradero *m*; (*of bus etc*) parada *f*.

stop-press [ˈstɒpˈpres] N (*also* **~ news**) noticias *fpl* de última hora; '**~**' (*as heading*) 'al cerrar la edición'.

stop sign [ˈstɒpsaɪn] N (*esp US*) stop *m*, señal *f* de stop.

stopwatch [ˈstɒpwɒtʃ] N cronógrafo *m*.

storage [ˈstɔːrɪdʒ] ① N almacenaje *m*, depósito *m*; (*Comput*) almacenamiento *m*; **to put sth into ~** poner algo en almacén.

② ATTR: **~ battery** acumulador *m*; **~ capacity** capacidad *f* de almacenaje; **~ charges** derechos *mpl* de almacenaje; **~ device** dispositivo *m* de almacenaje; **~ heater** acumulador *m*; **~ room** (*US*) trastero *m*; **~ space** depósito *m*; **~ tank** (*for oil etc*) tanque *m* de almacenamiento; (*for rainwater*) tanque *m* de reserva; **~ unit** (*furniture*) armario *m*.

store [stɔːʳ] ① N **(a)** (*stock*) provisión *f*; (*reserve*) reserva *f*; repuesto *m*; (*Brit: storehouse*) almacén *m*, depósito *m*; **to be in ~** estar en almacén, estar en depósito; **what is in ~ for sb** lo que le espera a uno, lo que la suerte tiene guardado para uno; **what has the future in ~ for us?** ¿qué guarda el futuro para nosotros?; **that is a treat in ~** eso es un placer que nos guarda el futuro; **to have** (*or* **keep**) **sth in ~** tener algo en reserva; **to lay in a ~ of** hacer provisión de, proveerse de; **to put** (*or* **set**) **great ~ by sth** conceder mucha importancia a algo, estimar algo en mucho; **to set little ~ by sth** conceder poca importancia a algo, estimar algo en poco.

(b) (*quantity*) abundancia *f*; tesoro *m*; **a great ~ of expertise** gran pericia *f*; **he has a ~ of knowledge about ...** tiene grandes conocimientos de ...

(c) **~s** (*Mil etc*) (*food*) víveres *mpl*, provisiones *fpl*, (*equipment*) pertrechos *mpl*; (**war**) **~s** material *m* bélico.

(d) (*shop: esp US*) tienda *f*, almacén *m*; **Bloggs's S~s** Almacenes *mpl* Bloggs; (*US*) **~ clerk** dependiente *m*, -a *f*; **to mind the ~*** (*US*) cuidar de los asuntos; V **department store**.

② ATTR (*US: also* **~-bought**) de confección, de serie.

③ VT almacenar; poner en reserva, tener en reserva, guardar; *documents* archivar; (*Comput*) almacenar.

④ VI conservarse (bien *etc*).

◆**store away** VT almacenar; poner en reserva, tener en reserva, guardar.

◆**store up** VT acumular, ir acumulando, amontonar; **a hatred ~d up over centuries** un odio almacenado durante siglos.

store card [ˈstɔːkɑːd] N tarjeta *f* de compra.

storefront [ˈstɔːfrʌnt] N (*US*) escaparate *m*.

storehouse [ˈstɔːhaʊs] N, PL **storehouses** [ˈstɔːˌhaʊzɪz] almacén *m*, depósito *m*; (*fig*) mina *f*, tesoro *m*.

storekeeper [ˈstɔːˌkiːpəʳ] N almacenero *m*; (*US*) tendero *m*; (*Naut*) pañolero *m*.

storeroom [ˈstɔːrʊm] N despensa *f*; depósito *m*; (*Naut*) pañol *m*.

storey, (US) **story²** ['stɔːrɪ] N piso m; **a 9-~ building** un edificio de 9 pisos.

storeyed, (US) **storied** ['stɔːrɪd] ADJ ending in compounds: **an 8-~ building** un edificio de 8 pisos.

stork [stɔːk] N cigüeña f.

storm [stɔːm] 1 N (a) (Met) tormenta f, tempestad f, temporal m; (Naut) borrasca f; (of wind) vendaval m, huracán m; **to brave the ~** aguantar la tempestad; **to ride out a ~** capear un temporal, hacer frente a un temporal.
(b) (fig) tempestad f, borrasca f; **a ~ in a teacup** (Brit) una tempestad en un vaso de agua; **~ of abuse** torrente m de injurias; **~ of criticism** vendaval m de críticas, nube f de críticas; **there were ~s of applause** sonaron fuertes aplausos, hubo repetidas salvas de aplausos; **there was a political ~** hubo un gran revuelo político; **it caused an international ~** levantó una polvareda internacional; **to bring a ~ about one's ears** atraer sobre sí una lluvia de protestas.
(c) (Mil) **to take a town by ~** tomar una ciudad por asalto; **the play took Paris by ~** la obra cautivó a todo París.
2 VT (Mil) asaltar, tomar por asalto.
3 VI rabiar, bramar; **to ~ at sb** tronar contra uno, enfurecerse con uno; **he came ~ing into my office** entró rabiando en mi oficina; **he ~ed on for an hour about the government** pasó una hora lanzando improperios contra el gobierno; **he ~ed out of the meeting** salió de la reunión como un huracán.

stormbound ['stɔːmbaʊnd] ADJ inmovilizado por el mal tiempo.

storm centre, (US) **storm center** ['stɔːm,sentə^r] N centro m de la tempestad; (fig) foco m de los disturbios, centro m de la agitación.

stormcloud ['stɔːmklaʊd] N nubarrón m.

storm-door ['stɔːmdɔː^r] N contrapuerta f.

storming ['stɔːmɪŋ] N asalto m (of a).

stormproof ['stɔːmpruːf] ADJ a prueba de tormentas.

storm-signal ['stɔːm,sɪgnl] N señal f de temporal.

storm-tossed ['stɔːmtɒst] ADJ sacudido por la tempestad.

storm-trooper ['stɔːm,truːpə^r] N guardia m de asalto.

storm-troops ['stɔːmtruːps] NPL tropas fpl de asalto.

stormwater ['stɔːm,wɔːtə^r] N agua f de lluvia.

storm window ['stɔːm,wɪndəʊ] N contraventana f.

stormy ['stɔːmɪ] ADJ tempestuoso, borrascoso (also fig); **~ petrel** (Orn) petrel m de la tempestad, (fig) persona f pendenciera, persona f de vida borrascosa.

story¹ ['stɔːrɪ] N (a) (account) historia f, relación f, relato m; (Liter) cuento m, historieta f; (joke) cuento m, chiste m; **the ~ of her life** la historia de su vida; **the ~ of their travels** la relación de sus viajes; **his ~ is that ...** según él dice ..., según lo que él cuenta ...; **that's another ~** eso es harina de otro costal; **that's not the whole ~** no te lo han contado en su totalidad, hay una parte que no te han contado; **it's the (same) old ~** es lo de siempre; **it's a long ~** es largo de contar; **to cut a long ~ short** para abreviar, en resumidas cuentas; **the ~ goes that ...** dice el cuento que ...; **to tell a ~** contar un cuento, narrar una historia; **the marks tell their own ~** las señales hablan por sí solas, las señales no necesitan interpretación; **the full ~ has still to be told** todavía no se ha hecho pública toda la historia; **what a ~ this house could tell!** ¡cuántas cosas nos diría esta casa!
(b) (plot) argumento m, trama f.
(c) (fig) cuento m, mentira f; embuste m; **a likely ~!** ¡puro cuento!, ¡qué cuento más inverosímil!; **to tell stories** contar embustes; **don't tell stories!** ¡no me vengas con tus embustes!
(d) (Press, TV) artículo m; reportaje m; noticia f.

story² ['stɔːrɪ] N (US Archit) = **storey.**

storyboard ['stɔːrɪ,bɔːd] N (Cine) dibujos mpl (or fotos fpl) secuenciales de imágenes, guión m gráfico.

storybook ['stɔːrɪbʊk] 1 N libro m de cuentos.
2 ATTR: **a ~ ending** una conclusión como el fin de una novela.

story-line ['stɔːrɪlaɪn] N argumento m.

storyteller ['stɔːrɪ,telə^r] N cuentista mf; (fibber) cuentista mf, embustero m, -a f.

story-writer ['stɔːrɪ,raɪtə^r] N narrador m, -ora f.

stoup [stuːp] N copa f, frasco m; (Eccl) pila f.

stout [staʊt] 1 ADJ (a) (solid) sólido, robusto, macizo, fuerte; person gordo, corpulento; (sturdy) fornido.
(b) (fig) (brave) valiente; (resolute) resuelto; resistance etc terco, tenaz; **~ fellow!** ¡muy bien!; **he's a ~ fellow** es un buen chico; **with ~ hearts** resueltamente.
2 N (Brit) especie de cerveza negra; ver también BEER.

stout-hearted ['staʊt'hɑːtɪd] ADJ valiente, resuelto.

stoutly ['staʊtlɪ] ADV: **~ built** de construcción sólida, fuerte; **to resist ~** resistir tenazmente; **he ~ maintains that ...** sostiene resueltamente que ...

stoutness ['staʊtnɪs] N gordura f, corpulencia f.

stove¹ [stəʊv] N (for heating) estufa f; (esp US: for cooking) hornillo m, cocina f (de gas etc), horno m (LAm), estufa f (Mex).

stove² [stəʊv] PRET AND PTP of **stave.**

stovepipe ['stəʊvpaɪp] 1 N tubo m de estufa.
2 ATTR: **~ hat** chistera f.

stow [stəʊ] VT meter, poner, colocar; (Naut) estibar, arrumar; (and hide: also **to ~ away**) esconder; **where can I ~ this?** ¿esto dónde lo pongo?; **~ it!** ¡déjate de eso!, ¡cállate!, ¡basta ya!

◆**stow away** 1 VT: **to ~ food away*** despachar rápidamente una comida, zamparse una comida.
2 VI viajar de polizón (on a ship en un buque), viajar sin pagar y clandestinamente.

stowage ['stəʊɪdʒ] N (act) estiba f, arrumaje m; (place) bodega f.

stowaway ['stəʊəweɪ] N polizón m, llovido m.

strabismus [strə'bɪzməs] N estrabismo m.

Strabo ['streɪbəʊ] NM Estrabón.

straddle ['strædl] VT esparrancarse encima de, estar con una pierna a cada lado de; horse montar a horcajadas; target horquillar.

strafe [strɑːf] VT bombardear, cañonear, atacar; destrozar a tiros.

strafing ['strɑːfɪŋ] N ametrallamiento m.

straggle ['strægl] VI (lag) rezagarse; (get lost) extraviarse; (spread) extenderse, estar esparcido; (wander) vagar, vagar en desorden, (Bot) lozanear; **the village ~s on for miles** el pueblo se extiende varios kilómetros (sin tener un plano fijo); **the guests ~d out into the night** los invitados salieron poco a poco y desaparecieron en la noche; **her hair ~s over her face** el pelo le cae en desorden por la cara.

◆**straggle away, straggle off** VI dispersarse.

straggler ['græglə^r] N rezagado m, -a f.

straggling ['stræglɪŋ] ADJ, **straggly** ['stræglɪ] ADJ disperso; rezagado; extendido; desordenado.

straight [streɪt] 1 ADJ (a) (not bent) derecho, recto; line recto; back erguido; hair lacio; **he carries himself as ~ as a ramrod** se mantiene perfectamente erguido; **~ razor** (US) navaja f de barbero.
(b) (honest) honrado; answer franco, directo; denial, refusal categórico, rotundo; **as ~ as a die** (fig) derecho como una vela, honrado a carta cabal; **is he ~?** ¿es de fiar?; **let me be ~ with you** te digo esto con toda franqueza, no hagamos confusiones.
(c) (plain, uncomplicated) sencillo; drink sin mezcla, puro; (Pol) fight de dos candidatos solamente; (Theat) part, play serio; **~ man** (Theat) actor m que da pie al cómico.
(d) (in order) en orden; **it's all ~ now** todo está en regla ya; **your tie isn't ~** tu corbata no está bien; **let's get this ~** pongamos las cosas claras, digámoslo claramente; vamos a concretar; **to put things ~** arreglar cosas, poner las cosas en orden; **to put the record ~** hacer constar la verdad, explicar los hechos; **are your affairs ~ at last?** ¿por fin has arreglado tus asuntos?
(e) (*: not gay) hetero*, heterosexual, no homosexual.
2 ADV (a) (in a ~ line) derecho, directamente, en línea recta; **to fly ~** volar en línea recta; **~ above us** directamente encima de nosotros; **it's ~ across the road from us** está exactamente enfrente de nosotros; **~ ahead, ~ on** todo seguido, todo recto, derecho (LAm); **keep ~ on for Toledo** vayan Vds todo seguido para Toledo; **I went ~ home** fui derecho a mi casa; **I went ~ to my room** fui derecho a mi cuarto, fui a mi cuarto sin detenerme para nada; **to look sb ~ in the eye** mirar directamente a los ojos de uno.
(b) (immediately, without diversion) directamente; inmediatamente; **~ after this** inmediatamente después de esto; luego; **~ away** en seguida, inmediatamente; **~ off** sin parar, sin interrupción; de un tirón; sin vacilar; **for 3 days ~ off** durante 3 días seguidos; **he read the whole of Proust ~ off** leyó toda la obra de Proust de un tirón; **she just went ~ off** se fue sin vacilar; **he said ~ off that ...** dijo sin vacilar que ...; **to come ~ to the point** ir directamente al grano; **to drink ~ from the bottle** beber de la misma botella.
(c) (frankly) francamente, con franqueza; (honestly) honradamente; **I tell you ~, I'll give it to you ~** te lo digo con toda franqueza; **~ out** francamente, sin rodeos; **he's always dealt very ~ with me** siempre se ha portado conmigo como hombre honrado, siempre me ha tratado con justicia; **~ up!** ¡te lo juro!
(d) (pure) sin mezcla; **we drink it ~** lo bebemos sin mezcla.
(e) (*) **to go ~** enmendarse, hacer nueva vida, vivir dentro de la ley; **he's been going ~ for a year now** lleva un año sin tener nada que ver con el crimen.
(f) (Theat) **he played the part ~** hizo el papel de manera seria; **we'll do 'Lear' ~ this time** esta vez haremos 'Lear' sin bromas.
3 N: **the ~** (Racing, Rail) la recta; **out of (the) ~** fuera de la plomada, no vertical; **to depart from the ~ and narrow** apartarse del buen camino; **to keep sb on the ~ and narrow** asegurar que uno no se aparte del buen camino.

straightaway ['streɪtə'weɪ] ADV en seguida, inmediatamente, luego, luego (Mex).

straightedge ['streɪtedʒ] N regla f de borde recto.

straighten ['streɪtn] 1 VT (also **to ~ out**) enderezar, poner derecho; (fig) arreglar, poner en orden; problem resolver; confused situation desenmarañar.

2 VI (*person*) enderezarse, ponerse derecho; erguirse.

◆**straighten out** VT = straighten 1.

◆**straighten up** 1 VT *room* arreglar.

2 VI enderezarse, ponerse derecho; erguirse.

3 VR: **to ~ o.s. up** = straighten 2.

straight-faced ['streɪt'feɪst] 1 ADJ serio, grave, solemne; **a ~ attitude** una actitud seria.

2 ADV: **he told the joke very ~** contó el chiste con cara muy seria.

straightforward [ˌstreɪt'fɔ:wəd] ADJ (*honest*) honrado; (*plain-spoken*) franco; (*simple*) sencillo; *answer* claro, franco.

straightforwardly [ˌstreɪt'fɔ:wədlɪ] ADV honradamente; francamente; sencillamente.

straightforwardness [ˌstreɪt'fɔ:wədnɪs] N honradez *f*; franqueza *f*; sencillez *f*; claridad *f*.

straightness ['streɪtnɪs] N (*honesty*) sinceridad *f*, honestidad *f*; (*frankness*) franqueza *f*.

straight-out* ['streɪtaʊt] ADJ *answer, refusal* sincero, franco; *supporter, enthusiast, thief* cien por cien.

strain[1] [streɪn] 1 N **(a)** (*Mech*) tensión *f*; esfuerzo *m*; (*damage*) deformación *f*; **the ~ on a rope** la tensión de una cuerda; **to take the ~ off a beam** disminuir la presión sobre una viga; **can you take some of the ~?** ¿me puedes ayudar a sostener (*etc*) esto?

(b) (*fig*) tensión *f*, tirantez *f*; esfuerzo *m* (grande, excesivo); (*mental*) agotamiento *m* nervioso, postración *f* nerviosa; **the ~s of international politics** las tensiones de la política internacional; **the ~s on the economy** las presiones sobre la economía; **the ~s of modern life** las tensiones de la vida moderna; **the ~ of 6 hours at the wheel** el agotamiento nervioso que producen 6 horas al volante; **to write without ~** escribir sin esfuerzo; **to put a great ~ on sb** someter a uno a un gran esfuerzo; exigir un gran esfuerzo a uno.

(c) (*Med*) torcedura *f*; distensión *f* (muscular).

(d) (*Mus*) ~s son *m*, compases *mpl*; **the ~s of a waltz** los compases de un vals; **the bride came in to the ~s of the wedding march** la novia entró a los acordes (*or* compases) de la marcha nupcial.

(e) (*tenor*) tenor *m*, estilo *m*, sentido *m*; **there was a lot else in the same ~** hubo mucho más a este tenor.

2 VT **(a)** (*stretch*) estirar, poner tirante, tender con fuerza.

(b) (*Med: overtax*) deformar, dañar por esfuerzo excesivo; *back, muscle etc* torcerse; *eyes* cansar; *heart* cansar (exigiendo un esfuerzo excesivo a); *patience etc* cansar, abusar de; *meaning, word* forzar, hacer violencia a; *friendship, relationship* pedir demasiado a; crear tensiones en, crear tirantez en; **to ~ one's ears to hear** esforzarse por oír; **to ~ the law to help sb** hacer violencia a una ley para ayudar a uno.

(c) **to ~ sb to one's breast††** (*liter*) abrazar a uno estrechamente, estrechar a uno entre los brazos.

(d) (*filter*) filtrar; (*Culin*) colar.

3 VI: **to ~ at sth** esforzarse tirando de algo, tirar con fuerza de algo; **don't ~ at it** no te esfuerces tanto, no te hagas daño tirando tanto; **they ~ed at the crate** manipularon el cajón con gran esfuerzo; **to ~ after sth** esforzarse por conseguir algo; **to ~ to do sth** esforzarse por hacer algo, hacer grandes esfuerzos por lograr algo.

◆**strain off** VT: **to ~ the water off** separar el agua, colar el agua.

strain[2] [streɪn] N (*breed*) raza *f*, linaje *m*; (*tendency*) tendencia *f*; **a ~ of weakness** un rasgo de debilidad; **a ~ of madness** una vena de locura.

strained [streɪnd] ADJ *muscle etc* torcido; *laugh, smile etc* forzado; *relations* tenso, tirante; *style* que muestra esfuerzo, afectado.

strainer ['streɪnər] N (*Culin*) colador *m*; (*Tech*) filtro *m*, coladero *m*.

strait [streɪt] N **(a)** (*Geog: also* ~s) estrecho *m*; **the S~ of Gibraltar** el Estrecho de Gibraltar.

(b) (*fig*) ~s estrecheces *fpl*; situación *f* apurada, apuro *m*; **to be in dire ~s** estar muy apurado; **the economic ~s we are in** el aprieto económico en que nos encontramos.

straitened ['streɪtnd] ADJ: **in ~ circumstances** en apuro, en la necesidad.

straitjacket ['streɪtˌdʒækɪt] N camisa *f* de fuerza; (*fig*) corsé *m*.

strait-laced ['streɪt'leɪst] ADJ gazmoño; remilgado.

strand[1] [strænd] N (*Naut*) 1 N (*liter*) playa *f*, ribera *f*.

2 VT *ship* varar, encallar; **to ~ sb without money in London** dejar a uno sin dinero ni recursos en Londres; **to be ~ed** (*person*) quedar solo, estar sin poderse ayudar, estar abandonado, (*by missing train etc*) quedarse colgado, (*car etc*) quedar inmovilizado; **to leave sb ~ed** dejar a uno desamparado, dejar a uno plantado.

3 VI varar, encallar.

strand[2] [strænd] N (*of rope*) ramal *m*; (*of thread*) hebra *f*, filamento *m*; (*of hair*) trenza *f*; (*of plant*) brizna *f*; **to tie up the loose ~s** (*fig*) atar cabos.

strange [streɪndʒ] ADJ (*unknown*) desconocido (*to* de); (*new*) nuevo (*to* para), no acostumbrado; (*odd*) extraño, raro, curioso; (*exotic*) exótico, peregrino; **how ~!** ¡qué raro!; **it is ~ that ...** es raro que + *subj*; **I find it ~ that ...** me extraña que + *subj*, para mí resulta incomprensible

que + *subj*; **I felt rather ~ at first** al principio no me sentí cómodo, me sentí algo molesto al principio; **I am ~ to the work** soy nuevo en el oficio, el trabajo es nuevo para mí; **~ to say ...** aunque parece mentira ...; **I never sleep well in a ~ bed** no duermo nunca bien en una cama que no sea la mía; **don't talk to any ~ men** no hables con ningún desconocido.

┌───┐
│ STRANGE, RARE   *see also main entries* │
│   │
│ **Position of "raro"**   │
│ You should generally put *raro* after the noun when you mean │
│ *strange* or *odd* and before the noun when you mean *rare*: │
│ He has a strange name   │
│ *Tiene un nombre raro*   │
│ ...a rare congenital syndrome...   │
│ *... un raro síndrome congénito...*   │
│ *For further uses and examples, see main entries at strange and rare.* │
└───┘

strangely ['streɪndʒlɪ] ADV extrañamente; de un modo raro; **it was ~ familiar to me** me era extrañamente familiar; **she acts somewhat ~** se comporta de un modo bastante raro; **~ (enough), I never met him** aunque parezca mentira, no le conocí nunca.

strangeness ['streɪndʒnɪs] N novedad *f*; extrañeza *f*, rareza *f*; lo exótico.

stranger ['streɪndʒər] N desconocido *m*, -a *f*; (*from another area etc*) forastero *m*, -a *f*; **he's a ~ to me** es un desconocido para mí; **I'm a ~ here** no soy de aquí, soy nuevo aquí; **hullo ~!** ¡cuánto tiempo sin vernos!; **you're quite a ~!** ¡apenas te dejas ver!; **he is no ~ to vice** conoce bien los vicios.

strangle ['stræŋgl] VT estrangular; (*fig*) *abuse, sob etc* ahogar; **a ~d cry** un grito entrecortado.

stranglehold ['stræŋglhəʊld] N (*Sport*) collar *m* de fuerza; (*fig*) dominio *m* completo; **to have a ~ on sth** dominar algo completamente.

strangler ['stræŋglər] N estrangulador *m*.

strangling ['stræŋglɪŋ] N estrangulación *f*.

strangulated ['stræŋgjʊleɪtɪd] ADJ estrangulado; **~ hernia** hernia *f* estrangulada.

strangulation [ˌstræŋgjʊ'leɪʃən] N estrangulación *f* (*also Med*).

strap [stræp] 1 N correa *f*; (*Sew etc*) tira *f*, banda *f*; (*shoulder ~*) tirante *m*, hombrera *f*; **to give sb the ~** azotar a uno, darle a uno con la correa.

2 VT **(a)** (*tie*) atar con correa.

(b) **to ~ sb** (*as punishment*) azotar a uno, darle a uno con la correa.

◆**strap down** VT: **to ~ sb down** sujetar a uno con correa.

◆**strap in** VT *object, child* sujetar con correas; **he isn't properly ~ped in** no está bien atado.

◆**strap on** VT *object* atar con correas; *watch* ponerse.

◆**strap up** VT = strap 2 (a).

strap-hang* ['stræphæŋ] VI viajar de pie (agarrado a la correa).

strap-hanger* ['stræphæŋər] N pasajero *m*, -a *f* que va de pie (agarrado, -a a la correa).

strapless ['stræplɪs] ADJ *dress* sin tirantes.

strapline ['stræpˌlaɪn] N (*Press*) titular *m*.

strapped [stræpt] ADJ: **to be ~ for funds** andar mal de dinero, tener dificultades económicas.

strapping ['stræpɪŋ] ADJ robusto, fornido.

Strasbourg ['stræzbɜ:g] N Estrasburgo *m*.

strata ['strɑ:tə] N, PL of **stratum.**

stratagem ['strætɪdʒəm] N estratagema *f*.

strategic(al) [strə'ti:dʒɪk(əl)] ADJ estratégico.

strategist ['strætɪdʒɪst] N estratega *mf*.

strategy ['strætɪdʒɪ] N estrategia *f*.

stratification [ˌstrætɪfɪ'keɪʃən] N estratificación *f*.

stratified ['strætɪfaɪd] ADJ estratificado.

stratify ['strætɪfaɪ] 1 VT estratificar.

2 VI estratificarse.

stratigraphic [ˌstrætɪ'græfɪk] ADJ estratigráfico.

stratigraphy [strə'tɪgrəfɪ] N estratigrafía *f*.

stratocumulus [ˌstreɪtəʊ'kju:mjʊləs] N, PL **stratocumuli** [ˌstreɪtəʊ'kju:mjʊlaɪ] estratocúmulo *m*.

stratosphere ['strætəʊsfɪər] N estratosfera *f*.

stratospheric [ˌstrætəʊs'ferɪk] ADJ estratosférico.

stratum ['strɑ:təm] N, PL **strata** ['strɑ:tə] estrato *m*; (*fig*) estrato *m*, capa *f*.

stratus ['streɪtəs] N, PL **strati** ['streɪtaɪ] estrato *m*.

straw [strɔ:] 1 N paja *f*; (*drinking ~*) pajita *f*, popote *m* (*Mex*), pitillo *m* (*And, Carib*), sorbete *m* (*Carib, SC*); **to drink through a ~** sorber con una pajita; **it's the last ~!** ¡es el colmo!, ¡no faltaba más!; **it's a ~ in the wind** sirve de indicio; **to clutch at ~s** agarrarse a un clavo ardiendo; **to draw** (*or* **get**) **the short ~** ser elegido para hacer algo desagradable; **the ~ that breaks the camel's back** la gota que colma el vaso.

2 ATTR de paja; (*colour*) pajizo, color paja; ~ **hat** sombrero *m* de paja, canotier *m*; ~ **man** hombre *m* de paja; ~ **poll**, ~ **vote** votación *f* de tanteo.

strawberry ['strɔːbərɪ] N (*fruit and plant*) fresa *f*, frutilla *f* (*LAm*); (*large, cultivated*) fresón *m*; ~ **blonde** rubia *f* fresa; ~ **mark** (*on skin*) mancha *f* de nacimiento, antojo *m*.

strawberry-bed ['strɔːbərɪbed] N fresal *m*.

straw-coloured, (*US*) **straw-colored** ['strɔːkʌləd] ADJ pajizo, color paja.

strawloft ['strɔːlɒft] N pajar *m*, pajera *f*.

stray [streɪ] **1** ADJ *animal etc* extraviado; mostrenco; *bullet* perdido; (*isolated*) aislado; (*scattered*) disperso; (*sporadic*) esporádico; **a ~ cat** un gato extraviado, un gato callejero; **in a few ~ cases** en algunos casos aislados; en algún que otro caso; **a few ~ thoughts** unos cuantos pensamientos inconexos.

2 N (**a**) (*animal*) animal *m* extraviado *m*; (*child*) niño *m* sin hogar, niño *m* desamparado, niña *f* sin hogar, niña *f* desamparada.

(**b**) ~**s** (*Rad*) parásitos *mpl*.

3 VI (*lose o.s.*) extraviarse, perderse; (*wander*) vagar, errar; **to ~ from** apartarse de (*also fig*) **we had ~ed 2 kilometres from the path** nos habíamos desviado 2 kilómetros del camino; **they ~ed into the enemy camp** erraron el camino y se encontraron en el campamento enemigo; **if the gate is left open the cattle ~** si se deja abierta la puerta las vacas se escapan; **my thoughts ~ed to the holidays** empecé a pensar en las vacaciones.

streak [striːk] **1** N raya *f*, lista *f*, línea *f* delgada; (*of mineral*) veta *f*, vena *f*; (*fig: of madness etc*) vena *f*; (*of luck*) racha *f*; ~ **of lightning** rayo *m* (*also fig*); **there is a ~ of Spanish blood in her** tiene una pequeña parte de sangre española; **he had a yellow ~** era un tanto cobarde; **he went past like a ~** (*of lightning*) pasó como un rayo.

2 VT rayar (*with* de).

3 VI (**a**) **to ~ along** correr a gran velocidad; **to ~ past** pasar como un rayo.

(**b**) (*) correr desnudo.

streaker ['striːkər] N corredor *m* desnudo, corredora *f* desnuda.

streaking ['striːkɪŋ] N carrera *f* desnudista.

streaky ['striːkɪ] ADJ (**a**) rayado, listado; (*Brit*) *bacon* veteado, entreverado; *rock etc* veteado. (**b**) *shot* afortunado.

stream [striːm] **1** N (*brook*) arroyo *m*, riachuelo *m*; (*river*) río *m*; (*current*) corriente *f*; (*jet etc*) chorro *m*, flujo *m*; (*fig*) torrente *m*; lluvia *f*, oleada *f*; (*of cars etc*) caravana *f*, riada *f*; ~**s of abuse** torrente *m* de injurias; ~**s of people** una multitud de gente, un sinfín de gente; ~ **of consciousness** monólogo *m* interior; **an unbroken ~ of cars** una riada de coches; **the B ~** (*Brit Scol*) el grupo B; **people were coming out in ~s** la gente salía en tropel; **in one continuous ~** ininterrumpidamente; **against the ~** contra la corriente; **with the ~** con la corriente; **to come on ~** (*oil-well etc*) empezar a producir; (*Comm*) entrar en (pleno) funcionamiento.

2 ATTR: ~ **feed** alimentación *f* continua.

3 VT (**a**) *water etc* derramar, dejar correr; *blood* manar; **his face ~ed blood** la sangre le corría por la cara.

(**b**) (*Scol*) clasificar, poner en grupos.

4 VI (*liquid*) correr, fluir; (*blood*) manar, correr; (*in wind etc*) ondear, flotar; **her eyes were ~ing** lloraba a mares; **the gas made my eyes ~** el gas me hizo lagrimear; **her cheeks were ~ing with tears** las lágrimas le corrían por las mejillas, tenía las mejillas bañadas en lágrimas; **to ~ out** (*liquid*) brotar, chorrear, salir a borbotones; **people came ~ing out** la gente salía en tropel; **the cars kept ~ing past** los coches pasaban ininterrumpidamente; **her hair ~ed in the wind** su pelo le ondeaba al viento.

streamer ['striːmər] N flámula *f*; (*Naut*) gallardete *m*; (*of paper, at parties etc*) serpentina *f*.

streaming ['striːmɪŋ] N (*Scol*) división *f* en grupos.

streamline ['striːmlaɪn] VT aerodinamizar; (*fig*) coordinar, perfeccionar, hacer más eficiente.

streamlined ['striːmlaɪnd] ADJ aerodinámico.

street [striːt] **1** N calle *f*; **it's right up my ~** (*Brit*) de eso sí sé algo; eso viene pintiparado para mí; **to be ~s ahead of sb** (*Brit*) llevar mucha ventaja a uno, haberse adelantado mucho a uno; **we are ~s ahead of them in design** les damos ciento y raya en el diseño; **they're ~s apart** les separa un abismo, no tienen color*; **they're not in the same ~ as us** (*Brit*) no están a nuestra altura, no admiten comparación con nosotros; **to be on the ~s** (*prostitute*) hacer la calle; V **walk 2** (**d**).

2 ATTR callejero, de la calle; ~ **accident** accidente *m* de circulación; ~ **arab** golfo *m*, chicuelo *m* de la calle; ~ **cred(ibility)** dominio *m* de la contracultura urbana; ~ **cry** pregón *m*; ~ **incident** incidente *m* callejero; **at ~ level** en el nivel de la calle; ~ **market** mercado *m* callejero; ~ **musician** músico *m* ambulante; ~ **photographer** fotógrafo *m* callejero; ~ **theatre** teatro *m* de calle; ~ **value** valor *m* en la calle; ~ **vendor** (*US*) vendedor *m* callejero, vendedora *f* callejera.

streetcar ['striːtkɑːr] N (*US*) tranvía *m*.

street-cleaner ['striːtkliːnər] N barrendero *m*, -a *f*.

street door ['striːt'dɔːr] N puerta *f* principal, puerta *f* de la calle.

street-fighting ['striːtfaɪtɪŋ] N luchas *fpl* en las calles.

street lamp ['striːtlæmp] N, **street light** ['striːtlaɪt] N farol *m*.

street-lighting ['striːtlaɪtɪŋ] N alumbrado *m* público.

street-map ['striːtmæp] N plano *m* (de la ciudad).

streetsmart ['striːtsmɑːt] ADJ (*US*) = **streetwise**.

street-sweeper ['striːtswiːpər] N barrendero *m*.

street-urchin ['striːtɜːtʃɪn] N golfo *m*, chicuelo *m* de la calle.

streetwalker ['striːtwɔːkər] N (prostituta *f*) callejera *f*.

streetwise ['striːtwaɪz] ADJ *child* pícaro; muy listo, de mucha mundología; experimentado en la vida callejera.

strength [streŋθ] N (**a**) (*gen*) fuerza *f*; (*toughness*) resistencia *f*; (*of person*) fuerzas *fpl*, vigor *m*; (*of colour, feeling etc*) intensidad *f*; (*of drink*) fuerza *f*; **the ~ of the pound** (*exchange value*) el valor de la libra; (*high value*) la fortaleza de la libra, el vigor de la libra; ~ **of character** carácter *m*, firmeza *f* de carácter; ~ **of will** resolución *f*; **on the ~ of** fundándose en, confiando en; **on the ~ of that success she applied for promotion** a base de ese éxito solicitó el ascenso; **with all one's ~** con todas sus fuerzas; **his ~ failed him** se sintió desfallecer, le abandonaron sus fuerzas; **give me ~!** ¡Dios me dé paciencia!; **it goes from ~ to ~** está cada vez más fuerte; **to save** (*or* **reserve**) **one's ~** reservarse.

(**b**) (*Mil etc*) número *m*, complemento *m*; efectivos *mpl*; **to be at full ~** tener todo su complemento; **to be below** (*or* **under**) ~ no tener suficiente mano de obra (*or* suficientes efectivos *etc*); **his supporters were there in ~** asistían muchos partidarios suyos; **they came in ~** vinieron en gran número; **to be on the ~** ser miembro del regimiento (*etc*); ser de plantilla; **to take sb on to the ~** dar a uno un puesto en el regimiento (*etc*).

strengthen ['streŋθən] **1** VT fortalecer, reforzar, hacer más fuerte; consolidar.

2 VI fortalecerse, reforzarse, hacerse más fuerte; consolidarse.

strengthening ['streŋθənɪŋ] **1** ADJ (*Med etc*) fortificante, tonificante.

2 N fortalecimiento *m*, refuerzo *m*; consolidación *f*.

strenuous ['strenjʊəs] ADJ (*energetic*) enérgico, vigoroso; (*tough*) arduo; (*exhausting*) agotador; *opposition etc* tenaz; *exercise* fuerte; **to make ~ efforts to** + *infin* esforzarse enérgicamente por + *infin*.

strenuously ['strenjʊəslɪ] ADV enérgicamente, vigorosamente, tenazmente; **to try ~ to** + *infin* procurar por todos los medios + *infin*.

streptococcus [ˌstreptəʊ'kɒkəs] N, PL **streptococci** [ˌstreptəʊ'kɒkaɪ] estreptococo *m*.

streptomycin [ˌstreptəʊ'maɪsɪn] N estreptomicina *f*.

stress [stres] **1** N (**a**) (*constraining force*) fuerza *f*, compulsión *f*; presión *f*; **under ~ of** bajo la compulsión de, impulsado por.

(**b**) (*strain*) tensión *f*; (*Med*) estrés *m*, tensión *f* nerviosa; **the ~es and strains of modern life** las presiones y tensiones de la vida moderna; **times of ~** tiempos *mpl* difíciles; **to be under ~** sufrir una tensión nerviosa; **to subject sb to great ~** someter a uno a grandes tensiones.

(**c**) (*emphasis*) énfasis *m*; (*Ling*) acento *m* tónico; ~ **mark** tilde *m*; ~ **system** sistema *m* de acentos, acentuación *f*; **the ~ is on the second syllable** el acento tónico cae en la segunda sílaba, la segunda sílaba está acentuada; **to lay great ~ on sth** insistir mucho en algo, subrayar algo, recalcar la importancia de algo.

(**d**) (*Mech*) tensión *f*, carga *f*; esfuerzo *m*.

2 VT (**a**) (*Ling*) acentuar.

(**b**) (*emphasize*) subrayar, recalcar; poner el énfasis en; insistir en; llamar la atención sobre; **I must ~ that ...** tengo que subrayar que ...

stressed [strest] ADJ acentuado.

stressful ['stresfʊl] ADJ lleno de tensión (nerviosa); que produce tensión (nerviosa), estresante.

stretch [stretʃ] **1** N (**a**) (*act of ~ing*) extensión *f*; estirón *m*; **for hours at a ~** durante horas enteras; **3 days at a ~** 3 días seguidos; **he read the lot at one ~** los leyó todos de un tirón; **to be at full ~**, **to go at full ~** esforzarse al máximo, emplear todas sus fuerzas (físicas *etc*); **when the engine is at full ~** cuando el motor rinde su potencia máxima; **with arms at full ~** con los brazos completamente extendidos; **by a ~ of the imagination** con un esfuerzo de imaginación; **not by any ~ of the imagination** aun haciendo un gran esfuerzo de imaginación.

(**b**) (*amount of ~*) elasticidad *f*; ~ **fabric** tela *f* elástica.

(**c**) (*distance*) trecho *m*; extensión *f*; (*of road etc*) tramo *m*; (*scope*) alcance *m*; (*of time*) período *m*; **in that ~ of the river** en aquella parte del río; **a splendid ~ of countryside** un magnífico paisaje; **for a long ~ it runs between ...** una extensión considerable corre entre ...; **for a long ~ of time** durante mucho tiempo.

(**d**) (:) **a ~** una condena de un año de prisión; **a 5-year ~** una condena de 5 años; **he's doing a ~** está en chirona:.

2 VT (**a**) (*also* **to ~ out**) (*pull out*) extender, estirar, alargar; (*widen*) ensanchar, dilatar; *arm* extender; *hand etc* tender, alargar; (*spread on* *ground etc*) extender; **to ~ one's legs** estirar las piernas, (*after stiffness*) desentumecerse las piernas, (*fig*) dar un paseíto; **the blow ~ed him (out) cold on the floor** el golpe le tumbó sin sentido en el suelo.

(**b**) *money, resources* estirar, hacer llegar; **our resources are fully ~ed** nuestros recursos están empleados a tope.

(**c**) *meaning* forzar, violentar; **that's ~ing it too far** eso va demasiado lejos; **to ~ the rules for sb** ajustar las reglas a beneficio de uno; *V* **point.**

(**d**) *athlete, student etc* exigir el máximo esfuerzo a; **the course does not ~ the students enough** el curso no exige bastante esfuerzo a los estudiantes.

3 VI (*also* **to ~ out**) extenderse, estirarse, alargarse; ensancharse, dilatarse; (*after sleep etc*) desperezarse, estirar los brazos (*etc*), desentumecerse las piernas; **this cloth won't ~** esta tela no se estira, esta tela no da de sí; **will it ~?** (*ie reach*) ¿llega?; **how far will it ~?** ¿hasta dónde llega?; ¿hasta dónde se extiende?; **it ~es for miles along the river** se extiende varios kilómetros a lo largo del río.

4 VR: **to ~ o.s.** (**a**) (*after sleep etc*) estirarse, estirarse los brazos.

(**b**) (*make effort*) esforzarse al máximo; **he doesn't ~ himself** no se esfuerza bastante, no se exige bastante esfuerzo a sí mismo.

◆ **stretch out** VT = **stretch 2** (**a**).

2 VI: **he ~ed out on the ground** se tendió en el suelo; **to ~ out to reach sth** alargar el brazo (*etc*) para tomar algo; *V also* **stretch 3.**

◆ **stretch up** VI: **to ~ up to reach sth** alargar el brazo (*etc*) para tomar algo.

stretcher ['stretʃəʳ] **1** N (*Tech*) (*for gloves etc*) ensanchador *m*; (*for canvas*) bastidor *m*; (*Archit*) soga *f*; (*Med*) camilla *f*.

2 VT: **to ~ sb away** (*or* **off**) llevar a uno en camilla.

stretcher-bearer ['stretʃə,beərəʳ] N camillero *m*.

stretcher-case ['stretʃəkeɪs] N enfermo *m*, -a *f* (*or* herido *m*, -a *f*) que tiene que ser llevado en camilla.

stretcher-party ['stretʃə,pɑːtɪ] N equipo *m* de camilleros.

stretch limo ['stretʃ,lɪməʊ] N limusina *f* larga.

stretchmark ['stretʃ,mɑːk] N estría *f*.

stretchy ['stretʃɪ] ADJ elástico.

strew [struː] (*irr*: PRET **strewed**, PTP **strewed** *or* **strewn**) VT (*scatter*) derramar, esparcir; (*cover*) cubrir, sembrar (*with* de); **to ~ one's belongings about the room** dejar sus cosas en desorden por todo el cuarto; **there were fragments ~n about everywhere** había fragmentos desparramados por todas partes; **to ~ sand on the floor** cubrir el suelo de arena, esparcir arena sobre el suelo; **the floors are ~n with rushes** los suelos están cubiertos de juncos.

strewth* [struːθ] EXCL (*Brit, Austral*) ¡por Dios!, ¡Dios santo!, ¡Virgen Santa!

striated [straɪ'eɪtɪd] ADJ estriado.

stricken ['strɪkən] ADJ (*and in some senses ptp of* **strike**) (*wounded*) herido; (*doomed*) condenado; (*suffering*) afligido; (*damaged*) destrozado; (*ill*) enfermo; **the ~ city** la ciudad condenada, la ciudad destrozada; **the ~ families** las familias afligidas; **to be ~ with** estar afligido por; **to be ~ with grief** estar agobiado por el dolor; **she was ~ with remorse** le remordió la conciencia.

-stricken ['strɪkən] ADJ *ending in compounds*: **drought~** aquejado de sequía, afectado por la sequía.

strict [strɪkt] ADJ (**a**) (*precise*) estricto; exacto, preciso; riguroso; **in the ~ sense of the word** en el sentido estricto de la palabra; **we need ~ accuracy here** aquí es necesario emplear la más rigurosa exactitud; **~ liability** (*Jur*) responsabilidad *f* absoluta; **~ neutrality** neutralidad *f* rigurosa; **in ~ confidence** en la más absoluta confianza (*and V* **confidence**).

(**b**) (*severe, stern*) *order, ban etc* terminante; *discipline* severo, riguroso; *person* severo, riguroso; escrupuloso; **they're terribly ~ here** aquí son terriblemente rigurosos; **to be ~ with sb** ser severo con uno, tratar a uno con severidad.

strictly ['strɪktlɪ] ADV (*V adj*) (**a**) estrictamente; exactamente; rigurosamente; **~ confidential** estrictamente confidencial; **'~ private'** (*notice*) 'propiedad privada', 'prohibido el paso'; **~ speaking** en rigor, **not ~ true** no del todo verdad; **~ between ourselves ...** en confianza entre los dos ...; **to be ~ accurate ...** para decirlo con toda precisión ...; **to remain ~ neutral** guardar la más rigurosa neutralidad.

(**b**) terminantemente; severamente; rigurosamente; **to treat sb very ~** tratar a uno con mucha severidad; **she was ~ brought up** se la educó estrictamente; **it is ~ forbidden to** + *infin* queda terminantemente prohibido + *infin.*

strictness ['strɪktnɪs] N (*V adj*) (**a**) exactitud *f*; rigor *m*. (**b**) severidad *f*; lo terminante.

stricture ['strɪktʃəʳ] N (**a**) (*Med*) constricción *f*. (**b**) (*fig*) censura *f*, crítica *f*, reparo *m*; **to pass ~s on sb** censurar a uno, poner reparos a uno.

stridden ['strɪdn] PTP *of* **stride.**

stride [straɪd] **1** N zancada *f*, tranco *m*, paso *m* largo; (*in measuring*) paso *m*; **he set off with big ~s** partió a grandes zancadas; **to get**

into one's ~, **to hit one's ~** (*US*) alcanzar el ritmo acostumbrado, cogerle el tranquillo a la tarea; **to make great ~s** hacer grandes progresos; **to take it in one's ~** sabérselo tomar bien, hacerlo sin cejar, estar a la altura de las circunstancias.

2 (*irr*: PRET **strode**, PTP **stridden**) VT *horse* montar a horcajadas; poner una pierna a cada lado de; (*cross*) cruzar de un tranco.

3 VI (*also* **to ~ along**) andar a trancos, andar a pasos largos, dar zancadas.

◆ **stride away, stride off** VI alejarse a grandes zancadas.

◆ **stride up** VI: **to ~ up and down** andar de aquí para allá a pasos largos; **to ~ up to sb** acercarse resueltamente a uno.

stridency ['straɪdənsɪ] N estridencia *f*, estridor *m*; lo chillón; lo estrepitoso.

strident ['straɪdənt] ADJ estridente; *colour, person* chillón; *protest* fuerte, estrepitoso.

stridently ['straɪdəntlɪ] ADV ruidosamente, de modo estridente; estrepitosamente.

strife [straɪf] N lucha *f*; (*not armed*) lucha *f*, contienda *f*; disensión *f*; **domestic ~** riñas *fpl* domésticas; **internal ~** disensión *f* interna; **to cease from ~** deponer las armas.

strife-ridden ['straɪf,rɪdn] ADJ conflictivo.

strike [straɪk] **1** N (**a**) (*of labour*) huelga *f*, paro *m* (*esp LAm*); **to be on ~** estar en huelga; **to come out on ~**, **to go on ~** ponerse en huelga, declarar la huelga.

(**b**) (*discovery*) descubrimiento *m* (*repentino*); **a big oil ~** un descubrimiento de petróleo en gran cantidad; **to make a ~** hacer un descubrimiento.

(**c**) (*Sport*) golpe *m*.

(**d**) (*Mil*) ataque *m*; **air ~** ataque *m* aéreo, bombardeo *m*.

2 ATTR: **~ ballot**, **~ vote** votación *f* a huelga; **~ committee** comité *m* de huelga; **~ force** fuerza *f* de asalto; fuerza *f* expedicionaria.

3 (*irr*: PRET **struck**, PTP **struck** *and in some senses* **stricken**) VT (**a**) (*hit*) golpear; (*with fist etc*) pegar, dar una bofetada a; (*wound*) herir; (*Tech*) percutir; (*with bullet etc*) alcanzar; *ball* golpear; *blow* asestar (*at* a); *chord, note* tocar; *instrument* herir, pulsar; tocar; **never ~ a woman** no pegar nunca a una mujer; **he struck her** (**a blow**) la pegó, le dio un golpe; **to ~ one's fist on the table**, **to ~ the table with one's fist** golpear la mesa con el puño; **the president was struck by two bullets** el presidente fue alcanzado por dos balas; **the tower was struck by lightning** cayó un rayo en la torre; **a fisherman was struck by lightning** un pescador fue alcanzado por un rayo; **the light ~s the window** la luz hiere la ventana.

(**b**) (*produce, make*) *coin, medal* acuñar; *a light, match* frotar, encender; **to ~ sparks from sth** hacer que algo eche chispas; **to ~ a cutting** hacer que un esqueje arranque; **to ~ root** echar raíces, arraigar; **to ~ terror into sb** infundir terror a uno.

(**c**) (*collide with, meet*) dar con; *rocks etc* chocar contra, estrellarse contra; *mine* chocar con; *difficulty, obstacle* encontrar, topar con; **a sound struck my ear** un ruido hirió mi oído; **what ~s the eye is the poverty** lo que más llama la atención es la pobreza; **his head struck the beam** dio con la cabeza contra la viga.

(**d**) (*of thoughts, impressions*) **it ~s me that ...**, **the thought ~s me that ...** se me ocurre que ...; **has it ever struck you that ...?** ¿has pensado alguna vez que ...?; **it ~s me as being most unlikely** se me hace muy poco probable; **at least that's how it ~s me** por lo menos eso es lo que pienso yo; **how does she ~ you?** ¿qué te parece (ella)?, ¿qué impresión te hace ella?; **I was much struck by his sincerity** su sinceridad me impresionó mucho; **I'm not much struck (with him)** no me hace buena impresión.

(**e**) (*find*) descubrir, encontrar; **to ~ oil** descubrir un yacimiento de petróleo, (*fig*) encontrar una mina; **he struck it rich** descubrió un buen filón, tuvo mucha suerte.

(**f**) (*take down*) **to ~ camp** levantar el campamento; **to ~ the flag** arriar la bandera.

(**g**) **to ~ work** abandonar el trabajo, declarar la huelga.

(**h**) *attitude* tomar, adoptar.

(**i**) (*arrive at, attain*) **to ~ an average** sacar el promedio; **to ~ a balance** (*Comm*) hacer balance, (*fig*) establecer un equilibrio (*between* entre); **to ~ a bargain** cerrar un trato; **to ~ a deal** llegar a un acuerdo, (*Comm*) cerrar un trato.

(**j**) (*delete*) borrar, tachar.

(**k**) (*cause to become*) **to ~ sb blind** cegar a uno; **to ~ sb dead** matar a uno; **may I be struck dead if ...** que me maten si ...; **to ~ sb dumb** (*fig*) dejar a uno sin habla.

4 VI (**a**) (*attack, Mil etc*) atacar; (*snake etc*) morder, atacar; **now is the time to ~** éste es el momento para atacar; **to ~ against sth** dar con algo, dar contra algo, chocar contra algo; **to ~ at sb** asestar un golpe a uno, tratar de golpear a uno; acometer a uno; (*Mil*) atacar a uno; **this ~s at our very existence** esto amenaza nuestra misma existencia; **when panic ~s** cuando cunde el pánico, cuando se extiende el pánico.

(**b**) (*clock*) dar la hora; **the clock has struck** ha dado la hora ya;

when one's hour ~s cuando llega la hora de uno.
(c) (*labour*) abandonar el trabajo, declarar la huelga; estar en huelga, huelguear (*And*); **to ~ for higher wages** hacer una huelga para conseguir un aumento de los sueldos.
(d) (*match*) encenderse.
(e) (*Naut: run aground*) encallar; tocar el fondo, dar contra las rocas.
(f) (*esp Naut: surrender*) arriar la bandera.
(g) (*Bot*) echar raíces, arraigar.
(h) (*move, go*) **to ~ across country** ir a campo traviesa; **to ~ into the woods** ir por el bosque, penetrar en el bosque; **the sun ~s through the mist** el sol penetra por entre la niebla.
(i) **to ~ (it) lucky** tener suerte, estar de suerte.
◆**strike back** VI devolver el golpe (*at* a); tomar represalias (*at* contra).
◆**strike down** VT derribar; (*kill*) matar; **he was struck down by paralysis** tuvo una parálisis, le acometió una parálisis; **he was struck down in his prime** se le llevó la muerte en la flor de la vida.
◆**strike off** ① VT **(a)** (*cut off*) cortar; cercenar, quitar de golpe; (*from list*) borrar, tachar.
(b) (*deduct*) rebajar.
(c) (*Typ*) tirar, imprimir.
② VI: **the road ~s off to the right** el camino tuerce a la derecha.
◆**strike on** VT: **to ~ on an idea** ocurrírsele a uno una idea.
◆**strike out** ① VT borrar, tachar.
② VI **(a)** empezar a repartir golpes; **to ~ out wildly** dar golpes sin mirar a quien.
(b) (*set off*) **to ~ out for the shore** (empezar a) nadar (resueltamente) hacia la playa; **to ~ out for o.s., to ~ out on one's own** hacerse independiente, hacer rancho aparte, obrar por cuenta propia.
◆**strike through** ① VT tachar.
② VI penetrar, pasar por.
◆**strike up** ① VT *music* iniciar, empezar a tocar; *conversation* entablar; *friendship* trabar.
② VI: **the orchestra struck up** la orquesta empezó a tocar.
◆**strike upon** VT = **strike on.**
strike-bound ['straɪkbaʊnd] ADJ paralizado por la huelga.
strikebreaker ['straɪk,breɪkər] N esquirol *m*.
strike fund ['straɪkfʌnd] N fondo *m* de huelga.
strike pay ['straɪkpeɪ] N subsidio *m* de huelga.
striker ['straɪkər] N **(a)** (*worker*) huelguista *mf*. **(b)** (*Sport*) ariete *m*.
striking ['straɪkɪŋ] ADJ **(a)** notable, impresionante; chocante, sorprendente; *contrast etc* acusado; *colour etc* llamativo; **of ~ appearance** de aspecto impresionante; **a ~ woman** una mujer imponente; **it is ~ that ...** es chocante que ... **(b)** **the ~ workers** los obreros que están de huelga.
strikingly ['straɪkɪŋlɪ] ADV notablemente; de modo sorprendente; **a ~ beautiful woman** una mujer de notable hermosura, una mujer extraordinariamente hermosa.
Strimmer ['strɪmər] ® N cortacéspedes *m invar* (*especial para los bordes*).
string [strɪŋ] ① N **(a)** (*cord*) cuerda *f*, mecate *m* (*Carib, Mex*); (*thin*) cordel *m*, bramante *m*; guita *f*; (*of beads*) hilo *m*, sarta *f*, collar *m*; (*of onions, garlic*) ristra *f*; (*of horses etc*) reata *f*; (*of lies*) sarta *f*; (*of curses*) serie *f*, retahíla *f*; (*row*) fila *f*, hilera *f*; (*of people*) hilera *f*, desfile *m*; (*of vehicles*) caravana *f*; **a whole ~ of errors** toda una serie de errores; **to have sb on a ~** dominar a uno completamente, tener a uno en un puño; **to have two ~s to one's bow** tener dos cuerdas en su arco; **to pull ~s** tocar resortes, mover palancas.
(b) (*Mus*) cuerda *f*; **~s** instrumentos *mpl* de cuerda.
(c) (*Bot*) fibra *f*, nervio *m*.
(d) (*fig*) condición *f*; **without ~s** sin condiciones; **there are no ~s attached** esto es sin compromiso alguno.
(e) (*Comput*) cadena *f*.
② ATTR: **~ bag** bolsa *f* de red; **~ beans** habichuelas *fpl*, judías *fpl* verdes, ejotes *mpl* (*Mex*), porotos *mpl* verdes (*SC*); **~ instrument** instrumento *m* de cuerda; **~ orchestra** orquesta *f* de cuerdas; **~ quartet** cuarteto *m* de cuerdas.
③ (*irr: PRET AND PTP* **strung**) VT **(a)** *pearls etc* (*also* **to ~ together**) ensartar; *bow, violin* encordar; **to ~ sentences together** ir ensartando frases; **they are just stray thoughts strung together** son pensamientos aislados que se han ensartado sin propósito*.
(b) *beans etc* desfibrar.
◆**string along*** ① VT: **to ~ sb along** embaucar a uno.
② VI ir también; venir también; **to ~ along with sb** pegarse a uno, acompañar a uno.
◆**string out** VT espaciar, escalonar; extender; **the posts are strung out across the desert** hay una serie de puestos aislados a través del desierto; **the convoy is strung out along the road** la caravana se extiende por la carretera; **his plays are strung out over 40 years** aparecieron sus obras a intervalos durante 40 años.
◆**string up** ① VT **(a)** *onions etc* colgar (con cuerda); *nets* extender; (*) *victim* ahorcar, linchar. **(b) to be all strung up** estar muy tenso, estar

muy nervioso.
② VR: **to ~ o.s. up to do sth** resolverse a hacer algo, cobrar ánimo para hacer algo.
stringed [strɪŋd] ADJ *instrument* de cuerda(s); **4-~** de 4 cuerdas.
stringency ['strɪndʒənsɪ] N (*V adj*) **(a)** rigor *m*, severidad *f*. **(b)** tirantez *f*, dificultad *f*; **economic ~** situación *f* económica apurada, estrechez *f*.
stringent ['strɪndʒənt] ADJ **(a)** riguroso, severo; **~ rules** reglas *fpl* rigurosas; **we shall have to be ~ about it** tendremos que obrar con rigor.
(b) (*Comm etc*) tirante, difícil.
stringently ['strɪndʒəntlɪ] ADV severamente, rigurosamente.
stringer ['strɪŋər] N (*journalist*) corresponsal *mf* local.
string-pulling ['strɪŋ,pʊlɪŋ] N enchufismo* *m*.
string vest [,strɪŋ'vest] N camiseta *f* de malla.
stringy ['strɪŋɪ] ADJ fibroso, lleno de fibras.
strip [strɪp] ① N **(a)** tira *f*; banda *f*, faja *f*; (*of land*) zona *f*, franja *f*; (*of metal*) cinta *f*, lámina *f*; (*cartoon*) tira *f*; (*Aer. landing ~*) pista *f*; **to tear sb off a ~*, to tear a ~ off sb*** poner a uno como un trapo*.
(b) (*Brit Sport*) camiseta *f*; colores *mpl*.
(c) (*) acto *m* de desnudarse, despelote* *m*; **~ club, ~ joint** (*US*), **~ show** (show *m* de) estriptise *f*, espectáculo *m* de desnudo; **to do a ~** desnudarse, despelotarse*.
② VT **(a)** (*denude*) desnudar, quitar la ropa (*etc*) a; **to ~ sb naked** desnudar a uno completamente, dejar a uno en cueros; **to ~ sb of sth** despojar a uno de algo; **to ~ a house of its furniture** dejar una casa sin muebles; **to ~ a company of its assets** despojar a una empresa de su activo; **~ped of all the verbiage, this means ...** sin toda la palabrería, esto quiere decir ...; **to ~ sb to the skin** dejar a uno en cueros.
(b) (*Tech: also* **to ~ down**) desmontar, desmantelar; *gears* estropear.
③ VI desnudarse, quitarse la ropa; **to ~ to the skin** quitarse toda la ropa; **to ~ to the waist** desnudarse hasta la cintura.
◆**strip down** VT = **strip 2 (b).**
◆**strip off** ① VT *paint etc* quitar; (*violently*) arrancar; **to ~ off one's clothes** quitarse (rápidamente) la ropa, despojarse de la ropa; **the wind ~ped the leaves off the trees** el viento arrancó las hojas de los árboles.
② VI desnudarse; (*paint etc*) desprenderse; separarse.
strip cartoon ['strɪpkɑ:'tu:n] N (*Brit*) historieta *f*, tira *f* cómica, banda *f* de dibujos.
stripe [straɪp] ① N raya *f*, lista *f*, banda *f*; (*Mil*) galón *m*; (*lash*) azote *m*, (*weal*) cardenal *m*; **of the worst ~** de la peor calaña.
② VT rayar, listar (*with* de).
striped [straɪpt] ADJ listado, rayado; *trousers etc* a rayas.
strip light ['strɪplaɪt] N tubo *m* fluorescente.
strip lighting ['strɪp,laɪtɪŋ] N (*Brit*) alumbrado *m* fluorescente, alumbrado *m* de tubos.
stripling ['strɪplɪŋ] N mozuelo *m*, joven *m* imberbe.
strip mine ['strɪpmaɪn] N (*esp US*) mina *f* a cielo abierto.
strip mining ['strɪpmaɪnɪŋ] N (*esp US*) minería *f* a cielo abierto.
stripped pine ['strɪpt'paɪn] N pino *m* natural, pino *m* desnudo
stripper* ['strɪpər] N estriptista* *mf*.
strip poker [,strɪp'pəʊkər] N strip poker *m*.
strip-search ['strɪpsɜ:tʃ] ① N (*also* **~ing**) registro *m* en el que la persona se ha de desnudar.
② VT: **he was ~ed at the airport** se tuvo que desnudar para ser registrado en el aeropuerto.
striptease ['strɪpti:z] N estriptise *f*, striptease *m*.
strip-wash ['strɪpwɒʃ] ① N lavado *m* por completo (de un inválido).
② VT lavar por completo (a un inválido).
stripy ['straɪpɪ] ADJ listado, rayado.
strive [straɪv] (*irr: PRET* **strove**, *PTP* **striven**) VI esforzarse, afanarse, luchar; **to ~ after sth, to ~ for sth** luchar por conseguir algo, afanarse por conseguir algo; **to ~ against sth** luchar contra algo; **to ~ to do sth** esforzarse por hacer algo, luchar por hacer algo.
striven ['strɪvn] PTP of **strive.**
striving ['straɪvɪŋ] N esfuerzos *mpl*, el esforzarse.
strobe [strəʊb] ① N *lights* estroboscópico.
② N **(a)** (*also* **~ light, ~ lighting**) luces *fpl* estroboscópicas. **(b)** = **stroboscope.**
stroboscope ['strəʊbəskəʊp] N estroboscopio *m*.
strode [strəʊd] PRET of **stride.**
stroke [strəʊk] ① N **(a)** (*blow*) golpe *m*; **10 ~s of the lash** 10 azotes; **~ of lightning** rayo *m*; **at a ~, at one ~** de un golpe; **with one ~ of his knife** de un solo cuchillazo; **with one fell ~** de un solo golpe fatal.
(b) (*Sport etc: Cricket, Golf*) golpe *m*; jugada *f*; (*Billiards*) tacada *f*; (*Rowing*) remada *f*, golpe *m*; (*Swimming: movement*) brazada *f*, (*type of ~*) estilo *m*; **with a total of 281 ~s** con un total de 281 golpes; **good ~!** ¡muy bien!; **he went ahead at every ~** se adelantaba con cada brazada; **they are rowing a fast ~** reman a ritmo rápido; **to**

put sb off his ~ hacer que uno falle con su golpe; **he hasn't done a ~ of work** no ha hecho absolutamente nada; **he doesn't do a ~** no da golpe; **~ of diplomacy** éxito *m* diplomático; **~ of genius** rasgo *m* de ingenio, genialidad *f*; **the idea was a ~ of genius** la idea ha sido genial; **~ of luck** racha *f* de suerte; **by a ~ of luck** por suerte; **then we had a ~ of luck** luego nos favoreció la suerte; **a good ~ of business** un buen negocio; **his greatest ~ was to ...** su golpe maestro fue ...

(c) (*of bell, clock*) campanada *f*; **on the ~ of 12** al acabar de dar las 12, a las 12 en punto; **to arrive on the ~** (*of time*) llegar a la hora justa.

(d) (*of piston*) carrera *f*; **two-~ engine** motor *m* de dos tiempos.

(e) (*Med*) ataque *m* fulminante, apoplejía *f*; **to have a ~** tener una apoplejía; *V* **heatstroke.**

(f) (*of pen*) trazo *m*; rasgo *m*, plumada *f*, plumazo *m*; (*of pencil*) trazo *m*; (*of brush*) pincelada *f*; (*Typ*) barra *f* oblicua; **at a ~ of the pen, with one ~ of the pen** de un plumazo; **with a thick ~ of the pen** con un trazo grueso de la pluma.

(g) (*Rowing: person*) primer remero *m*; **to row ~** ser el primer remero, remar en el primer puesto.

(h) (*caress*) caricia *f*; **she gave the cat a ~** acarició el gato; **with a light ~ of the hand** con un suave movimiento de la mano; con una leve caricia.

2 VT **(a)** (*caress*) acariciar; frotar suavemente; *chin* pasar la mano sobre, pasar la mano por.

(b) to ~ a boat ser el primero remero; **to ~ a boat to victory** ser el primero remero del bote vencedor.

stroll [strəʊl] **1** N paseo *m*, vuelta *f*; **to go for a ~, to have a ~, to take a ~** dar un paseo (*o* una vuelta).

2 VI pasear(se), dar un paseo, deambular, callejear; **to ~ up and down** pasearse de acá para allá; **to ~ up to sb** acercarse tranquilamente a uno.

stroller ['strəʊlə'] N paseante *mf*; (*US*) cochecito *m*, sillita *f* de ruedas.

strong [strɒŋ] **1** ADJ fuerte; recio, robusto; enérgico, vigoroso; sólido; (*Fin*) firme; *accent* marcado; *believer* fervoroso; *candidate* que tiene buenas posibilidades, respetable; *characteristic* acusado; *coffee* fuerte, cargado; *colour* intenso; *constitution* robusto; *conviction* profundo, sincero; *drink* fuerte, alcohólico; *emotion* fuerte, intenso; *evidence* fehaciente; *feature* acusado; *flavour* fuerte; *language* fuerte, indecente; *measure* enérgico; *personality* enérgico, fuerte; *point* (*of argument*) fuerte; *protest* enérgico; *reason* convincente; *situation* dramático, lleno de emoción; *smell* fuerte, penetrante, punzante; *solution* concentrado; *suit* (*Cards*) largo; *supporter* acérrimo; *tea* fuerte, cargado; *terms* enfáticos; *verb* irregular; *voice* fuerte; *wind* fuerte, recio, violento; **to be as ~ as a horse** ser tan fuerte como un toro; **to be ~ in the arm** tener los brazos fuertes; **to be ~ in** (*or* **on**) **chemistry** estar fuerte en química; **we are ~ in forwards** tenemos una buena línea delantera; **the gallery is ~ in Goya** el museo es rico en obras de Goya; **he's getting ~er every day** se va reponiendo poco a poco; **when you are ~ again** cuando te hayas repuesto del todo; **a group 20 ~** un grupo de 20 (miembros *etc*); **they were 50 ~** eran 50, contaban 50.

2 ADV: **the market closed ~** el mercado se cerró en situación firme; **to come on ~*** mostrarse demasiado severo; reaccionar demasiado; **she was coming on ~*** se veía que ella se sentía atraída por él (*etc*); **the firm is still going ~** la empresa todavía marcha bien; **she was still going ~ at 92** se encontraba todavía en forma a los 92 años; **he was still going ~ at the tape** al llegar a la cinta corría todavía con pleno vigor; **he pitches it pretty ~** exagera mucho, es un exagerado.

strong-arm ['strɒŋɑ:m] ADJ *policy, methods* de mano dura.

strong-armed ['strɒŋ'ɑ:md] ADJ de brazos fuertes.

strongbox ['strɒŋbɒks] N caja *f* de caudales, caja *f* fuerte.

stronghold ['strɒŋhəʊld] N fortaleza *f*, plaza *f* fuerte; (*fig*) baluarte *m*, centro *m*; **the last ~ of ...** el último reducto de ...

strongly ['strɒŋlɪ] ADV fuertemente, enérgicamente, vigorosamente; firmemente; fervorosamente; intensamente; **I ~ believe that ...** creo firmemente que ...; **he smelled ~ of beer** despedía fuerte olor a cerveza; **~ built** sólidamente construido, de construcción sólida; **~ marked** acusado, acentuado; **a ~ worded letter** una carta de tono enérgico.

strongman ['strɒŋmæn] N, PL **strongmen** ['strɒŋmen] (*Circus*) forzudo *m*, hércules *m*; (*Pol etc*) hombre *m* fuerte.

strong-minded ['strɒŋ'maɪndɪd] ADJ resuelto, decidido; de carácter.

strong-mindedly [,strɒŋ'maɪndɪdlɪ] ADV resueltamente.

strong-mindedness ['strɒŋ'maɪndɪdnɪs] N resolución *f*; carácter *m*.

strongpoint ['strɒŋpɔɪnt] N fuerte *m*, puesto *m* fortificado.

strongroom ['strɒŋrʊm] N cámara *f* acorazada.

strong-willed ['strɒŋ'wɪld] ADJ resuelto, de voluntad firme; (*pej*) obstinado.

strontium ['strɒntɪəm] N estroncio *m*; **~ 90** estroncio *m* 90.

strop [strɒp] **1** N suavizador *m*.

2 VT suavizar.

strophe ['strəʊfɪ] N estrofa *f*.

stroppy* ['strɒpɪ] ADJ: **to get ~** (*Brit*) cabrearse*, ponerse negro*, ponerse chulo*.

strove [strəʊv] PRET of **strive.**

struck [strʌk] PRET AND PTP of **strike.**

structural ['strʌktʃərəl] ADJ estructural.

structuralism ['strʌktʃərəlɪzəm] N estructuralismo *m*.

structuralist ['strʌktʃərəlɪst] **1** ADJ estructuralista.

2 N estructuralista *mf*.

structurally ['strʌktʃərəlɪ] ADV estructuralmente, desde el punto de vista de la estructura; **~ sound** de estructura sólida.

structure ['strʌktʃə'] **1** N estructura *f*; construcción *f*.

2 VT estructurar.

structured ['strʌktʃəd] ADJ estructurado; **~ activity** actividad *f* estructurada.

struggle ['strʌgl] **1** N lucha *f*; contienda *f*, conflicto *m*; (*effort*) esfuerzo *m*; **without a ~** sin luchar, (*bloodlessly*) sin efusión de sangre; **the ~ for survival** la lucha por la vida; **the ~ to find a flat** la lucha por encontrarse un piso.

2 VI luchar; esforzarse; bregar, forcejear, debatirse; **to ~ to do sth** luchar por hacer algo, esforzarse por hacer algo; **to ~ in vain** luchar en vano; **to ~ to one's feet** levantarse con esfuerzo; **he ~d up the rock** subió penosamente por la roca; **the light tries to ~ through the panes** la luz se esfuerza por penetrar por los cristales; **we ~d through the crowd** nos abrimos camino bregando por la multitud.

◆**struggle along** VI (*lit*) avanzar con dificultad, avanzar penosamente; (*fig: financially*) ir apurado.

◆**struggle back** VI (*return*) volver penosamente; **to ~ back to solvency** esforzarse por volver a ser solvente.

◆**struggle on** VI seguir luchando; seguir resistiendo; no cejar; **we ~d on another kilometre** avanzamos con dificultad un kilómetro más.

struggling ['strʌglɪŋ] ADJ *artist etc* poco reconocido; **a ~ novelist** un novelista que lucha por abrirse camino.

strum [strʌm] **1** VT *guitar etc* rasguear; tocar distraídamente.

2 VI cencerrear.

strumpet ['strʌmpɪt] N ramera *f*.

strung [strʌŋ] PRET AND PTP of **string;** *V* **highly.**

strut¹ [strʌt] VI (*also* **to ~ about, to ~ along**) pavonearse, contonearse; **to ~ into a room** entrar pavoneándose en un cuarto; **to ~ past sb** pasar delante de uno con paso majestuoso.

strut² [strʌt] N puntal *m*, riostra *f*, tornapunta *f*.

strychnine ['strɪkni:n] N estricnina *f*.

Stuart ['stjuːət] NM Estuardo.

stub [stʌb] **1** N (*of tree*) tocón *m*; (*of cigarette*) colilla *f*; (*of candle, pencil etc*) cabo *m*; (*of cheque, receipt*) resguardo *m*, talón *m*.

2 VT: **to ~ one's toe** dar con el dedo del pie contra algo, dar un tropezón.

◆**stub out** VT *cigarette* apagar.

◆**stub up** VT *tree trunks* desarraigar, quitar, arrancar.

stubble ['stʌbl] N rastrojo *m*; (*on chin*) barba *f* de tres días.

stubblefield ['stʌblfi:ld] N rastrojera *f*.

stubbly ['stʌblɪ] ADJ *chin* cerdoso, con barba de tres días; *beard* de tres días.

stubborn ['stʌbən] ADJ tenaz; *refusal* resuelto; inquebrantable; (*pej*) terco, testarudo, porfiado; **as ~ as a mule** terco como una mula.

stubbornly ['stʌbənlɪ] ADV tenazmente; tercamente, con porfía; **he ~ refused to + infin** se negó resueltamente a + infin.

stubbornness ['stʌbənnɪs] N tenacidad *f*; terquedad *f*, testarudez *f*, porfía *f*.

stubby ['stʌbɪ] ADJ achaparrado.

STUC N ABBR of **Scottish Trades Union Congress.**

stucco ['stʌkəʊ] **1** N estuco *m*.

2 ADJ de estuco.

3 VT estucar.

stuck [stʌk] PRET AND PTP of **stick.**

stuck-up* ['stʌk'ʌp] ADJ engreído, presumido; **to be very ~ about sth** presumir mucho a causa de algo.

stud¹ [stʌd] **1** N (*boot ~*) taco *m*; (*decorative*) tachón *m*, clavo *m* (de adorno); (*collar ~, shirt ~*) botón *m* (de camisa).

2 VT tachonar; adornar con clavos; (*fig*) sembrar (*with* de).

stud² [stʌd] N **(a)** (*~ farm*) caballeriza *f*, yeguada *f*. **(b)** (‡: *man*) semental‡ *m*.

studbook ['stʌdbʊk] N registro *m* genealógico de caballos.

student ['stjuːdənt] **1** N (*pupil*) alumno *m*, -a *f*; (*Univ*) estudiante *mf*; (*researcher*) investigador *m*, -ora *f*; **French ~** (*by nationality*) estudiante *m* francés, estudiante *f* francesa, (*by subject*) estudiante *mf* de francés; **old ~s' association** asociación *f* de ex alumnos.

2 ATTR estudiantil; **~ body** alumnado *m*; **~ driver** (*US*) aprendiz *m* de conductor, aprendiza *f* de conductora; **~ grant** beca *f*; **~ nurse** estudiante *mf* de enfermera (*or* de A.T.S.); **~ teacher** (*secondary*) profesor *m*, -a *f* en prácticas; (*primary*) maestro *m*, -a *f* en prácticas; **~ union** (*club*) club *m* de estudiantes universitarios; (*trade union*) sindicato *m* estudiantil.

studentship ['stjuːdəntʃip] N beca f.
stud farm ['stʌdfɑːm] N caballeriza f, yeguada f.
studhorse ['stʌdhɔːs] N caballo m padre.
studied ['stʌdɪd] ADJ calm etc calculado, deliberado, estudiado; insult premeditado; pose, style afectado.
studio ['stjuːdɪəʊ] **1** N (in most senses) estudio m; (sculptor's) taller m.
2 ATTR: **~ apartment, ~ flat** estudio m; **~ audience** público m de estudio; **~ couch** sofá-cama m; **~ director** director m, -ora f de interiores.
studious ['stjuːdɪəs] ADJ person estudioso; aplicado, asiduo; effort asiduo; politeness calculado, esmerado.
studiously ['stjuːdɪəslɪ] ADV con aplicación; **he ~ avoided mentioning the matter** evitó cuidadosamente aludir al asunto, se guardó de aludir al asunto.
studiousness ['stjuːdɪəsnɪs] N aplicación f.
stud mare ['stʌd,meəʳ] N yegua f de cría.
study ['stʌdɪ] **1** N (a) (in most senses) estudio m; **to be in a brown ~** estar absorto en la meditación, estar en Babia; **to make a ~ of sth** estudiar algo, investigar algo; **my studies show that ...** mis estudios demuestran que ...
(b) (room) despacho m, cuarto m de trabajo, estudio m.
2 VT estudiar; investigar; examinar, mirar detenidamente; escudriñar.
3 VI estudiar; **to ~ under sb** estudiar con uno, trabajar bajo la dirección de uno; **to ~ for an exam** prepararse para un examen; **to ~ to be an agronomist** estudiar para agrónomo.
study-group ['stʌdɪ'gruːp] N grupo m de estudio.
study-tour ['stʌdɪ,tʊəʳ] N viaje m de estudio.
stuff [stʌf] **1** N (a) (material in general) materia f; material m, sustancia f; **it's strange ~** es una sustancia singular; **there is some good ~ in that book** ese libro tiene cosas buenas; **there's good ~ in him** tiene buenas cualidades; **it's poor ~** no vale para nada; **do you call this ~ beer?** ¿llamas a esto cerveza?; **I can't read his ~** no alcanzo a leer sus libros; **I can't listen to his ~** no aguanto su música; **that's the ~!** ¡muy bien!; **have you brought the ~?** ¿lo has traído?, ¿has traído aquello?; **argument is the very ~ of politics** la discusión es la misma esencia de la política; **he is of the ~ that heroes are made of** tiene madera de héroe; **show him what ~ you are made of** demuéstrale tus cualidades, muéstrale si puedes o no.
(b) (material, cloth) tela f, paño m.
(c) (*: possessions) cosas fpl, chismes mpl; **he leaves his ~ scattered about** deja sus cosas de cualquier modo; **is this your ~?** ¿es tuyo esto?
(d) (*: nonsense) tonterías fpl; **all that ~ about Cervantes** todas esas tonterías acerca de Cervantes; **~ and nonsense!** ¡ni hablar!, ¡narices!*
(e) (*) hot **~*** cosa f maravillosa, persona f estupenda*; **she's hot ~** es cachonda, es de plan*; **he's hot ~ at chess** es un hacha para el ajedrez*.
(f) (*) **to do one's ~** actuar, trabajar etc; **do your ~!** ¡vamos!, ¡a ello!; **you do your ~ next** tú eres el próximo; **he doesn't do his ~** no trabaja (etc) como debiera; **he certainly knows his ~** conoce perfectamente su oficio, domina su especialidad.
(g) (US Drugs‡) polvo* m, droga f, chocolate‡ m.
2 VT (a) (fill) container llenar, hinchar, atiborrar (with de); (stow) contents meter sin orden, meter de prisa (into en); hole, leak etc tapar, atascar; (Culin) rellenar; animal (for exhibition) disecar; **he ~ed it into his pocket** lo metió de prisa en el bolsillo; **can we ~ any more in?** ¿cabe más?; **her head is ~ed with formulae** tiene la cabeza atiborrada de fórmulas; **two centuries ~ed with history** dos siglos prietos (or llenos) de historia. (b) (‡‡) joder; **get ~ed!‡‡** ¡vete a la porra!*, ¡vete al carajo!‡‡; **~ the government!‡‡** ¡que se joda el gobierno!‡‡; **you can ~ that idea‡‡** al carajo con esa idea‡‡.
3 (*) VI atracarse, comer a dos carrillos.
4 VR: **to ~ o.s. with food** darse un atracón, atiborrarse de comida; **I have to ~ myself with sedatives** me veo obligado a embutirme de calmantes.
♦ **stuff away*** VT food zampar, devorar.
♦ **stuff up** VT: **to get ~ed up** (pipe etc) atascarse, quedar obstruido; **to be ~ed up with** (a) cold* estar fuertemente acatarrado.
stuffed [stʌft] ADJ animal disecado; **~ shirt** (fig) persona f estirada; **~ toy** (US) muñeco m de peluche.
stuffily ['stʌfɪlɪ] ADV say en tono de desaprobación, con desaprobación.
stuffiness ['stʌfɪnɪs] N (a) (in room) mala ventilación f, falta f de aire.
(b) (fig) estrechez f de miras; lo estirado, lo remilgado, pesadez f.
stuffing ['stʌfɪŋ] N (of furniture, animal) relleno m, borra f; (Culin) relleno m; **he's got no ~** no tiene carácter, no tiene agallas; **he had the ~ knocked out of him by the blow** el golpe le dejó sin fuerzas ni ánimo; **to knock the ~ out of sb** dar una paliza a uno.
stuffy ['stʌfɪ] ADJ (a) room mal ventilado, donde falta el aire; atmosphere cargado, sofocante; **it's ~ in here** aquí falta el aire, aquí huele a encerrado.
(b) (narrow-minded) de miras estrechas; (stiff) estirado; (prudish) remilgado; (boring) pesado, poco interesante.
stultify ['stʌltɪfaɪ] VT hacer inútil, quitar valor a, anular; hacer (parecer) ridículo.
stultifying ['stʌltɪfaɪɪŋ] ADJ que hace inútil, que hace ineficaz; agobiador, opresivo, sofocante.
stumble ['stʌmbl] **1** N tropezón m, traspié m.
2 VI tropezar, dar un traspié; **to ~ against** tropezar contra, tropezar con; **to ~ on, to go stumbling on** avanzar dando traspiés; **to ~ over** tropezar en; **to ~ through a speech** pronunciar un discurso de cualquier manera, pronunciar torpemente un discurso.
♦ **stumble across, stumble (up)on** VT tropezar con, encontrar por casualidad.
stumbling-block ['stʌmblɪŋblɒk] N (fig) tropiezo m, piedra f de tropiezo, obstáculo m.
stump [stʌmp] **1** N (a) cabo m, fragmento m, último pedazo m; (of tree etc) tocón m; (of limb) muñón m; (of tooth) raigón m; (Cricket) poste m, palo m; (Art) esfumino m; (*: leg) pierna f; **to stir one's ~s*** menearse, moverse.
(b) **to be** (or go) **on the ~** (US) hacer (una) campaña.
(c) **to find o.s. up a ~*** (US) quedarse uno de piedra, estar perplejo.
2 VT (a) (*: puzzle) desconcertar, dejar perplejo, dejar confuso; **I'm properly ~ed** estoy totalmente perplejo; no sé qué hacer (or decir etc); no sé qué consejo darte; **he was ~ed for an answer** no sabía qué contestar.
(b) **to ~ the country** (US) recorrer el país pronunciando discursos.
3 VI: **to ~ about, to ~ along** andar pisando muy fuerte; (lamely) andar cojeando.
♦ **stump up** (Brit) **1** VT: **to ~ up £5** apoquinar 5 libras, desembolsar 5 libras (for sth para comprar algo, por algo).
2 VI apoquinar, soltar la guita (for sth para pagar algo).
stumpy ['stʌmpɪ] ADJ person etc achaparrado; pencil etc corto, reducido a casi nada, muy gastado.
stun [stʌn] VT (a) (Med) dejar sin sentido; aturdir de un golpe; animal aturdir. (b) (fig) aturdir, pasmar, dejar pasmado; **the news ~ned everybody** la noticia aturdió a todos; **this will ~ you** esto será una gran sorpresa para ti; **the family were ~ned by his death** la familia quedó anonadada a raíz de su muerte.
stung [stʌŋ] PRET AND PTP of **sting**.
stun grenade ['stʌngrə'neɪd] N granada f detonadora, granada f de estampida.
stunk [stʌŋk] PTP of **stink**.
stunned [stʌnd] ADJ (lit) aturdido, atontado; (fig) pasmado.
stunner* ['stʌnəʳ] N persona f maravillosa, cosa f estupenda*; **the picture is a ~** el cuadro es maravilloso; **she's a real ~** es francamente estupenda*.
stunning ['stʌnɪŋ] ADJ (a) blow que aturde. (b) news etc pasmoso; dress, girl etc estupendo, maravilloso.
stunningly ['stʌnɪŋlɪ] ADV dressed etc sensacionalmente.
stunt¹ [stʌnt] VT atrofiar, impedir el desarrollo de.
stunt² [stʌnt] **1** N (Aer) vuelo m acrobático, ejercicio m acrobático; (display) proeza f excepcional; maniobra f sensacional; (Comm) truco m publicitario, treta f publicitaria; **it's just a ~ to get your money** es solamente un truco para sacarte dinero; **to pull a ~** hacer algo peligroso (y tonto).
2 ATTR: **~ flier** aviador m acrobático, aviadora f acrobática.
3 VI hacer vuelos acrobáticos, hacer maniobras sensacionales.
stunted ['stʌntɪd] ADJ enano, achaparrado, mal desarrollado.
stuntman ['stʌntmæn] N, PL **stuntmen** ['stʌntmen], **stuntwoman** ['stʌntwʊmən] N, PL **stuntwomen** ['stʌntwɪmɪn] especialista mf, persona que se dedica a desempeñar los papeles peligrosos en el cine y otros espectáculos.
stupefaction [,stjuːpɪ'fækʃən] N estupefacción f.
stupefy ['stjuːpɪfaɪ] VT (a) (Med) causar estupor a, dejar sin conocimiento; **stupefied by drink** en estado de estupor después de haber bebido, (permanently) embrutecido por el alcohol.
(b) (fig) pasmar, causar estupor a, dejar estupefacto.
stupefying ['stjuːpɪfaɪɪŋ] ADJ (fig) pasmoso.
stupendous [stjuː'pendəs] ADJ estupendo, asombroso.
stupendously [stjuː'pendəslɪ] ADV estupendamente.
stupid ['stjuːpɪd] ADJ (with sleep etc) en estado de estupor, atontado; (silly) estúpido; **you ~ child!** ¡bobo!; **don't be ~** no seas bobo; **don't do that, ~!** ¡no hagas eso, imbécil!; **that was ~ of you, that was a ~ thing to do** eso fue una estupidez; **I've done a ~ thing** he hecho algo tonto; **to drink o.s. ~** beber tanto que uno queda en estado de estupor.
stupidity [stjuː'pɪdɪtɪ] N estupidez f.
stupidly ['stjuːpɪdlɪ] ADV estúpidamente.
stupidness ['stjuːpɪdnɪs] N = **stupidity**.
stupor ['stjuːpəʳ] N estupor m (also fig).
sturdily ['stɜːdɪlɪ] ADV fuertemente; vigorosamente; enérgicamente;

tenazmente; **~ built** de construcción sólida; *person* robusto.
sturdiness ['stɜːdɪnɪs] N robustez *f*, fuerza *f*; energía *f*; tenacidad *f*.
sturdy ['stɜːdɪ] ADJ robusto, fuerte; vigoroso; *opposition etc* enérgico; *resistance* tenaz; **~ independence** espíritu *m* fuerte de independencia.
sturgeon ['stɜːdʒən] N, PL INVAR esturión *m*.
stutter ['stʌtər] [1] N tartamudeo *m*; **he has a bad ~** tartamudea terriblemente; **to say sth with a ~** decir algo tartamudeando.
[2] VT (*also* **to ~ out**) balbucir, decir tartamudeando.
[3] VI tartamudear; balbucir.
stutterer ['stʌtərər] N tartamudo *m*, -a *f*.
stuttering ['stʌtərɪŋ] [1] ADJ tartamudo.
[2] N tartamudeo *m*.
stutteringly ['stʌtərɪŋlɪ] ADV: **he said ~** dijo tartamudeando.
sty¹ [staɪ] N **(a)** pocilga *f*, zahurda *f*. **(b)** (:) comisaría *f*.
sty², **stye** [staɪ] N (*Med*) orzuelo *m*.
Stygian ['stɪdʒɪən] ADJ estigio.
style [staɪl] [1] N **(a)** (*gen*) estilo *m*; (*Art, Liter etc*) estilo *m*; (*fashion*) estilo *m*; moda *f*; (*elegance*) elegancia *f*; **~ of living** estilo *m* de vida; **in the Italian ~** al estilo italiano, a la italiana; **that's the ~!** ¡bravo!, ¡muy bien!; **there's no ~ about him** no tiene elegancia en absoluto; **she has ~** tiene garbo, tiene aquél; lo hace todo con elegancia; **to cramp sb's ~** cortar los vuelos a uno; **to be in ~** estar de moda; **to do sth in ~** hacer algo con todo lujo, hacer algo como se debe; **to travel in ~** viajar con todo confort; **to live in ~** vivir en el lujo; **he won in fine ~** ganó de manera impecable, ganó limpiamente.
(b) (*of address*) tratamiento *m*; título *m*.
[2] VT **(a)** *dress* cortar a la moda, estilizar; *hair* marcar.
(b) (*entitle*) intitular, nombrar.
[3] VR: **to ~ o.s.** intitularse, darse el título de.
-style [staɪl] ADJ *ending in compounds*: **Western~ democracy** democracia al *or* de estilo occidental; **to dress 1920s~** vestir al estilo años veinte.
stylebook ['staɪlbʊk] N libro *m* de estilo.
stylesheet ['staɪlˌʃiːt] N hoja *f* de estilo.
styling ['staɪlɪŋ] N estilización *f*.
stylisation, stylization [ˌstaɪlaɪ'zeɪʃən] N estilización *f*.
stylish ['staɪlɪʃ] ADJ elegante; a la moda; garboso, estiloso.
stylishly ['staɪlɪʃlɪ] ADV elegantemente.
stylishness ['staɪlɪʃnɪs] N elegancia *f*.
stylist ['staɪlɪst] N estilista *mf*.
stylistic [staɪ'lɪstɪk] [1] ADJ estilístico.
[2] N: **~s** estilística *f*.
stylistically [staɪ'lɪstɪklɪ] ADV estilísticamente; **~ distinguished** distinguido en cuanto al estilo.
stylized ['staɪlaɪzd] ADJ estilizado.
stylus ['staɪləs] N (*pen*) estilo *m*; (*of record-player*) aguja *f*.
stymie* ['staɪmɪ] VT: **to ~ sb** bloquear a uno, poner obstáculos infranqueables delante de uno; **now we're properly ~d!** ¡la hemos pringado de verdad!*, ¡la liamos!*
styptic ['stɪptɪk] [1] ADJ estíptico; **~ pencil** lapicero *m* hemostático.
[2] N estíptico *m*.
Styrofoam ['staɪrəfəʊm] ®. [1] N (*US*) poliestireno *m*.
[2] ATTR de poliestireno.
Styx [stɪks] N Estigio *m*, Laguna *f* Estigia.
suasion ['sweɪʒən] N (*liter*) persuasión *f*.
suave [swɑːv] ADJ afable, cortés, fino; (*pej*) zalamero.
suavely ['swɑːvlɪ] ADV afablemente, cortésmente, con finura; (*pej*) con zalamería.
suavity ['swɑːvɪtɪ] N afabilidad *f*, cortesía *f*, finura *f*; (*pej*) zalamería *f*.
sub¹ [sʌb] N *and* VT ABBR *of* **subaltern**; **sub-edit**; **sub-editor**; **submarine**; **subscription**; **substitute**.
sub² [sʌb] VI: **to ~ for sb** hacer las veces de uno.
sub³* [sʌb] [1] N (*advance on wages*) avance *m*, anticipo *m*.
[2] VT anticipar dinero a.
sub... [sʌb] PREF sub...
subalpine [sʌb'ælpaɪn] ADJ subalpino.
subaltern ['sʌbltən] N (*Brit*) alférez *m*; subalterno *m*.
subaqua [ˌsʌb'ækwə] ADJ subacuático, de submarinismo.
subarctic [sʌb'ɑːktɪk] ADJ subártico.
subatomic [ˌsʌbə'tɒmɪk] ADJ subatómico.
sub-basement ['sʌbˌbeɪsmənt] N subsótano *m*.
sub-branch ['sʌbbrɑːntʃ] N subdelegación *f*.
subcommittee ['sʌbkəˌmɪtɪ] N subcomisión *f*.
subconscious [sʌb'kɒnʃəs] [1] ADJ subconsciente.
[2] N: **the ~** el subconsciente, la subconsciencia; **in one's ~** en el subconsciente.
subconsciously ['sʌb'kɒnʃəslɪ] ADV de modo subconsciente.
subcontinent ['sʌb'kɒntɪnənt] N subcontinente *m*.
subcontract [1] ['sʌb'kɒntrækt] N subcontrato *m*.
[2] [ˌsʌbkən'trækt] VT subcontratar.
subcontracting ['sʌbkɒn'træktɪŋ] [1] ADJ subcontratado.
[2] N subcontratación *f*.

subcontractor ['sʌbkən'træktər] N subcontratista *mf*.
subculture ['sʌbˌkʌltʃər] N subcultura *f*.
subcutaneous ['sʌbkjʊ'teɪnɪəs] ADJ subcutáneo.
subdivide ['sʌbdɪ'vaɪd] [1] VT subdividir.
[2] VI subdividirse.
subdivision ['sʌbdɪˌvɪʒən] N subdivisión *f*.
subdue [səb'djuː] VT (*conquer*) sojuzgar, dominar, avasallar; *passions etc* dominar; *colour, voice etc* suavizar.
subdued [səb'djuːd] ADJ *emotion etc* templado, suave; *voice* bajo; *colour* suave, apagado; *light* tenue; *lighting* disminuido; *person* (*docile*) sumiso, manso, (*depressed*) deprimido; **you were very ~ last night** anoche has mostrado poca animación, anoche estabas bastante callado; **he's very ~ these days** ahora es muy serio.
sub-edit ['sʌb'edɪt] VT (*Brit*) *article* corregir, preparar para la prensa.
sub-editor ['sʌb'edɪtər] N (*Brit*) redactor *m*, -ora *f*.
sub-entry ['sʌbentrɪ] N (*Book-keeping*) subasiento *m*, subapunte *m*.
sub-frame ['sʌbfreɪm] N (*Aut*) subchasis *m*.
subgroup ['sʌbgruːp] N subgrupo *m*.
subhead(ing) ['sʌbˌhed(ɪŋ)] N subtítulo *m*.
subhuman ['sʌb'hjuːmən] ADJ infrahumano.
subject [1] ['sʌbdʒɪkt] ADJ **(a)** *people* subyugado, esclavizado.
(b) **to be ~ to** (*at times*) estar propenso a, estar sujeto a; **this programme is ~ to change** este programa está sujeto a cambios; **all prices are ~ to alteration** todos los precios están sujetos a cambios.
(c) **to be ~ to** (*by nature*) ser propenso a; **he is very ~ to colds** es muy propenso a acatarrarse.
(d) (*conditional*) **~ to anything he may say** esto depende de lo que diga él; **~ to the approval of** sujeto a la aprobación de; (*liable*) **~ to change without notice** sujeto a cambio sin previo aviso; **~ to correction** bajo corrección.
[2] ['sʌbdʒɪkt] N **(a)** (*Pol*) súbdito *m*, -a *f*; **British ~** súbdito *m* británico, súbdita *f* británica; **liberty of the ~** libertad *f* del ciudadano; libertad *f* del individuo.
(b) (*Gram*) sujeto *m*.
(c) (*theme*) tema *m*, materia *f*; asunto *m*, cuestión *f*; (*Scol, Univ*) asignatura *f*; (*Art, Liter, Mus*) tema *m*; **on the ~ of ...** a propósito de ...; **it's a delicate ~** es un asunto delicado; **to change the ~** volver la hoja, cambiar de conversación; **to keep off a ~** no aludir a un tema, no discutir una cuestión; **to raise the ~ of the war** introducir el tema de la guerra, empezar a hablar de la guerra; **this raises the whole ~ of money** esto plantea el problema general del dinero.
(d) (*Med etc*) caso *m*; **he's a nervous ~** es un caso nervioso; **guinea pigs make excellent ~s** los conejillos son materia excelente (para los experimentos *etc*).
[3] ['sʌbdʒɪkt] ATTR: **~ heading** título *m* de materia; **~ index** (*in book*) índice *m* de materias; (*in library*) catálogo *m* de materias; **~ pronoun** pronombre *m* de sujeto.
[4] [səb'dʒekt] VT **(a)** (*conquer*) sojuzgar, dominar.
(b) (*submit*) someter (*to* a); **to ~ sb to a test** poner a uno a prueba; **to ~ a book to criticism** someter un libro a la crítica; **to be ~ed to inquiry** ser sometido a la investigación; **I will not be ~ed to this questioning** no tolero esta interrogación; **she was ~ed to much indignity** tuvo que aguantar muchas afrentas.
subjection [səb'dʒekʃən] N sujeción *f*; sometimiento *m*; **to bring a people into ~** subyugar a un pueblo; **to hold a people in ~** tener subyugado a un pueblo; **to be in ~ to sb** estar sometido a uno; **to be in a state of complete ~** estar completamente sumiso.
subjective [səb'dʒektɪv] ADJ subjetivo.
subjectively [səb'dʒektɪvlɪ] ADV subjetivamente.
subjectivism [səb'dʒektɪvɪzəm] N subjetivismo *m*.
subjectivity [ˌsʌbdʒek'tɪvɪtɪ] N subjetividad *f*.
subject-matter ['sʌbdʒɪktˌmætər] N materia *f*; tema *m*; (*of letter etc*) contenido *m*.
subjoin ['sʌb'dʒɔɪn] VT adjuntar.
sub judice [sʌb'djuːdɪsɪ] ADJ: **the matter is ~** el asunto está en manos del tribunal.
subjugate ['sʌbdʒʊgeɪt] VT subyugar.
subjugation [ˌsʌbdʒʊ'geɪʃən] N subyugación *f*; **to live in ~** vivir subyugado.
subjunctive [səb'dʒʌŋktɪv] [1] ADJ subjuntivo; **~ mood** modo *m* subjuntivo.
[2] N subjuntivo *m*.
sublease ['sʌb'liːs] [1] VT realquilar, subarrendar.
[2] ['sʌbˌliːs] N subarriendo *m*.
sublessee [ˌsʌble'siː] N subarrendatario *m*, -a *f*.
sublessor [ˌsʌble'sɔːr] N subarrendador *m*, -ora *f*.
sublet ['sʌb'let] (*irr: V* **let²**) VT realquilar, subarrendar.
sub-librarian ['sʌblaɪ'brɛərɪən] N subdirector *m*, -ora *f* de biblioteca.
sub-lieutenant ['sʌblef'tenənt] N (*Brit Naut*) alférez *m* de fragata; (*Mil*) subteniente *m*, alférez *m*.
sublimate [1] ['sʌblɪmɪt] N sublimado *m*.
[2] ['sʌblɪmeɪt] VT (*all senses*) sublimar.

sublimation [ˌsʌblɪ'meɪʃən] N sublimación f.

sublime [sə'blaɪm] ⒈ ADJ sublime.
⒉ N: **the ~** lo sublime; **to go from the ~ to the ridiculous** pasar de lo sublime a lo ridículo.

sublimely [sə'blaɪmlɪ] ADV sublimemente; **~ unaware of ...** completamente inconsciente de ..., demasiado exaltado para darse cuenta de ...

subliminal [sʌb'lɪmɪnl] ADJ subliminal, subliminar; **~ advertising** publicidad f subliminal.

subliminally [sʌb'lɪmɪnəlɪ] ADV subliminalmente.

sublimity [sə'blɪmɪtɪ] N sublimidad f.

submachine-gun ['sʌbmə'ʃiːŋɡʌn] N pistola f ametralladora, metralleta f.

submarine [ˌsʌbmə'riːn] ⒈ ADJ submarino.
⒉ N (a) submarino m. (b) (US•) sándwich m mixto de tamaño grande.

submarine-chaser [ˌsʌbmə'riːn,tʃeɪsəʳ] N cazasubmarinos m.

submariner [sʌb'mærɪnəʳ] N submarinista m.

sub-menu ['sʌb,menjuː] N submenú m.

submerge [səb'mɜːdʒ] ⒈ VT sumergir; (flood) inundar, cubrir.
⒉ VI sumergirse.

submerged [səb'mɜːdʒd] ADJ sumergido.

submergence [səb'mɜːdʒəns] N sumersión f, sumergimiento m, hundimiento m.

submersible [səb'mɜːsəbl] ADJ sumergible.

submersion [səb'mɜːʃən] N sumersión f.

submicroscopic ['sʌb,maɪkrəs'kɒpɪk] ADJ submicroscópico.

submission [səb'mɪʃən] N (a) (state) sumisión f. (b) (act) presentación f (of evidence de datos etc), entrega f. (c) (Jur etc) argumento m, alegato m; **in my ~** de acuerdo con mi tesis, según yo creo.

submissive [səb'mɪsɪv] ADJ sumiso.

submissively [səb'mɪsɪvlɪ] ADV sumisamente.

submissiveness [səb'mɪsɪvnɪs] N sumisión f.

submit [səb'mɪt] ⒈ VT someter; evidence presentar, aducir; report presentar; account rendir; **to ~ that ...** proponer que ..., sugerir que ...; **I ~ that ...** me permito decir que ...; **to ~ a play to the censor** someter una obra al censor; **to ~ a dispute to arbitration** someter una disputa a arbitraje.
⒉ VI someterse, rendirse; **to ~ to** someterse a; resignarse a, conformarse con; **he had to ~ to this indignity** tuvo que aguantar esta afrenta.

subnormal ['sʌb'nɔːməl] ⒈ ADJ subnormal.
⒉ NPL: **the ~** los subnormales.

suborbital ['sʌb'ɔːbɪtəl] ADJ suborbital.

subordinate ⒈ [sə'bɔːdnɪt] ADJ subordinado (also Gram); secundario, de importancia secundaria, menos importante; **A is ~ to B** A queda subordinado a B; A no tiene tanta importancia como B; A depende de B.
⒉ [sə'bɔːdɪnɪt] N subordinado m, -a f.
⒊ [sə'bɔːdɪneɪt] VT subordinar (to a).

subordination [sə,bɔːdɪ'neɪʃən] N subordinación f.

suborn [sʌ'bɔːn] VT sobornar.

subparagraph [sʌb'pærə,ɡrɑːf] N subpárrafo m.

subplot ['sʌb,plɒt] N intriga f secundaria.

subpoena [səb'piːnə] ⒈ N comparendo m, citación f (judicial), apercibimiento m.
⒉ VT mandar comparecer, citar a uno (para estrados).

subpopulation ['sʌb,pɒpjʊ'leɪʃən] N subgrupo m de población.

sub post-office [ˌsʌb'pəʊst,ɒfɪs] N subdelegación f de correos.

subrogate ['sʌbrəɡɪt] ADJ subrogado, sustituido; **~ language** lenguaje m subrogado.

sub rosa ['sʌb'rəʊzə] ⒈ ADJ secreto, de confianza; **it's all very ~** todo es de lo más secreto.
⒉ ADV en secreto, en confianza.

subroutine [ˌsʌbruː'tiːn] N subrutina f.

sub-Saharan ['sʌbsə'hɑːrən] ADJ subsahariano.

subscribe [səb'skraɪb] ⒈ VT (a) money suscribir, contribuir, dar; **~d capital** capital m suscrito.
(b) signature poner; document etc firmar, poner su firma en.
⒉ VI suscribir; **to ~ for sth** contribuir dinero para algo; **to ~ to a paper** suscribirse a un periódico, abonarse a un periódico; **to ~ to an opinion** suscribir una opinión, aprobar una opinión.

subscriber [səb'skraɪbəʳ] N suscriptor m, -ora f, abonado m, -a f; (St Ex) suscriptor m, -ora f.

subscript ['sʌbskrɪpt] N subíndice m.

subscription [səb'skrɪpʃən] ⒈ N suscripción f, abono m; (to club) cuota f; (St Ex) suscripción f; **to pay one's ~** suscribirse, abonarse, (to club) pagar su cuota; **to take out a ~ to a journal** abonarse a una revista.
⒉ ATTR: **~ fee, ~ rate** tarifa f de suscripción; **~ form** hoja f de suscripción.

subsection ['sʌb,sekʃən] N subsección f, subdivisión f.

subsequent ['sʌbsɪkwənt] ADJ subsiguiente; posterior, ulterior; **~ to** posterior a; **~ to this** (as prep) después de esto, a raíz de esto.

subsequently ['sʌbsɪkwəntlɪ] ADV después, más tarde, con posterioridad.

subserve [səb'sɜːv] VT ayudar, favorecer.

subservience [səb'sɜːvɪəns] N subordinación f (to a); servilismo m.

subservient [səb'sɜːvɪənt] ADJ (a) (secondary) subordinado (to a). (b) (cringing) servil.

subset ['sʌb,set] N subconjunto m.

subside [səb'saɪd] VI (water) bajar; (foundations, ground, pavement etc) hundirse; (wind) amainar, hacerse menos violento; (threat etc) disminuir, alejarse; (excitement etc) calmarse; **to ~ into a chair** dejarse caer en una silla.

subsidence [səb'saɪdəns] N bajada f; hundimiento m, (of pavement, road) socavón m; amaine m; disminución f; apaciguamiento m.

subsidiarity [sʌbsɪdɪ'ærɪtɪ] N (Pol) subsidiariedad f.

subsidiary [səb'sɪdɪərɪ] ⒈ ADJ subsidiario; secundario; auxiliar; (Fin) afiliado, filial; **~ company** empresa f filial.
⒉ N filial f, sucursal f.

subsidize ['sʌbsɪdaɪz] VT subvencionar; **~d** subvencionado, que tiene subvención (gubernamental etc).

subsidy ['sʌbsɪdɪ] N subvención f, subsidio m.

subsist [səb'sɪst] VI subsistir; sustentarse (on a food con una comida).

subsistence [səb'sɪstəns] ⒈ N subsistencia f; sustentación f; (allowance) dietas fpl.
⒉ ATTR: **~ allowance** dietas fpl; **~ economy** economía f de subsistencia; **~ farming** agricultura f de subsistencia; **~ wage** salario m de subsistencia; **to live at ~ level** vivir muy justo, poderse sustentar apenas.

subsoil ['sʌbsɔɪl] N subsuelo m.

subsonic ['sʌb'sɒnɪk] ADJ subsónico.

subspecies ['sʌb'spiːʃiːz] N, PL INVAR subespecie f.

substance ['sʌbstəns] N sustancia f; esencia f, parte f, parte f esencial; **in ~** en esencia, esencialmente; **an argument of ~** un argumento sólido; **man of ~** hombre m acaudalado; **the ~ is good but the style poor** la materia es buena pero el estilo malo.

substandard ['sʌb'stændəd] ADJ inferior, inferior al nivel normal, no del todo satisfactorio.

substantial [səb'stænʃəl] ADJ sustancial, sustancioso; part, proportion importante; sum considerable; loss importante; build etc sólido, fuerte; person acomodado; acaudalado; **~ damages** (Jur) daños mpl y perjuicios generales; **to be in ~ agreement** estar de acuerdo en gran parte.

substantially [səb'stænʃəlɪ] ADV sustancialmente; **~ built** de construcción sólida; **~ true** en gran parte verdadero; **it contributed ~ to our success** contribuyó materialmente a nuestro éxito.

substantiate [səb'stænʃɪeɪt] VT establecer, comprobar, justificar.

substantiation [səb,stænʃɪ'eɪʃən] N comprobación f, justificación f.

substantival [ˌsʌbstən'taɪvəl] ADJ sustantivo.

substantive ['sʌbstəntɪv] ⒈ ADJ sustantivo.
⒉ N sustantivo m.

substation [ˌsʌb,steɪʃən] N (Elec) subestación f.

substitute ['sʌbstɪtjuːt] ⒈ N (person) sustituto m, -a f, suplente mf (for de); (Sport) suplente mf; (thing) sustituto m, sucedáneo m; artículo m de reemplazo; **there is no ~ for petrol** la gasolina es insustituible; **this is a poor ~ for the real thing** esto no sustituye plenamente lo auténtico.
⒉ ADJ sucedáneo; de reemplazo; person suplente; **~ teacher** (US) profesor m suplente, profesora f suplente.
⒊ VT sustituir (A for B B por A); reemplazar (A for B A por B).
⒋ VI: **to ~ for sb** suplir a uno, hacer las veces de uno.

substitution [ˌsʌbstɪ'tjuːʃən] N sustitución f; reemplazo m.

substratum ['sʌb'strɑːtəm] N, PL **substrata** ['sʌb'strɑːtə] sustrato m.

substructure ['sʌb,strʌktʃəʳ] N infraestructura f.

subsume [sʌb'sjuːm] VT subsumir.

subsystem ['sʌb,sɪstəm] N subsistema m.

subteen• [ˌsʌb'tiːn] N preadolescente mf, menor mf de trece años.

subtenancy ['sʌb'tenənsɪ] N subarriendo m.

subtenant ['sʌb'tenənt] N subarrendatario m, -a f.

subterfuge ['sʌbtəfjuːdʒ] N subterfugio m.

subterranean [ˌsʌbtə'reɪnɪən] ADJ subterráneo.

subtext ['sʌbtekst] N subtexto m.

subtilize ['sʌtɪlaɪz] ⒈ VT sutilizar.
⒉ VI sutilizar.

subtitle ['sʌb,taɪtl] ⒈ N subtítulo m.
⒉ VT subtitular.

subtitling ['sʌb,taɪtlɪŋ] N subtitulado m.

subtle ['sʌtl] ADJ sutil; fino, delicado; charm misterioso; perfume delicado, sutil, tenue; irony etc fino; (crafty) astuto; **that wasn't very ~ of you** en eso te has mostrado poco fino.

subtlety ['sʌtltɪ] N sutileza f; finura f, delicadeza f; lo misterioso; astucia f.

subtly ['sʌtlɪ] ADV sutilmente; finamente, delicadamente; misteriosamente; astutamente.

subtopia [ˌsʌb'təʊpɪə] N (*hum*) (vida *f etc* de los) barrios *mpl* exteriores.

subtotal ['sʌbˌtəʊtl] N total *m* parcial.

subtract [səb'trækt] VT sustraer, restar; **to ~ 5 from 9** restar 5 a 9.

subtraction [səb'trækʃən] N sustracción *f*, resta *f*.

subtropical ['sʌb'trɒpɪkəl] ADJ subtropical.

subtype ['sʌbtaɪp] N (*Bio*) subtipo *m*.

suburb ['sʌbɜːb] N barrio *m*, barrio *m* exterior; colonia *f*; **new ~** barrio *m* nuevo, ensanche *m*; **a London ~** un barrio londinense, un distrito en las afueras de Londres; **the (outer) ~s** los barrios exteriores, las afueras.

suburban [sə'bɜːbən] ADJ suburbano; **train** de cercanías.

suburbanite [sə'bɜːbənaɪt] [1] ADJ surburbano.
[2] N habitante *mf* de los barrios exteriores.

suburbia [sə'bɜːbɪə] N (*freq pej*) los barrios exteriores, las afueras; manera *f* de vivir de los barrios exteriores.

subvention [səb'venʃən] N subvención *f*.

subversion [səb'vɜːʃən] N subversión *f*.

subversive [səb'vɜːsɪv] [1] ADJ subversivo.
[2] N subversor *m*; elemento *m* subversivo, persona *f* de dudosa lealtad política.

subvert [sʌb'vɜːt] VT subvertir, trastornar.

subway ['sʌbweɪ] [1] N (*esp Brit*) paso *m* subterráneo, paso *m* inferior; (*US Rail*) metro *m*.
[2] ATTR: **~ station** (*US*) estación *f* de metro.

sub-zero ['sʌb'zɪərəʊ] ADJ: **in ~ temperatures** a una temperatura bajo cero.

succeed [sək'siːd] [1] VT suceder a; **to ~ sb in a post** suceder a uno en un puesto; **spring is ~ed by summer** a la primavera le sigue el verano.
[2] VI (a) (*be successful: of person*) tener éxito, triunfar; (*of plan etc*) salir bien; **but he did not ~** (*in this*) pero no tuvo éxito (con esto), pero no lo consiguió; **to ~ in life** triunfar en la vida; **to ~ in one's hopes** ver logradas sus esperanzas; **to ~ in one's plan** llevar a cabo su proyecto; **to ~ in doing sth** lograr hacer algo, conseguir hacer algo.
(b) (*follow*) suceder; seguir; heredar; **who ~s?** ¿quién hereda?; **to ~ to the crown** suceder a la corona, heredar la corona; **to ~ to the throne** subir al trono; **to ~ to an estate** heredar una finca.

succeeding [sək'siːdɪŋ] ADJ futuro; subsiguiente; sucesivo; **on 3 ~ Saturdays** tres sábados seguidos; **in the ~ chaos** en la confusión subsiguiente; **~ generations will do better** las generaciones futuras harán mejor; **each ~ year brought** ... cada año sucesivo trajo ...

success [sək'ses] [1] N éxito *m*, buen éxito *m*; triunfo *m*; prosperidad *f*; **another ~ for our team** nuevo éxito *m* para nuestro equipo; **without ~** sin éxito, sin resultado; **to be a ~** (*person*) tener éxito; (*plan etc*) ser un acierto, dar resultado; **he was a great ~** tuvo mucho éxito; **he was not a ~ as Segismundo** no estuvo bien en el papel de Segismundo; **the play was a ~ in New York** la obra obtuvo un éxito en Nueva York; **the new car is not a ~** el nuevo coche no es satisfactorio; **the plan was a ~** el proyecto salió muy bien; **she had no ~** no tuvo éxito; **to make a ~ of sth** tener éxito en algo; **to meet with ~** tener éxito; prosperar.
[2] ATTR: **~ story** historia *f* de un éxito.

successful [sək'sesfʊl] ADJ person afortunado, feliz, que tiene éxito, exitoso; *attempt, plan etc* logrado, exitoso; *business etc* próspero; *effort* fructuoso; *candidate* elegido, afortunado; **to be ~** (*person*) tener éxito, triunfar; (*business etc*) prosperar; **to be entirely ~** tener un éxito completo; **to be ~ in doing sth** lograr hacer algo; **he was not ~ last time** no lo logró la última vez.

successfully [sək'sesfəlɪ] ADV con éxito; afortunadamente; prósperamente.

succession [sək'seʃən] [1] N (a) (*series*) sucesión *f*, serie *f*; **in ~** sucesivamente; **4 times in ~** 4 veces seguidas; **in quick ~** en rápida sucesión; rápidamente uno tras otro; **after a ~ of disasters** después de una serie de catástrofes.
(b) (*to post etc*) sucesión *f* (*to a*); **in ~ to sb** sucediendo a uno; como sucesor de uno; **Princess Rebecca is 7th in ~ to the throne** la princesa Rebeca ocupa el 7° puesto en la línea de sucesión a la corona.
(c) (*descendants*) descendencia *f*.
[2] ATTR: **~ duty** derechos *mpl* de sucesión.

successive [sək'sesɪv] ADJ sucesivo; consecutivo; **4 ~ days** 4 días seguidos.

successively [sək'sesɪvlɪ] ADV sucesivamente.

successor [sək'sesər] N sucesor *m*, -ora *f*.

succinct [sək'sɪŋkt] ADJ sucinto.

succinctly [sək'sɪŋktlɪ] ADV sucintamente.

succinctness [sək'sɪŋktnɪs] N concisión *f*.

succour, (*US*) **succor** ['sʌkər] [1] N socorro *m*.
[2] VT socorrer.

succubus ['sʌkjʊbəs] N, PL **succubi** súcubo *m*.

succulence ['sʌkjʊləns] N suculencia *f*.

succulent ['sʌkjʊlənt] [1] ADJ suculento; carnoso.
[2] N (*plant*) planta *f* carnosa.

succumb [sə'kʌm] VI sucumbir (*to a*).

such [sʌtʃ] [1] ADJ (a) (*of that sort*) tal; semejante; parecido; tanto; **~ a book** tal libro; **~ books** tales libros; **in ~ cases** en tales casos, en semejantes casos; **we had ~ a case last year** tuvimos un caso parecido el año pasado; **on just ~ a day in June** un día exactamente parecido de junio; **no ~ thing!** ¡no hay tal!, ¡ni hablar!; **there's no ~ thing** no hay tal cosa; **did you ever see ~ a thing?** ¿se vio jamás tal cosa?; **some ~ idea** alguna idea de este tipo, alguna idea por el estilo; **~ a plan is most unwise** un proyecto así es poco aconsejable, un proyecto de ese tipo no es aconsejable; **no ~ book exists** no existe tal libro; **X was ~ a one** X era así; **~ is life** así es la vida; **~ is not the case** esto no es así; **I am in ~ a hurry** tengo tanta prisa, estoy tan de prisa; **~ an honour!** ¡tanto honor!; **it caused ~ trouble that** ... dio lugar a tantos disgustos que ...
(b) (*gen*) **~ as** tal como; **~ a man as Ganivet** un hombre tal como Ganivet; **~ writers as Quevedo** los escritores tales como Quevedo; **~ money as I have** el dinero que tengo; **~ stories as I know** las historias que conozco; **there are no ~ things as giants** los gigantes no existen; **it is not ~ as to cause worry** no es tal que haya de causar inquietud; **it made ~ a stir as had not been known before** tuvo una repercusión como no se había conocido hasta entonces; **~ as?** ¿por ejemplo?
[2] ADV tan; **~ good food** comida *f* tan buena; **~ a clever girl** muchacha *f* tan inteligente; **it's ~ a long time ago** hace tanto tiempo ya.
[3] PRON los que, las que; **we took ~ as we wanted** tomamos los que queríamos; **I will send you ~ as I receive** te mandaré los que reciba; **and as ~ he was promoted** y como tal le ascendieron; **we know of none ~** no tenemos noticias de ninguno así; **there are no trees as ~** no hay árboles propiamente dichos, no hay árboles que digamos, no hay árboles árboles; **rabbits and hares and ~** conejos *mpl* y liebres y tal; **may all ~ perish!** ¡mueran cuantos hay como él!; **this is my car ~ as it is** tal como es, éste es mi coche; **he read the documents ~ as they were** leyó los documentos, los que había.

such-and-such ['sʌtʃənsʌtʃ] ADJ: **she lives in ~ a street** vive en tal o cual calle; **on ~ a day in May** a tantos de mayo; **I am not concerned with ~** no tengo que ver con aquello y lo otro.

suchlike ['sʌtʃlaɪk] [1] ADJ tal, semejante; **sheep and ~ animals** ovejas *fpl* y otros tales animales, ovejas *fpl* y otros animales de la misma clase.
[2] PRON: **thieves and ~** ladrones *mpl* y gente de esa calaña, ladrones *mpl* y otras tales personas; **buses and lorries and ~** autobuses *mpl* y camiones y tal.

suck [sʌk] [1] N chupada *f*; sorbo *m*; (*at breast*) mamada *f*; **to give ~ (to)** amamantar.
[2] VT (a) chupar; sorber; *breast* mamar; **to ~ one's fingers** chuparse los dedos. (b) **we were ~ed into the controversy** fuimos involucrados en la controversia sin querer.
[3] VI chupar; mamar; **to ~ at sth** chupar algo; **this ~s** es la mierda⁑, esto apesta‡.
◆ **suck down** VT tragar.
◆ **suck in** VT *liquid* sorber; *air, dust etc* aspirar.
◆ **suck off⁑** VT hacerle una mamada a‡.
◆ **suck out** VT succionar.
◆ **suck up** [1] VT aspirar; absorber.
[2] VI: **to ~ up to sb*** dar coba a uno*, hacer la pelotilla a uno*.

sucker ['sʌkər] N (a) (*Zool*) ventosa *f*.
(b) (*Bot*) serpollo *m*, mamón *m*.
(c) (‡: *person*) primo* *m*, bobo *m*; **some ~** algún pobre hombre; **to be a ~ for sth** no poder resistir algo; sucumbir pronto a los encantos de algo.
[2] VT (*US‡*) estafar, timar, embaucar; **to get ~ed out of 6 grand** ser objeto de un timo de 6.000 dólares.

sucking-pig ['sʌkɪŋpɪg] N lechón *m*, lechoncillo *m*, cochinillo *m*.

suckle ['sʌkl] [1] VT amamantar, dar el pecho a; (*fig*) criar.
[2] VI lactar.

suckling ['sʌklɪŋ] N mamón *m*, -ona *f*; **~ pig** cochinillo *m*.

sucks-boo* ['sʌks'buː] EXCL ¡narices!*

sucrose ['suːkrəʊz] N sacarosa *f*.

suction ['sʌkʃən] N succión *f*.

suction pump ['sʌkʃənpʌmp] N bomba *f* aspirante, bomba *f* de succión.

Sudan [suː'dɑːn] N Sudán *m*.

Sudanese [ˌsuːdə'niːz] [1] ADJ sudanés.
[2] N sudanés *m*, -esa *f*.

sudden ['sʌdn] ADJ (*rapid, hurried*) repentino, súbito; (*unexpected*) imprevisto, impensado; *change of temperature, curve etc* brusco; **~ death** (*Sport*) desempate *m* instantáneo, muerte *f* súbita; **~ infant death syndrome** síndrome *m* de la muerte infantil súbita; **all of a ~** de repente.

suddenly ['sʌdnlɪ] ADV de repente, de pronto; inesperadamente; bruscamente.

suddenness ['sʌdnnɪs] N lo repentino; lo imprevisto; brusquedad *f*.

suds [sʌdz] NPL **(a)** (*also* **soap ~**) jabonaduras *fpl*, espuma *f* de jabón. **(b)** (*US‡*) cerveza *f*.

Sue [suː] NF *familiar form of* Susan.

sue [suː] 1 VT: **to ~ sb** demandar a uno (*for sth* por algo), llevar a uno ante el tribunal; **to ~ sb for damages** demandar a uno por daños y perjuicios; **to be ~d for libel** ser demandado por calumnia. 2 VI **(a)** (*Jur*) presentar demanda; **to ~ for divorce** presentar demanda de divorcio, solicitar el divorcio. **(b) to ~ for peace** pedir la paz.

suède [sweɪd] N suecia *f*, ante *m*, gamuza *f* (*LAm*); **~ gloves** guantes *mpl* de ante, guantes *mpl* de cabritilla; **~ shoes** zapatos *mpl* de ante.

suet [suɪt] N sebo *m*; **~ pudding** pudín *m* a base de sebo.

Suetonius [swiː'təʊnɪəs] NM Suetonio.

suety ['suɪtɪ] ADJ seboso.

Suez Canal ['suːɪzkə'næl] N Canal *m* de Suez.

Suff N (*Brit*) ABBR of **Suffolk**.

suffer ['sʌfə^r] 1 VT **(a)** (*painfully*) sufrir, padecer; (*bear*) aguantar, sufrir; (*undergo*) sufrir, experimentar; **I can't ~ it a moment longer** no puedo aguantarlo un momento más; **it has ~ed a sharp decline** ha experimentado un brusco descenso; **to ~ a defeat** sufrir una derrota; **to ~ death** morir, ser muerto; **he doesn't ~ fools gladly** no tiene paciencia con los imbéciles. **(b)** (*allow*) permitir, tolerar; **to ~ sb to do sth** permitir a uno hacer algo; autorizar a uno para que haga algo; **to ~ sth to be done** permitir que se haga algo. 2 VI **(a)** sufrir, padecer; **did you ~ much?** ¿sufriste mucho?; **how I ~ed!** ¡lo que sufrí!; **the army ~ed badly** el ejército tuvo pérdidas importantes; **sales have ~ed badly** las ventas han sido afectadas seriamente; **the town ~ed in the raids** la ciudad sufrió grandes daños en los bombardeos; **we will see that you do not ~ by the changes** aseguraremos que Vd no pierda nada a consecuencia de estos cambios. **(b) to ~ for one's sins** sufrir las consecuencias de sus pecados; **you will ~ for it** lo pagarás después. **(c)** (*be afflicted*) **to ~ from** sufrir, padecer (de), estar afligido por; (*fig*) adolecer de; ser la víctima de; **to ~ from boils** tener diviesos; **to ~ from rheumatism** padecer de reumatismo; **to ~ from the effects of sth** resentirse de algo, estar resentido de algo; **she ~s from her environment** es la víctima de su ambiente; **the house is ~ing from neglect** la casa padece abandono; **your style ~s from overelaboration** su estilo adolece de una excesiva complicación.

sufferance ['sʌfərəns] N tolerancia *f*; **on ~** por tolerancia.

sufferer ['sʌfərə^r] N (*Med*) enfermo *m*, -a *f* (*from* de); víctima *f*; **~s from diabetes** los enfermos de diabetes, los diabéticos; **the ~s from the earthquake** las víctimas del terremoto.

suffering ['sʌfərɪŋ] 1 ADJ que sufre; (*Med*) doliente, enfermo. 2 N sufrimiento *m*, padecimiento *m*; (*grief etc*) dolor *m*; **after months of ~** después de sufrir durante meses; **the ~s of the soldiers** los padecimientos de los soldados.

suffice [sə'faɪs] 1 VT satisfacer; ser bastante para. 2 VI bastar, ser suficiente; **~ it to say that ...** basta decir que ...

sufficiency [sə'fɪʃənsɪ] N (*state*) suficiencia *f*; (*quantity*) cantidad *f* suficiente; **to have a ~** estar acomodado.

sufficient [sə'fɪʃənt] ADJ suficiente, bastante; **to be ~** ser suficiente, bastar.

sufficiently [sə'fɪʃəntlɪ] ADV suficientemente, bastante; **~ good** bastante bueno.

suffix ['sʌfɪks] 1 N sufijo *m*. 2 VT añadir como sufijo (*to* a).

suffocate ['sʌfəkeɪt] 1 VT ahogar, asfixiar, sofocar. 2 VI ahogarse, asfixiarse, quedar asfixiado, sofocarse.

suffocating ['sʌfəkeɪtɪŋ] ADJ sofocante, asfixiante; **~ heat** calor *m* sofocante.

suffocation [ˌsʌfə'keɪʃən] N sofocación *f*, asfixia *f*.

suffragan ['sʌfrəgən] 1 ADJ sufragáneo. 2 N obispo *m* sufragáneo.

suffrage ['sʌfrɪdʒ] N **(a)** (*franchise*) sufragio *m*; derecho *m* de votar; **to get the ~** obtener el derecho de votar. **(b)** (*formal: vote*) voto *m*; aprobación *f*.

suffragette [ˌsʌfrə'dʒet] N sufragista *f*.

suffuse [sə'fjuːz] VT bañar, cubrir (*with* de); difundirse por; **~d with light** inundado de luz, bañado de luz; **eyes ~d with tears** ojos *mpl* bañados de lágrimas.

suffusion [sə'fjuːʒən] N difusión *f*.

sugar ['ʃʊgə^r] 1 N **(a)** azúcar *m and f*. **(b)** (*US*•) hi, **~!** ¡oye, preciosidad!• **(c)** (*euph*) oh **~!** ¡caracoles!• 2 ATTR: **~ cube, ~ lump** terrón *m* de azúcar; **~ plantation** cañaveral *m*, plantación *f* de caña de azúcar; **~ refinery** refinería *f* de azúcar,

trapiche *m*, ingenio *m* azucarero. 3 VT azucarar; echar azúcar a (*or* en), añadir azúcar a; **~ed almonds** peladillas *fpl*, almendras *fpl* garapiñadas.

sugar-basin ['ʃʊgəˌbeɪsn] N (*Brit*) azucarero *m*.

sugar-beet ['ʃʊgəbiːt] N remolacha *f* azucarera.

sugar-bowl ['ʃʊgəbəʊl] N azucarero *m*.

sugar-candy ['ʃʊgəˌkændɪ] N azúcar *m* candi.

sugar-cane ['ʃʊgəkeɪn] N caña *f* de azúcar.

sugar-coated ['ʃʊgə'kəʊtɪd] ADJ azucarado, garapiñado.

sugar daddy• ['ʃʊgəˌdædɪ] N viejo *m* adinerado amante de una joven, protector *m* (de una joven).

sugared ['ʃʊgəd] ADJ = **sugary**.

sugar-free [ˌʃʊgə'friː] ADJ, **sugarless** ['ʃʊgəlɪs] ADJ sin azúcar.

sugarloaf ['ʃʊgələʊf] N pan *m* de azúcar.

sugarmill ['ʃʊgəmɪl] N ingenio *m* azucarero.

sugarplum ['ʃʊgəplʌm] N confite *m*.

sugar-tongs ['ʃʊgətɒŋz] NPL tenacillas *fpl* para azúcar.

sugary ['ʃʊgərɪ] ADJ **(a)** azucarado. **(b)** (*fig*) *style etc* meloso, almibarado; (*sentimental*) sensiblero, sentimental; romántico.

▼ **suggest** [sə'dʒest] 1 VT sugerir; (*point to*) indicar; (*advise*) aconsejar, indicar; (*hint*) insinuar; (*evoke*) evocar, hacer pensar en; **to ~ that ...** (*of person*) sugerir que ..., proponer que ...; **this ~s that ...** esto hace pensar que ..., esto lleva a pensar que ...; **I ~ to you that ...** (*in law speeches*) ¿no es cierto que ...?; **we ~ you contact X** les aconsejamos contactar con X; **it doesn't exactly ~ a careful man** no parece indicar un hombre prudente; **the coins ~ a Roman building** las monedas indican un edificio romano; **the symptoms ~ an operation** los síntomas aconsejan una operación; **prudence ~s a retreat** la prudencia nos aconseja retirarnos; **what are you ~ing?** ¿qué es lo que insinúa Vd?, ¿qué es lo que pretende Vd? 2 VR: **an idea ~s itself** se me ocurre una idea; **nothing ~s itself** no se me ocurre nada.

suggestibility [səˌdʒestɪ'bɪlɪtɪ] N sugestionabilidad *f*.

suggestible [sə'dʒestɪbl] ADJ *person* sugestionable.

▼ **suggestion** [sə'dʒestʃən] N **(a)** sugerencia *f*; indicación *f*; insinuación *f*; **~s box** buzón *m* de sugerencias; **if I may make** (*or* offer) **a ~** si se me permite proponer algo; **my ~ is that ...** yo propongo que ...; **that is an immoral ~** ésa es una idea inmoral; **following your ~ ...** siguiendo sus indicaciones ...; **I am writing at the ~ of Z** le escribo siguiendo la indicación de Z; **there is no ~ of corruption** nada indica la corrupción, no hay indicio de corrupción. **(b)** (*hypnotic*) sugestión *f*. **(c)** (*trace*) sombra *f*, traza *f*; **with just a ~ of garlic** con un poquitín de ajo; **with a ~ of irony in his voice** con un punto de ironía en la voz.

suggestive [sə'dʒestɪv] ADJ sugestivo; (*pej*) indecente; **~ of** que evoca, que hace pensar en; que trasciende a.

suggestively [sə'dʒestɪvlɪ] ADJ (*pej*) indecentemente.

suggestiveness [sə'dʒestɪvnɪs] N (*pej*) indecencia *f*.

suicidal [ˌsuɪ'saɪdl] ADJ suicida; **to have a ~ tendency** tener tendencia al suicidio; **I feel ~ this morning** esta mañana estoy por desesperarme; **he drives in a ~ way** es un suicida conduciendo; **it would be ~** sería peligrosísimo.

suicide ['suɪsaɪd] 1 N (*act*) suicidio *m*; (*person*) suicida *mf*; **to commit ~** suicidarse; **it would be ~ to say so** sería peligrosísimo decirlo. 2 ATTR: **~ attempt** tentativa *f* de suicidio; **~ note** nota *f* en la que se explica el motivo del suicidio; **~ pact** acuerdo *m* para suicidarse (dos personas al mismo tiempo); **~ squad** comando *m* suicida.

suit [suːt] 1 N **(a)** (*garment*) (*man's*) traje *m*; terno *m* (*LAm*); (*woman's*) traje *m* de chaqueta; **~ of armour** armadura *f*; **~ of clothes** traje *m*. **(b)** (*Jur*) pleito *m*, litigio *m*, proceso *m*; **to bring a ~** poner pleito; **to bring** (*or* file) **a ~ against sb** entablar demanda contra uno (*for sth* por algo). **(c)** (*request*) petición *f*; **at the ~ of** a petición de. **(d)** (*in marriage*) petición *f* de mano, oferta *f* de matrimonio; **to press one's ~** hacer una oferta de matrimonio. **(e)** (*Cards*) palo *m*, color *m*; **long ~, strong ~** palo *m* largo; **to have nothing in that ~** tener fallo a ese palo; **to follow ~** servir del (*or* el) palo, (*fig*) hacer lo mismo, seguir el ejemplo (de uno). 2 VT **(a)** (*adapt*) adaptar, ajustar, acomodar (*to* a); **to ~ one's style to one's audience** adaptar su estilo al público; **~ing the action to the word** uniendo la acción a la palabra; **the coat and hat are well ~ed** el abrigo y el sombrero van bien juntos; **they are well ~ed to each other** están hechos el uno para el otro; **he is not ~ed for** (*or* to be) **a doctor** no es apto para ser médico. **(b)** (*be suitable: clothes*) sentar a, ir bien a, caer bien a; (*in general*) convenir; gustar; **the coat ~s you** el abrigo te sienta, el abrigo te va bien; **the climate does not ~ me** el clima no me sienta bien; **the job ~s me nicely** el puesto me conviene perfectamente; **does this ~ you?** ¿te gusta esto?; **come when it ~s you** ven cuando quieras, ven cuando te convenga; **I know what ~s me best** sé lo que me conviene; **I shall do it when it ~s me** lo haré cuando me dé la gana.

3 VR: **he ~s himself** hace lo que le da la gana, hace lo que quiere; **~ yourself!** ¡haz lo que quieras!, ¡como quieras!

suitability [ˌsuːtəˈbɪlɪtɪ] N conveniencia *f*; idoneidad *f* (*for* para).

suitable ['suːtəbl] ADJ conveniente, apropiado; adecuado, idóneo; indicado; **the most ~ man for the job** el hombre más indicado para el puesto; **is this hat ~?** ¿me conviene este sombrero?; **the film is not ~ for children** la película no es apta para menores; **we didn't find anything at all ~** no encontramos nada a propósito, no encontramos nada que nos conviniera; **Tuesday is the most ~ day** el martes nos conviene más.

suitably ['suːtəblɪ] ADV convenientemente; apropiadamente; **~ dressed for tennis** convenientemente vestido para el tenis.

suitcase ['suːtkeɪs] N maleta *f*, valija *f* (*LAm*), veliz *m* (*Mex*).

suite [swiːt] N (*of retainers*) séquito *m*, comitiva *f*; (*of furniture*) juego *m*, mobiliario *m*; (*rooms*) serie *f* de habitaciones, grupo *m* de habitaciones; (*Mus*) suite *f*; **bedroom ~** (juego *m* de muebles para) alcoba *f*; **dining-room ~** comedor *m*.

suiting ['suːtɪŋ] N (*Comm*) tela *f* para trajes.

suitor ['suːtər] N pretendiente *m*; (*Jur*) demandante *mf*.

sulfa drug ['sʌlfədrʌg] N sulfamida *f*.

sulfate ['sʌlfeɪt] *etc* (*US*) = **sulphate** *etc*.

sulk [sʌlk] **1** N: **~s** mohína *f*, murria *f*, mal humor *m*; **to have the ~s** estar mohíno, estar de mal humor; **to get the ~s** amohinarse.

2 VI estar mohíno, estar amohinado, poner cara larga, estar de mal humor.

sulkily ['sʌlkɪlɪ] ADV con mohíno; *answer etc* con mal humor, de mala gana.

sulkiness ['sʌlkɪnɪs] N mohína *f*, murria *f*, mal humor *m*.

sulky ['sʌlkɪ] ADJ mohíno; malhumorado; resentido; **to be ~** estar mohíno, estar de mal humor.

sullen ['sʌlən] ADJ hosco, malhumorado; resentido; taciturno; *countryside* triste; *sky* plomizo.

sullenly ['sʌlənlɪ] ADV hoscamente; *answer* con mal humor; *look* con resentimiento.

sullenness ['sʌlənnɪs] N hosquedad *f*, mal humor *m*; resentimiento *m*; taciturnidad *f*.

sully ['sʌlɪ] VT (*liter*) manchar.

sulpha drug ['sʌlfədrʌg] = **sulfa drug**.

sulphate, (*US*) **sulfate** ['sʌlfeɪt] N sulfato *m*; **copper ~** sulfato *m* de cobre.

sulphide, (*US*) **sulfide** ['sʌlfaɪd] N sulfuro *m*.

sulphonamide, (*US*) **sulfonamide** [sʌlˈfɒnəmaɪd] N sulfamida *f*.

sulphur, (*US*) **sulfur** ['sʌlfər] N azufre *m*; **~ dioxide** dióxido *m* de azufre.

sulphureous, (*US*) **sulfureous** [sʌlˈfjʊərɪəs] ADJ sulfúrico.

sulphuric, (*US*) **sulfuric** [sʌlˈfjʊərɪk] ADJ sulfúrico; **~ acid** ácido *m* sulfúrico.

sulphurous, (*US*) **sulfurous** ['sʌlfərəs] ADJ sulfuroso, sulfúreo.

sultan ['sʌltən] N sultán *m*.

sultana [sʌlˈtɑːnə] N (a) (*person*) sultana *f*. (b) (*fruit*) pasa *f* de Esmirna.

sultanate ['sʌltənɪt] N sultanato *m*.

sultriness ['sʌltrɪnɪs] N bochorno *m*; calor *m* sofocante.

sultry ['sʌltrɪ] ADJ (a) *weather* bochornoso; *heat, atmosphere* sofocante. (b) (*fig*) apasionado; seductor, provocativo.

▼ **sum** [sʌm] N (*total*) suma *f*, total *m*; (*quantity*) suma *f*, cantidad *f*; (*Math*) problema *m* de aritmética; **~ total** total *m* (completo); **it is greater than the ~ of its parts** es mayor que la suma de sus partes; **the ~ total of my ambitions is ...** la meta de mis ambiciones es ...; lo único que ambiciono es ...; **in ~** en suma, en resumen; **to do ~s in one's head** hacer un cálculo mental; **I was very bad at ~s** era muy malo en aritmética.

◆ **sum up** **1** VT (*tot up*) sumar; (*review*) resumir; (*evaluate rapidly*) tomar las medidas a, evaluar (rápidamente), justipreciar; **to ~ up an argument** resumir un argumento, recapitular un argumento; **to ~ up a debate** recapitular los argumentos empleados en un debate; **she ~med me up at a glance** me tomó las medidas con una sola mirada; **he ~med up the situation quickly** se dio cuenta rápidamente de la situación.

2 VI recapitular, hacer un resumen; **to ~ up ...** en resumen ...

sumac(h) ['suːmæk] N zumaque *m*.

Sumatra [sʊˈmɑːtrə] N Sumatra *f*.

summarily ['sʌmərɪlɪ] ADV sumariamente.

summarize ['sʌməraɪz] VTI resumir.

summary ['sʌmərɪ] **1** ADJ sumario.

2 N resumen *m*, sumario *m*; **in ~** en resumen.

summat ['sʌmət] (*dialectal*) = **something**.

summation [sʌˈmeɪʃən] N (*act*) adición *f*; recapitulación *f*, resumen *m*; (*total*) suma *f*, total *m*.

summer ['sʌmər] **1** N verano *m*, estío *m*; **a girl of 17 ~s** una joven de 17 abriles; **a ~'s day** un día de verano; **to spend the ~** veranear, pasar el verano.

2 ATTR *day, clothing, residence* de verano; *season* veraniego; *resort* de veraneo; *weather, heat* estival; **~ camp** (*US*) colonia *f* veraniega infantil; **~ holidays** vacaciones *fpl* de verano, veraneo *m*; **~ school** escuela *f* de verano; **~ time** (*with reference to change of hour*) hora *f* de verano.

3 VI veranear, pasar el verano.

summerhouse ['sʌməhaʊs] N, PL **summerhouses** ['sʌməˌhaʊzɪz] cenador *m*, glorieta *f*.

summertime ['sʌmətaɪm] N (*Brit: season*) verano *m*.

summery ['sʌmərɪ] ADJ veraniego, estival.

summing-up ['sʌmɪŋ'ʌp] N resumen *m*, recapitulación *f*.

summit ['sʌmɪt] **1** N cima *f*, cumbre *f* (*also fig*).

2 ATTR: **~ conference** conferencia *f* (en la) cumbre; **~ meeting** cumbre *f*.

summitry ['sʌmɪtrɪ] N (*hum*) arte *m* de celebrar conferencias cumbre; política *f* en la cumbre.

summon ['sʌmən] VT *servant etc* llamar; *meeting* convocar; *aid* pedir, requerir; (*Jur*) citar, emplazar; **to be ~ed to sb's presence** ser llamado a la presencia de uno; **they ~ed me to advise them** me llamaron para que les diera consejos; **to ~ a town to surrender** hacer una llamada a una ciudad para que se rinda, intimar a una ciudad que se rinda.

◆ **summon up** VT *courage* armarse de, cobrar; *memory* evocar.

summons ['sʌmənz] **1** N llamamiento *m*, llamada *f*; requerimiento *m*; (*Jur*) citación *f*; **to serve a ~ on sb** entregar una citación a uno; **to take out a ~ against sb** entablar demanda contra uno, citar a uno (para estrados).

2 VT citar, emplazar.

sumo ['suːməʊ] N (*also ~ wrestling*) sumo *m*.

sump [sʌmp] N (*Brit Aut etc*) cárter *m*, colector *m* de aceite; (*Min etc*) sumidero *m*; (*fig*) letrina *f*.

sumptuary ['sʌmptjʊərɪ] ADJ suntuario.

sumptuous ['sʌmptjʊəs] ADJ suntuoso.

sumptuously ['sʌmptjʊəslɪ] ADV suntuosamente.

sumptuousness ['sʌmptjʊəsnɪs] N suntuosidad *f*.

sun [sʌn] **1** N sol *m*; **in the July ~** bajo el sol de julio; **to be out in the ~** estar al sol; **the milk stood in the ~ all day** la leche estuvo al sol todo el día; **he called me all the names under the ~** me dijo de todo; **there's nothing new under the ~** no hay nada realmente nuevo; **they stock everything under the ~** tienen de todo como en botica; **there's no reason under the ~** no hay razón alguna; **to bask in the ~** tomar el sol, estar tumbado al sol; **you've caught the ~** te ha dado el sol; **to have a place in the ~** (*fig*) tener una buena situación; **(put it) where the ~ do(es)n't shine!** (*US*) ¡(métetelo) donde te quepa!; **the ~ is shining** hace sol, el sol brilla.

2 ATTR de sol; solar.

3 VT asolear.

4 VR: **to ~ o.s.** asolearse, tomar el sol.

Sun. [sʌn] N ABBR *of* **Sunday** domingo *m*, dom.º.

sunbaked ['sʌnbeɪkt] ADJ endurecido al sol.

sunbath ['sʌnbɑːθ] N, PL **sunbaths** ['sʌnbɑːðz] baño *m* de sol.

sunbathe ['sʌnbeɪð] VI tomar el sol.

sunbather ['sʌnbeɪðər] N persona *f* que toma el sol.

sunbathing ['sʌnbeɪðɪŋ] N baños *mpl* de sol.

sunbeam ['sʌnbiːm] N rayo *m* de sol.

sunbed ['sʌnbed] N (*in garden etc*) tumbona *f*; (*with sunray lamp*) cama *f* de rayos infrarrojos, cama *f* solar.

sunbelt ['sʌnbelt] N (*US*) *franja del sur de Estados Unidos caracterizada por su clima cálido*.

┌─ **SUNBELT** ─┐

ⓘ *A los estados del sur de EE.UU. que van desde Carolina del Norte hasta California se les denomina sunbelt (cinturón del sol) por su clima cálido. Este nombre también se asocia con el reciente desarrollo económico de la zona, lo cual ha dado lugar a un aumento de población (por el movimiento demográfico de norte a sur) y a un mayor poder político. Por oposición a este término, a los estados del norte se les llama a veces frostbelt (cinturón de escarcha) o rustbelt (cinturón de óxido), por el número de fábricas ya en declive que hay en la zona.*

sunblind ['sʌnblaɪnd] N toldo *m*; store *m*.

sunblock ['sʌnblɒk] N filtro *m* solar.

sunbonnet ['sʌnˌbɒnɪt] N gorro *m* de sol.

sunburn ['sʌnbɜːn] N (*tan*) bronceado *m*; (*painful*) quemadura *f* del sol.

sunburned ['sʌnbɜːnd] ADJ, **sunburnt** ['sʌnbɜːnt] ADJ (*tanned*) tostado por el sol, bronceado; (*painfully*) quemado por el sol; **to get ~** broncearse; sufrir quemaduras del sol.

sundeck ['sʌndek] N cubierta *f* de sol.

sundae ['sʌndeɪ] N *helado con frutas, nueces etc*.

Sunday ['sʌndɪ] **1** N domingo *m*.

2 ATTR dominical, de domingo; ~ **best** ropa *f* dominguera; ~ **opening** = ~ **trading**; ~ **paper** periódico *m* del domingo; ~ **school** escuela *f* dominical, catequesis *f*; ~ **school teacher** profesor *m*, -ora *f* de escuela dominical; ~ **supplement** suplemento *m* dominical; ~ **trading** apertura *f* dominical; ~ **trading laws** leyes *fpl* reguladoras de la apertura dominical.

SUNDAY PAPERS

Los periódicos dominicales (**Sunday Papers**) *juegan un papel importante en el Reino Unido. Algunos de ellos, como* **The Observer** *o* **News of the World** *sólo se publican ese día, mientras que otros, como* **The Sunday Times, The Sunday Telegraph, The Independent on Sunday, The Sunday Express** *o* **The Sunday Mirror**, *son ediciones especiales de periódicos diarios. Los dominicales suelen tener distintas secciones, con espacios para cultura, viajes, deportes o negocios, además de incluir muchos de ellos una revista en color.*

En Estados Unidos se suelen comprar más los periódicos locales que los de tirada nacional. De éstos, el principal es el **New York Times**. *Al igual que en el Reino Unido, los periódicos dominicales tienen más secciones de lo habitual, con artículos más extensos, y venden más ejemplares. Pero a diferencia de los británicos, los estadounidenses suelen comprar un solo periódico los domingos.*

sunder [ˈsʌndəʳ] VT (*liter*) romper, dividir, hender; separar.
sundew [ˈsʌndjuː] N rocío *m* de sol.
sundial [ˈsʌndaɪəl] N reloj *m* de sol.
sundown [ˈsʌndaʊn] N puesta *f* del sol; anochecer *m*; **at** ~ al anochecer; **before** ~ antes del anochecer.
sundowner* [ˈsʌndaʊnəʳ] N (*Brit*) *trago de licor que se toma al anochecer.*
sun-drenched [ˈsʌndrentʃt] ADJ inundado de sol.
sundress [ˈsʌndres] N vestido *m* de playa.
sun-dried [ˈsʌndraɪd] ADJ secado al sol.
sundry [ˈsʌndrɪ] 1 ADJ varios, diversos; **all and** ~ todos y cada uno.
2 NPL: **sundries** (*Comm*) géneros *mpl* diversos; (*expenses*) gastos *mpl* diversos.
sun-filled [ˈsʌnfɪld] ADJ soleado.
sunfish [ˈsʌnfɪʃ] N peje-sol *m*.
sunflower [ˈsʌnˌflaʊəʳ] 1 N girasol *m*.
2 ATTR: ~ **oil** aceite *m* de girasol; ~ **seeds** pipas *fpl*.
sung [sʌŋ] PTP *of* **sing**.
sunglasses [ˈsʌnˌglɑːsɪz] NPL gafas *fpl* de sol.
sun-god [ˈsʌngɒd] N dios *m* del sol, divinidad *f* solar.
sunhat [ˈsʌnhæt] N pamela *f*, sombrero *m* ancho.
sunk [sʌŋk] PTP *of* **sink**.
sunken [ˈsʌŋkən] ADJ hundido.
sunlamp [ˈsʌnlæmp] N lámpara *f* de sol artificial, lámpara *f* ultravioleta.
sunless [ˈsʌnlɪs] ADJ sin sol.
sunlight [ˈsʌnlaɪt] N sol *m*, luz *f* del sol, luz *f* solar; **in the** ~ al sol; **the** ~ **is strong** el sol es fuerte; **hours of** ~ (*Met*) horas *fpl* de insolación.
sunlit [ˈsʌnlɪt] ADJ iluminado por el sol.
sun-lotion [ˈsʌnˌləʊʃən] N bronceador *m*.
sun-lounge [ˈsʌnlaʊndʒ] N solana *f*.
sunlounger [ˈsʌnˌlaʊndʒəʳ] N tumbona *f*.
Sunni [ˈsʌnɪ] 1 ADJ sunita.
2 N sunita *mf*.
sunny [ˈsʌnɪ] ADJ **(a)** *place, room etc* soleado; expuesto al sol; bañado de sol, iluminado por el sol; *day* de sol; **it is** ~ hace sol; **June is a** ~ **month** junio tiene mucho sol; **Málaga is sunnier than Manchester** Málaga tiene más sol que Manchester.
(b) (*fig*) *face* risueño; *smile, disposition* alegre; **to be on the** ~ **side of 40*** tener menos de 40 años; **eggs** ~ **side up** (*US*) huevos *mpl* al plato, huevos *mpl* fritos (*sin haberles dado la vuelta en la sartén*).
sun-parlour, (*US*) **sun-parlor** [ˈsʌnpɑːləʳ] N solana *f*.
sunray [ˈsʌnreɪ] ATTR: ~ **lamp** lámpara *f* ultravioleta; ~ **treatment** helioterapia *f*, tratamiento *m* con lámpara ultravioleta.
sunrise [ˈsʌnraɪz] 1 N salida *f* del sol; **from** ~ **to sunset** de sol a sol.
2 ATTR: ~ **industries** industrias *fpl* del porvenir, industrias *fpl* de alta tecnología.
sunroof [ˈsʌnruːf] N (*Aut*) techo *m* corredizo.
sunscreen [ˈsʌnskriːn] N bronceador *m* con filtro solar.
sunset [ˈsʌnset] 1 N puesta *f* del sol, ocaso *m*.
2 ATTR: ~ **industries** industrias *fpl* crepusculares.
sunshade [ˈsʌnʃeɪd] N (*portable*) quitasol *m*; (*over table*) sombrilla *f*; (*awning*) toldo *m*.
sunshine [ˈsʌnʃaɪn] 1 N **(a)** sol *m*, luz *f* del sol; **in the** ~ al sol; **hours of** ~ (*Met*) horas *fpl* de insolación; **daily average** ~ insolación *f* media diaria.
(b) (*) **hello,** ~**!** (*to child*) ¡hola, nena!*; **now look here,** ~ (*iro*) mira, macho*.
2 ATTR: ~ **laws** (*US*) *leyes que obligan a mantener informado al público*; ~ **roof** techo *m* corredizo.
sunspot [ˈsʌnspɒt] N mancha *f* solar.
sunstroke [ˈsʌnstrəʊk] N insolación *f*, asoleada *f* (*And*); **to have** ~ sufrir una insolación.
sunsuit [ˈsʌnsuːt] N traje *m* de playa.
suntan [ˈsʌntæn] 1 N bronceado *m*.
2 ATTR: ~ **lotion** bronceador *m*.
suntanned [ˈsʌntænd] ADJ bronceado.
suntrap [ˈsʌntræp] N solana *f*, lugar *m* muy soleado.
sunup [ˈsʌnʌp] N (*US*) salida *f* del sol.
sunworshipper [ˈsʌnwɜːʃɪpəʳ] N fanático *m*, -a *f* del sol.
sup [sʌp] 1 VT (*also* **to** ~ **up**) sorber, beber a sorbos.
2 VI cenar; **to** ~ **off sth, to** ~ **on sth** cenar algo.
super [ˈsuːpəʳ] 1 ADJ (*) estupendo*, bárbaro*, súper*; **how** ~**!** ¡qué bien!; **the new car is** ~ el nuevo coche es estupendo*; **we had a** ~ **time** lo pasamos bomba*.
2 N (*) (ABBR *Theat, Cine*) figurante *m*, -a *f*; comparsa *mf*; (*Tech: superintendent*) superintendente *m*, (*of police*) comisario *m*.
super... [ˈsuːpəʳ] PREF super..., sobre...; *eg* ~**-salesman** supervendedor *m*.
superabound [ˌsuːpərəˈbaʊnd] VI sobreabundar (*in, with* en).
superabundance [ˌsuːpərəˈbʌndəns] N sobreabundancia *f*, superabundancia *f*.
superabundant [ˌsuːpərəˈbʌndənt] ADJ sobreabundante, superabundante.
superannuate [ˌsuːpəˈrænjʊeɪt] VT jubilar.
superannuated [ˌsuːpəˈrænjʊeɪtɪd] ADJ jubilado; (*fig*) anticuado.
superannuation [ˌsuːpəˌrænjʊˈeɪʃən] 1 N jubilación *f*.
2 ATTR: ~ **contribution** cuota *f* de jubilación.
superb [suːˈpɜːb] ADJ magnífico, espléndido.
superbly [suːˈpɜːblɪ] ADV magníficamente; **a** ~ **painted picture** un cuadro de la mayor excelencia técnica; **a** ~ **fit man** un hombre en magnífico estado físico.
Super Bowl, Superbowl [ˈsuːpəbəʊl] N (*US: Sport*) *supercopa de fútbol americano.*
superbug* [ˈsuːpəbʌg] N bacteria *f* asesina.
supercargo [ˈsuːpəˌkɑːgəʊ] N sobrecargo *m*.
supercharged [ˈsuːpətʃɑːdʒd] ADJ sobrealimentado.
supercharger [ˈsuːpətʃɑːdʒəʳ] N sobrealimentador *m*.
supercilious [ˌsuːpəˈsɪlɪəs] ADJ desdeñoso, arrogante; suficiente.
superciliously [ˌsuːpəˈsɪlɪəslɪ] ADV desdeñosamente, con desdén; con aire de suficiencia.
superciliousness [ˌsuːpəˈsɪlɪəsnɪs] N desdén *m*, arrogancia *f*.
supercomputer [ˈsuːpəkəmˈpjuːtəʳ] N superordenador *m*.
superconductive [ˌsuːpəkənˈdʌktɪv] ADJ superconductor.
superconductivity [ˌsuːpəˌkɒndʌkˈtɪvɪtɪ] N superconductividad *f*.
superconductor [ˌsuːpəkənˈdʌktəʳ] N superconductor *m*.
super-duper* [ˈsuːpəˈduːpəʳ] ADJ estupendo*, magnífico, de aúpa*; ~**!** ¡magnífico!
superego [ˈsuːpərˌiːgəʊ] N superego *m*.
supererogation [ˌsuːpərˌerəˈgeɪʃən] N supererogación *f*.
superficial [ˌsuːpəˈfɪʃəl] ADJ superficial.
superficiality [ˌsuːpəˌfɪʃɪˈælɪtɪ] N superficialidad *f*.
superficially [ˌsuːpəˈfɪʃəlɪ] ADV superficialmente; en la superficie; ~ **this may be true** a primera vista esto puede ser verdad.
superfine [ˈsuːpəfaɪn] ADJ extrafino.
superfluity [ˌsuːpəˈflʊɪtɪ] N superfluidad *f*; **there is a** ~ **of ...** hay exceso de ...
superfluous [sʊˈpɜːflʊəs] ADJ superfluo; sobrante, que sobra, que está de más; **it is** ~ **to say that ...** no hace falta decir que ...
superfluously [sʊˈpɜːflʊəslɪ] ADV superfluamente; **he added** ~ añadió fuera de propósito.
superglue [ˈsuːpəˌgluː] N supercola *f*.
supergrass* [ˈsuːpəgrɑːs] N supersoplón* *m*, -ona *f*.
supergroup [ˈsuːpəgruːp] N grupo *m* estrella, superbanda *f*.
superhero [ˈsuːpəˌhɪərəʊ] N superhéroe *m*.
superheat [ˌsuːpəˈhiːt] VT sobrecalentar.
superhighway [ˈsuːpəˈhaɪweɪ] N (*US*) autopista *f* (de varios carriles).
superhuman [ˌsuːpəˈhjuːmən] ADJ sobrehumano.
superimpose [ˈsuːpərɪmˈpəʊz] VT sobreponer (*on* en).
superinduce [ˈsuːpərɪnˈdjuːs] VT sobreañadir, inducir por añadidura.
superintend [ˌsuːpərɪnˈtend] VT vigilar; supervisar, dirigir.
superintendence [ˌsuːpərɪnˈtendəns] N superintendencia *f*; supervisión *f*, dirección *f*.
superintendent [ˌsuːpərɪnˈtendənt] N superintendente *mf*; inspector *m*, -ora *f*; supervisor *m*, -ora *f*; (*in swimming pool etc*) vigilante *mf*; ~ **of police** comisario *m* de policía.
superior [sʊˈpɪərɪəʳ] 1 ADJ superior (*to* a); (*smug*) desdeñoso; satisfecho, suficiente; **she thinks herself very** ~ se da aires de suficiencia; **he said in that** ~ **tone** dijo en ese tono suficiente.
2 N superior *m*; (*Eccl*) superior *m*, -ora *f*; **Mother S~** (madre *f*) superiora *f*.

➤ LANGUAGE IN USE: **superior: 1 → 5.4**

superiority [sʊ,pɪərɪ'ɒrɪtɪ] N superioridad *f* (*to* a); desdén *m*; suficiencia *f*.

superlative [sʊ'pɜːlətɪv] **1** ADJ superlativo (*also Gram*), extremo. **2** N superlativo *m*.

superlatively [sʊ'pɜːlətɪvlɪ] ADV en sumo grado, extremadamente; ~ fit en óptimo estado físico.

superman ['suːpəmæn] N, PL **supermen** ['suːpəmen] superhombre *m*.

supermarket ['suːpə,mɑːkɪt] N supermercado *m*.

supernatural [,suːpə'nætʃərəl] **1** ADJ sobrenatural. **2** N: **the** ~ lo sobrenatural.

supernormal [,suːpə'nɔːməl] ADJ superior a lo normal.

supernova [,suːpə'nəʊvə] N (*Astron*) supernova *f*.

supernumerary [,suːpə'njuːmərərɪ] **1** ADJ supernumerario. **2** N supernumerario *m*, -a *f*; (*Theat, Cine*) figurante *m*, -a *f*, comparsa *mf*.

superordinate [,suːpər'ɔːdɪnɪt] **1** ADJ superior. **2** N (*Ling*) término *m* genérico, archilexema *m*.

superphosphate [,suːpə'fɒsfeɪt] N superfosfato *m*.

superpose ['suːpəpəʊz] VT sobreponer, superponer.

superposition ['suːpəpəzɪʃən] N superposición *f*.

superpower ['suːpə,paʊəʳ] N superpotencia *f*.

superscript [,suːpə'skrɪpt] N superíndice *m*.

superscription [,suːpə'skrɪpʃən] N sobrescrito *m*.

supersede [,suːpə'siːd] VT reemplazar, sustituir; suplantar.

supersensitive ['suːpə'sensɪtɪv] ADJ extremadamente sensible (*to* a).

supersonic ['suːpə'sɒnɪk] ADJ supersónico; ~ **bang**, ~ **boom** estampido *m* supersónico, bang *m* sónico.

supersonically ['suːpə'sɒnɪkəlɪ] ADV fly etc a velocidad supersónica.

superstar ['suːpəstɑːʳ] N superestrella *f*.

superstate ['suːpəsteɪt] N superestado *m*.

superstition [,suːpə'stɪʃən] N superstición *f*.

superstitious [,suːpə'stɪʃəs] ADJ supersticioso.

superstitiously [,suːpə'stɪʃəslɪ] ADV supersticiosamente.

superstore ['suːpəstɔːʳ] N (*Brit*) hipermercado *m*.

superstratum [,suːpə'strɑːtəm] N, PL **superstratums** or **superstrata** [,suːpə'strɑːtə] superstrato *m*.

superstructure ['suːpə,strʌktʃəʳ] N superestructura *f*.

supertanker ['suːpə,tæŋkəʳ] N superpetrolero *m*, petrolero *m* gigante.

supertax ['suːpətæks] N sobreimpuesto *m*; (*rate*) sobretasa *f*.

supervene [,suːpə'viːn] VI sobrevenir.

supervise ['suːpəvaɪz] VT supervisar; (*Univ*) thesis dirigir.

supervision [,suːpə'vɪʒən] N supervisión *f*: **to work under the** ~ **of** ... trabajar bajo la supervisión de ...

supervisor ['suːpəvaɪzəʳ] N supervisor *m*, -ora *f*; (*Univ*) director *m*, -ora *f*.

supervisory ['suːpəvaɪzərɪ] ADJ: **in a** ~ **post** en un cargo de supervisor; **in his** ~ **capacity** en su función de supervisor.

supine ['suːpaɪn] **1** ADJ supino; (*fig*) flojo, sin carácter, débil. **2** N supino *m*.

supper ['sʌpəʳ] N cena *f*; **the Last S~** la Última Cena; **to stay to** ~ quedarse a cenar; **to have** ~ cenar.

suppertime ['sʌpətaɪm] N hora *f* de cenar.

supplant [sə'plɑːnt] VT suplantar.

supple ['sʌpl] ADJ flexible.

supplement **1** ['sʌplɪmənt] N suplemento *m*; apéndice *m*; (*Press*) suplemento *m*. **2** [sʌplɪ'ment] VT suplir, complementar; **to** ~ **one's income by writing** aumentar sus ingresos escribiendo artículos (*etc*).

supplemental [,sʌplɪ'mentl] ADJ (*esp US: frm*) = **supplementary**.

supplementary [,sʌplɪ'mentərɪ] ADJ suplementario; adicional; *question* (*Parl*) adicional, oral; ~ **benefit** (*Brit formerly*) beneficio *m* suplementario.

suppleness ['sʌplnɪs] N flexibilidad *f*.

suppliant ['sʌplɪənt] **1** ADJ suplicante. **2** N suplicante *mf*.

supplicant ['sʌplɪkənt] N suplicante *mf*.

supplicate ['sʌplɪkeɪt] VTI suplicar.

supplication [,sʌplɪ'keɪʃən] N súplica *f*.

supplier [sə'plaɪəʳ] N suministrador *m*, -ora *f*; (*Comm*) proveedor *m*, -ora *f*; distribuidor *m*, -ora *f*; **from your usual** ~ de su proveedor habitual.

supply [sə'plaɪ] **1** N (**a**) suministro *m*, provisión *f*, abastecimiento *m*; (*stock: Comm*) surtido *m*, existencias *fpl*; (*Comm, Econ*) oferta *f*; **electricity** ~ suministro *m* de electricidad; **the** ~ **of fuel to the engine** el suministro de combustible al motor; ~ **and demand** oferta *f* y demanda; **new cars are in short** ~ hay pocos coches nuevos, hay escasez de coches nuevos; **we need a fresh** ~ **of coffee** hace falta proveernos de café; **to lay in a** ~ **of** proveerse de, hacer provisión de.
(**b**) **supplies** (*food*) provisiones *fpl*, víveres *mpl*; (*Mil*) pertrechos *mpl*; **electrical supplies** artículos *mpl* eléctricos; **office supplies** material

m para oficina; **supplies are running low** escasean las provisiones; se están agotando las existencias.
(**c**) (*Parl*) provisión *f* financiera; **Committee on S~** Comisión *f* del Presupuesto; **to vote supplies** votar créditos.
2 VT (**a**) *material etc* suministrar, facilitar, proporcionar; (*Comm*) surtir; *army, city etc* aprovisionar; **the tradesmen who** ~ **us** nuestros proveedores; **can you** ~ **this spare part?** ¿pueden facilitarme este repuesto?; **she supplied the vital clue** ella nos dio la pista esencial; **to** ~ **sb with sth** (*of supplies*) abastecer a uno de algo, proveer a uno de algo; **he supplied us with some facts** nos facilitó (*or* proporcionó) varios datos; **this supplied me with the chance** esto me brindó la oportunidad; **we are not supplied with a radio** no estamos provistos de radio.
(**b**) (*make good*) want suplir.

supply ship [sə'plaɪʃɪp] N buque *m* de abastecimiento.

supply-side [sə'plaɪ,saɪd] ATTR: ~ **economics** economía *f* de oferta.

supply teacher [sə'plaɪ'tiːtʃəʳ] N maestro *m*, -a *f* suplente.

▼ **support** [sə'pɔːt] **1** N (**a**) (*Tech*) soporte *m*, apoyo *m*; pilar *m*.
▼(**b**) (*fig*) apoyo *m*; (*person*) sostén *m*; **moral** ~ apoyo *m* moral; **financial** ~ ayuda *f* económica; **in** ~ **of** en apoyo de; **documents in** ~ **of an allegation** documentos *mpl* que confirman una alegación; **to speak in** ~ **of a candidate** apoyar la candidatura de uno; **I will give you every** ~ te apoyaré todo lo que pueda; **the proposal got no** ~ la propuesta no recibió apoyo alguno; **to lean on sb for** ~ apoyarse en uno; **they depend on him for financial** ~ dependen de él para mantenerse, reciben ayuda económica de él; **our** ~ **comes from the workers** nos apoyan los obreros, los obreros son partidarios nuestros; **liberal** ~ **got him elected** los votos de los liberales aseguraron su elección.
2 ATTR: ~ **buying** compra *f* proteccionista; ~ **hose**, ~ **stockings** venda *f* (*or* media *f*) elástica; ~ **price** precio *m* de apoyo.
3 VT (**a**) (*Tech*) apoyar, sostener; **it is** ~**ed on 4 columns** descansa sobre 4 columnas, está apoyado en 4 columnas.
(**b**) (*uphold*) apoyar; sostener, mantener; *campaign* apoyar, respaldar; *life* sostener; *motion* aprobar, votar por; *team* ser hincha de; (*corroborate*) confirmar; (*Comput*) apoyar; **I cannot** ~ **what you are doing** no apruebo lo que estás haciendo; **the liberals will** ~ **it** los liberales votarán en favor.
(**c**) (*financially*) mantener.
4 VR: **to** ~ **o.s.** (*physically*) apoyarse (*on* en); (*financially*) mantenerse; ganarse la vida.

supportable [sə'pɔːtəbl] ADJ soportable.

support band [sə'pɔːt,bænd] N grupo *m* telonero, teloneros *mpl*.

supporter [sə'pɔːtəʳ] N (**a**) (*Tech*) soporte *m*, sostén *m*; (*Her*) tenante *m*, soporte *m*. (**b**) (*person*) defensor *m*, -ora *f*; (*Pol etc*) partidario *m*, -a *f*; (*Sport*) seguidor *m*, -ora *f*, hincha *mf*; ~**s' club** peña *f* deportiva; **after the match** ~**s flooded on to the pitch** al terminar el partido los hinchas invadieron el campo de juego.

supporting [sə'pɔːtɪŋ] ADJ *film, role* secundario; ~ **feature** (*Cine*) complemento *m*.

supportive [sə'pɔːtɪv] ADJ (*esp US*) soportante; amable, compasivo; ~ **of** que apoya a; **a** ~ **role** un papel de apoyo, un papel fortalecedor; **I have a very** ~ **family** tengo una familia que me ayuda mucho.

supportively [sə'pɔːtɪvlɪ] ADV *act, behave* con actitud de apoyo.

supportiveness [sə'pɔːtɪvnɪs] N sustentación *f*.

support ship [sə'pɔːtʃɪp] N barco *m* de apoyo.

▼ **suppose** [sə'pəʊz] **1** VT (**a**) (*assume as hypothesis*) suponer; figurarse, imaginarse; **let us** ~ **that X equals 3** supongamos que X vale 3; **let us** ~ **that** ... pongamos por caso que ..., vamos a poner que ...; **let us** ~ **we are living in the 8th century** figurémonos que vivimos en el siglo VIII.
(**b**) (= *'if'*) ~ **he comes, supposing (that) he comes** y ¿si viene?; **even supposing it were true** aun en el caso de que fuera verdad; **always supposing he comes** siempre y cuando venga; ~ **they could see us now!** ¡si solamente pudieran vernos ahora!
(**c**) (*imperative: 'I suggest'*) ~ **we have a go** ¿probamos?; ~ **we buy it?** ¿qué te parece si lo compramos?; ~ **you have a wash?** ¿no crees que conviene a lavarte?
(**d**) (*presuppose*) suponer, presuponer; **that** ~**s unlimited resources** eso supone unos recursos ilimitados.
▼(**e**) (*take for granted, assume*) suponer, presumir; creer; **I** ~ **so** supongo que sí, creo que sí, (*unwillingly*) no hay más remedio, no cabe otra explicación; **it is not to be** ~**d that** ... no se ha de suponer que ..., no se imagine nadie que ...; **I** ~ **you are right** me supongo que tendrás razón, debes de tener razón; **I don't** ~ **he really means it** no creo que lo diga en serio; **do you** ~ **that** ...? ¿crees en serio que ...?; **who do you** ~ **was there?** ¿quiénes crees tú que estaban?; **you don't** ~ **he'll get lost?** ¿crees posible que se pierda?; **what's that** ~**d to mean?** ¿qué quieres decir con eso?; **I** ~ **you know that** ... me imagino que sabes que ...; **I don't** ~ **you could lend me a pound?**, **I** ~ **you couldn't lend me a pound?** ¿podrías por casualidad prestarme una libra?; **he is** ~**d to be coming** se cree que

va a venir, se supone que va a venir; **and he's ~d to be an expert!** ¡y él que tiene fama de experto!; **he's ~d to be in Wales** dicen que está en Gales.

(f) (of obligation) deber; **he's the one who's ~d to do it** él es quien debe hacerlo, le toca a él hacerlo; **you're ~d to be in bed** tú deberías estar en la cama; **you're not ~d to eat those** no deberías comer aquéllos, no se te permite comer aquéllos.

2 VI: **just ~!** ¡imagínate!; **you'll come, I ~?** ¿me imagino que vendrás?

supposed [sə'pəʊzd] ADJ supuesto, pretendido.

supposedly [sə'pəʊzɪdlɪ] ADV según cabe suponer; **he had ~ gone to Scotland** según lo que se creía había ido a Escocia; **the ~ brave James Bond** el James Bond que se suponía tan valiente; el supuesto valiente James Bond.

supposing [sə'pəʊzɪŋ] as CONJ si, en el caso de que; V **suppose (b)**.

supposition [ˌsʌpə'zɪʃən] N suposición f, hipótesis f; **that is pure ~** eso es una hipótesis nada más.

suppositional [ˌsʌpə'zɪʃənəl], **suppositious** [ˌsʌpə'zɪʃəs] ADJ hipotético.

suppositious [ˌsʌpə'zɪʃəs] ADJ, **supposititious** [sə,pɒzɪ'tɪʃəs] ADJ fingido, espurio, supositicio.

suppository [sə'pɒzɪtərɪ] N supositorio m.

suppress [sə'pres] VT (in most senses) suprimir; yawn etc ahogar; emotion contener; heckler etc reprimir, hacer callar; scandal etc disimular.

suppressant [sə'presənt] N (Med) inhibidor m; **appetite ~** inhibidor m del apetito.

suppressed [sə'prest] ADJ book etc suprimido; **with ~ emotion** con emoción contenida; **a half ~ laugh** una risa mal disimulada.

suppression [sə'preʃən] N supresión f; represión f; disimulación f.

suppressive [sə'presɪv] ADJ represivo.

suppressor [sə'presəʳ] N supresor m.

suppurate ['sʌpjʊəreɪt] VI supurar.

suppuration [ˌsʌpjʊə'reɪʃən] N supuración f.

supra... ['su:prə] PREF supra...; **~normal** supranormal; **~renal** suprarrenal.

supranational ['su:prə'næʃənl] ADJ supranacional.

suprasegmental [ˌsu:prəseg'mentl] ADJ suprasegmental.

supremacist [su'preməsɪst] N partidario m, -a f de la supremacía (de un grupo, raza etc).

supremacy [su'preməsɪ] N supremacía f.

supreme [sʊ'pri:m] ADJ supremo; sumo, eg **with ~ indifference** con suma indiferencia; **S~ Being** Ser m Supremo; **S~ Court** Tribunal m Supremo, Corte f Suprema (LAm); **to reign ~** (fig) estar en la cumbre (de su profesión etc), no tener rival alguno; ver también COURTS.

supremely [sʊ'pri:mlɪ] ADV sumamente.

supremo [sʊ'pri:məʊ] N jefe m.

Supt (Brit) ABBR of **Superintendent** comisario m de policía.

sura ['sʊərə] N sura m.

surcharge 1 ['sɜ:tʃɑ:dʒ] N sobrecarga f, sobretasa f; recargo m.

2 [sɜ:'tʃɑ:dʒ] VT sobrecargar.

surd [sɜ:d] N número m sordo.

▼ **sure** [ʃʊəʳ] **1** ADJ **(a)** (infallible, safe) seguro; cierto; aim etc certero; hand, touch firme; **as ~ as fate, as ~ as eggs** con toda seguridad; **~ thing!** (US) ¡por supuesto!

▼ **(b)** (certain) seguro; **to be ~!** ¡claro!; **and there he was, to be ~** y ahí estaba, efectivamente; **are you quite ~?** ¿estás seguro del todo?; **I'm perfectly ~** estoy perfectamente seguro; **to be ~ about sth** estar seguro de algo; **I'm not so ~ about that** no estoy del todo seguro, no diría yo tanto; **to be ~ of o.s.** estar seguro de sí mismo; **to be ~ that ...** estar seguro de que ...; **it is ~ that he will come** es seguro que vendrá; **I'm ~ I don't know** que me maten si lo sé; **it is ~ to rain** seguramente lloverá; **he is ~ to come** seguramente vendrá; **be ~ to turn the gas off** ten cuidado de cortar el gas; **be ~ to go and see her** no dejes de ir a verla, ve a verla sin falta.

(c) **I don't know for ~** no sé con seguridad, no sé a punto fijo; **that's for ~** eso es seguro; **he'll come next time for ~** vendrá la próxima vez sin falta.

(d) **to make ~ of** facts verificar, comprobar, cerciorarse de; **to make ~ of sb** asegurarse del apoyo de uno, asegurarse de poder contar con uno; **(in order) to make quite ~** para asegurarse del todo; **it's best to make ~** vale más estar seguro; **to make ~ that ...** asegurar que ..., cerciorarse de que ...

2 ADV **(a)** **~!** (esp US) sí; ¡claro!; ¡naturalmente!; ¡ya lo creo!; **~ enough** efectivamente, en efecto; **he'll come ~ enough** seguramente vendrá; **it's petrol ~ enough** en efecto es gasolina.

(b) (US) **that ~ was a rich man** ése sí que era rico; **that meat was ~ tough** esa carne esa fue verdaderamente dura.

sure-fire ['ʃʊə'faɪəʳ] ADJ de éxito seguro, seguro.

sure-footed ['ʃʊə'fʊtɪd] **1** ADJ de pie firme.

2 ADV con pie firme.

surely ['ʃʊəlɪ] ADV seguramente; ciertamente; por supuesto; **~!** (US: gladly) con mucho gusto; **~ not?** ¿será posible?; **~ you don't mean**

it? ¿seguramente no lo dices en serio?; **~ you don't expect me to do it?** ¿no querrás que lo haga yo?; **~ you don't believe him?** ¿no irás a creerle?; **it will ~ happen** seguramente pasará; **~ he's come (hasn't he?)** ¿será posible que no haya venido?; **~ he hasn't come (has he?)** ¿será posible que haya venido?; **~ to goodness** (or **God**) **you know that!** ¡no es posible que ignores eso!

sureness ['ʃʊənɪs] N seguridad f; certeza f; lo certero; firmeza f.

surety ['ʃʊərətɪ] N (sum) garantía f; fianza f; (person) fiador m, -ora f; garante mf; **to go** (or **stand**) **~ for sb** ser fiador de uno, salir garante por uno; **in his own ~ of £500** bajo su propia fianza de 500 libras.

surf [sɜ:f] **1** N (foam) espuma f; (waves) olas fpl, rompientes mpl; (swell) oleaje m.

2 VI hacer surf.

3 VT (Comput): **to ~ the Net*** navegar por Internet.

surface ['sɜ:fɪs] **1** N superficie f; exterior m; (of road) firme m; **we haven't done more than scratch the ~ yet** todavía no hemos ido al fondo de este problema (etc); **the tension below** (or **beneath**) **the ~** la tirantez que no se ve, la tensión oculta; **on the ~ it seems that ...** a primera vista parece que ...; **to come** (or **rise**) **to the ~** salir a la superficie.

2 ATTR de la superficie; **~ area** área f de la superficie; **~ noise** ruido m de la superficie; **~ tension** tensión f superficial; **~ water** aguas fpl superficiales; **~ workers** personal m del exterior, personal m que trabaja a cielo abierto; **by ~ mail** (land) por vía terrestre, (sea) por vía marítima.

3 VT poner superficie a; recubrir, revestir; (smoothe) alisar.

4 VI (submarine etc) salir a la superficie, emerger; **he ~s in London occasionally** de vez en cuando asoma la cara en Londres.

surface-(to)-air ['sɜ:fɪs(tu:)'eəʳ] ATTR: **~ missile** proyectil m tierra-aire.

surface-to-surface ['sɜ:fɪstə'sɜ:fɪs] ADJ tierra-tierra.

surfboard ['sɜ:fbɔ:d] N plancha f de surf, tabla f de surf.

surfboarder ['sɜ:f,bɔ:dəʳ] N surfista mf.

surfboarding ['sɜ:f,bɔ:dɪŋ] N surf m, acuaplano m.

surfeit ['sɜ:fɪt] **1** N (satiety) hartura f, saciedad f; (indigestion) empacho m; (excess) exceso m; superabundancia f; **there is a ~ of** hay exceso de; **he died of a ~ of lampreys** murió después de hartarse de lampreas.

2 VT hartar, saciar (on, with de).

3 VR: **to ~ o.s.** hartarse, saciarse (on, with de).

surfer ['sɜ:fəʳ] N tablista mf.

surfing ['sɜ:fɪŋ] N, **surfriding** ['sɜ:f,raɪdɪŋ] N (Brit) surf m, acuaplano m.

surge [sɜ:dʒ] **1** N **(a)** (Naut) oleaje m, oleada f; (fig) oleada f, ola f; **a ~ of people** una oleada de gente; **there was a ~ of sympathy for him** hubo una oleada de compasión por él.

(b) (Elec) sobretensión f transitoria.

2 VI (water) agitarse, hervir; **the crowd ~d into the building** la multitud entró a tropel en el edificio; **people ~d down the street** una oleada de gente avanzó por la calle; **blood ~d into her face** se le subió la sangre a la cara; **they ~d round him** se apiñaban en torno suyo.

surgeon ['sɜ:dʒən] N cirujano m, -a f; (Mil, Naut) médico m, oficial m médico; **S~ General** (Mil) cirujano m general.

surgery ['sɜ:dʒərɪ] **1** N **(a)** (art, operation) cirugía f. **(b)** (Brit: room) clínica f, consultorio m, gabinete m de consulta. **(c)** (Brit: period of consultation) consulta f; (: of MP) tiempo dedicado a las consultas y peticiones de los electores.

2 ATTR: **~ hours** horas fpl de consulta.

surgical ['sɜ:dʒɪkəl] ADJ quirúrgico; **~ dressing** vendaje m quirúrgico; **~ spirit** (Brit) alcohol m de 90°.

surgically ['sɜ:dʒɪklɪ] ADV quirúrgicamente; por medios quirúrgicos.

Surinam [ˌsʊərɪ'næm] N Surinam m.

Surinamese [ˌsʊərɪnæ'mi:z] **1** ADJ surinamés.

2 N surinamés m, -esa f.

surliness ['sɜ:lɪnɪs] N hosquedad f, mal humor m; falta f de educación; aspereza f.

surly ['sɜ:lɪ] ADJ hosco, malhumorado; maleducado; **of a ~ disposition** de genio áspero; **he gave me a ~ answer** contestó malhumorado.

surmise ['sɜ:maɪz] **1** N conjetura f, suposición f; **my ~ is that ...** lo que yo supongo es que ...

2 [sɜ:'maɪz] VT conjeturar, suponer; **I ~d as much** ya lo suponía; **as one could ~ from his book** según cabía entender en su libro.

surmount [sɜ:'maʊnt] VT **(a)** difficulty superar, vencer. **(b)** **~ed by** (Archit etc) coronado de.

surmountable [sɜ:'maʊntəbl] ADJ superable.

surname ['sɜ:neɪm] **1** N apellido m.

2 VT apellidar.

surpass [sɜ:'pɑ:s] **1** VT sobrepasar, superar, exceder; eclipsar; **it ~es anything we have seen before** supera a cuanto hemos visto antes.

2 VR: **to ~ o.s.** excederse a sí mismo.

surpassing [sɜ:'pɑ:sɪŋ] ADJ incomparable, sin par; **of ~ beauty** de hermosura sin par.

surplice ['sɜːpləs] N sobrepelliz f.

surplus ['sɜːpləs] **1** N excedente m, sobrante m, exceso m; (Fin, Comm) superávit m; **the 1995 wheat ~** el excedente de trigo de 1995.

2 ATTR excedente, sobrante; de sobra; **~ energy** energía f sobrante; **~ store** tienda f de excedentes; **my ~ socks** los calcetines que me sobran, los calcetines que no necesito; **American ~ wheat** el excedente de trigo norteamericano; **stocks ~ to requirements** existencias fpl que exceden de las necesidades; **sale of ~ stock** liquidación f de saldos; **have you any ~ sheets?** ¿tenéis sábanas que os sobren?

▼ **surprise** [sə'praɪz] **1** N sorpresa f; asombro m, extrañeza f; **~, ~!** ¡bomba!; **much to my ~, to my great ~** con gran sorpresa mía; **with a look of ~** con un gesto de extrañeza; **it was a ~ to find that ...** fue una sorpresa encontrar que ...; **imagine my ~** imaginaos cuál sería mi asombro; **it came as a ~ to us** nos cogió de nuevas; **to give sb a ~** dar una sorpresa a uno; **to take sb by ~** sorprender a uno, coger a uno desprevenido.

2 ATTR **~ attack** sorpresa f, ataque m por sorpresa, ataque m imprevisto; **~ defeat** derrota f sorpresa, derrota f sorpresiva; **~ package** sorpresa f; **~ party** fiesta f de sorpresa.

▼ **3** VT sorprender; asombrar, extrañar; (Mil) coger por sorpresa; **to ~ sb in the act** coger a uno in fraganti; **you ~ me!** ¡me asombras!; **it ~s me to learn that ...** me asombra saber que ...; **to be ~d** quedar asombrado; **to be ~d to see sb** asombrarse de ver a uno; **I should not be ~d if ...** no me sorprendería que + subj; **to look ~d** hacer un gesto de extrañeza.

▼ **surprising** [sə'praɪzɪŋ] ADJ sorprendente, asombroso.

surprisingly [sə'praɪzɪŋlɪ] ADV de modo sorprendente; asombrosamente; **he is ~ young** se asombra uno de descubrir que es tan joven; **and then ~ he left** y luego con asombro de todos partió; **~ enough, he agreed** cosa sorprendente, asintió.

surreal [sə'rɪəl] ADJ surreal, surrealista.

surrealism [sə'rɪəlɪzəm] N surrealismo m.

surrealist [sə'rɪəlɪst] **1** ADJ surrealista.

2 N surrealista mf.

surrealistic [sə,rɪə'lɪstɪk] ADJ surrealista.

surrender [sə'rendəʳ] **1** N rendición f, capitulación f; entrega f; renuncia f; cesión f; abandono m; **the ~ of Breda** la rendición de Breda; **~ of property** (Jur) cesión f de bienes; **no ~!** ¡no nos rendimos nunca!; **to make a ~ of one's principles** transigir con sus principios.

2 ATTR: **~ value** valor m de rescate.

3 VT (Mil) rendir, entregar; **goods** entregar; **claim, right** renunciar a; **lease, ownership** ceder; **insurance policy** rescatar; **hope** renunciar a, abandonar.

4 VI rendirse, entregarse; **to ~ to the police** entregarse a la policía; **I ~!** ¡me rindo!

5 VR: **to ~ o.s. to remorse** abandonarse al remordimiento.

surreptitious [,sʌrəp'tɪʃəs] ADJ subrepticio, clandestino.

surreptitiously [,sʌrəp'tɪʃəslɪ] ADV subrepticiamente, clandestinamente; a hurtadillas.

surrogacy ['sʌrəgəsɪ] N (in child-bearing) subrogación f, alquiler m de madres.

surrogate ['sʌrəgeɪt] N sustituto m, suplente m; (Brit Eccl) vicario m; **~ coffee** sucedáneo m de café; **~ mother** madre f portadora, madre f alquilada, concertada f; **~ motherhood** alquiler m de úteros.

surround [sə'raʊnd] **1** N marco m; borde m.

2 VT rodear, cercar, circundar; (Mil) copar, cercar; sitiar; **a town ~ed by hills** una ciudad rodeada de colinas; **she was ~ed by children** estaba rodeada de niños.

surrounding [sə'raʊndɪŋ] **1** ADJ circundante; **in the ~ hills** en las colinas vecinas, en las colinas de alrededor; **in the ~ darkness** en la oscuridad que le (etc) envolvía.

2 NPL: **~s** (of place) alrededores mpl, cercanías fpl, contornos mpl; (environment) ambiente m.

surround sound [sə'raʊnd,saʊnd] N (TV, Radio) sonido m envolvente, efecto m surround.

surtax ['sɜːtæks] N sobreimpuesto m; (rate) sobretasa f.

surtitle ['sɜːtaɪtl] N sobretítulo m.

surveil [sə'veɪl] VT (US) vigilar.

surveillance [sɜː'veɪləns] N vigilancia f; **to be under ~** estar vigilado, estar bajo vigilancia; **to keep sb under ~** vigilar a uno.

survey **1** ['sɜːveɪ] N inspección f, examen m; estudio m; reconocimiento m; (of land) apeo m, medición f; (of building, property) inspección f; (poll) encuesta f; (general view) vista f de conjunto; (as published report, to purchaser etc) informe m; **he gave a general ~ of the situation** hizo un informe general sobre la situación; **to make a ~ of housing in a town** estudiar la situación de la vivienda en una ciudad.

2 [sɜː'veɪ] VT (look at) mirar, contemplar; (inspect) inspeccionar, examinar; (study) estudiar, hacer un estudio de; **ground before battle etc** reconocer; **land** apear, medir; **town etc** levantar el plano de; (take

general view of) pasar en revista; obtener una vista de conjunto de; **he ~ed the desolate scene** miró detenidamente la triste escena; **monarch of all he ~s** monarca m de todo cuanto domina con la vista; **the report ~s housing in Slobodia** el informe estudia la situación de la vivienda en Eslobodia; **the book ~s events up to 1972** el libro pasa revista de los sucesos hasta 1972.

surveying [sɜː'veɪɪŋ] N agrimensura f; planimetría f; topografía f.

surveyor [sə'veɪəʳ] N (Brit: of land) agrimensor m, -ora f; topógrafo m, -a f; (of property) inspector m, -ora f.

survival [sə'vaɪvəl] **1** N **(a)** (act) supervivencia f; **~ of the fittest** supervivencia f de los más aptos.

(b) (relic) supervivencia f; vestigio m, reliquia f.

2 ATTR: **~ bag** saco m de supervivencia; **~ course** curso m de supervivencia; **~ kit** equipo m de emergencia.

survivalist [sə'vaɪvəlɪst] N (US) persona obsesionada por las catástrofes.

survive [sə'vaɪv] **1** VT (all senses) sobrevivir a; **he is ~d by his wife and 3 sons** le sobreviven su esposa y 3 hijos.

2 VI sobrevivir; (remain, persist) durar, perdurar, subsistir; **on my salary I can just ~** con mi sueldo vivo muy justo; **he ~d on nuts for several weeks** logró vivir durante varias semanas comiendo nueces.

surviving [sə'vaɪvɪŋ] ADJ **spouse, children etc** sobreviviente; **~ company** (Fin: after merger) compañía f resultante.

survivor [sə'vaɪvəʳ] N superviviente mf.

sus: [sʌs] N (= suspicion): **he was picked up on ~** la policía le detuvo por sospechoso.

Susan ['suːzn] NF Susana.

susceptibility [sə,septə'bɪlɪtɪ] N susceptibilidad f, sensibilidad f (to a); (Med) propensión f (to a); **to offend sb's susceptibilities** ofender las susceptibilidades (or la delicadeza) de uno.

susceptible [sə'septəbl] ADJ susceptible, sensible (to a); (Med) propenso (to a); (easily moved) impresionable; (to women) enamoradizo; **to be ~ of** admitir, dar lugar a.

sushi ['suːʃɪ] N sushi m.

Susie ['suːzɪ] NF familiar form of **Susan**.

▼ **suspect** **1** ['sʌspekt] ADJ sospechoso; **they are all ~** todos están bajo sospecha; **his fitness is ~** es sospechoso de no estar en buen estado físico, su estado físico deja lugar a dudas.

2 ['sʌspekt] N sospechoso m, -a f; **the chief ~ is the butler** el más sospechoso es el mayordomo.

▼ **3** [səs'pekt] VT (accusingly) sospechar; (fear) recelar, recelarse de; (believe) imaginar, figurar, creer; **to ~ sb of a crime** hacer a uno sospechoso de un crimen, sospechar a uno de haber cometido un crimen; **I ~ her of having stolen it** sospecho que ella lo ha robado; **I ~ him of being the author** sospecho que él es el autor; **are you ~ed?** ¿estás tú bajo sospecha?; **he never ~ed her** él nunca sospechó de ella; **he ~s nothing** no se recela de nada; **I ~ all Slobodians** me recelo de todos los eslobodios; **I ~ it may be true** tengo la sospecha de que puede ser verdad, creo que puede ser verdad; **it's not paid for, I ~** sospecho que no está pagado; **I ~ed as much** ya me lo figuraba.

suspected [səs'pektɪd] ADJ **thief etc** presunto; **X went off the field with a ~ fracture** X abandonó el campo con sospecha de fractura.

suspend [səs'pend] VT (all senses) suspender; **his licence was ~ed for 6 months, he was ~ed for 6 months** le retiraron el carnet por 6 meses, le quitaron la licencia por 6 meses; **to ~ sb from work** (or **his post**) suspender a uno de su empleo; **~ed animation** animación f suspendida; **2-year ~ed sentence** libertad f condicional de 2 años.

suspender [səs'pendəʳ] N liga f; **~s** ligas fpl, (US) tirantes mpl.

suspender-belt [səs'pendəbelt] N (Brit) liguero m, portaligas m.

suspense [səs'pens] **1** N **(a)** (uncertainty) incertidumbre f, duda f; ansiedad f; (Liter, Theat, Cine etc) suspense m; tensión f; **to keep sb in ~** dejar a uno en la incertidumbre; **the ~ became unbearable** la tensión se hizo inaguantable; **the ~ is killing me!** ¡no puedo con tanta emoción!

(b) (Jur etc) suspensión f; **it is in ~** está en suspenso; **the question is in ~** la cuestión está pendiente.

2 ATTR: **~ account** cuenta f transitoria (or de orden).

suspenseful ['səspensful] ADJ **story, situation** de suspense.

suspension [səs'penʃən] **1** N (gen, Tech) suspensión f; **~ of payments** suspensión f de pagos; **~ of driving licence** privación f del carnet de conducir.

2 ATTR: **~ bridge** puente m colgante; **~ file** archivador m colgante; **~ points** puntos mpl suspensivos.

suspensory [səs'pensərɪ] **1** ADJ suspensorio.

2 N (also **~ bandage**) suspensorio m.

suspicion [səs'pɪʃən] N **(a)** (mistrust etc) sospecha f; recelo m; **my ~ is that ...** sospecho que ...; **to be above ~** estar por encima de toda sospecha; **to be under ~** ser sospechoso, estar bajo sospecha; **to arouse ~** despertar recelos; **to arouse sb's ~s** despertar los recelos de uno; **to arrest sb on ~** detener a uno como sospechoso; **to cast ~s on sb's honesty** hacer que se dude de la honradez de uno; **to have one's ~s about sth** tener sospechas acerca de algo; **I had no ~**

that ... no sospechaba que ...; **to lay o.s. open to ~** hacerse sospechoso; **I was right in my ~s** resultaron ser ciertas mis sospechas; **~ fell on him** se empezó a sospechar de él.

(b) (*trace*) traza *f* ligera, sombra *f*, pizca *f*; (*aftertaste*) dejo *m*; **there is a ~ of corruption about it** esto tiene un dejo de corrupción, esto huele un poquito a corrupción; **there is just a ~ of a rigged game** hay cierto olorcillo a tongo.

suspicious [səs'pɪʃəs] ADJ **(a)** (*feeling suspicion*) suspicaz, desconfiado, receloso; **to be ~ about sth** recelarse de algo, tener sospechas acerca de algo; **that made him ~** eso le hizo sospechar.

(b) (*causing suspicion*) sospechoso; **it's highly ~** es sumamente sospechoso; **it looks very ~ to me** me parece muy sospechoso.

suspiciously [səs'pɪʃəslɪ] ADV **(a)** *look etc* con recelo, desconfiadamente.

(b) *behave etc* de modo sospechoso; **it looks ~ like measles to me** para mí tiene toda la apariencia de ser sarampión.

suspiciousness [səs'pɪʃəsnɪs] N (*V adj*) **(a)** recelo *m*. **(b)** lo sospechoso, carácter *m* sospechoso.

suss* [sʌs] VT (*Brit*): **to ~ sth out** investigar algo, explorar algo; (tratar de) aclarar algo, (procurar) entender algo; **we couldn't ~ it out at all** no logramos sacar nada en claro; **I ~ed him out at once** le calé en seguida.

sustain [səs'teɪn] VT **(a)** (*bear weight of*) sostener, apoyar; *body, life* sustentar; (*Mus*) sostener; *part* estar al nivel de; hacer dignamente; *pretence* continuar; *effort* sostener, continuar; *assertion* sostener; *objection* (*Jur*) confirmar la validez de; *charge, theory* confirmar, corroborar.

(b) (*suffer*) *attack* sufrir (y rechazar); *damage* sufrir; *injury* sufrir, tener, recibir; *loss* sufrir, tener.

sustainable [səs'teɪnəbl] ADJ sostenible; sustentable.

sustained [səs'teɪnd] ADJ *effort etc* sostenido, ininterrumpido, continuo; *note* sostenido; *applause* prolongado.

sustaining [səs'teɪnɪŋ] ADJ *food* nutritivo; **~ pedal** pedal *m* de sostenido.

sustenance ['sʌstɪnəns] N sustento *m*; **they depend for their ~ on, they get their ~ from** se sustentan de, se alimentan de.

suture ['suːtʃəʳ] **1** N sutura *f*.

2 VT suturar, coser.

suzerain ['suːzəreɪn] N soberano *m*, -a *f*.

suzerainty ['suːzəreɪntɪ] N soberanía *f*.

svelte [svelt] ADJ esbelto.

SVQ N (*Scot*) ABBR *of* **Scottish Vocational Qualification**; *ver también* NVQ - NATIONAL VOCATIONAL QUALIFICATION .

SW (a) ABBR *of* **south-west** suroeste *m*, *also* ADJ, SO. **(b)** N (*Rad*) ABBR *of* **short wave** onda *f* corta, OC.

swab [swɒb] **1** N (*cloth, mop*) estropajo *m*, trapo *m*; (*Naut*) lampazo *m*; (*Mil*) escobillón *m*; (*Med*) algodón *m*, torunda *f*.

2 VT (*also* **to ~ down**) limpiar (con estropajo *etc*), fregar.

swaddle ['swɒdl] VT envolver (*in* en); *baby* empañar, fajar; **he came out ~d in bandages** salió envuelto en vendas.

swaddling clothes ['swɒdlɪŋkləʊðz] NPL (*Liter*) pañales *mpl*; **to be still in ~** (*fig*) estar todavía en mantillas.

swag* [swæg] N botín *m*.

swagger ['swægəʳ] **1** N contoneo *m*, pavoneo *m*; **to walk with a ~** andar contoneándose, andar con paso jactancioso.

2 ADJ (*Brit**) muy elegante, muy pera*.

3 VI (*also* **to ~ about, to ~ along**) contonearse, pavonearse, andar pavoneándose; **he ~ed over to our table** se acercó a nuestra mesa con aire fanfarrón; **with that he ~ed out** con eso salió con paso jactancioso.

swaggering ['swægərɪŋ] ADJ *person* fanfarrón, jactancioso; *gait* importante, jactancioso.

Swahili [swɑː'hiːlɪ] N swahili *m*, suajili *m*.

swain [sweɪn] N (†† *or hum*) (*lad*) zagal *m*; (*suitor*) pretendiente *m*, amante *m*.

swallow¹ ['swɒləʊ] **1** N trago *m*; **at one ~, with one ~** de un trago.

2 VT **(a)** (*lit*) tragar; engullir, deglutir; *bait* tragarse; **he ~ed the lot** se lo tragó todo; **just ~ this pill** tómate esta píldora.

(b) (*fig*) tragar; **to ~ an insult** tragar un insulto; **to ~ one's pride** humillarse, olvidarse de su amor propio; **he ~ed the story** se tragó la bola; **to ~ one's words** desdecirse, retractarse.

3 VI: **to ~, to ~ hard** (*fig*) tragar saliva.

◆ **swallow down** VT tragar.

◆ **swallow up** VT **(a)** *food etc* tragar; acabar de comer.

(b) (*fig*) *savings etc* agotar, consumir; (*of the sea*) tragar; **the mist ~ed them up** la niebla les envolvió; **they were soon ~ed up in the darkness** desaparecieron pronto en la oscuridad.

swallow² ['swɒləʊ] N (*Orn*) golondrina *f*; **one ~ doesn't make a summer** una golondrina no hace verano.

swallow-dive ['swɒləʊdaɪv] N salto *m* de ángel.

swallowtail ['swɒləʊteɪl] N (*butterfly*) macaón *m*.

swam [swæm] PRET *of* **swim**.

swamp [swɒmp] **1** N pantano *m*, marisma *f*, ciénaga *f*.

2 ATTR: **~ fever** paludismo *m*.

3 VT **(a)** (*submerge*) sumergir, cubrir de agua (*etc*); (*flood*) inundar, llenar de agua; (*sink*) hundir.

(b) (*fig*) abrumar (*with* de), agobiar (*with* de); **towards the end of the game they ~ed us** hacia el fin del partido nos arrollaron completamente; **they have ~ed us with applications** nos han abrumado de solicitudes; **we are ~ed with work** estamos agobiados de trabajo, tenemos trabajo hasta encima de las cejas.

4 VI (*of field etc*) inundarse, quedar inundado, empantanarse.

swampland ['swɒmplænd] N ciénaga *f*, pantano *m*, marisma *f*.

swampy ['swɒmpɪ] ADJ pantanoso; **to become ~** empantanarse.

swan [swɒn] **1** N cisne *m*; **the S~ of Avon** (*Shakespeare*); **~ dive** (*US*) salto *m* de ángel; **'S~ Lake'** 'El lago de los cisnes'.

2 VI: **to ~ around*** gandulear, vivir en el ocio; darse buena vida; **to ~ off*** irse tranquilamente, partir con la mayor serenidad.

swank* [swæŋk] **1** N **(a)** (*vanity, boastfulness*) fachenda* *f*; ostentación *f*; **it's just a lot of ~** no es sino fachenda*; **he does it for ~** lo hace para darse tono.

(b) (*person*) currutaco *m*; fachendón* *m*, -ona *f*; **he's a terrible ~** es terriblemente fachendón*.

2 VI darse tono, darse humos, fachendear*, fanfarronear, presumir; **to ~ about** (ADV) pavonearse; **to ~ about sth** fachendear a causa de algo*, darse humos con motivo de algo.

swanky* ['swæŋkɪ] ADJ *person* ostentoso, fachendón*; fachendón*; *car etc* la mar de elegante*, muy pera*.

swannery ['swɒnərɪ] N colonia *f* de cisnes.

swansdown ['swɒnzdaʊn] N (*feathers*) plumón *m* de cisne; (*Texas*) fustán *m*, muletón *m*.

swansong ['swɒnsɒŋ] N canto *m* del cisne.

swap [swɒp] **1** N intercambio *m*, canje *m*; **~s** (*stamps*) duplicados *mpl*; **it's a fair ~** es un trato equitativo.

2 VT intercambiar, canjear; **to ~ stories (with sb)** contarse chistes; **we sat ~ping reminiscences** estábamos contando nuestros recuerdos; **will you ~ your hat for my jacket?** ¿quieres cambiar tu sombrero por mi chaqueta?; **to ~ places with sb** cambiar de silla (*etc*) con uno.

3 VI hacer un intercambio; cambiar con uno; **I wouldn't ~ with anyone** no cambio con nadie; **shall we ~?** ¿cambiamos?

◆ **swap (a)round, swap over** VTI cambiar.

SWAPO ['swɑːpəʊ] N ABBR *of* **South West Africa People's Organization.**

sward [swɔːd] N (*Liter*) césped *m*.

swarm¹ [swɔːm] **1** N (*of bees etc*) enjambre *m*; (*fig*) multitud *f*, muchedumbre *f*; **a ~ of mosquitoes** un enjambre de mosquitos; **a ~ of creditors** un enjambre de acreedores; **they came in ~s** vinieron en tropel; **there were ~s of women** hubo una multitud de mujeres, hubo millares de mujeres.

2 VI **(a)** (*bees*) enjambrar.

(b) (*other insects, people etc*) hormiguear, pulular; **to ~ with** (*of place*) hervir de, pulular de, estar plagado de; **the tourists ~ everywhere** en todas partes pululan los turistas; **Stratford ~s with Americans** Stratford hierve de americanos; **children ~ed all over the car** los niños hormigueaban por todo el coche.

swarm² [swɔːm] VI: **to ~ up a tree** trepar (rápidamente) a un árbol.

swarthiness ['swɔːðɪnɪs] N tez *f* morena, color *m* moreno; lo atezado.

swarthy ['swɔːðɪ] ADJ moreno, atezado.

swashbuckler ['swɒʃˌbʌkləʳ] N espadachín *m*, matón *m*.

swashbuckling ['swɒʃˌbʌklɪŋ] ADJ **(a)** (*gen*) valentón, fanfarrón. **(b)** (*Cine*) *hero* de película de aventuras; *film* de aventuras, de capa y espada.

swastika ['swɒstɪkə] N esvástica *f*, cruz *f* gamada.

SWAT [swɒt] N (*US*) ABBR *of* **Special Weapons and Tactics: ~ team** unidad especial de la policía.

swat [swɒt] **1** VT *fly* aplastar, matar.

2 VI: **to ~ at a fly** tratar de aplastar una mosca (con palmeta).

swath [swɔːθ] N, PL **swaths** [swɔːðs], **swathe¹** [sweɪð] N guadaña *f*, ringlera *f* (de heno segado *etc*); **to cut corn in ~s** segar el trigo y dejarlo en ringleras; **to cut ~s through sth** avanzar por algo a guadañadas.

swathe² [sweɪð] VT envolver; fajar; (*with bandage*) vendar; **~d in sheets** envuelto en sábanas.

swatter ['swɒtəʳ] N palmeta *f* matamoscas.

sway [sweɪ] **1** N **(a)** (*movement*) balanceo *m*, oscilación *f*; (*violent jerk*) sacudimiento *m*; vaivén *m*.

(b) (*rule*) imperio *m*, dominio *m*; (*influence*) influencia *f*, ascendiente *m*; (*power*) poder *m*; **his ~ over the party** su influencia con el partido, su dominio del partido; **to bring a people under one's ~** sojuzgar un pueblo, hacer que un pueblo reconozca el dominio de uno; **to hold ~ over a nation** gobernar una nación, dominar una nación.

2 VT **(a)** (*move*) balancear, hacer oscilar; sacudir; hacer tambalear.

(b) (*influence*) mover, influir en; inclinar; **these factors finally ~ed me** estos factores terminaron de convencerme; **he is not ~ed by any such considerations** tales cosas no influyen en él en absoluto; **I allowed myself to be ~ed** me dejé persuadir.

3 VI balancearse, oscilar (*in the wind* al viento); mecerse; bambolearse; tambalearse; **she ~s as she walks** se cimbrea al andar; **he was ~ing with drink** estaba tan borracho que se tambaleaba; **the train ~ed from side to side** el tren se bamboleaba de un lado para otro.

Swazi ['swɑːzɪ] **1** ADJ swazilandés, suazilandés.

2 N swazilandés *m*, -esa *f*, suazilandés *m*, -esa *f*.

Swaziland ['swɑːzɪlænd] N Swazilandia *f*, Suazilandia *f*.

swear [sweəʳ] (*irr:* PRET **swore**, PTP **sworn**) **1** VT **(a)** *oath* prestar, jurar; *fidelity* jurar; **I ~ it!** ¡lo juro!; **I ~ (that) I did not steal it** juro que no lo robé; **I could have sworn that was Lulu** juraría que ésa fue Lulú, que me maten si aquélla no fue Lulú; **to ~ sth on the Bible** jurar algo sobre la Biblia; **to ~ to do sth** jurar hacer algo.
(b) to ~ sb to secrecy hacer que uno jure no revelar algo.

2 VI **(a)** (*solemnly*) jurar; **to ~ to do sth** declarar algo bajo juramento; **I could ~ to it** juraría que fue así; **I can't ~ to it** no lo sé a punto fijo, no puedo afirmarlo con entera confianza.
(b) (*with swearwords*) jurar, decir tacos, soltar palabrotas, (*blasphemously*) blasfemar; **don't ~ in front of the children** no digas palabrotas estando los pequeños delante; **to ~ like a trooper** jurar como un carretero; **he swore most horribly** soltó unos tremendos tacos; **it's enough to make a bishop ~** esto bastaría para hacer blasfemar a un obispo; **to ~ at sb** maldecir a uno, echar pestes de uno; **he was ~ing about the police** echaba pestes de la policía.

3 N: **to have a good ~*** desahogarse soltando palabrotas.

◆ **swear by** VT: **to ~ by sth** jurar por algo, (*fig*) tener entera confianza en algo, creer ciegamente en algo.

◆ **swear in** VT: **to ~ sb in** tomar juramento a uno, juramentar a uno, hacer prestar juramento a uno; **to be sworn in** prestar juramento.

◆ **swear off** VT: **to ~ off alcohol** (jurar) renunciar al alcohol.

swearword ['sweəwɜːd] N taco *m*, palabrota *f*, grosería *f* (*LAm*).

sweat [swet] **1** N **(a)** sudor *m*; **by the ~ of one's brow** con el sudor de su frente; **to be in a ~** estar sudando, estar todo sudoroso, (*fig*) estar en un apuro, apurarse; **to be in a ~ about sth** estar muy preocupado por algo; **to get into a ~** empezar a sudar; **to get into a ~ about sth** apurarse por algo.
(b) (*) trabajo *m* difícil, trabajo *m* pesado; **what a ~ that was!** eso ¡cómo nos hizo sudar!; **we had such a ~ to do it** nos costó hacerlo; **no ~!** ¡no hay problema!, ¡está chupado!*
(c) **old ~*** veterano *m*.

2 VT **(a)** sudar; **to ~ blood** (*fig*) sudar la gota gorda.
(b) *workers* explotar.

3 VI sudar; **to ~ a lot, to ~ like a bull** (*or* **pig** *etc*) sudar la gota gorda.

◆ **sweat off** VT: **I ~ed off half a kilo** me quité medio kilo sudando.

◆ **sweat out** VT: **to ~ a cold out** quitarse un resfriado sudando; **to ~ it out*** aguantar todo; armarse de paciencia; **they left him to ~ it out*** no hicieron nada para ayudarle.

sweatband ['swetbænd] N (*on hat*) badana *f* del forro del sombrero, tafilete *m*; (*on head*) venda *f*, banda *f*; (*on wrist*) muñequera *f*.

sweated ['swetɪd] ADJ: **~ labour** trabajo *m* muy mal pagado.

sweater ['swetəʳ] N suéter *m*, jersey *m*.

sweat gland ['swetglænd] N glándula *f* sudorípara.

sweating ['swetɪŋ] **1** ADJ sudoroso.

2 N transpiración *f*; (*of workers*) explotación *f*.

sweatshirt ['swetˈʃɜːt] N niki *m*, camisa *f* floja (de deporte *etc*), sudadera *f*.

sweatshop ['swetˈʃɒp] N fábrica *f* donde se explota al obrero.

sweatsuit ['swetsuːt] N chandal *m*.

sweaty ['swetɪ] ADJ sudoroso; cubierto de sudor, mojado de sudor; **to be all ~** estar todo sudoroso.

Swede [swiːd] N sueco *m*, -a *f*.

swede [swiːd] N (*Brit Bot*) naba *f*, nabo *m* gallego.

Sweden ['swiːdn] N Suecia *f*.

Swedish ['swiːdɪʃ] **1** ADJ sueco.

2 N (*Ling*) sueco *m*.

sweep [swiːp] **1** N **(a)** (*act of ~ing*) barredura *f*, escobada *f*; **this room could do with a ~** hace falta barrer esta habitación; **we gave it a ~** lo limpiamos, lo barrimos; **to make a clean ~** (*Sport*) ganar todos los puntos, (*Cards*) copar, ganar todas las bazas; **to make a clean ~ of** cambiar completamente, hacer tabla rasa de.
(b) (*by police etc*) redada *f*; **they made a ~ for hidden arms** hicieron una redada buscando armas clandestinas.
(c) (*movement of arm*) gesto *m*, movimiento *m*; (*of scythe*) golpe *m*, guadañada *f*; (*of net*) redada *f*; (*of bean etc*) trayectoria *f*; (*of events etc*) marcha *f*.
(d) (*person*) deshollinador *m*.

(e) (*area*) extensión *f*; (*of wings*) envergadura *f*; (*range*) alcance *m*; (*curve*) curva *f*; **the whole ~ of the Thames at Putney** toda la extensión del Támesis en Putney; **a wide ~ of country** una ancha extensión de paisaje, un paisaje extenso; **the ~ of her lines** (*Naut etc*) su línea, su perfil (aerodinámico *etc*).
(f) = **sweepstake**.

2 (*irr:* PRET AND PTP **swept**) VT **(a)** *room, surface* barrer; *chimney* deshollinar; *channel etc* dragar; **to ~ a room clean** barrer un cuarto; **to ~ a channel clear of mines** barrer las minas de un canal; **the beach was swept by great waves** la playa fue barrida (*or* azotada) por olas gigantescas; **to ~ a road with bullets** barrer una carretera con balas; **to ~ the horizon with a telescope** examinar toda la extensión del horizonte con un telescopio.
(b) *dust* barrer, quitar barriendo; *mines* rastrear, barrer; *person, obstacle etc* arrastrar, llevarse; **a wave swept him overboard** fue arrastrado por una ola y cayó al mar; **he was swept off his feet by the water** fue arrastrado por la corriente; **to ~ a girl off her feet** arrebatar a una chica; **they swept him off to lunch** se lo llevaron con toda prisa a comer.

3 VI **(a)** (*with broom*) barrer.
(b) (*extend*) extenderse (*along, down etc* por); **the river ~s away to the east** el río hace una gran curva hacia el este; **the hills ~ down to the sea** las colinas bajan (majestuosamente) hacia el mar; **the road ~s up to the house** la carretera llega hasta la casa (de modo impresionante).
(c) (*of movement*) **to ~ into a room** entrar en una sala con paso majestuoso; **she swept past me angrily** pasó enfadada delante de mí; **it swept round the corner** dobló velozmente la esquina; **they swept down the slope** se lanzaron cuesta abajo; descendieron precipitadamente por la cuesta; **to ~ down on sb** abalanzarse sobre uno.

◆ **sweep along 1** VT arrastrar, llevar; **the crowd swept him along** le arrastró la multitud, desapareció arrastrado por la multitud.
2 VI: **the car swept along** el coche avanzó a gran velocidad.

◆ **sweep aside** VT *object* apartar bruscamente con la mano; *protest* desatender, no hacer caso alguno de; *suggestion* desechar bruscamente; *opposition* barrer; *difficulty* quitar de en medio.

◆ **sweep away 1** VT barrer; (*snatch*) arrebatar, arrastrar; (*remove*) quitar, eliminar, suprimir; *vestige etc* borrar.
2 VI irse rápidamente; irse con paso majestuoso.

◆ **sweep by** VI pasar rápidamente; pasar majestuosamente; (*nearly touch*) rozar.

◆ **sweep down 1** VT arrastrar, llevar; **the current ~s logs down with it** la corriente arrastra (*or* lleva) consigo los troncos.
2 VI V **sweep 3 (b)**, **3 (c)**.

◆ **sweep off** = **sweep away**.

◆ **sweep on** VI seguir su avance inexorable.

◆ **sweep out 1** VT *room* barrer.
2 VI salir (con paso majestuoso).

◆ **sweep up 1** VT barrer, recoger.
2 VI **(a)** (*clean up*) **to ~ up after sb** recoger la basura que ha dejado uno; **to ~ up after a party** limpiar después de un guateque.
(b) (*approach*) **to ~ up to sb** acercarse indignado a uno; acercarse con paso majestuoso a uno; **the car swept up to the house** el coche llegó con toda velocidad a la casa; V *also* **sweep 3 b.**

sweepback ['swiːpbæk] N (*of aircraft wing etc*) ángulo *m* de flecha.

sweeper ['swiːpəʳ] N (*person*) barrendero *m*, -a *f*; (*Ftbl*) escoba *m*; (*machine*) barredera *f*.

sweeping ['swiːpɪŋ] **1** ADJ **(a)** *gesture* dramático; *bow* profundo; *flight* majestuoso.
(b) *statement etc* general, tajante, terminante, dogmático; *change* radical, fundamental; **that's pretty ~** eso es mucho decir.
2 NPL: **~s** barreduras *fpl*; (*fig, of society etc*) heces *fpl*.

sweepstake ['swiːpsteɪk] N lotería *f* (*esp* de carreras).

sweet [swiːt] **1** ADJ **(a)** (*of taste*) dulce; azucarado; **this coffee is too ~** este café tiene demasiado azúcar; **is it ~ enough for you?** ¿te he puesto bastante azúcar?, ¿está bastante dulce?; **~ chestnut** (*fruit*) castaña *f*; (*tree*) castaño *m*; **~ oil** aceite *m* de oliva; **~ pea** guisante *m* de olor, alverjilla *f*: **~ potato** batata *f*, camote *m*, boniato *m* (*CAm*).
(b) (*fresh, pleasant*) *food* fresco, nuevo; *smell* fragante, agradable, bueno; *breath* sano; *land* fértil; en buen estado.
(c) (*of sounds*) dulce, melodioso.
(d) (*of person's character*) dulce, amable, simpático; **isn't he ~?** ¡es un ángel!; **that's very ~ of you** eres muy amable; **to be ~ on sb** estar un poco enamorado de uno; **to keep sb ~*** asegurarse de la amistad de uno, asegurarse de la buena voluntad de uno (mediante un regalo, propina *etc*).
(e) (*generally agreeable, charming*) *memory, revenge etc* dulce; *face* lindo; *dress etc* mono, majo, precioso; **it is ~ to be able to ...** es agradable poder ...; **it's ~ of you to say that** eres muy amable al decir eso; **you look so ~ in that hat** con ese sombrero eres un encanto; **what a ~ little hat!** ¡qué sombrerito más mono!; **to go one's own ~ way, to**

please one's own ~ self ir a su aire, ir a lo suyo.

(f) *running of car, machine etc* suave.

2 ADV: **to smell ~** tener buen olor, oler bien; **to taste ~** tener un sabor dulce, saber a dulce.

3 N (*esp Brit*) **(a)** dulce *m*, caramelo *m*; **~s** dulces *mpl*, bombones *mpl*, golosinas *fpl*; **the ~s of solitude** las dulzuras de la soledad; **the ~s of office** las ventajas materiales de estar en el poder, los premios que brinda el triunfo político.

(b) (*Brit*: *course*) postre *m*.

(c) **yes, my ~** sí, mi amor.

sweet-and-sour ['swiːtən'sauəʳ] **1** ADJ agridulce.

2 N (*Culin*) plato agridulce (*especialmente en la comida china*).

sweetbreads ['swiːtbredz] NPL lechecillas *fpl*, mollejas *fpl*.

sweetbriar, sweetbrier ['swiːtbraɪəʳ] N eglantina *f*, escaramujo *m* oloroso.

sweetcorn ['swiːtkɔːn] N maíz *m* tierno.

sweeten ['swiːtn] VT **(a)** endulzar (*also fig*); azucarar, poner azúcar a.

(b) (*) (*also to ~ up*) *person* (*bribe*) sobornar, (*win over*) asegurarse la buena voluntad de, captar la benevolencia de; *deal* hacer más atractivo.

sweetener ['swiːtnəʳ] N **(a)** edulcorante *m*, dulcificante *m*. **(b)** (*) astilla* *f*.

sweetening ['swiːtnɪŋ] N (*Culin*) dulcificante *m*.

sweetheart ['swiːthɑːt] N novio *m*, -a *f*; **yes, ~** sí, mi amor.

sweetie* ['swiːtɪ] N **(a)** (*person*) chica *f*, novia *f*; **she's a ~** es un encanto, es muy mona; **isn't she a ~?** ¡qué chica más mona!; **hi, ~!** ¡oye, preciosidad!* **(b)** (*Scot*: *sweet*) dulce *m*, caramelo *m*.

sweetish ['swiːtɪʃ] ADJ algo dulce.

sweetly ['swiːtlɪ] ADV dulcemente; amablemente; suavemente.

sweetmeats ['swiːtmiːts] NPL dulces *mpl*, confites *mpl*.

sweet-natured [,swiːt'neɪtʃəd] ADJ dulce, amable.

sweetness ['swiːtnɪs] N dulzura *f*; lo dulce, lo azucarado; fragancia *f*; buen olor *m*; fertilidad *f*; amabilidad *f*; suavidad *f*; **now all is ~ and light** reina ahora la más perfecta armonía; **to go around spreading ~ and light** ir por el mundo con una sonrisa amable para todos; **he was all ~ and light yesterday** ayer (contra costumbre) estuvo la mar de amable (*or razonable etc*).

sweet-scented ['swiːt'sentɪd] ADJ perfumado, fragante, de olor agradable.

sweetshop ['swiːtʃɒp] N (*Brit*) bombonería *f*, confitería *f*, dulcería *f* (*LAm*).

sweet-smelling ['swiːt'smelɪŋ] ADJ = **sweet-scented**.

sweet talk ['swiːt'tɔːk] **1** N halagos *mpl*, palabras *fpl* almibaradas, engatusamiento *m*.

2 **sweet-talk** VT engatusar, lisonjear; (*US*) enrollarse con.

sweet-tempered ['swiːt'tempəd] ADJ de carácter dulce, amable; **she's always ~** es siempre tan amable, no se altera nunca.

sweet-toothed ['swiːt'tuːθt] ADJ goloso.

sweet william ['swiːt'wɪljəm] N minutisa *f*.

swell [swel] **1** N **(a)** (*Naut*) mar *m* de fondo, marejada *f*, oleaje *m*.

(b) (*Mus*) crescendo *m*.

(c) (*Anat etc*) = **swelling**.

(d) (*†) (*stylish person*) guapo *m*, majo *m*; (*important person*) pez *m* gordo*, espadón* *m*; **the ~s** la gente bien, la gente de buen tono.

2 ADJ (*) (*in dress etc*) elegantísimo; (*fine, good*) estupendo*, bárbaro*, de órdago*; (*esp US*) **we had a ~ time** lo pasamos en grande*; **it's a ~ place** es un sitio estupendo*; **that's mighty ~ of you** eres muy amable.

3 (*irr*: PRET **swelled**, PTP **swollen**) VT **(a)** (*physically*) hinchar; abultar; inflar; (*Med*) hinchar; **to have a swollen hand** tener la mano hinchada; **eyes swollen with tears** ojos *mpl* hinchados de lágrimas; **the rains had swollen the river** las lluvias habían hecho crecer el río; **the river is swollen** el río está crecido.

(b) *sound* aumentar; *numbers etc* aumentar; engrosar; **this will go to ~ the numbers of ...** esto vendrá a aumentar el número de ...

4 VI **(a)** (*physically*: *also to ~ up*) hincharse; abultarse; inflarse; (*of river etc*) crecer; **her arm ~ed up** se le hinchó el brazo; **to ~ with pride** envanecerse, (*justifiably*) sentirse lleno de orgullo.

(b) (*in extent, numbers*) crecer, aumentar(se); **numbers have swollen greatly** el número se ha aumentado muchísimo; **the debt had swollen to ...** la deuda había aumentado mucho hasta alcanzar la cifra de ...; **the little group soon ~ed into a crowd** el pequeño grupo se transformó pronto en multitud.

◆ **swell up** VI V **swell 4 (a).**

swellhead* ['swelhed] N (*US*) vanidoso *m*, -a *f*.

swellheaded* ['swel'hedɪd] ADJ (*US*) vanidoso, engreído.

swelling ['swelɪŋ] N hinchazón *f*; protuberancia *f*; (*Med*) tumefacción *f*; (*bruise*) chichón *m*, bulto *m*; (*of gland etc*) ganglio *m*.

swelter ['sweltəʳ] VI abrasarse, sofocarse de calor; chorrear de sudor; **we ~ed in 40°** nos sofocábamos a una temperatura de 40 grados.

sweltering ['sweltərɪŋ] ADJ *day* de muchísimo calor; *heat* sofocante, abrasador; **it's ~ in here** está sofocante aquí.

---

swept [swept] PRET AND PTP of **sweep**.

sweptback ['swept'bæk] ADJ *wing* en flecha; *aircraft* con alas en flecha.

swerve [swɜːv] **1** N **(a)** (*dodge, turn*) desvío *m* brusco, viraje *m* repentino; (*of body, in sport etc*) esguince *m*, regate *m*.

(b) (*spin on ball*) efecto *m*; **to put a ~ on a ball** lanzar una pelota con efecto.

2 VT **(a)** desviar bruscamente, torcer (a un lado).

(b) *ball* dar efecto a, lanzar con efecto, sesgar.

3 VI desviarse bruscamente; hurtar el cuerpo; (*ball*) torcerse; **to ~ to the right** torcer repentinamente a la derecha.

swift [swift] **1** ADJ rápido, veloz; repentino; pronto; **~ of foot** de pies ligeros; **to be ~ to anger** tener prontos enojos; **we must be ~ to act** tenemos que obrar con toda prontitud.

2 N vencejo *m*.

swift-flowing ['swift'fləʊɪŋ] ADJ *current* rápido; *river* de corriente rápida.

swift-footed ['swift'fʊtɪd] ADJ de pies ligeros, veloz.

swiftly ['swiftlɪ] ADV rápidamente, velozmente; repentinamente; pronto.

swiftness ['swiftnɪs] N rapidez *f*, velocidad *f*; lo repentino; prontitud *f*.

swig* [swig] **1** N trago *m*, tragantada* *f*; **have a ~ of this** bébete un poco de esto; **he took a ~ at his flask** se echó un trago de la botella.

2 VT beber; beber a grandes tragos.

swill [swil] **1** N **(a)** bazofia *f*; (*pej*) bazofia *f*, aguachirle *f*; **how can you drink this ~?** ¿cómo te es posible beber esta basura?

(b) **to give sth a ~** (*out*) limpiar algo con agua.

2 VT **(a)** (*clean*: *also to ~ out*) lavar, limpiar con agua.

(b) (*drink*) beber (a grandes tragos).

3 VI emborracharse.

swim [swim] **1** N **(a)** nadada *f* (*LAm*); **after a 2-kilometre ~** después de nadar 2 km; **it's a long ~ back to the shore** nos costará llegar a la playa; **that was a long ~ for a child** eso fue mucho nadar para un niño; **that was a nice ~!** ¡cuánto me gusta nadar así!; **I like a ~** me gusta nadar, me gusta la natación; **to go for a ~, to have a ~** ir a nadar.

(b) **to be in the ~** estar al corriente; **to keep in the ~** mantenerse al día.

2 (*irr*: PRET **swam**, PTP **swum**) VT **(a)** *river etc* pasar a nado, cruzar a nado; **it was first swum in 1900** un hombre lo cruzó a nado por primera vez en 1900; **it has not been swum before** hasta ahora nadie lo ha cruzado a nado.

(b) **she can't ~ a stroke** no sabe nadar en absoluto; **before I had swum 10 strokes** antes de haber dado 10 brazadas; **he can ~ 2 lengths** puede nadar 2 largos; **can you ~ the crawl?** ¿sabes hacer el crol?

3 VI **(a)** nadar; **to ~ across a river** pasar un río a nado; **to ~ out to sea** alejarse nadando de la playa; **to ~ under water** nadar debajo del agua, bucear; **then we swam back** luego volvimos (nadando); **we shall have to ~ for it** tendremos que echarnos al agua, tendremos que salvarnos nadando; **to go ~ming** ir a nadar, ir a bañarse.

(b) **the meat was ~ming in gravy** la carne estaba inundada de salsa, la carne flotaba en salsa.

(c) (*head*) dar vueltas; **everything swam before my eyes** todo parecía estar girando alrededor de mí, todo parecía bailar ante mis ojos.

swimmer ['swiməʳ] N nadador *m*, -ora *f*.

swimming ['swimɪŋ] N natación *f*.

swimming-bath ['swimɪŋbɑːθ] N, PL **swimming-baths** ['swimɪŋbɑːðz] (*Brit*) piscina *f*, pileta *f*.

swimming-cap ['swimɪŋkæp] N gorro *m* de baño.

swimming-costume ['swimɪŋ,kɒstjuːm] N (*Brit*) traje *m* de baño, bañador *m*.

swimming gala ['swimɪŋ,gɑːlə] N exhibición *f* de natación.

swimmingly ['swimɪŋlɪ] ADV: **to go ~** ir a las mil maravillas.

swimming-pool ['swimɪŋpuːl] N piscina *f*, pileta *f*, alberca *f* (*Mex*).

swimming-trunks ['swimɪŋtrʌŋks] NPL pantalón *m* de baño, bañador *m*.

swimsuit ['swimsuːt] N traje *m* de baño, bañador *m*.

swimwear ['swimwɛəʳ] N trajes *mpl* de baño.

swindle ['swindl] **1** N estafa *f*, timo *m*; **it's a ~!** ¡nos han robado!

2 VT estafar, timar; **to ~ sb out of sth** estafar algo a uno, quitar algo a uno por estafa.

swindler ['swindləʳ] N estafador *m*, timador *m*.

swine [swain] **1** N **(a)** (*Zool pl*: **swine**) cerdos *mpl*, puercos *mpl*.

(b) (*) canalla *m*, cochino *m*; marrano* *m* (*LAm*); **you ~!** ¡canalla!; **what a ~ he is!** ¡es un canalla!; **they're a lot of ~** son unos cochinos.

2 ATTR: **~ fever** fiebre *f* porcina.

swineherd†† ['swainhɜːd] N porquero *m*.

swing [swiŋ] **1** N **(a)** (*movement*) balanceo *m*, oscilación *f*, vaivén *m*;

(*of pendulum*) oscilación *f*; (*Boxing*) golpe *m* lateral, swing *m*; **it has a ~ of 2 metres** tiene un recorrido de 2 metros; **to give the starting handle a ~** girar la manivela; **to give a hammock a ~** empujar una hamaca; **to give a child a ~** empujar a un niño en un columpio; balancear a un niño colgado de los brazos (*etc*); **he took a ~ at me** me asestó un golpe; **he took a ~ at me with the axe** trató de golpearme con el hacha.

(b) (*Pol: in votes etc*) movimiento *m*, desplazamiento *m*, viraje *m*; **a sudden ~ in opinion** un viraje repentino de la opinión; **the ~ of the pendulum** el flujo y reflujo de la popularidad (de los partidos); **there was a strong ~ in the election** en las elecciones se registró un fuerte viraje; **a ~ of 5% would give the opposition the majority** un 5 por 100 de desplazamiento de los votos daría a la oposición la mayoría.

(c) (*seat*) columpio *m*; **what you lose on the ~s you gain on the roundabouts** lo que no va en lágrimas va en suspiros.

(d) (*rhythm*) ritmo *m* (fuerte, agradable); (*kind of music*) swing *m*; **~ band** orquesta *f* de swing; **a tune that goes with a ~** una melodía que tiene un ritmo marcado; **it all went with a ~** todo fue sobre ruedas; **to walk with a ~** andar rítmicamente; **to be in full ~** estar en plena marcha, estar en plena actividad; **to get into the ~ of things** irse acostumbrando; coger el tino; ponerse al corriente de las cosas (*or* la situación).

② (*irr*: PRET AND PTP **swung**) VT **(a)** (*to and fro*) balancear; hacer oscilar; (*on a swing*) columpiar; (*brandish*) blandir, menear; *arms* menear; *propeller* girar; **to ~ a child** empujar a un niño en un columpio; balancear a un niño colgado de los brazos (*etc*); **he sat on the table ~ing his legs** estaba sentado sobre la mesa balanceando las piernas; **to ~ one's fist at sb** asestar un golpe (lateral) a uno con el puño; **he swung the case up on to his shoulders** haciendo un esfuerzo se echó la maleta sobre los hombros.

(b) (*fig*) *policy* cambiar; *outcome* determinar, decidir; influir en; *voters* hacer cambiar de opinión; **he swung the party behind him** obtuvo el apoyo del partido, logró la aprobación del partido; **eventually he managed to ~ it*** por fin lo logró.

(c) (*) **to ~ it** fingirse enfermo, racanear*, hacer el rácano*; **to ~ it on sb** embaucar a uno.

③ VI **(a)** (*to and fro*) balancearse; oscilar; (*on a swing*) columpiarse; (*hang*) colgar, pender; (*door etc*) girar; **to ~ at anchor** estar anclado; **the door ~s on its hinges** la puerta gira sobre sus goznes; **it swung open** de pronto se abrió; **it ~s in the wind** se balancea al viento; **a revolver swung from his belt** un revólver colgaba de su cinturón; **he'll ~ for it** le ahorcarán por ello.

(b) (*change direction*) cambiar de dirección; **the car swung into the square** el coche viró y entró en la plaza; **to ~ into action** ponerse en marcha; empezar a ponerse por obra; **the country has swung to the right** el país ha virado a la derecha.

(c) (*strike*) **to ~ at a ball** tratar de golpear una pelota; **he swung at me** me asestó un golpe.

④ VR: **to ~ o.s. into the saddle** subir a la silla con un solo movimiento enérgico.

◆**swing round** ① VT (*turn*) girar, hacer girar; **he swung the car round** hizo un viraje brusco; **they swung the gun barrel round** hicieron girar el cañon.

② VI (*change direction*) cambiar de dirección; **he swung round** giró sobre los talones, se volvió bruscamente; **it swung right round** dio una vuelta completa.

③ VR: **to ~ o.s. round** girar sobre los talones.

swing bin ['swɪŋbɪn] N *cubo de la basura con tapa oscilante*.

swing bridge ['swɪŋ'brɪdʒ] N puente *m* giratorio.

swing door ['swɪŋ'dɔːʳ] N (*Brit*) puerta *f* batiente.

swingeing ['swɪndʒɪŋ] ADJ *majority* abrumador; *penalty etc* severísimo.

swinger* ['swɪŋəʳ] N: **he's a ~** (*with it*) es muy mundano, es muy moderno; (*going to parties*) es un asiduo en las fiestas; (*sexually*) no tiene inhibiciones.

swinging ['swɪŋɪŋ] ADJ **(a)** (*) *city etc* alegre, movido, de vida alegre, lleno de diversiones. **(b)** **~ door** (*US*) puerta *f* giratoria.

swing-wing ['swɪŋwɪŋ] ATTR de geometría variable.

swinish ['swaɪnɪʃ] ADJ (*fig*) cochino, canallesco; brutal.

swipe [swaɪp] ① N golpe *m* fuerte; **to take a ~ at sb** asestar un golpe a uno.

② VT **(a)** golpear fuertemente; pegar; **he ~s her** la pega.

(b) (‡) apandar‡, guindar‡.

③ VI: **to ~ at sb** asestar un golpe a uno.

swirl [swɜːl] ① N remolino *m*, torbellino *m*; **it disappeared in a ~ of water** desapareció en el agua arremolinada; **the ~ of the dancers' skirts** el movimiento de las faldas de las bailadoras.

② VI arremolinarse; girar, girar confusamente.

swish [swɪʃ] ① N silbido *m*; crujido *m*.

② ADJ (*) (*smart*) elegantísimo; (*posh*) de buen tono.

③ VT **(a)** *cane* agitar (*or* blandir) produciendo un silbido; *tail* agitar, menear.

(b) (*) azotar.

④ VI silbar; sonar, crujir.

Swiss [swɪs] ① ADJ suizo; **~ roll** (*Culin*) brazo *m* de gitano.

② N suizo *m*, -a *f*.

switch [swɪtʃ] ① N **(a)** (*stick*) vara *f*, varilla *f*; (*whip*) látigo *m*.

(b) (*of hair*) trenza *f* postiza, trenza *f*, postizo *m*.

(c) (*Rail: points*) aguja *f*; (*change of line*) desviación *f*.

(d) (*Elec etc*) interruptor *m*, conmutador *m*, llave *f*, botón *m*.

(e) (*change*) cambio *m*; giro *m*; **a rapid ~ of plan** un cambio repentino de plan; **to do a ~, to make a ~** hacer un cambio.

② VT **(a)** *tail* agitar, menear.

(b) (*Rail*) desviar, cambiar de vía; **to ~ a train to another line** cambiar un tren a otra vía.

(c) (*change*) *position etc* cambiar; *policy etc* cambiar de; **to ~ the conversation** (**to another subject**) cambiar de tema; **so we ~ed hats** así que cambiamos los sombreros.

③ VI (*change*) cambiar; **to ~ (over) from Y to Z** cambiar de Y a Z, dejar Y para tomar Z.

◆**switch back** VI volver a su posición (*or* política *etc*) original; **to ~ back to** volver a, cambiar de nuevo a.

◆**switch off** ① VT (*Elec*) desconectar, quitar; *light* apagar; *engine* parar.

② VI desconectar la televisión (*etc*); (*fig*) dejar de prestar atención.

◆**switch on** ① VT (*Elec*) encender, conectar, poner; prender (*LAm*); (*Aut etc*) arrancar, poner en marcha; **please ~ the radio on** por favor, enciende la radio; **to leave the television ~ed on** dejar puesta la televisión.

② VI encender la radio, poner la televisión (*etc*); arrancar el motor.

◆**switch over** ① VT: **to ~ over A and B** cambiar A con B, invertir A y B.

② VI: **to ~ over to another station** cambiar a otra emisora; **we've ~ed over altogether to gas** lo hemos cambiado todo a gas; *see also* switch 3.

◆**switch round** ① VT cambiar, invertir; arreglar de otro modo.

② VI cambiar de sitio, cambiar de idea.

switchback ['swɪtʃbæk] N (*Brit*) (*at fair etc*) montaña *f* rusa, tobogán *m*; (*road*) camino *m* de fuertes altibajos, carretera *f* llena de baches.

switchblade ['swɪtʃˌbleɪd] N (*US*) navaja *f* de muelle, navaja *f* de resorte.

switchboard ['swɪtʃbɔːd] N (*Tech*) cuadro *m* de mandos; (*Elec*) tablero *m* de conmutadores, cuadro *m* de distribución; (*Telec: at exchange*) cuadro *m* de conexión manual, (*in office etc*) centralita *f*, conmutador *m* (*LAm*); **~ operator** telefonista *mf*.

switch-hit [ˌswɪtʃˈhɪt] (*US*) VI ser ambidextro en el bateo.

switch-hitter [ˌswɪtʃˈhɪtəʳ] N (*US*) (*Baseball*) bateador *m* ambidextro; (*) bisexual *m*.

switchman ['swɪtʃmən] N, PL **switchmen** ['swɪtʃmən] guardagujas *m*.

switch-over ['swɪtʃəʊvəʳ] N cambio *m* (to a); nuevo rumbo *m*, nuevo enfoque *m*.

switchtower ['swɪtʃˌtaʊəʳ] N (*US*) garita *f* de señales.

switchyard ['swɪtʃjɑːd] N (*US*) patio *m* de maniobras, estación *f* clasificadora.

Switzerland ['swɪtsələnd] N Suiza *f*.

swivel ['swɪvl] ① N eslabón *m* giratorio; pivote *m*.

② ATTR giratorio, movil; **~ seat** silla *f* giratoria.

③ VT (*also* **to ~ round**) girar.

④ VI (*also* **to ~ round**) girar; (*person*) volverse, girar sobre los talones.

◆**swivel round** ① VT = swivel 3.

② VI = swivel 4.

swizz* [swɪz] N, **swizzle*** ['swɪzl] N (*Brit*) = swindle.

swizzle-stick ['swɪzlstɪk] N paletilla *f* para cóctel.

swollen ['swəʊlən] PTP *of* swell.

swollen-headed ['swəʊlən'hedɪd] ADJ vanidoso, engreído.

swoon [swuːn] ① N desmayo *m*, desvanecimiento *m*; **to fall in a ~** desmayarse.

② VI (*also* **to ~ away**) desmayarse, desvanecerse; **she ~ed at the news** al saber la noticia se desmayó.

swoop [swuːp] ① N calada *f*, descenso *m* súbito; arremetida *f*; (*by police*) redada *f*; visita *f* de inspección; **at one fell ~, in one ~** de un solo golpe.

② VI (*bird: also* **to ~ down**) calarse, abatirse; abalanzarse; precipitarse; lanzarse (*on* sobre); **the plane ~ed low over the village** el avión picó y voló muy bajo sobre el pueblo; **the police ~ed on 8 suspects** en una redada la policía detuvo a 8 sospechosos; **he ~ed on this mistake** se lanzó sobre este error.

swoosh [swu(ː)ʃ] = swish.

swop [swɒp] = swap.

sword [sɔːd] N espada *f*; **to cross ~s with sb** habérselas con uno; reñir con uno; **to put people to the ~** pasar a cuchillo a unas gentes; **those that live by the ~ die by the ~** el que a hierro mata a hierro muere.

sword dance ['sɔːddɑːns] N danza *f* de espadas.

swordfish ['sɔːdfɪʃ] N pez *m* espada, emperador *m* (*Carib*).

swordplay ['sɔːdpleɪ] N esgrima *f*; manejo *m* de la espada; **the film has 5 minutes of ~** en la película se combate a espada durante 5 minutos.

swordsman ['sɔːdzmən] N, PL **swordsmen** ['sɔːdzmən] espada *f*, espadachín *m*; (*Fencing*) esgrimidor *m*; **a good ~** una buena espada.

swordsmanship ['sɔːdzmənʃɪp] N esgrima *f*, manejo *m* de la espada.

swordstick ['sɔːdstɪk] N bastón *m* de estoque.

sword-swallower ['sɔːd,swɒləʊəʳ] N tragasables *mf*.

sword-thrust ['sɔːdθrʌst] N estocada *f*.

swore [swɔːʳ] PRET *of* swear.

sworn [swɔːn] [1] PTP *of* swear. [2] ADJ *enemy* implacable; *evidence, statement* dado bajo juramento, jurado.

swot* [swɒt] (*Brit*) [1] N empollón* *m*, -ona *f*.
[2] VT empollar*.
[3] VI empollar*; **to ~ at sth** empollar algo*.
◆ **swot up*** VTI: **to ~ up (on) one's maths** empollar matemáticas*.

swotting* ['swɒtɪŋ] N: **to do some ~** empollar*; **too much ~ is a bad idea** empollar demasiado no es bueno*.

swum [swʌm] PTP *of* swim.

swung [swʌŋ] PRET AND PTP *of* swing.

sybarite ['sɪbəraɪt] N sibarita *mf*.

sybaritic [,sɪbə'rɪtɪk] ADJ sibarita, sibarítico.

sycamore ['sɪkəmɔːʳ] N (*also* ~ **tree**) sicomoro *m*.

sycophancy ['sɪkəfənsɪ] N adulación *f*; servilismo *m*.

sycophant ['sɪkəfənt] N sicofanta *m*, sicofante *m*, adulador *m*, -ora *f*, pelotillero *m*, -a *f*; persona *f* servil, sobón *f*.

sycophantic [,sɪkə'fæntɪk] ADJ *person* servil, sobón; *speech etc* adulatorio; *manner* servil.

Sydney ['sɪdnɪ] N Sidney *m*.

syllabi ['sɪlə,baɪ] NPL *of* **syllabus**.

syllabic [sɪ'læbɪk] ADJ silábico.

syllabication [sɪ,læbɪ'keɪʃən] N, **syllabification** [sɪ,læbɪfɪ'keɪʃən] N silabeo *m*, división *f* en sílabas.

syllabify [sɪ'læbɪfaɪ] VT dividir en sílabas.

syllable ['sɪləbl] N sílaba *f*; **I will explain it in words of one ~** te lo explico como a un niño.

syllabub ['sɪləbʌb] N *dulce frío hecho con nata o leche, licor y zumo de limón*.

syllabus ['sɪləbəs] N, PL **syllabuses** *or* **syllabi** ['sɪlə,baɪ] programa *m* (*esp de* estudios), plan *m* de estudios.

syllogism ['sɪlədʒɪzəm] N silogismo *m*.

syllogistic [,sɪlə'dʒɪstɪk] ADJ silogístico.

syllogize ['sɪlədʒaɪz] VI silogizar.

sylph [sɪlf] N (*Myth*) silfo *m*, sílfide *f*; (*woman*) sílfide *f*.

sylphlike ['sɪlflaɪk] ADJ *figure etc* de sílfide.

sylvan ['sɪlvən] ADJ selvático, silvestre; rústico.

Sylvia ['sɪlvɪə] NF Silvia.

symbiosis [,sɪmbɪ'əʊsɪs] N simbiosis *f*.

symbiotic [,sɪmbɪ'ɒtɪk] ADJ simbiótico.

symbol ['sɪmbəl] N símbolo *m*.

symbolic(al) [sɪm'bɒlɪk(əl)] ADJ simbólico; **symbolic logic** lógica *f* simbólica.

symbolically [sɪm'bɒlɪkəlɪ] ADV simbólicamente.

symbolism ['sɪmbəlɪzəm] N simbolismo *m*.

symbolist ['sɪmbəlɪst] [1] ADJ simbolista.
[2] N simbolista *mf*.

symbolize ['sɪmbəlaɪz] VT simbolizar.

symmetrical [sɪ'metrɪkəl] ADJ simétrico.

symmetrically [sɪ'metrɪkəlɪ] ADV simétricamente.

symmetry ['sɪmɪtrɪ] N simetría *f*.

sympathetic [,sɪmpə'θetɪk] ADJ (a) (*showing pity*) compasivo (*to* con), compadecido; (*kind*) amable, benévolo; (*understanding*) comprensivo; **we found a ~ policeman** encontramos a un policía que amablemente nos ayudó (*etc*); **they were ~ but could not help** se compadecieron de nosotros pero no podían hacer nada para ayudarnos; **they are ~ to actors** están bien dispuestos hacia los actores; **he wasn't in the least ~** no mostró compasión alguna.
(b) *ink, nerve, pain etc* simpático.

sympathetically [,sɪmpə'θetɪkəlɪ] ADV con compasión; amablemente, benévolamente; con comprensión; **she looked at me ~** me miró compasiva.

sympathize ['sɪmpəθaɪz] VI (*in sorrow etc*) compadecerse, condolerse; (*understand*) comprender; **I really do ~** lo siento de verdad; **to ~ with sb** compadecerse de uno, condolerse de uno; **I ~ with what you say, but ...** comprendo el punto de vista de Vd, pero ...; **those who ~ with our demands** los que apoyan nuestras reclamaciones; **to ~ with sb in his bereavement** dar el pésame a uno por la muerte de ...; **they called to ~** vinieron a dar el pésame.

sympathizer ['sɪmpəθaɪzəʳ] N simpatizante *mf*, partidario *m*, -a *f* (*with* de).

▼ **sympathy** ['sɪmpəθɪ] N (a) (*fellow-feeling*) simpatía *f*; solidaridad *f*; ~ **strike** huelga *f* de solidaridad; ~ **vote** voto *m* de consolación; **I am** **not in ~ with him** no comparto su criterio, no lo entiendo así; **the sympathies of the crowd were with him** la multitud estaba de lado de él, la multitud le apoyaba; **to strike in ~ with sb** declararse en huelga por solidaridad con uno.

▼ (b) (*pity*) compasión *f*, condolencia *f*; sentimiento *m*; (*kindness*) amabilidad *f*, benevolencia *f*; **he has my ~** le compadezco; **my sympathies are with her family** lo siento por la familia de ella; **have you no ~?** ¿no tiene compasión?; **to express one's ~** dar el pésame (*on the death of* por la muerte de); **his ~ for the underdog** su compasión por los desvalidos.

symphonic [sɪm'fɒnɪk] ADJ sinfónico.

symphony ['sɪmfənɪ] N sinfonía *f*; ~ **orchestra** orquesta *f* sinfónica.

symposium [sɪm'pəʊzɪəm] N, PL **symposiums** *or* **symposia** [sɪm'pəʊzɪə] simposio *m*.

symptom ['sɪmptəm] N síntoma *m*; indicio *m*.

symptomatic [,sɪmptə'mætɪk] ADJ sintomático (*of* de).

synagogue ['sɪnəgɒg] N sinagoga *f*.

synapse ['saɪnæps] N sinapsis *f*.

sync* [sɪŋk] N ABBR *of* **synchronization**: **in ~** en sincronización; **they are in ~** (*fig*) están sincronizados; **out of ~** (*fig*) desincronizado.

synchromesh ['sɪŋkrəʊ'meʃ] N (*also* ~ **gear**) cambio *m* sincronizado de velocidades.

synchronic [sɪŋ'krɒnɪk] ADJ sincrónico.

synchronism ['sɪŋkrənɪzəm] N sincronismo *m*.

synchronization [,sɪŋkrənaɪ'zeɪʃən] N sincronización *f*.

synchronize ['sɪŋkrənaɪz] [1] VT sincronizar (*with* con); ~**d swimming** natación *f* sincronizada.
[2] VI sincronizarse, ser sincrónico (*with* con); coincidir (*with* con).

synchronous ['sɪŋkrənəs] ADJ sincrónico, síncrono.

synchrotron ['sɪŋkrə,trɒn] N sincrotrón *m*.

syncopate ['sɪŋkəpeɪt] VT sincopar.

syncopation [,sɪŋkə'peɪʃən] N síncopa *f*.

syncope ['sɪŋkəpɪ] N (*Med*) síncope *m*; (*Ling, Mus*) síncopa *f*.

syncretism ['sɪŋkrətɪzəm] N sincretismo *m*.

syndic ['sɪndɪk] N síndico *m*.

syndicalism ['sɪndɪkəlɪzəm] N sindicalismo *m*.

syndicalist ['sɪndɪkəlɪst] [1] ADJ sindicalista.
[2] N sindicalista *mf*.

syndicate [1] ['sɪndɪkɪt] N (a) (*gen*) sindicato *m*; (*news agency*) agencia *f* de prensa; (*chain of papers*) cadena *f* de periódicos. (b) (*: *criminals*) banda *f* de malhechores, cuadrilla *f* de bandidos.
[2] ['sɪndɪkeɪt] VT sindicar; ~**d loan** préstamo *m* sindicado.

syndrome ['sɪndrəʊm] N síndrome *m*.

synecdoche [sɪ'nekdəkɪ] N sinécdoque *f*.

synergy ['sɪnədʒɪ] N sinergia *f*.

synod ['sɪnəd] N sínodo *m*.

synonym ['sɪnənɪm] N sinónimo *m*.

synonymous [sɪ'nɒnɪməs] ADJ sinónimo (*with* con).

synonymy [sɪ'nɒnəmɪ] N sinonimia *f*.

synopsis [sɪ'nɒpsɪs] N, PL **synopses** [sɪ'nɒpsiːz] sinopsis *f*.

synoptic(al) [sɪ'nɒptɪk(əl)] ADJ sinóptico.

synovial [saɪ'nəʊvɪəl] ADJ sinovial.

syntactic(al) [sɪn'tæktɪk(əl)] ADJ sintáctico.

syntagm ['sɪntæm] N, **syntagma** [sɪn'tægmə] N sintagma *m*.

syntagmatic [,sɪntæg'mætɪk] ADJ sintagmático.

syntax ['sɪntæks] [1] N sintaxis *f*.
[2] ATTR: ~ **error** error *m* sintáctico.

synthesis ['sɪnθəsɪs] N, PL **syntheses** ['sɪnθəsiːz] síntesis *f*.

synthesize ['sɪnθəsaɪz] VT sintetizar.

synthesizer ['sɪnθəsaɪzəʳ] N sintetizador *m*.

synthetic [sɪn'θetɪk] [1] ADJ sintético; ~ **fiber** (*US*), ~ **fibre** fibra *f* sintética; ~ **rubber** caucho *m* artificial.
[2] ~**s** NPL fibras *fpl* sintéticas.

synthetically [sɪn'θetɪkəlɪ] ADV sintéticamente.

syphilis ['sɪfɪlɪs] N sífilis *f*.

syphilitic [,sɪfɪ'lɪtɪk] [1] ADJ sifilítico.
[2] N sifilítico *m*, -a *f*.

syphon ['saɪfən] = **siphon**.

Syracuse ['saɪərəkjuːz] N Siracusa *f*.

Syria ['sɪrɪə] N Siria *f*.

Syrian ['sɪrɪən] [1] ADJ sirio.
[2] N sirio *m*, -a *f*.

syringe [sɪ'rɪndʒ] [1] N jeringa *f*, jeringuilla *f*.
[2] VT jeringar.

syrup ['sɪrəp] N jarabe *m*; almíbar *m*.

syrupy ['sɪrəpɪ] ADJ (a) parecido a jarabe, espeso como jarabe. (b) (*fig*) sensiblero, sentimentaloide*, dulzarrón.

system ['sɪstəm] N (a) (*gen*) sistema *m*; método *m*; (*Med*) organismo *m*, constitución *f*; (*Elec*) circuito *m*, instalación *f*; **the S~** (*Pol*) el Sistema; ~**s analysis** análisis *m* de sistemas; ~**s analyst** analista *mf* de sistemas; ~ **disk** disco *m* del sistema; ~**s engineer** ingeniero *m* de sistemas; ~**s engineering** ingeniería *f* de sistemas; ~**s programmer**

programador *m*, -ora *f* de sistemas; **~s software** software *m* del sistema; **a shock to the ~** una sacudida para el organismo; **to get sth out of one's ~** (*fig*) quitarse algo de encima.
(**b**) (*orderliness*) método *m*; **he lacks ~** carece de método.

systematic [ˌsɪstə'mætɪk] ADJ sistemático, metódico.

systematically [ˌsɪstə'mætɪkəlɪ] ADV sistemáticamente, metódicamente.

systematization ['sɪstəmətaɪ'zeɪʃən] N sistematización *f*.

systematize ['sɪstəmətaɪz] VT sistematizar.

systemic [sɪs'temɪk] ADJ (**a**) *changes, problems* sistémico. (**b**) (*Physiol*) sistémico, anabólico.

systole ['sɪstəlɪ] N (*Med*) sístole *f*.

T

T, t [tiː] N (letter) T, t; **T for Tommy** T de Tarragona; **T-bar lift** N remolque m T-bar; **T-bone steak** N entrecote m; **T-intersection** (US), **T-junction** cruce m en T; **T-shaped** en forma de T; **T-shirt** camiseta f, niki m, playera f (LAm), remera f (LAm); **T-square** doble escuadra f, escuadra f T; **that's it to a T** es eso exactamente; **it fits you to a T** te sienta perfectamente; **it suits you to a T** te viene de perlas.

TA N (a) (Brit) ABBR of **Territorial Army** ejército m de reserva; ver también TERRITORIAL ARMY . (b) (US Univ) ABBR of **teaching assistant**.

ta* [tɑː] INTERJ (Brit) ¡gracias!; **~ very much!** ¡muchas gracias!

tab¹ [tæb] N oreja f, lengüeta f; (label) etiqueta f; (of cheque) resguardo m; (US) cuenta f; **~s** (Theat) cortina f a la italiana; **to keep ~s on sb** echar un ojo sobre uno, vigilar a uno; **to keep ~s on sth** tener algo a la vista, tener cuenta de algo; **to pick up the ~** pagar la cuenta, (fig) asumir la responsabilidad.

tab² [tæb] 1 N tabulación f.
2 VT tabular.

tabard ['tæbəd] N tabardo m.

Tabasco [tə'bæskəʊ] ® N tabasco m.

tabby ['tæbɪ] 1 ADJ atigrado.
2 N (also ~ **cat**) gato m atigrado, gata f atigrada.

tabernacle ['tæbənækl] N tabernáculo m.

tab key ['tæbkiː] N tecla f de tabulación.

table ['teɪbl] 1 N (a) (furniture) mesa f; (Archit) tablero m; (of land) meseta f; **~ manners** modales mpl de mesa; **~ salt** sal f de mesa; **to keep a good ~** tener buena mesa; **to clear the ~** quitar la mesa; **the whole ~ laughed** se rieron todos los comensales; **to lay the ~**, **to set the ~** poner la mesa; **to put a proposal on the ~** (Brit) ofrecer una propuesta para discutir, (US) aplazar la discusión de una propuesta; **to rise from the ~** levantarse de la mesa; **to sit down to ~** sentarse a (or en) la mesa; **to turn the ~s on sb** devolver la pelota a uno, volver las tornas a uno.
(b) (Math etc) tabla f; (statistical etc) tabla f, cuadro m; (of prices) lista f, tarifa f; (league ~) liga f; clasificación f, escalafón m; **~ of contents** índice m de materias; **we are in fourth place in the ~** ocupamos el cuarto lugar en la clasificación.
2 VT (a) (Brit Parl etc) motion presentar, poner sobre la mesa.
(b) (set out) poner en una tabla, disponer en un cuadro; ordenar sistemáticamente.
(c) (US: postpone) aplazar, archivar, posponer; bill dar carpetazo a, dar largas a.

tableau ['tæbləʊ] N, PL **tableaus** or **tableaux** ['tæbləʊz] cuadro m (vivo).

tablecloth ['teɪblklɒθ] N, PL **tablecloths** ['teɪblklɒðs] mantel m.

tablecover ['teɪbl,kʌvəʳ] N mantel m.

table d'hôte ['tɑːbl'dəʊt] N menú m.

table-football [,teɪbl'fʊtbɔːl] N futbolín m.

table-lamp ['teɪbllæmp] N lámpara f de mesa.

tableland ['teɪbllænd] N meseta f, altiplano m (LAm).

table-leg ['teɪblleg] N pata f de mesa.

table-linen ['teɪbl,lɪnɪn] N mantelería f.

tablemat ['teɪblmæt] N salvaplatos m, salvamanteles m.

Table Mountain ['teɪbl'maʊntɪn] N Monte m de la Mesa.

table-napkin ['teɪbl,næpkɪn] N servilleta f.

table-runner ['teɪbl,rʌnəʳ] N mantelillo m, camino m de mesa.

tablespoon ['teɪblspuːn] N (spoon) cuchara f grande, cuchara f para servir; (quantity) cucharada f.

tablespoonful ['teɪbl,spuːnfʊl] N cucharada f.

tablet ['tæblɪt] N tabla f; tableta f; (Med) tableta f, comprimido m; (of soap etc) pastilla f; (stone, inscribed) lápida f; (writing ~) bloc m, taco m (de papel).

table-talk ['teɪbltɔːk] N conversación f de sobremesa.

table-tennis ['teɪbl,tenɪs] N tenis m de mesa, ping-pong m; **~ player** jugador m, -ora f de ping-pong (or de tenis de mesa).

table-top ['teɪbltɒp] N superficie f de la mesa.

tableware ['teɪblweəʳ] N vajilla f, servicio m de mesa.

tablewater ['teɪbl,wɔːtəʳ] N agua f mineral.

table wine ['teɪblwaɪn] N vino m de mesa.

tabloid ['tæblɔɪd] N (Med) tableta f, comprimido m; (newspaper) tabloide m; **the ~s** (pej) la prensa amarilla.

⌐ TABLOIDS AND BROADSHEETS ─

i En el Reino Unido hay dos tipos de periódicos, llamados, según su tamaño, *tabloids* o *broadsheets*. Los primeros son más grandes y suelen centrarse en noticias serias, artículos de contenido cultural y un análisis en profundidad de la actualidad, por lo que también se les denomina *quality press*. Algunos nombres muy conocidos son *The Daily Telegraph, The Times, The Guardian* y *The Independent*. Los llamados *tabloids* suelen tener grandes titulares, artículos cortos, muchas fotografías, opiniones espontáneas y muestran una clara preferencia por las historias escandalosas o sentimentales. Por sus contenidos sensacionalistas también reciben el nombre de *gutter press*. Los más conocidos de éstos son *The Sun, The Daily Mirror, The Daily Express, The Daily Mail* y *The Daily Star*.
En los Estados Unidos, el término *standard-sized newspapers* es el equivalente de *broadsheet*. El principal periódico de este tipo es la edición nacional del *New York Times*. Entre los *tabloids* más conocidos están el *New York Daily News* y el *Chicago Sun-Times*.

---

taboo [tə'buː] 1 ADJ tabú, prohibido; **the subject is ~** el asunto es tema tabú.
2 N tabú m; **all kinds of ~s** toda clase de tabúes.
3 VT declarar tabú, prohibir.

tabu [tə'buː] = **taboo**.

tabular ['tæbjʊləʳ] ADJ tabular.

tabulate ['tæbjʊleɪt] VT disponer en tablas, exponer en forma de tabla; contabilizar; (Comput) tabular.

tabulation [,tæbjʊ'leɪʃən] N disposición f en tablas, exposición f en forma de tabla; contabilización f.

tabulator ['tæbjʊleɪtəʳ] N tabulador m.

tachograph ['tækəgrɑːf] N tacógrafo m.

tachometer [tæ'kɒmɪtəʳ] N tacómetro m.

tachycardia [,tækɪ'kɑːdɪə] N taquicardia f.

tachymeter [tæ'kɪmɪtəʳ] N taquímetro m.

tacit ['tæsɪt] ADJ tácito.

tacitly ['tæsɪtlɪ] ADV tácitamente.

taciturn ['tæsɪtɜːn] ADJ taciturno.

taciturnity [,tæsɪ'tɜːnɪtɪ] N taciturnidad f.

Tacitus ['tæsɪtəs] NM Tácito.

tack [tæk] 1 N (a) (nail) tachuela f.
(b) (Brit Sew) hilván m.
(c) (Naut: rope) amura f; (course) virada f, bordada f; (fig) rumbo m, dirección f; línea f de conducta, política f; **to be on the right ~** (fig) ir por buen camino; **to be on the wrong ~** (fig) estar equivocado; **to try another ~** (fig) abordar un problema desde otro punto de partida; cambiar de política.
2 VT (a) (nail) clavar con tachuelas.
(b) (Brit Sew) hilvanar.
3 VI (Naut) virar, cambiar de bordada; **the ship ~ed this way and that** el buque daba bordadas.
◆ **tack down** VT: **to ~ sth down** afirmar algo con tachuelas, sujetar algo con tachuelas.
◆ **tack on** VT: **to ~ sth on to a letter** añadir algo a una carta; **somehow it got ~ed on** de algún modo u otro llegó a ser añadido a la parte principal.

tackle ['tækl] 1 N (a) (esp Naut: pulley) aparejo m; polea f; (ropes) jarcia f; cordaje m.
(b) (gear, equipment) equipo m, avíos mpl, aperos mpl; (fig) cosas fpl,

enseres *mpl*; (*fishing* ~) aparejo *m* de pescar.
(c) (*Ftbl etc*) entrada *f*; (*Rugby*) placaje *m*.
2 VT (*grapple with*) agarrar, asir; atacar; (*Ftbl*) entrar, atajar, blocar; (*Rugby*) placar; *problem* abordar, atacar; *task* emprender; **he had to ~ 3 intruders** tuvo que hacer frente a 3 intrusos; **he ~d Greek on his own** emprendió el estudio del griego sin ayuda de nadie; **did you ever ~ Mulacén?** ¿os atrevisteis alguna vez a escalar el Mulacén?; **can you ~ another helping?** ¿puedes comerte otra porción?; **I'll ~ him about it at once** lo discutiré con él en seguida (quiera o no quiera).

tacky[1] ['tækɪ] ADJ pegajoso.
tacky[2]* ['tækɪ] ADJ (*shabby*) raído; (*shoddy*) de pacotilla, malísimo; (*ostentatious*) cursi, vulgar; (*eccentric*) estrafalario; *house* feo, destartalado; *problem* peliagudo.
taco ['tɑːkəʊ] N (*US*) (*especie de*) *tortilla rellena hecha con harina de maíz*.
tact [tækt] N *tacto m*, discreción *f*.
tactful ['tæktfʊl] ADJ discreto, diplomático; **be as ~ as you can** use la mayor discreción; **that was not very ~ of you** pudieras haberlo hecho con más tacto.
tactfully ['tæktfəlɪ] ADV discretamente, diplomáticamente.
tactfulness ['tæktfʊlnɪs] N tacto *m*, discreción *f*.
tactic ['tæktɪk] N táctica *f*; maniobra *f*; **~s** (*collectively*) táctica *f*.
tactical ['tæktɪkəl] ADJ táctico; **~ voting** votación *f* táctica.
tactically ['tæktɪkəlɪ] ADV tácticamente.
tactician [tæk'tɪʃən] N táctico *m*.
tactile ['tæktaɪl] ADJ táctil.
tactless ['tæktlɪs] ADJ indiscreto, falto de tacto, poco diplomático.
tactlessly ['tæktlɪslɪ] ADV indiscretamente, de modo poco diplomático.
tactlessness ['tæktlɪsnɪs] N indiscreción *f*, falta *f* de tacto.
tad* [tæd] N: **a ~ big/small** un poco grande/pequeño.
Tadjikistan, Tadzhikistan [tɑːˌdʒɪkɪsˈtɑːn] = **Tajikistan**.
tadpole ['tædpəʊl] N renacuajo *m*.
taffeta ['tæfɪtə] N tafetán *m*.
taffrail ['tæfreɪl] N coronamiento *m*, pasamano *m* de la borda.
Taffy* ['tæfɪ] N galés *m*.
taffy ['tæfɪ] N (*US*) **(a)** = **toffee**. **(b)** (*) coba* *f*.
tag[1] [tæg] 1 N **(a)** (*loose end*) cabo *m*, rabito *m*; (*torn piece, hanging piece*) pingajo *m*; (*metal tip*) herrete *m*; (*label*) etiqueta *f*, marbete *m*, (*for identification etc*) chapa *f*; (*for criminal*) etiqueta *f* personal de control; **~ (question)** cláusula *f* final interrogativa.
(b) (*commonplace*) dicho *m*, lugar *m* común; muletilla *f*; (*quotation*) cita *f* trillada.
2 VT **(a)** (*follow*) seguir de cerca, pisar los talones a.
(b) (*label*) poner una etiqueta a, pegar una etiqueta a; *criminal* controlar electrónicamente.
♦**tag along** VI (*jog along*) seguir despacio su camino; proceder con calma; (*accompany*) ir también, venir después.
♦**tag on** 1 VT: **to ~ sth on to an article** pegar algo a un artículo; **can we ~ this on?** ¿podemos añadir esto?
2 VI: **to ~ on to sb** pegarse a uno.
tag[2] [tæg] N (*game*) marro *m*; **to play ~** jugar al marro.
tagliatelle [ˌtæljəˈtelɪ, ˌtæɡlɪəˈtelɪ] N tagliatelle *mpl*.
tagmeme ['tægmiːm] N tagmema *m*.
tagmemics [tægˈmiːmɪks] N tagmética *f*.
Tagus ['teɪgəs] N Tajo *m*.
tahini [təˈhiːnɪ] N *pasta hecha con semillas de sésamo*.
Tahiti [tɑːˈhiːtɪ] N Tahití *m*.
Tahitian [təˈhiːʃən] 1 ADJ tahitiano.
2 N **(a)** tahitiano *m*, -a *f*. **(b)** (*Ling*) tahitiano *m*.
tail [teɪl] 1 N **(a)** (*Anat*) cola *f*, rabo *m*; (*loose end*) cabo *m*; (*of hair*) trenza *f*; (*of comet*) cabellera *f*; (*Aer*) cola *f*; (*of procession etc*) cola *f*, parte *f* final; (*of coat*) faldón *m*, faldillas *fpl*; (*of shirt*) faldón *m*; **~s** (*coat*) frac *m*; (*of coin*) cruz *f*; **with its ~ between its legs** con el rabo entre las piernas; **~s you lose** cruz y pierdes; **to turn ~** volver la espalda, huir.
(b) (*: buttocks*) trasero *m*; **to work one's ~ off** sudar tinta*.
(c) (*US‡: girls*) jais‡ *fpl*; **a piece of ~‡** una jai‡, una tía*.
(d) (*: person following*) sombra *f*.
2 VT **(a)** (*follow*) seguir (de cerca), seguir y vigilar.
(b) *animal* descolar; *fruit* quitar el tallo a.
3 VI: **to ~ after sb** seguir a uno (de mala gana).
♦**tail away** VI ir disminuyendo (*into* hasta, hasta no ser más que), desaparecer poco a poco; **his voice ~ed away** su voz se fue debilitando; **after that the book ~s away** después de eso el libro ya no es tan bueno, después de eso el libro no tiene tantas cosas buenas.
♦**tail back** VI: **the traffic ~ed back to the bridge** la cola de coches se extendía atrás hasta el puente.
♦**tail off** VI = **tail away**.
tailback ['teɪlbæk] N (*Brit Aut*) caravana *f*, cola *f*, embotellamiento *m*.
tailboard ['teɪlbɔːd] N escalera *f*, tablero *m* posterior.
tailcoat ['teɪlkəʊt] N frac *m*.
-tailed [teɪld] ADJ con rabo ..., *eg* **long~** con rabo largo, rabilargo.

tail-end ['teɪl'end] N cola *f*; extremo *m*; parte *f* de atrás, parte *f* posterior; (*fig*) parte *f* que queda, porción *f* inservible; **at the ~ of the summer** en los últimos días del verano.
tailgate ['teɪlgeɪt] 1 N portón *m*.
2 VT ir a rebufo de.
3 VI ir a rebufo.
tail-gunner ['teɪlˌɡʌnəʳ] N artillero *m* de cola.
tail-lamp ['teɪllæmp] N piloto *m*, luz *f* trasera.
tailless ['teɪllɪs] ADJ sin rabo.
taillight ['teɪllaɪt] N piloto *m*, luz *f* trasera, calavera *f* (*Mex*).
tail-off ['teɪlɒf] N disminución *f* (paulatina).
tailor ['teɪləʳ] 1 N sastre *m*; **~'s (shop)** sastrería *f*; **~'s chalk** jabón *m* de sastre; **~'s dummy** maniquí *m*.
2 VT *suit* hacer, confeccionar; (*fig*) adaptar.
tailored ['teɪləd] ADJ: **~ dress** vestido *m* sastre; **a well-~ suit** un traje bien hecho, un traje que entalla bien.
tailoring ['teɪlərɪŋ] N (*craft*) sastrería *f*; (*cut*) corte *m*, hechura *f*.
tailor-made ['teɪləmeɪd] ADJ **(a)** *garment* hecho por sastre, de sastre; **~ costume** traje *m* hechura sastre.
(b) **~ for you** (*fig*) especial para Vd, creado especialmente para Vd.
tailor-make ['teɪlə'meɪk] VT diseñar a medida.
tailpiece ['teɪlpiːs] N (*Typ*) florón *m*; (*addition*) apéndice *m*, añadidura *f*.
tailpipe ['teɪlpaɪp] N (*US*) tubo *m* de escape.
tailplane ['teɪlpleɪn] N cola *f*, plano *m* de cola.
tailskid ['teɪlskɪd] N patín *m* de cola.
tailspin ['teɪlspɪn] N barrena *f* picada.
tailwheel ['teɪl'wiːl] N rueda *f* de cola.
tailwind ['teɪlwɪnd] N viento *m* de cola.
taint [teɪnt] 1 N **(a)** (*fig*) mancha *f*, tacha *f*; olor *m* (*of* a); **the ~ of sin** la mancha del pecado; **not free from the ~ of corruption** no sin cierto olor a corrupción.
2 VT *meat, food* contaminar; (*fig*) manchar, tachar (*LAm*).
tainted ['teɪntɪd] ADJ viciado, corrompido; *meat etc* pasado, contaminado; **a belief ~ with heresy** una creencia no exenta de herejía; **to become ~** (*meat etc*) echarse a perder.
Taiwan [ˌtaɪˈwɑːn] N Taiwán *m*.
Taiwanese [ˌtaɪwəˈniːz] 1 ADJ taiwanés.
2 N taiwanés *m*, -esa *f*.
Tajikistan [tɑːˌdʒɪkɪsˈtɑːn] N Tayikistán *m*.
take [teɪk] (*irr*: PRET **took**, PTP **taken**) 1 N **(a)** (*Cine, Phot*) toma *f*, vista *f*.
(b) (*money*) ingresos *mpl*; recaudación *f*; (*US Comm*) caja *f*, ventas *fpl* (del día *etc*).
(c) **to be on the ~*** (*US*) estar dispuesto a dejarse sobornar.
2 VT **(a)** (*gen*) tomar; (*by force*) coger (*Sp*), agarrar (*esp LAm*), asir, arrebatar; (*steal*) robar; (*keep*) quedarse con; **to ~ sth from sb** tomar algo a uno; **who took my beer?** ¿quién se ha llevado mi cerveza?; **to ~ a book from a shelf** sacar un libro de un estante; **to ~ a passage from an author** tomar un pasaje de un autor; **seeing that film took me out of myself** esa película me hizo olvidar mis propios problemas; **to ~ sb's arm** tomar del brazo a uno; **to ~ sb in one's arms** abrazar a uno, rodear a uno con los brazos; **with an attitude of ~ it or leave it** con actitud de lo toma o lo deja.
(b) (*capture*) *city etc* tomar, conquistar; *specimen, fish etc* coger; (*Chess etc*) comer; *prisoner* hacer; *suspect, wanted man* coger, detener; **to ~ sb alive or dead** coger a uno vivo o muerto; **the devil ~ it!** ¡maldición!, ¡que se lo lleve el diablo!; **to be ~n ill** ponerse enfermo, enfermar; **we were very ~n with him** le encontramos simpatiquísimo; **I'm not at all ~n with the idea** la idea no me gusta nada, la idea no me hace gracia.
(c) (*win*) *prize* ganar; *trick* ganar, hacer; **to ~ one's degree** recibir un título; **to ~ a degree in** licenciarse en; **to ~ £30 a day** cobrar 30 libras al día; **last year we took £30,000** el año pasado los ingresos sumaron 30.000 libras; **El Toboso took both points** El Toboso ganó los dos puntos; **V took a point from B** V sacó un punto a B.
(d) (*rent*) alquilar; **we shall ~ a house for the summer** alquilaremos una casa para el verano; **we took rooms at Torquay** alquilamos un piso en Torquay.
(e) (*occupy*) ocupar; **is this seat ~n?** ¿está ocupado este asiento?; **please ~ your seats!** ¡siéntense, por favor!
(f) (*go by*) *bus, train etc* coger (*Sp*), tomar (*LAm*); *road* tomar, ir por; *fence* saltar, saltar por encima de; **~ the first on the right** vaya por la primera calle a la derecha; **we took the wrong road** nos equivocamos de camino; **we ~ the golden road to Samarkand** vamos por el camino dorado de Samarkand.
(g) (*ingest*) *drink, food* tomar; **to ~ a meal** comer; **he took no food for 4 days** estuvo 4 días sin comer; **how much alcohol had he ~n?** ¿cuánto alcohol había ingerido?; **'not to be ~n'** (*Med*) 'para uso externo'; **will you ~ sth before you go?** ¿quieres tomar algo antes de irte?
(h) (*have, make, undertake etc*) *bath, bend, breath, decision, exercise, holiday, liberty, possession* tomar; *step, walk*, dar; *photo* sacar, tomar; *ticket*

sacar; *trip* hacer; *oath* prestar; *census* levantar, efectuar; *examination* presentarse para, sufrir; *opportunity* aprovechar; **~ five!***, **~ ten!*** (*US*) ¡haz una pausa!, ¡descansa un rato!

(i) (*receive*) recibir, tomar; *advice* seguir; *bet* aceptar, hacer; *responsibility* asumir; *lodger* recibir; *pupils* tomar; *course of study* seguir, cursar; *subject* estudiar; *newspaper etc* leer, abonarse a; **~ that!** ¡toma!; **~ it from me!** ¡escucha lo que te digo!; **you can ~ it from me that ...** puedes tener la seguridad de que ...; **to ~ the service** (*Tennis*) restar la pelota, ser restador; **he took the ball full in the chest** el balón le dio de lleno en el pecho; **what will you ~ for it?** ¿cuánto pides por él?; **to ~ a wife** casarse, contraer matrimonio; **to ~ sb into partnership** tomar a uno como socio; **to ~ (holy) orders** ordenarse de sacerdote; *V* **badly, ill** *etc*.

(j) (*tolerate*) aguantar, sufrir; **we can ~ it** lo aguantamos todo; **he took a lot of punishment** le dieron muy duro; **London took a battering in 1941** Londres recibió una paliza en 1941, Londres sufrió terriblemente en 1941; **his arrogance is hard to ~** su arrogancia es inaguantable; **I won't ~ no for an answer** no permito que digas no, no permito que me des una respuesta negativa; **I won't ~ that from you** no permito que digas eso; no acepto tal cosa de ti.

(k) (*consider*) tomar, considerar; **now ~ Ireland** consideren el caso de Irlanda, pongamos por caso Irlanda; **taking one thing with another ...** considerándolo todo junto ..., considerándolo en conjunto ...; **taking one year with another ...** tomando un año con otro ...

(l) (*contain*) tener cabida para; **a car that ~s 6 passengers** un coche con cabida para 6 personas, un coche donde caben 6 personas; **can you ~ 2 more?** ¿puedes llevar 2 más?, ¿caben otros 2?; **it won't ~ any more** no cabe(n) más; **it ~s weights up to 8 tons** soporta pesos hasta de 8 toneladas.

(m) (*experience*) experimentar; *illness* coger (*Sp*), agarrar (*LAm*); **to ~ cold** coger un resfriado (*Sp*), resfriarse; **to ~ fright** asustarse (*at* de); **to ~ a dislike to sb** coger antipatía a uno; **I do not ~ any satisfaction from ...** no experimento satisfacción alguna de ...; *V* **liking** *etc*.

(n) (*suppose*) suponer; **I ~ it that ...** supongo que ..., me imagino que ...; **I ~ her to be about 30** supongo que tiene unos 30 años; **I took him for a foreigner** creí que era extranjero, le tomé por extranjero; **what do you ~ me for?** ¿por quién me has tomado?, ¿crees que soy un tonto?; **we took A for B** equivocamos A con B.

(o) (*require*) necesitar; hacer falta; **a recipe that ~s 10 eggs** una receta en la que hacen falta 10 huevos; **it ~s a lot of courage** exige gran valor; **it ~s a brave man to do that** hace falta que un hombre tenga mucho valor para hacer eso; **he's got what it ~s*** tiene lo que hace falta; **it ~s 4 days** es cosa de 4 días; **a letter ~s 4 days to get there** una carta tarda 4 días en llegar allá; **it won't ~ long** no lleva mucho tiempo; **however long it ~s** el tiempo que sea; **it took 3 policemen to hold him down** se necesitaron 3 policías para sujetarle; **that verb ~s the dative** ese verbo rige el dativo; *V* **size** *etc*.

(p) (*lead, transport*) llevar; **to ~ sth to sb** llevar algo a uno; **to ~ sb somewhere** llevar a uno a un sitio; **we took her to the doctor** la llevamos al médico; **an ambulance took him to hospital** una ambulancia le llevó al hospital; **they took me over the factory** me mostraron la fábrica, me acompañaron en una visita a la fábrica; **to ~ sb for a walk** llevar a uno de paseo; **it took us out of our way** nos hizo desviarnos; **whatever took you to Miami?** ¿con qué motivo fuiste a Miami?, ¿para qué fuiste a Miami?

3 VI **(a)** (*stick*) pegar; (*set*) cuajar; (*vaccination*) prender; (*of plant*) arraigar; (*succeed*) tener éxito; resultar ser eficaz.

(b) **he ~s well** (*Phot*) sale bien (en fotografías), es muy fotogénico.

◆**take after** VT (*in looks*) salir a, parecerse a; (*in conduct*) seguir el ejemplo de.

◆**take against** VT cobrar antipatía a, encontrar antipático.

◆**take along** VT llevar, traer (consigo).

◆**take apart** **1** VT desmontar; (*) *room etc* destrozar, *person* dar una paliza a; **I'll ~ him apart!*** ¡le rompo la cara!; **the police took the place ~** la policía investigó minuciosamente el local.

2 VI: **it ~s apart easily** se desmonta fácilmente.

◆**take aside** VT llevar aparte.

◆**take away** **1** VT **(a)** (*carry away, lead away*) llevarse.

(b) (*remove*) quitar; llevarse.

(c) (*Math*) restar (*from* de); **7 ~ away 4 is 3** 7 menos 4 son 3.

2 VI: **that ~s away from its value** eso le quita valor, eso rebaja su valor.

◆**take back** VT **(a)** *words* retractar; *promise* desdecirse de; *husband* recibir otra vez; *object* recibir devuelto; **the company took him back** la compañía volvió a emplearle, la compañía le restituyó a su puesto.

(b) (*return*) devolver.

(c) (*Typ*) trasladar al renglón anterior.

(d) **the sight took me back many years** ver aquello me recordó cosas de hace muchos años; **it ~s you back, doesn't it?** ¡cuántos recuerdos (de los buenos tiempos)!

◆**take down** VT **(a)** *object* bajar; descolgar; *poster etc* despegar; *decora-*

tions quitar; *trousers* bajar; *V* **peg**.

(b) (*dismantle*) desmontar, desarmar.

(c) (*note*) apuntar; poner por escrito.

◆**take from** VT = **take away from**; *V* **take away 1** (c).

◆**take in** VT **(a)** *chairs, harvest* recoger; *sail* desmontar; *work* aceptar, admitir, recibir; *food* tomar; ingerir; *lodger* recibir, acoger (en casa).

(b) (*Sew*) achicar.

(c) (*include*) incluir, abarcar.

(d) (*grasp*) comprender.

(e) (*: *cheat*) embaucar, estafar; dar gato por liebre a; **I was properly ~n in by the disguise** el disfraz me despistó completamente; **don't let yourself be ~n in by appearances** no te dejes engañar por las apariencias.

◆**take off** **1** VT **(a)** (*remove*) *clothing* quitarse; *limb* amputar; *lid, wrapping, stain* quitar; (*unstick*) despegar; *discount* descontar, rebajar; **they took 2 names off the list** quitaron dos nombres de la lista, tacharon dos nombres de la lista; **the 5 o'clock train has been ~n off** han cancelado el tren de las 5.

(b) (*lead away*) llevarse; **they took him off to lunch** se lo llevaron a comer.

(c) (*imitate*) imitar; contrahacer, parodiar.

2 VI **(a)** (*depart*) salir (*for* para); largarse (*for* para); (*Aer*) despegar (*for* con rumbo a).

(b) (*succeed*) empezar a tener éxito, empezar a cuajar; **the idea never really took off** la idea no llegó a cuajar; **this style may ~ off** este estilo puede ponerse de moda.

◆**take on** **1** VT **(a)** *work* aceptar; emprender; *cargo* cargar, tomar; *duty* tomar sobre sí, cargar con, encargarse de; **he's ~n on more than he bargained for** le está resultando peor de lo que se creía, no contaba con tener que esforzarse tanto.

(b) (*in contest*) jugar contra; habérselas con; **I'll ~ you on!** ¡acepto (el desafío)!

(c) *employee* contratar.

(d) (*assume*) asumir, tomar.

2 VI **(a)** (*fashion etc*) establecerse, cuajar; ponerse de moda.

(b) (*Brit**) apurarse, excitarse, ponerse nervioso; quejarse; **don't ~ on so!** ¡no te apures!, ¡cálmate!

◆**take out** VT **(a)** (*lead out*) llevar fuera; *child, dog* llevar de paseo; *girl* invitar; escoltar, acompañar; salir con.

(b) (*remove*) quitar; (*extract*) sacar, extraer; (*Mil etc*) eliminar.

(c) *insurance* firmar; *licence, patent* obtener.

(d) (*tire*) **it took it out of me** me agotó, me rindió.

(e) **to ~ it out on sb** desahogarse riñendo a uno.

◆**take over** **1** VT **(a)** (*transport*) llevar.

(b) *control, responsibility* asumir; encargarse de; *leadership, office* asumir, tomar posesión de; *company* comprar; tomar el control de; **the tourists have ~n over the beaches** los turistas han acaparado las playas; **the army has ~n over power** el ejército se ha hecho cargo del poder, el ejército ha ocupado el poder.

2 VI (*in post*) tomar posesión; entrar en funciones; (*in relay race*) tomar el relevo, (*in lead*) tomar la delantera; (*at controls*) asumir el mando, (*Aut*) tomar el volante, (*Aer*) tomar los mandos; (*emotion*) cundir, dominar, llegar a dominar; **when the army ~s over** cuando el ejército se haga cargo del poder; **then panic took over** luego cundió el pánico.

◆**take to** VT **(a)** (*liking*) *person* coger simpatía a (*Sp*), tomar cariño a, encariñarse con (*LAm*); *thing* aficionarse a, cobrar afición a; **I didn't much ~ to him** no me resultó simpático; **I didn't ~ to the idea** la idea no me gustaba.

(b) **to ~ to** + *ger* (*start*) empezar a + *infin*; dedicarse a + *infin*; aficionarse a + *infin*.

(c) **to ~ to drink** darse a la bebida; *V* **bed, hill** *etc*.

◆**take up** **1** VT **(a)** (*carry up*) subir.

(b) (*lift*) coger (*Sp*), recoger; *carpet etc* quitar; *passengers* recoger; *arms* empuñar.

(c) (*occupy*) *room, time* ocupar, llenar; *residence* establecer, fijar; *post* tomar posesión de.

(d) (*absorb*) absorber.

(e) *study, career* empezar, emprender; dedicarse a; *case* emprender investigaciones acerca de; *story* empezar a contar, (*after break*) reanudar; *challenge* aceptar.

(f) **to ~ sb up on a point** censurar un punto a uno; expresar dudas acerca de algo que uno ha dicho; **I feel I must ~ you up on that** creo que es mi deber comentar lo que has dicho; **I'll ~ you up on that offer** acepto esa oferta; **I'll ~ you up on that some day** algún día recordaré lo que has dicho.

2 VI: **to ~ up with sb** relacionarse con uno, estrechar amistad con uno; empezar a alternar con uno; **he took up with a most unsuitable girl** entró en relaciones con una joven nada conveniente.

◆**take upon** VT: **to ~ sth upon o.s.** tomar algo sobre sí, encargarse de algo; **to ~ it upon o.s. to** + *infin* atreverse a + *infin*, (*pej*) tener bastante caradura como para + *infin*.

┌─ TAKE ─┐ ┌─ see also main entry ─┐

Both *tardar* and *llevar* can be used to translate *take* with *time*.

- Use *tardar* (*en*) + INFINITIVE to describe how long someone or something will take to do something. The subject of *tardar* is the person or thing that has to complete the activity or undergo the process:

  How long do letters take to get to Spain?
  ¿Cuánto (tiempo) tardan las cartas en llegar a España?
  How much longer will it take you to do it?
  ¿Cuánto más vas a tardar en hacerlo?
  It'll take us three hours to get to Douglas if we walk
  Tardaremos tres horas en llegar a Douglas si vamos andando

- Use *llevar* to describe how long an activity, task or process takes to complete. The subject of *llevar* is the activity or task:

  The tests will take at least a month
  Las pruebas llevarán por lo menos un mes
  How long will it take?
  ¿Cuánto tiempo llevará?

- Compare the different focus in the alternative translations of the following example:

  It'll take me two more days to finish this job
  Me llevará dos días más terminar este trabajo ◊ *Tardaré dos días más en terminar este trabajo*

  For further uses and examples, see main entry.

---

takeaway ['teɪkəweɪ] N (*Brit*) tienda *f* donde se venden comidas para llevar; **~ food, ~ meal** comida *f* para llevar; **a Chinese ~** una comida china para llevar.

take-home ['teɪkhəʊm] ATTR: **~ pay** sueldo *m* neto, sueldo *m* líquido.

taken ['teɪkən] PTP *of* **take**.

takeoff ['teɪkɒf] N (a) (*Aer*) despegue *m*; **short ~ aircraft** avión *m* de despegue corto. (b) (*imitation*) imitación *f*; parodia *f*; sátira *f*. (c) (*Mech*) **power ~** toma *f* de fuerza.

takeover ['teɪk,əʊvəʳ] N toma *f* de posesión; entrada *f* en funciones; relevo *m* (en el mando); **the ~ of company A by company Z** la adquisición (*or* compra) de la compañía A por la compañía Z; **~ bid** oferta *f* pública de adquisición (*de acciones*), OPA *f*.

taker ['teɪkəʳ] N: **~s of snuff** los que acostumbran tomar rapé; **~s of drink in moderation** los que beben con moderación; **at £5 there were no ~s** a un precio de 5 libras nadie se ofreció a comprarlo; **this challenge found no ~s** no hubo nadie que quisiera aceptar este desafío.

take-up ['teɪkʌp] N tasa *f* de aceptación, porcentaje *m* de personas que aceptan (*or* cobran *etc*).

taking ['teɪkɪŋ] [1] ADJ atractivo, encantador. [2] N (a) (*Mil*) toma *f*, conquista *f*. (b) **~s** (*Fin*) ingresos *mpl*; (*at show etc*) taquilla *f*, entrada *f*, recaudación *f*; **this year's ~s were only half last year's** este año se ha embolsado sólo la mitad de la recaudación del año pasado. (c) **it's yours for the ~** tómalo si quieres.

talc [tælk] N talco *m*.

talcum powder ['tælkəm,paʊdəʳ] N (polvos *mpl* de) talco *m*.

tale [teɪl] N cuento *m*; historia *f*, relación *f*; (*pej*) cuento *m*, patraña *f*; **'T~s of King Arthur'** 'Leyendas *fpl* del Rey Artús'; **old wives' ~** cuento *m* de viejas, patraña *f*; **I hear ~s about you** me cuentan cosas acerca de ti; **to tell ~s (out of school)** (*inform*) soplar, chismear; (*fib*) contar cuentos; **he told the ~ of his life** contó la historia de su vida; **he had quite a ~ to tell** tuvo bastante que contar; **sound the alarm, or we shan't live to tell the ~** toca el timbre, o no salimos vivos de esto; **it tells its own ~** habla por sí.

talebearer ['teɪl,bɛərəʳ] N soplón *m*, -ona *f*, chismoso *m*, -a *f*.

talent ['tælənt] N talento *m* (*for* para); **man of ~** hombre *m* de talento; **all the local ~** toda la gente de talento de la comarca; **there wasn't much ~ at the dance*** en el baile casi no había chicas atractivas; **he watches for ~ at away matches** busca jugadores de talento en los partidos fuera de casa.

talented ['tæləntɪd] ADJ de talento, talentoso, de talento.

talent-scout ['tælənt,skaʊt] N, **talent-spotter** ['tælənt,spɒtəʳ] N cazatalentos *mf*.

taletelling ['teɪl,telɪŋ] N chismorreo *m*.

talisman ['tælɪzmən] N talismán *m*.

talk [tɔːk] [1] N (*conversation*) conversación *f*, (*chat*) charla *f*, plática *f* (*Mex*); (*informal lecture*) charla *f*; (*gossip*) chismes *mpl*, habladurías *fpl*; **~s** (*negotiations*) negociaciones *fpl*; **it's just ~** son cosas que se dicen, son rumores; **with him it's all ~** con éste son palabras nada más; **she's the ~ of the town** todos hablan de ella, es la comidilla de la ciudad; **there is (some) ~ of** se habla de; **there has been some ~ of his going** se ha hablado de que va él; **to give a ~** dar una charla (*about* sobre); **to have a ~ to** (*or* **with**) **sb** hablar con uno; **we must have a ~ sometime** tenemos que citarnos un día para hablar. [2] VT hablar; **to ~ Arabic** hablar árabe; **~ some Arabic to me** dime

algo en árabe, dime unas palabras de árabe; **to ~ business** hablar de negocios; **to ~ nonsense** no decir más que tonterías; **to ~ sense** hablar con juicio, hablar razonablemente; *V* **shop** *etc*.

[3] VI hablar (*about, of* de; *to* con, a); charlar, platicar (*Mex*); **it's all ~ and no do** todo es hablar y no se hace nada; **'he's so untidy'** ... **'you can ~!'*** 'vive en el mayor desorden' ... '¡y tú que lo dices!'; **now you're ~ing!** ¡así se habla!; **it's easy for him to ~, but** ... es natural que lo diga él, pero ...; **look who's ~ing!** ¡quién lo dice!, ¡mira quien habla!; **to keep sb ~ing** entretener a uno en conversación; **to ~ through one's hat** decir tonterías; **~ about fleas!** ¡y las pulgas!; ¡Dios mío, qué pulgas!; **what shall we ~ about?** ¿de qué vamos a hablar?; **it is much ~ed about** se habla mucho de ello; **to get o.s. ~ed about in the papers** lograr que los periódicos hablen de uno; **he knows what he's ~ing about** habla con conocimiento de causa; **he doesn't know what he's ~ing about** no tiene la menor idea; **I'm not ~ing about you** no lo digo por ti; **~ing of bats, we** ... a propósito de los murciélagos, nosotros ...; **to ~ to o.s.** hablar consigo mismo; *V* **big**.

[4] VR: **to ~ o.s. hoarse** enronquecer a fuerza de hablar.

◆**talk away** [1] VT: **to ~ an hour away** pasar una hora charlando. [2] VI hablar mucho, no parar de hablar; **~ away!** ¡di lo que quieras!

◆**talk back** VI replicar; contestar con frescura.

◆**talk down** [1] VT (a) (*silence*) **to ~ sb down** reducir a uno al silencio, hacer callar a uno. (b) **to ~ a plane down** controlar el aterrizaje de un avión desde tierra. (c) *idea, plan* rebajar, quitar importancia a. [2] VI: **to ~ down to sb** darse aires de superioridad con uno, tratar a uno como un niño.

◆**talk into** VT: **to ~ sb into sth** convencer a uno para que haga algo; **to ~ o.s. into sth** convencerse a sí mismo, autosugestionarse; **you've ~ed me into it!** ¡me habéis convencido!

◆**talk on** VI no parar de hablar.

◆**talk out** VT (a) **to ~ out a bill** prolongar la discusión de un proyecto de ley de manera que no se pueda votar. (b) (*dissuade*) **to ~ sb out of sth** disuadir a uno de algo; **he ~ed himself out of the job** hizo tan mala impresión hablando que no le dieron el puesto. (c) *problem* discutir, examinar, resolver discutiendo.

◆**talk over** VT hablar de, discutir; pasar revista a; **I must ~ it over with my boss** tengo que discutirlo con mi jefe; **let's ~ it over** examinémoslo más detenidamente.

◆**talk round** VT (a) **to ~ sb round** llegar a convencer a uno; **she knows how to ~ him round** ella sabe cómo convencerle. (b) **they're only ~ing round the problem** están dando vueltas al problema sin resolverlo.

◆**talk through** VT: **to ~ a plan through** examinar un proyecto discutiéndolo; **let's ~ it through** discutámoslo.

◆**talk up** (*US*) [1] VT *product etc* dar bombo a*, hacer campaña en favor de; *sobrevalorar*; *person, possibility* mejorar la imagen de. [2] VI (*speak frankly*) decir las cosas como son, no callarse ni una.

talkative ['tɔːkətɪv] ADJ locuaz, hablador, platicón (*Mex*).

talkativeness ['tɔːkətɪvnɪs] N locuacidad *f*.

talked-of ['tɔːktɒv] ADJ: **a much ~ event** un suceso muy sonado.

talker ['tɔːkəʳ] N hablador *m*, -ora *f*; **to be a good ~** hablar bien; tener una conversación amena; **he's just a ~** habla mucho pero no hace nada.

talkie ['tɔːkɪ] N película *f* sonora; **the ~s** el cine sonoro.

talking ['tɔːkɪŋ] [1] ADJ parlante; *bird* parlero; **~ book** libro *m* hablado (*para ciegos*); **~ film, ~ picture** película *f* sonora; **~ head** (*TV*) locutor *m*, -ora *f*, busto *m* parlante. [2] N conversación *f*; palabras *fpl*; **'no ~'** 'prohibido hablar'; **no ~, please, ¡silencio, por favor!; she does all the ~** ella es quien habla.

talking-point ['tɔːkɪŋpɔɪnt] N tema *m* de conversación.

talking-shop ['tɔːkɪŋʃɒp] N *lugar donde se habla mucho pero no se hace nada*.

talking-to ['tɔːkɪŋtuː] N: **to give sb a ~** echar un rapapolvo a uno.

talk radio ['tɔːk'reɪdɪəʊ] N radio *f* hablada.

talk-show ['tɔːkʃəʊ] N programa *m* de entrevistas (informales).

tall [tɔːl] ADJ (a) alto; grande; **a building 30 metres ~** un edificio que tiene 30 metros de alto; **how ~ you've got!** ¡qué grande estás!; ¡cómo has crecido!; **how ~ are you?** ¿cuánto mides?; **I'm 6 feet ~** mido 6 pies; **to walk ~** andar con la cabeza alta. (b) (*fig*) **~ order** exigencia *f* exagerada, cosa *f* de mucho pedir; **~ story** cuento *m* exagerado, cuento *m* chino.

tallboy ['tɔːlbɔɪ] N (*Brit*) cómoda *f* alta.

tallness ['tɔːlnɪs] N altura *f*; talla *f*.

tallow ['tæləʊ] N sebo *m*.

tallowy ['tæləʊɪ] ADJ seboso.

tally ['tælɪ] [1] N (*stick*) tarja *f*; (*account*) cuenta *f*; (*fig*) número *m*, total *m*; **to keep a ~ of** llevar la cuenta de.

2 VI concordar, corresponder, cuadrar (*with* con).
tally clerk ['tælɪklɑːk] N medidor *m*, -ora *f*.
tallyho ['tælɪ'həʊ] INTERJ ¡hala! (*grito del cazador de zorras*).
Talmud ['tælmʊd] N Talmud *m*.
Talmudic [tæl'mʊdɪk] ADJ talmúdico.
talon ['tælən] N garra *f*.
tamable ['teɪməbl] ADJ domable, domesticable.
tamale [tə'mɑːlɪ] N tamal *m*.
tamarind ['tæmərɪnd] N tamarindo *m*.
tamarisk ['tæmərɪsk] N tamarisco *m*.
tambour ['tæmbʊəʳ] N tambor *m*.
tambourine [,tæmbə'riːn] N pandereta *f*.
Tamburlaine ['tæmbə,leɪn] NM Tamerlán.
tame [teɪm] **1** ADJ **(a)** (*tamed*) domesticado; (*by nature*) manso, dócil; **I'll ask my ~ psychiatrist** se lo preguntaré a mi psiquíatra de casa; **we have a ~ rabbit** tenemos un conejo doméstico (*or* casero); **the birds are growing ~** los pájaros se van domesticando.
(b) (*spiritless*) insípido, soso; (*boring, flat*) soso, aburrido.
2 VT *animal* domar, domesticar; amansar; *passion etc* reprimir, contener.
tamely ['teɪmlɪ] ADV sumisamente.
tameness ['teɪmnɪs] N mansedumbre *f*; insipidez *f*, sosería *f*; falta *f* de temor.
tamer ['teɪməʳ] N domador *m*, -ora *f*.
Tamil ['tæmɪl] **1** ADJ tamil.
2 N tamil *mf*.
taming ['teɪmɪŋ] N domadura *f*; 'The T~ of the Shrew' 'La fierecilla domada'.
tam o' shanter [,tæmə'ʃæntəʳ] N boina *f* escocesa.
tamp [tæmp] VT (*also* to ~ **down**, to ~ **in**) apisonar, afirmar; (*Min*) atacar.
Tampax ['tæmpæks] ® N Tampax *m invar* ®, támpax *m invar*.
tamper ['tæmpəʳ] VI: to ~ **with** (*mess up*) estropear, manosear, descomponer; ajar; *lock* tratar de forzar; *document* falsificar; interpolar; *witness* sobornar; (*meddle in*) entrometerse en; **my car had been ~ed with** algo se había hecho a mi coche; **they are ~ing with our plans** están estropeando nuestros planes.
tampon ['tæmpɒn] N tapón *m*; (*Med*) tampón *m*.
tan [tæn] **1** N (*sun*) bronceado *m*, tostado *m*; (*bark*) casca *f*; (*colour*) color *m* café claro, color *m* canela; **to acquire a ~, to get a ~** ponerse moreno, morenearse, broncearse (*LAm*).
2 ADJ color café claro, color canela, color marrón; *shoes* de color.
3 VT **(a)** (*of sun*) poner moreno, morenear, broncear, tostar.
(b) *leather* curtir, adobar; **to ~ sb*, to ~ the hide off sb*** zurrar a uno*.
4 VI ponerse moreno, morenearse, tostarse, broncearse (*LAm*).
tandem ['tændəm] **1** N tándem *m*.
2 ADJ, ADV en tándem; **to do sth in ~** hacer algo conjuntamente (*with sb* con uno).
tang [tæŋ] N **(a)** (*of knife*) espiga *f*. **(b)** (*taste*) sabor *m*, sabor *m* fuerte y picante; **it has the ~ of the soil** tiene fuerte sabor a tierra.
tangent ['tændʒənt] N tangente *f*; **to fly off at a ~, to go off at a ~** salirse por la tangente.
tangential [tæn'dʒenʃəl] ADJ tangencial.
tangerine [,tændʒə'riːn] N mandarina *f*, clementina *f*.
tangibility [,tændʒɪ'bɪlɪtɪ] N tangibilidad *f*.
tangible ['tændʒəbl] ADJ tangible; (*fig*) tangible, palpable, concreto, sensible; **~ assets** activo *m* tangible.
tangibly ['tændʒəblɪ] ADV de modo palpable, concretamente.
Tangier(s) [tæn'dʒɪə(z)] N Tánger *m*.
tangle ['tæŋgl] **1** N nudo *m*; enredo *m*, maraña *f*; (*of streets etc*) laberinto *m*; (*fig*) enredo *m*, lío *m*; confusión *f*; **to be in a ~** estar enmarañado, haberse formado un nudo; (*fig*) estar en confusión; **I'm in a ~ with the accounts** me he hecho un lío con las cuentas; **to get into a ~** hacerse un nudo, anudarse; (*fig*) enredarse, enmarañarse; **I got into a ~ with the police** me hice un lío con la policía.
2 VT (*also* to ~ **up**) enredar, enmarañar.
3 VI (*also* to ~ **up**) enredarse, enmarañarse; **to ~ with sb** pelearse con uno, meterse con uno; habérselas con uno.
tangled ['tæŋgld] ADJ enredado, enmarañado; (*fig*) enmarañado, complicado.
tango ['tæŋgəʊ] **1** N, PL **tangos** tango *m*.
2 VI bailar el tango; **it takes two to ~*** es cosa de dos.
tangy ['tæŋɪ] ADJ fuerte y picante.
tank [tæŋk] **1** N **(a)** tanque *m*, depósito *m*; (*large, water*) cisterna *f*, aljibe *m*. **(b)** (*Mil*) tanque *m*, carro *m* (de combate).
2 VT (‡) machacar, vapulear, dar una paliza a.
◆**tank along*** VI ir a toda pastilla*.
◆**tank up** VT (*Brit*): **to be ~ed up** ir como una moto, llevar una (buena) moto; **to get ~ed up‡** emborracharse (*on beer* bebiendo cerveza).

tankard ['tæŋkəd] N bock *m*, pichel *m*.
tank car ['tæŋkɑːʳ] N (*US*) vagón *m* cisterna.
tank-engine ['tæŋk,endʒɪn] N locomotora *f* ténder.
tanker ['tæŋkəʳ] N (*Naut*) petrolero *m*; (*Aut*) camión-tanque *m*, camión *m* cisterna.
tankful ['tæŋkfʊl] N contenido *m* (*or* capacidad *f*) de un depósito (*esp* de gasolina); **to get a ~ of petrol** llenar el depósito de gasolina; **a ~ is 25 litres** la capacidad del depósito es de 25 litros.
tank top ['tæŋktɒp] N chaleco *m* cerrado.
tank wagon ['tæŋk,wægən] N (*Rail*) vagón *m* cisterna; (*Aut*) camión *m* cisterna.
tanned [tænd] ADJ moreno.
tanner¹ ['tænəʳ] N curtidor *m*.
tanner²‡† ['tænəʳ] N (*Brit*) seis peniques *mpl*, moneda *f* de seis peniques (antiguos).
tannery ['tænərɪ] N curtiduría *f*, tenería *f*.
tannic ['tænɪk] ADJ: **~ acid** ácido *m* tánico.
tannin ['tænɪn] N tanino *m*.
tanning ['tænɪŋ] N **(a)** (*of leather*) curtido *m*. **(b)** (***) zurra* *f*; **to give sb a ~*** zurrar a uno*.
tannoy ['tænɔɪ] N sistema *m* de anuncios por altavoces.
tansy ['tænzɪ] N tanaceto *m*, atanasia *f*.
tantalize ['tæntəlaɪz] VTI atormentar (mostrando *or* prometiendo lo que no se puede conseguir), tentar (con cosas imposibles).
tantalizing ['tæntəlaɪzɪŋ] ADJ atormentador, tentador; seductor; **it is ~ to think that ...** es tentador pensar que ...; **with ~ slowness** con desesperante lentitud; **a most ~ offer** una oferta de lo más tentador.
tantalizingly ['tæntəlaɪzɪŋlɪ] ADV de modo atormentador, de modo tentador.
tantamount ['tæntəmaʊnt] ADJ: **~ to** equivalente a; **this is ~ to** esto equivale a.
tantrum* ['tæntrəm] N rabieta* *f*, berrinche* *m*; **to have (*or* throw) a ~** coger una rabieta*.
Tanzania [,tænzə'niːə] N Tanzania *f*.
Tanzanian [,tænzə'nɪən] **1** ADJ tanzano.
2 N tanzano *m*, -a *f*.
Tao [taʊ] N Tao *m*.
Taoism ['taʊɪzəm] N taoísmo *m*.
Taoist ['tɑːəʊɪst] **1** ADJ taoísta.
2 N taoísta *mf*.
tap¹ [tæp] **1** N **(a)** (*Brit: water~*) grifo *m*, llave *f* (*LAm*), canilla *f* (*LAm*); (*Brit: gas~*) llave *f*; (*Brit: of barrel*) espita *f*; (*tool*) macho *m* de terraja; (*Elec*) derivación *f*; **beer on ~** cerveza *f* (sacada) de barril, cerveza *f* servida al grifo; **to be on ~** (*fig*) estar a mano, estar disponible, estar listo.
(b) (*Elec*) derivación *f*; (*Telec*) escucha *f*, pinchazo* *m*.
2 VT **(a)** *barrel* espitar; *tree* sangrar; (*Med*) hacer una puntura en; *resources* explotar, utilizar; **to ~ sb for information*** tratar de sacar información de uno; **he tried to ~ me for £5*** quería que le prestase 5 libras.
(b) *wire* (*Elec*) hacer una derivación en; (*Telec*) intervenir, interceptar, pinchar*, escuchar clandestinamente.
3 VI: **to ~ into sb's supply** utilizar la provisión de otro; **to ~ into sb's ideas** aprovechar las ideas de otro, conectar con las ideas de otro.
tap² [tæp] **1** N palmadita *f*; golpecito *m*, golpe *m* ligero; (*on typewriter etc*) tecleo *m*, tic-tac *m*; **there was a ~ on the door** llamaron suavemente a la puerta; **I felt a ~ on my shoulder** sentí una palmadita en el hombro.
2 VT dar una palmadita a (*or* en); golpear suavemente, golpear ligeramente; *typewriter etc* pulsar; **to ~ in a nail** hacer que entre un clavo golpeándolo ligeramente.
3 VI dar golpecitos; (*on typewriter etc*) teclear; **to ~ at a door** llamar suavemente a una puerta; **he ~ped on the table several times** dio varios golpecitos en la mesa.
◆**tap out** VT **(a)** **to ~ out a message in morse** enviar un mensaje en Morse.
(b) **to ~ out one's pipe** vaciar la pipa golpeándola ligeramente.
tap-dance ['tæpdɑːns] **1** N zapateado *m*.
2 VI zapatear.
tap-dancer ['tæp,dɑːnsəʳ] N bailarín *m*, -ina *f* de zapateado.
tap-dancing ['tæp,dɑːnsɪŋ] N zapateado *m*, claqué *m*.
tape [teɪp] **1** N (*Sew etc*) cinta *f*; (*Sport*) cinta *f*; (*ceremonial*) cinta *f* simbólica; (*sticking*) cinta *f* adhesiva, (*Med*) esparadrapo *m*; (*recording ~*) cinta *f* de grabación, cinta *f* magnetofónica; (*~ measure*) cinta *f* métrica; **the Watergate ~s** las grabaciones de Watergate.
2 VT **(a)** (*seal*) poner una cinta a, cerrar con una cinta.
(b) (*record*) grabar en cinta, registrar en un magnetofón.
(c) **I've got him ~d*** (*Brit*) le tengo calado; **we've got it all ~d*** lo tenemos todo organizado, todo funciona perfectamente.
tape deck ['teɪpdek] N unidad *f* de cinta.
tape drive ['teɪpdraɪv] N accionador *m* de cinta.

tape-measure ['teɪp,meʒəʳ] N cinta *f* métrica.
taper ['teɪpəʳ] **1** N bujía *f*, cerilla *f*; (*Eccl*) cirio *m*.
  2 VT afilar, ahusar.
  3 VI ahusarse, rematar en punta.
♦ **taper away, taper off** VI ir disminuyendo.
tape-record ['teɪprɪ,kɔːd] VT grabar en cinta, registrar en un magnetofón.
tape-recorder ['teɪprɪ,kɔːdəʳ] N magnetofón *m*, magnetófono *m*, grabadora *f* de cinta (*LAm*).
tape-recording ['teɪprɪ,kɔːdɪŋ] N grabación *f* en cinta.
tapered ['teɪpəd] ADJ, **tapering** ['teɪpərɪŋ] ADJ ahusado, que termina en punta; (*Mech*) cónico; *finger* afilado.
tapestry ['tæpɪstrɪ] N (*object*) tapiz *m*; (*art*) tapicería *f*.
tape unit ['teɪpjuːnɪt] N unidad *f* de cinta.
tapeworm ['teɪpwɜːm] N tenia *f*, solitaria *f*.
tapioca [,tæpɪ'əʊkə] N tapioca *f*.
tapir ['teɪpəʳ] N tapir *m*.
tapper ['tæpəʳ] N (*Elec, Telec*) manipulador *m*.
tappet ['tæpɪt] N alzaválvulas *m*.
taproom ['tæprʊm] N (*Brit*) bodegón *m*.
taproot ['tæpruːt] N raíz *f* central.
tapwater ['tæp,wɔːtəʳ] N (*Brit*) agua *f* corriente, agua *f* de grifo.
tar[1] [tɑːʳ] **1** N alquitrán *m*, brea *f*.
  2 VT alquitranar, embrear; **to ~ and feather sb** emplumar a uno; **a newly ~red road** una carretera recién alquitranada; **he's ~red with the same brush** él es otro que tal, son lobos de la misma camada.
tar[2] [tɑːʳ] N (*also* **Jack T~**) marinero *m*.
taramasalata [,tærəməsə'lɑːtə] N taramasalata *f*, aperitivo griego a base de huevas de pescado ahumadas.
tarantella [,tærən'telə] N tarantela *f*.
tarantula [tə'ræntjʊlə] N tarántula *f*.
tardily ['tɑːdɪlɪ] ADV tardíamente; lentamente.
tardiness ['tɑːdɪnɪs] N tardanza *f*; lentitud *f*.
tardy ['tɑːdɪ] ADJ (*late*) tardío; (*slow*) lento.
tare[1] [teəʳ] N (*Bot: also* **~s**) arveja *f*; (*Bib*) cizaña *f*.
tare[2] [teəʳ] N (*Comm*) tara *f*.
target ['tɑːgɪt] **1** N (*Mil*) blanco *m*; (*fig*) blanco *m*, objetivo *m*; **our ~ is £100** nuestro objetivo es reunir (*etc*) 100 libras, nos proponemos reunir (*etc*) 100 libras; **the ~s for production in 2000** los objetivos previstos para la producción en 2000; **to be the ~ for criticism** ser el blanco de la crítica; **to be on ~** llevar la dirección que se había previsto, ir hacia el blanco.
  2 ATTR: **~ audience** público *m* objetivo; **~ date** fecha *f* tope, fecha *f* señalada; **~ figure** cifra *f* tope; **~ group** grupo *m* objeto; **~ language** (*study*) lengua *f* objeto de estudio; (*translation*) lengua *f* de llegada; (*Comput*) lenguaje *m* objeto; **~ market** mercado *m* objetivo; **~ practice** prácticas *fpl* de tiro, tiro *m* al blanco; **~ price** precio *m* indicativo.
  3 VT elegir como blanco; **the money should be ~ted on X** sería mejor dirigir el dinero hacia X, convendría invertir los fondos en X; **the factory is ~ted for closure** se propone cerrar la fábrica, se elige la fábrica para cerrar.
targetable ['tɑːgɪtəbl] ADJ dirigible.
tariff ['tærɪf] **1** N tarifa *f*, arancel *m*.
  2 ATTR arancelario; **~ barrier**, **~ wall** barrera *f* arancelaria; **~ reform** reforma *f* arancelaria.
tarmac ['tɑːmæk] ® N (*esp Brit*) alquitranado *m*; **the ~** (*Aer*) el asfaltado.
tarn [tɑːn] N lago *m* pequeño de montaña.
tarnation* [tɑː'neɪʃən] N (*US dialect*) ¡diablos!
tarnish ['tɑːnɪʃ] **1** VT deslustrar, quitar el brillo a; (*fig*) deslustrar, empañar.
  2 VI deslustrarse, perder su brillo, empañarse.
tarnished ['tɑːnɪʃt] ADJ deslustrado (*also fig*), sin brillo.
tarot ['tærəʊ] N tarot *m*.
tarp* [tɑːp] N (*US*) ABBR *of* **tarpaulin**.
tarpaulin [tɑː'pɔːlɪn] N alquitranado *m*, encerado *m*.
tarpon ['tɑːpɒn] N tarpón *m*.
tarragon ['tærəgən] N estragón *m*.
tarring ['tɑːrɪŋ] N asfaltado *m*.
tarry[1] ['tɑːrɪ] ADJ alquitranado, embreado; cubierto (*or* manchado *etc*) de alquitrán; **to taste ~** saber a alquitrán.
tarry[2] ['tærɪ] VI (*liter*) (*stay*) quedarse; (*dally*) entretenerse, quedarse atrás; (*be late*) tardar (en venir).
tarsus ['tɑːsəs] N, PL **tarsi** ['tɑːsaɪ] tarso *m*.
tart[1] [tɑːt] ADJ ácido, agrio; (*fig*) áspero.
tart[2] [tɑːt] N (**a**) (*esp Brit Culin*) tarta *f*; (*fruit*) pastelillo *m* de fruta, (*jam*) pastelillo *m* de mermelada. (**b**) (*) furcia* *f*, fulana* *f*.
♦ **tart up*** (*Brit pej*) **1** VT *house etc* renovar, rejuvenecer, remodelar.
  2 VR: **to ~ o.s. up** remozarse; ataviarse; (*with make-up*) pintarse, maquillarse.
tartan ['tɑːtən] N tartán *m*, (*diseño m a*) cuadros *mpl* escoceses; **a ~ scarf** una bufanda escocesa; *ver también* [KILT] .

Tartar ['tɑːtəʳ] **1** ADJ tártaro.
  2 N tártaro *m*, -a *f*; (*fig*) arpía *f*, fiera *f*; **to catch a ~** dar con la horma de su zapato.
tartar ['tɑːtəʳ] N (*Chem*) tártaro *m*; (*on teeth*) sarro *m*, tártaro *m*.
tartar(e) ['tɑːtəʳ] ATTR: **~ sauce** salsa *f* tártara; **~ steak** biftec crudo, picado y condimentado con sal, pimiento, cebolla etc.
tartaric [tɑː'tærɪk] ADJ: **~ acid** ácido *m* tartárico.
Tartary ['tɑːtərɪ] N Tartaria *f*.
tartlet ['tɑːtlɪt] N (*Brit*) tartaleta *f*, tartita *f*.
tartly ['tɑːtlɪ] ADV (*fig*) ásperamente.
tartness ['tɑːtnɪs] N acidez *f*, agrura *f*; (*fig*) aspereza *f*.
tarty* ['tɑːtɪ] ADJ putesco*.
Tarzan ['tɑːzən] NM Tarzán.
task [tɑːsk] **1** N tarea *f*, labor *f*; empresa *f*, cometido *m*, deber *m*; (*Comput*) tarea *f*; **to set sb the ~ of doing sth** encargar a uno hacer algo, dar a uno el encargo de hacer algo; **to take sb to ~** reprender a uno (*for sth* algo), llamar a uno a capítulo.
  2 VT: **to ~ sb to do sth** encargar a uno el deber de hacer algo.
task force ['tɑːskfɔːs] N (*Mil*) destacamento *m* especial; (*Naut*) fuerza *f* expedicionaria.
taskmaster ['tɑːsk,mɑːstəʳ] N amo *m* (severo); capataz *m* (severo); **he's a hard ~** es un tirano, es muy exigente.
Tasmania [tæz'meɪnɪə] N Tasmania *f*.
Tasmanian [tæz'meɪnɪən] **1** ADJ tasmanio.
  2 N tasmanio *m*, -a *f*.
tassel ['tæsəl] N borla *f*.
taste [teɪst] **1** N (**a**) (*flavour*) sabor *m* (*of* a); dejo *m* (*of* de); **it has an odd ~** tiene un sabor raro, sabe algo raro; **it has no ~** no sabe a nada, es insípido.
  (**b**) (*sense of ~*) paladar *m*; **sweet to the ~** con sabor dulce.
  (**c**) (*sample*) muestra *f*; (*sip*) sorbo *m*, trago *m*; **just a ~, then** pues un sorbito nada más, pues sólo un poquitín; **add a ~ of salt** añadir una pizca de sal; **may I have a ~?** ¿me permites probarlo?; **we got a ~ of what was to come** tuvimos una muestra de lo que había de venir después, se nos proporcionó un anticipo de lo que nos esperaba; **we had a ~ of his bad temper** tuvimos una muestra de su mal humor.
  (**d**) (*liking*) afición *f*, inclinación *f*, gusto *m*; **one's ~s in music** los gustos musicales de uno; **to acquire** (*or* **develop**) **a ~ for** tomar gusto a, cobrar afición a; **to have a ~ for** gustar de, ser aficionado a; **with sugar to ~** con azúcar al gusto, con azúcar a discreción; **it is to my ~** me gusta; **Wagner is not to my ~** no me gusta Wagner; **~s differ, each to his own ~** entre gustos no hay disputa.
  (**e**) (*good ~ etc*) **good ~** buen gusto *m*; **people of ~** gente *f* de buen gusto; **they certainly have ~** es cierto que tienen buen gusto; **to be in bad** (*or* **poor**) **~** ser de mal gusto.
  2 VT (**a**) (*sample*) probar; probar un bocado de, tomarse un trago de; (*professionally*) catar; **just ~ this** prueba un poco de esto; **I haven't ~ed salmon for years** hace años que no como salmón; **he hadn't ~ed food for 3 days** desde hacía 3 días no comía.
  (**b**) (*perceive flavour of*) percibir un sabor de; **I fancy I ~ garlic** creo notar un sabor a ajos; **I can't ~ anything when I have a cold** cuando estoy resfriado no noto sabor alguno.
  (**c**) (*experience*) experimentar, conocer; **at last we ~ed happiness** por fin conocimos la felicidad; **when he first ~ed power** cuando conoció por primera vez las delicias del poder.
  3 VI: **it doesn't ~ at all** no se nota sabor alguno; **it ~s good** es muy sabroso, está sabrosísimo, está muy rico; **it ~s all right to me** para mi gusto está bien; **to ~ of** saber a, tener sabor a; **it doesn't ~ of anything in particular** no sabe a nada en particular.
taste-bud ['teɪstbʌd] N papila *f* del gusto.
tasteful ['teɪstfʊl] ADJ elegante, de buen gusto.
tastefully ['teɪstfəlɪ] ADV elegantemente, con buen gusto; **a ~ furnished flat** un piso amueblado con buen gusto, un piso con muebles elegantes.
tastefulness ['teɪstfʊlnɪs] N elegancia *f*, buen gusto *m*.
tasteless ['teɪstlɪs] ADJ (*flat*) insípido, soso, insulso; (*in bad taste*) de mal gusto.
tastelessly ['teɪstlɪslɪ] ADV insípidamente; con mal gusto.
tastelessness ['teɪstlɪsnɪs] N insipidez *f*; mal gusto *m*.
taster ['teɪstəʳ] N (**a**) (*person*) catador *m*, -ora *f*. (**b**) (*fig*) muestra *f*.
tastily ['teɪstɪlɪ] ADV sabrosamente, apetitosamente.

tastiness ['teɪstɪnɪs] N sabor *m*, lo sabroso, lo apetitoso.
tasty ['teɪstɪ] ADJ sabroso, apetitoso.
tat¹ [tæt] VI (*Sew*) hacer encaje.
tat²* [tæt] N (*Brit*) ropa *f* vieja; objetos *mpl* viejos, (*fig*) basura *f*.
tata* ['tæ'tɑ:] INTERJ (*Brit*) adiós, adiosito*.
tattered ['tætəd] ADJ *person* andrajoso, harapiento; *dress, flag etc* en jirones.
tatters ['tætəz] NPL andrajos *mpl*; jirones *mpl*; **a tramp in ~** un vagabundo andrajoso; **his jacket hung in ~** su chaqueta estaba hecha jirones.
tatting ['tætɪŋ] N (trabajo *m* de) encaje *m*.
tattle ['tætl] 1 N (*chat*) charla *f*; (*gossip*) chismes *mpl*, habladurías *fpl*.
  2 VI (*chat*) charlar, parlotear; (*gossip*) chismear, contar chismes.
tattler ['tætlər] N charlatán *m*, -ana *f*; chismoso *m*, -a *f*.
tattletale* ['tætlteɪl] N (*US*) (*person*) acusica* *mf*; (*talk*) cotilleo *m*, chismes *mpl* y cuentos *mpl*.
tattoo¹ [tə'tu:] N (*Mil*) retreta *f*; (*Brit: pageant*) gran espectáculo *m* militar, exhibición *f* del arte militar; **to beat a ~ with one's fingers** tamborilear con los dedos.
tattoo² [tə'tu:] 1 N tatuaje *m*; *ver también* EDINBURGH FESTIVAL .
  2 VT tatuar.
tattooist [tə'tu:ɪst] N especialista *mf* en tatuaje, tatuador *m*, -ora *f*.
tatty* ['tætɪ] ADJ (*esp Brit*) raído, desaseado; poco elegante; en mal estado.
taught [tɔ:t] PRET AND PTP *of* **teach**.
taunt [tɔ:nt] 1 N mofa *f*, pulla *f*, dicterio *m*; sarcasmo *m*, dicho *m* sarcástico.
  2 VT mofarse de; insultar, reprochar con insultos; **to ~ sb with sth** echar algo en cara a uno.
taunting ['tɔ:ntɪŋ] ADJ insultante, mofador, burlón.
tauntingly ['tɔ:ntɪŋlɪ] ADV burlonamente, en son de burla.
taupe [təʊp] 1 ADJ de color marrón topo.
  2 N marrón *m* topo.
Taurean [ˌtɔː'riːən] N: **to be a ~** ser tauro.
tauromachy ['tɔ:rəmækɪ] N tauromaquia *f*.
Taurus ['tɔ:rəs] N (*Zodiac*) Tauro *m*.
taut [tɔ:t] ADJ tieso, tenso, tirante; (*fig*) tirante.
tauten ['tɔ:tn] 1 VT tensar, estirar; (*Naut*) tesar.
  2 VI tensarse, estirarse, ponerse tieso.
tautly ['tɔ:tlɪ] ADV (*lit*) *stretch* con tersura; (*fig*) *say* con voz tensa, con voz crispada.
tautness ['tɔ:tnɪs] N tiesura *f*, tirantez *f*.
tautological [ˌtɔ:tə'lɒdʒɪkəl] ADJ tautológico.
tautology [tɔ:'tɒlədʒɪ] N tautología *f*.
tavern ['tævən] N taberna *f*.
tawdriness ['tɔ:drɪnɪs] N lo charro; lo cursi; lo indigno.
tawdry ['tɔ:drɪ] ADJ charro; de oropel, de relumbrón, cursi; *motive etc* indigno, vergonzoso.
tawny ['tɔ:nɪ] ADJ leonado; (*wine parlance*) ámbar oscuro, tostado; **~ owl** cárabo *m*.
tax [tæks] 1 N (a) impuesto *m* (**on** sobre), contribución *f*; tributo *m*; derechos *mpl*; **free of ~** exento de contribuciones, no imponible; **profits after ~** beneficios *mpl* postimpositivos; **profits before ~** beneficios *mpl* preimpositivos; **to collect a ~** recaudar contribuciones; **to cut ~es** reducir impuestos; **to levy a ~ on sth** imponer contribución sobre algo.
  (b) (*fig*) carga *f* (**on** sobre), esfuerzo *m* (**on** para); **it is a ~ on his energies** exige un esfuerzo de él.
  2 ATTR: **~ accountant** contable *m* especializado, contable *f* especializada en asuntos tributarios; **~ allowance** desgravación *f* fiscal; **~ appraiser** tasador *m*, -ora *f* de impuestos; **the ~ authority** la Hacienda, el Fisco; **~ avoidance** evasión *f* fiscal; **~ base** base *f* imponible; **~ bracket** categoría *f* tributaria, categoría *f* fiscal; **~ burden** presión *f* fiscal; **~ code, ~ coding** código *m* impositivo; **~ disc** (*Brit*) pegatina *f* del impuesto de circulación; **~ evader** evasor *m*, -ora *f* de impuestos; **~ evasion** fraude *m* fiscal; **~ exemption** exención *f* contributiva, exención *f* de impuestos; **~ exile** persona *f* autoexiliada para evitar los impuestos; **~ form** impreso *m* de declaración de renta; **~ haven** paraíso *m* fiscal, refugio *m* fiscal; **~ incentive** incentivo *m* fiscal; **~ inspector** inspector *m*, -ora *f* de Hacienda; **~ law** derecho *m* tributario; **~ matters** asuntos *mpl* tributarios; **to declare sth for ~ purposes** declarar algo al fisco; **~ rebate** devolución *f* de impuestos, reembolso *m* fiscal; **~ reduction** reducción *f* de impuestos; **~ relief** desgravación *f* (de impuestos), desgravación *f* fiscal; **~ return** declaración *f* de renta; **~ shelter** protección *f* fiscal; **~ system** sistema *m* tributario, tributación *f*; **~ year** año *m* fiscal.
  3 VT (a) (*Fin*) *person* imponer contribuciones a, *thing* imponer contribución sobre, gravar con un impuesto; **the wife is separately ~ed** la esposa paga contribuciones por separado; **they are heavily ~ed** pagan unas fuertes contribuciones; **the rich are being ~ed out of**

existence los ricos pagan tantas contribuciones que dejarán pronto de existir.
  (b) (*Jur*) *costs* tasar.
  (c) (*fig*) cargar, abrumar (**with** de); *resources etc* exigir un esfuerzo excesivo a, someter a un esfuerzo excesivo; *patience* agotar; *tolerance* abusar de.
  (d) (*fig: accuse*) acusar (**with** de); interrogar (**with** acerca de); **to ~ sb with a fault** censurar una falta a uno.
taxable ['tæksəbl] ADJ imponible, gravable, sujeto a contribución, sujeto a impuesto; **~ income** renta *f* imponible.
taxation [tæk'seɪʃən] 1 N (*taxes*) impuestos *mpl*, contribuciones *fpl*; (*system*) sistema *m* tributario, tributación *f*, fiscalidad *f*.
  2 ATTR tributario; **~ system** sistema *m* tributario, tributación *f*.
tax-collecting ['tækskə,lektɪŋ] N recaudación *f* de impuestos.
tax-collector ['tækskə,lektər] N recaudador *m*, -ora *f* de impuestos.
tax-deductible ['tæksdɪ'dʌktəbl] ADJ desgravable.
taxeme ['tæksi:m] N taxema *m*.
tax-exempt ['tæksɪg'zempt] ADJ (*US*) exento de contribuciones; exento de impuesto.
tax-free ['tæks'fri:] (*Brit*) 1 ADJ exento de contribuciones, no imponible.
  2 ADV: **to live ~** vivir sin pagar contribuciones.
taxi ['tæksɪ] 1 N taxi *m*.
  2 VI (a) (*Aut*) ir en taxi. (b) (*Aer*) carretear, rodar de suelo.
taxicab ['tæksɪkæb] N taxi *m*.
taxidermist ['tæksɪdɜ:mɪst] N taxidermista *mf*.
taxidermy ['tæksɪdɜ:mɪ] N taxidermia *f*.
taxi-driver ['tæksɪ,draɪvər] N taxista *mf*.
taxi-fare ['tæksɪ,feər] N tarifa *f* de taxi.
taxi-man ['tæksɪmæn] N, PL **taxi-men** ['tæksɪmen] taxista *m*.
taximeter ['tæksɪ,mi:tər] N taxímetro *m*, contador *m* de taxi.
taxing ['tæksɪŋ] ADJ *problem* dificilísimo; *journey* duro, agotador; *task* absorbente.
taxi-rank ['tæksɪræŋk] N, **taxi-stand** ['tæksɪstænd] N parada *f* de taxis.
taxiway ['tæksɪweɪ] N (*Aer*) pista *f* de rodaje.
taxman* ['tæksmæn] N, PL **taxmen** ['tæksmen] recaudador *m* de impuestos.
taxonomist [tæk'sɒnəmɪst] N taxonomista *mf*.
taxonomy [tæk'sɒnəmɪ] N taxonomía *f*.
taxpayer ['tæks,peɪər] N contribuyente *mf*.
TB N ABBR *of* **tuberculosis** *f*.
TBC, tbc ABBR *of* **to be confirmed**.
tbsp(s) ABBR *of* **tablespoonful(s)**.
TD N (a) (*US Ftbl*) ABBR *of* **touchdown**. (b) (*US*) ABBR *of* **Treasury Department**. (c) (*Ireland*) ABBR *of* **Teachta Dála** miembro *mf* del parlamento irlandés.
te [ti:] N (*Mus*) si *m*.
tea [ti:] N (a) (*drink, plant*) té *m*; **not for all the ~ in China** por nada del mundo. (b) (*esp Brit: meal*) té *m*, merienda *f*; **to have ~** tomar el té, merendar.

┌─── TEA ──┐

ⓘ *Tomar el té sigue siendo un aspecto importante de la vida británica, aun cuando el café se ha hecho ya habitual en el país. Se bebe a cualquier hora y continúa siendo el acompañamiento tradicional de las comidas que se sirven en las cafeterías. Además de referirse a la bebida, la palabra* **tea** *también hace referencia a las comidas a las que éste acompaña. Por ejemplo,* **afternoon tea** *es una especie de merienda de media tarde que consiste en una taza de té acompañada de sandwiches y/o repostería, en especial los bollitos llamados* **scones***. El* **high tea** *es más sustancioso, pues incluye además platos calientes. En algunas partes del Reino Unido se usa también* **tea** *en lugar de* **dinner** *para hablar de la cena. En Estados Unidos una bebida muy corriente es el té helado (**iced tea**).*

└──┘

teabag ['ti:bæg] N bolsita *f* de té.
teabreak ['ti:breɪk] N (*Brit*) descanso *m* para el té; ≈ tiempo *m* del bocadillo.
tea-caddy ['ti:,kædɪ] N bote *m* para té.
teacake ['ti:keɪk] N (*Brit*) bollito *m*.
teach [ti:tʃ] (*irr*: PRET AND PTP **taught**) 1 VT enseñar; **to ~ sb how to do sth** enseñar a uno a hacer algo; **to ~ sb a language** enseñar una lengua a uno, instruir a uno en una lengua; **to ~ sb a lesson** (*fig*) hacer que uno vaya aprendiendo, escarmentar a uno; **that will ~ him!** ¡así irá aprendiendo!, ¡así escarmienta!; **he taught me a thing or two** me enseñó bastante, me enseñó cuántos son cinco; **I'll ~ you to leave the gas on!** ¡así aprenderás a no dejar encendido el gas!
  2 VI enseñar; ser profesor(a), dedicarse a la enseñanza.
teachability [ˌti:tʃə'bɪlɪtɪ] N (*esp US*) educabilidad *f*.
teachable ['ti:tʃəbl] ADJ (*esp US*) educable.
teacher ['ti:tʃər] N (*in general*) preceptor *m*, profesor *m*, -ora *f*; (*gram-*

mar school) profesor *m*, -ora *f* (de instituto), (*in other school*) maestro *m*, -a *f*; **our French ~** nuestro profesor de francés.

teacher-pupil ratio [ˌtiːtʃəˌpjuːplˈreɪʃɪəʊ] N proporción *f* profesor-alumnos.

teacher training ['tiːtʃəˌtreɪnɪŋ] ① N (*Brit*) formación *f* pedagógica.
② ATTR: **~ college** ≃ Instituto *m* de Ciencias de la Educación, ICE *m*.

tea-chest ['tiːtʃest] N caja *f* para té.

teach-in ['tiːtʃˌɪn] N reunión *f* de autoenseñanza colectiva.

teaching ['tiːtʃɪŋ] ① N (a) (*act*) enseñanza *f*. (b) (*belief*) enseñanza *f*, doctrina *f*; **~s** enseñanzas *fpl*, doctrinas *fpl*.
② ATTR docente; **~ aids** ayudas *fpl* pedagógicas, ayudas *fpl* para la enseñanza; **~ center** (*US*), **~ centre** centro *m* docente; **~ hospital** hospital *m* utilizado para la enseñanza de la medicina; **~ machine** autoprofesor *m*, profesor *m* robot; **~ materials** materiales *mpl* didácticos, materiales *mpl* pedagógicos; **~ practice** prácticas *fpl* de enseñanza; **~ profession** magisterio *m*; **~ staff** personal *m* docente, profesorado *m*.

teacloth ['tiːklɒθ] N (*Brit*) paño *m* de cocina.

tea-cosy ['tiːkəʊzɪ] N (*Brit*) cubretetera *f*, guardacalor *m* de la tetera.

teacup ['tiːkʌp] N taza *f* para té.

tea-dance ['tiːdɑːns] N té *m* bailable, té-baile *m*.

tea-garden ['tiːgɑːdn] N (*café*) café *m* al aire libre; (*Agr*) plantación *f* de té.

teahouse ['tiːhaʊs] N, PL **teahouses** ['tiːhaʊzɪz] salón *m* de té.

teak [tiːk] N teca *f*, madera *f* de teca.

teakettle ['tiːketl] N (*US*) tetera *f*.

teal [tiːl] N cerceta *f*.

tealeaf ['tiːliːf] N, PL **tealeaves** ['tiːliːvz] hoja *f* de té.

team [tiːm] ① N (*of persons*) equipo *m*, grupo *m*; (*Sport*) equipo *m*; (*in panel game*) jurado *m*; (*of horses*) tiro *m*; (*of oxen*) yunta *f*.
② ATTR: **~ championship** campeonato *m* por equipos; **~ game** juego *m* de equipos; **~ mate** compañero *m*, -a *f* de equipo; **~ member** miembro *mf* del equipo; **~ spirit** compañerismo *m*, espíritu *m* de equipo; **~ tournament** torneo *m* por equipos.
③ VT: **a film which ~s A with Z** una película que asocia A con Z, una película que ofrece juntamente A y Z.
◆**team up** VI asociarse, formar un equipo (*with* con).

teamster ['tiːmstər] N (*US*) camionero *m*, camionista *m*.

teamwork ['tiːmwɜːk] N labor *f* de equipo, trabajo *m* en equipo; cooperación *f*, colaboración *f*.

tea-party ['tiːpɑːtɪ] N té *m*.

teapot ['tiːpɒt] N tetera *f*.

tear¹ [teər] ① N rasgón *m*, desgarrón *m*; **it has a ~ in it** está roto.
② (*irr*: PRET **tore**, PTP **torn**) VT (a) (*rip*) rasgar, desgarrar; *flesh* lacerar, romper; (*to pieces*) romper, despedazar, hacer pedazos; **to ~ a hole in a cloth** rasgar un paño; **to ~ one's hair** mesarse el pelo; **to ~ a muscle** desgarrarse un músculo; **to ~ open** abrir apresuradamente, abrir violentamente.
(b) (*snatch*) arrancar; **to ~ sth from sb** arrancar algo a uno, quitar algo a uno violentamente.
(c) (*fig*) **the country was torn by civil war** el país fue desgarrado por una guerra civil; **she was torn by conflicting emotions** estaba atormentada por emociones opuestas, le desgarraban emociones opuestas; **I am very much torn** sigo sin saber a qué carta quedarme.
③ VI (a) (*cloth etc*) rasgarse, romperse; **it ~s easily** se rasga fácilmente.
(b) **to ~ at the earth with one's hands** tratar frenéticamente de remover la tierra con las manos; **she tore at my eyes** trató de arrancarme los ojos; **he tore at the paper wrapping** luchó violentamente por quitar la envoltura.
(c) (*rush*) lanzarse, precipitarse; **to ~ into a room** entrar precipitadamente en un cuarto; **the press tore into him** la prensa le puso un trapo*; **to ~ past** pasar como un rayo.
◆**tear along** VI correr precipitadamente, precipitarse; ir a máxima velocidad; **to ~ along the street** correr a todo gas por la calle.
◆**tear apart** VT *object* hacer trizas, destrozar; **he tore the theory apart** hizo la teoría pedazos; **the dispute was ~ing the company apart** la disputa dividía a la empresa en bandas opuestas; **nothing could ~ them apart** nada podía separarlos; **the conflicting loyalties were ~ing her apart** las lealtades opuestas le partían el corazón.
◆**tear away** ① VT arrancar, quitar violentamente; **the wind tore the flag away** el viento arrancó la bandera; **eventually we tore him away from the party** por fin le arrancamos de la fiesta.
② VI marcharse precipitadamente; salir disparado.
③ VR: **to ~ o.s. away** irse de mala gana; **I couldn't ~ myself away** no pude arrancarme de allí; **if you can ~ yourself away from that book** si puedes dejar ese libro de las manos un momento.
◆**tear down** VT *flag, hangings etc* quitar (arrancando), arrancar (de las paredes *etc*); *building* derribar, echar abajo.
◆**tear off** ① VT (a) (*remove*) arrancar.
(b) (*) *letter etc* escribir de prisa.
② VI = **~ away**.

◆**tear out** ① VT arrancar.
② VI salir disparado.
◆**tear up** ① VT *paper etc* romper; *plant* desarraigar (violentamente), arrancar.
② VI llegar a toda pastilla.

tear² [tɪər] N lágrima *f*; **to be in ~s** estar llorando; **to burst into ~s**, **to dissolve** (*or* **melt**) **into ~s** deshacerse en lágrimas; **to shed bitter ~s** llorar amargamente; **nobody is going to shed a ~ over that** nadie soltará una lágrima por eso; **to wipe away one's ~s** secarse las lágrimas.

tearaway ['tɛərəweɪ] N (*Brit*) alborotador *m*, -ora *f*, gamberro *m*, -a *f*.

teardrop ['tɪədrɒp] N lágrima *f*.

tear-duct ['tɪədʌkt] N conducto *m* lacrimal.

tearful ['tɪəfʊl] ADJ lloroso, llorón; lacrimoso; **to say in a ~ voice** decir llorando.

tearfully ['tɪəfəlɪ] ADV: **to say ~** decir lloroso, decir llorando.

teargas ['tɪəgæs] ① N gas *m* lacrimógeno.
② ATTR: **~ bomb** bomba *f* lacrimógena; **~ grenade** granada *f* lacrimógena.
③ VT *crowd etc* atacar con gas lacrimógeno.

tearing ['tɛərɪŋ] ADJ (a) **with a ~ noise** con un ruido de tela que se rasga. (b) (*fig*) **at a ~ speed** a una velocidad vertiginosa, a una velocidad peligrosa; **to be in a ~ hurry** estar muy de prisa.

tear-jerker* ['tɪəˌdʒɜːkər] N (*song*) canción *f* lacrimógena; (*play*) obra *f* lacrimógena, dramón *m* muy sentimental*; (*film*) película *f* lacrimógena.

tear-jerking* ['tɪəˌdʒɜːkɪŋ] ADJ lacrimógeno, muy sentimental.

tearless ['tɪəlɪs] ADJ sin lágrimas.

tearlessly ['tɪəlɪslɪ] ADV sin llanto, sin llorar.

tear-off ['tɛərɒf] ATTR (de) trepado; **~ calendar** calendario *m* de taco.

tearoom ['tiːrʊm] N salón *m* de té.

tea rose [ˌtiːˈrəʊz] N rosa *f* de té.

tearsheet ['tɛəʃiːt] N hoja *f* separable, página *f* recortable.

tear-stained ['tɪəsteɪnd] ADJ manchado de lágrimas.

tease [tiːz] ① N (a) (*person*) embromador *m*, -ora *f*, guasón *m*, -ona *f*; **he's a dreadful ~** es terriblemente guasón, le gusta atormentar a las personas.
(b) **to do sth for a ~** hacer algo para divertirse.
② VT (a) (*annoy*) jorobar, fastidiar, molestar; (*banter*) embromar, tomar el pelo a, guasearse con, (*cruelly*) atormentar; (*sexually*) atormentar, tentar; dar esperanzas a; **they ~ her about her hair** la molestan con chistes acerca de su pelo, la atormentan por lo de su pelo; **I don't like being ~d** no me gusta que se me tome el pelo.
(b) (*Tech*) cardar.
◆**tease out** VT *wool etc* desenredar, separar; *information* ir sacando (con dificultad), sonsacar.

teasel ['tiːzl] N (*Bot*) cardencha *f*; (*Tech*) carda *f*.

teaser ['tiːzər] N (a) (*person*) = **tease 1** (a). (b) (*puzzle*) rompecabezas *m*.

tea-service ['tiːˌsɜːvɪs] N, **tea-set** ['tiːset] N servicio *m* de té.

teashop ['tiːʃɒp] N (*Brit*) café *m*, cafetería *f*, (*strictly*) salón *m* de té.

teasing ['tiːzɪŋ] ① ADJ guasón, burlón.
② N guasa *f*, burlas *fpl*.

teasingly ['tiːzɪŋlɪ] ADV de manera burlona, de cachondeo*.

Teasmade, Teasmaid ['tiːzmeɪd] ® N tetera *f* automática (*que funciona al sonar el despertador*).

teaspoon ['tiːspuːn] N (*spoon*) cucharilla *f*, cucharita *f*; (*quantity*) cucharadita *f*.

teaspoonful ['tiːspʊnfʊl] N cucharadita *f*.

tea-strainer ['tiːˌstreɪnər] N colador *m* de té.

teat [tiːt] N (*of human*) pezón *m*; (*of animal*) teta *f*; (*Brit*: *of bottle*) chupador *m*, tetina *f*, pezón *m* de goma.

tea-table ['tiːˌteɪbl] N mesita *f* de té.

teathings ['tiːˌθɪŋz] NPL servicio *m* del té.

teatime ['tiːtaɪm] N hora *f* del té, hora *f* de la merienda.

tea-towel ['tiːˌtaʊəl] N (*Brit*) paño *m* de cocina, trapo *m* de cocina (*LAm*).

teatray ['tiːtreɪ] N bandeja *f* (del té).

tea-trolley ['tiːˌtrɒlɪ] N (*Brit*) carrito *m* (del té).

tea-urn ['tiːɜːn] N tetera *f* grande.

tea-waggon ['tiːˌwægən] N (*US*) carrito *m* (del té).

ʹtec* [tek] N = **detective**.

tech [tek] N (a) ABBR *of* **technology** tecnología *f*. (b) ABBR *of* **technical college**.

techie* ['tekɪ] N tecnologuillo *m*, -a *f*.

technetium [tek'niːʃɪəm] N tecnetio *m*.

technical ['teknɪkəl] ADJ técnico; **~ adviser** asesor *m* técnico, asesora *f* técnica; **~ college** (*Brit*) escuela *f* de artes y oficios, universidad *f* laboral; **~ drawing** dibujo *m* técnico; **~ hitch** problema *m* de carácter técnico; **~ knockout** K.O. *m* técnico; **~ offence** delito *m* técnico.

technicality [ˌteknɪˈkælɪtɪ] N (a) (*nature*) tecnicidad *f*, carácter *m*

técnico. (b) (*detail*) detalle *m* técnico, cosa *f* técnica; (*word*) tecnicismo *m*; **I don't understand all the technicalities** no entiendo todos los detalles técnicos; **it failed because of a ~** fracasó debido a una dificultad técnica.

technically ['teknɪkəlɪ] ADV técnicamente.

technician [tek'nɪʃən] N técnico *m*, -a *f*; (*Univ etc*) ayudante *mf* de laboratorio.

Technicolor ['teknɪ,kʌlər] ® ① N tecnicolor ® *m*; **in ~** en tecnicolor. ② ADJ en tecnicolor; de tecnicolor.

technique [tek'niːk] N técnica *f*.

techno... ['teknəu] PREF tecno...

technocracy [tek'nɒkrəsɪ] N tecnocracia *f*.

technocrat ['teknəukræt] N tecnócrata *mf*.

technocratic [,teknə'krætɪk] ADJ tecnocrático.

technological [,teknə'lɒdʒɪkəl] ADJ tecnológico.

technologically [teknə'lɒdʒɪklɪ] ADV tecnológicamente.

technologist [tek'nɒlədʒɪst] N tecnólogo *m*, -a *f*.

technology [tek'nɒlədʒɪ] N tecnología *f*; técnica *f*.

technophobe [,teknəu'fəub] N tecnófobo *m*, -a *f*.

technophobic [,teknəu'fəubɪə] ADJ tecnofóbico.

techy ['tetʃɪ] ADJ = **testy**.

tectonic [tek'tɒnɪk] ① ADJ tectónico; **~ movement** movimiento *m* tectónico; **~ plate** placa *f* tectónica. ② **~s** NPL tectónica *f*.

Ted [ted] NM *familiar form of* **Edward**.

tedder ['tedər] N heneador *m*.

Teddy ['tedɪ] NM *familiar form of* **Edward**.

teddy (bear) ['tedɪ(beər)] N osito *m* de felpa.

teddy-boy ['tedɪbɔɪ] N (*Brit*) gamberro *m* (de atuendo eduardiano).

tedious ['tiːdɪəs] ADJ aburrido, pesado.

tediously ['tiːdɪəslɪ] ADV aburridamente, de modo pesado.

tediousness ['tiːdɪəsnɪs] N, **tedium** ['tiːdɪəm] N tedio *m*, aburrimiento *m*, pesadez *f*.

tee [tiː] N tee *m*, soporte *m*; **third ~** salida *f* número 3.

◆ **tee off** VI golpear desde el tee.

◆ **tee up** VT (*Golf*) *ball* colocar en el tee; (*Football*) preparar.

tee-hee ['tiː'hiː] ① N risita *f* (tonta); **~!** ¡ji!, ¡ji!, ¡ji! ② VI reírse con una risita tonta, reírse un poquito.

teem [tiːm] VI abundar, pulular; **to ~ with** abundar en, hervir de; **the book ~s with errors** el libro está plagado de errores; **to ~ with rain** diluviar.

teeming ['tiːmɪŋ] ADJ numerosísimo; *rain* torrencial; **the ~ millions** los muchos millones; **a lake ~ with fish** un lago que rebosa de peces; **through streets ~ with people** por calles atestadas de gente.

teen* [tiːn] ① ADJ = **teenage**. ② N = **teenager**.

teenage ['tiːneɪdʒ] ADJ, ATTR *fashion etc* de los adolescentes, de los jóvenes (de 13 a 19 años); **he has ~ daughters already** tiene hijas adolescentes ya.

teenaged ['tiːneɪdʒd] ADJ: **~ boy** adolescente *m*; **~ girl** adolescente *f*.

teenager ['tiːn,eɪdʒər] N adolescente *mf*, joven *mf* de 13 a 19 años; **a club for ~s** un club para jóvenes (*de 13 a 19 años*).

teens [tiːnz] NPL edad *f* de adolescencia, edad *f* de 13 a 19 años; **to be in one's ~** ser adolescente, tener de 13 a 19 años; **to be still in one's ~** ser todavía adolescente, no haber cumplido aún los 20.

teensy(-weensy)* ['tiːnsɪ('wiːnsɪ)]   ['tiːnɪ('wiːnɪ)] ADJ, **teeny(-weeny)*** ['tiːnɪ('wiːnɪ)] ADJ chiquito, chiquitín.

teeny-bopper* ['tiːnɪ'bopər] N quinceañera *f* (apasionada de la música pop).

teepee ['tiːpiː] = **tepee**.

tee-shirt ['tiːʃɜːt] N = **T-shirt** (*in T*).

teeter ['tiːtər] VI balancearse, oscilar; (*US*) columpiarse; **to ~ on the edge of sth** balancearse en el borde de algo, (*fig*) estar sin resolverse sobre algo.

teeth [tiːθ] NPL *of* **tooth**.

teethe [tiːð] VI endentecer, echar los dientes.

teething ['tiːðɪŋ] ① N dentición *f*. ② ATTR: **~ troubles** (*fig*) problemas *mpl* de dentición.

teething-ring ['tiːðɪŋrɪŋ] N chupador *m*, mordedor *m*.

teetotal ['tiː'təutl] ADJ que no bebe alcohol, abstemio; *propaganda etc* antialcohólico.

teetotalism ['tiː'təutəlɪzəm] N abstinencia *f* (de bebidas alcohólicas).

teetotaller, (*US*) **teetotaler** ['tiː'təutlər] N abstemio *m*, -a *f*, persona *f* que no bebe alcohol.

TEFL ['tefəl] N ABBR *of* **Teaching (of) English as a Foreign Language**.

┌─ *TEFL/EFL, TESL/ESL, ELT, TESOL/ESOL* ─┐

🛈 *Los términos TEFL (Teaching (of) English as a Foreign Language: enseñanza del inglés como idioma extranjero) y EFL (English as a Foreign Language: inglés para extranjeros) se usan para hablar de la enseñanza del inglés a personas que no viven en un país de habla inglesa. TESL (Teaching (of) English as a Second Language: enseñanza del inglés*

como segunda lengua) y ESL (English as a Second Language: inglés como segunda lengua) se refieren a la enseñanza del inglés a personas que viven en un país de habla inglesa pero tienen otra lengua materna, por ejemplo, los miembros de las minorías étnicas. Este tipo de enseñanza intenta integrar el entorno cultural del alumno y aprovechar el conocimiento de su lengua materna en el proceso de aprendizaje.

ELT (English Language Teaching: enseñanza del inglés) es el término que se aplica a la enseñanza del inglés en general y, por tanto, engloba a los ya mencionados.

TESOL (Teaching (of) English to Speakers of Other Languages) es el término de inglés americano que equivale a TEFL y a TESL. ESOL (English for Speakers of Other Languages) es el equivalente a EFL y ESL.

Teflon ['teflɒn] ® N teflón ® *m*.

tegument ['tegjumənt] N tegumento *m*.

Teheran, Tehran [teə'rɑːn] N Teherán *m*.

tel. ABBR *of* **telephone** teléfono *m*, tel.

tele... ['telɪ] PREF tele...

telebanking ['telɪ,bæŋkɪŋ] N telebanca *f*.

telecast ['telɪkɑːst] ① N programa *m* de televisión. ② VTI transmitir por televisión.

telecommunication ['telɪkə,mjuːnɪ'keɪʃən] N telecomunicación *f*.

telecommute ['telɪkəm,juːt] VI teletrabajar, trabajar a distancia.

telecommuter ['telɪkəm,juːtər] N teletrabajador *m*, -ora *f*, trabajador *m*, -ora *f* a distancia.

telecommuting ['telɪkəm,juːtɪŋ] N teletrabajo *m*, trabajo *m* a distancia.

teleconference ['telɪ'kɒnfərəns] N teleconferencia *f*.

teleconferencing [,telɪ'kɒnfərensɪŋ] N teleconferencias *fpl*.

Telecopier ['telɪ,kɒpɪər] ® N telecopiadora *m*.

telecopy ['telɪ,kɒpɪ] N telecopia *f*.

telefax ['telɪfæks] N telefax *m*.

telefilm ['telɪfɪlm] N telefilm(e) *m*.

telegenic [,telɪ'dʒenɪk] ADJ televisivo, telegénico.

telegram ['telɪgræm] N telegrama *m*; **to send sb a ~** poner un telegrama a uno.

telegraph ['telɪgrɑːf] ① N telégrafo *m*. ② ATTR telegráfico; **~ pole** poste *m* telegráfico; **~ wire** hilo *m* telegráfico. ③ VTI telegrafiar.

telegraphese ['telɪgrɑː'fiːz] N estilo *m* telegráfico.

telegraphic [,telɪ'græfɪk] ADJ telegráfico.

telegraphically [,telɪ'græfɪkəlɪ] ADV telegráficamente.

telegraphist [tɪ'legrəfɪst] N telegrafista *mf*.

telegraphy [tɪ'legrəfɪ] N telegrafía *f*.

telekinesis [,telɪkɪ'niːsɪs] N telequinesia *f*.

telekinetic [,telɪkɪ'netɪk] ADJ telequinético.

telemarketing [,telɪ'mɑːkɪtɪŋ] N telemárketing *m*, ventas *fpl* telefónicas.

telematic [,telɪ'mætɪk] ADJ telemático.

telemessage ['telɪmesɪdʒ] N (*Brit*) telegrama *m*.

telemetric [,telɪ'metrɪk] ADJ telemétrico.

telemetry [tɪ'lemɪtrɪ] N telemetría *f*.

teleological [,telɪə'lɒdʒɪkl] ADJ teleológico.

teleology [,telɪ'ɒlədʒɪ] N teleología *f*.

teleordering ['telɪ,ɔːdərɪŋ] N pedido *m* telefónico.

telepath ['telɪpæθ] N telépata *mf*.

telepathic [,telɪ'pæθɪk] ADJ telepático.

telepathically [,telɪ'pæθɪklɪ] ADV telepáticamente, por telepatía.

telepathist [tɪ'lepəθɪst] N telepatista *mf*.

telepathy [tɪ'lepəθɪ] N telepatía *f*.

telephone ['telɪfəun] ① N teléfono *m*; **to be on the ~** (*subscriber*) tener teléfono, (*be speaking*) estar hablando por teléfono; **you're wanted on the ~** quieren hablar con Vd por teléfono, le llaman al teléfono. ② ATTR telefónico; **~ answering machine** contestador *m* automático; **~ book** guía *f* telefónica; **~ booth** (*US*), **~ box** (*Brit*) locutorio *m*, cabina *f* de teléfono; **~ call** llamada *f* (telefónica); **~ directory** guía *f* telefónica; **~ exchange** central *f* telefónica; **~ kiosk** (*Brit*) locutorio *m*, cabina *f* de teléfono; **~ line** cable *m* telefónico, línea *f* telefónica; **~ message** mensaje *m* telefónico; **~ number** número *m* de teléfono; **~ operator** telefonista *mf*; **~ sales** ventas *fpl* por teléfono; **~ salesperson** vendedor *m*, -ora *f* por teléfono; **~ sex** teléfono *m* erótico; **~ sex line** teléfono *m* erótico; **~ subscriber** abonado *m* telefónico, abonada *f* telefónica; **~ tapping** intervención *f* telefónica. ③ VTI llamar por teléfono, llamar al teléfono, telefonear.

telephonic [,telɪ'fɒnɪk] ADJ telefónico.

telephonist [tɪ'lefənɪst] N (*esp Brit*) telefonista *mf*.

telephony [tɪ'lefənɪ] N telefonía *f*.

telephoto ['telɪ'fəutəu] ADJ: **~ lens** objetivo *m* telefotográfico, teleobjetivo *m*.

telephotography [,telɪfə'tɒgrəfɪ] N telefotografía *f*.

teleport ['telɪpɔːt] VT teletransportar.
teleprint ['telɪˌprɪnt] N (*Brit*) transmitir por teletipo.
teleprinter ['telɪˌprɪntəʳ] N (*Brit*) teletipo *m*, teleimpresora *f*.
teleprocessing [ˌtelɪ'prəʊsesɪŋ] N teleproceso *m*.
teleprompter ['telɪˌprɒmptəʳ] N teleprompter *m*, chuleta* *f*.
telesales ['telɪˌseɪlz] NPL ventas *fpl* por teléfono.
telescope ['telɪskəʊp] ⓵ N telescopio *m*.
⓶ VT telescopar; enchufar; **to ~ sth into sth else** meter algo dentro de otra cosa.
⓷ VI telescoparse; enchufarse; **A ~s into B** A se mete dentro de B.
telescopic [ˌtelɪs'kɒpɪk] ADJ telescópico; enchufable, de enchufe; **~ lens** teleobjetivo *m*; **~ sight** mira *f* telescópica, visor *m* telescópico.
teleshopping ['telɪˌʃɒpɪŋ] N (*US*) compras *fpl* por teléfono.
teletex ['telɪteks] N teletexto *m*.
teletext ['telɪtekst] N teletex(to) *m*.
telethon ['teləθɒn] N telemaratón *m* (*con fines benéficos*).
Teletype ['telɪˌtaɪp] ⓡ N teletipo *m*.
teletypewriter [ˌtelɪ'taɪpraɪtəʳ] (*US*) N = **teleprinter**.
televangelist [ˌtelɪ'vændʒəlɪst] N evangelista *mf* de la tele.
teleview ['teləvjuː] VI (*US*) ver la televisión.
televiewer ['telɪˌvjuːəʳ] N televidente *mf*, telespectador *m*, -ora *f*.
televise ['telɪvaɪz] VT televisar.
television ['telɪˌvɪʒən] ⓵ N televisión *f*; **to be on ~** estar en la televisión; **to watch ~** mirar la televisión.
⓶ ATTR de televisión, televisivo; **~ aerial** antena *f* de televisión; **~ announcer** locutor *m*, -ora *f* de televisión; **~ broadcast** emisión *f* televisiva, **~ lounge** sala *f* de televisión; **~ network** cadena *f* (*or* red *f*) de televisión; **~ programme** programa *m* de televisión; **~ room** sala *f* de televisión; **~ screen** pantalla *f* de televisión; **~ set** televisor *m*, aparato *m* de televisión; **~ studio** estudio *m* de televisión; **~ tube** tubo *m* de rayos catódicos, cinescopio *m*.
televisual [telɪ'vɪzjʊəl] ADJ televisivo.
telework [ˌtelɪ'wɜːk] VI teletrabajar.
teleworker ['telɪwɜːkəʳ] N teletrabajador *m*, -ora *f*.
teleworking ['telɪwɜːkɪŋ] N teletrabajo *m*.
telex ['teleks] ⓵ N télex *m*; **~ number** número *m* de télex; **~ operator** operador *m*, -ora *f* de télex.
⓶ VT transmitir (*or* enviar) por télex.
tell [tel] (*irr*: PRET AND PTP **told**) ⓵ VT (a) (*gen*) decir; *adventure, story etc* contar; (*formally*) comunicar, informar; **to ~ a lie** mentir; **to ~ sb the news** comunicar las noticias a uno, contar novedades a uno; **to ~ the truth** decir la verdad (*see also* **truth**); **to ~ sb sth** decir algo a uno; **I have been told that ...** me han dicho que ..., se me ha dicho que ...; **I hear ~ that ...** dicen que ...; **I am glad to ~ you that ...** (*formal letter*) me es grato comunicarle que ...; **~ me all about it** cuéntame todo; **I'll ~ you all about it** te (lo) diré todo; **I told him about the missing money** le informé acerca del dinero perdido, le dije lo del dinero desaparecido; **I cannot ~ you how pleased I am** no encuentro palabras para expresar mi contento; **so much happened that I can't begin to ~ you** pasaron tantas cosas que no sé cómo empezar a contarlas; **I ~ you no!, I ~ you it isn't!** ¡te digo que no!; **I told you so!** ya lo decía yo; **didn't I ~ you so?** ¿no te lo dije ya?; **I ~ myself it can't be true** digo para mí que no puede ser verdad; **there were 3, I ~ you,** 3 había 3, ¿me oyes?, 3; **you can't ~ her anything she doesn't know about cars** no se le puede decir nada sobre coches que ella no sepa.
(b) (*gen: idiomatic uses*) **~ me another!** ¡vaya!; **~ that to the marines!** ¡a otro perro con ese hueso!; **you're ~ing me!** ¡a quién se lo cuentas!; **he's no saint, let me ~ you!** ¡no es ningún santo, te lo aseguro!; **he won't like it, I can ~ you** esto seguramente no le va a caer en gracia; **I could ~ you a thing or two about him** hay cosas de él que yo me sé; **I ~ you what!** ¡se me ocurre una idea!; **it hurt more than words can ~** dolió una barbaridad, dolió lo indecible.
(c) (*announce*) decir, anunciar; (*of clock, dial etc*) indicar, marcar; **the sign ~s us which way to go** la señal nos dice qué ruta conviene seguir; **the clock ~s the quarter hours** el reloj da los cuartos de hora; **to ~ sb's fortune** decir a uno la buenaventura.
(d) (*order*) **to ~ sb to do sth** decir a uno que haga algo, mandar a uno hacer algo; **I told you not to do it** te dije que no lo hicieras; **do as you are told!** ¡haz lo que te digo!; **he won't be told** no acepta las órdenes de nadie; no quiere hacer caso de ningún consejo.
(e) (*distinguish*) distinguir; (*recognize*) conocer, reconocer; **to ~ A from B** distinguir A de B; **to ~ right from wrong** (*saber*) distinguir el bien del mal; **one can ~ he's a German** se conoce que es alemán; **you can ~ him in any disguise** se le reconoce bajo cualquier disfraz; **can you ~ the time?** ¿sabes decir la hora?; **V apart**.
(f) (*know*) saber; **how can I ~ what she will do?** ¿cómo voy a saber lo que ella hará?; **I couldn't ~ how it was done** no sabía cómo se hizo; **I can't ~ the difference** no veo la diferencia; **you can't ~ much from his letter** su carta nos dice bien poco, su carta apenas sirve para aclarar el asunto; **we can't ~ much from this** no es posible deducir mucho de esto.

(g) (*count*) contar; **to ~ one's beads** rezar el rosario; **30 pigs all told** en total 30 cerdos.
⓶ VI (a) (*speak*) **to ~ of** hablar de; **I hear ~ of a disaster** oigo hablar de una catástrofe, tengo noticias de una catástrofe; **I have never heard ~ of it** no he oído nunca hablar de eso; **the ruins told of a sad history** las ruinas hablaban de una triste historia.
(b) (*: be talebearer*) soplar*.
(c) (*have an effect*) tener efecto, hacer mella; **blood will ~** la sangre cuenta; **words that ~** palabras *fpl* que hacen mella, palabras *fpl* que impresionan; **every blow told** cada golpe tuvo su efecto; **it told on his health** afectó su salud, se dejó ver en su salud; **the effort was beginning to ~ (on him)** el esfuerzo empezaba a afectarle de mala manera; **everything ~s against him** todo obra en contra de él; **stamina ~s in the long run** a la larga importa más la resistencia, a la larga vale más la resistencia.
(d) (*know*) saber; **how can I ~?** ¿cómo lo voy a saber?, ¿yo qué sé?; **who can ~?** ¿quién sabe?; **we cannot ~** (nos) es imposible saberlo; **it's hard for anyone to ~** es difícil que nadie lo sepa; **you never can ~** nunca se sabe; podría ser tanto lo uno como lo otro.
◆**tell off** VT (a) (*order*) ordenar, mandar. (b) (*: reprimand*) **to ~ sb off** reñir a uno, echar un rapapolvo a uno*.
◆**tell on** * VT: **to ~ on sb** soplarse a uno*, chivatear contra uno*.
teller ['teləʳ] N (*of story*) narrador *m*, -ora *f*; (*Parl*) escrutador *m*, -ora *f*; (*in bank*) cajero *m*, -a *f*.
telling ['telɪŋ] ⓵ ADJ eficaz; fuerte, enérgico; **a ~ argument** un argumento eficaz.
⓶ N narración *f*; **there is no ~** nunca se sabe, es imposible saberlo; **there is no ~ what he will do** es imposible saber qué va a hacer; **the story did not lose in the ~** el cuento no perdió en la narración.
telling-off * [ˌtelɪŋ'ɒf] N bronca *f*, reprimenda *f*.
telltale ['telteɪl] ⓵ ADJ revelador; indicador.
⓶ N soplón* *m*, -ona *f*; (*Naut*) axiómetro *m*.
tellurium [te'lʊərɪəm] N telurio *m*.
telly * ['telɪ] N (*Brit*) tele* *f*.
Temazepam [tɪ'mæzəpæm] ⓡ N Temazepam *m* ⓡ.
temblor ['tembləʳ] N (*US*) temblor *m* de tierra.
temerity [tɪ'merɪtɪ] N temeridad *f*; **to have the ~ to** + *infin* atreverse a + *infin*; **and you have the ~ to say ...!** ¡y Vd se atreve a decir que ...!, ¡y Vd me dice tan fresco que ...!
temp¹ [temp] (*Brit abbr of* **temporary**) ⓵ N empleado *m* eventual, empleada *f* eventual.
⓶ VI trabajar como empleado eventual (*or* empleada eventual).
temp.² ABBR **of temperature**.
temper ['tempəʳ] ⓵ N (a) (*nature, disposition*) disposición *f*, natural *m*; humor *m*, genio *m*; (*bad*) genio *m*, mal genio *m*; **~!** ¡qué mal genio!; **bad ~, hot ~, quick ~** genio *m*, mal genio *m*, genio *m* vivo; **good ~** buen humor *m*; **to be in a good ~** estar de buen humor; **he has a ~** tiene genio; **he has a foul** (*or* **vile** *etc*) **~** es un hombre de malas pulgas; **to have a quick ~** tener genio, tener prontos de enojo; **to keep one's ~** contenerse, no alterarse; **to fly into a ~, to lose one's ~** perder la paciencia, enojarse (*with* con); **to try sb's ~** probar la paciencia de uno.
(b) (*of metal*) temple *m*.
⓶ VT *metal* templar; (*fig*) templar, moderar, mitigar; **to ~ justice with mercy** templar la justicia con la compasión.
tempera ['tempərə] N pintura *f* al temple.
temperament ['tempərəmənt] N temperamento *m*, disposición *f*; (*moodiness, difficult ~*) excitabilidad *f*, tendencia *f* a cambiar repentinamente de humor; genio *m*; **he has a ~** tiene genio, tiene sus caprichos.
temperamental [ˌtempərə'mentl] ADJ (a) (*relating to temperament*) complexional, relativo al temperamento. (b) (*moody, difficult*) excitable, caprichoso, sujeto a impulsos repentinos.
temperamentally [ˌtempərə'mentəlɪ] ADV (*by nature*): **he's ~ suited/unsuited to this job** por naturaleza sirve/no sirve para hacer este trabajo; **~, he is more like...** en cuanto a temperamento, se parece más a....
temperance ['tempərəns] ⓵ N templanza *f*; moderación *f*; abstinencia *f* (*del alcohol*).
⓶ ATTR: **~ hotel** hotel *m* donde no se sirven bebidas alcohólicas; **~ movement** campaña *f* antialcohólica.
temperate ['tempərɪt] ADJ templado; moderado; (*in drinking*) abstemio; *climate, zone* templado; **to be ~ in one's demands** ser moderado en sus exigencias.
temperature ['temprɪtʃəʳ] N temperatura *f*; (*Med: high ~*) calentura *f*, fiebre *f*; **~ chart** gráfico *m* de temperaturas; **to have a ~, to run a ~** tener fiebre, tener calentura; **to take sb's ~** tomar la temperatura de uno.
tempered ['tempəd] ADJ templado.
-tempered ['tempəd] ADJ *ending in compounds*: de ... humor; *V* **bad, good** *etc*.
tempest ['tempɪst] N tempestad *f*.

tempestuous [tem'pestjʊəs] ADJ tempestuoso; (fig) tempestuoso, borrascoso.

Templar ['templər] N templario m.

template, (US) **templet** ['templɪt] N plantilla f.

temple¹ ['templ] N (Rel) templo m; **the T~** (London) el Colegio de Abogados.

temple² ['templ] N (Anat) sien f; (US: of spectacles) patilla f.

tempo ['tempəʊ] N, PL **tempi** ['tempiː] (Mus) tempo m (also fig); tiempo m; (fig) ritmo m.

temporal ['tempərəl] ADJ temporal.

temporarily ['tempərərɪlɪ] ADV temporalmente.

temporary ['tempərərɪ] ADJ temporáneo, provisional; transitorio, poco duradero, de poca duración; official interino; (of worker's status) temporero; **~ injunction** interdicto m temporal; **~ secretary** secretaria f eventual; **~ surface** firme m provisional; **these arrangements are purely ~** este arreglo es provisional nada más; **there was a ~ improvement** hubo una mejora temporal.

temporize ['tempəraɪz] VI contemporizar.

tempt [tempt] VT (a) tentar; atraer; seducir; **to ~ sb to do sth** tentar a uno a hacer algo, inducir a uno a hacer algo; **to be ~ed to do sth** (fig) estar tentado de hacer algo; **there was a time when he was ~ed to resign** hubo un momento en que estuvo tentado de dimitir; **to allow o.s. to be ~ed** ceder a la tentación; **I am ~ed** es una oferta atractiva, es una perspectiva agradable; **I am very ~ed** tengo muchas ganas; **doesn't the idea ~ you at all?** ¿la idea no te interesa siquiera un poquitín?; **can I ~ you to another cup?** ¿quieres otra taza?

(b) (†, Bib etc) poner a prueba; tentar; **one must not ~ fate** (or **providence**) no hay que tentar a la suerte.

temptation [temp'teɪʃən] N tentación f; atractivo m, aliciente m; **there is a ~ to** + infin es tentador + infin; hay tendencia a + infin; **to give way** (or **yield**) **to ~** ceder a la tentación; **to lead sb into ~** hacer que uno caiga en el pecado; **lead us not into ~** no nos dejes caer en la tentación; **to resist ~** resistir (a) la tentación (of + ger de + infin); **to put ~ in sb's way** exponer a uno a la tentación.

tempter ['temptər] N tentador m.

tempting ['temptɪŋ] ADJ tentador; atractivo; meal apetitoso, rico; theory etc seductor; **a ~ offer** una oferta tentadora; **it is ~ to think so** estamos tentados de considerarlo así; es fácil asentir a ello.

temptingly ['temptɪŋlɪ] ADV de modo tentador; de modo seductor; apetitosamente.

temptress ['temptrɪs] N tentadora f.

ten [ten] ① ADJ diez; **some ~ people** una decena de personas; **~ metre line** línea f de diez metros.

② N diez m; (as round number) decena f; **~s of thousands of Spaniards** decenas de miles de españoles; **~ to 1 you're right** seguro que tienes razón; **they're ~ a penny** son comunísimos; los hay baratísimos.

tenable ['tenəbl] ADJ defendible, sostenible.

tenacious [tɪ'neɪʃəs] ADJ tenaz; porfiado; **to be ~ of life** estar muy apegado a la vida, aferrarse a la vida.

tenaciously [tɪ'neɪʃəslɪ] ADV tenazmente; porfiadamente.

tenacity [tɪ'næsɪtɪ] N tenacidad f; porfía f.

tenancy ['tenənsɪ] N tenencia f; (of house) inquilinato m, ocupación f; (lease) arriendo m.

tenant ['tenənt] ① ADJ: **~ farmer** agricultor m arrendatario.
② N (inhabitant) habitante mf, morador m, -ora f; (paying rent) inquilino m, -a f, arrendatario m, -a f.

tenantry ['tenəntrɪ] N inquilinos mpl; (Agr) agricultores mpl arrendatarios.

tench [tentʃ] N, PL INVAR tenca f.

tend¹ [tend] VI tender; **to ~ to, to ~ towards** tender a, inclinarse a, tener tendencia a; **we ~ to think that ...** nos inclinamos a pensar que ...; **it ~s to be the case that ...** suele ser que ..., en general es que ...; **I rather ~ to agree with you** casi estoy por compartir ese criterio; **anything that ~s to help solve the problem** cualquier cosa que contribuya a resolver el problema, todo lo que conduzca a resolver el problema; **it is a blue ~ing to green** es un azul que tira a verde; **these clothes ~ to shrink** estas prendas tienen tendencia a encogerse; **which way is it ~ing?** ¿hacia qué lado se inclina?

tend² [tend] VT sick etc cuidar, atender; cattle guardar; machine manejar, operar, servir; mantener.

tendency ['tendənsɪ] N tendencia f, inclinación f, propensión f; proclividad f; **he has a ~ to say too much** tiene tendencia a decir demasiado; **there is a ~ for the ponds to dry up** los estanques tienden a secarse; **the present ~ to the left** la actual tendencia hacia la izquierda.

tendentious [ten'denʃəs] ADJ tendencioso.

tendentiously [ten'denʃəslɪ] ADV de modo tendencioso.

tendentiousness [ten'denʃəsnɪs] N tendenciosidad f.

tender¹ ['tendər] N (Rail) ténder m; (Naut) gabarra f, embarcación f auxiliar.

tender² ['tendər] ① N (a) (Comm) oferta f, proposición f; **~ documents** pliegos mpl de propuesta; **call for ~** propuesta f para licitación de obras; **to make a ~, to put in a ~** hacer una oferta (for para la construcción (etc) de), ofertar; **to put sth out to ~** solicitar ofertas para algo.
(b) **legal ~** moneda f corriente, moneda f de curso legal.
② VT ofrecer; resignation etc presentar; thanks dar.
③ VI (Comm) ofertar, hacer una oferta (for para).

tender³ ['tendər] ADJ (a) (soft) tierno, blando; spot delicado, sensible; (painful) dolorido; age etc tierno; conscience escrupuloso; problem, subject espinoso, delicado, difícil; **those of ~ years** los de tierna edad; **I still feel ~ there** ese sitio me duele todavía; **it is ~ to the touch** duele cuando se toca.
(b) (affectionate) tierno, afectuoso; compasivo; **I have ~ memories of her** la recuerdo con mucha ternura.

tenderfoot ['tendəfʊt] N (esp US) recién llegado m; principiante m, novato m.

tender-hearted ['tendə'hɑːtɪd] ADJ compasivo, bondadoso, tierno de corazón.

tender-heartedness ['tendə'hɑːtɪdnɪs] N compasión f, bondad f, ternura f.

tenderize ['tendəraɪz] VT ablandar.

tenderizer ['tendəraɪzər] N ablandador m.

tenderloin ['tendəlɔɪn] N (a) (meat) filete m. (b) (US*) barrio m de vicio y corrupción reconocidos.

tenderly ['tendəlɪ] ADV tiernamente, con ternura.

tenderness ['tendənɪs] N ternura f; lo delicado; sensibilidad f.

tendon ['tendən] N tendón m.

tendril ['tendrɪl] N zarcillo m.

tenement ['tenɪmənt] N vivienda f; habitación f; **~ house, ~s** casa f de pisos, casa f de vecindad.

Tenerife [ˌtenə'riːf] N Tenerife m.

tenet ['tenət] N principio m, dogma m.

tenfold ['tenfəʊld] ① ADJ décuplo, diez veces mayor.
② ADV diez veces.

ten-gallon ['ten'gælən] ATTR: **~ hat** sombrero m tejano.

Tenn. (US) ABBR of **Tennessee**.

tenner* ['tenər] N (Brit) billete m de diez libras, (US) billete m de diez dólares.

tennis ['tenɪs] N tenis m; **~ elbow** sinovitis f del codo, codo m de tenista.

tennis-ball ['tenɪsbɔːl] N pelota f de tenis.

tennis club ['tenɪsklʌb] N club m de tenis.

tennis-court ['tenɪskɔːt] N pista f de tenis, cancha f de tenis (LAm).

tennis match ['tenɪsmætʃ] N partido m de tenis.

tennis-player ['tenɪsˌpleɪər] N tenista mf.

tennis-racquet ['tenɪsˌrækɪt] N raqueta f de tenis.

tennis-shoe ['tenɪsʃuː] N zapatilla f de tenis.

tenon ['tenən] N espiga f, almilla f.

tenor ['tenər] ① ADJ instrument, part, voice de tenor; aria para tenor.
② N (a) (Mus) tenor m; (purport) tenor m, tendencia f; curso m.

tenpin bowling ['tenpɪn'bəʊlɪŋ] N, **tenpins** ['tenpɪnz] NPL (US) bolos mpl, bolera f.

tense¹ [tens] N (Gram) tiempo m.

tense² [tens] ① ADJ (stretched) tirante, estirado, tieso; (stiff) rígido, tieso; moment, nerves, situation etc tenso; **it has been a ~ day** la jornada ha sido muy tensa; **we waited with ~ expectancy** aguardamos con tensa expectación; **he looked rather ~** parecía estar algo tenso.
② VT tensar, tesar, estirar.

◆**tense up** VI tensarse.

tensely ['tenslɪ] ADV tensamente, con tensión.

tenseness ['tensnɪs] N tirantez f; tensión f.

tensile ['tensaɪl] ADJ tensor; extensible; de tensión, relativo a la tensión; **~ strength** resistencia f a la tensión.

tension ['tenʃən] N tirantez f; tensión f; **~ headache** dolor m de cabeza producido por la tensión.

tent [tent] N tienda f (de campaña), carpa f (LAm).

tentacle ['tentəkl] N tentáculo m.

tentative ['tentətɪv] ADJ provisional; experimental; de prueba, de ensayo; **these are ~ conclusions** son conclusiones provisionales; **everything is very ~ at the moment** por el momento todo es de carácter provisional; **she's a rather ~ person** es una persona bastante indecisa.

tentatively ['tentətɪvlɪ] ADV provisionalmente; en vía de prueba, como tanteo; **'yes', he said ~ 'sí'**, dijo sin gran confianza.

tenterhooks ['tentəhʊks] NPL: **to be on ~** estar sobre ascuas; tener el alma en vilo; **to keep sb on ~** tener a uno sobre ascuas.

tenth [tenθ] ① ADJ décimo.
② N décimo m; (part) décima parte f, décima f.

tentpeg ['tent,peg] N (Brit) estaquilla f, estaca f (de tienda).

tentpole ['tentpəʊl] N, (US) **tent stake** ['tentsteɪk] N mástil m de tienda, poste *m* de tienda.

tenuity [te'njʊɪtɪ] N tenuidad *f*; raridad *f*.

tenuous ['tenjʊəs] ADJ tenue; sutil; *connection* poco fuerte; *argument* poco sólido; *air* raro.

tenuously ['tenjʊəslɪ] ADV tenuemente, sutilmente.

tenure ['tenjʊəʳ] **1** N **(a)** (*of land etc*) posesión *f*, tenencia *f*, ocupación *f*. **(b)** (*Univ etc*) permanencia *f*; **teacher with ~** profesor *m*, -ora *f* de número, profesor *m* numerario, profesora *f* numeraria; **teacher without ~** profesor *m* no numerario, profesora *f* no numeraria; **~ track position** (*US*) puesto *m* con posibilidad de obtener la permanencia. **2** VT (*US*) conceder la permanencia a.

tepee ['ti:pi:] N (*US*) tipi *m*.

tepid ['tepɪd] ADJ tibio.

tepidity [te'pɪdɪtɪ] N, **tepidness** ['tepɪdnɪs] N tibieza *f*.

tequila [tɪ'ki:lə] N tequila *f*.

terbium ['tɜːbɪəm] N terbio *m*.

tercentenary [,tɜːsen'ti:nərɪ] N tricentenario *m*.

tercet ['tɜːsɪt] N terceto *m*.

Terence ['terəns] NM Terencio.

▼ **term** [tɜːm] **1** N **(a)** (*limit*) término *m*, límite *m*, fin *m*; (*Comm*) plazo *m*; **to put** (*or* **set**) **a ~ to** señalar un límite a; fijar un plazo para.
(b) (*period*) período *m*; duración *f*; plazo *m*; (*of president etc*) mandato *m*; **during his ~ of office** durante su mandato; **for a ~ of 6 years** durante (*or* para) un período de 6 años; **in the long ~** a la larga; **in the medium ~** a plazo medio; **in the short ~** en el futuro próximo.
(c) (*Scol, Univ*) trimestre *m*; **during ~, in ~** durante el curso; **out of ~** fuera del curso; **to keep ~s** residir, estar de interno, cumplir su período de residencia.
(d) (*Math, Logic*) término *m*; **A expressed in ~s of B** A expresado en términos de B; **in ~s of production we are doing well** por lo que se refiere a (*or* en cuanto a) la producción vamos bien; **he was talking in ~s of buying it** hablaba de la posibilidad de comprarlo; **he sees novels in ~s of sociology** considera la novela en su función sociológica, se explica la novela desde el punto de vista sociológico.
(e) (*word*) término *m*; vocablo *m*, voz *f*, expresión *f*; **in plain ~s, in simple ~s** en términos sencillos, en lenguaje sencillo; **in no uncertain ~s** en términos que no pueden ser más claros; **to choose one's ~s carefully** eligir sus palabras con cuidado; **she described it in glowing ~s** lo describió con mucho entusiasmo.
▼ **(f)** **~s** (*conditions*) condiciones *fpl* de pago; **~s of payment** condiciones *fpl* de pago; **~s of reference** puntos *mpl* de mandato, puntos *mpl* de consulta; **~s of sale** condiciones *fpl* de venta; **~s of surrender** capitulaciones *fpl*, condiciones *fpl* de la rendición; **~s of trade** términos *mpl* del intercambio; **according to the ~s of the contract** según las condiciones del contrato, conforme a lo estipulado en el contrato; **not on any ~s** bajo ningún concepto; **what are your ~s?** ¿cuáles son sus condiciones?; **to accept sb on his own ~s** aceptar a uno sabiendo lo que es, aceptar a uno sin esperar cambiar su naturaleza; **to come to ~s** llegar a un acuerdo, ponerse de acuerdo; **to come to ~s with a situation** adaptarse a una situación, conformarse con una situación; **to dictate ~s** dictar las condiciones; **you may name your own ~s** Vd puede estipular lo que quiera.
(g) **~s** (*Comm, Fin*) precio *m*, tarifa *f*; **our ~s for full board** nuestro precio para la pensión completa; **'inclusive ~s: £50'** '50 libras todo incluido', 'pensión completa: 50 libras'; **we bought it on advantageous ~s** lo compramos a buen precio; **we offer easy ~s** ofrecemos facilidades de pago.
(h) **~s** (*relationship*) relaciones *fpl*; **to be on easy** (*or* **familiar**) **~s with sb** tener confianza con uno; **to be on bad ~s with sb** llevarse mal con uno, estar en malas relaciones con uno; **to be on good ~s with sb** estar en buenas relaciones con uno; **we are on the best of ~s** somos muy amigos; **we're not on speaking ~s** no nos hablamos; **what ~s are they on?** ¿cuáles son sus relaciones?; **they were not competing on equal** (*or* **the same**) **~s** no competían en un pie de igualdad; **to fight sb on equal ~s** luchar con uno en iguales condiciones.
2 ATTR: **~ insurance** seguro *m* temporal; **~ loan** préstamo *m* a plazo fijo; **~ paper** (*US*) trabajo *m* escrito trimestral (*o* semestral).
3 VT llamar; nombrar, denominar; calificar de; **he ~s himself a businessman** se llama hombre de negocios; **I ~ it a disgrace** lo llamo una vergüenza, digo que es una vergüenza.

termagant ['tɜːməgənt] N arpía *f*, fiera *f*.

terminal ['tɜːmɪnl] **1** ADJ **(a)** terminal (*also Med*), final; **~ illness** enfermedad *f* terminal; **~ patient** enfermo *m*, -a *f* terminal. **(b)** (*Scol, Univ*) trimestral. **2** N **(a)** (*Elec*) borne *m*; polo *m*; (*Comput*) terminal *f*. **(b)** (*Aer, Naut, Rail*) terminal *f*.

terminally ['tɜːmɪnəlɪ] ADV: **the patient is ~ ill** el enfermo está en fase terminal.

terminate ['tɜːmɪneɪt] **1** VT terminar; *pregnancy* interrumpir.

2 VI terminar(se).

termination [,tɜːmɪ'neɪʃən] N terminación *f* (*also Gram*); (*of pregnancy*) interrupción *f*.

termini ['tɜːmɪnaɪ] NPL of **terminus**.

terminological [,tɜːmɪnə'lɒdʒɪkəl] ADJ terminológico.

terminologist [,tɜːmɪ'nɒlədʒɪst] N terminólogo *m*, -a *f*.

terminology [,tɜːmɪ'nɒlədʒɪ] N terminología *f*.

terminus ['tɜːmɪnəs] N, PL **termini** ['tɜːmɪnaɪ] *or* **terminuses** término *m*; (*Rail*) estación *f* terminal, término *m*.

termite ['tɜːmaɪt] N termita *f*, termes *m*, comején *m*.

termtime ['tɜːmtaɪm] N trimestre *m*.

tern [tɜːn] N golondrina *f* de mar; **common ~** charrán *m* común.

ternary ['tɜːnərɪ] ADJ ternario.

Terpsichore [tɜːp'sɪkərɪ] NF Terpsícore.

terpsichorean [,tɜːpsɪkə'ri:ən] ADJ coreográfico, de Terpsícore.

Ter(r). ABBR of **Terrace**.

terrace ['terəs] **1** N (*Agr*) terraza *f*; (*raised bank*) terraplén *m*; (*Brit: of houses*) hilera *f* de casas sin división entre sí; (*roof*) azotea *f*; **~s** (*Brit Sport*) gradas *fpl*, graderío *m*. **2** VT aterrazar, formar terrazas en; terraplenar.

terraced ['terəst] ADJ en terrazas; terraplenado; **~ gardens** jardines *mpl* colgantes; **~ house** casa que forma parte de una hilera de casas sin interrupción.

terracotta ['terə'kɒtə] **1** N terracota *f*. **2** ADJ terracota.

terra firma [,terə'fɜːmə] N tierra *f* firme.

terrain [te'reɪn] N terreno *m*.

terrapin ['terəpɪn] N tortuga *f* de agua dulce.

terrarium [te'reərɪəm] N terrario *m*.

terrazzo [te'rætsəʊ] N terrazo *m*.

terrestrial [tɪ'restrɪəl] ADJ terrestre.

terrible ['terəbl] ADJ terrible; horrible, malísimo, fatal; **it was just ~** fue sencillamente horrible; **I've been a ~ fool** yo he sido la mar de tonto; **his Spanish is ~** su español es fatal.

terribly ['terəblɪ] ADV **(a)** (*very*) terriblemente, espantosamente; **it's ~ dangerous** es tremendamente peligroso; **I think he's ~ nice** para mi gusto es simpatiquísimo. **(b)** (*very badly*) horriblemente; **she plays ~** toca malísimamente.

terrier ['terɪəʳ] N terrier *m*.

terrific [tə'rɪfɪk] ADJ tremendo; (*) bárbaro*, fabuloso*; **~!** ¡estupendo!*; **what ~ news!** ¡qué noticia más estupenda!*; **isn't he ~?** ¿es fabuloso, no?*; **we had a ~ time** lo pasamos en grande*.

terrifically [tə'rɪfɪkəlɪ] ADV tremendamente*; (*) tremendamente*, fabulosamente*.

terrified ['terɪfaɪd] ADJ: **to be ~** estar aterrorizado, estar aterrado; **to be ~ of sb/sth** tenerle terror *or* pavor a uno/algo; **to be ~ of doing sth: he was ~ of catching Aids** le aterrorizaba *or* le daba terror (la idea de) coger el sida; **I was ~ of her meeting another man** me daba terror que conociera a otro hombre; **to be ~ that: she was ~ (that) they'd lose their home** le aterrorizaba *or* le daba terror el pensar que pudieran perder su casa; **I was ~ that he might follow me** tenía terror de que pudiera seguirme.

terrify ['terɪfaɪ] VT aterrar, aterrorizar; **to ~ sb out of his wits** dar un susto mortal a uno.

terrifying ['terɪfaɪɪŋ] ADJ aterrador, espantoso.

terrifyingly ['terɪfaɪɪŋlɪ] ADV espantosamente.

terrine [te'ri:n] N terrina *f*.

territorial [,terɪ'tɔːrɪəl] **1** ADJ territorial; **T~ Army** ejército *m* de reserva; **~ waters** aguas *fpl* territoriales, aguas *fpl* jurisdiccionales. **2** N (*Brit*) reservista *m*.

TERRITORIAL ARMY

i *La organización británica* **Territorial Army** *o* **TA** *es un ejército de reserva formado exclusivamente por voluntarios civiles que reciben entrenamiento militar en su tiempo libre y están disponibles para ayudar al ejército profesional en tiempos de guerra o crisis. Como compensación por sus servicios, los voluntarios reciben una paga. En Estados Unidos el equivalente es la llamada* **National Guard**.

territoriality [,terɪ,tɔːrɪ'ælɪtɪ] N territorialidad *f*.

territory ['terɪtərɪ] N territorio *m*; **mandated ~** territorio *m* bajo mandato.

terror ['terəʳ] N **(a)** (*fear*) terror *m*, espanto *m*; **~ campaign** campaña *f* de terror; **to live in ~** vivir en el terror; **to sow ~ everywhere** sembrar el terror por todas partes; **he went** (*or* **was**) **in ~ of his life** temía por su vida, temía ser asesinado; **I have a ~ of bats** tengo horror a los murciélagos; **he had a ~ of flying** le daba miedo volar; **the headmistress holds no ~s for me** la directora no me infunde miedo a mí.
(b) (*person*) **a little ~, a ~ of a child** un niño terrible; **he's a ~ on the roads** es terrible conduciendo; **he was the ~ of the boys** fue el terror de los más pequeños.

terrorism ['terərɪzəm] N terrorismo *m*.
terrorist ['terərɪst] ①ADJ terrorista.
  ②N terrorista *mf*.
terrorize ['terəraɪz] VT aterrorizar.
terror-stricken ['terə,strɪkən] ADJ, **terror-struck** ['terə,strʌk] ADJ espantado, preso de pánico.
Terry ['terɪ] NMF *familiar form of* **Terence, Theresa**.
terry (cloth) ['terɪ(,klɒθ)] N (*US*) felpa *f*; toalla *f*.
terse [tɜːs] ADJ breve, conciso, lacónico; brusco.
tersely ['tɜːslɪ] ADV concisamente, lacónicamente; bruscamente.
terseness ['tɜːsnɪs] N brevedad *f*, concisión *f*, laconismo *m*; brusquedad *f*.
tertiary ['tɜːʃərɪ] ADJ terciario; ~ **production** producción *f* terciaria.
Tertullian [tɜː'tʌlɪən] NM Tertuliano.
Terylene ['terəliːn] ®N (*Brit*) terylene ® *m*.
TESL ['tes(ə)l] N ABBR *of* **Teaching (of) English as a Second Language**; *ver también* [TEFL/EFL, TESL/ESL, ELT, TESOL/ESOL] .
TESOL ['tesɒl] N (*US*) ABBR *of* **Teaching (of) English to Speakers of Other Languages**; *ver también* [TEFL/EFL, TESL/ESL, ELT, TESOL/ESOL] .
Tess [tes] NF, **Tessa** ['tesə] NF *familiar forms of* **Teresa**.
tessel(l)ated ['tesɪleɪtɪd] ADJ de mosaico; formado con teselas; ~ **pavement** mosaico *m*.
tessel(l)ation [,tesɪ'leɪʃən] N mosaico *m*.
test [test] ①N (a) prueba *f*; ensayo *m*; (*Scol, Univ etc*) examen *m*, test *m*; ejercicio *m*; (*Chem*) prueba *f*, análisis *m*; (*standard of judgement*) criterio *m*; **the ~ is whether** ... la piedra de toque es si ...; **to put sth to the ~** poner algo a prueba, someter algo a prueba; **to stand the ~** soportar la prueba; **it has stood the ~ of time** ha resistido el paso del tiempo.
  (b) (*Brit Sport*) = ~-**match**.
  ②ATTR de prueba(s); ~ **ban treaty** tratado *m* de suspensión de pruebas nucleares; ~ **bore** prueba *f* de sondeo.
  ③VT probar, poner a prueba, someter a prueba; examinar; *sight graduar*; (*Chem etc*) ensayar; *new drug etc* experimentar; **it severely ~ed our nerves** puso nuestros nervios a toda prueba; **the new weapon is being ~ed** se está sometiendo a prueba la nueva arma.
  ④VI: **to ~ for a gas leak** hacer investigaciones para ver si hay una fuga de gas; **how do you ~ for gas?** ¿cómo se comprueba la presencia de gas?; **~ing, ~ing!** (*microphone etc*) ¡uno, dos, tres!; **he ~ed positive** (*Med*) dio positivo.
◆**test out** VT comprobar.
testament ['testəmənt] N testamento *m*; **New T~** Nuevo Testamento *m*; **Old T~** Antiguo Testamento *m*.
testamentary [,testə'mentərɪ] ADJ testamentario.
testator [tes'teɪtəʳ] N testador *m*.
testatrix [tes'teɪtrɪks] N testadora *f*.
test-bed ['testbed] N banco *m* de pruebas.
test-bench ['testbentʃ] N banco *m* de pruebas.
test-card ['testkɑːd] N (*Brit*) carta *f* de ajuste.
test-case ['testkeɪs] N pleito *m* de ensayo (*para determinar la interpretación de una nueva ley*).
test-data ['test,deɪtə] N datos *mpl* de prueba.
test-drill ['test,drɪl] VI sondear.
test-drive ['test,draɪv] ①N prueba *f* de carretera.
  ②VT *car* someter a prueba de carretera.
tester¹ ['testəʳ] N (*person*) ensayador *m*, -ora *f*.
tester² ['testəʳ] N (†) baldaquín *m*.
testes ['testiːz] NPL testes *mpl*.
test-flight ['testflaɪt] N vuelo *m* de ensayo.
testicle ['testɪkl] N testículo *m*.
testify ['testɪfaɪ] ①VT atestiguar, dar fe de; **to ~ that** ... testificar que ...; declarar que ...
  ②VI (a) (*Jur*) prestar declaración, declarar.
  (b) **to ~ to sth** atestiguar algo, atestar algo; (*fig*) atestiguar algo, dar fe de algo.
testily ['testɪlɪ] ADV *answer etc* con enojo, malhumoradamente.
testimonial [,testɪ'məʊnɪəl] N (a) certificado *m*; (*reference about person*) recomendación *f*, carta *f* de recomendación; **as a ~ to** como testimonio a, en homenaje a.
  (b) (*gift*) regalo *m*, obsequio *m* (de jubilación *etc*).
testimony ['testɪmənɪ] N testimonio *m*, declaración *f*; **in ~ whereof** ... en fe de lo cual ...; **to bear ~ to sth** atestar algo.
testing ['testɪŋ] ①ADJ: **it was a ~ experience for her** fue una experiencia que la ponía a prueba; **it was a ~ time** fue un período difícil.
  ②N pruebas *fpl*; ensayo *m*; puesta *f* a prueba; comprobación *f*.
testing-ground ['testɪŋɡraʊnd] N zona *f* de pruebas, terreno *m* de pruebas.
testis ['testɪs] N, PL **testes** ['testiːz] testículo *m*, teste *m*.
test-match ['testmætʃ] N (*Brit*) partido *m* internacional.
testosterone [te'stɒstərəʊn] N testosterona *f*.
test-paper ['test,peɪpəʳ] N (a) (*Scol etc*) test *m*, examen *m*. (b) (*Chem*)

papel *m* reactivo.
test-piece ['testpiːs] N (*Mus*) obra *f* elegida para un certamen de piano (*etc*).
test-pilot ['test,paɪlət] N piloto *mf* de pruebas.
test-run ['testrʌn] N prueba *f*, ensayo *m*.
test-tube ['testtjuːb] N probeta *f*; ~ **baby** niño *m*, -a *f* (de) probeta, bebé *mf* (de) probeta.
testy ['testɪ] ADJ irritable, malhumorado.
tetanus ['tetənəs] N tétanos *m*.
tetchily ['tetʃɪlɪ] ADV malhumoradamente.
tetchiness ['tetʃɪnɪs] N malhumor *m*.
tetchy ['tetʃɪ] ADJ (*Brit*) = **testy**.
tête-à-tête ['teɪtɑː'teɪt] N conversación *f* íntima.
tether ['teðəʳ] ①N atadura *f*, traba *f*, cuerda *f*; V **end**.
  ②VT atar, atar con una cuerda (*to* a).
tetragon ['tetrəɡən] N tetrágono *m*.
tetrahedron ['tetrə'hiːdrən] N tetraedro *m*.
tetrameter [te'træmɪtəʳ] N tetrámetro *m*.
tetrathlon [te'træθlən] N tetratlón *m*.
Teuton ['tjuːtən] N teutón *m*, -ona *f*.
Teutonic [tjuː'tɒnɪk] ADJ teutónico.
Tex. (*US*) ABBR *of* **Texas**.
Texan ['teksən] ①ADJ tejano.
  ②N tejano *m*, -a *f*.
Texas ['teksəs] N Tejas *m*.
Texican ['teksɪkən] N (*hum*), **Tex-Mex** ['teks'meks] N *lengua mixta angloespañola de los estados del suroeste de EE.UU.*
text [tekst] N texto *m*; (*subject*) tema *m*; **to stick to one's ~** no apartarse de su tema.
textbook ['tekstbʊk] N libro *m* de texto; **a ~ case of** ... un caso clásico de ...
text editor ['tekst,edɪtəʳ] N (*Comput*) editor *m* de texto.
textile ['tekstaɪl] ①ADJ textil; ~ **industry** industria *f* textil.
  ②N textil *m*, tejido *m*.
text processing ['tekst'prəʊsesɪŋ] N proceso *m* de textos, tratamiento *m* de textos.
text processor ['tekst'prəʊsesəʳ] N procesador *m* de textos.
textual ['tekstjʊəl] ADJ textual; ~ **criticism** crítica *f* textual.
textually ['tekstjʊəlɪ] ADV textualmente.
texture ['tekstʃəʳ] N textura *f* (*also fig*).
TGIF* ABBR *of* **thank God it's Friday**.
TGWU N (*Brit*) ABBR *of* **Transport and General Workers' Union**; *ver también* [TRADE UNIONS] .
Thai [taɪ] ①ADJ tailandés.
  ②N (a) tailandés *m*, -esa *f*. (b) (*Ling*) tailandés *m*.
Thailand ['taɪlænd] N Tailandia *f*.
thalamus ['θæləməs] N tálamo *m*.
thalassaemia [,θælə'siːmɪə] N anemia *f* de Cooley.
thalidomide [θə'lɪdəʊmaɪd] ® N talidomida ® *f*.
thallium ['θælɪəm] N talio *m*.
Thames [temz] N Támesis *m*; **he won't set the ~ on fire** no descubrirá la pólvora, no es ningún genio.
▼ **than** [ðæn] CONJ (a) que; **I have more ~ you** yo tengo más que tú; **he swears less ~ her** él usa menos palabrotas que ella; **nobody is more sorry ~ I (am)** nadie lo siente más que yo; **he has more money ~ brains** tiene más dinero que inteligencia; **clothes come out whiter ~ white** sale la ropa más blanca que blanca; **it is better to phone ~ to write** más vale telefonear que escribir; **I'll do anything rather ~ that** haré cualquier cosa que no sea ésa, lo haré todo menos eso.
  (b) (*with numerals*) de; **more ~ 90** más de 90; ~ **than half** más de la mitad; **not less ~ 8** no menos de 8; **more ~ once** más de una vez; **it doesn't happen more ~ once** no ocurre más que una sola vez.
▼(c) (*with following clause*) **they have more money ~ we have** tienen más dinero del que nosotros tenemos, tienen más dinero que nosotros; **we have more chips ~ you have** nosotros tenemos más patatas fritas de las que vosotros tenéis (*or que vosotros*); **it was an even sillier play ~ we had thought** la obra fue aun más estúpida de lo que habíamos pensado; **the car went faster ~ we had expected** el coche fue más rápidamente de lo que habíamos esperado.
▼ **thank** [θæŋk] ①VT: **to ~ sb** dar las gracias a uno; ~ **you** gracias; ~ **you!** (*emphatic, reciprocating thanks*) ¡a usted!; ~ **you very much** muchas gracias; **no ~ you** (no) gracias; ~ **God!** ¡gracias a Dios!; **I cannot ~ you enough!** ¡cuánto te lo agradezco!; **to ~ sb for sth** agradecer algo a uno; ~ **you for the present** muchas gracias por el regalo; **did you ~ him for the flowers?** ¿le diste las gracias por las flores?; **you have him to ~ for that** eso tienes que agradecérselo a él, ese favor se lo debes a él; **he has himself to ~ for that** él mismo tiene la culpa de eso; **which he could never properly ~ you for** que nunca podría agradecerte bastante; **he won't ~ you for telling her** no te agradecerá el habérselo dicho a ella; **I'll ~ you not to do it** agradecería que no lo hicieras; **I'll ~ you to be more polite!** ¡conviene hablar con más educación!; **without so much as a '~ you'**

sin la menor señal de agradecimiento.

▼ **2** NPL: ~**s gracias** *fpl*; **many ~s!, ~s very much!, ~s a lot!** ¡muchas gracias!, ¡muchísimas gracias!; **my warmest ~s for your help** mis gracias más efusivas por tu ayuda; **that's all the ~s I get!** ¡como se me agradece!; **~s to the rain the game was abandoned** debido a la lluvia el partido fue anulado; **~s to you** gracias a ti; **no ~s to you** no te debo nada a ti; **it's all ~ to Brand X** todo lo debo (*etc*) a la marca X; **~ be to God** gracias a Dios; **to give ~s** dar las gracias (*for* por).

3 ATTR: ~**s offering** prueba *f* de gratitud.

thankful ['θæŋkfʊl] ADJ agradecido; **to be ~ to +** *infin* alegrarse de + *infin*; **let us be ~ that ...** agradezcamos que + *subj*; **how ~ we were for that umbrella!** ¡cuánto nos ayudó ese paraguas!, ¡cómo bendecimos ese paraguas!

thankfully ['θæŋkfəlɪ] ADV con gratitud, con agradecimiento; **he said ~** dijo agradecido; dijo con alivio.

thankfulness ['θæŋkfʊlnɪs] N gratitud *f*, agradecimiento *m*.

thankless ['θæŋklɪs] ADJ *person* ingrato; *task* ímprobo, ingrato.

thanksgiving ['θæŋks,gɪvɪŋ] N acción *f* de gracias; **T~ Day** (*Canada, US*) día *m* de Acción de Gracias; *ver también* MACY'S THANKSGIVING PARADE , PILGRIM FATHERS

┌─── THANKSGIVING ───┐

ⓘ *El Día de Acción de Gracias, en inglés* **Thanksgiving** *o* **Thanksgiving Day** *es un día de fiesta en Estados Unidos que se celebra el cuarto jueves de noviembre y que data de 1621. En esta fecha los primeros colonos norteamericanos* (**Pilgrim Fathers**) *celebraron un acto de acción de gracias por el éxito de su primera cosecha en suelo americano. La comida típica del Día de Acción de Gracias* (**Thanksgiving meal**) *consiste en pavo asado y pastel de calabaza. Muchas personas recorren largas distancias para estar junto a sus familias en este día.*

En Canadá se celebra una fiesta semejante el segundo lunes de octubre, aunque no está relacionada con dicha fecha histórica.

⇨ *Ver también* PILGRIM FATHERS , MACY'S THANKSGIVING PARADE

thankyou ['θæŋkju] N gracias *fpl*; **now a big ~ to John** ahora, nuestras gracias más sinceras para Juan; **it's a way of saying ~ to the nurses** es un modo de dar las gracias a las enfermeras.

that [ðæt] **1** DEM ADJ (PL **those**) *m*: ese, (*more remote*) aquel; *f*: esa, (*more remote*) aquella; **~ book** ese libro; **~ hill over there** aquella colina; **~ one** ése, aquél; **~ lad of yours** ese chico tuyo; **what about ~ cheque?** ¿y el cheque ese?

2 DEM PRON (PL **those**) *m*: ése, (*more remote*) aquél; *f*: ésa, (*more remote*) aquélla; '*neuter*': eso, aquello; **this car is new but ~ is old** este coche es nuevo pero ése es viejo; **~ is true** eso es verdad; **~ is all I can tell you** eso es todo lo que puedo decirte; **~'s what I say**

eso digo yo, lo mismo digo yo; **they all say ~** todos dicen lo mismo; **what is ~?** ¿qué es?, ¿eso qué es?; **who is ~?** ¿quién es?; **~ is Joe** es Pepe; **~ is** (**to say**) ... esto es ...; es decir ...; **bees and wasps and** (**all**) **~** abejas y avispas y cosas así; **~'s it, we've finished** ya está, hemos terminado; **they get their wages and ~'s it** tienen su sueldo y eso es todo; **~'s it! she can find her own gardener!** ¡se acabó! puede buscarse jardinero por su cuenta; **and ~'s ~!** ¡y eso es todo!, ¡y sanseacabó!, ¡y santas pascuas!; **you can't go and ~'s ~** no puedes ir y no hay más qué decir; **so ~ was ~** y no había más que hacer, y ahí terminó la cosa; **~'s odd!** ¡qué raro!, ¡qué cosa más rara!; **will he come? ... ~ he will!** ¿si vendrá? ... ¡ya lo creo!; **after ~** después de eso; **at ~** acto seguido, sin más; con eso, con lo cual; **and it was broken at ~** y además estaba roto; **it will cost $20, if ~** costará 20 dólares o algo menos; **do it like ~** hazlo de esa manera, hazlo de la manera que ves; **with ~** con eso; **if it comes to ~** en tal caso; si vamos a eso; **how do you like ~?** ¿qué te parece?, (*iro*) ¡vaya!

3 REL PRON (a) que; **the book ~ I read** el libro que leí; **the houses ~ I painted** las casas que pinté; **all ~ I have** todo lo que tengo.
(b) (*with prep*) que, el cual, la cual *etc*; **the box ~ I put it in** la caja en la cual lo puse, la caja donde lo puse; **the house ~ we're speaking of** la casa de que hablamos; **not ~ I know of** no que yo sepa.
(c) (*expressions of time*) **the evening ~ we went to the theatre** la tarde en que fuimos al teatro; **the summer ~ it was so hot** el verano cuando hacía tanto calor.

4 ADV tan; **~ far** tan lejos; **~ high** tan alto, así de alto; **~ many frogs** tantas ranas; **~ much money** tanto dinero; **it is ~ much better** es tanto mejor; **he can't be ~ clever** no puede ser tan inteligente como tú dices; **nobody can be ~ rich** nadie puede ser tan rico como eso; **I didn't know he was ~ ill** no sabía que estuviera tan enfermo; **he was ~ wild*** estaba tan furioso; **it was ~ cold!** ¡hacía tanto frío!

5 CONJ (a) que; **I believe ~ he exists** creo que existe; **~ he should behave like this!** ¡que se comporte así!; **~ he should behave like this is incredible** (el) que se comporte así es increíble; **~ he refuses is natural** (el) que rehúse es natural; **oh ~ we could!** ¡ojalá pudiéramos!, ¡ojalá!; V **would** etc.
(b) (*in order that*) para que + *subj, eg* **it was done (so) ~ he might sleep** se hizo para que pudiera dormir; V **so.**
(c) **in ~** en que, por cuanto.

thatch [θætʃ] **1** N (*straw*) paja *f*; (*roof*) techo *m* de paja; cubierta *f* de paja.
2 VT poner techo de paja a.

thatched [θætʃt] ADJ: **~ cottage** casita *f* con techo de paja; **~ roof** techo *m* de paja; cubierta *f* de paja; **the roof is ~** el techo es de paja.

thatcher ['θætʃər] N techador *m*.

Thatcherism ['θætʃərɪzəm] N thatcherismo *m*.

┌─── THAT ─── see also main entry ─┐

Demonstratives

Pronoun

• The pronoun *that* (*one*) can be translated by *ése* and *aquél* (masc), *ésa* and *aquélla* (fem) and *eso* and *aquello* (neuter). You can generally use *ése etc* when pointing to something near the person you are speaking to. Use *aquél etc* for something which is distant from both of you:
   Look at that
   Mira eso
   I prefer this picture to that one over there
   Prefiero este cuadro a aquél de allá

Adjective

• The adjective *that* can be translated by *ese* and *aquel* (masc) and *esa* and *aquella* (fem). The same distinctions apply as for the pronouns:
   That car is much better value than that sports model at the end
   Ese coche te sale a mejor precio que aquel modelo deportivo que hay al final
• Similarly *aquel etc* is used to refer to a time in the distant past. Use *ese etc* if you mention a concrete date, month, year, *etc*:
   Do you remember that holiday we had in Holland?
   ¿Te acuerdas de aquellas vacaciones que pasamos en Holanda?
   1988? That was the year you graduated, wasn't it?
   ¿1988? Ése fue el año en que acabaste la carrera, ¿no es así?
! Note that the masculine and feminine *pronouns* carry accents to distinguish them from the masculine and feminine *adjectives*, though these can be omitted if there is no ambiguity. Neuter pronouns never carry an accent.

Relative

• In relative clauses *that* is usually translated as *que*:
   ...the painting that won the Turner prize...
   ...el cuadro que ganó el premio Turner...

   The driver (that) he hired was Italian
   El chófer que contrató era italiano
! Unlike *that*, the Spanish relative cannot be omitted.
• If the *that* clause ends in a preposition, you can either translate *that* as *que* (usually preceded by the definite article) or as ARTICLE + *cual/cuales*. Use the second option particularly in formal language or after long prepositions or prepositional phrases:
   ...the actor (that) I was telling you about...
   ...el actor del que te hablaba...
   ...the car that she got into...
   ...el coche al que se subió...
   ...a planet that satellites go round...
   ...un planeta alrededor del cual giran satélites...

Conjunction

• When *that* introduces a clause, translate as *que*:
   He said (that) he would come today
   Dijo que vendría hoy
   I don't think (that) it will rain tomorrow
   No creo que llueva mañana
! Unlike *that*, *que* cannot be omitted here.
• Translate as *de que* in phrases like *the idea/belief/hope that*:
   The idea that I have committed a crime is absurd
   La idea de que he cometido un delito es absurda
• If the *that* CLAUSE is the subject of another verb it is usual to translate *that* as *el que* rather than *que* especially if it starts the sentence:
   That he did not know surprised me
   (El) que no lo supiera me extrañó ◊ *Me extrañó (el) que no lo supiera*
! In all these cases where an opinion is expressed, the verb which follows *that* will be in the subjunctive.
   For further uses and examples, see main entry.

Thatcherite ['θætʃəraɪt] **1** ADJ thatcheriano.
  2 N thatcheriano *m*, -a *f*.
thatching ['θætʃɪŋ] N paja *f* (para techar).
thaw [θɔː] **1** N deshielo *m*. **2** VT deshelar, derretir; *(fig)* ablandar, hacer menos severo; **to ~ out** *meat etc* deshelar.
  3 VI deshelarse, derretirse; *(fig)* ablandarse, hacerse menos severo; *(person)* hacerse más afable, ir perdiendo su reserva; **to ~ out** deshelarse; **it is ~ing** deshiela.
the [ðiː, ðə] **1** DEF ART **(a)** el, la, (PL) los, las *(masculine singular* a + el = al, *eg* **to the man** al hombre; *masculine singular* de + el = del, *eg* **of the cat** del gato).
  (b) *('neuter')* lo; **~ good and ~ beautiful** lo bueno y lo bello; **within the realms of ~ possible** dentro de lo posible; **it is ~ unusual which counts** es lo insólito lo que importa.
  (c) *(special uses)* **Charles ~ Fifth** Carlos Quinto; **Philip ~ Second** Felipe Segundo; **~ Browns** los Brown; **~ cheek of it!** ¡qué frescura!; **oh ~ pain!** ¡ay qué dolor!; **how's ~ leg?** ¿cómo va la pierna?; **he hasn't ~ sense to understand** no tiene bastante inteligencia para comprender; **the child has ~ measles** el niño tiene sarampión; **2 dollars ~ pound** 2 dólares la libra.
  (d) *(emphatic)* **he's ~ man for the job** es él hombre ideal para el puesto; es él hombre más indicado para el puesto; **you don't mean ~ Professor Bloggs?** ¿quieres decir el célebre profesor Bloggs?, ¿quieres decir el profesor Bloggs de que se habla tanto?; **it was ~ colour of 1991** fue el color que estaba tan de moda en 1991.
  2 ADV: **~ more he works the more he earns** cuanto más trabaja (tanto) más gana; **~ sooner ~ better** cuanto antes mejor; **it will be all ~ better** será tanto mejor.
theatre, *(US)* **theater** ['θɪətəʳ] N teatro *m (also fig, Mil etc)*; *(lecture ~)* aula *f*; **~ of the absurd** teatro *m* de lo absurdo; **to go to the ~** ir al teatro.
theatregoer, *(US)* **theatergoer** ['θɪətə,gəʊəʳ] N aficionado *m*, -a *f* al teatro.
theatre-in-the-round ['θɪətərɪnðə'raʊnd] N teatro *m* de escenario central.
theatreland ['θɪətəlænd] N teatrolandia *f*.
theatrical [θɪ'ætrɪkəl] **1** ADJ teatral; *company etc* de teatro; *person's manner* teatral; **~ agent** agente *mf* de teatro; **~ company** compañía *f* de teatro.
  2 NPL: **~s** funciones *fpl* teatrales; **amateur ~s** teatro *m* de aficionados.
theatricality [θɪ,ætrɪ'kælɪtɪ] N teatralidad *f*, lo teatral.
theatrically [θɪ'ætrɪkəlɪ] ADV teatralmente, de modo teatral; de modo exagerado.
theatrics [θɪ'ætrɪks] NPL *(fig: pej)* teatro *msg*.
Thebes [θiːbz] N Tebas *f*.
thee [ðiː] PRON (†† *or poet)* te; *(after prep)* ti; **with ~** contigo.
theft [θeft] N hurto *m*, robo *m*.
their [ðeəʳ] POSS ADJ su(s).
theirs [ðeəz] POSS PRON (el) suyo, (la) suya *etc*.
theism ['θiːɪzəm] N teísmo *m*.
theist ['θiːɪst] N teísta *mf*.
theistic [θiː'ɪstɪk] ADJ teísta.
them [ðem, ðəm] PRON *(acc)* los, las; *(dat)* les; *(after prep)* ellos, ellas.
thematic [θɪ'mætɪk] ADJ temático.
theme [θiːm] N tema *m*.
themed [θiːmd] ADJ *(esp Brit)* place, event temático.
theme-park ['θiːmpɑːk] N parque *m* museo.
themesong ['θiːmsɒŋ] N, **themetune** ['θiːmtjuːn] N motivo *m* principal.
themselves [ðəm'selvz] PRON *(subject)* ellos mismos, ellas mismas; *(acc, dat)* se; *(after prep)* sí (mismos, mismas); V **oneself**.
then [ðen] **1** ADV **(a)** *(at that time)* entonces; en ese momento; *(in those days)* en aquella época; **it was ~ 8 o'clock** eran las 8, eran las 8 ya; **he was ~ a little-known writer** en aquella época era un escritor poco conocido; **~ and there** en el acto, en seguida; **before ~** antes; hasta entonces, hasta ese momento; **by ~** para entonces, antes de eso; **even ~ it didn't work** aun así, no funcionaba; **from ~ on, since ~** desde entonces, desde aquel momento, a partir de entonces; **just ~** en ese mismo momento; precisamente entonces; **until ~** hasta entonces.
  (b) *(next, afterwards)* luego, después; **~ we went to Jaca** luego fuimos a Jaca; **first this ~ that** primero esto y luego aquello; **what ~?, and ~ what?** ¿qué pasó después?, y después ¿qué?
  (c) *(in that case)* pues, en ese caso; **what ~?** ¿y qué?, ¿qué más?; **can't you hear me, ~?** ¿es que no me oyes?; **~ what do you want?** ¿pues que es lo que quieres?; **but ~ we shall lose money** pero en ese caso perdemos dinero; **but ~, you can't tell** pero vamos, nadie lo sabe.
  (d) *(furthermore)* además; **and ~ again he's a red** y además es un rojo.
  2 CONJ pues, en ese caso; por tanto; entonces; **what do you want**

me to do ~? ¿pues qué quieres que haga yo?; **~ you don't want it?** ¿así que no lo quieres?, ¿con qué no lo quieres?; **well ~** ahora bien, pues; V **now 1 (d)**.
  3 ADV entonces, de entonces; **the ~ King of Slobodia** el entonces rey de Eslobodia, el rey de Eslobodia de entonces; **the ~ existing government** el gobierno que existía en esa época, el gobierno de entonces.

| THEN | *see also main entry* |

Time
- When *then* means "at that time", translate using *entonces*:
    It was then that she heard Gwen cry out
    Fue entonces cuando oyó gritar a Gwen
    I hadn't heard about it till then
    Hasta entonces no había oído hablar de ello
- Alternatively, use expressions like *en aquella época* to refer to a particular period or *en ese momento* to refer to a particular moment:
    ...my sister, who was then about 17...
    ...mi hermana, que en aquella época tenía unos 17 años... or *que tenía entonces unos 17 años...*
- When *then* is used in the sense of "next", translate using *luego* or *después*:
    At first he refused but then he changed his mind
    Primero se negó, pero luego o después cambió de opinión
    He went to Julián's house and then to the chemist's
    Fue a casa de Julián y luego o después a la farmacia

Reason
- When *then* means "so" or "in that case", translate using *entonces* (placed at the beginning of the sentence):
    "I have a headache" - "So you won't be coming to the theatre, then?"
    "Me duele la cabeza" - "¿Entonces no vienes al teatro?"
    Then you'll already know about the bomb
    Entonces ya sabrás lo de la bomba
- Alternatively, use *pues entonces*:
    Pues entonces ya sabrás lo de la bomba
- In more formal and written language, use *por (lo) tanto* or alternatively, *pues*, particularly when you are introducing a summary or a conclusion. These often appear between commas:
    Their decision, then, was based on a detailed analysis of the situation
    Su decisión, pues, or *Su decisión, por (lo) tanto, estaba basada en un análisis detallado de la situación*
    For further uses and examples, see main entry.

---

thence [ðens] ADV *(liter)* **(a)** *(from that place)* de allí, desde allí. **(b)** *(therefore)* por eso, por consiguiente.
thenceforth [,ðens'fɔːθ] ADV, **thenceforward** [,ðens'fɔːwəd] ADV *(liter)* desde entonces, de allí en adelante, a partir de entonces.
theocracy [θɪ'ɒkrəsɪ] N teocracia *f*.
theocratic [θɪə'krætɪk] ADJ teocrático.
theodolite [θɪ'ɒdəlaɪt] N teodolito *m*.
theologian [θɪə'ləʊdʒɪən] N teólogo *m*, -a *f*.
theological [θɪə'lɒdʒɪkəl] ADJ teológico; **~ college** seminario *m*.
theologist [θɪ'ɒlədʒɪst] N teólogo *m*, -a *f*.
theology [θɪ'ɒlədʒɪ] N teología *f*.
theorem ['θɪərəm] N teorema *m*.
theoretic(al) [θɪə'retɪk(əl)] ADJ teórico.
theoretically [θɪə'retɪkəlɪ] ADV teóricamente, en teoría.
theoretician [,θɪərə'tɪʃən] N, **theorist** ['θɪərɪst] N teórico *m*, -a *f*, teorizante *mf*.
theorize ['θɪəraɪz] VI teorizar.
theorizer ['θɪəraɪzəʳ] N teorizante *mf*.
▼ **theory** ['θɪərɪ] N teoría *f*; **in ~** teóricamente, en teoría.
theosophical [θɪə'sɒfɪkəl] ADJ teosófico.
theosophy [θɪ'ɒsəfɪ] N teosofía *f*.
therapeutic(al) [,θerə'pjuːtɪk(əl)] ADJ terapéutico.
therapeutics [,θerə'pjuːtɪks] N terapéutica *f*.
therapist ['θerəpɪst] N terapeuta *mf*.
therapy ['θerəpɪ] N terapia *f*, terapéutica *f*.
there [ðeəʳ] **1** ADV **(a)** *(place)* allí; allá; *(~ near you)* ahí; **back ~, down ~, over ~** allá; **12 kilometres ~ and back** 12 kilómetros ida y vuelta; **it's in ~** está allí dentro; **when we left ~** cuando partimos de allí.
  (b) *(less precisely)* ahí; **mind out ~!** ¡ojo!, ¡cuidado!; ¡cuidado ahí!; **make way ~!** ¡abran paso!, ¡atención!; **hurry up ~!** ¡despabílate!; ¡menearse!; **you ~!** ¡eh, usted!; **~ we differ** en eso no estamos de acuerdo, en eso discrepamos; **'~ you are'**, he said, handing the book over 'ahí lo tienes', dijo, entregando el libro; **if the demand is ~, the product will appear** si existe la demanda, aparecerá el producto; **~ and then** en el acto, en seguida; **~ again** por otra parte; **~ you go again**

vuelves a las tuyas; **it wasn't what I wanted, but ~ you go*** no era lo que buscaba, pero ¿qué le vamos a hacer?; **~ you are, what did I tell you!**, ¿ves? es lo que te dije; **~ you are wrong** en eso te equivocas; **~'s the bus** ahí está el autobús; ya viene el autobús; **~ she comes** ya viene; **~ we were, stuck** así que nos encontramos allí sin podernos mover.

(c) ~ **is**, ~ **are** hay; **~ will be** habrá; **~ were 10** había 10, hubo 10; **how many are ~?** ¿cuántos hay?; **~ was laughter at this** en esto hubo risas; **~ was singing and dancing** se cantó y se bailó; **~ is a pound missing** falta una libra; **~ is no wine left** no hay vino, no queda vino; **are ~ any bananas?** ¿hay plátanos?

(d) (*) **he's all ~** es la mar de listo*; **he's not all ~** le falta un tornillo*.

2 INTERJ ¡vaya!; **~**, **~** (comforting) ¡cálmate!, ¡ya, ya!, ¡no es nada!, ¡no te preocupes!; **~, drink this** bebe esto; **but ~, what's the use?** pero ¡vamos!, es inútil; **I'm not going, so ~!*** pues no voy, y fastídiate*.

┌───┐
│ ┌─ THERE IS, THERE ARE ─┐   ┌─ see also main entry ─┐ │

● Unlike *there is/are etc*, *hay, hubo, había, ha habido etc* do not change to reflect number:
    There were two kidnappings and a murder
    Hubo dos secuestros y un asesinato
    Will there be many students at the party?
    ¿Habrá muchos estudiantes en la fiesta?

● To translate *there must be, there may be, etc*, you can use *tiene que haber, debe (de) haber, puede haber, etc* although other constructions will also be possible:
    There may be a strike
    Puede haber or *Puede que haya huelga*
    There must be all sorts of things we could do
    Tiene que haber muchas cosas que podamos hacer

● If *there is/there are* is followed by *the*, you should normally not use *hay etc*. Use *estar* instead:
    And then of course there are the neighbours to consider
    Están también los vecinos, a los que hay que tener en cuenta
    There is also the question of the money transfer
    Está también la cuestión de la transferencia del dinero

● *Hay etc* should only be used to talk about existence and occurrence. Don't use it to talk about location. Use *estar* instead to say where things are:
    After the shop there's the bus station
    Después de la tienda está la estación de autobuses

● Don't use *hay etc* to translate phrases like *there are 4 of us, there will be 6 of them*. Instead, use *ser* in the relevant person:
    There are 4 of us
    Somos 4
    There will be 6 of them
    Serán 6

● Remember to use *que* in the construction *hay algo que hacer* (*there is sth to do*):
    There is a lot to do
    Hay mucho que hacer
    What is there to do?
    ¿Qué hay que hacer?
    For further uses and examples, see main entry at **there**.
└───┘

thereabouts [ˈðɛərəbaʊts] ADV por ahí, allí cerca; **12 or ~** 12 más o menos, alrededor de 12; **£5 or ~** 5 libras o así.

thereafter [ðɛərˈɑːftəʳ] ADV después, después de eso.

thereat [ðɛərˈæt] ADV (thereupon) con eso, acto seguido; (for that reason) por eso, por esa razón.

thereby [ˈðɛəˈbaɪ] ADV por eso, de ese modo; por esa razón; **it does not ~ become easier** no por eso se hace más fácil; **~ hangs a tale** eso tiene su cuento.

▼ **therefore** [ˈðɛəfɔːʳ] ADV por tanto, por lo tanto, por consiguiente; por esta razón; **~ X = 4** luego X vale 4; **I think, ~ I am** pienso, luego existo.

therefrom [ðɛəˈfrɒm] ADV de ahí, de allí.

therein [ðɛərˈɪn] ADV (inside) allí dentro; (in this regard) en eso, en esto, en este respecto; **~ lies the danger** ahí está el peligro, en eso consiste el peligro.

thereof [ðɛərˈɒv] ADV de eso, de esto; de lo mismo.

thereon [ðɛərˈɒn] ADV = thereupon.

there's [ðɛəz] = there is; there has.

Theresa [tɪˈriːzə] NF Teresa.

thereto [ðɛəˈtuː] ADV a eso, a ello.

thereunder [ˌðɛərˈʌndəʳ] ADV (formal) allí expuesto.

thereupon [ˌðɛərəˈpɒn] ADV (at that point) en eso, con eso; acto seguido, en seguida; (consequently) por tanto; por consiguiente.

therewith [ðɛəˈwɪθ] ADV con eso, con lo mismo.

therm [θɜːm] N termia f.

thermal [ˈθɜːməl] **1** ADJ termal; térmico; **~ baths**, **~ spring** termas

fpl; **~ blanket** manta f térmica; **~ paper** papel m térmico; **~ printer** termoimpresora f; **~ reactor** reactor m térmico; **~ underwear** ropa f interior térmica. **2** N térmica f, corriente f térmica.

thermic [ˈθɜːmɪk] ADJ térmico.

thermionic [ˌθɜːmɪˈɒnɪk] ADJ termiónico; **~ valve** lámpara f termiónica.

thermo... [ˈθɜːməʊ] PREF termo...

thermocouple [ˈθɜːməʊˌkʌpl] N termopar m, par m térmico.

thermodynamic [ˈθɜːməʊdaɪˈnæmɪk] **1** ADJ termodinámico. **2** N: **~s** termodinámica f.

thermoelectric [ˈθɜːməʊˈlektrɪk] ADJ termoeléctrico; **~ couple** par m termoeléctrico.

thermometer [θəˈmɒmɪtəʳ] N termómetro m.

thermonuclear [ˈθɜːməʊˈnjuːklɪəʳ] ADJ termonuclear.

thermopile [ˈθɜːməʊpaɪl] N termopila f.

thermoplastic [ˌθɜːməʊˈplæstɪk] N termoplástico m.

Thermopylae [θɜːˈmɒpɪliː] N Termópilas fpl.

Thermos [ˈθɜːməs] ® N (Brit: also **~ bottle**, **~ flask**) termos ® m, termo m.

thermosetting [ˌθɜːməʊˈsetɪŋ] ADJ: **~ plastics** plásticos mpl termoestables.

thermostat [ˈθɜːməstæt] N termostato m.

thermostatic [ˌθɜːməsˈtætɪk] ADJ termostático.

thesaurus [θɪˈsɔːrəs] N tesoro m; diccionario m; antología f.

these [ðiːz] (PL of **this**) **1** DEM ADJ m: estos; f: estas. **2** DEM PRON m: éstos; f: éstas; V also **this**.

Theseus [ˈθiːsjuːs] NM Teseo.

thesis [ˈθiːsɪs] N, PL **theses** [ˈθiːsiːz] tesis f.

Thespian [ˈθespɪən] (liter, hum) **1** ADJ de Tespis; (fig) dramático, trágico. **2** N actor m, actriz f.

Thespis [ˈθespɪs] NM Tespis.

Thessalonians [ˌθesəˈləʊnɪənz] NPL tesalonios mpl.

Thessaly [ˈθesəlɪ] N Tesalia f.

Thetis [ˈθiːtɪs] NF Tetis.

they [ðeɪ] PRON ellos, ellas; **~ who** los que, quienes.

they'd [ðeɪd] = they would; they had.

they'll [ðeɪl] = they will, they shall.

they're [ðɛəʳ] = they are.

they've [ðeɪv] = they have.

thiamine [ˈθaɪəmiːn] N tiamina f.

thick [θɪk] **1** ADJ **(a)** (of solid) espeso; thread, stroke etc grueso; book, file etc abultado; **it is 2 metres ~** tiene 2 metros de espesor; **on ice only 4 centimetres ~** sobre hielo de solamente 4 centímetros de espesor; **to give sb a ~ ear** (Brit*) pegar a uno.

(b) (dense) forest, vegetation etc espeso, denso; growth tupido; eyebrows, beard poblado; **the leaves were ~ on the ground** había una capa espesa de hojas en el suelo; **bodies lay ~ on the road** había cadáveres por doquier en la carretera; **the field is ~ with strawberries** el campo abunda en fresas; **the place will be ~ with tourists** el sitio estará atestado de turistas.

(c) (of liquid) (cloudy) turbio, (stiff) viscoso; cream, gravy etc espeso; fog, smoke denso, espeso; air viciado; voice velado, apagado, poco distinto; accent cerrado; **the air is pretty ~ in here** la atmósfera está bastante cargada aquí, aquí huele a encerrado; **the air was ~ with insults** el aire estaba lleno de insultos.

(d) (Brit*: stupid) torpe, lerdo; **he's as ~ as two (short) planks** es más corto que las mangas de un chaleco.

(e) (*: of relationship) íntimo; **they're very ~** son íntimos amigos, están a partir un piñón; **they're as ~ as thieves** son uña y carne; **A is ~ with B** A tiene mucha intimidad con B.

(f) (*: unjust) **it's a bit ~!** (Brit) ¡no hay derecho!, ¡esto es injusto!; **it's a bit ~ to have to** + infin es injusto tener que + infin.

2 ADV: **to spread butter ~** poner mucha mantequilla; **put the paint on ~** ponga una buena capa de pintura; **they cut the bread very ~** sirven el pan en trozos muy gruesos; **the blows fell ~ and fast upon him** le llovieron los golpes encima; **to lay it on ~*** V **lay on 1 (b)**.

3 N **(a)** in the **~ of battle** en lo más reñido de la batalla; **in the ~ of the crowd** en medio de la multitud; **he likes to be in the ~ of things** le gusta tener una vida muy activa, le gusta estar en el centro de las actividades, le gusta estar muy metido en todo.

(b) to **stick to sb through ~ and thin** apoyar a uno contra viento y marea, apoyar a uno incondicionalmente.

thicken [ˈθɪkən] **1** VT espesar, hacer más espeso. **2** VI **(a)** (lit) espesarse, hacerse más espeso; hacerse más denso; (Culin) espesarse. **(b)** (plot) complicarse, enmarañarse más.

thickener [ˈθɪkənəʳ] N espesador m.

thicket [ˈθɪkɪt] N matorral m, espesura f.

thickheaded* [ˈθɪkˈhedɪd] ADJ (Brit) torpe, lerdo; terco.

thickheadedness* [ˈθɪkˈhedɪdnɪs] N torpeza f; terquedad f.

thickie*, thicky* ['θɪkɪ] N bobo *m*, -a *f*.

thick-lipped ['θɪk'lɪpt] ADJ de labios gruesos, bezudo.

thickly ['θɪklɪ] ADV espesamente; gruesamente; *speak* con voz apagada, indistintamente; **~ populated areas** regiones *fpl* densamente pobladas; **bread ~ spread with butter** pan *m* con mucha mantequilla, pan *m* con una buena capa de mantequilla; **the snow was falling ~** nevaba muchísimo.

thickness ['θɪknɪs] N espesura *f*; densidad *f*; grueso *m*; (*in measuring*) espesor *m*; grosor *m*; **what is the ~ of the snow?** ¿cuánta nieve hay?; **boards of the same ~** tablas *fpl* del mismo espesor.

thicko* ['θɪkəʊ] = **thickie**.

thickset ['θɪk'set] ADJ rechoncho, grueso.

thickskinned ['θɪk'skɪnd] ADJ (*fig*) insensible, duro.

thief [θiːf] N, PL **thieves** [θiːvz] ladrón *m*, -ona *f*; **stop ~!** ¡al ladrón!; **to set a ~ to catch a ~** poner a pillo pillo y medio.

thieve [θiːv] VTI hurtar, robar.

thievery ['θiːvərɪ] N hurto *m*, robo *m*, latrocinio *m*.

thieving ['θiːvɪŋ] [1] ADJ ladrón, largo de uñas.

   [2] N hurto *m*, robo *m*, latrocinio *m*.

thievish ['θiːvɪʃ] ADJ ladrón; **to have ~ tendencies** ser largo de uñas.

thievishness ['θiːvɪʃnɪs] N propensión *f* a robar.

thigh [θaɪ] N muslo *m*.

thighbone ['θaɪbəʊn] N fémur *m*.

thimble ['θɪmbl] N (*Sew*) dedal *m*; (*Naut*) guardacabo *m*.

thimbleful ['θɪmblfʊl] N dedada *f*; **just a ~** unas gotas nada más.

thin [θɪn] [1] ADJ (a) *materials* delgado; *clothing, covering* ligero; *veil etc* transparente; diáfano; *layer* tenue, fino, delgado; *person* flaco; **with ~ legs** con piernas flacas; **to be as ~ as a rake** (*or* **lath** *or* **rail** *US*) estar en los huesos; **to get ~ner, to grow ~ner** enflaquecer.

(b) *hair* ralo; *crop, crowd, population* poco denso, escaso; **doctors are ~ on the ground** hay pocos médicos, escasean los médicos; **the wheat is ~ this year** este año hay poco trigo; **he's getting ~ on top** le escasea el pelo por encima, está un poco calvo.

(c) *liquid* poco denso; *soup, wine* aguado; que más bien parece ser agua; *scent, sound* tenue; *air, light* tenue, sutil; *voice* delgado; **in a ~ voice** con un hilo de voz; **at 20,000 metres the air is ~** a los 20.000 metros el aire está enrarecido; *see also* **air**.

(d) *excuse etc* poco convincente, flojo; **to have a ~ time*** pasarlo mal, pasar por un período difícil; **they gave him a ~ time of it*** hicieron sufrir al pobre, le hicieron sudar la gota gorda*; **my patience is wearing ~** se me agota la paciencia; **that excuse is wearing a bit ~** ese pretexto está resultando inaceptable; **the joke is wearing ~** el chiste ya no tiene gracia.

   [2] ADV: **to spread butter ~** poner poca mantequilla; **they cut the bread very ~** sirven el pan en trozos muy delgados.

   [3] VT: **to ~ paint (down)** desleír la pintura, diluir la pintura; **to ~ soup (down)** aguar la sopa.

   [4] VI (*slim*) adelgazar(se), (*and weaken*) enflaquecer; (*crowd etc*) hacerse menos denso, aclararse; (*number etc*) reducirse; **his hair is ~ning** está perdiendo el pelo.

◆**thin down** [1] VT: **to ~ sb down** adelgazar a uno, hacer que uno enflaquezca; *see also* **thin 3**.

   [2] VI adelgazar.

◆**thin out** [1] VT *plants etc* entresacar, aclarar; *crowd, number, army etc* reducir, mermar.

   [2] VI: **the forest starts to ~ out here** aquí el bosque empieza a ser menos denso.

thine [ðaɪn] POSS PRON (††) (el) tuyo, (la) tuya *etc*; **mine and ~** lo mío y lo tuyo; **for thee and ~** para ti y los tuyos; **what is mine is ~** lo que es mío es tuyo.

thing [θɪŋ] N (a) (*object*) cosa *f*; objeto *m*; artículo *m*; **~s** (*belongings*) cosas *fpl*, efectos *mpl*; (*equipment*) avíos *mpl*, equipo *m*; (*clothes*) ropa *f*, trapos *mpl*; (*luggage*) equipaje *m*; **~s of value** objetos *mpl* de valor; **a ~ of beauty** un objeto bello; **my painting ~s** mis avíos de pintar; **tea ~s** servicio *m* de té; **to wash up the tea ~s** lavar la vajilla; **where shall I put my ~s?** ¿dónde pongo mis cosas?; **to pack up one's ~s** hacer las maletas; **you must be seeing ~s** estás viendo visiones; **to take off one's ~s** desnudarse, quitarse la ropa.

(b) (*person*) ser *m*, criatura *f*; (*pej*) sujeto *m*; (*animal*) criatura *f*; **you poor ~!, poor old ~!** ¡pobrecito!; **he's a poor old ~ now** ahora no vale para nada; **you beastly** (*or* **horrid, rotten** *etc*) **~!** ¡canalla!; **how are you, old ~?†** ¿qué tal, hijo?

(c) (*matter, circumstance etc*) cosa *f*; asunto *m*; **the main ~** lo más importante, lo esencial; **above all ~s** ante todo, sobre todo; **for one ~** en primer lugar; **and for another ~** ... y además ..., y por otra parte ...; **a gentleman in all ~s** un caballero en todos los aspectos; **no such ~!** ¡no hay tal!; ¡ni hablar!; **what with one ~ and another** entre unas cosas y otras; **one ~ or the other** ... una de dos ...; **it's neither one ~ nor the other** no es ni lo uno ni lo otro; **first ~** (**in the morning**) a primera hora (de la mañana); **you don't know the first ~ about it** no sabes nada en absoluto de esto; **last ~** (**at night**) a última hora (de la noche); antes de acostarse; **the first ~ to do is**

... lo primero que hay que hacer es ...; **that's the last ~ we want** eso es lo que queremos menos; **the best ~ would be to** + *infin* lo mejor sería + *infin*; **the next best ~** lo mejor después de eso; (**the**) **next ~ I knew, he'd gone** de repente, resultó que se había ido; **it's a good ~ that** ... menos mal que ...; **the good ~ about it is that** ... lo bueno es que ...; **to be on to a good ~** haber encontrado algo bueno; ir por buen camino; **it's finished and a good ~ too** se acabó y me alegro de ello; **it was a close ~, it was a near ~** (*race*) fue una carrera muy reñida; (*accident*) por poco chocamos, casi chocamos; (*escape*) escapé (*etc*) por un pelo; **it's the real ~** es auténtico; **this is the real ~ at last** por fin lo tenemos sin trampa ni cartón; **it's the very ~!, it's just the ~!** ¡es exactamente lo que necesitábamos!; **it's one ~ to buy it, quite another to make it work** es fácil comprarlo, pero no es tan fácil hacerlo funcionar; **it's just one of those ~s** son cosas que pasan, son cosas de la vida; **that's the ~ for me** eso es lo que me hace falta; **he's got a ~ going with her*** se entiende con ella; **he's got a ~ for her*** está colado por ella*; **he had a ~ with her 2 years ago*** se lió con ella hace 2 años*; **the ~ is** ... el caso es que ..., es que ...; **the ~ is this** ... la dificultad es que ...; se trata de saber si ...; **the ~ is to sell your car first** conviene vender primero tu coche; **the only ~ is that** it no hay más remedio que pintarlo; **the play's the ~** lo que importa es la representación; **this is too much of a good ~** esto es demasiado; **as ~s are** tal como están las cosas; **how are ~s?** ¿qué tal?; **how are ~s with you?** ¿qué tal te va?; ¿cómo te va eso?; **~s are going badly** las cosas van mal; **that's how ~s are** así están las cosas; **with ~s as they are** tal como están las cosas; **I've done a silly ~** he hecho algo tonto; **we had hoped for better ~s** habíamos esperado algo mejor; **I don't know a ~ about cars** no sé nada en absoluto de coches; **I didn't know a ~ for that exam** para ese examen yo estaba pez; **she knows a good ~ when she sees it** sabe obrar de acuerdo con su propio interés; **he knows a ~ or two** sabe cuántos son cinco; **he makes a good ~ out of it** sabe sacar provecho de ello, con eso tiene un buen negocio; **he made a great ~ out of the accident** exageró mucho el accidente; explotó mucho las consecuencias del accidente; **don't make a ~ of it!** ¡no exageres!, ¡no es para tanto!; **to make a mess of ~s** estropearlo, hacerlo todo mal; **did you ever see such a ~?** ¿se vio jamás tal cosa?; **to try to be all ~s to all men** tratar de serlo todo para todos.

(d) (*fashion*) **the latest ~ in hats** la última moda del sombrero, el sombrero según la moda actual; **it's quite the ~** está muy de moda.

(e) (*socially acceptable ~*) **it's not the** (**done**) **~** eso no se hace, eso no está bien visto; **to do the right ~** obrar bien, obrar honradamente.

(f) (*obsession*) obsesión *f*; manía *f*; **she has a ~ about snakes** está obsesionada por las culebras, le obsesionan las culebras; **he's got a ~ about me** me tiene manía.

(g) (*: *activity, preference*) **his ~ is fast cars** lo suyo son los coches rápidos; **it's not my ~** no es lo mío; **you can see it's not her ~** se ve que no es lo suyo; **to do one's** (**own**) **~** ir a su aire, ir a lo suyo.

thingumabob* ['θɪŋəmɪbɒb] N, **thingamajig*** ['θɪŋəmɪdʒɪg] N, **thingummy*** ['θɪŋəmɪ] N, **thingy*** ['θɪŋɪ] N (*thing*) cosa *f*, chisme *m*; (*person*) fulano *m*, ése *m*, ésa *f*; **old ~ with the specs** fulano el de las gafas.

▼ **think** [θɪŋk] (*irr*: PRET AND PTP **thought**) [1] VT (a) (*believe*) pensar, creer; considerar; opinar; **I ~ so** creo que sí; **I ~ not** creo que no; **I thought so, I thought as much** ya me lo figuraba; lo había previsto ya; **I shouldn't ~ so** creo que no; **I should ~ so too!** ¡haces muy bien!; ¡ya era hora!; ¡buena falta te hacía!; **and it was free, I don't ~!*** ¿gratuito? ¡ni pensarlo!; **I ~** (**that**) **it is true** creo que es verdad; **I don't ~ it can be done** no creo que se pueda hacer, no creo que sea factible; **so you ~ that** ...? ¿así que crees que ...?; **that's what you ~!** ¡(que) te crees tú eso!; **what do you ~ I should do?** ¿qué crees (tú) que debiera hacer?, ¿qué me aconsejas hacer?; **I would have thought that** ... hubiera creído que ...; **I never thought that** ... nunca pensé que ...; **one might ~ that** ... podría creerse que ...; **anyone would ~ he was dying** cualquiera diría que se estaba muriendo; **who'd have thought it?** ¿quién lo diría?; **I ~ it very difficult** lo creo (*or* veo) muy difícil; **I don't ~ it at all likely** lo creo muy poco probable; **everyone thought him mad** todos le tenían por loco; **they are thought to be poor** se cree que son pobres; **you must ~ me very rude** vas a creer que soy muy descortés; **he ~s himself very clever** se cree la mar de listo; **she's very pretty, don't you ~?** es muy guapa, ¿no crees?

(b) (*conceive, imagine*) pensar, creer; imaginar; **who do you ~ you are?** ¿quién se cree Vd que es?; **who do you ~ you are to come marching in?** y Vd ¿qué derecho cree tener para entrar aquí tan fresco?; **~ what we could do with that house!** ¡imagina lo que podríamos hacer con esa casa!; **to ~ that** ...! ¡y pensar que ...!; **to ~ she once slept here!** ¡pensar que ella durmió aquí una vez!; **I can't ~ what you mean** no llego a entender lo que quieres decir; **I can't ~ what he can want** no llego a comprender su motivo; **to ~ great thoughts** pensar cosas profundas, tener pensamientos profundos.

▼**(c)** *(be of opinion)* pensar; **she didn't know what to ~** no sabía a qué carta quedarse; no sabía a qué atenerse; **now I don't know what to ~** ahora estoy en duda; **what do you ~?** ¿qué te parece?; **what do you ~ about it?** ¿qué te parece (de esto)?; **see what you ~ about it and let me know** estúdialo y dime luego tu opinión; **what do you ~ of him?** ¿qué piensas de él?, ¿qué te parece él?, ¿qué concepto tienes de él?; **to ~ highly of sb** tener en mucho a uno; **to ~ little of sb** tener en poco a uno; **to ~ well of sb** tener una buena opinión de uno; **he is well thought of here** aquí se le estima mucho; **we don't ~ much of X** tenemos un concepto más bien bajo de X; **I don't ~ much of that cheese** no me gusta nada ese queso; **I told him what I thought of him** le dije la opinión que tenía de él; le dije un par de cosas.

(d) *(intend)* pensar; **to ~ to** + *infin* pensar + *infin*; **I came here ~ing to question you** vine aquí con la intención de hacerte unas preguntas.

(e) *(expect)* esperar; contar con; **I never thought to hear that from you** no esperaba nunca escuchar tales palabras de ti; **we little thought that ...** estábamos lejos de pensar que ...; **I didn't ~ to see you here** no contaba con verte aquí.

(f) *(remember)* **I didn't ~ to tell him** me olvidé de decírselo.

(g) *(of ideas occurring)* **I was ~ing that ...** se me ocurrió pensar que ...; **I didn't ~ to do it** no se me ocurrió hacerlo.

2 VI **(a)** *(gen)* pensar; meditar, reflexionar; discurrir, razonar; **I ~, therefore I am** pienso, luego existo; **he doesn't ~ coherently** no discurre bien; **to ~ (long and) hard** pensar mucho; **to act without ~ing** obrar sin reflexionar; **~ before you reply** reflexiona antes de contestar; **give me time to ~** dame tiempo para reflexionar; **now let me ~** déjame pensar; veamos, vamos a ver; **I'm sorry, I wasn't ~ing** lo siento, no me había fijado; **to ~ again, to ~ twice** pensar dos veces; volver a pensar, reflexionar; **~ again!** ¡medítalo!; **we didn't ~ twice about it** no vacilamos un instante, no había lugar a dudas; **to ~ aloud** pensar en alta voz, expresar lo que uno piensa; **to ~ about sth** pensar algo bien, considerar algo detenidamente, reflexionar sobre algo; consultar algo con la almohada; **I'll ~ about it** lo pensaré; **you just ~ about it!** ¡medítalo!; **you ~ about money too much** le das demasiada importancia al dinero; **to ~ for o.s.** pensar por sí mismo.

(b) *(devote thought to, remember)* **to ~ about** pensar en; **that is worth ~ing about** eso vale la pena de pensarlo; **there is much to ~ about** hay tantas cosas que tener en cuenta; **you've given us a lot to ~ about** nos has dado mucho en que pensar; **~ (about) what you have done** recapacita en lo que acabas de hacer; **I ~ of you always, I am always ~ing of you** pienso constantemente en ti; **~ of a number** piensa en un número; **~ of me tomorrow in the exam** ayúdame mañana en el examen con tus pensamientos; **one can't ~ of everything** es imposible atender a todo, es imposible preverlo todo; **(now I come) to ~ of it ...** ahora que lo pienso ..., por cierto ...; **I couldn't ~ of the right word** no pude recordar la palabra exacta; **what(ever) can you have been ~ing of?** ¿qué demonios pensabas hacer?; ¿cómo se te ocurrió hacer (*etc*) eso?; **his style makes me ~ of Baroja** su estilo me hace pensar en el de Baroja, su estilo recuerda el de Baroja.

(c) *(be sympathetic to, take into account)* **to ~ of** considerar, tener en cuenta; **to ~ of other people's feelings** tener en cuenta los sentimientos de los demás; **one has to ~ of the expense** hay que considerar lo que se gasta; **he ~s of nobody but himself** no piensa más que en sí mismo; **but she has children to ~ about** pero ella tiene que pensar en sus hijos.

(d) *(imagine)* imaginar(se); **~ of me in a bikini!** ¡imagíname en bikini!; **~ of what might have happened!** ¡piensa en lo que podía ocurrir!; **~ of the cost of it all!** ¡piensa en lo que cuesta todo esto!; **and to ~ of her going there alone!** ¡y pensar que ella fue allí sola!; **have you ever thought of going to Cuba?** ¿has pensado alguna vez en ir a Cuba?; **just ~!** ¡fíjate!, ¡imagínate!

(e) *(of ideas occurring)* **I was ~ing that ...** se me ocurrió pensar que ...; **I thought of learning Basque** pensaba aprender el vasco, se me ocurrió aprender el vasco; **don't you ever ~ of washing?** ¿no se te ocurre alguna vez lavarte?; **I was the one who thought of it first** fui yo quien tuve la idea primero; **what(ever) will he ~ of next?** ¿qué se le va a ocurrir en lo sucesivo?

3 N (*) **I'll have a ~ about it** lo pensaré; **I'll have a good ~ about it** lo pensaré mucho, lo estudiaré; **I was just having a quiet ~** meditaba tranquilamente; **you'd better have another ~** conviene volver a pensarlo, conviene reconsiderarlo; **then she's got another ~ coming** tendrá que desengañarse, le espera una sorpresa desagradable.

◆**think back** VI recordar; **try to ~ back** trata de recordar; **I ~ back to that moment when ...** recuerdo ese momento cuando ...

◆**think out** VT *plan etc* imaginar, idear; elaborar; *answer* meditar a fondo; descubrir (después de pensarlo mucho); *problem* estudiar, resolver (después de pensarlo mucho); **this needs ~ing out** esto hay

que pensarlo mucho; **a well thought out answer** una respuesta estudiada, una contestación razonada; **he ~s things out for himself** razona por sí mismo.

◆**think over** VT: **to ~ sth over** considerar algo detenidamente; reflexionar sobre algo; consultar algo con la almohada; **I'll ~ it over** lo pensaré; **~ it over!** ¡medítalo!

◆**think through** VT considerar detalladamente, estudiar con la mayor seriedad; **this plan has not been properly thought through** este proyecto no ha sido pensado con el debido cuidado.

◆**think up** VT imaginar, idear; *excuse* inventar; **who thought this one up?** ¿quién ideó esto?, ¿a quién se le ocurrió esto?

thinkable ['θɪŋkəbl] ADJ concebible; **is it ~ that ...?** ¿es concebible que + *subj*?, ¿se concibe que + *subj*?

thinker ['θɪŋkəʳ] N pensador *m*, -ora *f*.

thinking ['θɪŋkɪŋ] **1** ADJ pensante, que piensa; inteligente, racional; serio; **to any ~ person** para cualquier persona racional, para el que piensa; **the ~ person's novelist** el novelista para el lector inteligente.

2 N pensamiento *m*; *(thoughts collectively)* pensamientos *mpl*; **good ~!** ¡muy bien!, ¡genial!; **his way of ~** su modo de pensar; **to my way of ~** a mi juicio, en mi opinión.

think-piece ['θɪŋkpiːs] N *(Press)* artículo *m* de opinión.

think-tank ['θɪŋktæŋk] N grupo *m* de expertos; gabinete *m* de estrategia.

thin-lipped ['θɪn'lɪpt] ADJ de labios apretados.

thinly ['θɪnlɪ] ADV: **~ disguised as ...** ligeramente disfrazado de ...; **with ~ spread butter** con una capa delgada de mantequilla.

thinner ['θɪnəʳ] N disolvente *m*, diluyente *m*.

thinness ['θɪnnɪs] N delgadez *f*; flaqueza *f*; tenuidad *f*.

thin-skinned ['θɪn'skɪnd] ADJ de piel fina; *(fig)* sensible, demasiado sensible.

third [θɜːd] **1** ADJ tercero; **~ degree** *(US)* V degree (e); **~ estate** estado *m* llano; **~ party** tercera persona *f*, tercero *m*; **~-party insurance** seguro *m* de responsabilidad social, seguro *m* contra terceros; **~ person** tercera persona *f*; **~ time lucky!** ¡a la tercera va la vencida!; **T~ World** Tercer Mundo *m*; **~ world** ATTR tercermundista.

2 N **(a)** tercio *m*, tercera parte *f*; **two-~s of the votes** dos tercios de los votos; **two-~s of those present** las dos terceras partes de los asistentes.

(b) *(Mus)* tercera *f*.

(c) *(Brit Univ)* tercera clase *f*.

(d) *(Aut)* tercera velocidad *f*; **in ~** en tercera.

3 ADV en tercer lugar; **to travel ~** viajar en tercera clase.

third-class ['θɜːd'klɑːs] **1** ADJ de tercera clase; *(pej)* de tercera clase, de baja categoría.

2 ADV: **to travel ~** viajar en tercera.

3 N *(US Post)* tarifa *f* de impreso.

thirdly ['θɜːdlɪ] ADV en tercer lugar.

third-rate ['θɜːd'reɪt] ADJ de baja categoría.

thirst [θɜːst] **1** N sed *f*; **the ~ for** *(fig)* la sed de, el ansia de, el afán de; **to quench one's ~** apagar la sed.

2 VI: **to ~ for** *(fig)* tener sed de, ansiar.

thirstily ['θɜːstɪlɪ] ADV: **he drank ~** bebió como si tuviera mucha sed.

thirsty ['θɜːstɪ] ADJ sediento; *land* árido, que necesita regarse mucho; **to be ~** tener sed; **how ~ I am!** ¡qué sed tengo!; **it's ~ work** es un trabajo que da sed.

thirteen ['θɜː'tiːn] ADJ trece.

thirteenth ['θɜː'tiːnθ] ADJ decimotercio, decimotercero.

thirtieth ['θɜːtɪɪθ] ADJ trigésimo, treinta; **the ~ anniversary** el treinta aniversario.

thirty ['θɜːtɪ] ADJ treinta; **the thirties** *(eg 1930s)* los años treinta; **to be in one's thirties** tener más de treinta años.

thirtyish ['θɜːtɪɪʃ] ADJ treintañero, de unos treinta años.

thirty-second ['θɜːtɪ'sekənd] ADJ: **~ note** *(US)* fusa *f*.

this [ðɪs] (PL **these**) **1** DEM ADJ *m*: este; *f*: esta; **~ evening** esta tarde; **~ coming week** esta semana que viene; **~ day last year** hoy hace un año; **~ day fortnight** hoy a quince días, de hoy en quince días.

2 DEM PRON *m*: éste; *f*: ésta; *'neuter'*: esto; **~ is new** esto es nuevo; **like ~** así, de este modo; **it was like ~** te contaré la cosa como pasó; te diré lo que pasó; **we talked about ~ and that** hablamos de esto y lo otro; **what with ~, that and the other** con esto, lo otro y lo demás; **what's all ~?** ¿qué pasa?; **who's ~?** ¿quién es?; **~ is Joe** *(on telephone etc)* aquí Pepe, soy Pepe; **~ is Joe Soap** *(introduction)* quiero presentarle al señor Joe Soap; **~ is Tuesday** hoy es martes; **but ~ is May** pero estamos en mayo; **'but he's nearly bald' ... '~ is it'** 'pero está casi calvo' ... 'ahí está la dificultad'.

3 ADV: **~ far** tan lejos; **~ high** tan alto, así de alto *(and* V that **4**).

thistle ['θɪsl] N cardo *m*.

thistledown ['θɪsldaʊn] N vilano *m* (de cardo).

thistly ['θɪslɪ] ADJ *(prickly)* espinoso; *(full of thistles)* lleno de cardos; *problem etc* espinoso, erizado de dificultades.

thither† ['ðɪðəʳ] ADV allá.

▶ LANGUAGE IN USE: **think: 1c → 1.2, 6.1**

> **THIS**
>
> The masculine and feminine *pronouns* **éste** and **ésta** usually carry accents. In theory, this is to distinguish them from the masculine and feminine *adjectives*, **este** and **esta**. When there is no ambiguity, the accent can be omitted. The neuter pronoun does not have an accent as there is no neuter adjective with which to confuse it.

tho'* [ðəʊ] CONJ = **though**.

thole [θəʊl] N escálamo *m*.

Thomas ['tɒməs] NM Tomás; **Saint ~** Santo Tomás; **~ More** Tomás Moro.

Thomism ['tɒmɪzəm] N tomismo *m*.

Thomist ['tɒmɪst] [1] ADJ tomista.

   [2] N tomista *mf*.

thong [θɒŋ] N correa *f*.

Thor [θɔːr] N Tor *m*.

thoracic [θɔːˈræsɪk] ADJ torácico.

thorax ['θɔːræks] N tórax *m*.

thorium ['θɔːrɪəm] N torio *m*.

thorn [θɔːn] N espina *f* (*also fig*); **to be a ~ in the flesh of sb** ser una espina en el costado de uno.

thornbush ['θɔːnbʊʃ] N espino *m*.

thornless ['θɔːnlɪs] ADJ sin espinas.

thorn-tree ['θɔːntriː] N espino *m*.

thorny ['θɔːnɪ] ADJ espinoso (*also fig*).

thorough ['θʌrə] ADJ (*complete*) completo, cabal; acabado; (*not superficial*) minucioso, concienzudo, meticuloso; **he's very ~** es muy cuidadoso, es muy concienzudo; **to have a ~ knowledge of a region** conocer una región a fondo; **we made a ~ search** lo registramos minuciosamente; **there will be a ~ investigation into the charges** las acusaciones serán investigadas a fondo; **I felt a ~ idiot** me sentía totalmente imbécil; **the man's a ~ rogue** es un bribón redomado.

thoroughbred ['θʌrəbred] [1] ADJ de pura sangre.

   [2] N pura sangre *mf*.

thoroughfare ['θʌrəfɛər] N vía *f* pública; carretera *f*, calle *f*; **'no ~'** 'prohibido el paso', 'paso prohibido'.

thoroughgoing ['θʌrə,gəʊɪŋ] ADJ *person* cien por cien, de cuerpo entero; *examination etc* minucioso, a fondo.

thoroughly ['θʌrəlɪ] ADV: **to know sth ~** conocer algo a fondo; **to investigate sth ~** investigar algo a fondo; **he works ~** trabaja cuidadosamente, trabaja concienzudamente; **a ~ bad influence** una influencia totalmente mala; **a ~ stupid thing to do** una acción completamente estúpida.

thoroughness ['θʌrənɪs] N minuciosidad *f*, meticulosidad *f*; perfección *f*; **with great ~** con el mayor esmero, con todo cuidado.

those [ðəʊz] (PL *of* **that**) [1] DEM ADJ *m*: esos, (*more remote*) aquellos; *f*: esas, (*more remote*) aquellas.

   [2] DEM PRON *m*: ésos, (*more remote*) aquéllos; *f*: ésas, (*more remote*) aquéllas; **~ of he de**, la de; **~ which** los que, las que; **~ who** los que, las que, quienes; *see also* **that**.

thou¹ [ðaʊ] PRON (†) tú.

thou²* [θaʊ] ABBR *of* **thousand**.

though [ðəʊ] [1] CONJ aunque; si bien; **~ it was raining at the time** aunque llovía entonces; (**even**) **~ he doesn't want to** aunque no quiera; **as ~** como si + *subj*; **~ small it's good** aunque (es) pequeño es bueno; **strange ~ it may appear** aunque parezca extraño, por extraño que parezca; **what ~ there is no money?** (*liter*) ¿qué importa que no haya dinero?

   [2] ADV sin embargo; **it's not so easy, ~** sin embargo no es tan fácil; **did he ~?** ¿de veras?

thought [θɔːt] [1] PRET AND PTP *of* **think**.

   2 N (**a**) (*gen*) pensamiento *m*; idea *f*, concepto *m*; reflexión *f*, meditación *f*; consideración *f*; (*thoughtfulness*) solicitud *f*; **the ~ of Sartre** el pensamiento de Sartre; **happy ~** idea *f* luminosa; **that's a ~!** eso hay que tenerlo en cuenta; **after much ~, on second ~s** después de pensarlo bien, después de mucho pensar; **my ~s were elsewhere** pensaba en otra cosa; **his one ~ is to** + *infin* su único propósito es de + *infin*; **the very ~ frightens me** sólo pensar en ello me da miedo; **to collect one's ~s** orientarse, concentrarse; **let me collect my ~s** déjame pensar; **to give ~ to sth** pensar algo, meditar algo; considerar algo detenidamente; **we must give some ~ to the others** hay que tener en cuenta a los demás, conviene tener presentes a los demás; **I didn't give it another** (*or* **a second**) **~** no volví a pensar en ello; **don't give it another ~** no vuelvas a pensar en eso; **I was too busy to give it another** (*or* **a second**) **~** estaba demasiado ocupado para volver a pensar en eso; **he hasn't a ~ in his head** no tiene nada en la cabeza; **I had no ~ of offending you** no tenía la intención de ofenderle; **I had no ~ of such a thing** no se me había ocurrido tal cosa; **I once had ~s of marrying her** hace

tiempo pensaba casarme con ella; **then I had second ~s** luego tuve otra idea, mudé luego de parecer; **to be lost in ~** estar absorto en meditación; **perish the ~!** ¡ni por pensamiento!, ¡Dios me libre!; **to read sb's ~s** adivinar el pensamiento de uno; **to take ~ how to do sth** pensar cómo hacer algo; **to take no ~ for the morrow** no pensar en mañana, no preparar para el futuro.

   (**b**) (*fig*) pizca *f*, poquito *m*; **it's a ~ too bright** es un poquito claro.

thoughtful ['θɔːtfʊl] ADJ (*pensive*) pensativo, meditabundo; (*in character*) serio; (*kind*) atento, solícito, considerado; (*far-sighted*) clarividente, previsor; **how ~ of you!, that's very ~ of you!** ¡qué detalle!, ¡es Vd muy amable!; **he's a ~ boy** es un chico serio.

thoughtfully ['θɔːtfəlɪ] ADV pensativamente; seriamente; atentamente, solícitamente, con consideración; con clarividencia, con previsión; **'Yes', he said ~** 'Sí', dijo pensativo; **sb had ~ provided a cup** alguien había puesto amablemente una taza.

thoughtfulness ['θɔːtfʊlnɪs] N seriedad *f*; carácter *m* reflexivo; atención *f*, solicitud *f*, consideración *f*; clarividencia *f*, previsión *f*.

thoughtless ['θɔːtlɪs] ADJ *act* irreflexivo, descuidado; *person* inconsiderado, desconsiderado, inconsciente.

thoughtlessly ['θɔːtlɪslɪ] ADV sin pensar, irreflexivamente; inconscientemente; impensadamente, insensatamente; **to act ~** obrar con poca consideración, obrar sin pensar.

thoughtlessness ['θɔːtlɪsnɪs] N irreflexión *f*, descuido *m*; inconsideración *f*, inconsciencia *f*.

thought-out [,θɔːt'aʊt] ADJ (bien) pensado.

thought police ['θɔːtpəliːs] N policía *f* política.

thought-process ['θɔːt,prəʊses] N proceso *m* mental.

thought-provoking ['θɔːtprə,vəʊkɪŋ] ADJ que hace reflexionar.

thought-reader ['θɔːt,riːdər] N lector *m*, -ora *f* (*or* adivinador *m*, -ora *f*) de pensamientos.

thought-reading ['θɔːt,riːdɪŋ] N adivinación *f* de pensamientos.

thought-transference ['θɔːt,trænsfərəns] N transmisión *f* de pensamientos.

thousand ['θaʊzənd] [1] ADJ mil; **a ~, one ~** mil; **4 ~ specimens** cuatro mil ejemplares; **I've got a ~ and one things to do** tengo la mar de cosas que hacer*.

   [2] N mil *m*; (*more loosely*) millar *m*; **they sell them by the ~** los venden a millares; **they were there in ~s** los había a millares; **I've told you ~s of times** te lo he dicho mil veces.

thousandfold ['θaʊzəndfəʊld] [1] ADJ multiplicado por mil; de mil veces.

   [2] ADV mil veces.

thousandth ['θaʊzəntθ] [1] ADJ milésimo.

   [2] N milésimo *m*.

thraldom ['θrɔːldəm] N (*liter*) esclavitud *f*.

thrall [θrɔːl] N (*liter*) (*person*) esclavo *m*, -a *f*; (*state*) esclavitud *f*; **to be in ~ to** ser esclavo de; **to hold sb in ~** retener a uno en la esclavitud.

thrash [θræʃ] [1] VT (**a**) (*beat*) golpear; *person* apalear, (*as punishment*) azotar, zurrar; (*Sport etc*) dar una paliza a, cascar.

   (**b**) *legs etc* mover violentamente, agitar mucho.

   (**c**) (*Agr*) trillar.

   [2] N (*Brit‡*) guateque *m*, party *m*.

◆**thrash about** VI sacudirse, dar revueltas; revolcarse; debatirse; **he ~ed about with his stick** daba golpes por todos lados con su bastón; **they were ~ing about in the water** se estaban revolcando en el agua.

◆**thrash out** VT *problem, difficulty* resolver mediante larga discusión, discutir largamente.

thrashing ['θræʃɪŋ] N zurra *f*, paliza *f*; **to give sb a ~** zurrar a uno, dar una paliza a uno; **to give a team a ~** dar una paliza a un equipo.

thread [θred] [1] N (**a**) (*Sew etc*) hilo *m*; (*fibre*) hebra *f*, fibra *f*; (*of silkworm, spider etc*) hebra *f*; **to hang by a ~** pender de un hilo; **to lose the ~** (*of what one is saying*) perder el hilo (de su discurso); **to pick** (*or* **take**) **up the ~ again** coger el hilo, tomar el hilo.

   (**b**) (*of screw*) filete *m*, rosca *f*.

   (**c**) **~s*** (*US*) trapos* *mpl*.

   [2] VT *needle* enhebrar; *beads etc* ensartar; **to ~ one's way through** colarse a través de, abrirse paso por, lograr pasar por.

threadbare ['θredbɛər] ADJ raído, gastado; *excuse etc* flojo, poco convincente.

threadworm ['θredwɜːm] N lombriz *f* intestinal.

threat [θret] N amenaza *f*; **it is a grave ~ to ...** constituye una grave amenaza para ...

threaten ['θretn] [1] VT amenazar, proferir amenazas contra; acechar; **to ~ violence** amenazar con (la) violencia, amenazar con ponerse violento; **to ~ sb with sth** amenazar a uno con algo; **a species ~ed with extinction** una especie amenazada de extinción; **to ~ to** + *infin* amenazar con + *infin*; **to ~ to kill sb** amenazar con matar a uno; **it is ~ing to rain** amenaza llover.

   [2] VI amenazar.

threatening [ˈθretnɪŋ] ADJ amenazador, amenazante.

threateningly [ˈθretnɪŋlɪ] ADV de modo amenazador; *say etc* en tono amenazador.

three [θriː] **1** ADJ tres.
2 N tres *m*; **~'s a crowd** tres es muchedumbre.

┌─────────────────┐
│ **THREE RS** │
└─────────────────┘

ⓘ *La expresión* **the three Rs** *hace referencia a los tres aspectos que se consideran fundamentales en educación:* **reading, writing, and arithmetic** *(lectura, escritura y aritmética). La expresión, que tiene su origen en la forma humorística en la que se escribe a veces la frase:* **reading,'riting, and 'rithmetic,** *se menciona a menudo cuando se habla de la necesidad de mejorar la calidad de la enseñanza.*

three-act [ˈθriːækt] ADJ *play* de tres actos, en tres actos.

three-colour(ed), (*US*) **three-color(ed)** [ˈθriːkʌləd] ADJ ATTR de tres colores, tricolor.

three-cornered [ˈθriːkɔːnəd] ADJ triangular; **~ hat** tricornio *m*, sombrero *m* de tres picos.

three-D [ˈθriːdiː] **1** ADJ tridimensional.
2 N: **in ~** en tres dimensiones.

three-day eventing [ˌθriːdeɪˈventɪŋ] N concurso *m* completo (de hípica).

three-decker [ˈθriːdekəʳ] N (*Naut*) barco *m* de tres cubiertas; (*Liter*) novela *f* de tres tomos; (*Culin*) sándwich *m* de tres pisos.

three-dimensional [ˈθriːdɪˈmenʃənl] ADJ (ABBR **3-D**) tridimensional.

threefold [ˈθriːfəʊld] **1** ADJ triple.
2 ADV tres veces.

three-legged [ˈθriːlegɪd] ADJ de tres piernas; *race, stool* de tres patas.

threepence [ˈθrepəns] N (*Brit*) 3 peniques *mpl*.

threepenny [ˈθrepənɪ] ADJ (*Brit*) de 3 peniques; (*fig*) de poca monta, despreciable; **~ bit, ~ piece** moneda *f* de 3 peniques; **T~ Opera** Ópera *f* de perra gorda.

three-phase [ˈθriːfeɪz] ADJ (*Elec*) trifásico.

three-piece [ˈθriːpiːs] ADJ: **~ costume, ~ suit** terno *m*; **~ suite** tresillo *m*.

three-ply [ˈθriːplaɪ] ADJ *wood* de tres capas; *wool* triple, de tres hebras.

three-point turn [ˌθriːpɔɪntˈtɜːn] N cambio *m* de sentido en tres movimientos.

three-quarter [ˌθriːˈkwɔːtəʳ] ADJ: **~-length sleeves** mangas *fpl* tres cuartos.

three-quarters [ˌθriːˈkwɔːtəz] **1** N tres cuartos *mpl*, tres cuartas partes *fpl*; **in ~ of an hour** en tres cuartos de hora; **I've done ~ of the work** he hecho las tres cuartas partes del trabajo.
2 ADV: **the tank is ~ full** quedan las tres cuartas partes en el depósito.

threescore [ˈθriːskɔːʳ] N sesenta; **~ years and ten** setenta años.

three-sided [ˈθriːsaɪdɪd] ADJ trilátero.

threesome [ˈθriːsəm] N grupo *m* de tres, conjunto *m* de tres.

three-way [ˈθriːweɪ] ADJ: **~ split** división *f* en tercios.

three-wheeler [ˈθriːwiːləʳ] N coche *m* de tres ruedas.

threnody [ˈθrenədɪ] N lamento *m*; canto *m* fúnebre.

thresh [θreʃ] VT trillar.

thresher [ˈθreʃəʳ] N trilladora *f*.

threshing [ˈθreʃɪŋ] N trilla *f*.

threshing-floor [ˈθreʃɪŋflɔːʳ] N era *f*.

threshing-machine [ˈθreʃɪŋməˌʃiːn] N trilladora *f*.

threshold [ˈθreʃhəʊld] **1** N umbral *m*; **to be on the ~ of** (*fig*) estar en los umbrales de, estar en la antesala de, estar al borde de; **to cross sb's ~** traspasar el umbral de uno; **to have a low pain ~** tener poca tolerancia del dolor.
2 ATTR: **~ agreement** convenio *m* de nivel crítico; **~ price** precio *m* umbral, precio *m* mínimo.

threw [θruː] PRET of **throw**.

thrice [θraɪs] ADV (††) tres veces.

thrift [θrɪft] N, **thriftiness** [ˈθrɪftɪnɪs] N economía *f*, frugalidad *f*.

thriftless [ˈθrɪftlɪs] ADJ malgastador, pródigo.

thriftlessness [ˈθrɪftlɪsnɪs] N prodigalidad *f*.

thrifty [ˈθrɪftɪ] ADJ (a) (*frugal*) económico, frugal, ahorrativo. (b) (*US*) próspero.

thrill [θrɪl] **1** N emoción *f*; sensación *f*; estremecimiento *m*; **with a ~ of excitement, he ...** estremecido de emoción, él ...; **what a ~!** ¡qué emoción!; **it's the ~ of the year** es la sensación del año; **he just does it for the ~** lo hace simplemente porque le emociona; **to get a ~ out of sth** emocionarse con algo; **it gives me a ~** me emociona; me hace mucha ilusión.
2 VT emocionar, conmover, estremecer; hacer ilusión a; **the film ~ed me** la película me emocionó; **I was ~ed to get your letter** tu carta me hizo mucha ilusión; **we were ~ed with** (*or* **about, at**) **your news** tu noticia nos emocionó muchísimo.
3 VI emocionarse, conmoverse, estremecerse; **to ~ to sb's touch** estremecerse al ser tocado por uno.

thriller [ˈθrɪləʳ] N novela *f* (*or* obra *f*, película *f*) escalofriante, novela *f* de suspense, novela *f* de misterio.

thrilling [ˈθrɪlɪŋ] ADJ emocionante, conmovedor; apasionante; sensacional; **an absolutely ~ journey** un viaje de lo más sensacional; **a ~ play** una obra muy emocionante; **how ~!** ¡qué emoción!

thrillingly [ˈθrɪlɪŋlɪ] ADV de modo emocionante; de modo sensacional.

thrive [θraɪv] (*irr*: PRET **thrived, throve,** PTP **thriven**) VI (*do well*) prosperar, medrar; florecer; (*grow*) crecer mucho, desarrollarse bien; **he ~s on hard work** le gusta estar muy ocupado, se encuentra perfectamente bien con un trabajo agotador; **the plant ~s here** la planta crece muy bien aquí; **children ~ on milk** a los niños les aprovecha la leche.

thriven [ˈθrɪvn] PTP of **thrive**.

thriving [ˈθraɪvɪŋ] ADJ próspero, floreciente.

throat [θrəʊt] N garganta *f*; (*from exterior*) cuello *m*; **they are at each other's ~s all the time** se atacan uno a otro todo el tiempo; **to clear one's ~** carraspear, aclarar la voz; **to cut one's ~** cortarse la garganta; **he's cutting his own ~** (*fig*) está actuando en perjuicio propio, se está haciendo daño a sí mismo; **to jump down sb's ~** lanzarse a criticar a uno en el acto, criticar a uno sin esperar razones; **to moisten one's ~** remojar el gaznate; **to thrust** (*or* **ram**) **sth down sb's ~** (*fig*) hacer que uno trague algo a la fuerza, meter algo a uno por las narices.

throaty [ˈθrəʊtɪ] ADJ gutural; ronco.

throb [θrɒb] **1** N (*of heart etc*) latido *m*, pulsación *f*; palpitación *f*; (*of engine*) vibración *f*; (*of emotion*) estremecimiento *m*.
2 VI latir; palpitar; vibrar; estremecerse; **the crowd ~bed with excitement** la multitud se estremeció emocionada.

throbbing [ˈθrɒbɪŋ] **1** ADJ palpitante; vibrante; *pain* pungente; *rhythm* marcado, fuerte.
2 N latido *m*, pulsación *f*; palpitación *f*; vibración *f*; estremecimiento *m*.

throes [θrəʊz] NPL (*of death*) agonía *f*; (*of childbirth etc*) dolores *mpl*; (*fig*) angustia *f*, agonía *f*; **to be in the ~ of** estar en medio de; estar sufriendo todas las molestias de.

thrombosis [θrɒmˈbəʊsɪs] N trombosis *f*.

throne [θrəʊn] N trono *m*; (*freq fig*) corona *f*, poder *m* real; **to ascend the ~, to come to the ~** subir al trono.

throneroom [ˈθrəʊnrʊm] N sala *f* del trono.

throng [θrɒŋ] **1** N multitud *f*, tropel *m*, muchedumbre *f*; **great ~s of tourists** multitudes *fpl* de turistas; **to come in a ~** venir en tropel.
2 VT atestar, llenar de bote en bote; **everywhere is ~ed** todo está lleno, todo está atestado; **the streets are ~ed with tourists** las calles están atestadas de turistas.
3 VI: **to come ~ing** venir en tropel, venir en masa; **to ~ round sb** apiñarse en torno a uno; **to ~ to hear sb** venir en tropel a escuchar a uno; **to ~ together** reunirse en tropel.

thronging [ˈθrɒŋɪŋ] ADJ *crowd etc* grande, apretado, nutrido.

throttle [ˈθrɒtl] **1** N (*Anat*) gaznate *m*; (*Mech*) regulador *m*, válvula *f* reguladora, estrangulador *m*; (*Aut, loosely*) acelerador *m*; **to give an engine full ~** acelerar un motor al máximo.
2 VT ahogar, estrangular; (*Mech*) estrangular.
3 VI asfixiarse, ahogarse.
◆**throttle back, throttle down** (*Mech*) **1** VT: **to ~ back** (*or* **~ down**) **the engine** moderar la marcha.
2 VI moderar la marcha.

through, (*US also*) **thru** [θruː] **1** ADV (a) (*of place*) de parte a parte, completamente; **the nail went right ~** el clavo penetró de parte a parte; **the wood has rotted ~** la madera se ha podrido completamente; **it's frozen (right) ~** está completamente helado; **the train goes ~ to Burgos** el tren va directo a Burgos; V **wet 1** (a).
(b) (*of time, process*) desde el principio hasta el fin; hasta el fin; **did you stay right ~?** ¿te quedaste hasta el final?; **we're staying ~ till Tuesday** nos quedamos hasta el martes; **to sleep the whole night ~** dormir la noche entera; **he knew it right ~** lo sabía todo, lo sabía de corrido.
(c) (*with* **to be**) **you're ~!** (*Telec*) ¡puede hablar!, ¡hable!; **you're ~!** (*US*) ¡queda Vd despedido!; **are you ~?** ¿has terminado?; **we'll be ~ at 7** terminaremos a las 7; **when I'm ~ with him** cuando haya terminado con él; **I'm not ~ with you yet** todavía no he terminado de decirte (*etc*) lo que tenía pensado; **are you ~ with that book?** ¿has terminado de leer ese libro?; **I'm ~ with bridge** renuncio al bridge, ya no vuelvo a jugar al bridge; **I'm ~ with her** he roto con ella; **she told him they were ~** ella le dijo que habían terminado sus relaciones.
(d) **a Catalan ~ and ~** catalán hasta los tuétanos, catalán por los cuatro costados; V **carry through, fall through** *etc*.
(e) **to put sb ~ to** (*Brit Telec*) poner a uno con.

2 PREP **(a)** (*of place*) por; a través de; de un lado a otro de; **to look ~ a telescope** mirar por un telescopio; **to walk ~ the woods** dar un paseo por el bosque; **the bullet went ~ 3 layers** la bala penetró 3 capas; **it went right ~ the wall** atravesó por toda la pared; **half-way ~ the film** a la mitad de la película.

(b) (*of time*) hasta, hasta e incluso; (*from*) **Monday ~ Friday** (*US*) desde el lunes hasta el viernes, de lunes a viernes; **all ~ our stay** durante toda nuestra estancia; **right ~ the year** durante el año entero.

(c) he's ~ the exam ha aprobado el examen.

(d) (*of means*) mediante, por medio de; por, por causa de; debido a; gracias a; **~ him I found out that ...** por él supe que ...; **~ not knowing the way** por no saber el camino; **he got it ~ friends** lo consiguió por medio de sus amigos; **it was ~ you that we were late** fue por vosotros por lo que llegamos tarde; **to act ~ fear** obrar movido por el miedo.

3 ADJ *carriage, train* directo; *traffic* de paso.

throughout [θruˈaʊt] **1** ADV **(a)** (*of place*) en todas partes, por todas partes; **the hull is welded ~** el casco está totalmente soldado; **the room has been cleaned ~** el cuarto ha sido limpiado completamente; **the house has electric light ~** la casa tiene luz eléctrica en todos los cuartos.

(b) (*of time, process*) todo el tiempo, desde el principio hasta el fin; **the weather was good ~** hizo buen tiempo todos los días; **it's a boring journey ~** es un viaje pesado en todo el recorrido, todo el viaje es monótono.

2 PREP **(a)** (*of place*) por todo, por todas partes de; **~ the country** por todo el país, en todo el país.

(b) (*of time, process*) durante todo, en todo.

throughput [ˈθruːpʊt] N rendimiento *m* total (de procesamiento); producto *m*, productividad *f*; capacidad *f* de ejecución.

throughway [ˈθruːweɪ] N (*US*) autopista *f* de peaje.

throve [θrəʊv] PRET of thrive.

throw [θrəʊ] **1** N echada *f*, tirada *f*, tiro *m*; (*move, at games*) jugada *f*; (*in wrestling*) derribo *m*; (*at dice*) lance *m*; **within a stone's ~** a tiro de piedra; **they're £5 a ~*** cuestan 5 libras cada uno.

2 (*irr:* PRET **threw**, PTP **thrown**) VT **(a)** (*gen*) echar, tirar, lanzar, arrojar; *dice* echar; *glance* lanzar, dirigir; *kiss* echar, tirar; **they threw a coat over her** le echaron encima un abrigo; **to ~ a ball 200 metres** lanzar (*LAm:* echar) una pelota 200 metros; **to ~ a bridge over a river** tender (*or* construir) un puente sobre un río; **to ~ a door open** abrir una puerta de golpe, abrir una puerta de par en par; **to ~ two rooms into one** unir dos cuartos; **to ~ the blame on sb** echar la culpa a uno; **to ~ the book at sb** acusar a uno de todo lo posible; castigar a uno con todo rigor; **to ~ temptation in sb's path** exponer a uno a la tentación; **to be ~n on one's own resources** tener que depender de sí mismo, no tener más que los propios recursos.

(b) (*direct*) *light, shadow, slides etc* proyectar; *punch* dar, asestar (*at* a); **to ~ light on** (*fig*) aclarar, arrojar luz sobre.

(c) *rider* desmontar, desarzonar; *opponent* derribar; *skin* mudar, quitarse; **to be ~n** (*rider*) ser derribado.

(d) (**: disconcert*) confundir, desconcertar, dejar perplejo; **this answer seemed to ~ him** esta respuesta parecía desconcertarle.

(e) (*Tech*) *pot* formar, dar forma a, hacer; tornear; *silk* torcer.

(f) (**: phrases*) **to ~ a fight** perder deliberadamente un encuentro; **to ~ a fit** sufrir un ataque (epiléptico); sufrir una crisis nerviosa; desmayarse; (*fig*) subirse por las paredes*; **to ~ a party** dar una fiesta (*for sb* en honor de uno).

3 VR: **to ~ o.s. at sb's feet** echarse a los pies de uno; **to ~ o.s. at sb** (*or* **at sb's head**) asediar a uno; **to ~ o.s. backwards** echarse hacia atrás; **to ~ o.s. down from a building** arrojarse desde un edificio; **to ~ o.s. into the fray** lanzarse a la batalla; **to ~ o.s. on sb** lanzarse sobre uno, precipitarse sobre uno; **to ~ o.s. to the ground** tirarse al suelo.

◆**throw about** VT tirar, esparcir; **to ~ money about** derrochar dinero; **to ~ one's arms about** agitar mucho los brazos; **to ~ o.s. about** agitar mucho los brazos; **they were ~ing a ball about** jugaban con una pelota.

◆**throw around** VT pasarse de uno a otro.

◆**throw aside** VT tirar, botar (*LAm*), tirar a un lado; apartar; desechar.

◆**throw away** VT **(a)** tirar, echar, botar (*LAm*); desechar; *money* malgastar, derrochar; *one's life* sacrificar inútilmente; *chance* desperdiciar; **it's old and can be ~n away** es viejo y se puede tirar.

(b) *line, remark* dejar caer; decir al azar; (*lose effect of*) perder todo el efecto de.

◆**throw back** VT **(a)** *ball* devolver; *fish* devolver al agua; *offer* rechazar (con desprecio).

(b) *hair, head* echar hacia atrás; **to ~ o.s. back** echarse hacia atrás.

(c) *enemy* rechazar, arrollar; **he was ~n back on his own resources** tuvo que depender de sus propios recursos.

◆**throw down** VT *ball etc* echar a tierra; lanzar hacia abajo; *building, defences* derribar, echar abajo; *arms, tools* dejar, abandonar; *glove* (*fig*)

arrojar; *challenge* lanzar; **to ~ o.s. down** echarse a tierra; **it's ~ing it down*** está lloviendo a cántaros.

◆**throw in** VT **(a)** (*Sport*) *ball* sacar; *remark* hacer, insertar, lanzar (de improviso); *cards* arrojar sobre la mesa (en señal de abandono).

(b) (*as addition*) añadir; dar de más, ofrecer de más; **with an extra meal ~n in** con una comida de más, con una comida gratis.

◆**throw off** VT **(a)** *burden, yoke* sacudirse, deshacerse de, quitarse de encima; *clothes* quitarse (de prisa); *disguise* abandonar; *habit* dejar, renunciar a; *pursuers* zafarse de; *infection* reponerse de; (*emit*) emitir, despedir, arrojar; **in order to ~ the dogs off the scent** para despistar a los perros; **in order to ~ the police off the trail** para despistar a la policía.

(b) *composition* hacer rápidamente; improvisar.

◆**throw on** VT *clothes* ponerse (de prisa); *coal etc* echar.

◆**throw out** VT **(a)** *rubbish* tirar; *defective article* desechar, tirar; *person* echar, expulsar; poner de patitas en la calle, correr (*Mex*); (*Parl*) *bill* rechazar; (*emit*) emitir, despedir, arrojar; **to ~ out one's chest** sacar el pecho, abultar el pecho; **it has ~n many men out of work** ha privado de trabajo a muchos hombres.

(b) *idea, suggestion* lanzar; hacer (de improviso); *challenge* lanzar.

(c) *calculation* falsear; perturbar, afectar mal; (*disconcert*) *person* desconcertar, desorientar.

◆**throw over** VT *intention etc* dejar, abandonar; *friend, lover* romper con.

◆**throw together** VT **(a)** (*make hastily*) hacer rápidamente; construir (*etc*) a la buena de Dios; (*assemble*) reunir de prisa, juntar de cualquier manera.

(b) *persons* poner juntos (por casualidad); **they were ~n together by chance** se conocieron por casualidad.

◆**throw up** **1** VT **(a)** (*cast up*) lanzar (*LAm:* echar) al aire; lanzar (*LAm:* echar) hacia arriba; *defences* levantar rápidamente, construir de prisa; *ideas etc* provocar; ofrecer, ocasionar.

(b) (*vomit*) vomitar, echar, devolver.

(c) (*give up*) *project etc* abandonar; *claim, post* renunciar a.

2 VI vomitar; **it makes me ~ up** (*fig*) me da asco, me repugna.

throwaway [ˈθrəʊəweɪ] ADJ **(a) ~ wrapping** envase *m* desechable, envase *m* a tirar. **(b) ~ line** palabras *fpl* al aire, observación *f* poco importante; **in a ~ tone** como quien no dice nada.

throwback [ˈθrəʊbæk] N salto *m* atrás, tornatrás *m*, reversión *f* (*to* a); **it's like a ~ to the old days** es como una reversión a los viejos tiempos.

thrower [ˈθrəʊəʳ] N lanzador *m*, -ora *f*.

throw-in [ˈθrəʊɪn] N saque *m* (de banda).

throwing [ˈθrəʊɪŋ] N (*Sport*) lanzamiento *m*.

thrown [θrəʊn] PTP of throw.

throw-out [ˈθrəʊaʊt] N cosa *f* desechada, cosa *f* inútil.

thru [θruː] (*US*) = through.

thrum [θrʌm] **1** VT *piano* teclear en; *guitar* rasguear, rasguear las cuerdas de.

2 VI teclear; rasguear las cuerdas.

thrush¹ [θrʌʃ] N (*Orn*) zorzal *m*, tordo *m*.

thrush² [θrʌʃ] N (*Med*) afta *f*; (*Vet*) arestín *m*.

thrust [θrʌst] **1** N **(a)** (*push*) empuje *m*; (*Mil*) avance *m*, ataque *m*; (*of sword*) estocada *f*; (*of dagger*) puñalada *f*; (*of knife*) cuchillada *f*.

(b) (*Mech*) empuje *m*.

(c) (*taunt*) pulla *f*; **a shrewd ~** un golpe certero, un golpe bien dado; **that was a ~ at you** eso lo dijo por ti, esa observación iba dirigida contra ti.

(d) (*thrustfulness*) empuje *m*, dinamismo *m*.

(e) (*basic meaning: of speech etc*) idea *f* clave.

2 (*irr:* PRET AND PTP **thrust**) VT (*push*) empujar; (*drive*) impeler, impulsar; (*insert*) introducir, meter (*into* en); (*insert piercingly*) clavar, hincar (*into* en); **to ~ a dagger into sb's back** clavar un puñal en la espalda de uno; **to ~ a stick into the ground** hincar un palo en el suelo; **to ~ one's hands into one's pockets** meter las manos en los bolsillos; **to ~ sb through with a sword** atravesar a uno (de parte a parte) con una espada; **with an arrow ~ through his hat** con una flecha que le atravesaba el sombrero; **to ~ one's way to the front** abrirse paso hacia adelante, empujar hacia adelante; **to ~ back** *crowd* hacer retroceder, *enemy* arrollar, rechazar, *thought* rechazar; **to ~ sth on sb** imponer algo a uno; obligar a uno a aceptar algo; **Spain had greatness ~ upon her** España recibió su grandeza sin buscarla, se le impuso la grandeza a España sin quererlo ella.

3 VI: **to ~ at sb** asestar un golpe a uno; **to ~ past sb** cruzar (empujando) delante de uno; **to ~ through** abrirse paso por la fuerza.

4 VR: **to ~ o.s. in** introducirse a la fuerza; (*fig*) entrometerse.

◆**thrust aside** VT *person* apartar bruscamente, *plan* rechazar.

◆**thrust forward** **1** VT empujar hacia adelante.

2 VI seguir adelante, proseguir su marcha (*etc*), (*Mil*) avanzar.

3 VR: **to ~ o.s. forward** (*fig*) ponerse delante de otros, darse importancia; ofrecerse (con poca modestia).

◆**thrust out** VT sacar, sacar fuera; *hand* tender; *tongue* sacar; *head* asomar; **to ~ sb out of a door** expulsar (or echar) a uno por una puerta.

thrustful ['θrʌstfʊl] ADJ, **thrusting** ['θrʌstɪŋ] ADJ emprendedor, vigoroso, dinámico; (pej) agresivo.

thrustfulness ['θrʌstfʊlnɪs] N empuje m, pujanza f, dinamismo m; (pej) agresividad f.

thruway ['θruːweɪ] N (US) autopista f de peaje.

Thucydides [θjuːˈsɪdɪdiːz] NM Tucídides.

thud [θʌd] [1] N ruido m sordo, golpe m sordo; **it fell with a ~** cayó ¡zas!

[2] VI hacer un ruido sordo, caer (etc) con un ruido sordo, caer ¡zas!; **to ~ across the floor** andar con pasos pesados; **he was ~ding about upstairs all night** pasó la noche andando con pasos pesados por el piso de arriba; **a shell ~ded into the hillside** una granada estalló en el monte.

thug [θʌg] N asesino m, gángster m; gorila m; gamberro m; (fig, as term of abuse etc) bruto m, bestia f, desalmado m.

thuggery ['θʌgərɪ] N gangsterismo m, matonismo m; brutalidad f.

thuggish ['θʌgɪʃ] ADJ person desalmado; behaviour propio de un matón, desalmado, canallesco.

thulium ['θjuːlɪəm] N tulio m.

thumb [θʌm] [1] N pulgar m; **I'm all ~s today** hoy soy un manazas, hoy estoy desmañado por completo; **to be under sb's ~** estar dominado por uno; **to twiddle one's ~s** (fig) estar mano sobre mano; **they gave it the ~s down** lo rechazaron, lo desaprobaron; **they gave it the ~s up** lo aprobaron; **he gave me a ~s up sign** me indicó con el pulgar que todo iba bien.

[2] VT (a) book, magazine manosear; **a well ~ed book** un libro muy manoseado.

(b) (*) **to ~ a lift, to ~ a ride** hacer autostop, hacer dedo (SC), pedir aventón (Mex); **to ~ a lift to London** viajar en autostop a Londres.

(c) **to ~ one's nose at sb** hacer un palmo de narices a uno.

◆**thumb through** VT: **to ~ through a book** hojear un libro.

thumb-index ['θʌmˈɪndeks] N índice m recortado, uñero m.

thumbnail ['θʌmneɪl] N uña f del pulgar; **~ sketch** dibujo m en miniatura.

thumbprint ['θʌmprɪnt] N impresión f del pulgar.

thumbscrew ['θʌmskruː] N empulgueras fpl.

thumbstall ['θʌmstɔːl] N dedil m.

thumbtack ['θʌmtæk] N (US) chinche f, chincheta f.

thump [θʌmp] (Brit) [1] N (blow) golpazo m, porrazo m; (noise of fall etc) ruido m sordo; **it came down with a ~** cayó ¡zas!

[2] VT golpear, aporrear; (as punishment) dar una paliza a; **to ~ the table** golpear la mesa, dar golpes en la mesa.

[3] VI (of heart) latir con golpes pesados; (of machine) funcionar con ruido sordo, vibrar con violencia; **it came ~ing down** cayó ¡zas!; **he ~ed across the floor** anduvo con pasos pesados.

◆**thump out** VT: **to ~ out a tune on the piano** tocar una melodía al piano golpeando las teclas.

thumping* ['θʌmpɪŋ] [1] ADJ enorme, enorme de grande; descomunal.

[2] ADV: **a ~ great book** un enorme libro, un librote.

thunder ['θʌndəʳ] [1] N trueno m; (loud report) tronido m; (of passing vehicle etc) rodar m pesado, estruendo m; (of applause) estruendo m; (of hooves) estampido m; **with a face like** (or **as black as**) **~** con cara de pocos amigos; **there is ~ about, there is ~ in the air** amenaza tronar; **to steal sb's ~** adelantarse a uno robándole una idea (or un chiste, una observación etc).

[2] VT: **to ~ threats against sb** fulminar amenazas contra uno; **to ~ out an order** dar una orden en tono muy fuerte; **'yes', he ~ed** 'sí', rugió.

[3] VI tronar; **the guns ~ed in the distance** los cañones retumbaban a lo lejos; **the train ~ed past** el tren pasó con gran estruendo.

thunderbolt ['θʌndəbəʊlt] N rayo m; (fig) rayo m, bomba f.

thunderclap ['θʌndəklæp] N tronido m.

thundercloud ['θʌndəklaʊd] N nube f tormentosa, nubarrón m.

thunderflash ['θʌndəflæʃ] N petardo m.

thundering* ['θʌndərɪŋ] [1] ADJ enorme, imponente; **it's a ~ nuisance** es una tremenda lata*; **it was a ~ success** obtuvo un tremendo éxito.

[2] ADV: **a ~ great row** un ruido de todos los demonios; **it's a ~ good film** es una película la mar de buena*.

thunderous ['θʌndərəs] ADJ applause etc atronador, ensordecedor.

thunderstorm ['θʌndəstɔːm] N tormenta f, tronada f.

thunderstruck ['θʌndəstrʌk] ADJ (fig) atónito, pasmado, estupefacto.

thundery ['θʌndərɪ] ADJ weather tormentoso, bochornoso.

thurible ['θjʊərɪbl] N incensario m.

thurifer ['θjʊərɪfəʳ] N monaguillo m que lleva el incensario.

Thuringia [θjʊəˈrɪndʒɪə] N Turingia f.

Thur(s). ABBR of **Thursday** jueves m, juev.

Thursday ['θɜːzdɪ] N jueves m.

thus [ðʌs] ADV así; de este modo; **~ far** hasta aquí; **~ it is that ...** así es

que ..., es por eso que ...; **~, when he got home ...** así que, cuando llegó a casa ...

thwack [θwæk] = **whack**.

thwart¹ [θwɔːt] VT frustrar; impedir, estorbar; plan etc frustrar, desbaratar; **to be ~ed at every turn** verse frustrado en todo.

thwart² [θwɔːt] N (Naut) bancada f.

thy†† [ðaɪ] POSS ADJ tu(s).

thyme [taɪm] N tomillo m.

thymus ['θaɪməs] N timo m.

thyroid ['θaɪrɔɪd] [1] ADJ tiroideo.

[2] N (also **~ gland**) tiroides m.

thyself†† [ðaɪˈself] PRON (subject) tú mismo, tú misma; (acc, dative) te; (after prep) ti (mismo, misma).

ti [tiː] N (Mus) si m.

tiara [tɪˈɑːrə] N diadema f; (pope's) tiara f.

Tiber ['taɪbəʳ] N Tíber m.

Tiberius [taɪˈbɪərɪəs] NM Tiberio.

Tibet [tɪˈbet] N el Tíbet.

Tibetan [tɪˈbetən] [1] ADJ tibetano.

[2] N (a) tibetano m, -a f. (b) (Ling) tibetano m.

tibia ['tɪbɪə] N tibia f.

tic [tɪk] N (Med) tic m.

tich* [tɪtʃ] N renacuajo* m.

tichy* ['tɪtʃɪ] ADJ pequeñito*, chiquitito*.

tick¹ [tɪk] [1] N (a) (of clock) tictac m.

(b) (Brit: moment) momento m, instante m; **at 6 o'clock on the ~** a las 6 en punto; **to arrive at** (or **on**) **the ~** llegar puntualmente; **half a ~!, just a ~!** ¡un momentito!; **I shan't be a ~** tardo dos minutos nada más, termino en seguida; **he won't take two ~s to do it** lo hará en menos de nada.

(c) (mark) señal f, marca f (de aprobación); palomita f; **to put a ~ against sb's name** poner una señal contra el nombre de uno.

[2] VT (Brit: also **to ~ off**) poner una señal contra; tildar.

[3] VI hacer tictac; **I wonder what makes him ~*** me pregunto de dónde saca tanta energía.

◆**tick away, tick by** VI: **time is ~ing away** or **by** el tiempo pasa.

◆**tick off** VT (a) = **tick¹** 2; (count) contar en los dedos.

(b) **to ~ sb off*** (Brit: reprimand) echar una bronca a uno, regañar a uno.

(c) **to ~ off*** (US: annoy) fastidiar, dar la lata a*.

◆**tick over** VI (Brit) (Aut, Mech) marchar al ralentí; (fig) ir tirando, mantenerse a flote; funcionar a ritmo lento.

tick² [tɪk] N (Zool) garrapata f.

tick³ [tɪk] N (cover) funda f.

tick⁴* [tɪk] N (Brit: credit) crédito m; **to buy sth on ~** comprar algo de fiado; **to live on ~** vivir de fiado.

ticker* ['tɪkəʳ] N (watch) reloj m; (heart) corazón m.

ticker-tape ['tɪkəteɪp] N cinta f de cotizaciones.

ticket ['tɪkɪt] [1] N (bus ~, Rail etc) billete m; boleto m (LAm); (Cine, Theat) entrada f; localidad f, boleto m (LAm), boleta f (LAm); (label) etiqueta f, rótulo m; (counterfoil) talón m; (at dry-cleaner's etc) resguardo m; (Aut) multa f (por infracción del código etc); (US Pol) lista f de candidatos, candidatura f; programa m político, programa m electoral; **that's the ~!*** ¡muy bien!, ¡eso es!; ¡así me gustas!; ¡es lo que hacía falta!

[2] VT (a) (label) rotular, poner etiqueta a. (b) (US) passenger expedir un billete a; **~ed passengers** viajeros mpl con billete, viajeros mpl que tienen billete.

ticket-agency ['tɪkɪtˌeɪdʒənsɪ] N (Rail etc) agencia f de viajes; (Theat) agencia f de localidades.

ticket-barrier ['tɪkɪtˌbærɪəʳ] N (Brit Rail) barrera más allá de la cual se necesita billete.

ticket-collector ['tɪkɪtkəˌlektəʳ] N, **ticket-inspector** ['tɪkɪtɪnˌspektəʳ] N revisor m, -ora f, controlador m, -ora f de boletos (LAm).

ticket-holder ['tɪkɪtˌhəʊldəʳ] N poseedor m, -ora f de billete; (season ~, at theatre etc) abonado m, -a f; (season ~, Ftbl) socio m, -a f; (of travelcard etc) titular mf.

ticket-office ['tɪkɪtˌɒfɪs] N (Rail) despacho m de billetes, despacho m de boletos (LAm); (Theat etc) taquilla f, boletería f (LAm).

ticket-of-leave ['tɪkɪtəvˈliːv] N (Brit) cédula f de libertad condicional; **~ man** hombre m bajo libertad condicional.

ticket-tout ['tɪkɪtˌtaʊt] N revendedor m (de entradas).

ticket-window ['tɪkɪtˌwɪndəʊ] N ventanilla f; (Rail etc) despacho m de billetes; (Theat etc) taquilla f.

ticking¹ ['tɪkɪŋ] N (material) cutí m, terliz m.

ticking² ['tɪkɪŋ] N (of clock) tictac m.

ticking-off* ['tɪkɪŋˈɒf] N (Brit) bronca f; **to give sb a ~** echar una bronca a uno, regañar a uno.

tickle ['tɪkl] [1] N: **to give the cat a ~** acariciar al gato; **to have a ~ behind one's ear** sentir cosquillas detrás de la oreja; **to have a ~ in one's throat** tener picor de garganta; **he never got a ~ all day** (Fishing) no picó pez alguno en todo el día; **at £5 he never got a ~***

a 5 libras nadie le echó un tiento*.

2 VT (**a**) cosquillear, hacer cosquillas a; *cat etc* acariciar.

(**b**) (*: *amuse*) divertir; hacer gracia a; (*delight*) chiflar*; **it ~d us no end** nos divirtió mucho, nos hizo mucha gracia; **we were ~d to death about it, we were ~d pink about it** nos moríamos de risa con eso*.

3 VI: **my ear ~s** siento cosquillas en la oreja, siento hormiguillo en la oreja; **don't, it ~s!** ¡por Dios, que me hace cosquillas!

tickler ['tɪklər] N (*Brit*) problema *m* difícil.

tickling ['tɪklɪŋ] N cosquillas *fpl*.

ticklish ['tɪklɪʃ] ADJ, **tickly*** ['tɪklɪ] ADJ (**a**) cosquilloso; **to be ~** tener cosquillas, ser cosquilloso.

(**b**) *problem etc* peliagudo, espinoso; delicado; **it's a ~ business** es un asunto delicado.

ticktack ['tɪktæk] N (*Racing*) lenguaje de signos utilizado por los corredores de apuestas en las carreras de caballos.

tick-tock ['tɪk'tɒk] N tictac *m*.

tic-tac-toe [,tɪktæk'təʊ] N (*US*) tres *m* en raya.

tidal ['taɪdl] ADJ de marea; **~ basin** dique *m* de marea; **~ energy** energía *f* de las mareas; **~ wave** maremoto *m*, ola *f* de marea; (*fig*) ola *f* gigantesca; **the river is ~ up to here** la marea sube hasta aquí; **the Mediterranean is not ~** en el Mediterráneo no hay mareas.

tidbit ['tɪdbɪt] (*US*) = **titbit**.

tiddler* ['tɪdlər] N (**a**) (*Brit*) (*stickleback*) espinoso *m*; (*small fish*) pececillo *m*. (**b**) (*child*) nene *m*, -a *f*.

tiddly* ['tɪdlɪ] ADJ (*esp Brit*) achispado*.

tiddlywink ['tɪdlɪwɪŋk] N pulga *f*; **~s** (*game*) juego *m* de pulgas.

tide [taɪd] N marea *f*; (*fig*) corriente *m*; marcha *f*, progreso *m*; tendencia *f*; **high ~** pleamar *f*, (*fig*) cumbre *f*, apogeo *m*; **low ~** bajamar *f*, (*fig*) punto *m* más bajo; **the rising ~ of public indignation** la creciente indignación pública; **the ~ of battle turned** cambió la suerte de la batalla; **the ~ of events** la marcha de los sucesos; **to go against the ~** ir contra la corriente; **to go with the ~** seguir la corriente.

◆**tide over** VT: **to ~ sb over** ayudar a uno a salvar el bache, ayudar a uno a salir de un apuro.

tideless ['taɪdlɪs] ADJ sin mareas.

tideline ['taɪdlaɪn] N, **tidemark** ['taɪdmɑːk] N lengua *f* del agua; (*hum*) cerco *m* (de suciedad, en bañera *etc*).

tiderace ['taɪdreɪs] N aguaje *m*, marejada *f*.

tidewater ['taɪd,wɔːtər] (*Brit*) **1** N agua *f* de marea.

2 ATTR drenado por las mareas, costero.

tideway ['taɪdweɪ] N canal *m* de marea.

tidily ['taɪdɪlɪ] ADV bien, en orden; aseadamente, pulcramente; metódicamente; **to be ~ dressed** ir bien vestido; **to arrange things ~** poner las cosas en orden.

tidiness ['taɪdɪnɪs] N buen orden *m*; limpieza *f*; aseo *m*, pulcritud *f*; carácter *m* metódico.

tidings ['taɪdɪŋz] NPL noticias *fpl*.

tidy ['taɪdɪ] **1** ADJ (**a**) *objects etc* en orden, ordenado; *room, desk* limpio; bien arreglado; *appearance, dress* aseado, pulcro; *person* metódico; **to get a room ~** limpiar un cuarto, arreglar un cuarto; **to make o.s. ~** asearse, arreglarse; **he has a ~ mind** tiene una mentalidad lógica, tiene una inteligencia metódica.

(**b**) (*) *pace* bastante rápido; *sum* considerable; **it cost a ~ bit** costó bastante; **he's a pretty ~ player** es un jugador bastante estimable.

2 VT arreglar, poner en orden, limpiar; **to ~ one's hair** arreglarse el pelo.

◆**tidy away** VT: **to ~ books away** devolver los libros a su lugar; **to ~ the dishes away** quitar los platos.

◆**tidy out** VT ordenar, limpiar, arreglar.

◆**tidy up 1** VT arreglar, poner en orden, limpiar.

2 VI arreglar las cosas, ponerlo todo en orden.

3 VR: **to ~ o.s. up** asearse, arreglarse.

tidy-out ['taɪdɪ'aʊt] N, **tidy-up** ['taɪdɪ'ʌp] N: **to have a ~** ordenar (la casa, la habitación *etc*).

tie [taɪ] **1** N (**a**) (*bond*) lazo *m*, vínculo *m*; **the ~s of friendship** los lazos de la amistad; **the ~s of blood** los lazos del parentesco.

(**b**) (*hindrance*) estorbo *m*; **the children are a ~ in the evenings** los pequeños son un estorbo para poder salir por las tardes; **he has no ~s here** no tiene nada que le retenga aquí, no tiene nada que le impida irse de aquí.

(**c**) (*cord etc*) atadura *f*, ligazón *f*; (*Brit*: *neck~*) corbata *f*; (*Archit*) tirante *m*; (*US Rail*) traviesa *f*; (*Mus*) ligado *m*.

(**d**) (*Sport*: *match*) encuentro *m*, partido *m*.

(**e**) (*draw*) empate *m*; **it ended in a ~ at 3-all** terminó en empate a 3; **there was a ~ in the voting** en la votación resultó un empate.

2 VT atar, liar; enlazar, unir; (*Mus*) ligar; *bow, knot, necktie* hacer; (*fig, with bond*) liar, ligar, vincular; **to ~ two things together** atar dos cosas; **to ~ a dog to a post** atar un perro a un poste; **to ~ sb's hands** atar las manos a uno (*also fig*); **to ~ one on*** emborracharse; **his hands are ~d** tiene las manos atadas (*also fig*); **to be ~d hand

and foot (*fig*) verse atado de pies y manos.

(**b**) (*hinder*) estorbar; (*limit*) limitar, restringir (*to* a); **we are very ~d in the evenings** por las tardes nos vemos bastante estorbados para salir; **are we ~d to this plan?** ¿estamos restringidos a este plan?; **the house is ~d to her husband's job** la casa está ligada al puesto que tiene su marido, la casa pertenece a la compañía en que trabaja su marido.

3 VI (*draw*) empatar; **we ~d with them 4-all** empatamos con ellos a 4.

◆**tie back** VT *hair etc* atar, liar.

◆**tie down** VT (**a**) atar; sujetar, afianzar (con cuerdas *etc*); inmovilizar.

(**b**) (*restrict etc*) limitar, restringir; obligar; **to ~ sb down to a task** obligar a uno a hacer una tarea; **to ~ sb down to a contract** obligar a uno a cumplir (*or* respetar) un contrato; **we can't ~ him down to a date** no podemos conseguir que fije una fecha; **we're ~d down for months to come** no podemos aceptar otro compromiso por muchos meses; **I refuse to be ~d down** me niego a atarme, no me dejaré atar; **I don't want to ~ myself down to attending** no quiero comprometerme a asistir.

◆**tie in 1** VT relacionar, asociar; **I'm trying to ~ that in with what was said earlier** trato de relacionar eso con lo que se dijo antes; **can you ~ in A with B?** ¿puedes compaginar A y B?

2 VI: **it all ~s in** todo concuerda, todo se encaja bien; **it doesn't ~ in with what he told us** no cuadra con lo que nos dijo.

◆**tie on** VT atar, pegar.

◆**tie together** VT atar, liar; *persons etc* liar, vincular.

◆**tie up 1** VT (**a**) (*bind*) atar, liar; envolver; (*Naut*) atracar (*to* a); **to get (o.s.) all ~d up** (*fig*) armarse un lío.

(**b**) (*esp US*: *block, stop*) obstruir, bloquear; *programme* interrumpir; *production etc* paralizar, parar; **the fog ~d up all the shipping** la niebla inmovilizó toda la navegación.

(**c**) *capital* inmovilizar; invertir (sin poder retirar); **he has a fortune ~d up in property** tiene una fortuna inmovilizada en bienes raíces.

(**d**) (*conclude*) *business* despachar, arreglar; *deal* concluir; *problem etc* resolver; **we'll soon have it all ~d up** pronto lo arreglamos todo.

(**e**) (*: *occupy*) **he's ~d up with the manager just now** ahora está conferenciando con el jefe, de momento está tratando un asunto con el jefe; **I'm ~d up tomorrow** mañana estoy liado; **he's ~d up with a girl in Lima** tiene un lío con una chica en Lima*.

(**f**) (*link*) **it's all ~d up with the fact that ...** todo depende del hecho de que ...; **the company is ~d up with a Spanish firm** la compañía tiene relaciones con una firma española.

2 VI (*Naut*) atracar, amarrar; (*fig*) llegar a puerto; **to ~ up at a wharf** atracar en un muelle; **to ~ up to a post** atracar a un poste.

tie-break(er) ['taɪbreɪk(ər)] N (*Tennis*) tiebreak *m*, desempate *m* (por muerte súbita); (*in quiz*) punto *m* decisivo.

tie-clip ['taɪklɪp] N pinza *f* de corbata.

tied [taɪd] ADJ (*Sport*) empatado; (*Mus*) ligado.

tie-in ['taɪɪn] N (*fig*) unión *f*; relación *f* estrecha (*between* entre).

tieless ['taɪlɪs] ADJ sin corbata.

tie-on ['taɪɒn] ADJ para atar.

tiepin ['taɪpɪn] N alfiler *m* de corbata.

tier [tɪər] N grada *f*, fila *f*; piso *m*; nivel *m*; **to arrange in ~s** disponer en gradas.

tiered ['tɪəd] ADJ con gradas, en una serie de gradas; **steeply ~** con gradas en fuerte pendiente; **a three-~ cake** un pastel de tres pisos.

tie-tack ['taɪtæk] N (*US*) = **tiepin**.

tie-up ['taɪʌp] N (*link*) enlace *m*; vinculación *f*; (*by strike etc*) paralización *f*; (*US*: *of traffic*) bloqueo *m*; embotellamiento *m*; (*US*: *stoppage*) interrupción *f*.

tiff* [tɪf] N riña *f*, pelea *f*.

tiffin ['tɪfɪn] N (*Indian*) almuerzo *m*.

tig [tɪg] N: **to play ~** jugar al marro.

tiger ['taɪgər] N tigre *mf*.

tigerish ['taɪgərɪʃ] ADJ (*fig*) salvaje, feroz.

tiger lily ['taɪgə,lɪlɪ] N tigridia *f*.

tiger moth [,taɪgə'mɒθ] N mariposa *f* tigre.

tiger's eye ['taɪgəz'aɪ] N (*Min*) ojo *m* de gato.

tight [taɪt] **1** ADJ (**a**) (*not leaky*) impermeable; a prueba de ...; *container* estanco; *joint* hermético.

(**b**) (*taut*) tieso, tirante; (*stretched*) estirado; *nut etc* apretado; *clothing* ajustado, ceñido, (*too ~*) apretado, estrecho; *embrace* estrecho; *box* bien cerrado; *curve* cerrado; *schedule* apretado; *control* riguroso, estricto; **as ~ as a drum** muy tirante; **it's a ~ fit** me (*etc*) viene muy estrecho; **to be in a ~ corner** (*or* situation) estar en un aprieto; **to keep ~ hold of sth** seguir fuertemente agarrado a algo; (*fig*) controlar algo rigurosamente.

(**c**) *money* escaso; *credit* difícil.

(**d**) (*close-fisted*) agarrado, tacaño.

(**e**) (*: *drunk*) borracho; **to be ~** estar borracho; **to get ~** emborracharse (*on gin* bebiendo ginebra).

2 ADV herméticamente; de modo tirante; apretadamente, estrechamente; **the door was shut ~** la puerta estaba bien cerrada; **shut the box ~** cierra bien la caja; **screw the nut up ~** aprieta la tuerca a fondo, apriete bien la tuerca; **to hold sth ~** agarrar algo fuertemente; **to hold sb ~** abrazar a uno estrechamente; **hold ~!** ¡agárrense bien!; **to sit ~** estarse quieto, no moverse, seguir en su lugar; seguir sin hacer nada; **sleep ~!** ¡que duermas bien!; **to squeeze sb's hand ~** apretar mucho la mano a uno.

③ NPL: **~s** (*Brit*) panti *m*, medias *fpl* (enteras); (*Theat*) mallas *fpl*; (*US*) traje *m* de malla.

tighten ['taɪtn] ① VT (*also* **to ~ up**) **(a)** (*tauten*) atiesar, estirar; estrechar; *nut etc* apretar.

(b) (*fig*) *regulations etc* hacer más severo; apretar; hacer observar, velar por la observancia de; *restrictions* reforzar, apretar, aplicar en forma más rigurosa.

② VI atiesarse, estirarse; estrecharse; apretarse; **to ~ up on** V 1.

◆**tighten up** VTI = **tighten**.

tightening ['taɪtnɪŋ] N tensamiento *m*.

tight-fisted ['taɪt'fɪstɪd] ADJ agarrado, tacaño.

tight-fitting ['taɪt'fɪtɪŋ] ADJ muy ajustado, muy ceñido.

tight-knit ['taɪt'nɪt] ADJ estrechamente unidos entre sí; *family etc* muy unido.

tight-lipped ['taɪt'lɪpt] ADJ (*fig*) callado; hermético; **to maintain a ~ silence** mantener un silencio absoluto; **he's being very ~ about it** sobre eso no dice nada en absoluto.

tightly ['taɪtlɪ] ADV V **tight** 2.

tightly- ['taɪtlɪ] PREF: **~packed** bien empaquetado; **~controlled** estrictamente controlado, rigurosamente controlado.

tightness ['taɪtnɪs] N impermeabilidad *f*; lo estanco; lo hermético; tensión *f*, tirantez *f*; lo apretado; estrechez *f*; escasez *f*; tacañería *f*; **to have a ~ in the chest** sentir opresión en el pecho.

tightrope ['taɪtrəʊp] N alambre *m* (de circo *etc*); **to be on a ~, to be walking a ~** (*fig*) andar a la cuerda floja, hacer equilibrios (*between A and B* entre A y B).

tightrope walker ['taɪtrəʊp,wɔːkər] N funámbulo *m*, -a *f*, volatinero *m*, -a *f*, equilibrista *mf*.

tightwad* ['taɪtwɒd] N (*US*) cicatero *m*.

tigress ['taɪgrɪs] N tigresa *f*, tigre hembra *f*.

Tigris ['taɪgrɪs] N Tigris *m*.

tilde ['tɪldɪ] N tilde *f*.

tile [taɪl] ① N (*roof ~*) teja *f*; (*floor ~*) baldosa *f*; (*wall ~, coloured, glazed*) azulejo *m*; (♣) sombrero *m*; **he's got a ~ loose*** le falta un tornillo*; **to spend a night on the ~s** (*Brit*) estar fuera toda la noche, pasar la noche de juerga*.

② VT *roof* tejar; cubrir de tejas; *floor* embaldosar; *wall* adornar con azulejos; **~d roof** techo *m* de tejas, tejado *m*.

tiling ['taɪlɪŋ] N tejas *fpl*, tejado *m*; baldosas *fpl*, embaldosado *m*; azulejos *mpl*.

till¹ [tɪl] VT (*Agr*) cultivar, labrar.

till² [tɪl] ① PREP hasta.

② CONJ hasta que; (*for usage* V **until**).

till³ [tɪl] N (*drawer*) cajón *m*; (*machine*) caja *f* registradora; **they caught him with his hand** (*or* **fingers**) **in the ~** le cogieron robando (dentro de la empresa *etc*).

tillage ['tɪlɪdʒ] N cultivo *m*, labranza *f*.

tiller ['tɪlər] N (*Naut*) caña *f* del timón.

tilt [tɪlt] ① N **(a)** (*sloping*) inclinación *f*; ladeo *m*; **it is on the ~, it has a ~ to it** está ladeado; **to give sth a ~** inclinar algo, ladear algo.

(b) (*Hist*) torneo *m*, justa *f*; (*at*) **full ~** a toda velocidad; **to run full ~ into a wall** dar de lleno contra una pared; **to have a ~ at** arremeter contra.

② VT inclinar, ladear; **~ it this way** inclínalo hacia este lado; **~ it back** inclínalo hacia atrás; **to ~ over a table** volcar una mesa.

③ VI **(a)** inclinarse, ladearse; **to ~ over** (*lean*) inclinarse, (*fall*) volcarse, caer; **lorry that ~s up** camión *m* que bascula, camión *m* basculante.

(b) (*Hist*) justar; **to ~ against** arremeter contra.

tilth [tɪlθ] N cultivo *m*, labranza *f*; condición *f* (cultivable) de la tierra.

Tim [tɪm] NM *familiar form of* **Timothy**.

timber ['tɪmbər] ① N (*material*) madera *f* (de construcción); (*growing trees*) árboles *mpl*, árboles *mpl* de monte; bosque *m*; (*beam*) madero *m*, viga *f*, (*Naut*) cuaderna *f*; **~!** ¡ojo, que cae!, ¡agua va!

② VT enmaderar.

timbered ['tɪmbəd] ADJ *house etc* enmaderado; *land* arbolado; **the land is well ~** el terreno tiene mucho bosque.

timbering ['tɪmbərɪŋ] N maderamen *m*.

timberland ['tɪmbəlænd] N (*US*) tierras *fpl* maderables.

timberline ['tɪmbəlaɪn] N límite *m* forestal.

timber merchant ['tɪmbə,mɜːtʃənt] N (*Brit*) maderero *m*.

timber-wolf ['tɪmbə,wʊlf] N, PL **timber-wolves** ['tɪmbə,wʊlvz] lobo *m* gris norteamericano.

timber-yard ['tɪmbəjɑːd] N (*Brit*) almacén *m* de madera.

timbre [tɛ̃mbr] N timbre *m*.

timbrel ['tɪmbrəl] N pandereta *f*.

time [taɪm] ① N **(a)** (*gen*) tiempo *m*; (**Father**) **T~** el Tiempo; **~ flies** el tiempo vuela; **~ presses** el tiempo apremia; **~ will show, ~ will tell** el tiempo lo dirá; **race against ~** carrera *f* contra (el) reloj; **for all ~** para siempre; **in** (**good**) **~, in process of ~, as ~ goes on** andando el tiempo, con el tiempo; **all in good ~** todo a su tiempo; **all in good ~!** ¡despacio!; **one of the best of all ~** uno de los mejores de todos los tiempos; **~ and motion study** estudios *mpl* de tiempo y movimiento, estudio *m* de desplazamientos y tiempos; **~!** ¡es la hora!, ¡la hora!; **~ gentlemen please!** ¡se cierra!; **half the ~ he's drunk** la mayor parte del tiempo está borracho; **it's only a matter** (*or* **question**) **of ~ before it falls** sólo es cuestión de tiempo antes de que caiga; **my ~ is my own** dispongo libremente de mi tiempo; **to find ~ for** encontrar tiempo para; **to gain ~** ganar tiempo; **we have ~, we have plenty of ~** tenemos tiempo de sobra; **to have no ~ to read** no tener tiempo para leer; (*fig*) **I've no ~ for him** no le aguanto; **I've no ~ for sport** (*fig*) desprecio los deportes, no apruebo los deportes; **to have ~ on one's hands** estar ocioso; no saber cómo ocuparse; tener tiempo de sobra; **to kill ~** entretener el tiempo, pasar el rato, matar el tiempo; **to lose ~** atrasarse; **to lose no ~ in + ger** no tardar en + *infin*; **there is no ~ to lose** (*or* **to be lost**) no hay que perder tiempo; **to make ~*** (*US*) ganar tiempo, apresurarse; **he's making ~ with his secretary*** (*US*) está tratando de acostarse con su secretaria; **to make up for lost ~** recuperar el tiempo perdido; **to play for ~** tratar de ganar tiempo; **to be pressed for ~** andar escaso de tiempo; **it takes ~** requiere tiempo, lleva su tiempo; **it takes ~ to + infin** se tarda bastante en + *infin*; **it took him all his ~ to find it** sólo encontrarlo le ocupó bastante tiempo; **to take one's ~** hacer las cosas con calma; ir despacio, no darse prisa; **he's certainly taking his ~** es cierto que tarda bastante ya; **take your ~!** tómate el tiempo que necesites, ¡no hay prisa!; **to take ~ by the forelock** tomar la ocasión por los pelos; V **waste** 3.

(b) (*period*) período *m*, tiempo *m*; plazo *m*; **~ deposit** depósito *m* a plazo; **~ loan** préstamo *m* a plazo fijo; **a long ~** mucho tiempo; **a long ~ ago** hace mucho tiempo, hace tiempo; **a short ~** poco tiempo, un rato; **a short ~ ago** hace poco; **a short ~ after** poco tiempo después, al poco tiempo; **for a ~** durante un rato, durante una temporada; **for a long ~ to come** hasta que haya transcurrido mucho tiempo; **for some ~ past** de algún tiempo a esta parte; **for the ~ being** por ahora; **he hasn't been seen for a long ~** hace mucho tiempo que no se le ve; **in** (**good**) **~** (*early*) a tiempo, con tiempo; **to arrive in good ~** llegar con bastante anticipación; **let me know in good ~** avíseme con anticipación; **he'll come in his own good ~** vendrá cuando le parezca conveniente; **we made good ~ on the journey** el viaje ha sido rápido; el viaje ha sido sin problemas; **in a short ~** en breve; con la mayor brevedad; **in a short ~ they were all gone** muy pronto habían desaparecido todos; **in 2 weeks'** ~ en 2 semanas; al cabo de 2 semanas; **in no ~ at all** en muy poco tiempo; **within the agreed ~** dentro del plazo convenido; dentro del límite de tiempo que se había fijado; **to do ~*** cumplir una condena; **it will last our ~** durará lo que nosotros; **to serve one's ~** hacer su aprendizaje; **to take a long ~ to + infin** tardar mucho en + *infin*.

(c) (*at work*) horas *fpl* de trabajo; jornada *f*; **he did the draft in** (*or* US **on**) **his own ~** preparó el borrador fuera de (las) horas de trabajo; **to be on** (*or* **to work**) **short ~** trabajar en jornadas reducidas; **on Saturdays they pay ~ and a half** los sábados pagan lo normal más la mitad; **~ and motion study** estudio *m* de tiempos y movimientos; V *also* **full-~, short-~** *etc*.

(d) (*epoch, period; often* **~s**) época *f*, tiempos *mpl*; **a sign of the ~s** un indicio de cómo cambian los tiempos; **the good old ~s** los buenos tiempos pasados; **the ~s we live in** los tiempos en que vivimos; **these naughty ~s** estos tiempos tan escandalosos; **that was all before my ~** todo eso fue antes de mis tiempos; **in my ~(s)** en mis tiempos; **in Victoria's ~(s)** en los tiempos de Victoria, en la época victoriana, bajo el reinado de Victoria; **in our ~** en nuestra época; **in ~s past, in former** (*or* **olden, older**) **~s** en otro tiempo, antiguamente; **in ~s to come** en los siglos venideros; **~s are somewhat hard** atravesamos un período bastante difícil; **those were tough ~s** fue un período de grandes dificultades; **what ~s they were!, what ~s we had!** ¡qué tiempos aquellos!; **how ~s change!** ¡cómo cambian las cosas!; **the ~s are out of joint** los tiempos actuales están revueltos; **one of the greatest footballers of our ~** uno de los mejores futbolistas de nuestros tiempos; **~ was when ...** hubo un tiempo en que ...; **to be behind the ~s** (*person*) ser un atrasado; estar atrasado de noticias; (*thing*) estar fuera de moda, haber quedado anticuado; **to fall on hard ~s** estar en el tiempo de las vacas flacas; **to keep abreast of** (*or* **up with**) **the ~s, to move with the ~s** ir con los tiempos, mantenerse al día.

(e) (*moment, point of* **~**) momento *m*; **any ~** en cualquier momento; **come (at) any ~ (you like)** ven cuando quieras; **it might happen (at) any ~** podría ocurrir de un momento a otro; **at the ~, at that ~**

por entonces; en aquella época, en aquel entonces; a la sazón; **at this particular ~** en este preciso momento; **at the present ~** en la actualidad, actualmente; **at one ~** en cierto momento, en cierta época; había momentos en que ...; **at one ~ ..., at another ~ ...** ora ..., ora ...; **Rodriguez, at one ~ minister of ...** Rodríguez, ministro que fue de ...; **at no ~** jamás, nunca; **at a given ~** en un momento convenido; **at a convenient ~** en un momento oportuno; **at the proper ~** en el momento oportuno; **at the same ~** al mismo tiempo; a la vez; **at ~s** a veces; **at all ~s** en todo momento, siempre; **at odd ~s** de vez en cuando; **at various ~s in the past** en determinados momentos del pasado; **between ~s** en los intervalos; **by this ~** ya, antes de esto; **(by) this ~ next year** para estas fechas del año que viene; **by the ~ we got there** antes de que llegásemos, antes de nuestra llegada, antes de llegar nosotros; cuando llegamos; **from ~ to ~** de vez en cuando; **from that ~ (on)** desde entonces, a partir de entonces; **until such ~ as he agrees** hasta que consienta; **now is the ~ to do it** éste es el momento en que conviene hacerlo; **now is the ~ to plant roses** ésta es la época para plantar las rosas; **the proper ~ to do it is ...** el momento más indicado para hacerlo es ...; **when the ~ comes** cuando llegue el momento; **the ~ has come to + infin** ha llegado el momento de + infin; **to choose one's ~ carefully** elegir con cuidado el momento más propicio; **her ~ was drawing near** se acercaba el momento de dar a luz; **his ~ was drawing near** se acercaba a la muerte; **this is no ~ for superstition** éste no es el momento para mostrarse supersticioso, tal momento no es para tomar en serio las supersticiones.

(f) (as marked on clock) hora f; **what's the ~?** ¿qué hora es?; **what do you make it?, what do you make the ~?** ¿qué hora tienes?; **have you the right ~?** ¿tienes la hora exacta?; **the ~ is 2.30** son las 2 y media; **a watch that keeps good ~** un reloj muy exacto; **to look at the ~** mirar su reloj.

(g) (as marked on clock: phrases with prep etc) **(and) about ~ too!, (and) not before ~!** ¡ya era hora!; **it is about ~ he was there** ya era hora que estuviera allí; **to be 23 minutes ahead of ~** llevar 23 minutos de adelanto; **to arrive ahead of ~** llegar temprano; **to die before one's ~** morir temprano; **to be behind ~** atrasarse, retrasarse; **the train is 8 minutes behind ~** el tren lleva 8 minutos de retraso; **to come in (good) ~ for lunch** venir con bastante anticipación a comer; **we were just in ~ to see it** llegamos justo a tiempo para verlo; **to start in good ~** partir a tiempo, partir pronto; **to be on ~** ser puntual, llegar (etc) puntualmente; llegar a la hora exacta; **to be up to ~** llegar sin retraso; **at any ~ of the day or night** en cualquier momento del día o de la noche; **at this ~ of day** a esta hora; **at any one ~ there is room for 12 readers** en un momento dado hay sitio para 12 lectores; **to pass the ~ of day with sb** detenerse a charlar un rato con uno; **I wouldn't give him the ~ of day** a mí él me tiene sin cuidado, me importa un rábano; **it's ~ for tea** es la hora del té; ha llegado la hora de servir el té; **it's coffee ~** es la hora del café; **it's ~ to go** ya es hora de marcharse; **it's high ~** ya era hora; **it's high ~ that ...** ya va siendo hora de + infin, es hora de que + subj; **there's a ~ and a place for everything** todo tiene su hora y su lugar debidos; éste no es ni el momento ni el lugar indicado.

(h) (as marked by calendar) época f; temporada f; estación f; **~ payment** (US) pago m a plazos; **at my ~ of life** a mi edad, con los años que yo tengo; **at this ~ of year** en esta época del año; **it's a lovely ~ of year** es una estación encantadora; **my favourite ~ is autumn** mi estación predilecta es el otoño.

(i) (good ~ etc) **to have a good ~ (of it)** pasarlo bien; **have a good ~!** ¡que lo pases bien!; **to give sb a good ~** hacer que uno se divierta; hacer que uno lo pase bien; **she's out for a good ~** se propone divertirse; **all they want to do is have a good ~** no quieren más que divertirse; **we had a high old ~*** lo hemos pasado en grande*; **we have a lovely ~** lo pasamos la mar de bien*; **I hope you have a lovely ~!** ¡que os divirtáis!; **to have a rough (or bad, thin etc) ~ of it** pasarlo mal, pasarlas negras; **what a ~ we'll have with the girls!** ¡vaya juergazo que nos vamos a correr con las chicas!*; **the big ~** (US) el gran mundo, la primera división; **to make it into the big ~*** abrirse paso y entrar en el gran mundo, ascender a primera división, triunfar.

(j) (occasion) vez f; **3 ~s** 3 veces; **this ~** esta vez; **last ~** la última vez; **next ~** la próxima vez; **the first ~ I did it** la primera vez que lo hice; **for the first ~** por primera vez; **for the last ~** por última vez; **~ after ~, ~ and again** repetidas veces; **each ~, every ~** cada vez; **each ~ that ...** cada vez que ...; **he won every ~** ganó todas las veces; **it's the best, every ~!** ¡es el mejor, no hay duda!; **give me beer every ~!** ¡para mí, siempre cerveza!; **many ~s** muchas veces; **many a ~ I saw him act, many's the ~ I saw him act** muchas veces le vi representar; **several ~s** varias veces; **the second ~ round** en la segunda vuelta; **third ~ lucky!** ¡a la tercera va la vencida!; **nine ~s out of ten, ninety-nine ~s out of a hundred** (fig) casi siempre; **I remember the ~ when ...** me acuerdo de cuando ...; **to bide one's ~**

esperar la hora propicia; **for weeks at a ~** durante semanas enteras, durante semanas seguidas; **to do 2 things at a ~** hacer 2 cosas a la vez; hacer 2 cosas al mismo tiempo; **to eat biscuits 4 at a ~** comer 4 galletas a la vez; **he ran upstairs 3 at a ~** subió la escalera de 3 en 3 escalones.

(k) (Math) **4 ~s 3** 4 por 3; **it's 4 ~s as fast as yours** es 4 veces más rápido que el tuyo.

(l) (ADV phrase) **at the same ~ you must remember that ...** de todas formas conviene recordar que ...; **at the same ~ as** (fig) al mismo tiempo que, al igual que, a la par que.

(m) (Mus) tiempo m; compás m; **in 3/4 ~** al compás de 3 por 4; **in ~ to the music** al compás de la música; **to beat (or keep) ~** llevar el compás; **to get out of ~** perder el ritmo, dejar de llevar el compás; **to mark ~** (Mil) marcar el paso; (fig) esperar, hacer tiempo.

(n) (Mech) **the ignition is out of ~** el encendido está fuera de fase, el encendido funciona mal.

2 VT **(a)** (reckon ~ of) medir el tiempo de, calcular la duración de; race cronometrar.

(b) (regulate) watch regular, poner en hora; **it is ~d to go off at midnight** debe estallar a medianoche, la espoleta está graduada para que explote a medianoche; **the train is ~d for 6** el tren debe llegar a las 6.

(c) (do at right ~) hacer en el momento oportuno; **you ~d that perfectly** elegiste a la perfección el momento para hacerlo (etc).

time-bomb ['taɪmbɒm] N bomba f de efecto retardado.
time-capsule ['taɪm,kæpsjuːl] N cápsula f del tiempo.
time-card ['taɪm,kɑːd] N tarjeta f de registro horario.
time-clock ['taɪm'klɒk] N reloj m registrador, reloj m de control de asistencia.
time-consuming ['taɪmkən,sjuːmɪŋ] ADJ que exige mucho tiempo.
time-exposure ['taɪmɪk,spəʊʒəʳ] N pose f, exposición f.
time frame, timeframe ['taɪmfreɪm] N margen m de tiempo; **to set a ~ for sth** poner fecha a algo.
time-fuse ['taɪmfjuːz] N temporizador m, espoleta f graduada, espoleta f de tiempo.
time-honoured, (US) time-honored ['taɪm,ɒnəd] ADJ sacramental, consagrado, clásico.
timekeeper ['taɪm,kiːpəʳ] N (watch) reloj m, cronómetro m; (person) cronometrador m, -ora f, apuntador m, -ora f del tiempo; **to be a good ~** ser puntual.
timekeeping ['taɪmkiːpɪŋ] N puntualidad f; **good/bad ~** puntualidad/impuntualidad or falta de puntualidad; **his ~ is good/bad** es muy puntual/impuntual.
time-lag ['taɪmlæg] N intervalo m; retraso m, pérdida f de tiempo; desfase m.
time-lapse photography ['taɪmlæpsfə'tɒgrəfɪ] N fotografía f de lapso de tiempo.
timeless ['taɪmlɪs] ADJ eterno; atemporal; race etc sin limitación de tiempo.
timelessness ['taɪmlɪsnɪs] N atemporalidad f.
time-limit ['taɪm,lɪmɪt] N limitación f de tiempo; (esp Comm) plazo m; (closing date) fecha f tope; **without a ~** sin limitación de tiempo; **to fix a ~ for sth** fijar un plazo para algo, señalar un plazo a algo.
timeliness ['taɪmlɪnɪs] N oportunidad f.
time-lock ['taɪmlɒk] N cerradura f de tiempo.
timely ['taɪmlɪ] ADJ oportuno.
time machine [,taɪmmə'ʃiːn] N máquina f de transporte a través del tiempo.
time-out [,taɪm'aʊt] N (US) tiempo m muerto.
timepiece ['taɪmpiːs] N reloj m.
timer ['taɪməʳ] N (Culin) avisador m, reloj m automático; (egg ~ etc) reloj m de arena; (Mech) reloj m automático; (Aut etc) distribuidor m de encendido.
timesaver ['taɪm,seɪvəʳ] N ahorrador m de tiempo.
time-saving ['taɪm,seɪvɪŋ] ADJ que ahorra tiempo.
time-scale ['taɪmskeɪl] N escala f de tiempo.
timeserver ['taɪm,sɜːvəʳ] N contemporizador m.
timeshare ['taɪmʃeəʳ] **1** N **(a)** (Comput) tiempo m compartido. **(b)** = time-sharing (b).
2 VT (Comput) utilizar colectivamente, utilizar en sistema de tiempo compartido.
time-sharing ['taɪmʃeərɪŋ] N **(a)** tiempo m compartido (also Comput). **(b)** (for holiday etc) multipropiedad f; **~ flat** piso m en edificio de multipropiedad.
time-sheet ['taɪmʃiːt] N hoja f de asistencia, hoja f de horas trabajadas.
time-signal ['taɪm,sɪgnl] N señal f horaria.
time-signature ['taɪm'sɪgnɪtʃəʳ] N compás m, signatura f de compás.
time-slice ['taɪmslaɪs] N fracción f de tiempo.
time-switch ['taɪmswɪtʃ] N interruptor m horario.
timetable ['taɪm,teɪbl] **1** N horario m; (programme of classes etc) programa m; (of negotiations) calendario m; (as booklet) guía f.

2 VT programar.
timetabling ['taɪmteɪblɪŋ] N programación f.
time trial ['taɪmtraɪəl] N prueba f contra reloj; cronometrada f.
timewarp ['taɪmwɔːp] N salto m en el tiempo, túnel m del tiempo.
time-wasting ['taɪmweɪstɪŋ] ADJ que hace perder tiempo.
timework ['taɪmwɜːk] N trabajo m a jornal; trabajo m por horas.
timeworn ['taɪmwɔːn] ADJ deteriorado por el tiempo.
time zone ['taɪmzəʊn] N huso m horario.
timid ['tɪmɪd] ADJ tímido.
timidity [tɪ'mɪdɪtɪ] N timidez f.
timidly ['tɪmɪdlɪ] ADV tímidamente.
timidness ['tɪmɪdnɪs] N timidez f.
timing ['taɪmɪŋ] 1 N (reckoning of time) medida f del tiempo, medida f de la duración: (rhythm) ritmo m, cadencia f, compás m; (Sport etc) cronometraje m; **the ~ of this is important** importa hacer esto en el momento exacto, importa elegir el momento más propicio para hacer esto.
2 ATTR (Mech) de distribución, de encendido; **~ device** (of bomb) temporizador m; **~ gear** engranaje m de distribución; **~ mechanism** dispositivo m para medir el tiempo.
timorous ['tɪmərəs] ADJ temeroso, tímido; animal huraño, asustadizo.
Timothy ['tɪməθɪ] NM Timoteo.
timpani ['tɪmpənɪ] NPL tímpanos mpl, atabales mpl.
timpanist ['tɪmpənɪst] N timbalero m.
tin [tɪn] 1 N (a) (element, metal) estaño m; (~plate) hojalata f.
(b) (esp Brit: container) lata f, bote m, pote m (Mex), tarro m (And, SC); **meat in ~s** carne f en lata, carne f enlatada.
2 ATTR de estaño; de hojalata; **~ can** lata f, bote m; **~ god** héroe m de cartón; **he has a ~ ear** (US Mus) tiene mal oído; **~ hat*** casco m de acero; **~ lizzie*** (Aut) genoveva f, viejo trasto m; **~ soldier** soldado m de plomo.
3 VT (a) (cover with ~) estañar.
(b) (can) envasar en lata, conservar en lata, enlatar; see also **tinned**.
tincture ['tɪŋktʃər] 1 N tintura f (also fig, Pharm).
2 VT tinturar, teñir (with de).
tinder ['tɪndər] N yesca f (also fig); **to burn like ~** arder como la yesca.
tinderbox ['tɪndəbɒks] N yescas fpl; (fig) polvorín m.
tinder-dry [ˌtɪndə'draɪ] ADJ muy seco, reseco.
tine [taɪn] N (fork) diente m; (pitchfork) púa f.
tinfoil ['tɪnfɔɪl] N papel m (de) estaño, papel m (de) aluminio.
ting [tɪŋ] = **tinkle**.
ting-a-ling ['tɪŋə'lɪŋ] N tilín m; **to go ~** hacer tilín.
tinge [tɪndʒ] 1 N tinte m; (fig) dejo m; matiz m; **not without a ~ of regret** no sin cierto sentimiento.
2 VT teñir (with de); (fig) matizar (with de); **pleasure ~d with sadness** placer m matizado de tristeza, placer m no exento de tristeza.
tingle ['tɪŋgl] 1 N comezón f; hormigueo m (de la piel); (thrill) estremecimiento m.
2 VI sentir comezón, sentir hormigueo; (ears) zumbar; (thrill) estremecerse (with de).
tingling ['tɪŋglɪŋ] N hormigueo m.
tingly ['tɪŋglɪ] ADJ: **~ feeling** sensación f de hormigueo; **my arm feels ~** siento hormigueo en el brazo; **I feel ~ all over** se me estremece todo el cuerpo.
tinker ['tɪŋkər] 1 N (a) (esp Brit) calderero m hojalatero; (gipsy) gitano m.
(b) (*) pícaro m, tunante m; **you ~!** ¡tunante!
2 VT (also **to ~ up**) remendar; (pej) remendar mal, remendar chapuceramente.
3 VI: **to ~ with** (mend) tratar de reparar; (play) jugar con, manosear; (and damage) estropear; **they're only ~ing with the problem** no se esfuerzan seriamente por resolver el problema; **he's been ~ing with the car all day** ha pasado todo el día tratando de reparar el coche.
tinkle ['tɪŋkl] 1 N (a) tilín m, retintín m; campanilleo m, cencerreo m.
(b) (Brit Telec*) llamada f; **I'll give you a ~** te llamaré.
2 VT hacer retiñir; hacer tintinar; hacer campanillear.
3 VI retiñir, tintinar; campanillear.
tinkling ['tɪŋklɪŋ] 1 ADJ que hace tilín (etc); **a ~ sound** un tilín (etc); **a ~ stream** un arroyo cantarín.
2 N tilín m, retintín m; campanilleo m, cencerreo m.
tin-mine ['tɪnmaɪn] N mina f de estaño.
tin-miner ['tɪnˌmaɪnər] N minero m de estaño.
tinned [tɪnd] ADJ (Brit) en lata, de lata; **~ tangerines** mandarinas fpl en conserva.
tinnitus [tɪ'naɪtəs] N zumbido m.
tinny ['tɪnɪ] ADJ (a) taste que sabe a lata; sound cascado, que suena a lata. (b) (*) inferior, de poco valor, de pacotilla; desvencijado.
tin-opener ['tɪnˌəʊpnər] N (Brit) abrelatas m.
Tin Pan Alley [ˌtɪnpæn'ælɪ] N industria f de la música pop.
tinplate ['tɪnpleɪt] N hojalata f.
tinpot* ['tɪnpɒt] ADJ de pacotilla, de poca monta.

tinsel ['tɪnsəl] 1 N oropel m (also fig); (cloth) lama f de oro (or de plata).
2 ADJ de oropel; (fig) de oropel, de relumbrón.
Tinseltown ['tɪnsəltaʊn] N (gen pej) Hollywood m.
tinsmith ['tɪnsmɪθ] N hojalatero m.
tint [tɪnt] 1 N tinte m, matiz m, color m; media tinta f.
2 VT teñir, matizar (blue de azul); **it's yellow ~ed with red** es amarillo matizado de rojo; **to ~ one's hair** teñirse el pelo.
tintack ['tɪntæk] N (Brit) tachuela f.
tinted ['tɪntɪd] ADJ glass, windscreen tintado; spectacles ahumado.
tintinnabulation ['tɪntɪˌnæbjʊ'leɪʃən] N campanilleo m.
tiny ['taɪnɪ] ADJ pequeñito, chiquitín, diminuto, minúsculo.
tip¹ [tɪp] 1 N (end) punta f, cabo m, extremidad f; (of stick etc) regatón m, casquillo m; (of finger) yema f, punta f; (of cigarette) boquilla f, embocadura f; **from ~ to toe** de pies a cabeza; **I had it on the ~ of my tongue** lo tenía en la punta de la lengua; **it's only the ~ of the iceberg** no es más que la punta del iceberg.
2 VT poner regatón a; **~ped with steel** con punta de acero.
tip² [tɪp] 1 N (a) (gratuity) propina f, gratificación f; **to give** (or **leave**) **sb a ~** dar una propina a uno.
(b) (hint) aviso m, advertencia f; consejo m, indicación f; (to police etc) soplo* m, chivatazo* m; (Racing) confidencia f; pronóstico m confidencial; **let me give you a ~** permítame darle un consejo; **if you take my ~** si sigues mi consejo; **the horse is a hot ~ for the 2.30** se pronostica con seguridad que el caballo ganará la carrera de las 2 y media.
2 VT (a) (tap, strike) golpear ligeramente, tocar ligeramente (al pasar), chocar ligeramente con; **to ~ one's hat to sb** tocarse el sombrero para saludar a uno.
(b) (reward) dar una propina a, dejar una propina para; **to ~ sb a pound** dar a uno una libra de propina; **to ~ sb generously** dar a uno una propina generosa.
(c) winner pronosticar, recomendar, elegir; **I ~ that horse to win** pronostico que ganará ese caballo; **he is being freely ~ped for the job** muchos creen que le darán el puesto; **he is strongly ~ped as prime minister** se pronostica con confianza que será primer ministro.
tip³ [tɪp] 1 N (Brit) (rubbish ~) vertedero m, basurero m, tiradero m (LAm); escombrera f; **this room is a ~*** este cuarto es un basurero.
2 VT (incline) inclinar, ladear; drinking vessel empinar; seat abatir, levantar; **to ~ away** liquid vaciar, verter, echar; **it's ~ping it down*** está lloviendo a cántaros; **to ~ sb off his seat** hacer que uno caiga de su asiento; **to ~ sb into the water** hacer caer a uno al agua (empujándole); **he ~s the scales at 100 kg** pesa 100 kg; **to ~ one's hand*** (US: **one's mitt‡**) delatarse a sí mismo involuntariamente.
3 VI (incline) inclinarse, ladearse; (topple) tambalearse; **he ~ped off into the sea** perdió el equilibrio y cayó al mar.
◆**tip back, tip backward(s)** 1 VT inclinar hacia atrás.
2 VI inclinarse hacia atrás.
◆**tip forward(s)** 1 VT inclinar hacia adelante.
2 VI inclinarse hacia adelante.
◆**tip off** VT avisar, notificar; **to ~ sb off** advertir a uno clandestinamente; **the police had been ~ped off** la policía había recibido un soplo.
◆**tip out** VT: **to ~ out the contents of a box** verter el contenido de una caja, vaciar una caja; **all the passengers were ~ped out** todos los pasajeros cayeron fuera.
◆**tip over** 1 VT volcar.
2 VI volcarse; caer.
◆**tip up** 1 VT (incline) inclinar, ladear; container volcar; person hacer perder el equilibrio; hacer caer, volcar; derribar.
2 VI volcarse; (seat) abatirse, levantarse; (lorry etc) bascular.
tip-cart ['tɪpkɑːt] N volquete m.
tip-off ['tɪpɒf] N advertencia f (clandestina), aviso m; soplo* m, chivatazo* m.
tipped [tɪpt] ADJ (Brit) cigarette emboquillado, con filtro.
tipper ['tɪpər] N volquete m.
tippet ['tɪpɪt] N esclavina f.
Tipp-Ex ['tɪpeks] ® 1 N Tippex ® m, corrector m.
2 VT (also **to ~ out**, **to ~ over**) corregir con Tippex.
tipple ['tɪpl] 1 N bebida f (alcohólica); **his ~ is Cointreau** él bebe Cointreau; **what's your ~?** ¿qué quieres tomar?
2 VI beber más de la cuenta; envasar, empinar el codo.
tippler ['tɪplər] N bebedor m, -ora f.
tippy-toe ['tɪpɪtəʊ] (US) = **tiptoe**.
tipsily ['tɪpsɪlɪ] ADV como borracho; **to walk ~** andar con pasos de borracho.
tipsiness ['tɪpsɪnɪs] N vinolencia f, chispa* f.
tipster ['tɪpstər] N pronosticador m.
tipsy ['tɪpsɪ] ADJ achispado*, bebido, tomado (LAm).
tiptoe ['tɪptəʊ] 1 N: **to walk on ~** caminar de puntillas; **to stand on ~** ponerse de puntillas.

2 VI: **to ~ across the floor** atravesar el suelo de puntillas; **to ~ to the window** ir de puntillas a la ventana; **to ~ in** entrar de puntillas; **to ~ out** salir de puntillas.

tiptop ['tɪp'tɒp] ADJ de primera, excelente; **in ~ condition** en excelentes condiciones; **a ~ show** un espectáculo de primerísima calidad.

tip-up ['tɪpʌp] ATTR *lorry* basculante; *seat* abatible.

tirade [taɪ'reɪd] N invectiva *f*, diatriba *f*.

tire[1] ['taɪə^r] **1** VT cansar, fatigar; (*bore*) aburrir.

2 VI cansarse, fatigarse; aburrirse; **to ~ of** cansarse de; aburrirse con; **she ~s easily** se cansa pronto.

◆**tire out** VT: **to ~ sb out** cansar a uno, rendir a uno de cansancio, agotar las fuerzas de uno.

tire[2] ['taɪə^r] N (*US*) = **tyre**.

tired ['taɪəd] ADJ (a) *movement, voice* cansado; **in a ~ voice** con voz cansada; **the ~ old clichés** los lugares comunes de siempre, los tópicos trillados.

(b) *person* cansado, fatigado; **to be ~** estar cansado; **to be ~ out** estar rendido, estar agotado; **to be ~ and emotional, to be as ~ as a newt** (*euph*) estar mareado; **I'm ~ of all that** estoy harto de todo eso; **to get** (*or* **grow**) **~ of doing sth** cansarse de hacer algo; **I get ~ of telling you** estoy harto de decírtelo; **you make me ~** me fastidias.

tiredly ['taɪədlɪ] ADV *walk etc* como cansado; *say* con voz cansada.

tiredness ['taɪədnɪs] N cansancio *m*, fatiga *f*.

tireless ['taɪəlɪs] ADJ infatigable, incansable.

tirelessly ['taɪəlɪslɪ] ADV infatigablemente, incansablemente.

tiresome ['taɪəsəm] ADJ molesto, fastidioso; *person* pesado; **how very ~!** ¡qué lata!; **he's a ~ sort** es un pesado; **he can be ~** a veces es un pesado.

tiresomeness ['taɪəsəmnɪs] N molestia *f*, fastidio *m*, lo fastidioso; pesadez *f*.

tiring ['taɪərɪŋ] ADJ molesto, fatigoso, que cansa, agotador; **after a ~ journey** después de un viaje cansado; **it's ~ work** es un trabajo agotador.

tiro ['taɪərəʊ] N novicio *m*, -a *f*, principiante *mf*.

Tirol [tɪ'rəʊl] = **Tyrol**.

tisane [tɪ'zæn] N tisana *f*.

tissue ['tɪʃuː] N (*cloth*) tisú *m*, lama *f*; (*handkerchief*) pañuelo *m* de papel; (*Anat etc*) tejido *m*; **a ~ of lies** una sarta de mentiras; **~ paper** papel *m* (de) seda.

tit[1] [tɪt] N (*Orn*) paro *m*; (*blue~*) herrerillo *m* común; (*coal~*) carbonero *m* garrapinos; (*long-tailed~*) mito *m*.

tit[2] [tɪt] N: **~ for tat!** ¡donde las dan las toman!; **so that was ~ for tat** así que ajustamos cuentas, así que le pagué en la misma moneda.

tit[3] [tɪt] N (a) (*Anat*) teta* *f*; pezón *m*; **~s** tetas* *fpl*; **to get on sb's ~s** sacar de quicio a uno, cabrear a uno*. (b) (*fool*) gilipollas‡ *m*.

Titan ['taɪtən] N titán *m*.

titanic [taɪ'tænɪk] ADJ titánico; inmenso, gigantesco.

titanium [tɪ'teɪnɪəm] N titanio *m*.

titbit ['tɪtbɪt] N, (*US*) **tidbit** ['tɪdbɪt] N golosina *f* (*also fig*); (*news*) pedazo *m*.

titch* [tɪtʃ], **titchy*** ['tɪtʃɪ] = **tich, tichy**.

titfer‡ ['tɪtfə^r] N (*Brit*) chapeo‡ *m*.

tithe [taɪð] N (*Eccl*) diezmo *m*.

Titian ['tɪʃən] NM Ticiano.

titillate ['tɪtɪleɪt] VT estimular, excitar, encandilar.

titillation [ˌtɪtɪ'leɪʃən] N estimulación *f*, excitación *f*, encandilamiento *m*.

titivate ['tɪtɪveɪt] **1** VT emperejilar, ataviar, adornar.

2 VI emperejilarse, ataviarse; arreglarse.

title ['taɪtl] **1** N (a) (*appellation, heading*) título *m*; (*Sport*) título *m*, campeonato *m*; **noble ~, ~ of nobility** título *m* de nobleza; **what ~ are you giving the book?** ¿qué título vas a dar al libro?, ¿cómo vas a titular el libro?; **what ~ should I give him?** ¿qué tratamiento debo darle?; **George V gave him a ~** Jorge V le ennobleció.

(b) (*Jur*) título *m*, derecho *m*; **his ~ to the property** su derecho a la propiedad.

2 VT titular, intitular.

titled ['taɪtld] ADJ con título de nobleza, noble.

title deed ['taɪtldiːd] N título *m* de propiedad.

title-fight ['taɪtlfaɪt] N combate *m* por un título.

title-holder ['taɪtlˌhəʊldə^r] N titular *mf*, campeón *m*, -ona *f*.

title-page ['taɪtlpeɪdʒ] N portada *f*.

title role ['taɪtl'rəʊl] N papel *m* principal.

title track ['taɪtltræk] N *canción que da título a un disco*.

titmouse ['tɪtmaʊs] N, PL **titmice** ['tɪtmaɪs] V **tit**[1].

titrate ['taɪtreɪt] VT valorar.

titration [taɪ'treɪʃən] N valoración *f*.

titter ['tɪtə^r] **1** N risa *f* disimulada.

2 VI reírse disimuladamente.

tittle ['tɪtl] N pizca *f*, ápice *m*; **there's not a ~ of truth in it** eso no tiene ni pizca de verdad.

tittle-tattle ['tɪtlˌtætl] N chismes *m*, chismografía *f*.

titty‡ ['tɪtɪ] N = **tit**[3]; **that's tough ~!** ¡mala suerte!

titular ['tɪtjʊlə^r] ADJ titular; nominal.

tiz* [tɪz] N, **tizzy*** ['tɪzɪ] N: **to be in a ~** estar nervioso, estar aturdido; **to get into a ~** ponerse nervioso, aturdirse.

TM N (a) ABBR *of* **transcendental meditation**. (b) (*Comm*) ABBR *of* **trademark**.

TN (*US Post*) ABBR *of* **Tennessee**.

TNT N ABBR *of* **trinitrotoluene** trinitrotolueno *m*.

to [tuː, tə] **1** PREP (a) (*dat*) a; **to give sth ~ sb** dar algo a uno; **I gave it ~ my friend** se lo di a mi amigo; **the person I sold it ~** la persona a quien lo vendí; **it belongs ~ me** me pertenece a mí, es mío; **it's new ~ me** es nuevo para mí; **I said ~ myself** dije para mí; **what is that ~ me?** y eso ¿qué me importa?; **they were kind ~ me** fueron amables conmigo.

(b) (*of movement, direction*) a; hacia; **to go ~ the town** ir a la ciudad; **to go ~ school** ir a la escuela; **to go ~ Italy** ir a Italia; **to go ~ Rome** ir a Roma; **to go ~ Peru** ir al Perú; **to go ~ the doctor** ir al médico; **let's go ~ John's** vamos a casa de Juan; **from door ~ door** de puerta en puerta; **the road ~ Zaragoza** la carretera de Zaragoza; **it's 90 kilometres ~ Lima** de aquí a Lima hay 90 kilómetros; **~ the left** a la izquierda; **~ the west** al oeste, hacia el oeste.

(c) (*as far as, right up to*) hasta; **to count up ~ 20** contar hasta 20; **~ this day** hasta hoy, hasta el día de hoy; **I'll see you ~ the door** te acompaño hasta la puerta; **funds ~ the value of ...** fondos *mpl* por valor de ...; **~ some degree** hasta cierto punto; **it's accurate ~ a millimetre** es exacto hasta el milímetro; **to be wet ~ the skin** estar mojado hasta los huesos; **they perished ~ a man** perecieron todos (sin excepción); **everybody down ~ the youngest** todos hasta el más joven.

(d) (*against*) a, contra; **to stand back ~ back** estar espalda con espalda; **to talk to sb man ~ man** hablar con uno de hombre a hombre; **to turn a picture ~ the wall** volver un cuadro contra la pared; **to clasp sb ~ one's breast** estrechar a uno contra su pecho.

(e) (*of time*) a, hasta; **from morning ~ night** de la mañana a la noche, desde la mañana hasta la noche; **8 years ago ~ the day** hoy hace exactamente 8 años; **at 8 minutes ~ 10** a las 10 menos 8; **a quarter ~ 5** las 5 menos cuarto.

(f) (*of*) de; **wife ~ Mr Milton** mujer *f* del Sr Milton; **secretary ~ the manager** secretaria *f* del gerente; **ambassador ~ King Cole** embajador *m* cerca del rey Cole; **he is heir ~ the duke** es heredero del duque; **he was heir ~ a million** había de heredar un millón de libras; **he has been a good friend ~ us** ha sido buen amigo nuestro.

(g) (*of dedications*) a; **greetings ~ all our friends!** ¡saludos a todos los amigos!; **welcome ~ you all!** ¡bienvenida a todos!, ¡bienvenidos todos!; **'~ Sue Atkins'** (*in book*) 'para Sue Atkins'; **to build a monument ~ sb** erigir un monumento en honor de uno; **here's ~ you!** ¡vaya por ti!, ¡por ti!; **to drink ~ sb** brindar por uno, beber a la salud de uno.

(h) (*in comparisons*) a; **inferior ~** inferior a; **that's nothing ~ what is to come** eso no es nada en comparación con lo que está todavía por venir.

(i) (*of proportion*) a; **A is ~ B as C is ~ D** A es a B como C es a D; **by a majority of 12 ~ 10** por una mayoría de 12 a 10; **Slobodia won by 4 goals ~ 2** ganó Eslobodia por 4 goles a 2; **the odds are 8 ~ 1** los puntos de ventaja son de 8 a 1; **200 people ~ the square mile** 200 personas por milla cuadrada.

(j) (*concerning*) a; **what do you say ~ this?** ¿qué contestación me das a esto?, ¿cómo contestas a esto?; **what would you say ~ a beer?** ¿qué te parece una cerveza?; **that's all there is ~ it** no hay nada más; no hay ningún misterio; todo queda tan sencillo como ves; **'~ repairing pipes: ...'** (*bill*) 'Reparación de los tubos: ...'; **'~ services rendered: ...'** 'Por los servicios que se han prestado: ...'

(k) (*according to*) según; **~ all appearances** al parecer, según todos los indicios; **~ my way of thinking** según mi modo de pensar; **it is not ~ my taste** no me gusta; **to write ~ sb's dictation** escribir al dictado de uno; **~ the best of my recollection** que yo recuerde; **it is sung ~ the tune of 'Tipperary'** se canta con la melodía de 'Tipperary'; **they came out ~ the strains of the national anthem** salieron a los compases del himno nacional.

(l) (*of purpose, result*) **~ this end** con este propósito; **to come ~ sb's aid** acudir en ayuda de uno; **to sentence sb ~ death** condenar a uno a muerte; **~ my great surprise** con gran sorpresa mía; **~ my lasting shame I did nothing** con gran vergüenza mía no hice nada; **to put an army ~ flight** poner en fuga a un ejército; **to go ~ ruin** arruinarse, echarse a perder; **to run ~ seed** granar, dar en grana (*and V* **seed**).

2 PREP (*before infin*) (a) (*with simple infin, not translated*) **~ know** saber, conocer; **'~ be or not ~ be'** 'ser o no ser'; (*following another verb a variety of constructions appears, for which see the verb in each case, eg*) **to**

forbid sb ~ do sth prohibir a uno hacer algo; **to begin ~ do sth** comenzar a hacer algo, empezar a hacer algo; **to try ~ do sth** tratar de hacer algo, procurar hacer algo; **I want you ~ do it** quiero que lo hagas; **I wanted you ~ do it** quería que lo hicieras; **they asked me ~ do it** me pidieron que lo hiciera.

(b) *(purpose)* para; **I did it ~ help you** lo hice para ayudarte.

(c) *(purpose, with verbs of motion)* a, para; **I came ~ see you** vine a verte; **I came specially ~ see you** vine expresamente para verte.

(d) *(result)* **I have done nothing ~ deserve this** no he hecho nada que mereciera esto.

(e) *(equivalent to* on + *ger)* **~ see him now one would never think that ...** al verle *(or* viéndole*)* ahora no creería nadie que ...

(f) *(expressing subsequent fact)* **I arrived ~ find she had gone** llegué para descubrir que ella se había ido; **it disappeared never ~ be found again** desapareció para no volver a encontrarse jamás.

(g) *(with ellipsis of verb)* **I don't want ~** no quiero; **you ought ~** debieras hacerlo *(etc)*; **I should love ~!** ¡ojalá!, ¡cuánto me gustaría hacerlo *(etc)*!; **we didn't want to sell it but we had ~** no queríamos venderlo pero tuvimos que hacerlo, no queríamos venderlo pero no había más remedio.

(h) **something ~ eat** algo de comer; **I have things ~ do** tengo cosas que hacer; **there is much ~ be done** hay mucho que hacer; **that book is still ~ be written** ese libro está todavía por escribir; **there was no-one for me ~ consult** no había nadie a quien yo pudiese consultar; **he is not ~ be trusted** no hay que fiarse de él; **he's not the sort ~ do that** no es capaz de hacer eso, tal cosa no cabe en él; **this is the time ~ do it** éste es el momento de hacerlo; **and who is he ~ protest?** ¿y quién es él para protestar?

(i) *(construction after adjs etc)* **to be ready ~ go** estar listo para partir; **it's hard ~ get hold of** es difícil de obtener; **he's slow ~ learn** es lento en aprender, aprende lentamente; **you are foolish ~ try it** eres un tonto si lo emprendes; **is it good ~ eat?** ¿es bueno de *(or* para*)* comer?, ¿se puede comer?; **to be the first ~ do sth** ser el primero en hacer algo; **who was the last ~ see her?** ¿quién fue el último en verla?; **he's a big boy ~** be still in short trousers es mayorcito ya para llevar todavía pantalón corto; **it's too heavy ~ lift** es demasiado pesado para levantar; **it's too hot ~ touch** no se puede tocar por el mucho calor; **he's too old ~ manage it** es demasiado viejo para poder hacerlo.

⑶ ADV: **to come ~** *(Naut)* fachear; *(Med)* volver en sí; **to lie ~** ponerse a la capa; **to push the door ~** cerrar la puerta (empujándola); *V* **fro.**

toad [təʊd] N sapo *m.*

toadflax ['təʊdflæks] N linaria *f.*

toad-in-the-hole [ˌtəʊdɪnðə'həʊl] N *(Brit)* empanada *f* de salchichas.

toadstool ['təʊdstuːl] N seta *f* (venenosa).

toady ['təʊdɪ] ⑴ N pelotillero* *m,* lameculos** *m.*

⑵ VI: **to ~ to sb** hacer la pelotilla a uno*, dar coba a uno*.

toadying ['təʊdɪɪŋ] N, **toadyism** ['təʊdɪɪzəm] N adulación *f* servil, coba* *f.*

toast [təʊst] ⑴ N (a) *(Culin)* pan *m* tostado, tostada *f*; **a piece of ~** un trozo de pan tostado.

(b) *(drink)* brindis *m* (to por); **to drink a ~ to sb** brindar por uno; **here's a ~ to all who ...** brindemos por todos los que ...; **A will propose a ~ to B** A pronunciará algunas palabras al brindar por B; **she was the ~ of the town** la celebraron mucho en toda la ciudad, en todas partes de la ciudad se brindó por ella.

⑵ VT (a) *(Culin)* tostar; **~ed sandwich** sándwich *m* tostado; **to ~ one's toes by the fire** calentar los pies cerca del fuego.

(b) *(drink to)* brindar por, beber a la salud de; **we ~ed the victory in champagne** celebramos la victoria con champán.

toaster ['təʊstər] N tostador *m.*

toasting-fork ['təʊstɪŋfɔːk] N tostadera *f.*

toast list ['təʊstlɪst] N lista *f* de brindis.

toastmaster ['təʊstˌmɑːstər] N oficial *m* que anuncia a los oradores en un banquete.

toastrack ['təʊstræk] N portatostadas *m.*

toasty ['təʊstɪ] N sándwich *m* tostado.

tobacco [tə'bækəʊ] N tabaco *m*; **~ industry** industria *f* tabacalera; **~ plant** planta *f* de tabaco; **~ plantation** tabacal *m.*

tobacco-jar [tə'bækəʊdʒɑːr] N tabaquera *f.*

tobacconist [tə'bækənɪst] N *(Brit)* estanquero *m,* -a *f,* tabaquero *m,* -a *f*; **~'s (shop)** estanco *m,* tabaquería *f.*

tobacco-pouch [tə'bækəʊpaʊtʃ] N petaca *f.*

Tobago [tə'beɪgəʊ] N Tobago *f.*

-to-be [tə'biː] ADJ *ending in compounds* futuro; *V* **be 11.**

toboggan [tə'bɒgən] ⑴ N tobogán *m,* trineo *m*; **~ run** pista *f* de tobogán.

⑵ VI ir en tobogán, deslizarse en tobogán.

toby jug ['təʊbɪdʒʌg] N *bock de cerveza en forma de hombre.*

toccata [tə'kɑːtə] N tocata *f.*

tocsin ['tɒksɪn] N campana *f* de alarma, rebato *m*; campanada *f* de alarma; *(fig)* voz *f* de alarma; **to sound the ~** *(fig)* dar la voz de alarma, tocar a rebato.

tod‡ [tɒd] N *(Brit)*: **on one's ~** a solas.

today [tə'deɪ] ⑴ ADV hoy; *(at the present time)* hoy día, hoy en día; **~ week, a week ~** de hoy en ocho días, dentro de una semana; **a fortnight ~** de hoy en quince días; **a year ago ~** hoy hace un año; **from ~** desde hoy, a partir de hoy; **early ~** hoy temprano; **all day ~** todo hoy; **what day is it ~?** ¿qué día es hoy?, ¿a cuántos estamos?; **here ~ and gone tomorrow** se cambia constantemente.

⑵ N hoy *m*; **~ is Monday** hoy es lunes; **~ is the 4th** estamos a 4; **~'s paper** el periódico de hoy; **the writers of ~** los escritores de hoy.

toddle ['tɒdl] VI *(begin to walk)* empezar a andar, dar los primeros pasos; *(walk unsteadily)* caminar sin seguridad; (*) *(go)* ir; *(stroll)* dar un paseo; *(depart: also* **to ~ off**) irse, marcharse; **we must be toddling*** es hora de irnos; **so I ~d round to see him*** así que fui a visitarle.

toddler ['tɒdlər] N pequeñito *m,* -a *f* (que aprende a andar, que da sus primeros pasos).

toddy ['tɒdɪ] N ponche *m.*

todger** ['tɒdʒər] N *(Brit)* chorra** *f.*

to-do* [tə'duː] N lío* *m,* follón* *m*; **there was a great ~** hubo un tremendo follón*; **what's all the ~ about?** ¿a qué tanto jaleo?; **she made a great ~** armó un lío imponente*.

toe [təʊ] ⑴ N *(Anat)* dedo *m* del pie; punta *f* del pie; *(of sock)* punta *f*; *(of shoe)* puntera *f*; **big ~** dedo *m* gordo del pie, dedo *m* grande del pie; **little ~** dedo *m* pequeño del pie; **to keep sb on his ~s** mantener a uno en estado de vigilancia, hacer que uno siga estando alerta; **you have to keep on your ~s** hay que estar alerta, hay que mantenerse bien despierto; **to tread on sb's ~s** ofender a uno; **to turn up one's ~s*** estirar la pata*.

⑵ VT tocar con la punta del pie; *V* **line¹.**

toecap ['təʊkæp] N puntera *f.*

toe-clip ['təʊklɪp] N calapiés *m.*

-toed [təʊd] ADJ *ending in compounds* de ... dedos del pie, *eg* **four~** de cuatro dedos del pie.

TOEFL ['təʊfəl] N ABBR *of* **Test of English as a Foreign Language.**

toehold ['təʊhəʊld] N punto *m* de apoyo (para el pie).

toenail ['təʊneɪl] N uña *f* del dedo del pie.

toe-piece ['təʊpiːs] N espátula *f,* punta *f.*

toerag‡ ['təʊræg] N mequetrefe *m.*

toff* [tɒf] N *(Brit)* currutaco *m,* chuleta* *m.*

toffee ['tɒfɪ] N *(Brit)* caramelo *m,* melcocha *f*; **he can't do it for ~*** no tiene la menor idea de cómo hay que hacerlo.

toffee-apple ['tɒfɪˌæpl] N manzana *f* acaramelada.

toffee-nosed* ['tɒfɪˌnəʊzd] ADJ presumido, engreído.

tofu ['təʊˌfuː] N tofu *m,* tofú *m.*

tog* [tɒg] ⑴ VT: **to ~ sb up** ataviar a uno *(in* de*)*, vestir a uno de modo impresionante *(or* ridículo *etc) (in* de*)*; **to get ~ged up** ataviarse, vestirse.

⑵ VR: **to ~ o.s. up** ataviarse, vestirse *(in* de*)*, emperejilarse.

⑶ NPL: **~s** ropa *f.*

toga ['təʊgə] N toga *f.*

together [tə'geðər] ⑴ ADV (a) *(in company)* junto, juntos; juntamente; **let's get it ~*** *(US)* organicémonos, pongamos manos a la obra; **now we're ~** ahora estamos juntos; **they were all ~ in the bar** todos estaban reunidos en el bar; **we're in this ~** en esto tenemos igual responsabilidad los dos; nos une la misma suerte; **they were both in it ~** resultó que los dos se habían confabulado, los dos estaban metidos en el asunto; **you can't all get in ~** no podéis entrar todos a la vez; **they managed it** entre los dos lo lograron; **they belong ~** están bien juntos, forman una pareja; **they work ~** trabajan juntos; *V* **bring, call** etc.

(b) **~ with** junto con; conjuntamente con; **~ with A, B is important** junto con A es importante B.

(c) *(simultaneously, in concert)* juntos, a la vez, a un tiempo; **all ~ now!** *(singing)* ¡todos en coro!; *(pulling)* ¡todos a la vez!; ¡bien, ahora!; **we'll do parts A and B ~** haremos juntamente las partes A y B; **don't all talk ~** no habléis todos a la vez.

(d) *(continuously)* seguido; sin interrupción; **for weeks ~** durante semanas seguidas.

⑵ ADJ *(esp US*)* equilibrado, cabal.

togetherness [tə'geðənɪs] N sentimiento *m* de estar todos estrechamente unidos; compañerismo *m*; espíritu *m* de familia *(or* de grupo *etc).*

toggle ['tɒgl] ⑴ N cazonete *m* de aparejo; fiador *m.*

⑵ ATTR: **~ key, ~ switch** conmutador *m* de palanca, tecla *f* de conmutación binaria.

Togo ['təʊgəʊ] N Togo *m.*

Togolese [ˌtəʊgəʊ'liːz] ⑴ ADJ togolés.

⑵ N togolés *m,* -esa *f.*

toil [tɔɪl] ⑴ N labor *f,* trabajo *m*; fatiga *f*; afán *m,* esfuerzo *m*; **after**

months of ~ después de meses de trabajo (agotador).
2 VI (a) (*work hard*) trabajar; fatigarse; apurarse, afanarse; **to ~ to do sth** esforzarse por hacer algo, afanarse por hacer algo; **we ~ed at it for hours** trabajamos en ello durante muchas horas (sin éxito); **they ~ed on into the night** siguieron trabajando hasta muy entrada la noche.

(b) (*labour*) **to ~ along** caminar con dificultad, avanzar penosamente; **to ~ up a hill** subir penosamente una colina; **the engine is beginning to ~** el motor empieza a funcionar con dificultad.

toilet ['tɔɪlɪt] **1** N (a) (*process of dressing*) tocado m; atavío m; (*dress*) vestido m.

(b) (*lavatory*) inodoro m, lavabo m, wáter m, sanitario m (*Mex*); 'T~s' 'Servicios', 'Baño'; **to go to the ~** ir al wáter, ir al baño (*LAm*).
2 ATTR de tocador; **~ articles**, **~ requisites** artículos mpl de tocador; **~ set** juego m de tocador.

┌─── TOILET ───┐

i El término británico más frecuente para referirse al aseo (no al cuarto de baño en su totalidad), es **toilet**. En los establecimientos públicos se usan también **the gents** (para el de caballeros) y **the ladies** (para el de señoras). **Loo** es un término más coloquial, aunque no tanto como **lav** y **bog**. **Lavatory**, **public convenience** y **WC** son términos más educados que también se ven en los letreros.
En inglés americano **bathroom** es el término estándar para el aseo. **John** o **can** son coloquiales; **rest room** y **washroom** son términos de más educación. En un establecimiento público también se usan los términos **men's room** para el de caballeros y **ladies' room** o **women's room** para el de señoras.

toilet-bag ['tɔɪlɪtbæg] N, **toilet-case** ['tɔɪlɪtkeɪs] N neceser m, estuche m de aseo, bolso m de aseo.
toilet-bowl ['tɔɪlɪtbəʊl] N, **toilet-pan** ['tɔɪlɪt,pæn] N taza f (de retrete).
toilet-paper ['tɔɪlɪt,peɪpəʳ] N papel m higiénico.
toiletries ['tɔɪlɪtrɪz] NPL artículos mpl de tocador.
toilet-roll ['tɔɪlɪt,rəʊl] N (rollo m de) papel m higiénico.
toilet-seat ['tɔɪlɪtsiːt] N asiento m de retrete.
toilet-soap ['tɔɪlɪt,səʊp] N jabón m de tocador.
toilette [twɑːˈlet] N = **toilet**.
toilet-tissue ['tɔɪlɪt,tɪʃuː] N papel m higiénico.
toilet-train ['tɔɪlɪttreɪn] VT: **to ~ a child** acostumbrar a un niño a no ensuciarse.
toilet-training ['tɔɪlɪt,treɪnɪŋ] N: **~ can be difficult** acostumbrar a un niño a no ensuciarse puede resultar difícil.
toilet-water ['tɔɪlɪt'wɔːtəʳ] N agua f de colonia.
toils [tɔɪlz] NPL red f, lazo m.
toilsome ['tɔɪlsəm] ADJ penoso, laborioso, arduo.
toilworn ['tɔɪlwɔːn] ADJ completamente cansado, rendido.
to-ing ['tuːɪŋ] N: **~ and fro-ing** ir m y venir, trajín m.
toke [təʊk] N (*US Drugs*) calada f.
token ['təʊkən] **1** N (a) (*sign, symbol*) señal f, muestra f, indicio m; (*remembrance*) prenda f, recuerdo m; (*of one's appreciation etc*) detalle m, señal f de agradecimiento; **as a ~ of**, **in ~ of** en señal de; como recuerdo de; **by the same ~** igualmente; del mismo modo; **love ~** prenda f de amor.
(b) (*disc etc*) ficha f, disco m (metálico); (*coupon*) bono m, vale m.
2 ADJ simbólico; **~ amount** cantidad f testimonial; **the ~ black** el negro simbólico; **~ payment** pago m nominal, pago m simbólico; **to put up a ~ resistance** oponer una resistencia simbólica, resistir por pura fórmula; **~ strike** huelga f simbólica; **~ woman** mujer-muestra f, representación f femenina.
tokenism ['təʊkənɪzəm] N programa m político de fachada.
Tokyo ['təʊkjəʊ] N Tokio m, Tokío m.
told [təʊld] PRET AND PTP of **tell**.
tolerable ['tɒlərəbl] ADJ (a) (*bearable*) tolerable, soportable. (b) (*fair*) regular, pasable.
tolerably ['tɒlərəblɪ] ADV bastante; pasablemente; **a ~ good player** un jugador bastante bueno, un jugador pasable; **it is ~ certain that ...** es casi seguro que ...
tolerance ['tɒlərəns] N (a) tolerancia f; paciencia f, indulgencia f. (b) (*margin*) tolerancia f.
tolerant ['tɒlərənt] ADJ tolerante; indulgente; **to be ~ of** tolerar, ser tolerante de.
tolerantly ['tɒlərəntlɪ] ADV con tolerancia; con indulgencia.
▼ **tolerate** ['tɒləreɪt] VT tolerar, soportar, aguantar; **are we to ~ this?** ¿hemos de soportar esto?; **I can't ~ any more** no aguanto más; **it is not to be ~d** es intolerable, es insoportable.
toleration [,tɒləˈreɪʃən] N tolerancia f; **religious ~** tolerancia f religiosa; libertad f de cultos.
toll¹ [təʊl] N (a) (*payment*) peaje m, portazgo m; (*on bridge*) pontazgo m; **~ motorway** autopista f de peaje; **to pay ~** pagar el peaje.
(b) (*losses, casualties*) mortalidad f, número m de víctimas, número m de pérdidas; **the ~ on the roads** el número de víctimas en

accidentes de circulación; **there is a heavy ~** hay muchas víctimas, son muchos los muertos; **the disease takes a heavy ~ each year** cada año la enfermedad se lleva a muchas víctimas, cada año la enfermedad causa gran número de muertes; **to take ~ of** causar bajas en, tener su efecto en; **the effort took its ~ on all of us** el esfuerzo tuvo un grave efecto en todos nosotros.
toll² [təʊl] **1** VT bell tañer, tocar, doblar (a muerto); **to ~ the hour** dar la hora.
2 VI doblar (a muerto); **the bells were ~ing in mourning for ...** doblaron las campanas en señal de duelo por ...; **'For whom the bell ~s'** 'Por quien doblan las campanas'.
tollbar ['təʊlbɑːʳ] N barrera f de peaje.
tollbooth ['təʊlbuːð] N cabina f de peaje.
tollbridge ['təʊlbrɪdʒ] N puente m de peaje.
toll call ['təʊlkɔːl] N (*US*) conferencia f.
toll-free [,təʊlˈfriː] ADV (*US*): **to call ~** llamar sin pagar.
tollgate ['təʊlgeɪt] N barrera f de peaje.
tolling ['təʊlɪŋ] N tañido m, doblar m.
tollkeeper ['təʊl,kiːpəʳ] N peajero m, portazguero m.
toll road ['təʊlrəʊd] N carretera f de peaje.
tollway ['təʊlweɪ] N (*US*) autopista f de peaje.
Tom [tɒm] NM familiar form of **Thomas**; **~ Dick and Harry** cada quisque m, cualquier hijo m de vecino; Fulano, Mengano y Zutano; **you shan't marry any ~ Dick or Harry** no te casarás con un cualquiera; **~ Thumb** Pulgarcito.
tom [tɒm] N gato m (macho).
tomahawk ['tɒməhɔːk] N tomahawk m; **to bury the ~** (*US*) echar pelillos a la mar, envainar la espada.
tomato [təˈmɑːtəʊ, (*US*) təˈmeɪtəʊ] **1** N, PL **tomatoes** [təˈmɑːtəʊz] (*fruit*) tomate m; (*plant*) tomatera f.
2 ATTR: **~ juice** jugo m de tomate; **~ ketchup** salsa f de tomate; **~ paste**, **~ purée** puré m de tomate; **~ plant** tomatera f; **~ sauce** salsa f de tomate.
tomb [tuːm] N tumba f, sepulcro m.
tombola [tɒmˈbəʊlə] N (*Brit*) tómbola f.
tomboy ['tɒmbɔɪ] N muchacha f hombruna, muchachota f, chica f poco femenina.
tomboyish ['tɒmbɔɪʃ] ADJ marimacho.
tombstone ['tuːmstəʊn] N lápida f sepulcral.
tomcat ['tɒmkæt] N (*cat*) gato m (macho); (*US:*) mujeriego m, calavera m.
tome [təʊm] N (*hum*) librote m.
tomfool ['tɒmˈfuːl] **1** ADJ tonto, estúpido.
2 N tonto m, imbécil m.
tomfoolery [tɒmˈfuːlərɪ] N pataratas fpl, payasadas fpl.
Tommy ['tɒmɪ] NM familiar form of **Thomas**; **~ (Atkins)** (*Brit*) el soldado raso inglés.
tommy-gun ['tɒmɪgʌn] N metralleta f, pistola f ametralladora.
tommy-rot* ['tɒmɪrɒt] N tonterías fpl.
tomography [təˈmɒgrəfɪ] N tomografía f.
tomorrow [təˈmɒrəʊ] **1** ADV mañana; **~ evening** mañana por la tarde; **~ morning** mañana por la mañana; **a week ~** de mañana en ocho días.
2 N mañana f; **the day after ~** pasado mañana; **~ is Sunday** mañana es domingo; **~ is another day** mañana es otro día; **he drank like there was no ~*** bebió como si fuera la última vez; **will ~ do?** ¿lo puedo dejar para mañana?; ¿te conviene mañana?; **~'s paper** el periódico de mañana.
tom-tit ['tɒmtɪt] N paro m, carbonero m común.
tom-tom ['tɒmtɒm] N tantán m.
ton [tʌn] N (a) (*weight*; *Brit*: = 1016 kg; *US: also* **short ~** = 907.18 kg) tonelada f; **it weighs a ~** pesa una tonelada.
(b) (*) **~s** montones* mpl; **we have ~s of it at home** en casa lo tenemos a montones*; **we have ~s of time** nos sobra tiempo, tenemos tiempo de sobra.
(c) (:) velocidad f de 100 millas por hora; **to do a ~** ir a 100 millas por hora (en moto); **~ up boys** (*Brit*) motoristas mpl que hacen 100 millas por hora.
tonal ['təʊnl] ADJ tonal.
tonality [təʊˈnælɪtɪ] N tonalidad f.
tone [təʊn] **1** N (a) (*in most senses*) tono m; (*of colour*) tono m, tonalidad f; matiz m; **in low ~s** en tono bajo; **in an angry ~** en tono de enojo.
(b) (*class*) clase f; dignidad f; buen tono m, elegancia f; **the place has ~** el sitio tiene buen tono, es un sitio elegante; **the clientèle gives the restaurant ~** la clientela da distinción al restaurante; **he lowers the whole ~ of the occasion** rebaja toda la dignidad de la ceremonia (*etc*).
(c) (*tendency*) tono m, nota f; **the ~ of the market** la nota dominante del mercado, el tono del mercado.
2 VT (*Mus*) entonar; (*Phot*) virar.
3 VI armonizar, ir bien juntos.

◆**tone down** VT (**a**) *noise* reducir, disminuir; *radio etc* reducir el volumen de; **~ it down!** ¡menos ruido! (**b**) *colour* hacer menos brillante. (**c**) *speech etc* moderar (el tono de).

◆**tone up** VT *muscles* poner en forma, fortalecer.

tone colour, (*US*) **tone color** ['təun,kʌlər] N (*Mus*) timbre *m*.

tone-control ['təunkən,trəul] N control *m* de tonalidad.

-toned [təund] ADJ *ending in compounds*: **sepia~** en tono sepia; **high~** en tono altisonante.

tone-deaf ['təun'def] ADJ que no tiene oído musical.

tone language ['təun,læŋgwɪdʒ] N lengua *f* tonal.

toneless ['təunlɪs] ADJ soso, flojo; *voice* monótono; apagado, inexpresivo.

tonelessly ['təunlɪslɪ] ADV monótonamente.

tone poem ['təun,pəuɪm] N poema *m* sinfónico.

toner ['təunər] N (*for photocopier*) virador *m*; (*for skin*) tonificante *m*.

ton(e)y* ['təunɪ] ADJ (*US*) de buen tono, elegante.

Tonga ['tɒŋə] N Tonga *f*.

tongs [tɒŋz] NPL (*for coal etc*) tenazas *fpl*; (*for sweets, sugar, hair*) tenacillas *fpl*; **a pair of ~** unas tenazas, unas tenacillas.

tongue [tʌŋ] N (**a**) (*Anat*) lengua *f*; (*of shoe etc*) lengüeta *f*; (*of bell*) badajo *m*; (*of flame, land*) lengua *f*; **with one's ~ in one's cheek** irónicamente, burla burlando; **a ~ in cheek remark** una observación irónica; **I can't get my ~ round these Ruritanian names** estos nombres ruritanios resultan impronunciables; **so you've found your ~?** ¿así que estás dispuesto por fin a hablar?; **to give ~** empezar a ladrar; **to give a ready ~** no morderse la lengua; **to hold one's ~** callarse; **hold your ~!** ¡a callarse!; **to loosen sb's ~** hacer hablar a uno; **wine loosens the ~** el vino suelta la lengua; **have you lost your ~?** ¿estás mudo o qué?; **the formula came tripping off her ~** pronunció la fórmula con la mayor facilidad.

(**b**) (*Ling*) lengua *f*, idioma *m*; **in the Slobodian ~** en eslobodiano, en la lengua eslobodia; **to speak in ~s** hablar en lenguas desconocidas.

tongue-and-groove [,tʌŋən'gru:v] N machihembrado *m*.

tongue-lashing ['tʌŋ'læʃɪŋ] N latigazo *m*, reprensión *f*; **to give sb a ~** poner a uno como un trapo.

tongue-tied ['tʌŋtaɪd] ADJ que tiene dificultad al hablar, que tiene defecto del habla; (*fig*) tímido, premioso, confuso.

tongue-twister ['tʌŋ,twɪstər] N trabalenguas *m*.

tonic ['tɒnɪk] ☐1 ADJ tónico; **~ accent** acento *m* tónico.

☐2 N (**a**) (*Mus*) tónica *f*.

(**b**) (*Med*) tónico *m*; (*as drink, with gin etc; also* **~ water**) (agua *f*) tónica *f*; (*fig*) tónico *m*; **this news will be a ~ for the market** esta noticia será un tónico para la bolsa.

tonicity [tɒ'nɪsɪtɪ] N tonicidad *f*.

tonic water ['tɒnɪk,wɔːtər] N agua *f* tónica.

tonight [tə'naɪt] ADV esta noche.

tonnage ['tʌnɪdʒ] N tonelaje *m*.

tonne [tʌn] N tonelada *f* (métrica) (= 1.000 kg).

-tonner ['tʌnər] N *ending in compounds* de ... toneladas; **a 1,000~** un barco de 1.000 toneladas.

tonometer [təu'nɒmɪtər] N tonómetro *m*.

tonsil ['tɒnsl] N amígdala *f*, angina *f* (*Mex*); **to have one's ~s out** sacarse las amígdalas.

tonsillectomy [,tɒnsɪ'lektəmɪ] N tonsilectomía *f*, amigdalotomía *f*.

tonsillitis [,tɒnsɪ'laɪtɪs] N amigdalitis *f*.

tonsorial [tɒn'sɔːrɪəl] ADJ (*esp hum*) barberil; relativo a la barba.

tonsure ['tɒnʃər] ☐1 N tonsura *f*.

☐2 VT tonsurar.

Tony ['təunɪ] NM *familiar form of* **Anthony**.

too [tuː] ADV (**a**) (*excessively*) demasiado; muy; **it's ~ hard** es demasiado duro, es muy duro; **it's ~ easy** es muy fácil, es muy sencillo; **it's ~ heavy for me to lift** es demasiado pesado para que lo levante; **~ often** con demasiada frecuencia, muy a menudo; **it's not ~ difficult** no es muy difícil; **I'm not ~ keen on the idea** la idea no me hace gracia que digamos; **it's ~ early for that** es (muy) temprano para eso; **~ right!**, **~ true!** ¡muy bien dicho!, ¡y cómo!; V **many, much, well**.

(**b**) (*also*) también; además, por otra parte; **I went ~** yo fui también; **and it's broken ~** y además está roto; **she is, ~!** ¡y tanto que lo es!

took [tuk] PRET *of* **take**.

tool [tuːl] ☐1 N (**a**) herramienta *f*; utensilio *m*; (*set of*) **~s** útiles *mpl*, utillaje *m*; **garden ~s** útiles *mpl* de jardinería; **plumber's ~s** útiles *mpl* de fontanero; **the ~s of one's trade** las cosas que uno necesita para su oficio; **to down ~s** suspender el trabajo; (*strike*) declararse en huelga; **give us the ~s and we will finish the job** dadnos las herramientas y nosotros terminaremos la obra.

(**b**) (*fig: person, book etc*) instrumento *m*; **the book is an essential ~** el libro es indispensable, el libro es instrumento imprescindible; **he was an unwilling ~ of the gang** sin quererlo fue un instrumento de la pandilla; **he is just the ~ of the minister** es la criatura del ministro nada más.

☐2 VT labrar con herramienta; *book* estampar en seco; filetear.

toolbag ['tuːlbæg] N bolsa *f* de herramientas.

toolbox ['tuːlbɒks] N, **tool chest** ['tuːltʃest] N caja *f* de herramientas.

tooled-up ['tuːld'ʌp] ADJ armado.

tooling ['tuːlɪŋ] N estampación *f* en seco; fileteado *m*.

toolkit ['tuːlkɪt] N juego *m* de herramientas.

toolmaker ['tuːl,meɪkər] N tallador *m* de herramientas.

toolmaking ['tuːl,meɪkɪŋ] N talladura *f* de herramientas.

toolroom ['tuːlrum] N departamento *m* de herramientas.

toolshed ['tuːlʃed] N cobertizo *m* para herramientas.

toot [tuːt] ☐1 N sonido *m* breve (de claxon *etc*); **he went off with a ~ on the horn** partió con un breve toque de bocina.

☐2 VT sonar, tocar.

☐3 VI sonar (la bocina *etc*); (*person*) tocar la bocina, dar un bocinazo.

tooth [tuːθ] N, PL **teeth** [tiːθ] (**a**) (*Anat*) diente *m*; (*esp molar*) muela *f*; **in the teeth of the wind** contra un viento violento; **in the teeth of great opposition** contra una resistencia de lo más terco; **to be armed to the teeth** estar armado hasta los dientes; **to cast sth in sb's teeth** echar algo en cara a uno; **to cut one's teeth** endentecer, echar los dientes; **to be fed up to the (back) teeth with** estar hasta la coronilla de; **to fight ~ and nail** luchar encarnizadamente; **to get one's teeth into** hincar el diente a (*also fig*); **the Commission must be given more teeth** hay que dar poderes efectivos a la Comisión; **to have a ~ out** hacerse sacar una muela; **she has a sweet ~** le gustan las cosas dulces; es golosa; **to lie in one's teeth** mentir descaradamente; **we've got to set our teeth and get on with it** tenemos que apretar los dientes e ir adelante; **to show one's teeth** enseñar los dientes.

(**b**) (*of saw, wheel*) diente *m*; (*of comb*) púa *f*.

toothache ['tuːθeɪk] N dolor *m* de muelas.

toothbrush ['tuːθbrʌʃ] N cepillo *m* de dientes; **~ moustache** bigote *m* de cepillo.

toothcomb ['tuːθkəum] N: **to go through sth with a fine ~** registrar algo minuciosamente.

toothed [tuːθt] ADJ *wheel etc* dentado; de dientes ..., *eg* **big-~** de dientes grandes.

tooth fairy ['tuːθfeərɪ] N ratoncito *m* Pérez.

toothless ['tuːθlɪs] ADJ desdentado, sin dientes; (*fig*) ineficaz, sin poder efectivo.

toothpaste ['tuːθpeɪst] N pasta *f* dentífrica, dentífrico *m*, crema *f* dental.

toothpick ['tuːθpɪk] N palillo *m* (mondadientes), mondadientes *m*.

tooth-powder ['tuːθ,paudər] N polvos *mpl* dentífricos.

toothsome ['tuːθsəm] ADJ sabroso.

toothy ['tuːθɪ] ADJ dentudo, dentón; **to give sb a ~ smile** sonreír a uno mostrando mucho los dientes.

tootle ['tuːtl] ☐1 N sonido *m* breve (de flauta, trompeta *etc*); serie *f* de notas breves; **give us a ~ on your trumpet** tócanos algo a la trompeta; *see also* **toot**.

☐2 VT *flute etc* tocar.

☐3 VI (**a**) tocar la flauta (*etc*); *see also* **toot**.

(**b**) (*Aut*) **we ~d down to Brighton** hicimos una escapada a Brighton, fuimos de excursión a Brighton; **we were tootling along at 60** íbamos a 60.

toots(y)* ['tuːts(ɪ)] N (*US*) chica *f*, gachí; *f*; **hey ~!** ¡oye, guapa!

top¹ [tɒp] ☐1 N (**a**) (*topmost point*) cumbre *f*, cima *f*; ápice *m*; (*of tree*) copa *f*; (*of head*) coronilla *f*; (*of building*) remate *m*; (*of wall*) coronamiento *m*; (*of wave*) cresta *f*; (*of stairs etc*) lo alto, parte *f* alta; (*of list, page, table, classification*) cabeza *f*; primer puesto *m*, primera posición *f*; (*of plant*) hojas *fpl*, parte *f* superior; (*further part*) otro extremo *m*; parte *f* más lejana; **at the ~ of the hill** en la cumbre de la colina; **at the ~ of the tree** en lo alto del árbol; **at the ~ of the list** a la cabeza de la lista, en la primera posición de la lista; **executives who are at the ~ of their careers** ejecutivos que están en la cumbre de sus carreras; **El Toboso is at the ~ of the league** El Toboso encabeza la liga, El Toboso va en primera posición de la liga; **he lives at the ~ of the house** ocupa el piso más alto de la casa; **I saw him at the ~ of the street** le vi al otro extremo de la calle; **he sits at the ~ of the table** se sienta a la cabecera de la mesa; **she's at the ~ of the bill** está en la cabecera del cartel; **from ~ to bottom** de arriba abajo, de cabo a rabo; **the system is rotten from ~ to bottom** el sistema entero está podrido; **from ~ to toe** de pies a cabeza; **I said it off the ~ of my head** lo dije sin pensar; **speaking off the ~ of my head, I would say ...** hablando así sin pensarlo, yo diría que ...; **on ~** encima; **to be on ~** estar encima; estar en la parte superior; (*fig*) llevar ventaja, estar ganando; **to come out on ~** salir ganando, salir ganancioso; **it's just one thing on ~ of another** es una cosa tras otra; **next second the lorry was on ~ of us** al instante el camión se nos echó encima; **the flat is so small we live on ~ of each other** el piso es tan pequeño que vivimos amontonados; **I'm on ~ of my work now** ahora puedo con el trabajo; **things are getting on ~ of her** los problemas empiezan a afectarla de mala manera; **and then on ~ of all that ...** y luego por añadidura ..., y como si eso fuera poco ...; y luego para colmo de desgracias ...; **over the ~** excesivo, desmesurado; **to go over the ~** (*Mil*) lanzarse al ataque (saliendo de las trincheras); (*fig*) pasarse (de lo razonable), desbordarse; **this proposal is really over the ~** esta propuesta pasa de la raya; **he doesn't have much up ~*** no es muy listo que digamos.

(b) (*surface*) superficie *f*; **on ~ of** sobre, encima de; **it floats on ~ of the water** flota sobre el agua; **oil comes to the ~** el aceite sube a la superficie; **the table ~ is damaged** la superficie de la mesa está deteriorada.

(c) (*Naut*) cofa *f*.

(d) (*cap of bottle*) cápsula *f*, tapa *f*; (*of pen*) capuchón *m*; (*lid*) tapa *f*, tapadera *f*; (*of carriage*) baca *f*; (*of bus*) piso *m* superior, imperial *f*; (*US Aut*) capota *f*; **with a sliding ~, with a sunshine ~** descapotable, con techo corredizo; **to blow one's ~*** subirse por las paredes‡.

(e) (*maximum, best*) lo mejor; **the ~ of the flood** (*or* **tide**) la pleamar; **the ~ of the morning to you!** (*Ir*) ¡buenos días!; **'T~ of the Pops'** ≃ 'Los cuarenta principales' (*Sp*); **to be at the ~ of one's form** estar en plena forma; **to shout at the ~ of one's voice** llamar a voz en grito; **it's the ~s*** es tremendo*, es fabuloso*, es la flor de la canela; **she's ~s*** es la reoca*.

2 ADJ (*highest*) más alto, el más alto; *cimero*; *part* superior, más alto; *floor, stair etc* más alto, último; (*first*) primero; (*greatest*) máximo; (*highest in rank*) principal, primero; puntero; *leader* supremo, máximo; *price* máximo, tope; **~ banana*** (*US*) pez *m* gordo*; **~ brass*** jefazos* *mpl*; **~ copy** original *m*; **to pay ~ dollar for sth*** (*US*) pagar una cosa a precio de oro; **~ executive** alto ejecutivo *m*; **~ gear** (*Brit*) directa *f*; **~ leaders** máximos dirigentes *mpl*; **~ management** alta gerencia *f*; **~ people** gente *f* bien; **~ secret document** documento *m* ultrasecreto; **~ security jail** cárcel *f* de alta (*or* máxima) seguridad; **~ spin** efecto *m* de avance, lift *m*; **~ team** equipo *m* líder; **the T~ 20** (*Mus*) los 20 principales; **at ~ speed** a máxima velocidad; **the ~ men in the party** los líderes del partido, los jerarcas del partido; **he was ~ boy** se clasificó primero (entre los muchachos); **to come ~** ganar, ganar el primer puesto, clasificarse primero; **he came ~ in maths** tuvo la mejor nota en matemáticas.

3 VT **(a)** *tree* desmochar; *plant* descabezar; *fruit etc* quitar las hojas (*etc*) de; (‡) *person* colgar.

(b) (*complete upper part of*) coronar, rematar; **the wall is ~ped with stone** el muro tiene un coronamiento de piedras; **and to ~ it all ...** y por añadidura ...; y para colmo de desgracias ...

(c) (*exceed*) exceder, aventajar; rebasar; salir por encima de; **to ~ sb in height** ser más alto que uno; **to ~ sb by a head** sacar a uno una cabeza; **this ~s everything** esto supera a todo lo demás; **we have ~ped last year's takings by £200** hemos recaudado 200 libras más que el año pasado, los ingresos exceden a los del año pasado en 200 libras; **sales ~ped the million mark** las ventas rebasaron el millón.

(d) (*reach summit of*) llegar a la cumbre de; *class, list* encabezar, estar a la cabeza de; llegar a ocupar la primera posición de; **the team ~ped the league all season** el equipo iba en cabeza de la liga toda la temporada; **to ~ the bill** (*Theat*) estar en la cabecera del cartel.

◆**top off** VT: **to ~ off a building** terminar el piso superior de un edificio; **he ~ped this off by saying that ...** esto lo remató diciendo que ...; **he ~ped off the 8th course with a cup of coffee** para completar el octavo plato se bebió una taza de café.

◆**top up** (*Brit*) **1** VT completar; rellenar; redondear; (*level up*) nivelar; **to ~ up sb's glass** acabar de llenar (*or* volver a llenar) el vaso de uno; **to ~ up a battery** recargar una batería hasta el nivel indicado; **shall I ~ you up?** ¿te doy más?

2 VI: **to ~ up with fuel** repostar combustible; **to ~ up with oil** poner aceite; **we ~ped up with a couple of beers** como remate nos bebimos un par de cervezas.

top² [tɒp] N (*spinning ~*) peonza *f*, peón *m*; (*humming ~, musical ~*) trompa *f*.

topaz [ˈtəʊpæz] N topacio *m*.

top boots [ˈtɒpbuːts] NPL botas *fpl* de campaña.

topcoat [ˈtɒpkəʊt] N sobretodo *m*.

top-down [ˌtɒpˈdaʊn] ADJ *approach, theory, leadership* verticalista.

top-drawer [ˌtɒpˈdrɔːr] ADJ de alta sociedad.

top dressing [ˈtɒpˈdresɪŋ] N abono *m* (aplicado a la superficie).

tope [təʊp] VI beber (más de la cuenta), emborracharse.

topee [ˈtəʊpiː] N salacot *m*.

toper [ˈtəʊpər] N borrachín *m*.

top-flight [ˈtɒpflaɪt] ADJ sobresaliente, de primera (clase).

topgallant [tɒpˈgælənt, *Naut* təˈgælənt] N (*also ~ sail*) juanete *m*.

top hat [ˈtɒpˈhæt] N chistera* *f*, sombrero *m* de copa.

top-hatted [ˈtɒpˈhætɪd] ADJ en chistera, enchisterado.

top-heaviness [ˈtɒpˈhevɪnɪs] N (*fig*) macrocefalia *f*.

top-heavy [ˈtɒpˈhevɪ] ADJ demasiado pesado por arriba; (*fig*) falto de equilibrio, mal equilibrado; macrocefálico; (*) tetuda*.

topiary [ˈtəʊpɪərɪ] N arte *m* de recortar los arbustos en formas de animales *etc*.

topic [ˈtɒpɪk] N asunto *m*, tema *m*.

topical [ˈtɒpɪkəl] ADJ **(a)** actual, de interés actual, corriente; **~ talk** charla *f* sobre cuestiones del día, charla *f* sobre actualidades; **a highly ~ question** una cuestión de palpitante actualidad. **(b)** (*US*) local.

topicality [ˌtɒpɪˈkælɪtɪ] N **(a)** actualidad *f*; importancia *f* actual, interés *m* actual. **(b)** (*US*) localidad *f*.

topknot [ˈtɒpnɒt] N moño *m* (*also Orn*); (*) cabeza *f*.

topless [ˈtɒplɪs] **1** ADJ top-less; **~ bar** bar *m* top-less; **~ swimsuit** monoquini *m*.

2 ADV: **to go ~** andar top-less.

top-level [ˈtɒpˈlevl] ADJ de primer nivel; **~ conference** conferencia *f* de alto nivel.

top-loader [ˌtɒpˈləʊdər] N lavadora *f* de carga superior.

topmast [ˈtɒpmɑːst] N mastelero *m*.

topmost [ˈtɒpməʊst] ADJ más alto, el más alto.

top-notch* [ˈtɒpˈnɒtʃ] ADJ de primerísima categoría.

top-of-the-range [ˌtɒpəvðəˈreɪndʒ] ADJ, **top-of-the-line** [ˌtɒpəvðəˈlaɪn] ADJ más alto de la gama.

topographer [təˈpɒgrəfər] N topógrafo *m*, -a *f*.

topographic(al) [ˌtɒpəˈgræfɪk(l)] ADJ topográfico.

topography [təˈpɒgrəfɪ] N topografía *f*.

topology [təˈpɒlədʒɪ] N topología *f*.

topper* [ˈtɒpər] N **(a)** (*hat*) chistera* *f*, sombrero *m* de copa. **(b)** **the ~ was that ...** (*US*) para colmo ..., para acabar de rematar ...*

topping* [ˈtɒpɪŋ] **1** ADJ (*Brit†*) bárbaro*, pistonudo*.

2 N (*Culin*) cubierta *f*.

topple [ˈtɒpl] **1** VT (*also* **to ~ over**) derribar, derrocar; tumbar; hacer caer; volcar.

2 VI (*also* **to ~ down**) caerse, venirse abajo; (*also* **to ~ over**) volcarse; (*lose balance*) perder el equilibrio; (*totter*) tambalearse; **he ~d over a cliff** cayó por un precipicio; **after the crash the bus ~d over** después del choque el autobús se volcó.

top-ranked [ˈtɒpˈræŋkt] ADJ *player, team* primero en el ránking.

top-rank(ing) [ˈtɒpˈræŋk(ɪŋ)] ADJ de primera categoría; *officer* de alta graduación.

top-rated [ˈtɒpˈreɪtɪd] ADJ *TV series* de más audiencia; *hotel, school* más prestigioso.

topsail [ˈtɒpsl] N gavia *f*.

top-secret [ˈtɒpˈsiːkrɪt] ADJ ultrasecreto, de reserva absoluta.

top-selling [ˈtɒpˈselɪŋ] ADJ = **best-selling**.

topside [ˈtɒpˌsaɪd] N lado *m* superior, superficie *f* superior; (*Culin*) tapa *f* y tajo redondo.

topsoil [ˈtɒpsɔɪl] N capa *f* superficial del suelo.

topsy-turvy [ˈtɒpsɪˈtɜːvɪ] **1** ADV en desorden, patas arriba; **everything is ~** todo está patas arriba.

2 ADJ confuso, desordenado.

top-up [ˈtɒpʌp] **1** N: **would you like a ~?** ¿quiere que se lo llene?

2 ATTR: **~ loan** (*Brit*) préstamo gubernamental a estudiantes.

toque [təʊk] N gorro *m* de cocinero

tor [tɔːr] N colina *f* abrupta y rocosa, pico *m* pequeño (*esp en el suroeste de Inglaterra*).

Torah [ˈtɔːrə] N: **the ~** la Torá.

torch [tɔːtʃ] N (*flaming*) antorcha *f*, tea *f*, hacha *f*; (*Brit: electric*) linterna *f* eléctrica, lámpara *f* de bolsillo; **to carry a ~ for sb** (*fig*) seguir enamorada de uno (*esp* a pesar de no ser correspondido por él).

torchbearer [ˈtɔːtʃˌbeərər] N persona *f* que lleva una antorcha.

torchlight [ˈtɔːtʃlaɪt] N luz *f* de antorcha; **~ procession** desfile *m* con antorchas.

torch song [ˈtɔːtʃsɒŋ] N canción *f* de amor.

tore [tɔːr] PRET of **tear**.

toreador [ˈtɒrɪədɔːr] N torero *m*.

torment **1** [ˈtɔːment] N tormento *m*; angustia *f*; suplicio *m*; **the ~s of jealousy** los tormentos de los celos; **to be in ~** estar sufriendo, sufrir mucho.

2 [tɔːˈment] VT atormentar, martirizar; torturar; **we were ~ed by thirst** sufrimos los tormentos de la sed; **she was ~ed by doubts** la atormentaron las dudas; **don't ~ the cat** no le des guerra al gato.

tormentor [tɔːˈmentər] N atormentador *m*, -ora *f*.

torn [tɔːn] PTP of **tear**.

tornado [tɔːˈneɪdəʊ] N, PL **tornadoes** [tɔːˈneɪdəʊz] tornado *m*.

torpedo [tɔːˈpiːdəʊ] **1** N, PL **torpedoes** [tɔːˈpiːdəʊz] torpedo *m*.

2 VT torpedear (*also fig*).

torpedo-boat [tɔːˈpiːdəʊbəʊt] N torpedero *m*, lancha *f* torpedera.

torpedo-tube [tɔːˈpiːdəʊtjuːb] N (tubo *m*) lanzatorpedos *m*.

torpid [ˈtɔːpɪd] ADJ aletargado, inactivo; (*fig*) torpe, apático; aburrido.

torpidity [tɔːˈpɪdɪtɪ] N, **torpor** [ˈtɔːpər] N letargo *m*, inactividad *f*; (*fig*) torpeza *f*, apatía *f*; aburrimiento *m*.

torque [tɔːk] **1** N par *m* de torsión.

2 ATTR: **~ wrench** llave *f* dinamométrica.

torrent [ˈtɒrənt] N torrente *m* (*also fig*); **to rain in ~s** llover a cántaros, diluviar.

torrential [tɒ'renʃəl] ADJ torrencial.
torrid ['tɒrɪd] ADJ tórrido.
torsion ['tɔːʃən] N torsión f.
torso ['tɔːsəʊ] N, PL **torsos** ['tɔːsəʊz] torso m.
tort [tɔːt] N agravio m, tuerto m.
tortilla [tɔː'tiːə] N tortilla f.
tortoise ['tɔːtəs] N tortuga f.
tortoiseshell ['tɔːtəsʃel] **1** N (a) carey m. (b) (butterfly: small ~) ortiguera f; (cat) gato m pardo.
2 ATTR: ~ **glasses** gafas fpl de carey.
tortuous ['tɔːtjʊəs] ADJ tortuoso.
torture ['tɔːtʃəʳ] **1** N tortura f; (fig) tormento m; **it was ~!** ¡lo que sufrí!; **to put sb to the ~** torturar a uno.
2 ATTR: ~ **chamber** cámara f de tortura.
3 VT torturar; (fig) atormentar; sense etc torcer, violentar; **to be ~d by doubts** ser atormentado por las dudas.
torturer ['tɔːtʃərəʳ] N verdugo m.
torturing ['tɔːtʃərɪŋ] ADJ torturador, atormentador.
Tory ['tɔːrɪ] (Brit) **1** ADJ conservador; **the T~ Party** el Partido Conservador.
2 N conservador m, -ora f.
Toryism ['tɔːrɪɪzəm] N (Brit) conservatismo m, conservadurismo m.
tosh* [tɒʃ] N música f celestial*; **~!** ¡tonterías!
toss [tɒs] **1** N (a) (movement: of head etc) movimiento m brusco; sacudida f, meneo m; (throw) echada f, tirada f; (by bull) cogida f; (fall from horse) caída f; **the ball came to him full ~** la pelota llegó a sus manos sin tocar la tierra; **he took a bad ~** sufrió una violenta caída; **I don't give a ~*** me la trae floja*.
(b) (of coin) echada f; sorteo m (para la elección de lado etc); **to argue the ~** andar en dimes y diretes, discutir; **to win the ~** ganar el sorteo.
2 VT head etc mover bruscamente, hacer un movimiento brusco de; sacudir, menear; (throw) echar, tirar; (of bull) coger (y lanzar al aire); coin echar a cara o cruz; **to ~ the caber** (Scot) lanzar troncos; **to ~ a salad** darle vueltas a una ensalada; **to ~ sb in a blanket** mantear a uno; **the horse ~ed its head** el caballo levantó airosamente la cabeza; ver también HIGHLAND GAMES .
3 VI (a) (also to ~ about, to ~ around) agitarse, sacudirse; (of plumes etc) ondear; (a boat: gently) balancearse sobre las ondas, (violently) ser sacudido por las ondas; **to ~ (in one's sleep), to ~ and turn** revolverse (en la cama).
(b) (also to ~ up) jugar a cara o cruz (for sth algo); (Sport) sortear (for sth algo); **we'll ~ up to see who does it** jugaremos a cara o cruz para decidir quién lo hará.
◆ **toss about, toss around** **1** VT lanzar acá y allá; **the currents ~ed the boat about** las corrientes zarandeaban la embarcación.
2 VI V toss 3 (a).
◆ **toss aside** VT echar a un lado, apartar bruscamente, abandonar.
◆ **toss away** VT echar, tirar.
◆ **toss off** **1** VT poem etc escribir rapidísimamente; **to ~ off a drink** beberse algo de un trago, beberse algo rápidamente.
2 VI (*) hacerse una paja*.
◆ **toss over** VT: **to ~ a book over to sb** tirar un libro a uno; **~ it over!** ¡dámelo!
◆ **toss up** **1** VT coin echar a cara o cruz.
2 VI = toss 3 (b).
tosser* ['tɒsəʳ] N (Brit) mamón* m, gilipollas* m.
toss-up ['tɒsʌp] N: **it's a ~** tanto puede ser lo uno como lo otro; **it's a ~ whether I go or stay** no me decido si irme o quedarme; **it was a ~ between X and Y** había iguales posibilidades para X e Y.
tot¹ [tɒt] N (a) (esp Brit: drink) trago m, copita f; **just a ~** unas gotitas nada más; **let's go in here for a ~** entremos aquí a tomar algo. (b) (child) nene m, -a f.
tot² [tɒt] (esp Brit) **1** VT: **to ~ up** sumar.
2 VI: **it ~s up to £5** suma 5 libras, viene a ser 5 libras; **what does it ~ up to?** ¿cuánto suma?
▼ **total** ['təʊtl] **1** ADJ (Math etc) total; (complete, utter) total, completo, entero; **the ~ losses amount to ...** las pérdidas suman un total de ...; **what is the ~ amount?** ¿cuánto es el importe total?; **~ assets** activo m total; **~ failure** fracaso m completo, fracaso m rotundo; **~ liabilities** pasivo m total; **~ loss** (Comm) pérdida f total; **~ output** producción f total; **~ war** guerra f total; **we were in ~ ignorance** lo ignorábamos por completo; **the disagreement is ~** el desacuerdo es total; V abstainer.
▼ **2** N total m; suma f; cantidad f global; **it comes to a ~ of ...** suma en total ..., asciende a ...; **the sum ~ of all this was that ...** el resultado de todo esto fue que ...
3 VT (a) (add up: also to ~ up) sumar.
(b) (amount to) ascender a, sumar, totalizar.
(c) (US*) car dejar hecho chatarra, destrozar, desguazar.
totalitarian [,təʊtælɪ'teərɪən] ADJ totalitario.
totalitarianism [,təʊtælɪ'teərɪənɪzəm] N totalitarismo m.

totality [təʊ'tælɪtɪ] N totalidad f.
totalizator ['təʊtəlaɪzeɪtəʳ] N totalizador m.
totalize ['təʊtəlaɪz] VT totalizar.
totalizer ['təʊtəlaɪzəʳ] = **totalizator**.
totally ['təʊtəlɪ] ADV totalmente, completamente.
tote¹* [təʊt] N totalizador m.
tote²* [təʊt] VT acarrear, llevar (con dificultad); **I ~d it around all day** cargué con él todo el día; (also in compounds): **gun-toting policemen** policías mpl pistoleros.
tote bag ['təʊtbæg] N (esp US) bolso m grande.
totem ['təʊtəm] N tótem m.
totemic [təʊ'temɪk] ADJ totémico.
totemism ['təʊtəmɪzəm] N totemismo m.
totem-pole ['təʊtəmpəʊl] N tótem m.
totter ['tɒtəʳ] VI (stagger) bambolearse, tambalearse; (be about to fall) tambalearse, estar para desplomarse.
tottering ['tɒtərɪŋ] ADJ, **tottery** ['tɒtərɪ] ADJ tambaleante; nada seguro; ruinoso; **he's getting tottery** empieza a andar con poca seguridad; **with tottering steps** con pasos inseguros, con pasos vacilantes.
totty* ['tɒtɪ] N (Brit) ganado* m; **a nice piece of ~** una tía buena.
toucan ['tuːkən] N tucán m.
touch [tʌtʃ] **1** N (a) (sense of ~) tacto m; **it feels rough to the ~** es áspero al tacto.
(b) (act of ~ing) toque m; contacto m; (light brushing) roce m; (Mus, of typist) pulsación f, toque m; (Art) pincelada f, toque m; **~ therapy** terapia f táctil; **final ~, finishing ~** última mano f, último toque m; **to give sth a finishing ~, to put the finishing ~ to sth** dar el último toque a algo; **common ~, human ~, personal ~** (in person's character) don m de gentes, (in contacts etc) nota f personal, nota f humana; **the master's ~** la mano del maestro; **it has the ~ of genius** lleva el sello de la genialidad; **it's the Nelson ~** es el estilo de Nelson; **the cold ~ of a dead fish** el contacto helado con un pez muerto; **at a ~ of her hand, I ...** al tocarme la mano de ella, yo ...; **with the barest ~ of a finger** con una ligerísima presión del dedo; **by ~** a tiento, tentándolo; **I felt a ~ on my neck** sentí que alguien me tocaba el cuello; **to give sb a ~ on the arm** tocar el brazo de uno.
(c) (contact) contacto m; **to be in ~ with sb** estar en contacto (or comunicación) con uno; **I'll be in ~** (writing) te escribiré, (phoning) te llamaré; **to be in ~ with new inventions** estar al tanto de los inventos, mantenerse al corriente de los inventos; **to be out of ~ with sb** haber perdido contacto con uno; **he's completely out of ~** sus ideas están completamente postergadas, está quedando anticuado; **we're very much out of ~ here** aquí casi no recibimos noticias de lo que pasa; **to get in ~ with sb** contactar a uno, ponerse en contacto con uno; **you can get into ~ with me at No. 7** puede contactarme en el número 7; **you ought to get in ~ with the police** conviene informar a la policía; **to keep in ~ with sb** mantener relaciones con uno; **well, keep in ~!** ¡bueno, no pierdas contacto!; **to lose ~ with sb** perder contacto con uno; **to put sb into ~ with another person** ayudar a uno a establecer contacto con otra persona.
(d) (*) **he's an easy** (or soft) **~** es la mar de generoso*; **he's good for a ~** seguramente nos dará (or prestará) algo; **to make a ~** lograr sacar dinero de uno, lograr dar un sablazo a uno*.
(e) (small quantity) pizca f; poquito m; (Med) ataque m leve; **a ~ of the sun** una insolación; **with a ~ of irony** con un dejo de ironía, con un punto de ironía; **to add a ~ of salt** agregar un poquitín de sal; **to have a ~ of 'flu** tener un ataque leve de gripe.
(f) (Sport) touche f, parte f fuera de juego; **to be in ~** estar fuera de juego; **to kick for ~, to kick the ball into ~** poner el balón fuera de juego.
(g) (as adv) **it's a ~ expensive** es un poquito caro.
2 VT (a) (come into contact with) tocar; (and explore) palpar; (brush against) rozar; (reach) alcanzar; **~ and move!** ¡pieza tocada, pieza jugada!; **to ~ sth with one's finger** tocar algo con el dedo; **sb ~ed me on the arm** alguien me tocó el brazo; **don't ~!** ¡no tocar!, ¡fuera las manos!; **his property ~es ours** su propiedad linda con la nuestra, su finca es contigua a la nuestra; **and the police can't ~ him** y la policía no puede tocarle; **I never ~ed her!** ¡no la toqué siquiera!; **I wouldn't ~ it (with a barge pole)** no lo quiero ver ni de lejos; **to ~ ground** tocar tierra, tomar tierra; **~ wood!** ¡toco madera!
(b) (eat, drink) tomar, probar; **I haven't ~ed a mouthful** no he probado bocado; **I never ~ onion** no como cebolla; **I never ~ gin** no bebo nunca ginebra.
(c) (equal) compararse con, igualar; **there's no violinist to ~ him, no one can ~ him as a violinist** no hay violinista que se le iguale, no hay violinista que pueda compararse con él.
(d) (make an impression on) hacer efecto en, hacer mella en; **this saw won't ~ it** esta sierra no le hace mella, esta sierra es inútil para esto; **I couldn't ~ the third question** no pude tocar siquiera la tercera pregunta.

(e) (*move*) conmover, enternecer; **I was deeply ~ed** me conmoví mucho, me emocioné profundamente; **it ~ed our hearts** enterneció nuestros corazones; **no one can see it without being ~ed** nadie lo ve sin conmoverse.

(f) (*concern*) afectar, tocar; **it ~es us all closely** nos toca de cerca a todos; **if it ~es the national interest** si afecta al interés nacional.

(g) (*) **to ~ sb for a loan** dar un sablazo a uno*, lograr sacar dinero de uno; **to ~ sb for £5** lograr que uno preste 5 libras.

3 VI (*come into contact*) tocarse; encontrarse; tocar al pasar, pasar rozando; (*collide*) chocar ligeramente; (*be adjacent*) lindar, estar contiguo; **our hands ~ed** se encontraron nuestras manos; **the subjects ~ at several points** los temas tienen varios aspectos en común.

◆**touch at** VI tocar en, hacer escala en.

◆**touch down** **1** VT (*Sport*) poner en tierra.

2 VI **(a)** (*Aer*) tocar tierra, aterrizar, (*loosely*) llegar; (*on sea*) amerizar, amarar.

(b) (*Sport*) tocar en tierra.

◆**touch off** VT *explosive* explotar, hacer estallar; *revolt* provocar, hacer estallar; *idea* dar origen a; *argument* causar, provocar.

◆**touch on** VT mencionar (de paso), referirse (brevemente) a.

◆**touch up** VT **(a)** (*Art, Phot etc*) retocar.

(b) (‡) meter mano a, manosear.

touch-and-go ['tʌtʃən'gəʊ] **1** ADJ *decision* difícil, dudoso.

2 N: **it's ~ whether ...** está en vilo si ..., es difícil decidir si ...; **3 hours of ~** 3 horas de tira y afloja.

touchdown ['tʌtʃdaʊn] N (*Aer*) aterrizaje *m*, (*loosely*) llegada *f*; (*on sea*) amerizaje *m*, amaraje *m*; (*Sport*) ensayo *m*, tanto *m*.

touché [tuː'ʃeɪ] EXCL ¡es verdad!; ¡dices bien!

touched* [tʌtʃt] ADJ chiflado*, tocado.

touchiness ['tʌtʃɪnɪs] N susceptibilidad *f*.

touching ['tʌtʃɪŋ] **1** ADJ conmovedor, patético.

2 PREP tocante a.

touchingly ['tʌtʃɪŋlɪ] ADV de modo conmovedor, patéticamente.

touch judge ['tʌtʃdʒʌdʒ] N juez *m* lateral.

touchline ['tʌtʃlaɪn] N (*Soccer etc*) línea *f* de banda; (*Rugby*) línea *f* de toque, línea *f* lateral.

touchpaper ['tʌtʃpeɪpər] N mecha *f*.

touch-sensitive ['tʌtʃ'sensɪtɪv] ADJ sensible al tacto.

touchstone ['tʌtʃstəʊn] N piedra *f* de toque (*also fig*).

touch-type ['tʌtʃtaɪp] VI mecanografiar al tacto.

touch-typing ['tʌtʃ,taɪpɪŋ] N mecanografía *f* al tacto.

touch-typist ['tʌtʃ,taɪpɪst] N mecanógrafo *m*, -a *f* al tacto.

touchy ['tʌtʃɪ] ADJ susceptible, quisquilloso; **to be ~** ofenderse por poca cosa, tener prontos enojos; **he's ~ about his weight** no le hacen gracia las referencias a su gordura, no le gusta que se le tome el pelo con motivo de su gordura.

touchy-feely ['tʌtʃɪ'fiːlɪ] ADJ (*pej*) sentimentaloide, sensiblero.

tough [tʌf] **1** ADJ **(a)** *materials* duro, fuerte, resistente; *meat* duro, estropajoso; (*leathery*) correoso; **it's as ~ as old boots** es duro como una suela.

(b) (*hardy*) resistente, fuerte, vigoroso; **~ guy*** machote* *m*; **the ~ sports** los deportes violentos; **he's pretty ~** tiene mucha resistencia.

(c) (*unyielding, stubborn*) tenaz, terco; *policy* duro, de mano dura; *person* (*pej*) duro, malvado; **we can expect ~ resistance** podemos contar con una resistencia tensa.

(d) (*difficult*) difícil, penoso; *problem* espinoso; *journey, work* arduo; **there's a ~ road ahead** el camino a recorrer es arduo; **to have a ~ time of it** pasar las de Caín.

(e) (*of luck etc*) malo; **~!, ~ luck!** ¡mala suerte!; **that's pretty ~** eso me parece muy injusto; **but it was ~ on the others** pero perjudicó a los demás, pero fue muy desagradable para los demás.

2 N (*) machote* *m*; (*pej*) gorila* *m*, forzudo *m*.

3 VT: **to ~ it out*** (*hold out*) no cejar, no ceder; mantenerse firme; (*rough it*) pasar estrecheces, vivir sin comodidades.

toughen ['tʌfn] (*also fig*) **1** VT endurecer, fortalecer.

2 VI endurecerse.

◆**toughen up** = **toughen**.

toughened ['tʌfnd] ADJ endurecido, fortalecido.

toughie* ['tʌfɪ] N (*difficult question*) pregunta *f* peliaguda; (*person*) bravucón *m*, -ona *f*.

toughly ['tʌflɪ] ADV vigorosamente; tenazmente, tercamente.

tough-minded ['tʌf'maɪndɪd] ADJ duro, severo; nada sentimental.

toughness ['tʌfnɪs] N dureza *f*, resistencia *f*; (*strictness*) inflexibilidad *f*; lo correoso; vigor *m*; tenacidad *f*, terquedad *f*; lo difícil, lo penoso; lo arduo; **the job needs a certain ~** el trabajo exige cierta resistencia.

Toulon [tuː'lɔ̃ːŋ] N Tolón *m*.

Toulouse [tuː'luːz] N Tolosa *f* (de Francia).

toupée ['tuːpeɪ] N casquete *m*, peluca *f*.

tour ['tʊər] **1** N (*journey*) viaje *m* (largo), excursión *f* (larga); (*by team, actors, musicians etc*) gira *f*; (*of building, exhibition*) visita *f*; inspección

f; **~ of duty** período *m* de servicio; **~ of inspection** visita *f*; recorrido *m* de inspección; **the Australian ~ of 1972** la gira australiana de 1972; **the ~ includes a week in Venice** el programa del viaje incluye una semana en Venecia; **to be on ~** estar de viaje; (*team etc*) estar de gira; **to go on ~** partir de viaje, (*team etc*) partir de gira; **to take a company on ~** llevar a una compañía de gira; **to take a play on ~** llevar una obra a una serie de teatros (de provincia *etc*).

2 ATTR: **~ guide** guía *m* turístico, guía *f* turística; **~ operator** (*Brit*) touroperador *m*, -ora *f*, operador *m* turístico, operadora *f* turística.

3 VT *country etc* viajar por, recorrer (como turista); *building, exhibition* visitar, recorrer.

4 VI viajar; estar de viaje, hacer viaje de turista; **we're just ~ing around** hacemos visitas de turismo aquí y allá.

Touraine [tʊ'reɪn] N Turena *f*.

tour de force ['tʊədə'fɔːs] N proeza *f*, hazaña *f*.

tourer ['tʊərər] N (coche *m* de) turismo *m*.

Tourette('s) syndrome [tʊə'rɛt(s),sɪndrəʊm] N síndrome *m* de Tourette.

touring ['tʊərɪŋ] **1** N turismo *m*; viajes *mpl* turísticos.

2 ATTR: **~ company** compañía *f* ambulante; **~ team** equipo *m* en gira; equipo *m* visitante.

tourism ['tʊərɪzəm] N turismo *m*.

tourist ['tʊərɪst] **1** N turista *mf*.

2 ATTR turista, turístico; para turistas; de viajes; **of ~ interest** de interés turístico; **~ agency** agencia *f* de viajes; **~ bureau, ~ office** oficina *f* de viajes; **~ class** clase *f* turística; **~ industry, ~ trade** industria *f* del turismo; **~ information centre** ≈ oficina *f* de información y turismo; **~ season** temporada *f* del turismo; **~ trap** trampa *f* de turistas, lugar *m* cazaturistas; **~ visa** visado *m* turístico, visa *f* turística (*LAm*).

touristy* ['tʊərɪstɪ] ADJ (demasiado) turístico, turistizado.

tournament ['tʊənəmənt] N torneo *m*; concurso *m*, certamen *m*.

tournedos ['tʊənə'dəʊ] N turnedó *m*, tournedós *m*.

tourney ['tʊənɪ] N torneo *m*.

tourniquet ['tʊənɪkeɪ] N torniquete *m*.

touse* [taʊz] VT dar una paliza a (*also fig*).

tousing* ['taʊzɪŋ] N paliza *f* (*also fig*).

tousle ['taʊzl] VT ajar, desarreglar; *hair* despeinar.

tousled ['taʊzld] ADJ ajado, desarreglado, en desorden; *hair* despeinado.

tout [taʊt] **1** N (*seller*) pregonero *m*; (*agent*) gancho *m*; (*ticket ~*) reventa* *m*, revendedor *m*; (*Racing*) pronosticador *m*.

2 VT *wares* ofrecer, pregonar; *tickets* revender.

3 VI: **to ~ for custom** solicitar clientes; tratar de hacer un negocio.

tout court ['tuː'kʊər] ADV: **his name is Rodríguez ~** se llama Rodríguez a secas.

tow¹ [təʊ] **1** N (*act*) remolque *m*; (*rope*) remolque *m*, cable *m* de remolque; (*thing towed*) vehículo *m* (*etc*) remolcado; **to be on** (*or US*) **in**) **~** ser remolcado, ir de remolque; **to have a car in ~** llevar un coche de remolque; **he had 3 girls in ~** iba acompañado de 3 chicas, (*fig*) andaba en relaciones con 3 chicas, tenía 3 chicas al retortero; **to take in ~** dar remolque a.

2 ATTR: **~ car** (*US*) grúa *f*, coche *m* de remolque.

3 VT remolcar, llevar a remolque; (*Naut*) atoar, toar; **to ~ sth about** (*fig*) llevar algo consigo.

◆**tow away** VT remolcar, quitar remolcando.

tow² [təʊ] N estopa *f*.

towage ['təʊɪdʒ] N (*act*) remolque *m*; (*fee*) derechos *mpl* de remolque.

toward(s) [tə'wɔːd(z)] PREP (*of direction*) hacia; (*of time*) hacia, cerca de; (*of attitude*) con, para con; **his feelings ~ the church** sus sentimientos para con la iglesia; **~ noon** hacia mediodía; **~ 6 o'clock** hacia las 6; **we're saving ~ our holiday** ahorramos dinero para nuestras vacaciones; **it helps ~ a solution** contribuye a la solución, ayuda en el esfuerzo por encontrar una solución.

towaway zone ['təʊəweɪ,zəʊn] N (*US Aut*) zona de aparcamiento prohibido donde la grúa procede a retirar los vehículos.

towbar ['təʊbɑːr] N barra *f* de remolque.

towboat ['təʊbəʊt] N (*US*) remolcador *m*.

towel ['taʊəl] **1** N toalla *f*; **to throw in the ~** tirar la toalla.

2 VT secar con toalla; frotar con toalla.

towelling, (*US*) **toweling** ['taʊəlɪŋ] N género *m* para toallas, felpa *f*.

towel-rack ['taʊəlræk] N, **towel-rail** ['taʊəlreɪl] N toallero *m*.

tower ['taʊər] **1** N torre *f*; (*bell~*) campanario *m*; **~ of strength** baluarte *m*, bastión *m*.

2 ATTR: **~ block** (*Brit*) torre *f* (de viviendas).

3 VI (*also* **to ~ up**) elevarse; encumbrarse; **to ~ above, to ~ over** dominar, destacarse sobre, (*fig*) descollar entre; **it ~s to over 300 metres** se eleva a más de 300 metros; **he ~s above his contemporaries** descuella fuertemente entre sus coetáneos.

towering ['taʊərɪŋ] ADJ *mountain* encumbrado; elevado, elevadísimo; *building* muy alto, imponente por su altura; *figure* destacado, dominante; *rage* muy violento.

tow-headed [ˌtəʊ'hedɪd] ADJ rubio, rubiacho.

towline ['təʊlaɪn] N (*Naut*) sirga *f*; (*Aut*) cable *m* de remolque.

town [taʊn] ⒈ N ciudad *f*; (*smaller, country ~*) pueblo *m*, población *f*; **~ and gown** ciudadanos *mpl* y universitarios, ciudad *f* y universidad; **to be on the ~*** estar en plan de juerga*; **to go (out) on the ~*** salir de juerga*; **to live in ~** vivir en la capital (*esp* Londres); **Jake's back in ~!** ¡ha vuelto Jake!; **to go up to ~** ir a la capital (*nacional or* local); **to go to ~** ir a la ciudad; **to go to ~ on*** dedicarse con entusiasmo a, entregarse de lleno a; **he certainly went to ~ on that mistake** de verdad sacó partido de ese error; **he's out of ~** está fuera, está de viaje; **he's from out of ~** (*US*) es forastero, no es de aquí; **to paint the ~ red** echar una cana al aire.

⒉ ATTR urbano; urbanístico; de (la) ciudad, municipal; **~ centre** centro *m* urbano; **~ clerk** secretario *m*, -a *f* del Ayuntamiento; **~ council** (*Brit*) concejo *m* municipal, ayuntamiento *m*; **~ councillor** (*Brit*) concejal *m*, -ala *f*; **~ crier** pregonero *m* público; **~-dweller** ciudadano *m*, -a *f*; **~ hall** (*Brit*) ayuntamiento *m*; **~ house** casa *f* adosada; (*not country*) residencia *f* urbana; **~ meeting** (*US*) pleno municipal; **~ plan** plan *m* de desarrollo urbano; **~ planner** (*Brit*) urbanista *mf*; **~ planning** (*Brit*) urbanismo *m*.

townee [taʊ'niː] N, (*US*) **townie** ['taʊnɪ] N habitante *mf* de la ciudad; hombre *m* (*or* mujer *f etc*) de la ciudad.

townsfolk ['taʊnzfəʊk] NPL ciudadanos *mpl*.

township ['taʊnʃɪp] N municipio *m*, término *m* municipal; pueblo *m*.

townsman ['taʊnzmən] N, PL **townsmen** ['taʊnzmən] ciudadano *m*; (*as opposed to countryman*) hombre *m* de la ciudad, habitante *m* de la ciudad.

townspeople ['taʊnzˌpiːpl] NPL ciudadanos *mpl*.

townswoman ['taʊnzwʊmən] N, PL **townswomen** ['taʊnzwɪmɪn] ciudadana *f*; (*as opposed to countrywoman*) habitante *f* de la ciudad.

towpath ['təʊpɑːθ] N camino *m* de sirga.

towrope ['təʊrəʊp] N remolque *m*, cable *m* de remolque; (*on canal*) sirga *f*.

tow truck ['təʊtrʌk] N (*US*) (camión *m*) grúa *f*, coche *m* de remolque.

toxaemia, (*US*) **toxemia** [tɒk'siːmɪə] N toxemia *f*.

toxic ['tɒksɪk] ⒈ ADJ tóxico; **~ alga** alga *f* tóxica; **~ substance** sustancia *f* tóxica; **~ waste** desechos *mpl* tóxicos, residuos *mpl* tóxicos. ⒉ N tóxico *m*.

toxicity [ˌtɒk'sɪsɪtɪ] N toxicidad *f*.

toxicological [ˌtɒksɪkə'lɒdʒɪkəl] ADJ toxicológico.

toxicologist [ˌtɒksɪ'kɒlədʒɪst] N toxicólogo *m*, -a *f*.

toxicology [ˌtɒksɪ'kɒlədʒɪ] N toxicología *f*.

toxin ['tɒksɪn] N toxina *f*.

toy [tɔɪ] ⒈ N juguete *m*; (*pej, iro*) juguete *m*, chuchería *f*. ⒉ ATTR *railway etc* de juguete, de jugar; **~ car** coche *m* de juguete; **~ dog** (*small*) perrito *m*, perro *m* faldero; **~ soldier** soldadito *m* de plomo; **~ theatre** teatro *m* de títeres; **~ train** tren *m* de juguete. ⒊ VI: **to ~ with** *object* jugar con, divertirse jugando con; *food* comiscar; *idea* dar vueltas a, acariciar; *sb's affections* divertirse con.

toybox ['tɔɪbɒks] N caja *f* de juguetes.

toyboy ['tɔɪbɔɪ] N amante *m* (de una mujer más vieja).

toy-maker ['tɔɪˌmeɪkəʳ] N fabricante *mf* de juguetes.

toyshop ['tɔɪʃɒp] N juguetería *f*.

toytown ['tɔɪtaʊn] ADJ (a) = **Mickey Mouse**. (b) **he's a ~ revolutionary** es un aspirante a revolucionario.

trace¹ [treɪs] ⒈ N rastro *m*, huella *f*; vestigio *m*; señal *f*, indicio *m*; (*small amount*) pequeñísima cantidad *f*, pizca *f*; (*Chem, Med*) indicio *m*; (*remaining taste etc*) dejo *m*; **without a ~ of ill feeling** sin asomo de rencor; **sunk without ~** desaparecido sin dejar el menor indicio; **to vanish without ~** desaparecer sin dejar rastro; **there is no ~ of it now** no queda vestigio alguno de ello ahora; **we looked all over but couldn't find a single ~** buscamos por todas partes pero sin encontrar el menor indicio. ⒉ VT (a) *curve, line etc* trazar; (*with tracing paper*) calcar. (b) (*follow trail of*) seguir, seguir la pista de; rastrear; (*find, locate*) encontrar; localizar, averiguar el paradero de; **I cannot ~ any reference to it** no he logrado encontrar ninguna referencia a ello; **she was finally ~d to a house in Soho** por fin la encontraron en una casa del Soho; **to ~ an idea for sb** exponer una idea a uno.

◆**trace back** VT: **to ~ one's ancestry back to Ferdinand III** hacer remontar su ascendencia hasta Fernando III; **to ~ a rumour back to its source** averiguar dónde se originó un rumor, seguir la pista de un rumor hasta llegar a su punto de partida.

trace² [treɪs] N tirante *m*, correa *f*; **to kick over the ~s** sacar los pies del plato, mostrar las herraduras.

traceable ['treɪsəbl] ADJ: **a person not now ~** una persona cuyo paradero actual es imposible de encontrar; **an easily ~ reference** una referencia fácil de encontrar.

trace element ['treɪsˌelɪmənt] N oligoelemento *m*.

tracer ['treɪsəʳ] ⒈ N (*Chem, Med*) indicador *m*, trazador *m*. ⒉ ATTR: **~ bullet** bala *f* trazadora; **~ element** elemento *m* trazador.

tracery ['treɪsərɪ] N tracería *f*.

trachea [trə'kɪə] N tráquea *f*.

tracheotomy [ˌtrækɪ'ɒtəmɪ] N traqueotomía *f*.

trachoma [træ'kəʊmə] N tracoma *m*.

tracing ['treɪsɪŋ] N calco *m*.

tracing-paper ['treɪsɪŋˌpeɪpəʳ] N papel *m* de calco.

track [træk] ⒈ N (a) (*mark: of animal*) huella *f*; pista *f*, rastro *m*; (*of person*) pista *f*; (*of vehicle*) huella *f*; (*of wheel*) rodada *f*; (*of boat*) estela *f*; (*of hurricane*) rastro *m*, marcha *f*; (*of bullet, rocket etc*) trayectoria *f*; **to be on sb's ~(s)** seguir la pista de uno; **he had the police on his ~** le buscaba la policía, le estaba cazando la policía; **they got on to his ~ very quickly** se pusieron sobre la pista muy pronto; **to cover up one's ~s** borrar sus huellas, procurar no dejar rastro de sí; **to follow in sb's ~** seguir el camino que ha marcado uno; **to keep ~ of sb** no perder de vista a uno; seguir la suerte a uno; **to keep ~ of new inventions** mantenerse al tanto de los nuevos inventos; **to lose ~ of sb** perder a uno de vista; **to lose ~ of what sb is saying** perder el hilo de lo que está diciendo uno; **to make ~s*** irse, largarse; **we must be making ~s*** tenemos que marcharnos; **to stop (dead) in one's ~s** pararse en seco; **to stop sb (dead) in his ~s** parar a uno en seco; **to throw sb off the ~** despistar a uno.

(b) (*path*) senda *f*, camino *m*; **to be on the right ~** ir por buen camino; **to be on the wrong ~** (*fig*) haberse equivocado, estar equivocado; **to be way off the ~** estar totalmente despistado; **to put sb on the right ~** mostrar a uno el camino que le conviene seguir.

(c) (*Sport*) pista *f*; (*lane*) carril *m*; **to be on the fast (or inside) ~** (*fig*) ser ambicioso, tener ganas de ascender.

(d) (*Rail*) vía *f*; **to cross the ~s** cruzar la vía; **to live on the wrong side of the ~s** (*esp US*) vivir en los barrios pobres; **to jump the ~(s),** **to run off the ~(s)** descarrilar.

(e) (*Mech*: also **caterpillar ~s**) oruga *f*.

(f) (*on tape*) banda *f*, canal *m*; (*Comput*) pista *f*.

⒉ ATTR: **~ activities, ~ athletics** (*US*) atletismo *m*; **~ event** prueba *f* atlética en pista; **~ record** (*Sport*) récord *m*; (*fig*) historial *m*, hoja *f* de servicios.

⒊ VT *animal* rastrear, seguir la pista de; *satellite etc* rastrear, seguir la trayectoria de.

⒋ VI: **to ~ along** avanzar por, ir por, seguir.

◆**track down** VT localizar, averiguar el paradero (*or* origen) de, buscar y encontrar; **finally we ~ed it down in the library** por fin lo encontramos en la biblioteca.

track and field [ˌtrækən'fiːld] ⒈ N atletismo *m*. ⒉ ADJ de atletismo.

tracked [trækt] ADJ: **~ vehicle** vehículo *m* con orugas.

tracker ['trækəʳ] N rastreador *m*.

tracker-dog ['trækədɒg] N perro *m* rastreador.

track events ['trækɪˌvents] NPL (*Sport*) pruebas *fpl* en pista.

tracking ['trækɪŋ] ⒈ N rastreo *m*; **~ device** dispositivo *m* de localización.

tracking-station ['trækɪŋˌsteɪʃən] N centro *m* de seguimiento, estación *f* de rastreo.

trackless ['træklɪs] ADJ sin caminos, impenetrable.

trackman ['trækmən] N, PL **trackmen** ['trækmən] (*US*) obrero *m* de ferrocarril.

track meet ['trækmiːt] N (*US*) concurso *m* de carreras y saltos.

track-race ['trækreɪs] N carrera *f* en pista.

track-racing ['trækˌreɪsɪŋ] N carreras *fpl* en pista, ciclismo *m* (*etc*) en pista.

trackshoes ['trækʃuːz] NPL zapatillas *fpl* para pista de atletismo (claveteadas).

tracksuit ['træksuːt] N chandal *m*.

tract¹ [trækt] N región *f*, zona *f*; extensión *f*; (*Anat*) región *f*.

tract² [trækt] N (*pamphlet*) folleto *m*; (*treatise*) tratado *m*.

tractable ['træktəbl] ADJ *person* tratable, dócil; *problem* soluble; *material* dúctil, maleable.

traction ['trækʃən] ⒈ N tracción *f*. ⒉ ATTR: **~ engine** locomóvil *f*, máquina *f* de tracción.

tractive ['træktɪv] ADJ tractivo.

tractor ['træktəʳ] N tractor *m*.

tractor-drawn ['træktədrɔːn] ADJ arrastrado por tractor.

tractor drive ['træktəˌdraɪv] N tractor *m*.

tractor-driver ['træktəˌdraɪvəʳ] N tractorista *mf*.

tractor feed ['træktəˌfiːd] N arrastre *m* de papel por tracción.

trad* [træd] ADJ ABBR *of* **traditional**.

trade [treɪd] ⒈ N (a) (*commerce*) comercio *m*; negocio *m*; tráfico *m* (*in* en); industria *f*; **the wool ~** la industria lanera; **the ~ in drugs, the drug ~** el tráfico en narcóticos, el comercio de narcóticos; **to be in ~** ser comerciante, tener un negocio, (*esp*) tener una tienda; **to do a good (or brisk, roaring) ~** hacer un buen negocio (*in* con); V **retail** *etc*.

(b) (*calling*) oficio *m*, profesión *f*; ramo *m*; empleo *m*; oficio *m* manual; **a butcher by ~** de oficio carnicero; **a lawyer by ~** (*hum*) de profesión abogado; **to carry on a ~** ejercer un oficio; **to put sb to a**

~ hacer que uno aprenda un oficio; **known in the ~ as** ... conocido por los que son del ramo como ...
(c) **~s** (*Geog*) vientos *mpl* alisios.
2 ATTR de comercio, comercial; mercantil; **~ agreement** acuerdo *m* comercial; **~ allowance**, **~ discount** descuento *m* comercial; **~ association** asociación *f* mercantil; **~ barriers** barreras *fpl* arancelarias; **~ cycle** ciclo *m* mercantil; **~ deficit** déficit *m* comercial; **T~ Descriptions Act** (*Brit*) ley sobre descripciones comerciales); **~ directory** guía *f* mercantil; **~ discount** descuento *m* para el comercio; **~ fair**, **~ show** feria *f* de muestras, feria *f* comercial; **~ figures** estadísticas *fpl* comerciales; **~ gap** déficit *m* del balance comercial; **~ journal** periódico *m* gremial; **~ mission** misión *f* comercial; **~ paper** revista *f* comercial; **~˙ press** prensa *f* especializada; **~ price** precio *m* al comerciante, precio *m* al por mayor, precio *m* al detallista; **~ reference** referencia *f* comercial; **~ restrictions** restricciones *fpl* comerciales; **~ route** ruta *f* comercial; **~ sanctions** sanciones *fpl* comerciales; **~ secret** secreto *m* de fábrica, secreto *m* profesional; **on ~ terms** con descuento para el comercio; **~ war** guerra *f* comercial.
3 VT (*fig*) vender; **to ~ A for B** cambiar A por B, trocar A por B.
4 VI comerciar (*in* en, *with* con); **we do not ~ with Ruritania** no tenemos relaciones comerciales con Ruritania; **to cease trading** dejar de existir, dejar de comerciar; **to ~ on an advantage** aprovecharse de una ventaja, explotar una ventaja.
◆**trade in** VT: **to ~ a car in** ofrecer un coche como parte del pago, devolver un coche usado al comprar otro nuevo.
◆**trade off** VT: **to ~ off one thing for another** renunciar a algo a cambio de otra cosa.
◆**trade up** VI vender lo que se tiene para comprar algo mejor; **they buy a house and then trade up as their income rises** compran una casa, luego cuando aumentan sus ingresos la venden para comprar otra mejor.
trade-in ['treɪdɪn] ATTR: **~ arrangements** sistema *m* de devolver un artículo usado al comprar otro nuevo; **~ price**, **~ value** valor *m* de un artículo usado que se descuenta del precio de otro nuevo.
trademark ['treɪdmɑːk] N marca *f* registrada, marca *f* de fábrica; (*fig*) marca *f*, sello *m*.
tradename ['treɪdneɪm] N nombre *m* comercial, nombre *m* de fábrica; marca *f*.
trade-off ['treɪdɒf] N intercambio *m*, canje *m*; concesiones *fpl* mutuas; compensación *f*.
trader ['treɪdər] N comerciante *m*; traficante *m*; (*street* ~) vendedor *m* ambulante; (*Hist*) mercader *m*.
tradescantia [ˌtrædəs'kæntɪə] N tradescantia *f*.
tradesman ['treɪdzmən] N, PL **tradesmen** ['treɪdzmən] (*shopkeeper*) tendero *m*; (*roundsman*) repartidor *m*, proveedor *m*; (*artisan*) artesano *m*; **~'s entrance** entrada *f* de servicio, puerta *f* de servicio.
tradespeople ['treɪdzˌpiːpl] NPL tenderos *mpl*.
trade(s) union ['treɪd(z)'juːnjən] **1** N sindicato *m*, gremio *m* (obrero); **to form a ~** formar un sindicato, agremiarse.
2 ATTR sindical, gremial; **~ labour** mano *f* de obra agremiada; **~ movement** movimiento *m* sindical; **~ shop** taller *m* donde todos los obreros son miembros de un sindicato.

┌─ *TRADE UNIONS* ─┐

ⓘ *Los sindicatos británicos (**trade unions**) son sindicatos profesionales, si bien existe una tendencia creciente a agruparse entre ellos y crear asociaciones mayores de varias profesiones. El llamado **Transport and General Workers' Union** o **TGWU** es el mayor de ellos. Todos los sindicatos importantes pertenecen a una confederación llamada **Trades Union Congress** o **TUC**, la cual siempre ha mantenido una estrecha relación con el Partido Laborista británico, hasta el punto de tener voto en la elección de un nuevo líder del partido. La organización de la patronal es la **Confederation of British Industry** o **CBI**.*

trade unionism ['treɪd'juːnjənɪzəm] N sindicalismo *m*, sistema *m* de sindicatos.
trade unionist ['treɪd'juːnjənɪst] N sindicalista *mf*, miembro *mf* de un sindicato.
trade winds ['treɪdwɪndz] NPL vientos *mpl* alisios.
trading ['treɪdɪŋ] **1** ATTR comercial, mercantil; **~ account** cuenta *f* comercial, cuenta *f* de compraventa; **~ estate** (*Brit*) zona *f* comercial; **~ floor** parqué *m*; **~ loss** pérdidas *fpl*; **~ nation** nación *f* con importante comercio exterior; **~ partner** socio *m*, -a *f* comercial; **~ port** puerto *m* comercial; **~ post** factoría *f*; **~ profits for 1995** beneficios *mpl* obtenidos en el ejercicio de 1995; **~ results** balance *m* comercial; **~ stamp** cupón *m*, sello *m* de prima.
2 N (a) (*Comm*) comercio *m*; tráfico *m*; **to stop ~**, **to suspend ~** dejar de comerciar. (b) (*St Ex*) operaciones *fpl* bursátiles.
tradition [trə'dɪʃən] N tradición *f*.
traditional [trə'dɪʃənl] ADJ tradicional; clásico, consagrado; **it is ~ for them to sing** por tradición cantan, cantan de acuerdo con la tradición.

traditionalism [trə'dɪʃnəlɪzəm] N tradicionalismo *m*.
traditionalist [trə'dɪʃnəlɪst] **1** ADJ tradicionalista.
2 N tradicionalista *mf*.
traditionality [trə,dɪʃə'nælətɪ] N tradicionalidad *f*.
traditionally [trə'dɪʃnəlɪ] ADV tradicionalmente; según tradición, de acuerdo con la tradición.
traduce [trə'djuːs] VT calumniar, denigrar.
traffic ['træfɪk] **1** N (a) (*Aut etc*) circulación *f*, tráfico *m*, tránsito *m* (*LAm*); movimiento *m*; **the ~ is heavy this morning** hay mucho tráfico esta mañana; **~ was quite light** había poco tráfico; **~ was blocked for some hours** la circulación quedó interrumpida durante varias horas.
(b) (*trade*) tráfico *m*, comercio *m* (*in* en); (*pej*) trata *f* (*in* de); **the drug ~** el tráfico en narcóticos.
2 ATTR de la circulación, del tráfico, del tránsito (*LAm*); **~ accident** accidente *m* de circulación; **~ circle** (*US*) cruce *m* giratorio, glorieta *f*, redondel *m*; **~ cone** cono *m* señalizador; **~ control** (*act*) control *m* del tráfico; (*lights*) semáforo *m*; **to be on ~ duty** estar en tráfico; **~ flow** flujo *m* de tráfico; **~ island** (*Brit*) refugio *m*; **~ offence** (*Brit*), **~ violation** infracción *f* de tránsito; **~ police** policía *f* de tráfico; **~ warden** (*Brit*) controlador *m*, -ora *f* de estacionamiento.
3 VI traficar, comerciar (*in* en); (*pej*) tratar (*in* en).
trafficator ['træfɪkeɪtər] N (*Brit*) indicador *m* de dirección, flecha *f* de dirección.
traffic-jam ['træfɪkdʒæm] N embotellamiento *m*, atasco *m*, aglomeración *f*; **a 5-mile ~** una cola de coches que se extiende hasta 5 millas; **there are always ~s here** aquí siempre se embotella el tráfico, aquí siempre hay atasco.
trafficker ['træfɪkər] N traficante *m* (*in* en), tratante *m* (*in* en).
traffic-lights ['træfɪklaɪts] NPL semáforo *m*, luces *fpl* (de tráfico), señales *fpl* (de tráfico).
traffic-sign ['træfɪksaɪn] N señal *f* de tráfico.
tragedian [trə'dʒiːdɪən] N trágico *m*.
tragedienne [trədʒiːdɪ'en] N trágica *f*, actriz *f* trágica.
tragedy ['trædʒɪdɪ] N tragedia *f*; **it is a ~ that** ... es trágico que ...; **what a ~!** ¡qué trágico!; **the ~ of it is that** ... lo trágico es que ...
tragic ['trædʒɪk] ADJ trágico.
tragically ['trædʒɪkəlɪ] ADV trágicamente; **don't take it too ~** no seas tan pesimista.
tragicomedy ['trædʒɪ'kɒmɪdɪ] N tragicomedia *f*.
tragicomic ['trædʒɪ'kɒmɪk] ADJ tragicómico.
trail [treɪl] **1** N (a) (*wake*) estela *f*; (*of comet, rocket*) cola *f*; **~ of fire** estela *f* de fuego; **the speech left a long ~ of comments** el discurso ha dejado larga estela de comentarios; **the hurricane left a ~ of destruction** el huracán dejó una estela de estragos.
(b) (*track of animal*) rastro *m*, pista *f*; **false ~** pista *f* falsa; **to be on the ~ of**, **to follow the ~ of** seguir la pista de; **to pick up the ~** encontrar la pista.
(c) (*path, road*) camino *m*, sendero *m*; (*Pol: of campaign*) recorrido *m*.
2 VT (a) (*drag*) arrastrar; *arms* bajar.
(b) (*track*) rastrear, seguir la pista de; seguir de cerca; (*of detective etc*) vigilar; **have that man ~ed** que vigilen (*or* sigan) a ese hombre.
(c) (*Cine*) poner un tráiler (*or* avance) de.
3 VI (a) (*be drawn along*) arrastrarse; **he walked with his coat ~ing on the ground** andaba arrastrando su abrigo por los suelos; **with a small boat ~ing behind** con un bote remolcado.
(b) (*of person*) **to ~ along** arrastrarse; caminar penosamente, ir con aire desanimado; **to ~ far behind** quedar muy a la zaga, rezagarse mucho; **El Toboso is ~ing at the foot of the league** El Toboso va en última posición de la liga; **the children ~ed home in the rain** los niños se fueron muy tristes a su casa bajo la lluvia.
(c) (*plant*) arrastrarse; trepar.
◆**trail away, trail off** VI esfumarse, ir desapareciendo (hasta perderse completamente), desvanecerse poco a poco.
trail bike ['treɪlbaɪk] N moto *f* de motocross, moto *f* de trial.
trailblazer ['treɪlbleɪzər] N pionero *m*, -a *f*.
trailblazing ['treɪlbleɪzɪŋ] **1** ADJ pionero.
2 N trabajo *m* (*or* viaje *etc*) pionero.
trailer ['treɪlər] **1** N (a) (*Aut etc*) remolque *m*; (*caravan*) caravana *f*. (b) (*Cine*) tráiler *m*, avance *m*.
2 ATTR: **~ park** (*US*) cámping *m* para remolques, cámping *m* para caravanas.
trailing ['treɪlɪŋ] ADJ colgado; *plant* rastrero, trepador; **~ edge** borde *m* de salida, borde *m* posterior.
trail mix ['treɪlmɪks] N revuelto *m* de frutos secos.
trail truck ['treɪltrʌk] N (*US*) tráiler *m*.
train [treɪn] **1** N (a) (*Rail*) tren *m*; **by ~** (*go*) en tren, (*send*) por ferrocarril; **to catch a ~** coger un tren (*Sp*), tomar un tren; **to change ~s** cambiar de tren, hacer transbordo.
(b) (*Mech*) tren *m*; **~ of gears** tren *m* de engranajes.
(c) (*series*) serie *f*, sucesión *f*; **a ~ of cars** una serie de coches; **~ of powder** reguero *m* de pólvora; **~ of events** serie *f* de sucesos; **~ of**

thought hilo *m* del pensamiento; **he began another ~ of thought** dejó discurrir el pensamiento en otra cosa, dirigió el pensamiento a otra cosa; **in an unbroken ~** en una serie ininterrumpida; sin solución de continuidad; **it is in ~** está en preparación; **to set sth in ~** poner algo en movimiento, empezar a poner algo en obra.
(d) (*of dress*) cola *f*; **to carry sb's ~** llevar la cola del vestido de una.
(e) (*entourage*) séquito *m*, comitiva *f*; (*of mules*) recua *f*, reata *f*; **it brought ruin in its ~** acarreó la ruina, trajo consigo la ruina.
2 ATTR: **~ attendant** (*US*) empleado *m*, -a *f* de coches-cama; **~ service** servicio *m* de trenes; **~ set** ferrocarril *m* de juguete; **~ station** estación *f* de ferrocarril.
3 VT (a) (*instruct etc*) adiestrar; preparar, formar; (*Mil*) adiestrar, ejercitar; disciplinar; (*in new technique*) capacitar; *child* enseñar; (*Sport*) entrenar, preparar; *animal* amaestrar; *horse* entrenar; *voice* educar; **they ~ boys for the Navy** preparan a los muchachos para la Marina; **to ~ sb in firearms** enseñar a uno el manejo de las armas de fuego; **where were you ~ed?** ¿dónde cursó Vd sus estudios?; **he was ~ed at Salamanca** tuvo su formación profesional en Salamanca; **to ~ sb to do sth** enseñar a uno a hacer algo, enseñar a uno el arte (*or* la técnica *etc*) de hacer algo; habituar a uno a hacer algo, acostumbrar a uno a hacer algo.
(b) (*direct*) *gun* apuntar (*on* a); *camera, telescope* enfocar (*on* a); *plant* guiar (*up, along* por).
4 VI (a) (*instruct o.s.*) adiestrarse; prepararse, formarse; educarse; (*Mil*) adiestrarse, ejercitarse; (*Sport etc*) entrenarse; **I ~ for 6 hours a day** me entreno 6 horas diarias, hago prácticas durante 6 horas cada día; **to ~ as a teacher, to ~ to become a teacher** estudiar para profesor; **we're ~ing for the cup game** nos entrenamos para el partido de copa; **where did you ~?** ¿dónde cursó Vd sus estudios?, ¿dónde se formó Vd?
(b) (*Rail*) ir en tren; **then we ~ed to Seville** luego fuimos en tren a Sevilla.
5 VR: **to ~ o.s. in a craft** enseñarse un arte, adiestrarse en un arte; **to ~ o.s. to do sth** enseñarse a hacer algo; habituarse a hacer algo, formarse la costumbre de hacer algo.
◆**train up** VT: **to ~ sb up** preparar a uno, formar a uno.

trained [treɪnd] ADJ *teacher etc* graduado, diplomado; *worker* cualificado, capacitado, especializado; *animal* amaestrado; **a well-~ child** un niño (bien) educado, un niño bien enseñado; **a well-~ horse** un caballo bien preparado; **a well-~ army** un ejército disciplinado; **a fully-~ nurse** una enfermera diplomada.

trainee [treɪ'niː] 1 N aprendiz *m* (profesional), aprendiza *f* (profesional); (*US Mil*) recluta *mf* en período de aprendizaje.
2 ATTR: **~ manager** aprendiz *m*, -iza *f* de administración.

trainer ['treɪnəʳ] N (a) (*Sport: person*) entrenador *m*, -ora *f*, preparador *m* físico, preparadora *f* física; (*of horses*) entrenador *m*, -ora *f*; (*of circus animals*) domador *m*, -ora *f*.
(b) (*plane*) entrenador *m*.
(c) **~s** (*shoes*) zapatillas *fpl* de deporte.

training ['treɪnɪŋ] 1 N adiestramiento *m*; preparación *f*, formación *f* (profesional); orientación *f*; instrucción *f*; (*Mil*) instrucción *f*, ejercicios *mpl*; (*Sport*) entrenamiento *m*, preparación *f* (física); (*of staff for new job*) capacitación *f*; **to be in ~** estar entrenado, estar en forma; **to be out of ~** estar desentrenado.
2 ATTR: **~ camp** campamento *m* de instrucción; **~ center** (*US*), **~ centre** centro *m* de instrucción; centro *m* de formación laboral; **~ course** curso *m* de entrenamiento; **~ manual** manual *m* de instrucción; **~ plane** entrenador *m*; **~ scheme** plan *m* de formación profesional; **~ shoes** zapatillas *fpl* de deporte.

training college ['treɪnɪŋ,kɒlɪdʒ] N escuela *f* normal.
training-ship ['treɪnɪŋʃɪp] N buque-escuela *m*.
trainman ['treɪnmæn] N, PL **trainmen** ['treɪnmen] (*US*) ferroviario *m*; guardafrenos *m*.
train-spotter ['treɪnspɒtəʳ] N aficionado *m*, -a *f* a locomotoras.
train-spotting ['treɪnspɒtɪŋ] N: **~ is very popular in Britain** el ir a ver trenes es muy popular en Gran Bretaña.
traipse* [treɪps] VI ir (a desgana), andar (penosamente); andar sin propósito fijo; **we ~d about all morning** pasamos toda la mañana yendo de acá para allá; **I had to ~ over to see him** tuve que tomarme la molestia de ir a verle.
trait [treɪt] N rasgo *m*.
traitor ['treɪtəʳ] N traidor *m*, -ora *f*; **to be a ~ to one's country** traicionar a la patria; **to turn ~** volverse traidor, volver la casaca.
traitorous ['treɪtərəs] ADJ traidor; traicionero.
traitorously ['treɪtərəslɪ] ADV traidoramente, con traición.
traitress ['treɪtrɪs] N traidora *f*.
Trajan ['treɪdʒən] NM Trajano.
trajectory [trə'dʒektərɪ] N trayectoria *f*.
tram [træm] N, **tramcar** (*Brit*) ['træmkɑːʳ] N tranvía *m*, tren *m* (*Mex*).
tramlines ['træmlaɪnz] NPL (*Brit*) carriles *mpl* de tranvía; (*Sport*) líneas *fpl* laterales.
trammel ['træməl] 1 VT poner trabas a, trabar, impedir.

2 NPL: **~s** trabas *fpl*.
tramp [træmp] 1 N (a) (*sound of feet*) marcha *f* pesada, pasos *mpl* pesados.
(b) (*hike*) paseo *m* largo, caminata *f*, excursión *f* a pie; **to go for a ~ in the hills** hacer una excursión a pie por la montaña; **after a ~ of many miles** después de recorrer muchos kilómetros a pie; **it's a long ~** es mucho camino.
(c) (*person: man*) vago *m*, vagabundo *m*; (*woman: US***) puta *f*, fulana *f*; **you (little) ~!** ¡lagarta!
(d) (*Naut: also* **~ steamer**) vapor *m* volandero.
2 VT (*stamp on*) pisar con fuerza; (*walk across*) recorrer a pie, hacer una excursión por; **to ~ the streets** andar (penosamente) por las calles, recorrer (de muy mala gana) las calles; **they had to ~ it** tuvieron que ir a pie.
3 VI marchar pesadamente, andar con pasos pesados; ir a pie; **sb ~ed up to the door** alguien se acercó con pasos pesados a la puerta; **to ~ along** caminar (con pasos pesados); **to ~ up and down** andar de acá para allá.
trample ['træmpl] 1 VT (*also* **to ~ underfoot**) pisar, pisotear, hollar.
2 VI (*also* **to ~ about, to ~ along**) pisar fuerte, andar con pasos pesados; **to ~ on sth** pisar algo, pisotear algo, hollar algo; **to ~ on sb** (*fig*) tratar a uno sin miramientos; **to ~ on sb's feelings** (*fig*) herir los sentimientos de uno.
trampoline ['træmpəlɪn] N trampolín *m*, cama *f* elástica.
trampolining ['træmpəliːnɪŋ] N salto *m* sobre cama elástica.
tramway ['træmweɪ] N (*Brit*) tranvía *m*.
trance [trɑːns] N rapto *m*, arrobamiento *m*, éxtasis *m*; (*Med*) catalepsia *f*; (*spiritualistic*) trance *m*; estado *m* hipnótico; **to go into a ~** entrar en un estado hipnótico, (*fig*) extasiarse.
tranche [trɑːnʃ] N parte *f*, tajada *f*.
tranny* ['trænɪ] N = **transistor**.
tranquil ['træŋkwɪl] ADJ tranquilo.
tranquillity, (*US*) **tranquility** [træŋ'kwɪlɪtɪ] N tranquilidad *f*.
tranquillize, (*US*) **tranquilize** ['træŋkwɪlaɪz] VT tranquilizar.
tranquillizer, (*US*) **tranquilizer** ['træŋkwɪlaɪzəʳ] N tranquilizante *m*.
trans... [trænz] PREF trans..., tras...
trans. (a) ABBR *of* **translation** traducción *f*. (b) ABBR *of* **translated** traducido, trad. (c) ABBR *of* **transferred**.
transact [træn'zækt] VT hacer, despachar; tramitar.
transaction [træn'zækʃən] N (*deal*) negocio *m*, transacción *f*, operación *f*; (*act*) negociación *f*, tramitación *f*; **~s** (*of society*) actas *fpl*, memorias *fpl*.
transactional [træn'zækʃənl] ADJ transaccional; **~ analysis** análisis *m* transaccional.
transalpine ['trænz'ælpaɪn] ADJ transalpino.
transatlantic ['trænzət'læntɪk] ADJ transatlántico.
transceiver [træn'siːvəʳ] N transceptor *m*, transmisor-receptor *m*.
transcend [træn'send] VT exceder, superar, rebasar.
transcendence [træn'sendəns] N, **transcendency** [træn'sendənsɪ] N superioridad *f*; lo sobresaliente; (*Philos*) trascendencia *f*.
transcendent [træn'sendənt] ADJ superior; sobresaliente.
transcendental [,trænsen'dentl] ADJ trascendental; **~ meditation** meditación *f* trascendental.
transcendentalism ['trænsen'dentlɪzəm] N trascendentalismo *m*.
transcontinental ['trænz,kɒntɪ'nentl] ADJ transcontinental.
transcribe [træn'skraɪb] VT transcribir, copiar.
transcript ['trænskrɪpt] N trasunto *m*, copia *f*; transcripción *f*; (*US Scol etc*) expediente *m*.
transcription [træn'skrɪpʃən] N (*act*) transcripción *f*; (*copy*) transcripción *f*, trasunto *m*, copia *f*; **phonetic ~** pronunciación *f* fonética.
transculturation [,trænzkʌltʃʊ'reɪʃən] N transculturación *f*.
transduce [trænz'djuːs] VT transformar, convertir.
transducer [trænz'djuːsəʳ] N transductor *m*.
transect [træn'sekt] N transecto *m*.
transept ['trænsept] N crucero *m*.
transfer 1 ['trænsfəʳ] N (a) (*act*) transferencia *f*, traspaso *m*; (*Jur*) transferencia *f*, cesión *f*; enajenación *f*; transbordo *m*; (*Sport*) traspaso *m*; traslado *m*; **~ of ownership** cesión *f* de propiedad.
(b) (*picture*) cromo *m*, calcomanía *f*.
2 ['trænsfəʳ] ATTR: **~ desk** mostrador *m* de transbordo; **~ fee** traspaso *m*; **~ list** lista *f* de traspasos; **~ lounge** sala *f* de tránsito; **~ rate, ~ speed** velocidad *f* de transferencia.
3 [træns'fɜːʳ] VT *property etc* transferir, traspasar, pasar (*to* a); (*Jur*) transferir, ceder; enajenar; *passenger etc* transbordar; (*Sport*) traspasar; (*to new post, place etc*) trasladar; (*in banking, accounting etc*) transferir; **to ~ one's affections to another** dar su amor a otro; **~red charge call** (*Brit*) conferencia *f* a cobro revertido, conferencia *f* por cobrar (*LAm*).
4 [træns'fɜːʳ] VI (*to a post etc*) trasladarse (*to* a); (*Rail etc*) cambiar, hacer transbordo (*to* a); **to ~ to a new course** cambiar a otra asignatura; **the firm is ~ring to Quito** la compañía se traslada a Quito.

transferable [træns'fɜːrəbl] ADJ transferible; **not ~** intransferible.

transference ['trænsfərəns] N transferencia *f*; traspaso *m*; traslado *m*.

transfiguration [ˌtrænsfɪgə'reɪʃən] N transfiguración *f*.

transfigure [træns'fɪgəʳ] VT transfigurar, transformar (*into* en).

transfix [træns'fɪks] VT traspasar, pasar de parte a parte; **to be ~ed, to stand ~ed** (*fig*) estar totalmente pasmado (*with* de), estar completamente paralizado (*with* de).

transform [træns'fɔːm] VT transformar (*into* en), convertir; metamorfosear (*into* en).

transformation [ˌtrænsfə'meɪʃən] N transformación *f*, conversión *f*; metamorfosis *f*.

transformational [ˌtrænsfə'meɪʃənl] ADJ transformacional.

transformer [træns'fɔːməʳ] 1 N transformador *m*. 2 ATTR: **~ station** estación *f* transformadora.

transfuse [træns'fjuːz] VT transfundir; *blood* hacer una transfusión de.

transfusion [træns'fjuːʒən] N transfusión *f*; **to give sb a blood ~** hacer a uno una transfusión de sangre.

transgenic [træns'dʒenɪk] ADJ transgénico.

transgress [træns'gres] 1 VT (*go beyond*) traspasar, exceder, ir más allá de; (*violate*) violar, infringir; (*sin against*) pecar contra. 2 VI pecar, cometer una transgresión.

transgression [træns'greʃən] N pecado *m*, transgresión *f*; infracción *f*.

transgressor [træns'gresəʳ] N transgresor *m*, -ora *f*; pecador *m*, -ora *f*; infractor *m*, -ora *f*.

tranship [træn'ʃɪp] VT tra(n)sbordar.

transhipment [træn'ʃɪpmənt] N tra(n)sbordo *m*.

transience ['trænzɪəns] N lo pasajero, transitoriedad *f*, fugacidad *f*.

transient ['trænzɪənt] 1 ADJ pasajero, transitorio, fugaz. 2 N (*US*) transeúnte *mf*.

transistor [træn'zɪstəʳ] N (*also* **~ set**) transistor *m*.

transistorized [træn'zɪstəraɪzd] ADJ transistorizado.

▼ **transit** ['trænzɪt] 1 N tránsito *m*, paso *m*; **in ~** de tránsito, de paso. 2 ATTR: **~ camp** campamento *m* de tránsito; **~ lounge** (*Brit*) sala *f* de tránsito; **~ visa** visado *m* de tránsito, visa *f* de tránsito (*LAm*).

transition [træn'zɪʃən] 1 N transición *f*, paso *m* (*from* de, *to* a); transformación *f*, evolución *f* (*to* en). 2 ATTR: **~ period** período *m* de transición.

transitional [træn'zɪʃənl] ADJ transicional, de transición.

transitive ['trænzɪtɪv] ADJ transitivo; **~ verb** verbo *m* transitivo.

transitively ['trænzɪtɪvlɪ] ADV transitivamente.

transitivity [ˌtrænsɪ'tɪvɪtɪ] N transitividad *f*.

transitory ['trænzɪtərɪ] ADJ transitorio.

translatable [trænz'leɪtəbl] ADJ traducible.

translate [trænz'leɪt] VT (a) (*Ling*) traducir (*from* de, *into* a); (*fig*) interpretar; **to ~ words into deeds** convertir palabras en acción; **to ~ centigrade into Fahrenheit** convertir grados centígrados en Fahrenheit; **how do you ~ 'posh'?** ¿cómo se traduce 'posh'? (b) (*change post of: esp Rel*) trasladar (*from* de, *to* a).

translation [trænz'leɪʃən] N (a) traducción *f*; versión *f*. (b) traslado *m*.

translator [trænz'leɪtəʳ] N traductor *m*, -ora *f*.

transliterate [trænz'lɪtəreɪt] VT transcribir.

transliteration [ˌtrænzlɪtə'reɪʃən] N transliteración *f*, transcripción *f*.

translucence [trænz'luːsns] N translucidez *f*.

translucent [trænz'luːsnt] ADJ translúcido.

transmigrate ['trænzmaɪgreɪt] VI transmigrar.

transmigration [ˌtrænzmaɪ'greɪʃən] N transmigración *f*.

transmissible [trænz'mɪsəbl] ADJ transmisible.

transmission [trænz'mɪʃən] 1 N (*all senses*) transmisión *f*. 2 ATTR: **~ shaft** árbol *m* de transmisión.

transmit [trænz'mɪt] VT (*all senses*) transmitir (*to* a).

transmitter [trænz'mɪtəʳ] N (*apparatus*) transmisor *m*; (*station*) estación *f* transmisora, emisora *f*.

transmogrify [trænz'mɒgrɪfaɪ] VT transformar (como por encanto; *into* en), metamorfosear (extrañamente; *into* en).

transmutable [trænz'mjuːtəbl] ADJ transmutable.

transmutation [ˌtrænzmjuː'teɪʃən] N transmutación *f*.

transmute [trænz'mjuːt] VT transmutar (*into* en).

transnational [trænz'næʃənəl] 1 ADJ transnacional. 2 N transnacional *f*.

transom ['trænsəm] N (*Archit*) travesaño *m*; (*US*) (montante *m* de) abanico *m*.

transparency [træns'pærənsɪ] N (a) (*quality*) transparencia *f*. (b) (*Brit Phot*) diapositiva *f*, filmina *f*, proyección *f*.

transparent [træns'pærənt] ADJ transparente, diáfano; (*fig*) claro, limpio; *excuse etc* transparente, clarísimo.

transparently [træns'pærəntlɪ] ADV de modo transparente; **~ clear** meridianamente claro; **~ false** a todas luces falso, obviamente falso.

transpiration [ˌtrænspɪ'reɪʃən] N transpiración *f*.

transpire [træns'paɪəʳ] 1 VT transpirar. 2 VI (a) (*of fluid, odour*) transpirar. (b) (*become known*) revelarse, divulgarse, saberse; **finally it ~d that ...**

por fin se supo que ..., por fin se desprendió que ... (c) (*happen*) tener lugar, pasar, ocurrir; **his report on what ~d** su informe acerca de lo que pasó.

transplant 1 ['trænsplɑːnt] N trasplante *m*. 2 [træns'plɑːnt] VT trasplantar (*also Med*).

transplantation [ˌtrænsplɑːn'teɪʃən] N trasplante *m* (*also Med*).

transponder [træn'spɒndəʳ] N transpondedor *m*.

transport 1 ['trænspɔːt] N (a) (*gen*) transporte *m*; acarreo *m*; **Ministry of T~** (*Brit*) Ministerio *m* de Transportes. (b) (*ship*) navío *m* de transporte; (*Aer*) avión *m* de transporte. (c) (*fig*) transporte *m*, éxtasis *m*; **to be in a ~ of delight** estar extasiado, extasiarse; **to be in a ~ of rage** estar fuera de sí (de rabia). 2 ['trænspɔːt] ATTR: **~ café** (*Brit*) restaurante *m* de carretera; **~ costs** gastos *mpl* de transporte, gastos *mpl* de acarreo. 3 [træns'pɔːt] VT (a) (*lit*) transportar; llevar, acarrear; (*Hist*) *convict* deportar. (b) (*fig*) transportar, embelesar; **to be ~ed with joy** estar extasiado, extasiarse.

transportable [træns'pɔːtəbl] ADJ transportable.

transportation [ˌtrænspɔː'teɪʃən] N transporte *m*, transportación *f*; transportes *mpl*; (*Hist: Jur*) deportación *f*; **the ~ system** el sistema de transportes.

transporter [træns'pɔːtəʳ] N transportista *m*, transportador *m*.

transpose [træns'pəʊz] VT transponer, cambiar (*into* a); (*Mus*) transportar.

transposition [ˌtrænspə'zɪʃən] N transposición *f*; (*Mus*) transporte *m*.

transputer [træns'pjuːtəʳ] N (*Comput*) transputor *m*.

trans-Pyrenean [trænzˌpɪrə'niːən] ADJ transpirenaico.

transsexual [trænz'seksjʊəl] 1 ADJ transexual. 2 N transexual *mf*.

transsexualism [trænz'seksjʊəlɪzəm] N transexualismo *m*.

transship [træns'ʃɪp] VT tra(n)sbordar.

transshipment [træns'ʃɪpmənt] N tra(n)sbordo *m*.

trans-Siberian [trænzsaɪ'bɪərɪən] ADJ transiberiano.

transubstantiate [ˌtrænsəb'stænʃɪeɪt] VT transubstanciar.

transubstantiation ['trænsəbˌstænʃɪ'eɪʃən] N transubstanciación *f*.

Transvaal ['trænzvɑːl] N Transvaal *m*.

transversal [trænz'vɜːsəl] ADJ transversal.

transverse ['trænzvɜːs] ADJ transverso, trasversal.

transversely [trænz'vɜːslɪ] ADV transversalmente.

transverse ['trænzvɜːs] ADJ transverso, trasversal.

transversely [trænz'vɜːslɪ] ADV transversalmente.

transvestism ['trænzˌvestɪzəm] N travestismo *m*.

transvestite [trænz'vestaɪt] 1 ADJ travestido. 2 N travestido *m*, -a *f*, travestí *mf*.

Transylvania [ˌtrænsəl'veɪnɪə] N Transilvania *f*.

trap [træp] 1 N (a) (*gen*) trampa *f*; (*fig*) trampa *f*, lazo *m*; **it's a ~** aquí hay trampa; **to catch an animal in a ~** coger (*LAm*: agarrar) un animal con una trampa; **he was caught in his own ~** cayó en su propia trampa; **we were caught like rats in a ~** estábamos como ratas en ratonera; **to lure sb into a ~** hacer que uno caiga en una trampa; **to set a ~ for sb** tender un lazo a uno. (b) (*:*) boca *f*; **to keep one's ~ shut** cerrar el buzón*:*; **you keep your ~ shut about this** de esto no digas ni pío; **shut your ~!** ¡callarse! (c) (*Tech*) sifón *m*; bombillo *m*. (d) (*~door*) escotilla *f*, trampa *f*; (*Theat*) escotillón *m*. (e) (*carriage*) tartana *f*, coche *m* ligero de dos ruedas. 2 VT (a) *animal* coger (*LAm*: agarrar) en una trampa, entrampar, atrapar; coger con trampas. (b) *person* atrapar, aprisionar; *vehicle, ship etc* aprisionar, bloquear; **the miners are ~ped** los mineros están aprisionados, los mineros están atrapados; **we were ~ped in the snow** estábamos aprisionados por la nieve; **the climbers were ~ped** los alpinistas estaban inmovilizados. (c) **to ~ a ball** parar el balón (con los pies); **to ~ one's foot in the door** cogerse (*LAm*: atraparse) el pie en la puerta. (d) (*fig*) hacer caer en el lazo, entrampar; **to ~ sb into an admission** lograr mediante un ardid que uno haga una confesión; **she ~ped him into marriage** logró mañosamente que se casara con ella; **to ~ sb into saying sth** lograr mañosamente que uno diga algo.

trapdoor ['træpdɔːʳ] N escotilla *f*, trampa *f*; (*Theat*) escotillón *m*.

trapes [treɪps] VI = **traipse**.

trapeze [trə'piːz] 1 N trapecio *m* (de circo, de gimnasia). 2 ATTR: **~ artist** trapecista *mf*.

trapezium [trə'piːzɪəm] N (*Math*) trapecio *m*.

trapezoid ['træpɪzɔɪd] N trapezoide *m*.

trapper ['træpəʳ] N cazador *m* (*esp* de animales de piel), trampero *m*.

trappings ['træpɪŋz] NPL arreos *mpl*; jaeces *mpl*; (*fig*) adornos *mpl*, galas *fpl*; **shorn of all its ~** sin ninguno de sus adornos, desprovisto de adorno; **that statement, shorn of its ~ ...** esa declaración, en términos escuetos ...; **with all the ~ of kingship** con todo el boato de la monarquía.

➤ LANGUAGE IN USE: **transit:** 1 → 20.5

trappist ['træpɪst] ☐1 ADJ trapense.
☐2 N trapense m.

trash [træʃ] ☐1 N pacotilla f, hojarasca f; trastos mpl viejos; (esp US) basura f; **the book is ~** el libro es una basura, el libro no vale para nada; **he talks a lot of ~** no dice más que tonterías; (human) ~ gente f inútil, gentuza f; **~!** ¡tonterías!
☐2 VT (US) (a) (wreck) hacer polvo, destrozar. (b) (rubbish) condenar como inútil, criticar duramente.

trash-can ['træʃkæn] N (US) cubo m de la basura, balde m de la basura (LAm).

trash-heap ['træʃhiːp] N basurero m.

trashy ['træʃɪ] ADJ inútil, baladí.

trattoria [ˌtræto'rɪə] N trattoria f.

trauma ['trɔːmə] N trauma m.

traumatic [trɔː'mætɪk] ADJ traumático.

traumatism ['trɔːmætɪzəm] N traumatismo m.

traumatize ['trɔːmətaɪz] VT traumatizar.

travail ['træveɪl] N (†† or hum) esfuerzo m penoso; (Med) dolores mpl del parto; **to be in ~** afanarse, azacanarse; (Med) estar de parto.

travel ['trævl] ☐1 N (a) viajes mpl, el viajar; **~s** viajes mpl; **to be on one's ~s** estar de viaje.
(b) (Mech) recorrido m.
☐2 ATTR de viajes, de turismo; **~ agency** agencia f de viajes; **~ agent** agente mf de viajes; **~ brochure** prospecto m de viaje; **~ bureau** oficina f de información (para turistas); **~ expenses** gastos mpl de viaje; **~ goods** artículos mpl de viaje; **~ insurance** seguro m de viaje.
☐3 VT (a) country etc viajar por (todas partes de), recorrer.
(b) distance recorrer, hacer, cubrir; **we ~led 50 miles that day** ese día cubrimos 50 millas.
☐4 VI (a) (make a journey) viajar; **to ~ by car** viajar en coche, ir en coche; **he ~s into the centre to work** se desplaza al centro a trabajar; **they have ~led a lot** han viajado mucho, han visto mucho mundo; **to ~ round the world** dar la vuelta al mundo; **to ~ over** viajar por, recorrer.
(b) (go at a speed etc) ir; **it ~s at 600 mph** tiene una velocidad de 600 mph; **we were ~ling at 30 mph** íbamos a 30 mph; **you were ~ling too fast** ibas a velocidad excesiva, ibas demasiado de prisa; **he was certainly ~ling** es cierto que iba a buen tren; **light ~s at a speed of ...** la luz viaja a una velocidad de ...; **news ~s fast** las noticias viajan rápido.
(c) (move, pass) correr; moverse, desplazarse; **it ~s along this wire** corre por este hilo; **it doesn't ~ freely on its rod** no corre lisamente por la varilla; **it ~s 3 centimetres** (Mech) tiene un recorrido de 3 centímetros; **his eye ~led slowly over the scene** examinó detenidamente la escena.
(d) (reach) llegar, extenderse; **will it ~ that far?** ¿llega hasta allí?, ¿se puede estirar hasta allí?
(e) (of wine etc) poderse transportar; **it's a nice wine but it won't ~** es un buen vino pero no viaja.
(f) (Comm) ser viajante; **he ~s for Pérez** es viajante de la compañía Pérez; **he ~s in underwear** es viajante de una compañía que fabrica ropa interior; **he ~s in soap** es viajante en jabones.

travelator ['trævəleɪtər] N (US) cinta f transbordadora, pasillo m móvil.

travelled, (US) **traveled** ['trævld] ADJ que ha viajado; **much ~, widely ~** que ha viajado mucho, que ha visto mucho mundo.

traveller, (US) **traveler** ['trævlər] N viajero m, -a f; (Comm: also **commercial ~**) viajante m; **a ~ in soap** un viajante en jabones; **~'s check** (US), **~'s cheque** cheque m de viaje; **~'s joy** (Bot) clemátide f.

travelling, (US) **traveling** ['trævlɪŋ] ☐1 ADJ, ATTR salesman, exhibition etc ambulante; expenses de viaje; crane etc corredero, corredizo; bag, clock, rug de viaje; **~ folk, ~ people** gitanos mpl.
☐2 N el viajar, viajes mpl.

travelogue, (US) **travelog** ['trævəlɒg] N película f de viajes; documental m de interés turístico.

travel-sick ['trævəlsɪk] ADJ mareado; **to get ~** marearse.

travel-sickness ['trævlˌsɪknɪs] N mareo m.

travel-worn ['trævlwɔːn] ADJ fatigado por el viaje, rendido después de tanto viajar.

traverse ['trævəs] ☐1 N (Tech) travesaño m; (Mil) través m; (Mountaineering) escalada f oblicua, camino m oblicuo.
☐2 VT atravesar, cruzar; recorrer; pasar por; **we are traversing a difficult period** atravesamos un período difícil.
☐3 VI (Mountaineering) hacer una escalada oblicua.

travesty ['trævɪstɪ] ☐1 N parodia f (also fig).
☐2 VT parodiar.

trawl [trɔːl] ☐1 N (a) (net) red f barredera. (b) (act) rastreo m; **a ~ through police files** una rastreo de los archivos policiales.
☐2 VT rastrear; dragar; **to ~ up** pescar, sacar a la superficie.
☐3 VI (a) pescar al arrastre, rastrear. (b) **to ~ through the files** rastrear los archivos; **to ~ for evidence** rastrear buscando pruebas.

trawler ['trɔːlər] N arrastrero m, barco m rastreador.

trawling ['trɔːlɪŋ] N pesca f a la rastra.

tray [treɪ] N bandeja f, charola f (Mex); (of balance) platillo m; (drawer) cajón m, batea f; (Phot, Tech) cubeta f.

traycloth ['treɪklɒθ] N cubrebandeja m.

treacherous ['tretʃərəs] ADJ traidor, traicionero; falso; (fig) engañoso, incierto, nada seguro; memory infiel; ground movedizo; ice etc peligroso, poco firme.

treacherously ['tretʃərəslɪ] ADV traidoramente, a traición; falsamente; engañosamente; peligrosamente.

treachery ['tretʃərɪ] N traición f, perfidia f; falsedad f; **an act of ~** una traición.

treacle ['triːkl] (Brit) ☐1 N melaza f.
☐2 ATTR: **~ tart** tarta f de melaza.

treacly ['triːklɪ] ADJ parecido a melaza; cubierto de melaza.

tread [tred] ☐1 N (a) (step) paso m, pisada f; (gait) andar m, modo m de andar; **with heavy ~** con pasos pesados, pisando fuertemente; **with measured ~** con pasos rítmicos.
(b) (of stair) huella f; (of shoe) suela f; (of tyre) banda f de rodaje.
☐2 (irr: PRET **trod**, PTP **trodden**) VT (also **to ~ down, to ~ underfoot**) pisar, pisotear, hollar; path batir; ir por, caminar por; (fig) abrir; grapes pisar; dance bailar; **to ~ water** pedalear en agua; **a place never trodden by human feet** un sitio no hollado por pie humano; **he trod his cigarette end into the mud** apagó la colilla pisándola en el lodo.
☐3 VI pisar; poner el pie; **to ~ on** pisar; **to ~ on sb's heels** pisar los talones a uno; **careful you don't ~ on it!** ¡ojo, que lo vas a pisar!; **to ~ carefully, to ~ warily** (fig) andar con pies de plomo; **we must ~ very carefully in this matter** en este asunto conviene andar con pies de plomo; **to ~ softly** pisar dulcemente, no hacer ruido al andar.
◆**tread down** VT pisar; see also **tread 2.**
◆**tread in** VT root, seedling asegurar pisando la tierra alrededor.

treadle ['tredl] N pedal m.

treadmill ['tredmɪl] N rueda f de andar; (fig) rutina f, monotonía f; tráfago m; **back to the ~!** ¡volvamos al trabajo!

Treas. ABBR of **Treasurer.**

treason ['triːzn] N traición f; **high ~** alta traición f.

treasonable ['triːzənəbl] ADJ traidor, desleal.

treasure ['treʒər] ☐1 N tesoro m; (fig) tesoro m; joya f, preciosidad f; **yes, my ~** sí, mi tesoro; **~s of Spanish art** joyas fpl del arte español; **our charlady is a real ~** nuestra asistenta es una verdadera joya.
☐2 VT (a) **to ~ up** (keep carefully) atesorar; guardar, acumular.
(b) (fig) guardar como un tesoro; apreciar muchísimo; memory etc guardar.

treasure chest ['treʒətʃest] N (a) (lit) cofre m del tesoro, tesoro m.
(b) (fig: of information, knowledge) tesoro m.

treasured ['treʒəd] ADJ memory etc entrañable; possession valioso, precioso.

treasure-house ['treʒəhaʊs] N, PL **treasure-houses** ['treʒəˌhaʊzɪz] tesoro m (also fig).

treasure-hunt ['treʒəhʌnt] N caza f al tesoro.

treasurer ['treʒərər] N tesorero m, -a f.

treasure-trove ['treʒətrəʊv] N tesoro m hallado; (fig) tesoro m (escondido).

treasury ['treʒərɪ] ☐1 N (a) tesoro m, tesorería f, fisco m, erario m, hacienda f; **T~,** (US) **T~ Department** Ministerio m de Hacienda.
(b) (anthology) tesoro m, antología f, florilegio m.
☐2 ATTR: **T~ Bench** (Brit) banco m azul, banco m del gobierno; **~ bill** (US), **~ bond** (US) pagaré m (or bono m) del Tesoro; **T~ promissory note** pagaré m del Tesoro; **T~ stock** (Brit) bonos mpl del Tesoro; (US) acciones fpl rescatadas; **~ warrant** autorización f para pago de fondos públicos.

┌─ **TREASURY** ─┐

🛈 **Her** o **His Majesty's Treasury** o simplemente **Treasury** es el ministerio británico responsable de la política fiscal y monetaria, del control del gasto público y de las relaciones financieras internacionales. Su departamento de cuentas es el **Exchequer** el cual se encarga de recibir y emitir los fondos públicos. A la cabeza del ministerio está el ministro (**Chancellor of the Exchequer**) encargado de las finanzas públicas y de preparar y presentar al Parlamento los Presupuestos Generales, normalmente conocidos como **the Budget**. Su residencia oficial es el número 11 de Downing Street, junto a la del Primer Ministro (el número 10). En Estados Unidos a la cabeza del ministerio **Department of the Treasury** se halla el **Secretary of the Treasury** y dentro de su departamento se encuentran también Hacienda (**Internal Revenue Service** o **IRS**), el Servicio Secreto (**Secret Service**), que protege al Presidente, Aduanas, y las secciones encargadas de la deuda pública y la regulación del tabaco, el alcohol y las armas de fuego.

⇨ Ver también BUDGET , DOWNING STREET

└──────────┘

treat [triːt] ☐1 N (a) (entertainment) convite m; (present) regalo m;

(*outing*) visita *f*; **it's my ~** invito yo; **to have a Dutch ~** pagar cada uno su cuota, ir a escote; **to stand sb a ~** invitar a uno.

(b) (*pleasure*) placer *m*, gusto *m*; recompensa *f* (especial); **a ~ in store** un placer futuro, un placer guardado para el futuro; **it is a ~ to hear you** da gusto escucharte, es un placer escucharte; **it's no sort of ~ for me** para mí no es ningún placer; **just to give them all a ~** sólo para darles placer a todos; **to give o.s. a ~** permitirse un lujo, permitirse hacer algo no acostumbrado.

(c) it suited us a ~* (*Brit*) nos convenía a las mil maravillas.

2 VT **(a)** (*behave towards*) tratar; **to ~ sb well** tratar bien a uno; **to ~ sb as if he were a child** tratar a uno como a un niño; **to ~ sth as a joke** tomar algo en broma, tomar algo en chunga.

(b) (*invite*) invitar, convidar (*to* a); **I'm ~ing you** invito yo; **they ~ed him to a dinner** le obsequiaron con un banquete; **let me ~ you to a drink** permíteme invitarte a tomar algo.

(c) (*Med*) tratar, curar; atender, asistir; **to ~ sb for a broken leg** curar la pierna rota de uno; **to ~ sb with X-rays** dar a uno un tratamiento de rayos X; **which doctor is ~ing you?** ¿qué médico te atiende?

(d) (*Tech*) tratar; **to ~ a substance with acid** tratar una sustancia con ácido.

(e) *subject, theme* tratar, discutir; **he ~s the subject objectively** trata el asunto con objetividad.

3 VI **(a)** (*negotiate*) **to ~ for peace** pedir la paz; **to ~ with sb** tratar con uno, negociar con uno.

(b) (*discuss*) **to ~ of** tratar de, discutir; versar sobre.

4 VR: **to ~ o.s. to sth** permitirse el lujo, permitirse algo no acostumbrado.

treatable ['triːtəbl] ADJ *condition, illness* tratable.

treatise ['triːtɪz] N tratado *m*.

treatment ['triːtmənt] N tratamiento *m*; (*Med*) tratamiento *m*, cura *f*, medicación *f*; **good ~** buen tratamiento *m*, buenos tratos *mpl*; **his ~ of his parents** su conducta con sus padres; **our ~ of foreigners** el trato que damos a los extranjeros; **to give sb the ~*** hacer sufrir a uno; **to respond to ~** responder al tratamiento.

treaty ['triːtɪ] N tratado *m*; **T~ of Accession** (*to EC*) Tratado *m* de Adhesión; **T~ of Rome** Tratado *m* de Roma; **T~ of Utrecht** Tratado *m* de Utrecht.

treble ['trebl] **1** ADJ **(a)** triple.

(b) (*Mus*) de tiple; **~ clef** clave *f* de sol.

2 N **(a)** (*Mus*) tiple *mf*; voz *f* de tiple. **(b)** (*drink*) triple *m*.

3 VT triplicar.

4 VI triplicarse.

trebly ['treblɪ] ADV tres veces; **it is ~ dangerous to ...** es tres veces más peligroso ...

tree [triː] **1** N **(a)** árbol *m*; **~ structure** estructura *f* arbórea; **~ of knowledge** árbol *m* de la ciencia; **to be at the top of the ~** estar en la cumbre de su profesión; **to be up a ~*** estar en un aprieto; **to be barking up the wrong ~** tomar el rábano por las hojas.

(b) (*for shoes*) horma *f*; (*of saddle*) arzón *m*.

2 VT *animal etc* ahuyentar por un árbol, hacer refugiarse en un árbol.

tree-covered ['triːˌkʌvəd] ADJ arbolado.

tree-creeper ['triːˌkriːpəʳ] N trepatroncos *m*.

tree-frog ['triːfrɒg] N rana *f* de San Antonio, rana *f* arbórea.

tree-house ['triːhaʊs] N, PL **tree-houses** ['triːˌhaʊzɪz] cabaña *f* (de niños) sobre un árbol.

tree hugger* ['triːhʌgəʳ] N (*esp US: hum*) fanático *m*, -a *f* del medioambiente.

treeless ['triːlɪs] ADJ pelado, sin árboles.

treeline ['triːlaɪn] N límite *m* forestal.

tree-lined ['triːlaɪnd] ADJ arbolado.

tree-planting ['triːˌplɑːntɪŋ] N plantación *f* de árboles; repoblación *f* forestal.

tree-surgeon ['triːˌsɜːdʒən] N arboricultor *m*, -ora *f* (que se ocupa de las enfermedades de los árboles).

treetop ['triːtɒp] N copa *f*, cima *f* de árbol.

treetrunk ['triːtrʌŋk] N tronco *m* de árbol.

trefoil ['trefɔɪl] N trébol *m*.

trek [trek] **1** N migración *f*; (*day's march*) jornada *f*; (*) viaje *m* largo y difícil; caminata *f*; excursión *f*; **it's quite a ~ to the shops*** las tiendas quedan muy lejos.

2 VI emigrar; viajar; (*) ir (de mala gana), caminar (penosamente); **we ~ked for days on end** caminamos día tras día; **I had to ~ up to the top floor** tuve que subir hasta el último piso.

Trekkie* ['trekɪ] N trekker *mf*, trekkie *mf*, fan de la serie televisiva "Star Trek".

trekking ['trekɪŋ] N trekking *m*.

trellis ['trelɪs] N enrejado *m*; (*Bot*) espaldera *f*, espaldar *m*.

trelliswork ['trelɪswɜːk] N enrejado *m*.

tremble ['trembl] **1** N temblor *m*, estremecimiento *m*; **to be all of a ~** estar todo tembloroso; **she said with a ~ in her voice** dijo tem-

blando.

2 VI temblar, estremecerse (*at* ante, *with* de); vibrar; agitarse; **to ~ all over** estar todo tembloroso; **to ~ like a leaf** temblar como un azogado.

trembling ['tremblɪŋ] **1** ADJ tembloroso.

2 N temblar *m*, temblor *m*, estremecimiento *m*; vibración *f*; agitación *f*.

tremendous [trəˈmendəs] ADJ tremendo, inmenso, formidable; (*) tremendo*, estupendo*; **that's ~!** ¡qué estupendo*!; **there was a ~ crowd** había una inmensa multitud.

tremendously [trəˈmendəslɪ] ADV tremendamente; **~ good** tremendamente bueno.

tremolo ['tremələʊ] N trémolo *m*.

tremor ['tremər] N temblor *m*; estremecimiento *m*; vibración *f*; **earth ~** temblor *m* de tierra; **he said without a ~** dijo sin inmutarse; **it sent ~s through the system** sacudió el sistema.

tremulous ['tremjʊləs] ADJ trémulo, tembloroso; tímido.

tremulously ['tremjʊləslɪ] ADV trémulamente; tímidamente.

trench [trentʃ] **1** N zanja *f*, foso *m*; (*Mil*) trinchera *f*.

2 ATTR: **~ warfare** guerra *f* de trincheras.

3 VT hacer zanjas (*or* fosos) en; (*Mil*) hacer trincheras en, atrincherar; (*Agr*) excavar.

trenchant ['trentʃənt] ADJ mordaz, incisivo.

trenchantly ['trentʃəntlɪ] ADV mordazmente.

trenchcoat ['trentʃkəʊt] N trinchera *f*, guerrera *f*.

trencher ['trentʃəʳ] N tajadero *m*.

trencherman ['trentʃəmæn] N, PL **trenchermen** ['trentʃəmən]: **to be a good ~** comer bien, tener siempre buen apetito.

trend [trend] **1** N tendencia *f*; curso *m*, dirección *f*, marcha *f*; (*fashion*) boga *f*, moda *f*; **now there is a ~ towards ...** ahora hay tendencia hacia ...; **~s in popular music** tendencias *fpl* de la música popular.

2 VI tender.

trendiness ['trendɪnɪs] N ultramodernismo *m*; tendencia *f* ultramodernista; afán *m* de estar al día.

trendsetter ['trendˌsetəʳ] N persona *f* que impone una moda.

trendsetting ['trendsetɪŋ] ADJ que impone la moda.

trendy ['trendɪ] **1** ADJ según la última moda, muy al día; de acuerdo con las tendencias actuales, modernísimo, marchoso*.

2 N persona *f* de tendencias ultramodernas, marchoso* *m*, -a *f*.

Trent [trent] N Trento *m*.

trepan [trɪˈpæn] VT trepanar.

trephine [treˈfiːn] **1** N trépano *m*.

2 VT trepanar.

trepidation [ˌtrepɪˈdeɪʃən] N turbación *f*, agitación *f*; **in some ~** algo turbado, agitado.

trespass ['trespəs] **1** N **(a)** (*illegal entry*) intrusión *f*, entrada *f* ilegal; entrada *f* sin derecho, penetración *f* en finca ajena. **(b)** (*transgression*) infracción *f*, violación *f*, ofensa *f*; (*Eccl*) pecado *m*; **forgive us our ~es** perdónanos nuestras deudas.

2 VI **(a)** entrar sin derecho (*on* en), entrar ilegalmente (*on* en); penetración *f* en finca ajena; **to ~ against** infringir, violar; **to ~ upon** (*fig*) abusar de; **to ~ upon sb's privacy** invadir la vida íntima de uno; **may I ~ upon your kindness to ask that ...** permítame molestarle pidiendo que ...; perdone Vd que le moleste pidiendo que ...

(b) (*Eccl*) pecar (*against* contra).

trespasser ['trespəsəʳ] N intruso *m*, -a *f*; **'T~s will be prosecuted'** 'se procederá contra los intrusos', (*loosely*) 'Prohibida la entrada'.

tress [tres] N trenza *f*; **~es** cabellera *f*, pelo *m*.

trestle ['tresl] **1** N caballete *m*.

2 ATTR: **~ bridge** puente *m* de caballetes; **~ table** mesa *f* de caballete.

trews [truːz] NPL (*Scot*) pantalón *m* de tartán.

tri... [traɪ] PREF tri...

triad ['traɪəd] N tríada *f*.

trial ['traɪəl] **1** N **(a)** (*Jur*) proceso *m*, juicio *m*, vista *f* de una causa; **~ by jury** juicio *m* con jurado; **detention without ~** detención *f* sin procesamiento; **new ~** revisión *f*; **to be on ~** estar en juicio; **to be on ~ for one's part in a crime** ser procesado por su complicidad en un crimen; **to be on ~ for one's life** ser acusado de un crimen capital; **to bring sb to ~** procesar a uno; **to commit sb for ~** remitir a uno al tribunal; **to go on ~, to stand one's ~** ser procesado.

(b) (*test*) prueba *f*, ensayo *m*; tentativa *f*; (*of sheepdogs etc*) concurso *m*; **~s** (*Sport, Tech*) pruebas *fpl*; **~ of strength** prueba *f* de fuerza; **by a system of ~ and error** por un sistema de tanteo, por un procedimiento empírico; **to be on ~** estar a prueba; **to give sb a ~** poner a uno a prueba.

(c) (*hardship*) aflicción *f*, adversidad *f*; desgracia *f*; (*nuisance*) molestia *f*; **~s and tribulations** aflicciones *fpl*; **the ~s of old age** las aflicciones de la vejez; **the child is a great ~ to them** el niño les amarga la vida.

2 ATTR (a) (*Jur*) procesal; relativo al proceso; *ver también* GRAND JURY .
(b) (*test, practice*) de prueba, de ensayo; **~ balance** balance *m* de comprobación; **~ balloon** (*US*) globo *m* sonda; **on a ~ basis** a prueba; **~ flight** vuelo *m* de prueba; **~ jury** (*US*) jurado *m* de juicio; **~ run, ~ trip** viaje *m* de ensayo.

triangle ['traɪæŋgl] N triángulo *m* (*also Mus*).

triangular [traɪ'æŋgjʊləʳ] ADJ triangular.

triangulate [traɪ'æŋgjʊleɪt] VT triangular.

triangulation [traɪˌæŋgjʊ'leɪʃən] N triangulación *f*.

triathlon [traɪ'æθlən] N triatlón *m*.

tribal ['traɪbəl] ADJ tribal.

tribalism ['traɪbəlɪzəm] N tribalismo *m*.

tribe [traɪb] N tribu *f* (*also Zool*); (*fig*) tropel *m*, masa *f*; ralea *f*.

tribesman ['traɪbzmən] N, PL **tribesmen** ['traɪbzmən] miembro *m* de una tribu; **to stir up the tribesmen** sublevar las tribus; **the tribesmen are friendly** las tribus son amistosas.

tribulation [ˌtrɪbjʊ'leɪʃən] N tribulación *f*; **~s** aflicciones *fpl*, dificultades *fpl*, sufrimientos *mpl*.

tribunal [traɪ'bjuːnl] N tribunal *m*.

tribune ['trɪbjuːn] N (*stand*) tribuna *f*; (*person*) tribuno *m*.

tributary ['trɪbjʊtərɪ] **1** ADJ tributario.
2 N (*person*) tributario *m*; (*Geog*) afluente *m*.

tribute ['trɪbjuːt] N (*payment, tax*) tributo *m*; (*fig*) homenaje *m*; elogio *m*; (*in flowers etc*) ofrenda *f*; **that is a ~ to his loyalty** eso acredita su lealtad, eso hace honor a su lealtad; **to pay ~ to** rendir homenaje a, elogiar, pronunciar elogios de.

trice [traɪs] N: **in a ~** en un santiamén.

tricentenary [ˌtraɪsen'tiːnərɪ] **1** ADJ (de) tricentenario; **~ celebrations** celebraciones *fpl* de(l) tricentenario.
2 N tricentenario *m*.

triceps ['traɪseps] N tríceps *m*.

trick [trɪk] **1** N (a) (*deceit*) engaño *m*, truco *m*; (*swindle*) estafa *f*; (*ruse*) trampa *f*, ardid *m*, estratagema *f*; (*harmless deception*) travesura *f*; (*hoax*) trastada *f*, primada *f*, burla *f*; **dirty ~, low ~, shabby ~** mala pasada *f*, faena *f*; **~s of the trade** trucos *mpl* del oficio, triquiñuelas *fpl* del oficio; **there must be a ~ in it** aquí debe haber trampa; **he's up to all the ~s, he knows a ~ or two** se lo sabe todo; **he's up to his old ~s again** ha vuelto a hacer de las suyas; **how's ~s?*** ¿cómo te va?, ¿cómo van las cosas?; **I know a ~ worth two of that** yo me sé algo mucho mejor; **to play a ~ on sb** hacer una mala pasada a uno, hacer una faena a uno; (*practical joke*) gastar una broma a uno; **his memory played him a ~** le falló la memoria; **unless my eyes are playing me ~s** a menos que me engañen mis ojos; **they tried every ~ in the book** emplearon todos los trucos.
(b) (*peculiarity*) peculiaridad *f* (personal); (*custom*) hábito *m*, manía *f*; **certain ~s of style** ciertas peculiaridades estilísticas, ciertos rasgos del estilo; **it's just a ~ he has** es una manía suya; **it's a ~ of the light, it was an illusion of the light; **history has a ~ of repeating itself** la historia tiene tendencia a repetirse.
(c) (*card ~*) juego *m* de naipes, truco *m* de naipes; (*conjuring ~*) juego *m* de manos; (*in circus*) número *m*; **the whole bag of ~s*** todo el rollo*; **that should do the ~** eso es lo que hace falta.
(d) (*Cards*) baza *f*; **to take all the ~s** ganar (*or* hacer) todas las bazas; **he doesn't miss a ~** (*fig*) no pierde ripio.
(e) (*knack*) tino *m*, truco *m*; **to get the ~ of it** coger el tino, aprender el modo de hacer algo.
(f) (‡: *of prostitute*) cliente *m*; **to turn a ~** ligar un cliente*.
2 ATTR: **~ photography** trucaje *m*; **~ question** pregunta *f* de pega; **~ riding** acrobacia *f* ecuestre.
3 VT (*deceive*) engañar; trampear; burlar; (*swindle*) estafar, timar; **we were ~d** nos engañaron, nos dejamos engañar; **to ~ sb into doing sth** lograr mañosamente que uno haga algo, inducir fraudulentamente a uno a hacer algo; **to ~ sb out of sth** quitar mañosamente algo a uno, estafar algo a uno.

◆ **trick out, trick up** VT (*decorate*) ataviar (*with* de).

trick-cyclist ['trɪk'saɪklɪst] N ciclista *mf* acróbata.

trickery ['trɪkərɪ] N astucia *f*, superchería *f*; mañas *fpl*; (*Jur*) fraude *m*; **to obtain sth by ~** obtener algo fraudulentamente.

trickle ['trɪkl] **1** N hilo *m*, chorro *m* delgado, goteo *m*; (*fig*) pequeña cantidad *f*; **a ~ of people** unas pocas personas; **we received a ~ of news** nos llegaba alguna que otra noticia; **what was a ~ is now a flood** lo que era un goteo es ya un torrente.
2 VT dejar caer gota a gota, dejar salir en un chorro delgado; **you're trickling blood** estás sangrando un poco.
3 VI (a) (*liquid*) gotear, salir gota a gota, salir en un chorro delgado; (*fig*) salir poco a poco; **blood ~d down his cheek** la sangre le corría gota a gota por la mejilla.
(b) (*of persons*) salir (*etc*) poco a poco; **people were trickling in** iban llegando unas cuantas personas; **shall we ~ over to the café?*** ¿nos trasladamos al café?

◆ **trickle away** VI: **our money is trickling away** nuestro dinero se consume poco a poco.

trickle-charger ['trɪkl,tʃɑːdʒəʳ] N cargador *m* de batería.

trick or treat [ˌtrɪkə'triːt] (*esp US*) **1** N frase que dicen los niños la noche de Halloween, que quiere decir: trastada o regalo (*me das algo o atente a las consecuencias*).
2 VI: **to go ~ing** ir de puerta en puerta diciendo "trick or treat"; *ver también* HALLOWEEN .

trickster ['trɪkstəʳ] N estafador *m*, -ora *f*, embustero *m*.

tricksy ['trɪksɪ] ADJ (*playful*) juguetón; guasón; (*crafty*) astuto, mañoso.

tricky ['trɪkɪ] ADJ *person* astuto; mañoso, tramposo; *situation etc* delicado, difícil; *problem* espinoso; **it's all rather ~** es un poco complicado, es un tanto difícil.

tricolour, (US) tricolor ['trɪkələʳ] N tricolor *f*, bandera *f* tricolor.

tricorn ['traɪkɔːn] **1** ADJ tricornio.
2 N tricornio *m*.

tricycle ['traɪsɪkl] N triciclo *m*.

trident ['traɪdənt] N tridente *m*.

Tridentine [traɪ'dentaɪn] ADJ tridentino.

tried [traɪd] ADJ probado, de toda garantía.

triennial [traɪ'enɪəl] ADJ trienal.

triennially [traɪ'enɪəlɪ] ADV trienalmente, cada tres años.

trier ['traɪəʳ] N persona *f* que se esfuerza mucho.

trifle ['traɪfl] **1** N (a) (*unimportant thing*) friolera *f*, bagatela *f*, fruslería *f*; **£5 is a mere ~** 5 libras son una bagatela; **he worries about ~s** se preocupa por pequeñeces (*or* nimiedades); **any ~ can distract her** le distrae cualquier tontería; **you could have bought it for a ~** hubieras podido comprarlo por una tontería.
(b) **a ~** (*as adv*) un poquito, un poquitín; algo; **it's a ~ difficult** es un tantico difícil; **it's a ~ too much** es un poquito demasiado; **we were a ~ put out** quedamos algo desconcertados.
(c) (*Culin*) dulce *m* de bizcocho borracho.
2 VI: **to ~ with one's food** comer melindrosamente, hacer melindres al comer; **to ~ with sb** jugar con uno, tratar a uno con poca seriedad; **he's not a person to be ~d with** es persona que hay que tratar con la mayor seriedad; **to ~ with a girl's affections** jugar con el amor de una joven.

◆ **trifle away** VT malgastar, desperdiciar.

trifler ['traɪfləʳ] N persona *f* frívola, persona *f* informal.

trifling ['traɪflɪŋ] ADJ insignificante, sin importancia, de poca monta.

triforium [traɪ'fɔːrɪəm] N triforio *m*.

trigger ['trɪgəʳ] **1** N (*Mil*) gatillo *m*; (*Tech*) disparador *m*, tirador *m*.
2 VT: **to ~ (off)** hacer estallar; (*Mech*) hacer funcionar, poner en movimiento; (*fig*) provocar, hacer estallar, desencadenar.

trigger finger ['trɪgə,fɪŋgəʳ] N índice *m* de la mano derecha (empleado para apretar el gatillo).

trigger-happy ['trɪgə,hæpɪ] ADJ pronto a disparar.

trigonometric(al) ['trɪgənə'metrɪk(əl)] ADJ trigonométrico.

trigonometry [ˌtrɪgə'nɒmɪtrɪ] N trigonometría *f*.

trijet ['traɪdʒet] N trirreactor *m*.

trike* [traɪk] N triciclo *m*.

trilateral ['traɪ'lætərəl] ADJ trilátero.

trilby ['trɪlbɪ] N (*Brit: also ~ hat*) (sombrero *m*) flexible *m*, sombrero *m* tirolés.

trilingual ['traɪ'lɪŋgwəl] ADJ trilingüe.

trill [trɪl] **1** N (*of bird*) trino *m*, gorjeo *m*; (*Mus*) trino *m*, quiebro *m*; (*of R*) vibración *f*.
2 VT pronunciar con vibración.
3 VI trinar, gorjear.

trillion ['trɪlɪən] N (*Brit*) trillón *m*; (*US*) billón *m*.

trilogy ['trɪlədʒɪ] N trilogía *f*.

trim [trɪm] **1** ADJ aseado, arreglado; elegante; en buen estado; **she has a ~ figure** tiene buen tipo.
2 N (a) (*condition*) estado *m*, condición *f*; buen estado *m*; (*of boat*) asiento *m*; (*of sails*) orientación *f*; **in good ~** en buen estado, en buenas condiciones, *person* en forma; **in fighting ~** listo para el combate, listo para entrar en acción; **to get things into ~** arreglar las cosas; hacer sus preparativos.
(b) (*cut*) recorte *m*; **to give one's hair a ~** recortarse el pelo.
(c) (*edging*) borde *m*, guarnición *f*.
3 VT (a) (*tidy*) arreglar, ordenar; disponer; ajustar, componer; *boat* equilibrar; *sails* orientar.
(b) (*Sewing*) *dress* adornar, guarnecer (*with* de); **sleeves ~med with lace** mangas *fpl* guarnecidas de encaje.
(c) (*cut*) cortar; *hair, hedge* recortar; *bush etc* podar; *lamp, wick* despabilar; *wood* desbastar, alisar.

◆ **trim away** VT cortar, quitar.

◆ **trim down** VT recortar.

◆ **trim off** VT = **trim away**.

◆ **trim up** **1** VT arreglar, componer.
2 VR: **to ~ o.s. up** arreglarse.

trimaran ['traɪməræn] N trimarán *m*.

trimester [trɪ'mestəʳ] N trimestre *m*.

trimming ['trɪmɪŋ] N adorno *m*, guarnición *f*; orla *f*; **~s** (*cuttings*) recortes *mpl*; (*adornments*) adornos *mpl*; accesorios *mpl*; (*pej*) arrequives *mpl*; **without all the ~s** sin todos aquellos adornos.

trimness ['trɪmnɪs] N aseo *m*; elegancia *f*; buen estado *m*.

trimphone ['trɪmfəʊn] N ≃ teléfono *m* góndola.

Trinidad ['trɪnɪdæd] N Trinidad *f*.

Trinidadian [ˌtrɪnɪ'dædɪən] **1** ADJ de Trinidad.

2 N nativo *m*, -a *f* (*or* habitante *mf*) de Trinidad.

trinitrotoluene [traɪ'naɪtrəʊ'tɒljuːiːn] N trinitrotolueno *m*.

Trinity ['trɪnɪtɪ] **1** N Trinidad *f*.

2 ATTR: **~ Sunday** Domingo *m* de la Santísima Trinidad; **~ term** trimestre *m* de verano.

trinket ['trɪŋkɪt] N dije *m*, chuchería *f*; **~s** (*pej*) baratijas *fpl*, chucherías *fpl*.

trinomial [traɪ'nəʊmɪəl] **1** ADJ trinomio.

2 N trinomio *m*.

trio ['triːəʊ] N trío *m*.

trip [trɪp] **1** N (**a**) (*journey*) viaje *m*; (*excursion*) excursión *f*; **he's away on a ~** está de viaje; **to take a ~** hacer un viaje; salir de excursión; **I must take a ~ into town** tengo que ir a la ciudad.

(**b**) (*stumble*) tropezón *m*, traspié *m*; (*in wrestling etc*) zancadilla *f*; (*fig*) desliz *m*, tropiezo *m*.

(**c**) (*Mech*) trinquete *m*, disparo *m*.

(**d**) (‡: *on drug*) viaje‡ *m*.

2 VT (*also* **to ~ up**) hacer tropezar, hacer caer, (*deliberately*) echar la zancadilla a; **to ~ sb up** (*fig*) coger a uno en una falta, hundir a uno; **the fourth question ~ped him up** la cuarta pregunta le confundió, la cuarta pregunta le desconcertó.

3 VI (**a**) **to ~ along, to go ~ping along** andar (*or* ir, correr *etc*) con paso ligero, andar airosamente.

(**b**) (*stumble*: *also* **to ~ up**) tropezar (*against, on, over* en), caer, dar un tropezón; (*fig*) tropezar, equivocarse.

(**c**) (‡: *on drug*) ir de viaje‡.

◆**trip over** VI tropezar, caer, dar un tropezón.

◆**trip up** **1** VI = **trip 3 (b)**.

2 VT = **trip 2**.

tripartite [traɪ'pɑːtaɪt] ADJ tripartito.

tripe [traɪp] N (**a**) (*Culin*) callos *mpl*; guata *f* (*Mex*), mondongo *m* (*SC*); **~s** (*Anat, hum*) tripas *fpl*.

(**b**) (*esp Brit**) tonterías *fpl*, bobadas *fpl*; **what utter ~!** ¡tonterías!; **he talks a lot of ~** no habla más que bobadas.

triphase ['traɪfeɪz] ADJ trifásico.

triphthong ['trɪfθɒŋ] N triptongo *m*.

triple ['trɪpl] **1** ADJ triple; **~ glazing** triple acristalamiento *m*; **~ jump** triple salto *m*; **~ the sum** el triple; **T~ Alliance** Triple Alianza *f*.

2 N triple *m*.

3 VT triplicar.

4 VI triplicarse.

triplet ['trɪplɪt] N (*Mus*) tresillo *m*; (*Poet*) terceto *m*; **~s** (*persons*) trillizos *mpl*, -as *fpl*.

triplicate **1** ['trɪplɪkɪt] ADJ triplicado.

2 ['trɪplɪkɪt] N: **in ~** por triplicado.

3 ['trɪplɪkeɪt] VT triplicar.

triply ['trɪplɪ] ADV tres veces; **~ dangerous** tres veces más peligroso.

tripod ['traɪpɒd] N trípode *m*.

Tripoli ['trɪpəlɪ] N Trípoli *m*.

tripper ['trɪpər] N (*Brit*) excursionista *mf*; (*day ~*) turista *mf* (que hace una visita de un día).

tripping ['trɪpɪŋ] ADJ ligero, airoso.

trippy‡ ['trɪpɪ] ADJ flipante‡.

triptych ['trɪptɪk] N tríptico *m*.

tripwire ['trɪpwaɪər] N cable *m* trampa.

trireme ['traɪriːm] N trirreme *m*.

trisect [traɪ'sekt] VT trisecar.

Tristan ['trɪstən] NM, **Tristram** ['trɪstrəm] NM Tristán.

trisyllabic ['trɪsɪ'læbɪk] ADJ trisilábico.

trisyllable ['traɪ'sɪləbl] N trisílabo *m*.

trite [traɪt] ADJ vulgar, trivial; gastado, trillado y llevado.

tritely ['traɪtlɪ] ADV vulgarmente, trivialmente.

triteness ['traɪtnɪs] N vulgaridad *f*, trivialidad *f*; lo gastado.

tritium ['trɪtɪəm] N tritio *m*.

Triton ['traɪtn] NM Tritón.

tritone ['traɪtəʊn] N tritono *m*.

triturate ['trɪtʃəreɪt] VT triturar.

trituration [ˌtrɪtʃə'reɪʃən] N trituración *f*.

triumph ['traɪʌmf] **1** N triunfo *m*; éxito *m*; **a new ~ for Slobodian industry** nuevo éxito de la industria eslobodia; **to achieve a great ~** obtener un gran éxito; **it is a ~ of man over nature** en esto el hombre triunfa de la naturaleza; **to come home in ~** volver a casa triunfalmente.

2 VI triunfar; **to ~ over a difficulty** triunfar de una dificultad; **to ~ over the enemy** triunfar sobre el enemigo.

triumphal [traɪ'ʌmfəl] ADJ triunfal; **~ arch** arco *m* triunfal.

triumphalism [traɪ'ʌmfəlɪzəm] N triunfalismo *m*.

triumphalist [traɪ'ʌmfəlɪst] ADJ triunfalista.

triumphant [traɪ'ʌmfənt] ADJ triunfante; victorioso; **he was ~** estaba jubiloso, estaba lleno de júbilo.

triumphantly [traɪ'ʌmfəntlɪ] ADV triunfalmente, de modo triunfal; **he said ~** dijo en tono triunfal.

triumvirate [traɪ'ʌmvɪrɪt] N triunvirato *m*.

triune ['traɪjuːn] ADJ trino.

trivet ['trɪvɪt] N (*US*) salvamanteles *m*.

trivia ['trɪvɪə] NPL trivialidades *fpl*.

trivial ['trɪvɪəl] ADJ trivial, insignificante; banal; superficial; *excuse, pretext etc* frívolo, poco serio.

triviality [ˌtrɪvɪ'ælɪtɪ] N (**a**) (*V adj*) trivialidad *f*, insignificancia *f*; banalidad *f*; superficialidad *f*; frivolidad *f*, falta *f* de seriedad; trivialidades *fpl*. (**b**) **a ~** una nimiedad; **to worry about trivialities** preocuparse por nimiedades.

trivialization [ˌtrɪvɪəlaɪ'zeɪʃən] N trivialización *f*, banalización *f*.

trivialize ['trɪvɪəlaɪz] VT trivializar, banalizar.

trivially ['trɪvɪəlɪ] ADV trivialmente, banalmente.

trochaic [trɒ'keɪɪk] ADJ trocaico.

trochee ['trɒkiː] N troqueo *m*.

trod [trɒd] PRET *of* **tread**.

trodden ['trɒdn] PTP *of* **tread**.

troglodyte ['trɒglədaɪt] N troglodita *m*.

troika ['trɔɪkə] N troica *f*.

Trojan ['trəʊdʒən] **1** ADJ troyano; **~ horse** caballo *m* de Troya; **~ War** Guerra *f* de Troya.

2 N troyano *m*, -a *f*.

troll [trəʊl] N gnomo *m*, duende *m*.

trolley ['trɒlɪ] N (**a**) (*esp Brit*) (*hand ~*) carretilla *f*; (*of supermarket*) carrito *m*; (*tea ~*) mesita *f* de ruedas; (*Med*) camilla *f* de ruedas; (*child's*) carretón *m*. (**b**) (*Tech*) corredera *f* elevada; (*Elec*) trole *m*, arco *m* de trole; **to be off one's ~*** (*US*) estar chiflado*. (**c**) (*US*) tranvía *m*.

trolleybus ['trɒlɪbʌs] N trolebús *m*.

trolleycar ['trɒlɪkɑːr] N (*US*) tranvía *m*.

trolley-pole ['trɒlɪpəʊl] N trole *m*.

trollop ['trɒləp] N marrana *f*; puta *f*.

trombone [trɒm'bəʊn] N trombón *m*.

trombonist [trɒm'bəʊnɪst] N (*orchestral*) trombón *mf*; (*jazz etc*) trombonista *mf*.

troop [truːp] **1** N (**a**) banda *f*, grupo *m*, compañía *f*; (*Mil*) tropa *f*, (*of cavalry*) escuadrón *m*; (*Theat*) V **troupe**; **~s** (*Mil*) tropas *fpl*; **to come in a ~** venir en tropel, venir en masa.

(**b**) **the steady ~ of feet** el ruido rítmico de pasos.

2 VT: **to ~ the colour** (*Brit*) presentar la bandera, desfilar con la bandera.

3 VI: **to ~ along** marchar (*todos juntos*); **to ~ away, to ~ off** marcharse en tropel; **to ~ out** salir todos juntos, salir en masa; **to ~ past** desfilar (*ante*); **to ~ together** reunirse en masa.

troop-carrier ['truːpˌkærɪər] N transporte *m* de tropas; camión *m* blindado.

trooper ['truːpər] N soldado *m* de caballería; (*US*) soldado *m* de reserva.

troopship ['truːpʃɪp] N transporte *m*.

troop train ['truːptreɪn] N tren *m* militar.

trope [trəʊp] N tropo *m*.

trophy ['trəʊfɪ] N trofeo *m*.

trophy wife* ['trəʊfɪwaɪf] N (*pej*) esposa *f* decorativa.

tropic ['trɒpɪk] N trópico *m*; **~s** trópicos *mpl*, zona *f* tropical; **T~ of Cancer** trópico *m* de Cáncer; **T~ of Capricorn** trópico *m* de Capricornio.

tropic(al) ['trɒpɪk(əl)] ADJ tropical.

troposphere ['trɒpəsfɪər] N troposfera *f*.

Trot* [trɒt] N ABBR *of* **Trotskyist**.

trot[1] [trɒt] **1** N (**a**) (*pace*) trote *m*; **at an easy ~, at a slow ~** a trote corto; **to break into a ~** echar a trotar; **for 5 days on the ~** durante 5 días seguidos; **Barataria won 5 times on the ~** Barataria ganó 5 veces de carrerilla; **to be always on the ~** no parar nunca, tener una vida ajetreada; **to keep sb on the ~** no dejar a uno descansar.

(**b**) **to have the ~s‡** tener el vientre descompuesto, tener cagueruelas‡ *fpl*.

2 VT *horse* hacer trotar.

3 VI (**a**) *horse* trotar, ir al trote.

(**b**) (*) ir; irse; marcharse; **we must be ~ting** es hora de marcharnos.

◆**trot along** VI (**a**) = **trot over**.

(**b**) = **trot away**.

◆**trot away, trot off** VI irse, marcharse; **we must be ~ting off** es hora de marcharnos.

◆**trot out** VT *excuses etc* ensartar; *arguments* sacar a relucir, presentar otra vez; *erudition* hacer alarde de.

◆**trot over, trot round** VI: **he ~s round to the shop** sale a la tienda en una carrera.

trot² [trɒt] N (US) chuleta f.

troth [trəʊθ] N (†† or hum) V **plight.**

Trotskyism ['trɒtskɪɪzəm] N trotskismo m.

Trotskyist ['trɒtskɪɪst] [1] ADJ trotskista.

[2] N trotskista mf.

trotter ['trɒtəʳ] N (a) (horse) trotón m, caballo m trotón. (b) (Culin) pie m de cerdo, manita f de cerdo.

trotting ['trɒtɪŋ] N (Sport) trote m.

troubadour ['truːbədɔːʳ] N trovador m.

▼ **trouble** ['trʌbl] [1] N (a) (grief, affliction) aflicción f; pena f, angustia f; (misfortune) desgracia f, desventura f; (worry) inquietud f, preocupación f; (difficult situation) apuro m, aprieto m; **my ~ and strife:** la parienta; **to be in ~** estar en un apuro; **to be in great ~** estar muy apurado; **now your ~s are over** ya no tendrás de que preocuparte, se acabaron las preocupaciones; **life is full of ~s** la vida está llena de aflicciones; **then this ~ came upon them** luego sufrieron esta aflicción; **to drown one's ~s** beber para olvidar sus aflicciones; **to lay up ~ for o.s.** hacer algo que causará pena en el futuro; **to tell sb one's ~s** contar sus desventuras a uno.

(b) (difficulty) dificultad f; disgusto m; (hindrance) estorbo m, inconveniente m; **family ~s** dificultades fpl domésticas; **money ~s** dificultades fpl económicas; **the ~ is that ...** la dificultad es que ..., lo malo es que ..., el inconveniente es que ...; **what's the ~?, what seems to be the ~?** ¿pasa algo?; **that's just the ~** ahí está (la madre del cordero); **their aunt is a great ~ to them** su tía constituye un gran estorbo para ellos; **it's just asking for ~** es buscarse complicaciones; **she never gave us any ~** nunca nos dio un disgusto; **to get into ~** meterse en un lío; **Peter got into ~ for saying that** Pedro se mereció una bronca diciendo eso; **he got into ~ with the police** tuvo una dificultad con la policía; **to get sb into ~** comprometer a uno, crear un lío a uno; **to get a girl into ~** dejar encinta a una joven; **to get out of ~** salir del apuro; **to get sb out of ~** ayudar a uno a salir del apuro; echar un cable a uno; **you'll have ~ with it** tendrás dificultades con eso; **did you have any ~?** ¿tuviste alguna dificultad?; **to make ~ for sb** crear un lío a uno; amargar la vida a uno.

▼ (c) (bother) molestia f; dificultad f; (effort) esfuerzo m; **with no little ~** con bastante dificultad, con no poca dificultad; **it's no ~** no es molestia; **it's no ~ to do it properly** no cuesta nada hacerlo bien; **it's more ~ than it's worth, it's not worth the ~** no vale la pena; **nothing is too much ~ for her** para ella todo es poco; **to give sb ~** causar molestia a uno; **to go to the ~ of + ger** darse la molestia de + infin; **we had ~ getting here in time** nos costó trabajo llegar aquí a tiempo; **we had all our ~ for nothing** todo aquello fue trabajo perdido; **to put sb to the ~ of doing sth** molestar a uno pidiéndole que haga algo; **I fear I am putting you to a lot of ~** me temo que esto te vaya a molestar bastante; **to save o.s. the ~** ahorrarse el trabajo; **to spare no ~ in order to + infin** no regatear medio para + infin; **to take the ~ to + infin** tomarse la molestia de + infin; **he didn't even take the ~ to say thank you** ni se dignó siquiera darme las gracias; **to take a lot of ~** esmerarse, trabajar (etc) con el mayor cuidado.

(d) (Med: upset) enfermedad f, mal m; **heart ~** enfermedad f cardíaca; **it's my old ~** ha vuelto lo de antes.

(e) (Mech: upset) avería f; fallo m; **engine ~** avería f del motor; **a mechanic put the ~ right** un mecánico reparó las piezas averiadas; **we drove 5,000 miles without ~ of any kind** cubrimos 5.000 millas sin la menor avería.

(f) (upset: between persons) disgusto m, desavenencia f, sinsabor m; **the Parnell ~** el caso Parnell; **there is constant ~ between them** riñen constantemente; **X caused ~ between Y and Z** X provocó un disgusto entre Y y Z.

(g) (unrest, Pol etc) conflicto m; trastorno m, disturbio m; **the Irish ~s** los conflictos de los irlandeses; **labour ~s** conflictos mpl laborales; **there's ~ at t'mill** hay un disturbio en la fábrica, hay huelga en la fábrica; **there's ~ brewing** soplan vientos de fronda; **to stir up ~** meter cizaña, revolver el ajo.

[2] VT (a) (afflict, grieve) afligir; (worry) inquietar, preocupar; (disturb) agitar, turbar; **the thought ~d him** el pensamiento le afligió; **the heat ~d us** nos molestó el calor; **his eyes ~ him** le duelen los ojos; **I am deeply ~d** estoy sumamente preocupado; **it's not that that ~s me** no me inquieto por eso, eso me trae sin cuidado.

(b) (bother) molestar, incomodar; (badger) importunar; **I'm sorry to ~ you** lamento tener que molestarle; **may I ~ you for a match?** ¿tienes fuego por favor?, ¿me haces el favor de darme fuego?; **may I ~ you to hold this?** ¿te molestaría tener esto?; **does it ~ you if I smoke?** ¿te molesta que fume?; **I shan't ~ you with all the details** no te molesto citando todos los detalles; **maths never ~d me at all** las matemáticas no me costaron trabajo en absoluto.

[3] VI preocuparse, molestarse; **please don't ~!** ¡no te molestes!, ¡no te preocupes!; **don't ~ to write** no te molestes en escribir; **he didn't ~ to shut the door** no se tomó la molestia de cerrar la puerta; **if**

you had ~d to find out si te hubieras tomado la molestia de averiguarlo.

[4] VR: **to ~ o.s. about sth** preocuparse por algo; **to ~ o.s. to do sth** tomarse la molestia de hacer algo; **don't ~ yourself!** ¡no te molestes!, ¡no te preocupes!

troubled ['trʌbld] ADJ person inquieto, preocupado; expression preocupado; period turbulento, agitado; life, story accidentado; waters revuelto, turbio; **to look ~** parecer estar preocupado.

trouble-free ['trʌblfriː] ADJ libre de inquietudes, totalmente tranquilo; (Pol etc) libre de disturbios; (Aut, Mech) exento de averías; **a thousand ~ miles** mil millas sin avería alguna.

troublemaker ['trʌbl,meɪkəʳ] N alborotador m, -ora f, buscarruidos m, elemento m perturbador.

troublemaking ['trʌbl,meɪkɪŋ] ADJ alborotador, perturbador.

trouble-shooter ['trʌbl,ʃuːtəʳ] N apagafuegos mf, bombero m.

troublesome ['trʌblsəm] ADJ molesto, fastidioso; importuno; dificultoso; **it's very ~** es terriblemente molesto; **now don't be ~** no seas difícil, no te pongas así.

trouble-spot ['trʌblspɒt] N centro m de fricción, lugar m turbulento, punto m conflictivo.

troubling ['trʌblɪŋ] ADJ inquietante, alarmante.

troublous ['trʌbləs] ADJ (liter) times turbulento, agitado, revuelto.

trough [trɒf] N (a) (depression) depresión f, hoyo m; (between waves) seno m; (channel) canal m; (Met) mínimo m de presión; (fig) parte f baja, punto m más bajo.

(b) (drinking ~) abrevadero m; (feeding ~) pesebre m, comedero m; (kneading ~) artesa f; (of stone) pila f.

trounce [traʊns] VT (thrash) pegar, zurrar, dar una paliza a; (defeat) derrotar, cascar; (castigate) fustigar.

troupe [truːp] N (Theat etc) compañía f, grupo m, conjunto m.

trouper ['truːpəʳ] N (Theat) miembro mf de una compañía de actores; **old ~** actor m veterano, actriz f veterana.

trouser ['traʊzəʳ] [1] NPL: **~s** (esp Brit) pantalones mpl, pantalón m; **a pair of ~s** un pantalón, unos pantalones; **to wear the ~s** (fig) llevar los pantalones.

[2] ATTR: **~ leg** pierna f de pantalón; **~ pocket** bolsillo m de pantalón; **~ suit** (Brit) traje-pantalón m.

trouser-press ['traʊzəpres] N prensa f para pantalones.

trousseau ['truːsəʊ] N, PL **trousseaus** or **trousseaux** ['truːsəʊz] ajuar m, equipo m (de novia).

trout [traʊt] N, PL INVAR trucha f; **old ~** arpía f, bruja* f.

trout-fishing ['traʊt,fɪʃɪŋ] N pesca f de truchas.

trove [trəʊv] N V **treasure-trove.**

trowel ['traʊəl] N (Agr) desplantador m, transplantador m; (builder's) paleta f, llana f.

Troy [trɔɪ] N Troya f.

troy (weight) ['trɔɪ('weɪt)] N peso m troy.

truancy ['truːənsɪ] N ausencia f sin permiso.

truant ['truːənt] [1] ADJ (slack) gandul, haragán, vago; (absent) ausente, desparecido.

[2] N (slacker) gandul m, vago m; (absentee) novillero m, -a f; **to play ~** ausentarse, (Scol) hacer novillos.

[3] VI (US) ausentarse (from de); (Scol) hacer novillos.

truce [truːs] N (Mil) tregua f; (fig) suspensión f, cesación f; **to call a ~ to sth** suspender algo.

truck¹ [trʌk] [1] N: **to have no ~ with sb** no tratar con uno, no tener relaciones con uno; **we want no ~ with that** no queremos tener nada que ver con eso.

[2] ATTR: **~ system** (Hist) pago m de salarios en especie.

truck² [trʌk] [1] N (esp US: waggon) carro m; (hand~) carretilla f; (Rail) vagón m (de mercancías); (lorry) camión m.

[2] VT (US) llevar, transportar.

truckage ['trʌkɪdʒ] N (US) acarreo m.

truck-driver ['trʌk,draɪvəʳ] N (esp US) camionero m, camionista m, conductor m de camión.

trucker ['trʌkəʳ] N (US) camionero m, camionista m.

truck farm ['trʌkˈfɑːm] N (US), **truck garden** ['trʌkˈgɑːdn] N (US) huerto m de hortalizas.

truck farmer ['trʌkˌfɑːməʳ] N (US) hortelano m, -a f.

truck farming ['trʌkˌfɑːmɪŋ] N (US) horticultura f.

trucking ['trʌkɪŋ] (US) [1] N acarreo m, transporte m.

[2] ATTR: **~ company** compañía f de transporte por carretera.

truckle ['trʌkl] VI: **to ~ to sb** someterse servilmente a uno.

trucklebed ['trʌklˈbed] N carriola f.

truckload ['trʌkləʊd] N carretada f; vagón m (lleno); **~s of soldiers** camiones mpl llenos de soldados; **by the ~** (fig) a carretadas, a montones.

truckman ['trʌkmən] N, PL **truckmen** ['trʌkmən] (US) camionero m, camionista m.

truckstop ['trʌkstɒp] N (US) restaurante m de carretera.

truculence ['trʌkjʊləns] N agresividad f; mal humor m, aspereza f.

truculent ['trʌkjʊlənt] ADJ agresivo; malhumorado, áspero.

▶ LANGUAGE IN USE: **trouble: 1c → 4, 18.5**

truculently ['trʌkjʊləntlɪ] ADV *behave* de modo agresivo; *answer* malhumorado, ásperamente.

trudge [trʌdʒ] ① N caminata *f* (difícil, larga, penosa). ② VT recorrer a pie (penosamente); **we ~d the streets looking for him** nos cansamos buscándole por las calles. ③ VI (*also* **to ~ along**) caminar penosamente, andar con dificultad.

▼ **true** [truː] ① ADJ (a) (*not false*) verdadero; **~!, too ~!** ¡es verdad!; **how (very) ~!** ¡es mucha verdad!; **it is ~ that ...** es verdad que ...; **can this be ~?** ¿es cierto esto?; **so ~ is this that ...** tan(to) es así que ...; **to come ~** realizarse, cumplirse, verificarse; **to hold sth to be ~** creer que algo es verdad; **it holds ~ of ...** también es cierto por lo que se refiere a ...

(b) (*genuine*) auténtico, verdadero, genuino; *account* verídico; *copy* fiel, exacto; **~ to life** realista, verista, conforme con la realidad; **~ to type** conforme con el tipo; **what is the ~ situation?** ¿cuál es la verdadera situación?; **it is not a ~ account of what happened** no es un informe verdadero de lo que pasó; **in a ~ spirit of service** en un auténtico espíritu de servicio; **like a ~ Englishman** como un inglés auténtico.

(c) *measures etc* exacto; *surface, join* uniforme, a nivel; *upright* a plomo; *wheel* centrado; *voice* justo, afinado; **the walls are not ~** las paredes no están a plomo.

(d) (*faithful*) fiel, leal; **a ~ friend** un fiel amigo; **all good men and ~** todos los buenos y leales; **to be ~ to sb** ser fiel a uno; **to be ~ to one's word** cumplir su promesa, cumplir lo prometido.

② ADV: **to aim ~** apuntar bien, acertar en la puntería; **to breed ~** reproducirse conforme con el tipo; **to run ~ to type** estar conforme con el tipo; **now tell me ~** dime la verdad.

③ N: **to be out of ~** (*things joining*) no estar a nivel, estar mal alineado, estar desalineado; (*things vertical*) no estar a plomo; (*wheel*) estar descentrado.

true-blue ['truːˈbluː] ① ADJ rancio, de lo más rancio. ② N partidario *m*, -a *f* de lo más leal, partidario *m* acérrimo, partidaria *f* acérrima.

true-born ['truːˈbɔːn] ADJ auténtico, verdadero.

true-bred ['truːˈbred] ADJ de casta legítima, de pura sangre.

true-life ['truːˈlaɪf] ADJ verdadero, conforme con la realidad.

truelove ['truːlʌv] N novio *m*, -a *f*, amor *m*, fiel amante *mf*.

truffle ['trʌfl] N trufa *f*.

trug [trʌg] N (*Brit*) cesto *m* de flores.

truism ['truːɪzəm] N perogrullada *f*, tópico *m*; **it is a ~ to say that ...** es un tópico decir que ...

truly ['truːlɪ] ADV verdaderamente; auténticamente; exactamente; fielmente; **and ~ it was tough** y efectivamente fue difícil; **a ~ great painting** un cuadro verdaderamente grande; **really and ~?** ¿de veras?; **yours ~** le saluda atentamente; **yours ~*** (*ie, myself*) este cura*, servidor, menda*; **nobody knows it better than yours ~** nadie lo sabe mejor que este servidor.

trump [trʌmp] ① N (*also* **~ card**) triunfo *m*; **hearts are ~s** triunfan corazones, pintan corazones; **what's ~s?** ¿a qué pinta?; **he always turns up ~s** (*Brit*) no nos falla nunca, es persona de la mayor confianza. ② VT (*Cards*) fallar. ③ VI triunfar, poner un triunfo.

◆**trump up** VT *charge* forjar, falsificar, inventar.

trumped-up ['trʌmptˈʌp] ADJ *accusation etc* forjado, inventado.

trumpery ['trʌmpərɪ] ① ADJ frívolo; (*valueless*) inútil, sin valor; (*insignificant*) sin importancia; (*trashy*) de relumbrón. ② N oropel *m*.

trumpet ['trʌmpɪt] ① N trompeta *f*; **to blow one's own ~** (*fig*) hacer autobombo, autobombearse. ② ATTR: **~ blast, ~ call** trompetazo *m*; (*fig*) clarinazo *m*. ③ VT trompetear; (*fig: also* **to ~ forth**) pregonar, anunciar (a son de trompeta). ④ VI (*elephant*) barritar.

trumpeter ['trʌmpɪtər] N (*orchestral*) trompetero *m*, trompeta *mf*; (*jazz etc*) trompetista *mf*.

trumpeting ['trʌmpɪtɪŋ] N bramido *m*.

truncate [trʌŋˈkeɪt] VT truncar.

truncated [trʌŋˈkeɪtɪd] ADJ truncado, trunco.

truncating [trʌŋˈkeɪtɪŋ] N (*Comput*) truncamiento *m*.

truncation [trʌŋˈkeɪʃən] N truncamiento *m*.

truncheon ['trʌntʃən] N porra *f*.

trundle ['trʌndl] ① VT hacer rodar, hacer correr (sobre ruedas); (*fig*) llevar, arrastrar (con dificultad). ② VI rodar (con mucho ruido, pesadamente).

◆**trundle on** VI avanzar (con mucho ruido, pesadamente).

trunk [trʌŋk] ① N (*Anat, Bot*) tronco *m*; (*case*) baúl *m*; (*US Aut*) maletero *m*, portaequipaje *m*, baúl *m* (*LAm*); maletera *f* (*LAm*); (*elephant's*) trompa *f*. ② ATTR: **~ call** (*Brit*) conferencia *f* (interurbana); **~ line** (*Rail*) línea *f* troncal; (*Telec*) línea *f* principal; **~ road** (*Brit*) carretera *f* nacional.

③ NPL: **~s** traje *m* de baño, bañador *m*.

trunnion ['trʌnɪən] N muñón *m*.

truss [trʌs] ① N (*bundle*) lío *m*, paquete *m*; (*of hay etc*) haz *m*, lío *m*; (*of fruit*) racimo *m*; (*Archit*) entramado *m*; (*Med*) braguero *m*. ② VT (*tie*) liar, atar; *fowl* espetar; (*Archit*) apuntalar, apoyar con entramado.

◆**truss up** VT: **to ~ sb up** atar a uno con cuerdas (*etc*).

trust [trʌst] ① N (a) (*belief, faith*) confianza *f* (*in* en); **to put one's ~ in** confiar en; **to take sth on ~** aceptar algo a ojos cerrados, creer algo sin tener (*or* pedir) pruebas de ello.

(b) (*Comm*) **to supply goods on ~** suministrar artículos al fiado, proveer artículos a crédito.

(c) (*charge*) cargo *m*, deber *m*, obligación *f*; responsabilidad *f*; **our sacred ~** nuestra sagrada obligación; **position of ~** puesto *m* de responsabilidad, puesto *m* de confianza; **to commit sth to sb's ~** confiar algo a uno; **to desert one's ~** faltar a su deber.

(d) (*Jur*) fideicomiso *m*; **to hold money in ~ for sb** tener dinero en administración a nombre de uno.

(e) (*Comm, Fin*) trust *m*; (*pej*) monopolio *m*, cartel *m*.

② ATTR: **~ account** cuenta *f* fiduciaria; **~ company** banco *m* fideicomisario; **~ fund** fondo *m* de fideicomiso; **~ territory** mandato *m*.

③ VT (a) (*believe in, rely on*) confiar en, fiarse de; tener confianza en; creer; **don't you ~ me?** ¿no te fías de mí?; **she is not to be ~ed** ella no es de fiar; **you can't ~ a word he says** es imposible creer ninguna palabra suya; **to ~ sb with sth** confiar algo a uno; **to ~ sb with a task** confiar un cometido a uno; **will you ~ me with your bike?** ¿me permites usar tu bicicleta?; **to ~ sb to do sth** confiar en que uno haga algo; **~ you!** ¡siempre igual!, ¡lo mismo que siempre!; **~ him to make a mess of it** no es sorprendente que lo haya hecho mal; **mother wouldn't ~ us out of her sight** mamá no permitía que nos alejásemos de ella, mamá nos tenía cosidos a sus faldas.

(b) (*Comm*) dar al fiado.

(c) (*hope*) esperar; **I ~ not** espero que no; **I ~ that all will go well** espero que todo vaya bien.

④ VI confiar; esperar; **to ~ in God** confiar en Dios; **to ~ to chance, to ~ to luck** confiar en tener suerte; hacer algo a la ventura.

trusted ['trʌstɪd] ADJ leal, de confianza.

trustee [trʌsˈtiː] N (*in bankruptcy*) síndico *m*; (*holder of property for another*) fideicomisario *m*, -a *f*, depositario *m*, -a *f*, administrador *m*, -ora *f*; (*of college*) regente *m*, -a *f*.

trusteeship [trʌsˈtiːʃɪp] N cargo *m* de síndico, cargo *m* de fideicomisario (*etc*); administración *f* fiduciaria.

trustful ['trʌstfʊl] ADJ, **trusting** ['trʌstɪŋ] ADJ confiado.

trustingly ['trʌstɪŋlɪ] ADV confiadamente.

trustworthiness ['trʌst‚wɜːðɪnɪs] N formalidad *f*, honradez *f*, confiabilidad *f*; carácter *m* fidedigno; exactitud *f*.

trustworthy ['trʌst‚wɜːðɪ] ADJ *person* formal, honrado, confiable, de confianza; *news, source etc* fidedigno; *statistics etc* exacto.

trusty ['trʌstɪ] ① ADJ *servant etc* fiel, leal; *weapon* seguro, bueno. ② N recluso *m*, -a *f* de confianza.

truth [truːθ] ① N, PL **truths** [truːðz] verdad *f*; realidad *f*; verosimilitud *f*; **the plain ~** la pura verdad, la verdad lisa y llana; **the whole ~** toda la verdad; **the ~ of the matter is that ...**, **~ to tell ...**, **to tell you the ~ ...** la verdad del caso es que ..., a decir verdad ...; **there is some ~ in this** hay una parte de verdad en esto; **~ will out** no hay mentira que no salga; **to tell the ~** decir la verdad; **to tell sb a few home ~s** decir a uno cuatro verdades; **in ~** en verdad, a la verdad. ② ATTR: **~ drug** suero *m* de la verdad.

truthful ['truːθfʊl] ADJ *account* verídico, exacto; *person* veraz; **are you being ~?** ¿es esto la verdad?

truthfully ['truːθfəlɪ] ADV con verdad; **now tell me ~** ahora bien, dime la verdad.

truthfulness ['truːθfʊlnɪs] N veracidad *f*; verdad *f*, exactitud *f*.

try [traɪ] ① N (a) (*attempt*) tentativa *f*; **to have a ~** hacer una tentativa, probar suerte; **to have a ~ for a job** presentarse como candidato a un puesto, solicitar un puesto; **have another ~!** ¡a probar otra vez!; **it's worth a ~** vale la pena probarlo; **he did it (at the) first ~** lo hizo la primera vez.

(b) (*Rugby*) ensayo *m*; **to score a ~** marcar un ensayo.

② VT (a) (*attempt*) intentar, probar; **shall we ~ it?** ¿lo probamos?; **you tried only 3 questions** has intentado 3 preguntas nada más.

(b) (*test*) probar, poner a prueba, ensayar; **to ~ one's strength** ensayar sus fuerzas; **to ~ one's strength against sb** ensayarse para determinar cuál de los dos es más fuerte; **we tried 3 hotels but they had no room** preguntamos en 3 hoteles pero no tenían habitación; **~ this door** a ver si esta puerta se abre; **he kept on ~ing the handle** siguió tirando del puño; **he was tried and found wanting** fue sometido a prueba y resultó ser deficiente.

(c) (*expose to suffering*) hacer sufrir; afligir; **his much-tried relations** sus familiares que tanto habían sufrido; **they have been sorely**

tried han sufrido mucho.

(d) (*tire*) *eyes* cansar; *person* irritar; **to ~ one's eyes by reading too much** cansarse los ojos leyendo demasiado; **you ~ my patience** me haces perder la paciencia.

(e) (*taste, sample*) probar; **have you tried these olives?** ¿has probado estas aceitunas?

(f) (*Jur*) *case* ver; *person* procesar (*for* por), juzgar; **to be tried for murder** ser procesado por asesino; **to be tried by one's peers** ser juzgado por sus iguales.

3 VI probar; esforzarse; **to ~ one's best, to ~ one's hardest** esforzarse mucho, poner todo su esfuerzo; **~ as he would ...** por más que se esforzase ...; **to ~ again** volver a probar; **you had better not ~** más vale no probarlo; le aconsejo no hacerlo; **to ~ for sth** tratar de obtener algo; **to ~ for a post** presentarse como candidato a un puesto, solicitar un puesto; **to ~ to do sth, to ~ and do sth** tratar de hacer algo, intentar hacer algo; procurar hacer algo; querer hacer algo; **he tried to get in but couldn't** quiso entrar pero no pudo; **it's ~ing to rain** empieza a llover, quiere llover; **~ not to cough** procura no toser, procura contener la tos; **do ~ to understand** trata de comprender; **it's no use ~ing to persuade him** no vale la pena tratar de convencerle.

◆**try on** VT **(a)** *dress* probarse, medirse (*Mex*).

(b) (*) **to ~ it on with sb** tratar de embaucar a uno; **he's just ~ing it on** lo hace nada más para ver si tragamos el anzuelo; **don't ~ anything on with me!** ¡no lo vayas a intentar conmigo!

◆**try out** VT probar, poner a prueba, someter a prueba, ensayar; **~ it out on the dog first** dáselo primero al perro (para ver qué pasa), pruébalo dándosele de comer al perro.

◆**try over** VT (*Mus etc*) ensayar.

trying ['traɪɪŋ] ADJ molesto; cansado; difícil.

try-on* ['traɪɒn] N trampa *f*, tentativa *f* de engañar, farol *m*.

try-out ['traɪaʊt] N prueba *f*; **to give a car a ~** someter un coche a prueba.

tryst [trɪst] N (*liter, hum*) cita *f*; lugar *m* de una cita.

tsar [zɑːʳ] N zar *m*.

tsarina [zɑːˈriːnə] N zarina *f*.

tsarism ['zɑːrɪsəm] N zarismo *m*.

tsarist ['zɑːrɪst] ADJ, N zarista *mf*.

tsetse fly ['tsetsɪflaɪ] N (mosca *f*) tsetsé *f*.

T-shirt ['tiːʃɜːt] N V T.

tsp(s) ABBR of **teaspoonful(s)**.

TT (a) ABBR of **teetotal**; **teetotaller**. **(b)** N (*Aut*) ABBR of **Tourist Trophy**. **(c)** (*Agr*) ABBR of **tuberculin-tested** a prueba de tuberculinas. **(d)** (*US Post*) ABBR of **Trust Territory**. **(e)** N (*Fin*) ABBR of **telegraphic transfer** transferencia *f* telegráfica.

TU N ABBR of **trade(s) union**.

tub [tʌb] **1** N tina *f*; cubo *m*, cuba *f*, balde *m* (*LAm*); artesón *m*; (*bath~*) baño *m*, bañera *f*, tina *f* (*LAm*); (*of washing-machine*) tambor *m*; (*Naut**) carcamán *m*; **to have a ~*** (*Brit*) tomar un baño. **2** VI tomar un baño.

tuba ['tjuːbə] N tuba *f*.

tubby* ['tʌbɪ] ADJ rechoncho.

tube [tjuːb] N **(a)** (*gen*) tubo *m*; (*TV*) tubo *m*; (*US Rad*) lámpara *f*; (*Aut*) cámara *f* de aire; (*Anat*) trompa *f*; **the ~*** la tele*; **it's all gone down the ~*** todo se ha perdido, todo se ha echado a perder. **(b)** (*Brit Rail*) metro *m*; **to go by ~** ir en el metro, viajar por metro.

tubeless ['tjuːblɪs] ADJ *tyre* sin cámara.

tuber ['tjuːbəʳ] N tubérculo *m*.

tubercle ['tjuːbəkl] N (*all senses*) tubérculo *m*.

tubercular [tjʊˈbɜːkjʊləʳ] ADJ tubercular; (*Med*) tuberculoso.

tuberculin [tjʊˈbɜːkjʊlɪn] N tuberculina *f*.

tuberculosis [tjʊˌbɜːkjʊˈləʊsɪs] N tuberculosis *f*.

tuberculous [tjʊˈbɜːkjʊləs] ADJ tuberculoso.

tube-station ['tjuːbˌsteɪʃən] N (*Brit*) estación *f* de metro.

tubing ['tjuːbɪŋ] N tubería *f*, cañería *f* (*LAm*); tubos *mpl*; **a piece of ~** un trozo de tubo.

tub-thumper ['tʌbˌθʌmpəʳ] N (*Brit*) orador *m* demagógico.

tub-thumping ['tʌbˌθʌmpɪŋ] (*Brit*) **1** ADJ demagógico. **2** N oratoria *f* demagógica.

tubular ['tjuːbjʊləʳ] ADJ tubular, en forma de tubo; *furniture* de tubo.

TUC N (*Brit*) ABBR of **Trades Union Congress**; *ver también* TRADE UNIONS .

tuck [tʌk] **1** N **(a)** (*Sew*) alforza *f*; pliegue *m*; **to take a ~ in a dress** hacer una alforza en un vestido.

(b) (*Brit**) (*food*) provisiones *fpl*, comestibles *mpl*; (*sweets*) dulces *fpl*, golosinas *fpl*.

2 VT (*Sew*) alforzar; plegar.

3 VI: **to ~ into sth*** comer algo vorazmente, zamparse algo.

◆**tuck away** VT **(a)** (*hide*) ocultar, esconder; **~ it away out of sight** ocúltalo para que no se vea; **the village is ~ed away among the woods** la aldea se esconde en el bosque; **he ~ed it away in his pocket** lo guardó en el bolsillo.

(b) (*: eat*) devorar, zampar; **he can certainly ~ it away** ése sí sabe

comer; **I can't think where he ~s it all away** no llego a comprender dónde lo almacena.

◆**tuck in** **1** VT: **to ~ in a flap** meter una solapa para dentro; **to ~ bedclothes in** remeter la ropa de la cama.

2 VI (*) comer con apetito, comer vorazmente; **~ in!** ¡a comer!, ¡a ello!

◆**tuck under** VT: **to ~ A under B** poner A debajo de B; esconder A debajo de B.

◆**tuck up** VT *skirt, sleeves* arremangar; **to ~ sb up in bed** arropar a uno en la cama; (*fig*) acostar a uno; **you'll soon be nicely ~ed up** pronto te verás metido cómodamente en la cama.

tucker* ['tʌkəʳ] VT (*US: also* **to ~ out**) cansar, agotar.

tuck-in* ['tʌkˈɪn] N banquetazo* *m*, comilona* *f*; **to have a good ~** darse un atracón*.

tuck-shop ['tʌkʃɒp] N (*Brit Scol*) bombonería *f*, confitería *f*.

Tudor ['tjuːdəʳ] ADJ Tudor; **the ~ period** la época de los Tudor.

Tue(s). ABBR of **Tuesday** martes, mart.

Tuesday ['tjuːzdɪ] N martes *m*.

tufa ['tjuːfə] N toba *f*.

tuft [tʌft] N (*of hair*) copete *m*; (*of hairs, wool*) mechón *m*; (*of feathers*) cresta *f*, copete *m*; (*on helmet etc*) penacho *m*; (*of plant*) mata *f*.

tufted ['tʌftɪd] ADJ copetudo.

tug [tʌg] **1** N **(a)** (*action*) tirón *m*; estirón *m*; **to give sth a ~** tirar de algo, dar un estirón a algo.

(b) (*Naut*) remolcador *m*.

2 VT **(a)** (*pull*) tirar de; dar un estirón a; **to ~ sth along** arrastrar algo, llevar algo arrastrándolo.

(b) (*Naut*) remolcar; **eventually they ~ged the boat clear** por fin sacaron el barco a flote.

3 VI: **to ~ at sth** tirar de algo; **somebody was ~ging at my sleeve** alguien me tiraba de la manga; **they ~ged their hardest** se esforzaron muchísimo tirando de él.

tugboat ['tʌgbəʊt] N remolcador *m*.

tug-of-love* [ˌtʌgəvˈlʌv] N litigio *m* entre padres por la custodia de los hijos (después de un divorcio *etc*).

tug-of-war ['tʌgə(v)'wɔːʳ] N lucha *f* de la cuerda; (*fig*) lucha *f*; tira *m* y afloja; **then comes the ~** luego es el momento crítico, luego se inicia la lucha decisiva.

tuition [tjʊˈɪʃən] **1** N enseñanza *f*, instrucción *f*; (*US*) matrícula *f*; **private ~** clases *fpl* particulares (*in* de).

2 ATTR: **~ fee** tasa *f* (de instrucción).

tulip ['tjuːlɪp] N tulipán *m*.

tulip-tree ['tjuːlɪptriː] N tulipanero *m*, tulipero *m*.

tulle [tjuːl] N tul *m*.

tum* [tʌm] N (*Brit*) panza *f*.

tumble ['tʌmbl] **1** N caída *f*; (*somersault*) voltereta *f*; **to have a ~, to take a ~** caerse; **to have a ~ in the hay** retozar, hacer el amor (en el pajar); **to take a ~** (*fig*) bajar de golpe, dar un bajón.

2 VT (*knock down*) derribar, abatir, tumbar; (*fig*) derrocar; (*upset*) derramar, hacer caer; (*disarrange*) desarreglar; **to ~ sb in the hay** tumbar a una (en el pajar).

3 VI **(a)** (*fall*) caer; (*stumble*) tropezar; **to toss and ~** (*in bed*) agitarse, revolverse mucho; **to ~ in, to ~ into bed** acostarse; acostarse del modo que sea.

(b) **to ~ to sth*** (*Brit*) caer en la cuenta de algo, comprender algo.

◆**tumble down** VI caer; desplomarse, hundirse, venirse abajo.

◆**tumble out** **1** VT echar en desorden.

2 VI salir en desorden; **to ~ out of a car** caerse de un coche; **to ~ out of bed** levantarse de prisa.

◆**tumble over** **1** VT derramar, hacer caer.

2 VI: **to go tumbling over and over** ir rodando, ir dando tumbas.

tumbledown ['tʌmbldaʊn] ADJ destartalado, ruinoso.

tumble-dry [ˌtʌmblˈdraɪ] VT meter en la secadora.

tumbledryer ['tʌmblˌdraɪəʳ] N secadora *f*.

tumbler ['tʌmbləʳ] N **(a)** (*glass*) vaso *m*. **(b)** (*of lock*) seguro *m*, fiador *m*; **~ switch** interruptor *m* de resorte. **(c)** (*person*) volteador *m*, -ora *f*; (*Orn*) pichón *m* volteador.

tumbleweed ['tʌmblwiːd] N (*US*) planta *f* rodadora.

tumbrel ['tʌmbrəl] N, **tumbril** ['tʌmbrɪl] N chirrión *m*, carreta *f*.

tumefaction [ˌtjuːmɪˈfækʃən] N tumefacción *f*.

tumescent [tjuːˈmesnt] ADJ tumescente.

tumid ['tjuːmɪd] ADJ túmido.

tummy* ['tʌmɪ] N barriguita* *f*, tripas* *fpl*; **~ tuck** cirugía *f* plástica anti-michelines*.

tummy-ache* ['tʌmɪeɪk] N dolor *m* de tripas*.

tumour, (*US*) **tumor** ['tjuːməʳ] N tumor *m*.

tumult ['tjuːmʌlt] N tumulto *m*, alboroto *m*.

tumultuous [tjuːˈmʌltjʊəs] ADJ tumultuoso.

tumultuously [tjuːˈmʌltjʊəslɪ] ADV tumultuosamente.

tumulus ['tjuːmjʊləs] N, PL **tumuli** ['tjuːmjʊlaɪ] túmulo *m*.

tun [tʌn] N tonel *m*.

tuna ['tjuːnə] N, (*US*) **tuna fish** ['tjuːnəfɪʃ] N atún *m*.

tundra ['tʌndrə] N tundra f.

tune [tjuːn] **1** N **(a)** (*melody*) aire m, melodía f, tonada f; (*fig*) tono m; **she calls the ~ in their house** ella lleva la voz cantante en su casa; **to change one's ~, to sing another ~** cambiar de disco•, mudar de tono; **it goes to the ~ of 'Greensleeves'** se canta con la melodía de 'Greensleeves'; **to the ~ of £500** por la bonita suma de 500 libras.
(b) to be in ~ (*Mus*) estar templado, estar afinado; **to sing in ~** cantar afinadamente, cantar bien; **to be in ~ with** (*fig*) armonizar con, concordar con; **to be out of ~** (*Mus*) estar destemplado, estar desafinado; **to sing out of ~** desafinar, cantar mal; **to be out of ~ with** (*fig*) desentonar con, estar en desacuerdo con; **to go out of ~** desafinar.
2 VT afinar, acordar, templar.
♦**tune in 1** VT: **to be ~d in•** estar en la onda•; estar al tanto (*to* de).
2 VI sintonizar; **to ~ in to a station** sintonizar una emisora.
♦**tune out** VI (*US*) desconectar la televisión (*etc*).
♦**tune up 1** VT (*Mus*) afinar, acordar, templar; (*Aut*) poner a punto, reglar, afinar.
2 VI (*Mus*) afinar el instrumento, acordar el instrumento; **we're still just tuning up** (*fig*) estamos todavía en la fase preliminar.

tuneful ['tjuːnfʊl] ADJ melodioso, armonioso.
tunefully ['tjuːnfəlɪ] ADV melodiosamente, armoniosamente.
tunefulness ['tjuːnfʊlnɪs] N lo melodioso, lo armonioso.
tuneless ['tjuːnlɪs] ADJ disonante, discordante.
tunelessly ['tjuːnlɪslɪ] ADV de modo disonante.
tuner ['tjuːnəʳ] N **(a)** (*person*) afinador m. **(b)** (*Rad, TV: knob*) botón m sintonizador.
tune-up ['tjuːnʌp] N (*Mus*) afinación f; (*Aut*) puesta f a punto, reglaje m.

tungsten ['tʌŋstən] N tungsteno m.
tunic ['tjuːnɪk] N túnica f; (*Brit Mil*) guerrera f, blusa f.
tuning ['tjuːnɪŋ] N (*Mus*) afinación f; (*Rad*) sintonización f; (*Aut*) afinación f, reglaje m.
tuning-coil ['tjuːnɪŋkɔɪl] N bobina f sintonizadora.
tuning-fork ['tjuːnɪŋfɔːk] N diapasón m.
tuning-knob ['tjuːnɪŋnɒb] N botón m sintonizador.
Tunis ['tjuːnɪs] N Túnez m (*ciudad*).
Tunisia [tjuːˈnɪzɪə] N Túnez m (*país*).
Tunisian [tjuːˈnɪzɪən] **1** ADJ tunecino.
2 N tunecino m, -a f.
tunnel ['tʌnl] **1** N túnel m; (*Min*) galería f.
2 VT construir un túnel bajo, construir un túnel a través de; **a mound ~led by rabbits** un montículo lleno de madrigueras de conejo; **wood ~led by beetles** madera f carcomida, madera f agujereada por coleópteros; **shelters ~led out in the hillsides** refugios mpl horadados en las colinas.
3 VT construir un túnel (*or* galería); (*animal*) excavar una madriguera; **they ~ into the hill** construyen un túnel bajo la colina; **to ~ down into the earth** perforar un túnel en la tierra; **the rabbits ~ under the fence** los conejos hacen madrigueras que pasan debajo de la valla; **they ~led their way out** escaparon excavando un túnel.
tunnel vision ['tʌnl'vɪʒən] N visión f de túnel; (*fig*) estrechez f de miras.
tunny ['tʌnɪ] N atún m; **striped ~** bonito m.
tuppence ['tʌpəns] N = **twopence.**
tuppenny ['tʌpənɪ] ADJ = **twopenny.**
turban ['tɜːbən] N turbante m.
turbid ['tɜːbɪd] ADJ túrbido.
turbine ['tɜːbaɪn] N turbina f.
turbo ['tɜːbəʊ] N (*fan*) turbosoplador m; (*in cars*) turbo(compresor) m.
turbo... ['tɜːbəʊ] PREF turbo...
turbocharged ['tɜːbəʊtʃɑːdʒd] ADJ turbocargado, turboalimentado.
turbocharger ['tɜːbəʊˌtʃɑːdʒəʳ] N turbocompresor m, turbo m.
turbofan ['tɜːbəʊfæn] N turboventilador m.
turbogenerator ['tɜːbəʊˈdʒenəreɪtəʳ] N turbogenerador m.
turbojet ['tɜːbəʊdʒet] **1** N turborreactor m.
2 ATTR turborreactor.
turboprop ['tɜːbəʊˈprɒp] **1** N turbohélice m.
2 ATTR turbohélice.
turbot ['tɜːbət] N rodaballo m.
turbulence ['tɜːbjʊləns] N turbulencia f; desorden m, disturbios mpl; (*Met*) turbulencia f.
turbulent ['tɜːbjʊlənt] ADJ turbulento; revoltoso.
turd⁺ [tɜːd] N **(a)** (*Brit⁺*) cagada⁑ f, zurullo⁑ m. **(b)** (*person*) mierda⁑ mf.
tureen [təˈriːn] N sopera f.
turf [tɜːf] **1** N, PL **turfs** *or* **turves** [tɜːvz] **(a)** (*sward*) césped m; (*clod*) tepe m, césped m; (*in turfing*) pan m de hierba; (*peat*) turba f; **the T~** el turf, las carreras de caballos.
(b) (*US⁺*) territorio m propio de uno.
2 ATTR: **~ accountant** (*Brit*) corredor m de apuestas.
3 VT (*also to ~ over*) encespedar, cubrir con céspedes.
♦**turf out•** VT: **to ~ sb out** (*Brit*) echar a uno, expulsar a uno.

turgid ['tɜːdʒɪd] ADJ turgente; (*fig*) hinchado; pesado, indigesto.
turgidity [tɜːˈdʒɪdɪtɪ] N turgencia f; (*fig*) hinchazón f; pesadez f.
Turin [tjʊˈrɪn] N Turín m.
Turk [tɜːk] N turco m, -a f; (*fig*) persona f incontrolable, elemento m alborotador; **little ~, young ~** tunante m.
Turkey ['tɜːkɪ] N Turquía f.
turkey ['tɜːkɪ] N **(a)** (*Orn*) pavo m, -a f, guajolote m (*Mex*), chompipe m (*CAm*); **to talk ~•** (*US*) hablar en serio. **(b)** (*US⁑*) patoso m, -a f, pato m mareado•. **(c)** (*Theat•*) fracaso m.
turkeycock ['tɜːkɪkɒk] N pavo m (*also fig*).
Turkish ['tɜːkɪʃ] **1** ADJ turco; **~ bath** baño m turco; **~ coffee** café m turco; **~ delight** rahat m lokum; **~ towel** (*US*) toalla f.
2 N turco m.
Turkish-Cypriot ['tɜːkɪʃˈsɪprɪət] **1** ADJ turcochipriota.
2 N turcochipriota mf.
Turkmenistan [ˌtɜːkmenɪsˈtɑːn] N Turkmenistán m.
turmeric ['tɜːmərɪk] N cúrcuma f.
turmoil ['tɜːmɔɪl] N confusión f, desorden m; alboroto m; tumulto m; (*mental*) trastorno m; **everything is in (a) ~** todo es confusión, todo está revuelto; **we had complete ~ for a week** durante una semana reinó la confusión.
turn [tɜːn] **1** N **(a)** (*revolution*) vuelta f, revolución f; (*of spiral*) espira f; **with a quick ~ of the hand** con un movimiento rápido de la mano; **he never does a hand's ~** no da golpe; **the meat is done to a ~** la carne está en su punto; **to give a screw another ~** apretar un tornillo una vuelta más.
(b) (*change of direction*) cambio m de dirección; (*Aut: by vehicle*) giro m, vuelta f; (*Aut: turning off*) salida f; (*Naut*) viraje m; (*Swimming*) vuelta f; (*in road*) curva f, vuelta f; recodo m; 'no left ~' (*Aut*) 'prohibido girar a la izquierda'; **~ of the tide** cambio m de la marea, vuelta f de la marea (*also fig*); **at every ~** a cada paso, a cada momento; **at the ~ of the century** al final del siglo; **the tide is on the ~** la marea está cambiando; **the milk is on the ~** la leche está cortándose; **to make a ~ to the left** girar a la izquierda; **to make a ~ to port** virar a babor; **I think we missed our ~ back there** creo que allí atrás nos hemos pasado de la salida; **things took a new ~** las cosas cambiaron de aspecto; **events took a tragic ~** los acontecimientos tomaron un cariz trágico; **events are taking a sensational ~** los acontecimientos vienen tomando un rumbo sensacional; **then things took a ~ for the better** luego las cosas empezaron a mejorar.
(c) (*Med: fainting fit etc*) vahído m, desmayo m; (*crisis*) crisis f, ataque m; (*fright*) susto m; **it gave me quite a ~** me dio todo un susto; **he had another ~ last night** anoche le dio otro ataque.
(d) (*short walk*) vuelta f; **to take a ~ in the park** dar una vuelta por el parque.
(e) (*successive opportunity*) turno m, vez f; oportunidad f; **~ and ~ about** cada uno por turno; ahora esto y luego aquello; **by ~s, in ~** por turnos, sucesivamente; **I felt hot and cold by ~s** tuve calor y luego frío en momentos sucesivos; **it's my ~** me toca a mí; **then it was my ~ to protest** luego protesté a mi vez; **it's her ~ next** le toca a ella después, ella es la primera en turno; **your ~ will come** tendrás tu oportunidad; **to give up one's ~** ceder la vez; **to go out of ~** jugar (*etc*) fuera de orden; **to miss one's ~** perder la vez; perder la ocasión; **the player shall miss two ~s** el jugador deberá perder dos jugadas; **to take one's ~** esperar su turno; turnar, alternar; **to take ~s at the controls** alternar a los mandos; **to take a ~ at the wheel** conducir por su turno; **to take ~s at doing sth, to take it in ~s to do sth** hacer algo por turnos, turnar para hacer algo.
(f) (*esp Brit Theat etc*) número m; **he came on and did a funny ~** salió a escena y presentó un número cómico.
(g) (*service*) **bad ~** mala jugada f, mala pasada f; **good ~** favor m, servicio m; **to do sb a bad ~** hacer una mala pasada a uno; **a scout does a good ~ each day** el explorador hace una buena acción cada día; **one good ~ deserves another** amor con amor se paga; **it will serve my ~** servirá para lo que yo quiero.
(h) (*inclination*) propensión f (*to* a); (*of mind*) disposición f, sesgo m; (*talent*) talento m, aptitud f; **to have a ~ for business** tener aptitud para los negocios; **it showed an odd ~ of mind** demostró una disposición de ánimo algo rara.
(i) (*form*) forma f; **the ~ of her arm** la configuración de su brazo, el contorno de su brazo; **~ of phrase** giro m, expresión f; **that's a French ~ of phrase** eso es un modismo francés; **the car has a good ~ of speed** el coche tiene buena aceleración.
2 VT **(a)** (*revolve*) girar, hacer girar; *handle* dar vueltas a, torcer; *key* dar vuelta a; *screw* atornillar, destornillar; **the belt ~s the wheel** la correa hace girar la rueda; **~ it to the left** dale una vuelta hacia la izquierda; **you can ~ it through 90°** se puede girarlo hasta 90 grados.
(b) (*~ to the other side*) volver; *ankle* torcer; *brain* trastornar; *pages of book* pasar, volver; *stomach, soil etc* revolver; *hay etc* volver al revés; **to ~ a page** volver una hoja; **to ~ a dress inside out** volver un vestido

del revés; **the plough ~s the soil** el arado revuelve la tierra.
(c) (*direct*) volver; dirigir; *blow* desviar; **to ~ one's head** volver la cabeza; **to ~ one's steps homeward** dirigirse a casa, volver los pasos hacia casa; **to ~ one's eyes in sb's direction** volver la mirada hacia donde está uno; **to ~ a gun on sb** apuntar un revólver a uno; **we managed to ~ his argument against him** pudimos volver su argumento contra él mismo; **to ~ A against B** predisponer a A en contra de B; **they ~ed him against his parents** le enemistaron con sus padres; **to ~ sb from doing sth** disuadir a uno de hacer algo; **we must ~ our thoughts to ...** hemos de concentrar nuestro pensamiento en ...; **if you will ~ your attention to ...** tengan la bondad de fijar la atención en ...
(d) (*pass*) *corner* doblar; **he has ~ed 50** ha cumplido los 50, ya tiene lo menos 50 años; **it's ~ed 11 o'clock** son las 11 dadas, ya dieron las 11.
(e) (*transform*) cambiar, mudar (*into, to* en); convertir, transformar (*into, to* en); *milk* agriar, volver agrio; **to ~ iron into gold** transformar el hierro en oro; **his admiration was ~ed to scorn** su admiración se transformó en desprecio; **to ~ verse into prose** verter verso en prosa; **to ~ a play into a film** hacer una versión cinematográfica de una obra dramática; **to ~ English into Spanish** traducir el inglés al español, verter el inglés en español; **to ~ colour** cambiar de color; **the heat ~ed the walls black** el calor volvió negras las paredes, el calor ennegreció las paredes.
(f) (*Tech*) tornear; **to ~ wood on a lathe** labrar la madera en un torno; **a well ~ed leg** una pierna bien formada, una pierna bien torneada; **a well ~ed sentence** una frase elegante.
⟨3⟩ VI **(a)** (*revolve*) girar, dar vueltas; (*of person*) volverse; girar sobre los talones; **my head is ~ing** mi cabeza está dando vueltas; **to toss and ~ in bed** revolverse en la cama; **everything ~s on whether ...** todo depende de si ...; **the conversation ~ed on newts** la conversación versaba sobre los tritones, el tema de la conversación era los tritones.
(b) (*change direction*) volver, volverse; (*Aer, Naut*) virar; (*Aut*) girar, torcer; (*tide*) repuntar; (*weather etc*) cambiar; **to ~ left** torcer a la izquierda; **right ~!** (*Mil*) derecha ... ¡ar!; **to ~ into a road** entrar en una calle; **to ~ to port** virar a babor; **to ~ for home** volver hacia casa; **please ~ to page 34** vamos a la página 34, por favor la página 34; **the wind has ~ed** el viento ha cambiado de dirección; **to wait for the weather to ~** esperar a que cambie el tiempo; **then our luck ~ed** luego mejoramos de suerte; **he ~ed to me and smiled** se volvió hacia mí y sonrió; **to ~ to sb for help** acudir a uno a pedir ayuda; **he ~ed to politics** se volvió a la política; **he ~ed to mysticism** recurrió al misticismo; empezó a estudiar el misticismo; **farmers are ~ing from cows to pigs** los granjeros cambian de vacas a cerdos; **our thoughts ~ to those who ...** pensamos ahora en los que ...; **I don't know which way to ~** estoy para volverme loco; **I don't know where to ~ for money** no sé en qué parte ir a buscar dinero; **to ~ against sb, to ~ on sb** volverse contra uno; **to ~ against sth** coger aversión a algo.
(c) (*change*) cambiar, cambiarse; convertirse, transformarse (*into, to* en); (+ ADJ) ponerse, volverse; (+ N) hacerse; (*leaves*) descolorarse; dorarse; (*milk*) agriarse, cortarse; **it ~s red** se pone colorado; **matters are ~ing serious** las cosas se ponen graves; **then he began to ~ awkward** luego empezó a ponerse difícil; **the princess ~ed into a toad** la princesa se transformó en sapo, la princesa quedó transformada en sapo; **it ~ed to stone** se convirtió en piedra; **to ~ soldier** hacerse soldado; **to ~ communist** hacerse comunista.
◆**turn about, turn around** ⟨1⟩ VT V **~ round**.
⟨2⟩ VI dar una vuelta completa; (*Pol*) cambiar completamente de política; **about~!** (*Mil*) media vuelta ... ¡ar!
◆**turn aside** ⟨1⟩ VT desviar, apartar.
⟨2⟩ VI desviarse (*from* de); apartarse del camino; **I ~ed aside in disgust** me aparté lleno de asco.
◆**turn away** ⟨1⟩ VT despedir; rechazar, no aceptar.
⟨2⟩ VI volver la cara.
◆**turn back** ⟨1⟩ VT **(a)** (*fold*) doblar.
(b) *clock* retrasar.
(c) *person* hacer volver; hacer retroceder; **they were ~ed back at the frontier** en la frontera les hicieron volver.
⟨2⟩ VI volverse (atrás); retroceder; volverse sobre sus pasos; **there can be no ~ing back now** ahora no vale volverse atrás.
◆**turn down** VT **(a)** (*bend, fold*) doblar, tornar; *case, glass etc* poner boca abajo; *thumb* volver hacia abajo.
(b) *gas, radio etc* bajar.
(c) *offer* rechazar; *candidate, suitor* no aceptar; **he was ~ed down for the job** no le dieron el puesto.
◆**turn in** ⟨1⟩ VT **(a)** (*fold*) doblar hacia adentro.
(b) *essay, report* entregar, presentar; *wanted man* entregar (a la policía).
⟨2⟩ VI **(a)** (*fold*) doblarse hacia adentro; apuntar hacia adentro.
(b) (*: *go to bed*) acostarse, ir a la cama.

◆**turn off** ⟨1⟩ VT **(a)** *light* apagar; (*Elec*) desconectar, quitar; cortar; *engine* parar; *tap* cerrar; *gas* cortar, cerrar la llave de.
(b) **it quite ~s me off*** me repugna, me deja frío.
⟨2⟩ VI desviarse (*from* del camino).
◆**turn on** VT **(a)** (*Elec*) encender, conectar, poner, prender (*LAm*); *tap* abrir; *gas* abrir la llave de; (*) *charm* desplegar, poner en juego; **to leave the radio ~ed on** dejar la radio encendida.
(b) (*: *excite*) emocionar; enrollar*; encandilar, chiflar*; **he doesn't ~ me on** no me chifla*; **whatever ~s you on** lo que te guste, lo que quieras; **to be ~ed on (with drugs)‡** estar iluminado‡.
◆**turn out** ⟨1⟩ VT **(a)** *light* apagar; *gas* cortar, cerrar la llave de.
(b) *person etc* echar, expulsar; poner en la calle; *rubbish* tirar, botar, vaciar.
(c) *pocket etc* vaciar; *room* limpiar, despejar.
(d) *product* hacer, producir, fabricar; **the college ~s out good secretaries** el colegio produce buenas secretarias.
(e) **to ~ out the guard** formar la guardia.
(f) **to be well ~ed out** ir bien vestido, estar bien trajeado.
⟨2⟩ VI **(a)** (*from bed*) levantarse, abandonar la cama; (*from house*) salir de casa, salir a la calle; (*guard*) formarse, presentarse para servicio.
(b) (*transpire*) **how are things ~ing out?** ¿cómo van tus cosas?; **it all ~ed out well** todo salió bien; **it ~s out to be harder than we thought** resulta más difícil de lo que pensábamos; **it ~s out that he's a vegetarian** resulta que es vegetariano; **as it ~s out** por fin; **as it ~ed out nobody went** por fin no fue nadie.
◆**turn over** ⟨1⟩ VT **(a)** *page etc* volver; *container, vehicle* volcar; (*upside down*) volver, poner al revés; **the thieves ~ed the place over*** los ladrones saquearon el local.
(b) (*Mech*) *engine* hacer girar; *matter in mind* revolver, meditar.
(c) (*hand over*) entregar, ceder, traspasar (*to* a).
(d) (*Comm*) *sum* mover, facturar; **they ~ over a million a year** su volumen de ventas (*or* producción *etc*) es de un millón al año.
⟨2⟩ VI **(a)** revolverse; (*Aut etc*) capotar, dar una vuelta de campana; **it ~ed over and over** fue dando tumbos; **my stomach ~ed over** se me revolvió el estómago.
(b) **please ~ over** véase al dorso.
◆**turn round** ⟨1⟩ VT **(a)** *object etc* volver, girar. **(b)** (*change*) cambiar; reformar; **it is time to ~ the economy round** es el momento de dar una nueva dirección a la economía.
⟨2⟩ VI (*revolve*) girar; dar vueltas; (*person*) volverse, girar sobre los talones; **I could hardly ~ round** apenas podía revolverme; **as soon as I ~ed round they were quarrelling again** en cuanto les volví la espalda se pusieron otra vez a reñir; **the government has ~ed right round** el gobierno ha cambiado completamente de rumbo; **to ~ round and round** seguir dando vueltas.
◆**turn to** VI empezar; empezar a trabajar (*etc*); **everyone had to ~ to and help** todos tuvieron que ayudar; **we must all ~ to** todos tenemos que poner manos a la obra.
◆**turn up** ⟨1⟩ VT **(a)** (*bend*) doblar hacia arriba; (*shorten*) acortar, hacer más corto.
(b) *gas* abrir (más); *radio etc* poner más fuerte.
(c) *earth* revolver; *buried object* desenterrar, hacer salir a la superficie.
(d) (*find*) encontrar; tropezar con; *reference* buscar, consultar.
(e) **~ it up!‡** ¡por favor!
⟨2⟩ VI **(a)** (*print upwards*) doblarse hacia arriba, apuntar hacia arriba.
(b) (*appear*) aparecer, surgir; (*card etc*) salir; (*arrive, show up*) llegar, acudir; presentarse; asomar la cara; (*be found again*) volver a aparecer; **we'll see if anyone ~s up** veremos si viene alguien; **he ~ed up 2 hours late** llegó con 2 horas de retraso; **he never ~s up at class** no asiste nunca a la clase; **sth is sure to ~ up** es seguro que surgirá alguna solución.
turnabout ['tɜːnəbaʊt] N, **turnaround** ['tɜːnəraʊnd] N **(a)** (*change*) cambio *m* completo, giro *m* en redondo, giro *m* total. **(b)** (*of ship etc*) tiempo *m* de descarga y carga, tiempo *m* en puerto (*etc*).
turncoat ['tɜːnkəʊt] N renegado *m*, -a *f*; **to become a ~** volver la chaqueta.
turned-down ['tɜːnd'daʊn] ADJ doblado hacia abajo.
turned-up ['tɜːnd'ʌp] ADJ doblado hacia arriba; *nose* respingona.
turner ['tɜːnəʳ] N tornero *m*.
turnery ['tɜːnərɪ] N tornería *f*.
turning ['tɜːnɪŋ] N vuelta *f*; ángulo *m*; recodo *m*; **the first ~ on the left** la primera bocacalle a la izquierda; **we parked in a side ~** aparcamos el coche en una calle que salía de la carretera.
turning-circle ['tɜːnɪŋ,sɜːkl] N (*Aut*) círculo *m* de viraje, diámetro *m* de giro.
turning-lathe ['tɜːnɪŋleɪð] N torno *m*.
turning-point ['tɜːnɪŋpɔɪnt] N (*fig*) punto *m* decisivo, coyuntura *f* crítica; **that was the ~** eso fue la vuelta de la marea, eso marcó el cambio decisivo.
turnip ['tɜːnɪp] N nabo *m*.
turnkey ['tɜːnkiː] ⟨1⟩ N **(a)** (*Hist*) llavero *m* (de una cárcel), carcelero *m*. **(b)** (*Comput*) llave *f* de seguridad.

2 ATTR: ~ **system** sistema *m* de seguridad.

turn-off ['tɜːnɒf] N **(a)** (*Aut*) salida *f* (de una carretera *etc*). **(b)** (*) **he's a real ~** ése me cae gordo*; **the film was a complete ~** la película fue asquerosa; **his breath is a big ~** su aliento me repugna.

turn-on* ['tɜːnɒn] N (*girl*) tía *f* buena*.

turnout ['tɜːnaʊt] N **(a)** (*attendance*) concurrencia *f*; número *m* de asistentes; (*paying spectators*) entrada *f*, público *m*; (*at election*) número *m* de votantes; **there was a poor ~** había poca gente, asistieron pocos; **we hope for a good ~ at the dance** esperamos que el baile sea muy concurrido. **(b)** (*output*) producción *f*. **(c)** (*dress*) atuendo *m*. **(d)** (*cleaning*) limpieza *f* (general).

turnover ['tɜːn,əʊvər] N **(a)** (*Comm*) volumen *m* de negocios, volumen *m* de ventas, facturación *f*; número *m* de transacciones; movimiento *m* de mercancías; rotación *f* de existencias; **there is a rapid ~ in staff** hay mucho movimiento de personal. **(b)** (*Culin*) empanada *f*.

turnpike ['tɜːnpaɪk] N (*Hist*) barrera *f* de portazgo; (*US Aut*) autopista *f* de peaje.

turn-round ['tɜːnraʊnd] N = **turnabout, turnaround**.

turn signal ['tɜːn,sɪgnl] N (*US*) indicador *m* (de dirección).

turnspit ['tɜːnspɪt] N mecanismo *m* que da vueltas al asador.

turnstile ['tɜːnstaɪl] N torniquete *m*.

turntable ['tɜːn,teɪbl] 1 N (*Rail*) placa *f* giratoria; (*of gramophone*) plato *m* giratorio, giradiscos *m*. 2 ATTR: ~ **ladder** escalera *f* de bomberos.

turn-up ['tɜːnʌp] N **(a)** (*Brit: of trousers*) vuelta *f*. **(b)** **that was a ~ for him** en eso tuvo mucha suerte; **what a ~ for the book!** ¡qué sorpresa más agradable!

turpentine ['tɜːpəntaɪn] N aguarrás *m*, trementina *f*.

turpitude ['tɜːpɪtjuːd] N (*liter*) infamia *f*, vileza *f*; **to be dismissed for gross moral ~** ser despedido por inmoralidad manifiesta, ser expulsado por conducta infame.

turps* [tɜːps] N ABBR *of* **turpentine**.

turquoise ['tɜːkwɔɪz] N turquesa *f*.

turret ['tʌrɪt] N (*Archit*) torreón *m*; (*Mil, Hist*) torre *f*, torrecilla *f*; (*of tank, warship, aircraft*) torreta *f*; (*US Tech*) cabrestante *m*.

turtle ['tɜːtl] N tortuga *f* marina; **to turn ~** volverse patas arriba, (*Naut*) zozobrar, (*Aut etc*) volcarse, dar una vuelta de campana.

turtledove ['tɜːtldʌv] N tórtola *f*.

turtleneck ['tɜːtlnek] N (*US: also ~* **sweater**) (jersey *m* de) cuello *m* de cisne.

Tuscan ['tʌskən] 1 ADJ toscano. 2 N **(a)** toscano *m*, -a *f*. **(b)** (*Ling*) toscano *m*.

Tuscany ['tʌskənɪ] N la Toscana.

tush [tʌʃ] EXCL: ~! ¡bah!

tusk [tʌsk] N colmillo *m*.

tussle ['tʌsl] 1 N (*struggle*) lucha *f* (*for* por); (*scuffle*) pelea *f*, agarrada *f*. 2 VI luchar (*with* con); pelearse, reñir (*about, over* por causa de); **they ~d with the police** se pelearon con la policía.

tussock ['tʌsək] N montecillo *m* de hierba.

tut [tʌt] (*also* **tut-tut**) 1 INTERJ ¡vamos!, ¡eso no!; ¡pche!; ¡qué horror! 2 VI hacer un gesto de desaprobación.

tutelage ['tjuːtɪlɪdʒ] N tutela *f*; **under the ~ of** bajo la tutela de.

tutelary ['tjuːtɪlərɪ] ADJ tutelar.

tutor ['tjuːtər] 1 N (*Hist*) ayo *m*; (*private teacher*) preceptor *m*, -ora *f*; profesor *m*, -ora *f* particular; (*Brit Univ, approx*) profesor *m*, -ora *f* que tiene a su cargo un pequeño grupo de estudiantes; (*teaching assistant*) profesor *m*, -ora *f* auxiliar; (*moral ~*) profesor *m* consejero, profesora *f* consejera; (*eg for OU, UNED*) tutor *m*, -ora *f*; (*Jur*) tutor *m*. 2 ATTR: ~ **group** (*Brit*) grupo *m* de tutoría. 3 VT enseñar, instruir; dar clase particular a; **to ~ a boy in French** dar a un muchacho clases particulares de francés.

tutorial [tjuːˈtɔːrɪəl] 1 ADJ preceptoral; tutorial; (*Jur*) tutelar. 2 N (*Univ*) clase *f* particular, clase *f* que consiste en un grupo pequeño de estudiantes; (*eg for OU, UNED*) tutoría *f*.

tutoring ['tjuːtərɪŋ] N clases *f* particulares (*in* de); (*remedial*) clases *fpl* de recuperación (*in* de).

tutti-frutti [,tʊtɪˈfrʊtɪ] N tutti-frutti *m*.

tutu ['tuːtuː] N tutú *m*.

tuwhit-tuwhoo [tʊˈwɪttəˈwuː] N ulular *m*.

tuxedo [tʌkˈsiːdəʊ] N (*US*) smoking *m*, esmoquin *m*.

TV N ABBR *of* **television** televisión *f*, TV.

TVA N (*US*) ABBR *of* **Tennessee Valley Authority**.

TVA - TENNESSEE VALLEY AUTHORITY

La Tennessee Valley Authority o TVA es un organismo independiente propiedad del gobierno estadounidense que distribuye electricidad a bajo precio a los hogares de siete estados del sur. Para los estadounidenses la TVA representa el mayor experimento con el socialismo que se ha hecho en el país. Este polémico organismo, libre de cargas fiscales y sin ánimo de lucro, fue creado por el presidente Roosevelt en 1933 después de la Gran Depresión, a pesar de la oposición de numerosas compañías de electricidad privadas. La TVA proporciona electricidad a 32 presas importantes, centrales hidroeléctricas, nucleares y de vapor y participa además en programas de conservación y sanidad.

TV dinner [,tiːviːˈdɪnər] N cena *f* precocinada.

TVEI N (*Brit*) ABBR *of* **technical and vocational educational initiative**.

TVP N ABBR *of* **texturized vegetable protein**.

twaddle ['twɒdl] N tonterías *fpl*, bobadas *fpl*.

twain [tweɪn] (††) N: **the ~** los dos; **to split sth in ~** partir algo en dos; **and ne'er the ~ shall meet** sin que el uno se acerque al otro jamás.

twang [twæŋ] 1 N (*Mus etc*) tañido *m*, punteado *m*; (*of bow etc*) ruido *m*, sonido *m* (de cuerda que se estira y se suelta); (*nasal ~*) gangueo *m*, timbre *m* nasal; **with an American ~** con voz gangosa americana. 2 VT (*Mus*) puntear; *bowstring* estirar y soltar repentinamente. 3 VI producir un sonido agudo; (*in speaking*) hablar con timbre nasal.

twangy ['twæŋɪ] ADJ *string etc* elástico, muy estirado; *accent* nasal, gangoso.

'twas [twɒz] (††) = **it was**.

twat** [twæt] N **(a)** (*Anat*) coño** *m*. **(b)** (*person*) gilipollas* *mf*.

tweak [twiːk] 1 N pellizco *m*; **to give sb a ~** dar un pellizco a uno. 2 VT pellizcar (retorciendo); **to ~ sth off** quitar algo pellizcándolo.

twee* [twiː] ADJ (*Brit*) *person* afectado, repipi*; *style etc* amanerado; dulzón, sensiblero.

tweed [twiːd] N tweed *m*, mezcla *f* de lana; **~s** (*suit*) traje *m* de tweed.

tweedy ['twiːdɪ] ADJ con traje de tweed, vestido de tweed; (*fig*) aristocrático (y rural).

'tween [twiːn] PREP (*liter*) = **between**.

tweet [twiːt] 1 N pío pío *m*. 2 VI piar.

tweeter ['twiːtər] N altavoz *m* para altas audiofrecuencias.

tweezers ['twiːzəz] NPL bruselas *fpl*, pinzas *fpl*; **a pair of ~** unas bruselas, unas pinzas.

twelfth [twelfθ] 1 ADJ duodécimo; **T~ Night** Noche *f* de Reyes, Epifanía *f*. 2 N duodécimo *m*; doceavo *m*, duodécima parte *f*.

twelve [twelv] 1 ADJ doce; **a ~ inch** (*Mus*) un maxisingle. 2 N doce *m*.

twelvemonth†† ['twelvmʌnθ] N año *m*; **this day ~** de hoy en un año; **we've not seen him for a ~** hace un año que no le vemos.

twelve-tone ['twelvtəʊn] ADJ dodecafónico.

twentieth ['twentɪɪθ] 1 ADJ vigésimo. 2 N vigésimo *m*, vigésima parte *f*.

twenty ['twentɪ] 1 ADJ veinte; **~-two metre line** (*Rugby*) línea *f* de veintidós metros; **~-~ vision** visión *f* normal. 2 N veinte *m*; **the twenties** (*eg 1920s*) los años veinte; **to be in one's twenties** tener más de veinte años.

twenty-first ['twentɪfɜːst] N (*birthday*) cumpleaños *m* veintiuno; (*party*) fiesta *f* del cumpleaños veintiuno.

twentyfold ['twentɪfəʊld] 1 ADV veinte veces. 2 ADJ veinte veces mayor.

twenty-four ['twentɪˈfɔːr] ATTR: **'~ hour service'** '24 horas de servicio', 'abierto 24 horas'.

twentyish ['twentɪɪʃ] ADJ de unos veinte años.

twerp* [twɜːp] N berzotas* *mf*; **you ~!** ¡imbécil!

twice [twaɪs] ADV dos veces; **~ as much** dos veces más; **A is ~ as big as B** A es dos veces más grande que B; **I am ~ as old as you are** tengo dos veces la edad de Vd, tengo el doble de la edad de Vd; **~ the sum, ~ the quantity** el doble; **at a speed ~ that of sound** a una velocidad dos veces superior a la del sonido; **he said 'she's ~ the woman you are'** dijo 'como mujer ella vale dos veces lo que tú'; **since the operation he is ~ the man he was** después de la operación vale dos veces lo de antes; **to do sth ~ over** hacer algo dos veces, volver a hacer algo; **to go to a meeting ~ weekly** ir a una reunión dos veces por semana; **he didn't have to be asked ~** no se hizo de rogar.

twiddle ['twɪdl] 1 N vuelta *f* (ligera); **to give a knob a ~** girar un botón. 2 VT girar, hacer girar; jugar con; revolver ociosamente. 3 VI: **to ~ round** dar vueltas, girar; **to ~ with sth** jugar con algo (entre los dedos).

twig¹ [twɪg] N ramita *f*; **~s** (*for fire*) leña *f* menuda.

twig²* [twɪg] (*Brit*) 1 VT comprender, caer en la cuenta de. 2 VI comprender, caer en la cuenta.

twilight ['twaɪlaɪt] 1 N crepúsculo *m*; (*fig*) crepúsculo *m*, ocaso *m*; **at ~** al anochecer; **in the ~** en el crepúsculo; **in the ~ of his room** en la media luz de su habitación. 2 ADJ crepuscular; **~ area, ~ zone** zona *f* gris; **~ sleep** sueño *m* crepuscular; **a ~ world** un mundo crepuscular.

twilit ['twaɪlɪt] ADJ: **in the ~ woods** en el bosque con luz crepuscular; **in some ~ area of the mind** en alguna zona crepuscular de la mente.

twill [twɪl] N tela *f* cruzada.

'**twill** [twɪl] = **it will.**

twin [twɪn] [1] ADJ gemelo; **~ beds** camas *fpl* gemelas; **~ brother** hermano *m* gemelo; **~ sister** hermana *f* gemela; **~ town** (*Brit*) ciudad *f* gemela.

[2] N gemelo *m*, -a *f*; **John and his ~** Juan y su hermano gemelo.

[3] VT: **the town with which Wigan is ~ned** la ciudad que tiene a Wigan como gemela.

twin-bedded ['twɪn'bedɪd] ADJ *room* con camas gemelas.

twin-carburettor ['twɪnkɑːbjʊ'retəʳ] [1] N carburador *m* de doble cuerpo.

[2] ADJ *engine* por carburador de doble cuerpo.

twin-cylinder ['twɪn'sɪlɪndəʳ] [1] ADJ de dos cilindros, bicilíndrico.

[2] N bicilindro *m*.

twine [twaɪn] [1] N guita *f*, hilo *m*, bramante *m*.

[2] VT (*weave*) tejer; (*encircle*) ceñir, rodear; (*roll up*) enrollar; **she ~d the string round her finger** enrolló la cuerda sobre el dedo; **she ~d her arms about his neck** le rodeó el cuello con los brazos.

[3] VI (*of spiral movement*) enroscarse; (*plant*) trepar, entrelazarse; (*road*) serpentear.

twin-engined ['twɪn'endʒɪnd] ADJ bimotor.

twinge [twɪndʒ] N punzada *f*, dolor *m* agudo; (*fig*) remordimiento *m*; **I've been having ~s of conscience** me ha estado remordiendo la conciencia.

twining ['twaɪnɪŋ] ADJ *plant* sarmentoso, trepador.

twin-jet ['twɪn'dʒet] [1] ADJ birreactor.

[2] N birreactor *m*.

twinkle ['twɪŋkl] [1] N centelleo *m*, parpadeo *m*; **in a ~** en un instante; '**No**', **he said with a ~** 'No', dijo maliciosamente, 'No' dijo medio riendo; **he had a ~ in his eye** se le reían los ojos; **when you were only a ~ in your father's eye** cuando tú no eras más que una vida en potencia.

[2] VI (*of light*) centellear, parpadear, titilar; (*of eyes*) brillar; (*of feet*) moverse rápidamente.

twinkling ['twɪŋklɪŋ] [1] ADJ *light* centelleante, titilante; *eye* brillante, risueño; *feet* rápido, ligero.

[2] N centelleo *m*, parpadeo *m*; **in the ~ of an eye** en un abrir y cerrar de ojos.

twinning ['twɪnɪŋ] N (*Brit*) hermanación *f* de dos ciudades.

twinset ['twɪnset] N (*Brit*) conjunto *m*.

twin-tub ['twɪn'tʌb] N lavadora *f* de dos tambores.

twirl [twɜːl] [1] N vuelta *f* (rápida), giro *m*; (*of pen etc*) rasgo *m*; (*of body*) pirueta *f*.

[2] VT girar rápidamente, dar vueltas rápidas a; voltear; (*twist*) torcer.

[3] VI girar rápidamente, dar vueltas rápidas; piruetear.

twirp* [twɜːp] N = **twerp.**

twist [twɪst] [1] N (a) (*of yarn*) torzal *m*; (*of hair*) mecha *f*; trenza *f*; (*of tobacco*) rollo *m*; (*of paper*) cucurucho *m*; (*coil*) vuelta *f*; (*spiral shape*) enroscadura *f*; (*in road etc*) vuelta *f*, recodo *m*; **~s and turns** vueltas *fpl*; **to take a ~ round a post with a rope** atar una cuerda alrededor de un poste; **the plot has an unexpected ~** la trama tiene un lance inesperado, la trama tiene un giro imprevisto; **he gave a new ~ to the old story** introdujo un nuevo giro en la vieja historia; **to be round the ~*** estar chiflado*.

(b) (*twisting action*) torsión *f*, torcimiento *m*; (*Med*) torcedura *f*; (*on ball*) efecto *m*; **to give one's ankle a ~** torcerse el tobillo; **to give a knob a ~** girar un botón; **with a quick ~ of the hand** torciendo rápidamente la mano.

(c) (*of mind*) rasgo *m* peculiar, sesgo *m*, peculiaridad *f*.

(d) (*Mus*) twist *m*.

(e) (*) estafa *f*, trampa *f*; **it's a ~!** ¡aquí hay trampa!; ¡me han robado!

[2] VT (a) (*wrench out of shape*) torcer, retorcer; *ball* dar efecto a, lanzar con efecto; (*turn*) dar vueltas a, girar; (*give spiral form to*) enroscar, formar en espiral; (*interweave*) trenzar, entrelazar; (*fig*) *sense, argument* forzar, retorcer, torcer; **to ~ sb's arm** torcer el brazo a uno (*and V* **arm¹** (a)); **to ~ one's arm** torcerse el brazo; **to ~ sth out of shape** deformar algo torciéndolo.

(b) (*) estafar, robar; **I've been ~ed!** ¡me han robado!

[3] VI (a) torcerse, retorcerse; (*coil up*) enroscarse, ensortijarse; (*of road etc*) serpentear, dar vueltas; (*writhe*) retorcerse, revolcarse.

(b) (*dance*) bailar el twist.

◆**twist off** VT: **to ~ a piece off** separar un trozo torciéndolo; **you ~ the top off like this** se quita la tapa dándole vueltas así.

◆**twist round** VT dar vueltas a, girar.

◆**twist up** VT: **to ~ paper up into a ball** retorcer un papel en forma de pelota.

twisted ['twɪstɪd] ADJ *idea, person* estrafalario, raro; pervertido.

twister ['twɪstəʳ] N (a) (*Brit*) tramposo *m*, estafador *m*. (b) (*US*)

huracán *m*.

twisting ['twɪstɪŋ] N retorcimiento *m*.

twisty ['twɪstɪ] ADJ *road, path* sinuoso, ondulante; *river, stream* ondulante, con meandros.

twit¹* [twɪt] N (*Brit*) imbécil *mf*, tonto *m*, -a *f*.

twit² [twɪt] VT embromar, tomar el pelo a, guasearse con; **to ~ sb about sth** tomar el pelo a uno con motivo de algo.

twitch [twɪtʃ] [1] N sacudida *f* repentina, tirón *m*; (*nervous*) tic *m*, contracción *f* nerviosa; movimiento *m* espasmódico.

[2] VT tirar bruscamente de, tirar ligeramente de; *hands* crispar, retorcer; *ears, nose etc* mover nerviosamente; **to ~ sth away from sb** quitar algo a uno con un movimiento rápido.

[3] VI crisparse; moverse nerviosamente.

twitcher* ['twɪtʃəʳ] N (*Brit*) observador *m*, -ora *f* de aves.

twitchy ['twɪtʃɪ] ADJ nervioso; **to get ~** ponerse nervioso, inquietarse.

twitter ['twɪtəʳ] [1] N (*bird*) gorjeo *m*; (*) agitación *f*, inquietud *f*, nerviosismo *m*; **to be all of a ~, to be in a ~** estar nerviosísimo, estar muy agitado.

[2] VI gorjear; (*) agitarse, estar inquieto, estar nervioso.

'**twixt** [twɪkst] PREP (*liter*) = **betwixt**; *V* **between.**

two [tuː] [1] ADJ dos.

[2] N dos *m*; **~ by ~, in ~s** de dos en dos; **to break sth in ~** romper algo en dos, partir algo por la mitad; **they're ~ of a kind** son tal para cual; **to put ~ and ~ together** atar cabos.

two-bit* ['tuːbɪt] ADJ (*US*) de poca monta, de tres al cuarto.

two-chamber ['tuː'tʃeɪmbəʳ] ADJ *parliament* bicamaral, de dos cámaras.

two-colour ['tuː'kʌləʳ] ADJ bicolor, de dos colores.

two-cycle ['tuː'saɪkl] ADJ *engine* de dos tiempos.

two-cylinder ['tuː'sɪlɪndəʳ] ADJ bicilíndrico, de dos cilindros.

two-decker ['tuː'dekəʳ] N autobús *m* de dos pisos.

two-dimensional ['tuːdaɪ'menʃənl] ADJ bidimensional.

two-door ['tuː'dɔːʳ] ADJ *car* de dos puertas.

two-edged ['tuː'edʒd] ADJ de doble filo.

two-engined ['tuː'endʒɪnd] ADJ bimotor.

two-faced ['tuː'feɪst] ADJ (*fig*) doble, falso.

two-fisted* [,tuː'fɪstɪd] ADJ (*US*) fortachón*, chicarrón*.

twofold ['tuːfəʊld] [1] ADV dos veces.

[2] ADJ doble.

two-handed ['tuː'hændɪd] ADJ de dos manos; *tool etc* para dos manos.

two-legged ['tuː'legɪd] ADJ de dos piernas, bípedo.

two-masted ['tuː'mɑːstɪd] ADJ de dos palos.

two-party ['tuː'pɑːtɪ] ADJ *state etc* de dos partidos.

twopence ['tʌpəns] NPL (*Brit*) 2 peniques *mpl*; *V* **care.**

twopenny ['tʌpənɪ] ADJ (*Brit*) de 2 peniques, que vale 2 peniques; (*fig*) insignificante, miserable, despreciable.

twopenny-halfpenny ['tʌpnɪ'heɪpnɪ] ADJ (*Brit fig*) insignificante, despreciable.

two-phase ['tuː'feɪz] ADJ bifásico.

two-piece ['tuː'piːs] [1] ADJ de dos piezas.

[2] N dos piezas *m*, conjunto *m*.

two-ply ['tuː'plaɪ] ADJ *wood* de dos capas; *wool* doble.

two-seater ['tuː'siːtəʳ] [1] ATTR biplaza, de dos plazas.

[2] N coche *m* (or avión *m* etc) biplaza.

twosome ['tuːsəm] N pareja *f*; grupo *m* de dos, partido *m* de dos.

two-star (petrol) ['tuːstɑː'(petrəl)] N (*Brit*) gasolina *f* normal.

two-step ['tuː'step] N paso *m* doble.

two-storey ['tuː'stɔːrɪ] ADJ *house* de dos pisos.

two-stroke ['tuː'strəʊk] [1] ADJ *engine* de dos tiempos.

[2] N (*also*: ~ **oil**) aceite *m* para motores de dos tiempos.

two-time* ['tuː'taɪm] VT (*US*) (*gen*) hacer una mala jugada a, traicionar; *lover* poner los cuernos a, engañar.

two-timer [,tuː'taɪməʳ] N (*US*) (a) (*gen: traitor*) traidor *m*, -ora *f*, traicionero *m*. (b) (*in marriage*) marido *m* (or mujer *f*) infiel.

two-tone ['tuː'təʊn] ADJ *car* bicolor, de dos colores.

'**twould** [twʊd] = **it would.**

two-way ['tuː'weɪ] ADJ: **~ radio** transmisor-receptor *m*; **~ street** calle *f* de doble sentido; **~ switch** conmutador *m* de dos direcciones; **~ traffic** circulación *f* en ambas direcciones.

two-wheeler ['tuː'wiːləʳ] N bicicleta *f*.

TX (*US Post*) ABBR of **Texas.**

Tx ABBR of **telex.**

tycoon [taɪ'kuːn] N magnate *m*.

tyke [taɪk] N (a) (*) (*dog*) perro *m* de la calle; (*child*) chiquillo *m*; **you little ~!** ¡tunante! (b) (*pej*: *also* **Yorkshire ~**) hombre *m* de Yorkshire.

tympani ['tɪmpənɪ] NPL (*Mus*) = **timpani.**

tympanum ['tɪmpənəm] N (*Anat, Archit*) tímpano *m*.

type [taɪp] [1] N (a) (*characteristic specimen*) tipo *m*; **to deviate from the ~** apartarse del tipo; **to revert to ~** saltar atrás en la cadena natural; **she was the very ~ of Spanish beauty** era el tipo exacto de la belleza española.

(b) (*: person*) tipo* *m*, sujeto* *m*; **he's an odd ~** es un tipo raro.

(c) (*class*) tipo *m*, género *m*; **people of that ~** la gente de ese tipo; **he's not my ~** ese tipo de hombre no me gusta, no me gustan los hombres así; **what ~ of car is it?** ¿qué modelo de coche es?
(d) (*Typ*) tipo *m* (de letra), letra *f*, carácter *m*; (*collectively*) tipos *mpl*.
2 VT (*also* **to ~ out, to ~ up**) escribir a máquina, hacer a máquina, mecanografiar.
3 VI escribir a máquina; '**secretary ... must be able to ~'** 'secretaria ... sabiendo mecanografía'.
typecast ['taɪpkɑːst] (*irr: V* **cast**) **1** VT *actor* encasillar.
2 ADJ *actor* encasillado.
typeface ['taɪpfeɪs] N = **type 1 (d)**; área *f* de texto impreso, (*loosely*) tipografía *f*.
typescript ['taɪpskrɪpt] **1** ADJ mecanografiado.
2 N mecanografiado *m*.
typeset ['taɪpset] VT componer.
typesetter ['taɪp,setəʳ] N (*person*) cajista *m*; (*machine*) máquina *f* de componer.
typesetting ['taɪp,setɪŋ] N composición *f* (tipográfica).
typewrite ['taɪpraɪt] (*irr: V* **write**) VT = **type 2**.
typewriter ['taɪp,raɪtəʳ] **1** N máquina *f* de escribir.
2 ATTR: **~ ribbon** cinta *f* para máquina de escribir.
typewriting ['taɪp,raɪtɪŋ] N mecanografía *f*.
typewritten ['taɪp,rɪtn] ADJ mecanografiado, escrito a máquina.
typhoid ['taɪfɔɪd] N tifoidea *f*, fiebre *f* tifoidea.
typhoon [taɪ'fuːn] N tifón *m*.
typhus ['taɪfəs] N tifus *m*.
typical ['tɪpɪkəl] ADJ típico; característico; clásico; **the ~ Spaniard** el español típico; **wearing the ~ beret** con la clásica boina; **it is ~ of him that ...** es característico de él que ...; **isn't that just ~!** ¡eso es muy de él!
typically ['tɪpɪkəlɪ] ADV típicamente; **all that is ~ Spanish** todo lo que es típico de España; **a ~ smug person** una persona típicamente satisfecha.
typify ['tɪpɪfaɪ] VT tipificar; simbolizar; representar, ser ejemplo de.

typing ['taɪpɪŋ] **1** N mecanografía *f*.
2 ATTR: **~ agency** agencia *f* mecanográfica; **~ error** error *m* mecanográfico; **~ paper** papel *m* para máquina de escribir; **~ pool** sala *f* de mecanógrafas; servicio *m* de mecanógrafas; **~ speed** palabras *fpl* por minuto (mecanografiadas).
typist ['taɪpɪst] N mecanógrafo *m*, -a *f*.
typo* ['taɪpəʊ] N errata *f*.
typographer [taɪ'pɒgrəfəʳ] N tipógrafo *m*, -a *f*.
typographic(al) [,taɪpə'græfɪk(əl)] ADJ tipográfico.
typography [taɪ'pɒgrəfɪ] N tipografía *f*.
typology [taɪ'pɒlədʒɪ] N tipología *f*.
tyrannic(al) [tɪ'rænɪk(əl)] ADJ tiránico.
tyrannically [tɪ'rænɪkəlɪ] ADV tiránicamente.
tyrannicide [tɪ'rænɪsaɪd] N (*act*) tiranicidio *m*; (*person*) tiranicida *mf*.
tyrannize ['tɪrənaɪz] **1** VT tiranizar.
2 VI: **to ~ over a people** tiranizar un pueblo.
tyranny ['tɪrənɪ] N tiranía *f*.
tyrant ['taɪrənt] N tirano *m*, -a *f*.
Tyre ['taɪəʳ] N Tiro *m*.
tyre ['taɪəʳ] **1** N (*Aut etc*) neumático *m*, llanta *f* (*LAm*); (*outer cover*) cubierta *f*; (*inner tube*) cámara *f* (de aire); (*of cart*) llanta *f*, calce *m*; (*of pram etc*) rueda *f* de goma.
2 ATTR: **~ pressure** presión *f* de los neumáticos.
tyre-burst ['taɪəbɜːst] N pinchazo *m*, reventón *m*.
tyre valve ['taɪəvælv] N válvula *f* de neumático.
tyro ['taɪərəʊ] N = **tiro**.
Tyrol [tɪ'rəʊl] N el Tirol.
Tyrolean [,tɪrə'lɪ(ː)ən], **Tyrolese** [,tɪrə'liːz] **1** ADJ tirolés.
2 N tirolés *m*, -esa *f*.
Tyrrhenian [tɪ'riːnɪən] ADJ: **the ~ Sea** el mar Tirreno.
tzar [zɑːʳ] N zar *m*.
tzarina [zɑːˈriːnə] N zarina *f*.
tzarist ['zɑːrɪst] N = **tsarist**.

U

U¹, u [ju:] N (*letter*) U, u *f*; **U for Uncle** U de Uruguay; **U-bend** (*Brit*) codo *m*, curva *f* en U; **U-boat** submarino *m* (alemán); **U-shaped** en forma de U; **U-turn** viraje *m* en U, giro *m* de 180 grados (*also fig*).

U² ADJ (**a**) (*Brit*) ABBR of **upper-class**. (**b**) (*Cine*) ABBR of **universal** todos los públicos.

UAE NPL ABBR of **United Arab Emirates** Emiratos *mpl* Árabes Unidos, EAU *mpl*.

UB40 [,ju:bi:'fɔ:tɪ] N (*Brit*) ABBR of **Unemployment Benefit 40** tarjeta *f* de desempleo, carné *m* del paro; **~s*** (*unemployed people*) los parados.

ubiquitous [ju:'bɪkwɪtəs] ADJ ubicuo, omnipresente, que se encuentra en todas partes; **it is ~ in Spain** se encuentra en toda España; **the secretary has to be ~** el secretario tiene que estar constantemente en todas partes.

ubiquity [ju:'bɪkwɪtɪ] N ubicuidad *f*, omnipresencia *f*.

UCAS N (*Brit*) ABBR of **Universities and Colleges Admissions Service**.

UCCA ['ʌkə] N (*Brit: formerly*) ABBR of **Universities Central Council on Admissions**.

UDA N (*Brit*) ABBR of **Ulster Defence Association** *organización paramilitar protestante en Irlanda del Norte*.

UDC N (*Brit*) ABBR of **Urban District Council**.

udder ['ʌdər] N ubre *f*.

UDF N (*Brit*) ABBR of **Ulster Defence Force** *organización paramilitar protestante en Irlanda del Norte*.

UDI N (*Brit*) ABBR of **unilateral declaration of independence**.

UDP N (*Brit*) ABBR of **Ulster Democratic Party**.

UDR N (*Brit*) ABBR of **Ulster Defence Regiment** *fuerza de seguridad de Irlanda del Norte*.

UEFA [ju'eɪfə] NPL ABBR of **Union of European Football Associations**.

UFC N (*Brit*) ABBR of **Universities' Funding Council** *entidad que controla las finanzas de las universidades*.

UFF N (*Brit*) ABBR of **Ulster Freedom Fighters** *organización paramilitar protestante en Irlanda del Norte*.

UFO N ABBR of **unidentified flying object** objeto *m* volante (*or* volador) no identificado, OVNI *m*.

ufologist [,ju:'fɒlədʒɪst] N ufólogo *m*, -a *f*.

ufology [,ju:'fɒlədʒɪ] N ufología *f*.

Uganda [ju:'gændə] N Uganda *f*.

Ugandan [ju:'gændən] 1 ADJ ugandés.
2 N ugandés *m*, -esa *f*.

ugh [ɜ:h] INTERJ ¡puf!

ugli fruit ['ʌglɪ'fruːt] N *fruto parecido a un pomelo, híbrido de tres cítricos*.

uglify ['ʌglɪfaɪ] VT afear.

ugliness ['ʌglɪnɪs] N fealdad *f*, lo feo; lo peligroso; lo repugnante.

ugly ['ʌglɪ] ADJ *appearance, person* feo; *custom, vice etc* feo, repugnante, asqueroso; *situation, wound* peligroso; *rumour etc* nada grato, inquietante; *mood* peligroso, violento; **~ duckling** patito *m* feo (*also fig*); **to be as ~ as sin** ser más feo que Picio; **to turn ~*** ponerse violento, amenazar violencia.

UHF N ABBR of **ultra high frequency** frecuencia *f* ultraelevada, UHF *f*.

uh-huh ['ʌ,hʌ] EXCL (*agreeing*) a-ha.

UHT ADJ ABBR of **ultra heat-treated** uperizado.

UK N ABBR of **United Kingdom** Reino *m* Unido, R.U. *m*.

Ukraine [ju:'kreɪn] N Ucrania *f*.

Ukrainian [ju:'kreɪnɪən] 1 ADJ ucranio.
2 N ucranio *m*, -a *f*.

ukulele [,ju:kə'leɪlɪ] N ukulele *m*.

ulcer ['ʌlsər] N úlcera *f*; (*fig*) llaga *f*.

ulcerate ['ʌlsəreɪt] 1 VT ulcerar.
2 VI ulcerarse.

ulceration [,ʌlsə'reɪʃən] N ulceración *f*.

ulcerous ['ʌlsərəs] ADJ ulceroso.

ullage ['ʌlɪdʒ] N (*loss*) merma *f*; (*amount remaining*) atestadura *f*.

ulna ['ʌlnə] N, PL **ulnae** ['ʌlniː] cúbito *m*.

ULSI N ABBR of **ultra-large-scale integration** integración *f* a ultra gran escala.

Ulster ['ʌlstər] N Ulster *m*.

Ulsterman ['ʌlstəmən] N, PL **Ulstermen** ['ʌlstəmən] nativo *m* (*or* habitante *m*) de Ulster.

ult. [ʌlt] ADV (*Comm*) ABBR of **ultimo; the 5th ~** el 5 del mes pasado.

ulterior [ʌl'tɪərɪər] ADJ ulterior; **~ motive** motivo *m* oculto, segunda intención *f*.

ultimate ['ʌltɪmɪt] ADJ (*furthest*) más remoto, extremo; (*final*) último, final; *destination etc* definitivo; *purpose, reason, truth etc* fundamental, esencial; **it's the ~ in hair-styling** es el último grito del peinado.

ultimately ['ʌltɪmɪtlɪ] ADV (*in the end*) por último, al final; (*in the long run*) a la larga; (*fundamentally*) en el fondo, fundamentalmente.

ultimatum [,ʌltɪ'meɪtəm] N, PL **ultimata** [,ʌltɪ'meɪtə] *or* **ultimatums** ultimátum *m*.

ultimo ['ʌltɪməʊ] ADV = **ult**.

ultra... ['ʌltrə] PREF ultra...

ultra-fashionable ['ʌltrə'fæʃnəbl] ADJ muy de moda, elegantísimo.

ultrafine [,ʌltrə'faɪn] ADJ ultrafino.

ultralight ['ʌltrə'laɪt] 1 ADJ ultraligero.
2 N (*Aviat*) ultraligero *m*.

ultramarine [,ʌltrəmə'riːn] 1 ADJ ultramarino.
2 N azul *m* ultramarino, azul *m* de ultramar.

ultramodern ['ʌltrə'mɒdən] ADJ ultramoderno.

ultra-red [,ʌltrə'red] ADJ ultrarrojo, infrarrojo.

ultrasensitive ['ʌltrə'sensɪtɪv] ADJ ultrasensitivo.

ultra-short wave ['ʌltrə,ʃɔːt'weɪv] 1 N onda *f* ultracorta.
2 ATTR de onda ultracorta.

ultrasonic ['ʌltrə'sɒnɪk] ADJ ultrasónico.

ultrasound ['ʌltrəsaʊnd] N ultrasonido *m*.

ultraviolet ['ʌltrə'vaɪəlɪt] ADJ ultravioleta; **~ light** luz *f* ultravioleta; **~ radiation** radiación *f* ultravioleta; **~ rays** rayos *mpl* ultravioleta; **~ treatment** tratamiento *m* de onda ultravioleta.

ululate ['juːljʊleɪt] VI ulular.

ululation [juːljʊ'leɪʃən] N ululato *m*.

Ulysses [ju:'lɪsiːz] NM Ulises.

um [ʌm] INTERJ pues, es decir, esto ...; **to ~ and err** vacilar.

umber ['ʌmbər] 1 N tierra *f* de sombra.
2 ADJ color ocre oscuro, pardo oscuro.

umbilical [,ʌmbɪ'laɪkəl] ADJ umbilical; **~ cord** cordón *m* umbilical.

umbilicus [,ʌmbɪ'laɪkəs] N ombligo *m*.

umbrage ['ʌmbrɪdʒ] N resentimiento *m*; **to take ~** ofenderse (*at* por), resentirse (*at* de).

umbrella [ʌm'brelə] N paraguas *m*; (*on beach etc*) quitasol *m*; (*Mil: of fire*) cortina *f* de fuego antiaéreo; (*of aircraft*) sombrilla *f* protectora; **~ organization** organización *f* paraguas.

umbrella stand [ʌm'breləstænd] N paragüero *m*.

umlaut ['ʊmlaʊt] N (*phenomenon*) metafonía *f*; (*symbol*) diéresis *f*.

umpire ['ʌmpaɪər] 1 N árbitro *mf*.
2 VTI arbitrar.

umpteen* ['ʌmptiːn] ADJ tantísimos, muchísimos.

umpteenth* ['ʌmptiːnθ] ADJ enésimo; **for the ~ time** por enésima vez.

UMW N (*US*) ABBR of **United Mineworkers of America**.

'un* [ʌn] PRON = **one; that's a good ~** (*joke etc*) ¡qué bueno!; **he did well, for an old ~** lo hizo bien, para ser un viejo; **she's got two little ~s** tiene dos críos.

un... [ʌn] PREF in...; des...; no ...; nada ...; poco ...; sin ...; anti...

UN NPL ABBR of **United Nations** Naciones *fpl* Unidas, NN.UU.

unabashed ['ʌnə'bæʃt] ADJ descarado, desvergonzado; desenfadado; **'Yes', he said quite ~** 'Sí', dijo sin alterarse.

unabated ['ʌnə'beɪtɪd] ADJ sin disminución, no disminuido.

unabbreviated ['ʌnə'briːvɪeɪtɪd] ADJ íntegro, completo.

▼ **unable** [ʌnˈeɪbl] ADJ: **to be ~ to do sth** no poder hacer algo, estar sin poder hacer algo; ser incapaz de hacer algo; verse imposibilitado de hacer algo; **I am ~ to see why** no veo por qué, no comprendo cómo; **those ~ to go** los que no pueden ir.
unabridged [ʌnəˈbrɪdʒd] ADJ íntegro, integral.
unaccented [ʌnækˈsentɪd] ADJ inacentuado, átono.
▼ **unacceptable** [ʌnəkˈseptəbl] ADJ inaceptable.
unacceptably [ʌnəkˈseptəblɪ] ADV inaceptablemente.
unaccommodating [ʌnəˈkɒmədeɪtɪŋ] ADJ poco amable, poco servicial, poco acomodaticio.
unaccompanied [ʌnəˈkʌmpənɪd] ADJ (Mus) sin acompañamiento, no acompañado; **to go somewhere ~** ir a un sitio sin compañía, ir solo a un sitio.
unaccomplished [ʌnəˈkʌmplɪʃt] ADJ (a) task incompleto, sin acabar. (b) person sin talento.
unaccountable [ʌnəˈkaʊntəbl] ADJ inexplicable.
unaccountably [ʌnəˈkaʊntəblɪ] ADV inexplicablemente; **~ annoyed** extrañamente enfadado, enfadado sin motivo.
unaccounted [ʌnəˈkaʊntɪd] ADJ: **two passengers are ~ for** no hay noticias de dos de los pasajeros, se ignora la suerte de dos de los pasajeros; **two books are ~ for** faltan dos libros.
unaccustomed [ʌnəˈkʌstəmd] ADJ (a) **to be ~ to sth** no estar acostumbrado a algo; **to be ~ to doing sth** no acostumbrar hacer algo, no tener la costumbre de hacer algo; **~ as I am to public speaking** aunque no tengo experiencia de hablar en público. (b) **with ~ zeal** con un entusiasmo insólito.
unacknowledged [ʌnəkˈnɒlɪdʒd] ADJ no reconocido; letter etc no contestado, sin contestar.
unacquainted [ʌnəˈkweɪntɪd] ADJ: **to be ~ with sth** desconocer algo, ignorar algo.
unadaptable [ʌnəˈdæptəbl] ADJ inadaptable.
unadapted [ʌnəˈdæptɪd] ADJ inadaptado.
unaddressed [ʌnəˈdrest] ADJ letter sin señas.
unadjusted [ʌnəˈdʒʌstɪd] ADJ no corregido; **seasonally ~ employment figures** estadísticas de desempleo con variaciones estacionales no corregidas.
unadopted [ʌnəˈdɒptɪd] ADJ (Brit) road no oficial (siendo de los vecinos la responsabilidad de su mantenimiento).
unadorned [ʌnəˈdɔːnd] ADJ sin adorno, sencillo; **beauty ~** la hermosura sin adorno; **the ~ truth** la verdad lisa y llana.
unadulterated [ʌnəˈdʌltəreɪtɪd] ADJ sin mezcla, puro.
unadventurous [ʌnədˈventʃərəs] ADJ poco atrevido.
unadvisable [ʌnədˈvaɪzəbl] ADJ poco aconsejable; **it is ~ to + infin** es poco aconsejable + infin.
unaesthetic, (US) **unesthetic** [ʌniːsˈθetɪk] ADJ antiestético.
unaffected [ʌnəˈfektɪd] ADJ (a) person etc sin afectación. (b) **to be ~ by** no ser afectado por.
unaffectedly [ʌnəˈfektɪdlɪ] ADV sin afectación; sinceramente, hondamente.
unaffiliated [ʌnəˈfɪlɪˌeɪtɪd] ADJ no afiliado.
unafraid [ʌnəˈfreɪd] ADJ sin temor, impertérrito.
unaided [ʌnˈeɪdɪd] 1 ADV sin ayuda, por sí solo.
2 ADJ: **by his own ~ efforts** por sí solo, sin ayuda de nadie.
unalike [ʌnəˈlaɪk] ADJ no parecido.
unalloyed [ʌnəˈlɔɪd] ADJ sin mezcla, puro.
unalterable [ʌnˈɒltərəbl] ADJ inalterable.
unalterably [ʌnˈɒltərəblɪ] ADV de modo inalterable; **we are ~ opposed to it** nos oponemos rotundamente a ello.
unaltered [ʌnˈɒltəd] ADJ inalterado, sin cambiar, sin alteración.
unambiguous [ʌnæmˈbɪgjʊəs] ADJ inequívoco.
unambiguously [ʌnæmˈbɪgjʊəslɪ] ADV de modo inequívoco.
unambitious [ʌnæmˈbɪʃəs] ADJ poco ambicioso, poco emprendedor.
un-American [ʌnəˈmerɪkən] ADJ antiamericano, poco americano.
unamiable [ʌnˈeɪmɪəbl] ADJ poco simpático.
unanimity [juːnəˈnɪmɪtɪ] N unanimidad f.
unanimous [juːˈnænɪməs] ADJ unánime.
unanimously [juːˈnænɪməslɪ] ADV unánimamente; por unanimidad; **the motion was passed ~** la moción fue aprobada por unanimidad.
unannounced [ʌnəˈnaʊnst] ADJ: **to arrive ~** llegar sin dar aviso.
unanswerable [ʌnˈɑːnsərəbl] ADJ question incontestable; (attack etc) irrebatible, irrefutable.
unanswered [ʌnˈɑːnsəd] ADJ question incontestado, sin contestar; letter no contestado, sin contestar.
unappealable [ʌnəˈpiːləbl] ADJ inapelable.
unappealing [ʌnəˈpiːlɪŋ] ADJ poco atractivo.
unappetizing [ʌnˈæpɪtaɪzɪŋ] ADJ poco apetitoso, poco apetecible; (fig) repugnante, nada atractivo.
unappreciative [ʌnəˈpriːʃɪətɪv] ADJ desagradecido; **to be ~ of sth** no apreciar algo.
unapproachable [ʌnəˈprəʊtʃəbl] ADJ inaccesible; person intratable, inabordable.
unappropriated [ʌnəˈprəʊprɪeɪtɪd] ADJ balance etc no asignado, sin asignar.

unarguable [ʌnˈɑːgjʊəbəl] ADJ indiscutible, incuestionable.
unarguably [ʌnˈɑːgjʊəblɪ] ADV indiscutiblemente; **it is ~ true that ...** es una verdad incuestionable que ...
unarmed [ʌnˈɑːmd] ADJ que no lleva armas, desarmado; (defenceless) inerme; **~ combat** combate m sin armas.
unashamed [ʌnəˈʃeɪmd] ADJ desvergonzado, descarado; **he was quite ~ about it** no tuvo remordimiento alguno por esto, no sintió el menor remordimiento.
unashamedly [ʌnəˈʃeɪmɪdlɪ] ADV desvergonzadamente; **to be ~ proud of sth** enorgullecerse sin remordimiento de algo.
unasked [ʌnˈɑːskt] ADJ: **to do sth ~** hacer algo motu proprio; **they came to the party ~** vinieron al guateque sin ser invitados.
unassailable [ʌnəˈseɪləbl] ADJ fortress inexpugnable; position inatacable; argument irrebatible; **he is quite ~ on that score** no se le puede atacar por ese lado.
unassisted [ʌnəˈsɪstɪd] ADJ sin ayuda, por sí solo.
unassuming [ʌnəˈsjuːmɪŋ] ADJ modesto, sin pretensiones.
unassumingly [ʌnəˈsjuːmɪŋlɪ] ADV modestamente.
unattached [ʌnəˈtætʃt] ADJ part etc suelto, separable; disponible; person libre, no prometido, soltero; (Mil) de reemplazo; (Jur) no embargado.
unattainable [ʌnəˈteɪnəbl] ADJ inasequible; record etc inalcanzable.
unattended [ʌnəˈtendɪd] ADJ descuidado; sin guardia, sin personal; **to leave sth ~** dejar algo sin vigilar.
unattractive [ʌnəˈtræktɪv] ADJ poco atractivo.
unattractiveness [ʌnəˈtræktɪvnɪs] N falta f de atractivo.
unattributable [ʌnəˈtrɪbjʊtəbl] ADJ news de fuente que no se puede revelar.
unattributed [ʌnəˈtrɪbjʊtɪd] ADJ quote, remarks de fuente desconocida, anónimo; source anónimo, no revelado.
unauthorized [ʌnˈɔːθəraɪzd] ADJ no autorizado.
unavailable [ʌnəˈveɪləbl] ADJ indisponible, inasequible; (Comm) agotado; person que no puede atender a uno, que no está libre.
unavailing [ʌnəˈveɪlɪŋ] ADJ inútil, vano, infructuoso.
unavailingly [ʌnəˈveɪlɪŋlɪ] ADV inútilmente, en vano.
unavoidable [ʌnəˈvɔɪdəbl] ADJ inevitable, ineludible; **it is ~ that ...** es inevitable que ...
unavoidably [ʌnəˈvɔɪdəblɪ] ADV inevitablemente; **he is ~ detained** tiene un retraso inevitable.
unaware [ʌnəˈweəʳ] ADJ inconsciente; **to be ~ that ...** ignorar que ...; **I am not ~ that ...** no ignoro que ...; **to be ~ of sth** ignorar algo, no darse cuenta de algo.
unawareness [ʌnəˈweənɪs] N inconsciencia f (of de).
unawares [ʌnəˈweəz] ADV de improviso, inopinadamente; **to catch sb ~** coger a uno desprevenido.
unbacked [ʌnˈbækt] ADJ sin respaldo; (Fin) al descubierto.
unbalance [ʌnˈbæləns] N desequilibrio m.
unbalanced [ʌnˈbælənst] ADJ desequilibrado; (mentally) trastornado, desequilibrado; (Fin) que no está en equilibrio.
unban [ʌnˈbæn] VT levantar la prohibición de; despenalizar.
unbandage [ʌnˈbændɪdʒ] VT desvendar, quitar las vendas a.
unbaptized [ʌnˈbæptaɪzd] ADJ sin bautizar.
unbar [ʌnˈbɑːʳ] VT door etc desatrancar; (fig) abrir, franquear.
unbearable [ʌnˈbeərəbl] ADJ inaguantable, insufrible, insoportable.
unbearably [ʌnˈbeərəblɪ] ADV insoportablemente; **it is ~ hot** hace un calor inaguantable; **she is ~ vain** es vanidosa en un grado inaguantable.
unbeatable [ʌnˈbiːtəbl] ADJ insuperable; team etc imbatible; price, offer inmejorable.
unbeaten [ʌnˈbiːtn] ADJ team imbatido; army invicto; price no mejorado.
unbecoming [ʌnbɪˈkʌmɪŋ] ADJ indecoroso, impropio; dress etc que sienta mal a uno; **it is ~ to + infin** no es elegante + infin.
unbeknownst [ʌnbɪˈnaʊnst] ADV: **~ to me** sin saberlo yo.
unbelief [ʌnbɪˈliːf] N (Rel: in general) descreimiento m, (of person) falta f de fe; escepticismo m; (astonishment) incredulidad f.
▼ **unbelievable** [ʌnbɪˈliːvəbl] ADJ increíble; **it is ~ that ...** es increíble que + subj.
unbelievably [ʌnbɪˈliːvəblɪ] ADV increíblemente.
unbeliever [ʌnbɪˈliːvəʳ] N no creyente mf, descreído m, -a f.
unbelieving [ʌnbɪˈliːvɪŋ] ADJ incrédulo.
unbelievingly [ʌnbɪˈliːvɪŋlɪ] ADV watch, stare sin dar crédito a sus etc ojos.
unbend [ʌnˈbend] (irr: V bend) 1 VT desencorvar, enderezar.
2 VI (fig) suavizarse; (person) hacerse más afable.
unbending [ʌnˈbendɪŋ] ADJ inflexible, rígido; person inflexible; poco afable.
unbias(s)ed [ʌnˈbaɪəst] ADJ imparcial.
unbidden [ʌnˈbɪdn] ADJ: **to do sth ~** hacer algo espontáneamente; **they came to the party ~** vinieron al guateque sin ser invitados.
unbind [ʌnˈbaɪnd] (irr: V bind) VT desatar; (unbandage) desvendar.

unbleached ['ʌn'bliːtʃt] ADJ sin blanquear.
unblemished [ʌn'blemɪʃt] ADJ sin tacha, intachable, sin mancha.
unblinking [ʌn'blɪŋkɪŋ] ADJ imperturbable; (pej) desvergonzado.
unblock ['ʌn'blɒk] VT pipe etc desatascar, desobstruir; road etc desbloquear, abrir, franquear.
unblushing [ʌn'blʌʃɪŋ] ADJ desvergonzado, fresco.
unblushingly [ʌn'blʌʃɪŋlɪ] ADV desvergonzadamente; he said ~ dijo tan fresco.
unbolt ['ʌn'bəʊlt] VT desatrancar.
unborn ['ʌn'bɔːn] ADJ no nacido aún, nonato; generations yet ~ generaciones fpl que están todavía por nacer (or que están por venir).
unbosom [ʌn'bʊzəm] VR: to ~ o.s. of sth desahogarse de algo, confesar algo espontáneamente; to ~ o.s. to sb abrir su pecho a uno, desahogarse con uno.
unbound ['ʌn'baʊnd] ADJ sin encuadernar, en rústica.
unbounded [ʌn'baʊndɪd] ADJ ilimitado, infinito.
unbowed ['ʌn'baʊd] ADJ: with head ~ con la cabeza erguida; orgullosamente.
unbreakable ['ʌn'breɪkəbl] ADJ irrompible, inquebrantable.
unbribable ['ʌn'braɪbəbl] ADJ insobornable.
unbridgeable [ʌn'brɪdʒəbl] ADJ gap etc abismal, infranqueable.
unbridled [ʌn'braɪdld] ADJ (fig) desenfrenado.
unbroken ['ʌn'brəʊkən] ADJ crockery etc entero, intacto; seal intacto; time, silence no interrumpido; series continuo, sin solución de continuidad; sheet of ice etc continuo; soil sin labrar; record imbatido; horse no domado; spirit indómito.
unbuckle ['ʌn'bʌkl] VT deshebillar.
unbudgeted [ʌn'bʌdʒɪtɪd] ADJ no presupuestado.
unburden ['ʌn'bɜːdn] [1] VT person aliviar; to ~ sb of a load aliviar a uno quitándole un peso; to ~ one's heart abrir su pecho.
[2] VR: to ~ o.s. abrir su pecho (to sb a uno); to ~ o.s. of sth desahogarse de algo, confesar algo abiertamente.
unburied ['ʌn'berɪd] ADJ insepulto.
unbusinesslike [ʌn'bɪznɪslaɪk] ADJ poco práctico, poco metódico; informal; que carece de instinto comercial.
unbutton ['ʌn'bʌtn] [1] VT desabotonar, desabrochar.
[2] VI (*) hacerse más afable.
uncalled-for [ʌn'kɔːldfɔːʳ] ADJ gratuito, inmerecido; fuera de lugar; impertinente.
uncannily [ʌn'kænɪlɪ] ADV misteriosamente; it is ~ like the other one tiene un extraño parecido con el otro, se parece extraordinariamente al otro.
uncanny [ʌn'kænɪ] ADJ misterioso, extraño, extraordinario; it's quite ~ es extraordinario; it's ~ how he does it no llego a comprender cómo lo hace.
uncap ['ʌn'kæp] VT destapar.
uncapped [ʌn'kæpt] ADJ (Sport) debutante; ~ player debutante mf (en la selección nacional).
uncared-for ['ʌn'kɛədfɔːʳ] ADJ descuidado; person abandonado, desamparado; appearance desaseado, de abandono; building etc abandonado.
uncaring ['ʌnkɛərɪŋ] ADJ poco compasivo; he went on all ~ siguió sin hacer caso.
uncarpeted ['ʌn'kɑːpɪtɪd] ADJ no enmoquetado.
uncashed ['ʌn'kæʃt] ADJ cheque no cobrado, sin cobrar.
uncatalogued ['ʌn'kætəlɒgd] ADJ no catalogado.
unceasing [ʌn'siːsɪŋ] ADJ incesante.
unceasingly [ʌn'siːsɪŋlɪ] ADV incesantemente, sin cesar.
uncensored ['ʌn'sensəd] ADJ no censurado.
unceremonious ['ʌn,serɪ'məʊnɪəs] ADJ descortés, brusco, poco formal.
unceremoniously ['ʌn,serɪ'məʊnɪəslɪ] ADV sin miramientos.
uncertain [ʌn'sɜːtn] ADJ incierto, dudoso; person (of character) indeciso, vacilante; temper vivo; to be ~ of no estar seguro de; I am ~ whether ... no estoy seguro si ...
uncertainly [ʌn'sɜːtnlɪ] ADV inciertamente; he said ~ dijo indeciso.
uncertainty [ʌn'sɜːtntɪ] N incertidumbre f, duda f; indecisión f, irresolución f; in view of this ~ ... teniendo en cuenta estas dudas ...; in order to remove any ~ para disipar cualquier duda.
uncertificated ['ʌnsə'tɪfɪkeɪtɪd] ADJ teacher etc sin título.
unchain ['ʌn'tʃeɪn] VT desencadenar.
unchallengeable ['ʌn'tʃælɪndʒəbl] ADJ incontestable, incuestionable.
unchallenged ['ʌn'tʃælɪndʒd] ADJ incontestado; we cannot let that go ~ eso no lo podemos dejar pasar sin protesta.
unchangeable [ʌn'tʃeɪndʒəbl] ADJ inalterable, inmutable.
unchanged ['ʌn'tʃeɪndʒd] ADJ sin alterar; everything is still ~ todo sigue igual.
unchanging [ʌn'tʃeɪndʒɪŋ] ADJ inalterable, inmutable.
uncharacteristic [,ʌnkærəktə'rɪstɪk] ADJ poco característico, nada típico.
uncharacteristically [,ʌnkærɪktə'rɪstɪklɪ] ADV: ~ rude/generous de

una grosería/generosidad inusitada; to behave ~ comportarse de manera inusual.
uncharitable [ʌn'tʃærɪtəbl] ADJ poco caritativo, duro.
uncharitably [ʌn'tʃærɪtəblɪ] ADV poco caritativamente.
uncharted ['ʌn'tʃɑːtɪd] ADJ inexplorado, desconocido.
unchaste ['ʌn'tʃeɪst] ADJ impúdico; spouse infiel.
unchecked ['ʌn'tʃekt] [1] ADV continue etc libremente, sin estorbo, sin restricción.
[2] ADJ abuse etc desenfrenado; fact etc no comprobado.
unchivalrous ['ʌn'ʃɪvəlrəs] ADJ poco caballeroso, poco caballeresco.
unchristian ['ʌn'krɪstɪən] ADJ poco cristiano, indigno de un cristiano.
uncial ['ʌnsɪəl] [1] ADJ uncial.
[2] N uncial f.
uncircumcised ['ʌn'sɜːkəmsaɪzd] ADJ incircunciso.
uncivil ['ʌn'sɪvl] ADJ descortés, grosero, incivil; to be ~ to sb ser grosero con uno.
uncivilized ['ʌn'sɪvɪlaɪzd] ADJ incivilizado, inculto.
unclad ['ʌn'klæd] ADJ desnudo.
unclaimed ['ʌn'kleɪmd] ADJ sin reclamar, sin dueño.
unclasp ['ʌn'klɑːsp] VT dress etc desabrochar; hands soltar, separar.
unclassifiable [,ʌn'klæsɪfaɪəbl] ADJ inclasificable.
unclassified ['ʌn'klæsɪfaɪd] ADJ sin clasificar.
uncle ['ʌŋkl] N (a) tío m; my ~ and aunt mis tíos; U~ Sam el tío Sam (personificación de EE.UU.); U~ Tom negro m que trata de congraciarse con los blancos; to cry (or say) ~* (US) rendirse, darse por vencido. (b) (‡) perista* m.
unclean ['ʌn'kliːn] ADJ sucio, inmundo; (fig) deshonesto; (ritually) impuro.
uncleanliness ['ʌn'klenlɪnɪs] N suciedad f; (fig) deshonestidad f.
unclear [,ʌn'klɪəʳ] ADJ poco claro, nada claro; to be ~ about no estar seguro de.
unclench ['ʌn'klentʃ] VT desapretar, soltar, aflojar.
unclimbed ['ʌn'klaɪmd] ADJ no escalado.
unclog ['ʌn'klɒg] VT desobstruir, desatrancar.
unclothe ['ʌn'kləʊð] VT desnudar.
unclothed ['ʌn'kləʊðd] ADJ desnudo.
unclouded ['ʌn'klaʊdɪd] ADJ despejado, sin nubes.
uncoil ['ʌn'kɔɪl] [1] VT desenrollar.
[2] VI desenrollarse; desovillarse; (snake) desanillarse.
uncollected [,ʌnkə'lektɪd] ADJ goods, luggage sin recoger; tax no recaudado, sin cobrar.
uncoloured, (US) uncolored ['ʌn'kʌləd] ADJ sin color, incoloro; account etc objetivo.
uncombed ['ʌn'kəʊmd] ADJ despeinado, sin peinar.
uncomely ['ʌn'kʌmlɪ] ADJ desgarbado.
uncomfortable [ʌn'kʌmfətəbl] ADJ (physically) incómodo; feeling molesto; to be ~ (chair etc) ser incómodo; (person) estar inquieto, sentirse molesto; I feel ~ about the change el cambio me trae preocupado; we had an ~ few minutes pasamos un mal rato; to make life ~ for sb amargar la vida a uno, crear dificultades a uno.
uncomfortably [ʌn'kʌmfətəblɪ] ADV incómodamente; he thought ~ pensaba con cierto remordimiento, pensaba algo inquieto; the shell fell ~ close cayó el proyectil inquietantemente cerca.
uncommitted ['ʌnkə'mɪtɪd] ADJ no comprometido; nation no alineado.
uncommon [ʌn'kɒmən] [1] ADJ poco común, nada frecuente; fuera de lo común; extraño, insólito.
[2] ADV (*) sumamente, extraordinariamente.
uncommonly [ʌn'kɒmənlɪ] ADV raramente, rara vez; extraordinariamente; that's ~ kind of you ha sido Vd amabilísimo; not ~ con cierta frecuencia.
uncommunicative ['ʌnkə'mjuːnɪkətɪv] ADJ poco comunicativo, reservado.
uncomplaining ['ʌnkəm'pleɪnɪŋ] ADJ resignado, sumiso.
uncomplainingly ['ʌnkəm'pleɪnɪŋlɪ] ADV con resignación, sumisamente.
uncompleted ['ʌnkəm'pliːtɪd] ADJ incompleto, inacabado.
uncomplicated [ʌn'kɒmplɪkeɪtɪd] ADJ person etc sin complicaciones, sencillo.
uncomplimentary ['ʌn,kɒmplɪ'mentərɪ] ADJ nada lisonjero, poco halagüeño.
uncomprehending ['ʌn,kɒmprɪ'hendɪŋ] ADJ incomprensivo.
uncompromising [ʌn'kɒmprəmaɪzɪŋ] ADJ intransigente, inflexible.
uncompromisingly [ʌn'kɒmprəmaɪzɪŋlɪ] ADV inflexiblemente, intransigentemente.
unconcealed ['ʌnkən'siːld] ADJ abierto, no disimulado; with ~ glee con abierta satisfacción.
unconcern ['ʌnkən'sɜːn] N (calm) calma f, tranquilidad f, (in face of danger) sangre f fría; (lack of interest) indiferencia f, despreocupación f.
unconcerned ['ʌnkən'sɜːnd] ADJ tranquilo; indiferente, despreocupado; he went on speaking ~ siguió hablando sin inmutarse;

to be ~ about sth no inquietarse por algo.

unconcernedly [ˈʌnkənˈsɜːnɪdlɪ] ADV con calma, tranquilamente; con sangre fría; con indiferencia; sin preocuparse, sin inquietarse.

unconditional [ˈʌnkənˈdɪʃənl] ADJ incondicional, sin condiciones; **~ surrender** rendición *f* sin condiciones.

unconditionally [ˈʌnkənˈdɪʃnəlɪ] ADV incondicionalmente.

unconfessed [ˈʌnkənˈfest] ADJ *sin* no confesado; *die* sin confesar.

unconfined [ˈʌnkənˈfaɪnd] ADJ ilimitado, no restringido, libre; **let joy be ~** que se regocijen todos, que la alegría no tenga límite.

unconfirmed [ˈʌnkənˈfɜːmd] ADJ no confirmado, inconfirmado.

uncongenial [ˈʌnkənˈdʒiːnɪəl] ADJ antipático; desagradable.

unconnected [ˈʌnkəˈnektɪd] ADJ inconexo; **~ with** no relacionado con.

unconquerable [ʌnˈkɒŋkərəbl] ADJ inconquistable, invencible.

unconquered [ʌnˈkɒŋkəd] ADJ invicto.

unconscionable [ʌnˈkɒnʃnəbl] ADJ desmedido, desrazonable.

unconscious [ʌnˈkɒnʃəs] **1** ADJ **(a)** (*unaware*) inconsciente, no intencional; **to be ~ of** estar inconsciente de, ignorar, no darse cuenta de; **to remain blissfully ~ of the danger** continuar tan tranquilo sin darse cuenta del peligro.
(b) (*Med*) sin sentido, desmayado, inconsciente; **to be ~** estar sin sentido, estar desmayado; **to be ~ for 3 hours** pasar 3 horas sin sentido; **to become ~** perder el sentido, perder el conocimiento, desmayarse; **to fall ~** caer sin sentido; **they found him ~** le encontraron inconsciente.
2 N: **the ~** el inconsciente.

unconsciously [ʌnˈkɒnʃəslɪ] ADV inconscientemente; **~ funny** cómico sin querer.

unconsciousness [ʌnˈkɒnʃəsnɪs] N inconsciencia *f*; (*Med*) insensibilidad *f*, pérdida *f* de conocimiento, falta *f* de sentido.

unconsidered [ˈʌnkənˈsɪdəd] ADJ desatendido; irreflexivo; **~ trifles** pequeñeces *fpl* de ninguna importancia.

unconstitutional [ˈʌnˌkɒnstɪˈtjuːʃənl] ADJ inconstitucional, anticonstitucional.

unconstitutionally [ʌnˌkɒnstɪˈtjuːʃnəlɪ] ADV inconstitucionalmente, anticonstitucionalmente.

unconstrained [ˈʌnkənˈstreɪnd] ADJ libre, espontáneo, franco.

unconsummated [ʌnˈkɒnsəmeɪtɪd] ADJ *marriage* no consumado.

uncontested [ˈʌnkənˈtestɪd] ADJ incontestado; (*Parl*) *seat* ganado sin oposición, no disputado.

uncontrollable [ˈʌnkənˈtrəʊləbl] ADJ incontrolable; *temper* ingobernable; *laughter* incontenible; *terror etc* irrefrenable.

uncontrollably [ˈʌnkənˈtrəʊləblɪ] ADV incontrolablemente; ingobernablemente; inconteniblemente; irrefrenablemente.

uncontrolled [ˈʌnkənˈtrəʊld] ADJ incontrolado, libre, desenfrenado.

uncontroversial [ˈʌnˌkɒntrəˈvɜːʃəl] ADJ no controvertido, nada conflictivo.

unconventional [ˈʌnkənˈvenʃənl] ADJ poco convencional; *person* poco formalista, original, despreocupado.

unconventionality [ˈʌnkənˌvenʃəˈnælɪtɪ] N originalidad *f*.

unconversant [ˈʌnkənˈvɜːsənt] ADJ: **to be ~ with** no estar al tanto de, estar poco versado en.

unconverted [ˈʌnkənˈvɜːtɪd] ADJ no convertido (*also Fin*).

unconvertible [ˌʌnkənˈvɜːtɪbl] ADJ *currency* inconvertible.

unconvinced [ˈʌnkənˈvɪnst] ADJ: **to remain ~** seguir siendo escéptico, seguir sin convencerse.

unconvincing [ˈʌnkənˈvɪnsɪŋ] ADJ poco convincente.

unconvincingly [ˈʌnkənˈvɪnsɪŋlɪ] ADV *argue etc* sin convencer a nadie.

uncooked [ˈʌnˈkʊkt] ADJ sin cocer, crudo.

uncool* [ʌnˈkuːl] ADJ **(a)** (*unsophisticated*) nada sofisticado; (*unfashionable*) fuera de moda, anticuado. **(b)** (*excitable*) excitable, emocionado; (*tense*) nervioso.

uncooperative [ˈʌnkəʊˈɒpərətɪv] ADJ poco dispuesto a ayudar, nada servicial.

uncoordinated [ˈʌnkəʊˈɔːdɪneɪtɪd] ADJ no coordinado, incoordinado.

uncork [ˈʌnˈkɔːk] VT descorchar, destapar.

uncorrected [ˈʌnkəˈrektɪd] ADJ sin corregir.

uncorroborated [ˈʌnkəˈrɒbəreɪtɪd] ADJ no confirmado, sin corroborar.

uncorrupted [ˈʌnkəˈrʌptɪd] ADJ incorrupto; **~ by** no corrompido por.

uncount [ˈʌnˈkaʊnt] ADJ: **~ noun** sustantivo *m* no contable.

uncountable [ˈʌnˈkaʊntəbl] ADJ incontable.

uncounted [ˈʌnˈkaʊntɪd] ADJ sin cuenta.

uncouple [ˈʌnˈkʌpl] VT desacoplar, desenganchar.

uncouth [ʌnˈkuːθ] ADJ grosero, ineducado, inculto.

uncover [ʌnˈkʌvər] VT descubrir; (*remove lid of*) destapar; (*remove coverings of*) dejar al descubierto; (*disclose*) descubrir, dejar al descubierto, dejar patente.

uncovered [ʌnˈkʌvəd] ADJ descubierto, sin cubierta; destapado; (*Fin*) *loan* en descubierto; *person* sin seguro, no asegurado.

uncritical [ˈʌnˈkrɪtɪkəl] ADJ falto de sentido crítico.

uncritically [ˈʌnˈkrɪtɪkəlɪ] ADV sin sentido crítico.

uncross [ˈʌnˈkrɒs] VT *legs* descruzar.

uncrossed [ˈʌnˈkrɒst] ADJ *cheque* sin cruzar.

uncrowned [ˈʌnˈkraʊnd] ADJ sin corona; **the ~ king of Slobodia** el rey sin corona de Eslobodia.

UNCTAD [ˈʌŋktæd] N ABBR *of* **United Nations Conference on Trade and Development.**

unction [ˈʌŋkʃən] N (*unguent*) unción *f*, ungüento *m*; (*fig*) unción *f*; celo *m*, fervor *m*; (*pej*) efusión *f*, celo *m* fingido, fervor *m* afectado; zalamería *f*; **extreme ~** (*Eccl*) extremaunción *f*; **he said with ~** dijo efusivo.

unctuous [ˈʌŋktjʊəs] ADJ (*fig*) afectadamente fervoroso; sobón, zalamero; **in an ~ voice** en tono efusivo, en tono meloso.

unctuously [ˈʌŋktjʊəslɪ] ADV efusivamente, melosamente, zalameramente.

unctuousness [ˈʌŋktjʊəsnɪs] N (*fig*) efusión *f*, celo *m* fingido, fervor *m* afectado; zalamería *f*.

uncultivable [ˈʌnˈkʌltɪvəbl] ADJ incultivable.

uncultivated [ˈʌnˈkʌltɪveɪtɪd] ADJ inculto (*also fig*).

uncultured [ˈʌnˈkʌltʃəd] ADJ inculto, iletrado.

uncurl [ˈʌnˈkɜːl] **1** VT desrizar, desenrollar, abrir.
2 VI desrizarse, desenrollarse, abrirse; desovillarse.

uncut [ˈʌnˈkʌt] ADJ sin cortar; *stone* sin labrar; *diamond* en bruto, sin tallar; *book* sin abrir; *film, text* integral, sin cortes.

undamaged [ʌnˈdæmɪdʒd] ADJ indemne, intacto; sin sufrir desperfectos.

undamped [ˈʌnˈdæmpt] ADJ *enthusiasm etc* no disminuido.

undated [ˈʌnˈdeɪtɪd] ADJ sin fecha.

undaunted [ˈʌnˈdɔːntɪd] ADJ impávido, impertérrito; **he carried on quite ~** siguió sin inmutarse; **with ~ bravery** con valor indomable; **to be ~ by** no dejarse desanimar por.

undeceive [ˈʌndɪˈsiːv] VT desengañar, desilusionar.

undecided [ˈʌndɪˈsaɪdɪd] ADJ *question* pendiente, no resuelto; *person's character* indeciso; **we are still ~ whether to** + *infin* no hemos decidido todavía si + *infin*; **that is still ~** eso queda por resolver.

undecipherable [ˈʌndɪˈsaɪfərəbl] ADJ indescifrable.

undeclinable [ˈʌndɪˈklaɪnəbl] ADJ indeclinable.

undefeated [ˈʌndɪˈfiːtɪd] ADJ invicto, imbatido; **he was ~ at the end** siguió invicto al final.

undefended [ˈʌndɪˈfendɪd] ADJ indefenso; (*Jur*) *suit* ganado por incomparecencia del demandado.

undefiled [ˈʌndɪˈfaɪld] ADJ puro, inmaculado; **~ by any contact with ...** no corrompido por contacto alguno con ...

undefinable [ˌʌndɪˈfaɪnəbl] ADJ indefinible.

undefined [ˌʌndɪˈfaɪnd] ADJ indefinido, indeterminado.

undelivered [ˌʌndɪˈlɪvəd] ADJ *goods, letters* sin entregar, no entregado.

undemanding [ˌʌndɪˈmɑːndɪŋ] ADJ *person* poco exigente; *job* que exige poco esfuerzo.

undemocratic [ˌʌndeməˈkrætɪk] ADJ antidemocrático.

undemonstrative [ˈʌndɪˈmɒnstrətɪv] ADJ reservado, cohibido, poco expresivo.

▼ **undeniable** [ˌʌndɪˈnaɪəbl] ADJ innegable; **it is ~ that ...** es innegable que ...

undeniably [ˌʌndɪˈnaɪəblɪ] ADV indudablemente; **it is ~ true that ...** es innegable que ...; **an ~ successful trip** un viaje de éxito innegable.

undenominational [ˈʌndɪˌnɒmɪˈneɪʃənl] ADJ no sectario.

undependable [ˈʌndɪˈpendəbl] ADJ poco formal, poco confiable.

under [ˈʌndər] **1** ADV **(a)** debajo; abajo; *V* **down** *etc*. **(b) he was ~ for several hours*** estuvo sin conocimiento durante varias horas.
2 PREP **(a)** (*place: precise*) debajo de, *eg* **~ the table** debajo de la mesa; (*less precise*) bajo, *eg* **~ the sky** bajo el cielo, **~ the water** bajo el agua.
(b) (*place, fig*) **~ the Romans** bajo los romanos; **~ Ferdinand VII** bajo Fernando VII, durante el reinado de Fernando VII; **~ the command of** bajo el mando de; **~ lock and key** bajo llave; **~ oath** bajo juramento; **~ full sail** a todo trapo, a vela llena; a toda vela; **the field is ~ wheat** el campo está sembrado de trigo.
(c) (*number etc*) **~ 50** menos de 50; **any number ~ 90** cualquier número inferior a 90; **in ~ 2 hours** en menos de 2 horas; **aged ~ 21** que tiene menos de 21 años; **it sells at ~ £5** se vende a menos de 5 libras.
(d) (*according to, by*) con arreglo a, de acuerdo con, conforme a, según; **~ Article 25 of the Code** conforme al Artículo 25 del Código; **his rights ~ the contract** sus derechos según el contrato.

under- [ˈʌndər] PREF **(a)** (*insufficiently*) insuficientemente; *eg* **~prepared** insuficientemente preparado.
(b) (*less than*) **an ~15** un joven de menos de 15 años, una persona que tiene menos de 15 años; **the Spanish ~21 team** la selección española sub-21.
(c) *part etc* bajo, inferior; *clothing* inferior; (*in rank*) subalterno, segundo; **the ~cook** la segunda cocinera; **the ~gardener** el mozo de huerto.

under-achieve [ˌʌndərə'tʃiːv] vɪ no desarrollar su potencial, no rendir (como se debe).

under-achievement [ˌʌndərə'tʃiːvmənt] N bajo rendimiento *m*.

under-achiever [ˌʌndərə'tʃiːvəʳ] N (*Brit*) persona *f* que no desarrolla su potencial, persona *f* que no rinde (como se debe).

underact ['ʌndər'ækt] vɪ no dar de sí, hacer un papel sin el debido brío.

under-age [ˌʌndər'eɪdʒ] ADJ menor de edad.

underarm ['ʌndərɑːm] [1] N sobaco *m*, axila *f*.
[2] ATTR (*Anat*) sobacal, del sobaco; *service etc* hecho con la mano debajo del hombro; ~ **deodorant** desodorante *m*.
[3] ADV: **to serve** ~ sacar con la mano debajo del hombro.

underbelly ['ʌndə,belɪ] N panza *f*; (*fig*) parte *f* indefensa, parte *f* más expuesta al ataque.

underbid ['ʌndə'bɪd] (*irr: V* bid) [1] vᴛ ofrecer precio más bajo que.
[2] vɪ (*Bridge*) declarar menos de lo que tiene uno.

underbody ['ʌndəbɒdɪ] N (*Aut*) bajos *mpl* del chasis.

underbrush ['ʌndəbrʌʃ] N (*US*) maleza *f*, monte *m* bajo.

undercapitalized ['ʌndə'kæpɪtəlaɪzd] ADJ subcapitalizado, descapitalizado.

undercarriage ['ʌndə,kærɪdʒ] N, **undercart•** ['ʌndəkɑːt] N tren *m* de aterrizaje.

undercharge ['ʌndə'tʃɑːdʒ] vᴛ cobrar menos del precio justo a.

underclass ['ʌndəklɑːs] N clase *f* inferior.

underclothes ['ʌndəkləʊðz] NPL, **underclothing** ['ʌndə,kləʊðɪŋ] N ropa *f* interior, ropa *f* íntima (*LAm*); **to be in one's** ~ estar en paños menores.

undercoat ['ʌndəkəʊt] [1] N primera capa *f*; (*paint itself*) pintura *f* preparatoria.
[2] vᴛ poner una primera capa a; (*US Aut*) proteger contra la corrosión.

undercooked ['ʌndə'kʊkt] ADJ medio crudo.

undercover ['ʌndə,kʌvəʳ] ADJ secreto, clandestino.

undercurrent ['ʌndə,kʌrənt] N corriente *f* submarina, contracorriente *f*; (*fig*) nota *f* callada; tendencia *f* oculta; **an** ~ **of criticism** una serie de críticas calladas.

undercut ['ʌndəkʌt] (*irr: V* cut) vᴛ *competitor* vender más barato que.

underdeveloped ['ʌndədɪ'veləpt] ADJ infradesarrollado, subdesarrollado; (*Phot*) insuficientemente revelado.

underdevelopment ['ʌndədɪ'veləpmənt] N infradesarrollo *m*, subdesarrollo *m*.

underdog ['ʌndədɒg] N (*socially*) desvalido *m*; (*in game*) perdidoso *m*, el que está perdiendo; **the** ~**s** los de abajo, los débiles, los desamparados.

underdone ['ʌndə'dʌn] ADJ poco hecho.

underdrawers ['ʌndə'drɔːəz] NPL (*US*) calzoncillos *mpl*.

underdress ['ʌndə'dres] vɪ vestirse sin la debida elegancia, no vestirse de forma apropiada.

underemphasize [ˌʌndər'emfəsaɪz] vᴛ subenfatizar.

underemployed ['ʌndərɪm'plɔɪd] ADJ subempleado.

underemployment [ˌʌndərɪm'plɔɪmənt] N subempleo *m*.

underestimate [1] ['ʌndər'estɪmɪt] N estimación *f* demasiado baja; infraestimación *f*, infravaloración *f*.
[2] ['ʌndər'estɪmeɪt] vᴛ subestimar; infraestimar, infravalorar.

under-expose ['ʌndərɪks'pəʊz] vᴛ subexponer, exponer insuficientemente.

under-exposed ['ʌndərɪks'pəʊzd] ADJ subexpuesto.

under-exposure ['ʌndərɪks'pəʊʒəʳ] N subexposición *f*.

underfed ['ʌndə'fed] ADJ subalimentado, desnutrido.

underfeed ['ʌndə'fiːd] (*irr: V* feed) vᴛ alimentar insuficientemente.

underfeeding ['ʌndə'fiːdɪŋ] N subalimentación *f*, desnutrición *f*.

underfelt ['ʌndəfelt] N arpillera *f*.

underfinanced [ˌʌndəfaɪ'nænst] ADJ insuficientemente financiado.

underfloor ['ʌndəflɔːʳ] ADJ de debajo del suelo.

underfloor heating [ˌʌndəflɔː'hiːtɪŋ] N calefacción *f* por suelo (radiante).

underfoot ['ʌndə'fʊt] ADV debajo de los pies; **it's very wet** ~ el suelo está mojado.

underfund [ˌʌndə'fʌnd] vᴛ infradotar.

underfunded [ˌʌndə'fʌndɪd] ADJ infradotado.

underfunding [ˌʌndə'fʌndɪŋ] N infradotación *f*.

undergarment ['ʌndə,gɑːmənt] N prenda *f* de ropa interior (*LAm:* íntima); ~**s** ropa *f* interior, ropa *f* íntima (*LAm*).

undergo ['ʌndə'gəʊ] (*irr: V* go) vᴛ sufrir, experimentar; *operation* someterse a; *treatment* recibir; **to** ~ **repairs** ser reparado.

undergrad• [ˌʌndə'græd] ADJ, N ABBR *of* **undergraduate**.

undergraduate ['ʌndə'grædjuɪt] [1] N estudiante *mf* (*no licenciado*).
[2] ATTR *student* no licenciado; *study* de licenciatura, para estudiantes no licenciados; ~ **humour** humor *m* estudiantil; **70** ~ **rooms** 70 habitaciones para estudiantes.

underground ['ʌndəgraʊnd] [1] ADJ (**a**) (*lit*) subterráneo; ~ **railway** ferrocarril *m* subterráneo.

(**b**) (*fig*) clandestino, secreto; ~ **cinema** cine *m* underground.
[2] ADV (**a**) (*lit*) bajo tierra; **it's 6 feet** ~ está a 6 pies bajo tierra.
(**b**) (*Pol etc*) clandestinamente, en la clandestinidad; **this may drive the party** ~ esto puede obligar al partido a pasar a la clandestinidad.
[3] N (**a**) (*Brit Rail*) metro *m*.
(**b**) (*Mil, Pol*) resistencia *f*; movimiento *m* clandestino.

undergrowth ['ʌndəgrəʊθ] N maleza *f*, monte *m* bajo.

underhand ['ʌndəhænd] ADJ (*Sport*) *service etc* hecho con la mano debajo del hombro; (*fig*) *method* turbio, poco limpio; *trick* malo; *attack* solapado.
[2] ADV: **to serve** ~ sacar con la mano debajo del hombro.

underhanded [ˌʌndə'hændɪd] = **underhand**.

underhandedly [ˌʌndə'hændɪdlɪ] ADV bajo mano.

underinsure [ˌʌndərɪn'ʃʊəʳ] vᴛ asegurar por debajo del valor real; **to be** ~**d** estar infraasegurado.

underinvestment [ˌʌndərɪn'vestmənt] N infrainversión *f*.

underlay ['ʌndəleɪ] N (*for carpet*) refuerzo *m* (de alfombra).

underlie [ˌʌndə'laɪ] (*irr: V* lie²) vᴛ estar debajo de, extenderse debajo de; servir de base a; (*fig*) subyacer a, estar a la base de, ser la razón fundamental de.

underline [ˌʌndə'laɪn] vᴛ subrayar (*also fig*).

underling ['ʌndəlɪŋ] N subordinado *m*, inferior *m*.

underlining [ˌʌndə'laɪnɪŋ] N subrayado *m*.

underlip ['ʌndəlɪp] N labio *m* inferior.

underlying [ˌʌndə'laɪɪŋ] ADJ subyacente; (*fig*) fundamental, esencial; **the** ~ **problem is that ...** el problema de fondo es que ...

undermanned [ˌʌndə'mænd] ADJ: **to be** ~ estar sin la debida plantilla, no tener el debido personal.

undermanning [ˌʌndə'mænɪŋ] N escasez *f* de mano de obra, falta *f* de personal.

undermentioned ['ʌndə'menʃənd] ADJ abajo citado.

undermine [ˌʌndə'maɪn] vᴛ socavar, minar (*also fig*); **his health is being** ~**d by overwork** el exceso de trabajo le está arruinando la salud.

undermost ['ʌndəməʊst] ADJ (el) más bajo.

underneath ['ʌndə'niːθ] [1] ADV debajo, por debajo.
[2] PREP bajo, debajo de, por debajo de.
[3] ADJ inferior, de abajo; **the** ~ **one** el de abajo.
[4] N superficie *f* inferior.

undernourished ['ʌndə'nʌrɪʃt] ADJ desnutrido.

undernourishment ['ʌndə'nʌrɪʃmənt] N desnutrición *f*.

underpaid ['ʌndə'peɪd] ADJ insuficientemente retribuido, mal pagado.

underpants ['ʌndəpænts] NPL calzoncillos *mpl*, calzones *mpl* (*LAm*).

underpart ['ʌndəpɑːt] N parte *f* inferior.

underpass ['ʌndəpɑːs] N paso *m* inferior.

underpay ['ʌndə'peɪ] (*irr: V* pay) vᴛ pagar mal, pagar un sueldo insuficiente a.

underperform [ˌʌndəpə'fɔːm] vɪ (**a**) (*St Ex*) comportarse mal, tener un mal comportamiento; **the stock has** ~**ed on the Brussels stock market** las acciones han tenido un mal comportamiento en la bolsa de Bruselas. (**b**) *at work, in school* rendir poco.

underpin [ˌʌndə'pɪn] vᴛ (*Archit*) apuntalar; (*fig*) *argument, case* secundar, sostener.

underpinning [ˌʌndə'pɪnɪŋ] N apuntalamiento *m*.

underplay [ˌʌndə'pleɪ] [1] vᴛ: **to** ~ **a part** hacer flojamente un papel.
[2] vɪ (*Theat*) hacer flojamente su papel, estar muy flojo en su papel.

underpopulated ['ʌndə'pɒpjʊleɪtɪd] ADJ poco poblado, con baja densidad de población.

underprice [ˌʌndə'praɪs] vᴛ señalar un precio demasiado bajo a; **at 5 dollars it is** ~**d** el precio de 5 dólares es más bien bajo.

underpricing ['ʌndə'praɪsɪŋ] N asignación *f* de precios demasiado bajos.

underprivileged ['ʌndə'prɪvɪlɪdʒd] ADJ desvalido, desfavorecido, desamparado.

underproduction ['ʌndəprə'dʌkʃən] N producción *f* insuficiente.

underqualified ['ʌndə'kwɒlɪ,faɪd] ADJ: **to be** ~ no estar suficientemente cualificado (*for* para).

underrate [ˌʌndə'reɪt] vᴛ subestimar.

underrated [ˌʌndə'reɪtɪd] ADJ subestimado; infravalorado.

underripe [ˌʌndə'raɪp] ADJ poco maduro, verde.

underscore [ˌʌndə'skɔːʳ] vᴛ subrayar, recalcar.

undersea ['ʌndəsiː] [1] ADJ submarino.
[2] ADV bajo la superficie del mar.

underseal ['ʌndəsiːl] vᴛ (*Brit*) impermeabilizar (por debajo), proteger contra la corrosión.

undersealing ['ʌndəsiːlɪŋ] N (*Brit*) impermeabilización *f* de los bajos.

undersecretary ['ʌndə'sekrətərɪ] N subsecretario *m*, -a *f*.

undersecretaryship ['ʌndə'sekrətərɪʃɪp] N subsecretaría *f*.

undersell ['ʌndə'sel] (*irr: V* sell) vᴛ *person* vender a precio más bajo que; *article* malvender; **Burnley has been undersold as a tourist centre** no se ha hecho la debida publicidad de Burnley como centro turístico.

undersexed [ˌʌndəˈsekst] ADJ de libido floja.

undershirt [ˈʌndəʃɜːt] N (US) camiseta f.

undershoot [ˌʌndəˈʃuːt] (irr: V **shoot**) **1** VT target (fig) no alcanzar, no llegar a.
2 VI no alcanzar el blanco; **we have undershot by £80** nos faltan 80 libras para alcanzar el objetivo.

undershorts [ˈʌndəʃɔːts] NPL (US) calzoncillos mpl.

underside [ˈʌndəsaɪd] N superficie f inferior; (of small object) envés m, cara f inferior.

undersigned [ˈʌndəsaɪnd] ADJ: **the ~** el abajofirmante, el infraescrito, (PL) los abajofirmantes, los infraescritos.

undersized [ˈʌndəˈsaɪzd] ADJ pequeño, no bastante grande, de tamaño insuficiente; person sietemesino.

underskirt [ˈʌndəskɜːt] N (Brit) enaguas fpl.

underslung [ˈʌndəslʌŋ] ADJ (Aut) colgante.

undersoil [ˈʌndəsɔɪl] **1** N subsuelo m.
2 ATTR: **~ heating** calefacción f subterránea.

underspend [ˌʌndəˈspend] VI gastar menos de lo previsto.

understaffed [ˈʌndəˈstɑːft] ADJ: **to be ~** estar falto de personal, no tener el debido personal.

understaffing [ˈʌndəˈstɑːfɪŋ] N escasez f de mano de obra, falta f de personal.

▼ **understand** [ˌʌndəˈstænd] (irr: V **stand**) **1** VT **(a)** (grasp) comprender, entender; **I don't ~ Arabic** no entiendo el árabe; **I don't ~ you** no te entiendo; **I don't ~ why** no entiendo por qué; **we ~ each other** nos entendemos, nos comprendemos; **as I ~ it** según tengo entendido.
(b) (assume) sobreentender; **one has to ~ 3 words here** aquí se sobreentienden 3 palabras; V also **understood**.
(c) (believe) entender; **I ~ that ...** (formal declarations) quedo informado de que ...; **I ~ (that) you have been absent** tengo entendido que has estado ausente; **to give sb to ~ that ...** dar a uno a entender que ...; **I was given to ~ that ...** me dieron a entender que ..., me hicieron creer que ...
2 VI comprender, entender; **I ~** lo comprendo; **I quite ~** lo comprendo perfectamente; **do you ~?** ¿me entiendes?, ¿comprendes?

understandable [ˌʌndəˈstændəbl] ADJ comprensible; **it is ~ that ...** se comprende que ...; **it is very ~ that ...** se comprende perfectamente que ...

understandably [ˌʌndəˈstændəblɪ] ADV naturalmente; (lit) comprensiblemente; **he ~ refused** naturalmente se negó, se comprende que rehusara.

understanding [ˌʌndəˈstændɪŋ] **1** ADJ comprensivo, compasivo; **they were very ~ about it** se mostraron muy comprensivos; **he gave me an ~ look** me miró compasivo.
2 N **(a)** (intelligence) entendimiento m, inteligencia f; (grasp) comprensión f; **he has good ~** tiene una inteligencia fina; **his ~ of these problems** su comprensión de estos problemas, su capacidad para comprender estos problemas.
(b) (agreement) acuerdo m, arreglo m; **to come to an ~ with sb** ponerse de acuerdo con uno, llegar a un acuerdo con uno; **to have an ~ with sb** tener un acuerdo (esp verbal) con uno; **I have an ~ with the milkman** tengo un arreglo con el lechero, nos entendemos el lechero y yo; **on the ~ that ...** con tal que + subj, bien entendido que + subj.
(c) (sympathy) comprensión f mutua, inteligencia f; simpatía f; **this will encourage good ~ between peoples** esto ha de fomentar la buena inteligencia entre los pueblos.

understandingly [ˌʌndəˈstændɪŋlɪ] ADV con comprensión, compasivamente; **he looked at me ~** me miró compasivamente.

understate [ˈʌndəˈsteɪt] VT minimizar; situation describir quitándole importancia; gravity atenuar; needs subestimar; (Gram) atenuar.

understated [ˌʌndəˈsteɪtɪd] ADJ comedido.

understatement [ˈʌndəˈsteɪtmənt] N atenuación f; descripción f insuficiente; (Gram) atenuación f; (quality) moderación f, modestia f excesiva; **the ~ of the year** el eufemismo del año.

understood [ˌʌndəˈstʊd] ADJ AND PTP **(a)** **~?** ¿comprendido?; **it is ~ that ...** (believed) se cree que ..., tenemos entendido que ...; (understandable) se comprende que ...; **that is ~** eso se entiende; **it being ~ that ...** con tal que + subj; **I wish it to be ~ that ...** entiéndase que ..., quiero decir bien claro que ...; **to make o.s. ~** hacerse entender.
(b) (assumed) **with 3 words ~** con 3 palabras que se sobreentienden; **it is an ~ thing that ...** se entiende que ..., se acepta el que ...

understorey [ˈʌndəˌstɔːrɪ] N monte m bajo.

understudy [ˈʌndəˌstʌdɪ] **1** N suplente mf, sobresaliente mf.
2 VT doblar a, aprender un papel para poder suplir a.

undertake [ˌʌndəˈteɪk] (irr: V **take**) VT task etc emprender; acometer; duty etc encargarse de; **to ~ to do sth** comprometerse a hacer algo, prometer hacer algo; **to ~ that ...** comprometerse a que ..., prometer que ...

undertaker [ˈʌndəˌteɪkər] N director m de pompas fúnebres; **~'s**

funeraria f.

undertaking [ˌʌndəˈteɪkɪŋ] N **(a)** (Comm) empresa f; (task) empresa f, tarea f. **(b)** (pledge) garantía f, compromiso m, promesa f; **to give an ~ that ...** prometer que ..., asegurar que ...; **I can give no such ~** no puedo comprometerme a eso, no puedo dar esa promesa.

under-the-counter* [ˌʌndəðəˈkaʊntər] ADJ goods etc adquirido por la trastienda*.

underthings* [ˈʌndəθɪŋz] NPL paños mpl menores; **to be in one's ~** estar en paños menores.

undertone [ˈʌndətəʊn] N (sound) voz f baja, sonido m suave; (Art) matiz m suave; (of criticism etc) nota f callada, trasfondo m, corriente f oculta, sentimiento m no expresado; **in an ~** en voz baja; **there are ~s of protest here** aquí hay notas calladas de protesta.

undertook [ˌʌndəˈtʊk] PRET of **undertake**.

undertow [ˈʌndətəʊ] N resaca f.

under-use 1 [ˌʌndəˈjuːs] N infrautilización f.
2 [ˌʌndəˈjuːz] VT infrautilizar.

under-utilization [ˌʌndəˈjuːtəlaɪzeɪʃən] N infrautilización f.

underutilize [ˌʌndəˈjuːtɪlaɪz] VT infrautilizar.

under-utilized [ˌʌndəˈjuːtəlaɪzd] ADJ infrautilizado.

undervalue [ˈʌndəˈvæljuː] VT subvalorar, minusvalorar, valorizar incompletamente, apreciar en menos de su justo valor; (fig) subestimar; menospreciar; **he has been ~d as a writer** como escritor no se le ha apreciado debidamente.

underwater [ˈʌndəˈwɔːtər] ADJ submarino; **~ archaeology** arqueología f submarina; **~ diver** submarinista mf; **~ exploration** exploración f submarina; **~ fisherman** submarinista mf; **~ fishing** pesca f submarina.

underway [ˌʌndəˈweɪ] ADJ V **way 1(o)**.

underwear [ˈʌndəweər] N ropa f interior, ropa f íntima (LAm).

underweight [ˌʌndəˈweɪt] ADJ de peso insuficiente; **to be ~** (person) no pesar bastante, estar flaco.

underwent [ˌʌndəˈwent] PRET of **undergo**.

underwhelm [ˈʌndəˈwelm] VT (hum) impresionar muy poco; **this left us somewhat ~ed** esto apenas nos impresionó.

underwhelming* [ˌʌndəˈwelmɪŋ] ADJ (hum) response, applause poco entusiasta; results, performance poco satisfactorio.

underworld [ˈʌndəwɜːld] **1** ADJ **(a)** (of hell) infernal. **(b)** (criminal) criminal, del hampa.
2 N **(a)** (hell) infierno m; (of spirits) inframundo m. **(b)** (criminal) hampa f, mundo m del hampa, bajos fondos mpl.

underwrite [ˈʌndəraɪt] (irr: V **write**) VT asegurar, asegurar contra riesgos; (on 2nd insurance) reasegurar; (fig) apoyar, respaldar, aprobar, garantizar.

underwriter [ˈʌndəˌraɪtər] N asegurador m, -ora f, reasegurador m, -ora f.

underwritten [ˈʌndəˌrɪtn] PTP of **underwrite**.

underwrote [ˈʌndərəʊt] PRET of **underwrite**.

undeserved [ˈʌndɪˈzɜːvd] ADJ inmerecido.

undeservedly [ˈʌndɪˈzɜːvɪdlɪ] ADV inmerecidamente.

undeserving [ˈʌndɪˈzɜːvɪŋ] ADJ indigno, de poco mérito.

undesirable [ˈʌndɪˈzaɪərəbl] **1** ADJ indeseable; **it is ~ that ...** no es recomendable que + subj, es poco aconsejable que + subj.
2 N indeseable mf.

undetected [ˈʌndɪˈtektɪd] ADJ no descubierto; **to go ~** pasar inadvertido.

undetermined [ˈʌndɪˈtɜːmɪnd] ADJ (unknown) indeterminado; (uncertain) incierto.

undeterred [ˈʌndɪˈtɜːd] ADJ: **he was ~ by ...** no se dejó intimidar por ...; **he carried on ~** siguió sin inmutarse.

undeveloped [ˈʌndɪˈveləpt] ADJ subdesarrollado; fruit etc verde, inmaturo; film sin revelar; land sin cultivar; resources sin explotar.

undeviating [ʌnˈdiːvɪeɪtɪŋ] ADJ directo, constante; **to follow an ~ path** seguir un curso recto.

undeviatingly [ʌnˈdiːvɪeɪtɪŋlɪ] ADV directamente, constantemente; **to hold ~ to one's course** seguir su curso sin apartarse para nada de él.

undiagnosed [ʌnˈdaɪəgˌnəʊzd] ADJ sin diagnosticar.

undid [ˌʌnˈdɪd] PRET of **undo**.

undies* [ˈʌndɪz] NPL paños mpl menores.

undigested [ˈʌndaɪˈdʒestɪd] ADJ indigesto.

undignified [ʌnˈdɪgnɪfaɪd] ADJ act, position etc indecoroso; person sin dignidad, informal, poco serio.

undiluted [ˈʌndaɪˈluːtɪd] ADJ sin diluir, puro; (fig) puro.

undiminished [ˈʌndɪˈmɪnɪʃt] ADJ no disminuido.

undimmed [ˈʌnˈdɪmd] ADJ (fig) no empañado.

undiplomatic [ˈʌnˌdɪpləˈmætɪk] ADJ poco diplomático, indiscreto.

undiscernible [ˈʌndɪˈsɜːnəbl] ADJ imperceptible.

undiscerning [ˈʌndɪˈsɜːnɪŋ] ADJ sin discernimiento, poco discernidor.

undischarged [ˈʌndɪsˈtʃɑːdʒd] ADJ debt impagado, por pagar; promise no cumplido; **~ bankrupt** quebrado m no rehabilitado, persona f que sigue en estado de quiebra.

undisciplined [ʌnˈdɪsɪplɪnd] ADJ indisciplinado.

undisclosed ['ʌndɪs'kləʊzd] ADJ no revelado, sin revelar.

undiscovered ['ʌndɪs'kʌvəd] ADJ no descubierto; **he remained ~ for 3 days** siguió durante 3 días sin descubrir.

undiscriminating ['ʌndɪs'krɪmɪneɪtɪŋ] ADJ sin discernimiento, poco discernidor.

undisguised ['ʌndɪs'gaɪzd] ADJ sin disfraz; (*fig*) franco, abierto; **with ~ satisfaction** con abierta satisfacción.

undismayed ['ʌndɪs'meɪd] ADJ impávido; **he was ~ by this** no se dejó desanimar por esto; **he said ~** dijo sin inmutarse.

undisposed-of ['ʌndɪs'pəʊzdɒv] ADJ (*Comm*) no vendido.

undisputed ['ʌndɪs'pjuːtɪd] ADJ incontestable, indiscutible.

undistinguished ['ʌndɪs'tɪŋgwɪʃt] ADJ más bien mediocre.

undistributed [,ʌndɪs'trɪbjutɪd] ADJ: **~ profit** beneficios *mpl* no distribuidos.

undisturbed ['ʌndɪs'tɜːbd] ADJ tranquilo, sin molestar; **to leave things ~** dejar las cosas como están, dejar las cosas sin tocar; **he was ~ by this** no se perturbó con esto; **to go on with one's work ~** continuar su trabajo en paz; **he likes to be left ~** no quiere que le interrumpan las visitas (*or* llamadas *etc*).

undivided ['ʌndɪ'vaɪdɪd] ADJ indiviso, íntegro, entero; **I want your ~ attention** quiero que me presten toda su atención.

undo ['ʌn'duː] (*irr: V* **do**) VT *arrangement etc* anular; *work* deshacer; *knot* desatar; *clasp* desabrochar; *packet* abrir; *mischief* reparar; *command* cancelar; *V also* **undone.**

undocumented [ʌn'dɒkjʊmentɪd] ADJ (a) *event* indocumentado. (b) (*US*) *person* indocumentado.

undoing ['ʌn'duːɪŋ] N ruina *f*, perdición *f*; **that was his ~** aquello fue su ruina.

undomesticated ['ʌndə'mestɪkeɪtɪd] ADJ indomado, no domesticado.

undone ['ʌn'dʌn] ADJ: **I am ~!** (*liter*) ¡estoy perdido!, ¡es mi ruina!; **to come ~** *knot etc* desatarse; **to leave sth ~** *task* dejar algo sin hacer.

undoubted [ʌn'daʊtɪd] ADJ indudable.

undoubtedly [ʌn'daʊtɪdlɪ] ADV indudablemente, sin duda.

undreamt-of [ʌn'dremtɒv] ADJ no soñado, inimaginable, nunca pensado.

undress ['ʌn'dres] **1** N traje *m* de casa, desabillé *m*; (*Mil*) uniforme *m* (de diario); **in a state of ~** desnudo.
2 VT desnudar.
3 VI desnudarse.

undressed [ʌn'drest] ADJ *hide* sin adobar, sin curtir; *salad etc* sin salsa; **to get ~** desnudarse, quitarse los vestidos.

undrinkable ['ʌn'drɪŋkəbl] ADJ no potable, imbebible.

undue ['ʌn'djuː] ADJ indebido, excesivo.

undulate ['ʌndjʊleɪt] VI ondular, ondear.

undulating ['ʌndjʊleɪtɪŋ] ADJ ondulante, ondeante; *land* ondulado.

undulation [,ʌndjʊ'leɪʃən] N ondulación *f*.

undulatory ['ʌndjʊlətərɪ] ADJ ondulatorio.

unduly ['ʌn'djuːlɪ] ADV indebidamente, excesivamente, con exceso; **we are not ~ worried** no estamos mayormente preocupados.

undying [ʌn'daɪɪŋ] ADJ (*fig*) imperecedero, inmarcesible.

unearned ['ʌn'ɜːnd] ADJ no ganado; **~ income** renta *f* (no salarial), rentas *fpl*; **~ increment** plusvalía *f*.

unearth ['ʌn'ɜːθ] VT desenterrar; (*fig*) desenterrar, descubrir.

unearthly [ʌn'ɜːθlɪ] ADJ sobrenatural; *light etc* misterioso, fantástico; *hour etc* intempestivo, inverosímil.

unease [ʌn'iːz] N malestar *m*.

uneasily [ʌn'iːzɪlɪ] ADV inquietamente, con inquietud; **I noted ~ that ...** me inquieté al observar que ...

uneasiness [ʌn'iːzɪnɪs] N inquietud *f*; desasosiego *m*, intranquilidad *f*.

uneasy [ʌn'iːzɪ] ADJ *calm, peace, etc* inseguro; *sleep* poco tranquilo; *conscience* desasosegado, intranquilo; **to be ~** estar inquieto (*about* por), sentirse mal a gusto; **to become ~** empezar a inquietarse (*about* por); **I have an ~ feeling that ...** me inquieta la posibilidad de que + *subj*; **to make sb ~** intranquilizar a uno, turbar a uno.

uneatable ['ʌn'iːtəbl] ADJ incomible, que no se puede comer.

uneaten ['ʌn'iːtn] ADJ no comido, sin comer.

uneconomic(al) ['ʌn,iːkə'nɒmɪk(əl)] ADJ antieconómico.

unedifying ['ʌn'edɪfaɪɪŋ] ADJ indecoroso, poco edificante.

unedited [ʌn'edɪtɪd] ADJ inédito.

uneducated ['ʌn'edjʊkeɪtɪd] ADJ inculto, ignorante.

unemotional ['ʌnɪ'məʊʃənl] ADJ *character* impasible, reservado; *person* que no se deja emocionar; *account etc* objetivo.

unemotionally ['ʌnɪ'məʊʃnəlɪ] ADV: **to look on ~** mirar impasible, mirar sin dejarse emocionar.

unemployable ['ʌnɪm'plɔɪəbl] ADJ inútil para el trabajo.

unemployed ['ʌnɪm'plɔɪd] **1** ADJ *person* parado, sin empleo, desempleado; *capital etc* sin utilizar, no utilizado.
2 N: **the ~** los parados, los sin trabajo, los desempleados.

unemployment ['ʌnɪm'plɔɪmənt] **1** N paro *m* (forzoso), desempleo *m*, desocupación *f*.
2 ATTR: **~ benefit** (*Brit*) subsidio *m* de paro; **~ figures** cifras *fpl* del

paro.

unencumbered ['ʌnɪn'kʌmbəd] ADJ suelto, sin trabas; (*estate etc*) libre de gravamen; **~ by** no impedido por, sin el estorbo de.

unending [ʌn'endɪŋ] ADJ interminable, sin fin.

unendurable ['ʌnɪn'djʊərəbl] ADJ inaguantable, insufrible.

unengaged ['ʌnɪn'geɪdʒd] ADJ libre; sin compromiso.

un-English ['ʌn'ɪŋglɪʃ] ADJ poco inglés, indigno de un inglés.

unenlightened ['ʌnɪn'laɪtnd] ADJ *person, age* ignorante, poco instruido; *policy etc* poco ilustrado.

unenterprising ['ʌn'entəpraɪzɪŋ] ADJ *person* falto de iniciativa, poco emprendedor; *policy etc* tímido.

unenthusiastic ['ʌnɪn,θuːzɪ'æstɪk] ADJ poco entusiasta; **everybody seemed rather ~ about it** nadie se mostró mayormente entusiasmado con la idea.

unenthusiastically ['ʌnɪn,θuːzɪ'æstɪkəlɪ] ADV sin entusiasmo.

unenviable ['ʌn'envɪəbl] ADJ poco envidiable.

unequal ['ʌn'iːkwəl] ADJ desigual; desproporcionado; **to be ~ to a task** no estar a la altura de una tarea, no tener fuerzas para una tarea.

unequalled, (*US*) **unequaled** ['ʌn'iːkwəld] ADJ inigualado, sin par; **a record ~ by anybody** un historial mejor que el de nadie.

unequally ['ʌn'iːkwəlɪ] ADV desigualmente; desproporcionadamente.

unequivocal ['ʌnɪ'kwɪvəkəl] ADJ inequívoco.

unequivocally ['ʌnɪ'kwɪvəkəlɪ] ADV de modo inequívoco, sin dejar lugar a dudas.

unerring ['ʌn'ɜːrɪŋ] ADJ infalible.

UNESCO [juː'neskəʊ] N ABBR *of* **United Nations Educational, Scientific and Cultural Organization** Organización *f* de las Naciones Unidas para la Educación, la Ciencia y la Cultura, UNESCO *f*.

unescorted [,ʌnɪs'kɔːtɪd] ADJ sin escolta; sin compañía, sin compañero.

unessential ['ʌnɪ'senʃəl] **1** ADJ no esencial.
2 NPL: **the ~s** las cosas (*or* los aspectos *etc*) no esenciales.

unesthetic [,ʌniːs'θetɪk] ADJ (*US*) antiestético.

unethical ['ʌn'eθɪkəl] ADJ inmoral; poco honrado.

uneven ['ʌn'iːvən] ADJ desigual; *road etc* quebrado, ondulado, lleno de baches; *land* accidentado, escabroso.

unevenly ['ʌn'iːvənlɪ] ADV desigualmente.

unevenness ['ʌn'iːvənnɪs] N desigualdad *f*; escabrosidad *f*.

uneventful ['ʌnɪ'ventfʊl] ADJ sin incidentes notables, sin accidentes, tranquilo.

uneventfully ['ʌnɪ'ventfʊlɪ] ADV tranquilamente.

unexampled ['ʌnɪg'zɑːmpld] ADJ sin igual, sin precedente.

unexceptionable [,ʌnɪk'sepʃnəbl] ADJ intachable, impecable.

unexceptional [,ʌnɪk'sepʃənl] ADJ usual, corriente, normal.

unexciting ['ʌnɪk'saɪtɪŋ] ADJ poco emocionante, de poco interés.

unexpected ['ʌnɪks'pektɪd] ADJ inesperado, inopinado.

unexpectedly ['ʌnɪks'pektɪdlɪ] ADV inesperadamente, inopinadamente.

unexpended ['ʌnɪks'pendɪd] ADJ no gastado.

unexpired ['ʌnɪks'paɪəd] ADJ *bill* no vencido; *lease, ticket* no caducado.

unexplained ['ʌnɪks'pleɪnd] ADJ inexplicado.

unexploded ['ʌnɪks'pləʊdɪd] ADJ sin explotar.

unexploited ['ʌnɪks'plɔɪtɪd] ADJ inexplotado, sin explotar.

unexplored ['ʌnɪks'plɔːd] ADJ inexplorado.

unexposed ['ʌnɪks'pəʊzd] ADJ no descubierto; (*Phot*) inexpuesto.

unexpressed ['ʌnɪks'prest] ADJ no expresado; tácito.

unexpressive ['ʌnɪks'presɪv] ADJ inexpresivo.

unexpurgated ['ʌn'ekspɜːgeɪtɪd] ADJ sin expurgar, íntegro.

unfading [ʌn'feɪdɪŋ] ADJ (*fig*) inmarcesible, imperecedero.

unfailing [ʌn'feɪlɪŋ] ADJ indefectible; *zeal* infalible; *supply* inagotable.

unfailingly [ʌn'feɪlɪŋlɪ] ADV indefectiblemente; infaliblemente; inagotablemente; **to be ~ courteous** ser siempre cortés, no faltar en ningún momento a la cortesía.

▼ **unfair** ['ʌn'feə'] ADJ *comment, practice etc* injusto, no equitativo; *dismissal* improcedente; *competition* desleal; *play* sucio; *tactics* no aprobado, no permitido por las reglas; **that's very ~** eso es muy injusto; **how ~!** ¡no hay derecho!; **it was ~ of him to** + *infin* era injusto que él + *subj*.

unfairly ['ʌn'feəlɪ] ADV injustamente; deslealmente; de modo contrario a las reglas; **he was ~ condemned** se le condenó injustamente.

unfairness ['ʌn'feənɪs] N injusticia *f*; deslealtad *f*; suciedad *f*.

unfaithful ['ʌn'feɪθfʊl] ADJ infiel (*to a* to).

unfaithfulness ['ʌn'feɪθfʊlnɪs] N infidelidad *f*.

unfaltering [ʌn'fɔːltərɪŋ] ADJ resuelto, firme.

unfalteringly [ʌn'fɔːltərɪŋlɪ] ADV resueltamente, decididamente, firmemente.

unfamiliar ['ʌnfə'mɪlɪə'] ADJ *subject etc* desconocido, nuevo; **to be ~ with** desconocer, ignorar.

unfamiliarity ['ʌnfə,mɪlɪ'ærɪtɪ] N no familiaridad *f*, desconocimiento *m*.

➤ LANGUAGE IN USE: **unfair → 26.3**

unfashionable ['ʌn'fæʃnəbl] ADJ pasado de moda, fuera de moda; poco elegante; **it is now ~ to talk of ...** no está de moda ahora hablar de ...

unfasten ['ʌn'fɑːsn] VT (*untie*) desatar; *dress* desabrochar; *door* abrir; (*get free*) soltar; (*loosen*) aflojar.

unfathomable [ʌn'fæðəməbl] ADJ insondable.

unfathomed ['ʌn'fæðəmd] ADJ no sondado.

unfavourable, (*US*) **unfavorable** ['ʌn'feɪvərəbl] ADJ desfavorable, adverso; *outlook etc* poco propicio; *weather* malo.

unfavourably, (*US*) **unfavorably** ['ʌn'feɪvərəblɪ] ADV desfavorablemente; **to be ~ impressed** formarse una impresión desfavorable.

unfazed* ['ʌn'feɪzd] ADJ (*esp US*): **her criticism left him quite ~** sus críticas le dejaban tan pancho*; **she was completely ~ by the extraordinary events** se quedó como si nada ante unos sucesos tan extraordinarios.

unfeasible [ʌn'fiːzɪbl] ADJ no factible, inviable.

unfeeling [ʌn'fiːlɪŋ] ADJ insensible.

unfeelingly [ʌn'fiːlɪŋlɪ] ADV insensiblemente.

unfeigned [ʌn'feɪnd] ADJ sincero, no fingido, verdadero.

unfeignedly [ʌn'feɪnɪdlɪ] ADV sin fingimiento, verdaderamente.

unfeminine ['ʌn'femɪnɪn] ADJ poco femenino.

unfermented ['ʌnfə'mentɪd] ADJ no fermentado.

unfettered ['ʌn'fetəd] ADJ sin trabas.

unfilled ['ʌn'fɪld] ADJ: **~ orders** pedidos *mpl* pendientes.

unfinished ['ʌn'fɪnɪʃt] ADJ incompleto, inacabado, inconcluso, sin terminar; **I have 3 ~ letters** tengo 3 cartas por terminar; **we have ~ business** tenemos asuntos pendientes.

unfit ① ['ʌn'fɪt] ADJ (*incompetent*) incapaz, incompetente; (*unsuitable*) no apto (*for* para); (*useless*) inservible, inadecuado (*for* para); (*unworthy*) indigno (*to* de); (*ill*) enfermo, indispuesto, (*injured*) lesionado; **~ to eat** impropio para el consumo humano; **~ for publication** indigno de publicarse, no apto para publicar; **~ for military service** no apto para el servicio militar; **he is quite ~ to hold office** es totalmente incapaz de ocupar ningún cargo; **the road is ~ for lorries** el camino es intransitable para los camiones.
② [ʌn'fɪt] VT: **to ~ sb for sth** inhabilitar a uno para algo, incapacitar a uno para algo; **he is ~ted for such a career** no es apto para tal carrera.

unfitness ['ʌn'fɪtnɪs] N incapacidad *f*, incompetencia *f*; falta *f* de aptitud; inadecuación *f*; (*Med*) mala salud *f*, falta *f* de salud.

unfitting [ʌn'fɪtɪŋ] ADJ impropio.

unflagging [ʌn'flægɪŋ] ADJ incansable.

unflaggingly [ʌn'flægɪŋlɪ] ADV incansablemente.

unflappability* [ˌʌnflæpə'bɪlɪtɪ] N imperturbabilidad *f*.

unflappable* ['ʌn'flæpəbl] ADJ imperturbable.

unflattering ['ʌn'flætərɪŋ] ADJ poco lisonjero, poco grato.

unflatteringly ['ʌn'flætərɪŋlɪ] ADV de modo poco lisonjero.

unfledged ['ʌn'fledʒd] ADJ implume.

unflinching ['ʌn'flɪntʃɪŋ] ADJ impávido, resuelto.

unflinchingly ['ʌn'flɪntʃɪŋlɪ] ADV impávidamente, resueltamente.

unfocus(s)ed ['ʌn'fəʊkəst] ADJ *eyes* desenfocado; *desires* sin objetivo concreto, nada concreto; *energies* que carece de dirección.

unfold [ʌn'fəʊld] ① VT desplegar, desdoblar, abrir; *idea, plan* exponer; *secret* revelar; **to ~ a map on a table** extender un mapa sobre una mesa.
② VI desplegarse, desdoblarse, abrirse; (*view etc*) revelarse, extenderse.

unforced [ʌn'fɔːst] ADJ *style etc* natural, sin artificialidad; *error* no forzado.

unforeseeable ['ʌnfɔː'siːəbl] ADJ imprevisible.

unforeseen ['ʌnfɔː'siːn] ADJ imprevisto.

unforgettable ['ʌnfə'getəbl] ADJ inolvidable.

unforgettably ['ʌnfə'getəblɪ] ADV de manera inolvidable; **~ beautiful** tan hermoso que resulta inolvidable.

▼ **unforgivable** ['ʌnfə'gɪvəbl] ADJ imperdonable, indisculpable.

unforgiving ['ʌnfə'gɪvɪŋ] ADJ implacable.

unforgotten ['ʌnfə'gɒtn] ADJ no olvidado.

unformatted ['ʌn'fɔːmætɪd] ADJ no formateado, sin formatear.

unformed ['ʌn'fɔːmd] ADJ informe, sin formar aún.

unforthcoming ['ʌnfɔːθ'kʌmɪŋ] ADJ poco comunicativo.

unfortified ['ʌn'fɔːtɪfaɪd] ADJ no fortificado; *town* abierto.

▼ **unfortunate** [ʌn'fɔːtʃnɪt] ① ADJ *person* desgraciado, desdichado, desventurado; *event* funesto, desgraciado; *manner, remark* infeliz, inoportuno; **how very ~!** ¡qué mala suerte!, ¡qué desgracia!; **it is most ~ that ...** es muy de lamentar que + *subj*; **you have been most ~** has tenido muy mala suerte.
② N desgraciado *m*, -a *f*.

▼ **unfortunately** [ʌn'fɔːtʃnɪtlɪ] ADV por desgracia, desgraciadamente, desafortunadamente; **it is ~ true that ...** desgraciadamente es verdad que ...; **an ~ phrased statement** una declaración expresada en términos infelices.

unfounded ['ʌn'faʊndɪd] ADJ infundado, que carece de fundamento.

unframed ['ʌn'freɪmd] ADJ sin marco.

unfreeze ['ʌn'friːz] ① VT descongelar.
② VI descongelarse.

unfrequented ['ʌnfrɪ'kwentɪd] ADJ poco frecuentado.

unfriendliness ['ʌn'frendlɪnɪs] N hostilidad *f*.

unfriendly ['ʌn'frendlɪ] ADJ poco amistoso.

unfrock ['ʌn'frɒk] VT degradar, expulsar; *priest* secularizar, exclaustrar.

unfruitful [ʌn'fruːtfʊl] ADJ infructuoso.

unfulfilled [ʌnfʊl'fɪld] ADJ incumplido.

unfulfilling [ʌnfʊl'fɪlɪŋ] ADJ: **he finds his job ~** su trabaja no le llena (lo suficiente).

unfunny* [ʌn'fʌnɪ] ADJ nada divertido.

unfurl [ʌn'fɜːl] VT desplegar.

unfurnished ['ʌn'fɜːnɪʃt] ADJ desamueblado, sin muebles.

ungainliness [ʌn'geɪnlɪnɪs] N desgarbo *m*, torpeza *f*.

ungainly [ʌn'geɪnlɪ] ADJ desgarbado, torpe.

ungallant ['ʌn'gælənt] ADJ falto de cortesía, descortés.

ungenerous [ʌn'dʒenərəs] ADJ poco generoso.

ungentlemanly [ʌn'dʒentlmənlɪ] ADJ poco caballeroso, indigno de un caballero.

un-get-at-able* ['ʌnget'ætəbl] ADJ inaccesible.

ungird ['ʌn'gɜːd] (*irr: V* **gird**) VT desceñir.

unglazed ['ʌn'gleɪzd] ADJ no vidriado; *window* sin cristales.

ungodliness [ʌn'gɒdlɪnɪs] N impiedad *f*.

ungodly [ʌn'gɒdlɪ] ADJ impío, irreligioso; (*) atroz; **at this ~ hour** a hora tan inverosímil, a hora tan poco católica*.

ungovernable [ʌn'gʌvənəbl] ADJ ingobernable; *temper* incontrolable, irrefrenable.

ungracious ['ʌn'greɪʃəs] ADJ descortés, grosero; **it would be ~ to refuse** sería descortés no aceptarlo.

ungraciously [ʌn'greɪʃəslɪ] ADV descortésmente.

ungrammatical ['ʌngrə'mætɪkəl] ADJ incorrecto, agramatical, antigramatical.

ungrammatically ['ʌngrə'mætɪkəlɪ] ADV incorrectamente; **to talk Spanish ~** hablar español con poca corrección.

ungrateful [ʌn'greɪtfʊl] ADJ desagradecido, ingrato.

ungratefully [ʌn'greɪtfəlɪ] ADV desagradecidamente.

ungrudging ['ʌn'grʌdʒɪŋ] ADJ liberal, generoso; sin escatimar; *support etc* incondicional.

ungrudgingly ['ʌn'grʌdʒɪŋlɪ] ADV liberalmente, generosamente; de buena gana, incondicionalmente.

unguarded ['ʌn'gɑːdɪd] ADJ (*Mil*) indefenso, no defendido, sin protección; *remark etc* imprudente; **in an ~ moment** en un momento de descuido.

unguent ['ʌŋgwənt] N ungüento *m*.

ungulate ['ʌŋgjʊleɪt] ① ADJ ungulado.
② N ungulado *m*.

unhampered ['ʌn'hæmpəd] ADJ libre, sin estorbos; **~ by** no estorbado por.

unhand [ʌn'hænd] VT soltar; **~ me, sir!** ¡suélteme, señor!

unhandy [ʌn'hændɪ] ADJ *person* desmañado; *thing* incómodo; **to be ~ with sth** ser desmañado en el manejo de algo.

unhappily [ʌn'hæpɪlɪ] ADV (*miserably*) infelizmente; (*unfortunately*) desgraciadamente.

unhappiness [ʌn'hæpɪnɪs] N desdicha *f*, tristeza *f*; desgracia *f*.

▼ **unhappy** [ʌn'hæpɪ] ADJ *person* infeliz, desdichado; *childhood etc* desgraciado; (*ill-fated*) malhadado, infausto; *remark etc* infeliz, inoportuno; **that ~ time** aquella triste época; **to be ~ about sth** inquietarse por algo, no aceptar algo de buena gana; **we are ~ about the decision** no nos gusta la decisión; **to make sb ~** poner triste a uno, amargar la vida a uno; **she was ~ in her marriage** era desgraciada en su matrimonio.

unharmed ['ʌn'hɑːmd] ADJ *person* ileso, incólume; *thing* indemne; **to escape ~** salir ileso.

unharness [ʌn'hɑːnɪs] VT desguarnecer.

UNHCR N ABBR *of* **United Nations High Commission for Refugees** Alta Comisión *f* de las Naciones Unidas para los Refugiados.

unhealthy [ʌn'helθɪ] ADJ *person* enfermizo; *place* malsano, insalubre; *complexion* de aspecto poco sano; *curiosity* morboso.

unheard [ʌn'hɜːd] ADJ: **to condemn sb ~** condenar a uno sin oírle.

unheard-of [ʌn'hɜːdɒv] ADJ inaudito.

unheated ['ʌn'hiːtɪd] ADJ sin calentar; sin calefacción.

unheeded [ʌn'hiːdɪd] ADJ desatendido; **the warning went ~** nadie prestó atención a la advertencia, nadie hizo caso de la advertencia.

unheeding [ʌn'hiːdɪŋ] ADJ desatento, sordo; **they passed by ~** pasaron sin prestar atención.

unhelpful ['ʌn'helpfʊl] ADJ *person* poco servicial; nada simpático; *advice etc* inútil.

unhelpfully ['ʌn'helpfʊlɪ] ADV poco servicialmente.

unhelpfulness ['ʌn'helpfʊlnɪs] N falta *f* de espíritu servicial; falta *f* de simpatía; inutilidad *f*.

unheralded ['ʌn'herəldɪd] ADJ: **to arrive ~** llegar sin dar aviso.

unhesitating [ʌn'hezɪteɪtɪŋ] ADJ *person etc* resuelto; *reply etc* pronto.

➤ LANGUAGE IN USE: **unforgivable** → 18.3   **unfortunate:** 1 → 18.1   **unfortunately** → 18.2   **unhappy** → 14

unhesitatingly [ʌn'hezɪteɪtɪŋlɪ] ADV: **he said ~** dijo sin vacilar, dijo decidido.

unhindered ['ʌn'hɪndəd] ADJ libre, sin estorbos; **~ by** no estorbado por.

unhinge [ʌn'hɪndʒ] VT desquiciar; (fig) mind trastornar; person trastornar el juicio de.

unhinged ['ʌn'hɪndʒd] ADJ (mad) loco.

unhip* [ˌʌn'hɪp] ADJ fuera de onda*, que no está en la onda*.

unhistorical ['ʌnhɪs'tɒrɪkəl] ADJ antihistórico, que no tiene nada de histórico.

unhitch ['ʌn'hɪtʃ] VT desenganchar.

unholy [ʌn'həʊlɪ] ADJ impío; (*) atroz.

unhook ['ʌn'hʊk] VT desenganchar; (from wall etc) descolgar; dress desabrochar.

unhoped-for [ʌn'həʊptfɔːʳ] ADJ inesperado.

unhopeful [ʌn'həʊpfʊl] ADJ prospect poco alentador, poco prometedor; person pesimista.

unhorse ['ʌn'hɔːs] VT desarzonar.

unhurried ['ʌn'hʌrɪd] ADJ lento, pausado, parsimonioso.

unhurriedly ['ʌn'hʌrɪdlɪ] ADV lentamente, pausadamente, con parsimonia.

unhurt ['ʌn'hɜːt] ADJ ileso, incólume; **to escape ~** salir ileso.

unhygienic ['ʌnhaɪ'dʒiːnɪk] ADJ antihigiénico.

uni... ['juːnɪ] PREF uni...

unicameral ['juːnɪ'kæmərəl] ADJ unicameral.

UNICEF ['juːnɪsef] N ABBR of **United Nations International Children's Emergency Fund** Fondo m Internacional de las Naciones Unidas de Socorro a la Infancia, UNICEF m.

unicellular ['juːnɪ'seljʊləʳ] ADJ unicelular.

unicorn ['juːnɪkɔːn] N unicornio m.

unicycle ['juːnɪˌsaɪkl] N monociclo m.

unidentifiable ['ʌnaɪˌdentɪ'faɪəbl] ADJ no identificable.

unidentified ['ʌnaɪ'dentɪfaɪd] ADJ sin identificar, no identificado aún.

unidirectional [ˌjuːnɪdɪ'rekʃənl] ADJ unidireccional.

unification [ˌjuːnɪfɪ'keɪʃən] N unificación f.

uniform ['juːnɪfɔːm] [1] ADJ uniforme; igual, constante; **to make sth ~** hacer algo uniforme, uniformar algo.
[2] N uniforme m; **in ~** (fig) en filas; **in full ~** de gran uniforme.

uniformed ['juːnɪfɔːmd] ADJ uniformado.

uniformity [ˌjuːnɪ'fɔːmɪtɪ] N uniformidad f.

uniformly ['juːnɪfɔːmlɪ] ADV uniformemente, de modo uniforme.

unify ['juːnɪfaɪ] VT unificar, unir.

unifying ['juːnɪfaɪɪŋ] ADJ factor etc unificador.

unilateral ['juːnɪ'lætərəl] ADJ unilateral; **~ disarmament** desarme m unilateral.

unilateralism ['juːnɪ'lætərəlɪzəm] N opinión f (or campaña f etc) a favor del desarme unilateral.

unilateralist ['juːnɪ'lætərəlɪst] N persona f que está a favor del desarme unilateral.

unilaterally ['juːnɪ'lætərəlɪ] ADV unilateralmente.

unilingual [ˌjuːnɪ'lɪŋgwəl] ADJ monolingüe.

unimaginable [ˌʌnɪ'mædʒməbl] ADJ inconcebible, inimaginable.

unimaginably [ˌʌnɪ'mædʒməblɪ] ADV inimaginablemente, inconcebiblemente.

unimaginative ['ʌnɪ'mædʒmətɪv] ADJ poco imaginativo.

unimaginatively ['ʌnɪ'mædʒmətɪvlɪ] ADV poco imaginativamente.

unimaginativeness ['ʌnɪ'mædʒnətɪvnɪs] N falta f de imaginación.

unimpaired ['ʌnɪm'pɛəd] ADJ no disminuido; no afectado; intacto, entero.

unimpeachable [ˌʌnɪm'piːtʃəbl] ADJ irrecusable, intachable; **from an ~ source** de fuente fidedigna.

unimpeded ['ʌnɪm'piːdɪd] ADJ sin estorbo.

unimportant ['ʌnɪm'pɔːtənt] ADJ sin importancia, insignificante.

unimposing ['ʌnɪm'pəʊzɪŋ] ADJ (not big) poco impresionante; (drab, boring) con poca gracia.

unimpressed ['ʌnɪm'prest] ADJ no impresionado; **he remained ~** no se convenció; **I remain ~ by the new building** el nuevo edificio no me impresiona.

unimpressive ['ʌnɪm'presɪv] ADJ poco impresionante, poco convincente; person soso, insignificante.

unimproved [ˌʌnɪm'pruːvd] ADJ land (not drained) sin drenar; (not treated) sin abonar.

uninfluenced ['ʌn'ɪnflʊənst] ADJ: **~ by any argument** no afectado por ningún argumento; **a style ~ by any other** un estilo no influido por ningún otro.

uninformative ['ʌnɪn'fɔːmətɪv] ADJ poco informativo.

uninformed ['ʌnɪn'fɔːmd] ADJ character desinformado, poco instruido, ignorante; **to be ~ about sth** no estar enterado de algo, desconocer algo.

uninhabitable ['ʌnɪn'hæbɪtəbl] ADJ inhabitable.

uninhabited ['ʌnɪn'hæbɪtɪd] ADJ deshabitado, inhabitado; desierto.

uninhibited ['ʌnɪn'hɪbɪtɪd] ADJ nada cohibido, desinhibido,

totalmente libre.

uninitiated ['ʌnɪ'nɪʃɪeɪtɪd] [1] ADJ no iniciado.
[2] N: **the ~** los no iniciados.

uninjured ['ʌn'ɪndʒəd] ADJ ileso; **to escape ~** salir ileso.

uninspired ['ʌnɪn'spaɪəd] ADJ sin inspiración, soso, mediocre.

uninspiring ['ʌnɪn'spaɪərɪŋ] ADJ nada inspirador.

uninsured ['ʌnɪn'ʃʊəd] ADJ no asegurado.

unintelligent ['ʌnɪn'telɪdʒənt] ADJ ininteligente, poco inteligente.

unintelligibility ['ʌnɪnˌtelɪdʒə'bɪlɪtɪ] N ininteligibilidad f, incomprensibilidad f.

unintelligible ['ʌnɪn'telɪdʒəbl] ADJ ininteligible, incomprensible.

unintelligibly ['ʌnɪn'telɪdʒəblɪ] ADV de modo ininteligible, de modo incomprensible.

unintended ['ʌnɪn'tendɪd] ADJ, **unintentional** ['ʌnɪn'tenʃənl] ADJ involuntario, no intencional; **it was ~** fue sin querer.

unintentionally ['ʌnɪn'tenʃnəlɪ] ADV sin querer.

uninterested [ʌn'ɪntrɪstɪd] ADJ sin interés; **to be ~ in a subject** no tener interés en un asunto.

uninteresting ['ʌn'ɪntrɪstɪŋ] ADJ poco interesante, falto de interés.

uninterrupted ['ʌnˌɪntə'rʌptɪd] ADJ ininterrumpido, sin interrupción.

uninterruptedly ['ʌnˌɪntə'rʌptɪdlɪ] ADV ininterrumpidamente.

uninvited ['ʌnɪn'vaɪtɪd] ADJ guest no invitado; comment gratuito; **to do sth ~** hacer algo sin ser rogado; **they came to the party ~** vinieron al guateque sin ser invitados.

uninviting ['ʌnɪn'vaɪtɪŋ] ADJ poco atractivo.

union ['juːnjən] [1] N unión f; (marriage) enlace m; (Pol) sindicato m, gremio m obrero; (Mech) unión f, manguito m de unión; **the U~** (USA) la Unión.
[2] ATTR sindical, de los sindicatos, gremial; **~ catalog(ue)** catálogo m colectivo, catálogo m conjunto; **~ member** miembro mf del sindicato, sindicalista mf; **~ membership** sindicalización f; **~ shop** (US) taller m de obreros agremiados, taller m de afiliación (sindical) obligatoria; **~ suit** (US) prenda f interior de cuerpo entero.

unionism ['juːnjənɪzəm] N (a) V trade(s) unionism. (b) U~ (Brit Pol) unionismo m.

unionist ['juːnjənɪst] [1] N (a) V trade(s) unionist. (b) U~ (Brit Pol) unionista mf.
[2] ADJ (Brit Pol) unionista.

unionize ['juːnjənaɪz] [1] VT sindicar, agremiar.
[2] VI sindicarse, agremiarse.

Union Jack ['juːnjən'dʒæk] N (Brit) bandera del Reino Unido.

Union of South Africa ['juːnjənˌsaʊθ'æfrɪkə] N Unión f Sudafricana.

Union of Soviet Socialist Republics ['juːnjənəv'səʊvɪət-'səʊʃəlɪstrɪ'pʌblɪks] N Unión f de Repúblicas Socialistas Soviéticas.

unique [juː'niːk] ADJ único.

uniquely [juː'niːklɪ] ADV especialmente.

uniqueness [juː'niːknɪs] N unicidad f.

unisex ['juːnɪseks] ADJ unisex(o).

unison ['juːnɪzn] N armonía f; (Mus) unisonancia f; **to sing in ~** cantar al unísono; **to act in ~ with sb** obrar de acuerdo con uno.

unissued ['ʌn'ɪʃuːd] ADJ: **~ capital** capital m no emitido.

unit ['juːnɪt] [1] N unidad f (also Math, Mil); (Elec measurement) unidad f; (Mech, Elec) grupo m; (Univ) unidad f de valor; **~ of account** unidad f de cuenta.
[2] ATTR: **~ charge**, **~ cost** costo m por unidad; costo m unitario; **~ furniture** muebles mpl de elementos adicionables, muebles mpl combinados; **~ price** precio m unitario; **~ trust** (Brit) fondo m de inversión mobiliaria.

UNITA [juː'niːtə] N ABBR of **União Nacional para a Independencia Total de Angola** UNITA f, Unita f.

Unitarian [ˌjuːnɪ'tɛərɪən] [1] ADJ unitario.
[2] N unitario m, -a f.

Unitarianism [ˌjuːnɪ'tɛərɪənɪzəm] N unitarismo m.

unitary ['juːnɪtərɪ] ADJ unitario; **~ labour costs** costes mpl laborales unitarios.

unite [juː'naɪt] [1] VT unir, juntar; (marry) casar; parts of country unificar.
[2] VI unirse, juntarse; **to ~ against sb** unirse para hacer frente a uno; **to ~ in doing sth** unirse para hacer algo, concertarse para hacer algo.

united [juː'naɪtɪd] ADJ unido.

United Arab Emirates [juː'naɪtɪd'ærəbe'mɪərɪts] NPL Emiratos mpl Árabes Unidos.

United Arab Republic [juː'naɪtɪd'ærəbrɪ'pʌblɪk] N República f Árabe Unida.

United Kingdom [juː'naɪtɪd'kɪŋdəm] N Reino m Unido (Inglaterra, Gales, Escocia, Irlanda del Norte).

United Nations [juː'naɪtɪd'neɪʃənz] NPL Naciones fpl Unidas.

United States (of America) [juː'naɪtɪd'steɪts(əvə'merɪkə)] NPL (Los) Estados mpl Unidos (de América).

unity ['juːnɪtɪ] N unidad *f*; unión *f*; armonía *f*; ~ **of place** unidad *f* de lugar; ~ **of time** unidad *f* de tiempo.

Univ. ABBR *of* **University.**

univalent ['juːnɪ'veɪlənt] ADJ univalente.

univalve ['juːnɪvælv] 1 ADJ univalvo.

2 N molusco *m* univalvo.

universal [ˌjuːnɪ'vɜːsəl] 1 ADJ universal; ~ **heir** heredero *m* único; ~ **joint** junta *f* cardán, junta *f* universal; **U~ Postal Union** Unión *f* Postal Universal; ~ **product code** (*US*) código *m* de barras; ~ **suffrage** sufragio *m* universal; **its use has been ~ since 1900** desde 1900 tiene un empleo general; **soap is now ~** el jabón se emplea ahora en todas partes; **to become ~** universalizarse, generalizarse; **to make ~** universalizar, generalizar.

2 N universal *m*.

universality [ˌjuːnɪvɜː'sælɪtɪ] N universalidad *f*.

universalize [ˌjuːnɪ'vɜːsəlaɪz] VT universalizar.

universally [ˌjuːnɪ'vɜːsəlɪ] ADV universalmente; generalmente, comúnmente; ~ **known** mundialmente conocido.

universe ['juːnɪvɜːs] N universo *m*.

university [ˌjuːnɪ'vɜːsɪtɪ] 1 N universidad *f*; **to be at ~** estar en la universidad; **to go to ~** ir a la universidad.

2 ATTR *degree, library, year etc* universitario; *professor, student etc* de universidad; ~ **entrance** acceso *m* a la universidad; ~ **town** ciudad *f* que tiene universidad.

unjust ['ʌn'dʒʌst] ADJ injusto.

unjustifiable [ʌn'dʒʌstɪfaɪəbl] ADJ injustificable.

unjustifiably [ʌn'dʒʌstɪfaɪəblɪ] ADV injustificadamente.

unjustified ['ʌn'dʒʌstɪfaɪd] ADJ injustificado; *text* no alineado, no justificado.

unjustly ['ʌn'dʒʌstlɪ] ADV injustamente.

unkempt ['ʌn'kempt] ADJ *appearance* desaseado, descuidado; *hair* despeinado.

unkind [ʌn'kaɪnd] ADJ (*of person etc*) poco amable, nada amistoso; poco compasivo; cruel, despiadado; *remark, word, blow* cruel; *climate* riguroso; **that was very ~ of him** en eso no se mostró nada amable; **he was ~ enough to** + *infin* fue lo bastante cruel como para + *infin*.

unkindly [ʌn'kaɪndlɪ] ADV cruelmente; **don't take it ~ if ...** no lo tome a mal si ...

unkindness [ʌn'kaɪndnɪs] N (**a**) (*quality*) falta *f* de amabilidad; crueldad *f*, rigor *m*, severidad *f*. (**b**) (*act*) acto *m* de crueldad.

unknowable ['ʌn'nəʊəbl] ADJ inconocible; insondable, impenetrable; **the ~** lo inconocible.

unknowing ['ʌn'nəʊɪŋ] ADJ inconsciente.

unknowingly ['ʌn'nəʊɪŋlɪ] ADV sin querer; sin saberlo; **he did it all ~** lo hizo sin darse cuenta.

unknown ['ʌn'nəʊn] 1 ADJ desconocido, ignorado; ignoto; incógnito; **the ~ soldier** el soldado desconocido; **towards ~ regions** hacia regiones desconocidas; **a substance ~ to science** una sustancia ignorada por la ciencia; ~ **quantity** (*Math, fig*) incógnita *f*.

2 ADV: ~ **to me** sin saberlo yo.

3 N (*person*) desconocido *m*, -a *f*; (*Math, also fig*) incógnita *f*; **the ~** lo desconocido; **to go out into the ~** salir a explorar tierras incógnitas.

unlace ['ʌn'leɪs] VT desenlazar; *shoes* desatar los cordones de.

unladen ['ʌn'leɪdn] ADJ vacío, sin cargamento.

unladylike ['ʌn'leɪdɪlaɪk] ADJ vulgar, ordinario, impropio de una señora.

unlamented ['ʌnlə'mentɪd] ADJ no llorado, no lamentado.

unlatch ['ʌn'lætʃ] VT *door* abrir, alzar el pestillo de, abrir levantando el picaporte de.

unlawful ['ʌn'lɔːfʊl] ADJ ilegal, ilícito.

unlawfully ['ʌn'lɔːfəlɪ] ADV ilegalmente, ilícitamente.

unleaded [ˌʌn'ledɪd] 1 ADJ *petrol* sin plomo.

2 N gasolina *f* sin plomo.

unlearn ['ʌn'lɜːn] VT desaprender, olvidar.

unlearned ['ʌn'lɜːnɪd] ADJ indocto, ignorante.

unleash ['ʌn'liːʃ] VT *dog* desatraillar, soltar; (*fig*) desencadenar, desatar.

unleavened ['ʌn'levnd] ADJ ázimo, sin levadura; ~ **bread** pan *m* ázimo, pan *m* cenceño.

unless [ən'les] CONJ a menos que + *subj*; a no ser que + *subj*; ~ **you can find another one** a menos que puedas encontrar otro; ~ **I am mistaken** si no me equivoco; ~ **I hear to the contrary** a menos que me digan lo contrario.

unlettered ['ʌn'letəd] ADJ indocto.

unlicensed ['ʌn'laɪsənst] ADJ sin permiso, sin licencia, no autorizado.

▼ **unlike** ['ʌn'laɪk] 1 ADJ desemejante, distinto; (*Math*) de signo contrario; **they are quite ~** son muy distintos, no se parecen en nada.

▼ 2 PREP a diferencia de; **it's quite ~ him** no es nada característico de él; **the photo is quite ~ him** la foto no le representa en absoluto; **I, ~ others, ...** yo, a diferencia de otros ...

unlikeable ['ʌn'laɪkəbl] ADJ antipático.

unlikelihood [ʌn'laɪklɪhʊd] N, **unlikeliness** [ʌn'laɪklɪnɪs] N im-

probabilidad *f*.

▼ **unlikely** [ʌn'laɪklɪ] ADJ improbable, poco probable; difícil; (*odd*) inverosímil; **it is most ~** no es nada probable; **I think it very ~** lo creo muy poco probable; **it is ~ that he will come, he is ~ to come** no es probable que venga; **wearing a most ~ hat** con un sombrero inverosímil.

unlimited [ʌn'lɪmɪtɪd] ADJ ilimitado, sin límite; ~ **company** compañía *f* ilimitada; ~ **liability** (*Comm*) responsabilidad *f* ilimitada.

unlined ['ʌn'laɪnd] ADJ *coat* sin forro; *face* sin arrugas; *paper* sin rayar.

unlisted ['ʌn'lɪstɪd] ADJ: ~ **company** sociedad *f* sin cotización oficial, compañía *f* no cotizable; ~ **number** (*US*) número *m* que no figura en la guía telefónica; ~ **securities** valores *mpl* no inscritos en bolsa.

unlit ['ʌn'lɪt] ADJ oscuro, sin luz; *street* sin alumbrado, sin faroles.

unload ['ʌn'ləʊd] 1 VT descargar; (*get rid of*) deshacerse de.

2 VI descargar.

unloaded ['ʌn'ləʊdɪd] ADJ *gun* descargado; *truck, ship* descargado, sin carga.

unloading ['ʌn'ləʊdɪŋ] N descarga *f*.

unlock ['ʌn'lɒk] VT abrir (con llave); *mystery etc* resolver.

unlooked-for [ʌn'lʊktfɔːr] ADJ inesperado, inopinado.

unloose ['ʌn'luːs] VT, **unloosen** [ʌn'luːsn] VT aflojar, desatar, soltar.

unlovable ['ʌn'lʌvəbl] ADJ antipático, poco amable.

unloved ['ʌn'lʌvd] ADJ no amado; **to feel ~** sentirse rechazado.

unlovely ['ʌn'lʌvlɪ] ADJ feo, desgarbado, sin atractivo.

unloving ['ʌn'lʌvɪŋ] ADJ nada cariñoso.

unluckily [ʌn'lʌkɪlɪ] ADV: ~ **I couldn't go** desgraciadamente no pude ir; **it was ~ left at the station** por desgracia quedó olvidado en la estación.

unluckiness [ʌn'lʌkɪnɪs] N mala suerte *f*; lo nefasto.

unlucky [ʌn'lʌkɪ] ADJ *person, stroke etc* desgraciado; (*ill-omened*) funesto, nefasto; **a very ~ day** un día de los menos propicios; **to be ~** (*person*) tener mala suerte; **I've been ~ all my life** toda la vida he sido desgraciado; **how very ~!** ¡qué mala suerte!; **it's ~ to go under ladders** pasar por debajo de las escaleras trae mala suerte.

unmade ['ʌn'meɪd] ADJ *bed* deshecho; *road* sin alquitranar.

unmake ['ʌn'meɪk] (*irr: V* **make**) VT deshacer.

unman ['ʌn'mæn] VT (**a**) (*cow*) acobardar. (**b**) *post etc* desguarnecer.

unmanageable [ʌn'mænɪdʒəbl] ADJ (*unwieldy*) inmanejable, difícil de manejar; *person* indócil, ingobernable.

unmanly ['ʌn'mænlɪ] ADJ afeminado; cobarde.

unmanned ['ʌn'mænd] ADJ no tripulado.

unmannerly [ʌn'mænəlɪ] ADJ descortés, mal educado.

unmarked ['ʌn'mɑːkt] ADJ sin marcar; *police-car* camuflado; (*uninjured*) ileso; (*Sport*) desmarcado.

unmarketable ['ʌn'mɑːkɪtəbl] ADJ invendible.

unmarriageable ['ʌn'mærɪdʒəbl] ADJ incasable.

unmarried ['ʌn'mærɪd] ADJ soltero; ~ **mother** madre *f* soltera; **the ~ state** el estado de soltero, el celibato.

unmask ['ʌn'mɑːsk] 1 VT desenmascarar (*also fig*).

2 VI quitarse la máscara, descubrirse.

unmast ['ʌn'mɑːst] VT desarbolar.

unmatched ['ʌn'mætʃt] ADJ incomparable, sin par.

unmemorable [ʌn'memərəbl] ADJ nada memorable, indigno de ser recordado.

unmentionable [ʌn'menʃnəbl] 1 ADJ que no se puede mencionar; indescriptible, indecible.

2 NPL: ~**s** (*hum*) prendas *fpl* íntimas, pantalones *mpl*.

unmerciful [ʌn'mɜːsɪfʊl] ADJ despiadado.

unmercifully [ʌn'mɜːsɪfəlɪ] ADV despiadadamente.

unmerited ['ʌn'merɪtɪd] ADJ inmerecido.

unmet [ʌn'met] ADJ *needs, demands* insatisfecho, incumplido; **to go ~** dejar insatisfecho, quedar sin cumplir.

unmethodical ['ʌnmɪ'θɒdɪkəl] ADJ poco metódico, desordenado.

unmindful [ʌn'maɪndfʊl] ADJ: **to be ~ of** no pensar en; ~ **of the danger, he ...** él, sin pensar en el peligro ...

unmissable* [ˌʌn'mɪsəbəl] ADJ (*Brit*) *event, film* que no se lo puede uno perder; **it was an ~ chance/opportunity** era una oportunidad que no podíamos perder.

unmistak(e)able [ˌʌnmɪs'teɪkəbl] ADJ inconfundible, inequívoco.

unmistak(e)ably [ˌʌnmɪs'teɪkəblɪ] ADV de modo inconfundible; **it is ~ mine** sin duda alguna es mío.

unmitigated [ʌn'mɪtɪgeɪtɪd] ADJ no mitigado, absoluto; *dislike etc* implacable; *rogue etc* redomado; **it was an ~ disaster** fue un desastre total.

unmixed ['ʌn'mɪkst] ADJ sin mezcla, puro.

unmolested ['ʌnmə'lestɪd] ADJ tranquilo, seguro; sin ser abordado; **to do sth ~** hacer algo sin ser molestado por otros.

unmotivated ['ʌn'məʊtɪveɪtɪd] ADJ inmotivado, sin motivo.

unmounted ['ʌn'maʊntɪd] ADJ *rider* desmontado; *stone* sin engastar; *photo, stamp* sin pegar.

unmourned ['ʌn'mɔːnd] ADJ no llorado.

unmoved ['ʌn'muːvd] ADJ impasible; **to remain ~ by** no dejarse conmover por, seguir siendo insensible a; **it leaves me ~** me trae sin cuidado.

unmoving [ʌn'muːvɪŋ] ADJ inmóvil.

unmusical ['ʌn'mjuːzɪkəl] ADJ (*Mus*) inarmónico; *person* poco aficionado a la música; sin oído para la música.

unmuzzle [,ʌn'mʌzl] VT *dog* quitar el bozal a; (*fig*) *press etc* quitar la mordaza a; **~d** sin bozal; (*fig*) libre, sin mordaza.

unnamed ['ʌn'neɪmd] ADJ sin nombre, innominado.

unnatural [ʌn'nætʃrəl] ADJ antinatural, no natural, contrario a la naturaleza; anormal; *habit, vice* perverso; *person's manner* afectado.

unnaturally [ʌn'nætʃrəlɪ] ADV de manera poco natural; anormalmente; perversamente; **not ~ he was cross** era lógico que se enfadara, lógicamente se enfadó.

unnavigable ['ʌn'nævɪgəbl] ADJ innavegable.

unnecessarily [ʌn'nesɪsərɪlɪ] ADV innecesariamente, sin necesidad.

unnecessary [ʌn'nesɪsərɪ] ADJ innecesario, inútil; **it is ~ to add that ...** huelga añadir que ...

unneighbourly, (*US***) unneighborly** ['ʌn'neɪbəlɪ] ADJ poco amistoso, impropio de un buen vecino.

unnerve ['ʌn'nɜːv] VT acobardar, amilanar.

unnerved ['ʌn'nɜːvd] ADJ acobardado, desanimado.

unnerving ['ʌn'nɜːvɪŋ] ADJ desconcertante.

unnervingly ['ʌn'nɜːvɪŋlɪ] ADV: **~ quiet/calm** de una frialdad/calma desconcertante.

unnoticed ['ʌn'nəʊtɪst] ADJ inadvertido, desapercibido; **to go ~, to pass ~** pasar inadvertido.

unnumbered ['ʌn'nʌmbəd] ADJ sin numerar; (*countless*) innumerable.

UNO N ABBR *of* **United Nations Organization** Organización *f* de las Naciones Unidas, ONU *f*.

unobjectionable ['ʌnəb'dʒekʃnəbl] ADJ intachable, impecable; aceptable; *person etc* inofensivo.

unobservant ['ʌnəb'zɜːvənt] ADJ poco observador; distraído, que no se fija.

unobserved ['ʌnəb'zɜːvd] ADJ desapercibido; **to get away ~** lograr escapar inadvertido.

unobstructed ['ʌnəb'strʌktɪd] ADJ libre, sin obstáculos, despejado.

unobtainable ['ʌnəb'teɪnəbl] ADJ (*Comm etc*) agotado, que no se puede conseguir.

unobtrusive ['ʌnəb'truːsɪv] ADJ discreto, modesto.

unobtrusively ['ʌnəb'truːsɪvlɪ] ADV discretamente, modestamente.

unoccupied ['ʌn'ɒkjʊpaɪd] ADJ *house* deshabitado; *territory* despoblado, sin habitantes, (*Pol*) libre, sin colonizar; *seat, place* libre; *post* vacante; *person* desocupado, ocioso.

unofficial ['ʌnə'fɪʃəl] ADJ extraoficial, no oficial, oficioso; **~ strike** huelga *f* no oficial; **from an ~ source** de fuente oficiosa.

unofficially ['ʌnə'fɪʃəlɪ] ADV de modo extraoficial.

unopened ['ʌn'əʊpənd] ADJ sin abrir.

unopposed ['ʌnə'pəʊzd] ADJ sin oposición; sin contrincante; (*Mil*) sin encontrar resistencia; **to be returned ~** (*Parl*) ganar un escaño por ser el único candidato que se presenta.

unorganized ['ʌn'ɔːgənaɪzd] ADJ no organizado.

unoriginal ['ʌnə'rɪdʒɪnəl] ADJ poco original.

unorthodox ['ʌn'ɔːθədɒks] ADJ poco ortodoxo, nada convencional; (*Eccl*) heterodoxo.

unostentatious ['ʌn,ɒsten'teɪʃəs] ADJ modesto, sin ostentación.

unpack ['ʌn'pæk] **1** VT desembalar, desempaquetar, desempacar (*LAm*); *suitcase* vaciar, deshacer.

2 VI deshacer las maletas, desempacar (*LAm*).

unpacking ['ʌn'pækɪŋ] N desembalaje *m*; desempaquetado *m*.

unpaid ['ʌn'peɪd] ADJ *bill* por pagar, no pagado; *debt* no liquidado; *work, person* no retribuido.

unpalatable [ʌn'pælɪtəbl] ADJ *food* incomible, de mal sabor; (*fig*) desagradable, intragable, nada grato; **the ~ truth** la verdad lisa y llana.

unparalleled [ʌn'pærəleld] ADJ sin paralelo, incomparable, sin par; sin precedentes; **this is ~ in our history** esto no tiene precedentes en nuestra historia.

unpardonable [ʌn'pɑːdnəbl] ADJ imperdonable, indisculpable.

unpardonably [ʌn'pɑːdnəblɪ] ADV imperdonablemente.

unparliamentary ['ʌn,pɑːlə'mentərɪ] ADJ antiparlamentario.

unpatented ['ʌn,peɪtntɪd] ADJ sin patentar.

unpatriotic ['ʌn,pætrɪ'ɒtɪk] ADJ antipatriótico.

unpatriotically ['ʌn,pætrɪ'ɒtɪkəlɪ] ADV de modo antipatriótico.

unpaved ['ʌn'peɪvd] ADJ sin pavimentar.

unperceived ['ʌnpə'siːvd] ADJ inadvertido, desapercibido.

unperturbed ['ʌnpɜː'tɜːbd] ADJ impertérrito; **he carried on ~** continuó sin alterarse, siguió sin inmutarse; **~ by this disaster ...** sin dejarse desanimar por esta catástrofe ...

unpick ['ʌn'pɪk] VT *seam* descoser.

unpin ['ʌn'pɪn] VT desprender; quitar los alfileres de.

unplaced ['ʌn'pleɪst] ADJ (*Sport*) no colocado.

unplanned ['ʌn'plænd] ADJ sin planear; imprevisto.

unplayable ['ʌn'pleɪəbl] ADJ *pitch* en condiciones tan malas que está

inservible.

▼ **unpleasant** [ʌn'pleznt] ADJ desagradable; repugnante; *person* (*by character*) antipático, (*in words etc*) grosero, mal educado; **he was ~ to her** se portó groseramente con ella; **he had some very ~ things to say** hizo unas observaciones de las más desagradables; **it was a most ~ hour** fue una hora muy desagradable.

unpleasantly [ʌn'plezntlɪ] ADV desagradablemente; **'No', he said ~** 'No', dijo en tono nada amistoso; **the bomb fell ~ close** cayó la bomba lo bastante cerca como para inquietarnos.

unpleasantness [ʌn'plezntnɪs] N lo desagradable; lo repugnante; antipatía *f*; (*quarrel*) desavenencia *f*, disgusto *m*; **that ~ with the conductor** aquel disgusto con el cobrador; **there has been a lot of ~** ha habido muchos disgustos.

unpleasing [ʌn'pliːzɪŋ] ADJ poco atractivo, antiestético; poco grato (*to* a).

unplug ['ʌn'plʌg] VT desenchufar, desconectar.

unplugged ['ʌn'plʌgd] ADJ (*Mus*) unplugged, *sin efectos acústicos ni elementos electrónicos*.

unplumbed ['ʌn'plʌmd] ADJ no sondado, insondable.

unpoetic(al) ['ʌnpəʊ'etɪk(əl)] ADJ poco poético.

unpolished ['ʌn'pɒlɪʃt] ADJ sin pulir; *diamond* en bruto; (*fig*) grosero, tosco, inculto.

unpolluted ['ʌnpə'luːtɪd] ADJ impoluto; no contaminado.

unpopular ['ʌn'pɒpjʊlər] ADJ impopular, poco popular; **it is ~ with the miners** los mineros no lo quieren; **the decision is ~** la decisión no es popular; **to make o.s. ~** hacerse detestar; **you will be very ~ with me** no te lo agradeceré.

unpopularity ['ʌn,pɒpjʊ'lærɪtɪ] N impopularidad *f*.

unpopulated ['ʌn'pɒpjʊleɪtɪd] ADJ deshabitado, desierto.

unpractical [ʌn'præktɪkəl] ADJ falto de sentido práctico, poco práctico, desmañado.

unpractised, (*US***) unpracticed** [ʌn'præktɪst] ADJ inexperto.

unprecedented [ʌn'presɪdəntɪd] ADJ sin precedentes, inaudito.

unpredictability ['ʌnprɪ,dɪktə'bɪlɪtɪ] N imprevisibilidad *f*, incertidumbre *f*; carácter *m* caprichoso, volubilidad *f*.

unpredictable ['ʌnprɪ'dɪktəbl] ADJ *thing* imprevisible, incierto; *person* caprichoso, voluble, de reacciones imprevisibles, desconcertante.

unpredictably ['ʌnprɪ'dɪktəblɪ] ADV de manera imprevisible; caprichosamente, de manera voluble; de manera desconcertante.

unprejudiced [ʌn'predʒʊdɪst] ADJ imparcial.

unpremeditated ['ʌnprɪ'medɪteɪtɪd] ADJ impremeditado.

unprepared ['ʌnprɪ'peəd] ADJ no preparado; *speech etc* improvisado; **to be ~ for sth** no contar con algo, no esperar algo; **to catch sb ~** coger (*LAm*: agarrar) a uno desprevenido.

unpreparedness ['ʌnprɪ'peərɪdnɪs] N desapercibimiento *m*, desprevención *f*.

unprepossessing ['ʌn,priːpə'zesɪŋ] ADJ poco atractivo.

unpresentable ['ʌnprɪ'zentəbl] ADJ mal apersonado.

unpretentious ['ʌnprɪ'tenʃəs] ADJ modesto, nada pretencioso, sin pretensiones.

unpriced ['ʌn'praɪst] ADJ sin precio.

unprincipled [ʌn'prɪnsɪpld] ADJ poco escrupuloso, cínico, sin conciencia.

unprintable ['ʌn'prɪntəbl] ADJ intranscribible, indecente.

unproductive ['ʌnprə'dʌktɪv] ADJ *capital, soil etc* improductivo; *meeting etc* infructuoso.

unprofessional ['ʌnprə'feʃnl] ADJ (*ethically*) indigno de su profesión; contrario a la ética profesional; (*unskilled*) inexperto.

unprofitable [ʌn'prɒfɪtəbl] ADJ *enterprise* improductivo; *meeting etc* infructuoso; (*useless*) inútil; (*financially*) antieconómico, poco provechoso, nada lucrativo.

UNPROFOR, Unprofor N ABBR *of* **United Nations Protection Force** Fuerza(s) *f(pl)* de Protección de las Naciones Unidas, FORPRONU *f*, Unprofor *f*.

unpromising ['ʌn'prɒmɪsɪŋ] ADJ poco prometedor; **it looks ~** no promete mucho.

unprompted ['ʌn'prɒmptɪd] ADJ espontáneo.

unpronounceable ['ʌnprə'naʊnsəbl] ADJ impronunciable.

unpropitious ['ʌnprə'pɪʃəs] ADJ impropicio, poco propicio.

unprotected ['ʌnprə'tektɪd] ADJ sin protección, desprotegido, indefenso.

unproved ['ʌn'pruːvd] ADJ no probado.

unprovided ['ʌnprə'vaɪdɪd] ADJ: **~ for** (*unforeseen*) imprevisto; (*person*) desamparado, desvalido; **~ with** desprovisto de.

unprovoked ['ʌnprə'vəʊkt] ADJ no provocado, sin provocación.

unpublished ['ʌn'pʌblɪʃt] ADJ inédito, sin publicar.

unpunctual ['ʌn'pʌŋktjʊəl] ADJ poco puntual; **this train is always ~** este tren siempre llega con retraso.

unpunctuality ['ʌn,pʌŋktjʊ'ælɪtɪ] N falta *f* de puntualidad; atraso *m*.

unpunished ['ʌn'pʌnɪʃt] ADJ impune; **to go ~** (*crime*) quedar sin castigo; (*person*) escapar sin castigo, salir impune.

unputdownable ['ʌnpʊt'daʊnəbl] ADJ que no se puede dejar de la mano, absorbente.

unqualified ['ʌn'kwɒlɪfaɪd] ADJ *person* incompetente; sin título; *workman* no cualificado; *success, assertion* incondicional; *praise* grande; **to be ~ to do sth** no reunir las condiciones para hacer algo.

unquenchable [ʌn'kwentʃəbl] ADJ (*fig*) inextinguible; *thirst* inapagable; *desire etc* insaciable.

unquestionable [ʌn'kwestʃənəbl] ADJ incuestionable, indiscutible.

▼ **unquestionably** [ʌn'kwestʃənəblɪ] ADV indudablemente.

unquestioned [ʌn'kwestʃənd] ADV indiscutido, incontestable.

unquestioning [ʌn'kwestʃənɪŋ] ADJ incondicional; *faith etc* ciego.

unquestioningly [ʌn'kwestʃənɪŋlɪ] ADV incondicionalmente; ciegamente.

unquiet ['ʌn'kwaɪət] ADJ inquieto.

unquote ['ʌn'kwəʊt] N: '~' 'fin *m* de la cita'.

unquoted ['ʌn'kwəʊtɪd] ADJ *share etc* no cotizado, sin cotización oficial.

unravel [ʌn'rævəl] VT desenmarañar; (*fig*) desenmarañar, desembrollar.

unread ['ʌn'red] ADJ no leído; **to leave sth ~** dejar algo sin leer.

unreadable ['ʌn'riːdəbl] ADJ ilegible; (*fig*) imposible de leer, de lectura muy pesada; **I found the book ~** el libro me resultó pesadísimo.

unreadiness ['ʌn'redɪnɪs] N desapercibimiento *m*; desprevención *f*.

unready ['ʌn'redɪ] ADJ desapercibido, desprevenido.

unreal ['ʌn'rɪəl] ADJ **(a)** irreal; imaginario, ilusorio. **(b)** (*esp US**) (*extraordinary*) increíble; (*difficult*) dificilísimo.

unrealistic ['ʌnrɪə'lɪstɪk] ADJ ilusorio, fantástico; irrealista; *estimate etc* no basado en los hechos, disparatado; *scheme* impracticable; *person* poco realista.

unrealistically ['ʌnrɪə'lɪstɪkəlɪ] ADV ilusoriamente; impracticablemente; poco realistamente.

unreality ['ʌnrɪ'ælɪtɪ] N irrealidad *f*.

unrealizable ['ʌnrɪə'laɪzəbl] ADJ irrealizable.

unrealized ['ʌn'riːəlaɪzd] ADJ no realizado, que ha quedado sin realizar; *objective* no logrado.

unreason ['ʌn'riːzn] N insensatez *f*.

unreasonable [ʌn'riːznəbl] ADJ irrazonable, poco razonable; *demand etc* excesivo; **he was most ~ about it** se negó a considerarlo razonablemente; **don't be so ~!** ¡no seas tan porfiado!; ¡no te pongas así!

unreasonableness [ʌn'riːznəblnɪs] N irracionalidad *f*; exorbitancia *f*, lo excesivo; (*of person*) porfía *f*.

unreasonably [ʌn'riːznəblɪ] ADV: **to be ~ difficult about sth** porfiar estúpidamente en algo.

unreasoning [ʌn'riːznɪŋ] ADJ irracional.

unreceptive ['ʌn'septɪv] ADJ poco receptivo.

unreclaimed ['ʌnrɪ'kleɪmd] ADJ *land* no rescatado, no utilizado.

unrecognizable ['ʌn'rekəgnaɪzəbl] ADJ irreconocible, desconocido.

unrecognized ['ʌn'rekəgnaɪzd] ADJ no reconocido; **he went ~ through the market** atravesó el mercado sin que nadie le conociese.

unreconstructed [,ʌnriːkəns'trʌktɪd] ADJ (*fig*) no reformado, sin reformar; tradicional.

unrecorded ['ʌnrɪ'kɔːdɪd] ADJ no registrado, de que no hay constancia.

unredeemed ['ʌnrɪ'diːmd] ADJ no redimido; *promise* sin cumplir, incumplido; *pledge* no desempeñado; *bill* sin redimir; *debt* sin amortizar; **~ by** no compensado por.

unreel [ʌn'rɪəl] VT desenrollar.

unrefined ['ʌnrɪ'faɪnd] ADJ *material* no refinado; (*fig*) inculto.

unreflecting ['ʌnrɪ'flektɪŋ] ADJ irreflexivo.

unreformed ['ʌnrɪ'fɔːmd] ADJ no reformado.

unregarded ['ʌnrɪ'gɑːdɪd] ADJ desatendido, no estimado; **those ~ aspects** aquellos aspectos de los que nadie hace caso.

unregenerate ['ʌnrɪ'dʒenərɪt] ADJ empedernido.

unregistered ['ʌn'redʒɪstəd] ADJ no registrado; *letter* sin certificar.

unregretted ['ʌnrɪ'gretɪd] ADJ no llorado, no lamentado.

unrehearsed ['ʌnrɪ'hɜːst] ADJ *speech etc* improvisado; *incident* imprevisto.

unrelated ['ʌnrɪ'leɪtɪd] ADJ inconexo.

unrelenting ['ʌnrɪ'lentɪŋ] ADJ inexorable, implacable.

unreliability ['ʌnrɪ,laɪə'bɪlɪtɪ] N falta *f* de fiabilidad.

unreliable ['ʌnrɪ'laɪəbl] ADJ *person* informal, de poca confianza; *news* nada fidedigno; *machine etc* que no es de fiar.

unrelieved ['ʌnrɪ'liːvd] ADJ absoluto, monótono, total; **~ by** no aliviado por, no mitigado por; **3 hours of ~ boredom** 3 horas de aburrimiento total.

unremarkable ['ʌnrɪ'mɑːkəbl] ADJ ordinario, corriente.

unremarked ['ʌnrɪ'mɑːkt] ADJ inadvertido.

unremitting ['ʌnrɪ'mɪtɪŋ] ADJ infatigable, incansable; cansante, incesante.

unremittingly ['ʌnrɪ'mɪtɪŋlɪ] ADV incansablemente.

unremunerative ['ʌnrɪ'mjuːnərətɪv] ADJ poco remunerador, poco lu-

crativo.

unrepealed ['ʌnrɪ'piːld] ADJ no revocado.

unrepeatable ['ʌnrɪ'piːtəbl] ADJ que no puede repetirse; **what he said is quite ~** no me atrevo a repetir lo que me dijo.

unrepentant ['ʌnrɪ'pentənt] ADJ impenitente.

unreported [,ʌnrɪ'pɔːtɪd] ADJ *crime* no denunciado, sin denunciar; **the news went ~** la noticia no fue comunicada.

unrepresentative ['ʌn,reprɪ'zentətɪv] ADJ *assembly etc* poco representativo; (*untypical*) poco típico, nada característico.

unrepresented ['ʌn,reprɪ'zentɪd] ADJ sin representación; **they are ~ in the House** no tienen representación en la Cámara.

unrequited ['ʌnrɪ'kwaɪtɪd] ADJ no correspondido.

unreserved ['ʌnrɪ'zɜːvd] ADJ no reservado, libre.

unreservedly ['ʌnrɪ'zɜːvɪdlɪ] ADV sin reserva, incondicionalmente.

unresisting ['ʌnrɪ'zɪstɪŋ] ADJ sumiso.

unresolved ['ʌnrɪ'zɒlvd] ADJ *problem* no resuelto, pendiente.

unresponsive ['ʌnrɪs'pɒnsɪv] ADJ insensible, sordo (*to* a).

unrest [ʌn'rest] N malestar *m*, inquietud *f*; (*Pol*) conflictividad *f*, desasosiego *m*, (*active*) desorden *m*; **the ~ in the Congo** los disturbios del Congo.

unrestrained ['ʌnrɪ'streɪnd] ADJ desenfrenado, desembarazado (de trabas); *language, remarks* libre.

unrestrainedly ['ʌnrɪ'streɪnɪdlɪ] ADV desenfrenadamente, con desenfreno; sin trabas; libremente.

unrestricted ['ʌnrɪ'strɪktɪd] ADJ sin restricción, libre.

unrevealed ['ʌnrɪ'viːld] ADJ no revelado.

unrewarded ['ʌnrɪ'wɔːdɪd] ADJ sin recompensa, sin premio; **his work went ~** su labor quedó sin recompensa.

unrewarding ['ʌnrɪ'wɔːdɪŋ] ADJ sin provecho, infructuoso, inútil.

unrighteous [ʌn'raɪtʃəs] **1** ADJ malo, perverso.

2 NPL: **the ~** los malos, los perversos.

unripe ['ʌn'raɪp] ADJ verde, inmaturo.

unrivalled, (*US*) **unrivaled** [ʌn'raɪvəld] ADJ sin par, incomparable; **Bilbao is ~ for food** la cocina bilbaína es incomparable.

unroadworthy ['ʌn'rəʊd,wɜːðɪ] ADJ en condiciones no aptas para circular.

unrobe ['ʌn'rəʊb] **1** VI desvestirse, desnudarse.

2 VT (*frm*) desvestir, desnudar.

unroll ['ʌn'rəʊl] **1** VT desenrollar.

2 VI desenrollarse.

unromantic ['ʌnrə'mæntɪk] ADJ poco romántico.

unroof ['ʌn'ruːf] VT destechar, quitar el techo de.

unrope ['ʌn'rəʊp] **1** VT desatar.

2 VI desatarse.

unruffled ['ʌn'rʌfld] ADJ *person* imperturbable, ecuánime; *hair, surface* liso; **he carried on quite ~** siguió sin inmutarse.

unruled ['ʌn'ruːld] ADJ *paper* sin rayar.

unruly [ʌn'ruːlɪ] ADJ revoltoso, ingobernable; *hair* despeinado.

UNRWA ['ʌnrə] N ABBR *of* United Nations Relief and Works Agency.

unsaddle ['ʌn'sædl] VT *rider* desarzonar; *horse* desensillar, quitar la silla a.

unsafe ['ʌn'seɪf] ADJ *machine, car etc* inseguro; *policy, journey* peligroso, arriesgado; **~ to eat** malo para comer; **~ to drink** malo para beber; **it is ~ to rely on it** no se puede contar con eso; **it is ~ to let him have a gun** es peligroso permitirle llevar escopeta.

unsaid ['ʌn'sed] ADJ sin decir, sin expresar; **to leave sth ~** callar algo, dejar de decir algo; **to leave nothing ~** no dejar nada en el tintero; **much was left ~** se dejaron de decir muchas cosas.

unsalaried ['ʌn'sælərɪd] ADJ sin sueldo, no remunerado.

unsal(e)able ['ʌn'seɪləbl] ADJ invendible.

unsalted [,ʌn'sɒltɪd] ADJ sin sal.

unsanitary [,ʌn'sænɪtərɪ] ADJ insalubre, antihigiénico.

unsatisfactory ['ʌn,sætɪs'fæktərɪ] ADJ insatisfactorio.

unsatisfied ['ʌn'sætɪsfaɪd] ADJ insatisfecho.

unsatisfying ['ʌn'sætɪsfaɪɪŋ] ADJ que no satisface, insuficiente.

unsaturated ['ʌn'sætʃəreɪtɪd] ADJ no saturado, insaturado.

unsavoury, (*US*) **unsavory** ['ʌn'seɪvərɪ] ADJ desagradable, repugnante; *person* indeseable.

unsay ['ʌn'seɪ] (*irr: V say*) VT desdecirse de.

unscathed ['ʌn'skeɪðd] ADJ ileso; **to get out ~** salir ileso.

unscheduled ['ʌn'ʃedjuːld] ADJ no programado; no previsto.

unscholarly ['ʌn'skɒləlɪ] ADJ *person* nada erudito; poco metódico; *work* indigno de un erudito.

unschooled ['ʌn'skuːld] ADJ indocto; no instruido, sin instrucción; **to be ~ in a technique** no haber aprendido nada de una técnica.

unscientific ['ʌn,saɪən'tɪfɪk] ADJ poco científico.

unscramble ['ʌn'skræmbl] VT *message* descifrar; (*TV*) descodificar.

unscrew ['ʌn'skruː] VT destornillar.

unscripted ['ʌn'skrɪptɪd] ADJ improvisado; sin guión.

unscrupulous [ʌn'skruːpjʊləs] ADJ poco escrupuloso, sin escrúpulos, desaprensivo.

unscrupulously [ʌn'skruːpjʊləslɪ] ADV de modo poco escrupuloso.

unscrupulousness [ʌn'skruːpjʊləsnɪs] N falta f de escrúpulos, desaprensión f.

unseal ['ʌn'siːl] VT desellar, abrir.

unseasonable [ʌn'siːznəbl] ADJ intempestivo; fuera de estación.

unseasonably [ʌn'siːznəblɪ] ADV inoportunamente.

unseasoned ['ʌn'siːznd] ADJ no sazonado.

unseat ['ʌn'siːt] VT rider desarzonar; passenger etc echar de su asiento; (Parl) hacer perder su escaño.

unseaworthy ['ʌn'siːˌwɜːðɪ] ADJ innavegable.

unsecured ['ʌnsɪ'kjʊəd] ADJ (Fin) no respaldado, sin aval; ~ creditor acreedor m común; ~ debt deuda f sin respaldo.

unseeded ['ʌn'siːdɪd] ADJ player no preseleccionado.

unseeing ['ʌn'siːɪŋ] ADJ (fig) ciego.

unseemliness [ʌn'siːmlɪnɪs] N lo indecoroso, falta f de decoro, impropiedad f.

unseemly [ʌn'siːmlɪ] ADJ indecoroso, impropio.

unseen ['ʌn'siːn] 1 ADJ invisible; secreto, oculto; inadvertido; translation hecho a primera vista; **he managed to get through ~** logró pasar inadvertido.
2 N (a) (esp Brit) traducción f hecha a primera vista. (b) **the ~** lo invisible, lo oculto.

unsegregated ['ʌn'sɛgrɪgeɪtɪd] ADJ no segregado, sin segregación (racial etc).

unselfconscious ['ʌnˌsɛlf'kɒnʃəs] ADJ natural.

unselfconsciously ['ʌnˌsɛlf'kɒnʃəslɪ] ADV de manera desenfadada.

unselfish [ʌn'sɛlfɪʃ] ADJ desinteresado; abnegado; altruista.

unselfishly [ʌn'sɛlfɪʃlɪ] ADV desinteresadamente; abnegadamente; de modo altruista, con altruismo.

unselfishness [ʌn'sɛlfɪʃnɪs] N desinterés m; abnegación f; altruismo m.

unsentimental ['ʌnˌsɛntɪ'mɛntəl] ADJ nada sentimental.

unserviceable ['ʌn'sɜːvɪsəbl] ADJ inservible, inútil.

unsettle ['ʌn'sɛtl] VT perturbar, agitar, inquietar.

unsettled ['ʌn'sɛtld] ADJ inquieto, intranquilo; weather variable; state, market inestable; land inhabitado, despoblado, no colonizado, sin poblar; question pendiente; account por pagar; **he's feeling ~ in his job** no está del todo contento en su puesto, se siente algo molesto en su puesto.

unsettling ['ʌn'sɛtlɪŋ] ADJ influence etc perturbador, inquietante.

unsex ['ʌn'sɛks] VT privar de la sexualidad, suprimir el instinto sexual de.

unshackle ['ʌn'ʃækl] VT desencadenar, quitar los grillos a.

unshaded ['ʌn'ʃeɪdɪd] ADJ place sin sombra; con luz directa; bulb sin pantalla.

unshak(e)able ['ʌn'ʃeɪkəbl] ADJ resolve inquebrantable; **he was ~ in his resolve** se mostró totalmente resuelto; **after 3 hours he was still ~** después de 3 horas siguió tan resuelto como antes.

unshaken ['ʌn'ʃeɪkən] ADJ impertérrito; **he was ~ by what had happened** no se dejó amedrentar por lo que había pasado.

unshaven ['ʌn'ʃeɪvn] ADJ sin afeitar.

unsheathe ['ʌn'ʃiːð] VT desenvainar.

unship ['ʌn'ʃɪp] VT goods desembarcar; rudder, mast etc desmontar.

unshockable ['ʌn'ʃɒkəbl] ADJ: **she's ~** no se escandaliza por nada, no es fácil que se asombre.

unshod ['ʌn'ʃɒd] ADJ descalzo; horse desherrado.

unshrinkable ['ʌn'ʃrɪŋkəbl] ADJ inencogible.

unshrinking [ʌn'ʃrɪŋkɪŋ] ADJ impávido.

unsighted ['ʌn'saɪtɪd] ADJ: **I was ~ for a moment** por un momento no pude ver, por un momento tuve la vista impedida.

unsightliness [ʌn'saɪtlɪnɪs] N fealdad f.

unsightly [ʌn'saɪtlɪ] ADJ feo, repugnante.

unsigned ['ʌn'saɪnd] ADJ sin firmar.

unsinkable ['ʌn'sɪŋkəbl] ADJ insumergible.

unskilled ['ʌn'skɪld] ADJ worker no cualificado; work no especializado.

unskil(l)ful ['ʌn'skɪlfʊl] ADJ inexperto, desmañado.

unskimmed ['ʌn'skɪmd] ADJ sin desnatar.

unsmiling ['ʌn'smaɪlɪŋ] ADJ sin sonrisa.

unsmilingly ['ʌn'smaɪlɪŋlɪ] ADV sin sonreír; con gesto severo.

unsociability ['ʌnˌsəʊʃə'bɪlɪtɪ] N insociabilidad f.

unsociable [ʌn'səʊʃəbl] ADJ insociable; person poco sociable, huraño.

unsocial [ʌn'səʊʃəl] ADJ: **to work ~ hours** trabajar fuera de las horas normales.

unsold ['ʌn'səʊld] ADJ sin vender; **to remain ~** quedar sin vender.

unsoldierly ['ʌn'səʊldʒəlɪ] ADJ indigno de un militar, impropio de un militar.

unsolicited ['ʌnsə'lɪsɪtɪd] ADJ no solicitado.

unsolvable ['ʌn'sɒlvəbl] ADJ irresoluble, insoluble.

unsolved ['ʌn'sɒlvd] ADJ no resuelto; ~ crime crimen m que sigue sin resolver.

unsophisticated ['ʌnsə'fɪstɪkeɪtɪd] ADJ sencillo, cándido, ingenuo.

unsought ['ʌn'sɔːt] ADJ no solicitado; no buscado; **the offer came quite ~** se hizo la oferta sin que se hubiera pedido nada.

unsound ['ʌn'saʊnd] ADJ (in construction) defectuoso; fruit podrido; argument, opinion falso, erróneo; **of ~ mind** mentalmente incapacitado; **the book is ~ on some points** no hay que fiarse del libro en ciertos aspectos, el libro tiene algunas cosas erróneas.

unsoundness ['ʌn'saʊndnɪs] N lo defectuoso; falsedad f, lo erróneo.

unsparing [ʌn'spɛərɪŋ] ADJ (generous) generoso, pródigo; effort incansable; (cruel) despiadado; **to be ~ of praises** no escatimar las alabanzas; **to be ~ in one's efforts to** + infin no regatear esfuerzos por + infin.

unsparingly [ʌn'spɛərɪŋlɪ] ADV generosamente, pródigamente; incansablemente.

unspeakable [ʌn'spiːkəbl] ADJ indecible; (very bad) incalificable.

unspeakably [ʌn'spiːkəblɪ] ADV: **to suffer ~** sufrir lo indecible; **it was ~ bad** fue horroroso.

unspecified ['ʌn'spɛsɪfaɪd] ADJ no especificado.

unspectacular [ˌʌnspɛk'tækjʊlər] ADJ poco aparatoso; nada llamativo.

unspent ['ʌn'spɛnt] ADJ no gastado.

unsplinterable ['ʌn'splɪntərəbl] ADJ inastillable.

unspoiled ['ʌn'spɔɪld] ADJ, **unspoilt** ['ʌn'spɔɪlt] ADJ intacto; no estropeado; child natural, no mimado; countryside que conserva sus encantos, que sigue en su estado natural.

unspoken ['ʌn'spəʊkən] ADJ no expresado, tácito.

unsporting ['ʌn'spɔːtɪŋ] ADJ, **unsportsmanlike** ['ʌn'spɔːtsmənlaɪk] ADJ antideportivo.

unstable ['ʌn'steɪbl] ADJ inestable.

unstamped ['ʌn'stæmpt] ADJ sin sello, sin franquear.

unstated [ʌn'steɪtɪd] ADJ wish etc no expresado; understanding tácito.

unstatesmanlike ['ʌn'steɪtsmənlaɪk] ADJ indigno (or impropio) de un estadista.

unsteadily ['ʌn'stɛdɪlɪ] ADV inestablemente, inseguramente; inconstantemente.

unsteadiness ['ʌn'stɛdɪnɪs] N inestabilidad f, inseguridad f; inconstancia f; lo movedizo, falta f de firmeza.

unsteady ['ʌn'stɛdɪ] ADJ inestable, inseguro; inconstante; (shaky) movedizo, poco firme; **to be ~ on one's feet** no poder estar de pie sin tambalearse, titubear.

unstick ['ʌn'stɪk] VT despegar.

unstinted [ʌn'stɪntɪd] ADJ praise etc generoso; effort incansable.

unstinting [ʌn'stɪntɪŋ] ADJ: **to be ~ in one's praise** ser pródigo de alabanzas, no escatimar sus alabanzas; **to be ~ in one's efforts to** + infin no regatear esfuerzo por + infin.

unstintingly [ˌʌn'stɪntɪŋlɪ] ADV sin escatimar esfuerzos, de manera infatigable y generosa.

unstitch ['ʌn'stɪtʃ] VT descoser; **to come ~ed** descoserse.

unstop ['ʌn'stɒp] VT desobstruir, desatascar.

unstoppable ['ʌn'stɒpəbl] ADJ incontenible, irrefrenable; (Sport) shot etc imparable.

unstrap ['ʌn'stræp] VT quitar la correa de; soltar.

unstressed ['ʌn'strest] ADJ átono, inacentuado.

unstring ['ʌn'strɪŋ] (irr: V string) VT (Mus) desencordar; nerves trastornar; pearls desensartar.

unstructured ['ʌn'strʌktʃəd] ADJ sin estructura, no estructurado.

unstuck ['ʌn'stʌk] ADJ: **to come ~** despegarse, desprenderse, soltarse; (fig) fracasar; sufrir un revés; **where he comes ~ is ...** a él lo que le pierde es ...

unstudied ['ʌn'stʌdɪd] ADJ natural, sin afectación.

unsubdued ['ʌnsəb'djuːd] ADJ indomado.

unsubmissive ['ʌnsəb'mɪsɪv] ADJ insumiso.

unsubstantial ['ʌnsəb'stænʃəl] ADJ insustancial.

unsubstantiated ['ʌnsəb'stænʃɪeɪtɪd] ADJ no probado, no corroborado.

unsuccessful ['ʌnsək'sesfʊl] ADJ person, negotiation etc fracasado; effort etc infructuoso, inútil, ineficaz; infeliz; **to be ~** fracasar, malograrse, no tener éxito; no poder; **to be ~ in doing sth** no lograr hacer algo, fracasar en sus esfuerzos por hacer algo, no poder hacer algo.

unsuccessfully ['ʌnsək'sesfəlɪ] ADV en vano, sin éxito, inútilmente.

unsuitability ['ʌnˌsuːtə'bɪlɪtɪ] N impropiedad f; inconveniencia f; lo inadecuado; lo inoportuno; incompetencia f; ineptitud f.

unsuitable ['ʌn'suːtəbl] ADJ inapropiado; inconveniente; inadecuado; inoportuno; (in a post etc) inepto, no apto; **a most ~ word** una palabra sumamente impropia; **he married a most ~ girl** se casó con una chica nada conveniente; **the film is ~ for children** la película no es apta para menores.

unsuitably ['ʌn'suːtəblɪ] ADV inapropiadamente; ~ **dressed** vestido de manera inapropiada.

unsuited ['ʌn'suːtɪd] ADJ: ~ **for** inepto para, no apto para; ~ **to do sth** inepto para hacer algo; **they are ~ to each other** son incompatibles (el uno con el otro).

unsullied ['ʌn'sʌlɪd] ADJ inmaculado, no corrompido; ~ **by** no corrompido por.

unsung ['ʌn'sʌŋ] ADJ desconocido, no celebrado.

unsupported ['ʌnsə'pɔːtɪd] ADJ statement etc que carece de base firme, no apoyado por datos; *candidate* sin apoyo, no respaldado por nadie.

unsure ['ʌnˈʃʊəʳ] ADJ inseguro, poco seguro; **he seemed very ~ about it** no parecía estar muy seguro de ello.

unsurmountable ['ʌnsəˈmaʊntəbl] ADJ insuperable.

unsurpassable ['ʌnsəˈpɑːsəbl] ADJ inmejorable, insuperable.

unsurpassed ['ʌnsəˈpɑːst] ADJ insuperado, sin par; **~ in quality** de calidad inmejorable; **~ by anybody** no superado por nadie.

unsurprising ['ʌnsəˈpraɪzɪŋ] ADJ nada sorprendente.

unsurprisingly ['ʌnsəˈpraɪzɪŋlɪ] ADV: **the news was received, ~, in silence** la noticia fue recibida, naturalmente, en silencio.

unsuspected ['ʌnsəsˈpektɪd] ADJ insospechado.

unsuspecting ['ʌnsəsˈpektɪŋ] ADJ nada suspicaz, sin recelo, confiado, desprevenido.

unsweetened ['ʌnˈswiːtnd] ADJ sin azucarar.

unswerving [ʌnˈswɜːvɪŋ] ADV *resolve* inquebrantable; *loyalty* inquebrantable, firme; *course* sin vacilar.

unswervingly [ʌnˈswɜːvɪŋlɪ] ADV: **to be ~ loyal to sb** seguir totalmente leal a uno; **to hold ~ to one's course** seguir sin vacilar.

unsympathetic ['ʌn,sɪmpəˈθetɪk] ADJ incompasivo, poco compasivo; falto de comprensión; indiferente; **he was totally ~** no mostró la más mínima comprensión; **they were ~ to my plea** no hicieron caso de mi ruego; **I am not ~ to your request** no veo con malos ojos su petición.

unsystematic ['ʌn,sɪstɪˈmætɪk] ADJ poco sistemático, poco metódico.

unsystematically ['ʌn,sɪstɪˈmætɪkəlɪ] ADV de modo poco metódico.

untainted ['ʌnˈteɪntɪd] ADJ inmaculado, no corrompido; *food* no contaminado; **~ by** no corrompido por.

untam(e)able ['ʌnˈteɪməbl] ADJ indomable.

untamed ['ʌnˈteɪmd] ADJ indomado.

untangle ['ʌnˈtæŋgl] VT desenmarañar.

untanned ['ʌnˈtænd] ADJ sin curtir.

untapped ['ʌnˈtæpt] ADJ *resources* sin explotar.

untarnished ['ʌnˈtɑːnɪʃt] ADJ *reputation etc* sin tacha.

untasted ['ʌnˈteɪstɪd] ADJ sin probar.

untaught ['ʌnˈtɔːt] ADJ no enseñado; (*ignorant*) sin instrucción.

untaxed ['ʌnˈtækst] ADJ libre de impuestos, no sujeto a contribuciones.

unteachable ['ʌnˈtiːtʃəbl] ADJ incapaz de aprender.

untempered ['ʌnˈtempəd] ADJ *steel etc* sin templar.

untenable ['ʌnˈtenəbl] ADJ insostenible.

untenanted ['ʌnˈtenəntɪd] ADJ desocupado, vacío.

untended ['ʌnˈtendɪd] ADJ no atendido, no vigilado; **he left the car ~** dejó el coche sin vigilar.

untested ['ʌnˈtestɪd] ADJ no probado.

unthinkable [ʌnˈθɪŋkəbl] **1** ADJ inconcebible, impensable; **it is ~ that ...** es inconcebible que + *subj*. **2** N: **the ~** lo inconcebible.

unthinking [ʌnˈθɪŋkɪŋ] ADJ irreflexivo.

unthinkingly [ʌnˈθɪŋkɪŋlɪ] ADV irreflexivamente, sin pensar.

unthought-of [ʌnˈθɔːtɒv] ADJ inimaginable, inconcebible.

unthread ['ʌnˈθred] VT *cloth* deshebrar, descoser; *needle* desenhebrar; *pearls* desensartar.

unthrifty ['ʌnˈθrɪftɪ] ADJ manirroto; impróvido.

untidily [ʌnˈtaɪdɪlɪ] ADV desaliñadamente; sin método; en desorden; **she does everything ~** todo lo hace de cualquier modo.

untidiness [ʌnˈtaɪdɪnɪs] N desaliño *m*; falta *f* de método; desorden *m*.

untidy [ʌnˈtaɪdɪ] ADJ (*in dress, appearance*) desaliñado, desaseado; *work* poco metódico; *room* en desorden, desordenado; **she's a very ~ person** es una persona que vive sin método, es una persona que hace las cosas (*or* deja sus cosas) de cualquier modo, es una persona desordenada.

untie [ʌnˈtaɪ] VT desatar.

until [ənˈtɪl] **1** PREP (*also* **up ~**) hasta; **~ 10** hasta las 10; **~ his arrival** hasta su llegada. **2** CONJ (**a**) (*of future time*) hasta que + *subj, eg* **wait ~ I get back** espera hasta que yo vuelva. (**b**) (*of past time*) hasta que + *indic, eg* **he did nothing ~ I told him** no hizo nada hasta que yo se lo dije.

untilled ['ʌnˈtɪld] ADJ sin cultivar.

untimely [ʌnˈtaɪmlɪ] ADJ intempestivo, inoportuno; prematuro.

untiring [ʌnˈtaɪərɪŋ] ADJ incansable.

untiringly [ʌnˈtaɪərɪŋlɪ] ADV incansablemente.

unto ['ʌntʊ] PREP (††) *V* to; towards.

untold ['ʌnˈtəʊld] ADJ *story* nunca contado, inédito; *secret* nunca revelado; *loss, wealth etc* incalculable, fabuloso; *suffering* indecible.

untouchable [ʌnˈtʌtʃəbl] (*India*) **1** ADJ intocable. **2** N intocable *mf*.

untouched ['ʌnˈtʌtʃt] ADJ intacto; (*safe*) incólume, indemne; **a product ~ by human hand** un producto que ninguna mano humana ha tocado; **he is ~ by any plea** es insensible a todas las súplicas; **to leave one's food ~** dejar su comida sin probar; **those peoples ~ by civilization** esos pueblos no alcanzados por la civilización.

untoward [ˌʌntəˈwɔːd] ADJ desfavorable; adverso; *event etc* fatal, funesto.

UNTIL	see also main entry

- As with other time conjunctions, *hasta que* is used with the *subjunctive* if the action which follows hasn't happened yet or hadn't happened at the time of speaking:
  - Go on stirring until the sauce is cold
  - *Sigue removiendo hasta que se enfríe la salsa*
  - I shan't be happy until you come
  - *No estaré contenta hasta que (no) vengas*
  - NOTE: When the main clause is negative, *no* can optionally be given in the *hasta que* clause without changing the meaning.
- *Hasta que* is used with the *indicative* when the action in the *hasta que* clause has already taken place:
  - He lived in this house until he died
  - *Vivió en esta casa hasta que murió*
  - I didn't see her again until she returned to London
  - *No volví a verla hasta que (no) regresó a Londres*
- *Hasta que* is also used with the *indicative* when describing habitual actions:
  - I never wake up until the alarm goes off
  - *Nunca me despierto hasta que (no) suena el despertador*
- Instead of *hasta que* + VERB, you can use *hasta* with an *infinitive* when the subject of both clauses is the same:
  - Go on stirring until you get a thick creamy mixture
  - *Sigue removiendo hasta obtener una crema espesa*
  - *For further uses and examples, see main entry.*

---

untrained ['ʌnˈtreɪnd] ADJ *person* inexperto; (*unskilled*) no cualificado; *teacher etc* sin título, que no tiene título; (*Sport*) no entrenado; *soldier* desentrenado; *animal* sin amaestrar, no adiestrado.

untrammelled, (*US*) **untrameled** [ʌnˈtræməld] ADJ ilimitado.

untransferable ['ʌntræns'fɜːrəbl] ADJ intransferible.

untranslatable ['ʌntrænzˈleɪtəbl] ADJ intraducible.

untravelled, (*US*) **untraveled** ['ʌnˈtrævld] ADJ *place* inexplorado; *road etc* no trillado, poco frecuentado; *person* que no ha viajado.

untreated [ʌnˈtriːtɪd] ADJ *injury* no tratado, no curado; *effluent* no tratado, sin tratar.

untried ['ʌnˈtraɪd] ADJ (**a**) *method etc* no probado; *person* novicio, no puesto a prueba; *soldier* bisoño. (**b**) (*Jur*) *person* no procesado, *case* no visto.

untrimmed ['ʌnˈtrɪmd] ADJ *hedge* sin recortar, sin podar; *wood* sin desbastar; *dress* sin guarnición.

untrodden ['ʌnˈtrɒdn] ADJ no trillado, sin pisar.

untroubled ['ʌnˈtrʌbld] ADJ tranquilo; **~ by thoughts of her** sin pensar en ella para nada, no afectado por ningún recuerdo de ella.

untrue ['ʌnˈtruː] ADJ *statement* falso; *world etc* ficticio, imaginario; *person* infiel, desleal; **that is wholly ~** eso es completamente falso.

untrustworthy ['ʌnˈtrʌst,wɜːðɪ] ADJ *person* informal, indigno de confianza; *source etc* no fidedigno; *book etc* de dudosa autoridad; *machine, car* inseguro.

untruth ['ʌnˈtruːθ] N, PL **untruths** ['ʌnˈtruːðz] mentira *f*.

untruthful ['ʌnˈtruːθfʊl] ADJ mentiroso, falso.

untruthfully ['ʌnˈtruːθfəlɪ] ADV falsamente.

untruthfulness ['ʌnˈtruːθfʊlnɪs] N falsedad *f*.

untutored ['ʌnˈtjuːtəd] ADJ indocto, poco instruido; *mind, taste* no formado.

untwine ['ʌnˈtwaɪn] VT, **untwist** ['ʌnˈtwɪst] VT destorcer.

untypical ['ʌnˈtɪpɪkəl] ADJ atípico.

unusable ['ʌnˈjuːzəbl] ADJ inservible, inútil.

unused ADJ (**a**) ['ʌnˈjuːzd] *stamp etc* nuevo, sin usar; sin estrenar. (**b**) ['ʌnˈjuːst] **to be ~ to** no estar acostumbrado a.

unusual [ʌnˈjuːʒʊəl] ADJ insólito, poco común, inusual; inusitado.

unusually [ʌnˈjuːʒʊəlɪ] ADV: **an ~ awkward matter** un asunto extraordinariamente difícil; **an ~ gifted man** un hombre de talentos poco comunes; **he arrived ~ late** llegó más tarde que de costumbre.

unutterable [ʌnˈʌtərəbl] ADJ indecible.

unutterably [ʌnˈʌtərəblɪ] ADV indeciblemente.

unvaried [ʌnˈveərɪd] ADJ sin variación, constante; (*pej*) monótono.

unvarnished ['ʌnˈvɑːnɪʃt] ADJ sin barnizar; (*fig*) sencillo, llano, sin adornos; **the ~ truth** la verdad lisa y llana.

unvarying [ʌnˈveərɪŋ] ADJ invariable, constante.

unveil [ʌnˈveɪl] VT quitar el velo a; *statue etc* descubrir.

unveiling [ʌnˈveɪlɪŋ] N descubrimiento *m* (de una estatua); (*ceremony*) inauguración *f*.

unventilated ['ʌnˈventɪleɪtɪd] ADJ sin ventilación, sin aire.

unverifiable ['ʌnˈverɪfaɪəbl] ADJ no comprobable, que no puede verificarse.

unverified ['ʌnˈverɪfaɪd] ADJ sin verificar.

unversed ['ʌnˈvɜːst] ADJ: **~ in** poco ducho en.

unvisited ['ʌnˈvɪzɪtɪd] ADJ no visitado, no frecuentado.

unvoiced [ʌnˈvɔɪst] ADJ no expresado; (*Gram*) sordo.

unwaged [ʌnˈweɪdʒd] **1** ADJ sin sueldo.
2 N: **the ~** los que no tienen sueldo.

unwanted [ˈʌnˈwɒntɪd] ADJ superfluo; *child* no deseado; *pregnancy* no deseado, involuntario.

unwarily [ʌnˈwɛərɪlɪ] ADV imprudentemente, incautamente.

unwariness [ʌnˈwɛərɪnɪs] N imprudencia *f*.

unwarlike [ʌnˈwɔːlaɪk] ADJ pacífico, poco belicoso.

unwarranted [ʌnˈwɒrəntɪd] ADJ injustificado.

unwary [ʌnˈwɛərɪ] ADJ imprudente, incauto.

unwashed [ʌnˈwɒʃt] **1** ADJ sin lavar, sucio.
2 NPL: **the Great U~** (*hum*) la plebe.

unwavering [ʌnˈweɪvərɪŋ] ADJ *loyalty, resolve* inquebrantable, firme; *course* constante; *gaze* fijo.

unwaveringly [ʌnˈweɪvərɪŋlɪ] ADV firmemente; constantemente; **to hold ~ to one's course** seguir su curso sin apartarse para nada de él.

unweaned [ˈʌnˈwiːnd] ADJ no destetado.

unwearable [ˈʌnˈwɛərəbl] ADJ *clothes, colour* imposible de llevar.

unwearying [ʌnˈwɪərɪŋ] ADJ incansable.

unwed [ˈʌnˈwed] ADJ soltero.

unwelcome [ʌnˈwelkəm] ADJ importuno, molesto, inoportuno; desagradable; **a most ~ piece of news** una noticia excepcionalmente desagradable (*to* para); **the change is not ~** el cambio no es del todo molesto para nosotros.

unwelcoming [ʌnˈwelkəmɪŋ] ADJ *person* nada simpático, poco cordial; *place* poco acogedor.

unwell [ˈʌnˈwel] ADJ: **to be ~** estar indispuesto; **to feel ~** sentirse mal; **I felt ~ on the ship** me mareé en el barco.

unwholesome [ˈʌnˈhəʊlsəm] ADJ insalubre, nocivo; (*morally*) indeseable.

unwieldy [ʌnˈwiːldɪ] ADJ pesado, abultado, difícil de manejar.

unwilling [ˈʌnˈwɪlɪŋ] ADJ desinclinado; no querer; **to be ~ to do sth** no querer hacer algo, estar poco dispuesto a hacer algo; **to be ~ for sb to do sth** no querer que uno haga algo, estar poco dispuesto a permitir que uno haga algo.

unwillingly [ˈʌnˈwɪlɪŋlɪ] ADV de mala gana.

unwillingness [ˈʌnˈwɪlɪŋnɪs] N falta *f* de inclinación, desgana *f*; **his ~ to help us** su desgana para ayudarnos, su resistencia para ayudarnos.

unwind [ʌnˈwaɪnd] (*irr: V* **wind²**) **1** VT desenvolver; *thread* desovillar.
2 VI desenvolverse; desovillarse; (*fig: relax*) esparcirse, relajarse.

unwisdom [ʌnˈwɪzdəm] N imprudencia *f*.

unwise [ˈʌnˈwaɪz] ADJ imprudente; poco aconsejable, desaconsejado; **it would be ~ to +** *infin* sería poco aconsejable + *infin*; **that was most ~ of you** en eso has sido muy imprudente.

unwisely [ʌnˈwaɪzlɪ] ADV imprudentemente.

unwitting [ʌnˈwɪtɪŋ] ADJ inconsciente.

unwittingly [ʌnˈwɪtɪŋlɪ] ADV inconscientemente; sin saber, sin darse cuentar.

unwomanly [ʌnˈwʊmənlɪ] ADJ poco femenino.

unwonted [ʌnˈwəʊntɪd] ADJ insólito, inusitado.

unworkable [ˈʌnˈwɜːkəbl] ADJ impracticable; (*Min*) inexplotable.

unworldly [ˈʌnˈwɜːldlɪ] ADJ poco mundano, poco realista.

unworn [ˈʌnˈwɔːn] ADJ nuevo, sin estrenar.

unworthiness [ʌnˈwɜːðɪnɪs] N indignidad *f*, falta *f* de mérito.

unworthy [ʌnˈwɜːðɪ] ADJ indigno (*of* de); **to be ~ to do sth** ser indigno de hacer algo; **it is ~ of attention** no merece atención.

unwound [ˌʌnˈwaʊnd] PRET, PTP *of* **unwind**.

unwounded [ʌnˈwuːndɪd] ADJ ileso.

unwrap [ʌnˈræp] VT desenvolver; *parcel* deshacer, desempaquetar.

unwritten [ˈʌnˈrɪtn] ADJ no escrito.

unyielding [ʌnˈjiːldɪŋ] ADJ inflexible.

unyoke [ˈʌnˈjəʊk] VT desuncir.

unzip [ˈʌnˈzɪp] VT abrir la cremallera (*LAm*: el cierre) de.

up [ʌp] **1** ADV **(a)** (*gen*) hacia arriba; arriba, para arriba; en el aire, en lo alto; **~!** ¡arriba!, (*from bed*) ¡levántate!; **~ (with) the revolution!** ¡viva la revolución!; **all the way ~** durante toda la subida, en todo el recorrido; en toda su extensión; **halfway ~** a mitad de camino; **'this side ~'** 'este lado hacia arriba'; **'road ~'** 'cerrado por obras'; **~ above** allí arriba; **to be ~ above sth** estar por encima de algo; **~ in London** allá en Londres; **my office is 5 floors ~** mi oficina está en el quinto piso; **we're ~ for the day** hemos venido a pasar el día; **when I was ~** (*Univ*) cuando yo estaba en la universidad, cuando yo era estudiante; **to throw sth ~ (in the air)** lanzar algo al aire, lanzar algo por alto; **to walk ~ and down** pasearse, andar de un lado para otro, andar de acá para allá.
(b) (*out of bed*) **to be ~** estar levantado; **we were ~ at 7** nos levantamos a las 7; **to be ~ and about again** estar levantado ya; estar mucho mejor; **to be ~ and doing** ser activo; **to be ~ all night** no acostarse en toda la noche; **we were still ~ at midnight** a medianoche seguíamos sin acostarnos.
(c) (*fig*) **when the sun is ~** después de la salida del sol; cuando bri-

lla el sol; **the river is ~** el río ha subido; **the tide is ~** la marea está alta.
(d) (*of price, quantity etc*) **potatoes are ~** han subido las patatas; **the thermometer is ~ 2 degrees** ha subido el termómetro 2 grados; **Ceuta were 3 goals ~** Ceuta tenía 3 goles de ventaja; **we were 20 points ~ on them** les llevábamos una ventaja de 20 puntos.
(e) (*upwards*) **from £2 ~** de 2 libras para arriba; **from the age of 13 ~** desde los 13 años para arriba; a partir de los 13 años.
(f) (*on a level*) **put it ~ beside the other one** ponlo junto al otro; **to be ~ with sb** estar a la altura de uno, haber alcanzado el nivel de uno; **is he ~ to advanced work?** ¿tiene capacidad para estudios superiores?; **to be ~ to a task** estar a la altura de un cometido; **I don't feel ~ to it** no me siento con fuerzas para ello; **it's not ~ to much** no vale gran cosa; **to be well ~ in maths** ser fuerte en matemáticas.
(g) **to be ~ against difficulties** tener dificultades, haber tropezado con dificultades; **to be ~ against it** estar en un aprieto; **now we're really ~ against it!** ¡con la iglesia hemos topado!; **to be ~ against sb** tener que habérselas con uno; *V* **hard** *etc*.
(h) (*: wrong*) **what's ~?** ¿qué pasa?; **what's ~ with John?** ¿qué le pasa a Juan?; **there's sth ~** pasa algo malo, (*of a plot*) están tramando algo.
(i) (*finished*) **time is ~** se ha terminado el tiempo permitido, es la hora; se ha agotado el tiempo; **when the period is ~** cuando termine el plazo; **his holiday is ~** han terminado ya sus vacaciones; **our time here is ~** no podemos estar más tiempo aquí, se ha acabado nuestra estancia aquí; *V* **all**.
(j) (*as far as*) **~ to** hasta; **~ to now** hasta ahora; **~ to here** hasta aquí; **~ to this week** hasta esta semana; **~ to £10** hasta 10 libras; **to count ~ to 100** contar hasta 100; **they advanced ~ to the wood** avanzaron hasta el bosque.
(k) (*busy doing*) **they're ~ to sth** están tramando algo; **what are you ~ to?** ¿qué haces ahí?; **what are you ~ to with that knife?** ¿qué haces con ese cuchillo?; **what does he think he's ~ to?** ¿qué diablos piensa hacer?; **I see what you're ~ to** te veo venir.
(l) (*incumbent on*) **it is ~ to you to decide** te toca a ti decidir; **I feel it is ~ to me to tell him** creo que me incumbe a mí decírselo; **if it was ~ to me** si yo tuviera que decidirlo.
(m) (*US**) **a bourbon (straight) ~** un bourbon sin hielo; **two fried eggs ~** un par de huevos fritos boca arriba.
(n) **to be ~ and running** estar en funcionamiento; **to get sth ~ and running** poner algo en funcionamiento.
2 PREP **(a)** en lo alto de; encima de; **~ a tree** en lo alto de un árbol; **halfway ~ the stairs** a mitad de la escalera; **halfway ~ the mountain** a mitad de la subida del monte; **they live further ~ the road** viven en esta calle pero más arriba; **he went off ~ the road** se fue calle arriba; **~ (the) river** río arriba.
(b) **~ yours!⁑** ¡vete a hacer puñetas!⁑, ¡vete a hacer morcillas!⁑
3 ADJ **(a) the ~ train** (*Brit*) el tren ascendente.
(b) to be ~* (*elated*) estar en plena forma.
4 N **(a) ~s and downs** vicisitudes *fpl*, alternativas *fpl*, altibajos *mpl*, peripecias *fpl*; **after many ~s and downs** después de mil peripecias; **the ~s and downs that every politician has** las alternativas a que está sometido todo político.
(b) it's on the ~ and ~ (*Brit*) va cada vez mejor; (*US*) eso está en regla, eso es legítimo.
5 VT *price* subir, aumentar; **to ~ an offer** aumentar una oferta, ofrecer más.
6 VI (*) **to ~ and +** *inf* ponerse de repente a + *infin*; **he ~ped and hit her** sin más la pegó; **he ~ped and offed** sin más se largó*; **she ~ped and left** se levantó y se marchó.

up-and-coming [ˈʌpənʤˈkʌmɪŋ] ADJ joven y prometedor, nuevo y emprendedor.

up-and-down [ˈʌpənˈdaʊn] ADJ *movement* vertical, perpendicular; *business, progress etc* poco uniforme, variable; (*eventful*) accidentado, con altibajos.

up-and-under [ˌʌpənˈʌndər] N (*Rugby*) patada *f* a seguir.

upbeat [ˈʌpˈbiːt] **1** ADJ (*) optimista, animado, alegre.
2 N (*Mus*) tiempo *m* débil, tiempo *m* no acentuado; (*fig: in prosperity*) aumento *m*.

up-bow [ˈʌpbəʊ] N (*Mus*) movimiento *m* ascendente del arco.

upbraid [ʌpˈbreɪd] VT reprender, censurar; **to ~ sb with sth** censurar algo a uno.

upbringing [ˈʌpˌbrɪŋɪŋ] N educación *f*, crianza *f*.

upcast [ˈʌpkɑːst] N (*Min; also ~ shaft*) pozo *m* de ventilación.

upchuck⁑ [ˈʌptʃʌk] VI (*US*) echar los hígados por la boca⁑, vomitar.

upcoming [ˈʌpkʌmɪŋ] ADJ (*US*) venidero, futuro; que se acerca.

upcountry [ˈʌpˈkʌntrɪ] **1** ADV: **to be ~** estar tierra adentro, estar en el interior; **to go ~** ir hacia el interior, penetrar en el interior.
2 ADJ del interior.

up-current [ˈʌpˈkʌrənt] N (*Aer*) corriente *f* ascendente.

update **1** [ˈʌpdeɪt] N puesta *f* al día; actualización *f*; últimas noticias *fpl*; (*~d version*) versión *f* actualizada; **he gave me an ~ on ...** me puso al día con respecto a ...

2 [ʌp'deɪt] VT modernizar, actualizar; **to ~ sb on a matter** poner a uno al tanto de un asunto, dar a uno los últimos detalles de un asunto.

updating [ʌp'deɪtɪŋ] N puesta *f* al día; actualización *f*.

updraught, (*US*) **updraft** ['ʌpdræft] N corriente *f* ascendente.

upend [ʌp'end] VT poner vertical; volver de arriba abajo, poner al revés; *person* volcar.

up-front* [ʌp'frʌnt] **1** ADJ (a) (*esp US: frank*) abierto, franco, sincero. (b) (*US: important*) importante. (c) (*paid in advance*) pagado por adelantado. **2** ADV (a) **to pay ~ for sth** pagar algo por adelantado. (b) (*esp US: frankly*) sinceramente, abiertamente.

upgrade 1 ['ʌpgreɪd] N (a) (*slope*) cuesta *f*, pendiente *f*; **to be on the ~** ir cuesta arriba, prosperar, estar en auge; (*Med*) estar mejor, estar reponiéndose. (b) (*of system etc*) mejoramiento *m*, reforma *f*; (*Comput*) modernización *f*, potenciamiento *m*. **2** [ʌp'greɪd] VT *person* ascender; *job* asignar a un grado más alto; valorar en más; *system etc* mejorar, reformar; (*Comput*) modernizar, potenciar, mejorar las prestaciones de.

upgrad(e)able [ʌp'greɪdəbl] ADJ mejorable, modernizable.

upheaval [ʌp'hiːvəl] N (*Geol*) solevantamiento *m*; (*fig*) cataclismo *m*, sacudida *f*, convulsión *f*.

upheld [ʌp'held] PRET, PTP of **uphold**.

uphill ['ʌp'hɪl] **1** ADV cuesta arriba; **to go ~** ir cuesta arriba; **the road goes ~ for 2 miles** la carretera sube durante 2 millas. **2** ADJ: **it's an ~ task** es una labor ardua, es un trabajo ímprobo.

uphold [ʌp'həʊld] (*irr: V* **hold**) VT (*hold up*) sostener, apoyar; (*maintain*) sostener, defender; (*Jur*) confirmar.

upholder [ʌp'həʊldəʳ] N defensor *m*, -ora *f*.

upholster [ʌp'həʊlstəʳ] VT tapizar, entapizar (*with* de); **well ~ed*** atocinado*.

upholsterer [ʌp'həʊlstərəʳ] N tapicero *m*, -a *f*.

upholstery [ʌp'həʊlstərɪ] N tapicería *f*, tapizado *m*; (*cushioning etc*) almohadillado *m*; (*Aut etc*) guarnecido *m*, tapizado *m*.

UPI N (*US*) ABBR of **United Press International**.

upkeep ['ʌpkiːp] N conservación *f*; (*of car, house etc*) mantenimiento *m*; (*cost*) gastos *mpl* de mantenimiento.

upland ['ʌplənd] **1** N tierra *f* alta, meseta *f*; **~s** tierras *fpl* altas. **2** ADJ de la meseta.

uplift 1 ['ʌplɪft] N sustentación *f*; (*fig*) inspiración *f*, edificación *f*; **moral ~** edificación *f*. **2** [ʌp'lɪft] VT (*fig*) inspirar, edificar.

uplifted [ʌp'lɪftɪd] ADJ *face* vuelto hacia arriba; **with ~ arms** con los brazos en alto.

uplifting [ʌp'lɪftɪŋ] ADJ inspirador, ennoblecedor, edificante.

up-market [ʌp'mɑːkɪt] **1** ADJ *product* superior, para la sección superior del mercado (*or* de la clientela). **2** ADV: **to go ~** buscar clientela en la sección superior.

upmost ['ʌpməʊst] = **uppermost**.

upon [ə'pɒn] PREP *V* **on**.

upper ['ʌpəʳ] **1** ADJ superior, más alto; de arriba; *class* alto; *deck, floor etc* superior, de arriba; (*in Geog names*) alto; **~ atmosphere** atmósfera *f* superior; **~ chamber** (*Parl*) cámara *f* alta; **the ~ class** (*Brit Theat*) galería *f* superior; **~ class** clase *f* alta; **~ crust*** flor *f* y nata, clase *f* alta; **U~ Egypt** Alto Egipto *m*; **U~ House** (*Parl*) Cámara *f* Alta; **~ lip** labio *m* superior; **~ school** cursos *mpl* superiores. **2** N (a) (*of shoe*) pala *f*; **to be on one's ~s*** no tener un céntimo. (b) (‡: *drug*) estimulante *m*. (c) (*: US Rail*) litera *f* de arriba.

upper-case ['ʌpə'keɪs] ATTR mayúsculo, de letra mayúscula.

upper-class ['ʌpə'klɑːs] ADJ de la clase alta.

upper-crust* ['ʌpə'krʌst] ADJ de categoría (social) superior, de buen tono.

uppercut ['ʌpəkʌt] N uppercut *m*, gancho *m* a la cara.

uppermost ['ʌpəməʊst] **1** ADJ (a) (*highest*) (el) más alto; **to put sth face ~** poner algo cara arriba. (b) (*fig*) principal, predominante; **what is ~ in sb's mind** lo que ocupa el primer lugar en el pensamiento de uno; **it was ~ in my mind** pensé en eso antes que en otra cosa. **2** ADV encima.

Upper Volta [ˌʌpə'vɒltə] N Alto Volta *m*.

uppish* ['ʌpɪʃ] ADJ, **uppity*** ['ʌpɪtɪ] ADJ (*Brit*) engreído; fresco; **to get ~** engreírse.

upraise [ʌp'reɪz] VT levantar; **with arm ~d** con el brazo levantado.

upright ['ʌpraɪt] **1** ADJ vertical; derecho; *piano* vertical, recto; (*fig*) honrado, recto, probo. **2** ADV: **to hold o.s. ~** mantenerse erguido; **to sit bolt ~** (*state*) estar muy derecho en su silla. **3** N montante *m*; (*goalpost*) poste *m*.

uprightly ['ʌp,raɪtlɪ] ADV (*fig*) honradamente, rectamente.

uprightness ['ʌp,raɪtnɪs] N (*fig*) honradez *f*, rectitud *f*.

uprising ['ʌpraɪzɪŋ] N alzamiento *m*, sublevación *f*.

up-river [ʌp'rɪvəʳ] ADV = **upstream**.

uproar ['ʌprɔːʳ] N alboroto *m*, tumulto *m*; escándalo *m*; **at this there was ~** en esto estallaron ruidosas las protestas, en esto se armó un escándalo; **the whole place was in ~** la sala estaba alborotada.

uproarious [ʌp'rɔːrɪəs] ADJ tumultuoso, estrepitoso; *laughter* tumultuoso, escandaloso; *joke etc* divertidísimo; *success* clamoroso.

uproariously [ʌp'rɔːrɪəslɪ] ADV tumultuosamente, con estrépito; **to laugh ~** estar para morirse de risa.

uproot [ʌp'ruːt] VT desarraigar, arrancar; (*destroy*) eliminar, extirpar; **whole families have been ~ed** se han desplazado familias enteras.

upsa-daisy ['ʌpsə,deɪzɪ] EXCL ¡aúpa!

upset 1 ['ʌpset] N (*accident*) vuelco *m*; (*in plans etc*) revés *m*, contratiempo *m*; (*Med*) trastorno *m*, desarreglo *m*; **to have a stomach ~** tener un trastorno estomacal, tener el estómago trastornado. **2** [ʌp'set] (*irr: V* **set**) VT (*overturn*) volcar, trastornar; (*spill*) derramar; *stomach* trastornar, hacer daño a; *plans etc* dar al traste con; *person* (*emotionally*) desconcertar, alterar, perturbar; **garlic ~s me** el ajo no me sienta bien; **the news ~ her a lot** la noticia le causó gran pesar; **I didn't intend to ~ her** no tenía la intención de alterarla. **3** [ʌp'set] VR: **to ~ o.s.** acongojarse, apurarse; preocuparse; **don't ~ yourself!** ¡no te acongojes!, ¡no te preocupes! **4** [ʌp'set] ADJ: **to be ~** estar perturbado, estar acongojado, estar preocupado; sentirse molesto; **to get ~** alterarse, perturbarse; **she looked terribly ~** parecía estar apuradísima; **she is easily ~** se apura por cualquier cosa; **what are you so ~ about?** ¿qué te preocupa tanto?, ¿a qué se debe tanto sentimiento?; **I have an ~ stomach** tengo el estómago trastornado. **5** ['ʌpset] ATTR: **~ price** (*esp Scot, US*) precio *m* mínimo, precio *m* de salida.

upsetting [ʌp'setɪŋ] ADJ inquietante, desconcertante.

upshot ['ʌpʃɒt] N resultado *m*; **in the ~** al fin y al cabo; **the ~ of it all was ...** resultó por fin que ...

upside-down ['ʌpsaɪd'daʊn] **1** ADV al revés; **to turn a box ~** volver una caja al revés, invertir una caja; **to turn a room ~** introducir el desorden en un cuarto; **we turned everything ~ looking for it** al buscarlo lo revolvimos todo, en la búsqueda lo registramos todo de arriba abajo. **2** ADJ al revés; **to be ~** estar al revés, tener lo de arriba abajo; **the room was ~** reinaba la mayor confusión en el cuarto, en el cuarto todo estaba patas arriba.

upstage ['ʌpsteɪdʒ] **1** ADV: **to be ~** estar en el fondo de la escena; **to go ~** ir hacia el fondo de la escena. **2** ADJ (*) engreído. **3** VT: **to ~ sb** lograr captar la atención del público a costa de otro; (*fig*) eclipsar a uno.

upstairs ['ʌp'steəz] **1** ADV arriba; **to go ~** ir arriba, subir al piso superior; **to walk slowly ~** subir lentamente la escalera. **2** ADJ de arriba; **we looked out of an ~ window** nos asomamos a una ventana del piso superior. **3** N: **the ~** el piso superior, la parte de arriba.

upstanding [ʌp'stændɪŋ] ADJ (a) **a fine ~ young man** un buen mozo gallardo. (b) **be ~!** (*Jur etc*) ¡levántense!; ¡de pie, por favor!

upstart ['ʌpstɑːt] **1** ADJ arribista; advenedizo; **some ~ youth** algún joven presuntuoso. **2** N arribista *mf*; advenedizo *m*, -a *f*; insolente *mf*.

upstate ['ʌpsteɪt] ADJ (*US, esp of New York*) interior, septentrional.

upstream ['ʌpstriːm] ADV aguas arriba, río arriba (*from* de); **to go ~** ir río arriba; **to swim ~** nadar contra la corriente; **a town ~ from Windsor** una ciudad más arriba de Windsor; **about 3 miles ~ from Seville** unas 3 millas más arriba de Sevilla.

upstretched ['ʌpstretʃt] ADJ extendido hacia arriba.

upstroke ['ʌpstrəʊk] N (*with pen*) trazo *m* ascendente; (*Mech*) carrera *f* ascendente.

upsurge ['ʌpsɜːdʒ] N acceso *m*, aumento *m* grande; **a great ~ of interest in Góngora** un gran renacimiento del interés por Góngora; **there has been an ~ of feeling about this question** ha aumentado de pronto la preocupación por esta cuestión.

upswept ['ʌpswept] ADJ *wing* elevado, inclinado hacia arriba; **with ~ hair** con peinado alto.

upswing ['ʌpswɪŋ] N movimiento *m* hacia arriba; (*fig*) alza *f*, auge *m*, curva *f* ascensional, mejora *f* notable (*in, of* de).

uptake ['ʌpteɪk] N (a) (*acceptance*) recepción *f*, aceptación *f*; (*intake*) consumo *m*; admisión *f*, cantidad *f* admitida. (b) **to be quick on the ~** verlas venir, cogerlas al vuelo; **to be a bit slow on the ~** ser algo torpe.

up-tempo [ˌʌp'tempəʊ] ADJ *tune* con ritmo rápido.

upthrust ['ʌp'θrʌst] **1** ADJ empujado hacia arriba, dirigido hacia arriba; (*Geol*) solevantado. **2** N empuje *m* hacia arriba; (*Geol*) solevantamiento *m*.

uptight* [ʌp'taɪt] ADJ tenso, nervioso; **to get ~ about sth** ponerse nervioso por algo.

uptime ['ʌptaɪm] N tiempo m de operación.

up-to-date ['ʌptə'deɪt] ADJ moderno, actual; al día; *see also* **date**.

up-to-the-minute ['ʌptəðə'mɪnɪt] ADJ de última hora.

uptown ['ʌp'taʊn] (*US*) ① ADV hacia las afueras, hacia los barrios exteriores.

② ADJ exterior, de las afueras.

uptrend ['ʌptrend] N (*Econ*) tendencia f al alza; **in** *or* **on an ~** en alza.

upturn ① ['ʌptɜ:n] N mejora f, aumento m (*in* de); (*Econ etc*) repunte m.

② [ʌp'tɜ:n] VT volver hacia arriba; (*overturn*) volcar.

upturned ['ʌptɜ:nd] ADJ vuelto hacia arriba; *nose* respingón.

UPU N ABBR *of* **Universal Post Union** Unión f Postal Universal, UPU.

UPVC ABBR *of* **unplasticized polyvinyl chloride**.

upward ['ʌpwəd] ADJ *curve, movement etc* ascendente, ascensional; *slope* en pendiente; *tendency* al alza; **~ mobility** (posibilidades *fpl* de) ascenso m social.

upwardly ['ʌpwədlɪ] ADV: **~ mobile** emprendedor, dinámico, que va en alza.

upward(s) ['ʌpwəd(z)] ADV hacia arriba; **to lay sth face ~** poner algo con la cara hacia arriba; **to look ~** mirar hacia arriba; **£50 and ~** de 50 libras para arriba; **from the age of 13 ~** desde los 13 años para arriba; a partir de los 13 años; **~ of 200** más de 200.

upwind ['ʌp'wɪnd] ADV: **to stay ~** quedarse en la parte de donde sopla el viento.

URA N (*US*) ABBR *of* **Urban Renewal Administration**.

uraemia [jʊ'ri:mɪə] N uremia f.

uraemic [jʊ'ri:mɪk] ADJ urémico.

Urals ['jʊərəlz] NPL Urales *mpl*, Montes *mpl* Urales.

uranalysis [jʊərə'nælɪsɪs] N = **urinalysis**.

uranium [jʊə'reɪnɪəm] N uranio m.

Uranus [jʊə'reɪnəs] N Urano m.

urban ['ɜ:bən] ADJ urbano; **~ area** zona f urbana; **~ flight** éxodo m rural; **~ guerrilla** guerrillero m urbano, guerrillera f urbana; **~ renewal** renovación f urbana; **~ sprawl** extensión f urbana.

urbane [ɜ:'beɪn] ADJ urbano, cortés, fino.

urbanity [ɜ:'bænɪtɪ] N urbanidad f, cortesía f, fineza f.

urbanization ['ɜ:bənaɪ'zeɪʃən] N urbanización f.

urbanize ['ɜ:bənaɪz] VT urbanizar.

urchin ['ɜ:tʃɪn] N galopín m, pilluelo m, golfillo m.

Urdu ['ʊədu:] N urdu m.

urea ['jʊərɪə] N urea f.

uremia [jʊə'ri:mɪə] (*US*) = **uraemia**.

uremic [jʊə'ri:mɪk] (*US*) = **uraemic**.

ureter [jʊə'ri:tər] N uréter m.

urethra [jʊə'ri:θrə] N uretra f.

urge [ɜ:dʒ] ① N impulso m; instinto m, deseo m; ansia f; ambición f; **the ~ to win** el afán de victoria; **the ~ to write** el deseo apremiante de escribir, la ambición de hacerse escritor; **to feel an ~ to do sth** ansiar hacer algo, sentirse impulsado a hacer algo; **to get the ~, to have the ~** entrarle a uno ganas (*to* +*infin* de +*infin*).

② VT (a) **to ~ sb to do sth** instar a uno a hacer algo, incitar a uno a hacer algo, recomendar a uno encarecidamente que haga algo; **to ~ that sth should be done** recomendar encarecidamente que se haga algo.

(b) **to ~ sth on sb** incitar a uno a algo, recomendar encarecidamente algo a uno; **to ~ a policy on the government** hacer presión en el gobierno para que adopte una política.

◆**urge on** VT: **to ~ sb on** animar a uno, instar a uno a ir adelante.

urgency ['ɜ:dʒənsɪ] N urgencia f; **with a note of ~ in his voice** en tono algo perentorio, con una nota de perentoriedad; **is there much ~ about this?** ¿corre prisa esto?; **it is a matter of ~** es un asunto urgente.

urgent ['ɜ:dʒənt] ADJ urgente; *tone etc* apremiante, perentorio; *entreaty etc* insistente, apremiante; **it is ~ that ...** urge que + *subj*; **is this ~?** ¿corre prisa esto?

urgently ['ɜ:dʒəntlɪ] ADV urgentemente; de modo apremiante, con insistencia.

uric ['jʊərɪk] ADJ úrico; **~ acid** ácido m úrico.

urinal [jʊə'raɪnl] N (*building*) urinario m; (*vessel*) orinal m.

urinalysis [jʊərə'nælɪsɪs] N análisis m de orina.

urinary ['jʊərɪnərɪ] ADJ urinario.

urinate ['jʊərɪneɪt] ① VT orinar.

② VI orinar(se).

urine ['jʊərɪn] N orina f, orines *mpl*.

urn [ɜ:n] N urna f; (*for tea*) tetera f (grande).

urogenital [jʊərəʊ'dʒenɪtl] ADJ urogenital.

urological [jʊərəʊ'lɒdʒɪkl] ADJ urológico.

urologist [jʊə'rɒlədʒɪst] N urólogo m, -a f.

urology [jʊə'rɒlədʒɪ] N urología f.

Ursa Major ['ɜ:sə'meɪdʒər] N Osa f Mayor.

Ursa Minor ['ɜ:sə'maɪnər] N Osa f Menor.

urticaria [,ɜ:tɪ'kεərɪə] N urticaria f.

Uruguay ['jʊərəgwaɪ] N el Uruguay.

Uruguayan [,jʊərə'gwaɪən] ① ADJ uruguayo.

② N uruguayo m, -a f.

US N ABBR *of* **United States** Estados *mpl* Unidos, EE.UU.

us [ʌs] PRON nos; (*after prep*) nosotros, nosotras.

USA N (a) ABBR *of* **United States of America** Estados *mpl* de América, EE.UU. (b) ABBR *of* **United States Army**.

usable, useable ['ju:zəbl] ADJ utilizable, aprovechable; **~ space** espacio m útil; **it is no longer ~** ya no sirve.

USAF N ABBR *of* **United States Air Force**.

usage ['ju:zɪdʒ] N (a) (*custom*) uso m, costumbre f; **in the ~ of railwaymen** en el lenguaje de los ferroviarios, en el uso ferroviario; **an ancient ~ of the Celts** una antigua usanza de los celtas.

(b) (*treatment*) tratamiento m; trato m, tratos *mpl*; (*handling*) manejo m; **kind ~** buenos tratos *mpl*, buen tratamiento m; **it's had some rough ~** ha sido manejado con bastante dureza.

USCG N (*US*) ABBR *of* **United States Coast Guard**.

USD ABBR *of* **US Dollars**.

USDA N ABBR *of* **United States Department of Agriculture**.

USDAW ['ʌzdɔ:] N ABBR *of* **Union of Shop, Distributive and Allied Workers** *sindicato de empleados de comercio*.

USDI N ABBR *of* **United States Department of the Interior**.

use ① [ju:s] N (a) (*employment*) uso m, empleo m; manejo m; **a new ~ for old tyres** nuevo método m para utilizar los neumáticos viejos; **'directions for ~'** 'modo m de empleo'; **for the ~ of the blind** para uso de los ciegos, para los ciegos; **fit for ~** servible, en buen estado; **ready for ~** listo para usar; **care in the ~ of guns** cuidado m en el manejo de las armas de fuego; **word in ~** palabra f en uso, palabra f que se usa; **it is not now in ~** ya no se usa; **it has not been in ~ for 5 years** hace 5 años que no se usa; **an article in everyday ~** un artículo de uso diario; **it is now out of ~** ya no se usa; eso ha quedado anticuado, eso está fuera de moda ya; **to find a ~ for sth** utilizar algo, aprovechar algo; **it improves with ~** mejora con el uso; **to make ~ of** servirse de; utilizar, aprovechar, explotar; (*right etc*) valerse de, ejercer; **to make good ~ of** aprovecharse debidamente de; **to put sth to good ~** servirse de algo, sacar partido de algo; hacer que algo trabaje (*or* rinda *etc*); **to put sth into ~** poner algo en servicio.

(b) (*usage*) **'the carpark is for the ~ of customers only'** 'sólo para clientes'; **to have the ~ of a garage** poder usar un garaje; **I have the ~ of it on Sundays** me permiten usarlo los domingos; **I should like to have the ~ of it** quisiera poderlo usar; **he lost the ~ of his arm** se le quedó inútil el brazo.

(c) (*usefulness*) utilidad f; **to be of ~** servir (*for* para); **to be of no ~ no servir; can I be of any ~?** ¿puedo ayudar?; **it's (of) no ~** es inútil; **it's no ~ your protesting** de nada sirve quejarse, es inútil quejarse; **it's no ~ discussing it further** no vale la pena discutirlo más; **he's no ~** no vale para nada; **he's no ~ as a goalkeeper** no sirve como portero; **what's the ~ of all this?** ¿de qué sirve todo esto?, ¿qué utilidad tiene todo esto?, ¿qué finalidad tiene todo esto?; **to have no ~ for sth** no tener uso para algo, no poder usar algo; **to have no ~ for sb** despreciar a uno; **I've no ~ for those who ...** detesto a los que ...; **to have no further ~ for sth** no poder usar algo más; **it has its ~s** tiene sus aspectos útiles; de algo nos sirve.

(d) (*custom*) uso m, costumbre f.

② [ju:z] VT (a) (*employ*) *object, tool etc* usar, emplear; servirse de, utilizar; manejar; **he ~d a knife** empleó un cuchillo; **are you using this book?** ¿te hace falta este libro?, ¿estás trabajando con este libro?; **which book did you ~?** ¿qué libro consultaste?; **I could ~ a drink!** ¡no me vendría mal un trago!; **this room could ~ some paint** no le vendría mal a este cuarto una mano de pintura; **careful how you ~ that razor!** ¡cuidado con la navaja esa!; **have you ~d a gun before?** ¿has manejado alguna vez una escopeta?; **the money is ~d for the poor** el dinero se dedica a los pobres, el dinero se emplea en los pobres; **the word is no longer ~d** la palabra ya no se usa; **may I ~ your name?** ¿puedo dar su nombre?; **to ~ sth as a hammer** emplear algo como martillo; **to ~ sth for a purpose** servirse de algo con un propósito.

(b) (*employ*) *abstract things* emplear; **to ~ force** emplear la fuerza; **to ~ every means** emplear todos los medios; no perdonar esfuerzo (*to* + *infin* por + *infin*); **to ~ one's influence** ejercer su influencia.

(c) (*treat*) tratar; **to ~ sb well** tratar bien a uno; **to ~ sb roughly** tratar a uno brutalmente; **she had been cruelly ~d by ...** había sido tratada con crueldad por ...

③ [ju:z] VT (*in Drugs*) drogarse.

④ [ju:s] V AUX: **I ~d to go** iba, solía ir, acostumbraba (a) ir, tenía la costumbre de ir; **but I ~d not to** pero antes no; **things aren't what they ~d to be** las cosas ya no son lo que eran.

◆**use up** VT: **to ~ sth up** consumir algo, agotar algo; **it's all ~d up** todo está agotado; **when we've ~d up all our money** cuando hayamos gastado todo nuestro dinero; **please ~ up all the coffee** que no quede café sin beber.

| USED TO | | *see also main entry* |

- To describe what someone *used to do* or what *used to happen*, you should generally just use the imperfect tense of the main verb:
  We used to buy our food at the corner shop
  Comprábamos la comida en la tienda de la esquina
  ...as my mother used to say...
  ...como decía mi madre...
- Alternatively, to describe someone's habits you can use *solía* + INFINITIVE or *acostumbraba (a)* + INFINITIVE:
  He used to go for a walk every day
  Solía or Acostumbraba (a) dar un paseo todos los días
  NOTE: A further option is *tener la costumbre de*:
  Tenía la costumbre de dar un paseo todos los días
- To emphasize the contrast between what *used to* happen previously and what happens now, use *antes* + IMPERFECT:
  He used to be a journalist
  Antes era periodista
  She didn't use to or She used not to drink alcohol
  Antes no tomaba alcohol
  For further uses and examples, see main entry at *use*.
---

useable ['ju:zəbl] = **usable**.

used ADJ **(a)** [ju:zd] usado; gastado, viejo; *stamp* usado; **~ car** coche *m* de ocasión; **~ literature** (*US*) libros *mpl* de segunda mano.
(b) [ju:st] (*accustomed*) **to be ~ to** estar acostumbrado a; **to be ~ to** + *ger* estar acostumbrado a + *infin*; **to get ~ to** acostumbrarse a; **I still haven't got ~ to the lifts** todavía no me he acostumbrado a los ascensores.

useful ['ju:sfʊl] ADJ útil; provechoso; **a ~ player** un buen jugador, un jugador que vale; **~ capacity** capacidad *f* útil; **it is very ~ to be able to ...** es muy útil poder ...; **he's ~ with his fists** sabe defenderse con los puños; **he's ~ with a gun** sabe manejar un fusil; **would it be ~ to buy two?** ¿sería bueno comprar dos?; **to come in ~** servir, ser útil; venir a propósito; **to make o.s. ~** ayudar, trabajar (*etc*); **come on, make yourself ~!** ¡vamos, a trabajar!; **we had a ~ time in Spain** nuestra estancia en España fue muy provechosa.

usefully ['ju:sfəlɪ] ADV útilmente; provechosamente, con provecho; **there was nothing that could ~ be said** no había nada provechoso que se pudiese decir.

usefulness ['ju:sfʊlnɪs] N utilidad *f*; valor *m*; provecho *m*; **it has outlived its ~** ha dejado de tener utilidad.

useless ['ju:slɪs] ADJ inútil; inservible; inoperante; *person* inepto, incompetente; **he's ~** no vale para nada; **he's ~ as a forward** no vale como delantero; **it is ~ to shout** de nada sirve gritar, es inútil gritar; **to make** (*or* **render**) **sth ~** inutilizar algo.

uselessly ['ju:slɪslɪ] ADV inútilmente, en vano.

uselessness ['ju:slɪsnɪs] N inutilidad *f*.

user ['ju:zər] N usuario *m*, -a *f*; (*Drugs*) drogadicto *m*, -a *f*; **heroin ~** heroinómano *m*, -a *f*; **~ identification** identificación *f* del usuario; **~ language** lenguaje *m* del usuario.

user-definable [ˌju:zədɪ'faɪnəbl] ADJ, **user-defined** [ˌju:zədɪ'faɪnd] ADJ definido por el usuario.

user-friendliness [ˌju:zə'frendlɪnɪs] N facilidad *f* de uso, facilidad *f* de manejo.

user-friendly [ˌju:zə'frendlɪ] ADJ amistoso, fácil de utilizar, fácil para el usuario.

user software ['ju:zə'sɔftweər] N software *m* del usuario.

USES N ABBR of **United States Employment Service**.

USGS N ABBR of **United States Geological Survey**.

usher ['ʌʃər] **1** N ujier *m*, portero *m*; (*Theat*) acomodador *m*; (*at public meeting etc*) guardia *m* de sala, encargado *m* del orden.
2 VT **to ~ sb into a room** hacer pasar a uno a un cuarto, hacer entrar a uno en un cuarto; **to ~ sb out** acompañar a uno a la puerta.
♦**usher in** VT: **to ~ sb in** (*Theat etc*) acomodar a uno; **I was ~ed in by the butler** me hizo pasar el mayordomo; **it ~ed in a new reign** anunció un nuevo reinado, marcó el comienzo del reinado nuevo; **summer was ~ed in by storms** el verano empezó con tormentas.

usherette [ˌʌʃə'ret] N acomodadora *f*.

USIA N ABBR of **United States Information Agency**.

USM N **(a)** ABBR of **United States Mail**. **(b)** (*Fin*) ABBR of **unlisted securities market** mercado *m* de valores no cotizados en la Bolsa. **(c)** ABBR of **United States Mint**.

USN N ABBR of **United States Navy**.

USO N (*US*) ABBR of **United Service Organization**.

USP N ABBR of **unique sales** (*or* **selling**) **proposition**.

USPHS N ABBR of **United States Public Health Service**.
USPO N ABBR of **United States Post Office**.
USPS N ABBR of **United States Postal Service**.
USS N ABBR of **United States Ship** (*or* **Steamer**).
USSR N ABBR of **Union of Soviet Socialist Republics** Unión *f* de Repúblicas Socialistas Soviéticas, URSS *f*.
UTC ABBR of **Universal Time Coordinated**.
usu. **(a)** ABBR of **usual**. **(b)** ABBR of **usually**.

usual ['ju:ʒʊəl] **1** ADJ usual; acostumbrado, habitual; corriente; normal; **as ~** como de costumbre, como siempre; **as per ~!*** ¡lo de siempre!; **more than ~** más que de costumbre, más que lo normal; **his ~ restaurant** su restaurante habitual; **to come earlier than ~** venir antes de la hora (*or* fecha *etc*) acostumbrada; **it's not ~** no es normal; **it's not ~ for people to leave so soon** no es normal marcharse tan pronto.
2 N: **my ~ please!*** ¡lo de siempre!, ¡como de costumbre!

usually ['ju:ʒʊəlɪ] ADV por lo general, por regla general; **we ~ wash it ourselves** acostumbramos lavarlo nosotros mismos; **what do you do ~?** ¿qué hacen Vds normalmente?; **we have to be more than ~ careful** tenemos que tomar más cuidado que de costumbre; **not ~** por lo general no.

usufruct ['ju:zjʊfrʌkt] N usufructo *m*.

usufructuary [ˌju:zjʊ'frʌktərɪ] N usufructuario *m*, -a *f*.

usurer ['ju:ʒərər] N usurero *m*.

usurious [ju:'zjʊərɪəs] ADJ usurario.

usurp [ju:'zɜ:p] VT usurpar.

usurpation [ˌju:zɜ:'peɪʃən] N usurpación *f*.

usurper [ju:'zɜ:pər] N usurpador *m*, -ora *f*.

usurping [ju:'zɜ:pɪŋ] ADJ usurpador.

usury ['ju:ʒʊrɪ] N usura *f*.

UT (*US Post*) ABBR of **Utah**.

utensil [ju:'tensl] N utensilio *m*; **kitchen ~s** utensilios *mpl* de cocina, (*set*) batería *f* de cocina.

uterine ['ju:təraɪn] ADJ uterino.

uterus ['ju:tərəs] N útero *m*.

utilitarian [ˌju:tɪlɪ'teərɪən] **1** ADJ utilitario.
2 N utilitarista *mf*.

utilitarianism [ˌju:tɪlɪ'teərɪənɪzəm] N utilitarismo *m*.

utility [ju:'tɪlɪtɪ] **1** N **(a)** utilidad *f*. **(b)** **public ~** (empresa *f* de) servicio *m* público.
2 ATTR *car, clothing etc* utilitario; **~ room** office *m*; trascocina *f*; **~ vehicle** furgoneta *f*, camioneta *f*.

utilizable ['ju:tɪˌlaɪzəbl] ADJ utilizable.

utilization [ˌju:tɪlaɪ'zeɪʃən] N utilización *f*.

utilize ['ju:tɪlaɪz] VT utilizar.

utmost ['ʌtməʊst] **1** ADJ mayor; supremo; **of the ~ importance** de primerísima importancia; **with the ~ ease** con suma facilidad.
2 N: **the ~ that one can do** todo lo que puede hacer uno; **to do one's ~** hacer todo lo posible (*to* + *infin* por + *infin*); **200 at the ~** 200 a lo más, 200 a lo sumo; **to the ~** al máximo, hasta más no poder; **to the ~ of one's ability** lo mejor que sepa uno.

Utopia [ju:'təʊpɪə] N Utopía *f*.

Utopian [ju:'təʊpɪən] **1** ADJ *dream etc* utópico; *person* utopista.
2 N utopista *mf*.

Utopianism [ju:'təʊpɪənɪzəm] N utopismo *m*.

utricle ['ju:trɪkl] N utrículo *m*.

utter¹ ['ʌtər] ADJ completo, total, absoluto; *fool, madness etc* puro; **~ nonsense!** ¡tonterías!; **it was an ~ disaster** fue un desastre total; **he was in a state of ~ depression** estaba completamente abatido.

utter² ['ʌtər] VT **(a)** *words* pronunciar; *cry etc* dar; *threat, insult etc* proferir; *libel* publicar; **she never ~ed a word** no dijo nada, no dijo ni pío; **don't ~ a word about it** de esto no digas ni pío.
(b) *counterfeit money* poner en circulación, expender.

utterance ['ʌtərəns] N **(a)** (*remark*) palabras *fpl*, declaración *f*. **(b)** (*expression*) expresión *f*; **to give ~ to** expresar, manifestar, declarar. **(c)** (*style*) pronunciación *f*; articulación *f*.

utterly ['ʌtəlɪ] ADV completamente, totalmente, del todo.

uttermost ['ʌtəməʊst] ADJ más remoto, más lejano; extremo; *V* utmost.

UV ADJ ABBR of **ultraviolet** ultravioleta, UV.

UVF N (*Brit*) ABBR of **Ulster Volunteer Force** *organización paramilitar protestante en Irlanda del Norte*.

uvula ['ju:vjələ] N úvula *f*.

uvular ['ju:vjələr] ADJ uvular.

uxorious [ʌk'sɔ:rɪəs] ADJ muy enamorado de su mujer, enamorado con exceso (*or* con ostentación) de su mujer.

Uzbek ['ʊzbek] **1** ADJ uzbeko.
2 N **(a)** uzbeko *m*, -a *f*. **(b)** (*Ling*) uzbeko.

Uzbekistan [ˌʊzbekɪs'tɑ:n] N Uzbekistán *m*.

V

V, v [viː] N (*letter*) V, v *f*; **V for Victor** V de Valencia; **V for victory** V de la victoria; **V-neck** cuello *m* en V; escote *m* en V; **V-necked** con cuello en V; con escote en V; **V-shaped** en forma de V; **V-sign** V *f* de la victoria; (*obscene*) corte *m* de mangas; **to give sb the V-sign** hacer un corte de mangas a uno; **V1** (*flying bomb*) bomba *f* volante (1944-45); **V2** (*rocket*) cohete *m* (1944-45).

v. (a) (*Liter*) ABBR of **verse** estrofa *f*.
(b) (*Bible*) ABBR of **verse** versículo *m*, vers.º.
(c) PREP (*Sport, Jur etc*) ABBR of **versus, against** contra, versus, v.
(d) (*Elec*) ABBR of **volt(s)** voltío(s) *m(pl)*.
(e) ABBR of **vide, see** véase, vid., vide, v.
(f) ABBR of **very**.
(g) ABBR of **volume**.

V&A N (*Brit*) ABBR of **Victoria and Albert Museum.**

VA (*US Post*) ABBR of **Virginia.**

vac* [væk] N (*Brit*) (a) = **vacation.** (b) = **vacuum.**

vacancy ['veɪkənsɪ] N (a) (*emptiness*) lo vacío; (*of mind etc*) vaciedad *f*, vacuidad *f*.
(b) (*in boarding-house etc*) cuarto *m* vacante; **have you any vacancies?** ¿hay algún cuarto libre?, ¿tiene algo disponible?; **we have no vacancies for August** para agosto no hay nada disponible, en agosto todo está lleno.
(c) (*in post*) vacante *f*; **'vacancies'** 'se ofrece trabajo', 'se necesita mano de obra'; **'~ for keen young man'** 'búscase joven enérgico'; **to fill a ~** proveer una vacante.

vacant ['veɪkənt] ADJ (a) *seat, room etc* libre, desocupado; disponible; *space* vacío, desocupado; **~ lot** (*US*) solar *m*; **~ post** vacante *f*; **is this seat ~?** ¿está libre este asiento?; **have you a room ~?** ¿tienen algo disponible?; **to become ~, to fall ~** (*post*) vacar.
(b) *look etc* distraído, vago, (*stupid*) de bobo.

vacantly ['veɪkəntlɪ] ADV *look etc* distraídamente, vagamente, (*stupidly*) sin comprender, boquiabierto.

vacate [vəˈkeɪt] VT *house* desocupar; *post* dejar, dejar vacante, salir de; *throne etc* renunciar a.

vacation [vəˈkeɪʃən] ⚊1⚊ N (a) (*esp Brit*) (*Jur*) vacaciones *fpl*; **long ~** (*Univ*) vacación *f* de verano.
(b) (*US*) vacaciones *fpl*; **to be on ~** estar de vacaciones.
⚊2⚊ ATTR: **~ course** curso *m* de vacaciones, (*esp*) curso *m* de verano; **~ job** empleo *m* de verano; **~ pay** paga *f* de las vacaciones; **~ resort** centro *m* turístico; **~ season** temporada *f* de las vacaciones.
⚊3⚊ VI (*US*) estar de vacaciones; tomarse unas vacaciones; pasar las vacaciones; *see also* **holiday.**

vacationer [vəˈkeɪʃənəʳ] N, **vacationist** [vəˈkeɪʃənɪst] N (*US*) veraneante *mf*.

vaccinate ['væksɪneɪt] VT vacunar.

vaccination [ˌvæksɪˈneɪʃən] N vacunación *f*.

vaccine ['væksiːn] N vacuna *f*.

vacillate ['væsɪleɪt] VI (*sway, vary*) oscilar (*between* entre); (*hesitate*) vacilar, dudar; **to ~ about a course of action** no resolverse a seguir una política determinada.

vacillating ['væsɪleɪtɪŋ] ADJ vacilante, irresoluto.

vacillation [ˌvæsɪˈleɪʃən] N vacilación *f*.

vacuity [væˈkjuːɪtɪ] N (a) vacuidad *f*. (b) (*silly remarks*) **vacuities** vaciedades *fpl*.

vacuous ['vækjʊəs] ADJ bobo, necio.

vacuum ['vækjʊm] ⚊1⚊ N (a) vacío *m*; **it can't exist in a ~** no puede existir en el vacío. (b) (*) **to give a room a ~** limpiar un cuarto con aspiradora.
⚊2⚊ ATTR de vacío; al vacío.
⚊3⚊ VT (*) pasar la aspiradora por.

vacuum bottle ['vækjʊmˌbɒtl] N (*US*) termo(s) *m*.

vacuum-cleaner ['vækjʊmˌkliːnəʳ] N aspiradora *f*.

vacuum-flask ['vækjʊmflɑːsk] N (*Brit*) termo(s) *m*.

vacuum-packed ['vækjʊmˈpækt] ADJ empaquetado al vacío, envasado al vacío.

vacuum-pump ['vækjʊmˈpʌmp] N bomba *f* al vacío.

vade mecum ['vɑːdɪˈmeɪkʊm] N vademécum *m*.

vagabond ['vægəbɒnd] ⚊1⚊ ADJ vagabundo.
⚊2⚊ N vagabundo *m*, -a *f*.

vagary ['veɪgərɪ] N (*whim*) capricho *m*, extravagancia *f*; (*of thermometer etc*) irregularidad *f*, variación *f*; (*of the mind*) divagación *f*; **the vagaries of taste** lo caprichoso del gusto, la inconstancia de la moda.

vagina [vəˈdʒaɪnə] N vagina *f*.

vaginal [vəˈdʒaɪnəl] ADJ vaginal; **~ smear** frotis *m* vaginal.

vagrancy ['veɪgrənsɪ] N vagancia *f*, vagabundaje *m*; **~ in 16th century Spain** los vagabundos (*or* el vagabundeo) en España en el siglo XVI.

vagrant ['veɪgrənt] ⚊1⚊ ADJ vagabundo, vagante; (*fig*) errante.
⚊2⚊ N vagabundo *m*, -a *f*.

vague [veɪg] N (a) (*unclear*) vago; indistinto, borroso; incierto; impreciso; **the ~ outline of a ship** el perfil indistinto de un buque; **the outlook is somewhat ~** la perspectiva es algo incierta; **it is a ~ concept** es un concepto impreciso; **he made some ~ promises** hizo varias promesas imprecisas; **I haven't the ~st** no tengo la más remota idea.
(b) (*of person: in giving details etc*) impreciso, equívoco; (*by nature*) de ideas poco precisas; de actitud poco concreta; (*absent-minded*) despistado, distraído; **he was ~ about the date** no quiso precisar la fecha, no dijo concretamente cuál era la fecha; **he's terribly ~** tiene un tremendo despiste, es un despistado; **you mustn't be so ~** hay que decir las cosas con claridad, hay que concretar; **I am ~ on the subject of ants** sé muy poca cosa en concreto de las hormigas; **then he went all ~** luego comenzó a hablar vagamente; **to look ~** tener aire distraído.

vaguely ['veɪglɪ] ADV vagamente; indistintamente; imprecisamente; distraídamente; **a picture ~ resembling another** un cuadro que tiene cierto parecido vago con otro; **he talks very ~** habla en términos muy vagos; **she looked at me ~** me miró distraída, me miró sin comprender.

vagueness ['veɪgnɪs] N (*V adj*) (a) vaguedad *f*; lo indistinto, lo borroso. (b) incertidumbre *f*, imprecisión *f*; despiste *m*, distracción *f*.

vain [veɪn] ADJ (a) (*useless*) vano, inútil; **in ~** en vano; **it is ~ to try** es inútil intentarlo; **all our efforts were in ~** todos nuestros esfuerzos resultaron ser infructuosos; **to take sb's name in ~** hablar con poco respeto de uno.
(b) (*conceited*) vanidoso; presumido, engreído; **she is very ~ about her hair** es muy orgullosa de su cabello, se enorgullece de su cabello.

vainglorious [veɪnˈglɔːrɪəs] ADJ vanaglorioso.

vainglory [veɪnˈglɔːrɪ] N vanagloria *f*.

vainly ['veɪnlɪ] ADV (a) vanamente, inútilmente; infructuosamente; sin éxito. (b) vanidosamente.

valance ['væləns] N cenefa *f*, doselera *f*.

vale [veɪl] N valle *m*; **~ of tears** valle *m* de lágrimas.

valediction [ˌvælɪˈdɪkʃən] N despedida *f*.

valedictory [ˌvælɪˈdɪktərɪ] ⚊1⚊ ADJ *address etc* de despedida.
⚊2⚊ N (*US*) oración *f* de despedida.

valence ['veɪləns] N valencia *f*.

Valencian [vəˈlensɪən] ⚊1⚊ ADJ valenciano.
⚊2⚊ N (a) valenciano *m*, -a *f*. (b) (*Ling*) valenciano *m*.

valency ['veɪlənsɪ] N valencia *f*.

valentine ['væləntaɪn] N (a) **St V~'s Day** día *m* de San Valentín, día *m* de los enamorados (*14 febrero*).
(b) (*also* **~ card**) tarjeta *f* del día de San Valentín (*enviada por jóvenes, sin firmar, de tono amoroso o jocoso*).
(c) (*person*) novio *m*, -a *f* (*escogido el día de San Valentín*).

valerian [vəˈlɪərɪən] N valeriana *f*.

valet ['væleɪ] N ayuda m de cámara; '~ **parking'** (US) 'con servicio de aparcamiento a cargo del hotel'; **~ing service** servicio m de planchado.

valetudinarian ['vælɪ,tjuːdɪ'nɛərɪən] ⓵ ADJ valetudinario.
　⓶ N valetudinario m, -a f.

Valhalla [væl'hælə] N Valhala m.

valiant ['vælɪənt] ADJ (liter) esforzado, denodado.

valiantly ['vælɪəntlɪ] ADV esforzadamente, denodadamente, con denuedo.

valid ['vælɪd] ADJ válido; ticket etc valedero; law vigente; **a ticket ~ for 3 months** un billete valedero para 3 meses; **that ticket is no longer ~** ese billete ya no vale, ese billete ha caducado ya; **that argument is not ~** ese argumento no vale, ese argumento no es válido.

validate ['vælɪdeɪt] VT convalidar.

validation [,vælɪ'deɪʃən] N convalidación f.

validity [və'lɪdɪtɪ] N validez f; vigencia f.

valise [və'liːz] N valija f, maleta f.

Valium ['vælɪəm] ⓡ N valium ⓡ m.

Valkyrie ['vælkɪrɪ] N Valquiria f.

valley ['vælɪ] N valle m.

valorous ['vælərəs] ADJ (liter) esforzado, denodado.

valour, (US) **valor** ['vælər] N valor m, valentía f.

valuable ['væljʊəbl] ⓵ ADJ valioso; estimable; costoso; **a ~ contribution** una valiosa aportación; **is it ~?** ¿vale mucho?
　⓶ **~s** NPL objetos mpl de valor, valores mpl.

valuation [,væljʊ'eɪʃən] N valuación f, valorización f; tasación f; **to make a ~ of sth** valorar algo, valorizar algo; **to take sb at his own ~** aceptar todo lo que dice uno acerca de sí mismo.

valuator ['væljʊ,eɪtər] N valuador m, -ora f, tasador m, -ora f.

value ['væljuː] ⓵ N **(a)** (gen) valor m; estimación f; importancia f; (Gram, Mus etc) valor m; **~ of money** valor m del dinero; **things of ~** cosas fpl de valor; **of great ~** de gran valor, muy valioso (to para); **of no ~** sin valor; **to be of ~ to sb** ser de valor para uno, ser útil a uno; **to be of little ~ to sb** ser de poco valor para uno, servir poco a uno; **of what ~ is Greek nowadays?** ¿qué valor tiene el griego hoy?, ¿qué utilidad tiene el griego hoy?; **to the ~ of** por valor de; **this dress is good ~ (for the money)** este vestido bien vale lo que pagué por él; **to get good ~ for one's money** gastar su dinero bien; sacar jugo al dinero; **to set a ~ of £200 on sth** tasar algo en 200 libras; **to set a high ~ on sb** estimar a uno en mucho, tener un concepto muy bueno de uno; **to attach no ~ to** no conceder importancia a.
(b) (moral) **~s** valores mpl morales, principios mpl; **sense of ~s** sentido m de los valores morales; **~ judgement** juicio m de valor.
　⓶ VT (financially) valorar, valorizar, tasar (at en); (morally etc) estimar, apreciar; (~ highly) tener en mucho, tener un buen concepto de, apreciar; **it is ~d at £8** está valorado en 8 libras; **I ~ my leisure** para mí son muy importantes mis ratos de ocio; **he doesn't ~ his life** desprecia su vida, no hace estimación de su vida; **she sent her jewellery to be ~d** envió sus joyas para que se las tasaran.

value-added ['væljuː'ædɪd] ADJ: **~ tax** (Brit) impuesto m sobre el valor añadido.

valued ['væljuːd] ADJ estimado, apreciado; **my ~ colleague** mi estimado colega.

valueless ['væljʊlɪs] ADJ sin valor.

valuer ['væljʊər] N tasador m, -ora f.

valve [vælv] N (Anat, Mech) válvula f; (Rad) lámpara f, válvula f; (Bot, Zool) valva f.

valve-tester ['vælv,testər] N comprobador m de válvulas.

vamoose: [və'muːs] VI largarse*; desaparecer.

vamp¹ [væmp] ⓵ N (of shoe) empella f, pala f; (patch) remiendo m.
　⓶ VT shoe poner empella a; remendar; (Mus) improvisar, improvisar un acompañamiento para; **to ~ up an engine** (repair) componer un motor, (supercharge) sobrealimentar un motor.
　⓷ VI (Mus) improvisar (un acompañamiento).

vamp²* [væmp] ⓵ N vampiresa f, vampi* f.
　⓶ VT coquetear con, flirtear con; **to ~ sb into doing sth** engatusar a uno para que haga algo.

vampire ['væmpaɪər] N **(a)** (Zool) vampiro m. **(b)** (fig) vampiro m; (woman) vampiresa f.

van¹ [væn] N (Mil, fig) vanguardia f; **to be in the ~** ir a la vanguardia; **to be in the ~ of progress** estar en la vanguardia del progreso.

van² [væn] N (Brit Aut) camioneta f, furgoneta f; (for removals) camión m de mudanzas; (Brit Rail) furgón m.

vanadium [və'neɪdɪəm] N vanadio m.

Vandal ['vændəl] ⓵ ADJ vándalo, vandálico.
　⓶ N **(a)** (Hist) vándalo m, -a f. **(b)** **v~** gamberro m, vándalo m, -a f.

Vandalic [væn'dælɪk] ADJ vándalo, vandálico.

vandalism ['vændəlɪzəm] N vandalismo m, gamberrismo m; **piece of ~** acto m de vandalismo.

vandalize ['vændəlaɪz] VT destruir, estropear, arruinar.

van-driver ['væn'draɪvər] N conductor m, -ora f de camioneta.

vane [veɪn] N (weathercock) veleta f; (of mill) aspa f; (of propeller) paleta

f; (of feather) barbas fpl.

vanguard ['vængɑːd] N vanguardia f; **to be in the ~** ir a la vanguardia; **to be in the ~ of progress** estar en la vanguardia del progreso.

vanilla [və'nɪlə] N vainilla f.

vanish ['vænɪʃ] VI desaparecer, desvanecerse; **to ~ without trace** desaparecer sin dejar rastro.

vanishing-cream ['vænɪʃɪŋ,kriːm] N crema f de día.

vanishing-point ['vænɪʃɪŋ,pɔɪnt] N punto m de fuga.

vanishing trick ['vænɪʃɪŋ,trɪk] N desaparición f, fuga f.

vanity ['vænɪtɪ] N vanidad f; **all is ~** todo es vanidad; **to do sth out of ~** hacer algo por vanidad.

vanity-case ['vænɪtɪ,keɪs] N neceser m de belleza, polvera f (de bolsillo).

vanity plates ['vænɪtɪ,pleɪts] NPL (esp US: Aut) matrícula fsg personalizada.

vanity unit ['vænɪtɪ'juːnɪt] N lavabo m empotrado.

vanpool ['vænpuːl] N (US) furgonetas fpl de uso compartido.

vanquish ['væŋkwɪʃ] VT (liter) vencer, derrotar.

vantage ['vɑːntɪdʒ] N ventaja f.

vantage-point ['vɑːntɪdʒ,pɔɪnt] N posición f ventajosa, lugar m estratégico; (for views) punto m panorámico; **from our modern ~ we can see that ...** desde nuestra atalaya moderna vemos que ...

vapid ['væpɪd] ADJ insípido, soso.

vapidity [væ'pɪdɪtɪ] N insípidez f, sosería f.

vaporization [,veɪpəraɪ'zeɪʃən] N vaporización f.

vaporize ['veɪpəraɪz] ⓵ VT vaporizar, volatilizar.
　⓶ VI vaporizarse, volatilizarse.

vaporizer ['veɪpəraɪzər] N vaporizador m; (for inhalation) inhalador m; (for perfume) atomizador m.

vaporous ['veɪpərəs] ADJ vaporoso.

vapour, (US) **vapor** ['veɪpər] ⓵ N vapor m; vaho m, exhalación f; **the ~s** (Med†) los vapores.
　⓶ ATTR: **~ trail** estela f de humo.
　⓷ VI (US) fanfarronear; **to ~ about** decir disparates de.

variability [,vɛərɪə'bɪlɪtɪ] N variabilidad f.

variable ['vɛərɪəbl] ⓵ ADJ variable; **~ costs** costes mpl variables; **~ yield securities** valores mpl de renta variable.
　⓶ N variable f.

variance ['vɛərɪəns] N: **to be at ~** estar en desacuerdo (with con), desentonar (with con), estar reñidos (with con).

variant ['vɛərɪənt] ⓵ ADJ variante.
　⓶ N variante f.

variation [,vɛərɪ'eɪʃən] N variación f (also Mus); (variant form) variedad f.

varicoloured, (US) **varicolored** ['vɛərɪ'kʌləd] ADJ abigarrado, multicolor.

varicose ['værɪkəʊs] ADJ varicoso; **~ veins** varices fpl.

varied ['vɛərɪd] ADJ variado.

variegated ['vɛərɪgeɪtɪd] ADJ abigarrado; jaspeado.

variegation [,vɛərɪ'geɪʃən] N abigarramiento f.

variety [və'raɪətɪ] ⓵ N variedad f (also Bio); diversidad f; (Comm: of stock) surtido m; **in a ~ of colours** en varios colores, de diversos colores, (Comm) en diversos colores; **in a ~ of ways** de diversas maneras; **a ~ of opinions was expressed** se expresaron diversas opiniones; **for ~** por variar; **to lend ~ to sth** servir para variar algo, dar diversidad a algo; **~ is the spice of life** en la variedad está el gusto.
　⓶ ATTR: **~ artist(e)** artista mf de variedades; **~ show** revista f, show m; **~ store** (US) tienda f barata que vende de todo, bazar m; **~ theatre** teatro m de variedades.

varifocal [vɛərɪ'fəʊkl] ⓵ ADJ progresivo.
　⓶ NPL: **~s** gafas fpl progresivas, lentes fpl progresivas.

variola [və'raɪələ] N viruela f.

various ['vɛərɪəs] ADJ vario, diverso; **for ~ reasons** por diversas razones; **in ~ ways** de diversos modos; **at ~ times in the past** en determinados momentos del pasado.

variously ['vɛərɪəslɪ] ADV diversamente, de diversos modos; **she stated her age ~** declaraba su edad de diversos modos.

varmint ['vɑːmɪnt] N (Hunting) bicho m; (*) golfo m, bribón m.

varnish ['vɑːnɪʃ] ⓵ N barniz m; (for nails) esmalte m para las uñas, laca f para las uñas; (fig) barniz m, capa f, apariencia f.
　⓶ VT barnizar; nails laquear, esmaltar; (fig: also to ~ over) colorear, encubrir, disimular, paliar; **~ed wood** madera f barnizada, madera f con barniz.

varnishing ['vɑːnɪʃɪŋ] N barnizado m, esmaltado m.

varsity ['vɑːsɪtɪ] N (Brit*) universidad f.
　⓶ ATTR: **V~ Match** partido m entre las Universidades de Oxford y Cambridge.

vary ['vɛərɪ] ⓵ VT variar; decision etc cambiar, modificar.
　⓶ VI variar; (disagree) estar en desacuerdo; discrepar (from de); (deviate) desviarse (from de); **it varies** depende; **it varies from 2 to 10**

varía de 2 a 10; **it varies a lot from the norm** se desvía mucho de la norma; **authors ~ about the date** los autores discrepan acerca de la fecha; **it varies in price** varía de precio; **they ~ in price** los hay de diversos precios; **it varies inversely with ...** varía en razón inversa según ...

varying ['veərɪɪŋ] ADJ cambiante; diverso; **with ~ results** con resultados diversos.

vascular ['væskjʊlər] ADJ vascular.

vase [vɑːz] N florero *m*, jarrón *m*.

vasectomy [væ'sektəmɪ] N vasectomía *f*.

Vaseline ['væsɪliːn] ® N vaselina ® *f*.

vasoconstrictor [,veɪzəʊkən'strɪktər] N vasoconstrictor *m*.

vasodilator [,veɪzəʊdaɪ'leɪtər] N vasodilatador *m*.

vassal ['væsəl] N vasallo *m*.

vassalage ['væsəlɪdʒ] N vasallaje *m*.

vast [vɑːst] ADJ vasto; inmenso, enorme; dilatado; *majority* abrumador.

vastly ['vɑːstlɪ] ADV enormemente; **~ improved** muy mejorado; **~ superior to** con mucho superior a; **we were ~ amused** nos reímos muchísimo con eso; **~ different** muy distinto.

vastness ['vɑːstnɪs] N inmensidad *f*.

VAT [viːeɪ'tiː, væt] N (*Brit*) ABBR of **value-added tax** impuesto *m* sobre el valor añadido, IVA *m*; **~-registered company** compañía *f* declarante del IVA.

vat [væt] N tina *f*, tinaja *f*, cuba *f*.

Vatican ['vætɪkən] ① N Vaticano *m*.
② ADJ vaticano, del Vaticano; **~ City** Ciudad *f* del Vaticano.

vatman* ['vætmæn] N, PL **vatmen** ['vætmen] recaudador *m* del impuesto de valor añadido.

vaudeville ['vəʊdəvɪl] N (*esp US*) vodevil *m*, vaudeville *m*.

vault¹ [vɔːlt] ① N (*Archit*) bóveda *f*; (*for wine*) bodega *f*; (*of bank*) sótano *m*, cámara *f* acorazada; (*tomb*) tumba *f*; (*of church*) cripta *f*; **family ~** panteón *m* familiar; **~ of heaven** bóveda *f* celeste.
② VT abovedar.

vault² [vɔːlt] ① N salto *m*; **at one ~, with one ~** de un solo salto.
② VI saltar; **to ~ into the saddle** colocarse de un salto en la silla; **to ~ over a stream** cruzar un arroyo de un salto.
③ VT saltar.

vaulted ['vɔːltɪd] ADJ abovedado.

vaulting ['vɔːltɪŋ] N abovedado *m*; (*Sport*) salto *m* con pértiga.

vaulting-horse ['vɔːltɪŋ,hɔːs] N potro *m* (de madera).

vaunt [vɔːnt] ① VT jactarse de, hacer alarde de; lucir, ostentar.
② VI jactarse.

vaunted ['vɔːntɪd] ADJ cacareado, alardeado; **much ~** tan cacareado.

vaunting ['vɔːntɪŋ] ① ADJ jactancioso.
② N jactancia *f*.

VC N (a) (*Brit Mil*) ABBR of **Victoria Cross** condecoración británica. (b) (*Univ*) ABBR of **Vice-Chancellor**. (c) ABBR of **vice-chairman**.

VCR N ABBR of **video-cassette recorder**.

VD N ABBR of **venereal disease** enfermedad *f* venérea.

VDT N (*esp US*) ABBR of **visual display terminal**.

VDU N ABBR of **visual display unit** unidad *f* de despliegue visual, UDV *f*, unidad *f* de presentación visual, UPV *f*; **~ operator** operador *m*, -ora *f* de UDV.

veal [viːl] N ternera *f*.

vector ['vektər] N vector *m*.

Veda ['veɪdə] N Veda *m*.

V-E Day [,viːiː'deɪ] N ABBR of **Victory in Europe Day** día *m* de la victoria en Europa.

┌─── **V-E DAY** ───┐

ⓘ *El 8 de mayo se celebra en el Reino Unido y Estados Unidos el Día de la Victoria Europea o **V-E Day: Victory in Europe Day**. En este día se conmemora la victoria del ejército aliado en Europa en la Segunda Guerra Mundial en 1945. El 15 de agosto se conmemora el Día de la Victoria sobre Japón o **V-J Day**, **Victory over Japan Day**, que ocurrió también en 1945.*

Vedic ['veɪdɪk] ADJ védico.

veep* [viːp] N (*US*) vicepresidente *m*, -a *f*.

veer [vɪər] VI (*also* **to ~ round**) (*ship, also fig*) virar; (*wind*) girar, cambiar; **the country has ~ed to the left** el país ha virado hacia la izquierda; **it ~s from one extreme to the other** oscila desde un extremo al otro; **people are ~ing round to our point of view** la gente está empezando a aceptar nuestro criterio.

veg* [vedʒ] N ABBR of **vegetable(s)** verdura *f*, vegetales *mpl*.
♦**veg out*** VI (*US*) relajarse, descansar; tumbarse.

vegan ['viːgən] N vegeteriano *m* estricto, vegetariana *f* estricta.

veganism ['viːgənɪzəm] N vegetarianismo *m* estricto.

vegeburger* ['vedʒɪ,bɜːgər] N = **veggie burger**.

vegetable ['vedʒɪtəbl] ① N (a) (*Bot*) vegetal *m*; (*edible plant*) legumbre *f*, hortaliza *f*; **~s** (*on sale as food, as item of diet*) legumbres *fpl*, hortalizas *fpl*, (*cooked, greens*) verduras *fpl*.
(b) (*human ~*) vegetal *mf*.

② ATTR: **~ dish** plato *m* de legumbres, (*vessel*) fuente *f* de legumbres; **~ fat** grasa *f* vegetal; **~ garden** huerto *m* (de hortalizas); **~ kingdom** reino *m* vegetal; **~ marrow** (*esp Brit*) calabacín *m*; **~ matter** materia *f* vegetal; **~ oil** aceite *m* vegetal; **~ patch** huerto *m*, huertecito *m*; **~ salad** ensalada *f* verde; macedonia *f* de verduras con mayonesa, ensaladilla *f* rusa; **~ soup** sopa *f* de hortelano.

vegetarian [,vedʒɪ'teərɪən] ① ADJ vegetariano.
② N vegetariano *m*, -a *f*.

vegetarianism [,vedʒɪ'teərɪənɪzəm] N vegetarianismo *m*.

vegetate ['vedʒɪteɪt] ① VT: **the land is sparsely ~d** la tierra tiene escasa vegetación.
② VI vegetar (*also fig*).

vegetation [,vedʒɪ'teɪʃən] N vegetación *f*.

vegetative ['vedʒɪtətɪv] ADJ vegetativo.

veggie* ['vedʒɪ] ① ADJ vegetariano; **~ burger** hamburguesa *f* vegetal, hamburguesa *f* vegetariana.
② N vegetariano *m*, -a *f*.

vehemence ['viːɪməns] N vehemencia *f*; violencia *f*, pasión *f*.

vehement ['viːɪmənt] ADJ vehemente; violento, apasionado; **a ~ speech** un discurso apasionado; **there was ~ opposition** hubo una resistencia violenta.

vehemently ['viːɪməntlɪ] ADV con vehemencia; violentamente, apasionadamente; **we are ~ opposed to it** nos oponemos totalmente a ello, estamos cien por cien en contra.

vehicle ['viːɪkl] N vehículo *m*; (*means*) vehículo *m*, medio *m*, instrumento *m* (*for* de).

vehicular [vɪ'hɪkjʊlər] ADJ *road etc* de vehículos, para coches; **~ traffic** circulación *f* rodada.

veil [veɪl] ① N velo *m* (*also Phot and fig*); **under a ~ of secrecy** en el mayor secreto; **to draw a ~ over sth** correr un velo sobre algo, encubrir algo; **we had better draw a ~ over that** es mejor no hablar de eso; **to take the ~** tomar el hábito, meterse monja.
② VT velar (*also fig*); **eyes ~ed by tears** ojos *mpl* empañados por lágrimas; **the town was ~ed by mist** la ciudad estaba cubierta por un velo de niebla.

veiled [veɪld] ADJ velado; encubierto; **with ~ irony** con velada ironía; **that was a ~ reference to the bishop** fue una referencia velada al obispo.

veiling ['veɪlɪŋ] N (*Phot*) velo *m*.

vein [veɪn] N (*Anat, Bot*) vena *f*; (*Min: of ore etc*) filón *m*, veta *f*; (*in stone*) vena *f*; (*in wood*) fibra *f*; hebra *f*, veta *f*; (*fig*) vena *f*, rasgo *m*; **a ~ of madness** una vena de loco, un rasgo de locura; **to be in ~** estar en vena; **to be in the ~ for** estar de humor para.

veined [veɪnd] ADJ veteado, jaspeado.

veining ['veɪnɪŋ] N (*Anat etc*) venas *fpl*; (*Min*) vetas *fpl*, veteado *m*.

velar ['viːlər] ADJ velar.

Velasquez, Velazquez [vɪ'læskwɪz] NM Velázquez.

Velcro ['velkrəʊ] ® N velcro ® *m*.

veld(t) [velt] N sabana *f*.

vellum ['veləm] ① N vitela *f*.
② ATTR: **~ paper** papel *m* vitela.

velocipede†† [və'lɒsɪpiːd] N velocípedo†† *m*.

velocity [vɪ'lɒsɪtɪ] N velocidad *f*.

velodrome ['viːlə,drəʊm] N velódromo *m*.

velour(s) [və'lʊər] N terciopelo *m*.

velum ['viːləm] N velo *m* del paladar.

velvet ['velvɪt] ① N terciopelo *m*; (*on antlers*) piel *f* velluda, vello *m*; **to be on ~*** estar en situación muy ventajosa, vivir en Jauja; **a skin like ~** una piel aterciopelada.
② ADJ, ATTR (*velvety*) aterciopelado; (*of ~*) de terciopelo.

velveteen ['velvɪtiːn] N pana *f*.

velvety ['velvɪtɪ] ADJ aterciopelado; (*fig*) *voice etc* de terciopelo.

venal ['viːnl] ADJ venal.

venality [viː'nælɪtɪ] N venalidad *f*.

vend [vend] VT vender.

vendee [ven'diː] N comprador *m*, -ora *f*.

vendetta [ven'detə] N enemistad *f* mortal, odio *m* de sangre; disputa *f*; **to carry on a ~ against sb** hacer una campaña contra uno; hostigar a uno, perseguir a uno.

vending ['vendɪŋ] N venta *f*, distribución *f*.

vending-machine ['vendɪŋmə,ʃiːn] N vendedora *f* automática.

vendor ['vendɔːr] N vendedor *m*, -ora *f*; (*pedlar*) buhonero *m*.

veneer [və'nɪər] ① N chapa *f*, enchapado *m*; (*fig*) barniz *m*, apariencia *f*; **with a ~ of culture** con un barniz de cultura; **it's just a ~** es un barniz superficial nada más.
② VT chapear.

venerable ['venərəbl] ADJ venerable.

venerate ['venəreɪt] VT venerar, reverenciar.

veneration [,venə'reɪʃən] N veneración *f*; **his ~ for ...** la veneración que sentía por ...; **to hold sb in ~** reverenciar a uno.

venereal [vɪ'nɪərɪəl] ADJ venéreo; **~ disease** enfermedad *f* venérea.

Venetian [vɪ'niːʃən] ① ADJ veneciano; **~ blind** persiana *f*.

2 N veneciano *m*, -a *f*.

Venezuela [ˌveneˈzweɪlə] N Venezuela *f*.

Venezuelan [ˌveneˈzweɪlən] **1** ADJ venezolano.

2 N venezolano *m*, -a *f*.

vengeance [ˈvendʒəns] N venganza *f*; **with a ~** con creces; de verdad; **it's raining with a ~** está lloviendo de verdad; **to take ~ on sb** vengarse de (*or* en) uno.

vengeful [ˈvendʒfʊl] ADJ (*liter*) vengativo.

venial [ˈviːnɪəl] ADJ venial.

veniality [ˌviːnɪˈælɪtɪ] N venialidad *f*.

Venice [ˈvenɪs] N Venecia *f*.

venison [ˈvenɪzn] N carne *f* de venado.

venom [ˈvenəm] N veneno *m*; (*fig*) virulencia *f*, malignidad *f*; **he spoke with real ~ in his voice** habló en tono de verdadero odio.

venomous [ˈvenəməs] ADJ venenoso; (*fig*) virulento, maligno; *tongue* viperino.

venomously [ˈvenəməslɪ] ADV (*fig*) con malignidad, con odio.

venous [ˈviːnəs] ADJ (*Med*) venoso.

vent [vent] **1** N (*opening*) abertura *f*; válvula *f*; (*Mech*) válvula *f* de purga, orificio *m*, lumbrera *f*; (*airhole*) respiradero *m*; (*in pipe*) ventosa *f*; (*Zool*) cloaca *f*; **to give ~ to** dar salida a, desahogar, expresar; **to give ~ to one's feelings** desahogarse; **to give ~ to a sigh** exhalar un suspiro.

2 VT (*Mech*) purgar; (*discharge*) descargar, emitir, dejar escapar; (*pierce*) agujerear; *feelings etc* desahogar, descargar; **to ~ one's anger** desahogar su cólera, desahogarse; **to ~ one's spleen** descargar la bilis (*on* contra).

ventilate [ˈventɪleɪt] VT ventilar (*also fig*).

ventilation [ˌventɪˈleɪʃən] **1** N ventilación *f*.

2 ATTR: **~ shaft** pozo *m* de ventilación.

ventilator [ˈventɪleɪtəʳ] N ventilador *m*.

ventral [ˈventrəl] ADJ ventral.

ventricle [ˈventrɪkl] N ventrículo *m*.

ventriloquism [venˈtrɪləkwɪzəm] N ventriloquia *f*.

ventriloquist [venˈtrɪləkwɪst] N ventrílocuo *m*, -a *f*.

▼ **venture** [ˈventʃəʳ] **1** N aventura *f*, empresa *f* (arriesgada); **at a ~** a la ventura; **his ~ into business** su aventura en el mundo de los negocios; **it seemed a stupid ~ at the time** en aquel momento parecía ser una empresa descabellada; **a new ~ in publishing** un nuevo rumbo en la edición de libros, una nueva empresa editorial.

2 ATTR: **~ capital** capital-riesgo *m*.

3 VT aventurar; (*stake*) jugar; *opinion etc* osar expresar; **they ~d everything** lo jugaron todo; **if I may ~ an opinion** si me permite expresar mi opinión; **may I ~ a guess?** ¿puedo hacer una conjetura?; **he ~d to remark that ...** se permitió observar que ...; **nothing ~ nothing gain** quien no se arriesga no pasa la mar.

4 VI (**a**) **to ~ on sth** arriesgarse en algo, osar emprender algo, lanzarse a algo; **when we ~d on this** cuando emprendimos esto; **to ~ into a wood** (osar) penetrar en un bosque; **to ~ out of doors** osar salir fuera, arriesgarse fuera.

▼ (**b**) **to ~ to** + *infin* osar + *infin*, atreverse a + *infin*; permitirse + *infin*; **I ~ to add that ...** me permito agregar que ...; **I ~ to write to you** me tomo la libertad de dirigirme a Vd; **but he did not ~ to speak** pero no osó hablar.

◆ **venture forth** VI (*liter*) aventurarse a salir.

venturesome [ˈventʃəsəm] ADJ *person* atrevido, audaz; *enterprise* arriesgado, azaroso.

venue [ˈvenjuː] N punto *m* de reunión, lugar *m* de reunión; **the ~ for the next match** el campo para el próximo partido; **change of ~** (*Jur*) cambio *m* de jurisdicción; **the ~ has been changed** se ha cambiado de lugar.

Venus [ˈviːnəs] N (*Myth*) Venus *f*; (*Astron*) Venus *m*.

veracious [vəˈreɪʃəs] ADJ veraz.

veracity [vəˈræsɪtɪ] N veracidad *f*.

veranda(h) [vəˈrændə] N veranda *f*, terraza *f*, galería *f*.

verb [vɜːb] N verbo *m*.

verbal [ˈvɜːbəl] ADJ verbal.

verbalize [ˈvɜːbəlaɪz] **1** VT expresar en palabras; exteriorizar hablando.

2 VI expresarse en palabras; **he does not ~ easily** no se expresa con facilidad.

verbally [ˈvɜːbəlɪ] ADV verbalmente; de palabra, por boca.

verbatim [vɜːˈbeɪtɪm] **1** ADJ palabra por palabra, literal.

2 ADV palabra por palabra, literalmente.

verbena [vɜːˈbiːnə] N verbena *f*.

verbiage [ˈvɜːbɪɪdʒ] N verbosidad *f*, palabrería *f*.

verbose [vɜːˈbəʊs] ADJ verboso, prolijo.

verbosely [vɜːˈbəʊslɪ] ADV prolijamente.

verbosity [vɜːˈbɒsɪtɪ] N verbosidad *f*.

verdant [ˈvɜːdənt] ADJ verde.

verdict [ˈvɜːdɪkt] N (*Jur*) veredicto *m*, fallo *m*, sentencia *f*, juicio *m*; (*fig*) opinión *f*, juicio *m*; **a ~ of guilty** una sentencia de culpabilidad;

open ~ juicio *m* en el que se determina el crimen sin designar el culpable; **what's your ~?** ¿qué opinas de esto?, ¿qué juicio te has formado sobre esto?; **his ~ on the wine was unfavourable** hizo un juicio desfavorable acerca del vino; **to bring in a ~, to return a ~** pronunciar una sentencia, fallar, dar un fallo; **to bring in a ~ of guilty** pronunciar una sentencia de culpabilidad.

verdigris [ˈvɜːdɪɡriːs] N verdete *m*, cardenillo *m*.

verdure [ˈvɜːdjʊəʳ] N verdor *m*.

verge [vɜːdʒ] N borde *m*, margen *m*; **to be on the ~ of disaster** estar a dos dedos del desastre, estar en el mismo borde de la catástrofe; **to be on the ~ of a nervous breakdown** estar al borde de una crisis nerviosa; **to be on the ~ of a great discovery** estar en la antesala de un gran descubrimiento; **we are on the ~ of war** estamos al borde de la guerra; **she was on the ~ of tears** estaba para deshacerse en lágrimas; **to be on the ~ of** + *ger* estar a punto de + *infin*.

◆ **verge on** VI acercarse a, rayar en; estar a un paso mínimo de; **a state verging on madness** un estado que raya en la locura.

verger [ˈvɜːdʒəʳ] N sacristán *m*.

Vergil [ˈvɜːdʒɪl] NM Virgilio.

Vergilian [vəˈdʒɪlɪən] ADJ virgiliano.

verifiability [ˌverɪfaɪəˈbɪlɪtɪ] N verificabilidad *f*.

verifiable [ˈverɪfaɪəbl] ADJ comprobable, verificable.

verification [ˌverɪfɪˈkeɪʃən] N comprobación *f*, verificación *f*.

verifier [ˈverɪfaɪəʳ] N (*Comput*) verificador *m*.

verify [ˈverɪfaɪ] VT comprobar, verificar; (*Comput*) verificar.

verily [ˈverɪlɪ] ADV (†) en verdad.

verisimilitude [ˌverɪsɪˈmɪlɪtjuːd] N verosimilitud *f*.

veritable [ˈverɪtəbl] ADJ verdadero; **a ~ monster** un verdadero monstruo.

veritably [ˈverɪtəblɪ] ADV verdaderamente.

verity [ˈverɪtɪ] N verdad *f*; **the eternal verities** las verdades eternas.

vermicelli [ˌvɜːmɪˈselɪ] N fideos *mpl*.

vermicide [ˈvɜːmɪsaɪd] N vermicida *m*.

vermifuge [ˈvɜːmɪfjuːdʒ] N vermífugo *m*.

vermilion [vəˈmɪlɪən] **1** N bermellón *m*.

2 ADJ bermejo.

vermin [ˈvɜːmɪn] N (*insects etc*) bichos *mpl*, sabandijas *fpl*; parásitos *mpl*; (*mammals*) alimañas *fpl*; (*fig*) sabandijas *fpl*; (*persons*) chusma *f*.

verminous [ˈvɜːmɪnəs] ADJ verminoso, piojoso; (*fig*) vil.

vermouth [ˈvɜːməθ] N vermú *m*, vermut *m*.

vernacular [vəˈnækjʊləʳ] **1** ADJ (**a**) (*Ling*) vernáculo, vulgar; **in ~ Persian** en persa vulgar, en la lengua vernácula de Persia. (**b**) *architecture etc* típico; local, regional; doméstico.

2 N lengua *f* vernácula; (*fig*) lenguaje *m* corriente, lenguaje *m* vulgar.

vernal [ˈvɜːnl] ADJ *equinox* de invierno; (*liter*) *flowers* de primavera.

Veronica [vəˈrɒnɪkə] NF Verónica.

veronica [vəˈrɒnɪkə] N (*Bot*) verónica *f*.

verruca [vəˈruːkə] N verruga *f*.

Versailles [veəˈsaɪ] N Versalles *m*.

versatile [ˈvɜːsətaɪl] ADJ versátil.

versatility [ˌvɜːsəˈtɪlɪtɪ] N versatilidad *f*.

verse [vɜːs] **1** N (**a**) (*stanza*) estrofa *f*; (*of Bible*) versículo *m*; 'The Satanic V~s' 'Los versículos satánicos'. (**b**) (*genre*) verso *m*; (*poetry*) poesías *fpl*, versos *mpl*; **is it in ~?** ¿está en verso?

2 ATTR: **~ drama** teatro *m* en verso, drama *m* poético; **a ~ version of the 'Celestina'** una versión en verso de la 'Celestina'.

versed [vɜːst] ADJ: **to be well ~ in** estar versado en, conocer, ser conocedor de.

versification [ˌvɜːsɪfɪˈkeɪʃən] N versificación *f*.

versifier [ˈvɜːsɪfaɪəʳ] N versificador *m*, -ora *f*, versista *mf*.

versify [ˈvɜːsɪfaɪ] **1** VT versificar.

2 VI versificar, escribir versos.

version [ˈvɜːʃən] N versión *f*; **in Lope's ~ of the story** en la versión que hizo Lope de la historia; **my ~ of events is as follows ...** yo veo los sucesos del siguiente modo ..., así es como yo veo los hechos; **according to his ~** según su interpretación; **that's a different ~ again** ése es otro modo distinto de contarlo.

verso [ˈvɜːsəʊ] N verso *m*.

versus [ˈvɜːsəs] PREP contra.

vertebra [ˈvɜːtɪbrə] N, PL **vertebrae** [ˈvɜːtɪbriː] vértebra *f*.

vertebral [ˈvɜːtɪbrəl] ADJ vertebral.

vertebrate [ˈvɜːtɪbrɪt] **1** ADJ vertebrado.

2 N vertebrado *m*.

vertex [ˈvɜːteks] N, PL **vertices** [ˈvɜːtɪsiːz] vértice *m*.

vertical [ˈvɜːtɪkəl] **1** ADJ vertical; **~ integration** integración *f* vertical; **~ section** sección *f* vertical, corte *m* vertical.

2 N vertical *f*.

vertically [ˈvɜːtɪkəlɪ] ADV verticalmente.

vertiginous [vɜːˈtɪdʒɪnəs] ADJ vertiginoso.

vertigo [ˈvɜːtɪɡəʊ] N vértigo *m*.

➤ LANGUAGE IN USE: venture: **4b** → 26.3

verve [vɜːv] N energía f, empuje m; brío m; entusiasmo m.

very ['verɪ] 1 ADV (a) (extremely) muy; ~ **good** muy bueno; 'That will be all' — 'V~ good, sir' 'Nada más' — 'Muy bien, señor'; ~ **well** muy bien; **he couldn't ~ well refuse** no pudo muy bien negarse a hacerlo; ~ **much** mucho, muchísimo; 'Did you enjoy it?' — 'V~ much so' '¿Te ha gustado?' — 'Sí, mucho'; **she felt ~ much better** se encontró muchísimo mejor; **I was ~ (much) surprised** me sorprendió mucho, para mí era una gran sorpresa; **it's not so ~ diffi-cult** no es tan difícil, la dificultad no es tan grande; **that's ~ kind of you** eres muy amable; **you're not being ~ helpful** realmente no nos ayudas nada; **it is ~ cold** (object) está muy frío, (weather) hace mucho frío.
(b) (absolutely) **the ~ first** el primero, el primero de todos; **the ~ best** el mejor, el mejor que haya; **we did our ~ best** hicimos todo lo que pudimos; **try your ~ hardest** esfuércese al máximo; **at the ~ most** a lo más, a lo sumo, todo lo más; **the ~ most we can offer** el límite de lo que podemos ofrecer; **the ~ next day** precisamente el día siguiente; **the ~ same hat** el idéntico sombrero, el mismísimo sombrero.
(c) (alone, in reply to question) mucho; **are you tired?** — ~ ¿estás cansado? — mucho.
(d) (emotional use) **they are so ~ poor** son pobrísimos; **it is a ~ good wine** es un vino rebueno, es un vino requetebueno.
2 ADJ (a) (precise, exact) mismo; **in this ~ house** en esta misma casa; **at that ~ moment** en ese mismo momento; **to the ~ bone** hasta el mismo hueso; **he's the ~ man we want** es precisamente el hombre que buscamos; **it's the ~ thing!** ¡es exactamente lo que necesitamos!; **at the ~ beginning** ya en los comienzos; **the ~ bish-op himself was there** el mismísimo obispo estaba allí, hasta el propio obispo estaba allí; **the ~ idea!** ¡ni hablar!, ¡qué cosas dices!; **the ~ thought frightens me** sólo pensar en ello me da miedo.
(b) (liter) **the veriest rascal** el mayor bribón; **the veriest simpleton** el más bobo.

vesicle ['vesɪkl] N vesícula f.

vespers ['vespəz] NPL vísperas fpl.

vessel ['vesl] N (a) (Anat, Bot) vaso m; (receptacle) vasija f, recipiente m; **he's a weak ~** es una persona sin carácter.
(b) (Naut) buque m, barco m.

vest¹ [vest] N (Brit) camiseta f; (US) chaleco m.

vest² [vest] VT (frm) (a) **to ~ sb with sth** investir a uno de algo.
(b) **to ~ rights in sb** conferir derechos a uno, conceder derechos a uno, revestir a uno de derechos; **by the authority ~ed in me** en virtud de la autoridad que se me ha concedido; **to ~ property in sb** ceder una propiedad a uno, hacer a uno titular de una propiedad.

vesta ['vestə] N cerilla f.

vestal ['vestl] 1 ADJ vestal.
2 N vestal f.

vested ['vestɪd] ADJ right inalienable; ~ **interest** interés m personal; ~ **interests** intereses mpl creados.

vestibule ['vestɪbjuːl] N vestíbulo m; (hall of house) zaguán m; (anteroom) antecámara f.

vestige ['vestɪdʒ] N vestigio m, rastro m; (Bio) rudimento m; **not a ~ of it remains** no queda rastro de ello, de ello no queda ni el menor vestigio; **without a ~ of decency** sin la menor decencia; **if there is a ~ of doubt** si hay una sombra de duda.

vestigial [ves'tɪdʒɪəl] ADJ vestigial; rudimentario.

vestment ['vestmənt] N vestidura f.

vest-pocket [vest'pɒkɪt] ADJ (US) de bolsillo.

vestry ['vestrɪ] N sacristía f.

vesture ['vestʃəʳ] N (liter) vestidura f.

Vesuvius [vɪ'suːvɪəs] N Vesubio m.

vet [vet] 1 N (a) ABBR of veterinary surgeon, veterinarian veterinario mf (also -a f).
(b) (US*) ABBR of veteran ex combatiente m.
2 VT repasar, revisar; examinar, investigar; aprobar; (give clearance to) acreditar; **he's ~ting the proofs** está corrigiendo las pruebas; **we'll have it ~ted by the boss** haremos que el jefe lo revise; **he was ~ted by Security** fue investigado por la Seguridad, (and cleared) fue acreditado por la Seguridad.

vetch [vetʃ] N arveja f.

veteran ['vetərən] 1 ADJ veterano.
2 N veterano m; (esp US) ex combatiente m.

veterinarian [ˌvetərɪ'neərɪən] N (US) veterinario mf (also -a f).

veterinary ['vetərɪnərɪ] ADJ veterinario; ~ **medicine**, ~ **science** medicina f veterinaria, veterinaria f; ~ **school** escuela f de veterinaria; ~ **surgeon** (esp Brit) veterinario mf (also -a f).

veto ['viːtəu] 1 N, PL **vetoes** ['viːtəuz] veto m; **to have a ~** tener veto; **to put a ~ on sth** poner su veto a algo.
2 VT vedar, vetar, prohibir; **he ~ed it** lo prohibió, lo vedó; **the president ~ed it** el presidente le puso su veto.

vetting ['vetɪŋ] N (check) examen m previo; investigación f; (clearance) acreditación f; (test of loyalty) prueba f de lealtad.

vex [veks] VT (anger) fastidiar, irritar, contrariar; (make impatient) impacientar, sacar de quicio; (afflict) afligir; **the problems that are ~ing the country** los problemas que afligen el país, los problemas que alteran el país.

vexation [vek'seɪʃən] N irritación f, contrariedad f; impaciencia f; aflicción f; **he had to put up with numerous ~s** tuvo que soportar muchos disgustos.

vexatious [vek'seɪʃəs] ADJ fastidioso, molesto, engorroso.

vexed [vekst] ADJ (a) (annoyed) **to be ~ about sth** estar enfadado de (or por) algo, estar enojado por algo (LAm); **to be ~ with sb** estar enfadado con uno; **to be very ~** estar muy enfadado; **to get ~** enfadarse, impacientarse; **in a ~ tone** en tono ofendido, en tono de enojo. (b) ~ **question** cuestión f batallona.

vexing ['veksɪŋ] ADJ fastidioso, molesto, engorroso; **it's very ~** es una lata.

VFD N (US) ABBR of **voluntary fire department**.

v.g. ABBR of **very good** muy bueno, sobresaliente, S.

VGA N ABBR of **video graphics array**.

VHF N ABBR of **very high frequency** frecuencia f muy alta, VHF.

VHS N ABBR of **video home system**.

VI (US Post) ABBR of **Virgin Islands**.

via ['vaɪə] PREP por, por vía de; **we came ~ London** pasamos por Londres.

viability [ˌvaɪə'bɪlɪtɪ] N viabilidad f.

viable ['vaɪəbl] ADJ viable.

viaduct ['vaɪədʌkt] N viaducto m.

vial ['vaɪəl] N frasquito m.

viands ['vaɪəndz] NPL (liter) manjares mpl (exquisitos).

viaticum [vaɪ'ætɪkəm] N viático m.

vibes* [vaɪbz] NPL (a) (ABBR of vibrations) (from band, singer) vibraciones fpl, ambiente m; **I got good ~ from her** me cayó muy bien. (b) (Mus: ABBR of vibraphone) vibráfono m.

vibrancy ['vaɪbrənsɪ] N energía f, dinamismo m; vitalidad f.

vibrant ['vaɪbrənt] 1 ADJ vibrante (also fig; with de).
2 N vibrante f.

vibraphone ['vaɪbrə,fəun] N vibráfono m.

vibrate [vaɪ'breɪt] VTI vibrar.

vibration [vaɪ'breɪʃən] N vibración f.

vibrato [vɪ'brɑːtəu] N vibrato m.

vibrator [vaɪ'breɪtəʳ] N vibrador m.

vibratory ['vaɪbrətərɪ] ADJ vibratorio.

viburnum [vaɪ'bɜːnəm] N viburno m.

Vic [vɪk] (a) NM familiar form of Victor. (b) NF ABBR of **Victoria**.

vicar ['vɪkəʳ] N vicario m; (Anglican) párroco m, cura m.

vicarage ['vɪkərɪdʒ] N casa f del párroco.

vicar-general ['vɪkə'dʒenərəl] N vicario m general.

vicarious [vɪ'keərɪəs] ADJ experimentado por otro; indirecto; responsibility delegado; **to get ~ pleasure out of sth** sentir placer por lo que está haciendo otro; **I got a ~ thrill** me emocioné mucho sin tener nada que ver con lo que pasaba.

vicariously [vɪ'keərɪəslɪ] ADV: **to feel excitement ~** emocionarse por lo que está haciendo otro, emocionarse a través de la emoción de otro.

vice¹ [vaɪs] 1 N vicio m.
2 ATTR: ~ **squad** brigada f contra el vicio.

vice², (US) **vise** [vaɪs] N (Mech) torno m de banco, tornillo m de banco.

vice³ ['vaɪsɪ] PREP en lugar de, sustituyendo a.

vice... [vaɪs] PREF vice...

vice-admiral ['vaɪs'ædmərəl] N vicealmirante m.

vice-chairman ['vaɪs'tʃeəmən] N, PL **vice-chairmen** ['vaɪs'tʃeəmən] vicepresidente m.

vice-chairmanship ['vaɪs,tʃeəmənʃɪp] N vicepresidencia f.

vice-chancellor ['vaɪs'tʃɑːnsələʳ] N (Univ) ≃ rector m.

vice-consul ['vaɪs'kɒnsəl] N vicecónsul m.

vice-presidency ['vaɪs'prezɪdənsɪ] N vicepresidencia f.

vice-president ['vaɪs'prezɪdənt] N vicepresidente m, -a f.

vice-principal ['vaɪs'prɪnsɪpəl] N (US Scol) subdirector m, -ora f.

viceroy ['vaɪsrɔɪ] N virrey m.

viceroyalty ['vaɪs'rɔɪəltɪ] N virreinato m.

vice versa ['vaɪsɪ'vɜːsə] ADV viceversa, a la inversa; **and ~** y viceversa, y a la inversa.

vicinity [vɪ'sɪnɪtɪ] N (a) (area) vecindad f, región f; **and other towns in the ~** y otras ciudades de la región, y otras ciudades cercanas; **we are in the ~ of Wigan** estamos en la región de Wigan, estamos cerca de Wigan; **in the ~ of 90** unos 90, alrededor de 90.
(b) (nearness) proximidad f (to de).

vicious ['vɪʃəs] ADJ (related to vice) vicioso; person depravado, perverso; cruel; dog bravo; horse resabiado, arisco; blow cruel, sañudo; crime atroz; criticism virulento, cruel, rencoroso; ~ **circle** círculo m vicioso; **with ~ intent** con mala intención, con intención criminal.

viciously ['vɪʃəslɪ] ADV viciosamente; perversamente, cruelmente; con virulencia, con rencor, rencorosamente.

viciousness ['vɪʃəsnɪs] N viciosidad *f*; perversidad *f*, crueldad *f*; bravura *f*, resabios *mpl*; atrocidad *f*; virulencia *f*, rencor *m*.

vicissitudes [vɪ'sɪsɪtjuːdz] NPL vicisitudes *fpl*; altibajos *mpl*, peripecias *fpl*.

vicissitudinous [vɪ,sɪsɪ'tjuːdɪnəs] ADJ agitado, accidentado.

Vicky ['vɪkɪ] NF *familiar form of* **Victoria**.

victim ['vɪktɪm] N víctima *f*; **the ~s** (*suffering survivors*) los damnificados; **to be the ~ of an accident** ser víctima de un accidente, morir (*etc*) en un accidente; **to be the ~ of a swindle** ser víctima de una estafa; **to fall a ~ to flu** enfermar con la gripe; **to fall a ~ to sb's charms** rendirse (*or* sucumbir) a los encantos de uno.

victimization [,vɪktɪmaɪ'zeɪʃən] N sacrificio *m*; persecución *f*; (*of striker etc*) castigo *m*, represalias *fpl*.

victimize ['vɪktɪmaɪz] VT victimizar; escoger y castigar, tomar represalias contra; **the strikers should not be ~d** no hay por qué castigar a los huelguistas; **she feels she has been ~d** ella cree que ha sido escogida como víctima.

victimless ['vɪktɪmlɪs] ADJ sin víctimas.

Victim Support ['vɪktɪmsə'pɔːt] N (*Brit*) organización de ayuda a las víctimas de actos delictivos.

Victor ['vɪktər] NM Victor.

victor ['vɪktər] N vencedor *m*, -ora *f*.

Victoria [vɪk'tɔːrɪə] NF Victoria.

Victoria Cross [vɪk'tɔːrɪə'krɒs] N (*Brit*) la condecoración más alta de las fuerzas armadas británicas y de la Commonwealth.

Victoria Falls [vɪk'tɔːrɪə'fɔːlz] NPL Cataratas *fpl* de Victoria.

Victorian [vɪk'tɔːrɪən] ① ADJ victoriano.
　② N victoriano *m*, -a *f*.

🛈 |▔VICTORIAN▔|
El adjetivo **Victorian** *se usa para referirse a la época del reinado de la reina Victoria (1837-1901), así como a la cultura y a las personas de dicha época, en frases como, por ejemplo,* **they live in a Victorian house** *o* **the Victorian Prime Minister, Gladstone***. Las actitudes o cualidades llamadas victorianas son las que se consideran características de la época, tales como el interés por la respetabilidad social, una estricta moralidad represiva, la falta de sentido del humor, la intolerancia y la hipocresía. El término* **Victorian values** *(valores victorianos) se usa en política para abogar por cualidades positivas como la decencia, la superación personal, el respeto a la autoridad y la importancia de la familia, cualidades que muchos opinan que faltan en la sociedad actual. En Estados Unidos también se utiliza el adjetivo* **Victorian** *para describir la arquitectura, muebles, actitudes, etc., contemporáneas de la época victoriana en el Reino Unido.*

Victoriana [vɪk,tɔːrɪ'ɑːnə] NPL objetos *mpl* victorianos, antigüedades *fpl* victorianas.

victorious [vɪk'tɔːrɪəs] ADJ victorioso; **the ~ team** el equipo vencedor, los vencedores; **to be ~** triunfar (*over* sobre), salir victorioso, vencer.

victoriously [vɪk'tɔːrɪəslɪ] ADV victoriosamente, triunfalmente.

victory ['vɪktərɪ] N victoria *f*; triunfo *m*; **∨ V** *f* de la victoria; **to win a famous ~** obtener un triunfo señalado.

victual ['vɪtl] ① VT abastecer, avituallar.
　② VI abastecerse, avituallarse, tomar provisiones.
　③ NPL: **~s** víveres *mpl*, provisiones *fpl*.

victualler ['vɪtlər] N: *V* **license²** 1.

vicuña [vɪ'kjuːnə] N vicuña *f*.

vide ['vɪdeɪ] VT vea, véase.

videlicet [vɪ'diːlɪset] ADV a saber.

video ['vɪdɪəʊ] ① N vídeo *m*.
　② ATTR vídeo, de vídeo; **~ arcade** salón *m* recreativo de videojuegos; **~ camera** videocámara *f*; **~ cassette** casete *m* de vídeo, videocasete *m*; **~ cassette recorder** videograbadora *f*; **~ club** videoclub *m*; **~ disc**, (*US*) **~ disk** videodisco *m*; **~ film** película *f* de vídeo, videofilm *m*; **~ frequency** videofrecuencia *f*; **~ game** videojuego *m*; **~ library** videoteca *f*; **~ magazine** videorrevista *f*; **~ nasty*** videofilm *m* de horror; videofilm *m* porno*; **~ piracy** videopiratería *f*; **~ projector** videoproyector *m*; **~ recorder** vídeo *m*, videograbadora *f*; **~ recording** (*act*) videograbación *f*, (*object*) videograma *m*; **~ shop** tienda *f* de vídeo; **~ terminal** terminal *m* de vídeo, videoterminal *m*; **~ wall** vídeo-panel *m*, panel *m* de vídeo.
　③ VT hacer un vídeo de.

video... ['vɪdɪəʊ] PREF vídeo...

videophone ['vɪdɪəʊ,fəʊn] N videófono *m*, videoteléfono *m*.

videotape ['vɪdɪəʊ,teɪp] ① N cinta *f* de vídeo, videocinta *f*.
　② ATTR: **~ library** videoteca *f*; **~ recorder** videograbadora *f*.
　③ VT grabar en (cinta de) vídeo.

videotaping ['vɪdɪəʊ,teɪpɪŋ] N videograbación *f*.

videotex ['vɪdɪəʊ,teks] N vídeotex *m*.

videotext ['vɪdɪəʊ,tekst] N videotexto *m*.

vie [vaɪ] VI competir, ser rivales; **to ~ for sth** disputarse algo; **to ~ with sb for sth** disputar algo a alguien, luchar contra uno para

conseguir algo; **to ~ with sb** competir con uno, rivalizar con uno.

Vienna [vɪ'enə] N Viena *f*.

Viennese [,vɪə'niːz] ① ADJ vienés.
　② N vienés *m*, -esa *f*.

Vietcong [,vjet'kɒŋ] ① ADJ del Vietcong.
　② N vietcong *mf*.

Vietnam ['vjet'næm] N Vietnam *m*.

Vietnamese [,vjetnə'miːz] ① ADJ vietnamita.
　② N (a) vietnamita *mf*. (b) (*Ling*) vietnamita *m*.

vieux jeu ['vɪɜː'ʒɜː] ADJ anticuado, fuera de moda.

▼ **view** [vjuː] ① N (a) (*gen*) vista *f*; panorama *m*; (*Art, Phot*) panorama *m*; (*landscape*) paisaje *m*; **it's a beautiful ~** es un bello panorama; **there is a fine ~ from the top** desde la cumbre se ofrece un magnífico panorama; **50 ~s of Venice** 50 vistas de Venecia; **a ~ of Toledo from the north** Toledo en su aspecto norte, Toledo visto desde el norte; **to be in ~** ser visible; **to be in full ~** ser totalmente visible; **he did it in full ~ of hundreds of people** lo hizo estando delante centenares de personas, lo hizo a plena vista de centenares de personas; **to have (*or* keep) sb in ~** no perder a uno de vista; **to be on ~** estar expuesto; **to come into ~** aparecer, presentarse; **the house will be on ~ to the public on Saturdays** la casa estará abierta al público los sábados.

▼ **(b)** (*opinion etc*) opinión *f*, parecer *m*; criterio *m*; actitud *f*; **in my ~** en mi opinión; **in ~ of this** en vista de esto; **with a ~ to doing sth** con miras a hacer algo, con el propósito de hacer algo; **our ~ of the problem** nuestro modo de enfocar el problema; **what is the government's ~?** ¿cuál es el parecer del gobierno?; **it is not easy to form a ~** no es fácil llegar a una conclusión; **to have (*or* keep) sth in ~** tener algo en cuenta, tener algo presente; **I do not share that ~** no comparto ese criterio; **to take the ~ that ...** opinar que ...; **to take the long ~** considerar un asunto a largo plazo; **we take a different ~** nosotros pensamos de otro modo; **to take a dim (*or* poor) ~ of sb** tener un concepto desfavorable de uno, ver a uno con malos ojos; **I should take a dim ~ if ...** no me agradaría que + *subj*.
　② VT (a) (*see, examine*) mirar; ver, contemplar; examinar, inspeccionar; **we went to ~ the house** fuimos a ver la casa; **Cadiz ~ed from the sea** Cádiz visto desde el mar.
　(b) (*TV*) ver, mirar.
　(c) (*consider*) considerar, ver, mirar; **we ~ it with some alarm** para nosotros es motivo de cierta alarma; **how does the government ~ it?** ¿cuál es el parecer del gobierno?
　③ VI (*TV*): **were you ~ing last night?** ¿estabas viendo la televisión anoche?; **do you spend much time ~ing?** ¿pasas mucho tiempo viendo televisión?

viewdata ['vjuː,deɪtə] NPL vídeodatos *mpl*.

viewer ['vjuːər] N (a) (*onlooker*) espectador *m*, -ora *f*; (*TV*) televidente *mf*, telespectador *m*, -ora *f*. (b) (*apparatus*) visionador *m*, visionadora *f*.

viewfinder ['vjuː,faɪndər] N visor *m* (de imagen).

viewing ['vjuːɪŋ] ① ADJ: **~ habits** hábitos *mpl* de los telespectadores; **the ~ public** los telespectadores, la audiencia televisiva; **TV ~ figures** cifras *fpl* de audiencia televisiva; *V* **peak 2**.
　② N (a) (*gen*) visita *f*, inspección *f*.
　(b) (*TV: act*) ver *m* la televisión; (*programmes*) programas *mpl*, programación *f*; **your ~ for the weekend** sus programas para el fin de semana; **late-night ~** programas *mpl* para las altas horas; **tennis makes good ~** el tenis va bien en televisión, el tenis es muy televisivo.

viewpoint ['vjuː,pɔɪnt] N (a) (*Geog*) mirador *m*, punto *m* panorámico.
　(b) (*fig*) punto de vista; criterio *m*; **from the ~ of the economy** desde el punto de vista de la economía.

vigil ['vɪdʒɪl] N vigilia *f*; **to keep ~** velar.

vigilance ['vɪdʒɪləns] ① N vigilancia *f*; **to escape sb's ~** burlar la vigilancia de uno.
　② ATTR: **~ committee** (*US*) comité *m* de autodefensa.

vigilant ['vɪdʒɪlənt] ADJ vigilante; desvelado, alerta.

vigilante ['vɪdʒɪ'læntɪ] N vigilante *m*.

vigilantism [,vɪdʒɪ'læntɪzəm] N vigilancia *f* callejera.

vigilantly ['vɪdʒɪləntlɪ] ADV vigilantemente.

vignette [vɪ'njet] N (*Phot, Typ*) viñeta *f*; (*character sketch etc*) esbozo *m* en miniatura, esbocito *m*; estampa *f*.

vigorous ['vɪgərəs] ADJ vigoroso, enérgico, pujante.

vigorously ['vɪgərəslɪ] ADV vigorosamente, con vigor, enérgicamente.

vigour, (*US*) **vigor** ['vɪgər] N vigor *m*, energía *f*, pujanza *f*; **in the full ~ of manhood** en la flor de la edad viril.

Viking ['vaɪkɪŋ] N vikingo *m*.

vile [vaɪl] ADJ vil, infame, detestable; (*very bad*) horrible, asqueroso; **the weather was ~** el tiempo fue horrible; **it's a ~ play** es una obra malísima; **he has a ~ temper** tiene un genio de perro, es un hombre de malas pulgas; **that was a ~ thing to say** eso fue infame.

vilely ['vaɪllɪ] ADV vilmente; de modo infame, de modo detestable; malísimamente, horriblemente; **he treated her ~** la trató de modo infame.

vileness ['vaɪlnɪs] N vileza f, infamia f; lo horrible, lo asqueroso; **the ~ of the weather** el tiempo tan horrible que hace.

vilification [ˌvɪlɪfɪ'keɪʃən] N vilipendio m.

vilify ['vɪlɪfaɪ] VT vilipendiar.

villa ['vɪlə] N (Roman etc) villa f; (seaside) chalet m; (country house) casa f de campo, quinta f.

village ['vɪlɪdʒ] [1] N (small) aldea f, pueblecito m; lugar m; (large) pueblo m.
[2] ATTR aldeano; pueblerino; de aldea, de la aldea; ~ **cricket** criquet m pueblerino; ~ **green** césped m comunal; ~ **hall** sala f del pueblo; ~ **idiot** tonto m del lugar; ~ **store** tienda f del pueblo.

villager ['vɪlɪdʒər] N aldeano m, -a f.

villain ['vɪlən] N malvado m; (Liter) malo m, traidor m; (criminal) ladrón m, criminal m; (hum) tunante m, bribón m; **you ~!** ¡ladrón!; **the ~ of the piece is X** el que debiera cargar con la culpa de esto es X, el verdadero responsable es X.

villainous ['vɪlənəs] ADJ malvado, vil, infame; (very bad) malísimo, horrible; **and other ~ characters** y otros personajes infames.

villainously ['vɪlənəslɪ] ADV vilmente; ~ **ugly** feísimo.

villainy ['vɪlənɪ] N maldad f, vileza f.

villein ['vɪlɪn] N (Hist) villano m, -a f.

vim [vɪm] N energía f, empuje m, vigor m.

VIN N ABBR of **vehicle identification number**.

vinaigrette [ˌvɪner'gret] N vinagreta f.

Vincent ['vɪnsənt] NM Vicente.

vindaloo [ˌvɪndə'lu:] N plato indio muy picante.

vindicate ['vɪndɪkeɪt] [1] VT vindicar, justificar.
[2] VR: **to ~ o.s.** justificarse.

vindication [ˌvɪndɪ'keɪʃən] N vindicación f, justificación f.

vindictive [vɪn'dɪktɪv] ADJ vengativo; rencoroso; **to feel ~ about sth** guardar rencor por algo; **to feel ~ towards sb** guardar rencor a uno.

vindictively [vɪn'dɪktɪvlɪ] ADV rencorosamente, con rencor.

vindictiveness [vɪn'dɪktɪvnɪs] N deseo m de venganza, espíritu m de venganza; rencor m.

vine [vaɪn] N vid f; (climbing, trained) parra f.

vine arbour, (US) **vine arbor** ['vaɪn,ɑːbər] N emparrado m.

vinegar ['vɪnɪgər] N vinagre m.

vinegary ['vɪnɪgərɪ] ADJ vinagroso.

vinegrower ['vaɪn,grəʊər] N viticultor m, -ora f, viñador m, -ora f.

vinegrowing ['vaɪn,grəʊɪŋ] N viticultura f.

vineleaf ['vaɪnli:f] N, PL **vineleaves** ['vaɪnli:vz] hoja f de parra, hoja f de vid, pámpana f.

vineyard ['vɪnjəd] N viña f, viñedo m.

viniculture ['vɪnɪkʌltʃər] N vinicultura f.

vino* ['vi:nəʊ] N vino m, tintorro* m, purrela f.

vinous ['vaɪnəs] ADJ vinoso.

vintage ['vɪntɪdʒ] [1] N (season, harvest) vendimia f; (with reference to quality or year) cosecha f; **the 1990 ~** la cosecha de 1990; **it will be a good ~** la cosecha promete ser buena.
[2] ADJ clásico; ~ **wine** vino m añejo, vino m de calidad; vino m de crianza; ~ **car** coche m de época, coche m antiguo, coche m clásico; **it was a ~ year** fue un año famoso, fue un año clásico; **it has been a ~ year for plays** en el teatro ha sido una temporada excelente.

vintner ['vɪntnər] N vinatero m.

vinyl ['vaɪnl] [1] N vinilo m; ~ **acetate** acetato m de vinilo.
[2] ADJ vinílico.

viol ['vaɪəl] N viola f.

viola¹ ['vaɪələ] N (Bot) viola f, violeta f.

viola² [vɪ'əʊlə] [1] N (Mus) viola f; ~ **da gamba** viola f de gamba; ~ **d'amore** viola f de amor.
[2] ATTR: ~ **player** viola mf.

violate ['vaɪəleɪt] VT (rape) violar; (Jur) violar, quebrantar, infringir; privacy invadir.

violation [ˌvaɪə'leɪʃən] N violación f; **in ~ of a law** violando así una ley; **in ~ of sb's privacy** invadiendo la vida privada de uno.

violator ['vaɪəleɪtər] N violador m, -ora f; (of law) infractor m, -ora f.

violence ['vaɪələns] N violencia f; **there was ~** se recurrió a la fuerza; **there has been ~ on the streets** ha habido violencia en las calles; **to die by ~** morir violentamente; **to do sb a ~** agredir a uno, herir a uno; **to do ~ to** violentar; **to do ~ to a theory** torcer una teoría; **to offer ~** mostrarse violento; **to resort to ~** recurrir a la fuerza, venirse a las manos; tomar medidas violentas; **to rob sb with ~** robar algo a uno a mano airada.

violent ['vaɪələnt] ADJ violento; feeling etc intenso, acerbo; pain intenso; colour chillón; **to become ~** mostrarse violento; apelar a la fuerza; **to lay ~ hands on sb** agredir a uno; **to take a ~ dislike to sb** tomar un odio intenso a uno.

violently ['vaɪələntlɪ] ADV violentamente, con violencia; **to die ~** morir violentamente; **to fall ~ in love with sb** enamorarse perdidamente de uno; **he expresses himself rather ~** se expresa en términos algo violentos.

violet ['vaɪəlɪt] [1] N (Bot) violeta f; (colour) violado m, violeta f.
[2] ADJ violado, violeta; ~ **color** (US), ~ **colour** color m violeta.

violin [ˌvaɪə'lɪn] [1] N violín m.
[2] ATTR: ~ **case** maletín m de violín.

violinist [ˌvaɪə'lɪnɪst] N violinista mf.

violist [vɪ'əʊlɪst] N (US) viola mf.

violoncellist [ˌvaɪələn'tʃelɪst] N violonchelista mf.

violoncello [ˌvaɪələn'tʃeləʊ] N violonchelo m.

VIP N (freq hum) ABBR of **very important person** personaje m, figura f, VIP m; **to give sb the ~ treatment** tratar a uno como VIP.

viper ['vaɪpər] N víbora f.

viperish ['vaɪpərɪʃ] ADJ (fig) viperino.

virago [vɪ'rɑːgəʊ] N fiera f, arpía f.

viral ['vaɪərəl] ADJ vírico.

Virgil ['vɜːdʒɪl] NM Virgilio.

Virgilian [vɜː'dʒɪlɪən] ADJ virgiliano.

virgin ['vɜːdʒɪn] [1] ADJ virgen; cork, forest, soil etc virgen.
[2] N virgen f; **the V~** la Virgen; **the Blessed V~** la Santísima Virgen.

virginal ['vɜːdʒɪnl] [1] ADJ virginal.
[2] ~**s** NPL (Mus) espineta f.

Virginian [və'dʒɪnɪən] [1] ADJ virginiano.
[2] N (a) virginiano m, -a f. (b) (also ~ **tobacco**) tobaco m rubio.

Virgin Isles ['vɜːdʒɪn,aɪlz] NPL Islas fpl Vírgenes.

virginity [vɜː'dʒɪnɪtɪ] N virginidad f.

Virgo ['vɜːgəʊ] N (Zodiac) Virgo f.

virgule ['vɜːgjuːl] N (US Typ) barra f oblicua.

virile ['vɪraɪl] ADJ viril.

virility [vɪ'rɪlɪtɪ] N virilidad f.

virologist [ˌvaɪə'rɒlədʒɪst] N virólogo m, -a f.

virology [ˌvaɪə'rɒlədʒɪ] N virología f.

virtual ['vɜːtjʊəl] ADJ virtual; ~ **memory**, ~ **storage** memoria f virtual; ~ **reality** realidad f virtual; **the ~ dictator of the country** el que es en efecto el dictador del país; **it was a ~ defeat** era prácticamente una derrota; **he made a ~ admission of guilt** en efecto se confesó culpable.

virtuality [vɜːtjʊ'ælɪtɪ] N realidad f virtual, virtualidad f.

virtually ['vɜːtjʊəlɪ] ADV virtualmente; prácticamente; **it is ~ impossible to do anything** es prácticamente imposible hacer nada, es casi imposible hacer nada; **it ~ destroyed the building** destruyó virtualmente el edificio.

virtue ['vɜːtjuː] N virtud f; (of woman) honra f; **a woman of easy ~** una mujer de vida alegre, una mujer de moralidad laxa; **by ~ of, in ~ of** en virtud de; **he had designs on her** ~ iba a tratar de seducirla; **her ~ was in no danger** su honra no estaba en peligro; **to make a ~ of necessity** hacer de la necesidad (una) virtud; **I see no ~ in that** no encuentro ninguna ventaja en eso; **I see no ~s in trams** no comprendo el porqué de los tranvías.

virtuosity [ˌvɜːtjʊ'ɒsɪtɪ] N virtuosismo m.

virtuoso [ˌvɜːtjʊ'əʊzəʊ] N, PL **virtuosos** or **virtuosi** [ˌvɜːtjʊ'əʊzɪ] virtuoso m.

virtuous ['vɜːtjʊəs] ADJ virtuoso.

virtuously ['vɜːtjʊəslɪ] ADV virtuosamente.

virulence ['vɪrʊləns] N virulencia f.

virulent ['vɪrʊlənt] ADJ virulento.

virulently ['vɪrʊləntlɪ] ADJ con virulencia.

virus ['vaɪərəs] [1] N virus m (also Comput).
[2] ATTR: ~ **disease** enfermedad f vírica.

visa ['viːzə] [1] N visado m, visa m, visa f (LAm).
[2] VT visar.

visage ['vɪzɪdʒ] N (liter) semblante m.

vis-à-vis ['viːzəviː] PREP respecto de, con relación a; para con; frente a.

viscera ['vɪsərə] NPL vísceras fpl.

visceral ['vɪsərəl] ADJ visceral.

viscid ['vɪsɪd] ADJ viscoso.

viscose ['vɪskəʊs] [1] ADJ viscoso.
[2] N viscosa f.

viscosity [vɪs'kɒsɪtɪ] N viscosidad f.

viscount ['vaɪkaʊnt] N vizconde m.

viscountcy ['vaɪkaʊntsɪ] N vizcondado m.

viscountess ['vaɪkaʊntɪs] N vizcondesa f.

viscous ['vɪskəs] ADJ viscoso.

vise [vaɪs] N (US) = **vice²**.

visibility [ˌvɪzɪ'bɪlɪtɪ] N visibilidad f (also Aer etc); **in good ~** en buenas condiciones de visibilidad; **there was a ~ of 500 metres** la visibilidad era de 500 metros; ~ **is down to nil** la visibilidad queda reducida a cero.

visible ['vɪzəbl] ADJ visible; ~ **exports** exportaciones fpl visibles; ~ **imports** importaciones fpl visibles; ~ **reserve** reserva f visible.

visibly ['vɪzəblɪ] ADV visiblemente; **he had got ~ thinner** había adelgazado visiblemente; **she was ~ moved** patentizó su emoción, acusó una fuerte conmoción.

Visigoth ['vɪzɪgɒθ] N visigodo m, -a f.

Visigothic [ˌvɪzɪˈgɒθɪk] ADJ visigodo, visigótico.

vision [ˈvɪʒən] N **(a)** visión f (also Eccl); (eyesight) vista f; **to have normal** ~ tener la vista normal.
(b) (farsightedness) clarividencia f; **a man of** ~ un hombre clarividente; **he had the** ~ **to see that ...** era lo bastante clarividente como para ver que ...
(c) (dream) sueño m; **my** ~ **of the future** mi sueño del porvenir, mi manera de imaginar el futuro; **to have** ~**s of wealth** soñar con ser rico; **I had** ~**s of getting lost** me veía ya perdido.

visionary [ˈvɪʒənərɪ] **1** ADJ visionario.
2 N visionario m, -a f.

vision-mixer [ˈvɪʒənˌmɪksər] N (TV) mezclador m, -ora f de imágenes.

visit [ˈvɪzɪt] **1** N visita f; **on an official** ~ en visita oficial; **on a private** ~ en visita privada; **to be on a** ~ **to ...** estar de visita en ...; **to pay sb a** ~ hacer una visita a uno; **to return a** ~ devolver una visita.
2 VT **(a)** (go and see) visitar, hacer una visita a; ir a; conocer; **when we first** ~**ed the town** cuando conocimos la ciudad por primera vez; **to** ~ **the sick** visitar a los enfermos.
(b) (†: inflict, afflict) **to** ~ **a punishment on sb** castigar a uno con algo, mandar un castigo a uno; **they were** ~**ed with the plague** sufrieron el azote de la peste.
3 VI (also **to go** ~**ing**) hacer visitas; **to** ~ **with sb** (US) visitar a uno; charlar con uno.

visitation [ˌvɪzɪˈteɪʃən] N **(a)** (Eccl) visitación f; (inspection) inspección f; (•) visitón* m. **(b)** (punishment) castigo m.

visiting [ˈvɪzɪtɪŋ] ADJ de visita; ~ **card** (Brit) tarjeta f de visita; ~ **hours**, ~ **time** horas fpl de visita; ~ **nurse** (US) enfermera f que visita a domicilio; ~ **professor** profesor m, -ora f visitante; ~ **team** equipo m visitante; **we're on** ~ **terms** nos visitamos.

visitor [ˈvɪzɪtər] N visitante mf; (to one's home) visita f; (tourist) turista mf, visitante mf; (tripper) excursionista mf; (stranger) forastero m, -a f; ~**'s book** libro m de visitas, libro m de honor; ~ **center** (US), ~ **centre** centro m de información; **the museum had 900** ~**s** el museo recibió a 900 visitantes; **we can't invite you because we have** ~**s** no podemos invitarte pues tenemos visita; **sorry, we're just** ~**s here** lo siento, estamos aquí de visita nada más; **the summer** ~**s bring a lot of money** los veraneantes aportan mucho dinero.

visor [ˈvaɪzər] N visera f.

VISTA [ˈvɪstə] N (US) ABBR of **Volunteers in Service to America** programa m de ayuda voluntaria a los necesitados.

vista [ˈvɪstə] N vista f, panorama m; (fig) perspectiva f; **there are new** ~**s** hay perspectivas nuevas; **it opened up** ~**s of wealth** ofreció perspectivas de riqueza.

visual [ˈvɪzjʊəl] ADJ visual; ~ **aid** ayuda f visual; ~ **display unit** unidad f de despliegue visual; ~ **effects** efectos mpl visuales.

visualization [ˌvɪzjʊəlaɪˈzeɪʃən] N visualización f.

visualize [ˈvɪzjʊəlaɪz] VT **(a)** (form a picture of) representarse (en la mente), imaginarse.
(b) (foresee) prever; **the government** ~**s that ...** el gobierno prevé que ...; **we do not** ~ **any great change** no prevemos ningún cambio de importancia; **that is not how we** ~**d it** eso no corresponde a lo que nosotros preveíamos.

visually [ˈvɪzjʊəlɪ] ADV visualmente; ~ **handicapped person** invidente mf.

▼ **vital** [ˈvaɪtl] **1** ADJ **(a)** (essential) esencial; imprescindible; de suma importancia, trascendental; **of** ~ **importance** de primerísima importancia, de importancia primordial (to para); **the book is** ~ el libro es esencial; **it is** ~ **that ...** es esencial que + subj, importa muchísimo que + subj.
(b) (critical) decisivo, crítico; **at the** ~ **moment** en el momento decisivo.
(c) person (of character) enérgico, vivo, lleno de vida; **she's a very** ~ **person** es una persona que rebosa de energía.
(d) (relating to life) vital; ~ **parts** partes fpl vitales; ~ **statistics** estadísticas fpl demográficas, bioestadística f; (hum) medidas fpl vitales, mensuraciones fpl.
2 ~**s** NPL partes fpl vitales.

vitality [vaɪˈtælɪtɪ] N vitalidad f, energía f.

vitalize [ˈvaɪtəlaɪz] VT vitalizar, vivificar, infundir nueva vida a.

vitally [ˈvaɪtəlɪ] ADV: ~ **important** de primerísima importancia; **it is** ~ **important that ...** es esencial que + subj.

vitamin [ˈvɪtəmɪn] **1** N vitamina f.
2 ATTR content etc vitamínico; ~ **deficiency** avitaminosis f; ~ **enriched** enriquecido con vitaminas; ~ **tablet** pastilla f de vitaminas.

vitaminize [ˈvɪtəmɪnaɪz] VT vitaminar.

vitaminized [ˈvɪtəmɪnaɪzd] ADJ vitamin(iz)ado, reforzado con vitaminas.

vitiate [ˈvɪʃɪeɪt] VT viciar (also Jur); estropear, destruir; quitar valor a.

viticulture [ˈvɪtɪkʌltʃər] N viticultura f.

vitreous [ˈvɪtrɪəs] ADJ vítreo.

vitrifaction [ˌvɪtrɪˈfækʃən] N vitrificación f.

vitrify [ˈvɪtrɪfaɪ] **1** VT vitrificar.
2 VI vitrificarse.

vitriol [ˈvɪtrɪəl] N vitriolo m.

vitriolic [ˌvɪtrɪˈɒlɪk] ADJ (fig) mordaz, vitriólico.

vitro [ˈvɪtrəʊ] V in vitro.

vituperate [vɪˈtjuːpəreɪt] VT vituperar, llenar de injurias.

vituperation [vɪˌtjuːpəˈreɪʃən] N vituperio m, injurias fpl.

vituperative [vɪˈtjuːpərətɪv] ADJ vituperioso, injurioso.

viva¹ [ˈvaɪvə] N (Brit) examen m oral.

viva² [ˈviːvə] INTERJ: ~ **Diana!** ¡viva Diana!

vivacious [vɪˈveɪʃəs] ADJ animado, vivaz, alegre, lleno de vida.

vivaciously [vɪˈveɪʃəslɪ] ADJ animadamente, alegremente.

vivacity [vɪˈvæsɪtɪ] N animación f, vivacidad f, vida f, alegría f.

vivarium [vɪˈveərɪəm] N vivero m.

viva voce [ˈvaɪvəˈvəʊsɪ] **1** ADV de viva voz.
2 ADJ exam oral.
3 N (Brit) examen m oral.

vivid [ˈvɪvɪd] ADJ vivo; colour, light intenso; flash súbito; impression, memory etc vivo; description gráfico, enérgico, pintoresco.

vividly [ˈvɪvɪdlɪ] ADV intensamente; súbitamente; vivamente; enérgicamente, con rasgos enérgicos, de modo pintoresco.

vividness [ˈvɪvɪdnɪs] N viveza f; intensidad f; vivacidad f; energía f.

vivify [ˈvɪvɪfaɪ] VT vivificar.

viviparous [vɪˈvɪpərəs] ADJ vivíparo.

vivisection [ˌvɪvɪˈsekʃən] N vivisección f.

vivisectionist [ˌvɪvɪˈsekʃənɪst] N vivisector m, -ora f.

vixen [ˈvɪksn] N zorra f, raposa f; (woman) arpía f.

viz. [vɪz] ADV ABBR of videlicet, namely verbigracia, v.gr.

vizier [vɪˈzɪər] N visir m; **grand** ~ gran visir m.

V-J Day [ˌviːˈdʒeɪˌdeɪ] N ABBR of **Victory over Japan Day** Brit: 15 agosto 1945; US: 2 septiembre 1945; ver también V-E DAY .

VLF N ABBR of **very low frequency.**

VLSI N ABBR of **very large-scale integration** integración f a muy gran escala.

VOA N ABBR of **Voice of America** Voz f de América.

vocab* [ˈvəʊkæb] N ABBR of **vocabulary.**

vocable [ˈvəʊkəbl] N vocablo m.

vocabulary [vəˈkæbjʊlərɪ] N vocabulario m, léxico m.

vocal [ˈvəʊkəl] **1** ADJ **(a)** (Anat) vocal; ~ **cords** cuerdas fpl vocales; ~ **organs** órganos mpl vocales, órganos mpl de la voz.
(b) (Mus) vocal; ~ **score** partitura f vocal.
(c) (noisy) ruidoso; chillón, gritón; **they're getting rather** ~ **about it** están empezando a protestar; **there was some** ~ **opposition** hubo alguna oposición ruidosa.
2 ~**s** NPL voz f, canto m; **backing** ~**s** voz f auxiliar; **lead** ~**s** voz f principal.

vocalic [vəʊˈkælɪk] ADJ vocálico.

vocalisation [ˌvəʊkəlaɪˈzeɪʃən] N vocalización f.

vocalist [ˈvəʊkəlɪst] N cantante mf; (in cabaret etc) vocalista mf.

vocalize [ˈvəʊkəlaɪz] **1** VT vocalizar.
2 VI vocalizarse.

vocally [ˈvəʊkəlɪ] ADV vocalmente; ruidosamente.

vocation [vəʊˈkeɪʃən] N vocación f; **to have a** ~ **for art** tener vocación por el arte; **he has missed his** ~ se ha equivocado de carrera.

vocational [vəʊˈkeɪʃənl] ADJ vocacional, profesional; ~ **guidance** guía f vocacional, orientación f profesional; ~ **training** formación f vocacional (or profesional).

vocative [ˈvɒkətɪv] **1** ADJ vocativo; ~ **case = 2.**
2 N vocativo m.

vociferate [vəʊˈsɪfəreɪt] VTI vociferar, gritar.

vociferation [vəʊˌsɪfəˈreɪʃən] N vociferación f.

vociferous [vəʊˈsɪfərəs] ADJ vinglero, clamoroso; vociferante; ruidoso; **there were** ~ **protests** hubo protestas ruidosas, se protestó ruidosamente.

vociferously [vəʊˈsɪfərəslɪ] ADV a gritos, clamorosamente; ruidosamente.

vodka [ˈvɒdkə] N vodka m.

vogue [vəʊg] **1** N boga f, moda f; **the** ~ **for short skirts** la moda de la falda corta; **to be in** ~ estar de moda, estar en boga.
2 ATTR: ~ **word** palabra f que está de moda.

voice [vɔɪs] **1** N (gen) voz f; **in a gentle** ~ en tono dulce; **in a loud** ~ en voz alta; **in a low** ~ en voz baja; **with one** ~ a una voz, al unísono; **to be in (good)** ~ estar en voz; **to find one's** ~ volver a poder hablar; **to give** ~ **to** expresar, hacerse eco de; **to have no** ~ **in a matter** no tener voz en capítulo; **to keep one's** ~ **down** seguir hablando en tono bajo; **to lower one's** ~ bajar el tono; **to raise one's** ~ levantar el tono, (protest) protestar.
(b) (Ling, Gram) voz f; **active** ~ voz f activa; **passive** ~ voz f pasiva.
2 ATTR: ~ **box** caja f laríngea; ~ **mail** fonobuzón m; ~ **parts** melodía f; ~ **recognition** reconocimiento m de la voz; ~ **synthesis** síntesis f

de la voz; **~ synthesizer** sintetizador *m* de la voz humana; **~ train-ing** educación *f* de la voz.
③ VT **(a)** (*express*) expresar, hacerse eco de.
(b) (*Ling*) sonorizar.
voice-activated ['vɔɪs'æktɪveɪtəd] ADJ activado por sonido.
voiced [vɔɪst] ADJ sonoro.
voiceless ['vɔɪslɪs] ADJ sordo.
voice-over ['vɔɪs,əʊvər] N voz *f* en off.
voiceprint ['vɔɪs,prɪnt] N impresión *f* vocal.
voicing ['vɔɪsɪŋ] N sonorización *f*.
void [vɔɪd] ① ADJ (*empty*) vacío; desocupado; *post* vacante; (*Jur*) nulo, inválido; **to be ~ of** estar falto de, estar desprovisto de; **to make a contract ~** anular un contrato, invalidar un contrato; **to make sb's efforts ~** hacer inútiles los esfuerzos de uno; *V* **null**.
② N **(a)** (*lit, fig*) vacío *m*; hueco *m*, espacio *m*; **the ~** la nada; **to fill the ~** llenar el hueco; **to have an aching ~** tener mucha hambre.
(b) (*Cards*) fallo *m*; **to have a ~ in hearts** tener fallo a corazones.
③ VT **(a)** evacuar, vaciar.
(b) (*Jur*) anular, invalidar.
voile [vɔɪl] N gasa *f*.
vol., vols ABBR *of* **volume(s)** tomo(s) *m(pl)*, t.
volatile ['vɒlətaɪl] ADJ volátil (*also fig*); **~ memory** memoria *f* no per-manente.
volatility [,vɒlə'tɪlɪtɪ] N volatilidad *f* (*also fig*).
volatilize [vɒ'lætəlaɪz] ① VT volatilizar.
② VI volatilizarse.
vol-au-vent ['vɒləʊvã] N volován *m*.
volcanic [vɒl'kænɪk] ADJ volcánico.
volcano [vɒl'keɪnəʊ] N, PL **volcanoes** [vɒl'keɪnəʊz] volcán *m*.
vole [vəʊl] N campañol *m*.
volition [və'lɪʃən] N volición *f*; **of one's own ~** por voluntad propia, espontáneamente, motu propio.
volley ['vɒlɪ] ① N **(a)** (*of shots*) descarga *f*, descarga *f* cerrada; (*of stones etc*) lluvia *f*; (*of applause*) salva *f*; (*of abuse etc*) torrente *m*, retahíla *f*.
(b) (*Tennis*) voleo *m*.
② VT **(a)** (*Tennis*) volear.
(b) *abuse etc* dirigir (*at* a).
③ VT (*Mil*) lanzar una descarga.
volleyball ['vɒlɪbɔːl] N vol(e)ibol *m*, balonvolea *m*.
volleyer ['vɒlɪər] N especialista *mf* en voleas.
volt [vəʊlt] N voltio *m*.
voltage ['vəʊltɪdʒ] N voltaje *m*.
voltaic [vɒl'teɪɪk] ADJ voltaico.
volte-face ['vɒlt'fɑːs] N viraje *m*, cambio *m* súbito de opinión.
voltmeter ['vəʊlt,miːtər] N voltímetro *m*.
volubility [,vɒljʊ'bɪlɪtɪ] N locuacidad *f*.
voluble ['vɒljʊbl] ADJ *person* locuaz, hablador; **in ~ French** en francés suelto y rápido; **a ~ protest** una protesta larga y enérgica.
volubly ['vɒljʊblɪ] ADV de modo locuaz, con locuacidad; con soltura, rápidamente; larga y enérgicamente.
volume ['vɒljuːm] ① N **(a)** (*book*) volumen *m*; (*number in series*) tomo *m*; **in the third ~** en el tercer tomo; **an edition in 4 ~s** una edición en 4 tomos; **it speaks ~s** es sumamente significativo; **it speaks ~s for it** lo evidencia de modo inconfundible; **it speaks ~s for him** es un testimonio muy significativo acerca de él.
(b) (*size*) volumen *m*; **production ~** cantidad *f* de producción.
(c) (*sound*) volumen *m* (sonoro); **to turn the ~ up** aumentar el sonido.
(d) (*large amount*) cantidad *f*, masa *f*; (*of water*) cantidad *f* de agua; caudal *m* (de un río *etc*).
② ATTR: **~ business** empresa *f* que comercia sólo en grandes cantidades; **~ control** control *m* de volumen; **~ discount** descuento *m* por volumen de compras; **~ sales** ventas *fpl* a granel.
volumetric [,vɒljʊ'metrɪk] ADJ volumétrico.
voluminous [və'luːmɪnəs] ADJ voluminoso.
voluntarily ['vɒləntərɪlɪ] ADV voluntariamente, espontáneamente, sin ser forzado.
voluntarism ['vɒləntərɪzəm] N voluntariado *m*.
voluntary ['vɒləntərɪ] ① ADJ voluntario; espontáneo; libre; **~ controls** controles *mpl* voluntarios; **~ liquidation** liquidación *f* voluntaria; **~ redundancy, ~ severance** baja *f* incentivada, baja *f* por incentiva; **~ worker** trabajador *m* voluntario, trabajadora *f* voluntaria.
② N solo de órgano; **trumpet ~** solo *m* de trompeta.
volunteer [,vɒlən'tɪər] ① N voluntario *m*.
② ADJ, ATTR *force etc* de voluntarios.
③ VT **(a)** *information, services* ofrecer; *remark* hacer.
(b) (*) **they ~ed him for the job** le señalaron contra su voluntad para el puesto.
④ VI ofrecerse (voluntario); (*Mil*) alistarse voluntario; **to ~ for ser-vice overseas** ofrecerse para servir en ultramar; **to ~ to do a job** ofrecerse a hacer un trabajo; **he wasn't forced to, he ~ed** nadie le obligó a ello, se ofreció libremente.

voluptuary [və'lʌptjʊərɪ] N voluptuoso *m*, -a *f*.
voluptuous [və'lʌptjʊəs] ADJ voluptuoso.
voluptuously [və'lʌptjʊəslɪ] ADJ voluptuosamente.
voluptuousness [və'lʌptjʊəsnɪs] N voluptuosidad *f*.
vomit ['vɒmɪt] ① N vómito *m*.
② VT vomitar, arrojar.
③ VI vomitar, tener vómitos.
vomiting ['vɒmɪtɪŋ] N vómito *m*.
voodoo ['vuːduː] N vudú *m*.
voracious [və'reɪʃəs] ADJ voraz.
voraciously [və'reɪʃəslɪ] ADV vorazmente.
voracity [vɒ'ræsɪtɪ] N voracidad *f*.
vortex ['vɔːteks] N, PL **vortices** ['vɔːtɪsiːz] vórtice *m*.
Vosges [vəʊʒ] NPL Vosgos *mpl*.
votary ['vəʊtərɪ] N (*Rel*) devoto *m*, -a *f*; (*fig*) partidario *m*, -a *f*.
vote [vəʊt] ① N **(a)** (*gen*) voto *m*; sufragio *m*; **to cast one's ~, to give one's ~** dar su voto (*for, to* a); **how many ~s did he get?** ¿cuántos votos obtuvo?; **he won by 89 ~s** ganó por 89 votos.
(b) (*voting*) votación *f*; (*election*) elección *f*, elecciones *fpl*; **~ of cen-sure** voto *m* de censura; **~ of confidence** voto *m* de confianza; **~ of no confidence** voto *m* de censura; **~ of thanks** palabras *fpl* de agradecimiento; **by popular ~** por votación popular, (*fig*) en la opinión de muchos; **by secret ~** por votación secreta; **to allow a free ~** dejar libertad de voto; **as the 1931 ~ showed** según demos-traron las elecciones de 1931; **to put a motion to the ~, to take a ~ on a motion** someter una moción a votación; **let's take a ~ on it** ¡votémoslo!
(c) (*right to ~*) derecho *m* de votar, sufragio *m*; **when women got the ~** cuando se concedió a las mujeres el derecho de votar; **to have the ~** tener el derecho de votar.
② VT: **to ~ a sum for defence** votar una cantidad para la defensa; **she was ~d Miss Granada 1995** fue elegida como Miss Granada 1995; **we ~d it a failure** opinamos que fue un fracaso; **the team ~d it a hit** el equipo pronosticó que tendría éxito; **to ~ that ...** resolver por votación que ...; **I ~ that ...*** propongo que ..., sugiero que ...; **to ~ sb into office** elegir a uno para ocupar un puesto.
③ VI votar; (*go to polls*) ir a votar, acudir a las urnas; **to ~ for sb** votar por uno; **to ~ Socialist** votar socialista, votar por los socialistas; **to ~ with one's feet** expresar su opinión no acudiendo (*or* abandonando la organización *etc*).
◆**vote down** VT: **to ~ a proposal down** rechazar una propuesta por votación; **we ~d that idea down** rechazamos esa idea.
◆**vote in** VT: **to ~ a government in** elegir un gobierno.
◆**vote out** VT rechazar (por votación, en elecciones).
◆**vote through** VT aprobar (por votación).
vote-catching ['vəʊtkætʃɪŋ] ① ADJ electoralista.
② N electoralismo *m*.
voter ['vəʊtər] N votante *mf*.
voting ['vəʊtɪŋ] ① N votación *f*.
② ATTR: **~ booth** cabina *f* de votación; **~ machine** (*US*) máquina *f* de votar; **~ paper** papeleta *f* (de votación); **~ pattern** tendencia *f* de la votación; **~ power** potencia *f* electoral; **~ register** registro *m* electoral; **~ right** derecho *m* a voto; **~ share** acción *f* con derecho a voto.
votive ['vəʊtɪv] ADJ votivo.
vouch [vaʊtʃ] ① VT garantizar, atestiguar; confirmar; **to ~ that ...** afirmar que ..., asegurar que ...
② VI: **to ~ for sth** garantizar algo; confirmar algo; responder de algo; **I cannot ~ for its authenticity** no puedo responder de su autenticidad; **to ~ for sb** responder por uno.
voucher ['vaʊtʃər] N documento *m* justificativo; (*Comm*) comprobante *m*; vale *m*, cupón *m*.
vouchsafe [vaʊtʃ'seɪf] VT conceder, otorgar; *reply etc* servirse hacer, dignarse hacer; **to ~ to + infin** dignarse + *infin*.
vow [vaʊ] ① N voto *m* (*also Eccl*); promesa *f* solemne; **lovers' ~s** promesas *fpl* solemnes de los amantes; **the ~ of poverty** el voto de pobreza; **to be under a ~ to do sth** haber hecho voto de hacer algo, haber prometido solemnemente hacer algo; **to take a ~ to + infin** hacer voto de + *infin*, jurar + *infin*; **to take ~s** profesar.
② VT: **to ~ vengeance against sb** jurar vengarse (de uno); **to ~ that ...** jurar que ..., prometer solemnemente que ...; **to ~ to + infin** hacer voto de + *infin*, jurar + *infin*.
vowel [vaʊəl] ① N vocal *f*.
② ATTR vocálico; **~ shift** cambio *m* vocálico; **~ sound** sonido *m* vocálico; **~ system** sistema *m* vocálico.
vox pop ['vɒks'pɒp] N (*Brit*) voz *f* de la calle.
voyage ['vɔɪɪdʒ] ① N viaje *m* (por mar, en barco); (*crossing*) travesía *f*; **the ~ out** el viaje de ida; **the ~ home** el viaje de regreso.
② VI viajar (por mar); navegar; **to ~ across unknown seas** viajar por mares desconocidos.
voyager ['vɔɪədʒər] N viajero *m*, -a *f* (por mar).
voyeur [vwɑːˈjɜːr] N voyer *m*, mirón *m*.

voyeurism [vwɑːˈjɜːrɪzəm] N voyerismo *m*, mironismo *m*.
voyeuristic [vwɑːjɜːˈrɪstɪk] ADJ voyeurista.
V.P. N ABBR *of* **Vice-President** Vicepresidente *mf*, V.P.
VR N ABBR *of* **virtual reality** realidad *f* virtual.
vs ABBR *of* **versus** contra, versus, vs.
VSO N (*Brit*) ABBR *of* **Voluntary Service Overseas.**
VSOP ABBR *of* **very special** (*or* **superior**) **old pale.**
VT (*US Post*) ABBR *of* **Vermont.**
VTOL [ˈviːtɒl] N ABBR *of* **vertical take-off and landing** (*aircraft*) avión *m* de despegue y aterrizaje cortos, ADAC.
VTR N ABBR *of* **videotape recorder.**
Vulcan [ˈvʌlkən] NM Vulcano.
vulcanite [ˈvʌlkənaɪt] N vulcanita *f*, ebonita *f*.
vulcanization [ˌvʌlkənaɪˈzeɪʃən] N vulcanización *f*.
vulcanize [ˈvʌlkənaɪz] VT vulcanizar.
vulcanologist [ˌvʌlkənˈɒlədʒɪst] N vulcanólogo *m*, -a *f*.
vulcanology [ˌvʌlkəˈnɒlədʒɪ] N vulcanología *f*.
vulgar [ˈvʌlgəʳ] ⒈ ADJ (**a**) (*of the people*) vulgar; **V~ Latin** latín *m* vulgar; **in the ~ tongue** en la lengua vulgar, en la lengua vernácula; **that is a ~ error** eso es un error vulgar. (**b**) (*indecent*) ordinario, grosero; (*in bad taste*) de mal gusto, cursi; *joke, song* verde, colorado

(*LAm*); *person* ordinario.
⒉ NPL: **the ~** el vulgo.
vulgarian [vʌlˈgɛərɪən] N persona *f* ordinaria; (*wealthy*) ricacho *m*, -a *f*.
vulgarism [ˈvʌlgərɪzəm] N vulgarismo *m*.
vulgarity [vʌlˈgærɪtɪ] N (*V* **vulgar**) vulgaridad *f*; ordinariez *f*, grosería *f*; mal gusto *m*, cursilería *f*; lo verde, indecencia *f*; **such ~!** ¡qué ordinario!, ¡qué indecente!; **no ~, please** por favor, nada de indecencias.
vulgarize [ˈvʌlgəraɪz] VT vulgarizar.
vulgarly [ˈvʌlgəlɪ] ADV vulgarmente; de modo ordinario; groseramente; con mal gusto, de modo cursi; indecentemente; **X, ~ known as Y** X, vulgarmente llamado Y.
Vulgate [ˈvʌlgɪt] N Vulgata *f*.
vulnerability [ˌvʌlnərəˈbɪlɪtɪ] N vulnerabilidad *f*.
vulnerable [ˈvʌlnərəbl] ADJ vulnerable (*to* a).
vulpine [ˈvʌlpaɪn] ADJ vulpino (*also fig*).
vulture [ˈvʌltʃəʳ] N buitre *m* (*also fig*).
vulva [ˈvʌlvə] N vulva *f*.
vv. ABBR *of* **verses**; *V* **v.** (**a**), (**b**).
v.v. ABBR *of* **vice versa.**
vying [ˈvaɪɪŋ] GER *of* **vie.**

W, w ['dʌblju] N (*letter*) W, w *f*; **W for William** W de Washington.
W ABBR *of* **west** oeste *m*, O; *also adj.*
w. ABBR *of* **watt(s)** vatio(s) *m(pl)*, v.
WA (*US Post*) ABBR *of* **Washington** (*estado*).
WAAF [wæf] N ABBR *of* **Women's Auxiliary Air Force.**
wacko* ['wækəʊ] ADJ colgado*, excéntrico.
wacky* ['wækɪ] ADJ (*US*) *person* chiflado*; *thing* absurdo.
wad [wɒd] **1** N (*stuffing*) taco *m*, tapón *m*; (*in gun, cartridge*) taco *m*; (*of cotton wool etc*) bolita *f* de algodón; (*of papers*) lío *m*; (*of banknotes: US*) fajo *m*.
2 VT (*stuff*) rellenar; (*Sew*) acolchar.
wadding ['wɒdɪŋ] N (*wad*) taco *m*, tapón *m*; relleno *m*; (*lining*) entretela *f*, forro *m*; (*Med*) algodón *m* hidrófilo.
waddle ['wɒdl] **1** N anadeo *m*; **to walk with a ~** andar como pato, anadear.
2 VI anadear; **she ~d over to the window** fue anadeando a la ventana.
wade [weɪd] **1** VT vadear.
2 VI (*also* **to ~ along**) caminar por el agua (*or* nieve, lodo *etc*), (*waist-deep etc*) caminar con el agua hasta la cintura (*etc*); **we shall have to ~** tendremos que meternos en el agua; **to ~ across a river** vadear un río; **to ~ ashore** llegar a tierra vadeando; **to ~ into sb** (*fig*) emprenderla con uno, arremeter contra uno; **to ~ into a meal** echarse sobre una comida; **to ~ through the water** caminar por el agua; **to ~ through a book** leerse un libro a pesar de lo aburrido (*or* lo difícil *etc*); **it took me an hour to ~ through your essay** tardé una hora en leer tu ensayo.
◆**wade in** VI entrar en el agua; (*fig*) entrar pisando fuerte.
wader ['weɪdər] N (**a**) (*Orn*) ave *f* zancuda. (**b**) **~s** botas *fpl* altas de goma.
wadge [wɒdʒ] N = **wodge.**
wadi ['wɒdɪ] N *cauce de río en el norte de África.*
wading bird ['weɪdɪŋ,bɜːd] N ave *f* zancuda.
wading pool ['weɪdɪŋ,puːl] N (*US*) estanque *m* para chapotear, estanque *m* (*or* piscina *f*) para niños.
wafer ['weɪfər] N (**a**) (*biscuit*) galleta *f*; (*with ice cream*) barquillo *m*; (*for sealing*) oblea *f*; (*Eccl*) hostia *f*. (**b**) (*Comput*) oblea *f*, microplaqueta *f*.
wafer-thin ['weɪfə'θɪn] ADJ delgadísimo, finísimo.
wafery ['weɪfərɪ] ADJ delgado, ligero.
waffle ['wɒfl] **1** N (**a**) (*Culin*) gofre *m*; **~ iron** molde *m* para hacer gofres.
(**b**) (*Brit**) palabras *fpl* inútiles, palabrería *f*; (*in essay etc*) paja *f*.
2 VI (*Brit*: *also* **to ~ on**) dar el rollo*, ser muy charlatán, parlotear; (*in essay etc*) poner mucha paja.
waffler* ['wɒflər] N (*Brit*) charlatán *m*, -ana *f*, pico *mf* de oro*.
waft [wɑːft] **1** N soplo *m*, ráfaga *f* de olor.
2 VT llevar por el aire; hacer flotar; (*stir*) mecer, mover.
3 VI moverse (de un sitio a otro); ser llevado por el aire; flotar.
wag¹ [wæg] **1** N meneo *m*, movimiento *m*; (*of tail*) coleada *f*.
2 VT mover, menear, agitar; **the dog ~ged its tail** el perro meneó la cola.
3 VI moverse, menearse, agitarse; **tongues were ~ging about their relationship** las malas lenguas se ocupaban de sus relaciones; **this will make the tongues ~** esto dará en qué hablar.
wag² [wæg] N (*joker*) bromista *m*, zumbón *m*.
wage [weɪdʒ] **1** N (*also* **~s**) salario *m*; (*esp day* **~**) jornal *m*; (*fig*) pago *m*; premio *m*.
2 ATTR salarial; **~s bill** gastos *mpl* de nómina; **~ claim** (*Brit*) reivindicación *f* salarial; **~ differential** diferencia *f* salarial; **~ freeze** congelación *f* de los salarios; **~ increase** aumento *m* salarial; **~ packet** sobre *m* de la paga; **~-price spiral** espiral *f* de precios y salarios; **~ rates** escala *f* salarial; **~ restraint** restricción *f* salarial, moderación *f* salarial; **~ rise** aumento *m* salarial; **~ scale** escala *f* salarial; **~ settle-**

ment acuerdo *m* salarial; **~s slip** hoja *f* salarial, papeleta *f* de salario.
3 VT *war* hacer; *battle* librar, dar; *campaign* proseguir.
wage-earner ['weɪdʒ,ɜːnər] N asalariado *m*, -a *f*.
waged [weɪdʒd] **1** ADJ con sueldo.
2 N: **the ~** los que tienen sueldo.
wager ['weɪdʒər] **1** N apuesta *f*; **to lay a ~** hacer una apuesta; **to lay a ~ on a horse** apostar dinero a un caballo.
2 VT apostar; **to ~ £20 on a horse** apostar 20 libras a un caballo; **to ~ that ...** apostar a que ...; **he won't do it, I ~ !** ¡a que no lo hace!
wages ['weɪdʒɪz] NPL V **wage.**
wage slave ['weɪdʒsleɪv] N currante* *mf*.
wage-worker ['weɪdʒ,wɜːkər] N (*US*) asalariado *m*, -a *f*.
waggish ['wægɪʃ] ADJ zumbón, bromista.
waggishly ['wægɪʃlɪ] ADV: **he said ~** dijo zumbón.
waggle ['wægl] = **wag¹.**
wag(g)on ['wægən] N carro *m*; (*Brit Rail*) vagón *m*; (*US: also* **station ~**) furgoneta *f*, rubia *f*, camioneta *f*; (*US: police van*) furgón *m* policial; **to be on the (water) ~*** no beber; **to go on the (water) wagon*** resolverse a no beber; **to hitch one's ~ to a star** picar muy alto.
wag(g)onage ['wægənɪdʒ] N acarreo *m*; transporte *m* en vagones (*etc*).
wag(g)onload ['wægənləʊd] N carretada *f*, carga *f* de un carro (*etc*); **50 ~s of coal** 50 vagones de carbón.
Wagnerian [vɑːg'nɪərɪən] ADJ wagneriano.
wagtail ['wægteɪl] N lavandera *f*.
waif [weɪf] N niño *m* abandonado, niña *f* abandonada; **~s and strays** niños *mpl* desamparados.
wail [weɪl] **1** N (*cry*) lamento *m*, gemido *m*; (*baby's first cry*) vagido *m*; (*complaint*) queja *f*, protesta *f*; **a great ~ went up** pusieron el grito en el cielo.
2 VI lamentarse, gemir; (*child*) gimotear; llorar; (*complain*) quejarse, protestar.
wailing ['weɪlɪŋ] N lamentación *f*, lamentaciones *fpl*, gemidos *mpl*; vagidos *mpl*; quejas *fpl*, protestas *fpl*; **W~ Wall** Muro *m* de las Lamentaciones.
wain [weɪn] N carro *m*; **the W~** (*Astron*) el Carro.
wainscot ['weɪnskət] N friso *m*; entablado *m*, revestimiento *m* (de la pared).
wainscotting ['weɪnskətɪŋ] N revestimiento *m*.
waist [weɪst] N (*Anat etc*) cintura *f*, talle *m*; (*fig, narrow part*) cuello *m*; (*Naut*) combés *m*.
waistband ['weɪs.bænd] N pretina *f*, cinturón *m*.
waistcoat ['weɪskəʊt] N (*Brit*) chaleco *m*.
waist-deep ['weɪst'diːp] ADV hasta la cintura.
-waisted ['weɪstɪd] ADJ de cintura ..., de talle ..., *eg* **slim-~** de cintura delgada.
waist-high ['weɪst'haɪ] **1** ADV hasta la cintura; al nivel de la cintura.
2 ADJ: **~ vegetation** vegetación *f* que crece hasta la altura de la cintura.
waistline ['weɪstlaɪn] N talle *m*, cintura *f*.
wait [weɪt] **1** N (**a**) espera *f*; (*pause*) pausa *f*, intervalo *m*; **there was a ~ of 10 minutes** tuvimos que esperar 10 minutos; **to have a long ~** tener que esperar mucho tiempo; **to be** (*or* **lie**) **in ~** acechar (*for sb* a uno).
(**b**) **~s** (*Brit*) murga *f* (de Nochebuena).
2 VT esperar; aplazar; guardar para después; **to ~ one's chance** esperar su ocasión; **we'll ~ dinner for you** no empezaremos a cenar hasta que vengas.
3 VI (**a**) esperar; aguardar; **~ a moment!** ¡un momento!, ¡momentito! (*LAm*); (*fig, querying*) ¡oiga!; **~ and see!** espera y verás; **there's a parcel ~ing to be collected** hay un paquete que recoger; **the dishes can ~** no hay prisa con los platos; **all that can ~ till tomorrow** todo eso lo podemos dejar para mañana; **'repairs while**

you **~'** 'reparaciones en el acto', 'reparaciones instantáneas'; **just you ~!** ¡me las pagarás!; **just you ~ till your father finds out!** ¡a ver qué pasa cuando se entere tu padre!; **I can't ~** estoy impaciente (to + infin por + infin); **~ till you're asked** espera hasta que te inviten; **~ till you're older** eso es para cuando seas algo mayor; **to keep sb ~ing** hacer esperar a uno; **to ~ for sb** esperar a uno, (in ambush) acechar a uno; **to ~ for sb to do sth** esperar hasta que uno haga algo; **we are ~ing for you to decide** estamos pendientes de la decisión de Vd; **what are you ~ing for?** (hurry up) ¡vamos ya!, ¡date prisa!; **~ for it!** (guess what) ¡a ver si lo adivinas!; (not yet) ¡todavía no!

(b) (as servant etc) servir; **to ~ at table** servir a la mesa.
◆**wait about, wait around** VI esperar, perder el tiempo.
◆**wait behind** VI quedarse; **to ~ behind for sb** quedarse para esperar a uno.
◆**wait in** VI: **to ~ in for sb** estar en casa (etc) esperando a uno.
◆**wait on** VT **(a)** **to ~ on sb** servir a uno; **to ~ on sb hand and foot** desvivirse por uno, mimar a uno.
(b) (frm) = **wait upon (a).**
◆**wait out** VT quedarse hasta el final de; **to ~ sb out** esperar más que uno.
◆**wait up** VI velar, no acostarse, seguir sin acostarse; **don't ~ up for me!** ¡idos (LAm: váyanse) a la cama sin esperarme!
◆**wait upon** VT **(a)** **to ~ upon sb** (frm) cumplimentar a uno, presentar sus respetos a uno.
(b) = **wait on (a).**
waiter ['weɪtəʳ] N camarero m, mesero m (LAm).
waiting ['weɪtɪŋ] **1** ADJ: **~ time** tiempo m de espera; **to play a ~ game** dejar pasar el tiempo.
2 N **(a)** espera f; **all this ~!** ¡tanto esperar! **(b)** (frm) servicio m; **to be in ~ on sb** estar de servicio con uno, servir a uno.
waiting-list ['weɪtɪŋ'lɪst] N lista f de espera.
waiting-room ['weɪtɪŋrʊm] N sala f de espera.
waitress ['weɪtrɪs] N camarera f, mesera f (LAm); **~!** ¡señorita!
waitressing ['weɪtrɪsɪŋ] N: **to get a job/do ~** obtener un trabajo de/trabajar de camarero.
waive [weɪv] VT renunciar a; prescindir de.
waiver ['weɪvəʳ] N renuncia f.
wake¹ [weɪk] N (Naut) estela f; **in the ~ of** (fig) como consecuencia de, tras, después de, a raíz de; **wars bring misery in their ~** las guerras acarrean la miseria; **they came in the ~ of the invaders** siguieron a los invasores.
wake² [weɪk] **1** N (over corpse) vela f, velatorio m, velorio m (esp LAm).
2 (irr: PRET **woke**, PTP **woken, waked**) VT (also **to ~ up**) despertar; corpse velar; **a noise which would ~ the dead** un ruido que despertaría a un muerto.
3 VI (also **to ~ up**) despertar, despertarse; **~ up!** ¡despierta!; **she woke up with a start** despertó sobresaltada; **he woke up (to find himself) in prison** amaneció en la cárcel; **he woke up to find himself rich** a la mañana siguiente amaneció rico; **to ~ up to reality** despertar a la realidad; **to ~ up to the truth** darse cuenta de la verdad.
wakeful ['weɪkfʊl] ADJ (awake) despierto; (alert) vigilante; desvelado; (unable to sleep) insomne; **to have a ~ night** pasar la noche sin dormir, pasar la noche en blanco.
wakefulness ['weɪkfʊlnɪs] N vigilancia f, desvelo m; insomnia f.
waken ['weɪkən] **1** VT despertar.
2 VI despertar, despertarse.
wakey-wakey ['weɪkɪ'weɪkɪ] EXCL ¡arriba!
waking ['weɪkɪŋ] **1** ADJ: **in one's ~ hours** en las horas en que uno está despierto.
2 N despertar m; **on ~** al despertar.
Waldorf salad [,wɔːldɔːf'sæləd] N ensalada f Waldorf, ensalada de manzanas, nueces y apio con mayonesa.
Wales [weɪlz] N Gales f.
walk [wɔːk] **1** N **(a)** (spell of ~ing: stroll) paseo m; (hike) caminata f, excursión f a pie; (Sport) marcha f; **it's only a 10-minute ~ from here** ir desde aquí a pie es sólo cosa de 10 minutos; **from there you have a short ~ to his house** desde allí a su casa se va a pie en muy poco tiempo; **to go for (or have, take) a ~** dar un paseo, dar una vuelta; **to take sb for a ~** llevar a uno de paseo; **take a ~!*** ¡lárgate*!
(b) (gait) andar m, paso m; **he has an odd sort of ~** tiene un modo de andar algo raro; **to know sb by (or from) his ~** conocer a uno por su modo de andar; **he went at a quick ~** caminó a un paso rápido.
(c) (route) **there's a nice ~ by the river** se pasea muy bien a lo largo del río, es encantador pasearse a lo largo del río; **this is my favourite ~** éste es mi paseo favorito.
(d) (fig) **~ of life** profesión f; esfera f; clase f social; **people from every ~ of life** gente f de toda condición.
(e) (avenue) paseo m, alameda f.
2 VT **(a)** person llevar a paseo, pasear; **to ~ sb off his legs** dejar a

uno rendido caminando; **to ~ a girl home** acompañar a una joven a su casa; **I'll ~ you to the station** te acompaño a la estación; **she ~s the dog every day** lleva al perro de paseo todos los días.
(b) **to ~ a horse** llevar un caballo al paso.
(c) (distance) cubrir, recorrer a pie, andar; **we ~ed 40 kilometres yesterday** ayer anduvimos 40 kilómetros.
(d) **to ~ the streets** andar por las calles, callejear, (aimlessly) vagar por las calles; (prostitute) hacer la carrera; (be homeless) no tener hogar, estar sin techo; **to ~ the boards** salir a escena; **to ~ the wards** hacer prácticas de clínica.
(e) (*) **don't worry, you'll ~ it** no te preocupes, será facilísimo.
3 VI **(a)** (gen) andar, caminar (LAm); **'W~'** (US Aut) 'Cruzar'; **'Don't W~'** (US Aut) 'No cruzar'; **can the boy ~ yet?** ¿sabe andar el niño ya?; **~ a little with me** ven a acompañarme un poco; **to ~ in one's sleep** ser sonámbulo, pasearse dormido; **to ~ downstairs** bajar la escalera; **to ~ upstairs** subir la escalera; **to ~ slowly** andar despacio.
(b) (not ride) andar, ir a pie; (stroll) pasearse; **we had to ~** tuvimos que ir andando; **to ~ home** ir andando hasta casa; **you can ~ there in 5 minutes** en 5 minutos se va allá andando; **we were out ~ing** nos estábamos paseando.
(c) (ghost) andar, aparecer.
(d) (*: disappear) volar*.
◆**walk about** VI pasearse; ir y venir.
◆**walk across** VI cruzar.
◆**walk around** VI dar una vuelta, pasearse.
◆**walk away** VI **(a)** (lit) irse; alejarse (from sb de uno); **to ~ away from a problem** negarse a afrontar un problema; **you can't just ~ away from it!** ¡no puedes irte como si no hubiera nada!
(b) **to ~ away with** prize llevarse, copar, largarse con; (steal) robar.
◆**walk back** VI volver a pie, regresar andando.
◆**walk down** VI bajar (a pie).
◆**walk in** VI entrar; **'please ~ in'** 'entren sin llamar'; **who should ~ in but Joe** y ¡bomba! entra Pepe; **to ~ in on sb** interrumpir a uno.
◆**walk into** VT **(a)** **to ~ into a room** entrar en un cuarto; **to ~ into an ambush** caer en una trampa; **you really ~ed into that one!*** ¡te has dejado embaucar por las buenas!
(b) (collide with) chocar con, dar con, dar contra; (*: meet) topar, tropezar con.
(c) (*) food devorar, zampar.
(d) **to ~ into sb*** (attack) atacar a uno, arremeter contra uno.
(e) (*) **to ~ into a job** conseguir fácilmente un puesto.
◆**walk off** **1** VT: **to ~ off a headache** quitarse un dolor de cabeza dando un paseo, dar una vuelta para quitarse un dolor de cabeza; **to ~ off one's lunch** bajar la comida dando un paseo.
2 VI **(a)** irse; alejarse; **he ~ed off angrily** se fue enfadado.
(b) **to ~ off with** prize llevarse, copar, largarse con; (steal) robar.
◆**walk on** VI **(a)** (continue) seguir andando (or caminando (LAm)).
(b) (Theat) salir de figurante.
◆**walk out** VI **(a)** salir; (from meeting) salir, retirarse; (on strike) declararse en huelga; **you can't ~ out now!** ¡no puedes marcharte ahora!
(b) **to ~ out on sb** abandonar a uno; **to ~ out on a girl** dejar plantada a una chica, plantar a una chica.
◆**walk over** **1** VT (treat badly) **to ~ all over sb** atropellar a uno, tratar a uno a coces; **they ~ed all over us in the second half** nos cascaron en el segundo tiempo.
2 VI (Sport) ganar; ganar la carrera por ser el único caballo (etc) que participa.
◆**walk through** VT (Theat) ensayar (por primera vez).
◆**walk up** VI subir (a pie); **~ up!, ~ up!** ¡vengan!, ¡acérquense!; **to ~ up to sb** acercarse a uno, abordar a uno; **to ~ up and down** pasearse (de acá para allá).
walkabout ['wɔːkəbaʊt] N paseo m entre el público; **to go ~** pasearse entre el público.
walkaway ['wɔːkəweɪ] N (US) victoria f fácil.
walker ['wɔːkəʳ] N **(a)** (stroller) paseante mf; (not rider) peatón m; (Sport) marchador m, -ora f; (hiker) andarín m, -ina f; **to be a great ~** ser gran andarín; ser aficionado a las excursiones a pie.
(b) (apparatus) pollera f, andador m.
walker-on ['wɔːkər'ɒn] N (Theat) figurante m, -a f, comparsa mf; (Cine) extra mf.
walkies ['wɔːkɪz] N SING paseo m; **to take the dog ~** llevar al perro de paseo.
walkie-talkie ['wɔːkɪ'tɔːkɪ] N transmisor-receptor m portátil, walki-talki m.
walk-in ['wɔːkɪn] **1** ADJ **(a)** furniture empotrado; **~ cupboard** alacena f ropera. **(b)** **in ~ condition** en condiciones de habitabilidad, habitable.
2 N (US) **(a)** = **~ cupboard.** **(b)** (victory) victoria f fácil.
walking ['wɔːkɪŋ] **1** ADJ ambulante; **~ delegate** (US) delegado m, -a f sindical; **~ pace** paso m de andar; **~ papers*** (US) pasaporte* m, aviso m de despido; **~ race** carrera f pedestre; **~ shoes** zapatos mpl para caminar; **~ tour** viaje m a pie, excursión f a pie; **the ~ wound-**

ed los heridos que pueden ir de pie; **it's within ~ distance** se puede ir allí andando; **he's a ~ encyclopaedia** es una enciclopedia ambulante.
2 N paseo *m*, pasearse *m*; *(as exercise)* marcha *f*; *(Sport)* marcha *f* (atlética).
walking frame ['wɔːkɪŋfreɪm] N andador *m*.
walking-on [,wɔːkɪŋ'ɒn] ADJ: = **walk-on.**
walking-stick ['wɔːkɪŋstɪk] N bastón *m*.
Walkman ['wɔːkmən] ® N, PL **Walkmans** ['wɔːkmənz] Walkman ® *m*.
walk-on ['wɔːkɒn] ADJ: **~ part** *(Theat)* papel *m* de figurante, papel *m* de comparsa; *(Cine)* papel *m* de extra.
walkout ['wɔːkaʊt] N *(from conference)* salida *f*, retirada *f*; *(strike)* huelga *f*; **to stage a ~** *(leave)* salir, retirarse, *(strike)* declarar la huelga, salir del trabajo.
walkover ['wɔːk,əʊvəʳ] N *(Sport)* walkover *m*; *(fig)* triunfo *m* fácil, pan *m* comido; **it won't be a ~** no va a ser un paseo.
walk-through ['wɔːkθruː] N ensayo *m*.
walk-up ['wɔːkʌp] N *(US)* pisos *mpl* sin ascensor.
walkway ['wɔːkweɪ] N pasarela *f*.
wall [wɔːl] 1 N muro *m*; *(interior, Anat etc)* pared *f*; *(city ~)* muralla *f*; *(garden ~)* tapia *f*; *(fig)* barrera *f*; *(Sport: of players)* barrera *f*; **the Great W~ of China** la Gran Muralla China; **the north ~ of the Eiger** la pared norte del Eiger; **to break the ~ of silence** romper el muro del silencio; **to climb the ~***, **to go up the ~*** subirse por las paredes*; **to come up against a blank** *(or* **brick)** **~** *(fig)* tener por delante una barrera infranqueable; **to do sth off the ~*** *(US)* hacer algo espontáneamente, hacer algo de improviso; **it drives** *(or* **sends)** **me up the ~*** me vuelve loco, me hace subir por las paredes*; **to go to the ~** ser desechado por inútil, *(Comm)* quebrar, ir a la bancarrota; **to push sb to the ~** poner a uno en una situación muy difícil; **~s have ears** las paredes oyen.
2 ATTR *map etc* de pared, mural.
3 VT murar; cerrar con muro; *city* amurallar; *garden* tapiar, cercar con tapia.
◆**wall in** VT cerrar con muro; *garden* tapiar, cercar con tapia.
◆**wall off** VT amurallar; separar con un muro.
◆**wall up** VT *person* emparedar; *opening* cerrar con muro, tabicar.
wallaby ['wɒləbɪ] N ualabí *m*.
wallah* ['wɒlə] N hombre *m*; *(pej)* tío* *m*, sujeto* *m*; **the ice-cream ~** el hombre de los helados; **the ~ with the beard** él de la barba.
wallbars ['wɔːlbɑːz] NPL espalderas *fpl*.
wallboard ['wɔːlbɔːd] N *(US)* cartón *m* de yeso; fibra *f* prensada (para paredes).
wall-clock ['wɔːlklɒk] N reloj *m* de pared.
wall-covering ['wɔːl,kʌvərɪŋ] N material *m* de decoración de paredes.
walled [wɔːld] ADJ *city* amurallado; *garden* con tapia.
wallet ['wɒlɪt] N cartera *f*, billetera *f* *(LAm)*.
wall-eyed ['wɔːl'aɪd] ADJ de ojos incoloros; estrábico.
wallflower ['wɔːl,flaʊəʳ] N alhelí *m*; **to be a ~** *(fig)* ser la fea del baile, comer pavo.
wall-map ['wɔːlmæp] N mapa *m* mural.
Walloon [wɒ'luːn] 1 ADJ valón.
2 N (a) valón *m*, -ona *f*. (b) *(Ling)* valón *m*.
wallop* ['wɒləp] 1 N (a) *(blow)* golpe *m*, golpazo *m*; **~!** ¡zas!; **to give sb a ~** pegar a uno; **it packs a ~*** *(US)* es muy fuerte, tiene mucho efecto.
(b) *(speed)* velocidad *f*; **to go at a fair ~** correr rápidamente.
(c) *(Brit: beer)* cerveza *f*.
2 VT golpear fuertemente; *(punish)* zurrar*.
walloping* ['wɒləpɪŋ] 1 ADJ colosal, grandote.
2 N zurra* *f*, paliza *f*; **to give sb a ~** dar una paliza a uno *(also fig)*.
wallow ['wɒləʊ] 1 N: **I had a good ~ in the bath** descansé bañándome largamente.
2 VI revolcarse *(in* en); **to ~ in** *(fig)* revolcarse en, sumirse en; **to ~ in money** nadar en la opulencia; **to ~ in vices** revolcarse en los vicios.
wall-painting ['wɔːl,peɪntɪŋ] N pintura *f* mural.
wallpaper ['wɔːl,peɪpəʳ] 1 N papel *m* pintado, papel *m* de paredes.
2 VT empapelar.
wall-socket ['wɔːl,sɒkɪt] N enchufe *m* de pared.
Wall Street ['wɔːlstriːt] N *(US)* calle de la Bolsa y de muchos bancos en Nueva York; *(fig)* mundo *m* bursátil, mundo *m* financiero; **shares rose sharply on ~** las acciones subieron bruscamente en la Bolsa (de Nueva York).
wall-to-wall ['wɔːltə'wɔːl] ADJ: **~ carpet** moqueta *f* de pared a pared.
wally ['wɒlɪ] N gili* *mf*, criajo* *m*.
walnut ['wɔːlnʌt] N *(nut)* nuez *f*; *(tree, wood)* nogal *m*.
walnut-tree ['wɔːlnʌttriː] N nogal *m*.
walrus ['wɔːlrəs] 1 N morsa *f*.
2 ATTR: **~ moustache** bigotes *mpl* de foca.
Walter ['wɔːltəʳ] NM Gualterio.

waltz [wɔːlts] 1 N vals *m*; **it was a ~!*** *(US)* ¡fue tirado!*, ¡fue coser y cantar!
2 VI valsar; **to ~ in*** entrar tan fresco*; **to ~ out*** salir tan fresco*.
◆**waltz off with***, **waltz away with*** VT (a) *person* largarse con*. (b) *title, championship* hacerse fácilmente con.
◆**waltz through*** VT *match, game* ganar sin mover un dedo.
wan [wɒn] ADJ pálido, macilento; *(sad)* triste.
wand [wɒnd] N *(of office)* vara *f*; **magic ~** varilla *f* de virtudes.
wander ['wɒndəʳ] 1 VT vagar por, recorrer; **to ~ the streets** vagar por las calles, pasearse por las calles, callejear; **to ~ the world** vagar por el mundo.
2 VI vagar, pasearse sin propósito fijo, deambular; ir a la deriva, viajar al azar; andar perdido; *(get lost)* extraviarse; **to ~ aimlessly** deambular; **to ~ (in one's mind)** divagar, delirar; **to ~ from the path** desviarse camino, descaminarse; **to ~ from the point** salirse del tema; **to ~ off** irse (distraído); **the children ~ed off into the woods** los niños se alejaron sin rumbo y entraron en el bosque; **his speech ~ed on and on** continuó incansable su discurso tan confuso; **to ~ round a shop** curiosear en una tienda; **to let one's mind ~** dejar que la imaginación fantasee.
3 N paseo *m*; **to take** *(or* **go for)** **a ~** pasearse, dar un paseo.
◆**wander about, wander around** VI deambular.
wanderer ['wɒndərəʳ] N hombre *m* errante, mujer *f* errante; *(traveller)* viajero *m*, -a *f*; *(pej)* vagabundo *m*, -a *f*; *(tribesman etc)* nómada *mf*; **I've always been a ~** nunca he querido establecerme de fijo en un sitio.
wandering ['wɒndərɪŋ] 1 ADJ errante, errabundo; *stream* sinuoso; *salesman etc* ambulante; *tribesman* nómada; *mind, thoughts* distraído.
2 NPL: **~s** viajes *mpl*; errabundeo *m*; andanzas *fpl*; *(pej)* vagabundeo *m*; *(Med)* delirio *m*.
wanderlust ['wɒndəlʌst] N pasión *f* de viajar, ansia *f* de ver mundo.
wane [weɪn] 1 N: **to be on the ~** menguar, estar menguando; *(fig)* decaer, menguar, disminuir; declinar, estar en decadencia.
2 VI = **to be on the ~.**
wangle* ['wæŋgl] 1 N chanchullo* *m*, trampa *f*, truco *m*; **it's a ~** aquí hay trampa; **he got in by a ~** se las arregló para ser admitido.
2 VT (a) *job etc* mamarse*, agenciarse, conseguir; **he ~d his way in** logró entrar gracias a un truco; **he'll ~ it for you** te lo procurará por el sistema que él se sabe; **can you ~ me a free ticket?** ¿puedes procurarme una entrada de favor?
(b) *accounts etc* amañar.
wangler* ['wæŋgləʳ] N chanchullero* *m*, trapisondista *mf*.
wangling* ['wæŋglɪŋ] N chanchullos* *mpl*, trampas *fpl*; **there's a lot of ~ goes on** hay muchas trampas.
waning ['weɪnɪŋ] 1 ADJ *moon* menguante; *(fig)* decadente.
2 N *(of moon)* menguante *f*; *(fig)* mengua *f*; disminución *f*; decadencia *f*.
wank*⁑ [wæŋk] *(Brit)* 1 N: **to have a ~ = 2.**
2 VI hacerse una paja⁑.
wanker⁑ ['wæŋkəʳ] N *(fig)* tío *m* tonto*.
wanky⁑ ['wæŋkɪ] ADJ *(Brit)* de puta pena⁑, mierdoso⁑, cutre*.
wanly ['wɒnlɪ] ADV pálidamente; *(sadly)* tristemente.
wanna* ['wɒnə] = **want to.**
wannabe* ['wɒnəbiː] 1 N imitador *m* barato, imitadora *f* barata.
2 ATTR amateur, aspirante.
wanness ['wɒnnɪs] N palidez *f*.
▼ **want** [wɒnt] 1 N (a) *(lack)* falta *f*; ausencia *f*; *(shortage)* carencia *f*, escasez *f*; **~ of judgement** falta *f* de juicio; **for ~ of** por falta de; **for ~ of anything better** por falta de algo mejor; **for ~ of sth to do** por no tener nada que hacer; **to feel the ~ of** sentir la falta de.
(b) *(poverty)* miseria *f*, pobreza *f*, indigencia *f*; **to be in ~** estar necesitado.
(c) *(need)* necesidad *f*; **my ~s are few** necesito poco; **to be in ~ of** necesitar; **to attend to sb's ~s** atender a las necesidades de uno; **it fills a long-felt ~** viene a llenar un vacío hace tiempo sentido; **~ ad*** *(US)* anuncio *m* clasificado.
2 VT (a) *(Brit: need: of person)* necesitar; **all I ~ is sleep** lo único que necesito es dormir; **children ~ lots of sleep** los niños necesitan dormir mucho; **we have all we ~** tenemos todo lo que necesitamos; **you ~ to be careful*** hay que tener mucho ojo; **what you ~ is a good hiding*** no te vendría mal una paliza de las buenas; **those ~ing a job** los que buscan trabajo; **'~ed'** *(police notice)* 'se busca'; **the ~ed man** el hombre buscado; **the most ~ed man** el hombre más buscado; **'~ed: general maid'** *(advert)* 'necesítase criada para todo'; **he is ~ed for murder** se le busca por asesino.
(b) *(need: of thing)* exigir, requerir; **it ~s some doing** no es nada fácil hacerlo; **that work ~s a lot of time** ese trabajo exige mucho tiempo; **does my hair ~ cutting?** ¿me hace falta cortar el pelo?; **the house will ~ painting next year** el año que viene será necesario pintar la casa.
▼ (c) *(wish)* querer, desear; **she knows what she ~s** ella se sabe lo que quiere; **I ~ to see the manager!** ¡quiero ver al gerente!; **to ~ sb**

➤ LANGUAGE IN USE: **want: 2c** → 8.3, 8.4

to do sth querer que uno haga algo; **I ~ him sent away at once** quiero que se le despida en seguida; **I was ~ing to leave** estaba deseando marcharme; **what does he ~ with me?** ¿qué quiere de mí?, ¿qué tiene que ver conmigo?; **he ~s £200 for the picture** pide 200 libras por el cuadro; **you don't ~ much!** (*iro*) ¡eso no es mucho pedir!; **you're ~ed on the 'phone** te llaman al teléfono.

(d) (*lack*) carecer de; **he ~s talent** carece de talento; **he ~s enterprise** le falta iniciativa; **the contract ~s only his signature** sólo hace falta que firme el contrato; **it ~s 2 for a complete set** faltan 2 para hacer una serie completa; **it ~ed only this last step to** + *infin* sólo hacía falta este último paso para + *infin.*

3 VI **(a)** (*lack*) **to ~ for** necesitar, carecer de; **they ~ for nothing** no carecen de nada, lo tienen todo.

(b) **he ~s out*** quiere dejarlo, quiere terminar con eso.

wanting ['wɒntɪŋ] ADJ defectuoso; deficiente (*in* en), falto (*in* de); **charity is ~ in the novel** a la novela le falta caridad, la novela es deficiente en caridad; **there is sth ~** falta algo; **he is ~ing in enterprise** le falta iniciativa, está falto de iniciativa; **he was tried and found ~** se le sometió a la prueba y resultó que le faltaban las cualidades indispensables.

wanton ['wɒntən] ADJ **(a)** (*playful*) juguetón; (*wayward*) travieso; caprichoso; (*unrestrained*) desenfrenado; (*licentious*) lascivo.

(b) (*motiveless*) sin motivo, inmotivado; *destruction* sin propósito, sin sentido; *cruelty* gratuito.

wantonly ['wɒntənlɪ] ADV (*V adj*) **(a)** caprichosamente; dessenfrenadamente; lascivamente. **(b)** sin motivo; sin propósito; gratuitamente.

wantonness ['wɒntənnɪs] N (*V adj*) **(a)** lo caprichoso; desenfreno *m*; lascivia *f.* **(b)** falta *f* de motivo; lo gratuito.

war [wɔːʳ] **1** N guerra *f*; **~ of nerves** guerra *f* de nervios; **~ of words** guerra *f* de propaganda; **~ to the knife** guerra *f* a muerte; **Great W~** (*1914-18*) Primera Guerra *f* Mundial; **Second World W~** (*1939-45*) Segunda Guerra *f* Mundial; **the period between the ~s** (*1918-39*) el período de entreguerras; **to be at ~** estar en guerra (*with* con); **you've been in the ~s!** (*to child*) ¡vuelve el guerrero herido!; **to declare ~** declarar la guerra (*on* a); **to go to ~** emprender la guerra; hacer la guerra; **we shall not go to ~ over the Slobodian question** no emprenderemos la guerra por la cuestión de Eslobodia; **they went to ~ singing** fueron a la guerra cantando; **to make ~** hacer la guerra (*on* a).

2 ATTR (*in most senses*) de guerra; **~ clouds** nubes *fpl* de guerra; **~ correspondent** corresponsal *mf* de guerra; **~ crime** crimen *m* de guerra; **~ criminal** criminal *mf* de guerra; **~ dead** muertos *mpl* en campaña; **~ debt** deuda *f* de guerra; **~ effort** esfuerzo *m* bélico; **on a ~ footing** en pie de guerra; **~ material** material *m* bélico; **~ memorial** monumento *m* a los caídos; **W~ Office** (†) Ministerio *m* de Guerra; **~ widow** viuda *f* de guerra.

3 VI (*liter*) guerrear (*on* con).

warble ['wɔːbl] **1** N trino *m*, gorjeo *m.*

2 VT *song etc* cantar trinando, cantar con trinos.

3 VI trinar, gorjear.

warbler ['wɔːbləʳ] N mosquitero *m*, curruca *f.*

warbling ['wɔːblɪŋ] N gorjeo *m.*

warcry ['wɔːkraɪ] N grito *m* de guerra.

ward [wɔːd] **1** N **(a)** (*~ship*) tutela *f*, custodia *f*; **in ~** bajo tutela.

(b) (*person*) pupilo *m*, -a *f*; **~ of court** persona *f* bajo la protección del tribunal.

(c) (*Brit Pol*) distrito *m* electoral.

(d) (*of hospital*) sala *f*, crujía *f*; **'W~ 7'** 'Sala 7'; **to walk the ~s** hacer prácticas de clínica.

(e) (*of key*) guarda *f.*

2 ATTR: **~ round** (*Med*) visita *f* de salas.

♦ **ward off** VT *blow* desviar, parar; *danger* evitar; *attack* rechazar, defenderse contra; *cold* protegerse de.

-ward(s) [wəd(z)] SUF hacia; **townward(s)** hacia la ciudad; **pubward(s)** hacia la taberna.

war-dance ['wɔːdɑːns] N danza *f* guerrera.

warden ['wɔːdn] N guardián *m*; vigilante *mf*; (*Univ etc*) director *m*, -ora *f*; (*Aut*) controlador *m*, -ora *f* de estacionamiento; (*of castle etc*) alcaide *m.*

warder ['wɔːdəʳ] N (*esp Brit*) celador *m*, -ora *f.*

ward heeler ['wɔːd'hiːləʳ] N (*US Pol*) muñidor *m.*

wardress ['wɔːdrɪs] N celadora *f.*

wardrobe ['wɔːdrəʊb] **1** N (*clothes*) vestidos *mpl*, trajes *mpl*; (*Theat*) vestuario *m*; (*cupboard*) guardarropa *m*, armario *m* (ropero); ropero *m* (*LAm*); (*in hall*) gabanero *m.*

2 ATTR: **~ dealer** ropavejero *m*; **~ mistress** guardarropa *f*; **~ trunk** baúl *m* ropero.

wardroom ['wɔːdrum] N (*Naut*) cámara *f* de oficiales.

wardship ['wɔːdʃɪp] N tutela *f.*

warehouse **1** ['wɛəhaʊs] N, PL **warehouses** ['wɛə,haʊzɪz] almacén *m*, depósito *m.*

2 ATTR: **~ keeper** almacenista *m*; **~ loan** préstamo *m* de almacén; **~ manager** gerente *m* de almacén; **~ price** precio *m* en almacén; **~ receipt** recibo *m* de almacén; **~ warrant** duplicado *m* del certificado de almacén.

3 ['wɛəhaʊz] VT almacenar.

warehouseman ['wɛəhaʊsmən] N, PL **warehousemen** ['wɛəhaʊsmən] almacenista *m.*

warehousing ['wɛəhaʊzɪŋ] N almacenamiento *m.*

wares [wɛəz] NPL mercancías *fpl*; **to cry one's ~** pregonar sus mercancías.

warfare ['wɔːfɛəʳ] N guerra *f*; (*as study*) arte *m* militar, arte *m* de la guerra.

war-fever ['wɔːˌfiːvəʳ] N psicosis *f* de guerra.

war-game ['wɔːgeɪm] N simulacro *m* de guerra; juego *m* de guerra.

warhead ['wɔːhed] N (*of torpedo*) punta *f* de combate; (*of rocket*) cabeza *f* de guerra; **nuclear ~** cabeza *f* nuclear.

warhorse ['wɔːhɔːs] N caballo *m* de guerra; (*fig*) veterano *m.*

warily ['wɛərɪlɪ] ADV con cautela, cautelosamente; **to tread ~** (*also fig*) andar con pies de plomo.

wariness ['wɛərɪnɪs] N cautela *f*, precaución *f*; recelo *m.*

Warks N (*Brit*) ABBR of **Warwickshire**.

warlike ['wɔːlaɪk] ADJ guerrero, belicoso.

war-loan ['wɔːləʊn] N empréstito *m* de guerra.

warlock ['wɔːlɒk] N brujo *m*, hechicero *m.*

warlord ['wɔːlɔːd] N señor *m* de la guerra; jefe *m* militar.

warm [wɔːm] **1** ADJ **(a)** caliente (*pero no con exceso*); (*not too hot*) templado, tibio; *climate* cálido; *day, summer* caluroso, de calor; *blanket, clothing etc* cálido; **~ front** frente *m* caliente; **to be ~** (*person*) tener calor, (*thing*) estar caliente, (*weather*) hacer calor; **to be very ~** (*person*) tener mucho calor, (*thing*) estar muy caliente, (*weather*) hacer mucho calor; **to get ~** (*thing*) calentarse, (*weather*) empezar a hacer calor; **to get ~** (*person*) entrar en calor; **I still haven't got ~** todavía no he entrado en calor; **you're getting ~!** (*in games*) ¡te quemas!; **to keep o.s. ~** mantener el calor del cuerpo; **to keep sth ~** tener algo caliente, mantener el calor de algo; **to be as ~ as toast** estar muy bien de caliente.

(b) (*fig*) *scent* fresco; *tint* cálido; *thanks* efusivo; *heart, temperament* afectuoso; *dispute* acalorado; *greeting, welcome* caluroso; *hope* ardiente, sincero; *applause* cálido, entusiasta; *supporter* entusiasta; **it's ~ work** es un trabajo que hace sudar.

2 N: **to be in the ~** estar al calor, estar donde hay un calor agradable; **come and have a ~ by the fire** ven a calentarte junto a la lumbre.

3 VT calentar; *heart etc* alegrar, regocijar; (*) zurrar*.

4 VI **I** (*or my heart*) **~ed to him** le fui cobrando simpatía; **to ~ to one's subject** entusiasmarse con su tema.

5 VR: **to ~ o.s. at the fire** calentarse junto a la lumbre.

♦ **warm over** VT (*US*) *food* calentar; (*) *idea etc* recrear.

♦ **warm through** VT *food* calentar.

♦ **warm up** **1** VT *food* recalentar; *engine* calentar; *atmosphere etc* avivar, reanimar.

2 VI precalentarse (*also Sport*); (*argument*) acalorarse; **things are ~ing up** hay más actividad, hay más animación; **the game is ~ing up** el partido se está animando.

warm-blooded ['wɔːm'blʌdɪd] ADJ de sangre caliente; (*fig*) ardiente, apasionado.

warmed-up ['wɔːmd'ʌp] ADJ recalentado.

warm-hearted ['wɔːm'hɑːtɪd] ADJ bondadoso, afectuoso.

warming ['wɔːmɪŋ] N **(a)** recalentamiento *m.* **(b)** (*) zurra* *f.*

warming-pan ['wɔːmɪŋpæn] N calentador *m* (de cama).

warmly ['wɔːmlɪ] ADV **(a)** **the sun shone ~** brillaba el sol y hacía calor; **to dress ~** arroparse, ir bien abrigado; **the flat was very ~ heated** el piso tenía buena calefacción.

(b) (*fig*) efusivamente, con efusión; afectuosamente; calurosamente; con entusiasmo; **he thanked me most ~** me dio las más efusivas gracias; **he shook my hand ~** me estrechó la mano afectuosamente; **we ~ welcome it** nosotros lo acogemos con entusiasmo.

warmonger ['wɔːˌmʌŋgəʳ] N belicista *m.*

warmongering ['wɔːˌmʌŋgərɪŋ] **1** ADJ belicista.

2 N belicismo *m.*

warmth [wɔːmθ] N **(a)** calor *m*; lo cálido, lo caluroso.

(b) (*fig*) efusión *f*; afecto *m*; lo caluroso; entusiasmo *m*; **the ~ of their greeting** su acogida calurosa; **he replied with some ~** contestó bastante indignado.

warm-up ['wɔːmʌp] **1** N (*Sport*) precalentamiento *m*, calentamiento *m* previo; actividad *f* preliminar, preparativos *mpl.*

2 ATTR: **~ suit** (*US*) chandal *m.*

▼ **warn** [wɔːn] VT avisar, advertir; amonestar; prevenir; **to ~ the police** avisar a la policía; **the bell is to ~ the workmen** el timbre es para dar aviso a los obreros; **~ me before you blow it up** avísame antes de volarlo; **you have been ~ed!** ¡está Vd prevenido!; **to ~ sb not to do sth** advertir a uno que no haga algo; **to ~ sb about sth** amonestar a uno acerca de algo; **to ~ sb against sb else** prevenir a uno contra otra persona; **to ~ sb of a danger** prevenir a uno contra un peligro; **to ~ sb off** expulsar a uno; **to ~ sb off a subject** advertir a uno que no se meta en un asunto; **I ~ed him off Espronceda** le dije que no le convenía estudiar a Espronceda.

warning ['wɔːnɪŋ] **1** N aviso *m*, advertencia *f*; **without ~** sin dar aviso, sin previo aviso; **it fell without ~** cayó de repente, cayó inesperadamente; **they came without ~** vinieron sin avisar; **let this be a ~ to you** que esto te sirva de escarmiento; **thank you for the ~** gracias por la advertencia; **the bell gives ~** el timbre da la alarma; **to give sb a week's ~** avisar a uno con ocho días de anticipación; **to give sb due ~** avisar a uno con mucha antelación; **you were given due ~** te avisamos debidamente; **I give you due ~ that ...** le advierto en serio que ...; **to send a ~ to the police** avisar a la policía; **to sound a ~** dar un aviso; dar la voz de alarma; **to take ~ from** aprender la lección de, escarmentar en.

2 ADJ: **~ device** dispositivo *m* de alarma; **~ light** luz *f* de advertencia; **~ notice** aviso *m*; **~ shot** cañonazo *m* de advertencia, disparo *m* de advertencia; **~ sign** señal *f* de peligro; **in a ~ tone** en tono amonestador; **~ triangle** (*Aut*) triángulo *m* señalizador; **~ voices** voces *fpl* admonitorias.

warp [wɔːp] **1** N (**a**) (*in weaving*) urdimbre *f*. (**b**) (*of wood*) deformación *f*, alabeo *m*, comba *f*; (*fig*) sesgo *m*. **2** VT *wood* deformar, alabear, torcer; *mind* pervertir, torcer, afectar. **3** VI deformarse, alabearse, torcerse.

war-paint ['wɔːpeɪnt] N pintura *f* de guerra.

warpath ['wɔːpɑːθ] N: **to be on the ~** estar en pie de guerra, estar preparado para la guerra; (*fig*) estar dispuesto a armar un lío; estar buscando pendencia.

warped [wɔːpt] ADJ *wood* deformado, torcido; *character, sense of humour etc* pervertido.

warping ['wɔːpɪŋ] N (*of wood*) deformación *f*, alabeo *m*; (*Aer*) torsión *f*.

warplane ['wɔːpleɪn] N avión *m* militar.

warrant ['wɒrənt] **1** N (**a**) (*justification*) autorización *f*, justificación *f*. (**b**) (*certificate*) cédula *f*, certificado *m*; (*Comm*) garantía *f*; (*Jur*) mandamiento *m* judicial; mandato *m*, orden *f*; **~ of arrest** orden *f* de prisión; **~ issue** emisión *f* de cédula; **there is a ~ out for his arrest** se ha ordenado su detención. **2** VT (**a**) (*justify*) autorizar, justificar; **nothing ~s such an assumption** no hay nada que justifique tal suposición; **this order ~s your immediate attention** esta orden exige que Vd le preste atención en seguida; **the facts do not ~ it** los hechos no lo justifican. (**b**) (*Comm etc*) garantizar, certificar; **I ~ (you)** te lo aseguro.

warrantable ['wɒrəntəbl] ADJ justificable.

warranted ['wɒrəntɪd] ADJ (**a**) (*justified*) justificado. (**b**) (*guaranteed*) garantizado; **~ 18 carat gold** certificado de oro de 18 quilates.

warrant officer ['wɒrəntˌɒfɪsəʳ] N (*Mil*) brigada *m*; (*Naut*) contramaestre *m*.

warrantor ['wɒrəntɔːʳ] N garante *mf*.

warranty ['wɒrəntɪ] N garantía *f*; **without ~** sin garantía.

warren ['wɒrən] N madriguera *f* (de conejos); (*fig*) (*house etc*) conejera *f*, casa *f* con muchísimos inquilinos; casa *f* laberíntica; (*area of town*) barrio *m* densamente poblado; **it is a ~ of little streets** es un laberinto de callejuelas.

warring ['wɔːrɪŋ] ADJ *interests, nations etc* opuestos, reñidos entre sí, en lucha abierta entre sí.

warrior ['wɒrɪəʳ] N guerrero *m*; **the Unknown W~** el Soldado Desconocido.

Warsaw ['wɔːsɔː] **1** N Varsovia *f*. **2** ATTR: **~ Pact** Pacto *m* de Varsovia.

warship [wɔːʃɪp] N buque *m* de guerra, barco *m* de guerra.

wart [wɔːt] N (*Med, Bot*) verruga *f*; **~s and all** con todas sus imperfecciones.

wart-hog ['wɔːthɒg] N jabalí *m* verrugoso, facochero *m*.

wartime ['wɔːtaɪm] **1** N tiempo *m* de guerra; **in ~** en tiempos de guerra, en la guerra. **2** ATTR de tiempos de guerra, de guerra.

war-torn ['wɔːtɔːn] ADJ destrozado por la guerra.

warty ['wɔːtɪ] ADJ verrugoso.

war-weary ['wɔːˌwɪərɪ] ADJ cansado de la guerra.

war-wounded ['wɔːˌwuːndɪd] NPL: **the ~** los heridos de guerra.

wary ['wɛərɪ] ADJ cauteloso, cauto; **it's best to be ~ here** aquí conviene andar con pies de plomo; **I was ~ about it** tuve mis dudas acerca de ello, me recelé, desconfié de ello; **to keep a ~ eye on sb** vigilar a uno con recelo, tener cuidado con uno.

war-zone ['wɔːzəun] N zona *f* de guerra.

was [wɒz, wəz] V be.

wash [wɒʃ] **1** N (**a**) (*act of ~ing*) lavado *m*; baño *m*; **to give sth a ~** lavar algo; **to have a ~** lavarse; **to have a ~ and brush-up** lavarse y arreglarse; **my shirt is at (or in) the ~** mi camisa se está lavando, mi camisa está en la lavandería; **to send sheets to the ~** mandar sábanas a la lavandería; **it will all come out in the ~** todo saldrá en la colada.
(**b**) (*clothes:* dirty) ropa *f* sucia, ropa *f* para lavar; (*hung to dry*) tendido *m*, colada *f*; **the Monday ~** la ropa para lavar el lunes.
(**c**) (*of ship*) remolinos *mpl*; (*Aer*) disturbio *m* aerodinámico; **the ~ of the water** (*sound*) el movimiento del agua, el chapoteo del agua.
(**d**) (*liquid:* hair~) champú *m*; (*mouth~*) enjuague *m*; (*of distemper, paint*) capa *f*; pintura *f*; (*of insecticide etc*) baño *m*; (*liquid remains*) lavazas *fpl*, despojos *mpl* líquidos; (*pej*) aguachirle *f*; **a coat of blue ~** una capa de pintura azul.
2 VT (**a**) (*clean with water etc*) lavar; *dishes* fregar; *clothes* lavar; **to ~ one's hair** lavarse el pelo; **to ~ one's hands** lavarse las manos; **to ~ sth clean** limpiar algo lavándolo, lavar algo hasta dejarlo limpio; **the sea ~ed it clean of oil** el mar le quitó todo el aceite.
(**b**) **to ~ the walls with distemper** dar una capa de pintura (al temple) a las paredes; **to ~ a metal with gold** dar una capa de oro a un metal, bañar un metal en oro.
(**c**) **an island ~ed by a blue sea** una isla bañada por el mar azul.
(**d**) (*of river, sea:* carry) llevar, llevarse; **the house was ~ed downstream** la casa fue llevada aguas abajo; **the sea ~ed it ashore** el mar lo echó a la playa; **he was ~ed overboard** fue arrastrado por las olas.
3 VI (**a**) (*have a ~*) lavarse; (*do the ~ing*) lavar la ropa.
(**b**) **a cloth that ~es well** una tela que puede lavarse; **it's nice but it won't ~** es atractivo pero no se puede lavar; **that excuse won't ~!*** (*Brit*) ¡esa excusa no cuela!
(**c**) (*of sea etc*) moverse; chapotear; **the river was ~ing against the top of the bridge** el río estaba a la altura de la parte alta del puente; **the sea ~ed over the promenade** el mar inundó el paseo marítimo.
◆**wash away** VT (**a**) *dirt* quitar (lavando).
(**b**) **the boat was ~ed away** el bote fue arrastrado por la corriente; **the river ~ed away part of the bank** el río se llevó una parte de la orilla.
◆**wash down** VT (**a**) *car, wall* lavar.
(**b**) **to ~ one's dinner down with wine** regar la cena con vino.
(**c**) (*by flood etc*) llevar, arrastrar.
◆**wash off** **1** VT quitar (lavando), hacer desaparecer (lavando). **2** VI: **it ~es off easily** se quita fácilmente (lavándolo); **it won't ~ off** no se quita, no sale.
◆**wash out** **1** VT (**a**) *vessel* lavar, enjuagar; *stain* lavar.
(**b**) **to feel ~ed out** no estar bien de salud; estar muy cansado; **to look ~ed out** estar ojeroso.
(**c**) (*ruin*) arruinar, acabar con; **the game was ~ed out** el partido fue cancelado debido a la lluvia; **it ~ed out our last chance** acabó con nuestra última posibilidad; **let's ~ it all out** abandonémoslo todo, renunciemos a la empresa.
2 VI: **the colour ~es out** el color se destiñe.
◆**wash through** VT *clothes* lavar rápidamente.
◆**wash up** **1** VT (**a**) (*Brit*) *dishes* fregar, lavar.
(**b**) **the sea ~ed it up** el mar lo echó, el mar lo arrojó (a la playa).
(**c**) (*) **that's all ~ed up** eso es un fracaso total, eso ya se acabó; **he's all ~ed up** está hecho una calamidad.
2 VI (**a**) (*Brit*) fregar los platos.
(**b**) (*US*) lavarse, lavarse las manos.

Wash. (*US*) ABBR of Washington.

washable ['wɒʃəbl] ADJ lavable.

wash-and-wear ['wɒʃən'wɛəʳ] ADJ *clothing* de no planchar, de lava y pon.

wash bag ['wɒʃbæg] N (*US*) esponjera *f*.

washbasin ['wɒʃˌbeɪsn] N (*Brit*), **washbowl** ['wɒʃbəul] N palangana *f*, jofaina *f*.

washboard ['wɒʃbɔːd] N tabla *f* de lavar; (*US*) rodapié *m*, zócalo *m*.

washcloth ['wɒʃklɒθ] N, PL **washcloths** ['wɒʃklɒθs, 'wɒʃklɒðz] (*US*) paño *m* para lavarse, manopla *f*.

washday ['wɒʃdeɪ] N día *m* de colada.

washed-out ['wɒʃ'taut] ADJ deslavazado.

washer ['wɒʃəʳ] N (**a**) (*Tech*) arandela *f*; (*on tap*) arandela *f*, zapatilla *f*. (**b**) (*washing-machine*) lavadora *f*.

washer-dryer, washer-drier ['wɒʃə'draɪəʳ] N lavadora-secadora *f*.

washerwoman ['wɒʃəˌwumən] N, PL **washerwomen** ['wɒʃəˌwɪmɪn] lavandera *f*.

wash-hand basin ['wɒʃˌhænd,beɪsn] N lavabo *m*, lavamanos *m invar*.

wash-house ['wɒʃhaus] N, PL **washhouses** ['wɒʃˌhauzɪz] lavadero *m*.

washing ['wɒʃɪŋ] N (**a**) (*act*) lavado *m*, el lavar. (**b**) (*clothes:* dirty) ropa *f* sucia, ropa *f* para lavar; (*hung to dry*) tendido *m*, colada *f*; **to take in ~** ser lavandera.

washing-day ['wɒʃɪŋdeɪ] N día *m* de colada.

washing-line ['wɒʃɪŋ'laɪn] N cuerda *f* de tender la ropa.

washing-machine ['wɒʃɪŋmə,ʃiːn] N lavadora *f*.

washing-powder ['wɒʃɪŋ,paudəʳ] N (*Brit*) jabón *m* en polvo.

washing-soda ['wɒʃɪŋ,səudə] N sosa *f*, carbonato *m* sódico.

Washington ['wɒʃɪŋtən] N Washington *m*.

washing-up ['wɒʃɪŋ'ʌp] N (*Brit*) (*act*) fregado *m*, el fregar (los platos); (*dishes: to be washed*) platos *mpl* para lavar; (*washed*) platos *mpl* lavados; ~ **liquid** detergente *m* líquido, lavavajillas *m*; **he did all the** ~ fregó todos los platos.

wash-leather ['wɒʃˌleðəʳ] N (*Brit*) gamuza *f*.

wash-out* ['wɒʃaʊt] N desastre *m*, fracaso *m*; **it was a** ~ fue un fracaso total; **he's a** ~ es una calamidad*.

washrag ['wɒʃræg] N (*US*) paño *m* de cocina; = **washcloth**.

washroom ['wɒʃrʊm] N lavabo *m*, aseos *mpl*, sanitarios *mpl* (*LAm*), baño *m* (*LAm*); *ver también* TOILET.

wash sale ['wɒʃseɪl] N (*US*) venta *f* ficticia.

washstand ['wɒʃstænd] N lavabo *m*, lavamanos *m*.

washtub ['wɒʃtʌb] N tina *f* de lavar; (*bath*) bañera *f*.

washy ['wɒʃɪ] ADJ aguado, diluido; débil; (*fig*) flojo, soso.

wasn't ['wɒznt] = **was not**.

WASP* [wɒsp] N (*US*) ABBR for **White Anglo-Saxon Protestant**.

┌─── WASP ───┐

ⓘ *La expresión WASP o White Anglo-Saxon Protestant se usa para referirse a los norteamericanos originarios del norte de Europa. Esta expresión fue acuñada en los años sesenta por E. Digby Baltzell, un escritor de Philadelphia. Es un término peyorativo para los miembros de este grupo étnico y religioso, a los que se considera como los más poderosos, privilegiados e influyentes de Estados Unidos. Este término también se utiliza por extensión para hacer referencia a toda persona blanca de clase media descendiente de los primeros colonos y que cree en los valores tradicionales estadounidenses.*

wasp [wɒsp] N avispa *f*; **~s' nest** avispero *m* (*also fig*).

waspish ['wɒspɪʃ] ADJ *character* irascible; *person* de prontos enojos, fácil de enojar; *comment* mordaz, punzante.

waspishly ['wɒspɪʃlɪ] ADV mordazmente.

wasp waist ['wɒsp'weɪst] N (*fig*) talle *m* de avispa.

wasp-waisted ['wɒsp'weɪstɪd] ADJ (*fig*) con talle de avispa.

wassail†† ['wɒseɪl] **1** N (*drink*) cerveza *f* especiada; (*festivity*) juerga *f*, fiesta *f* de borrachos.
2 VI beber mucho.

wastage ['weɪstɪdʒ] N desgaste *m*, desperdicio *m*; pérdida *f*; (*from container*) merma *f*; **the ~ of our resources** el desperdicio de nuestros recursos; **the ~ rate among students** la proporción de estudiantes que no terminan su licenciatura (*etc*); **the ~ rate among entrants to the profession** el porcentaje de los que abandonan la profesión poco tiempo después de ingresar en ella.

waste [weɪst] **1** ADJ (*rejected*) desechado, de desecho; (*left over*) sobrante, superfluo; (*useless*) inútil; *land* baldío; yermo; ~ **disposal unit** triturador *m* de basuras; ~ **material** material *m* de desecho; ~ **paper** papel *m* viejo, papel *m* de desecho, papeles *mpl* usados; ~ **products** (*Bio*) desperdicios *mpl*, (*of industry*) residuos *mpl*; ~ **steam** vapor *m* de escape; **'The W~ Land'** 'Tierra *f* baldía'; **to lay** ~ asolar, devastar; **to lie** ~ quedar sin cultivar; quedar sin utilizar.

2 N (**a**) (*act*) despilfarro *m*, derroche *m*; (*of time etc*) pérdida *f*; (*wastage*) desgaste *m*, desperdicio *m*; merma *f*; **it's a ~ of time** es tiempo perdido; **it's a ~ of effort** es un esfuerzo inútil; **there's a lot of ~ here** hay mucho desperdicio aquí; **to go to** ~, **to run to** ~ echarse a perder, perderse.

(**b**) (~ *material*) desperdicios *mpl*, desechos *mpl*; (*rubbish*) basura *f*; (*industrial*) residuos *mpl*, vertidos *mpl*.

(**c**) (*land*) yermo *m*, tierra *f* baldía; desierto *m*; **lost in the ~s of Siberia** perdido en la inmensidad de Siberia; **to plough the ~s of Siberia** cultivar la tierra baldía de Siberia.

3 VT (**a**) (*squander*) despilfarrar, derrochar; malgastar; *time etc* perder; (*not use*) desperdiciar; *opportunity etc* desaprovechar, desperdiciar; (*use up*) agotar, consumir; **a ~d life** una vida desperdiciada; **nothing is ~d** no queda nada sin aprovechar; **we ~d 3 litres of petrol** perdimos 3 litros de gasolina; **to ~ no time in doing sth** hacer algo cuanto antes; **we must ~ no time** no hay que perder tiempo; **you're wasting your time talking to him** es tiempo perdido hablar con él; **don't ~ your efforts on him** no te canses tratando de hacer cosas por él.

(**b**) *body etc* consumir, gastar, debilitar.

(**c**) (*US‡: kill*) mandar al otro mundo*, cargarse*.

4 VI (**a**) ~ **not, want not** la economía protege de la necesidad. (**b**) (~ *away*) gastarse, perderse.

◆ **waste away** VI consumirse, mermar; (*person*) consumirse; **you're not exactly wasting away** (*iro*) no pareces haber enflaquecido de modo peligroso que digamos.

wastebasket ['weɪstˌbɑːskɪt] N (*US*) cesto *m* de los papeles, papelera *f*.

wastebin ['weɪstbɪn] N (*Brit*) cubo *m* de la basura.

wasted ['weɪstɪd] ADJ *opportunity* desaprovechado; *effort* inútil, vano; *person* (*thin*) demacrado; *limb* atrofiado; (*: *from drugs*) destrozado.

wasteful ['weɪstfʊl] ADJ *person etc* pródigo, despilfarrado, derrochador;

process antieconómico, dispendioso; *expenditure* pródigo, excesivo; **it is ~ of effort** no utiliza debidamente el esfuerzo.

wastefully ['weɪstfəlɪ] ADV pródigamente; antieconómicamente; excesivamente.

wastefulness ['weɪstfʊlnɪs] N prodigalidad *f*, despilfarro *m*; falta *f* de economía, lo antieconómico; lo excesivo.

wasteland ['weɪstlænd] N tierra *f* baldía, yermo, erial *m*.

wastepaper-basket [weɪst'peɪpəˌbɑːskɪt] N cesto *m* de los papeles, papelera *f*.

waste-pipe ['weɪstpaɪp] N tubo *m* de desagüe.

waster ['weɪstəʳ] N (*person*) derrochador *m*, perdido *m*.

wasting ['weɪstɪŋ] ADJ *disease* debilitante; *asset* agotable.

wastrel ['weɪstrəl] N derrochador *m*, perdido *m*.

watch [wɒtʃ] **1** N (**a**) (*vigilance*) vigilancia *f*; (*act of ~ing*) vigilia *f*, vela *f*; **to be on the** ~ estar a la mira (*for* de), estar al acecho, vigilar; **they're on the ~ for smugglers** están al acecho por si hay contrabandistas, están al acecho de los contrabandistas; **we have the place under** ~ estamos vigilando el local; **to keep** ~ estar de guardia; **to keep ~ all night** velar toda la noche; **to keep a close ~ on sth** vigilar algo con mucho cuidado; **to keep ~ over** *person* velar, vigilar; *thing* velar por; **to set a ~ on sb** poner a uno bajo vigilancia.

(**b**) (*period of duty*) guardia *f*; **to have a 4-hour** ~ estar de guardia durante 4 horas.

(**c**) (*persons: Hist*) ronda *f*; (*Mil: persons*) guardia *f*, (*1 man*) guardia *m*, centinela *m*; (*Naut: persons*) guardia *f*, vigía *f*, (*1 man*) vigía *m*; **officer of the** ~ oficial *m* de guardia.

(**d**) (*timepiece*) reloj *m* (de bolsillo, de pulsera); **what does your ~ say?** ¿qué hora tienes?

2 VT (**a**) (*guard*) guardar, vigilar; proteger.

(**b**) (*observe*) observar, mirar; (*at length*) contemplar; (*spy on*) espiar, acechar; (*TV etc*) ver; **did you ~ the programme?** ¿viste el programa?; **to ~ sb doing sth** ver a uno hacer algo, observar mientras uno hace algo, observar a uno hacer algo; **now ~ this closely** ahora observen esto detenidamente; **we are being ~ed** nos están observando; **have you ever ~ed an operation?** ¿has visto alguna vez una operación?; **Big Brother is ~ing you** el Gran Hermano te vigila.

(**c**) (*be careful with*) ser cuidadoso con, prestar atención a, tener ojo a; ~ **it!** ¡ojo!, ¡cuidado!, ¡abusado! (*Mex*); **you'd better ~ it** conviene tener más cuidado; mejor será que tengas cuidado; (*Aut: slogan*) ~ **your speed!** ¡atención a la velocidad!; ~ **your language!** ¡cuida tu vocabulario!; **we shall have to ~ the expenses** tendremos que estudiar detalladamente los gastos; convendrá tener ojo con los gastos; ~ **how you go!** ¡anda con cuidado!; *V* **step** *etc*.

(**d**) *chance etc* esperar, aguardar; **he ~ed his chance and slipped out** esperó el momento propicio y se escabulló.

3 VI ver, mirar; observar; (*vigilantly*) vigilar; **you ~!** (*wait and see*) ¡espera y verás!; (*see this*) ¡mira esto!, ¡a ver esto!; **to ~ for sb** esperar a uno, aguardar a uno; **to ~ for sth to happen** esperar a que pase algo; **to ~ over sb** velar a uno; **to ~ over the safety of the country** velar por la seguridad de la patria; **to ~ over a property** vigilar una propiedad.

◆ **watch out** VI tener ojo, tener cuidado; estar alerta; ~ **out!** ¡ojo!, ¡abusado! (*Mex*); ~ **out for thieves!** ¡cuidado con los ladrones!; **to ~ out for trouble** estar alerta por si hay problemas, estar al acecho por si hay disturbios; **then you'd better ~ out!** ¡pues aténgase a las consecuencias!

watchband ['wɒtʃbænd] N (*US*) pulsera *f* de reloj, correa *f* de reloj.

watchcase ['wɒtʃkeɪs] N caja *f* de reloj.

watchdog ['wɒtʃdɒg] **1** N perro *m* guardián; (*fig*) perro *m* vigilante, guardián *m*, -ana *f*.
2 ATTR: ~ **committee** comisión *f* de vigilancia, comisión *f* de seguimiento.

watcher ['wɒtʃəʳ] N observador *m*, -ora *f*; espectador *m*, -ora *f*; (*pej*) mirón *m*, -ona *f*.

-watcher ['wɒtʃəʳ] N *ending in compounds, eg* **China-~** especialista *mf* en asuntos chinos, sinólogo *m*, -a *f*; *V* **bird-~** *etc*.

watchful ['wɒtʃfʊl] ADJ vigilante; observador; (*esp fig*) desvelado; **under the ~ gaze of ...** bajo la vigilante mirada de ...

watchfully ['wɒtʃfəlɪ] ADV vigilantemente.

watchfulness ['wɒtʃfʊlnɪs] N vigilancia *f*; desvelo *m*.

watchglass ['wɒtʃglɑːs] N cristal *m* de reloj.

watchmaker ['wɒtʃˌmeɪkəʳ] N relojero *m*; ~'s (*shop*) relojería *f*.

watchman ['wɒtʃmən] N, PL **watchmen** ['wɒtʃmən] guardián *m*; (*night ~*) (*in street, flats*) sereno *m*, (*in factory etc*) vigilante *m* nocturno.

watch night service ['wɒtʃ'naɪt'sɜːvɪs] N (*Rel*) servicio *m* de fin de año.

watchstem ['wɒtʃstəm] N (*US*) cuerda *f*.

watchstrap ['wɒtʃstræp] N pulsera *f* de reloj, correa *f* de reloj.

watchtower ['wɒtʃˌtaʊəʳ] N atalaya *f*, vigía *f*, torre *f* de vigilancia.

watchword ['wɒtʃwɜːd] N (*Mil etc*) santo *m* y seña; (*motto*) lema *m*, consigna *f*.

water ['wɔːtəᵣ] **1** N **(a)** agua *f*; **like ~** (*fig*) como agua, pródigamente, en abundancia; **like ~ off a duck's back** como si nada; **the square is under ~** la plaza está inundada; **a lot of ~ has flowed** (*or* **passed**) **under the bridge** (*fig*) ya ha llovido desde entonces; **that's all ~ under the bridge now** todo eso queda ya a la espalda; **to be in hot ~*** estar metido en un lío*; **to get into hot ~*** cargársela* (*for, over* en el asunto de); meterse en un lío*; **to hold ~** retener el agua, (*fig*) estar bien fundado, ser lógico; **that excuse won't hold ~** esa excusa no vale; **to pour cold ~ on an idea** echar un jarro de agua fría a una idea; **to spend money like ~** derrochar dinero; **to swim under ~** nadar bajo el agua; **to test the ~(s)** (*fig*) probar la temperatura del agua; **to turn on the ~** hacer correr el agua; (*from tap*) abrir el grifo; **still ~s run deep** la procesión va por dentro; no te fíes del agua mansa.

(b) (*urine*) orina *f*, orines *mpl*; **to make** (*or* **pass**) **~** hacer aguas, mear.

(c) (*Med*) **~s** aguas *fpl*; **to drink** (*or* **take**) **the ~s at Harrogate** tomar las aguas en Harrogate.

(d) (*of sea etc*) agua *f*; **the ~s of the Ebro** las aguas del Ebro; **by ~** por mar; **on land and ~** por tierra y por mar; **to back ~** ciar; **to fish in troubled ~s** pescar en río revuelto; **to get into deep ~(s)** meterse en honduras; **low ~** *etc* V **tide**.

(e) (*Med*) **~ on the brain** hidrocefalía *f*; **~ on the knee** derrame *m* sinovial.

(f) **of the first ~** de lo mejor, de primerísima calidad.

2 ATTR acuático; de agua; para agua; **~ biscuit** galleta *f* de soda; **~ blister** ampolla *f*; **~ buffalo** búfalo *m* de agua, carabao *m*; **~ chestnut** castaña *f* de agua; **~ cooler** enfriadora *f* de agua; **~ plants** plantas *fpl* acuáticas; **~ purification plant** estación *f* depuradora de aguas residuales; **~ supply** abastecimiento *m* de agua.

3 VT *garden, plant* regar; *horses* abrevar; *wine* aguar; diluir; (*moisten*) mojar, humedecer; **to ~ a plant with an insecticide** regar (*or* rociar) una planta con insecticida; **the river ~s the provinces of ...** el río riega las provincias de ...; **to ~ capital** emitir un número excesivo de acciones; **to ~ down** aguar; diluir; (*fig*) mitigar; suavizar; **I should ~ the abuse down a bit** conviene suavizar un poco las injurias.

4 VI (*of eyes*) hacerse agua, lagrimear, llorar; **my mouth ~ed** se me hizo la boca agua; **it's enough to make your mouth ~** se hace la boca agua.

waterage ['wɔːtərɪdʒ] N transporte *m* por barco.

waterbed ['wɔːtə'bed] N cama *f* de agua.

water bird ['wɔːtəbɜːd] N ave *f* acuática.

waterborne ['wɜːtəbɔːn] ADJ llevado por barco (*etc*); **~ traffic** tráfico *m* fluvial, tráfico *m* marítimo.

waterbottle ['wɔːtə,bɒtl] N cantimplora *f*.

water-butt ['wɔːtə'bʌt] N tina *f* para agua.

water-cannon ['wɔːtə'kænən] N cañón *m* de agua.

water-carrier ['wɔːtə,kærɪəʳ] N aguador *m*.

water-cart ['wɔːtəkɑːt] N cuba *f* de riego, carro *m* aljibe; (*motorized*) camión *m* de agua.

water-closet ['wɔːtə,klɒzɪt] N (*freq abbr* WC) wáter *m*, inodoro *m*.

watercolour, (*US*) **watercolor** ['wɔːtə,kʌləʳ] N acuarela *f*.

watercolourist, (*US*) **watercolorist** ['wɔːtə,kʌlərɪst] N acuarelista *mf*.

water-cooled ['wɔːtəkuːld] ADJ refrigerado por agua.

water-cooling ['wɔːtəkuːlɪŋ] N refrigeración *f* por agua.

watercourse ['wɔːtəkɔːs] N (*stream*) arroyo *m*; (*canal*) canal *m*; (*bed*) lecho *m*, cauce *m*.

watercress ['wɔːtəkres] N berro *m*, mastuerzo *m*.

water-diviner ['wɔːtədɪ,vaɪnəʳ] N zahorí *m*.

water-divining ['wɔːtədɪ,vaɪnɪŋ] N arte *m* del zahorí.

watered ['wɔːtəd] ADJ aguado; **~ stock** acciones *fpl* diluidas.

watered-down ['wɔːtəd'daʊn] ADJ *wine etc* aguado, bautizado; (*fig*) *account, version* saneado.

waterfall ['wɔːtəfɔːl] N cascada *f*, salto *m* de agua, catarata *f*.

waterfowl ['wɔːtəfaʊl] NPL aves *fpl* acuáticas.

waterfront ['wɔːtəfrʌnt] N (*esp US*) terreno *m* ribereño; (*harbour area*) puerto *m*, muelles *mpl*, dársenas *fpl*.

water-heater ['wɔːtə'hiːtəʳ] N calentador *m* de agua.

waterhole ['wɔːtəhəʊl] N charco *m*; abrevadero *m*.

water-ice ['wɔːtəraɪs] N (*Brit*) sorbete *m*, helado *m*.

watering ['wɔːtərɪŋ] N riego *m*; **frequent ~ is needed** hay que regar con frecuencia.

watering-can ['wɔːtərɪŋkæn] N regadera *f*.

watering-hole ['wɔːtərɪŋ'həʊl] N (*for animals*) abrevadero *m*; (*) pub *m*.

watering-place ['wɔːtərɪŋpleɪs] N (*spa*) balneario *m*; (*seaside resort*) playa *f*, ciudad *f* marítima de veraneo; (*Agr*) abrevadero *m*.

water-jacket ['wɔːtə,dʒækɪt] N camisa *f* de agua.

water-jump ['wɔːtə'dʒʌmp] N foso *m* (de agua).

waterless ['wɔːtəlɪs] ADJ sin agua, árido.

water-level ['wɔːtə,levl] N nivel *m* del agua; (*Naut*) línea *f* de agua.

water-lily ['wɔːtə,lɪlɪ] N nenúfar *m*.

waterline ['wɔːtəlaɪn] N línea *f* de flotación.

waterlogged ['wɔːtəlɒgd] ADJ *ground etc* anegado, inundado; *wood etc* empapado; **to get ~** anegarse; empaparse.

Waterloo [,wɔːtə'luː] N Waterloo *m* (*1815*); **he met his ~** se le llegó su San Martín.

water main ['wɔːtəmeɪn] N cañería *f* principal.

waterman ['wɔːtəmən] N, PL **watermen** ['wɔːtəmən] barquero *m*.

watermark ['wɔːtəmɑːk] N filigrana *f*.

water-meadow ['wɔːtə,medəʊ] N prado *m* (junto al río *or* sujeto a inundaciones).

watermelon ['wɔːtə,melən] N sandía *f*.

water meter ['wɔːtə,miːtəʳ] N contador *m* del agua.

watermill ['wɔːtəmɪl] N molino *m* de agua.

waterpark ['wɔːtəpɑːk] N parque *m* acuático.

waterpipe ['wɔːtəpaɪp] N caño *m* de agua.

water-pistol ['wɔːtə'pɪstl] N pistola *f* de agua.

water-polo ['wɔːtə'pəʊləʊ] N polo *m* acuático, water-polo *m*.

water power ['wɔːtə,paʊəʳ] N fuerza *f* hidráulica.

waterproof ['wɔːtəpruːf] **1** ADJ impermeable.
2 N impermeable *m*.
3 VT impermeabilizar.

waterproofing ['wɔːtə'pruːfɪŋ] N (*process*) impermeabilización *f*; (*material*) impermeabilizante *m*.

water-pump ['wɔːtəpʌmp] N bomba *f* de agua.

water-rat ['wɔːtəræt] N rata *f* de agua.

water rate ['wɔːtəreɪt] N (*Brit*) tarifa *f* de agua; impuesto *m* sobre el agua.

water-repellent ['wɔːtərɪ'pelənt] **1** ADJ hidrófugo.
2 N hidrófugo *m*.

water-resistant ['wɔːtərɪ'zɪstənt] ADJ a prueba de agua; *ink* indeleble; *material* impermeable.

watershed ['wɔːtəʃed] N (*Geog*) línea *f* divisoria de las aguas, parteaguas *m*; cuenca *f*; (*fig*) división *f*, línea *f* divisoria; **the ~ of the Duero** la cuenca del Duero.

waterside ['wɔːtəsaɪd] **1** N orilla *f* del agua, ribera *f*.
2 ATTR ribereño; situado en la orilla.

water-ski ['wɔːtəskiː] VI esquiar en el agua.

water-skier ['wɔːtə,skiːəʳ] N esquiador *m* acuático, esquiadora *f* acuática.

water-skiing ['wɔːtə,skiːɪŋ] N esquí *m* acuático.

water-snake ['wɔːtə'sneɪk] N culebra *f* de agua.

water-softener ['wɔːtə'sɒfnəʳ] N ablandador *m* de agua.

water-soluble ['wɔːtə'sɒljubl] ADJ soluble en agua, hidrosoluble.

watersports ['wɔːtəspɔːts] NPL deportes *mpl* acuáticos.

waterspout ['wɔːtəspaʊt] N tromba *f* marina.

water-table ['wɔːtə,teɪbl] N capa *f* freática, nivel *m* de agua freática.

water-tank ['wɔːtətæŋk] N cisterna *f*, depósito *m* de agua; aljibe *m*.

watertight ['wɔːtətaɪt] ADJ *compartment etc* estanco; hermético; (*fig*) irrecusable, completamente lógico.

water-tower ['wɔːtə,taʊəʳ] N arca *f* de agua, alcubilla *f*.

water-vapour, (*US*) **water-vapor** ['wɔːtə,veɪpəʳ] N vapor *m* de agua.

water-vole ['wɔːtəvəʊl] N rata *f* de agua.

water-waggon ['wɔːtə'wægən] N (*US*) vagón-cisterna *m*.

waterway ['wɔːtəweɪ] N vía *f* fluvial; (*inland ~*) canal *m*, canal *m* navegable.

waterweed ['wɔːtə'wiːd] N planta *f* acuática.

waterwheel ['wɔːtəwiːl] N rueda *f* hidráulica; (*Agr*) noria *f*.

water-wings ['wɔːtəwɪŋz] NPL nadaderas *fpl*, flotadores *mpl*.

waterworks ['wɔːtəwɜːks] N **(a)** central *f* depuradora; (*loosely*) (sistema *m* de) abastecimiento *m* de agua. **(b)** (‡) (*Anat*) vías *fpl* urinarias. **(c)** (*) **to turn on the ~** echar a llorar.

watery ['wɔːtərɪ] ADJ *substance* acuoso; (*wet*) húmedo, mojado; *eye* lagrimoso; *sky* que amenaza lluvia, lluvioso; *soup, wine* débil, flojo.

WATS ['wɒts] N (*US*) ABBR *of* **Wide Area Telecommunications Service**.

watt [wɒt] N vatio *m*.

wattage ['wɒtɪdʒ] N vataje *m*.

wattle[1] ['wɒtl] N zarzo *m*; **~ and daub** zarzos *mpl* y barro.

wattle[2] ['wɒtl] N (*Orn*) barba *f*.

wave [weɪv] **1** N **(a)** (*of water*) ola *f*; **~ energy** energía *f* de las ondas; **to make ~s** (*fig: rock the boat*) hacer olas, (*play up*) dar guerra, (*make a fuss*) armar un lío.

(b) (*Phys, Rad*) onda *f*; **long ~** onda *f* larga; **medium ~** onda *f* media; **short ~** onda *f* corta.

(c) (*in hair, on surface*) ondulación *f*.

(d) (*fig*) oleada *f*; **~ of enthusiasm** oleada *f* de entusiasmo; **~ of panic** oleada *f* de pánico; **~ of strikes** oleada *f* de huelgas; **cold ~** oleada *f* de frío; **the first ~ of the attack** la primera oleada de asalto; **the attackers came in ~s** las tropas atacaron en oleadas.

(e) (*movement of hand*) movimiento *m*, ademán *m* (de la mano), señal *f* (hecha con la mano); **with a ~ of his hand** con un movimiento de la mano, haciendo una señal con la mano; **with a ~ he was gone** hizo una señal con la mano y desapareció.

(f) (*Liter etc*) **new ~** nueva ola *f*.

2 VT **(a)** (*brandish*) agitar, (*threateningly*) blandir; *flag etc* ondear, agitar; **don't ~ it about!** ¡no lo agites!; **he ~d the ticket under my nose** agitó el billete en mis narices; **to ~ one's hand to sb** hacer una señal a uno con la mano; **to ~ one's arms about** agitar mucho los brazos; **to ~ sb goodbye** decir adiós a uno con la mano; **to ~ a handkerchief to sb** agitar el pañuelo para dar una señal a uno; **he ~d a greeting to the crowd** saludó a la multitud con un movimiento de la mano.

(b) *hair etc* ondular; **to have one's hair ~d** hacerse ondular el pelo, hacerse una permanente.

3 VI **(a)** (*person*) hacer señales con la mano, agitar el brazo; **to ~ to sb** hacer señales con la mano a uno; **we ~d as the train drew out** cuando partió el tren nos dijimos adiós con la mano.

(b) (*flag etc*) ondear; flotar; (*arm etc*) agitarse.

◆**wave aside**, **wave away** VT *offer etc* rechazar; **to ~ sb aside** hacer una señal a uno para que se aparte; **he ~d my help aside** indicó con un movimiento de la mano que no necesitaba mi ayuda.

◆**wave down** VT: **to ~ a car down** hacer señales a un coche para que pare.

◆**wave off** VT: **to ~ sb off** decir adiós a uno con la mano.

◆**wave on** VT: **to ~ sb on** hacer señales a uno para que avance.

waveband ['weɪvbænd] N banda *f* de ondas; **long ~** banda *f* de onda larga.

wavelength ['weɪvleŋθ] N longitud *f* de onda; **we are not on the same ~** (*fig*) no estamos en la misma onda.

wavelet ['weɪvlɪt] N pequeña ola *f*, olita *f*, rizo *m*.

waver ['weɪvəʳ] VI (*oscillate*) oscilar (*between* entre); (*hesitate*) dudar, vacilar; (*weaken*) flaquear; **I ~ed for some days** durante varios días no me resolví; **he's beginning to ~** está empezando a vacilar.

wave range ['weɪvreɪndʒ] N (*Rad*) gama *f* de ondas.

waverer ['weɪvərəʳ] N indeciso *m*, -a *f*, irresoluto *m*, -a *f*.

wavering ['weɪvərɪŋ] **1** ADJ indeciso, irresoluto, vacilante.

2 N oscilación *f*; vacilación *f*, irresolución *f*.

wavy ['weɪvɪ] ADJ *hair*, *surface* ondulado; *motion* ondulante.

wavy-haired ['weɪvɪ'heəd] ADJ de pelo ondulado.

wax[1] [wæks] **1** N cera *f*; (*in ear*) cera *f* de los oídos, cerumen *m*, cerilla *f*.

2 ADJ de cera; **~ paper** papel *m* encerado; **~ seal** sello *m* de lacre.

3 VT encerar.

wax[2] [wæks] VI (*moon*) crecer; (*with adj*) ponerse, hacerse; **to ~ enthusiastic** entusiasmarse; **to ~ talkative** empezar a hablar mucho; **to ~ and wane** crecer y descrecer.

waxed [wækst] ADJ *paper etc* encerado; *jacket* impermeabilizado.

waxen ['wæksən] ADJ (*of wax*) de cera; (*like wax*) ceroso, parecido a cera; como color de cera.

waxing ['wæksɪŋ] **1** ADJ *moon* creciente.

2 N crecimiento *m*.

waxwork ['wækswɜːk] N figura *f* de cera; **~s** museo *m* de (figuras de) cera.

waxy ['wæksɪ] ADJ = **waxen**.

way [weɪ] **1** N **(a)** (*road*) camino *m*, vía *f*; carretera *f*; calle *f*; **W~ of the Cross** Vía *f* Crucis, viacrucis *m*; **permanent ~** vía *f*; **the public ~** la vía pública; **across the ~**, **over the ~** enfrente (*from* de); **by ~ of** vía, por vía de; pasando por.

(b) (*route*) camino *m*, ruta *f* (*to* de); **the ~ to the station** el camino de la estación; **which is the ~ to the station, please?** por favor, ¿qué camino tomo para ir a la estación?, ¿cómo se llega a la estación? (*LAm*); **this isn't the ~ to Lugo!** ¡por aquí no se va a Lugo!; **the ~ is hard** el camino es duro; **the ~ of virtue** el camino de la virtud; **to go the shortest ~** ir por el camino más corto; **to go the ~ of all good things** desaparecer como todo lo bueno; **to go the ~ of all flesh** fenecer como todo ser humano; **to lead the ~** ir primero, (*fig*) dar el ejemplo, mostrar el camino; **to prepare the ~** preparar el terreno (*for* a, para); **on the ~** en el camino; durante el viaje; **on the ~ here** mientras veníamos aquí; **on the ~ to Aranjuez** camino de Aranjuez; **it's on the ~ to Murcia** está en la carretera de Murcia; **they have another child on the ~** tienen otro niño en camino; **you pass it on your ~ home** cae de camino para tu casa; **your house is on my ~** tu casa me viene de camino; **the place is very out of the ~** el lugar es muy remoto, el sitio es bastante aislado; **the subject is rather out of the ~** el tema es algo insólito; **her painting is nothing out of the ~** su pintura no tiene nada de particular; **to go out of one's ~** desviarse del camino; **to go out of one's ~ to +** *infin* (*fig*) tomarse la molestia de + *infin*; desvivirse por + *infin*.

(c) (*route, with adv*) **~ down** bajada *f*, ruta *f* para bajar; **~ in** entrada *f*; **'~ in'** 'entrada'; **Spain's ~ into the United Nations** el camino que siguió España para ingresar en las Naciones Unidas; **to find a ~ in** encontrar un modo de entrar; **~ out** salida *f*; **'~ out'** 'salida'; **you'll find it on the ~ out** lo encontrarás cerca de la salida; **it's on its ~ out** está en camino de desaparecer, ya está pasando de moda; **there's no ~ out** (*fig*) no hay salida, no hay solución, esto no tiene solución; **there's no other ~ out** (*fig*) no hay más remedio; **~ through** paso *m*; **'no ~ through'** 'cerrado el paso'; **~ up** subida *f*, ruta *f* para subir.

(d) (*route, with personal associations*) **he is well on his ~ to finishing it** lo tiene casi terminado; **to ask the ~** preguntar cómo se llega a un lugar, preguntar una dirección; **if the chance comes my ~** si se presenta la oportunidad; **to feel one's ~** andar a tientas, (*fig*) proceder con tiento; **to find one's ~ into a building** encontrarse un modo de entrar en un edificio; **the cat found the ~ into the pantry** el gato logró introducirse en la despensa; **can you find your ~ home?** ¿sabes por dónde ir a tu casa?; **to go the wrong ~** equivocarse de camino; **to go one's own ~** (*fig*) ir a la suya; hacer rancho aparte; **I know my ~ about town** conozco el plano de la ciudad; **she knows her ~ about** (*fig*) tiene bastante experiencia; no es que sea una inocente; **to lose one's ~** extraviarse, errar el camino; **to make one's ~ to** dirigirse a; **to make one's ~ home** ir a casa, volver a casa; **to make one's ~ through a crowd** abrirse camino por la gente; **to make one's ~ in the world** hacer progresos en su profesión, hacerse (una) carrera; valerse por sí mismo; **he had to make his own ~ in the art world** tuvo que abrirse camino por sus propios medios en el mundo del arte; **to pay one's ~** (*in restaurant*) pagar su parte; (*Fin*) ser solvente; **the company isn't paying its ~** la compañía tiene un saldo negativo; **the department pays its ~** la sección tiene beneficios suficientes; **Britain must pay her ~** Gran Bretaña tiene que lograr la solvencia; **to see one's ~ (clear) to +** *ger or infin* ver la forma de + *infin*; **could you possibly see your ~ to +** *infin*? ¿tendrías la amabilidad de + *infin*?; **we're on our ~!** ¡vamos para allá!; (*Sport etc*) **we're on our ~ up** estamos en fase ascendente; **to start on one's ~** ponerse en camino; **to work one's ~ up a rock** escalar a duras penas una roca, escalar poco a poco una roca; **to work one's ~ to the front** abrirse camino hacia la primera fila (*etc*); **he worked his ~ up in the company** a fuerza de trabajar llegó a ocupar un alto puesto en la sociedad; logró ser ascendido en la sociedad gracias a sus esfuerzos personales; **he worked his ~ up from nothing** empezó sin nada y fue muy lejos por sus méritos personales.

(e) (*path*) camino *m*, vía *f*; **the middle ~** el camino de en medio; **to be in sb's ~** estorbar a uno; **am I in the ~?** ¿estorbo?; **to get in the ~** estorbar; **to get in one another's ~** estorbarse uno a otro; **to put difficulties in sb's ~** crear dificultades a uno; **to stand in sb's ~** estorbar; **now nothing stands in our ~** ahora no hay obstáculo alguno; **his age stands in his ~** su edad es una desventaja para él; **to stand in the ~ of progress** estorbar el progreso, ser un estorbo para el progreso; **out of my ~!** ¡quítese de delante!; **it's out of the ~ of the wind** está al abrigo del viento; **to get out of the ~** quitarse de en medio; **to get sth out of the ~** quitar algo de en medio; **to get sb out of the ~** quitar a uno de en medio; **as soon as I've got my exams out of the ~** en cuanto esté libre de exámenes; **one should keep matches out of the ~ of children** no se debe dejar las cerillas al alcance de los niños; **I kept well out of the ~** me mantuve muy lejos; **I try to keep out of his ~** procuro evitar cualquier contacto con él; **he wants his wife out of the ~** quiere deshacerse de su mujer; **to bar the ~**, **to block the ~** cerrar el paso; **to clear a ~ for** abrir camino para; **to clear the ~** despejar el camino; **to fight one's ~ out** lograr salir luchando; **to fight one's ~ to the sea** abrirse paso luchando hacia el mar; **to force one's ~ through** abrirse paso luchando; **to force one's ~ in** introducirse a la fuerza; **to hack one's ~ through** abrirse paso por algo a fuerza de tajos; **to leave the ~ open for further talks** dejar la vía libre para otra conferencia; **to leave the ~ open to abuse** dejar vía libre al desafuero; **make ~!** ¡calle!; **to make ~** hacer sitio (*for* para); **to take the easy ~ out** optar por la solución más fácil.

(f) (*distance*) distancia *f*; trayecto *m*, recorrido *m*; **there are flowers all the ~** por todo el recorrido hay flores; **it rained all the ~ there** durante todo el viaje llovió; **I was sick part of the ~** me mareé durante una parte del viaje; **a little ~ away, a little ~ off** no muy lejos, a poca distancia; **a long ~ away, a long ~ off** muy lejos, a gran distancia; a lo lejos; **spring is a long ~ off** la primavera queda muy lejos; **it's a long (or good) ~** es mucho camino; **it's a long ~ from here** está muy lejos de aquí; **you're a long ~ out** Vd se ha extraviado bastante, (*fig*) Vd está muy errado; **we've come a long ~ since then** hemos hecho muchos progresos desde entonces; **to go the long ~ round** ir por rodeos; **he'll go a long ~** irá lejos; **we have a long ~ to go** tenemos mucho camino por delante; **it should go a long (or some) ~ towards +** *ger* ha de contribuir mucho a + *infin*; **a little help goes a long ~** una pequeña ayuda puede ser muy valiosa; **that's a long ~ from the truth** eso queda muy lejos de la verdad, dista mucho de ser verdad; **better by a long ~** mucho mejor, mejor pero con mucho; **not by a long ~** ni con mucho; **a short ~ off** no muy lejos, a poca distancia; **I can swim quite a ~ now** ahora puedo nadar bastante bien.

(g) (*direction*) dirección *f*, sentido *m*; **this ~** por aquí; **'this ~ for the lions'** 'a los leones'; **this ~ and that** por aquí y por allá, en todas direcciones; **down our ~** en nuestro barrio; allí donde vivimos nosotros; **it's out Windsor ~** está en la región de Windsor, está cerca de Windsor; **which ~ are you going?** ¿por dónde vas?; **which ~ did it go?** ¿hacia dónde fue?; **which ~ do we go from here?** ¿por dónde vamos desde aquí?; **which ~ is the wind blowing?** ¿de dónde sopla el viento?; **she didn't know which ~ to look** no sabía adónde poner los ojos; **to look the other ~** (*fig*) hacer la vista gorda; no darse por aludido; **it doesn't matter to me one ~ or the other** me es igual, me da lo mismo; **it doesn't often come my ~** no se me ofrece muy a menudo; **if the chance comes your ~** si tienes la oportunidad; **are you going my ~?** ¿vas por donde voy yo?

(h) (*of position*) **turn it the other ~ round** vuélvelo al revés; **it was you who invited her, not the other ~ round** eres tú quien la invitaste, no al revés; **it's the wrong ~ up** está al revés, lo de abajo está arriba; **put it right ~ up** ponlo bien, enderézalo; **to rub an animal up the wrong ~** frotar a un animal a contrapelo; **to rub sb up the wrong ~** irritar a uno, sacar a uno de quicio; **they seem to rub each other up the wrong ~** parecen irritarse mutuamente; **we'll split it 3 ~s** lo dividiremos en 3 partes iguales.

(i) (*means*) medio *m*; **~s and means** medios *mpl*; **Committee on W~s and Means** Comité *m* del Presupuesto; **W~s and Means Committee** (*US*) Comité *m* de Medios y Arbitrios; **that's not the right ~** no es ése el método correcto; **we'll find a ~ of doing it** buscaremos el modo de hacerlo; **love will find a ~** el amor encontrará el camino; **no ~!** ¡ni hablar!; **no ~ was that a goal!** ¡imposible que fuera eso un gol!; **there is no ~ I am going to agree** no hay posibilidad de que yo consienta.

(j) (*manner*) manera *f*, modo *m*; forma *f*; método *m*, sistema *m*; **~ of life** estilo *m* de vida; **each ~** (*Racing*) (a) ganador y colocado; **this ~, in this ~** de este modo; **it doesn't matter one ~ or the other** no importa ni para esto ni para aquello; **one ~ or another I'm going back** de algún modo u otro voy a volver; **a week one ~ or the other won't matter** no importa que sea una semana más o una semana menos; **you can't have it both ~s** tienes que optar por lo uno o lo otro; **an odd ~ of talking** un extraño modo de hablar; **the only ~ of doing it** la única forma de hacerlo; **there are many ~s of ...** hay muchas maneras de ...; **her ~ of looking at things** su modo de ver las cosas; **my ~ is to** + *infin* mi sistema consiste en + *infin*; **he has his own ~ of doing it** tiene su sistema particular para hacerlo; **that's the ~!** ¡así!; ¡eso es!; **that's the ~ the money goes** así se gasta el dinero; **the ~ things are** tal como están las cosas; **to leave things the ~ they are** dejar las cosas como están; **the ~ things are going we shall have nothing left** si esto continúa así nos vamos a quedar sin nada; **it was this ~ ...** lo que pasó fue esto ...; **that ~ it won't disturb anybody** si lo hacemos (*etc*) así, no molestará a nadie; **it looks that ~** así parece; **she's clever that ~** para esas cosas es muy lista; **that's always the ~ with him** siempre le pasa igual; **there are no two ~s about it** no cabe otra posibilidad, no le encuentro otra posibilidad; yo lo veo perfectamente claro.

(k) (*manner: phrases with* in) **in a ~** hasta cierto punto; en cierto modo; **in this ~** de este modo; **in one ~ or another** de algún modo; **in the same ~** del mismo modo; **in more ~s than one** de más de una manera; **he had little in the ~ of education** tuvo poca educación formal, hizo pocos estudios; **in a general ~ this is true** en general esto es verdad; **without in any ~ wishing to** + *infin* sin querer en lo más mínimo + *infin*, sin tener intención alguna de + *infin*; **I'll do it in my own ~** lo haré según mi método particular; **he's a good sort in his ~** tiene sus rarezas pero es buena persona; a pesar de todo es buena persona; **they interpret it each in his own ~** lo interpretan cada uno a su modo; **he said in his rough ~** dijo en ese tono suyo un poco brusco; **to go on in the same old ~** continuar como siempre, seguir empleando los viejos métodos; **to be in a small ~ of business** tener un negocio modesto.

(l) (*custom*) costumbre *f*; **the ~s of the Spaniards** las costumbres de los españoles; **the ~s of good society** los modales de la buena sociedad, la etiqueta de la buena sociedad; **that is our ~ with traitors** así tratamos a los traidores; **he has a ~ with him** tiene atractivo personal, es simpático; tiene dotes de persuasión; **he has his little ~s** tiene sus manías, tiene sus rarezas; **he has a ~ with children** sabe captarse a los niños, los niños le encuentran muy simpático; **he had his wicked (*or* evil) ~ with her** se la llevó al huerto, la sedujo; **the child has some pretty ~s** el niño hace cosas que encantan; **to mend one's ~s** enmendarse, reformarse; **to be out of the ~ of** + *ger* haber perdido la costumbre de + *infin*; **to get out of the ~ of** + *ger* perder la costumbre de +

infin; **to get into the ~ of** + *ger* (*by habit*) adquirir la costumbre de + *infin*, (*by learning*) aprender el modo de + *infin*.

(m) (*of will*) **to get one's (own) ~** salirse con la suya; **they had it all their own ~ in the second half** en el segundo tiempo hicieron lo que les dio la gana; **have it your own ~!** ¡como quieras!; ¡tú te lo has buscado!; **they didn't have things all their own ~** no dominaron el partido (*etc*) completamente, su dominio no fue completo; **he wants his own ~ all the time** todo el tiempo insiste en su punto de vista, siempre quiere salirse con la suya.

(n) (*respect*) respecto *m*; **in a ~** en cierto modo, hasta cierto punto; **in no ~** de ningún modo; **in every possible ~** en todos los respectos; desde todos los puntos de vista; **I will help in every possible ~** ayudaré por todos los medios a mi disposición; **in many ~s** en muchos respectos, por muchas cosas; **in some ~s** en ciertos modos; **in a big ~** en grande*, en gran escala; **we lost in a really big ~** perdimos de modo realmente espectacular; **in a small ~** en pequeña escala; **we help in a small ~** ayudamos un poco, prestamos una modesta ayuda; **he's not a plumber in the ordinary ~** no es de esos fontaneros corrientes; no es un fontanero de profesión; **in the ordinary ~ we go out once a week** en general salimos una vez por semana.

(o) (*Naut etc*) **to be under ~** estar en marcha, (*fig*) avanzar, estar en curso; **to gather ~** empezar a moverse; acelerar, ir más rápidamente; **to get under ~** (*Naut*) zarpar, hacerse a la vela; (*Aut etc*) ponerse en marcha; (*person*) partir, ponerse en camino; **things are getting under ~ at last** por fin las cosas están haciendo progresos; **to get a ship under ~** hacer navegar un barco; **to give ~** (*break*) hundirse, ceder, romperse; (*Brit Aut etc*) ceder el paso; **'give ~'** 'ceda el paso'; **to give ~ to the left** ceder el paso a la izquierda; **the radio gave ~ to a television set** la radio cedió el paso a un televisor; **you gave ~ too easily** abandonaste demasiado pronto, te dejaste vencer demasiado fácilmente; **she gave ~ to tears** se deshizo en lágrimas; **he never gives ~ to despair** nunca se abandona a la desesperación.

(p) (*state*) estado *m*; **things are in a bad ~** las cosas van mal; **the car is in a bad ~** el coche está en mal estado; **he's in a very bad ~** (*Med*) está grave, está de cuidado; **he's in a fair ~ to succeed** tiene buenas posibilidades de lograrlo.

(q) (*with by*) **by the ~** a propósito; por cierto; entre paréntesis, de paso; **by the ~!** ¡eh!; ¡oiga!; **oh, and by the ~ ...** hay otra cosa ..., antes que se me olvide ...; **all this is by the ~** todo esto está un poco al margen, todo esto está entre paréntesis; **by ~ of** como, a modo de; **by ~ of an answer** a título de respuesta; **by ~ of a warning** a modo de advertencia; **he's by ~ of being a painter** tiene algo de pintor, tiene sus ribetes de pintor.

2 ADV: **~ back in 1900** allá en 1900; **that was ~ back** eso fue hace mucho tiempo ya; **~ down (below)** muy abajo; **~ out to sea** mar afuera; **you're ~ out in your sum** te has equivocado mucho en el cálculo; **~ up in the sky** muy alto en el cielo.

-way [weɪ] *in compounds, eg* **a five-~ split** una división en cinco partes.

waybill ['weɪbɪl] N hoja *f* de ruta.

wayfarer ['weɪ,feərər] N caminante *mf*; viajero *m*, -a *f*.

wayfaring tree ['weɪfeərɪŋ,triː] N viburno *m*.

waylay [weɪ'leɪ] (*irr V* lay) VT acechar; salir al paso a; detener; **they were waylaid by thieves** les atacaron unos ladrones; **I was waylaid by the manager** me detuvo el gerente.

way-out* ['weɪ'aʊt] ADJ ultramoderno, revolucionario, nueva ola.

wayside ['weɪsaɪd] **1** N borde *m* del camino, borde *m* de la carretera; **by the ~** al borde de la carretera; **to fall by the ~** caer en el camino. **2** ATTR del borde del camino; *inn etc* de camino, de carretera; *flower* silvestre.

way station ['weɪ,steɪʃən] N (*US*) apeadero *m*; (*fig*) paso *m* intermedio.

wayward ['weɪwəd] ADJ (*self-willed*) voluntarioso; (*naughty*) travieso; rebelde; (*capricious*) caprichoso; (*freakish*) caprichoso, variable, inexplicable.

waywardness ['weɪwədnɪs] N voluntariedad *f*; travesura *f*; rebeldía *f*; lo caprichoso; variabilidad *f*.

W/B N ABBR *of* **waybill**.

WBA N ABBR *of* **World Boxing Association**.

WC N (*Brit*) ABBR *of* **water closet** wáter *m*, WC; *ver también* TOILET .

WCC N ABBR *of* **World Council of Churches**.

wdv ABBR *of* **written-down value** valor *m* amortizado.

we [wiː] PRON nosotros, nosotras.

w/e ABBR *of* **week ending** semana *f* que termina el día ...

WEA N (*Brit*) ABBR *of* **Workers' Educational Association**.

weak [wiːk] **1** ADJ débil; flojo; *argument etc* flojo, poco convincente; *market etc* flojo; *sound* débil, tenue; *character, currency* débil; *tea etc* claro, no muy cargado; **to grow ~** debilitarse; **to have ~ eyes** ser corto de vista; **to have a ~ stomach** tener el estómago delicado; **her maths is ~, she is ~ at maths** es floja en matemáticas. **2 the ~** NPL los débiles.

weaken ['wiːkən] **1** VT debilitar; (*lessen*) disminuir, reducir; (*mitigate*) atenuar, mitigar; **this fact ~s your case** este dato quita fuerza a su argumento; **his resignation ~ed the party** su dimisión debilitó el partido.

2 VI debilitarse; flaquear, desfallecer; (*give way*) ceder, abandonar; **his influence is ~ing** su influencia flaquea; **we must not ~ now** ahora tenemos que mantenernos firmes; **prices have ~ed** las cotizaciones han aflojado.

weak-kneed ['wiːk'niːd] ADJ (*fig*) sin resolución, sin carácter, débil.

weakling ['wiːklɪŋ] N ser *m* delicado, persona *f* débil; cobarde *m*; (*of litter etc*) redrojo *m*; (*in health*) persona *f* enfermiza; **he's no ~** no es ningún debilucho.

weakly ['wiːklɪ] **1** ADJ enclenque, achacoso, enfermizo.

2 ADV débilmente; flojamente; tenuemente.

weak-minded ['wiːk'maɪndɪd] ADJ mentecato, imbécil; (*irresolute*) vacilante, sin carácter.

weakness ['wiːknɪs] N (*quality*) debilidad *f*; flojedad *f*; tenuidad *f*; (*weak point*) flaco *m*, lado *m* débil; desventaja *f*; (*of character*) falta *f* de voluntad; falta *f* de carácter; **to have a ~ for** tener gusto por, ser muy aficionado a; **to make allowances for human ~** tener en cuenta la flaqueza humana.

weak-willed ['wiːk'wɪld] ADJ de voluntad débil, indeciso.

weal[1] [wiːl] N (††) bienestar *m*; **the common ~** el bien público.

weal[2] [wiːl] N (*Med*) verdugón *m*.

wealth [welθ] **1** N riqueza *f*; abundancia *f*; **for all his ~** a pesar de su riqueza; **por rico que sea**; **with a ~ of details** con abundantes detalles, con acopio de datos.

2 ATTR: **~ tax** impuesto *m* sobre el patrimonio.

wealthy ['welθɪ] **1** ADJ rico; acaudalado, pudiente.

2 NPL: **the ~ los ricos.**

wean [wiːn] VT destetar; **to ~ sb from sth** (*fig*) ir apartando a uno de algo, desacostumbrar a uno de algo.

weaning ['wiːnɪŋ] N destete *m*, ablactación *f*.

weapon ['wepən] N arma *f*.

weaponry ['wepənrɪ] N armas *fpl*.

wear [wɛər] **1** N (a) (*use*) uso *m*; **for evening ~** para la noche, para llevar de noche; **for everyday ~** para uso diario, para todos los días, para todo trote; **for hard ~** resistente, duradero; **he got 4 years' ~ out of it** la prenda la duró 4 años; **you will get plenty of ~ out of this** esto le ha de durar muchos años, esto tiene gran durabilidad.

(b) (*~ and tear*) deterioro *m*, desgaste *m*, uso *m*; **the ~ on the engine** el desgaste del motor; **one has to allow for ~ and tear** hay que tener en cuenta el desgaste natural; **to look the worse for ~, to show signs of ~** mostrarse deteriorado, dar indicios de deterioro; **she looks the worse for ~*** parece algo desmejorada.

(c) (*clothing*) ropa *f*; prenda *f*; **children's ~** ropa *f* para niños; **summer ~** ropa *f* de verano; **light ~ for hot countries** ropa *f* ligera para países cálidos; **it is compulsory ~ for schoolboys** la prenda es obligatoria para los colegiales.

2 (*irr*: PRET **wore**, PTP **worn**) VT (a) *objects in general* llevar, usar, gastar; *clothing* llevar; traer, traer puesto; vestir; *shoes* calzar; *look, smile etc* tener; (*put on*) ponerse; **she wore her blue dress** llevaba el vestido azul; **she wore blue** se vestía de azul, vestía un vestido azul; **what shall I ~?** ¿qué me pongo?; **I have nothing to ~ to the dinner** no tengo qué ponerme para ir a la cena; **I haven't worn that for ages** hace siglos que no me pongo eso; **were you ~ing a watch?** ¿llevabas reloj?; **my uncle wore a beard** mi tío llevaba barba; **Eskimos don't ~ bikinis** los esquimales no usan bikini; **what size do you ~?** ¿qué número tiene Vd.?; **to ~ one's hair long** llevar el pelo largo, dejarse el pelo largo; **he wore a big smile** sonreía alegremente; **he wore a serious look** parecía grave, tenía el gesto grave.

(b) (*~ out*) desgastar, deteriorar; **to ~ sth into holes, to ~ holes in sth** hacer agujeros en algo (rayéndolo *etc*); **to ~ sth to a threadbare state** dejar algo raído.

(c) (*Brit**) aguantar; consentir, permitir; **he won't ~ that** eso no lo permitirá; **we'll see if he'll ~ it** veremos si consiente en ello.

3 VI (a) (*last*) durar; **they will ~ for years** le durarán muchos años; **that dress has worn well** ese vestido ha durado mucho; **she's worn well*** se ha conservado muy bien, no representa su edad; **the theory has worn well** la teoría ha resistido muy bien, la teoría ha sido muy duradera.

(b) (*rub etc thin*) **the cloth has worn into holes** al paño le han salido agujeros con el uso; **the rock has worn smooth** la roca se ha alisado.

4 VR: **to ~ o.s. to death** matarse (trabajando *etc*).

◆**wear away** **1** VT gastar, desgastar; raer; consumir; **he's worn away to a shadow** está hecho una sombra.

2 VI gastarse, desgastarse; consumirse.

◆**wear down** **1** VT *material* gastar, desgastar; *resistance* agotar; rendir; *patience* agotar, cansar; *enemy* cansar hasta rendir.

2 VI (*material*) gastarse, desgastarse.

◆**wear off** VI quitarse; pasar, desaparecer; **the pain is ~ing off** está

desapareciendo el dolor, ya duele menos; **it soon wore off** pronto desapareció; **when the novelty ~s off** cuando la novedad deje de serlo.

◆**wear on** VI (*time*) pasar, ir pasando, transcurrir; **the year is ~ing on** están pasando los meses; **as the evening wore on** a medida que avanzaba la noche.

◆**wear out** **1** VT *clothes etc* usar, desgastar; romper con el uso; **you can ~ them out next winter** los acabarás de gastar el invierno que viene.

2 VI usarse, romperse con el uso, quedar inservible; consumirse.

3 VR: **to ~ o.s. out** agotarse, matarse.

◆**wear through** **1** VT gastar.

2 VI (*clothing etc*) gastarse, desgastarse.

┌─ **WEAR** ──────────── *see also main entry* ─┐

● Don't translate the *a* in sentences like *was she wearing a hat?, he wasn't wearing a coat* if the number of such items is not significant since people normally only wear one at a time:

    Was he wearing a hat?
    ¿Llevaba sombrero?
    He wasn't wearing a coat
    No llevaba abrigo

● Do translate the *a* if the garment, item of jewellery *etc* is qualified:

    Queen Sofía is wearing a long dress
    Doña Sofía lleva un vestido largo
    For further uses and examples, see main entry.

└──────────────────────────────┘

wearable ['wɛərəbl] ADJ que se puede llevar; **it's still ~** todavía se puede llevar.

wearer ['wɛərər] N el (*or* la) que lleva puesto algo; **~s of bowler hats** los que llevan hongo; **straight from maker to ~** directamente del fabricante al cliente.

wearily ['wɪərɪlɪ] ADV cansadamente, fatigadamente; **he said ~** dijo cansado, dijo en tono de hastío.

weariness ['wɪərɪnɪs] N cansancio *m*, fatiga *f*; abatimiento *m*, hastío *m*; aburrimiento *m*.

wearing ['wɛərɪŋ] ADJ cansado, pesado, molesto.

wearisome ['wɪərɪsəm] ADJ cansado, pesado; fatigoso, agotador.

weary ['wɪərɪ] **1** ADJ (*tired*) cansado, fatigado; (*dispirited*) abatido, hastiado; (*tiring*) aburrido, pesado; (*annoying*) fastidioso; **to be ~ of** estar cansado de, estar harto de; **to grow ~ of** cansarse de; **three ~ hours** tres horas aburridas; **five ~ miles** cinco millas pesadas.

2 VT cansar, fatigar; aburrir.

3 VI cansarse, fatigarse; **to ~ of** cansarse de; aburrirse de; **to ~ of +** *ger* cansarse de + *infin*.

weasel ['wiːzl] **1** N comadreja *f*.

2 ATTR: **~ words** ambages *mpl*, palabras *fpl* equívocas.

weather ['weðər] **1** N tiempo *m*; (*harsh ~*) intemperie *f*; **~ permitting** si el tiempo no lo impide; **in the hot ~** cuando hace calor; **in this ~** con el tiempo que hace; **it is fine ~** hace buen tiempo, el tiempo es bueno; **what's the ~ like?** ¿qué tiempo hace?; **he has to go out in all ~s** tiene que salir en todo tiempo; **it gets left outside in all ~s** está fuera a la intemperie; **to be under the ~** (*Med*) estar mal, estar indispuesto, (*with drink*) estar con la turca*; **to make heavy ~ of sth** encontrar algo difícil; crearse dificultades al tratar de hacer algo.

2 ATTR meteorológico, del tiempo; (*Naut*) de barlovento; **~ balloon** globo *m* meteorológico; **~ bureau** (*US*) oficina *f* meteorológica; **~ conditions** estado *m* del tiempo; **to keep a ~ eye on sth** observar algo con atención; **~ forecast** pronóstico *m* del tiempo, boletín *m* meteorológico; **~ forecaster** meteorólogo *m*, -a *f*; **~ map** mapa *m* meteorológico; **~ report** boletín *m* meteorológico; **~ side** costado *m* de barlovento.

3 VT (a) *storm etc* (*also* **to ~ out**) aguantar, hacer frente a; superar, sobrevivir a; **the government has ~ed many storms** el gobierno ha aguantado muchas tempestades.

(b) (*Naut*) *cape* doblar; pasar a barlovento.

(c) (*Geol etc*) *wood* curar; *skin* curtir.

4 VI (*Geol*) desgastarse; (*skin etc*) curtirse a la intemperie.

weather-beaten ['weðə,biːtn] ADJ deteriorado por la intemperie; *skin* curtido.

weatherboard ['weðəbɔːd] N (*Brit*) tabla *f* de chilla; **~ house** (*US*) casa *f* de madera.

weather-bound ['weðəbaʊnd] ADJ bloqueado por el mal tiempo.

weathercock ['weðəkɒk] N veleta *f*.

weathered ['weðəd] ADJ *oak etc* maduro, curado.

weatherman ['weðəmæn] N, PL **weathermen** ['weðəmen] hombre *m* del tiempo, meteorólogo *m*.

weatherproof ['weðəpruːf] ADJ a prueba de la intemperie; *clothing* impermeable, impermeabilizado.

weathership ['weðəʃɪp] N barco *m* del servicio meteorológico.

weather-station ['weðə,steɪʃən] N estación f meteorológica.
weather-strip ['weðəstrɪp] N burlete m.
weather-vane ['weðəveɪn] N veleta f.
weave [wiːv] [1] N tejido m; textura f.
[2] (irr: PRET **wove**, PTP **woven**) VT (a) tejer; trenzar; entretejer, entrelazar; (fig) plot urdir, tramar; **to ~ details into a story** entretejer detalles en un cuento; **to ~ episodes into a plot** ir entretejiendo episodios para formar un argumento.
(b) **to ~ one's way through** abrirse paso (por entre).
[3] VI (a) tejer.
(b) **to ~ in and out** (boxer etc) evadirse torciendo rápidamente a derecha e izquierda; **the plane was weaving in and out among the clouds** el avión serpenteaba (or zigzagueaba) entre las nubes; **to ~ in and out among traffic** serpentear por entre el tráfico (para adelantarse a toda prisa); **the road ~s about a lot** el camino serpentea mucho; **let's get weaving!*** ¡vamos!
weaver ['wiːvəʳ] N tejedor m, -ora f.
weaving ['wiːvɪŋ] [1] N tejeduría f.
[2] ATTR de tejer, para tejer; de tejidos.
weaving-machine ['wiːvɪŋməˌʃiːn] N telar m.
weaving-mill ['wiːvɪŋmɪl] N tejeduría f.
web¹ [web] N (fabric) tela f, tejido m; (spider's) telaraña f; (membrane) membrana f; (fig) red f; **a ~ of intrigue** un tejido de intrigas; **a ~ of spies** una red de espías.
Web, web² [web] (Comput) [1] N: **the ~** el Web.
[2] ATTR: **web browser** navegador m de Internet; **web site** web site m.
webbed [webd] ADJ foot palmeado.
webbing ['webɪŋ] N cincha f, (Tech) pretina f de reps.
web-footed ['web'fʊtɪd] ADJ palmípedo.
wed [wed] [1] VT casarse con; (of priest etc, also fig) casar.
[2] VI casarse.
we'd [wiːd] = **we would; we had**.
wedded ['wedɪd] ADJ (a) (person) casado; bliss, life etc conyugal; **his ~ wife** su legítima esposa.
(b) **to be ~ to** estar casado con; (fig: connected) estar relacionado con, estar unido a; **to be ~ to an opinion** aferrarse a una opinión, estar aferrado a una opinión; **to be ~ to a pursuit** ser aficionado a una actividad, ser entusiasta de un pasatiempo.
wedding ['wedɪŋ] [1] N boda f; casamiento m; bodas fpl; (fig) unión f, enlace m; **civil ~** matrimonio m civil; **to have a civil ~** casarse por lo civil; **to have a church ~** casarse por la iglesia; **to have a quiet ~** casarse en la intimidad, casarse en privado.
[2] ATTR de boda, de bodas; nupcial.
wedding anniversary ['wedɪŋ,ænɪ'vɜːsərɪ] N aniversario m de bodas.
wedding band ['wedɪŋ'bænd] N = **wedding-ring**.
wedding breakfast ['wedɪŋ'brekfəst] N banquete m de boda.
wedding-cake ['wedɪŋkeɪk] N tarta f de boda, pastel m de boda.
wedding-day ['wedɪŋdeɪ] N día m de (la) boda; ver también BEST MAN .
wedding-dress ['wedɪŋdres] N traje m de novia.
wedding-march ['wedɪŋmɑːtʃ] N marcha f nupcial.
wedding-night ['wedɪŋnaɪt] N noche f de (la) boda, noche f de bodas.
wedding-present ['wedɪŋ,preznt] N regalo m de boda.
wedding-ring ['wedɪŋrɪŋ] N anillo m de boda, alianza f.
wedge [wedʒ] [1] N cuña f; calce m, calza f; (of cake etc) porción f, pedazo m (grande); (Golf) wedge m, cucharilla f; **it's the thin end of the ~** por ahí empieza, esto puede ser el principio de muchos males; **to drive a ~ between two people** romper el vínculo que une a dos personas, enemistar a dos personas, separar a dos personas.
[2] VT acuñar, calzar; **to ~ a door open** mantener abierta una puerta con calza; **it's ~d** está sin poderse mover, se ha agarrado; **I was ~d between two bishops** me encontré apretado entre dos obispos, estuve inmovilizado entre dos obispos.
◆**wedge in** [1] VT: **can we ~ a few more in?** ¿podemos introducir algunos más (por apretados que estén)?
[2] VR: **to ~ o.s. in** introducirse con dificultad.
wedge-heeled [,wedʒ'hiːld] ADJ: **~ shoes** topolinos mpl.
wedge-shaped ['wedʒʃeɪpt] ADJ de forma de cuña.
wedlock ['wedlɒk] N matrimonio m; **to be born out of ~** nacer fuera del matrimonio.
Wednesday ['wenzdeɪ] N miércoles m.
Wed(s). ABBR of **Wednesday** miércoles m, miérc.
wee¹ [wiː] ADJ (Scot*) pequeñito, diminuto; **a ~ bit** un poquitín, un poquito; **I'm a ~ bit worried** estoy un poco inquieto.
wee²‡ [wiː] N, VI: **to (have a) ~** hacer pipí‡.
weed [wiːd] [1] N (a) (Bot) mala hierba f; **the ~** (hum) el tabaco; **~s** malas hierbas fpl, hierbajos mpl.
(b) (*: person) madeja mf.
[2] VT ground escardar, desherbar, sachar; **to ~ out** plant arrancar; (fig) suprimir, quitar, eliminar.

weeding ['wiːdɪŋ] N escarda f.
weed-killer ['wiːd,kɪləʳ] N herbicida m.
weeds [wiːdz] NPL: **widow's ~** ropa f de luto.
weedy ['wiːdɪ] ADJ (a) ground lleno de malas hierbas. (b) (*) person flaco, desmirriado; **~ youth** mozalbete m.
week [wiːk] N semana f; **~ in, ~ out** semana tras semana; **twice a ~** dos veces a la semana; **this day ~, a ~ today** de hoy en ocho días, dentro de ocho días; **tomorrow ~, a ~ from tomorrow** (US) de mañana en ocho días; **Tuesday ~** del martes en ocho días; **in a ~ or so** dentro de unos ocho días; **in the middle of the ~** a mitad de semana; **it changes from ~ to ~** esto cambia cada semana; **I haven't seen her for** (or in) **~s** hace tiempo que no la veo; **allow 4 ~s for delivery** dejar 4 semanas para entrega; **to knock sb into the middle of next ~*** dar una tremenda paliza a uno.
weekday ['wiːkdeɪ] N día m laborable; **on a ~** entre semana.
weekend ['wiːk'end] [1] N fin m de semana, weekend m; **a ~ trip** una excursión de fin de semana; **~ case** maletín m de viaje; **~ cottage** casita f de fin de semana; **to stay over the ~** pasar el fin de semana; **to take a long ~** hacer puente.
[2] as ADV: **they are away ~s** están fuera los fines de semana.
[3] VI pasar el fin de semana.
weekender ['wiːk'endəʳ] N persona f que va a pasar solamente el fin de semana (en una casa de campo etc).
weekly ['wiːklɪ] [1] ADJ semanal; de cada semana; **~ paper** semanario m; **~ report** informe m semanal; **~ statement** (Fin) balance m semanal, estado m de cuenta semanal.
[2] ADV semanalmente, cada semana; **£15 ~** 15 libras por semana.
[3] N semanario m.
weeknight ['wiːknaɪt] N noche f de entresemana.
weenie ['wiːnɪ] N (US Culin) salchicha f de Frankfurt.
weeny* ['wiːnɪ] ADJ chiquitito*, minúsculo.
weeny-bopper* ['wiːnɪ'bɒpəʳ] N doceañera f (aficionada de la música pop).
weep [wiːp] (irr: PRET AND PTP **wept**) [1] VT tears llorar, derramar; **to ~ one's eyes out** llorar a mares.
[2] VI llorar; **I could have wept** era para desesperarse; **to ~ for sb** llorar a uno; **to ~ for joy** llorar de alegría; **to ~ for one's sins** llorar sus pecados; **to ~ for what has happened** llorar por lo que ha pasado; **to ~ to see sth** llorar al ver algo.
[3] N: **to have a good ~** aliviarse llorando.
weeping ['wiːpɪŋ] [1] ADJ lloroso; **~ willow** sauce m llorón.
[2] N llanto m, lágrimas fpl.
weepy ['wiːpɪ] [1] ADJ llorón, que llora por poca cosa; (*) film etc lacrimógeno.
[2] N (*) (Brit) película f (etc) lacrimógena.
weever ['wiːvəʳ] N peje m araña.
weevil ['wiːvl] N gorgojo m.
weewee‡ ['wiːwiː] [1] N pipí‡ m.
[2] VI hacer pipí‡.
w.e.f. ABBR of **with effect from**.
weft [weft] N trama f; (fig) red f.
weigh [weɪ] [1] VT (a) (lit) pesar; **to ~ sth in one's hand** pesar algo en la mano.
(b) (fig) pesar, ponderar; **to ~ sth in one's mind** ponderar algo, meditar algo; **to ~ A against B** contraponer A y B, considerar A con relación a B; **to ~ the pros and cons** pesar las ventajas y las desventajas; **to ~ one's words** medir las palabras.
(c) **to ~ anchor** levar anclas.
[2] VI (a) (lit) pesar; **it ~s 4 kilos** pesa 4 kilos; **how much does it ~?** ¿cuánto pesa?; **it ~s heavy** pesa mucho.
(b) **it ~s on his mind** pesa sobre su mente, le preocupa, le inquieta; **her absence began to ~ (up)on me** su ausencia empezaba a inquietarme; **these factors do not ~ with him** estos factores no tienen importancia para él, estos factores no influyen en él.
◆**weigh down** VT sobrecargar; (fig) abrumar, agobiar (with de); **she was ~ed down with parcels** iba muy cargada de paquetes; **a branch ~ed down with fruit** una rama doblada bajo el peso del fruto; **to be ~ed down with sorrow** estar agobiado de dolor.
◆**weigh in** VI (a) (jockey) pesarse; **to ~ in at 65 kilos** pesar 65 kilos.
(b) (pej) entrar pisando fuerte; intervenir (sin ser llamado); **to ~ in with an argument** intervenir afirmando que ...
◆**weigh out** VT pesar.
◆**weigh up** VT (a) (lit) = **weigh 1(a)**.
(b) (fig) = **weigh 1(b)**; **to ~ sb up** formar un juicio sobre uno.
weighbridge ['weɪbrɪdʒ] N báscula-puente f, báscula f de puente.
weigh-in ['weɪɪn] N peso m, pesaje m.
weighing-machine ['weɪɪŋməˌʃiːn] N báscula f.
weight [weɪt] [1] N (a) peso m; (heaviness) peso m, pesadez f; **~ note** certificado m de peso; **3 kilos in ~** que pesa 3 kilos, de 3 kilos; **it is worth its ~ in gold** vale su peso en oro; **to feel the ~ of, to test** (or **try**) **the ~ of sth** sopesar algo; **he carries too much ~** pesa demasiado; **to gain ~, to put on ~** engordar, hacerse más gordo; **to**

lose ~ adelgazar; **sold by ~** vendido a peso; **to take the ~ off one's feet** sentarse y descansar, dejar descansar los pies.
(b) (*of clock; disc etc used on scales*) pesa *f*; **system of ~s and measures** sistema *m* de pesos y medidas; **to put the ~** lanzar el peso; **putting the ~** lanzamiento *m* del peso.
(c) (*fig: of worries etc*) peso *m*, carga *f*; (*of blow*) fuerza *f*; (*importance*) peso *m*, autoridad *f*, importancia *f*; **the ~ of the years** la carga de los años; **a blow without much ~ behind it** un golpe de poca fuerza; **a person of no ~** una persona de poca monta, una persona de escasa importancia; **these are arguments of some ~** son argumentos de cierto peso; **that's a ~ off my mind** es un gran alivio para mí; **he carries no ~** no tiene autoridad; **those arguments carry great ~ with the minister** esos argumentos influyen poderosamente en el ministro; **to chuck*** (*or* **throw**) **one's ~ about** darse importancia; hablar (*etc*) en tono autoritario; **to give due ~ to an argument** conceder la debida importancia a un argumento; **he doesn't pull his ~ in the section** no trabaja en la sección tanto como debiera; **to throw one's ~ behind sb** apoyar a uno con toda su fuerza.
[2] VT cargar (*with* de), añadir peso a; (*hold down*) sujetar con un peso; (*statistically*) ponderar; **this is ~ed in your favour** esto se inclina del lado de Vd, esto le favorece a Vd.
◆**weight down** VT sujetar con un peso (*or* una piedra *etc*).
weighted [weɪtɪd] ADJ compensado, ponderado; **~ average** media *f* ponderada; **~ index** índice *m* compensado.
weightiness ['weɪtɪnɪs] N peso *m*; (*fig*) peso *m*, importancia *f*; influencia *f*.
weighting ['weɪtɪŋ] N (*on salary*) aumento *m* por coste de vida; (*Scol*) factor *m* de valoración; (*Statistics*) ponderación *f*; **London ~** subsidio *m* por residir en Londres.
weightless ['weɪtlɪs] ADJ ingrávido.
weightlessness ['weɪtlɪsnɪs] N ingravidez *f*.
weightlifter ['weɪt,lɪftəʳ] N levantador *m* de pesas, halterófilo *m*, haltera *m*.
weightlifting ['weɪt,lɪftɪŋ] N levantamiento *m* de pesas, halterofilia *f*.
weight limit ['weɪtlɪmɪt] N límite *m* de peso.
weight-train ['weɪt,treɪn] VI entrenar con pesas.
weight-training ['weɪt,treɪnɪŋ] N entrenamiento *m* con pesas.
weight-watcher ['weɪt,wɒtʃəʳ] N persona *f* que quiere evitar engordar.
weight-watching ['weɪt,wɒtʃɪŋ] N conciencia *f* de la necesidad de no engordar; campaña *f* pro adelgazamiento, régimen *m* para adelgazar.
weighty ['weɪtɪ] ADJ pesado; (*fig*) importante, de peso, influyente.
weir [wɪəʳ] N vertedero *m*, vertedor *m*; cañal *m*, encañizada *f*; (*fish-trap*) presa *f*, pesquera *f*.
weird [wɪəd] ADJ misterioso, fantástico, sobrenatural; (*odd*) raro, extraño; **how ~!** ¡qué raro!
weirdly ['wɪədlɪ] ADV misteriosamente, fantásticamente; extrañamente; **~ dressed** vestido de un modo raro.
weirdness ['wɪədnɪs] N misterio *m*, lo fantástico, lo sobrenatural; rareza *f*.
weirdo* ['wɪədəʊ] N, **weirdy*** ['wɪədɪ] N bicho *m* raro.
welch* [welʃ] VI = **welsh.**
▼**welcome** ['welkəm] [1] ADJ **(a)** bienvenido; **~!** ¡bienvenido!; **~ on board!** ¡bienvenidos a bordo!; **~ to Spain!** ¡bienvenido a España!; **to make sb ~** recibir a uno afectuosamente, dar una buena acogida a uno; **I didn't feel very ~ there** no creía que mi presencia allí les fuera muy grata; **to put out the ~ mat for sb** recibir a uno con todos los honores.
(b) (*pleasing*) grato, agradable; **that is ~ news** es una noticia grata; **it's a ~ change** es un cambio muy aceptable; **a glass of sherry is always ~** siempre se agradece una copita de jerez, una copita de jerez siempre viene bien.
(c) you're ~! (*answer to thanks*) ¡de nada!, ¡no hay de qué!; (*iro*) ¡buen provecho te haga!; **you are ~ to it** está a tu disposición; **you are ~ to try** eres muy dueño de probarlo, tienes permiso para probarlo; **you will always be ~ here** estás en tu casa.
[2] N bienvenida *f*; (buena) acogida *f*, recepción *f*; **to bid sb ~** dar la bienvenida a uno; **to give sb a hearty ~** acoger a uno con entusiasmo; **the crowd gave him an enthusiastic ~** el público le dispensó una calurosa acogida; **to meet with a cold ~** ser recibido fríamente; **what sort of a ~ will this product get?** ¿qué aceptación tendrá este artículo?
▼[3] VT dar la bienvenida a; acoger, recibir; aprobar; **they went to the airport to ~ him** fueron a recibirle al aeropuerto; **to ~ sb with open arms** recibir a uno con los brazos abiertos; **we should ~ this tendency** deberíamos dar la bienvenida a esta tendencia; **we ~ this step** aprobamos esta medida; **I'd ~ a cup of coffee** no me vendría mal una taza de café.
◆**welcome back** VT: **to ~ sb back** dar una buena acogida a uno cuando regresa.

> *WELCOME WAGON*
>
> *Se llama* **welcome wagon** *a un acto de bienvenida a los recién llegados a una ciudad, los cuales reciben la visita de un habitante de la misma que les entrega una carpeta informativa sobre ella, pequeños regalos, muestras de productos y vales de descuento para tiendas de la ciudad. Es un acto que tiene lugar en muchas poblaciones estadounidenses y que está normalmente organizado por la Cámara de Comercio o por alguna empresa.*

welcoming ['welkəmɪŋ] ADJ acogedor, cordial.
weld [weld] [1] VT **(a)** (*Tech*) soldar; **to ~ parts together** soldar unas piezas; **the hull is ~ed throughout** el casco es totalmente soldado.
(b) (*fig*) **to ~ together** soldar, unir, unificar; **we must ~ them together into a new body** hemos de soldarlos para formar un nuevo organismo.
[2] VI soldarse.
welder ['weldəʳ] N soldador *m*.
welding ['weldɪŋ] [1] N soldadura *f*.
[2] ATTR de soldar, de soldadura, soldador; **~ torch** soplete *m* soldador.
welfare ['welfɛəʳ] [1] N **(a)** (*well-being*) bienestar *m*, bien *m*; prosperidad *f*; **child ~** bienestar *m* de los niños; **to work for the nation's ~** trabajar en bien de la nación.
(b) (*social aid etc*) asistencia *f* social, beneficencia *f* social; **to be on ~, to live on ~** vivir a cargo de la asistencia social.
[2] ATTR: **~ centre** centro *m* de asistencia social; **~ state** estado *m* de bienestar, estado *m* asistencial, estado *m* benefactor; **~ work** trabajos *mpl* de asistencia social; **~ worker** asistente *mf* social.
Welfarism ['welfɛərɪzəm] N (*US*) *teoría y práctica de la protección de la salud y del bienestar públicos.*
well[1] [wel] [1] N pozo *m*; (*fig*) fuente *f*, manantial *m*; (*of stairs*) hueco *m*, caja *f*; **to sink a ~** perforar un pozo.
[2] VI (*also* **to ~ out, to ~ up**) brotar, manar.
well[2] [wel] [1] ADV **(a)** bien; **~ and good** muy bien; **the child speaks ~** el niño habla bien; **it's ~ painted** está bien pintado; **you would do ~ to think seriously about our offer** le convendría considerar seriamente nuestra oferta; *V* **speak, think** *etc.*
(b) (*intensive*) **we got ~ and truly wet** nos mojamos de verdad; **~ over a thousand** mucho más de mil; **they may ~ be lying** es muy posible que mientan; **it was ~ worth the trouble** realmente valió la pena; **we were ~ beaten** nos derrotaron fácilmente; **you may ~ ask** con razón preguntas.
(c) (*with qualifying adv*) **very ~** muy bien; **very ~, I'll do it** bueno, lo haré; **that's all very ~, but ...** todo eso está muy bien, pero ...; **all too ~, only too ~** de sobra, sobradamente.
(d) as ~ también; **it's just as ~ you've come** menos mal que has venido; **she cried, as ~ she might** lloró, y con razón; **it is as ~ to remember that ...** conviene recordar que ...; **in cars as ~ as on bikes** en coches así como en bicicletas; **she swims as ~ as she walks** nada tan bien como anda; **you might as ~ tell me the truth** más valdría decirme la verdad; **A as ~ as B** A además de B, tanto A como B.
(e) (*concessive*) pues; **~ now** ahora bien; **~, it was like this** bueno, te lo diré; bueno, pasó lo siguiente; **~?** ¿y entonces?; **~ then** pues bien; **~ then?** ¿y qué?
[2] EXCL: **~!** ¡vaya!, ¡caramba!; **~, ~!** ¡vaya, vaya!; **~, that's that!** ¡bueno, asunto concluido!
[3] ADJ bien, bien de salud; **are you ~?** ¿qué tal estás?; **I'm very ~, thanks** estoy muy bien, gracias; **I'm fairly ~** estoy regular; **she's not been ~ lately** recientemente ha estado algo indispuesta; **I don't feel at all ~** no me siento nada bien; **to get ~** reponerse (*after* de); **to make sb ~** curar a uno, devolver la salud a uno.
[4] N: **to leave ~ alone** no tocar, dejar las cosas como están; **to speak ~ of sb** hablar de uno en términos elogiosos; **to think ~ of sb** tener un buen concepto de uno; **to wish sb ~** desear todo lo mejor a uno.
well- [wel] ADV *in compounds*: bien ..., *eg* **~-preserved** bien conservado.
we'll [wiːl] = **we will, we shall.**
well-adjusted ['welə'dʒʌstɪd] ADJ equilibrado.
well-aimed ['wel'eɪmd] ADJ certero.
well-appointed ['welə'pɔɪntɪd] ADJ bien amueblado.
well-argued ['wel'ɑːgjuːd] ADJ razonado.
well-attended ['welə'tendɪd] ADJ muy concurrido.
well-baby clinic [wel'beɪbɪklɪnɪk] N clínica *f* de revisión pediátrica.
well-balanced ['wel'bælənsd] ADJ bien equilibrado.
well-behaved ['welbɪ'heɪvd] ADJ bien educado, formal; *animal* manso.
wellbeing ['wel,biːɪŋ] N bienestar *m*.
wellborn ['wel'bɔːn] ADJ bien nacido.
well-bred ['wel'bred] ADJ bien educado, culto, cortés; *accent etc* culto; *animal* de raza, pura sangre.
well-brought-up ['wel'brɔːtʌp] ADJ *child* educado.

➤ LANGUAGE IN USE: **welcome: 3 → 13**

well-built ['wel'bɪlt] ADJ sólidamente construido, de construcción sólida; *person* fornido.

well-chosen ['wel'tʃəʊzn] ADJ elegido con cuidado; *remarks, words etc* acertado.

well-cooked ['wel'kʊkt] ADJ (*tasty*) bien preparado; (*cooked long*) muy hecho.

well-defined ['weldɪ'faɪnd] ADJ bien definido.

well-deserved ['weldɪ'zɜːvd] ADJ merecido.

well-developed ['weldɪ'veləpt] ADJ *arm, muscle etc* bien desarrollado; *sense* agudo, fino.

well-disposed ['weldɪs'pəʊzd] ADJ favorable, benévolo; bienintencionado; **to be ~ towards sth** estar bien dispuesto hacia algo.

well-documented ['wel'dɒkjʊ,mentɪd] ADJ documentado.

well-dressed ['wel'drest] ADJ bien vestido.

well-earned ['wel'ɜːnd] ADJ merecido.

well-educated ['wel'edjʊkeɪtɪd] ADJ instruido, culto.

well-endowed [,welɪn'daʊd] ADJ (a) *institution* bien dotado de fondos, con buena dotación monetaria. (b) *woman* bien dotada, bien despachada*; *man* bien dotado, bien despachado*.

well-equipped ['welɪ'kwɪpt] ADJ bien equipado.

well-established ['welɪ'stæblɪʃt] ADJ sólidamente establecido; *custom* muy arraigado; *firm* sólido, de buena reputación.

well-favoured, (*US*) **well-favored** ['wel'feɪvəd] ADJ bien parecido.

well-fed ['wel'fed] ADJ bien alimentado, que come bien; (*in appearance*) regordete.

well-fixed* ['wel'fɪkst] ADJ (*US*): **to be ~** nadar en la abundancia, estar boyante; **we're ~ for food** tenemos comida de sobra.

well-formed ['wel'fɔːmd] ADJ (*Ling*) gramatical.

well-formedness ['wel'fɔːmdnɪs] N gramaticalidad *f*.

well-founded ['wel'faʊndɪd] ADJ (bien) fundado.

well-groomed ['wel'gruːmd] ADJ acicalado.

well-grown ['wel'grəʊn] ADJ grande, maduro, adulto.

wellhead ['welhed] N fuente *f*, manantial *m*.

well-heeled* ['wel'hiːld] ADJ ricacho*.

well-hung ['wel'hʌŋ] ADJ (a) (‡) *man* bien dotado, bien despachado‡, con un buen paquete‡. (b) (*Culin*) *game* bien manido.

wellies* ['welɪz] NPL (*Brit*) = **wellingtons.**

well-informed ['welɪn'fɔːmd] ADJ (*in general*) enterado, instruido; **to be ~ about sth** estar muy enterado de algo, estar al corriente de algo.

Wellington ['welɪŋtən] N Wellington *m*.

wellingtons ['welɪŋtənz] NPL, **wellington boots** ['welɪŋtən'buːts] NPL (*Brit*) botas *fpl* de goma.

well-intentioned ['welɪn'tenʃnd] ADJ bienintencionado; *lie* piadoso.

well-judged ['wel'dʒʌdʒd] ADJ bien calculado.

well-kept ['wel'kept] ADJ (muy) cuidado, bien conservado, en buen orden; **a ~ secret** un secreto bien guardado.

well-knit ['wel'nɪt] ADJ *body* robusto, fornido; *scheme etc* lógico, bien razonado; *speech etc* bien pensado, de estructura lógica.

well-known ['wel'nəʊn] ADJ (muy) conocido.

well-liked ['wel'laɪkt] ADJ querido, apreciado.

well-loved ['wel'lʌvd] ADJ muy querido, amado.

well-made ['wel'meɪd] ADJ bien hecho, fuerte.

well-managed ['wel'mænɪdʒd] ADJ bien administrado; bien dirigido.

well-man clinic [wel'mænklɪnɪk] N clínica *f* de salud (*para hombres*).

well-mannered ['wel'mænəd] ADJ educado, culto, cortés.

well-marked ['wel'mɑːkt] ADJ bien marcado.

well-matched ['wel'mætʃt] ADJ muy iguales.

well-meaning ['wel'miːnɪŋ] ADJ bienintencionado.

well-meant ['wel'ment] ADJ bienintencionado.

well-nigh ['welnaɪ] ADV casi; punto menos que; **it's ~ finished** está casi terminado; **this is ~ impossible** esto es punto menos que imposible.

well-nourished ['wel'nʌrɪʃt] ADJ bien alimentado.

well-off ['wel'ɒf] ADJ (a) (*financially*) acomodado; pudiente; adinerado; **the less ~** las gentes menos pudientes; **he spoke with a ~ accent** habló con acento culto, (*pej*) habló con acento afectado. (b) (*in circumstances*) **she's ~ without him** está mejor sin él; **you don't know when you're ~** no sabes los muchos beneficios que tienes.

well-oiled* ['wel'ɔɪld] ADJ hecho una cuba*.

well-padded* ['wel'pædɪd] ADJ gordo.

well-paid ['wel'peɪd] ADJ bien pagado, bien retribuido.

well-preserved ['welprɪ'zɜːvd] ADJ = **well-kept;** *person* bien conservado.

well-proportioned ['welprə'pɔːʃnd] ADJ bien proporcionado, de forma elegante; *person* de talle elegante.

well-read ['wel'red] ADJ leído, instruido; culto; **to be ~ in history** haber leído mucha historia, estar muy documentado en historia.

well-respected ['welrɪ'spektɪd] ADJ respetado, estimado.

well-rounded ['wel'raʊndɪd] ADJ redondeado, acabado.

well-spent ['wel'spent] ADJ bien empleado, fructuoso.

well-spoken ['wel'spəʊkən] ADJ bienhablado, con acento culto.

wellspring ['wel,sprɪŋ] N (*fig*) fuente *f*.

well-stacked* ['wel'stækt] ADJ de buen tipo, curvilínea.

well-stocked ['wel'stɒkt] ADJ bien provisto, bien surtido; **~ shelves** estantes *mpl* llenos.

well-thought-of ['wel'θɔːtəv] ADJ bien reputado, de buena reputación.

well-thought-out ['wel,θɔːt'aʊt] ADJ bien planeado.

well-timed ['wel'taɪmd] ADJ oportuno.

well-to-do ['weltə'duː] ADJ acomodado, pudiente; **the ~** la gente pudiente, (*also pej*) la gente bien.

well-travelled, (*US*) **well-traveled** ['wel'trævld] ADJ *person* que ha viajado mucho, que ha visto mucho mundo; *path* trillado.

well-tried ['wel'traɪd] ADJ *method* comprobado.

well-trodden ['wel'trɒdn] ADJ trillado.

well-turned ['wel'tɜːnd] ADJ elegante.

well-wisher ['wel,wɪʃər] N partidario *m*, -a *f*.

well-woman clinic ['welwʊmənklɪnɪk] N clínica *f* de salud (*para mujeres*).

well-worn ['wel'wɔːn] ADJ *garment* raído; *path* trillado; *cliché* traído y llevado, trillado, manoseado.

well-written ['wel'rɪtn] ADJ bien escrito.

Welsh [welʃ] [1] ADJ galés, de Gales; **~ rabbit, ~ rarebit** pan *m* con queso tostado.
[2] N (a) **the ~** PL los galeses.
(b) (*Ling*) galés *m*.

welsh* [welʃ] VI (*bookmaker*) largarse sin pagar*; dejar de cumplir una obligación (*on sb* contraída con uno).

Welshman ['welʃmən] N, PL **Welshmen** ['welʃmən] galés *m*.

Welshwoman ['welʃ,wʊmən] N, PL **Welshwomen** ['welʃ,wɪmɪn] galesa *f*.

welt [welt] [1] N (a) (*of shoe*) vira *f*; (b) (*weal*) verdugón *m*.
[2] VT (a) poner vira a. (b) pegar, zurrar, hacer verdugones a.

welter ['weltər] [1] N confusión *f*, mezcla *f* confusa, mescolanza *f*, revoltijo *m*; **in a ~ of blood** en un mar de sangre.
[2] VI revolcarse; **to ~ in** estar bañado en, bañarse en.

welterweight ['weltəweɪt] N wélter *m*; **light ~** wélter *m* ligero.

wen [wen] N lobanillo *m*, quiste *m* sebáceo; **the Great W~** el gran tumor (*Londres*).

wench [wentʃ] [1] N mozuela *f*, muchacha *f*; (*pej*) moza *f*; (*whore*) puta *f*.
[2] VI (*also to go ~ing*) ir de fulanas, putañear.

wend† [wend] VT: **to ~ one's way to** enderezar sus pasos a.

Wendy house ['wendɪ,haʊs] N, PL **Wendy houses** ['wendɪ,haʊzɪz] (*Brit*) casa *f* de muñecas (suficientemente grande para entrar).

went [went] PRET *of* **go.**

wept [wept] PRET AND PTP *of* **weep.**

were [wɜːr] PRET *of* **be.**

we're [wɪər] = **we are.**

weren't [wɜːnt] = **were not.**

werewolf ['wɪəwʊlf] N, PL **werewolves** ['wɪəwʊlvz] hombre-lobo *m*.

wert†† [wɜːt] V **be.**

Wesleyan ['wezlɪən] [1] ADJ metodista.
[2] N metodista *mf*.

Wesleyanism ['wezlɪənɪzəm] N metodismo *m*.

west [west] [1] N oeste *m*, occidente *m*; **the W~** el Oeste, el Occidente; **tales of the American W~** cuentos *mpl* del Oeste americano.
[2] ADJ del oeste, occidental; *wind* del oeste; **W~ Africa** África *f* Occidental; **W~ Bank** (*Middle East*) Cisjordania *f*; **W~ Berlin** (*Hist*) Berlín *m* Oeste; **W~ German** (*Hist*: N) alemán *m*, -ana *f* occidental, (ADJ) germanooccidental; **W~ Germany** (*Hist*) Alemania *f* Occidental; **to go ~*** (*object, machine*) romperse, estropearse; (*plan etc*) fracasar; (*person*) estirar la pata*.

westbound ['westbaʊnd] ADJ *traffic* que va hacia el oeste; *carriageway* dirección oeste.

westerly ['westəlɪ] ADJ oeste; *wind* del oeste.

western ['westən] [1] ADJ occidental, del oeste.
[2] N western *m*.

westerner ['westənər] N habitante *mf* del Oeste; (*Pol etc*) occidental *mf*.

westernization ['westənaɪ'zeɪʃən] N occidentalización *f*.

westernize ['westənaɪz] VT occidentalizar.

westernized ['westənaɪzd] ADJ occidentalizado, influido por el Occidente; **to become ~** occidentalizarse.

westernmost ['westənməʊst] ADJ (el) más occidental, situado más al oeste.

west-facing ['west'feɪsɪŋ] ADJ con cara al oeste, orientado hacia el oeste; **~ slope** vertiente *f* oeste.

West Indian ['west'ɪndɪən] [1] ADJ antillano.
[2] N antillano *m*, -a *f*.

West Indies ['west'ɪndiːz] NPL Antillas *fpl*.

Westminster ['west,mɪnstə^r] N (*Brit*) Westminster *m* (*el parlamento británico*).

┌─ **WESTMINSTER** ─┐

(i) **Westminster**, *también llamado* **City of Westminster**, *es el distrito del centro de Londres que comprende el Parlamento* (**Houses of Parliament**), *la Abadía de Westminster* (**Westminster Abbey**) *y el Palacio de Buckingham* (**Buckingham Palace**). *Este nombre se usa también normalmente en los medios de comunicación para referirse al Parlamento o a los parlamentarios británicos.*

westward ['westwəd] ☐1 ADJ *advance etc* hacia el oeste, en dirección oeste.
☐2 ADV (*also* **~s**) hacia el oeste, en dirección oeste.

wet [wet] ☐1 ADJ (a) (*naturally*) húmedo; (*accidentally, temporarily*) mojado; *paint etc* fresco; **~ blanket*** aguafiestas *mf*; **~ dream** polución *f* nocturna; **~ fish** pescado *m* fresco; (*) tío *m* tonto*; **the ~ look** acabado *m* con apariencia de mojado; **in ~ clothes** en ropa mojada; **cheeks ~ with tears** mejillas *fpl* bañadas de lágrimas; **to be ~ through, to be ~ to the skin** estar mojado hasta los huesos; **the ink is still ~** la tinta no se ha secado todavía; **the baby's ~** el bebé se ha meado; **to be ~ behind the ears*** estar con la leche en los labios; **to get ~** mojarse; **to get one's feet ~** mojarse los pies; **it grows in ~ places** se encuentra en lugares húmedos.
(b) (*weather*) lluvioso; **a ~ day** un día de lluvia; **a ~ climate** un clima lluvioso; **the ~ season** la estación de las lluvias; **in ~ weather** cuando llueve; **it was ~ in the night** llovió durante la noche; **it was too ~ for us to go out** llovió tanto que no pudimos salir.
(c) (*Brit**: *stupid*) soso, bobo; **don't be so ~!** ¡no seas bobo!
(d) (*Brit Pol**) derechista moderado, de la derecha moderada.
(e) (*US**) antiprohibicionista.
(f) **you're all ~*** (*US*) estás totalmente equivocado, estás metiendo la pata a fondo*.
☐2 N (a) humedad *f*; (*rain*) lluvia *f*; **it's out in the ~** está fuera a la intemperie.
(b) (*US**) = **wetback**.
(c) (*Brit Pol**) político *mf* de la derecha moderada.
☐3 VT mojar, humedecer; *tea* hacer; echar agua hirviente a; (*) *bargain* cerrar con un brindis; **to ~ the bed** orinarse en la cama; **to ~ one's pants** orinarse en las bragas.
☐4 VR: **to ~ o.s.** mearse.

wetback ['wetbæk] N (*US*) inmigrante *m* (mejicano) ilegal; bracero *m*.

wether ['weðə^r] N carnero *m* castrado.

wetland ['wetlənd] N pantano *m*, zona *f* húmeda, zona *f* acuosa; **~s** pantanos *mpl*, tierras *fpl* pantanosas.

wetness ['wetnɪs] N humedad *f*; (*raininess*) lo lluvioso.

wet-nurse ['wetnɜːs] N nodriza *f*, ama *f* de cría.

wetsuit ['wetsuːt] N vestido *m* isotérmico.

wetting ['wetɪŋ] N mojada *f*; **to get a ~** mojarse; **to give sb a ~** mojar a uno.

WEU N ABBR *of* **Western European Union**.

we've [wiːv] = **we have**.

WFP N ABBR *of* **World Food Programme**.

WFTU N ABBR *of* **World Federation of Trade Unions** Federación *f* ▼ Sindical Mundial, FSM *f*.

whack [wæk] ☐1 N (a) (*blow*) golpe *m* grande, golpe *m* ruidoso; porrazo *m*; **to give sb a ~** darle a uno ¡zas!; **to give sth a ~** golpear algo ruidosamente.
(b) (*: *attempt*) tentativa *f*; **to have a ~ at sth** intentar algo, probar algo; **let's have a ~** probemos, vamos a ver.
(c) (*Brit**: *share*) parte *f*, porción *f*; **you should get your ~** seguramente recibirás lo tuyo; **top ~** salario *m* máximo.
(d) **out of ~*** (*US*) estropiciado*, fastidiado.
☐2 VT (a) (*beat*) golpear, aporrear; (*defeat*) dar una paliza a.
(b) (*fig*) **the problem has me ~ed** todavía el problema me trae perplejo; **we've got the problem ~ed at last** por fin hemos resuelto el problema.

whacked* ['wækt] ADJ (*Brit*): **to be ~** estar agotado, estar hecho polvo*.

whacking ['wækɪŋ] ☐1 ADJ (*esp Brit*) grandote, enorme, imponente.
☐2 ADV (*: *esp Brit*): **a ~ big book** un libro enorme de grande, un tomazo*.
☐3 N zurra *f*; **to give sb a ~** zurrar a uno, pegar a uno.

whacky* ['wækɪ] ADJ (*US*) = **wacky**.

whale [weɪl] N ballena *f*; **a ~ of a difference*** una enorme diferencia; **to have a ~ of a time*** divertirse en grande*, pasarlo bomba*.

whalebone ['weɪlbəʊn] N ballena *f*, barba *f* de ballena.

whale-oil ['weɪlɔɪl] N aceite *m* de ballena.

whaler ['weɪlə^r] N (*person, ship*) ballenero *m*.

whaling ['weɪlɪŋ] N pesca *f* de ballenas.

whaling-ship ['weɪlɪŋʃɪp] N ballenero *m*.

whaling-station ['weɪlɪŋ,steɪʃən] N estación *f* ballenera.

wham [wæm] (a) = **whang**. (b) INTERJ: **~!** ¡zas!

whammy* ['wæmɪ] N (*US*) mala sombra *f*, mala suerte *f*, mala pata *f*.

whang [wæŋ] ☐1 N golpe *m* resonante.
☐2 VT golpear de modo resonante.
☐3 VI: **to ~ against sth, to ~ into sth** chocar ruidosamente con algo.

wharf [wɔːf] N, PL **wharfs** *or* **wharves** [wɔːvz] muelle *m*; **ex ~** franco en el muelle; **price ex ~** precio *m* franco de muelle.

wharfage ['wɔːfɪdʒ] N muellaje *m*.

what [wɒt] ☐1 ADJ (a) (*rel*) el ... que, la ... que, lo ... que *etc*; **~ little I had** lo poco que tenía; **with ~ money I have** con el dinero que tengo; **buy ~ food you like** compra los comestibles que quieras.
(b) (*interrog*) qué; cuál de ...; **~ book do you want?** ¿qué libro quieres?, ¿cuál de los libros quieres?; **~ news did he bring?** ¿qué noticias trajo?
(c) (INTERJ) qué; **~ a man!** ¡qué hombre!; **~ luck!** ¡qué suerte!; **~ a fool I've been!** ¡qué tonto he sido!; **~ an ugly dog!** ¡qué perro más (*or* tan) feo!
(d) (*interj, iro*) lindo, valiente, bueno; **~ a general!** ¡valiente general!; **~ an excuse!** ¡buen pretexto!
☐2 PRON (a) (*rel, = that which*) lo que; **~ I like is tea** lo que me gusta de verdad es el té; **that is not ~ I asked for** eso no es lo que pedí; **~ is done is done** lo que está hecho no se puede cambiar; **and ~ not, and ~ have you, and I don't know ~** y qué sé yo qué más; **and ~ is more ...** y además ...; **~ with the weather and the crisis** entre el mal tiempo y la crisis; **~ with one thing and another** entre una cosa y otra; **come ~ may** venga lo que viniere; **say ~ he will** diga lo que diga; **business is not ~ it was** los negocios no son lo que eran; **not a day but ~ it rains** no hay día que no llueva; **to give sb ~ for*** cargarse a uno*.
(b) (*interrog*) ¿qué?; (*please repeat*) ¿cómo?; **~ is it?** ¿qué es?; **~'s that?** ¿y eso qué es?; **~ is that to you?** y eso ¿qué te importa?; **'I'm going to be an actress' — 'You ~?'*** 'Voy a hacerme actriz' — ¿Qué dices?'; **do you want it or ~?** ¿lo quieres o qué?; **~ is the reason?** ¿cuál es la razón?; **~ is the formula for ...?** ¿cuál es la fórmula de ...?; **~ is this called?** ¿cómo se llama esto?; **~ can we do?** ¿qué podemos hacer?; **~ do 4 and 3 make?** ¿cuánto suman 4 y 3?; **so ~?** ¿y qué?; **so ~ if it does rain?** y si llueve, ¿qué?; **so ~ if he is gay?** y ¿nos importa que sea gay?; **~ if ...?** ¿y si ...?, ¿qué será si ...?; **~ of it?, ~ of that?** y eso ¿qué importa?; **(do) you know ~, I think he's drunk** creo que está borracho, ¿sabes?; **I know ~, let's ring her up** se me ocurre una idea: llamémosla al teléfono; **I know ~ you're after** sé lo que buscas; **I don't know ~ to do** no sé qué hacer; **I'll tell you ~** se me ocurre una idea, tengo una idea; **he knows ~'s ~** sabe cuántas son cinco; **rats and mice and God knows ~** ratas y ratones y Dios sabe qué más; V **about, for** *etc*.
(c) (INTERJ) ¡cómo!; **~! you sold it!** ¡cómo! ¡lo has vendido!; **~! a man in your room?** ¿un hombre en tu cuarto?; **shameful, ~?** (*esp Brit*) vergonzoso, ¿no?

what-d'ye-call-him* ['wɒtdʒʊ,kɔːlɪm] PRON fulano; **old ~ with the red nose** ése que tiene la nariz tan coloradota.

what-d'ye-call-it* ['wɒtdʒʊ,kɔːlɪt] PRON cosa *f*, chisme *m*; **he does it with the ~** lo hace con el chisme ese; **that green ~ on the front** esa cosa verde en la parte delantera.

whatever [wɒt'evə^r] ☐1 PRON lo que; todo lo que; **~ you like** lo que quieras; **~ you find** cualquier cosa que encuentres; **~ I have is yours** todo lo que tengo es tuyo; **~ it may be** sea lo que sea; **~ he says** diga lo que diga; **~ you say** (*acquiescing*) lo que quieras; **~ happens** pase lo que pase; **or ~ they're called** o como quiera que se llamen; **~ do you mean?** pero ¿qué diablos quieres decir?; **or ~** o lo que sea; **~ did you do?** ¿pues qué hiciste?
☐2 ADJ (a) **~ book you choose** cualquier libro que elijas; **~ books you choose** cualquier libro de los que elijas; **every book of ~ size** todo libro tamaño que sea; **~ time is it?** ¿qué hora podrá ser?
(b) (*negative*) **no man ~** ningún hombre sea quien sea; **nothing ~** nada en absoluto; **he said nothing ~ of interest** no dijo nada en absoluto que tuviera interés; **it's of no use ~** no sirve para nada en absoluto.

what-ho* ['wɒt'həʊ] INTERJ (*surprise*) ¡caramba!, ¡vaya!; (*greeting*) ¡hola!, ¡oye!

whatnot ['wɒtnɒt] ☐1 N (a) (*furniture*) juguetero *m*. (b) (*) (*whatsit*) chisme *m*.
☐2 PRON: **and ~*** y qué sé yo, y un largo etcétera.

what's-his-name* ['wɒtsɪz,neɪm] PRON fulano; **old ~ with the limp** fulano el cojo.

whatsit* ['wɒtsɪt] N chisme *m*.

whatsoever [,wɒtsəʊ'evə^r] PRON, ADJ = **whatever**.

wheat [wiːt] ☐1 N trigo *m*; **to separate the ~ from the chaff** (*fig*) separar la cizaña del buen grano.
☐2 ATTR de trigo, trigueño; **~ loaf** pan *m* de trigo.

wheatear ['wiːtɪə^r] N (*Orn*) collalba *f*.

wheaten ['wiːtn] ADJ de trigo, trigueño; de color de trigo.

wheatfield ['wiːtfiːld] N trigal *m.*

wheatgerm ['wiːtdʒɜːm] N germen *m* de trigo.

wheatmeal ['wiːtmiːl] N harina *f* de trigo.

wheatsheaf ['wiːtʃiːf] N gavilla *f* de trigo.

wheedle ['wiːdl] VT engatusar; **to ~ sb into doing sth** engatusar a uno para que haga (*or* para hacer) algo, conseguir por medio de halagos que uno haga algo; **to ~ sth out of sb** sonsacar algo a alguien.

wheedling ['wiːdlɪŋ] ① ADJ mimoso.
② N mimos *mpl,* halagos *mpl.*

wheel [wiːl] ① N (a) rueda *f;* (*steering ~*) volante *m;* (*potter's*) torno *m;* (*Naut*) timón *m;* **~ of fortune** rueda *f* de fortuna; **the ~s of government** el mecanismo del gobierno; **big ~** (*at fair*) noria *f,* (**: person*) personaje *m,* pez *m* gordo*; **to be at** (*or* **behind**) **the ~** estar al volante, estar conduciendo; **there are ~s within ~s** esto es más complicado de lo que parece, esto tiene su miga; **a basket on ~s** una cesta con ruedas; **are you on ~s?*** (*US*) ¿tienes coche?, ¿estás motorizado?*; **to oil the ~s** (*fig*) lubricar el mecanismo; **to take the ~** tomar el volante.
(b) (*Mil*) vuelta *f,* conversión *f;* **a ~ to the right** una vuelta hacia la derecha.
② ATTR (*Aut*) **four ~ drive** tracción *f* a las cuatro ruedas; **front ~ drive** tracción *f* delantera; **rear ~ drive** tracción *f* trasera.
③ VT (*turn*) hacer girar; hacer rodar; *bicycle, pram* empujar; *child* pasear en cochecito; **we ~ed it over to the window** lo empujamos hasta la ventana; **when it broke down I had to ~ it** cuando se averió tuve que empujarlo.
④ VI (*turn*) girar; rodar; dar vueltas; (*birds*) revolotear; (*Mil*) dar una vuelta, cambiar de frente; **to ~ left** dar una vuelta hacia la izquierda; **to ~ round** (*person*) girar sobre los talones; (*fig*) cambiar de rumbo, cambiar de opinión.

◆**wheel out*** [ˌwiːl'aut] VT *supporter, expert* traer; *idea, cliché* desempolvar.

wheelbarrow ['wiːlˌbærəu] N carretilla *f.*

wheelbase ['wiːlbeɪs] N batalla *f,* distancia *f* entre ejes.

wheelbrace ['wiːlbreɪs] N llave *f* de ruedas en cruz.

wheelchair ['wiːltʃɛəʳ] N silla *f* de ruedas.

wheel-clamp ['wiːlklæmp] ① N cepo *m.*
② VT poner cepo a, inmovilizar con el cepo; **I found I was ~ed** me encontré inmovilizado con el cepo.

wheeled [wiːld] ADJ: **~ traffic** tránsito *m* rodado; **~ transport** transporte *m* rodado.

-wheeled [wiːld] ADJ *ending in compounds: eg* **four~** de cuatro ruedas.

wheeler-dealer* ['wiːləˌdiːləʳ] N comerciante *m* poco escrupuloso.

wheel horse* ['wiːlhɔːs] N (*US*) trabajador *m,* -ora *f* infatigable, mula *f* de carga.

wheelhouse ['wiːlhaus] N, PL **wheelhouses** ['wiːlˌhauzɪz] timonera *f,* cámara *f* del timonel.

wheeling ['wiːlɪŋ] N: **~ and dealing*** negocios *mpl* sucios, intrigas *fpl.*

wheelwright ['wiːlraɪt] N ruedero *m,* carretero *m.*

wheeze [wiːz] ① N (a) resuello *m* (ruidoso), resuello *m* asmático; respiración *f* sibilante.
(b) (*Brit**) truco *m,* treta *f;* idea *f;* **that's a good ~** es buena idea; **to think up a ~** idear una treta.
② VT: **'Yes,' he ~d** 'Sí', dijo en voz asmática.
③ VI resollar (con ruido), jadear; respirar con silbido.

wheezing ['wiːzɪŋ] ADJ, **wheezy** ['wiːzɪ] ADJ *breath* ruidoso, difícil; *pronunciation* sibilante.

whelk [welk] N buccino *m.*

whelp [welp] ① N cachorro *m.*
② VI parir (*la perra etc*).

when [wen] *see also* WHEN *on next page* ① ADV cuándo?; **~ did it happen?** ¿cuándo ocurrió?; **I know ~ it happened** yo sé cuándo ocurrió; **~ is the interview?** ¿cuándo es la entrevista?; **say ~** (*in pouring drink*) dime cuándo; **since ~?** ¿desde cuándo?; **since ~ do you have a car?** ¿de cuándo acá tienes tú coche?; **till ~?** ¿hasta cuándo?
② CONJ (a) cuando; **~ I came in** cuando yo entré; al entrar (yo); **~ I was young** cuando era joven; en mi juventud; **you can go ~ I have finished** puedes irte en cuanto yo termine; **~ the bridge is built** cuando se construya el puente; **he's only happy ~ drunk** es feliz únicamente cuando está borracho; **he did it ~ a child** lo hizo de niño, lo hizo siendo niño.
(b) (*rel*) cuando; **this is ~ it always rains** esto es cuando llueve siempre; **at the very moment ~ ...** en el mismo momento en que (*or* cuando) ...; **one day ~ the tide is out** un día cuando la marea esté baja.

whence [wens] ADV (*liter*) (a) (*of place*) ¿de dónde?; **~ comes it that ...?** ¿cómo es que ...?
(b) (*fig*) por lo cual, y por consiguiente; **~ I conclude that ...** por lo cual concluyo que ...

whenever [wen'evəʳ] ① CONJ siempre que, cuandoquiera que; cuando, todas las veces que; **come ~ you like** ven cuando quieras; **I go ~ I can** voy todas las veces que puedo; **~ you see one of those, stop** siempre que veas uno de ésos, para; **we will help ~ possible** ayudaremos siempre cuando sea posible.
② ADV: **~ can he have done it?** ¿cuándo demonios ha podido hacerlo?; **~ do I have the time for such things?** ¿cuándo crees que tengo tiempo para estas cosas?; **Monday, Tuesday, or ~** el lunes o el martes o cuando sea, el lunes o el martes o algún día de éstos.

where [wɛəʳ] ADV (a) (*interrog*) ¿dónde?; **~ am I?** ¿dónde estoy?; **I know ~ he is** yo sé dónde está; **~ are you going?** ¿adónde vas?; **~ are you from?** ¿de dónde eres?; **~ should we be if ...?** ¿dónde estaríamos nosotros si ...?; **~ is the sense of it?** ¿qué sentido tiene?
(b) (*rel*) donde; **~ possible** donde sea posible; **go ~ you like** ve donde quieras; **this is ~ we got to** éste es el punto al que habíamos llegado; **this is ~ we got out** nos apeamos aquí, aquí es donde nos apeamos; **we are at the stage ~ we have to be careful** estamos en el punto en que tenemos que andar con cuidado; **the house ~ I was**

Pronoun

In direct questions

● In direct questions, *what* can generally be translated by *qué*:
  What is the matter with you?
  ¿Qué te pasa?

● But only use *¿qué es...?/¿qué son...?* to translate *what is/are* when asking for a *definition*:
  What is metaphysics?
  ¿Qué es la metafísica?
  What are endocrines?
  ¿Qué son las endocrinas?

● In other contexts use *¿cuál es?/¿cuáles son?*:
  What was the result?
  ¿Cuál fue el resultado?
  What is the address?
  ¿Cuál es la dirección?

● However, not all expressions with *what* should be translated literally. Some require *qué* used adjectivally:
  What is the difference?
  ¿Qué diferencia hay?
  What are your plans?
  ¿Qué planes tienes?

In indirect questions

● In most cases translate the pronoun *what* using either *lo que* (without an accent) or *qué* (with an accent):
  He asked me what we were going to do
  Me preguntó (qué es) lo que íbamos a hacer ◊ Me preguntó qué íbamos a hacer
  She asked me what a brake pad was
  Me preguntó lo que or Me preguntó qué era una pastilla de frenos

  Do you know what she's done?
  ¿Sabes lo que or ¿Sabes qué ha hecho?

● However, use *cuál era/cuáles son etc* instead of *lo que era/lo que son etc* if *what was/are etc* does not relate to a definition:
  He was asked what his favourite pastime was
  Le preguntaron cuál era su pasatiempo favorito

In ordinary statements

● Translate the pronoun *what* using *lo que*:
  I heard what you said
  He oído lo que has dicho
  It depends on what you mean by that
  Depende de lo que quieras decir con eso

● Translate *what* before an infinitive using *qué*:
  I'm not sure what to do
  No sé muy bien qué hacer

Adjective

● *What* used adjectivally is always *qué*:
  What time shall we meet?
  ¿A qué hora nos vemos?
  Tell me what colour you like best
  Dime qué color te gusta más

Accents

● Remember to put an accent on question words in direct and indirect questions as well as in exclamations:
  What do they want?
  ¿Qué quieren?
  What dreadful weather!
  ¡Qué tiempo más or tan horrible!
  For further uses and examples, see main entry.

see also main entry

born la casa donde nací, la casa en la que nací; **from ~ I'm sitting** desde aquí, desde donde estoy sentado; **that's just ~ you're wrong** en eso te equivocas; **that's ~ I disagree with you** en eso no estoy de acuerdo contigo; **~ this book is dangerous is in suggesting that ...** el aspecto peligroso de este libro es la sugerencia de que ...; **~ husband and wife both work, benefits are ...** en el caso de que los dos esposos trabajan, los beneficios son ...

```
┌─[ WHEN ]─────────────────────────[ see also main entry ]─┐
```

In direct and indirect questions
- *When* in direct and indirect questions as well as after expressions of (un)certainty and doubt (e.g. *no sé*) translates as *cuándo* (with an accent) and is used with the indicative:
    When will they arrive?
    ¿Cuándo llegarán?
    She was asked when she had seen him last
    Le preguntaron cuándo lo había visto por última vez
    I have no idea when they'll come
    No tengo idea de cuándo vendrán
    NOTE: The accented form should also be used in exclamations:
    When will we learn to keep our mouths shut!
    ¡Cuándo aprenderemos a callar la boca!

In statements
- In statements other than the above, *when* can be translated by *cuando* (without an accent) followed by either the indicative or the subjunctive. Use the *indicative* when talking about the past or making general statements about the present. Use the *subjunctive* when the action is or was in the future:
    We met her when she was living in Barcelona
    La conocimos cuando vivía en Barcelona
    He always cries when I leave
    Siempre llora cuando me voy
    Call me when you get there
    Llámame cuando llegues
    She said she would call me when she got home
    Dijo que me llamaría cuando llegase or llegara a casa

After nouns
- If *when* follows a noun (e.g. *day*, *time*) and defines the noun, translate using *en que* not *cuando*:
    She can't remember a time when she wasn't happy
    No recuerda una época en que no fuese feliz
- If the *when* clause provides additional information that does not define or restrict the noun - in English as in Spanish commas are obligatory here - translate using *cuando*:
    Some days, when we're very busy, we don't finish work till very late
    Algunos días, cuando tenemos mucho trabajo, no acabamos hasta muy tarde
    NOTE: You can test whether *cuando* or *en que* is required by reading the sentence *without* the *when* clause. If it still makes sense, *cuando* is the likely translation. If it does not make sense, *en que* is needed.
- If *when* + VERB can be substituted by *on* + -ING in English and describes an action that either happens at the same time as or closely follows another one, you can use *al* + INFINITIVE:
    When he went out he saw it was raining
    Al salir vio que estaba lloviendo
    For further uses and examples, see main entry.

---

whereabouts [1] ['weərə'bauts] ADV ¿dónde?
  [2] ['weərəbauts] N paradero *m*; **nobody knows his ~** se desconoce su paradero actual.
▼**whereas** [weər'æz] CONJ visto que, por cuanto, mientras; (*in legal parlance*) considerando que.
whereat [weər'æt] ADV (*liter*) con lo cual.
whereby [weər'baɪ] ADV (*frm*) por lo cual, por donde; **the rule ~ it is not allowed to** + *infin* la regla según (*or* mediante) la cual no se permite + *infin*.
wherefore†† ['weəfɔːr] [1] ADV (*why*) por qué; (*and for this reason*) y por tanto, por lo cual.
  [2] N: **the whys and ~s** las razones, el por qué; los detalles, la explicación detallada.
wherein†† [weər'ɪn] ADV en donde.
whereof†† [weər'ɒv] ADV de que.
whereon [weər'ɒn] ADV (*liter*) en que.
wheresoever [,weəsəu'evər] ADV (*liter*) dondequiera que.
whereto [,weə'tuː] ADV (*frm*, ††) adonde.
whereupon ['weərəpɒn] ADV con lo cual, después de lo cual.
wherever [weər'evər] [1] CONJ dondequiera que; **~ you go I'll go too** dondequiera que vayas yo te acompañaré; **~ I am** (esté) donde esté; **~ possible** donde sea posible; **he follows me ~ I go** me sigue por

donde vaya; **~ they went they were cheered** por dondequiera que fueron se les aplaudió; **sit ~ you like** siéntate donde te parezca bien; **I'll buy them ~ they come from** los compraré no importa su procedencia, los compraré vengan de donde vengan.
  [2] ADV: **~ did you put it?** ¿dónde demonios lo pusiste?; **~ can they have got to?** ¿dónde diablos se habrán metido?; **in Madrid or Barcelona or ~** en Madrid o Barcelona o donde sea.

```
┌─[ WHERE ]────────────────────────[ see also main entry ]─┐
```

In direct and indirect questions
- *Where* in direct questions as well as after report verbs and expressions of (un)certainty and doubt (e.g. *no sé*) usually translates as *dónde* (with an accent), sometimes preceded by a preposition:
    Where are you going (to)?
    ¿A dónde or Adónde or Dónde vas?
    Where can I have put my keys (down)?
    ¿En dónde or Dónde puedo haber puesto las llaves?
    They asked where he had been
    Le preguntaron dónde había estado
    They don't know where he is
    No saben dónde está

In statements
- *Where* in statements other than those mentioned above is usually translated as *donde* (without accent), again often preceded by a preposition:
    I live where I've always lived
    Vivo donde siempre he vivido
    We went to visit the house where Diego was born
    Fuimos a visitar la casa en donde nació Diego
    NOTE: In informal speech, you can use *donde* + NOUN PHRASE to translate examples like the following:
    Go to where my parents are ◊ Go to my parents' place
    Vete donde mis padres
    For further uses and examples, see main entry.

---

wherewith [weə'wɪθ] ADV con lo cual.
wherewithal ['weəwɪðɔːl] N medios *mpl*, recursos *mpl*, cónquibus *m* (*hum*); **they haven't got the ~** no tienen los medios.
wherry ['werɪ] N chalana *f*.
whet [wet] VT *tool* afilar, amolar; *appetite, curiosity* estimular, despertar, aguzar.
whether ['weðər] CONJ si; **I do not know ~ ...** no sé si ...; **I doubt ~ ...** dudo que + *subj*; **~ he is here or in Madrid** que esté aquí o en Madrid; **~ she sings or dances** que cante o baile; **~ they come or not** vengan o no (vengan).
whetstone ['wetstəun] N piedra *f* de amolar, afiladera *f*.
whew [hwjuː] INTERJ ¡vaya!, ¡caramba!
whey [weɪ] N suero *m*.
whey-faced ['weɪ'feɪst] ADJ pálido.
whf ABBR of **wharf**.
which [wɪtʃ] *see also* ⌐WHICH⌐ *on next page* [1] ADJ (a) (*interrog*) ¿qué?; ¿cuál?; **~ picture do you prefer?** ¿qué cuadro prefieres?, ¿cuál de los cuadros prefieres?; **I don't know ~ tie he wants** no sé qué corbata quiere; **~ way did she go?** ¿por dónde se fue?; **~ one?** ¿cuál?; **~ one of us?** ¿cuál de nosotros?; **~ house do you live in?** ¿en qué casa vives?, ¿qué casa es la tuya?
  (b) (*rel*) **in ~ case** en cuyo caso; **he used 'peradventure', ~ word is now archaic** dijo 'peradventure', palabra que ha quedado anticuada; **look ~ way you will ...** mires por donde mires ...
  [2] PRON (a) (*interrog*) ¿cuál?; **~ do you want?** ¿cuál quieres?; **~ of you did it?** ¿cuál de vosotros lo hizo?; **I don't mind ~** no me importa cuál; **I can't tell ~ is ~** no sé cuál es cuál.
  (b) (*rel*) que; lo que; **the bear ~ I saw** el oso que vi; **two forms are to be filled in** dos formularios que deberán llenarse; **the meeting ~ we attended** la reunión a que asistimos; **it rained hard ~ upset her** llovió mucho, lo que la desconcertó; **... ~ God forbid ...** lo que Dios no quiera.
  (c) (*rel governed by prep*) el que (*etc*), el cual (*etc*); lo cual; **the hotel at ~ we stayed** el hotel en el que nos hospedamos; **the cities to ~ we are going** las ciudades a las que vamos; **the bull ~ I'm talking about** el toro del que hablo; **at ~** con lo cual, sobre lo cual; **from ~ we deduce that ...** de lo cual deducimos que ...; **after ~ we went to bed** después de lo cual nos acostamos.
whichever [wɪtʃ'evər] [1] ADJ cualquier; **~ possibility you choose** cualquier posibilidad que elijas; **~ way you look at it** se mire como se mire; **you can choose ~ system you want** puedes elegir el sistema que quieras; **~ system you have there are difficulties** hay dificultades no importa el sistema que tengas.
  [2] PRON cualquiera; el que, la que; **choose ~ is easiest** elige el que sea más fácil; **~ of the methods you choose** cualquiera de los métodos que elijas, no importa el método que elijas; **~ can he**

▶ LANGUAGE IN USE: **whereas** → 26.3

mean? ¿cuál demonios querrá decir?

whiff [wɪf] **1** N soplo *m,* soplo *m* fugaz; vaharada *f;* bocanada *f;* (*smell*) olorcillo *m;* **a ~ of grapeshot** un poco de metralla; **not a ~ of wind** ni el menor soplo de viento; **to catch a ~ of sth** percibir un olorcillo de algo, oler algo brevemente; **to go out for a ~ of air** salir a tomar el fresco; **what a ~!** ¡qué olor!

2 VI (*) oler (mal); **to ~ of** oler a.

Whig [wɪg] (*Pol Hist*) **1** N político liberal de los siglos XVII y XVIII.

2 ADJ liberal.

▼ **while** [waɪl] **1** N (a) rato *m,* tiempo *m;* **after a ~** poco tiempo después, al poco tiempo; **for a ~** durante algún tiempo; **a good ~, a great ~, a long ~** largo rato, mucho tiempo; **a long ~ ago** hace mucho; **it will be a good ~ before he gets here** tardará bastante en llegar; **it will be a good ~ before they finish** tardarán bastante en terminar; **a little ~ ago** hace poco; **it takes quite a ~** es cosa de bastante tiempo, exige mucho tiempo; **in a short ~** dentro de poco; **stay a ~ with us** quédate un rato con nosotros.
(b) **the ~** entretanto, mientras tanto; **all the ~** todo el tiempo; **he looked at me the ~** mientras tanto me estaba mirando.
(c) **it is worth ~ to ask whether ...** vale la pena preguntar si ...; **it's not worth my ~** desde mi punto de vista no vale la pena; **we'll make it worth your ~** le pagaremos bien, le compensaremos.

2 CONJ (a) (*time*) mientras; **~ this was happening** mientras pasaba esto; **~ you are away** mientras estés fuera; **she fell asleep ~ reading** se durmió leyendo; **to drink ~ on duty** beber estando de servicio.
(b) (*concessive*) aunque, bien que; **~ I admit it is awkward** aunque confieso que es difícil.
▼ (c) (*whereas*) mientras; **I have a blue car ~ you have a red one** yo tengo un coche azul y el tuyo es rojo.
(d) (*contrast*) si bien; **~ this used to be true, it is no longer so** si bien esto era verdad, ya no es así.

◆ **while away** VT: **to ~ away the time** pasar el rato, entretener el tiempo.

whilst [waɪlst] CONJ = **while.**

whim [wɪm] N capricho *m,* antojo *m,* manía *f;* **a passing ~** un capricho; **her every ~** todos sus antojos y fantasías; **it's just a ~ of hers** es un capricho suyo; **as the ~ takes me** según se me antoja.

whimbrel ['wɪmbrəl] N zarapito *m.*

whimper ['wɪmpəʳ] **1** N quejido *m,* gemido *m;* **without a ~** sin quejarse.

2 VT: **'Yes', she ~ed** 'Sí', dijo lloriqueando.

3 VI lloriquear; quejarse, gemir.

whimpering ['wɪmpərɪŋ] **1** ADJ que lloriquea.

2 N lloriqueo *m,* gimoteo *m.*

whimsical ['wɪmzɪkəl] ADJ *person* caprichoso; antojadizo; *idea* caprichoso, fantástico; **to be in a ~ mood** estar de humor para dejar volar la fantasía.

whimsicality [wɪmzɪ'kælɪti] N capricho *m,* fantasía *f;* **a novel of a pleasing ~** una novela de agradable fantasía.

whimsically ['wɪmzɪkəli] ADV caprichosamente; fantásticamente.

whimsy ['wɪmzi] N (*whim*) capricho *m,* antojo *m;* (*whimsicality*) fantasía *f,* extravagancia *f.*

whin [wɪn] N tojo *m.*

whine [waɪn] **1** N (*complaining cry*) quejido *m,* gimoteo *m,* (*of dog*)

gañido *m;* (*of bullet*) silbido *m.*

2 VT: **'Yes', he ~d** 'Sí', dijo gimoteando.

3 VI quejarse, gimotear; gañir; silbar; (*fig*) quejarse; **don't come whining to me about it** no venga a mí a quejarse; **the dog was whining to be let in** el perro estaba gañendo para que le abrieran.

whinge* [wɪndʒ] VI (a) (*complain*) quejarse. (b) = **whine 2.**

whinger* ['wɪndʒəʳ] N (*Brit*) quejica* *mf,* llorica* *mf.*

whining ['waɪnɪŋ] **1** ADJ quejumbroso; que gimotea.

2 N quejidos *mpl,* gimoteo *m;* el silbar.

whinny ['wɪni] **1** N relincho *m.*

2 VI relinchar.

whip [wɪp] **1** N (a) (*riding ~*) látigo *m;* (*used in punishment*) azote *m,* zurriago *m.*
(b) (*Brit Parl: call*) llamada *f;* **three-line ~** llamada *f* apremiante (*para que un diputado acuda a votar en un debate importante*).
(c) (*Parl: person*) diputado encargado de la disciplina de partido; **Chief W~** diputado jefe encargado de la disciplina de partido; *ver también* LEADER OF THE HOUSE .
(d) (*Culin*) postre *m* de nata y huevos batidos.

2 VT (a) azotar; dar con un látigo; (*Culin*) batir; (*defeat*) batir, cascar; (*criticize etc*) fustigar.
(b) *rope* ligar, envolver con cuerda; (*Sew*) sobrecoser.
(c) (*Brit**) birlar*.
(d) **to ~ sb off to a meeting** llevar a uno con toda prisa a una reunión.
(e) **he was ~ping the crowd into a frenzy** provocaba el frenesí en la multitud.

3 VI moverse rápidamente; ir con toda prisa; **the car ~ped past** el coche pasó como un rayo.

┌─── WHIP ───
ⓘ *En el Parlamento británico la disciplina de partido está a cargo de un grupo de parlamentarios llamados* **whips,** *encabezados por el* **Chief Whip.** *Su deber es informar a los miembros del partido de los asuntos del Parlamento, comunicar a los líderes del partido las opiniones de los parlamentarios y asegurarse de que todos ellos asistan a la Cámara de los Comunes (**House of Commons**) y emitan su voto en asuntos importantes. Este último aspecto puede ser crucial cuando el gobierno sólo posee una escasa mayoría. Tanto el gobierno como la oposición tienen sus propios* **Whips** *y por lo general todos ellos tienen también altos cargos en la Administración del Estado si pertenecen al partido en el poder.*
└────────────

◆ **whip away** **1** VT: **to ~ sth away from sb** arrebatar algo a uno.
2 VI: = **whip 3.**

◆ **whip back** VI (*return*) volverse de golpe; (*bounce back*) rebotar de repente hacia atrás.

◆ **whip in** VT (*Hunting*) *hounds* llamar, reunir; (*Parl*) *member* llamar para que vote; *electors* hacer que acudan a las urnas.

◆ **whip off** VT *lid etc* quitar con un movimiento brusco; *dress* quitarse bruscamente.

◆ **whip on** VT *lid etc* poner con un movimiento brusco; *dress* ponerse bruscamente.

◆ **whip out** VT sacar de repente.

◆ **whip round** VI (a) (*turn*) volverse de repente.

┌─ WHICH ─────────────────────────────────────── *see also main entry* ─┐

In direct and indirect questions

As pronoun

• *Which/which one/which ones* in direct and indirect questions and after expressions of (un)certainty and doubt (e.g. *no sé*) usually translates as *cuál/cuáles:*
   Which of you is Kathleen?
   ¿Cuál de vosotras es Kathleen?
   I don't know which (one) to choose
   No sé cuál escoger
   Tell me which (ones) you like best
   Dime cuáles te gustan más

As adjective

• When *which* is used as an interrogative adjective, translate using *qué* + NOUN when the possibilities are very open or *cuál/cuáles de* + ARTICLE + PLURAL NOUN when the possibilities are limited:
   Which day are they coming?
   ¿Qué día vienen?
   Which option do you prefer?
   ¿Cuál de las alternativas prefieres?

As relative

• In relative clauses where *which* defines the noun it refers to, you can usually translate it as *que.* Note that in this type of sentence *which* can be substituted by *that* in English:
   The letter which *or* that came this morning was from my niece
   La carta que llegó esta mañana era de mi sobrina

   Do you remember the house (which *or* that) we saw last week?
   ¿Te acuerdas de la casa que vimos la semana pasada?
  ! Unlike *which,* the Spanish relative cannot be omitted.

• If *which* is the object of a preposition, you can either translate it as *que* (usually preceded by the definite article) or as ARTICLE + *cual/cuales.* Use the second option particularly in formal language or after long prepositions or prepositional phrases:
   This is the time (which *or* that) they usually come at
   Ésta es la hora a la que or a la cual suelen venir
   He explained the means by which we could achieve our objective
   Explicó los medios a través de los cuales podíamos alcanzar nuestro objetivo

• If instead of defining the noun the *which* clause merely adds additional information, you can use ARTICLE + *cual/cuales* as an alternative to *que:*
   The oak dining-table, which was a present from my father, seats 10 people comfortably
   La mesa de roble, que or la cual fue un regalo de mi padre, admite cómodamente diez comensales

• When *which* refers to the whole of a preceding sentence or idea, translate as *lo que* or *lo cual:*
   They left early, which my wife did not like at all
   Se marcharon pronto, lo cual or lo que no agradó nada a mi mujer
   For further uses and examples, see main entry.

└──┘

➤ LANGUAGE IN USE: **while: 2c → 5.1, 26.3**

(b) (*) **I'll ~ round to the shop** voy corriendo a la tienda; **the car ~ped round the corner** el coche dobló la esquina a gran velocidad.
(c) **to ~ round for sb*** hacer una colecta para uno.
◆**whip through** VT *book* leer rápidamente; *task, homework* realizar de un tirón.
◆**whip up** VT **(a)** *feeling* avivar, estimular; *support* procurar.
(b) (*Culin*) *cream etc* batir.
(c) (*pick up*) coger de repente; arrebatar.
whipcord ['wɪpkɔːd] N tralla *f*.
whip-hand ['wɪp'hænd] N: **to have the ~** llevar la ventaja (*over sb* a uno); llevar la batuta, mandar.
whiplash ['wɪplæʃ] **1** N tralla *f*, latigazo *m*.
2 ATTR: **~ injury** desnucamiento *m*, latigazo *m*.
whipped [wɪpt] ADJ *cream etc* batido.
whipper-in ['wɪpər'ɪn] N (*Hunting*) montero *m* que cuida los perros de caza.
whippersnapper ['wɪpə,snæpər] N (*also* **young ~**) mequetrefe *m*.
whippet ['wɪpɪt] N lebrel *m*.
whipping ['wɪpɪŋ] N azotamiento *m*; flagelación *f*; (*defeat*) derrota *f*; (*criticism etc*) paliza *f*; **to give sb a ~** azotar a uno, (*fig*) dar una paliza a uno.
whipping-boy ['wɪpɪŋbɔɪ] N cabeza *f* de turco.
whipping cream ['wɪpɪŋ,kriːm] N nata *f* para montar.
whipping-top ['wɪpɪŋtɒp] N peonza *f*, trompo *m*.
whippy ['wɪpɪ] ADJ flexible, dúctil.
whip-round* ['wɪpraʊnd] N (*Brit*) colecta *f*; **to have a ~ for sb** hacer una colecta para uno.
whipsaw ['wɪpsɔː] N sierra *f* cabrilla.
whir [wɜːr] = **whirr**.
whirl [wɜːl] **1** N **(a)** (*turn*) giro *m*, vuelta *f*; (*turning*) rotación *f*; el girar; (*of dust, water etc*) remolino *m*; **a ~ of pleasures** un torbellino de placeres; **my head is in a ~** mi cabeza está dando vueltas; **he disappeared in a ~ of dust** desapareció en una polvareda. **(b)** (*) **let's give it a ~** vamos a probarlo.
2 VT (*make turn*) hacer girar, hacer dar vueltas, dar vueltas a; (*wave, shake*) agitar; (*transport*) llevar con toda rapidez; **he ~ed his hat round his head** agitaba el sombrero alrededor de la cabeza; **he ~ed her off to the dance** la llevó con toda rapidez al baile; **the train ~ed us off to Paris** el tren nos llevó muy rápidamente a París.
3 VI (*spin*) girar rápidamente, dar vueltas; (*of dust, water*) arremolinarse; **my head ~s** mi cabeza está dando vueltas; **they ~ed past us in the dance** pasaron delante de nosotros girando alegremente en el baile.
◆**whirl round** VI girar rápidamente, dar vueltas; (*dust, water*) arremolinarse.
whirligig ['wɜːlɪgɪg] N (*toy*) molinete *m*; (*roundabout*) tiovivo *m*; (*Ent*) girino *m*; (*fig*) vicisitudes *fpl*; movimiento *m* confuso.
whirlpool ['wɜːlpuːl] N torbellino *m*, remolino *m*, (*fig*) vorágine *f*.
whirlwind ['wɜːlwɪnd] **1** N torbellino *m*, manga *f* de viento; **like a ~** como un torbellino, como una tromba; **to reap the ~** segar lo que se ha sembrado, padecer las consecuencias.
2 ATTR rapidísimo; **a ~ courtship** un noviazgo brevísimo; **they took us on a ~ tour** nos llevaron en una gira relámpago.
whirlybird* ['wɜːlɪbɜːd] N (*US*) helicóptero *m*.
whirr [wɜːr] **1** N (*of bird's wings*) ruido *m*, aleteo *m*, batir *m*, (*of insect's wings*) zumbido *m*; (*of machine: quiet*) zumbido *m*, runrún *m*, (*louder*) rechino *m*.
2 VI hacer ruido, batir; zumbar, runrunear; rechinar; **the cameras ~ed** runruneaban las cámaras.
whisk [wɪsk] **1** N **(a)** (*brush*) escobilla *f*; (*fly ~*) mosqueador *m*; (*Culin*) espumadera *f*, batidor *m*, (*electric etc*) batidora *f*.
2 VT **(a)** (*Brit Culin*) batir.
(b) (*fig*) **they ~ed him off to a meeting** le llevaron con toda prisa a una reunión; **we were ~ed up in the lift to the 9th floor** el ascensor nos llevó con toda rapidez al piso 9.
3 VI moverse rápidamente.
◆**whisk away 1** VT **(a)** *dust etc* quitar con un movimiento brusco; **the horse ~ed the flies away with its tail** el caballo ahuyentó las moscas con un movimiento brusco de la cola.
(b) she ~ed it away from me me lo arrebató; me lo quitó de repente; **the waiter ~ed the dishes away** el camarero quitó los platos en un periquete.
2 VI desaparecer de repente.
◆**whisk off** VT *dust etc* quitar con un movimiento brusco.
◆**whisk up** VT (*Culin*) batir.
whisker ['wɪskər] N pelo *m* (de la barba); **~s** barbas *fpl*; (*moustache*) bigotes *mpl*; (*side ~s*) patillas *fpl*; (*Zool*) bigotes *mpl*; **by a ~** por un pelo; **he was within a ~ of ...** estaba a dos dedos de ...
whiskered ['wɪskəd] ADJ bigotudo.
whisky, (*Ireland, US*) **whiskey** ['wɪskɪ] N whisk(e)y *m*, güisqui *m*; **~ and soda** whisky *m* con sifón, whisky *m* con soda.
whisper ['wɪspər] **1** N **(a)** (*low tone*) cuchicheo *m*; (*of leaves*) susurro

m; **to say sth in a ~** decir algo en tono muy bajo; **to speak in a ~** hablar muy bajo; **her voice scarcely rose above a ~** apenas pudo hablar sino en tono muy bajo.
(b) (*rumour*) rumor *m*, voz *f*; **at the least ~ of scandal** al menor indicio del escándalo; **there is a ~ that ...** corre la voz de que ..., se rumorea que ...
2 VT **(a)** decir en tono muy bajo; **to ~ sth to sb, to ~ a word in sb's ear** decir algo al oído de uno.
(b) (*fig*) **it is ~ed that ...** corre la voz de que ..., se rumorea que ...
3 VI cuchichear, hablar muy bajo; (*leaves*) susurrar; **to ~ to sb** cuchichear a uno, decir algo al oído de uno; **just ~ to me** dímelo al oído; **stop ~ing!** ¡silencio!; **it's rude to ~ in company** es de mala educación cuchichear en compañía.
whispering ['wɪspərɪŋ] **1** N **(a)** cuchicheo *m*; (*of leaves*) susurro *m*.
(b) (*gossip*) chismes *mpl*, chismografía *f*; (*rumours*) rumores *mpl*.
2 ATTR: **~ campaign** campaña *f* de rumores; campaña *f* de difamación; **~ gallery** galería *f* con eco.
whist [wɪst] N (*Brit*) whist *m*.
whist-drive ['wɪstdraɪv] N certamen *m* de whist.
whistle ['wɪsl] **1** N **(a)** (*sound*) silbido *m*, silbo *m*, pitido *m*; **final ~** pitido *m* final.
(b) (*instrument*) silbato *m*, pito *m*; **blast on the ~** pitido *m*; **the referee blew his ~** el árbitro pitó; **to blow the ~ on sb*** llamar a uno al orden; delatar a uno; poner fin a las actividades de uno; **to wet one's ~*** remojar el gaznate*, beber un trago.
2 VT silbar; **to ~ a tune** silbar una melodía.
3 VI silbar; (*Sport etc*) pitar; **it ~d past my ear** pasó (silbando) muy cerca de mi oreja, me rozó casi la oreja al pasar; **the car ~d past us** el coche pasó como una bala; **the boys ~ at the girls** los chicos silban a las chicas; **the crowd ~d at the referee** el público silbó al árbitro; **he ~d for a taxi** llamó un taxi con un silbido; **the referee ~d for a foul** el árbitro pitó falta; **he can ~ for it*** lo pedirá en vano, que espere sentado.
◆**whistle up** VT **(a) to ~ up one's dog** llamar a su perro con un silbido.
(b) (*fig*) (*find*) encontrar, hacer aparecer; *meal* preparar, servir; *people* reunir.
whistle-blower* ['wɪslbləʊər] N persona que tira de la manta, persona que desvela una situación ilegal.
whistle-stop ['wɪslstɒp] **1** N (*US*) población *f* pequeña.
2 ATTR: **~ tour** gira *f* electoral muy rápida.
Whit [wɪt] **1** N Pentecostés *m*.
2 ATTR de Pentecostés; **~ Sunday** domingo *m* de Pentecostés; **~ week** semana *f* de Pentecostés.
whit [wɪt] N: **never a ~, not a ~** ni pizca; **without a ~ of** sin pizca de; **every ~ as good as** de ningún modo inferior a.
white [waɪt] **1** ADJ blanco; *hair, meat, wine etc* blanco; *face (of complexion)* blanco, (*with fear*) pálido; (*fig*) honorable, decente; **~ blood-cell** célula *f* sanguínea blanca; **~ bread** pan *m* blanco, pan *m* candeal; **~ Christmas** Navidad *f* nevada; **~ coffee** (*Brit*) café *m* con leche; **to show the ~ feather** mostrarse cobarde; **~ flag** bandera *f* blanca; **~ flour** harina *f* blanca; **~ goods** (*linens*) ropa *f* blanca; (*US: domestic appliances*) (aparatos *mpl*) electrodomésticos *mpl*; **~ heat** candencia *f*; **~ hope** esperanza *f* dorada; **~ horses** (*waves*) palomas *fpl*; **W~ House** (*US*) Casa *f* Blanca; **~ lead** albayalde *m*; **~ lie** mentirilla *f*, mentira *f* piadosa (or caritativa); **~ magic** magia *f* blanca; **~ meat** carne *f* blanca; **~ noise** sonido *m* blanco, sonido *m* uniforme; **~ paper** (*Parl*) libro *m* blanco; **~ pepper** pimienta *f* blanca; **~ slave trade** trata *f* de blancas; **~ tie** corbatín *m* blanco; **~ trash** (*US:, pej*) término ofensivo contra la clase blanca pobre estadounidense; **~ water** aguas *fpl* bravas; **~ wedding** boda *f* de iglesia (en la que la novia viste de blanco); **to be as ~ as a sheet** estar pálido como la muerte; **to go ~, to turn ~** (*thing*) blanquear, (*person*) palidecer, ponerse pálido.
2 N **(a)** (*colour*) blanco *m*, color *m* blanco; (*whiteness*) blancura *f*; (*of egg*) clara *f* del huevo, blanquillo *m* (*LAm*); **the ~ of the eye** el blanco del ojo.
(b) (*person*) blanco *m*, -a *f*.
(c) ~s PL traje *m* blanco de deporte.

┌─ **WHITE TRASH** ─┐

White trash (basura blanca) es un término peyorativo que se usa en Estados Unidos para referirse a los pobres de raza blanca con un nivel cultural bajo, especialmente en los estados del sur, y a menudo se les considera torpes, sucios y perezosos. Sus perspectivas de futuro son por lo tanto comparables a las de los colectivos más pobres de hispanos, indios americanos o negros. La expresión la utilizó por primera vez la población negra de los estados del sur a mediados del siglo XIX para describir a los blancos que vivían sumidos en la pobreza pero que se sentían superiores a los negros simplemente por el color de su piel.

whitebait ['waɪtbeɪt] N (*gen pl*) espadines *mpl*, chanquetes *mpl*.

whitebeam ['waɪtbiːm] N mojera f.

whiteboard ['waɪtbɔːd] N pizarra f vileda, pizarra f blanca.

white-collar ['waɪtˌkɒləʳ] ADJ *worker* de cuello blanco; *crime* de guante blanco.

white elephant ['waɪt'elɪfənt] N maula f, cosa f dispendiosa e inútil.

white-faced ['waɪt'feɪst] ADJ blanco (como papel).

whitefish ['waɪtfɪʃ] N (*species*) corégono m; (*collectively*) pescado m magro, pescado m blanco.

whitefly ['waɪtˌflaɪ] N mosca f blanca.

whole-grain ['həʊlgreɪn] ADJ *bread, cereal* integral.

white-haired ['waɪt'hɛəd] ADJ, **white-headed** ['waɪt'hedɪd] ADJ de cabeza blanca, de pelo blanco; **~ boy*** favorito m, protegido m.

Whitehall [ˌwaɪt'hɔːl] N (*fig*) el gobierno británico.

WHITEHALL

ⓘ **Whitehall** *es la calle de Londres que va desde* **Trafalgar Square** *al Parlamento* (**Houses of Parliament**), *calle en la que se hallan la mayoría de los ministerios. Su nombre se usa con frecuencia para referirse conjuntamente a la Administración* (**Civil Service**) *y a los ministerios, cuando se trata de sus funciones administrativas.*

---

white-hot ['waɪt'hɒt] ADJ candente, calentado al blanco.

whiten ['waɪtn] 1 VT blanquear.
2 VI blanquear; (*person*) palidecer, ponerse pálido.

whitener ['waɪtnəʳ] N blanqueador m.

whiteness ['waɪtnɪs] N blancura f.

whitening ['waɪtnɪŋ] N (*chalk etc*) tiza f; (*for shoes*) blanco m para zapatos; (*whitewash*) jalbegue m.

whiteout ['waɪtaʊt] N (*Met*) resplandor m sin sombras; (*block*) bloqueo m total causado por la nieve; (*fig*) masa f confusa.

white sauce ['waɪt'sɔːs] N salsa f bechamel.

white spirit ['waɪt'spɪrɪt] N (*Brit*) trementina f.

whitethorn ['waɪtθɔːn] N espino m.

whitethroat ['waɪtθrəʊt] N curruca f zarcera.

whitewash ['waɪtwɒʃ] 1 N (a) jalbegue m.
(b) (*fig*) blanqueo m.
2 VT (a) enjalbegar, encalar, blanquear.
(b) (*fig*) blanquear.
(c) (*Sport**) dejar en blanco, dar un baño a*.

whither ['wɪðəʳ] ADV (*liter*) ¿adónde?

whiting¹ ['waɪtɪŋ] N (*colouring*) tiza f, blanco m de España; blanco m para zapatos.

whiting² ['waɪtɪŋ] N, PL INVAR (*Fish*) pescadilla f.

whitish ['waɪtɪʃ] ADJ blanquecino, blancuzco.

whitlow ['wɪtləʊ] N panadizo m.

Whitsun ['wɪtsn] 1 N Pentecostés m.
2 ATTR de Pentecostés.

Whitsuntide ['wɪtsntaɪd] 1 N Pentecostés m.
2 ATTR de Pentecostés.

whittle ['wɪtl] VT cortar pedazos a (con un cuchillo), tallar.
◆**whittle away, whittle down** VT reducir poco a poco, rebajar gradualmente.

whiz(z)* [wɪz] N as* m; **he's a ~ at tennis** es un as del tenis.

whizz [wɪz] 1 N silbido m, zumbido m.
2 VI silbar, zumbar; (*arrow*) rehilar; **to ~ along, to go ~ing along** ir como una bala; **it ~ed past my head** pasó (silbando) muy cerca de mi cabeza; **me rozó casi la cabeza al pasar; the sledge ~ed down the slope** el trineo bajó la cuesta a gran velocidad.

whizzkid* ['wɪzkɪd] N chico m prodigio.

WHO N ABBR of **World Health Organization** Organización f Mundial de la Salud, OMS f.

who [huː] PRON (a) (*interrog*) quién; **~ is it ?** ¿quién es?; **~ are they ?** ¿quiénes son?; **I know ~ it was** yo sé quién fue; **~ do you think you are?** ¿quién se cree Vd que es?; **~ does she think she is?** ¿qué derecho se cree tener para hacer (*etc*) eso?; **'W~'s W~'** 'Quién es Quién'; **you'll soon get to know ~'s ~ in the office** pronto sabrás quién es quién en la oficina; **~ should it be but Jaimito?** y henos aquí a Jaimito, y como por milagro aparece Jaimito.
(b) (= *whom*) **~ are you looking for?** ¿a quién buscas?
(c) (*rel*) que; el (*etc*) que, quien; **my cousin ~ plays the accordion** mi primo que toca el acordeón; **he ~ wishes to ...** el que quiera ...; **those ~ swim** los que nadan; **deny it ~ may** niéguelo quien quiera, aunque habrá quien lo niegue.

whoa [wəʊ] INTERJ ¡so!

who'd [huːd] = **who had; who would**.

whodun(n)it* [huːˈdʌnɪt] N novela f policíaca.

whoever [huːˈevəʳ] PRON (a) (*rel*) quienquiera que, cualquiera que; **~ finds it can keep it** quienquiera que lo encuentre puede quedarse con él; **I'll talk to ~ it is** hablaré con quien sea; **~ said that was an idiot** el que dijo eso fue un imbécil; **ask ~ you like** pregúntaselo a cualquiera, pregúntaselo a quien te parezca bien; **I was told as much by Count A or Baron B or ~** me lo dijo el conde A o el barón

---

┌─ **WHO, WHOM** ──────────────────────────────── *see also main entries* ─┐

In direct and indirect questions

• In direct and indirect questions as well as after expressions of (un)certainty and doubt (e.g. *no sé*), translate *who* using *quién/quiénes* when it is the subject of a verb:

  Who broke the window?
  ¿Quién rompió la ventana?
  She had no idea who her real parents were
  Ignoraba quiénes eran sus verdaderos padres

• When *who/whom* is the object of a verb or preposition, translate using *quién/quiénes* preceded by personal *a* or another preposition as relevant:

  Who(m) did you call?
  ¿A quién llamaste?
  Who(m) is she going to marry?
  ¿Con quién se va a casar?
  You must tell me who you are going to go out with
  Tienes que decirme con quién/quiénes vas a salir

In exclamations

• Translate using *quién/quiénes* with an accent as in the interrogative form:

  Who would have thought it!
  ¡Quién lo hubiera pensado!

As relative

• When *who/whom* follows the noun it refers to, the most common translation is *que*:

  Do you recognize the three girls who have just come in?
  ¿Reconoces a las tres chicas que acaban de entrar?
  Peter, who was at the match, has told me all about it
  Pedro, que estuvo en el partido, me lo ha contado todo
  That man (who) you saw wasn't my father
  El hombre que viste no era mi padre

! Unlike *who(m)*, *que* cannot be omitted. Personal *a* is not used before *que*.

"Who" as subject of a verb

• When *who* is the subject, *que* can sometimes be substituted by *el cual/la cual* or *quien* (singular) and *los cuales/las cuales* or *quienes* (plural). This can help avoid ambiguity:

  I ran into Ian and Sue, who had just come back from Paris
  Me encontré con Ian y con Sue, la cual or quien acababa de regresar de París

• You can only substitute *quien* or *el cual etc* for *que* in cases where the *who* clause provides additional information rather than defining the person in question. In these cases the sentence still makes sense if you omit the *who* clause:

  In Leeds, I bumped into Paul and Dorothy

• Only *que* is possible in cases where subject *who* can be substituted by *that*, i.e. where *who* defines the person in question and the sentence does not make sense if you omit the *who* clause:

  The little boy who won the cycle race is Sarah's nephew
  El niñito que ganó la carrera ciclista es el sobrino de Sarah

"Who(m)" as object of a verb or preposition

• When *who(m)* is the object of a verb, you can translate it using *que* as above. Alternatively, especially in formal language, use personal *a + quien/quienes* or personal *a + ARTICLE + cual/cuales etc* or personal *a + ARTICLE + que*:

  The woman (who or whom) you're describing is my music teacher
  La señora que or a quien or a la cual or a la que describes es mi profesora de música

"Who(m)" as object of a preposition

• After prepositions, you should usually use *que* or *cual* preceded by the article or *quien*:

  This is the girl (who or whom) I talked to you about
  Ésta es la chica de la que or de la cual or de quien te hablé

The one(s) who, those who

• Translate using *el que/la que* in the singular and *los que/las que* in the plural:

  This officer is the one who helped me
  Este policía es el que me ayudó
  Those who don't book ahead won't get seats
  Los que no hagan la reserva con tiempo se quedarán sin entradas

NOTE: *Quien/quienes* are usually also possible, but are used less commonly.

For further uses and examples, see main entry at **who** *and* **whom**.

B o el que fuera.
(b) (*interrog*) ¿quién?; **~ can have told you that?** ¿quién diablos te dijo eso?
whole [həʊl] **1** ADJ **(a)** (*entire*) todo, entero; total; íntegro; **~ milk** leche *f* sin desnatar; **~ note** (*US*) semibreve *f*; **~ number** número *m* entero; **the ~ world** el mundo entero; **she swallowed it ~** se lo tragó entero; **a pig roasted ~** un cerdo asado entero; **along its ~ length** por todo el largo; **is that the ~ truth?** ¿me has contado toda la verdad?; **but the ~ man eludes us** pero el hombre en su totalidad se nos escapa; **but the ~ purpose was to ...** pero la única finalidad era de ...; **a ~ lot of people will be glad** muchísimas personas se alegrarán.
(b) (*unbroken*) sano; ileso, intacto; **not a cup was left ~ after the party** después de la fiesta no quedó copa sana; **to our surprise he came back ~** con gran sorpresa nuestra volvió ileso.
2 N todo *m*; total *m*; conjunto *m*, totalidad *f*; **nearly the ~ of our production** casi toda nuestra producción; **the ~ of Madrid** todo Madrid; **the ~ of his works** todas sus obras, la totalidad de sus obras; **the ~ and its parts** el todo y sus partes; **as a ~** en su totalidad, en conjunto; **on the ~** en general, por regla general.
wholefood(s) [ˈhəʊlfuːd(z)] **1** N comida *f* naturista, alimentos *mpl* integrales.
2 ATTR: **~ restaurant** restaurante *m* naturista.
whole-grain [ˈhəʊlɡreɪn] ADJ *bread, cereal* integral.
wholehearted [ˈhəʊlˈhɑːtɪd] ADJ entusiasta, incondicional, cien por cien.
wholeheartedly [ˈhəʊlˈhɑːtɪdlɪ] ADV con entusiasmo, incondicionalmente, cien por cien.
wholeheartedness [ˈhəʊlˈhɑːtɪdnɪs] N entusiasmo *m*.
wholemeal [ˈhəʊlmiːl] ADJ (*Brit*) integral; **~ bread** pan *m* integral; **~ flour** harina *f* integral.
wholeness [ˈhəʊlnɪs] N totalidad *f*; integridad *f*.
▼ **wholesale** [ˈhəʊlseɪl] **1** N venta *f* al por mayor.
▼ **2** ATTR **(a)** **~ dealer**, **~ trader** comerciante *mf* al por mayor, mayorista *mf*; **~ price** precio *m* al por mayor; **~ price index** índice *m* de precios al por mayor; **~ trade** comercio *m* al por mayor.
(b) (*fig*) en masa; general; **~ destruction** destrucción *f* general.
3 ADV **(a) to buy ~** comprar al por mayor; **to sell sth ~** vender algo al por mayor.
(b) (*fig*) masivo, en masa; sin hacer distinción de personas (*etc*); **the books were burnt ~** los libros fueron quemados en masa.
wholesaler [ˈhəʊlˌseɪlər] N comerciante *mf* al por mayor, mayorista *mf*.
wholesaling [ˈhəʊlseɪlɪŋ] N venta *f* al por mayor.
wholesome [ˈhəʊlsəm] ADJ sano, saludable.
wholesomeness [ˈhəʊlsəmnɪs] N lo sano, lo saludable.
whole-wheat [ˈhəʊlwiːt] ADJ de trigo integral, hecho con trigo entero.
who'll [huːl] = who will; who shall.
wholly [ˈhəʊlɪ] ADV enteramente, completamente.
whom [huːm] PRON **(a)** (*interrog*) a quién; **~ did you see?** ¿a quién viste?; **of ~ are you talking?** ¿de quién hablas?; **I know of ~ you are talking** sé de quién hablas; **from ~ did you receive it?** ¿de quién lo recibiste?
(b) (*rel*) que, a quien; **the lady ~ I saw** la señora a quien vi; **the lady with ~ I was talking** la señora con quien hablaba; **three policemen, all of ~ were drunk** tres policías, todos borrachos; **three policemen, none of ~ wore a helmet** tres policías, ninguno de los cuales llevaba casco.
whomever [huːmˈevər] PRON V **whoever**.
whoop [huːp] **1** N alarido *m*, grito *m*; **with a ~ of joy** con un grito de alegría.
2 VT: **to ~ it up*** divertirse ruidosamente; echar una cana al aire.
3 VI gritar, dar alaridos.
whoopee [wʊˈpiː] **1** EXCL ¡estupendo!
2 N juerga *f*, guateque *m*; **to make ~*** divertirse una barbaridad*; **~ cushion** artículo de broma (cojín *m* de ventosidades).
whooping-cough [ˈhuːpɪŋˌkɒf] N tos *f* ferina, coqueluche *f*.
whoops [wuːps] EXCL ¡epa!, ¡lep!
whoosh [wʊ(ː)ʃ] N ruido del agua etc que sale bajo presión, o del viento fuerte; **it came out with a ~** salió con mucho ruido; salió de repente.
whop: [wɒp] VT pegar.
whopper* [ˈwɒpər] N (*big thing*) cosa *f* muy grande; (*lie*) mentirón *m*, embuste *m*; **that fish is a ~** ese pez es enorme; **what a ~!** ¡qué enorme!
whopping* [ˈwɒpɪŋ] ADJ enorme, muy grande, grandísimo.
whore [hɔːr] **1** N puta *f*.
2 VI (*also* **to go whoring**) putañear, putear.
who're [huːər] = who are.
whorehouse [ˈhɔːhaʊs] N, PL **whorehouses** [ˈhɔːˌhaʊzɪz] (*US*) casa *f* de putas.
whorl [wɜːl] N (*of shell*) espira *f*; (*Bot*) verticilo *m*; (*Tech*) espiral *f*.

whortleberry [ˈwɜːtlˌbərɪ] N arándano *m*.
who's [huːz] = who is; who has.
whose [huːz] **1** PRON (*interrog*) ¿de quién; **~ is this?** ¿de quién es esto?, ¿a quién pertenece esto?; **I know ~ it was** sé de quién era.
2 ADJ **(a)** (*interrog*) ¿de quién?; **~ car did you go in?** ¿en qué coche fuiste?; **~ fault was it?** ¿quién tuvo la culpa?; **~ umbrella did you take?** ¿de quién es el paraguas que tomaste?
(b) (*rel*) cuyo; **the man ~ hat I took** el hombre cuyo sombrero tomé; **the man ~ seat I sat in** el hombre en cuya silla me senté; **those ~ passports I have** aquellas personas cuyos pasaportes tengo.

| **WHOSE** | *see also main entry* |

In direct and indirect questions
- *Whose* in direct questions as well as after report verbs and expressions of doubt (e.g. *no sé*) translates as *de quién/de quiénes*, (*never cuyo*):
  Whose coat is this?
  ¿De quién es este abrigo?
  He asked us whose coats they were
  Nos preguntó de quiénes eran los abrigos
  I don't know whose umbrella this is
  No sé de quién es este paraguas

As a relative
- In relative clauses *whose* can be translated by *cuyo/cuya/cuyos/cuyas* and must agree with the following noun:
  The man whose daughter is a friend of Emily's works for the Government
  El señor cuya hija es amiga de Emily trabaja para el Gobierno
  ...the house whose roof collapsed...
  ...la casa cuyo tejado se hundió...
  NOTE: When *whose* refers to more than one noun, make *cuyo* agree with the first:
  ...a party whose policies and strategies are very extremist...
  ...un partido cuya política y tácticas son muy extremistas...
- However, *cuyo* is not much used in spoken Spanish. Try using another structure instead:
  My daughter, whose short story won a prize in the school competition, wants to be a journalist
  Mi hija, a quien premiaron por su relato en el concurso de la escuela, quiere ser periodista
  ! There is no accent on *quien* here, as it is a relative pronoun.
  For further uses and examples, see main entry.

---

whosis [ˈhuːzɪs] N (*US*) **(a)** (*thing*) cosa *f*, chisme *m*, chifurrio* *m*. **(b)** (*person*) fulano *m*, -a *f*, cómo-se-llame *m*.
whosoever [ˌhuːsəʊˈevər] = **whoever**.
who've [huːv] = who have.
whozis [ˈhuːzɪs] N (*US*) = **whosis**.
whse ABBR of **warehouse**.
▼ **why** [waɪ] **1** ADV ¿por qué?, ¿para qué?; ¿por qué razón?; ¿con qué objeto?; **~ not?** ¿por qué no?, ¿cómo no?; **~ did you do it?** ¿por qué lo hiciste?; **~ on earth didn't you tell me?** ¿por qué demonios no me lo dijiste?; **I know ~ you did it** sé por qué lo hiciste; **~ he did it we shall never know** no sabremos nunca por qué razón lo hizo; **that's ~ I couldn't come** por eso no pude venir, ésa es la razón por la que no pude venir; **which is ~ I am here** razón por la cual estoy aquí.
2 INTERJ ¡cómo!, ¡toma!; **~, what's the matter?** bueno, ¿qué pasa?; **~, it's you!** ¡toma, eres tú!; **~, there are 8 of us!** ¡si somos 8!; **~, it's easy!** ¡vamos, es muy fácil!
3 N porqué *m*; causa *f*, razón *f*.
whyever [ˈwaɪˈevər] ADV: **~ did you do it?** ¿por qué demonios lo hiciste?
WI (a) ABBR of **West Indies** Antillas *fpl*. **(b)** N (*Brit*) ABBR of **Women's Institute**. **(c)** (*US Post*) ABBR of **Wisconsin**.
wick [wɪk] N mecha *f*; **he gets on my ~:** me hace subir por las paredes*; **to dip one's ~:** echar un polvo:.
wicked [ˈwɪkɪd] ADJ **(a)** (*iniquitous*) malo, malvado; perverso; inicuo; **you're a ~ man** (*hum*) eres muy malo; **that was a ~ thing to do** eso fue inicuo.
(b) (*fig*) *satire etc* muy mordaz, cruel; *temper* muy vivo; (*very bad*) horroroso, horrible, malísimo; **a ~ waste** un despilfaro escandaloso; **it's ~ weather** hace un tiempo horrible; **it's a ~ car to start** este coche es horrible para arrancar.
(c) (:) de puta madre:.
wickedly [ˈwɪkɪdlɪ] ADV mal; perversamente; inicuamente; cruelmente; horriblemente.
wickedness [ˈwɪkɪdnɪs] N maldad *f*; perversidad *f*; iniquidad *f*; crueldad *f*; **all manner of ~** toda clase de maldades.
wicker [ˈwɪkər] **1** N mimbre *m or f*.
2 ATTR de mimbre.

➤ LANGUAGE IN USE: **wholesale: 2a** → 20.1   **why: 1** → 1.1, 17.1, 26.3

wickerwork ['wɪkəwɜːk] **1** N artículos *mpl* de mimbre; cestería *f*; (*of chair etc*) rejilla *f*.
2 ATTR de mimbre.

```
┌─WHY──────────────────────────────┤see also main entry├─┐
```

- *Why* can usually be translated by *por qué*:
  Why didn't you come?
  ¿Por qué no viniste?
  . They asked her why she hadn't finished her report
  Le preguntaron por qué no había terminado el informe
  ! Remember the difference in spelling between *por qué* (why) and *porque* (because).

- To ask specifically about the *purpose* of something, you can translate *why* using *para qué*, more commonly used to translate *what* :
  Why go if we are not needed?
  ¿Para qué vamos a ir si no nos necesitan?

- In statements, you can translate (*the reason*) *why* using *por qué*, *la razón* (*por la que*) or *el motivo* (*por el que*):
  Tell me (the reason) why you don't want to accept the proposal
  Dime por qué o la razón por la que o el motivo por el que no quieres aceptar la propuesta

- Translate *that's why* using *por eso* or *ésa es la razón por la que* or *ése es el motivo por el que*:
  That's why they wouldn't pay
  Por eso no quisieron pagar ◊ Ésa es la razón por la que o Ése es el motivo por el que no quisieron pagar

- Like all question words in Spanish, *porqué* can function as a masculine noun. Note that in *el porqué*, *porqué* is written as one word:
  I'd like to know why he's absent *or* the reason for his absence
  Me gustaría saber el porqué de su ausencia
  For further uses and examples, see main entry.

```
└──────────────────────────────────────────────────────┘
```

---

wicket ['wɪkɪt] N (*gate*) postigo *m*, portillo *m*; (*Cricket*: *stumps*) palos *mpl*, (*pitch*) área *f*, terreno *m*; **to be on a sticky ~** estar en una situación difícil; *ver también* CRICKET .
wicket keeper ['wɪkɪt'kiːpəʳ] N (*Cricket, Baseball*) guardameta *m*.
wide [waɪd] **1** ADJ **(a)** ancho; extenso, vasto; *gap* grande, muy abierto; *difference* grande, considerable; *understanding etc* amplio; **it is 3 metres ~** tiene 3 metros de ancho; **how ~ is it?** ¿cuánto tiene de ancho?; **eyes ~ with fear** ojos muy abiertos de miedo; **the ~ plains of Castile** las extensas llanuras de Castilla; **the ~ world** el ancho mundo; **his ~ knowledge of the subject** sus amplios conocimientos del tema.
(b) **~ boy*** (*Brit*) astuto *m*, taimado *m*.
2 ADV lejos; extensamente; **far and ~** por todas partes; **to be ~ open** estar muy abierto, (*door etc*) estar abierto de par en par; **to be ~ open to criticism** estar expuesto a ser criticado de todos lados; **to open one's eyes ~** abrir mucho los ojos; **to fling the door ~** abrir la puerta de par en par; **they are set ~ apart** están puestos muy lejos uno de otro, están muy apartados; **the shot went ~** el tiro no dio en el blanco.
-wide [waɪd] ADJ *ending in compounds*: **nation-~** por toda la nación, a escala nacional; de toda la nación; **a country-~ inquiry** una investigación a escala nacional.
wide-angle ['waɪdˌæŋgl] ADJ *lens etc* granangular.
wide-awake ['waɪdə'weɪk] ADJ completamente despierto; (*fig*) despabilado; vigilante, alerta.
wide-bodied ['waɪd'bɒdɪd] ADJ (*Aer*) de fuselaje ancho.
wide-eyed ['waɪd'aɪd] ADJ con los ojos desorbitados, con los ojos desmesuradamente abiertos; (*fig*) inocente, cándido.
widely ['waɪdlɪ] ADV extensamente; generalmente; **to travel ~** viajar extensamente; viajar por muchos países (*etc*); **it is ~ believed that ...** por todas partes se cree que ...; **the opinion is ~ held** es una creencia general; **a ~-known author** un autor generalmente conocido; **a ~-read student** un estudiante que ha leído mucho.
widen ['waɪdn] **1** VT ensanchar; ampliar, extender.
2 VI (*also ~ out*) ensancharse; **the passage ~s out into a cave** el pasillo se ensancha para formar una caverna.
wideness ['waɪdnɪs] N anchura *f*; extensión *f*, amplitud *f*.
wide-ranging ['waɪdˌreɪndʒɪŋ] ADJ *survey etc* de gran alcance, de amplia extensión; *interests* múltiples, muy diversos.
wide-screen ['waɪdskriːn] ADJ *film* para pantalla ancha; **~ TV** televisión *f* con pantalla panorámica.
widespread ['waɪdspred] ADJ **(a)** extendido; **with arms ~** con los brazos extendidos, con los brazos abiertos.
(b) (*fig*) extenso, amplio; muy difundido, general; **to become ~** extenderse, generalizarse; **there is ~ fear that ...** muchos temen que ...; **knowledge of this is now ~** el conocimiento de esto está muy difundido ahora.
widgeon ['wɪdʒən] N ánade *m* silbón.

widget* ['wɪdʒɪt] N (*esp US*: *device*) artilugio *m*; (*thingummy*) ingenio *m*, cacharro* *m*.
widow ['wɪdəu] **1** N viuda *f*; **~'s pension** viudedad *f*; **W~ Twankey** la viuda de Twankey; **I'm a golf ~** paso mucho tiempo sola mientras mi marido juega al golf; **all the cricket ~s got together for tea** las mujeres cuyos maridos estaban jugando al críquet se reunieron para tomar el té; **to be left a ~** enviudar, quedar viuda.
2 VT dejar viuda (*or* viudo); **she was twice ~ed** quedó viuda dos veces; **his ~ed mother** su madre viuda; **she has been ~ed for 5 years** enviudó hace 5 años, lleva 5 años de viuda.
widowed ['wɪdəud] ADJ viudo.
widower ['wɪdəuəʳ] N viudo *m*.
widowhood ['wɪdəuhud] N viudez *f*.
width [wɪdθ] N anchura *f*; extensión *f*, amplitud *f*; (*of cloth*) ancho *m*; **to be 6 centimetres in ~** tener 6 centímetros de ancho; **to swim a ~** hacer un ancho (de la piscina).
widthways ['wɪdθweɪz] ADV, **widthwise** ['wɪdθwaɪz] ADV de canto.
wield [wiːld] VT *pen, sword etc* manejar; *sceptre* empuñar; *power* ejercer, poseer; **to ~ a pen in the service of ...** menear cálamo al servicio de ...
wiener schnitzel ['viːnəʳʃnɪtsəl] N escalope *m* de ternera con guarnición.
wienie ['wiːnɪ] N (*US Culin*) = **weenie**.
wife [waɪf] N, PL **wives** [waɪvz] mujer *f*, esposa *f*; **the ~*** la parienta*; **'The Merry Wives of Windsor'** 'Las alegres comadres de Windsor'; **~'s earned income** ingresos *mpl* de la mujer; **this is my ~** ésta es mi mujer; **my boss and his ~** mi jefe y su esposa; **to take a ~** casarse; **to take sb to ~** casarse con una, contraer matrimonio con una.
wifely ['waɪflɪ] ADJ de esposa, de mujer casada.
wife-swapping ['waɪfˌswɒpɪŋ] N cambio *m* de pareja.
wig [wɪg] N peluca *f*.
wigeon ['wɪdʒən] N ánade *m* silbón.
wigging* ['wɪgɪŋ] N (*Brit*) peluca* *f*, rapapolvo* *m*, bronca *f*; **to give sb a ~** echar una peluca a uno*.
wiggle ['wɪgl] **1** N meneo *m*; (*in walking*) contoneo *m*; **to walk with a ~** contonearse, caminar contoneándose.
2 VT menear; *hips etc* mover mucho.
3 VI menearse rápidamente; moverse mucho; (*in walking*) contonearse, caminar contoneándose.
wiggly ['wɪglɪ] ADJ que se menea, que se mueve mucho; *line* ondulado.
wight [waɪt] N (†† *or hum*) criatura *f*; (*luckless ~, sorry ~*) pobre hombre *m*.
wigmaker ['wɪgˌmeɪkəʳ] N peluquero *m*.
wigwam ['wɪgwæm] N wigwam *m*, tipi *m*.
wilco [ˌwɪl'kəu] ADV (*Telec*) ¡procedo!
wild [waɪld] **1** ADJ **(a)** (*not domesticated*) *animal, man* salvaje; *flower, plant* silvestre; campestre, de los campos; *country* agreste, difícil, bravo; **~ beast** fiera *f*; **~ beast show** espectáculo *m* de fieras; **~ card** comodín *m* (*also Comput*); **~ character** carácter *m* comodín; **~ child** (*Brit*) niña-mujer *f* rebelde, lolita* *f*; **~ oat** avena *f* silvestre; **to sow one's ~ oats** (*fig*) correrla, pasar las mocedades; **~ rabbit** conejo *m* de monte; **~ and woolly** rústico, tosco; **to grow ~** crecer libre, crecer sin cultivo; **to run ~** (*plant*) volver al estado silvestre.
(b) (*of cruel disposition*) feroz, fiero, bravo; *horse* sin domar, cerril.
(c) (*rough*) *wind etc* furioso, violento; *weather* tormentoso; *sea* bravo; **it was a ~ night** fue una noche de tormenta.
(d) (*unrestrained, disordered*) *child* desmandado, desgobernado; *laughter, party, enthusiasm etc* loco; **W~ West** el oeste norteamericano (*bajo su aspecto heroico*); **he was ~ in his youth, he had a ~ youth** tuvo una juventud desordenada; **to lead a ~ life** vivir desenfrenadamente; **the room was in ~ disorder** el cuarto estaba en el mayor desorden; **they were ~ times** fue un período turbulento, fueron años alborotados; **to run ~** (*children*) vivir como salvajes; **that dog is running ~** ese perro está sin controlar.
(e) *person* loco, insensato; frenético; **to be ~ about sb** andar loco por uno; **to be ~ with joy** estar loco de alegría; **to be ~ with sb** estar furioso contra uno; **it drives me ~, it makes me ~** me saca de quicio, me hace rabiar; **it drives them ~ with desire** las pone muy cachondas; **to get ~** ponerse furioso, ponerse negro; **he has ~ eyes** tiene ojos de loco; **the crowd went ~** la multitud se puso loca (*with excitement* de emoción); **I'm not exactly ~ about it*** la idea no me llena de entusiasmo que digamos.
(f) (*rash, ill-judged*) extravagante, estrafalario; disparatado, descabellado; fantástico; **there was some ~ talk** se propusieron unas ideas estrafalarias, se dijeron cosas insensatas; **it's a ~ exaggeration** es una enorme exageración; **to make a ~ guess** hacer una conjetura extravagante; **he had some ~ scheme for ...** tuvo algún proyecto disparatado de ...
2 N tierra *f* virgen, tierra *f* poco poblada (*or poco conocida*); soledad *f*, yermo *m*; **the call of the ~** la atracción de la soledad, el encanto de las tierras vírgenes; **it's a pet and couldn't live in the ~** es un

animal doméstico que no podría vivir en la naturaleza; **when do they breed in the ~?** ¿cuándo se reproducen en estado natural?; **to go out into the ~s** ir a vivir en tierras poco conocidas; **they live out in the ~s of Berkshire** viven en lo más remoto de Berkshire.

wildcat ['waɪld'kæt] **1** N **(a)** (*Zool*) gato *m* montés. **(b)** (*for oil*) perforación *f* de sondaje en tierra virgen.

2 ATTR: **~ strike** huelga *f* salvaje; **~ scheme** proyecto *m* descabellado, proyecto *m* arriesgado; **~ venture** proyecto *m* arriesgado.

3 VI (*US*) hacer perforaciones para extraer petróleo.

wildebeest ['wɪldɪbiːst] N ñu *m*.

wilderness ['wɪldənɪs] N desierto *m*, yermo *m*, soledad *f*; (*virgin land*) tierra *f* virgen; **a ~ of ruins** un desierto de ruinas, una infinidad de ruinas; **he spent 4 years in the ~ before returning to power** pasó 4 años en el desierto antes de volver al poder.

wild-eyed ['waɪld'aɪd] ADJ de mirada salvaje.

wildfire ['waɪld,faɪər] N: **to spread like ~** propagarse como la pólvora, correr como un reguero de pólvora.

wildfowl ['waɪldfaʊl] NPL aves *fpl* de caza, (*esp*) ánades *mpl*.

wildfowler ['waɪld,faʊlər] N cazador *m* de ánades.

wildfowling ['waɪld,faʊlɪŋ] N caza *f* de ánades.

wild-goose chase [,waɪld'guːstʃeɪs] N empresa *f* desatinada, búsqueda *f* inútil.

wildlife ['waɪldlaɪf] N fauna *f* (y flora *f*); **~ park**, **~ reserve** reserva *f* natural; **~ trust** asociación *f* protectora de la naturaleza.

wildly ['waɪldlɪ] ADV *blow etc* (*of wind*) furiosamente, violentamente; *live* desordenadamente, de modo alborotado; *behave* de modo indisciplinado; (*madly*) locamente, insensatamente; frenéticamente; *act* sin reflexión; **to be ~ happy** estar loco de contento; **to shoot ~** disparar sin apuntar; **to hit out ~** repartir golpes a tontas y a locas; **to talk ~** (*loosely*) hablar sin ton ni son, hablar incoherentemente, (*extravagantly*) hablar como un loco; **she looked ~ from one to another** miró con ojos espantados a uno y a otro; **you're guessing ~** haces conjeturas sin pensar; **to clap ~** aplaudir frenéticamente; **to dash about ~** correr como un loco de aquí para allá.

wildness ['waɪldnɪs] N (*V adj*) **(a)** estado *m* salvaje, lo salvaje; estado *m* silvestre; lo agreste, lo difícil; braveza *f*.

(b) ferocidad *f*, fiereza *f*.

(c) furia *f*, violencia *f*.

(d) desgobierno *m*, desenfreno *m*; turbulencia *f*, lo alborotado.

(e) locura *f*, insensatez *f*; frenesí *m*.

(f) extravagancia *f*, lo estrafalario; lo disparatado; lo fantástico.

wiles [waɪlz] NPL engaños *mpl*, tretas *fpl*, ardides *mpl*.

wilful, (*US*) **willful** ['wɪlfʊl] ADJ *person* voluntarioso; testarudo; *child* travieso; *act* intencionado, deliberado; *murder etc* premeditado; **you have been ~ about it** has sido testarudo en esto.

wilfully, (*US*) **willfully** ['wɪlfəlɪ] ADV voluntariamente; intencionadamente; deliberadamente; con premeditación; **you have ~ ignored ...** te has obstinado en no hacer caso de ...

wilfulness, (*US*) **willfulness** ['wɪlfʊlnɪs] N voluntariedad *f*; testarudez *f*; lo travieso; lo intencionado; lo premeditado.

wiliness ['waɪlɪnɪs] N astucia *f*.

Will [wɪl] NM *familiar form of* **William**.

▼**will¹** [wɪl] V AUX **(a)** (*forming future tense*) **he ~ come** vendrá; **you won't lose it, ~ you?** ¿no lo vas a perder, eh?; **you ~ come to see us, won't you?** ¿vendrás a vernos, no?

(b) (*future emphatic*) **I ~ do it!** ¡sí lo haré!; **no he won't!** ¡no lo hará!; **I ~** (*marriage service*) sí quiero.

(c) (*wish*) querer; **no, he won't** no, no quiere; **come when you ~** ven cuando quieras; **do as you ~** haz lo que quieras, haz lo que te parezca bien; **look where you ~** mires donde mires.

(d) (*conjecture*) **that ~ be the postman** será el cartero; **she'll be about 50** tendrá como 50 años.

▼**(e)** (*consent*) **the engine won't start** el motor no arranca, el motor no quiere arrancar; **a man who ~ do that ~ do anything** un hombre que es capaz de eso es capaz de todo; **despite the doctor she ~ smoke** a pesar del médico, se empeña en fumar; **wait a moment, ~ you?** espera un momento, ¿quieres?; **won't you sit down?** ¿quiere sentarse?, siéntese, por favor; **I ~ not have it!** ¡no lo permito!; **he ~ have none of it** no lo aprueba de ningún modo, no quiere ni siquiera pensarlo; **I ~ not have it that ...** no permito que se diga que + *subj*; *see also* **have 1 (i)**.

(f) (*habit, potentiality*) **the car ~ do up to 220 kph** el coche hará hasta 220 kph; **accidents ~ happen** siempre pueden ocurrir accidentes, ocurren inevitablemente accidentes; **boys ~ be boys** así son los chicos; juventud no conoce virtud.

will² [wɪl] **1** N **(a)** (*faculty*) voluntad *f*; (*free ~*) albedrío *m*; (*wish*) voluntad *f*, placer *m*, deseo *m*; **iron ~, ~ of iron** voluntad *f* de hierro; **the ~ to win** el afán de triunfar, la voluntad de ganar; **the ~ of God** la voluntad de Dios; **against one's ~** contra su voluntad; mal de su grado; a pesar suyo, a desgana; **at ~** a voluntad; **of one's own free ~** por voluntad propia; **it is my ~ that you should do it** quiero que lo hagas; **where there's a ~ there's a way** querer es poder; **to**

do sb's ~ hacer la voluntad de uno; **Thy ~ be done** hágase tu voluntad; **she has a ~ of her own** tiene voluntad propia; **to set to work with a ~** empezar a trabajar con ilusión (*or* con entusiasmo), emprender resueltamente una tarea.

(b) V **good ~**, **ill ~**.

(c) (*testament*) testamento *m*; **the last ~ and testament of ...** la última voluntad de ...; **to make one's ~** hacer su testamento, otorgar testamento.

2 VT (PRET, PTP **willed**) **(a)** (*dispose*) querer; ordenar, disponer; **God has so ~ed it** Dios lo ha ordenado así; **if God ~s** si lo quiere Dios; **having ~ed the end we must ~ the means** quien desea el fin ordena los medios.

(b) (*urge by willpower*) lograr por fuerza de voluntad; sugestionar; **to ~ sb to do sth** sugestionar a uno para que haga algo; **I was ~ing you to win** estaba deseando mucho que ganaras, te estaba ayudando a ganar con la fuerza de mi voluntad.

(c) (*by testament*) legar, dejar en testamento; **he ~ed his pictures to the nation** legó sus cuadros a la nación.

willful ['wɪlfʊl] ADJ (*US*) *etc* = **wilful** *etc*.

William ['wɪljəm] NM Guillermo; **~ the Conqueror** Guillermo el Conquistador.

willie* [wɪlɪ] N (*Brit*) = **willy**.

willies* ['wɪlɪz] NPL: **to get the ~** pegarse un susto*, pasar horrores*; **I get the ~ whenever I think about it** me horroriza pensar en ello; **it gives me the ~** me da horror.

▼**willing** ['wɪlɪŋ] **1** ADJ **(a)** (*helpful*) servicial; complaciente; de buena voluntad, de buen corazón; (*voluntary*) espontáneo; **a ~ boy** un chico de buen corazón, un chico que trabaja (*etc*) de buena gana; **we need ~ helpers** necesitamos personas dispuestas a ayudarnos; **there were plenty of ~ hands** hubo muchos que no ayudaron espontáneamente.

▼**(b)** **to be ~** querer, querer hacerlo (*etc*); **are you ~ ?** ¿quieres?; **God ~** si Dios quiere; **I asked her and she was quite ~** se lo pedí y ella asintió gustosa; **to be ~ to do sth** estar dispuesto a hacer algo, consentir en hacer algo; **he was ~ for me to take it** me permitió llevarlo, consintió en que me lo llevase; **to be ~ that ...** consentir en que + *subj*, permitir que + *subj*.

2 N: **to show ~*** demostrar su buena voluntad.

willingly ['wɪlɪŋlɪ] ADV de buena gana, con gusto; **they ~ helped us** nos ayudaron de buena gana; **did he come ~ or by force?** ¿vino libremente o a la fuerza?; **yes, ~** sí, con mucho gusto.

willingness ['wɪlɪŋnɪs] N buena voluntad *f*, complacencia *f*; deseo *m* de servir (*or* ayudar *etc*); consentimiento *m*; **in spite of his ~ to buy it** a pesar de que estaba dispuesto a comprarlo.

will-o'-the-wisp ['wɪləðə'wɪsp] N fuego *m* fatuo; (*fig*) quimera *f*, ilusión *f*, sueño *m* imposible.

willow ['wɪləʊ] N (*also* **~-tree**) sauce *m*.

willowherb ['wɪləʊhɜːb] N adelfa *f*.

willow-pattern ['wɪləʊ,pætən] ADJ: **~ plate** plato *m* de estilo chino.

willow-warbler ['wɪləʊ,wɔːblər] N mosquitero *m* musical.

willowy ['wɪləʊɪ] ADJ (*fig*) esbelto, cimbreño.

willpower ['wɪlpaʊər] N fuerza *f* de voluntad.

Willy ['wɪlɪ] NM *familiar form of* **William**.

willy* [wɪlɪ] N colita* *f*.

willy-nilly ['wɪlɪ'nɪlɪ] ADV de grado o por fuerza, quiera o no quiera.

wilt¹†† ** [wɪlt] V **will¹.

wilt² [wɪlt] **1** VT marchitar; (*fig*) debilitar, hacer decaer.

2 VI marchitarse; (*fig*) debilitarse, decaer; (*lose courage*) perder el ánimo, desanimarse; (*of effort etc*) languidecer.

Wilts [wɪlts] N ABBR *of* **Wiltshire**.

wily ['waɪlɪ] ADJ astuto, mañoso.

WIMP* [wɪmp] N ABBR *of* **windows, icons, menus** (*or* **mice**), **pointers**.

wimp* [wɪmp] N pobre hombre *m*, burro *m*; endeble *mf*, enclenque *mf*.

◆**wimp out*** VI rajarse*, echarse para atrás*.

wimpish* ['wɪmpɪʃ] ADJ endeble, débil.

wimpishness* ['wɪmpɪʃnɪs] N lo endeble, debilidad *f*.

wimple ['wɪmpl] N griñon *m*.

wimpy* ['wɪmpɪ] = **wimpish**.

win [wɪn] **1** N victoria *f*, triunfo *m*; éxito *m*; **another ~ for Castroforte** nueva victoria del Castroforte; **their fifth ~ in a row** su quinta victoria consecutiva; **to back a horse for a ~** apostar dinero a un caballo para el primer puesto; **to have a ~** ganar, vencer; **to play for a ~** jugar para ganar.

2 (*irr*: PRET AND PTP **won**) VT **(a)** *race, cup, prize etc* ganar; *victory* llevarse; **it won him the first prize** le valió el primer premio.

(b) (*obtain*) lograr, conseguir; *sympathy, support* atraerse, captar; **how to ~ friends and influence people** cómo ganar amigos e influenciar a las personas; **to ~ sb's esteem** llegar a ser estimado por uno; **to ~ sb's favour** alcanzar el favor de uno; **to ~ sb's love** enamorar a uno; **to ~ glory** laurearse; **to ~ a reputation for honesty** granjearse una reputación de honrado.

(c) *metal* extraer (*from* de); arrancar (*from* a).

(d) he won his way to the top alcanzó la cumbre, llegó (a duras penas) a la cumbre.

⦿ **3** VI ganar; triunfar; tener éxito; **to ~ by a head** ganar por una cabeza; **if you're up against the minister you can't ~** si tienes el ministro en contra no hay manera de salir ganando; **OK, you ~** muy bien, tú ganas.

♦ **win back** VT *land etc* reconquistar, volver a conquistar; *gambling loss etc* recobrar; *support etc* volver a ganar.

♦ **win out** VI ganar, tener éxito.

♦ **win over, win round** VT *supporters etc* atraerse, conquistar; (*to an opinion*) convencer; **eventually we won him round to our point of view** por fin le persuadimos a adoptar nuestro punto de vista.

♦ **win through** VI triunfar por fin, tener al fin el éxito deseado; **to ~ through to a place** alcanzar un sitio, llegar por fin a un sitio.

wince [wɪns] **1** N mueca *f* de dolor; **he said with a ~** dijo con una mueca de dolor.

2 VI hacer una mueca de dolor, estremecerse; (*flinch*) retroceder, asustarse; **without wincing** sin pestañear.

winceyette [ˌwɪnsɪˈet] N (*Brit*) franela *f* de algodón.

winch [wɪntʃ] **1** N cabrestante *m*, torno *m*.

2 VT: **to ~ up** levantar con un torno (*etc*).

Winchester disk [ˈwɪntʃɪstəˈdɪsk] ® N disco *m* Winchester ®.

wind¹ [wɪnd] **1** N **(a)** (*gen*) viento *m*; **high ~** viento *m* fuerte; **west ~** viento *m* del oeste; **~s of change** aires *mpl* de cambio, vientos *mpl* nuevos; **that's all a lot of ~** todo eso son chorradas*; **where is the ~?, which way is the ~?** ¿de dónde sopla el viento?; **it's an ill ~ that blows nobody any good** no hay mal que por bien no venga; a río revuelto, ganancia de pescadores; **to be in the ~** (*fig*) estar en el aire, estar en preparación; **there's sth in the ~** algo flota en el aire; están tramando algo; **to get ~ of sth** llegar a saber algo, husmear algo; **to get** (*or* **have**) **the ~ up*** (*Brit*) encogérsele a uno el ombligo*; **to put the ~ up sb*** (*Brit*) meter a uno el ombligo para dentro; **it properly put the ~ up me*** (*Brit*) me dio un susto de los buenos; **to raise the ~*** conseguir fondos; **to see which way the ~ blows** esperar para ver por dónde van los tiros.

(b) (*Naut*) viento *m*; **between ~ and water** cerca de la línea de flotación; **in the teeth of the ~** contra el viento; **to run before the ~** navegar viento en popa; **to sail close to the ~** (*fig*) decir (*etc*) cosas algo peligrosas, correr riesgo de provocar un escándalo; **to take the ~ out of sb's sails** bajar los humos a uno.

(c) (*Med*) flato *m*, flatulencia *f*; (*from bowel*) pedo *m*, (*from stomach*) eructo *m*; **to break ~** ventosear, soltar un pedo; **to bring up ~** eructar.

(d) (*breath*) aliento *m*, resuello *m*; **to be short of ~** respirar con dificultad, estar corto de aliento; **to get one's second ~** volver a respirar normalmente, cobrar el aliento; (*fig*) renovar fuerzas.

(e) (*Mus*) **the ~** los instrumentos de viento.

2 ATTR: **~ energy, ~ power** energía *f* del viento, energía *f* eólica; **~ farm** parque *m* eólico; **~ instrument** instrumento *m* de viento; **~ machine** máquina *f* de viento; **~ turbine** aerogenerador *m*.

3 VT: **to ~ sb** dejar a uno sin aliento; **to be ~ed by a ball** quedar sin aliento después de ser golpeado por un balón; **to be ~ed after a race** quedar sin aliento después de una carrera.

wind² [waɪnd] (*irr*: PRET AND PTP **wound²**) **1** N **(a)** (*bend*) curva *f*, recodo *m*.

(b) to give one's watch a ~ dar cuerda al reloj; **give the handle another ~** dale otra vuelta a la manivela.

2 VT **(a)** (*wrap etc*) enrollar, envolver; *wool etc* devanar, ovillar; **to ~ one's arms round sb** enlazar a uno con los brazos, abrazar a uno estrechamente; **to ~ in a fishing line** ir cobrando sedal; **to ~ wool into a ball** ovillar lana, hacer un ovillo de lana; **~ this round your head** envuélvete la cabeza con esto, líate esto a la cabeza; **with a rope wound tightly round his waist** con una cuerda que le ceñía estrechamente la cintura.

(b) *handle* (*also* **to ~ round, to ~ up**) dar vueltas a, girar; *clock, watch, clockwork toy etc* dar cuerda a, remontar.

(c) the road ~s its way through the valley la carretera serpentea por el valle.

3 VI (*also* **to ~ along, to ~ round**) (*road etc*) serpentear; **the road ~s up the valley** el camino serpentea por el valle; **to ~ round** (*snake etc*) enroscarse; **the procession wound round the town** el desfile serpenteaba por la ciudad; **the car wound slowly up the hill** el coche subió lentamente la colina culebreando.

♦ **wind back** VT *tape etc* girar hacia atrás, rebobinar.

♦ **wind down 1** VI (*lit*) (*clock*) pararse; (*: *relax*) relajarse; desconectar; (*fig: activity, event*) tocar a su fin.

2 VT **(a)** *car window* bajar. **(b)** (*fig*) *company, department etc* reducir las actividades de (antes de cerrar); *operation* limitar progresivamente.

♦ **wind forward** VT *tape etc* girar hacia adelante.

♦ **wind off** VT devanar; desenrollar.

♦ **wind on** = **wind forward**.

♦ **wind up 1** VT **(a) to ~ sth up with a winch** levantar algo con cabrestante.

(b) *handle etc* V **wind² 2 (b)**.

(c) (*fig: nervously*) agitar, emocionar con exceso; **she's dreadfully wound up** está muy tensa; **it gets me all wound up (inside)** con esto me pongo nervioso, esto me emociona terriblemente.

(d) (*: *pull sb's leg*) tomar el pelo a*.

(e) (*end*) terminar, concluir; (*Comm*) liquidar; **he wound up his speech by saying that ...** terminó su discurso diciendo que; **the company was ordered to be wound up** se ordenó la liquidación de la sociedad.

2 VI (*handle*) V **wind² 3**.

(b) (*close*) terminar, acabar; **how does the play ~ up?** ¿cómo termina la obra?; **we wound up in Santander** fuimos a parar en Santander; **he ~s up for the government** cierra el debate por el gobierno.

windbag [ˈwɪndbæg] N saco *m* de aire; (*person*) charlatán *m*, -ana *f*.

windblown [ˈwɪndbləʊn] ADJ *leaf etc* llevado por el viento, arrancado por el viento; *hair* despeinado por el viento.

windborne [ˈwɪndbɔːn] ADJ llevado por el viento.

windbreak [ˈwɪndbreɪk] N abrigada *f*; protección *f* contra el viento, barrera *f* rompevientos, cortavientos *m*.

windbreaker [ˈwɪndˌbreɪkəʳ] N (*US*) cazadora *f*.

windburn [ˈwɪndbɜːn] N: **to get ~** curtirse al viento.

windcheater [ˈwɪndˌtʃiːtəʳ] N cazadora *f*.

windchill [ˈwɪndtʃɪl] ATTR: **the ~ factor** el efecto enfriador del viento.

wind-chimes [ˈwɪndtʃaɪmz] NPL móvil *m* de campanillas.

windcone [ˈwɪndkəʊn] N manga *f*, indicador *m* cónico de la dirección del viento.

winder [ˈwaɪndəʳ] N devanadera *f*; carrete *m*, bobina *f*.

windfall [ˈwɪndfɔːl] **1** N fruta *f* caída; (*fig*) ganancia *f* inesperada, golpe *m* de suerte inesperado, cosa *f* llovida del cielo.

2 ATTR: **~ profits** beneficios *mpl* imprevistos; **~ tax** impuesto *m* sobre los beneficios extraordinarios.

windgauge [ˈwɪndgeɪdʒ] N anemómetro *m*.

winding [ˈwaɪndɪŋ] **1** ADJ tortuoso, sinuoso, serpentino; **~ staircase** escalera *f* de caracol.

2 N (*of watch*) cuerda *f*; (*of road*) tortuosidad *f*; (*Elec*) bobinado *m*, devanado *m*; **the ~s of a river** las vueltas de un río, los meandros de un río.

winding-gear [ˈwaɪndɪŋgɪəʳ] N manubrio *m*, cabrestante *m*.

winding-sheet [ˈwaɪndɪŋʃiːt] N mortaja *f*.

winding-up [ˈwaɪndɪŋˈʌp] N conclusión *f*; (*Comm*) liquidación *f*.

windjammer [ˈwɪndˌdʒæməʳ] N buque *m* de vela (grande y veloz).

windlass [ˈwɪndləs] N torno *m*, maquinilla *f*; cabrestante *m*.

windless [ˈwɪndlɪs] ADJ sin viento.

windmill [ˈwɪndmɪl] N molino *m* (de viento); (*toy*) molinete *m*.

window [ˈwɪndəʊ] **1** N ventana *f*; (*shop ~*) escaparate *m*, vidriera *f* (*LAm*); (*of booking office etc, of envelope*) ventanilla *f*; (*of train*) ventanilla *f*; (*of car*) ventanilla *f*, cristal *m*, luna *f*, luneta *f*; (*Comput*) ventana *f*; **good sense flies out of the ~** se desvanece el buen sentido; **to lean out of the ~** asomarse a la ventana; **to look out of the ~** mirar por la ventana.

2 ATTR: **~ envelope** sobre *m* de ventanilla.

windowbox [ˈwɪndəʊbɒks] N jardinera *f* de ventana.

window-cleaner [ˈwɪndəʊˌkliːnəʳ] N limpiacristales *m*.

window-dresser [ˈwɪndəʊˌdresəʳ] N escaparatista *mf*, decorador *m*, -ora *f* de escaparates.

window-dressing [ˈwɪndəʊˌdresɪŋ] N decoración *f* de escaparates, escaparatismo *m*; (*fig*) camuflaje *m*; fachada *f*; (esfuerzo *m* por salvar las) apariencias *fpl*; (*in accounts etc*) presentación *f* de información especiosa.

window-frame [ˈwɪndəʊfreɪm] N marco *m* de ventana.

window-ledge [ˈwɪndəʊledʒ] N antepecho *m*, alféizar *m*, repisa *f* (*LAm*).

windowpane [ˈwɪndəʊpeɪn] N cristal *m*, vidrio *m* (*LAm*).

window-seat [ˈwɪndəʊsiːt] N asiento *m* junto a una ventana, (*Rail etc*) asiento *m* junto a una ventanilla.

window-shop [ˈwɪndəʊʃɒp] VI ir de escaparates.

window-shopping [ˈwɪndəʊˌʃɒpɪŋ] N: **I like ~** me gusta ir de escaparates.

windowsill [ˈwɪndəʊsɪl] N alféizar *m*, antepecho *m*.

windpipe [ˈwɪndpaɪp] N tráquea *f*.

wind-powered [ˈwɪndˌpaʊəd] ADJ impulsado por el viento, que funciona con energía eólica.

windproof [ˈwɪndpruːf] ADJ a prueba de viento.

windscreen [ˈwɪndskriːn] N, (*US*) **windshield** [ˈwɪndʃiːld] N parabrisas *m*.

windscreen-washer [ˈwɪndskriːnˈwɒʃəʳ] N, (*US*) **windshield washer** [ˈwɪndʃiːldˈwɒʃəʳ] N lavaparabrisas *m*.

windscreen-wiper [ˈwɪndskriːnˌwaɪpəʳ] N, (*US*) **windshield wiper** [ˈwɪndʃiːldˌwaɪpəʳ] N limpiaparabrisas *m*, escobilla *f*.

windsleeve ['wɪndsliːv] N, **windsock** ['wɪndsɒk] N manga *f* (de viento).

windstorm ['wɪndstɔːm] N ventarrón *m*, huracán *m*.

windsurf ['wɪndsɜːf] VI practicar el windsurf.

windsurfer ['wɪndsɜːfəʳ] N tablista *mf*, surfista *mf*.

windsurfing ['wɪndsɜːfɪŋ] N windsurf *m*, surf *m* a vela; **to go ~** hacer windsurf.

windswept ['wɪndswept] ADJ azotado por el viento, barrido por el viento; *person* despeinado.

wind-tunnel ['wɪnd,tʌnl] N túnel *m* aerodinámico, túnel *m* de pruebas aerodinámicas.

wind-up ['waɪndʌp] N (a) (*: joke) tomadura* *f* de pelo. (b) = **winding up**.

windward ['wɪndwəd] ⨐1⨐ ADJ de barlovento.
⨐2⨐ N barlovento *m*; **to ~ a** barlovento.

Windward Isles ['wɪndwəd,aɪlz] NPL Islas *fpl* de Barlovento.

windy ['wɪndɪ] ADJ (a) ventoso; *day* de mucho viento; *place* expuesto al viento; **it is ~ today** hoy hace viento; **it's ~ out here** aquí fuera el viento sopla fuerte, aquí fuera hay mucho viento; **the W~ City** Chicago *m*; *ver también* ⨐CITY NICKNAMES⨐.
(b) *speech, style etc* pomposo, hinchado.
(c) (*Brit**) **to be ~** pasar miedo; **to get ~** encogérsele a uno el ombligo*; **are you ~?** ¿tienes mieditis?*

wine [waɪn] ⨐1⨐ N vino *m*; **good ~ needs no bush** el buen paño en el arca se vende.
⨐2⨐ ATTR (*colour*) color vino.
⨐3⨐ VT: **to ~ and dine sb** dar a uno muy bien de comer y de beber, hacer grandes agasajos a uno.

wine-bar ['waɪnbɑːʳ] N bar *m* especializado en servir vinos.

winebibber ['waɪn,bɪbəʳ] N bebedor *m*, -ora *f*.

wine-bottle ['waɪn,bɒtl] N botella *f* de vino.

wine-cask ['waɪnkɑːsk] N tonel *m* de vino, barril *m* de vino.

winecellar ['waɪn,seləʳ] N bodega *f*.

wineglass ['waɪnglɑːs] N copa *f* (para vino), vaso *m* (para vino).

wine-grower ['waɪn,grəʊəʳ] N viñador *m*, -ora *f*, vinicultor *m*, -ora *f*.

wine-growing ['waɪn,grəʊɪŋ] ⨐1⨐ ADJ vinícola.
⨐2⨐ N vinicultura *f*.

winelist ['waɪnlɪst] N lista *f* de vinos.

winemanship ['waɪnmənʃɪp] N pericia *f* en vinos, oenofilia *f*.

wine-merchant ['waɪn,mɜːtʃənt] N (*Brit*) vinatero *m*, -a *f*.

winepress ['waɪnpres] N prensa *f* de uvas, lagar *m*.

winery ['waɪnərɪ] N (*US*) lagar *m*.

wineskin ['waɪnskɪn] N pellejo *m*, odre *m*.

wine-taster ['waɪn,teɪstəʳ] N catavinos *mf*, probador *m*, -ora *f* de vinos, catador *m*, -ora *f* de vinos.

wine-tasting ['waɪn,teɪstɪŋ] N cata *f* de vinos.

wine vinegar [,waɪn'vɪnɪgəʳ] N vinagre *m* de vino.

winewaiter ['waɪn,weɪtəʳ] N escanciador *m*, sumiller *m*.

wing [wɪŋ] ⨐1⨐ N ala *f*; (*Archit*) ala *f*; (*Brit Aut*) aleta *f*, guardabarros *m*; (*of chair*) cabecera *f*, oreja *f*; (*Sport: position*) ala *f*, exterior *m*, (*player*) extremo *m*, -a *f*; (*Aer: section*) escuadrilla *f*; **~s** (*Theat*) bastidores *mpl*; **left ~** (*Pol*) ala *f* izquierda; **right ~** (*Pol*) ala *f* derecha; **on the ~s of fantasy** en alas de la fantasía; **to be on the ~** estar volando; **to be on the left ~, to belong to the left ~** (*Pol*) ser de izquierdas; **to clip sb's ~s** cortar las alas a uno; **to shoot a bird on the ~** matar un pájaro al vuelo; **to stretch** (*or* **spread**) **one's ~s** (*fig*) empezar a volar; **to take ~** irse volando, alzar el vuelo; **to take sb under one's ~** tomar a uno bajo su protección; **to be waiting in the ~s** (*fig*) esperar entre bastidores.
⨐2⨐ VT (a) *bird* tocar, herir en el ala; *person* herir en el brazo.
(b) **to ~ one's way** volar, ir volando.
⨐3⨐ VI volar.

wingcase ['wɪŋkeɪs] N (*Zool*) élitro *m*.

wingchair ['wɪŋtʃeəʳ] N butaca *f* de orejas, butaca *f* orejera.

wing-collar ['wɪŋ,kɒləʳ] N cuello *m* de puntas.

wing commander ['wɪŋkə,mɑːndəʳ] N teniente *m* coronel de aviación.

wingding* ['wɪŋ,dɪŋ] N (*US*) fiesta *f* animada, guateque *m* divertido.

winged [wɪŋd] ADJ (*Zool*) alado; *seed* con alas.

-winged [wɪŋd] ADJ *ending in compounds* de alas; **brown-~** de alas pardas; **four-~** de cuatro alas.

winger ['wɪŋəʳ] N extremo *m*, -a *f*, ala *mf*.

wingless ['wɪŋlɪs] ADJ sin alas.

wing-mirror ['wɪŋ,mɪrəʳ] N (*Brit*) retrovisor *m*.

wingnut ['wɪŋnʌt] N tuerca *f* mariposa.

wingspan ['wɪŋspæn] N, **wingspread** ['wɪŋspred] N envergadura *f* (de alas).

wingtip ['wɪŋtɪp] N punta *f* del ala.

wink [wɪŋk] ⨐1⨐ N (*blink*) pestañeo *m*; (*meaningful*) guiño *m*; **I didn't get a ~ of sleep** no pegué ojo; **to give sb a ~** guiñar el ojo a uno; **to have 40 ~s** descabezar un sueño, echarse una siestecita; **he said with a ~** dijo guiñándome el ojo; **I didn't sleep a ~** no pegué ojo;

to tip sb the ~* avisar a uno clandestinamente.
⨐2⨐ VT *eye* guiñar.
⨐3⨐ VI (*blink*) pestañear; (*meaningfully*) guiñar el ojo; (*of light, star etc*) titilar, parpadear; **to ~ at sb** guiñar el ojo a uno; **to ~ at sth** (*fig*) hacer la vista gorda a algo, fingir no ver algo.

winker ['wɪŋkəʳ] N (*Brit Aut*) intermitente *m*.

winking ['wɪŋkɪŋ] ⨐1⨐ N pestañeo *m*; **it was as easy as ~** era facilísimo.
⨐2⨐ ADJ pestañeante.

winkle ['wɪŋkl] ⨐1⨐ N (*Brit*) bígaro *m*, bigarro *m*.
⨐2⨐ VT: **to ~ sb out** hacer salir a uno; **to ~ a secret out of sb** sonsacar un secreto a uno; **to ~ sth out of a crevice** sacar algo con dificultad de una grieta.

winkle-pickers ['wɪŋkl'pɪkəz] NPL (*Brit*) zapatos o botas de puntera muy estrecha.

winner ['wɪnəʳ] N (*person, horse etc*) ganador *m*, -ora *f*, vencedor *m*, -ora *f*; (*book, entry etc*) obra *f* premiada; (*Tennis: ball*) pelota *f* imposible de restar; **this disc is a ~!** ¡este disco es fabuloso!; **the tune is bound to be a ~** la melodía obtendrá seguramente un éxito; **he knew he was on** (**to**) **a ~** sabía que con ese producto (*etc*) tenía asegurado el triunfo.

winning ['wɪnɪŋ] ⨐1⨐ ADJ (a) *person, horse, team etc* vencedor, victorioso; *book, entry etc* premiado; *hit, shot* decisivo.
(b) *smile, ways etc* atractivo, encantador.
⨐2⨐ NPL: **~s** ganancias *fpl*.

winning-post ['wɪnɪŋpəʊst] N poste *m* de llegada, meta *f*.

winnow ['wɪnəʊ] VT aventar.

winnower ['wɪnəʊəʳ] N, **winnowing machine** ['wɪnəʊɪŋmə,ʃiːn] N aventadora *f*.

wino* ['waɪnəʊ] N alcohólico *m*, -a *f*.

winsome ['wɪnsəm] ADJ atractivo, encantador.

winter ['wɪntəʳ] ⨐1⨐ N invierno *m*.
⨐2⨐ ATTR de invierno, invernal; **~ clothes** ropa *f* de invierno; **~ Olympics** Olimpíada *f* de invierno; **~ quarters** cuarteles *mpl* de invierno; **~ solstice** solsticio *m* invernal; **~ sports** deportes *mpl* de invierno; **~ sports centre** (*or* **resort**) estación *f* invernal; **~ time** (*hour*) hora *f* de invierno.
⨐3⨐ VI invernar.

wintergreen ['wɪntəgriːn] N aceite *m* de gualteria.

winterize ['wɪntəraɪz] VT (*US*) adaptar para el invierno.

winterkill ['wɪntəkɪl] (*US*) ⨐1⨐ VT matar de frío.
⨐2⨐ VI perecer a causa del frío.

wintertime ['wɪntətaɪm] N invierno *m*.

wintry ['wɪntrɪ] ADJ de invierno, invernal; frío, glacial; (*fig*) glacial.

wipe [waɪp] ⨐1⨐ N (a) limpión *m*, limpiadura *f*; **to give sth a ~** (**down** *etc*) limpiar algo, pasar un trapo (*etc*) sobre algo.
(b) (:) cate* *m*, lapo* *m*.
⨐2⨐ VT limpiar; enjugar; *dishes* secar; **to ~ a table dry** secar una mesa con un trapo, enjugar una mesa; **to ~ one's brow** enjugarse la frente; **to ~ one's eyes** enjugarse las lágrimas; **to ~ a child's eyes** enjugar las lágrimas a un niño; **to ~ one's nose** sonarse (las narices).
⨐3⨐ VI secar los platos.

◆**wipe at** VT secar, enjugar.

◆**wipe away, wipe off** VT quitar con un trapo, quitar frotando.

◆**wipe down** VT limpiar.

◆**wipe out** VT (*erase*) borrar; (*suppress*) borrar, cancelar; suprimir; *debt* liquidar; *memory* borrar; (*destroy*) destruir, extirpar; (*kill off completely*) aniquilar.

◆**wipe up** VT limpiar; **to ~ up the dishes** secar los platos.

wipe-out ['waɪpaʊt] N (a) (*destruction*) aniquilación *f*, destrucción *f*.
(b) (*windsurfing*) caída *f*.

wiper ['waɪpəʳ] N (a) (*cloth*) paño *m*, trapo *m*. (b) (*Brit Aut*) limpiaparabrisas *m*, escobilla *f*.

wire ['waɪəʳ] ⨐1⨐ N (a) alambre *m*; **down to the ~*** (*US*) hasta el final, hasta la última; **to come** (*or* **get**) **in** (**just**) **under the ~*** (*US*) llegar justo a tiempo; **to get one's ~s crossed** (*fig*) sufrir un malentendido; **to pull ~s*** tocar resortes; **he can pull ~s*** tiene muchos enchufes*, tiene buenas agarraderas*.
(b) (*Telec*) telegrama *m*; **to send sb a ~** poner un telegrama a uno.
⨐2⨐ VT (a) *house* instalar el alambrado de; *fence* alambrar; **it's ~d for sound** tiene el alambrado para el sonido; **it's ~d to the alarm** está conectado a la alarma; **~d, ~ up*** (*US*) tenso, malhumorado, de mal genio.
(b) **to ~ sb** poner un telegrama a uno; **to ~ information to sb** enviar información a uno por telegrama.
⨐3⨐ VI (*poner un telegrama*) (*for sth* pidiendo algo, *to sb* a uno).

◆**wire up** VT instalar el alambrado de, cablear, alambrar; **it's all ~d up for television** se ha completado la instalación eléctrica para la televisión; *V* **wire 2**.

wire brush ['waɪə'brʌʃ] N cepillo *m* de alambre.

wirecutters ['waɪə,kʌtəz] NPL cizalla *f*, cizallas *fpl*, cortaalambres *m*.

wire-haired ['waɪəhɛəd] ADJ *dog* de pelo áspero.

wireless ['waɪəlɪs] (*esp Brit*) ① N (a) (*as science etc*) radio *f*, radiofonía *f*.
(b) (†: *set*) radio *f*, receptor *m* de radio, radiorreceptor *m*; **by ~, on the ~, over the ~** por radio; **to talk on the ~** hablar por radio.
② ATTR de radio, radiofónica; **~ message** radiograma *m*.
③ VT radiar, transmitir por radio.
④ VI: **to ~ to sb** enviar un mensaje a uno por radio.

wireless cabin ['waɪəlɪs,kæbɪn] N cabina *f* de radio.

wireless operator ['waɪəlɪs,ɒpəreɪtəʳ] N radiotelegrafista *mf*, radio *mf*.

wireless set ['waɪəlɪsset] N radio *f*, receptor *m* de radio, radio-rreceptor *m*.

wireless station ['waɪəlɪs,steɪʃən] N emisora *f*.

wire mesh ['waɪəmeʃ] N tela *f* metálica.

wire netting ['waɪə'netɪŋ] N red *f* de alambre, alambrada *f*, tela *f* metálica.

wirepuller⁕ ['waɪə,pʊləʳ] N enchufista⁕ *mf*.

wirepulling⁕ ['waɪə,pʊlɪŋ] N empleo *m* de resortes, enchufismo⁕ *m*.

wire service ['waɪə'sɜːvɪs] N (*esp US*) agencia *f* de noticias.

wiretap ['waɪətæp] VI intervenir las conexiones telefónicas, practicar escuchas telefónicas.

wiretapping ['waɪə'tæpɪŋ] N intervención *f* de las conexiones telefónicas.

wire wool ['waɪə'wʊl] N lana *f* de alambre.

wireworm ['waɪəwɜːm] N gusano *m* de elatérido.

wiring ['waɪərɪŋ] ① N alambrado *m*, cableado *m*, instalación *f* eléctrica.
② ATTR: **~ diagram** esquema *m* del alambrado.

wiry ['waɪərɪ] ADJ *person, build* delgado pero fuerte; *hand* nervudo, nervioso.

Wis., Wisc. (*US*) ABBR *of* **Wisconsin**.

wisdom ['wɪzdəm] ① N sabiduría *f*; saber *m*; prudencia *f*, juicio *m*; lo acertado, acierto *m*; **doubts were expressed about the ~ of the visit** se dudaba si era prudente hacer esta visita; **in her ~ she decided not to go** muy prudentemente decidió no ir.
② ATTR: **~ tooth** muela *f* del juicio.

▼ **wise¹** [waɪz] ADJ (a) (*learned*) sabio; (*prudent*) prudente, juicioso; *move, step etc* acertado; **a ~ man** un sabio; **~ guy**⁕ sabelotodo⁕ *m*, vivo *m*; **~ guy, huh?**⁕ ¿Vd se lo sabe todo, eh?; **the (Three) W~ Men (of the East)** los Reyes Magos; **it does not seem ~ to** + *infin* no parece aconsejable + *infin*; **you would be ~ to ask him first** sería aconsejable preguntarle primero; **the ~st thing to do is ...** lo más prudente es ...; **I'm none the ~r** sigo sin entenderlo, ahora lo entiendo menos que antes; **nobody will be any the ~r** nadie sabrá de esto, nadie se dará cuenta; **that wasn't very ~ of you** en eso no has sido muy prudente.
(b) (⁕) **to be ~ to sb** conocer el juego de uno, calar a uno; **to get ~ to sth** caer en la cuenta de algo; **to put sb ~ to sth** poner a uno al tanto de algo, informar a uno acerca de algo.
◆ **wise up**⁕ VI (*esp US*) informarse, enterarse (*to* de); ponerse al tanto (*to* de); caer en la cuenta (*to* de).

wise² [waɪz] N (††) guisa *f*, modo *m*; **in this ~** de esta guisa; **in no ~** de ningún modo.

-wise [waɪz] SUFFIX con respecto a, en cuanto a, relativo a, por lo que se refiere a; **profitwise** en cuanto a las ganancias; **how are you off money-wise?** ¿cómo estás en cuanto a dinero?

wiseacre ['waɪz,eɪkəʳ] N sabihondo *m*.

wisecrack ['waɪzkræk] ① N cuchufleta *f*, chiste *m*, salida *f*.
② VI cuchufletear; **'you weigh a ton', he ~ed** 'pesas más que un burro en brazos' dijo bromeando.

wisely ['waɪzlɪ] ADV sabiamente; prudentemente, con prudencia; acertadamente.

▼ **wish** [wɪʃ] ① N (a) (*desire, will*) deseo *m* (*for* de); ruego *m*; **according to one's ~es** según los deseos de uno; **her ~ to do it** su deseo de hacerlo; **your ~ is my command** sus deseos son órdenes para mí; **it has long been my ~ to** + *infin* desde hace mucho tiempo vengo deseando + *infin*, desde hace mucho tengo la intención de + *infin*; **to go against sb's ~es** oponerse a los deseos de uno; **the fairy granted her 3 ~es** el hada le concedió 3 deseos; **you shall have your ~** se hará lo que pides, se cumplirá tu deseo; **I have no great ~ to go** me apetece poco ir, realmente no tengo ganas de ir; **to make a ~** pensar un deseo, formular un deseo.
▼(b) **with best ~es** (*in letter*) saludos de tu amigo ..., un abrazo de ...; **with best ~es for the future** con mis augurios para el porvenir; **I went to give him my best ~es** fui a darle la enhorabuena; **please give him my best ~es** por favor dale recuerdos míos, salúdale de mi parte; **we sent a message of good ~es on Slobodian independence day** enviamos un mensaje de buenos augurios el día de independencia de Eslobodia.
② VT (a) (*desire*) desear, querer; **I do not ~ it** no lo quiero, no quiero que se haga.
▼(b) **to ~ sb good luck, to ~ sb well** desear a uno mucha suerte; **I ~ you all possible happiness** os deseo la más completa felicidad; **I**

don't ~ her ill, I don't ~ her any harm no le deseo ningún mal; **to ~ sb good morning** dar los buenos días a uno; **to ~ sb goodbye** despedirse de uno; **to ~ sb a happy Christmas** desear a uno unas Pascuas muy felices, felicitarle a uno las Pascuas.
▼(c) (*with verb complement*) **to ~ to do sth** querer hacer algo, desear hacer algo; **to ~ sb to do sth** querer que uno haga algo; **what do you ~ me to do?** ¿qué quieres que haga?; **I do ~ you'd let me help me** gustaría muchísimo que me dejaras ayudar; **I ~ she'd come** estoy deseando que venga; **I ~ed after that I had stayed till the end** después de eso sentí no haberme quedado hasta el fin; **I ~ I could!** ¡ojalá!, ¡ojalá pudiera!; **I ~ it were not so** ojalá no fuera así; **I ~ I could be there!** ¡ojalá estuviera allí!
(d) (⁕) **to ~ sth on sb** lograr que uno acepte algo que no desea; **the job was ~ed on me** me dieron el cometido sin quererlo yo, me impusieron el trabajo; **she was ~ed on us as a guest** nos impusieron que la invitáramos; **I wouldn't ~ that on anybody** eso no lo desearía para nadie.
③ VI hacer un voto; **to ~ for sth** desear algo, anhelar algo; **what more could you ~ for?** ¿qué más podría desear?; **she has everything she could ~ for** tiene todo cuanto podría desear.

wishbone ['wɪʃbəʊn] N espoleta *f*.

wishful ['wɪʃfʊl] ADJ deseoso (*to* + *infin* de + *infin*); ilusionado; **~ thinking** ilusiones *fpl*, ilusionismo *m*, espejismo *m*.

wish-fulfilment ['wɪʃfʊl'fɪlmənt] N ilusiones *fpl*, ilusionismo *m*, espejismo *m*.

wishing-bone ['wɪʃɪŋbəʊn] N espoleta *f*.

wishing well ['wɪʃɪŋ,wel] N pozo *m* de los deseos.

wish-wash⁕ ['wɪʃwɒʃ] N aguachirle *f*.

wishy-washy⁕ ['wɪʃɪ,wɒʃɪ] ADJ soso, flojo, insípido.

wisp [wɪsp] N (*fragment*) trozo *m* ligero, pedazo *m* menudo; (*trace*) vestigio *m*; (*of grass*) manojito *m*; brizna *f*; (*of hair*) mechón *m*; (*of cloud*) jirón *m*; **~ of smoke** columna *f* delgada, espiral *f* ligera.

wispy ['wɪspɪ] ADJ delgado, sutil, tenue.

wisteria [wɪs'tɪərɪə] N vistaria *f*, glicina *f*.

wistful ['wɪstfʊl] ADJ triste, melancólico; pensativo.

wistfully ['wɪstfəlɪ] ADV tristemente, con melancolía; pensativamente, **she looked at me ~** me miró pensativa.

wistfulness ['wɪstfʊlnɪs] N tristeza *f*, melancolía *f*; lo pensativo.

wit¹ [wɪt] N: **to ~** (*Jur or hum*) a saber, esto es.

wit² [wɪt] N (a) (*understanding*) inteligencia *f*, entendimiento *m*, juicio *m*; talento *m*; **a battle of ~s** una contienda entre dos inteligencias; **to be at one's ~'s end** estar para volverse loco (*wondering what to do* pensando qué hacer); **to be out of one's ~s** estar fuera de sí; **to collect** (*or* **gather**) **one's ~s** reconcentrarse; **to frighten sb out of his ~s** dar a uno un susto mortal; **to have** (*or* **keep**) **one's ~s about one** tener mucho ojo; conservar su presencia de ánimo; **he hadn't the ~ to see that ...** no tenía bastante inteligencia para comprender que ...; **to live by one's ~s** vivir del cuento, ser caballero de industria; **to sharpen one's ~s** aguzar el ingenio, despabilarse; **to use one's ~s** usar su sentido común; valerse de su ingenio.
(b) (*humour, wittiness*) ingenio *m*, agudeza *f*; sal *f*; gracia *f*; **the ~ and wisdom of Joe Soap** las agudezas y sabiduría de Joe Soap; **to have a ready** (*or* **pretty**) **~** ser ingenioso, tener chispa; **there's a lot of ~ in the book** el libro tiene mucha sal; **a story told without ~** un cuento narrado sin gracia; **in a flash of ~ he said ...** con un rasgo de ingenio dijo ...
(c) (*person*) chistoso *m*, -a *f*, persona *f* de mucha sal; (*Hist*) ingenio *m*; **an Elizabethan ~** un ingenio de la época isabelina.

witch [wɪtʃ] N bruja *f*, hechicera *f*; **~es' sabbath** aquelarre *m*.

witchcraft ['wɪtʃkrɑːft] N brujería *f*.

witchdoctor ['wɪtʃ,dɒktəʳ] N hechicero *m*.

witchery ['wɪtʃərɪ] N brujería *f*; (*fig*) encanto *m*, magia *f*.

witch-hazel ['wɪtʃ,heɪzl] N olmo *m* escocés.

witch-hunt ['wɪtʃhʌnt] N caza *f* de brujas, cacería *f* de brujas.

witching ['wɪtʃɪŋ] ATTR: **~ hour** (*hum*) hora *f* de las brujas.

with [wɪð, wɪθ] PREP (a) (*gen*) con; en compañía de; **I was ~ him** yo estaba con él; **she stayed with friends** se hospedó con unos amigos; **I'll be ~ you in a moment** un momento y estoy con vosotros; **to leave sth ~ sb** dejar algo en manos de uno; **to leave a child ~ sb** dejar a un niño al cuidado de uno; **that problem is always ~ us** ese problema sigue afectándonos, ese problema no se resuelve; **the fashion ended ~ the century** la moda terminó al terminar el siglo, la moda terminó cuando el siglo; **~ the Alcántara it is the biggest ship of its class** junto con el Alcántara es el mayor buque de su tipo; **she's good ~ children** sabe manejar a los niños, es muy buena con los niños; **I am ~ you there** en eso estoy de acuerdo contigo; **he took it away ~ him** se lo llevó consigo; **~ no sin, *eg* ~ no trouble at all** sin dificultad alguna; **I'm sorry, I'm not ~ you**⁕ lo siento, pero te he perdido⁕; **are you ~ me?**⁕ ¿me entendéis?
(b) (*descriptive*) de, con; **a house ~ big windows** una casa con grandes ventanas; **the fellow ~ the big beard** él de la barba grande; **you can't speak to the queen ~ your hat on** no se puede hablar

con la reina llevando puesto el sombrero.
(c) (*in spite of*) con; **~ all his faults** con todos sus defectos.
(d) (*according to*) según, de acuerdo con; **it varies ~ the season** varía según la estación.
(e) (*manner*) con; **~ all his might** con todas sus fuerzas; **~ all speed** a toda prisa; **~ one blow** de un solo golpe; **to cut wood ~ a knife** cortar madera con un cuchillo; **to welcome sb ~ open arms** recibir a uno con los brazos abiertos; **to walk ~ a stick** andar con un bastón.
(f) (*cause*) de; **to jump ~ joy** saltar de alegría; **to shake ~ fear** temblar de miedo; **to shiver ~ cold** tiritar de frío; **the hills are white ~ snow** las colinas están cubiertas de nieve; **to be ill ~ measles** tener sarampión; **it's pouring ~ rain** está lloviendo a cántaros; **to fill a glass ~ wine** llenar un vaso de vino.
(g) (*construction with certain words*) **the trouble ~ Harry** la dificultad con Enrique; el disgusto que hubo con Enrique; **it's a habit ~ him** es una costumbre que tiene, es cosa de él; **be honest ~ me** cuéntamelo con toda franqueza; **be honest ~ yourself** no te forjes ilusiones; **you must be patient ~ her** hay que tener paciencia con ella; **we agree ~ you** estamos de acuerdo contigo; **to fill sb ~ fear** infundir miedo a uno; llenar a uno de miedo.
(h) (*) **to be ~ it** estar al tanto, estar al día; tener ideas modernas; comprender el mundo actual, estar de acuerdo con las tendencias actuales; (*of dress etc*) estar de moda; **to get ~ it** ponerse al día, (*in dress etc*) ponerse a la moda.
withal†† [wɪ'ðɔːl] ADV además, también; por añadidura.
withdraw [wɪθ'drɔː] (*irr: V draw*) **1** VT *object* retirar, sacar, quitar (*from* de); *troops, money, stamps, ambassador etc* retirar (*from* de); *words* retractar; (*Jur*) *charge* apartar.
2 VI (*Mil etc*) retirarse (*from* de, *to* a), replegarse; (*Sport*) abandonar; (*move away*) apartarse, alejarse, irse; (*before orgasm*) dar marcha atrás; **he withdrew a few paces** se retiró unos pasos, se apartó un poco; **then they all withdrew** luego se retiraron todos; **to ~ from business** retirarse de los negocios; **to ~ from a contest** abandonar, renunciar a tomar parte en una contienda; **to ~ in favour of sb else** renunciar en favor de otro; **to ~ into o.s.** ensimismarse; **you can't ~ now** no puedes abandonar ahora.
withdrawal [wɪθ'drɔːəl] **1** N retirada *f*; retiro *m*; abandono *m*; retractación *f*; renuncia *f*; (*before orgasm*) marcha *f* atrás; **to make a ~ of funds from a bank** efectuar una retirada de fondos de un banco; **they made a rapid ~** se retiraron rápidamente.
2 ATTR: **~ notice** (*Fin*) aviso *m* de retirada de fondos; **~ symptoms** síndrome *m* de la abstinencia.
withdrawn [wɪθ'drɔːn] **1** PTP *of* **withdraw**.
2 ADJ reservado, encerrado en sí mismo, introvertido.
withe [wɪθ] N mimbre *m or f*.
wither ['wɪðəʳ] **1** VT marchitar, secar; (*fig*) aplastar; **to ~ sb with a look** aplastar (*or* fulminar) a uno con la mirada.
2 VI marchitarse, secarse.
◆**wither away** VI extinguirse.
withered ['wɪðəd] ADJ marchito, seco.
withering ['wɪðərɪŋ] ADJ *heat* abrasador; *gunfire etc* arrollador; *look, tone* fulminante; *criticism* mordaz.
witheringly ['wɪðərɪŋlɪ] ADV *say, look* desdeñosamente.
withers ['wɪðəz] NPL cruz *f* (de caballo).
withhold [wɪθ'həʊld] (*irr: V hold*) VT (*keep back*) retener; (*refuse*) negar; (*refuse to reveal*) ocultar; no revelar; **to ~ a pound of sb's pay** retener una libra del pago a uno; **to ~ one's help** negarse a ayudar a uno; **to ~ the truth from sb** no revelar la verdad a uno.
▼ **within** [wɪð'ɪn] **1** ADV dentro; **from ~** desde dentro, desde el interior.
▼**2** PREP (*inside*) dentro de; (*~ range of*) al alcance de; **here ~ the town** aquí dentro de la ciudad; **~ a radius of 10 kilometres** en un radio de 10 kilómetros; **we were ~ 100 metres of the summit** estábamos a menos de 100 metros de la cumbre, nos faltaban sólo 100 metros para llegar a la cumbre; **the village is ~ a mile of the river** el pueblo dista poco menos de una milla del pueblo; **to be ~ an inch of** estar a dos dedos de; **to be ~ call** estar al alcance de la voz; **~ the week** antes de terminar la semana; **~ a year of her death** menos de un año después de su muerte; **~ the stipulated time** dentro del plazo señalado; **to keep ~ the law** obrar dentro de la ley; **to live ~ one's income** vivir con arreglo a los ingresos; **a voice ~ me said ...** una voz interior me dijo ...
with-it* ['wɪðɪt] ADJ: **a ~ dress** un vestido a la moda.
without [wɪð'aʊt] **1** ADV (*liter*) fuera; por fuera; **from ~** desde fuera.
2 PREP sin; a falta de, en ausencia de; **~ a tie** sin corbata; **3 days ~ food** 3 días sin comer; **~ speaking** sin hablar, sin decir nada; **~ my noticing it** sin verlo yo, sin que yo lo notase; **not ~ some difficulty** no sin alguna dificultad.
with-profits ['wɪθ'prɒfɪts] ADJ: **~ endowment assurance** seguro *m* dotal con beneficios.
withstand [wɪθ'stænd] (*irr: V stand*) VT resistir a; oponerse a; aguantar.
withy ['wɪðɪ] N mimbre *m or f*.

witless ['wɪtlɪs] ADJ estúpido, tonto; **to scare sb ~** dar un susto mortal a uno.
witness ['wɪtnɪs] **1** N **(a)** (*evidence*) testimonio *m*; **in ~ of** en fe de; **in ~ whereof** en fe de lo cual; **to bear ~ to** dar fe de, atestiguar.
(b) (*person*) testigo *mf* (*also Jur*); espectador *m*, -ora *f*; **~ for the defence** testigo *mf* de descargo; **~ for the prosecution** testigo *mf* de cargo; **there were no ~es** no hubo testigos; **we want no ~es to this** no queremos que nadie vea esto, no queremos que haya testigos; **I was (a) ~ to this event** yo presencié este suceso; **to call sb as ~** citar a uno como testigo.
2 VT **(a)** (*see*) asistir a, presenciar, ser espectador de; ver; **the accident was ~ed by two people** hay dos testigos del accidente, dos personas vieron el accidente; **I have never ~ed such scenes before** no he visto nunca tales escenas; **this period ~ed important changes** este período fue testigo de cambios importantes; **to ~ sb doing sth** ver a uno que hace algo, ver cómo uno hace algo.
(b) **~ what happened when ...** ved lo que pasó cuando ..., consideren lo que pasó cuando ...; **~ the case of X** según quedó demostrado en el caso de X; **~ my hand** en fe de lo cual firmo.
(c) **to ~ a document** firmar un documento como testigo.
3 VI: **to ~ to sth** dar testimonio de algo.
witness-box ['wɪtnɪsbɒks] N, (*US*) **witness stand** ['wɪtnɪsstænd] N barra *f* de los testigos, puesto *m* de los testigos, tribuna *f* de los testigos.
witter* ['wɪtəʳ] VI (*Brit*) parlotear; **to ~ on about sth** hablar de algo sin cesar; **stop ~ing (on)!** ¿quieres callarte de una vez?
witticism ['wɪtɪsɪzəm] N agudeza *f*, chiste *m*, ocurrencia *f*, dicho *m* gracioso.
wittily ['wɪtɪlɪ] ADV ingeniosamente; con gracia, de modo divertido.
wittiness ['wɪtɪnɪs] N agudeza *f*, viveza *f* de ingenio; gracia *f*, lo divertido.
wittingly ['wɪtɪŋlɪ] ADV a sabiendas.
witty ['wɪtɪ] ADJ *person* ingenioso, chistoso, salado; *remark, speech etc* gracioso, divertido, ocurrente; **he's very ~** tiene mucha gracia, es un tipo muy salado.
wives [waɪvz] NPL *of* **wife**.
wizard ['wɪzəd] **1** N **(a)** (*magician*) hechicero *m*, brujo *m*, mago *m*. **(b)** (*: expert*) as* *m*, genio *m*; experto *m*.
2 ADJ (*esp Brit**) estupendo*, maravilloso.
wizardry ['wɪzədrɪ] N hechicería *f*, brujería *f*.
wizened ['wɪznd] ADJ seco, marchito; *person, skin etc* arrugado, apergaminado.
wk ABBR *of* **week** semana *f*, sem.
W/L ABBR *of* **wavelength** longitud *f* de onda.
Wm ABBR *of* **William**.
WMO N ABBR *of* **World Meteorological Organization** Organización *f* Meteorológica Mundial, OMM *f*.
WNW ABBR *of* **west-north-west** oesnoroeste, ONO.
WO N (*Mil*) ABBR *of* **Warrant Officer**.
wo [wəʊ] INTERJ, **woa** [wəʊ] INTERJ = **whoa**.
woad [wəʊd] N hierba *f* pastel, glasto *m*.
wobble ['wɒbl] **1** N bamboleo *m*, tambaleo *m*; **to walk with a ~** tambalearse al andar, andar tambaleándose; **this chair has a ~** esta silla está coja, esta silla cojea.
2 VI **(a)** bambolear, tambalearse; vacilar, oscilar; (*rock*) balancearse; (*of chair etc*) cojear, ser poco firme.
(b) (*be indecisive*) vacilar.
wobbly ['wɒblɪ] **1** ADJ inseguro, poco firme, cojo.
2 N: **to throw a ~*** ponerse histérico.
wodge* [wɒdʒ] N trozo *m*.
woe [wəʊ] N (*liter*) aflicción *f*, dolor *m*; mal *m*, infortunio *m*; **~ is me!** ¡ay de mí!; **~ betide him who ...!** ¡ay del que ...!; **to tell sb one's ~s** contar a uno sus males; **it was such a tale of ~** fue una historia tan triste, fue una historia tan llena de desgracias.
woebegone ['wəʊbɪˌgɒn] ADJ desconsolado, angustiado.
woeful ['wəʊfʊl] ADJ *person etc* triste, afligido, desconsolado; *sight, story etc* triste, lamentable.
woefully ['wəʊfəlɪ] ADV tristemente; lamentablemente.
Wog* [wɒg] N (*Brit pej*) negro *m*, -a *f*.
wok [wɒk] N *cazuela china de base redonda*.
woke [wəʊk] PRET *of* **wake**[2].
woken ['wəʊkn] PTP *of* **wake**[2].
wold [wəʊld] N (*approx*) rasa *f* ondulada.
wolf [wʊlf] **1** N, PL **wolves** [wʊlvz] lobo *m*, a *f*; (*) tenorio *m*; **lone ~** (*fig*) solitario *m*; **~ in sheep's clothing** lobo *m* en piel de cordero; **to cry ~** gritar al lobo; **to keep the ~ from the door** guardarse del hambre, evitar caer en la miseria; **to throw sb to the wolves** arrojar a uno a los lobos.
2 VT (*also* **to ~ down**) *food* zamparse, comer vorazmente.
wolfcub ['wʊlfkʌb] N lobato *m*, lobezno *m*.
wolfhound ['wʊlfhaʊnd] N perro *m* lobo.
wolfish ['wʊlfɪʃ] ADJ lobuno.

wolfpack ['wʊlfpæk] N manada f de lobos.
wolfram ['wʊlfrəm] N volframio m, wolfram m.
wolf-whistle ['wʊlf͵wɪsl] N silbido m de admiración.
wolverine ['wʊlvəriːn] N carcayú m, glotón m.
wolves [wʊlvz] NPL of **wolf**.
woman ['wʊmən] [1] N, PL **women** ['wɪmɪn] mujer f; (*servant*) criada f; **as one ~** unánimemente; **como una sola mujer, todas a una; my good ~** buena mujer; **I'm not a drinking ~** no bebo, no soy de las que beben; **~ to ~** de mujer a mujer; **she's her own ~** es una mujer muy fiel a sí misma; **young ~** joven f; **old ~** vieja f; **my old ~*** la parienta*, mi media naranja; **he's rather an old ~** es una persona bastante sosa; se queja por poca cosa; se inquieta sin motivo; **~ of the town** prostituta f; **~ of the world** mujer f mundana; **women's football** fútbol m para mujeres, fútbol m femenino; **women's group** grupo m femenino; **women's movement** movimiento m feminista; **his ~** (*lover*) su querida, su amante; **X and all his women** X y todas sus queridas; **Z and his kept ~** Z y su querida; **to make an honest ~ of sb** casarse con una (a causa de haberla dejado encinta); **he runs after women** se dedica a la caza de mujeres.
[2] ATTR: **~ doctor** médica f; **~ driver** conductora f; **~ pilot** piloto f; **~ priest** mujer f sacerdote; **~ writer** escritora f.
woman-hater ['wʊmən͵heɪtəʳ] N misógino m.
womanhood ['wʊmənhʊd] N (**a**) (*women in general*) mujeres fpl, sexo m femenino. (**b**) (*age*) edad f adulta (de mujer); **to reach ~** llegar a la edad adulta (de mujer). (**c**) (*womanliness*) feminidad f.
womanish ['wʊmənɪʃ] ADJ mujeril, propio de mujer; *man* afeminado.
womanize ['wʊmənaɪz] VI ser mujeriego, dedicarse a la caza de mujeres.
womanizer ['wʊmənaɪzəʳ] N mujeriego m.
womanizing ['wʊmənaɪzɪŋ] N el ser mujeriego; caza f de mujeres.
womankind ['wʊmən'kaɪnd] N mujeres fpl, sexo m femenino.
womanlike ['wʊmənlaɪk] ADJ mujeril.
womanliness ['wʊmənlɪnɪs] N feminidad f.
womanly ['wʊmənlɪ] ADJ femenino.
womb [wuːm] N matriz f, útero m; (*fig*) seno m.
wombat ['wɒmbæt] N wombat m.
women ['wɪmɪn] NPL of **woman**, **~'s doubles** dobles mpl femeninos, dobles mpl de damas; **w~'s libber*** liberacionista f, feminista f; **~'s page** sección f para la mujer; **~'s refuge** hogas m para mujeres maltratadas; **~'s studies** (*Univ*) estudios mpl de la mujer; **~'s rights** derechos mpl de la mujer; **~'s room** (*US*) servicio m de señoras; **~'s team** equipo m femenino; *ver también* TOILET .
womenfolk ['wɪmɪnfəʊk] NPL las mujeres.
won [wʌn] PRET AND PTP of **win**.
▼ **wonder** ['wʌndəʳ] [1] N (**a**) (*object*) maravilla f; prodigio m; portento m, milagro m; **the ~ of electricity** el milagro de la electricidad; **~s of science** maravillas fpl de la ciencia; **the 7 ~s of the world** las 7 maravillas del mundo; **a nine-days' ~** un prodigio que deja pronto de serlo; **no ~!** ¡no me extraña!; **and no ~** y con razón, como era lógico, como era de esperar; **he paid cash, for a ~** pagó al contado, por milagro; **~s never cease!** ¡todavía hay milagros!; **the ~ of it was that ...** lo asombroso fue que ...; **it is a ~ that ...** es un milagro que ...; **it is no** (*or* **little, small**) **~ that ...** no es sorprendente que + *subj*, no es mucho que + *subj*; **to do ~s with sth** hacer maravillas con algo; **it did ~s for her health** tuvo efectos milagrosos en su salud; **he promised ~s** prometió el oro y el moro; **to work ~s** hacer milagros.
(**b**) (*sense of ~*) admiración f, asombro m; **to be lost in ~** quedar asombrado.
[2] ATTR: **~ boy** joven m prodigio; **~ drug** remedio m milagroso.
▼ [3] VT desear saber, preguntarse; **I ~ what he'll do now** me pregunto qué hará ahora; **I ~ if she'll come** me pregunto si viene, ¿si vendrá?; **I ~ who first said that** ¿quién habrá dicho eso por primera vez?; **I ~ if you really love me** a veces me pregunto si me quieres de verdad; **I ~ whether the milkman's been** a ver si el lechero habrá venido; **she ~ed whether to go on** no sabía si seguir adelante; **if you're ~ing how to do it** si no sabes cómo hacerlo.
[4] VI (**a**) (*reflect*) **I ~!** ¡quizá!, ¡quién sabe!; **I often ~** me lo pregunto mucho; **it set me ~ing** me hizo pensar; **I ~ed about that for a long time** le di muchas vueltas a eso; **I'm ~ing about buying some** pienso en la conveniencia de comprar algunos.
(**b**) (*marvel*) admirarse, asombrarse, maravillarse (*at* de); **I ~ at your rashness** me admiro de tu temeridad, me asombra tu temeridad; **that's hardly to be ~ed at** eso no tiene nada de extraño, no hay que asombrarse de eso; **I shouldn't ~!** ¡sería lógico!; **I shouldn't ~ if ...** no me sorprendería que + *subj*; **she's married by now, I shouldn't ~** se habrá casado ya como sería lógico, cabe presumir que está casada ya; **can you ~?** ¿natural, no?
wonderful ['wʌndəfʊl] ADJ maravilloso; estupendo; **~!** ¡estupendo!
wonderfully ['wʌndəfəlɪ] ADJ maravillosamente.
wondering ['wʌndərɪŋ] ADJ *tone, look etc* perplejo, sorprendido.
wonderingly ['wʌndərɪŋlɪ] ADV: **to look ~ at sb** mirar a uno per-

plejo, mirar a uno sorprendido.
wonderland ['wʌndəlænd] N país m de las maravillas, mundo m maravilloso.
wonderment ['wʌndəmənt] N = **wonder 1 (b)**.
wonderstruck ['wʌndəstrʌk] ADJ asombrado, pasmado.
wonder-worker ['wʌndə͵wɜːkəʳ] N (*Med etc*) droga f (*etc*) milagrosa.
wondrous ['wʌndrəs] [1] ADJ (*liter*) maravilloso.
[2] ADV (*liter*, ††) = **wondrously**.
wondrously ['wʌndrəslɪ] ADV (*liter*) maravillosamente; **~ beautiful** extraordinariamente hermoso, hermoso en extremo.
wonga: ['wɒŋgə] N (*Brit*) pasta* f, guita: f.
wonky* ['wɒŋkɪ] ADJ (*Brit*) (*unsteady*) poco firme, poco seguro; flojo; (*broken down*) descompuesto.
wont [wəʊnt] [1] ADJ: **to be ~ to** + *infin* soler + *infin*, acostumbrar + *infin*; **as he was ~** (**to**) como solía (hacer).
[2] N costumbre f; **it is his ~ to** + *infin* suele + *infin*, acostumbra + *infin*.
won't [wəʊnt] = **will not**.
wonted ['wəʊntɪd] ADJ (*liter*) acostumbrado.
woo [wuː] VT (*liter*) pretender, cortejar; (*fig*) procurar ganarse la amistad de, solicitar el apoyo de; *fame etc* buscar, procurar.
wood [wʊd] [1] N (**a**) (*forest*) bosque m; **~s** bosque m, bosques mpl, monte m; **we're not out of the ~ yet** todavía está la pelota en el tejado; **he can't see the ~ for the trees** los árboles no le están dejando ver el bosque; **to take to the ~s** echarse al monte.
(**b**) (*material*) madera f; (*fire ~*) leña f; **dead ~** ramas fpl muertas; leña f seca; (*fig*) material m inútil, personas fpl inútiles; **to knock on ~** (*US*), **to touch ~** tocar madera; **we shall manage it, touch ~** lo lograremos si Dios quiere (*or* Dios mediante).
(**c**) (*in winemaking etc*) barril m; **drawn from the ~** de barril.
(**d**) (*Mus*) instrumentos mpl de viento de madera.
(**e**) (*Bowls*) bola f.
[2] ATTR (**a**) (*of forest*) de los bosques, selvático.
(**b**) (*of material*) de madera; **~ alcohol, ~ spirit** alcohol m metálico.
wood anemone ['wʊdən'eməni] N anémona f de los bosques.
woodbine ['wʊdbaɪn] N madreselva f.
wood-block ['wʊdblɒk] N bloque m de madera; (*in paving*) adoquín m de madera, tarugo m.
wood-carving ['wʊd͵kɑːvɪŋ] N escultura f en madera, talla f (en madera).
woodchuck ['wʊdtʃʌk] N marmota f de América; *ver también* GROUNDHOG DAY .
woodcock ['wʊdkɒk] N becada f, chocha f, chochaperdiz f.
woodcraft ['wʊdkrɑːft] N conocimiento m de la vida del bosque.
woodcut ['wʊdkʌt] N grabado m en madera, xilografía f.
woodcutter ['wʊd͵kʌtəʳ] N leñador m.
wooded ['wʊdɪd] ADJ arbolado, enselvado.
wooden ['wʊdn] ADJ (**a**) de madera; de palo; **~ nickel*** (*US*) baratija f, objeto m sin valor; **to try to sell sb ~ nickels*** (*US*) intentar darle a uno gato por liebre, tratar de engañar a uno; **~ spoon** cuchara f de palo; (*fig*) premio m para el peor, premio m para el último.
(**b**) (*fig*) *face etc* sin expresión, inexpresivo; de estatua; *personality* soso, poco imaginativo, sin animación; *response etc* inflexible.
wood engraving ['wʊdɪn'greɪvɪŋ] N grabado m en madera.
wooden-headed ['wʊdn'hedɪd] ADJ cabezahueca.
woodenly ['wʊdnlɪ] ADV *say etc* sin expresión, inexpresivamente.
woodland ['wʊdlənd] [1] N bosque m, monte m, arbolado m.
[2] ATTR de los bosques, selvático.
woodlark ['wʊdlɑːk] N totovía f, cogujada f.
woodlouse ['wʊdlaʊs] N, PL **woodlice** ['wʊdlaɪs] cochinilla f.
woodman ['wʊdmən] N, PL **woodmen** ['wʊdmən] leñador m; trabajador m forestal.
woodpecker ['wʊd͵pekəʳ] N pájaro m carpintero, pito m, pico m; **green ~** pito m real; **lesser spotted ~** pico m menor.
woodpigeon ['wʊd͵pɪdʒən] N paloma f torcaz.
woodpile ['wʊdpaɪl] N montón m de leña.
wood-pulp ['wʊdpʌlp] N pulpa f de madera, lignocelulosa f, pasta f celulosa.
wood shavings ['wʊd͵ʃeɪvɪŋz] NPL virutas fpl.
woodshed ['wʊdʃed] N leñera f.
woodsy ['wʊdzɪ] ADJ (*US*) selvático.
woodwind ['wʊdwɪnd] N (*also* **~ instruments**) instrumentos mpl de viento de madera.
woodwork ['wʊdwɜːk] N (**a**) (*wood*) maderaje m; molduras fpl; (*of goal*) madera f; **they come crawling out of the ~** (*fig*) salen de la madera como carcomas. (**b**) (*craft*) carpintería f, ebanistería f, artesanía f en madera.
woodworm ['wʊdwɜːm] N carcoma f; **the table has ~** la mesa está carcomida.
woody ['wʊdɪ] ADJ *tissue etc* leñoso.
woof¹ [wuːf] N trama f.
woof² [wʊf] [1] N (*bark*) ladrido m.

[2] VI ladrar.

woofer ['wu:fə^r] N altavoz *m* para sonidos graves.

woofter‡ ['wʊftə^r] N, **wooftah‡** ['wʊftə] N (*Brit: pej*) marica‡ *m*.

wooing ['wu:ɪŋ] N galanteo *m*.

wool [wʊl] [1] N lana *f*; (•) pelo *m*; **a dyed in the ~ supporter** un partidario fanático, un partidario acérrimo; **to pull the ~ over sb's eyes** dar a uno gato por liebre; **all ~ and a yard wide** (*US*) de lo bueno lo mejor, auténtico, sin trampa ni cartón.
[2] ATTR de lana; lanar; **~ trade** comercio *m* de lana.

wool-gathering ['wʊl,gæðərɪŋ] N: **to go ~** estar en la luna, estar en Babia.

woollen, (*US*) **woolen** ['wʊlən] [1] ADJ de lana; lanar, lanero; **~ industry** industria *f* de la lana.
[2] NPL: **~s** ropa *f* (*esp* interior) de lana; (*Comm*) géneros *mpl* de lana.

woolliness, (*US*) **wooliness** ['wʊlɪnɪs] N lanosidad *f*; (*fig*) lo borroso; confusión *f*.

woolly, (*US*) **wooly** ['wʊlɪ] [1] ADJ lanudo, lanoso; de lana; *outline etc* borroso; *idea, thinking* confuso.
[2] NPL: **woollies**, (*US*) **woolies** ropa *f* (*esp* interior) de lana.

woolly-minded ['wʊlɪ'maɪndɪd] ADJ confuso.

woolman ['wʊlmən] N, PL **woolmen** ['wʊlmen] (*trader*) comerciante *m* en lanas; (*manufacturer*) dueño *m* de una fábrica textil, lanero *m*.

wool-merchant ['wʊl,mɜːtʃənt] N comerciante *m* en lanas, lanero *m*.

woolsack ['wʊlsæk] N: **the W~** (*Brit Parl*) saco *m* de lana (*silla del Gran Canciller en la Cámara de los Lores*).

woops• [wʊps] = **whoops**.

woozy• ['wu:zɪ] ADJ aturdido, confuso; (*Med*) ligeramente indispuesto, mareado.

Wop‡ [wɒp] N italiano *m*, -a *f*.

Worcester sauce ['wʊstə'sɔ:s] N, **Worcestershire sauce** ['wʊstə,ʃə'sɔ:s] N salsa *f* Worcester, salsa *f* Worcestershire.

Worcs. ABBR *of* **Worcestershire**.

word [wɜːd] [1] N **(a)** (*gen*) palabra *f*; vocablo *m*; voz *f*, término *m*; **~s** (*of song*) letra *f*; **~ for** ~ palabra por palabra; **~ of honour** palabra *f*, palabra *f* de honor; **high ~s** palabras *fpl* airadas, palabras *fpl* mayores; **fine ~s** palabras *fpl* elocuentes (pero quizá poco sinceras); **a man of few ~s** un hombre nada locuaz; **never a ~** ni una palabra; **by ~ of mouth** de palabra; **too funny for ~s** tremendamente divertido; **too stupid for ~s** de lo más estúpido; **in a ~** en una palabra; **in other ~s** en otros términos; es decir ..., esto es; **in the ~s of Calderón** con palabras de Calderón, como dice Calderón; **in his own ~s** con sus propias palabras; **without a ~** sin decir palabra; **a ~ to the wise is sufficient** al buen entendedor pocas palabras le bastan; **that's not the ~ I would have chosen** yo no me hubiera expresado así; **the ~ is going round that ...** se dice que ..., corre la voz de que ...; **his ~ is law** su palabra es ley; **it's his ~ against mine** es su palabra contra la mía; **it's the last ~ in luxury** es el último grito del lujo; **rough isn't the ~ for it** brutal no basta, brutal es poco; **there is no other ~ for it** no se puede llamar de otro modo; **~s fail me** no encuentro palabras para expresarme; **~s failed me** me quedé de una pieza; **~s passed between them** cambiaron algunas palabras injuriosas; **not to breathe a ~** no decir palabra, no decir ni pío; **to eat one's ~s** tragarse lo dicho, desdecirse, retractarse; **I can't get a ~ out of him** no logro sacarle una palabra; **not to let sb get a ~ in edgeways** no dejar a uno meter baza; **to have a ~ with sb** cambiar unas palabras con uno; **I'll have a ~ with him about it** hablaré con él, lo discutiré con él, se lo mencionaré; **could I have a (short) ~ with you?** ¿me permite una palabra?; **to have ~s with sb** tener palabras con uno, reñir con uno; **the referee had ~s with him** el árbitro le dijo cuatro palabras; **I had a few ~s with him yesterday** cambié algunas palabras con él ayer; **to have the last ~ in an argument** decir la última palabra en una discusión; **I won't hear a ~ against him** no permito que se le critique; **not to mince one's ~s** no tener pelos en la lengua, no morderse la lengua; **to put in a (good) ~ for sb** defender a uno, hablar por uno; **you're putting ~s into my mouth** te refieres a cosas que yo no he dicho; **she didn't say so in so many ~s** no lo dijo exactamente así, no lo dijo así concretamente; **he never said a ~** no dijo una sola palabra; **don't say a ~ about this** de esto no digas ni una palabra; **nobody had a good ~ to say for him** nadie quería defenderle, nadie habló en su favor; **I now call on Mr X to say a few ~s** ahora le cedo la palabra al Señor X, ahora le invito al Sr X a hacer uso de la palabra; **many a true ~ is spoken in jest** las bromas a veces pueden ser veras; **you took the ~s right out of my mouth** me quitaste la palabra de la boca; **to weigh one's ~s** medir las palabras.
(b) (*message*) aviso *m*, recado *m*; noticia *f*; **~ came that ...** llegó noticia de que ..., se supo que ...; **to bring ~ of sth to sb** dar a uno la noticia de algo; **to leave ~** dejar recado; **to leave ~ that ...** dejar dicho que ...; **pass the ~ that it's time to go** diles que es hora de marcharnos; **to send ~** mandar recado; **to send sb ~ of sth** avisar a uno de algo; **to spread the ~** propagar la noticia.
(c) (*promise*) palabra *f*; (**upon**) **my ~!** ¡caramba!; **he is a man of his**

~ es hombre de entera confianza; **his ~ is as good as his bond** su palabra merece entera confianza; **to be as good as one's ~** cumplir lo prometido; **to break one's ~** faltar a la palabra; **to give sb one's ~ that ...** prometer que ...; **to go back on one's ~** faltar a la palabra; **to hold** (*or* **keep**) **sb to his word** coger a uno la palabra; **to keep one's ~** cumplir su promesa, cumplir lo prometido; **take my ~ for it** te lo aseguro; **I take your ~ for it** acepto lo que me dices, lo creo; **to take sb at his ~** aceptar lo que uno dice.
(d) (*order*) orden *f*; (*pass~*) santo *m* y seña; **~ of command** voz *f* de mando; **the ~ has gone round that ...** se ha transmitido la orden de que ...; **to give the ~** dar la orden; **you have only to say the ~** solamente hace falta que des la orden.
(e) (*Rel*) Verbo *m*; **the W~ of God** el Verbo de Dios.
[2] VT redactar; expresar; **a simply ~ed refusal** una negativa sencilla; **it is not very clearly ~ed** los términos no son muy claros; **a well-~ed declaration** una declaración bien expresada; **how shall we ~ it?** ¿cómo lo expresamos?

wordage ['wɜːdɪdʒ] N número *m* de palabras, recuento *m* de palabras.

word-blind ['wɜːd,blaɪnd] ADJ aléxico.

word-blindness ['wɜːd,blaɪndnɪs] N alexia *f*.

wordbook ['wɜːdbʊk] N vocabulario *m*.

word-class ['wɜːdklɑːs] N categoría *f* gramatical (de las palabras).

word-count ['wɜːdkaʊnt] N recuento *m* de vocabulario.

word-formation ['wɜːdfɔː,meɪʃən] N formación *f* de palabras.

word-game ['wɜːdgeɪm] N juego *m* de formación (*or* adivinación *etc*) de palabras.

wordiness ['wɜːdɪnɪs] N verbosidad *f*, prolijidad *f*.

wording ['wɜːdɪŋ] N fraseología *f*, estilo *m*; términos *mpl*.

wordless ['wɜːdlɪs] ADJ sin palabras; silencioso.

wordlist ['wɜːdlɪst] N lista *f* de palabras, vocabulario *m*.

word-of-mouth ['wɜːdəv'maʊθ] ADJ verbal, oral; *see also* **word 1 (a)**.

word-order ['wɜːd,ɔːdə^r] N orden *m* de palabras.

word-perfect ['wɜːd'pɜːfɪkt] ADJ: **to be ~** saber perfectamente su papel.

word-picture ['wɜːd,pɪktʃə^r] N descripción *f*.

wordplay ['wɜːdpleɪ] N juego *m* de palabras.

word-process ['wɜːd'prəʊses] VT procesar.

word-processing ['wɜːd'prəʊsesɪŋ] N proceso *m* de textos, tratamiento *m* de textos.

word-processor ['wɜːd'prəʊsesə^r] N procesador *m* de textos, procesador *m* de palabras.

wordsmith ['wɜːdsmɪθ] N (*hum*) artífice *mf* de la palabra, (*esp*) poeta *mf*.

wordwrap ['wɜːdræp] N salto *m* de línea automático.

wordy ['wɜːdɪ] ADJ verboso, prolijo.

wore [wɔː^r] PRET *of* **wear**.

▼ **work** [wɜːk] [1] N **(a)** (*gen*) trabajo *m*; empleo *m*, ocupación *f*; **to be at ~** estar trabajando; estar en la fábrica, estar en la oficina (*etc*); tener trabajo; **there are forces at ~** hay fuerzas en movimiento; **to be in ~** tener trabajo, tener un empleo; **to be out of ~** estar desempleado; estar parado, no tener trabajo; **to put** (*or* **throw**) **sb out of ~** privar a uno de trabajo; **to make short ~ of sth** despachar algo rápidamente, (*fig*) zamparse algo; **to go the right way to ~** empezar correctamente; **to set to ~** ponerse a trabajar, (*fig*) poner manos a la obra; **to set sb to ~** poner a uno a trabajar.
(b) (*task, ~ to be done*) trabajo *m*; labor *f*; **a piece of ~** un trabajo, una labor; **the dictator and all his ~s** el dictador y todo lo suyo; **day's ~** jornal *m*; **it's all in a day's ~** estamos acostumbrados a eso; **it was grim ~** (*fig*) fue una cosa repugnante; **it's nice ~ if you can get it** es muy agradable para los que tienen esa suerte; **~ in progress** trabajo *m* en curso; **~ has begun on the new dam** se han comenzado las obras del nuevo embalse; **it's closed for ~ on the steeple** está cerrado debido a las obras del campanario; **I have my ~ cut out as it is** ya tengo trabajo hasta por encima de las cejas; **I had my ~ cut out to stop it** me costó detenerlo; **you'll have your ~ cut out trying to stop him** te costará muchísimo trabajo impedirle; **to do one's ~** hacer su trabajo; **the medicine had done its ~** la medicina había tenido efecto.
(c) (*product: Art, Liter etc*) obra *f*; **the ~s of God** las obras de Dios; **good ~s** buenas obras *fpl*; **a literary ~** una obra literaria; **~ of art** obra *f* de arte; **the ~s of Cervantes** las obras de Cervantes; **~ of reference** libro *m* de consulta.
(d) **~s** (*Mil*) obras *fpl*, fortificaciones *fpl*; (*public*) obras *fpl*; **Ministry of W~s** Ministerio *m* de Obras Públicas.
(e) **~s** (*Mech*) mecanismo *m*; motor *m*; **to bung** (*or* **gum**) **up the ~s** paralizar el motor.
(f) **~s** (*Brit: factory*) fábrica *f*; taller *m*; **gas~s** fábrica *f* de gas.
(g) (•) **~s** todo, la totalidad; **they gave him the ~s** le hicieron sufrir, le sometieron a un severo interrogatorio (*etc*); **let's give it the ~s** vamos a probarlo, probemos.
(h) **~s** (‡ *syringe*) chuta‡ *f*.
[2] ATTR: **~ camp** campamento *m* laboral; **~s council** consejo *m* de

obreros, comité *m* de empresa; ~ **experience** experiencia *f* laboral; ~ **factor** factor *m* laboral; **~s manager** gerente *m* de fábrica; **~s outing** excursión *f* del personal; ~ **relief** trabajo *m* para asistencia a los parados; ~ **study** estudio *m* del trabajo, (*US Scol*) práctica *f* estudiantil; ~ **week** (*US*) semana *f* laboral.

3 VT **(a)** (*cause to* ~) *men* hacer trabajar; **they ~ed us from 8 till 6** nos hicieron trabajar de 8 a 6.

(b) (*Mech etc*) *machine* hacer funcionar; manejar, operar; *brake* accionar; *moving part* mover; **it is ~ed by electricity** funciona con electricidad, es accionado por electricidad; **can you ~ it?** ¿sabes manejarlo?; **can we ~ that scheme again?** ¿podemos volver a emplear ese sistema?; **he ~ed the lever up and down** movió la palanca hacia arriba y hacia abajo.

(c) (*bring about*) *change* producir, motivar; *miracle, cure etc* hacer, efectuar, operar; *mischief* hacer; **to ~ it*** lograrlo, conseguirlo, manejar las cosas; **they ~ed it so that she could come*** se las arreglaron para que ella pudiese venir; **they ~ed his promotion*** agenciaron su ascenso, hicieron diligencias para asegurar su ascenso.

(d) (*Sew*) bordar; **~ed with blue thread** bordado de hilo azul.

(e) *wood etc* tallar; *metal* trabajar; **~ed flint** piedra *f* tallada.

(f) *mine* explotar; *land* cultivar; **he ~s the eastern part of the province** trabaja en la parte este de la provincia; se dedica a cubrir la parte este de la provincia; **we ~ed the river bank looking for the plant** recorrimos la orilla del río buscando la planta; **this land has not been ~ed for many years** estas tierras hace mucho tiempo que no se cultivan.

(g) to ~ one's passage on a boat costear el viaje trabajando.

(h) (*manoeuvre etc*) *ship* maniobrar; **to ~ an incident into a book** introducir un episodio en un libro; **we'll try to ~ in a reference somewhere** trataremos de insinuar una referencia en alguna parte; **can't you ~ me into your plans?** ¿no sería posible dejarme entrar a formar parte de tus proyectos?; **to ~ one's hands free** lograr soltar las manos; **to ~ one's way to the top of the company** llegar a ocupar un alto puesto en la sociedad a fuerza de trabajar; **to ~ one's way up a cliff** escalar a duras penas un precipicio, escalar poco a poco un precipicio (*and V* **way (d)**).

▼**4** VI **(a)** (*gen*) trabajar (*at, on* en); (*be in a job*) tener trabajo, tener un empleo; **to ~ hard** trabajar mucho; **to ~ like a slave** (*or Trojan etc*) trabajar como un demonio; **what are you ~ing at** (*or* **on**) **now?** ¿en qué trabajas ahora?, (*more generally*) ¿a qué te dedicas ahora?; **they're ~ing on the car now** están trabajando en el coche ahora; **they will get ~ing on it at once** empezarán la reparación (*etc*) en seguida; **the police are ~ing on it** la policía lo está investigando; **have you any clue to ~ on?** ¿tienes alguna pista que seguir?; **there are few facts to ~ on** apenas hay datos en que basarse; **we ~ on the principle that ...** nos atenemos al principio de que ..., nos guiamos por el principio de que ...; **we'll ~ on him*** trataremos de convencerle.

(b) (*Mech etc*) funcionar, marchar; **it won't ~** no funciona; **'not ~ing'** (*lift etc*) 'no funciona'; **to get sth ~ing** hacer funcionar algo; reparar algo para que funcione; **it ~s off the mains** funciona con electricidad de la red, se conecta con la red; **the motor ~s with gas** el motor funciona con gas; **it's ~ing as planned** funciona de acuerdo con el plan.

(c) (*medicine etc*) ser eficaz, surtir efecto, obrar; **how long does it take to ~?** ¿cuánto tiempo hace falta para que empiece a surtir efecto?; **this can ~ both ways** esto puede ser un arma de doble filo, esto puede ser contraproducente; **the scheme won't ~** el proyecto no es práctico, esto no será factible, el proyecto no tendrá resultados útiles; **it won't ~, I tell you!** ¡te digo que no se puede (hacer)!

(d) (*yeast*) fermentar.

(e) (*mouth, face*) torcerse, moverse.

(f) (*be* ~ *loose*) V **loose**.

5 VR: **to ~ o.s. to death** matarse trabajando, matarse con exceso de trabajo; **to ~ o.s. into a frenzy** excitarse hasta el frenesí, exaltarse en grado extremo.

◆**work away** VI seguir trabajando, trabajar sin parar.

◆**work in 1** VT *screw etc* introducir poco a poco; meter con esfuerzo; *quotation etc* deslizar.

2 VI **(a)** (*substance*) penetrar poco a poco, calarse; introducirse.

(b) it ~s in quite well with our plans esto se ajusta bastante bien a nuestros planes, esto cuadra bastante bien con nuestros planes.

◆**work off 1** VT **(a)** *debt etc* pagar con su trabajo.

(b) to ~ off one's feelings desahogarse, aliviarse; **to ~ off surplus fat** quitarse las grasas excesivas trabajando; **don't ~ your bad temper off on me!** ¡no te desahogues riñendo conmigo!

2 VI (*part*) separarse, soltarse (con el uso); (*pain*) desaparecer.

◆**work on** VI seguir trabajando.

◆**work out 1** VT **(a)** *problem* resolver; *sum* calcular, hacer; *idea* desarrollar, elaborar; *plan* trazar, elaborar; **to ~ out one's own solution** determinar su propia suerte.

(b) *mine* agotar.

(c) to ~ out one's time servir el aprendizaje; (*in prison*) cumplir su condena.

2 VI **(a)** resultar; resolverse; **it doesn't ~ out** (*sum*) no sale; **it ~s out at £8** llega a 8 libras, asciende a 8 libras, viene a sumar 8 libras; **how much does it ~ out at?** ¿cuánto suma?; **everything ~ed out well** todo resultó perfecto, la cosa salió bien; **how did it ~ out?** ¿qué tal salió?

(b) (*athlete*) entrenarse, prepararse.

◆**work over*** VT (*beat up*) dar una paliza a, apalizar.

◆**work round** VI: **eventually he ~ed round to the price** por fin llegó a mencionar el precio; **what are you ~ing round to?** ¿adónde va a parar todo esto?

◆**work up 1** VT **(a)** *business* desarrollar; fomentar; *theme* elaborar; **together they ~ed the business up from nothing** entre los dos crearon el negocio de la nada; **you could ~ this story up into a film** podrías elaborar este cuento para hacer una película.

(b) *feelings* excitar; *crowd etc* emocionar, encandilar; **it gets me properly ~ed up** (*moved*) me emociona mucho, con esto me emociono mucho; (*with anger*) me saca de quicio; **now don't get ~ed up!** ¡no te pongas nervioso!, ¡cálmate!; **the speaker was ~ing them up into a frenzy** el orador excitaba los ánimos hasta el frenesí.

2 VI: **what are you ~ing up to?** ¿adónde va a parar todo esto?, ¿qué propósito tiene todo esto?; **I thought he was ~ing up to a proposal** creía que estaba preparando el terreno para hacerme una declaración.

3 VR: **to ~ o.s. up** exaltarse, sofocarse; emocionarse mucho; ponerse nervioso.

workable ['wɜːkəbl] ADJ práctico, factible.

workaday ['wɜːkədeɪ] ADJ de cada día; (*fig*) rutinario, prosaico.

workaholic [,wɜːkə'hɒlɪk] N trabajador *m* obsesivo, trabajadora *f* obsesiva, curroadicto* *m*, -a *f*.

workbasket ['wɜːk,bɑːskɪt] N neceser *m* de costura.

workbench ['wɜːkbentʃ] N obrador *m*, banco *m* de trabajo.

workbook ['wɜːkbʊk] N libro *m* de trabajo; (*Scol*) cuaderno *m*.

workbox ['wɜːkbɒks] N neceser *m* de costura.

workday ['wɜːkdeɪ] N (*US*) día *m* laborable.

work ethic ['wɜːk,eθɪk] N ética *f* del trabajo.

worker ['wɜːkəʳ] N trabajador *m*, -ora *f*; obrero *m*, -a *f* (*also Pol*); operario *m*, -a *f*; (*ant, bee*) obrera *f*; **all the ~s in the industry** todos los trabajadores de la industria; **what about the ~s?** ¿y los obreros?, ¡justicia para los obreros!; **he's a fast ~** trabaja con toda prisa; (*fig*) trabaja rápido.

worker-ant ['wɜːkərænt] N hormiga *f* obrera.

worker-bee ['wɜːkəbiː] N abeja *f* obrera.

worker-priest ['wɜːkəpriːst] N sacerdote *m* obrero.

work file ['wɜːkfaɪl] N fichero *m* de trabajo.

workflow ['wɜːkfləʊ] N volumen *m* de trabajo.

workforce ['wɜːkfɔːs] N mano *f* de obra, personal *m*.

workhorse ['wɜːk,hɔːs] N caballo *m* de tiro; (*fig*) persona *f* muy trabajadora.

workhouse ['wɜːkhaʊs] N, PL **workhouses** ['wɜːk,haʊzɪz] (*Brit Hist*) asilo *m* de pobres; asilo *m* de ancianos; asilo *m* para desamparados.

work-in ['wɜːkɪn] N ocupación *f* laboral (de una fábrica *etc*), encierro *m*.

working ['wɜːkɪŋ] **1** ADJ: ~ **assets** activo *m* circulante; ~ **capital** capital *m* de explotación; **the ~ class** la clase obrera; ~ **clothes** ropa *f* de trabajo; ~ **conditions** condiciones *fpl* de trabajo; ~ **control** control *m* efectivo; ~ **day** (*Brit*) (*weekday*) día *m* laborable, (*time*) jornada *f*; ~ **environment** ambiente *m* laboral; ~ **expenses** gastos *mpl* de explotación; ~ **face** cara *f* de trabajo; ~ **hypothesis** hipótesis *f* de guía; ~ **lunch** almuerzo *m* de trabajo; **to have a ~ knowledge of French** tener ciertos conocimientos de francés; ~ **majority** mayoría *f* suficiente; ~ **man** obrero *m*; ~ **model** modelo *m* que funciona; ~ **mother** madre *f* trabajadora; ~ **paper** documento *m* de trabajo; ~ **partner** socio *m* activo; ~ **party** (*Brit*) grupo *m* de trabajo; ~ **population** población *f* ocupada, población *f* activa; ~ **relationship** relación *f* laboral; **to have a good ~ relationship with sb** tener una buena relación laboral con uno, trabajar bien con uno; ~ **week** semana *f* laborable; ~ **woman** mujer *f* trabajadora.

2 N **(a)** trabajo *m*, el trabajar; funcionamiento *m*; explotación *f*; manejo *m*, operación *f*; labra *f*, laboreo *m*.

(b) ~**s** (*Min etc*) labores *fpl* .

working-class ['wɜːkɪŋklɑːs] ADJ de la clase obrera.

working holiday [,wɜːkɪŋ'hɒlədɪ] N, (*US*) **working vacation** N *vacaciones en las que se trabaja un poco.*

workload ['wɜːkləʊd] N cantidad *f* de trabajo.

workman ['wɜːkmən] N, PL **workmen** ['wɜːkmən] obrero *m*; trabajador *m*; **workmen's compensation insurance** seguro *m* de compensación por accidentes laborales; **to be a good ~** ser buen trabajador, trabajar bien.

workmanlike ['wɜːkmənlaɪk] ADJ competente, concienzudo.

workmanship ['wɜːkmənʃɪp] N hechura *f*; arte *m*, artificio *m*; destreza *f*, habilidad *f*; **of fine ~** esmerado, exquisito.

workmate ['wɜːkmeɪt] N compañero *m*, -a *f* de trabajo.

workout ['wɜːkaʊt] N (período *m* de) entrenamiento *m*, ejercicios *mpl*.

workpeople ['wɜːkˌpiːpl] N obreros *mpl*; personal *m*, mano *f* de obra.

work-permit ['wɜːkˌpɜːmɪt] N permiso *m* de trabajo.

workplace ['wɜːkˌpleɪs] N lugar *m* de trabajo.

workroom ['wɜːkrʊm] N taller *m*, sala *f* de trabajo.

work-sharing ['wɜːkˌʃeərɪŋ] N repartimiento *m* del trabajo.

worksheet ['wɜːkʃiːt] N hoja *f* de trabajo.

workshop ['wɜːkʃɒp] N taller *m*; (*at congress etc*) taller *m* de trabajo.

workshy ['wɜːkʃaɪ] ADJ gandul, holgazán, vago.

workspace ['wɜːkspeɪs] N **(a)** (*area to work in*) espacio *m* para trabajar. **(b)** (*Comput*) área *m* de trabajo

workstation ['wɜːkˌsteɪʃən] N puesto *m* de trabajo, estación *f* de trabajo.

worktable ['wɜːkˌteɪbl] N mesa *f* de trabajo.

work therapy ['wɜːkˌθerəpɪ] N laborterapia *f*, terapia *f* laboral.

worktop ['wɜːktɒp] N encimera *f*.

work-to-rule ['wɜːktə'ruːl] N (*Brit*) huelga *f* de celo, paro *m* técnico.

work-worn ['wɜːkwɔːn] ADJ agotado (por el trabajo).

world [wɜːld] **1** N **(a)** (*gen, Geog*) mundo *m*, tierra *f*; **all the ~ over** en todas partes del mundo; **are there ~s other than ours?** ¿existen otros mundos aparte de éste nuestro?; **it's a small ~** el mundo es un pañuelo; **to feel on top of the ~** estar como un reloj; **to go round the ~** dar la vuelta al mundo; **to knock about the ~, to see the ~** ver mundo; **he lives in a ~ of his own** habita un pequeño mundo suyo, queda absorto en sus cosas sin prestar atención a otros; **the ~ and his wife** todos, todo quisque; **the Joe Soaps of this ~ always lose out** los Rodríguez de este mundo siempre salen perdiendo.
(b) **New W~** Nuevo Mundo *m*; **Old W~** Viejo Mundo *m*.
(c) (*realm*) mundo *m*; **the ~ of sport, the sporting ~** el mundo deportivo, el mundo de los deportes; **the business ~** el mundo comercial, los negocios; **the animal ~** el reino animal; **the Roman ~** el mundo romano; **the ~ of dreams** el mundo de la fantasía, el mundo de los sueños.
(d) (*society*) **man of the ~** hombre *m* de mundo; **to come down in the ~** venir a menos; **to go up in the ~** prosperar, hacer progresos en su carrera, ser ascendido; **to have the ~ at one's feet** triunfar, estar en la cumbre de la fama (*etc*); **to take the ~ as it is** adaptarse a la realidad, aceptar la vida como es.
(e) (*this life, Rel etc*) mundo *m*; siglo *m*; **the other ~, the next ~, the ~ to come** el otro mundo; **~ without end** por los siglos de los siglos; **in the ~** (*Eccl*) en el siglo; **in this ~** en esta vida; **it's out of this ~** es tremendo, es increíble; **he's not long for this ~** le queda poco tiempo de vida; **to bring into the ~** echar al mundo; **to come into the ~** nacer.
(f) (*emphatic idioms etc*) **not for all the ~** por nada del mundo; **nothing in the ~ would make me do it, I wouldn't do it for the ~** no lo haría por nada del mundo; **what in the ~ can I do about it?** ¿qué demonios puedo hacer?; **it's what she most wants in the ~** es lo que ella más desea sobre todas las cosas; **to be alone in the ~** estar totalmente solo, estar completamente desamparado; **it was for all the ~ as if ...** fue exactamente como si + *subj*; **I'm the ~'s worst cook** soy el peor cocinero del mundo; **she's** (*or* **she means**) **all the ~ to me** para mí ella es el mundo entero; **their views are ~s apart** sus opiniones están totalmente opuestas; **they're ~s apart politically** en política los separa un abismo; **there is a ~ of difference between A and X** A y X son totalmente distintos; **there is a ~ of difference between buying one and using one** de comprarlo a usarlo hay gran trecho; **since the ~ began** desde que el mundo es mundo; **to be dead to the ~** (*asleep*) estar profundamente dormido, (*drunk*) estar completamente borracho; **it did him the ~ of good** le hizo la mar de bien; le fue muy provechoso; **he'll never set the ~ on fire** nunca hará nada extraordinario; **to think the ~ of sb** tener un altísimo concepto de uno.
2 ATTR mundial; universal; **W~ Bank** Banco *m* Mundial; **~ championship** campeón *m*, -ona *f* mundial; **~ championship** campeonato *m* mundial; **W~ Cup** Copa *f* Mundial; **~ dealer network** red *f* de tratantes mundiales; **~ fair** feria *f* mundial; **~ language** lengua *f* universal; **~ leader** (*Pol, Comm*) líder *m* mundial; **~ market** mercado *m* mundial; **~ market price** precio *m* de mercado mundial; **~ power** potencia *f* mundial; **on a ~ scale** a escala mundial; **W~ Series** (*US*) campeonato *m* nacional de béisbol; **W~ title** título *m* mundial; **~ war** guerra *f* mundial; **W~ War One** la Primera Guerra Mundial; **W~ War Two** la Segunda Guerra Mundial; **the W~ Wide Web** (*WWW*) = the Web.

world-beater ['wɜːldˌbiːtəʳ] N campeón *m*, -ona *f* mundial.

world-class ['wɜːldklɑːs] ADJ de calidad mundial.

world-famous ['wɜːld'feɪməs] ADJ mundialmente conocido, famosísimo.

worldliness ['wɜːldlɪnɪs] N mundanería *f*.

worldly ['wɜːldlɪ] ADJ mundano; **all my ~ goods** todo lo que tengo, todo lo mío.

worldly-wisdom ['wɜːldlɪ'wɪzdəm] N mundología *f*; astucia *f*.

worldly-wise ['wɜːldlɪ'waɪz] ADJ que tiene mucho mundo; astuto.

world-shaking ['wɜːld,ʃeɪkɪŋ] ADJ, **world-shattering** ['wɜːld,ʃætərɪŋ] ADJ pasmoso.

world view ['wɜːld'vjuː] N cosmovisión *f*.

world-weariness ['wɜːld'wɪərɪnɪs] N hastío *m*.

world-weary ['wɜːld'wɪərɪ] ADJ hastiado, cansado de la vida.

world-wide ['wɜːld'waɪd] **1** ADV mundialmente, en (*or* por) todo el mundo.
2 ADJ mundial, universal.

World-Wide Web [ˌwɜːldwaɪd'web] N: **the ~** el World Wide Web.

WORM [wəːm] ABBR *of* **write once read many times**.

worm [wɜːm] **1** N **(a)** (*grub*) gusano *m*; (*earth~*) lombriz *f*; (*person*) canalla *m*, persona *f* de lo más vil; **~s** (*Med*) lombrices *fpl*; **to have ~s** (*animal*) tener lombrices; **the ~ will turn** la paciencia tiene límite. **(b)** (*Mech*) tornillo *m* sin fin.
2 VT **(a)** **to ~ one's way along** serpentear, avanzar serpenteando; **to ~ one's way into a group** insinuarse en un grupo, introducirse astutamente en un grupo; **to ~ a secret out of sb** sonsacar un secreto a uno.
(b) *animal* quitar las lombrices a.
3 VR: **to ~ o.s. along** arrastrarse como un gusano; **to ~ o.s. through sth** atravesar algo serpenteando.

worm-eaten ['wɜːm,iːtn] ADJ *wood* carcomido; *cloth* apolillado.

wormhole ['wɜːmhəʊl] N agujero *m* de gusano, picadura *f* de polilla.

worm(ing) powder ['wɜːm(ɪŋ),paʊdəʳ] N polvos *mpl* antigusanos.

wormwood ['wɜːmwʊd] N ajenjo *m*; (*fig*) hiel *f*, amargura *f*.

wormy ['wɜːmɪ] ADJ gusanoso, agusanado, lleno de gusanos; carcomido; apolillado.

worn [wɔːn] **1** PTP *of* **wear**.
2 ADJ *carpet etc* gastado, deteriorado; *face, person* cansado; **he's looking very ~** tiene aspecto de muy cansado.

worn-out ['wɔːn'aʊt] ADJ gastado; estropeado; inservible; inútil; anticuado; **to be ~** (*person*) estar rendido.

worried ['wʌrɪd] ADJ *tone, look etc* inquieto, preocupado; **to be ~ about sth** inquietarse por algo, estar preocupado por algo; **I'm not ~ either way** me es igual con cualquiera; **that's got them ~** eso les ha dado en qué pensar; **you had me ~ for a moment** empezabas a preocuparme; **to look ~** tener aire preocupado, parecer estar inquieto.

worrier ['wʌrɪəʳ] N aprensivo *m*, -a *f*; **he's a terrible ~** es muy aprensivo, se inquieta por cualquier cosa.

worrisome ['wʌrɪsəm] ADJ inquietante, preocupante; aprensivo.

▼ **worry** ['wʌrɪ] **1** N inquietud *f*, preocupación *f*; cuidado *m*; problema *m*; **~ line** arruga *f* de preocupación; **financial worries** preocupaciones *fpl* financieras; **he had business worries** tenía problemas con sus negocios; **it's a great ~ to us all** nos trae a todos muy preocupados; **what's your ~?** ¿qué mosca te ha picado?, ¿qué problema es éste?; **the ~ of having to + infin** el problema de tener que + *infin*; **to settle sb's worries** resolver los problemas de uno.
2 VT **(a)** (*make anxious*) inquietar, intranquilizar, preocupar; molestar; **that photo worries me** esa foto me inquieta; no estoy satisfecho con esa foto; **what worries me is not that at all** no es eso lo que me preocupa; **it worries me terribly** me tiene preocupadísimo; **that doesn't ~ me in the least** eso me tiene absolutamente sin cuidado.
(b) (*dog etc*) *prey* pillar, sacudir y morder, morder sacudiendo; **that dog worries sheep** el perro ese ataca las ovejas; **is this man ~ing you, madam?** ¿le molesta este hombre, señora?
▼ **3** VI inquietarse, preocuparse (*about, over* por); apurarse; molestarse; **he worries a lot** se apura por cualquier cosa; **not to ~!** ¡no hay problema!; ¡todos tranquilos!; **don't ~!** ¡no te preocupes!; ¡descuida!; **it's all right, don't ~** está bien, no te molestes; **don't ~ about me** no te preocupes por mí; **that's nothing to ~ about** no hay que preocuparse por eso; **I've got quite enough to ~ about without that** tengo bastante problema sin preocuparme de eso; **I should ~!** y a mí ¿qué?
◆ **worry at** VT *bone etc* V **worry 2 (b)**; *problem* V **worry out**.
◆ **worry out** VT: **to ~ out a problem** esforzarse por resolver un problema, devanarse los sesos para resolver un problema; **finally we worried it out** por fin lo resolvimos a costa de mucho trabajo.

worry beads ['wʌrɪbiːdz] NPL *hilo de cuentas con que se juguetea para calmar la tensión nerviosa*.

worrying ['wʌrɪɪŋ] ADJ inquietante, preocupante.

▼ **worse** [wɜːs] **1** ADJ COMP *of* **bad**; peor; inferior; **A is ~ than B** A es peor que B, A es inferior a B; **~ and ~!** ¡peor todavía!; **it gets ~ and ~** va de mal en peor; **it's ~ than ever** es peor que nunca; **it could have been ~!** ¡menos mal!; **it would have been ~ if ...** hubiera sido más grave si ...; **it will be the ~ for you** será peor para ti; **so much** the **~ for him** tanto peor para él; **to be the ~ for drink** estar algo borracho, estar tomado (*LAm*); **to be the ~ for wear** estar deteriorado (*and V* **wear**); **he is none the ~ for it** no se ha hecho daño; la experiencia no le ha hecho mal (*see also* **none**); **to get ~**, **to grow ~** empeorar, hacerse peor, (*Med*) ponerse peor, empeorar; **to make a situation ~** agravar una situación, hacer una situación más difícil; **to make matters ~** para colmo de desgracias; **I don't think any the ~ of you** esto no afecta la opinión que tengo de ti.

2 ADV COMP *of* **badly**; **it hurts ~** me duele más; **she behaves ~ than ever** se comporta peor que nunca; **you might do ~** hay cosas peores; **you might do ~ than to** + *infin* sería quizá posible + *infin*, quizá sea aconsejable + *infin*; **he is now ~ off than before** ahora está peor que antes; **we are ~ off than them for books** en cuanto a libros nosotros estamos peores que ellos.

3 N el peor, lo peor; **there is ~ to come** hay más, todavía no te he dicho (*etc*) lo peor; **it's changed for the ~** ha empeorado.

worsen ['wɜːsn] **1** VT agravar, hacer peor; hacer más difícil.

2 VI empeorar, hacerse peor; agravarse; hacerse más difícil; (*Med*) ponerse peor, empeorar.

worsening ['wɜːsnɪŋ] **1** ADJ *situation* que empeora, que va de mal en peor.

2 N empeoramiento *m*.

worship ['wɜːʃɪp] **1** N **(a)** (*adoration*) adoración *f*, veneración *f*; (*organized ~*) culto *m* (*of* a); (*church service*) culto *m*, oficio *m*; **with a look of ~** con una mirada llena de adoración; **place of ~** edificio *m* de culto.

(b) (*esp Brit: in titles*) **His W~ the Mayor of X** el señor alcalde de X; **Your W~** (*to judge*) señor juez, (*to mayor*) señor alcalde; **if your w~ wishes** (*iro*) si el caballero lo desea, si su señoría quiere.

2 VT adorar (*also fig*), venerar.

3 VI asistir al culto, ir a misa (*etc*); **to ~ at the shrine of ...** rezar en el santuario de ...

worshipful ['wɜːʃɪpfʊl] ADJ (*esp Brit: in titles*) excelentísimo.

worshipper, (*US*) worshiper ['wɜːʃɪpəʳ] N adorador *m*, -ora *f*, devoto *m*, -a *f*; **~s** (*collectively*) fieles *mpl*.

worst [wɜːst] **1** ADJ SUPERL *of* **bad**; (el) peor; **the ~ film of the three** la peor película de las tres; **~ case analysis** análisis *m* del peor de los casos.

2 ADV SUPERL *of* **badly**; peor; **I did it ~** yo lo hice peor.

3 N lo peor; **in the ~ of the winter** en lo peor del invierno; **in the ~ of the storm** en el peor momento de la tormenta; **when the crisis was at its ~** en el momento más grave de la crisis; **at (the) ~** en el peor de los casos; **that's the ~ of it** ésa es la peor parte; **the ~ of it is that ...** lo peor del caso es que ...; **if the ~ comes to the ~** si pasa lo peor; **do your ~!** ¡haga todo lo que quiera!; **to get the ~ of it** salir perdiendo, llevar la peor parte, sufrir más que su contrincante; **to give sb the ~ of it** derrotar a uno; **we're over (*or* past) the ~ of it now** lo peor ha pasado, hemos vencido la cuesta ya; **once you get the ~ over** en cuanto salves el bache; **to think the ~ of sb** pensar lo peor de uno; tener una opinión bajísima de uno.

4 VT vencer, derrotar; salir superior a, quedar por encima de.

worsted ['wʊstɪd] N estambre *m*.

worth [wɜːθ] **1** ADJ **(a)** (*in monetary senses*) equivalente a, que vale, del valor de; **it's ~ £5** vale 5 libras; **what's this ~?** ¿cuánto vale esto?; **it's not ~ much** no vale mucho; apenas tiene valor; **he was ~ a million when he died** murió millonario, murió dejando una fortuna de un millón; **what's the old man ~?** ¿cuánto dinero tiene el viejo?; **one Ruritanian is ~ 3 Slobodians** un ruritano vale por (*or* equivale a) 3 eslobodios; **I tell you this for what it's ~** te digo esto sin poder afirmar que sea cierto, te digo esto por si acaso el dato te interesa; **it's more than my job's ~ to tell you** me costaría mi empleo decirle eso; **to run for all one is ~** correr a todo correr; **to sing for all one is ~** cantar con toda el alma.

(b) (*deserving*) digno de, que merece; **it's not ~ it, it's not ~ the trouble** no vale la pena; **a thing ~ having** una cosa digna de ser poseída, una cosa que vale la pena adquirir; **is the book ~ buying?** ¿me vale la pena comprar el libro? **it's ~ thinking about** merece que se considere, merece consideración; *V* **while**.

2 N (*monetary*) valor *m*; (*fig*) valía *f*, mérito *m*; **£30's ~ of books** libros *mpl* por valor de 30 libras; **50 pesetas' ~ of sweets** 50 pesetas de bombones; **he had no chance to show his true ~** no tuvo ocasión de demostrar su verdadera valía; **his moral ~ is not in question** no se trata de su valor moral; **what's the ~ of this table?** ¿cuánto vale esta mesa?; *V* **money's-worth**.

worthily ['wɜːðɪlɪ] ADV dignamente; **to respond ~ to an occasion** estar a la altura de las circunstancias.

worthiness ['wɜːðɪnɪs] N mérito *m*, merecimiento *m*.

worthless ['wɜːθlɪs] ADJ sin valor; inútil, que no vale para nada; **~ cheque** cheque *m* sin fondos; **a ~ individual** una persona despreciable; **he's not completely ~** no es que carezca absolutamente de buenas cualidades.

worthlessness ['wɜːθlɪsnɪs] N falta *f* de valor; inutilidad *f*; lo des-

preciable.

▼ **worthwhile** ['wɜːθ'waɪl] ADJ valioso, útil; digno de consideración; que vale la pena; **a ~ film** una película seria, una película que merece atención; *see also* **while**.

worthy ['wɜːðɪ] **1** ADJ **(a)** (*meritorious*) meritorio; benemérito; respetable; loable, plausible; *motive etc* honesto, honrado; **a ~ person** una persona respetable; **your ~ newspaper** (*letter to editor*) su estimado periódico.

(b) (*deserving*) **~ of** digno de; **~ of remark** notable, digno de notar; **~ of respect** digno de respeto, respetable; **to be ~ of sth** ser digno de algo, merecer algo; **it is ~ of note that ...** vale observar que ...; es notable que ...; **that comment was not ~ of you** esa observación fue indigna de Vd; **the car is ~ of a better driver** el coche merece tener mejor conductor.

2 N (*freq hum*) personaje *m*; dignatario *m*.

wossname* ['wɒsneɪm] PRON fulano; **old ~ with the glasses** fulano el de las gafas.

wot: [wɒt] PRON INTERROG = **what 2 (b)**.

wotcher: ['wɒtʃəʳ] EXCL (*Brit*) ¡hola!

▼ **would** [wʊd] V AUX **1 (a)** (*used to form conditional tense*) **she ~ come** vendría; **if you asked him he ~ do it** si se lo pidieras lo haría; **if you had asked him he ~ have done it** si se lo hubieras pedido lo habría hecho (*or* lo hubiera hecho); **I thought you ~ want to know** se me figuraba que desearías saber; **I ~ have a word with him** (*if I were you*) sería aconsejable discutirlo con él; **I ~n't worry too much if I were you** yo en tu lugar no me preocuparía mucho de eso; **you'd never know she was not a native Spanish speaker** nadie diría que el español no es su lengua materna.

(b) (*conditional, emphatic*) **you ~ be the one to forget** desde luego eres tú el que se olvida; **it ~ be you!** ¡tú tenías que ser!; **well he ~, ~n't he?** es lógico que dijera (*etc*) eso.

(c) (*conditional, probability*) **it ~ seem so** así parece ser; **it ~ be about 8 o'clock** serían las 8.

(d) (*conjecture*) **what ~ this be?** ¿qué será esto?

2 (a) (*wish*) querer; **what ~ you have me do?** ¿qué quieres que haga?; **try as he ~** por mucho que se esforzara, por más que intentase; **the place where I ~ be** el lugar donde me gustaría estar; **~ (that) it were not so!** (*liter*) ¡ojalá no fuera así!; **~ to God!, ~ to heaven!** (*liter*) ¡ojalá!

▼ **(b)** (*consent*) querer; **~ you care for some tea?** ¿quieres una taza de té?; **~ you tell me your name?** ¿me hace el favor de darme su nombre?; **he ~ not do it** no quería hacerlo, se negó a hacerlo; **he ~n't say if it was true** no quiso decir si era verdad.

(c) (*habit*) **he ~ paint it each year** solía pintarlo cada año, lo pintaba cada año.

would-be ['wʊdbiː] ADJ: **a ~ poet** un aspirante a poeta, uno que presume de poeta, uno que quiere ser poeta.

wouldn't ['wʊdnt] = **would not**.

would've ['wʊdəv] = **would have**.

wound¹ [wuːnd] **1** N herida *f*; **to lick one's ~s** lamer sus heridas; **to open up old ~s** renovar la herida.

2 VT herir (*also fig*); **to ~ sb's feelings** herir los sentimientos de uno.

wound² [waʊnd] PRET AND PTP *of* **wind²**.

wounded ['wuːndɪd] **1** ADJ herido (*also fig*).

2 NPL: **the ~** los heridos.

wounding ['wuːndɪŋ] ADJ *remark, tone* hiriente, mordaz.

wove [wəʊv] PRET *of* **weave**.

woven ['wəʊvən] PTP *of* **weave**.

wow* [waʊ] **1** EXCL ¡caramba!, ¡caray*!

2 VT chiflar*, cautivar.

3 N (*Acoustics*) lloro *m*, bajón *m* del volumen.

WP (a) N ABBR *of* **word processing, word processor**. **(b)** ABBR *of* **weather permitting** si lo permite el tiempo.

wpb* N ABBR *of* **wastepaper-basket** papelera *f*.

WPC N ABBR *of* **Woman Police Constable**.

WPI N ABBR *of* **wholesale price index**.

wpm ABBR *of* **words per minute** palabras *fpl* por minuto, p.p.m.

WR N (*Sport*) ABBR *of* **World Record**.

WRAC N (*Brit*) ABBR *of* **Women's Royal Army Corps**.

wrack¹ [ræk] N (*Bot*) fuco *m*, alga *f*.

wrack² [ræk] = **rack¹** *and* **rack²**.

WRAF N (*Brit*) ABBR *of* **Women's Royal Air Force**.

wraith [reɪθ] N fantasma *m*.

wrangle ['ræŋgl] **1** N altercado *m*, riña *f* (indecorosa), pelea *f* (*LAm*).

2 VI reñir (indecorosamente), pelear (*LAm*) (*about, over* a causa de, *with* con); (*in bargaining*) regatear.

wrangling ['ræŋglɪŋ] N riña *f*, discusión *f*.

wrap [ræp] **1** N (*indoor*) bata *f*, (*outdoor*) abrigo *m*; **to keep sth under ~s** (*fig*) guardar algo secreto, no revelar algo.

2 VT (*also to ~ up*) envolver; (*for warmth*) arropar; (*cover*) cubrir; **shall I ~ it (up) for you?** ¿se lo envuelvo?; **he does so ~ it up** (*fig*) lo dice con tal exceso de palabras, lo expone de manera tan enmarañada; **to be ~ped up in** estar envuelto en; (*fig*) estar absorto en, estar completamente dedicado a; **he is ~ped up in her** no quiere pensar en nada sino en ella, está absorto en ella; **they are ~ped in each other** están absortos el uno en el otro.

◆**wrap up** ① VT = **wrap 2**.
② VI arroparse, arrebujarse; **~ up!*** ¡cállate!; **see that you ~ up warm** cuida de arroparte bien.

wraparound ['ræpə,raʊnd] N reciclado *m*, bucle *m*.

wraparound sunglasses ['ræpə,raʊnd'sʌŋglɑːsɪs] NPL, **wraparound shades** ['ræpə,raʊnd'ʃeɪdz] NPL gafas *fpl* de sol envolventes.

wrapper ['ræpəʳ] N (*of packet etc*) envoltura *f*, envase *m*; (*of book*) sobrecubierta *f*, camisa *f*; (*postal*) faja *f*.

wrapping ['ræpɪŋ] N envoltura *f*, envase *m*.

wrapping-paper ['ræpɪŋ,peɪpəʳ] N papel *m* de envolver.

wrath [rɒθ] N (*lit*) cólera *f*, ira *f*; (*fig, of storm etc*) ira *f*, furia *f*.

wrathful ['rɒθfʊl] ADJ (*liter*) colérico, iracundo.

wrathfully ['rɒθfʊlɪ] ADV coléricamente, airadamente.

wreak [riːk] VT (*liter*) ejecutar; *destruction etc* hacer, causar; *vengeance* tomar (*on* en); *anger* descargar (*on* en); *punishment* infligir (*on* en); **to ~ havoc** hacer (*or causar*) estragos.

wreath [riːθ] N, PL **wreaths** [riːðz] (*of flowers etc*) guirnalda *f*, (*funeral ~*) corona *f* (mortuoria); (*of smoke*) espiral *f*; **laurel ~** corona *f* de laurel.

wreathe [riːð] ① VT (*encircle*) ceñir, rodear (*with* de); (*plait*) trenzar; entrelazar; (*garland*) enguirnaldar (*with* con); **to ~ flowers into one's hair** ponerse flores en el pelo; **a face ~d in smiles** una cara envuelta en sonrisas, una cara muy risueña; **trees ~d in mist** árboles *mpl* envueltos en niebla.
② VI (*of smoke etc; also to ~ upwards*) enroscarse, formar espirales, elevarse en espirales.

wreck [rek] ① N (**a**) (*Naut: act*) naufragio *m*; (*ship*) buque *m* naufragado, buque *m* hundido; **the ship was a total ~** el buque se consideró como totalmente perdido.
(**b**) (*Rail etc*) colisión *f*, accidente *m*.
(**c**) (*fig*) ruina *f*, destrucción *f*; **the ~ of one's hopes** la ruina de las esperanzas de uno; **he's a** (*or an old*) **~** es un carcamal; **I'm a ~, I feel a ~** estoy hecho polvo; **she's a nervous ~** tiene los nervios destrozados; **I'm a nervous ~** tengo los nervios de punta; **if this goes on I shall be a nervous ~** si las cosas siguen así acabaré con los nervios destrozados; **she looks a ~** está hecha una pena.
② VT (**a**) *ship* hacer naufragar, hundir, destruir; *train* descarrilar; *car, plane, mechanism etc* estropear, destrozar; **you've ~ed my gears** has estropeado la caja de cambios; **to be ~ed** (*Naut*) naufragar, irse a pique, ser hundido; **the ship was ~ed on those rocks** el buque naufragó en aquellas rocas.
(**b**) (*fig*) *hopes etc* arruinar, destruir, acabar con.

wreckage ['rekɪdʒ] N (**a**) (*act*) naufragio *m*; (*fig*) naufragio *m*, ruina *f*, destrucción *f*.
(**b**) (*remains: Naut*) pecios *mpl*, restos *mpl* de un buque naufragado; (*of car etc*) restos *mpl*; (*of house etc*) escombros *mpl*, ruinas *fpl*.

wrecked [rekt] ADJ *ship* naufragado, hundido; *car etc* estropeado, averiado; (‡) colocado‡.

wrecker ['rekəʳ] N (*gen*) destructor *m*, -ora *f*; (*Hist: of ships*) provocador *m* de naufragios; (*esp US: person*) demoledor *m*; (*US: tow truck*) camión-grúa *m*.

wrecking ball ['rekɪŋ,bɔːl] N martillo *m* de demolición.

wren [ren] N (**a**) (*Orn*) troglodito *m*. (**b**) W~ (*Brit Navy*) miembro de la sección femenina de la marina británica.

wrench [rentʃ] ① N (**a**) arranque *m*, tirón *m*; (*Med*) torcedura *f*; **to give sth a ~** tirar violentamente de algo, torcer algo violentamente; **to give one's arm a ~** torcerse el brazo.
(**b**) (*tool*) llave *f* inglesa.
(**c**) (*fig*) dolor *m*; sacudida *f*; choque *m*; **the ~ of parting** el dolor de la separación, la angustia de la separación; **it was a ~ to have to leave** fue angustioso tener que partir.
② VT arrancar, tirar violentamente de; **to ~ one's arm** torcerse el brazo, dislocarse el brazo; **to ~ sth (away) from sb** arrebatar algo a uno; **to ~ sth off** arrancar algo; **to ~ a door open** abrir una puerta con un tirón (violento); **to ~ a bulb out** arrancar una bombilla.
③ VI AND VR: **he ~ed (himself) free** haciendo un gran esfuerzo se soltó.

wrest [rest] ① VT: **to ~ sth from sb** arrebatar (*or arrancar*) algo a uno, arrancar algo a uno; **to ~ gold from the rocks** extraer a duras penas oro de las rocas; **to ~ a living from the soil** vivir penosamente cultivando la tierra.
② VR: **to ~ o.s. free** (*lograr*) libertarse tras grandes esfuerzos; **try to ~ yourself free** procura soltarte haciendo un esfuerzo.

wrestle ['resl] ① N lucha *f*; partido *m* de lucha; **to have a ~ with sb** luchar con uno.
② VT luchar con, luchar contra; **to ~ sb to the ground** tumbar a uno, derribar a uno.

③ VI luchar (*with* con, contra); **to ~ with** (*fig*) luchar con; **we are wrestling with the problem** estamos luchando con el problema, nos esforzamos por resolver el problema; **the pilot ~d with the controls** el piloto luchaba con los mandos.

wrestler ['resləʳ] N luchador *m*, -ora *f*.

wrestling ['reslɪŋ] ① N lucha *f*; (*freestyle ~*) lucha *f* libre.
② ATTR: **~ match** partido *m* de lucha.

wretch [retʃ] N desgraciado *m*, -a *f*, infeliz *mf*; **little ~** (*often hum*) tunante *m*, picaro *m*, -a *f*; **some poor ~** algún desgraciado, algún pobre diablo; **you ~!** (*hum*) ¡canalla!, ¡granuja!

wretched ['retʃɪd] ADJ (*unfortunate*) desgraciado, desdichado; (*contemptible*) miserable, despreciable; pobre, lamentable; (*very bad*) horrible; (*ill*) malo, enfermo; **that ~ dog** ese maldito perro; **where's that ~ stick?** ¿dónde está el condenado bastón ese?; **it's ~ weather** hace un tiempo de perros; **what ~ luck!** ¡qué perra suerte!; **I'm a ~ player** juego malísimamente; **to feel ~** (*Med*) sentirse muy mal; (*depressed*) estar deprimido, estar abatido; **I felt ~ about it** me daba grandes remordimientos.

wretchedly ['retʃɪdlɪ] ADV lamentablemente; horriblemente; muy mal; **to be ~ unlucky** tener malísima suerte; **she plays ~** toca horriblemente mal; **they treated her ~** la trataron de modo infame.

wretchedness ['retʃɪdnɪs] N desgracia *f*, desdicha *f*; lo despreciable; lo lamentable; lo horrible; infamia *f*; depresión *f*, abatimiento *m*.

wrick [rɪk] ① N torcedura *f*.
② VT (*Brit*) torcer; **to ~ one's neck** darse un tortícolis.

wriggle ['rɪgl] ① N meneo *m*; serpenteo *m*, culebreo *m*.
② VT menear; *ears, hips etc* mover; **to ~ one's way into** deslizarse en, introducirse (con dificultad) en; **to ~ one's way through** lograr pasar (con dificultad) por.
③ VI menearse; (*also to ~ along*) culebrear, moverse culebreando, avanzar serpenteando; **to ~ away** escaparse culebreando; **to ~ out of a difficulty** escaparse mañosamente de un apuro; **to ~ through a hole** pasar (culebreando, con dificultad) por un agujero; **to ~ with pain** retorcerse de dolor.

◆**wriggle about, wriggle around** VI culebrear, serpentear; (*snake, worm*) culebrear; (*fish*) colear; (*person*) moverse mucho.

wriggly ['rɪglɪ] ADJ sinuoso, tortuoso.

wring [rɪŋ] (*irr: PRET AND PTP wrung*) ① VT (**a**) (*squeeze, twist*) torcer, retorcer; *clothes* escurrir; *hands* retorcer; *animal's neck* torcer; **to ~ clothes out** escurrir la ropa; **to ~ water out of clothes** exprimir el agua de la ropa.
(**b**) (*fig*) *heart etc* acongojar, apenar; **to ~ money out of sb** sacar dinero a uno; **to ~ a concession out of sb** arrancar una concesión a uno; **eventually we wrung the truth out of them** por fin pudimos arrancarles la verdad.
② N: **to give clothes a ~** exprimir el agua de la ropa.

◆**wring out** VT = **wring 1 (a), 1 (b)**.

wringer ['rɪŋəʳ] N escurridor *m*, máquina *f* de exprimir; **to put sb through the ~*** hacer sufrir a uno.

wringing ['rɪŋɪŋ] ADJ: **to be ~ (wet)** estar empapado, (*person*) estar calado hasta los huesos.

wrinkle ['rɪŋkl] ① N (**a**) arruga *f*; pliegue *m*. (**b**) (‡) (*idea*) idea *f*, noción *f*; (*tip*) indicación *f*; (*dodge*) truco *m*.
② VT (*also to ~ up*) *fabric etc* arrugar; *brow* fruncir.
③ VI (*also to ~ up*) arrugarse; plegarse, ajarse; fruncirse.

wrinkled ['rɪŋkld] ADJ, **wrinkly** ['rɪŋklɪ] ADJ arrugado, lleno de arrugas.

wrinklies* ['rɪŋklɪz] NPL viejos *mpl*.

wrist [rɪst] N muñeca *f*.

wristband ['rɪstbænd] N (*of shirt*) puño *m*; (*of watch*) pulsera *f*; (*Sport*) muñequera *f*.

wrist joint ['rɪst,dʒɔɪnt] N articulación *f* de la muñeca.

wristlet ['rɪstlɪt] ① N pulsera *f*, muñequera *f*, brazalete *m*.
② ATTR: **~ watch** reloj *m* de pulsera.

wristwatch ['rɪstwɒtʃ] N reloj *m* de pulsera.

writ [rɪt] ① N escritura *f*; (*Jur*) orden *f*, mandato *m*, decreto *m* judicial; requisitoria *f*, citación *f*; (*fig*) autoridad *f*; **~ for an election** autorización *f* para celebrar elecciones; **~ of attachment** orden *f* de embargo; **~ of execution** auto *m* de ejecución; **~ of restraint** inhibitoria *f*; **to issue a ~** dar orden, hacer un decreto judicial; **to issue a ~ against sb** demandar a uno en juicio; **to issue a ~ for slander against sb** demandar a uno por calumnia; **to serve a ~ on sb** entregar una orden (*etc*) a uno; **his ~ does not run here** aquí él no tiene autoridad, su autoridad no se extiende hasta aquí.
② (†) PTP: **it's just the old policy ~ large** es solamente la vieja política con adornos; es la misma política en forma exagerada; **guilt was ~ large on his face** se hacía patente la culpa en su cara.

▼**write** [raɪt] (*irr: PRET wrote, PTP written*) ① VT (**a**) (*gen*) escribir; redactar; poner por escrito; **did I ~ that?** ¿lo escribí yo así?; ¿fui capaz de escribir eso?; **how is that written?** ¿cómo se escribe eso?; **she ~s a good hand** tiene buena letra; **his guilt was written all over his face** tenía aspecto de culpable, delataba su culpabilidad; **he** had **'policeman' written all over him** llevaba 'policía' escrito por todas partes.

(b) (*compose*) escribir; componer.

▼**2** VI (**a**) (*gen*) escribir; **as I ~** mientras escribo estas líneas; **we ~ to each other** nos escribimos, nos carteamos; **will you ~ to me?** ¿me escribirás?; **I wrote to him to come** le escribí diciéndole que viniera; **that's nothing to ~ home about** eso no tiene nada de particular, no es nada del otro mundo; **I'll ~ for it at once** lo pediré por escrito en seguida, escribiré para pedirlo en seguida.

(b) (*as profession*) escribir, ser escritor; **he ~s for a living** se gana la vida escribiendo, es escritor de profesión; **he ~s as a hobby** escribe como distracción; **to ~ for a paper** colaborar en un periódico, escribir en un periódico.

◆**write away** VI = **write off 2**.

◆**write back** VI contestar.

◆**write down** VT (**a**) (*note*) apuntar, anotar; (*put in writing*) poner por escrito; (*record*) registrar, hacer constar; **we wrote him down as useless** decidimos que era inútil; **written-down value** valor *m* rebajado, valor *m* amortizado.

(b) (*Comm*) rebajar, bajar el precio de; reducir el valor nominal de.

◆**write in** **1** VT escribir, insertar; (*US Pol*) *candidate* añadir a la lista oficial.

2 VI escribir (*for sth* solicitando algo).

◆**write into** VT incluir en, hacer constar en; **the details will be written into the contract** se harán constar los detalles en el contrato.

◆**write off** **1** VT (**a**) (*write quickly*) escribir rápidamente, escribir en seguida.

(b) (*Comm, fig*) *debt etc* borrar, cancelar, anular; **to ~ sth off as a total loss** considerar algo como totalmente perdido; **the car had to be written off** el coche se consideró como sin valor alguno; **to ~ £1000 off for depreciation** quitar 1000 libras al valor nominal por depreciación; **he had been written off as a failure** se le había considerado como un fracasado.

2 VI escribir (con prontitud) (*for sth* solicitando algo).

◆**write out** VT (**a**) escribir; *cheque* escribir, extender; (*transcribe*) copiar, transcribir; (*in full*) escribir en su forma completa, escribir sin abreviar.

(b) **he was written out of the series** suprimieron el papel que tenía en la telenovela (*etc*).

◆**write up** VT (**a**) *report* escribir; *event* escribir una crónica, hacer un reportaje de; *diary, ledger* poner al día.

(b) (*) **to ~ sb up (in a big way)** dar bombo a uno*, describir a uno en términos elogiosos; **to ~ sth up (in a big way)** describir algo exageradamente.

write-off ['raɪtɒf] N (*Comm*) depreciación *f*; (*of debt*) cancelación *f*; (*fig*) pérdida *f* total; (*person*) fracasado *m*, -a *f*, caso *m* desahuciado; **the car is a complete ~** el coche no sirve para nada.

write-protect ['raɪtprə'tekt] VT proteger contra escritura.

writer ['raɪtəʳ] N escritor *m*, -ora *f*; autor *m*, -ora *f*; **the (present) ~** el que esto escribe; **~ to the signet** (*Scot*) notario *m*; **a ~ of detective stories** un autor de novelas policíacas; **~'s cramp** calambre *m* de los escribientes; **to be a poor ~** (*in handwriting*) tener mala letra.

write-up ['raɪtʌp] N (*report*) crónica *f*, reportaje *m*; (*pej*) bombo *m*, descripción *f* exagerada, descripción *f* muy elogiosa.

writhe [raɪð] VI retorcerse, contorcerse; debatirse; **to ~ with pain, to ~ in pain** retorcerse de dolor; **to make sb ~** (*painfully*) hacer sufrir a uno, atormentar a uno, (*with disgust*) dar asco a uno; **it made me ~ with embarrassment** con eso me sentí terriblemente molesto.

◆**writhe about, writhe around** VI retorcerse.

writing ['raɪtɪŋ] **1** N (**a**) (*art in general*) escribir, escritura *f*; **in ~** por escrito; **evidence in ~** declaración *f* escrita, testimonio *m* por escrito; **at the time of ~** en el momento de escribir esto; **to commit sth to ~, to put sth in ~** poner algo por escrito.

(b) (*hand~*) escritura *f*, letra *f*; **in one's own ~** de su propia letra, de su puño y letra; **in Góngora's own ~** de puño y letra de Góngora; **~ on the wall** advertencias *fpl* graves, profecías *fpl* terribles; **the ~ is on the wall for them** es una advertencia muy clara para ellos; **he had seen the ~ on the wall** se había dado cuenta de que era un aviso del cielo.

(c) (*thing written*) escrito *m*; obra *f*; **the ~s of Cela** las obras de Cela.

(d) (*profession*) profesión *f* de autor; trabajo *m* literario; **he earns a bit from his ~** gana algo con su trabajo literario.

2 ATTR de escribir; **~ materials** artículos *mpl* de escritorio.

writing-case ['raɪtɪŋkeɪs] N (*Brit*) recado *m* de escribir.

writing-desk ['raɪtɪŋdesk] N escritorio *m*.

writing-pad ['raɪtɪŋpæd] N taco *m* de papel, bloc *m*.

writing-paper ['raɪtɪŋˌpeɪpəʳ] N papel *m* de escribir.

written ['rɪtn] **1** PTP of **write**.

2 ADJ escrito; **~ offer** oferta *f* por escrito; **~ statement** declaración *f* escrita; **the ~ word** la palabra escrita.

WRNS [renz] N (*Brit*) ABBR of **Women's Royal Naval Service**.

▼**wrong** [rɒŋ] **1** ADJ (**a**) (*morally: wicked*) malo, inicuo; (*unfair*) injusto;

it's ~ to steal malo es robar; **that was very ~ of you** en eso has hecho muy mal; **you were ~ to** + *infin* hiciste mal en + *infin*; **what's ~ with a drink now and again?** ¿será pecado tomar algo de vez en cuando?; **what's ~ in cuddling?** ¿qué tiene de malo abrazarse?, ¿es que es un pecado abrazarse?

▼(b) (*incorrect*) erróneo, incorrecto, inexacto, equivocado; **the ~ use of drugs** el uso impropio de las drogas; **to be ~** (*person*) no tener razón; equivocarse, estar equivocado; **that is ~** eso no es exacto, eso no es cierto; **the answer is ~** la respuesta es inexacta; **is that still ~?** ¿eso está mal todavía?; **that clock is ~** ese reloj anda mal, ese reloj no marcha bien.

(c) (*improper, not sought, not wanted*) impropio, inoportuno; **it's the ~ one** no es el que buscaba (*or* quería), no es el que hacía falta; **~ side** (*of cloth etc*) revés *m*, envés *m*; **to be ~ side out** estar al revés; **he was driving on the ~ side (of the road)** conducía por el lado prohibido (de la carretera); **at the ~ time** inoportunamente; **it's in the ~ place** está mal situado, está mal colocado; **I'm in the ~ job** tengo un puesto que no me conviene, soy miembro de una profesión que no me conviene; me he equivocado de profesión; **we were on the ~ train** nos habíamos equivocado de tren; **is this the ~ road?** ¿nos habremos equivocado de camino?; **to play a ~ note** tocar una nota falsa; **to say the ~ thing** decir algo inoportuno; **you have the ~ number** (*Telec*) Vd se ha equivocado de número; *V* **way** etc.

(d) (*amiss*) **sth is ~** hay algo que no está bien; **is anything ~?, is sth ~?** ¿pasa algo?; **what's ~ with you?** ¿qué te pasa?; **I hope there's nothing ~ at home** espero que no pase nada en casa; **sth's ~ with my watch** le pasa algo a mi reloj, mi reloj no anda bien; **there is sth ~ with my lights** los faros tienen una avería, pasa algo a los faros.

2 ADV mal; sin razón; injustamente; incorrectamente, equivocadamente; al revés; **to answer ~** contestar mal, contestar incorrectamente; **you did ~** hiciste mal; **you're doing it all ~** no se hace así, no comprendes el modo de hacerlo; **to get it ~** (*misunderstand*) comprender mal; no acertar; (*Math etc*) calcular mal, equivocarse (en el cálculo); **don't get me ~** entiéndame bien; **to go ~** (*on route*) equivocarse de camino; extraviarse; (*in calculation*) equivocarse; (*morally*) extraviarse, caer en el vicio; (*of affair*) ir mal, salir mal; (*Mech*) fallar; estropearse, averiarse; dejar de funcionar; **sth went ~ with the gears** pasó algo a la caja de cambios, se averió la caja de cambios; **sth went ~ with their plans** algo falló en sus planes, fracasaron sus planes; **sth is seriously ~** pasa algo grave; **you can't go ~!** ¡no tiene pérdida!

3 N (**a**) (*evil*) mal *m*; **to know right from ~** saber distinguir el bien del mal; **two ~s do not make a right** no se subsana un error cometiendo otro.

(b) (*injustice*) injusticia *f*; agravio *m*, entuerto *m*; **to do sb a great ~** ser muy injusto con uno, agraviar seriamente a uno; **to labour under a sense of ~** sentirse agraviado; **to right a ~** deshacer un agravio, acabar con un abuso.

(c) **to be in the ~** no tener razón, estar equivocado; tener la culpa; **to put sb in the ~** hacer quedar mal a uno, echar la culpa a uno.

4 VT agraviar; ser injusto con; **you ~ me** eso no es justo; **to feel that one has been ~ed** sentirse agraviado.

wrongdoer ['rɒŋˌduːəʳ] N malhechor *m*, -ora *f*; pecador *m*, -ora *f*.

wrongdoing ['rɒŋˌduːɪŋ] N maldad *f*; pecado(s) *m(pl)*; perversidad *f*; crimen *m*, crímenes *mpl*.

wrong-foot ['rɒŋ'fʊt] VT poner en situación violenta (*or* desfavorable); **that left us ~ed** eso nos dejó en una situación violenta.

wrongful ['rɒŋfʊl] ADJ injusto; ilegal; **~ arrest** detención *f* ilegal; **~ dismissal** despido *m* arbitrario, despido *m* improcedente.

wrongfully ['rɒŋfəlɪ] ADV injustamente; ilegalmente.

wrong-headed ['rɒŋ'hedɪd] ADJ obstinado, terco, perversamente equivocado; **to be ~ about sth** obstinarse perversamente en sostener (*etc*) algo.

wrong-headedly ['rɒŋ'hedɪdlɪ] ADV obstinadamente, perversamente.

wrong-headedness ['rɒŋ'hedɪdnɪs] N obstinación *f*, terquedad *f*; error *m* perverso.

wrongly ['rɒŋlɪ] ADV mal; injustamente; incorrectamente; equivocadamente; al revés; **he ~ maintains that ...** sostiene equivocadamente que ...; **to put a screw in ~** poner un tornillo mal; **she had been very ~ treated** la habían tratado muy injustamente.

wrongness ['rɒŋnɪs] N iniquidad *f*; injusticia *f*; inexactitud *f*, error *m*, falsedad *f*; impropiedad *f*, inoportunidad *f*.

wrote [rəʊt] PRET of **write**.

wrought [rɔːt] **1** (††) PRET AND PTP of **work**; **he ~ valiantly** (*liter*) luchó denodadamente, trabajó con esfuerzo; **great changes have been ~** se han efectuado grandes cambios; **destruction ~ by the floods** daños *mpl* causados por las inundaciones.

2 ADJ (**a**) **~ iron** hierro *m* forjado, hierro *m* batido. (b) **to be ~ (up)** (*person*) estar muy agitado, estar muy nervioso.

wrought-up ['rɔːt'ʌp] ADJ agitado, nervioso.

WRU N (*Wales*) ABBR of **Welsh Rugby Union**.

wrung [rʌŋ] PRET AND PTP of **wring**.

WRVS N (*Brit*) ABBR of **Women's Royal Voluntary Service**.

wry [raɪ] ADJ torcido; *sense of humour, joke etc* pervertido, raro; *speech etc* irónico, lleno de ironía; **to make a ~ face** hacer una mueca, torcer el gesto.

wryly ['raɪlɪ] ADV irónicamente, con ironía.

wryneck ['raɪnek] N torcecuello *m*.

WSW ABBR of **west-south-west** oessudoeste, OSO.

wt ABBR of **weight** peso *m*.

W/T ABBR of **wireless telegraphy** radiotelegrafía *f*.

WTO N ABBR of **World Trade Organisation** Organización *f* Mundial del Comercio, OMC *f*.

wuss* [wʌs] N (*US*) pavo* *m*, -a *f*, gallina* *mf*.

WV (*US Post*) ABBR of **West Virginia**.

W. Va. (*US*) ABBR of **West Virginia**.

WWI N ABBR of **World War One**.

WW2 N ABBR of **World War Two**.

WWF N ABBR of **World Wildlife Fund** Fundación *f* Mundial para la Naturaleza.

WWW N (*Comput*) ABBR of **World Wide Web**.

WY (*US Post*) ABBR of **Wyoming**.

wych-elm ['wɪtʃˈelm] N olmo *m* escocés, olmo *m* de montaña.

Wyo. (*US*) ABBR of **Wyoming**.

WYSIWYG ['wɪzɪˌwɪg] ABBR of **what you see is what you get**.

X

X, x [eks] N (*letter*) X, x *f*; (*Math, fig*) x *f*; incógnita *f*; **X for Xmas** X de Xiquena; **X marks the spot** el sitio está señalado con una X; **if you have X pesetas a year** si tienes equis pesetas al año; **for X number of years** por equis años; **~ chromosome** cromosoma *m* X; **X-rated** (*US*) para mayores de 18 años.

Xavier ['zeɪvɪəʳ] NM Javier.

X-certificate ['eksə,tɪfɪkɪt] ADJ (*Brit: Cine*) para adultos, clasificado X, de dos rombos †, no apto para menores de 18 años.

xenon ['zenɒn] N xenón *m*.

xenophobe ['zenəfəʊb] N xenófobo *m*, -a *f*.

xenophobia [,zenə'fəʊbɪə] N xenofobia *f*.

xenophobic [,zenə'fəʊbɪk] ADJ xenófobo.

Xenophon ['zenəfən] NM Jenofonte.

xerography [zɪə'rɒgrəfɪ] N xerografía *f*.

Xerox ['zɪərɒks] ® ⃞ N (*machine*) fotocopiadora *f*; (*copy*) fotocopia *f*.
2⃞ VT fotocopiar.

Xerxes ['zɜːksiːz] NM Jerjes.

XL ABBR *of* **extra large** super grande, SG.

Xmas ['eksməs] N ABBR *of* **Christmas.**

X-ray ['eks'reɪ] 1⃞ N radiografía *f*; **~s** rayos *mpl* X.
2⃞ ATTR radiográfico; **~ examination** examen *m* con rayos X; **~ photograph** radiografía *f*; **~ treatment** tratamiento *m* de rayos X.
3⃞ VT radiografiar.

xylograph ['zaɪləgrɑːf] N xilografía *f*, grabado *m* en madera.

xylographic [zaɪlə'græfɪk] ADJ xilográfico.

xylography [zaɪ'lɒgrəfɪ] N xilografía *f*.

xylophone ['zaɪləfəʊn] N xilófono *m*.

xylophonist [zaɪ'lɒfənɪst] N xilofonista *mf*.

Y

Y, y [waɪ] N (*letter*) Y, y *f*; **Y for Yellow, Y for Yoke** (*US*) Y de Yegua; **~ chromosome** cromosoma *m* Y.

yacht [jɒt] ① N (*esp large, seagoing*) yate *m*, velero *m*, balandra *f*; (*small, model*) balandro *m*.
② VI pasear en yate, navegar en yate; tomar parte en regatas de balandros; dedicarse al balandrismo.

yacht club ['jɒtklʌb] N club *m* náutico.

yachting ['jɒtɪŋ] ① N deporte *m* de la vela, balandrismo *m*; pasear *m* en yate, navegar *m* en yate; regatas *fpl* de balandros.
② ATTR de yates, de balandros; de balandristas; **in ~ circles** entre los aficionados al deporte de la vela, entre balandristas; **it's not a ~ coast** en esa costa no se practica el deporte de la vela.

yacht race ['jɒtreɪs] N regata *f* de yates, regata *f* de balandros.

yachtsman ['jɒtsmən] N, PL **yachtsmen** ['jɒtsmən] deportista *m* náutico; yatista *m*, balandrista *m*.

yachtsmanship ['jɒtsmənʃɪp] N arte *m* de navegar en yate (*or* balandro).

yachtswoman ['jɒtswumən] N, PL **yachtswomen** ['jɒtswɪmɪn] deportista *f* náutica; yatista *f*, balandrista *f*.

yack* [jæk], **yackety-yak*** ['jækɪtɪ'jæk] ① N (*chatter*) palabreo *m*, cháchara *f*; (*argument*) dimes and diretes *mpl* y diretes; (*insistence*) machaqueo *m*.
② VI (*pej*) hablar como una cotorra.

yah [jɑː] INTERJ ¡bah!

yahoo [jɑːˈhuː] N patán *m*.

yak [jæk] N yac *m*, yak *m*.

Yakuza [jəˈkuːzə] N Yakuzas *mpl*.

Yale [jeɪl] ® ATTR **~ lock** cerradura *f* de cilindro.

yam [jæm] N batata *f*, ñame *m*, camote *m*.

yammer* ['jæmər] VI quejarse, gimotear.

yang [jæŋ] N yang *m*.

Yank* [jæŋk] N yanqui *mf*.

yank [jæŋk] ① N tirón *m*; **to give a rope a ~** tirar de una cuerda.
② VT tirar de.
♦**yank off*** VT (a) (*detach*) quitar de un tirón.
(b) **to ~ sb off to jail** coger y meter a uno en la cárcel.
♦**yank out*** VT: **to ~ a nail out** sacar un clavo de un tirón.

Yankee ['jæŋkɪ] ① ADJ yanqui.
② N yanqui *mf*.

yap [jæp] ① N ladrido *m* agudo.
② VI dar ladridos agudos; (*: *chat*) charlar; (*: *protest*) quejarse, protestar (sin razón).

yapping ['jæpɪŋ] N ladridos *mpl* agudos.

yard¹ [jɑːd] N (a) yarda *f* (= 91,44 cm); **an essay ~s long** un ensayo kilométrico; **he pulled out ~s of handkerchief** sacó un enorme pañuelo; **with a face a ~ long** con una cara muy larga; **a few ~s off** a unos metros, a poca distancia.
(b) (*Naut*) verga *f*.

yard² [jɑːd] N (*of house*) patio *m*; (*of farm etc*) corral *m*; (*Scol*) patio *m* de recreo; (*US*) jardincito *m*; **the Y~, Scotland Y~** (*Brit*) oficina central

de la policía de Londres.

yardage ['jɑːdɪdʒ] N ≃ metraje *m*.

yardarm ['jɑːdɑːm] N verga *f*, penol *m*.

Yardie ['jɑːdɪ] N (*Brit*) Yardy *m* (*miembro de una organización criminal de Jamaica*).

yardstick ['jɑːdstɪk] N (*fig*) criterio *m*, norma *f*.

yarn [jɑːn] ① N (a) (*thread etc*) hilo *m*, hilaza *f*.
(b) (*tale*) cuento *m*, historia *f*; **to spin a ~** contar una historia; contar cosas inverosímiles; **to spin sb a ~** disculparse con un pretexto inverosímil.
② VI contar historias; contar cosas inverosímiles; contar chistes.

yarrow ['jærəʊ] N milenrama *f*.

yashmak ['jæʃmæk] N velo *m* (de musulmana).

yaw [jɔː] (*Naut*) ① N guiñada *f*.
② VI guiñar, hacer una guiñada.

yawl [jɔːl] N yol *m*, yola *f*.

yawn [jɔːn] ① N bostezo *m*; **it was a ~ from start to finish*** fue aburridísimo; **to say sth with a ~** decir algo bostezando.
② VT (*also* **to ~ out**) decir bostezando; **to ~ one's head off** bostezar mucho; bostezar abriendo muchísimo la boca.
③ VI bostezar; (*fig*) abrirse.

yawning ['jɔːnɪŋ] ADJ *gap etc* muy abierto, grande.

yd ABBR *of* **yard** yarda *f*, yda.

ye¹ [jiː] PRON (††, *liter, dial*) vosotros, vosotras.

ye² [jiː] DEF ART (††) = **the**.

yea†† [jeɪ] ① ADV (*yes*) sí; (*indeed*) sin duda, ciertamente; (*moreover*) además.
② N sí *m*; **the ~s and the nays** los votos a favor y los votos en contra.

yeah* [jɛə] ADV = **yes**.

year ['jɪər] N (a) año *m*; **~ of grace** año *m* de gracia; **~ end** final *m* del año; **in the ~ of our Lord ...** en el año del Señor ...; **all the ~ round** durante todo el año; **~ in, ~ out** año tras año; todos los años sin falta; **3 times a ~** 3 veces al año; **100 dollars a ~** 100 dólares al año; **to reckon by the ~** calcular por años; **in after ~s** en los años siguientes, años después; **in the ~ dot** en el año de la nana; **since the ~ dot** desde el año de la nana, desde siempre; **not from one year's end to the other** nunca jamás; **of late ~s** en estos últimos años; **last ~** el año pasado; **the ~ before last** el año antepasado; **next ~** (*looking to future*) el año que viene, (*in past time*) el año siguiente; **he got 10 ~s** le condenaron a 10 años de prisión; **it takes ~s** es cosa de años y años; **we waited ~s** esperamos una eternidad.
(b) (~s *of person*) **in my early ~s** en mi infancia, en mi juventud; **in his late ~s** en sus últimos años; **he died in his 89th ~** murió en el año 89 de su vida; **she's very spry for a woman of her ~s** para una mujer de su edad es muy ágil; **he looks old for his ~s** aparenta más años de los que tiene; **he's getting on in ~s** va para viejo, es bastante viejo; **the work has put ~s on him** el trabajo le ha hecho envejecer bastante; **that hairdo takes ~s off you** ese peinado te quita muchos años; **to reach ~s of discretion** llegar a la edad adulta.
(c) (*Scol, Univ*) año *m*, curso *m*; **he's in (the) second ~** está en el segundo curso; **the fellows in my ~** los chicos de mi curso; **he's in fourth ~ Law** estudia cuarto de Derecho.

yearbook ['jɪəbʊk] N anuario *m*; *ver también* │HIGH SCHOOL│ .

*fotografías de grupos y organizaciones estudiantiles. Una sección se dedica a las estudiantes más atractivas, entre las cuales se incluye la **Homecoming Queen**, reina de las fiestas de antiguos alumnos. También hay secciones dedicadas a los estudiantes con más probabilidades de éxito en la vida y a aquéllos que gozan de mayor popularidad. Es tradición que los estudiantes escriban dedicatorias en los anuarios de sus compañeros de clase.*

yearling [ˈjɪəlɪŋ] **1** ADJ primal.
2 N primal *m*, -ala *f*.
yearlong [ˈjɪəˈlɒŋ] ADJ que dura un año (entero).
yearly [ˈjɪəlɪ] **1** ADJ anual; ~ **payment** anualidad *f*.
2 ADV anualmente, cada año; (**once**) ~ una vez al año.
yearn [jɜːn] VI suspirar; **to ~ for** anhelar, añorar, ansiar, suspirar por; *person* suspirar por; **to ~ to** + *infin* anhelar + *infin*, suspirar por + *infin*.
yearning [ˈjɜːnɪŋ] **1** ADJ ansioso, anhelante; *look, tone etc* tierno, amoroso.
2 N ansia *f*, anhelo *m*, añoranza *f* (**for** de).
yearningly [ˈjɜːnɪŋlɪ] ADV ansiosamente, con ansia; tiernamente, amorosamente.
year-round [ˈjɪəˈraʊnd] ADJ que dura todo el año, de todo un año.
yeast [jiːst] N levadura *f*.
yeast extract [ˈjiːstˈekstrækt] N extracto *m* de levadura.
yeasty [ˈjiːstɪ] ADJ (**a**) *smell, taste* a levadura. (**b**) (*fig*) frívolo, superficial.
yell [jel] **1** N grito *m*, alarido *m*, chillido *m*; **to give a ~, to let out a ~** dar un alarido.
2 VT (*also* **to ~ out**) gritar, decir a gritos, vociferar.
3 VI (*also* **to ~ out**) gritar, dar un alarido.
yelling [ˈjelɪŋ] N gritos *mpl*, alaridos *mpl*, chillidos *mpl*.
yellow [ˈjeləʊ] **1** ADJ (**a**) amarillo; *hair* rubio; ~ **fever** fiebre *f* amarilla; ~ **jersey** jersey *m* (*or* maillot *m*) amarillo; ~ **journalism** (*US*) amarillismo *m*; ~ **line** línea *f* amarilla (de estacionamiento limitado); ~ **pages** (*Telec*) páginas *fpl* amarillas; ~ **press** prensa *f* sensacional; **Y~ Sea** Mar *m* Amarillo; **to go ~, to turn ~** amarillear, amarillecer.
(**b**) (*cowardly*) cobarde.
2 N amarillo *m*.
3 VT volver amarillo.
4 VI amarillecer, amarillear, ponerse amarillo.
yellow belly [ˈjeləʊˌbelɪ] N cagueta; *mf*.
yellow card [ˈjeləʊˈkɑːd] N tarjeta *f* amarilla.
yellowhammer [ˈjeləʊˌhæməʳ] N ave *f* tonta, verderón *m*.
yellowish [ˈjeləʊɪʃ] ADJ amarillento.
yellowness [ˈjeləʊnɪs] N amarillez *f*.
yellow peril [ˈjeləʊˈperɪl] N peligro *m* amarillo.
yellowy [ˈjeləʊɪ] ADJ amarillento, que tira a amarillo.
yelp [jelp] **1** N gañido *m*.
2 VI gañir; (*person*) gritar, dar un grito.
yelping [ˈjelpɪŋ] N gañidos *mpl*.
Yemen [ˈjemən] N Yemen *m*.
Yemeni [ˈjemənɪ] **1** ADJ yemenita.
2 N yemenita *mf*.
yen¹ [jen] N (*coin*) yen *m*.
yen²* [jen] N deseo *m* vivo; **to have a ~ to** + *infin* desear vivamente + *infin*, anhelar + *infin*.
yeoman [ˈjəʊmən] **1** N, PL **yeomen** [ˈjəʊmən] (*Brit Hist*) (**a**) (*also* ~ **farmer**) labrador *m* rico, pequeño propietario *m* rural, pequeño terrateniente *m*.
(**b**) (*Mil*) soldado *m* (voluntario) de caballería; ~ **of the guard** (*Brit*) alabardero *m* de la Casa Real.
2 ATTR: **to give ~ service** (*fig*) prestar grandes servicios.
yeomanry [ˈjəʊmənrɪ] N (**a**) clase *f* de los labradores ricos, pequeños propietarios *mpl* rurales. (**b**) (*Brit Mil*) caballería *f* voluntaria.
yep* [jep] ADV (*esp US*) sí.
yes [jes] **1** ADV sí; ~? (*doubtfully*) ¿es cierto eso?, ¿ah sí?; ~? (*awaiting further reply*) ¿y qué más?; ~? (*answering knock at door*) ¿quién es?, ¡adelante!; ~ **and no** (*sort of*) un poco sí y un poco no; **to say ~** decir que sí, (*to marriage proposal*) dar el sí; **he says ~ to everything** se allana a todo, se conforma con cualquier cosa.
2 N sí *m*; **he gave a reluctant ~** asintió pero de mala gana.
yes man* [ˈjesmæn] N, PL **yes men** [ˈjesmen] pelotillero* *m*.
yes-no question [ˌjesˈnəʊˌkwestʃən] N pregunta *f* de sí o no.
yesterday [ˈjestədeɪ] **1** ADV ayer; ~ **afternoon** ayer por la tarde; ~ **morning** ayer por la mañana; **late ~** ayer a última hora; **no later than ~** ayer mismo, ayer precisamente; **he wasn't born ~** no es ningún niño.
2 N ayer *m*; **the day before ~** anteayer; ~ **was Monday** ayer era lunes; **all our ~s** todos nuestros ayeres.
yesteryear [ˈjestəˈjɪəʳ] ADV (*poet*) antaño.
yet [jet] **1** ADV (**a**) todavía, aún; **as ~** hasta ahora, todavía; **not ~, not just ~** todavía no; **I hear it ~** lo oigo todavía; **need you go ~?** ¿tienes que irte ya?; **I don't have to go ~** me puedo quedar todavía

un poco; **it is ~ to be settled** eso queda por resolver; **half is ~ to be built** la mitad queda todavía por construir; **it hasn't happened ~** todavía no ha ocurrido; no ha ocurrido aún; **it's not time ~** todavía no es hora.
(**b**) (*emphatic*) todavía; ~ **again** otra vez (más); ~ **more** todavía más, más todavía, más aún.
2 CONJ con todo, a pesar de todo; **and ~** y sin embargo, pero con todo; **we'll do it ~** a pesar de todo lo lograremos.

YET | *see also main entry*

In questions
● When *yet* is used in affirmative questions, translate using *ya*:
Is Mary here yet?
¿Está aquí María ya?
Have they arrived yet?
¿Han llegado ya?

In negatives
● When *not ... yet* is used in statements or questions, translate using *todavía no*. *Todavía* can go at either the beginning or the end of the sentence:
My parents haven't got up yet
Mis padres no se han levantado todavía or aún ◊ *Todavía or Aún no se han levantado mis padres*
Haven't they done it yet?
¿No lo han hecho todavía or aún? ◊ *¿Todavía or Aún no lo han hecho?*

Meaning "to date"
● When *yet* follows a superlative or *never* and means "to date", translate using *hasta ahora*:
It's the best (one) yet
Es el mejor hasta ahora
I've never been late yet
Hasta ahora no he llegado nunca con retraso

Meaning "still"
In predictions
● When *yet* is used in predictions about the future, translate using *todavía*:
The economic crisis will go on for some time yet
La crisis económica continuará todavía or aún algún tiempo
They will be a long time yet
Todavía or Aún tardarán bastante en venir

With to-INFINITIVE
● When *yet* is followed by *to* + VERB, translate using *todavía por* or *sin* + INFINITIVE or *aún por* or *sin* + INFINITIVE:
The house is yet to be cleaned
La casa está todavía por or sin limpiar

Meaning "even"
● When *yet* precedes a comparative and means "even", translate using *todavía* or *aún*:
There is yet more rain to come in the north
Todavía or Aún habrá más precipitaciones en el norte
Yet bigger satellites will be sent up into orbit
Se pondrán en órbita satélites todavía or aún más grandes

---

yeti [ˈjetɪ] N yeti *m*.
yew [juː] N (*also* ~-**tree**) tejo *m*.
Y-fronts [ˈwaɪfrʌnts] ® NPL (*Brit*) calzoncillos *mpl*.
YHA N (*Brit*) ABBR of **Youth Hostels Association**.
Yid; [jɪd] N (*pej*) judío *m*, -a *f*.
Yiddish [ˈjɪdɪʃ] **1** ADJ judío.
2 N (y)iddish *m*, yíd(d)ish *m*, judeo-alemán *m*.
yield [jiːld] **1** N producción *f*; productividad *f*; (*Agr*) cosecha *f*; (*Fin, Comm*) rendimiento *m*, renta *f*, (*on capital*) rédito *m*; **net ~** rédito *m* neto; **a ~ of 5%** un rédito de 5 por cien; **what is the ~ on the shares?** ¿cuánto rinden las acciones?
2 VT (**a**) *crop, result* producir, dar; *profit* rendir; *opportunity etc* ofrecer, dar, deparar; **the shares ~ 5%** las acciones rinden el 5 por cien, las acciones dan un rédito de 5 por cien.
(**b**) (*give up*: *also* **to ~ up**) entregar, ceder.
3 VI (*submit*) rendirse, someterse; (*give way*) ceder; (*US Aut*) ceder el paso; **to ~ to a plea** ceder a un ruego; **to ~ to temptation** ceder a la tentación; **I ~ to nobody in my admiration for ...** admiro como todos a ..., no me quedo corto en mi admiración por ...; **finally the door ~ed** por fin cedió la puerta; **the ice began to ~** el hielo empezó a ceder; el hielo empezó a romperse; **we shall never ~** no nos rendiremos nunca.
yielding [ˈjiːldɪŋ] ADJ flexible, blando; (*fig*) dócil, complaciente; tierno, amoroso.
yin [jɪn] N yin *m*.
yippee* [jɪˈpiː] INTERJ ¡estupendo!*

YMCA N ABBR of **Young Men's Christian Association.**
yob* ['jɒb] N, **yobbo*** ['jɒbəʊ] N (Brit) gamberro m.
yobbish ['jɒbɪʃ] ADJ (Brit) behaviour de gamberro; person salvaje, incívico.
yod [jɒd] N yod f.
yodel, yodle ['jəʊdl] **1** N canto m a la tirolesa.
    2 VT cantar a la tirolesa.
    3 VI = **2.**
yoga ['jəʊgə] N yoga m.
yoghourt, yog(h)urt ['jəʊgət] N yogur m.
yogi ['jəʊgɪ] N yogui m.
yogic flying [,jəʊgɪk'flaɪɪŋ] N levitación f yóguica.
yo-heave-ho [jəʊ'hiːv'həʊ] INTERJ = **heave-ho.**
yoke [jəʊk] **1** N (of oxen) yunta f; (carried on shoulder) balancín m, percha f; (Mech) horquilla f; (Sew) canesú m; (fig) yugo m; **under the ~ of the Nazis** bajo el yugo de los nazis, bajo la férula de los nazis; **to throw off the ~** sacudir el yugo.
    2 VT (also **to ~ together**) uncir, acoplar; (fig) unir.
yokel ['jəʊkəl] N palurdo m, patán m.
yolk [jəʊk] N yema f (de huevo).
Yom Kippur [,jɒmkɪ'pʊəʳ] N Yom Kip(p)ur m.
yomp [jɒmp] VI caminar penosamente (a través del campo).
yon [jɒn] ADV (†† or prov) aquel.
yonder†† ['jɒndəʳ] **1** ADJ aquel.
    2 ADV allá, a lo lejos.
yonks* [jɒŋks] N: **for ~** hace siglos; **I haven't seen you for ~** hace siglos que no te veo.
yoo-hoo* ['juː'huː] EXCL ¡yu-hu!*
yore†† [jɔːʳ] N: **of ~** (liter) de antaño, de otro tiempo, de hace siglos.
Yorks [jɔːks] N ABBR of **Yorkshire.**
Yorkshire pudding ['jɔːkʃɪə'pʊdɪŋ] N (Brit) especie de buñuelo que se sirve acompañando al rosbif.
you [juː] PRON **1** in familiar use, with second person verb: (subject: SING) tú, (PL) vosotros, vosotras, ustedes (LAm); (acc, dat: SING) te, (PL) os, les (LAm); (after prep: SING) ti, (PL) vosotros, vosotras, ustedes (LAm); **with ~** (SING, reflexive) contigo, (PL, reflexive) con vosotros, con vosotras, con ustedes (LAm).
    2 in formal use, with third person verb: (subject: sing) usted, (PL) ustedes; (acc, dat: sing) le, la, (PL) les; (after prep: sing) usted, (PL) ustedes; **with ~** (sing and pl, reflexive) consigo.
    3 when impersonal or general, often translated by (a) reflexive: **~ can't do that** eso no se hace, eso no se permite; **~ can't smoke here** no se puede fumar aquí, no se permite fumar aquí, se prohibe fumar aquí; **when ~ need one it's not here** cuando se necesita uno, no está aquí.
    (b) uno: **~ never know whether ...** uno nunca sabe si ...
    (c) impersonal constructions: **~ need to check it every day** hay que comprobarlo cada día, conviene comprobarlo cada día; **~ must paint it** hace falta pintarlo.
    4 phrases and special uses: **~ rogue!** ¡canalla!; **~ there!** ¡eh! ¡usted!; **~ doctors** vosotros los médicos; **~ Spaniards** vosotros los españoles; **poor ~!, poor old ~!, ~ poor old thing!** ¡pobrecito!; **away with ~!** ¡vete!, ¡fuera de aquí!; **between ~ and me** entre tú y yo; **if I were ~** yo que tú, yo en tu lugar; **there's a pretty girl for ~!** ¡mira que chica más guapa!

YOU   *see also main entry*

When translating you, even though you often need not use the pronoun itself, you will have to choose between using familiar *tú/vosotros* verb forms and the polite *usted/ustedes* ones.
- In Spain, use *tú* and the plural *vosotros/vosotras* with anyone you call by their first name, with children and younger adults. Use *usted/ustedes* with people who are older than you, those in authority and in formal contexts.
- In Latin America usage varies depending on the country and in some places only the *usted* forms are used. Where the *tú* form does exist, only use it with people you know very well. In other areas *vos*, used with verb forms that are similar to the *vosotros* ones, often replaces *tú*. This is standard in Argentina and certain Central American countries while in other countries it is considered substandard. Use *ustedes* for all cases of *you* in the plural.
For further uses and examples, see main entry.

---

you'd [juːd] = **you would; you had.**
you-know-who* [,juːnəʊ'huː] N tú ya sabes quien, fulano.
you'll [juːl] = **you will, you shall.**
young [jʌŋ] **1** ADJ joven; nuevo, reciente; brother etc menor; **a ~ man**

un joven; **a ~ woman** una joven; **'Portrait of the Artist as a Y~ Man'** 'Retrato del artista adolescente'; **~ offender** (Brit) delincuente mf juvenil; **the ~er son** el hijo menor; **Pitt the Y~er** Pitt el Joven, Pitt hijo; **the ~ idea, Y~ England** las nuevas generaciones, la juventud de hoy; **~ Turk** (Pol etc) joven turco m; **in my ~ days** en mi juventud; **if I were 10 years ~er** si tuviera 10 años menos; **you're only ~ once** no se es joven más que una vez en la vida, hay que aprovechar la juventud mientras dure; **I'm not so ~ as I was** empiezo a notar los efectos de la edad, ya no soy lo que fui en mis veinte; **the night is ~** la noche es joven; **the pile is like a ~ mountain** el montón se parece a una montaña menor de edad; **to marry ~** casarse joven.
    2 NPL (a) **the ~** los jóvenes, la juventud; **old and ~** grandes y pequeños. (b) (Zool) cría f, hijuelos mpl.
youngish ['jʌŋɪʃ] ADJ bastante joven, más bien joven.
young-looking ['jʌŋ,lʊkɪŋ] ADJ de aspecto joven.
youngster ['jʌŋstəʳ] N joven mf, jovencito m, -a f.
your [jɔːʳ] POSS ADJ **1** in familiar use, second person: tu(s); vuestro(s), vuestra(s).
    2 in formal use, third person: su(s).
you're ['jʊəʳ] = **you are.**
yours ['jʊəz] POSS PRON **1** in familiar use, second person: (SING) (el) tuyo, (la) tuya etc; (PL) (el) vuestro, (la) vuestra etc, el de ustedes, la de ustedes (LAm).
    2 in formal use, third person: el suyo, (la) suya etc; **you and ~** Vd y los suyos.
    3 in ending letters: **~ faithfully** le saluda atentamente; V **sincerely** etc.
yourself [jə'self] PRON **1** in familiar use, second person: (subject) tú mismo, tú misma; (acc, dat) te; (after prep) ti (mismo, misma).
    2 in formal use, third person: (subject) usted mismo, usted misma; (acc, dat) se; (after prep) sí (mismo, misma); V **oneself.**
yourselves [jə'selvz] PRON PL **1** in familiar use, second person: (subject) vosotros mismos, vosotras mismas, ustedes mismos, ustedes mismas (LAm); (acc, dat) os, se (LAm); (after prep) vosotros (mismos), vosotras (mismas), ustedes mismos, ustedes mismas (LAm).
    2 in formal use, third person: (subject) ustedes mismos, ustedes mismas; (acc, dat) se; (after prep) sí (mismos, mismas); V **oneself.**
youth [juːθ] **1** N, PL **youths** [juːðz] (a) (gen) juventud f. (b) (person) joven m. (c) (persons collectively) jóvenes mpl, juventud f; **present-day British ~** la juventud actual inglesa; **Hitler Y~** Juventudes fpl Hitlerianas.
    2 ATTR: **~ club** club m juvenil, casal m de jóvenes; **~ employment scheme** plan m de empleo juvenil.
youthful ['juːθfʊl] ADJ juvenil; joven; **to look ~** tener aspecto joven, parecer joven.
youthfulness ['juːθfʊlnɪs] N juventud f.
youth hostel ['juːθ,hɒstl] N albergue m para jóvenes.
youth hostelling ['juːθ,hɒstəlɪŋ] N: **to go ~** pasar las vacaciones en albergues para jóvenes.
you've [juːv] = **you have.**
yowl [jaʊl] **1** N aullido m, alarido m.
    2 VI aullar, dar alaridos.
yo-yo ['jəʊjəʊ] ® N (a) yoyó ® m. (b) (US*) bobo m, -a f, imbécil mf.
yr (a) ABBR of **year** año m, a. (b) ABBR of **your** su etc.
yrs (a) ABBR of **years** años mpl. (b) ABBR of **yours** suyo etc.
YT (Canada) ABBR of **Yukon Territory.**
YTS N (Brit) ABBR of **Youth Training Scheme** plan de promoción de empleo para jóvenes.
ytterbium [ɪ'tɜːbɪəm] N iterbio m, yterbio m.
yttrium ['ɪtrɪəm] N itrio m.
yuan ['juː'æn] N INVAR yuan m.
yucca ['jʌkə] N yuca f.
yuck* [jʌk] EXCL ¡puaj!*, ¡puaf!*
yucky* ['jʌkɪ] ADJ asqueroso.
Yugoslav ['juːgəʊ'slɑːv] **1** ADJ yugo(e)slavo.
    2 N yugo(e)slavo m, yugo(e)slava f.
Yugoslavia ['juːgəʊ'slɑːvɪə] N Yugo(e)slavia f.
Yugoslavian ['juːgəʊ'slɑːvɪən] ADJ yugo(e)slavo.
yuk* [jʌk] EXCL = **yuck.**
Yule(tide) ['juːl(taɪd)] N (liter) Navidad f; **at ~** por Navidades; **~ log** leño m de Navidad.
yum* [jʌm] INTERJ: **~-~!** ¡ñam, ñam, ñam!*
yummy* ['jʌmɪ] ADJ de rechupete*.
yup* [jʌp] (US) sss*, sí.
yuppie* ['jʌpɪ] N ABBR of **young upwardly mobile professional** yuppie mf; **~ disease, ~ flu** síndrome m vírico.
YWCA N ABBR of **Young Women's Christian Association.**

Z

Z, z [zed, (*US*) ziː] N (letter) Z, z *f*; **Z for Zebra** Z de Zaragoza.
zaftig* ['zæftɪg] ADJ (*US*) *woman* regordeta y mona.
Zaire [zɑːˈiːəʳ] N Zaire *m*.
Zairean [zɑːˈiːərɪən] [1] ADJ zaireño.
　[2] N zaireño *m*, -a *f*.
Zambesi [zæmˈbiːzɪ] N Zambeze *m*.
Zambia ['zæmbɪə] N Zambia *f*.
Zambian ['zæmbɪən] [1] ADJ zambiano.
　[2] N zambiano *m*, -a *f*.
zany ['zeɪnɪ] ADJ *car* tonto; *humour etc* estrafalario, surrealista.
Zanzibar ['zænzɪbɑːʳ] N Zanzíbar *m*.
zap* [zæp] [1] EXCL ¡zas!
　[2] VT *person* cargarse*; (*Comput*) borrar, suprimir.
　[3] VI ir corriendo.
◆ **zap along*** VI ir a toda pastilla*.
zappy* ['zæpɪ] ADJ *car* alegre, respondón; *computer* veloz; *prose, style approach* vivaz.
Z-bed ['zedbed] N cama *f* plegable.
zeal [ziːl] N celo *m*, entusiasmo *m* (*for* por), ardor *m*.
zealot ['zelət] N fanático *m*, -a *f*.
zealotry ['zelətrɪ] N fanatismo *m*.
zealous ['zeləs] ADJ celoso (*for* de), entusiasta (*for* de); apasionado (*for* por).
zealously ['zeləslɪ] ADV con entusiasmo.
zebra ['ziːbrə] [1] N cebra *f*.
　[2] ATTR: ~ **crossing** (*Brit*) paso *m* de cebra.
zebu ['ziːbuː] N cebú *m*.
zed [zed] N, (*US*) **zee** [ziː] N zeta *f*.
Zen [zen] [1] N Zen *m*.
　[2] ATTR: ~ **Buddhism** budismo *m* Zen; ~ **Buddhist** budista *mf* Zen.
zenana [zeˈnɑːnə] N harén *m* indio.
zenith ['zenɪθ] N cenit *m*; (*fig*) cenit *m*, apogeo *m*, punto *m* culminante; **to be at the ~ of one's power** estar en el apogeo de su poder.
Zeno ['ziːnəʊ] N Zenón *m*.
Zephaniah [ˌzefəˈnaɪə] N Sofonías *m*.
zephyr ['zefəʳ] N céfiro *m*.
zeppelin ['zeplɪn] N zepelín *m*.
zero ['zɪərəʊ] [1] ADJ cero, nulo; ~ **gravity** gravedad *f* nula; ~ **growth** crecimiento *m* cero; ~ **hour** hora *f* H; ~ **option** opción *f* cero; **to be ~-rated for VAT** tener tipo cero del IVA; ~ **rating** tasa *f* cero.
　[2] N cero *m*; **absolute ~** cero *m* absoluto; **it is 5° below ~** hace cinco grados bajo cero.
◆ **zero in** VI: **to ~ in on** (*move in on*) dirigirse de cabeza a; (*fig: identify*) identificar; (*concentrate on*) dirigir todos sus esfuerzos a; **he ~ed in on those who ...** (*fig*) reservó sus críticas más acérrimas para los que ...

┌─ **ZERO** ─┐

ⓘ *Existen varias palabras que pueden usarse en lugar de* **zero** *según el contexto.* **Zero** *es el término más general en inglés americano, que se usa en la mayoría de los casos. En inglés británico se usa normalmente en matemáticas y ciencias para referirse a temperaturas u otras escalas de valores, como por ejemplo en las frases* **zero population growth** *(crecimiento de población cero), o* **zero inflation** *(índice de inflación cero).*
Nought *se usa en inglés británico para leer números decimales, como por ejemplo* **nought point nought seven**: 0.07 *(en inglés se usa el punto en vez de la coma como separador decimal) y en las calificaciones:* **nought out of ten** *(cero sobre diez).*
O *(pronunciado igual que la letra o) se usa en inglés británico en los números de teléfono:* **O one four one** : 0141. *También se usa en secuencias de dígitos que no representan cantidades numéricas, como por ejemplo en tarjetas de crédito o números de cuentas bancarias.*

Nil se usa normalmente en el Reino Unido en los tanteos deportivos:
Liverpool won five nil *(Liverpool ganó cinco a cero).*
　Nothing *es el equivalente americano de* **nil**, *aunque también se usa a veces en inglés británico.*

---

zest [zest] N gusto *m*, entusiasmo *m*; **to do sth with ~** hacer algo con entusiasmo; **to eat with ~** comer con gusto.
zestful ['zestfʊl] ADJ entusiasta.
zestfully ['zestfəlɪ] ADV con entusiasmo.
zesty ['zestɪ] ADJ *wine* garboso, enérgico.
Zeus [zjuːs] NM Zeus.
ziggurat ['zɪgʊræt] N zigurat *m*.
zigzag ['zɪgzæg] [1] N zigzag *m*.
　[2] ADJ en zigzag.
　[3] VI zigzaguear, moverse en zigzag; (*person*) hacer eses.
zilch* [zɪltʃ] N (*US*) nada de nada, cero; **he's a real ~** es un cero a la izquierda.
zillion* ['zɪljən] (*US*) [1] ADJ: **a ~ dollars** tropecientos dólares*; **a ~ problems** tropecientos problemas*, problemas a montones*.
　[2] N: ~**s of dollars** tropecientos dólares*.
Zimbabwe [zɪmˈbɑːbwɪ] N Zimbabue *m*.
Zimbabwean [zɪmˈbɑːbwɪən] [1] ADJ zimbabuo.
　[2] N zimbabuo *m*, -a *f*.
Zimmer ['zɪməʳ] ['zɪməʳ] ® N andador *m*.
zinc [zɪŋk] N cinc *m*.
　[2] ATTR: ~ **ointment** pomada *f* de zinc; ~ **oxide** óxido *m* de zinc.
zine*, **'zine*** [ziːn] N fanzine *m*, revistilla *f*.
zing [zɪŋ] [1] N silbido *m*; (*) gusto *m*, entusiasmo.
　[2] VI (*bullet, arrow*) silbar; **the bullet ~ed past his ear** la bala le pasó silbando cerca de la oreja; **the cars ~ed past** los coches pasaron estruendosamente.
zinnia ['zɪnɪə] N rascamoño *m*, zinnia *f*.
Zion ['zaɪən] N Sión *m*.
Zionism ['zaɪənɪzəm] N sionismo *m*.
Zionist ['zaɪənɪst] [1] ADJ sionista.
　[2] N sionista *mf*.
zip [zɪp] [1] N (**a**) (*sound*) silbido *m*, zumbido *m*.
　(**b**) (*Brit: also* ~-**fastener**) cremallera *f*, cierre *m* (de cremallera).
　(**c**) (*) energía *f*, vigor *m*.
　[2] VT (**a**) **to ~ open** abrir (la cremallera *or* el cierre de).
　(**b**) (*close: also* **to ~ up**) cerrar (la cremallera *or* el cierre de).
　[3] VI: **to ~ past** pasar silbando; (*fig*) pasar como un rayo.
◆ **zip up** [1] VT = **zip 2**.
　[2] VI cerrar.
zipcode ['zɪpkəʊd] N (*US Post*) código *m* postal.
zip-fastener ['zɪpˌfɑːsnəʳ] N cremallera *f*, cierre *m* (de cremallera).
zipgun ['zɪpgʌn] N (*US*) arma *f* de fuego de fabricación casera.
zipper ['zɪpəʳ] N (*esp US*) = **zip-fastener**.
zippy* ['zɪpɪ] ADJ enérgico, vigoroso; pronto, rápido.
zircon ['zɜːkən] N circón *m*.
zirconium [zɜːˈkəʊnɪəm] N circonio *m*.
zit* [zɪt] N grano *m*.
zither ['zɪðəʳ] N cítara *f*.
zloty ['zlɒtɪ] N zloty *m*.
zodiac ['zəʊdɪæk] N zodíaco *m*.
zodiacal [zəʊˈdaɪəkəl] ADJ zodiacal, del zodíaco.
zombie ['zɒmbɪ] N zombi *m* (*also fig*).
zonal ['zəʊnl] ADJ zonal.
zone [zəʊn] [1] N zona *f*.
　[2] VT dividir por zonas, distribuir en zonas.
zone therapy ['zəʊnˌθerəpɪ] N reflexoterapia *f*, reflejoterapia *f*.
zoning ['zəʊnɪŋ] N división *f* por zonas, distribución *f* en zonas.
zonked: [zɒŋkt] ADJ (*on drink, drugs*) colocado:; (*exhausted*) hecho

polvo*.

zoo [zuː] N zoo *m*, jardín *m* zoológico, parque *m* zoológico; (*small, private*) colección *f* de fieras.

zookeeper [ˈzuːkiːpəʳ] N guarda *mf* de parque zoológico.

zoological [ˌzəʊəˈlɒdʒɪkəl] ADJ zoológico; ~ **gardens** *V* **zoo**.

zoologist [zəʊˈɒlədʒɪst] N zoólogo *m*, -a *f*.

zoology [zəʊˈɒlədʒɪ] N zoología *f*.

zoom [zuːm] ①︎ N (a) (*sound*) zumbido *m*. (b) (*Aer*) empinadura *f*.
②︎ VI (a) zumbar; **it ~ed past my ear** pasó zumbando cerca de mi oído. (b) (*Aer*) empinarse.
◆ **zoom in** VI (*Cine*) dar un golpe de zoom (*on* para captar).

zoom-lens [ˈzuːmˈlenz] N zoom *m*, teleobjetivo *m*.

zoomorph [ˈzəʊəʊmɔːf] N zoomorfo *m*.

zoomorphic [ˌzəʊəʊˈmɔːfɪk] ADJ zoomórfico.

zoophyte [ˈzəʊəˌfaɪt] N zoófito *m*.

zooplankton [ˌzəʊəʊˈplæŋktən] N zooplancton *m*.

zoot-suit* [ˈzuːtsuːt] N *traje de espaldas anchas y de pantalones anchos de los años 40.*

Zoroaster [ˌzɒrəʊˈæstəʳ] NM Zoroastro.

Zoroastrianism [ˌzɒrəʊˈæstrɪənˌɪzəm] N zoroastrismo *m*.

zouk [zuːk] N (*Mus*) zouk *m*.

zucchini [zuːˈkiːnɪ] N, PL INVAR (*US*) calabacín *m*, calabacines *mpl*, calabacita *f* (*LAm*).

Zulu [ˈzuːlʊ] ①︎ ADJ zulú.
②︎ N zulú *mf*.

Zululand [ˈzuːlʊlænd] N Zululandia *f*.

zygote [ˈzaɪɡəʊt] N cigoto *m*, zigoto *m*.

APPENDICES
APÉNDICES

THE SPANISH VERB

THE SPANISH VERB

Each verb entry in the Spanish-English section of the Dictionary includes a reference by number and letter to the tables below, in which the simple tenses and parts of the three conjugations and of irregular verbs are set out. For verbs having only a slight irregularity the indication of it is given in the main text of the dictionary (eg **escribir** [3a; *ptp* **escrito**]) and is not repeated here. Certain other verbs have been marked in the main text as *defective* and in some cases indications of usage have been given there, but for further information it is best to consult a full grammar of the language.

Certain general points may be summarized here:

The **imperfect** is regular for all verbs except *ser* (*era* etc) and *ir* (*iba* etc).

The **conditional** is formed by adding to the stem of the future tense (in most cases the infinitive) the endings of the imperfect tense of *haber*: *contaría* etc. If the stem of the future tense is irregular, the conditional will have the same irregularity: *decir – diré, diría; poder – podré, podría*.

Compound tenses are formed with the auxiliary *haber* and the past participle:

perfect	he cantado (*subj*: haya cantado)
pluperfect	había cantado (*subj*: hubiera cantado, hubiese cantado)
future perfect	habré cantado
conditional perfect	habría cantado
perfect infinitive	haber cantado
perfect gerund	habiendo cantado

The **imperfect subjunctives** I and II can be seen as being formed from the 3rd person plural of the preterite, using as a stem what remains after removing the final -*ron* syllable and adding to it -*ra* (I) or -*se* (II), eg:

cantar: canta/ron – cantara, cantase
perder: perdie/ron – perdiera, perdiese
reducir: reduje/ron – redujera, redujese

The form of the **imperative** depends not only on number but also on whether the person(s) addressed is (are) treated in familiar or in formal terms. The 'true' imperative is used only in familiar address in the affirmative:

cantar: canta (tú), cantad (vosotros)
vender: vende (tú), vended (vosotros)
partir: parte (tú), partid (vosotros)

(There are a few irregular imperatives in the singular – *salir* – *sal, hacer* – *haz,* etc, but all the plurals are regular.) The imperative affirmative in formal address requires the subjunctive: *envíemelo, háganlo, conduzca Vd con más cuidado, ¡oiga!* The imperative negative in both familiar and formal address also requires the subjunctive: *no me digas, no os preocupéis, no grite tanto Vd, no se desanimen Vds.*

Continuous tenses are formed with *estar* and the gerund: *está leyendo, estaba lloviendo, estábamos hablando de eso.* Other auxiliary verbs may occasionally replace *estar* in certain senses: *según voy viendo, va mejorando, iba cogiendo flores, lo venía estudiando desde hacía muchos años.* Usage of the continuous tenses does not exactly coincide with that of English.

The **passive** is formed with tenses of *ser* and the past participle, which agrees in number and gender with the subject: *las casas fueron construidas, será firmado mañana el tratado, después de haber sido vencido.* The passive is much less used in Spanish than in English, its function often being taken over by a reflexive construction, by *uno,* etc.

SPANISH VERB CONJUGATIONS

INFINITIVE	PRESENT INDICATIVE	PRESENT SUBJUNCTIVE	PRETERITE
[1a] cantar (regular: see table at end of list) Gerund: *cantando*			
[1b] cambiar **i** of the stem is not stressed and the verb is regular Gerund: *cambiando*	cambio cambias cambia cambiamos cambiáis cambian	cambie cambies cambie cambiemos cambiéis cambien	cambié cambiaste cambió cambiaron cambiasteis cambiaron
[1c] enviar **i** of the stem stressed in parts of the present tenses Gerund: *enviando*	envío envías envía enviamos enviáis envían	envíe envíes envíe enviemos enviéis envíen	envié enviaste envió enviamos enviasteis enviaron
[1d] evacuar **u** of the stem is not stressed and the verb is regular Gerund: *evacuando*	evacuo evacuas evacua evacuamos evacuáis evacuan	evacue evacues evacue evacuemos evacuéis evacuen	evacué evacuaste evacuó evacuamos evacuasteis evacuaron
[1e] situar **u** of the stem stressed in parts of the present tenses Gerund: *situando*	sitúo sitúas sitúa situamos situáis sitúan	sitúe sitúes sitúe situemos situéis sitúen	situé situaste situó situamos situasteis situaron
[1f] cruzar Stem consonant **z** written **c** before **e** Gerund: *cruzando*	cruzo cruzas cruza cruzamos cruzáis cruzan	cruce cruces cruce crucemos crucéis crucen	crucé cruzaste cruzó cruzamos cruzasteis cruzaron
[1g] picar Stem consonant **c** written **qu** before **e** Gerund: *picando*	pico picas pica picamos picáis pican	pique piques pique piquemos piquéis piquen	piqué picaste picó picamos picasteis picaron
[1h] pagar Stem consonant **g** written **gu** (with **u** silent) before **e** Gerund: *pagando*	pago pagas paga pagamos pagáis pagan	pague pagues pague paguemos paguéis paguen	pagué pagaste pagó pagamos pagasteis pagaron

INFINITIVE	PRESENT INDICATIVE	PRESENT SUBJUNCTIVE	PRETERITE
[1i] averiguar **u** of the stem written **ü** (so that it is pronounced) before **e** Gerund: *averiguando*	averig**u**o averig**u**as averig**u**a averig**u**amos averig**u**áis averig**u**an	averi**gü**e averi**gü**es averi**gü**e averi**gü**emos averi**gü**éis averi**gü**en	averi**gü**é averiguaste averiguó averiguamos averiguasteis averiguaron
[1j] cerrar Stem vowel **e** becomes **ie** when stressed Gerund: *cerrando*	c**ie**rro c**ie**rras c**ie**rra cerramos cerráis c**ie**rran	c**ie**rre c**ie**rres c**ie**rre cerremos cerréis c**ie**rren	cerré cerraste cerró cerramos cerrasteis cerraron
[1k] errar As [1j], but diphthong written **ye-** at the start of the word Gerund: *errando*	**ye**rro **ye**rras **ye**rra erramos erráis **ye**rran	**ye**rre **ye**rres **ye**rre erremos erréis **ye**rren	erré erraste erró erramos errasteis erraron
[1l] contar Stem vowel **o** becomes **ue** when stressed Gerund: *contando*	c**ue**nto c**ue**ntas c**ue**nta contamos contáis c**ue**ntan	c**ue**nte c**ue**ntes c**ue**nte contemos contéis c**ue**nten	conté contaste contó contamos contasteis contaron
[1m] agorar As [1l], but diphthong written **üe** (so that the **u** is pronounced) Gerund: *agorando*	ag**üe**ro ag**üe**ras ag**üe**ra agoramos agoráis ag**üe**ran	ag**üe**re ag**üe**res ag**üe**re agoremos agoréis ag**üe**ren	agoré agoraste agoró agoramos agorasteis agoraron
[1n] jugar Stem vowel **u** becomes **ue** when stressed; stem consonant **g** written **gu** (with **u** silent) before **e** Gerund: *jugando*	j**ue**go j**ue**gas j**ue**ga jugamos jugáis j**ue**gan	j**ue**gue j**ue**gues j**ue**gue ju**gu**emos ju**gu**éis j**ue**guen	ju**gu**é jugaste jugó jugamos jugasteis jugaron
[1o] estar Irregular. Imperative: *está (tú)* Gerund: *estando*	estoy estás está estamos estáis están	esté estés esté estemos estéis estén	estuve estuviste estuvo estuvimos estuvisteis estuvieron
[1p] andar Irregular. Gerund: *andando*	ando andas anda andamos andáis andan	ande andes ande andemos andéis anden	anduve anduviste anduvo anduvimos anduvisteis anduvieron

INFINITIVE	PRESENT INDICATIVE	PRESENT SUBJUNCTIVE	PRETERITE
[1q] dar Irregular. Gerund: *dando*	doy das da damos dais dan	dé des dé demos deis den	di diste dio dimos disteis dieron
[2a] temer (regular: see table at end of list)			
[2b] vencer Stem consonant **c** written **z** before **a** and **o** Gerund: *venciendo*	venzo vences vence vencemos vencéis vencen	venza venzas venza venzamos venzáis venzan	vencí venciste venció vencimos vencisteis vencieron
[2c] coger Stem consonant **g** written **j** before **a** and **o** Gerund: *cogiendo*	cojo coges coge cogemos cogéis cogen	coja cojas coja cojamos cojáis cojan	cogí cogiste cogió cogimos cogisteis cogieron
[2d] conocer Stem consonant **c** becomes **zc** before **a** and **o** Gerund: *conociendo*	conozco conoces conoce conocemos conocéis conocen	conozca conozcas conozca conozcamos conozcáis conozcan	conocí conociste conoció conocimos conocisteis conocieron
[2e] leer Unstressed **i** between vowels is written **y**. Past Participle: *leído* Gerund: *leyendo*	leo lees lee leemos leéis leen	lea leas lea leamos leáis lean	leí leíste leyó leímos leísteis leyeron
[2f] tañer Unstressed **i** after **ñ** (and also after **ll**) is omitted Gerund: *tañendo*	taño tañes tañe tañemos tañéis tañen	taña tañas taña tañamos tañáis tañan	tañí tañiste tañó tañimos tañisteis tañeron
[2g] perder Stem vowel **e** becomes **ie** when stressed Gerund: *perdiendo*	pierdo pierdes pierde perdemos perdéis pierden	pierda pierdas pierda perdamos perdáis pierdan	perdí perdiste perdió perdimos perdisteis perdieron
[2h] mover Stem vowel **o** becomes **ue** when stressed Gerund: *moviendo*	muevo mueves mueve movemos movéis mueven	mueva muevas mueva movamos mováis muevan	moví moviste movió movimos movisteis movieron

INFINITIVE	PRESENT INDICATIVE	PRESENT SUBJUNCTIVE	PRETERITE
[2i] oler As [2h], but diphthong is written **hue-** at the start of the word Gerund: *oliendo*	**hue**lo **hue**les **hue**le olemos oléis **hue**len	**hue**la **hue**las **hue**la olamos oláis **hue**lan	olí oliste olió olimos olisteis olieron
[2j] haber (see table at end of list)			
[2k] tener Irregular. Future: *tendré* Imperative: *ten (tú)* Gerund: *teniendo*	tengo tienes tiene tenemos tenéis tienen	tenga tengas tenga tengamos tengáis tengan	tuve tuviste tuvo tuvimos tuvisteis tuvieron
[2l] caber Irregular. Future: *cabré* Gerund: *cabiendo*	quepo cabes cabe cabemos cabéis caben	quepa quepas quepa quepamos quepáis quepan	cupe cupiste cupo cupimos cupisteis cupieron
[2m] saber Irregular. Future: *sabré* Gerund: *sabiendo*	sé sabes sabe sabemos sabéis saben	sepa sepas sepa sepamos sepáis sepan	supe supiste supo supimos supisteis supieron
[2n] caer Unstressed **i** between vowels written **y**, as [2e]. Past Participle: *caído* Gerund: *cayendo*	caigo caes cae caemos caéis caen	caiga caigas caiga caigamos caigáis caigan	caí caíste ca**y**ó caímos caísteis ca**y**eron
[2o] traer Irregular. Past Participle: *traído* Gerund: *trayendo*	traigo traes trae traemos traéis traen	traiga traigas traiga traigamos traigáis traigan	traje trajiste trajo trajimos trajisteis trajeron
[2p] valer Irregular. Future: *valdré* Gerund: *valiendo*	valgo vales vale valemos valéis valen	valga valgas valga valgamos valgáis valgan	valí valiste valió valimos valisteis valieron
[2q] poner Irregular. Future: *pondré* Past Participle: *puesto* Imperative: *pon (tú)* Gerund: *poniendo*	pongo pones pone ponemos ponéis ponen	ponga pongas ponga pongamos pongáis pongan	puse pusiste puso pusimos pusisteis pusieron

INFINITIVE	PRESENT INDICATIVE	PRESENT SUBJUNCTIVE	PRETERITE
[2r] hacer Irregular. Future: *haré* Past Participle: *hecho* Imperative: *haz (tú)* Gerund: *haciendo*	hago haces hace hacemos hacéis hacen	haga hagas haga hagamos hagáis hagan	hice hiciste hizo hicimos hicisteis hicieron
[2s] poder Irregular. In present tenses like [2h]. Future: *podré* Gerund: *pudiendo*	puedo puedes puede podemos podéis pueden	pueda puedas pueda podamos podáis puedan	pude pudiste pudo pudimos pudisteis pudieron
[2t] querer Irregular. In present tenses like [2g]. Future: *querré* Gerund: *queriendo*	quiero quieres quiere queremos queréis quieren	quiera quieras quiera queramos queráis quieran	quise quisiste quiso quisimos quisisteis quisieron
[2u] ver Irregular. Imperfect: *veía* Past Participle: *visto* Gerund: *viendo*	veo ves ve vemos veis ven	vea veas vea veamos veáis vean	vi viste vio vimos visteis vieron

[2v] **ser** (see table at end of list)

[2w] **placer.** Exclusively 3rd person singular. Irregular forms: Present subj. *plazca* (less commonly *plega* or *plegue*); Preterite *plació* (less commonly *plugo*); Imperfect subj. I *placiera*, II *placiese* (less commonly *plugiera*, *plugiese*).

[2x] **yacer.** Archaic. Irregular forms: Present indic. *yazco* (less commonly *yazgo* or *yago*), *yaces* etc; Present subj. *yazca* (less commonly *yazga* or *yaga*), *yazcas* etc; Imperative *yace (tú)* (less commonly *yaz*).

[2y] **raer.** Present indic. usually *raigo, raes* etc (like *caer* [2n]), but *rayo* occasionally found; Present subj. usually *raiga, raigas* etc (also like *caer*), but *raya, rayas* etc occasionally found.

[2z] **roer.** Alternative forms in present tenses: Indicative, *roo, roigo* or *royo*; *roes, roe* etc. Subjunctive, *roa, roiga* or *roya*. First persons usually avoided because of the uncertainty. The gerund is *royendo*.

[3a] **partir** (regular: see tables at end of list)

INFINITIVE	PRESENT INDICATIVE	PRESENT SUBJUNCTIVE	PRETERITE
[3b] esparcir Stem consonant **c** written **z** before **a** and **o** Gerund: *esparciendo*	esparzo esparces esparce esparcimos esparcís esparcen	esparza esparzas esparza esparzamos esparzáis esparzan	esparcí esparciste esparció esparcimos esparcisteis esparcieron
[3c] dirigir Stem consonant **g** written **j** before **a** and **o** Gerund: *dirigiendo*	dirijo diriges dirige dirigimos dirigís dirigen	dirija dirijas dirija dirijamos dirijáis dirijan	dirigí dirigiste dirigió dirigimos dirigisteis dirigieron

INFINITIVE	PRESENT INDICATIVE	PRESENT SUBJUNCTIVE	PRETERITE
[3d] distinguir u after the stem consonant g omitted before a and o Gerund: *distinguendo*	distingo distingues distingue distinguimos distinguís distinguen	distinga distingas distinga distingamos distingáis distingan	distinguí distinguiste distinguió distinguimos distinguisteis distinguieron
[3e] delinquir Stem consonant **qu** written **c** before **a** and **o** Gerund: *delinquiendo*	delinco delinques delinque delinquimos delinquís delinquen	delinca delincas delinca delincamos delincáis delincan	delinquí delinquiste delinquió delinquimos delinquisteis delinquieron
[3f] lucir Stem consonant **c** becomes **zc** before **a** and **o** Gerund: *luciendo*	luzco luces luce lucimos lucís lucen	luzca luzcas luzca luzcamos luzcáis luzcan	lucí luciste lució lucimos lucisteis lucieron
[3g] huir A **y** is inserted before endings not beginning with **i**. Gerund: *huyendo*	huyo huyes huye huimos huís huyen	huya huyas huya huyamos huyáis huyan	huí huiste huyó huimos huisteis huyeron
[3h] gruñir Unstressed **i** after **ñ** (and also after **ch** and **ll**) omitted Gerund: *gruñendo*	gruño gruñes gruñe gruñimos gruñís gruñen	gruña gruñas gruña gruñamos gruñáis gruñan	gruñí gruñiste gruñó gruñimos gruñisteis gruñeron
[3i] sentir The stem vowel **e** becomes **ie** when stressed; **e** becomes **i** in 3rd persons of Preterite, 1st and 2nd persons pl. of Present Subjunctive. Gerund: *sintiendo* In *adquirir* the stem vowel **i** becomes **ie** when stressed	siento sientes siente sentimos sentís sienten	sienta sientas sienta sintamos sintáis sientan	sentí sentiste sintió sentimos sentisteis sintieron
[3j] dormir The stem vowel **o** becomes **ue** when stressed; **o** becomes **u** in 3rd persons of Preterite, 1st and 2nd persons pl. of Present Subjunctive. Gerund: *durmiendo*	duermo duermes duerme dormimos dormís duermen	duerma duermas duerma durmamos durmáis duerman	dormí dormiste durmió dormimos dormisteis durmieron
[3k] pedir The stem vowel **e** becomes **i** when stressed, and in 3rd persons of Preterite, 1st and 2nd persons pl. of Present Subjunctive. Gerund: *pidiendo*	pido pides pide pedimos pedís piden	pida pidas pida pidamos pidáis pidan	pedí pediste pidió pedimos pedisteis pidieron

INFINITIVE	PRESENT INDICATIVE	PRESENT SUBJUNCTIVE	PRETERITE
[3l] reír	río	ría	reí
Irregular.	ríes	rías	reíste
Past Participle: *reído*	ríe	ría	rió
Gerund: *riendo*	reímos	riamos	reímos
Imperative: *ríe (tú)*	reís	riáis	reísteis
	ríen	rían	rieron
[3m] erguir	yergo	yerga	erguí
Irregular.	yergues	yergas	erguiste
Gerund: *irguiendo*	yergue	yerga	irguió
Imperative: *yergue* (*tú*) and less	erguimos	yergamos	erguimos
commonly *irgue (tú)*	erguís	yergáis	erguisteis
	yerguen	yergan	irguieron
[3n] reducir	redu**zc**o	redu**zc**a	redu**j**e
The stem consonant **c** becomes **zc** before	reduces	redu**zc**as	redu**j**iste
a and **o** as [3f]; irregular preterite in **-uj-**	reduce	redu**zc**a	redu**j**o
Gerund: *reduciendo*	reducimos	redu**zc**amos	redu**j**imos
	reducís	redu**zc**áis	redu**j**isteis
	reducen	redu**zc**an	redu**j**eron
[3o] decir	digo	diga	dije
Irregular.	dices	digas	dijiste
Future: *diré*	dice	diga	dijo
Past Participle: *dicho*	decimos	digamos	dijimos
Gerund: *diciendo*	decís	digáis	dijisteis
Imperative: *di (tú)*	dicen	digan	dijeron
[3p] oír	oigo	oiga	oí
Irregular.	oyes	oigas	oíste
Unstressed **i** between vowels becomes **y**	oye	oiga	oyó
Past Participle: *oído*	oímos	oigamos	oímos
Gerund: *oyendo*	oís	oigáis	oísteis
	oyen	oigan	oyeron
[3q] salir	salgo	salga	salí
Irregular.	sales	salgas	saliste
Future: *saldré*	sale	salga	salió
Imperative: *sal (tú)*	salimos	salgamos	salimos
Gerund: *saliendo*	salís	salgáis	salisteis
	salen	salgan	salieron
[3r] venir	vengo	venga	vine
Irregular.	vienes	vengas	viniste
Future: *vendré*	viene	venga	vino
Gerund: *viniendo*	venimos	vengamos	vinimos
Imperative: *ven (tú)*	venís	vengáis	vinisteis
	vienen	vengan	vinieron
[3s] ir	voy	vaya	fui
Irregular.	vas	vayas	fuiste
Imperfect: *iba*	va	vaya	fue
Gerund: *yendo*	vamos	vayamos	fuimos
Imperative: *ve (tú), id (vosotros)*	vais	vayáis	fuisteis
	van	vayan	fueron

[1a] **cantar** (regular verb)

INDICATIVE	CONDITIONAL
Present	cantaría
canto	cantarías
cantas	cantaría
canta	cantaríamos
cantamos	cantaríais
cantáis	cantarían
cantan	*Imperative*
Imperfect	canta (tú)
cantaba	cantad (vosotros)
cantabas	*Past Participle*
cantaba	cantado
cantábamos	SUBJUNCTIVE
cantabais	*Present*
cantaban	cante
Preterite	cantes
canté	cante
cantaste	cantemos
cantó	cantéis
cantamos	canten
cantasteis	*Imperfect*
cantaron	cantara/-ase
Future	cantaras/-ases
cantaré	cantara/-ase
cantarás	cantáramos/-ásemos
cantará	cantarais/-aseis
cantaremos	cantaran/-asen
cantaréis	
cantarán	
Gerund	
cantando	

[3a] **partir** (regular verb)

INDICATIVE	CONDITIONAL
Present	partiría
parto	partirías
partes	partiría
parte	partiríamos
partimos	partiríais
partís	partirían
parten	*Imperative*
Imperfect	parte (tú)
partía	partid (vosotros)
partías	*Past Participle*
partía	partido
partíamos	SUBJUNCTIVE
partíais	*Present*
partían	parta
Preterite	partas
partí	parta
partiste	partamos
partió	partáis
partimos	partan
partisteis	*Imperfect*
partieron	partiera/-iese
Future	partieras/-ieses
partiré	partiera/-iese
partirás	partiéramos/-iésemos
partirá	partierais/-ieseis
partiremos	partieran/-iesen
partiréis	
partirán	
Gerund	
partiendo	

[2a] **temer** (regular verb)

INDICATIVE	CONDITIONAL
Present	temería
temo	temerías
temes	temería
teme	temeríamos
tememos	temeríais
teméis	temerían
temen	*Imperative*
Imperfect	teme (tú)
temía	temed (vosotros)
temías	*Past Participle*
temía	temido
temíamos	SUBJUNCTIVE
temíais	*Present*
temían	tema
Future	temas
temeré	tema
temerás	temamos
temerá	temáis
temeremos	teman
temeréis	*Imperfect*
temerán	temiera/-iese
Preterite	temieras/-ieses
temí	temiera/-iese
temiste	temiéramos/-iésemos
temió	temierais/-ieseis
temimos	temieran/-iesen
temisteis	
temieron	
Gerund	
temiendo	

[2j] **haber**

INDICATIVE	CONDITIONAL
Present	habría
he	habrías
has	habría
ha	habríamos
hemos	habríais
habéis	habrían
han	SUBJUNCTIVE
Imperfect	*Present*
había	haya
habías	hayas
había	haya
habíamos	hayamos
habíais	hayáis
habían	hayan
Preterite	*Imperfect*
hube	hubiera/-iese
hubiste	hubieras/-ieses
hubo	hubiera/-iese
hubimos	hubiéramos/-iésemos
hubisteis	hubierais/-ieseis
hubieron	hubieran/-iesen
Future	
habré	
habrás	
habrá	
habremos	
habréis	
habrán	
Gerund	
habiendo	
Past Participle	
habido	

[2v] **ser**

INDICATIVE	CONDITIONAL
Present	sería
soy	serías
eres	sería
es	seríamos
somos	seríais
sois	serían
son	*Imperative*
Imperfect	sé (tú)
era	sed (vosotros)
eras	SUBJUNCTIVE
era	*Present*
éramos	sea
erais	seas
eran	sea
Preterite	seamos
fui	seáis
fuiste	sean
fue	*Imperfect*
fuimos	fuera/-ese
fuisteis	fueras/-eses
fueron	fuera/-ese
Future	fuéramos/-ésemos
seré	fuerais/-eseis
serás	fueran/-esen
será	
seremos	
seréis	
serán	
Gerund	
siendo	
Past Participle	
sido	

EL VERBO INGLÉS

EL VERBO INGLÉS

El verbo inglés es bastante más sencillo que el español, a lo menos en cuanto a su forma. Hay muchos verbos fuertes o irregulares (damos una lista de ellos a continuación) y varias clases de irregularidad ortográfica (véanse las notas al final); pero hay una sola conjugación, y dentro de cada tiempo no hay variación para las seis personas excepto en el presente (tercera persona de singular). Por tanto, no es necesario ofrecer para el verbo inglés los cuadros y paradigmas con que se suele explicar el verbo español; la estructura general y las formas del verbo inglés se resumen en las siguientes notas.

Indicativo

(a) Presente: tiene la misma forma que el infinitivo en todas las personas menos la tercera del singular; en ésta, se añade una **-s** al infinitivo, p.ej. **he sells**, o se añade **-es** si el infinitivo termina en sibilante (los sonidos [s], [z], [ʃ] y [tʃ]; en la escritura **-ss, -zz, -sh** y **-ch**, etc). Esta **-s** añadida tiene dos pronunciaciones: tras consonante sorda se pronuncia sorda [s], p.ej. **scoffs** [skɒfs], **likes** [laɪks], **taps** [tæps], **waits** [weɪts], **baths** [bɑːθs]; tras consonante sonora se pronuncia sonora, p.ej. **robs** [rɒbz], **bends** [bendz], **seems** [siːmz], **gives** [gɪvz], **bathes** ['beɪðz]; **-es** se pronuncia también sonora tras sibilante o consonante sonora, o letra final del infinitivo, p.ej. **races** ['reɪsɪz], **urges** ['ɜːdʒɪz], **lashes** ['læʃɪz], **passes** ['pɑːsɪz].

Los verbos que terminan en **-y** la cambian en **-ies** en la tercera persona del singular, p.ej. **tries, pities, satisfies**; pero son regulares los verbos que en el infinitivo tienen una vocal delante de la **-y,** p.ej. **pray – he prays, annoy – she annoys.**

El verbo **be** es irregular en todas las personas:

I am	we are
you are	you are
he is	they are

Cuatro verbos más tienen forma irregular en la tercera persona del singular:

do – he does [dʌz]	go – he goes [gəʊz]
have – he has [hæz]	say – he says [sez]

(b) Pretérito (o **pasado simple**) **y participio de pasado:** tienen la misma forma en inglés; se forman añadiendo **-ed** al infinitivo, p.ej. **paint – I painted – painted**, o bien añadiendo **-d** a los infinitivos terminados en **-e** muda, p.ej. **bare – I bared – bared, move – I moved – moved, revise – I revised – revised.** (Para los muchos verbos irregulares, véase la lista abajo.) Esta **-d** o **-ed** se pronuncia por lo general [t]: **raced** [reɪst], **passed** [pɑːst]; pero cuando se añade a un infinitivo terminado en consonante sonora o en **r**, se pronuncia [d], p.ej. **bared** [bɛəd], **moved** [muːvd], **seemed** [siːmd], **buzzed** [bʌzd]. Si el infinitivo termina en **-d** o **-t,** la desinencia **-ed** se pronuncia como una sílaba más, [ɪd], p.ej. **raided** ['reɪdɪd], **dented** ['dentɪd]. Para los verbos cuyo infinitivo termina en **-y,** véase **Verbos débiles (e)** abajo.

(c) Tiempos compuestos del pasado: se forman como en español con el verbo auxiliar **to have** y el participio de pasado: perfecto **I have painted,** pluscuamperfecto **I had painted.**

(d) Futuro y condicional (o **potencial**): se forma el futuro con el auxiliar **will** o **shall** y el infinitivo, p.ej. **I will do it, they shall not pass**; se forma el condicional (o potencial) con el auxiliar **would** o **should** y el infinitivo, p.ej. **I would go, if she should come.** Como en español y de igual formación existen los tiempos compuestos llamados futuro perfecto, p.ej. **I shall have finished,** y potencial compuesto, p.ej. **I would have paid.**

(e) Para cada tiempo del indicativo existe una forma continua que se forma con el tiempo apropiado del verbo **to be** (equivalente en este caso al español **estar**) y el participio de presente (véase abajo): **I am waiting, we were hoping, they will be buying it, they would have been waiting still, I had been painting all day.** Conviene subrayar que el modo de emplear estas formas continuas no corresponde siempre al sistema español.

Subjuntivo

Este modo tiene muy poco uso en inglés. En el presente tiene la misma forma que el infinitivo en todas las personas, **(that) I go, (that) she go** etc. En el pasado simple el único verbo que tiene forma especial es **to be,** que es **were** en todas las personas, **(that) I were, (that) we were** etc. En los demás casos donde la lógica de los tiempos en español pudiera parecer exigir una forma de subjuntivo en pasado, el inglés emplea el presente, p.ej. **he had urged that we do it at once.** El subjuntivo se emplea obligatoriamente en inglés en **if I were you, if he were to do it, were I to attempt it** (el indicativo **was** es tenido por vulgar en estas frases y análogas); se encuentra también en la frase fosilizada **so be it,** y en el lenguaje oficial de las actas, etc, p.ej. **it is agreed that nothing be done, it was resolved that the pier be painted** (pero son igualmente correctos **should be done, should be painted**).

Gerundio y participio de presente

Tienen la misma forma en inglés; se añade al infinitivo la desinencia **-ing,** p.ej. **washing, sending, passing.** Para las muchas irregularidades ortográficas de esta desinencia, véase la sección **Verbos débiles** abajo.

Voz pasiva

Se forma exactamente como en español, con el tiempo apropiado del verbo **to be** (equivalente en este caso a **ser**) y el participio de pasado: **we are forced to, he was killed, they had been injured, the company will be taken over, it ought to have been rebuilt, were it to be agreed.**

Imperativo

Hay solamente una forma, que es la del infinitivo: **tell me, come here, don't do that.**

VERBOS FUERTES (O IRREGULARES)

INFINITIVO	PRETÉRITO	PARTICIPIO DE PASADO	INFINITIVO	PRETÉRITO	PARTICIPIO DE PASADO
abide	abode *or* abided	abode *or* abided	**gild**	gilded	gilded *or* gilt
arise	arose	arisen	**gird**	girded *or* girt	girded *or* girt
awake	awoke	awaked	**give**	gave	given
be	was, were	been	**go**	went	gone
bear	bore	(*llevado*) borne, (*nacido*) born	**grind**	ground	ground
			grow	grew	grown
beat	beat	beaten	**hang**	hung, (*Law*) hanged	hung, (*Law*) hanged
become	became	become			
beget	begot, (††) begat	begotten	**have**	had	had
			hear	heard	heard
begin	began	begun	**heave**	heaved, (*Naut*) hove	heaved, (*Naut*) hove
bend	bent	bent			
beseech	besought	besought	**hew**	hewed	hewed *or* hewn
bet	bet *or* betted	bet *or* betted	**hide**	hid	hidden
bid (*ordenar*)	bade	bidden	**hit**	hit	hit
(*licitar etc*)	bid	bid	**hold**	held	held
bind	bound	bound	**hurt**	hurt	hurt
bite	bit	bitten	**keep**	kept	kept
bleed	bled	bled	**kneel**	knelt	knelt
blow	blew	blown	**know**	knew	known
break	broke	broken	**lade**	laded	laden
breed	bred	bred	**lay**	laid	laid
bring	brought	brought	**lead**	led	led
build	built	built	**lean**	leaned *or* leant	leaned *or* leant
burn	burned *or* burnt	burned *or* burnt			
burst	burst	burst	**leap**	leaped *or* leapt	leaped *or* leapt
buy	bought	bought			
can	could	–	**learn**	learned *or* learnt	learned *or* learnt
cast	cast	cast			
catch	caught	caught	**leave**	left	left
choose	chose	chosen	**lend**	lent	lent
cleave[1] (*vt*)	clove *or* cleft	cloven *or* cleft	**let**	let	let
cleave[2] (*vi*)	cleaved, (††) clave	cleaved	**lie**	lay	lain
			light	lit *or* lighted	lit *or* lighted
cling	clung	clung	**lose**	lost	lost
come	came	come	**make**	made	made
cost (*vt*)	costed	costed	**may**	might	–
(*vi*)	cost	cost	**mean**	meant	meant
creep	crept	crept	**meet**	met	met
cut	cut	cut	**mow**	mowed	mown *or* mowed
deal	dealt	dealt	**pay**	paid	paid
dig	dug	dug	**put**	put	put
do	did	done	**quit**	quit *or* quitted	quit *or* quitted
draw	drew	drawn	**read** [ri:d]	read [red]	read [red]
dream	dreamed *or* dreamt	dreamed *or* dreamt	**rend**	rent	rent
			rid	rid	rid
drink	drank	drunk	**ride**	rode	ridden
drive	drove	driven	**ring**	rang	rung
dwell	dwelt	dwelt	**rise**	rose	risen
eat	ate	eaten	**run**	ran	run
fall	fell	fallen	**saw**	sawed	sawed *or* sawn
feed	fed	fed	**say**	said	said
feel	felt	felt	**see**	saw	seen
fight	fought	fought	**seek**	sought	sought
find	found	found	**sell**	sold	sold
flee	fled	fled	**send**	sent	sent
fling	flung	flung	**set**	set	set
fly	flew	flown	**sew**	sewed	sewn
forbid	forbad(e)	forbidden	**shake**	shook	shaken
forget	forgot	forgotten	**shave**	shaved	shaved *or* shaven
forsake	forsook	forsaken	**shear**	sheared	sheared *or* shorn
freeze	froze	frozen	**shed**	shed	shed
get	got	got, (*US*) gotten	**shine**	shone	shone

INFINITIVO	PRETÉRITO	PARTICIPIO DE PASADO	INFINITIVO	PRETÉRITO	PARTICIPIO DE PASADO
shoe	shod	shod	**stick**	stuck	stuck
shoot	shot	shot	**sting**	stung	stung
show	showed	shown *or* showed	**stink**	stank	stunk
shrink	shrank	shrunk	**strew**	strewed	strewed *or* strewn
shut	shut	shut			
sing	sang	sung	**stride**	strode	stridden
sink	sank	sunk	**strike**	struck	struck
sit	sat	sat	**string**	strung	strung
slay	slew	slain	**strive**	strove	striven
sleep	slept	slept	**swear**	swore	sworn
slide	slid	slid	**sweep**	swept	swept
sling	slung	slung	**swell**	swelled	swollen
slink	slunk	slunk	**swim**	swam	swum
slit	slit	slit	**swing**	swung	swung
smell	smelled *or* smelt	smelled *or* smelt	**take**	took	taken
			teach	taught	taught
smite	smote	smitten	**tear**	tore	torn
sow	sowed	sowed *or* sown	**tell**	told	told
speak	spoke	spoken	**think**	thought	thought
speed (*vt*)	speeded	speeded	**thrive**	throve *or* thrived	thriven *or* thrived
(*vi*)	sped	sped			
spell	spelled *or* spelt	spelled *or* spelt	**throw**	threw	thrown
spend	spent	spent	**thrust**	thrust	thrust
spill	spilled *or* spilt	spilled *or* spilt	**tread**	trod	trodden
spin	spun, (††) span	spun	**wake**	woke *or* waked	woken *or* waked
spit	spat	spat	**wear**	wore	worn
split	split	split	**weave**	wove	woven
spoil	spoiled *or* spoilt	spoiled *or* spoilt	**weep**	wept	wept
spread	spread	spread	**win**	won	won
spring	sprang	sprung	**wind**	wound	wound
stand	stood	stood	**wring**	wrung	wrung
stave	stove *or* staved	stove *or* staved	**write**	wrote	written
steal	stole	stolen			

N.B. – No constan en esta lista los verbos compuestos con prefijo etc; para ellos véase el verbo básico, p.ej. para **forbear** véase **bear,** para **understand** véase **stand.**

VERBOS DÉBILES CON IRREGULARIDAD ORTOGRÁFICA

(a) Hay muchos verbos cuya ortografía varía ligeramente en el participio de pasado y en el gerundio. Son los que terminan en consonante simple precedida de vocal simple acentuada; antes de añadirles la desinencia **-ed** o **-ing,** se dobla la consonante:

Infinitivo	Participio de pasado	Gerundio
sob	sobbed	sobbing
wed	wedded	wedding
lag	lagged	lagging
control	controlled	controlling
dim	dimmed	dimming
tan	tanned	tanning
tap	tapped	tapping
prefer	preferred	preferring
pat	patted	patting

(pero **cook-cooked-cooking, fear-feared-fearing, roar-roared-roaring,** donde la vocal no es simple y por tanto no se dobla la consonante).

(b) Los verbos que terminan en **-c** la cambian en **-ck** al añadirse las desinencias **-ed, -ing:**

frolic	frolicked	frolicking
traffic	trafficked	trafficking

(c) Los verbos terminados en **-l, -p,** aunque precedida de vocal átona, tienen doblada la consonante en el participio de pasado y en el gerundio en el inglés británico, pero simple en el de Estados Unidos:

grovel	(*Brit*) grovelled	(*Brit*) grovelling
	(*US*) groveled	(*US*) groveling
travel	(*Brit*) travelled	(*Brit*) travelling
	(*US*) traveled	(*US*) traveling
worship	(*Brit*) worshipped	(*Brit*) worshipping
	(*US*) worshiped	(*US*) worshiping

Nota – existe la misma diferencia en los sustantivos formados sobre tales verbos: (*Brit*) traveller = (*US*) traveler, (*Brit*) worshipper = (*US*) worshiper.

(d) Si el verbo termina en **-e** muda, se suprime ésta al añadir las desinencias **-ed, -ing:**

rake	raked	raking
care	cared	caring
smile	smiled	smiling
move	moved	moving
invite	invited	inviting

(Pero se conserva esta **-e** muda delante de **-ing** en los verbos **dye, singe** y otros, y en los pocos que terminan en **-oe: dyeing, singeing, hoeing.**)

(e) Si el verbo termina en **-y** (con las dos pronunciaciones de [ɪ] y [aɪ]) se cambia ésta en **-ied** (con las pronunciaciones respectivas de [ɪd] y [aɪd]) para formar el pretérito y el participio de pasado: **worry-worried-worried; pity-pitied-pitied; falsify-falsified-falsified; try-tried-tried.** El gerundio de tales verbos es regular: **worrying, trying** etc. Pero el gerundio de los verbos monosílabos **die, lie, vie** se escribe **dying, lying, vying.**

ASPECTS OF WORD FORMATION
IN SPANISH

ASPECTS OF WORD FORMATION IN SPANISH

Processes of word formation in Spanish are in some respects far richer and more complex than those of English, and users of the dictionary may find the following notes of interest as guides which both draw together and extend information conveyed in the main alphabetic list.

1 Prefixes and prefixed elements

These very largely correspond to those of English when drawn, as so many are, from the common Graeco-Latin stock: **contra-**, **des-**, **dis-**, **ex-**, **hiper-**, **hipo-**, **para-**, **re-**, **ultra-** and so on, with **auto-** representing both English **auto-** and **self-**. There is normally total correspondence also in the immense range of scientific elements, allowance being made for phonetic and orthographic adjustments such as **lympho-/linfo-**. Elements may build up in blinding-with-science advertisements such as that for **electrofisiohidroterapias**. There are a few traditional Spanish intensifying prefixes which have no corresponding English forms: see **re-**, **requete-**, **recontra-**, also **archi-** which is much more used than **arch-** in English. These may be combined for exceptional emphasis: **archirrequetedicho** 'oft-repeated'.

2 Formation by suffix

(a) In both languages many suffixes of Latin origin correspond perfectly and will not be discussed here: **-al/-al**, **-ific(al)/-ífico**, **-ity/-idad**, **-ous/-oso**, **-tion/-ción**, and others. It is probable but not wholly predictable that in both languages on any one base the full range of forms can be built: for example **-izar**, **-izado**, **-izante**, **-izaje**, **-ización**, **-izacionar**, **-izacionismo**, though Spanish with its greater degree of latinity may much exceed English in this regard (**tecnocratizarse** 'to become technocratic'; 'to become dominated by technocrats'; **desgubernamentalización**, **destrascendentalización**). See further remarks below on **-able**, **-abilidad**.

(b) For other suffixes, hundreds of items have been listed in the main body of the dictionary because they are sufficiently common to warrant this. They are of two types. In the first group are those words which have become fully 'lexicalized' and need separate treatment, such as **casita**, **españolito**, **lentillas**, **librote**, **mujeraza**, **mujerzuela**, **palabrota**. In the second group, an occasional series has been included in the main dictionary as an illustration of the process here under discussion: see for example **amigacho-amigazo-amiguete-amigote-amiguito**. In any case, the notion of what may be considered 'lexicalized' is very unsure.

(c) Identification of the base word is easy in most cases. Normally, but far from always, the suffixed form retains the gender of the original noun. Certain changes of what is or becomes with suffix a medial consonant need to be borne in mind: **lazo-lacito**, **voz-vocecita**, **barco-barquito**, **loco-loquillo**. Sometimes two or even more suffixes are built on a base: **facilonería** consists of **fácil** + **-ón** + **-ería**, **hombrachón** consists of **hombre** + **-acho** + **-ón**, **tristoncete** consists of **triste** + **-ón** + **ete**, **gentucilla** consists of **gente** + **-uza** + **-illa**, while real complexities are offered by **es una marisabidilla** and **hay peces pero son chiquititecillos**. The need for a compounding consonant is seen in some formations: **hombre** will not make *hombrito or *hombrillo, but **hombrecito**, **hombrecillo**.

(d) Nearly all the suffixes to be listed below are nouns and adjectives. There is little one can say about the formation of verbs except to note that it is less free than in English (in which one can all too readily say 'the troops will be helicoptered in', 'the match was weathered off', 'please have this text word-processed and the data accessed'). New verbs almost always belong to the first **-ar** conjugation (including **-ear**, **-ificar**, **-izar**) and may themselves be built on noun or adjectival suffixes or related to them (eg **mariconear** supposing noun suffix **-eo**).

(e) Few adverbs are listed below; they are readily formed in the standard way from the feminine form of the adjective + **-mente**. Speakers and writers of Spanish in ordinary colloquial registers tend to avoid these forms (this does not refer to such ordinary forms as eg **rápidamente**), preferring less pretentious circumlocutions ('de una manera ...', etc), but the **-mente** forms appear powerfully in literary and journalistic writing and are often much more expressive than the English adverbial form in **-ly**. Thus we find **obrar maquiavélicamente** 'to act in a Machiavellian fashion', **pintar goyescamente** 'to paint in the manner of Goya', **una fruta gustativamente superior** 'a fruit which is superior in terms of flavour', **generacionalmente hablando** 'speaking in terms of generations', **solicitar improrrogablemente** 'apply with no possible extension of the deadline', **una republiquilla mafiosamente organizada** 'a potty republic organized on Mafia lines', and even – as an imaginative nonce-word – **huyó gacelamente** 'she fled with the grace of a gazelle' (there being no base adjective *gacelo).

(f) The usage discussed below is that of Spain. Latin-American Spanish offers notable differences from this: some suffixes of Spain are hardly used in Latin America, while **-ito** is used far more and often without any perceptible diminutive or emotive function (eg **Con permiso** 'May I come in?' in Spain may be **Con permisito** in Venezuela). See eg **ahorita**, **lueguito**.

(g) While some of the suffixes listed below present no semantic problem, being wholly objective or neutral (when designating largeness or smallness), some of these and many others may carry an emotive charge (intensifying, belittling, self-deprecatory, ironical, admiring ...) for the speaker or writer and this is often a subtle one. It follows that to give an English translation or even an impression in a few words is difficult: the reader should try to form his own sense by inspecting a wide range of examples of the same suffix, including some which are cross-referenced to the main dictionary. The expressive wealth of formation by suffix can be illustrated by the following collection of forms all based on **rojo** in its political sense and gathered from the press in recent years: **rojamen, rojazo, rojeras, rojería, rojerío. rojete, rojillo, rojismo, rojista, rojoide**. For English readers the best study is that of Anthony Gooch, **Diminutive, Augmentative and Pejorative Suffixes in Modern Spanish** (Oxford etc, Pergamon Press, 1967, 2nd ed. 1970), with thousands of examples and English versions which are both sensitive and lively. What follows is a selection only, of common and current items, and is in no way to be taken as a comprehensive survey.

-able, -abilidad (*also* -ible, -ibilidad)

This suffix often expresses more than the corresponding English **-able, -ability** (or English does not tolerate the corresponding forms). Examples are **idolatrable** 'that can be idolatrized', **indeglutible** 'that cannot be swallowed, unswallowable', **jubilable** 'of pensionable age', **tanques largables** 'tanks that can be jettisoned'. The latinate nature of Spanish permits such formations as **inasequibilidad, inconsultabilidad, la indescarrilabilidad del nuevo tren.**

-aco, -aca

Pejorative noun suffix: **hombraco** 'contemptible fellow, horrible chap', **tiparraco** 'odious individual, creep'. Compare in the dictionary **libraco, pajarraco.**

-acho, -acha

Pejorative noun suffix: **vulgacho** 'the common herd'. Compare in the dictionary **hombracho, populacho, ricacho.**

-ada

(i) A noun suffix expressing 'an act by or typical of': **carlistada** 'Carlist uprising', **escocesada** 'typically Scottish thing to do', 'just what one might expect of a Scot'; compare in the dictionary **bobada, perrada, puñalada.**

(ii) A noun suffix implying some notion of collectivity, as in **extranjerada** 'group of foreigners', **parrafada** 'good long chat', and compare in the dictionary **camada, hornada, indiada, muslada.** Beyond these one finds also an intensifying function, as in **gozada, liada, riada,** with which perhaps belong **panzada, tripada** 'bellyful'.

-ado, -aje

These noun suffixes of similar function are enjoying some popularity at the moment in new formations which express a process (often rendered by English **-ing**): **blanqueado** and **lavado (del dinero)** 'laundering (of money)', **lastrado** 'ballasting', **clonaje, gemelaje** 'cloning', **matonaje** 'bully-boy behaviour', **reciclaje.** A particular function of **-ado** is to express a collectivity, in English 'the body of ...': see in the dictionary **alumnado, campesinado, estudiantado, profesorado.**

-ajo, -aja

Strongly pejorative noun suffix: **muñecajo** 'rotten old doll', **papelajo** 'dirty old bit of paper'; see further in the dictionary **pintarrajo.** Among adjectives one finds **pequeñajo** 'wretchedly small'.

-amen

A humorous augmentative: **barrigamen** 'grossly fat belly', **labiamen** 'great red gash of a made-up mouth', **papelamen** 'lots of paper'. Compare in the dictionary **caderamen, culamen, muslamen, tetamen,** whose tone is warmly appreciative. In **ladrillamen** 'brickwork' and **maderamen** 'woodwork' there is a collective connotation.

-ante

A neutral adjectival suffix which generally corresponds to English **-ing**. Self-explanatory are eg **destripante, gimoteante, lastrante, masificante, mistificante, mitificante:** less transparent are the **crónicas masacrantes** 'vicious reports' which a journalist wrote about an event. Compare in the dictionary **golfante, hilarante, pimpante, preocupante,** and see also **-izante.**

-ata

See in the dictionary the group **bocata, drogata, fumata, tocata,** colloquial variations created by young people.

-azo, -aza

(i) Augmentative of more or less neutral tone: **animalazo** 'huge creature, whacking great brute', **generalazo** 'important general', **golpazo** 'heavy blow', **jovenazo** 'big lad, strapping youth'.

(ii) Augmentative of favourable tone: **hembraza** 'magnificent figure of a woman', **soy madrileñazo** 'I'm from Madrid and proud of it', **morenazo** 'man with dark good looks'; 'man with a lovely tan', **talentazo** 'immense talent'.

(iii) Augmentative of unfavourable tone: **cochinaza** 'dirty sow of a woman', **locaza** 'outrageous old queen', **melenaza** 'great mop of long hair'; **¡ostiazo!** (see **hostia (d)**).

(iv) The suffix may signify 'a blow with ...': **ladrillazo** 'blow with a brick', **misilazo** 'missile strike'; compare in the dictionary **aldabonazo,**

codazo, etc. **Cristazo** 'blow with a crucifix' is rumoured to exist, and one can readily imagine a **diccionariazo**.

(v) The suffix may signify 'a sound made with ...': **cornetazo** 'bugle-call, blast on the bugle'; compare in the dictionary **telefonazo** and (with probable sounds) **frenazo**.

(vi) The (attempted) blow may be a military one, a coup or attack: in the past a **gibraltarazo** may have been contemplated, and there was certainly a **malvinazo**. See in the dictionary **cuartelazo**, **tejerazo**.

-e

This is increasingly used as a noun suffix to refer to a process: **manduque** 'eating', **tueste** 'roasting' (of coffee). Compare in the dictionary **cuelgue**, **derrame**, **desfase**, **desmadre**.

-ejo, -eja

Mostly a pejorative suffix: **discursejo** 'rotten speech', **grupejo** 'insignificant little group', **nos costó un milloncejo** 'it cost us all of a million', **todo por unas cuantas pesetejas** 'all for a few measly pesetas'. See in the dictionary **animalejo**, **caballejo**, **palabreja**. Sometimes the sense is simply diminutive, eg **gracejo**, **rinconcejo**.

-eo

This like **-e** refers to a process or continuing act, and is much commoner: **guitarreo** 'strumming on the guitar', **ligoteo** 'chatting-up', **mariposeo** 'flirting', **marisqueo** 'gathering shellfish'. See in the dictionary **cachondeo**, **gimoteo**, **musiqueo**, **papeleo**.

-eras

A strongly intensifying masculine singular suffix: **guarreras** 'filthy person', **macheras** 'over-the-top macho man'. Compare **boceras**, **golferas**, **guaperas**.

-ería

Among a very wide variety of applications of this common suffix one may distinguish a general notion of quality inherent in the base noun or adjective: **marchosería**, **matonería**, **mitinería**, **milagrería**, **pelmacería** (compare in the dictionary **chiquillería**, **nadería**, **patriotería**, **tontería**). The suffix may also indicate 'place where', as in **floristería**, **frutería**; a recent invention is **liguería**, 'pick-up joint'.

-ero

The wide application of this mainly adjectival suffix may be gauged from eg **cafetero**, **carero**, **etiquetero**, **faldero**, **futbolero**, **patriotero**, **pesetero** in the dictionary. A **barco atunero/bacaladero/camaronero/marisquero** will fish for tunny, cod, shrimps, and shellfish respectively.

-esco

English **-esque** is only a pale equivalent of this adjectival suffix. Self-explanatory are **chaplinesco**, **tarzanesco**, and in the dictionary **goyesco**, **mitinesco**, **oficinesco**. One notes **con lentitud notariesca** 'with all a lawyer's dreary deliberation', **Madrid se va poniendo pulpesco** (Gooch) 'Madrid is extending its tentacles in all directions', and of London, **el ambiente minifaldesco de los años 60** 'the swinging '60s scene'.

-ete, -eta

Mildly diminutive noun and adjectival suffix: **alegrete** 'a bit merry', **guapete** 'quite handsome'; **unos duretes** 'a few measly pesetas', **tartaleta** 'small cake'. Compare in the dictionary **galancete**, **palacete**, **pobrete**.

-ez

A noun suffix which can often be translated by the English abstract **-ness**: **grisez**, **majez**, **menudez**, **modernez**, **muchachez**, and in the dictionary eg **gelidez**, **morenez**, **testarudez**.

-iano

A common adjectival suffix which English **-ian** might but usually cannot represent when attached to personal names: not only, in the dictionary, native **calderoniano**, **galdosiano**, **lorquiano**, but also **galbraithiano**, **goethiano**, **grouchiano**, **joyciano** (and **joyceano**), **una novela lampedusiana**. Some forms may puzzle foreign learners: eg **la poesía juanramoniana** refers to the work of the Spanish poet Juan Ramón Jiménez.

-ico, -ica

As an adjective, this is a regional (Aragon and Navarre, Granada, Murcia) variant of **-ito**: **me duele un tantico, ¿te han dejado solico?** As a noun it is a contemptuous diminutive: **cobardica**, **llorica**, **miedica**, **mierdica**, **sólo me pidió medio milloncico**. Compare in the dictionary **acusica**, **roñica**.

-il

An adjectival suffix which is not specially pejorative but conveys a mildly ironical tone. Senses are transparent: **caciquil**, **curanderil**, **una dieta garbancil**, **machil** 'a bit too macho', **ministeril**, **ratonil**. Very expressive are **urraquil**, which depends on the word **urraca**, 'magpie', with its thievish propensities, and **sus encantos cleopatriles** 'her *femme fatale* (-like) charms'.

-illo, -illa

A noun and adjectival suffix, gently diminutive and often implying a degree of good-humoured condescension. For adjectives, consider **un vino ligerillo** 'a pleasantly light wine', **una sevillana guapilla** 'a pretty and provocative Sevillian girl', **es dificilillo** 'it's a wee bit tricky'. For nouns, **un lugarcillo** 'a nice little place', **jefecillo** 'local boss, petty boss', **jequecillo** 'petty sheik', **un olorcillo a corrupción** 'a slight smell of corruption'. More plainly pejorative are **empleadillo, ministrillo, personajillo**.

-ín, -ina

A mildly approving suffix for nouns and adjectives, quite widely used but specially attached to Asturias and Granada: **guapín, guapina, jovencina, monín, pequeñín**; **cafetín** is in part demeaning but also affectionate, and **tontín** to a child will not cause alarm.

-ísimo

This suffix is not one of the degrees of comparison but implies 'very' with various nuances:

(i) 'Very', neutral in tone: **un asunto importantísimo** 'a very important matter, a most important matter'; **una cuestión discutidísima** 'a highly controversial question'; **un desarrolladísimo sentido de orgullo** 'a very highly developed sense of pride'; **es dificilísimo** 'it is extremely difficult'.

(ii) More emotionally: **es simpatiquísimo** 'he's terribly nice, he's awfully kind'; **es guapísima** 'she really is pretty'.

(iii) Exaggerating somewhat in order to impress: **un libro grandísimo** 'an enormous great book, a megatome'; **una comida costosísima**. There may be humour or irony, depending on context: **la superfinísima actriz, esta cursilísima costumbre**.

(iv) Passionately patriotic: **aquel españolísimo plato** 'that most Spanish of all dishes'; **la madrileñísima plaza de Santa Ana** St Anne's Square which is so (endearingly) typical of Madrid'.

(v) Exceptionally, one finds this suffix attached to a noun: **aquí ella es la jefísima** 'she's the only real boss round here'.

(vi) Adverbs may be formed in the usual way on some of these forms, eg **brillantísimamente, riquísimamente**.

-ismo

In hundreds of simple cases, Spanish words in **-ismo** naturally correspond to English **-ism**. But Spanish uses the suffix much more and in creations which English has to express in a circumlocutory way: while **japonesismo** might just be 'Japaneseness', and **ilegalismo** is hardly more than **ilegalidad** 'illegality', **el guitarrismo moderno** has to be 'modern guitar-playing' and **gorilismo** 'rule by bully-boys'. **El felipismo** sums up criticism of the Spanish Prime Minister Felipe González. Real complications start with such examples as **gaudinismo** 'style and practices of the architect Gaudí', **gubernamentalismo** 'government interventionism, tendency for the government to intervene in everything', **el paragüismo de los gallegos** 'devotion of the Galicians to their umbrellas', **importanadismo** and in America **quemimportismo** 'couldn't-care-less attitude', while **el lolitismo** has to be left to the imagi-

nation of the reader.

-ista

This forms nouns of common gender and adjectives also. Simple cases such as **comunista** again correspond precisely to English, but many do not: an **independista** supports an independence movement, that is **un movimiento independentista**; a **madridista** is a supporter of Real Madrid football club, and many Spanish teams acquire similarly-designated supporters; a **maximarquista** and a **plusmarquista** are record-holders, a **pluriempleísta** is a moonlighter having two or more jobs, and a **mariposista** specializes in the butterfly stroke. Compare in the dictionary **congresista, juerguista, ordenancista**.

-itis

A few formations on this adopt the suffix of eg **bronquitis** and humourously imply a medical condition: **barriguitis** 'tendency to get a paunch, paunchiness', **concursitis** 'obsessive wish to enter competitions', **empatitis** 'tendency to draw games', **mudancitis** 'disease which leads one to move house perpetually'. See in the dictionary **gandulitis, holgazanitis**.

-ito, -ita

This suffix is the commonest of all. One can discern at least three categories:

(i) The purely diminutive: **Juanito** 'Johnny', **su hijito** 'her small son, her baby', **es más bien bajita** 'she's rather on the short side'. Among adverbs one finds **salimos tempranito, pues hazlo prontito**.

(ii) Diminutive with added affective (usually kindly) nuance: **jugosito** 'nice and juicy', **limpito** 'clean as a new pin', **un golito** 'a nice little goal', **iban cogiditos de la mano, ¡pobrecito!** 'poor old chap!', 'poor little fellow!', etc. One may be self-deprecating: **te traigo un regalito, ofrecemos una fiestecita en casa**, or one may need to apologize for troubling others: **¿me echas una firmita aquí?** 'could you please sign here?' To small children it is natural to say **hay que ser educaditos** 'we must be on our best behaviour'.

(iii) Other uses express a kind of superlative: **ahora mismito** 'this very instant', **estaba solito** 'he was all on his own', **están calentitos** 'they're piping hot', **lo mejorcito que haya** 'the very best there is'.

-izante

This adjectival and noun suffix may correspond to English **-izing**, as in **medida liberalizante, tendencia modernizante**, but sometimes goes beyond this: **idiotizante** 'stupefying', **colores mimetizantes, hormona masculinizante**. Compare **teorizante** and others in the dictionary.

-izo

This adjectival suffix expresses the 'quality' of the

base word: see in the dictionary eg **acomodadizo, huidizo, quebradizo, rollizo**.

-ocracia

Spanish **meritocracia** = English 'meritocracy', but Spanish seems to have a greater capacity for rather bitterly humorous formations with this suffix: **gorilocracia** 'reign of the strong-arm men', **mojigatocracia** 'rule by hypocritical establishment circles'. See further in the dictionary **dedocracia, falocracia, yernocracia**.

-oide

This adjectival and noun suffix implies 'somewhat, rather', and is always pejorative: **extranjeroide** 'somewhat foreign', **locoide** and **tontoide, estas tramas fascistoides** 'these quasi-fascist schemes', while a **liberaloide** is a 'pseudo-liberal' who might well indulge in **sentimentaloidería**.

-ón, -ona

This very frequent noun and adjectival suffix has several differing connotations:

(i) purely augmentative: **muchachón, generalón** 'really important general', **pistolón, liberalón, lingotón** 'big shot of whisky' (etc), **doncellona** 'unmarried lady of a certain age'; among adjectives, **grandón** 'tall and solidly built', **gastón** 'free-spending', **docilón** 'extremely placid'.

(ii) augmentative with a strongly approving tone: **mimosón, simpaticón, guapetón** (see **guapetona** in the dictionary: a word so rich that it has formed the subject of a learned article).

(iii) augmentative with unpleasant or strongly ironic nuances: **britanicón** 'overbearing Brit of the old school', **hombrón** 'hulking great brute', **milagrón** 'great miracle', **movidón** (see **movida** in the dictionary).

-osis

Like **-itis**, this is for jocular formations which echo the common suffix of medical terms. Recently noted: **ligosis** 'obsessive womanizing'.

-ote, -ota

An adjectival and noun augmentative, with varying nuances. Among adjectives, **gordote, guapote, liberalote, mansote** (of a bull) carry little extra charge, as is the case also with nouns **aldeota, drogota, muchachote, pasota**. Stronger feelings emerge with **presumidote** 'impossibly vain', **militarote** 'overblown braggart soldier', **britanicote** 'Colonel-Blimpish Brit'. One man who stole a glance at an attractive girl took a longer look, explaining that his **miradita** became a **miradota**.

-uco, -uca

This is a diminutive suffix, not common except per-haps in Santander province (**niñuco** 'very small boy'), and more especially a pejorative one: **frailuco** 'contemptible little priest', **mujeruca** 'very odd little woman'.

-ucho, -ucha

Much like the preceding, and commoner: **debilucho** 'weakish', **delicaducho** 'rather delicate', **delgaducho** 'terribly thin, scrawny', **morenucho** 'extremely swarthy'; a **hotelucho** would be classed as minus two stars. See in the dictionary **cuartucho, novelucha**.

-udo, -uda

This adjectival suffix expresses the notion of 'possessing (the base quality) in abundance': **mostachudo, patilludo, talentudo; una caligrafía garrapatuda** 'nasty scrawled writing', Compare in the dictionary **concienzudo, huesudo, linajudo, melenudo, suertudo**.

-uelo, -uela

A diminutive and sometimes affectionate suffix: **gordezuelo, pequeñuelo; muchachuelo, tontuela**.

-ujo, -uja

A strongly pejorative suffix for adjective and noun: **papelujo** 'wretched bit of paper'; **estrechujo, pequeñujo**.

-uzo, -uza

A very strongly pejorative suffix for adjective and noun: **marranuzo** 'filthy, stinking'; **carnuza** 'rotten awful meat'.

3 Designations of women in the professions etc.

(a) In recent decades the entry of women into many professions previously more or less closed to them has caused developments and problems for Spanish with its consistent gender-marking of nouns (in contrast to English with its very restricted perception of gender in such usages as 'she will dock tomorrow' and 'she's been a very good car', together, naturally, with the full range of biological pairs 'fox/vixen', 'bull/cow' and so on). What follows is an attempt to outline aspects of usage and problems in Spanish, without recommendations which it would be perilous to offer in a time of rapid change. Alternative possibilities have been offered in many entries in the main text of the dictionary. The remarks relate to Peninsular Spanish; usage in Latin America, especially in countries with strongly conservative social structures, is very varied and often different from that of Spain.

(b) There is generally no problem about the morphology (forms) of the feminine. A noun whose masculine ends in **-o** has a feminine in **-a**; **la médica, la ministra, la bióloga, la bioquímica**. The same is true of **-or -ora**: **la instructora**, **la lectora**, **la embajadora**, **la conductora**, and of other pairs such as **alcalde/alcaldesa**, **coronel/coronela**, **capitán/ capitana**, **presidente/presidenta**, **jefe/jefa**, while all nouns in **-ista** are of common gender anyway, **el/la periodista** etc. (note however the special case of **el modisto**). There is doubt as between **la juez** and **la jueza**.

(c) Usage, however, often invalidates any automatic application of forms mentioned above. On the one hand, some women in the professions may feel that they have attained full status and equality with men colleagues only when the established standard word is applied to them: one may expect **la abogada** and this will often be correct, but sometimes a woman prefers to be **la abogado** and equally **la médico**, **la arquitecto**, **la dramaturgo**. It was noticeable that for a time the Spanish press referred to **la primer ministro** in several countries and then passed to **la primera ministra**. There seems to be resistance to the adoption of **la soldada**.

(d) There is a special problem when a feminine form already exists in a pejorative sense which may for a time preclude, for some speakers and writers, its use about a woman with a newly-attained professional or other status: such words as **jefa** and **socia** are concerned here. It was noticed that the woman circulation manager of a Spanish newspaper sent out subscription forms for some years signing her name over the words **Jefe de Márketing** and then changing the first to **Jefa**. The women members of a society will more likely be **las miembros** but one notes a tendency for them to be **las socias**, showing that the old pejorative sense is no longer a bar to this. There is also a group of words for sciences whose existence may in some contexts cause doubt: because **la física** is 'physics' there may be uncertainty about whether a woman physicist should be **una física** or **una físico**. A few special cases cause difficulties of other kinds: since **la policía** is established as 'the police force', it is not readily applicable to a policewoman in case confusion should arise, and informants specify that while they will refer to **una policía** 'a policewoman' and **unas policías** 'several policewomen', they would avoid such usage with the definite article and say **la mujer policía** 'the policewoman' or possibly take refuge in the safely bi-gender **la agente**. If there is doubt a woman should naturally be asked which designation she herself prefers. It may also be the case that organizations have their house-rules too, though these may be very haphazardly applied: thus **El País** of 9 May 1990 headlines a report **Sanción ratificada contra una médica**, but in the body of the article the woman concerned is twice referred to as **la médico**.

(e) In the category of military and similar ranks older senses have been relegated as archaisms: **la coronela** was 'the colonel's lady' but is now '(woman) colonel', **la embajadora** is not 'the ambassador's wife' but '(woman) ambassador', and **la alcaldesa** is '(woman) mayor'. In other walks of life a woman poet is **una poeta**, since **poetisa** is as unthinkable as English 'poetess', and a woman writer is **una autora**, to be translated as 'author' rather than 'authoress'. A woman minister in a nonconformist church may safely be called **la pastora**, but it is wholly unsure by what term women priests in the Anglican Church are or will be known.

4 Attributive use of nouns

(a) Examples of such formations as **el patrón oro** go back to the 17th century, but remained rare until recent times when there has been an explosion of the attributive use of nouns (defined as the use of a noun in a qualifying or adjectival function but without concord of number or gender). Much of this is owed to the influence of English, but some formations now go well beyond any possible pattern existing in English. **Buque fantasma** translates English 'ghost ship' and **gobierno fantasma** was once formed as a calque on English 'shadow cabinet', but the usage then develops a momentum of its own in Spanish and we find **empresa fantasma**, **gol fantasma** and other expressive formations.

(b) Well-established usages are covered in many cases by entries in the dictionary. Such are **cuestión clave**, **programa coloquio**, **reunión cumbre**, **fecha límite**, **cárcel modelo**, **mitín monstruo**, **emisión pirata**, **planta piloto**, **peso pluma**, **niña prodigio**, **país satélite**, **coches sport**, **precio tope**. There is a range of attributives which may go with eg **efecto**: **efecto avalancha/ boomerang/ dominó/ Doppler/embudo/ escoba/pistón/túnel**), and **efecto invernadero** seems to have displaced earlier **efecto de invernadero**. Formations such as **faros antiniebla**, **manifestaciones antihuelga**, **medidas antipolución** are now standard, as are many others in the domains of fashion (**falda pantalón**, **falda tubo**) and cuisine, etc. These correspond closely to English models. Statements about colour in attributive form are also standard usage, eg **un vestido color (de) lila**, **uniformes verde oliva**, **cortinas verde oscuro** (but naturally **cortinas verdes** with concord). The same is true of phrases with **modelo**, **tipo**, and similar words: **un coche modelo Tiburón 1500**, **aviones tipo Concorde**, **el factor Rhesus**, **un sombrero estilo Bogart**, and also of biological definitions such as **el pájaro hembra**, **las musarañas macho**.

(c) Creativity in this aspect in journalistic Spanish has now gone well beyond any possible English model, however: examples are **un jugador promesa**, **horas punta**, **tecnología punta**, **tránsito punta**, **el grupo revelación de 1992**, **una teoría puente**. Abbreviations may figure too in a kind of journalistic shorthand: **tres aviones USA**, **dos agentes CIA**.

(d) While the principle of non-concord is the soundest one, as above, speakers may occasionally treat the attributive element as an adjective and assign it concord for number (but never for gender): **hay dos palabras claves**, **pedimos pagos extras**. One finds both **hombres rana** and **hombres ranas**. In the press those who compose headlines may not always agree with those who write articles: **Cambio 16** on 11 August 1986 carried the headline **Matilde Fernández explica por qué no ha habido mujeres ministro en el nuevo gobierno**, while the body of the report below included the words **no se han conseguido**

mujeres ministros.

(e) Confusion reigns in the use or absence of the hyphen in such combinations: **hombre rana**, **hombre-rana**. If the combination is brief there is a tendency to use the hyphen: **granja-escuela, grúa-puente, dos grúas-puente**. The Academy appears to rule against the hyphen but has hardly put its mind as yet to this relatively new and rapidly-developing usage.

Note: * preceding a word denotes an invented form.

NUMERALS
LOS NÚMEROS

NUMERALS

CARDINAL NUMBERS

NÚMEROS CARDINALES

nought, zero	0	cero
one	1	(*m*) uno, (*f*) una
two	2	dos
three	3	tres
four	4	cuatro
five	5	cinco
six	6	seis
seven	7	siete
eight	8	ocho
nine	9	nueve
ten	10	diez
eleven	11	once
twelve	12	doce
thirteen	13	trece
fourteen	14	catorce
fifteen	15	quince
sixteen	16	dieciséis
seventeen	17	diecisiete
eighteen	18	dieciocho
nineteen	19	diecinueve
twenty	20	veinte
twenty-one	21	veintiuno (*see note* **b**)
twenty-two	22	veintidós
twenty-three	23	veintitrés
thirty	30	treinta
thirty-one	31	treinta y uno
thirty-two	32	treinta y dos
forty	40	cuarenta
fifty	50	cincuenta
sixty	60	sesenta
seventy	70	setenta
eighty	80	ochenta
ninety	90	noventa
ninety-nine	99	noventa y nueve
a (*or* one) hundred	100	cien, ciento (*see note* **c**)
a hundred and one	101	ciento uno
a hundred and two	102	ciento dos
a hundred and ten	110	ciento diez
a hundred and eighty-two	182	ciento ochenta y dos
two hundred	200	(*m*) doscientos, (*f*) –as
three hundred	300	(*m*) trescientos, (*f*) –as
four hundred	400	(*m*) cuatrocientos, (*f*) –as
five hundred	500	(*m*) quinientos, (*f*) –as
six hundred	600	(*m*) seiscientos, (*f*) –as
seven hundred	700	(*m*) setecientos, (*f*) –as
eight hundred	800	(*m*) ochocientos, (*f*) –as
nine hundred	900	(*m*) novecientos, (*f*) –as
a (*or* one) thousand	1000	mil
a thousand and two	1002	mil dos
two thousand	2000	dos mil
ten thousand	10000	diez mil
a (*or* one) hundred thousand	100000	cien mil
a (*or* one) million	1000000	un millón (*see note* **d**)
two million	2000000	dos millones (*see note* **d**)

LOS NÚMEROS

Notes on usage of the cardinal numbers

(a) One, and the other numbers ending in one, agree in Spanish with the noun (stated or implied): *una casa, un coche, si se trata de pagar en libras ello viene a sumar treinta y una, había ciento una personas.*

(b) 21: In Spanish there is some uncertainty when the number is accompanied by a feminine noun. In the spoken language both *veintiuna peseta* and *veintiuna pesetas* are heard; in 'correct' literary language only *veintiuna pesetas* is found. With a masculine noun the numeral is shortened in the usual way: *veintiún perros rabiosos.* These remarks apply also to 31, 41 *etc.*

(c) 100: When the number is spoken alone or in counting a series of numbers both *cien* and *ciento* are heard. When there is an accompanying noun the form is always *cien: cien hombres, cien chicas.* In the compound numbers note 101 = *ciento uno,* 110 = *ciento diez,* but 100000 = *cien mil.*

(d) 1000000: In Spanish the word *millón* is a noun, so the numeral takes *de* when there is a following noun: *un millón de fichas, tres millones de árboles quemados.*

(e) In Spanish the cardinal numbers may be used as nouns, as in English; they are always masculine: *jugó el siete de corazones, el once nacional de Ruritania, éste es el trece y nosotros buscamos el quince.*

(f) To divide the larger numbers clearly a point is used in Spanish where English places a comma: English 1,000 = Spanish 1.000, English 2,304,770 = Spanish 2.304.770. (This does not apply to dates: see below.)

ORDINAL NUMBERS

NÚMEROS ORDINALES

first	1	primero (*see note* **b**)
second	2	segundo
third	3	tercero (*see note* **b**)
fourth	4	cuarto
fifth	5	quinto
sixth	6	sexto
seventh	7	séptimo
eighth	8	octavo
ninth	9	noveno, nono
tenth	10	décimo
eleventh	11	undécimo
twelfth	12	duodécimo
thirteenth	13	decimotercio, decimotercero
fourteenth	14	decimocuarto
fifteenth	15	decimoquinto
sixteenth	16	decimosexto
seventeenth	17	decimoséptimo
eighteenth	18	decimoctavo
nineteenth	19	decimonoveno, decimonono
twentieth	20	vigésimo
twenty-first	21	vigésimo primero, vigésimo primo
twenty-second	22	vigésimo segundo
thirtieth	30	trigésimo
thirty-first	31	trigésimo primero, trigésimo primo
fortieth	40	cuadragésimo
fiftieth	50	quincuagésimo
sixtieth	60	sexagésimo

seventieth	**70**	septuagésimo
eightieth	**80**	octogésimo
ninetieth	**90**	nonagésimo
hundredth	**100**	centésimo
hundred and first	**101**	centésimo primero
hundred and tenth	**110**	centésimo décimo
two hundredth	**200**	ducentésimo
three hundredth	**300**	trecentésimo
four hundredth	**400**	cuadringentésimo
five hundredth	**500**	quingentésimo
six hundredth	**600**	sexcentésimo
seven hundredth	**700**	septingentésimo
eight hundredth	**800**	octingentésimo
nine hundredth	**900**	noningentésimo
thousandth	**1000**	milésimo
two thousandth	**2000**	dos milésimo
millionth	**1000000**	millonésimo
two millionth	**2000000**	dos millonésimo

Notes on usage of the ordinal numbers

(**a**) All these numbers are adjectives in *-o*, and therefore agree with the noun in number and gender: *la quinta vez, en segundas nupcias, en octavo lugar.*

(**b**) *primero* and *tercero* are shortened to *primer, tercer* when they directly precede a masculine singular noun: *en el primer capítulo, el tercer hombre* (but *los primeros coches en llegar, el primero y más importante hecho*).

(**c**) In Spanish the ordinal numbers from 1 to 10 are commonly used; from 11 to 20 rather less; above 21 they are rarely written and almost never heard in speech (except for *milésimo*, which is frequent). The custom is to replace the forms for 21 and above by the cardinal number: *en el capítulo treinta y seis, celebran el setenta aniversario* (or *el aniversario setenta*), *en el poste ciento cinco contando desde la esquina.*

(**d**) **Kings, popes and centuries.** The ordinal numbers from 1 to 9 are employed for these in Spanish as in English: *en el siglo cuarto, Eduardo octavo, Pío nono, Enrique primero.* For 10 either the cardinal or the ordinal may be used: *siglo diez* or *siglo décimo, Alfonso diez* or *Alfonso décimo.* For 11 and above it is now customary to use only the cardinal number: *Alfonso once* (but *onceno* in the Middle Ages), *Juan veintitrés, en el siglo dieciocho.*

(**e**) **Abbreviations.** English 1st, 2nd, 3rd, 4th, 5th *etc* = Spanish 1º *or* 1er, 2º, 3º *or* 3er, 4º, 5º and so on (*f*: 1era, 2ª).

(**f**) See also the notes on Dates, below.

DECIMALS / LAS DECIMALES

In Spanish a comma is written where English writes a point: English 3·56 (three point five six) = Spanish 3,56 (*tres coma cinco seis*); English ·07 (point zero seven) = Spanish ,07 (*coma cero siete*). The recurring decimal 3·3333 may be written in English as 3·3 and in Spanish as 3,3.

FRACTIONS / NÚMEROS QUEBRADOS

one half, a half	$\frac{1}{2}$	(m) *medio,* (f) *media*
one and a half helpings	$1\frac{1}{2}$	(*una*) *porción y media*
two and a half kilos	$2\frac{1}{2}$	*dos kilos y medio*
one third, a third	$\frac{1}{3}$	*un tercio, la tercera parte*
two thirds	$\frac{2}{3}$	*dos tercios, las dos terceras partes*
one quarter, a quarter	$\frac{1}{4}$	*un cuarto, la cuarta parte*
three quarters	$\frac{3}{4}$	*tres cuartos, las tres cuartas partes*
one sixth, a sixth	$\frac{1}{6}$	*un sexto, la sexta parte*
five and five sixths	$5\frac{5}{6}$	*cinco y cinco sextos*
one twelfth, a twelfth	$\frac{1}{12}$	*un duodécimo; un dozavo, la duodécima parte*
seven twelfths	$\frac{7}{12}$	*siete dozavos*
one hundredth, a hundredth	$\frac{1}{100}$	*un centésimo, una centésima parte*
one thousandth, a thousandth	$\frac{1}{1000}$	*un milésimo*

UNITS / NOMENCLATURA

3,684 is a four-digit number
It contains 4 units, 8 tens, 6 hundreds and 3 thousands
The decimal ·234 contains 2 tenths, 3 hundredths and 4 thousandths

3.684 es un número de cuatro dígitos (or *guarismos*)
Contiene 4 unidades, 8 decenas, 6 centenas y 3 unidades de millar
la fracción decimal, 234 contiene 2 décimas, 3 centésimas y 4 milésimas

PERCENTAGES / LOS PORCENTAJES

$2\frac{1}{2}\%$ two and a half per cent

$2\frac{1}{2}$ *por 100,* (less frequently) $2\frac{1}{2}\%$; *dos y medio por cien, dos y medio por ciento* (in spoken usage and among the authorities there is disagreement about *cien/ciento* here).

18% of the people here are over 65

el dieciocho por cien de la gente aquí tienen más de 65 años.

Production has risen by 8%
(*See also* per, hundred *in the main text.*)

la producción ha aumentado en un 8 por 100.
(*Vése también* por, cien/ciento *en el diccionario*)

CALCULATIONS

8 + 6 = 14 eight and (*or* plus) six are (*or* make) fourteen
15 − 3 = 12 fifteen take away three are (*or* equals) twelve, three from fifteen leaves twelve
3 × 3 = 9 three threes are nine, three times three is nine
32 ÷ 8 = 4 thirty-two divided by eight is (*or* equals) four
$3^2 = 9$ three squared is nine
$2^5 = 32$ two to the fifth (*or* to the power of five) is (*or* equals) thirty-two
$\sqrt{16} = 4$ the square root of sixteen is four

SIGNS

+	addition sign
+	plus sign (*eg* + 7 = plus seven)
−	subtraction sign
−	minus sign (*eg* − 3 = minus three)
×	multiplication sign
÷	division sign
√	square root sign
∞	infinity
≡	sign of identity, is exactly equal to
=	sign of equality, equals
≃	is approximately equal to
≠	sign of inequality, is not equal to
>	is greater than
<	is less than

EL CÁLCULO

8 + 6 = 14 *ocho y* (or *más*) *seis son catorce*
15 − 3 = 12 *quince menos tres resta doce, de tres a quince van doce*
3 × 3 = 9 *tres por tres son nueve*

32 ÷ 8 = 4 *treinta y dos dividido por ocho es cuatro*
$3^2 = 9$ *tres al cuadrado son nueve*
$2^5 = 32$ *dos a la quinta potencia son treinta y dos*

$\sqrt{16} = 4$ *la raíz cuadrada de dieciséis es cuatro.*

LOS SIGNOS

+	signo de adición
+	signo de más (*p.ej.* + 7 = 7 de más)
−	signo de sustracción
−	signo de menos (*p.ej.* − 3 = 3 de menos)
×	signo de multiplicación
:	signo de división
√	signo de raíz cuadrada
∞	infinito
≡	signo de identidad, es exactamente igual a
=	signo de igualdad, es igual a
≈	es aproximadamente igual a
≠	signo de no identidad, no es igual a
>	es mayor que
<	es menor que

WEIGHTS AND MEASURES

PESOS Y MEDIDAS

METRIC SYSTEM – SISTEMA MÉTRICO

Measures formed with the following prefixes are mostly omitted:

Se omiten la mayor parte de las medidas formadas con los siguientes prefijos:

deca-	10 times	10 veces	*deca-*
hecto-	100 times	100 veces	*hecto-*
kilo-	1000 times	1000 veces	*kilo-*
deci-	one tenth	una décima	*deci-*
centi-	one hundredth	una centésima	*centi-*
mil(l)i-	one thousandth	una milésima	*mili-*

Linear measures – medidas de longitud

1 millimetre (milímetro)	=	0·03937 inch (pulgada)
1 centimetre (centímetro)	=	0·3937 inch (pulgada)
1 metre (metro)	=	39·37 inches (pulgadas)
	=	1·094 yards (yardas)
1 kilometre (kilómetro)	=	0·6214 mile (milla) *or* almost exactly five-eighths of a mile

Square measures – medidas cuadradas o de superficie

1 square centimetre (centímetro cuadrado)	=	0·155 square inch (pulgada cuadrada)
1 square metre (metro cuadrado)	=	10·764 square feet (pies cuadrados)
	=	1·196 square yards (yardas cuadradas)
1 square kilometre (kilómetro cuadrado)	=	0·3861 square mile (milla cuadrada)
	=	247·1 acres (acres)
1 are = 100 square metres (área)	=	119·6 square yards (yardas cuadradas)
1 hectare = 100 ares (hectárea)	=	2·471 acres (acres)

Cubic measures – medidas cúbicas

1 cubic centimetre (centímetro cúbico)	=	0·061 cubic inch (pulgada cúbica)
1 cubic metre (metro cúbico)	=	35·315 cubic feet (pies cúbicos)
	=	1·308 cubic yards (yardas cúbicas)

Measures of capacity – medidas de capacidad

1 litre (litro) = 1000 cubic centimetres	=	1·76 pints (pintas)
	=	0·22 gallon (galón)

Weights – pesos

1 gramme (gramo)	=	15·4 grains (granos)
1 kilogramme (kilogramo)	=	2·2046 pounds (libras)
1 quintal (quintal métrico) = 100 kilogrammes	=	220·46 pounds (libras)
1 metric ton (tonelada métrica) = 1000 kilogrammes	=	0·9842 ton (tonelada)

BRITISH SYSTEM – SISTEMA BRITÁNICO

Linear measures – medidas de longitud

1 inch (pulgada)	=	2,54 centímetros
1 foot (pie) = 12 inches	=	30,48 centímetros
1 yard (yarda) = 3 feet	=	91,44 centímetros
1 furlong (estadio) = 220 yards	=	201,17 metros
1 mile (milla) = 1760 yards	=	1.609,33 metros
	=	1.609 kilómetros

Surveyors' measures – medidas de agrimensura

1 link = 7·92 inches	=	20,12 centímetros
1 rod (or pole, perch) = 25 links	=	5,029 metros
1 chain = 22 yards = 4 rods	=	20,12 metros

Square measures – medidas cuadradas o de superficie

1 square inch (pulgada cuadrada)	=	6,45 cm^2
1 square foot (pie cuadrado) = 144 square inches	=	929,03 cm^2
1 square yard (yarda cuadrada) = 9 square feet	=	0,836 m^2
1 square rod = 30·25 square yards	=	25,29 m^2
1 acre = 4840 square yards	=	40,47 áreas
1 square mile (milla cuadrada) = 640 acres	=	2,59 km^2

Cubic measures – medidas cúbicas

1 cubic inch (pulgada cúbica)	=	16,387 cm^3
1 cubic foot (pie cúbico) = 1728 cubic inches	=	0,028 m^3
1 cubic yard (yarda cúbica) = 27 cubic feet	=	0,765 m^3
1 register ton (tonelada de registro) = 100 cubic feet	=	2,832 m^3

Measures of capacity – medidas de capacidad

(a) Liquid—para líquidos

1 gill	=	0,142 litro
1 pint (pinta) = 4 gills	=	0,57 litro
1 quart = 2 pints	=	1,136 litros
1 gallon (galón) = 4 quarts	=	4,546 litros

(b) Dry—para áridos

1 peck = 2 gallons	=	9,087 litros
1 bushel = 4 pecks	=	36,36 litros
1 quarter = 8 bushels	=	290,94 litros

Weights – pesos (Avoirdupois system – sistema avoirdupois)

1 grain (grano)	=	0,0648 gramo
1 drachm or dram = 27,34 grains	=	1,77 gramos
1 ounce (onza) = 16 dra(ch)ms	=	28,35 gramos
1 pound (libra) = 16 ounces	=	453,6 gramos
	=	0,453 kilogramo
1 stone = 14 pounds	=	6,348 kilogramos
1 quarter = 28 pounds	=	12,7 kilogramos
1 hundredweight = 112 pounds	=	50,8 kilogramos
1 ton (tonelada) = 2240 pounds= 20 hundredweight	=	1.016 kilogramos

US MEASURES – MEDIDAS NORTEAMERICANAS

In the US the same system as that which applies in Great Britain is used for the most part; the main differences are mentioned below.

En EE.UU. se emplea en general el mismo sistema que en Gran Bretaña; las principales diferencias son las siguientes:

Measures of capacity – medidas de capacidad

(a) Liquid—para líquidos

1 US liquid gill	=	0,118 litro
1 US liquid pint = 4 gills	=	0,473 litro
1 US liquid quart = 2 pints	=	0,946 litro
1 US gallon = 4 quarts	=	3,785 litros

(b) Dry—para áridos

1 US dry pint	=	0,550 litro
1 US dry quart = 2 dry pints	=	1,1 litros
1 US peck = 8 dry quarts	=	8,81 litros
1 US bushel = 4 pecks	=	35,24 litros

Weights – pesos

1 hundredweight (*or* short hundredweight) = 100 pounds	=	45,36 kilogramos
1 ton (*or* short ton) = 2000 pounds = 20 short hundredweights	=	907, 18 kilogramos

TRADITIONAL SPANISH WEIGHTS AND MEASURES – PESOS Y MEDIDAS ESPAÑOLES TRADICIONALES

These are the measures which were standard until the introduction of the metric system in Spain in 1871, and they are still in use in some provinces and in agriculture.

Son éstas las medidas que se emplearon hasta la introducción del sistema métrico en España en 1871. Se emplean todavía en algunas provincias y en la agricultura

Linear measures – medidas de longitud

1 vara	=	0·836 metre
1 braza	=	1·67 metres
1 milla	=	1·852 kilometres
1 legua	=	5·5727 kilometres

Square measure – medida cuadrada o de superficie

1 fanega = 6460 square metres = 1·59 acres

Measures of capacity – medidas de capacidad

(a) Liquid—para líquidos

1 cuartillo	=	0·504 litre
1 azumbre = 4 cuartillos	=	2·016 litres
1 cántara = 8 azumbres	=	16·128 litres

(b) Dry – para áridos

1 celemín	=	4·625 litres
1 fanega = 12 celemines	=	55·5 litres = 1·58 bushels

Weights – pesos

1 onza	=	28·7 grammes
1 libra = 16 onzas	=	460 grammes
1 arroba = 25 libras	=	11·502 kilogrammes = 25 pounds
1 quintal = 4 arrobas	=	46 kilogrammes

TIME

2 hours 33 minutes and 14 seconds
half an hour
a quarter of an hour
three quarters of an hour
what's the time?
what do you make the time?
have you the right time?
I make it 2.20
my watch says 3.37
it's 1 o'clock
it's 2 o'clock
it's 5 past 4
it's 10 to 6
it's half-past 8
it's a quarter past 9
it's a quarter to 2
at 10 a.m.
at 4 p.m.
at 11 p.m.
at exactly 3 o'clock, at 3 sharp, at 3 on the dot
the train leaves at 19.32
(at) what time does it start?
it is just after 3
it is nearly 9
about 8 o'clock
at (or by) 6 o'clock at the latest
have it ready for 5 o'clock
it is full each night from 7 to 9
'closed from 1.30 to 4.30'
until 8 o'clock
it would be about 11
it would have been about 10
at midnight
before midday, before noon

LA HORA

2 horas 33 minutos y 14 segundos
media hora
un cuarto de hora
tres cuartos de hora
¿qué hora es?
¿qué hora tienes?
¿tiene Vd la hora exacta?
yo tengo las dos veinte
mi reloj marca las tres treinta y siete
es la una
son las dos
son las cuatro y cinco
son las seis menos diez
son las ocho y media
son las nueve y cuarto
son las dos menos cuarto
a las diez de la mañana
a las cuatro de la tarde
a las once de la noche
a las tres en punto
el tren sale a las diecinueve treinta y dos
¿a qué hora comienza?
son un poco más de las tres
son casi las nueve
cerca de las ocho, hacia las ocho, a eso de las ocho
a las seis a más tardar
téngalo listo para las cinco
está lleno todas las noches de siete a nueve
'cerrado de 1.30 a 4.30'
hasta las ocho
serán las once
serían las diez
a medianoche
antes del mediodía

DATES

N.B. The days of the week and the months are written with small letters in Spanish: *lunes, martes, febrero, mayo.*

the 1st of July, July 1st
the 2nd of May, May 2nd

on the 21st (of) June
on Monday
he comes on Mondays
'closed on Fridays'
he lends it to me from Monday to Friday
from the 14th to the 18th

what's the date?, what date is it today?
today's the 12th
one Thursday in October
about the 4th of July
Heading of letters: 19th May 1984
1975, nineteen (hundred and) seventy-five
4 B.C., B.C. 4
70 A.D., A.D. 70
in the 13th Century
in (or during) the 1930s
in 1940 something

LAS FECHAS

el 1º de julio, el primero de julio
el 2 de mayo, el dos de mayo (the cardinal numbers are used in Spanish for dates from 2nd to 31st)
el 21 de junio, el día veintiuno de junio
el lunes
viene los lunes
'cerrado los viernes'
me lo presta de lunes a viernes
desde el 14 hasta el 18, desde el catorce hasta el dieciocho
¿qué día es hoy?
hoy es el doce, estamos a doce
un jueves en octubre
hacia el cuatro de julio
19 de mayo de 1984
mil novecientos setenta y cinco
4 a. de J.C. (see main text)
70 d. de J.C. (see main text)
en el siglo XIII, en el siglo trece
en el decenio de 1930 a 40, durante los años treinta
en el año 1940 y tantos

(See also in the main text of the dictionary **week, year** *etc.)*

abbreviation	*abbr, abr*	abreviatura
Academy	*Acad*	Academia
accusative	*acc, ac*	acusativo
adjective	*adj*	adjetivo
administration	*Admin*	administración
adverb	*adv*	adverbio
aeronautics	*Aer*	aeronáutica
agriculture	*Agr*	agricultura
surveying	*Agrimen*	agrimensura
anatomy	*Anat*	anatomía
Andean usage	*And*	zona andina
approximately	*approx, aprox*	aproximadamente
architecture	*Archit, Arquit*	arquitectura
article	*art*	artículo
astronomy	*Astron*	astronomía
attributive	*attr, atr*	atributivo
automobiles	*Aut*	automóviles
auxiliary	*aux*	auxiliar
biblical	*Bib*	bíblico
biology	*Bio*	biología
botany	*Bot*	botánica
British	*Brit*	Inglés británico
Central America	*CAm*	Centroamérica
Caribbean usage	*Carib*	zona del Caribe
carpentry	*Carp*	carpintería
chemistry	*Chem*	química
cinema	*Cine*	cinema, cinematográfico
commerce	*Comm, Com*	comercio
comparative	*comp*	comparativo
compound element	*cpd*	compuesto
computing	*Comput*	informática
building trade	*Constr*	construcción
sewing	*Cos*	costura
cookery	*Culin*	culinario, cocina
dative	*dat*	dativo
definite	*def*	definido
demonstrative	*dem*	demostrativo
sport	*Dep*	deportes
direct	*dir*	directo
ecclesiastical	*Eccl, Ecl*	eclesiástico
economics	*Econ*	economía
education	*Educ*	educación
United States	*EE.UU.*	Estados Unidos
for example	*eg*	por ejemplo
electricity, electronics	*Elec*	electricidad, electrónica
entomology	*Ent*	entomología
school	*Escol*	escuela
Spanish usage	*Esp*	español de España
especially	*esp*	especialmente
etcetera	*etc*	etcétera
euphemism	*euph, euf*	eufemismo
exclamation	*excl*	exclamación
feminine	*f*	femenino
pharmacy	*Farm*	farmacia
railways	*Ferro*	ferrocarriles
figurative	*fig*	figurado
philosophy	*Fil*	filosofía
finance	*Fin*	finanzas
physics	*Fis*	física
physiology	*Fisiol*	fisiología
phonetics	*Fon*	fonética
photography	*Fot*	fotografía
frequently	*freq, frec*	frecuentemente
formal usage	*frm*	uso formal
football	*Ftbl*	fútbol
generally	*gen*	generalmente
geography	*Geog*	geografía
geology	*Geol*	geología
gerund	*ger*	gerundio
grammar	*Gram*	gramática
heraldry	*Her*	heráldica
history	*Hist*	historia
horticulture	*Hort*	horticultura
humorous	*hum*	humorístico
that is	*ie*	esto es, es decir
impersonal	*impers*	impersonal
indefinite	*ind*	indefinido
indicative	*indic*	modo indicativo
infinitive	*infin*	infinitivo
computing	*Inform*	informática
interjection	*interj*	interjección
interrogative	*interrog*	interrogativo
invariable	*invar*	invariable
Ireland, Irish	*Ir*	Irlanda, irlandés
ironic	*iro, iró*	irónico
irregular	*irr*	irregular
law, legal	*Jur*	derecho, jurídico
Latin America	*LAm*	Latinoamérica